KANKAKEE VALLEY HIGH SCHOOL

REF 427 DIC

31095 DICTIONARY OF AMERICAN

P9-CRP-927

DATE DUE

31095

REF
427
DIC

Dictionary of
American regional
English, volume I,
introduction and A-
C.

KANKAKEE VALLEY HIGH SCHOOL

857139 06092 54086C 04157F

Dictionary of American Regional English

Dictionary of American Regional English

Volume I   Introduction and A-C

Frederic G. Cassidy
Chief Editor

The Belknap Press of Harvard University Press
Cambridge, Massachusetts, and London, England

Copyright © 1985 by the President and Fellows of Harvard College
All rights reserved
Printed in the United States of America
10 9 8 7 6 5

This book is printed on acid-free paper, and its binding materials
have been chosen for strength and durability.

Designed by Marianne Perlak

Library of Congress Cataloging in Publication Data
Main entry under title:
Dictionary of American regional English.
    Contents: v. 1. Introduction and A-C.
    1. English language—Provincialisms—United States—
Dictionaries. 2. English language—Dialects—United
States—Dictionaries. 3. English language—United
States—Dictionaries. I. Cassidy, Frederic Gomes,
1907–
PE2843.D52 1985   427′.973   84-29025
ISBN 0-674-20511-1 (v. 1: alk. paper)

DARE Staff, Volume I

CHIEF EDITOR
Frederic G. Cassidy

ADJUNCT EDITOR
Audrey R. Duckert

ASSOCIATE EDITOR
Joan H. Hall

SENIOR ASSOCIATE EDITORS
John C. McGalliard
Margaret Waterman

ASSISTANT EDITORS
Martha Bateson
Craig M. Carver, *Managing Editor*
John F. Clark
Jennifer K. Ellsworth
Carrie A. Estill
George H. Goebel
James W. Hartman
Michael M. T. Henderson
Edward C. Hill
Jeffrey A. Hirshberg
Matt Hogan, *Science Editor*
Sheila Y. Kolstad, *Senior Science Editor*
David Vander Meulen
Luanne von Schneidemesser, *Production Editor*
Lois Wood

BIBLIOGRAPHER
Goldye Mohr

COMPUTING STAFF
Jean Anderson
Thomas Johnson
William Katke
Richard Venezky
William Woodson

WORD PROCESSORS, PROOFREADERS
Diane Balmer
Dolores Fries
Mary Ann Pels
Lida Wagner
Michael Williamson

OFFICE MANAGER
Carol Wilson

FIELDWORKERS
Leslie Anderson (CA)
Frank Anshen (NJ)
Donald Boyd (TX)
James Breuer (PA)
Charlotte Brown (AL, GA, IL, OH, WV)
Peter Brunette (PA)
David Carlson (MA)
F. G. Cassidy (AK, DC, HI, WI)
Tom Clark (OH)
Lurline Coltharp (TX)
Stanley J. Cook (KS, NE)
Robert L. Cowser (NY)
L. Benjamin Crane (AR, MS)
Lawrence M. Davis (IL)
Audrey R. Duckert (MA)
Warren L. P. Dwyer (IL, TX)
Jon Erickson (UT)
Jean Ehrenkranz (NJ, RI)
George Ferger (WI)
Lawrence Foley (AL)
Virginia Foscue (AL)
Charles W. Foster (AL, TN)
Timothy Frazer (IL)
David Goldberg (CT, NJ, NY, OR, PA, TX, VT, WA)
Leonard Goldberg (MA)
Susan Goldberg (NY)
Bonnie Greatman (MD)
Iris Greenberg (NY)
Michael Grossinger (AZ)
Steve Halpern (NJ)
Robert Hausmann (AL, PA, WI)
Kirk Hegbloom (ID, MT, ND, SD, TX, WY)
Lois Hood (RI)
Sharon Huizenga (KY, VA)
Michele McKeegan Jacobs (CA)
Robert Jacobs (NY)
Mary Jay Jones (CA)
Jay H. Kendall (VT)
Robert Keenan (WV)
B. J. Keene (AR)
Sheila Y. Kolstad (KY, IL)
Hans Krichels (CT)
Diane Kutzko (IL)
Michael Lampman (GA, PA)
Mary Lee (CA)
Maurice Lee (IL, OK)
Peter Lee (WI)
Albert Logan (IL, IN, PA)
Reino Maki (ME, NH, NM, OK, VT)
Charles McCabe (IA, MN)
Robert McCracken (MI)
Marsha McKeldin (KY, MS, MO, TN)
W. C. Middleton (IL)
Charlotte J. Miller (NY, VA)
Cynthia Milne (TX)
Laura Murray (FL, NC, SC, VA)
Barbara Myhre (CA, IL)
Geoffrey Needler (NY)
Evelyn Nimz (IL, IA, KS, WI)
Raymond O'Cain (IN, SC)
Ruth Porter (FL, NC)
John Reddington (MI)
Sally Rentschler (GA, MI, TN)
August Rubrecht (AR, DE, LA, NY, TN)
Dale Ruff (CA, IL, MI, NH, NY, NC, OH, TX)
Geoffrey Russom (NY)
Gladys Saunders (DC, PA, MA, NY)
Barbara Scott (TN)
Charles Seastone (IN, NY)
Toby Sindt (NJ)
Timothy Sloan (NY, PA)
Thomas Smith (NC)
Detlef Stark (GA)
L. C. Suddarth (IN)
Martin Todaro (TX)
Gerald Udell (MO)
Patt Van Dyke (CA, CO, IA, MN, NV)
Elizabeth Van Guilder (MA)
Nancy Williamson (CA, NC)
James Wood (NJ)
Joan Zink (MA)
Terry Zwigoff (IL, TN)

A complete list of *DARE* staff will appear in the final volume.

Contents

Acknowledgments

It would be quite impossible to thank by name the hundreds of people from every walk of life who have contributed in one way or another, to one degree or another, to this first volume of *DARE*. We have shared an interest in the English language in America, especially in its regional varieties, which, in the spirit of our national motto, make unity out of diversity. The project has been helped in countless ways, including financial support, contributions of collections of data, volunteered reading, access granted to many kinds of source materials, and single items of data from every part of the country.

DARE has received financial support from both government and nongovernment sources. The first grant, from the U.S. Office of Education (1965–1970), paid for the basic fieldwork. Thereafter, the National Endowment for the Humanities has supported the processing of data and the editing (1971–1984), and the National Science Foundation has also helped materially (1980–1984). Other assistance has come from the Rockefeller Foundation (1976), the Andrew W. Mellon Foundation (1978–1984), the Brittingham Foundation (1980–1984), the Evjue Foundation (1980), the Johnson Foundation of Racine (1972), the Gramercy Foundation (1980–1981), and the Marathon Oil Company. Private donors have also provided substantial support: Margaret Bryant, William Card, Audrey R. Duckert, Philip H. Gray, A. Murray Kinloch, John B. McFarland, James B. McMillan, Barbara Richmond, I. Willis Russell, Mr. and Mrs. Merton M. Sealts, Peter Tamony, Francis Lee Utley, and Eugene B. Vest.

The University of Wisconsin–Madison, as Cooperating Institution, has supported the project steadily from the beginning. Officers who deserve special mention are Presidents Fred Harvey Harrington and Robert O'Neil; Chancellor Irving Shain; and Deans Eric Rude, Robert M. Bock, Mark H. Ingraham, Robert B. Doremus, and E. David Cronon.

The Wisconsin Foundation has handled funds and given advice as to funding. The Department of English has been generous with its facilities and personal interest taken in the work, especially by Chairmen Helen C. White, Walter B. Rideout, Simon Heninger, Charles T. Scott, Phillip Harth, William T. Lenehan, Sargent Bush, Jr., and Joseph J. Wiesenfarth. Professor and Mrs. Merton M. Sealts have given generous help and useful criticism. Foreign scholars who wrote at a critical time, urging the National Endowment to give *DARE* essential support, were A. J. Aitken, R. W. Burchfield, Robert D. Eagleson, Guy Jean Forgue, and Pierre Michel. Thanks are also due the scholars who acted as members of *DARE*'s advisory boards: Harold B. Allen, Audrey R. Duckert, Einar Haugen, Hans Kurath, Raven I. McDavid, Jr., James B. McMillan, Albert H. Marckwardt, Thomas Pyles, Allen Walker Read, I. Willis Russell; and later, John Algeo, Richard W. Bailey, Larry D. Benson, Charles A. Ferguson, John H. Fisher, Eric Hamp, Winfred P. Lehmann, Robert Lumiansky, Fred C. Robinson, and Robert D. Stevick.

Special compilations, some comprising decades of data collecting, have been contributed to *DARE* (see Introduction). Chief among these are the Gordon Wilson and Joseph Hall collections; the Carleton, Hand, Hench, McDavid, Tabbert, and Tamony collections are also of special value.

In the early years a reading program was launched in which volunteers marked possible examples of regionalisms in more than two hundred American novels, short stories, plays, and poems. Useful information also came from correspondents all over the United States who wrote in response to articles about *DARE* and television appearances by the Chief Editor.

Thanks go also to the 2777 informants interviewed by *DARE* fieldworkers, who generously contributed their time and knowledge. They were promised that their names would be kept confidential.

DARE has also benefited greatly from contributions of other individuals. In the lexicographic community, special thanks must go to Frederick Mish (Merriam-Webster) and Robert Burchfield (Oxford English Dictionaries). Clarence L. Barnhart has furnished wise inspiration. J. Edward Gates has given aid through the Dictionary Society of North America; Laurence Urdang through *Verbatim* and in other ways. The staffs of the University of Wisconsin–Madison libraries and the Wisconsin Historical Society library have been consistently helpful. John Nitti, director of the *Dictionary of the Old Spanish Language,* has given unstinting aid of many kinds, especially with our computer problems. Generous computing assistance has also come from James E. Hallen, William H. Kelly, and Paul R. Stevens, and Michael von Schneidemesser has contributed more time and computer expertise than anyone can reckon.

It was through the good offices of Howard Mumford Jones initially, and of W. V. Quine, Einar Haugen, and Morton M. Bloomfield, that Harvard University Press became acquainted with *DARE* and in 1974 accepted it for publication. Their help is acknowledged with warm thanks, as is also the contribution of the Press staff, especially Maud Wilcox, Susan M. Hayes, and Camille Smith, and Darby Jo Campbell of Progressive Typographers.

Lexicography, which by its nature demands a high degree of accuracy in detail, is not a rapid science. The *DARE* project, begun in 1965, has advanced steadily in these twenty years. Data have been collected and prepared. Problems of limitation and presentation have been worked out. Volume I is now complete, and considerable work has been done toward the remaining volumes. With continued support, it should be possible to complete these within a few years. *DARE* has had the great benefit of popular interest all along — the warm collaboration without which such a piece of work could hardly be accomplished. To all who have helped in any way, our grateful thanks.

As a personal note, the Chief Editor adds the following lines of dedication to his wife, Professor Hélène Monod Cassidy (1909–1980):

Līf wæs þe līhtre   þonne Lēoht eastan cwōm
Fronclonde from,   faemne welēadig,
wīs ond wittig,   wīfmonna swētost,
glēaw in glīwstōlas.   Ðæt wæs gōde ides.

Life was brighter when   Ἑλένη came from the east,
from the land of France,   a bride well-blest,
wise and learned,   of women most dear,
keen in joyous places.   That was a good spouse.

Introduction

History

A scholarly project that has required many years of work, involving hundreds of people and considerable expense, cannot be fully understood without taking account of its inception, its aims, its progress. The history of the *Dictionary of American Regional English (DARE)* goes back almost a hundred years, to the founding in 1889 of its sponsoring body, the American Dialect Society (ADS). It is no coincidence that in the same year Joseph Wright took the first step toward editing his *English Dialect Dictionary (EDD);* that fact was well known to the eminent American philologists who founded ADS, whose purpose evidently was to do, for the English language in America, what the English Dialect Society had done in gathering materials for Wright and sponsoring his work.

The list of names, though a century old, is still a roll of honor, deserving remembrance. Among the most eminent members were Edward S. Sheldon, Charles H. Grandgent, George L. Kittredge, Francis J. Child, James B. Greenough, John M. Manly, Benjamin I. Wheeler, and William D. Whitney. They stated, as the purpose of the Society, "the investigation of the English Dialects of America with regard to pronunciation, grammar, vocabulary, phraseology, and geographical distribution." The first issue of the Society's publication, *Dialect Notes (DN),* appeared in 1890. It continued publication for forty-nine years and produced six volumes, chiefly of word lists but also including other apposite studies.

Though production of a dictionary was evidently foreseen from the first, collecting was left to individual initiative; there was never a real campaign or an adequately planned effort to cover the country. Word lists, besides, often lacked the kind of precise information necessary for compiling a dictionary. When the Society was seventeen years old, William E. Mead made this point in no uncertain terms:

> The most ardent admirer of the achievements of the Society must admit that all the investigation that has been done, however thorough for certain districts, is fragmentary in the extreme . . . To one who has reviewed the whole situation it seems clear that the time has come when we should definitely abandon the drifting policy which we have followed and set out on a systematic investigation. If our chief aim is to publish detached studies of a district here and there as chance may offer them, we shall doubtless accomplish something of value . . . but if we cherish the hope that by such means we shall, within a reasonable time, succeed in preparing an adequate dialect map of our vast country and in bringing together a sufficient amount of trustworthy

material for an *American Dialect Dictionary* worthy to stand beside the *English Dialect Dictionary,* we are optimistic indeed. (*DN* 3, 168–169.)

Mead estimated that "the work of the Dialect Society must be multiplied twenty-fold before a dialect dictionary can be safely undertaken." Pointing to the rich fields, especially the South, at that time but scantily studied, he outlined a plan of organized collecting, state by state. He deplored the daily disappearance of material as speakers of dialect died. And he insisted that this kind of investigation could not be made without *money*— more money than the Society was taking in from its membership. Hoping for the support of some wealthy individual, he concluded: "If such assistance can be obtained, we may hope to accomplish a work of lasting importance." That was in 1906.

The chief moving force in the following years was Percy W. Long, who in 1917 began the formation of a master file. Yet only two years later he warned that, despite some progress made, "the Society's chief enterprise may be said to be in a critical position" (*DN* 5, 74–75). It was the period of the First World War; the making of the file had been delayed; Mead's hoped-for Maecenas had not been found.

A new step was taken in 1929 when the office of Editor of the Dictionary was created and Long was elected to fill it. In his report, however, the new Editor remarked, "there is no immediate prospect of beginning work on the Dictionary itself." The lists of words and expressions already printed in *Dialect Notes,* he said,

> now total over 30,000 entries . . . No doubt it seems to many that the Society's dictionary should without much further delay begin to assume some form practicable of publication. An examination of the data now available shows that a dictionary of a kind could be prepared from them. It would probably include the greater number of existent dialect words and locutions. It would probably indicate with some approach to accuracy the sections in which they primarily appear. On the other hand, it could not compare at all favorably with the *English Dialect Dictionary.*

Even to equal the *EDD* it would still be necessary to gather dialect materials from literature, to have many county glossaries, and to have local correspondents to whom questions could be submitted during the process of editing. That was in 1930. The time was not yet ripe for the kind of effort necessary to produce the kind of dictionary that had been envisioned.

Meanwhile, the Society took part in two other projects of a related sort: the Linguistic Atlas of the United States and

Canada, whose first publication was the *Linguistic Atlas of New England*;[1] and the *Dictionary of American English.*[2] *Dialect Notes* ceased publication in 1939 but was succeeded in 1944 by the *Publication of the American Dialect Society (PADS),* which has continued to print word lists and special studies. For a time, the hope of producing the dictionary was greatly weakened. During her presidency, Louise Pound revived it to the extent of personally encouraging Harold Wentworth to produce his *American Dialect Dictionary,* a small compilation based chiefly on *Dialect Notes* and his own extensive reading.[3] But no field collecting was undertaken, large parts of the subject area remained unexamined, and the resulting volume was never accepted as the Society's intended dictionary. The dictionary was not forgotten, however: in the late 1940s two meetings were held especially to plan it. At last, the present writer, asked to say how he would go about it, replied in "The ADS Dictionary—How Soon?" (*PADS* 39) and in 1962 found himself appointed Editor and encouraged to get on with the work.

Preparatory Steps

Studies already made were ready to be used. First, the new Editor had done fieldwork for the Linguistic Atlas, completing fifty workbooks in Wisconsin. This work had proved clearly that numerous local differences in Wisconsin speech could be correlated with settlement history and other social factors. Second was a statewide study, the Wisconsin English Language Survey (WELS), in which, by means of a mailed questionnaire, fifty Wisconsin natives in twenty-five chosen communities had returned a large number of variant responses. This questionnaire ultimately became the basis of that used by *DARE.* The purpose of WELS was, within the limits of practicability, to gather as much of the local lexicon as possible, in all its variations. This could not be done efficiently by random questioning. For WELS, therefore, the items printed up to that time in the *DN* and *PADS* word lists—approximately forty thousand of them—were analyzed and sorted by semantic categories. The questionnaire was then constructed of questions covering those categories which had proved to be the most fruitful in regional variation.[4] Collecting could thus be undertaken with some assurance of maximal results. As noted, WELS became the pilot study on which the *DARE* Questionnaire was based.

The Editor had laid down two essential conditions for production of the Dictionary: full-time direction and full-scale financing. Fortunately for the latter, the U.S. Office of Education, just at this time, was supporting a few projects of research in the humanities. The Dictionary received support for five years, during which field collecting over the entire United States could be accomplished. The hope was that in another five years the collections could be edited and the Dictionary produced. But the success of the first step was so resounding—such a huge and valuable corpus was collected—that the years of editing stretched from five to ten and beyond.

The *DARE* Questionnaire

In the summer of 1964 the Chief Editor and Audrey R. Duckert worked out the essentials of the project and gave it its name.[5] The acronym was taken to be a hopeful augury. For the essential nationwide campaign of data collecting, the primary tool required was a series of questions to be asked uniformly in all areas so that results would be comparable. The WELS questions were therefore completely revised, made over from their postal form for use in direct oral interviews, and put into a fixed phrasing which the fieldworkers were instructed not to alter.

Intended for use in personal interviews, the *DARE* Questionnaire (QR) begins with the neutral subject of time in order to allay possible suspicions of some hidden purpose on the part of the investigator. Next come weather and topography, equally neutral and safely concrete. Houses, furniture, and household utensils follow, with dishes, foods, vegetables, and fruits. And so the questions continue to more abstract topics: honesty and dishonesty, beliefs, emotions, relationships among people, manner of action or being, and so on—41 categories in all with a total of 1847 questions. (The entire set of questions, with all the different responses made to them, will be presented as the Data Summary in the final volume of *DARE.*) In all, 1002 QRs were completed in as many communities.

In an attempt to avoid prompting specific replies, questions were phrased without using words that might possibly be given as answers. For example, the word *rise* is not used in asking about the sun, though *sun* itself is unavoidable: "What do you call the time early in the day before the sun comes into sight?" would not prompt *sunrise* rather than *sunup, dawn,* or some other word. (By far the most frequent response was *dawn.*) The language of the questions was kept as simple and common as possible, in order to elicit an immediate, spontaneous response. Secondary and other responses, though not sought, were carefully recorded when given. The immediate, spontaneous response, however, is as close to normal local usage as an investigator can hope to come. It avoids inhibitions and second thoughts on the part of the informant; he or she does not have time to change the answer under the influence of educational or other social pressures. That the informants are aware of such pressures is revealed by such secondary responses as "I don't know if that's correct, but it's what we say here" or "I shouldn't have said *snuck; sneaked* is the right word." Fieldworkers were instructed to record all such self-critical remarks; they are of great sociolinguistic value, especially when used alongside the informants' biographies.

Most of the questions seek to establish the regional or local name for a single object or idea. For example, qu. R2 briefly describes a dragonfly and asks for its name. To this question 79 different replies were given, among them *snake feeder* (chiefly N Midl, also S Midl), *snake doctor* (chiefly Midl, Sth),

1. *Linguistic Atlas of New England (LANE),* by Hans Kurath et al. (Providence: Brown University, 1939–1943).

2. *A Dictionary of American English on Historical Principles (DAE),* ed. Sir William A. Craigie and James R. Hulbert (Chicago: University of Chicago Press, 1938–1944).

3. *American Dialect Dictionary (ADD),* by Harold Wentworth (New York: Crowell, 1944).

4. The WELS questionnaire, revised, was published in 1953: Frederic G. Cassidy and Audrey R. Duckert, *A Method for Collecting Dialect, PADS* 20.

5. The ADS had referred to the projected dictionary, over the years, as "American Dialect Dictionary," but in 1944 Harold Wentworth had preempted this title. Actually, the state of dialect in the United States makes the present title more appropriate.

mosquito hawk (chiefly Sth), *spindle* (coastal NJ), *ear-cutter* (NH, WI). Open questions were necessary when a whole class of objects had to be referred to: "What different kinds of oak trees grow around here?" (qu. T10). Informants might name as many as 20, or none at all, but at least the best-known kinds of oak in each region would usually be mentioned, including a number of local folk names, such as *pin, post, Spanish, chinquapin, overcup, shim, chair bark oak.* More than 130 names for oaks were proffered.[6]

Because the phrasing was so important, the questions were printed in a preliminary form and tried out in the first 75 QRs. In the final revision, some low-yield questions were dropped, a small number of new ones added, some troublesome ones rephrased. The QR was then printed and used without further change in the remaining 927 communities. As noted, the yield was enormous; the data gathered on living American speech are unequaled elsewhere. Nor does *DARE* exhaust them as a linguistic resource: they contain a great deal of unexploited data on syntax, for example.

The QR is not perfect, however. As Jules Gilliéron noted after making the *Atlas Linguistique de la France,* a questionnaire, to be appreciably better, would have to be made *after* the fieldwork had been done.[7] In the nature of questionnaires, the question, if properly phrased and understood, and the answer, if responsibly given, should ideally produce a reversed definition. For example: "What do you call a container for coal to use in a stove?" Responses: *coal bucket, hod, pail, scuttle,* and so on. Reversed, this becomes a definition: *scuttle,* a container for coal to use in a stove. The method works relatively well for simple material objects like coal scuttles, less well for abstract things or emotional matters.

Questions intended to elicit one part of speech, or one form of a verb, were often answered in another: qu. GG34a, "To feel depressed or in a gloomy mood: He has the _____ today," aiming at a noun, got the reply "feels blue" or "in low cotton." To qu. X6, "If a person's lower jaw sticks out prominently, you say he's _____," one informant replied "box chin"; the question, intended to elicit an adjective, produced a noun. This kind of switched response served as a check in making the questions: they had to be simple and idiomatic to keep from misleading the respondent, whose reply, unless hesitant or obviously uncertain, was a sound guide to his or her normal syntax or idiom.

The section of the questionnaire covering wildflowers proved unsatisfactory: it is difficult to describe a wildflower briefly in nontechnical terms with assurance that the informant will visualize the intended one. To compensate, a special questionnaire was devised, keyed to color photographs.[8] Each picture was shown to the informant and the response recorded in a special list. Since this greatly increased the fieldworker's burden, it could not be carried out in more than a few communities, but it did furnish a substantial and more accurate body of regional wildflower names.

Communities

It was decided that one thousand communities could be investigated in the five years for which support was assured. (This is a somewhat looser mesh than that of the Linguistic Atlases, but in areas where they can be compared, findings have corresponded well.)[9] Communities were chosen in each state, the number proportional to the population and taking

settlement history into account. (The planners of *DARE* were fully aware that linguistic variation does not go by states. Population statistics and settlement history are usually published by state, however.) The aim was to choose relatively stable communities, distributed according to the states' composition, and communities of various types, so that the aggregate would reflect the makeup of each state's population. Five community types were established:

1. *Urban:* a specific section within a metropolitan area, with a population usually in the thousands within a total of a million or more.
2. *Large city:* a section within a large nonmetropolitan city with a total population in the hundreds of thousands.
3. *Small city:* a city independent of any metropolitan attachment, with a population in the tens of thousands.
4. *Village:* an independent town closely attached to its surrounding rural area, with a population in the thousands.
5. *Rural:* an area with unconcentrated population — farm dwellings, small crossroads settlements — and a population in the hundreds.

DARE recognized as a "community" any group of people living fairly close to each other and sharing the same commercial facilities, social organizations, and the like. Even within metropolitan areas such communities, or subcommunities, exist with a sense of focus based on ethnic, religious, and other characteristics. Contrariwise, quite small independent rural communities, though close together, may keep themselves apart on similar grounds. (For details about the *DARE* communities see the List of Informants.)

Fieldworkers

After a short period of preparation, data gatherers were sent to the chosen communities to find informants and get them to answer the QRs. These fieldworkers were chiefly graduate students trained in English language and linguistics and able to handle phonetic transcription; a few undergraduates and faculty members were also among them. The Chief Editor used the QR and interview method himself, comparing them with Atlas practices and seeing what details needed revision.

It was the task of the fieldworker, sent to the designated community, to find an informant who would answer the questions in the QR. It usually required more than one informant to complete the QR, but since each was given a personal identifying number and every response is coded, responses cannot be misattributed. For each informant a page of biographical information was made, including name, address, social factors (sex, race, age, education), amount of

6. In such lists there is much duplication of widespread names such as *white oak, black oak, red oak, live oak;* many others are named only once. The coverage is therefore not as full as for questions about a single object. Nevertheless, open questions collect classes of words that could not be covered singly.

7. "Le questionnaire . . . pour être sensiblement meilleur, aurait dû être fait après l'enquête." *Etude de Géographie Linguistique,* Pathologie et Thérapeutique Verbales, 1. (Bern: Librairie Beerstecher, 1915), 45.

8. The photographs were taken from the best book available at the time: Homer House, *Wild Flowers* (New York: Macmillan, 1961).

9. *DARE* averages 20 communities per state, ranging from 86 (NY) to 2 (NV); 20 states have more than the average, and 31 have fewer than the average. The Linguistic Atlas coverage is more intensive and affords the less populous states more than their proportional share.

travel, chief occupations, associations, family background on both sides, a brief description of the community, and a description of the informant's speech and attitudes toward language. These facts have greatly helped the editors to evaluate the data. It was also the responsibility of the fieldworker, in choosing informants, to attempt to balance social factors overall for his or her geographic area. Fieldworkers were closely monitored so that such matters could be controlled, and each fieldworker's first QR was checked critically before the worker was permitted to continue. The total number of fieldworkers was 80: 51 men and 29 women.

One question—a minor one as it proved—had to do with Black informants and fieldworkers. Would a Black fieldworker establish a closer relationship with a Black informant than a White fieldworker could? To test the possibility, Black informants were interviewed by both White and Black fieldworkers, but no significant difference in the results was detected.

The *DARE* interview method was based on that of the Linguistic Atlas but with some innovations. It served remarkably well. Fieldworkers were instructed to avoid suggesting responses. When, rarely, they had to prompt an answer, they were to mark it *sugg* for suggested. If they heard something of linguistic interest in an informant's free speech, they were to mark it *con* for conversational. If the informant said "We don't have that here," the fieldworker wrote *NH* for not here; if there was no response, he wrote *NR*. If the fieldworker had doubts about the response, he marked it with a question mark. If he was quite certain of something that others might doubt, he double-underlined it or wrote [*sic*]. Informants almost always took the procedure seriously, but a few were occasionally tempted to invent or to give humorous replies. Sometimes an informant misunderstood and answered at cross purposes. Fieldworkers were encouraged to make notes of any kind beyond the limits of the questions; their marginalia, quoted as *FW Addit* (fieldworker's additional information) have often proved quite valuable.

The fieldworker was also required to make a tape recording of each of his or her chief informants from each community speaking freely for twenty minutes or more—preferably on a familiar topic so that the speech would be relaxed and normal. To check on more formal pronunciation, the informant was also asked to read the children's tale "Arthur the Rat" (famous among phoneticians), in *DARE*'s revised version.[10] These two types of recordings permitted comparisons, often highly instructive, between an informant's speaking and reading styles. Tapes were made not only of the regular informants who answered the QR but also, as opportunity offered, by a number of auxiliary informants. In all, 1843 audiotapes were made; they constitute a unique record of American pronunciation, drawn from many levels of life and all fifty states. The tapes were studied over a two-year period not only for regional pronunciation but for other features, especially lexical ones that might go into the *DARE* files.

Informants

As with communities, the attempt was made to choose informants so that the aggregate would reflect the native population of the United States in its diversity. To qualify as a *DARE* informant, a man or woman had to have been born in the community represented or very close by, and could not have

traveled or stayed away long enough for his or her speech to be affected. If the family had been in the community for generations, so much the better. Informants with foreign-language backgrounds had to use English as their home language, whatever else they might be able to speak in the community. Biographical information was compiled for every informant who completed at least one section of a QR, but not always for auxiliary informants who happened to be present during an interview and furnished an occasional word. The choice of informants was generally balanced with an eye to the five social factors already mentioned—community type, sex, race, age, and education—but with a deliberate weighting toward older people. Folk language is traditional, and older people remember many things that young ones have never heard of. *DARE*'s 2777 informants included 1368 men and 1409 women, ranging in age from about 18 to over 90. Old informants (60 years and over) made up 66 percent of the total, middle-aged (40–59 years) 24 percent, young informants 10 percent. The levels of education were as follows: less than fifth grade, 3 percent; at least fifth grade, 24 percent; at least two years of high school, 41 percent; at least two years of college, 31 percent; unknown, 1 percent. The racial distribution was Whites 92.7 percent, Blacks 6.7 percent, American Indians .3 percent, Orientals .3 percent. In addition, 244 informants made tapes but did not answer the QR, and 21 answered the wildflower QR only. These people are listed separately at the end of the List of Informants.

It must be understood that no attempt was made to prorate every one of these factors state by state; to have attempted to use such precise criteria would have made the task virtually impossible. Further, neither the choice of communities nor that of informants was randomized; on the contrary, the intention was to maximize the collection of materials by going to the places and people most likely to furnish the largest amount of appropriate data.

Processing the Data

By 1970 the 1002 QRs had been completed, but the sheer quantity of material gathered had become a problem. If every question had elicited one response each time it was asked, there would have been 1,850,694 responses—but multiple answers brought the total closer to 2,500,000. The planners of *DARE* had realized from the first that the mass of data would be large and that computer processing must be considered. In 1965, however, though numerical computing was well advanced, the handling of alphabetic material was only beginning. Nevertheless, the collections were coded for sorting, filing, and other forms of processing, and fortunately, as the collection grew, computing methods also advanced. *DARE* was ultimately able to save much time because of this, and to develop its unique map-making capacity.

As the completed QRs began to come back from field-

10. The story was first used for phonetic study over a century ago in England by Henry Sweet. In this century it was adopted by W. C. Greet at Columbia University, who made phonograph recordings of it with his students from many parts of the United States (Victor and Victrola, "American Speech," Under the Direction of H. M. Ayres and Cabell Greet, Columbia University, nos. 65–76). At some point, the young rat, né Grip, was renamed Arthur, because phonetic variation would be greater in the latter name. For the *DARE* version of the text, see the Guide to Pronunciation, p. xliii.

workers, a group of graduate students — the modern counterparts of Dr. Johnson's amanuenses — were employed to prepare them for computer input. Every page of every QR had to be numbered and stamped with the informant's code, which consists of the two-letter state abbreviation plus the individual's designated number. Thus, for example, OH47 is informant 47 from Ohio; VA3 is informant 3 from Virginia. Also marked were the sections of the QR that each informant had answered. Assuming no undiscovered typographical errors, every response can thus be traced back to the QR in which the fieldworker first recorded it. Data from the QRs were then fed into the computer, and ultimately the entire collection was printed out, question by question, with the responses listed alphabetically and the codes given by state and numerical sequence. The editors then condensed this mass of printout, removing anomalies,[11] and it became the Data Summary, which will appear in the final volume. It still lists the QR questions in code sequence but now gives the responses in descending order of frequency.[12]

While the QRs were being processed, the other part of the *DARE* corpus was being gathered and put in order to form the Main File. This contains both oral and written, published and unpublished materials. Chief among published sources were *DN; PADS; American Speech;* the *Journal of American Folklore* and other folklore journals; the Federal Writers' Project state guides series; more than five hundred books of regional literature; and selected newspapers from every state, especially county and small-town newspapers. Under a grant from the American Council of Learned Societies, a special program was carried out in which 114 diaries were excerpted. These sources are generally accessible in good libraries.

In addition, *DARE* has used a large body of materials that are not generally accessible. Notable are the personal collections of Gordon Wilson and Joseph Hall, made over periods of about 35 years each and generously given outright to the project. They contain records of local speech respectively from the areas of Mammoth Cave in Kentucky and the Great Smoky Mountains in Tennessee and North Carolina, gathered directly from lifelong residents before the communities were dispersed and the areas made into national parks — communities therefore now forever gone. Other personal collections given to *DARE* include those of Atcheson L. Hench, Kelsie B. Harder, and Russell Tabbert.[13]

Special mention should be made of materials gathered for but not used in the *Linguistic Atlas of New England (LANE)*. Thanks to Raven I. McDavid, Jr., the original *LANE* workbooks were furnished to *DARE*. Similarly, the aluminum disks of New England (and other) speech recorded by Miles L. Hanley and Guy S. Lowman, Jr., in 1932–1934, among the earliest of such recordings, were transferred to audiotapes and the lexical items added to the *DARE* Main File.[14] (In 1984 these disks were archived in the Library of Congress.)

DARE also has several special files that are not otherwise accessible:

1. The WELS file, covering 50 Wisconsin speakers, with audiotape recordings of their speech.

2. The "Northup File" of natural history, with the folk names of plants and animals cross-referenced to their scientific names, and with bibliographical references to a large number of published sources.

3. The "Latest File" — an ongoing file of everything that continued to come in from a variety of sources after the compilation and computer indexing of the Main File. This began in a very small way but over the years grew to more than 70,000 items.

4. Letters from the public, often in response to news articles or radio or television appearances. Replies of this kind, though of varying quality, are often useful sources of information.

DARE fostered two studies of special vocabularies in the hope of gaining understanding of certain questions concerning regionality. The lexicon unquestionably varies regionally in widespread activities such as farming, housekeeping, fishing, and lumbering. It was decided to study two extensively practiced activities to check on possible connections with geography. The activities chosen were coal mining and tobacco growing and marketing. Mary Ritchie Key collected for *DARE* the vocabulary of tobacco growing in eight states, and Dennis R. Preston carried out the study of coal mining in nine states.[15] Both studies give evidence that certain features of occupational vocabulary are affected by general regional usage.

The *DARE* Maps

The method of coding every question in the QR, every response, every community investigated, every informant, and the most relevant social facts about each made it possible to

11. This was done always on the basis of the QRs. No evidence was rejected. Editors made spellings consistent, removed differences in fieldworkers' practices, and unified matters of form, such as the proper form for multiword phrases. The condensation was achieved by grouping together all responses with nine or more informants and itemizing only those with eight or fewer.

12. In general, the most frequent response is considered standard. When two alternate terms are used with nearly equal frequency, neither can be considered the exclusive standard. Examples are *twilight* and *dusk* (370 vs. 365 responses), and *neigh* and *whinny* (387 vs. 383 responses). All are used in every state; no one clearly dominates. All must be considered standard. With such synonymous pairs, however, there is usually a difference of geographical concentration: the areas of use overlap but are not congruent. Thus *whinny* is strong in the North, weak in the Southeastern and Southern states; *neigh* is much weaker in the North, more evenly distributed through the country as a whole. What we have here are regionally standard words.

13. Gordon Wilson, Sr., had made a card file of about 9000 lexical items, gathered orally from more than 225 local people, with exact biographical information, and with phonetic transcriptions, definitions and usage notes, and annotations showing in what dictionaries they were treated. In the 1940s he made many recordings of the regional speech. All his materials were put into the *DARE* Main File; the original cards and audiotapes are in Bowling Green at the Kentucky Folklore Society.

Joseph Sargent Hall's card file, also put into the Main File, consists of material from interviews with about 230 informants, with brief biographies and transcripts of audiotapes. Also very useful was his monograph, "The Phonetics of Great Smoky Mountain Speech," *American Speech* 1942, no. 2, pt. 2.

The Hench Collection may be consulted in the University of Virginia Library, Charlottesville. Kelsie Harder not only answered the WELS questions but also excerpted letters his mother had written to him during his army service — a valuable source for linguistic evidence from central-western Tennessee. Russell Tabbert, collecting data for a Dictionary of Alaskan English, put his collection at *DARE*'s disposal in 1980.

14. The tapes are in A. L. Davis's collection, with a copy in the ADS Archive, University of Massachusetts, Amherst. A full account is in the *DARE* archive: Margaret Waterman, "The Hanley Tapes," 1974.

15. The study of coal mining has been published, with an annotated glossary, in *PADS* 59.

display the data in ways helpful to the editors and to the user of the Dictionary. The most innovative of these computer-aided features are the maps that appear in the Dictionary as part of the treatment of strikingly regional words or phrases. Where a feature was found, and where it was not found, can be very quickly understood from a map. Manual mapmaking is laborious; mapmaking by the *DARE* computer method is so rapid and easy that it became an investigative tool of great value in the editing process.

The *DARE* maps are populational, not areal — that is, they say nothing about square miles of territory but show the number and distribution of the informants' (speakers') communities, this number having been prorated to density of population, state by state. The states appear on the *DARE* map as nearly as possible in their proper spatial relation to one another, and in something like their proper shape, but each is enlarged or diminished according to the prorated number of communities in it. Within each state a rectangular space is assigned to each community; these too are placed generally in their proper relative positions. The symbol indicating a specific response is then printed in the rectangle assigned to the community where that response was given. This means that empty spaces are also significant: in those communities some other response was given (unless, as occasionally happened, the question was not answered). For further detail, see The *DARE* Map and Regional Labels, pp. xxiii–xxxv.

Maps are used only when the data warrant them; if responses are very few or very many, a map is not a useful means of dealing with them. Each map is placed as close as possible to the treatment of the word or phrase being illustrated. The map is an aid to visualizing the region of use; details of use are in the accompanying text.

Maps are based on information derived from field collecting using the *DARE* questionnaire. They are always geographical, but some are also used to show social features. Some social maps, and some contrastive maps showing more than one word or phrase, appear in the Map Section of the final volume.

Inclusions and Exclusions

The title of *DARE,* had it been made in the seventeenth century, might have been "A Dictionary of That Part of the English Language that is commonly spoken in the Colonies of North America in Sundry Regions, Provinces, Tracts, Districts, and smaller Settlements, but not in that People as a Whole, Detailing its Varieties as Projected by the Native Folk." Condensed rather drastically for twentieth-century digestion, it came out as *Dictionary of American Regional English.* This leaves the key word "regional" in need of sharper definition. What does *DARE* include, what exclude, and how are the lines drawn?

DARE does not treat technical, scientific, or other learned words or phrases — or anything else that could be considered standard.[16] Beyond that general exclusion, two criteria have guided the editors: (1) Any word or phrase whose form or meaning is not used generally throughout the United States but only in part (or parts) of it, or by a particular social group, is to be included. (2) Any word or phrase whose form or meaning is distinctively a folk usage (regardless of region) is to be included. Some terms are widespread without prevailing

nationally (compare the maps for *baby carriage* and *baby buggy*),[17] while others may be current in a single community (for example, *arab,* street vendor, is used only in and around Baltimore). Regionality, then, as defined in *DARE,* bears no relation to the size of the area of use, so long as it is less than total.

For *DARE,* folk usage is that which is learned in the home and in the community, from relatives and friends, not from schooling, books, or other outside forms of communication. It is traditional and largely oral; it includes anything that can be called "dialect" in the United States. But here the definitions of traditional scholarship break down. For the *English Dialect Dictionary,* and for the European dialect atlases, especially in the nineteenth century when the folk speech was being collected, a large part of the population was still firmly localized away from cities, not greatly affected by schooling, living in traditional ways, and keeping traditional speech. Not so in the United States, and less and less so in the twentieth century, when easy communication, mechanized farming, public education, the growth of cities, widespread migration, and most recently the tremendous success of radio and television, have disrupted even the more traditional communities, blurring former lines of dialectal division and creating a relative uniformity in speech. Even if most people still stay in one place and keep up their former ways of life, change, or pressure for change, is everywhere. And change in ways of life brings with it accelerated change in language. In the old-world sense there is little "dialect" spoken in the United States. Yet it is possible to see more "uniformity" than actually exists. In both city and countryside, distinctive regional and social differences in pronunciation, vocabulary, and syntax persist, as *DARE* shows.[18]

DARE does not cover artificial forms of speech such as Boontling (the private language used by the inhabitants of Boonville, California, and its environs) or any whose purpose or effect is to exclude the general listener. Criminal argot is of this kind, an in-group code intentionally separated from the general idiom. *DARE* includes such terms only if they have escaped into wider use. The same policy is followed with occupational language, sometimes called trade jargon, which only its users understand. For example, the hobo word *gump,* a chicken, is not known otherwise, but the jazz musician's *cool* has long since come into wider use. *DARE* does not

16. In a relatively small number of instances a standard word is entered (though not itself illustrated) so that nonstandard terms may be listed together under it. Examples: *anhinga, blue jay, fringed polygala.*

17. *Baby carriage* clearly prevails throughout New England and is found, though less commonly, in the rest of the country; *baby buggy,* also widespread, though sparse in the Atlantic states, becomes the prevalent form from the longitude of Ohio westward to the Pacific. In other words, the areas of use overlap: people who say *baby buggy* probably have heard and would understand *baby carriage,* and vice versa. One term is no more standard than the other. Yet there is a significant regional difference in their areas of concentration, and *DARE* must include them. Such borderline cases are relatively few, however: the great majority of the words and phrases treated in *DARE* are more narrowly local, and many are totally unknown outside their own small areas. Not many people outside New York City know that a *sliding-pond* is a playground slide; not many readers of these lines would be able to gloss *skillypot, grass onions, jockey-box, work brickle, genavy.*

18. Dialect differences are most distinctive as to pronunciation, secondarily as to vocabulary; syntactic differences are relatively few and less conspicuous.

attempt to cover restricted occupational vocabularies—especially when the occupation is highly specialized or esoteric, such as the sexing of chicks or the wrapping of cigars. On the other hand, the vocabularies of widespread occupations such as farming, housekeeping, mining, lumbering, cattle-raising, which involve entire communities and even entire regions, are necessarily included.

Regionality is affected also by the nature of some occupations. The language of sailors, for example, folk-created and traditional, is geographically limited to use on ships wherever they go. Along seacoasts it is brought ashore and enters landsmen's usage. But on ships sailing all over the world it becomes to some extent international. In reading sea literature for *DARE* the attempt was made to collect only such nautical usages as were distinctly American. Even so, regional labels that normally apply ashore do not apply to sea terms. To a lesser degree, perhaps, the language of other kinds of transportation—railmen's, truckers', even airline employees' talk—is not regionally limited and is likely to be much the same everywhere, a mixture influenced by the geographical sources of its practitioners. Again, treatment in *DARE* depends upon whether such occupational terms are known only within the groups or have escaped into more general usage.

The language of children's games has been treated fully in *DARE* because it is almost entirely of folk origin and of oral preservation, and because it shows considerable regional variation. It represents a notable combination of the traditional with many local differences. The same game, judging by the name, may be played by different rules, whereas the same game, judging by the manner of play, may have several different names. An example of the latter is the once familiar stick-and-peg game, variously called *cricket, jippy-sticks, kitty-cat, knick-knock, peeny, peewee, tee-toe, whip-stick,* and so on. There is no question that many variants are regional—see, for example, the maps for *Andy-over, Annie-over, anti-i-over,* and *Antony-over.* The language of children's games preserves, in disguise, many quite ancient words and ways of speech.

The language to be collected was, then, any form of American English as spoken in the various regions of the United States. This necessarily included American "Black English," but *DARE* went further and included Gullah, the only creole English now surviving in the continental United States, and Hawaiian "pidgin," actually creole. As English-based folk dialects spoken by native Americans, these deserve inclusion.

A persistent problem was that natural regionality often comes into counterplay or conflict with linguistic regionality. A topographic feature, a kind of plant, a climatic condition, a bird or other animal form not found everywhere in the country, cannot have variant names where it does not exist. Folk names will be found for it only where it does exist. The most common folk name will usually become the standard one outside its natural area or for those who hear or read about it but do not know it directly. Within a natural area, however, there are often several local folk names (not always clearly distinguished), and *DARE* includes these. For example, the *pasqueflower* is also called *windflower, gosling, badger,* and other names; the most common name for *Cathartes aura* is *buzzard,* but it is also called *carrion crow, turkey vulture, red-neck buzzard,* and so on. The scientific

identification of folk names is not always possible, but *DARE,* assigning special editors to this task, has corrected many vague or erroneous attributions of the past (see, for example, the entries for *apache plume, congo snake, fly poison plant,* and *rosemary pine*).

The widespread confusion in the use of the term *slang* has led to its rejection by *DARE.* Popularly, *slang* is used to cover any kind of unconventional usage, especially if it has been condemned in schoolrooms. Attempts to define it are as numerous as their attempters, and while there is some core of agreement, the word remains so imprecise that its use as a scientific term has been challenged. Finding *slang* too indefinite and too often used merely to condemn, *DARE* dispenses with it and uses more definitive and objective labels.

Some other distinctions need to be noted. Speakers of all kinds have, in the well-known phrase, a vocabulary of use and a vocabulary of recognition. That is, everyone has some acquaintance with a great many more words than he or she habitually uses. *DARE* seeks, through the spontaneous immediate answer to a QR question, to find out what word the informant (and presumably others in his or her community) does habitually use. For the country as a whole these may be relics or innovations, commonplaces or rarities. *DARE* attempts to label them appropriately. Obsoleteness is difficult to prove; many present folk terms were once standard or literary, but have gone out of general use. Yet some are revived, or, like the coelacanth, are thought to be extinct and then are suddenly discovered alive and well. Accordingly, *DARE* uses the label *obs* sparingly, normally if the most recent example found is a century or more old. With few exceptions, terms have not been entered unless they are in current or recent use. As a part of *DARE*'s function as a historical dictionary, changes of status are also attended to: the decay of formerly widespread usages, the spread of formerly restricted usages, folk terms that have made their way into written or literary use.

It need hardly be said that borderline cases have been numerous. Most teasing have been questions arising from insufficient evidence. A single word or phrase given by an informant, not followed up at the time by the fieldworker, and nowhere found again, may nevertheless have the ring of genuineness. Here the decision to keep or to reject must rest on the editors' "feel" for the language, their experience and judgment. At the collecting stage it was appropriate to err on the side of inclusiveness; the collector could not know what other support for a strange form might be waiting in the files. At the editing stage, however, forms had to demonstrate their right to inclusion. Putative loanwords had to be found in actual use in English-language contexts. Apparent individualisms had to have analogs that made them seem likely to be more generally used. In the *DARE* entries, a double dagger (‡) is prefixed to entries that may well be folk usages but for which conclusive evidence has not been found.

Finally, because *DARE*'s purpose is to describe regional and folk language as it is, there has been no bowdlerizing or expurgation. What has been found has been entered if it meets the general criteria for inclusion. One recalls the story of the ladies who commended Dr. Johnson for omitting from his Dictionary all *naughty* words. "What, my dears!" replied the Doctor, "then you have been looking for them?" If the reader sets out to look for them, he will certainly find in *DARE* the normal vulgarities and crudenesses of everyday American speech. To have rejected these would have been to distort the picture. Ethnic nicknames and epithets, often derogatory but also used humorously or, among friends, even affectionately, have been included or excluded according to the same criteria as any others. Usage notes often call attention to the social status and emotional effect of such expressions. The reader is enjoined to distinguish firmly between what *DARE* labels say and opinions that may be expressed in quoted sources. Quotations must be read historically, in light of their dates; many express attitudes that are now obsolete. In any case, *DARE* quotations are chosen for their linguistic value, not for the opinions their authors may express.

Treatment of Entries

DARE entries are normally presented in three parts: the opening section, the definition, and the supporting quotations. The first part, using many abbreviations, conveys the basic information about each entry: headword or -words, part of speech, pronunciation, variant forms, etymology, geographic range, usage, cross-references, and editorial notes. In the second part, meanings (if there are more than one) are numbered, with alphabetic subdivisions if necessary (see, for example, the treatment of *be*). Because standard senses are not normally treated, the historical sequence of senses is sometimes not obvious. Editorial notes are included when deemed necessary. Boldface type is used for cross-references and to give prominence to dates and regionality.

Entry Form

Most entry forms are single words, but there are also numerous compounds and phrases. All are entered under the standard spellings or under established dialect spellings, with cross-references at variant spellings.[19] Entries for which there was no established spelling—those recorded by phonetic transcription or on disks or audiotapes—have been spelled by analogy with the most similar standard spellings and with due attention to etymology. Examples: *ooch over,* to move oneself along (as on a bench); *patalca* and *kitarber,* variants of *catalpa.*

Entries are strictly alphabetical, except for spaces or punctuation marks, which are taken into account only as they move an otherwise identical form down the alphabet.

As to the vexing question of whether to spell compounds open, hyphenated, or solid *(coal hod, coal-hod, coalhod),* *DARE* follows Webster's *Third New International Dictionary* except in the rare instances when new evidence indicates that a form should be spelled otherwise. (Quotations from written sources of course reproduce the spelling of the source.)

When variant forms are almost equal in frequency, they are equally usable as the headword. The choice then rests on such considerations as etymology, alphabetic convenience, and clarity of presentation. When one variant is clearly more frequent, it is taken as the headword; the others are listed after part of speech and pronunciation, preceded by "also." Example: *cabbage pea . . .* Also *cabbage bean.*

Such entries as the plant name *angel's-trumpet* raise the problem of the apostrophe. Attested written forms are *angel's,*

angels', and *angel;* spoken forms are ambiguous—there is no way of knowing how the speaker would have written them, and the fieldworker's spelling only reflects personal graphic habits. To present all these small variants economically, *DARE* uses swung dashes and parentheses to indicate repeated and optional elements. Example: *angel's-trumpet . . .* Also ~ *trumpets, angel(s') trumpet(s).*

Phrases are entered under the word or words that form the stable core, though other parts of the phrase may vary. For example, *he wouldn't know beans from barley* may also have other initial pronouns *(she, they),* other auxiliaries *(can't, doesn't),* other verbs *(tell),* and especially other contrasters *(beans from butter, B from a bull's foot,* and several more). The phrases are entered with the core words first, as *beans, not to know* and *B from (a) bull's foot, not to know,* with appropriate references to other phrases of the same meaning entered elsewhere in the alphabet, such as *A from B, not to know.*

Parts of Speech

The traditional nine parts of speech are indicated by abbreviations immediately following the entry forms: *n* noun, *pron* pronoun, *adj* adjective, *v* verb, *adv* adverb, *art* article, *prep* preposition, *conj* conjunction, *intj* interjection. Other labels used occasionally in this position are *exclam* exclamation, *part* particle, and *phr* phrase.

Noun includes single words and also compound nouns and those derived by conversion from other parts of speech. Examples: *arrow, arrow chase, Adam-and-Eve root, boiled owl, carry-in.* Phrasal nouns are treated simply as nouns. Virtually any noun can be used attributively; *DARE* notes attributive uses that seem significant.

Verb is a general label; transitivity or intransitivity is not indicated unless there is immediate need to note the distinction. The definition makes it evident whether the use being illustrated is transitive or intransitive. Nonfinite verb forms are labeled *infin* infinitive, *pple* participle, *vbl n* verbal noun, *ppl adj* participial adjective.

Verb phrase is the label for a verb regularly construed with an adverb and forming a loose unit with it: *fall away, hog down.* It is also used for set verb-plus-object phrases, such as *eat dried apples,* to become pregnant.

Adjective phrase, adverb phrase, preposition phrase, and *conjunction phrase* are so labeled. Examples: *dry-headed,* adj phr; *side by each,* adv phr; *over against,* prep phr; *as how,* conj phr.

Distinction is made between *interjection* and *exclamation:* the interjection stands apart from syntactic context and has no formal syntax of its own, whereas the exclamation has its own syntax, surface or underlying, and may be joined to the adjacent contextual unit. Examples of interjections: *ooch! phooey! Crimanetly!* Examples of exclamations: *Andy-over! King's ex! Carry me out with the tongs!*

A few entries could not be classified with any of these labels. They have morphological status as affixes (prefix, infix, suffix) or inert phonetic units. Examples: *a, ker-, -ma-.*

---

19. Except in rare cases, the headword spellings follow those of Webster's *Third New International Dictionary of the English Language* (Springfield, MA: Merriam, 1961).

Pronunciation

Pronunciation is indicated for entries only when *DARE* has supporting oral data, recorded in phonetically written form or on phonograph disks or audiotapes. No pronunciations inferred from spellings are given. Pronunciations follow the indication of part of speech and are given in broad International Phonetic Association (IPA) characters enclosed in vertical lines. Pronunciation-spellings—those in which writers have sought to suggest actual pronunciation through spelling—are also listed fully. The reader may infer the pronunciation from these, up to a point; but such inferences must not be taken as equivalent to recorded speech.

Pronunciations given phonetically or by various kinds of respelling in the quotations are generally retained. Forms of transcription earlier than IPA are updated to it; otherwise, as with other quotations, they are unchanged. The only variances from IPA characters are č, ǰ, š, ž, used respectively for IPA tʃ, dʒ, ʃ, ʒ according to current widespread American practice. Instead of the IPA shift signs ⊥, ⊤, ⊢, ⊣, *DARE* uses ˆ, ˇ, ˒, ˓, following Linguistic Atlas practice, to indicate positions of articulation respectively higher, lower, farther back, and farther forward from the positions of "cardinal" vowels. Narrow IPA transcriptions, when given, are placed in brackets. Occasionally, to avoid misunderstanding, a hyphen is used to indicate that a disyllabic vowel cluster rather than a diphthong is intended, as in *carry* |ˈkæ-i|.

Variant Spellings

Variant spellings from written sources are recorded in *DARE* for reasons of both pronunciation and orthography. Up to a point, as noted, past pronunciations can be inferred from past spellings; sometimes, also, variant spellings make it possible to follow the stages through which new or unfamiliar words acquire settled forms.

DARE differentiates among spelling-pronunciations, pronunciation-spellings, and eye-dialect spellings. A *spelling-pronunciation* is one in which a speaker follows the written form of a word, pronouncing all the letters even though some of them are properly silent or have other values than the ones he or she gives them. For example, the speaker may pronounce the *l* in *palm, calm, balk, chalk,* or give full value to all the letters of *boatswain* and *colonel*. Spelling-pronunciations are a byproduct of the shortcomings of English orthography, which has more than one value for many letters or combinations of letters and more than one way of spelling the same sound. Past methods of teaching spelling in the schools by letters and syllables have contributed to the production of many spelling-pronunciations in folk and regional speech. In this instance, writing brings about changes in speech.

Pronunciation-spellings are those in which a writer tries to represent the nonstandard pronunciation of a speaker. The word *calm,* with the regional variants |kɑm|, |kæm|, |kam|, |kɑrm|, |kɔlm|, appears in writing not only in the standard way (which will do for any variant but does not specify the one used) but also as *cam, ca'm, carm, cyaam.* Some of these may merely indicate that the writer was a bad speller. Others may be attempts to reflect some nuance of a specific variant. Most often the writer is trying to characterize an individual, fictional or not, through his speech. Some writers do this very badly, with apostrophes sprinkled wherever the pronunciation does not agree with standard spelling; others succeed better by using a simple "phonetic" representation. To indicate an "r-less" pronunciation of *through,* for example, *th'ough* signals to the eye, which then translates for the ear—a two-step process; *thoo,* by contrast, signals directly to the ear. In each case, of course, context confirms the intended meaning.

Eye-dialect spellings are those which an author uses intentionally to suggest that a character's speech is substandard and that the person is illiterate, even though those spellings correspond to pronunciations that are perfectly standard. *Cum, slay, thawt* for *come, sleigh, thought* are phonetically correct but suggest that the character has had little schooling. Eye-dialect was widely used as a device of folksy or popular humor by such nineteenth-century writers as Artemus Ward and Petroleum V. Nasby, and in this century by Ring Lardner.

The gradual settling down of a new word, often a loanword from a foreign language, into an accepted American form may sometimes be followed through variant spellings. For example, Spanish *vaquero,* borrowed into southwestern usage, includes among its variant spellings: 1827 *bakhara;* 1847 *baccaro;* 1862 *bukkarer;* 1873 *buccahro;* 1889, 1910 *buckayro;* 1890 *buckhara;* 1900 *buccaroo;* 1907, 1919 *buckaroo.* These are pronunciation-spellings that attempt to render the foreign word as said by speakers of American English. Its form varies until a standard spelling becomes established—in this case with a peculiar adaptation to the influence of *-aroo* or *-eroo,* a suffix that became popular in the early part of the twentieth century.

Though some of the spelling variants recorded may individually seem trivial (and a few no doubt are), they have value in the aggregate. As noted, they may help to show changes in pronunciation, naturalization of loanwords, processes of word formation, and other historical developments in the language. Alternate spellings are usually listed alphabetically, but are sometimes grouped by similarity of form.

Etymology

DARE does not give etymologies for all entries. Those well treated in general dictionaries need not be repeated. Compounds or phrases whose components are standard in form and sense, such as *Abolition War, about to die, acting pole, bullneck, bluejoint,* need no formal etymology. When appropriate, *DARE* indicates how the phrase differs from the sum of its components. Here etymology and definition work together.

Etymologies and explanations of origins appear in square brackets. They are given, when possible, for certain types of entries:

1. Words and phrases that most other dictionaries do not treat. Examples: *Abe Lincoln fence, bobbasheely.*

2. Foreign loans—words or phrases—usually traced only to the proximate source language. Examples: *aber nit, abri, aguardiente, apee.*

3. Any entry in which an existing etymology can be improved. Examples: *abiselfa, appaloosa.*

4. Entries in which nonstandard forms or meanings require explanation. Examples: *ace-boon-coon, amarugian, anchor ice.*

A distinction is sometimes made between *echoic* and *imitative* (abbreviated *imit*), echoic referring to names derived by similarity of sounds, imitative referring to instances in which some feature other than sound is prominent. Thus *zoom* would be called echoic; *zig-zag* would be called imitative.

When an origin is unknown but *DARE*'s research has turned up possibly relevant information, this is guardedly recorded as an aid to future research.

If a headword has been found to be a trademark, listed in *The Trademark Register of the United States,* this fact is stated in the etymology or in a note. *DARE*'s entries reflect actual observed usage and make no judgments as to the legal status of the word.

Geographical Labels

Areas within the United States are popularly understood in different ways; there is no general agreement on what such terms as *North, South, Middle West* include or exclude. In the interest of uniformity, the editors of *DARE* devised a list of geographical divisions for use in the entries. These geographic labels are often qualified with *esp* (for *especially*) or the somewhat stronger *chiefly.* In quoted matter, of course, the authors' labels have been respected. (See The *DARE* Map and Regional Labels, pp. xxiii–xxxv, for the list of geographical divisions and their abbreviations.)

Usage Labels

As noted earlier, the editors of *DARE* have sought to keep usage labels and notes factual and objective, to describe usage as it is (or as it was during the period of primary data collecting, 1965–1970), never to say how it should be or to express the editors' opinions about it. (Other people's opinions, frequently expressed in the quotations, often throw light on changes of attitude over the years.) Emotionally loaded labels such as *illiterate, vulgar, provincial* have not been used.

Labels give information of four kinds: (1) amount of use, as *rare, occas, freq, usu;* (2) currency, as *obs, arch, old-fash, hist;* (3) type of user, as *rural, Gullah, grade-school educ;* (4) manner of use, as *joc, derog.*[20] (All abbreviations are identified in the List of Abbreviations, pp. clii–clvi.)

The basis of many of *DARE*'s usage labels is furnished by the social factors mentioned earlier: the informants' age, sex, race, level of education, and type of community. When these correlate in some notable way, varying from the average, a label is called for. For example, in qu. H35, for *dropped eggs,* 83 percent of the responses were from old informants, whose percentage in the total of informants answering was 70 percent; thus the label *somewhat old-fash* was clearly called for. In qu. U27, for *beau dollar,* 79 percent of the responses were from Black informants; thus the label *esp freq among Black speakers* was justified. These are statistical statements with no further overtones.[21]

Labels are given to help the reader to a clearer sense of the geographic or social status of a word or phrase: they cannot be expected to be exhaustive or absolute. They are valid as far as *DARE* evidence goes — no farther. Fuller detail can be found in the data base in the *DARE* archive.

Quotations

Like other historical dictionaries, *DARE* uses dated quotations to support the definitions. In choosing which examples to use, the editors have preferred "defining" quotations to those in which the word or phrase being illustrated is merely mentioned or used in passing. Original sources have been preferred to derivative ones. As to the choice and number of quotations, the editors have sought to give the earliest example found in American use, at least one per century, and a late or recent one. Quotations should also illustrate and justify the geographical label or note. Quotations are placed in brackets (as in *OED*) when they do not exactly illustrate the entry because of differences in form, sense, or region of use.

An important feature of the documentation is the use of oral sources. Examples taken from *Dialect Notes* are among the earliest obtainable; these and the *PADS* word lists have all been taken into the files. *American Speech* has been fully read. The Linguistic Atlas materials (including unpublished workbook notes taken by the fieldworkers) have been used copiously, as have the Hanley recordings and the *DARE* audiotapes. But of course the most valuable part of the entire corpus is the Data Summary made from the *DARE* QRs. These oral sources are examples of unedited, genuine American usage by native speakers throughout the nation whose regional and social attachments are known.

Next in value are such written materials as diaries, personal letters, unedited accounts of travel, adventure, and daily life; these are as close to actual usage as any written materials can be. After these come regional literature written by authors who knew their regions thoroughly and did not romanticize or stereotype their characters. Among older writers of this kind might be mentioned Edward Eggleston and Joel Chandler Harris; among more recent ones Marjorie Kinnan Rawlings, Julia Peterkin, and William Faulkner. But many regional writers have accepted stereotypes and clichés, have exaggerated or overdone the regional speech, or, worse, have got it wrong. The editors have been wary of this class of literature and have quoted from it cautiously if at all.

With travel accounts a difficulty arises. Suppose a native of Massachusetts writes about his journey to Texas. Two regions and two kinds of usage are involved here: the traveler's home idiom as he writes, and the Texan usages on which he comments. The editor must keep these apart.

Quotations of data from *DARE* QRs are necessarily formulaic, and therefore may not be immediately easy to read. But one soon becomes accustomed to them, and as they contain the most valuable data, the reader is advised to be patient. They give the question asked in the QR, with its code, and list the responses, with the codes of the informants responding so. The question is sometimes given in full, sometimes abbreviated, sometimes only referred to, according to evident need.

20. *Jocular* implies intentional or self-aware joking by an individual; *humorous* implies a wider consensus.

21. The computerized map-making program works out statistics on which quite exact application of usage labels may be based. For example, it sorts on the exact numbers and identities of informants responding with the specific word or phrase being examined, and on each of the five social factors about each informant. For examples of the use of such statistics, see *animal* 1, *all in, all the,* and their usage notes.

(For the full text of the QR, see pp. lxii–lxxxv.) Every question code is an implicit cross-reference to the Data Summary in the final volume, which lists every question and every response. *DARE* quotations therefore display in condensed form the best oral evidence, to which other sources are additional.

The Bibliography in the final volume lists every source quoted in *DARE*, giving the reader all the facts necessary to track a quotation back to its origin. To save space, short-titles are used in the *DARE* entries. Short-titles retain the first or most important noun or verb and enough other words to ensure identification. Examples: Simon Ansley O'Ferrall, *A Ramble of Six Thousand Miles through the United States of America,* becomes **1832** O'Ferrall *Ramble;* William Prince, *A Short Treatise on Horticulture,* becomes **1828** Prince *Horticulture.*

Dating of Quotations

No problem of dating arises in quoting from a book that was printed only once, but other situations are more difficult. For example, one may want to quote from a record dated 1695 that was first printed in 1705 and is now accessible only in a 1970 facsimile of an 1870 printing. The Bibliography in the final volume will tell all this, but the *DARE* entry will never give more than two dates, the earliest and latest: here 1695 (1970). This is enough to identify the source and say that the original record was not used, but the facsimile. Any single date tells the reader that the original source was used. When a single date is given, pagination of the quotation is from that edition; otherwise it is from the edition published at the second date.

This is the general rule, but a number of complexities had to be dealt with. *DARE* uses five standard forms for indicating dates:

1. **date**
2. **date** (date)
3. **date** in date
4. **date** Author *Title [for/of date]*
5. **[any of the above]** Author *Title* (as of [date])

1. The date of the earliest edition in which the quotation appeared. Also used for microform reproductions. Example: **1938** FWP *Guide MN.*

2. The date of the first edition of a work plus that of the later edition from which the *DARE* quote was taken. Situations in which this format is used include: (*a*) a later printing from the same plates (not from reset type); (*b*) a new edition with complete resetting of type, therefore usually with different pagination and possible revisions in the text; (*c*) a photofacsimile edition of an earlier work; (*d*) a posthumous edition of undated material, using *ante* with the author's date of death as the date of composition, as in **a1862** (1865) Thoreau *Cape Cod;* (*e*) a diary, with the two dates referring to the dated entry and the date of publication.

3. Matter quoted in a later publication: the first date is that of the quoted matter, the second that of the work in which it is quoted. Examples: **1789** in 1889 Washington *Writings;* **1637** in 1850 CT (Colony) *Pub. Rec.* This form is used for letters or speeches quoted in a biography, collections of government documents and historical society publications, collections of

an author's works known to have been published earlier, and in similar situations.

4. A work in which the title contains a date other than the date of publication. This occurs in almanacs and in the annual publications of societies and governmental departments. In the *DARE* reference the first date given is the date of publication. Examples: **1869** *TX Almanac for 1870;* **1850** MI State Ag. Soc. *Trans. for 1849.*

5. Material recollected from a time considerably earlier than the date of the publication. Example: **1962** Morison *One Boy's Boston* 54 **MA** (as of 1900).

Cross-references

In a dictionary that pays special attention to variance of forms, there is necessarily a high proportion of cross-references. In *DARE*, variants are cross-referred to the entry under which they are treated. Many cross-references within entries call the reader's attention to synonyms, related forms, or analogous forms. Any cross-reference in bold type is to a *DARE* entry.

Definitions and Sense Divisions

The intention in *DARE* definitions is to use standard but simple words, to avoid the technical or recondite. When, as occasionally happens, a word of popular speech suits the purpose better than a standard one, it may be used as well. Natural objects (plants, animals) are defined in everyday terms and also, when identifiable, with their Latin genus-species names. When the only evidence is in a single quoted source, or when the source gives an adequate definition, no other is usually given.

Definitions may be preceded by: (1) grammatical notes such as *also attrib, constr as pl, in passive usage;* (2) delimiters such as *In marble play, Of cattle, Among loggers;* (3) semantic or stylistic indicators such as *fig, transf, in ironic use.* Synonyms may be defined simply by cross-reference to the best-known equivalent elsewhere in the Dictionary.

The division of senses is a necessity of presentation. Most sense divisions are easily set up on the basis of the quotations at hand. But there are inevitably a number of borderline cases, which must be put on one side or the other of the line. Where they are put rests ultimately on the editors' perception, experience, and feel for the language.

The sequence of senses is ideally historical and logical, but many terms, especially those of everyday speech, exist in use long before their first known appearance in writing. Senses may also develop simultaneously in more than one direction. When dated evidence is lacking and more than one sequence of development seems logical, it is often impossible to establish the exact filiation of senses. Clear presentation is then the best resort.

James Hulbert, second editor of the *Dictionary of American English,* wrote in his almost poetic "Consolation of Lexicography":

I know of no more enjoyable intellectual activity than working on a dictionary. Unlike most research, lexicography rarely sends one on fruitless quests. One does not devote days, months, or even years to testing an hypothesis only to decide that it is not tenable, or to attempting to collect evidence to prove a theory only to have to conclude that sufficient facts are no longer in existence to clinch it. It does not make one's life anxious, nor build up hopes only to have them collapse. Every day one is confronted by new problems, usually small but absorbingly interesting; at the end of the day one feels healthily tired, but content in the thought that one has accomplished something and advanced the whole work towards its completion.[22]

This picture is broadly true, but the tint is too rosy. To attempt a work of the scope of *DARE* is to give hostages to imperfection. The task of covering all the regional variation in American English is beyond human accomplishment. Compromise is inescapable. On occasion, contrary to Hulbert's optimistic words, editors have spent days, months, and even years in tracking down individual items, correcting bibliographic references, finding original editions, establishing correct authorship, dates, pagination, the exact wording and spelling of entries — only to have the findings condensed into a few inconspicuous lines no different, in appearance, from the easy and obvious entries. The editors have repeatedly had to settle for inconclusiveness when in their hearts they felt that further evidence could be found "out there somewhere" if only they could abandon all else and go in pursuit of it. But that way madness lies — or at least the guarantee that a tangible, published dictionary will never be made. One of the things a lexicographer must learn — sometimes painfully — is how and when to let go. If all facts are equal in the eyes of Science, the realities of the world are fraught with inequality.

In *DARE* the editors have sought to produce a work of useful scholarship, one also that will testify to the wondrous variety and creativeness of human language, and specifically of the English language as it is used regionally in the United States. To this task they have given many years, much thought, and much hope. May *DARE* prove a worthy monument to their labors.

22. J. R. Hulbert, *Dictionaries British and American* (London: Deutsch, 1955), 42–43.

The *DARE* Map and Regional Labels

by Craig M. Carver

How to Read a *DARE* Map

The *DARE* map is designed to illustrate visually the regional distributions of words and phrases elicited by the questionnaire. Though it resembles the conventional areal map of the United States, it appears distorted because it displays population density rather than land area (see figure 1).[1] This makes Nevada, for example, a tiny wedge of a state, while New York, in reality half the size of Nevada, is a large elongated shape one quarter of which is the bulb-like protrusion of New York City. Despite their abstracted shapes, the states have the same general spatial relationship to each other on the *DARE* map as they do in reality, with a few exceptions, such as Maine's boundary with Massachusetts and the missing boundary between Wisconsin and Iowa. Also, Alaska and Hawaii are joined to the mainland.

The overall area of the map is almost completely filled in by the 1002 *DARE* communities, which are usually symbolized as large dots (figure 2), each dot representing a single community where one questionnaire was completed. Each community is assigned a position on the map defined by a set of x-y coordinates, which the computer uses to locate and plot the individual informant responses.

Figure 3 displays the communities on a conventional map and, when compared with figure 2, shows how the *DARE* map is distorted. On the conventional map, the communities are concentrated in the most populous areas of the country, so much so that to fit them all on the map we have had to enlarge the scale of the northeast. At the same time the communities of the western states are widely scattered. The *DARE* map, by contrast, compresses the western states while expanding the more populous eastern states, creating a relatively uniform distribution of communities across the map. This makes it easier to see the clustering of the communities where a given response is recorded.

Figure 4 shows, in their relative positions, the informant numbers for all 1002 communities where questionnaires were answered. Although there is only one questionnaire per community, more than one informant was usually involved, each answering different sections. For example, Colorado informants 11–16 each answered parts of the questionnaire for Durango. The informants' numbers were assigned arbitrarily as the questionnaires were returned and have no other significance.

In some rural areas more than one village or post office address constitutes a single community. For example, informants 34 and 35 in Maryland, who answered different sections of the same questionnaire, were from the towns of Still Pond and Chestertown in Kent County. At the same time,

large cities constitute many communities. New York City, for example, has 22 *DARE* communities and thus 22 questionnaires (see figure 9).

Because most of the map's area is composed of juxtaposed communities, the space that normally exists between towns is absent. Durango, for example, is sandwiched between Moab, Utah (UT11–15) to the west and Trinidad, Colorado (CO22–27) to the east (see figure 4), when in reality they are hundreds of miles apart. Not every space on the *DARE* map, however, indicates a community. There are empty areas that do not correspond to any actual geographical feature, such as the gap to the south of Durango. These gaps are created by the inherent difficulty of superimposing a horizontal-vertical arrangement of communities on a map shaped to resemble the United States. With the exceptions of the small areas in southwestern Ohio and to the east of Tennessee and the stylized portions of Maine and Massachusetts, the largest empty spaces on the map occur in the West, where this difficulty is increased by the higher ratio of land area to population. Although the empty areas are apparent when the map is filled, as in figure 2, they are virtually invisible on the maps in the body of the Dictionary (which are never completely filled), and they are not large enough to interfere with the regional distributions.

Though the *DARE* map roughly retains the relative locations of the communities, there is some inevitable deformation. Figure 5 gives an idea of the degree to which some communities have been displaced from their actual locations. The numbers on the *DARE* inset in figure 5 are not informant numbers but place markers for the 28 communities in Virginia and the 5 in the District of Columbia and its suburbs; they correspond to the numbers on the geographical map.

Although the *DARE* map is generally oriented according to the compass points, the specific spatial relationships among the communities are occasionally skewed. For example, in the *DARE* version of Virginia in figure 5, Charlottesville (9) is east of Buckingham (8), whereas in reality it is almost directly north of Buckingham. Perhaps the greatest distortion occurs in the relationship between Fredericksburg (11) and Capron (12), which on the *DARE* map are displaced east and west of each other separated by Washington, D.C., when in actuality Fredericksburg is more than a hundred miles north of Capron.

Such distortions at the local level, however, become less important at the regional level. From *DARE*'s satellite view,

1. To be more specific, the map is distorted to reflect the number of *DARE* Informants in each state, this number being roughly proportional to the state populations as of the 1960 census.

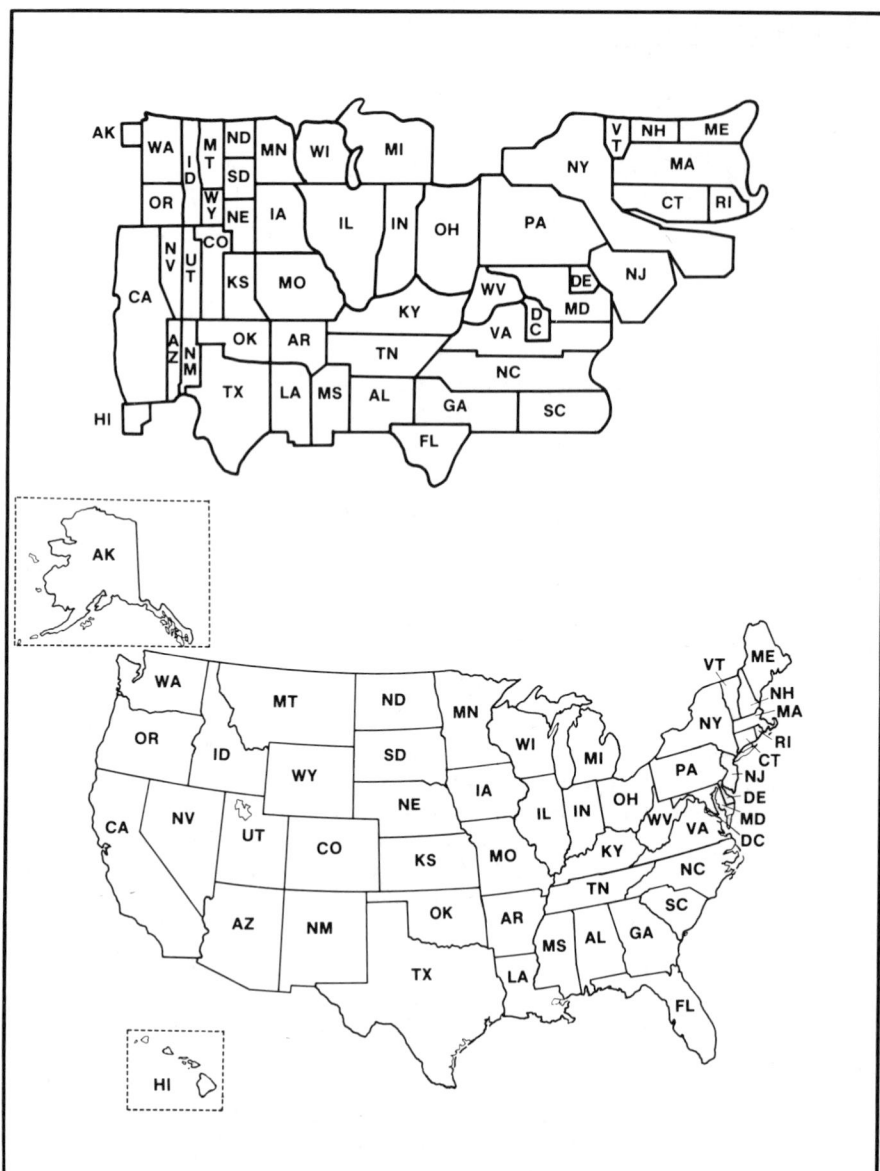

Figure 1. The *DARE* map of the United States with a conventional map for comparison.

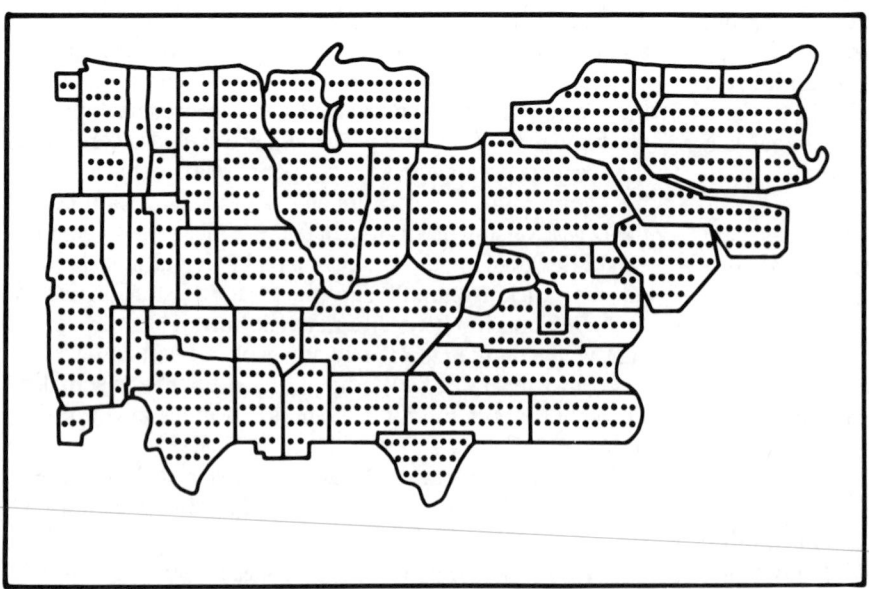

Figure 2. *DARE*'s 1002 communities on the *DARE* map.

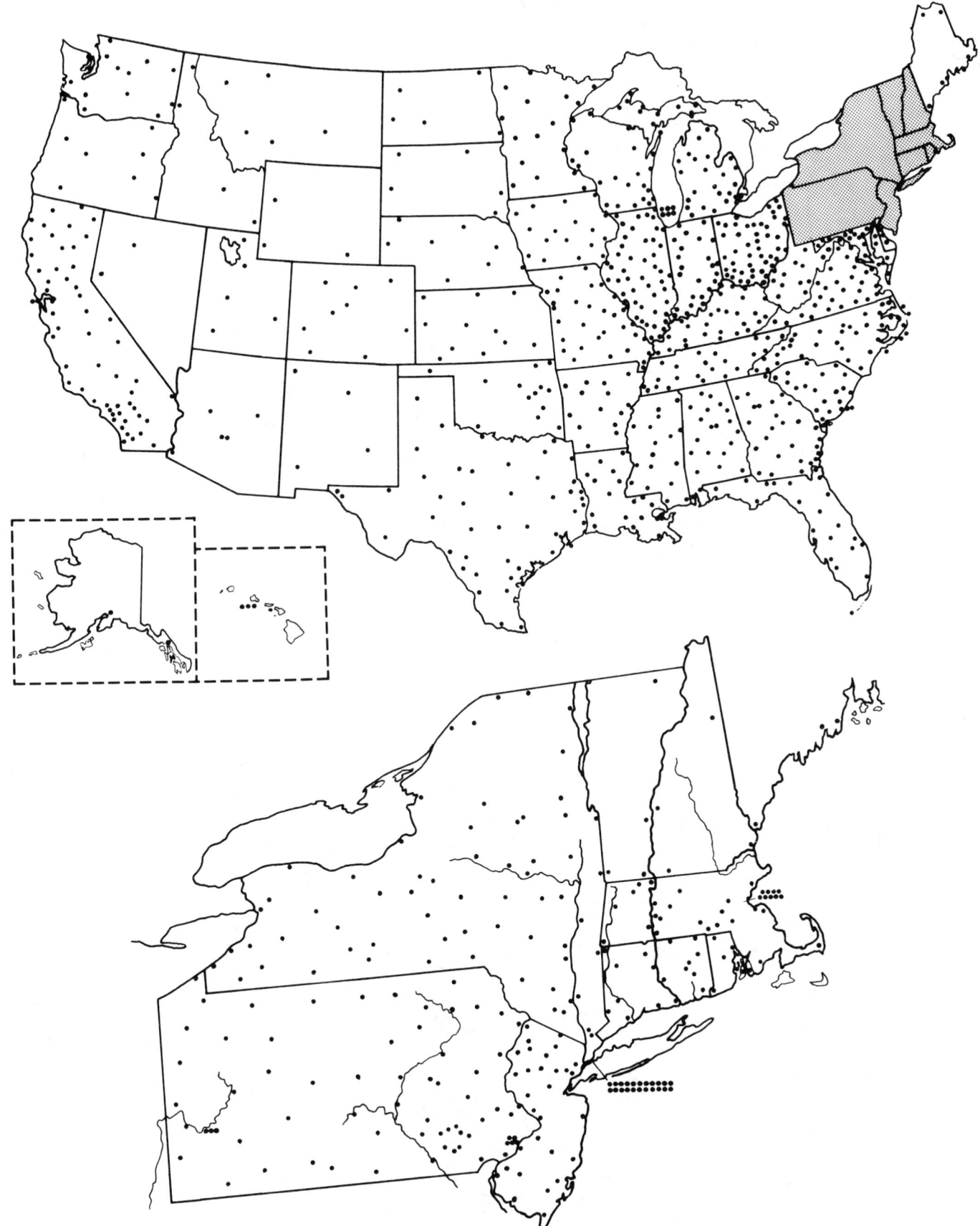

Figure 3. *DARE*'s 1002 communities on a conventional map.

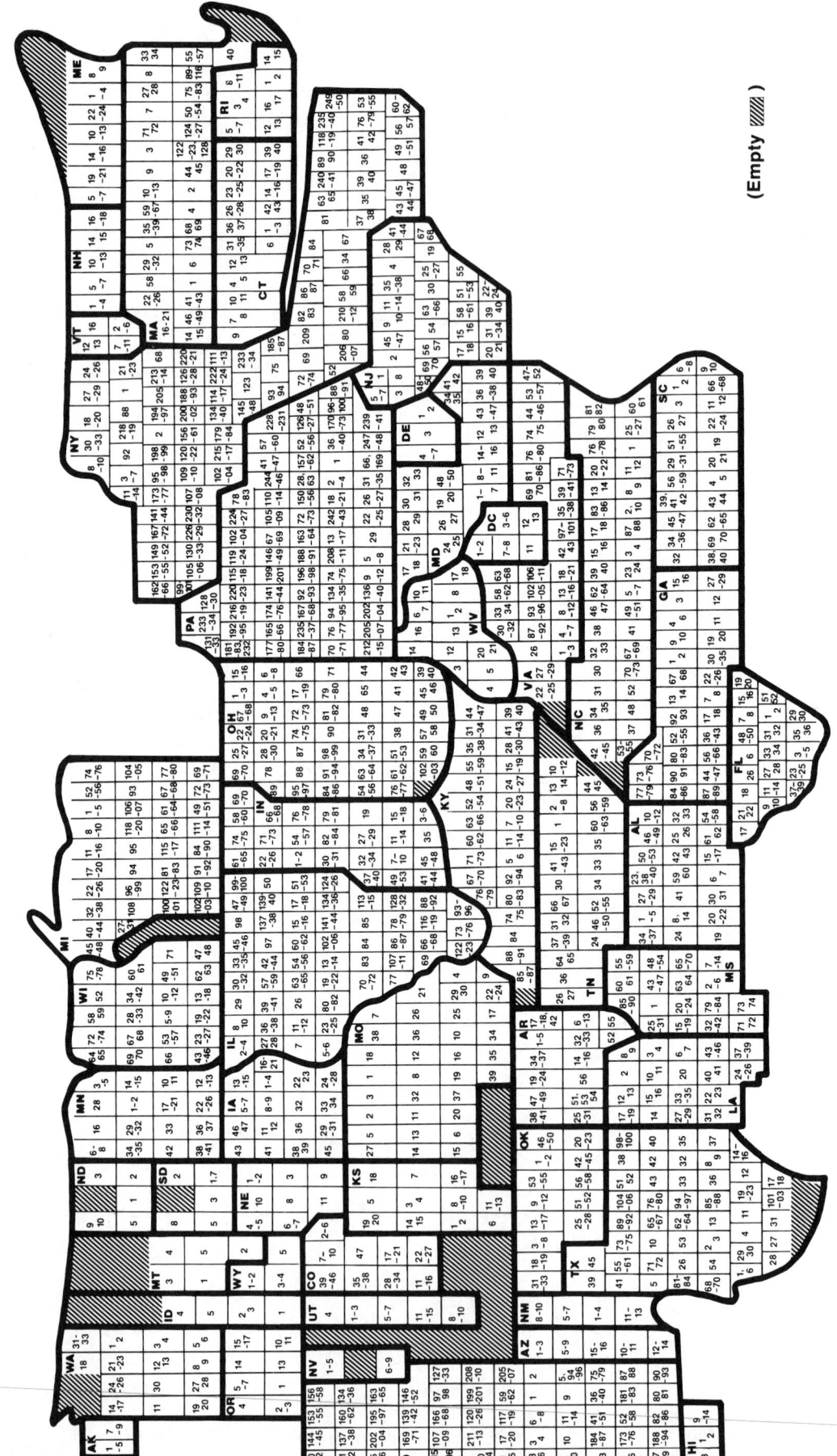

Figure 4. Informant numbers for the *DARE* communities.

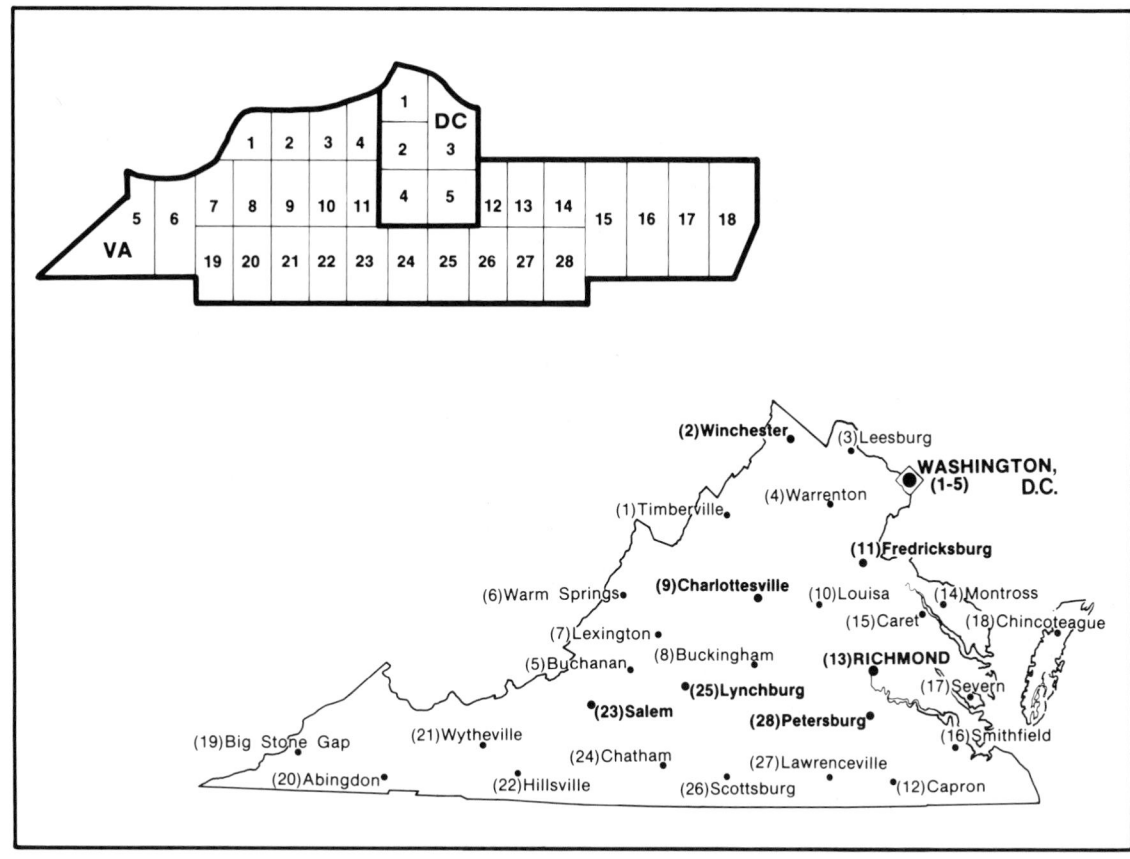

Figure 5. The relative positions of *DARE* communities in Virginia and Washington, D.C. The numbers correspond to the same communities on both the *DARE* map and the conventional map.

the details recede and a new picture unique in linguistic geography emerges—a view of the *nationwide* distribution of American speech. It is at this level that the *DARE* Map is intended to be used in conjunction with descriptive labels to give a reliable impression of the overall regionality of a word. For purposes that require a more exact picture, such as the drawing of isoglosses (lines showing boundaries formed by the distribution of particular features), community locations can be transferred to a conventional map with the aid of figure 4 and the List of Informants.

Figure 6 illustrates the general reliability of the *DARE* map by comparing the ways a regional expression is plotted on it and on a conventional map. Both show the distribution of informants who gave the response *mosquito hawk* (= dragonfly) and those who gave the response *skeeter hawk* to question R2. The distribution of this expression is a paradigm for the southern dialect region. The *DARE* map gives a concise visual statement of the overall clustering of responses. For example, it is just as easy, if not easier, to see on the *DARE* map as on the conventional map that the variant *skeeter hawk* is especially concentrated in the South Atlantic states from North Carolina to northern Florida. The *DARE* map is essentially a scatter diagram that economically illustrates degrees of clustering—that is, degrees of regionality.

The clustering of *mosquito hawk* is a notably tight one, but even here the map reveals some stray responses deep in

Yankee territory. As the user of this Dictionary will soon realize, language refuses to stay within strict geographical boundaries and almost always ignores political or state boundaries. Some of the apparent anomalies here, however, can be explained using the field records.

Occasionally, when an informant was slow in responding to a question, the fieldworker would mention a number of possible responses. The fieldworker was instructed, in such cases, to mark "sugg" (suggested) beside the response in the questionnaire. The two anomalous instances of *skeeter hawk* in Ohio are both marked "sugg" in the questionnaires. The unexpected occurrence of *mosquito hawk* in Minnesota, Wisconsin, and Michigan is explained by the biographies of the informants: four of these informants frequently vacationed or wintered in Florida or other parts of the South; it was there, very probably, that they picked up this memorable name for the dragonfly. Such supplemental information is provided in the *DARE* entries when appropriate.

Figure 7 shows the relationship between the two maps for a regionally more complex set of responses. It also illustrates a fairly common situation in linguistic geography: the complementary distribution of synonymous expressions. In this example the synonyms are folk names for any of various wasps that build a nest of mud: *mud dauber, dirt dauber,* and *mud wasp* (qu. R20). Each of these expressions is used in a more or less distinct region which forms the counterpart of the other

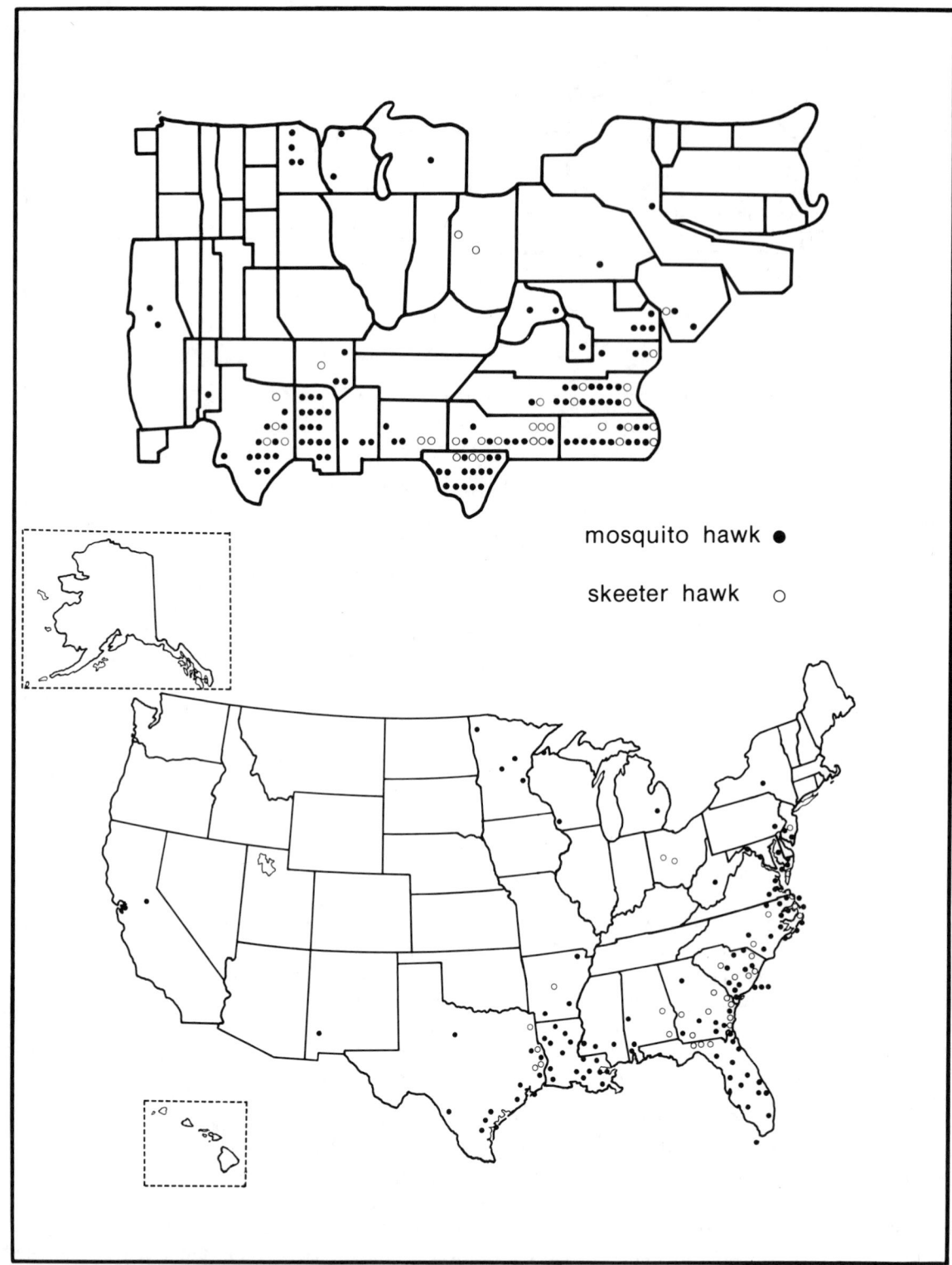

Figure 6. The distribution of *mosquito hawk* and *skeeter hawk* on
the *DARE* map and a conventional map.

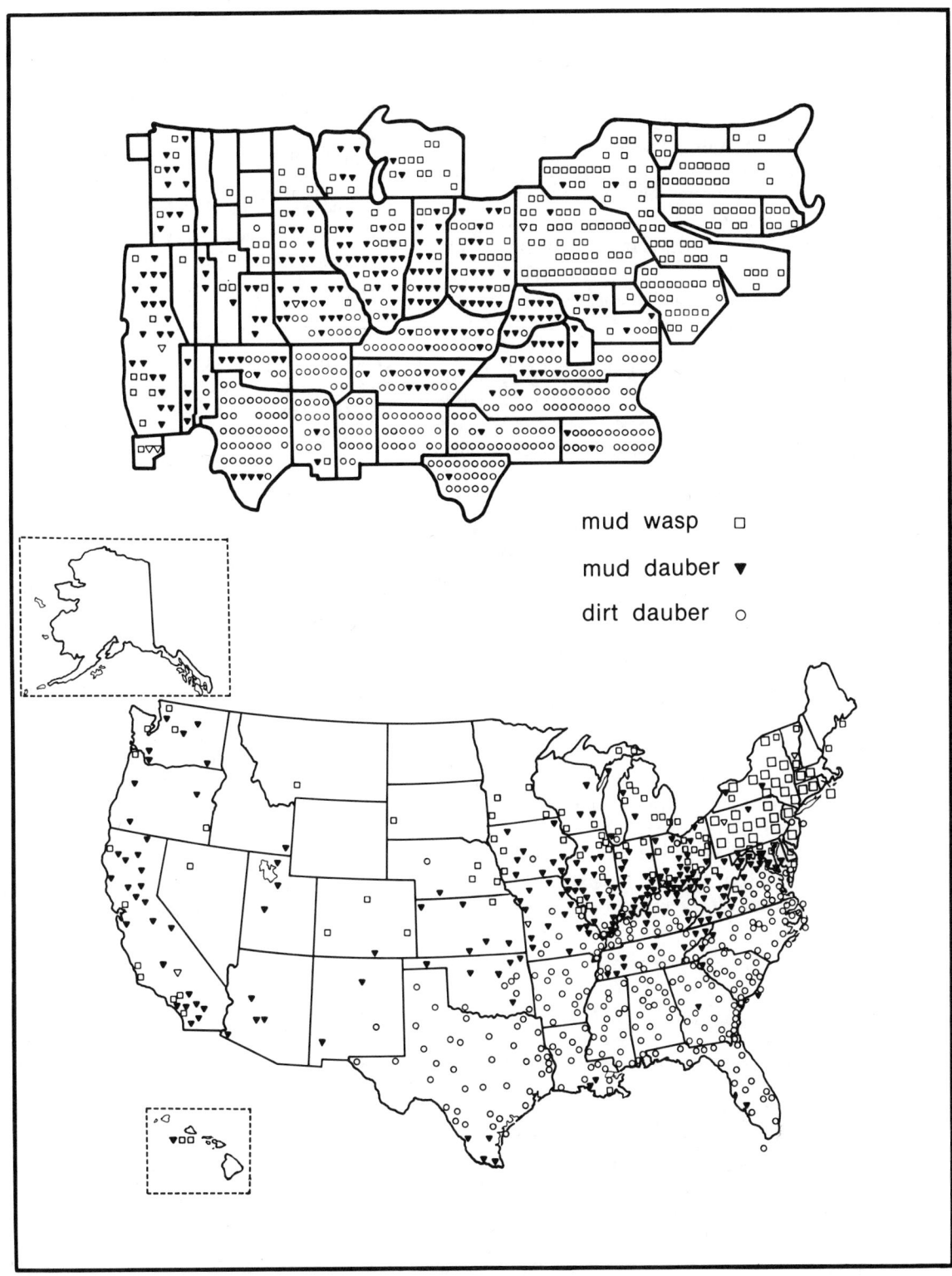

Figure 7. The distribution of *mud wasp, mud dauber,* and *dirt dauber* on the *DARE* map and a conventional map. When *mud wasp* and *mud dauber* occur in the same community, an open triangle is used. If *dirt dauber* occurs in the same community as either of the two other responses, only *dirt dauber* is indicated. On the conventional map, the largest square symbol represents four or more communities where *mud wasp* was recorded; the smaller square (as in Vermont) represents two or three communities.

two.[2] In this case, *mud wasp* is primarily used in the North and North Midland; *mud dauber* primarily in the Midland and West; and *dirt dauber* in the South and South Midland.

DARE handles complementary regionalisms with a combination of cross-references and contrast maps. In the entry for *mud dauber,* for example, both *dirt dauber* and *mud wasp* are cross-referenced. In addition, the reference "See Map and Map Section" directs the user not only to the map accompanying the entry but also to the Map Section of the final volume. That section of the Dictionary contains maps that plot two or three regionally contrasting terms like those in figure 7. It also contains maps that illustrate the regionality of a response in terms of one of the five social variables: community type, age, education, race, and sex.

Figure 8 maps the response for *beau dollar* (= a silver dollar) in terms of the race of the informants. It shows that this expression is used primarily by Black speakers, since 27 of the 34 informants were Black compared to the much smaller percentage of Blacks in the entire sample of *DARE* informants. But more important, it reveals that the spread of this term northward is the result of the migration of southern Blacks into the urban North. All of the informants in the North who gave the response *beau dollar* are Black and live in large cities, namely, Chicago, Cincinnati, Philadelphia, and Trenton.

Figure 9 shows the locations of three types of *DARE* communities: urban, coastal, and mountain, as well as selected geographical landmarks, relating the *DARE* map to the conventional map of the United States. For example, what appear on the *DARE* map to be coastal communities in Mississippi are not, and what appears to be inland territory is sometimes actually coastline, as in North Carolina. In addition, unified geographic features sometimes appear to be split, as is the case with the Missouri Ozarks, the South Carolina Appalachians, and New York's Hudson Valley. Some cities—Boston, Charleston, New Orleans, St. Louis, and Los Angeles—are also divided on the map.

DARE Regional Labels

A *DARE* entry may present evidence of regionality in two ways: with a selection of quotations, which also illustrate history and usage; and with the findings of the fieldwork as represented in maps accompanying certain entries. The maps do this by plotting the locations of all the informants who gave the same or closely variant responses to the questionnaire as summarized in the *DARE* quotation.[3] When their locations, represented by dots, cluster together or are clearly denser in one area than others, the response is considered regional. In this way the maps give a visual definition of the specific region of use.

DARE uses 37 basic labels to indicate regionality. In the Dictionary entries these regional designations appear in bold type. Because few regional expressions strictly confine themselves within sharp boundaries, *DARE* labels are often modified by such terms as *chiefly, esp* (especially), or a combination of formulas, such as *widespread, but esp common in* a particular region, or *throughout U.S., exc* (except) *in* a particular region. These modifiers cannot be quantified precisely: they merely serve to indicate generally the degree to which a particular distribution of informants conforms to the regional designation. They can be defined only in relation to one another.

Chiefly means that most of the evidence, of which there is a significant amount, is confined to a particular area; consequently, on the maps the informant responses tend to cluster

2. Although this situation occurs with some frequency, the reader should beware of assuming that for every expression used in only one part of the country there is a regional counterpart in other sections of the country. Often a nonregional term, one that is standard or widely known, is a counterpart.

3. When the number of informants given is greater than the number of dots on the map, this is usually because some informants gave the same response to more than one question, and are thus counted more than once. On the map, however, the community of each informant is represented by only one dot.

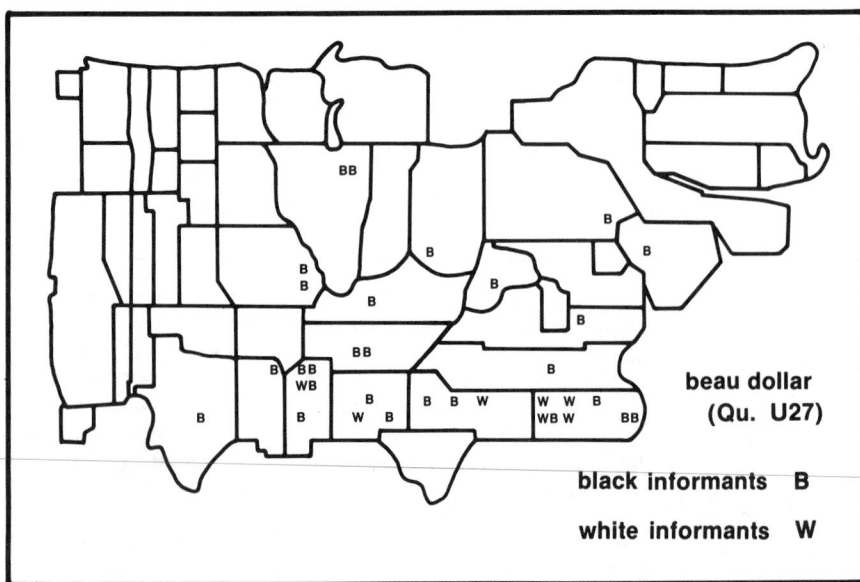

Figure 8. Social map of the distribution of *beau dollar.*

beau dollar
(Qu. U27)

black informants   B

white informants   W

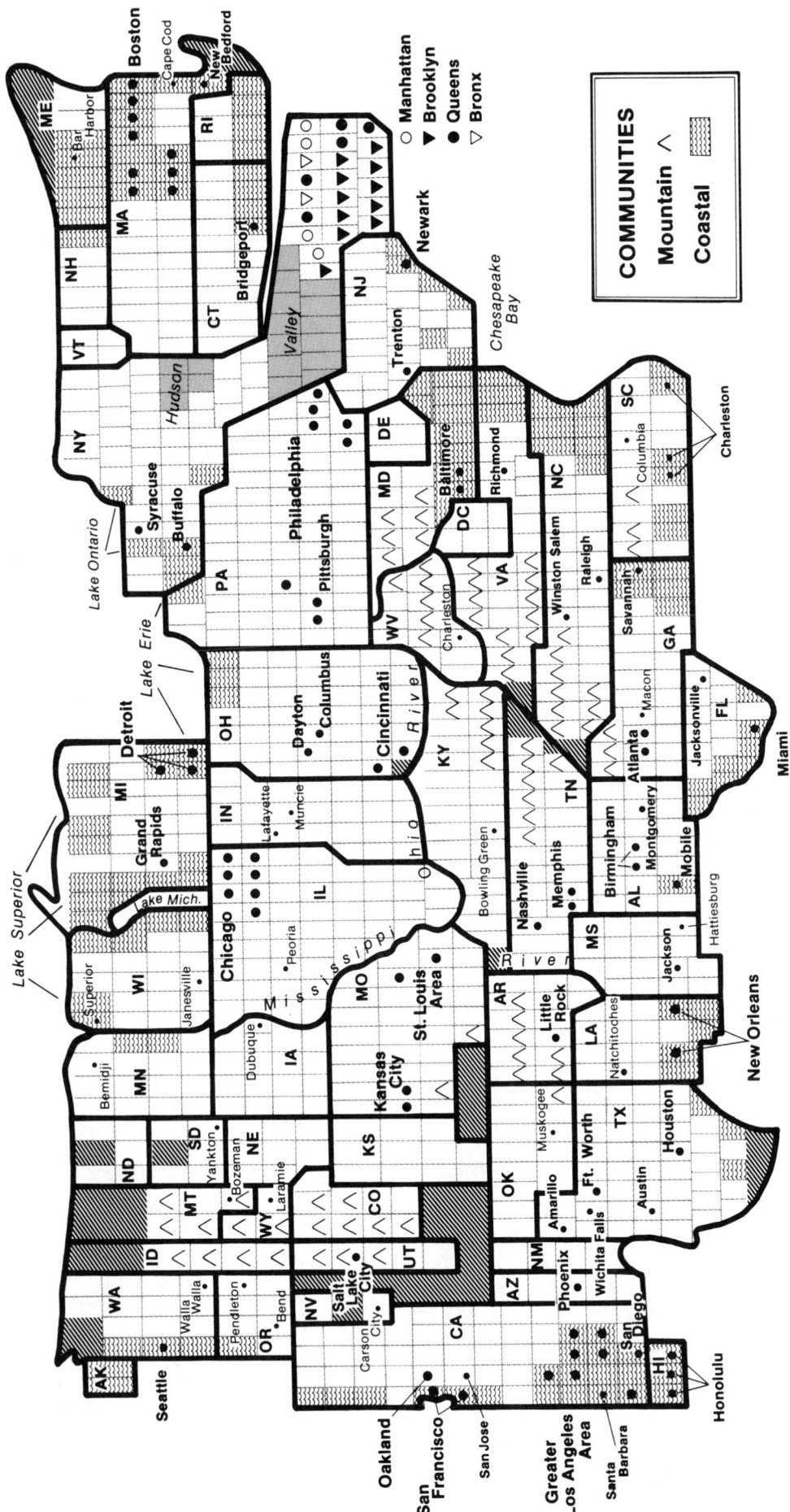

Figure 9. Locations of urban, coastal, and mountain *DARE* communities.

in a relatively dense pattern, and even the more scattered locations are generally near the area of high density. For example, *mosquito hawk* is labeled *chiefly Sth.*

Especially (abbreviated *esp*) indicates somewhat weaker regionality than *chiefly,* because there is less evidence confined to the given area. For the maps this means that the clustering is not as dense. The exceptions are often distant or widely scattered. *Esp,* however, is only occasionally used by itself to modify a label. More often it is used in formula with other modifiers to designate a subregion within a larger context, as *chiefly Nth, esp NEast.* It is also often used with *widespread* or *scattered,* as in *widespread, but esp Sth, S Midl. Widespread* means that an expression has considerable currency virtually everywhere in the United States. *Scattered* indicates wide dispersion but low density.

To designate subdivisions of states the following scheme is used:

North

nw	cn	ne
cw	c	ce
sw	cs	se

West ← → East

South

Each state is thought of as having three divisions in each of the four compass directions, plus a central area. The state code is two capital letters, as used by the U.S. Postal Service; the subdivisions are in lower-case letters preceding the state code. For example, the subdivisions of Ohio can be referred to as nwOH, cnOH, neOH, and so on. These abbreviations are often used with the quotations, to name a speaker's home area or to indicate the locale of the quotation. They are rarely used as regional generalizations for the whole entry. Because the states are not rectangular, the scheme is only approximate, but for purposes of *DARE* it takes the reader reasonably close. With a living language, and without knowing the responses of every speaker, it would be misleading to pretend to any higher degree of exactness.

The definitions of the regional labels themselves are primarily based on the organization and evidence of the Linguistic Atlas projects and on general regional patterns that commonly occur in the *DARE* maps. For example, Upper Midwest and North Central States are based on the organization of the Linguistic Atlas; North, North Midland, South Midland, Midland, and South (among others) are based both on *DARE* maps and Linguistic Atlas fieldwork; and South Atlantic, Appalachians, Mississippi Valley, and West Midland are based almost exclusively on the *DARE* maps. Settlement patterns and the geographical evidence from quotations are also used in defining areas.

For those regional labels which are inductively derived from fieldwork, the intent is to define broadly the geography of particular usages, not to discover the specific boundaries of dialect regions. In other words, the regional label in an entry is a description of the actual distribution of a usage (insofar as it is known) *in terms of predefined sections of the country.*

Maps 1–8 illustrate the regions specified by *DARE* labels. The following alphabetical list defines all the regional labels and tells which map illustrates each region.

Appalachians: neAL, nGA, eKY, wMD, wNC, cPA, wSC, eTN, wVA, WV. Map 3

Atlantic: CT, DC, DE, FL, GA, MA, MD, ME, NC, NH, NJ, NY, PA, RI, SC, VA, VT. Map 5

C Atl (Central Atlantic): DC, DE, eMD, sNJ, ePA, eVA. Map 4

Cent (Central): AR, KS, MO, NE, OK. Map 7

Delmarva: DE, eMD, eVA. Map 2

Desert SW (Desert Southwest): AZ, seCA, NM. Map 3

Gt Lakes (Great Lakes): nIL, nIN, MI, MN, nwNY, nOH, nwPA, WI. Map 7

Gulf States: AL, FL, LA, MS, eTX. Map 4

Inland Nth (Inland North): Nth except NEng. Map 8

Inland Sth (Inland South): AL, KY, MS, TN. Map 7

Lower Missip Valley (Lower Mississippi Valley): AR, sIL, wKY, LA, MS, sMO, wTN. Map 5

Mid Atl (Middle Atlantic): MD, NC, SC, VA. Map 6

Midl (Midland): N Midl, S Midl, DC. Map 8

Missip-Ohio Valleys: IA, IL, IN, KY, MN, MO, OH, WI. Map 6

Missip Valley (Mississippi Valley): AR, IA, IL, wKY, LA, MN, MO, MS, wTN, WI. Map 5

N Atl (North Atlantic): NEng, nNJ, seNY. Map 7

N Cent (North Central): IL, IN, KY, MI, OH, WI. Map 4

NEast (Northeast): NEng, NJ, NY, nPA. Map 2

NEng (New England): CT, MA, ME, NH, RI, VT (eNEng = east of Connecticut R.; wNEng = west of Connecticut R). Map 8

N Midl (North Midland): nDE, c,sIA, cIL, nMD, NE, sNJ, cOH, c,sPA, sSD, nWV. Map 1

Nth (North): nIA, nID, nIL, nIN, MI, MN, MT, ND, NEng, nNJ, NY, nOH, OR, nPA, nSD, WA, WI, nWY. Map 1

NW (Northwest): ID, OR, WA (MT, WY). Map 2

Ozarks: nwAR, swMO, neOK. Map 3

Pacific: CA, OR, WA. Map 5

Pacific NW (Pacific Northwest): nCA, OR, WA. Map 4

Plains States: eCO, KS, NE. Map 3

Rocky Mts (Rocky Mountains): wCO, ID, MT, NV, UT, WY. Map 3

S Atl (South Atlantic): FL, GA, NC, SC. Map 7

SE (Southeast): S Atl, AL, MS, TN. Map 2

S Midl (South Midland): nAL, AR, nGA, sIL, sIN, KY, nLA, nMD, c,sMO, nMS, wNC, sOH, neOK, TN, wSC, wVA, sWV. Map 1

Sth (South): c,sAL, sDE, FL, c,sGA, c,sLA, e,sMD, c,sMS, c,eNC, c,eSC, eTX, eVA. Map 1

SW (Southwest): AZ, sCA, NM, OK, TX. Map 2

Upper MW (Upper Midwest): IA, MN, NE, ND, SD. Map 4

Upper Missip Valley (Upper Mississippi Valley): c,nIL, IA, MN, nMO, WI. Map 5

Upstate NY (Upstate New York): all NY except NYC metropolitan area. Map 6

West (west of 100th parallel): wND, wSD, wNE, wKS, wOK, wTX, and all points west. Map 6

W Midl (West Midland): Midl except DC, DE, MD, sNJ, sPA. Map 8

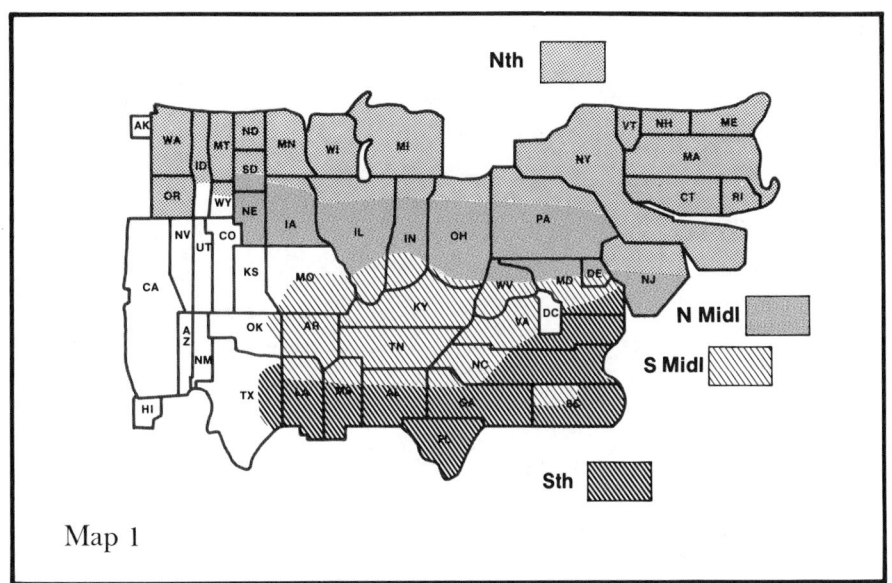

Map 1

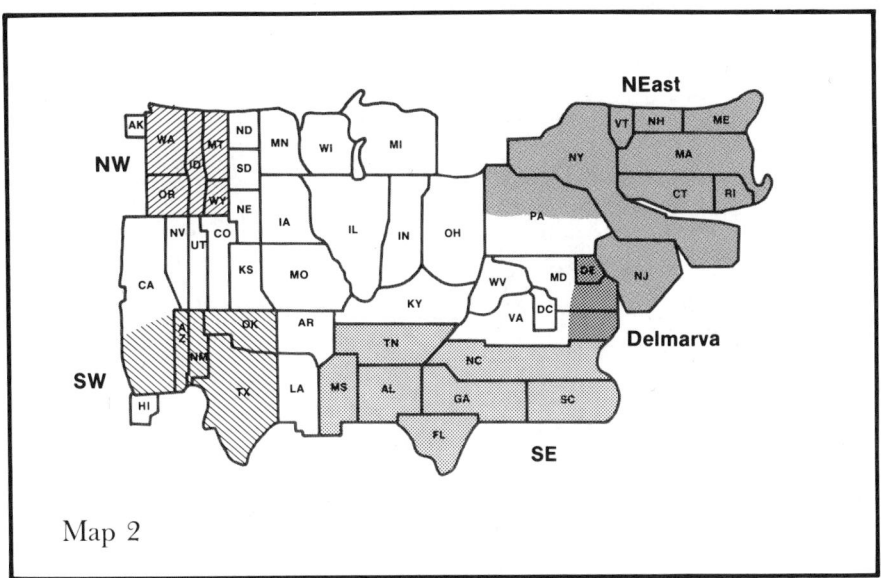

Map 2

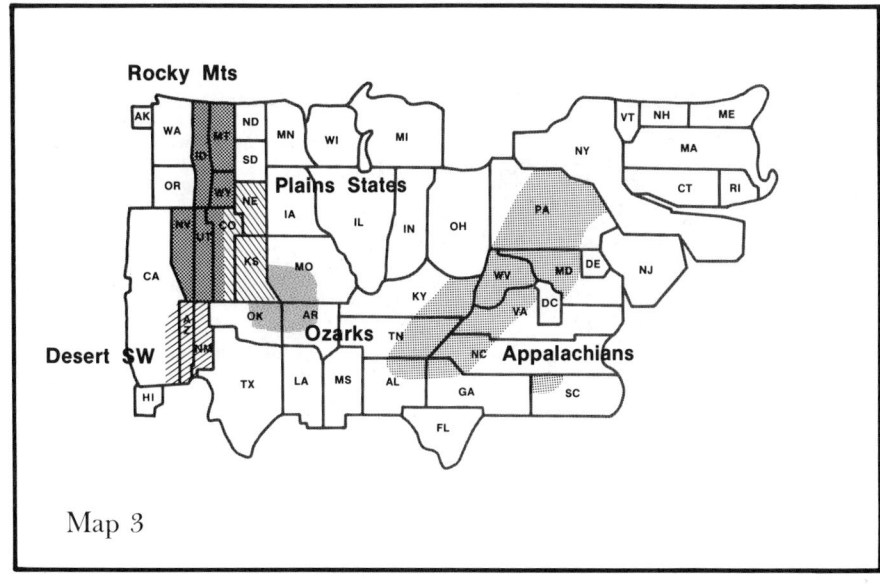

Map 3

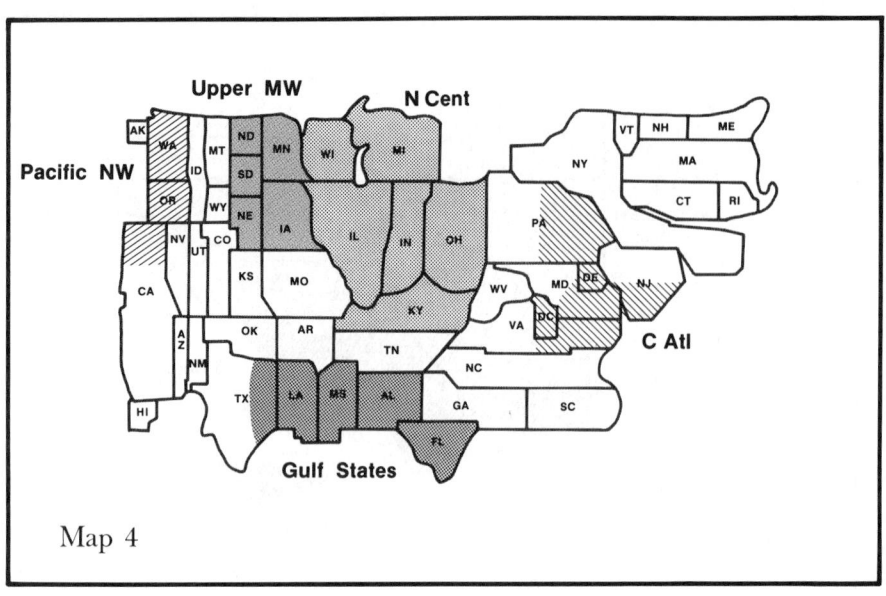

Map 4

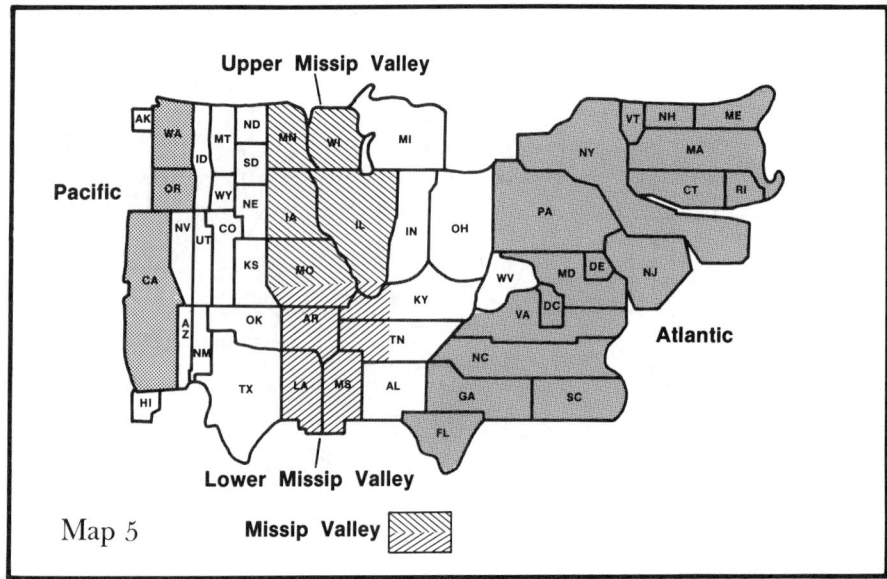

Map 5

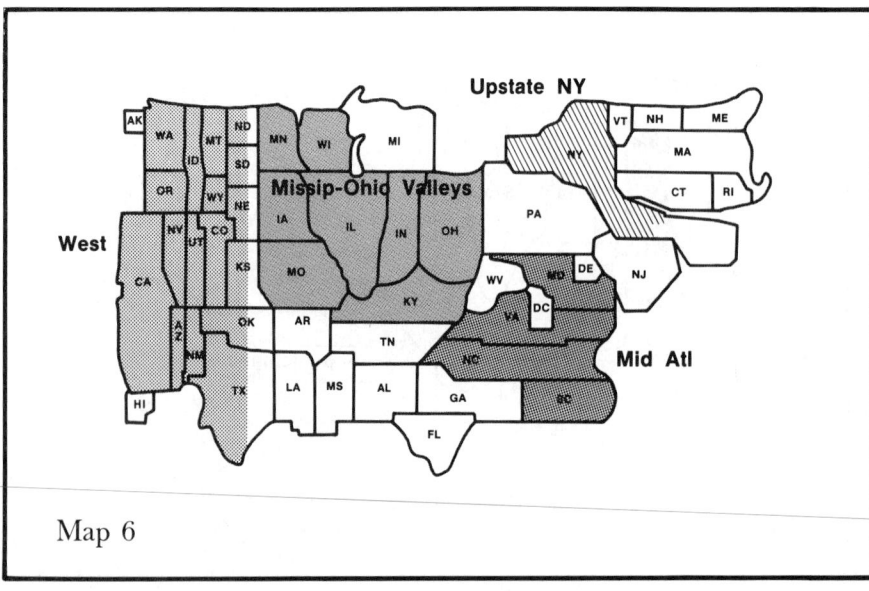

Map 6

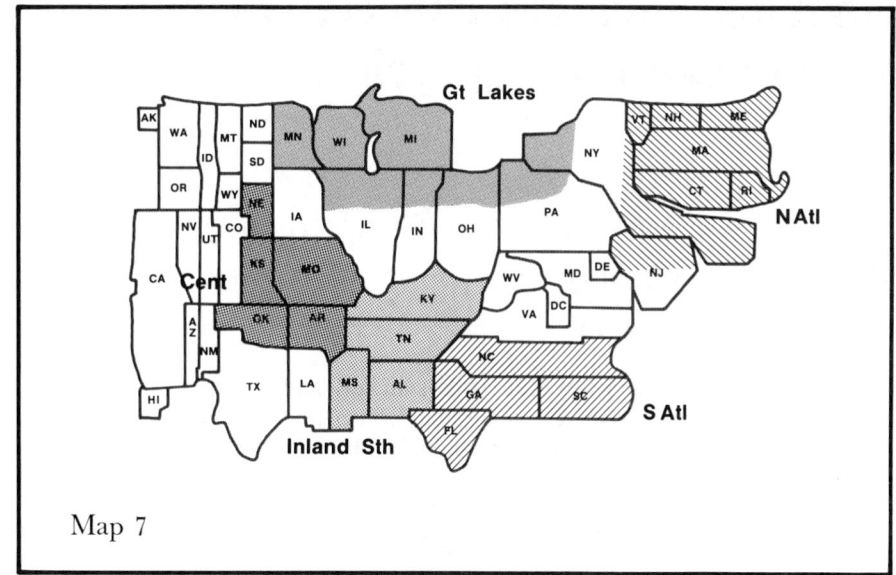

Map 7

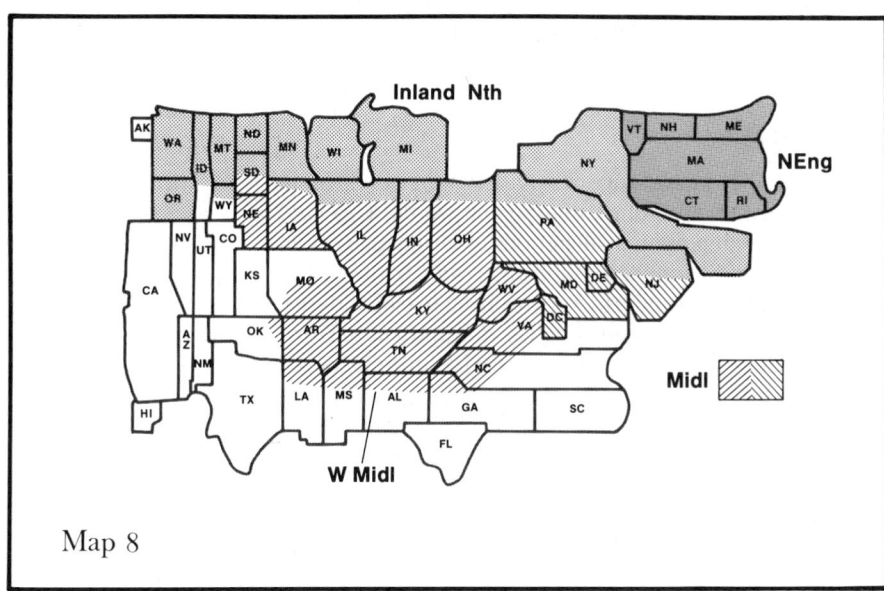

Map 8

Language Changes Especially Common in American Folk Speech

by Frederic G. Cassidy

Language is always changing. Within both standard and nonstandard vocabulary, certain changes of sound, form, and syntactic structure occur unpredictably, though following known processes. Many of these changes occur more often in folk usage than otherwise, to the point where they become characteristic of folk speech. They fall roughly into four main types, which are not mutually exclusive and are sometimes concurrent. These types are changes of word form, grammatical changes, derivational changes, and changes in pronunciation.

I. Changes of Word Form

1. *Metathesis:* The interchange of sounds within words, or, in compounds, the reversal of the component words. This kind of change has been present at all periods of the language. Old English (or Anglo-Saxon) had *acsian* and *crudd.* In the course of time the sounds [ks] and [ru] were reversed to [sk] and [ur], ultimately producing Modern English *ask* and *curd.* However, the ancient forms *ax* and *crud* survive in folk speech today. Other folk examples: *calvary* cavalry, *crips* crisp, *cupalo* cupola, *waps* wasp, *purty* pretty, *lectren* lectern, *aglore* galore, *prespire* perspire, *dientical* identical. Examples of reversed compounds: *hoppergrass* grasshopper, *peckerwood* woodpecker, *ticktacks* tactics, *right-down* downright, *picktooth* toothpick, *pourdown* downpour, *everwhich* whichever, *cropout* outcrop.

2. *Metanalysis:* The result of a shift in the juncture point or syllable division within a word so that a sound belonging to one word is lost or transferred to an adjoining word. Middle English *a nadder* became *an adder;* similarly *a napron* became *an apron* and *a numpere, an umpire.* The shift can go in the other direction: Middle English *an ewte* became *a newt; then once* produced *the nonce; an eke name* became *a nickname.* Modern examples are disguised by established spelling, but pronunciation-spellings, such as *not-a-tall* for *not at all* and *I-mo(n)* +infinitive for *I'm going* (or *gonna*) +infinitive, reveal that the process is still active. Other examples: *an aggie* (marble) has produced *a naggie; a nigh horse* has produced *an eye horse.* A good current example is the common phrase, "That's *a* whole *nother* ballgame."

3. *Iteration* or *reduplication:* The kind of word-formation in which a first component is echoed in the second. This process is found all over the world. In English there are three distinct types: simple, in which the same sound is repeated, as in *pooh-pooh, goody-goody;* graded, in which the internal stressed vowel changes, as in *ding-dong, tick-tock, zigzag;* and rhyming, in which only the initial consonants of the two parts

differ, as in *hocus-pocus, mumbo-jumbo, roly-poly.* Examples from folk speech: *dumdum, flip-flap, hokey-pokey, jeepers-creepers, streakity-strikity, super-duper.*

4. *Redundancy:* Adding to a word or phrase another that is synonymous or nearly so, as in *plentiful abundance, musical tune, period of time.* The purpose is to ensure that the communication is made, or to give emphasis. Redundancy is a property of all natural language structure, but since it is easily overused it is often condemned by stylists. Examples from folk speech: *bare-naked, cabbage-kraut, dry drouth, ford crossing, grape-vineyard, hawk-bird, horn bugle, ocean sea, rifle-gun, tooth-dentist, tumbler-glass, viper snake, widow-woman.*

5. *Stretching:* Lengthening the pronunciation of a word by adding heavy stress to the initial syllable, which normally is weakly stressed. This is a device for emphasis, and examples are recorded from the past, but it has not permanently affected the written forms of words. Some current folk examples: *bée-yútiful, dée-líghted, ón-réasonable, ré-dickilous.*

6. *Folk-etymology* or *popular etymology:* The change of an unfamiliar word or phrase into a more familiar form by semantic reanalysis (not always logical). Many examples from the past are found in plant names, as Old English *wermōd* becoming *wormwood,* Latin *ros marinus* (sea dew) becoming *rosemary,* but the process is in wide current use. Sometimes it is indulged in humorously. Some current folk examples: *high-bred* hybrid, *our beauties* arbutus, *shoemake* sumac, *very close* or *very coarse veins* varicose veins, *sandy Pete* centipede, a *fist-to-cuff fight* fisticuff, *brown kitties* bronchitis, *colored marbles* cholera morbus, *gamble (stick)* gambrel.

7. *Aphetism* or *aphaeresis:* The cutting off of a weakly stressed initial syllable from a word. Many words so shortened have become standard, as *fence* from *defense, tend* from *attend, cute* from *acute, sport* from *disport.* This process was formerly common in poetic use: *neath* for *beneath, lone* for *alone, spite* for *despite.* Folk examples are still numerous: *casion* occasion, *lasses* molasses, *ceptin* excepting, *pinion* opinion, *deed* indeed, *timidatin* intimidating, *larmin* alarming.

8. *Epenthesis:* The addition to a word of an "inorganic" sound, that is, one unsupported by etymology. Such a sound (also called intrusive, excrescent, or parasitic) usually develops as a byproduct of the phonetic environment but may also come in by analogy. This type of change has been in progress throughout the history of English; many words so produced have become established, standard forms. Intrusive

sounds are generally homorganic with adjoining sounds: they share one or more features of articulation, though differing in others. Thus *b* and *m* are bilabial, though *b* has no nasal quality. Examples of intrusive consonants:

/b/ Old English *þȳmel* is now *thimble.* Present folk words: *chimbly* chimney, *fambly* family.

/d/ Middle English *soun* is now *sound.* Present folk words: *oild* oil, *gownd* gown, *liard* liar.

/l/ Present folk speech: *conflab, dumbfloundered.*

/m/ Present folk speech: *ampron* apron.

/n/ Present folk speech: *agnate* agate, *antic* attic, *minety* mighty, *minge* midge, *spink and span.*

/r/ Added internally: *crursh, daurter, horspital, porched egg, warsh, womern.* Added finally: *ager* ague, *chinar, dror* draw, *Emmar, potater.*

/s/ Prefixed to words beginning with /k/ or /t/: *screak, scringe, scrunch, squench, strollop, strull.*

/t/ Added to words ending with /f/, /s/, /š/, /k/, or /n/: *acrost, attackt, chanst, orphant, skifft, varmint, wisht.*

/w/ *twang* tang, *twile* toil, *twill* or *twell* till, *wooze* ooze, *wuxtry* extra.

/y/ *million* melon, *year* ear, *yearly* early, *yearth* earth.

Examples of intrusive vowels:

/ə/ spelled *a: a-growed, a-make, a-many, athaletic, cycalone, parairie, thataway, thisaway.*

/ə/ spelled *e: umberella.*

/ə/ spelled *u: ellum* elm, *fillum* film.

/ɪ/ spelled *i: grievious* grievous, *heinious* heinous, *mischievious* mischievous.

9. *Ellipsis* or *telescoping:* Omission of internal sounds from words (rather than of words from syntactic structures). This phenomenon of phonetic simplification is responsible for the present standard form of many words: Old English *hlæfdīge* became *lady, hēafod* became *head;* for centuries *boatswain* has been pronounced *bosun* and *forecastle, fo'c'sle.* Pronunciation-spellings show that the process is much alive in present folk speech: *a'ter* after, *cal'late* calculate, *cap'm* captain, *chirren* children, *consid'able, comf'table, gov'ment, pres'dent.*

10. *Malapropism:* The blundering substitution, for the intended word, of another similar to it in sound but having an altogether different meaning. Malapropism has seldom furnished new words to standard usage, but a number are found in folk usage: *emancipated* for *emaciated, surrogated* for *corrugated, ministrating* for *menstruating, expire* for *perspire, mitigate* for *militate; calvary* for *cavalry* (which also illustrates metathesis).

11. *Euphemism:* The substitution of a softer word or phrase for one considered painful, obscene, profane, or otherwise offensive. Examples of avoiding the subject of death are very numerous: instead of *die* people say *pass over, join one's ancestors, cross the great divide, cash in one's checks* or *check out, kick the bucket,* and so on. Another type works by "mincing"—that is, by altering the offensive word or phrase just enough to avoid actually saying it. Examples: *I vum* I vow (nineteenth century), *goldurn, jeepers criminy, son of a biscuit.*

12. *Onomatopoeia* or *echoism:* The formation of words by imitation of sounds heard in nature. This is a basic word-forming method in all known languages. Standard English contains thousands of examples, and new ones are created every day in both speech and literature. Folk examples (some of which have rapidly moved into broader popular use): *barf* vomit, *burp* belch, *chookee* the orchard oriole, *ooch* push or slide sideways, *whop* strike hard, *zap* smack or squash suddenly, *zoon* fly with a humming buzz.

13. *False-learned words:* Learned words, frequently from medical or legal Latin, adopted into folk speech, are altered, sometimes with conscious humor. Examples: *affidavy* affidavit, *collywobbles* or *golly marbles* cholera morbus, *epizoodick* or *epizooty* epizoötic, *gumbo whackum* gum guiacum, *maniaporchia* mania à potu, *suppeeny* subpoena.

II. Grammatical Changes

1. *Multiple negatives:* The use of negative words added to an already negative statement to intensify it is present in all historical phases of the language. It had literary status in the past: Chaucer: "He *never* yet *no* vileynie *ne* sayde . . . unto *no* maner wight." Shakespeare: "Love no man in good earnest; *nor no* further in sport *neither.*" In the eighteenth century, however, under the influence of Latin grammar, this was replaced in the standard language by the "logical" principle, according to which "not never" is equivalent to "sometimes." This principle is the basis of the widespread belief that "two negatives make a positive" (as in algebra), which is sometimes used to condemn even such unexceptionable examples of litotes as *not unfriendly* and *not unlikely.*

The multiple negative, though now nonstandard, survives as one of the chief markers of folk speech. It serves to give emphasis, to show determination, and the like. Examples: "I ain't got nary none"; "I ain't never seen no men-folks of no kind do no washin'" (**1926** Kephart *Highlanders* 361); "I can't do nothin'"; "It's not here noplace." It is also found in some single words: *unthoughtless,* a blend of *unthoughtful* and *thoughtless; irregardless* (since *ir-* means *not*).

2. *Multiple comparatives and superlatives:* Use of either the inflectional *-(e)r, -(e)st* or the periphrastic *more, most* markers of comparison together. Chaucer: "As thilke love is the more grevous to perfourne, the *more gretter* the merite." Shakespeare: "This was the *most* unkind*est* cut of all." This is no longer acceptable in standard English but survives to some extent in folk speech. Examples: *betterer, more better, more beautifuller, more lonesomer, worser; bestest, bestmost, most loveliest, best-naturedest, worsest.* A famous American example, "Get there fustest with the mostest," attributed to General Nathan Bedford Forrest, is used humorously today but was said seriously in its time as the highly emphatic statement of a practical soldier.

3. *Multiple plurals:* Though double pluralization has never had literary status, it has been common in folk speech. Examples: *antses, centses, folkses, galluses, geeses, gentlemens, jeanses, mices, oxens, tomatoeses.* A triple plural is *feetses.* (It will be noted that many of these occur with the mutation plurals, which, taken as singulars, are overcorrected with plural inflections.)

4. *Pleonastic subjects:* A noun subject followed by an agreeing pronoun. It is found in all stages of English and in other languages as a device of identification. Examples: "*Hosy he*

cum down stares" (**1846** in 1848 Lowell *Biglow Papers* 2); "Th' ol *Doctor, he*'s got a gre't cur'osity t' see ye" (**1861** Holmes *Elsie Venner* 2.175); "So *him and Tom they* hitched up the mules" (**1884** Lanier *Poems* 172); "*Jim he* hid in back o' th' jail-house" (**1927** *American Speech* 3.10); "My second *mister, he* was took" (**1938** Matschat *Suwannee River* 86); "*Maw, she* knows"; "The *woman she* bakes us a pone" (**1926** Kephart *Highlanders* 112, 122).

5. *Double* -ed *and* -ing*:* When a formerly separate syllable *-ed* of past tense or past participle was reduced, in early Modern English, to *-d* or *-t* (as *lovèd* becoming *loved, leavèd* becoming *left*) the new reduced ending was sometimes not recognized for what it was, so a new *-ed* was often added to make past tense or past participle. Examples are numerous in present folk speech: *attackted, belongded, crepted, drownded, equipted, foalded* foaled, *ruinded, spaded* spayed, *stunded* stunned, *tossted; bornded* is a triple participle.

Double *-ing* occurs in folk speech only, with the older form of the participial suffix [ɪn]. Examples: *fiddlinin, fishinin, huntinin, loadinin, ridinin.*

6. *Use of plural for singular:* A number of nouns singular in meaning are plural in form. In general American usage, *a woods, a falls, a barrens, a narrows* are plurally inflected though agreeing with a singular article and being singular in meaning. These are also well established in folk speech. Other folk examples: a *forks* of a tree, a *stretchers,* a *teethache.* (*Feetsore,* an adjective, is changed similarly.)

7. *Use of singular for plural:* In terms of measurement such as *foot, mile, pound, fathom,* the apparently singular form is of ancient lineage, preserving in disguise the Old English possessive plural: *fōta, mīla, punda, fæþma.* Folk examples: "I walked five mile"; "She gained ten pound"; "Eight foot deep." Shakespeare: "Full fathom five thy father lies." A very similar occurrence is found with a few other words: "He has six cartridge left."

When mass nouns are treated as count nouns in folk speech, a singular form may be used with plural syntax: "Will you have a few cabbage or squash?" "Pass me them cabbage." Contrariwise, a mass noun may be pluralized: "I wisht they wouldn't give us so many of them celeries" (**1941** Faulkner *Men Working* 198).

8. *Use of adjective for adverb:* In Old English such adjectives as *brād* broad, *glæd* glad, *prætig* pretty, *prūd* proud, *smōð* smooth, *soft* soft, *lang* long, *sceort* short, *lȳtel* little, had corresponding adverbs ending in *-e: brāde* broadly, *glæde* gladly, etc. Being so much alike, they were sometimes confused and, to avoid the confusion, *-līce* (like) was often added to the adjective: *brādlīce, glædlīce,* etc. This has survived to some extent in the folk speech, as *easy-like, smooth-like, soft-like.* More often *-like* was reduced phonetically to *-ly,* which has become a regular mark of the adverb in standard English.

A few words have never submitted to the pattern: He worked *long* (not *longly*), She stands *tall* (not *tally*), and colloquially (in informal standard usage) some of the old forms are regularly used without *-ly:* Take it *easy,* sitting *pretty,* cut it *short.* (For all of these, *-ly* forms also exist, but the meaning is different: Take it *easily* means "without difficulty"; take it *easy* means "without fuss or excitement.")

In folk speech, the pattern of making adverbs from adjectives without change of form is widespread and affects many words not of Old English origin. Examples: It's *actual* true, *amazing* good, *awful* nice, do it *careful,* love me *tender. Real* (good, cold, nice) has gone to the point of becoming established as informal standard usage in many parts of the country.

9. *Infinitive used for participle:* After the verb *despise,* and some others not so construed in standard use, folk speech often uses the infinitive: "I despise *to go* out nights" (**1903** *Dialect Notes* 2.311); "I despise *to see* a fence growed up like that" (**1942** *American Speech* 17.53); they wouldn't mind *to fight* us; I admire *to get* letters. (This evidently depends on the use of particular verbs; it would be good standard usage to say *hate* to go, *refuse* to fight, *like* to get.)

10. *Strong and weak verbs:* In the course of development from Old English to Modern English, the tendency has been for verbs to change over from the "strong" pattern (with internal vowel gradation to show tense differences, as *sing, sang, sung* or *break, broke, broken*) to the "weak" pattern (in which *-(e)d* or *-t* is added to the base, as *walk, walked* or *send, sent*). Though all strong verbs have been subject to this tendency, various ones have developed differently. Folk usage has been generally more conservative than standard, but not altogether so. Many Old English verbs have become weak in standard English. Examples:

flēon flee, past participle *flogen;* standard form *fled*
ceorfan carve, past participle *corfen;* standard form *carved*
gieldan yield, past participle *golden;* standard form *yielded.*

In some of these, the strong form survives in folk usage:

helpan help, part participle *holpen;* folk form *holp*
creopan creep, past participle *cropen;* folk form *crope*
climban climb, past participle *clomben;* folk form *clomb*
dragan drag, past participle *drogen;* folk form *drug*

For some Old English weak verbs, however, strong forms have developed in folk usage:

dyfan dive, *dyfede* dived; new folk form *dove* (now regionally established in the northern United States)
wafian wave, *wafode* waved; new folk form *wove*
þencan think, *þuhte* thought; new folk form *thunk.*

This proves the vitality of the strong pattern, as does also its effect on foreign loanwords, such as French *arrive:*

standard *arrive, arrived;* folk form *arrove.*

11. *The unmarked reflexive dative:* The Old English reflexive dative of nouns and pronouns, meaning *to* or *for,* has come down to Modern English in disguise. In OE it had a form distinct from that of the accusative: for example, accusative *mec,* dative *mē.* In present English, the direct and indirect objects are no longer distinct in form; *me* is used for both. Standard English reflexive dative pronouns have added *-self:* I bought *myself* a hat; but in folk speech the old reflexive dative without *-self* survives: I bought *me* a hat; he kilt *him* a bear; they built *them* a house.

12. *Overcorrection* (or *hyperurbanism*): A change of grammatical or pronunciation form made in an attempt to avoid supposed incorrectness. Examples: *an awfully lot; highfaluting* for *highfalutin;* adding false *-ing* to words like *chicken, mountain, muslin,* making them *chicking, mounting, musling.* Edward Eggleston, in *The Hoosier Schoolmaster,* de-

picted an Indiana "lady" who prided herself on having "been at Bosting" (Boston).

III. Derivational Changes

1. *Suffixation:* At every stage in the language, new words may be made by derivation, the addition of affixes to words or word bases. Many such formations are accepted without question, but others, formed by the same rules, remain oddities not generally accepted, used only locally or only by the occasional individual. The eighteenth-century prejudice against innovation or neologisms, though now greatly modified, still holds against many such formations in folk speech. Suffixes so used include:

-*able,* as in *ageable* on in years, *biddable* obedient, *fightable* eager to fight.

-*ation,* as in *botheration, darnation, flinderation, murderation, tarnation, thunderation, twitteration.*

-*fy, -ify, -ified,* as in *airified, argufy, fitified, happify, speechify, weakified.*

-*ment,* especially with extra stress on the suffix, as in *appearment, botherment, disgracement, fixment, foolishment, hustlement, needments, reasonment, revengement, studyment, worriment.*

-*some,* as in *beautysome, bettersome, boresome, dangersome, hindersome, idlesome, pestersome, queersome, tellsome, youthsome.*

-*(e)ty, -dy, -y,* on adjective base: *biggety, fadedy, fainty, jaggedy, pleggity, raggedy, ramshacklety.*

on verb base: *crinklety, crumplety, fixy, itchety, mincy, rockety, wrinkledy.*

on noun base: *compushency, conceity, ficety, filey, roguey, spasmy, spitey, strengthy.*

2. *Prefixation:* Folk use of prefixes is less distinctive than that of suffixes, but the continued use of *a-* is characteristic. This prefix, a worn-down form of the preposition *on,* is no longer a free form in standard English, though it survives as a bound form in such common words as *abed, about, afoot, ahead, ashore, asleep,* and many more. In folk speech it is common preceding participles, especially present participles: *a-comin, a-goin, a-laughin, a-walkin.* Apart from poetic survivals, it has been lost in this context in standard English; the sense of *on* is expressed, when necessary, with *on:* folk *a-purpose,* standard *on purpose.*

3. *Back-formation:* A new word is formed from an existing one by false derivation. Examples: the verb *diagnose* is actually back-formed from *diagnosis,* not the other way around, as one might think. Similarly, *edit* is back-formed from *editor* and *burgle* from *burglar.* All these are now fully accepted as standard. Some examples from folk speech: *jink* bad luck, taken as the singular of *jinx; sull,* taken as the infinitive of *sullin'* (mistaken for *sullen*); *mize* to act stingily, from *miser.*

4. *Omission of suffix:* The suffix -*er* expressing agency is sometimes dropped, as in *fly bat, fly flap, fly spat, fly swat, flycatch* (the bird), *salt-shake, fertilize* (noun), *drain* colander, *frogstick* pocket knife. All the corresponding forms with -*er* are attested.

5. *Abbreviation or shortening:* This has always been a means of reducing the length and complexity of phrases or compounds, producing shorter words. Sometimes it is due to the operation of phonetic laws, a well-known example being Old English *hlāf-weard* becoming Middle English *lord* (initial *hl* was reduced to *l*; internal *fs* were often labialized, as also in *hawk* from OE *hafoc;* and *w* was vocalized). Most often, however, a part of the phrase or compound is simply dropped, standard English examples being *bus* from *omnibus, fan* from *fanatic, mob* from Latin *mobile vulgus, wig* from *periwig.* The same forces are at work in popular speech, producing such words as *copter* helicopter, *math* mathematics, *prof* professor, which are generally accepted as informal standard English. Folk examples are not numerous: *cat fever* catarrhal fever, *con* consumption (tuberculosis), *igg* to ignore, *ticky* particular.

IV. Pronunciations

A number of pronunciation patterns exist that go against the rules of standard English and spelling but that nevertheless may be strong regionally.

1. *Final unstressed vowels:* Most widespread are the variations in treating a final unstressed vowel, [i], [ɪ] or [ə], in disagreement with standard spelling.

   a. The endings of *Cincinnati, Missouri, prairie* are locally pronounced [ə], and in pronunciation-spellings are spelled *a: Cincinnata, Missoura, paraira.* In many other words spelled with final *i,* this has not happened.

   b. *Africa, Alabama, algebra, America, arnica, cholera, Martha, Ora, Sara,* and dozens more—a very common change during the nineteenth century—end in /i/ or /ɪ/, with pronunciation-spellings using *y: Africky, Alabamy, algebry.* The force of standard spelling has changed most of these to standard pronunciations in /ə/, but many have at the same time acquired an intrusive *r,* as *Atlanter, bannanner, umbreller,* etc.

   c. Words ending in *ow* very frequently reduce /o/ to /ə/ and often add an *r: medda, medder* meadow, *meller* mellow, *shadder* shadow, *shaller* shallow, *swoller* swallow, *waller* wallow.

2. *Recessive stress:* Words of Germanic origin (as are the majority of Old English words) normally bore stress on the first syllable. Folk speech frequently applies the rule to non-Germanic loanwords, stressing the first syllable when standard pronunciation does not. The effect is to give primary stress to the first syllable, often with lengthening of the vowel, and to reduce the second-syllable stress to secondary stress. Examples: *ad*vice, *De*cember, *de*cide, *de*fend, *de*liberate, *dis*rupt, *dis*turb, *e*lope, *en*courage, *en*force, *i*dea, *in*vest, *in*vite, *mis*take, *po*lice, *re*duce, *Sep*tember, *sub*tract.

3. *Unreduced suffixes:* In the Middle English period the -*es* of noun plurals and of verb third-person singulars was pronounced as a separate syllable. In early Modern English the majority lost this separateness and were assimilated directly to the base: *walkes,* two-syllable noun or verb, became *walks; dreades* became *dreads.* Words ending in *s, sh, z, zh* resisted this change: *buzzes, fishes, garages, passes.* Many more words of the older form have survived in folk speech after -*sp, -st,* or -*sk: beastes, claspes, deskes, frostes, ghostes, nestes, postes, tuskes, trustes, waspes, wristes.*

A very similar reduction of the -*(e)d* of past-tense verbs took place at the same period, the separate syllable being lost. A few words failed to follow this pattern of change: standard are *agèd* old, *belovèd, blessèd.* A few more survive in folk speech: *streakèd, stripèd,* formed from verb plus participial *-ed,* and the similar *forkèd, peakèd,* formed from noun plus *-ed* having, characterized by.

4. *Sound substitutions:* Folk speakers may substitute sounds or sound clusters for others in general use. Like intrusive consonants, these are usually homorganic with the sounds they replace. Examples:

k for *t: turkle* turtle, *bickle* victuals, *bunk* (verb) bunt, *clouk* (noun) clout, *buck* (verb) butt, *ecksetra* etcetera.

k for *p: plunk* (verb) plump, *chonk* (verb) chomp, champ.

r for *l: jagger* (verb) jaggle, *kitarber* catalpa.

l for *r: clumbly* crumbly.

The word *catalpa* has undergone an unusual number of such substitutions, with forty variant forms recorded, including *patalca* (*p* for *k, k* for *p*); *macaltha* (*m* for *k, k* for *t, th* for *p*); *catalba* (*b* for *p*); *catalfa* (*f* for *p*).

Guide to Pronunciation

by James W. Hartman

1. Introduction

The treatment of pronunciation in *DARE* differs from that in standard dictionaries in several ways. First, pronunciation is not included in the heading for words that are widely used in American English (AE) and have little or no variation in pronunciation (such as *slap*), or that vary by well-known regular processes (for example, presence or absence of postvocalic /r/, as in *brier*). At the other extreme, pronunciation is not included when there is no oral evidence at all for the pronunciation (as with *cadulix*), when there is too little information from which to generalize (as with *cadarup*), or when *DARE* quotations are solely from written sources that give no indication of pronunciation even though the word is obviously well known in a region (as is *caballero*). The last case results in seeming inconsistency, since words such as the Spanish loans *caballada* and *caballero* are treated quite differently; however, the principle of providing pronunciations only from oral evidence or phonetic transcriptions has been adhered to despite the resulting variability in treatment.

A second way in which *DARE*'s treatment differs from that in other dictionaries is that pronunciation may be indicated in any of several ways: it may be given in the heading immediately following the part of speech; it may be provided in one or more of the quotations; it may be suggested by inclusion of pronunciation-spellings; or some combination of these alternatives may be used. As to accuracy, *DARE* is responsible only for transcriptions in the headings.

Third, *DARE*'s use of symbols to indicate pronunciation varies depending on whether a generalization (a "broad" transcription) or a precise rendering (a "narrow" transcription) is called for (see further below). The purposes of this Guide to Pronunciation are to give the reader information that will suggest the likely or possible regional pronunciation of words for which transcriptions are not given in *DARE,* and to provide a basic outline of the kinds and patterns of variation that occur in AE pronunciation in general.

The Guide to Pronunciation has three major parts: Section 1 gives the reader basic information about the symbols used to indicate pronunciation. Section 2 presents a brief overview of the nature of regional and social pronunciation variation in AE, its historical development, and some present-day influences on it. Section 3, the *DARE* Pronunciation Key, has three major divisions: 3.I describes the use of different sound units in the same word; 3.II describes the most important variations heard in each of the sound units; and 3.III summarizes the most notable regional patterns of pronunciation and provides maps to illustrate some of them. Section 3 is intended to be used as a reference. *DARE* entries refer the reader to the appropriate subheadings in section 3 for general descriptive information on geographical variants in pronunciation.

AE has been described, abstractly, as having a set of distinctive sound units (phonemes), a reservoir that is drawn upon and assigned a reality (articulation) and a sequence to produce the pronunciation of a word or string of words. AE speakers can distinguish *bit* from *pit* because, although *b* and *p* are similar in articulation, there are differences between them that native speakers hear as being fundamental or distinctive. But not all sound differences are distinctive. For example, the final *t* on *bit* and *pit* may be articulated with or without a strong puff of air (aspiration), but AE speakers treat either of these as being fundamentally the same sound, a *t*. The English spelling system goes far in identifying what is distinctive and what is not. For example, *b* and *p* are distinct not only in function to distinguish words but also in the alphabet, whereas the two kinds of *t* are distinct in neither. But traditional spelling cannot be relied on to represent distinctive differences, or not to represent nondistinctive differences. The *th* spelling, for example, covers two distinct units, as in *thigh* and *thy.* Although these two words otherwise sound alike, they are kept separate by two distinct sounds, both represented by *th* in conventional spelling. On the other hand, for many AE speakers words like *cot* and *caught* sound the same, even though the spelling differs. Likewise, for some, *god* and *guard* sound alike. Therefore traditional orthography cannot be relied upon to represent the many phonetic variations that occur in AE.

In order to indicate pronunciation unambiguously in writing, it is necessary to have a system with a one-to-one correspondence between written symbols and speech sounds. Because there are more speech sounds than there are letters in the alphabet, certain additional symbols must be used. (At the same time, a few letters of the alphabet are *not* used, because their sounds are adequately represented by other letters.) The additional symbols are taken for the most part from the International Phonetic Alphabet, along with a few other symbols that are in regular use among American linguists. The basic symbols used in *DARE* are shown below, between diagonal slashes, each one accompanied by an illustrative word.

I   Vowels

/i/	b*ea*t	/o/	b*oa*t
/ɪ/	b*i*t	/ɔ/	c*au*ght
/e/	b*ai*t	/ɑ/	f*a*ther
/ɛ/	b*e*t	/ə/	*a*bove
/æ/	b*a*t	/ɝ/	b*ir*d, fath*er*

/u/	b*oo*t	/aɪ/	b*i*te
/ʊ/	b*oo*k	/aʊ/	b*ou*t
		/ɔɪ/	b*oy*

II Consonants

/p/	*p*o*p*	/v/	*v*al*v*e
/b/	*b*o*b*	/s/	*s*a*ss*
/t/	*t*o*t*	/z/	*z*eroe*s*
/d/	*d*i*d*	/š/	*sh*ip, wi*sh*
/k/	*k*i*ck*	/ž/	mea*s*ure
/g/	*g*a*g*	/č/	*ch*ur*ch*
/m/	*m*o*m*	/ǰ/	*j*u*dg*e
/n/	*n*o*n*e	/h/	*h*ot
/ŋ/	si*ng*, i*n*k	/w/	*w*eb
/θ/	*th*imble, e*th*er	/j/	*y*es
/ð/	*th*em, ei*th*er	/r/	*r*un
/f/	*f*i*f*e	/ə/	fa*r* (in *r*-less areas)
		/l/	*l*itt*l*e

Although the illustrative words used above were chosen to indicate the correspondence between the symbols and speech sounds, because of regional differences in pronunciation not everyone will pronounce these words in exactly the same manner. To this extent, the indication of the speech sound associated with each symbol is necessarily somewhat imprecise. For example, many people in the North and South pronounce *cot* and *caught* so that they sound different; that is, they distinguish between the vowels /ɑ/ and /ɔ/. In the West, however, *cot* and *caught* are often pronounced so that they sound the same; that is, many speakers do not distinguish between /ɑ/ and /ɔ/, lacking the vowel /ɔ/ entirely. But, on the whole, the illustrative words are pronounced similarly by speakers throughout the country.

The symbols shown above are used in two basic ways: simply to indicate particular sounds; or to show more detail about the way those sounds were produced. For example, the pronunciation of the word *pep* can be represented by the set of symbols /pɛp/; it can also be represented by the set [pʻɛ˕p̚]. The first transcription shows the three distinctive sounds used in saying the word; it is enclosed in diagonal slashes that indicate a "broad" or general rendering. The second transcription not only gives the three basic sounds but also shows that the first sound was articulated with a puff of air, the vowel was pronounced with the tongue in a slightly lower position than usual, and the last sound was unreleased (that is, the lips did not open immediately after coming together); this "narrow" or more detailed set is enclosed in square brackets. The set of modifying signs used to indicate such details of articulation is shown below. (Additional symbols and combinations used to indicate variants of the basic symbols are discussed in section 3.II.)

- ˜ (over a symbol) = nasalized
- – (through the middle of a symbol) = articulated toward the center of the mouth
- : (following a symbol) = length
- ‹ (following a symbol) = forward in the mouth
- › (following a symbol) = back in the mouth
- ˆ (following a symbol) = higher in the mouth
- ˇ (following a symbol) = lower in the mouth
- ʻ (following a symbol) = aspirated
- ̄ (following a symbol) = unreleased

- ̥ (beneath a symbol) = voiceless
- ̬ (beneath a symbol) = voiced
- ̫ (beneath a symbol) = labialized
- ̪ (beneath a consonant) = dentalized
- ̯ (beneath /ə/) = unsyllabic
- ̩ (beneath a consonant) = syllabic
- ̣ (beneath a vowel) = retroflex

In the dictionary entries, narrow transcriptions may occur in quotations, especially those from such sources as the *Linguistic Atlas of New England,* where great care was taken to transcribe utterances as precisely as possible; they also occur in *DARE* quotations, in cases where fieldworkers felt that minute detail was useful. For the sake of uniform presentation, however, all of the *DARE* transcriptions, whether narrow or broad, are enclosed within brackets. Quotations from written sources of course follow the practice of the author with respect to brackets or diagonal slashes. For sources written before transcription practices had been standardized (such as early volumes of *Dialect Notes*), the editors have regularized the transcriptions. Pronunciations given in the headings of entries are generalizations based primarily on evidence in the quotations. Because the evidence includes both narrow and broad transcriptions, the symbols in the headings are enclosed in vertical strokes to signal a middle ground between the detailed and the general.

Although *DARE*'s use of diagonal slashes and brackets is similar to that favored by linguists to represent phonemic and subphonemic levels, it should not be viewed as representing a unified phonemic-phonetic system for all of AE, or even for one region within the whole. Because the data were not analyzed with the goal of actually setting up phonemic systems, the symbols, as used here, are to be taken as indicators of the speech sounds themselves, without reference to their place in an overall system.

The details of variation in AE pronunciation are highly complex. The amount of data needed to establish patterns in individuals, social groups, regions, and circumstances of style and linguistic context is enormous. Constant change, moreover, rapidly or slowly erodes the applicability of data collected at any given time. And there are local, even neighborhood, pronunciations that are yet unrecorded. The pronunciation features discussed here should not be unduly generalized—they are, of necessity, taken from individual speakers at a particular time. Nevertheless, patterns of pronunciation do tend to be stable, as evidenced by the fact that many young speakers still exhibit the same regional features described in studies done nearly three generations ago.

Variation is implicit in the use of any spoken language. To document this variation is to reveal historical and social ties that run deep in the culture of the groups involved; to share forms of language is to share values. The more broadly pronunciation data are viewed, the more consistency and stability are seen. Beyond the intrinsic interest of "knowing what is there for its own sake," the social and regional differences of AE have a larger significance. The American past, linguistic and cultural, is embedded in contemporary variation. And not only do users of the forms attach social meaning to them, but nonusers often make judgments—positive or negative—about them. Some features are considered quaint, some colorful, some ignorant, some cultivated, some irritating, some pleasing. These attitudes can be very strong and often subtly affect our judgments about the speakers. The native who claims "we don't have any accents around here" reveals the tenacity of our perceptions of "us" and "them." In truth, of course, every speaker is from somewhere, regionally, educationally, and emotionally, and it is impossible not to reveal through pronunciation some part of that background. It is useful to remember that AE is the sum total of its variation and that all its varieties are the current results of complex historical and linguistic developments.

The information presented below is derived from many sources: studies of American speech that deal with small neighborhoods as well as large regions; with single features as well as entire systems; with social class, race, educational and generational differences; with theories of change and histories of development. In addition, the sources include a unique body of pronunciation data, the *DARE* audiotapes, a collection of 1843 field recordings of the *DARE* informants. These tapes average approximately one half-hour each. Each tape has two major sections: a reading of a set passage, "Arthur the Rat," in which each word is chosen to indicate known variations in pronunciation; and a period of free conversation in which the informant is encouraged to speak casually on familiar topics. The set passage elicits more formal speech ("reading style"), while the free conversation samples more informal speech. From the total number of field recordings a nationwide sampling representing the geographical and social grouping of the informants was taken for analysis. These tapes were transcribed phonetically, charted, and plotted on maps to provide much of the basic data presented here. Intonation data (pitch, stress), the consequences of intonation (for example, vowel length), and many narrow phonetic qualities (such as palatalization and lip rounding) were excluded as being too technical for a general treatment. The text of the *DARE* version of "Arthur the Rat" is as follows:

Once upon a time there was a young rat who couldn't make up his mind. Whenever the other rats asked him if he would like to come out hunting with them, he would answer in a hoarse voice, "I don't know." And when they said, "Would you rather stay inside?" he wouldn't say yes, or no either. He'd always shirk making a choice.

One fine day his aunt Josephine said to him, "Now look here! No one will ever care for you if you carry on like this. You have no more mind of your own than a greasy old blade of grass!"

The young rat coughed and looked wise, as usual, but said nothing.

"Don't you think so?" said his aunt, stamping with her foot, for she couldn't bear to see the young rat so cold-blooded.

"I don't know," was all he ever answered, and then he'd walk off to think for an hour or more, whether he would stay in his hole in the ground or go out into the loft.

One night the rats heard a loud noise in the loft. It was a very dreary old place. The roof let the rain come washing in, the beams and rafters had all rotted through, so that the whole thing was quite unsafe.

At last one of the joists gave way, and the beams fell with one edge on the floor. The walls shook, the cupola fell off, and all the rats' hair stood on end with fear and horror.

"This won't do," said their leader. "We can't stay cooped up here any longer." So they sent out scouts to search for a new home.

A little later on that evening the scouts came back and said they had found an old-fashioned horse-barn where there would be room and board for all of them.

The leader gave the order at once, "Company fall in!" and the rats crawled out of their holes right away and stood on the floor in a long line.

Just then the old rat caught sight of young Arthur — that was the name of the shirker. He wasn't in the line, and he wasn't exactly outside it — he stood just by it.

"Come on, get in line!" growled the old rat coarsely. "Of course you're coming too?"

"I don't know," said Arthur calmly.

"Why, the idea of it! You don't think it's safe here any more, do you?"

"I'm not certain," said Arthur undaunted. "The roof may not fall down yet."

"Well," said the old rat, "we can't wait for you to join us." Then he turned to the others and shouted, "Right about face! March!" and the long line marched out of the barn while the young rat watched them.

"I think I'll go tomorrow," he said to himself, "but then again, perhaps I won't — it's so nice and snug here. I guess I'll go back to my hole under the log for a while just to make up my mind."

But during the night there was a big crash. Down came beams, rafters, joists — the whole business.

Next morning — it was a foggy day — some men came to look over the damage. It seemed odd that the old building was not haunted by rats. But at last one of them happened to move a board, and he caught sight of a young rat, quite dead, half in and half out of his hole.

Thus the shirker got his due, and there was no mourning for him.

2. Pronunciation Variation in American English

American folklore includes observations about a southern drawl, a Yankee whine, a midwestern twang, and other labels for perceived regional differences in speech. For these differences various fanciful explanations are offered: southerners talk slowly because of the heat; Philadelphians sometimes drop their *r*'s because the humid climate produces such widespread sinus problems that the articulation of that sound is hindered. Popular attitudes toward social and regional versions of AE tend to be stereotyped. A certain kind of Boston speech is perceived as "classy," whereas the speech of other regions provokes laughter or disapproval. How much of this folklore corresponds to fact? Is there really a southern drawl? A midwestern twang? As with other matters of folk or popular knowledge — medical treatments, for example — there is some truth and some fiction in such regional stereotyping. For example, contrary to the common belief, southern speech is not necessarily slower than that found elsewhere. The use of a rising pitch by some southern speakers where others would use level or falling pitches (making a southern statement sound like a question to outsiders) draws attention. Likewise, the lengthening of vowels at given places in sentences contributes to an impression of slowness. The amount of silence allowed in various types of discourse may also be greater for some southern speakers. But the latter characteristic is not unique to the South, nor do all southerners utilize pauses to the same degree. Although it is clear that different regions do have characteristic mannerisms of speech, which include the characteristics just mentioned and also such things as use of vocal qualifiers (nasality, aspiration, "rough" or "smooth" use of vocal cords), articulation habits, and so on, adequate documentation of the differences is lacking. Many other aspects of social and regional variation of AE have been documented, however, as will be detailed later in this section. But first, there are some general matters whose introduction will aid in the understanding of details.

Dialect. Although this term is popularly applied to speech that is heard as odd or "nonstandard," most scholars use it to refer to any defined variety of speech, social or regional. From this point of view, every speaker has a dialect, one that reflects social and regional characteristics.

Standard English. Difficult to define, this term usually refers to the forms of English found in edited writing. Pronunciation, however, is much less subject to a recognized norm in American speech. It is normal for standard speakers in Atlanta to differ from their counterparts in Chicago, San Francisco, New Orleans, Boston, and so on. Broadcast (American) English as heard from professional announcers on radio and television has been developing as an informal norm, but it is far from having the force that Received Pronunciation has had in England. In other words, the United States tends to have regional standards of pronunciation.

General American. This much used and abused term most frequently refers to the speech of the western half of the country (excluding Texas and, perhaps, Oklahoma) and most of the territory east of the Mississippi that is north of the Ohio River (excluding the East Coast). Of course there are differences in pronunciation within this large area, but they are often less striking than those of the South or the East. There is some evidence that younger, college-educated speakers in the South and East are adopting some features from the General American area. And, in fact, this term occasionally is used to refer to educated speech across the country. To avoid possible misunderstanding, the term "General American" will not be used in the following discussion.

Urban vs. Rural. In pronunciation, as in other characteristics of AE, urban areas differ from their surrounding rural areas. Generally speaking, the larger and older cities of the eastern half of the United States are more differentiated than those of the western half, but even in the latter differences exist and seem to be increasing. Smaller, younger cities are more likely to represent an amalgam of features to be found in their rural environs, whereas older, larger cities may contain pronunciation characteristics that are relatively rare in the surrounding territory.

Social Factors. Social pressures to adopt one form of pronunciation or another are real and pervasive. American children very early begin modifying their speech away from that of the home to that of their peers. As their world expands they encounter new varieties of English from which they may choose features. Their choices are based on such influences as frequency of occurrence and their attitudes toward other speakers. The latter influence, sometimes termed "prestige," is easily misunderstood. What the culture in general holds to be "good" is not necessarily what the individual will choose.

In fact, there is evidence that many speakers knowingly use nonprestigious forms in order to separate themselves from standard social norms and solidify their identification with subgroups. Indeed, all speakers adjust their speech, including pronunciation, to fit the situation and the audience. These shifts are often so natural that they go unnoticed unless a speaker uses inappropriate forms. Not all pronunciation is affected by social class or situation; only some features, which have become markers within a given region, will vary across social groups and social contexts.

Social forces are constantly shaping the direction and nature of American English pronunciation. Some are national in scope, others regional or local. The degree to which these forces are balanced governs the degree to which speech is homogeneous. It is commonly argued that as such pervasive institutions as education and the media become more national, and as more people travel or change their place of residence, regional and local features of speech are weakened. This contention has some support. For example in the "*r*-less" areas of the country (where *r*'s after vowels are not strongly articulated) some younger speakers have more postvocalic /r/ articulation than their counterparts had a generation ago. Contacts among speakers from diverse areas in large regional universities may be encouraging such standardizing trends. Reservoirs of regional and local speech exist in most communities, however, and, with the possible exception of folk pronunciation of individual words, they are likely to remain indefinitely. Furthermore, various appeals to regional, local, ethnic, and other kinds of pride may lead to resurgence and growth of variation. Even though pronunciation possibilities are limited and guided by biological and linguistic forces, degrees of homogenization and variation are also reflections of cultural developments.

Despite its complex patterns of variation, AE pronunciation is remarkably homogeneous over an area of approximately 3 million square miles containing more than 200 million speakers from diverse language backgrounds. Indeed, few sharp regional or social distinctions mark variant pronunciations; more often, gradient transitions and overlapping mixtures characterize what are commonly referred to as the dialects or "accents" of AE. Popular stereotyping of such features as Brooklyn's "boid" and "toid" for *bird* and *third* notwithstanding, very few pronunciation characteristics are unique to an area or social group. Rather, a group's unique pronunciation can usually be defined only by a *set* of features, any single feature in the set being shared with one or more other areas that may or may not be contiguous with it. It is the *combinations* of pronunciation features that best reveal the unique character of any given area or social group. In fact, this sharing of individual characteristics extends beyond the boundaries of the United States. Many of the variant pronunciations found in the United States may be found in British English as well, although the proportional number of speakers in the two countries who use a certain pronunciation may differ dramatically, as may the social status of any given feature. Moreover, the combination of features for any individual speaker of British English will differ from those of any given American.

In spite of the high degree of homogeneity of AE, it is clear even to the casual observer that distinctive differences, geographical and social, do exist. Not surprisingly, the earlier-set-tled East Coast and South have more distinct regional and social differences than do the more recently settled Midwest, Southwest, and Pacific Coast. (We use these regional terms about language with only general boundaries in mind; language differences have little or nothing to do with state boundaries or administrative divisions.) Urban areas, in particular, are internally quite complex and are often distinct from the surrounding rural areas, even in the West where speech is generally more uniform.

Though the members of a group of speakers may sound much the same to an outsider, no area, large or small, achieves complete uniformity of pronunciation: there are likely to be subareal differences (neighborhoods, suburbs, communities) and social differences as well. The social groupings most likely to be reflected in pronunciation differences are age, sex, social class (as seen in education, income, occupation, and community type), and ethnic background. Even informal social groupings, however, may be marked by identifiable differences in pronunciation, many of them so subtle that group members themselves may not be aware of them. Pronunciation becomes even more complex when individual variation is taken into account. Speakers may shift pronunciation to fit the situation and the audience. They may change some pronunciations as they grow older and come into contact with other varieties of the language. In brief, regional, social, and individual variation in pronunciation is not exceptional: it is the norm. Moreover, all of these factors change through time. The reader would do well to keep this complexity in mind when consulting the information on pronunciation given later in this discussion and in the dictionary entries.

Nearly all present-day phonological variations are products of historical processes, recent or past. Many are the result of a sound being influenced by neighboring sounds—a process called assimilation, in which one sound becomes more like another. When such a process has affected one word, the change may then spread to rhymes or near rhymes of that word. This spread may occur rapidly or slowly, sometimes taking generations. Moreover, a process that begins in one regional or social group may spread to other groups. The total set of words involved in the process may not be the same among all groups and may vary over time.

In *wash,* for example, the /š/ has influenced the way sounds preceding it are articulated by some speakers. One result is an intrusive /r/, that is, an *r* sound that intervenes between the vowel and the /š/. Thus, many AE speakers pronounce *wash* as [wɑrš]. Many of these also say [wɑršɪŋ] *washing* and [wɑršt] *washed.* But these speakers may or may not pronounce *Washington* as [wɑršɪŋtən]: not all those who say [wɑrš] also have the intrusive sound in all similar words. The same sound pattern, a vowel plus intrusive /r/ before /š/, occurs in other words, such as *mush* [mɝš], *mushroom* [mɝšrum], and *brush* [brɝš], but the vowel that is most likely to invite intrusive /r/ is /ʌ/.

Another example of uneven distribution of phonological processes across regional and social groups is the influence of /š/ and the similar /ž/. Some speakers have only tense or diphthongized vowels before /š/ or /ž/: *fish* and *dish* are [fiš], [diš]; *bush* and *push* are [buš], [puš]; *measure* and *special* are [mežɚ], [spešəl]; *rush* and *mush* are [rʌɪš], [mʌɪš]; *ash* and *mash* are [æɪš], [mæɪš]; and *wash* and *Washington* are [wɔɪš], [wɔɪšɪŋtən]. But many speakers do not have this process for all possible words in a rhyming set; some will say [mežɚ] or [spešəl], for example, but lack similar variants for other words.

In brief, a phonological process may start with one word for one group (or one individual). It may then spread to other similar words and to other members of the speech community, but the growth of both kinds may be uneven in generalization or in rapidity. Furthermore, if the new variant encounters resistance—for example, if it is made fun of and becomes stigmatized—it may recede, and this shrinking may be as uneven as its spread. The first utterance of the new form may be treated as a peculiarity (good or bad) or may go unnoticed; it will be treated as a variant until it has spread to all (or almost all) members of the word set and throughout the population. (Those words to which it fails to spread become relics.)

Although the types of phonological processes are many and complex, most variations noted in *DARE* can be accounted for by loss, addition, modification, and change. *Loss* of a sound (or syllable) may occur in any part of a word and may affect sets of words, clearly revealing a pattern, or perhaps only a single word. One of the outstanding examples of patterned loss is that of postvocalic /r/. In some areas of the United States the *r* after a vowel in the spelling of many words is not pronounced. Thus *farm* may be [fɑ:m], *rare* [rɛ:ə], *cord* [kɔ:d]. Another patterned loss occurs when consonant clusters are reduced, most often finally in a word but also initially and medially. Some speakers thus may have [wel] for *whale,* [wil] for *wheel,* [wɑpɚ] for *whopper,* while others begin those words with /hw/. Similarly, *huge, humor,* and *Hubert* can begin with /j/ rather than /hj/. Some examples of nonpatterned loss are [laɪbɛri] for *library,* [ˈgʌvmənt] for *government,* [ˈklʌmbəs] for *Columbus.* For additional examples see sections 3.I.19, 3.I.22, and 3.II.26.

Addition of a sound can be illustrated by the intrusive /r/ in *wash* [wɑrš] and *idea* [aɪˈdiɚ], the /ə/ in *athlete* [ˈæθəlit] and *elm* [ˈɛləm], and the /t/ in *across* [əkrɔst] and *once* [wʌnst]. For further detail, see section 3.I.23.

Modification results in what native speakers would perceive as variants of the "same" sound. Modification is very common in AE and provides much of the subtle variation to be heard from one region to another. In some areas, postvocalic /r/, rather than being either lost or fully articulated, has an intermediate nature, producing what others hear as a "weak r." Similarly, some speakers have a velar (strongly backed) postvocalic /l/ that is heard not as a completely different sound but as a different version of *l.* These kinds of variation are detailed in section 3.II.

Change or *alternation* involves the use of one distinctive unit rather than another in a word or set of words. For example, the vowels in *fish* [fiš] and *bush* [buš], compared with the more usual [fɪš] and [bʊš], show the use of different sound units in those words by speakers of different regions or social groups. This kind of variation is examined in section 3.I.

To summarize: phonological variation in the United States is usually the result of sound changes that have spread irregularly through the population, being limited to given regions or social groups and affecting different word sets. The changes have numerous causes, including the influence of neighboring sounds. Of the four types of processes discussed, three (loss, addition, change) work across the sound units of the language, while the fourth (modification) involves slightly different articulation of a given sound unit. The number and kinds of words affected by these processes may produce patterned variation or more limited variation.

Some general comments about systematic approaches to AE pronunciation, discussed in section 1, bear restatement. The number of actual sounds produced by speakers of AE is incalculable, for pronunciation varies with each articulation of every individual. Some abstraction is necessary to deal with this very prolific reality. For the purpose of discussing phonological variation, linguistic scholarship has produced no completely satisfactory system of analysis. The scheme presented here sees AE as having altogether forty sound units or phonemes; all the phonetic elements (articulated sounds) that are taken to be variants of the "same sound" by native speakers (and that meet certain formal criteria) are considered to be a single sound unit and are represented by a single symbol. (These symbols are enclosed in diagonal slashes.) For example, in *bite* the vowel is represented by /aɪ/, but the phonetic elements that AE speakers actually produce (for which /aɪ/ stands) can be represented (in square brackets) by [aɪ], [ʌɪ], [ɒɪ], [a:], and others. It is at this phonetic level that much variation in AE takes place, with two exceptions. First, there is one phoneme, /ɔ/, that not all AE speakers have, and second, some processes produce differences of sound-unit occurrence in given words or word-sets. That is, sound units differ in their phonetic manifestations from region to region and group to group and in their incidence in words. No attempt is made in *DARE* to present all possible or known variants; some, because of the number of words or speakers affected, are of more interest than others. Judicious selection rather than exhaustive listing is the practice followed here.

History

Much variation in contemporary AE pronunciation is linguistic change working through social and regional variation. This situation is complicated by the fact that AE is, historically, a displaced language. That is, regional and social variations existing in British English were uprooted and mixed in various ways with one another and with other languages in a new context, producing American English. Some pronunciations that were quite limited either socially or regionally in British English became widespread in AE; others remained limited in North America as in Great Britain; still others died out. And, of course, North American innovations have occurred during the three hundred and fifty years since English was brought to the New World. Many, if not most, of the variations found in the United States may also be found in Great Britain; the outstanding difference between British English and AE pronunciation is the mixture of features to be found in any one place and in any one speaker.

The English that was brought to North America in the early seventeenth century was in the latter stages of a period that had already seen great changes in pronunciation. The tense ("long") vowels had all raised their points of articulation, a process that simplified the vowel system by eliminating several distinctive sound contrasts but also produced two wide diphthongs, /aɪ/ and /aʊ/. Furthermore, most of the signifi-

cant changes that were later to appear in Standard London English were probably well under way among some speakers in England. For example, loss of postvocalic /r/ in certain phonological environments is evidenced as early as the sixteenth century in areas within and around London (the source of much early migration to North America). Rural migrants brought it into the speech of lower-class London, where it rose socially, became part of Standard London English, then spread outward again. It was probably indigenous to colonial North American speakers but was later brought more forcefully into AE through those regions which had kept continuous cultural contact with London English.

There is reason to believe that other features that later became standard pronunciations in London English were present in the speech of the lower classes. The seventeenth- and eighteenth-century change in which some words with /ʊ/ (such as *must*) became pronounced with /ə/ must have begun much earlier, for it is nearly universal in AE, whereas in England some northern dialects retain the older form even today. Likewise most AE speakers have an unround vowel, for example [a] or [ɑ], in "short *o*" words like *hot* and *stock* where most English speakers have a round vowel, [ɔ]. The common AE form, however, does exist in British English, and there is written evidence for its occurrence in Britain as early as the seventeenth century. Again, it must have been brought to North America during early settlement to have spread so thoroughly in AE; at the same time, it became ridiculed as a foppish pronunciation in England and failed to gain general acceptance there. Similarly, the voiced (or flapped) medial *t* heard as /d/ in words like *butter, latter, metal,* which has become nearly universal in colloquial AE, has remained quite restricted regionally in England. Other pronunciation changes that took place in England were imported into America with more limited usage. The "broad *a*," /ɑ/, of standard British English, rather than /æ/, in words like *bath* and *can't,* attained widespread usage only in eastern New England, with much more limited and sporadic use farther south.

It is not impossible that some of these features shared by American and British English are of independent origin. That is, as a result of contact with other languages or for purely phonetic reasons, features parallel with those of British English may have appeared independently in AE. Until more is known about language development, however, it is probably best to assume the simplest hypothesis for the shared feature: importation.

AE pronunciation began in the seventeenth century as a mixture of contemporary British English forms, but not all regional varieties were equally represented. The early colonists came mainly from southeastern England; settlers from other sections came in greater numbers later in the seventeenth century and early in the eighteenth. Nor were all social varieties of British English equally represented. The bulk of the colonial settlers were the more ambitious, dissatisfied, or unlucky members of the lower and middle classes. Thus the composition of the American population favored some social and regional speech varieties over others. This helped to bring about a simplification in AE, compared to the complexity of variation in British English, which remains to the present. The first two or three generations of North Americans probably further reduced variation by permitting some of the less usual forms to lapse. At the same time, some ongoing changes in standard British English were paralleled by those in AE. For example, the diphthongs in words like *nice* and *now,* which were probably [ʌɪ] and [ʌʊ] at the time of settlement, moved (for many speakers) to their present [aɪ] and [aʊ]. (Some speakers in parts of the East Coast and in Canada retain these earlier forms in such words as *nice* and *about.*) The influence of northern British English speakers became significant, especially in the South Midland area of the colonies, with the eighteenth-century immigration of the Ulster Scots, who brought many of the same pronunciations with them.

The eighteenth century was a period of language scrutiny both in England and in the New World. Regularization and formalization according to standards of correctness dictated by logic, Latin structure, and educated usage began to shape popular attitudes toward language. At the same time, the middle class was expanding and efforts toward public education were under way. Late in the century came attempts in the new United States to Americanize the language—especially through the efforts of Noah Webster with his speller and dictionary (1806). Educated use of English, American style, took root. By the late eighteenth century regional distinctions as well as an "American" accent were noticeable. Though the growing regional centers (Boston, New York, Philadelphia, Richmond, Charleston) had developed their own local differences reflecting their unique histories, they were still American. As an educated standard emerged, some peculiarities of pronunciation were probably excluded from the speech of the educated, but regional variations of the standard were tolerated (as they are today).

The American language was also influenced by the great numbers of speakers of other languages with whom the English settlers came into early contact. American Indian, Dutch, Swedish, French, and African languages, among others, were part of the colonial linguistic milieu. The influence of these languages on the lexicon and syntax of regional and standard AE has not been adequately documented. Equally problematic is non-English influence on AE pronunciation. Evidence for any early influence is ambiguous at best, since most of the possibly influential forms also occur in British English. Whether such features as /t/ and /d/ for /θ/ and /ð/ in parts (both north and south) of the East Coast, or lack of postvocalic /r/, are independently derived is open to question. The influence of African speakers, especially in the South where their relative numbers were high, is particularly controversial. Creole English, derived from African and Caribbean languages, was certainly present. How long it lasted and the degree of influence it has had (even on present generations of Blacks) is also open to question. Creole English lacks postvocalic /r/ as well as /θ/ and /ð/; it also lacks /æ/ and the contrast between /ɑ/ and /ɔ/. Neither of the last two characteristics is much evidenced in the current pronunciation of Black or White southerners, whereas the first two are (as also in British English and elsewhere in AE). However, various British English dialects not only have /æ/ and a contrast between /ɑ/ and /ɔ/ but also have speakers who lack postvocalic /r/ and substitute other sounds for /θ/ and /ð/. Thus, no final judgment about non-English influences on early seventeenth- and eighteenth-century AE pronunciation can be made at present.

The question of non-English influence is even more troublesome for the nineteenth and early twentieth centuries. Large numbers of Germanic, Slavic, and Romance-language speakers, Chinese and Japanese, and Protestant and Catholic Irish poured into already settled areas as well as the newly developing agricultural areas. Again the question arises whether identical features in widely separated areas are of independent and coincidental origins or come from a common source. Such cities as Milwaukee, Chicago, Cleveland, Buffalo, New York, Philadelphia, and Baltimore, for example, have numerous speakers who use /t/ and /d/ for /θ/ and /ð/, a common substitution in foreign-accented English. Outside the South, however, these forms are not common in nonurban areas, even those heavily settled by non-English speakers. It is possible that density of population and particular economic and language situations leading to differing patterns of assimilation produced the difference. Other variants such as [ŋg] in the common local pronunciation [lɔŋ'gaɪlənd] for *Long Island* or [ɛ] rather than [æ] in such words as *that* and *ask* in New York City have been attributed to the influence of Eastern European Jews. Yet the same features are found elsewhere in both AE and British English.

Some variations of AE pronunciations do, however, seem likely to be results of non-English settlement. In Wisconsin, Minnesota, and the Dakotas, for example, the tense vowels for many speakers have much less diphthongization than elsewhere, so that /e/ is [e] rather than [eɪ], thus closer to its pronunciation by German, Norwegian, and Swedish speakers who settled the area in great numbers. The same lack of diphthongization exists in parts of eastern Pennsylvania, also heavily settled by German speakers. There are other influences in the Cajun area of Louisiana, in the Pennsylvania German area, the Georgia–South Carolina islands and Low Country, and other communities, urban and rural, where non-English features are still noticeable. In general, however, enough of the evidence for possible non-English influence on majority AE pronunciation is coincidental and ambiguous that prudence dictates withholding judgment on its effect for the present.

The nineteenth-century westward movement of English-speaking Americans and new immigrants established the basic geographical patterning of phonological variation that to a large extent continues today (although developments since World War I have begun to modify it). Except in the South, most of the westward migration began in inland areas, with successive overlapping waves starting from ever more westerly points of departure. Settlers had a tendency to seek out living conditions similar to those they left behind. Thus settlers from western New England moved into New York state, northern Pennsylvania, northern Ohio, Indiana, Illinois, Michigan, Wisconsin, and, more thinly, westward to the Pacific Coast. Those who left northern Maryland, Delaware, and eastern Pennsylvania moved across central Pennsylvania into central Ohio, Illinois, Indiana, and parts of Nebraska, Iowa, Missouri, Arkansas, and Oklahoma. Southern plantation culture moved across the rich Gulf Plains area into eastern Texas. But once these movements reached far enough westward (about the 98th parallel of longitude) their character changed. The lack of navigable rivers in the West made overland travel necessary; moreover, rainfall could not be counted upon to sustain traditional crops. Thus many settlers either doubled back or leaped to the Pacific Coast.

During the mid-nineteenth century, foreign settlements, supplemented by a burgeoning cattle industry moving from northern Texas into the high Plains region, led to a more thorough mixing of settlement, and consequently of speech patterns, through the Rocky Mountains and the length of the Pacific Coast. The penetration of eastern regional pronunciations into the interior, where they came in contact with other varieties as well as with immigrant and American Indian speech, was one of the most important occurrences in the development of AE and its regional patterning. During this period regional consciousness reached a peak from which it is still descending. Inland urban centers with socially complex speech patterns were being formed, a trend greatly accelerated toward the end of the nineteenth century and on into the twentieth.

Another influence affecting pronunciation was that of the schoolmarm and the schoolmaster. Public education for an ever-growing portion of the population was increasing in importance. Along with it came a heightened desire for "correctness" in language usage. Regional standards of pronunciation were still tolerated, but increasing attention was being paid to "better speech," especially in school activities like reading and spelling aloud, and this brought about spelling-pronunciations that in some cases reversed historical trends. Earlier, the *-ing* endings had been pronounced, in standard as well as nonstandard speech, *-n* (as in Shakespeare's normal usage). Except in parts of the South, the *-ing* pronunciation was reinstated as, at least, the formal pronunciation. Similarly *forehead* regained a lost *h*. During the same period the United States came close to having one regional pronunciation become the standard for the country (as has happened in England). The influence of Boston, which enjoyed a cultural flowering in the mid-nineteenth century and which had long been the seat of the highest education, was felt across large parts of the country. New England-bred and -influenced teachers, ministers, and elocutionists spreading across the land left many an [ɑnt] *aunt* and ['rɑðɚ] *rather* behind them.

A combination of sloth, indifference, hostility, and good sense put limitations to this trend, but the influence of public schooling should not be underestimated. Many non-English speakers were to be made American. Many English speakers were rising into the middle class and needed standards to speak by. This became especially important in the developing urban melting pot centers, where class consciousness was very strong. There is some reason to believe that foreign-language communities often adopt a kind of schoolbook English before complete language assimilation takes place. In general, public schooling has done much to reduce variation within regions. American Blacks, who as a group were long denied adequate public schooling, show some marked departures from regional and national norms, retaining older forms derived from British English and, perhaps, early Creole. Likewise, in Appalachia, where until recently public schooling was less constant than elsewhere, many older speakers still retain what are seen today as unusual forms (although the view that some pure Old, Middle, or Elizabethan English is still spoken there is an exaggeration and rests only on the survival of a handful of archaic words and phrases). In addition, the rise of large regional universities, by mixing many young speakers, has done much to level variations of pronunciation not only within but across regions. As a result, many college-educated, socially mobile speakers retain less regional and local pronunciation than their parents do.

Other twentieth-century developments have also modified the regional patterns established during the nineteenth century. Many southerners, Black and White, have moved to large northern cities, coming in sufficient numbers to prevent ready linguistic assimilation. The Detroit area, for example, though a northern city with a majority of northern speakers, also has many speakers with southern pronunciations. Meanwhile many northerners have moved to places like Florida and Arizona, altering the historically expectable patterns there. The development of huge urban centers with their rings of suburbs peopled by a highly mobile, socially selected population also is modifying older patterns. These urban areas, in time, also affect one another, with the result that two widely separated cities can be more like one another than like their closer rural neighbors. And finally, a familiarity with both the artificial standard of national radio and television and the speech of other regions, through the media and through travel, is also having an influence.

In brief, the process that began with London English assimilating many British English regional variations, turning them into urban, socially restricted patterns, some of which became part of the standard pronunciation, has been repeated (short of producing a "national standard") in American cities. Moreover, through public education, great mobility, and communication, this process is happening nationally. Even as new variants appear and spread, and as many speakers become aware of the developing national standard, they come to view the older regional and local patterns as social liabilities. One casualty of this process is folk speech, the language of continuing local tradition unaffected by schooling. Formerly widespread, folk pronunciation now occurs less frequently, although conservative usage among some Black and Appalachian speakers gives the appearance of social and regional patterning. Pronunciations like [drin] for *drain,* [nɑri] for *narrow,* [jaɪn] for *join,* [æks] for *ask,* [ɛləm] for *elm,* all of which date to the eighteenth century or earlier, are now considered rustic even though some of them like [jaɪn], were at one time fashionable, even literary. Meanwhile, even as some changes in regional and social AE pronunciation can be observed, more general changes continue to occur largely beyond conscious comprehension and control, responsive to social movement as well as to internal linguistic pressures.

AE variation is uneven in its density and complexity. The Eastern Seaboard and the South are more diverse than other parts of the United States; greater homogeneity occurs farther west. Not only are local and regional variation greater but urban social diversity is greater in older cities; moreover, western cities tend to reflect the speech of their surrounding regions more directly than do eastern cities. This too is changing, as the older cities extend their influence outward and the western cities begin to differentiate themselves from their rural areas. New York metropolitan speech is pushing into parts of Connecticut and New Jersey and up the Hudson Valley. Greater Los Angeles is beginning to differentiate itself from the rest of southern California (San Francisco has been separate for some time, for other reasons, from northern California). St. Louis, is, in a number of ways, different from its surrounding area, whereas the newer and more western Kansas City is still a good reflection of its environs, with only some younger speakers beginning to initiate change. Similarly, between Boston and Richmond, a driving distance of little over five hundred miles, many differences of pronunciation are encountered. In contrast, from Seattle to Los Angeles, more than twice that distance, relative homogeneity exists. If an east-west view is taken, as opposed to a north-south one, a somewhat different picture appears. Starting at the Eastern Seaboard, it is possible to move directly westward finding decreasing variation the farther one proceeds.

The foregoing account needs qualification, however. Some pronunciation features, especially on the East Coast, do run north and south, though with regional pockets and disjunctures. Social features may modify or even override regional ones. Furthermore, lines that separate users of one feature from those of another are seldom clear-cut. If regions and groups are to be defined by their pronunciation, the definitions must be in terms of sets of often overlapping features, and at times they must incorporate quantitative and social qualifications. The more detailed the set of features, the more limited is the social or regional group being described. For example, if the first feature in a set is full articulation of postvocalic /r/, the possible area is very large, excluding only parts of the East Coast and the South. If a fronted pronunciation of /aʊ/ as [æʊ] is added, the likely area has been reduced to the South Midland, the western part of the Midwest, and much of the Southwest. If a lack of a contrast between /ɑ/ and /ɔ/ is added and the speaker is middle-aged or old, the area is further reduced to part of the high Plains and Rocky Mountain states. If full articulation of the wide diphthongs is added, it is likely to be an urban area. If alternation of /ɛ/ for /æ/, and a rounded vowel in "short o" words, are added, the set is typical of, for example, Wichita, Kansas. Again, to be fully specific it is often necessary to build social and quantitative data into the set. Ultimately, of course, each individual speaker has sets that themselves contain variables.

Although overviews of regional variations in AE are somewhat risky, they can be valid and useful if properly qualified. One such overview is that derived from data gathered by a series of projects known collectively as the Linguistic Atlas of the United States and Canada. Based on both lexical and phonological data collected over nearly fifty years to the present, it is particularly revealing of the effects of nineteenth-century migrations. The general areas established by Atlas researchers include four basic regions: (1) the North, representing New England and its westward extensions; (2) the North Midland, representing the Central Atlantic states and their westward extensions; (3) the South Midland, representing the Middle Atlantic states and their westward extensions; and (4) the South, representing the spread of plantation culture. There are, of course, numerous subareas within each of these regions. The data gathered for *DARE* often corroborate the regions described by Atlas fieldwork, but they also show mixing of features across "boundaries" and suggest the existence of still more subareas.

Two social groups, the young and the Black, are differentiated from those around them sufficiently to warrant special attention. Regional generalizations such as those in the following sections do not always account for pronunciations that are common in Black communities. In the South, the races share many pronunciation features, though the proportions of Black and White speakers having any single feature may vary. For example, /θ/ and /ð/ are frequently pronounced /t/ and /d/ in Black speech, less frequently, though not rarely, among Whites. It is possible that if social and educational

backgrounds were held constant a greater similarity of use would be revealed. Another example is the pronunciation of *aunt*. Although both races have both /ænt/ and /ɑnt/ in the South, Blacks are most likely to have /ɑnt/ and Whites /ænt/. Outside the South, Blacks show varying degrees of assimilation to local and regional patterns. When the Black population is small and dispersed, as in a city like Minneapolis or in many small midwestern towns, assimilation is nearly complete. When numbers are larger or the concentration is great, as in many northern cities, preservation of southern features is common—for example, as in the greater likelihood of dropping of postvocalic /r/, preservation of the contrast between /ɑ/ and /ɔ/ (when Whites in the same community are losing it), and lack of a contrast between *pin* and *pen*. Here, too, of course, differing social and educational backgrounds produce marked variation. (Although details of pronunciation are different, these generalizations are also true for Appalachian Whites who have moved to northern and western areas.)

Young speakers, especially socially mobile ones, appear to be breaking with local speech patterns in favor of broader regional and perhaps even newly developing national ones. As the United States becomes more completely urbanized (integrated) in its social structure, the language will necessarily reflect that trend. The movement seems to be toward articulation of vowels farther forward in the mouth; continued loss of marginal contrasts such as /ɑ/ – /ɔ/ (*cot* vs. *caught*) or /ɔ/ – /o/ before /r/ (*for* vs. *four*); reinstatement of postvocalic /r/; and lowering of /i/ and /e/ to /ɪ/ and /ɛ/ before /l/, threatening the contrast between *feel* and *fill, sale* and *sell*. These and other adjustments appear to be spreading (although trends can change quickly and unexpectedly). Thus, many of the features discussed in succeeding sections may be inconsistent in young speakers' use, more stable among older speakers.

3. The *DARE* Pronunciation Key

This section has three major divisions: I. Alternations between Sound Units, II. Variation within Sound Units, III. Summary of Major Regional Variants.

The purpose of section 3.I is to describe particular phonological contexts and to show how more than one sound unit can be used in such contexts without changing the meaning of a word. For example, in the words *near, cheer,* and *beer,* two vowels, /i/ and /ɪ/, occur frequently in AE. The words mean the same thing no matter which vowel sound is used. In other contexts, however, the two vowels are not interchangeable: in such word pairs as /bit/ *beat* and /bɪt/ *bit,* /sip/ *seep* and /sɪp/ *sip,* /liv/ *leave* and /lɪv/ *live,* /pič/ *peach* and /pɪč/ *pitch,* the vowel is the sound unit that signals a difference in meaning, and to use a different vowel is to confuse the listener. Section 3.I describes many contexts in which more than one vowel can occur without altering the meaning of a word. This kind of alternation between vowels can vary either by geographic region or by social group.

Section 3.II describes the kinds of variation that can occur within individual sound units. For example, the diphthong /aʊ/ of *about* occurs as [aʊ], [ɑʊ], or [æʊ] in most parts of the country but is often [ʌʊ] in parts of Virginia, Maryland, and North Carolina and the coastal areas of South Carolina,

Georgia, and Florida. All three variants, however, are understood as signifying the same word—that is, though they are recognizably different, they all represent the same sound unit. This kind of alternation of sounds within individual units can also vary by geographic region, social group, or individual speaker.

Because both variation between units and variation within units can be the result of the conditioning effects of neighboring sounds, the distinctions may seem somewhat artificial. For example, the phonological context of a vowel followed by /š/ yields variation between [æš] and [æɪš] in the word *ash*, with both [æ] and [æɪ] being considered variants of the same sound unit. But before /š/ in the word *push*, many speakers who have [æɪ] in *ash* will have [puš] rather than [pʊš]—/u/ and /ʊ/ being considered two different sound units. Since the conditioning effect of the following /š/ determines the vowel in both cases, to consider one variation to be within a unit and the other to be between units may seem inconsistent. But it is the behavior of the sounds in all of their environments—not just one—that determines the classification of sound units; and while the divisions used here may overlap on occasion, the basic framework reflects as accurately as possible the functioning of the sound units in AE as a whole.

Section 3.III describes some of the major alternations considered in 3.I and 3.II in terms of their broad regional patterns.

Even though geographical areas where variants are used frequently are listed, the reader should keep in mind the following caveats: (1) Not all speakers within the given area can be expected to use any given form; social and localized restrictions are numerous and complex. (2) The frequency of occurrence of any form relative to its variants may be very high in some geographical locations but low in others. For example, the tensing of all lax vowels before /š/ and /ž/ occurs in the speech of a diminishing minority of speakers from Delaware through the Ohio River Valley. But the use of the vowel /e/ rather than /ɛ/, as in *measure* [meža˞], *treasure* [treža˞], is much more widespread geographically and in terms of the number of speakers using it than alternations between other vowels before /š/ and /ž/. (3) The sound described may well occur outside the designated geographical area; these areas should be taken as broad designators of relatively frequent occurrence of a variant. (4) No study is likely to discover all possible pronunciation variants. Especially in a wide area survey such as the *DARE* survey, done largely to collect lexical variants, there are limitations on both the number and the social types of speakers interviewed. The complexities become greater but more identifiable in intensive local studies. In brief, the following sections describe the *most notable* variants and their *major* geographical limitations. They are to be used as a pronunciation key to the dictionary entries and for general interest and information.

3.I   *Alternations between Sound Units*

3.I.0   Vowels.

3.I.1   Vowels before retroflex /r/ in monosyllabic words.

a. *fear, beard, near*, etc.   Both /i/ and /ɪ/ are found nationwide, varying in complex ways. /i/ occurs most strongly in the Southeast and as far west as Texas, less

strongly in the Northeast, North, and urban West Coast. /ɪ/, more general geographically, appears to predominate in the West and eastward through the center of the country into Pennsylvania. Infrequently the sounds /e/, /ɛ/, /ɜ/ occur, particularly among older speakers in parts of the South Midland, such as the Ozark region.

b. *bear, chair, hair*, etc.   /ɛ/ predominates, with /e/, /æ/, /ɪ/, /ɑ/, and /ɜ/ as alternates. Word incidence (*chair, care, dare*, etc.) is highly variable. /e/ is most frequent in the northeastern and southeastern quarters of the country. /æ/ occurs, especially in older speakers, in the South Midland from southern Delaware into Texas and rarely in the rural West. The rarer /ɪ/, /ɑ/, and /ɜ/ appear sporadically but most commonly on the Atlantic and Gulf coasts.

c. *barn, farm, car*, etc.   The vowel /ɑ/ occurs throughout the country (though variants have some differences in distribution: see 3.II.10). The rounded low-back vowel /ɔ/ sometimes occurs, in Delmarva and in parts of the rural West (as Utah).

d. *poor, sure, moor*, etc.   Variation in words of this type appears to be no less complicated than each word's historical development. The vowels /u/, /ʊ/, /o/, /ɔ/, and /ɜ/ are the major alternants. Both /ʊ/ and /ɔ/ can be found in all parts of the country, with /ʊ/ and /u/ most frequent in the northeastern quarter, /o/ and /ɔ/ in the southeastern quarter, /ʊ/ and /ɔ/ in much of the West. /ɜ/ is the least common vowel in this context, occurring mainly in the word *sure* (where it is quite general), and varying both by speaker and by social context.

e. *horse, hoarse, morning, mourning*, etc.   /ɔ/ predominates in both word types, but /o/ is a major variant, /ɑ/ an infrequent one. A distinction between /ɔ/ in *horse* and *morning* and /o/ in *hoarse* and *mourning* occurs inconsistently along the East Coast (becoming more frequent in the South) and even less consistently in inland areas, such as central New York state, St. Louis, and perhaps the rural west. It appears to be retained mostly by older speakers. When no distinction is made between /o/ and /ɔ/, these words appear to have /o/ most strongly in the Northeast and the Southeast, with some currency in the rural West. /ɑ/ occurs sporadically, occasionally as a stigmatized feature, in the South Midland extending from North Carolina into Texas and the rural West; in the St. Louis area it is characteristic of urban speech.

f. *learn, earth, service*, etc.   Constricted variants of /ɜ/ are usual here, but /ɑ/ also occurs sporadically, as in *learn* /lɑrn/, *burn* /bɑrn/, *earth* /ɑrθ/. It is less common today than formerly and occurs most frequently among older speakers and those with little formal education.

g. *fire, tire, wire*, etc.   The diphthong /aɪ/ is the most frequent vowel in these words, although /ɑ/ also occurs frequently in the South Midland and adjacent areas, and occasionally in the rural West. /ɔ/ sometimes occurs in Delmarva.

h. *flower, shower, hour*, etc.   The /aʊ/ diphthong occurs most frequently in these words, though occasionally /ɑ/ is heard, especially in Pennsylvania, and /æ/ occurs occasionally in the South Midland.

3.I.2   Vowels before intersyllabic /r/.

Because of the strong influence on vowels of an /r/ following in the same syllable, in polysyllabic words (e.g., *carry,
horrible*) vowel variation depends, in part, on whether the
medial /r/ articulation is present at the end of the stressed
syllable or at the onset of the next syllable only. (The possible
effects of presence or absence of this "linking" sound apply to
/l/ as well.) However, variants produced by other influences
also occur in these word types.

   a. *carry, parent, merry, Mary, bury,* etc.   /ɛ/ occurs most
   frequently in these words overall, with some striking
   variation in word incidence and in regional patterning.
   In words like *carry, parent,* and *marry* /æ/ also occurs
   frequently, especially in those areas of the East Coast
   and the South which lack postvocalic /r/ in monosyllables, but also in the Inland North through the Great
   Lakes region to the West, where word incidence complicates description. The word *parent,* for example, appears
   to have /æ/ more frequently than other words of the
   type. In *Mary, various, area,* and several other words, /e/
   is frequent in the South, occasional in some words in the
   North. In *merry, bury,* /ɛ/ predominates, but /ɜ/ also
   occurs sporadically, especially in such areas as Philadelphia and Texas.

   b. *forest, orange, tomorrow,* etc.   /ɔ/ probably predominates, but /ɑ/ is very frequent on the East Coast, extending westward through the southern half of the country,
   lessening in frequency in the rural West. Word incidence, however, complicates this generalization. *To-
   morrow* and *sorry,* for example, have /ɑ/ generally; but
   some speakers in the North, particularly the western
   Great Lakes area (Wisconsin, northern Illinois) have /ɔ/
   in those words. The word *orange* has /ɑ/ among some
   younger speakers who otherwise have /ɔ/.

   c. *hurry, curry, furry,* etc.   /ɜ/ predominates, but /ə/ also
   occurs, especially in areas of the East and South that lack
   postvocalic /r/ in monosyllables. The Inland North and
   West have both vowels.

3.I.3   Vowels before /l/.

   a. *milk, pillow, Illinois,* etc.   While /ɪ/ is the usual vowel
   in these words, /ɛ/ also occurs, especially in the Great
   Lakes area.

   b. *television, yellow, help,* etc.   /ɛ/ predominates, but /æ/
   alternates, especially in the speech of those who have /ɛ/
   rather than /ɪ/ in *milk, pillow, Illinois,* etc.

   c. *really, steel, wheel,* etc.   Although /i/ is the most common vowel, younger speakers throughout the West and
   speakers of all ages across the southern half of the country frequently have /ɪ/. The alternation does not affect all
   words of this type equally: a speaker who pronounces
   really as ['rɪlɪ] will not necessarily pronounce *steel* as
   [stɪl].

   d. *sale, jail, mailer,* etc.   /e/ is most common, but a variant of /ɛ/ also occurs, especially among younger
   speakers in the West. Because of variation within the
   two sound units /e/ and /ɛ/, words such as *sale* and *sell*
   do not usually sound alike for those who have /ɛ/ in *sale.*

   e. *call, doll, fall,* etc.   /ɑ/ predominates, but /ɔ/ is a frequent alternate. These vowels are highly variable in

nearly all contexts, making generalizations somewhat
unreliable, but it can be said that /ɔ/ is especially frequent in the Boston area and also occurs irregularly,
particularly among older speakers, from western Pennsylvania into the rural West.

   f. *pile, mild, child,* etc.   The /aɪ/ diphthong is usual in
   these words (with much variation within the unit itself;
   see 3.II.13), but the monophthong /ɑ/ also occurs in the
   South and South Midland.

   g. *howl, prowl, growl,* etc.   The /aʊ/ diphthong is the most
   common vowel in these words, but occasionally /æ/ and
   /ɑ/ occur.

   h. *result, bulk,* etc.   /ə/ predominates, with /ʊ/ also occurring fairly frequently in the South Midland and adjacent
   areas and sporadically in the West, especially in nonmetropolitan areas. /ɑ/ occurs occasionally.

   i. *cool, fool, pool,* etc.   The tense vowel /u/ is most common, but the lax vowel /ʊ/ also occurs occasionally,
   especially among younger speakers in the West.

3.I.4   Vowels before /n/.

   a. *pen, ten, mentor,* etc.   While /ɛ/ occurs most frequently, the higher vowel /ɪ/ is also very common,
   especially in the southern half of the country and in the
   rural West. For some speakers, /ɪ/ and /ɛ/ are not distinguished before /n/, while for others the coalescence is
   restricted to particular words. (The word *been,* which is
   regularly pronounced /bɪn/ in much of the country, is
   occasionally /bɛn/ in the South even for those who have
   /ɪ/ in *pen, men, send,* etc.) /e/ and /æ/ also occur occasionally, especially in the South Midland, in such words
   as *bench.*

   b. *onion, country, un-,* etc.   /ə/ occurs most frequently,
   but the lower central vowel /ɑ/ also occurs, especially as
   a prefix, as in *uncommon, uncertain, unequal,* etc. /ɑ/
   seems to be most frequent in the Mid Atlantic, Upper
   Midwest, and parts of the South. It results in spellings
   such as "oncommon" and has been stigmatized as a
   "wrong" pronunciation.

   c. *on, dawn,* etc.   Both /ɑ/ and /ɔ/ occur frequently, with
   /ɔ/ being more common in the East and South and /ɑ/
   predominating in the Inland North and the urban areas
   of the West.

3.I.5   Vowels before /š/, /ž/, /č/, /ǰ/.

   a. *fish, dish, itch,* etc.   /ɪ/ is most common, but /i/ also
   occurs, especially from Delaware and Maryland westward through the Ohio River Valley into northwestern
   Missouri; it also occurs occasionally in the rural West
   and in the South Midland. /i/ is most frequent among
   older speakers.

   b. *measure, treasure, fresh, edge,* etc.   /ɛ/ predominates,
   but /e/ also occurs. The distribution of /e/ is similar to
   that of /i/ in *fish* (above), except that it occurs more
   extensively in the South and West and is more frequent
   among speakers of all age groups.

   c. *bush, push, butcher,* etc.   /ʊ/ predominates, but /u/
   also occurs, especially in the South Midland and into the
   rural West. Use of /u/ seems to be receding. Infrequently, /ɜ/ occurs.

   d. *rush, mush, begrudge,* etc.   /ə/ is by far the most common vowel, but /ɛ/ also occurs, especially in the South Midland, and /ɜ/ occurs sporadically, especially among older, less educated speakers in the rural Ohio Valley.

   e. *gosh, wash, botch,* etc. Both /ɑ/ and /ɔ/ occur frequently, with /ɑ/ being usual in the South, parts of the Northeast, and much of the West, and /ɔ/ occurring regularly in the South Midland. Occasionally the diphthong /ɔɪ/ occurs, especially in the Ohio River Valley and in parts of the South Midland. Pronunciations with intrusive /r/—[warš], [worš], [garš], [gorš]—also occur, with widespread though sporadic evidence from Pennsylvania westward and southward (except in areas without postvocalic /r/), and occasional occurrence on the West Coast.

3.I.6   Vowels before /g/, /ŋ/.

   a. *egg, leg, keg,* etc. /ɛ/ predominates, but /e/ is also frequent, sometimes alternating with /ɛ/ even within the speech of individuals. Across the North /ɛ/ dominates, becoming mixed with /e/ in the rural West; from the South Midland into the Southwest, /e/ is most frequent; in the South and the lower Ohio Valley, both vowels occur. *Cag,* with /æ/, was once very common for *keg.*

   b. *log, frog, fog,* etc. Both /ɑ/ and /ɔ/ are current, but they vary more by word incidence than the vowels in other classes, making generalizations somewhat tenuous. On the whole, /ɑ/ is most frequent across the North and in the urban West; /ɔ/ is most frequent through the Ohio River Valley, the South Midland, and into the rural West. The South and eastern New England have /ɔ/ most frequently, with /ɑ/ occurring not infrequently. As with the low vowels in other contexts, younger speakers appear to be adopting the more fronted vowel.

   c. *long, song, strong,* etc. Variation between /ɑ/ and /ɔ/ is complex, but /ɔ/ probably predominates in terms of both geographic range and use throughout different age groups. The unrounded /ɑ/ occurs on the Atlantic Coast from Virginia southward to Florida, and in the urban West. It also occurs from Pennsylvania westward, often varying with /ɔ/. The South Midland has /ɔ/, often varying with /ɑ/ in its western regions. In the North, /ɑ/ and /ɔ/ are mixed in eastern New England, /ɑ/ is frequent in the western Great Lakes area, and /ɔ/ is common further west.

   d. *ring, thing, think,* etc. While /ɪ/ is most frequent, both /ɛ/ and /æ/ also occur, especially in the South Midland extending into Texas, with sporadic occurrences in the South and the rural West.

3.I.7   /æ/ and /ɑ/ ("broad *a*").

   aunt, rather, dance, path, etc. /æ/ predominates, with /ɑ/ (including both fronted [a] and retracted [ɑˑ] as variants) also occurring, especially in New England and on the Atlantic Coast. Word incidence appears to be highly variable in those areas that have [a] and [ɑˑ]. Word incidence is a stylistic factor among older speakers in much of the country, including Hawaii, where /ɑ/ may be used in *aunt* and *rather* in reading style, but /æ/ appears in conversational usage. *Aunt* and *rather* have frequent incidence of /ɑ/ (articulated as [ɑˑ]) sporadically down the East Coast to Florida, and (articulated as [a]) in New England, but are quite variable in incidence.

Younger speakers appear to have /æ/ forms more frequently and regularly across the word set.

3.I.8   /u/ and /ʊ/ before front consonants: /p/, /t/, /f/, /v/, /m/.

   coop, root, roof, hooves, room, etc. These words exemplify a limited set that gives evidence of variation of /u/ and /ʊ/. /u/ dominates in the usage of younger speakers and those in urban areas, although any word may prove an exception. The rural, the older, and the less educated often have variable usage, even for a single word. The less frequent vowel /ʊ/ has its most frequent occurrence in the Northeast, sporadically west through the Great Lakes into Minnesota, and on the South Atlantic and Gulf Coasts into Texas, with scattered occurrences in the rural West (being most frequent there in Washington and Hawaii).

3.I.9   /ɑ/ and /ɔ/ after /w/.

   wash, water, watch. These words have both /ɑ/ and /ɔ/, with variation among words and even word-forms (e.g., *wash, Washington*) being common. In *water* most of the East Coast and the South have /ɔ/. Other areas frequently have /ɑ/, but /ɔ/ (particularly when articulated as [ɒ]) is not infrequent. /ə/ occurs occasionally in Pennsylvania and New Jersey. In *wash,* /ɑ/ occurs along most of the East Coast (except for eastern New England) and throughout the South into Texas, and often in the West; /ɔ/ is frequent elsewhere; /ə/ occurs sporadically. *Watch* appears to have /ɑ/ more frequently than /ɔ/ everywhere, but backed or rounded forms occur sporadically.

3.I.10   /u/, /ju/, /ɪu/ after /t/, /d/, /n/.

   tube, due, new, etc. Following an alveolar consonant, the vowel /u/, the palatalized glide /ju/, and the back-gliding vowel /ɪu/ all occur. /u/ is most common, occurring through most of the country. In addition to /u/, /ju/ also occurs frequently on the Atlantic Coast from Delaware and Maryland south into Florida, then westward into Arkansas and eastern Texas, as well as in the San Francisco area and in Hawaii. There is also scattered usage in the rural West. In New England, /ɪu/ occurs alongside /u/, though less frequently than formerly. It is most common in the speech of those with little formal education. The vowel [ɪu], probably to be considered a variant of /ju/, also occurs in word sets with *o* spellings. For example, *do* and *too* occur as [dɪu] and [tɪu] sporadically, not only in areas with /ju/ in *due* and *tube,* but also in the South and the rural West, even among speakers who lack the glide in *new, due,* etc.

3.I.11   Alternation of /ɔɪ/ and /aɪ/ before /l/, /n/, /s/, /z/.

   joint, point, boil, oil, poison, hoist, etc. The most frequent vowel in these words is the diphthong /ɔɪ/. In parts of eastern New England, in the southern Appalachians, in scattered areas of the Mid and South Atlantic, and sporadically elsewhere, /aɪ/ also occurs. /aɪ/ is especially common among older people in folk speech and is also retained as a jocular form among some speakers of standard English. Word incidence varies, with /aɪ/ occurring more frequently in *hoist* than in other words, with *heist* perhaps being understood as a distinct word.

3.I.12   Vowels in weakly stressed final syllables.

   a. *haunted, bucket, houses,* etc. In the final syllable of such words the front vowel /ɪ/ (often articulated as a retracted variant [ɨ]) appears to predominate over mid-central /ə/. /ə/ is most common from the Mid Atlantic states westward to Ohio, alternating with /ɪ/ into the West and Southwest. The North, most of the South, and the West have /ɪ/ predominantly.

b. *sofa, china, California, Florida,* etc. Words of this type usually end in /ə/, but the vowel /i/ also occurs in folk speech (especially in northern New England and parts of the South Midland and South), and /ɝ/ (articulated as [ɚ]) also appears occasionally.

c. *Missouri, Cincinnati,* etc. Both /i/ and /ə/ occur in these place names, with widely mixed usage. In general, natives of these places tend to have /ə/, while outsiders tend to use spelling-pronunciations with /i/.

d. *meadow, window, follow, tomato,* etc. Words of this group may end in /o/, /ə/, or /ɝ/ (articulated as [ɚ]). In general, /o/ predominates in the North, North Midland, and West, while /ə/ is most frequent in the South Midland, South, and their settlement areas. Especially among folk speakers in the South Midland and South, /ɝ/ also occurs. In words like *borrow,* /i/ occurs alongside /o/ and /ə/. Like /ɝ/, /i/ occurs most frequently in folk speech in the South Midland and South.

3.I.13 Consonants.

Alternations between consonants tend to be somewhat less systematic in geographic distribution than those for the vowels, and often occur less regularly in all the words in a set.

3.I.14 Alternations among voiceless stops: /p/, /t/, /k/.

These consonants occasionally alternate with one another, though not always in regular or reciprocal patterns. In such words as *ask, desk,* and *stark,* /t/ can occur for usual /k/; the reverse is true in words such as *turtle, blast,* and *credit,* where /k/ sometimes occurs. Infrequently /t/ occurs where /p/ is usual in words such as *wasp* [wɔst]; and /p/ for /t/ has been observed in such forms as *catnip* [kæpnɪp]. The velar stop /k/ can alternate with the bilabial /p/, as in *baptize* ['bæk,taɪz].

3.I.15 Alternations between voiced and voiceless consonant pairs: /p~b/, /t~d/, /f~v/, /s~z/, /θ~ð/, /č~ǰ/.

Alternations between voiced and voiceless counterparts occur with some frequency. In a word such as *Baptist,* for example, the pronunciations [bæbdɨs(t)] and [bæbtɨs(t)], rather than [bæptɨs(t)], are common, especially in the South and South Midland. The use of /z/ in such words as *greasy, blouse,* (and perhaps *absurd*) is characteristic of most of the South, the Midland, and much of the Southwest, while /s/ in those words occurs regularly in the North (with a few exceptions, such as New York City) and on the West Coast. In the words *with* and *without,* both voiced /ð/ and voiceless /θ/ occur, with /ð/ generally dominating in the North and usage being mixed elsewhere. Some alternation between /f/ and /v/ takes place, as in *nephew* ['nɛvju] and *fascinator* ['væsɪnetɚ], but this seems to be a relic pattern occurring in scattered isolated communities rather than in broad regional patterns. The use of /č/ where /ǰ/ is usual, as in *college* ['kɑlɪč], occurs infrequently, being largely restricted to areas of dense foreign-language settlement.

3.I.16 Alternation between /k~kj/, /g~gj/.

In words such as *car, garden,* and *cow,* where the low vowel or diphthong is usually preceded by a velar stop, alternation between the stop and the stop plus a palatal glide occurs. The clusters /kj/, /gj/ occur most often in the South Midland and in parts of the South. Less frequently the clusters occur before front vowels, as in *care* and *carry,* often articulated as [kɪ] rather than [kj]. These clusters occur most often on the Atlantic Coast between the Potomac and Savannah Rivers, sporadically westward to the Mississippi River, and occasionally in the West.

3.I.17 Alternations among stops and fricatives.

Use of the stops /t/ and /d/ rather than the fricatives /θ/ and /ð/, as in *thing* [tɪŋ] and *this* [dɪs], is fairly widespread, especially in northern urban areas (where it is often characteristic of working-class speech), in the South (especially among Blacks), and in areas such as the Upper Midwest and the Southwest that have had dense settlement by foreign-language speakers. These alternations are common even within an individual's speech. Others are much less common: use of /f/ for /θ/ and /v/ for /ð/ as in *tooth* [tuf] and *with* [wɪv] occurs occasionally, especially among conservative Black speakers; the use of /b/ where /v/ is expected, as in *seven* ['sɛbn̩], ['sɛbm̩] or *drive* [draɪb] also occurs especially frequently among Blacks; the reverse alternation, of /v/ for /b/, as in *February* ['fɛvə,wɛri], occurs much less frequently. Occurrence of the stop /d/ where the fricative /z/ is expected, as in *business* ['bɪdnɨs], or *wasn't* ['wʌdnt], is especially frequent in the South but is not restricted to that area.

3.I.18 Alternations among fricatives and affricates.

Alternation of /s/ for /š/ occurs most frequently before /r/, as in *shrimp, shrink,* and *shrivel,* with pronunciations [srɪmp], [srɪŋk], ['srɪvəl] occurring most often in the South and South Midland, often among Blacks. Scattered instances occur elsewhere. (A further substitution, yielding [swɪmp], [swɪŋk], [swɪvəl], also occurs most frequently among Blacks in the South.) In such words as *measure, garage, beige,* and *television,* /ž/ and /ǰ/ alternate, but stylistic and social variation are more prominent than regional patterning. In *garage,* both [gə'raž] and [gə'raǰ] are frequent, though the former pronunciation is often a learned one. Pronunciations of the type ['meǰɚ], [beɪǰ], and ['tɛlə,vɪǰən] occur most frequently among speakers with little formal education. The same is true for words such as *rinse, lance,* and *wince,* where /č/ can occur for /s/ in contexts following a nasal consonant ([rɪnč], [rɛnč], [lænč], [wɪnč]); such forms illustrate the preservation of older pronunciations.

3.I.19 Alternations among fricatives and frictionless continuants.

Use of the frictionless continuant /w/ where the fricative /v/ is expected, as in *varmint* ['wɑ(r)mɨ(n)t], *very* ['wɛri], and *November* [no'wɛmbɚ] is a characteristic both of English Cockney speech and of creolized varieties of English; it occurs most frequently among Blacks in the South Carolina–Georgia Low Country, and also occurs occasionally in Hawaii. The reverse alternation, of /v/ for /w/ as in *wax* [væks] occurs, but rarely.

The articulation of /h/ before /w/, as in *wheel* [hwil], *where* [hwɛr], *why* [hwaɪ], seems to be receding in favor of the pronunciations [wil], [wɛr], and [waɪ]. Use of /hw/ is highly subject to style shifting, occurring much more frequently in reading and formal speech than in conversational speech.

Regional patterns of use of /hw/ and /w/ were identifiable several generations ago but are much less so today, with use varying greatly within regions and even within the speech of many individuals. Retention of /h/ before /j/, as in *humor* and *huge*, also varies widely within regions, with /hj/ probably dominant. The New York City metropolitan area often has /j/, as do other parts of the East Coast, but this varies from word to word as well as within and across regions.

3.I.20 Nasal consonants.

Alternations among nasal consonants vary less by region than by phonological context, often being affected by contiguous consonants. In words such as *length* and *precinct,* for example, the usual /ŋ/ sometimes varies with /n/, as [lɛnθ], ['pri,sɪnt], under the influence of the following interdental and dental consonants. Similarly, *conversation* becomes [kɑmvɚ'sešən], and is sometimes further assimilated to [kɑmpɚ'sešən]. Use of /n/ for /ŋ/ in words with final *-ing* is widespread, though it occurs more regularly in the South and South Midland than elsewhere. Its obverse, use of /ŋ/ for /n/, occurs among speakers who, having been corrected for saying *runnin'* rather than *running,* carry that "correction" to words that may seem analogous, but are not, so that words such as *mountain* and *button* become [maʊntɪŋ] and [bʌtɪŋ]. Alternation of /n/ with /m/, as in *palm* [pɑn], [pæn] and *mushroom* ['mʌš,run] occurs sporadically; it is especially frequent among older speakers.

3.I.21 Alternation of /r/ and /ɚ/.

In words having an *r* spelling after a vowel in the same syllable (such as *fire, course, board*), the consonant /r/ varies with a vowel-like unsyllabic consonant /ɚ/ according to fairly distinct regional and social patterns. Therefore, the use of /ɚ/ (also understood as the loss or "dropping" of /r/) is one of the most easily recognized features of variation in AE. Postvocalic /r/ is regularly retained in all of the Midland and North (except for eastern New England and the New York City metropolitan area) and in the West and Southwest. It is also retained in some areas of the Atlantic Coast, as in Delmarva and parts of the Carolinas. On most of the Atlantic Coast, however, and through most of the South (with the exception of many areas in Florida), and sporadically elsewhere, postvocalic /r/ is not retained but occurs as /ɚ/. That is, words such as *fort, charm,* and *fire* are pronounced not as [fɔɚt], [čɑɚm], and [faɪɚ], but as [fɔət], [čɑəm], and [faɪə], where the /ɚ/ is neither a part of the preceding vowel nor the nucleus of a second syllable. Within the geographic patterns outlined above, some social distinctions can be made. Particularly in northern cities with large numbers of Black residents, the /ɚ/ consonant occurs alongside /r/. In areas of predominant use of /ɚ/, the adoption of /r/ seems to be spreading among younger and better-educated speakers.

3.I.22 Reduction of consonant clusters.

In syllables with two or more contiguous consonants, the cluster is often "reduced," or pronounced without the distinct articulation of each sound. In words such as *ground, boiled, last, width, loaves,* for instance, many speakers articulate only one final consonant, producing [graʊn], [bɔɪl], [læs], [wɪθ], [loz]. Similarly, in words with three final consonant sounds, the clusters are often reduced to two or even one consonant: *asked* [æskt] may become [æst] or [æs]; *wolves* may become

[wʊlz] or [wʊvz]; *fifths* may become [fɪθs] or [fɪfs]; and words such as *wasps, desks,* and *fists* may be reduced to [wɑsp], [dɛsk], [fɪst], or even further to [wɑs], [dɛs], [fɪs], or may have a vowel added between consonants to facilitate articulation, as [wɑs(p)ɪz], [dɛs(k)ɪz], [fɪs(t)ɪz]. Cluster reduction can also occur initially and medially, as in *scratch* [kræč], *library* ['laɪbɛrɪ], *government* ['gʌvɚmənt], ['gʌvmənt]. While reduction of consonant clusters occurs in all regions, it is somewhat more frequent in the South and South Midland than elsewhere.

3.I.23 Excrescent sounds.

The introduction of sounds where there is no historic basis for them occurs frequently, with regional and social patterns varying from word to word. Such "intrusive" or "excrescent" sounds may be either vowels or consonants. They may occur initially, medially, or finally, and appear in such varied words as *across* [ə'krɔst], *anything* ['ɛnɪθɪŋk], *apron* ['emprən], *athlete* ['æθəlit], *attic* [æntɪk], *balance* ['bælənst], *breakfast* [brɛkfrəst], *curl* [kwɝl], *earth* [jɝθ], *elm* [ɛləm], *family* ['fæmblɪ], *percolate* ['pɝkjulet], and *wash* [wɔrš]. (See also Language Changes Especially Common in American Folk Speech.)

3.II *Variation within Sound Units*

This division treats each of the forty sound units, with the major variants, recognized in American English. No given variant can be exhaustively treated here: occurrence outside the stated limitations is possible, and not every speaker who fits the stated limitations necessarily has the given variant. To a certain extent, what one hears in a given place depends on who the speaker is and under what conditions he or she is speaking. And finally, some variants may be used by a majority of the speakers in one region, by a minority in another; estimates of probable proportions can only be general. All phonetic variation is probably governed by context—neighboring sounds, stress, grammatical category, usage level, even word meaning—as well as by the location and social characteristics of the speaker, but detailed, narrow studies would have to be done to establish these characteristics firmly. The following discussions are based on a wider network and represent broader patterns of use. They should provide the information necessary for a reader to infer the most likely pronunciations for particular regions.

3.II.0 The stressed vowels.

The key words given illustrate only some of the possible phonetic contexts for each vowel.

3.II.1 /i/ *beat, dream, feel,* etc.

The principal variants are [i], lengthened [i:], upgliding [ɪi], and ingliding [iə]. Though these variations are subtle, they show some regional and social patterning. [ɪi] occurs in all regions, but competes with the other variants in given areas. The ingliding vowel (when not produced by stress patterns) occurs most prominently in the South Carolina Low Country (approximately the eastern third of the state); it is receding in favor of [ɪi] and [i(:)]. Monophthongal [i(:)] is found in New York City, eastern Pennsylvania, sporadically across western New England, New York, Ohio, Michigan, and Illinois, more often in Wisconsin, Minnesota, and the Dakotas, and sporadically in the Northwest. It is occasional throughout the South Midland into Texas. It appears to be strongest in areas heavily settled by speakers of Germanic languages.

3.II.2 /ɪ/ *bit, him, pill,* etc.

The principal phonetic variants are [ɪ], lengthened [ɪ:], ingliding [ɪə], retracted [ɨ], and lowered [ɪˇ]. [ɪ(:)] and [ɪə] are the most common, occurring throughout the country. South of a line from Philadelphia to Kansas City, [ɪə] is quite common except in coastal areas. Younger speakers in the Inland North also are making increased use of this form. In both areas, stress and phonological context variably control the use of [ɪə]. In the South into Texas, [ɨ] occurs in *scissors, sister,* and several other words. Across the North, sporadic occurrence of a lowered [ɪˇ] (approaching [ɛ]) occurs, particularly but not exclusively in younger speakers.

3.II.3 /e/ *bait, main, tail,* etc.

The principal phonetic variants are [e], lengthened [e:], upgliding [eɪ], ingliding [eə], and upgliding [ɛɪ] with a lowered onset. [eɪ] predominates generally, but in some regions other variants are frequent. [e] and [e:] occur in nonurban areas of New England and westward through the Great Lakes area to the West Coast, including Alaska; they are particularly strong in Wisconsin, Minnesota, and the Dakotas. They also occur in eastern Pennsylvania and sporadically westward into the Great Plains. They compete with [eə] in eastern South Carolina, and may also occur in areas with concentrated non-English settlement, such as Hawaii. The upglide [ɛɪ] occurs in both Philadelphia and Pittsburgh and sporadically in central Pennsylvania and Ohio. It appears to be receding in favor of other variants.

3.II.4 /ɛ/ *bet, men, help,* etc.

The principal phonetic variants are [ɛ], ingliding [ɛə], raised [ɛˆ], lowered [ɛˇ], and upgliding [ɛɪ]. Throughout most of the country, [ɛ] is the most common, with other variants prevailing only in specific phonological contexts. In the southern half of the country as far west as New Mexico, however, ingliding [ɛə] tends to dominate, especially before /l/ and /r/. It also occurs sporadically in the North and seems to be increasing among young speakers. The raised variant [ɛˆ] occurs widely before nasal consonants (and sometimes alternates with the /ɪ/ sound unit; see 3.I.4). The lowered [ɛˇ] occurs mainly among young speakers in northern urban areas, in words like *desk* and *best.* The upglide occurs most often in the South and South Midland.

3.II.5 /æ/ *bat, sand, pal,* etc.

The principal phonetic variants are [æ], a raised and nasalized [æˆ], ingliding [æə], and upgliding [æɪ]. Although [æ] occurs in all parts of the United States, most areas also have at least one of the other variants in some phonological environments. The upgliding [æɪ], as in *ash* and *bag,* occurs most frequently south of a line from Delaware through southern Missouri, being less common in coastal areas than inland. Scattered instances occur in New England and the rural West. Raised and nasalized variants are common from New England and New York City westward to the Pacific Coast (including San Francisco). This feature appears to be spreading among the young, even in areas outside those listed above. In the South the raised variant without nasalization can be

heard. The ingliding diphthong [æə] occurs occasionally in the South and South Midland.

3.II.6 /u/ *boot, fool, moon,* etc.

The principal phonetic variants are [u], upgliding [ʊu] and [ʌu], ingliding [uə], and centralized [ʉ]. The upgliding diphthong [ʊu] is the most widespread variant. In parts of the northern Midwest, eastern Pennsylvania, the Georgia–South Carolina coast, and sporadically elsewhere, the monophthong [u] occurs, often being attributable to foreign-language influence. Younger speakers in these areas tend to use this form less frequently than their parents. [uə] and [ʌu] occur in the South and several adjacent areas: the former especially near Charleston, South Carolina, the latter throughout the South, especially in the east. The centralized [ʉ] occurs in the South, the lower Midwest, and the rural West, and seems to be increasing among younger speakers.

3.II.7 /ʊ/ *good, pull, push,* etc.

The principal phonetic variants are [ʊ], ingliding [ʊə], frontgliding [ʊɪ], and centralized [ʊ̵]. The most widespread variant is [ʊ]. The inglide occurs frequently throughout the South Midland, the lower Midwest, and the rural West and occasionally in New England and the South. The centralized variant is heard frequently in the South Midland and adjacent areas of the Midwest and the Southwest, and is also found in the rural West. Particularly before /š/, as in *push,* the frontgliding variant [ʊɪ] occurs, being most frequent in parts of New England and the South.

3.II.8 /o/ *boat, rose, gold,* etc.

The principal phonetic variants are an upgliding [oʊ], ingliding [oə], upgliding [ɤʊ], monophthongal [o], and midback [ɵ] (traditionally called the "New England short *o*"). Upgliding [oʊ] occurs through most of the country. The monophthong [o] occurs most frequently in the Upper Midwest, along the Georgia–South Carolina coast, and sporadically elsewhere, especially where foreign-language settlement has been dense. It is becoming a conservative pronunciation. The ingliding variant occurs most often in coastal South Carolina, Georgia, and Florida, but also in eastern Virginia and the southernmost part of Maryland. Formerly found chiefly in the Baltimore-Philadelphia area, western Pennsylvania, eastern Ohio, and northeastern North Carolina, the upglide [ɤʊ], with centralized start, seems to be gaining currency, occurring sporadically across the North and into the West. It appears to be increasing particularly among younger speakers. The New England [ɵ], by contrast, has been receding rapidly and is becoming rare even in northeastern New England, where it was still common a generation ago.

3.II.9 /ɔ/ *caught, bought, August,* etc.

Not all speakers have the raised low-back rounded vowel /ɔ/. In areas in which it occurs, it often contrasts with /ɑ/ in such word pairs as *cot–caught* /kɑt/–/kɔt/ and *tot–taught* /tɑt/–/tɔt/. For those who do not make the distinction between /ɑ/ and /ɔ/, the retracted variant [ɑ] of the /ɑ/ vowel may occur where other speakers have /ɔ/. The variants of /ɑ/ and /ɔ/ are among the most complex pronunciation variables in AE, governed by phonetic context and by social and geographic factors, and involving the separation or nonseparation of word classes. See 3.III.4.

The principal phonetic variants of /ɔ/ are a low-back round

[ɔ] and a raised variant [ɔˆ], a lower low-back round [ɒ], upgliding diphthongs [ɑʊ] and [ɔʊ], and an ingliding [ɔə]. [ɔ] is most common, occurring widely throughout the East and the South and in much of the North. In eastern New England both [ɒ] and [ɔ] are current; in the New York metropolitan area [ɔˆ] is common; [ɒ] is frequent in western Pennsylvania and into Ohio. The diphthongal variants occur throughout the South into Texas and are occasional in the rural West.

3.II.10   /ɑ/   *father, stock, college,* etc.

The principal phonetic variants are fronted [a] and [aᶜ], central [ɑ], and retracted [ɑ]. [a] occurs most frequently from New England across the Great Lakes area to the West Coast. It is most frequent in those areas before a spelled *r* as in *car, yard, scarf,* but is also common in other phonological environments, especially among younger speakers. [aᶜ], even approaching [æ] for some speakers, is especially common in New England. The central [ɑ] occurs in at least some phonological contexts over most of the United States but often alternates with one or more of the other variants, usually controlled by phonetic context. The retracted variant [ɑ] is frequent on the East Coast, although the controlling contexts differ from north to south. Where postvocalic /r/ is not articulated, a lengthened [ɑ:] is often heard in words like *car* [kɑ:] in metropolitan New York, Virginia and adjacent areas of Maryland and North Carolina, and coastal South Carolina and Georgia. Where postvocalic /r/ is articulated, [ɒ], a variant of /ɔ/, can also be heard, especially in the South Midland and the rural West. It is most frequent there among older and poorly educated speakers. In other phonological contexts, [ɑ] also occurs frequently in western Pennsylvania and sporadically elsewhere.

3.II.11   /ə/   *cut, sun, judge,* etc.

The principal phonetic variants are [ʌ], raised [ʌˆ], ingliding [ʌə], and upgliding [ʌɪ]. [ʌ] prevails throughout the North and is fairly common in parts of the South. Raised and ingliding variants are also found in the South Midland and South. The upgliding [ʌɪ] is a positional variant, occurring before /š/ and /ǰ/ (as in *brush, judge*) in parts of the South. In unstressed position, as in the first syllable of *about,* the symbol [ə], corresponding to stressed [ʌ], is used.

3.II.12   /ɜ/   *bird, sermon, further,* etc.

The principal phonetic variants are a fully constricted [ɝ] (articulated with the tongue curled back), a slightly constricted [ɜ], an unconstricted [ɜ], and an unconstricted upgliding diphthong [ɜɪ]. The constricted variant prevails throughout most of the Inland North, the Midland, and the West. The unconstricted vowel is generally confined to eastern New England, the New York City metropolitan area, tidewater Virginia, and coastal South Carolina and Georgia (areas that lack postvocalic /r/ in general). In the areas where unconstricted [ɜ] prevails, a partially constricted variant may also occur sporadically. The upgliding diphthong [ɜɪ], which occurs in metropolitan New York and in parts of the South, is sometimes stigmatized, having been characterized in literature as a Brooklyn lower-class feature. While for most speakers it is not homophonous with [ɔɪ] (as suggested by such spellings as *boid* and *toid* for *bird* and *third*), it is sufficiently different from [ɝ] and [ɜ] to sound strange to many Americans. In unstressed position, as in *father, mother,* the symbols [ɚ] and [ə] are used, corresponding in articulation and distribution to stressed [ɝ] and [ɜ].

3.II.13   /aɪ/   *nice, ride, wire,* etc.

The diphthongs typically vary by both onset and glide elements. The principal phonetic variants of /aɪ/ are upgliding [aɪ], [ɑɪ], [ɔɪ], and [ʌɪ] (for onset varieties) and ingliding [aə] and [ɑə] (for glide varieties, also called "weakened diphthongs"). The lengthened monophthong [a:] (sometimes called a "flattened" diphthong) also occurs for /aɪ/. Both [aɪ] and [ɑɪ] (particularly the former), are widespread, occurring across the United States. [ɔɪ] occurs most frequently on the East Coast, especially in Philadelphia and eastern North Carolina but occasionally elsewhere. The "fast" diphthong [ʌɪ] (starting from a more central position, so having a shorter glide), is most common on the East Coast, and is occasional along the Canadian border. It is especially frequent among conservative speakers in northeastern New England, tidewater Virginia and adjoining parts of Maryland and North Carolina, and coastal areas of South Carolina, Georgia, and Florida. There are scattered instances in the Gulf states. This variant occurs most often before voiceless consonants. The ingliding variants are more widespread, occurring especially frequently in the South and South Midland, and also in the lower Midwest and the Plains states as well as the Rocky Mountain area. Monophthongal [a:] is heard most frequently throughout the South and South Midland west to New Mexico, but is not restricted to that area. It occurs most often before /r/ and /l/ (as in *wire, mile*), before other voiced consonants (as in *wide, five*), and in final position (as in *high, my, try*).

3.II.14   /aʊ/   *about, loud, flour,* etc.

The principal phonetic variants are [aʊ], [ɑʊ], [æʊ], and [ʌʊ]; additionally, diphthongs with fronted [ʉ] as the second element are heard, and monophthongal [a:] also occurs. The major variant is [aʊ], with [æʊ] occurring next most frequently and probably increasing among young speakers. [ɑʊ] is heard most frequently in the Upper Midwest and in other places that have had substantial Germanic-language settlement. Centralized [ʌʊ] occurs most often among conservative speakers on the East Coast, and is especially frequent (occurring in all social groups) in tidewater Virginia. It is also an occasional variant in the North near the Canadian border. In the Southeast, diphthongs having centralized [ʉ] as the second element are also heard. Flattened or monophthongal [a:] occurs, especially in parts of the Midland and Midwest; it is particularly common before /r/ and /l/.

3.II.15   /ɔɪ/   *boy, moist, soil,* etc.

The principal phonetic variants are [ɔɪ], [oɪ], [ɒɪ], [ɔə], and [ɔ:]. The major variant is [ɔɪ], occurring throughout the country. [oɪ], having a higher onset element, occurs most frequently on the East Coast, especially in the Philadelphia area, and is occasional in the South. The diphthong [ɒɪ], with a low onset vowel, is a conservative variant, heard especially among older speakers and limited in its word incidence. Ingliding [ɔə] and monophthongal [ɔ:] occur frequently in the South and Midland, being especially common in contexts preceding /l/, as in *oil* [ɔ:l] or [ɔəl].

3.II.16　The consonants are on the whole less variable, at least in geographically generalizable ways, than the vowels. Their variability often is limited to specific words or tends to be stylistic rather than regional. Their influence on contiguous vowels, however, is great, as can be seen in the preceding sections. Two consonants, /l/ and /r/, have particularly strong influence over nearby vowels and some consonants and have some vowel-like characteristics themselves. Because they are very complex, they are treated in greater detail than the other consonants, but even so the descriptions outline only their major characteristics. For each sound unit, key words illustrating its occurrence in initial, medial, and final position are provided.

3.II.17　/p/　*poor, spring, sleep,* etc.

The principal phonetic variants are [p], aspirated [pʻ], unreleased [p⁻], and partially voiced [p̬]. In initial position, the aspirated variant is usual, except when followed by /r/ or /l/ (as in *preach, place*) in which case [p] often occurs. As the second element in a prevocalic consonant cluster (as in *spring, spigot*), [p] is usual. In final position, [p] is most common, but it alternates frequently with unreleased [p⁻]. [p̬] also occurs infrequently, most often in intervocalic position, as in *stopper, popple.*

3.II.18　/b/　*birds, labs, job,* etc.

The principal phonetic variant is [b]. Occasionally [b̥], a variant without full voicing, occurs, especially in final position and especially in areas that have had dense foreign (particularly German) settlement. A third variant, [β], articulated with some friction rather than complete stoppage, occurs infrequently; it is most likely in such words as *February, seven,* and *eleven,* where /b/ and /v/ alternate for some speakers (see 3.I.17).

3.II.19　/t/　*tap, stop, pet,* etc.

The principal phonetic variants are [t], [tʻ], [t⁻], and [t̬] (whose occurrences parallel those of the corresponding variants of /p/), and a flapped [ɾ], a dentalized [t̪], and a glottal stop [ʔ]. The voiced variant and flap usually occur intervocalically, especially in rapid speech in words such as *water, city, Saturday.* The dental stop, which occurs most frequently as the initial sound of an unstressed syllable (as in *hunter* [ˈhʌnt̪ə(r)]) has widest occurrence in the New York metropolitan area. The glottal stop, heard in words like *mountain* [ˈmaʊnʔn̩], *bottle* [ˈbɑʔl̩], and *eighteen* [ˈeɪʔˈtiɪn], is usually in syllable-final but not word-final position. It occurs sporadically throughout the country, with somewhat greater frequency in urban areas such as Boston, New York, and New Orleans.

3.II.20　/d/　*dog, pads, lad,* etc.

The principal phonetic variant is [d]. A partially devoiced variant [d̥] also occurs occasionally; like [b̥], it occurs especially in areas of heavy foreign-language settlement.

3.II.21　/k/　*cat, sketch, talk,* etc.

The principal phonetic variants are [k], [kʻ], and [k⁻] (whose occurrences parallel those of the corresponding variants of /p/ and /t/), and [x], articulated with velar friction. The [x] variant usually occurs in final position and is most common in areas of Germanic settlement.

3.II.22　/g/　*get, dragged, dog,* etc.

The principal phonetic variant is [g]. A partially devoiced variant [g̥] also occurs occasionally and, like [b̥] and [d̥], is most common in areas of heavy foreign-language settlement.

3.II.23

/f/	*fist, gift, puff*	/v/	*vice, wives, thrive*
/θ/	*thing, laths, myth*	/ð/	*this, scythes, lathe*
/s/	*sleep, wrist, toss*	/z/	*zero, housed, rise*
/š/	*sheet, washed, brush*	/ž/	*measure, garage*
/č/	*chin, reached, watch*	/ǰ/	*jump, nudged, badge,* etc.

The fricatives and affricates have little variation, usually being articulated [f], [v], [θ], [ð], [s], [z], [š], [ž], [č], [ǰ]. The primary exceptions are that the voiceless sounds can be articulated with partial voicing, [f̬], [θ̬], [s̬], [š̬], [č̬], and each of the voiced sounds has a partially devoiced variant, [v̥], [ð̥], [z̥], [ž̥], [ǰ̥], that occurs most often in areas of heavy German settlement. In addition, a fronted variant [š̠] occasionally occurs for /š/, particularly before front vowels and before /r/ as in *shrink* and *shrimp.* The /ž/ sound has a unique limitation: it occurs regularly in medial and final position but occurs in initial position only in proper names and loanwords (*Zsa Zsa, genre*).

3.II.24　/m/　*mad, bump, rum*
　　　　　　/n/　*now, dent, ran*
　　　　　　/ŋ/　*skunk, spring,* etc.

The principal articulations of the nasal consonants are [m], [n], [ŋ]. Each can occur as the syllabic nucleus, as in *bottom, button, Washington,* and in postvocalic position each can be assimilated, resulting in the nasalization of the preceding vowel, as in *jumping* [ˈǰʌ̃pɪŋ], *mantle* [mæ̃tl̩], *skunk* [skʌ̃k]. The velar nasal /ŋ/ occurs only in medial and final positions.

3.II.25　/h/　*high*
　　　　　　/w/　*wide, white, twenty*
　　　　　　/j/　*yesterday, funeral,* etc.

These consonants have very little variation in articulation, being pronounced [h], [w], [j] in most instances.

3.II.26　/r/　*run, pretty, spring, three, farther, car,* etc.
　　　　　　/ɚ/　*farther, car, fort, ear, mare,* etc.

In initial and medial positions, as in *rice, spruce,* /r/ is usually articulated [r], an alveolar frictionless continuant. In medial position following /θ/, however, as in *three* or *thrift,* a flapped variant [ɾ] also occurs. It is in postvocalic position, as in *car, fort, farm, ear,* that /r/ has significant variation in articulation. It can be pronounced, like [r], with full retroflexion or turning back of the tongue tip, as [ɚ]; with only partial retroflexion [ɝ]; or with no retroflexion at all, in which case it sounds like the weakly stressed vowel /ə/ but is sometimes considered a vowel-like unsyllabic consonant /ə̯/ (articulated [ə̯]). Alternatively, if there is no retroflexion, the preceding vowel may simply be lengthened. In general, the West, Southwest, Inland North, and Midland have full retroflexion. There are a few pockets in those areas, however, where variants with partial retroflexion can be heard, as in San Francisco and Seattle (among conservative speakers) and sporadically in the Upper Midwest. Most of the Atlantic Coast and all of the South are the regions where postvocalic /r/ is most regularly "dropped" or pronounced without retroflexion, though the feature also occurs elsewhere, particularly in northern urban areas where large numbers of Blacks have moved. However, even in the speech of a single individual, this articulation is not necessarily consistent, and lack of retroflexion can alternate with full or partial retroflexion. When postvocalic /r/ is also in word-final position (as in *ear, hair, door*), speakers in those regions which regularly "drop" the /r/ usually have articulations such as [ɪɪə̯], [hɛə̯], [doə̯]. In the South and among some Blacks elsewhere, however, lengthening of the preceding vowel may occur instead. This is a conservative feature, which is sometimes socially stigmatized. In both the Northeast and the South, young speakers appear to have less *r*-dropping than older speakers, indicating that fuller retroflexion may gradually spread through areas where /r/ is now regularly lost.

In the Northeast, where loss of postvocalic /r/ is the norm, when final /r/ is followed by a word beginning with a vowel, as in the phrase *mother and,* full retroflexion of /r/ usually occurs. In the South, this "linking" /r/ may also be heard but is less frequent than in the Northeast. It is probably the analogical source of the intrusive /r/ that occurs in phrases like *idea of,* which becomes [aɪˈdiə˞ˌəv]; this occurs most often in the Northeast.

Intervocalic /r/ exhibits a pattern related to that of postvocalic /r/. In words like *hurry, hairy, marry, horrible,* and *during,* some speakers have what could be described as two *r*'s, while others have only one. That is, the first type of speaker ends the first syllable with a postvocalic /r/ and begins the second syllable with an initial /r/, as in *hurry* [ˈhɝˌrɪ]. The second type ends the first syllable with a vowel, with /r/ occurring only in the second syllable, as [ˈhʌrɪ]. The "one *r*" pronunciation is most frequent along the East Coast and in the South; the "two *r*" pronunciation dominates through most of the rest of the country, though the Great Lakes region and the far West show mixed usage.

The influence of /r/ on preceding vowels is very strong, tending to pull vowels to the center of the mouth. Thus the "two *r*" speakers have neutralized some vowel distinctions kept by other speakers; for example, "two *r*" speakers usually have the pronunciation [ˈhɛə˞rɪ] for both *Harry* and *hairy,* while "one *r*" speakers distinguish between [ˈhærɪ] and [ˈhɛrɪ]. Similarly, in words like *forest* and *horrible,* many "two *r*" speakers maintain the historical low-back /ɔ/, [ˈfɔə˞rɪst], [ˈhɔə˞rɪˌbəl], while others have fronted, lowered, and unrounded the vowel to /ɑ/, [ˈfɑrɪst], [ˈhɑrɪbəl].

3.II.27 /l/ *light, blue, milk, ankle, fool,* etc.

The principal variants are [l] (articulated near the center of the mouth), [l̟] (a "light" variant pronounced toward the front of the mouth), and [ɫ] (a "dark" variant articulated toward the back of the mouth). The light /l/ usually occurs in contiguity with front vowels or with bilabial or labiodental consonants (as in *leaf, place, flee*), while the dark /l/ is usually contiguous with a back vowel or a velar consonant (as in *bowl, gloom, ankle*). Occasionally [ɫ] occurs initially, as in *love* [ɫʌv], particularly in the Northeast and most especially in the Philadelphia area. Additionally, a completely vocalized variant [ɯ], which sounds very much like the vowel [ʊ] or the consonant /w/, sometimes occurs in words such as *milk* [mɪɯk], *twelve* [twɛɯv], and *elbow* [ˈɛɯboʊ]. This vocalization of /l/, which occurs most often in the South and the upper Ohio Valley, is

analogous to the articulation of postvocalic /r/ in words such as *fire* [faɪə̯] and *poor* [pʊə̯]. And just as /r/ can be "lost" in words such as *far* [fɑː], /l/ can be lost in such words as *help* [hɛːp] or [hɛəp] and *wolf* [wʊːf]. In both cases, the loss is usually compensated for by a lengthened or ingliding vowel. The loss of /l/ is less frequent than that of /r/. It seems to occur most often in the South and among Blacks, but its regional and social patterns are less distinct than those for the loss of /r/, and its word incidence is less regular.

Intervocalic /l/, like intervocalic /r/, has two usage types. The first type closes one syllable with [ɫ] and begins the next with [l], as in *cooler* [ˈkuɫlə˞]. The second type ends the first syllable with a vowel and begins the next with [l], [ˈkulə˞]. In general, the East Coast, South, South Midland, and interior West have the "one *l*" usage, the interior Northeast and the North Central states have the "two *l*" type, and the coastal West has mixed usage.

Like /r/, /l/ has a strong influence on preceding vowels. Diphthongs are "flattened" or monophthongized more frequently before /l/, as in *file* [faːl], than elsewhere. Lax vowels tend to alternate with tense, as when *steel, pail, fool* are pronounced [stɪl], [pɛl], [fʊl] rather than [stil], [pel], [ful]. (This pattern is most common in the West, but is not restricted to that area.) Additionally, lower lax vowels alternate with higher lax vowels before /l/, as when *milk* is pronounced [mɛlk] and *Philadelphia* becomes [ˌfɪləˈdælfɪə].

3.III *Summary of Major Regional Variants*

This section takes some of the more significant pronunciation variations and summarizes them in terms of their regional and social distributions.

3.III.1 Presence or absence of postvocalic /r/.

Probably the most readily noticed feature of variation in AE, this feature is nevertheless a linguistically and socially complex matter. Most speakers of AE have a retroflex /r/ (articulated with the tip of the tongue turned back) following vowels in the same syllable, as in *car, floor, farm, work, course.* Most network radio and television professionals also have this feature. In most of the South and along much of the East Coast, however, postvocalic /r/ is not articulated as /r/ but rather as a vowel-like unsyllabic /ə/. But within these broad areas there is significant variation in practice; not all speakers "drop" the /r/, nor do all speakers follow the same practices in dropping it. Variation within these regions is affected by age, social class, and word incidence, and pronunciation within the speech of particular individuals also varies. Map 1 illustrates the areas (1) where medial postvocalic /r/ (as in *course, work*) is regularly dropped, and (2) where medial postvocalic /r/ is weakened, or articulated with less than full retroflexion of the tongue.

3.III.2 Weakened variants of diphthongs.

The "wide" diphthongs, /aɪ/ (*bite*), /aʊ/ (*bout*), /ɔɪ/ (*boy*) all have varying degrees of weakening of the second element, to the point of becoming "flattened" diphthongs (that is, lengthened monophthongs). Thus, the sound unit /aɪ/ may be articulated as [aɪ] (the full diphthongal upglide), [aᶦ] (a weakened upglide), [aə] (an inglide), or [aː] (a flattened variant). The diphthongs /aʊ/ and /ɔɪ/ have corresponding variants. Some phonological environments encourage weakening

Map 1

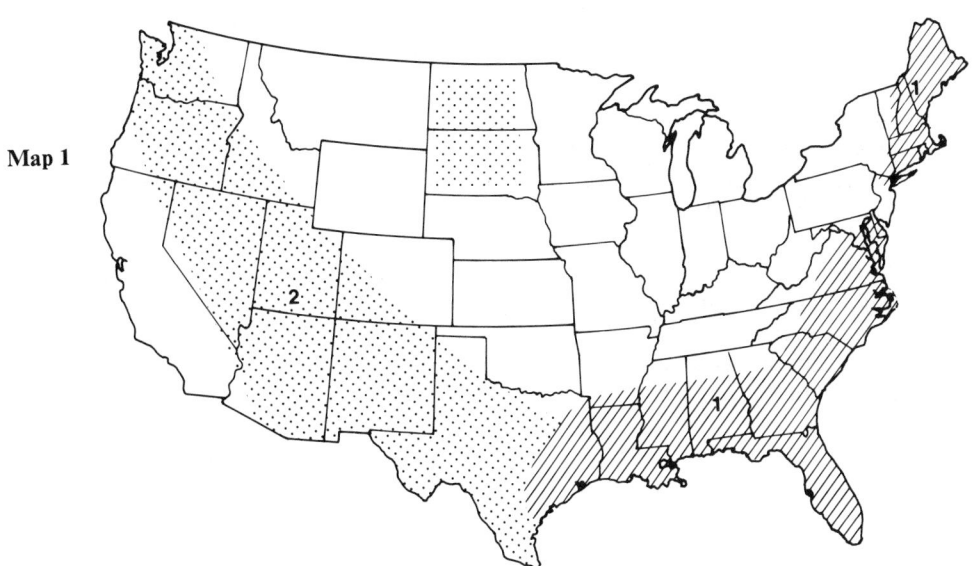

more than others: voiced consonants following the diphthong are more likely to promote weakening than are voiceless consonants, and /r/ and /l/ encourage it more than other voiced consonants. Further, different areas of the country (and different social groups within the areas) have weakened variants of the diphthongs under different conditions. In final position (as in *by, high, try*), the South, South Midland, and part of the Southwest frequently have both weakened and flattened variants. The Plains states, Rocky Mountain area, and southern parts of the Midwest have the weakened variants [aˈ] and [aə], most frequently before voiced consonants, especially /r/ and /l/. The South tends to have monophthongal variants of /aɪ/ before voiced consonants; the South Midland has them in even more environments. In other parts of the country, if /aɪ/ is weakened at all it is most likely to be so before /l/.

The /aʊ/ diphthong is less likely to have monophthongal variants than /aɪ/. However, it too is most likely to weaken before /r/ and /l/, and before voiced rather than voiceless consonants. The geographic area of most frequent occurrence

includes northern Maryland and southern and western Pennsylvania, but extends basically from the upper Ohio Valley southward into the Southwest (especially before /r/ and /l/), with occasional usage elsewhere in the East.

Although /ɔɪ/ is less consistently weakened than the other two diphthongs, weakened or flattened variants (such as [ɔəl] or [ɔːl] for *oil*) occur across the South and South Midland into the Southwest.

Map 2 shows the approximate areas of (1) weakening and flattening of /aɪ/ in word-final position (as in *by, high*), and (2) weakening of /aɪ/ before a final voiced consonant (as in *ride, mile, fire*).

3.III.3　Diphthongized variants of monophthongs.

Sound units that are usually monophthongs may be articulated as diphthongs in any of several patterns. The most common is the addition of the inglide, as in *pit* [pɪət], *bell* [bɛəl]. This is most frequent in the South Midland and adjacent areas and in the South, but it does occur occasionally in western New England and westward in a slightly "faster"

Map 2

version (that is, with shorter and weaker articulation of the inglide). Parts of the South and the South Midland and adjacent areas also have upgliding variants of /æ/, /ɛ/, and /ə/, especially before /š/, as in *ash* [æɪš], *mesh* [mɛɪš], and *mush* [mʌɪš]. The same upglides occur in some parts of the South and South Midland in other phonological environments as well, as in *bag* [bæɪg], *egg* [ɛɪg]. Also in the South Midland and in adjacent western areas, less frequently in the South, and as far north as Philadelphia in the East, /ɔ/ has diphthongized variants [ɑɔ] and [ɔʊ], as in *dog* [dɑɔg], [dɔʊg], *loft* [lɑɔft], [lɔʊft], *August* ['ɑɔgəst], ['ɔʊgəst]. Map 3 shows the area of most frequent diphthongization of one vowel, /ɔ/, before voiceless consonants (as in *loft*).

3.III.4   Alternations among vowels.

Some systematic alternations among vowel sets can be described in terms of tongue height and front-to-back articulation in the mouth. That is, if two vowels can both occur in a particular environment, one part of the country may regularly favor the lower over the higher vowel, while in another context speakers of one region may use a front vowel while others prefer a back vowel. Lower vowels are most frequent before /r/ and /l/, though they can also occur in other contexts: the articulation of *Coors* (brand name) as /kɜz/ ([kɝz]) rather than /kʊrz/ and of *there* as /ðar/ rather than /ðɛr/ is heard most often in the South Midland and adjacent western areas; *milk* and *pillow* become /mɛlk/ and /'pɛlo/ most often in the Great Lakes region; the South and parts of the West are most likely to have lowered vowels in *feel, sale,* and *school,* yielding /fil/, /sɛl/, /skʊl/; the lowering of /ɪ/ to /ɛ/ or even to /æ/, as in *thing* /θɛŋ, θæŋ/, occurs most often in the South Midland but also sporadically in the South and the West.

The use of a higher vowel than the norm occurs most frequently in the South Midland and parts of the South and rural West before nasal consonants, as in *pen* /pɪn/, *hem* /hɪm/, and *length* /lɪŋθ/. A similar alternation, that of /ɛ/ for /æ/ as in *bat,* occurs especially in the Northeast and the South. Before /r/, where the vowels /i~ɪ/, /e~ɛ/, /u~ʊ/, /o~ɔ/ alternate in pairs, the higher vowel occurs most frequently in the

South while the lower vowel is generally heard more often in the North. Much of the West has the lower vowel, but both can be heard frequently.

Variation between back vowels and more centralized vowels is most obvious in AE in the occurrence of /ɔ/ and /ɑ/. The low vowels as a group are highly variable in terms of their basic structure, their phonetic conditioning, social articulation, and the word sets that manifest a given sound, and the distinction between "short *o*" words like *cot, tot,* and *rot,* and *au* or *ou* words like *caught, taught,* and *wrought* is especially problematic. In general, AE has tended to front, lower and unround the vowel in historical "short *o*" words from [ɔ] to [ɑ]. However, for some speakers, especially those in the northern tier of states, the fronting has gone to [a], even approaching [æ] in some cases. For others, the shift has been to a lower, rounded variant [ɒ]. This last occurs in eastern New England, western Pennsylvania, occasionally on the southern coast, and sporadically across the country into the Rocky Mountains and the Southwest. Before /r/, /ɔ/ is general (except for frequent /o/ forms in the South). However, some speakers have /ɑ/ here, too: the East Coast and the South have [ɑ] in words like *forest* ['fɑrɪst], *horror* ['hɑrə], while some historically related but noncontiguous areas in Delaware, Maryland, North Carolina, southern Missouri, west Texas, and rural Utah have [ɒ] or [ɑ] in monosyllabic words (such as *fork, horse, born*) as well. The other environments are highly variable, even for the individual speaker.

A similar process of fronting of the vowel appears to be taking place for words like *taught, sought, wrought.* The South and much of the North generally maintain /ɔ/ in these words, so that there is a distinction between *caught* /kɔt/ and *cot* /kɑt/. In much of the West and in parts of the Southwest and Midwest, however, /ɑ/ occurs in *caught,* with the result that *caught* and *cot* sound alike. This is especially prevalent among younger speakers. In eastern New England and western Pennsylvania the vowel of *caught* is articulated [ɒ], but since the vowel of "short *o*" words is also [ɒ], the words sound alike in these regions too. Thus *cot-caught* word pairs may have contrasting low vowels, may have a single low vowel, or may

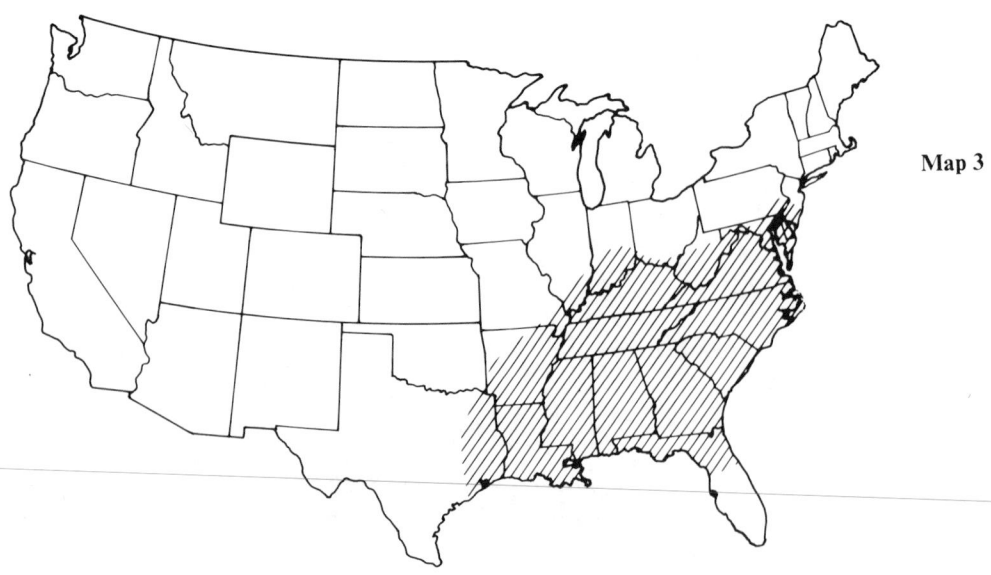

Map 3

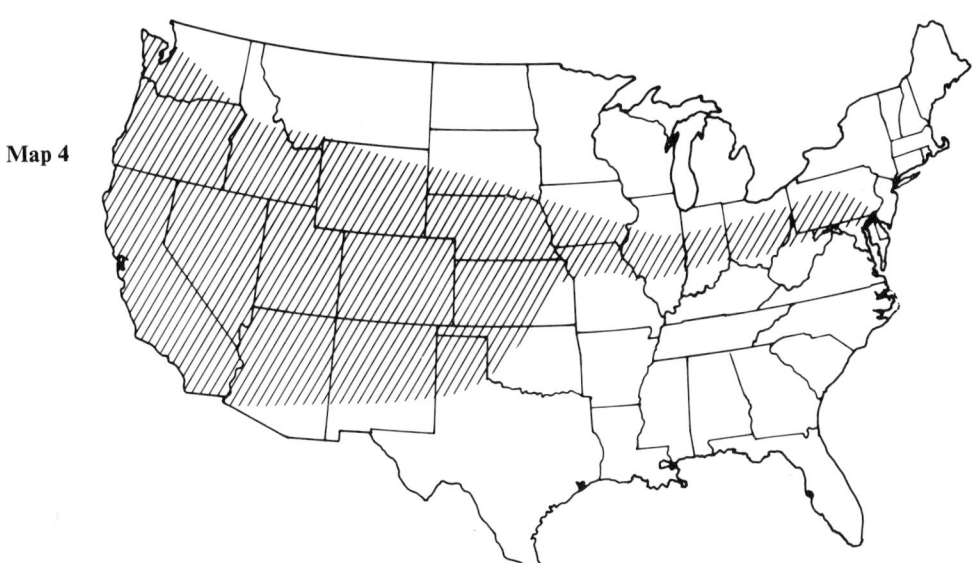

Map 4

vary by word or word subsets. Map 4 shows the general area where the distinction between /ɔ/ and /ɑ/ is not maintained, that is, where *cot* and *caught* sound alike.

3.III.5   Strictly speaking, each feature of pronunciation has a unique pattern even when considered in a general way, that is, when minimizing complexities of social groups, geographical discontinuities, and phonological environments. Some features, however, have similar enough distributions that, taken together, they form a recognizable pattern of overlap. Each of the maps in this section represents such a pattern. It is important to remember that the "boundaries" for each feature are necessarily fuzzy, and that individual speakers within each area may vary in their use of particular features that make up the pattern. Furthermore, since language is always changing, the patterns must be seen as representing the situation at a particular time and not as a static picture of what will always be.

Text of Questionnaire

The following questions, 1847 in all, were prepared for use by the *DARE* fieldworkers in direct interview with local informants in chosen communities in the fifty states. They are divided into 41 categories, each with a heading broadly describing the topics covered in that section. To avoid the effect of a 'school exercise,' however, the questions on verb forms (section OO) were not asked in a sequence by themselves but were interspersed among the other questions wherever they seemed appropriate to the subject.

Fieldworkers were instructed to ask each question as it is written here so that the responses would be comparable. Parenthetic instructions to the fieldworkers, however, were not read aloud. The questions in the last section, marked "Questions in Early Questionnaire Only," were asked in the first 75 Questionnaires completed; they were deleted thereafter as generally unproductive. Informants who answered the early Questionnaires are marked with an asterisk in the List of Informants, and their responses to these 223 questions are marked in a quotation with the phrase "total Infs questioned, 75."

Time

A1 What do you call the time in the early morning before the sun comes into sight?

A2 The time when the sun first comes into sight, that's _____.

A3 The time between the middle of the day and supper time:

A4 The time of day when the sun goes out of sight:

A5 The time right after the sun goes out of sight, before it becomes all dark:

A6 What time is this? (Show picture of clock face at 10:45.)

A7 And what time is this? (Show picture of clock face at 10:30.)

A9 What do you call wasting time by not working on the job?

A10 And doing little unimportant things: Somebody asks, "What are you doing?" and you answer, "Nothing in particular --- I'm just _____."

A11 When somebody takes too long about coming to a decision, you might say, "I wish he'd quit _____."

A12 When somebody keeps you waiting, you might say, "Hurry up! I don't have all day to _____ you!"

A13 When something needs to be done immediately, you might say, "I'll do it _____!"

A14 Referring to a very short period of time: "I'll be ready in _____." or "It won't take any longer than _____."

A15 Something that happens only occasionally: "He comes around _____."

A16 A very long period of time: "I haven't seen him _____."

A17 If it was 1960 and you were speaking of something that happened in 1950, you might say, "That was ten _____."

A18 Words or expressions used around here about a very slow person: "What's keeping him? He certainly is _____!"

A19 Other ways of saying "I'll have to hurry": "I'm late, I'll have to _____."

A20 Joking ways of telling somebody to hurry: You might say, "_____!"

A21 When someone is in too much of a hurry you might say, "Now just slow down! Don't _____."

A22 Other ways of saying 'to start working hard': "She had only ten minutes to clean the room, but she _____ (and had it done in no time)."

A23 To do something at the very first try: "He got the right answer _____."

A24 Speaking of someone who has always been the same way: "He's been hot-tempered from _____."

A26 Talking about the past: "People used to walk a lot, but everybody drives a car _____."

Weather

B1 If a day is very pleasant, you say it's a _____ day.

B2 If the weather is very unpleasant, you say it's a _____ day.

B3 If a day is very hot, you say it's (a) _____.

B4 A day when the air is very still, moist, and warm --- it's _____

B5 When the weather looks as if it will become bad, you say it's _____.

B6 When clouds begin to increase, you say it's _____.

B7 When clouds begin to decrease, you say it's _____.

B8 When clouds come and go all day, you say it's _____.

B9 What do you call the big clouds that roll up high before a rainstorm?

B10 What do you call the long trailing clouds high in the sky?

B11 Are there any other kinds of clouds that come often around here? (Open question --- answers not necessarily comparable. Get descriptions.)

B12 When the wind begins to increase, you say it's _____.

B13 When the wind begins to decrease, you say it's _____.

B14 When the wind is blowing unevenly, sometimes strong and sometimes weak, you say it's _____.

B15 When the wind suddenly begins to blow in a different direction, you say it _____.

B16 A destructive wind that comes with a funnel-shaped cloud:

B17 A destructive wind that blows straight:

B18 Are there any special kinds of wind that you get around here? (Open question)

B19 When fog begins to go up into the air, you say it's _____.

B21 When fine drops of moisture are falling, you say it's doing what?

B22 Rain accompanied by thunder and lightning --- you call that a _____.

B23 Speaking of a light rain that doesn't last, you would say it's just a _____.

B24 What do you call a sudden, very heavy rain?

B25 Any joking names around here for a very heavy rain? You might say, "It's a regular _____."

B26 When it's raining very heavily, you say, "It's raining _____."

B27 A sudden rush of water coming from heavy rain:

B28 When there is no rain for a long time, that's a _____.

B29 A frost that does not kill plants is a _____.

B30   A frost that kills plants is a _____.
B32   A period of warm weather late in the fall:
B33a   The first thin ice that forms over the surface of a pond or pool: "There's just a _____ of ice."
B33b   Talking about the first thin ice that forms over the surface of a pond or pool: "The pond is just _____ over."
B34   When a pond or lake becomes entirely covered with ice, you say it is _____.
B35   Ice that will bend when you step on it, but not break:
B36   Patterns formed by ice inside a window glass in winter:
B39   A very light fall of snow:

Topography

C1   What do you call a small stream of water not big enough to be a river?
C3   A place in a swift stream where the surface of the water is broken:
C4a   What do you call a fairly large body of fresh water? (Give the names of some around here.)
C4b   Is there any difference in the size of a lake and a pond? In the use? For example, would people go fishing or swimming in a pond?
C6   What do you call a piece of land that's often wet, and has grass and weeds growing on it?
C7   What do you call land that usually has some standing water with trees or bushes growing in it?
C8   What do you call a place in a stream where water flows round and round and draws things in toward the center?
C9   Water from a river that comes up and covers low land when the river is high:
C11   Soft, wet sand in streams or wet places, that draws people and things down into it:
C13   A piece of land that sticks out noticeably into a body of water:
C14   A stretch of still water going off to the side from a river or lake:
C15   A place in mountains or high hills where you can get through without climbing over the top:
C16   When a mass of earth and rock comes loose from a high place and rushes down, you call it a _____.
C17   Around here, what do you call a small, rounded hill? (Get dimensions!)
C19   What do you call low land running between hills? (With and without water) (Get local names and specific differences of those mentioned.)
C21   A deep place cut in sloping ground by running water:
C22   A piece of stone too big for one person to move easily:
C24a   A small piece of stone that you could easily throw:
C24b   "The dog wouldn't go away, so he took a stone/rock and (Make gesture) _____ (it at it.)" (Get past tense.)
C25   Other kinds of stone around here: about so big (Show size of a person's head), smooth and hard --- what do you call these?
C26   What special kinds of stone or rock are there in this part of the state? (Open question)
C28   A place where underbrush, weeds, vines and small trees grow together so that it's nearly impossible to get through:
C29   A good-sized stretch of level land with practically no trees:
C30   What do you call loose, dark soil?
C31   What do you call heavy, sticky soil?
C33   What joking names do you have for an out-of-the-way place, or a very unimportant place?
C34   Nicknames for nearby settlements, villages, or districts: (Open question)
C35   Nicknames for the different parts of your town or city: (Open question)

Houses

D4   The space up under the roof, usually used for storing things:
D6   To get to the second floor, you walk up the _____.

D7   A small space anywhere in a house where you can hide things or get them out of the way:
D8   The small room next to the kitchen (in older houses) where dishes and sometimes foods are kept:
D9   To prevent bread and cake from drying, you put them in a _____. (See article --- make sure what it is.)
D10a   The place to keep food cool, usually with ice, so that it won't spoil:
D10b   The place to keep food cool if it is run by electricity or gas:
D11   When you go into a house, the part just beyond the front door is the _____.
D12   The part that's put on in winter around an outside door to give extra protection from the cold:
D13   The room where you entertain company:
D16   Names used around here for parts added on to the main part of a house: (Open question)
D17   What do you call the platform, sometimes with a roof, that's built on the front or the side of a house? (Differences?)
D18   The part of the house below the ground floor:
D19   Referring to the part of the house below the ground floor, you might say, "I'm going _____." (Gesture downward.)
D20   Names for a sloping outside cellar door:
D21   A small, poorly-built house, or one in rundown condition:
D22   Underground place to go to in case of a violent windstorm:
D23   A house that is divided in two through the middle so that two families can live in it:
D24   Living quarters in a building where several other families live:
D26   What names do you have for different kinds of apartments? (Especially, small apartments)
D27   Strips of wood used to cover the outside of a frame house:
D28   What hangs below the edge of the roof to carry off rain-water?
D29   The pipe that takes the collected rain-water down to the ground or to a storage tank:
D30   The strip of wood or metal that covers the ridge of a roof:
D31   In front of a fireplace there's usually stonework on the floor --- what do you call this?
D32   The metal stands in a fireplace that the logs are laid on:
D33   When you build a fire in the fireplace, what do you call the big log that goes behind the others?
D34   What do you call the small pieces of wood and other stuff that are used to start a fire?
D36   What do you call the shelf over the fireplace?
D37   The strip of wood about eight inches high along the bottom of the wall (inside a room) joining to the floor: (Point at it.)
D39   What nicknames do people have around here for a small eating place where the food is not especially good?
D40   Names and nicknames around here for the upper balcony in a theater:

Furniture

E1   A piece of furniture that stands against the wall, and you hang clothes in/on it:
E2   A built-in space in a room for hanging clothes:
E3   A piece of furniture in which you lay clothes flat:
E4   Section in a piece of furniture that you pull in and out: (Point to one.)
E5   A piece of furniture with a flat top for keeping tablecloths, dishes, and such:
E6   A small shelf hanging on the wall with small decorative articles on it:
E7   The piece of upholstered furniture that you can stretch out on to rest:
E9   A piece of upholstered furniture that seats three people: (Differences?)
E10   Knitted or crocheted pieces placed on the back and arms of a chair for decoration and cleanliness:
E12   Pieces of stiff material that you pull down on the inside of a window to keep the sun out: (Gesture or point to them.)
E13   Words meaning to pull the shades (or other word) down:

"When the sun is too bright, you go to the window and _____." (Gesture.)

E14   Wooden slats built into a window frame that shut out the sun but let in light and air: (Only in Deep South)

E15   The cloth that is put on top of a bed, mostly for decoration:

E16   A padded covering used on a bed, mostly for warmth:

E17   The removable cover for a bed pillow:

E18   A temporary or emergency bed made up on the floor:

E20   Soft rolls of dust that collect on the floor under beds or other furniture:

E21   Talking about a room that needs to be put in order, you might say, "I'm just going to _____ this room."

E22   If a house is untidy and everything is upset, you might say, "It's a _____!" or "It looks like _____."

Utensils

F1   What do you call a heavy metal pan that's used to fry foods?

F3   When you're frying things --- for example, eggs --- you turn them over with a _____.

F4   What do you call the deep metal container used to boil foods?

F6   The kitchen utensil with holes punched through the sides and bottom, to drain off liquid from foods:

F7   The kitchen utensil with wire mesh, used to separate the fine part of food from the coarse:

F8   The kitchen utensil that you pass flour through:

F9   To get a liquid through a narrow opening --- for example, the neck of a bottle --- you'd pour it through a _____.

F10   If you are familiar with wood-burning stoves --- what do you call the round flat pieces that you take out to put in the wood?

F11   The thing you use to remove the lids (or other word) from a wood-burning stove when it is hot:

F12   The flat metal piece below a wood-burning stove, to catch the ashes:

F15   What you turn to let the vinegar or cider run out of a barrel:

F17   What peaches come in --- different kinds:

F19   A cloth container for grain:

F20   A cloth container for feed:

F21   A cloth or paper container that you buy flour in:

F22a   A smaller paper container for bringing groceries home from the store:

F22b   A smaller paper container for carrying a lunch: "He had his lunch in a _____."

F23   A container made of rough, loosely woven, brown cloth; commonly used for potatoes, etc:

F24   The container for kitchen parings and scraps --- inside the kitchen:

F25   The container for kitchen parings and scraps --- out of doors:

F27a   What you turn on and off inside the house to get running water:

F27b   What you turn on and off outside the house to get running water:

F28   The utensil with a small cup on a long handle, used to take water or milk out of a pail:

F29   Different kinds of irons --- not electric --- used around here for smoothing clothes after they're washed: (Differences?)

F30   What is a pail made of? What is it used for?

F31   What is a bucket made of? What is it used for?

F32   Talking about a sudden flood in the cellar, you might say, "A water pipe must have _____."

F33   A small tool that you hold in one hand, with 'jaws' for gripping things: (Show picture.)

F34   The wooden cross-pieces that you put your feet on when you go up a ladder: (Not a stepladder)

F35   A small broom that you hold in one hand, and use it in places that are hard to get at: (Show picture.)

F36   Other kinds of brooms that people use around here:

F37   Names for an indoor toilet:

F38   Utensil kept under the bed for use at night:

F39   A large pocket knife with blades that fold in and out:

F42   A woman who washes clothes for other people:

F43   After clothes have been washed, what do you do to get the soap off?

F44   What do you call a container for coal to use in a stove?

F45   What do you call the fuel that's used in an ordinary lamp?

F46   What do you call the kind of matches you can strike anywhere?

F47   What do you call the wire or rubber device with a handle, that is used to kill flies?

F48   What do you call pages of writing paper glued together at the top with a cardboard back?

F49   What do you call this? (Show rubber band.)

Dishes

G2   What names are used around here for a glass that you drink water from?

G3   A container for salt that's put on the table --- if it's open (without a cover):

G4   A container for salt that has a cover with holes in it:

G6   Other dishes that you might have on the table for a big dinner or special occasion --- for example, Thanksgiving: (Open question)

G8   A bunch of cut flowers: "The bride carried a pretty _____."

G9   When you have to get the table ready for a meal, you say "It's time to _____."

G10   When the meal is all over, what do you have to do to the table?

G11   Other names or nicknames for a toothpick:

G14   The rough metal pad that's used to scour pots and pans:

G15   When you pour hot water on the dishes to get the soap off, you _____ them.

G16   What do you dry the dishes with? (Differences --- size? material?)

G17   Other kinds of towels that people use around here: (Open question)

Foods

H2   The meal that people eat around the middle of the day:

H3   The meal that people eat at the end of the day: (The same every day?)

H5   What do you call a small amount of food eaten between regular meals?

H6   Words for food in general: "He certainly enjoys his _____."

H7   When a housewife is about to prepare a meal --- for example, supper --- she might say, "I have to go and _____ supper."

H9   If somebody always eats a considerable amount of food, you say he's a _____.

H11a   If somebody eats rapidly and noisily, you say he _____.

H11b   If he makes a noise with his food, he _____.

H12   If somebody eating a meal takes little bits of food and leaves most of it on his plate, you say he _____.

H13   Bread that is not made at home:

H14   Bread that's made with cornmeal: (Explain differences.)

H15   Bread made with wheat flour:

H16   What do people use to raise the bread before it's baked?

H17   What different kinds (of yeast) are used around here? (Describe differences.)

H18   Are there any special kinds of bread made now or in past years around here? (Open question)

H19   What do you mean by a biscuit? How are they made? (Description; different kinds; different terms)

H20a   Do you use the word 'pancakes' around here?

H20b   What other names do you have for pancakes?

H21   What do you call the sweet stuff that's poured over these cakes?

H23   What do you call hot cooked breakfast cereal?

H24   What names or nicknames do people have around here for boiled cornmeal?

H25   What names or nicknames do people have around here for fried cornmeal?

H26   A round cake of dough, cooked in deep fat, with a hole in the center:

H27   Do you have any joking names for doughnuts (or other word)?
H28   Different shapes or types of doughnuts (or other word)?
H29   A round cake, cooked in deep fat, with jelly inside:
H30   An oblong cake, cooked in deep fat:
H32   Names used around here for fancy rolls and pastries: (According to shapes, etc.): (Open question)
H34   What are the parts of an egg?
H35   When eggs are taken out of the shells and cooked in boiling water, you call them _____ eggs.
H36   Kinds of soup favored around here --- any specialties? (Open question)
H37   What words do you have for gravy? Any joking ones?
H38   Other words for bacon (including joking ones):
H40   A small sausage that is put into a long roll or bun to make a sandwich:
H41   Other kinds of roll or bun sandwiches favored around here --- in a round bun or roll:
H42   The kind in a much larger, longer bun, that's a meal in itself:
H43   Foods made from parts of the head and inner organs of an animal: Different kinds: (With and without cornmeal)
H44   Beef that has been dried to preserve it:
H45   Dishes made with meat, fish, or poultry that everybody around here would know, but that people in other places might not:
H46   When meat begins to go bad, so that you can't eat it, you say it's _____.
H47   Kinds of fried potatoes favored around here: (Describe kinds.)
H48   Baked dishes made of potatoes cut up with meat or cheese:
H49   Dishes made by boiling potatoes with other foods:
H50   Dishes made with beans, peas, or corn that everybody around here knows, but people in other places might not:
H52   Dishes made with fresh cabbage:
H56   Names for different kinds of pickles favored around here:
H57   Tasty or spicy side-dishes served with meats:
H58   Milk that's just beginning to become sour is _____.
H59   Milk that becomes thick as it turns sour:
H60   The lumpy white cheese that is made from sour milk:
H63   Kinds of desserts especially favored by people around here: (Describe; if any unusual, get recipe.) (Open question)
H64   The sweet covering spread on top of a cake:
H65   Foreign foods favored by people around here: (Open question)
H66a   The sweet liquid that you pour over a pudding:
H66b   The sweet liquid that you pour over ice cream:
H67   Food that was not finished at one meal but saved for another:
H68   When food remains over from one meal and you heat it again for another meal, you call it _____. For example, "She got out Sunday's roast and _____ (it)."
H69   When food is hard on your stomach, you say that it _____.
H70   When people bring baked dishes, salads, and so forth to a meeting-place and share them together, that's a _____ meal.
H71   Words for the last piece of food left on a plate:
H72   Words for preparing tea: "Pour on the water and let it _____."
H73   Words for preparing coffee: the housewife says, "I think I'll go and _____ some coffee."
H74a   Different words for coffee according to how it's made --- very strong:
H74b   Different words for coffee according to how it's made --- very weak:
H75   When a housewife is going to preserve fruit in jars, she says she's going to _____ some fruit.
H78   Ordinary soft drinks, usually carbonated --- what are they called?
H79   What do you call the exact directions for cooking a certain dish, making a cake, and so on?
H80   Kinds of candy often made at home around here: (Open question)
H81   Candy on a stick for children to lick:
H82a   Cheap candies sold especially for schoolchildren around here: (Open question)

H82b   Kinds of cheap candy that used to be sold years ago: (Open question)

Vegetables and Fruits

I1   What do you call the garden where you grow carrots, beans, and such things, to eat at home?
I3   What do you call the large yellowish root vegetable, similar to a turnip, with a strong taste?
I4   What vegetables are less commonly grown around here?
I5   The kind of onions that keep coming up without replanting year after year:
I6   The kind of onions that come up fresh early in the year, and you eat them raw:
I7   The small plants like onions with hollow green leaves that are cut up in a salad:
I8   When root vegetables get old and tough and are not good to eat, you say they are _____.
I9   Other names (including nicknames) for potatoes:
I10   The outside covering of green peas that you break open to get the peas out:
I11   When somebody takes peas out of the covering like that, you say, "She's _____ peas."
I12   The outside covering of dry beans:
I13   When you take dry beans out of the cover you are _____ them.
I14   Kinds of beans that you eat in the pod before they're dry:
I15   Some of the beans that you eat in the pod have yellow pods; you call these _____.
I16   The large flat beans that are not eaten in the pod:
I17   Beans (not pods) that are dark red when they are dry:
I18   The smaller beans that are white when they are dry:
I19   Small white beans with a black spot where they were joined to the pod:
I20   Other kinds of beans that are grown around here: (Open question)
I22a   Names for different kinds of peppers --- small hot:
I22b   Names for different kinds of peppers --- large hot:
I22c   Names for different kinds of peppers --- small sweet:
I22d   Names for different kinds of peppers --- large sweet:
I23   What kinds of squash do people grow around here? (Draw shape or describe.)
I25   Names or nicknames for cucumbers (growing):
I26   What kinds of melons do people grow around here? (Open question)
I28a   What kinds of things do you call 'greens' around here? Those that are eaten raw:
I28b   Kinds of greens that are cooked:
I29   Names or nicknames for asparagus:
I30   Other names for rhubarb:
I31   When a corn stalk is well grown, what comes out at the top?
I33   What do you call ears of corn that are just right for eating?
I34   If you don't have sweet corn, you can always eat young _____.
I35   What kitchen herbs are grown and used in cooking around here?
I37   Small plants shaped like an umbrella that grow in woods and fields --- which are safe to eat: (Any nicknames?)
I38   Small plants shaped like an umbrella that grow in woods and fields --- which are not safe to eat:
I39   What do you call the thick outside covering of a walnut?
I40   The hard part inside the husk (or other word) of a walnut that you have to break:
I41   The part of the nut that you eat:
I42   Other names or nicknames used around here for peanuts:
I43   What kinds of nuts grow wild around here? (Open question)
I44   What kinds of berries grow wild around here? (Open question)
I46   Other kinds of fruits that grow wild around here? (Open question)

I47 When you pull the stem out of a strawberry, what do you call the green part that comes off with the stem?

I48 The hard center of a cherry: you call that a cherry _____.

I49 And the hard center of a plum: that's a plum _____.

I50 And the hard center of a peach: that's a peach _____.

I51 The kind of a peach where the hard center is loose:

I52 The kind of a peach where the hard center is tight to the flesh:

I53 Other fruits grown around here: any special varieties? (Open question)

Domestic Animals

J1 What do you call a dog of mixed breed?

J2 What joking or uncomplimentary words do you have for dogs?

J3a To make a female dog so that she can't breed, she must be _____.

J3b To make a female cat so that she can't breed, she must be _____.

J5 A cat with fur of mixed colors:

J6 A cat that catches lots of rats and mice --- you'd say, "She's a good _____."

J8 To tell a dog to attack an animal or a person, you'd say, "_____."

J9a To tell a dog to lie down on the ground and keep still:

J9b To tell a dog to stand without moving:

J10 To call a cat to make it come, you say "_____."

Farm Animals

K1 A cow that is giving milk is a _____.

K3a When a cow stops giving milk, you say she _____.

K3b When a cow stops giving milk, you say she's a _____.

K4 The cow's udder is called the _____.

K6 And taking the last of the milk from the udder:

K7 What sickness can a cow get in her udder --- for example, if she's left unmilked too long?

K8 Joking terms for milking a cow: A farmer might say, "Well, it's time to go out and _____."

K9 If one quarter of a cow's udder does not give milk, you say she's _____.

K10 Words used about a cow that is going to have a calf:

K11 When a cow has a calf, you say she _____.

K12 A cow that has never had horns:

K13 A cow that has had her horns cut off:

K14 Milk that has a taste from something the cow ate in the pasture --- you say, "That milk is _____."

K15 A thin, bony, or poor-looking cow:

K16 A cow with a bad temper:

K18 What kind of mark is used around here to identify a cow? (Describe; where is it put?)

K19 Noise made by a calf that's taken away from its mother:

K20 A calf that is sold for meat:

K21 The noise a cow makes, calling for her calf:

K22 Words used for a bull:

K23 Words used by women or in mixed company for a bull:

K24 What does the word 'ox' mean around here?

K25 What is a 'steer'?

K26 If six oxen are hitched together two and two, you have three _____.

K27 What do you call the sharp-pointed stick used to get oxen to move?

K28 What are the chief diseases that cows have around here? (Open question)

K32a With a team of horses, what do you call the horse on the driver's right hand?

K32b The horse on the left side in plowing or hauling:

K34 What do you say to make the horses stop? (Get actual exclamation.)

K36a What do you say to make a horse go faster?

K36b What do you say to make a horse go backwards?

K37 What do you call a horse of mixed colors?

K38 A horse of a dirty white color:

K39 What other names do you have for horses according to their colors? (Open question)

K40 The sound that a horse makes:

K41 A horse with its tail cut short is called a _____.

K42 A horse that is rough, wild, or dangerous:

K43 A horse that was not intentionally bred, or bred by accident:

K44 A bony or poor-looking horse:

K45 When a mare has had a young horse, you say she has just _____.

K47 What diseases do horses or mules commonly get around here? (Open question)

K48 When a horse is short of breath, you say it's _____.

K49 You take a horse to the blacksmith to have it _____.

K50 Joking nicknames for mules:

K51 Talking about pigs, a very young one is called a _____.

K52 A male pig kept for breeding is a _____. (Any hesitation about using words like this before women?)

K54 Names used around here for the smallest pig in a litter:

K55 A pig that doesn't grow well and is not worth keeping:

K57 The big teeth that stick out of a boar's mouth:

K58 A castrated pig is a _____.

K59 What do pigs eat out of?

K60 When somebody is going to give the pigs food, he says, "I'm going to _____."

K61 What do you call the pig's nose?

K62 What do you call a female sheep?

K63 What do you call a male sheep?

K66 The noise made by a sheep:

K68 What do you call a goat that habitually strikes people with its horns?

K70 Words used around here for castrating an animal:

K72 When the hen stops laying and begins to sit on the eggs to hatch them, she's a _____.

K73 What names do you have for the rump of a cooked chicken?

K74 A bone from the breast of a chicken, shaped like a horseshoe:

K75 A male turkey is called a _____.

K76 What other kinds of poultry are raised around here? (Open question)

K78 What diseases do chickens commonly get around here? (Open question)

K79 How do you call the chickens to you at feeding time?

K80 The call that's used around here to get the cows in from the pasture:

K81 To make a cow stand still --- for example, when milking her --- you say, "_____."

K82 The call used around here to get horses in from the pasture:

K83 To call a calf to you at feeding time:

K84 The call used around here to get the pigs in at feeding time:

K85 The call to sheep to come in from the pasture:

Farming

L1 A man who is employed to help with work on a farm:

L2 The extra house on a large farm where a hired man and his family live:

L3 A man who lives on the farm and does the work, but divides the expenses and profits with the owner:

L4b What do you call the time early in the morning and at night when you have to feed livestock, clean stalls, and so on? A person might say, "I've got to go now, it's _____."

L5 When a farmer gets help on a job from his neighbors in return for his help on their farms later on, you call it _____.

L6a What do you call a piece of land under cultivation --- less than an acre?

L6b A piece of land under cultivation --- if it's several acres:

L7 A piece of land with a hay crop planted on it:

L8 Hay that grows naturally in damp places:

L9a What kinds of grass are grown for hay around here? (Open question)

L9b Hay from other kinds of plants (not grass): (Open question)

L10   After hay has been cut, then it grows back and you cut it again, you'd call that _____.

L11   What do you do to hay in the field after it's cut?

L12   What do you call the small piles of hay standing in the field?

L13   The kind of wagon used for carrying hay: (Note: special wagon, or frame put on ordinary wagon?)

L14   A large pile of hay stored outdoors: (Do names differ according to shape?)

L15   When you are putting hay into a building for storage, you say you are _____.

L16   Machines used around here in handling hay: (Open question)

L17   Other names around here for manure used in the fields: (Also joking names)

L18   Kinds of plows used around here, at present and in the past: (Get descriptions.) (Open question)

L20   The implement used in a field after it's been plowed to break up the lumps: (Different kinds?)

L22   When talking about a crop he intends to plant --- for example, oats --- a farmer might say, "This year, I'm going to _____ a crop of oats/corn/cotton, etc." (Name the local crops in turn and record the verb.)

L23   What machinery is used around here in putting in the seed? (Which machine for which crop?)

L24   A crop or part of a crop that springs up and grows by itself from old seed:

L25   The implement used to clean out weeds and loosen the earth between rows of corn:

L28   Tools used in the past for cutting grain:

L29   Machines now used for cutting grain:

L30a   When grain is cut it is (or used to be) tied up in _____.

L30b   Then these sheaves (or other word) are set together in piles called _____.

L31   What do you call the top bundle of a shock (or other word)?

L32a   In early days, how was the grain separated from the straw?

L32b   In early days, how was the grain separated from the chaff? (Describe methods.)

L33   How is the grain separated from the straw nowadays?

L34   What are the most important crops grown around here? (Open question)

L35   Hand tools used for cutting underbrush and digging out roots:

L36   What do you call it around here when you dig out roots and underbrush to make a new field? (New methods: bulldozing, etc.)

L37   A hand tool used for cutting weeds and grass:

L38   What do you use around here to sharpen tools in the field?

L39   An iron bar with a bent end, used for pulling nails, opening boxes, and so on: (Be sure of object named.)

L40   A long iron bar used to move rocks and other heavy things:

L41   A device for moving dirt and other loads, with one wheel in front and handles to lift and push it behind:

L42   Do you use the word 'rig' around here? What kind of thing do you call a 'rig'?

L43a   When somebody is going to get horses ready to work, he might say, "I'll _____ the horses."

L43b   To get a horse ready to ride:

L44   On a buggy, two long pieces of wood stick out in front and the horse goes between them. You call them the _____.

L45   The long piece of wood that sticks out in front of a wagon, and you put a horse on each side:

L46   Behind each horse there's a movable bar (the leathers or ropes from the collar are fastened to it) --- what would you call this?

L47   The two movable bars behind a team of horses are fastened to a longer piece; this is a _____.

L48   The part of a wagon that goes crosswise underneath and has a wheel at each end:

L49   Leathers or ropes, fastened to the collar, that a horse or mule pulls by:

L51   The leathers or ropes that a driver holds to guide a horse:

L52   Pieces of leather used to cover the sides of a horse's eyes:

L53a   The band that goes under a horse's middle to hold a saddle on:

L53b   The band that goes under a horse's middle to hold a saddle on --- what is it called if it's a part of a work harness?

L54   If someone was transporting firewood (or dirt) in a wagon, you'd say he was _____ firewood.

L55   If the wagon was only partly full, you'd say he had a _____.

L56   The amount of wood a person can carry in both arms: "We're out of firewood --- I'll just get in a _____."

L57   A low wooden platform used for bringing stones or heavy things out of the fields:

L58   An implement with an A-shaped frame (Make gesture) that you put boards on to saw them:

L59   An implement with an X-frame (Gesture) to hold firewood for sawing:

L60   A fence made of stone or rock without mortar:

L61   Fences made of solid logs, now or in the past: (Describe construction.)

L62   A fence made of split logs: (Describe differences.)

L63   Kinds of fences made with wire: (Open question)

L64   The kind of wooden fence that's built around a garden or near a house:

L65   What other kinds of fences, past or present, do you have around here? (Describe construction.) (Open question)

Farm Buildings

M1   What different or special kinds of barns do you have around here according to their use or the way they are built? (Open question)

M2   What do you call the small wooden construction on top of a barn with slats for ventilation? (It sometimes has a weathervane on it.)

M3   The place inside a barn for storing hay:

M5   What do you call the hole for throwing hay down below?

M6   The place where grain is kept in a barn:

M8   The building where corn is kept:

M9   The part of a barn where horses are kept:

M10   The part of the barn where cows are kept:

M11   What do you put the cow's head through when she stands in the barn?

M12   What do you keep food for the cattle in over winter?

M13   The space near the barn with a fence around it where you keep the livestock:

M14   The open area around or next to the barn:

M15   The place outdoors where pigs are kept:

M16   The small shelter for a hen that can be moved about from place to place:

M17   A building where chickens or hens are kept:

M18   The separate building where milk is kept cool:

M19   A place for keeping carrots, turnips, potatoes, and so on over the winter:

M20   A small building where meat or fish are smoked and cured:

M21a   An outside toilet building:

M21b   Joking names for an outside toilet building:

M22   What other kinds of buildings would there be on farms around here? (Open question)

Vehicles and Transportation

N1   Other names for an ambulance:

N2   The car used to carry a dead body for burial:

N3   The car or wagon that takes arrested people to the police station or to jail:

N4   A police vehicle with a red, blue, or yellow flashing light on top:

N5   Nicknames for an automobile, especially an old or broken-down car:

N6   An old car that has been fixed up to make it go fast or make a lot of noise:

N7   If you had made a trip by car to a city (Supply local name) you might say, "We _____ to X last week."

N8   If somebody gave you lessons in driving a car, you might say, "He _____ me how to drive."

N9   The colored lights that control the cars at busy road crossings:

N10   What other words are used around here for the bright and dim lights on a car?

N11   A very large truck used to haul freight, new cars, and other big loads:

N12   Names for somebody who drives carelessly or not well:

N13   If someone has been drinking and then drives a car, he may be arrested for:

N14   The place where you go to get gasoline put into a car:

N15a   Gas stations (or other word) usually have two kinds of gasoline: A cheaper kind that's called _____.

N15b   Gas stations (or other word) usually have two kinds of gasoline: A more expensive kind that's called _____.

N16a   Names for a highway with two lanes on each side and a separation down the middle:

N16b   Names for a highway with two lanes on each side and a separation down the middle --- if you have to pay to drive on it:

N17   What do you call the separating area in the middle of a four-lane road?

N18   How do you speak of roads that have numbers or letters? For example, if someone asked directions to get to (Supply local city name), you might say, "Take _____."

N19   What do you call a structure that carries a road above railroad tracks, or above another road or a deep gully?

N20   What do you call a circular arrangement on one level at a big intersection, where cars can go around till they come to the road they want?

N21   Roads that are surfaced with smooth black pavement:

N22   When a road that is surfaced with smooth pavement gets wet so that cars slip or skid on it, you say it's _____.

N23   Other kinds of paved roads around here:

N24   A ditch along the side of a graded road:

N25   The unpaved part of a graded road along the edge of the pavement:

N27a   Names around here for different kinds of unpaved roads: (Open question)

N27b   When unpaved roads get very rough, you call them _____.

N28   A road that connects a big highway with stores and business places set back from it:

N29   What names are used around here for a less important road running back from a main road?

N30   What do you call a sudden short dip in a road?

N31   A place in a road where animals regularly go across:

N32   A place where roads cross at right angles: (Gesture.)

N33   A man whose job is to take care of roads in a certain locality:

N34   An electric car that runs on tracks in a city --- any around here?

N35   A fast train that goes from one big city to another without stopping at all the stations:

N37   Joking names for a branch railroad that is not very important or gives poor service:

N38   On a trip when you have to change trains and wait a while between them, you might say, "I have a two-hour _____ in Chicago."

N39   The place where you go to begin a trip and where you get off at the end:

N40a   (In snow areas) What different kinds of sleighs do you have around here for hauling loads?

N40b   Different kinds of sleighs for carrying people:

N40c   Different kinds of sleighs for carrying other things:

N41a   What kinds of horse-drawn vehicles are used around here, or used to be, to carry people?

N41b   Horse-drawn vehicles to carry heavy loads:

N41c   Horse-drawn vehicles to carry light loads:

N42   Vehicles for a baby or small child --- the kind it can lie down in:

N43   Vehicles for a small child --- the kind it has to sit up in:

N44   In a town, the strip of grass and trees between the sidewalk and the curb:

Boats and Sailing

O1   What do you call a small rowboat, not big enough to hold more than two people?

O2   Nicknames around here for an old, clumsy boat:

O3   A small platform sticking out into the water where boats can tie up, and people can get into them:

O4   A much larger and solider structure where ships can come to land:

O5   The posts standing in the water which these platforms rest on:

O6   If a wooden boat is leaking, what do you have to do to stop the leaks?

O7   What do you call a place where boats can be rented?

O8   The devices on the sides of a boat that hold the oars in place:

O9   What kinds of sailboats are used around here? (Open question)

O10   What other kinds of boats are used around here? (Open question)

O11   What other names do you have for an outboard motor?

O12   A disturbance caused by wind which seems to run and spread quickly along the surface of water:

O13   A heavy stone structure, often with masonry work, that encloses and protects a harbor:

O14a   A floating structure out in a large lake or the sea usually marking a channel for boats:

O14b   What different kinds of buoys are there? (Open question)

O15   What names do you have for different kinds of waves around here, referring to how the water acts? (Open question)

O16   What do you call the stirred-up water following a boat?

O17   When the water is very smooth and still, you call that a _____.

O18   Different currents or actions of the water that are important when you're in a boat: (Get explanations.)

O19   Different kinds or degrees of wind that are important when you're in a boat: (Open question)

O21   When men out in seagoing boats get together for a visit and a cup of hot coffee, that's called a _____.

Fishing, Hunting, Wildlife

P1   What kinds of freshwater fish are caught around here that are good to eat? (Open question)

P2   (In saltwater areas) What kinds of saltwater fish caught around here are good to eat? (Open question)

P3   Freshwater fish that are not good to eat: (Open question)

P4   Saltwater fish that are not good to eat: (Open question)

P5   What do you call the common worm used as bait?

P6   Other kinds of worms also used for bait: (Open question)

P7   Small fish used as bait for bigger fish:

P9   When you're fishing but not catching any, you might say, "_____."

P13   What other ways of fishing do you have around here besides the ordinary hook and line? (Special kinds of bait, hooks, lures, nets, traps, spears, etc.?) (Open question)

P14   If commercial fishing is done around here, what do the fishermen go out after? (Open question)

P15   What do you call fishing that's done from a slowly moving boat?

P16   When fishermen throw bits of bait in the water to attract fish --- what do you call this?

P17   What do you call it around here when the people fish by lowering a line and sinker close to the bottom of the water?

P18   What kinds of shellfish are common around here? (Open question)

P19   What do you call the small, freshwater crayfish around here?

P20   Very young frogs --- when they still have tails but no legs:

P21   Small frogs that sing or chirp loudly in spring:

P22   Names or nicknames for a very large frog that makes a deep, loud sound:

P23   Names for the animal similar to the frog that lives away from water:

P24   What kinds of turtles are found around here? (Open question)
P25   What kinds of snakes are found around here? (Open question)
P26   Names and nicknames around here for a skunk:
P27   What kinds of squirrels do you have around here? (Open question)
P29   Do you have 'gophers' around here? If yes, what other name do they have, or what other animal are they most like? (The term is applied differently in different places.)
P30   Do you have wild rabbits around here? What kinds?
P31   What other names or nicknames do you have around here for the groundhog, muskrat, opossum, panther, porcupine, raccoon, wildcat?
P32   What other kinds of wild animals do you have around here? (Open question)
P35a   Names or nicknames for any deer shot illegally:
P35b   Illegal methods of shooting deer:
P36   When a hunter sees a deer or other game animal and gets so excited he can't shoot, he has _____.
P37a   Nicknames for a rifle:
P37b   Nicknames for a shotgun:
P38   What do you put into a rifle to shoot?
P39a   When a hunter or a dog finds a game animal and makes it start running, you'd say he _____ it.
P39b   If the dog makes a bird or a covey fly, you'd say he _____.

Birds

Q1   What do you call the kind of owl that makes a shrill, trembling cry?
Q2   Other kinds of owls found around here: (Open question)
Q3   Other birds that come out only after dark: (Open question)
Q4   What kinds of hawks are found around here? (Open question)
Q5   What kinds of wild ducks do you have around here? (Open question)
Q6   What kinds of wild geese do you have around here? (Open question)
Q7   Names and nicknames for other kinds of game birds around here: (Open question)
Q8   A water bird that makes a booming sound before rain and often stands with its beak pointed almost straight up:
Q9   The bird that looks like a small, dull-colored duck and is commonly found on ponds and lakes:
Q10   Other water birds and marsh birds common around here: (Open question)
Q11   What kinds of blackbirds do you have around here? (Open question)
Q13   Names around here for the vulture:
Q14   What other names do you have around here for these birds: bobolink, brown thrasher, catbird, cowbird, cuckoo, goldfinch, killdeer, kingbird, martin, mockingbird, shrike, thrush?
Q15   What different kinds of larks do you have around here? (Open question)
Q16   What kinds of jays do you have around here? (Open question)
Q17   What kinds of woodpeckers do you have around here? (Open question)
Q18   Joking names and nicknames for woodpeckers:
Q20   What kinds of swallows and birds like them do you have around here?
Q21   Different kinds of sparrows around here:
Q22   Joking names or nicknames for the common sparrow:
Q23   The insect-eating bird that goes headfirst down a tree trunk:

Insects

R1   What do you call the small insect that flies at night and flashes a light at its tail?
R2   What other names do you have around here for the dragonfly?
R4   A large winged insect that hatches in summer in great numbers around lakes or rivers, crowds around lights, lives only a day or so, and is good fish bait:

R5   A big brown beetle that comes out in large numbers in spring and early summer, and flies with a buzzing sound: (Note: some are green.)
R6   What other names do people have around here for grasshoppers?
R7   Insects that sit in trees or bushes in hot weather and make a sharp, buzzing sound:
R8   Other kinds of creatures that make a clicking or shrilling or chirping kind of sound: (Open question)
R9a   An insect from two to four inches long that lives in bushes and looks like a dead twig:
R9b   An insect that holds up its front feet as if saying a prayer:
R10   Very small flies that don't sting, often seen hovering in large groups or bunches outdoors in summer:
R11   A very tiny fly that you can hardly see, but that stings:
R12   What other kinds of flies are common around here --- for example, those that fly around animals? (Open question)
R13   Flies that come to meat or fruit:
R14   Small worm-like things (seen in rain barrels or standing water) that hatch into mosquitoes:
R15a   What other names or nicknames do you have around here for mosquitoes?
R15b   Any names for an extra-big mosquito?
R17   What names do you have for the big black ants that sting?
R18   What other kinds of ants do you have around here? (Open question)
R19a   The place where bees live and store their honey --- tame bees:
R19b   And the place where wild bees live and store their honey:
R20   Wasps that build their nests of mud: (Get description of insect and nest: color, size, and shape.)
R21   Are there any other kinds of stinging insects around here? (Open question)
R22   Very small red insects, almost too small to see, that get under your skin and cause itching:
R23a   Insects or other creatures that fasten themselves to the skin and suck blood --- on land:
R23b   Blood-sucking creatures --- in water:
R24   What other names are used around here for a bedbug?
R25   Joking names for a head louse, or body louse:
R26   Any other names for the small greenish lice that come on plants?
R27   What kinds of caterpillars or similar worms do you have around here? (Open question)
R28   What different kinds of spiders do you have around here? (Open question)
R29a   What do you call the thing that a spider spins and lives in? --- If it is indoors:
R29b   What the spider spins --- if it is outdoors:
R30   What other kinds of beetles are known around here --- for example, because of their odor or color or something else? (Open question)

Wildflowers, Weeds

S1   What other names do you have around here for the jack-in-the-pulpit?
S2   What do you call the flower that comes up in the woods early in spring, with three white petals that turn pink as the flower grows older?
S3   A flower like a large violet with a yellow center and small ragged leaves --- it comes up early in spring on open, stony hilltops:
S4   Other names around here for the mayapple: (Woodside plant, not a tree, with two large spreading leaves; they grow in patches and have a small yellow fruit late in summer.)
S5   Other names around here for the wild morning glory:
S6   Other names around here for Queen Anne's lace: (Summertime roadside weed two feet high or so with a lacy white top)

S7   A kind of daisy, bright yellow with a dark center, that grows along roadsides in late summer:

S8   A common kind of wild grass that grows in fields: it spreads by sending out long underground roots, and it's hard to get rid of:

S9   Other kinds of grass that are hard to get rid of: (Open question)

S11   What other names do you have around here for: bachelor's button, blue violet, bluets, dandelion, dog-tooth violet, peony, wild snapdragon, zinnia?

S13   There's a common wild bush with bunches of round, prickly seeds; when they get dry they stick to your clothing --- what are these called around here?

S14   Other prickly seeds, small and flat, with two prongs at one end, that cling to clothing:

S15   Do you have any other weed seeds that cling to clothing? (Open question)

S16   A three-leaved plant that grows in woods and countryside and makes people's skin itch and swell:

S17   What other kinds of plants do you have around here that will cause itching and swelling?

S18   A kind of mushroom that grows like a globe (Gesture) --- sometimes gets as big as a man's head:

S19   Mushrooms that grow out like brackets from the sides of trees:

S20   A common weed that grows on open hillsides: It has velvety green leaves close to the ground, and a tall stalk with small yellow flowers on a spike at the top:

S21   What other weeds do you have around here that are a trouble in gardens and fields? (Open question)

S22   What do you call the bright yellow flowers that bloom in clusters in marshes in early springtime?

S23   Pale blue flowers with downy leaves and cups that come up on open, stony hillsides in March or early April:

S24   A wild flower that grows in swamps and marshes and looks like a small blue iris: (Sometimes other colors)

S25   What do you call the small wild chrysanthemum-like flowers (blue, purple, white) that bloom in fields late in the fall?

S26a   What other wildflowers do you have around here, not yet mentioned? Roadside flowers: (Open question)

S26b   Wildflowers that grow in water or wet places: (Open question)

S26c   Wildflowers that grow in woods: (Open question)

S26d   Wildflowers that grow in meadows: (Open question)

S26e   Other wildflowers not yet mentioned: (Open question)

Trees, Bushes, etc.

T1   What do you call a bunch of trees growing together in open country, especially on a hill?

T2a   What do you call a piece of land covered with trees --- if it's only a few acres?

T2b   What do you call a piece of land covered with trees --- if it's a large acreage?

T3   The tree that produces syrup and sugar:

T4   The place where these trees grow together and sap is gathered:

T5   What kinds of evergreens, other than pine, do you have around here? (Open question)

T6   The pointed leaves that fall from pine trees:

T7   The sticky stuff that comes out of pine trees:

T8   Joints of pine wood that burn easily and make good fuel:

T9   The common shade tree with large heart-shaped leaves, clusters of white blossoms, and long thin seed pods or 'beans':

T10   What different kinds of oak trees grow around here? Any special kinds? (Open question)

T11   What different kinds of elm trees grow around here? (Open question)

T12   The kind of poplar tree that has sticky, sweet-smelling buds:

T13   What other names do you have around here for these trees: box elder, hackberry, linden, osage orange, poplar, sumac, sycamore, tamarack, tulip tree?

T14   What different kinds of maples do you have around here? (Open question)

T15   What kinds of swamp trees do you have? (Open question)

T16   What kinds of trees are 'special' around here? (Open question)

T17   What different kinds of pine trees do you have around here? (Open question)

Buying and Selling, Money

U1a   When you are going to a store or several stores to buy things, you say, "I'm going _____."

U1b   Do you use a different expression if you're buying groceries?

U2   What do you call a piece of clothing not made at home --- one that you buy?

U3   A coat, dress, or other garment that is passed on from one person to another (or an older child to a younger one):

U4   A place where you can take something valuable and borrow money on it:

U5   Someone who sells small articles on a street corner:

U6   Someone who sells vegetables or other articles from a wagon or truck, going from house to house:

U7   A man who goes from town to town selling things:

U8a   Other ways of saying "It cost me ten dollars."

U8b   Similar expressions meaning "I paid ten dollars for it."

U9   If you buy something for much less than it usually costs, you say, "At ten dollars it was a _____!"

U11   If you buy something but don't pay cash for it, you might say, "I _____."

U12   If you were buying something and you argued with the person selling it till you made him lower the price, you might say, "I _____."

U13   When buying or exchanging something that you have not seen, you say you're getting it _____.

U14   When you're exchanging with somebody when neither one has seen what the other has (children often do this) you'd call that a _____.

U15   When you're buying something, if the seller puts in a little extra to make you feel that you're getting a good bargain, you call that _____.

U16   If somebody was caught short of money and went to a friend to get some, he might say, "I need five dollars before Saturday, will you _____ it to me?"

U17   Names or nicknames for a person who doesn't pay his bills:

U18   If you force somebody to pay money that he owes you, but that he did not want to pay, you might say, "I finally made him _____."

U19a   Words used around here for money in general: "He's certainly got the _____."

U19b   Talking of paper money: "He always carries a big _____."

U20   Words used for dollars around here: "It cost a hundred _____."

U21   Other words for 'one cent':

U22   Other words around here for a five-cent piece:

U23   Other words for a 25-cent piece:

U24   Other words for a 50-cent piece:

U26   Names or nicknames around here for a paper dollar:

U27   Names for a silver dollar:

U28a   Names for other kinds of paper money --- a five-dollar bill:

U28b   Names for other kinds of paper money --- a ten-dollar bill:

U28c   Names for other kinds of paper money --- a twenty-dollar bill:

U29   Names or nicknames around here for worthless money:

U30   What do you keep money in when you carry it around with you? (Different shapes, different for men and women, etc.)

U32   Words and expressions used about a very generous person: "He's _____."

U33   Names or nicknames for a stingy person:

U35   Words meaning thrifty but not in a complimentary way: "She's not a bad housekeeper, but very _____."

U36a   Words and expressions about a person who saves in a mean way or is greedy in money matters: "He's an awful _____."

U36b   Words and expressions used to describe a person who saves

in a mean way or is greedy in money matters: "She certainly
is _____."

U37　Words and expressions about somebody who has plenty of
money:

U38a　Words referring to a great deal of money: "He's got _____
(of money)."

U38b　Words referring to a great deal of money: "He made a
_____ (of money)."

U39　Somebody who has lost all his money: "During the depression he _____."

U40　Somebody who is temporarily out of money: You might say,
"At the moment he's _____."

U41a　Somebody who has lost everything and is very poor: "He's
_____."

U41b　Somebody who has lost everything and is very poor: "He's
poor as _____."

U43　What do you call the kind of store where most articles cost
(or used to cost) only five or ten cents?

Honesty and Dishonesty

V1　When you suspect that somebody is trying to deceive you, or
that something is going on behind your back, you say,
"There's _____."

V2a　What do you call a deceiving person, or somebody that you
can't trust?

V2b　About a deceiving person, or somebody that you can't trust,
you might say: "I wouldn't trust him _____."

V2c　About a deceiving person, or somebody that you can't trust,
you might say: "I wouldn't trust him any further than I
could _____."

V4　Other words for stealing something valuable --- for example,
a watch: "Yesterday somebody _____ my watch."

V5a　To take something of small value that doesn't belong to you
--- for example, a child taking cookies: "Who's been
_____ the cookies?"

V5b　If you take something that nobody seems to own, you might
say, "Before anybody else gets it, I'm going to _____ this."

V6　What words are used around here for a thief --- any kind of
thief?

V7　A person who sets out to cheat others while pretending to be
honest:

V8a　What do you call a paper ordering somebody to appear in
court? "The sheriff came with a _____ for him."

V8b　Of a person who has been given a paper ordering him into
court you might say: "He was _____ into court."

V9　What nicknames do people have around here for a policeman?

V10a　And what joking names are there for a sheriff?

V10b　And what joking names for a marshal?

V10c　And what joking names for a constable?

V11　What joking names do you have around here for a county or
city jail?

V12　Words for the amount of time a person has to spend in jail
--- for example, "He's in for a ten-year _____."

Clothing --- Men's and Women's

W1a　What do you open up and hold over your head when it rains?

W1b　If you use an umbrella (or other word) when the sun is too
hot, you call it a _____.

W1c　What joking names do people have for an umbrella around
here?

W2　What do you call a cloth bonnet worn by women for protection from the sun?

W3　A piece of cloth that a woman folds over her head and ties
under her chin:

W4　What names do you have around here for men's coats or
jackets for work and outdoor wear?

W6　What do you mean by the word 'blouse' --- for women, and
for men?

W7　If a man doesn't use a belt, what does he wear over his
shoulders to hold up his trousers?

W8　Names and nicknames for low canvas-top shoes with rubber
soles:

W9　A work garment, usually of blue cloth, covering the legs and
sometimes the chest, worn by farmers:

W10　Work trousers made of rough cloth, usually blue, --- different
names and kinds:

W11　Men's low, rough work shoes --- what names do you have for
them around here?

W12a　Heavy pieces of metal fastened under the soles of boots to
keep them from slipping:

W12b　Metal pieces under the tips of shoes to prevent wear:

W14　Names for underwear, including joking names. Men's ---
long, men's --- short, women's --- long, women's --- short:

W15　A shirt-length undergarment worn by women:

W16a　The full-length garment that a woman wears under her dress:

W16b　The garment worn by a woman under her dress --- if it only
goes from the waist down:

W19　Names and nicknames for the folded cloth worn by a baby
in place of pants:

W20　If somebody has no clothes on at all --- for example, "There
was Johnny, _____." or, "They went in swimming
_____."

W21　Soft shoes that people wear only inside the house:

W22　What do you call a loose, full housedress that ties at the waist?

W24a　What expressions are used around here to warn a woman
slyly that her slip is showing?

W24b　Sayings to warn a man that his pants are torn or split:

W24c　Sayings to warn a man that his trouser-fly is open:

W25　When a woman is cutting out a dress to sew, what do you
call the little scraps of cloth left over?

W27　What do you call a three-cornered tear in a piece of clothing
from catching it on something sharp?

W28　When a woman is in a hurry and has to sew up a torn place
quickly, she might say, "I'll just _____."

W29　What expressions do you have around here for things that
are sewn carelessly? "They're _____."

W30　When a woman adds decorations to make something more
attractive --- for example, a hat, she might say, "It's too plain
--- I think I'll put on a few flowers to _____ it up."

W32　What names do you have around here for a group of women
that meet to sew together?

W33　What do you call the jewelry that goes around a woman's
forearm?

W34　Jewelry that a woman wears on her ears: (Gesture.)

W35　A piece of jewelry that a woman wears fastened at the neck
of her dress:

W36　What do people say around here about a woman who uses a
lot of cosmetics?

W37　When a woman puts on her good clothes and tries to look
her best, you say she's _____.

W38　When a man dresses himself up in his best clothes, you say
he's _____.

W39　Joking ways of referring to a person's best clothes:

W40　What do people say about a woman who overdresses or who
spends too much on clothes?

W41　What expressions do you have for someone whose clothes
never look right or who always dresses carelessly?

W42a　What nicknames do you have around here for men's sharp-
pointed shoes?

W42b　And what nicknames for men's square-toed shoes?

W43　What joking words do you have for clothes in general?

Parts of the Body

X1a　Names used around here for false hair, worn by men:

X1b　False hair worn by women:

X2　When a woman divides her hair into three strands and twists
them together, you say she is _____ (her hair).

X3   When a woman puts her hair up on her head in a bunch, you call this a ———.

X4a   If you were speaking of somebody's hair getting gray, you might say, "His ——— is/are getting gray."

X4b   A person might say, "On Saturday I have to wash my ——— (hair/hairs)."

X5   What names do you have around here for different kinds of men's haircuts?

X6   If a person's lower jaw sticks out prominently, you say he's ———.

X7   Other names for the throat: "Some food got stuck in his ———."

X8   What general words do you have for the organs inside the body?

X9   Joking or uncomplimentary words for a person's mouth --- for example, you might say, "I wish he'd shut his ———."

X10b   To tell a person to stop talking --- not very politely:

X11   What do you call the flesh that the teeth are set in?

X12   What do you call large front teeth that stick out of the mouth?

X13a   What joking names do you have around here for teeth?

X13b   Joking names for false teeth:

X14   Joking words for the nose:

X15   What names do you have for different kinds of noses, according to shape or size?

X16   Sticky mucus that forms in the nose --- children's words for this:

X17   Talking about smells: A damp cellar that had been shut up for some time would smell ———.

X18   And talking about listening: When one person doesn't quite hear what another person said, what does he say?

X19a   When a person's hearing is not very good, you say he's ———.

X19b   And if a person's hearing is very bad, you say he's ———.

X20   What other words do you have for a black eye?

X21a   What words are used to describe people according to their eyes --- for example, if they stick out?

X21b   If the eyes are very sharp or piercing:

X21c   If the eyes are very round:

X22   To stare at something with your mouth open:

X23   What joking words do you have around here for eyeglasses?

X24   When a person opens and closes his eyes quickly, he ———.

X25   To close your eyes part way --- for example, when looking at the sun:

X26a   If a person's eyes look in different directions, looking inward, he's ———.

X26b   If a person's eyes look in different directions, looking outward, he's ———.

X28   Joking words used around here for a person's head:

X29   Joking or uncomplimentary words for a person's face:

X31   Other words used around here for a woman's breasts:

X32   Joking or uncomplimentary words for the hands --- you might say, "Those are mine. You keep your ——— (out of them)."

X33   The place in the elbow that gives you a strange feeling if you hit it against something:

X34   Other names and nicknames for the navel:

X35   Joking words for the part of the body that you sit on --- for example, "He slipped and came down hard on his ———."

X37   What words do you have to describe people's legs if they're noticeably bent, or uneven, or not right?

X38   Joking names for unusually big or clumsy feet:

X39   A mark on the skin where somebody has sucked it hard and brought the blood to the surface:

X40   What other ways do you have of saying "I'm going to bed"?

X41   When you're going to sleep for a very short while, you might say, "I'm just going to ———."

X42   What other way do you have to say "I stopped sleeping at six o'clock."

X43a   If you sleep later than usual one day by accident, you'd say, "I ———."

X43b   If you sleep later than usual one day on purpose, you'd say, "I ———."

X45   What joking expressions do you have around here about snoring?

X46   When a person's getting sleepy and opens his mouth wide and takes a deep breath, that's a ———.

X47   What other ways do you have of saying "I'm very tired, at the end of my strength"?

X48a   Expressions meaning that a person is not so young any more --- for example, "She must be ——— sixty."

X48b   Or if a person is not so young any more, you might say, "He's ———."

X49   Expressions used about a person who is very thin:

X50   Names or nicknames for a person who is very fat:

X51   To lose weight because of sickness: "He was sick all winter and ——— (quite a bit)."

X52   And you'd say that a person like that who had been sick was looking ———.

X53a   What do you call an oversize stomach?

X53b   An oversize stomach that results from drinking:

X54   When a person gets a spell of going 'hic' (Make the sound!) he's got the ———.

X55b   Words for breaking wind from the bowels:

X56a   Other words for sweat:

X56b   Expressions about sweating very heavily:

X57   A person with light-colored hair and skin, "He's fair ———."

X58   When you are cold, and little points of skin begin to come on your arms and legs, you have ———.

X59   What do you call the small infected pimples that form usually on the face?

X60   What do you call a lump that comes up on your head when you get a sharp blow or knock?

Physical Actions

Y1   What expressions are used around here for a person suddenly falling down: "He slipped on the steps and took quite a ———."

Y2   Other words for upsetting or disturbing somebody: "Losing all that money didn't seem to ——— him a bit."

Y3   To say uncomplimentary things about somebody:

Y4   Other words for a very uncomplimentary remark:

Y5   Words meaning to urge somebody to do something he shouldn't: "Johnny wouldn't have tried that if the other boys hadn't ———."

Y6   Words meaning to put pressure on somebody to do something he ought to have done but hasn't: "He's a whole week late. I'm going to ———."

Y7   When one person never misses a chance to be mean to another or to annoy another: "I don't know why she keeps ——— me all the time!"

Y9   Somebody who always follows along behind others: "His little brother is an awful ———."

Y10   To throw something --- for example, "The dog came at him, so he picked up a stone and ——— it at him."

Y11   Other words for a very hard blow: "You should have seen Bill go down. Joe really hit him a ———."

Y12a   A fight between two people, mostly with words:

Y12b   A real fight in which blows are struck:

Y13   A fist fight with several people in it:

Y14a   To hit somebody hard with the fist:

Y14b   To hit somebody with the open hand:

Y15   To beat somebody thoroughly: "John really ——— that fellow!"

Y16   A thorough beating: "He gave the bully an awful ———."

Y17   When two people agree to stop fighting and not be enemies any more, you might say, "I hear they ———."

Y18   To leave in a hurry: "Before they find this out, we'd better ———!"

Y19   To begin to go away from a place: "It's about time for me to ———."

Y20   To run fast: "You should have seen him _____!"

Y21   To move about slowly and without energy:

Y22   To move around in a way to make people take notice of you: "Look at him _____."

Y23   Expressions meaning to move yourself or get yourself in motion: "I was so stiff I could hardly _____."

Y24   Expressions meaning to walk, to go on foot: "I can't get a ride, so I'll just have to _____."

Y25   To walk heavily, making a lot of noise: "He came _____ into the house."

Y26a   To walk very quietly: "She came _____ to the baby's bed."

Y26b   To walk very quietly: "The children filled their pockets and _____ out the back way."

Y27   To go about aimlessly, with nothing to do: "He's always _____ around the drugstore."

Y28   A person who loiters about with nothing to do:

Y29a   To 'go out' a great deal, not to stay at home much: "She's always _____."

Y29b   Or, about a man who doesn't stay home much: "He's always _____."

Y30a   To take something up and move it from one place to another --- for example, a paper sack of groceries:

Y30b   To take something heavy up and move it from one place to another --- for example, a bushel of apples:

Y31   If a child asked his father to carry him on his back, he might say, "Give me a _____."

Y32   To squeeze yourself into a small space: "If you're going to fit in there you'll have to _____." (Gesture.)

Y33   Other words for squeezing or crushing something --- for example, your finger in a door: "I _____ my finger in the door."

Y34a   When somebody moves on his hands and knees: "He was down in the bushes, _____ around."

Y34b   What babies do before they walk:

Y35   To spoil something so that it can't be used --- for example, a new coffee pot: "My new coffee pot --- it's completely _____."

Y36   To spill something over the sides of a container: "See if you can carry that water without _____ (it all over)."

Y37   To make a place untidy or disorderly: "I wish they wouldn't _____ the room so." (Gesture.)

Y38   Mixed together, confused: "The things in the drawer are all _____."

Y39   To get something sticky or smeared up: "The children have been eating candy and they've got their faces all _____."

Y40a   Other words referring to sticky stuff: "I've got to wash my hands. They're all _____."

Y40b   Other words referring to sticky stuff: "I've got to wash my hands. They're all covered with _____."

Y41a   Expressions used around to tell someone to light a lamp or lantern: "_____ the lamp."

Y41b   Expressions used around here to tell someone to light an electric light: "_____ the light."

Y42   Expressions for putting out a lamp or light:

Y43a   Expressions meaning to light a fire: "_____ the fire."

Y43b   Expressions meaning to put out a fire:

Y44   A very small, sharp piece of wood: "His finger is sore --- he ran a _____ into it."

Y45   Talking of a liquid --- to scatter in all directions: "When he opened the can, the beer _____ (all over the kitchen)."

Y46a   To get hurt with something sharp --- for example a thorn: "He _____ a thorn into his hand."

Y46b   To get hurt with something sharp, like a needle: "She _____ herself with a needle."

Y47   To hide something away for future use: "I know he's got it _____ somewhere."

Y48   To look in every possible place for something you've mislaid --- for example, a pair of gloves: "I've _____ (the house looking for them)."

Y50   To undertake or carry out a job: "That's a big job for just one person to _____."

Y51   Other ways of saying 'to avoid' things or people --- for example: "He's not your kind --- you'd better _____ him."

Y52   To move over --- for example on a long bench: "We have to make room for one more. Can you _____ (a little)?"

Family Relationships

Z1   What words do people around here use for 'father' within the family?

Z2   What words do people around here use for 'mother'?

Z3   What words do people around here use for 'grandfather'?

Z4   What words do people around here use for 'grandmother'?

Z5   Nicknames and affectionate words meaning 'brother':

Z6   Nicknames and affectionate words meaning 'sister':

Z7   Nicknames and affectionate words for any other relatives: (Open question)

Z8   General word for your own immediate family group:

Z9   General word for others related to you by blood:

Z10   If a child looks very much like his father, you might say, "He _____ his father."

Z11a   Words for a child whose parents were not married --- serious words:

Z11b   Nicknames and joking words for a child of unwed parents:

Z12   Nicknames and joking words meaning 'a small child': "He's a healthy little _____."

Z13   If a mother has to leave her baby for a little while, she might ask a neighbor, "While I'm gone, will you _____ the baby for me?"

Z14a   To give a child its own way or pay too much attention to it: "Everyone _____ that child."

Z14b   If a child expects to have its own way or have too much attention, you might say, "That child is _____."

Z16   A small child who is rough, misbehaves, and doesn't obey, you'd call him a _____.

Z17   To take care of or bring up a child: "All her children were _____ (on the farm)."

Courtship, Marriage, Childbearing

AA1   When a man goes to see a girl often and seems to want to marry her, he's _____ her.

AA2   If a man is going to a dance and a girl is going with him, you might say, "John is going to _____ Mary to the dance."

AA3   Nicknames or affectionate names for a sweetheart:

AA4a   What words and expressions are used around here about a man who is very eager to get married? "He's _____."

AA4b   And what expressions about a woman who is very eager to get married? "She's _____."

AA5   If a woman seems to be going after one certain man that she wants to marry: "She's _____ him."

AA6a   What do you call a man who is fond of being with women and tries to attract their attention --- if he's nice about it?

AA6b   What do you call a man who is fond of being with women and tries to attract their attention --- if he's rude or not respectful?

AA7a   What words do you have for a woman who is very fond of men and is always trying to know more --- if she's nice about it?

AA7b   What words do you have for a woman who is very fond of men and is always trying to know more --- if she's not respectable about it?

AA8   When people make too much of a show of affection in a public place --- for example, "There they were at the church supper _____ (with each other)."

AA9   Other words used around here for a loud or vigorous kiss:

AA10   A very special liking that a boy may have for a girl (or the other way round) --- you'd say, "He _____ her." or "She _____ him."

AA11   If a man asks a girl to marry him and she refuses, you'd say she _____.

AA12   If a man loses interest in a girl and stops seeing her, you'd say he _____.

AA13   When two people who have been 'going steady' or were engaged, stop going together, you might say, "I guess they _____."

AA15a   What joking ways do you have around here of saying that people got married? "They _____."

AA15b   What joking ways do you have around here of saying that a man is getting married? "He _____."

AA15c   What joking ways do you have around here of saying that a woman is getting married? "She _____."

AA17   What other people beside the bride and groom do you usually have in a wedding party around here? (Open question)

AA18   What do you call a noisy neighborhood celebration after a wedding, where the married couple is expected to give a treat?

AA19   Words or expressions about a man and woman who are not married but live together as if they were:

AA20   A marriage that takes place because a baby is on the way:

AA21   What joking expressions do you have about a wife who gives the orders and a husband who takes them from her?

AA22   Joking names that a man may use to refer to his wife: "I have to go down and pick up my _____."

AA23   Joking names that a woman may use to refer to her husband: "It's time to go and get supper for my _____."

AA24   A man whose wife is dead:

AA25   A woman whose husband is dead:

AA26   A divorced woman:

AA27   What other names or expressions are used for a woman's menstruation?

AA28   What joking or sly expressions do women use to say that another is going to have a baby? "She('s) _____."

AA29   What do you call the blue, swollen veins that a woman often gets on her legs while expecting a baby?

AA30   An older woman who comes in (or used to come in) to help when a baby is going to be born:

Health and Disease

BB1   When a person has been injured so that when he walks he steps more heavily on one foot than the other: "He _____."

BB2   If a person is careful not to put much weight on his injured leg, you might say he was _____ that leg.

BB3a   What do you call a pain that strikes you suddenly in the neck?

BB3b   A sudden pain that strikes you in the back:

BB3c   A sudden pain that comes in the side: (Gesture.)

BB4   Other words for a pain --- for example, in the arm: "He's had a _____ in his arm for a week."

BB5   A general feeling of discomfort or illness that isn't any one place in particular:

BB6   A sudden feeling of weakness, when sometimes the person loses consciousness:

BB7   A feeling that lasts for a short while, with difficult breathing and heart beating fast:

BB8   When a person's joints and muscles ache and sometimes swell up, especially in damp weather, he may have _____.

BB9   A sickness in which you have a severe cough and difficult breathing --- it often starts with a cold, and lasts a week or two:

BB10   What other names or nicknames are used, or used to be used, around here for tuberculosis?

BB11   Speaking of a deep cough that you can't seem to get rid of: "Listen to him _____."

BB12   The kind of cough that comes with bronchitis: "He has a _____ cough."

BB13   Other words used around here for chills and fever:

BB14   To suddenly become unconscious and fall: "Just as she came to the door she _____."

BB15   Somebody who is unconscious from a hard blow: "He's been _____ for ten minutes."

BB16a   If something a person ate didn't agree with him, he might be sick _____ his stomach. (Gesture.)

BB16b   If something a person ate didn't agree with him, he might just feel a bit _____.

BB17   Other words or expressions used around here for vomiting:

BB18   To vomit a great deal at once:

BB19   Joking names for looseness of the bowels:

BB20   Joking names or expressions for overactive kidneys:

BB21   Other words for being constipated:

BB22   What home remedies do you have around here for constipation? (Open question)

BB23   The disease where the skin becomes a yellowish color:

BB24   Other names for a rash that comes out suddenly --- from hives or something else: "He's got some kind of _____ all over his chest."

BB25   What are some common skin diseases around here? (Open question)

BB27   When somebody pretends to be sick (often to get out of doing something) you'd say he's _____.

BB28   Joking names that people make up for imaginary diseases: "He must have the _____."

BB29   What do you call the red flesh that sometimes grows in a wound and keeps it from healing right?

BB30   What do you call a hard, painful swelling (often on a finger) that seems to come from deep under the skin?

BB32   If somebody had a swelling --- for example, in his whole face --- you might say, "Last week his face was all _____."

BB33a   What do you call a swelling under the skin, bigger than a pimple, that comes to a head?

BB33b   What do you call a swelling under the skin --- if it is very big or serious?

BB35   The yellowish stuff that comes out of a boil when the head breaks:

BB36   When there's an open sore and this yellowish stuff is coming out of it, you say it's _____.

BB37   When yellowish stuff comes out of a person's ear, he has a _____.

BB38   When a person doesn't look healthy, or looks as if he hadn't been well for some time, you'd say, "He looks _____."

BB39   On a day when you don't feel just right, though not actually sick, you might say, "I'll be all right tomorrow --- I'm just feeling _____ today."

BB40   If you're inquiring about somebody acting strangely: "All of a sudden he got up and left. What do you suppose _____ him?"

BB41   Not seriously ill, but sick enough to be in bed: "He's been _____ for a week."

BB42   If a person is very sick you say he's _____.

BB43   A person who has to stay in bed all the time: "For two years now he's been _____."

BB44   Words used around here about a person just starting some sickness --- for example, pneumonia: "He _____ pneumonia."

BB45   The time that an illness lasts --- for example, stomach trouble: "He's been having a long _____ of stomach trouble."

BB46   Words and expressions about someone who has been very sick but now is getting better: "He's _____."

BB47   Feeling in the best of health and spirits: "I'm feeling _____!"

BB48   When a person has too much sugar in his blood and may have to take insulin for it, you'd say he has _____.

BB49   What other kinds of diseases are common around here, or used to be common? (Open question)

BB50a   What are the favorite remedies around here for a cough? (Open question)

BB50b   Remedies for chest colds: (Open question)

BB50c   Remedies for infections: (Open question)

BB50d   Favorite spring tonics around here: (Open question)

BB51a   What cures for corns or warts do you have around here? (Open question)

BB51b   Are there any 'magical' cures for corns or warts, like rubbing them with something special, or in a special way?

BB52   What joking words do you have around here for a dentist?

BB53a   What joking names do you have for a doctor?
BB53b   What do you call a doctor who is not very capable or doesn't have a very good reputation?
BB54   When a sick person is past hope of recovery, you'd say he's (a) _____.
BB56   Joking expressions for dying: "He _____."
BB57   If someone committed suicide, you'd say he _____.
BB60   When friends and relatives gather together at the place where the body is, usually the night before the funeral, you call that:
BB61a   Other words used around here for a cemetery:
BB61b   Any joking names for a cemetery?

Religion and Beliefs

CC1   On a church building, what do you call the part that sticks up high?
CC2   What are the predominant religious denominations around here?
CC3   Are there any religions that have come in recently around here or are a bit different from the common ones?
CC4   What nicknames do you have around here for various religions or religious groups?
CC5   Names for seats in a church, especially near the front:
CC6   The place where the preacher stands to give the sermon:
CC7   Words for a person who goes to church very seldom or not at all:
CC8   Other names for the devil:
CC9   Other words or expressions for hell: "That man is headed straight for _____."
CC10   What words do you have around here for an unprofessional, part-time lay preacher?
CC11   When somebody has had a lot of good luck, you say he _____.
CC12a   Expressions used about bad luck, or about somebody who has had a lot of it: "Poor Joe. He's really been having _____."
CC12b   Or if a person has a lot of bad luck you might say, "He's been _____."
CC13a   What names do you have around here for a forked stick that's used to show where there's water underground? (What kind of wood?)
CC13b   And what do you call the person who knows how to use a forked stick to find water?
CC14   Words or expressions used here, where one person supposedly casts a spell over another:
CC15   When people say there are ghosts in a certain place, or when it gives you a creepy feeling to go near it: "They say that the old house is _____."
CC16   A small light that seems to dance or flicker over a marsh or swamp at night:
CC17   Imaginary animals or monsters that people around here tell tales about --- especially to tease greenhorns: (What are they like? What do they do?)

Tobacco, Liquor

DD1   What different forms does chewing tobacco come in around here?
DD2   The portion or quantity of tobacco chewed at one time: "He's always got a big _____ in his cheek."
DD3a   What do you call a person who uses snuff?
DD3b   How do people take snuff around here?
DD4   Moisture in the mouth, colored brown by snuff or chewing tobacco:
DD5   A metal or earthenware receptacle on the floor that tobacco-chewers use, or used to use:
DD6a   Other names or nicknames for cigars:
DD6b   Nicknames for cigarettes:
DD7   Different names for cigars around here according to size, shape, or the way they're made:
DD8   The part left over when a cigar or cigarette is smoked:

DD9a   What expressions are used about a person who smokes a great deal? "He's a _____."
DD9b   Of a person who smokes a great deal you might say, "He smokes like a _____."
DD10   When somebody gives up smoking: "He isn't smoking any more --- a month ago he _____."
DD11   When somebody gives up drinking: "I hear he _____."
DD12   What words or expressions do you have around here for a person who drinks steadily or a great deal?
DD13   When a drinker is just beginning to show the effects of the liquor, you say he's _____.
DD14   When a person is partly drunk, "He's _____."
DD15   A person who is thoroughly drunk:
DD16   To have a drinking bout and get drunk is to go on a _____.
DD17   To drink a great deal, or too fast: "He doesn't just drink, he _____."
DD18   A drink of liquor, or the amount of liquor taken in one swallow: "He took a good _____."
DD21a   General words used around here for any kind of liquor:
DD21b   General words used around here for bad liquor:
DD21c   Nicknames for whiskey, especially illegally made whiskey:
DD22   Other expressions meaning delirium tremens:
DD24   Other diseases that come from continual drinking:
DD25   What nicknames are used around here for beer?
DD27   What nicknames are used around here for wine?
DD28b   What fermented drinks are made at home around here?
DD30   Joking names for a place where liquor is (or was) sold and consumed illegally:
DD32   A person who sells illegal liquor is called a _____.
DD33a   A person who drinks no liquor at all:
DD33b   A person who is actively against drinking:
DD34   A party at which there is considerable drinking:
DD35   What are the favorite card games that people play around here? (Open question)
DD37   Other table games played a lot by adults around here: (Open question)

Children's Games

EE1   What games do children play around here, in which they form a ring, and either sing or recite a rhyme?
EE2   Games that have one extra player --- when a signal is given, the players change places, and the extra one tries to get a place:
EE3   Games in which you hide an object and then look for it:
EE4   Games in which one player's eyes are bandaged and he has to catch the others and guess who they are:
EE5   Games where you try to make a jackknife stick in the ground:
EE6a   Names for different kinds of marbles --- the big one that's used to knock others out of the ring:
EE6b   Small marbles or marbles in general:
EE6c   Cheap marbles:
EE6d   Special marbles:
EE7   What kinds of marble games are played or used to be played around here? (Open question)
EE8   The line toward which the players roll their marbles before beginning a game, to determine the order of shooting:
EE9a   The children's trick of turning over rapidly straight forward close to the ground: (Gesture.)
EE9b   If children jump forward, land on the hands, and turn over: (Gesture.)
EE9c   What if children spread their arms and turn over sideways? (Gesture.)
EE10   A game in which a short stick lying on the ground is flipped into the air and then hit with a longer stick, that's _____.
EE11   Bat-and-ball games for just a few players (when there aren't enough for a regular game):
EE12   Games in which one captain hides his team and the other team tries to find it:
EE13a   Games in which every player hides except one, and that one must try to find the others:

EE13b   In games in which all the others hide, the one who must try to find them, he's _____.

EE14   What do you call the place where the player who is 'it' has to wait and count while the others hide?

EE15   When he has caught the first of those that were hiding what does the player who is 'it' call out to the others?

EE16   Hiding games that start with a special, elaborate method of sending the players out to hide:

EE17   In a game of tag, if a player wants to rest, what does he call out so that he can't be tagged?

EE18   Games in which the players set up a stone, a tin can, or something similar, and then try to knock it down:

EE19   The game in which children mark a 'court' on the ground or sidewalk, throw a flat stone in one section, then go on one foot and try to kick it or carry it out:

EE20   When two boys are fighting, and the one who is losing wants to stop, he calls out, "_____."

EE21b   When boys were fighting very actively, you might say, "For a while those fellows really _____."

EE22   What do you call the game in which they throw a ball over a building (a house or a barn) to a player on the other side?

EE23a   In the game of andy-over (or other word) what do you call out when you throw the ball?

EE23b   In the game of andy-over (or other word) if you fail to get the ball over the building and it rolls back, what do you call out?

EE24a   When there's snow, children go down the hill on a _____.

EE24b   When children go down hill on a sled (or other word) they say they're _____.

EE25   When a child picks up his sled (or other word), runs with it, and then throws himself down on it, that's a _____.

EE26   What games do children play in the snow around here? (Open question)

EE27   Games played on the ice: (Open question)

EE28   Games played in the water: (Open question)

EE29   When swimmers are diving and one comes down flat onto the water, that's a _____.

EE30   Throwing a flat stone over the surface of water so that it jumps several times:

EE31   Playground equipment with a long board for two children to sit on and go up and down in turn:

EE32   A homemade merry-go-round:

EE33   Other outdoor games not yet mentioned that children play now, or that were played in your childhood: (Open question)

EE34   Other words used around here meaning a child's toy:

EE35   Long wooden poles with a footpiece that children walk around on to make them tall:

EE36   To climb the trunk of a tree by holding on with your legs while you pull yourself up with your hands:

EE37   The game where you try to throw metal rings or something similar over a stake in the ground:

EE38a   A game played with pencil and paper where the players try to get three X's or three O's in a row:

EE38b   If the game of tick-tack-toe (or other word) comes out so that neither X nor O wins, you call that _____.

EE39   Other games played on paper by two people: (Open question)

EE40   What table games are played around here, using dice? (Open question)

EE41   A hobgoblin that is used to threaten children and make them behave:

Entertainments and Celebrations

FF1   Do you have around here a kind of group meeting called a 'social' or 'sociable'? What kinds are there? (What goes on?)

FF2   What kinds of parties do people favor around here? (Open question)

FF3   Do people give 'showers' or 'gift parties' around here? What kinds?

FF4   Names and joking names for different kinds of dancing parties:

FF5a   Names for different steps and figures in dancing --- in past years:

FF5b   More recent dance steps:

FF6   Expressions used around here meaning 'to be asked to go to a party': "Did you get a _____ to the party?"

FF7   A small musical instrument that you blow on, and move from side to side in your mouth:

FF8   Another small instrument that you hold between the teeth and pluck on:

FF9   A Christmas gathering, at church or at someone's home, where there are songs and presents: "Are you going to the _____?"

FF10   What do people around here say to greet each other on Christmas morning?

FF11   What do you call the night of December 31st?

FF12a   What do you call the first day of May around here?

FF12b   What do you call the night of May first? (Do children give May baskets? Is there a Maypole? When?)

FF14   What different kinds of firecrackers do you have around here?

FF15   When a firecracker doesn't go off, and you break it in the middle and light the powder, you call it a _____.

FF16   What other local contests or celebrations do you have? What goes on? (Open question)

FF17   Words meaning that people had a very good or enjoyable time: "We all had a _____ last night."

FF18   Joking words or expressions about a noisy or boisterous celebration or party: "They certainly _____ last night."

FF19   Words used about a very dull or unenjoyable time: "The party was _____."

FF21a   A joke that is so old it doesn't seem funny any more: "His jokes are all _____."

FF21b   Or about old jokes people say: "The first time I heard that one I _____."

FF22a   Names for clubs and societies around here --- for women: (Open question)

FF22b   Names for clubs and societies around here --- for men: (Open question)

FF23   What joking names do people have for any of these clubs or lodges?

FF24   The place or building where people go to see motion pictures:

FF25   Joking names for motion pictures:

FF26   Words meaning a large group of people at a public gathering --- for example, an auction: "There was quite a _____ at the auction."

FF27   Joking names and nicknames for television:

FF28   What other kinds of fireworks do you have? (Open question)

Emotional States and Attitudes

GG2   Expressions meaning 'confused, mixed up': "So many things were going on at the same time that he got completely _____."

GG3   To tease: "See those big boys trying to _____ (that little one)."

GG4   Stirred up, angry: "When he saw them coming he got _____."

GG5   When someone does something unexpectedly bold or forward, you might say: "Well, she certainly has a lot of _____."

GG6   Talking about a person's feelings being hurt: "When she said she couldn't go with him, he was quite _____."

GG7   Words meaning annoyed or upset: "Though we were only ten minutes late, she was all _____."

GG8   When a person is very easily offended: "Be careful what you say to him, he's _____."

GG9   To suddenly embarrass somebody and throw him off balance: "When they told him what she had said about him, it certainly did _____ him."

GG11   To be quite anxious about something --- for example, waiting for a letter: "The letter hasn't come and he's _____."

GG12   To have an inner feeling that something is about to happen: "There she comes now, I _____ she would."

GG13a   When something keeps bothering a person and makes him nervous, he may say, "It _____ me."

GG13b   When something keeps bothering a person and makes him nervous, he may say: "It gives me the _____."

GG14   Names and nicknames for someone who fusses or worries a lot, especially about little things:

GG15   Talking about a person who became over-excited and lost control, "At that point he really _____."

GG16   Words for finding fault, or complaining: "You just can't please him --- he's always _____."

GG17   Other words for longing (to see somebody who has been away): "She had been so lonely --- she was really _____ (to see him)."

GG18   Other words meaning 'obstinate': "Why does he have to be so _____."

GG19a   When you can see from the way a person acts that he's feeling important or independent: "He surely is _____ these days."

GG19b   When you can see from the way a person acts that he's feeling important or independent: "He seems to think he's _____."

GG20   Words or expressions meaning 'very much surprised': "When those two got married, I was certainly _____."

GG21a   If you don't care what a person does, you might tell him, "You can go ahead and do it _____."

GG21b   If you don't care what a person does, you might say, "Go ahead --- I don't give a _____."

GG22a   When you have come to the end of your patience, you might say, "Well that's the _____."

GG22b   When you have come to the end of your patience, you might say, "Well, that certainly _____."

GG23a   If you speak sharply to somebody to make him be patient, you say, "Now just keep your _____."

GG23b   If you speak sharply to somebody to make him be patient, you might say, "Hold _____!"

GG23c   Any other expressions (to tell someone to be patient):

GG24   Other words meaning to frighten: "Now don't let those fellows _____ you."

GG25   To become frightened: "The children were _____ he was going to hurt them."

GG26   A feeling of weakness from fear: "When she saw the dog coming at her she got _____."

GG27a   To get somebody out of an unhappy mood, you might say to him, "Everything's going to be all right, so _____."

GG27b   To get somebody out of an unhappy mood, you might say to him, "Don't _____."

GG28   To be very pleased or happy about something: "She managed to come home for Christmas, and everybody was _____ to see her."

GG29   To be in a good or pleasant mood: "This morning he seems to be feeling _____."

GG30   To suddenly break out laughing: "When he told her that, she just _____."

GG31   To laugh very hard: "I thought I'd _____."

GG32a   To habitually play tricks or jokes on people: "He's always _____."

GG32b   To habitually play tricks or jokes on people: "He's an awful _____."

GG34a   To feel depressed or in a gloomy mood: "He has the _____ today."

GG34b   To feel depressed or in a gloomy mood: "She's feeling _____ today."

GG35a   To sulk or pout: "It won't do any good to _____ about it."

GG35b   Of a person who acts annoyed or disappointed you might say, "Because she couldn't go, she's been _____ all day."

GG36a   The kind of person who is always poking into other people's affairs: "She's an awful _____."

GG36b   The kind of person who is always poking into other people's affairs: "She's the _____ person I know!"

GG37   Somebody who is very brave or courageous: "He's got plenty of _____."

GG38   Somebody who is usually mean and bad tempered: "He's an awful _____."

GG39   Somebody who seems to be looking for reasons to be angry: "He's a _____."

GG40   Words or expressions meaning violently angry:

GG41   To lose patience easily: "You never did see such a _____ person."

GG42   A reckless person, one who takes foolish chances:

Types and Attitudes of People

HH1   Names and nicknames for a rustic or countrified person:

HH2   Names and nicknames for a citified person:

HH3   A dull and stupid person:

HH4   Someone who has odd or peculiar ideas or notions:

HH5   Someone who is queer but harmless:

HH6   Someone who is out of his mind:

HH7a   Someone who talks too much, or too loud: "He's an awful _____."

HH7b   Someone who talks too much, or too loud: "He's always _____."

HH8   A person who likes to brag:

HH9   A very silly or light-headed person:

HH10   A very timid or cowardly person: "He's _____."

HH11a   Someone who is too particular or fussy --- if it's a man:

HH11b   Someone who is too particular or fussy --- if it's a woman:

HH12   A person who is always finding fault about unimportant things:

HH13   Expressions meaning that a person is not very alert or not aware of things: "He's certainly _____."

HH14   Ways of teasing a beginner or inexperienced person --- for example, by sending him for a 'left-handed monkey wrench': "Go get me _____."

HH15   A very inexperienced person, one who is just learning how to do a new thing:

HH16   Uncomplimentary words with no definite meaning --- just used when you want to show that you don't think much of a person: "Don't invite him. He's a _____."

HH17   A person who tries to appear important, or who tries to lay down the law in his community: "He'd like to be the _____ around here."

HH18   Very insignificant or low-grade people:

HH19   Other words or nicknames for a tramp:

HH20a   An idle, worthless person: "He's a _____."

HH20b   Of an idle, worthless person you might say, "He doesn't amount to _____."

HH20c   Of an idle, worthless person you might say, "He isn't worth _____."

HH21   A very awkward, clumsy person:

HH22b   Talking about a very mean person, you might say, "He's meaner than _____."

HH22c   Talking about a very mean person, you might say, "He's mean enough to _____."

HH24   Somebody who doesn't talk very much, who keeps his thoughts to himself:

HH25   One who never has anything to say: "What's the matter with him?" "_____?"

HH26   A person who is always ready to stir up trouble:

HH27a   A very able and energetic person who gets things done:

HH27b   Of a very able and energetic person who gets things done you might say, "He's got lots of _____."

HH28   Names and nicknames around here for people of foreign background: (Get only those appropriate in your area.)

HH29a   Names around here for people of mixed blood --- part Indian:

HH29b   Names for people of mixed blood --- part Negro:

HH30   Things that are nicknamed for different nationalities --- for example, a 'Dutch treat': (Open question)

HH31   Somebody who is not from your community, and doesn't belong:

HH34   General words around here for a woman, not necessarily uncomplimentary:

HH35   A woman who puts on a lot of airs: "She's too _____ for me."

HH36   A careless, slovenly woman: "She's just an old _____."

HH37   An immoral woman:

HH38   A womanish man:

HH39   A homosexual man:

HH40   Uncomplimentary words for an old man:

HH43a   The top person in charge of a group of workmen, the _____.

HH43b   The assistant to the top person in charge of a group of workmen is called the _____.

HH44   Joking or uncomplimentary names for lawyers:

Relationships among People

II1   Words meaning a close friend (or other ways of saying "He's my friend."): "He's my _____."

II2a   When two people begin to be friendly: "He has just recently _____ with John."

II2b   When two people have become friendly you might say, "It's been quite a while that Mary and Jane have been _____."

II3   Expressions to say that people are very friendly toward each other: "They're _____."

II4   When people around here ask to be introduced to someone --- for example: "I'd like to _____ John Smith."

II5a   When you don't want to have anything to do with a certain person because you don't like him, you might say, "I'd certainly like to get _____ of him."

II5b   When you don't want to have anything to do with a certain person because you don't like him, you might say, "I'd certainly like to give him the _____."

II6   If you meet somebody who used to be a friend, and he pretends not to know you: "When I met him on the street he _____."

II7   Somebody who doesn't seem to 'fit in' or to get along very well, you might say about him, "He's kind of a _____."

II8   When one person wants to share or divide something with another person, he might say, "Let's _____ (on that)."

II9   If several people have to contribute in order to pay for something, you say, "Let's all _____."

II10a   Asking directions of somebody on the street when you don't know his name --- what you'd say to a boy: "Say, _____, where's the post office?"

II10b   Asking directions of somebody on the street when you don't know his name --- what you'd say to a man: "Say, _____, how far is it to the next town?"

II11a   If two people don't get along well together, you'd say, "They don't _____."

II11b   If two people can't bear each other at all, you'd say, "Those two are _____."

II12   Talking about meeting somebody on the street and speaking only a few words with him: "We just _____."

II14   To pay a short visit: "Last night our new neighbors _____."

II15   When somebody is passing by and you want him or her to stop and talk a while, you might say, "_____."

II17   If you happen to meet someone that you haven't seen for a while: "Guess who I _____ this morning."

II18   Someone who joins himself on to you and your group without being asked and won't leave:

II19   When you think somebody has been put ahead of you or has been given something you deserved, you might say, "I'd rather quit than _____."

II20a   A person who tries too hard to gain somebody else's favor: "He's an awful _____."

II20b   A person who tries too hard to gain somebody else's favor: "He's always trying to _____ the boss."

II21   When somebody behaves unpleasantly or without manners: "The way he behaves, you'd think he was _____."

II22   Expressions to tell somebody to keep to himself and mind his own business:

II23   Joking names for the people who are, or think they are, the best society of a community: The _____.

II24   Names or nicknames for the part of a town where the well-off people live:

II25   Names or nicknames for the part of a town where the poorer people, special groups, or foreign groups live:

II26   Joking ways of saying that you would not know who somebody is: "I wouldn't know him from _____."

II27   If somebody gives you a very sharp scolding, you might say, "I certainly got a _____ for that."

II28   An unexplainable dislike that you feel from the first moment you meet a person: "I took a _____ to him."

II29a   An unexplainable dislike that you feel from the first moment you meet a person: "I don't know why, but I just can't _____ him."

II29b   Or you might try to explain the unpleasant effect that person has on you: "He just _____."

II31   In an argument between two people, when one of them claims too much and the other shows him up: "He saw that he was wrong, so he started to _____."

II32   To manage some way to shift the responsibility: "He said it wasn't his fault and tried to _____."

II33   To get an advantage over somebody by tricky means: "I don't trust him, he's always trying to _____."

II34   If you think somebody is trying to use you to his advantage: "I'm not going to be his _____."

II35   A person who is disliked because he seems to think he knows everything:

II36a   Somebody who talks back or gives rude answers: "Did you ever see such a _____?"

II36b   Of somebody who talks back or gives rude answers you might say, "She certainly is _____!"

II39   What other ways do you have of saying 'Thank you'?

Schoolgoing, Mental Actions

JJ1a   Other words for a schoolteacher --- a woman:

JJ1b   Other words for a schoolteacher --- a man:

JJ2a   A child going to school, one in the lower grades:

JJ2b   A person who attends high school:

JJ3a   When a school child makes a special effort to 'get in good' with the teacher in hopes of getting a better grade: "He's trying to _____ again."

JJ3b   When a school child makes a special effort to 'get in good' with the teacher in hopes of getting a better grade: "She's an awful _____."

JJ4   A child who is always telling on other children:

JJ5   A time-out of about 10 or 15 minutes in the middle of the morning or afternoon: (Note stress.)

JJ6   To stay away from school without an excuse:

JJ7   Words or expressions for cheating in school examinations:

JJ8   To study very hard the last minute before an exam:

JJ9   Somebody who studies too hard or all the time:

JJ10a   Different kinds of pens and pencils:

JJ10b   Parts of an ink pen:

JJ11   Joking names for handwriting that's hard to read: "I can't make anything out of his _____."

JJ12   Little flourishes that some people put on their handwriting or signature to make it look fancy:

JJ13   What joking words do you have for a name signed to a paper? "I'll put my _____ on that."

JJ14   To write a person's name and where he lives on a letter you are sending to him: "I'll mail this letter as soon as I _____ it."

JJ15a   Sayings about a person who seems to you very stupid: "He hasn't sense enough to _____."

JJ15b   Sayings about a person who seems to you very stupid: "He doesn't know _____."

JJ16   When there was something you didn't understand, then suddenly you do understand it, you might say, "Oh, now I _____."

JJ17   When you know that somebody has been trying to deceive you, you might say, "He's not fooling me one bit, I'm _____ (him)."

JJ18   If you want to have time to think about something before you make a decision: "Give me till tomorrow, I'd like to _____."

JJ19 If somebody has dishonest intentions, or is up to no good, you might say, "I think he's got _____."

JJ20 If you felt very sure about something, and wanted to show it: "I'm so sure, I'd _____ it."

JJ21 If you want to be very positive: Somebody asks you "Are you really going to do that?" And you answer, "You _____."

JJ22 To express your opinion --- for example, at a public meeting: "I went to the meeting, and _____."

JJ23 To refuse to give in or yield: "He tried to scare me off but I _____."

JJ24 To refuse firmly: "He wanted to get some more money, but this time I _____."

JJ25 To show somebody that you're the boss: "He thought he could take the place over, but I made him _____."

JJ26 If somebody has been doing poor work or not enough, the boss might say, "If he wants to keep his job he'd better _____."

JJ27 To give somebody a hint for his own good: "He had no idea that she was up to anything, but I put _____."

JJ28 If you are afraid you may forget something, you may tell another person, "Before I leave tonight, be sure and _____ (me to do it)."

JJ29 Talking of something that may have happened in the past: "Have you met him before?" "Not that I _____."

JJ30a Other words or expressions for forgetting something: "I _____."

JJ30b Other expressions for forgetting: "It _____."

JJ31a What you'd say to a bus driver: "Please stop at the next corner --- I want _____."

JJ31b Or you might say, "The dog is scratching at the door, he wants _____."

JJ32 If you have to make up your mind between two things --- for example, a dog and a cat, you might say, "I'd _____ (have a dog)."

JJ33 When you can't choose, but have to take what you're given: "I'll take a cat, but if I had my _____ I'd take a dog."

JJ34 When you decide it would be to your advantage to do something, you might say, "Yes, I _____ I'll be better off that way."

JJ35a When you have just about reached the point of telling somebody what you think of him: "By gosh, I have a _____ (to tell him what I think of him)."

JJ35b Other expressions you might use when you have lost patience and are just about ready to tell somebody what you think of him:

JJ36 To work out a plan, especially a secret plan: "Mary knows more about that, you and she can _____ together."

JJ40 When you admit that you did something wrong and are willing to take the consequences, you might say: "It was my fault and I'm willing to _____."

JJ41 An embarrassing mistake: "Last night she made an awful _____."

JJ42 To make an error in judgment and get something quite wrong: "He usually handles things well, but this time he certainly _____."

JJ43 To give away a secret or tell a piece of news too soon: "He wasn't supposed to know. Somebody must have _____."

JJ44 Expressions about someone who can be trusted to keep a secret: "Don't worry about him, he'll _____."

JJ45 When someone avoids giving a definite answer: "We tried to pin him down, but he just kept _____."

JJ46 Other ways of saying to pretend: "Let's _____ we don't know a thing about it."

Manner of Action or Being

KK1a Other words meaning very good --- for example, food: "That pie was _____."

KK1b Words meaning 'in the very best condition': "His farm is _____."

KK3a Words for the perfect condition --- for example, in cooking: "It's done to _____."

KK3b Something done perfectly --- for example, a piece of work: "It's done to _____."

KK4 When things turn out just right, you might say, "Everything is _____ now."

KK5 A very skilled or expert person --- for example, at woodworking: "He's a _____."

KK6 Something low-grade or of poor quality --- for example, a piece of merchandise: "I wouldn't buy that, it's _____."

KK7 When wood --- for example, a tree stump --- is starting to decay inside, you'd say, "It's _____ inside."

KK8 Other words for succeeding, especially in spite of difficulty: "He had a hard time, but at last he _____."

KK9 When someone undertakes something too big for him to handle: "This time you've _____."

KK10 Other words for something failing --- for example, a plan: "He didn't work it out carefully enough, and his plan _____."

KK11 To make great objections or a big fuss about something: "When we asked him to do that, he _____."

KK12 A meeting where there's a lot of talking: "They got together yesterday and had a real _____."

KK13 Other words for arguing: "They stood there for an hour _____."

KK14 Something that people disagree about: "I have a _____ to pick with you."

KK15 A disagreement or quarrel: "They had _____ about where the fence was to be."

KK16 A great noise or disturbance: "I wish they'd stop making that awful _____."

KK19 If a machine or appliance is temporarily out of order: "My sewing machine _____."

KK20a Something that looks as if it might collapse any minute: "That old shed is certainly _____."

KK20b Something that looks as if it might collapse any minute: "Our old washing machine is _____."

KK21 When something hollow is crushed by a heavy weight, or by a fall: "They ran the wagon over the coffee pot and _____."

KK22 Other ways of saying completely shattered: "The jug fell out of the window and was _____."

KK23 Weak or unsteady: "I think the footbridge will hold but it is a bit _____."

KK24 Something that breaks easily: "She broke her arm again: Her bones must be _____."

KK25 Something that bends or yields easily: "That willow branch is very _____."

KK26 Something that makes no difference at all to you: "He can think what he likes, it _____ me."

KK27 A very lively, active old person: "For his age, he's _____."

KK28 Feeling ambitious and eager to work:

KK29 To start working very hard: "He was slow at first but now he's really _____."

KK30 Feeling slowed up or without energy: "I certainly feel _____."

KK31 To go about aimlessly looking for distraction: "He doesn't have anything to do, so he's just _____ around."

KK32 Do you use the word 'busywork' around here? What does it mean?

KK33 Other ways of saying 'in succession': "He had a cold, then the measles, then chicken pox _____."

KK34 Other expressions meaning very neat and clean: "Her house always looks _____."

KK35 When someone wants to pass on a compliment about you, in exchange for one about himself, he says, "I have a _____ for you."

KK36 Talking about a person who is easily fooled: "It's easy to _____."

KK37   Words to describe a very sly person: "He's _____."

KK38   To put preparations on the hair to hold it close to the head and make it shiny: "I wish he wouldn't _____ his hair down so!"

KK39   Stirred up, upset: "Because of the storm, the pond was all _____."

KK40   Other words meaning 'usually': "They come twice a month, _____."

KK41   Something that is very difficult to do: "I managed to get through with it, but it was _____."

KK42a   Expressions about a person who does something very easily: "For him that would be _____."

KK42b   Expressions about a person who does something very easily: "He could do that _____."

KK43   When the hardest part of a task is finished: "We've still a long way to go, but at least we _____."

KK45   Other words for a narrow escape: "That time, he really had a _____."

KK46   Other expressions for taking things as they come and not worrying: "The whole family was sort of _____."

KK47   Something that is left undecided or unfinished: "Perhaps we'd better just _____."

KK48   When you work something out as you go, without having a plan or pattern to follow: "I didn't have anything to go by, so I just did it _____."

KK49   When you don't have the time or ambition to do something thoroughly: "I'm not going to give the place a real cleaning, I'll just _____."

KK50   When something is planned out carefully, down to the last detail: "He had it all worked out _____."

KK51   Very plainly or abruptly: "I asked him _____ what he meant by that."

KK52   To do something in an indirect and complicated way: "I don't know why he had to go _____ to do that."

KK53   When one thing suddenly hits hard against something else: "He ran _____ into a car."

KK54   Just about equal, very close: "They were both fast runners and it was _____ all the way."

KK55a   To deny something very firmly: "No, not by a _____."

KK55b   To deny something very firmly: "Would you work for him?" "Not on your _____."

KK55c   Other expressions of strong denial:

KK56   Wood that is heavy from being in water a long time: It's _____.

KK57   To take a thing up so as to judge its weight: "That suitcase must weigh forty pounds. Just _____ it."

KK58   An excuse that looks as if it would not stand up under questioning: "His story won't _____."

KK59   To have a mistaken idea, or to be quite wrong about something: "If he thinks she'll help him, he's _____."

KK60   Having nothing in particular to do: "I'd just as soon go with you this afternoon --- I'm _____ anyway."

KK61   Food taken alone, with nothing added: "Would you like milk or lemon in your tea?" "No thanks, I'll take it _____."

KK62   When you want to make it clear that you will not do something: "I wouldn't do that for _____."

KK63   To do a clumsy or hurried job of repairing something: "It will never last --- he just _____."

KK64   Speaking of the part of a city that was once very fine, but isn't any more: "The neighborhood is sort of _____."

KK65   Expressions meaning 'the same sort': "If you like Bob, I'm sure you'll like his brother --- they're _____."

KK66   When you are showing somebody the right way to do something: "No, not like that --- do it _____."

KK67   When people think alike about something: "On that particular thing, we _____."

KK68   When people don't think alike about something: "We agree on most things, but on politics we're _____."

KK70   Something that has got out of proper shape: "That house is all _____."

Size, Quantity and Number

LL1   Something very small: "I only took a _____ one." (Gesture with two fingers.)

LL2   Other words meaning too small to be worth much: "I don't want that little _____ potato."

LL3a   Shrunk, dried up: "These apples are all _____."

LL3b   Shrunk, dried up: "He's a little _____ old man."

LL4   Very large: "He took a _____ helping of potatoes."

LL5   Something impressively big: "That cabbage is really a _____."

LL6a   A small, indefinite amount --- for example, of cream: "I'll take just a _____ of cream in my coffee."

LL6b   A small, indefinite amount --- for example, of butter: "I'll put in just a _____ of butter."

LL6c   A small, indefinite amount --- for example, of cinnamon: "It still needs just a _____ of cinnamon."

LL7   In small amounts, by small degrees: "She didn't get the money all at once, they sent it to her _____."

LL8a   A large amount or number: More than enough --- for example, of time: "He's got _____ of time."

LL8b   Or, a large number --- for example, of cousins: "She has a whole _____ of cousins."

LL9a   As much as you need or more --- for example, of apples: "We've got _____ of apples."

LL9b   Or, all you need or more --- for example, of clothes: "She's got clothes _____."

LL10   A whole group of people: "They made too much noise, so he sent the whole _____ home."

LL11a   In short supply --- hard to get: "Good men are _____ these days."

LL11b   In short supply --- hard to get: "There's a _____ of seed corn this year."

LL12   Not to have enough --- for example, of money needed to pay for something: "I'm fifty cents _____ of the price."

LL13   Not full or sufficient: "She gave us a _____ meal."

LL14   None at all, not even one: "This pond used to be full of fish but now there's _____ left."

LL15   To write ten (10), what figure do you put after '1'?

LL17   Ways of saying there's no more of something: "The potatoes are _____."

LL18   To do no work at all, not even make any effort: "She hasn't _____ all day."

LL19   A few, anywhere from two to four: "Just put in _____ onions."

LL20   Beads to wear around the throat: "She wore a _____ of green beads."

LL21   Two things --- one and also the other: "Do you want the red one or the blue one?" "I want _____ of them."

LL22   Less than you should get: "They'll try to give you _____ every time."

LL23   Cheated, treated dishonestly: "These apples are wormy, I think you got _____."

LL24   To keep firewood neat you have to cut it, split it, and _____ it up.

LL25   Expressions meaning entirely, completely: "He sold out the whole place, _____."

LL26a   Other words for 'all the way': "He drove _____ to the end of the road."

LL26b   Other words meaning 'entirely' --- for example, "He's Irish _____."

LL28   Expressions meaning entirely full: "The box of apples was _____."

LL29   Any sign or trace: "He left last week, and nobody's seen _____ of him since."

LL30   Words and expressions meaning 'nearly' or 'almost': "He fell off the ladder and _____ (broke his neck)."

LL31   Other ways of saying all but one: "Everybody's here now, _____ John."

LL32   Expressions meaning that one man's ability is not nearly as great as another man's: "John can't (or doesn't, or isn't) _____ Bill."

LL33   A longer distance: New York or California --- which is _____ from here?

LL34   When a road is blocked: "This is all _____ we can go."

LL35   Words used to make a statement stronger: "This cake tastes _____ good."

LL36   To make a statement much stronger: "Poor fellow. I think it's a _____ shame."

LL37   To make a statement as strong as you can: "I could have wrung her neck, I was so _____ mad."

Position

MM1   Words meaning 'opposite to': Suppose the barn is here (Gesture with hands) and the shed is here, you could say, "The shed is _____ the barn."

MM2   Suppose a little girl accidentally gets her dress on wrong so that the back part is turned around, you could say, "Look, you've got your dress on _____."

MM3   When someone does something the wrong way round you might tell him: "This is the front, you've got the whole thing turned _____."

MM4   Words for a short distance past --- for example, the mail box, a short distance past the pine tree, you could say: "The mail box is just _____ the pine tree."

MM5   When you're pointing out a house that's not far away: "The house is over _____." (Gesture.)

MM6   Other words meaning 'very close' or 'only a short distance away': "The house is _____ the park."

MM7   If there's a house on each side of the school (Set up an object and use both hands) you'd say, "The school is _____ the houses."

MM8   A bad housekeeper sweeps the dirt either under the rug or _____ the door.

MM9   If you are standing in line, and a man named John is in the position before you, you might say, "We stood in line and John was _____ me."

MM10   The opposite of 'behind': "Is the car behind the house?" "No, I left it _____."

MM11   When you're trying to find something --- you don't know where it is --- you might say, "I must have left it _____."

MM12a   Other ways of saying 'in all directions' --- for example, you might say, "He shot into a flock of birds and they went _____."

MM12b   Other ways of saying 'in all directions' --- for example, you might say, "When she was out on the dance floor, she broke her beads and they went _____."

MM13   The table was nice and straight until he came along and knocked it _____.

MM14   If a drugstore is on one corner of a square and a gas station is on the far corner you might say, "The drugstore is _____ the gas station."

MM15   If a carpenter nails a board crossing another board at an angle, you might say, "He nailed the board on _____."

MM16   If you're walking with somebody to the other corner of a square, and you want to save steps, you might say, "It'll be shorter if we _____."

MM17   If two things are next to each other, you might say, "He put the two boxes on the table (Gesture with hands) _____."

MM18   "Going from the kitchen to the back steps, he walked _____ the door." (Pointing gesture)

MM19   "He took the letter _____ his pocket." (Gesture.)

MM20   "So that she could sit down, he took his coat _____ the chair." (Gesture.)

MM22   If you are talking to a friend who lives in another place and you want to inquire about his neighborhood, you might ask, "How are things _____?"

MM23   Do you use 'uptown' and 'downtown' around here? What do they mean?

MM24   Other expressions meaning 'a short distance': "The river is just a _____ from the house."

MM25   Expressions meaning a long distance: "Texas is a _____ (from here)."

Exclamations

NN1   Other words like 'yes': "Are you coming along too?" (Give response in IPA; include the 'grunts'.)

NN2   Exclamations of very strong agreement: Somebody says, "I think Smith is absolutely right," and you reply, "_____."

NN3   Words and expressions meaning 'Don't you agree?': "She's a nice-looking woman, _____?" or "We ought to come back here again, _____?"

NN4   Other ways of answering 'no': "Would you lend him ten dollars?" "_____."

NN5   Other ways of saying 'Do you understand?': "You take hold of it this way, _____?"

NN6a   Exclamations of joy --- for example, when somebody gets a pleasant surprise, he might shout "_____."

NN6b   Expressions of joy used mostly by children:

NN7   Exclamations of surprise: "They're getting married next week? Well, _____."

NN8a   Exclamations of annoyance or disgust: "Oh _____. I've lost my glasses again."

NN8b   Other expressions of annoyance: "This jar won't come open, _____ it."

NN9a   Exclamations showing great annoyance: "_____. The electric power is off again."

NN9b   Exclamations showing great annoyance: "He's run off with my hammer again, _____!"

NN10a   Expressions (such as 'hello') used when you meet somebody you know quite well:

NN10b   Greetings used when you meet somebody you do not know well:

NN11   Informal ways of saying 'good-bye' to people you know quite well: (Include humorous expressions.)

NN12a   Things that people say to put a child off when he asks too many questions: "What's that for?" (Pronounce 'fur'.)

NN12b   Things that people say to put off a child when he asks, "What are you making?"

NN13   When you think that the thing somebody has just said is silly or untrue: "Oh, that's a lot of _____."

NN17   Something that keeps on annoying you --- for example, a fly that keeps buzzing around you: "That _____ fly won't go away."

NN18   When somebody sneezes, what do people say to him?

NN19   When you want people to stop talking for a moment so that you can listen for something, you say: (Gesture, raising finger and cocking head.)

NN20a   Exclamations caused by sudden pain --- a blow on the thumb:

NN20b   Exclamations caused by sudden pain --- a slight burn:

NN21a   Exclamations caused by sudden pain --- a pinched finger:

NN21b   Exclamations caused by sudden pain --- a hard blow on the chest:

NN21c   Exclamations caused by sudden pain --- a twisted ankle:

NN22a   Expressions used to drive away people or animals --- for example, flies:

NN22b   Expressions used to drive away children:

NN22c   Expressions used to drive away a dog:

NN22d   Expressions used to drive away animals other than dogs:

NN23   Exclamations when people smell a very bad odor:

NN24   Humorous substitutes for stronger exclamations: "Why the son of a _____!"

NN25a   Weakened substitutes for 'damn' or 'damned': "_____ it all!"

NN25b   Weakened substitutes for 'damn' or 'damned': "Well, I'll be _____!"

NN26a   Weakened substitutes for 'hell': "Oh _____!"

NN26b   Weakened substitutes for 'hell': "Go to _____!"

NN26c Weakened substitutes for 'hell': "What the _____!"
NN27a Weakened substitutes for 'god': "My _____!"
NN27b Weakened substitutes for 'god': "For _____ sakes!"
NN28a Exclamations beginning with 'good': "Good _____!"
NN28b Exclamations beginning with 'goodness': "Goodness _____!"
NN29a Exclamations beginning with 'great': "Great _____!"
NN29b Exclamations beginning with 'land': "Land _____!"
NN29c Exclamations beginning with 'holy': "Holy _____!"
NN30 Exclamations beginning with the sound of 'j': (Make the sound 'jee-', get all variants.)
NN31 Exclamations beginning with the sound of 'cr-', for example, 'cripes':
NN32 Exclamations like 'I swear' or 'I vow': "I _____."

Verb Forms (Within Text)

OO2a Talking about eating: "He feels sick --- he must have _____ something (that disagreed with him)."
OO2b Talking about eating: "I don't feel right --- I think I _____ too much."
OO3a Speaking about drinking coffee: "The coffee's all gone --- we must have _____ (a lot)."
OO3b Speaking about drinking coffee: "There's not a drop left --- we _____ (it all)."
OO5a Talking about heating houses: "Before furnaces came in, our house was _____ (with a stove)."
OO5b Talking about heating houses: "Years ago they _____ (the house) with a stove."
OO6a Talking about dough with yeast in it: "The room was warm, so the dough _____ (quickly)."
OO6b Talking about dough with yeast in it: "She put the dough in the oven too soon --- before it had _____ enough."
OO7a Talking about giving presents: "Yesterday was John's birthday so everybody _____ (him presents)."
OO7b Talking about giving presents: "I didn't know about it in time or I would've _____ (one too)."
OO8a Talking about hanging a criminal: "Before the electric chair came in, a murderer would be _____."
OO8b If a man committed suicide by hanging, you'd say he _____ (himself).
OO10a Talking about climbing trees: "When we were children we often _____ (trees)."
OO10b Talking about climbing trees: "Some trees were dangerous --- we shouldn't have _____ (those)."
OO11a Talking about catching mice: "Some mice got into the cellar but our cat _____ (them)."
OO11b Talking about catching mice: "That makes five she's _____ (this week)."
OO12a Talking about dogs biting: "Some dogs will bite --- last week the mailman was _____."
OO12b Talking about dogs biting: "It was a big black dog that _____ him."
OO13a About breaking a leg: "He limps ever since he _____ his leg."
OO13b About breaking a leg: "That's the second time he has _____ (that leg)."
OO14a About the wind blowing hard: "Last night the wind _____ (very hard)."
OO14b About the wind blowing hard: "One of my apple trees was _____ (down)."
OO15a About freezing your ears: "I was so cold my ears nearly _____."
OO15b About freezing your ears: "If he had been out last night he would have _____ (his ears)."
OO16a Talking about bringing tools: "I was supposed to bring the nails --- you should have _____ (the hammer)."
OO16b Talking about bringing tools: "I did bring the hammer, and I also _____ (a saw)." (Gesture of sawing)

OO17a Talking about someone coming home: "Yesterday her son _____ home."
OO17b Talking about someone coming home: "He was late; he should have _____ (days ago)."
OO18a Talking about drawing a plan: "Last year the plan for the new school was _____ (up)."
OO18b Talking about drawing a plan: "I know that man _____ (it)."
OO19a Talking about stretching out to rest: "He felt tired, so he went to the couch (or other word) and _____ (down for a while)."
OO19b Talking about stretching out to rest: "He'll feel better after he has _____ (down a while)."
OO20a About the school bell ringing: "When it was time for school, the bell _____."
OO20b About the school bell ringing: "It's eight o'clock. Has the bell _____ (yet)?"
OO22a About knowing people: "He used to live next door. At that time I _____ (him well)."
OO22b About knowing people, "For the past twenty years I've _____ (him well)."
OO23a About a child growing: "Billy has to have new clothes --- during the summer he _____ (two inches)."
OO23b About a child growing: "You wouldn't think a child could have _____ (so fast)."
OO25a Talking about diving: "The water is deep enough --- the children have often _____ (there)."
OO25b Talking about diving: "Only yesterday the children _____ (there)."
OO26a Talking about drowning: "The current is very strong. Several people have _____ (there)."
OO26b Talking about drowning: "Only last week a boy was _____ (there)."
OO27a Talking about riding horses: "When she was a girl she _____ horseback."
OO27b Talking about riding horses: "All my life I've _____ (horses)."
OO28a Talking about running: "John was so scared he _____ (all the way home)."
OO28b Talking about running: "He was out of breath because he had _____ (so fast)."
OO29a Talking about swimming: "The water is clean --- we have always _____ (there)."
OO29b Talking about swimming: "When we were children we _____ (there too)."
OO30a Talking about a horse throwing the rider: "John got a bad horse and was _____ (off)."
OO30b Talking about a horse throwing the rider: "Last week the same horse _____ (his brother)."
OO32b If a person can't sleep steadily but keeps on waking, he might say, "Every night this week I've _____ (several times)."
OO33a Talking about doing chores: "Seven days a week, chores have to be _____."
OO33b Talking about doing chores: "This morning as usual we _____ (the chores)."
OO34a Talking about writing a letter home: "It's weeks since she last _____ (us a letter)."
OO34b Talking about writing a letter home: "She should have _____ (long ago)."
OO35a Talking about vegetables thriving: "Last year we fertilized the garden, and the plants really _____."
OO35b Talking about vegetables thriving: "That land is poor --- nothing has ever _____ there."
OO37a Talking about clothes shrinking: "The first time my wool socks were washed they _____."
OO37b Talking about clothes shrinking: "I can't get them on because they've _____ (too much)."
OO38a About shoes fitting just right: "When I tried these shoes on, they _____ (just right)."

OO38b   About shoes fitting just right: "I wouldn't have bought them if they hadn't _____ (just right)."

OO39a   Talking about a meeting beginning: "Has the meeting _____ (yet)?"

OO39b   Talking about a meeting beginning: "Yes, it _____ (an hour ago)."

OO40a   About driving a car: "They borrowed our car last night and John _____."

OO40b   About driving a car: "That was the first time John had ever _____ (our car)."

OO41a   About taking too many chances: "He got hurt because he _____ (too many chances)."

OO41b   About taking too many chances: "He would be alive today if he hadn't _____ (so many chances)."

OO42a   About stealing money: "He admitted that he _____ (the money)."

OO42b   About stealing money: "He says it's the first time he has ever _____ (money)."

OO43a   About pleading with somebody: "She said she was afraid to be alone and _____ (with me to stay)."

OO43b   About pleading: "I wouldn't have stayed if she hadn't _____ (so hard)."

OO44a   About somebody in a chair: "He did nothing at all --- he just _____ (there)."

OO44b   About somebody in a chair: "All day long he has just _____ (in that chair)."

OO45a   About seeing somebody: "He thought nobody was looking but I _____ (him hide it)."

OO45b   About seeing somebody: "Many's the time I've _____ him hide things."

OO46a   Talking about dragging something heavy: "We hitched the log on and _____ it out (of the woods)."

OO46b   Talking about dragging something heavy: "Half a mile or so we must have _____ (it)!"

OO47a   Talking about horses sweating: "It was a warm day and the horses _____ (a lot)."

OO47b   Talking about horses sweating: "They wouldn't have caught cold if they hadn't _____ (so much)."

Questions in Early Questionnaire Only

A8   What joking names do you have for an alarm clock?

A25   When something goes on for a very long time: "That sermon yesterday was certainly _____."

B20   If fog goes up very fast: "It's _____."

B31   A period of cold weather that comes early in the fall, after the first frost:

B37   Long pointed pieces of ice that hang down from the roof:

B38   When rain falls half-frozen you say, "It's _____."

B40   A severe snowstorm:

B41   When there's a wet mixture of snow and water on the ground in spring, you say, "It's _____ weather."

C2   After a heavy rain or a quick thaw, when you see the water in a stream getting higher, you say it's _____.

C5   What are the names of some of the lakes and ponds around here?

C10   When a river is dammed and the water backs up and spreads out above a dam, you call that:

C12   A section of a river where the banks are much farther apart, and the water widens out for some distance:

C18   What do you call a mass of rock that stands up high above the level of the land around it?

C20   What if it's broader or larger?

C23   A piece of stone that one person could lift but is too big to throw:

C27   A hillside or deep hole where stone is taken out:

C32   When soil breaks up easily in your fingers, it's _____.

C36   Nicknames for special communities or groups of people living around here: (Open question)

D1   What do you call the upper part of a two-story house?

D2   A sleeping room in a house:

D3   A room for visitors to sleep in:

D5   When you go from one floor of a house to the floor above: "I'm going _____."

D14   The room where members of the family spend most of their time together when they are at home:

D15a   Other rooms in your house besides the living room (or other word):

D15b   Other rooms (not already mentioned) in other people's houses:

D25   Nicknames for buildings where several families live:

D35   After a large wood fire has burned out, you have to take away a lot of _____.

D38   The strip of wood along the bottom of the wall (inside a room) --- if it is quite a bit higher than eight inches:

E8   A piece of upholstered furniture that holds two people:

E11   Pieces of cloth that hang alongside a window to dress it up:

E19   What do you call a bed that is made up wrong as a joke?

F2   What do you call the light metal pan for frying?

F5   What is used around here to stir a large pot, to prevent lumping or sticking?

F13   Talking about different kinds of containers --- a small wooden container that nails come in:

F14   A large wooden container for vinegar or cider:

F16   The container apples come in:

F18   The container grapes come in:

F26   The place where dishes are washed:

F37b   Joking names for an indoor toilet:

F40a   What do you put into a bottle to close it --- if it's made of cork?

F40b   What do you put in a bottle to close it --- if it's made of glass?

F41   A girl or woman who comes in to do general work around the house:

G1   A general word meaning cups, saucers, and plates: "When she has company, she always uses her good _____."

G5   A large, flat dish for serving the meat at table:

G7   If you have cut flowers in the house, you put them in a _____.

G12   After the meal, you have to go to the kitchen and _____ the dishes.

G13   The cloth that you use to wash the dishes with:

H1   The first meal in the morning is _____.

H4   Are the names of meals the same on Sundays as on weekdays?

H8   When you are having company for a meal and you want them to take their places at the table, you say _____.

H10   If somebody never eats very much food, you say he's a _____.

H22   What do you call flat pieces of food dipped in batter and fried in deep fat?

H31   Other foods made with dough and cooked in deep fat:

H33   Joking names for eggs:

H39   Kinds of sausage that people around here especially favor:

H51   Dishes made with cooked cabbage:

H53   Dishes made with tomatoes:

H54   Dishes made with greens: (What kinds of 'greens' are eaten?)

H55   Different kinds of stew:

H61   Other kinds of homemade cheese besides cottage cheese (or other word):

H62   What would 'peach sauce' mean around here? (Describe.)

H72a   Names for tea according to how it's made --- very strong tea:

H72b   Names for tea according to how it's made --- very weak tea:

H76a   When clear, sweetened fruit juice is cooked and it begins to thicken, you say it's starting to _____.

H76b   Then when it becomes hard, you call it _____.

H77   When you are making jam, what do you call the stuff that has to be skimmed off the top?

I2   What general word do you have for vegetables?

I4a   Do you have any other names around here for carrots?

I4b   Do you have any other names around here for beets?

I4c   Do you have any other names around here for turnips?

I4d   Do you have any other names around here for lettuce?

I21	Names or nicknames for tomatoes:
I24	What kinds of pumpkins do people grow around here?
I27	Do you have any other names or nicknames for cabbage?
I32	How do you know when corn is ready to eat?
I36	What do you call a bunch of kitchen herbs --- for example, used in soup?
I45	If berries are not safe to eat, you'd say, "Don't eat those berries, they're _____."
J4	A cat with a very short tail:
J7	How do people around here call to a dog to make it come?
K2	A cow that gives good milk or a lot of milk --- she's _____.
K5	Milk comes out of the _____.
K17	How is the word 'heifer' used around here?
K29	A male horse kept for breeding:
K30	A castrated horse:
K31	A horse that's only partly castrated:
K33	When you're driving horses (or mules), how do you make them start?
K35a	What do you say to make the horses or mules turn right?
K35b	What do you say to make the horses or mules turn left?
K46	If a horse or cow is deformed, what words are used about it?
K51b	A half-grown pig is a _____.
K51c	A full-grown pig is a _____.
K53	Words used by women or in mixed company for a male breeding-pig:
K56	What do you call the stiff hairs on a pig?
K63b	What do you call a male sheep that has been castrated?
K64	Words used by women or in mixed company for a male sheep:
K65	A sheep that's kept as a pet:
K67a	Words for a male goat:
K67b	Words for a female goat:
K69	The noise that a goat makes:
K71	A hen that is producing eggs is called a _____.
K77	What does the word 'fowl' refer to around here?
L4a	A general word for work done every morning and evening on a farm, such as feeding livestock, cleaning stalls, etc.:
L19	When you plow land or sod that has never been plowed before, you're _____.
L21	What kinds of grain are grown around here --- anything special? (Open question)
L26	Sayings about corn and other important crops around here --- when to put it in, how fast it should grow, etc.:
L27	When you turn the pigs into a cornfield to finish it off, you _____.
L50	What does the word 'team' mean on farms around here?
L60b	A fence of stone built with mortar:
M4a	What do you call the spaces or sections between the joists in a barn?
M4b	What do you call the spaces or sections between the joists in a shed?
M7	A separate building where grain is kept:
N26	A road that follows surveyors' divisions:
N36	Names for a slow train or one that stops at every station:
O20	Winds from particular directions:
P8	Do fishermen around here use 'white bait'? If answer is 'yes', what is it?
P10	When the fishing is very good, you might say:
P11	When the fish just begins to take the bait, you say:
P12	When the fish takes the bait with a quick pull:
P28	What other names do you have for the chipmunk?
P33	When an animal goes into its hole to sleep all winter, it _____. (What animals?)
P34	Names or nicknames for a female deer:
P38b	What do you put into a shotgun?
Q12	What kinds of crows do you have around here? (Open question)
Q19	Other birds similar to the whippoorwill:
R3	Whitish, worm-like creatures, found in ponds, that hatch into dobsonflies, and are commonly used for fish bait:
R16	What do you call the fine, thin cloth that lets air in but keeps mosquitoes and other insects out?
S10	A shrub that gets covered with bright yellow, spicy-smelling flowers early in spring:
S12a	What do you call the sharp points along the stems of rose bushes, berry bushes, and so on? --- large ones:
S12b	What do you call the sharp points along the stems of rose bushes, berry bushes, and so on? --- small ones:
U10	If something costs a great deal, or more than you think it's worth, you might say, "That's _____."
U25	Other words for seventy-five cents:
U31	What you might say about a person who spends money very freely: "He's certainly _____."
U34	Other words and expressions around here meaning 'stingy,' especially when a person saves money in a mean way:
U42	When somebody pretends to be poor but you know he's not, you say he's _____.
V3	And about a thoroughly dishonest person, you might say, "He's a _____."
W5	The garment without sleeves that a man wears under his coat:
W13	What kinds of rubber footwear are worn around here?
W17a	Names and nicknames for clothes men wear to sleep in:
W17b	Names and nicknames for clothes women wear to sleep in:
W18a	The long, coat-like garment often worn by men around the house over pajamas:
W18b	The long, coat-like garment often worn by women around the house over nightclothes:
W23	When a collar or other clothing works itself up out of place, you might say, "It's _____."
W26	When a piece of clothing has been used until it gets thin and breaks, you'd say it was _____.
W31	What kinds of fancywork do women around here generally do? (Local specialties?)
X10a	To tell a person to stop talking --- politely:
X27	A person whose eyesight is failing: "He's getting _____."
X30	What do you call the back part of the neck?
X36	Joking names for the knees:
X44	To get somebody out of bed early in the morning: "I had to _____."
X55	The sound that gas makes when it comes up from the stomach after a meal:
Y8	To keep after a person so as to get him to do things: "He never gets a minute's peace --- she's always _____."
Y49	A sudden pull on something: "If you want to get that string out, just _____ it."
AA14a	Names or nicknames for a woman who never married:
AA14b	Names or nicknames for a man who never married:
AA16	What kinds of parties or celebrations do you have around here before a wedding?
BB26	About a disease that spreads easily from one person to another: "Scarlet fever is very _____."
BB31	When a swelling begins to get less, you say it's _____.
BB34a	What remedies do you use to bring a boil to a head?
BB34b	What is a poultice made with?
BB55	What other expressions are used around here to say that a person died? --- Serious expressions:
BB58	The person who prepares a dead body for burial:
BB59	The box that a body is put into for burial:
DD6c	Nicknames for a pipe:
DD19	A little drink: "I'll just take _____."
DD20	A big drink: "He always takes _____."
DD23	Sickness that comes the day after a drinking bout:
DD26a	Other words for a beer mug:
DD26b	Other words for a beer glass:
DD28a	Names and nicknames for kinds of liquor other than beer, wine, or whiskey:
DD29	Common containers for liquor (now and in the past):
DD31	Joking names for homemade hard liquor:
DD36	What expressions do you have around here that come from card games --- for example, 'an ace up your sleeve'?

EE21a   When somebody goes into a fight very actively: "You should have seen Jack _____ Bob."

FF13   What other words do you have around here to mean 'firecrackers'?

FF20   Short humorous stories that people tell to make others laugh: "He's always telling _____."

GG1a   Words meaning 'very fond of' something --- for example, card playing: "People here are _____ about playing cards."

GG1b   Or very fond of something to eat: "He _____ ice cream."

GG10   To be very eager to do something: "He certainly seems _____ to marry that girl."

GG33a   To feel very sad and upset about something: "When he got the news he was _____."

GG33b   To feel very sad and upset about something: "I never saw a woman _____ so."

HH22a   A mean or disagreeable person:

HH23   A person who gets along well with everybody: "Now there's a _____."

HH32   Other words meaning 'a person' --- for example, "In a case like that, what's _____ to do?"

HH33   Other words meaning 'people' --- for example, "When they hear that, what are _____ going to say?"

HH41   Someone who has a very high opinion of himself:

HH42   Names and nicknames for a common laborer:

II13   When you are friendly with people who live near you, and you do little things for each other, you might say, "We've always _____ with them."

II16   When a visitor stays too long or comes too often: "He _____."

II30   What other ways do you have of saying that you are firmly opposed to someone? "I'm _____ him."

II37   Somebody who is very courteous or polite: "He's such a _____."

II38   To be indebted to somebody for a favor or kindness (not money): "I'm very much _____ to him."

JJ37   When you have reason to believe that someone is not honest: "I'm not sure, but I _____ that man is a thief."

JJ38   When somebody agreed to do something, then changed his mind, you might say, "At the last minute he _____."

JJ39   When somebody is being accused who doesn't deserve it, you might say, "He couldn't help it, so don't _____ him."

JJ47   If there is something you can't do --- for example, for fear of the consequences, you might say, "Doctor's orders --- I _____ eat any."

KK2   Other words meaning 'very likeable or popular': "He's _____."

KK17   Words and expressions meaning 'worthless': "It isn't worth _____."

KK18   If something is in good running order: "This sewing machine is _____."

KK44   To continue doing something even though it is difficult: "For five winters we've _____."

KK54b   Just about equal, very close: "It doesn't matter to me --- it's _____."

KK69   What other words do you have for 'sort' or 'kind'? "What _____ rifle is that?"

LL16   The most basic thing, the simplest thing: "He doesn't know _____ thing about plumbing."

LL27   Other words meaning 'thoroughly': "The boss bawled him out _____."

LL38   Very much, to a great degree: "He wasn't _____ willing to come."

MM21   Other ways of saying 'off': "Get _____ my land."

NN14   When you doubt something that somebody has said, and you want to be sure that it is true, you say: "Is that really so?" He answers "_____."

NN15   An oath or profane word: "Every time he opens his mouth a _____ comes out."

NN16   Swearing or using obscene language: "He's always _____."

OO1a   To buy: "Have you _____ your groceries?"

OO1b   To buy: "Yes, I _____ them an hour ago."

OO4a   To knit: "When we were young, she _____ all our socks."

OO4b   To knit: "She has also _____ sweaters and mittens."

OO9a   To ask: "He won't tell me even though I've _____ him many times."

OO9b   To ask: "Today I'm going to ask him the same question I _____ him yesterday."

OO21a   To learn: "Even as a child, he _____ fast."

OO21b   To learn: "He has always _____ quicker than the others."

OO24a   To fight: "Bill _____ hard, but Jack beat him."

OO24b   To fight: "Bill has _____ with every boy in school."

OO31a   To dream: "Last night I _____ I was going away."

OO31b   To dream: "I have _____ that same thing often."

OO32a   To wake: "Last night I _____ three times."

OO36a   To wear: "He went dancing and _____ his new shoes."

OO36b   To wear: "His new shoes were no good. He has _____ a hole in them already."

List of Informants

Key

Informant Code
See List of Abbreviations for state codes. An asterisk indicates that the Informant answered the early version of the Questionnaire (see further pp. lxii, xiii).

Community Type
1. Urban: A section within a metropolis; population of 1,000,000 or more.
2. Large city: Large nonmetropolitan city; population in the 100,000s.
3. Small city: Small independent city; population in 10,000s.
4. Village: Independent town or village in rural area; population in 1,000s.
5. Rural: Rural area; unconcentrated population in 100s.

Note: Within the entries of the Dictionary, these are referred to by number.

Age-group
Old: 60 or over at the time of the interview.
Middle: 40 – 59.
Young: 18 – 39.

Education
Unknown: No information.
Some schooling: Less than grade 5.
Grade school: At least grade 5.
High school: At least 2 years of high school.
College: At least 2 years of college or vocational school.

Occupation
Labels refer to broad categories rather than specific job titles.

Sex
M: Male
F: Female

Audiotape
+: Made
−: None made

Note: See also the List of Informants Who Made Audiotapes Only (pp. cxlv – cli), and the addendum on p. cli.

Informant Code	Community	Community Type	Age-group	Year of Birth	Year of Interview	Education	Occupation	Sex	Race	Audio-tape
AL001	Jasper	small city	old	1905	1966	grade school	domestic, maid	F	Black	+
AL002	Jasper	small city	old	1904	1966	college	storekeeper	M	White	+
AL003	Jasper	small city	old	1887	1966	high school	storekeeper	M	White	+
AL004	Jasper	small city	old	1903	1966	college	educational administrator	M	White	+
AL005	Jasper	small city	old	1902	1966	college	local government	M	White	−
AL006	Greenville	village	old	1880	1966	college	homemaker	F	White	+
AL007	Greenville	village	middle	1926	1966	college	farmer, rancher	M	White	−
AL008	Tuscaloosa	small city	young	1947	1967	college	student	F	White	+
AL010	Anniston	small city	old	1895	1966	high school	clerical	M	White	+
AL011	Oxford	village	old	1883	1966	unknown	farmer, rancher	M	Black	+
AL012	Anniston	small city	old	1905	1966	college	clerical	F	White	+
AL014	Tuscaloosa	small city	young	1928	1966	grade school	domestic, maid	F	Black	+
AL015	Dothan	small city	old	1904	1967	grade school	farmer, rancher	F	White	+
AL016	Dothan	rural	old	1896	1967	high school	wholesale, retail sales	M	White	+
AL017	Dothan	rural	old	1905	1967	high school	service station operator	M	White	−
AL019	Dickinson	rural	young	1946	1967	college	student	M	White	+
AL020	Mobile	large city	old	1888	1967	high school	farm woman	F	White	+
AL021	Mobile	large city	old	1895	1967	high school	homemaker	F	White	+

Informant Code	Community	Community Type	Age-group	Year of Birth	Year of Interview	Education	Occupation	Sex	Race	Audio-tape
AL022	Mobile	large city	middle	1919	1967	high school	engineer	M	White	+
AL023	Huntsville	large city	old	1900	1966	college	homemaker	F	White	+
AL024	Coatopa	rural	middle	1907	1966	grade school	domestic, maid	F	Black	+
AL025	Montgomery	large city	middle	1912	1967	high school	service station operator	F	White	+
AL026	Montgomery	large city	old	1899	1967	grade school	small business: owner, manager	M	White	+
AL027	Athens	small city	old	1903	1967	high school	homemaker	F	White	+
AL028	Athens	small city	old	1890	1967	college	teacher	M	White	+
AL029	Athens	small city	old	1879	1967	grade school	homemaker	F	White	−
AL030	Bay Minette	village	old	1905	1967	college	clerical	F	White	+
AL031	Bay Minette	village	old	1887	1967	high school	clerical	M	White	+
AL032	Cullman	small city	old	1901	1967	grade school	food services	M	White	+
AL033	Holly Pond	rural	old	1884	1967	grade school	farm woman	F	White	+
AL034	Russellville	village	old	1890	1967	grade school	lodging trades	F	White	+
AL035	Russellville	village	old	1895	1967	grade school	laborer	M	White	+
AL036	Russellville	village	old	1892	1967	high school	storekeeper	F	White	−
AL037	Russellville	village	old	1889	1967	high school	homemaker	F	White	−
AL038	Brownsboro	rural	middle	1928	1968	high school	wholesale, retail sales	M	White	−
AL039	New Market	rural	middle	1917	1968	grade school	small business: owner, manager	M	White	+
AL040	New Market	rural	middle	1922	1968	high school	homemaker	F	White	−
AL041	Birmingham	large city	middle	1928	1968	college	real estate	M	White	+
AL042	Selma	small city	middle	1915	1968	high school	homemaker	F	White	+
AL043	Selma	small city	middle	1915	1968	high school	farmer, rancher	M	White	+
AL046	Gadsden	small city	old	1900	1968	grade school	clerical	F	White	−
AL047	Gadsden	small city	old	1887	1968	high school	clerical	M	White	+
AL048	Gadsden	small city	middle	1910	1968	high school	homemaker	F	White	+
AL049	Gadsden	small city	old	1908	1968	high school	skilled trades	M	White	−
AL050	Albertville	rural	old	1888	1969	grade school	farmer, rancher	M	White	−
AL051	Hustlerville	rural	old	1908	1969	high school	farmer, rancher	M	White	−
AL052	Boaz	village	old	1900	1969	high school	religion	M	White	+
AL053	Boaz	village	old	1897	1969	high school	farmer, rancher	M	White	−
AL054	Langdale	rural	old	1883	1969	college	storekeeper	M	White	−
AL055	Lafayette	village	old	1900	1969	high school	storekeeper	M	White	−
AL056	Lafayette	village	old	1909	1969	high school	postal service	M	White	+
AL057	Lafayette	village	middle	1919	1969	high school	homemaker	F	White	−
AL058	Lafayette	rural	old	1902	1969	high school	homemaker	F	White	−
AL059	Birmingham	large city	old	1910	1970	grade school	postal service	M	Black	+
AL060	Birmingham	large city	middle	1917	1970	high school	seamstress	F	Black	−
AL061	Tuskegee	small city	young	1946	1970	college	medicine	F	Black	+
AL062	Tuskegee	small city	old	1906	1970	grade school	local government	M	Black	+
AK001	Juneau	village	middle	1911	1968	college	journalism	M	White	−
AK002	Juneau	village	old	1897	1968	college	small business: owner, manager	M	White	−
AK003	Sitka	village	old	1901	1968	college	journalism	F	White	−
AK004	Juneau	village	middle	1923	1968	high school	wholesale, retail sales	M	White	+
AK005	Sitka	village	old	1907	1968	college	librarian	F	White	−
AK007	Anchorage	small city	old	1880	1968	grade school	homemaker	F	White	−
AK008	Palmer	village	old	1896	1968	grade school	farm woman	F	White	+
AK009	Anchorage	small city	old	1906	1968	college	skilled trades	M	White	+
AZ001	Prescott	village	old	1899	1967	grade school	farmer, rancher	F	White	+
AZ002	Prescott	village	middle	1908	1967	high school	medicine	F	White	+
AZ003	Prescott	village	old	1906	1967	unknown	museum staff	F	White	−

Informant Code	Community	Community Type	Age-group	Year of Birth	Year of Interview	Education	Occupation	Sex	Race	Audio-tape
AZ005	Snowflake	rural	young	1937	1967	high school	homemaker	F	White	+
AZ006	Snowflake	rural	middle	1910	1967	high school	postal service	M	White	+
AZ007	Taylor	rural	old	1889	1967	some schooling	farmer, rancher	M	White	+
AZ008	Snowflake	rural	middle	1919	1967	high school	homemaker	F	White	+
AZ009	Taylor	rural	middle	1927	1967	college	farmer, rancher	M	White	+
AZ010	Mesa	small city	old	1894	1969	high school	farm woman	F	White	−
AZ011	Mesa	small city	old	1893	1969	college	teacher	F	White	+
AZ012	Yuma	small city	young	1939	1970	high school	homemaker	F	White	−
AZ013	Yuma	small city	old	1883	1970	college	medicine	M	White	+
AZ014	Yuma	small city	middle	1915	1970	college	storekeeper	M	White	+
AZ015	Phoenix	large city	old	1894	1969	grade school	farm woman	F	White	+
AZ016	Phoenix	large city	old	1895	1969	college	homemaker	F	White	+
*AR001	Mountain View	rural	old	1899	1966	some schooling	farm woman	F	White	−
*AR002	Mountain View	rural	old	1893	1966	high school	homemaker	F	White	−
*AR003	Mountain View	rural	old	1897	1966	high school	homemaker	F	White	−
*AR004	Allison	rural	old	1899	1966	grade school	storekeeper	M	White	−
*AR005	Mountain View	rural	old	1885	1966	grade school	farmer, rancher	M	White	−
AR006	Helena	small city	middle	1907	1966	high school	homemaker	F	White	−
AR007	Helena	small city	old	1899	1966	grade school	domestic, maid	F	Black	−
AR008	Helena	small city	old	1905	1966	high school	homemaker	F	White	−
AR009	Helena	small city	old	1894	1966	college	small business: owner, manager	M	White	−
AR010	Helena	small city	old	1904	1966	high school	homemaker	F	White	+
AR011	Helena	small city	old	1896	1966	college	homemaker	F	White	−
AR012	Helena	small city	old	1886	1966	high school	homemaker	F	White	−
AR013	Helena	small city	old	1894	1966	high school	homemaker	F	White	−
AR014	Star City	rural	old	1894	1966	college	farm woman	F	White	−
AR015	Star City	rural	old	1891	1966	grade school	farmer, rancher	M	White	+
AR016	Star City	rural	old	1876	1966	high school	farmer, rancher	M	White	−
*AR017	Childress	rural	old	1890	1966	unknown	farm woman	F	White	−
*AR018	Greene Co.	rural	old	1897	1966	grade school	laborer	M	White	−
*AR019	Jasper	rural	old	1898	1966	high school	homemaker	F	White	−
*AR020	Jasper	rural	old	1885	1966	some schooling	farm woman	F	White	−
*AR021	Jasper	rural	old	1888	1966	high school	farmer, rancher	M	White	−
*AR022	Jasper	rural	old	1886	1966	grade school	skilled trades	M	White	−
*AR023	Jasper	rural	old	1890	1966	some schooling	farm woman	F	White	−
*AR024	Jasper	rural	old	1884	1966	some schooling	homemaker	F	White	−
*AR025	Mena	village	middle	1915	1966	high school	clerical	F	White	−
*AR026	Mena	village	old	1881	1966	unknown	homemaker	F	White	−
*AR027	Cherry Hill	rural	old	1885	1966	grade school	farm woman	F	White	−
*AR028	Mena	rural	old	1890	1966	grade school	farmer, rancher	M	White	−
*AR029	Mena	rural	old	1886	1966	some schooling	farmer, rancher	M	White	−
*AR030	Mena	village	old	1892	1966	high school	small business: owner, manager	M	White	−
*AR031	Cherry Hill	rural	old	1891	1966	high school	teacher	M	White	−
*AR032	Stuttgart	rural	old	1887	1966	high school	farm woman	F	White	+
*AR033	Stuttgart	rural	old	1886	1966	unknown	farmer, rancher	M	White	+
*AR034	Heber Springs	village	old	1883	1966	grade school	homemaker	F	White	−
*AR035	Heber Springs	village	old	1885	1966	high school	homemaker	F	White	−

Informant Code	Community	Community Type	Age-group	Year of Birth	Year of Interview	Education	Occupation	Sex	Race	Audio-tape
*AR036	Heber Springs	village	old	1879	1966	high school	storekeeper	M	White	+
*AR037	Heber Springs	village	old	1889	1966	high school	storekeeper	M	White	−
*AR038	Farmington	rural	old	1876	1966	high school	homemaker	F	White	−
*AR039	Prairie Grove	rural	old	1883	1966	high school	farmer, rancher	M	White	−
*AR040	Prairie Grove	rural	old	1887	1966	unknown	farmer, rancher	M	White	−
*AR041	Prairie Grove	rural	old	1899	1966	high school	farm woman	F	White	+
*AR042	Blue Cane	rural	young	1946	1966	college	student	M	White	+
AR047	Clarksville	village	old	1899	1967	grade school	lodging trades	M	White	+
AR048	Clarksville	village	old	1887	1967	college	clerical	M	White	−
AR049	Clarksville	village	old	1891	1967	high school	clerical	F	White	−
AR051	Murfreesboro	rural	old	1897	1967	grade school	farmer, rancher	M	White	+
AR052	Magnolia	village	old	1901	1967	college	homemaker	F	White	+
AR053	Murfreesboro	rural	old	1885	1967	some schooling	farmer, rancher	M	White	−
AR054	Murfreesboro	rural	old	1887	1967	some schooling	farm woman	F	White	−
AR055	Monticello	village	old	1883	1967	high school	storekeeper	M	White	+
AR056	Little Rock	large city	middle	1911	1970	grade school	clerical	M	White	+
CA001	Victorville	small city	young	1942	1967	college	clerical	F	White	+
CA002	Barstow	small city	old	1895	1966	college	homemaker	F	White	+
CA003	San Bernardino	large city	old	1897	1967	high school	small business: owner, manager	M	White	+
CA004	San Bernardino	large city	middle	1911	1967	college	teacher	F	White	+
CA005	Needles	village	old	1887	1968	high school	railroad	M	White	+
CA006	Redlands	small city	old	1881	1967	college	journalism	F	White	+
CA007	Redlands	small city	old	1905	1967	college	agricultural services	M	White	+
CA008	Redlands	small city	old	1906	1967	college	teacher	F	White	+
CA009	Thermal	rural	old	1894	1967	high school	lodging trades	F	White	+
CA010	Glendale	urban	middle	1915	1967	college	educational administrator	F	White	+
CA011	Palm Springs	small city	middle	1921	1967	college	homemaker	F	White	−
CA012	Palm Springs	small city	old	1886	1967	grade school	lodging trades	F	White	+
CA013	Palm Springs	small city	old	1893	1967	college	educational administrator	F	White	+
CA014	Palm Springs	small city	middle	1917	1967	high school	homemaker	F	White	−
CA015	San Francisco	urban	old	1902	1967	high school	real estate	M	White	+
CA016	Berkeley	urban	middle	1918	1967	college	homemaker	F	White	−
CA017	San Juan Bautista	village	old	1889	1967	high school	clerical	F	White	−
CA018	San Juan Bautista	village	old	1903	1967	high school	homemaker	F	White	−
CA019	San Juan Bautista	village	old	1887	1967	high school	wholesale, retail sales	F	White	−
CA020	Hollister	village	old	1901	1967	college	teacher	F	White	−
CA021	Lompoc	village	old	1885	1967	grade school	farm woman	F	White	+
CA022	Lompoc	village	old	1887	1967	high school	farm woman	F	White	−
CA023	Lompoc	village	old	1879	1967	grade school	farmer, rancher	M	White	+
CA024	San Luis Obispo	small city	old	1889	1967	high school	clerical	F	White	−
CA025	San Luis Obispo	small city	middle	1914	1967	high school	ranger, guide	M	White	−
CA026	San Luis Obispo	small city	young	1949	1967	college	student	F	White	−
CA027	San Luis Obispo	small city	old	1907	1967	college	financial services	M	Oriental	−

Informant Code	Community	Community Type	Age-group	Year of Birth	Year of Interview	Education	Occupation	Sex	Race	Audio-tape
CA028	San Luis Obispo	small city	old	1891	1967	college	surveyor	M	White	−
CA029	San Luis Obispo	small city	old	1902	1967	high school	clerical	F	White	−
CA030	San Luis Obispo	small city	old	1886	1967	high school	homemaker	F	White	−
CA031	Carmel Valley	village	old	1887	1967	grade school	farmer, rancher	M	White	−
CA032	Carmel Valley	village	young	1935	1967	college	storekeeper	M	White	−
CA033	Carmel Valley	village	young	1933	1967	high school	farmer, rancher	M	White	−
CA034	Monterey	small city	old	1905	1967	college	journalism	F	White	−
CA035	Monterey	small city	old	1900	1967	high school	police	M	White	−
CA036	Yorba Linda	village	old	1896	1968	grade school	farmer, rancher	M	White	+
CA037	Placentia	small city	young	1944	1968	college	clerical	F	White	−
CA038	Whittier	small city	middle	1928	1968	college	homemaker	F	White	−
CA039	Placentia	village	old	1895	1968	grade school	farmer, rancher	M	White	−
CA040	Yorba Linda	village	old	1898	1968	college	teacher	F	White	−
CA041	Altadena	urban	old	1900	1968	college	educational administrator	F	White	−
CA042	Altadena	urban	old	1894	1968	college	librarian	F	White	−
CA043	Pasadena	urban	old	1897	1968	college	teacher	F	White	−
CA044	Pasadena	urban	old	1894	1968	college	teacher	F	White	−
CA045	Altadena	urban	old	1897	1968	college	financial services	M	White	−
CA046	Altadena	urban	old	1897	1968	college	homemaker	F	White	−
CA047	Pasadena	urban	middle	1915	1968	college	foreman, supervisor	M	White	−
CA048	Pasadena	urban	middle	1918	1968	college	homemaker	F	White	−
CA049	Pasadena	urban	young	1942	1968	college	unemployed	M	White	−
CA050	Pasadena	urban	old	1900	1968	college	teacher	F	White	−
CA051	Duarte	urban	old	1891	1968	college	teacher	F	White	−
CA052	Whittier	small city	old	1901	1968	college	farmer, rancher	M	White	+
CA053	Whittier	small city	old	1898	1968	college	homemaker	F	White	+
CA054	Whittier	small city	old	1895	1968	college	homemaker	F	White	−
CA055	Whittier	small city	old	1888	1968	college	medicine	M	White	−
CA056	Whittier	small city	middle	1926	1968	high school	homemaker	F	White	−
CA057	Whittier	small city	old	1888	1968	college	farmer, rancher	M	White	−
CA058	Whittier	small city	old	1903	1968	college	small business: owner, manager	F	White	−
CA059	Cantil	rural	old	1904	1968	college	teacher	F	White	−
CA060	Mojave	village	old	1905	1968	college	teacher	F	White	−
CA061	Mojave	village	middle	1915	1968	high school	homemaker	F	White	−
CA062	Cantil	rural	old	1902	1968	high school	postal service	M	White	−
CA063	Santa Barbara	rural	old	1889	1968	unknown	farmer, rancher	M	White	+
CA064	Santa Barbara	small city	old	1906	1968	high school	homemaker	F	White	−
CA065	Santa Barbara	small city	old	1904	1968	grade school	firefighter	M	White	−
CA066	Santa Barbara	small city	middle	1926	1968	high school	military	M	White	+
CA070	San Francisco	urban	old	1888	1968	grade school	homemaker	F	White	−
CA071	San Francisco	urban	old	1890	1968	high school	homemaker	F	White	−
CA072	San Francisco	urban	old	1893	1968	high school	homemaker	F	White	+

Informant Code	Community	Community Type	Age-group	Year of Birth	Year of Interview	Education	Occupation	Sex	Race	Audio-tape
CA073	San Francisco	urban	old	1893	1968	high school	homemaker	F	White	+
CA074	San Francisco	urban	old	1895	1968	high school	homemaker	F	Oriental	+
CA075	Escondido	small city	old	1901	1968	high school	homemaker	F	Am Ind	−
CA076	Escondido	small city	middle	1915	1968	high school	homemaker	F	White	−
CA077	Escondido	rural	old	1896	1968	grade school	farmer, rancher	M	White	−
CA078	Escondido	small city	old	1886	1968	high school	administrative, managerial	M	White	−
CA079	Escondido	small city	old	1880	1968	college	homemaker	F	White	+
CA080	El Cajon	small city	young	1931	1968	high school	homemaker	F	White	+
CA081	El Cajon	small city	middle	1925	1968	high school	homemaker	F	Black	−
CA082	La Jolla	urban	middle	1928	1968	college	homemaker	F	White	−
CA083	La Jolla	urban	middle	1923	1968	high school	homemaker	F	White	−
CA084	La Jolla	urban	old	1906	1968	college	homemaker	F	White	−
CA085	La Jolla	urban	middle	1918	1968	college	teacher	F	White	−
CA086	Pacific Beach	urban	old	1895	1968	high school	administrative, managerial	M	White	−
CA087	Julian	rural	old	1901	1968	grade school	homemaker	F	White	+
CA088	Julian	rural	young	1930	1968	college	laborer	M	White	−
CA090	El Centro	village	old	1894	1968	grade school	farmer, rancher	M	White	+
CA091	El Centro	village	middle	1918	1968	high school	lodging trades	F	White	−
CA092	El Centro	village	young	1935	1968	high school	farm woman	F	White	−
CA093	El Centro	village	young	1941	1968	high school	homemaker	F	White	−
CA094	Needles	village	middle	1925	1968	high school	homemaker	F	Am Ind	+
CA095	Needles	village	middle	1915	1968	high school	railroad	M	White	−
CA096	Needles	village	middle	1921	1968	college	wholesale, retail sales	M	White	−
CA097	St. Helena	village	old	1885	1968	college	teacher	M	White	+
CA098	St. Helena	village	old	1880	1968	high school	unemployed	F	White	+
CA099	Cloverdale	village	old	1885	1968	high school	homemaker	F	White	+
CA101	Piercy	rural	old	1894	1968	grade school	homemaker	F	White	+
CA102	Piercy	rural	old	1898	1968	high school	farmer, rancher	M	White	−
CA105	Fort Bragg	village	old	1887	1968	grade school	railroad	M	White	+
CA106	Fort Bragg	village	middle	1913	1968	high school	clerical	F	White	−
CA107	Walnut Creek	urban	old	1898	1969	grade school	small business: owner, manager	M	White	+
CA108	Walnut Creek	urban	old	1908	1969	college	financial services	M	White	−
CA109	Orinda	village	young	1935	1969	college	wholesale, retail sales	M	White	−
CA110	Eureka	small city	old	1903	1969	college	journalism	F	White	+
CA111	Eureka	small city	old	1891	1969	grade school	skilled trades	M	White	+
CA112	Eureka	small city	middle	1918	1969	college	homemaker	F	White	+
CA113	Bakersfield	small city	old	1898	1969	college	administrative, managerial	M	White	+
CA114	Bakersfield	small city	old	1908	1969	college	journalism	M	White	−
CA115	Bakersfield	small city	old	1885	1969	college	social & community services	F	White	−
CA116	Bakersfield	small city	old	1884	1969	college	homemaker	F	White	−
CA117	Fresno	large city	young	1937	1969	college	teacher	M	White	+
CA118	Fresno	large city	young	1937	1969	college	teacher	F	White	−
CA119	Fresno	large city	middle	1914	1969	high school	clerical	M	White	−
CA120	Angels Camp	village	middle	1910	1969	high school	miner	M	White	+
CA121	Angels Camp	village	middle	1915	1969	college	wholesale, retail sales	M	White	−
CA122	Angels Camp	village	young	1944	1969	college	skilled trades	M	White	−
CA123	Angels Camp	village	old	1894	1969	grade school	skilled trades	M	White	+

Informant Code	Community	Community Type	Age-group	Year of Birth	Year of Interview	Education	Occupation	Sex	Race	Audio-tape
CA124	San Andreas	village	old	1908	1969	college	farmer, rancher	M	White	−
CA125	Angels Camp	village	old	1892	1969	college	lodging trades	M	White	−
CA126	Angels Camp	village	old	1894	1969	high school	teacher	F	White	−
CA127	Sutter Creek	village	old	1886	1969	grade school	unemployed	F	White	+
CA128	Amador City	rural	old	1901	1969	grade school	miner	M	White	+
CA129	Sutter Creek	village	old	1893	1969	grade school	miner	M	White	−
CA130	Jackson	village	young	1937	1969	high school	skilled trades	M	White	−
CA131	Sutter Creek	village	old	1887	1969	grade school	farmer, rancher	M	White	−
CA132	Jackson	village	old	1902	1969	high school	homemaker	F	White	−
CA133	Sutter Creek	village	middle	1915	1969	college	teacher	F	White	−
CA134	Cassel	rural	old	1898	1969	grade school	farm woman	F	White	+
CA135	Hat Creek	rural	middle	1911	1969	high school	farm woman	F	White	+
CA136	Hat Creek	rural	middle	1910	1969	grade school	farmer, rancher	M	White	+
CA137	Weaverville	village	old	1897	1969	grade school	miner	M	White	+
CA138	Weaverville	village	old	1897	1969	high school	social & community services	F	White	+
CA139	Folsom	village	old	1891	1969	high school	homemaker	F	White	−
CA140	Carmichael	small city	young	1944	1969	college	ranger, guide	M	White	−
CA141	Folsom	village	old	1896	1969	high school	storekeeper	M	White	−
CA142	Folsom	village	young	1944	1969	college	teacher	F	Oriental	+
CA142A	Folsom	village	old	−	1969	unknown	−	F	Oriental	+
CA144	Weed	village	old	1883	1969	grade school	farm woman	F	White	+
CA145	Weed	village	old	1909	1969	college	foreman, supervisor	M	White	−
CA146	Nevada City	village	old	1899	1969	college	teacher	F	White	−
CA147	Nevada City	village	old	1904	1969	high school	firefighter	M	White	+
CA148	Nevada City	village	middle	1914	1969	grade school	domestic, maid	F	White	−
CA149	Nevada City	village	old	1905	1969	college	lodging trades	F	White	−
CA150	Nevada City	village	young	1937	1969	college	teacher	F	White	−
CA151	Nevada City	village	old	1903	1969	grade school	homemaker	F	White	+
CA152	Penn Valley	rural	old	1893	1969	high school	farmer, rancher	M	White	−
CA153	Tulelake	rural	old	1906	1969	high school	foreman, supervisor	M	White	−
CA154	Tulelake	rural	young	1937	1969	college	farm woman	F	White	+
CA155	Tulelake	rural	middle	1928	1969	high school	farmer, rancher	M	White	+
CA156	Alturas	village	old	1886	1969	grade school	farmer, rancher	M	White	+
CA157	Alturas	village	old	1886	1969	grade school	homemaker	F	White	+
CA158	Alturas	village	old	1891	1969	high school	farmer, rancher	M	White	+
CA160	Red Bluff	village	old	1895	1969	grade school	farmer, rancher	M	White	+
CA161	Red Bluff	village	old	1886	1969	high school	farmer, rancher	M	White	+
CA162	Red Bluff	rural	middle	1925	1969	high school	homemaker	F	White	+
CA163	Susanville	village	old	1900	1969	college	farmer, rancher	M	White	+
CA164	Susanville	village	old	1887	1969	high school	storekeeper	F	White	+
CA165	Susanville	village	old	1889	1969	high school	homemaker	F	White	+
CA166	Vallejo	large city	middle	1919	1969	high school	homemaker	F	White	+
CA167	Vallejo	large city	old	1887	1969	high school	social & community services	F	White	−
CA168	Vallejo	large city	middle	1915	1969	high school	foreman, supervisor	M	White	+
CA169	Colusa	village	young	1935	1969	college	medicine	M	White	+
CA170	Colusa	village	old	1909	1969	college	homemaker	F	White	+
CA171	Colusa	village	middle	1925	1969	high school	farmer, rancher	M	White	+
CA173	Oxnard	small city	old	1907	1970	high school	librarian	F	White	−
CA174	Oxnard	small city	old	1900	1970	college	teacher	F	White	+
CA175	Oxnard	small city	young	1931	1970	college	wholesale, retail sales	M	White	+
CA176	Oxnard	small city	young	1945	1970	college	wholesale, retail sales	M	White	−

Informant Code	Community	Community Type	Age-group	Year of Birth	Year of Interview	Education	Occupation	Sex	Race	Audio-tape
CA177	Long Beach	urban	young	1949	1970	college	student	M	White	−
CA178	Long Beach	urban	young	1944	1970	high school	skilled trades	M	White	−
CA179	Los Angeles	urban	old	1906	1970	high school	wholesale, retail sales	F	White	+
CA181	Trabuco Oaks	rural	old	1906	1970	high school	ranger, guide	M	White	+
CA182	Trabuco Canyon	rural	middle	1925	1970	college	homemaker	F	White	+
CA183	Trabuco Canyon	rural	young	1955	1970	grade school	student	F	White	+
CA184	Hollywood	urban	young	1943	1970	college	clerical	F	White	+
CA185	Hollywood	urban	old	1899	1970	college	small business: owner, manager	M	White	+
CA187	Hollywood	urban	young	1950	1970	college	student	M	White	−
CA188	San Juan Capistrano	village	young	1949	1970	college	food services	F	White	−
CA189	San Juan Capistrano	village	middle	1925	1970	high school	clerical	F	White	+
CA190	San Juan Capistrano	village	young	1952	1970	college	student	F	White	+
CA191	San Juan Capistrano	village	middle	1914	1970	high school	nautical, fishing	M	White	+
CA192	San Juan Capistrano	village	middle	1915	1970	college	teacher	F	White	+
CA193	San Juan Capistrano	village	old	1885	1970	unknown	farmer, rancher	M	White	+
CA194	San Juan Capistrano	village	old	1902	1970	high school	homemaker	F	White	−
CA195	Quincy	rural	middle	1924	1970	high school	farmer, rancher	M	White	−
CA196	Quincy	rural	old	1903	1970	grade school	homemaker	F	White	+
CA197	Quincy	village	old	1895	1970	high school	wholesale, retail sales	M	White	+
CA199	Mariposa	rural	old	1896	1970	grade school	farmer, rancher	M	White	+
CA200	Mariposa	rural	old	1891	1970	grade school	homemaker	F	White	+
CA201	Mariposa	rural	old	1898	1970	college	homemaker	F	White	+
CA202	Paradise	small city	old	1891	1970	high school	homemaker	F	White	+
CA203	Paradise	small city	old	1882	1970	high school	small business: owner, manager	M	White	+
CA204	Paradise	small city	old	1895	1970	college	financial services	F	White	+
CA205	Lone Pine	village	old	1901	1970	grade school	food services	F	White	+
CA206	Lone Pine	village	old	1909	1970	high school	clerical	F	White	+
CA207	Lone Pine	village	middle	1913	1970	high school	skilled trades	M	White	+
CA208	Bishop	village	old	1904	1970	high school	farmer, rancher	M	White	+
CA209	Bishop	village	old	1891	1970	high school	postal service	F	White	+
CA210	Bishop	village	middle	1915	1970	high school	farmer, rancher	M	White	+
CA211	San Jose	large city	old	1909	1970	college	police	M	White	+
CA212	Santa Clara	large city	old	1900	1970	grade school	homemaker	F	White	+
CA213	Santa Clara	large city	middle	1911	1970	college	legal	M	White	+
CO002	Sterling	rural	old	1889	1967	grade school	farmer, rancher	M	White	+
CO003	Sterling	rural	old	1888	1967	grade school	farmer, rancher	M	White	−
CO004	Sterling	small city	old	1884	1967	grade school	farmer, rancher	M	White	+
CO005	Sterling	small city	old	−	1967	grade school	farmer, rancher	M	White	+
CO006	Sterling	small city	old	1883	1967	high school	homemaker	F	White	+
CO007	Loveland	small city	old	1894	1967	college	storekeeper	M	White	+
CO008	Loveland	small city	young	1935	1967	high school	homemaker	F	White	−
CO009	Loveland	rural	middle	1911	1967	college	ranger, guide	M	White	−
CO010	Loveland	small city	old	1878	1967	grade school	homemaker	F	White	−
CO011	Durango	small city	old	1907	1967	high school	homemaker	F	White	+

Informant Code	Community	Community Type	Age-group	Year of Birth	Year of Interview	Education	Occupation	Sex	Race	Audio-tape
CO012	Durango	small city	old	1903	1967	grade school	farmer, rancher	M	White	−
CO013	Durango	small city	old	1901	1967	high school	clerical	F	White	−
CO014	Durango	small city	middle	1925	1967	college	teacher	M	White	−
CO015	Durango	small city	old	1906	1967	high school	homemaker	F	White	−
CO016	Durango	small city	middle	1920	1967	college	small business: owner, manager	M	White	−
CO017	Cheyenne Wells	rural	middle	1908	1967	grade school	homemaker	F	White	−
CO018	Cheyenne Wells	rural	middle	1908	1967	high school	farmer, rancher	M	White	−
CO019	Cheyenne Wells	rural	old	1892	1967	high school	farmer, rancher	M	White	+
CO020	Cheyenne Wells	rural	middle	1912	1967	high school	local government	F	White	−
CO021	Cheyenne Wells	rural	old	1903	1967	college	teacher	F	White	−
CO022	Trinidad	small city	old	1898	1967	high school	real estate	M	White	+
CO023	Trinidad	small city	old	1897	1967	college	legal	M	White	−
CO024	Trinidad	small city	old	1869	1967	grade school	wholesale, retail sales	M	White	+
CO025	Trinidad	small city	middle	1912	1967	college	homemaker	F	White	−
CO026	Trinidad	small city	middle	1918	1967	college	homemaker	F	White	−
CO027	Trinidad	small city	middle	1909	1967	college	homemaker	F	White	−
CO028	Delta	village	old	1885	1967	high school	postal service	M	White	−
CO029	Delta	village	middle	1922	1967	college	farm woman	F	White	−
CO030	Delta	village	old	1888	1967	high school	homemaker	F	White	−
CO031	Delta	village	old	1888	1967	high school	homemaker	F	White	−
CO032	Delta	rural	middle	1920	1967	high school	farmer, rancher	M	White	−
CO033	Delta	village	old	1886	1967	grade school	farmer, rancher	M	White	+
CO034	Delta	village	middle	1912	1967	college	homemaker	F	White	−
CO035	Leadville	village	old	1892	1967	college	teacher	F	White	−
CO036	Leadville	village	young	1941	1967	high school	homemaker	F	White	−
CO037	Leadville	village	old	1886	1967	high school	educational administrator	F	White	−
CO038	Leadville	rural	young	1933	1967	high school	farm woman	F	White	−
CO039	Steamboat Springs	village	young	1932	1967	high school	homemaker	F	White	−
CO040	Steamboat Springs	village	old	1893	1967	grade school	homemaker	F	White	−
CO041	Steamboat Springs	village	old	1882	1967	some schooling	railroad	M	White	−
CO042	Steamboat Springs	village	middle	1914	1967	high school	wholesale, retail sales	F	White	−
CO043	Steamboat Springs	village	old	1907	1967	college	storekeeper	F	White	−
CO044	Steamboat Springs	village	old	1897	1967	grade school	farmer, rancher	M	White	−
CO045	Steamboat Springs	village	old	1883	1967	college	homemaker	F	White	−
CO046	Steamboat Springs	village	old	1884	1967	high school	storekeeper	M	White	−
CO047	Georgetown	rural	middle	1922	1967	high school	trucking, transportation	M	White	+
CT001	Southbury	village	old	1890	1968	college	teacher	F	White	+
CT002	South Britain	rural	old	1899	1968	high school	farmer, rancher	M	White	+
CT003	Southbury	village	middle	1915	1968	college	wholesale, retail sales	M	White	+
CT004	Wethersfield	small city	old	1891	1968	high school	storekeeper	M	White	+
CT005	Wethersfield	small city	middle	1909	1968	college	homemaker	F	White	+
CT006	Danbury	small city	old	1892	1968	grade school	storekeeper	M	White	+

Informant Code	Community	Community Type	Age-group	Year of Birth	Year of Interview	Education	Occupation	Sex	Race	Audio-tape
CT007	Litchfield	village	old	1895	1968	grade school	storekeeper	M	White	+
CT008	Litchfield	village	old	1905	1968	high school	clerical	F	White	+
CT009	Salisbury	village	middle	1915	1968	college	legal	M	White	+
CT010	Simsbury	village	old	1902	1968	college	real estate	M	White	+
CT011	Simsbury	village	middle	1915	1968	college	clerical	F	White	+
CT012	East Hampton	village	old	1898	1968	grade school	factory worker	F	White	+
CT013	East Hampton	village	old	1905	1968	college	lodging trades	M	White	+
CT014	Guilford	rural	old	1890	1968	high school	farmer, rancher	M	White	+
CT015	Guilford	village	old	1889	1968	high school	storekeeper	M	White	+
CT016	Guilford	village	old	1890	1968	high school	clerical	F	White	+
CT017	Centerbrook	village	old	1890	1968	grade school	farmer, rancher	M	White	+
CT018	Ivoryton	village	old	1890	1968	college	teacher	F	White	+
CT019	Ivoryton	village	middle	1914	1968	high school	clerical	F	White	+
CT020	Brooklyn	village	old	1887	1969	college	teacher	F	Black	+
CT021	Brooklyn	village	middle	1913	1969	grade school	clerical	F	White	+
CT022	Brooklyn	village	old	1896	1969	grade school	custodial, maintenance	M	White	−
CT023	Jewett City	village	old	1898	1969	high school	clerical	M	White	−
CT024	Jewett City	rural	old	1904	1969	grade school	farmer, rancher	M	White	−
CT025	Jewett City	rural	old	1907	1969	college	farmer, rancher	M	White	+
CT026	Scotland	rural	old	1890	1969	grade school	farmer, rancher	M	White	−
CT027	Scotland	village	old	1895	1969	grade school	skilled trades	M	White	−
CT028	Scotland	rural	old	1906	1969	grade school	logging	M	White	−
CT029	Woodstock	village	old	1905	1969	grade school	administrative, managerial	M	White	+
CT030	Woodstock	village	old	1899	1969	grade school	homemaker	F	White	+
CT031	Stafford Springs	rural	middle	1913	1969	grade school	farmer, rancher	M	White	−
CT032	Stafford Springs	village	old	1898	1969	grade school	wholesale, retail sales	M	White	−
CT033	Stafford Springs	village	old	1906	1969	college	teacher	F	White	−
CT034	Stafford Springs	village	young	1935	1969	college	clerical	M	White	−
CT035	Stafford Springs	village	old	1907	1969	grade school	homemaker	F	White	−
CT036	Lebanon	rural	old	1898	1969	unknown	farmer, rancher	M	White	+
CT037	Lebanon	village	old	1907	1969	unknown	clerical	F	White	−
CT039	Old Mystic	village	old	1884	1969	grade school	farm woman	F	White	−
CT040	Old Mystic	village	middle	1918	1969	high school	postal service	F	White	−
CT042	Bridgeport	large city	old	1902	1970	grade school	seamstress	F	Black	+
CT043	Bridgeport	large city	middle	1927	1970	college	social & community services	F	Black	+
DE001	Georgetown	village	old	1906	1968	high school	service station operator	M	White	+
DE002	Georgetown	village	middle	1909	1968	high school	homemaker	F	White	+
DE003	Dover	small city	old	1889	1968	grade school	skilled trades	M	White	+
DE004	Leipsic	rural	old	1908	1968	high school	nautical, fishing	M	White	+
DE005	Smyrna	rural	old	1899	1968	grade school	farmer, rancher	M	White	−
DE006	Smyrna	rural	old	1901	1968	high school	farm woman	F	White	−
DE007	Dover	rural	old	1900	1968	grade school	farmer, rancher	M	White	+
*DC001	Washington DC	urban	old	1897	1967	college	librarian	F	White	+
*DC002	Silver Spring MD	urban	old	1905	1967	college	teacher	F	White	+

Informant Code	Community	Community Type	Age-group	Year of Birth	Year of Interview	Education	Occupation	Sex	Race	Audio-tape
*DC003	Washington DC	urban	old	1892	1966	college	teacher	F	Black	+
*DC004	Washington DC	urban	old	1892	1966	grade school	skilled trades	M	Black	−
*DC005	Brandywine MD	rural	old	1904	1966	grade school	farmer, rancher	M	Black	+
*DC006	Washington DC	urban	old	1896	1966	high school	laborer	M	Black	−
*DC007	Washington DC	urban	old	1895	1966	grade school	skilled trades	M	White	−
*DC008	Silver Spring MD	urban	old	1901	1966	high school	skilled trades	M	White	+
DC011	Washington DC	urban	middle	1930	1970	college	teacher	F	Black	+
DC012	Washington DC	urban	middle	1914	1970	high school	clerical	M	Black	+
DC013	Washington DC	urban	middle	1925	1970	high school	homemaker	F	Black	+
*FL001	Palatka	small city	old	1896	1966	college	postal service	M	Black	+
*FL002	Palatka	small city	old	1878	1966	grade school	domestic, maid	F	Black	+
*FL003	Miami	large city	old	1900	1966	college	librarian	F	White	+
*FL004	Miami	large city	middle	1921	1966	high school	postal service	F	White	+
*FL005	Miami	large city	middle	1926	1966	college	homemaker	F	White	+
*FL006	Chiefland	village	old	1895	1966	high school	homemaker	F	White	+
*FL007	Madison	village	old	1898	1966	college	educational administrator	M	White	+
*FL008	Madison	village	old	1897	1966	college	food services	F	White	+
*FL009	Elfers	rural	old	1891	1966	grade school	medicine	F	White	+
*FL010	Elfers	rural	old	1883	1966	grade school	homemaker	F	White	+
*FL011	Boca Grande	rural	young	1930	1966	high school	wholesale, retail sales	F	White	+
*FL012	Punta Gorda	village	old	1901	1966	college	agricultural services	M	White	+
*FL013	Boca Grande	rural	old	1882	1966	grade school	nautical, fishing	M	White	+
*FL014	Boca Grande	rural	old	1901	1966	grade school	domestic, maid	F	White	+
*FL015	Jacksonville	large city	old	1900	1966	college	legal	M	White	+
*FL016	Jacksonville	large city	middle	1917	1966	college	agricultural services	M	White	+
*FL017	Milton	village	old	1876	1965	college	clerical	M	White	+
*FL018	Campbellton	rural	old	1896	1965	college	teacher	F	White	+
*FL019	Hilliard	village	old	1898	1966	college	homemaker	F	White	+
*FL020	Hilliard	village	old	1892	1966	college	teacher	F	White	+
*FL021	Apalachicola	village	old	1886	1965	grade school	nautical, fishing	M	White	+
*FL022	Apalachicola	village	old	1905	1965	high school	skilled trades	M	White	+
*FL023	Key West	small city	middle	1910	1966	high school	librarian	F	White	+
*FL024	Key West	small city	old	1889	1966	unknown	nautical, fishing	M	White	+
*FL025	Key West	small city	old	1900	1966	college	real estate	F	White	+
*FL026	Quincy	rural	old	1891	1966	grade school	farm woman	F	White	+
*FL027	Bartow	village	old	1897	1966	college	agricultural services	M	White	+
*FL028	Bartow	village	old	1903	1966	college	farmer, rancher	M	White	+
*FL029	Fort Pierce	small city	old	1895	1966	high school	local government	M	White	+
*FL030	Eden	small city	old	1891	1966	high school	teacher	F	White	+
*FL031	Kissimmee	village	middle	1908	1966	grade school	laborer	F	White	+
*FL032	Kissimmee	rural	old	1890	1966	some schooling	farmer, rancher	M	White	+
*FL033	Ocala	small city	old	1895	1966	college	teacher	F	Black	+
*FL034	Ocala	rural	middle	1917	1966	high school	farmer, rancher	M	White	+
*FL035	Okeechobee	village	old	1893	1966	grade school	farmer, rancher	M	White	+
*FL036	Basinger	rural	old	1894	1966	grade school	farmer, rancher	M	White	+

Informant Code	Community	Community Type	Age-group	Year of Birth	Year of Interview	Education	Occupation	Sex	Race	Audio-tape
*FL037	Buckingham	rural	old	1886	1966	some schooling	farm woman	F	White	+
*FL038	Fort Myers	small city	middle	1918	1966	high school	medicine	F	White	+
*FL039	Fort Myers	small city	old	1902	1966	high school	journalism	F	White	+
FL048	Havana	village	middle	1930	1970	college	teacher	M	Black	+
FL049	Havana	rural	old	1905	1970	unknown	farm woman	F	Black	+
FL050	Havana	rural	old	1880	1970	grade school	farmer, rancher	M	Black	+
FL051	Gifford	village	middle	1929	1970	college	teacher	F	Black	+
FL052	Gifford	village	young	1942	1970	college	administrative, managerial	M	Black	+
*GA001	Elbert Co.	rural	old	1906	1966	grade school	farmer, rancher	M	White	+
*GA002	Elbert Co.	rural	middle	1909	1966	high school	homemaker	F	White	−
*GA003	Richmond Hill	rural	middle	1926	1966	grade school	skilled trades	M	White	+
*GA004	Louisville	rural	old	1903	1966	some schooling	domestic, maid	F	Black	+
*GA005	Louisville	village	old	1880	1966	some schooling	farmer, rancher	M	White	+
*GA006	Matthews	rural	young	1944	1966	grade school	homemaker	F	White	−
*GA007	Telfair Co.	rural	middle	1916	1966	grade school	farmer, rancher	M	White	+
*GA008	Telfair Co.	rural	young	1929	1966	grade school	homemaker	F	White	+
*GA009	Washington	rural	old	1897	1966	grade school	farmer, rancher	M	White	+
*GA010	Washington	village	old	1891	1966	high school	wholesale, retail sales	F	White	+
*GA011	St. Simons Island	village	old	1905	1966	high school	homemaker	F	White	+
*GA012	Darien	rural	middle	1907	1966	high school	homemaker	F	White	+
*GA013	Athens	small city	old	1906	1966	high school	wholesale, retail sales	M	White	+
*GA014	Athens	rural	old	1904	1966	some schooling	farmer, rancher	M	Black	−
*GA015	Savannah	large city	old	1885	1966	high school	homemaker	F	White	+
*GA016	Rincon	rural	old	1889	1966	grade school	farmer, rancher	M	White	−
GA017	Tifton	small city	middle	1919	1968	high school	factory worker	F	White	−
GA018	Tifton	small city	middle	1913	1968	college	teacher	F	White	+
GA019	Folkston	village	old	1904	1968	high school	financial services	M	White	+
GA020	Folkston	village	middle	1923	1968	high school	ranger, guide	M	White	+
GA022	Fargo	rural	old	1893	1968	some schooling	logging	M	White	+
GA023	Fargo	rural	middle	1920	1968	grade school	clerical	M	White	+
GA024	Fargo	rural	middle	1913	1968	grade school	small business: owner, manager	F	White	−
GA025	Fargo	rural	old	1897	1968	some schooling	ranger, guide	M	White	+
GA026	Fargo	rural	old	1884	1968	grade school	farmer, rancher	M	White	−
GA027	Midway	rural	old	1903	1968	high school	museum staff	F	White	−
GA028	Midway	rural	old	1901	1968	grade school	homemaker	F	White	−
GA029	Midway	rural	old	1901	1968	grade school	postal service	F	White	−
GA030	Waycross	rural	old	1896	1968	some schooling	ranger, guide	M	White	+
GA031	Waycross	rural	old	1904	1968	college	administrative, managerial	M	White	+
GA032	Waycross	small city	old	1888	1968	high school	clerical	F	White	−
GA033	Waycross	small city	old	1903	1968	high school	medicine	F	White	−
GA034	Waycross	rural	old	1901	1968	grade school	logging	M	White	−
GA035	Waycross	rural	middle	1923	1968	high school	ranger, guide	M	White	+
GA036	Cairo	village	old	1900	1968	college	administrative, managerial	M	White	+
GA037	Cairo	village	old	1908	1968	some schooling	homemaker	F	Black	−
GA038	Cairo	village	middle	1913	1968	college	librarian	F	White	−
GA039	Cairo	village	middle	1913	1968	college	agricultural services	M	White	+
GA040	Cairo	village	middle	1913	1968	grade school	custodial, maintenance	M	Black	−
GA041	Cairo	village	middle	1910	1968	high school	barber, beautician	M	Black	−

Informant Code	Community	Community Type	Age-group	Year of Birth	Year of Interview	Education	Occupation	Sex	Race	Audio-tape
GA042	Cairo	village	young	1931	1968	college	librarian	F	Black	−
GA043	Cairo	village	middle	1928	1968	high school	seamstress	F	Black	−
GA044	Donalson-ville	village	old	1901	1968	college	clerical	F	White	+
GA045	Donalson-ville	village	middle	1917	1968	college	teacher	F	Black	−
GA046	Donalson-ville	village	middle	1913	1968	college	librarian	F	White	−
GA047	Donalson-ville	village	young	1930	1968	college	teacher	M	Black	−
GA052	Macon	large city	middle	1919	1968	some schooling	homemaker	F	Black	−
GA053	Macon	large city	middle	1911	1968	high school	clerical	F	White	+
GA054	Macon	large city	young	1948	1968	college	student	M	White	+
GA055	Macon	large city	middle	1917	1968	college	teacher	F	White	+
GA056	Marshallville	village	middle	1922	1968	high school	librarian	F	White	−
GA057	Marshallville	village	middle	1923	1968	high school	librarian	F	White	−
GA058	Marshallville	village	old	1906	1968	high school	librarian	F	White	−
GA059	Marshallville	village	middle	1912	1968	college	teacher	F	White	−
GA060	Marshallville	village	middle	1909	1968	high school	teacher	M	White	−
GA061	Marshallville	village	middle	1915	1968	college	educational administrator	M	Black	+
GA062	Marshallville	village	young	1930	1968	college	teacher	F	White	+
GA063	Marshallville	village	young	1948	1968	college	student	M	White	−
GA065	Marshallville	village	old	1903	1968	grade school	laborer	M	White	−
GA066	Marshallville	village	old	1900	1968	unknown	teacher	F	White	−
GA067	Milledgeville	small city	old	1895	1968	college	teacher	F	White	+
GA068	Milledgeville	small city	old	1896	1968	college	journalism	F	White	−
GA070	Rabun Gap	rural	middle	1910	1969	high school	domestic, maid	F	White	−
GA071	Rabun Gap	rural	old	1906	1969	grade school	farmer, rancher	M	White	+
GA072	Dillard	rural	middle	1911	1969	grade school	farmer, rancher	M	White	+
GA073	Ball Ground	rural	middle	1919	1969	college	postal service	M	White	−
GA074	Ball Ground	rural	old	1897	1969	high school	administrative, managerial	M	White	+
GA075	Ball Ground	rural	middle	1921	1969	college	teacher	F	White	−
GA076	Ball Ground	rural	middle	1925	1969	college	skilled trades	M	White	−
GA077	Rome	small city	middle	1913	1969	some schooling	custodial, maintenance	M	White	+
GA078	Mount Berry	small city	old	1904	1969	college	teacher	F	White	−
GA079	Rome	small city	old	1899	1969	high school	food services	F	Black	+
GA080	Austell	village	old	1901	1969	college	skilled trades	M	White	−
GA081	Atlanta	large city	middle	1910	1969	high school	clerical	F	White	+
GA082	Atlanta	large city	middle	1914	1969	high school	storekeeper	M	White	+
GA083	Atlanta	large city	young	1933	1969	high school	skilled trades	M	Black	−
GA084	Hogansville	village	old	1902	1969	high school	insurance	M	White	+
GA085	Hogansville	village	old	1906	1969	college	teacher	F	White	−
GA086	Hogansville	rural	middle	1916	1969	college	farmer, rancher	M	White	+
GA087	Richland	rural	old	1900	1969	grade school	farmer, rancher	M	White	−
GA088	Richland	rural	old	1906	1969	high school	farm woman	F	White	−
GA089	Richland	rural	middle	1916	1969	college	logging	M	White	+
GA090	Atlanta	large city	young	1954	1970	high school	student	F	Black	+
GA091	Atlanta	large city	young	1940	1970	college	postal service	M	Black	+
GA092	Eatonton	village	young	1951	1970	college	student	F	Black	+
GA093	Eatonton	village	young	1955	1970	high school	student	M	Black	+
HI001	Honolulu	large city	old	1902	1967	college	teacher	F	White	+
HI002	Honolulu	large city	old	1903	1967	college	agricultural services	F	White	+

Informant Code	Community	Community Type	Age-group	Year of Birth	Year of Interview	Education	Occupation	Sex	Race	Audio-tape
HI003	Hauula	rural	old	1902	1967	grade school	farmer, rancher	M	White	−
HI004	Waianae	large city	old	1897	1967	some schooling	nautical, fishing	M	White	+
HI005	Honolulu	urban	middle	1917	1967	grade school	skilled trades	M	White	−
HI006	Honolulu	large city	young	1929	1967	grade school	domestic, maid	F	White	−
HI007	Honolulu	urban	young	1945	1967	high school	artist, craftsman	M	White	+
HI008	Honolulu	large city	young	1945	1967	high school	homemaker	F	White	+
HI009	Honolulu	large city	old	1907	1967	grade school	laborer	M	Oriental	+
HI010	Honolulu	urban	young	1945	1967	high school	clerical	F	Oriental	+
HI011	Honolulu	large city	middle	1908	1967	high school	farmer, rancher	M	Oriental	−
HI012	Honolulu	large city	middle	1909	1967	college	agricultural services	M	Oriental	−
HI013	Honolulu	large city	young	1943	1967	college	social & community services	F	Oriental	−
HI014	Honolulu	large city	middle	1915	1967	college	agricultural services	M	White	−
ID001	Montpelier	village	old	1892	1966	high school	farmer, rancher	M	White	+
ID002	Arco	rural	old	1893	1966	high school	farmer, rancher	M	White	+
ID003	Arco	rural	old	1897	1966	high school	farmer, rancher	M	White	+
ID004	Bonners Ferry	village	old	1900	1966	high school	postal service	M	White	+
ID005	Moscow	village	old	1901	1967	college	homemaker	F	White	+
IL002	Galena	village	old	1905	1967	high school	storekeeper	F	White	+
IL003	Galena	village	middle	1914	1967	college	librarian	F	White	−
IL004	Galena	village	middle	1915	1967	grade school	farmer, rancher	M	White	+
IL005	Nauvoo	village	old	1897	1967	college	homemaker	F	White	+
IL006	Nauvoo	village	old	1902	1967	grade school	ranger, guide	M	White	−
IL007	Galesburg	small city	old	1901	1967	high school	storekeeper	M	White	+
IL008	Savanna	village	young	1938	1967	college	clerical	M	White	−
IL009	Savanna	village	old	1904	1967	high school	small business: owner, manager	M	White	+
IL010	Savanna	village	old	1897	1967	college	storekeeper	M	White	+
IL011	Galva	village	middle	1909	1967	college	storekeeper	M	White	+
IL012	Galva	village	middle	1913	1967	high school	police	M	White	+
IL013	Havana	village	old	1899	1967	college	storekeeper	M	White	+
IL014	Havana	rural	old	1893	1967	grade school	farmer, rancher	M	White	+
IL015	Mahomet	village	old	1885	1967	grade school	homemaker	F	White	+
IL016	Mahomet	rural	old	1890	1967	grade school	farmer, rancher	M	White	+
IL017	Urbana	small city	middle	1925	1967	high school	homemaker	F	White	+
IL018	Urbana	small city	old	1906	1967	high school	wholesale, retail sales	F	White	−
IL019	Petersburg	village	middle	1924	1967	high school	homemaker	F	White	+
IL020	Petersburg	village	old	1904	1967	high school	homemaker	F	White	+
IL021	Petersburg	village	middle	1920	1967	college	legal	M	White	+
IL022	Petersburg	village	old	1885	1967	college	storekeeper	M	White	−
IL023	Carthage	village	old	1892	1967	high school	clerical	F	White	+
IL024	Carthage	village	old	1905	1967	college	librarian	F	White	−
IL025	Carthage	village	old	1900	1967	high school	homemaker	F	White	+
IL026	Peoria	large city	old	1883	1967	grade school	homemaker	F	White	+
IL027	Prophets-town	village	young	1941	1968	high school	skilled trades	F	White	+
IL028	Prophets-town	village	middle	1917	1968	high school	librarian	F	White	+
IL029	Grand Detour	rural	old	1906	1968	grade school	homemaker	F	White	+
IL030	Belvidere	small city	old	1905	1969	college	teacher	F	White	+
IL031	Belvidere	small city	old	1908	1969	college	social & community services	F	White	−

Informant Code	Community	Community Type	Age-group	Year of Birth	Year of Interview	Education	Occupation	Sex	Race	Audio-tape
IL032	Belvidere	small city	old	1886	1969	high school	artist, craftsman	M	White	−
IL033	Algonquin	rural	old	1895	1969	grade school	farmer, rancher	F	White	−
IL034	West Dundee	village	middle	1923	1969	high school	homemaker	F	White	−
IL035	West Dundee	village	old	1890	1969	high school	journalism	F	White	+
IL036	Ottawa	small city	old	1902	1969	high school	foreman, supervisor	F	White	+
IL037	Ottawa	small city	old	1906	1969	college	local government	F	White	−
IL038	Ottawa	rural	old	1896	1969	college	farmer, rancher	M	White	+
IL039	Morris	village	old	1902	1969	high school	clerical	F	White	+
IL040	Morris	village	old	1893	1969	college	local government	M	White	−
IL041	Morris	rural	young	1934	1969	high school	farmer, rancher	M	White	−
IL042	Downers Grove	small city	old	1878	1969	high school	small business: owner, manager	M	White	−
IL043	Downers Grove	small city	old	1901	1969	high school	homemaker	F	White	−
IL044	Downers Grove	rural	middle	1915	1969	high school	farmer, rancher	F	White	+
IL045	Zion	small city	young	1935	1969	high school	homemaker	F	White	+
IL046	Zion	rural	old	1886	1969	college	farmer, rancher	M	White	−
IL047	Winnetka	urban	old	1893	1969	college	teacher	F	White	−
IL048	Winnetka	urban	old	1891	1969	college	architect	M	White	+
IL049	Winnetka	urban	old	1908	1969	college	journalism	M	White	−
IL050	Chicago	urban	old	1891	1966	college	teacher	F	White	+
IL051	South Holland	small city	old	1893	1969	high school	homemaker	F	White	−
IL052	South Holland	small city	old	1894	1969	college	teacher	F	White	+
IL053	South Holland	small city	old	1894	1969	college	medicine	F	White	−
IL054	Towanda	rural	middle	1911	1969	college	storekeeper	M	White	−
IL055	Towanda	rural	old	1885	1969	college	teacher	F	White	+
IL056	Towanda	rural	middle	1926	1969	high school	farmer, rancher	M	White	−
IL057	Bourbonnais	village	old	1894	1969	high school	postal service	M	White	−
IL058	Bourbonnais	village	old	1909	1969	college	financial services	M	White	+
IL059	Bourbonnais	rural	old	1897	1969	college	food services	M	White	−
IL060	Forrest	village	old	1897	1969	high school	journalism	F	White	+
IL061	Forrest	village	old	1896	1969	high school	librarian	F	White	−
IL062	Forrest	rural	old	1901	1969	college	farm woman	F	White	−
IL063	Mount Pulaski	village	old	1907	1969	college	teacher	F	White	+
IL064	Mount Pulaski	village	old	1888	1969	high school	storekeeper	M	White	−
IL065	Mount Pulaski	village	old	1883	1969	college	farmer, rancher	M	White	−
IL066	Chester	rural	old	1891	1969	grade school	farmer, rancher	M	White	+
IL067	Chester	village	young	1931	1969	high school	skilled trades	M	White	−
IL068	Chester	village	old	1909	1969	high school	librarian	F	White	+
IL069	Kaskaskia	rural	old	1897	1969	grade school	farmer, rancher	M	White	+
IL070	Quincy	small city	old	1896	1969	college	teacher	F	White	+
IL071	Quincy	small city	middle	1915	1969	college	storekeeper	M	White	−
IL072	Quincy	small city	old	1883	1969	college	administrative, managerial	M	White	−
IL073	Metropolis	village	old	1902	1969	high school	farmer, rancher	F	White	+
IL074	Metropolis	village	old	1900	1969	grade school	farmer, rancher	M	White	+
IL075	Metropolis	village	old	1905	1969	college	homemaker	F	White	+
IL076	Metropolis	village	old	1901	1969	high school	teacher	F	White	+

Informant Code	Community	Community Type	Age-group	Year of Birth	Year of Interview	Education	Occupation	Sex	Race	Audio-tape
IL077	Prairie du Rocher	rural	old	1889	1969	high school	farmer, rancher	M	White	+
IL078	Mount Vernon	rural	old	1890	1969	college	farmer, rancher	M	White	+
IL079	Mount Vernon	rural	old	1897	1969	high school	homemaker	F	White	+
IL080	Beardstown	village	middle	1929	1969	college	teacher	F	White	+
IL081	Beardstown	village	old	1902	1969	college	artist, craftsman	M	White	−
IL082	Beardstown	village	middle	1912	1969	high school	administrative, managerial	F	White	−
IL083	Hardin	village	old	1882	1969	grade school	homemaker	F	White	+
IL084	Carlinville	village	middle	1911	1969	college	nautical, fishing	M	White	+
IL085	Pana	village	middle	1924	1969	college	food services	M	White	+
IL086	Highland	village	old	1907	1969	college	financial services	M	White	+
IL087	Highland	village	middle	1913	1969	high school	financial services	M	White	+
IL088	Shawnee-town	village	old	1904	1969	high school	medicine	F	White	+
IL089	Shawnee-town	village	old	1884	1969	grade school	surveyor	M	White	−
IL090	Shawnee-town	rural	old	1909	1969	grade school	farmer, rancher	M	White	−
IL091	Shawnee-town	village	old	1900	1969	high school	homemaker	F	White	+
IL092	Shawnee-town	village	old	1897	1969	college	farm woman	F	White	+
IL093	Elizabeth-town	rural	old	1903	1969	grade school	miner	M	White	+
IL094	Elizabeth-town	rural	middle	1911	1969	grade school	homemaker	F	White	−
IL095	Elizabeth-town	rural	old	1907	1969	some schooling	skilled trades	M	White	+
IL096	Elizabeth-town	rural	old	1898	1969	grade school	postal service	M	White	−
IL097	Arlington Heights	urban	middle	1923	1969	college	homemaker	F	White	+
IL098	Chicago (North Side)	urban	young	1947	1969	college	student	M	White	+
IL099	Evanston	urban	middle	1919	1969	college	homemaker	F	White	+
IL100	Evanston	urban	young	1948	1969	college	student	F	White	−
IL102	St. Elmo	village	old	1900	1969	high school	homemaker	F	White	+
IL103	St. Elmo	village	old	1898	1969	high school	homemaker	F	White	−
IL104	St. Elmo	village	old	1888	1969	high school	railroad	M	White	−
IL105	St. Elmo	village	middle	1919	1969	high school	homemaker	F	White	+
IL106	St. Elmo	village	old	1886	1969	grade school	homemaker	F	White	−
IL107	Edwardsville	small city	old	1902	1969	college	teacher	F	White	−
IL108	Edwardsville	small city	old	1908	1969	high school	homemaker	F	White	−
IL109	Edwardsville	small city	old	1903	1969	high school	journalism	M	White	+
IL110	Edwardsville	small city	old	1904	1969	high school	clerical	F	White	−
IL111	Edwardsville	small city	old	1903	1969	high school	clerical	M	White	−
IL113	Charleston	small city	old	1910	1970	college	homemaker	F	White	+
IL114	Charleston	small city	old	1897	1970	college	real estate	M	White	+
IL115	Charleston	rural	middle	1912	1970	high school	ranger, guide	M	White	+
IL116	Carterville	village	middle	1917	1970	high school	miner	M	White	−
IL117	Marion	small city	old	1908	1970	grade school	miner	M	White	−
IL118	Marion	small city	middle	1917	1970	college	legal	M	White	+
IL119	Marion	small city	young	1945	1970	college	student	M	White	−
IL122	Cairo	village	old	1905	1970	high school	librarian	F	White	+

Informant Code	Community	Community Type	Age-group	Year of Birth	Year of Interview	Education	Occupation	Sex	Race	Audio-tape
IL123	Cairo	village	old	1889	1970	high school	skilled trades	M	White	+
IL124	Paris	rural	old	1900	1970	high school	farm woman	F	White	−
IL125	Paris	rural	old	1897	1970	college	farmer, rancher	M	White	−
IL126	Paris	rural	middle	1930	1970	high school	farmer, rancher	M	White	+
IL128	Carmi	village	old	1905	1970	college	journalism	M	White	+
IL129	Carmi	village	old	1890	1970	high school	homemaker	F	White	−
IL130	Carmi	village	old	1900	1970	grade school	postal service	M	White	+
IL131	Carmi	village	old	1902	1970	college	lodging trades	F	White	+
IL132	Carmi	village	young	1948	1970	college	student	M	White	−
IL134	Greenup	village	old	1898	1970	college	homemaker	F	White	−
IL135	Greenup	village	middle	1919	1970	college	homemaker	F	White	+
IL136	Greenup	village	middle	1927	1970	high school	homemaker	F	White	+
IL137	Chicago	urban	young	1943	1970	high school	factory worker	F	Black	+
IL138	Chicago	urban	young	1942	1970	college	teacher	F	Black	−
IL139	Chicago	urban	young	1927	1970	high school	homemaker	F	Black	−
IL140	Chicago	urban	young	1947	1970	high school	homemaker	F	Black	+
IL141	Olney	village	middle	1926	1970	college	homemaker	F	White	+
IL142	Olney	rural	middle	1922	1970	college	farmer, rancher	M	White	+
IL143	Olney	village	old	1905	1970	high school	homemaker	F	White	+
IL144	Olney	village	middle	1922	1970	college	small business: owner, manager	M	White	−
IN001	Lafayette	small city	young	1943	1966	college	teacher	F	White	+
IN002	Lafayette	small city	middle	1911	1966	high school	homemaker	F	White	−
IN003	Corydon	village	old	1901	1968	grade school	homemaker	F	White	+
IN004	Corydon	village	old	1902	1968	high school	farmer, rancher	M	White	−
IN005	Corydon	village	middle	1913	1968	college	homemaker	F	White	+
IN006	Corydon	village	old	1902	1968	grade school	farmer, rancher	M	White	−
IN007	Salem	village	old	1894	1968	college	homemaker	F	White	+
IN008	Salem	village	old	1879	1968	college	farmer, rancher	M	White	+
IN009	Salem	village	old	1903	1968	grade school	skilled trades	M	White	+
IN010	Salem	village	old	1888	1968	college	homemaker	F	White	+
IN011	Hanover	rural	old	1899	1968	grade school	farmer, rancher	M	White	+
IN012	Hanover	rural	old	1883	1968	grade school	homemaker	F	White	+
IN013	Hanover	rural	old	1899	1968	grade school	trucking, transportation	M	White	+
IN014	Hanover	rural	old	1907	1968	high school	homemaker	F	White	+
IN015	Vevay	village	middle	1910	1968	college	wholesale, retail sales	F	White	+
IN016	Vevay	village	old	1908	1968	college	teacher	F	White	+
IN017	Vevay	village	old	1903	1968	college	teacher	M	White	+
IN018	Vevay	village	old	1886	1968	grade school	skilled trades	M	White	+
IN019	Versailles	village	old	1890	1968	college	teacher	F	White	+
IN022	Delphi	village	old	1907	1968	college	teacher	M	White	−
IN023	Delphi	village	old	1890	1968	grade school	homemaker	F	White	+
IN024	Delphi	village	old	1900	1968	high school	homemaker	F	White	−
IN025	Delphi	rural	old	1917	1968	high school	farmer, rancher	M	White	−
IN026	Delphi	village	middle	1910	1968	grade school	social & community services	M	White	−
IN027	Nashville	rural	middle	1912	1968	grade school	domestic, maid	F	White	+
IN028	Nashville	rural	old	1894	1968	high school	lodging trades	F	White	−
IN029	Nashville	rural	old	1884	1968	grade school	local government	M	White	−
IN030	Waveland	rural	old	1903	1968	high school	homemaker	F	White	+
IN031	Waveland	rural	old	1903	1968	high school	farmer, rancher	M	White	−
IN032	Mitchell	village	old	1899	1968	college	teacher	F	White	+
IN033	Mitchell	village	old	1880	1968	college	teacher	F	White	−

Informant Code	Community	Community Type	Age-group	Year of Birth	Year of Interview	Education	Occupation	Sex	Race	Audio-tape
IN034	Mitchell	rural	old	1880	1968	college	farmer, rancher	F	White	−
IN035	St. Meinrad	rural	old	1907	1968	grade school	homemaker	F	White	+
IN037	Rockville	village	middle	1912	1968	college	homemaker	F	White	−
IN038	Rockville	village	old	1883	1968	high school	journalism	F	White	−
IN039	Rockville	village	middle	1913	1968	college	homemaker	F	White	−
IN040	Rockville	rural	old	1899	1968	college	farmer, rancher	M	White	−
IN041	Mount Vernon	rural	middle	1911	1968	grade school	farm woman	F	White	+
IN042	Mount Vernon	rural	old	1907	1968	high school	farmer, rancher	M	White	+
IN043	Mount Vernon	rural	young	1943	1968	college	farmer, rancher	M	White	−
IN044	Mount Vernon	rural	old	1889	1968	grade school	farmer, rancher	M	White	−
IN045	Rockport	rural	old	1903	1968	high school	farmer, rancher	M	White	+
IN046	Rockport	rural	old	1898	1968	grade school	farmer, rancher	M	White	−
IN047	Rockport	rural	middle	1911	1968	college	homemaker	F	White	−
IN048	Rockport	village	old	1891	1968	high school	farm woman	F	White	−
IN049	New Harmony	rural	old	1896	1968	grade school	farmer, rancher	M	White	−
IN050	New Harmony	rural	old	1898	1968	grade school	farm woman	F	White	−
IN051	New Harmony	village	old	1889	1968	grade school	farmer, rancher	M	White	+
IN052	New Harmony	village	old	1896	1968	grade school	homemaker	F	White	−
IN053	New Harmony	rural	old	1892	1968	college	farmer, rancher	M	White	−
IN054	Muncie	small city	old	1884	1969	grade school	homemaker	F	White	+
IN055	Muncie	small city	old	1883	1969	college	storekeeper	M	White	−
IN056	Muncie	small city	middle	1918	1969	high school	skilled trades	M	White	+
IN057	Muncie	small city	middle	1915	1969	high school	skilled trades	M	White	−
IN058	Culver	village	old	1901	1969	high school	postal service	M	White	+
IN059	Culver	village	old	1896	1969	high school	laborer	M	White	−
IN060	Culver	village	middle	1922	1969	high school	librarian	F	White	−
IN061	Rensselaer	village	middle	1925	1969	high school	administrative, managerial	M	White	+
IN062	Rensselaer	village	young	1948	1969	college	student	M	White	+
IN063	Rensselaer	rural	middle	1915	1969	high school	farmer, rancher	M	White	−
IN064	Rensselaer	village	young	1949	1969	high school	librarian	F	White	−
IN065	Rensselaer	village	old	1906	1969	grade school	homemaker	F	White	−
IN066	Berne	village	old	1909	1969	college	homemaker	F	White	+
IN067	Berne	rural	old	1901	1969	high school	farmer, rancher	M	White	−
IN068	Berne	village	old	1909	1969	college	wholesale, retail sales	M	White	+
IN069	Lagrange	village	old	1896	1969	college	agricultural services	M	White	+
IN070	Lagrange	village	old	1894	1969	high school	homemaker	F	White	−
IN071	Wabash	small city	old	1893	1969	college	small business: owner, manager	M	White	−
IN072	Urbana	rural	young	1933	1969	college	teacher	M	White	−
IN073	Wabash	small city	old	1897	1969	college	financial services	M	White	−
IN074	Michigan City	small city	old	1889	1969	high school	railroad	M	White	−
IN075	Michigan City	small city	young	1949	1969	high school	food services	M	White	−
IN076	Dublin	village	middle	1912	1969	high school	librarian	F	White	+
IN077	Dublin	village	old	1908	1969	high school	custodial, maintenance	F	White	+

Informant Code	Community	Community Type	Age-group	Year of Birth	Year of Interview	Education	Occupation	Sex	Race	Audio-tape
IN078	Dublin	village	old	1880	1969	high school	factory worker	M	White	−
IN079	Richmond	small city	old	1889	1969	some schooling	homemaker	F	White	+
IN080	Richmond	small city	old	1905	1969	grade school	clerical	M	White	−
IN081	Richmond	small city	middle	1917	1969	high school	clerical	F	White	−
IN082	Metamora	rural	old	1893	1969	high school	homemaker	F	White	+
IN083	Metamora	rural	old	1891	1969	college	skilled trades	M	White	+
IN084	Metamora	rural	old	1889	1969	some schooling	farmer, rancher	M	White	−
IA001	Grundy Center	rural	old	1898	1967	high school	farmer, rancher	M	White	+
IA002	Grundy Center	village	old	1897	1967	high school	teacher	F	White	+
IA003	Grundy Center	small city	old	1895	1967	college	teacher	F	White	+
IA004	Grundy Center	rural	old	1892	1967	college	farmer, rancher	M	White	+
IA005	Mason City	small city	middle	1908	1967	college	clerical	M	White	+
IA006	Mason City	rural	young	1928	1967	college	farmer, rancher	M	White	+
IA007	Mason City	small city	old	1894	1967	college	teacher	F	White	+
IA008	Boone	small city	old	1897	1967	high school	skilled trades	M	White	+
IA009	Boone	small city	old	1891	1967	college	teacher	F	White	+
IA011	Guthrie Center	village	old	1888	1967	high school	skilled trades	M	White	+
IA012	Guthrie Center	rural	old	1892	1967	high school	farm woman	F	White	+
IA013	Lansing	village	old	1897	1967	college	teacher	F	White	+
IA014	Lansing	rural	old	1898	1967	grade school	farmer, rancher	M	White	+
IA015	Lansing	village	old	1896	1967	high school	storekeeper	M	White	+
IA016	Dubuque	small city	old	1896	1968	college	librarian	F	White	−
IA017	Dubuque	small city	old	1883	1968	high school	homemaker	F	White	−
IA018	Dubuque	small city	old	1887	1968	grade school	homemaker	F	White	−
IA019	Dubuque	small city	old	1887	1968	college	administrative, managerial	M	White	+
IA020	Dubuque	small city	old	1898	1968	college	teacher	F	White	−
IA021	Dubuque	small city	old	1898	1968	college	teacher	F	White	−
IA022	Muscatine	small city	old	1900	1968	grade school	lodging trades	M	White	+
IA023	Muscatine	small city	middle	1914	1968	high school	lodging trades	F	White	−
IA024	Mount Pleasant	village	old	1894	1968	high school	homemaker	F	White	−
IA025	Mount Pleasant	village	old	1907	1968	college	homemaker	F	White	−
IA026	Mount Pleasant	rural	old	1889	1968	college	farmer, rancher	M	White	−
IA027	Mount Pleasant	village	young	1939	1968	high school	barber, beautician	F	White	+
IA028	Mount Pleasant	village	middle	1916	1968	high school	lodging trades	M	White	−
IA029	Mystic	rural	old	1903	1968	grade school	miner	M	White	−
IA030	Mystic	rural	old	1891	1968	high school	homemaker	F	White	+
IA031	Mystic	rural	old	1881	1968	high school	small business: owner, manager	M	White	−
IA031A	Mystic	rural	young	1931	1968	high school	food services	F	White	−
IA032	Amana	village	young	1951	1968	high school	student	F	White	−
IA033	What Cheer	rural	old	1900	1968	college	storekeeper	F	White	+
IA034	What Cheer	rural	old	1901	1968	high school	homemaker	F	White	+
IA036	Newton	small city	old	1897	1968	grade school	homemaker	F	White	+
IA038	Council Bluffs	small city	old	1903	1968	college	homemaker	F	White	+

Informant Code	Community	Community Type	Age-group	Year of Birth	Year of Interview	Education	Occupation	Sex	Race	Audio-tape
IA039	Council Bluffs	rural	old	1897	1968	college	farmer, rancher	M	White	−
IA041	Ida Grove	village	old	1899	1968	college	clerical	F	White	+
IA043	Orange City	village	young	1947	1968	high school	clerical	F	White	+
IA045	Villisca	village	young	1950	1968	high school	student	M	White	+
IA046	Emmetsburg	village	young	1929	1968	high school	homemaker	F	White	+
IA047	Emmetsburg	village	middle	1928	1968	college	homemaker	F	White	+
KS001	Dodge City	small city	middle	1892	1967	college	museum staff	F	White	+
KS002	Dodge City	small city	middle	1924	1967	college	museum staff	F	White	+
KS003	Victoria	village	young	1932	1967	high school	homemaker	F	White	+
KS004	Victoria	village	young	1931	1967	high school	clerical	F	White	+
KS005	Smith Center	village	old	1888	1967	college	farmer, rancher	M	White	+
KS006	Liberal	small city	old	1888	1967	college	storekeeper	M	White	+
KS007	Lindsborg	village	old	1885	1968	college	teacher	F	White	+
KS008	Newton	small city	middle	1910	1968	college	seamstress	F	White	+
KS009	Newton	rural	old	1902	1968	high school	farmer, rancher	M	White	−
KS010	Newton	small city	middle	1916	1968	college	homemaker	F	White	+
KS011	Medicine Lodge	village	old	1898	1968	high school	homemaker	F	White	−
KS012	Medicine Lodge	village	old	1895	1968	college	small business: owner, manager	M	White	+
KS013	Medicine Lodge	village	old	1892	1968	high school	teacher	F	White	+
KS014	Sharon Springs	village	old	1894	1968	high school	financial services	M	White	+
KS015	Sharon Springs	village	middle	1921	1968	high school	homemaker	F	White	+
KS016	Yates Center	village	old	1891	1968	high school	homemaker	F	White	+
KS017	Yates Center	village	old	1891	1968	college	real estate	M	White	−
KS018	Marysville	village	old	1900	1968	high school	farm woman	F	White	+
KS019	St. Francis	village	old	1893	1968	college	financial services	F	White	+
KS020	St. Francis	village	old	1900	1968	college	teacher	F	White	+
KY005	Bowling Green	rural	old	1890	1969	grade school	homemaker	F	White	+
KY006	Bowling Green	rural	old	1893	1969	grade school	farmer, rancher	M	White	+
KY007	Center	rural	old	1892	1969	grade school	homemaker	F	White	−
KY008	Center	rural	middle	1929	1969	college	homemaker	F	White	−
KY009	Center	rural	old	1908	1969	grade school	farmer, rancher	M	White	+
KY010	Center	rural	young	1946	1969	high school	storekeeper	F	White	−
KY011	Falls of Rough	rural	middle	1916	1969	grade school	farmer, rancher	M	White	−
KY012	Falls of Rough	rural	old	1906	1969	grade school	homemaker	F	White	−
KY013	Falls of Rough	rural	old	1895	1969	grade school	logging	M	White	+
KY014	Falls of Rough	rural	old	1893	1969	grade school	farmer, rancher	M	White	+
KY015	Honeybee	rural	middle	1911	1969	high school	homemaker	F	White	−
KY016	Sawyer	rural	old	1900	1969	grade school	storekeeper	M	White	+
KY017	Sawyer	rural	old	1902	1969	grade school	homemaker	F	White	+
KY018	Sawyer	rural	middle	1916	1969	grade school	farmer, rancher	M	White	−
KY019	Sawyer	rural	middle	1926	1969	grade school	farm woman	F	White	−
KY020	Tompkins-ville	rural	middle	1924	1969	grade school	homemaker	F	White	−
KY021	Tompkins-ville	rural	middle	1912	1969	grade school	farmer, rancher	M	White	+

Informant Code	Community	Community Type	Age-group	Year of Birth	Year of Interview	Education	Occupation	Sex	Race	Audio-tape
KY022	Tompkins-ville	rural	old	1903	1969	grade school	homemaker	F	White	−
KY023	Tompkins-ville	rural	old	1904	1969	grade school	farmer, rancher	M	White	+
KY024	London	rural	old	1883	1969	college	farmer, rancher	M	White	+
KY025	London	village	old	1887	1969	college	homemaker	F	White	−
KY026	London	village	middle	1917	1969	college	educational administrator	M	White	−
KY027	London	rural	old	1907	1969	high school	farmer, rancher	M	White	−
KY028	Walker	rural	middle	1915	1969	grade school	homemaker	F	White	+
KY029	Walker	rural	old	1908	1969	grade school	miner	M	White	−
KY030	Barbourville	village	middle	1921	1969	college	small business: owner, manager	M	White	−
KY031	Clayhole	rural	middle	1918	1967	college	social & community services	M	White	−
KY032	Clayhole	rural	old	1902	1967	some schooling	farm woman	F	White	−
KY033	Clayhole	rural	middle	1926	1967	grade school	homemaker	F	White	−
KY034	Hardshell	rural	middle	1908	1967	grade school	homemaker	F	White	+
KY035	Berea	rural	old	1909	1969	grade school	farmer, rancher	M	White	+
KY036	Berea	rural	old	1902	1969	high school	homemaker	F	White	−
KY037	Berea	rural	old	1895	1969	grade school	farm woman	F	White	−
KY038	Berea	rural	middle	1912	1969	high school	farm woman	F	White	−
KY039	Hindman	rural	old	1899	1969	grade school	skilled trades	M	White	+
KY040	Hindman	rural	middle	1914	1969	grade school	homemaker	F	White	−
KY041	Viper	rural	old	1894	1969	grade school	homemaker	F	White	+
KY042	Hazard	village	old	1904	1969	grade school	farm woman	F	White	−
KY043	Jeff	rural	old	1896	1969	high school	storekeeper	M	White	−
KY044	Adams	rural	old	1894	1969	grade school	farm woman	F	White	+
KY045	Adams	rural	old	1908	1969	high school	homemaker	F	White	−
KY046	Adams	rural	old	1890	1969	grade school	farmer, rancher	M	White	−
KY047	Adams	rural	old	1889	1969	grade school	farmer, rancher	M	White	−
KY048	Washington	rural	old	1896	1969	grade school	storekeeper	F	White	−
KY049	Washington	rural	old	1897	1969	grade school	farmer, rancher	M	White	−
KY050	Washington	rural	old	1902	1969	high school	clerical	F	White	+
KY051	Washington	rural	middle	1919	1969	grade school	postal service	F	White	−
KY052	Falmouth	village	old	1900	1969	grade school	homemaker	F	White	−
KY053	Falmouth	rural	middle	1911	1969	grade school	farmer, rancher	M	White	+
KY054	Butler	rural	old	1901	1969	grade school	homemaker	F	White	−
KY055	Owingsville	village	old	1900	1969	grade school	homemaker	F	Black	−
KY056	Owingsville	rural	old	1896	1969	grade school	farm woman	F	White	+
KY057	Owingsville	village	middle	1918	1969	grade school	homemaker	F	Black	−
KY058	Owingsville	village	old	1895	1969	grade school	farmer, rancher	M	White	−
KY059	Owingsville	village	middle	1920	1969	college	homemaker	F	White	−
KY060	Carrollton	village	middle	1911	1969	college	small business: owner, manager	M	White	+
KY061	Carrollton	village	old	1902	1969	college	teacher	F	White	−
KY062	Worthville	rural	middle	1919	1969	grade school	farm woman	F	White	−
KY063	Harrodsburg	village	middle	1913	1969	college	homemaker	F	White	+
KY064	Harrodsburg	village	middle	1915	1969	college	farmer, rancher	M	White	+
KY065	Burgin	rural	old	1902	1969	grade school	farmer, rancher	M	White	−
KY066	Burgin	rural	old	1907	1969	grade school	homemaker	F	White	−
KY067	Eastview	rural	old	1904	1969	grade school	farmer, rancher	M	White	−
KY068	Eastview	rural	old	1901	1969	grade school	farmer, rancher	M	White	−
KY069	Eastview	rural	old	1903	1969	grade school	farm woman	F	White	−

Informant Code	Community	Community Type	Age-group	Year of Birth	Year of Interview	Education	Occupation	Sex	Race	Audio-tape
KY070	Eastview	rural	middle	1924	1969	high school	homemaker	F	White	+
KY071	Bardstown	rural	middle	1919	1970	grade school	homemaker	F	White	−
KY072	Cox's Creek	rural	old	1906	1970	high school	farmer, rancher	M	White	+
KY073	Cox's Creek	rural	young	1942	1970	college	homemaker	F	White	−
KY074	Calhoun	rural	middle	1914	1970	college	farm woman	F	White	−
KY075	Calhoun	rural	middle	1911	1970	grade school	farmer, rancher	M	White	+
KY076	Henderson	small city	old	1890	1970	college	farmer, rancher	M	White	−
KY077	Henderson	small city	old	1906	1970	grade school	homemaker	F	White	+
KY078	Henderson	small city	old	1895	1970	high school	homemaker	F	White	−
KY079	Henderson	small city	middle	1912	1970	high school	small business: owner, manager	F	White	+
KY080	Pembroke	rural	old	1915	1970	college	farmer, rancher	M	White	+
KY081	Pembroke	rural	old	1907	1970	grade school	farm woman	F	Black	−
KY082	Pembroke	rural	young	1947	1970	high school	skilled trades	M	Black	−
KY083	Pembroke	rural	old	1904	1970	grade school	farmer, rancher	M	White	−
KY084	Smithland	rural	middle	1919	1970	grade school	laborer	M	White	+
KY085	Hickman	village	old	1899	1970	grade school	farm woman	F	White	+
KY086	Hickman	village	old	1895	1970	grade school	farmer, rancher	M	White	−
KY087	Hickman	village	young	1934	1970	high school	teacher	F	Black	−
KY088	Farmington	rural	old	1907	1970	grade school	farmer, rancher	F	White	−
KY089	Farmington	rural	old	1892	1970	college	homemaker	F	White	−
KY090	Murray	rural	old	1892	1970	grade school	farmer, rancher	M	White	+
KY091	Murray	rural	old	1904	1970	grade school	farmer, rancher	M	White	−
KY092	Hopkinsville	small city	old	1905	1970	college	teacher	M	Black	−
KY093	Hopkinsville	small city	middle	1914	1970	unknown	farmer, rancher	M	Black	+
KY094	Hopkinsville	small city	old	1908	1970	college	librarian	F	Black	+
LA002	Grayson	rural	old	1895	1967	grade school	logging	M	White	+
LA003	St. Francis-ville	village	old	1914	1967	high school	medicine	M	White	+
LA004	St. Francis-ville	village	young	1928	1967	college	teacher	F	White	−
LA006	Clinton	village	old	1895	1967	some schooling	farm woman	F	Black	+
LA007	Clinton	village	old	1891	1967	some schooling	farmer, rancher	M	Black	+
LA008	Lake Providence	rural	middle	1913	1967	high school	laborer	M	Black	+
LA009	Lake Providence	village	old	1894	1967	grade school	domestic, maid	F	Black	−
LA010	Jonesville	rural	old	1897	1967	college	farmer, rancher	M	White	+
LA011	Jonesville	rural	old	1900	1967	college	teacher	F	White	+
LA012	Ruston	small city	old	1879	1967	high school	homemaker	F	White	+
LA013	Ruston	rural	old	1881	1967	high school	teacher	F	White	−
LA014	Natchitoches	small city	middle	1910	1967	college	journalism	M	White	+
LA015	Lecompte	rural	old	1893	1968	grade school	farmer, rancher	M	White	+
LA016	Lecompte	rural	old	1895	1968	grade school	farm woman	F	White	+
LA017	Mansfield	village	young	1938	1968	college	journalism	F	White	+
LA018	Mansfield	rural	old	1898	1968	high school	farmer, rancher	M	White	−
LA019	Mansfield	village	old	1908	1968	high school	homemaker	F	White	−
LA020	Donaldson-ville	rural	old	1901	1968	grade school	foreman, supervisor	M	White	+
LA022	New Orleans	urban	old	1906	1968	grade school	custodial, maintenance	M	Black	+
LA023	Metairie	urban	young	1935	1968	high school	homemaker	F	White	+
LA024	Franklin	village	old	1895	1968	grade school	small business: owner, manager	M	White	−
LA025	Franklin	rural	old	1893	1968	grade school	farm woman	F	White	+

Informant Code	Community	Community Type	Age-group	Year of Birth	Year of Interview	Education	Occupation	Sex	Race	Audio-tape
LA026	Franklin	village	middle	1918	1968	high school	service station operator	M	White	−
LA027	De Quincy	village	old	1888	1968	grade school	police	M	White	+
LA028	De Quincy	village	old	1900	1968	grade school	homemaker	F	White	+
LA029	De Quincy	village	old	1892	1968	some schooling	food services	M	White	+
LA030	De Quincy	village	old	1896	1968	grade school	farmer, rancher	M	White	−
LA031	Cameron	rural	old	1895	1968	college	farmer, rancher	M	White	+
LA032	Cameron	rural	young	1933	1968	high school	homemaker	F	White	+
LA033	St. Martin-ville	village	middle	1909	1968	college	clerical	F	White	+
LA034	St. Martin-ville	village	young	1944	1968	high school	police	M	White	+
LA035	St. Martin-ville	village	middle	1923	1968	college	homemaker	F	White	+
LA037	Grand Isle	village	young	1950	1968	high school	student	M	White	+
LA038	Grand Isle	village	young	1948	1968	high school	clerical	F	White	−
LA039	Grand Isle	village	middle	1918	1968	high school	small business: owner, manager	M	White	
LA040	Hammond	village	old	1888	1968	high school	farmer, rancher	M	White	+
LA041	Hammond	village	old	1905	1968	grade school	homemaker	F	White	−
LA043	New Orleans	urban	young	1931	1968	high school	nautical, fishing	M	White	−
LA044	New Orleans	urban	middle	1919	1968	grade school	factory worker	M	White	−
LA045	New Orleans	urban	middle	1928	1968	grade school	trucking, transportation	M	White	−
LA046	New Orleans	urban	young	1941	1968	high school	skilled trades	M	White	+
ME001	Allagash	rural	old	1887	1966	some schooling	farmer, rancher	M	White	+
ME002	Allagash	rural	old	1877	1966	grade school	homemaker	F	White	+
ME003	Allagash	rural	old	1874	1966	grade school	logging	M	White	−
ME004	Allagash	rural	old	1900	1966	grade school	logging	M	White	−
*ME005	North Ber-wick	rural	old	1883	1966	high school	farmer, rancher	M	White	+
*ME006	North Ber-wick	rural	old	1895	1966	grade school	farmer, rancher	M	White	+
*ME007	North Ber-wick	rural	old	1899	1966	high school	farm woman	F	White	−
ME008	Presque Isle	rural	old	1893	1966	high school	farmer, rancher	M	White	+
ME009	Presque Isle	rural	middle	1908	1966	high school	farmer, rancher	M	White	+
ME010	Bar Harbor	village	old	1897	1966	high school	laborer	M	White	+
ME011	Bar Harbor	village	old	1904	1966	high school	homemaker	F	White	−
ME012	Bar Harbor	village	old	1885	1966	grade school	farmer, rancher	M	White	−
ME013	Bar Harbor	village	old	1900	1966	high school	wholesale, retail sales	M	White	−
*ME014	Rockland	rural	old	1885	1966	grade school	farmer, rancher	M	White	−
*ME015	Rockland	village	middle	1914	1966	high school	homemaker	F	White	−
*ME016	Rockland	village	old	1886	1966	high school	nautical, fishing	M	White	−
*ME019	Augusta	small city	old	1888	1966	high school	skilled trades	M	White	+
*ME020	Augusta	small city	middle	1910	1966	high school	skilled trades	M	White	−
*ME021	Augusta	small city	old	1889	1966	grade school	skilled trades	M	White	−
ME022	Beals	rural	middle	1907	1966	high school	homemaker	F	White	+
ME023	Beals	rural	old	1892	1966	grade school	nautical, fishing	M	White	−
ME024	Beals	rural	middle	1916	1966	high school	nautical, fishing	M	White	−
MD001	Baltimore	large city	old	1877	1968	college	teacher	F	White	+
MD002	Baltimore	large city	middle	1914	1968	high school	clerical	F	White	−
MD003	Baltimore	large city	old	1895	1968	high school	homemaker	F	White	+
MD004	Baltimore	large city	old	1905	1968	grade school	custodial, maintenance	M	White	−
MD005	Baltimore	large city	middle	1926	1968	high school	skilled trades	M	White	−
MD006	Baltimore	large city	old	1907	1968	high school	small business: owner, manager	M	White	−

Informant Code	Community	Community Type	Age-group	Year of Birth	Year of Interview	Education	Occupation	Sex	Race	Audio-tape
MD007	Baltimore	large city	old	1901	1968	college	educational administrator	F	White	−
MD008	Baltimore	large city	middle	1920	1968	high school	homemaker	F	White	+
MD009	Baltimore	large city	old	1908	1968	high school	firefighter	M	White	+
MD010	Baltimore	large city	middle	1918	1968	high school	firefighter	M	White	−
MD011	Baltimore	large city	old	1908	1968	grade school	firefighter	M	White	−
MD012	Leonardtown	village	old	1887	1968	grade school	clerical	F	White	+
MD013	Leonardtown	rural	old	1889	1968	grade school	farmer, rancher	M	White	+
MD014	Annapolis	small city	old	1885	1968	grade school	homemaker	F	White	+
MD015	Annapolis	small city	middle	1913	1968	grade school	local government	M	White	+
MD016	Annapolis	small city	middle	1923	1968	high school	food services	M	White	−
MD017	Deer Park	rural	old	1899	1968	grade school	farm woman	F	White	+
MD018	Oakland	rural	old	1895	1968	grade school	farmer, rancher	M	White	+
MD019	Frederick	rural	old	1901	1968	grade school	farm woman	F	White	+
MD020	Frederick	rural	old	1893	1968	some schooling	farmer, rancher	M	White	+
MD021	Mount Savage	rural	old	1900	1968	some schooling	homemaker	F	White	+
MD022	Frostburg	rural	old	1895	1968	grade school	farmer, rancher	M	White	+
MD023	Frostburg	rural	old	1904	1968	grade school	farm woman	F	White	+
MD024	Oldtown	rural	old	1904	1968	high school	homemaker	F	White	+
MD025	Cumberland	small city	old	1894	1968	grade school	railroad	M	White	+
MD026	Sharpsburg	rural	old	1901	1968	high school	clerical	F	White	+
MD027	Hagerstown	small city	old	1902	1968	grade school	farmer, rancher	M	White	+
MD028	Emmitsburg	village	old	1895	1968	high school	homemaker	F	White	+
MD029	Emmitsburg	rural	old	1901	1968	high school	farmer, rancher	M	White	+
MD030	Westminster	rural	old	1890	1968	college	farmer, rancher	F	White	+
MD031	Westminster	rural	old	1904	1968	grade school	farmer, rancher	M	White	+
MD032	Elkton	village	old	1888	1968	grade school	clerical	M	White	+
MD033	Elkton	village	old	1907	1968	high school	storekeeper	F	White	+
MD034	Chestertown	village	old	1900	1968	high school	farmer, rancher	M	White	+
MD035	Still Pond	rural	old	1896	1968	grade school	homemaker	F	White	+
MD036	Crisfield	village	old	1898	1968	grade school	skilled trades	M	White	+
MD037	Crisfield	village	middle	1923	1968	high school	storekeeper	F	White	+
MD038	Marion Station	rural	old	1895	1968	some schooling	farmer, rancher	M	White	−
MD039	Princess Anne	village	middle	1918	1968	high school	homemaker	F	White	+
MD040	Princess Anne	village	old	1897	1968	grade school	skilled trades	M	White	+
MD041	Oxford	rural	old	1888	1968	high school	homemaker	F	White	+
MD042	Easton	rural	old	1899	1968	grade school	farmer, rancher	M	White	+
MD043	Ewell, Smith Island	village	middle	1913	1968	some schooling	nautical, fishing	M	White	+
MD044	Tylerton	village	middle	1910	1968	grade school	homemaker	F	White	+
MD045	Ewell, Smith Island	village	old	1886	1968	grade school	nautical, fishing	M	White	+
MD046	Rhodes Point	village	old	1903	1968	grade school	homemaker	F	White	−
MD047	Rhodes Point	village	young	1939	1968	high school	homemaker	F	White	−
MD048	Monkton	rural	old	1891	1968	high school	farmer, rancher	M	White	+
MD049	Bel Air	rural	middle	1916	1968	high school	farmer, rancher	M	White	−
MD050	Bel Air	village	old	1892	1968	high school	lodging trades	F	White	+
MA001	Amherst	small city	young	1947	1967	college	student	M	White	+
MA002	Framingham	large city	middle	1926	1967	college	clerical	F	White	+
MA003	Boston (West Roxbury)	urban	young	1931	1967	high school	homemaker	F	White	+

Informant Code	Community	Community Type	Age-group	Year of Birth	Year of Interview	Education	Occupation	Sex	Race	Audio-tape
MA004	Auburn	small city	old	1905	1967	high school	homemaker	F	White	+
MA005	Montague/ North Leverett	rural	old	1884	1967	college	food services	F	White	+
MA006	Prescott	rural	old	1900	1966	grade school	homemaker	F	White	+
MA007	Boston (North End)	urban	middle	1917	1968	grade school	firefighter	M	White	−
MA008	Boston (Roxbury)	urban	young	1935	1967	high school	clerical	F	Black	+
MA009	Boston (Back Bay)	urban	young	1946	1968	college	student	M	White	+
MA010	Waltham	large city	old	1880	1966	college	educational administrator	F	White	+
MA011	Waltham	large city	old	1888	1966	college	skilled trades	M	White	+
MA012	Waltham	large city	old	1888	1966	college	medicine	F	White	+
MA013	Waltham	large city	old	1891	1966	college	medicine	F	White	+
MA014	Sheffield	village	old	1892	1969	grade school	domestic, maid	F	White	+
MA015	Sheffield	village	old	1893	1969	grade school	farmer, rancher	M	White	−
MA016	Dalton	village	old	1893	1969	college	farmer, rancher	M	White	+
MA017	Dalton	village	old	1880	1969	high school	engineer	M	White	−
MA018	Dalton	village	old	1886	1969	high school	farm woman	F	White	−
MA019	Becket	village	middle	1911	1969	high school	farmer, rancher	M	White	−
MA020	Dalton	village	old	1900	1969	high school	homemaker	F	White	−
MA021	Dalton	village	old	1889	1969	college	teacher	F	White	−
MA022	Charlemont	rural	old	1901	1969	high school	storekeeper	M	White	+
MA023	Shelburne Falls	rural	middle	1918	1969	high school	farmer, rancher	M	White	−
MA024	Heath	rural	old	1893	1969	high school	homemaker	F	White	−
MA025	Charlemont	rural	old	1895	1969	grade school	farmer, rancher	M	White	+
MA026	Charlemont	rural	old	1907	1969	high school	skilled trades	M	White	−
MA027	Boston (South Boston)	urban	old	1899	1967	grade school	storekeeper	M	White	+
MA028	Boston (South Boston)	urban	young	1932	1967	high school	police	M	White	+
MA029	Gill	village	old	1885	1969	high school	homemaker	F	White	+
MA030	Gill	village	old	1896	1969	high school	farmer, rancher	M	White	+
MA031	Gill	village	old	1887	1969	high school	storekeeper	M	White	−
MA032	Gill	village	old	1894	1969	high school	farmer, rancher	M	White	+
MA033	Boston (Dorchester)	urban	middle	1927	1967	high school	firefighter	M	White	−
MA034	Boston (Dorchester)	urban	old	1892	1967	high school	homemaker	F	White	+
MA035	Petersham	village	old	1897	1969	grade school	factory worker	M	White	−
MA036	Petersham	village	old	1902	1969	high school	skilled trades	M	White	−
MA037	Petersham	village	old	1889	1969	grade school	farmer, rancher	M	White	+
MA038	Petersham	village	old	1894	1969	high school	homemaker	F	White	+
MA039	Petersham	village	old	1895	1969	high school	homemaker	F	White	−
MA040	New Bedford	large city	old	1886	1969	high school	wholesale, retail sales	M	White	+
MA041	Ludlow	small city	old	1895	1969	high school	postal service	M	White	−
MA042	Ludlow	small city	old	1879	1969	high school	farmer, rancher	M	White	+
MA043	Ludlow	small city	old	1891	1969	high school	homemaker	F	White	−
MA044	Boston (Roslindale)	urban	middle	1924	1967	college	clerical	F	White	+
MA045	Boston (West Roxbury)	urban	old	1902	1967	high school	skilled trades	M	White	−
MA046	South-ampton	village	old	1891	1969	high school	small business: owner, manager	M	White	−

Informant Code	Community	Community Type	Age-group	Year of Birth	Year of Interview	Education	Occupation	Sex	Race	Audio-tape
MA047	South-ampton	village	old	1885	1969	high school	farmer, rancher	M	White	+
MA048	South-ampton	village	old	1892	1969	college	homemaker	F	White	+
MA049	South-ampton	village	old	1895	1969	high school	clerical	F	White	−
MA050	Walpole	small city	old	1907	1967	college	medicine	F	White	+
MA051	Walpole	small city	old	1899	1967	high school	homemaker	F	White	+
MA052	Norwood	small city	old	1900	1967	grade school	skilled trades	M	White	+
MA053	Norwood	small city	middle	1910	1967	high school	barber, beautician	M	White	−
MA054	Norwood	small city	middle	1913	1967	high school	storekeeper	M	White	+
MA055	Chatham	village	old	1881	1969	grade school	small business: owner, manager	M	White	+
MA056	Chatham	village	old	1873	1969	grade school	nautical, fishing	M	White	+
MA057	Chatham	village	old	1893	1969	high school	seamstress	F	White	+
MA058	Colrain	village	old	1893	1969	high school	farmer, rancher	M	White	+
MA059	Gardner	small city	old	1886	1969	college	insurance	M	White	+
MA060	Gardner	small city	old	1896	1969	grade school	homemaker	F	White	−
MA061	Gardner	small city	old	1894	1969	high school	clerical	M	White	−
MA062	Gardner	small city	old	1887	1969	high school	foreman, supervisor	M	White	+
MA063	Gardner	small city	old	1887	1969	high school	homemaker	F	White	−
MA064	Gardner	small city	old	1897	1969	college	homemaker	F	White	−
MA065	Gardner	small city	old	1893	1969	college	homemaker	F	White	−
MA066	Westminster	rural	old	1904	1969	high school	farmer, rancher	M	White	−
MA067	Gardner	small city	old	1887	1969	college	social & community services	F	White	−
MA068	Douglas	village	old	1889	1969	high school	local government	M	White	+
MA069	Douglas	village	old	1892	1969	college	homemaker	F	White	+
MA071	Lynn	large city	old	1903	1967	college	legal	M	White	+
MA072	Lynn	large city	old	1887	1967	unknown	railroad	M	White	−
MA073	Mendon	village	old	1893	1969	college	clerical	F	White	+
MA074	Uxbridge	rural	old	1894	1969	grade school	farmer, rancher	M	White	+
MA075	Weymouth	large city	old	1894	1970	grade school	farmer, rancher	M	White	−
MA076	Weymouth	large city	old	1890	1970	high school	local government	M	White	−
MA077	Weymouth	large city	old	1892	1970	college	clerical	F	White	−
MA078	East Wey-mouth	small city	old	1908	1970	high school	factory worker	M	White	−
MA079	Weymouth	large city	middle	1914	1970	high school	journalism	F	White	+
MA080	Weymouth	large city	old	1900	1970	grade school	storekeeper	M	White	+
MA081	North Wey-mouth	large city	old	1895	1970	college	educational administrator	M	White	−
MA082	South Wey-mouth	small city	old	1884	1967	high school	homemaker	F	White	−
MA083	South Wey-mouth	small city	old	1902	1967	high school	homemaker	F	White	+
MA089	Plymouth	small city	young	1940	1969	college	student	M	Black	+
MA097	Plymouth	small city	old	1905	1970	high school	custodial, maintenance	M	White	+
MA098	Plymouth	small city	old	1908	1970	high school	homemaker	F	White	+
MA099	Plymouth	small city	old	1894	1970	college	administrative, managerial	M	White	+
MA100	Plymouth	small city	old	1893	1970	high school	museum staff	F	White	+
MA106	Plymouth	small city	old	1904	1967	high school	journalist	F	White	+
MA116	Plymouth	small city	old	1895	1967	college	financial services	M	White	+
MA122	Boston (Ja-maica Plain)	urban	middle	1912	1970	college	social & community services	F	Black	+

Informant Code	Community	Community Type	Age-group	Year of Birth	Year of Interview	Education	Occupation	Sex	Race	Audio-tape
MA123	Boston (Mattapan)	urban	middle	1925	1970	college	librarian	M	Black	+
MA124	Boston (Back Bay)	urban	old	1903	1970	college	—	F	Black	—
MA125	Everett	urban	old	1919	1970	college	social & community services	F	Black	—
MA126	Boston (Roxbury)	urban	old	1910	1970	college	teacher	F	Black	—
MA127	Cambridge	large city	young	1942	1970	college	librarian	F	Black	—
MA128	Boston (Roxbury)	urban	middle	1925	1970	high school	social & community services	F	Black	+
MI001	Sault Ste. Marie	small city	old	1890	1966	high school	postal service	F	White	+
MI002	Brimley	rural	old	1896	1966	grade school	farmer, rancher	M	White	+
MI003	Sault Ste. Marie	small city	young	1932	1966	high school	homemaker	F	White	+
MI004	Sault Ste. Marie	small city	old	1897	1966	college	small business: owner, manager	M	White	+
MI005	Brimley	rural	middle	1921	1966	high school	laborer	M	White	—
MI006	Brimley	rural	middle	1911	1966	grade school	homemaker	F	White	—
MI008	Newberry	rural	old	1905	1966	high school	farmer, rancher	M	White	+
MI009	Newberry	village	middle	1911	1966	college	homemaker	F	White	+
MI010	Newberry	village	middle	1920	1966	college	logging	M	White	+
MI011	Munising	village	old	1901	1966	high school	small business: owner, manager	M	White	+
MI012	Limestone	rural	middle	1922	1966	high school	farmer, rancher	M	White	+
MI013	Munising	village	young	1931	1966	high school	homemaker	F	White	+
MI014	Munising	village	old	1892	1966	high school	skilled trades	M	White	+
MI015	Munising	village	middle	1925	1966	college	homemaker	F	White	+
MI016	Munising	village	old	1906	1966	college	homemaker	F	White	+
MI017	Marquette	small city	old	1899	1966	grade school	medicine	F	White	+
MI018	Marquette	small city	young	1940	1966	college	homemaker	F	White	+
MI019	Marquette	small city	middle	1914	1966	grade school	farm woman	F	White	+
MI020	Marquette	small city	old	1899	1966	grade school	miner	M	White	+
MI022	Ishpeming	village	middle	1911	1966	grade school	homemaker	F	White	+
MI023	Ishpeming	rural	old	1901	1966	grade school	farmer, rancher	M	White	+
MI024	Ishpeming	village	old	1894	1966	high school	insurance	M	White	+
MI025	Ishpeming	village	middle	1923	1966	high school	clerical	F	White	+
MI026	Ishpeming	village	old	1903	1966	college	legal	M	White	+
MI027	Gladstone	village	old	1898	1966	grade school	laborer	M	White	+
MI028	Gladstone	village	old	1902	1966	high school	wholesale, retail sales	F	White	+
MI029	Gladstone	village	old	1887	1966	grade school	homemaker	F	White	+
MI030	Gladstone	village	old	1893	1966	grade school	skilled trades	M	White	—
MI031	Gladstone	village	middle	1907	1966	college	educational administrator	M	White	+
MI032	Calumet	village	young	1935	1966	high school	trucking, transportation	M	White	+
MI033	Mohawk	rural	young	1947	1966	college	homemaker	F	White	+
MI034	Mohawk	rural	old	1897	1966	high school	homemaker	F	White	+
MI035	Mohawk	rural	middle	1909	1966	high school	homemaker	F	White	+
MI036	Eagle River	rural	old	1896	1966	grade school	miner	M	White	+
MI037	Eagle River	rural	old	1906	1966	high school	clerical	F	White	—
MI038	Mohawk	rural	old	1900	1966	grade school	skilled trades	M	White	—
MI039	Calumet	village	young	1937	1966	high school	homemaker	F	White	—
MI040	Chassell	rural	middle	1907	1967	college	farmer, rancher	M	White	+
MI041	Houghton	village	old	1898	1967	college	small business: owner, manager	M	White	+

Informant Code	Community	Community Type	Age-group	Year of Birth	Year of Interview	Education	Occupation	Sex	Race	Audio-tape
MI042	Houghton	village	old	1903	1967	college	postal service	M	White	+
MI043	Baltic	rural	middle	1919	1967	high school	homemaker	F	White	+
MI044	Houghton	village	old	1892	1967	high school	wholesale, retail sales	M	White	+
MI045	Ontonagon	village	old	1896	1967	college	teacher	F	White	−
MI046	Ontonagon	village	middle	1908	1967	high school	clerical	F	White	+
MI047	Ontonagon	rural	old	1889	1967	grade school	logging	M	White	+
MI048	Ontonagon	village	old	1903	1967	high school	postal service	F	White	−
MI049	Dexter	rural	old	1905	1967	college	farmer, rancher	M	White	+
MI050	Ann Arbor	small city	old	1897	1967	college	teacher	F	White	+
MI051	Ann Arbor	small city	old	1887	1967	high school	teacher	F	White	+
MI052	St. Ignace	village	old	1906	1967	high school	homemaker	F	White	+
MI053	St. Ignace	village	old	1893	1967	high school	skilled trades	M	White	+
MI054	St. Ignace	village	old	1903	1967	grade school	laborer	M	White	+
MI055	St. Ignace	village	middle	1914	1967	grade school	lodging trades	M	White	+
MI056	Moran	rural	old	1904	1967	grade school	farmer, rancher	M	White	+
MI061	Romeo	village	old	1902	1967	high school	homemaker	F	White	+
MI062	Romeo	village	old	1907	1967	high school	homemaker	F	White	+
MI063	Romeo	village	old	1906	1967	high school	farmer, rancher	M	White	−
MI064	Romeo	village	old	1880	1967	high school	farmer, rancher	M	White	−
MI065	Walled Lake	village	old	1887	1967	grade school	farmer, rancher	M	White	+
MI066	Walled Lake	village	old	1898	1967	high school	homemaker	F	White	+
MI067	Detroit	urban	old	1899	1967	college	teacher	F	White	+
MI068	Detroit	urban	old	1891	1967	college	homemaker	F	White	+
MI069	Detroit	urban	middle	1923	1967	college	homemaker	F	White	+
MI070	Detroit	urban	young	1943	1967	college	medicine	F	White	+
MI071	Wayne	small city	old	1885	1967	grade school	skilled trades	M	White	+
MI072	Detroit	urban	middle	1926	1967	high school	clerical	F	Black	+
MI073	Bloomfield Hills	village	middle	1921	1967	college	engineer	M	White	−
MI074	Bad Axe	village	young	1947	1968	high school	clerical	F	White	−
MI075	Bad Axe	village	middle	1920	1968	college	social & community services	F	White	−
MI076	Bad Axe	village	old	1895	1968	high school	museum staff	M	White	+
MI077	Port Sanilac	rural	old	1905	1968	high school	homemaker	F	White	−
MI078	Port Sanilac	rural	old	1895	1968	high school	farm woman	F	White	−
MI079	Port Sanilac	rural	old	1903	1968	college	homemaker	F	White	−
MI080	Port Sanilac	rural	old	1903	1968	high school	storekeeper	M	White	+
MI081	Owosso	small city	old	1887	1968	high school	homemaker	F	White	+
MI082	Owosso	small city	old	1887	1968	high school	homemaker	F	White	−
MI083	Owosso	rural	middle	1912	1968	high school	farmer, rancher	M	White	−
MI084	Battle Creek	small city	old	1880	1968	high school	financial services	M	White	+
MI085	Battle Creek	small city	middle	1915	1968	college	homemaker	F	White	−
MI086	Battle Creek	small city	middle	1920	1968	high school	storekeeper	F	White	−
MI087	Battle Creek	small city	old	1885	1968	grade school	homemaker	F	White	−
MI088	Battle Creek	small city	middle	1922	1968	high school	food services	F	White	−
MI089	Battle Creek	small city	middle	1916	1968	high school	homemaker	F	Black	−
MI090	Battle Creek	small city	old	1906	1968	college	teacher	F	White	−
MI091	Dowagiac	village	young	1932	1969	college	small business: owner, manager	M	White	+
MI092	Dowagiac	village	old	1891	1969	college	educational administrator	F	White	+
MI093	Frankenmuth	village	old	1895	1969	college	teacher	M	White	+
MI094	Cadillac	small city	old	1900	1968	college	medicine	F	White	−

Informant Code	Community	Community Type	Age-group	Year of Birth	Year of Interview	Education	Occupation	Sex	Race	Audio-tape
MI095	Mount Pleasant	small city	old	1896	1968	high school	homemaker	F	White	−
MI096	Buckley	rural	old	1888	1968	college	medicine	F	White	+
MI097	Buckley	rural	middle	1914	1968	high school	storekeeper	M	White	−
MI098	Interlochen	rural	old	1899	1968	grade school	food services	F	White	−
MI099	Interlochen	rural	old	1894	1968	grade school	custodial, maintenance	M	White	−
MI100	Pentwater	village	old	1892	1969	college	teacher	F	White	+
MI101	Pentwater	village	old	1904	1969	high school	skilled trades	M	White	+
MI102	Holland	small city	middle	1917	1969	high school	clerical	F	White	+
MI103	Holland	small city	old	1904	1969	college	artist, craftsman	M	White	+
MI104	West Branch	village	middle	1912	1969	college	homemaker	F	White	+
MI105	West Branch	village	old	1895	1969	college	local government	F	White	+
MI106	Onaway	village	old	1881	1969	grade school	logging	M	White	−
MI107	Onaway	village	middle	1912	1969	college	teacher	F	White	+
MI108	Manistee	village	old	1904	1969	college	librarian	F	White	+
MI109	Saugatuck	village	old	1897	1969	high school	skilled trades	M	White	+
MI110	Saugatuck	village	old	1899	1969	high school	homemaker	F	White	+
MI111	Hillsdale	village	old	1892	1970	college	teacher	F	White	−
MI112	Hillsdale	village	middle	1914	1970	grade school	custodial, maintenance	M	White	+
MI113	Hillsdale	village	old	1910	1970	college	small business: owner, manager	M	White	+
MI114	Hillsdale	rural	middle	1921	1970	high school	homemaker	F	White	−
MI115	Howell	village	old	1883	1970	college	legal	M	White	+
MI116	Howell	rural	middle	1922	1970	high school	farmer, rancher	M	White	+
MI117	Howell	rural	young	1940	1970	college	medicine	F	White	−
MI118	Gaylord	village	young	1944	1970	high school	skilled trades	M	White	−
MI119	Gaylord	village	old	1905	1970	college	teacher	F	White	−
MI120	Gaylord	rural	middle	1920	1970	grade school	skilled trades	M	White	+
MI122	Grand Rapids	large city	middle	1916	1970	college	librarian	F	White	+
MI123	Grand Rapids	large city	young	1940	1970	college	librarian	M	White	−
MN001	Virginia	small city	middle	1910	1967	high school	postal service	M	White	+
MN002	Virginia	small city	middle	1908	1967	high school	barber, beautician	F	White	+
MN003	Baudette	village	old	1889	1967	college	clerical	F	White	+
MN004	Baudette	rural	middle	1917	1967	high school	farmer, rancher	M	White	+
MN005	Baudette	village	middle	1910	1967	college	storekeeper	M	White	−
MN006	Moorhead	small city	middle	1915	1967	college	librarian	F	White	+
MN007	Moorhead	rural	old	1905	1967	high school	farmer, rancher	M	White	+
MN008	Moorhead	rural	old	1896	1967	high school	farmer, rancher	M	White	+
MN009	Moorhead	rural	old	1897	1967	high school	farmer, rancher	M	White	−
MN010	Two Harbors	village	old	1898	1967	college	storekeeper	M	White	+
MN011	Two Harbors	village	old	1907	1967	college	teacher	F	White	+
MN012	Harmony	rural	old	1883	1968	grade school	farmer, rancher	M	White	+
MN013	Harmony	rural	old	1891	1968	grade school	farm woman	F	White	+
MN014	Grand Marais	rural	old	1886	1968	grade school	ranger, guide	M	White	−
MN015	Grand Marais	rural	old	1906	1968	grade school	farmer, rancher	M	White	+
MN016	Newfolden	rural	middle	1918	1968	high school	farmer, rancher	M	White	+
MN017	Taylors Falls	rural	old	1889	1968	grade school	farmer, rancher	F	White	−
MN018	Taylors Falls	rural	old	1906	1968	high school	skilled trades	M	White	−
MN019	Taylors Falls	rural	old	1896	1968	college	postal service	M	White	+
MN020	Taylors Falls	rural	old	1887	1968	high school	librarian	F	White	−

Informant Code	Community	Community Type	Age-group	Year of Birth	Year of Interview	Education	Occupation	Sex	Race	Audio-tape
MN021	Taylors Falls	rural	middle	1924	1968	high school	storekeeper	M	White	−
MN022	Red Wing	small city	old	1904	1968	high school	homemaker	F	White	−
MN023	Red Wing	rural	old	1891	1968	grade school	farmer, rancher	M	White	−
MN024	Red Wing	small city	old	1905	1968	high school	local government	M	White	−
MN025	Red Wing	small city	middle	1925	1968	college	postal service	M	White	−
MN026	Red Wing	small city	old	1898	1968	college	librarian	F	White	−
MN028	Bemidji	small city	young	1944	1968	college	teacher	F	White	+
MN029	Aitkin	village	old	1888	1968	grade school	journalism	M	White	+
MN030	Aitkin	village	old	1896	1968	high school	homemaker	F	White	−
MN031	Aitkin	rural	old	1900	1968	grade school	farmer, rancher	M	White	−
MN032	Aitkin	village	old	1896	1968	high school	homemaker	F	White	−
MN033	Little Falls	village	middle	1914	1968	high school	homemaker	F	White	+
MN034	Elbow Lake	village	young	1932	1968	high school	homemaker	F	White	+
MN035	Elbow Lake	village	middle	1916	1968	high school	wholesale, retail sales	M	White	−
MN036	New Ulm	village	old	1894	1968	college	medicine	M	White	+
MN037	New Ulm	village	old	1898	1968	high school	teacher	F	White	−
MN038	Pipestone	village	old	1891	1968	college	financial services	M	White	+
MN039	Pipestone	village	old	1891	1968	high school	homemaker	F	White	−
MN040	Pipestone	rural	old	1887	1968	grade school	farmer, rancher	M	White	−
MN041	Pipestone	village	old	1898	1968	high school	homemaker	F	White	−
MN042	Watson	rural	middle	1927	1968	grade school	food services	F	White	+
*MS001	Taylor	village	middle	1906	1965	grade school	skilled trades	M	White	+
*MS002	Lincoln Co.	rural	old	1901	1966	grade school	farmer, rancher	M	White	−
*MS003	Johnson's Station	rural	middle	1914	1966	high school	farm woman	F	White	−
*MS004	McComb	small city	old	1891	1966	grade school	clerical	M	White	−
*MS005	McComb	small city	middle	1913	1966	high school	religion	M	White	−
*MS006	McComb	small city	old	1891	1966	high school	homemaker	F	White	−
*MS007	Hattiesburg	small city	old	1888	1966	college	teacher	F	White	−
*MS008	Hattiesburg	small city	middle	1917	1966	high school	homemaker	F	White	−
*MS009	Hattiesburg	rural	old	1904	1966	grade school	farmer, rancher	M	White	−
*MS010	Hattiesburg	small city	old	1889	1966	high school	homemaker	F	White	−
*MS011	Hattiesburg	small city	old	1904	1966	high school	custodial, maintenance	M	Black	−
*MS012	Hattiesburg	small city	old	1891	1966	grade school	homemaker	F	White	−
*MS013	Hattiesburg	small city	old	1897	1966	some schooling	domestic, maid	F	Black	−
*MS014	Hattiesburg	small city	middle	1909	1966	college	homemaker	F	White	+
*MS015	Vicksburg	small city	old	1883	1966	high school	teacher	F	White	+
*MS016	Vicksburg	rural	old	1895	1966	grade school	farm woman	F	White	−
*MS017	Vicksburg	small city	middle	1909	1966	high school	storekeeper	F	White	−
*MS018	Vicksburg	small city	old	1897	1966	high school	storekeeper	F	White	−
*MS019	Vicksburg	rural	old	1899	1966	high school	farmer, rancher	M	White	−
*MS020	Deasonville	rural	old	1905	1966	high school	farmer, rancher	M	White	−
*MS021	Vaughan	rural	old	1894	1966	high school	storekeeper	M	White	−
*MS022	Deasonville	rural	old	1877	1966	unknown	homemaker	F	White	+
*MS023	Deasonville	rural	old	1894	1966	high school	teacher	F	White	+
*MS024	Vaughan	rural	middle	1914	1966	grade school	farmer, rancher	F	Black	−
*MS025	Grenada	village	young	1940	1965	college	insurance	M	White	−
*MS026	Grenada	village	old	1894	1965	college	homemaker	F	White	−
*MS027	Grenada	village	old	1875	1965	college	homemaker	F	White	−
*MS028	Grenada	rural	old	1887	1965	some schooling	farmer, rancher	M	White	−
*MS029	Grenada	village	old	1896	1965	some schooling	homemaker	F	White	−
*MS030	Holcomb	rural	old	1883	1965	grade school	farm woman	F	White	−

Informant Code	Community	Community Type	Age-group	Year of Birth	Year of Interview	Education	Occupation	Sex	Race	Audio-tape
*MS031	Holcomb	rural	old	1885	1965	high school	farmer, rancher	M	White	−
*MS032	Natchez	small city	old	1883	1966	high school	clerical	M	White	−
*MS033	Natchez	small city	old	1902	1966	high school	homemaker	F	White	−
*MS034	Natchez	rural	old	1899	1966	some schooling	farmer, rancher	M	Black	−
*MS035	Natchez	small city	old	1894	1966	grade school	clerical	M	White	−
*MS036	Natchez	small city	old	1905	1966	college	unemployed	F	White	−
*MS037	Natchez	small city	old	1906	1966	college	teacher	F	White	−
*MS038	Pine Ridge	rural	old	1894	1966	high school	homemaker	F	White	−
*MS039	Natchez	small city	old	1893	1966	college	librarian	F	White	−
*MS040	Natchez	rural	old	1895	1966	high school	farmer, rancher	M	White	−
*MS041	Natchez	small city	old	1902	1966	high school	clerical	M	White	−
*MS042	Natchez	small city	middle	1913	1966	college	teacher	F	White	+
*MS043	Starkville	small city	middle	1923	1966	grade school	custodial, maintenance	M	Black	−
*MS044	Starkville	rural	old	1896	1966	grade school	farmer, rancher	M	Black	−
*MS045	Starkville	small city	middle	1913	1966	grade school	domestic, maid	F	Black	+
*MS046	Starkville	small city	old	1878	1966	grade school	homemaker	F	Black	−
*MS047	Starkville	small city	middle	1914	1966	grade school	custodial, maintenance	M	Black	−
*MS048	Columbus	small city	old	1894	1966	college	homemaker	F	White	−
*MS049	Columbus	small city	old	1875	1966	college	unemployed	F	White	−
*MS050	Columbus	small city	old	1896	1966	college	homemaker	F	White	−
*MS051	Columbus	small city	young	1932	1966	college	homemaker	F	White	−
*MS052	Columbus	small city	middle	1917	1966	college	administrative, managerial	M	White	−
*MS053	Artesia	rural	middle	1916	1966	college	homemaker	F	White	−
*MS054	Columbus	village	old	1892	1966	college	homemaker	F	White	−
*MS055	Iuka	rural	old	1897	1965	grade school	homemaker	F	White	−
*MS056	Iuka	rural	old	1896	1965	some schooling	farmer, rancher	M	White	+
*MS057	Iuka	rural	old	1900	1965	some schooling	homemaker	F	White	−
*MS058	Iuka	rural	old	1894	1965	some schooling	farmer, rancher	M	White	−
*MS059	Iuka	village	old	1884	1965	high school	railroad	M	White	−
*MS060	Holly Springs	village	middle	1916	1965	grade school	domestic, maid	F	Black	−
*MS061	Oxford	village	old	1895	1965	some schooling	skilled trades	M	Black	+
*MS062	Holly Springs	village	middle	1906	1965	unknown	custodial, maintenance	M	Black	−
*MS063	Durant	rural	old	1881	1965	grade school	farmer, rancher	M	White	−
*MS064	Durant	village	old	1898	1965	high school	laborer	M	White	−
*MS065	Meridian	small city	old	1894	1966	high school	homemaker	F	White	−
*MS066	Meridian	rural	old	1876	1966	some schooling	farm woman	F	White	−
*MS067	Meridian	small city	old	1889	1966	high school	homemaker	F	White	−
*MS068	Meridian	small city	old	1888	1966	grade school	homemaker	F	White	+
*MS069	Meridian	small city	middle	1913	1966	high school	homemaker	F	White	−
*MS070	Meridian	small city	old	1886	1966	grade school	homemaker	F	White	−
*MS071	Picayune	village	old	1882	1966	unknown	police	M	White	+
*MS072	Picayune	village	old	1887	1966	grade school	homemaker	F	White	+
*MS073	Gautier	village	old	1899	1966	high school	artist, craftsman	F	White	+
*MS074	Gautier	rural	old	1901	1966	some schooling	farmer, rancher	M	White	−
MS079	Jackson	small city	old	1905	1970	high school	skilled trades	F	Black	+
MS080	Jackson	small city	middle	1925	1970	high school	domestic, maid	F	Black	−
MS081	Jackson	small city	middle	1925	1970	college	teacher	M	Black	+
MS082	Jackson	small city	old	1904	1970	high school	medicine	F	Black	−
MS083	Jackson	small city	middle	1927	1970	high school	barber, beautician	F	Black	−
MS084	Jackson	small city	young	1945	1970	college	clerical	F	Black	−
MS085	Mound Bayou	village	middle	1913	1970	high school	clerical	F	Black	−

Informant Code	Community	Community Type	Age-group	Year of Birth	Year of Interview	Education	Occupation	Sex	Race	Audio-tape
MS086	Mound Bayou	village	old	1897	1970	high school	clerical	F	Black	+
MS087	Mound Bayou	rural	old	1889	1970	grade school	farmer, rancher	M	Black	−
MS088	Mound Bayou	village	old	1893	1970	college	surveyor	M	Black	−
MS089	Mound Bayou	village	old	1898	1970	high school	small business: owner, manager	M	Black	−
MS090	Mound Bayou	village	old	1896	1970	college	farmer, rancher	F	Black	−
MO001	Lancaster	rural	old	1893	1966	grade school	lodging trades	F	White	+
MO002	Bethany	village	middle	1922	1967	high school	clerical	F	White	+
MO003	Arrow Rock	rural	old	1906	1967	high school	farmer, rancher	M	White	+
MO004	Cape Girardeau	small city	old	1882	1968	grade school	homemaker	F	White	+
MO005	Cameron	rural	old	1897	1967	high school	farmer, rancher	M	White	+
MO006	Carthage	small city	old	1884	1969	high school	homemaker	F	White	+
MO007	Clarksville	rural	middle	1916	1967	high school	homemaker	F	White	+
MO008	Columbia	small city	old	1897	1967	grade school	domestic, maid	F	Black	+
MO009	Cooter	rural	old	1895	1968	grade school	homemaker	F	White	+
MO010	Frederick-town	village	old	1898	1968	grade school	real estate	F	White	+
MO011	Harrisonville	rural	middle	1917	1967	high school	farmer, rancher	M	White	+
MO012	Hermann	village	middle	1908	1967	high school	storekeeper	F	White	+
MO013	Independence	small city	old	1899	1967	high school	administrative, managerial	M	White	+
MO014	Kansas City	urban	young	1945	1967	college	student	M	White	+
MO015	Nevada	village	old	1907	1969	high school	wholesale, retail sales	F	White	+
MO016	Old Mines	rural	middle	1909	1968	grade school	trucking, transportation	M	White	+
MO017	Portageville	rural	old	1891	1968	grade school	farmer, rancher	M	White	+
MO018	Shelbina	rural	middle	1927	1967	high school	farmer, rancher	M	White	+
MO019	Rolla	rural	old	1900	1969	grade school	farmer, rancher	M	White	+
MO020	Springfield	small city	middle	1919	1969	high school	food services	F	White	+
MO021	St. Charles	rural	old	1900	1967	grade school	farmer, rancher	M	White	+
MO022	New Madrid	village	old	1901	1970	college	teacher	F	Black	+
MO023	New Madrid	village	middle	1926	1970	grade school	homemaker	F	Black	+
MO024	New Madrid	village	old	1905	1970	grade school	skilled trades	M	Black	−
MO025	Ste. Genevieve	village	old	1905	1968	high school	homemaker	F	White	+
MO026	University City	village	young	1944	1967	college	student	M	White	+
MO027	St. Joseph	small city	middle	1925	1969	high school	firefighter	M	White	+
MO029	St. Louis	large city	middle	1927	1970	college	artist, craftsman	F	Black	+
MO030	St. Louis	large city	young	1945	1970	college	clerical	F	Black	−
MO032	Versailles	rural	middle	1915	1969	high school	homemaker	F	White	+
MO033	Versailles	rural	middle	1912	1969	grade school	farmer, rancher	M	White	−
MO034	Ellsinore	rural	middle	1912	1968	grade school	homemaker	F	White	+
MO035	West Plains	village	middle	1918	1968	high school	wholesale, retail sales	M	White	+
MO036	Washington	village	old	1906	1968	high school	seamstress	F	White	+
MO037	Waynesville	village	old	1902	1969	grade school	homemaker	F	White	+
MO038	Hannibal	rural	old	1887	1967	grade school	farmer, rancher	M	White	+
MO039	Purdy	rural	old	1906	1969	grade school	farmer, rancher	M	White	+
MT001	Walkerville	village	old	1901	1966	grade school	miner	M	White	+
MT002	Bozeman	small city	old	1887	1966	high school	local government	M	White	+
MT003	Shelby	village	old	1903	1966	college	small business: owner, manager	M	White	+

Informant Code	Community	Community Type	Age-group	Year of Birth	Year of Interview	Education	Occupation	Sex	Race	Audio-tape
MT004	Rollins	rural	old	1901	1966	grade school	storekeeper	M	White	+
MT005	Roundup	rural	old	1896	1966	grade school	farmer, rancher	M	White	+
NE001	Bassett	village	old	1907	1967	grade school	insurance	M	White	+
NE002	Bassett	village	middle	1910	1967	college	librarian	F	White	+
NE003	Aurora	village	old	1897	1967	college	agricultural services	F	White	+
NE004	Chadron	village	old	1906	1967	college	medicine	F	White	+
NE005	Chadron	village	old	1901	1967	high school	homemaker	F	White	+
NE006	Scottsbluff	small city	old	1903	1967	college	homemaker	F	White	+
NE007	Scottsbluff	small city	old	1905	1967	high school	homemaker	F	White	+
NE008	Madison	village	middle	1908	1967	high school	homemaker	F	White	+
NE009	Nebraska City	village	old	1906	1967	college	homemaker	F	White	+
NE010	Mullen	rural	middle	1915	1967	college	social & community services	F	White	+
NE011	Cambridge	village	middle	1922	1967	college	engineer	F	White	+
NV001	Winnemucca	rural	old	1889	1967	grade school	farmer, rancher	M	White	+
NV002	Winnemucca	rural	old	1885	1967	grade school	farmer, rancher	M	White	+
NV003	Winnemucca	village	young	1937	1967	college	homemaker	F	White	−
NV004	Winnemucca	village	middle	1923	1967	high school	small business: owner, manager	M	White	−
NV005	Winnemucca	rural	old	1890	1967	grade school	farm woman	F	White	−
NV006	Carson City	small city	old	1887	1968	college	legal	M	White	−
NV007	Carson City	small city	old	1898	1968	high school	clerical	F	White	−
NV008	Carson City	rural	old	1885	1968	some schooling	farmer, rancher	M	White	+
NV009	Carson City	rural	old	1906	1968	high school	farm woman	F	White	−
NH001	Jaffrey	village	middle	1910	1966	grade school	custodial, maintenance	M	White	−
NH002	Jaffrey	village	middle	1914	1966	grade school	laborer	M	White	−
NH003	Jaffrey	rural	old	1899	1966	grade school	farmer, rancher	M	White	−
NH004	Jaffrey	village	old	1890	1966	grade school	lodging trades	M	White	+
NH005	Lebanon	rural	old	1886	1966	high school	farmer, rancher	M	White	+
NH006	Lebanon	village	old	1898	1966	grade school	homemaker	F	White	−
NH007	Lebanon	village	middle	1907	1966	high school	wholesale, retail sales	M	White	−
NH010	Concord	small city	old	1905	1966	high school	wholesale, retail sales	M	White	−
NH011	Concord	small city	old	1881	1966	grade school	homemaker	F	White	−
NH012	Concord	small city	old	1895	1966	grade school	laborer	M	White	−
NH013	Concord	small city	middle	1910	1966	grade school	factory worker	M	White	−
NH014	Berlin	small city	middle	1916	1968	grade school	logging	M	White	+
NH015	Berlin	small city	middle	1922	1968	high school	homemaker	F	White	−
NH016	Seabrook	village	old	1892	1969	grade school	skilled trades	M	White	−
NH017	Seabrook	village	middle	1915	1969	high school	librarian	F	White	+
NH018	Seabrook	village	young	1939	1969	high school	laborer	M	White	+
NJ001	Newton	village	old	1889	1967	high school	railroad	M	White	+
NJ002	Washington	village	old	1900	1967	college	teacher	F	White	+
NJ003	Blairstown	rural	old	1895	1967	grade school	homemaker	F	White	+
NJ004	Rockaway	village	old	1897	1967	high school	clerical	F	White	+
NJ005	Montague	rural	old	1908	1968	college	teacher	F	White	+
NJ006	Montague	rural	old	1902	1968	grade school	farmer, rancher	M	White	+
NJ007	Montague	rural	old	1897	1968	high school	laborer	F	White	+
NJ008	Andover	rural	old	1889	1968	high school	clerical	M	White	+
NJ009	Long Valley	village	old	1889	1968	grade school	homemaker	F	White	+
NJ010	Long Valley	rural	young	1930	1968	high school	homemaker	F	White	+
NJ011	Mendham	village	old	1896	1968	college	medicine	F	White	+
NJ012	Mendham	village	middle	1910	1968	high school	wholesale, retail sales	F	White	+

Informant Code	Community	Community Type	Age-group	Year of Birth	Year of Interview	Education	Occupation	Sex	Race	Audio-tape
NJ013	Mendham	village	old	1902	1968	college	teacher	F	White	+
NJ014	Mendham	village	old	1889	1968	high school	homemaker	F	White	−
NJ015	Salem	village	old	1893	1968	high school	clerical	F	White	+
NJ016	Salem	village	old	1908	1968	high school	farmer, rancher	M	White	−
NJ017	Swedesboro	rural	old	1896	1968	grade school	farmer, rancher	M	White	+
NJ018	Swedesboro	village	old	1900	1968	grade school	police	M	White	+
NJ019	Newark	urban	old	1897	1968	high school	unemployed	F	White	+
NJ020	Greenwich	rural	old	1888	1968	college	homemaker	F	White	+
NJ021	Greenwich	rural	old	1904	1968	grade school	trucking, transportation	M	White	+
NJ022	Cape May Court House	village	old	−	1968	grade school	small business: owner, manager	M	White	+
NJ023	Cape May Court House	village	young	1939	1968	college	medicine	F	White	+
NJ024	Cape May Court House	village	−	−	1968	high school	homemaker	F	White	−
NJ025	Carlstadt	village	old	1892	1968	grade school	journalism	M	White	+
NJ026	Carlstadt	village	middle	1923	1968	high school	small business: owner, manager	F	White	+
NJ027	Carlstadt	village	old	1899	1968	high school	financial services	M	White	+
NJ028	Butler	village	old	1892	1968	high school	foreman, supervisor	M	White	+
NJ029	Butler	village	old	1898	1968	college	social & community services	F	White	−
NJ030	Maplewood	small city	middle	1911	1968	college	teacher	F	White	+
NJ031	Mays Land-ing	village	old	1898	1968	unknown	laborer	M	White	+
NJ032	Mays Land-ing	village	old	1897	1968	high school	homemaker	F	White	+
NJ033	Mays Land-ing	village	old	1900	1968	high school	clerical	M	White	+
NJ034	Mays Land-ing	village	young	1939	1968	high school	homemaker	F	White	+
NJ035	Bound Brook	small city	old	1904	1968	high school	postal service	M	White	+
NJ036	Bound Brook	small city	old	1890	1968	college	insurance	M	White	+
NJ037	Bound Brook	small city	old	1891	1968	grade school	homemaker	F	White	−
NJ038	Bound Brook	small city	old	1892	1968	college	homemaker	F	White	−
NJ039	Port Repub-lic	rural	old	1904	1968	high school	logging	M	White	+
NJ040	Port Repub-lic	rural	old	1904	1968	high school	homemaker	F	White	+
NJ041	Ringwood	village	old	1895	1968	high school	miner	M	White	+
NJ042	Ringwood	village	old	1896	1968	high school	financial services	F	White	+
NJ043	Ringwood	village	old	1900	1968	college	teacher	F	White	−
NJ044	Ringwood	village	young	1932	1968	high school	trucking, transportation	M	White	−
NJ045	Flemington	village	middle	1910	1968	high school	homemaker	F	White	+
NJ046	Flemington	village	old	1898	1968	college	homemaker	F	White	−
NJ047	Flemington	rural	old	1892	1968	high school	homemaker	F	White	+
NJ048	Pennington	village	old	1895	1968	college	logging	M	White	−
NJ049	Pennington	village	old	1895	1968	college	clerical	F	White	−
NJ050	Pennington	village	old	1889	1968	some schooling	logging	M	White	+
NJ051	Chatsworth	rural	old	1892	1968	grade school	ranger, guide	M	White	+
NJ052	Chatsworth	rural	old	1891	1968	grade school	logging	M	White	+
NJ053	Chatsworth	rural	old	1887	1968	grade school	wholesale, retail sales	M	White	+
NJ054	Mount Holly	small city	middle	1917	1969	college	storekeeper	M	White	+
NJ055	Barnegat	rural	old	1897	1969	college	insurance	M	White	+
NJ056	Collingswood	small city	old	1887	1969	high school	skilled trades	M	White	+

Informant Code	Community	Community Type	Age-group	Year of Birth	Year of Interview	Education	Occupation	Sex	Race	Audio-tape
NJ057	Collingswood	small city	old	1899	1969	high school	teacher	F	White	−
NJ058	Glassboro	small city	old	1909	1969	college	teacher	F	White	−
NJ059	Glassboro	small city	middle	1929	1969	high school	skilled trades	F	White	−
NJ060	Glassboro	small city	middle	1911	1969	grade school	firefighter	M	White	+
NJ061	Glassboro	small city	old	1883	1969	college	teacher	F	White	−
NJ063	Madison	small city	old	1905	1970	high school	storekeeper	M	White	−
NJ064	Chatham	village	old	1888	1970	high school	local government	M	White	+
NJ065	Madison	rural	old	1885	1970	high school	farmer, rancher	M	White	+
NJ066	Madison	small city	old	1890	1970	high school	homemaker	F	White	−
NJ067	Asbury Park	small city	old	1898	1970	grade school	lodging trades	F	Black	+
NJ068	Asbury Park	small city	old	1909	1970	grade school	domestic, maid	F	Black	+
NJ069	Trenton	large city	old	1906	1970	some schooling	laborer	M	Black	+
NJ070	Trenton	large city	middle	1924	1970	college	social & community services	M	Black	+
*NM001	Roswell	rural	middle	1908	1966	grade school	farm woman	F	White	−
*NM002	Roswell	rural	old	1885	1966	grade school	homemaker	F	White	+
*NM003	Roswell	rural	old	1895	1966	grade school	farmer, rancher	M	White	+
*NM004	Roswell	rural	middle	1912	1966	grade school	homemaker	F	White	−
*NM005	Las Vegas	small city	old	1896	1966	high school	homemaker	F	White	+
*NM006	Las Vegas	small city	old	1892	1966	grade school	postal service	M	White	+
*NM007	Las Vegas	small city	old	1894	1966	high school	homemaker	F	White	+
*NM008	Kirtland	rural	old	1903	1966	grade school	homemaker	F	White	+
*NM009	Kirtland	rural	old	1901	1966	grade school	homemaker	F	White	+
*NM010	Kirtland	rural	old	1898	1966	grade school	farmer, rancher	M	White	−
*NM011	Silver City	village	old	1897	1966	grade school	social & community services	M	White	−
*NM012	Silver City	village	old	1886	1966	high school	homemaker	F	White	+
*NM013	Silver City	rural	old	1891	1966	grade school	farmer, rancher	M	White	+
NY001	Pottersville	rural	middle	1913	1967	college	unemployed	M	White	+
NY002	Gloversville	small city	old	1894	1967	grade school	artist, craftsman	M	White	+
NY003	Old Forge	rural	old	1888	1967	high school	storekeeper	M	White	−
NY004	Old Forge	rural	old	1889	1967	high school	farmer, rancher	M	White	+
NY005	Old Forge	rural	old	1895	1967	high school	ranger, guide	M	White	−
NY006	Old Forge	rural	middle	1916	1967	high school	ranger, guide	M	White	−
NY007	Old Forge	rural	young	1945	1967	college	administrative, managerial	F	White	+
NY008	Ogdensburg	small city	old	1882	1967	grade school	wholesale, retail sales	M	White	−
NY009	Ogdensburg	small city	old	1896	1967	grade school	factory worker	M	White	−
NY010	Ogdensburg	small city	old	1890	1967	high school	wholesale, retail sales	M	White	−
NY011	Sackets Harbor	village	old	1886	1967	high school	postal service	M	White	−
NY012	Sackets Harbor	village	old	1889	1967	college	teacher	F	White	−
NY013	Sackets Harbor	rural	middle	1918	1967	high school	farmer, rancher	M	White	−
NY014	Sackets Harbor	village	old	1886	1967	grade school	homemaker	F	White	−
NY018	Hogansburg	rural	young	1932	1967	high school	homemaker	F	White	−
NY019	Hogansburg	rural	old	1905	1967	some schooling	trucking, transportation	M	White	−
NY020	Hogansburg	rural	old	1902	1967	high school	homemaker	F	White	−
NY021	Upper Jay	rural	old	1878	1967	high school	librarian	F	White	−
NY022	Upper Jay	rural	old	1903	1967	high school	teacher	F	White	−
NY023	Upper Jay	rural	old	1902	1967	high school	wholesale, retail sales	M	White	−
NY024	Plattsburgh	small city	old	1880	1967	some schooling	skilled trades	M	White	−

Informant Code	Community	Community Type	Age-group	Year of Birth	Year of Interview	Education	Occupation	Sex	Race	Audio-tape
NY025	Plattsburgh	small city	young	1929	1967	college	social & community services	F	White	+
NY026	Plattsburgh	rural	middle	1915	1967	high school	farmer, rancher	M	White	+
NY027	Chateaugay	rural	old	1896	1967	grade school	farmer, rancher	M	White	+
NY028	Chateaugay	rural	middle	1919	1967	high school	homemaker	F	White	+
NY029	Chateaugay	rural	young	1929	1967	college	religion	M	White	−
NY030	Potsdam	village	old	1899	1967	college	librarian	F	White	+
NY031	Potsdam	village	old	1888	1967	college	religion	M	White	−
NY032	Potsdam	rural	old	1887	1967	some schooling	farmer, rancher	M	White	+
NY033	Potsdam	village	old	1897	1967	high school	teacher	F	White	−
NY034	Brooklyn	urban	old	1904	1967	college	librarian	F	White	+
NY035	Brooklyn	urban	old	1904	1967	high school	clerical	F	White	+
NY036	Brooklyn	urban	old	1904	1968	high school	foreman, supervisor	M	White	+
NY037	Brooklyn	urban	old	1899	1968	high school	clerical	M	White	+
NY038	Brooklyn	urban	old	1908	1968	college	unemployed	F	White	+
NY039	Brooklyn	urban	middle	1911	1968	grade school	homemaker	F	White	+
NY040	Brooklyn	urban	middle	1919	1968	high school	skilled trades	M	White	+
NY041	Brooklyn	urban	old	1898	1968	high school	homemaker	F	White	+
NY042	Brooklyn	urban	old	1903	1968	college	financial services	M	White	+
NY043	Brooklyn	urban	old	1877	1968	grade school	teacher	F	White	+
NY044	Brooklyn	urban	middle	1912	1968	high school	insurance	M	White	+
NY045	Brooklyn	urban	old	1898	1968	college	homemaker	F	White	+
NY046	Brooklyn	urban	middle	1918	1968	college	clerical	F	White	+
NY047	Brooklyn	urban	middle	1918	1968	unknown	nautical, fishing	M	White	−
NY048	Brooklyn	urban	old	1900	1968	college	social & community services	F	White	+
NY049	Brooklyn	urban	old	1902	1968	high school	homemaker	F	White	+
NY050	Brooklyn	urban	middle	1925	1968	high school	clerical	F	White	−
NY051	Brooklyn	urban	middle	1911	1968	high school	clerical	F	White	+
NY052	Goshen	rural	old	1895	1968	college	farmer, rancher	M	White	+
NY053	Queens	urban	old	1886	1968	high school	unemployed	F	White	+
NY054	Queens	urban	old	1900	1968	high school	clerical	F	White	+
NY055	Queens	urban	middle	1920	1968	high school	homemaker	F	Black	+
NY056	Brooklyn	urban	middle	1918	1968	high school	journalism	M	White	−
NY057	Brooklyn	urban	old	1892	1968	some schooling	skilled trades	M	White	+
NY058	Tarrytown	small city	old	1902	1968	high school	homemaker	F	White	−
NY059	Tarrytown	small city	old	1900	1968	high school	skilled trades	M	White	−
NY060	Queens	urban	old	1899	1968	college	homemaker	F	White	+
NY061	Queens	urban	old	1884	1968	grade school	domestic, maid	F	Black	+
NY062	Queens	urban	old	1887	1968	college	financial services	M	White	−
NY063	Queens	urban	middle	1911	1968	college	small business: owner, manager	M	White	−
NY064	Queens	urban	middle	1924	1968	high school	clerical	F	White	+
NY065	Queens	urban	old	1886	1968	college	financial services	F	White	−
NY066	North Tarry-town	small city	old	1890	1968	high school	nautical, fishing	M	White	+
NY067	Manhattan	urban	middle	1918	1968	college	homemaker	F	White	+
NY068	Granville	rural	old	1888	1968	grade school	storekeeper	M	White	+
NY069	White Sul-phur Springs	rural	old	1896	1968	grade school	homemaker	F	White	+
NY070	Kinderhook	village	old	1892	1968	grade school	homemaker	F	White	−
NY071	Valatie	rural	old	1888	1968	high school	ranger, guide	M	White	+
NY072	Roxbury	rural	old	1888	1968	grade school	farmer, rancher	M	White	−

Informant Code	Community	Community Type	Age-group	Year of Birth	Year of Interview	Education	Occupation	Sex	Race	Audio-tape
NY073	Roxbury	rural	old	1888	1968	grade school	farmer, rancher	M	White	+
NY074	Roxbury	rural	old	1887	1968	high school	—	M	White	−
NY075	Oxford	rural	old	1897	1968	grade school	skilled trades	M	White	+
NY076	Queens	urban	middle	1909	1968	high school	foreman, supervisor	F	White	−
NY077	Queens	urban	middle	1921	1968	high school	homemaker	F	White	−
NY078	Queens	urban	middle	1911	1968	high school	homemaker	F	White	+
NY079	Queens	urban	old	1904	1968	high school	food services	M	White	+
NY080	Newburgh	small city	middle	1912	1968	high school	police	M	White	+
NY081	Manhattan	urban	young	1948	1968	college	student	M	White	+
NY082	Saugerties	village	old	1904	1968	grade school	factory worker	M	White	+
NY083	Saugerties	village	old	1898	1968	high school	food services	F	White	−
NY084	Millerton	rural	old	1897	1968	grade school	skilled trades	M	White	−
NY086	Kingston	small city	middle	1914	1968	high school	firefighter	M	White	−
NY087	Kingston	small city	middle	1918	1968	high school	firefighter	M	White	+
NY088	Warrensburg	village	middle	1916	1968	high school	wholesale, retail sales	F	White	+
NY089	Queens	urban	young	1939	1968	high school	homemaker	F	White	+
NY090	Queens	urban	old	1893	1968	high school	teacher	F	White	+
NY092	Lake Pleasant	rural	middle	1912	1968	high school	custodial, maintenance	M	White	+
NY093	Windsor	village	middle	1914	1968	high school	local government	M	White	+
NY094	Windsor	village	middle	1925	1968	high school	homemaker	F	White	+
NY095	Boonville	village	middle	1910	1968	college	storekeeper	M	White	−
NY096	Boonville	village	old	1894	1968	grade school	skilled trades	M	White	+
NY097	Boonville	village	middle	1911	1968	high school	ranger, guide	M	White	−
NY098	Boonville	village	young	1947	1968	college	student	M	White	−
NY099	Fredonia	small city	old	1898	1968	college	homemaker	F	White	+
NY100	Fredonia	small city	old	1897	1968	college	teacher	F	White	+
NY101	Fredonia	small city	old	1892	1968	grade school	factory worker	M	White	+
NY102	Ripley	rural	old	1899	1968	high school	farmer, rancher	M	White	+
NY103	Ripley	village	old	1886	1968	college	engineer	M	White	+
NY104	Ripley	village	old	1889	1968	high school	seamstress	F	White	+
NY105	Gowanda	village	old	1889	1968	high school	wholesale, retail sales	F	White	+
NY106	Gowanda	village	old	1883	1968	high school	homemaker	F	White	+
NY107	Geneseo	village	old	1895	1968	college	farm woman	F	White	+
NY108	Geneseo	village	old	1894	1968	high school	homemaker	F	White	+
NY109	Seneca Falls	rural	middle	1934	1968	high school	farmer, rancher	M	White	+
NY110	Seneca Falls	village	old	1887	1968	grade school	skilled trades	M	White	−
NY111	Montour Falls	village	old	1908	1968	high school	homemaker	F	White	+
NY112	Montour Falls	village	old	1886	1968	grade school	engineer	M	White	−
NY113	Montour Falls	village	old	1896	1968	high school	homemaker	F	White	+
NY114	Wayland	village	young	1931	1968	grade school	unemployed	M	White	+
NY115	Wayland	village	old	1892	1968	high school	homemaker	F	White	+
NY116	Wayland	rural	old	1893	1968	grade school	farm woman	F	White	+
NY117	Wayland	village	old	1880	1968	high school	storekeeper	M	White	+
NY118	Bronx	urban	young	1941	1968	college	teacher	M	White	+
NY119	Bronx	urban	young	1938	1968	college	teacher	M	White	−
NY120	Skaneateles	village	old	1904	1968	college	homemaker	F	White	+
NY121	Skaneateles	village	middle	1928	1968	college	medicine	F	White	+
NY122	Skaneateles	rural	middle	1924	1968	high school	farmer, rancher	M	White	+
NY123	Owego	village	middle	1916	1968	college	service station operator	F	White	+
NY126	Schoharie	village	old	1902	1969	high school	storekeeper	F	White	+

Informant Code	Community	Community Type	Age-group	Year of Birth	Year of Interview	Education	Occupation	Sex	Race	Audio-tape
NY127	Schoharie	village	old	1908	1969	high school	storekeeper	M	White	−
NY128	Schoharie	village	old	1904	1969	college	teacher	F	White	−
NY130	Buffalo	large city	middle	1919	1969	high school	real estate	F	White	−
NY131	Buffalo	large city	old	1895	1969	unknown	wholesale, retail sales	M	White	+
NY132	Buffalo	large city	old	1906	1969	college	insurance	M	White	−
NY133	Buffalo	large city	young	1935	1969	college	financial services	M	White	−
NY134	Wellsville	village	old	1888	1969	college	storekeeper	M	White	−
NY135	Wellsville	village	old	1900	1969	high school	wholesale, retail sales	F	White	−
NY136	Wellsville	village	old	1902	1969	college	administrative, managerial	M	White	−
NY137	Wellsville	village	old	1893	1969	high school	clerical	F	White	−
NY138	Wellsville	village	middle	1925	1969	college	medicine	M	White	−
NY139	Wellsville	village	old	1888	1969	college	homemaker	F	White	+
NY140	Wellsville	rural	young	1948	1969	high school	farmer, rancher	M	White	−
NY141	Fayetteville	village	middle	1911	1969	college	homemaker	F	White	+
NY142	Fayetteville	rural	middle	1911	1969	college	farmer, rancher	M	White	−
NY143	Fayetteville	village	old	1909	1969	college	librarian	F	White	−
NY144	Fayetteville	village	young	1930	1969	college	homemaker	F	White	+
NY145	Corning	small city	middle	1910	1969	high school	clerical	F	White	+
NY146	Corning	small city	old	1902	1969	high school	factory worker	F	White	+
NY148	Corning	rural	old	1909	1969	high school	farmer, rancher	M	White	+
NY149	Oswego	small city	old	1906	1969	high school	wholesale, retail sales	F	White	−
NY150	Oswego	rural	old	1897	1969	grade school	farmer, rancher	M	White	+
NY151	Oswego	small city	young	1932	1969	college	wholesale, retail sales	M	White	−
NY152	Oswego	small city	middle	1917	1969	college	homemaker	F	White	−
NY153	Palmyra	village	old	1890	1969	grade school	homemaker	F	White	+
NY154	Palmyra	village	middle	1924	1969	high school	homemaker	F	White	−
NY155	Palmyra	village	middle	1910	1969	high school	farmer, rancher	M	White	−
NY156	Homer	village	young	1949	1969	high school	skilled trades	M	White	+
NY157	Homer	village	middle	1920	1969	college	wholesale, retail sales	M	White	+
NY158	Homer	village	old	1893	1969	high school	homemaker	F	White	+
NY159	Homer	rural	old	1890	1969	grade school	farmer, rancher	M	White	+
NY160	Homer	village	middle	1924	1969	high school	farmer, rancher	M	White	−
NY161	Homer	village	middle	1924	1969	high school	homemaker	F	White	+
NY162	Albion	village	middle	1915	1969	high school	social & community services	F	White	−
NY163	Albion	rural	old	1898	1969	high school	farmer, rancher	M	White	+
NY164	Albion	rural	old	1895	1969	college	farmer, rancher	M	White	−
NY165	Albion	village	old	1899	1969	college	teacher	F	White	−
NY166	Albion	village	old	1904	1969	college	homemaker	F	White	−
NY167	Syracuse	large city	middle	1911	1969	college	clerical	F	White	+
NY168	Syracuse	large city	middle	1923	1969	college	teacher	F	White	+
NY169	La Fayette	large city	old	1891	1969	college	homemaker	F	White	−
NY170	La Fayette	large city	middle	1911	1969	high school	postal service	M	White	−
NY171	De Witt	large city	young	1931	1969	college	architect	M	White	−
NY172	Fayetteville	village	young	1935	1969	college	homemaker	F	White	−
NY173	Yorkville	village	old	1891	1969	high school	homemaker	F	White	+
NY174	Yorkville	village	old	1896	1969	high school	homemaker	F	White	−
NY175	Yorkville	village	middle	1928	1969	high school	homemaker	F	White	+
NY176	Whitesboro	rural	old	1885	1969	grade school	farmer, rancher	M	White	−
NY177	New Hartford	small city	old	1902	1969	college	engineer	M	White	−
NY179	Salamanca	village	old	1892	1969	grade school	homemaker	F	White	−

Informant Code	Community	Community Type	Age-group	Year of Birth	Year of Interview	Education	Occupation	Sex	Race	Audio-tape
NY180	Salamanca	village	middle	1910	1969	high school	homemaker	F	White	−
NY181	Salamanca	village	old	1899	1969	high school	homemaker	F	White	−
NY182	Salamanca	rural	old	1897	1969	high school	farmer, rancher	M	White	−
NY183	Salamanca	village	middle	1915	1969	high school	skilled trades	M	White	+
NY184	Salamanca	village	young	1930	1969	high school	homemaker	F	White	+
NY185	Oneonta	small city	old	1898	1969	high school	storekeeper	M	White	−
NY186	Oneonta	small city	young	1932	1969	college	homemaker	F	White	+
NY187	Oneonta	small city	middle	1924	1969	college	storekeeper	M	White	−
NY188	Cooperstown	village	old	1897	1969	college	teacher	F	White	−
NY189	Cooperstown	village	old	1899	1969	grade school	museum staff	M	White	−
NY190	Cooperstown	village	old	1906	1969	college	storekeeper	F	White	+
NY191	Cooperstown	village	old	1901	1969	grade school	ranger, guide	M	White	−
NY192	Cooperstown	village	old	1906	1969	high school	clerical	F	White	−
NY193	Cooperstown	village	old	1895	1969	grade school	local government	M	White	−
NY194	Canajoharie	village	old	1892	1969	college	teacher	F	White	+
NY195	Canajoharie	village	old	1890	1969	high school	homemaker	F	White	+
NY196	Canajoharie	village	old	1888	1969	college	teacher	M	White	−
NY197	Fort Plain	village	middle	1920	1969	high school	homemaker	F	White	−
NY198	Little Falls	village	old	1885	1969	grade school	small business: owner, manager	M	White	−
NY199	Little Falls	village	old	1902	1969	college	teacher	F	White	+
NY200	Hamilton	rural	old	1901	1969	unknown	farmer, rancher	M	White	+
NY201	Hamilton	village	old	1904	1969	college	clerical	M	White	−
NY202	Hamilton	village	old	1909	1969	college	teacher	M	White	+
NY205	Saratoga Springs	village	old	1891	1969	high school	farmer, rancher	M	White	+
NY206	Monroe	rural	old	1889	1969	grade school	farmer, rancher	M	White	−
NY207	Monroe	village	middle	1924	1969	high school	financial services	M	White	−
NY209	Pine Bush	rural	old	1887	1969	grade school	farmer, rancher	M	White	+
NY210	Newburgh	small city	middle	1921	1969	high school	wholesale, retail sales	M	White	−
NY211	Newburgh	small city	old	1905	1969	college	farmer, rancher	M	White	+
NY212	Newburgh	small city	old	1907	1969	high school	insurance	M	White	−
NY213	Hoosick Falls	village	old	1895	1969	high school	homemaker	F	White	+
NY214	Hoosick Falls	village	old	1898	1969	grade school	foreman, supervisor	M	White	−
NY215	Jamestown	small city	old	1904	1969	grade school	skilled trades	M	White	+
NY216	Falconer	rural	young	1951	1969	high school	student	M	White	−
NY217	Jamestown	small city	old	1890	1969	high school	wholesale, retail sales	M	White	−
NY218	Speculator	rural	old	1895	1969	college	postal service	F	White	−
NY219	Speculator	rural	old	1896	1969	grade school	custodial, maintenance	M	White	+
NY220	Voorheesville	village	old	1894	1969	high school	teacher	F	White	+
NY221	Voorheesville	rural	old	1886	1969	college	farmer, rancher	M	White	−
NY222	Bath	village	old	1869	1969	high school	clerical	F	White	+
NY223	Bath	village	old	1893	1969	high school	clerical	F	White	+
NY224	Bath	rural	old	1891	1969	grade school	farmer, rancher	M	White	−
NY226	Alden	village	old	1887	1969	college	medicine	M	White	+
NY227	Alden	village	old	1905	1969	high school	small business: owner, manager	M	White	−
NY228	Alden	village	old	1898	1969	college	farmer, rancher	M	White	−
NY229	Alden	village	old	1890	1969	high school	skilled trades	M	White	−
NY230	Arcade	village	old	1904	1970	college	teacher	F	White	−
NY231	Arcade	village	old	1895	1970	high school	skilled trades	M	White	−
NY232	Arcade	village	old	1890	1970	high school	homemaker	F	White	+
NY233	Whitney Point	village	old	1894	1970	grade school	insurance	M	White	−

Informant Code	Community	Community Type	Age-group	Year of Birth	Year of Interview	Education	Occupation	Sex	Race	Audio-tape
NY234	Whitney Point	village	middle	1920	1970	high school	farm woman	F	White	+
NY235	Manhattan	urban	middle	1914	1970	college	educational administrator	F	Black	−
NY236	Manhattan	urban	young	1937	1970	high school	unemployed	F	Black	+
NY237	Manhattan	urban	young	1940	1970	high school	clerical	F	Black	−
NY238	Manhattan	urban	middle	1929	1970	college	educational administrator	F	Black	−
NY239	Manhattan	urban	young	1942	1970	college	teacher	M	Black	−
NY240	Bronx	urban	old	1897	1970	high school	firefighter	M	Black	+
NY241	Bronx	urban	young	1951	1970	high school	social & community services	M	Black	−
NY248	Manhattan	urban	middle	1924	1970	high school	skilled trades	M	Black	−
NY249	Manhattan	urban	middle	1925	1970	college	architect	M	Black	−
NY250	Manhattan	urban	middle	1916	1970	high school	homemaker	F	Black	−
NC001	Cedar Island	rural	old	1898	1966	grade school	nautical, fishing	M	White	+
NC002	New Bern	rural	old	1889	1966	grade school	farm woman	F	White	+
NC003	Chinquapin	rural	old	1906	1966	high school	teacher	F	White	+
NC004	Wallace	village	old	1892	1966	college	teacher	F	White	+
NC005	Raleigh	large city	middle	1912	1966	high school	homemaker	F	White	+
NC006	Raleigh	large city	middle	1891	1966	high school	homemaker	F	White	+
NC007	Raleigh	large city	old	1903	1966	high school	homemaker	F	White	+
NC008	Bath	rural	old	1905	1966	high school	teacher	F	White	+
NC009	Bath	rural	middle	1881	1966	high school	homemaker	F	White	+
NC010	New Bern	rural	old	1886	1966	grade school	farm woman	F	White	+
NC011	Beaufort	village	old	1895	1966	college	teacher	F	White	+
NC012	Beaufort	rural	middle	1917	1966	grade school	farmer, rancher	M	White	+
*NC013	Elizabeth City	small city	old	1891	1966	high school	police	M	White	+
*NC014	Elizabeth City	small city	old	1896	1966	college	teacher	F	White	+
*NC015	Halifax	rural	old	1890	1966	unknown	wholesale, retail sales	M	White	+
*NC016	Halifax	rural	old	1882	1966	high school	museum staff	F	White	+
*NC017	Edenton	village	old	1898	1966	high school	homemaker	F	White	+
*NC018	Edenton	village	old	1903	1966	college	homemaker	F	White	+
NC020	Columbia	rural	old	1891	1966	grade school	lodging trades	F	White	+
NC021	Columbia	rural	old	1891	1966	grade school	farmer, rancher	M	White	+
NC022	Columbia	rural	middle	1907	1966	high school	farm woman	F	White	+
NC023	Old Dock	rural	old	1898	1966	high school	farmer, rancher	F	White	+
NC024	Old Dock	rural	middle	1915	1966	high school	farmer, rancher	M	White	+
NC025	Ocracoke	rural	middle	1913	1966	grade school	homemaker	F	White	+
NC026	Ocracoke	rural	old	1902	1966	grade school	military	M	White	+
NC027	Ocracoke	rural	old	1884	1966	some schooling	ranger, guide	M	White	+
NC030	Linville	rural	middle	1924	1966	high school	lodging trades	M	White	+
NC031	Spruce Pine	village	middle	1908	1966	college	homemaker	F	White	+
NC032	Boone	rural	old	1886	1966	college	farmer, rancher	M	White	−
NC033	Boone	village	old	1892	1966	college	real estate	M	White	+
NC034	Burnsville	village	middle	1911	1966	college	lodging trades	M	White	+
NC035	Pensacola	rural	old	1892	1966	grade school	farmer, rancher	M	White	+
NC036	Asheville	small city	middle	1911	1966	college	clerical	F	White	+
NC037	Highlands	rural	young	1940	1966	high school	storekeeper	F	White	+
NC038	Winston-Salem	large city	old	1891	1967	college	teacher	F	White	+
NC039	Durham	small city	old	1902	1967	college	librarian	F	Black	+

Informant Code	Community	Community Type	Age-group	Year of Birth	Year of Interview	Education	Occupation	Sex	Race	Audio-tape
NC040	Durham	small city	old	1894	1967	grade school	homemaker	F	White	+
NC041	Pinehurst	village	old	1897	1967	grade school	skilled trades	M	White	+
NC042	Cherokee	rural	old	1889	1966	grade school	museum staff	M	Am Ind	−
NC043	Cherokee	rural	old	1898	1966	grade school	railroad	M	Am Ind	−
NC044	Cherokee	rural	middle	1890	1966	grade school	homemaker	F	Am Ind	−
NC045	Cherokee	rural	middle	1908	1966	high school	storekeeper	M	White	−
NC046	Chapel Hill	small city	middle	1915	1967	college	insurance	M	White	+
NC047	Chapel Hill	small city	young	1934	1967	college	homemaker	F	White	+
NC048	Brevard	village	old	1886	1967	college	legal	M	White	
NC049	Maxton	rural	old	1902	1968	some schooling	farmer, rancher	M	Am Ind	
NC050	Maxton	rural	middle	1928	1968	grade school	farmer, rancher	F	Am Ind	
NC051	Maxton	rural	young	1929	1968	college	farmer, rancher	M	White	+
NC052	Gastonia	small city	old	1898	1968	high school	engineer	M	White	+
NC053	Brasstown	rural	young	1952	1968	grade school	student	M	White	+
NC054	Brasstown	rural	middle	1915	1968	grade school	farmer, rancher	M	White	+
NC055	Brasstown	rural	old	1896	1968	grade school	artist, craftsman	F	White	+
NC060	Buxton	rural	old	1889	1969	high school	homemaker	F	White	+
NC061	Hatteras	rural	middle	1921	1969	high school	homemaker	F	White	−
NC062	Hillsborough	village	old	1907	1969	college	storekeeper	M	White	+
NC063	Hillsborough	village	young	1938	1969	college	insurance	M	White	−
NC064	Hillsborough	village	middle	1924	1969	grade school	homemaker	F	Black	−
NC067	Jugtown	rural	young	1933	1969	grade school	skilled trades	M	White	−
NC068	Seagrove	rural	middle	1917	1969	grade school	artist, craftsman	M	White	+
NC069	Robbins	village	old	1901	1969	high school	storekeeper	M	White	−
NC070	Salisbury	small city	old	1904	1969	grade school	laborer	M	Black	−
NC071	Salisbury	small city	middle	1916	1969	college	journalism	M	White	+
NC072	Salisbury	small city	old	1904	1969	high school	journalism	M	White	+
NC073	Salisbury	small city	old	1897	1969	high school	financial services	M	White	−
NC076	Salvo	rural	young	1945	1969	high school	skilled trades	M	White	+
NC077	Rodanthe	rural	middle	1920	1969	high school	lodging trades	F	White	−
NC078	Rodanthe	rural	old	1891	1969	some schooling	nautical, fishing	M	White	−
NC079	Kitty Hawk	rural	old	1887	1968	college	teacher	F	White	−
NC080	Kitty Hawk	rural	old	1896	1968	high school	military	M	White	−
NC081	Manteo	rural	old	1894	1968	grade school	military	M	White	−
NC082	Wanchese	rural	old	1903	1968	college	homemaker	F	White	−
NC083	Elizabeth City	small city	old	1882	1970	college	teacher	F	Black	+
NC084	Elizabeth City	small city	old	1912	1970	grade school	seamstress	F	Black	+
NC085	Elizabeth City	small city	middle	1918	1970	grade school	religion	M	Black	+
NC086	Elizabeth City	small city	old	1902	1970	college	teacher	F	Black	+
NC087	Rocky Mount	rural	old	1907	1970	grade school	farmer, rancher	M	Black	+
NC088	Princeville	rural	old	1910	1970	college	teacher	F	Black	+
ND001	Mandan	rural	old	1891	1966	grade school	farmer, rancher	M	White	+
ND002	Wahpeton	village	old	1889	1966	grade school	homemaker	F	White	+
ND003	Walhalla	rural	old	1906	1966	grade school	custodial, maintenance	M	White	+
ND005	Medora	rural	old	1897	1966	grade school	farmer, rancher	M	White	+
ND009	Stanley	village	middle	1912	1966	high school	skilled trades	M	White	+
ND010	Stanley	village	middle	1909	1966	high school	homemaker	F	White	+
OH001	Chagrin Falls	small city	old	1898	1967	college	homemaker	F	White	+
OH002	Chagrin Falls	small city	middle	1924	1967	college	homemaker	F	White	+

Informant Code	Community	Community Type	Age-group	Year of Birth	Year of Interview	Education	Occupation	Sex	Race	Audio-tape
OH003	Chagrin Falls	rural	old	1896	1967	college	farm woman	F	White	−
OH004	Twinsburg	rural	old	1897	1967	college	farmer, rancher	M	White	+
OH005	Twinsburg	village	old	1895	1967	college	teacher	F	White	−
OH006	Burton	village	old	1892	1967	high school	real estate	M	White	+
OH007	Burton	village	old	1888	1967	high school	homemaker	F	White	−
OH008	Burton	village	old	1890	1967	high school	museum staff	F	White	+
OH009	Hudson	rural	old	1878	1967	high school	farmer, rancher	M	White	−
OH010	Hudson	rural	middle	1910	1967	college	farmer, rancher	M	White	+
OH011	Hudson	village	old	1880	1967	high school	homemaker	F	White	+
OH012	Hudson	rural	old	1881	1967	grade school	farmer, rancher	M	White	−
OH013	Hudson	village	old	1904	1967	college	financial services	F	White	−
OH015	Madison	rural	old	1878	1967	high school	homemaker	F	White	+
OH016	Madison	rural	old	1891	1967	high school	insurance	M	White	+
OH017	Leroy	rural	old	1887	1967	high school	clerical	F	White	+
OH018	Leroy	rural	old	1889	1967	high school	homemaker	F	White	+
OH019	Leroy	rural	old	1892	1967	high school	custodial, maintenance	M	White	−
OH020	Wellington	village	middle	1920	1967	college	small business: owner, manager	M	White	+
OH021	Wellington	village	middle	1921	1967	college	homemaker	F	White	+
OH022	Custar	rural	old	1906	1967	high school	small business: owner, manager	M	White	+
OH023	Bowling Green	small city	old	1892	1967	high school	homemaker	F	White	+
OH024	Bowling Green	small city	old	1896	1967	high school	homemaker	F	White	+
OH025	Napoleon	village	old	1877	1967	grade school	storekeeper	M	White	−
OH026	Napoleon	village	old	1890	1967	college	journalism	M	White	−
OH027	Napoleon	village	old	1890	1967	college	small business: owner, manager	M	White	−
OH028	Norwalk	small city	old	1884	1967	high school	museum staff	F	White	+
OH029	Norwalk	small city	old	1890	1967	high school	clerical	F	White	+
OH030	Norwalk	rural	middle	1920	1967	grade school	farmer, rancher	M	White	−
OH031	Circleville	rural	old	1902	1967	college	farm woman	F	White	+
OH032	Circleville	rural	old	1902	1967	high school	farmer, rancher	M	White	+
OH033	Circleville	small city	middle	1912	1967	high school	local government	M	White	+
OH034	Chillicothe	small city	old	1906	1967	college	administrative, managerial	M	White	+
OH035	Chillicothe	rural	old	1904	1967	college	farmer, rancher	M	White	−
OH036	Chillicothe	small city	old	1903	1967	college	small business: owner, manager	M	White	+
OH037	Chillicothe	small city	old	1906	1967	high school	homemaker	F	White	+
OH038	Wellston	village	old	1896	1968	college	homemaker	F	White	+
OH039	Long Bottom	rural	young	1933	1968	grade school	food services	F	White	+
OH040	Long Bottom	rural	young	1950	1968	high school	clerical	F	White	+
OH041	McConnelsville	village	old	1890	1968	high school	journalism	F	White	+
OH042	Marietta	small city	old	1897	1968	college	real estate	M	White	+
OH043	Marietta	small city	young	1938	1968	college	teacher	M	White	+
OH044	Clarington	rural	old	1904	1968	college	teacher	M	White	+
OH045	Gallipolis	village	middle	1915	1968	high school	homemaker	F	White	+
OH046	Gallipolis	village	young	1947	1968	high school	barber, beautician	F	White	+
OH047	The Plains	village	middle	1920	1968	high school	skilled trades	M	White	+
OH048	Somerset	rural	old	1904	1968	grade school	farm woman	F	White	+
OH049	Ironton	small city	old	1903	1968	college	teacher	F	White	+
OH050	Ironton	small city	old	1902	1968	college	legal	M	White	+

Informant Code	Community	Community Type	Age-group	Year of Birth	Year of Interview	Education	Occupation	Sex	Race	Audio-tape
OH051	Peebles	village	old	1908	1968	college	teacher	F	White	+
OH052	Peebles	village	middle	1924	1968	high school	homemaker	F	White	+
OH053	Peebles	rural	old	1905	1968	high school	teacher	M	White	−
OH054	Oxford	small city	old	1884	1968	college	clerical	M	White	+
OH055	Oxford	small city	old	1901	1968	college	homemaker	F	White	+
OH056	Oxford	rural	old	1899	1968	college	farmer, rancher	M	White	−
OH057	Ripley	village	old	1900	1968	college	artist, craftsman	F	White	+
OH058	Ripley	village	old	1897	1968	high school	storekeeper	M	White	+
OH059	Georgetown	village	old	1899	1968	college	homemaker	F	White	+
OH060	Georgetown	rural	old	1900	1968	college	farm woman	F	White	+
OH061	Leesburg	rural	old	1906	1968	high school	farm woman	F	White	+
OH062	Leesburg	rural	old	1879	1968	grade school	farm woman	F	White	−
OH063	Lebanon	village	old	1909	1968	college	homemaker	F	White	+
OH064	Lebanon	rural	old	1891	1968	grade school	farmer, rancher	M	White	+
OH065	Cambridge	small city	old	1908	1968	high school	homemaker	F	White	+
OH066	Salem	small city	old	1895	1968	high school	homemaker	F	White	+
OH067	Port Clinton	village	old	1884	1968	high school	farmer, rancher	M	White	−
OH068	Port Clinton	village	old	1901	1968	college	clerical	M	White	+
OH069	Bryan	rural	old	1907	1968	high school	farm woman	F	White	+
OH070	Bryan	rural	old	1906	1968	high school	farmer, rancher	M	White	+
OH071	East Liverpool	small city	old	1888	1968	college	real estate	M	White	+
OH072	Bellville	village	old	1885	1968	high school	architect	F	White	+
OH073	Bellville	village	old	1885	1968	high school	insurance	M	White	+
OH074	Mount Vernon	small city	old	1892	1968	high school	financial services	M	White	+
OH075	Mount Vernon	small city	old	1899	1968	college	storekeeper	F	White	+
OH076	Cheviot	urban	middle	1919	1968	high school	storekeeper	M	White	+
OH077	Cheviot	urban	middle	1915	1968	high school	custodial, maintenance	M	White	−
OH078	Mount Pleasant	rural	old	1895	1968	high school	clerical	F	White	+
OH079	New Philadelphia	small city	old	1897	1968	high school	engineer	M	White	+
OH080	Dover	small city	old	1887	1968	grade school	journalism	M	White	+
OH081	Berlin	rural	old	1893	1968	grade school	financial services	M	White	+
OH082	Millersburg	village	old	1907	1968	college	teacher	M	White	+
OH084	Greenville	small city	young	1935	1968	college	teacher	F	White	+
OH085	Greenville	small city	old	1904	1968	high school	homemaker	F	White	+
OH086	Greenville	rural	old	1901	1968	high school	farm woman	F	White	−
OH087	Delaware	rural	middle	1912	1968	high school	farm woman	F	White	+
OH088	Upper Sandusky	rural	middle	1915	1969	grade school	farm woman	F	White	+
OH089	Delphos	village	old	1894	1969	grade school	skilled trades	M	White	+
OH090	Granville	village	middle	1921	1969	high school	lodging trades	F	White	+
OH091	Dayton	large city	young	1948	1970	high school	clerical	F	White	+
OH092	Dayton	large city	old	1899	1970	high school	homemaker	F	White	−
OH093	Dayton	large city	old	1898	1970	college	homemaker	F	White	+
OH094	Dayton	large city	middle	1922	1970	college	librarian	F	White	+
OH095	Urbana	rural	old	1900	1970	high school	farmer, rancher	M	White	+
OH096	Urbana	small city	old	1883	1970	college	medicine	F	White	+
OH097	Urbana	small city	young	1950	1970	college	student	M	White	−
OH098	Columbus	large city	old	1907	1970	college	librarian	F	White	+
OH099	Columbus	large city	young	1942	1970	college	student	M	White	−

Informant Code	Community	Community Type	Age-group	Year of Birth	Year of Interview	Education	Occupation	Sex	Race	Audio-tape
OH102	Cincinnati	urban	young	1935	1970	high school	food services	F	Black	+
OH103	Cincinnati	urban	young	1953	1970	high school	student	M	Black	+
*OK001	Watova	rural	old	1887	1965	grade school	farmer, rancher	M	White	+
*OK002	Watova	rural	old	1897	1965	grade school	homemaker	F	White	−
*OK003	Cushing	rural	old	1895	1965	grade school	farm woman	F	White	−
*OK004	Cushing	rural	old	1895	1965	grade school	farmer, rancher	M	White	−
*OK006	Cushing	village	middle	1907	1965	grade school	skilled trades	M	White	+
*OK007	Cushing	rural	middle	1915	1965	high school	farmer, rancher	M	White	−
*OK008	Cushing	rural	old	1902	1965	grade school	farmer, rancher	M	White	−
*OK009	Okmulgee	small city	middle	1915	1965	high school	museum staff	F	White	−
*OK010	Okmulgee	small city	old	1898	1965	grade school	wholesale, retail sales	M	White	−
*OK011	Okmulgee	small city	old	1904	1965	grade school	police	M	White	−
*OK012	Okmulgee	small city	old	1881	1965	grade school	seamstress	F	White	−
*OK013	Boley	rural	old	1882	1965	some schooling	farmer, rancher	M	Black	−
*OK014	Boley	rural	old	1891	1965	high school	postal service	F	Black	−
*OK015	Boley	rural	old	1886	1965	college	farmer, rancher	F	Black	−
*OK016	Boley	rural	old	1889	1965	college	homemaker	F	Black	−
*OK017	Boley	rural	old	1895	1965	high school	homemaker	F	Black	−
*OK018	Fairview	rural	old	1900	1966	grade school	farmer, rancher	M	White	+
*OK019	Fairview	rural	old	1904	1966	grade school	farm woman	F	White	+
*OK020	Broken Bow	village	old	1900	1966	high school	clerical	F	Am Ind	−
*OK021	Eagletown	rural	old	1874	1966	grade school	storekeeper	F	White	+
*OK022	Broken Bow	village	old	1896	1966	high school	financial services	F	Am Ind	+
*OK023	Broken Bow	village	old	1900	1966	high school	storekeeper	M	White	+
*OK025	Frederick	village	middle	1922	1966	high school	firefighter	M	White	+
*OK026	Frederick	village	middle	1914	1966	grade school	wholesale, retail sales	F	White	−
*OK027	Frederick	village	young	1927	1966	high school	firefighter	M	White	+
*OK028	Frederick	village	old	1901	1966	grade school	wholesale, retail sales	M	White	−
*OK031	Guymon	village	middle	1912	1966	grade school	homemaker	F	White	+
*OK032	Guymon	village	old	1900	1966	college	homemaker	F	White	+
*OK033	Guymon	village	middle	1909	1966	grade school	farmer, rancher	M	White	−
*OK042	Canadian	rural	old	1906	1966	grade school	storekeeper	M	White	+
*OK043	Canadian	rural	middle	1906	1966	high school	farmer, rancher	M	White	+
*OK044	Canadian	rural	middle	1918	1966	high school	homemaker	F	White	−
*OK045	Canadian	rural	old	1897	1966	high school	farmer, rancher	M	White	−
*OK046	Miami	rural	old	1887	1965	grade school	farmer, rancher	M	White	−
*OK047	Miami	rural	old	1898	1965	grade school	homemaker	F	White	−
*OK048	Miami	rural	old	1889	1965	grade school	homemaker	F	White	+
*OK049	Miami	rural	old	1887	1965	grade school	homemaker	F	White	−
*OK050	Miami	rural	old	1884	1965	grade school	homemaker	F	White	−
*OK051	McAlester	rural	old	1893	1966	high school	farmer, rancher	M	White	+
*OK052	McAlester	village	old	1904	1966	some schooling	miner	M	White	+
OK053	Taft	rural	old	1890	1970	unknown	local government	M	Black	+
OK054	Taft	rural	young	1947	1970	college	social & community services	M	Black	+
OK055	Taft	rural	middle	1915	1970	high school	postal service	M	Black	+
OK056	Muskogee	small city	middle	1928	1970	high school	food services	F	Black	+
OK057	Muskogee	small city	middle	1933	1970	college	social & community services	M	Black	+
OK058	Muskogee	small city	old	1883	1970	high school	homemaker	F	Black	+
OR001	Bend	small city	middle	1918	1967	high school	journalism	F	White	+
OR002	Jacksonville	village	old	1893	1967	grade school	skilled trades	M	White	+
OR003	Jacksonville	village	old	1883	1967	grade school	farmer, rancher	M	White	+

Informant Code	Community	Community Type	Age-group	Year of Birth	Year of Interview	Education	Occupation	Sex	Race	Audio-tape
OR004	Astoria	small city	old	1894	1967	grade school	homemaker	F	White	−
OR005	Junction City	rural	old	1889	1967	grade school	farmer, rancher	M	White	−
OR006	Junction City	village	old	1900	1967	grade school	homemaker	F	White	+
OR007	Junction City	rural	old	1894	1967	grade school	farmer, rancher	M	White	−
OR010	Jordan Valley	rural	middle	1924	1967	college	homemaker	F	White	−
OR011	Jordan Valley	rural	old	1892	1967	some schooling	farmer, rancher	M	White	+
OR013	Burns	village	old	1892	1967	college	wholesale, retail sales	M	White	+
OR014	John Day	village	young	1928	1967	grade school	trucking, transportation	M	White	−
OR015	Pendleton	small city	middle	1909	1967	college	medicine	M	White	+
OR016	Pendleton	small city	old	1896	1967	college	homemaker	F	White	−
OR017	Pendleton	small city	middle	1915	1967	grade school	laborer	M	White	−
PA001	Ephrata	village	old	1902	1966	grade school	homemaker	F	White	+
PA002	Lititz	village	middle	1915	1967	college	homemaker	F	White	+
PA003	Lititz	village	old	1894	1967	college	wholesale, retail sales	M	White	+
PA004	Lititz	village	old	1898	1967	college	teacher	F	White	+
PA005	Paradise	rural	old	1894	1967	high school	homemaker	F	White	+
PA006	Paradise	rural	old	1881	1967	high school	farmer, rancher	M	White	+
PA007	Paradise	rural	middle	1912	1967	college	homemaker	F	White	+
PA008	Paradise	rural	old	1894	1967	high school	teacher	F	White	−
PA009	Lancaster	small city	old	1895	1967	unknown	homemaker	F	White	+
PA010	Millersville	village	old	1893	1967	grade school	laborer	M	White	−
PA011	Millersville	village	old	1906	1967	college	skilled trades	M	White	+
PA012	Millersville	village	old	1895	1967	high school	homemaker	F	White	−
PA013	Carlisle	rural	old	1883	1967	grade school	farm woman	F	White	+
PA014	Carlisle	rural	old	1899	1967	grade school	homemaker	F	White	+
PA015	New Bloomfield	rural	old	−	1967	unknown	homemaker	F	White	+
PA016	Carlisle	rural	middle	1915	1967	high school	homemaker	F	White	−
PA017	Carlisle	small city	old	1884	1967	grade school	factory worker	M	White	+
PA018	Manheim	village	middle	1911	1967	high school	homemaker	F	White	+
PA019	Manheim	village	middle	1916	1967	high school	homemaker	F	White	+
PA020	Manheim	village	old	1884	1967	high school	unemployed	F	White	+
PA021	Manheim	rural	middle	1909	1967	some schooling	farmer, rancher	M	White	−
PA022	Terre Hill	rural	old	1907	1967	college	teacher	F	White	+
PA023	New Holland	village	old	1896	1967	high school	wholesale, retail sales	M	White	−
PA024	Terre Hill	rural	old	1906	1967	college	teacher	F	White	+
PA025	Brownstown	village	old	1901	1967	college	custodial, maintenance	M	White	−
PA026	Honey Brook	village	middle	1909	1967	college	clerical	F	White	+
PA027	Honey Brook	village	old	1897	1967	college	journalism	M	White	+
PA028	Annville	village	old	1899	1967	high school	factory worker	F	White	+
PA029	Strasburg	village	old	1899	1967	high school	wholesale, retail sales	M	White	+
PA031	Kennett Square	small city	old	1889	1967	high school	postal service	F	White	+
PA032	Kennett Square	small city	old	1895	1967	college	clerical	F	White	−
PA033	Kennett Square	rural	middle	1922	1967	college	farm woman	F	White	−
PA034	Kennett Square	small city	old	1885	1967	high school	lodging trades	M	White	−
PA035	Kennett Square	small city	old	1896	1967	high school	clerical	M	White	+
PA036	Pottstown	small city	old	1895	1967	grade school	clerical	F	White	−
PA037	Spring City	rural	old	1890	1967	grade school	trucking, transportation	M	White	−
PA038	Pottstown	small city	old	1903	1967	high school	surveyor	F	White	−

Informant Code	Community	Community Type	Age-group	Year of Birth	Year of Interview	Education	Occupation	Sex	Race	Audio-tape
PA039	Pottstown	small city	old	1893	1967	high school	storekeeper	M	White	−
PA040	Pottstown	small city	old	1899	1967	high school	homemaker	F	White	−
PA041	Lehighton	village	old	1894	1967	grade school	unemployed	F	White	−
PA042	Lehighton	village	old	1902	1967	high school	clerical	M	White	+
PA043	Lehighton	rural	old	1904	1967	high school	farmer, rancher	M	White	−
PA044	Lehighton	village	old	1899	1967	high school	journalism	M	White	+
PA045	Lehighton	village	old	1899	1967	high school	homemaker	F	White	−
PA046	Palmerton	village	young	1938	1967	college	medicine	M	White	−
PA047	Lehighton	village	middle	1916	1967	high school	trucking, transportation	M	White	+
PA048	Doylestown	small city	old	1893	1967	high school	administrative, managerial	M	White	−
PA049	Doylestown	small city	old	1902	1967	college	librarian	F	White	+
PA050	Doylestown	small city	middle	1922	1967	high school	skilled trades	M	White	−
PA051	Hatfield	rural	middle	1909	1967	grade school	farmer, rancher	M	White	−
PA052	Quakertown	village	old	1884	1967	grade school	foreman, supervisor	F	White	−
PA053	Quakertown	village	old	1897	1967	college	teacher	F	White	−
PA054	Quakertown	village	old	1895	1967	college	teacher	F	White	+
PA055	Quakertown	village	old	1892	1967	high school	small business: owner, manager	M	White	+
PA056	Quakertown	rural	middle	1914	1967	high school	unemployed	M	White	−
PA057	East Strouds-burg	village	old	1887	1967	high school	laborer	M	White	−
PA058	East Strouds-burg	village	old	1895	1967	high school	local government	M	White	−
PA059	East Strouds-burg	village	old	1892	1967	college	teacher	F	White	−
PA060	East Strouds-burg	village	old	1882	1967	high school	teacher	F	White	+
PA063	Annville	village	old	1895	1967	high school	factory worker	F	White	−
PA066	Chester	small city	young	1948	1968	high school	clerical	F	Black	+
PA067	Laporte	rural	old	1889	1968	college	teacher	F	White	+
PA068	Laporte	rural	middle	1920	1968	high school	clerical	F	White	+
PA069	Laporte	rural	middle	1913	1968	high school	engineer	M	White	+
PA070	Washington	small city	old	1885	1968	grade school	skilled trades	M	White	+
PA071	Washington	rural	old	1898	1968	college	farmer, rancher	M	White	+
PA072	Lewistown	small city	young	1943	1968	high school	homemaker	F	White	+
PA073	Lewistown	small city	young	1938	1968	college	skilled trades	M	White	−
PA074	Greensburg	small city	middle	1918	1968	high school	homemaker	F	White	+
PA075	Greensburg	rural	old	1888	1968	grade school	farmer, rancher	M	White	−
PA076	Pittsburgh	large city	young	1945	1968	college	student	M	White	+
PA077	Pittsburgh	large city	old	1892	1968	some schooling	homemaker	F	White	+
PA078	Hawley	village	old	1878	1968	high school	wholesale, retail sales	F	White	−
PA079	Hawley	village	old	1899	1968	high school	homemaker	F	White	−
PA080	Hawley	rural	old	1892	1968	grade school	farmer, rancher	M	White	−
PA081	Hawley	rural	middle	1916	1968	high school	farm woman	F	White	+
PA082	Hawley	village	old	1892	1968	high school	railroad	M	White	−
PA083	Hawley	village	old	1901	1968	high school	administrative, managerial	M	White	−
PA088	Philadelphia	urban	old	1890	1968	high school	clerical	F	White	+
PA089	Philadelphia	urban	middle	1921	1968	high school	agricultural services	F	White	−
PA090	Philadelphia	urban	old	1886	1968	grade school	homemaker	F	White	+
PA091	Philadelphia	urban	old	1886	1968	high school	unemployed	F	White	+
PA092	Pittsburgh	large city	old	1882	1968	grade school	factory worker	M	White	−
PA093	Pittsburgh	large city	young	1947	1968	college	student	F	White	+

Informant Code	Community	Community Type	Age-group	Year of Birth	Year of Interview	Education	Occupation	Sex	Race	Audio-tape
PA094	Pittsburgh	large city	young	1941	1968	college	student	M	White	+
PA095	Pittsburgh	large city	old	1908	1968	college	journalism	M	White	+
PA096	Philadelphia	urban	old	1889	1968	grade school	homemaker	F	White	+
PA097	Philadelphia	urban	old	1888	1968	grade school	homemaker	F	White	+
PA098	Philadelphia	urban	old	1894	1968	high school	skilled trades	M	White	−
PA099	Philadelphia	urban	−	−	1968	unknown	−	F	White	−
PA100	Philadelphia	urban	old	−	1968	unknown	−	F	White	−
PA102	Montrose	village	old	1888	1968	high school	librarian	F	White	−
PA103	Montrose	village	old	1886	1968	college	medicine	M	White	−
PA104	Montrose	village	old	1883	1968	high school	journalism	M	White	+
PA105	Berwick	small city	old	1894	1968	high school	homemaker	F	White	+
PA106	Berwick	small city	old	1894	1968	college	teacher	M	White	−
PA107	Berwick	small city	old	1894	1968	high school	factory worker	M	White	−
PA108	Berwick	small city	old	1903	1968	college	teacher	M	White	+
PA109	Berwick	small city	old	1894	1968	unknown	storekeeper	M	White	−
PA110	Centralia	village	middle	1916	1968	high school	homemaker	F	White	−
PA111	Mount Carmel	village	−	−	1968	grade school	postal service	M	White	−
PA112	Ashland	village	old	1906	1968	college	teacher	F	White	+
PA113	Centralia	village	middle	1909	1968	high school	homemaker	F	White	+
PA114	Mount Carmel	village	middle	1915	1968	high school	foreman, supervisor	M	White	−
PA115	Laceyville	rural	old	1894	1968	high school	wholesale, retail sales	F	White	+
PA116	Wyalusing	rural	old	1886	1968	high school	farmer, rancher	M	White	−
PA117	Laceyville	rural	old	−	1968	unknown	ranger, guide	M	White	+
PA118	Wyalusing	rural	old	1898	1968	high school	homemaker	F	White	−
PA119	Nicholson	rural	old	1900	1968	high school	homemaker	F	White	−
PA120	Tunkhannock	village	old	1883	1968	college	agricultural services	M	White	−
PA121	Tunkhannock	village	old	1883	1968	high school	railroad	M	White	−
PA122	Nicholson	rural	old	1887	1968	college	homemaker	F	White	−
PA123	Tunkhannock	village	old	1894	1968	high school	homemaker	F	White	−
PA124	Nicholson	rural	old	1905	1968	college	homemaker	F	White	+
PA126	New Hope	rural	old	1894	1968	college	clerical	F	White	+
PA127	New Hope	rural	old	1885	1968	high school	farmer, rancher	M	White	+
PA128	North East	village	old	1896	1968	high school	homemaker	F	White	−
PA129	North East	village	old	1908	1968	college	teacher	F	White	+
PA130	North East	village	old	1897	1968	grade school	homemaker	F	White	+
PA131	Meadville	small city	old	1899	1968	college	journalism	F	White	+
PA132	Meadville	rural	middle	1909	1968	high school	farmer, rancher	M	White	−
PA133	Meadville	small city	young	1950	1968	high school	student	M	White	+
PA134	Hopwood	village	old	1902	1968	grade school	homemaker	F	White	+
PA135	Hopwood	village	old	1896	1968	college	medicine	F	White	+
PA136	Red Lion	village	old	1898	1968	grade school	factory worker	F	White	−
PA137	Red Lion	rural	old	1892	1968	grade school	farmer, rancher	M	White	−
PA138	Red Lion	village	old	1901	1968	grade school	wholesale, retail sales	M	White	−
PA139	Red Lion	village	old	1886	1968	high school	factory worker	M	White	−
PA140	Red Lion	village	old	1901	1968	grade school	factory worker	F	White	−
PA141	Aaronsburg	rural	old	1904	1968	high school	storekeeper	M	White	+
PA142	Aaronsburg	rural	old	1905	1968	high school	skilled trades	M	White	+
PA143	Aaronsburg	rural	middle	1912	1968	high school	homemaker	F	White	−
PA144	Aaronsburg	rural	middle	1923	1968	high school	clerical	M	White	−

Informant Code	Community	Community Type	Age-group	Year of Birth	Year of Interview	Education	Occupation	Sex	Race	Audio-tape
PA146	Sunbury	small city	old	1906	1968	high school	teacher	F	White	+
PA147	Sunbury	small city	old	1901	1968	grade school	skilled trades	M	White	+
PA148	Sunbury	small city	old	1892	1968	high school	postal service	M	White	+
PA149	Sunbury	rural	old	1904	1968	grade school	farmer, rancher	M	White	−
PA150	Millersburg	village	old	1890	1968	high school	homemaker	F	White	−
PA151	Millersburg	village	old	1894	1968	college	teacher	M	White	−
PA152	Millersburg	village	middle	1922	1968	high school	homemaker	F	White	−
PA153	Millersburg	rural	old	1897	1968	grade school	farmer, rancher	M	White	−
PA154	Millersburg	village	old	1900	1968	grade school	small business: owner, manager	M	White	−
PA155	Millersburg	village	middle	1923	1968	high school	factory worker	M	White	−
PA156	Millersburg	village	old	1904	1968	grade school	clerical	M	White	−
PA157	Kutztown	village	old	1893	1968	high school	teacher	M	White	−
PA158	Kutztown	rural	old	1890	1968	grade school	farmer, rancher	M	White	−
PA159	Kutztown	village	old	1894	1968	grade school	homemaker	F	White	−
PA160	Kutztown	village	old	1901	1968	high school	clerical	M	White	+
PA161	Kutztown	village	young	1945	1968	college	student	M	White	−
PA162	Kutztown	village	old	1908	1968	college	homemaker	F	White	−
PA163	Loretto	rural	middle	1918	1968	grade school	farmer, rancher	M	White	+
PA164	Loretto	rural	old	1907	1968	grade school	trucking, transportation	M	White	+
PA165	Ridgway	village	young	1934	1968	college	teacher	M	White	+
PA166	Ridgway	rural	old	1904	1968	grade school	farmer, rancher	M	White	−
PA167	Ambridge	small city	young	1948	1968	college	student	F	White	+
PA168	Ambridge	small city	middle	1912	1968	high school	factory worker	M	White	−
PA169	Swarthmore	village	old	1905	1968	college	teacher	F	White	−
PA170	Philadelphia	urban	young	1939	1968	college	police	M	White	+
PA171	Philadelphia	urban	middle	1926	1968	high school	artist, craftsman	F	White	+
PA172	Philadelphia	urban	middle	1919	1968	high school	clerical	F	Black	−
PA173	Philadelphia	urban	middle	1916	1968	college	financial services	M	White	−
PA174	Morrisdale	rural	old	1897	1968	grade school	farmer, rancher	M	White	−
PA175	Philipsburg	village	old	1903	1968	high school	clerical	F	White	+
PA176	Philipsburg	village	old	1905	1968	high school	custodial, maintenance	M	White	−
PA177	Tionesta	rural	old	1901	1969	college	teacher	F	White	−
PA178	Tionesta	rural	old	1905	1969	grade school	farmer, rancher	M	White	+
PA179	Tionesta	rural	young	1936	1969	high school	wholesale, retail sales	F	White	−
PA180	Tionesta	rural	middle	1923	1969	college	small business: owner, manager	M	White	+
PA181	Warren	small city	old	1907	1969	college	teacher	F	White	+
PA182	Warren	small city	middle	1915	1969	college	medicine	M	White	+
PA183	North Warren	village	old	1896	1969	high school	homemaker	F	White	−
PA184	Mercer	village	middle	1923	1969	high school	homemaker	F	White	+
PA185	Mercer	village	middle	1920	1969	high school	service station operator	M	White	+
PA186	Mercer	village	old	1879	1969	high school	homemaker	F	White	+
PA187	Mercer	village	old	1880	1969	high school	skilled trades	M	White	−
PA188	Punxsutawney	village	old	1879	1969	grade school	storekeeper	M	White	+
PA189	Punxsutawney	village	old	1905	1969	high school	homemaker	F	White	+
PA190	Punxsutawney	village	old	1899	1969	college	teacher	F	White	−
PA191	Punxsutawney	rural	old	1897	1969	grade school	farmer, rancher	M	White	−
PA192	Coudersport	village	old	1895	1969	college	ranger, guide	M	White	+

Informant Code	Community	Community Type	Age-group	Year of Birth	Year of Interview	Education	Occupation	Sex	Race	Audio-tape
PA193	Coudersport	rural	old	1903	1969	grade school	farmer, rancher	M	White	+
PA194	Coudersport	village	old	1903	1969	high school	homemaker	F	White	−
PA195	Coudersport	village	young	1938	1969	high school	storekeeper	M	White	−
PA196	Kittanning	village	middle	1914	1969	high school	homemaker	F	White	+
PA197	Kittanning	village	old	1899	1969	grade school	insurance	M	White	−
PA198	Kittanning	village	old	1890	1969	grade school	farmer, rancher	M	White	+
PA199	Williamsport	small city	middle	1912	1969	high school	postal service	M	White	+
PA200	Williamsport	small city	old	1906	1969	college	social & community services	F	White	+
PA201	Williamsport	small city	middle	1912	1969	high school	skilled trades	M	White	−
PA202	Gettysburg	village	old	1900	1969	college	storekeeper	M	White	+
PA203	Gettysburg	village	old	1905	1969	grade school	homemaker	F	White	+
PA204	Gettysburg	rural	middle	1927	1969	high school	farmer, rancher	M	White	−
PA205	McConnells-burg	rural	middle	1918	1969	high school	storekeeper	M	White	+
PA206	McConnells-burg	rural	middle	1919	1969	high school	homemaker	F	White	−
PA207	McConnells-burg	rural	middle	1916	1969	high school	farmer, rancher	M	White	−
PA208	Somerset	village	young	1936	1969	college	storekeeper	M	White	+
PA209	Somerset	village	middle	1929	1969	high school	service station operator	M	White	+
PA210	Somerset	village	old	1905	1969	high school	homemaker	F	White	−
PA211	Rockwood	rural	old	1902	1969	grade school	miner	M	White	−
PA212	Everett	rural	middle	1920	1969	college	farmer, rancher	M	White	+
PA213	Everett	village	middle	1912	1969	grade school	homemaker	F	White	−
PA214	Everett	village	middle	1922	1969	high school	financial services	M	White	+
PA215	Everett	village	middle	1915	1969	high school	homemaker	F	White	+
PA216	Wellsboro	village	middle	1924	1969	college	financial services	M	White	+
PA217	Wellsboro	village	old	1889	1969	high school	homemaker	F	White	−
PA218	Crooked Creek	rural	old	1900	1969	grade school	farmer, rancher	M	White	−
PA219	Wellsboro	village	young	1931	1969	college	storekeeper	M	White	−
PA220	Troy	village	middle	1924	1969	high school	homemaker	F	White	−
PA221	Troy	village	middle	1914	1969	high school	homemaker	F	White	+
PA222	Troy	village	old	1889	1969	grade school	farmer, rancher	M	White	−
PA223	Troy	village	middle	1918	1969	college	small business: owner, manager	M	White	+
PA224	Carbondale	small city	middle	1919	1969	high school	homemaker	F	White	−
PA225	Carbondale	small city	middle	1920	1969	high school	homemaker	F	White	+
PA226	Carbondale	small city	old	1905	1969	high school	skilled trades	M	White	−
PA227	Carbondale	small city	middle	1919	1969	college	storekeeper	M	White	−
PA228	Milford	village	middle	1916	1969	high school	service station operator	M	White	−
PA229	Milford	village	young	1940	1969	college	homemaker	F	White	−
PA230	Milford	rural	middle	1916	1969	high school	farm woman	F	White	−
PA231	Milford	village	middle	1916	1969	grade school	skilled trades	M	White	+
PA232	Warren	rural	young	1943	1969	high school	farmer, rancher	M	White	−
PA233	Union City	village	old	1896	1969	grade school	police	M	White	+
PA234	Union City	village	old	1900	1970	high school	teacher	F	White	+
PA235	Beaver Falls	small city	old	1896	1970	grade school	custodial, maintenance	M	White	+
PA236	Beaver Falls	small city	young	1952	1970	high school	student	M	Black	−
PA237	Beaver Falls	small city	old	1892	1970	high school	storekeeper	M	White	−
PA239	Philadelphia	urban	young	1943	1970	high school	homemaker	F	Black	+
PA240	Philadelphia	urban	young	1939	1970	high school	skilled trades	M	Black	+
PA241	Philadelphia	urban	young	1948	1970	high school	clerical	F	Black	+

Informant Code	Community	Community Type	Age-group	Year of Birth	Year of Interview	Education	Occupation	Sex	Race	Audio-tape
PA242	Elizabeth-town	village	old	1900	1970	college	teacher	F	White	+
PA243	Elizabeth-town	village	young	1939	1970	college	teacher	M	White	−
PA244	Saint Clair	village	old	1886	1970	grade school	homemaker	F	White	+
PA245	Saint Clair	village	old	1899	1970	high school	police	M	White	+
PA246	Saint Clair	village	old	1908	1970	some schooling	miner	M	White	−
PA247	Philadelphia	urban	young	1941	1970	high school	homemaker	F	Black	+
PA248	Philadelphia	urban	middle	1930	1970	college	teacher	F	Black	+
RI001	Middletown	small city	old	1890	1969	high school	wholesale, retail sales	F	White	+
RI002	Middletown	rural	old	1897	1969	high school	farmer, rancher	M	White	−
RI003	Hope	rural	middle	1910	1969	high school	postal service	F	White	+
RI004	Hope	rural	old	1904	1969	grade school	storekeeper	M	White	+
RI005	Bridgton	village	old	1904	1969	grade school	seamstress	F	White	+
RI005A	Bridgton	village	old	1905	1969	grade school	skilled trades	M	White	+
RI006	Bridgton	village	middle	1911	1969	grade school	factory worker	M	White	−
RI007	Pascoag	rural	middle	1910	1969	grade school	farm woman	F	White	−
RI008	Bristol	rural	middle	1917	1969	grade school	farmer, rancher	M	White	+
RI009	Bristol	small city	old	1884	1969	high school	museum staff	F	White	+
RI010	Bristol	small city	old	1893	1969	college	teacher	F	White	+
RI011	Bristol	small city	young	1948	1969	college	student	M	White	−
RI012	Westerly	small city	old	1897	1969	college	engineer	M	White	+
RI013	Westerly	small city	middle	1916	1969	college	legal	M	White	−
RI014	Little Compton	village	old	1884	1969	grade school	homemaker	F	White	+
RI015	Little Compton	rural	middle	1910	1969	college	farm woman	F	White	+
RI016	Jamestown	village	old	1893	1969	college	domestic, maid	F	White	+
RI017	Jamestown	village	old	1894	1969	high school	postal service	M	White	+
SC001	Cheraw	village	old	1897	1966	grade school	small business: owner, manager	M	White	−
SC002	Cheraw	village	old	1880	1966	grade school	homemaker	F	White	+
SC003	Kershaw	rural	old	1902	1966	grade school	homemaker	F	White	+
SC004	Charleston	small city	old	1880	1966	college	financial services	M	White	−
SC005	Charleston	small city	old	1880	1966	college	homemaker	F	White	+
SC006	Marion	village	old	1903	1966	grade school	medicine	F	White	−
SC007	Marion	village	old	1900	1966	high school	homemaker	F	White	+
SC008	Marion	village	young	1944	1966	college	student	F	White	+
SC009	Georgetown	rural	old	1890	1966	some schooling	farmer, rancher	M	Black	+
SC010	Georgetown	rural	old	1900	1966	some schooling	farmer, rancher	M	Black	+
SC011	Kingstree	village	old	1889	1966	high school	homemaker	F	White	+
SC012	Kingstree	village	old	1899	1966	high school	homemaker	F	White	+
SC019	Cross	rural	old	1894	1966	grade school	small business: owner, manager	M	White	+
SC020	Charleston	small city	middle	1921	1966	grade school	police	M	White	−
SC021	Charleston	small city	middle	1908	1966	high school	postal service	M	White	+
SC022	Davis Station	rural	old	1901	1966	high school	homemaker	F	White	−
SC023	Davis Station	rural	old	1903	1966	high school	storekeeper	F	White	−
SC024	Davis Station	rural	old	1883	1966	high school	homemaker	F	White	+
SC026	Orangeburg	small city	middle	1908	1966	grade school	domestic, maid	F	Black	+
SC027	Orangeburg	small city	middle	1915	1966	college	medicine	M	White	−
SC028	Orangeburg	small city	young	1943	1966	college	student	M	White	−
SC029	York	village	old	1890	1967	college	homemaker	F	White	+
SC030	York	rural	old	1882	1967	grade school	farmer, rancher	M	White	−

Informant Code	Community	Community Type	Age-group	Year of Birth	Year of Interview	Education	Occupation	Sex	Race	Audio-tape
SC031	York	village	old	1898	1967	high school	homemaker	F	White	+
SC032	Westminster	village	middle	1914	1967	grade school	custodial, maintenance	M	White	+
SC034	Lebanon	rural	old	1900	1967	high school	homemaker	F	White	+
SC035	Lebanon	rural	old	1894	1967	unknown	skilled trades	M	White	+
SC036	Lebanon	rural	middle	1910	1967	college	teacher	F	White	−
SC038	New Ellenton	village	old	1900	1967	college	teacher	F	White	+
SC039	Greenville	small city	old	1895	1967	grade school	homemaker	F	White	+
SC040	New Ellenton	village	young	1929	1967	high school	farmer, rancher	M	White	+
SC041	Greenville	small city	old	1904	1967	high school	food services	F	White	−
SC042	Piedmont	village	middle	1916	1967	high school	factory worker	M	White	+
SC043	Walterboro	village	old	1880	1967	some schooling	farmer, rancher	M	White	+
SC044	Walterboro	village	young	1933	1967	high school	homemaker	F	White	+
SC045	Greenwood	small city	young	1943	1967	college	student	M	White	+
SC046	Bradley	rural	old	1883	1967	high school	homemaker	F	White	+
SC047	Callison	rural	old	1883	1967	unknown	farmer, rancher	M	White	+
SC051	Columbia	large city	middle	1924	1968	high school	postal service	M	White	−
SC052	Columbia	rural	young	1944	1968	high school	farmer, rancher	M	White	−
SC053	Columbia	rural	young	1943	1968	high school	farm woman	F	White	−
SC054	Columbia	large city	middle	1920	1967	college	journalism	F	White	+
SC055	Columbia	large city	old	1900	1967	college	real estate	M	Black	+
SC056	Peak	rural	old	1892	1968	grade school	postal service	F	White	+
SC057	Irmo	rural	old	1896	1968	high school	farmer, rancher	M	White	+
SC058	Little Mountain	rural	old	1899	1968	grade school	skilled trades	M	White	+
SC059	Pomaria	rural	old	1892	1968	college	teacher	F	White	+
SC062	Beaufort	village	middle	1925	1967	high school	homemaker	F	White	−
SC063	Seabrook	rural	middle	1908	1967	college	farmer, rancher	M	White	−
SC064	Beaufort	village	young	1950	1968	high school	student	M	Black	+
SC065	Beaufort	village	young	1950	1968	high school	student	M	Black	+
SC066	Charleston	small city	old	1902	1970	college	teacher	F	Black	+
SC067	Charleston	small city	middle	1920	1970	college	agricultural services	M	Black	+
SC068	Charleston	small city	middle	1915	1970	college	real estate	M	Black	+
SC069	Port Royal	village	middle	1914	1970	high school	small business: owner, manager	M	Black	+
SC070	Port Royal	village	middle	1918	1970	high school	medicine	F	Black	+
SD001	Yankton	small city	old	1886	1966	high school	financial services	M	White	+
SD002	Eureka	village	middle	1909	1966	grade school	skilled trades	M	White	+
SD003	Baltic	rural	old	1892	1966	high school	postal service	M	White	+
SD005	Deadwood	village	old	1893	1966	high school	railroad	M	White	+
SD007	Yankton	small city	old	−	1966	unknown	−	M	White	−
SD008	Ludlow	rural	old	1899	1966	some schooling	farmer, rancher	M	White	+
TN001	Cumberland Gap	rural	old	1900	1967	grade school	skilled trades	M	White	+
TN002	Rogersville	village	old	1893	1967	college	clerical	F	White	+
TN003	Rogersville	village	old	1890	1967	college	teacher	F	White	+
TN004	Rogersville	village	old	1897	1967	college	teacher	F	White	+
TN005	Rogersville	village	old	1900	1967	college	teacher	F	White	+
TN006	Rogersville	village	old	1901	1967	college	teacher	F	White	+
TN007	Rogersville	village	middle	1910	1967	college	legal	M	White	+
TN008	Rogersville	village	middle	1913	1967	college	teacher	F	White	+
TN010	Telford	rural	middle	1916	1967	college	farmer, rancher	M	White	+
TN011	Jonesboro	village	old	1892	1967	high school	insurance	M	White	−
TN012	Jonesboro	village	old	1882	1967	college	teacher	F	White	+

Informant Code	Community	Community Type	Age-group	Year of Birth	Year of Interview	Education	Occupation	Sex	Race	Audio-tape
TN013	Gatlinburg	village	old	1901	1967	grade school	homemaker	F	White	+
TN014	Gatlinburg	village	old	1897	1967	some schooling	farmer, rancher	M	White	+
TN015	Maryville	rural	old	1905	1967	grade school	farmer, rancher	M	White	+
TN016	Maryville	rural	old	1895	1967	grade school	farmer, rancher	M	White	+
TN017	Maryville	rural	old	1894	1967	some schooling	farmer, rancher	M	White	−
TN018	Maryville	small city	middle	1911	1967	high school	domestic, maid	F	White	−
TN019	Maryville	rural	old	1900	1967	some schooling	farmer, rancher	M	White	−
TN020	Maryville	rural	middle	1916	1967	high school	homemaker	M	White	−
TN022	Maryville	rural	old	1885	1967	high school	laborer	M	White	+
TN023	Maryville	small city	old	1891	1967	high school	homemaker	F	White	+
TN024	Raleigh	large city	old	1895	1968	grade school	homemaker	F	White	+
TN026	Martin	rural	old	1908	1968	grade school	laborer	M	White	+
TN027	Martin	rural	middle	1909	1968	high school	homemaker	F	White	−
TN030	Smithville	village	young	1931	1969	high school	financial services	M	White	+
TN031	Castalian Springs	rural	old	1890	1969	grade school	farmer, rancher	M	White	+
TN032	Castalian Springs	rural	middle	1922	1969	high school	homemaker	F	White	−
TN033	Selmer	village	young	1935	1969	high school	homemaker	F	White	+
TN034	Somerville	village	old	1889	1969	college	local government	M	White	+
TN035	Parsons	small city	middle	1914	1969	college	storekeeper	F	White	+
TN036	Camden	rural	old	1896	1969	grade school	farmer, rancher	M	White	−
TN037	Springfield	village	old	1904	1969	college	agricultural services	M	White	+
TN038	Springfield	village	young	1942	1969	college	educational administrator	M	White	+
TN039	Springfield	village	young	1946	1969	college	teacher	F	White	+
TN041	Dayton	village	middle	1914	1970	college	clerical	F	White	+
TN042	Dayton	village	old	1910	1970	high school	local government	M	White	+
TN043	Dayton	village	middle	1928	1970	college	educational administrator	M	White	+
TN044	Jasper	village	middle	1916	1970	high school	small business: owner, manager	M	White	+
TN045	Jasper	village	young	1950	1970	college	student	F	White	−
TN046	Memphis	large city	young	1947	1970	college	social & community services	F	Black	+
TN047	Memphis	large city	old	1910	1970	high school	lodging trades	M	Black	−
TN048	Memphis	large city	old	1888	1970	college	religion	M	Black	+
TN049	Memphis	large city	middle	1914	1970	college	teacher	F	Black	−
TN050	Memphis	large city	young	1939	1970	high school	lodging trades	M	Black	−
TN052	Brownsville	village	old	1892	1970	grade school	−	F	Black	+
TN053	Brownsville	village	old	1910	1970	college	educational administrator	M	Black	+
TN054	Brownsville	village	young	1948	1970	college	financial services	M	Black	−
TN055	Brownsville	village	middle	1911	1970	high school	social & community services	F	Black	−
TN056	Cornersville	rural	old	1891	1970	college	teacher	M	White	+
TN057	Pulaski	village	old	1894	1970	college	unemployed	F	White	+
TN058	Pulaski	village	young	1946	1970	college	student	F	White	+
TN059	Pulaski	village	young	1938	1970	high school	homemaker	F	White	+
TN060	Columbia	small city	old	1907	1970	college	farm woman	F	White	+
TN061	Culleoka	rural	middle	1921	1970	college	homemaker	F	White	+
TN062	Columbia	small city	old	1874	1970	grade school	farmer, rancher	M	White	+
TN063	Columbia	small city	young	1939	1970	college	teacher	M	White	+
TN064	Nashville	large city	old	1913	1970	college	educational administrator	F	White	+

Informant Code	Community	Community Type	Age-group	Year of Birth	Year of Interview	Education	Occupation	Sex	Race	Audio-tape
TN065	Nashville	large city	young	1948	1970	college	student	M	White	−
TN066	Murfreesboro	small city	middle	1928	1970	college	social & community services	M	White	+
TN067	Murfreesboro	small city	middle	1928	1970	college	homemaker	F	White	+
TX001	Crystal City	village	old	1888	1967	college	local government	M	White	+
TX002	Del Rio	rural	old	1898	1967	high school	farmer, rancher	M	Black	−
TX003	Del Rio	small city	old	1892	1967	grade school	real estate	F	White	+
TX004	Uvalde	small city	old	1899	1967	college	journalism	F	White	+
TX005	El Paso	rural	middle	1910	1967	college	farmer, rancher	M	White	+
TX006	Crystal City	village	old	1887	1967	college	legal	M	White	−
TX008	Mauriceville	rural	middle	1920	1967	college	farmer, rancher	M	White	+
TX009	Orange	small city	old	1902	1967	high school	storekeeper	M	White	+
TX010	Clint	rural	old	1895	1967	college	homemaker	F	White	+
TX011	Goliad	village	old	1905	1967	high school	storekeeper	M	White	+
TX012	Bay City	rural	old	1886	1967	college	farm woman	F	White	+
TX013	Karnes City	village	old	1895	1967	high school	small business: owner, manager	M	White	+
TX014	Port Bolivar	rural	middle	1915	1967	high school	laborer	M	White	+
TX015	Galveston	small city	old	1907	1967	college	homemaker	F	White	+
TX016	Galveston	rural	young	1928	1967	college	skilled trades	M	White	−
TX017	Rockport	village	old	1891	1967	college	homemaker	F	White	+
TX018	Rockport	village	middle	1908	1967	high school	storekeeper	M	White	+
TX019	Refugio	village	old	1903	1967	grade school	laborer	M	White	+
TX020	Refugio	village	old	1907	1967	high school	homemaker	F	White	−
TX021	Refugio	village	old	1889	1967	high school	clerical	F	White	+
TX022	Refugio	village	old	1907	1967	college	farmer, rancher	M	White	+
TX023	Refugio	village	old	1899	1967	college	medicine	M	White	+
TX026	Austin	large city	old	1896	1967	grade school	skilled trades	M	Black	+
TX027	Mission	small city	young	1948	1967	high school	homemaker	F	White	+
TX028	Laredo	small city	middle	1918	1967	college	legal	M	White	+
TX029	Cotulla	village	middle	1909	1967	college	librarian	F	White	+
TX030	Cotulla	village	old	1904	1967	college	medicine	M	White	+
TX031	Brownsville	small city	old	1893	1967	high school	financial services	M	White	+
TX032	San Augustine	village	middle	1914	1967	grade school	homemaker	F	White	+
TX033	Nacogdoches	small city	young	1934	1967	high school	homemaker	F	White	+
TX035	Brookeland	rural	old	1889	1967	high school	teacher	M	White	+
TX036	Woodville	village	old	1891	1967	grade school	homemaker	F	White	+
TX037	Jasper	village	middle	1921	1967	high school	police	M	White	+
TX038	Marshall	small city	old	1880	1967	high school	clerical	F	White	+
TX039	Amarillo	large city	old	1891	1967	some schooling	police	M	White	+
TX040	Cisco	rural	old	1888	1967	grade school	homemaker	F	White	+
TX041	Lubbock	large city	young	1949	1967	high school	student	M	White	+
TX042	Abilene	small city	old	1892	1967	high school	insurance	F	White	−
TX043	San Angelo	small city	old	1891.	1967	high school	financial services	M	White	+
TX045	Turkey	rural	old	1892	1967	grade school	homemaker	F	White	−
TX051	Clarksville	village	middle	1912	1968	college	educational administrator	M	White	+
TX052	Clarksville	village	middle	1913	1968	college	teacher	F	White	+
TX053	Waco	small city	middle	1923	1968	college	wholesale, retail sales	M	White	+
TX054	Fredericksburg	village	old	1908	1968	grade school	police	M	White	+
TX055	Wichita Falls	large city	middle	1920	1969	high school	lodging trades	F	White	−
TX056	Wichita Falls	large city	middle	1921	1969	high school	barber, beautician	M	White	−

Informant Code	Community	Community Type	Age-group	Year of Birth	Year of Interview	Education	Occupation	Sex	Race	Audio-tape
TX057	Wichita Falls	large city	old	1891	1969	some schooling	wholesale, retail sales	M	White	−
TX058	Wichita Falls	large city	old	1893	1969	high school	wholesale, retail sales	F	White	−
TX059	Wichita Falls	large city	middle	1919	1969	unknown	storekeeper	M	White	+
TX060	Wichita Falls	large city	middle	1919	1969	college	clerical	F	White	−
TX061	Wichita Falls	large city	young	1940	1969	high school	clerical	F	White	−
TX062	Dime Box	rural	old	1895	1969	high school	homemaker	F	White	+
TX063	Dime Box	rural	old	1893	1969	high school	medicine	M	White	−
TX064	Dime Box	rural	old	1903	1969	college	teacher	M	White	−
TX065	Alpine	village	old	1887	1969	college	real estate	F	White	+
TX066	Alpine	rural	old	1900	1969	college	farmer, rancher	M	White	−
TX067	Alpine	village	old	1898	1969	high school	farmer, rancher	F	White	−
TX068	Ozona	village	old	1897	1969	high school	farmer, rancher	M	White	+
TX069	Ozona	rural	old	1908	1969	college	homemaker	F	White	+
TX070	Ozona	rural	young	1952	1969	high school	student	M	White	+
TX071	Mentone	rural	old	1904	1969	grade school	homemaker	F	White	+
TX072	Mentone	rural	middle	1922	1969	college	small business: owner, manager	M	White	+
TX073	Fort Worth	large city	old	1903	1969	college	teacher	F	White	+
TX074	Fort Worth	large city	middle	1919	1969	high school	storekeeper	F	White	−
TX075	Fort Worth	large city	old	1905	1969	college	homemaker	F	White	+
TX076	Big Spring	small city	old	1909	1970	grade school	trucking, transportation	M	White	−
TX077	Big Spring	small city	old	1905	1970	high school	homemaker	F	White	−
TX078	Big Spring	rural	young	1935	1970	college	farmer, rancher	M	White	+
TX079	Big Spring	small city	middle	1914	1970	high school	journalism	F	White	+
TX080	Big Spring	small city	old	1906	1970	college	librarian	F	White	−
TX081	Brady	village	middle	1917	1970	high school	wholesale, retail sales	M	White	+
TX082	Brady	village	old	1890	1970	college	homemaker	F	White	+
TX083	Brady	village	young	1941	1970	college	journalism	M	White	−
TX084	Brady	village	old	1891	1970	grade school	clerical	M	White	−
TX085	Houston	large city	old	1899	1970	grade school	seamstress	F	White	+
TX086	Houston	large city	middle	1927	1970	high school	seamstress	F	Black	−
TX087	Houston	large city	middle	1919	1970	college	librarian	F	White	+
TX088	Houston	large city	young	1953	1970	high school	student	M	White	−
TX089	Sulphur Springs	village	old	1905	1970	college	wholesale, retail sales	M	White	+
TX090	Sulphur Springs	village	young	1951	1970	college	student	F	White	−
TX091	Sulphur Springs	village	old	1904	1970	college	teacher	F	White	−
TX092	Sulphur Springs	village	young	1952	1970	high school	student	M	Black	−
TX094	Kennard	rural	old	1893	1970	grade school	farm woman	F	White	+
TX095	Crockett	village	middle	1913	1970	college	legal	M	White	−
TX096	Crockett	rural	old	1889	1970	grade school	farmer, rancher	M	White	+
TX097	Crockett	village	middle	1925	1970	college	teacher	F	Black	−
TX098	Timpson	village	middle	1917	1970	high school	insurance	M	White	−
TX099	Timpson	village	old	1906	1970	college	teacher	F	White	+
TX100	Timpson	rural	middle	1912	1970	high school	farmer, rancher	M	White	+
TX101	Kingsville	village	old	1898	1970	college	teacher	M	White	+
TX102	Kingsville	rural	old	1889	1970	college	farmer, rancher	F	White	+
TX103	Kingsville	village	old	1887	1970	high school	homemaker	F	White	−
TX104	Athens	village	old	1890	1970	grade school	lodging trades	F	White	+
TX105	Athens	rural	old	1908	1970	unknown	farmer, rancher	M	White	−
TX106	Athens	rural	old	1908	1970	some schooling	laborer	M	Black	−

Informant Code	Community	Community Type	Age-group	Year of Birth	Year of Interview	Education	Occupation	Sex	Race	Audio-tape
*UT001	Salt Lake City	large city	old	1884	1965	grade school	homemaker	F	White	+
*UT002	Salt Lake City	large city	old	1882	1965	grade school	engineer	M	White	−
*UT003	Salt Lake City	large city	middle	1909	1965	high school	foreman, supervisor	M	White	+
UT004	Corinne	rural	old	1905	1968	grade school	skilled trades	M	White	+
UT005	Fillmore	village	old	1899	1968	high school	postal service	M	White	−
UT006	Fillmore	village	old	1905	1968	college	teacher	F	White	+
UT007	Fillmore	village	old	1897	1968	college	teacher	F	White	+
UT008	Cedar City	village	old	1898	1968	high school	homemaker	F	White	+
UT009	Cedar City	village	middle	1910	1968	college	teacher	F	White	−
UT010	Cedar City	village	young	1932	1968	college	clerical	F	White	−
UT011	Moab	village	old	1904	1968	high school	storekeeper	F	White	+
UT012	Moab	village	old	1906	1968	high school	homemaker	F	White	+
UT013	Moab	village	old	1885	1968	high school	homemaker	F	White	−
UT014	Moab	village	young	1933	1968	college	journalism	M	White	−
UT015	Moab	village	young	1933	1968	college	financial services	M	White	−
VT002	Brattleboro	rural	old	1906	1968	grade school	farmer, rancher	M	White	−
VT003	Brattleboro	rural	middle	1915	1968	high school	local government	F	White	−
VT004	West Brattle-boro	rural	old	1892	1968	high school	farmer, rancher	M	White	−
VT005	Vernon	rural	old	1906	1968	grade school	homemaker	F	White	−
VT006	Vernon	rural	old	1886	1968	grade school	farm woman	F	White	−
VT007	Arlington	rural	old	1895	1968	high school	farmer, rancher	M	White	+
VT008	Arlington	village	middle	1910	1968	grade school	food services	F	White	−
VT009	Arlington	rural	old	1894	1968	high school	farmer, rancher	M	White	−
VT010	Arlington	village	old	1895	1968	high school	logging	M	White	−
VT011	Arlington	rural	middle	1914	1968	high school	farm woman	F	White	−
VT012	Woodstock	rural	old	1889	1969	college	farmer, rancher	M	White	−
VT013	Woodstock	village	old	1884	1969	high school	clerical	F	White	+
VT016	Newport	village	middle	1914	1969	high school	storekeeper	M	White	+
VT017	Newport	village	old	1896	1969	high school	teacher	F	White	−
VA001	Big Stone Gap	rural	middle	1915	1968	some schooling	homemaker	F	White	−
VA002	Big Stone Gap	rural	young	1931	1968	grade school	homemaker	F	White	+
VA003	Big Stone Gap	village	middle	1926	1968	grade school	laborer	M	White	−
VA004	Abingdon	village	middle	1919	1968	high school	homemaker	F	White	−
VA005	Abingdon	village	old	1898	1968	high school	administrative, managerial	M	White	+
VA006	Abingdon	village	middle	1907	1968	college	storekeeper	M	White	−
VA007	Abingdon	rural	middle	1926	1968	high school	homemaker	F	White	−
VA008	Wytheville	village	old	1893	1968	high school	postal service	M	White	−
VA009	Wytheville	rural	old	1895	1968	grade school	homemaker	F	White	+
VA010	Wytheville	rural	middle	1909	1968	high school	farmer, rancher	M	White	−
VA011	Wytheville	rural	old	1902	1968	high school	homemaker	F	White	−
VA012	Wytheville	village	old	1904	1968	high school	journalism	F	White	+
VA013	Laurel Fork	rural	old	1903	1968	college	teacher	F	White	−
VA014	Hillsville	rural	old	1889	1968	college	teacher	M	White	−
VA015	Hillsville	rural	old	−	1968	college	teacher	F	White	−
VA016	Hillsville	rural	old	1891	1968	college	teacher	F	White	−
VA018	Salem	small city	old	1887	1968	college	teacher	F	White	+
VA019	Catawba	rural	old	1881	1968	college	farmer, rancher	M	White	−
VA020	Catawba	rural	old	1905	1968	high school	farmer, rancher	M	White	−
VA021	Catawba	rural	old	1908	1968	college	farm woman	F	White	−

Informant Code	Community	Community Type	Age-group	Year of Birth	Year of Interview	Education	Occupation	Sex	Race	Audio-tape
VA022	Springwood	rural	old	1904	1968	high school	homemaker	F	White	−
VA023	Buchanan	village	old	1885	1968	college	teacher	F	White	+
VA024	Buchanan	rural	young	1931	1968	high school	farmer, rancher	M	White	−
VA025	Buchanan	rural	old	1893	1968	high school	farm woman	F	White	+
VA026	Lexington	rural	old	1896	1968	college	farmer, rancher	M	White	+
VA027	Warm Springs	rural	old	1897	1968	some schooling	farmer, rancher	M	White	+
VA028	Warm Springs	rural	old	1899	1968	college	teacher	F	White	−
VA029	Warm Springs	rural	old	1896	1968	high school	clerical	F	White	−
VA030	Timberville	rural	old	1899	1968	college	teacher	F	White	+
VA031	New Market	rural	old	1906	1968	college	teacher	F	White	−
VA032	Timberville	rural	old	1906	1968	high school	farmer, rancher	M	White	−
VA033	Winchester	small city	old	1895	1968	college	administrative, managerial	M	White	+
VA034	Winchester	small city	middle	1916	1968	college	teacher	F	White	−
VA035	Scottsburg	rural	middle	1915	1970	high school	farm woman	F	White	−
VA036	Scottsburg	rural	old	1891	1970	grade school	farm woman	F	White	−
VA037	Scottsburg	rural	middle	1921	1970	high school	farmer, rancher	M	White	−
VA038	Scottsburg	rural	middle	1915	1970	some schooling	farmer, rancher	M	White	+
VA039	Alberta	rural	middle	1926	1970	high school	homemaker	F	Black	−
VA040	Lawrence-ville	rural	old	1890	1970	some schooling	farmer, rancher	M	Black	+
VA041	Lawrence-ville	village	middle	1913	1970	high school	storekeeper	F	Black	−
VA042	Chatham	rural	old	1908	1970	high school	homemaker	F	White	−
VA043	Chatham	rural	old	1904	1970	high school	farmer, rancher	M	White	+
VA044	Smithfield	rural	old	1897	1970	high school	farmer, rancher	M	White	−
VA045	Smithfield	rural	old	1894	1970	high school	farm woman	F	White	−
VA046	Smithfield	rural	old	1902	1970	high school	farmer, rancher	M	Black	+
VA047	Chincoteague	village	middle	1928	1970	high school	nautical, fishing	M	White	+
VA048	Chincoteague	village	old	1894	1970	some schooling	homemaker	F	White	−
VA049	Parksley	rural	old	1891	1970	high school	farmer, rancher	M	White	−
VA050	Chincoteague	village	middle	1916	1970	college	clerical	F	White	−
VA051	Accomac	rural	old	1892	1970	college	journalism	M	White	−
VA052	Chincoteague	village	old	1901	1970	grade school	nautical, fishing	M	White	+
VA053	Hayes	rural	old	1894	1970	grade school	homemaker	F	White	−
VA054	Hayes	rural	young	1944	1970	high school	laborer	F	White	−
VA055	Severn	rural	old	1889	1970	some schooling	nautical, fishing	M	White	+
VA056	Maryus	rural	middle	1913	1970	grade school	storekeeper	F	White	−
VA057	Gloucester	rural	old	1898	1970	high school	farmer, rancher	F	White	−
VA058	Leesburg	village	old	1898	1970	college	clerical	F	White	−
VA059	Leesburg	rural	young	1935	1970	high school	farmer, rancher	M	White	+
VA060	Leesburg	village	old	1905	1970	college	teacher	F	White	−
VA061	Leesburg	rural	old	1900	1970	high school	farmer, rancher	M	White	−
VA062	Leesburg	village	young	1936	1970	high school	homemaker	F	White	+
VA063	Warrenton	village	middle	1920	1970	college	homemaker	F	White	−
VA064	Warrenton	village	old	1904	1970	college	small business: owner, manager	M	White	+
VA065	Warrenton	village	middle	1925	1970	high school	homemaker	F	White	+
VA066	Warrenton	village	old	1881	1970	high school	unemployed	F	White	+
VA067	Warrenton	village	young	1934	1970	high school	homemaker	F	White	−
VA068	Casanova	rural	old	1905	1970	grade school	farmer, rancher	M	White	−

Informant Code	Community	Community Type	Age-group	Year of Birth	Year of Interview	Education	Occupation	Sex	Race	Audio-tape
VA069	Capron	rural	middle	1917	1970	high school	homemaker	F	Black	+
VA070	Capron	rural	old	1909	1970	grade school	farmer, rancher	M	Black	+
VA071	Petersburg	small city	old	1909	1970	high school	domestic, maid	F	Black	+
VA072	Petersburg	small city	old	1905	1970	college	teacher	F	Black	+
VA073	Petersburg	small city	young	1942	1970	high school	trucking, transportation	M	Black	+
VA074	Caret	rural	old	1907	1970	college	teacher	F	White	−
VA075	Caret	rural	middle	1920	1970	grade school	farmer, rancher	M	White	+
VA076	Montross	rural	middle	1918	1970	grade school	homemaker	F	White	−
VA077	Warsaw	rural	middle	1912	1970	grade school	farmer, rancher	M	White	−
VA078	Montross	rural	middle	1918	1970	high school	storekeeper	F	White	−
VA079	Warsaw	rural	young	1943	1970	high school	wholesale, retail sales	M	White	+
VA080	Warsaw	rural	middle	1919	1970	high school	homemaker	F	White	+
VA081	Richmond	large city	young	1941	1970	high school	homemaker	F	White	+
VA082	Richmond	rural	old	1905	1970	college	farmer, rancher	M	White	−
VA083	Richmond	large city	young	1936	1970	college	homemaker	F	White	+
VA084	Richmond	large city	middle	1919	1970	college	financial services	M	White	−
VA085	Richmond	large city	young	1938	1970	college	real estate	M	White	−
VA086	Richmond	large city	young	1942	1970	college	homemaker	F	White	−
VA087	Dillwyn	rural	old	1891	1970	high school	farmer, rancher	M	White	−
VA088	Dillwyn	rural	old	1898	1970	high school	farm woman	F	White	−
VA089	Buckingham	rural	old	1904	1970	college	agricultural services	M	White	−
VA090	Buckingham	rural	middle	1923	1970	high school	teacher	F	White	+
VA091	Buckingham	rural	middle	1925	1970	high school	homemaker	F	White	+
VA092	Dillwyn	rural	middle	1927	1970	high school	homemaker	F	White	−
VA093	Charlottes-ville	small city	middle	1923	1970	high school	homemaker	F	White	+
VA094	Charlottes-ville	small city	old	1897	1970	college	financial services	F	White	−
VA095	Charlottes-ville	rural	old	1901	1970	some schooling	farmer, rancher	M	White	−
VA096	Scottsville	rural	middle	1913	1970	high school	farmer, rancher	M	White	+
VA097	Lynchburg	small city	old	1902	1970	grade school	small business: owner, manager	M	White	+
VA098	Lynchburg	small city	young	1931	1970	college	homemaker	F	White	+
VA099	Lynchburg	small city	middle	1930	1970	college	homemaker	F	White	−
VA100	Monroe	rural	middle	1916	1970	high school	farmer, rancher	M	White	−
VA101	Madison Heights	rural	middle	1917	1970	high school	homemaker	F	White	−
VA102	Bumpass	rural	middle	1928	1970	high school	homemaker	F	White	−
VA103	Louisa	rural	old	1887	1970	high school	homemaker	F	White	−
VA104	Pendletons	rural	old	1895	1970	high school	homemaker	F	White	+
VA105	Bumpass	rural	old	1902	1970	high school	farmer, rancher	M	White	+
VA106	Fredericks-burg	small city	old	1897	1970	college	medicine	F	White	+
VA107	Fredericks-burg	small city	young	1938	1970	college	homemaker	F	White	+
VA108	Fredericks-burg	small city	old	1886	1970	college	teacher	F	White	−
VA109	Fredericks-burg	small city	young	1936	1970	college	homemaker	F	White	−
VA110	Fredericks-burg	small city	old	1899	1970	high school	local government	M	White	−
VA111	Fredericks-burg	rural	old	1905	1970	high school	farmer, rancher	M	White	−
WA001	Chewelah	rural	old	1901	1966	high school	farm woman	F	White	+
WA002	Chewelah	village	old	1872	1966	grade school	food services	M	White	+

Informant Code	Community	Community Type	Age-group	Year of Birth	Year of Interview	Education	Occupation	Sex	Race	Audio-tape
WA003	Pullman	small city	old	1896	1966	college	postal service	M	White	+
WA004	Pullman	small city	old	1894	1966	college	financial services	M	White	−
WA005	Walla Walla	small city	old	1901	1966	college	homemaker	F	White	−
WA006	Walla Walla	small city	old	1887	1966	high school	librarian	F	White	+
WA007	Walla Walla	small city	old	1887	1966	high school	postal service	M	White	+
WA008	Yakima	rural	old	1890	1966	college	farm woman	F	White	+
WA009	Yakima	small city	old	1901	1966	high school	homemaker	F	White	+
WA011	Seattle	large city	old	1900	1966	high school	skilled trades	M	White	+
WA012	Cashmere	village	old	1891	1966	high school	homemaker	F	White	+
WA013	Cashmere	village	old	1897	1966	high school	farmer, rancher	M	White	+
WA014	Port Town-send	village	old	1882	1966	high school	small business: owner, manager	M	White	−
WA015	Port Town-send	village	old	1887	1966	high school	farmer, rancher	F	White	+
WA016	Port Town-send	village	old	1896	1966	college	journalism	M	White	+
WA017	Port Town-send	village	old	1892	1966	high school	laborer	M	White	+
WA018	Lynden	village	old	1881	1966	college	financial services	M	White	−
WA019	Raymond	village	old	1906	1967	high school	librarian	F	White	+
WA020	Raymond	village	old	1904	1967	high school	logging	M	White	+
WA021	Skykomish	rural	old	1883	1967	grade school	laborer	M	White	−
WA022	Skykomish	rural	young	1939	1967	college	teacher	M	White	−
WA023	Skykomish	rural	middle	1920	1967	college	teacher	F	White	+
WA024	Arlington	village	old	1889	1967	grade school	logging	M	White	+
WA025	Arlington	rural	old	1891	1967	high school	farm woman	F	White	+
WA026	Arlington	village	old	1897	1967	grade school	teacher	F	White	−
WA027	Vancouver	small city	middle	1926	1967	high school	financial services	F	White	−
WA028	Hazel Dell	village	middle	1917	1967	high school	farm woman	F	White	+
WA030	Castle Rock	rural	old	1907	1967	high school	logging	M	White	+
WA031	Okanogon	rural	old	1880	1966	grade school	farmer, rancher	M	White	−
WA032	Okanogon	village	old	1890	1966	grade school	homemaker	F	White	−
WA033	Okanogon	village	middle	1921	1966	high school	artist, craftsman	F	White	−
WV001	Marlinton	village	old	1899	1968	grade school	clerical	F	White	+
WV002	Marlinton	village	old	1900	1968	college	educational administrator	M	White	+
WV003	Spencer	village	old	1888	1968	high school	police	M	White	+
WV004	Milton	village	old	1881	1968	grade school	logging	M	White	+
WV005	Logan	village	old	1901	1968	grade school	miner	M	White	+
WV006	Westover	village	old	1888	1968	grade school	homemaker	F	White	+
WV007	Westover	rural	old	1882	1968	grade school	farmer, rancher	M	White	+
WV008	Moorefield	rural	old	1908	1968	some schooling	farmer, rancher	M	White	+
WV010	Romney	village	young	1947	1968	college	student	F	White	+
WV011	Romney	village	old	1881	1968	grade school	homemaker	F	White	+
WV012	Lewisburg	village	young	1938	1968	high school	factory worker	M	White	+
WV013	Richwood	village	old	1902	1968	grade school	logging	M	White	+
WV014	Salem	village	middle	1912	1970	college	teacher	M	White	+
WV016	Buckhannon	village	old	1890	1970	college	small business: owner, manager	M	White	+
WV017	Charles Town	village	old	1897	1969	high school	farmer, rancher	M	White	−
WV018	Charles Town	village	middle	1925	1969	high school	administrative, managerial	M	White	+
WV020	Charleston	small city	young	1944	1970	college	student	F	Black	+
WV021	Charleston	small city	young	1952	1970	high school	student	M	Black	+

Informant Code	Community	Community Type	Age-group	Year of Birth	Year of Interview	Education	Occupation	Sex	Race	Audio-tape
WI005	Portage	village	old	1893	1968	college	educational administrator	F	White	−
WI006	Portage	rural	old	1900	1968	grade school	farmer, rancher	M	White	−
WI007	Portage	village	old	1894	1968	college	administrative, managerial	M	White	+
WI008	Portage	village	old	1900	1968	college	teacher	F	White	+
WI009	Portage	village	old	1895	1968	college	journalism	M	White	−
WI010	Juneau	rural	old	1898	1968	grade school	farmer, rancher	M	White	+
WI011	Juneau	rural	old	1908	1968	high school	homemaker	F	White	+
WI012	Hustisford	rural	middle	1919	1968	college	ranger, guide	M	White	+
WI013	Jefferson	village	middle	1926	1968	college	journalism	F	White	+
WI014	Jefferson	village	old	1901	1968	high school	financial services	M	White	−
WI015	Jefferson	rural	old	1885	1968	grade school	farmer, rancher	M	White	−
WI016	Jefferson	rural	old	1889	1968	grade school	farmer, rancher	M	White	−
WI017	Jefferson	rural	middle	1918	1968	high school	farmer, rancher	M	White	+
WI018	Jefferson	village	middle	1914	1968	high school	homemaker	F	White	+
WI019	Janesville	small city	old	1892	1968	college	wholesale, retail sales	M	White	+
WI020	Janesville	small city	old	1908	1968	college	museum staff	F	White	+
WI021	Janesville	small city	old	1892	1968	college	teacher	F	White	+
WI022	Milton	rural	old	1888	1968	grade school	skilled trades	M	White	+
WI023	Belmont	rural	old	1905	1968	high school	homemaker	F	White	+
WI024	Belmont	rural	old	1898	1968	college	farmer, rancher	F	White	+
WI025	Belmont	rural	old	1894	1968	high school	medicine	F	White	+
WI026	Belmont	rural	old	1888	1968	grade school	trucking, transportation	M	White	+
WI027	Belmont	rural	old	1898	1968	high school	trucking, transportation	M	White	+
WI028	Necedah	rural	old	1891	1968	college	teacher	F	White	−
WI029	Necedah	rural	middle	1911	1968	high school	librarian	F	White	+
WI030	Necedah	rural	middle	1910	1968	grade school	farmer, rancher	M	White	+
WI031	Necedah	rural	old	1895	1968	high school	farm woman	F	White	+
WI032	Necedah	rural	old	1888	1968	high school	foreman, supervisor	M	White	−
WI033	Necedah	rural	old	1903	1968	college	small business: owner, manager	M	White	−
WI034	Wautoma	village	young	1938	1968	college	teacher	F	White	+
WI035	Wautoma	village	young	1941	1968	high school	homemaker	F	White	−
WI036	Wautoma	village	old	1880	1968	college	legal	M	White	−
WI037	Wautoma	village	young	1937	1968	college	legal	M	White	−
WI038	Wautoma	village	young	1935	1968	college	food services	M	White	−
WI039	Wautoma	village	young	1938	1968	college	teacher	F	White	−
WI040	Wautoma	village	middle	1919	1968	high school	postal service	M	White	+
WI041	Wautoma	village	old	1895	1968	high school	teacher	F	White	−
WI042	Wautoma	rural	middle	1913	1968	grade school	farmer, rancher	M	White	−
WI043	Lancaster	rural	old	1900	1968	high school	farmer, rancher	M	White	+
WI044	Lancaster	rural	old	1885	1968	grade school	farmer, rancher	M	White	+
WI045	Lancaster	village	old	1883	1968	high school	financial services	M	White	+
WI046	Lancaster	village	old	1889	1968	high school	homemaker	F	White	+
WI047	New Berlin	small city	young	1933	1968	college	homemaker	F	White	+
WI048	Greenfield	small city	middle	1920	1968	college	administrative, managerial	M	White	+
WI049	Menomonee Falls	small city	old	1890	1968	high school	clerical	F	White	+
WI050	Menomonee Falls	small city	middle	1923	1968	high school	homemaker	F	White	+
WI051	Menomonee Falls	small city	old	1894	1968	high school	skilled trades	M	White	−

Informant Code	Community	Community Type	Age-group	Year of Birth	Year of Interview	Education	Occupation	Sex	Race	Audio-tape
WI052	Florence	rural	old	1896	1968	college	teacher	F	White	+
WI053	La Crosse	small city	old	1901	1968	college	homemaker	F	White	−
WI054	Onalaska	rural	middle	1912	1968	high school	wholesale, retail sales	F	White	−
WI055	La Crosse	small city	young	1943	1968	college	teacher	M	White	+
WI056	Medary	small city	old	1903	1968	college	homemaker	F	White	+
WI057	La Crosse	small city	young	1947	1968	college	artist, craftsman	M	White	−
WI058	Polar	village	middle	1918	1968	college	teacher	F	White	+
WI059	Antigo	village	old	1888	1968	college	insurance	M	White	+
WI060	Algoma	village	old	1901	1968	high school	administrative, managerial	M	White	+
WI061	Algoma	village	old	1908	1968	high school	administrative, managerial	M	White	+
WI062	Burlington	village	old	1890	1968	college	homemaker	F	White	+
WI063	Burlington	village	middle	1910	1968	high school	homemaker	F	White	−
WI064	Superior	small city	middle	1914	1968	college	medicine	F	White	+
WI065	Superior	small city	middle	1912	1968	high school	homemaker	F	White	+
WI066	Pepin	rural	old	1896	1968	high school	homemaker	F	White	+
WI067	Jim Falls	rural	old	1901	1968	grade school	homemaker	F	White	+
WI068	Jim Falls	rural	middle	1926	1968	high school	homemaker	F	White	+
WI069	River Falls	village	old	1891	1968	college	teacher	F	White	−
WI070	River Falls	village	old	1890	1968	high school	domestic, maid	F	White	+
WI071	Manitowoc	small city	middle	1916	1968	high school	clerical	F	White	+
WI072	Bayfield	rural	old	1899	1968	college	homemaker	F	White	+
WI073	Bayfield	rural	old	1887	1968	college	administrative, managerial	M	White	−
WI074	Bayfield	rural	old	1891	1968	college	teacher	F	White	−
WI075	Washington Island	rural	old	1904	1969	grade school	nautical, fishing	M	White	+
WI076	Washington Island	rural	old	1896	1969	grade school	homemaker	F	White	+
WI077	Washington Island	rural	middle	1915	1969	grade school	farmer, rancher	M	White	+
WI078	Washington Island	rural	old	1887	1969	grade school	nautical, fishing	M	White	−
WY001	Jackson	rural	old	1906	1967	high school	ranger, guide	M	White	+
WY002	Jackson	village	old	1897	1967	grade school	ranger, guide	M	White	+
WY003	Hilliard Flat	rural	old	1896	1967	grade school	farm woman	F	White	+
WY004	Hilliard Flat	rural	old	1891	1967	grade school	farmer, rancher	M	White	+
WY005	Laramie	village	old	1892	1967	high school	farmer, rancher	M	White	+

Informants Who Made Audiotapes Only

Informant Code	Community	Community Type	Age-group	Year of Birth	Year of Interview	Education	Occupation	Sex	Race	Audio-tape
AL009	Mobile	large city	young	1945	1967	high school	teacher	F	White	+
AL013	Anniston	small city	middle	1911	1966	some schooling	domestic, maid	F	Black	+
AL018	Dothan	small city	middle	1917	1967	high school	homemaker	F	White	+
AL045	Scottsboro	village	−	−	1968	unknown	wholesale, retail sales	M	White	+
AK006	Juneau	village	old	1892	1968	unknown	ranger, guide	M	White	+
AK010	Sitka	village	old	1877	1968	unknown	−	M	White	+
AK011	Juneau	village	old	−	1968	unknown	−	F	White	+
AK012	Anchorage	small city	old	−	1968	unknown	artist, craftsman	M	Am Ind	+
AK013	Anchorage	small city	old	−	1968	unknown	food services	F	White	+
AZ004	Prescott	village	old	1887	1967	some schooling	farmer, rancher	M	White	+
AR050	Cale	rural	middle	1912	1967	grade school	logging	M	White	+
CA067	San Luis Obispo	small city	old	1897	1967	high school	museum staff	F	White	+
CA068	Carmel	village	young	1954	1967	grade school	student	F	White	+

Informant Code	Community	Community Type	Age-group	Year of Birth	Year of Interview	Education	Occupation	Sex	Race	Audio-tape
CA068A	Carmel	village	young	1958	1967	some schooling	student	F	White	+
CA069	Carmel	village	young	1929	1967	college	insurance	M	White	+
CA069B	Carmel	village	young	1958	1967	some schooling	student	F	White	+
CA089	Julian	rural	old	1897	1968	some schooling	farmer, rancher	M	White	+
CA100	Garberville	rural	old	1882	1968	grade school	logging	M	White	+
CA103	Fort Bragg	village	old	1878	1968	high school	logging	M	White	+
CA104	Fort Bragg	village	old	1894	1968	college	logging	M	White	+
CA143	Folsom	village	old	1906	1969	unknown	small business: owner, manager	M	Oriental	+
CA159	Tulelake	rural	old	1893	1969	high school	farmer, rancher	M	White	+
CA172	Crescent City	village	old	—	1969	unknown	—	M	White	+
CA172A	Crescent City	village	old	—	1969	unknown	—	F	White	+
CA172B	Crescent City	village	old	—	1969	unknown	—	M	White	+
CA180	Long Beach	urban	young	1947	1970	high school	student	M	White	+
CA186	San Diego	urban	old	1895	1970	unknown	small business: owner, manager	M	White	+
CA198	Quincy	village	old	1910	1970	college	homemaker	F	White	+
CO001	Sterling	small city	old	1878	1967	grade school	farmer, rancher	M	White	+
CT038	Stafford Springs	village	old	—	1969	unknown	trucking, transportation	M	White	+
CT041	Old Mystic	village	old	1873	1969	unknown	factory worker	F	White	+
DC009	Potomac MD	village	middle	—	1966	unknown	—	M	White	+
DC010	Potomoc MD	rural	old	1882	1966	unknown	farmer, rancher	M	White	+
DC014	Washington DC	urban	middle	1914	1970	high school	trucking, transportation	M	Black	+
DC015	Washington DC	urban	middle	1915	1970	unknown	domestic, maid	F	Black	+
FL040	Key West	small city	old	1899	1966	high school	teacher	F	White	+
FL041	Interlachen	rural	old	1883	1966	some schooling	homemaker	F	Black	+
FL042	Milton	village	old	1880	1965	some schooling	small business: owner, manager	M	White	+
FL043	Port St. Joe	village	middle	1919	1965	high school	small business: owner, manager	M	White	+
FL044	Graceville	village	middle	1918	1965	college	skilled trades	M	White	+
FL045	Fort Pierce	small city	old	1903	1966	high school	insurance	M	White	+
FL046	Grove City	village	old	1894	1966	some schooling	nautical, fishing	M	White	+
FL047	Fort Myers	small city	old	1878	1966	grade school	nautical, fishing	M	White	+
GA021	Folkston	rural	young	1935	1968	grade school	homemaker	F	White	+
GA048	Hoboken	rural	old	1884	1968	unknown	farmer, rancher	M	White	+
GA050	Fargo	rural	old	—	1969	unknown	logging	M	White	+
GA050A	Fargo	rural	old	—	1969	unknown	homemaker	F	White	+
GA051	Folkston	village	old	1892	1969	unknown	ranger, guide	M	White	+
GA069	Montezuma	village	—	—	1968	unknown	farmer, rancher	M	White	+
ID006	Pocatello	small city	old	1895	1967	high school	railroad	M	White	+
ID007	Pocatello	small city	middle	1925	1967	college	agricultural services	M	White	+
ID008	Jerome	village	middle	1922	1967	college	teacher	M	White	+
ID009	Pocatello	small city	middle	1917	1967	college	railroad	M	White	+
ID010	Pocatello	small city	middle	1915	1967	high school	homemaker	F	White	+
ID011	Pocatello	small city	—	—	1967	unknown	—	F	White	+
ID012	Pocatello	small city	middle	1914	1967	unknown	teacher	F	White	+
ID013	Pocatello	small city	middle	1914	1967	college	teacher	F	White	+
ID014	Preston	village	old	1889	1967	grade school	homemaker	F	White	+
IL001	Kankakee	small city	—	—	1965	unknown	—	M	White	+
IL039A	Morris	village	young	—	1969	high school	—	F	White	+

Informant Code	Community	Community Type	Age-group	Year of Birth	Year of Interview	Education	Occupation	Sex	Race	Audio-tape
IL101	Chicago (South Side)	urban	middle	1917	1969	high school	clerical	F	White	+
IL112	Chicago (South Side)	urban	middle	1924	1969	high school	homemaker	F	White	+
IL120	Marion	small city	middle	1925	1970	grade school	police	M	White	+
IL121	Marion	small city	young	1933	1970	high school	police	M	White	+
IL127	Paris	village	middle	1927	1970	college	local government	M	White	+
IL133	Carmi	village	young	1950	1970	college	student	F	White	+
IL145	Chicago	urban	young	1949	1969	high school	laborer	M	Black	+
IN020	Rockport	village	old	1886	1968	college	teacher	M	White	+
IN021	Richland	rural	old	1903	1968	grade school	homemaker	F	White	+
IN036	Marshall	rural	middle	1915	1968	unknown	farmer, rancher	M	White	+
IN054A	Muncie	small city	old	1886	1969	high school	—	F	White	+
IN079A	Richmond	small city	old	1887	1969	high school	—	F	White	+
IA010	Boone	rural	middle	1912	1967	some schooling	farmer, rancher	M	White	+
IA035	What Cheer	village	young	1929	1968	high school	small business: owner, manager	M	White	+
IA037	Newton	small city	middle	1921	1968	high school	insurance	M	White	+
IA040	Council Bluffs	small city	middle	1910	1968	college	social & community services	M	White	+
IA042	Ida Grove	village	middle	1926	1968	high school	custodial, maintenance	M	White	+
IA044	Orange City	village	young	1950	1968	high school	student	M	White	+
IA048	Emmetsburg	village	young	1933	1968	high school	wholesale, retail sales	M	White	+
KY001	Hindman	rural	old	—	1965	unknown	—	M	White	+
KY002	Booneville	rural	old	1875	1965	unknown	—	F	White	+
KY002A	Booneville	rural	old	—	1965	unknown	librarian	F	White	+
KY003	Pine Mountain	rural	—	—	1965	unknown	teacher	M	White	+
KY003A	Pine Mountain	rural	middle	—	1965	unknown	farmer, rancher	M	White	+
KY003B	Pineville	village	old	1902	1965	college	administrative, managerial	M	White	+
LA001	Grayson	rural	middle	1927	1967	high school	logging	M	White	+
LA005	St. Francisville	village	middle	1926	1967	grade school	nautical, fishing	M	White	+
LA036	Grand Isle	village	young	1957	1968	some schooling	student	M	White	+
LA042	New Orleans	urban	middle	1915	1968	some schooling	laborer	M	White	+
ME017	Port Clyde	rural	old	1904	1966	grade school	nautical, fishing	M	White	+
ME018	Readfield	rural	old	1885	1966	high school	farmer, rancher	M	White	+
ME025	Beals	rural	old	1889	1966	grade school	nautical, fishing	M	White	+
ME026	Masardis	rural	old	—	1966	unknown	logging	M	White	+
MD051	Baltimore	urban	young	—	1968	unknown	—	M	White	+
MA005C	Montague/ North Leverett	rural	old	1885	1966	unknown	farmer, rancher	M	White	+
MA006B	Prescott	rural	old	1892	1966	unknown	teacher	F	White	+
MA070	Lynn	small city	middle	1914	1967	college	librarian	F	White	+
MA084	Colrain	village	old	1880	1965	unknown	—	F	White	+
MA085	East Colrain	village	old	—	1965	unknown	farmer, rancher	M	White	+
MA086	Westhampton	rural	old	—	1967	unknown	skilled trades	M	White	+
MA086A	Westhampton	rural	—	—	1967	unknown	—	F	White	+
MA090	Colrain	village	middle	—	1967	unknown	teacher	F	White	+
MA091	Petersham	village	—	—	1966	unknown	wholesale, retail sales	F	White	+
MA092	Chesterfield	rural	old	—	1965	unknown	artist, craftsman	M	White	+

Informant Code	Community	Community Type	Age-group	Year of Birth	Year of Interview	Education	Occupation	Sex	Race	Audio-tape
MA093	Boston (Beacon Hill)	urban	old	1876	1966	high school	unemployed	F	White	+
MA094	Topsfield	village	young	1946	1966	unknown	student	F	White	+
MA096	South Chatham	village	old	—	1967	unknown	teacher	F	White	+
MA099A	Plymouth	small city	young	1942	1970	college	teacher	M	White	+
MA101	Plymouth	small city	old	1895	1970	grade school	museum staff	M	White	+
MA102	Plymouth	small city	old	—	1967	unknown	financial services	M	White	+
MA103	Salem	small city	old	—	1966	unknown	—	F	White	+
MA104	Charlemont	small city	old	—	1966	unknown	—	F	White	+
MA105	Dedham	small city	—	—	1967	unknown	museum staff	F	White	+
MA107	Moore's Corner	rural	old	1892	1967	unknown	logging	M	White	+
MA108	Moore's Corner	rural	old	1897	1967	unknown	postal service	F	White	+
MA110	North Eastham	rural	old	—	1966	unknown	—	M	White	+
MA111	Weymouth	large city	old	—	1966	unknown	teacher	F	White	+
MA112	Bedford	small city	—	—	1966	unknown	police	M	White	+
MA113	Longmeadow	village	old	1886	1966	unknown	agricultural services	F	White	+
MA114	North Leverett	rural	old	—	1967	unknown	custodial, maintenance	M	White	+
MA115	Montague/ North Leverett	village	old	—	1967	unknown	farmer, rancher	M	White	+
MA117	Colrain	village	old	1876	1967	unknown	—	F	White	+
MA118	Westhampton	rural	old	1902	1966	unknown	—	F	White	+
MA119	Boston	urban	old	—	1966	unknown	laborer	M	White	+
MA120	Dartmouth	village	young	1944	1966	unknown	teacher	F	White	+
MA121	Malden	small city	—	—	1966	unknown	—	F	White	+
MI021	Marquette	small city	old	1900	1966	grade school	skilled trades	M	White	+
MI121	Gaylord	village	old	1888	1970	college	insurance	M	White	+
MI124	Grand Rapids	large city	old	1886	1970	high school	skilled trades	M	White	+
MI125	Dorr	rural	old	1895	1970	grade school	farmer, rancher	M	White	+
MI125A	Byron Center	rural	middle	1919	1970	grade school	farmer, rancher	M	White	+
MS075	Meridian	small city	old	1906	1966	some schooling	domestic, maid	F	Black	+
MS076	Oak Top	rural	old	1870	1966	unknown	laborer	F	Black	+
MS077	Redwood	rural	old	1896	1966	unknown	farmer, rancher	F	Black	+
MS078	Columbus	small city	middle	1917	1966	college	teacher	F	White	+
MO031	St. Louis	urban	old	1900	1970	college	teacher	F	Black	+
NJ062	Glassboro	small city	—	—	1969	unknown	clerical	F	White	+
NM014	Roswell	rural	old	1890	1966	grade school	farmer, rancher	M	White	+
NM015	Silver City	village	old	1903	1966	college	miner	M	White	+
NY085	Millerton	village	middle	1916	1968	high school	teacher	M	White	+
NY124	Brooklyn	urban	middle	1918	1966	college	small business: owner, manager	M	White	+
NY125	Manhattan	urban	old	1870	1968	college	social & community services	F	White	+
NY129	Buffalo	large city	middle	1914	1969	unknown	small business: owner, manager	M	White	+
NY147	Corning	small city	middle	1913	1969	unknown	farm woman	F	White	+
NY178	Orleans	village	old	1889	1969	high school	teacher	M	White	+
NY203	Little Falls	village	old	1904	1969	high school	clerical	M	White	+
NY204	Binghamton	large city	young	1952	1969	unknown	student	F	White	+
NY208	Monroe	village	—	—	1969	unknown	—	F	White	+

Informant Code	Community	Community Type	Age-group	Year of Birth	Year of Interview	Education	Occupation	Sex	Race	Audio-tape
NY225	Jamestown	small city	young	1938	1969	college	social & community services	M	White	+
NY242	New York City	urban	middle	1916	1970	unknown	wholesale, retail sales	M	Black	+
NY243	Brooklyn	urban	old	1871	1965	some schooling	skilled trades	M	White	+
NY244	Brooklyn	urban	old	1886	1965	high school	homemaker	F	White	+
NY245	Brooklyn	urban	old	1887	1965	high school	wholesale, retail sales	M	White	+
NY246	Manhattan	urban	old	1894	1966	college	homemaker	F	White	+
NY247	Brooklyn	urban	middle	1924	1966	high school	clerical	M	White	+
NC019	Elizabeth City	small city	old	1887	1966	college	religion	M	White	+
NC029	Crossnore	rural	middle	—	1966	unknown	artist, craftsman	F	White	+
NC051A	Maxton	village	young	1956	1968	grade school	student	F	Am Ind	+
NC056	Kitty Hawk	rural	old	1887	1968	unknown	teacher	F	White	+
NC057	Kitty Hawk	rural	old	—	1968	unknown	nautical, fishing	M	White	+
NC058	Roanoke Island	rural	old	1903	1968	unknown	service station operator	F	White	+
NC059	Roanoke Island	rural	old	1894	1968	unknown	nautical, fishing	M	White	+
NC065	Hatteras	rural	old	1883	1969	some schooling	nautical, fishing	M	White	+
NC066	Hillsborough	village	old	1909	1969	college	teacher	F	Black	+
NC074	Robbins	rural	young	1939	1969	grade school	skilled trades	M	White	+
NC089	Princeville	village	young	1950	1970	college	student	F	Black	+
NC090	Rocky Mount	rural	old	1906	1970	grade school	farmer, rancher	M	Black	+
OH014	Madison	rural	middle	1911	1967	unknown	architect	F	White	+
OH083	Port Clinton	village	middle	1919	1968	high school	nautical, fishing	M	White	+
OH100	Columbus	large city	young	1954	1970	high school	student	F	White	+
OH101	Columbus	large city	young	1953	1970	high school	student	F	Black	+
OK024	Eagletown	rural	old	1897	1966	some schooling	farmer, rancher	M	White	+
OK029	Guymon	village	middle	1919	1966	high school	skilled trades	M	White	+
OK030	Guymon	village	old	1885	1966	high school	farmer, rancher	M	White	+
OK037	Miami	rural	old	—	1965	unknown	farmer, rancher	M	White	+
OK039	Fairview	village	old	1864	1966	grade school	farmer, rancher	M	White	+
OK040	Frederick	village	old	1889	1966	grade school	farmer, rancher	M	White	+
OR018	Jordan Valley	rural	middle	1914	1967	unknown	storekeeper	M	White	+
PA030	New Holland	village	middle	1926	1967	high school	small business: owner, manager	M	White	+
PA061	Quakertown	village	old	1893	1967	grade school	farmer, rancher	M	White	+
PA062	Kennett Square	village	old	1884	1967	grade school	wholesale, retail sales	M	White	+
PA064	Pottstown	small city	old	1888	1967	high school	teacher	M	White	+
PA065	Kennett Square	village	middle	1920	1967	college	homemaker	F	White	+
PA084	Honesdale	village	old	1901	1968	high school	educational administrator	M	White	+
PA085	Honesdale	village	old	1878	1968	grade school	journalism	M	White	+
PA086	Honesdale	village	old	1894	1968	unknown	farmer, rancher	M	White	+
PA087	West Newton	village	young	1949	1968	high school	student	F	White	+
PA101	Montrose	village	middle	1913	1968	unknown	—	M	White	+
PA125	Tunkhannok	village	old	1868	1968	grade school	storekeeper	M	White	+
PA145	Pittsburgh	urban	young	1929	1968	high school	homemaker	F	White	+
PA238	Beaver Falls	small city	old	1908	1970	unknown	custodial, maintenance	M	White	+
PA249	Elizabeth-town	village	old	1890	1970	grade school	storekeeper	F	White	+
SC013	Cheraw	village	old	1894	1966	high school	agricultural services	M	White	+

Informant Code	Community	Community Type	Age-group	Year of Birth	Year of Interview	Education	Occupation	Sex	Race	Audio-tape
SC014	Georgetown	small city	old	1891	1966	some schooling	farmer, rancher	M	Black	+
SC015	Georgetown	rural	old	1903	1966	some schooling	farmer, rancher	M	Black	+
SC016	Plantersville	rural	old	1883	1966	some schooling	farmer, rancher	M	Black	+
SC017	Kingstree	village	old	1895	1966	grade school	farmer, rancher	M	White	+
SC018	McClellan-ville	rural	young	1944	1966	college	student	M	White	+
SC025	Eutawville	rural	young	1935	1966	college	farmer, rancher	M	White	+
SC033	Westminster	village	middle	1924	1967	unknown	small business: owner, manager	M	White	+
SC037	York	village	young	1938	1967	college	legal	M	White	+
SCO50	Seabrook	rural	middle	1908	1967	college	farmer, rancher	M	White	+
SC060	Peak	rural	old	1891	1968	grade school	farmer, rancher	M	White	+
SC061	Peak	rural	old	1894	1968	grade school	farm woman	F	White	+
SC071	Charleston	small city	young	—	1970	unknown	homemaker	F	Black	+
SD004	Deadwood	village	old	1902	1966	grade school	farmer, rancher	M	White	+
TN009	Greenville	rural	middle	1914	1967	grade school	food services	M	White	+
TN021	Maryville	rural	middle	1912	1967	grade school	farmer, rancher	M	White	+
TN025	Athens	village	old	—	1968	unknown	—	F	White	+
TN028	Athens	village	—	—	1968	unknown	—	F	White	+
TN029	Athens	village	—	—	1968	unknown	museum staff	M	White	+
TN040	Camden	village	young	1941	1968	college	administrative, managerial	M	White	+
TN051	Memphis	large city	old	1894	1970	some schooling	food services	F	Black	+
TX001A	Crystal City	village	old	1891	1967	grade school	food services	F	White	+
TX024	Comstock	rural	old	1888	1967	grade school	farmer, rancher	M	White	+
TX025	Del Rio	small city	young	1946	1967	college	student	M	White	+
TX046	Uvalde	rural	old	1903	1966	grade school	farmer, rancher	M	White	+
TX047	San Angelo	small city	old	1883	1967	some schooling	skilled trades	M	White	+
TX048	Laredo	small city	young	1936	1967	college	small business: owner, manager	M	White	+
TX049	Nacogdoches	small city	old	1875	1967	high school	wholesale, retail sales	M	White	+
TX050	Nacogdoches	small city	old	1897	1967	high school	financial services	M	White	+
TX093	Sulphur Springs	village	old	1902	1970	college	teacher	F	White	+
TX107	Athens	rural	middle	—	1970	unknown	laborer	M	Black	+
VT001	Brattleboro	rural	old	1887	1967	unknown	educational administrator	F	White	+
VT014	Woodstock	village	old	1905	1969	unknown	custodial, maintenance	M	White	+
VT015	Woodstock	village	old	—	1969	unknown	service station operator	M	White	+
VT018	Quechee	rural	old	—	1966	unknown	wholesale, retail sales	M	White	+
VA017	Hillsville	rural	old	1889	1968	grade school	homemaker	F	White	+
VA052A	Chincoteague	village	old	—	1969	unknown	small business: owner, manager	M	White	+
VA052B	Chincoteague	village	old	1891	1969	unknown	—	F	White	+
VA112	Tangier	rural	middle	1915	1970	grade school	nautical, fishing	M	White	+
VA113	Tangier	rural	—	—	1970	unknown	—	F	White	+
VA113A	Tangier	rural	—	—	1970	unknown	—	F	White	+
VA113B	Tangier	rural	—	—	1970	unknown	—	F	White	+
VA114	St. Charles	rural	old	1879	1965	unknown	storekeeper	F	White	+
WA029	Vancouver	small city	middle	1909	1967	grade school	small business: owner, manager	M	White	+
WV009	Petersburg	village	young	1946	1968	high school	skilled trades	M	White	+
WV015	Salem	village	old	1908	1969	college	teacher	F	White	+
WV019	Charles Town	village	young	1951	1969	high school	student	F	White	+

Informant Code	Community	Community Type	Age-group	Year of Birth	Year of Interview	Education	Occupation	Sex	Race	Audio-tape
WV022	Charles Town	village	old	1900	1969	high school	museum staff	F	White	+
WV023	Bluefield	village	old	—	1965	unknown	railroad	M	White	+
WI001	Verona	village	old	—	1965	unknown	farm woman	F	White	+
WI002	Verona	village	old	—	1966	unknown	skilled trades	M	White	+
WI003	Cottage Grove	village	old	1894	1965	grade school	farm woman	F	White	+

Wildflower Questionnaire

Informant Code	Community	Community Type	Age-group	Year of Birth	Year of Interview	Education	Occupation	Sex	Race	Audio-tape
AR044	Clarksville	village	old	1897	1967	college	homemaker	F	White	—
AR045	Rogers	village	old	1893	1967	grade school	medicine	F	White	—
AR046	Garfield	rural	middle	1919	1967	some schooling	small business: owner, manager	M	White	—
LA021	Mansfield	village	old	1898	1968	college	homemaker	F	White	—
MI007	Sault Ste. Marie	small city	old	1894	1966	high school	teacher	F	White	—
MI057	Ann Arbor	small city	old	1880	1967	college	teacher	F	White	—
NY015	Sackets Harbor	village	—	—	1966	unknown	—	F	—	—
NY016	Parishville	village	—	—	1966	unknown	—	F	—	—
NY017	Martinburg	village	middle	1912	1967	high school	small business: owner, manager	M	White	—
NY091	Maine	village	old	1890	1968	college	teacher	M	White	—
NC028	Tar Landing	rural	old	1877	1966	high school	farm woman	F	White	—
ND004	Wahpeton	village	middle	1910	1966	high school	homemaker	F	White	—
OH014	Madison	rural	middle	1911	1967	college	architect	F	White	—
OR008	Bend	small city	middle	1911	1967	college	administrative, managerial	M	White	—
OR009	Junction City	village	young	1933	1967	high school	wholesale, retail sales	F	White	—
OR012	Burns	village	middle	1911	1967	college	homemaker	F	White	—
SC049	York	village	old	1907	1967	college	teacher	F	White	—
SD006	Deadwood	village	old	1894	1966	unknown	homemaker	F	White	—
TX034	Chireno	rural	old	1904	1967	high school	homemaker	F	White	—
TX044	Laredo	small city	middle	1922	1967	college	teacher	M	White	—
WA010	Pullman	small city	old	1881	1966	college	skilled trades	F	White	—

Additions to General List of Informants

Informant Code	Community	Community Type	Age-group	Year of Birth	Year of Interview	Education	Occupation	Sex	Race	Audio-tape
NJ015A	Salem	village	old	1898	1968	high school	clerical	F	White	+
SC038A	New Ellenton	village	old	1898	1967	college	homemaker	F	White	+

Additions to List of Informants Who Made Audiotapes Only

Informant Code	Community	Community Type	Age-group	Year of Birth	Year of Interview	Education	Occupation	Sex	Race	Audio-tape
AR043	Fort Worth	rural	—	—	—	unknown	—	M	—	+
GA021A	Folkston	rural	—	—	1968	unknown	—	M	—	+
KY034A	Hardshell	rural	—	—	1967	unknown	—	M	—	+
MA085A	East Colrain	village	—	—	1965	unknown	—	F	—	+
NY046A	Brooklyn	urban	old	—	1968	unknown	—	F	White	+
NY118A	Brooklyn	urban	—	—	1968	unknown	—	M	—	+

List of Abbreviations

Note: Periods are used for abbreviations in short-titles, but are generally omitted elsewhere.

a	ante (before)
A	auxiliary informant
abbr	abbreviated, abbreviation
absol	absolute(ly)
abstr	abstract
acad	academy
acc	accusative
accd	according to
acct	account
ADD	Wentworth, *American Dialect Dictionary*
addit	additional
adj(s)	adjective(s), adjectival
adv(s)	adverb(s), adverbial
advent	adventure(s)
advt	advertisement(s), advertiser
Afr	African
Afro-Amer	Afro-American
ag	agricultural, agriculture
agric	agriculturalist
AHD	*American Heritage Dictionary*
alt	alternation, alternative
alter(s)	alteration(s)
Amer	America(n)
AmFr	American French
AmInd	American Indian
AmSp	*American Speech*
AmSpan	American Spanish (language)
anon	anonymous
anthol	anthology
anthro	anthropological, anthropology
antiq	antiquarian, antiquity
aphet	aphetic
apoc	apocopated, apocopation
app	appendix
appar	apparent(ly)
approx	approximate(ly)
Apr	April
arch	archaic
archeol	archeological, archeology
art	article
assim	assimilated, assimilation
assoc	associate, association
asst	assistant
astron	astronomical, astronomy
attrib	attribution, attributive
Aug	August
Austr	Australia(n)
autobiog	autobiographical, autobiography
aux	auxiliary
BBC	British Broadcasting Corporation
bd	board
betw	between
bib	bibliographical, bibliography

biog	biographical, biography
biol	biological, biology
bot	botanical
Brit	Britannica, British
bur	bureau
c	central; circa (about)
Can	Canadian
CanFr	Canadian French (language)
cap	capital
Capt	Captain
CB	citizens band
cent	central; century
Cent D	Whitney, *Century Dictionary*
cf	confer (compare)
ch	church
chem	chemical, chemistry
Chr	Christian
chron	chronicle(s)
co	company
Co	county
cogn	cognate
Col	Colonel
coll	collected, collection, collective; college
colloq	colloquial
comb(s)	combination(s), combine(s)
comm(s)	commission(ers); committee(s); community, -ies
comp	composition
compar	comparative
concr	concrete(ly)
conj	conjunction
conjug	conjugation
cons	consonant
conserv	conservancy, conservation
constr(s)	construct(ed), construction(s); construed
contemp	contemporary
contr	contracted, contraction
contrib	contribution(s)
conv	conversation(al)
coop	cooperative
Corn	Cornish, Cornwall
corr	correct, corrected, correction
correl	correlated, correlation, correlative
corresp	correspondence
cpd	compound, compounded, compounding
crit	critical
cyclop	cyclopedia
DA	Mathews, *Dictionary of Americanisms*
DAE	Craigie-Hulbert, *Dictionary of American English*
Dan	Danish
DARE	*Dictionary of American Regional English*
DAS	Wentworth-Flexner, *Dictionary of American Slang*
dat	dative

DBE	Holm, *Dictionary of Bahamian English*		fig	figurative, figure
DCan	Avis, *Dictionary of Canadianisms*		Fin	Finnish
Dec	December		folk-etym	folk-etymological, folk-etymology
def art	definite article		folkl	folklore
defin	defining, definition, definitive		foll	follow(s), followed, following
dem	demonstrative		Fr	French
dept	department		Franco-Amer	Franco-American
deriv	derivation, derived, derivative		FrCan	French Canadian (people)
derog	derogatory		freq	frequent(ly)
descr	description, descriptive		Fri	Friday
dial	dialect(al)		Fris	Frisian
dicc	diccionario		ft	foot (measures)
dict	dictionary		Ft	Fort
dimin(s)	diminutive(s)		funct	function(al)
diss	dissertation(s)		fut	future
dissim	dissimilated, dissimilation		*F&W*	*Funk and Wagnalls Standard Dictionary*
distrib	distributed, distribution, distributive		FW	fieldworker
div	division			
DJE	Cassidy-Le Page, *Dictionary of Jamaican English*		Gael	Gaelic
DN	*Dialect Notes*		gaz	gazette(er)
DNE	Story-Kirwin-Widdowson, *Dictionary of Newfoundland English*		gen	general(ly); genitive
			geneal	genealogical, genealogy
doc	document(ary)		genl	general
DOST	Craigie-Aitken, *Dictionary of the Older Scottish Tongue*		geog	geography
			geogr	geographer, geographic(al)
Dr	Doctor		geol	geological, geology
DS	Data Summary (see Introduction)		Ger	German
DSL	Jamieson, *Dictionary of the Scottish Language*		Gk	Greek
			gloss	glossary
Du	Dutch		Gmc	Germanic
			gov	governor
e	east(ern)		govt	government
ed	edition, editor, editorial		gram	grammar, grammatical
EDD	Wright, *English Dialect Dictionary*		Gt Lakes	Great Lakes
EDG	Wright, *English Dialect Grammar*			
educ	educated, education(al)		Haw	Hawaiian
ellip	ellipsis, elliptical(ly)		hdbk	handbook
EModE	Early Modern English		Heb	Hebrew
encycl	encyclopedia		herb	herbaceous
engin	engineering		hist	historic, historical(ly), history
Engl	England, English		horticult	horticultural(ist), horticulture
entomol	entomological, entomologist, entomology		hs	high school
epenth	epenthesis, epenthetic		Hung	Hungarian
Episc	Episcopal		hydrog	hydrographical, hydrography
equiv	equivalence, equivalent			
erron	erroneous(ly)		*ibid*	ibidem
esp	especially		idiom	idiomatic
est	established		i.e.	id est (that is)
et al	et alii (and others)		illit	illiterate
etc	et cetera		illustr	illustrated, illustration
etym(s)	etymological, etymology, -ies		imit	imitation, imitative
euphem(s)	euphemism(s), euphemistic(ally)		imper	imperative(ly)
eve	evening		imperf	imperfect(ly)
evid	evidently		impers	impersonal(ly)
ex(x)	example(s)		in.	inch
exag	exaggerated		inc	incorporated
exc	except		incl	include, including, inclusive
exclam	exclamation, exclamatory		indef	indefinite(ly)
excr	excrescent		indic	indicative(ly)
exped	expedition(s)		inf(s)	informant(s)
exper	experiment(al)		infin	infinitive(ly)
expl(s)	explain(ed), explanation(s)		infl	influence(d)
explor	exploration(s)		info	information
expr(s)	expression(s)		infreq	infrequent(ly)
ext	extended, extension		init	initial(ly)
eye-dial	eye-dialect		inst	institute, institution
			interp	interpretation, interpreter
f., ff.	and following		interrog	interrogative(ly)
famil	familiar(izing)		intj	interjection
Feb	February		intr	intransitive(ly)
fem	feminine			

intro	introduced, introducing, introduction	newsl	newsletter
Ir	Irish	newsp	newspaper(s)
irreg	irregular(ly)	Nfld	Newfoundland
Is.	Island(s)	no.	number
Ital	Italian	nom	nominative
iter	iteration, iterative	non-std	nonstandard
		Norw	Norwegian
Jan	January	Nov	November
Jct	Junction	np	no page
joc	jocular(ly)	ns	new series
jrl(s)	journal(s)	Nth(n)	North(ern)
		NYC	New York City
L	Lake	*NYT*	*New York Times*
l., ll.	line(s)		
lab	laboratory	obj	objective
LaFr	Louisiana French	obs	obsolete
LAGS	*Linguistic Atlas of the Gulf States*	occas	occasional(ly)
LAMSAS	*Linguistic Atlas of the Middle and South Atlantic States*	Oct	October
LANCS	*Linguistic Atlas of the North Central States*	OE	Old English
LANE	*Linguistic Atlas of New England*	*OED(S)*	Murray et al, *Oxford English Dictionary (Supplement)*
lang	language	OF	Old French
Lat	Latin	old-fash	old-fashioned
LAUM	*Linguistic Atlas of the Upper Midwest*	ON	Old Norse
LGer	Low German	orig	origin, original(ly)
lib	library	ornith	ornithological, ornithology
ling	linguistic(s)	Oxfd	Oxford
lit	literature; literary		
Luth	Lutheran(s)	p	post (after)
		p., pp.	page(s)
M	Monsieur	*PADS*	*Publication of the American Dialect Society*
m	meter(s)	PaGer	Pennsylvania German
mag	magazine	pejor	pejorative
malaprop	malapropism	perf	perfect
Mar	March	perh	perhaps
masc	masculine	pers	person
math	mathematical, mathematics	pert	pertaining
ME	Middle English (in etymologies; elsewhere = Maine)	petrol	petroleum
MED	*Middle English Dictionary*	philol	philological, philology
med	medical, medicinal, medicine	philos	philosopher, philosophical, philosophy
mem	memorial(s)	phon	phonetic
metall	metallurgical, metallurgy	phr(r)	phrase(s)
metaph	metaphor, metaphorical(ly)	phys	physical
metath	metathesis, metathetic(ally)	pl	plural
Mex	Mexican, Mexico	poet	poetical
MexSpan	Mexican Spanish	Pol	Polish
mfg(r)(s)	manufacture, manufacturer(s), manufacturing	pop	popular(ly)
mid-aged	middle-aged (of Infs: 40-59)	Port	Portuguese
Midl	Midland	poss	possessive; possible
Midwest	Midwestern	ppl	participial
misc	miscellaneous, miscellany	pple	participle
mispronc	mispronunciation	prec	preceded, preceding
MLG	Middle Low German	pred	predicate, predication, predicative(ly)
mod	modern	pref	prefix(ation)
ModE	Modern English	prehist	prehistoric, prehistory
Mon	Monday	prelim	preliminary
monogr	monograph(s)	prep(s)	preposition(s)
MS(S)	manuscript(s)	pres	present
Mt(s)	Mountain(s)	pret	preterite
mth	monthly	prob	probable, probably
		proc	proceedings
n	noun; north(ern)	progr	progressive
N Amer	North America(n)	pron	pronoun
narr(s)	narrative(s)	pronc	pronounced, pronunciation
nat	natural	Pronc Intro	Guide to Pronunciation, pp. xli–lxi
natl	national	pronc-sp	pronunciation-spelling
naut	nautical	Prot	Protestant
NB	New Brunswick	prov	proverb(ial); provincial
nd	no date	psych	psychological, psychology
neg	negative	Pt	Port
neut	neuter	pub	public; publication(s)
		punct	punctuation

Qq	questions
QR	Questionnaire
qrly	quarterly
Qu	question
quot	quotation
R	River
r	recto
rec	record(s)
recoll	recollections
redund	redundant
redup	reduplicated, reduplication, reduplicative
ref(s)	refer, reference(s)
refl	reflexive
reg	register; regular(ly)
rel	related, relation, relative
relig	religious
repet	repetition, repetitive
repr	representative(s); represent(s), representing; reprint(ed)
rept	report(s)
resp(s)	response(s)
rev	review
revol	revolution(ary)
RR	railroad(s)
Russ	Russian
s	south(ern)
Sat	Saturday
Scan	Scandinavian
sci	science(s)
Scotl	Scotland
Scots	Scottish
sec(s)	section(s)
secy	secretary
Sept	September
ser	series
serv	service
sg	singular
sig	signature
SND	Grant, *Scottish National Dictionary*
soc	society
sociol	sociological, sociology
sp(p)	spelling(s); species
Span	Spanish
SpanAm	Spanish American (people)
spec	specific(ally)
sp-pronc	spelling-pronunciation
St	Saint; Street
Sta	Station
statist	statistical
std	standard
StdE	Standard English
Sth(n)	South(ern)
subj	subject
subjunc	subjunctive
subseq	subsequent
subsp(p)	subspecies
suff	suffix(ation)
sugg	suggest(ed), suggestion
Sun	Sunday
superl	superlative
suppl	supplement(ary)
surv	survey
Sw	Swedish
syll	syllable
syn	synonym(ous)
tech	technological, technology
Terr	Territories

Thu	Thursday
topog	topographic
tr	transitive
trans	transactions
transcr	transcribe, transcription
transf	transfer(red)
transl	translate(d), translation
treas	treasury
Tue	Tuesday
ult	ultimate(ly)
uncert	uncertain
uncom	uncommon
uncult	uncultivated
univ	university
unpub	unpublished
unstr	unstressed
US(A)	United States (of America)
usu	usual(ly)
v	verb; verso
var(r)	variant(s), various, varying; variety
vbl	verbal
vd	various dates
vet	veterinarian, veterinary
viz	videlicet (namely)
vocab	vocabulary
vol	volume
w	west(ern); weekly
W2	Merriam-Webster *Webster's New International Dictionary*, 2nd ed
W3	Merriam-Webster *Webster's Third New International Dictionary*
wd	word
Wed	Wednesday
WELS	Cassidy-Duckert, *Wisconsin English Language Survey*
Wildfl	Wildflower
wks	works
WNID	Merriam-Webster *Webster's New International Dictionary*
Wrn	Western
yd	yard
yr(s)	year(s)
zool	zoological, zoology

State Abbreviations

AK	Alaska
AL	Alabama
AR	Arkansas
AZ	Arizona
CA	California
CO	Colorado
CT	Connecticut
DC	Washington DC
DE	Delaware
FL	Florida
GA	Georgia
HI	Hawaii
IA	Iowa
ID	Idaho
IL	Illinois
IN	Indiana
KS	Kansas
KY	Kentucky
LA	Louisiana

MA	Massachusetts		SD	South Dakota
MD	Maryland		TN	Tennessee
ME	Maine		TX	Texas
MI	Michigan		UT	Utah
MN	Minnesota		VA	Virginia
MO	Missouri		VT	Vermont
MS	Mississippi		WA	Washington
MT	Montana		WI	Wisconsin
NC	North Carolina		WV	West Virginia
ND	North Dakota		WY	Wyoming
NE	Nebraska			
NH	New Hampshire			
NJ	New Jersey			
NM	New Mexico			
NV	Nevada			
NY	New York			
OH	Ohio			
OK	Oklahoma			
OR	Oregon			
PA	Pennsylvania			
RI	Rhode Island			
SC	South Carolina			

Signs and Symbols

~   is used to avoid repetition of a previously spelled-out word or phrase

‡   is used to indicate a word or sense of questionable genuineness

*   is used to indicate unattested or hypothetical forms

+   is used for "and"

→   is used with dates to indicate first or last attestation

<   is used for "derived from"

>   is used for "from which is derived"

=   is used for "equals"

Dictionary of American Regional English

a indef art Usu |ə, e(ɪ)| Also eye-dial *er, ur*

A Forms.

1888 Jones *Negro Myths* 37 **GA coast,** Buh Tiger come out in er hurry, an dey graff hold er one anurrer. **1892** Smith *Day at Laguerre's* 181 **VA** [Black], She want ur steel one. An' she sez ef yer ain't got no steel one she want ur squart o' molasses. **1893** in 1944 *ADD, A . . .* [ʌ]. Generally written *er* by dial. writers, but no sound of *r* is ever apparent in the negro pron. **1894** Riley *Armazindy* 52 **IN,** Flick ye wid er buggy-whirp yer spit er little blacker. **1944** Kenyon–Knott *Pronc. Dict., A . . .* The use of [e] . . in places where the unstressed [ə] belongs, often gives an artificial effect to public address. **1944** *AmSp* 14.44 **TX,** [wʌn 'naɪt dɪ 'ræts 'hɚd e 'greɪt 'nɔɪz . . . ðeɪ 'sɛnt aut 'skaʊts tu sɚč fɔɚ ʔeɪ 'nju houm].

B Sense.

Before words beginning with a vowel sound: an. **freq throughout US**

1794 (1936) Parry *Jrl.* 379 **PA,** With about a hours work we got off. **1843** (1916) Hall *New Purchase* 227 **IN,** Sker'd to hear a Injin holler. *Ibid* 366, A body in a exercise. *Ibid passim.* **1889** Edwards *Runaways* 26 **GA,** Did n' he sen' you like er aingil? **1899** Chesnutt *Conjure Woman* 136 **NC,** Dey is a' easy way ter prove it. **1902** *DN* 2.227 **sIL,** *A . . .* The article is not used. 'A apple,' 'A hour,' 'A image.' **1903** *DN* 2.295 **Cape Cod MA** (as of 1850s). **1903** *DN* 2.304 **seMO. 1906** *DN* 3.114 **sIN. 1907** *DN* 3.228 **nwAR. 1908** *DN* 3.285 **eAL, wGA. 1916** Howells *Leatherwood God* 19 **OH,** Like it was a earthquake. **1954** Harder *Coll.* **cwTN,** Got me a oil cloth. **c1960** Wilson *Coll.* **csKY,** He had a old horse.

a vbl aux See **have** v[1], v[2]

a prep[1] [OE *on, an;* cf *OED a* prep.[1] and note] Usu hyphened to following word, but also separate or joined solid

1a Prefixed to nouns of place and forming adv phrr. [*OED a* prep.[1] 5; cf such now std combinations as *ashore, away*] See also **ahorse(back), aside (of), aslew**

1622 Mourt's *Relation* *Iournall Plimoth* 23, That night we returned againe aship boord. **1669** in 1884 *Archives of MD* 2.160, Sett a Beggar a horse back & he will Run. **1674** in 1880 Brookhaven NY *Records* 1.34, Whosoever shall Run . . a hors back in the streetes . . shall forfet 10s. **1910** Hart *Vigilante Girl* 315 **CA,** The rogue who was a-ship had divided the swag with the rogue who was ashore.

b in phr *a-one-side:* To one side. [*OED* →1684] *obs*

1823 Cooper *Pioneers* 2.225 **nNY,** Knocking that carpenter's face a-one-side, as you call it. **1845** (1968) Simms *Wigwam & Cabin* (1st ser) 56 **sNC,** And there, a little a one side, . . was a woman.

2 Prefixed to days or dates and forming adv phrr. [*OED a* prep.[1] 8, "Obs. exc. in a few archaic phrases."] See also **adays**

1686 (1878) S. Sewall *Diary* 1.134 **MA,** Seeing the warrants to arrive a Thorsday night. **1707** in 1875 *VA Calendar State Papers* 1.117, We had taken five or more of them a Monday. **1849** *Knickerbocker* 34.151/1 **NY,** This lady read a play to Bunkum a-Monday week. **1871** Eggleston *Hoosier Schoolmaster* 108 **IN,** "We'll tend to his case a Christmas." Christmas was two days off. **1871** (1882) Stowe *Fireside Stories* 242 **MA,** They'd even race hosses a Sunday. **1926** Roberts *Time of Man* 124 **KY,** Like I said a Sunday to Elmer. **1939** *Hall Coll.* **wNC,** I went back down a-Sunday. **1966–69** *DARE* Tape **KY16A,** I want you to marry me a-Thursday night; **NC21,** And a-Monday he carried her over to [the] doctor.

3 Prefixed to nouns and forming advs or adv phrr of manner. [*OED a* prep.[1] 9, "Obs."] **chiefly Sth** See also **apurpose, afeet**

1899 (1912) Green *VA Folk-Speech, A-purpose . . .* "You knocked that child down a-purpose." **1903** *DN* 2.300 **Cape Cod MA** (as of 1850s), *Purpose . . .* In expression, 'a purpose,' or 'on a purpose,' purposely. **1908** *DN* 3.285 **eAL, wGA,** *A . . .* Very commonly used for *on* in such expressions as 'a purpose,' . . 'a credit.' **1915** *DN* 4.180 **swVA,** *A.* Used for *on,* as 'a purpose.' **1968–70** *DARE* (Qu. U11) Inf **GA77,** Bought it a-credit; **LA15,** Got it a-credit; (Qu. X43b, *If you sleep later than usual*) Inf **LA2,** Stayed in bed a-purpose.

4 Prefixed to a noun and forming an adj of state. [*OED a* prep.[1] 11; cf std *asleep, afloat,* etc] See also **akink**

1818 (1937) Guild *Jrl.* 288 **VT,** So much beyond my expectations it set me all ahue. **1823** Cooper *Pioneers* 1.194 **nNY,** An Indian will drink cider, though he niver be athirst. **1932** Faulkner *Light in August* 364 **MS,** And the doctor's Jezebel come running from her lustful bed, still astink with sin and fear. **1940** *Sat. Eve. Post* 30 Mar 62/2 **Sth,** He's a-plague with worry. **1944** (1967) McNichols *Crazy Weather* 116 **SW,** The horse had been a-lather, but it was dry now. **1967–69** *DARE* (Qu. B27) Inf **IA8,** The crick's aflood; (Qu. Y38, *Mixed together . . "The things in the drawer are all _____."*) Inf **KY24,** A-gaum; **NV5, WV18,** A-jumble; (Qu. GG11, . . *"The letter hasn't come and he's _____."*) Inf **MD36,** All a-stew; (Qu. OO47a, . . *Sweating: "It was a warm day and the horses _____."*) Inf **WA31,** Were all a-lather; (Qu. MM13, *The table was nice and straight until he came along and knocked it _____*) Inf **RI5,** A-tilt; (Qu. X56b, . . *Sweating very heavily*) Inf **ME10,** A-reek o' sweat.

5 Also sp *er-.* Prefixed to any pres pple. [*OED a* prep.[1] 13, "*Arch.* or *dial.* save in a few phrases."] Found in resps of *DARE* Infs with over 125 different verbs: see quot 1965–70 for representative exx. **throughout US, but esp freq in Midl, SW; less freq Sth, NEng** *chiefly among less educ and rural speakers; somewhat old-fash* See also 1943 *LANE* Map 671

1637 in 1868 *Essex Inst. Coll.* 9.49, Giles . . said I was the strangest troublesome man a falling out and quarrelling. **1648** (1908) Winthrop *Jrl.* 2.346, The *Welcome,* of Boston, about 300 tons . . . fell a rolling. **1757** in 1899 Hamilton *Letters to Washington* 2.62 **VA,** Order them out in Parties with some of Your Men a Scalping. **1846** (1934) Boynton *Jrl.* 364 **VT,** If I could hold out, long enough to get a-going. **1893** Shands *MS Speech, A.* By illiterate whites the letter *a* is almost always used before the present participle. **1899** Edwards *Defense* 11 **GA,** Thar she was er-sewin' on 'er sewin'-machine. **1942** Hall *Smoky Mt. Speech* 52 **eNC, wTN,** I'm a-tellin' you the truth . . . We didn't do no good a-bear-huntin' . . . We heerd somep'n a-hollerin. **1953** *Survey of Verb Forms* 34, Various verbs with *a-* occur throughout N. Eng . . . there is no area of any extent where the *a-* forms do not occur at least occasionally. In the M[iddle] A[tlantic] S[tates] . . . these forms are fairly common everywhere except in metropolitan New York City and part of c. and w. Pa.; they are particularly common in W. Va . . . In the S[outh] A[tlantic] S[tates] the form *a-laughing* is given by some seven eighths of the Type I informants and over half of the Type II. **c1960** Wilson *Coll.* **csKY,** Pappy went a-visiting yesterday. **1965–70** *DARE* (Numerous Qq.) 167 Infs, **throughout US but esp Midl, SW,** A-baiting, a-bawling, a-biting, a-blowing, a-coming, a-going, a-kidding, a-laughing, etc. [Of all *DARE* Infs, 28% had less than hs educ, 69% were from comm-types 4 and 5, and 66% were old; of those giving these responses, 57% had less than hs educ, 86% were from comm-types 4 and 5, and 80% were old.] **1965–70** *DARE* FW Addit **swAR,** A-tryin', a-doin', etc.: schwa always precedes present participle after verb *be;* **ceKY,** A-fixing to, a-laying-off to: when a person is anticipating or preparing, or postponing doing something; **swNC,** They's a-swimmin'; **neOK,** He's a-chunkin' [rocks] at me; **TN17,** Them chickens was a-mouldin' [FW:=moulting]; **TN17A,** While Jesus was a-crucifyin'. **1966** *DARE* Tapes **OK24,** That's the only way you knowed where you was a-goin'; **SC**16, Cotton been a-goin' [ə'gwɔɪn] on a little ahead of the tobacco. **1975** Allen *LAUM* 2.45 **Upper MW**, The regional distribution of *a-* seems to be Midland oriented, with its greater frequency in Iowa, Nebraska, and South Dakota. But although *a-* is still more common among the least educated, its incidence even in that group has dropped to one-third and in Type II to only one-tenth . . . The *a-* prefix is probably on the way toward obsolescence.

a prep[2] See **of**

a prep[3] See **to**

a conj See **or**

a inert vowel |ə| [Excrescent] Sp separately, hyphened, or joined solid **now chiefly Sth, Midl** *esp among old and less educ speakers* Note: unlike **a** prep[1], the presence of this vowel alters neither the part of speech nor the meaning of the word to which it is attached.

1 Prefixed to a past pple. [Prob < ME *y-* < OE *ȝe-*] See also **aknown, ascared**

1759 in 1882 Essex Inst. *Coll.* 19.65, I . . found that we was abelated out at 4 pence per Day. **1788** (1925) Washington *Diaries* 3.295 **VA**, The house [was] a good deal a dangered. **1871** (1882) Stowe *Fireside Stories* 161 **MA**, Two great elm-trees that's a grown now each side o' the front gate. *Ibid* 183, Bill had a got him out o' the house. **1926** Kephart *Highlanders* 299 **sAppalachians**, Pringle's a-been horse-throwed. **1933** Miller *Lamb in His Bosom* 5 **GA**, "Gittin' tired?" . . "No, I ain't a-tired." **1965–70** *DARE* (Qq. J3a, b, *To make a female dog* [or *cat*] *so that she can't breed, she must be _____*) Inf **MO**9, A-spayed; (Qu. AA24, *A man whose wife is dead*) Inf **TN**15, A-widowed; (Qu. GG26, . . *"When she saw the dog coming at her she got _____."*) Inf **MO**2, Afroze; (Qu. JJ35b) Inf **GA**28, Going to get afouled of him; (Qu. KK39, . . *"Because of the storm, the pond was all _____."*) Inf **MO**15, Kind of a-muddled.

2 Prefixed to an adv or adv phr.

1829–30 in 1927 *DN* 5.424 **VA** (Dunglison's Glossary), A traveller, hearing the above expression [="the wind is brief"] in Virginia, inquired of the driver what the word meant. It meant, he replied, "that the wind was a sort a [=of] peart." **1834** *Life Andrew Jackson* 110 **TN**, The gineral look'd a kinder thoughtful. **1846** in 1848 Lowell *Biglow* 1 'Upcountry' **MA**, He looked a kindo's though he'd jest com down. **1871** (1882) Stowe *Fireside Stories* 163 **MA**, When a body was a least thinkin' on't. **1967** *DARE* (Qu. X56b, . . *Sweating heavily*) Inf **IA**8, Sap's areally runnin'.

3 Prefixed to a preposition. See also **anear, anigh, apast** prep

1942 Hall *Smoky Mt. Speech* 52 **eTN, wNC**, He run right a-towards home. **1963** Edwards *Gravel* 154 **eTN** (as of 1920s), On this side of the mountain in abelow the Carr Gap.

4 As a linking or transition sound. See also **thataway, thisaway, whichaway, lookyhere** Cf **-ma-** infix

1908 *DN* 3.285 **eAL, wGA**, Ahere . . . "Look *ahere*, what I found." This intrusive *a* . . . occurs frequently in such expressions as 'look ayonder,' 'look athere.' **1926** Kephart *Highlanders* 351 **sAppalachians**, The hillsmen . . . are fond of grace syllables: "I gotta me a deck o' cyards." **1928** Peterkin *Scarlet Sister Mary* 214 **SC**, Ben is gwine to stop sayin so much-a sinful words. *Ibid* 282, I ain' gwine let you get away wid any such-a doins in my house.

5 Prefixed to a finite verb form.

1938 Matschat *Suwannee R.* 29 **nFL, sGA**, The black one a-tolls people in to whar the rattler can nip 'em. **1939** Cheney *Lightwood* (*ADD*) **GA**, You most like a-don't recollect Pa & me a-seein' you. *Ibid*, We might as well a-make camp some'ers. **1967** *DARE* (Qu. Z14a, *To give a child its own way* . . *"Everyone _____ that child."*) Inf **MO**8, Aspoils.

6 Prefixed to an adj. See also **ahungry, aloose, aweary.**

1931–33 *LANE Worksheets* **VT**, I shipped a forty barrels of apples every year. **1967** *DARE* (Qu. X17, . . *A damp cellar that had been shut up for some time would smell*) Inf **TN**13, Afunky. **1972** *Courier-Jrl.* (Louisville KY) 4 May A12, Hit was February, and . . I was late getting back and ascarce of firewood.

-a |ə| Also *-ah, -aw* Representing a pronc of *-i* in such words as *Cincinnati, gladioli, Miami, Missouri, spaghetti* [Once thought to be hypercorrection (as quot 1944), but perh from earlier [aɪ], altered when word-final stress was reduced: see 1960 *AmSp* 35.175–187] **chiefly wNEng south through NC (exc NYC and Philadelphia areas), Cent and SW:** See 1939 *LANE* Maps 17,

23; 1961 Kurath–McDavid *Pronc. Engl.* Map 150. Note: this pronc has been common since c1840 despite opposition from purists: addit quots in 1933 *AmSp* 8.4.22–36.

1808 (1910) Aẏer *Diary* 54 **MA**, Went over the river to see a family, who have come . . from Canada and are going on to Albana [=Albany]. **1838** in 1933 *AmSp* 8.4.32 **MO**, Missoura. **1884** *Critic* ns 2.73/1 **NY**, *Cincinnati* . . . Sinsinnah'ta. **1889** Field *Western Verse* 36 **MO**, He lives here in Mizzoora where the people are so set. **1893** *Chicago Daily Tribune* (IL) 6 Aug 29b/2 **MO**, And every boy here that respects his parents and the Constitution of the United States will always say Mizzouraw. **1944** *PADS* 2.32 **NC**, Southern uneducated persons of the lowest class tend to change the pronunciation of a final (unstressed) syllable in *-a* or *-e* to [ɪ]. The class just above the lowest mocks at the pronunciation of the lowest, and by over-correction avoids the [ɪ] where it is correct to pronounce it: thus "Miam*i*" is carefully changed to "Miam*a*," "Cincinnat*i*" to "Cincinnat*a*," etc. **1954** *Harder Coll.* **cwTN**, Cola, Ana, Sophia, etc., but Miama, Cincinnata. **1961** Kurath– McDavid *Pronc. Engl.* 169, *Missouri, Cincinnati* . . . These place names end in [ə] or in [ɨ ~ ɪ], the former predominating in Western New England, New Jersey, Pennsylvania, Virginia, and parts of North Carolina, the latter in Eastern New England, Metropolitan New York, Philadelphia, and the Lower South. Elsewhere the two pronunciations are rather evenly matched. There is no marked class cleavage in usage. **1966–70** *DARE* (Qu. H63, *Kinds of desserts*) Inf **MO**26, Spimona ice cream; (Qu. H65, *Foreign foods*) Inf **FL**1, Raviola [rævi'olə]; **NY**233, Raviola; **NJ**11, Manicotta.

aa n |'ʔɑ,ʔɑ| [Haw *'a'a* < *'ā* fiery, burning] **orig and still chiefly HI; now also on mainland US where volcanic activity has occurred**

Rough lava. Cf **pahoehoe**

1859 *Amer. Jrl. Science* 2d ser 28.70 **HI**, We . . saw '*pahoihoi*' or solid lava forming, and also '*aa*' or clinkers. **1873** in 1966 Bishop *Sandwich Is.* 52, We travelled . . over an immense expanse of lava of the kind called *pahoehoe,* or satin rock, to distinguish it from the *a-a,* or jagged, rugged, impassable rock. Savants all use these terms in the absence of any equally expressive in English. **1935** in 1967 Reinecke–Tsuzaki *Hawaiian Loanwords, Aa, a-a* . . . "Beds of dense basalt containing irregular stretched and deflated vesicles, lying between and in places including beds of clinkers." **1955** Longwell *Phys. Geol.* 73 **HI**, Rough, porous lava called *aa.* **1967** *DARE* (Qu. C26, . . *Special kinds of stone or rock*) Inf **HI**4, Aa [ʔɑʔɑ]—dry lava. **1972** Carr *Da Kine Talk* 86 [In list of "Hawaiian Words Commonly Heard in Hawaii's English"], '*a'ā*. A rough kind of lava. **1980** *DARE* File **ID**, In southern Idaho the lava is of the type called aa—sharp and jagged. We found none of the rope-like pahoehoe.

aaay-yuh See **ayuh**

aafter See **after**

aa'gyfy See **argufy**

aa'gyment See **argument**

-aah See **-ah** intj

a-aint v Also *int* [a prep[1] + *aint,* var of *oint* anoint (*OED* "Obs. or *arch.*"); *EDD* 1823 →, from ceEngl] See also **ant** v[2]
To anoint.

1899 (1912) Green *VA Folk-Speech* 60, Aaint . . . To smear with fatty matter. *Ibid* 240, *Int* . . . To annoint [sic]. *Aaint.*

aale See **aole**

A and B n

In gospel singing: see quot.

1977 Smitherman *Talkin* 257 [Black], *A & B,* Gospel soul reference to singing of two songs by a group on a musical program, "giving an A & B."

A and izzard See **izzard**

Aaron's rod n [See *Numbers* 17:8]

1 Any of several plants with tall, often yellow-flowering stems, but esp the common **mullein** (*Verbascum thapsus*), **goldenrod,** and, in the Southeast, a **false lupine** (here: *Thermopsis mollis*).

1891 *Century Dict., Aaron's–rod* . . A popular name of several plants with tall flowering stems, as the goldenrod, the hag-taper [=mullein], etc. **1933** Small *Manual SE Flora* 673, *T[hermopsis] caroliniana* . . . *Aaron's–rod* . . . Often grown as a garden plant. **1953** Greene–Blomquist *Flowers South* 55, *Aaron's–Rod* (*Thermopsis caro-*

liniana) . . . grows . . from sandy pinelands of the Coastal Plain to clayey soils of open woods in the Blue Ridge Mountains. **1960** Williams *Walk Egypt* 15 **GA,** Most of all Aunt Baptist liked to toll out the names of plants. "Adam's–flannel, Aaron's–rod, Noah's–ark, [etc.]." **1971** Krochmal *Appalachia Med. Plants* 264, *Verbascum thapsus* . . . Common mullein, Aaron's rod . . . A tea made from the leaves is used in Appalachia for colds.

2 Either of two related succulent plants: **houseleek 1** or esp **orpine** (here: *Sedum telephium*). **NEng**

    1891 *Jrl. Amer. Folkl.* 4.148, *Sedum telephium* we knew correctly as *houseleek;* but in other places in New Hampshire I have found it called . . *Aaron's Rod.* **1910** Graves *Flowering Plants* 214 **CT,** *Sedum Telephium* . . . Aaron's Rod. **1911** *Century Dict.* 5463, *S[edum] Telephium* . . [is] known as *Aaron's rod* because sometimes growing when pressed and apparently dried. **1929** *Torreya* 150 **ME,** *Sempervivum tectorum* . . "*Aaron's Rod.*"

A–B–Ab n, usu pl |'ei 'bi 'æb| Similarly, *B–A–Ba* [From schoolroom repetition of letters and syllables: see quot 1894] *old-fash* Cf **abiselfa**

1 The first step in learning to spell by syllables. Also called **abb and ebb**

    1830 Ames *Mariner's Sketches* 264 **MA,** The outside of my head has often been adorned in the same room where the inside first received its literary bias from an initiation into the mysteries of a–b, ab. **1835** Crockett *Account* 86 **TN,** As far as my learning went, I would stand over it, and spell a strive or two with any of them, from *a–b–ab* to *crucifix,* which was where I left off at school. **1848** Lowell *Biglow* 23 **'Upcountry' MA,** I see / The humble school-house of my A, B, C, / Where well-drilled urchins . . / Discharged their *a–b abs.* **1894** in 1901 *DN* 2.135 **NY,** Of course, the a, b, c's, were first, then a, b, abs, and when the child could put two syllables together and form a word, as ba–ker, baker, it was a proud day to the little fellow. **1899** (1912) Green *VA Folk-Speech,* Ab, ab's and ba, ba's. The beginnings of spelling lessons; used to show that a person is in the very beginning of things, and has everything to learn. "Why he is hardly in his *ab* and *ab's,* and *ba ba's* yet." **c1939** in 1977 *Amer. Slave Suppl. 1* 1.19 **NC,** Muh showed me my 'a–b–abs' and my numbers and when I was fifteen I went to school. **1967** *DARE* Tape **TX35,** The old Webster blueback speller was a good way to teach children their a–b–c's and teach them to sound letters. Now, they say that you didn't give words . . but you give sounds, they'd have a–b–ab. But if a child knew two letters he could begin to spell, you know.

2 in var phrr: The most rudimentary forms of knowledge.

    1899 [see **A–B–Ab 1**]. **1901** *DN* 2.135 **c,eNY,** *Abs* . . . "He doesn't know his a b abs" (of a stupid boy). **1906** *DN* 3.142 **nwAR,** *I know my a, b, ab's* ['ei 'bi 'æbz]. I am sophisticated. Used by the older generation. **1938** Stuart *Dark Hills* 393 **KY,** Sweet Bird don't know a letter of the A, B, abs.

aback adv [**a** *prep*[1] + *back*]

1 also *aback of:* Behind. [*DAE* "*Obs.* or *dial.*"]

    1783 (1916) Fleming *Travels KY* 663, Fern Creek is lost in ponds and low flat land a back of the Falls. **1836** Edward *Hist. TX* 79, Those districts . . aback of the older settled ones. **1938** Matschat *Suwannee R.* 162 **nFL, sGA,** He heerd somethin' gruntin' a-back of some gallberry bushes. **1943** *LANE* Map 723 **seMA,** 1 Inf, A-back of [for "behind"].

2 Ago. [*EDD* aback 4, 1768]

    1967 *DARE* (Qu. A17, *If it was 1960 and you were speaking of something that happened in 1950, you might say "That was ten _____."*) Inf **TN11,** Years aback.

aback adj [Transf from naut sense: with the front of the sail(s) turned toward the wind]

Immobilized; at a standstill.

    1903 *DN* 2.293 **Cape Cod MA,** *Aback* . . . 'You run your business that way and first thing you know you're all aback.' [**1945** Colcord *Sea Language* 19 **ME, Cape Cod MA, Long Island NY,** *Aback.* Of a vessel, unmanageable, due to a sudden shift of wind striking the sails from the side opposite to that to which they are trimmed.]

abaft prep [Transf from naut use]

Behind.

    1945 Colcord *Sea Language* 19 **ME, Cape Cod, Long Island,** *Abaft.* Behind (but on board the vessel; behind and outboard is astern). The word is common in coastal speech: "You'll find my valise up attic just abaft the chimney."

abalone v **CA**

To fish for abalone.

    1968 *DARE* Tape **CA**100, I've abaloned ['æbə,lonid]. **1975–76** *DARE* File **cwCA,** [Sign near beach:] Restricted Area: Keep Out. No Fishing or Abaloning; **cwCA,** To go abaloneing [æbə'lonijɪŋ]. General.

abanded pple [Contr of *abandoned;* cf *OED* aband "*Obs* . . . An artificial contraction of *Abandon.*" The present example is prob historically unrelated, a fresh contraction.]

Abandoned.

    1941 in 1944 *ADD* **cwWV,** The factory was abanded.

abaout See **about**

abasicky intj Also *anbasicky* [Etym unknown]

Among children: Naughty! Shame on you!

    1954 *Hench Coll.* **cVA,** *A–ba–sicky* . . . Expostulation of teasing or scorn, used by children . . . Heard this discussed by three persons . . the exclamation is often accompanied by the gesture of moving the index finger of one hand along, and at right angles to the index finger of the other hand, in the direction of the person teased or scorned. **1958** Babcock *I Don't Want to Shoot an Elephant* 18 **cSC** *(Hench Coll.),* "Anbasicky!" Stud retorted.

abb and ebb n, usu pl *obs*

=**A–B–Ab 1.**

    1821 Howison *Upper Canada* 294 **NY,** Yes, sir, only three years old, and knows his letters.—He was in the *abbs* and *ebbs* last week.—He must be awfully smart!

‡**abbers** exclam |'æbəz| [Prob var of **evers**]

In marbles play: a call entitling the caller to move his marble a short distance to improve its position.

    1967 *DARE* (QR, near Qu. EE7) Inf **CO4,** Abbers ['æbəz]—call you used to move a bad lie, a small move only.

abbuhtize See **advertise**

a.b.c. n See **ace-boon-coon.**

‡**ABC bug** n

    1969 *DARE* (Qu. P6, *. . Worms . . used for bait*) Inf **GA80,** ABC bug—has markings on back that look like ABC.

Abe n

1 See **Abie.**

2 See **Abraham Lincoln.**

abeah See **abear**

abeam adj [Transf from nautical use] **coastal NEng**

At a right angle to one's line of motion.

    1942 *ME Univ. Studies* 56.43 **ME,** When you've brought the meetin' house abeam you'll see the Town Hall round the bend. **1945** Colcord *Sea Language* 19 **ME, Cape Cod and Long Island,** *Abeam.* At right angles to the length of the ship, and some distance off. Common in coastal dialect.

abear v Also pronc-sp *abeah* [OE *āberan;* in mod use perh infl by *abide*] *old-fash or arch*

Usu in neg constr: to bear, endure, suffer.

    1891 Page *Elsket* 129 **VA** [Black], I nuver could abeah chillern ner women to be sullen roun' me. **1916** Lowell *Men* 290 **NEng,** Seem's ef I couldn't abear to see the golden-rod bloomin'. *Ibid* 292, Don't turn from me like that. I can't abear it. **1950** *WELS* (*To dislike a person: "I don't know why, but I just can't _____ him."*) 1 Inf, **cwWI,** Abear. Rare. [FW: Inf thinks she has heard here.]

Abe Kabibble, Abe Kabiblish See **Abie Kabibble**

abelated See **a inert vowel 1**

Abe Lincoln bug n

=**harlequin cabbage bug.**

    1901 Howard *Insect Book* 313, Many species possess an extremely bad odor and taste . . . The harlequin cabbage bug . . . in parts of Georgia . . is still known as the "Abe Lincoln bug."

Abe Lincoln fence n Also *Lincoln fence* [Ref to Lincoln's sobriquet "the rail-splitter"]

A split-rail fence.

1931–33 *LANE* Worksheets **ceRI,** Abe Lincoln fence — same as old farmer's fence. **1967–68** *DARE* (Qu. L62) Inf **CT6,** Zig-zag fence — also called a "Lincoln fence"; **OR1,** Lincoln fence — same as zigzag.

Abe Lincoln War n [Cf *DA* Lincoln 1 for var combinations alluding to the Civil War] **NEng** *arch or obs*
The Civil War.

    1943 *LANE* Map 551, 1 Inf, **csME,** Abe Lincoln War. **1969** McDavid *Unpleasantness* 202, Only in abolitionist New England do we find names that reflect the slavery issue . . *The Nigger War, The Abe Lincoln War, The War for the Blacks.*

abelow See **a inert vowel 3**

abel-wackit n [Transf from *able-whackets* a now obs sailors' card game, in which the loser's hands would be beaten or "whacked" by a twisted handkerchief. Cf 1890 Farmer–Henley *Slang*] *obs*
A light blow.

    1834 *Life Andrew Jackson* 26 **TN,** At it they went. Their blows warn't no abel-wackits I can tell ye. Every click tell'd.

abeout See **about**

aber nit adv phr [Ger *aber nicht*] See also **nit** Cf **left, over the**
Definitely not!

    1896 *DN* 1.421 **nOH,** *Nit:* a decided negative . . . In [nOH] also *aber nit.* **1897** *KS Univ. Qrly.* 6.85 **neKS,** Aber nit: "over the left." General. **1920** *DN* 5.77, German words or phrases are employed to contribute to folk-humor in phrases like *'raus mit em, aber nit,* etc., but this usage is not so widespread [as that of jocularizing French words], is of another type, and it does not emerge from so cultivated a class. **1927** Lewis *Elmer Gantry* 59 **KS** (as of 1903), Prexy Quarles and Juanita! Aber nit! Never get them two together!

Abe's picture See **Abraham Lincoln**

abide v intr [*OED* abide 2 →1535, "obs."] *old-fash*
To tarry; to wait before proceeding further.

    1967 *DARE* (Qu. II15, *When somebody is passing by and you want him or her to stop and talk a while, you might say*) Inf **IL5,** Abide a bit.

Abie n Also *Abe, Aby* [Abbr for *Abraham* Jewish patriarch and still a common Jewish name] *usu derog* See also **Abie Kabibble, Ikey.**
1 A Jew.

    1914 *DN* 4.158 **ePA,** *Aby* . . . Jew. **1941** *LANE* Map 455 (*Nicknames for a Jew*) 1 Inf, **nME,** [eɪbɪ]. **1942** Berrey–Van den Bark *Amer. Slang* 385.2, *Jew.* Abe, Abie. **1950** *WELS* (*Names and nicknames for people of foreign backgrounds . . Jewish*) 1 Inf, **ceWI,** Aby. **1970** Tarpley *Blinky* 254 **neTX,** *Nicknames for Jewish people* . . . Abie [in list of "other responses"].

2 A stingy person. [From the stereotype of the Jew as parsimonious]

    1968 *DARE* (Qu. U36a, . . *A person who saves in a mean way or is greedy in money matters: "He's an awful _____."*) Inf **WI43,** Shylock; Abie — a Jewish name.

Abie Kabibble n Also *Abe ~* [From the character in Harry Hershfield's popular comic strip *Abie the Agent,* 1914–1940] See also **Abie, ish kabibble**
An unassimilated Jewish immigrant. Hence adj *Abe Kabiblish.*

    1932 Farrell *Young Lonigan* 163 **Chicago IL,** You got to soft soap some of these Abie Kabibbles. **1937** (1958) Levin *Old Bunch* 102 **Chicago IL,** "Hullo, Pisano!" "Hullo, you Abe Kabibble!" **1938** Farrell *No Star* 115 **Chicago IL,** Danny thought it was funny, all right, old men talking Yiddish. They were Abie Kabibbles, that's what they were. **1970** Feinsilver *Yiddish* 317, "Abe (or Abie) Kabibble" was presumably a derivative [of *ish kabibble*]. I've seen this as an adjective: "Abe Kabiblish."

abiselfa n Also *abisselfa* [Contr of *a-by-itself-a* the first formula in the "cumulative" method of spelling once popular in the US and Engl: see quot 1848 and cf *ampersand < and-per-se-and*] *obs*
The letter *a.*

    1840 (1847) Longstreet *GA Scenes* 73, In the good old days of *fescues, abisselfas,* and *anpersants,* terms which used to be familiar in this country during the Revolutionary war, and which lingered in some of our county schools for a few years afterward. **1848** Bartlett *American-*

isms, Abisselfa. A, by itself, A . . . In the olden time, the first letter of the alphabet was denominated "abisselfa" when it formed a syllable by itself, as in the word *able.* The scholar . . was taught to say, "*a,* by itself *a* (rapidly, *abisselfa,*) b, l, e, able." [**1908** *Uncle Remus's Mag.* Mar 17 (*DN* 4.435) **GA,** It was customary to say *a – by-itself – a, b – by-itself – b,* and so on.] **1917** *DN* 4.435 **cGA,** *Abiselfa* . . . in use in Middle Georgia, until about 1835.

able adj
1 Wealthy; influential. [*OED* able 6, →1863, "*Obs.*"]

    1899 (1912) Green *VA Folk-Speech,* Able . . . "He is an *able* man." **1952** Brown *NC Folkl.* 1.512. **c1960** Wilson *Coll.* **csKY,** Able . . . Rich, well-to-do, powerful.

2 foll by *for:* Fit to cope with. [*EDD* able 2]

    1940 Stuart *Trees of Heaven* 55 **neKY,** You act like you air tired. You won't be able fer the dance.

Abolition War n [Cf *DA* abolition for var combinations alluding to the Civil War] **nNEng**
The Civil War.

    1943 *LANE* Map 551, 1 Inf, **csME,** Abolition War; 1 Inf, **seNH,** Abolition War, older term. **1969** McDavid *Unpleasantness* 202, Only in abolitionist New England do we find names that reflect the slavery issue: *The Abolition War.*

aboon prep, adv [*SND* abune; *EDD* aboon. A Northern British form] **wNC** *rare*
Above; higher than.

    1891 Maitland *Amer. Slang Dict.* **1944** *PADS* 2.38 **cwNC,** *Aboon* . . . Above; to think oneself superior. "That 'omern's *aboon* her own kinnery." . . Rare. **1952** Brown *NC Folkl.* 1.513 **wNC,** *Aboon* . . . Rare.

about prep, adv Usu |(ə)'baʊt, (ə)'baʊt|; also, **chiefly Sth, Midl** |ə'bæʊt|; in **MD, eVA, eSC,** often |ə'boːʊt, ə'b(ə)ʊt, ɑ'bʊt|; rarely |ə'bɑt|. See Pronc Intro 3.II.14 Pronc-spp *abaout, abeout, abowoot, 'bout, erbout*
A Forms.

    1861 Holmes *Venner* 152 **wMA,** What'y' been dreamin' abaout? **1895** *DN* 1.372 **wNC, eTN, seKY,** *Let go* . . . "The road is back yander, let go abeout a mile." **1901** *DN* 2.181 **KY** [Black], 'Bout. **1903** *DN* 2.291 **Cape Cod MA** (as of 1850s), *Ou, ow* were always *au,* never *æu:* how, . . about. **1917** Torrence *Granny Maumee* 51 [Black], I got er-bout—fifty er so. **1919** *DN* 5.40 **VA,** *Out,* . . pronounced *ow-oot.* Similarly, "a-bowoot." **1927** Shewmake *Engl. Pronc. VA* 24, In typical Eastern Virginia speech, diphthongal ou or ow is given the dialectal sound represented by (uh–oo) . . . Examples of words in which dialectal *ou* is heard are *about, couch, doubt,* [etc.]. **1930** *AmSp* 5.347 **cSC,** [æʊ] in *scouts, out, about.* **1930** *AmSp* 6.94 **VA,** In the Tidewater . . *about* . . [əbaʊt] or [əbut]. **1934** *AmSp* 9.213 **eVA, eSC,** Along the coast . . the diphthong in *about* and *out* tends to become . . [u] or [ʊ]. **1937** *AmSp* 12.290 **wVA,** [əbæʊt feɪs]. **1938** *AmSp* 13.369 **nePA,** *About* [ə'bɑt]. **1941** *AmSp* 16.7 **eTX** [Black], In Negro speech this diphthong is not often flattened to [æʊ] as in 'hill type' speech, but retains its standard form, with lengthening of the first element . . . *about* . . [ba:ʊt]. **1967–68** *DARE* FW Addits **MD,** About [ə'bʊt]; **cnNY,** About [ə'bot].

B As prep.
Foll by a vbl n (where an infin is now common): on the point of. [*OED* about A13, →1865] *?obs*

    1802 (1941) Tucker *Diary* 313 **MA,** With the air of one about conferring a great favor. **1831** (1927) Rodman *Diary* 89 **MA,** Engaged part of the forenoon relative to a cottage which I am about building on the south side . . of School St. **1837** in 1926 *AmSp* 2.31 **IL,** An effort is being made. **a1853** (1890) Cutler *Life & Times* 86 (as of 1806) **CT,** My brother . . was here on his first visit to Ohio, and was about returning on horseback to Massachusetts.

C As adv.
Alternately, in turns: see quots. [*OED* about B5b →1851] *arch*

    1834 in 1956 Eliason ~~Tarheel Talk~~ 257 **NC,** I give . . unto my son Rezin . . his own choice of horse beast him and my son Henry chooseing one about. **1953** Randolph *Down in Holler* 166 **swMO,** A man in Forsyth . . said: "Maw used to call me an' Fred up *a morning about* to make the fire." That is, she called the two boys on alternate mornings, so that the task was evenly divided. Which reminds me of the two men in Christian County . . . "By God, I'll chop the damn' thing to pieces!" one yelled. "Good idea, Tom," cried the other. "Fetch the ax, an' we'll *take a lick about!*" He meant that they would take turns a-chopping.

about east See **east, about**

abouten prep [*about* + -*en* suff[1]] *arch* Cf **withouten**

About.

   1925 Glasgow *Barren Ground* 423 **VA,** I'se gwine out agin about'n sunup. **1941** Faulkner *Men Working* 199 **MS,** Never knowed a thing abouten it.

about house adj phr [Cf *EDD about* 9] *obs*

Of one's physical condition or health: well enough to move about the house; up and around.

   1829 (1941) Jones *Jrls.* 2.19 **NJ,** Found all well except Mary E. and she is about house and goes out. **1839** Walker in 1940 Drury *Pioneers Spokanes* 257 **ME,** But for this trouble I think I would have been about house in a week.

abouts adv [*OED*→1553; cf std *hereabouts, thereabouts, where-abouts*] *old-fash*

About, near. Cf **along 1**

   1960 Williams *Walk Egypt* 17 **GA,** "You want off here?" "Along abouts." **1970** *DARE* Tape MI112, There are some flowers around, here and there and abouts.

about to die adj phr Also ~ *kick the bucket,* ~ *pass* **chiefly Sth, S Midl**

Taken seriously or suddenly ill.

   1902 *DN* 2.227 **sIL,** *About to die.* An expression in constant use, of persons taken suddenly or violently ill. **1903** *DN* 2.304 **seMO,** *About to die . . .* "He was about to die yesterday." **1906** *DN* 3.114 **sIN.** **1907** *DN* 3.228 **nwAR.** **1908** *DN* 3.285 **eAL, wGA.** **c1960** *Wilson Coll.* **csKY.** **1965–70** *DARE* (Qu. BB42, *If a person is very sick you say he's*) 13 Infs, **Sth, S Midl, SW,** About to die; Inf **OK**7, About to kick the bucket; **VA**69, About to pass.

above one's bend adv phr Also *above one's huckleberry* [*OED bent* sb.[2] 9] **esp Sth, West** *obs* Cf **huckleberry above one's persimmon**

Beyond one's abilities.

   1835 Crockett *Account* 44 **TN,** I shall not attempt to describe the curiosities here; it is above my bend. **1859** (1968) Bartlett *Americanisms, Above one's bend . . .* A common expression in the Western States. *Above one's huckleberry* is a vulgarism of the same signification. **1872** Schele de Vere *Americanisms* 577. **1977** Watts *Dict. Old West.*

above snakes adj phr

Above the ground; tall.

   1855 Stuart–Wortley *Travels U.S.* 154 **NY,** Look at those two tall Kentuckians, with their tufted chins, somewhere about seven feet "above snakes." **1877** Bartlett *Americanisms, Above Snakes,* Exaggerated cant for "from the ground," or more than above the ground. **1977** Watts *Dict. Old West.*

abowoot See **about**

abra n [Span] **SW, esp TX**

A narrow pass or defile; a valley.

   1892 *DN* 1.243 **TX,** *Abra:* a narrow pass between mountains; in Texas, more specifically, a break in a *mesa . .* or in a range of hills. **1912** Lumholtz *New Trails* 17 **sAZ,** The intervening valleys, or *abras,* as the Mexicans call them, are rather flat. **1933** *AmSp* 8.3.9 **SW,** The open spaces between very old, worn-down mountains, which have filled in flat with detritus, are called *abras* (openings). **1977** Watts *Dict. Old West.*

Abraham n
=**Adam 1.**

   1968 *DARE* (Qu. II26, . . *"I wouldn't know him from _____."*) Inf **IN**35, Abraham.

Abraham Lincoln n Also *Abe, Abe's picture, picture of Abe* [From the portrait on the bill] **chiefly Sth, Midl** *freq among Black speakers*

A five-dollar bill.

   1965–70 *DARE* (Qu. U28a, . . *A five-dollar bill*) Infs **DC**4, 12, **GA**92, **IL**21, **KY**80, Abraham Lincoln; **AL**8, **MS**6, 88, Abe; **AR**32, Abe's picture; **MI**76, Picture of Abe. [Of all Infs responding to the question, 6% were Black; of the 10 Infs giving this response, 4 were Black.]

Abraham's cabbage n *?obs*

The redroot pigweed *(Amaranthus retroflexus).*

   1891 *Jrl. Amer. Folkl.* 4.148 **seMA,** Amaratus [sic] retroflexus we called *Abraham's Cabbage.*

Abraham's tree n [Perh an allusion to Gen 21:33]

   1959 *Western Folkl.* 18.49 **IL,** Abraham's tree . . . A cloud form, consisting of an assemblage of long feathers and plumes of cirrus clouds, which seem to radiate from a single point on the horizon.

‡**abram** n |'ebrəm|

A large black stinging ant (prob Myrmicinae).

   1966 *DARE* (Qu. R17) Inf **SC**9 [Gullah speaker], Abram ['ebrəm].

abreast (of) prep (phr) [Transf from naut use]

Across from; opposite to.

   [**1857** (1973) Perry *Amer. in Japan* 356, The Island of Oho-sima, about two miles distant abreast the ships.] **1931–33** *LANE Worksheets* **seMA,** Nantucket is right abreast of Chatham. **1968** *DARE* (Qu. MM1, . . *"Opposite to" . . "The shed is _____ the barn"*) Inf **IN**35, Abreast.

abri n |ɑ'bri| [Fr *abri* shelter]

   1968 *DARE* FW Addit **seLA,** *Abri*—wooden protector for the north side of cucumber hills in the first weeks after planting. Consists of two one-by-eights joined at right angles [and set on edge]. In [the local] French this noun is feminine . . . In English its construction is regular, including plural [ˌɑ'briz].

abroad adv

1 Out; away from one's home but in the community. [*OED abroad* 3 →1859] *?old-fash*

   1940 *Hench Coll.* **cVA,** A questioner was asked . . if so-and-so were at home. "No," was the reply. "He's abroad." Further questioning showed that the person . . was away from home for the day. **1944** *PADS* 2.38 **sVA,** *Abroad . . .* "Finny isn't at home just now; she's gone abroad." . . Rare. **1963** Edwards *Gravel* 175 **eTN** (as of 1920s), "He wuzent at home," said his neighbor; "I don't know where he wuz." "Jist as I thought," said Uncle Eph; "they usually catch it abroad." **1969** *DARE* (Qu. U1, *When you're going to a store . . "I'm going _____."*) Inf **NY**205, Abroad.

2 See quot 1905.

   1905 *DN* 3.68 **nwAR,** *Abroad . . .* At or to a distance of approximately fifty miles or more. 'Mr. Jones has returned from his trip *abroad.'* Common in the newspapers. **c1940** in 1944 *ADD* **FL.**

abroad n [**abroad** adv] See also **broad** n

A trip or visit.

   1938 in 1941 *AmSp* 16.21 **swIN,** *Abroad.* Used as a noun for a trip or visit to another locality. 'I see Mrs. Brown's back from her abroad.'

abrojo n **SW**

Any of var related chaparral shrubs, esp **lotebush** and **squaw-bush** (here: *Condalia globosa*).

   1931 U.S. Dept. Ag. *Misc. Pub.* 101.114, Texas jujube . . of western Texas, locally known as abrojo, lote-bush, and Texas buckthorn, . . is often of value in preventing erosion. **1941** Jaeger *Wildflowers* 138 **Desert SW,** *Gray-leaved Abrojo. Condalia lycioides canescens . . . Parry Abrojo. Condalia Parryi . . . Spiny Abrojo. Condalia spathulata.* **1960** Vines *Trees* **SW** 695, *Condalia obtusifolia . . .* Vernacular names are Texas Buckthorn . . and abrojo. *Ibid* 696, *Condalia spathulata . . .* It is known under the vernacular names of . . Squaw-bush, Chamis, Abrojo.

abscess of the bowels n (Cf *DS* BB49 and the once common *inflammation of the bowels* in the same sense) *old-fash*

   c1960 *Wilson Coll.* **csKY,** Abscess of the bowels, older name for appendicitis.

abscess (root) n
=**Jacob's ladder** (here: *Polemonium reptans*).

   1873 in 1976 Miller *Shaker Herbs* 125 **ceNY,** *Abscess. Polemonium reptans.* Greek Valerian. Blue Bells. Jacob's Ladder. Serviceable in pleurisy, fevers, and inflammatory diseases. **1931** Clute *Common Plants* 122, A number of the ancient plant names recall afflictions which have happily gone quite out of style . . . abscess root (*Polemonium reptans*).

abscond v tr [*OED abscond* 2, →1721] *arch*

Foll by a reflexive pron: to hide or conceal.

   1899 (1912) Green *VA Folk-Speech* 60, *Abscond . . .* "I immediately absconded myself."

‡absentmind adj

Absentminded.

　1967 *DARE* (Qu. JJ30a, . . *Forgetting something*) Inf **TN**1, I'm absentmind.

absey book n [*absey* obs form of *ABC (OED)*] *obs*

A hornbook or primer.

　1899 (1909) Earle *Child Life* 124, The hornbook was called by other names, horn-gig, horn-bat, battledore-book, absey-book, etc.

absolute auction n **KY**

An auction of property in which the highest bid must be accepted. See quot 1976.

　1966 *Cynthiana Democrat* (KY) 5 May 1.8/1 [Advt], *Absolute Auction* at Lebus Tobacco Whse. No. 1. *Ibid* 9 June 8/1 [Advt], 6 Room House—Full Basement *Absolute Auction* . . . to settle the estate of the late W.T. Ecklar we have been authorized to sell his house and lot. **1976** *DARE* File **neKY**, An absolute auction means just that: If you bid highest on that particular property, it will be yours. This . . Kentucky statute . . has been in existence for at least 100 years. The owner and auctioneer can be sued and be made to deliver the deed to the property.

absotoot(e)ly adv [Blend of *absolutely* + *toot* (as in *you're darn tootin'*)] *humorous*

Absolutely.

　1955 *NY Times* (NY) 25 May 36/1 **TN** [Quoting a film actor's rendition of Davy Crockett], There's jest about no nuthin' so absotootely onresistible as an old-fashioned, good-natured grin. **1968** *DARE* (Qu. JJ21, . . *Very positive: Somebody asks you "Are you really going to do that?" And you answer*) Inf **WI**47, Absotootly.

absquatulate v Also *obsquatulate, obsquotulate* [Fanciful pseudo-Lat formation] See *DA* for addit varr and deriv forms; for addit quots see also 1912 Thornton *Amer. Gloss. formerly widespread, now old-fash; joc*

A Intr senses.

1a Of persons or animals: to leave, depart, esp hastily or furtively; to abscond. Fig, to die.

　1830 *Telegraph* (Painesville OH) 15 June 1/5 *(DA)*, Obsquatulate—To mosey, to abscond. **1834** *Life Andrew Jackson* 36 **TN**, By golly, if you obsquotulate, you are ded before you can say Jack Robinson. **1851** (1969) Burke *Polly Peablossom* 184 **IL**, I'm done—I'll absquatulate. **1853** Bird *Nick of Woods* 69 **KY**, "Your . . horse has absquatulated!" "*Absquatulated!*" echoed Forrester, amazed as much at the word as at the fierce visage of his friend, — "what is that? Is the horse hurt?" "Stolen away, sir, by the etarnal Old Scratch!" **1873** Perrie *Buckskin* 18 **eWI**, The vagabond had "absquatulated" with the whole of the joint-stock funds. **1950** *WELS* (To leave in a hurry: "*Before they find this out, we'd better＿＿＿＿*.") 1 Inf, **cwWI**, Absquatulate—old-fashioned. [Old Inf.]

b Of things: to part, separate, fall away.

　1842 *Spirit of the Times* 29 June *(DA)*, When Mr. F. again called, the shingle had absquatulated from the shutter. **1858** *Advocate* (Salem IL) 17 Feb 1/2 *(DA)*, She might . . give him a kiss. Ah, and a good one, too—not one of the touches that wouldn't make a dew drop absquatulate from a rose leaf.

2 To squabble.

　1976 *Harper's Weekly* 65.18 **Midwest**, We always thought it was a perfectly legitimate word—everybody in the Midwest used it and understood it . . . When one of my colleagues here in the effete East [Irvington NJ] was making a big fuss over nothing, and I innocently asked, "What are you obsquatulating about?" I started a real linguistic hassle. Nobody . . had ever heard the word.

B Tr sense.

To send away, to dismiss.

　1887 *Fargo Argus* (ND) 10 Jan, It is rumored that the present grand jury is to be absquatulated—and another called.

‡absquinchiated ppl adj [Fanciful creation on pattern of **absquatulate**]

Used up, finished.

　1967 *DARE* (Qu. LL17, *Ways of saying there's no more of something: "The potatoes are＿＿＿＿."*) Inf **ID**5, Absquinchiated [əb'skwɪnšɪ‚etəd].

absurd adj Usu |æb'sɝd, əb–,–zɝd|; occas |æb'sɝb, æb'zɝb|

Std senses, var forms.

　1937 *AmSp* 12.126 **Upstate NY**, *Absurd* occasionally ends in [b],

apparently by remote assimilation. **1940** *AmSp* 15.85 **neTN**, [ən əbzɝb lukən spænjəl pʌpɪ]. **1942** *AmSp* 17.156 **seNY**, In *absurd* the records show—final [d] 188 [responses], [b] 14.

abuji n [Korean] **HI**

A father.

　1972 Carr *Da Kine Talk* 109 **HI**, Among loanwords of wide circulation are . . terms of respectful address: *abuji* 'father.'

abvertize See **advertise**

Aby See **Abie**

ac' See **act**

acadami(z)ed See **macadamize**

Acadian owl n Also ~ *night* ~ esp **NEng**

=saw-whet owl.

　1839 Audubon *Synopsis Birds* 24, *Ulula Acadica*, . . Acadian Night-Owl . . . Saw-whet. **1872** Coues *Key to N. Amer. Birds* 206, *Acadian Owl. Saw-whet Owl.* **1939** *LANE* Map 230, 1 Inf, **seCT**, [ə'kedjən ɛul] = barn owl, very small. **1966** *DARE* (Qu. Q1) Inf **ME**8, Acadian owl or saw-whet.

acause conj |ə'kɔz| [Cf *EDD*, with exx chiefly from nEngl]

Because.

　1871 (1882) Stowe *Fireside Stories* 245 **NEng**, These 'ere ungodly fellers gettin' the laugh on him, and all acause o' that 'are hoss. **1922** Rollins *Cowboy* 191 **West**, I've warmed up this bit, acause I'm riding the finest little cow horse this State has ever seen. **1950** *PADS* 13.22 **sKY**, *Acause* [ə'kɔz] . . . Heard occasionally among uneducated . . . "Why did you do that?" "Jist *acause.*"

accaount See **account**

accident n

An unexpected turn of events.

　1923 *DN* 5.199 **swMO**, 'Ithout a accident hit'll rain ag'in mornin'.

accommodation n, freq attrib, as in *accommodation car*, ~ *stage*, ~ *train*, etc *old-fash*

A public vehicle, esp a train, which stops at every station to accommodate its passengers.

a A train.

　1838 *Boston Almanac* 49 *(DA)*, Depots on the Providence Rail Road. Accommodation Train. **1911** *Southern Reporter* 55.595 **MS**, A "mixed or accommodation train" is a train equipped and having the appliances and facilities for the carriage of passengers as well as freight. **1950** *WELS* (A train that stops at every station) 1 Inf, **cWI**, Accommodation train. **c1960** *Wilson Coll.* **csKY**, *Accommodation* . . . A local train, one that stops at every station or flag stop; now practically unknown. **1963** Haywood *Yankee Dict.* 1 **NEng**, *Accommodation*—The train that made every station on the line, dropping off mail for each village post office, taking aboard the outgoing pouch and unloading from the express car various items. **1965–70** *DARE* (Qu. N37, . . *Branch railroad*) Inf **IN**13, Accommodation ['kɔmə‚dešən]—because it stopped everyplace; **LA**3, The accommodation—ran from Woodville to New Orleans and back in one day; **PA**235, Accommodation—stops at any stop it comes to and anything in between; (Qu. N36) Inf **FL**17, Accommodation train—used to come through here. [All Infs are old.] **1977** Adams *Lang. Railroader*, Accommodation train.

b Any other vehicle which stops at the passengers' convenience.

　1811 *Columbian Centinel. MA Federalist* (Boston MA) 25 Sep 3/1, The *Accommodation Stage* Will run . . on the Trenton Turnpike Road. Leaves Boston every Monday, Wednesday, and Friday. **1829** Royall *Pennsylvania* 2.9 *(DA)*, I . . intended to take the Accommodation in the morning. **1892** *Harper's Mag.* 84.426/1 **Chicago IL**, What may be called accommodation cars [of an elevator] halt at the lower floors. **1907** *St. Nicholas* May 669/1 **PA**, When the miners go down into the mines, they get into a car called the accommodation. **1909** *DN* 4.55 **seMA**, *Accommodation* . . . A horse-drawn public conveyance travelling over a fixed route, stopping on signal to take or leave passengers . . . "Shall we walk up-along, or take the accommodation?" **1937** FWP *Guide MA* 330 **seMA**, The Boston steamers whistle a last farewell, the 'accommodation' (street bus) is converted back into a fish truck . . and Provincetown settles down again to a 'nice quiet winter.'

accommodation street n *?obs*

A street of small shops and businesses conveniently catering to local residences.

1899 (1977) Norris *McTeague* 2 **San Francisco CA,** He had . . opened his "Dental Parlors" on Polk Street, an "accommodation street" of small shops in the residence quarter of the town.

accordion n Cf **buck** v² **1**
Among loggers: see quot.
 1958 McCulloch *Woods Words* **Pacific NW** *Accordion*—A bucked log with a series of shallow shelves across the end, caused by poor bucking.

account n Usu |ə'kaʊnt|; also, **esp Sth, Midl** |(ə)'kæʊnt|; in **eVA,** occas |ə'kɔʊnt| See Pronc Intro 3.II.14 Pronc-spp *accaount, 'count*
A Forms.
 1861 Holmes *Venner* 2.299 **wMA,** Here is your accaount, Miss Darley. **1916** *DN* 4.344 **NE,** *'Count* [kæʊnt] . . for *account:* used by a white boy. **1927** Shewmake *Engl. Pronc. VA* 24 **eVA,** On the Virginia peninsula [some speakers] regularly [say ə'kɔʊnt].] **1942** Hall *Smoky Mt. Speech* 45 **eTN, wNC,** The following words almost always have [æʊ] . . About, account.
B Sense.
Value, use. [From the std phr *of no account* of no value] *?old-fash* See also **no-account** adj
 1850 Garrard *Wah-to-yah* 2 **OH,** Your money's no account. **1852** Stowe *Uncle Tom's Cabin* 1.185 **KY,** "Then it's no account talking," said the woman. **1878** Beadle *Western Wilds* 187 **UT,** Little Si Duvall, a splintery feller with no legs to speak of, and everybody said no account. **1899** Garland *Boy Life* 15 **nwIA,** But Mr. Jennings . . only sucked his pipe and said, "They're no account, I guess, on account of the stagnant water." **1940** Richter *Trees* 32 **OH,** But now that he greased it with bear's oil, he reckoned it might be of some account. **1970** *DARE* FW Addit **neKY,** "Was it any count?" That is, any good. Common.

account of conj phr
On account of; because.
 1938 Rawlings *Yearling* 31 **FL,** He ain't full weight right now, account of his stomach bein' shrunk up. **1942** *Horizon* (London) 6.62 **Sth,** Fred's five foot ten . . but I tell him he's till [sic] a shrimp, account of I'm so tall.

accoutrements n pl [*EDD* 1880, from wCornwall; cf *DJE kruchument* (< *accoutrement)* in same sense] Cf **clatterment**
 1944 *PADS* 2.38 **NC,** *Accoutrements* . . . Inconsequential things—odds and ends—that collect in one's household. Used . . by a man and his sister, who originally came from sw. Va. Very rare.

accumulate v Usu |ə'kjumjələt|; occas |(ə)'kjumə,let| Pronc-sp *accumalate*
Std senses, var forms.
 1936 *AmSp* 11.159 **eTX,** In another group, the medial *u* is pronounced both [jə] and [ə], the latter sound being especially characteristic of less literate speech: *accumulate. Ibid* 310 **Upstate NY,** *Accumulate* . . may occasionally be heard as [ə'kjumjələt]. **1942** Hall *Smoky Mt. Speech* 67 **wNC, eTN,** Accumulate ['kjuməlet]. **1942** *New Yorker* 11 July 20/3 **sCA,** Me stuck with all the restront bills the two accumalated.

accumy See **alchemy**

ace n, freq attrib [From *ace* any person outstandingly good (*OEDS* 1919 → "U.S. Slang")] *among Black speakers* See also **ace-boon-coon**
A very close friend.
 1958 Hughes–Bontemps *Negro Folkl.* 481 **NYC** [Glossary of Harlem Jive], *Ace:* Bosom friend. *He's my ace boy.* **1970** Bullins *Electronic* 85 **sCA** [Black], What could she gain by messin' 'round on me with my ace buddy? **1970** Knight *Black Voices* 78 **IN,** You know me, baby . . . I am your ace man. **1970** Major *Afro–Amer. Slang, Ace* . . . One's best friend; a first-rate person; one's lover. **1970** *DARE* (Qu. II1, . . *A close friend* . . "He's my _____.") Infs **FL52, MO29, NC84,** Ace; **SC68,** Ace-buddy; (Qu. II3, . . *Very friendly*) Inf **DC11,** My ace. [All Infs Black] **1971** Roberts *Third Ear.*

ace adv See **yes**

ace-boon-coon n For varr see quots [*ace* first rate, infl by **ace** n + *boon* good or intimate, as *boon companion* + **coon** n¹ **2**] *among Black speakers* Cf **ace-coon**
A very close friend.
 1962 Crump *Burn* 200 **Chicago IL** [Black], We're ace-boon-coons, remember? **1965** Brown *Manchild* 77 **NYC** [Black], I knew K.B. about

a year before we became ace boon coons. K.B. was the first cat I locked with up at Wiltwyck. **1970** *DARE* (Qu. II1, . . *A close friend*) Infs **FL48, 52, KY94, MS88, NY241, SC69,** Ace-boon-coon; **SC68,** Boon-coon; (Qu. II3) Inf **DC11,** Ace-spoon-coon. [All Infs Black] **1971** Roberts *Third Ear.* **1980** Folb *Runnin' Down* 35 [Black], One of the closest levels of friendship is reflected in a term like *ace* and its variants *ace coon, ace boon coon, ace coon poon, ace boom boom, a.b.c.*

ace-coon n [*ace* first rate + **coon** n¹ **2**] *among Black speakers*
1 See **ace-boon-coon.**
2 An important person; a big shot.
 1970 *DARE* (Qu. HH17, *A person who tries to appear important . . "He'd like to be the _____ around here."*) Inf **VA71,** Ace-coon.

ace-over-apex adv phr Var of **ass-over-teakettle** *euphem*
 1969 *DARE* (Qu. X35, . . "He slipped and came down _____.") Inf **PA202,** Ace-over-apex [laughter].

acequia n Usu, as in Span |ə'sekjə|, also |ə'sik,wiə, ə,se'kwiə| [Span] **SW** Also called **sequia, zanja**
An irrigation ditch. Hence *acequia madre* mother ditch; *acequiador* local official in charge of *acequias.*
 1844 (1954) Gregg *Commerce* 285 **SW,** I followed up the *acequia* that led from the spring—a ditch four or five feet wide, through which flowed a stream three or four feet in depth. *Ibid* 107, One *acequia madre* (mother ditch) suffices generally to convey water for the irrigation of an entire valley. **1860** in 1948 *Western Folkl.* 7.3 **sCA,** Persons throwing earth or any filthy matter into . . the canals or *Acequias* of the city . . shall be fined. **1892** *DN* 1.186 **TX,** I have heard . . *acequia* . . pronounced *acéquia* (the normal pronunciation), *acequía,* or even *assay-kwía. Ibid* 243, *Acequiador:* The officer in charge of the *acequias* . . in a community, who, between planting time and harvest, ranks everybody, even the *alcalde.* **1932** *DN* 6.223 **NM. 1932** Bentley *Spanish Terms, Acequia* . . (Spanish, a:sé:ki:a:; *English, the same and . . also* ə se: kwía) A canal or ditch for irrigation purposes or for the water supply of [a] pueblo or village. **1940** Fergusson *Our Southwest* 278 **NM,** They have saved . . its *acequias* running clear mountain water, its trees, and a respect for its Spanish-speaking folk. **1962** Atwood *Vocab. TX* 41, *Main irrigation ditch* . . . An older term, *acequia* . . , recalling the days of gravity irrigation, is still in occasional use, chiefly in Southwest Texas. **1966** *DARE* (Qu. C1, . . *A small stream of water*) Inf **NM6,** Acequia [ə'seɪkjə]—irrigation ditch.

ace-spoon-coon See **ace-boon-coon**

acetonemia n For varr see quot; folk-etym *acid anemia*
Std sense, var forms.
 1968–70 *DARE* (Qu. K28, *The chief diseases that cows have around here*) Inf **CT9,** Azetonemia; **MI116,** Astinemia; **MA66,** Acid anemia; **OH81,** Acigenema; **PA163,** Acetomenia; **PA193,** Estimenia [ɛstə'miniə]—cow quits eating.

achemy See **alchemy**

achies See **aikie(s)**

achins exclam
=**aikie(s).**
 1940 *Qrly. Jrl. Speech* 26.266 **VA,** What children in the North call "dibs on it," meaning *I claim a share,* Virginia children may call . . [eɪkənz] on it . . or [eɪčənz].

ach (ja) adv, intj Also *ach yes* [Ger] **Ger settlement areas** See also **ach ja** n
Oh yes! Yes indeed!
 1968 *DARE* (Qu. NN1, *Other words like 'yes'*) Inf **MN37,** Ach ja ['ɑkjɑ]. **1973** Allen *LAUM* 1.387, 1 Inf, **neNE,** Ach, ach yes.

ach ja n |'ɑk jɑ| [Ger, lit "oh yes!", phr used in song and game]
A children's ring game: see quot 1940.
 1940 *Handy Play Party Book* 114, *Ach Ja* . . . Partners join adjacent hands . . . They walk to the right around the circle four slow steps; partners then face each other, release hands and bow very simply by bending at the hips, on "Ja," then turn back to back and bow again on "Ja." . . Repeat from the beginning. **1968–70** *DARE* (Qu. EE33) Inf **NY123,** Ach ja—children pair up and dance in a circle; **PA242,** Ach ja ['ɑkjɑ]—song and moving around, bow and say, "Ach ja."

acid anemia See **acetonemia**

acid bumps n pl Also *acid rash*
Hives.
    1966–67 *DARE* (Qu. BB25, . . *Common skin diseases*) Inf **SC**39, Acid bumps—allergy to tomatoes, oranges, etc; **FL**25, Heat rash, acid rash, fish poisoning.

acigenema See **acetonemia**

acion n [Span] **SW**
Stirrup leather: the strap suspending a stirrup.
    1944 Adams *Western Words* 3, *Ación* . . . Stirrup leather. A Spanish term sometimes used on the southern border and in California. **1961** Adams *Old-Time Cowhand* 112. **1977** Watts *Dict. Old West.*

aciteria, acituria See **azoturia**

ack v See **act**

ack n Also *ackey* [Perh var of **Ikey**] *derog* Cf **Itie**
An Italian.
    1941 *LANE* Map 453 (*[An] Italian*) 2 Infs, **cMA**, Ack, Ackey [æk, ækɪ].

ackempucky n [Prob Algonkian; perh rel to *achpunk?siin* to place on hot ashes, bake, roast. This does not, however, agree with *ADD's* definitions. The unidentified quots were apparently Wentworth's observations.] **WV**
    1944 *ADD,* Ackempucky . . . a Any food mixture of unknown ingredients. *c.1928 w.cent.W.Va. Charleston.* b A food of jellylike consistency, as gelatine. *1943 n.W.Va. Monongalia Co.*

acker fortis, ackie fortis See **aggie forti(e)s**

acknowledge n Pronc-sp *ecknowledge* [*OED* →1555, "*obs.*"] **SC, GA coasts** *Gullah*
Knowledge, understanding.
    1922 Gonzales *Black Border* 28 **sSC, GA coasts** [Gullah], Him hab uh sonny-law wuh hab uh berry good ecknowledge fuh git money out'uh buckruh'; *Ibid* 42, Uh got uh ecknowledge fuh look t'ru 'e face; *Ibid* 299 [Gullah glossary], *Ecknowledge*—knowledge, ability, understanding.

acknowledge the corn v phr Also *confess ~, own ~; acknowledge the coin, ~malt* [*acknowledge* admit + *corn* corn liquor (*DA corn* 2, 1820 →); see *AmSp* 51.102–08] Addit quots and varr in 1912 Thornton *Amer. Gloss.* **formerly widespread, now chiefly Midl** *old-fash, joc*
Orig, to admit to being drunk; by ext, to admit to any mistake, fault, or impropriety.
    1839 *Times–Picayune* (New Orleans LA) 5 Apr 2/3 (*AmSp* 51.107) **VA,** We "acknowledge the corn." . . The people there [=in Mississippi] do not drink one-tenth part of what they do in this state. **1842** *Spirit of the Times* 16 Mar (in 1912 Thornton *Amer. Gloss.*), Your honor, I confess the corn. I was royally drunk. **1861** *Harper's Mag.* 23.280/2 **AR,** Sure enough it was his own house . . . He 'owned the corn,' flung Cæsar a dollar to pay for the information, and passed the remainder of the night *at home* with his guests. **1865** Derby *Squibob* 171, Amos acknowledged the malt by a cheerful guffaw. **1908** *DN* 3.285 **eAL, wGA,** *Acknowledge the corn* . . . Sometimes *acknowledge the coin* is heard. **1923** *DN* 5.199 **swMO. 1927** *AmSp* 2.347 **WV. 1936** *AmSp* 11.316 **Ozarks,** Own the corn. **1940** in 1944 *ADD* **nWV.**

acme n |ˈækmi| Pronc var of *acne*
    1966–69 *DARE* (Qu. X59, . . *Small infected pimples that form, usually on the face*) Infs **FL**19, **NJ**59, **NC**30, **PA**195, 197, Acme [ˈækmi].

acorn calf n [From the belief that the calf's condition is the result of an excess of acorns in the mother's prenatal diet] **chiefly West** Also called **deacon**
A congenitally weak calf; a runt. Also transf to other animals and humans.
    1929 *AmSp* 5.16 **Ozarks,** Acorn calf . . . A poor specimen, a runt, a weakling. Refers to human beings as well as to cattle, swine and other animals. **1934** Weseen *Dict. Amer. Slang* 92 **West,** *Acorn calf*—A runt; a weakling. **1961** Adams *Old-Time Cowhand* 155 **West,** A poor, runty, and weak calf was called an "acorn calf." **1977** Watts *Dict. Old West.*

acorn-cracker n Cf **corncracker** 1 and *DS* HH1
A countrified person.
    1905 *DN* 3.68 **nwAR,** Acorn [ˈekn̩]-*cracker* . . . Uncouth countryman. 'Country jakes are sometimes called *acorn-crackers.*' Rare.

acorn duck n [From its feeding on acorns]
=**wood duck.**
    1888 Trumbull *Names of Birds* 34, *Wood Duck* . . . At Pocomoke City . . , Maryland, and in the vicinity of Charleston, S.C., Acorn Duck. **1888** (1890) Warren *Birds PA* 40. **1932** Bennitt *Check-list* 19 **MO. 1955** Forbush–May *Birds* 70, *Wood Duck* . . . Summer Duck; Wood Widgeon; Acorn Duck. **1967–70** *DARE* (Qu. Q5, . . *Kinds of wild ducks*) Inf **AL**31, Summer or acorn duck; **MS**87, Acorn [ˈekən] ducks.

acorn tree n [*EDD* 1881 →]
An oak tree.
    1954 Roberts *I Bought Dog* 19 **seKY,** A acorn had fallen in the horse's back and made a acorn tree. **1967** *DARE* (QR near Qu. I43) Inf **CO**8, Acorn tree—oak tree [conv]. **1975** Newell *If Nothin' Don't Happen* 159 **FL,** Mr. Jenkins . . , lookin' as pleased as a blind hog findin' an acorn tree.

acquaint v intr [*OED acquaint* 2 →1774 "*obs.*"; *W3* "*archaic*"; *EDD* 1818 →]
Usu foll by *with:* to become acquainted.
    1966–69 *DARE* (Qu. II2a, *When two people begin to be friendly: "He has just recently _____ with John.*") Infs **AR**51, **CA**15A, **DC**8, **NY**73, 92, Acquainted; **NY**200, Socialized, became social, acquainted; **WI**47, Acquainted, started going around.

acquainted ppl adj [*OED acquainted* 4, "*obs.*"]
Made familiar by experience with; knowledgeable about.
    1965 *DARE* Tape **MA**92, Stevensville, if you're acquainted up that way.

acquaintun ppl adj Also aphet *quaintun* [Perh back-formation from *acquaintance* or *acquainting*] **SC, GA coasts** *Gullah*
Acquainted.
    1888 Jones *Negro Myths* 63 **GA Coast,** Wid dem people wuh no quaintun wid um eh pass ehself off fuh er fus-class cook. *Ibid* 69, Eh mek um quaintun bout wen de Ring tuk, an who eh tink tief um. **1922** Gonzales *Black Border* 79 **sSC, GA coasts** [Gullah], He is berry well acquaintun wid uh sutt'n annimel dat eenhabit de jungle.

a-credit See **a** *prep¹* 3

acre-foot adj Cf **forty acres** and *DS* X38
Big-footed.
    1908 *DN* 3.285 **eAL, wGA,** *Acre-foot* . . . "Look at that acre-foot nigger." Rare.

across prep **HI**
Opposite; across from.
    1972 Carr *Da Kine Talk* 120 **HI,** "I sat across you at church las' Sunday." . . "Meet me at the bus stop across the library." . . Certain pairs of expressions . . cause problems in Hawaii, and one of the most typical is the pair *across* and *across from.*

across-lot adj [*across lot(s)* adv phr 1] *?nonce lit use*
Direct; efficient.
    1867 Lowell *Biglow* 100 "Upcountry" **MA,** Their mission-work with Afrikins hez put 'em up . . / To all the mos' across-lot ways o' preachin' an' convartin.

across lot(s) adv phr See also **cross-lot(s)** adv
1 By the shortest route: directly. **chiefly NEng and settlement area**
    1858 (1894) Lowell *Biglow* 28 "Upcountry" **MA,** Joe looked roun'/ And see (acrost lots in a pond . .)/ A goose. **1881** Pierson *In the Brush* 30 **KY,** On their way to the graveyard they climbed the fences and went across-lots by a shorter route, leaving the hearse to go around the road. **1905** *DN* 3.2 **cCT. 1907** *DN* 3.208 **nwAR. 1908** Lincoln *Cy Whittaker* 396 **NEng,** He went across lots, in the rear of the barns and orchards, wading through drifts and climbing fences. **1947** Chalfant *Gold* 74 **wNV,** Palmer, Dexter, and one more man, each with Springfield rifle and fixed bayonet, went across lots to the bar of the Exchange Hotel. **1957** Beck *Folkl. ME* 75, The old man arose, took his lunch and strolled "across lots" as they say in Maine, following the landmarks of his dream. **1966–69** *DARE* (Qu. MM16, *If you're walking with somebody to the other corner of a square, and you want to save steps, . . "It'll be shorter if we _____.*") Infs **CT**9, **LA**40, **MA**29, **NH**5, 13, **RI**15, Go (or cut) across lots; **MA**14, Went across-lot this way.

2 in phr *go* (or *send*) *to hell* (or *the devil*) *across lots:* Go straight to hell. **chiefly UT**

1853 in 1854 *Jrl. of Discourses* 1.83 **UT,** I [=Brigham Young] dreamed that I . . . cut one of their throats from ear to ear, saying, "Go to hell across lots." **1859** (1968) Bartlett *Americanisms* 3, I swore in Nauvoo, when my enemies were looking me in the face, that I would send them to hell across lots if they meddled with me. —*Speech of Brigham Young,* 1857. **1862** Winthrop *John Brent* 195 **UT,** You may go to the devil across lots, on that runt pony of yourn, with your new friends, for all I care. **1959** Robertson *Ram* 244 **sID** (as of 1875), As for me, if I didn't have some place to put my money I would go to hell across lots.

across-the-track adj [Attrib use of *across the tracks* adv phr, where poor people live (*DA track,* 1929 →)] Cf *DS* II25
Indigent; low-grade.
1967 *DARE* (Qu. HH18) Inf **SC**45, Across-the-track people.

acrost adv, prep |əˈkrɔst| [*across* + excrescent *t*: see Pronc Intro 3.I.23] **throughout US** *esp among speakers with less than coll educ* See also **crost** adv, prep Addit quots in 1944 *ADD*
Across.
1759 in 1882 Essex Inst. *Coll.* 19.145, Ye Enemy fird at our men a Crost ye River. **1779** in 1886 MA Hist. Soc. *Proc.* 2d ser 2.467 **MA,** The Lake . . is . . about 8 miles acrost. **1852** Stowe *Uncle Tom's Cabin* 2.60 **OH,** A good, round, school-boy hand, that Tom said might be read "most acrost the room." **1891** *DN* 1.165 **cNY,** [əˈkrɔst]. **1892** *DN* 1.237 **wMO, MI, NEng.** **1905** *DN* 3.102 **nwAR.** **1907** *DN* 3.240 **eME.** **1908** *DN* 3.285 **eAL, wGA,** (A)crost. **1915** *DN* 4.178 **swVA,** (A)crost. **1938** Rawlings *Yearling* 47 **FL,** The old Spanish trail clear acrost Floridy. **1965–70** *DARE* (Qu. MM16, . . *"It'll be shorter if we _____."*) 17 Infs, Cut (go, walk, etc) acrost; (Qu. MM15, . . *"He nailed the board on _____."*) Infs **MI**117, **MO**4, Acrost; (Qu. MM14, . . *"The drugstore is _____ the gas station."*) Infs **CT**22, **MA**56, **NY**234, (Diagonally, directly) acrost (from); (Qu. MM1, . . *"The shed is _____ the barn."*) Infs **IA**23, **NJ**28, **NY**219, 234, **OH**45, **PA**122, Acrost (from); (Qu. II17) Infs **IL**44, **NY**27, **WA**20, Came (ran, run) acrost; (Qu. U18) Infs **NM**8, **NY**96, 219, Come acrost; (Qu. X50) Inf **WI**47, Five ax-handles acrost; (Qu. MM5) Inf **WI**27, Acrost. [Of 29 Infs, 25 have less than college educ.] **1968** *DARE* FW Addit **NY**75, Acrost [əˈkrɔst]. **1976** Allen *LAUM* 3.301, After /s/ four infs. add the /t/ to *once* . . and thirty to *across* . . as /əkrɔst/.

act v Usu |ækt|, also freq |æk| Pronc-spp *ac', ack*
A Forms.
1894 in 1941 Warfel–Orians *Local-Color Stories* 737 **sAR** [Black], How I gwine ac' in dis heah trouble. **1899** Garland *Prairie Folks* 95 **IA,** What makes ma ac' so? **1923** *DN* 5.211 **swMO,** He ac's mighty ill. **1927** Kennedy *Gritny* 56 **sLA** [Black], Go set down an' ack like people. **1940** *Sat. Eve. Post* 20 July 55/1 **GA** [Black], They ack that way. **1954** Harder *Coll.* **cwTN,** Act [æk].

B Senses.
1 To personate, assume the character of. [*OED act* 7, 1651 →] (note that the noun complement is usu sg regardless of the subject of the verb) **chiefly Sth, Midl** *old-fash*
1908 *DN* 3.285 **eAL, wGA,** Act the nigger . . . Do menial work, drudge. "I don't perpose to act the nigger no longer." **1937** Hall Coll. **eTN, wNC,** Act the fool . . . To act foolish; to play the clown . . very much used in some sections. **1954** Harder *Coll.* **cwTN,** He's actin' the fool. **1956** Gipson *Old Yeller* 6, **TX,** Then he'd had to go act a fool and get himself killed. **1966–70** *DARE* (Qu. AA8, *When people make too much of a show of affection in a public place*) Infs **LA**16, **NC**41, Acting a (or the) fool; (Qu. BB27, *When somebody pretends to be sick*) Inf **PA**142, Actin' the possum; (Qu. DD14, *When a person is partly drunk*) Inf **LA**11, Acting a fool; (Qu. FF18, . . *Noisy or boisterous . . party: "They certainly _____ last night."*) Inf **TX**104A, Acted the fool; (Qu. GG32a, *To habitually play tricks . . "He's always _____."*) Infs **NM**9, **OH**65, Acting a (or the) fool; (Qu. LL4) Inf **NC**41, He acted the hog. [All Infs old] **1967** *DARE* FW Addit **LA**6, Acting a rascal — being mischievous. Common.

2 also *act out:* To misbehave, act up. Cf **act off**
1903 *DN* 2.295 **Cape Cod MA** (as of 1850s), Act . . . To misbehave. **1913** *DN* 4.3 **seME,** Act out. To misbehave, of children in school.

3 To perform gymnastic feats, esp on an **acting pole.**
1950 *PADS* 14.11 **SC,** Act . . . To perform on a horizontal bar; to perform on any gymnastic paraphernalia, as parallel bars . . . Used before the days of gymnasiums. **c1960** *Wilson Coll.* **csKY,** "Little Jimmy shore kin act on the poles." . . This usage is virtually unknown among [cultured speakers].

4 also *act out:* To pretend. **?Midl**
1966–70 *DARE* (Qu. JJ46, . . *Pretend: "Let's _____ we don't know a thing about it."*) Infs **MO**9, 15, **NC**33, **OH**84, **TN**53, **TX**62, Act; **KY**90, Act out like.

‡actable adj
Active, capable of lively activity.
1966 *DARE* (Qu. KK27, *A very lively, active old person: "For his age, he's _____."*) Inf **SC**10, Actable [ˈæktəbəl].

act-ass n Cf **act off**
A smart-aleck.
1970 *DARE* (Qu. II36a, *Somebody who talks back or gives rude answers*) Inf **MA**127, Act-ass [ˈækˌæs].

actchelly See **actual(ly)**

acting pole n Also *acting bar, action bar* See also **act B3**
A horizontal pole used for performing gymnastic feats.
1950 *PADS* 14.11 **SC,** Acting pole . . . An improvised horizontal bar, such as was formerly put up by school boys, and on which they *acted* during recess. Also called *acting bar, action bar.* **c1960** *Wilson Coll.* **csKY,** Acting pole . . . A pole put between two trees or posts and used for boys to perform on. "He can hang by his toes on the acting pole." Not widely used as a term.

act'lly See **actual(ly)**

act off v phr [Cf **act B 2** and common *act up*]
To behave in an unruly or capricious manner.
1946 *PADS* 6.4 **eNC,** Act off . . . To cut up, to act silly before company. Said of children. "You decided to try to act off." **1950** *WELS* (*When children or young people are full of mischief or tricks: "They're always _____."*) 1 Inf, **swWI,** Acting off. **1968** *DARE* (QR p282) Inf **GA**45, "You're acting off" (acting strange).

act out See **act B 2, 4**

actual adv
Actually.
1940–44 in 1944 *ADD* **AR,** We don't actual know much about him . . . He don't actual do it. Radio.

actual(ly) adj, adv Usu |ˈækšəl(i), ˈækčəl(i)|, also |æktl(i)| Pronc-spp *actchelly, act'lly*
Std senses, var forms.
1867 Lowell *Biglow* (*ADD*), Act'lly. **1887** *Scribner's Mag.* 2.478 **AR,** Actchelly, Jeff, my bones is wearin' out waitin' ter dance at yo' weddin'! **1891** *DN* 1.166 **cNY,** [t] is also common in words pronounced with [č] by educated people . . . [æktl] < *actual.* **1942** Hall *Smoky Mt. Speech* 95 **wNC, eTN,** Actual [ˈækčəl]. **1940–44** in 1944 *ADD* **AR,** Actual . . . [ˈækšəl]. Radio.

Adam n [*Adam* the first man, the archetypal man]
1 also *Adams:* A person one does not know — usu emphatic. **widespread** Also called **Abraham, Adam's apple 2, Adam's housecat, Adam's off-ox 1, Eve**
1787 (1841) Smith *Jrl. & Corresp.* 1.140, In a country [=France] where I am not known from Adam — without the *s* — *alias* the husband of Eve. **1844** Stephens *High Life in NY* 1.191, He don't know me from Adam. **1938** Farrell *No Star* 241 **Chicago IL** (as of 1914–15), Walk by him as if you didn't know him from Adam. **1965–70** *DARE* (Qu. II26, *Joking ways of saying that you would not know who somebody is: "I wouldn't know him from _____."*) 649 Infs, **throughout US,** Adam; **MD**19, **MA**56, **MO**3, 16, **NY**70, **RI**4, Adams.
2 In humorous phrr suggesting a very remote or primitive time. Cf **Hector**
1839 *Spirit of Times* 26 Oct 397/1 **Ohio R Valley,** As great races . . as has ever been run since Adam was a yearling. **1935** Davis *Honey* 105 **OR,** He said he hadn't heard a word about Wade Shively since Adam was a cowboy. **1939** (1962) Thompson *Body & Britches* 499 **NY,** That horse is old enough to have been born in Adam's stable. **1942** ME Univ. *Studies* 56.80, "Since Adam was an oakum-boy." From time immemorial. **1959** *VT Hist.* ns 27.123, Since Adam was a rag doll . . . As long as one can remember. Occasional. **1967–70** *DARE* (Qu. FF21b, . . *About old jokes . . "The first time I heard that one _____."*) Infs **LA**14, **PA**68, Adam was a pup; **TX**11, Adam was a kid; **MD**8, Adam wore short pants; (Qu. A24, . . *Someone who has always been the same way: "He's been hot-tempered from _____."*) Inf **OH**99, Adam's birth.

3 In phrr suggesting a person's complete ignorance of the obvious or elementary. [Ext of **Adam 1**]

    1966–69 *DARE* (Qu. JJ15b, . . *A person who seems to you very stupid: "He doesn't know _____."*) Infs **IL**100, **WI**34, From Adam; **NJ**25, Himself from Adam; **WA**3, His name from Adam.

4 In exprs suggesting the state of nature, nakedness. Cf **outward Adam.**

    1967–68 *DARE* (Qu. W20, . . *No clothes on at all . . "There was Johnny, _____", or "They went in swimming _____."*) Inf **IL**5, Dressed like Adam; **WI**74, In Adam's original dress.

Adam-and-Eve n [See quots senses **1** and **3**; *OEDS* 1789 →; see also *EDD*]

1 also ∼ *root:* Esp **puttyroot** (eastern two-thirds US; see also **Adam-and-Eve-and-their-son**), but also any of var similar plants, as of the genera *Arethusa* and *Corallorhiza*.

    1807 Scott *Geog. MD & DE* 25, Adam and Eve; this plant has two bulbous roots, joined together by a small filament, about two inches in length; when put into water, one of the roots swims, and the other sinks. **1840** MA Zool. & Bot. Surv. *Herb. Plants & Quadrupeds* 199, Adam and Eve. A singular plant with a single leaf sheathed, and bearing a few flowers towards the summit. The form of the flower originates the popular name. **1872** Schele de Vere *Americanisms* 398, *Putty-Root . . ,* more generally known by its familiar name of *Adam and Eve.* **1901** Lounsberry *S. Wild Flowers* 96, When the plant is uprooted there are to be found as in a chain several old corms attached in succession to the one of the present season. It was perhaps a young plant that had borne but two which suggested to the donor of its popular name, Adam and Eve, hand in hand. **1931** *Jrl. Amer. Folkl.* 44.413 Sth [Black], Adam and Eve roots (pair). Sew together in bag and carry on person for protection. **1940** Steyermark *Flora MO* 100, *Adam-and-Eve . . (Aplectrum hyemale) . . .* Stem from a rounded bulb-like base (Adam) connected by a horizontal attachment to a similar one (Eve). **1959** Carleton *Index Herb. Plants* 1, Adam and Eve: Aplectrum hyemale . . ; Corallorrhiza [sic] odontorrhiza; . . Also applied to many other flowers with an upright spadix or pistil, and to a number of orchids. **1969–70** *DARE* (Qu. S26b) Inf **SC**67, Adam-and-Eve root—used in witchcraft; (Qu. S26e) Inf **KY**47, Adam-and-Eve—small white flower, like last-of-the-summer.

2 also *Adam-and-Eve-in-the-bower, Adam-and-Eve's-chariot:* The common monkshood *(Aconitum napellum).* **esp ME**

    1893 *Jrl. Amer. Folkl.* 6.136, Aconitum napellus, Adam and Eve, Washington Co., Me. **1896** *Jrl. Amer. Folkl.* 9.179, Aconitum Napellus . . Adam-and-Eve-in-the-bower, Deering, Me. **1959** Carleton *Index Herb. Plants* 1, Adam and Eve's chariot: Aconitum (v).

3 =**dogtooth violet. CA**

    1897 Parsons *Wild Flowers CA* 136, The dog's-tooth violets . . . in Mendocino County . . are commonly known as "chamise-lilies." Another name is "Adam and Eve," bestowed because the plant often bears a large and a small flower at the same time. **1915** (1926) Armstrong *Western Wild Flowers* 28, In California they [*Erythronium* spp] are often called Chamise Lily, and sometimes Adam and Eve.

4 A yucca (here: *Yucca filamentosa).* Cf **Adam's needle (and thread)**

    1967 *DARE* FW Addit **PA**162, Adam-and-Eve—Yucca plants.

5 =**Adam 1.**

    1966–70 *DARE* (Qu. II26, . . *"I wouldn't know him from _____."*) Infs **LA**20, 35, **NV**4, **NJ**64, **ND**3, **OK**27, **VA**25, Adam and Eve; **IA**22, **MN**15, Adam or Eve.

Adam-and-Eve-and-their-son n

A **puttyroot** with three corms. Cf **Adam-and-Eve 1**

    1970 Hyatt *Hoodoo* 410, One informant calls this root . . *Adam-and-Eve-and-Their-Son . . .* When there are two [corms], we have *Adam* and *Eve;* when three, the *son* is added. This could suggest The Trinity or The Holy Family, but as often as I heard the plant named I remember the *son* once.

Adam-and-Eve-in-the-bower See Adam-and-Eve 2

Adam-and-Eve root See Adam-and-Eve 1

Adam-and-Eve's chariot See Adam-and-Eve 2

Adam-and-Eve's needle and thread n Also ∼ *thread and needle, Adam and Eve thread*

=**Adam's needle (and thread).**

    1831 *Boston Eve. Transcript* (MA) 5 June 2/1 *(DA),* Yucca filamentosa, or Adam and Eve's thread and needle. **1966** *DARE* FW Addit **MA**6, Adam and Eve's needle and thread—yucca. **1970** *DARE* (Qu. S26e) Inf **VA**77, Adam and Eve thread—a soap-plant. [FW drawing in QR: silkgrass, a yucca, prob yucca filamentosa.]

Adam apple n

The Adam's apple.

    1943 Writers' Program NC *Bundle of Troubles* 106, He is skinny and runty, and he got a big Adam apple in his guzzle what bob up and down when he talk. **1968–70** *DARE* (Qu. X7, . . *The throat: "Some food got stuck in his _____."*) Infs **KY**85, **SC**58, Adam apple. [Both Infs have grade-school educ]

Adam or Eve See Adam-and-Eve 5

Adams See Adam 1

Adam's ale n [*OED* 1643 →; *EDD:* "Dial. slang in *gen.* use."] *joc*

Water.

    1708 (1865) Cook *Sot-weed Factor* 21 MD, And was in fact but *Adam's Ale.* [**1857** Hawthorne *Twice-Told* 1.171 **MA,** The unadulterated ale of father Adam.] **1899** (1912) Green *VA Folk-Speech, Adam's ale . . .* Water. **1939** *AmSp* 14.89 c**TN. 1941** *AmSp* 16.21 **IN, MO. 1943** *AmSp* 18.66 **AL, LA, NC, SC, TN. 1944** in 1957 Old Farmer's Almanac *Sampler* 134 **NEng,** When the water is pouring off you in the hayfield, get the womenfolk to bring out a gallon of oatmeal water—two handfuls of oatmeal with Adam's ale from the spring. **1949** Brown *Amer. Cooks* 677 **OH,** Ohio water is so good that Buckeye football teams take gallons of Adam's ale from home when touring the country, to keep the team healthy. **c1960** *Wilson Coll.* cs**KY. 1966** *DARE* (QR p225) Inf **MA**11, Adam's ale—nickname for water.

Adam's all fox n Also *Adam's fox,* ∼ *old fox* [Metanalysis of **Adam's off-ox**]

=**Adam's off-ox 1.**

    1950 *WELS* ("*I wouldn't know him from _____."*) 1 Inf, cn**WI,** Adam's all fox. **1968** *DARE* (Qu. II26, . . *"I wouldn't know him from _____."*) Inf **OH**63, Adam's off-ox—my grandmother said that, and for most of my life I said, "Adam's all fox"; **CA**53, **IN**22, Adam's old fox; **LA**32, Adam's fox.

Adam's apple n

1 =**jack-in-the-pulpit 1.**

    1944 *PADS* 2.17 sAppalachians, *Adam's-apple . . .* The Indian turnip or jack-in-the-pulpit, known for its acrid or pungent taste.

2 =**Adam 1. chiefly Sth, Midl**

    1966–69 *DARE* (Qu. II26, . . *"I wouldn't know him from _____."*) Infs **FL**5, **GA**82, **IL**26, **IN**19, **IA**11, **MO**15, 21, **NC**24, **TX**29, 32, 38, Adam's apple.

Adam's brother n

=**Adam's off-ox 1.**

    1967 *DARE* (Qu. II26, . . *"I wouldn't know him from _____."*) Inf **SC**45, Adam's brother.

Adam's cat See Adam's housecat

Adam's cup n chiefly NEng

=**pitcher plant 1** (here: *Sarracenia purpurea).*

    1840 Phelps *Lectures on Botany* (1) 169, Side-saddle flower . . is sometimes called Adam's cup, in reference also to the shape of the leaf. **1892** *Bot. Gaz.* 17.366, Adam's cup, Dudley, Mass. **1910** Graves *Flowering Plants* 213 **CT,** Adam's . . cup . . . The roots and leaves are medicinal. **1959** Carleton *Index Herb. Plants* 1.

Adam's flannel n [See quot 1957; *EDD* 1828 →]

=**mullein** (here: *Verbascum thapsus).*

    1891 *AN&Q* 7.210/1, Numerous fanciful names have been bestowed on the Mullen, such as *flannel-flower, hare's beard, Adam's flannel, Jupiter's staff.* **1931** Clute *Common Plants* 80, Even Adam and Eve have been remembered, but such names as Adam's flannel . . and Eve's darning needle *(Yucca filamentosa)* must have been invented after the pair left the garden; at least they apparently had no use for flannel and darning needles earlier. **1965** Teale *Wandering Through Winter* 55, Adam's flannel . . . On the American frontier, the thick, grey-green wooly leaves of the mullein provided a substitute for flannel in binding up sore throats.

Adam's foot n
=**Adam's off-ox 1.**
    1967 *DARE* (Qu. II26, . . *"I wouldn't know him from _____."*) Inf
TN13, Adam's foot.

Adam's fox See **Adam's all fox**

Adam's fruit n pl
1 Among loggers: apples.
    1972 *Yesterday* 1.2.26 **Nth,** The loggers called apples "Adam's fruit"
while prunes were either "anchor brand strawberries" or "raisins with
the mumps."
2 Transf: pregnant women. Cf **eat dried apples**
    1969 Sorden *Lumberjack Lingo* 1 **NEng & Great Lakes,** *Adam's
fruit*—Dried apples, pregnant women.

Adam's hat(band) n [Perh by assoc with **Dick's hatband**]
=**Adam's off-ox 1.**
    1967 *DARE* (Qu. II26, . . *"I wouldn't know him from _____."*) Inf
MA8, Adam's hat; LA14, Adam's hatband.

Adam's housecat n Also *~ cat, ~ house* **chiefly S Atl, Gulf
States** See Map
=**Adam's off-ox 1.**
    1908 *DN* 3.285 **eAL, wGA,** *Adam's (house-)cat* . . . "He wouldn't
know me from Adam's house-cat." **1965–70** *DARE* (Qu. II26, . . *"I
wouldn't know him from _____."*) 83 Infs, **chiefly S Atl, Gulf States,**
Adam's housecat; Infs LA25, OH90, VA69, 71, Adam's cat; AL10,
Adam's house; FL48, A housecat, [corr to] Adam's housecat. [Of all Infs
responding to the question, 26% had less than hs educ; of those giving
these responses, 56% had less than hs educ]

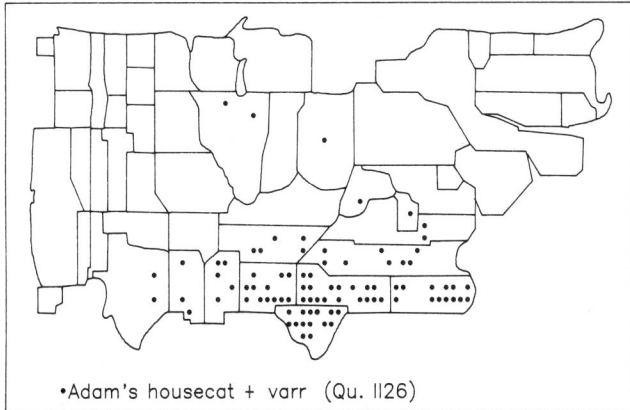

•Adam's housecat + varr (Qu. II26)

Adam's needle (and thread) n [See quot 1891; *OEDS* 1760 →]
Any of several spp of **yucca,** chiefly of the eastern half US, but esp
Yucca filamentosa which is also called **Adam-and-Eve 4, Adam-
and-Eve's needle and thread, bear grass, bear's thread, curly
hair, devil's shoestring, Eve's darning needle, Eve's thread 1,
ghost bush, needle and thread 2, silk aloe, silk grass, Spanish
bayonet, thread and needle.**
    1765 (1942) Bartram *Diary of a Journey* 15 July **NC,** Ye other tree if we
may so call it thay call adams needle. **1828** Rafinesque *Med. Flora*
2.276, *Y. filamentosa* called *Adam's needle, Silk aloes, Beargrass,* useful, . . . furnishing a silky thread, fine strong flax, twisted ropes, traces,
and even cables. **1876** Hobbs *Bot. Hdbk.* 1, Adam's needle, Yucca
gloriosa. **1891** *Century Dict.* 7026/2, *Yucca* . . . From their sharp-
pointed leaves with threads hanging from their edges, *Y. filamentosa* and
Y. aloifolia are known as *Adam's needle and thread* and as *Eve's thread.*
1936 Winter *Plants NE* 11, *Y. glauca* . . . Bear-grass. Soap-weed.
Adam's-needle . . . Common in western Nebr., also found . . in eastern
Nebr. **1949** Moldenke *Amer. Wild Flowers* 368, Probably best known is
the *Adamsneedle* or *threadandneedle, Y. filamentosa.* **1973** Stephens
Woody Plants 18, *Y. filamentosa* . . . Yucca, Adam's needle and thread,
Spanish bayonet . . . Florida to Louisiana, north to Kansas (intro-
duced), east to Tennessee and North Carolina.

Adam's off-bull n
=**Adam's off-ox 1.**
    1956 *Harder Coll.* **cwTN,** I wouldn't a knowed 'im from Adam's off
bull.

Adam's off-ox n [off-ox]
1 also *~ (old) ox:* A person or thing one does not know and
cannot identify. [Var of **Adam 1**] **chiefly west of Appalachians** See Map and cf **Adam's housecat.** Also called **Adam's
all fox, Madam's off-ox; Adam's brother, ~ foot, ~ hat(band), ~
off-bull; Beltashazur's off-ox, devil's off-ox, Gabe's off-ox**
    1894 in 1950 *PADS* 13.11 **GA,** He didn't know me from Adam's
off-ox. **1912** *DN* 3.570 **wIN,** *Adam's off ox* . . . used only in . . "He
wouldn't know me (or somebody or something) from Adam's off ox."
1914 *DN* 4.102 **KS.** **1931** *PMLA* 46.1304 **sAppalachians.** **1933** Charlottesville *Daily Progress* 1 Apr 4/3 (Hench Coll.) **VA,** I've been speaking
for years to three men I do not know from Adam's off-ox. **1950** *WELS*
("*I wouldn't know him from _____.*") 15 Infs, **throughout WI,** Adam's
off-ox. **1956** *Harder Coll.* **cwTN.** **1965** Needham–Mussey *Country
Things* 76 **sVT,** If a man says he don't know you from Adam's off ox, he
means the right-hand ox. **1965–70** *DARE* (Qu. II26, *Joking ways of
saying that you would not know who somebody is: "I wouldn't know him
from _____."*) 165 Infs, **chiefly west of Appalachians,** Adam's off-ox;
Infs IN60, LA8, MO10, OK45, Adam's ox; OH45, Adam's old ox.

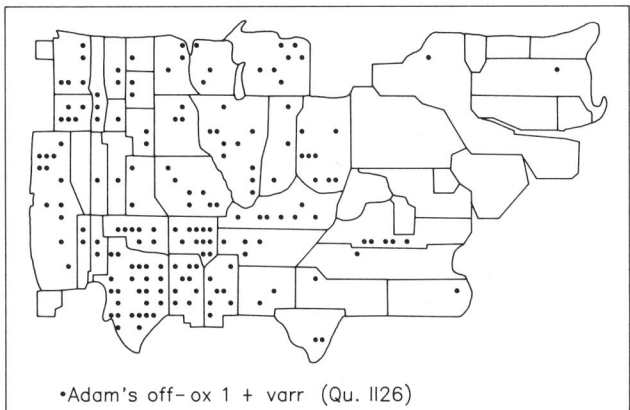

•Adam's off- ox 1 + varr (Qu. II26)

2 in proverbial comparisons: Someone who is extremely slow, ·
poor, odd, stubborn or stupid. See also **God's off-ox, Job's
off-ox.**
    1966–69 *DARE* (Qu. A18) Inf MN38, Slow as Adam's off-ox; (Qu.
U41b, . . "*He's poor as _____.*") Inf WA33, Adam's off-ox; (Qu.
HH5, *Someone who is queer but harmless*) Inf MA58, Adam's off-ox.
1967 Wilson *Folkways Mammoth Cave No. 2* 33, Stubborn as Adam's
off ox. **1975** Preston *Proverbial Comparisons* **sIN,** Crazy as Adam's off
ox. **1978** *Yankee* Mar 18 **NY,** One of my mother's expressions was, "He
doesn't know any more than Adam's off-ox." Never could figure out
what it was all about.

3 Anyone or anything: see quot.
    1967 *DARE* (Qu. KK62, *When you want to make it clear that you will
not do something: "I wouldn't do that for _____."*) Inf TX26, Adam's
off-ox.

Adam's old fox See **Adam's all fox**

Adam's (old) ox See **Adam's off-ox**

Adam's pet monkey n
=**Adam's off-ox 1.**
    1966 *DARE* (Qu. II26, . . *"I wouldn't know him from _____."*) Inf
MS15, Adam's pet monkey.

Adam's pitcher n
=**pitcher plant 1** (here: *Sarracenia purpurea*).
    1933 Small *Manual SE Flora* 581, *S. purpurea* . . . *Adam's-pitcher.*
1961 *W3.*

Adamstown Indian n [See quot 1963; the ref is prob to nearby
Adamstown MD, no Adamstown VA having been identified]
One of a group of people of mixed racial ancestry, partly
Indian. Cf **issue B1**
    1946 *Social Forces* 24.447 **VA,** There are many other mixed Indian
peoples . . . [including, in Virginia:] Adamstown Indians, Chickaho-
miny, Issues. **1963** Berry *Almost White* 35, Sometimes it is the nearby
town which gives the people their name. Hence we have . . Adamstown
Indians in Virginia.

ad ax n [*ad* back-formation from *adz* taken as pl + *ax*] Cf **mad ax**

An adz.

1969 *DARE* Tape **MA**40, They probably used an ad ax in those days. That was an ax that, well, instead of haddin' a blade that run along with the handle, the blade went just opposite the way the handle did . . . And they would take that an' cut the bark off the trees.

adays adv [*a* prep[1] 2; *OED* →1765 "Obs."] *arch* Cf **anights**

1899 (1912) Green *VA Folk-Speech*, *Adays* . . . By day; in the daytime.

ad burn intj [Alter of *dad burn*] Cf **dad** n

1897 *KS Univ. Qrly.* 6.85 **neKS**, *Ad burn* . . . A mild oath.

adder n

1 A snake—used as a generic term (often in comb). **scattered, but esp Sth, NEast; rare in West** See Map

a**1864** (1874) Hawthorne *Passages Amer. Note-Books* 2.228, She called it an adder, but it appears to have been a striped snake. **1965–70** *DARE* (Qu. P25) 204 Infs, **scattered, but esp Sth, NEast**, Adder, chicken adder, milk adder, puff adder (and many other names).

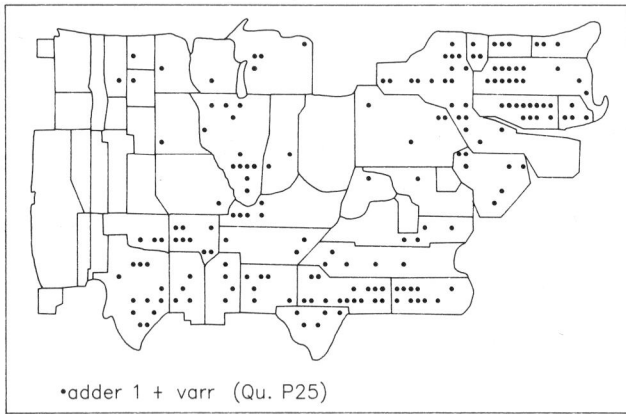

•adder 1 + varr (Qu. P25)

2 See **adder's tongue 1**.

3 In proverbial comparr:

a *deaf as a(n)* ~, *deafer than a(n)* ~ [Ref to Psalms 58:4, "like the deaf adder that stoppeth her ear"] **chiefly east of Missip R, esp NEast**

1770 in 1965 Adams *Legal Papers* 3.270 **MA**, Deaf as an adder to the clamours of the populace. **1811** Graydon *Memoirs* 314 **PA**, They were, every where deaf as adders, to the claims of a general interest. **1848** (1968) Cooper *Letters & Jrls.* 5.310 **nNY**, Poor old Mrs. De Lancey, who was as deaf as an adder. **1929** *AmSp* 5.130 **ME**, Deaf as an adder. **1938** *AmSp* 13.75, She [from Maine coast] says: 'Deaf as an adder,' we say [in Ohio] 'deaf . . as a post.' **1943** *LANE* Map 502 **CT, NH, ME,** 6 Infs, Deaf as an adder; **CT, MA,** 2 Infs, Deafer than an adder. **1965** Barbour *Proverbs IL* 4. **1965–70** *DARE* (Qu. X19a, *When a person's hearing is not very good, . . he's*) Inf NC61, Deafer than an adder; (Qu. X19b, . . *If a person's hearing is very bad*) 10 Infs, Deaf as an adder [9 of 10 Infs are **NEast**]; Infs CT30, NC1, 61, VT8, Deafer than an adder; **CT**20, **MA**73, NC9, NY21, Deaf as a adder; NY209, Deef as an adder; NY75, Deefer than an adder.

b *dumb as an* ~.

1952 Brown *NC Folkl.* 1.360.

adder mouth See **adder's mouth**

adder's flower n **prob NEast**

Red campion (*Lychnis dioica*).

1931 Clute *Common Plants* 111, Adder's flower, with no reason for being so named, is *Lychnis dioica*.

adder's leaf See **adder's tongue 1**

adder's mouth n Also *adder mouth* [Perh from the configuration of the flower]

1 An orchid of the genus *Malaxis* (esp *M. unifolia*).

1808 Rafinesque in 1901 Mohr *Plant Life AL* 457, *Achroanthes unifolia* . . Green Addersmouth. **1840** *MA Zool. & Bot. Surv. Herb. Plants & Quadrupeds* 202 **MA**, *Microstylis ophioglossoides* . . Adder-mouth . . root bulbous; roots of trees. **1903** Small *Flora SE U.S.* 386,

Malaxis . . . Adders-mouths. **1975** Duncan–Foote *Wildflowers SE* 278, *Adder's-mouth*—*Malaxis unifolia*.

2 =**rose pogonia**.

1900 Lyons *Plant Names* 297, Adder's-mouth Pogonia or Orchis. **1910** Graves *Flowering Plants* 132 **CT**, *Pogonia ophioglossoides* . . Adder's Mouth. **1936** Eaton *Wild Gardens New Engl.* 119, Adder's mouth . . (moist meadows and swamps).

3 =**chickweed** (here: *Stellaria media*).

1876 Hobbs *Bot. Hdbk.* 1, Adder's mouth . . Stellaria media. **1971** Krochmal *Appalachia Med. Plants* 242, *Stellaria Media* . . Common names: . . adder's mouth.

adder's tongue n

1 also occas *adder tongue*, rarely *adder*; also *adder's leaf*: =**dogtooth violet** (in the eastern half US usu *Erythronium americanum* or *E. albidum;* in the West, esp OR, usu *E. montanum*). **chiefly NEast and N Cent** See Map

1822 (1832) *MA Hist. Soc. Coll.* 2d ser 9.150 **VT**, Plants, which are indigenous in the township of Middlebury . . . Erythronium lanceolatum . . Adder's tongue. **1857** Gray *Manual of Botany* 471, *E. Americanum* . . . Yellow Adder's-tongue . . . Low copses, &c.; common. May. **1876** Hobbs *Bot. Hdbk.* 1, Adder's leaf, Adder's tongue, Erythronium Americanum. **1894** Burroughs *Riverby* 26, *Erythronium* . . . How it came to be called adder's-tongue I do not know; probably from the spotted character of the leaf, which might suggest a snake, though it in no wise resembles a snake's tongue. **1937** Stemen *OK Flora* i, Many of the Oklahoma wild flowers are . . . "choice wildflowers for transplanting": Adder's-tongue [etc.]. **1949** Moldenke *Amer. Wild Flowers* 331, The common name of "adderstongue" is applied to these plants [*Erythronium* spp] because of the sharp purplish leaf points which push up above ground in earliest spring, reminding some imaginative folks of the dark-colored, sharp, and darting tongues of snakes. **1949** Peattie *Cascades* 252 **OR**, The white avalanche lily. Erythronium montanum, is sometimes called deertongue, adder's tongue, and dogtooth violet. **1965–70** *DARE* (Qq. S3, S11, S26a, b, c, e) 105 Infs, **chiefly NEast and N Cent**, Adder's tongue; 22 Infs, **esp MI and NY**, Adder tongue; TN11, Spotted adder's tongue; **OH**2, Yellow adder's tongue; MI64, Spotted adders. **1966** *DARE* Wildfl. QR Pl. 15a Infs **AR**46, **MI**57, Adder's tongue.

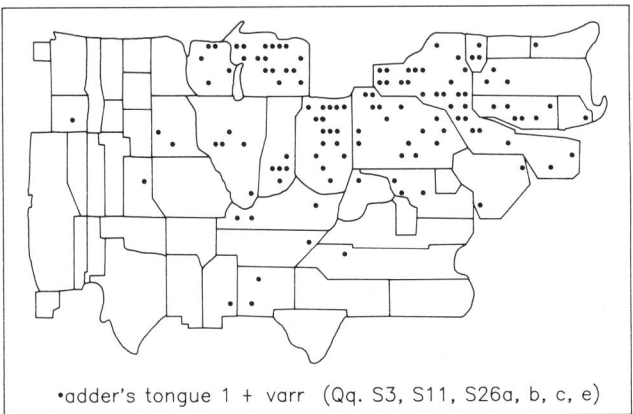

•adder's tongue 1 + varr (Qq. S3, S11, S26a, b, c, e)

2 also *adder-tongue cactus*: =**rattlesnake plantain** (here: *Goodyera pubescens*).

1898 *Jrl. Amer. Folkl.* 11.281, *Goodyera pubescens* . . adder's tongue, Turner, M[ain]e. Adder-tongue cactus, Swan's Island, Kennebec River, Me.

adder's violet n Cf **rattlesnake violet**

1 =**rattlesnake plantain** (here: *Goodyera pubescens*).

1876 Hobbs *Bot. Hdbk.* 1, Adder's violet, Net leaf plantain, Goodyera pubescens.

2 =**dogtooth violet** (here: *Erythronium americanum*).

1900 Lyons *Plant Names* 151, *E[rythronium] Americanum* . . . Adder's Violet.

adder tongue See **adder's tongue 1**

adder-tongue cactus See **adder's tongue 2**

add-iron n [Var of **andiron**, perh infl by folk-etym] *old-fash*

1965–70 *DARE* (Qu. D32, . . *Metal stands in a fireplace that the logs are laid on*) 14 Infs, **throughout US**, Add-iron(s). [All Infs old]

addition n

Usu prec by a noun attrib or poss: a future suburban residential area; an area near a city, town, or village marked out into streets and lots as an extension of the residential section. **chiefly Missip–Ohio Valley**

1786 *MD Jrl. & Baltimore Advt.* (MD) 6 Jan 4/1, Found . . in Howard's new Addition to Baltimore-Town, One Hundred and Twenty-seven panes of glass. **1895** *DN* 1.384 **nMissip Valley**, *Addition:* part of village or city laid out in addition to original plot; *e.g.* Knox's addition to the city of _____. Used in legal papers, etc. **1904** *DN* 2.416 **nwAR**, *Addition . . .* Territory annexed to a city or town. 'I bought a lot in the Leverett addition.' **1923** Herrick *Lilla* 24 **IL**, The new Addition . . . was a new strip of prairie [near Chicago] which the Porter Realty Company was preparing to put on the market. **1941** *Post* (Morgantown WV) 18 Mar 1 *(ADD)*, A lot in Norwood Addition. Town of Sabraton . . her new home in Suncrest Addition. **1965–70** *DARE* (Qu. C34, *Nicknames for nearby settlements*) Inf **OK**56, Caesar addition; (Qu. C35, . . *Different parts of your town*) 13 Infs, **chiefly Missip–Ohio Valley**, (Barnes, Berria, Carney, etc.) addition; (Qu. II24, . . *Where the well-off people live*) Inf **WV**5, Middleburg addition; (Qu. II25, . . *Where the poorer people . . live*) Inf **LA**28, Lower-bracket addition; **WV**5, Draper addition.

addle v [*OED* addle v.², "*Obs.* or *dial.*"; cf *EDD*]

1969 Sorden *Lumberjack Lingo* **NEng, Gt Lakes**, *Addle*—To earn by labor.

add out See out

adge See edge

adios intj, n [Span: lit *to God,* as Eng *good-bye* < *God be with you*] **scattered, but esp SW** See Map

Good-bye! An expression of farewell.

1837 *New York Mirror* 23 Dec 208/1 *(DA),* An overworked, spavined, broken-down set—but adios, Amigo. **1844** (1954) Gregg *Commerce* 156 **SW**, The attentive host, who gently waves, with his hand, a final '*ádios'* from a window. **c1871** Twain *Screamers* 58 **MO**, "*You* are the loser by this rupture, not me, Pie-plant. Adios." I then left. **1892** *DN* 1.243 **TX**. **1929** *AmSp* 5.76 **NE**. **1932** Bentley *Spanish Terms* 86, *Adios* is commonly made use of in the border region and is heard in light conversation in other parts of the United States. It is heard in U.S. army parlance and has been adopted also by radio announcers. **1965–70** *DARE* (Qu. NN11, *Informal ways of saying 'good-bye' to people you know quite well*) 56 Infs, **scattered, but esp SW**, Adios; **NH**18, **FL**52, Adios amigo(s); (Qu. Y19, *To begin to go away*) Inf **TX**103, Say adios.

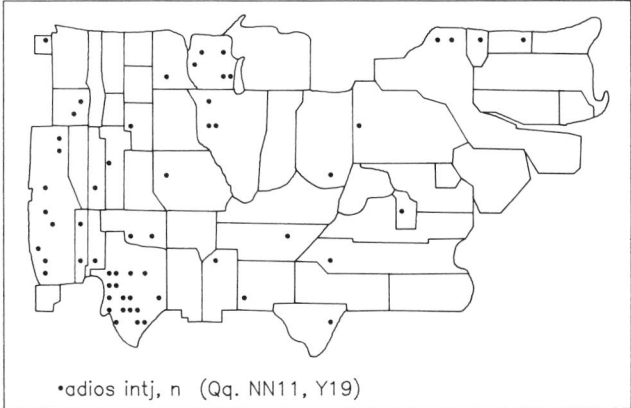

•adios intj, n (Qq. NN11, Y19)

adios v [adios intj, n]

=**vamoose** v.

1970 *DARE* (Qu. Y18, . . "*Before they find this out, we'd better _____.*") Inf **TX**103, Adios; get up and go.

Adirondack steak n Also ~ goat Cf DS P35a

=**mountain lamb.**

1954 White *Adirondack Country* 118 **neNY**, Hotels served venison in and out of season; out of season, the name changed to "Adirondack Steak" or "mountain lamb." *Ibid* 40, Game is still killed out of season

and a doe may be dragged out of the woods at night to be cut up quickly and put in the freezer . . . "Lamb without horns" or "Adirondack goat" turns up at Sunday dinner in back country homes now and then.

admiration n [*OED* admiration 1, →1852, "*arch.*"] Cf **admire A, miration**

Wonderment, surprise.

1952 Brown *NC Folkl.* 1.513, *Admiration, to make* . . . To show surprise. **1953** Randolph *Down in Holler* 85 **Ozarks**, Admiration, usually shortened to *miration,* still means wonderment or surprise in the Ozarks.

admire v

A Intr sense.

Usu foll by *at:* to marvel, to regard with wonder or astonishment. [*OED* admire 1b,c →1865] **chiefly NEng, S Midl** *arch or old-fash* See also **admiration**

1638 Hooker *Unbeleevers* 1.8 **NEng**, Thus the people admired at Gods great goodnesse. **1774** in 1865 MA Hist. Soc. *Proc.* 8.349, I . . could not but admire at the *subservient* honors paid his Excellency. **1853** Bird *Nick of Woods* 370 **KY**, Roland did not admire long at the unlooked-for resurrection of his old ally of the ruin. **1859** (1968) Bartlett *Americanisms, To Admire* . . . To wonder at; to be affected with slight surprise . . . In New England, particularly in Maine, the word is used in this sense. **1865** Dodge *Skirmishes* 437 **NEng**, Sound Orthodox piety . . is a thing to be admired (at) in this Mammon-worshipping age. **1940** *AmSp* 15.45 **sAppalachians**, Their [=mountain people's] use of *sight* is shared by Gower; . . *admire* for to be astonished by Milton.

B Tr senses.

1 usu followed by infin: To like, enjoy (something, or doing something). [*OED* admire 1d "*Obs.* or *dial.*"] **chiefly NEng, S Midl, and settlement areas**

a1770 in 1859 Duane *Letters to Franklin* 194 **Boston MA**, I should admire to come and see and hear all about every thing. **1829** in 1927 *DN* 5.423 **NEng** [Dunglison's Glossary], I should admire to go to Boston. **1831** (1940) Motte *Charleston to Harvard* 88, After drinking a glass of soda water, which he admired (Yankeeism), we started for Boston. **1859** (1968) Bartlett *Americanisms, To Admire* . . . To like very much. This verb is often and very absurdly used in New England in such expressions as, "I should *admire* to see the President." **1864** in 1926 Harte *Sketches* 128 **PA**, My comrade said he did not admire to smell a whale; and I adopt his sentiments while I scorn his language. **1873** Harte *Mrs. Skaggs* 63 **CA**, Thar's dried appils too on the shelf, but I don't admire 'em. Appils is swellin'. **1903** *DN* 2.304 **seMO**. **1913** *DN* 4.1 **swME**, *Admire* . . . "I just admire to get letters, but I don't admire to answer them." **1926** *AmSp* 2.82 **ME**, I'd admire to go. **1927** *AmSp* 2.347 **cwWV**, She would admire for to see your mother. **1973** Allen *LAUM* 1.408 **SD**, She admired to smell a skunk. **1976** Garber *Mountain-ese* 1 **sAppalachians**, I'd really admire to have youens eat dinner with us next Sunday.

2 To wish, to desire strongly.

1876 Harte *Gabriel Conroy* 190 **CA**, "Why didn't you come into the parlor?" she said . . . "I didn't admire to to-night," returned Gabriel. **c1960** *Wilson Coll.* **csKY**, I'd sure admire to see that girl. **1967** *DARE* FW Addit **TN**11, I would admire to have been somewheres else. [FW: Inf has heard]

admiring vbl n

The act of casting an "evil eye."

1970 Anderson *TX Folk Med.* 30, *Evil eye* . . . To cure soreness or injury to the body caused by admiring (looking over), have the victim assume a prone position and rub the body with a raw egg.

admittance, give one the v phr [Folk-etym] Var of **mitten, give one the**

1941 *LANE* Map 406 **swCT**, 'She refused . . to go with him to a party or a dance.' . . Gave him the admittance [gev im ði admɪtənts], used by the informant and his wife.

ado See a inert vowel 5

adobe n, often attrib Usu |(ə)'do̞ˌbi| Pronc-sp *adobie* [Span] **SW, West, and Spanish settlement areas** See also **dobe** and its compounds

1a Sun-dried mud or clay, or a crude cement made of this; also, a brick of such material used in building.

1759 Venegas *Hist. CA* 1.77, Some, to please the fathers, have made themselves houses, if they may be called such, of adobe or unburnt bricks, covered with sedge; but few live in them. **1844** (1954) Gregg *Commerce* 144 **NM,** The materials generally used for building are . . unburnt bricks, about eighteen inches long by nine wide and four thick, laid in mortar of mere clay and sand. These bricks are called *adobes,* and every edifice, from the church to the palacio, is constructed of the same stuff. *Ibid* 277, Some inferior houses of *adobe* were so much soaked by the rains, that they tumbled to the ground. **1856** Derby *Phoenixiana* 133 **sCA,** We have . . Indians employed . . in mixing adobe for the type moulds. **1892** *DN* 1.187 **TX,** *Adóbe:* sun-baked tile or large brick . . . By extension the tenacious clay used as material . . . Often pronounced by Americans *ad-ōb;* on the border it is *ad-ō-bé* or even simply *dōb-é.* **1968** Adams *Western Words.* **1972** Carr *Da Kine Talk* 105 **HI,** Spanish words were acquired by both the English and the Hawaiian languages . . between 1830 and 1840 . . around Waimea, Hawaii . . . Much more important than the word *poncho* . . was the word *adobe,* and the new method of building houses and schools introduced with it by the Spaniards at Waimea.

b attrib uses.

1839 (1973) Farnham *Travels Prairies* 2.96 **OR,** We spent the 2d and 3d most agreeably with Mr. Walker, in his hospitable adobie castle. **1867** Lowell *Biglow* 157 **NEng,** He goes to plast'rin' his adobë house. **1907** White *AZ Nights* 21, The roof of the shack had fallen in, and the floor was six inches deep in adobe mud. **1970** *DARE* Tape **CA206,** Adobe brick . . brick made out of adobe clay.

2 An adobe house.

1821 in 1858 Dewees *Letters TX* 21, The remainder of the buildings are adobes, except a few which are made of wood. **1883** *Harper's Mag.* 66.491/1 **sAZ,** The town is a collection of inferior adobes. **1948** *Popular Western* 44/1 *(DA),* In the squat, thick-walled adobe, he lighted a reflector wall lamp.

3 In mining: see quot 1889.

1873 *Mining & Scientific Press* 21 Mar *(DA),* The screenings and fine stuff is called 'tierras.' These 'tierras' are made into 'adobes' before being burnt. **1889** *Century Dict., Adobe* . . . In the quicksilver-mines of the Pacific coast, a brick made of the finer ores mixed with clay, for more convenient handling in the furnace.

4 Heavy, clay-like soil; clay. **SW, esp CA**

1858 *Hutching's Mag.* Sept 138/1 *(DA),* What vegetables flourish best in the different Adobe soils? . . Big dornicks and scrubby cedars. **1891** *AN&Q* 6.216 **CA,** Another use of the word *adobe* . . is that which makes it the name of a kind of clay. So distinguished a writer as Prof. E.W. Hilgard often speaks of *adobe* soils. **1897** *Land of Sunshine* 7.187 **cCA,** There is no hardpan, alkali, or adobe to vex the tiller of the soil. **1922** Bryan *Routes to Desert* 106 **AZ,** Orchard-like forests of mesquite are common on adobe flats. **1965–70** *DARE* (Qu. C31, . . *Heavy, sticky soil*) 21 Infs, **SW, CA,** Adobe. [16 of 21 Infs **CA**]

adobe dollar n **SW** See also **dobe**
A Mexican peso.

1909 (1930) *WNID* **SW,** *Adobe* . . . Made of adobe;—hence applied colloquially by Americans to any of various Mexican things; as, an *adobe* dollar. *Colloq.* **1936** McKenna *Black Range* 271 **SW,** I made big winnings—adobe silver dollars by the gallon . . . And that sack of adobe dollars acted just like a cork lifesaver. **1960** Wentworth–Flexner *Slang.*

adobe-maker n **SW** *derog* Cf *DS* HH28
1970 *Current Slang* 4.3.12 **NM,** *Adobe-maker* . . . A Mexican or Mexican-American.

adone intj [**a** vbl aux + *done: OED* have done! under *do* 17, →1803; cf *EDD adone*] *arch*
Stop! Enough!

1903 *DN* 2.295 **Cape Cod MA** (as of 1850s), *Adone* . . . No more of that. Expression generally repeated as 'Adone, adone.'

adopt v[1], also ppl adj *adopted*
To adapt.

1895 *DN* 1.395. **1967** *DARE* FW Addit **TN17,** They wasn't adopted to this climate.

adopt v[2]
To contract (a disease).

1917 *DN* 4.407 **wNC,** *Adopt* . . . "He adopted a rheumatiz." **1926** Kephart *Highlanders* 296 **sAppalachians,** Sooner or later he "adopts a rheumatiz," and the adoption lasts till he dies.

A-drag n |'e‚dræg|
=**A-harrow.**
1868 IA State Ag. Soc. *Report* 151, When the [corn] plants are one or

two inches in hight [sic] the ground is harrowed between the rows to destroy the small weeds . . . This is done with an A drag, after the front teeth have been removed, one-half passing on each side of a row. **1968** *DARE* (Qu. L20, . . *Implement used in the field after it's been plowed to break up the lumps*) Inf **NY96,** A-drag—had an A-shaped frame with square teeth — peg-teeth, they called 'em. **1968** *DARE* FW Addit **sDE,** *A-drag*—a harrow with an A-shaped frame and spikes the size of railroad spikes, used to break up clods.

adrift adj [Transf from naut use] **chiefly coastal NEng**
Loose, unfastened; unclaimed: see quots.

1916 Macy–Hussey *Nantucket Scrap Basket* 123, "Adrift"—Nantucketers use this word constantly in the sense of loose or unfastened; as "a blind on the house got adrift in the gale." **1942** ME Univ. *Studies* 56.30, There was danger everything was *adrift,* that is, loose and out of place or *ramshackle.* [Footnote to *adrift:*] Fig. Rickety, crazy, coming apart or undone. **1945** Colcord *Sea Language* 21 **ME, Cape Cod, Long Island,** In coastal speech, to break, come, fetch or strike, adrift is to become untied or to come apart. "You can't mail this here passel; it's all adrift." To cut, cast, set or turn, adrift means to abandon. **1975** Gould *ME Lingo* 32, *Adrift*—Afloat, but meaning something that should be moored or in its right place. Hence, a flapping shirt tail, a barn door off its hinges, or a lady who doesn't do all her work at home . . . The cadets use the term "gear *adrift*" for something they have found; particularly if 'twern't lost until they found it. Gear *adrift* is up for salvage.

adswocate v Pronc-sp for *advocate*
1922 Gonzales *Black Border* 287 **sSC, GA coasts** [Gullah glossary], *Adswocate*—advocate, advocates, advocated, advocating.

advantage v Pronc-sp *'vantage* [Cf *DJE advantage* in same sense]
To take advantage of; cheat.

1929 Sale *Tree Named John* 106 **MS** [Black], He didn' want Brer Frawg t' think he 'uz tryin' t' 'vantage 'im.

adverage See **average**

adverse n
An uphill railroad grade.

1958 McCulloch *Woods Words* **Pacific NW,** *Adverse*—A grade on a logging road or railroad, against the movement of loaded logs. **1977** Adams *Lang. Railroader.*

advertise v Pronc-spp *abbuhtize, abvertize*
A Forms.

1884 Harrison *Negro Engl.* 240, *Abvertize.* **1922** Gonzales *Black Border* 287 **sSC, GA coasts** [Gullah glossary], *Abbuhtize*—advertise, advertises, advertised, advertising.

B Sense.

1982 *Barrick Coll.* **sePA,** *Advertise*—Publish legal notice that one is no longer responsible for his wife's debts. "He advertised her in the paper and she left him."

adz n Usu |ædz| rarely |æj| or, by back-formation, |æd|
Std sense, var forms.

1893 *DN* 1.278 **wCT** (as of c1850), The word [*adz*] on account of its form was looked on as a plural, and always took a plural verb . . *them adz.* **1965–68** *DARE* FW Addit **cnOK,** Foot [æj]; **TN26,** Foot [æd]. [Cf **foot adz**]

adz v *humorous*
Fig: to bite.

1975 Gould *ME Lingo* 33, References to it [=the *adz*] in everyday Maine speech are obvious as to derivation and meaning: "Migod, you should have seen him *adz* into that punkin pie!"

adzac(k)ly, adzactly See **exactly**

ae adv |'ɑe| [Haw, prob infl by Engl *aye,* Japanese *hai* yes] **HI**
Yes.

c1833 in 1934 Frear *Lowell and Abigail* 78 **HI,** "Do you think you can learn?" "Ae, paha" (Yes, perhaps). **1938** Reinecke *Hawaiian Loanwords* 7, *Ae* . . . Yes; the expression of affirmation, approbation, or consent. **1972** Carr *Da Kine Talk* 86 **HI,** [Hawaiian words commonly heard in Hawaii's English:] *'Ae.* Yes; agreement.

aebleskive(r) See **appleskiver**

aeroplane See **fandango** n

afear(e)d adj Also sp *afeer(e)d, aferd* [*OED* c1000 →; *EDD,* "In . . dial. use throughout Sc. Irel. and Eng."; *SND,* "chiefly

archaic."] **once widespread, now chiefly Sth, Midl** *somewhat old-fash* See also **feared**
Afraid.

1815 Humphreys *Yankey in England* 103 **NEng**, [Glossary:] *Afeard,* afraid. **1843** (1916) Hall *New Purchase* 227 **IN**, so powerful he was afeer'd to come down. **1861** Holmes *Venner* 1.56 **wMA**, Put him aout y'rself, 'f ye a'n't afeard on him. **1871** Eggleston *Hoosier Schoolmaster* 128 **sIN**, "But come on," cried Bud, "ef you a'n't afeared to fight somebody besides a poor, little, sickly baby." **1890** *DN* 1.69 **LA**, *Afeared.* **1892** *DN* 1.214 **MA**. *Ibid* 234 **KY**. **1893** Shands *MS Speech* 16, *Afeard* . . . is still in very common use by the negroes and uneducated whites. **1894** *DN* 1.327 **NJ**. **1895** *DN* 1.375 **TN**. **1900** Harris *On the Wing* 142 **eAL**, I ain't afeard of his capers. **1902** *DN* 2.227 **sIL**. **1906** *DN* 3.114 **sIN**. **1907** *DN* 3.220 **nwAR**. **1908** *DN* 3.285 **eAL**, **wGA**. **1923** *DN* 5.200 **swMO**, *Afeerd.* **1927** *DN* 5.470 **sAppalachians**. **1930** *AmSp* 6.97 **cNY**, You ain't aferd. **1940** *Sat. Eve. Post* 20 Jan 39/4 **FL**, I'm a-feered. **1941** *LANE* Map 475 **VT, NH, ME,** *Afeard* is regarded as old-fashioned by . . [25 Infs]. **1965–70** *DARE* (Qu. GG25, . . *"The children were _____ he was going to hurt them.")* 12 Infs, Afeard [11 of 12 Infs **Sth, Midl**]; (Qu. BB2, *If a person is careful not to put much weight on his injured leg)* Inf **KY**81, Afeard of hurting it again. **1966–67** *DARE* FW Addit **cwNC**, Afeared [ə'fɪrd]—old-fash. **1973** Allen *LAUM* 1.354 **swMN**, *Afeard:* Inf. says some people . . who moved . . from the Ozarks say this.

afeet adv [**a** prep¹ **3** + *feet*]
Afoot.
1966 *DARE* (Qu. Y24, . . *To walk)* Inf **AR**31, Go afeet.

affected ppl adj Cf **affection**
Infected.
1937 *Hall Coll.* **eTN**, His hand got affected.

affection n [*OED affection* 10; but here perh a malaprop for *affliction* or *infection*] *infreq*
Disease.
1960 Williams *Walk Egypt* 116 **GA**, He'll give you affection of the brain, you mess with it long enough. **1968** *DARE* (Qu. DD24, *Other diseases . . from continual drinking)* Inf **OH**41, Affection of the liver.

affidavy n Pronc-sp for *affidavit*
1843 (1916) Hall *New Purchase* 411 **IN**, It would be most powerful onfair to ask folks to believe anybody without swearin', who couldn't take a legal affidavy. **1884** Lanier *Poems* 170 **GA**, They tuck affidavy without no bones.

Affikin See **African** n¹, adj **A**

Aff'iky See **Africa A**

afflicted ppl adj [*OED afflicted* 2, here used as euphem for var disorders] **chiefly Sth, Midl**
Affected with disease of body or mind; subnormal.
1895 *DN* 1.384 **seMD**, *Afflicted:* mentally deficient, or deformed. **1905** *DN* 3.68 **nwAR**, *Afflicted* . . . Defective mentally or physically . . . General. **1908** *DN* 3.285 **eAL, wGA**. **1912** *DN* 3.570 **wIN**, *Afflicted* . . . Idiotic or feeble-minded. "They don't go out much because they have a daughter that is afflicted." **1952** Brown *NC Folkl.* 1.513, *Afflicted* . . . Idiotic.—Rare.

Affrishy See **Africa A**

affrishy town n
=**nigger town.**
1936 in 1977 *Amer. Slave Suppl. 1* 1.237 **AL**, The remainder remained in the neighborhood of Mobile river above Mobile on Meaher's land and that part of the suburb of Plateau known as "Affrishy Town."

Af'ican See **African** n¹, adj **A**

aflood See **a** prep¹ **4**

afoot adj [Ext of *OED afoot* 1, on foot, as against *on horseback*] See also **afeet**
Without horse or vehicle: hence, by implication, destitute, poor.
1848 (1855) Ruxton *Life Far West* 98 **SW**, La Bonté now found himself without animals, and fairly "afoot;" consequently nothing remained for him but to seek some of the trapping bands, and hire himself for the hunt. **1941** Smith *Going to God's Country* 13 **MO** (as of 1890), The bresh whackers would make raids through Missouri and burn houses and kill the cows and take the teams. Some people were left a foot and out

of doors. **1954** *Harder Coll.* **cwTN**, Afoot: Not owning any means of travel. [Letter:] "he is afoot." **1965** *DARE* (Qu. U41a, *Somebody who has lost everything and is very poor: "He's _____.")* Inf **MS**63, Afoot. **1968** Adams *Western Words, Afoot*—Said of a man without a horse in the cattle country. A man afoot on the range is looked upon with suspicion by most ranchers . . unless he can prove . . that his being afoot is the result of some misfortune . . . "There's only two things the old-time puncher was afraid of, a decent woman and bein' left afoot."

afoot or (a)horseback adj phr
In phr *not to know whether* (or *if*) *one is* ~: to be confused; to be somewhat stupid.
1895 *Century Illustr. Mag.* ns 28.570/1 **SC**, Sam he had on a keg hat, all shiny silk, and a red necktie thet Car' Jane hed made him git, and he did n't know whether he was afoot or a-hossback. **1927** *Collier's* 22 Oct 7/3 **sCA**, 'Fay Daniels!' gasps the girl, which don't know if she's afoot or horseback—and neither did I. **1950** *WELS (A dull and stupid person)* 1 Inf, **ceWI**, Doesn't know whether he's afoot or horseback. **1951** West *Witch Diggers* 256 **IN**, With the one hand he works them to death and with the other hand coddles them. They don't know whether they're afoot or horseback. **1963** Haywood *Yankee Dict.* 2 **NEng**, When a Yankee says "He don't know whether he's afoot or ahossback," he means that the person . . is in a bemused and bepuzzled state . . . Or . . the fellow lacks sufficient mental acuity to know where he is going or how. **1967** *DARE* (Qu. JJ15b, . . *Very stupid: "He doesn't know _____.")* Inf **MI**55, Whether he's afoot or ahorseback.

afore adv, conj, prep **once widespread, now chiefly Sth, Midl** *old-fash* Addit quots in *ADD*
Before.
1815 Humphreys *Yankey in England* 103 **NEng**, [Glossary:] *Afore,* before. **1844** Thompson *Major Jones's Courtship* 75 **GA**, She gin her galls a rite good talkin to rite afore me. **1861** Holmes *Venner* 57 **wMA**, I won't go afore I'm ready. **1872** Schele de Vere *Americanisms* 432, *Afore* and *aforehand* . . still survive in remoter regions of the New England States. **1887** *Scribner's Mag.* 2.482 **AR**, I walked frum Hoxie's on the track; started afore sun up. **1894** *DN* 1.327 **NJ**. **1897** *KS Univ. Qrly.* 6.85 **neKS**. **1899** (1912) Green *VA Folk-Speech* 61, *Afore* . . . Before. "A little *afore* day." "Night *afore* last." **1908** *DN* 3.285 **eAL, wGA**. **1909** *DN* 3.392 **nwAR**. **1911** *DN* 3.537 **eKY**. **1930** *AmSp* 6.97 **cNY**, *Afore* . . . "He ought to be hitched afore he breaks loose." **1931** *AmSp* 7.90 **eKY**. **1938** Matschat *Suwannee R.* 186 **nFL, sGA**, Git hisself 'nough meat to et all the days hit might take afore the runs brung him to the river. **1958** *PADS* 29.6 **cTN**. **1969** *DARE* (Qu. MM9, . . *"We stood in line and John was _____ me.")* Inf **NC**72, Afore. **1976** Garber *Mountain-ese* 1 **sAppalachians**, Lizzie wants to git the house swept afore company comes.

afore-day See **before-day**

afoul of prep [Transf from naut use] **chiefly coastal NEng**
In phrr *run, fall* or *get* ~: to meet, esp to meet accidentally.
1941 *LANE* Map 422 *(I ran across him)*, 8 Infs, **chiefly coastal NEng**, Afoul of, 1 Inf, **seCT**, Fell afoul of. **1945** Colcord *Sea Language* 21 **ME, Cape Cod, Long Island,** *Afoul.* Entangled, or in collision . . . To fall, get or run, afoul of are common in shore speech for meet accidentally. **1970** *DARE* (Qu. II17, . . *"Guess who I _____ this morning!")* Inf **WV**16, Run afoul of.

afraid adj Usu |ə'fred| Also, **esp in eVA** |ə'frεd|; rarely |ə'freɪt| Pronc-spp *afred, afreed* See also **faid, fraid; afear(e)d**
Std senses, var forms.
1843 (1916) Hall *New Purchase* 227 **IN**, I was afreed he'd run in and git drownded. **1856** in 1956 Eliason *Tarheel Talk* 306 **NC**, Afred. **1919** *DN* 5.39 **VA**, *Afred* . . . Afraid. **1937** in 1944 *ADD* **VA**, *Afraid, afred* . . . |əfred|. c[VA] 18 & 17 instances respectively of 36 & 34 test prons. In w.Va., 1 instance in 31. **1937** *AmSp* 12.286 **wVA**, *Afraid* and *great* usually have [e], in spite of the influence of eastern Virginia towards [ə'fred] and [gret]. **1938** Std, *Afraid* . . —|ε|—. Freq. **1951** *VA Univ. Univ. Studies* 5.116 **eVA**, [ə'frεd]. The incidence of this form marks what might be regarded as the approximate normal limits of the eastern Virginia dialect. The feature is well established in both Piedmont and Tidewater. It occurs on the Western Shore of Maryland and in the Norfolk area; only on the Eastern Shore is it of rare occurrence . . . [ə'fred] . . is perfectly standard within its area, being used by all categories of informants. [Map in text] **1970** *DARE* (Qu. GG25) Inf **KY**83, Afraid [ə'freɪt].

afraidly adj
Afraid.

1940 Qrly. Jrl. Speech 26.264 **wVA,** Two colloquial adverbs are "kindly," meaning *rather . . ,* and "afraidly," as in "I'm afraidly so."

afred, afreed See **afraid**

Africa n, also attrib Usu |ˈæfrɪkə|, also |ˈæːfrɪkɪ| *somewhat old-fash* Pronc-spp *Aff'iky, Affrishy, Afric(k)y, Afriky*
A Forms.

1851 Hooper *Widow Rugby's Husband* 50 **AL,** His d——d heathen dumb brute of *Afriky.* *1867* Lowell *Biglow* 96 **"Upcountry" MA,** The bes' blood in Europe, yis, an' *Afriky* an' Ashy. *1891 DN* 1.157 **cNY,** [æːfrɪkɪ], 'Africa.' *1922* Gonzales *Black Border* 36 **sSC, GA coasts** [Gullah], Lion en' nigguh alltwo come f'um *Aff'iky.* *Ibid* 79, De jungle ub *Aff'iky.* *1933* Miller *Lamb in His Bosom* 43 **GA,** The men spoke of *Africky,* where folks was black like razor-back hogs. *1934 WV Review* Dec 79, At one time *Asye* was the accepted way of pronouncing *Asia,* as *Africy* was of *Africa,* both of which we very frequently hear. *1936* in *1977 Amer. Slave Suppl. 1* 1.237 **AL,** *Affrishy Town.*

B Sense.

See **African** n[1], adj **B1.**

African n[1], adj Pronc-spp *Affikin, Af'ican*
A Forms.

1922 Gonzales *Black Border* 36 **sSC, GA coasts** [Gullah], Dem *Aff'ikin* king en' t'ing hab lion een dem cage.

B As noun.

1 also *Africky:* Fighting spirit; temper, dander. **Sth** Also called **Dutch, Indian, Irish**

1838 S. Lit. Messenger 4.162/1 **VA,** Well, it sort o' raised his *Africky,* at first. *1880* Harris *Uncle Remus Songs* 231, Well, you des oughter see me git my *Affikin* up. *1884* Harrison *Negro Engl.* 263, To git de *Affikin* up = to evoke the African nature. *1928* Bradford *Ol' Man Adam* 199 **Sth,** So de people kept right on laughin' and passin' remarks about old Samson to finally old Samson got his *Af'ican* up.

2 in pl: See quot and **African black fats.**

1940 AmSp 15.133 **KY,** *Africans.* Tobacco grown mostly in Kentucky, prepared principally for West African Trade.

C As adj, noun.

1 (A) Negro. **now chiefly Sth,** exc in ref to certain societies and churches. See also **African dominoes, ~ golf, ~ goose**

1797 Morse *Amer. Gaz.* s.v. *Philadelphia,* The African church is a large, neat building. It is supplied with a negro clergyman, who has been lately ordained by the bishop. They are of the Episcopalian order. *1818* Fearon *Sketches* 168 **sePA,** The three "African Churches," as they are called, are for all those native Americans who are black, or have any shade of colour darker than white. *1922* Gonzales *Black Border* 80 **sSC, GA coasts** [Gullah], Dis defenseless female ub de *Aff'ikin* race. *1965–70 DARE* (Qu. HH28, *Names . . for people of foreign background: Negro*) Infs **AR55, MS6, NC87, TX37,** African; **SC32,** Africans–joking; **LA46,** African ape; (Qu. CC2) Inf **NY249,** African Nationalist Party; (Qu. CC3) Inf **PA104,** Zion African Methodist.

2 Used euphemistically in allusion to **nigger in the woodpile.** Cf **Ethiopian**

1865 Daily Democrat (Cairo IL) 4 Oct 4/3 *(DA),* The house filled, the audience became anxious for a little gushing melody, but not a gush was heard, and it was soon evident that a 'free American of African "scent"' had become secreted in the woodpile. *1879 Congressional Record* 11 June 1931/1 **CT,** There is a gigantic African here [i.e., in the Army Appropriation Bill] . . . I want the African taken out of the bill. *1892 Ibid* 19 Jan 431/1 **MO,** It is indeed difficult to know just how many Africans are hid away in this wood pile [i.e., a public printing bill]. *1980 DARE* File **csWI** (as of 1930–40), There's an African in the cordwood . . . Said without any rancor or meanness.

African n[2] [Malaprop or folk-etym]
An afghan, shawl.

1967–68 DARE (Qu. E10, *Knitted or crocheted pieces placed on the back and arms of a chair*) Inf **KS5,** Africans [ˈæfrɪˌkænz]; **NY72,** On the back of the davenport is a knitted thing called an African.

African ape See **ape** n **1**

African black fats n pl, constr as sg Cf **African** n[1], adj **B2** and **black tobacco**
Tobacco prepared for export to the West Indies.

1940 AmSp 15.133 **KY,** *African Black Fats.* A misnomer. This tobacco is prepared for the West Indies and British Guiana, not for Africa.

African cue n [**African** n[1], adj **C1** + *cue (ball)*]
A closely cropped **Afro.**

1970 DARE (Qu. X5, . . *Men's haircuts*) Inf **KY94,** Afro, African cue.

African dominoes n pl, often constr as sg [See quot 1960] *joc* Cf **African golf 1**
Dice; spec, the game of craps.

1919 in *1980* Lighter *Hist. Dict. Amer. Slang,* First in popularity is the ancient and honorable game of . . "African dominoes." *1922 Outing* Dec 120/3 **VA,** For one, to become proficient in African Dominoes has not been my lot, although the right arm has developed inches from exercise of rolling bones, while the left has increased in the same proportion from reaching for my pocket-book. *1942* Berrey–Van den Bark *Amer. Slang* 750.2. *1960* Wentworth–Flexner *Slang, African dominoes . . .* Commonly used in ref. to craps, thus implying the game's popularity among Negroes. Game of "coups" was first introduced from France in New Orleans, where large Negro and Creole population quickly accepted it. *1962 Western Folkl.* 21.29 **sCA,** African dominoes —dice.

African golf n [Because the game is believed to be a favorite pastime among Blacks] *joc* Cf **Amish golf, Zulu golf**
1 The game of craps. Also called **African dominoes**

1919 A. Kauffman in *1980* Lighter *Hist. Dict. Amer. Slang,* The great pastime of African golf. *1920 Collier's* 5 June 10/2, I got in that African golf tourney because I thought I could grab off enough doubloons to take us to New York *right.* *1930 Sun* (Baltimore MD) 1 Aug 6/3 *(Hench Coll.),* Three crap-shooting Negroes "rolled their own" sentences on the Police Court bench . . after being found guilty of playing African golf. *1932 AmSp* 7.328 **Baltimore MD** [Johns Hopkins Jargon]. *1967 DARE* Tape **IL11,** Poker and African golf.

2 A children's outdoor game: see quot.

1967 DARE (Qu. EE33, *Other outdoor games*) Inf **TX18,** African golf—bat small can around with stick.

African goose n Cf **nigger-goose**
=white-winged scoter.

1956 AmSp 31.184 **SD,** African goose . . . White-winged scoter . . . From its black color and large size among ducks.

African twist n
A dance step.

1967–68 DARE (Qu. FF5b, . . *Different steps in dancing . . more recent ones*) Infs **LA6A, PA66, 93,** African twist. [All Infs are young; 2 of 3 are Black] [*1968* Stearns *Jazz Dance* 1, The swaying motion of the Twist was employed long ago in Africa and by the Negro folk in the South.]

African wiggler n Cf **Georgia wiggler**

1968 DARE (Qu. P6, *Other kinds of worms . . used for bait*) Inf **AL41,** African wiggler.

Africky See **Africa** n **A, African** n[1] **B1**

Africy, Afriky See **Africa** n **A**

Afro n, also attrib |ˈæfro| *esp among young Black speakers* See Map Section Also called **'fro, natural** Cf **African cue**
A bushy haircut modeled on African styles.

1965–70 DARE (Qu. X5, . . *Men's haircuts*) 26 Infs, **chiefly Sth, Black, young,** Afro. [Of all Infs responding to the question, 6% were Black, 12% young; of those giving this response, 88% were Black, 43% young. Of all Blacks in *DARE* sample, 23% were young; of those Blacks giving this response, 43% were young.] *1968 DARE* FW Addit **PA66,** Afro—haircut worn by Negro males, long, unstraightened and without a part. *1970 New Yorker* 6 May 110 **MO,** At Burroughs, there were several black students, wearing Afro haircuts and dashikis. *1970* Updike *Bech* 113, The girl was rather light-skinned with an Afro hair-do cut like an upright loaf of bread. *1970* Major *Afro–Amer. Slang* 19, *Afro:* a "natural" hair style that became popular among Afro-Americans in the early 1960's. The hair is allowed to grow long and is left woolly. *1971 Time* 14 June 64 **Los Angeles CA,** Michael, with the loveliest, fullest, twelve-year-old Afro you'll hope to see, has the history of the group down pat. *1972* Claerbaut *Black Jargon.*

Afro adv

In **Afro** style.

1970 *Time* 6 Apr 46 **IL**, Since last June, Laura has been wearing her hair Afro.

Afroed adj

Wearing the hair in **Afro** style.

1970 *Time* 26 Oct 28, In Manhattan . . Afroed young blacks and a scattering of long-haired whites demonstrated in Angela's [=Angela Davis'] support.

A from B, not to know v phr For varr see quots. See also **B from (a) bull's foot, not to know; izzard**

To be ignorant; not to have the most rudimentary knowledge.

1952 Brown *NC Folkl.* 1.362, He doesn't know A from a bull's foot. **1953** Brewer *Word Brazos* 43 **eTX** [Black], He don' know "A" from "Bullfrog," but he raily preach de Word. **1965–70** *DARE* (Qu. JJ15b, *Sayings about a person who seems to you very stupid: "He doesn't know _____."*) 38 Infs, **scattered**, A. from B.; 10 Infs, **chiefly N Midl**, A. from Z.; **CA**59, **FL**18, **IN**30, **LA**12, **NC**52, **PA**7, A. from izzard; **CT**8, **DC**2, **SC**69, **VT**16, A. from beans; **LA**12, **MS**71, **TX**37, A. from (a) bull's foot; **NY**92, A. from asshole; **TN**53, A. from bull; **TX**86, A. from bullfrog.

afromobile n Palm Beach FL

A three-wheeled passenger vehicle usu pedaled by a Black person sitting in back: see quot 1953.

1939 FWP *Guide FL* 229 **Palm Beach FL**, For many years no wheeled vehicles, with the exception of bicycles and afromobiles, were allowed in the city. **1953** *Sun* (Baltimore MD) 23 Oct B16/2 *(Hench Coll.)*, Mrs. Jackson Boyd . . saw a man she recognized—the colored operator of a Palm Beach "afromobile." This vehicle, which is one of the prides of Palm Beach, is a combination of a two-seated chair in front and the business end of a Negro-pedaled bicycle behind. **1976** Jahoda *Florida* 150, When the hotel's guests wished to make a tour of the city of Palm Beach . . , they were propelled by Afromobiles—two-seated wicker chairs pedalled by a bicycle mechanism driven by a deferential black. **1981** *Wall St. Jrl.* (New York NY) 13 Mar 12/1 **Palm Beach FL**, Transportation . . for rich whites in the early 1900s was provided by "Afromobiles," wicker vehicles pedaled by blacks.

after prep, adv, conj, n Usu |'æftɚ|; also, **esp NEng, Sth** |'a(f)tə(r)|; **chiefly Sth, Midl** *esp among older speakers* |'ætə(r), 'ædə(r)|; less freq |'æeftɚ, 'etɚ| Pronc-spp *aäfter, afteh, ahter, arfter, arter, a'ter, atter, attuh, ayfter, efter*

A Forms (isolated and in comb).

1 *ar(f)ter.*

1815 Humphreys *Yankey in England* 103 [Glossary], *Arter,* after. **1835** (1955) *Crockett Almanacks* 3 **wTN**, Arter the great fuss the public have made about an individual of my humble pretensions. **1836** *Ibid* 54, The feller . . was never heered on arterwards. **1837** Sherwood *Gaz. GA* 69 [In list of Provincialisms to be avoided], *Arter,* for after. **1871** (1892) Johnston *Dukesborough Tales* 60 **GA**, I always feels some better arfter he's been of a-paddlin' me. **1871** (1882) Stowe *Fireside Stories* 69 **NEng**, He didn't come till most the middle of the arternoon. **1884** Murfree *TN Mts.* 253, A good while arterward. **1893** Shands *MS Speech* 17, *Arter* [atə] Negro for *after.* **1933** Rawlings *South Moon* 10 **FL**, A 'possum or sich arter the chicks.

2 *a'ter, atter, ahter, attuh.*

1758 Virginia *Calendar . . State Papers* 1.258 *(DAE)*, Soon ater we had come to a conclusion about it. **1803** Fessenden *Terrible Tractoration* 20 **NY**, Not one soul took small pox a'ter. **1841** (1952) Cooper *Deerslayer* 131 **NY**, The one most sought e'ter. **1867** Lowell *Biglow* lxxi 'Up-country' **MA** [Intro], *Afterwurds* always retains its locative *s,* and is pronounced always *afterwurds',* with a strong accent on the last syllable. **1904** *DN* 2.423 **Cape Cod MA** (as of 1850s), *Afternoon . . .* Rare. **1908** *DN* 3.288 **eAL, wGA**, *Atter . .* chiefly among negroes. **1917** *DN* 4.407 **wNC, IL, NEng**, *Atter, afterwards.* **1922** Gonzales *Black Border* 130 **sSC, GA coasts** [Gullah], Attuh Buh John done dead. **1926** Kephart *Highlanders* 353 **sAppalachians**, The same man, at different times, may say . . atter and arter or after. **1936** *AmSp* 11.234 **eTX**, But ['æ⊥tɚ] for *after* and ['sæːdɪ] for *Saturday* are heard only among the illiterate. (The last two are typical Negro pronunciations.) **1941** Stuart *Men of Mts.* 343 **neKY**, I've melted down ten pounds this afternoon. **1950** Faulkner *Stories* 78 **MS** [Black], Dey jest went down de road a piece en atter a while hyer he come a-hickin' en a-blumpin' up de road. **c1960** Wilson *Coll.* **csKY**, After ['ætə]. **1966–68** *DARE* FW Addit **GA**30, After [ætɚ]; **cwNC**, After ['ædɚ]. Among older folks. **1969** *DARE* Tape **KY**16A, I wrote her a letter the next day after ['ædɚ] Lucy died.

3 *aäfter, afteh, ayfter, efter,* ['etɚ].

1861 Holmes *Venner* 172 **wMA**, I been aäfter ye f'r a week. **1887** *Scribner's Mag.* 2.484 **AR**, He won' git pneumony ayfter all. **1914** *DN* 4.158 **cVA**, "John Henry belongs to folla afteh Sayrah." **1938** Liebling *Back Where* 140 **NYC**, Efter all, you should know. **1942** Hall *Smoky Mt. Speech* 23 **eTN, wNC**, After ['æeftɚ] . . . ['etɚ] . . ['ætɚ] . . . ['etɚ] . . is fairly common in the speech of old-timers. *Ibid* 100, [t] becomes the flapped voiced consonant [t̬] . . in *after* ['ætr].

B As prep.

1 foll by pres pple: on the point of; having just; about to be; intending to be. [*W3 after* 5, *"chiefly Irish";* cf quot 1792]

1792 Brackenridge *Mod. Chivalry* 1.99 **wPA**, The Irishman . . utterly refused to be after fighting in any such manner. **1800** in 1929 Weems *Mason Locke Weems* 2.137 **NJ**, I fear you'll be after printing too many. **c1890** in 1910 Twain *Speeches* 81, If yez want to see Mr. Daly, yez'll have to be after going to the front door and buy a ticket. **1898** Lloyd *Country Life* 138 **AL**, He was after savin lost souls and was willin to let other men save the country. **1899** (1912) Green *VA Folk-Speech, After . .* about. "That hen is after laying." **1926** Vollmer *Sun-Up* 68 **wNC**, I ain't after botherin' ye . . . I ain't after touchin' ye. **1926** (1927) Black *You Can't Win* 69, I was just after gettin' a six months' floater out of Denver an' went down to Pueblo.

2 Added, often without evident function, to certain verbs; sometimes equivalent to *at, from,* or *to.* **chiefly S Midl**

1824 Knight *Letters* 106 **KY**, Some words are used, even by genteel people, from their imperfect educations, in a new sense; . . as: . . best book I ever read after. **1850** in 1953 Randolph *Down in Holler* 65 **St. Louis MO**, We recommend it [=a musical composition] as a beautiful piece to waltz after, and easily executed. **1917** *DN* 4.416 **wNC, SC**, *Read after . . .* To read. "You write the nicest English I ever read after." **1919** *DN* 5.34 **seKY**, *Read after . . .* To read, or read about. "My boy's a pyore scholar, and *reads atter* Shakespeare, and this war." **1926** *DN* 5.399 **Ozarks**, *Eat after . .* Used with reference to the preparation of food. "Thet ol' woman's the best cook I ever *et atter.*" **1953** Randolph *Down in Holler* 65 **Ozarks**, After is combined with certain verbs in a peculiar fashion . . . "Lon Jordan is the best fiddler I ever danced after." A prominent woman in southwest Missouri told reporters that she "liked to read after Wright," meaning that she enjoyed Harold Bell Wright's novels . . . When a boy says "I study after Professor Baines," he means that Mr. Baines is his teacher. **1953** Goodwin *It's Good* 152 **sIL** [Black], "You gonna come up dead, eatin' after all these strange niggers."

C As adv.

Later, afterwards.

1969 *DARE* FW Addit **NYC**, "I'll do it after"—meaning later . . . Used often in New York City. **1970** *DARE* File **cMA** (as of c1915), "I can't tell you now, but I'll tell you after." Common in my childhood.

D As noun. [Abbr]

Afternoon.

1915–20 in 1944 *ADD* **cNY**, 'What a'you goin to do this after?' [ðɪs 'æftɚ]. In freq. serious use among boys. **1934** (1947) O'Hara *Appointment* 46 **PA**, Tonight, or this after', when Ed showed up at the Apollo, he probably would be in a bad humor. **1942** McAtee *Dial. Grant Co. IN* (as of 1890s), *Atter . . .* "This _____"; used facetiously, at least as a rule. **1981** *DARE* File **csWI**, Hey, . . are ya comin' to my room this after?

afterclap n

1 An unexpected subsequent stroke or event; a surprising (and esp disagreeable) sequel. *old-fash*

1650 (1965) Bradstreet *Tenth Muse* 185 **MA**, This is the fore-runner of my Afterclap. **1654** (1974) Johnson *Wonder-Working* 139, But let *N. England* beware of an after-clap, & provoke the Lord no longer. **1851** (1976) Melville *Moby-Dick* 90, He got so frightened about his plaguy soul, that he shrinked and sheered away from whales, for fear of after-claps. **1899** (1912) Green *VA Folk-Speech* 61, *Afterclap . . .* Something happening after an affair is supposed to be at an end. **1953** *AmSp* 28.247 **csPA**, 'Make sure there won't be any afterclap.' Popular speech. Older residents.

2 An unjust or additional demand beyond the terms of a bargain or agreement. *obs*

1840 (1847) Longstreet *GA Scenes* 29, I'm a man that, when he makes a bad trade, makes the most of it until he can make a better. I'm for no rues and after-claps. **1843** (1846) Haliburton *Attaché* (1st ser) 2.227 **NEng,** I'll give up and swap even; and there shall be no after claps, nor ruein [sic] bargains, nor recantin', nor nothin'. **1872** Schele de Vere *Americanisms* 577, *Afterclap* represents in Pennsylvania and the Western States an additional and generally unjust demand beyond the agreement or bargain originally made. "None of your afterclaps!" **1880** in 1971 Farmer *Americanisms,* His blamed afterclaps raised my rile, and made me rip. I was na' goin' to stan' that rush anyhow, as I had agreed afore to pay fifty dollars for the trade.

3 See quot. [Transf from **afterclap 1;** see also *EDD after-cleckin, -clep, -cleth* under *after* 9, a second brood of chickens]
1930 Shoemaker *1300 Words* 1 **cPA Mts** (as of c1900), *Afterclap* — A child born long after its brothers and sisters.

aftercrop n [*OEDS* →1831]
=**aftermath.**
1806 (1970) Webster *Compendious Dict.* 7/2, Aftermath, Aftercrop . . . the second crop. **1939** *LANE* Map 125 *(Second crop)* 1 Inf, **csME,** Aftercrop. **1949** Kurath *Word Geog.* Fig 112 *(Second Crop)* 2 Infs, **nePA,** Aftercrop. **1968** *DARE* (Qu. L24, *A crop or part of a crop that springs up and grows by itself*) Inf **VA7,** Aftercrop.

aftercurrent See **afterwash**

after cut n
Among loggers: =**back cut.**
1958 McCulloch *Woods Words* **Pacific NW,** *After-cut* — A less-used term for back cut, the final cut made in falling a tree.

after cutting n **NEng** and settlement areas
=**aftermath.**
1949 Kurath *Word Geog.* 67, Scattered cases of *aftercrop, aftercutting,* . . in the New England settlement area. **1967** *PADS* 47.5 **NEng,** Aftercutting.

afterdinner n [*OED* →1618, obs exc in attrib use] **chiefly S Midl**
The afternoon.
1927 *DN* 5.472 **Ozarks,** *After-dinner* . . . "Caint you-all come over this after-dinner?" **1953** Randolph *Down in Holler* 212 **Ozarks,** The term *afternoon* is seldom heard, but the period just after the noon meal is sometimes called the *afterdinner.* **1966–70** *DARE* (Qu. A3, *The time between the middle of the day and supper time*) Infs **SC4, TX104,** Afternoon, afterdinner.

afterfeed(ing) n now **chiefly nNY** *old-fash*
Aftermath used for grazing.
1714 *Boston News-Letter* (MA) 30 Aug 1/1 **MA,** A sore scorching Drought . . threatening a great Diminution of the Ungathered Corn and Fruits, and total Deprivation of the After-Feed. **1803** *Lit. Mag.* (Phila.) Dec 210 *(DAE),* The after-feed has been generally cut off, which is much against the farmers; as the crop of hay was short. **1831** MA General Court *Acts & Resolves* 19 Mar 687 **MA,** The number of acres of pasture land . . with the after feed of the whole farm. **1968–70** *DARE* (Qu. L10, *After hay has been cut, then it grows back and you cut it again, you'd call that* _____) Infs **CT26, NY189, 219, 233,** Afterfeed; **NY96,** Afterfeeding — this was not cut; it was grass left for cattle to eat like pasture. [All Infs old]

afterflow See **afterwash**

aftergrass n chiefly **neME, nPA,** and settlement areas *old-fash*
(Cf 1974 Orton – Wright *Word Geog. England* Map 97, showing the distribution of *aftergrass* chiefly in swEngl)
=**aftermath.**
1939 *LANE* Map 125 *(Second crop)* 5 Infs, **neME, cNH,** Aftergrass. [Commentary:] **cwNH,** Aftergrass, heard in Chateaugay, N.Y. [Note also 7 Infs from New Brunswick, Canada.] **1940–41** Cassidy *WI Atlas* **csWI,** Aftergrass. [Inf old] **1949** Kurath *Word Geog.* 67, Rare relics . . of historical interest [include] . . *aftergrass* in New Brunswick and northeastern Maine. *Ibid* Fig 112, 3 Infs, **ne,cnPA, nwNH,** Aftergrass. **1966–68** *DARE* (Qu. L10, *After hay has been cut, then it grows back and you cut it again*) Inf **NY69,** Aftergrass; **ME14,** One old person from down east — the provinces — called it aftergrass. [Both Infs old] **1973** Allen *LAUM* 1.273 **cwIA,** Only one [of the New England terms for a "second cutting"], *aftergrass,* appeared in the field interviews — that from an Iowan whose father came from Pennsylvania.

aftergrowth n
=**aftermath.**

[**1939** *LANE* Map 125 *(Second crop)* **New Brunswick, Canada,** 1 Inf, Aftergrowth.] **1949** Kurath *Word Geog.* Fig 112 *(Second crop)* 2 Infs, **nePA, cwNY,** Aftergrowth. **1967–70** *DARE* (Qu. L10, *After hay has been cut, then it grows back and you cut it again*) Infs **NE2, NJ69,** Aftergrowth; (Qu. L24, *A crop or part of a crop that springs up and grows by itself*) Inf **NJ69,** Aftergrowth? **1973** Allen *LAUM* 1.273 **NE,** *Aftergrowth,* a relic in northern Pennsylvania, is the term of two Nebraskans . . , one whose paternal grandfather came from Pennsylvania and another with German ancestry.

aftermath n Usu |'æftə(r),mæθ|, rarely |-mæt| **chiefly NEng, Delmarva** *old-fash; occas considered a book word* See map in 1949 Kurath *Word Geog.* Fig 112. Also called **aftercrop, ~ cutting, ~ grass, ~ growth, lattermath, rowen** See also **afterfeed(ing)**
A second growth of grass after the first has been cut for hay.
1786 (1925) Washington *Diaries* 3.96 **VA,** The aftermath is more valuable, and the Second growth quicker. **1858** (1867) Flint *Milch Cows* 180, The tall Oat Grass . . after being mown . . shoots up a very thick aftermath. **1939** *LANE* Map 125 *(Second crop)* 23 Infs, **throughout NEng,** Aftermath. [Commentary:] **swCT,** 'Recently the State Colleges have tried to get the farmers to say *Aftermath*'; **nwCT,** [æftrmæt]; **cCT,** *Aftermath,* learned from the dictionary; **ceMA,** Aftermath — father's term. **1949** Kurath *Word Geog.* 67/1, Rare relics . . of historical interest [include] *aftermath* in the New England area and on Delmarvia. **1950** *WELS* (*Hay that grows again after it has been cut once*) 1 Inf, **nwWI,** Aftermath — old-fash. **c1960** *Wilson Coll.* **csKY,** *Aftermath* . . . A second cutting of hay. Very rarely used. **1968–70** *DARE* (Qu. L10, *After hay has been cut, then it grows back and you cut it again, you'd call that* _____) Infs **KY76, NY72A, 176,** Aftermath; **MA16,** Rowen; [in] some parts of the country it's called aftermath; **NY205,** Aftermath; also second cutting, but aftermath is most common; **VA25,** Some call it aftermath. [All Infs old] **1971** Wood *Vocab. Change* 188, 299 **AL, TN,** [A second growth of hay or clover:] 5 Infs, Aftermath. **1973** Allen *LAUM* 1.273 **MN, NE,** *Aftermath* . . is the term of two Minnesotans . . , one with Massachusetts and New Hampshire parents and the other with Vermont parents, and of two Nebraskans . . , one of English parentage and the other with Canadian and New York state parents.

after night adv phr chiefly **PA** *obs*
In the evening.
1804 (1898) Hunt *Diary* 10 **sePA,** After night came on rain. **1847** Hurd *Grammatical Corrector* 103, *After night,* for *evening;* as, "A meeting will be held in the court house, *after night.*" "Being otherwise engaged through the day, he reads *after night.*" This singular expression is believed to be peculiar to Pennsylvania. **1848** Bartlett *Americanisms.* **1872** Schele de Vere *Americanisms* 432, *After night* is a local expression, peculiar to Pennsylvania and some of the Border States, where *night* is very commonly used for the hours of the afternoon, and hence, "Court will open again *after night,*" means simply "after candlelight," as it is expressed everywhere else.

afternight n [From the adv phr]
Evening; the time after it gets dark.
1899 (1912) Green *VA Folk-Speech* 62, *After-night* . . . The time after it becomes night. **1902** *DN* 2.227 **sIL.** *Ibid* 233, Evening . . . And when night finally closes in, the phrase — 'after night' is employed. **1907** *DN* 3.220 **nwAR.** **1942** in 1944 *ADD* Midwest.

afternoon farmer n *joc*
1928 *Ruppenthal Coll.* **KS,** Immigrants from New York if not elsewhere brought to pioneer Kansas the term 'afternoon farmer' for those rising late.

aftersupper n [Cf *OEDS afters* in same sense]
1972 *Atlanta Letters* **nwGA,** Aftersupper — dessert.

afterswell See **afterwash**

aftertimes adv
Afterward, later.
1960 Williams *Walk Egypt* 8 **GA,** The side porch-and-kitchen was a wooden tail tacked on after-times.

afterwash n Also *aftercurrent, afterflow, afterswell, aftertow* **Atl**
The wake of a boat; backwash.
1966–69 *DARE* (Qu. O16, . . *The stirred-up water following a boat*) Inf **FL1,** Aftertow; **GA72,** Afterwash, afterflow; **NJ21,** Afterswell; **NJ24,** Aftercurrent.

afterwhile adv [Ellip for *after a while*]   **chiefly Sth, Midl**
Later on.
1926 *DN* 5.392, *After while* (without *a*), "Not after while." — advertisement in Lawrence (Kansas) Journal–World. **1926** Roberts *Time of Man* 378 **cKY**, Afterwhile I'll send for you-all if you're of a mind to come where I am. **1935** Hurston *Mules & Men* 128 **FL** [Black], Well, 'way after while somebody kilt him. *Ibid passim.* **c1960** *Wilson Coll.* **csKY**, *After while* . . . After a while, in a little while. Very old people said |'ætɚ·|. **1966–69** *DARE* (Qu. A13, *When something needs to be done immediately, . . "I'll do it _____!"*) Inf **OH63**, After while, pretty soon; **OK25**, Directly, afterwhile; **NC70**, Not after while. Now! **1967** Green *Horse Tradin'* 38 **MS**, I think her mother wants her in heah aftah while for something. **1975** Newell *If Nothin' Don't Happen* 33 **nwFL**, Me and Tarley went on out to the oyster bars and loaded up the skiff . . . After while Tarley said . . [etc].

afunky See **a** inert vowel **6**

ag v See **egg** v

ag n [Abbr for **agate 1**]
1921 *DN* 5.109 **CA**, *Ag* . . . An agate marble. Boy's usage. **1965–68** *DARE* (Qu. EE6d) Infs **MS64, MO4**, Ags.

again prep, adv, conj Usu |ə'gɛn|;   **freq in Atl States, less freq elsewhere** |ə'gen|, which may be considered affected in some areas where it is least freq; **throughout US** *esp among older and less educ speakers* |ə'gɪn|;   **chiefly Nth, N Midl**, occas |ə'gæn|. See Kurath–McDavid *Pronc. Engl.* Maps 60, 61. Pronc-spp *agen, agin*

A Forms. Addit quots in *ADD*.
1815 Humphreys *Yankey in England* 103 **NEng** [Glossary], *Agin*, again. **1843** (1916) Hall *New Purchase* 134 **IN**, They stops agin. **1861** Holmes *Venner* 187 **wMA**, Ag'in. **1891** *PMLA* 6.164 **WV**, In addition to . . [əgen] . . [əgen] . . , we find . . [əgɪn] . . , though only as [a] vulgarism. **1899** (1912) Green *VA Folk-Speech, Again . . . Agen, agin.* **1905** *DN* 3.101 **nwAR**, [ə'gen]. **1933** *AmSp* 8.2.44 **neNY**, [ə'gɪn]. **1936** *AmSp* 11.15 **eTX**, Among the less literate the use of [ə'gɪn] is widespread. **1961** Kurath–McDavid *Pronc. Engl.* 131, *Again* . . . The /ɛ/ of *pen* is in fairly general use in cultivated speech throughout the Eastern States . . . /ɪ/ of *pin* is widely used in folk speech in nearly all parts of the Eastern States . . . In middle-class speech, /əgɪn/ is much more restricted; it predominates over /əgen/ in large parts of the South, in West Virginia, and in Western Pennsylvania, but is uncommon to rare elsewhere. The vowel /e/ of *pain* is decidedly uncommon in *again* and exhibits no marked social dissemination. It occurs especially in parts of New England, on Delaware Bay, in Tidewater Virginia and northeastern North Carolina . . , and again in the Savannah Valley; only scattered instances are found elsewhere. Rare cases of /əgæn/ . . occur in the North and the North Midland. **1967–68** *DARE* FW Addit **LA3**, Again [ə'geɪn]; **New Orleans LA**, [ə'geɪn] common in uptown University District; **csLA**, Both [ə'gæn] and [ə'geɪn] are heard here; **LA17**, [ə'geɪn] —occas, [əgen]—frequent. **1976** Allen *LAUM* 3.270, The form |əgɪn| . . is recorded in the U[pper] M[idwest] by only two [fieldworkers], . . in Duluth, Minnesota, and . . in southern Iowa, where its Midland background is obvious . . . An ingliding diphthong, [eə] or [ɪə], appears in Midland speech territory in the speech of . . [27 Infs].

B As adv.
1 usu in neg constr, implying that the appropriate time for an action has passed: Now, anymore, after all. [Cf *DJE again* 1, *OED again* 4]
1872 Twain *Roughing It* 250 **MO**, "Yes, you see he's dead again — " "*Again?* Why, has he ever been dead before?" "Dead before? No! Do you reckon a man has got as many lives as a cat? But you bet you he's awful dead now." **1954** *PADS* 21.19 **SC**, *Again* . . . There is no idea of repetition implied. "John is fifty and still a bachelor. Do you think he will ever marry?" "No, not again." "If you haven't sent that letter, I wouldn't send it again." "I've changed my mind about that trip. It's too expensive. I won't go again." "If he hasn't come by now, he certainly will not come again."
2 Back to the starting point; esp with *go, come, leave.* [*OED again* A1b "*Obs.*"]
1968 *Budget* (Sugarcreek OH) 25 July 15 **ceOH** [Mennonite community], They are from Lanc. Co. They had dinner at Iddo Yoder's and left for their home Sun. eve. again.

C As prep.
1 usu [ə'gɪn]: Against. [See *OED again*, headnote and B1-11;

see also *OEDS*]   **now chiefly Sth, Midl** exc in such set phrr as *agin the government* (or *law*), *dead set agin him*
a Std senses of *against.*
1836 (1955) *Crockett Almanacks* 43 **wTN**, Adam Huntsman, who run agin me for Congress last election. **1840** (1847) Longstreet *GA Scenes* 31, He'd *jist as leve* go agin the house with you, or in a ditch, as any how. **1843** (1916) Hall *New Purchase* 216 **IN**, I'll bet old Nan —(his rifle)— again two-shot gun! **1915** *DN* 4.224 **wTX**. **1923** *DN* 5.200 **swMO**, He run ag'in a stump. **1926** Vollmer *Sun-Up* 48 **wNC**, I ain't got nothin' agin ye. *Ibid* 62, Ain't ye fitten to use yo' law agin' nothin' but wimen, and men folks whut's without guns? **1939** *Hall Coll.* **eTN**, It's strictly agin the law to set a trap out in a trail. **1954** *Harder Coll.* **cwTN**, I allus stick my head agin the cow when I [meək] [=milk]. **1966–69** *DARE* (Qu. CC12b) Infs **LA12, 28**, Up agin it [əp ə'gɪn ɪt]; (Qu. DD33b) Inf **CT23**, Dead set agin it; (Qu. JJ26) Inf **MO38**, Put his shoulder agin the wheel; (Qu. II30, . . *Firmly opposed to someone: "I'm _____ him."*) Infs **FL8, NM4**, Agin; **FL15, MS69**, Agin [ə'gɪn]; **FL19**, Against, agin [laughter]. **1967–68** *DARE* Tape **SC32**, You could go around all these bootleggers and they was agin liquor stores as bad as any church organization; **IL29**, The water would run [ə'gɪn] that. **1967–68** *DARE* FW Addit **TN17**, Hit's standin' [ə'gɪn] the wall; **PA142**, It was leaning again the house; **nwMD**, *Agin* [ə'gɪn] for against—occasional.
b Towards the front of; near, adjoining. [*OED against* 4, "*dial.*"]
1950 *PADS* 14.11 **SC**, Over agin the river. **1967** *DARE* (Qu. MM6, . . *"The house is _____ the park."*) Inf **CO33**, Right agin. **1976** Garber *Mountain-ese* **sAppalachians**, *Agin* . . . next to . . . His land lays agin the mountain.
c In place of, by mistake for. [*OED against* 14, "now only *lit.*"]
1940–41 Cassidy *WI Atlas*, 1 Inf, **swWI**, Like somebody pickin' up a snake agin a worm.
2 By, before, in anticipation of. [*OED again* B11 c1230–a1450] See Kurath *Word Geog.* Fig 160 **chiefly Midl** See also **gin** prep
1838 in 1956 Eliason *Tarheel Talk* 258 **NC**, 4 bsls. of wheet at $1.00. If paid again Christmas if not $1.25. **1902** *DN* 2.228 **sIL**, Agin four o'clock. **1923** *DN* 5.20 **swMO**, Hit'll rain ag'in mornin'. **1967** *DARE* FW Addit **NC**, I'll be there again daylight.
3 Of time: towards, drawing near.
1906 *DN* 3.114 **sIN**, It's agin noon.
D As conj.
By the time (that). **chiefly Sth, Midl** *somewhat old-fash* See also **against C1**
1887 (1967) Harris *Free Joe* 102 **GA**, Ag'in bullaces is ripe you'll git your heart sot on 'possum. **1899** (1912) Green *VA Folk-Speech, Agen; agin . . .* "I'll have it ready *agin* you come." **1902** *DN* 2.228 **sIL**, We will get there agin he does. **1917** *DN* 4.407 **wNC**. **1923** *DN* 5.200 **swMO**. **1931** Hannum *Thursday April* 166 **Appalachians**, I aimed to give you yore pick of 'em ag'in you got married. **1949** Kurath *Word Geog.* 79, The greater part of the Midland and the South . . have retained in their folk speech the expression *agin I get there . . . Agin* is most common in the Appalachians, but it has considerable currency among the simple folk, white and black, in the Southern piedmont and along the coast as well. In Pennsylvania *agin* is not unusual west of the Alleghenies. Farther east it is heard now only on the upper Susquehanna and along the Maryland line. **c1960** *Wilson Coll.* **csKY**. **1961** *Mt. Life* Fall 9 **Appalachians**, They'll be larrupin' good . . agin ye can step on the head o' yer shadder.

against prep, conj Usu |ə'gɛnst|;   freq |(ə)'gɪnst| **throughout US** *esp among less educ speakers;* less freq |ə'geɪnst| Pronc-spp *aginst, angainst, ginst*
A Forms.
1867 Lowell *Biglow* 88 'Upcountry' **MA**, Cov'nants o' works go 'ginst my grain. **1890** *DN* 1.67 **KY**, Against [əgɪnst]. **1891** *PMLA* 6.164 **WV**, In addition to . . [ə'genst] . . and [ə'genst], we find the pronunciation . . [ə'gɪnst], though only as [a] vulgarism. **1906** *DN* 3.114 **sIN**, Aginst. **1908** *DN* 3.285 **eAL, wGA**, (A)ginst. **1916** *DN* 4.355 **NE**, All were used persistently, not as nonce-formations . . . *Angainst*, against. "He did it angainst his will." **1936** *AmSp* 11.15 **eTX**, Among the less literate the use of [ə'gɪnst] is widespread. **1941** *AmSp* 16.5 **eTX** [Black], *Against* is [gĩĩns(t)].

B As prep. See also **again C**
1 In expr of time: by; before; until.   *old-fash*

1804 (1898) Hunt *Diary* 10 **sePA**, This day fell a considerable snow. After night came on rain. Against morning snow all gone. **1858** in 1956 Eliason *Tarheel Talk* 258 **swNC**, Beter make sum arangements to have your tax paid a ginest the 18th. **1916** *DN* 4.340 **se,neOH**, Be there against nine o'clock. **1926** Roberts *Time of Man* 237 **KY**, I got a long piece to go against sundown. **1927** *AmSp* 2.347 **cwWV**, "Mr. Jones will hold the cattle against your arrival." **1953** *PADS* 19.8 **Appalachians, NC Piedmont**, I'll have this sewing done against dinner time.

2 In response to, toward.

1945 Beck *Jersey Genesis* 201 **NJ**, Of course the first decoys were crude — soot and oil were used to color 'em. Now — well, ducks is more eddicated. They just don't come down against something that doesn't look real.

3 Opposite to. [*OED against* 1 "now generally *over against*"]
1967 *DARE* (Qu. MM1, . . *"The shed is_____ the barn.'*) Inf **MO5**, Against.

C As conj. [*OED against* B: used with relative, "*obs."*; used simply, "*arch or dial."*] See also **again D**

1 By the time (that); before. **chiefly sAppalachians, Ozarks**

1813 in 1956 Eliason *Tarheel Talk* 258 **nwNC**, I expecte to get up the two Lower fiedds [sic] against you gite these fewe Lines. **1909** *DN* 3.392 **nwAR**, I must get my work done against Pop comes home, or he'll give me a whalin'. **1910** *DN* 3.456 **seKY**. **1911** *DN* 3.537 **eKY**, I'll get there against you do. **1916** *DN* 4.289 **sAppalachians**. **1937** *Hall Coll.* **eTN**, We'd orta do plenty of fishin' against the season closes. **1943** Chase *Jack Tales* 91 **wNC** (as of 1880s), And against ye get that done, I'll come up there with somethin' to help ye. **c1960** *Wilson Coll.* **csKY**, Against [əˈgɪnst] . . By the time that.

2 In case, in the event that.

1905 *DN* 3.60 **NE**, Sweep the porch against some one comes. **1931** *AmSp* 7.19 **swPA**, *Against.* In case of, if. "May I leave this here against I come again?"

againster n ["Corrected" var of **aginner**]

1945 Chicago *Times* 25 Aug Editorial (*AmSp* 21.68), The againsters have dragged out the old slogan: The full employment bill would bring about a Government-managed national economy. **1954** *Sun* (Baltimore MD) 14 Jun ed B 8/3 *(Hench Coll.)*, [Headline] Citizens For Ike Not 'Againsters.' [Text] Washington, June 13 (AP) — Chairman James L. Murphy said today the National Citizens for Eisenhower Congressional Committee is "not against anybody" in seeking to elect Republican members of Congress.

agarita n, also attrib Also commonly *algerita* For other var forms see quots [MexSpan, from Span *agrito* sorrel] **SW esp TX** Cf **algeredo**

Any of several **barberries** native to the southwestern US, and/or their fruit, but esp *Berberis trifoliata* which is also called **agrillo 1, agrito 1, barberry, chaparral berry 2, currant 2, palo amarillo, wineberry.**

1891 *TX Geol. Surv. Report* 485, The most abundant berry is the algireta . . . The berry resembles the cranberry of the North, in color, but is entirely different. **1892** *DN* 1.243 **TX**, *Algiréta* or *algeréta:* a small, red berry; the fruit of a species of berberis not identified, probably identical with the *chaparral* . . berry . . . The forms *algaríte, aguirite,* and *alguiritte* have been met with. **1916** *Torreya* 16.237, *Berberis trifoliolata* . . . Currants, New Braunfels, Tex . . ; algeritas, Austin, Tex. **1936** McKenna *Black Range* 291 **swNM**, He told me he had lately gathered bushels of alderita berries to make wine. **1937** U.S. Forest Serv. *Range Plant Hdbk.* B99, Frémont holly grape *(Odostemon fremontii)* and red holly grape *(O. hæmatocarpus)* . . are known in the Southwest as algerita, agarita, agrillo, and yellow wood. **1951** *PADS* 15.32 **TX**, *Berberis trifoliata* . . Agarito or agarita . . . Good for jellies, preserves, wine making, though tedious to pick; and delicious raw . . . Wood and roots, under their outer skins, yellow, were used for making a dye almost as yellow as the exquisite little fragrant rosettes of flowers that crowd stems of the 'wild currant' bushes. **1960** Vines *Trees SW* 273, *Laredo Mahonia* . . . Vernacular names are Wild Currant, Chaparral Berry, Agarita, Agrito, Algerita, Agrillo, and Palo Amarillo. **1967–70** *DARE* (Qu. H63) Inf **TX4**, Agarita cobbler, agarita — a wild plum; (Qu. I44) Infs **TX3, 4, 11, 43**, Agarita berries; **TX102**, Agaritas; **TX5**, Algerita [ælˈjəˈritə] berry — some kind of curran'; **TX42**, Algerita — same thing that is called agarita in south Texas; **TX69**, [ælˈjəˈridə] berries; (Qu. I46) Inf **TX40**, Algerita berry; **TX73**, [ˌælˈjəˈridə] berry; (Qu. T5) Infs **TX1, 3, 4**, Agarita; **TX5, 42**, Algerita.

agate n, also attrib Usu |ˈægət, ˈægɪt|, rarely |ˈeɪgət| Pronc-sp *egget* **widespread** Also called **ag, agatey, aggie, agnate, agnes**

1 A playing marble, orig made of agate stone but since early 20th century commonly replaced by glass imitating agate in color and pattern (see **immie**). Note: the agate is freq considered "special," larger ones being used as taws.

1889 *Century Dict.* **1890** *DN* 1.76 **ME, MA**, "Alleys" and "agates" were used in Maine some thirty years ago . . , and "agates" . . in Boston fifteen years ago. **1933** *Hanley Disks* **Boston MA**. **1934** *AmSp* 9.75 **csND**, *Agates* or *aggies*. Marbles made of agate and usually used as shooters. **1945** *Good Housekeeping* Mar 137/1 *(DA)*, The revolutionary automatic machine that made this country supreme in the manufacture of marbles was brought out by the Akro Agate Company. **1955** *PADS* 23.34 **ceKY**, *Egget* . . . Variant of *agate.* **1965–70** *DARE* (Qu. EE6a, . . *Marbles — the big one that's used to knock others out of the ring)* 66 Infs, **scattered, but esp Nth, N Midl**, Agate; (Qu. EE6d, *Special marbles*) 327 Infs, Agates. **1970** *DARE* Tape **KY80**, We used to call it a agate. That was a great big marble an' usually striped or somethin'. That was what they always shot with.

2 A marble of any kind, regardless of material. See also **agate-agate**

1958 *PADS* 29.29 **GA, IA, MA, MO, NY, OH, WA, WI**, Agate. **1962** *PADS* 37.1 **cKS**. **1963** *KY Folkl. Rec.* 9.58 **neKY**, *Large marbles:* agate [1 Inf]. **1965–70** *DARE* (Qu. EE6b, *Small marbles or marbles in general*) 16 Infs, **throughout US**, Agates. **c1970** Wiersma *Marbles Terms* **swMI** (as of 1955), Agate [ˈeɪgət]. A playing marble containing at least two colors intermingled.

3 A cheap marble; specif, a marble made of glazed clay or stone. **chiefly Sth, Midl** Also called **dobe, jug**

1908 *DN* 3.285 **eAL, wGA**, *Agate* . . . A marble made of glazed clay . . . The regular agate is called stone-glass. **1963** *KY Folkl. Rec.* 9.58 **neKY**, *Stone marble:* agate [2 Infs]. **1965–67** *DARE* (Qu. EE6c, *Cheap marbles*) Infs **MS52, MO7, OK1**, Agates.

4 Transf. See quot.

1941 *AmSp* 16.236 **ceNE**, Pig testicles are *agates*, sheep testicles *mountain oysters.*

agate-agate n Cf **alley-alley**

Marble stone, or a playing marble, of genuine agate.

1896 *DN* 1.411 **NYC**, In marbles . . *agate-agate.* **1901** *DN* 2.135 **Detroit MI**, *Agate-agate* . . A very fine variegated marble from Lake Superior.

agate-eye n **chiefly Nth, esp Gt Lakes**

A playing marble having markings like an eye, considered to be special.

1965–70 *DARE* (Qu. EE6d, *Special marbles*) Infs **CA202, IL4, IN13, MI61, NY126, 139, 199, 228**, Agate-eyes; **FL22**, Agate-eyes — the big ones with a blue dot on them.

agatey n

In marble play: =**agate 1.**

1892 *DN* 1.219 **DC**, *Agatey:* a marble made of material supposed to resemble agate.

agatine n

A playing marble of cheap material.

1968 *DARE* (Qu. EE6c) Inf **IN45**, Agatines [ægəˈtinz].

agaum See **a *prep*¹ 4, gaum**

agave n |əˈgave, əˈgavi| **chiefly SW**

A genus of apparently stemless plants which have a basal cluster of large, fleshy, toothed leaves and a tall scape with a loose panicle of flowers. Also called **amole 1, century plant, lechuguilla, maguey, mescal.** For names of particular species see **dagger-grass, false aloe 1, palmilla, rattlesnake master 2**

1842 Ganilh *Ambrosio* 1.10 **swTX**, Hardly can one find . . a sturdy agave, or a half withered opuntia, sadly vegetating in the rocky crevices. **1843** (1845) Green *Jrl. Texian Exped.* 260, While the juice of the agave inspired the soul, the ass's milk filled the stomach. **1865** *Atlantic Mth.* 15.424/1 **eGA**, The deserted house was embowered in . . Mexican agaves and English ivies. **1910** Hart *Vigilante Girl* 189 **CA**, I want to show you that agave plant; it's just about to burst into blossom. **1951** Corle *Gila R.* 348, A desert plant that is not a cactus but is as well known as any and is often mistaken for one is the agave. It is also known as mescal, amole, maguey, and lechuguilla.

age n

1 also (because of phonetic similarity) *edge:* Orig the advantage held by the player to the left of the dealer in poker; by ext, any advantageous position held by one person over another. [*age* player to the left of the dealer *(DA)*] *old-fash*

1844 in 1883 Shields *Life S. Prentiss* 334, You can't expect me to take a hand in this game when he . . holds two bullets and a bragger and has the age of me to boot. **1891** Maitland *Amer. Slang Dict., Age, or Edge . . .* The player next to the dealer holds the "age" and is not compelled to bet until all the players have signified their intentions. **1907** Twain in *N. Amer. Rev.* 184.569, How could I talk when he was talking? He 'held the age,' as the poker clergy say.

2 Among railroad workers: seniority in service.

1945 Hubbard *Railroad Ave.* 331, *Age — Seniority, length of service.* **1947** Beebe *Mixed Train* 353. **1977** Adams *Lang. Railroader* 3.

ageable adj chiefly Sth

Advanced in years.

1845 Hooper *Advent. Simon Suggs* 153 **AL**, Judy Tompkins, ageable woman, and four children. **1888** Jones *Negro Myths* 131 **GA coast**, De soldier . . massacree all de ageable people een de lan. **1899** (1912) Green *VA Folk-Speech*, They are right *ageable* people. **1945** FWP *Lay My Burden Down* 84 **AL** [Black], My own daddy lived to be very ageable, but I don't know when he died. **1950** *PADS* 14.11 **SC**. **1955** *DE Folkl. Bulletin* 1.17, When he matures and reaches his twilight years he is referred to as "bein' ageable." **1962** *Hench Coll.* **cVA**, Informant reports that his brother-in-law, if he is not feeling good and someone asks him how he is, may reply, 'I'm getting ageable.' **1969** Emmons *Deep Rivers* 58 **eTX** [Black], I asked particularly about his age, and was told, "No'm, he ain't so old. He's just sorta ageable. He's got grown children, but he can work good."

ageful adj

1944 *PADS* 2.38 **cnNC**, *Ageful . . .* Old, getting old . . . Rare. **1952** Brown *NC Folkl.* 1.513.

ageing See edging

agen See again

agent n

1 also *traveling agent:* An itinerant salesman. *somewhat old-fash*

1950 *WELS* (A man who goes from town to town selling things) 7 Infs, **throughout WI**, Agent; 1 Inf, **cWI**, Agent — old-fash. **c1960** *Wilson Coll.* **csKY**, *Agent . . .* House-to-house seller of small articles or subscriptions. **1965–70** *DARE* (Qu. U7) 14 Infs, **chiefly Sth, Upper MW, Gt Lakes**, Agent; **VA70**, Traveling agent. [13 of 15 Infs are old, 2 mid-aged]

2 A straw boss.

1967–70 *DARE* (Qu. HH43b, *The assistant to the top person in charge of a group of workmen)* Infs **LA8, MS88**, Agent. [Both Infs are Black.]

age of years n Cf DS and std month of Sundays

A very long time.

1969 *DARE* (Qu. A16, . . *"I haven't seen him _____."*) Inf **MA17**, In an age of years.

age out v phr

To grow too old to continue in a particular vocation.

1971 Green *Last Trail Drive* 14 **TX** (as of 1920s), During this horse scuffle, old Friole couldn't keep his eyes off the fun, and, like all top hands that have aged out, he hollered lots of advice and funny conversation. **1971** Green *Village Horse Doctor* 59 **TX**, A transplanted Vermonter who had come to the Far Southwest as a very young man and had aged out in the business.

ager See ague

ager bumps n pl

Gooseflesh.

1954 *Harder Coll.* **cwTN**, I so cold, ager bumps a-poppin' out all over me. *Ibid*, I git ager bumps ever' time we pass 'at old graveyard. **1966** *DARE* (Qu. X58) Inf **GA3**, Ager |ega-| bumps.

agered (up) adj (phr) Also sp agured Cf aguefied

Afflicted with the symptoms of **ague**.

1966 *PADS* 46.24 **cnAR**, *Agured . . .* "It got me kindly agured." **1966** *DARE* Tape **GA25**, I been ['ɛkərd 'ʌp], crippled up.

agerwatin See aggravating

ager worm See fever-and-ague worm

ageways See edgeways

agey adj |'eʤi| Also sp agy [OEDS "arch."] somewhat old-fash

Old.

1899 (1912) Green *VA Folk-Speech, Agy.* **1967** *Hall Coll.* **eTN**, Bruce is bound to be gettin' agy. Because Bruce at that time [c1940] was up in thirty. Bruce is gettin' age on him. **1968** *DARE* (Qu. X48b) Inf **OH61**, He's getting agey.

agg n See egg n

agg v See egg v

agg'avate See aggravate

aggerfret See aggrafret

aggerpervoke v, hence also ppl adj aggerpervoking [Blend of metath forms of aggravate + provoke] Cf aggervex, aggravoke =aggravate.

1923 *DN* 5.200 **swMO**, *Agger-pervokin' . . .* Aggravating, exasperating, annoying, irritating. **1953** Randolph *Down in Holler* 223 **Ozarks**, Aggerpervoke . . . To irritate, to provoke, to annoy.

aggervate See aggravate

aggervex v [Blend of aggravate + vex] Cf aggerpervoke =aggravate.

1933 *AmSp* 8.1.47 **Ozarks**, *Aggervex . . .* To vex, to aggravate, to provoke.

aggie n |'ægɪ; rarely |'eɪgɪ|. Also sp aggy [agg- from agate + -ie familiarizing suff] widespread Cf crystal B

In marble play: an **agate**.

1921 *DN* 5.109 **CA**. **1934** *AmSp* 9.75 **Bismarck ND**, *Aggies . . .* usually used as shooters. **1944** *PADS* 2.53 **cnMO**. **1945** *Sat. Review* 4 Aug 22, She pounced upon the "aggies" and carried them off for her grandson. **1951** *PADS* 15.65 **cwNH**. **1955** *PADS* 23.10 **AL**, *Aggie (aggy).* **1958** *PADS* 29.29, **AR, GA, IL, IN, KS, KY, ME, MA, NE, SD.** **c1960** *Wilson Coll.* **csKY**, What'll you give me for this aggie? **1962** *PADS* 37.1 **cKS**. **1965–70** *DARE* (Qu. EE6a) 127 Infs, **widespread**, Aggie; (Qu. EE6b) 17 Infs, **chiefly east of Missip R**, Aggies; (Qu. EE6c) Infs **MD49, MA8, 52, 128**, Aggies; (Qu. EE6d, *Special marbles*) 234 Infs, **widespread**, Aggies. **1967** *DARE* Tape **IL11**, There were those they called aggies, were supposed to be made out of agates . . . glassies really. **c1970** Wiersma *Marbles Terms* **MI, NY, PA**, Aggie [eɪgɪ]. A target marble.

aggie forti(e)s n Also acker fortis, ackie fortis, agur forty [aqua fortis strong water, the Lat name for nitric acid] chiefly Sth, S Midl old-fash See also forty axes

Any very strong drink; see also quot 1947.

1859 (1968) Bartlett *Americanisms* 4, *Agur-forty.* Aqua-fortis, vulgarly so called at the South-west. *The doctors fed me on lodlum tea and epecac . . ; they then tried agur-forty — if it had been agur-hundred, 't would n't have done — N.Y. Spirit of the Times, Frontier Tale.* **1867** New Orleans *Picayune, Police Reports* 25 Dec (in Schele De Vere *Americanisms* 577), Your Honor need't say another word; I knock under; this man's whiskey ain't Red Eye, it ain't Chain Lightnin' either, it's regular *Agur-forty*, and there isn't a man living can stand a glass and keep his senses. **1944** *PADS* 2.38 **VA, NC**, *Aggie forties* ['ægɪ 'fɔtɪz] . . . Anything very strong; generally used in reference to something to drink. S.Va; Johnston Co., N.C. Rare now. *Ackie fortis* ['æki 'fortɪs]: Swain Co., N.C. **1947** (1964) Randolph *Ozark Superstitions* 109, In Pineville, Missouri, my old neighbors asked the druggist for "a dime's worth of acker fortis an' a nickel's worth of quicksilver," by which they meant nitric acid and mercury, to make some kind of itch medicine. **1967–68** *DARE* (Qu. H74a, *Different words for coffee according to how it's made: very strong)* Inf **TX3**, Strong as aggie fortis; (Qu. DD1) Inf **NC80**, Red Apple [chewing tobacco was] stronger than [æki 'fortɪsɪs].

aggrafret v Also, by metath, aggerfret [Blend of aggravate + fret]

See quot 1919.

1919 *DN* 5.32 **ceKY**, *Aggerfret . . .* To aggravate, or fret. Slang. **1920** *DN* 5.119 **KY**, *Aggerfret*, aggravate. **1941** *AmSp* 16.21 **sIN**, *Aggrafret.* Aggravate.

aggravate v Usu |'ægrə,ve(ɪ)t|, freq metath |'ægɚ,ve(ɪ)t|, occas |'ægə,ve(ɪ)t| Pronc-spp *agg'avate, aggervate*

A Forms.

1936 *AmSp* 11.244 **eTX,** Aggravate . . . *Hill-type* ['ægɚ,veɪt], *Negro* ['ægəveɪt]. **1942** Hall *Smoky Mt. Speech* 98 **eTN, wNC,** Aggravate ['ægɚ,veɪt]. **1952** Brown *NC Folkl.* 1.513, *Agg'avate.* **1954** *Harder Coll.* **cwTN,** She aggervates 'em all time! **c1960** *Wilson Coll.* **csKY,** "He is so stingy that he aggravates me." ['ægə–] . . Almost universal pronunciation. **c1970** *Thompson Coll.* **GA,** |'ægə,vet|.

B Sense.

To annoy, tease, provoke. **scattered, but esp Sth, S Midl** *largely avoided as nonstd in NEast*

1836 (1955) *Crockett Almanacks* 59 **wTN,** The young eagles . . thereupon set up such a scream as aggravated the mother to a much higher degree. **1841** (1952) Cooper *Deerslayer* 40 **nNY,** My advice to you is, never to aggravate Judith; though you may tell anything to Hetty, and she'll take it as meek as a lamb. **1859** Elwyn *Glossary* 14, "He *aggravated* my temper," I have often heard in New England. **1950** *PADS* 14.11 **SC.** **1965–70** *DARE* (Qu. Y7, . . *To be mean to another or to annoy another: "I don't know why she keeps _____ me all the time."*) 86 Infs, **scattered, but esp Sth, S Midl,** Aggravating; (Qu. GG3, *To tease: "See those big boys trying to _____ (that little one)."*) 65 Infs, **chiefly Sth, S Midl,** Aggravate. [For addit *DARE* exx, see *DS* A11, Y2, 5, 6, GG24, II29b, NN12a, NN17.] **1975** Morris *Usage* 18, [In response to the question whether to accept *aggravate* in the sense of "to vex," a usage panel responded as follows:] In writing Yes: 43%. No: 57%. In speech Yes: 53%. No: 47% . . . Here are typical opinions . . . "No down-east North Carolinian like me can be 'aggravated' by this use. It is the authentic music of home." . . "No. I'm reacting to having been born and brought up in Brooklyn, where children, butchers, in-laws, and everything else aggravated everyone."

aggravated ppl adj Pronc-sp *aggrevated* **widespread, though esp freq in Sth, Midl**

Annoyed, provoked.

c1871 Twain *Screamers* 16, He'd got the blues, and feel kind o' scruffy, aggravated, and disgusted. **1891** Page *Elsket* 139 **VA,** De jedge settin' up in he pulpit, lookin' mighty aggrevated. **1956** Gipson *Old Yeller* 37 **TX,** I was half aggravated with myself because I hadn't thought of it. **1965–70** *DARE* (Qu. GG4, *Stirred up, angry: "When he saw them coming he got _____."*) 41 Infs, **scattered,** Aggravated; (Qu. GG7, . . *"Though we were only a few minutes late, she was all _____."*) Infs **GA6, IN14, KY74, LA17, OH48, SC21,** 45, **TN24, VA11,** Aggravated; (Qu. GG6) Infs **IL11, WI60,** Aggravated; (Qu. GG8) Inf **CA87,** Easily aggravated; (Qu. GG11) Inf **IA15,** Aggravated; **WA11,** Very aggravated; (Qu. GG41) Inf **MD36,** Easily aggravated; (Qu. LL37) Infs **MO17,** 19, Aggravated. **1967** *DARE* FW Addit **neLA,** He was so ['ægrə,veɪtɪd] at what they was doin'. **1970** Tarpley *Blinky* 244 **neTX,** *When you lose your temper you become _____.* [In list of "other responses":] Aggravated.

aggravating ppl adj Pronc-sp *agerwatin* [**aggravate** + *ing*] **chiefly Sth, S Midl** See Map

Annoying, troublesome.

1880 Twain *Tramp Abroad* 263, No sound is quite so inane, and silly, and aggravating as the "hoo' hoo" of a cuckoo clock. **1880** *Scribner's Mth.* Feb 572/1 **VA** [Black], Feels as if I could bust into ten thousand

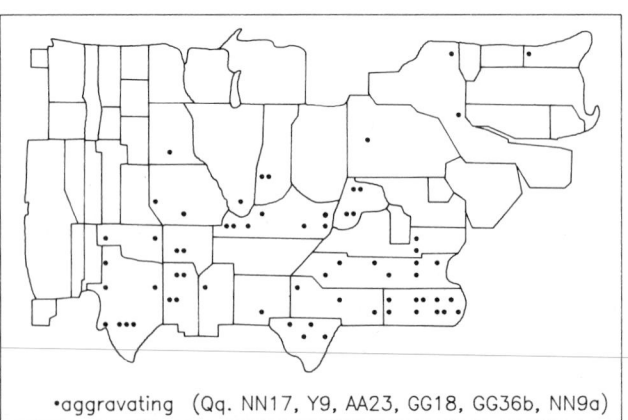

•aggravating (Qq. NN17, Y9, AA23, GG18, GG36b, NN9a)

emptin's, dey's so agerwatin. **1949** Perry *Granny Van* 159 **TX,** He . . looked on her as an utterly spoiled and aggravating but lovable child. **1965–70** *DARE* (Qu. NN17, *Something that keeps on annoying you: "That _____ fly won't go away"*) 60 Infs, **chiefly Sth, S Midl,** Aggravating; (Qu. Y9, . . *"His little brother is an awful _____."*) Inf **LA12,** Aggravating piece; (Qu. AA23, . . *"It's time for me to go and get supper for my _____."*) Inf **KY44,** Aggravating man; (Qu. GG18, . . *"Why does he have to be so _____."*) Inf **PA167,** Aggravating; (Qu. GG36b, . . *"She's the _____ person I know."*) Inf **LA2,** Most aggravating; (Qu. NN9a) Inf **MO39,** Aggravating stuff; **IL75,** How aggravating.

aggravoke v [Blend of **aggravate** + *provoke;* cf *aggrivoking* reported from Somerset Engl in *N & Q* 170.75] See also **aggerpervoke**

To provoke, incite.

1967 Faulkner *Wishing Tree* 44 **MS,** Him and his army! I'll war him, I will: he ain't never seen no war like what I can aggravoke.

aggress v intr [*OED* "Obs."]

To move forward, progress, advance (oneself).

1967 Cerello *Dakota Co. MN* 43, "He'll get along and will agress in life till he's ahead." Fairly common usage among all [45] informants.

aggrevated See **aggravated**

aggy See **aggie**

agin See **again**

aginner n |ə'gɪnɚ| Also sp *aginer, ag'in'er* [*agin* pronc-sp for **again** prep **C1** + *-er*] See also **againster**

One who opposes some specific position or point of view, or who tends to disfavor anything unfamiliar.

1941 *NYT Book Rev.* 20 July 15, [Shaw's] bad taste, ineptitudes and sporadic insults have raised up an army of 'aginers.' **1944** Morgantown [WV] *Post* 9 Feb 6/2 *(ADD),* We hope [the Republican Party] doesn't become a grab bag for all the aginners in the country—at least, not to the extent of letting the aginners formulate the party policies. **1953** *Sun* (Baltimore MD) 27 Aug ed B 5/2 *(Hench Coll.),* Clare Hoffman . . rallied some die-hards from both parties against it . . . The committee's disapproval was pure, instinctive obstructionism. Clare is a natural "ag'in'er." **1966–68** *DARE* (Qu. HH4, *Someone who has odd or peculiar ideas or notions*) Inf **MI26,** An Aginner; (Qu. GG39, *Somebody who seems to be looking for reasons to be angry: "He's a _____."*) Inf **PA69,** Aginner [ə'gɪnɚ].

aginst See **against**

agitate up a storm v phr *joc*

To create a commotion (mental or physical) over something.

1954 *Harder Coll.* **cwTN,** He's agitatin' up a storm over the 'lection.

aglee adj [*a* prep¹ **3** + *glee*] *old-fash*

Gleeful.

1899 (1912) Green *VA Folk-Speech,* The children were all *aglee* at the idea of going to the play.

agley adv |ə'gle| [Scots *agley* squinting, awry]

Awry, off the straight; fig, wrong morally.

1928 Chapman *Happy Mt.* 52 **seTN,** I never aimed to fall in the water and send your fish agley. *Ibid* 181, Only if a matter went agley would he dart out and see to it. **1944** *PADS* 2.38 **VA, NC,** Agley [ə'gle] . . Wrong morally. "Ef Sally don't watch that gal, she's apt to go *agley.*"

aglore adj |ə'gloɚ| [Metath from *galore;* cf **aglory**]

Aplenty, in abundance.

1967–70 *DARE* (Qu. LL9b, . . *"She's got clothes _____."*) Infs **KY85, PA135** |ə'gloɚ|; **NJ3,** Aglore; **NY105,** Aglore—old-fashioned. [All Infs are old]

aglory adj [Blend of **aglore** + *glory*]

Aplenty, in abundance.

1969–70 *DARE* (Qu. LL9b, . . *"She's got clothes _____."*) Infs **KY41,** 85, Aglory.

agnail n Also *angnail* [*EDD* agnail 1; *OED* agnail 3 →1882, ult from OE *angnægl*] *? obs*

A hangnail.

1899 (1912) Green *VA Folk-Speech, Agnail . . .* Angnail. A hangnail. A small piece of partly separated skin at the root of the nail or beside it.

agnate n |'ægnət, –nɛt| [*agate* + intrusive *n*] See also **agnes**
=**agate 1.**
   1969 *DARE* (Qu. EE6d, *Special marbles*) Inf **KY**47, Agnate ['ægnɛt];
KY66, Agnates ['æɪgnəts].

agnes n |'ægnɪs| [Prob from pl of **agnate** + folk-etym personifi-
cation]
A playing marble which is considered special.
   1969 *DARE* (Qu. EE6d) Inf **KY**29, Agnes ['ægnɪs].

Agnes, goodness See **goodness Agnes**

agog adj Cf **antigoglin**
Askew, awry, out of line.
   1969 *DARE* (Qu. MM13, *The table was nice and straight until he came
along and knocked it _____.*) Inf **NY**169, Agog [ə'gag].

agoment n [Prob |'ægə|–as in **agony** or pronc var of *aggravate* +
-ment]
Aggravation, annoyance, frustration.
   1957 Faulkner *Town* 255 **MS,** I bear the worry and the risk and the
agoment for years and years, and I get sixty dollars a head for them
[mules].

agone adj [*OED* under *ago:* "agone has remained dialectally,
and as an archaic and poetic variant."] *old-fash*
Ago.
   1823 Cooper *Pioneers (ADD),* 30 years agone. **1937** in 1944 *ADD*
cn**VA,** 'Bout 10 year agone. **1943** in 1944 *ADD* w**PA,** nW**V.** **1967–68**
DARE (Qu. A17, . . *"That was ten _____."*) Infs **PA**156, **TX**11, Years
agone. [Both Infs are old] **1969** Kantor *MO Bittersweet* 232 **MO,** When
I was a little girl, many many years agone.

agony n
   1 usu in phr *pile on the agony:* Theatrically or emotionally
exaggerated behavior.
   1839 Marryat *Diary* 1.199, Well, I don't go much to theatricals, that's a
fact; but I do think *he piled the agony up a little too high* in that last
scene. **1859** Shillaber *Knitting-Work* 55 **Boston MA,** This was putting
the agony on too thick; it was the grain that broke the back of the camel.
1872 Locke *Struggles Nasby* 309 **Sth,** What in thunder . . did they mean
by pilin on the agony over the Yanks we killed? **1889** Twain *CT Yankee*
203, A band . . opened the proceedings with what seemed to be the crude
first-draft or original agony of the wail "In the Sweet Bye and Bye."
   2 Style, fashion, fad. Esp in phr *put on (the) agony:* to dress
according to the latest fashion; to overdress.
   1906 *DN* 3.124 nw**AR,** It's the latest agony. **1929** *AmSp* 5.130 **ME,**
He's dressed in agony. **1942** McAtee *Dial. Grant Co. IN* 6 (as of 1890s),
Agony, put on: overdress, overact. **1949** Randolph *Ozark Folksongs*
229, [Informant] says it [=song, "Putting on the style"] was in all the
popular songbooks in the late 90's . . . [Lyrics:] Put-ting on the ag-o-ny,
put-ting on the style, What the sty-lish people are a-do-ing all the while.
1950 *WELS* (When a woman puts on her good clothes and tries to look
her best, you say she's _____.) 1 Inf cs**WI,** Putting on the agony,
putting on the style. **1968–70** *DARE* (Qu. W37) Infs **IN**13, **NC**86,
[Reported "heard"] Putting on the agony.

agony (pan) n [Etym unknown]
A pan used to hold fermenting fruit in the making of wine.
   1966 *DARE* Tape **SC**26, Inf: What kinda container put it in? You must
put it in—if you can find a agony, stuff like that. F.W.: Stone? Inf: Yeah.
Somethin' like that. But something wide, you know. It make it be better.
I never have make it in these aluminum things 'cause I don't know how it
is. I make it [in] *agony* pan, sit in [?] agony pan? Boy, that thing—in
three days time. Strain it. If you got a wooden container, now put it [in] a
wooden container.

agreeable adj Pronc-sp *agribble*
   A Form. *? joc*
   1952 Brown *NC Folkl.* 1.514, *Agribble by me . . Agreeable with me;*
suitable, pleasing.
   B Sense. [*OED agreeable* 3, "*Obs.*"]
In agreement.
   1968 *DARE* (Qu. KK67, *When people think alike about something,
"On that particular thing, we _____."*) Inf **CT**6, Are agreeable; (Qu.
KK68, . . *"We agree on most things, but on politics we're _____."*) Inf
WI73, Not agreeable.

agree to agree v phr
To cease quarreling and determine to make amends. Also in neg
constr, *agree not to disagree.*
   1967–70 *DARE* (Qu. Y17) Inf **MI**68, Agree to agree; Infs **MI**68,
CA173, Agreed not to disagree.

agree to disagree v phr
   1 To hold differing opinions while retaining an amicable relationship. **chiefly Nth, West** Cf **agree to agree**
   [**1770** in 1948 *N&Q* 193.172, In a sermon by John Wesley . . I find
'agree to disagree' in quotation marks.] **1942** Berrey–Van den Bark
Amer. Slang 347.2. **1965–70** *DARE* (Qu. KK68, . . *"We agree on most
things, but on politics we're _____."*) 22 Infs, **chiefly Nth, West,**
Agreed to disagree; **MI**15, 46 [FW Sugg], We agree to disagree; (Qu. Y17,
When two people agree to stop fighting . . "I hear they _____.") Infs
CA201, **IN**61, Agreed to disagree; **NH**14, Didn't agree to disagree.
   2 To end a romance. *esp freq among women, joc*
   c1960 *Wilson Coll.* cs**KY,** Agree to disagree . . . A humorous way of
saying that two lovers have broken up. **1965–70** *DARE* (Qu. AA13,
*When two people who have been 'going steady' or were engaged, stop
going together . . "I guess they _____."*) 26 Infs, **scattered,** Agreed to
disagree. [Of all Infs responding to the question, 58% were women; of
those giving this response, 74% were women.]

agregado n [Span] **SW** *? obs*
A farmhand who lives on the farm of another: see quots.
   1871 *Republican Review* (Albuquerque, N. Mex.) 14 Jan. 2/1 *(DA),*
Then again there are others who are simply *agregados* or persons
permitted by the consent of the rest to settle on the lands. **1977** Watts
Dict. Old West, Agregado . . . A farmhand or a man allowed to work for
himself on part of the landowner's soil.

agribble See **agreeable A**

agricultural ant n [See quot 1879]
Any of var western **harvester ants,** but esp *Pogonomyrmex
barbatus* of the Southwest.
   1868 *Amer. Naturalist* 2.157, Such structures [beaver dams] are remarkable . . reminding us of the intelligence shown by the Agricultural
Ant of Texas. **1879** McCook *Nat. Hist. Ag. Ant* 33 **TX,** One of these
appears to be the . . ant-rice, to which Lincecum has given such wide
notoriety by the statement that it is actually planted, cultivated, and
harvested by the ants, who have received the name "Agricultural Ants"
from this fact. *Ibid* 68, It has been stated that the flat disk seems to be the
normal form of the agricultural ant nest. **1911** *Century Dict., Agricultural ant,* a kind of ant which clears the ground of verdure in the vicinity
of its nest. Such a species is *Pogonomyrmex barbatus* of Texas, which
cuts down all the herbage within ten or twelve feet of its nest. **1935** Natl.
Geog. Soc. *Insect Friends* 136, From the train window the traveler in the
Southwest sees large ant hills dotted over the desert. These are usually
nests of the bearded agricultural ants, Pogonomyrmex. **1964** Borror–
DeLong *Intro. Insects* 578, The ants of the genera *Pogonomyrmex* and
Pheidole are often called harvester ants or agricultural ants; they feed on
seeds and store seeds in their nests.

agrillo n [MexSpan, from Span *agrilla* sorrel] **SW**
   1 =**agarita.**
   1937 U.S. Forest Serv. *Range Plant Hdbk.* B99, *Odostemon fremontii . .* and *O. Haematocarpa* are large shrubs characteristic of brush types
on dry slopes and in ridges of the piñon-juniper belt in the Southwest . . . Both species are known in the Southwest as algerita, agarita,
agrillo and yellowwood. **1957** Jaeger *N. Amer. Deserts* 266, *Three-leaf
Barberry* or *Argillo* [sic] . . . The round, red to bluish-black fruit has
several seeds and is edible. **1960** Vines *Trees SW* 273, Vernacular
names are . . Algerita, Agrillo, and Palo Amarillo. The red, acid berries
make excellent jellies and wine.
   2 =**sumac** (here: *Rhus aromatica* and *R. microphylla*).
   1960 Vines *Trees SW* 630, *Rhus aromatica . . .* Other vernacular
names are . . Quail-bush, Agrillo, and Lemita. The acid fruit is eaten.
Ibid 637, *Rhus microphylla . . .* Vernacular names are . . Correosa,
Agrito, and Agrillo. The reddish orange hairy drupe is edible, but sour.

agrito n [Span "sorrel"] **SW**
   1 =**agarita,** esp *Berberis trifoliata.*
   1892 *DN* 1.243 **TX,** *Agrito.* **1936** Whitehouse *TX Flowers* 30, Agarita.
Texas Barberry . . known also as agrito (meaning "little sour"). **1960**
Vines *Trees SW* 273, Vernacular names are . . Agrito, Algerita [etc.].
The red, acid berries make excellent jellies and wine.

2 =**sumac** (here: *Rhus microphylla*).

1960 Vines *Trees SW* 637, Vernacular names are Winged Sumac, . . Agrito, and Agrillo. The reddish orange hairy drupe is edible, but sour.

3 =**wood sorrel** (here: *Oxalis corniculata* and *O. Dichondraefolia*).

1970 Correll *Plants TX* 895, *Oxalis dichondraefolia . . . Agrito. Ibid* 896, *Oxalis corniculata . . . Creeping lady's-sorrel, agrito, jocoyote.*

4 =**bee brush** (here: *Aloysia lycioides*).

1960 Vines *Trees SW* 888, Vernacular names are Bee-brush, Bee-blossom, Agrito [etc.].

agropelter n [*agro-* of fields, soil + *pelter,* one who pelts] *joc*

1969 Sorden *Lumberjack Lingo* 2 **Gt Lakes,** *Agropelter*—A horrible animal that lived in hollow trees mostly in Minnesota. Any lumberjack walking near its abode was killed by a falling limb.

agrown See **a** inert vowel **1**

aguardiente n, also attrib Also sp *agua ardiente, aguadiente, aguadinte, aguardent, aquadiente, aquadinte, aquedent, argadent, awerdenty* [Span "brandy"] **chiefly SW, Gulf States** Addit exx in *DAE*

Any strong alcoholic drink.

1818 *N.-Eng. Palladium* (Boston) 28 Sept 3/2 *(DA),* Isaac McLellan & Co . . . Have for sale . . . 100 pipes Spanish Rum or Aquedent, entitled to debenture. **1825** in 1970 Paulding *Jrl.* 11, Our host indulged himself freely with the use of aquadiente. **1834** Pike *Prose Sketches* 103 **NM,** The first glass of the aguadiente, or white brandy, or of the vino del Paso, generally touched her lips. **1847** *Times–Picayune* (New Orleans LA) 12 Sept 2/1 *(DA),* Many of the Mexicans were pretty well *corned,* [for] . . *aguadinte* was plentiful. **1850** Garrard *Wah-to-yah* 193 **NM,** I swar' you look tired; come in and take a 'horn'—a little of the *awerdenty.* **1854** (1932) Bell *Log TX–CA Trail* 309, The most unpalatable article of aquadinte is sold by the pound . . at the rate of one dollar for a libro. **1857** in 1941 *AmSp* 16.265 **CA,** Aguardiente, Brandy. **1892** *DN* 1.187 **TX,** *Aguardiente.* **1941** Faherty *Big Old Sun* 107 *(Hench Coll.)* **FL,** I'll go with you to the beer places. We'll set and drink argadent rum, and dance. **1967** Will *Dredgeman* 28 **FL,** "We ain't got nothin' here but steam engine oil and that ain't scarcely fittin' for drinkin' purposes." "Steam engine hell! This here is tonsil oil! Cape Sable aguardent!" **1968** Adams *Western Words* 4, *Agua ardiente. Ibid* 10, *Awerdenty*—In trapping, an early name for whisky. Undoubtedly a corruption of *aguardiente.*

ague n, often pl |'eˌgju, 'egˌju|, occas |'eˌgu|; in **Sth, Midl** *esp among older speakers* |'egə(r), 'ɛgə(r)|—See Map; in **N Midl** occas |'ægˌju, 'egˌju|; sp-pronc |eg| freq among those for whom this is a book-word only.   Pronc-spp *ager, aguer, agur, agy, eager*

A Forms.

1794 (1914) Clark *Jrl.* 435 **VA,** A sickly Camp mostly eagers & fevers. **1805** in 1956 Eliason *Tarheel Talk* 306 **NC,** Ager. **1823** Cooper *Pioneers* 1.164 **nNY,** I've been watching the deer-licks, when the fever-an-agy seeds was to be seen in it, as plain . . as you can see the rattlesnakes on old Crumhorn. **1837** Sherwood *Gaz. GA* 69 [In list of Provincialisms to be avoided], *Ager,* for ague. **1845** Kirkland *Western Clearings* 69 **MI,** *You* thought he had the agur, but I know'd well enough

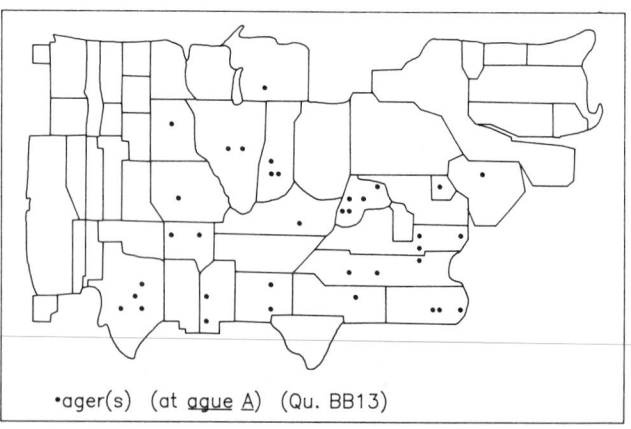

•ager(s) (at ague A) (Qu. BB13)

what ailded him. **1891** *DN* 1.162 **cNY,** [egu, egər]. **1894** *DN* 1.327 **NJ** [eɪgər]. **1907** *DN* 3.228 **nwAR, seMO,** *Aguer, ager.* **1908** *DN* 3.285 **eAL, wGA. 1914** Furman *Sight* 61 **eKY,** And though my heart shuck like a ager, I laid down on that table same as a soldier. **1922** *DN* 5.183 **GA. 1923** *DN* 5.200 **swMO. 1950** *WELS (Other words for chills and fever)* **throughout WI,** 13 Infs, Ague; 4 Infs, Ague ['ɛgju]; 2 Infs ['eg]; 1 Inf, Fever and ague. **1964** Faulkner *As I Lay Dying* 179 **MS,** "You wont help me?" Jewel says, them white eyes of hisn kind of blaring and his face shaking like he had a aguer. **1965–70** *DARE* (Qu. BB13, . . *Chills and fever*) 34 Infs, **chiefly Sth, Midl,** Ager(s); **IN**13, Ager, agers chills ['ɛgɚ, 'ɛgɚz čɪlz]. [Of all Infs responding to the question, 68% were old; of those giving this response, 88% were old.]

B Senses.

1 A violent fever, esp malarial fever, usu accompanied by severe chills; symptoms associated with such a fever.   *somewhat old-fash*

1650 (1965) Bradstreet *Tenth Muse* 36, Unto diseases not inclin'd as ye: /Nor cold, nor hot, Ague nor Plurisie. **1786** (1925) Washington *Diaries* 3.109 **VA,** Taken with an Ague . . which . . confined me to the House till evening. **1836** (1930) Phelps *Diary* 229 **IL,** My two youngest children had the ague and fevor every other day. **1871** Philadelphia *Age* 3 April *Correspondence* (in 1872 Schele De Vere *Americanisms*), Lansing, Michigan, is a very healthy locality for the *ague.* It comes creeping up a fellow's back like a ton of wild oats, goes crawling through his joints like iron spikes, and is followed by a fever, which prohibits the patient from thinking of anything but the Independent Order of Good Templars. It isn't the every-other-day kind, but gets up with a man at daylight and sleeps in the small of his back all night. His teeth feel about six inches long, his joints wobble like a loose wagon-wheel, and the shakes are so steady that one can't hold any kind of conversation except by putting in dashes. **1946** *PADS* 6.16 **eNC** (as of 1900–10), *Hard ague . . .* A severe chill . . . Common. **1965–70** *DARE* (Qu. BB13, . . *Chills and fever*) 199 Infs, **throughout US,** Ague; 35 Infs, **chiefly Sth, Midl,** Ager(s); **ME**5, **WA**6, Fever and ague; **MA**5, Ague and bones; **CA**87, Dumb ague; **MN**12, Fever ague; **OH**15, Shaking of ague. [Of all Infs responding to the question, 68% were old, 8% young; of those giving this response, 80% were old, 2% young.]

2 A general feeling of discomfort.

1966–70 *DARE* (Qu. BB5) Inf **WA**18, Ague; **KY**94, Pains and ague.

3 =**buck fever 1.** See also **buck ague**

1935 *AmSp* 10.12 [In gangster argot c1900], *Ague.* Loss of nerve under stress; *cold feet.* Obs. **1967** *DARE* (Qu. P36, *When a hunter sees a deer or other game animal and gets so excited he can't shoot, he has_____*) Inf **AL**17, Ague; **LA**29, **SC**43, **WV**5, Agers.

ague bark n [From its common use in treating **ague**]

The **hoptree** and/or its bark.

1889 *Century Dict.,* Ague-bark . . . The bark of the wafer-ash, *Ptelea trifoliata.* **1931** Clute *Common Plants* 121, Among the other plants reputed to be a cure for malaria were . . the ague-bark or quinine tree. **1973** Meyer *Amer. Folk Med.* 20, There were also ague bark *(Ptelea trifoliata) . .* and other plants for ague.

ague cake n [*OED* →1801] *? obs*

An enlarged spleen resulting from ague.

1775 (1962) Romans *Nat. Hist. FL* 242, The use of bark is generally blamed as productive of dropsy; jaundice, the ague cake, and other inveterate chronical disorders . . . [Footnote: Ague cake] A hardness in the region of the spleen, one of the consequences of long continued fevers. **1832** O'Ferrall *Ramble* 216 **sMS,** I have seen many, particularly females, who had immense swellings or protuberances on their stomachs, which they denominate 'ague-cakes.' **1899** (1912) Green *VA Folk-Speech,* Aguecake . . . An enlarged and hardened spleen, the consequence of intermittent fever.

ague-faced adj

1912 *DN* 3.570 **wIN,** *Ague-faced . . .* Twitchy. "Well, why doesn't the ague-faced snob say something?"

aguefied adj [**ague** + *-ified*] Cf **agered (up)**

Pained, stiff, sore, as with ague.

1939 *Hench Coll.* 1 Jan, I heard a brakeman in the Washington, D.C., Union Station say, "I've been aguefied in my joints these cold nights."

ague grass n Also *ague root,* rarely *~horn* [From its supposed efficacy in treating **ague**]

=**colicroot 2.**

1687 in 1739 Royal Soc. London *Philos. Trans.* 41.158 **VA**, Some call it *Ague-grass,* other [sic] *Ague-root,* others *Star-grass.* **1876** Hobbs *Bot. Hdbk.* 2, Ague grass, Unicorn root, Aletris farinosa. **1931** Clute *Common Plants* 121, Among other plants reputed to be a cure for malaria were the ague-root or ague-grass. **1966** *DARE* Wildfl QR Pl. 16 Inf **MI**57, Ague root. **1971** Krochmal *Appalachia Med. Plants* 40, Ague grass, ague horn, agueroot . . . In Appalachia a mixture of roots and brandy is drunk as a treatment for rheumatism.

aguer See **ague**

ague root See **ague grass**

ague tree n [See quot 1917; *OED* →1753]
=**sassafras**.
   1900 Lyons *Plant Names* 335, Sassafras . . . Ague-tree. **1917** (1923) Rogers *Trees Worth Knowing* 131, The name "Ague Tree" originated with the use of sassafras bark tea as a stimulant that warmed and brought out the perspiration freely for victims of the malarial "ague," or "chills and fever." **1971** Krochmal *Appalachia Med. Plants* 228.

agueweed n [From its supposed efficacy in treating **ague**]
1 =**boneset 1** (here: *Eupatorium perfoliatum*).
   1828 Rafinesque *Med. Flora* 174, *Eupatorium Perfoliatum* . . . Vulgar Names . . Agueweed. **1907** Lyons *Plant Names* 189. **1971** Krochmal *Appalachia Med. Plants* 118, Ague-weed . . . In Appalachia, a tea made of the leaves is used to treat coughs and consumption, and it is used as a laxative.
2 =**gentian** (here: *Gentiana quinquefolia*.).
   1889 *Century Dict.* 119/2, Ague-weed . . . 2. A species of gentian, *Gentiana quinqueflora*. **1901** Lounsberry *S. Wild Flowers* 428, Through these parts of the country the mountain people call it . . ague-weed on account of the extract they make from its roots and employ for curing fever. **1931** Clute *Common Plants* 121, Among other plants reputed to be a cure for malaria . . the ague-weed (*Gentiana quinquefolia*). **1967** Borland *Hill Country* 298 **nwCT**, Close by, in the edge of the thicker woods, we found a number of lesser gentians commonly called ague-weed.
3 =**colicroot 2** (here: *Aletris farinosa*).
   1959 Carleton *Index Herb. Plants* 2, Ague Weed: Aletris farinosa.

aguirite See **agarita**

agur See **ague**

agured See **agered (up)**

agur forty See **aggie forti(e)s**

agvice See **exwice**

agy adj See **agey**

agy n See **ague**

Ah See **I**

-ah See **-a**

-ah intj Also sp *-aah*
   A syllable conventionally added for emphasis after words in Primitive Baptist sermon style: see quots.
   1843 (1916) Hall *New Purchase* 386 **IN**, Fervent heat-ah!—and the trumpit a soundin-ah!—and the dead arisin-ah! . . . Sinner-sinner-sinner-ah! **1871** Eggleston *Hoosier Schoolmaster* 105 **IN**, In reporting a single specimen passage of Mr. Bosaw's sermon, I . . shall give that which can be vouched for. "You see, my respective hearers," he began . . . "My respective hearers-ah, you see-ah as how-ah as my tex'-ah says that the ox-ah knoweth his owner-ah." **1931** *PMLA* 46.1303 **sAppalachians**, Intensely hortatory and polemic, the preacher's words are spoken rapidly and often incoherently. In a sing-song fashion, *-ah* is added at the end of most clauses and sentences. **1942** in 1959 Lomax *Rainbow Sign* 189 **nMS** [Black], O Lord, we need you this evenin, /Sin is causin men to die—AAH /Hitler needs you this evenin—AAH /Hitler needs you this evenin—AAH /You know the world . . . There is no shame here—AAH.

ah-ah n [Prob repr a "grunt" of negation]
   A stupid person.
   1928 McKay *Home to Harlem* 30 **NYC** [Black], Oh what a big Ah-Ah I was! *Ibid* 27, I was a fool not to go back right then . . . A grand Ah-Ah I is. Feet in mah hands!

ahana intj |ɑhɑnɑ| For varr see quots [Haw, in which this is used as a taunting intj and as a verb, to tease; perh ult from Engl

aha!: see quot 1938] **HI**
   See quots.
   1938 Reinecke *Hawaiian Loanwords,* Ahana, ahana kokole, ahana kohole, ahanakole, ahanagole, ahanagogole, ahahanakole, . . ahanka . . . [Reinecke: Of unknown origin; possibly not Hawaiian. Lee suggests that *ahana* may have originated from Eng. *aha!* with *na* added for its rhythmic appeal.] Look out!, You'll catch it!—a warning to naughty children, mostly confined to childish speech. It is sometimes used in a derisive rhyme . . . V[ery] F[requent]. **1972** Carr *Da Kine Talk* 86 **HI**, *Ahahana* or *ahana*. Shame on you!

A-harrow n Also called **A-drag** See also **V-harrow**
   A harrow with an A-shaped frame.
   1868 IA State Ag. Soc. *Report for 1867* 169, As soon as the corn appears in the row, drag with an A harrow with the front tooth out. **1872** (1876) Knight *Amer. Mech. Dict.* 2.1068/1, The letter 'A' harrow . . is very handy in ground from which stumps have not been eradicated. It is easily lifted by the corner or by the bow. **1907** Bailey *Cyclop. Amer. Ag.* 1.394/2, Later, a cross-arm was attached and the implement was known as the 'A' harrow. **c1960** *Wilson Coll.* **csKY**, A-harrow . . a home-made harrow shaped like the capital A. Sometimes it is called a V-harrow, looked at from the other direction. **1966–70** *DARE* (Qu. L20, *The implement used in a field after it's been plowed to break up the lumps*) Infs **OK**52, **SC**26, A-harrow; **IL**142, A-harrow—wooden beams in an A-frame, with spikes driven through; **OK**43, An A-harrow (home-made) used to be commonly used for breaking up new ground. It was made with eight-inch spikes run through logs or four-by-fours. This was used around stumps, etc.; very maneuverable; (Qu. L18) Inf **AR**56, A-harrow; (Qu. L25), Inf **OK**52, A-harrow.

‡ahead on adv
   Head on.
   1969 *DARE* (Qu. KK53, *When one thing suddenly hits hard against something else: "He ran ___ into a car."*) Inf **NC**72, Ahead-on.

ahere See **a** inert vowel **4**

ahi n, also attrib [Haw] **HI**
   A tuna (*Thunnus* spp).
   1933 Bryan *Hawaiian Nature* 226, In Hawaiian waters these include the skipjack or shore bonito; the tunny, the albacore, and the yellow-finned albacore, all three called ahi. **1955** Day *HI People* 254, Smaller sampans, usually called "ahi" boats, may range for a thousand miles and stay out for days at a time . . . The crew use aku to catch mackerel, which in turn become bait for the ahi (the prized yellowfin tuna or albacore). **1960** Gosline–Brock *Hawaiian Fishes* 260, The Hawaiian name "'ahi" is used for all species of large tunas. **1967** *Honolulu Star–Bulletin* (HI) 31 May F 1/4, Ahi . . Tuna . . There are three kinds—yellow fin, blue fin, albacore. Best for sashimi. Also good fried or boiled.

ahina adj [See quot] **HI**
   1967 Reinecke–Tsuzaki *Hawaiian Loanwords,* Ahina; ['ɑhinɑ]; . . [Probably a shortened form of *'ɑhinahina,* very light blue-gray or gray.] Used in the phrase "ahina pants," blue denim trousers, which are *ahinahina* in color after a few washings. F[requent].

ahind prep, adv |ə'haɪn(d), (ə)'haɪnt| Pronc-sp *ahint* [Engl dial: see *EDD* for exx, chiefly from nEngl, Scotl] **chiefly Midl old-fash**
   Behind.
   1843 (1916) Hall *New Purchase* 81 **IN**, Lay down ahind an ole-log. **1884** Murfree *TN Mts.* 250, He war a-ridin' a-hint him. **1934** *WV Review* Dec 78/1, Sir Walter Scott's stories contain a number of our commonly used archaic words . . [including] *gin* for *if, ahint* for *behind.* **1952** Brown *NC Folkl.* 1.514, *Ahint.* **1958** *PADS* 29.6 **se,cwTN**, *Ahint:* Behind. Rep. from Hamilton [Co]. Pronounced *hine* [haɪn] rep. from Perry [Co]. **1969** *DARE* (Qu. MM8, *A bad housekeeper sweeps the dirt either under the rug or ___ the door.*) Inf **MA**58, Ahind—old-fashioned.

ahiu n [Haw *'ahiu* wild, untamed] **HI** *? not fully naturalized*
   A wild and dangerous horse.
   1967 *DARE* (Qu. K42) Inf **HI**3, Ahiu [ɑ'hiu].

ahkio n, also attrib |'ɑkio| Also sp *akio* [See quot 1955] **AK**
   A type of light cargo sled.
   1955 U.S. Arctic Info. Center *Gloss.* 2, Ahkio . . A Finnish term, derived from the Lappish word 'akja,' for an open, canoe-shaped sled. Diffused through Scandinavia, the ahkio was adopted by the military as an item of equipment for over-snow movement. The form currently

used by the U.S. Army is constructed of light wood, aluminum, or fiberglass; it weighs approximately 25 pounds. Loaded with 100 to 200 pounds, it can be pulled easily by a man on skis or snowshoes. **1973** *Fairbanks Daily News–Miner* (AK) 27 Nov, [Advt:] Do you need a new Akio Sled? We build them tough [of fiberglass]. **1974** *Fairbanks News–Miner* (AK) 10 Dec, [Advt:] New *Ahkios* (cargo sleds) 6 different models ranging from 4'–8' . . shallow and high sidewall models.

Ahlabahm See **Alabama**

ahn See **iron**

aho n |ɑho| [Haw] **HI**

    1967 Reinecke–Tsuzaki *Hawaiian Loanwords, Aho* . . . A cord, esp. fishcord or, among children, kite-string.

ahold n |ə'hold, ə'holt| Pronc-sp *aholt* [Prob *a* indef art, now usu reduced to inert vowel + *hold* grasp; *OEDS* "colloq. or *dial.*"; *W3* "*dial.*"]

    After such verbs as *catch, get, lay* or *take:* a firm grasp. Also fig. **1872** Eggleston *End of the World* 77, You gripped a-holt of the truth. **1884** (1958) Twain *Huck. Finn* 70 [Black speaker], I swum to de stern uv it, en tuck aholt. **1905** *DN* 3.58 **eNE**, Catch-a-holt. **1925** (1958) Hemingway *In Our Time* 70 **MI**, Nick dropped his wrist. 'Listen,' Ad Francis said. 'Take ahold again.' **1933** Rawlings *South Moon* 141 **FL**, I'll git aholt o' Syl Jacklin and Luke Saunders. **1961** Adams *Old-Time Cowhand* 269 **SW**, He starts right in tryin' to flank that yearlin'. The boys all grab a-holt, too. **1965–70** *DARE* (Qu. V5b, . . *"Before anybody else gets it, I'm going to* _____ *this."*) Infs **AR**37, **IL**117, **NY**82, Get ahold of; **WV**5, 13, Lay ahold of; (Qu. DD13) Inf **MD**30, It's got ahold of him and he can't let go; (Qu. KK29) Inf **GA**31, Took ahold; (Qu. BB40, . . *"What do you suppose* _____ *him?"*) Inf **NJ**69, Got ahold to; (Qu. LL11a) Inf **MO**11, Hard to git ahold of. **1966** *Wilson Coll.* **csKY**, He got aholt of me. **1968** *DARE* Tape **OH**69, The younger women don't take a-holt to it. They'd rather do other things than quilt.

ahold of adj phr [**ahold** n]

    After nouns which it modifies: having a firm grasp upon. **1879** *Scribner's Mth.* May 17/1, The drone makes no resistance except to pull back and try to get away; but . . with one bee a-hold of your collar or the hair of your head, and another a-hold of each arm or leg . . the odds are greatly against you. **1887** *Century Illustr. Mag.* 35.110 **LA**, "De plow gang had to be in de field long befo' sun up, . . ebery man a-hold of his plow." **1954** Roberts *I Bought Dog* 6 **KY**, And the giant aholt of him whispered and said, "We're goin to throw you up on top of the wall."

aholehole n Also *ahole* [Haw]

    A large-eyed, silvery, inshore food fish (*Kuhlia sandvicensis*), with a single dorsal fin, which is found chiefly in the Hawaiian Islands. **1926** Pan-Pacific Research Inst. *Jrl.* 1.9, Kuhlia sandvicensis . . . Aholehole. **1960** Gosline–Brock *Hawaiian Fishes* 159, The aholehole is very adaptable, and there is little that it does not feed on. **1967** *Honolulu Star–Bulletin* (HI) 31 May F1/4, Aholehole. **1967** *DARE* (Qu. P1) Inf **HI**4, Aholehole—fresh and salt water. **1971** Pukui–Elbert *Hawaiian Dict.* 7/2, The mature stage is āhole, the young stage āholehole. Because of the meaning of *hole*, to strip away, this fish was used for magic, as to chase away evil spirits and for love magic.

aholt See **ahold**

ahoo adv Also sp *ahuh* [Engl dial *ahuh* awry: cf *EDD*]

    Aslant, out of plumb: see quots. **1899** (1912) Green *VA Folk-Speech, Ahoo* . . . Ahuh; when anything is out of perpendicular; or lopsided; or a wheel runs not true, it is said to be *ahoo*, "all *ahoo*." **1952** Brown *NC Folkl.* 1.514, Ahoo . . . Awry— Chapel Hill.

ahorse(back) adv [**a** prep¹ **1a** + *horse(back)*] *somewhat old-fash* See also **afoot or (a)horseback**

    On or by horseback. **1669** in 1884 *Archives of MD* 2.160, Sett a Beggar a horse back & he will Ride, soe sett a childe a horse back & he will be afrade to guide the horse. **1834** Smith *Letters Jack Downing* 131, And then get on to the horses and ride awhile a horseback. **1857** Willis *Paul Fane* 74 **IN**, One of those men recognized as a class in the West, and defined as "born a-horseback." **1946** Faulkner *Sound & Fury* App 3 **MS**, To proceed in peace, by whatever means he and his people saw fit, afoot or ahorse. **1967** *DARE* Tape **AZ**4, Everything I ever done was ahorseback. **1967–70** *DARE*

(Qu. JJ15b, . . *A person who seems . . very stupid: "He doesn't know* _____ .*"*) Inf **MI**55, Whether he's afoot or a-horseback; (Qu. OO27a, . . *"When she was a girl she* _____ .*"*) Infs **KY**53, **VA**49, Rode a-horseback.

ahrn See **iron**

ahter See **after**

ahue See **a** prep¹ **4**

ahuh See **ahoo**

ahun See **iron**

ahungry adj [**a** prep¹ or **a** inert vowel **6** + *hungry*]

    Hungry, troubled with hunger. **1926** Vollmer *Sun-Up* 13 **wNC**, The most of 'em wuz a hungry. **1933** Miller *Lamb in His Bosom* 91 **GA**, Jasper found that he was not a-hungry.

ahunky See **hunky**

ahupuaa n [See quot 1967] **HI**

    A unit of land: see quots and cf **ili**. **1954–60** Hance *Hawaiian Sugar*, Ahupuaa . . one of the smaller land divisions of a kalana or district. **1967** Reinecke–Tsuzaki *Hawaiian Loanwords*, Ahupuaa; [ahupua'a] . . [Reinecke-Tsuzaki: *Ahu*, collection, heap of stones, or altar; and *pua'a*, hog.] The Hawaiian unit of land, often extending from the sea to some place high up the mountain and having roughly the shape of a sector of a circle . . . The usual word by which it is translated is *land*.

ai' See **aunt** A2

aiah n¹ See **air** n

aiah n² See **hour**

aiah adv See **ayuh**

aideah See **idea**

aidge See **edge**

aig See **egg** n, v

aige See **edge**

aihue adj, v [Haw *'ai* food + *hue* to steal] **HI**

    1967 Reinecke–Tsuzaki *Hawaiian Loanwords, Aihue;* ['aihue] . . 1. Thievish. 2. To thieve. F[requent].

aikane n |aɪ'kɑne| [Haw] **HI**

    A friend. **1938** Reinecke *Hawaiian Loanwords, Aikane* . . . 1. A friend . . . 2. An intimate friend. F[requent]. **1954–60** Hance *Hawaiian Sugar*, Aikane, . . Friend. **1967** *DARE* (Qu. II1) Inf **HI**1, Aikane [ˌaɪ'kɑne].

aikie(s) intj |'eki(z)| Also sp *akey(s), achies* [Etym uncertain; perh from Engl dial ['ekl] 'equal' or *hake* 'To hanker or gape after' (*EDD*); discussion in *AmSp* 56.28–30] **chiefly NYC** Cf **achins, eggies, yakers,** and *DS* II8

    A child's expression used to lay claim to something or to demand equal division of something found; also, a response to such a demand. Hence also *no aikie(s)*. **1934** Roth *Call it Sleep* 364 **NYC**, "We're goin fishin'." Maxey drew out a large black gob of grease. "On Tent' Stritt. We're potners. We seen id foist." . . And with a "No akey! No akey!" flung over their shoulders, the two partners raced toward Avenue D. *Ibid* 366, "Yuh god it! Betcha million! Slow! Slow!" Maxey murmured exultingly. **1956** *AmSp* 31.37, Then there is the negative form, . . in which . . the claimant fends off all other claims, down to the smallest: *fen dibs, fen shackies, no dibs, no aikies, no chips, no divvies,* and . . *no halveens. Ibid* 38, Aikies, evreese, and possy . . I got from college students from New York City, Tennessee, and Maryland, respectively. **1968** *DARE* FW Addit **NY**34, Achies on the toilet—I'm the first one, when there is a line up. **1970** *DARE* File **Brooklyn NY** (as of c1915), "I want to go akeys ['ekiz] on that," expresses desire for equal division of something found. Also "no akeys," meaning a refusal. **1981** *AmSp* 56.31 **Chicago IL** (as of 1920s–30s), This form was most often used by a possessor in acceding to a claim, for example: "Gimme some!" "OK, |'eki 'ekiz|, here's half."

ail along v phr Also *ail around*

    To be or seem to be slightly ill.

1933 *Sun* (Baltimore MD) 26 Oct 16/8 *(Hench Coll.),* [In an advt] Low mentally and physically. Pepless . . irritable . . yet nothing really wrong . . *just ailing along.* **1967** *DARE* (Qu. BB41) Inf **LA8,** He's been ailing around for a week.

aild v tr [Back-formation from **ailded**] *old-fash*
To ail: to make mildly ill, to trouble or upset.

1903 *DN* 2.305 **seMO,** I don't know what ailds the child. **1906** *DN* 3.114 **sIN,** What ailds the boy?

ailded v, past tense and past pple Pronc-sp *ailted* [*ail* + *-ed* past tense marker + *-ed* 1] Cf **aild**
Ailed.

1845 Kirkland *Western Clearings* 69 **MI,** I know'd well enough what ailded him. **1887** (1895) Robinson *Uncle Lisha* 41 **wVT,** Then I god daown on all fours, an' peeked in to see what the matter was ailded it. **1914** *DN* 4.102 **KS,** What ailted him? **1917** *DN* 4.387 **neOH,** Ailded, v. Preterit of *ail,* though *aild* was not used, so far as I know, for the present. "He didn't know what *ailded* him." **1923** *DN* 5.200 **swMO.** **1927** *AmSp* 2.347 **cwWV,** *Ailded* (v.t.), used only as the past tense of the verb ail. "Sally didn't know what ailded her mother." **1929** *AmSp* 5.16 **Ozarks.** **1938** Rawlings *Yearling* 89 **nFL,** I don't figger there was nothin' ailded me but green brierberries. *Ibid* 207, You ain't et your biscuit nor drinked your milk, boy. What ailded 'em? **c1960** *Wilson Coll.* **csKY,** What ailed (or ailded) him? **1965–70** *DARE* (Qu. BB40, . . *"All of a sudden he got up and left. What do you suppose _____ him?")* Inf **NC82,** Ailded. **1967–68** *DARE* Tape **GA25,** Alum was good for anythin' what ailded you.

ailish adj [*ail* v intr + *-ish*] See also **aily**
Slightly ill.

1941 Faulkner *Men Working* 26 **MS,** "Maw's kind of ailing." "Hot weather, I 'spec'," said Mrs. Taylor. "Hit makes us all feel ailish and complainy sort of."

ailted See **ailded**

ailwife See **alewife**

aily adj See also **ailish**
Slightly ill.

1952 Brown *NC Folkl.* 1.514 **wNC,** *Aily* . . . Not well, ailing, complaining. **c1960** *Wilson Coll.* **csKY.**

aim v *formerly widespread, now chiefly Sth, S Midl*
Usu foll by infin: To intend, to plan.

1650 (1965) Bradstreet *Tenth Muse* 74 **MA,** Not so content, but aiming to be great. **1874** Long *Wild-Fowl* 15 *(DAE),* I have aimed to instruct rather than to amuse. **1895** *DN* 1.370 **seKY, eTN.** **1902** *DN* 2.228 **sIL.** **1903** *DN* 2.305 **seMO.** **1904** *DN* 2.316 **nwAR.** **1908** *DN* 3.285 **eAL, wGA.** **1912** *DN* 3.570 **wIN.** **1917** *DN* 4.407 **wNC, AZ, IL, KY, MA, ND, neOH, SC.** **1923** *DN* 5.200 **swMO.** **1926** *DN* 5.385 **ME,** "I aim to do it sometime." Obsol[escent]. **1926** Roberts *Time of Man* 310 **KY,** He did not aim that his child should want some small thing and not have it. **1958** Humphrey *Home from the Hill* 99 **TX,** I aimed to get up a little ahead and get a bite of breakfast. **1958** *PADS* 29.6 **TN,** Comments from informants, however, show the use *he was aimin to go* as uncultivated. **c1960** *Wilson Coll.* **csKY,** "He's a-aiming to plant peas there." . . Very commonly used. **1965** *DARE* (Qu. JJ38) Inf **MS61,** Didn't aim to do it. **1967** *DARE* FW Addit **LA6,** "I aimed to go back to the house, but . . ." Common usage. **1969** *DARE* Tape **NC56,** He didn't aim to let her go when it was real bad.

aimbition n Pronc-sp for *ambition* [Perh **aim** + *ambition*]
1941 *Amer. Mercury* 52.663/2 **nGA,** Since the day her parents brought her to these mountains from North Carolina . . she's never seen beyond them. "Th' aimbition of my life is ter see Dalton (thirty-five miles west.)"

ain' See **ain't** v[1]

aina See **ainna**

aingern See **onion**

ainna interrog exclam Usu |'ɛnə| Also sp *aina, enna* [Contr of *ain't it,* infl in its use as a tag question by Ger *nicht wahr*] **chiefly German settlement areas** *somewhat old-fash, occas joc* Cf **ain't v[2], enty, inso, isn't it**
As a tag question: Isn't that so? Don't you agree?

1947 *WELS Suppl.* **Milwaukee WI,** Will you please explain Milwaukee's dialect in ending numerous statements with a sound something like

enna? **1950** *WELS (Words and expressions meaning "Don't you agree?")* 12 Infs, **chiefly eWI, esp Milwaukee,** Ain(n)a ['ɛnə]; 1 Inf, **seWI,** Enna—Polish version of Milwaukee "aina." **1968–69** *DARE* (Qu. NN3, . . *"She's a nice-looking woman, _____?")* Infs **CT25, NJ57, 61,** Ainna; **WI48,** Ainna hey [Inf heard]. **1976** *St. Louisan* Oct 60/2, But there is one [old-world] word that is heard occasionally on the south side [of St. Louis]: *aina.* It's a contraction of *ain't it*—("hot today, *aina?"*)—and it is used by an aging population.

ainshen See **ancient**

ain't v[1] Usu |e(ɪ)nt|, occas |ɛnt, int| Also sp *ain', aint, a'n't, an't, ant, een't, ent* [Contr of *am not, are not* (*OED* 1778 → *"dial."*); used also for *is not, have not, has not,* and among Blacks also for *do not, does not*] Generally considered non-std, though some cultivated speakers in **Mid Atl, S Atl** use sense **1** in conversation with peers (see quot 1953). Rare in writing unless used facetiously or to indicate educ status of a speaker. See also **hain't** v

1 Am not, are not, is not. See also **be** C1
1723 *New-Engl. Courant* (Boston MA) 16–23 Sept 1/1, An't you an impudent, saucy, sorry Fellow. **1818** Fessenden *Ladies Monitor* 171 **VT,** Some provincial words and phrases which ought to be avoided . . . *Ant,* for am not. **1835** Crockett *Account* 114 **TN,** This an't the way with private people. **1860** Holmes *Professor* 151 **NEng,** And marryin' a'n't for them. **1867** in 1919 Hale *Letters* 31 **Boston MA,** Ain't it fun to be Consuls. **1890** *DN* 1.67 **KY,** Ain't [eɪnt]. For *am not, is not, are not* [also in New England]: as "I aint goin'," . . . Well nigh universally used here and farther south. **1908** *DN* 3.285 **eAL, wGA.** **1922** Gonzales *Black Border* 287 **sSC, GA coasts,** [Gullah glossary], Ain' . . Is not, isn't. **1953** Atwood *Survey of Verb Forms* 31, Nearly one third of the cultured informants in the M[iddle] A[tlantic] S[tates] and the S[outh] A[tlantic] S[tates] use *ain't I?,* usually alongside some other form. There are about a dozen occurrences of the form *een't* /int/, nearly all in the coastal areas of Va. and N.C. . . Informants in the South seem to be least inhibited about the use of *ain't,* those in R.I. and the New York City area, most inhibited. **1954** *Harder Coll.* **cwTN,** Ain't goin' git stomped for woolly worm [said by one who needs a haircut]. **1966** *DARE* Tape **ME26,** They ain't many that will. **1967–69** *DARE* FW Addits **MS,** Ain't fittin—It is not proper or appropriate; **nw Forks NY,** Ain't much of a hand for listening—common; **GA25,** Ain't never done nary thing; **LA14,** "You ain't never." That's the way we use ain't around here—a joking intensive.

2 Has not, have not.
1838 (1852) Gilman *S. Matron* 52, They began to twit me, and I an't hearn the last of it yit. **1843** (1916) Hall *New Purchase* 55 **IN,** Maybe they aint got more silver than Squire Snoddy. **1851** Burke *Polly Peablossom* 21 **GA,** An't we honest? An't we raised our children decent . . ? **1871** Eggleston *Hoosier Schoolmaster* 15 **IN,** You can begin right off a Monday. They a'n't been no other applications. **1891** Harris *Balaam* 432 **GA** [Black speaker], You ain't never is bin ter Sander'ville, is you, boss? **1908** *DN* 3.285 **eAL, wGA.** **1923** *DN* 5.200 **swMO.** **c1960** *Wilson Coll.* **csKY.** **1966** *DARE* (Qu. LL18) Inf **SC26,** She ain't hit a lick at a snake . . . She ain't turned a hand to do nothing . . . She ain't lift a broom; **SC9,** She ain't done nothing.

3 Do not, does not, did not. *among Black speakers*
1894 Stuart in 1941 Warfel–Orians *Local-Color Stories* 742 **AR,** I ain't keer who play de music. **1899** Edwards *Defense* 115 **GA,** "Do you think so, Isam?" A shadow fell upon her face. "Ain' I know hit?" [Isam replied]. **1922** Gonzales *Black Border* 139 **sSC, GA coasts** [Gullah], Ent you know suh 'ooman lub uh freehan' man? *Ibid* 261, Ent you know dat dey ent uh Chryce' hom'ny een de house fuh eat? **1927** Kennedy *Gritny* 87 **sLA** [Black], Ain't you know Felo bin stay'n wid me . . ? **1930** *DN* 6.79 **cSC,** "I ain' know." Negroism. **1966** *DARE* Tape **SC10,** I ain't feel so good. **1976** Wolfram–Christian *Appalachian Speech* 114, In some varieties, such as Vernacular Black English, a third correspondence developed—the use of *ain't* for *didn't,* so that we have constructions such as *He ain't go to the store* in this variety.

4 esp in phr *ain't only:* To be or have no more than.
1926 Faulkner *Soldiers' Pay* 14, He ain't only going to Buffalo. **1942** Whipple *Joshua* 18 **UT** (as of c1850), Come in an' set a spell! . . We ain't got only "bread-and-with it," but—. **1943** *LANE* MAP 718 **cVT,** I ain't got only six. **1959** Faulkner *Mansion* 56 **MS,** I'd like to hold the bank offen you myself, but I aint only vice-president of it, and I cant do nothing with Manfred de Spain.

5 following a modal aux: Not be. *among Black speakers* See also **ain't must**

1967 *DARE* (Qu. P9) Inf **LA7**, Fish must ain't bitin'; (Qu. U17) Inf **LA6**, I'd say he must ain't gon' [=going to] pay me. [Both Infs Black] **1970** *Thompson Coll.* **AL** [Black], You mus ain't so much of a man, all you kin do is flunky fuh a white lady.

6 in phr *ain't no* (or *nothing*): There is not any(thing).

1965 *AmSp* 40.176 [Black], Ain't nothing decent in our lives. **1968–69** *DARE* FW Addit **csNC**, Ain't no telling—an answer to the question "Why?" if one doesn't know the answer. **1976** Warner *Beautiful Swimmers* 60 **eShore MD**, Ain't no one person knows all about crabs.

ain't v[2] Also *ain't it, ain't not, ain't so* [Perh < *ain't it* (by syncope of internal *t*), by analogy with Ger *nicht wahr*] **Pa Ger and other Ger settlement areas** *freq considered uncult* Cf **ainna, enty, inso; ain't it** interrog exclam[2]

1 Isn't it? Isn't it true? Right?

1886 *Amer. Philol. Assoc. Proc.* 17.xiii **Pa Ger area**, "Ain't" . . when it is used introducing, or by way of introducing a sentence, implying "isn't it so?" or when it assumes the still more barbarous form of "ain't not?" persuasively entreating another's concession to the views of the person speaking, some sectional peculiarity may be claimed for it. **1907** (1970) Martin *Betrothal* 158 **sePA**, I ain't half eat yet. I guess you're eat a'ready, ain't? **1914** *DN* 4.157 **sePA**, Questions frequently contain an ain't: "It's a nice day, ain't?" (or ain't it). **1935** *AmSp* 10.167 **sePA**, He don't know what for [=what sort of] bonnet I have on, ain't not? **1939** Aurand *Quaint Idioms* 32 **PA**, John, I'm so proud of you; you're a college graduate now, ain't. **1948** *AmSp* 23.109 **IL**, Come to see us Sunday, ain't it? **1950** *WELS* (*Words and expressions meaning "Don't you agree?"*) 6 Infs, **c,eWI**, Aint it?; 15 Infs, **chiefly eWI**, Ain't so?

2 introducing an interrogative clause: Isn't it true that _____?

1914 *DN* 4.157 **sePA**, You'll do that, ain't you won't? He's been gone a long time, ain't he has?

aint See **aunt A2**

ain't done See **it ain't done it**

ain't it interrog exclam[1] See **ain't** v[2]

ain't it interrog exclam[2] [Prob var of **enty**, but see also **ain't** v[2]] *chiefly among Black speakers*
Isn't that so?

1927 Kennedy *Gritny* 35 **sLA** [Black], Nobody but Roxy an' you in de house to bother 'bout, ain't it? **1963** Wright *Lawd Today* 86 **Chicago IL** [Black], There's a nasty taste in yo' *mouth,* ain't it?

aintment See **ointment**

ain't much See **much adj**

ain't must modal aux Cf **ain't** v[1] **5**
Must not.

1927 Adams *Congaree* 7 **cSC** [Black], He cuss, an' steal, an' make game at God's work, an' do everything de Bible say he ain't mus' do.

ain't not, ain't so See **ain't** v[2]

air n Usu |e(ɪ)r, ɛ(ɪ)r|; in **Sth** freq |ær, æə, eə| Pronc-spp *aiah, a'r* See Pronc Intro 3.I.1.b
Std senses, var forms.

1884 Lanier *Poems* 180 **GA** [Black], When folks starts prayin', answer-angels drops down th'u' de a'r./ Yas, Dinah, Whar'ould you be now, jes' 'ceptin' fur dat pra'r? **1890** *DN* 1.67 **KY**, Are . . . Pronounced like *air* [æə]. **1914** *DN* 4.158 **VA**, Air and hour pronounced alike. "Ah don't mean aiah like a clock; ah means *aiah* like this heah (waving his hand before his face)." **1927** Shewmake *Engl. Pronc.* VA 42, *Air. Ae-uh* represents Virginia usage. **1942** Hall *Smoky Mt. Speech* 24 **eTN, wNC**, [æ] occurs in: Air, barely, [etc.]. **1966** *Wilson Coll.* **csKY**, Air foam ['eə fom]. **1982** *DARE* File **neGA** (as of c1960), About *air* and *hour:* when I was an undergraduate at Piedmont . . I thought I heard those words pronounced alike . . . I believe out of context you could not tell the difference.

air v[1] Also *air up*
To fill with air.

1967 *DARE* FW Addit **MI9**, Let's go down to the gas station and air up the tires. **c1974** Jones *Ozark Hill Boy* 32 **AR** (as of c1930), The first Sunday afternoon I aired the tires, filled it with gas and drove to the . . State Park.

air v[2] See **be A1, B4**

air v[3] See **heir** v

air adj See **ary**

air bridge n Also called **overcast**
In coal mining: an insulated wall between one **air course** and another.

1973 *PADS* 59.24 **VA**.

‡air castle flower n
=**mariposa lily.**

1968 *DARE* (Qu. S26c) Inf **CA87**, Fairy lanterns or air castle flowers.

air course n [*OEDS* 1882 →] Also called **back entry, blind entry, light entry**
In mining: an airway; an opening through which air can circulate to workers under ground.

1969 *DARE* Tape **CA128** [In gold mining], The raise is more for air course because it gets pretty hot down there. **1973** *PADS* 59.24 [In bituminous coal mining], *Air course* . . an underground passage opened to carry air to and from the working sections of a *mine*.

air-cure v, hence *air-cured* ppl adj, *air-curing* vbl n Cf **fire-cure, flue-cure**
Of tobacco: to dry by exposure to air rather than by use of artificial heat.

1933 *Sun* (Baltimore MD) 15 Sept 3/2 *(Hench Coll.)*, The tax rates for the various types are: Cigar leaf, 3 cents a pound farm sales weight; . . dark air-cured, 3.3, 3.8, and 5.1. **1940** *AmSp* 15.133 **KY**, *Air-cured.* Tobacco cured by air and with little or no artificial heat. **1944** *PADS* 2.64 **sVA**, *Air-cure* . . . To cure [tobacco] in the open air—for use or for storage. **1960** Heimann *Tobacco* 109, In general, cigar leaf is air-cured. **1966** *PADS* 45.6 **Lexington KY**, Our tobacco is air-cured. **1967** Key *Tobacco Vocab.* **CT, KY, MO, TN**, Air-cured. **1969–70** *DARE* Tapes **KY35**, It'll be cured to where we can strip it the middle of November, just through the natural process of air-curin'; **KY75**, Air-cured . . . Dark type tobacco.

aire See **ary**

airesipelus See **erysipelas**

air foam n Also called **sheepskin, skeelings, skimmings**
Froth which forms on the surface of boiling jam.

1966 *Wilson Coll.* **csKY**, Air foam ['eə fom].

air, go by v phr joc
To go on foot in the open air (rather than in a vehicle).

1968 *DARE* (Qu. Y24, . . *To walk*) Inf **CA59**, Go by air: "I'm going by air; air [=are] you going my way?"—old-fashioned.

air hook n joc Cf *DS* X14, 15, and **air, (up) in the 3**
One's nose.

1950 *WELS* (*Joking words for the nose*) 1 Inf, **cwWI**, Air hook.

airified adj Also sp *airyfied* [*OED* 1864 →; *air* demeanor, haughtiness + **-ified**] *somewhat old-fash* Cf **airish 2, airy** adj[1] **1**
Given to putting on airs; conceited.

1933 *AmSp* 8.1.47 **Ozarks**, *Airyfied* . . . Inclined to put on airs, stuck-up, *fine-haired.* **1968** *DARE* (Qu. HH35) Inf **SC59**, She's too airified ['arɪfaɪd] for me. [Old Inf.]

‡airify v [Prob back-formation from **airified**, but cf **-ify**]
To put on airs.

1898 Westcott *Harum* 239 **nNY**, What'll your wife say to seein' me airifyin' 'round in your git-up?

air, in the See **air, (up) in the**

airish adj Also sp *arsh, arrish*

1 Chilly, cool. **chiefly Sth, S Midl** Note: The form is still current in Scots though obs in std Engl *(SND).*

1878 Beadle *Western Wilds* 609, Going westward on any line one will find the winters growing dryer, also more 'airish.' **1912** Green *VA Folk-Speech.* **1918** *DN* 5.39 **VA**, Arsh . . cool, brisk (of the air). **1926** *DN* 5.397 **Ozarks**. **1947** *Hench Coll.* **VA**, Conversation . . with a Negro workman . . at an auto store and filling station: The Negro said to me, 'a bit arrish this morning.' Not catching him for sure, I said, 'What did you say?' 'A bit arrish outside.' I later realized he was giving his own pronunciation of 'airish.' **c1960** *Wilson Coll.* **csKY**, It's kinder airish ['ærɪš] this morning. **1972** *Atlanta Letters* 22, "It's getting airish" means the weather is getting cooler.

2 Inclined to put on airs. **chiefly Sth, Midl** *chiefly among Blacks* See Map Cf **airified, airy** adj **1, arnchy**

1943 Writers' Program NC *Bundle of Troubles* 26 **NC,** Miss Muskrat got so airish 'cause Mr. Bullfrog pay her mind that she act like none the other woods folks good enuf for her to 'sociate with. **1947** Ballowe *The Lawd* 240 **LA** [Black], Ah sees huccome them quarters frawgs [=work hands on a French-speaking plantation] so airish. The quality done showed 'em. **1965–70** *DARE* (Qu. HH35, *A woman who puts on a lot of airs: "She's too _____ for me."*) 18 Infs, **chiefly Sth, Midl,** Airish. [10 Infs Black]

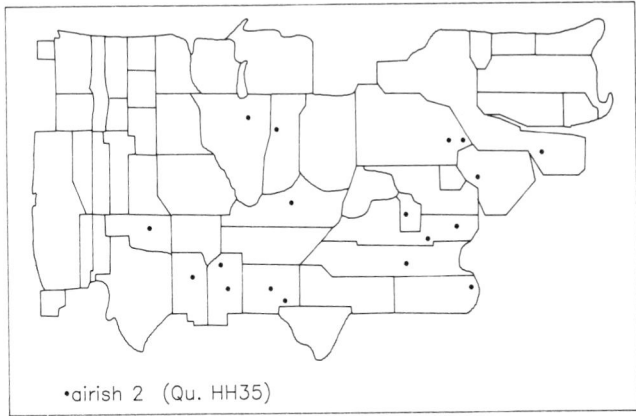

•airish 2 (Qu. HH35)

‡3 also *airy:* Effeminate in manner.

1968 *DARE* (Qu. HH38, *A womanish man*) Inf **MD35,** Airish, airy, girlish.

airjammer n *joc* Cf *DS* HH7a

=**windjammer.**

1966 *Daily Oklahoman* (Oklahoma City OK) 11 Dec Mag sec 11 [Among oil workers], "Airjammers" . . are know-it-all types.

airly See **early**

air monkey See **monkey**

airn pron Also sp *ary'n* [Contr of **ary** + *one*] **Sth, S Midl** Cf **nairn**

Usu in neg constrs: Any; even one.

1905 *DN* 3.68 **nwAR,** Airn *(airy 'un)* . . . 'I ain't got airn.' Common among the uneducated. **1908** *DN* 3.285 **eAL, wGA,** Airn . . . Any one, e'er a one. Only heard among the illiterate. **1915** *DN* 4.180 **swVA.** **1952** Brown *NC Folkl.* 1.514, Airn [ærn, æən] . . . "Have you got a knife?" "No, I ain't got *airn* with me." . . Illiterate. **1976** Garber *Mountain-ese* 4 **sAppalachians,** We expected a crowd but not ary'n showed up fer the class.

airn v See **earn**

airnest See **earnest**

air one's lungs v phr

1 To swear.

1911 in 1968 Fletcher *Up the Trail* 7, He aired his lungs by cussing everything from his cow pony to the minister we met in the road. **1944** Adams *Western Words,* Airin' the lungs—What the cowboy calls "cussin'," which seems to be a natural part of his language. **1961** Adams *Old-Time Cowhand* 24.

2 To argue or talk at length.

1969 *DARE* (Qu. KK13, *Other words for arguing: "They stood there for an hour _____."*) Inf **IL96,** Airing their lungs.

air one's paunch v phr Also ~*belly*

1 To vomit.

1920 Hunter *Trail Drivers TX* 300, Of vomiting, [the cowboy says] "airing the paunch". **1960** Wentworth–Flexner *Slang, Air [one's] belly.* **1968** Adams *Western Words,* Airin' the paunch—What the cowboy calls vomiting.

2 To boast.

1928 (1964) Santee *Cowboy* 137, Pretty Dick had been airin' his paunch about Canada an' tellin' what good horses he had rode up there.

air out v phr *among Black speakers*

1 To stroll in the open air.

1942 *Amer. Mercury* 55.85 **NYC** [Black], So this day he was airing out on the Avenue. **1960** Wentworth–Flexner *Slang, Air out* . . . To stroll; to saunter. *Orig. Negro use.* **1970** Major *Afro–Amer. Slang, Air out:* to go for a walk.

2 To flee, escape.

1942 *Amer. Mercury* 55.94 **NYC** [Glossary of Harlem Slang], Air out—leave, flee, stroll. **1960** Wentworth–Flexner *Slang, Air out* . . . To leave; to flee. *Not common.*

airplane n

1 also ~*bug,* ~*fly:* =**dragonfly.**

1967–69 *DARE* (Qu. R2) Inf **CA137,** Airplanes; **DE1, WA28,** Airplane fly; **WA28,** Airplane bug. **1973** Allen *LAUM* 1.318 **neSD,** Airplane [Heard in the community].

‡2 A very large mosquito.

1966 *DARE* (Qu. R15b) Inf **ND3,** Airplanes.

airplane tail n

A vapor trail or contrail left by an airplane.

1968 *DARE* (Qu. B10, . . *Long trailing clouds high in the sky*) Inf **MN28,** Airplane tails.

air potato n, also attrib **Sth**

=**wild yam** (here: *Dioscorea bulbifera*).

1895 Gray–Bailey *Field Botany* 431, Air potato . . . Somewhat cult. in Gulf States for the large angular edible gray tubers. **1942** Amer. Joint Comm. Horticult. Nomenclature *Std. Plant Names,* Airpotato Yam. **1953** Greene–Blomquist *Flowers South* 151, Beware of the air-potato! It was introduced into this country by the . . USDA, hoping that its many bitter, aerial tubers could be used medicinally. It was not only found useless, but the vine has become a nuisance because of its aggressive growth and rapid propagation by the aerial tubers.

air puncher See **puncher**

air shot n **all bituminous coal-mining areas**

In coal mining: a weak explosion: see quot 1973.

1920 Fay *Gloss. Mining* 22, Air shot. A shot prepared . . for the purpose of lessening its shattering effect. **1973** *PADS* 59.25 **AL, IL, IN, KY, OH, PA, TN, VA, WV,** Air shot . . a weak explosion in which the end of the drill hole has been expanded so that a pocket of air surrounds the charge.

airspring n

=**handspring** n.

1968 *DARE* (Qu. EE9b, *If children jump forward, land on their hands, and turn over*) Inf **NJ28,** Airspring—same thing [as] handspring.

airth See **earth**

airtight n [Absol, from the adj]

1 A heating stove that admits very little air. **chiefly NEast** *obsolescent*

1844 Stephens *High Life in NY* 2.227 **NYC,** Speakin' of stoves, Par, I got . . what they call an air tight, and a little teenty tointy handful of wood keeps 'em warm as blazes a hull day and night tu. **1850** Judd *Richard Edney* 87 **ME,** I want you to kindle a fire in the air-tight in the parlor. **1862** (1882) Stowe *Pearl of Orr's Is.* 65 **eME,** The advent of those sullen gnomes, the "air-tights," or even those more sociable and cheery domestic genii, the cooking stoves. **1902** Sears *Catalogue* 827/1. **1951** Hough *Singing in Morning* 209 **Martha's Vineyard MA,** An airtight . . is a type of stove used for heating. The barrel is made of sheet iron and there is usually a good-sized feed door. The fittings are airtight . . . It burns wood.

2 An airtight container, a can.

1961 Adams *Old-Time Cowhand* 14 **West,** Even when a cowboy'd learned to read he didn't get much chance to put it into practice. In the first place, he didn't have the material to practice with, except the air-tights and bakin'-soda cans.

3 Transf: Canned food. **West** *old-fash*

1897 Lewis *Wolfville* 330 **AZ,** What's air-tights? Which you Eastern shorthorns is shore ignorant. Air-tights is can peaches, can tomatters, an' sim'lar bluffs. **1907** White *AZ Nights* 219, On top of a few incidental pounds of *chile con,* baked beans, soda biscuits, 'air tights,' and other delicacies. **1923** *Outing* Mar 263/1, One afternoon I decided the party had been on airtight (canned meat) long enough. **1951** Grant *Cowboy Encycl.* 13, Airtights. Any kind of canned goods, but particularly canned peaches. **1977** Watts *Dict. Old West.*

air up See **air** v[1]

air, (up) in the adj phr

1 Annoyed, irritated; anxious, upset.

1906 *Evening Post* (New York NY) 13 Jan 4/1, Representatives . . have . . 'gone up in the air' because they could not "land" their men. **1914** *Living Age* 282, **NEast** ["Business Slang"], You will rouse his anger, and he may "go up in the air." **1965–70** *DARE* (Qu. GG7, . . *"Though we were only ten minutes late, she was all _____."*) 28 Infs, **scattered,** (Up) in the air; (Qu. GG11, . . *"The letter hasn't come and he's _____."*) Infs **AR3, IL28, OH29, OK31, TN12, TX101,** Up in the air; **IN73,** All up in the air; (Qu. GG13a) Inf **IN54,** I'm all up in the air; (Qu. GG16) Inf **MO13,** Up in the air; (Qu. GG35b) Inf **GA7,** Up in the air. (Qu. GG15, . . *A person who became over-excited and lost control: "At that point he really _____."*) Infs **MI66, MS15,** Flew up in the air; **MD26,** Got up in the air about it; **TX35,** Went up in the air; (Qu. GG40) Inf **MO38,** All up in the air; **NY153,** Right up in the air; (Qu. GG4) Inf **PA82,** Up in the air; (Qu. A21, . . *"Now just slow down! Don't _____."*) Inf **KY67A,** Get up in the air.

2 In a good mood; in good health.

1967–69 *DARE* (Qu. BB47) Infs **CA127, TN12,** Up in the air; (Qu. GG29) Infs **GA74, NY38,** Up in the air.

3 Cocky, snobbish; brazen. [Prob ref to having one's *nose in the air*] **chiefly Gulf States** Cf **air hook, walk on air**

1966–69 *DARE* (Qu. GG19a, . . *He's feeling important or independent: "He surely is _____ these days."*) Infs **FL35, GA3, 54, 74, IL28, OH8,** Up in the air; (Qu. HH35) Infs **AL8, LA28,** Up in the air; **GA83,** Much in the air; (Qu. II36b) Inf **OH43,** Up in the air.

airy adj[1]

1 Inclined to put on airs. **chiefly Sth, NEast** See Map See also **airified, airish 2**

1869 Twain *Innocents* 479, If we chance to discover that from Dan to Beersheba seemed a mighty stretch of country to the Israelites, let us not be airy with them, but reflect that it *was* and *is* a mighty stretch when one can not traverse it by rail. **1891** Maitland *Amer. Slang Dict.* 15 *Airy,* conceited. **1954** Armstrong *Satchmo* 139 **LA,** He had an airy way about him that'd make one think he was stuck up. **1965–70** *DARE* (Qu. HH35, *A woman who puts on a lot of airs: "She's too _____ for me."*) 23 Infs, **chiefly Sth, less freq NEast,** Airy.

2 See **airish 3.**

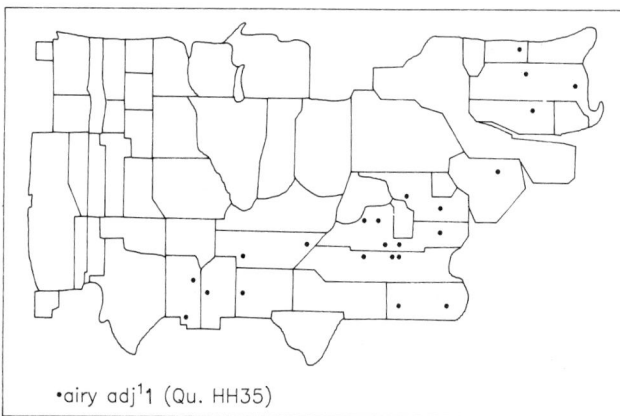

•airy adj[1]1 (Qu. HH35)

airy adj[2], pron See **ary**

airy n See **area**

airyfied See **airified**

airy-way n Also *area* [Prob folk-etym: see **area** for var proncs and *DA* for *areaway*] **Brooklyn NY**

An areaway; a subsurface space between the front of a building and the street-side railings.

1968 *DARE* File **Brooklyn NY** (as of 1930s), I first heard this as *airy way* . . which seemed unlikely, for it was where rubbish was put to be picked up. **1968** *DARE* FW Addit **Brooklyn NY,** [ˈɛæri,we], space between front porch of house and fence. **1980** *DARE* File **Brooklyn NY** (as of c1920), In a Brooklyn Brownstone the stone entrance with the iron gate into the basement is the "air ree" — pronunciation not spelling. It is also the space under the front stoop where the ash cans were kept and the burlap bag, "trash bag" for paper hung on the door . . . I think it is spelled Area, but don't remember ever seeing it, only hearing it.

aix See **ex** n

aje See **edge** A

ajo n Also *ajo lily* [Span *ajo* garlic] **AZ, CA** Cf **false garlic**

The desert lily *(Hesperocallis undulata);* also its edible bulbs formerly used by desert Indians.

1880 Darlington *Amer. Weeds* 355, Ajo . . . Cultivated as an article of medicine and used by some to season food, for which purpose it is extensively used in the Spanish American parts of our continent. **1908** Hornaday *Camp-Fires* 77, The Ajo—which for convenience we may call the Ajo *Lily,* was found from Wall's Well to the Pinacate lava region. **1917** Saunders *W. Flower Guide* 4, The plant is reputed responsible for the name of the Ajo Mountains in Southwestern Arizona —*ajo,* the Spanish for garlic, being also the term applied locally to the Hesperocallis, which is very abundant in that vicinity. **1941** Jaeger *Wildflowers* 11, The Indians found their onion flavor agreeable, as did the early Spanish explorers, who called them *ajo,* garlic.

ajumble See **a** prep[1] **4**

ajusi n [Korean] **HI**

An uncle.

1972 Carr *Da Kine Talk* 109 **HI,** Among loanwords of wide circulation are two terms of respectful address: *abuji* 'father' and *ajusi* 'uncle'.

A.K. n

1 An old fogy. [Abbr for **alter kocker**]

[**1942** Berrey–Van den Bark *Amer. Slang* 583.6 *Veteran Actor.* A.K. *(antediluvian knight).*] **1943** *AmSp* 18.45 **NYC,** 'A.K.'—*Variety,* I think, is credited with having introduced the term in print and with having concocted that delicious definition, "antediluvian knight," which took in so many of the unsuspecting, among whom, I fear, Berrey and Van den Bark must be included . . . Actually, the term may refer to any old-fogey or has-been, whether he is an actor, a husband, or a superannuated athlete . . . The abbreviation of the Yiddish expression *[alte kacker]* gives to the American term 'A.K.' its peculiar piquancy. **1948** *AmSp* 23.315 **NYC and other Jewish settlement areas,** A.K. . . is one of the most often heard [of "American–Jewish alphabetical expressions"] and has ordinarily a semihumorous derogatory connotation, although it can be used in an honestly derogatory sense, usually in application to an old man, or one old in his ways. Speaking of the members of a certain group one might hear: 'What a bunch of A.K.'s those guys are!' **1968** Rosten *Yiddish* 14, A.K. is a testimonial to the ineradicable earthiness and vigor of Yiddish. (My mother *never* let me use such a phrase, or employ such vulgarity.) A.K. is as often used in mild, fond condescension as it is in derision: "Let him alone: He's just an A.K." . . I certainly prefer A.K. to its English equivalent, "old fart." **1970** Feinsilver *Yiddish* 355, I recall a letter to "Dear Abby" in 1963 which was signed, "Stuck with an A.K." Some months ago I saw a Connecticut license plate "AK902" and remarked to my companion that the owner probably wasn't Jewish: if he were and these were his initials, he would certainly not have asked for them for his car!

2 One who curries favor. [Abbr for *ass kisser*] See also **A.K.** v

1939 *AmSp* 14.24 **SC** [Among students at The Citadel Military College:], A.K. . . A cadet who indulges in the practice [of currying favor with a superior]. **1960** Wentworth–Flexner *Slang,* A.K. . . [taboo] . . . *ass kisser.* This use is now the more common. **1966** *DARE* (Qu. JJ3b, *When a school child makes a special effort to 'get in good' with the teacher . . . "She's an awful _____."*) Inf **FL28,** A.K. (ass-kisser) [laughter]. **1971** Landy *Underground Dict.*

A.K. v, also vbl n *A.K.-ing* [**A.K.** n 2] **S Atl** See also **ass up to**

To curry favor with, play up to.

1939 *AmSp* 14.24 **SC** [Among students at The Citadel Military College:], A.K., . . To curry favor with a superior. **1959** *AmSp* 34.154 **FL** [Among students at Univ of Florida:], *A-K-ing* (apple-polishing). **1969** *DARE* (Qu. II20b, *A person who tries too hard to gain somebody else's favor: "He's always . . _____ the boss."*) Inf **GA82,** A.K.'in'. [FW: ass-kissing.]

akamai adj |ˈɑkəˈmaɪ| [Haw] **HI**

Smart, clever, skillful.

1840 in 1934 Frear *Lowell & Abigail* 149 **HI,** Brother Bliss has a neat adobe house. He appears to be rather *akamai* . . in fitting up things. **1938** Reinecke *Hawaiian Loanwords* 7, Akamai . . . Learned or skilled; expert; ingenious; clever . . F[requent]. **1967** *DARE* (Qu. JJ15a) Inf **HI1,** Akamai—clever at whatever one does. A much used word; (Qu. KK5, *A very skilled or expert person*) Inf **HI1,** Akamai—very good at anything. Applied specifically, very widely. **1967** *DARE* Tape **HI2**, You have to work up to be a forelady by being especially akamai. **1969** *DARE* File **Honolulu HI**, Akamai ['ɑkə,maɪ]—clever. Common. **1972** Carr *Da Kine Talk* 86 [Words common in Hawaiian English], *Akamai.* Smart, clever.

akern n Pronc-sp for *acorn*

[**1891** *DN* 1.128 **cNY** ['ekɚn] .. 'acorn.'] **1923** *DN* 5.200 **swMO**, Akern. **1956** *AmSp* 31.146 **cnIN**.

akey(s) See **aikie(s)**

‡**akimbo** adj [Fig use of *akimbo* with elbows bent and hands on hips]

Crooked, out of alignment.

1968 *DARE* (Qu. KK70, .. *Out of proper shape: "That house is all _____."*) Inf **CA80**, Akimbo.

akimbo v

To saunter with one's hands on one's hips.

1946 in 1958 Brewer *Dog Ghosts* 55 **TX** [Black], "Well," 'low [=allowed] Myra, akimboin' 'fo' Willie Word .. , "Ah sho would lack to hab me some venison for mah dinnuh tomorruh."

‡**akink** adj [a prep[1] **4** + *kink* bend]

Kinked, bent (as at the "elbow" or bend of wing); not fully extended.

1960 Williams *Walk Egypt* 16 **GA**, The hawk soared with elbows a-kink like the boogy-bird it was to chickens and rats.

akinned adj |ə'kɪnd| [*akin* + *-ed* ppl suff as if *akin* were a verb; cf *OED* akind, "Obs."] *old-fash*

Akin, related.

1937 *Hall Coll.* **eTN**, I told the German doctor that we was akinned |ə'kɪnd|. **1942** Hall *Smoky Mt. Speech* 92 **eTN, wNC**, [d] is added by most elderly speakers to *akin* and *born*: [ə'kɪnd], [bɔɚnd].

akio See **ahkio**

akkes, akkie See **bakkes**

‡**aknown** ppl adj [a inert vowel **1** + *known;* cf *OED* acknow, aknow "Very rare after OE period exc. in pa. pple."]

Known; acquainted.

1938 Matschat *Suwannee R.* **nFL, GA**, Let's set, and git a-known. Whar be ye from?

aku n, also attrib |'ɑku| [Haw] **HI**

Skipjack tuna *(Katsuwonus pelamis).*

1933 Bryan *Hawaiian Nature* 228, The Hawaiian name for the fish is *aku.* **1951** *AmSp* 26.20 **HI**, Many terms for varieties of fish have been borrowed; among these are *aku* (bonito). **1955** Day *HI People* 253, "Aku" (skipjack or ocean bonito), a light-meated tuna. **1967** *DARE* (Qu. P2) Inf **HI2**, Aku; **HI4**, Aku-tuna, skipjack; **HI14**, Aku [ɑku]—bonito; (Qu. P14, .. *Commercial fishing*) Inf **HI2**, Mostly aku; (Qu. H36, .. *Soup favored around here*) Inf **HI6**, Aku-head soup. **1967** *DARE* Tape **HI9**, Tuna they call ['aku]. **1967** *Honolulu Star–Bulletin* (HI) 31 May F 1/4, Aku .. can be eaten raw, steamed, fried, baked, or boiled. Dried aku is a favorite with poi. **1968** *Jrl. Engl. Ling.* 2.80. **1972** Carr *Da Kine Talk* 12, Some common loanblends of Hawaii [include] *aku boat* .. Seagoing vessel used in fishing for *aku* (bonito or skipjack).

akua n [Haw] **HI**

A god, spirit, supernatural being; see quot 1967.

1873 in 1966 Bishop *Sandwich Is.* 92, Kaluna wanted to sleep on the lounge here, probably because he is afraid of 'akuas,' or spirits. **1940** Von Tempski *Paradise* 234 **HI** (as of 1900–25), We children used to watch the sea and sky for days before Christmas, praying to God and propitiating *akuas* with *leis.* **1967** Reinecke–Tsuzaki *Hawaiian Loanwords, Akua,* /akua/ . . . Any supernatural being, the object of fear or worship; a spirit of Hawaiian mythology (still widely believed in); a ghost; a term applied by modern Hawaiians in referring to the Deity . . . F[requently] used].

akualele n [Haw **akua** spirit + *lele* flying, jumping] **HI**

A fireball or meteor.

1938 Reinecke *Hawaiian Loanwords, Akualele* . . . A will-o'-the-wisp, or fireball. (Such a phenomenon is regarded as supernatural by many.) V[ery] S[eldom]. **1967** *DARE* Tape **HI4**, That [=kawila, a black wood] can protect your home from anything. Like this akualele ['aku'lele], they

can fly it . . . They make it fly .. through the air .. to kill his enemy . . . When he fly it, it looks like a fireball.

akule n [Haw] **HI**

=**big-eyed scad.**

1902 Jordan–Evermann *Amer. Fishes* 303, Among the Hawaiian Islands it is an abundant and important food-fish and is known as the akule. **1960** Gosline–Brock *Hawaiian Fishes* 173, (Akule, Hahalalu [young], Aji, Bigeye scad) The akule may be easily identified by its large eyes . . . The akule .. is an important commercial species in Hawaii. **1967** *DARE* (Qu. P2) Inf **HI14**, [a'kule]—mackerel; (Qu. P7) Inf **HI4**, Akule—[fished for] with light threads looking like shrimp. **1967** *DARE* Tape **HI9**, They caught about a ton, I guess, .. [of] akule . . . Akule .. is something like a salmon .. [but they're] smaller, weigh about three-quarter pound.

Al See **Old Al**

ala n [Haw] **HI** See also **alanui**

A path, a road.

1951 *AmSp* 26.22 **HI**, Other common Hawaiian words are .. *ala* (path, road). **1955** Day *HI People* 310, Many Hawaiian words have been taken into English .. [including] *ala:* road. **1967** *DARE* Tape **HI2**, Ala is a path.

Alabama n, also attrib Usu |ælə'bæmə| Also, **chiefly Sth**, |ælə'bæm|—*now old-fash or self-conscious usage;* occas |ælə'bæmi|, for which cf **-y**, |'bæmɚ|. Pronc-spp *Ahlabahm, Alabam, Alabamy,* 'Bam, 'Bama, 'Bammy, 'Bamy

A Forms.

1827 (1939) Sherwood *Gaz. GA* 139, [In list of provincialisms to be avoided:] *Alabam,* for Alabama. **1873** Harte *Mrs. Skaggs* 134, [He] recalled some lovely nights in the South in Alabama ("in the South in Ahlabahm" was the way the old man heard it). **1893** Shands *MS Speech* 17, *Alabam* . . . Negro and illiterate white for *Alabama.* **1908** *DN* 3.285 **eAL, wGA** [æləbæm(ə)]. **1940** in 1944 *ADD* **swPA, nWV**, Alabamy. **1940** *Post* (Morgantown WV) 27 Jan *(ADD)*, [Headline:] 'Bama. **c1940** in 1944 *ADD*, 'Bamy. Radio "Ain't that Good News," negro song. **1942** in 1944 *ADD*, ['ælə'bæ'mɪ] bound. (Song.) **1942** Hall *Smoky Mt. Speech* 77 **eTN, wNC**, *Alabama* occasionally loses its final vowel. **1942** [see **B1** below]. **1970** *DARE* (Qu. HH1) Inf **DC11**, [bæmɚ]. **1979** *DARE* File, [A Connecticut youth speaking of his father's Alabama speech:] I sure hate to hear him use that " 'Bammy" talk!

B Senses. *chiefly among Black speakers*

1 The South.

1942 *Amer. Mercury* 55.91 **NYC** [Black], Youse from right down in 'Bam your ownself! *Ibid* 94 [Glossary of Harlem Slang], Bam, and down in Bam—down South. **1960** Wentworth–Flexner *Slang, Alabama* . . . The South, those states which were part of the Southern Confederacy . . . *Not now common; associated with Negro use.*

2 also *'Bama chukker:* A rustic or countrified person, esp one from the South.

1966 *Current Slang* 1.2.1 **DC** [Black], *'Bama chukker* . . . A Southern white rustic . . . He some ol' *'bama chukker.* **1970** *Ibid* 5.2.5 **SD** [Black], *Bama* . . . A rustic; an "un-hip" person. **1970** *DARE* (Qu. HH1) Inf **DC11**, [bamɚ].

Alabama clover n

=**Mexican clover.**

1933 *Torreya* 33.84 **MS**, *Richardia scabra* . . . Alabama clover.

Alabama egg n Also called **hobo egg, Rocky Mountain egg**

An egg fried in the hollow center of a piece of bread.

1951 Brown *Southern Cook Book* 149 **SC**, *Alabama Eggs* . . . Cut a round center out of a slice of bread about the size of egg yolk . . . Lay bread in pan and break egg carefully over it, being careful that the yolk slips into the center of the bread. Fry to golden brown.

Alabama whippoorwill See **whippoorwill**

Alabama wool n *joc*

1958 McCulloch *Woods Words* **Pacific NW**, *Alabama wool*—Cotton clothing, especially underwear.

Alabamy See **Alabama**

alabaster n

A playing marble made to resemble alabaster. Usu called **alley** n[2]

1967 *DARE* (Qu. EE6d, *Special marbles*) Inf **LA8**, Alabaster [ˌæləˈbæstə].

alabia n [Perh conn with Haw *'ālapa* athletic, athlete] **HI**
A children's game: see quot.
   1967 *DARE* (Qu. EE33) Inf **HI6**, [ˌalaˈβia] — Bull Durham bags stuffed with grass; each side tossed bags back and forth; [if you] hit someone, he's dead (out of the game); then run across and pick up your own bag without being hit by other bag. Only two bags no matter how many players.

à la Comanche adv phr [Fr *à la* in the manner of + *Comanche* an Indian tribe] **SW**
Of horseback riding: see quots.
   [**1844** (1954) Gregg *Commerce* 436 **SW,** They always fight on horseback . . . On such occasions a Comanche will often throw himself upon the opposite side of his charger, so as to be protected from the darts of the enemy; and, while clinging there, he will discharge his arrows with extraordinary dexterity from underneath his horse's neck.] **1850** Garrard *Wah-to-yah* 161 **NM,** Motioning to us to ride *a la camanche*—with our bodies so that nothing is seen on the opposite side but part of the leg with which, and the heel of the same, we held on the saddle cant. **1968** Adams *Western Words, À la Comanche*—Hanging on on the side of a horse as the Comanche Indian did in battle.

alacran n Also *alacrany, alicran* [Span *alacrán*] **SW**
A scorpion.
   1844 (1954) Gregg *Commerce* 282, As an expedient to deliver the city [=Durango, Mexico] from this terrible pest, a society has actually been formed, which pays a reward . . for every *alacran* (or scorpion) that is brought to them. **1848** Hughes *Doniphan's Exped.* 128/2, The soldiers [while in Chihuahua] would sometimes shake their blankets, toss the scorpions and lizards, and alacrans, . . exclaiming angrily, "d— — n the scorpion family." **1887** in 1921 Thorp *Songs Cowboys* 93 **SW,** In my little adobe casa on the plains. Alacranies on the ceiling, cucarachas on the wall. **1891** *DN* 1.243 **TX,** *Alacrán:* a scorpion. Different species of the genus *scorpio,* common in Texas and Mexico. **1932** Bentley *Spanish Terms* 89, *Alacran* English modification *alicran* . . . The word is seldom used in English even in the most Spanish sections along the border. English "scorpion" is preferred.

alae salt n [Haw *'alaea* + Engl *salt:* see quot] **HI**
A coarse, red salt.
   1972 Carr *Da Kine Talk* 112 **HI,** Some common loanblends of Hawaii [include] . . *'alae salt* . . . A coarse-grained, red salt used in Hawaiian food. The Hawaiian word *'alaea* is defined as "water-soluble colloidal ocherous earth, used for coloring salt, for medicine, and for dye."

‡**alamagoozlum** n [A fanciful formation, perh from Fr *à la* + *-ma-* infix + **goozlum** thick liquid]
   1895 *DN* 1.384 **seNY,** *Alamagoozlum:* maple syrup made by melting down the sugar.

alameda n [Span, from *alamo* poplar] **SW** Cf **allée**
A public park or walk lined with trees—now used chiefly in place names.
   [**1824** Poinsett *Notes on Mexico* 50, The Alameda, a public walk, or rather park, laid out in lines diverging from different centres, and planted with a great variety of trees.] **1872** Schele de Vere *Americanisms* 120 **SW,** The *alamo* (Populus monilifera) represents in Texas and all the formerly Spanish states the *Cottonwood* of the older part of the union . . . [It is found] growing wild, and carefully planted in the public walks of Southern and Western towns, which hence derive the name of *Alameda.* **1878** in 1942 *CA Folkl. Qrly.* 1.269 **AZ,** The alameda long and wide/ With cottonwoods to shade each side/ Stretched out a good long mile or more. **1970** Stewart *Amer. Place-Names, Alameda* . . used loosely for a grove of any kind of shade-giving trees. The county (hence, the city) in CA was named for the fine growth of oaks.

alamo n, also attrib Also dimins *alamillo, alamito* [Span] **SW**
1 Any of several poplars, such as the cottonwood.
   1854 in 1856 U.S. Congress *Serial Set* 794.1.11 **AZ,** The alamos grow to a good large size and are quite abundant. **1860** in 1948 *Western Folkl.* 7.3, On the Colorado River. There is abundance of mesquit and alamo timber. **1892** *DN* 1.187 **TX.** **1916** Peixotto *Hispanic SW* 164, It is known locally as "Old Town", and centres about a placeta, set out with tamarisks and alamitos. **1964** Hymes *Lang. in Culture* 467, The Spanish word *âlamo,* meaning the European poplar, and thus applied to American cottonwoods, has come to be the usual word for any deci-

duous tree not specifically identified. **1967** *DARE* (Qu. T13, . . *Poplar trees*) Inf **TX22,** Cottonwood—not poplar; called alamo. **1970** Correll *Plants TX* 455, *Populus Wislizenii . . Alamillo.*
2 The Arizona sycamore.
   1953 Little *Native Trees U.S.* 278, *Platanus wrightii . . . Other Common Names . . .* álamo. *Range.*—Southwestern New Mexico and southeastern to central Arizona. Local in southeastern California.

alanui n [Haw **ala** path + **nui** large] **HI**
A main path.
   1938 Reinecke *Hawaiian Loanwords, Alanui* . . . A highway, road, or wide and frequented path, as distinguished from a mere trail. **1954–60** Hance *Hawaiian Sugar,* Alanui. **1967** *DARE* Tape **HI2,** As you go along in this tremendously long block [in a pineapple field] . . , every once in a while they have a cut-through, which takes the Hawaiian word *alanui* [ɑlɑˈnuɪ] . . . *Ala* is a path, and I don't know what the *nui* means.

al'a's See **always**

Alaska cotton n, also attrib [See quot 1938]
=**cotton grass 1.**
   1938 (1958) Sharples *AK Wild Flowers* 56, "Alaska Cotton." . . Flowers in dense heads, the perianth bristles very numerous and elongated, producing a fluffy ball of "cotton." **1939** FWP *Guide AK* 225, A Chugach love potion was made of 'Alaska cotton,' thoroughly dried and powdered. **1942** *Alaska Sportsman* Sept 27 (Tabbert *Alaskan Engl.*), Then Mr. Atmik illustrated the old method of lighting a pipe with flint and steel and fuzz from the Alaska cotton plant. **1971** Bailey *Field Work of a Museum Naturalist* 84 (Tabbert *Alaskan Engl.*), The tundra was covered sparsely with willow but grasses grew in profusion—the white heads of "Alaska cotton", blown gently by a cool breeze, making the summer flats look like shimmering snow fields. **1976** Hobbs *Tisha* 19 **AK** (as of 1927), "What's that?" I asked Mr. Strong . . . I didn't think it could be cotton, but it was. " 'Alaska cotton,' " Mr. Strong said. *Ibid* 20, We rode through acres and acres of silvery bolls, their long silky fibers waving like pom-poms atop a slender stem.

Alaskan tea See **Alaska tea**

‡**Alaskan trade** n [Folk-etym based on **last-go-trade,** var of **trade-last**] Cf **lasso trade**
=**trade-last.**
   1966 *DARE* (Qu. KK35, *When someone wants to pass on a compliment about you, in exchange for one about himself, . . "I have a _____ for you.")* Inf **GA13,** Alaskan trade.

Alaska pine n **Pacific NW**
The mountain hemlock *(Tsuga mertensiana).*
   1897 Sudworth *Arborescent Flora* 45, *Tsuga mertensiana* . . . Alaska Pine (Northwestern lumbermen). **1958** McCulloch *Woods Words* 2 **Pacific NW,** *Alaska pine*—Western hemlock.

Alaska robin n **Pacific NW**
=**varied thrush.**
   1917 (1923) *Birds Amer.* 239, Varied Thrush *Ixoreus nævius nævius . . Other Names.*—Oregon Robin; Alaska Robin. **1940** Writers' Program OR *Mt. Hood* 18, The Western thrush or robin, a summer resident, differs only slightly from the varied thrush or Alaska robin, a shy resident seldom seen. **1967** *DARE* (Qu. Q14) Inf **WA30,** Alaska robin . . thrush.

Alaska tea n Also *Alaskan tea*
=**Labrador tea.**
   1933 Marshall *Arctic Village* 124 (Tabbert *Alaskan Engl.*), We tore down long aisles between dark green spruce trees, were brushed by the willow branches and the evergreen leaves of the Alaska Tea. **1935** *Alaska Sportsman* April 28 (Tabbert *Alaskan Engl.*), To complete your indigenous dinner try the wild and wooly beverage of the northland, the Wooly Alaska tea. **1967** *Alaska Sportsman* July 10 (Tabbert *Alaskan Engl.*), Great areas were covered by cotton sedge, salmonberry, and the white showy blossoms of Alaskan tea.

Alaska time n Cf **colored people's time, farmers' time, Jewish time**
   1976 Hobbs *Tisha* 77 **AK,** "You're going to have to get used to Alaska time." "What's Alaska time?" "An hour or two early or an hour or two late. Maybe more depending on the weather."

Alaska turkey n Cf **Cape Cod Turkey** *joc*
Salmon.
   1948 Rowe *Maritime Hist.* 235 **ME,** Other Maine ships . . made them-

selves useful in the later days [=1890s] carrying . . Chinese cannery workers north through the Unimax Pass to the fishing stations, returning when the canning season was over with full cargoes of "choice Alaska turkey."

alather See **a** prep[1] **4**

al'ays See **always**

Albany beechdrops n
=**pinedrops 1.**
    1822 Eaton *Botany* 414, *Pterospora—andromeda* . . Albany beech-drops. **1847** Wood *Class-Book* 380, Albany Beech-drops [is found] in various parts of N.Y. and Vt. . . . First discovered . . near Niagara Falls. **1915** (1926) Armstrong *Western Wild Flowers* 360, It is also called Giant Bird's-nest and Albany Beech-drops.

Albany beef n [From the former abundance of sturgeon near Albany NY] **NY** *joc; now hist* Cf **Cape Cod turkey**
The flesh of the sturgeon.
    1791 (1971) Long *Indian Interpreter* 118, This fish [=sturgeon] is very common in Albany, and is sold at 1d. per lb. York currency. The flesh is called Albany beef. **1848** Bartlett *Americanisms, Albany Beef.* Sturgeon; a fish which abounds in the Hudson river; so called by the people in the State of New York. **1872** Schele de Vere *Americanisms* 348, The former [=sturgeon] coming up the Hudson River as far as Albany, and being highly esteemed there, especially when roasted in the form of steaks, are popularly known as *Albany Beef.* **1883** in 1909 Ware *Passing Engl.* 4/1, The *New York Herald* concludes by observing that 'ioukkà,' which it calls 'really the national soup of Russia,' to 'one of simple tastes, must resemble Hudson River sturgeon, otherwise known as Albany beef, struck by Jersey lightning.' **1949** Brown *Amer. Cooks* 616 **NY,** That fine caviar producer, the sturgeon was once so plentiful up the Hudson River that it was called 'Albany beef.'

Albany hemp n [See quot 1859]
The Canada nettle *(Laportea canadensis).*
    1859 (1968) Bartlett *Americanisms, Albany Hemp.* (*Urtica canadensis.)* Canada nettle, so called from the use made of its fibrous bark. **1910** Graves *Flowering Plants* **CT** 155, *Laportea canadensis* . . Albany Hemp.

Albany sleigh n Also ~*cutter* [See quot 1977] **Nth** *now hist*
Also called **swell-body sleigh** Cf **Portland sleigh**
A popular horse-drawn sleigh of the latter half of the nineteenth century.
    1934 *Hanley Disks* **csCT,** [One style of] gentleman's driving sleigh . . was called an Albany sleigh. That was rather low-back, [with a] higher dash, more . . like a boat. **1976** *WI Then & Now* December 2, The classic Albany (or Swellbody) and Portland (or Kimball) sleighs designed and built by craftsmen were latter-day city cousins of the homemade, utilitarian sledges that provided most of the winter overland transportation in Wisconsin before railroads and roads. **1977** Berkebile *Amer. Carriages* 148 [Caption], This plate, drawn from ambrotypes furnished by the James Goold firm in Albany, N.Y., shows the ever-popular Albany cutter, also known as a swell-body or Goold cutter. Though originated by Goold nearly a quarter of a century earlier, this sleigh was also built by hundreds of other builders until the end of the carriage era. [Plate reprinted from] *The New York Coach-maker's Magazine,* vol. 1, Nov. 1858.

albedritsch See **elbedritsch**

alberca n [Span "pond, pool"] **SW**
See quot 1892.
    1892 *DN* 1.187 **TX,** *Albérca:* a water hole, water pocket, watering place. Used only in Western Texas. *Ibid* 243, Also permanent water in a *cañon* or *barranca.* Originally in Spanish, a water basin. From Arabic. **1934** (1975) Mawson *Dict. Foreign Terms, Alberca* . . water hole; water pocket: southwestern U.S.

albertwitsch See **elbedritsch**

Alberty See **-y**

albetritsch See **elbedritsch**

albondigas n pl, also attrib [Span *albóndiga* ball of forcemeat] **SW**
Meatballs, usu served in a soup.
    1940 FWP *Guide NM* 110, *Albondigas*—Meat balls. [**1968** Bradford *Red Sky* 110 **SW,** She and Amadeo and I stuffed ourselves on venison chile for a week, and then she made *sopa de albondigas* with what was left.] **1970** *DARE* (Qu. H36) Inf **CA**194, Albondigas [æl'bɔndəgəs]—meatball soup. Common among those of Spanish background; also known by some others of long standing in the area. **1981** *DARE* File **sCA,** Lots of people around here like to eat albondigas soup. That's vegetable soup that's got little meatballs in it along with the vegetables—carrots, celery, and potatoes, usually. [**1982** *Capital Times* (Madison WI) 20 Oct 35/3, Here's an ethnic California soup, heavy on the garlic: *Sopa De Albondigas or Meatball Soup California Style.*]

album quilt n [Transf from *album* book in which to collect autographs and inscriptions] Cf **friendship quilt, presentation quilt**
A quilt in which each block, usu bearing an autograph or brief verse, is contributed by a different person.
    1947 Botkin *Treas. New Engl. Folkl.* 695, Out of the autograph album with its varying sentiments both wise and maudlin, emerged the "Album" quilt, each block bearing an embroidered text or verse and signed by the donor . . . To be the recipient of an "Album" quilt was considered a distinguished honor. **1949** Ickis *Quilt Making* 207, Album quilts have no set pattern, except that they are made in blocks or squares; each block has a different design created from materials by the woman who made it. **1970** GA Dept. Ag. *Farmers Market Bulletin* 12 Aug 7/2, [Advt:] Quilt patterns; pc. Maple Leaf, Milky Way, . . Album. **1979** *WI Then & Now* 25.7, One of the most striking appliquéd quilts . . is the "Oak Leaf" album quilt (any quilt with autographs or verses written in the plain blocks is termed an album quilt) made in 1846 in Pennsylvania.

albur n [Span *albures*] **SW** *obs*
A card game.
    1851 in 1942 *AmSp* 17.64 **NM,** All gambling at albur shall be prohibited. **1892** *DN* 1.243 **TX,** *Albúr:* a game of cards. From Spanish *albures,* of Arabic origin.

alcabala n [Span] **SW** *obs*
A tax, esp a sales tax.
    [**1824** Poinsett *Notes on Mexico* 14, They [=the goods] are charged with a further duty, or alcabala, of twelve and a half per cent. ad valorem.] **1836** (1935) Holley *Texas* 213, All the produce of agriculture or industry of the new settlers, shall be free from excise duty, *Alcabala,* or other duties.

alcalde n |ˌɑlˈkɑlde, ˌælˈkældi| Also *alcade, alcaide* (but see quot 1932) [Span] **SW** *somewhat old-fash*
A local official; now also any important or self-important person.
    1803 U.S. Congress *Debates & Proc.* 14.1506 **LA,** There are two Alcaldes, whose jurisdiction, civil and criminal, extends through the city of New Orleans. **1806** Berquin–Duvallon *Travels* 150 **LA,** This council [=cabildo] distributes among its members several important offices, such as . . alcalde provincial, attorney general, &c. **1821** (1904) Austin *Jrl.* **TX** 298, Wrote to the alcade that he could not spare any soldiers. **1860** in 1948 *Western Folkl.* 7.3 **Los Angeles CA,** The robbers carry a list . . . of thirty-three persons who are to lose their goods and lives . . . all the alcaldes and judges. **1892** *DN* 1.187 **TX,** *Alcálde* . . . This word is often applied to justices of the peace, more specifically to O.M. Roberts, governor of Texas, who was a justice of the peace in the early days of Texas, as an affectionate nickname, "the Old Alcalde." **1932** Bentley *Spanish Terms* 90, *Alcalde* (*Spanish,* [ɑːlˈkɑːldeː]; *English* [ælˈkældi]) . . . was used throughout the Spanish territory of America and only recently has been replaced in parts of New Mexico. It is sometimes confused with Spanish *alcaide* meaning the officer charged with the defense of a fort or castle. **1967** *DARE* (Qu. HH17, . . "He'd like to be the _____ around here." ') Inf **TX**43, Alcalde [ælˈkældi].

alcaldia n Also anglicized as *alcaldeship* [Span] **SW** *arch or old-fash*
The court or domain over which an **alcalde** had jurisdiction.
    1885 Shinn *Mining-Camps* 97, The most important alcaldeship in California . . was that of San Francisco. **1968** Adams *Western Words, Alcaldía*—The territory in which an *alcalde* . . has jurisdiction; also, the office in which he conducts business.

alcamy See **alchemy**

‡**alcapoga** n Cf *DS* T9 and **catalpa**
    1968 *DARE* (Qu. T9, *The common shade tree with large heart-shaped leaves, clusters of white blossoms, and long thin seed pods*) Inf **MD**34, Alcapoga [ˈælkəpogə].

alcatraz n [*Alcatraz,* the penitentiary]
A marble game: see quot.

c1970 Wiersma *Marbles Terms* **Cleveland OH,** Alcatraz . . . A circle 3 to 6 feet in diameter is surrounded by a trench 2 to 3 inches wide and 2 to 3 inches deep; a shooter marble is rolled through the ditch toward a target marble in the center of the circle.

alchemy n, usu attrib Also pronc-spp *accumy, achemy, alcamy, alchimy, alchymy, alcomy, alcumy, alkomy, occomy* [*OED alchemy* 3 →1812 *"Obs."*] arch
A mixed metal resembling brass.

1638 in 1857 New Haven (Colony) *Records* 4 **CT,** Twelve alcumy spoones. **1645** in 1914 Essex Inst. *Coll.* 50.336 **eMA,** Dozen alcamy spoones, 3s. 4d. **1651** in 1908 *Mayflower Descendant* 10.39 **MA,** I give my Daughter Jane . . two alchymy spoones. **1689** in 1904 Manwaring *Digest CT Probate* 1.469, The inventory of William Hooker [included] 1-2 doz. accumy spoons. **1714** (1879) S. Sewall *Diary* 2.419 **MA,** I presented my Son and daughter with . . 6 Alchimy spoons. **1899** (1912) Green *VA Folk-Speech* 61, *Achemy* . . . Alcamy, alcomy, alkomy, occomy. A mixed metal used for utensils, a modification of brass.

alder bird n
=**goldfinch** (here: *Spinus tristis*).
1966 *DARE* (Qu. Q14) Inf **ME22,** Wild canary . . alder bird.

alderita See **agarita**

alderman n Also *alderman's belly* **Nth** *somewhat old-fash* Cf **corporation**
An enlarged abdomen.

1934 Farrell *Young Manhood* 394 **Chicago IL,** Slob Lonigan! . . Got an alderman. Alderman on your gut, and couldn't even get yourself a decent girl. Slob! **1950** *WELS* (An oversize stomach) 1 Inf, **seWI,** Alderman. **1966–68** *DARE* (Qu. X53a, . . *An oversize stomach*) Infs **MA13, NY105,** Alderman; **MA72,** Alderman—[used] in the old days; **WI33,** Alderman's belly; (Qu. X53b, *An oversize stomach . . from drinking*) Inf **WI33,** Alderman's belly. [All Infs old]

alderman in chains n
A roast turkey garnished with link sausages.

[**1890** Farmer–Henley *Slang* 1.29/2, *An alderman in chains; i.e.,* a roast turkey well stuffed and garnished with sausages. The latter are said to be emblematical of the gold chain worn by the civic dignitary—what then about the stuffing?] **1954** Forbes *Rainbow* 342 **NEng,** Tite would be regulating the heat in the brick oven so it would be just right at midnight—which is the time to pop in "the alderman in chains" as we called our turkeys, because of the link sausages over them.

aldermite n
The larva of the alderfly (Sialidae).
1967 *DARE* (Qu. R4) Inf **PA58,** Aldermite—after they get wings, they live only a short time.

alder tag n, also attrib [Reversal of *tag alder*] **Sth**
Smooth alder (*Alnus oblongifolia*).
1966 *DARE* Tape **AL1,** Alder tag [ˈɔltəˈteɪg] vine; it's full of leaves and . . long fuzzy things . . that was tea for colds. [Inf Black] **1970** *DARE* (Qu. T15, . . *Swamp trees*) Inf **VA40,** Tag alder or alder tag; (Qu. BB22 . . *Home remedies . . for constipation*) Inf **VA41,** Alder tag tea [ˈɔltɚˈtæg]—old-fash. [Infs Black]

aleby trout n obs
=**burbot.**
1884 Goode *Fisheries U.S.* 1.236 **Gt Lakes,** Professor Jordan gives the names "Aleby-trout" and "Mother of Eels" as in use in the Upper Great Lake region.

aleck n [*smart aleck* bumptious person]
A rat.
1934 *Sun* (Baltimore MD) 16 Jan 22/3 (Hench Coll.), In the next building, closer to the water front, they caught an "aleck." The "Aleck" is a roof rat . . . The "Aleck" and the black rat, the trappers explained, were long-tailed rodents . . . "Alecks are the smartest of them all," Arthur explained.

alefish n Cf **alewife**
1970 *DARE* (Qu. P7, *Small fish used as bait for bigger fish*) Inf **VA55,** Alefish.

alegria n [MexSpan *alegría*] **SW**
An **amaranth** (here: *Amaranthus paniculatus*).

1844 (1954) Gregg *Commerce* 153 **NM,** The belles of the ranchos and villages have a disgusting habit of besmearing their faces with the crimson juice of a plant or fruit called *alegría,* which is not unlike blood. **1848** (1855) Ruxton *Life Far West* 192 **SW,** Coated with cosmetic *alegría*—an herb, with the juice of which the women of Mexico hideously bedaub their faces. **1947** (1976) Curtin *Healing Herbs* 24, *Alegria* Amaranthus paniculatus . . . was brought into this region by the Spaniards. **1968** Adams *Western Words, Alegría*—Pigweed, an herb used as a cosmetic; . . The leaves can be chewed or squeezed to produce a bright-red juice.

alewife n Usu |ˈelˌwaɪf, ˈɛlˌwaɪf|, infreq |ˈæl–|; **esp** in CT |ˈelˌwɒp, ˈɛlˌwɒp, –(h)wɒp|; rarely |ˈɛlˌwaɪ| Also sp *ailwife, alewhap, alewop, ellw(h)op, ellwife, elwife, elwop* For arch spp and addit varr see *DAE* and *LANE* Map 233 [Orig uncert; perh *ale + wife* (see quot 1674), or perh an Engl dial fish name (cf *EDD alley³, OED allice*); once thought to be derived from an AmInd term; discussion in 1945 AmSp 20.107] **chiefly C Atl, N Atl, Gt Lakes** See also **alefish, old wife**
Any of various fish generally of the Atlantic coast such as **round pompano,** a pilchard (*Harengula pensacolæ*), or **menhaden,** but esp a fish of the herring family (*Alosa pseudoharengus*) used commercially for oil and in feed products. This last is also called **big-eyed herring, blueback herring, branch herring, gaspereau, kyack, river herring, sawbelly, skipjack, spring herring.**

1633 in 1855 New Plymouth Colony *Records* 1.17, Whereas God . . hath cast the ffish (called) alewives or herringes in the middest of the place appointed for the town of New Plymouth. **1674** Josselyn *Two Voyages* 107, The *Alewife* is like a *herrin,* but has a bigger bellie therefore called an *Alewife.* **1765** Rogers *N. Amer.* 67, In the before-mentioned rivers [Hudson, Mohock] is great plenty of fish, such as shad, ail-wives, sturgeon. **a1870** Chipman (*DAE*), Alewife is called Alewhap, pl. alewhaps—Conn. **1884** Goode *Fisheries U.S.* 1.580, [The river herring] is pre-eminently the "Alewife" of New England; the "Ellwife" or "Ellwhop" of the Connecticut River. **1895** Brown *Meadow-Grass* 117 **NH,** He ketched 'em [=mumps] down to Portsmouth, when he went off on that fool's arrant arter elwives. **1905** *DN* 3.2 **cCT,** *Alewives,* . . Pronounced commonly *elwops.* **1907** *DN* 3.187 **seNH,** Ellwives are cheap now. **1939** *LANE* Map 1.233, *Alewives, Elwives, Alewops* . . Names for the *alewife* . . incidentally recorded from a number of informants. **1947** Coffin *Yankee Coast* 297, Herring we have, . . from the little brothers of seraphs that we call sardines and immortalize in olive oil in flat cans, up to the fat seraphs of alewives. (Pronounced L-Y's.) **1965–70** *DARE* (Qu. P3, *Freshwater fish . . not good to eat*) 20 Infs, Alewife. [18 of 20 Infs Gt Lakes]; (Qu. P4) Inf **NJ69,** Alewife—mostly for fertilizer and oil; **DE4,** [ˈelˌwaɪvz]; **ME10,** Alewife; **VA79,** Bunker = alewife; (Qu. P7) Inf **DC2,** [ˈelˌwaɪz] . . [are] fry of fish, minnow-like, close to surface of water, making it ripple; **ME22,** Alewives; (Qu. P14) Inf **VA79,** Alewife—used for fertilizer in Reedville plant; **MI123,** Alewives—formerly . . for dog food; **WI48,** Alewives; (Qu. P2) Inf **MD36,** Alewife . . some people eat, others use commercially for oil or manure. **1970** *DARE* Tape **VA112,** [ˈelˌwaɪvz]; **NJ67,** [ˈelˌwaɪ].

alewife bird n **MA**
=**Wilson's snipe.**
1888 Trumbull *Names of Birds* 157 **MA,** Nuttall (1834) speaks of its [*Gallinago delicata*] being in the vicinity of Cambridge, Mass., as the *alewife bird,* "from its arrival with the shoals of that fish." **1925** (1928) Forbush *Birds MA* 1.391, *Gallinago delicata* . . . Wilson's snipe. *Other names:* . . alewife-bird. **1955** *MA Audubon* 39.446 **MA,** *Wilson's snipe.* Alewife Bird.

alewop See **alewife**

Alexander Hamilton n
1 A ten-dollar bill. [Ref to portrait of Hamilton on the bill]
1967–70 *DARE* (Qu. U28b) Infs **DC12, IL21,** Alexander Hamilton.
‡2 One's signature. [By confusion or analogy with *John Hancock*]
1966 *DARE* (Qu. JJ13) Inf **FL25,** Alexander Hamilton.

alfalfa n, also attrib Usu |ˌælˈfælfə|; occas |–fi|, cf **-y;** rarely |–θə, –θi| or |ˌælˈfæsθə| Pronc-spp *alfalfy, alfalthy*
A Forms.
1914 *DN* 4.102 **KS,** Alfalthy. **1928** Ruppenthal *Coll.* **KS,** Alfalfy, alfalthy . . alfalfa. Large numbers of persons use the -i or -y sound instead of "short Italian a" at the end of words such as: alfalfa, Dora. **1930** *AmSp* 5.268 **Ozarks,** The hillman turns the *a* into *y,* just as he does

the final *a* in *soda, extra, alfalfa* and the like. **1965–70** *DARE* (Qu. L9b) Infs **KY**86, **LA**8, **MI**71, 107, **NJ**53, **PA**120, **VA**24, 46, [,æl'fælθə]; **KY**58, [,æl'fælfɪ]; (Qu. L9a) Inf **DC**5, [,æl'fæsθə]; (Qu. R30) Inf **KY**53, [,æl'fælfɪ] beetle. **1968** *DARE* Tape **IN**13, Alfalfa [,æl'fælfɪ].

B Senses.

1 Tobacco. *joc*

1940 *AmSp* 15.335 **Lincoln NE**, Tobacco is . . *the weed, . . hay, alfalfa, corn-shucks* [etc]. **1960** Wentworth–Flexner *Slang, Alfalfa* . . Smoking tobacco. *Underworld use. Obs.*

2 See quot. *joc*

1950 *Western Folkl.* 9.158 **cCA** ["Mountaineering Vocabulary"], *Alfalfa.* Dried spinach.

alforja n Also Americanized and sp *alfarga, alfarge, alfarky, alforche, alforga, alforge, alforka, alforki, alforkus, allforche* [Span *alforja*] **West** Cf **sawbuck**

A saddlebag; see also quot 1932.

[**1841** Stephens *Incidents Central Amer.* 1.88, And when she saw that our servant had pineapples in his alforgas, she asked why he brought them.] **1892** *DN* 1.187 **TX**, *Alfárga, -s, alforjas:* saddlebags. Used almost exclusively in the plural. The forms *alforge, alfarge,* etc., are also used in Texas. **1922** Rollins *Cowboy* 155, All or a part of the parcels might have been stuffed into 'alforjas,' which were wide, leathern or canvas bags . . hanging from the crosses on the saddle's top. **1932** Bentley *Spanish Terms* 91, *Alforjas,* is, in fact, commonly interpreted as "saddlebags." But it has been used also to designate a leather container not of saddle-bag nature. *Alforjas* is not nearly so commonly used, even by those whose borrowings from Spanish are most extensive, as is the English "saddle-bags." **1936** Adams *Cowboy Lingo* 48, The wide leathern or canvas bags, one on either side of a 'pack-saddle' and hanging from the crosses on the saddle's top, were called 'alforki.' This was a Spanish word which suffered much from American spelling, having been forced to appear as 'alforge,' 'alforka,' 'allforche,' and many other forms. **1942** Berrey–Van den Bark *Amer. Slang* 915.7, [Western slang] *Saddle bag.* Allforche, alforche, alforge, alforka, alforki. **1958** *AmSp* 33.268 **eWA**, *Alforkus* [æl'forkɪs] . . . A packsaddle; a corruption by folk etymology of the Spanish *alforja,* saddlebag. **1958** McCulloch *Woods Words* **Pacific NW**, *Alfarky*—A mule or horse pack . . . Unknown to latter day loggers and woodsmen; and many an old timer who has lost a rasslin' match with mules and alfarkies is also glad to forget the word.

‡algamite n [Prob var of **hellgrammite**]

1968 *DARE* (Qu. P6, *Other kinds of worms*) Inf **OH**87, Algamites.

algarite See **agarita**

algaroba n, also attrib Also sp *algarroba,* rarely *algarola* [See quots 1920, 1937] **SW, HI**

=**mesquite 1** (here: *Prosopis glandulosa* and *P. juliflora*).

1896 *Bot. Gaz.* 22.480 **AZ**, *Prosopis juliflora* . . algarola. **1920** Saunders *Useful Wild Plants* 61 **SW**, The Spanish term algarroba applied in Mexico and our Southwest to the Mesquit bean, is a case of transference, *algarrobo* being the word used in Spain for the carob tree. **1934** Frear *Lowell & Abigail* 116 **HI**, A picturesque symbol of the time [=1837] is the planting . . of the first algaroba tree. **1937** U.S. Forest Serv. *Range Plant Hdbk.* B112, When the Spanish conquistadores arrived in Mexico and the Southwest they called the mesquite "algaroba", as it reminded them of the closely related carob tree . . of their native land. The name algaroba is often used for mesquite in this country, and is universal in Hawaii, but is a misapplication of a Spanish–Arabic plant name. **1967** *DARE* Tape **HI**2, What we call kiawe or algaroba [ælJərobə]. Used for charcoal. **1967** *DARE* (Qu. I20, . . *Beans . . grown around here*) Inf **HI**11, Algaroba—fed to animals; (Qu. T16, *What kinds of trees are 'special' around here*) Inf **HI**11, Algaroba [ælJirobə].

algeredo n, also attrib Also sp *algerado* **SW** Cf **agarita**

=**granjeno**.

1937 Parks *Plants TX* 25, *Celtis pallida* . . a bush-like shrub which . . bears numerous berries . . which are collected for jellies and in many places sold under the name of algeredo. **1942** Friend *Plants Rio Grande* 53, *Celtis pallida.* Granjeno . . . These fruits are used in making 'Algerado' jelly.

algerita, algireta See **agarita**

algodon n [Span *algodón* cotton]

A southwestern species of **cottonwood.**

1878 Beadle *Western Wilds* 76 **TX**, A little grove of algodones beyond

the hacienda. **1977** Watts *Dict. Old West, Algodon* . . . In the Southwest this word for cotton was sometimes applied to the *cottonwood* tree.

alguacil n Also sp *alguazil* [Span] **SW** *now hist*

A constable or justice of the peace.

1888 Wallace *Land of Pueblos* 42 **NM, AZ**, The *Alguacil,* or Sheriff [of a pueblo village], carries out the orders of the Governor, and is overseer and director of the public works. **1931** *Amer. Mercury* 23.221 **NM**, Sosa then appointed from among the Indians themselves an *alcalde* and an *alguazil,* which were two essential officers of a Spanish village.

alguiritte See **agarita**

alibi v

1 usu with *out* or *away:* To excuse oneself speciously.

1917 *Collier's* 13 Oct 16/1 **sCA**, I ain't trying to alibi: it was a solid bone play. **1926** (1927) Black *You Can't Win* 3 **CA**, I am not lugging in the fact . . to alibi myself away from anything. **1963** Hohn *Dutchman on Brazos* 37 **TX**, I alibied out of it by deciding to wait and see how Mama reacted. **1966–70** *DARE* (Qu. II32, *To manage some way to shift the responsibility: "He said it wasn't his fault and tried to _____."*) Inf **CA**174, Alibi out; **FL**38, **NC**45, Alibi out of it.

2 To hedge; to avoid an issue.

1967 *DARE* (Qu. JJ45, . . *"We tried to pin him down, but he just kept _____."*) Infs **OH**5, **PA**39, Alibiing.

3 To malinger. Cf **alibi day**

1968–69 *DARE* (Qu. BB27, *When somebody pretends to be sick . . you'd say he's _____*) Infs **IL**43, **VA**18, Alibiing.

alibi day n *joc* Cf **alibi 3**

Among loggers: payday.

1958 McCulloch *Woods Words* 2 **Pacific NW**, *Alibi day*—Pay day in camp. This was the time when loggers suddenly developed toothache or thought up some other alibi which required a trip to town. **1969** Sorden *Lumberjack Lingo* **NEng, Gt Lakes.**

alicia n

An erect, hairy, yellow-flowered perennial plant *(Chapmannia floridana)* of the pea family native to Florida.

1933 Small *Manual SE Flora* 730, *Alicia* . . Dry pinelands, pen[insular] Fl[orid]a. **1942** Amer. Joint Comm. Horticult. Nomenclature *Std. Plant Names* 108, *Chapmannia* . . Alicia . . Florida A[licia]. **1953** Greene–Blomquist *Flowers South* 60, Alicia, Chapman's pea *(Chapmannia floridana)* . . Grows in dry pinewoods, peninsular Florida.

alicran See **alacran**

alight and look at one's saddle v phr For varr see quots *somewhat old-fash*

Come in and sit a spell—an invitation to stop and talk, and perhaps to share a meal.

1912 *DN* 3.570 **wIN**, Used only in the expression, "Won't you alight and look at your saddle?" **1937** *DN* 6.621 **csTX**, His cheery greeting to a horseman to *light and look at his saddle* is about the most hospitable invitation to dinner to be encountered. **1969–70** *DARE* (Qu. II15, *When somebody is passing by and you want him or her to stop and talk a while, you might say, "_____"*) Infs **MA**58, **WV**16, Alight and look to your beast. [Both Infs over 75 years old.]

alii n |ɑ'li(ʔ)i| [Haw *ali'i*] **HI**

A noble person, a chief.

1938 Reinecke *Hawaiian Loanwords* 3, Terms so rooted in the native culture that exact translation is difficult or impossible . . . [include:] *poi, pa'iai, ali'i. Ibid* 8, *Ali'i* [a–liʔi] . . . Properly, one of tabu rank; one of the ruling caste of early Hawaii. More recently, a Hawaiian chief of high rank. **1951** *AmSp* 26.20, Alii (chief). *Ibid* 117, They must inevitably have come upon the word *ali'i,* which is used indiscriminately in the Hawaiian language to mean 'chief,' 'chiefess,' 'king,' and 'queen.' **1955** Day *HI People* 19, The young chief . . had already assumed a leading role among the Hawaiian *alii,* or nobility. **1972** Carr *Da Kine Talk* 86 [In a list of Hawaiian words common in Hawaiian English], Ali'i.

alisier n [Fr *alisier* whitebeam *(Sorbus aria)*] **chiefly LA**

Either **black haw 1** or a **hawthorn.**

1897 Sudworth *Arborescent Flora* 339, *Viburnum prunifolium* . . . Common names . . . Alisier (La.). **1911** *Century Dict.,* Alisier . . . Creole F[rench] . . . The stag-bush, *Viburnum prunifolium.* [Louisiana]. **1931** Read *LA French* 2, Alisier . . . Blackhaw *(Viburnum rufidulum* Raf.). **1937** *Torreya* 37.101, *Viburnum rufidulum* . . Alisier, the fruit alise, Louisiana; in Missouri these names are applied to either black *(Viburnum)* or red *(Crataegus)* haws.

aliso n [Span "alder tree"]

1 =**sycamore** (here: *Platanus racemosa*). **CA**

1860 *Star* (Los Angeles CA) 22 Sept 2/3 (*Western Folkl.* 7.4), Over all spreads the mammoth tree known as the "Aliso." **1948** *Pacific Discovery* July–Aug 31/1 *(DA)*, The name *El Aliso* is the Spanish–Californian for the sycamore or plane tree which is a conspicuous feature in the canyons and along the watercourses on the rancho. **1948** *Western Folkl.* 7.4, *Aliso* . . . in California, frequently a sycamore. **1979** Little *Checklist U.S. Trees* 202, *Platanus racemosa* . . California sycamore . . . Other common names . . aliso (Spanish).

2 An alder.

1908 Ingersoll *Century Hist.* [xiii] **sCA,** Glossary . . Aliso, Alder tree. **1948** *Western Folkl.* 7.4, *Aliso.* An alder.

alive adj

Of bread or fruit: retaining freshness.

1912 Green *VA Folk-Speech* 63, Bread made from newly ground meal, being soft and elastic, instead of dry and crumbly, is said to be *alive.* **1947** *Daily Progress* (Charlottesville VA) 4 Feb 6/1 *(Hench Coll.),* Instead of joining the growing number of frozen food producers, Martin went up 20 degrees or so [above freezing] to box vegetables with a new "chilling process" that allows them to be picked vine-ripe and stored "alive" and fresh until the housewife uses them.

alkali n |'ælkə,laı| **West**

1 freq attrib: A soluble salt obtained from the ashes of plants; a type of soil rendered unfit for agriculture by the presence of such salt; also, a region where the soil is of this kind. (References are often indistinguishable.)

1848 Clayton *Emigrants' Guide* 3, Emigrants have lost many of their teams in the neighborhood of the *Alkali lakes,* in consequence of not knowing the distance from any one of these lakes to good water. **1869** Bowles *New West* 275, The alkali dust, dry with a season's sun, . . was thick and constant. *Ibid* 276, Bare alkali plains stretch out . . for miles. **1879** Twain *Sketches* 272 **NV,** That awful five days' journey, through alkali, sagebrush, peril of body, and imminent starvation. **1928** Wister *Virginian* 78, Sunrise found the white stage lurching eternally on across the alkali. **1951** Grant *Cowboy Encycl.* 15, Alkali dust opens bleeding cuts on the face. Old-time cowboys rubbed canned tomatoes on the cuts and also on the lips of the horses after they had drunk the water. **1966** *DARE* (Qu. C31) Inf **ND3,** ['ælkə,laı]. **1971** Bright *Word Geog. CA & NV* 164, *Badlands* /unfit for cultivation/ . . . alkali + (flats), (bed), (land), (ground), (soil) . . [Scattered usage, among 22% of Infs].

2 A person who lives, usu by choice, in an alkali region.

1904 White *Mountains* 239, The cave . . . is inhabited by an old "alkali" and half a dozen bear dogs. **1907** White *AZ Nights* 66, A man can do a heap with that much money. And yet an old 'alkali' is never happy anywhere else. **1977** Watts *Dict. Old West.*

3 See quot. [Absol, from *alkali poisoning*]

1971 Green *Village Horse Doctor* 32 **TX** (as of 1940s), One of the other constant questions was, "What do you know about alkali?" This was the local name for livestock that were poisoned by eating goldenrod in the wintertime.

alkali buttercup n

A **buttercup 1** (here: *Ranunculus cymbalaria*).

1953 Nelson *Plants Rocky Mt. Park* 71, Alkali buttercup or shore buttercup . . . It grows in moist meadows, especially on alkali or salty soil, and has been found in Horseshoe Park and along Cow Creek. **1966** Barnes–Jensen *Dict. UT Slang, Alkali Buttercup* . . a name often given to the Strawberry or Trailing Buttercup *(Ranunculus cymbalaria)* which grows along ditches.

alkali cordgrass n [From the habitat] **West**

=**cordgrass** (here: *Spartina gracilis*).

1950 Hitchcock *Manual Grasses* 513, *Spartina grácilis* . . Alkali cordgrass. **1956** St. John *Flora SE WA* 58, *Spartina gracilis* . . Alkali Cord Grass.

alkalied adj **West, esp Rocky Mts**

1 Saturated with, or affected by, **alkali,** usu by having drunk alkaline water.

1858 Stone *Put's Golden* 53, I joined a train and travelled on,/ And all seemed satisfied,/ Until our grub was nearly gone,/ And I got alkalied.

1870 Beadle *Utah* 444 *(DA),* It is only where small streams have run some distance across the plain that they are, in local phrase, 'alkalied.' **1907** White *AZ Nights* 126, "The trouble with you fellows," he proffered, "is that you're so plumb alkalied you don't know the real thing when you see it." **1942** Lillard *Desert Challenge* 140, Water was an ever-present problem . . . A cure for alkalied cattle was a plug of tobacco between two slices of bacon. [*DARE* Ed: *Alkalied* is a misnomer: "alkali disease" in cattle is now known to be caused by a toxic alcohol found in certain plants.]

2 Experienced in living in the West. Cf **alkali 2**

1936 Adams *Cowboy Lingo* 27, A man old in the ways of the West was sometimes called a 'rawhide,' and was said to be 'bone-seasoned' or 'alkalied,' the latter term meaning he was acclimated to the country. **1977** Watts *Dict. Old West, Alkalied* . . . Said of a man who was a veteran of the big dry country . . , much as in the desert fighting of World War II one would remark that a man had sand behind his ears.

alkali grass n

1 also *alkaline grass, alkali saltgrass:* A **saltgrass** (here: *Distichlis* spp).

1870 Pine *Beyond the West* 376 **NV,** Our horses recruited with a few blades of alkali grass about the spring. **1889** *Century Dict., Alkaligrass* . . . A name given to several species of grass growing in alkaline localities in the western portions of the United States, especially to *Distichlis spicata.* **1889** Vasey *Ag. Grasses* 61, *Distichlis maritima* (Salt Grass; Akaline [sic] Grass) . . . A perennial grass, growing . . . in alkaline soil throughout the arid districts of the Rocky Mountains. **1918** Visher *Geog. SD* 90, On the somewhat alkaline soil of many "blow-outs" and other undrained depressions, alkali grass replaces wheat grass. **1940** Gates *Flora KS* 126, Distichlis stricta . . . Alkaligrass, Saltgrass. **1973** Hitchcock–Cronquist *Flora Pacific NW* 636, Alkali s[altgrass] . . . D[is-tichlis] stricta.

2 A grass of the genus *Puccinellia.* Also called **goose grass** For other names of var spp see **salt meadow grass, sea speargrass**

1940 Gates *Flora KS* 136, Nuttall Alkaligrass. Moist usually alkalin [sic] or saline soil. **1950** Stevens *ND Plants* 57, *Alkali-grass* . . . Common, usually in scattered tufts at edges of ponds or on saline, wet flats. **1967** Braun *Monocotyledoneae* 75, *Puccinellia* . . . *Alkali Grass.* About 30 species of temperate and cold regions, chiefly of saline habitats. **1970** in 1983 *Carleton Coll.,* Alkali grass = *Puccinelia* [sic] *airoides.* **West. 1973** Hitchcock–Cronquist *Flora Pacific NW* 664.

3 A **death camas** (here: *Zigadenus elegans*).

1894 *Jrl. Amer. Folkl.* 7.102, *Zygadenus elegans* . . alkali-grass, Minn. **1950** Gray–Fernald *Manual of Botany* 427, *Alkali-grass* . . . Prairies, meadows and calcareous rocks. **1960** Correll *Plants TX* 381, *White camas, alkali-grass* . . . On wet ledges and seepage in canyons.

alkaline grass See **alkali grass 1**

alkali sacaton See **sacaton**

alkali saltgrass See **alkali grass 1**

alkali spot n **West**

=**hardpan 1.**

1918 Visher *Geog. SD* 27, Small gumbo areas, often popularly called "alkali spots," are found here and there even in the glaciated part of the state. **1948** *Ardmoreite* (Ardmore OK) 30 Mar 10/2 *(DA),* Long a primary problem to farmers is the appearance of alkali spots after a field has been in cultivation for years. **1966** *DARE* FW Addit **OK42,** Alkali spots . . Hard spots in a field where nothing will grow.

alkali weed n

1 A plant of the genus *Cressa.* **SW**

1913 *Pacific Coast Avifauna* 9.26 **CA,** Imagine a salt-grass pasture, . . the odor of alkali weeds, and half a dozen long-legged, black and white waders. **1959** Munz–Keck *CA Flora* 458, Alkali weed . . . saline and alkaline places, mostly below 4000 ft. **1967** *DARE* (Qu. S21, . . *Other weeds*) Inf **CO4,** Alkali weed.

2 A plant of the genus *Nitrophila.* **SW**

1941 Jaeger *Wildflowers* 48, Alkali-weed. *Nitrophila occidentalis* . . . Deserts east of the Sierra Nevada; to Ore. and Nev.

3 =**yerba mansa. CA**

1911 *Century Dict. Suppl, Alkali-weed* . . The yerba mansa, *Anemopsis Californica.*

alkomy See **alchemy**

all adj[1]

1 preceding *the* + a singular noun: The only. **chiefly Sth, Midl**
1908 *DN* 3.286 **eAL, wGA,** This is all the coat I've got. **1915** *DN* 4.180
VA, All the friend I've got. **1946** *PADS* 6.4 **neNC,** [Reported heard]
"That's all the pencil I have." . . Occasional among children. **1949**
PADS 11.16 **CO,** This is all the doll I have. **c1960** *Wilson Coll.* **csKY,**
That's all the brother I've got.

2 followed by a noun: Covered with—used esp in ref to substances that stick or cling; see quot 1976. **chiefly NEng** Cf **all over** adv phr **2**
1927 *Harper's Mag.* Nov 673/1 **CT,** Hang on to 'em, idiot; don't you
dare let 'em get all sand again. **1931–33** *LANE Worksheets* **cnCT,**
Don't pick that rag up, it's all grease. *Ibid* **nwMA,** My hands is all
grease. *Ibid* **ceMA,** All gudgeon [means] greasy. Gudgeon is the grease
that comes off the end of the axle mixed with iron filings. **1976** *DARE*
File **cnMA,** My hands could be all butter, all flour, all paint—"all"
anything that sticks or clings. Not, I think, "all milk," "all water." **1979**
Stegner *Recapitulation* 34 **UT,** "I was all *muddy!*" . . He said once more,
"I'm all *mud!*"

all adj[2] [PaGer *all* from Ger *alle* all gone] **chiefly PA, also N Cent** See Map Addit quots in 1944 *ADD.* See also **all anymore**
Of quantifiable nouns, esp food or drink: consumed, used up, gone. Of persons: dead.
1859 (1968) Bartlett *Americanisms* 5 **PA,** A servant will say, "The
potatoes is *all any more,*" . . or she will say simply, "They's all." **1892**
KS Univ. Qrly. 1.95 **KS, IN, PA,** *All:* all gone, as, The corn is all. **1914**
DN 4.157 **sePA.** **1916** *DN* 4.271 **NE, PA, MI, KS.** **1916** *DN* 4.337
scPA, OH, sNE. **1928** *AmSp* 3.463 **ncPA.** **1931** *AmSp* 7.19 **swPA.**
1937 *AmSp* 12.287 **cnVA,** The Shenandoah German may say, 'The salt
is all,' meaning the salt is all gone. **1939** Aurand *Quaint Idioms* 22
sePA, The ginger-ale is *all* but the soda is *yet.* Sort o' far-fetched—but
one can hear it rendered thus. **1941** *AmSp* 16.21 **sIN.** **1942** Warnick
Garrett Co. MD (as of 1900–18). **1942** Greene *Papa is All* [A Comedy
In Three Acts]. **1950** *WELS* ("The potatoes are ———.") 10 Infs,
c,sWI, All. [Marked *German* by 3 Infs, *colloquial* by 1.] *Ibid,* 1 Inf,
seWI, There used to be lots of fish here, but now they're all. **1965–70**
DARE (Qu. LL17, . . *There's no more of something: "The potatoes are
———.")* 34 Infs, **chiefly PA, also N Cent,** All; (Qu. H74b) Inf **PA203,**
The coffee must be all.

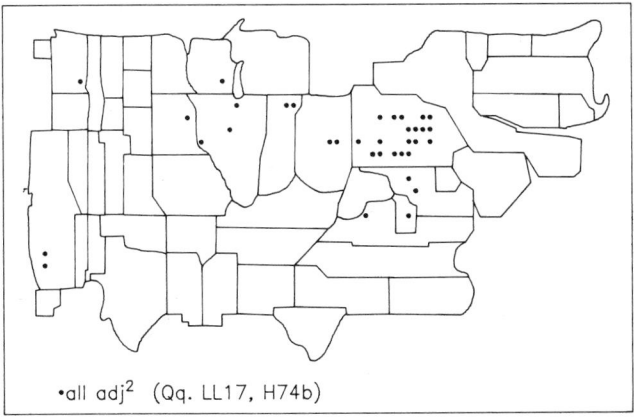
•all adj[2] (Qq. LL17, H74b)

all n
The whole; entirety.
1965 *DARE* (Qu. GG22a, *When you have come to the end of your
patience . . , "Well, that's the ———."*) Inf **OK1,** That's the all of it.

-all pron suff
Used as a pluralizing suffix with a personal, relative, or interrogative pronoun: see **I-all, they-all, we-all, you-all, you-all's; whatall, where-all, who-all, why-all**

all along of See **along of 1**

all-and-all n *joc*
1 One's wife.
1970 *DARE* (Qu. AA22, . . *"I have to go down and pick up my
———."*) Inf **NJ64,** All-and-all.
2 One's best clothes.
1970 *DARE* (Qu. W39) Inf **CT43,** All-and-all.

all and each, all and every See **each and every**

all anyhow adv phr [Cf *OEDS* anyhow "in random fashion"]
In a confused or disorderly manner.
1942 Berrey–Van den Bark *Amer. Slang* 5.5, In confusion. All anyhow. **1950** Moore *Candlemas Bay* 38 **ME,** Guy came to his feet in a
horrified scramble, all anyhow, pulling himself up by the boat's cheeserind.

all anymore adj phr [Redund: all adj[2] + anymore] **PA, NJ**
=**all** adj[2].
1859 (1968) Bartlett *Americanisms* 5, *All any more.* A common expression in Pennsylvania among the illiterate to mean "all gone." Thus a
servant will say, "The potatoes is *all any more.*" **1872** Schele de Vere
Americanisms 578, *All any more* . . is a Pennsylvania vulgarism . . . The
waiter at the hotel will say, "The pies are *all any more,* Sir," meaning that
there are no more. **1902** (1968) Clapin *Americanisms* 12, *All any
more* . . . A Pennsylvania vulgarism signifying "all gone." . . This curious piece of jargon is also frequently heard in New Jersey. **c1940** in
1944 *ADD* **sePA,** 'It's all any more' = The train has gone by.

all arms and legs See **all thumbs**

all around adv phr **S Atl**
Near, close to.
1938 Rawlings *Yearling* 344 **nFL,** I come all around courtin' her, 'fore I
married your Ma. **1950** *PADS* 14.11 **SC,** He came all around winning . . . He was all around passing out. **1964** Will *Hist. Okeechobee* xi
FL, *Come all around to*—nearly succeed.

‡all-around n
=**runaround.**
1967 *DARE* (Qu. JJ45, *We tried to pin him down, but he just kept
———*) Inf **LA12,** Giving us the all-around.

all around one's elbow See **go around one's elbow to get to one's thumb**

all at once adv phr [Cf *OED* at once 1, "at one stroke . . *Obs.*"]
All of a sudden; suddenly.
1929 *AmSp* 5.122 **ME,** One who died suddenly "died all at once."

all both pron [Perh an African calque: see **all two** etym note]
chiefly coastal SC *Gullah* See also **both two**
Both.
1927 Adams *Congaree* 8 **cSC** [Black], White folks an' niggers, all both
of them, an' all lined up 'side of de road. **1955** *PADS* 23.41 **SC,** Forms
characteristic of the entire South, such as *all two, all both* 'both'.
1966–67 *DARE* (Qu. LL21, *Two things . . "Do you want the red one or
the blue one?" "I want ——— of them."*) Infs **SC9, 19, 26,** All both
[FW: in conv]; **SC11, 21,** All both [Reported heard but not used]; **SC24,
45,** All both [Resp sugg by FW]; **SC65,** All both—countrified but still in
use; going out of use; **SC44,** All both—kids would use this. **1967** *DARE*
FW Addit **SC,** If you hurt a snake so he can't go, a green snake or doctor
snake will be there shortly to help him and all both of them gone.

all by one's lone(some) See **all (of) one's lone**

all change places n
A children's game: =**fruit basket upset.**
1954 *Harder Coll.* **cwTN.**

all clear exclam
=**all (in) free.**
1968–70 *DARE* (Qu. EE15) Infs **CT42, PA66,** All clear.

all come in (home) (free) See **all (in) free**

all-day(er) n [Absol, from *all-day sewing, all-day rain,* etc] Cf
all-nighter
An activity or occurrence expected to last an entire day.
1931 *AmSp* 7.19 **swPA,** All-day sewing at a church. "The ladies will
have an all-day on Tuesday." **1968** *DARE* (Qu. B25, *Any joking names
around here for a very hard rain?*) Inf **NJ31,** All-dayer.

all-day meeting n Cf **big meeting**
1912 Green *VA Folk-Speech,* All-day meeting. In the summer-time in
the country; there was a sermon in the morning; rest in the middle of the
day for dinner; then service again; in the Baptist and Methodist churches.

all-day singing n Also *singing-all-day;* similarly *all-night singing* **Sth**

A festive day-long church gathering; in conjunction with **dinner on the ground.**

   1909 *DN* 3.370 **eAL, wGA,** *Singing, (all day)* . . . A gathering of singers to spend the day in practising. Dinner is served on the ground, and a general good time for all is the order of the day. **1933** (1965) Jackson *White Spirituals* 3 **sAppalachians,** [He] described one of the fasola "singin'-all-day-and-dinner-on-the-grounds" conventions which he had observed in Texas. **1942** (1960) Robertson *Red Hills* 160 **SC,** We can . . lay the crop by and go off to camp meetings and all-day singings and fish fries. **1954** *PADS* 21.19 **GA,** An all-day religious songfest with picnic lunch on the grounds . . . *All-day singing* is a custom of long standing . . . An *all-night singing* was recently reported from Florida. **c1965** *Thompson Coll.* **Birmingham AL** (as of 1920s), All day sayngin with dinner own the groun(d)s, whiskey's in the bushes an the devil's all aroun. **1967** *DARE* (Qu. FF1) Inf **TX33,** All-day singings and eating on the ground.

all day with one, be v phr **chiefly NEast** *old-fash*

To be a hopeless situation for someone.

   1836 *Knickerbocker* 8.205 **NY,** Marlinspike now swore that it was all day with him; and . . he might as well content himself. **1840** Haliburton *Clockmaker* (3d ser) 204 **NEng,** Corcoran, the head of our sect is in jail. They are a-goin' to give him a birth in the states prison. It's all day with him now; and I must say it kinder sarves him right. **1856** Whitcher *Bedott Papers* 328 **NY,** If 'Daddy-long-legs' . . once gets his dander up it'll be all day with the parson; for some how or other, he's contrived to git considerable influence in the parish. **1889** Munroe *Golden Days* 153 **CA,** If you hadn't toed the mark, good and square, . . 'twould have been all day with me.

‡all ease adv phr

Without difficulty; easily.

   1969 *DARE* (Qu. KK42, . . *"He could do that _____."*) Inf **KY36,** All ease.

allée n [Fr *allée* path, passage]

A tree-lined promenade: see quot and cf **alley** n¹, **alameda.**

   1941 FWP *Guide LA* 685, *Allée* . . . A double row of trees leading from the road or river to a plantation house.

all-ee all-ee (all) in free exclam Usu |ˈɔli, ˈɑli|, less freq |ˈæli| (repr here by pronc-sp *allie*) For var phrr see quots (Note: the final vowel sound in *all-ee* is added for audibility and rhythm; for similar usage in Engl see 1959 (1967) Opie *Lore Schoolchildren* 143.) **chiefly Nth** See Map See also **Ole Ole Olson all in free**

In the children's game of hide and seek: =**all (in) free.**

   1965–70 *DARE* (Qu. EE15) 25 Infs, **chiefly Nth,** All-ee all-ee in free; 20 Infs, **Nth,** All-ee all-ee all in free; 9 Infs, **chiefly NEast,** Allie allie in free; **PA213, WA22,** Allie allie in come free; **IA34,** All-ee all-ee all-ee in free; **OH37,** All-ee all-ee alls in free; **CO26,** All-ee all-ee alts comes in free; **MA64,** All-ee in free; **WI77,** Allie all in free; **MA71,** Allie allie; **CA112,** Allie allie all's in free; **IL97,** Allie allie all come free; **IL116,** Allie allie free. **1977–78** Foster *Lexical Variation* 79 **NJ,** *Allie allie in free* (20 responses), *allie allie in come free* (2), and *allie allie in clear* (1).

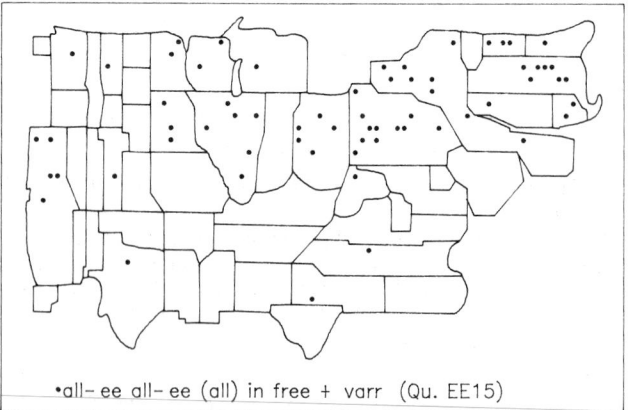

•all-ee all-ee (all) in free + varr (Qu. EE15)

all-ee all-ee auction free exclam Also ~*come out free,* ~*free-free-free* Varr of **all-ee all-ee oxen (all in) free** **sCA, HI**

   1967–68 *DARE* (Qu. EE15) Inf **HI4,** All-ee all-ee auction [ɔkšǝn] come out free; **CA37,** All-ee all-ee auction free; **CA87,** All-ee all-ee auction free-free-free. **1980** *DARE* File **sCA** (as of c1955), After the person who was "it" couldn't find any more people, he would call, "Ally, Ally, auction free!"

all-ee all-ee out(s) in free exclam For varr see quots Varr of **all's out('s) (come) in free** **chiefly Inland Nth, West** See Map See also **allsie allsie outs in free**

   1950 *WELS* (Games in which every player hides except *"it"*) 1 Inf, **csWI,** Hide and go seek — ["It" calls out] to get the players back after one is caught, [ˈoli ˈɔli] outs in free. **1965–70** *DARE* (Qu. EE15) 39 Infs, **chiefly wPA, nwIL, and west of Missip R,** All-ee all-ee (*or* allie allie) outs in free; **IA38, KS15, MT4, NY184, RI15,** All-ee all-ee's out(s) in free; **CA9, 14,** All-ee all-ee all outs (in) free; **MN30,** All-ee all-ee out come in; **OR1,** All-ee all-ee outs come in free; **WY4,** All-ee all-ee outs in; **NY234,** Allie allie out in free; **NV3,** All-ees all-ees outs in free; **DC2, IL43, MI44, NE6, OH65, TX68, WA22,** All-ee all-ee (*or* allie-allie) oops in free; **CA174, MI44,** Allie allie opes in free; **IL27, 47, OH93, WI47,** Allie allie otts (*or* oats) in free; **IL100,** All-ee all-ee osh in free; **MI118, TX88,** All-ee all-ee ump (in) free. **1977–78** Foster *Lexical Variation* 79 **NJ,** Allie allie out in free . . 1 [Inf].

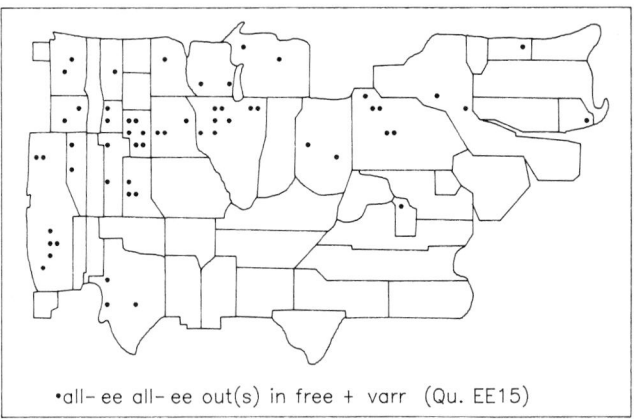

•all-ee all-ee out(s) in free + varr (Qu. EE15)

all-ee all-ee oxen (all in) free exclam For varr see quots [Var of **all-ee all-ee out(s) in free**] **chiefly West and Gt Lakes, esp CA** See Map

In the childen's game of hide and seek: =**all (in) free.**

   1965–70 *DARE* (Qu. EE15) 11 Infs, **chiefly Upper MW, CA,** All-ee all-ee ox in free; 10 Infs, **chiefly West, esp CA,** Allie allie oxen free; **CA59, 107, 182, 190, 207, MT1, PA185,** Allie allie ox in free; **AL41, CA82, 93, IN39, PA7,** All-ee all-ee oxen free; **UT7, 12,** Allie allie oxen all in free; **CA169, FL5,** All-ee all-ee oxen all in free; **OR10,** All-ee ox in free; **CA94, MO26,** Allie all(ie) ax in free; **VT16,** All-ee all-ee ex in free; **IL9,** Allie allie awk in free; **UT10,** Allie allie oxford all in free. **1972** *Yesterday* 1.4.28 **WI,** You would start walking down the alley very carefully . . . Then you spotted someone . . . Thereupon, you both raced back toward the telephone pole and the first one there yelled: "Alle, alle, oxen free!" **1977–78** Foster *Lexical Variation* 79 **NJ,** *Allie allie oxen free* . . 12 [Infs]. **1980** *DARE* File **csNE,** Ally ally oxen free.

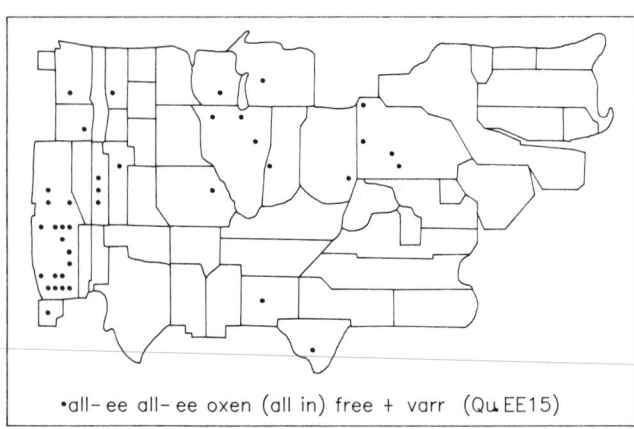

•all-ee all-ee oxen (all in) free + varr (Qu. EE15)

allee samee adv phr Also ~ *in Dutch* [Imit of presumed Pidgin English] *joc*

All the same; nevertheless; see also quot 1945.

1883 in 1909 Ware *Passing Engl.* 6/2 **NYC,** It appeared that they were not quite married, but that they lived together allee samee. **1897** *KS Univ. Qrly.* 6.85 **KS,** *Allee samee* (sometimes *"allee samee in Dutch"*): all the same, for emphasis; nevertheless. **1929** Ruppenthal *Coll.* **KS,** *Allee samee* . . . nevertheless . . . in imitation of Chinese brogue. **1945** Colcord *Sea Language* 22 **ME, Cape Cod MA, Long Island NY,** *Allee samee.* Like. "Allee samee hell you will!" Pidgin English, brought home by sailors.

Alleghany foamflower See **foamflower**

Alleghany fringe See **Alleghany vine**

Allegheny hellbender See **hellbender**

Allegheny oilnut See **oilnut 2**

Allegheny skiff n *now hist* Cf **Mississippi skiff**

A shallow-draft cargo boat used on or associated with the Allegheny River.

1826 Flint *Recollections* 14 **PA,** Then there are what the people call 'covered sleds,' or ferry-flats, and Allegany-skiffs, carrying from eight to twelve tons. **1941** Baldwin *Keelboat Age* 42 (as of c1800), The smaller bateaux were sometimes called skiffs, and this name was also applied occasionally to the larger bateaux, usually with the prefix 'Allegheny' or 'Mackinaw,' which probably had little to do with the origin of the particular boat named.

Allegheny vine n Also sp *Alleghany ~; also Alleghany fringe* **eUS**

=**mountain fringe 1.**

1850 Cooper *Rural Hours* 170 **cNY,** The Alleghany vine, with its pale pink clusters and very delicate foliage, is very common in some places. **1876** Hobbs *Bot. Hdbk.* 24, Climbing fumitory, Alleghany fringe, Adlumia cirrhosa. **1900** Lyons *Plant Names* 16, Mountain-fringe, wood-fringe, Alleghany-fringe, Alleghany-vine. **1910** Graves *Flowering Plants* 197 **CT,** Mountain or Wood Fringe. Alleghany or Canary Vine . . . Local or occasional northward in the western half of our area. **1953** Strausbaugh–Core *Flora WV* 414, *Alleghany Vine.* Handsome slender vines . . . principally in the Alleghenies.

alleluia n [Origin uncert, perh from its flowering during the Easter season when 'alleluia' is sung: see *OED* quots 1543 →] **chiefly sAppalachians**

The common **wood sorrel 1** *(Oxalis acetosella).*

1900 Lyons *Plant Names* 271, *O[xalis] Acetosella* . . . Alleluia. **1901** Lounsberry *S. Wild Flowers* 288, White wood-sorrel . . . In some places even it is known by the delightful name of "Alleluia." **1932** *Country Life* 62.67, **NC, TN,** One of the Appalachian wild plants, known locally as Alleluia, is none other than the White Wood Sorrel. **1959** Carleton *Index Herb. Plants* 2.

Allen plow n [?Mfgr's name]

=**turnplow.**

1949 *AmSp* 24.106 **cSC.**

allerickstix adv [See quot 1890] *?obs*

All right.

1890 *DN* 1.60 **Cincinnati OH,** *Allerickstix* (used in common schools of Cincinnati): all right. *E.g.:* Qu. "How did you get through examination?" Ans. "Allerickstix." Presumably a corruption of German *alles richtig,* used as an equivalent for the English *all right.* **1892** *DN* 1.234 **KY.** **1902** (1968) Clapin *Americanisms.* **1980** *DARE* File **neOH,** *Allerickstix*—I heard this used in Akron, Ohio, in an English context, about 1922 by a young male, about 14–15 yrs old.

allers See **always**

allers ago See **always-ago** adv

alley n[1] [Fr *allée* journey, passage, going, track] Cf **allée**

1 also *alleyway:* A road of secondary importance, often private or unpaved. **chiefly Nth, N Midl**

1788 (1975) Freneau *Poems & Misc. Wks.* 2.223 **C Atl,** The *article* stipulated expressly, that the alley-way should be *sufficient for the passing and repassing* of the plaintiff. **1931** *AmSp* 7.19 **swPA,** *Alleys.* Private lanes or drives. **1968** *DARE* (QR p99) Inf **CA71 San Francisco,** In the city [small streets used to be] called *alleys;* there was no negative

connotation then. They are called *lanes* now. **1968–69** *DARE* (Qu. N27a, . . *Kinds of unpaved roads*) Infs **IL48, 98, PA93, 94,** Alley(s); (Qu. N29, . . *A less important road running back from a main road*) Infs **IL32, NY226, OH87, PA134,** Alley(s).

2 A passage between rows of planted vegetation. **chiefly S Atl**

1833 Silliman *Man. Sugar Cane* 17 (*DA*), There is great danger of disturbing the roots, which . . extend far into the alleys. **1857** in 1969 Turner *Cotton Planter's Manual* 133 **eSC,** The beds for cotton, corn, and potatoes, are all made in the same manner and distance apart, and reversed every other crop; that is, changed into the alleys of the preceding one. **1899** (1912) Green *VA Folk-Speech* 64, *Alley* . . . In a garden between a row of flowers. **1946** *PADS* 6.4 **ceNC,** *Alley* . . The space between two rows of corn, cotton, etc.; the sloping, concave area made by plowing out the middle or balk. The space is called an *alley* after the crop is laid by. **1949** Turner *Africanisms* 283 **eSC,** From top of the bed you bring the grass all down to the alley till all the land done fix that way.

3 A narrow lane or back street in a city, often suggesting darkness, poverty and crime. See *DS* C 33–35, II25, and headwords, e.g., **hog-pen alley, mortgage alley, pig alley**

1841 *Knickerbocker* 18.521, He was busy about the village, penetrating every grog-hole and gambling-alley. **1865** Stowe *House & Home* 38 **NEng,** We have been eating in a little dingy den, with a window looking out on a back-alley. **1931** *AmSp* 7.22 **WY,** [At Yellowstone Park:] *Savage Alley*—row or street on which employees' cabins are located. **1948** *AmSp* 23.250 **neTX** [At North Texas Agricultural College:], *Tin Can Alley* . . . one of the parking lots on the campus.

4 An empty track in a railroad yard.

1932 *Santa Fe Employes' Mag.* 26.2 Jan 34/1, A clear track in a yard is an alley. **1945** Hubbard *Railroad Ave.* 331. **1969** *AmSp* 44.253 **Chicago IL.**

5 also *alleyway:* A relatively narrow conduit; spec a trough, an **eaves trough,** or a **hay chute.**

1950 *WELS* (*What do cows and horses eat out of?*) 1 Inf, **csWI,** Feed alley. **1965–70** *DARE* (Qu. D28, *What hangs below the edge of the roof to carry off rain-water?*) Infs **FL18, MA124, OH78,** Alley; (Qu. M5, . . *The hole for throwing hay down below*) Inf **MS66,** Alley; **OH35,** Alleyway.

6 =**driveway.**

1955 Stong *Blizzard* 13 **IA,** I'll have the heifers in the hay alley.

7 also *alleyway:* Among loggers: a covered passage between two buildings. Also called **dingle, midway** n Cf **dogtrot**

1956 Sorden–Ebert *Logger's Words* **Gt Lakes.** **1969** Sorden *Lumberjack Lingo* 1 **Gt Lakes, NEng,** *Alley* or *alley way*—The roofed-over space between the kitchen and sleeping quarters where meat and wood were stored. Same as dingle, midway.

8 In logging: see quot.

1958 McCulloch *Woods Words* 2 **Pacific NW,** *Alley*—The space between two pockets in a booming ground. A long, narrow float on which the swifter machine [=winch] is placed.

9 See **alleyway 1.**

alley n[2] Also sp *allie, ally* [Abbr for **alabaster** + -ie 3] **chiefly NEast** See Map

1 A playing marble, orig of alabaster and subsequently of glass in imitation of alabaster, considered a favorite marble to be used as a shooter or taw.

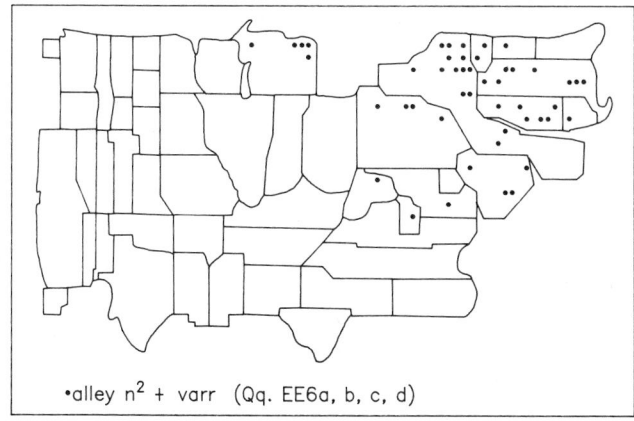

•alley n[2] + varr (Qq. EE6a, b, c, d)

1848 Bartlett *Americanisms* 7, *Alley*. . . An ornamental marble, used by boys for shooting in the ring . . ; also called in England, a *taw*. It is often made of white marble or of painted clay. **1876** Twain *Tom Sawyer* 27 **MO,** I'll give you a marvel. I'll give you a white alley . . . White alley, Jim! And it's a bully taw. **1890** *DN* 1.76 **NY, NJ.** **1958** *PADS* 29.29 **WI,** *Alley, shooter*. . . A shooter or taw. **1965–70** *DARE* (Qu. EE6a, . . *Marbles—the big one that's used to knock others out of the ring*) 27 Infs **chiefly NEast,** Allie; **DC3,** Glass allie; **NJ53,** Shooting allie.

2 Any playing marble.

1892 *DN* 1.219 **DC,** *Allies:* marbles. *Marbles* is never used. **1950** *WELS* (*Small marbles*) 1 Inf, **csWI,** Allies. **1951** *PADS* 15.65 **cwNH** (as of 1920s) *Alley*. . . Glass marble. Commonly this term means merely marble. **1951** Johnson *Resp. to PADS 20* **DE,** (*Nicknames for marbles*) Allies. **1955** *PADS* 23.10 **1958** *PADS* 29.29 **NJ, PA, WI.** **c1960** *Wilson Coll.* **csKY.** **1965–70** *DARE* (Qu. EE6b, *Small marbles or marbles in general*) Infs **CT3, MA52, 64, NY18,** Allies; **MD12,** [ˈæləz]; (Qu. EE6c, *Cheap marbles*) Inf **CT11,** Allies; (Qu. EE6d, *Special marbles*) 11 Infs, **chiefly NEast,** Allies; Infs **MI44, MA42,** Glass allies; **NY213,** Steel allies.

alley-alley n [alley n²] Cf **agate-agate**

A playing marble of real alabaster.

1896 *DN* 1.411 **NYC,** *Ally-ally:* a term in marbles, equivalent to *agate-agate.*

alley(-alley)-over n, exclam Also sp *olly-olly-over* Cf **illy-ally-over** and *DS* EE22, 23a

=**Antony-over** n, exclam.

1950 *WELS* (*Game in which you throw a ball over a low building*) 1 Inf, **ceWI,** Olly-olly over—Common. *Ibid* (*What do you say or call out when you throw the ball*) **ceWI,** [Same Inf:] Olly-olly over. **1967–69** *DARE* (Qu. EE22, . . *The game in which they throw a ball over a building*) Infs **MO27, OH40, PA152, TX11,** Alley over; **IL51, NY94,** Alley-alley over; (Qu. EE23, . . *What do you call out when you throw the ball*) Infs **NY94, 228,** Alley-alley over!; **PA152,** Alley-over!

alley apple n [alley n¹ 3 + apple] *joc*

1 A brick, rock or stone, usu when used as a missile. Cf **Irish confetti**

1927 *AmSp* 2.390 ["Argot of the Vagabond"], A rock is an *alley-apple.* **1934** *Sun* (Baltimore MD) 7 Dec 28/3 (*Hench Coll.*), For the next sixty days . . a brick-tossing seaman can sit in a cell in the City Jail and regret his marksmanship with an "alley apple." **1946** D. Runyon (synd. newsp. col.) 14 Sept (*DAS*), A fellow's blonde usually stepped in . . and slugged the other gee with an alley apple or a ground biscuit, meaning a rock done up in a stocking. **1960** Partridge *Slang* 422, *Alley Apple.* A stone or brickbat employed in street fighting ([from] 1860). **1970** *DARE* (Qu. C26) Inf **PA239,** Alley apple—a new slang word for *brick.*

2 A piece of horse manure. Cf **road apple,** and *DS* L17.

1960 Wentworth–Flexner *Slang.* **1967** *DARE* Tape **PA29.** **1967** *DARE* FW Addit **sePA,** Alley apples—horse droppings. Old-fashioned term, used chiefly by males. Also called *street apples*. [FW note: Amish people drive horses in this area.]

alley bat n [alley n¹ 3 + bat prostitute *(DAS)*; cf the common *alley cat* in similar use *(DAS, OEDS)*]

A promiscuous, careless or slovenly woman—sometimes used as a general term of abuse.

1968–69 *DARE* (Qu. AA7b, . . *A woman who is very fond of men and is always trying to know more—if she's not respectable about it*) Inf **GA77,** Alley-bat; (Qu. HH37, *An immoral woman*) Inf **GA19,** Alley-bat; (Qu. HH36) Inf **GA77,** Alley-bat.

alley-cat v [From *alley cat* promiscuous woman *(DAS, OEDS)*] Cf **alley bat, alley cat** n, **eave cat, tomcat** v

To behave in a sexually promiscuous manner.

1958 Voelker *Anatomy of Murder* 292 **nMI,** You mean, Officer, [you tried] to find out whether it might not have been her husband who beat her up for staying out alley-catting? **1966** *DARE* (Qu. Y29b, *Or, about a man who doesn't stay home much: "He's always _____"*) Inf **WA3,** Alley-catting.

alley cat n Cf **alley-cat** v

An illegitimate child.

1966 *DARE* (Qu. Z11b) Inf **SC3,** Woods colt, bastard, alley cat.

alley dog n [By analogy with the now std *alley cat*]

A mongrel dog.

1967–70 *DARE* (Qu. J1, . . *A dog of mixed breed*) Infs **IL15, IN69,**

PA242, TN20, TX62, Alley dog; (Qu. J2, . . *Joking or uncomplimentary words . . for dogs*) Infs **IL26, MI72, TN52, TX13,** Alley dog.

alley line n

In marble play: =**starting line,** toward which alleys are thrown to begin the game.

1968 *DARE* (Qu. EE8) Inf **MD12,** Alley line.

alley oop(s) n, exclam Cf *DS* EE22, 23a

=**Antony-over** n, exclam.

1967–70 *DARE* (Qu. EE22, . . *The game in which they throw a ball over a building*) Inf **TX68,** Alley-oop; **MI67,** Alley-oops; (Qu. EE23a, . . *What do you call out when you throw the ball*) Inf **TX68,** Alley-oop; **IL128,** Alley-oops [ˈɑli ˈups].

alley-over See **alley(-alley)-over**

alley taw n Also *~tor* Cf **shooting taw** and *DS* EE6a–d

In marble play: a shooter.

1955 *PADS* 23.10 **cwTN,** *Alley taw (-tor, -taw)* . . . (tautological compound). The offensive marble, or the marble used as a shooter.

alley-waiter n Also sp *ally-waiter* [Folk-etym, perh infl by *dumbwaiter*]

An elevator.

1896 *DN* 1.411 **nwMD,** *Ally waiter:* pop. etym for *elevator*. **1942** Berrey–Van den Bark *Amer. Slang* 81.21, *Elevator*. Alley-waiter.

alleyway n

1 also *alley:* A long hall or corridor; a narrow passage within a house, building, or train.

1854 *Harper's Mag.* 9.849/2 **GA,** I was taken to the Auburn state-prison. And as I walked along the concealed alley-ways, . . I bethought me of my theft of fruit. **1926** *DN* 5.385 **ME,** "Hang your coat in the alley-way." Rare. **1970** Major *Afro–Amer. Slang, Alley:* corridor in a hospital. **1977** Adams *Lang. Railroader* 6, *Alleyway:* A corridor. The narrow passage at the side of staterooms and compartments in sleeping and parlor cars.

2 A side yard.

1916 *DN* 4.346 **New Orleans LA.**

3 See **alley** n¹ 1, 5, 7.

all feet, all fingers See **all thumbs**

all-fire n [Back-formation from **all-fired** adj or adv] *old-fash, euphem*

Hellfire.

1899 Edwards *Defense* 20 **GA,** Hit did rain like all-fire. **1968** *DARE* (Qu. GG40) Inf **SC58,** Mad as all-fire [fɑr].

all-fired ady Also (by assim of final [d]) *all-fire* [Euphem for *hell-fired*] **widespread** *somewhat old-fash*

Extremely.

1837 *Yale Lit. Mag.* 2.149 *(DAE),* Star's an all-fired good ox. **1854** Stephens *High Life in NY* 1.26, My eyes begun to grow allfired bright. **1865** *Atlantic Mth.* 15.671, I didn't feel so all-fired cold as I hev sometimes. **1905** *DN* 3.2 **CT.** *Ibid* 3.60 **eNE.** **1907** *DN* 3.208 **nwAR.** **1908** *DN* 3.286 **eAL, wGA.** **1910** *DN* 3.436 **wNY.** **1914** *DN* 4.68 **ME, nNH.** **1927** *AmSp* 3.140 **ME coast.** **1940** Faulkner *Hamlet* 44 **MS,** Looking a right smart less easy in the face and most all-fired watchful. **1950** (1965) Richter *Town* 30 **OH,** Where folks were so all-fired clean and white of their sins that a person from another settlement couldn't stand looking at them till he smoked up a piece of glass. **1965–70** *DARE* (Qu. LL37, . . *"I could have wrung her neck, I was so _____ mad."*) 36 Infs, **scattered,** All-fired. [Of all Infs responding to the question, 63% were old; of those giving this response, 89% were old.]; Inf **FL22,** All-fire; (Qu. GG40) Inf **WV3,** All-fired mad.

all-fired adj Also superl *all-firedest* [Euphem for *hell-fired*] *somewhat old-fash*

Extreme, severe—often used as an intensifier or mild oath.

1835 *Boston Pearl* 28 Nov 81/1, He made so many stupid mistakes that his boss . . got out of patience with him, and gin him a most all-fired cut with a horsewhip. **1864** Lowell *Fireside Travels* 185, This 'ere's the allfiredest, powerfullest moon 't ever you *did* see. **1898** Westcott *Harum* 182, I had the all-firedist lickin' ahead of me 't I'd ever got. **1905** *DN* 3.2 **cCT.** **1907** *DN* 3.208 **nwAR.** **1908** *DN* 3.286 **eAL, wGA.** **1944** *AmSp* 19.243. **c1960** *Wilson Coll.* **csKY,** He's such an all-fired smart alec.

allforche See **alforja**

all free See **all (in) free**

all get-out n Pronc-sp ~ *git-out* See also **get-out**

In compar phrr following *like, as,* or *than:* an extreme or high degree.

1884 (1958) Twain *Huck. Finn* 325, We got to dig in like all git-out. **1908** Lincoln *Cy Whittaker* 13 **MA,** Stubborn as all get-out to the end, he was, and willed the place, all he had left, to them Howes folks. **1912** *DN* 3.581 **wIN,** He was working like all get out. **1914** *DN* 4.68 **ME, nNH,** "He hypered like all git aout!" He departed very rapidly. **1914** *DN* 4.102 **KS,** As rich (tired, easy, etc.) as all get out. **1916** Wilson *Somewhere* 197 **West,** When I got into the parlour she had them on, pleased as all get-out. **1929** *AmSp* 4.204 **Ozarks,** Clever an' biddable as all git-out. **1965-70** *DARE* (Qu. HH22b, . . "*He's meaner than _____.*") 113 Infs, **widespread,** All get-out. **1966** Barnes–Jensen *Dict. UT Slang* 3, He was as drunk as all get out.

‡**all get-outdoors** n [Blend of **all get-out** + **all outdoors 2**]
=**all get-out.**

1970 *DARE* (Qu. GG40, *Words or expressions meaning violently angry*) Inf **TX86,** Mad as all get-outdoors.

all-gone adj Cf **all in** adj

Fatigued, weak, somewhat ill.

1950 *WELS* (*Feeling lifeless or without energy:* "*I certainly feel _____ today.*") 1 Inf, **csWI,** All gone. **1967-69** *DARE* (Qu. BB5, *A general feeling of discomfort or illness*) Infs **NJ58, OH15,** All-gone feeling; (Qu. BB6, *A sudden feeling of weakness*) Inf **NJ39,** All-gone feeling.

all hair by the nose See **hair on the nose**

all hands (and feet) See **all thumbs**

all hands and the cook (and the whiskey-jacks) n, often used as an exclam [*all hands,* orig nautical, here transf] Cf **Hannah Cook**

All members of a working group without exception—usu used as an exclam announcing an emergency requiring everyone's help.

1942 *ME Univ. Studies* 56.11, The whole ship's company . . was somewhat facetiously called all hands and the cook. **1942** *AmSp* 17.130 **IN.** **1944** Adams *Western Words.* **1958** McCulloch *Woods Words* **Pacific NW,** All hands and the cook and the whiskey-jacks—Everybody turn out, big trouble coming up. **1969** Sorden *Lumberjack Lingo* 1 **Gt Lakes,** All Hands and the Cook—The call or cry that a log jam had occurred and that every one of the river crew was needed to help break it. Also used in other emergencies when help was needed. **1970** Halpert *Coll.* **wKY,** It took all hands and the cook to get the job finished.

all-heeled adj
=**well-heeled.**

1908 *DN* 3.286 **eAL, wGA,** Don't you worry about me. I'm all-heeled.

all hid n [From the rhyme called out by "it"; *all hid* was the name of this game as played in Elizabethan England (*OED* 1608)] *among Black speakers*

The children's game of hide-and-seek.

1959 Lomax *Rainbow Sign* 39 **AL** [Black], We was playing All Hid at our house . . . *It* was singin . . . All hid . . . Everybody hollered: No, no!/ Is it all hid?/ No, no./ Corn bread rough and Corn bread tough,/ Niggers down yonder don't never get enough . . . / All hid? . . . This time, we all said, "Yes." So *it* start out from the base, not far, though, because all us watchin him to see if we could beat him back to the base to get our hundreds. **1964** Lomax *Penguin Amer. Folk Songs* 98 **Sth** [Black], When the rhymes and games of American children are put together in one book, the most original chapter will be that of Negro children of the deep South. 'All Hid' is a hide-and-go-seek rhyme known in Mississippi and Alabama, recorded by us in numerous versions for the Library of Congress.

all hollow adv phr Also *all to hollow,* pronc-sp ~*holler* [*OED hollow* adv B2, 1762 →; sugg emptiness, what was inside having been beaten out]

Completely, thoroughly—now usu in phr *beat (one)* ~.

1815 in 1856 Adams *Works* 10.125, Burr . . had a copy of this list brought to him immediately. He read it over, with great gravity folded it up, put it in his pocket, and, without uttering another word said, 'Now I have him all hollow.' **1824** Irving *Tales of a Traveller* 2.39, Her blood carried it all hollow; there was no withstanding a woman with such blood in her veins. **1835** (1955) *Crockett Almanacks* 8 **wTN,** I saw she preferred me all holler. **1871** Eggleston *Hoosier Schoolmaster* 50 **IN,** "Gewhilliky crickets! . . " said Bud, rubbing his hands on his knees. "That beats my time all holler!" **1908** *DN* 3.286 **eAL, wGA,** I beat him all-hollow the last time I played him. **1912** *DN* 3.570 **wIN.** **1977** *DARE* File **cnMA** (as of c1915), The expression *all to hollow* is familiar to me as well as *all hollow.* "The Orange baseball team beat ours all to hollow."

all home (free) exclam Var of **home free**

In the children's game of hide-and-seek: see quot.

1965-70 *DARE* (Qu. EE15, . . *What does the player who is "it" call out to the others?*) Infs **MI55, OH61,** All home free; **MA14,** All home.

all horns and rattles adj phr [Ref to cattle's *horns* and snakes' *rattles*] **West**

Very angry: see quot.

1944 Adams *Western Words,* All horns and rattles—Said of one displaying a fit of temper. A man in this mood, as one cowboy said, "maybe don't say nothin', but it ain't safe to ask questions."

all how adv phr Cf **as how**

How; in what way.

1952 Brown *NC Folkl.* 1.514, He told *all how* he beat that fellow up. **1976** Warner *Beautiful Swimmers* 138 **eShore MD,** That's all how we get the big peelers from the middle of May through the second week of June.

all-hunky (dory) See **hunky**

allicomgreenzie n [Scots *SND,* 1824 →]

A children's ring-game similar to *drop the handkerchief.*
1956 *AmSp* 31.35 **MA.**

allie See **alley** n²

allie allie (in) free and varr See **all-ee all-ee (all) in free**

allies exclam [*all* + *-ies*]

In marbles play: =**evers 3.**

1963 *KY Folkl. Rec.* 9.63 **neKY,** *Demand for possession of all marbles knocked off square or out of ring when a shot is taken . . : allies:* Greenup (County).

alligator n¹ Usu |ˈælɪˌɡeɪtɚ|

A Form.

1968 *DARE* Tape **GA35,** [ˈɔlɪˌɡeɪtɚ].

B Senses. [From a resemblance to the reptile]

1 Any of three usu large salamanders: the **hellbender,** the **siren 1** (here: *Siren lacertina*), or the **tiger salamander.**

1859 (1968) Bartlett *Americanisms, Alligator* . . . In the Western States, the name is applied . . to the *Menopoma alleghaniensis,* a salamandroid animal. **1892** IN Dept. Geol. & Nat. Resources *Report for 1891* 417, Where it abounds [*Siren lacertina*] it is, according to Barton, called "Alligator" and "Water-lizard." **1926** TX Folkl. Soc. *Pub.* 5.63, In the plains region of Western Texas the large tiger salamander is a common animal . . . Large ones are called "alligators." *Ibid* 5.72, The name *alligator,* a corruption of the Spanish *lagarto* (lizard) is frequently used in West Texas to indicate the large tiger salamander. **1930** Shoemaker *1300 Words* 2 **cPA Mts** (as of c1900), *Alligator*—A large salamander formerly numerous in West Branch of Susquehanna; destroyed by industrial pollution.

2 =**fence lizard.** Cf **alligator lizard**

1911 *Century Dict., Alligator* . . . A local name of the little brown fence-lizard, *Sceloporus undulatus,* common in many parts of the United States.

3 The larva of the **dobsonfly.**

1894 *DN* 1.339 **wCT,** *Alligator:* larva of the hellgramite *[corydalus cornutus],* an aquatic insect used as bait for bass. **1901** Howard *Insect Book* 212, In 1889 . . the names in use in Rhode Island alone for the insect . . . are: Dobsons, crawlers, . . alligators, Ho Jack [etc.].

4 In mining: see quot 1881. *obs*

1881 Raymond *Gloss. Mining, Alligator* . . . A rock-breaker operating by jaws. **1968** Adams *Western Words.*

5 A person, usu non-Black, who listens to rather than plays jazz music. (Note: this is the probable source for the non-regional catch-phrase *see you later, alligator.*) *orig among Black speakers and derog, though not always recognized as such*

1937 *Etude* 55.835 **NYC,** *Alligator:* A non-playing swing devotee, a listener. **1938** *New Yorker* 8 Jan 34 *(Hench Coll.),* In the jargon of swingmen, these appreciative listeners are termed "alligators." **1955** Shapiro *Hear Me Talkin'* 97 **Chicago IL** [Black], Some guys would come in to sit in with you and learn what you were doing. We'd call them alligators. That was our tip-off word, because they were guys who came up to swallow everything we had to learn. **1958** *AmSp* 33.223. **1958** Hughes–Bontemps *Negro Folkl.* 481 **NYC** [Black], *Alligator:* A jitterbug. **1970** Major *Afro–Amer. Slang* 20, *Alligator:* (1930's) term used by black jazzmen, particularly in New Orleans, referring to white jazz musicians, jive people or jitterbugs.

6 See **alligator horse.**

7 A resident of Florida — used as a humorous nickname. See also **gator**

1937 Shankle *Nicknames* 188, *Floridians . . .* are nicknamed *Alligators, Crackers,* and *Fly-up-the Creeks.* **1949** *AmSp* 24.29.

8 In logging: a boat or sled used for transporting logs: see quots.

1942 Berrey–Van den Bark *Amer. Slang* 512.9 [In logging], Alligator, *a boat provided with windlass and cable for hauling logs, also a sled, often the fork of a tree, used in skidding logs.* **1956** Sorden–Ebert *Logger's Words* **Gt Lakes,** *Alligator,* 1. A boat used in handling floating logs. It can be moved overland from one body of water to another by its own power . . . 2. A device, often made from the fork of a tree, on which the front end of a log is placed to facilitate skidding on swampy ground. **1968** Adams *Western Words.* **1975** Gould *ME Lingo* 34, *Alligator* — A flat-bottomed scow or raft used on inland lakes for moving boomed logs. (Tow boats came later.) The alligator would be rowed out ahead of the *boom* of logs and anchored. A capstan or wench then pulled the *boom* up to the *alligator* by a cable. The *alligator* would be advanced to a new position and the process repeated until the *boom* had been brought to its destination.

9 A device used in shoeing a horse: see quot.

1961 Adams *Old-Time Cowhand* 243, With the clinchin' block, or "alligator," held on the outside wall [of the hoof] underneath the nail, the head of the nail should be hammered down into the crease of the shoe.

10 A tag game played in the water. **Sth** Also called **gator**

1967–68 *DARE* (Qu. EE28) Inf **GA**58, Alligator — a type of tag; **SC**44, Alligator (or gator) — a tag game. If you're out of the water you can't be tagged; **TX**32, Alligator — one tries to catch the others, and each one he catches helps him catch the rest; **LA**34, Alligator — one pretends to be an alligator, the other to be Tarzan. **1981** *DARE* File **cnOK** (as of c1960), A swimming game, like tag, played in Choctaw County.

11 also *alligator walk:* A dance step popular among young adults in the late 1960s: see quot 1980.

1967–69 *DARE* (Qu. FF5b, . . *Recent dance steps*) Inf **SC**65, Alligator walk; **NY**211B, Alligator. [Both Infs are young, Black] **1980** *DARE* File **cPA** (as of 1969), Our fraternity used to hire a Black singer to play for a full weekend of partying once a year. One of the more grotesque dances he introduced us to was called the "alligator." The dancers would wiggle and writhe on their bellies on the floor.

12 A type of pastry: see quot.

1968 *DARE* FW Addit **Madison WI** [Heard in restaurant], Alligator — a type of sweet roll which is long and narrow.

alligator n² [By error for *delegate:* see quot]
A member of the Virginia House of Delegates.

a1883 (1911) Bagby *VA Gentleman* 290, In peace times this bell struck the hours of the day and night . . and called the truant "Alligators" from their haunts in the barrooms and faro-banks when there was a close vote in the General Assembly. [Footnote: Explanation that "alligator" was a Dutchman's blunder for "delegate" in the Virginia House of Delegates, and became a well-known nickname. "Ever since the term "Alligator" has been a household word in Virginia."]

‡alligator n³ [Perh folk etym from **gaiter**]
A man's low, rough work shoe.

1968 *DARE* (Qu. W11) Inf **MO**17, Alligators.

alligator apple n [From the habitat and applelike shape; *DJE* 1756 →]
=**pond apple.**

1933 Small *Manual SE Flora* 532, *Annona glabra . . .* Alligator-apple . . . Swamps, ponds, and low hammocks, S. pen. Fla. and the Keys. **1979** Little *Checklist U.S. Trees* 54, *Pond-apple . . . Other common name* — alligator-apple.

alligator bait n

1 Unpalatable food, esp liver.

1926 *AmSp* 1.650 ["Hobo Lingo"], *Alligator-bait* — fried or stewed liver. **1927** *DN* 5.437 [Among construction workers], Alligator bait . . Stewed or fried liver. This is a staple article of food at construction camps. Bull's liver is kept until rotten in order to make it tender. **1930** Irwin *Amer. Tramp, Alligator Bait.* — Fried liver, so called from its unpalatable, indigestible character as served in construction camps and cheap lunch rooms. The term is often applied to any poor food or meal.

2 A Black person, esp a Black child. **chiefly Sth** *derog*

1901 Oliver *Roughing It* 75, Pickaninnies, or as they are most commonly known, "alligator bait," swam around the boat. **1930** Irwin *Amer. Tramp, Alligator Bait . . .* A generic term for negro children, this largely through the South, where it is considered humorous in the extreme to frighten the pickaninnies by threatening to throw them to the " 'gators" which they fear. **1960** Wentworth–Flexner *Slang, Alligator-bait . . .* A Negro, esp. one from Florida or Louisiana. *Dial.* **1968** *DARE* (Qu. HH28) Infs **NY**76, **LA**23, Alligator-bait. **1970** Major *Afro–Amer. Slang* 20, *Alligator-bait:* (1940's) a Negro in or from Florida. **1970** Tarpley *Blinky* 265 **neTX,** Teasing and derogatory names for Negroes . . . 'gator bait.

alligator bark n Cf **alligator juniper**

1961 Douglas *My Wilderness* 187 **MD,** The bark of the persimmon is deeply divided into so many square plates that local people call it alligator bark.

alligator bark juniper See **alligator juniper**

alligator blankets n Cf **alligator bonnet(s), alligator buttons**
A water lily 1 of the genus *Nymphaea.*

1913 *Torreya* 13.230, Alligator blankets, Santee Club, S.C.

alligator bonnet(s) n Also *gator bonnet* [From the bonnet-shaped leaf] **Sth**

1 =**white water lily** (here: *Nymphaea odorata*).

1920 *Torreya* 20.21, Alligator bonnet, Cameron Parish, La. **1933** Small *Manual SE Flora* 543, *Nymphaea odorata . . .* Alligator-bonnet. Star-lotus . . . Ponds, lakes, slow streams, and ditches, . . Fla. to La., Man., and N.S. **1953** Greene–Blomquist *Flowers South* 38, Water-Lilies . . . One of the most widely distributed of these is the white to pinkish "alligator-bonnet" . . *(N. odorata).* **1970** Correll *Plants TX* 632, White Water-lily, Alligator-bonnet, Ninfa acuática . . . flowers very fragrant.

2 A spatterdock.

1900 Lyons *Plant Names* 262, *N[ymphaea] sagittæfolia . .* southeastern U.S. . . is called also Alligator-bonnets. **1968** *DARE* (Qq. S26a,b) Inf **GA**28, Gator bonnet (also called waterlily).

alligator bread n

1968 *DARE* (Qu. H18, . . *Special kinds of bread made now or in past years around here*) Inf **IL**27, Alligator bread — A big round loaf [with a] rough surface on top.

alligator buttons n sg or pl **SE**
=**water chinquapin.**

1920 *Torreya* 20.21, *Nelumbo lutea . . .* Alligator buttons, Goose Creek, S.C. **1933** Small *Manual SE Flora* 540, *Alligator-buttons . . .* The fruits were used as food by the aborigines. **1959** Carleton *Index Herb. Plants* 2.

alligator cooter n chiefly **S Atl** Cf **cooter** n
=**alligator turtle.**

1842 DeKay *Zool. NY* 3.9, *The Snapping Turtle. Chelonura serpentina . .* is known under the names of *Loggerhead, Alligator Turtle* and *Couta.* **1942** Rawlings *Cross Creek* 227 **FL,** The alligator cooter is the most highly prized of all inland turtle meats. He is very dangerous, a virulent fighter encased in a ridged, scaly shell from which he takes his name, with a fierce hooked beak at the end of his head and long neck that can make mincemeat of an enemy. **1966** *DARE* (Qu. P24, . . *Kinds of turtles*) Infs **SC**7, 9, 26, 43, Alligator cooter. **c1970** Pederson *Dial. Survey Rural GA,* 2 Infs, **seGA,** Alligator cooter. [Both Infs Black]

alligator corn n Also ~ *pea*
The edible seed of **water chinquapin.**

1941 *Torreya* 41.47, *Nelumbo lutea . . .* Alligator peas . . Oakley, S.C. **1950** *PADS* 14.11 **SC,** *Alligator corn . . .* The seed pods of the water lily.

alligator effect See **alligatoring**

alligator gar n [From its size and general aspect]

A large freshwater gar *(Lepisosteus spatula)* of the central and southern US.

1820 Rafinesque *Ohio R. Fishes* 73, This fish *[Lepisosteus spatula]* bears . . the names of . . Alligator Gar, Alligator fish, Jack or Gar Pike, &c. **1841** Kennedy *Texas* 1.132, The alligator gar . . is armed with almost impenetrable scales, and, from its strength and voracity, may be termed the river-shark. **1851** (1969) Burke *Polly Peablossom* 129 **cwMS,** I was nearly thrown into the lake by the plunge of a monster alligator gar. **1920** Forbes–Richardson *Fishes of IL* 35, Alligator-gar . . . Formerly made into oil, by the people of Arkansas, for use as a lotion to prevent attack by the buffalo-gnat. **1933** LA Dept. of Conserv. *Fishes* 402, The Mississippi Alligator Gar . . . This formidable fresh water fish, attaining a length of as much as twenty feet, ranges from completely salt to completely fresh water. **1955** Carr–Goin *Guide Reptiles* 39, Alligator Gar . . . Mouth extended into a bill-like structure, with two rows of large teeth on each side in the upper jaw. **1965–70** *DARE* (Qu. P3) Infs **GA84, IL41, OK42, 52, TX27, 78, 96,** Alligator gar; (Qu. P4) Inf **TX14,** Alligator gar.

alligator grass n Also *alligator weed* [Perh because often in alligator habitats] **chiefly SE**

A usu aquatic perennial plant *(Alternanthera philoxeroides)* of the southeastern US and CA which has opposite grasslike leaves and a spike of white flowers and which clogs waterways with its dense masses.

1933 *Torreya* 33.83, Alligator grass, Mississippi Delta, La . . . Alligator grass as at present recorded is an introduced species that has shown considerable tendencies toward "taking the place" much in the manner of water hyacinth. **1944** AL Geol. Surv. *Bulletin* 53.98, *A. philoxeroides* . . is called "alligator weed" in southern Louisiana, where it is a pest in bayous. **1958** Grau *Hard Blue Sky* 17 **LA,** The edges of this side of the island were marshy: he could see the alligator grass and the cattails and the saw grass. **1959** Munz-Keck *CA Flora* 388. **1970** Correll *Plants TX* 568, *Alligator-weed* . . . is rapidly clogging the streams, canals, ponds and other such places in coastal Texas.

alligator hole n Also *gator hole* **S Atl**

A retreat or "nest" made by alligators in swampy land.

1791 (1958) Bartram *Travels* 150 **FL,** Our chief conducted me another way to shew me a very curious place, called the Alligator-Hole, which was lately formed by an extraordinary eruption or jet of water; it is one of those vast circular sinks . . . about sixty yards over, and the surface of the water [is] six or seven feet below the rim of the funnel or bason: the water is transparent, cool, and pleasant to drink, and well stored with fish; a very large alligator at present is lord or chief. **1842** Buckingham *Slave States* 1.155, In their retreats, or nests, called alligator-holes, as large a brood as a hundred are seen at a time. **1873** in 1953 McMullen *Topog. Terms FL* 63, The alligator makes large holes in these swamps and savannas. He covers the holes with dried cane, grass and whatever he can find of a similar nature. This covering is raised like a cone, and is two or three feet in height. There is a hole in one side of the covering, through which the 'gator crawls out and in . . . The greatest alligator hole in Florida is on the ocean side of the Indian River. **1922** Gonzales *Black Border* 120 **sSC, GA coasts** [Gullah], The yawning mouth of the big 'gator hole, ordinarily covered with water, now disclosed a parched throat wide enough to have taken in a [rifle] barrel. **1934** *Natl. Geog. Mag.* 65.598/1 **GA,** In these morasses are many areas of open water, varying from lakes a quarter of a mile in diameter to "alligator holes" a rod in width. **1938** Matschat *Suwannee R.* 70 **nFL, sGA,** A miner's lamp . . made a flood of light to pierce the dark waters of the run and the near-by gator holes, but their owners were not at home.

alligator horse n Also *alligator* obs

=**half horse, half alligator.**

1826 in 1861 Woodworth *Poet. Wks.* 2.8 **KY,** We'll show him that Kentucky boys/ Are "alligator horses." **1850** *Quincy Whig* (Quincy IL) 9 Apr 4/1 *(DA),* 'Eh! hem, a horse, eh!' said the Judge. 'Yes, sir, an alligator horse.' **1945** Le Sueur *North Star Country* 248 **MN, WI** [Among lumberjacks, as of 1860s], His crew were often tough men—"alligator horses"—of short lives and violent ends . . . I'm the toughest goldarned alligator in the North Woods.

alligatoring vbl n Also n *alligator effect* [See quot 1936]

The cracking of paint into patches as a result of contraction or uneven drying.

1911 *Engin. News* 27 July 121 *(DA)* **NY,** Many of the paints which lack

any evidence of cracking, checking, or alligatoring. **1936** *The Pathfinder* 14 Mar 18 (Hench Coll.) **DC,** Painters use the term alligatoring to describe paint which has cracked into large segments because of its resemblance to an alligator's skin. **1969** *AmSp* 44.9 **Pacific NW,** *Alligator* . . . (The unfortunate result of) painting a dark paint over a light color. The dark paint holds (attracts) heat, which causes it to crack in an "alligator" effect.

alligator juniper n Also *alligator bark juniper*

An evergreen tree *(Juniperus deppeana),* native to Texas, Arizona and New Mexico, which has gray bark divided into conspicuous squarish plates. Also called **checkered-bark juniper, oak-barked cedar, oak-barked juniper**

1897 Sudworth *Arborescent Flora* 98, *Juniperus pachyphloea* . . . Alligator Juniper (Ariz.). **1909** AZ Ag. Exp. Sta. *Timely Hints* 79.6, The one-seeded juniper *(Juniperus monosperma)* grows at altitude somewhat lower than the alligator-bark juniper *(Juniperus pachyphlaea).* **1925** Bryan *Papago Country* 45, With these oaks are associated . . the Mexican piñon . . and the alligator juniper. **1947** *Primitive Man* Jan–Apr 9 **AZ,** "What kind of juniper?" he asked, "Alligator bark juniper?" **1960** Vines *Trees SW* 31, The thick, square-plated bark has been compared to the rough plates on an alligator's back and the vernacular name, Alligator Juniper, has been given the tree. **1970** Correll *Plants TX* 78, Alligator juniper . . . from w. Tex., w. to cen. Ariz. and s. to cen. Mex. The wood of this species is used for fence posts and fuel.

alligator lily n [Prob reference to its prevalence in alligator habitat but possibly referring to the black, somewhat alligatorlike scales covering the bulb] **SE, esp FL**

A **spider lily,** here *Hymenocallis* spp esp *H. palmeri.*

1933 Small *Manual SE Flora* 324, *H. Palmeri* . . . Alligator-lily . . . Prairies and Everglades, pen. Fla.—Spr[ing]. **1934** *Torreya* 34.136, In the more prairie-like parts of the Everglades . . . perhaps the most striking of all is the Alligator Lily, *Hymenocallis.* **1938** Rawlings *Yearling* 421 **nFL,** The first rays of the sun lay on the river. Alligator lilies on the far bank caught them like white cups. **1970** *DARE* (Qu. S26b, *What other wildflowers do you have around here . . that grow in wet places?)* Inf **VA52,** Alligator lily—a water lily.

alligator lizard n Cf **alligator** n¹ B2

1 =**fence lizard.**

1892 IN Dept. Geol. & Nat. Resources *Report for 1891* 540, *Sceloporus undulatus* . . . Alligator Lizard; Pine Tree Lizard.

2 Any of several long-tailed, slow-moving, chiefly terrestrial lizards *(Gerrhonotus* spp) native to the western US.

1931 *Copeia* 14 **CA,** For several days . . a silvery footless lizard . . was kept in the cage with the alligator lizard, but was not eaten. **1935** in 1946 Smith *Lizards* 438, Recorded methods of self-protection used by alligator lizards include hiding in holes or among dry leaves. **1958** Conant *Reptiles & Amphibians* 107, *Texas Alligator Lizard* . . . Scales large and platelike (suggesting the Alligator). **1964** Lowe *Vertebrates* 166, Arizona Alligator Lizard . . . Occasionally in wood rat nests and rodent burrows.

‡**alligator nephew** n

Prob =**alligator turtle 1.**

c**1970** Pederson *Dial Survey Rural GA (A creature with a very hard shell that lives in water. It can draw its four legs and head and tail completely inside its shell.)* 1 Inf, **seGA,** Cooter, soft shell turtle, alligator nephew.

alligator pea See **alligator corn**

alligator pear n [*DJE* 1696 →]

An avocado *(Persea* spp).

1766 Stork *E. Florida* 61 *(DAE),* The plantane-tree and allegator pear, the tenderest of the tropical plants, are in full perfection at Augustine. **1859** (1968) Bartlett *Americanisms,* Alligator Pear . . . A West Indian fruit, resembling a pear in shape. **1900** Lyons *Plant Names* 282, Avocado . . Alligator Pear, Holy-ghost Pear. **1933** Small *Manual SE Flora* 921, Avocado. Alligator-pear . . . Hammocks and pinelands, S pen. Fla. and the Keys. **1966–67** *DARE* (Qu. I46, . . *Fruits that grow wild)* Infs **FL15, IL17,** Alligator pear(s); (Qu. I53) Inf **HI1,** "Alligator pear" was my regular term; "avocado" has now largely displaced it. **1969** *DARE* FW Addit **Honolulu HI.**

alligator root n Cf **alligator tree**

See quot.

1970 Hyatt *Hoodoo* 412 **NC** [Black], They tell me that chew can wear some *roots*—*High John the Conker, alligator root*, and *'coon root*, and put a little salt in that, a little cayenne pepper, and make a sack out of it . . and wear it round your neck with a little bluestone and alum in it, and that the individual can't *hurt* yah. [Hyatt's note: *Alligator root* is either shaped like an alligator or root from the sweet gum tree, often called alligator tree in Southern U.S.A.]

alligator snapper n Also ~*snapping turtle, gator snapper* **Gulf States and Missip Valley**
=alligator turtle esp **2.**

1884 Goode *Fisheries U.S.* 1.153, I have myself seen an 'Alligator Snapper,' of perhaps forty pounds weight, bite the handle of a broom in two when enraged. **1938** Matschat *Suwannee R.* 24 **sGA,** Swamp folk are as much afraid of the ferocious alligator snappers as they are of the real alligators . . . Many an unsuspecting waterfowl is caught and dragged down to furnish a meal for the gator snapper. **1946** *Outdoor Life* Oct 124/3, I nominate the alligator snapping turtle, vicious, hard-shelled, reptilian devil of the southern rivers. **1958** Conant *Reptiles & Amphibians* 35, Alligator Snapper . . . often lies at bottom of lake or river with mouth wide open. A curious pink process on floor of mouth resembles a worm, wriggles like one, and serves as a lure for fishes. **1968–70** *DARE* (Qu. P24) Infs **IL119, LA34,** Alligator snapper. **1972** Ernst–Barbour *Turtles* 30, The alligator snapper occurs most frequently in the deep water of rivers, canals, lakes, and oxbows.

alligator soap n
Soap made from alligator fat.

1943 Pratt *Barefoot Mailman* 152 **seFL,** Linda worked Steven hard at making alligator soap . . . [After the lye was] placed in a kettle under which another fire was built, Linda then threw in the clear white fat of an alligator Jesse had killed. This finally set into a hard coarse soap.

alligator terrapin n **S Atl**
=alligator turtle.

1835 Simms *Partisan* 317 **SC,** Three enormous terrapins of that doubtful brood which the vulgar in the southern country describe as the alligator terrapin. **1855** Simms *Forayers* 545 **SC,** What we call the alligator terrapin is the best of the tribe—the fattest, richest, best flavored. **1934** *Natl. Geog. Mag.* 65.610 **sGA,** The turtle fauna . . with aquatic preferences range in size from the musk turtle, with a carapace between three and four inches in length, to the mighty 75-pound alligator terrapin, with a head practically as large as a man's. **1966** *DARE* (Qu. P24, *What kinds of turtles are found around here?*) Inf **FL32,** Alligator turtle or terrapin. **1969** *DARE* Tape **GA51,** Alligator terrapins ['æl₁ɪˌgɛtɚ 'tærəpɪnz] [we] call 'em. They have a tail about that long an' it looks just like a alligator's.

alligator tree n Also *alligator wood* [From the ridges of the bark which resemble those of an alligator's hide] **chiefly Sth** See also **alligator root**
=sweet gum.

1889 *Century Dict.,* Alligator-tree. **1893** *Bot. Gaz.* 18.427 **WV,** Alligator-wood. **1897** Sudworth *Arborescent Flora* 205 **NJ,** Sweet Gum . . . Alligator Wood. **1901** Lounsberry *S. Wild Flowers* 230, Sweet Gum. Star-Leaved Gum. Bilsted. Alligator Tree. Through the Alleghany ridges it is not so frequently seen as in the Mississippi basin, where it attains to a great size. **1916** Seton *Woodcraft Manual Girls* 288, Alligator Tree, or Liquidambar . . . A tall tree . . remarkable for the corky ridges on its bark. **1933** Small *Manual SE Flora* 601, Sweet-gum . . . Alligator-tree . . . Coastal Plain and adj. provinces, C. Fla. to Tex., Mo., and Conn . . . The wood is used for cabinet work. **1960** Vines *Trees SW* 325, *Liquidambar styraciflua* . . . Bark. Very rough, deeply furrowed, ridges rounded, brown to gray . . . Alligator-tree.

alligator turtle n Also *gator ~* [From some resemblance to the alligator's scaly head and long tail]

1 A freshwater snapping turtle, *Chelydra serpentina*, common throughout the U.S. east of the Rockies. Also called **alligator cooter, ~nephew, ~snapper, ~terrapin, caouane, loggerhead**

1798 in 1930 Dunbar *Life* 92 **Sth, Missip Valley,** One of them is called the Alligator Turtle on account of his overgrown head and tail being covered with a species of scales resembling those which form the armour of the Crocodile. **1842** DeKay *Zool. NY* 3.8, The Snapping Turtle . . . is one of our largest turtles . . . In other sections, it is known under the names of *Loggerhead, Alligator Turtle* and *Couta*. **1884** Goode *Fisheries U.S.* 1.153, The southern species, *Macrochelys lacertina*, known as the 'Alligator Turtle,' or 'Loggerhead,' is found in western Georgia, and in all the states bordering on the Gulf, from Florida to

Texas. It also occurs in Missouri, where it is said to receive the name 'Caouane.' **1966–70** *DARE* (Qu. P24) Inf **FL27,** Alligator turtle—mean, have a long tail; **SC40,** Alligator turtle—brown, good to eat; **FL35, 51, SC66,** Alligator turtle; **FL32,** Alligator turtle or terrapin; **FL4,** Gator.

2 A voracious freshwater snapping turtle, *Macroclemys temminkii*, found in the Gulf States and Missip River Valley which may grow to a size of more than 200 lb. Also called **alligator snapper, ~terrapin, loggerhead**

1934 *W2, Alligator snapper . .* or *turtle . . .* A voracious snapping turtle (*Macrochelys temminckii*). **1966–70** *DARE* (Qu. P24) Infs **FL48, GA25, 41,** Alligator turtle. [Note: These Infs may have referred instead to **1** above, as the ranges of the two turtles overlap in this area.] **c1970** Pederson *Dial. Survey Rural GA, (A creature with a very hard shell that lives in water)* 1 Inf, **seGA,** Alligator turtle; 1 Inf, **seGA,** Gator turtle.

alligator walk See alligator n¹ **B11**

alligator wampee n [*alligator* + *wampee*] **S Atl**
=pickerelweed.

1916 *Torreya* 16.237, Alligator wampee . . Santee Club, S.C.,; wild gentian, Cat. Id., S.C. **1952** Taylor *Plants Colonial Days* 66 **VA,** An aquatic plant native to eastern North America, pickerel-weed grows in shallow water at the margins of lakes that may or may not contain pickerel! Alligator wampee is another common name sometimes used.

alligator weed See alligator grass

alligator wood See alligator tree

all in adj See also **all-gone, all out**

1 used predicatively: Exhausted. **chiefly Nth, Midl** *somewhat old-fash* See Map (Addit map in 1941 *LANE* 2.482.)

1902 McFaul *Ike Glidden* 201 *(DA)* **ME,** The horse was holding steady up to his clip, but it could be easily seen that he was 'all in.' **1927** *AmSp* 2.347 **cwWV,** The men were all in when the fire was under control. **1928** Ruppenthal *Coll.* **KS,** After struggling against the wind for a mile she was all in. **1950** *WELS (Very tired)* 27 Infs, **WI,** All in; *(Feeling lifeless or without energy: "I certainly feel _____ today.")* 6 Infs, **WI,** All in. **c1960** Wilson *Coll.* **csKY,** I'm all in after working at the mill. **1965–70** *DARE* (Qu. X47, *. . Other ways . . of saying "I'm very tired, at the end of my strength.")* 162 Infs, **scattered, but esp Nth, Midl,** All in; (Qu. KK30, *Feeling slowed up or without energy)* 43 Infs, **chiefly Inland Nth,** All in. [Of all Infs responding to Qq. X47 and KK30, 64% and 63% respectively were old; of those giving this response, 82% and 93% were old.] **1973** Allen *LAUM* 1.361, *All in* is used by one-half of all infs.

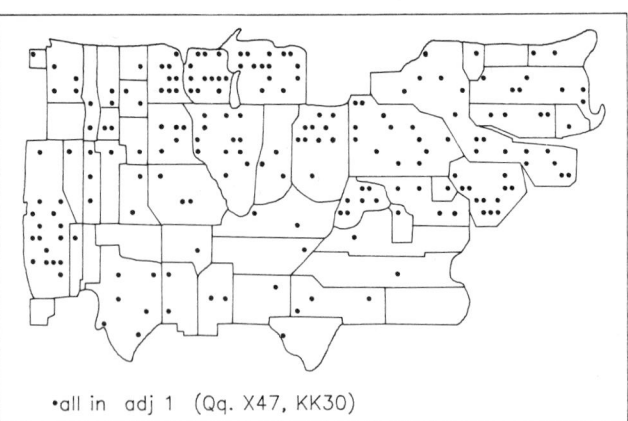

•all in adj 1 (Qq. X47, KK30)

2 Characterized by a general feeling of discomfort. Cf **all-ins, the**

1965–70 *DARE* (Qu. BB39, *On a day when you don't feel just right . . , "I'll be all right tomorrow—I'm just feeling _____ today.")* 14 Infs, **scattered,** All in; Inf **DE2,** All in and pooped [12 of 15 Infs are old]; (Qu. BB5) Infs **CA148, MI68, 115, NY57, 105, OH29, PA234,** All in; (Qu. GG26, *A feeling of weakness from fear)* Inf **MI78,** All-in feeling.

3 Very sick; drunk.

1967–70 *DARE* (Qu. BB42, *If a person is very sick you say he's _____)* Infs **CA113, IL143,** All in; (Qu. X52, *. . A person . . who had been sick was looking _____)* Inf **CA113,** All in; (Qu. DD5, *. . Thoroughly drunk)* Inf **OH11,** All in.

4 Transf, of machinery: run-down, dilapidated.
  1967 *DARE* (Qu. KK20b, *Something that looks as if it might collapse any minute: "Our washing machine is _____."*) Inf **OR**1, All in.

all in exclam
1 See **all (in) free**.
‡**2** Time out!
  1968 *DARE* (Qu. EE17, *In a game of tag, if a player wants to rest, what does he call out so that he can't be tagged?*) Inf **MN**16, All in.

all in but one's shoestrings adj phr Also ~*shoelaces*, ~*bootstraps* **Nth** Cf **all in** adj
1 Exhausted.
  1940–41 Cassidy *WI Atlas* **ceWI**, All in but my shoestrings. **1941** *LANE* Map 482 **cnVT**, 1 Inf, I'm all in but my shoestrings. **1950** *WELS* (*Very tired*) 1 Inf, **seWI**, All in but my shoe strings; 1 Inf, **cWI**, All in but my boot straps. **1966–69** *DARE* (Qu. X47) Infs **IL**5, **NY**219, All in but my shoestrings; **WA**1, All in but my shoestrings, and they're hanging out; (Qu. KK30) Inf **NY**109, All in but my shoelaces.
2 Characterized by a general feeling of discomfort.
  1968 *DARE* (Qu. BB5) Inf **WI**24, All in but the shoestrings.

all (in) free exclam Also *all come in (free)*, *all come in home free* [Abbr for *all who are out may come in free*] **throughout US** in this and numerous other forms: see *DS* EE15 and separate entries.
  In the children's game of hide and seek: the phrase called out by the seeker ("it") after he has caught the first of the hiders (who will succeed him as "it").
  1956 [see **Ole Ole Olson all in free**]. **1965–70** *DARE* (Qu. EE15) 61 Infs, **throughout US**, All free; 29 Infs, **chiefly east of Missip R**, All in free; **AL**26, **DC**8, **FL**10, **MD**46, **PA**49, **TX**101, **VA**93, All come in free; **CT**23, **MA**57, **NJ**57, **OK**52, **PA**36, All in; **MO**15, All come free; **NM**12, All come in; **IN**81, All come in home free; **PA**152, All all in free.

all-ins, the n pl [**all-in** adj 2]
=**all-overs** n 2.
  1967 *DARE* (Qu. BB5) Inf **PA**36, The all-ins.

all is adv phr Similarly *all was* **chiefly NEng, Appalachians** *old-fash*
  Everything considered; in any case.
  1869 Stowe *Oldtown Folks* 239 **NEng**, All is, when I begin a thing I like to go through with it. **1871** (1882) Stowe *Fireside Stories* 36 **NEng**, Nobody rightly knew where he hed ben or where he hadn't: all was, he turned up at last all alive, and chipper as a skunk blackbird. *Ibid* 87, She kep' her veil down so we couldn't get sight o' her face. All was, she must see Cap'n Tucker alone right away. **1891** (1967) Freeman *New Engl. Nun* 199, All is, I don't feel much like it, you know. **1914** *DN* 4.68 **ME**, **nNH**, All is, she's plumb wuthless. **1928** Chapman *Happy Mt.* 222 **seTN**, All is, . . I aim to go where is good pasturings. **1931** Hannum *Thursday April* 108 **WV Mts**, "All is, hit'll be a heap sight better'n havin' him make cheer bottoms the rest of his days."

all-jaw n
  A biting midge of the family Ceratopogonidae.
  1967 *DARE* (Qu. R11, *A very tiny fly that you can hardly see, but that stings*) Inf **NY**1, All-jaws—small stinging flies, bigger than no-see-ums.

all kinds of a time n Also ~*of times* *old-fash*
  A very good time.
  1905 *DN* 3.68 **nwAR**, Did you enjoy yourself? Why, I had all kinds of times. **1908** *DN* 3.286 **eAL**, **wGA**, All kinds of times . . . A good time. Also *all kinds of a time*.

all knees and elbows See **all thumbs**

‡**all leather** adj phr Cf **all wool and a yard wide**
  Genuine, reliable.
  1922 Knibbs *Saddle Songs* 40 (in 1939 Carlisle *Southwestern Dict.*), But he's all leather, sure enough.

all left feet See **all thumbs**

‡**all mines** exclam Cf **dibs, hosey**
  They're all mine!—a children's expression used to lay entire claim to something found or won.
  1956 *AmSp* 31.36, *Fin dibs* . . . means 'No divisions on what is mine!' or, as Chuck Albert, from Providence, Rhode Island, says, 'All mines, fellas, all mines!'

all more See **all (the) more**

allmouth n
1 =**goosefish**.
  1882 U.S. Natl. Museum *Bulletin* 16.844, *L[ophius] piscatorius.*—Fishing-frog; . . Goose-fish; All-mouth; . . Angler. **1933** LA Dept. of Conserv. *Fishes* 294, The first impression one gets of it [the *angler, Lophius piscatorius*] is that it is all mouth. References to its lack of beauty are expressed in such popular names for it as Bellowsfish and Allmouth. **1960** Amer. Fisheries Soc. *List Fishes* 51, Allmouth—see goosefish. *Ibid* 49, Goosefish—*Lophius americanus*. **1969** *DARE* FW Addit **eNC**, Allmouth—a pretty big fish, but almost all of it is mouth.
2 =**butter-and-eggs**.
  1968 *DARE* (Qu. S11) Inf **NJ**31, *Allmouth*—wild snapdragon.

all-nighter n Cf **all-day(er)**
1 An animal which prowls throughout the night.
  1895 *Outing* 26.436/2 **Sth**, Most of his [=the American racoon's] habits are bad. He is an "all-nighter" and a "rounder," a robber of hen-roosts and nests, and a destroyer of game birds and their eggs.
2 usu in phr *pull an* ~: An activity which lasts all night; spec, studying all night for an examination. *among young speakers*
  1966 *Current Slang* 1.1.1 **SD**, *All-nighter.* A long, tedious job, esp. studying for a test.—College students, upper classes and graduate. Midwest.—This paper is going to be an *all-nighter.* **1967** *Melody Maker* 28 Jan 11 (*OEDS*), 'It's an all-nighter,' he revealed. 'And I want you to play three 45 minute spots.' **1968** *DARE* (Qu. JJ8, *To study very hard the last minute before an exam*) Inf **NY**81, Pull an all-nighter. **1969** *Current Slang* 3.4.3 **KY**. **1980** *NYT Mag.* 8 **PA**, Staying awake the whole night through to 'cram' is called 'pulling an all-nighter.' . . An 'all-nighter' is never 'spent,' never 'had,' but only 'pulled.'

all-night singing See **all-day singing**

all not hid can't hide over exclam [From a longer rhyme with numerous varr: see quot 1952 and **bushel of wheat, bushel of rye**] Cf **all (in) free**
  In the children's game of hide and seek: a phrase called out by the seeker ("it") before or after he has caught the first hider.
  1952 Brown *NC Folkl.* 1.38, When he [='it'] has finished counting . . [and] if there is no response, he calls: "Bushel of wheat, bushel of clover,/ All not hid can't hide over . . . " **1967–68** *DARE* (Qu. EE15) Infs **IN**32, **TX**37, All ain't hid can't hide over.

all oak and iron bound adj phr Var of **all wool and a yard wide**
  1969 *DARE* (Qu. BB47, *Feeling in the best of health and spirits: "I'm feeling _____."*) Inf **TX**65, All oak and iron bound.

all of a phr **chiefly Nth, esp NEng** Cf **a** prep[1] 4
  Usu foll by a noun to form a predicate adj or adv phr, as *all of a shiver* "shivering," *all of a rush* "suddenly": see quots.
  1875 (1886) Woolson *Castle Nowhere* 116 **Mackinac Is MI**, You're all of a tremble. I would n't stray so far from home if I was you, child. **1895** Brown *Meadow-Grass* 119 **NH**, I was all of a shiver. **1899** (1912) Green *VA Folk-Speech* 464, All of a *twitter*. **1914** *DN* 4.68 **ME**, **nNH**, All of a *biver* . . . Excited. *All of a high* . . . Very anxious . . . *All of a scatter* . . or *scatteration* . . . Broadcast; widely scattered. **1929** *AmSp* 5.126 **ME**, A person might be . . "all of a washing sweat," "wet as sop," "all of a lather." **1938** *Sun* (Baltimore MD) 8 June 8/8 (*Hench Coll.*), Later in the season they [=crabs] drop off almost altogether until late July or in August, when they seem to come back all of a rush.

all (of) one's lone adj phr Also ~*by one's lone(some)* [*EDD* 1894, *OEDS* 1899 →]
  By oneself, alone.
  1890 Farmer–Henley *Slang*, All of my lone . . . (American).—A negro vulgarism for *'alone.'* **1905** *DN* 3.60 **NE**, I was all by my lonesome. **1910** Raine *Bucky O'Connor* 21 (*OEDS*), But why for do they let a sick man like you travel all by his lone? **1917** in 1944 *ADD* **sWV**, I was here all my lone.

all one's born days See **born days**

allot v **chiefly NEng** *old-fash* now usu aphet: see **lot** v
  Usu with *on, upon*: to count upon, expect; to determine or intend (to do something); to be of the opinion.
  1816 Pickering *Vocab.*, I *allot upon* going to such a place. This verb is used only in conversation, and that, chiefly in the *interior* of New England. But it is never heard among people of education. **1836** (1838) Haliburton *Clockmaker* (1st ser) 188 **NEng**, My dear, says she, I ordered

it — you know they are a goin to set you up for Governor next year, and I allot we must economise or we will be ruined. **1847** Hurd *Grammatical Corrector* 16, *Allot on,* or *'lot on,* for *rely on . . as,* "I *allot on,* or *'lot on* his ability and readiness to aid me." **1889** (1971) Farmer *Americanisms, Allot Upon, To . .* A New England colloquialism. "Senator W. seems to have allotted upon a course that is hardly to be commended." *Banner of Light* (Boston). **1931–33** *LANE Worksheets* **nwRI,** I'm lottin' to go . . . I'm allottin'.

all out adj Cf **all in**

1 Exhausted, lacking energy.

1941 *LANE* Map 482 *(Exhausted)* 1 Inf, **cnCT,** All out. **1966–70** *DARE* (Qu. X47) Infs **FL**25, **NJ**69, All out; (Qu. KK30) Inf **MS**1, All out.

2 Out of sorts; having a feeling of general discomfort.

1967–69 *DARE* (Qu. BB5) Inf **KY**28, Feel all out today; (Qu. BB39) Infs **SC**58, **TN**12, All out.

3 Drunk.

1969 *DARE* (Qu. DD15) Inf **IL**35, All out.

all out come in free exclam For varr see quots

In the children's game of hide and seek: =**all (in) free.**

1965–70 *DARE* (Qu. EE15) 8 Infs, All outs in free; Infs **KS**13, **MI**19, **OH**71, All out come in free; **IL**16, **OR**3, All out are in free; **WV**5, 13, All out in free; **TX**61, **WI**60, All that are out come in free; **IL**135, **TN**61, All the other outs in free; **IA**41, All outs free; **WI**29, All that's on the outside come in free; **OK**9, All that's out's in free; **CO**26, All who are out comes in free.

all outdoors n Also *all out-o(f)-doors*

1a The whole world; everything; everyone.

1846 *Quincy* (IL) *Whig* 17 Feb 2/2 *(DA),* I was going to speak of the President's messige — Jimmy K's statement to all out-doors, and some parts of Ashey [=Asia]. **1867** Lowell *Biglow* 23 **MA,** Ourn's the fust thru-by-daylight train, with all ou'doors for deepot. **c1960** *Wilson Coll.* **csKY,** All out-of-doors, also *all outdoors . . .* Everything. **1968** *DARE* (Qu. GG19b, *When you can see from the way a person acts that he's feeling important or independent: "He seems to think he's _____."*) Inf **CT**13, All outdoors.

b An exorbitant fee.

1969 *DARE* FW Addit **neCT,** They charge you all outdoors — huge prices. **1982** *DARE* File **cMA,** I said it this morning at the post office when I mailed a package to England: "This is going to cost all outdoors."

2 in compar phrr, e.g., *as big (hard, slow) as all outdoors:* Something in the extreme. Cf **all get-outdoors**

1825 Neal *Brother Jonathan* 1.III *(DA),* Stuffy feller (that bear) as ever you see'd; big as all out o' doors. **1840** Haliburton *Clockmaker* (3d ser) 78, A-lookin' as big as all out doors. **1941** *AmSp* 16.21 **sIN, MO,** Big as all outdoors. **1942** McAtee *Dial. Grant Co. IN* 5 (as of 1890s), The natural man . . was not content merely to say something was big; no, it was "as big as a whale" or "as big as all out doors." **1952** Brown *NC Folkl.* 1.514, It's as hard as all-outdoors to make money now. **1966–68** *DARE* (Qu. HH22b, *Talking about a very mean person, you might say, "He's meaner than _____."*) Infs **DC**8, **LA**17, **MS**71, All outdoors; (Qu. A18) Inf **MD**14, Slow as all outdoors.

all over adv phr

1 Thoroughly, completely.

1844 in 1930 Meine *Tall Tales* 152 **GA,** I felt all over in spots [=gooseflesh?], for I spected every minit he'd nip me. **1942** (1971) Campbell *Cloud-Walking* 112 **seKY,** Two blankets, one all over red and one purple and black in stripes. **1950** *WELS,* 1 Inf, **seWI,** I've got to wash my hands; they're all over sticky, all over messy.

2 followed by a noun: Entirely covered with. [*OEDS* 1855 →] Cf **all** adj[1] **2**

1890 Howells *Boy's Town* 113 **sOH,** You got somebody . . to sew an egg up in [new calico]; and when the egg was boiled it came out all over the pattern of the calico. **1904** (1969) Robins *Magnetic North* 132 **AK,** When he asked me to hand it to him I nearly stuck fast to it. It's all over syrup. **1916** *DN* 4.272 **NE,** Hand me that blursh [=brush], I'm all over cat hairs. **1954** Forbes *Rainbow* 107 **NH** (as of 1800s), He . . had put on . . one of those heavy blue and white aprons, all over pockets, workmen sometimes wear to keep their tools and oil cans in. **1954** *Harder Coll.* **cwTN,** All-over fidgets . . . extremely nervous and impatient. **c1960** *Wilson Coll.* **csKY,** He is all over sores. **1968** *DARE* (Qu. X58) Inf **CA**87, All over goose bumps.

‡**all-over** exclam

=**anti-over** exclam.

1968 *DARE* (Qu. EE23a) Inf **MO**36, All-over.

all-over-fidges See **fidget** n **1**

all-overish adj *somewhat old-fash*

Physically or mentally uneasy; apprehensive.

1833 *Sketches D. Crockett* 52 **TN,** I wish I may be shot if I know how I felt; but I tell you what, it made me feel quite all-overish. **a1894** Brewer *Dict. Phrase & Fable* 22, All-overish. A familiar expression meaning . . . not exactly ill, but by no means well. **1899** (1912) Green *VA Folk-Speech,* All-overish . . . Feeling confused or abashed. **1916** Howells *Leatherwood God* 15 **OH** (as of c1850), [The mysterious appearance and then disappearance of a strangely dressed, unusual figure at a religious revival] — Made me feel all-overish.

all-overishness n *? obs*

=**all-overs** n **2.**

1846 Smith *Theatr. Apprent.* 216 *(DAE),* A feeling of all-over-ish-ness, like that experienced by a timid child while enjoying (?) the luxury of a cold shower-bath. **1874** (1895) Eggleston *Circuit Rider* 61 **IN** (as of c1800), I feel a kind of all-overishness myself. I 'low we'll have the fever in the bottoms this year.

all-overness n

1 =**all-overs** n **3.**

1820 in 1965 *AmSp* 40.127, [Song verse, from "Oh, What a Row!":] I'm seized with an alloverness, I faint! I die!

2 =**all-overs** n **2.**

1969 *DARE* (Qu. BB5) Inf **IL**66, The all-overness [laughter].

all-overs n pl, usu prec by *the;* rarely sg *the all-over*

1 Feelings of uneasiness, apprehension, or nervousness. chiefly **Sth, S Midl** See Map See also **all-ins, the**

1884 Harris *Mingo* 127 **GA,** She looks lonesome, an' she's got one er them kinder fur-away looks in her eyes that gives me the all-overs. **1891** (1900) French *Otto* 165 **AR,** I jes' take the all-overs every time I see paw gatherin' his gun to go out. **1917** *DN* 4.407 **wNC, MA,** Every time I go to studyin' about it I git the all-overs. **1942** Rawlings *Cross Creek* 167 **FL,** I came to Cross Creek with such a phobia against snakes that a picture of one in the dictionary gave me what Martha calls "the all-overs." **1942** *AmSp* 17.130 **IN.** **1951** Craig *Singing Hills* 218 **swVA, NC,** It gives me the all-overs to have a gun pointed in my ribs. **1952** Brown *NC Folkl.* 1.514 **wNC.** **1965–70** *DARE* (Qu. GG13b, *When something keeps bothering a person and makes him nervous, he may say, "It gives me the _____."*) 22 Infs, esp **Inland Sth, GA, IL, TX,** All-overs; (Qu. GG26, . . *Weakness from fear: "When she saw the dog coming at her she got _____."*) **IN**5, The all-overs; **GA**74, She took the all-overs; (Qu. II29b, . . *The unpleasant effect that person has on you: "He just _____."*) Inf **TX**35, Gives me the all-overs.

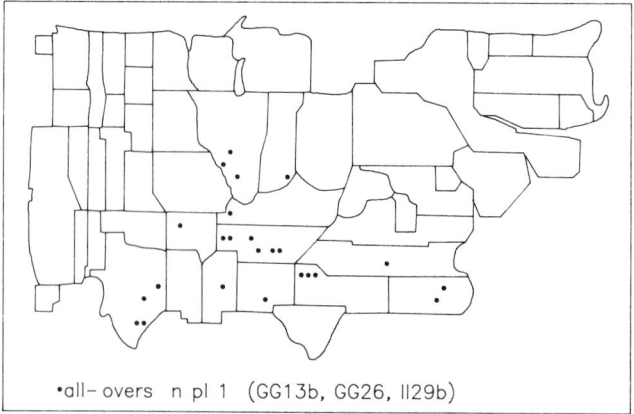

•all-overs n pl 1 (GG13b, GG26, II29b)

2 General feelings of discomfort, illness, or vexation. chiefly east of Missip R See also **all-overishness, all-overness 2, all-ins, the**

1893 Shands *MS Speech* 70, All-overs . . A term employed by all classes to mean *a feeling of extreme annoyance or vexation;* as, "That man is so trifling it gives me the all-overs to look at him." **1965–70** *DARE* (Qu. BB5, *A general feeling of discomfort or illness that isn't any one place in* *particular*) 13 Infs, The all-overs; 9 Infs, All-overs; **GA8,** The all-over. [22 of 23 Infs are **east of Missip R.**].

3 Feelings of exhilaration; thrills.   See also **all-overness 1**

1895 J.C. Harris in 1938 *SW Rev.* 23.220 **GA,** It [=*The Vicar of Wakefield*] touches me more deeply — it gives me the "all-overs" more severely — than all others.

4 Long underwear.

1926 Roberts *Time of Man* 67 **cKY,** I saw your white all-overs the day you went washing in the creek.

all overs adv phr

All over; in every direction.

1968 *DARE* (Qu. MM12a,b, . . *"In all directions," . . "He shot into a flock of birds and they went _____."*) Inf **NJ50,** All overs.

all-overst adj [See quot 1942]

Most extreme: worst; best.

1937 *Hall Coll.* **wNC,** It was the all-overst sight I ever seed!   **1942** Hall *Smoky Mt. Speech* 31 **wNC, eTN,** [All-overst] Not heard in natural speech, but reported in such uses as . . 'the all-overst achin' I ever had,' 'the all-overst cow I ever seen,' (i.e., the most 'no account' cow). This expression evidently developed from the adverb *all over* . . and is apparently not semantically related to *all-overs* 'nervousness.'   **1972** Hall *Sayings Old Smoky* 36, All-overst. Apparently a generalized intensive for 'best' or 'worst,' with a notion of 'best over all,' or 'worst of all.' "He's the all-overst fellow I ever saw," said of one "who's full of fun, a practical joker"; can mean, "There's no one like him."

all over the floor adj phr Cf *DS* X47, BB39

1959 *VT Hist.* ns 27.136, All over the floor . . . Tired; exhausted. Occasional.

allow v often aphet *'low*

1 To suppose, think, consider. [*OED* 1580 →; perh because of ironic use, senses **1** and **2** are often difficult to distinguish: see quot 1892] **chiefly Sth, Midl** *somewhat old-fash*

1794 (1936) Parry *Jrl.* 388 **PA,** We did not start until 10: having another Wilderness of ridges, mountains, hills . . allowed to be somewhat dangerous.   **1801** *Thomas' MA Spy or Worcester Gaz.* (MA) 11 Nov 2/3, We allow it was merit for Mr. Jefferson not to hinder it.   **1892** Eggleston *Hoosier Schoolmaster* 71 **IN,** [Footnote:] *Allow* . . is nearly the equivalent of *guess* in the Northern and Middle States, and of *reckon* in the South. It agrees precisely with the New England *calk'late*. Like all the rest of these words it may have a strong sense by irony. When a man says, "I 'low that is a purty peart sort of a hoss," he understates for the sake of emphasis.   **1894** *Century Illustr. Mag.* 26.872, On the north side of the Ohio River, "guess" is genteel enough for colloquial use, but " 'low" is lower class. Bartlett's "Dictionary of Americanisms" gives this word as "allow," which it rarely is except when pressed and laid away in an herbarium.   **1895** *DN* 1.372 **seKY, eTN, wNC.**   **1902** *DN* 2.228 **sIL.** **1905** *DN* 3.87 **nwAR,** I 'lowed they said 'crazy as a loom' [sic].   **1918** *DN* 5.18 **NC.**   **1923** *DN* 5.200 **swMO,** "I don't 'low I'll go."   "I 'low he shorely must be sick."   **1930** *AmSp* 5.388.   **1931** *AmSp* 7.90 **KY,** We allow he's straight.   **1937** *Hall Coll.* **eTN.**   **1940** *AmSp* 15.45 **sAppalachians and Ozarks.**   **1943** *LANE* Map 592 **ME,** *Allow* [is] rare; **VT,** *Allow* [is] old-fashioned.   **1950** *PADS* 14.11 **SC,** We 'lowed you wudden [=wasn't] comin', so we left.   **1952** Brown *NC Folkl.* 1.514.   **c1960** *Wilson Coll.* **csKY.**   **1968–69** *DARE* (Qu. JJ34, *When you decide it would be to your advantage to do something, you might say, "Yes, I _____ I'll be better off that way"*) Inf **IN32,** Allow; (Qu. GG12, . . *"There she comes now, I _____ she would."*) Inf **AZ10,** Allowed.   **c1970** *Halpert Coll.* **wKY,** I 'low that is true.

2 To assert, remark, opine, declare.

1825 Neal *Brother Jonathan* 28 **NEng,** Her large eyes would sparkle — so the men "allowed" — like the mischief.   **1843** (1916) Hall *New Purchase* 51 **IN,** She "allowed" we had better stop where we were. *Ibid* 432, I allows I kin a sort a pint out the course n'er on about as well as Bill himself kin.   **1903** *DN* 2.305 **seMO,** He allowed I couldn't do it.   **1905** *DN* 3.2 **cCT.**   **1907** *DN* 3.208 **nwAR.**   **1909** *DN* 3.347 **eAL, wGA.**   **1929** Sale *Tree Named John* 107 **MS,** Rabbit 'low, he did, dat he wa'n't skeered uv 'im ner nobody ilse.   **1931–33** *LANE Worksheets* **seMA,** They allowed as how they'd be there on time.   **1980** *DARE* File **DC** [National news commentator:], But he [=Senator Henry Jackson] did allow that he thought Kennedy had a better chance of beating Reagan than President Carter.

3 Acknowledge, admit, concede.

1884 (1958) Twain *Huck. Finn* 214 **MO,** "Why, Biljy, it beats the

Nonesuch, *don't* it?" The duke allowed it did.   **1943** *LANE* Map 592 **CT,** The other fellow'd never allow 'twas a fact.   **1949** Guthrie *Way West* 160 **MO** (as of 1847), "Ma was scared to walk." "Not afeared exactly," she answered, "but offish. I'll allow to being offish."   **c1960** *Wilson Coll.* **csKY.**

4 To plan, intend.   **chiefly Sth, Midl**

1873 Twain – Warner *Gilded Age* 21 **eTN,** Hit warn't no time for to sell, he say, so he fotch it back agin 'lowin' to wait tell fall.   **1875** Harte *Tales of Argonauts* 11 **MO,** I allowed to go to bed.   **1891** Ryan *Pagan* 235 **Allegheny Mts PA,** Now what you decide to allow to do about it?   **1892** Eggleston *Hoosier Schoolmaster* 71 **IN** [Footnote:], *Allow* . . has sometimes a sense of purpose or expectation, as when a man says, "I 'low to go to town to-morry."   **1902** *DN* 2.228 **sIL.**   **1906** *DN* 3.114 **sIN,** I don't 'low to go.   **1909** *DN* 3.347 **eAL, wGA.**   **1941** Williams *Strange Woman* 235 **ME** (*Hench Coll.*), I don't allow to be made a fool of by the two of you.

5 To attribute.

1953 Goodwin *It's Good* 143 **sIL** [Black], She should just allow it to their ignorance.

all-possessed adv

Extremely.

1881 *Harper's Mag.* 63.750/2 **MI,** You needn't be so all-possessed poor that you can't pay an honest woman for . . cooking your venison.

all-possessed, like adv phr

As if bewitched.

1833 Smith *Life Jack Downing* 209 **ME,** [He] struck his fists together like all possessed.   **1856** Whitcher *Bedott Papers* 30 **NY,** Bill Jenkins . . . was a dreadful mean man, used to git drunk every day of his life and . . used to swear like all possest when he got mad.   **1878** Beadle *Western Wilds* 184 **IL,** She dropped a pan o' hot oysters into the lap of a customer, and set him to swearin' and dancin' like all possessed.   **1904** *DN* 2.426 **Cape Cod MA** (as of 1850s).   **1905** *DN* 3.2 **cCT.**   **1907** *DN* 3.207 **nwAR.**   **1908** *DN* 3.286 **eAL, wGA.**   **1909** *DN* 3.407 **ME,** *Act like all possessed* . . . To misbehave.   **1916** Porter *Just David* 280 **NEng,** He danced and laughed and clapped his hands, . . an' carried on like all possessed.

alls n pl [*OED* all B1b, 1721–1763, "still a common phrase in Scotland"] **?Sth** *old-fash*

Usu in phr *pack up one's ~:* All one's possessions.

1830 Royall *Southern Tour* 1.153 (*DAE*), I shall not go without you, so pack up your alls and be ready.   **1912** Green *VA Folk-Speech,* We packed up our alls.

all's pron Also *al(l)st* [Contr of *all* + **as** pron (+ *that*)]

All that.

1967 *DARE* FW Addit **cwMA,** All's [ɔlz] I get is . . , all's he can do is . . . Heard used by 3 or 4 natives of Amherst in their middle or late twenties. All use it fairly frequently.   **1975** Gould *ME Lingo* 35, *Alst* — Perhaps *allst*. It means all or "everything that." "*Alst* I know is what they tell me." "*Alst* you do to fix that leak is buy a new bilge pump."

all sail set, (with) adv phr [Abbr for *with all sails set*]

In a hurried and determined manner: see quots.

1916 Macy – Hussey *Nantucket Scrap Basket* 124, "All Sail Set" — Hurriedly; sometimes, fully dressed. "He was going 'all sail set' for home."   **1945** Colcord *Sea Language* 155 **ME, Cape Cod MA, and Long Island NY,** The process of handling sails has contributed many phrases to shore speech. To make sail for somewhere is to start off in a hurry; with all sail set, full sail ahead, . . means proceeding fast, determinedly.

all set See **all('s) set**

all setting adj phr [Prob *all* + *set* ready; but cf *OED setting* 1, "Becoming, suitable, graceful. *Obs.* exc. *Sc.*," and *SND set* v 12]

All ready, in good condition.

1874 Uncle Bob *Letters to the Children* 154 (*Hench Coll.*), I took him by the hand, and said, "Well, Sam, how do you do?" He grinned, and, in the most careless way imaginable, said, "O I'm all settin'."   **1889** (1971) Farmer *Americanisms,* All-a-setting. — In good condition — a term of barnyard origin. Western in usage. "On the first good grass which they (oxen) strike, they halt a few days, and allow the teams to graze undisturbed, which makes them all-a-setting again." *Overland Monthly.*   **1902** (1968) Clapin *Americanisms.*   **1977** Watts *Dict. Old West.*

all she wrote, that's phr [Perh ref to *Dear John letter* (*OEDS dear* a.[1] 2c)] **chiefly Sth, West** *gaining currency esp among younger speakers*

1 That's all there is; there is no more.

1948 *AmSp* 23.250 **nTX,** [College jargon] *That's all she wrote.* An expression of termination. **1951** Jones *Here to Eternity* 35, All she'd have to do, if she got caught with you, would be to holler rape and it would be Dear John, that's all she wrote. **1967–69** *DARE* (Qu. LL34, *When a road is blocked: "That is all _____."*) Infs **AR**51, **KY**53, **LA**2, **MS**1, **TX**18, She wrote. [3 Infs mid-aged, 2 old] **c1970** *Halpert Coll.* **wKY,** "That's all she wrote" = something is over and done. **1970** *DARE* File **cIA** (as of 1940s), That's all she wrote. **1976** *DARE* File **nCA,** [Response after pouring the last drop from a coffee pot:] That's all she wrote! **1977** Smitherman *Talkin* 258 [Black], *All she wrote,* the end of something, as after finishing a huge serving of chitlins, the Sister said, "Well, that's all she wrote!" **1979** *DARE* File, In the last year I've heard *that's all she wrote* in conversation, used by people from California, Idaho, and Washington. In these contexts it simply means used up, or over (as a slide show). **1981** *WI State Jrl.* (Madison) 25 Oct 6.4/4 **sCA,** "It hurts to lose this kind of game," [Los Angeles Dodgers'] Manager Bob Lemon said . . . "Usually it's one or two innings out of Davis, then the Goose . . and that's all she wrote."

2 That's the end of my patience! — An expression of frustration.

1965–70 *DARE* (Qu. GG22a, *When you have come to the end of your patience, you might say, "Well that's _____."*) Infs **MS**8, **OK**6, **TX**95, All she wrote. [All Infs are mid-aged]

allsie allsie outs in free exclam

In the children's game of hide and seek: = **all-ee all-ee out(s) in free**

1977–78 Foster *Lexical Variation* 79 **NJ,** Allsie allsie outs in free . . 1 [Inf].

all's left See **all's out('s) (come) in free**

all sorts of adj phr **chiefly Sth, S Midl** *old-fash*

Thoroughgoing; excellent.

1841 in **1898** Griswold *Corresp.* 93 **VA,** I wish you to write "all sorts" of an article for the Messenger. **1847** (1962) Robb *Squatter Life* 133 **MO,** She was all sorts of a gal—thar warn't a sprinklin' too much of her. **1852** Haliburton *Traits* 1.229 **NEng,** If you can only get Kit rid of them little failings, you'll find him all sorts of a horse. **1859** (1968) Bartlett *Americanisms,* All sorts of. A Southern expression, synonymous with expert, acute . . . It is a prevalent idiom of low life, and often heard in the colloquial language of the better informed. A man who in New England would be called a *curious* or a *smart* fellow, would in the South be called *all sorts of* a fellow. **1899** (1912) Green *VA Folk-Speech* 65, *All sorts of* . . . Expert; excellent; acute; capital; expert in many ways.

all's out('s) (come) in free exclam For var phrr see quot **chiefly west of Appalachian Mts** See Map See also **all-ee all-ee out(s) in free**

In the children's game of hide and seek: =**all (in) free.**

1965–70 *DARE* (Qu. EE15) 33 Infs, **chiefly west of Appalachian Mts, esp WV, OH,** All's out come in free; 12 Infs, **11 west of Missip R,** All's out's in free; Infs **AZ**12, 15, **PA**1, 229, **TX**28, All's free; **CA**114, **IL**24, **WI**62, All's out in free; **IL**143, **SD**5, All's in; **ID**5, **MI**92, All's out are in free; **CA**2, 136, All's out is in free; **CA**166, All's in free; **MN**42, All's left; **OK**55, **TX**33, All's out (come home free); **MO**7, All's out that's in free.

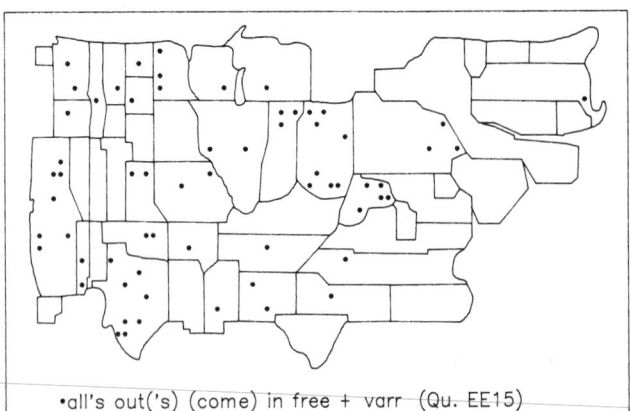

•all's out('s) (come) in free + varr (Qu. EE15)

allspice See **Carolina allspice**

all-spine n **SW**

=**allthorn 1.**

1957 Jaeger *N. Amer. Deserts* 46, Here one also finds . . the broad-leafed Torrey yucca . ., all-spine (*Koeberlinia spinosa . .),* and the thorny condalia.

all('s) set exclam

Everything is ready! Let's go!

1844 (1954) Gregg *Commerce* 35 **SW,** Each teamster vies with his fellows who shall be soonest ready; and it is a matter of boastful pride to be the first to cry out—"All's set!" . . . "All's set!" is finally heard from some teamster—"All's set," is directly responded from every quarter. **1947** *Trail & Timberline* June 92/1 *(DA),* His "All set!" is the signal for the lead man to move smoothly out along the ledge. **1968** Adams *Western Words, All's set! . .* The call of the freighting teamster in answer to the wagon master's *Catch up!* signifying that the teamster is ready to pull out.

allst See **all's** pron

all standing adv [Transf from naut use: *all standing* left without dismantling or unrigging (*OED stand* v 24, 1791 →)] **NEng** *old-fash*

Fully clothed.

1840 (1841) Dana *Two Years* 373, He [the mate] turned-in 'all standing,' and was always on deck the moment he was called. **1846** Levinge *Echoes from Backwoods* 1.235, He had turned in with all his clothes on, as he had done during the three nights on board the schooner, what the Yankees term 'all standing,' viz., in boots, great coat, &c. **1938** Tripp *Flukes* 218 **MA** (as of 1925), The men left their work at midnight, or whatever hour they were relieved, and tumbled into the bunks, "all standing" as the sailors say, that is, with all their clothes on, just saturated with oil.

all talk and no cider See **cider** n

all tanto See **ataunto**

all the foll by an adj or adv usu of positive or compar degree, e.g. *far* or *farther,* to form an adj phr of superl degree meaning *as far as* or *the farthest.* **chiefly Sth, S Midl** when the adj is of positive degree; **chiefly Inland Nth, N Midl** when the adj is comparative. See Maps

1891 *PMLA* 6.175 **TN,** That's all the high (or higher) he can jump. **1893** Shands *MS Speech* 17, The general use of *all* in such expressions as, "All the far he can run," "All the fast it can fly," . . is peculiar . . . *All the far* means entirely as far. **1901** *DN* 2.135 **seNY, seIA, eNY,** Here's all the deeper I can go . .; that's all the far I got . .; that's all the farther I got. **1904** *DN* 2.416 **nwAR,** That's all the far I've read. **1905** *DN* 3.60 **NE. 1908** *DN* 3.286 **eAL, wGA,** All the . . . This is a very common usage, found even among the well educated in such expressions as 'all the far,' . . . "That's all the fast I can run." **1909** *DN* 3.392 **nwAR,** All the farther. **1911** *DN* 3.537 **eKY. 1912** *DN* 3.570 **wIN. 1914** *DN* 4.158 **ePA,** All the further. **1927** *AmSp* 2.347 **wcWV. 1931** *AmSp* 7.19 **swPA. 1946** *PADS* 6.4 **Salem VA. 1950** *PADS* 14.11 **SC. 1951** *PADS* 15.51 **cnIN. 1953** *AmSp* 28.247 **csPA. c1960** *Wilson Coll.* **csKY,** "That's all the fast this horse can run." "That's all the further I can go." *As far . .* is probably less common than *all the far* or *all the further.* **1962** Atwood *Vocab.* **TX** 49, The Midland construction *all the further (farther) . .* is not in general use. **1965–70** *DARE* (Qu. LL34, *When a road*

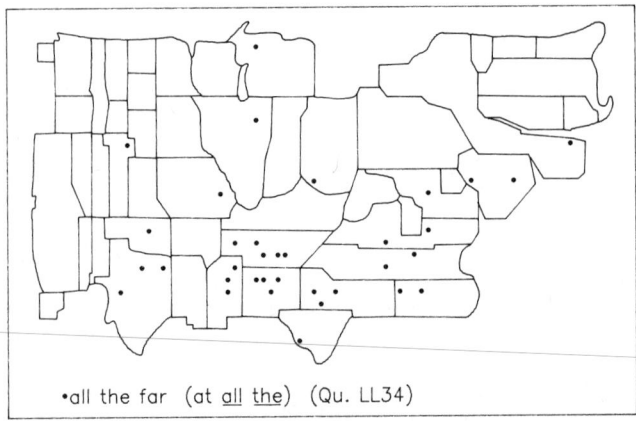

•all the far (at all the) (Qu. LL34)

is blocked: "This is all _____ we can go.") 36 Infs, **chiefly Sth, S Midl,** (The) far. [Of all Infs responding to this question, 34% were coll-educ; of those giving this response, 19% were coll-educ]; 189 Infs, **chiefly Inland Nth, N Midl,** (The) farther [49% were coll-educ]; 137 Infs, **chiefly Inland Nth, N Midl,** (The) further; **DE**7, **FL**7, **TN**36, **WA**1, (The) futher [40% were coll-educ.] **1973** Allen *LAUM* 1.275 **Upper MW,** Phrases with initial *all*— *all the far, all the farther, all the farthest, all the furthest*—are sometimes listed in usage handbooks as unacceptable but in the U[pper] M[idwest] reveal no distinctive contrasts among the inf. levels . . . They are evenly distributed except for their absence in Nebraska.

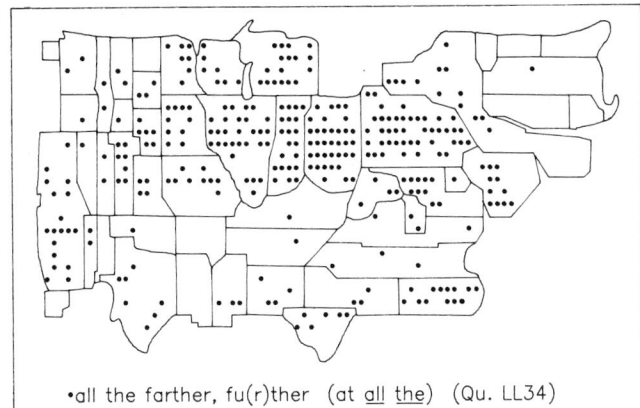

•all the farther, fu(r)ther (at <u>all</u> <u>the</u>) (Qu. LL34)

all the birds in the wood See **feathers, feathers, animal's feathers**

all the go See **go** *n*

all the horns in the wood See **feathers, feathers, animal's feathers**

all (the) more *adj phr*

All that, as much as: see quots.

1929 *AmSp* 4.304 **IA,** A man of my acquaintance . . said contemptuously, "That's all the more you know." **1938** Rawlings *Yearling* 184 **nFL,** Now a wash tub o' biscuits is all more is needed.

all the tea in China See **tea in China**

all (the) time *adv phr* **chiefly Sth, S Midl** Cf **all the way**

Before a verb (where std usage places the adv phr after the verb): always, constantly.

1927 Kennedy *Gritny* 223 **sLA** [Black], W'at make you all time wan' be so scoffish? **1932** (1974) Caldwell *Tobacco Road* 16 **GA,** This raft of women and children is all the time bellowing for snuff and rations. **c1960** *Wilson Coll.* **csKY,** He's all the time a-talking about his folks. **1967** *DARE* Tape **AZ**4, He was all time singin' that song. **1968** *DARE* (Qu. Y9) Inf **GA**28, He's all the time tagging after him; (Qu. GG14) Inf **GA**30, He's all the time gripin'. **1976** Wolfram–Christian *Appalachian Speech* 99, Adverbial phrases of time (typically referring to frequency) may be moved within the verb phrase (usually before the main verb, but they may . . precede the auxiliary) . . . We'd all the time get in fights . . . She's all the time wantin' to watch something.

all the way *adv phr* [Perh from *alway* arch form of *always*] Cf **all (the) time**

Always, constantly.

1976 Wolfram–Christian *Appalachian Speech* 99, We's all the way talkin'.

all the way through *adv phr* Also *all through* **chiefly Nth, N Midl, TX** See Map

Through and through; in every respect.

1965–70 *DARE* (Qu. LL26b, *. . Words meaning 'entirely' . . . "He's Irish _____."*) 33 Infs, **chiefly Nth, N Midl, TX,** All the way through; 10 Infs, **chiefly Nth, N Midl,** All through.

allthorn *n,* also attrib

1 A usu leafless, much-branched and very spiny green-stemmed shrub/tree *(Koeberlinia spinosa)* native to arid regions of the Southwest. Also called **all-spine, corona de Cristo, crucifixion thorn 2, junco** *n*[2] **1**

1908 Hornaday *Camp-Fires* 226 **AZ,** Of greater interest than they were the All-Thorn Bushes with large, fleshy stems for the storage of water,

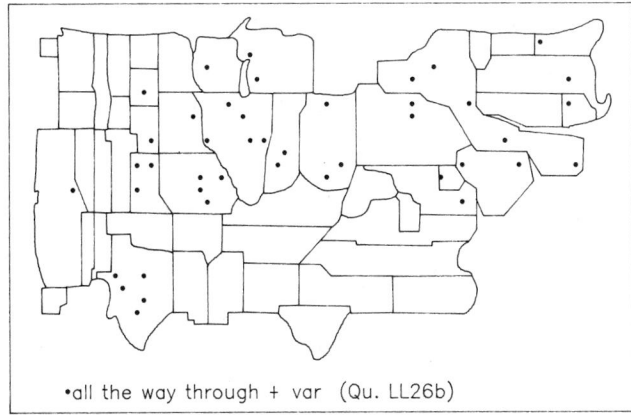

•all the way through + var (Qu. LL26b)

and many thorns but no leaves. **1942** Castetter *Pima & Papago Ag.* 22 **seAZ,** Commonly associated shrubs are lotebush *(Zizyphus lycoides)* . . and allthorn *(Koeberlinia spinosa).* **1960** Vines *Trees SW* 299, Spiny Allthorn . . . is a perfect example of adjustment to desert conditions, with the green thorns and twigs carrying on the photosynthetic process. **1967** *DARE* FW Addit **wTX,** Allthorn . . It is said that Christ's crown was made from this bush.

2 =**goatbush. TX**

1942 Amer. Joint Comm. Horticult. Nomenclature *Std. Plant Names* 93, *Castela texana* . . Allthorn C. **1960** Vines *Trees SW* 600, *Allthorn Castela* . . . Young twigs grayish green . . ending in slender, sharp, straight spines which give rise to numerous lateral spines. **1970** Correll *Plants TX* 911, *Castela texana* . . . Allthorn . . . Low . . shrub with spinescent branchlets and axillary spines.

3 =**junco** *n*[2] **2. TX**

1960 Vines *Trees SW* 687, Texas Adolphia *(Adolphia infesta)* . . . Also known under the names of Junco or Allthorn, but these names also apply to *Koeberlinia spinosa,* which this shrub somewhat resembles.

all through See **all the way through**

all thumbs *adj phr* Similarly *all arms and legs, all feet, ~fingers, ~left feet, ~hands (and feet), ~knees and elbows* [*OED thumb* 5c 1546 →]

Orig and still freq in phr, *one's fingers are ~,* but also said of the person: clumsy, awkward.

1838 Neal *Charcoal Sketches* 117 **Philadelphia PA,** He . . could do almost anything . . if, by a singular fatality, all his fingers were not thumbs. **1850** Melville *White-Jacket* 48, Clumsy seamen, whose fingers are all thumbs. **1939** *AmSp* 14.261 **sIN,** A clumsy individual is 'as awkward as a cow,' or 'His fingers are all thumbs.' **1950** *WELS* (A very awkward or clumsy person) 3 Infs, **WI,** All feet; 1 Inf, All hands; 1 Inf, All thumbs; 1 Inf, All hands and feet, all arms and legs. **1952** Brown *NC Folkl.* 1.407, My fingers are all thumbs (of a clumsy person). **c1960** *Wilson Coll.* **csKY,** All thumbs—a very awkward person. **1965–70** *DARE* (Qu. HH21, *A very awkward, clumsy person)* 27 Infs, **scattered,** All thumbs; Inf **GA**53, All arms and legs [laughter]; **ME**6, **TN**15, All feet; **ID**5, **NY**54, All left feet; **MN**16, All fingers; **MI**120, All hands; **MN**30, All hands and feet; **CA**169, All knees and elbows; **CA**2, All thumbs and no fingers; (Qu. HH15) Infs **CA**106, **IN**70, All thumbs.

all time See **all (the) time**

all to *adv* [*OED all* 15 →1684; *W3* "obs."] *relic*

Completely, thoroughly.

1950 *WELS,* 1 Inf, **ceWI,** Our team beat the visitors all to.

all to hollow See **all hollow**

all-to-pieces *adj obs*

Thorough-going; excessive.

1856 Whitcher *Bedott Papers* 123 **cNY,** She was an all-to-pieces snuff-taker.

‡**all-turner** *n*

A type of **scrub** baseball.

1968 *DARE* (Qu. EE11, *Bat and ball games for just a few players)* Inf **VA**33, All-turners—two batters; they ran all the way around reduced base lines.

all two *adj, pron, conj* Also occas in redund phr *all two both* [*OED all* A11 lists *all two* without example alongside *all both* c1420, and derives both from Fr *tous les deux.* These forms are prob unrelated to U.S. *all two,* which in **S Atl, esp SC, GA coasts** is prob an African calque; in **Nth,** examples from speakers of Ger background are prob calques of *alle beide*—an example of coincidental borrowing from unrelated sources] See also **all both, both two**

Both.

   1838 (1852) Gilman *S. Matron* 94 [Gullah], Sister Nelly begin for sing till Maus Ben and him fell asleep, all two. **1867** Allen *Slave Songs* xxvii SC [Gullah], *Both* they seldom use; generally "all-two," or emphatically, "all-two boff togedder." **1888** Jones *Negro Myths* 17 GA coast [Gullah], Buh Wolf an Buh Rabbit all two bin a spark at um an a cote um. *Ibid* 78, Dem all two lub fish. **1922** Gonzales *Black Border* 139 **sSC, GA coasts** [Gullah], Alltwo come out de same nes' en' alltwo hatch out de same time. *Ibid* 287 [Glossary], Alltwo—both, also each. **1938** Rawlings *Yearling* 289 **nFL,** He says do he meet Twink and Oliver, he'll kill 'em all two. *Ibid* 227, I couldn't watch him and grind corn, all two. **1941** Writers' Program SC *Folk Tales* 30 [Gullah], En all two bot' 'e foots stick! **1950** *PADS* 14.11 SC, *All two* . . . Gullah. **1966–69** *DARE* (Qu. LL21, *Two things . . . 'Do you want the red one or the blue one?' 'I want _____ of them.'*) Infs **GA**28, **MA**58, **MS**7, **SC**9, All two; **SC**11, All two [Reported heard but not used]; **SC**19, 40, All two [Resp sugg by FW]; **CO**7, All two, "for fun"; **PA**149, All two [laughter]. **1982** *DARE* File **csWI** (as of c1945), We're going out tomorrow with all two both of our tractors. [Young male speaker of Ger descent]

allus See **always**

allus-ago See **always-ago** adv, n

allust, alluz See **always**

all was See **all is**

all which(a)way(s) adv phr Var of **every whichaway(s)**
   1966–69 *DARE* (Qu. MM12a, . . *"He shot into a flock of birds and they went _____."*) Inf **IL**39, All which ways; **SC**2, All whichaway.

all wool and a yard wide adj phr *somewhat old-fash* See also **all leather, all oak and iron bound, all wool and no shoddy**

Orig of cloth, but transf generally: of high quality, genuine, reliable, in the best condition.
   1882 Peck *Peck's Sunshine* 85 WI, You want to pick out a thoroughbred, that is, all wool, a yard wide, but just right. **1891** Maitland *Amer. Slang Dict.* **1892** *Congressional Record* 10 Feb 1038/1 NY, I desire this House to understand that the people of the State of Ohio are "all wool and a yard wide" on the subject of sustaining this Government, its glory, and its character. **1908** *DN* 3.286 **eAL, wGA,** All wool and a yard wide . . . All right, having or practising no deception, straight, honest, genuine. **1912** *DN* 3.570 **wIN.** **1915** *DN* 4.180 **swVA.** **1922** *DN* 5.155 **IN, AL, VA, NE.** **1927** *AmSp* 2.347 **cwWV.** **1929** *AmSp* 5.120 **ME,** A stingy man was said to be "tighter than the bark on a tree," an especially fine one to be "all wool and a yard wide." **1946** *CA Folkl. Qrly.* 5.235 **wOR.** **1966** Barnes–Jensen *Dict. UT Slang* 3, I tell you the man is all wool and a yard wide—we can depend on him. **1966–69** *DARE* (Qu. U32, . . *About a very generous person: "He's _____."*) Infs **AZ**11, **NE**8, All wool and a yard wide; (Qu. BB47, . . *In the best of health and spirits: "I'm feeling _____."*) Inf **ID**5, All wool and a yard wide; (QR p144) Inf **NC**6, "He's all wool and a yard wide"—said of someone real nice and kind.

all wool and no shoddy adj phr [*shoddy* inferior fabric manufactured from reclaimed wool]
=**all wool and a yard wide.**
   1946 *CA Folkl. Qrly.* 5.235 **wOR,** It's all wool and no shoddy. It is trustworthy; genuine stuff; not filled or adulterated.

ally See **alley** n²

ally-waiter See **alley-waiter**

almanac n Usu |'ɔlmə,næk, 'al–|, also chiefly **NEng, S Midl** |'ɔlmə,nɪk, –nɛk, 'ælmənɪk| rarely |'amə,nɛk, –nɪk| Pronc-spp *almanick, amanik*

Std sense, var forms.
   1695 in 1897 ME Hist. Soc. *Doc. Hist.* 5.429, [The Indians] Left behind them . . a small bag in which was his beads Crusefix Almanick: & som other trompery. **1768** in 1912 Augusta Co. VA *Chronicles* 1.462, To . . 2 alminicks, 1 alminick. **1891** *DN* 1.123 **cNY,** ['ælmənɪk, 'ɔlmənɪk]. **1899** (1912) Green *VA Folk-Speech, Almanick.* **1917** *DN* 4.407 **wNC, NEng, KY, neOH, IL.** **1923** *DN* 5.200 **swMO.** **1926**

Kephart *Highlanders* 326 **sAppalachians,** "Git the almanick and see when that feller'll full!" (as though she were bidding him look to see when the moon would be full). **1942** Hall *Smoky Mt. Speech* 59 **eTN, wNC,** Almanac ['ɔlmənɪk]. **1949** *AmSp* 24.106 GA, Amanik ['amənɪk] . . Almanac. **1968** *DARE* Tape GA25, Almanac ['ɔlmənɛk]. **1968** *DARE* Tape IN20, Take an almanac ['amə,nɛk], see where the moon is.

Almighties n pl Cf *DS* II23, GG19b.
   1966 *DARE* (Qu. II23, *Joking names for the people who are, or think they are, the best society of a community: The _____*) Inf **SC**21, Almighties.

almighty adj Usu |ɔl'maɪti|, also |ə'maɪti, ɔ'maɪti|, occas |ɔl'maɪnti| Pronc-spp *a'mighty, almighnty*

Std senses, var forms.
   1910–25 in 1944 *ADD* **cNY,** [ɔl'maɪnti]. 'Gosh Almighnty.' . . Common. **1914** *DN* 4.73 **ME, nNH,** Gosh a'mighty! **1926** Vollmer *Sun-Up* 54 **wNC,** This country belonged to us 'cose God A'mighty let us be born here. **1936** *AmSp* 11.247 **eTX,** [ə'maɪtɪ], [ɔ'maɪtɪ] in the phrase 'God almighty' are widespread and are by no means limited to illiterate speech. **1942** McAtee *Dial. Grant Co. IN* 11 (as of 1890s), Gosh-a-mighty.

almighty adv Cf **mighty**

Extremely.
   1833 Jones *Green Mt. Boy* I.iii VT (*DAE*), I shall look almighty fierce. **1878** (1977) Stowe *Poganuc People* 35 CT, "Yis," said Hiel, "but Sim's almighty plucky." **1941** *LANE* Map 426, 1 Inf, **nwCT,** Almighty glad. **1942** McAtee *Dial. Grant Co. IN* 12 (as of 1890s), "Almighty hot." Slang. **c1960** *Wilson Coll.* **csKY,** "It's almighty hot today." Almost a cuss-word.

almond n Usu |'æmən(d), 'amən(d)|, infreq |'ɔmən(d)|; sp-proncs |'ælmənd, 'al–| esp common where the fruit is known only commercially. Pronc-sp *ammon* See also 1941 *LANE* Map 278

Std sense, var forms.
   1847 Hurd *Grammatical Corrector* 78, Almonds . . . [Incorrectly pronounced:] ['ælmʊnz]. **1899** (1912) Green *VA Folk-Speech* 66, *Ammon . . . Almond.* **1933** *AmSp* 8.2.45 **neNY,** There is a general tendency to sound the [l] in . . *almond.* **1936** *AmSp* 11.23 **eTX,** *Almond* . . ['æ:mən]. **1965–70** *DARE* (Qu. I53) Infs **CA**113, 118, ['æmənz]; **CA**97, ['æməndz]; **CA**69, ['aməndz]; **AL**11, ['ɔlmənz]; **MO**11, ['almənd]; (Qu. H80) Inf **TX**85, ['ɔlmən] candy; (Qu. H82) Inf **NJ**37, ['ælmənd] bars; (Qu. T16) Inf **CA**119, ['æmən]; (Qu. X21c) Inf **MO**14, ['a:lmənd] eyed; (Qu. X28) Inf **NY**75, ['ælmən] headed.

almond letter See **letter**

almud n [Span] **SW** *arch*

A unit of dry measure of approximately one peck; see also quot 1892.
   1849 (1906) Audubon *Western Jrl.* 113, Beans are seventy-five cents an "Almud." **1892** *DN* 1.244 **swTX,** *Almud:* a dry measure, one-twelfth of a *fanega* . . , about a peck. Also as much as may be sowed with an *almud* of wheat or corn. **1900** Smithwick *Evolution of a State* 42 **TX,** An act prohibiting any one person from planting more than an almud (one-sixth of a bushel) of tobacco seed. **1934** (1975) Mawson *Dict. Foreign Terms, Almud* . . a measure of capacity of varying content, equal in Texas to about a peck.

aloe n

1 Either of two **agaves:** *Agave americana* and esp **false aloe 1.**
   1828 Rafinesque *Med. Flora* 187, *Agave Americana, . . Flowering Aloes.* **1876** Hobbs *Bot. Hdbk.* 1, *Aloe,* American . . Agave, Americana [sic]. **1901** Lounsberry *S. Wild Flowers* 66, *False aloe—Agave Virginica . . .* Although the custom is very prevalent, it is quite improperly that the agaves are called aloes and century plants. **1975** Hamel–Chiltoskey *Cherokee Plants* 23, Aloe, false aloe—*Agave virginica.*

2 See **aloeroot.**

aloeroot n Also *aloe*
=**colicroot 2.**
   1828 Rafinesque *Med. Flora* 37, *Aletris Farinosa* . . Vulgar names . . Aloroot [sic] . . . The root contains an intense bitter emulsive resin, soluble in Alcohol, somewhat similar to Aloes, but less cathartic. **1892** (1974) Millspaugh *Amer. Med. Plants* 172, Aloe root . . is indigenous to North America, where it frequents the borders of wet, sandy or swampy woods from Florida northward, especially at the seaboard.

1971 Krochmal *Appalachia Med. Plants* 40, *Aletris Farinosa . . . Common Names:* Whitetube stargrass, . . aloe, aloeroot.

aloes to catch meddlers n [Metath of *layoes* ~, for which see **layovers** ~]
=layovers to catch meddlers.
1927 *AmSp* 2.409 **GA, TN.**

aloha n |ɑˈlohɑ| [Haw] **chiefly HI though recognized throughout US**

1 Love, kindness, sympathy, good feeling; often used as a greeting, hence also, the greeting itself.
1820 in 1931 Bernice P. Bishop Museum *Special Pub.* 17.18 **HI,** The first salutation was similar to our manner of introduction, that of giving the hand and Alohah, i.e., how do you do, or good morning. **1833** in 1934 Frear *Lowell & Abigail* 55 **HI,** Their [the Hawaiians'] word for salutation is "aloha." **1951** *AmSp* 26.19 **HI,** *Aloha,* the Hawaiian greeting, is known around the world . . . *Aloha* means 'love, sympathy'; it can be used for 'hello' or 'good-by' and is a frequent reminder of the spirit of Hawaiian hospitality. **1954–60** Hance *Hawaiian Sugar.* **1965** Krauss *Grove Farm* xv **HI.** **1967** Reinecke–Tsuzaki *Hawaiian Loanwords, Aloha . .* probably the most important blanket word in Hawaii. According to context, it may mean anything from "love" to "mere kindly feeling of the political or commercialized variety." Among native Hawaiians and occasionally among others, it is used as a salutation at meeting or parting. **1967–69** *DARE* (Qu. NN11, *Informal ways of saying 'good-bye' to people you know quite well:*) Infs AZ11, [əˈloɑ]; CA105, GA84, Aloha [laughter]; HI1, Aloha is said a great deal. On Maui, children wave and say this, but it is being institutionalized; MN41, Aloha; (Qu. NN10b, *Greeting used when you meet somebody you do not know well*) Inf HI6, Aloha.

2 In var other borrowed phrr of common currency in **HI:** *aloha ino,* ~ *kakou,* ~ *nui (kakou, loa),* ~ *oe:* see quots.
1843 in 1934 Frear *Lowell & Abigail* 169, The British Commission has taken French leave — *aloha ino* [Frear: profound sympathy] for a man in his predicament. **1967** Reinecke–Tsuzaki *Hawaiian Loanwords* 92, *Aloha kakao* [əˈlohɑ ˈkaːkou] . . . Good feeling among us all! V[ery] F[requent]. *Aloha nui . . .* Great regard. VF . . . *Aloha nui kakou . . .* Great good feeling among us all! F[requent] *Aloha nui loa . . .* Very great regard. VF . . . *Aloha oe . . .* 1. May you be loved or greeted. 2. As the well-known song "Aloha Oe" is frequently sung at the end of parties, the words have come to connote in some contexts "farewell to you." VF.

aloha party n **HI**
1972 Carr *Da Kine Talk* 112 **HI,** *Aloha party . . .* A farewell party given for someone about to leave the Islands. The word *aloha* itself may be a greeting or a farewell, but an *aloha party* is almost always for leave-taking.

aloha shirt n **HI but recognized throughout US**
A loose, brightly colored and often flowered sport-shirt, especially popular in Hawaii.
1968 *Jrl. Engl. Ling.* 2.80. **1972** Carr *Da Kine Talk* 112 **HI,** *Aloha shirt . . .* A bright-colored, short-sleeved shirt, open at the neck — the informal attire of men in Hawaii.

along adv Also aphet *'long*

1 often foll by *about, back:* somewhere or sometime. See also **abouts, back along, down along, up along**
1851 (1914) Kingsley *Diary* 165 **CA,** Worked as usual today, took-out 50 ounces and 4 dollars, which gains on our days along back. **1879** Twain *Sketches* 135, In the one case you start out with a friend along about eleven o'clock on a summer's night. **1905** *DN* 3.2 **cCT,** It's been quite wet along back. **c1960** *Wilson Coll.* **csKY,** "Along in May I'm going to buy me a horse" (or *'long*). **1966** Barnes–Jensen *Dict. UT Slang* 3, It was along back in January when he left the camp. **1976** Garber *Mountain-ese* 3 **sAppalachians,** I'm not sure, but I think we got home along about sundown.

2 Continuously over an indefinite period of time.
1856 *MI State Ag. Soc. Trans.* 7.806, The result was, his corn grew right along, for it could not help it. **1913** Wharton *Custom of Country* 112 **NY,** You're *living* in New York, then — you're going to live here right along? **1940** *Sat. Eve. Post* 6 April 17/1 **Sthn plantation,** 'What you been eating?' 'Different things along. Blackberries, and palmetto cabbage, and robins.' **1966** *DARE* (Qu. LL7, *In small amounts, by small degrees: "She didn't get the money all at once; they sent it to her _____."*) Infs AR18, 33, A little along; SC8, Along and along.

along of prep Also aphet *'long of*

1 also *all along of:* Because of. [Ult from OE *gelang on* because of, owing to; *OED:* "Common in London and southern dialects generally"; *EDD* 1846 →] **chiefly Midl, Sth** *somewhat old-fash*
1862 Winthrop *John Brent* 190 **OR,** We was a little late one morning, along of our horses havin' strayed off from camp. **1875** (1886) Woolson *Castle Nowhere* 130 **Mackinac Is MI,** He took all we had, and we've gone cold and hungry 'long of him. **1903** Wiggin *Rebecca* 67 **ME,** Rebecca never'll come to grief along of her beauty, that's certain. **1909** *DN* 3.346 **eAL, wGA,** "It was *long* o' them Smith boys that we didn't come on time." Rare. **1912** Green *VA Folk-Speech.* **1931** *AmSp* 7.91 **eKY,** I came early long of wantin' to get it done afore the rain. **1936** Morehouse *Rain on Just* 79 **NC,** Not one of us ought to be at licker . . . Rease just now buried. Dead along of that same poison. **1939** Hench Coll., *All along of* is used in Albermarle County, Va. to mean "because of, dependent upon."

2 With. [*EDD* 1890 →]
1884 Murfree *TN Mts.* 262, 'Pears ter me ez ye mought hev brought him hyar ter eat his supper along of we-uns. **1903** *DN* 2.299 **Cape Cod MA** (as of 1850s), *Long of:* Along with. **1931** *AmSp* 6.272 **KY Mts,** Go along of me as fur as my cabin. **1942** Chamberlain *Laverack* 53/4, Just a ole dawg come here as a pup along of a swipe named One-eye Tuppy.

alongst prep [*OED:* "*Along* with advb. genitive *-es* . . very early corrupted to *alongest, alongst,* as if it were a superlative form." Cf *EDD*] *relic*
Along, alongside of.
1899 (1912) Green *VA Folk-Speech, Alongst . . .* Along; through or by the length of. **1964** *Mt. Life* Spring 54 **sAppalachians,** *Alongst* (alongside of).

aloose adj [a inert vowel **6** + *loose*] **Sth, Midl**
Loose.
1884 Harrison *Negro Engl.* 244. **1908** *DN* 3.286 **eAL, wGA,** Turn that hoss a-loose. **1934** Stribling *Unfinished Cathedral* 8 **AL,** A dern Yankee is jest as li'able to turn a nigger aloose as hold him. **1966** *Wilson Coll.* **csKY,** He got aholt of me and would not turn me aloose. **1966** *DARE* Tape NC13, The government is turning . . needlings [i.e., small fish] aloose every year. **1967** *DARE* FW Addit LA11, Turn aloose our dogs, cats, and chickens. **1968** *DARE* (Qu. MM13, . . . *He came along and knocked it*) Inf PA66, Aloose.

a lots adv, adj [Blend of *a lot* + *lots* much]
Much, many; often.
1968 *DARE* Tape GA48A, I've killed 'em a lots; GA50A, That's another thing we'd eat a lots of — we'd eat a lot of ducks. *Ibid,* If he's been bothering a lots. **1970** *Thompson Coll.* **GA,** I need a lots of them. *Ibid* **GA,** I shore done a lots a surveying with that old mule.

alow and aloft adv phr [Transf from naut use, lit below and above the deck] **chiefly NEng** *arch*
Throughout, completely.
[**1827** Cooper *Red Rover* 55, I think you said something concerning the manner in which yonder ship has anchored, and of the condition in which they keep things alow and aloft?] **1851** (1976) Melville *Moby-Dick* 177, A row a'low, and a row aloft — gods and men — both brawlers! **1945** Colcord *Sea Language* 23 **ME, Cape Cod MA, Long Island NY,** *Alow.* Down, downwards . . . The word is now obsolete except in the phrase, alow and aloft, meaning completely, all over. **1963** Haywood *Yankee Dict.* 4 **NEng,** What concerned the ship from deck to keel was 'alow' and when life was completely satisfactory the windjammer sailor said "all's well alow and aloft."

alphabet n, also attrib [Calque from Japanese or Korean: see quot] **HI**
Any letter of the alphabet.
1972 Carr *Da Kine Talk* 121 **HI,** "My name begins with the alphabet *A,* so I have to go first in line." As used very widely by speakers in all nonstandard types, *alphabet* covers the meaning 'a single letter' as well as 'a set or system of letters.' There are parallel usages . . : the Japanese word *kana* means not only a single *kana* symbol but also the total syllabary . . ; in Korean, there is no distinction between the words meaning 'alphabet' and 'letter.'

‡**alphabet slinger** n *joc* Cf **inkslinger**
A schoolteacher.
1969 *DARE* (Qu. JJ1) Inf GA72, Alphabet-slinger.

alphabets, the n [Prob a ref to abbr *T.B.*]
Tuberculosis.
   1970 *DARE* (Qu. BB10) Inf **FL**51, "The alphabets"—not at all common, but still has been used.

alpine fir n
An evergreen tree *(Abies lasiocarpa)* of the Rocky Mountains, found at altitudes of 2700 feet and upwards. Also called **balsam 5, balsam fir, corkbark fir, pumpkin tree, white fir**
   1897 Sudworth *Arborescent Flora* 52, Abies lasiocarpa—Alpine Fir. **1967** *DARE* (Qu. T5) Inf **CO**9, Alpine fir; (Qu. T16) Inf **WA**22, Alpine fir.

alpine forget-me-not n
A dwarf, perennial Rocky Mountain plant *(Eritrichium elongatum)* with usually blue flowers similar to forget-me-nots.
   1953 Nelson *Plants Rocky Mt. Park* 132, Alpine forget-me-not . . Eritrichium argenteum **1961** Douglas *My Wilderness* 18 **CO,** Low to the ground in thick mats grows the alpine forget-me-not. The flowers are tiny and fragrant. They are as blue as the sky, and in their center is a touch of gold fringed by white.

already adv Usu |ˌɔl'rɛdɪ|, also chiefly **Sth, S Midl** *esp among less educ speakers* |ɔ'rɛdɪ, ə'rɛdɪ| Pronc-sp *a'ready*
A Forms.
   1861 Holmes *Venner* 1.118 **wMA,** I'm pretty nigh beat out a'ready. **1899** (1912) Green *VA Folk-Speech* 68, Have you came back a'ready. **1899** Chesnutt *Conjure Woman* 139 **NC** [Black], Fer he owed ez much ez he could borry a'ready on de skyo'ity he could gib. **1936** *AmSp* 11.247 **eTX,** [ə'rɛdɪ] and [ˌɔ'rɛdɪ] are . . widely used, with [ˌɔl'rɛdɪ] as a more elegant form. **1954** Harder *Coll.* **cwTN,** That road's done filled with holes a-ready. **c1960** *Wilson Coll.* **csKY,** Already is often [ə'rɛdɪ]. **1976** Allen *LAUM* 3.315 **ceNE,** 1 Inf [ɔ'rɛdɪ].
B Senses.
1 also *already yet:* Previously; before; ago. [Calque: through PaGer from Ger *schon* already, yet, so far] **chiefly sePA and other Ger settlement areas**
   1907 (1970) Martin *Betrothal* 104 **sePA,** It's five years back already that he died for me. **1935** *AmSp* 10.167 **sePA,** He has lost his respect for her long already. **1942** Berrey–Van den Bark *Amer. Slang* 2.5, Formerly; Before. Already yet. **1948** *AmSp* 23.109 **sIL** [Ger settlement area], He didn't have it already. **1953** *AmSp* 28.246 **csPA.** **1958** *AmSp* 33.232, In the case of *already,* too, the Yiddish and Pennsylvania German influences seem somewhat different. Contrast, for example, 'He has lost his respect for her long already,' cited from Pennsylvania-German American speech . . with 'Finish up, already!' from Jewish American speech. **1968** *DARE* FW Addit **PA**142, Have you eaten dandelion already?
2 also *already yet, yet already:* An intensifier used to indicate emphasis, annoyance, or immediacy. [Calque: ult from Ger *schon* as transmitted independently by PaGer *schun* and Yidd *shoyn*] **chiefly in Jewish and Ger settlement areas**
   1907 (1970) Martin *Betrothal* 109 **sePA,** Lizzie thought that's what made her teeth go so fast, so 's he had to get his store ones already. **1939** Aurand *Quaint Idioms* 29 **sePA,** I seen him yet a'ready! **1958** *AmSp* 33.232, 'Finish up, already!' from Jewish American speech. **c1960** *DARE* File **KS,** In a poem [Walt] Mason wrote: "the sports are hedging already yet" . . . the usage in Kansas was not far less than common and the usage is similar to what one hears around Lancaster, Pa. **1967** *DARE* (Qu. EE20) Inf **MO**14, I give up already. [Inf Jewish] **1968** *DARE* FW Addit **PA**142, What wonders me, already, is why he did it. **1970** Feinsilver *Yiddish* 297, The use of "already" at the end of a sentence is a direct translation of the Yiddish *shoyn,* as in *kum, shoyn!* (Come, already!) . . . "Enough, already!" and "Let's go, already!" have been widely used on TV and seem to be making inroads into general speech. **1976** *Capital Times* (Madison WI) 9 Mar 12/1 **FL,** One octogenarian, with a yarmulke on his head . . didn't sit down when Jackson started to speak. He continued to clap . . until an annoyed neighbor shouted "Sit down, already."
3 Yet—sometimes used simply for emphasis. **HI** *(in creolized speech)*
   1934 *AmSp* 9.123 **HI,** *You been eat lunch already?—Yes, I been eat. Already* is frequently added to strengthen the idea of completed action. **1960** *Social Process* 24.66 [In "List of Pidgin Errors"], Already . . . Used sometimes to express simple past time, sometimes redundantly for emphasis. *Ibid* 67, Spotty went kill one pussy already. **1972** Carr *Da*

Kine Talk 121, "I called you up but you weren't there already." . . In Hawaii *already* is used widely in both affirmative and negative expressions. This may be because *already* has long been a very common word, used as a tense-marker in reduced English without regard to finer points . . . There is no word in the Hawaiian language equivalent to *already,* and native speakers of Hawaiian must have had difficulty with this much-used English word.

already yet See **already 1, 2**

alsike n Usu |'æl,saɪk|, freq |'æl,sæk|, occas |'æl,saɪt|; for less freq varr see quots
Std sense, var forms.
   1950 *WELS* (. . *Kinds of grass* . . *grown for hay)* 2 Infs, **WI,** Alsake; 1 Inf, Alsac. [Informants' spp] **1965–70** *DARE* (Qu. L9a) Inf **CO**38 ['ɔl,saɪt]; **MN**7, ['ɛl,sæk]; (Qu. L9b) Inf **MI**56, ['æl,sæk]; **TN**62, Alsack; **MI**2, ['æl,sæk] Clover—Horses like it better than any other feed growed; **MI**47, ['æl,sæk] clover; **MD**29 ['ælə,saɪk]; **WI**10, ['ɔl,saɪk]; **WI**44, ['æl,saɪt] clover.

alst See **all's** pron

altar-bound adj Also ~*conscious,* ~*crazy*
Eager to get married.
   1965–70 *DARE* (Qu. AA4a) Infs **AL**27, **MA**69, **MT**3, Altar-bound; (Qu. AA4b) **IL**97, **IA**7, **MS**51, **WV**18, Altar-conscious; **SC**69, Altar-crazy.

alte kacker See **alter kocker**

alter v *somewhat old-fash, sometimes euphem*
To castrate or spay a domestic or farm animal.
   1821 (1930) Hazard *Jrl.* 555/2 **RI,** Worner Knowles oltered my four Boar Piggs. **1852** *Florida Plantation Records* 62 *(DA),* I have sheared the sheep and altered the Lambs. **1905** *DN* 3.2 **cCT.** **1908** *DN* 3.286 **eAL, wGA.** **1923** *DN* 5.200 **swMO.** **1939** *LANE* Map 210, *Alter* is described as the usual term [for male domestic animals] by . . [12 informants]; as the polite term by . . [22 informants]; as 'proper' by . . [1 informant]; as a farmers' term by . . [3 informants]; as rare by . . [3 informants]; and as old-fashioned by . . [4 informants]. **1944** *PADS* 2.39 **sVA, LA.** **1946** *PADS* 5.9 **VA.** **1950** *PADS* 14.11 **SC.** **1952** Brown *NC Folkl.* 1.514. **1958** *AmSp* 33.268 **eWA.** **c1960** *Wilson Coll.* **csKY,** "We're going to alter that calf today." Euphemism, often among men. **1965–70** *DARE* (Qu. K70, *Words . . for castrating an animal)* 212 Infs, **throughout US,** Alter [of all Infs responding to the question, 73% were old; of those giving this response, 81% were old]. (Qu. J3a, *To make a female dog so that she can't breed, she must be* _____) 21 Infs, **chiefly Nth,** Altered [All Infs old]; (Qu. J3b, *To make a female cat so that she can't breed)* 29 Infs, **chiefly Nth,** Altered [24 Infs were old, 4 mid-aged, 1 young].

alter n [Ger *Alte* old man] *PaGer* Cf **alter kocker**
An old man.
   1939 Aurand *Quaint Idioms* 11 **sePA,** Hi, ya, *alter* (. . endearing term)!

‡**alterated** ppl adj [Blend of *altered* + *castrated,* or perh *alterate* (back-formation from *alteration*) + *-ed*]
   1968 *DARE* (Qu. K25, *What is a 'steer'?)* Inf **CA**101, An alterated cow.

alter kocker n Also facetious *alter coyote,* pronc-spp *alte kacker, alter kaker* [Yidd, ult from Ger *alter* old + *kocker* excrement] **NYC and other Jewish settlement areas** *often derisive but also used familiarly* See also **A.K.** n **1, alter** n
An old fogy.
   1943 *AmSp* 18.44 **NYC,** A Jewish person who would not hesitate to say . . *alte kacker* (the latter word being pronounced the way New Yorkers would say *cocker* spaniel) . . would quite possibly be shocked to hear them even spoken by another. **1968** Rosten *Yiddish* 14, *Alter kocker* . . . Pronounced *oll-ter kock-er,* to rhyme with "Sol the mocker." From the German: *alter,* "old"; *Der Alter* [sic], "the old man." What *kocker* means I had rather not tell you in street argot, but *kock* means "defecate." . . "He lies in bed all day, like an *alter kocker.*" I make no special plea for *alter kocker,* but I certainly prefer *A.K.* to its English equivalent, "old fart." **1970** Feinsilver *Yiddish* 355, *Alter kaker* . . . is roughly equivalent to "Old Goat" and is sometimes spoken in full or in the bilingual euphemism "*Alter* Coyote." **1976** Flexner *America Talking* 222, *Alter kocker* . . literally "old shit" . . old man, old fogey, . . mid 1930s.

alto n [Span] **SW** *now rare exc in place names*
   1892 *DN* 1.244 **TX,** *Alto:* a hill, an eminence, generally without trees.

altone n [Blend of *alto* + *baritone*]

1927 Kennedy *Gritny* 5 **sLA** [Black], Three "good altone songsters" were coming to lend added luster to the meeting.

alum bloom n [See **alumroot**]

=**cranesbill 1** (here: *Geranium maculatum*).

1896 *Bot. Gaz.* 22.478, Old maids' night-caps, Madison, Wis. alum root, alum bloom, crow foot. **1930** Sievers *Amer. Med. Plants* 62, *Geranium maculatum* . . . Alum-bloom . . . flourishes in low grounds and open woods from Newfoundland to Manitoba and south to Georgia and Missouri. **1971** Krochmal *Appalachia Med. Plants* 134, Alum bloom . . . Harvest: Leaves and rhizomes in spring, just before plant flowers, or in late summer.

aluminum n Usu |ə'lumɪnəm, ə'lumənəm|, freq aphet |'lumənəm|; occas in **Sth, S Midl** |(ə)'lumɪəm, (ə)'lumjəm|; rarely |ə'lumənə, ə'lumɪən| Pronc-sp *alumium*

Std sense, var forms.

1942 in 1944 *ADD* **nWV,** |'lu,mɪəm|. **1949** *PADS* 11.3 **wTX,** *Alumium* [ə'lumjəm] . . . Occasional. Uneducated. **1965–68** *DARE* Tape **GA22,** They use ['lumɪən] cups; **TN15,** I use the gut strings . . wound with ['lumjəm]; **AL14,** Tin pails . . . They didn't have [ə'lumənə]; **MS56,** [ə'lumɪən]. **1966–67** *DARE* (QR, near Qu. F1) Inf **AL24,** Aluminum [ə'lumɪən]; (Qu. F31) Inf **AL14,** Aluminum [ə'lumənə].

alumroot n [From the astringent properties of the root]

1 Any of several spp of the genus *Heuchera* (but esp *H. americana*) which have geraniumlike basal leaves and tall slender stalks with panicles of small bell-shaped flowers. Also called **cliffweed, coral bells, crag-jangle, cranesbill 2, ground maple, rock geranium, sanicle, split rock, wild geranium 2**

1813 Muhlenberg *Catal. Plantarum* 29 *(DA),* American Heuchera (alum root). **1848** Gray *Manual of Botany* 149, *Heuchera,* L. Alumroot . . . Flowers in small clusters disposed in a . . panicle. **1901** Lounsberry *S. Wild Flowers* 218, *H[euchera] Americana,* alum-root, raises a stout and high stem . . . Its leaves, however, are its prominent feature of beauty. **1931** Harned *Wild Flowers Alleghanies* 218, Alum Root . . . The root is strongly astringent, producing an alum-like effect when applied to the tongue. **1971** GA Dept. Ag. *Farmers Market Bulletin* 1 Sept 8/1, Alum-root, Heuchera americana, is an attractive foliage plant which mixes well with ferns in woodland gardens . . . The common name of the plant is derived from its thick root which is an astringent.

2 =**cranesbill** (here: *Geranium maculatum*).

1830 Lindley *Nat. Syst. Bot.* 140 *(OED),* The root of *Geranium maculatum* is considered a valuable astringent in North America, where it is sometimes called Alum root. **1901** Lounsberry *S. Wild Flowers* 285, Country people also call it *[Geranium maculatum]* alum root in reference to that part's bitter flavor. **1930** Sievers *Amer. Med. Plants* 62, Wild Geranium . . . Other common names.— . . alumroot [etc.]. **1971** Krochmal *Appalachia Med. Plants* 134, *Geranium maculatum* . . . alumroot . . . The roots and rhizomes . . are very astringent.

always adv Usu |'ɔlwe(ɪ)z, 'ɔlwiz|; often *esp in rapid speech and among less educ speakers* |'ɔlə(r)z, 'ɔlə(r)s|; less freq |'ɔlɛz, 'ɔlɪz, 'ɔ(w)ɪz| Freq pronc-spp *allers, allus;* less freq pronc-spp *al'a's, al'ays, allust, alluz, alus, alwez, alwuz, awluz, ollers*

Std senses, var forms.

1847 Hurd *Grammatical Corrector* 78, *Always . . . Incorectly pronounced:* ['alʊrs]. **1867** Lowell *Biglow* 24 'Upcountry' **MA,** Ignorant folks is ollers sot an' wun't git used to takin' on 'em. **1871** Eggleston *Hoosier Schoolmaster* 63 **IN,** You allers take sides with that air hussy. **1871** (1882) Stowe *Fireside Stories* 56 **MA,** The young fellers was allers 'mazin' anxious to be sent after Huldy. **1887** in 1941 Warfel–Orians *Local-Color Stories* 454 **VA** [Black], He al'ays handled heself to he raisin. **1891** (1967) Freeman *New Engl. Nun* 45, I allers believed in goin' dressed suitable for the occasion. **1891** *DN* 1.164 **cNY,** [ɔlərz] . . *always.* **1894** *DN* 1.327 **NJ, CT,** *Alluz.* **1906** *DN* 3.114 **sIN,** He allus goes. **1908** *DN* 3.286 **eAL, wGA,** *Allus.* **1909** *DN* 3.392 **nwAR,** *Allus.* **1930** *AmSp* 5.350 **IL,** [ɔlez] for *always.* **1931** *AmSp* 7.90 **eKY,** The chillern allers kept their mouths shet in the presence o' their neighbors. **1934** Carmer *Stars Fell on AL* 177, He wuz alwez a-wantin' to be big 'stead of little. *Ibid* 180, Brer Rabbit wa'n't al'a's de prankin' tricky fellow he is now. **1938** Matschat *Suwannee R.* 268 **GA,** She comes alus in time of very bad storm. **1939** *AmSp* 14.287 **ceIL,** [hid 'ɔɪz 'šɔ˞k 'meɪkɪŋ ə 'čɔːɪs]. **1942** *AmSp* 17.176, [In Mark Twain's representation of Black speech:] *Alwuz* is the stressed, *awluz* the unstressed form of

always. **1954** *PADS* 21.20 **cnSC,** Allust. **1976** Allen *LAUM* 3.315 **NE,** Loss of /l/ occurs in . . ['ɔweˑz] or ['ɔwɪˑz] for always, heard from [8 Infs] . . . A loss of /w/ in *always* produces such a pronunciation as is exemplified with [ɔulu:z], [ɔɫəz], and [ɔɫˑz], heard chiefly in the conversation of 12 scattered Type I infs. but only one Type II and no Type III's. It is clearly a minor social marker.

always-ago adv Usu pronc-spp *allus-ago, allers ago* **sAppalachians** *somewhat old-fash*

Long ago.

1914 Furman *Sight* 70 **eKY,** Beseeched of her to forgive and forgit . . which of course, being Marthy, she had already done allus-ago. **1922** Cobb *Kinfolks* 59 **sAppalachians,** Allus-ago I yearned to view the sea. **1931** *PMLA* 36.1320 **sAppalachians,** "Always ago" (long ago) is corrupted into "allus ago," or "allers (sharp *s*) ago." **1937** (1963) Hyatt *Kiverlid* 113 **sAppalachians,** Granny lurnt me that allus-ago.

always-ago n Pronc-sp *allus-ago* [From the adv] **sAppalachians** *somewhat old-fash*

A long time ago.

1922 Cobb *Kinfolks* 3 **sAppalachians,** Dulcimer over the fireboard, hanging sence allus-ago. **1931** *AmSp* 7.92 **eKY,** Mama's been gone since allus-a-go.

alwez, alwuz See **always**

am See **be**

ama-ama n [Haw *'ama'ama*] **HI**

The striped mullet *(Mugil cephalus).*

1960 Gosline–Brock *Hawaiian Fishes* 154, *Mugil cephalus ('Ama 'ama)* . . . The young are silvery pelagic fishes that may be taken at a night light well offshore in spring. **1967** *Honolulu Star–Bulletin* (HI) 31 Mar, *Ama ama* . . . Mullet. Two kinds—fresh and salt-water. Bake, steam. **1967** *DARE* (Qu. P1) Inf **HI4,** Mullet—Ama-ama . . fresh and salt water.

amadama bread See **anadama bread**

amake See **a inert vowel 5**

amakihi n [Haw]

A small yellowish-green honeycreeper *(Loxops virens)* common in the Hawaiian Islands.

1972 Berger *Hawaiian Birdlife* 19, Although the Apapane *(Himatione sanguinea)* is undoubtedly the most common species of living honeycreeper, the Amakihi *(Loxops virens)* appears to be the most adaptable. **1980** Bushnell *Water of Kane* 394 **HI,** The youth would . . follow the amakihi, the nukupuu and iiwi, and the rare ou in their excursions among the forest trees.

amanik See **almanac**

a many quasi-n [*OED many* B1a 1590 →, now std with a modifier before *many,* as *a great many, a good many*] *arch*

A great number of.

1884 Murfree *TN Mts.* 251, Thar hev been sech a many folks killed on the T'other Mounting.

a many adj phr

Foll by a sg n: many a; more than one.

1965–70 *DARE* FW Addits **OK40,** I've gone to a many dance with him; **OK52,** There's a many man had a rock pulled on him in the mines, a many one; **ceNJ,** I've had a many one come in.

a many a adj phr [Blend of **a many** adj phr + *many a* (*OED many* A1b, c1250 →), now std in *many a day, many a time,* without a preceding indef art] **chiefly Sth, S Midl** *somewhat old-fash*

Many a; more than one.

1893 in 1901 *Independent* 53.2765/2 **NEng,** I have went hungry a many a time almost starved. **1899** (1912) Green *VA Folk-Speech, A-many* . . . Many people; a multitude; "a-many a one;" a great many. **1905** *DN* 3.68 **nwAR,** 'A many a poor tired woman has set up and doctored and worried over a sick baby! Common. **1940** Stuart *Trees of Heaven* 38 **neKY,** I've kilt a-many a squirrel in that tree, son. **1946** *PADS* 6.4 **NC,** "I've seen him a many a time." Pamlico. Common. **1950** *PADS* 15.51 **Grant Co IN,** A many a . . . First "a," an expletive. "I've been there a many a time." **1966** *DARE* (QR, near Qu. K50) Inf **NM3,** I've tied down a many a [horse]. **1968–70** *DARE* Tape **VA17,** I've churned a many of a gallon of milk; **VA52b,** I really shedded a many a tear; **VA55,** He killed a many a one.

amaranth n

Std: a plant of the genus *Amaranthus.* Also called **alegria, beetroot, borax, careless weed, caterpillar, cockscomb 2, curls, light-houses, love-lies-bleeding, matweed, pigweed, prince's-feather, purslane, redroot, spleen amaranth, tumbleweed, tumbling pigweed, waterhemp, wild beet**

Amar'ca See **America**

amargoso n, also attrib Also sp *amargosa* [MexSpan < Span *amargoso* bitter, referring to the bark] **TX**
=goatbush.

1878 U.S. Natl. Museum *Proc.* 1.122, This little bird perched upon the topmost twig of an amargosa bush. **1885** *Ibid* 8.515 *Castela erecta . . .* the Amargoso of the Mexicans . . . [is] common on the gravelly bluffs of the lower Rio Grande. **1892** *DN* 1.187, 244 **TX,** *Amargóso.* **1942** Friend *Plants Rio Grande* 53, Amargosa [is] a spiny native shrub. **1960** Vines *Trees SW* 600, . . . Vernacular names are Bisbirinda, Amargosa, and Goat-bush. **1967** *DARE* (Qu. T16 *What kinds of trees are "special" around here?*) Inf **TX22,** Amargoso.

amarugian n, often cap Also sp *amerugian, anaroogian, annarugian, arnarougen* (?misprint) [Prob factitious quasi-group name (with *-ian*): cf **Scandihoovian** and phonetically similar **hoosier** |'huʒɚ| and **hoojin.** Note also *Aberginian (DA),* a general term in early Massachusetts Bay settlement for wild northern Indians]

A crude, unruly person; a member of a rough party of funmakers — orig applied to residents of Fulton Co., Illinois.

1856 Hall *College Words* 10 **KY,** At Centre College, Kentucky, is a society called the *Annarugians,* "composed," says a correspondent, "of the wildest of the College boys, who, in the most fantastic disguises, are always on hand when a wedding is to take place, and join in a most tremendous Charivari, nor can they be forced to retreat until they have received a due proportion of the sumptuous feast prepared." **1879** *Hist. Fulton Co. IL* 970, *Amarugia.* — Near the center of the township [=Young Hickory] is the spot where in early days some of the settlers would congregate for sport, such as horse-racing, shooting matches, prize fights, etc. Some of them would take a little too much bourbon, and appeared very ridiculous, to say the least, which on one occasion brought forth the following remark from one of the old settlers: "They look more like Amarugians than anything else." The people took up the name and christened the place Amarugia, by which that vicinity is known even to this day, and the time was when all persons living in Young Hickory were known as Amarugians for twenty to thirty miles around. **1912** *DN* 3.570 **wIN,** *Anaroogian . . .* A very rural old fellow. "The old anaroogian never comes to town except upon election day." [**1925** *IL State Hist. Soc. Jrl.* 18.423 **cwIL** (as of 1844), Seven miles to the North was the Cline settlement, which was somewhat similar, but generally known as Arnarougen . . . The people generally were illiterate and in our section schools and churches were unknown.] **1969** *Hist. Fulton Co. IL* (ed. Clark) 271, Somebody, sometime, somewhere thrust the name Amarugians on the people of Young Hickory Township and surrounding area . . . The whole area became known as Amarugia, and until very recently London Mills was thought of as being a rough town. **1983** *DARE* File **cwIL,** I have not heard the word "amerugian" used lately . . in this community [Fulton Co.]. I remember my wife's folks used it quite often . . as a term of mild reproach for their children, after they had been in mischief . . . "You little Amerugian." *Ibid* **cwIL,** According to the President of the Fulton County Historical Society, the people of London Mills still refer to themselves as Amarugians.

amazing adv Pronc-sp *'mazin'*

Amazingly, extremely.

1805 in 1940 Criswell *Lewis & Clark* 8, In the afternoon their arose a storm of hard wind and rain and amazeing large hail. **1871** (1882) Stowe *Fireside Stories* 56 **MA,** The young fellers was allers 'mazin' anxious to be sent after Huldy. **1878** *Harper's Mag.* Sept 574 **NEng,** Parson he reckoned he'd be amazin' fore-handed this year. **1905** *DN* 3.2 **cCT.** **c1960** *Wilson Coll..* **csKY.**

‡**ambacker juice** n [Blend of **ambeer** + *'backer* pronc var of *tobacco*] *rare* See also **amber juice**
=ambeer.

1930 *Herald–Advt.* (Huntington WV) 30 Nov **ceKY,** The hill-man . . . expectorates not tobacco juice but "ambeer" — or, as one said, "ambacker juice."

ambeer n Usu |'æm,bɪr, 'æm,bɪə|, less freq |'æmbə(r)|, occas |'embə(r)| Pronc-spp *amber, ambia, ambier* [Alter of *amber,* for the color, infl by *beer,* with ref to color and foam of the spittle] **chiefly Sth, S Midl** See Map See also **ambacker juice, amber juice**

1 Juice from tobacco trash: see quot.

a1763 in 1775 *VA Gaz.* (Williamsburg) [Purdie] 4 Aug 1, The floor [of the tobacco-house] being thus prepared, sprinkle strong ambeer over it, made from tobacco trash, and cover it with wet ground leaves, or other tobacco trash, for a fortnight.

2 Saliva colored by chewing tobacco or snuff.

1848 Bartlett *Americanisms* 391, *Ambia,* Used in Virginia and the Carolinas for tobacco juice. It is a euphemism for the spittle produced by this voluntary ptyalism. **1902** *DN* 2.228 **sIL,** *Ambeer . . .* Tobacco juice. The saliva when chewing tobacco. **1903** *DN* 2.305 **seMO,** *Ambeer . . .* Tobacco juice. "They spit ambeer all over the floor." **1907** *DN* 3.220 **nwAR.** **1908** *DN* 3.286 **eAL, wGA.** **1914** *DN* 4.102 **KS.** *Ibid* 180, **VA.** **1923** *DN* 5.200 **swMO.** **1927** Adams *Congaree* 24 **cSC** [Black], Wid ambier drippin' off her bill jes like it drip off her tongue in dis world. **1944** Howard *Walkin' Preacher* 125 **MO,** She spat a mouthful of amber directly over the bare toe and into the fire. "Ya kotched me achawin' my terbaccy." **1950** *PADS* 14.11 **SC,** Ambeer ['æmbɛə, 'æmbjɛə]. **c1960** *Wilson Coll.* **csKY.** **1965–70** *DARE* (Qu. DD4, *Moisture in the mouth, colored brown by snuff or chewing tobacco*) 113 Infs, **chiefly Sth, S Midl,** Ambeer ['æm,bɪə, 'æm,bɪr]; 21 Infs, **chiefly Sth, S Midl,** Amber ['æmbə(r)]; Infs **KY92, MS88,** Amber ['embə(r)].

3 The residue that gathers in the stem of a smoker's pipe.

1899 (1912) Green *VA Folk-Speech, Ambeer . . .* Thick nicotine in a pipe stem. **1967** *DARE* FW Addit **ceSC,** Ambeer . . . The tars, etc. that collect in the pipe stem — not the same as tobacco spittle.

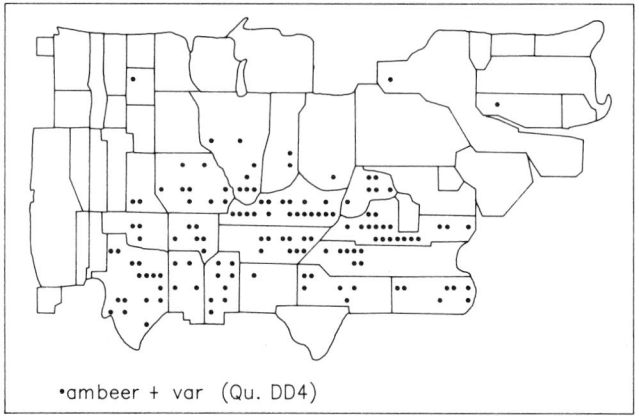

•ambeer + var (Qu. DD4)

amber bell n [From the color and shape of the flower]

1 **=bead lily** (here: *Clintonia borealis*).

1943 Peattie *Great Smokies* 265, Clintonia . . the "bluebead lily" of the north woods; the "amber bell" of the southern highlands.

2 **=dogtooth violet** (here: *Erythronium americanum*).

1933 Small *Manual SE Flora* 292, *E[rythronium] americanum . . .* Amberbell. **1949** Moldenke *Amer. Wild Flowers* 329, Best known of our fawnlilies is the yellow fawnlily or amberbell.

amberfish n [From its color] **S Atl** See also **amberjack 2, horse mackerel**

Any of var fish of the genus *Seriola* or related genera.

1674 Josselyn *Two Voyages* 107 **NEng,** The Sea-bream, Dorado, or Amber-fish, they follow ships . . and are good meat. **1775** (1962) Romans *Nat. Hist. FL* App 19, A little to the north here of is a small reef . . where vast quantities of groopers, snappers, amber-fish, . . may be taken. **1799** (1803) Ellicott *Jrl.* 255, Along the Florida Reef, and among the Keys, a great abundance and variety of fish may be taken: such as . . amber-fish. **1881** U.S. Bur. Fisheries *Report* 42, The Amberfish is quite common off the West Florida coast . . . It is a good food-fish.

amberjack n

1 Yellow sphalerite.

1888 *Harper's Mag.* June 48/1 **KS,** Along the line of Spring River, lead, . . galena, and zinc, as blende, or black-jack and amber-jack, are abundant.

2 A species of **amberfish**, esp *Seriola dumerili*. **S Atl**

1895 *Std. Dict. Engl. Lang.* (Funk), *Amberjack, n.* An amberfish (*Seriola lalandi*). *Amberfish, n.* A carangoid (genus *Seriola*), usually bright-colored, of warm seas, as *S. carolinensis* of the southern United States. **1897** *Outing* 29.330/2 **FL**, Not inferior to the kingfish for sport is the amber fish or 'amberjack.' **1966–68** *DARE* (Qu. P2, . . *Saltwater fish . . good to eat*) Inf **NC**12, Amberjack; (Qu. P4, *Saltwater fish that are not good to eat*) Inf **NC**52, Amberjack. **1975** Evanoff *Catch More Fish* 215, The amberjack . . is also called the great amberfish, amberfish, coronado, and great jack.

amber juice n Cf **ambacker juice**
=**ambeer 2.**

1968 *DARE* (Qu. DD4) Infs **IN**45, **TN**26, Amber juice.

ambia, ambier See **ambeer**

ambition n **chiefly Mid Atl and settlement areas** Cf **ambitious 1**
Malice, vindictiveness; hatred; irascibility.

1826 *VA Herald* 19 Aug. 1/4 *(DA)*, Ambition, is used to express malice—an ambitious man means in common parlance a vindictive man. **1829–30** *Dunglison's Glossary* in 1927 *DN* 5.423 **VA**, *Ambition* —"spite"—a Virginianism. "He has brought the action against me, for ambition." **1859** (1968) Bartlett *Americanisms, Ambition.* In North Carolina this word is used instead of . . *grudge* . . "I had an *ambition* against that man." I am credibly informed, that it is even employed in this manner by educated men. **1901** *Scribner's Mag.* 29.395/1 **KY**, His friends . . kept urging him to revenge. A woman wanted them to stop. "Hit jes' raises the ambition in him and *don't do no* good *nohow.*" **1903** *DN* 2.305 se**MO**, *Ambition* . . enmity. "He has had ambition against me for years." **1950** *PADS* 14.11 **SC**, *Ambition* . . . A quick temper.

ambition v
To propose or opine assertively.

1898 Westcott *Harum* 153 **nNY**, He ambitioned that if his mother 'd raise a thousan' dollars on her place he'd be sure to take care of the int'rist, an' prob'ly pay off the princ'ple in almost no time.

ambitious adj

1 Of persons or animals: spirited, unruly; vicious; angry. **Sth, Midl** Cf **ambition n**

1853 Bird *Nick of Woods* 1.23 **KY**, The fight had made him as ambitious as a wild-cat. [Footnote:] *Ambitious,*—in Western parlance, vicious. *Ibid* 54, He's never ambitious, except among Injuns and horses. **1859** (1968) Bartlett *Americanisms, Ambitious.* Angry, enraged. A native of Georgia was heard to say, "I was powerful *ambitious* and cussed snortin'." The word is used in the West in a similar sense. They say an "*ambitious* horse" meaning . . a horse that is fiery and unmanageable. **1902** *DN* 2.228 s**IL**, *Ambitious* . . . Mettlesome; full of animal spirits. A fiery horse is called *ambitious,* or a vivacious person. **1907** *DN* 3.220 nw**AR**. **1919** *DN* 5.33 se**KY**, *Cut a skive* . . . To prance about considerably. Applied to an "ambitious" (fiery) horse. **1931** *PMLA* 46.1310 s**Appalachians**, An "ambitious" horse is an unruly horse. **1950** *PADS* 14.11 **SC**, *Ambitious* . . hot tempered, quick tempered. **1952** Brown *NC Folkl.* 1.514, *Ambitious* . . . Vicious. "That dog is mighty ambitious."

2 Energetic, lively. [From *ambition* energy (*W3* sense *3*), which evidence from *DARE* Qu. HH27b suggests is not regional] **chiefly Inland Nth, N Midl** See Map

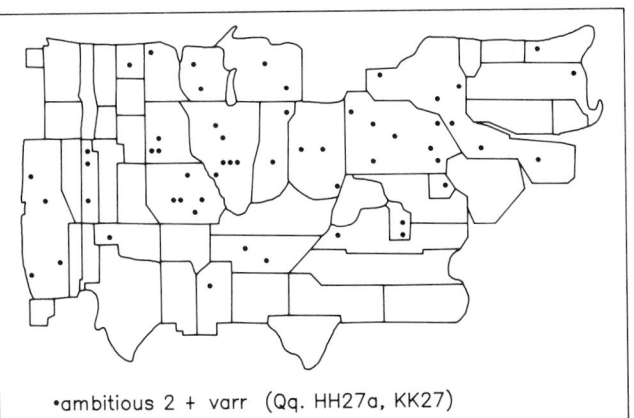

•ambitious 2 + varr (Qq. HH27a, KK27)

1889 (1971) Farmer *Americanisms, Ambitious* . . . in Massachusetts and Connecticut . . . it is indicative of energy, industry and moral worth as regards human beings, and is descriptive of good points where animals are concerned. **1901** *DN* 2.135 sc**NY**, *Ambitious* . . Industrious. **1909** *Atlantic Mth.* 104.137/1 **NW**, The word 'ambitious' is used in a sense for which I can find no Southern parallel unless it be in the old word 'pert.' **1917** *DN* 4.387 ne**OH**, *Ambitious* . . . Full of energy, industrious. "I don't feel very ambitious today." Also N. Eng., N. Car., Ill., Ky., N.Y. **c1960** *Wilson Coll.* cs**KY**, *Ambitious.* Energetic rather than trying to dominate. **1965–70** *DARE* (Qu. HH27a, *A very able and energetic person who gets things done*) 52 Infs, **chiefly Inland Nth, N Midl**, (Very) ambitious (person); **MA**8, Ambitious and gets things done; **OK**18, Ambitious guy; (Qu. KK27, . . *Lively, active* . . *"For his age, he's awfully _____."*) Inf **OH**91, Very ambitious. **1973** Allen *LAUM* 1.353 **Upper MW**, A person with unusual vigor and vitality is described in many ways in the UM . . . ambitious [by 10 Infs].

‡ambleshoot n *joc* Cf *DS* W1a,b,c
An umbrella.

1968 *DARE* (Qu. W1c, . . *Joking names . . for an umbrella*) Inf **NY**73, Ambleshoot, bumbleshoot.

ambrelluh, ambril See **umbrella**

ambrosia n

1 also *ambrose:* Usu **Jerusalem oak 1**; sometimes **Mexican tea 1.**

1847 Wood *Class-Book* 469, *C. ambrosioides. Ambrosia Goose-foot.* **1894** *Jrl. Amer. Folkl.* 7.97, *Chenopodium Botrys, . .* ambrosia, Concord, Mass. **1900** Lyons *Plant Names* 95, *C. ambrosioides . . .* Mexican Tea . . Ambrosia. *Ibid, C. Botrys . . .* Jerusalem oak, Ambrose. **1910** Graves *Flowering Plants* 165 **CT**, *Chenopodium Botrys . .* Ambrosia. Ambrose. **1918** *DN* 5.32 se**KY**, Ambrosia, an odorific yard flower, sometimes called "seasash." **1971** Krochmal *Appalachia Med. Plants* 86, *Chenopodium ambrosioides* . . . Common Names: . . . *ambrosia.*

2 A dessert containing oranges and shredded coconut, sometimes nuts and other fruit. [Cf *OED* ambrosia 4, 5] **chiefly Sth** Cf **embroidery B**

1932 (1946) Hibben *Amer. Regional Cookery* 262 **MS**, *Ambrosia* . . . 6 large oranges . . sugar . . 2 cups freshly grated cocoanut. **1941** Percy *Lanterns* 29 **MS**, Imagine ice-cream *and* pudding, ambrosia *and* pie. **1942** Rawlings *Cross Creek Cookery* 195 **FL**. **1964** Amer. Heritage *Cookbook* 565, Ambrosia . . is familiarly known to Americans as a combination of oranges and coconut—a very popular dessert in the South. In some sections it is traditionally served for Christmas dinner. **1965–70** *DARE* (Qu. H63, *Kinds of desserts specially favored . . around here*) Infs **AL**25, **CO**5, **GA**32, 55, 85, **LA**14, **MS**54, 63, **NM**5, **NY**181, **SC**51, **VA**66, 98, Ambrosia.

ambulance n Usu |'æmbjǝlǝn(t)s|, often *esp among less educ speakers* |'æmbǝlǝns, æmbɪlǝns, æmbɪlǝns, –æn(t)s|; occas, perh for humorous effect, metath |'æmblɪǝn(t)s, –æn(t)s|, or syncopated |'æm(b)lɪns, –ǝns|; addit varr in quot 1965–70

A Forms.

1942 Hall *Smoky Mt. Speech* 67 e**TN**, w**NC**, Ambulance ['æmbǝlǝns]. **1954** *Harder Coll.* cw**TN**, Ambulance |'æǝm,lǝns|. **c1960** *Wilson Coll.* cs**KY**, Ambulance [æmblǝns]. **1965–70** *DARE* (Qu. N1) Infs **IA**47, **MD**26, **NC**67, **SC**19, 32, **UT**15, **VA**59, 64, 96, ['æmbǝlǝns, æmbɪlǝns, æmbǝlǝns, –æn(t)s]; **KY**42, **MI**105, **VA**84, ['æmblɪ,æns, 'æmblǝ,æns]; **FL**31 ['æmblǝnts]; **MO**3, ['æmblɪns]; (Qu. N2) Inf **GA**40, ['æmǝ,lænts]; **LA**29, ['æmblǝnts], **MS**63 ['æmlǝns]; **MO**1, ['æmbɪlǝnts]; **MO**19, ['æmblɪnts]. **1968** *DARE* Tape **MD**9, Ambulance ['æmǝ'læns]. **1969** *DARE* FW Addit **Baltimore MD**, Ambulance ['æmbjɪ'læns]—common, not by highly educated.

B Senses.

1 A prairie wagon; a passenger vehicle resembling a hospital ambulance. **SW** *now hist* Cf **dougherty wagon, avalanche 1**

1854 (1932) Bell *Log TX–CA Trail* 213 **TX**, I can with difficulty keep my eyes open and am compelled to get a Mexican to ride her [=a mule] and I get in the ambulance. **1856** *NY Herald* 9 Jan 2/1 *(DA)*, The vehicle, which, like most ambulances, or 'prairie wagons,' as they call them here, proved rather airy, was made comfortable by wrapping ourselves in buffalo robes and moccasins. **1893** (1958) Wister *Out West* 174, At Birkenshaw's an ambulance met us, and off got a respectable person who shook hands, and I remembered the Rev. Coolidge, Indian and clergyman. *Ibid* 175, I asked promptly for an ambulance to go and get ourselves clean at the Hot Springs. **1936** *Hench Coll.* **Charlottesville**

VA, A . . woman told me of a week's cross-country trip that her father and mother took her and some friends on in the late 1880's. "We went in two large, covered spring-wagons," she said, "which were called 'ambulances.'" **1943** Wood *Walter Reed* 92 *(DA),* The road had turned out to be so rough that any progress faster than a walk threatened to shake both the ambulance (as the doherty wagon was also called) and its occupants apart. **1968** Adams *Western Words.*

2 Among railroad workers: a caboose.
1977 Adams *Lang. Railroader* 6.

ambulanter n *?obs* Cf **ambulance 1**
An itinerant worker or tramp: see quot.
1927 *DN* 5.437 **NC,** *Ambulanter* . . . A tramp who travels in a wagon with his family picking up odd jobs as he goes.

ambuscade n *?obs*
A disagreement.
1895 *DN* 1.370 **eTN, seKY, wNC,** Him an' me had several little ambuscades.

ambush v [*OED ambush* 1b →1814] *arch*
To hide (oneself).
1905 *DN* 3.68 **nwAR,** He ambushed himself along the road to see if anyone was following him.

amen bench See **amen pew**

amen corner n, also attrib

1 also *amens corner, amen section:* A section in certain churches or religious meeting places, usu the front seats to the right or left of the preacher, occupied by those leading the responsive amens; hence a corner occupied by highly vocal worshippers. **chiefly Sth, Midl** See Map Cf **awomen corner, mourner's bench**
1860 *Harper's Mag.* Jan 279/2, The Rev. Judson Nott, a local Methodist preacher in the town of _____, in Southern Kentucky . . . was a good singer, could pray long and loud, and was one of the best "Scotchers" that occupied the "Amen corner" [at a church in another town]. **1889** Edwards *Runaways* 145 **GA,** Elder Hamlin ceased, and amid the shuffling of feet that followed the deep "Amen" which rolled from the prompt "Amen corner" back into the dilatory recess beyond the last post, the congregation resumed their seats. **1903** *DN* 2.305 **seMO,** *Amen corner* . . Seats near the pulpit in a church. **1906** *DN* 3.114 **sIN.** **1907** *DN* 3.228 **nwAR.** **1918** *DN* 5.18 **NC.** **1944** *PADS* 2.24 **cwNC.** **1950** *PADS* 13.16 **cTX.** **c1960** *Wilson Coll.* **csKY,** *Amen corner* . . . Largely humorous now. **1965–70** *DARE* (Qu. CC5, . . *Seats in a church, especially near the front)* 135 Infs, **chiefly Sth, Midl,** Amen corner(s); **MA1, SC64, VA41,** Amens corner; **NJ46,** Amen section. **1979** *TriQuarterly* Spring 182, So he made a special show of . . booming out some gibberish mumbo-jumbo in his best amen-corner baritone.

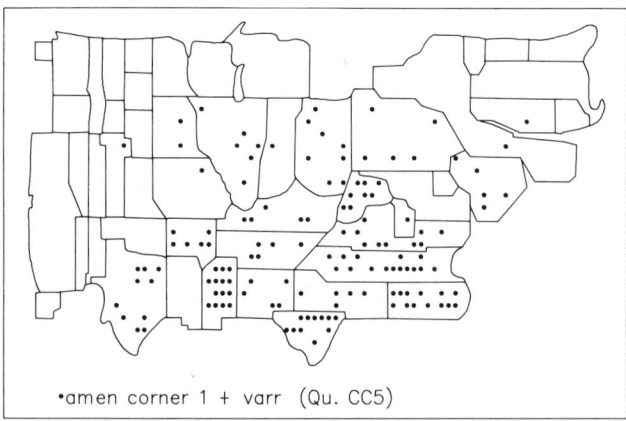

•amen corner 1 + varr (Qu. CC5)

2 =**anxious bench 1.**
1944 *PADS* 2.24 **wNC,** *Amen corner* . . . That part of the church where seekers kneel at a revival.

3 Among loggers: see quot.
1969 Sorden *Lumberjack Lingo* **NEng, Gt Lakes,** *Amen Corner*—A corner in the bunkhouse where the old-timers reminisced, or a place where sky pilots [=preachers] spoke, or entertainers told their stories.

amen pew n Also ~*bench,* ~*row,* ~*seat* **chiefly Sth and Atl States** Cf **confession seat**
A bench or seat in the **amen corner** of a church; in pl, the **amen corner** itself.
1877 Habberton *Jericho Road* 128 **Missip Valley,** In an "amen" seat sat an old half-breed. **1950** *WELS (Seats in a church or meeting house . . especially those near the front)* 1 Inf, **cWI,** "Amen row"—front row—old-fashioned. **1965–70** *DARE* (Qu. CC5, . . *Seats in a church, especially near the front)* Infs **AL6, CT11, 37, GA89, NC79, 82, NH6, NJ4, OH15, PA185, SC5, TX20, 51,** Amen pew(s); **AR21, CT6, 16, 23, GA74, TX1,** Amen seats; **CA79, NJ41, PA175,** Amen row; **GA9, 12,** Amen bench(es).

America n Usu |ə'mɛrəkə|; often *esp among less educ speakers* |ə'mɛrəki, ə'mɛrəki, ə'mɛrəkɚ|; *occas* |ə'mʌrɪkə|; *rarely* |ə'mɑrkə| Pronc-spp *Amar'ca, Americee, Ameriky, Amurrica*
A Forms.
1643 in 1827 *RI Hist. Soc. Coll.* 1.57, [In rhymed verse by Roger Williams:] Yet I have found lesse noyse, more peace / In wilde America, / Where women quickly build the house, / And quickly move away. **1926** *DN* 5.385 **ME,** -*a* (final). Pronounced like -*y* or -*er* in such words as Amelia, America, Augusta. **1926** *AmSp* 2.81 **ME,** Final *a* in proper nouns is usually *y* . . . "Ameriky." **1933** *AmSp* 8.4.61 **DE, MD, VA,** On several records *America* is pronounced [əmɑrɪkə]. One of the first gentlemen of the Delaware says [əmɑrɪkə]. **1934** (1970) Wilson *Backwoods Amer.* 111 **Ozarks,** They was havin' a quilt sewin' at Uncle Ameriky Henstep's. **1934** *AmSp* 9.236, The 20th century phonetic change is at bottom the same as that of the 16th century; namely, the prevalence over the preceding vowel of the [ə] glide before the [r]—the same, too, that gives us "Amurrica." **1940** in 1944 *ADD* 'Middle Border,' *Amar'ca.* Old-fashioned. **1941** *Sat. Eve. Post* 10 May 111/1 **eKY,** The finest cellar in *Americee.* **1950** (1965) Richter *Town* 36 **OH,** It minded her when she was a girl . . . Hardly anybody then . . said America. No, they said Ameriky.

B Senses.

1 From the point of view of isolated or backcountry dwellers: the outside civilized and urban world, hardly known to them.
1848 Cooper *Oak-Openings* 2.111 **MI,** But you can never find the food of a pale-face kitchen out here in the Openings of Michigan. When a body comes to reckon up all the good things of Ameriky, she don't know where to begin, or where to stop. **1938** Matschat *Suwannee R.* 197 **nFL, sGA,** Her heart thumped with excitement over . . the major thrill of having a sister married to a fureen man and going away to live in far Ameriky!

2 The eastern states, or those east of the Mississippi River. **West** *now hist* Cf **American**
1857 in 1912 Thornton *Amer. Gloss.* 855, A man writing from Southern Oregon to the *N.Y. Tribune* says that some of the people are going to California, and "others are talking of going back to America." **1867** Dixon *New Amer.* 10, The current jest, everywhere to be heard from Atchison to Salt Lake, says, that a man who means to cross the Missouri is going on a trip to America. **1931** Willison *Here They Dug* 50 **CO** (as of c1860), On every canvas top can still be read *Pike's Peak or Bust!* But to this has been added *Busted, by God!*—or some such sentiment as *Bound for America!*

3 The mainland of the US.
1977 *UpCountry* July 7/1 **Martha's Vineyard MA,** Walp, goin' over to America Thursday to get my damn teeth fixed agin'.

American adj [**America B2**] **West, esp SW** *now chiefly hist* but see also **American jack**
Of a cow or horse: Eastern; of a breed from the eastern states as opposed to inferior ones early found on the plains.
1837 in 1908 *Amer. Hist. Assoc. Annual Rept. for 1907* 2.187 **TX,** A large number of fine American horses . . , which there is no doubt had been stolen by the Indians from Citizens of Texas. **1846** (1848) Bryant *What I Saw in CA* 52, Such [Indians] as rode ponies were desirous of *swapping* them for the American horses of the emigrants. **1862** Winthrop *John Brent* 2.14, He was an American horse,—so they distinguish in California one brought from the old States. **1875** *Cimarron News* 7 Aug 4/4 *(DA)* **NM,** What are cattle worth? . . Texas cows, $12 to $16 per head; American cows, $25 to $50 per head. **1940** Fergusson *Our Southwest* 62 **TX,** Mounts ranged from nimble Spanish ponies to big American horses.

American banana See **banana B1**

American beauty n Cf **American fried**

A red, white, and blue playing marble: see quot.

c1970 Wiersma *Marbles Terms* **MI** (as of 1940), American beauty . . a red, white, and blue colored marble; (as of 1960) American beauty . . a multicolored playing marble with interlacing or swirling patterns. Considered very valuable.

American coffee bean See **coffee bean 1**

American fence See **American wire fence**

American fried n Cf **American beauty, fried marble**

1973 Ferretti *Marble Book* 39 **seNY**, *American fried.* Larger than average marbles, of glass, that have been heated, then iced, creating inner cracks. Used as shooters.

American fried potatoes n pl Also *American fries*

1 Boiled potatoes sliced and then fried in a shallow pan. **chiefly Upper MW, N Cent** See Map Cf **hash browns, raw fried potatoes**

1950 *WELS (Kinds of fried potatoes)* 5 Infs, **WI**, American fried; 1 Inf, **cnWI**, American—slices (thick) of cooked potatoes; 1 Inf, **cwWI**, American fried—fried in pan with just enough fat; 1 Inf **seWI**, American fried—sliced fried in little fat in pan; 1 Inf **ceWI**, American fried—fried in bacon grease or lard; 1 Inf **cWI**, American—cooked first then fried in shallow grease; 1 Inf, **swWI**, American fried—cooked, fried with some fat to flavor (as ham or bacon); 1 Inf, **cWI**, American fried—boiled and fried; 1 Inf, **cnWI**, American—plain fried in slices. **1960** Bailey *Resp. to PADS 20* **KS**, American fries: boiled first. **1965–70** *DARE* (Qu. H47, *Kinds of fried potatoes*) 84 Infs, **chiefly Upper MW, N Cent**, American fried; Infs **IA**17, 43, **IL**27, 122, **IN**60, 73, **MI**43, **TN**1, American fries; **MO**19, Old American fried.

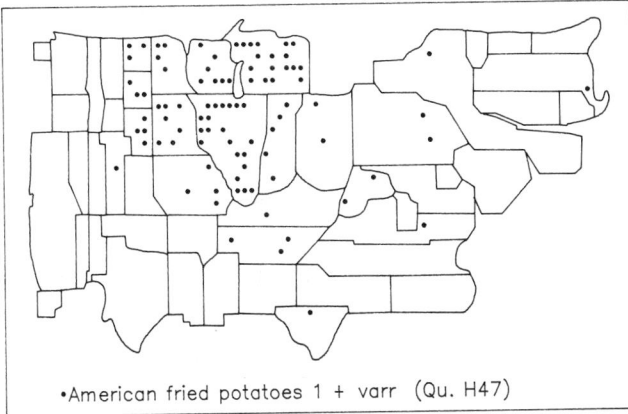

•American fried potatoes 1 + varr (Qu. H47)

2 =**raw fried potatoes.** Cf **American raw fry**

c1960 *Wilson Coll.* **csKY**, American fried potatoes . . . Raw potatoes cut crosswise and fried. **1968** *DARE* FW Addit **cwLA**, American fried potatoes—potatoes fried like French fries but cut into discs instead of long strips.

American ipecac See **milk ipecac**

American jack n [**American** + **jack** donkey]

A large donkey used for breeding.

1967 *DARE* Tape **TX**26, They got what they call a American jack. That's a great big fellah. He's . . usually the stud jack, will weigh up around twelve- or fourteen-hundred pounds. And the little ordinary jack won't weigh more than six- or seven-hundred pounds. So the big American jack is the one that they usually bred to the mare to get big American mules. They used to do a lot of that up in Missouri.

American raw fry n Cf **American fried potatoes 1, 2**

=**raw fried potatoes.**

1950 *WELS (Kinds of fried potatoes)* 1 Inf, **ceWI**, American raw fry—thinly sliced potatoes fried slowly in a little fat and seasoning.

American wire fence n For varr see quots **chiefly Atl States**

See also **hog wire fence**

A fence made from a square-meshed heavy woven wire, sometimes called *American wire.*

1923 *DN* 5.200 **swMO**, *American wire* . . . Any variety of heavy, woven fence wire. **1965–70** *DARE* (Qu. L63, . . *Fences made with wire*) Inf **FL**6, American wire fence—woven; **FL**34, Woven fence or American wire—old-fashioned; **FL**37, Barb wire, American hog wire; **MD**20, American wire fence—square pattern, heavy wire [illustr in text]; **MD**31, American wire—square mesh; **MD**34, American wire—square weave; **NJ**50, American steel wire; **NY**122, American wire fence; **TN**26, American wire fence—a brand name of woven wire fence [but see quot 1980]; **NY**109, American fence; **VT**9, American fence—four-foot woven wire; **NY**206, American field fence. [**1980** *DARE* File **Madison WI** [Conv with fence salesman], The kind of fence that is heavy and square is called a field wire fence. Some people call it hog fence or sheep fence, but it's just a plain, heavy square fence. I have never heard of an "American" wire fence.]

Americee, Ameriky See **America**

amerugian See **amarugian**

ami ami ami See **hommie**

a'mighty See **almighty** adj

amigo n [Span] **SW, but recognized throughout US**

A friend.

1837 *N.Y. Mirror* 23 Dec 208/1 *(DA)*, An overworked, spavined, broken-down set—but *adios,* Amigo. **1854** *Harper's Mag.* 8.580/1 **NM**, These [=foods] they were willing to dispose of to their *'amigos.'* **1932** Bentley *Spanish Terms* 92, *Amigo* is commonly used by Americans in the Southwest. **1967–70** *DARE* (Qu. II1, . . *Close friend*) Infs **NM**6, **TX**4, 5, 68, 72, Amigo; (Qu. NN11, . . *Saying 'good-bye' to people you know quite well*) Infs **FL**52, **NH**18, Adios amigo(s).

aminah See **go** v

a mind adj phr [Engl dial, ellip from *of a mind (to):* see *EDD mind* sb. 1] **chiefly NEng, Sth** Cf **mind** n

Following *to be* and usu preceding an infinitive: disposed (to do something).

1805 (1904) White *Jrl.* 17 **MA**, The girls were a mind to have me stay a week. **1865** (1868) Trowbridge *3 Scouts* 2 **TN**, He could work, though, boys, if he was a mind to. **1890** *DN* 1.74, Note the New England phrase, "if he was a mind to." **1909** *DN* 3.400 **nwAR**, I ain't a mind to do it, and that is all there is about it. **1926** *DN* 5.385 **ME**, "I'll do as I'm a mind to." Common. **1933** Rawlings *South Moon* 8 **FL**, You-all kin set up if you're a mind to. **1942** (1971) Campbell *Cloud-Walking* 75 **seKY**, Would they be a-mind to hear her sing.

amint n Pronc-sp for *amount.* arch

1914 *DN* 4.73 **ME, nNH**, They's *any God's amint . .* o' woodchucks in them woods!

Amish bean soup See **Amish preaching soup**

Amish blue n

A blue color commonly used in Amish settlement areas.

1938 Hark *Hex* 18, Into many a neat and tidy barnyard my car has poked its nose; past many a spruce and spotless home with gates and blinds and shutters of vivid 'Amish blue.' **1950** Klees *PA Dutch* 43, This lack of draperies gives the houses a certain austerity, a quality that is little relieved by the cool light blue with which so many of the rooms are painted. The blue is so widely used by the Amish that among the Pennsylvania Dutch it is often called Amish blue.

Amish golf n [Because the game is believed to be a favorite pastime among the Amish] joc Cf **African golf, Zulu golf**

Croquet.

1969 *Current Slang* 3.3.3 **OH**, *Amish golf* . . . [In use among] High school students, both sexes.

Amish preaching soup n Also ~*bean soup* **PA, OH, and other Amish settlement areas**

A thick bean soup served in Amish homes after or between religious services.

c1965 Randle *Cookbooks* (Plain Cookery) 3.4 **ceOH**, Amish Bean Soup—8 lb. dry beans, 1 gallon home made butter, 30 gallons milk, 15 to 20 loaves day old bread . . . Yield 150 servings and is served following Amish Church services in the home. **1968** *DARE* (Qu. H36, . . *Soup favored around here*) Inf **OH**81, Amish bean soups. **1975** Jones *Amer. Food* 72, The so-called "Amish Preaching Soup" is a rib-sticking mélange which belongs to the Old Order of Amish who hold their religious services in various homes and serve this mixture of beans and ham or smoked pork butts between their two Sunday preachings.

amly n
=**hellgrammite.**

1901 Howard *Insect Book* 212, In 1889 Professor W.W. Bailey . . collected the names in use in Rhode Island alone for this insect, and they are . . . amly, conniption bugs [etc.]. **1911** *Century Dict.* Suppl.

ammon See **almond**

Ammy Dammy bread See **anadama bread**

amole n, also attrib |ə'mole, ə'moli| Also sp *ammole* [Mex-Span] **SW**

1 Any of var plants, or parts thereof, used like soap, as:
a =**soap plant 1. CA**

1831 Beechey *Narrative* 2.43 **CA,** They had also collected in great quantities a very useful root called in that country [California] *amoles.* **1845** Frémont *Rept. Rocky Mts.* 249, Near the river . . are great quantities of *ammole,* (soap plant) . . used in California. **1915** (1926) Armstrong *Western Wild Flowers* 12, Amole, Soap Plant . . . The bulbs form a lather in water. **1974** Munz *Flora S. CA* 926, Soap Plant. Amole . . . *C[hlorogalum] pomeridianum.*

b A yucca, usu **soapweed.**

[1833 (1847) Lundy *Life & Travels* 75, A plant called Amole, which possesses the properties of soap, grows spontaneously in this vicinity [Mexico].] **1920** Saunders *Useful Wild Plants* 168 **NM,** The root was a sort of vegetable soap and answered to that strange word . . *amole.* **1937** U.S. Forest Serv. *Range Plant Hdbk.* B157 **SW,** The roots of soap tree yucca are used locally (under the name *amole*) as soap by both Indians and white men. **1962** Sweet *Plants of West* 16, Yuccas, Amoles, Yucca sp.

c Either of two **agaves,** esp **lechuguilla,** but also *Agave schottii.*

1886 Havard *Flora W. & S. TX for 1885* 518, Lechuguilla is the most important of the soap or 'amole' plants of Southwestern Texas and Northern Mexico. **1951** Corle *Gila R.* 348, A desert plant . . is the agave. It is also known as . . amole, . . and lechuguilla. **1960** Vines *Trees SW* 81, *Agave lechuguilla* . . . The root, under the name "amole," is extensively used as a substitute for soap. *Ibid* 84, *Agave . . . schottii* . . . The plant is sometimes known as "Amole," and the crown is used for soap.

2 The soap obtained from an amole plant.

1900 Lyons *Plant Names* 401, Yucca . . . The stems of some species are used . . as a substitute for soap, called . . Amole. **1941** Jaeger *Wildflowers* 13 **Desert SW,** The roots yield a soap, called *amole,* used especially in ceremonial hair-washings. **1968** Adams *Western Words* 6, *Amole,* The root of a soap plant, or the soap obtained from it; from the Spanish.

amongst (hands of) them pron Also aphet *'mongst~* [Cf *OED among the hands of,* "*Obs.* or *dial.*"] Cf **and them**

The others; the rest of them.

1913 *DN* 4.54 **seNH,** *'Mongst 'em* . . . Others; the rest, et cetera. "Who was there?" "Oh, Mis Brown, an' Mis Jones, an' 'mongst 'em." **1942** *AmSp* 17.130 **IN,** *Amongst hands of 'em.* "Jim and Bob and 'mongst hands of 'em helped me out today."

amongst you pron Also *among you* Pronc-sp *mongst-ye* chiefly **C Atl**

=**you-all.**

1890 *AN&Q* 5.8/2, I am told that in some parts of Maryland *amongst* is used for *all,* as in this example: "Amongst you going to town?" meaning, "Are all of you going to town?" Can this be a survival of an obsolete use? *Among* originally meant a *mingling,* a crowd. **1892** *KS Univ. Qrly.* 195, *Among:* all of, as, Where are you going among you? **1918** *DN* 5.20 **neNC,** "Amongst ye come to see us," before you come to see us. [*DARE* ed questions interpretation] **1949** Kurath *Word Geog.* 67, **DE, MD, VA,** All these [plural] forms have a possessive case: *you'ns's, you-all's, mongst-ye's* . . . The form *mongst-ye* is common in the folk speech of the central part of Delamarvia, and rare instances are found from the mouth of Chesapeake Bay to Albemarle Sound.

among the willows adj phr, adv phr **West**

1968 Adams *Western Words,* Among the willows — Dodging the law; on the dodge.

among you See **amongst you**

amost adv Also *a'most* Pronc-spp for *almost* [*OED* "still used dial"] chiefly **NEng, Midl** See also **eenamost**

Almost.

1758 in 1881 *Essex Inst. Coll.* 18.105 **MA,** The Regulars . . were a most all swept off by grape Shot. **1843** (1916) Hall *New Purchase* 162 **sIN,** We rested and blowed, uttering between the puffs — "plaguey heavy!" "a'most too long" and the like. **1887** Cooke *Happy Dodd* 69 **NEng,** I call that a most an excellent sermon. **1899** (1912) Green *VA Folk-Speech,* Amost. **1908** *DN* 3.286 **eAL, wGA. 1914** *DN* 4.68 **ME, nNH,** A'most. **1926** Kephart *Highlanders* 358 **sAppalachians.**

ampron See **apron** n

amputate v Usu |'æmpjə,te(ɪ)t|; also |'æmp(ə),te(ɪ)t, 'æmpɪte(ɪ)t|, occas |'æmpɚ,te(ɪ)t|

Std senses, var forms.

1891 *DN* 1.159 **cNY,** [æmptet]. **1936** *AmSp* 11.159 **eTX,** Medial *u* is pronounced both [jə] and [ə], the latter sound being especially characteristic of less literate speech: *accumulate, accurate,* . . *amputate* . . . An old country doctor . . says ['æpɪteɪt], ['æmpɚ-te(ɪ)t], for *amputate.*

amuddled See **a** inert vowel **1**

Amurrica See **America**

amyroot n [Etym unknown] prob **SE**

=**Indian hemp 1.**

1892 (1974) Millspaugh *Amer. Med. Plants* 133, American Indian Hemp, Dog's Bane, Old-Amy Root. **1901** Lounsberry *S. Wild Flowers* 433, Indian hemp. Amy-root . . . grows mostly in fields and thickets and is especially a favorite with honey-bees. **1907** Hodge *Hdbk. Amer. Indians* 1.605, *Indian hemp* . . . The army-root (*Apocynum cannabinum*) [is] called also black Indian hemp. [Note: 'Army-root' is prob either a printer's error or a pronc-sp.] **1930** U.S. Dept. Ag. *Misc. Pub.* 77.34, Amy-root . . . Part used. — The root, collected in autumn. **1971** Krochmal *Appalachia Med. Plants* 52, Hemp dog bane, American hemp, amyroot, bitter root . . . This plant is a cardiotonic drug that is extremely poisonous. It has been used as a diuretic, diaphoretic, expectorant, and emetic.

an conj See **and** conj, **than**

an' n See **aunt A3**

anacahuita n [MexSpan] **sTX**

A small aromatic tree, *Cordia boissieri,* of Texas and Mexico, the wood, leaf and fruit of which are occas used medicinally.

1886 Havard *Flora W. & S. TX for 1885* 510, *Cordia Boissieri* . . (Anacahuita.) A small tree on the bluffs of the Lower Rio Grande, with hard, close-grained wood. Its various parts . . are popularly used by Mexicans in bronchial affections. **1892** *DN* 1.244 **TX. 1938** *AmSp* 13.111 **sTX. 1951** *PADS* 15.39 **TX. 1967** *DARE* (Qu. T5, 16) Inf **TX29,** Anacahuita [a,naka'wi:tə].

anacua See **anaqua**

anadama bread n Usu |,ænə'dæmə|, occas |,æmə'dæmə| Pronc-spp *amadama ~, Ammy Dammy ~* [Etym unknown; for folk-etym, see quots] **NEng**

A loaf bread made from corn meal, flour, and molasses.

1915 *DN* 4.239 **MA,** Ammy Dammy bread. A kind of loaf bread. Recipe from Old Salem Tavern. **1939** Wolcott *Yankee Cook Book* 145. **1956** Crocker *Picture Cook Book,* An amusing story of the origin of Anadama Bread relates — The name *Anadama* comes from a New England fisherman whose lazy wife always served him corn meal mush and molasses for dinner. One day he came home and found the same corn meal and molasses. Tired of it, he mixed it with flour and yeast and baked it as bread, saying: "Anna damn her." **1964** Amer. Heritage *Cookbook* **MA. 1965** *DARE* Tape MA85A, This woman was always baking this certain kind of bread, years and years ago, and her name was Anna . . . Her husband got to the point that was all he was getting . . so he said, "I had some of Anna's damn bread," and they called it Anadama bread. **1967–70** *DARE* (Qu. H14) Infs **MA5, NY94, RI**1A, Anadama; **VT**13, |æmədæmə| bread [is] white with a sprinkling of cornmeal; (Qu. H18) Inf **MA**72, |ænə'dæmə|, from "Anna damn her!"; **MA**83, Anadama — cornmeal, white flour.

anagua See **anaqua**

anan intj Also *anen, anend, anon, nan* [Orig a response indicating one's intention to attend to a remark or request; later, a request that the remark or order be repeated. See *OED* anan headnote.] chiefly **N Atl** *now prob obs*

What? What did you say?

1789 Webster *Dissertations Engl. Lang.* 188, A word . . which is sometimes pronounced *nan*, and sometimes *anan* . . is used for *what*, or *what do you say.* **1826** Cooper *Last of Mohicans* 1.119 **nNY**, 'I am an unworthy instructor in the art of psalmody.' 'Anan!' **1829** Kirkham *Engl. Grammar* 192 [In list of provincialisms to be avoided], *New England* . . nan . . what. **1843** (1916) Hall *New Purchase* 212 **IN**, "Nan!" (she *heard* well enough). **1859** Elwyn *Glossary* 16, *Anan.* Is used often by Natty Bumppo; but only occasionally heard, so far as my experience goes, among his countrymen of the present day. It is common in England . . , and I have heard it in Chester County, Pennsylvania. **1870** *Nation* 28 July 56/2 **PA**, In 'strict' families the younger folks must not use the brusque "what?" in addressing their elders and betters, but the word "nan?" ("anan"). **1894** *DN* 1.327 **NJ**, *Anen, anend, anan, nan:* interrogative word used to a limited extent in S[outh] J[ersey]. **1960** McAtee *Studies Vocab. Hall* 34, *Nan* . . . In America, this term has been recorded most frequently from Pennsylvania; thus Hall [in quot 1843] may have placed it from his own early recollections in the mouth of a Hoosierine.

anaqua n Also sp *anacua, anagua;* pronc-spp *knackaway, knockaway, nockaway* [MexSpan *anacua*]
A half-evergreen tree *(Ehretia anacua)* native to central and sthn TX which has usu multiple trunks, thick furrowed bark, and edible yellowish-orange fruit. Also called **sugarberry 3**
1884 Sargent *Forests of N. Amer.* 114 **sTX**, *Ehretia elliptica . . . Knackaway. Anaqua.* **1896** *Garden and Forest* 9.282, *Knackaway* . . A corruption of Mexican-Spanish anaqua, shortened from anacahuite, which is from Aztec *nanahuaquahuitl,* "lues venera tree," so called from the medicinal use of its roots. **1934** (1975) Mawson *Dict. Foreign Terms, Anaqua* . . found in Mexico and southwestern Texas. Called also *knockaway.* **1960** Vines *Trees SW* 883, *Anaqua* . . . Other vernacular names are . . Knackaway, Nockaway [etc.]. **1967** *DARE* (Qu. T5) Inf **TX22** ['nakə,we]; (Qu. T16) Inf **TX18**, [ə'nakə,we]; Illiterate persons would probably spell it *knockaway;* (Qu. I46) Inf **TX28**, [ɑ'nɑkwə]. **1979** *Little Checklist U.S. Trees* 125, *Anacua* . . . Spelled also anaqua and anagua. Other common names—sugarberry, knackaway, knockaway.

anaroogian See **amarugian**

anbasicky See **abasicky**

ancey See **antsy**

anchor n
1 Among railroad workers: a brake, esp a hand brake. See also **anchor v**
1942 Berrey–Van den Bark *Amer. Slang* 773.9, [*Railroad*] *Brakes* . . . anchors. **1945** [see **anchor v**]. **1977** Adams *Lang. Railroader* 6, *Anchor:* A hand brake.
2 A caboose.
1977 Adams *Lang. Railroader* 6.

anchor v [**anchor** n 1]
Among railroad workers: to set the brakes.
1931 *Writer's Digest* 11.41 ["Lingo of Locale"], *Anchor them*—Set the brakes on still cars. **1945** Hubbard *Railroad Ave.* 331, *Anchor them* . . the opposite is *release anchors.* **1947** Beebe *Mixed Train* 353. **1977** Adams *Lang. Railroader* 6, *Anchor her:* To set the brakes. To set hand brakes on a standing car.

anchor (and chain) n [Var of the more common *ball and chain*] *joc* Cf **anchored**
One's spouse.
1942 Berrey–Van den Bark *Amer. Slang* 446.15, *Wife.* Anchor, ball-and, ball-and-chain. **1966** *DARE* (Qu. AA22, *Joking names that a man may use to refer to his wife*) Inf **MI19**, Anchor; **WA11**, Anchor and chain.

anchor brand strawberry n *joc*
Among loggers: a prune.
1969 Sorden *Lumberjack Lingo* 2 **Gt Lakes**, *Anchor Brand Strawberries*—Prunes. A term used on Great Lakes lumber ships. **1972** *Yesterday* Mar–Apr 26/2 **Nth**, The loggers called apples "Adam's fruit" while prunes were either "anchor brand strawberries" or "raisins with the mumps."

anchor cattle n [From their use as the stable or fixed part of a herd being formed] Also called **decoy herd**
A small group of cattle used as a nucleus around which a larger herd or group is gathered.

1890 *Stock Grower* 11 Jan 11/2 (1942 *AmSp* 17.64), All 'anchor' cattle belonging to this company are tally branded and all increase of 1884 is in the same brand. **1961** Adams *Old-Time Cowhand* 249 **West**, A "cut" was a group of cattle separated from the main herd . . , and this was usually started with a "decoy herd" or "anchor cattle," a few cows used in startin' a cut of cattle.

anchored adj *joc* Cf **anchor (and chain)**
Married.
1968 *DARE* (Qu. AA15a . . *Joking ways . . of saying that people got married*) Inf **NH14**, Got anchored.

anchor fishing vbl n
Bottom fishing.
1967–68 *DARE* (Qu. P17, . . *When the people fish by lowering a line and sinker close to the bottom of the water*) Infs **MA35, NY92**, Anchor fishing.

anchor ice n [Because it fastens or anchors itself to river or lake bottoms or banks.] **Nth**
1 Ice which forms below the surface of a body of water and which can become attached to the bottom.
1815 *Niles' Natl. Reg.* 201/1 **PA**, On the same day the anchor-ice began to run a little. **1945** Colcord *Sea Language* **ME, Cape Cod, Long Island**, *Anchor ice.* Ice that forms on the bottom of a lake or pond. **1969** Sorden *Lumberjack Lingo* 2 **Gt Lakes, NEng**, *Anchor Ice*—Ice in shady places and along banks of streams that stayed after ice in center of the stream had broken up. An unexplained phenomenon whereby ice forms on the bottom of rapids in a fast flowing stream.
2 Detached chunks of ice floating on a pond, lake, or river.
1907 *DN* 3.240 **eME**, *Anchor ice* . . . Detached ice (for the most part, *surface* ice) which floats down a river. "A jam of anchor ice now fills the river for two miles." **1943** *LANE* Map 648 **VT**, [Of a pond lightly frozen] It's full of [æŋkər ɐɪs]. **c1950** *Atlas Checklists* **WI**. **1968** *DARE* (Qu. B33a) Inf **NY88**, Anchor ice. **1968** *DARE* Tape **NH14**, In the Fall of the year around here. It'll freeze over, you know, and then it'll warm up, say, the next day. That ice'll freeze on the shore . . . Next day . . that'll let go, and you'll see chunks of anchor ice, small pieces, you know, won't be more 'en that thick [about an inch] . . [and] three feet square.

anchor off v phr [Perh for *ankle off;* see **ankle**]
To amble.
c1970 *Halpert Coll.* **wKY**, I'm going to anchor off down to her house.

anchor the can n
A children's game: see quot and cf **duck on a rock, kick the can.**
1968 *DARE* (Qu. EE18, *Games in which the players set up a stone, a tin can, or something similar, and then try to knock it down*) Inf **NJ28**, Anchor the can.

anchus See **anxious**

ancient adj, n Usu |'e(ɪ)nšənt|; in **S Midl** often |'æn(t)š(ə)nt, 'anšənt| Pronc-sp *ainshen*
A Forms.
1891 *PMLA* 6.32 **WV**, *Ancient* . . is here often pronounced [anšənt]. **1905** *DN* 3.103 **nwAR**, [ænšnt] . . ancient. **1927** Kennedy *Gritny* 98 **sLA** [Black], Quit reachin' way back yonder in ainshen days. **1942** Hall *Smoky Mt. Speech* 18 **eTN, wNC**, *Ancient* . . heard only with [æ]: ['æntšənt].
B Sense.
A rustic.
1970 *DARE* (Qu. HH1, . . *A rustic or countrified person*) Inf **NC84**, Ancient ['ænšənt].

ancón n [Span *ancón* corner] **SW** Cf **rincón**
See quot 1892.
1892 *DN* 1.244 **TX**, *Ancón:* a piece of land on the banks of a river, generally in a bend, which is cultivated by irrigation. Very common on the lower Rio Grande. In Spanish the name applies to a small anchorage or roadstead. **1934** (1975) Mawson *Dict. Foreign Terms, Ancón* . . irrigated land on the banks of a river: *southwestern U.S.*

and conj In stressed or emphatic position, usu |ænd, æn|, occas |and|; under weak stress, |ənd, ən, n̩| **throughout US** Also sp *an, an', en', 'n'*
A Forms.

1867 Allen *Slave Songs* xxxiii **SC** [Gullah], De morest part ob de mens dey git heaps o' clo'—more'n 'nuff; 'n I ain't git nuffin. **1888** Jones *Negro Myths* 134 **seGA,** Wen de rain stop, Buh Wolf heng up eh fiddle an gone git eh knife . . en sharpen eh knife on de pot rim. **1899** (1912) Green *VA Folk-Speech,* An. **1917** *DN* 4.387 **neOH, cIN, VA, PA, CA,** And [and] . . . This pronunciation in pause and under some stress occurs occasionally (regularly with some individuals) . . . It is spoken by people who never affect the "broad a." **1921** Thorp *Songs Cowboys* 142 **NM,** He was little en peaked en thin, en narry a no-account horse. **1937** *AmSp* 12.289 **wVA,** [æn].

B Senses.

1 If. [*OED and* conj[1] C1, *an* conj 2 *"arch and dial"*; W3, *"obs."*] *arch or old-fash*

1909 *DN* 3.419 **Cape Cod MA,** I shouldn't wonder *'n* I got back before it snowed. **1913** *DN* 4.3 **csME,** I wouldn't wonder an you could get down to Jordan's. **1914** *DN* 4.68 **ME, nNH. 1916** *DN* 4.285 **sAppalachians,** And you go, I won't stay, nary a step! **1936** Morehouse *Rain on Just* 124 **NC,** "Mammy, you daren't strike them," Least Dolly called, cold-white and furious. "They're little fellows. Whop me and you have to be whopping." **1958** Grau *Hard Blue Sky* 356 **LA,** "And he went slower," Mike said softly, "he go better."

2 In numbers, esp dates, between hundreds and tens. **chiefly Sth, Midl** *somewhat old-fash* See also **eighteen-hundred-and-froze-to-death**

1896 Bunner *Poems* 65 **West,** I brung the original pair f'm the States in eighteen-n-fifty. **1944** *PADS* 2.6 **MS, TN, VA,** "Nineteen hundred and forty-two." . . Common. **1959** Lomax *Rainbow Sign* 154 **LA** [Black], It was in 18 and 92 that I stopped in Coffeysville, Kansas. **c1960** *Wilson Coll.* **csKY,** Nineteen and sixty has been a very odd year. **1966–68** *DARE* Tapes **AL31, 33, GA22, LA28, NC29, SC46, WA12. 1969** *DARE* FW Addit **NC. 1976** Wolfram–Christian *Appalachian Speech* 172, Well, in nineteen and I believe it was fifty-six is about the worst one [=a flood] I can remember around here.

3 After certain verbs, esp *try,* with the effect of creating a logical infinitive: to. [*OED and* conj 10, 1671 →] **throughout US** *informal:* See quot 1969.

1847 McCallum *ME Letters,* I will try and answer your letter. **1955** *College English* 16.360/1, "We try and sort out all the mail from Wisconsin" ([Senator Joseph] McCarthy). *Ibid* 17.178, Although in American there is some prejudice against *try and* . . , the idiom . . continues to be used. **c1960** *Wilson Coll.* **csKY,** Try and come. **1967–69** *DARE* (Qu. II39) Inf **ME5,** I'll try and do as much; (Qu. KK57) Inf **IL98,** Try and lift; (Qu. LL22) Inf **CA133,** Try and hook you, try and sting you; **MO3,** Try and skin you. **1969** *Amer. Heritage Dict.* 1378, *Try and* is common in speech for *try to,* especially in such established combinations as *try and stop me* or *try and make me* (defiance) and *try and get some rest* (exhortation). In most contexts . . it is usually not interchangeable with *try to* unless the level is expressly informal. As an example in writing, the following is unacceptable to 79 percent of the Usage Panel: *It is a mistake to try and force compliance with something so unpopular.* **1977** *Capital Times* (Madison WI) 25 June 19/1, If you're wondering whatever happened to someone, drop us a note and we'll try and find out.

4 What with; at a time when; with. [Perh orig an Irish or Scots locution: see *EDD and* conj 2 "To introduce a nominative absolute, sometimes with ellipsis of *v.*"]

1866 (1946) George *Cap'n's Wife* 58 **MA,** Uriel's birthday and he down on his beam ends seasick. **1926** (1927) Black *You Can't Win* 68, Tell her you're ashamed to be settin' there wasting time and the other boys starvin' under the bridge. **1931** *AmSp* 6.272 **KY Mts,** Will ye worm-eat the flower of my Noration, and hits petals jist onfoldin' to the world? **1936** (1947) Mencken *Amer. Lang.* (4th ed) 451 [Footnote:], The familiar Irish "John is dead and *him* always so hearty" shows the same [=Gaelic] influence. **1938** Rawlings *Yearling* 13 **FL,** A pity to waste light, ain't it, . . and the full moon shinin'. **1942** (1971) Campbell *Cloud-Walking* 153 **seKY,** Some folks made bold to ask where was Shy keeping hisself and a crowd gathered at his house. **1943** Chase *Jack Tales* 14 **wNC** (as of 1880s), Jack knowed he couldn't even tip one of them things over and hit empty. **1976** Warner *Beautiful Swimmers* 172 **eMD,** It ain't a nice way to put it, but crabs will eat a drownded man and him all swollen.

5 In combinatory phrr in which the second element is not stated but implied. See also **coffee and** Cf **with**

1875 Twain *Sketches New & Old* (Hartford) 74, His last acts was to go his pile on "Kings-*and*" (calklatin' to fill, but which he didn't fill), when there was a "flush" out agin him. **1899** Twain *Man Hadleyburg* 100.50,

He saw my deuces-*and* with a straight flush, and by rights the pot is his. **1932** *World's Work* Feb 26/2, Lunch wagons . . now serve more than one million meals a day, a majority of which are, of course, "coffee and" (doughnuts, sandwich, beans, pie, and so on) orders. **1946** *AmSp* 21.87 **CA,** *And*—and eggs (when following ham, bacon, or sausage; as, 'ham and'); but 'coffee and' . . means 'with cream and sugar.' In skidroad restaurants, 'coffee and' is still sometimes used for coffee and doughnuts. **1963** Ramsay–Emberson *Twain Lexicon* 6, Neither 'kings-*and*' nor 'deuces-*and*' . . seems to be any longer in use. Present-day poker experts . . are far from agreed in their interpretations. 'Kings-*and*', . . would clearly seem to mean two pair, one pair being kings . . . By analogy, 'deuces-*and*' should be two pair also, one of the pairs being deuces . . . With this emphatic use of *and* compare the common American tennis expressions "game-*and*" and "thirty-*and*."

and indef art [Perh by overcorrection]

An.

1891 *PMLA* 6.171 **TN,** Consonants are sometimes inserted in a word, or added to the end . . . *and old man.*

and prep [By corr of homophonous *in* [n̩], perh infl by *now and then:* cf *DS* A15]

In phr *once and a while:* In.

1852 Stowe *Uncle Tom's Cabin* 2.45, The horrid cruelties and outrages that once a while find their way into the papers. **1871** (1882) Stowe *Fireside Stories* 28 **NEng,** I like once and a while to sort o' gravel her. **1909** *DN* 3.401 **nwAR,** Once and awhile . . . Popular etymology for "once in a while."

ándale v phr Usu |ˈɑndəˌle|, occas |ˈɑndəˌli|; addit less freq proncs in quot 1966–70. Also sp *ódale* [Span] **chiefly SW**

Get going! Hurry!

1932 Bentley *Spanish Terms, Andale* is common in colloquial usage . . . Americans native to the Southwest use the word . . as naturally, at least in the colloquial language, as they do an English phrase or word of the same meaning. A mother sending a child or servant on an errand might be expected to conclude her instructions with "Now, andale." **1966–70** *DARE* (Qu. A20, *Joking ways of telling somebody to hurry*) Infs **CA117A, TX5, 66,** [ˈɑndəˌle]; **CA87,** [ˈɑndəˌli]; **NM1,** [ˈʌndɪˌli]; **TX29** [ˈɑndeˌle]; **TX1, 2,** Andale pronto; (Qu. A19, *Other ways of saying, "I'll have to hurry."*) Inf **CA207,** [ˈʌndɑli], a Mexican word used quite a lot around here. **1968** Adams *Western Words, Andale*— An expression commonly used by Spanish-speaking cowboys, meaning *hurry up, get a move on, get going* . . . Cowboys frequently yell this word at cattle being driven. **1979** Homer *Jargon* 214 [Street Talk], *Ándale*— An expression . . that can mean either agreement with a proposed plan or a strong suggestion to get out of the vicinity . . . Also *ódale.*

and all like (of) that, and along like (of) that See and like (of) that

and-bush n

An ambush.

1841 (1952) Cooper *Deerslayer* 49 **NY,** "This is a nat'ral and-bush," half whispered Hurry, as if he felt that the place was devoted to secresy [sic] and watchfulness. **1950** Faulkner *Stories* 684 **MS,** Spoils of war! I brought them here! I tolled them in here: a military and-bush!

‡and else conj [Perh by metath of [ənlɛs]]

Unless.

1942 Whipple *Joshua* 7 **UT,** I'm afeared an' else the scouts finds more water, it's gonna be, "Give Me Three Grains of Corn, Mother, Honly Three Grains of Corn!"

andiron n, usu pl Usu |ˈændˌaɪə(r)n|, occas |ˈænˌaɪə(r)n| or metath |ˈændˌaɪrən| Cf **iron** A Arch spp *anderens, and irons* [*OED* a1300 →] **formerly chiefly Nth; now throughout US** in coexistence with numerous regional and non-regional synonyms: see *DS* D32 and headwords.

One of a pair of iron supports for wood in a fireplace.

1640 in 1916 **MA** (Colony) Probate Court (Essex Co.) *Records* 1.12, I give unto Elizabeth Nicksone my payer of Anderens. **1798** in 1956 Eliason *Tarheel Talk* 258 **NC,** I am realy sorry to say that all the and Irons Shovels Tongs &c was melted. **1845** *Knickerbocker* 15.444, The andirons, with lions-heads for tops, still rested in the old fire-place. **1946** *PADS* 5.9 **VA,** Andirons . . common. **1949** Kurath *Word Geog.* 51, The usual expression in Pennsylvania and the North is *andirons,* which has also become well established on Chesapeake Bay and on the Potomac. As a literary term *andirons* is current also in Southern cities. **1958**

PADS 29.6 **TN.** **c1960** *Wilson Coll.* **csKY,** "Pappy got us a new set of andirons." [The word is] now fairly common. **1962** Atwood *Vocab. TX* 45, The iron devices used in a fireplace are known variously as *andirons* (43) [numbers indicate percent of occurrence], *dog irons* (40), and *fire dogs* (14) . . . All of these are older usages, no doubt because of the decline of the fireplace in favor of gas heating. *Andirons* has a higher frequency among better-educated informants. **1965–70** *DARE* (Qu. D32) 642 Infs, **throughout U.S.,** Andirons.

and like (of) that conj phr Also *and all* (or *along*) *like (of) that* **?esp Nth** Cf **and that**

And that sort of thing; and so forth — sometimes used without precise meaning.

1965–70 *DARE* Tape **AL6,** Sheets and cloth and like that; **AZ5,** They thought it was the Mormon Bible so to speak and like that; **GA10,** Coats and raincoats and all like that; **MI27,** If they [=deer] got two prongs on a side, they call that a four-point, three on a side a six and along like that; **MA92,** We shipped away to paper mills and like that and drag sawing. **1969** *DARE* FW Addit **seNY,** He made a great thing of watching birds and like of that; **ceVT,** And like of that — and so on. **1970** *Eaton Coll.* **neWI,** We taught them to bake — bread, rolls, and like that. **1979** *DARE* File **Madison WI,** The classes we had [in beautician's school] were in perms, and hair styles, and like that. **1980** Folb *Runnin' Down* 94 [Black], Everybody's trippin', call 'im names 'n like dat.

andog n, usu pl [Prob blend of **andiron** + **firedog** or **dog iron**; *EDD* chiefly from cwEngl, 1790 →]
=**andiron.**

1969 *DARE* (Qu. D32) Inf **AL55,** Andogs ['ændɔgz].

and over n Var of **Andy-over** n Cf **hand-over** exclam

1966 *DARE* Tape **AL1,** [The game was called] and over. And over . . over the house.

Andrew-over n Var of **Andy-over**

1950 *WELS* (Game in which you throw a ball over a low building) 1 Inf, **ceWI,** Andrew over.

and that conj phr Also *and this* Cf **and like (of) that, and thing**

And other similar things or places.

1966–69 *DARE* Tape **MI2,** Some of the bigger cities like Detroit and that; **WI75,** That's . . for fishing off piers and that. **1976** Wolfram – Christian *Appalachian Speech* 174, And there's alot of them don't like the mines and they'll go somewhere and work at different jobs, construction working, factories and this.

and them conj phr Also *and those* [Cf *DJE* an' *dem*] **chiefly Sth** Cf **and thing, and that; amongst (hands of) them**

Plus the others (of a group) or the other member (of a pair).

1898 Westcott *Harum* 343 **nNY,** I hain't took no active part, an' Purse an' them thinks I'm goin' to be on their side when it comes to a pinch. **1944** *PADS* 2.39 **NC, SC, VA,** *And those* . . . This phrase when following a (generally singular) substantive may refer to two or more persons, to one person, or even to no one at all. "Mary *and those* came to see me" may mean that only Mary came. [*DARE* ed. questions "or even to no one at all".] **1950** *PADS* 14.67 **SC,** "I saw Mr. Smith and those at church today," meaning Mr. Smith and the others of his family. **1952** Brown *NC Folkl.* 1.515 **c, eNC,** *And those.* **1968** *DARE* Tape **GA21D,** What was that you said the other night whenever . . Jean and them was here? **1970** *Thompson Coll.* **Sth** (as of 1920s–70s), *And them* . . And his group. "Joe an thimm oughtta be comin along mos inny minute now." Also used of groups of animals. **1972** *Thompson Coll.* **GA,** I just gotta get over there and see Mama and them [i.e. Papa] before we leave for Ft. Lauderdale. [Spoken by a Negro chauffeur.] **1975** *DARE* File **swCA,** [Heard on television:] George and them [=his wife] just had a baby. **1979** Stegner *Recapitulation* 133 **UT,** "Will it be a lot of noisy drunks?" "Probably." "Jack Bailey and those."

and thing conj phr Pronc-spp *an' ting, en' t'ing'* [*and* + *thing* ellip for *such,* or *similar things.* Cf *OED thing* 14a.] **sSC, GA coast** *Gullah* Cf **and that, and them**

Plus similar things or actions.

1922 Gonzales *Black Border* 20 **sSC, GA coasts** [Gullah], 'E ride hawss, 'e eat ricebu'd en' summuh duck en' t'ing'. *Ibid* 129, Dem kin lick muskittuh', fly en' t'ing' same lukkuh hawss. *Ibid* 300 [Gullah Glossary] *en' t'ing'* — and things, and everything. **1925** *DN* 5.357 **swSC, eGA** [Black], All he oddah cloes al fole up an ah put dey in de daid box wiv he, an al de ting an ting dat he ebber had.

and this See **and that**

and those See **and them**

Andy n *euphem* Cf *DS* M21a,b

An outhouse, privy.

1947 Adams *Banner* 287 **Erie Canal NY** (as of 1817–1847), This type of architecture was known in the northern counties as an "Andy," whence the juvenile euphemism, "Going to the Andes."

Andy-come-back See **anti-come-back**

Andy Gump chin n Also *Andy Gump,* ~*Goom* and adj *Andy-Gump jawed* [*Andy Gump,* chinless comic strip character created by Sidney Smith in 1917 and widely popular during the 1920s]

A conspicuously receding chin; by ext, any unusual chin or jaw, or, ironically, a person with a prominent jaw.

1968–70 *DARE* (QR p163) Inf **LA15,** Andy Gump chin — if he hasn't got any chin; (Qu. X6, *If a person's lower jaw sticks out prominently, you say he's___*) Inf **NY50,** Andy-Gump jawed; **IL41, 45,** Andy Gump; **NJ63,** Andy Goom ['gum] — old-fashioned.

Andy Gump snake n [See **Andy Gump chin**]

The banded sand snake (*Chilomeniscus cinctus*).

1974 Shaw – Campbell *Snakes West* 159 **AZ,** The banded sand snake is highly adapted . . . The lower jaw is so deeply countersunk that this snake has been called the "Andy Gump" snake after the chinless cartoon hero.

Andy-i-over See **anti-i-over**

Andy-iron n, usu pl Usu |'ændi–, 'ændɨ, aɪ(ə)rnz|, addit proncs in quot 1965–70. [Folk-etym] **esp Mid Atl** See also **anty-iron, handy iron**
=**andiron.**

1958 *PADS* 29.6 **cnTN,** *Andirons* . . . Occasional pronunciation *andy irons.* **1965–70** *DARE* (Qu. D32) Inf **AR55,** ['ænd,aənz] or occasionally ['ændɪ,aənz]; **IL48,** One little girl in [the] neighborhood calls them Andy-irons after her brother, whose name is Andy; **NY80,** ['ændɪ,aɪrənz]; **NC43,** ['ændɪ,a:rn]; **NC99,** ['ɛndɪ,aɚnz]; **SC6, 38, 47,** ['ændɨ,a(ə)rnz]; **RI5, VA26,** ['ændi,aɪɚnz].

Andy-over n, exclam For varr see quots **chiefly W Midl** See Map See also **Andrew-over**
=**Antony-over.**

1905 *DN* 3.69 **nwAR,** *Andy-over.* **1937** in 1972 *Amer. Slave* 2.55 **SC,** When I was a little girl I played 'Andy-over' with a ball, in the moonlight. **1950** *PADS* 14.11 **SC,** *Andy-over* . . . This boy's ball game is played by two sides, one on each side of a building, such as the schoolhouse. The side in possession of the ball shouts: *Andy-over!* to denote that the ball is in play. It is then thrown over the house, and if it is caught, the one catching it is entitled to go with his team around to the other side and throw the ball at anyone of the other team. If the ball is not caught, it must be thrown back. **1950** *WELS* (Games in which you throw a ball over a low building) 2 Infs, **WI,** Andy-over; (*What do you shout when you throw the ball?*) 4 Infs, **WI,** Andy-Andy-over; 2 Infs, Andy-over. **c1960** *Wilson Coll.* **csKY.** **1965–70** *DARE* (Qu. EE22) 85 Infs, **chiefly W Midl,** Andy-over; **IL70, IN35, IA27, NY107, 228, PA185, 194, 213,** Andy-Andy-over; (Qu. EE23a, . . *What do you call out when you throw the ball?*) 67 Infs **chiefly W Midl,** Andy-over; **IL70, IA27, NY107, 120, OH18, PA71, 185, 194, 234,**

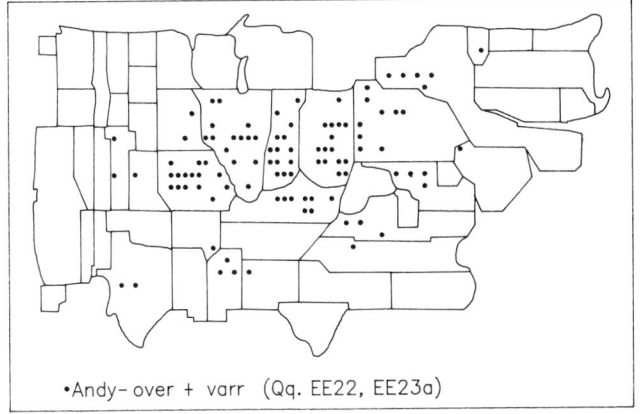

•Andy- over + varr (Qq. EE22, EE23a)

Andy-Andy-over; **KY**17, Andy-Andy-Olin-coming over; **OH**66, Andy-over-the-coal-house; **PA**68, Andy-over, Andy-back; **VA**26, Andy-over, here it comes; **MA**1, 60, **MO**11, **TX**26, Andy. **1967** *DARE* Tape **KY**34, A ball is thrown back and forth over a building while the players shout "Andy-over!"

Andy up See **Annie up**

anear prep [a inert vowel 3 + *near; OED* →1879] Cf **anigh** prep

Near, close to.

1899 (1912) Green *VA Folk-Speech,* Don't come anear me. **1903** *DN* 2.295 **Cape Cod MA** (as of 1850s), He never come *anear* me. **1913** *DN* 4.3 csME. **1950** Stuart *Hie Hunters* 237 **eKY** (as of c1920), The bullets stung the trees a-near me and singed off into space!

aneath prep [Scots and nEngl form of *beneath:* cf *OED, EDD, SND*] *rare*

Beneath.

1952 Brown *NC Folkl.* 1.515.

anend adv

1 To the end; straight-on; continuously. [*OED an-end* 2 →1785] *?obs*

1867 Lowell *Biglow* xxxi '**Upcountry**' **MA**, End, which the Yankee more often makes *eend,* still using familiarly the old phrase "right anend" for "continuously." **1899** (1912) Green *VA Folk-Speech, An-end . . .* Onwards; forwards; to go *an-end,* to go straight on without delay in any project.

2 On end; vertically. [*OED an-end* 4 →1850] *?obs*

1899 (1912) Green *VA Folk-Speech, An-end . . .* Upright; not lying down; on one end.

3 Endways; on the end. *old-fash*

1917 *DN* 4.387 **neOH**, An end . . . "Drive this timber an end a little." "Strike it an end." Distinct in sound from *on end.*

anen(d) intj See **anan**

anent prep [*OED anent* 7, "arch. or *dial.*"] *old-fash*

1 Opposite; against; near. Cf **fornent**

1895 *DN* 1.370 **eTN**, *Anent . . .* "It was anent two houses." **1904** Day *Kin o' Ktaadn* 70 **ME**, With 'High, diddy-di,' and your vulgar strain / Anent some female, coarse and vain. **1926** *DN* 5.397 **Ozarks**, *Anent . . .* "He was a-layin' in th' road down anent th' springhouse." . . It is rather rare in the Ozarks. **1930** Shoemaker *1300 Words* **cPA Mts** (as of c1900). **1953** Randolph *Down in Holler* 67 **Ozarks**, *Anent* means near, beside, or even against, in such a sentence as "Will's hat was layin in the weeds, down anent the smokehouse."

2 Concerning.

1908 White *Riverman* 37 **MI**, He departed, catching fragments of vows anent never going on any more errands for nobody.

anether See **another**

angainst See **against**

angel n

1 An innocent; a prospective victim of a swindle.

1935 *AmSp* 10.12 [Underworld argot as of c1900], *Angel.* The victim or prospective victim of criminals. (Obs.). **1964** Jackman–Long *OR Desert* 394, An angel—a greenhorn buyer at an auction, who can be depended upon to buy unsound horses.

2 A gold coin: see quot. [Perh rel to *OED angel* 6, an old English gold coin, but sugg as well charity from a divine messenger] *obs*

1930 Shoemaker *1300 Words* **cPA Mts** (as of c1900), *Angels*—Gold coins occasionally put in the collection boxes at churches by rural aristocrats.

‡3 A dustball. Cf **dust devil** and *DS* E20

1950 *WELS* (Soft rolls of dust that collect on the floor under beds or other furniture) 1 Inf, **cwWI**, Angels—[they're] soft and cottony.

4 Also *angel wings, angel's wings:* **=snow angel. chiefly Nth, West**

1950 *WELS* (Games played in the snow) 7 Infs, **throughout WI**, Make (or making) (an) angel(s); 1 Inf, **ceWI**, Angel; 1 Inf, **csWI**, Angels—lie stretched out in snow—arms extended above [the] head and move through snow from top to sides—legs from side-to-side to make bottom of robe. **1965–70** *DARE* (Qu. EE26, . . Games . . children play in the *snow*) 29 Infs, **chiefly Nth, West**, Angels; Infs **CT**8, **IL**50, **IA**3, 41, **MI**95, 123, **MN**6, **NY**24, Make (an) angel(s); **MI**19, Angel in the snow; **AK**5, Laying down angels; **KS**2, **MN**37, **OH**87, **PA**165, Angel wings; **NM**5, Angel's wings.

5 pl: In phrr referring to clouds or rain: see quots.

[**1909** *Baseball Magazine* Aug 51/1 (*AmSp* 26.29), Pitilessly the sun beats down from a sky, broken only by the fleecy-white clouds that the players call "angels," because they afford so benevolent a background for the batted ball.] **1950** *WELS* (When the first drops of rain begin to fall, you say) 1 Inf, **swWI**, Angels are crying. **1968** *DARE* (Qu. B10, *What do you call long trailing clouds high in the sky*) Inf **AK**2B, "The angels are sweeping," children said.

angel bird n

The common egret (*Casmerodius albus*).

1959 *Names* 7.114, For its white color, the American egret is known as angel bird in Florida.

angel-devil n Cf *DS* EE19

In the game of hopscotch: see quot 1967.

[**1953** Brewster *Amer. Nonsinging Games* 114, Both of the latter ideas associate [hopscotch] with the soul's progress from earth to heaven . . . the goal toward which the block is propelled is frequently termed "Heaven" or "Paradise" and . . the space just before it is often "Purgatory" or "Fire."] **1967** *DARE* FW Addit **NYC** (as of 1950s), Angel-devil . . . Part of a hop-scotch game. At the end, after you have finished going forwards and backwards on both feet, throwing potsie in each box, then do the same on one foot, with the potsie. Then, with eyes shut, without throwing the potsie, jump through it on both feet. The opponent calls out on each jump "angel" (if you do not step on a line), and "devil" (if you do).

Angeleno n |ˌænjəˈlino| Also sp *Angeleño, Angelino* [From *Los Angeles* + Span *-eño* resident of] **formerly sCA, now more widespread**

1 A resident of Los Angeles, California.

1857 *Star* (Los Angeles CA) 14 Mar 2/2 (*Western Folkl.* 7.4), We have to go abroad to fully appreciate the varied blessings showered on the *Angelinos.* **1888** Lindley *Calif. of South* 79 *(DA)*, Governor Pico is still a resident of Los Angeles, and any Angeleño will cheerfully [sic] point him out to the inquiring stranger. **1948** *AmSp* 23.162 **Los Angeles CA.** **1948** *L.A. Times* 10 May 1/6 *(DA)*, Angelenos upheld summer traditions and went to the beach yesterday. **1966** *Time* 2 Sept 15/1, Like a majority of adult Angelenos, he [Mayor Sam Yorty] comes from "back East"—anywhere east of the Sierras. **1969** *DARE* (Qu. HH2) Inf **CA**160, Angelenos.

2 See **angels on horseback.**

angeleyes n pl, constr as sg Also *angel's tears*

=bluet 2.

1892 *Jrl. Amer. Folkl.* 5.97, *Houstonia cærulea,* . . . angel-eyes. **1948** Wherry *Wild Flower Guide* 124, *Bluets . . .* Also known as . . Angel-eyes. **1969** *DARE* (Qu. S11) Inf **MA**58, Angel's tears.

angelfish n

1 **=angel shark.**

1882 U.S. Natl. Museum *Bulletin* 16.35, *S[quatina] angelus . .* Angelfish; monk-fish; Angel Shark. **1911** *Century Dict., Angel-fish . . .* Also called *monk-fish* and *fiddle-fish.* **1933** John G. Shedd Aquarium *Guide* 21, *Squatina squatina*—Monkfish; Angelfish.

2 **=spadefish** (here: *Chaetodipterus faber*).

1873 in 1878 Smithsonian Inst. *Misc. Coll.* 14.2.29, *Parephippus faber . .* angel-fish (South Carolina). **1887** Goode *Amer. Fishes* 146, The Moon-fish, *Chætodipterus faber . .* is called . . from Florida to Charleston the "Angel-fish," a name which, according to Schoepf, appears to have been current during the last century at Beaufort, N.C. **1933** LA Dept. of Conserv. *Fishes* 261, The Spadefish [*Chaetodipterus faber*] is often also called Moonfish or Angelfish.

angel grass n Cf *DS* I29

1950 *WELS* (Names or nicknames for asparagus) 1 Inf, **cWI**, Angel grass.

angel hair See **angels' hair**

angelica n Also *angelico*

1a Std: a plant of the genus *Angelica.* For other names of var spp see **archangel 1, Aunt Jericho, bellyache root, dead nettle 4, masterwort 2, sea watch, white root, wild parsnip**

b Transf: see quot.

1936 IL Nat. Hist. Surv. *Wildflowers* 223; Candied sweetmeats called Angelica are made from young stems of this giant Parsley *[A. atropurpurea]* and command a high price.

2 also *wild angelica:* =**lovage**, esp *Ligusticum canadense.*

1848 Gray *Manual of Botany* 160, *L[igusticum] actæifolium, . .* (. . Angelico.). **1906** Rydberg *Flora CO* 253, *Ligusticum . .* Lovage, Angelica. **1940** Steyermark *Flora MO* 393, Wild Angelica *(Ligusticum canadense . .).*

angelica tree n [Prob from the similarity of the medicinal properties and/or the flowers to those of *Angelica* spp.]

1 =**Hercules club 1.**

1785 Marshall *Arbustrum* 11, *Virginian Angelica Tree . .* rises with a thick woody stem to the height of ten or twelve feet. **1830** Rafinesque *Med. Flora* 116, Many ignorant herbalists . . call likewise Prickly Ash, the *Aralia Spinosa*, whose true name is Prickly Elder or Angelica tree. **1880** Darlington *Amer. Weeds* 156, Angelica Tree . . . The bark, root, and berries have been used in medicine; they are aromatic and stimulant. **1910** Maury *Trees KY* 114, Sometimes called Angelica Tree . . a small, slightly spreading tree, having its trunk thickly set with sharp, stout prickles. **1950** Moore *Trees AR* 100, Angelica Tree . . . Extremely spiny tree often confused with the prickly ash. **1979** Little *Checklist U.S. Trees* 55, *Devils-walkingstick . . . Other common names*—Hercules-club, prickly-ash, angelica-tree.

2 =**prickly ash 1** (here: *Zanthoxylum americanum*).

1900 Lyons *Plant Names* 399, *X[anthoxylum] Americanum . . .* Angelica-tree . . . *Berries* used to flavor beer, etc. **1930** Sievers *Amer. Med. Plants* 47, *Zanthoxylum americanum . . .* Other common names . . . Angelica tree [etc.]. **1960** Vines *Trees SW* 594, Angelica-tree, Northern Prickly-ash, . . . has some use as a honey plant and as food for wildlife.

angeliferous adj Also obs sp *anngelliferous* [*angel* + *iferous* humorous adj-forming suff popular in 19th cent: cf **eujifferous, splendiferous**] *old-fash*

Angelic; splendid.

1840 Haliburton *Clockmaker* (3d ser) 148 **NEng**, I have got a'most an angeliferous craft, a rael screemer, and I'm the man that sez it. **1853** Bird *Nick of Woods* 179 **KY**, H'yar am I, come to do anngelliferous madam's fighting agin all critturs human and inhuman. *Ibid passim.* **1856** *Town Talk* 20 July 1/1 **San Francisco CA** *(DA),* I didn't see . . . no nothin', 'cept one of the most splendifferous, angeliferous, . . female critters I ever set my two gooseberry eyes onto. **1913** *DN* 4.20, What *angeliferous* music! **1942** Berrey–Van den Bark *Amer. Slang* 29.4, *Excellent; first-rate . . .* angeliferous. *Ibid* 37.10, *Beautiful.* Angeliferous. *Ibid* 277.6, *Pleasant; delightful.* Angeliferous.

Angelino See **Angeleno**

angeliquor n Also *angel liquor* [Blend of *angelica* + *liquor*]

Angelica wine.

1942 *Jrl. Amer. Folkl.* 55.214 **LA** [Among Blacks], Each sanct [participating in an **Easter rock**] receives . . a glass of "angeliquor" (angelica wine). **1966** *DARE* (Qu. DD27) Inf **MS33**, Angel liquor.

angel leaves n [Perh from the more-or-less wing-shaped leaf] **Pacific coast**

=**vanillaleaf 1.**

1919 *DN* 5.80 **WA**, *Angel leaves.* Achlys leaves. **1941** *Torreya* 41.48, *Achlys triphylla* DC.—Angel-leaves, elkhorn, smell-leaves, Washington State.

angel liquor See **angeliquor**

angel of death See **death angel**

angelo on horseback See **angels on horseback 1**

angels are crying, angels are sweeping See **angel 5**

angels' hair n Also *angel('s)~* [From the many hairlike curling yellow tendrils of the plant] **LA, TX**

=**dodder.**

1897 *Jrl. Amer. Folkl.* 10.51 **LA**, *Cuscuta Gronovii, . .* angels' hair. **1898** *Bot. Gaz.* 20.249 **LA**, Angels' hair. **1951** *PADS* 15.38 **TX**, Love vine; strangle-weed; angel-hair; robber vine; devil vine. **1970** Correll *Plants TX* 1255, *Cuscuta . . .* Additional vernacular names to those above are "angel's hair" [etc.].

angel shark n **Atlantic coast**

A fish of the genus *Squatina*, six to eight feet long, which has a

flat, roundish head and winglike fins. Also called **angelfish 1, fiddlefish, monkfish, squato**

1882 U.S. Natl. Museum *Bulletin* 16.35, *S[quatina] angelus . .* Angelfish; Monk-fish; Angel Shark. **1896** U.S. Natl. Museum *Bulletin* 47.58, *Squatinidæ.*—(The Angel Sharks.) . . *Squatina squatina, . .* (Monkfish; Angel Fish; Squato.)

angel's lace n Cf *DS* B36

The pattern formed by ice on the inside of a window pane.

1968 *DARE* (Qu. B36) Inf **OH45**, Angel's lace.

angels on horseback n pl [Loan-transl of Fr *anges à cheval;* cf *OEDS*]

1 also *angelenos, angelo on horseback:* Oysters rolled in bacon and served on toast.

1909 Ware *Passing Engl.,* Angels on Horseback (Virginia). Fricaseed oysters—meaning exquisite. **1933** LA Dept. of Conserv. *Fishes* 579, *Angels (Angelo) on Horseback . . .* Wrap each oyster in bacon, arrange on steel skewers . . . Serve hot . . on triangular pieces of buttered toast. **1971** Leonard *Amer. Cooking West* 19, Foods for a Western cocktail party fill a table of offbeat culinary treats . . . At bottom right are bacon-wrapped oysters called *angelenos. Ibid* 200 [Index], *Angelenos* (angels on horseback, California style).

2 Transf: see quot.

1981 *DARE* File **nCA** (as of 1950s), When I went to summer camp, a traditional "cook-out" meal included angels on horseback—hot dogs sliced so that a piece of cheese could be inserted, then wrapped 'round with a piece of bacon and cooked over the fire.

angel's seat n

Among railroad workers: the cupola of a caboose.

1946 in 1953 Botkin *Treas. Railroad Folkl.* 350, The shack was in the angel's seat of the ape wagon. **1977** Adams *Lang. Railroader* 6.

angel's slipper n

=**jewbush.**

1955 *S. Folkl. Qrly.* 19.232 **FL**, Pedalantus [sic] . . . One variety bears bright red slipper-shaped flowers, fancifully supposed to resemble the slipper an angel would wear, hence the name *Angel's Slipper.*

angel's tears See **angeleyes**

angel('s) teat n

A type of mellow whiskey.

1946 *AmSp* 21.194 [Stillers' argot], 'Angel teat,' a mellowed whiskey with a rich bouquet. **1960** Wentworth–Flexner *Slang.*

angel's-trumpet n Also *~trumpets, angel(s') trumpet(s)* [From the shape of the white flowers]

1 Any of several, usu cultivated, spp of *Datura*, esp *D. arborea.* **Sth, CA and HI** Cf **devil's trumpet, jimson weed**

1889 *Century Dict.,* Angel's-trumpets . . . The large trumpet-shaped flowers of the *Datura suaveolens.* **1897** Parsons *Wild Flowers CA* 96, *D[atura] suaveolens . . .* is common in Californian gardens, and is known popularly as . . "angels' trumpets." **1929** Neal *Honolulu Gardens* 277, The angel's trumpet . . gained its common name from the large white trumpet-shaped flowers that hang vertically from its branches. **1953** Greene–Blomquist *Flowers South* 160, *Angel's Trumpet (Datura arborea) . .* is periodically covered with . . flowers 8″–9″ long, resembling trumpets. **1967** *DARE* (Qu. S26e) Inf **AR49**, Angeltrumpet—like jimson-weed . . . Cultivated. **1974** (1977) Coon *Useful Plants* 249, *Datura Stramonium*—Jimson weed, . . angel's trumpet.

2 =**trumpets 3** (here: *Acleisanthes longiflora*). **SW**

1936 Whitehouse *TX Flowers* 20, Angel's Trumpet . . . The flowers are over an inch broad with a tube 4–6 in. long. **1961** Wills–Irwin *Flowers TX* 107, True to the character of the Four-o'clock Family, Angel's-trumpet is nocturnal, opening at dusk and closing the following morning. **1965** Teale *Wandering Through Winter* 150 **TX**, All across Texas, a host of . . names have been bestowed on the wild plants . . . They run from angel's trumpet . . to shame vine. **1970** Correll *Plants TX* 590, *Angel trumpets . . .* In s. and w. Tex., spring–fall; w. to Riverside Co., Calif., s. to Mex.

angel's turnip n

=**spreading dogbane.**

1926 (1968) Puckett *S. Negro* 245, Angel's Turnip *(Apocymum androsoemifolium)*—Wrap in red flannel—brings good luck. **1942** *Torreya* 42.164, *Apocynum androsaemifolium . . .* Angel's turnip, N.N. Puckett

(Folk beliefs of the southern negro,* 1926, p. 245) . . . *Some obvious misidentifications in this book have been excluded, and possibly the records under Nos. 43 and 168 [*Apocynum androsaemifolium*] also should have been rejected. **1977** Dillard *Lexicon* 126 [Black, in list of conjure potions], More or less miscellaneous terms are *hogs hoof, red coon root, . . Angel's turnip.*

angel's wand n
=**blazing star 2.**

1953 Greene–Blomquist *Flowers South* 6, *Fairy-* or *Angel's-Wand (Chamaelirium luteum) . . .* Flowers are borne in spike-like racemes.

angel('s) wing n

1 Any of var wing-shaped bivalve mollusks (genera *Barnea, Cyrtopleura, Pholas*) of the South Atlantic coast and Gulf of Mexico. Cf **false angel wing**

1908 Rogers *Shell Book* 316, The Angel's Wings are found . . in Florida . . . northward to Cape Cod . . The white valves conform strikingly in outline, colour and sculpture to the conventional representation of angels' wings. **1949** Palmer *Nat. Hist.* 360, *Angel's Wing Shell. Barnea costata.* **1968** *DARE* (Qu. P18) Inf **MD36**, Angel wing—looks like a . wing. Very rare. **1974** Abbott *Seashells* 543, *Barnea truncata . .* Fallen Angel Wing. *Ibid* 544, *Cyrtopleura costata . .* Angel Wing . . . *Pholas campechiensis . .* Campeche Angel Wing.

2 See **angel 4.**

angel-trumpet(s) See **angel's-trumpet**

angel wreath See **feather crown**

angle n

1961 Sackett–Koch *KS Folkl.* 111, Angle . . . A diagonal road from one section line road to another.

angledog n [*angle* to fish + *dog* in uncert sense, perh rel to Engl dial *dog-crowler* "a small kind of shore-crab used by fishermen for bait" (*EDD*); cf *EDD* **angledog** and varr recorded from Devonshire] **chiefly NEng, esp CT and swMA, and settlement areas** *somewhat old-fash*
=**angleworm.**

1867 Hill *Homespun* 96 **NEng**, We pocketed the well-scoured angle-dogs, shouldered our birch fishing-rod, and sallied forth. **1891** *AN&Q* 7.127/2 **cwMA**, When I was a youth, in Western-Central Massachusetts, a very common name for the earthworm was Angle-dog. Angle-twitch and Angle-touch are common enough names in England, . . but angle-dog so far as I know is quite local. **1931–33** *LANE Worksheets* 9 Infs, **chiefly CT, sMA, swVT**, Angledog. **1933** *AmSp* 8.4.14 **NEng**, *Angle-dog . .* is the usual word in the sections of Connecticut centered about and settled from the 'river town' of Windsor . . It is not surprising to find that *angledog* is still in use in southwestern Vermont . . and in the Connecticut Valley. [Footnote:] In [areas mentioned above] *angledog* is considered an old-fashioned term . . . This term is still used in the Western Reserve in Ohio. **1967–69** *DARE* (Qu. P5) Infs **CT**23, 36, **IA**4, **MA**15, Angledog. [All Infs are old.] **1971** Wood *Vocab. Change* 237 **TN** [Rare instances of] angledog.

angle-godlin adv Var of **antigodlin**

1970 Tarpley *Blinky* 22 **neTX**, *To go from one corner of a field to another is to walk . .* angle-godlin [in list of "other responses"].

angle grass n [Prob so called from the triangular scape]
A bulrush (here: *Scirpus robustus*).

1941 *Torreya* 41.46 **seSC**, Angle grass.

angler n [See quot 1911]
=**goosefish.**

1815 Lit. & Philos. Soc. NY *Trans.* 1.465, *Bellows-fish,* or common *Angler. Lophius piscator.* **1862** Acad. Nat. Sci. Philadelphia *Proc. of 1861* 46, *Lophius americanus . .* "Angler." **1911** *Century Dict.,* *Angler . . .* The name . . [is] in allusion to its attracting small fish . . by the movement of certain filaments attached to the head and mouth. **1933** John G. Shedd Aquarium *Guide* 162, *Lophius piscatorius . .* Angler.

angler worm n Also **angler** Var of **angleworm**

1896 *DN* 1.411 **NYC**, Angler-worm ['æŋgləwɚm]. **1933** *AmSp* 8.4.14 **ME**, *Angler* appears in Gardner, Maine. **1940–41** Cassidy *WI Atlas* **Prairie Du Chien**, Angler. **1968** *DARE* (Qu. P5) Inf **PA**134, Angler.

angleworm n [*angle* to fish + *worm*] **chiefly Nth and West** See Map Addit maps in 1933 *AmSp* 8.4.13, 1939 *LANE* Map 236,

1949 Kurath *Word Geog* Fig 140. Also called **angledog, angler worm, angling worm**

An **earthworm** used as bait for fishing.

1832 Williamson *Hist. ME* 1.168, We have among us, in summer, a variety of native *Worms, . .* the *Earthworm,* the *Brandling,* the *Angle worm.* **1894** *DN* 1.339 **wCT.** **1900** *Everybody's Mag.* 3.521/2 **IN**, He collected a small gourdful of angle-worms. **1912** *DN* 3.566 **cNY, VT, MO.** **1925** Stuart *40 Yrs.* 1.65 **CA**, Having no shortening they dug angleworms and crushed them up with the acorns. **1949** Kurath *Word Geog.* 14, *Angle worm* has spread to the entire Northern area. *Ibid* 45, Two other expressions that are widely used in New England appear in scattered sections of the Southern coast: *angleworm . .* on the Potomac, the lower Neuse, and the lower Peedee. **1961** *AmSp* 36.31 **nOH**, *Angleworm . . .* Its use declines as the informants become younger and more cultivated. **1965–70** *DARE* (Qu. P5, . . *The common worm used as bait*) 300 Infs, **chiefly Nth and West**, Angleworm; **MI**101, Ringed angleworm; (Qu. P6) Infs **GA**80, **IA**8, **KS**5, **MA**42, **OH**3, **OK**1, 11, Angleworm; (Qu. R27) Infs **MI**67, **NY**66, **WA**15, Angleworm. **1971** Wood *Vocab. Change* 237, Angleworm [occurs occasionally throughout the South]. **1973** Allen *LAUM* 1.326, *Angleworm,* dominant in New England and New York, so increased its dominance that it became the distinctively Northern form in the U[pper] M[idwest].

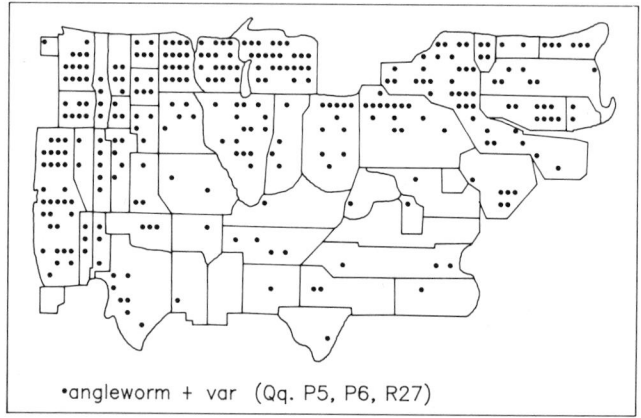

·angleworm + var (Qq. P5, P6, R27)

angling worm n Var of **angleworm**

1933 *AmSp* 8.4.14 **ME**, *Angling worm . .* appears in Gardner, Maine.

Anglo n, also attrib **formerly SW, now widely recognized**

1 =**Anglo-American.**

1940 Fergusson *Our Southwest* 70, *Los ricos* accepted the incoming Anglos as friends, as wives or husbands. **1943** *NM Qrly. Rev.* Spring 33, Native Anglos and Spanish Americans of New Mexico. **1949** *AmSp* 24.312 **NM**, The pair of words I seemed to hear most frequently [to distinguish people of English-speaking and Spanish-speaking descent] was *Anglos* and *Hispanos.* **1967–69** *DARE* Tape **TX**5, The first Anglo-Saxon type, commonly referred to as Anglos, started drifting into this country in the early 1800s . . . Most of the Anglos, or as they were referred to, the Gringos, used chili; **TX**69, Anglo. **1974** Cicourel *Lang. Use* 3 **sCA**, The population of the other school . . was more evenly mixed between Anglo, Black, and Chicano children.

2 The English language.

1968 Fulbright *Cow-Country Counselor* 71 **AZ** (as of 1930s–1960s), She was a middle-aged woman, plump, and talked poor Anglo.

Anglo-American n, also attrib [See *DA* for historical treatment of related senses] **formerly SW, now recognized throughout US** Also called **Anglo 1**
A white English-speaking American who is not of Spanish or Indian descent.

1834 Pike *Prose Sketches* 1 **NM**, And south of the river Arkansas and its branches, has been rarely, and parts of it never, trodden by the foot or beheld by the eye of an Anglo-American. **1857** *TX Almanac for 1858* 114, The Anglo-Americans of Texas were threatened with subjection to military despotism. **1948** *Seventeen* June 4/4 (*OEDS*), We had a Chinese boy cheerleader, a Mexican girl cheerleader, and three Anglo-Americans. **1948** *Sat. Eve. Post* 2 Oct 51/1 **TX**, One of the things that help exclude the Mexicans from a fuller part of Anglo-American doings is a residual Indian shyness that manifests itself in their clannishness.

angnail See **agnail**

angora n Usu |æŋ'gɔrə|, occas |æŋ'gorɪ|. Cf **-y**

A Form.

1968 *DARE* (Qu. J5) Inf **NY**72, Angora [æŋgorɪ].

B Sense.

In pl: chaps made from angora goat hide. **West** Also called **woolies**

1944 Adams *Western Words, Angoras*—A frequently used slang name for chaps made of goat hide with the hair left on. **1946** Mora *Trail Dust* 88 s**CA**, At our early rodeo shows, I saw some enthusiasts with their angoras dyed green and pink . . . When those buckaroos waddled along as dismounted bipeds with those mammoth contraptions on, they sure looked funny. **1955** Harris *Look of Old West* 213, The American cowboy didn't really go for fur chaps, angoras (made from Angora goat hide), or woolies (sheepskin) until he got up on the northern ranges in Montana, Wyoming, and the Dakotas.

‡**Angorian** adj

Angora.

1966 *DARE* Tape **SC**3, He had the Angorian [æn'goriən] goats. He sheared 'em and sold the hair.

angry adj [*OED* 1579 →] **chiefly NEng, Midl**

Of a sore or wound: inflamed.

1899 (1912) Green *VA Folk-Speech, Angry, adj.* Inflamed, as a sore. Red. **1902** *DN* 2.228 s**IL**. **1903** *DN* 2.305 se**MO**. **1907** *DN* 3.220, 228 sw**IL**, nw**AR**, se**MO**. **1908** *DN* 3.286 e**AL**, w**GA**, The sore looks right angry. **1931–33** *LANE Worksheets* 4 Infs, **MA**, 2 Infs, **VT**, 1 Inf, **CT**. **1943** *LANE* Map 514 throughout **NEng**, Several informants who offer the adjective *angry* use it of a wound only in predicative position (*It looks angry*) . . . *Angry* is described as an older term than *inflamed*, though still in use, by [17 Infs]. **1950** *WELS* (*When the skin around a sore . . is red and hot, you say it is*) 2 Infs, **WI**, Angry. **1954** *Harder Coll.* cw**TN**. c**1960** *Wilson Coll.* cs**KY**, That cut place on my leg is angry-looking today, Doc. **1968** *DARE* (Qu. BB29, *What do you call the red flesh that sometimes grows in a wound and keeps it from healing right?*) Inf**OH**38, Angry flesh. **1969** *DARE* FW Addit **KY**44.

angry acacia n Also *angry tree* [See quots] **AZ, CA, NV**

An acacia, prob **cat's claw** (here: *Acacia gregii*. Note: Only this sp has the size and range indicated in the quots. Mimosas in the US do not range into Nevada.).

1892 *AN&Q* 8.131/2, The "angry tree," a woody plant, which grows from ten to twenty-five feet high, and was formerly supposed to exist only in Nevada, has recently been found both in eastern California and in Arizona. If disturbed, this peculiar tree shows every sign of vexation, even to ruffling up its leaves like the hair on an angry cat, and giving forth an unpleasant, sickening odor. **1930** *Sun* (Baltimore MD) 13 Feb 14/3 (*Hench Coll.*) **NV**, The "angry acacia" of Nevada quivers violently when disturbed and emits an unpleasant odor. It takes this bad-tempered tree an hour or two to go back to good humor.

anhinga n [*OEDS* 1769 →]

Std: a dark water bird (*Anhinga anhinga*) resembling a cormorant but with long slender neck, small head, and turkey-like tail, found chiefly in the South Atlantic and Gulf States. Also called **bec-a-lance, darter, negro goose, snakebird, water crow, water turkey**

anigh prep [a inert vowel **3** + *nigh; OED* 1773 →; cf *EDD*] **esp Sth, S Midl** *old-fash* Cf **anear**

Near, close to.

1856 Holmes *Lena Rivers* 64 **NEng**, I charge you never to go a nigh 'em. **1888** Jones *Negro Myths* 123 se**GA**, Soon as Buh Wolf come anigh um, Buh Rabbit biggin fuh sing. **1891** Ryan *Pagan* 271 **Allegheny Mts**, Him up there on the mountain, and not a-nigh her. **1899** (1912) Green *VA Folk-Speech*, Don't go anigh him. **1908** *DN* 3.286 e**AL**, w**GA**, Don't come anigh me. **1952** Brown *NC Folkl.* 1.515, Anigh . . . Near. c**1960** *Wilson Coll.* cs**KY**, "Don't you come anigh me, or I'll smack you right betwixt the eyes." Rare, used by old people.

anigh adv [*OED*, 1868 →] *old-fash*

Nearby, close by.

1856 Cary *Married* 63 (*DAE*) **OH**, There ain't a brute beast in Woodside that don't foller after him if he goes a nigh. **1869** Whitney *Hitherto* 420 **NEng**, If, haply, I might be worthy yet to dwell anigh. **1974** *AmSp* 49.61 se**ME** (as of c1910, in the works of George Savary Wasson). **1976**

Garber *Mountain-ese* 3 s**Appalachians**, He slept while the horses grazed anigh.

anights adv [a prep¹ **2** + *nights* from OE genitive *nihtes; OED* →1838] *arch or obs* Cf **adays**

At night; by night.

1663 in 1887 East Hampton NY *Records* 1.205 **NY**, It is ordered that there shall 12 men goe to Meantaquit to make a yard to put up the drie Cattell a nights. **1705** Beverley *Hist.* VA 4.66, Chinches are a sort of flat Bug, which lurks in the Beadsteads [sic] and Bedding, and disturbs People's rest a-nights. **1759** in 1882 Essex Inst. *Coll.* 19.150 **MA**, Our Duty Very heard at work a days and on gaurd [sic] a Nights and our Provision only Pork and Bread. **1899** (1912) Green *VA Folk-Speech*, When we go out anights.

animal n Usu |'ænəməl|, occas |'ænəmɪl|; often humorously |'ænə,maɪl, 'ænə,mjul| Pronc-sp *annimel* See also **animule.**

A Forms.

1891 *DN* 1.121 c**NY**, [ænəmɪl]. **1914** *DN* 4.151 w**ME**, *Animil*, pronounced *animĭl*. **1922** *DN* 5.134 c**West**, Intentional mispronunciations . . . Students and others often make these words oxytones: . . ani'mule or ani'mile (ai). **1922** Gonzales *Black Border* 42 s**SC, GA coasts** [Gullah], Uh look 'gen 'e come close, en' uh see 'e duh annimel eye!

B Senses.

1 A bull or, occas, a stallion. **chiefly NEng, N Midl, West** *euphem, esp among rural and male speakers; somewhat old-fash*

1912 *DN* 3.570 w**IN**. **1933** *AmSp* 8.1.29 **TX**, *Animal.* A bull. The cowboy and ranchman would use any amount of circumlocution to avoid calling a spade a spade in the presence of ladies. **1939** *LANE* Map 190, The reluctance of women and of men in the presence of women to mention the word *bull* appears to be less widespread than formerly . . . [For ex, one Inf remarked,] *Animal*, only in the presence of 'high-toned women from a village.' **1957** *AmSp* 32.114 **NEng**, [In frequency table, "animal" fifth of ten euphemisms for "bull."] c**1960** *Wilson Coll.* cs**KY**, Grandpa's old animal chased me and Mary across the pasture field. **1965–70** *DARE* (Qu. K22, *Words used for a bull*) 22 Infs, **chiefly N Midl, West**, Animal; (Qu. K23, *Words used by women or in mixed company for a bull*) 9 Infs, **chiefly N Midl, West**, Animal. [Of 26 Infs giving this response, 22 were old, 15 rural, and 20 male.] **1969** *WV Hist.* 30.2.471, A stallion was either a "stable horse" or else rather ominously, "The animal." **1973** Allen *LAUM* 1.244 **Upper MW**, Bull . . . *Animal* and *male animal* appear 29 times rather evenly distributed.

2 A word-for-word translation used by students as an aid in learning a foreign language. [By analogy with *pony*: see *DA pony* 1, 1827 →. For similar varr see 1942 Berrey–Van den Bark *Amer. Slang* 838.2]

1900 *DN* 2.15, The literal translation has already been mentioned as furnishing numerous student words, most of them zoological, from the specific *pony, horse,* to the quite general *animal, beast. Ibid* 21, *Animal* . . . A literal translation [in use at 7 Northeastern Colleges]. **1922** *DN* 5.155.

3 An inexperienced logger.

1958 McCulloch *Woods Words* **Pacific NW**, *Animal* . . . A green hand in the woods.

‡**animal ball** n Also *farmer ball*

A children's game: see quot.

1968 *DARE* (Qu. EE33) Inf **PA**163, Animal ball—two teams are on opposite sides of a demilitarized area. Teams throw at one another in the middle area. Also called "farmer ball."

animal car n *joc* Cf **ape wagon**

Among railroad workers: a caboose.

1942 Berrey–Van den Bark *Amer. Slang* 774.15, *Caboose.* Animal car. **1977** Adams *Lang. Railroader* 7.

animal fertilizer n *euphem*

Manure.

1966–68 *DARE* (Qu. L17) Infs **MA**6, **WI**63, Animal fertilizer.

‡**animal hunt** n

A children's game: see quot.

1968 *DARE* (Qu. EE3) Inf **PA**133, Animal hunt—various leaders or captains have broods whom they must call to them; these must get to the nest before the fox gets them.

animal pass n

A place in a road where animals cross regularly.

1966–69 *DARE* (Qu. N31) Infs **CA**63, **IL**48, **ME**19, **NY**117, 226, **OH**58, Animal pass.

animule n [Blend of *animal* + *mule*] *facetious*

Any animal, not necessarily a mule.

c1834 in 1890 Farmer–Henley *Slang* 1.55, Them animules is too beat to do that. **1872** Schele de Vere *Americanisms* 578, *Animules* is, in California and the Southwestern Territories, a favorite substitute for *Animals,* with a sly pun upon *mules*. **1905** *DN* 3.67 **NE**, Folk etymology . . *animule.* **1908** *DN* 3.286 **eAL, wGA**, *Animule* . . . Animal: often used facetiously of a mule. "Wait till I ketch this here animule" **1922** *DN* 5.136 **cWest**, A word is transformed into a conscious blend in a folk-etymologizing way: . . animule. **1930** Shoemaker *1300 Words* **cPA** (as of c1900), *Animule*—A crippled, aged horse; less than a horse but four-legged. **c1960** *Wilson Coll.* **csKY**.

anise root n [From the fragrance and taste of the root] **chiefly Nth**

=**sweet cicely**.

1876 Hobbs *Bot. Hdbk.* 4, Anise root, Sweet Cicely, Osmorrhiza longistylis. **1910** Graves *Flowering Plants* 298 **CT**. **1936** IL Nat. Hist. Surv. *Wildflowers* 218, Anise roots . . are perennial herbs and have clusters of thick edible roots which possess the fragrance and flavor of anise. **1963** Conserv. Council PA *Native Plants* 53.

ank See **ink A**

ankety-over n, exclam

In the game of **Antony-over**: see quot.

1968 *DARE* (Qu. EE22, . . *The game in which they throw a ball over a building . . to a player on the other side*) Inf **MD**26, Ankety-over; (Qu. EE23a, . . *What do you call out when you have the ball?*) Inf **MD**26, Ankety-over; (Qu. EE23b, *If you fail to get the ball over the building . . what do you call out?*) Inf **MD**26, Ankety-over.

ankish See **anxious**

ankle v Cf **anchor off, ankle express**

To walk.

1920s in 1944 *ADD* **cNY**. **1934** *AmSp* 9.26 [Prison slang], Ankle. To walk. **1938** *AmSp* 13.195. **1940** *AmSp* 15.446 **TN**, He ankled up to the mailbox. **1951** *AmSp* 26.238, There she goes ankling along the pavement, her skirts swishing. **1959** Robertson *Ram* 296 **ID**, We tried to avoid the popular magazine jargon such as "ankled" for walked, and "hair-pinning" for mounting. **1970** Major *Afro–Amer. Slang* 20. **1971** Jennings *Cowboys* 11 **West**, Come on and ankle over to Miss Fanny Zook's with me 'fore school lets out.

ankle-biter n Cf **rug-rat, DS Z12, 16**

An unruly or disobedient child.

1967 *DARE* (Qu. Z16, *A small child who is rough, misbehaves, and doesn't obey*) Inf **AL**19, Ankle-biter. **1979** *DARE* File **wOR**, *Ankle-biter* can be used affectionately in addressing a small child, as in "Where are you going, you little ankle-biter?"

ankle express n esp **West, Sth** Cf **ankle v, shank's mare**

Transportation by foot; walking.

1920 Hunter *Trail Drivers TX* 219, From Brenham I went by stage to Austin, and from Austin I took the "ankle express" for my home in Llano county, seventy-five miles away. **1966–69** *DARE* (Qu. Y24, *Expressions meaning to walk*) Infs **GA**82, **MA**4, Go by ankle express; **TX**18, Ankle express; **LA**2A, Go ankle express; **GA**72, Go on ankle express; **IN**1, Take the ankle express. **1968** Adams *Western Words*. **1971** Jennings *Cowboys* 134 **West**, It was a good hour back to camp by ankle express; with a limping horse, three.

ankles from elbows, not to know v phr Var of **ass from one's elbow, not to know one's**

1968 *DARE* (Qu. JJ15b, . . *A person who seems to you very stupid: "He doesn't know _____."*) Inf **OH**68, Ankles from elbows.

ankle-tie n, usu pl **chiefly NEng** *old-fash*

A women's or girls' low dress shoe which fastens around the ankles.

1874 Ward *Trotty's Wedding* 13 **NEng**, Her little ankle-ties swung tormentingly and carelessly to and fro against the wood-pile. **1909** *DN* 3.407 **neME**, *Ankle tie* . . . A low shoe with a strap buttoning across the ankle. **1923** Wiggin *Garden of Memory* 5 **ME**, A very dim and evasive

memory of a "dame school," where I see myself sitting on a low bench in the company of three or four other children, with brief legs, white stockings, and ankle-ties. **1941** *LANE* Map 366 **ME, MA**, 4 Infs, Ankle-ties [for "low shoes"]. **1976** *DARE* File **cnMA** (as of c1910), Ankle-ties were the same as Mary Janes. They were "proper" dress up shoes for little girls, usually black, with a flat bow. They did not tie but buttoned with one button.

‡anligodlin adj [Var of **antigodlin**]

1970 *DARE* (Qu. MM13) Inf **AR**56, ['ænlɪˌgɑdlɪn].

annarugian See **amarugian**

anngelliferous See **angeliferous**

Annie See **Annie Oakley, Annie-over**

Annie-come-back See **anti-come-back**

Annie-i-over See **anti-i-over**

Annie-nover, Annie-novo See **Annie-over**

Annie Oakley n, also attrib Also *Annie* [After Annie Oakley, markswoman; see quots 1922, 1940; for discussion, see also 1933 *AmSp* 8.1.76ff] *orig circus cant, now more widespread*

1 A complimentary ticket.

1922 *New York World* 28 June 7/3 (1933 *AmSp* 8.1.76) **NYC**, Miss Oakley explained that Ban Johnson is the man who invented the term "Annie Oakley" for free passes. . "A man was brought to him . . who had rented out his baseball pass. Ban Johnson looked at it, filled with neat holes, and suggested that the man had been letting me use it as a target." **1926** *AmSp* 1.437. **1931** *AmSp* 6.329. **1931** *Sun* (Baltimore MD) 5 Mar 14/1 (*Hench Coll.*), Miami, Fla., Chilly weather, a law-suit for damages and a substantial rush for 'Annie Oakleys' at fistic headquarters today were the only noteworthy developments . . . Partly as a consequence, the market for 'Annies,' or complimentary tickets, was much heavier than the activity on the part of cash customers. **1932** *AmSp* 7.314. **1933** *AmSp* 8.76. **1940** FWP *Guide OH* 558, She could pierce a playing card tossed into the air several times before it touched the ground—whence came the term 'Annie Oakleys' for complimentary passes filled with punch marks. **1977** Adams *Lang. Railroader*, Annie Oakley: A railroad pass.

2 By ext: anything with many holes punched in it.

1934 *Sun* (Baltimore MD) 22 Sept 13/8 (*Hench Coll.*), Vanderbilt immediately broke it out in place of the "Mae West" spinnaker that had been running a bad second to Endeavour's ingenious "Annie Oakley" spinnaker, a much larger balloon of canvas with holes punched in it like a complimentary ticket.

3 Transf: in baseball: a base on balls. [Because the batter gets a "free" trip to first base.]

1940 *Richmond News Leader* 2 July 23/7 (*Hench Coll.*) Newson's Annie Oakley average last season while winning twenty games and losing eleven for the Browns and Tigers was 3.85. **1943** *AmSp* 18.105, When the batter obtains a base on balls . . he is said to . . *get an Annie Oakley.*

Annie-over n, exclam Also *Annie-nover, Annie-novo,* and simplex *Annie* **widespread, but least freq in NEng, S Atl** See Map

A As noun.

=**Antony-over** n.

1949 *PADS* 11.16 **CO**, Annie, annie over. **1950** *WELS* (Game in

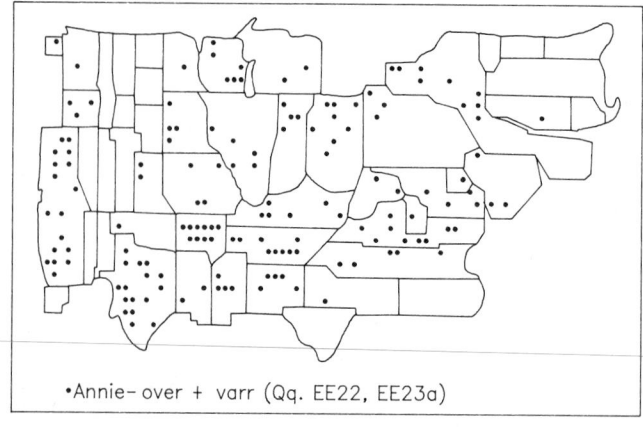

•Annie-over + varr (Qq. EE22, EE23a)

which you throw a ball over a low building) 2 Infs, **WI**, Annie-over; 2 Infs, Annie-Annie-over. **1951** Johnson *Resp. to PADS 20* **DE.** **1965–70** *DARE* (Qu. EE22), 113 Infs, **widespread, but least freq in NEng, S Atl,** Annie-over; 21 Infs **chiefly Inland Nth,** Annie-Annie-over; **AR9,** Annie-over-Annie; **LA6,** Annie-nover.

B As exclamation.

1 =**Antony-over** exclam.
1950 *WELS (What do you shout when you throw the ball?)* 3 Infs, **WI,** Annie-over; 1 Inf, Annie-Annie-over. **1965–70** *DARE* (Qu. EE23a) 80 Infs, **widespread, but least freq in NEng, S Atl,** Annie-over; 17 Infs, **chiefly Inland Nth,** Annie-Annie-over; **WI68,** Annie-Annie; **LA6,** Annie-novo [–ˈnovoʊ]; **TX104,** Annie-over, here she come; 16 Infs, **all S Midl, TX,** Annie.

2 See **anti-come-back.**

Annie up v phr Also *Andy up* [Folk-etym varr of *ante up*]
To contribute one's share; to pay a debt.
1968–70 *DARE* (Qu. U18, *If you force somebody to pay money that he owes you, . . "I finally made him _____."*) Inf **PA126,** Annie up; (Qu. II9, . . "*Let's all _____."*) Inf **PA234,** Andy up.

annigodlin See **antigodlin**

annigoglin See **antigoglin**

annimel See **animal**

Anniversary Day n [Cf *DA anniversary* →1860] *old-fash*
A day on which annual church meetings and celebrations were held. Hence *anniversary sermon,* sermon delivered on anniversary day.
1953 Brewer *Word Brazos* 17 **eTX** [Black], De annuhversury sermon come oncet a yeah so de membuhship kin help de pastuh 'long wid his duds ez well ez his grub. **1966** *DARE* Tape **NY247,** Like Anniversary Day, you know, when all the churches used to parade. Now they call it Brooklyn Day.

annudder See **another**

‡**anny** n [Perh a var of *ante:* see **ante up 2**]
1958 *PADS* 29.29 **CT,** *Anny* . . A choice marble.

anoder See **another**

anoint v Usu |əˈnɔɪnt|; also, **esp in eVA** |(ə)ˈnaɪnt| *somewhat old-fash* Pronc-spp *noint, nint* See also **a-aint, ant** v²
A Forms.
1899 (1912) Green *VA Folk-Speech* 300 *Noint, . . . Nint.* To annoint [sic]. To beat severely. "Ninted scoundrel." **1927** Shewmake *Engl. Pronc. VA* 17, *Anoint* [əˈnaɪnt] . . . The prevailing sound was that of *i* as in *pint* . . . Some of these early pronunciations are heard still in illiterate speech.
B Sense.
To flog, beat. *joc*
1859 Matsell *Vocabulum* 8, *Anointed.* Flogged. **1889** (1971) Farmer *Americanisms.* **1927** *DN* 5.437.

anon See **anan**

anoodling See **noodling**

another adj Pronc-spp, esp in representation of Black speech: *anether, annudder, anoder, anud(d)er, anurr(er), anuther, ernurther,* aphet *nother, nothuh, nuder, nuther* See also **nother**
A Forms.
1823 Cooper *Pioneers* 1.243 **cNY** [Black], Gib anoder shillin, Billy, and hab anudder shot. **1888** Jones *Negro Myths* 5 **seGA** [Gullah], Deese yer Cooter am all so much like one anurrer you cant tell one from turrer. **1893** Shands *MS Speech, Anudder* . . . A negro form for *another.* **1899** (1912) Green *VA Folk-Speech, Anuder.* **1905** Culbertson *Banjo Talks* 69 **Sth,** Jes' you tetch anu'rr sip. **1909** *DN* 3.353 **eAL, wGA,** *Nude(r)n* . . . Another one. **1916** Howells *Leatherwood God* 76 **OH,** Abel will find her some time or 'nother. **1928** Peterkin *Scarlet Sister Mary* 161 **SC** [Black], Dey ain' never see one annudder. **1941** Percy *Lanterns* 294 **nwMS** [Black], Ernurther one cum, still bigger, en ernurther, en ernurther. **1978** *AP Letters* **swPA,** Anĕther.
B Sense.
Following *somehow, something:* or other.
1843 (1916) Hall *New Purchase* 145 **IN,** Then I hears somethin a nuther in the beech above. **1848** Lowell *Biglow* 2 "Upcountry" **MA,** Hosee's

gut the chollery or suthin anuther. **1887** (1967) Harris *Free Joe* 125 **GA,** I know in reason they must be somep'n 'nother wrong. **1914** *DN* 4.113 **KS,** *Something another . . .* Something or other. **1937** in 1958 Brewer *Dog Ghosts* 72 **TX** [Black], Crawlin' 'roun' on his han's an' knees lack he lookin' for sump'n' 'nothuh he done lose. **1942** in 1944 *ADD* **nKS,** *Somehow another.*

another-guess adj Also sp *-gess* [*OED* →1860: reduced from *anothergets, anothergates* (*OED* →1693), lit 'of another way, manner, or fashion.'] *?obs*
Different (in kind).
1865 Crockett *Life* 242 **TN,** So I walked away from the shantee, but in another guess sort from the way I entered it. **1899** (1912) Green *VA Folk-Speech, Another-gess* . . . Another kind; of a different sort. "He is another-gess man."

anquera n [MexSpan] **SW**
See quots 1968, 1977.
1881 Farrow *Mt. Scouting* 139, The Mexican or California saddles . . [are] usually furnished with wool-lined bastos, llama skin anqueras, sudaderos, tapaderos, and stirrup leathers handsomely cut-stamped. **1910** Hart *Vigilante Girl* 180 **nCA,** The remaining bandits . . selected half a dozen of the prettiest women there, seated them behind their saddles, strapped them to the *anqueras,* and dashed away into the night. **1968** Adams *Western Words, Anquera*—A round covering for the hindquarters of a horse; . . Americans use this term for the broad leather sewn to the base of the cantle when there is no rear jockey and extending beyond the cantle. **1977** Watts *Dict. Old West, Anquera* . . . It was sometimes used "simply for looks." Rossi identifies the anquera as a flanker fastened back of the saddle and adds that though some were small, others, highly decorated, extended over the horse's rump and reached almost to the ground.

ansenberg See **osnaburg**

answer n Pronc-sp *ansuh* **seSC, nGA coast** *Gullah*
A message.
1922 Gonzales *Black Border* 288 **sSC, GA coasts** [Gullah], *Ansuh* . . . Also used for message, especially for one requiring an answer; as: "Uh sen' uh ansuh to de gal fuh tell'um uh wan' hab'um fuh wife"—I sent a message to the girl to tell her that I wanted to marry her. **1950** *PADS* 14.12 **SC,** "Cap'n, de answer we git wuz come cut crossties for wunnuh. Dat de right, enti?" The message we got was to come and cut crossties for you. That is right, is it not? Gullah and coastal Negro usage.

answer the last call v phr Also *answer the (last) roll call* *euphem* Cf *DS* BB56
To die.
1915 Hall *Claib Jones* 38 **KY,** I am now nearly 90 years old and will soon have to answer the roll-call across the border. **1942** *AmSp* 17.213 **SW,** Other euphemisms I noticed were in headlines: ' "California Frank" Hafley *Answers Last Call*' and 'Bill Steele *Rides to Last Roundup.*' **1942** Berrey–Van den Bark *Amer. Slang* 117.11, *Die.* Answer the . . last roll call.

ant n Usu |ænt|; in **Sth,** also |eɪnt, ẽɪ̃|; elsewhere occas |ɑnt| Cf **aunt**
A Forms.
1941 *AmSp* 16.5 **TX** [Black], *Ant, can't* are usually [ẽɪ̃], [kjẽɪ̃], though [æ̠ɪnt], [kjæ̠ɪnt] are heard as well. **1968–69** *DARE* FW Addits **MA29,** Ants [ɑnts]; **TN17A,** [eɪnts].
B Sense.
=**jimmie.**
1982 *NY Times* (NY) 25 Nov A22, What do you call the tiny multicolored flecks of candy that are sometimes scattered on chocolate cakes, or into which ice cream cones are dipped? . . To a Rhode Islander, they are ants. **1982** *DARE* File **nCA** (as of c1950), As children, we called the chocolate sprinkles on cakes and cookies "ants."

a'n't, an't, ant v¹ See **ain't** v¹

ant v² [Var of *oint* (*OED,* "Obs. or arch.")] See also **a-aint**
To anoint.
1965 Teale *Wandering Through Winter* 131 **TX,** The green jay . . [has] been observed "anting with fire," anointing [its] . . plumage with smoke from smoldering logs.

ant bed n
An anthill.

1907 *DN* 3.180 **seNH,** Look out! You're stepping on an ant-bed. **1908** *DN* 3.286 **eAL, wGA.**

ant bug n

An ant.

1944 *PADS* 2.17 **sAppalachians,** *Ant-bug* . . . The ant. A survival of the O.E. fondness for compounds.

ant cow n Also *ant's cow* [See quots 1889, c1960]

Usu an aphid (Aphididae) but also any of various similar insects, as those of the family Coccidae.

1875 *Encycl. Brit.* (9th ed) 2.98/1, The *Coccidæ* in America take the place of the European *aphides* as ant-cows. 1889 *Century Dict., Ant-cow* . . . An aphid, plant-louse, or some similar insect, kept and tended by ants. 1950 *WELS (Other names for plant lice)* **WI,** 2 Infs, Ant cows; 2 Infs, Ant's cows. c1960 *Wilson Coll.* **csKY,** *Ant cow*—aphid from which ants get honeydew. 1965–70 *DARE* (Qu. R26) Infs **CA80, GA25, HI14, IL26, 119, 143, IA45, KY5, LA14, SC2, 69, VA15, WI37, 43,** Ant cows; **TN6,** Ant's cows—children's term.

ante n |ænti| Cf **ante line, ante up 2, at-it, bait** n **4**

In marble play: the stakes in a game of **keeps.**

1942 Berrey–Van den Bark *Amer. Slang* 665.3, "Ante." *(Marbles put in the ring as a stake).* 1955 *PADS* 23.11 **cwTN,** *Ante:* The preliminary wager in a marble game of chance. 1958 *PADS* 29.29 **OK.** 1963 *KY Folkl. Rec.* 9.61 **eKY,** *The marbles of an individual being played for in a game:* ante [reported in 5 of 18 counties]. 1973 Ferretti *Marble Book* 39 **seNY,** *Ante.* The number of marbles agreed upon as stakes for the winner or to put into an enclosure and shot at—for keeps.

ante v See **ante up**

ante-come-back See **anti-come-back**

‡**anteen** n [Etym unknown]

1966 *DARE* (Qu. K38, *What do you call a horse of a dirty white color?*) Inf **DC5,** ['æn'tin].

antegoddlin' See **antigodlin**

antegogglin' See **antigoglin**

ante line n Cf **ante** n

In marble play: the **starting line.**

1967 *DARE* (Qu. EE8) Inf **NE1,** Ante line.

antelope brush n **West**

1 also *antelope bitterbrush,* ∼*brittlebrush,* ∼*bush:* =**bitterbrush 1.**

1915 *Nat. & Science on Pac. Coast* 151 *(DA),* The most abundant species are the sagebrush, . . antelope brush *(Purshia tridentata),* and in alkaline soil black greasewood. 1931 U.S. Dept. Ag. *Misc. Pub.* 101.52, *Bitterbrush (Purshia tridentata)* . . . Other . . names often applied to it are antelope-brush [etc.]. 1953 Nelson *Plants Rocky Mt. Park* 94, *Antelope-brush* or *antelope brittlebrush.* 1960 Vines *Trees SW* 423, Antelope Bitter-brush is considered to be a very important browse plant for cattle and sheep, but is usually not eaten by horses. It is important also as a food for wildlife. 1974 Munz *Flora S. CA* 758, Antelope Bush.

2 also *antelope sage:* =**wild buckwheat** (here: *Eriogonum jamesii*).

1937 U.S. Forest Serv. *Range Plant Hdbk.* W70, James eriogonum . . , known locally as antelope sage, . . . is almost worthless as forage. 1960 Vines *Trees SW* 233, James Eriogonum . . . Also known by the vernacular name of Antelope-brush. The root is reported to be used medicinally by certain Indians.

antelope bush See **antelope brush 1**

antelope chipmunk n **SW**

=**antelope ground squirrel.**

1915 *Nat. & Science on Pac. Coast* 111 *(DA),* Daylight-roaming rodents . . include the striped antelope chipmunk which holds its short, flat, white-lined tail closely appressed to its back.

antelope ground squirrel n Also *antelope squirrel* [See quot 1952] **SW**

A small, grayish, white-lined ground squirrel, esp *Citellus leucurus.* Also called **antelope chipmunk**

1908 Hornaday *Camp-Fires* 66 **AZ,** During the day we saw . . one coyote, two Harris's antelope squirrels . . [etc]. 1928 Anthony *N. Amer. Mammals* 215, Antelope Ground Squirrel.—*Ammospermophilus leucurus* . . Names . . . White-tailed Chipmunk. 1939 Pickwell *Deserts* 3/1 **Desert SW,** For six weeks the Desert Antelope Ground Squirrel lived without a drop of water, yet it had water. 1941 Jaeger *Wildflowers* 139, The little white-tailed antelope ground squirrels *[Citellus leucurus],* nicknamed "ammos," store the fresh seeds. 1952 Burt *Field Guide Mammals* 69, Whitetail antelope squirrel. *Citellus leucurus* . . . When running, the tail is curled over the back, exposing the white undersurface, and all one really sees is a *white patch* going away. 1957 Jaeger *N. Amer. Deserts* 216, *Antelope Ground Squirrel,* or *Desert "Chipmunk." Ammospermophilus leucurus.*

antelope horn(s) n [From the curved upright pods] **chiefly KS, OK, TX**

=**spider milkweed** (here: *Asclepias asperula* and *A. viridis*).

1941 Jaeger *Wildflowers* 185 **Desert SW,** *Antelope Horns* . . . Eastern Mohave D.; to Ark. and Tex. The common name is derived from an appropriate Navaho name referring to the form of the green pods. 1948 Stevens *KS Wild Flowers* 184, Green Antelopehorn . . . Pods erect, with or without soft, sharp processes. *Ibid,* Spider Antelopehorn . . . Pods erect on recurved pedicels. 1951 *PADS* 15.19 **OK,** Antelope-horns. 1970 Correll *Plants TX* 1223, *Asclepias viridis* . . . Antelope-horn . . . Flowers large and rather showy.

antelope jackrabbit n **Desert SW**

A white-sided jackrabbit *(Lepus alleni).*

1909 Nelson *Rabbits N.A.* 117 *(DA),* Antelope Jack Rabbit . . is the handsomest . . of the North American hares. 1925 Bryan *Papago Country* 50 **swAZ,** The antelope jack rabbit *(Lepus alleni)* is one of the most interesting of the desert animals. 1928 Anthony *N. Amer. Mammals* 488, White-sided Jack Rabbits . . Antelope Jack Rabbit.—*Lepus alleni alleni.*

antelope sage See **antelope brush 2**

antelope squirrel See **antelope ground squirrel**

antem n Also sp *ant'em* [OED →1530; cf Pronc Intro 3.I.17] *relic*

An anthem.

1942 (1965) Parrish *Slave Songs* 5 **seGA,** The slave songs or "ant'ems," as they were sometimes called in Georgia before the Civil War and are called in the Bahamas to this day. 1965 *DARE* File **AR** [Newspaper item], Uncle Finner . . can't abide hearing a scritchy voiced woman a singing antems.

ante-over See **anti-over**

anteroom n Also *ante-shed*

=**storm shed.**

1969 *DARE* (Qu. D12) Inf **MO6,** Anteroom; **MI106,** Ante-shed.

ante up v Also *ante, anty up*

By ext from std sense:

1 To do one's share.

1927 *AmSp* 2.347 **cwWV,** Ante up . . , to do one's part or share. "I'm not afraid but that he'll ante up." 1969 *DARE* (Qu. JJ26, *If somebody has been doing poor work or not enough, the boss might say, "If he wants to keep his job he'd better _____."*) Inf **CA138,** Ante; **VA65,** Ante up.

2 In marble play:

a See quots.

1942 Berrey–Van den Bark *Amer. Slang* 665.4, *Ante up* . . to put marbles in a ring as a stake. 1955 *PADS* 23.11 **cwTN,** To ante up. To place the preliminary wager in a marble game of chance.

b as exclam: Let's begin!

1955 *PADS* 23.11 **cwTN,** Ante up. *Heard.* 1958 *PADS* 29.29 **WV,** *Ante up* . . . A call to start playing marbles.

3 To hurry up.

1917 *DN* 4.387 **neOH,** Anty up.

‡**4** To submit.

1969 *DARE* (Qu. JJ25, *To show somebody that you're the boss: "He thought he could take the place over, but I made him _____."*) Inf **CA135,** Ante.

ant heap n [From its shape] **NEng**

An abscess, carbuncle.

1943 *LANE* Map 512, **cMA,** ['æntˌhɹip] is a carbuncle; **cnMA,** ['aˑntˌhip], with several openings. 1966 *DARE* (Qu. BB33b) Inf **MA6,** Ant heap.

Anthony-over n, exclam [Prob orig a spelling var only for **Antony-over**, there being no clear evidence of early pronc [θ] for *th;* now a sp-pronc] **chiefly C Atl, N Midl**
=**Antony-over.**

1883 Eggleston *Hoosier Schoolboy* 41 **IN,** Let Jack play two-hole cat or Anthony-over with the little fellows. **1904** *DN* 2.394. **1940** *Sun* (Baltimore MD) 10 Dec 10/5 *(Hench Coll.),* He let himself get kindergartened into such games as Anthony Over. By the way, we called it Ante Over. **1951** Johnson *Resp. to PADS 20* **DE.** **1965–70** *DARE* (Qu. EE22) Infs **GA68, MO34, NJ48, NY98,** 120, Anthony-over; **OH47, PA163,** Anthony-Anthony-over; (Qu. EE23a, . . *What do you call out when you throw the ball?*) Infs **NY120, OH47, PA163,** Anthony-Anthony-over; **NJ48, NY98,** Anthony-over.

‡**anthrash** n [Pronc var of *anthrax,* perh with folk-etym]
Anthrax.

1967 *DARE* (Qu. K28) Inf **LA8,** Anthrash [ænθræš].

anti See **anti-over** n, exclam

anti-by-godlin adv [Blend of **antigodlin** adv + *by god*] Cf **antisigodlin**
=**antigodlin.**

1968 *DARE* FW Addit **LA18,** *Anti-by-godlin*—angled, diagonal.

antic adj Also sp *antick*

1 Clownish, amusing. **chiefly S Midl**

1902 *DN* 2.228 **sIL,** 'He is antic,' instead of 'he is full of antics.' **1917** *DN* 4.407 **wNC,** He's as antic as a jaybird when he takes the notion. **1930** Shoemaker *1300 Words* 1 **cPA Mts** (as of c1900), *Antic*—Odd, full of tricks. **1944** *PADS* 2.17 **sAppalachians,** *Antic* . . . Given to fun, capers, pranks. "Old Lige is feeble, but he's plum' antic." **1974** Fink *Mountain Speech* 1 **wNC, eTN,** *Antic* . . joking, playful. "He was an antic sort of feller."

2 Frisky, lively, irrepressible.

1903 *DN* 2.305 **seMO,** Your horse is mighty antic this morning. **c1908** in 1974 *AmSp* 49.61 **seME** [In the writings of George Savary Wasson], *Antic* . . . Active, spry "He felt young and antic." **1931** *AmSp* 7.90 **eKY,** That's an antic calf. **1949** Hornsby *Lonesome Valley* 89 **KY,** "You're so antic," she said, "I reckon you're well enough to plow my late bean patch."

3 Irresponsible, ungovernable. **Ozarks**

1936 *AmSp* 11.314 **Ozarks,** *Antic* . . . Clownish, wild, irresponsible . . . At Fayetteville, Ark., it means *ungovernable.* **1953** Randolph *Down in Holler* 223 **Ozarks,** "Charley's gettin' too *antick* round them Burton gals" generally means only that he pinched the girls' legs, or something of the sort.

antic n Also sp *antick* [Cf *EDD*] **S Midl**
A clown, buffoon.

1895 *DN* 1.370 **eTN mts,** Ab Deel's a natchul (natural) antic. **1927** *DN* 5.472 **Ozarks,** *Antick.*

antic v
To fool around, play.

1976 Garber *Mountain-ese* 3, Jim ain't too serious, he likes to antic with the boys.

anti-come-back exclam Also *Andy~, Annie~, ante~* For addit varr see quots See also **auntie-broke-her-leg**
In the game of **Antony-over:** =**pigtail** exclam.

1950 *WELS (What do you shout if the ball does not go over the building, but comes back)* 2 Infs, **WI,** Ante-back; 1 Inf, Anti-back-again; 1 Inf, Annie-come-back; 1 Inf, Annie-came-back-again. **1965–70** *DARE* (Qu. EE23b) 21 Infs, **scattered,** Annie-come-back; **CA65, IL78, SC32, UT12,** Annie-back; **KY74, MD20, MO35, OK31,** Annie-over; **MO3,** Annie; **WY1,** Annie-comes-back; **TN1,** Annie-over-again; **IN49, MO5,** Andy-back; **IL14, MO37,** Andy-come-back; **IN39,** Andy-over-the-pigpen; **AZ8, CA105, IN14, MD38,** Anti-over; **CA2,** 201, **IL61,** Anti-back; **KS13, MI61, WI52,** Anti-come-back; **AZ11,** Anti-came-back; **NY186,** Anti-come-down; **CO21,** Anti-come-over; **SC19,** Anti-gone-back; **MI78,** Anti-i-over-again; **CA209,** Anti-over, all-in-free.

antifogmatic(k) n [Pseudo-medical] *arch*
Any alcoholic drink taken, usu in the mornings, supposedly to counteract the bad effects of fog or dampness.

1789 *Thomas' MA Spy or Worcester Gaz.* (MA) 12 Nov 4/2, Rum. Its great utility in preserving the planters from the effects of the damp and

unwholesome air of the morning, has given it the medical name of an *Antifogmatick.* **1832** *Fraser's Mag.* 5.518 **PA,** Why does not somebody write us a philosophical, philological, and peripatetical treatise on the art of drinking, as practised in America? — of the various degrees and kinds of drams, anti-fogmatics, gall-breakers, gum-ticklers. **1899** (1940) Douglas *I Rode with Stonewall* 269 **VA,** Upon the first invitation I reversed my decision not to take an "antifogmatic" so early in the morning . . . We took "morning bitters" with one, "an eye-opener" with another, a "pre-prandial" with another, and then an appetizer all together, and when breakfast was ready at daylight so were we. **1947** Adams *Banner* 172 **NY** (as of 1817–1847), That whimwhamsical fellow, Mr. Tim Baggo, was sipping his morning antifogmatic at the bar of the Farmer's Hotel in Geneva.

antigadlin See **antigodlin**

‡**antiganglin** adj [Var or alter of **antigoglin 1**]
Bent, out of shape.

1929 *AmSp* 4.204 **Ozarks,** Thet 'ar pore . . woman o' hisn was . . a-scrunchin' cheenches on th' punch'on 'ith a antiganglin noodle-hook [=a crude hand-held fish hook].

antigod(d)le v [Var of **antigogle** or back-formation < **antigodlin**]

1 To stagger.

1933 *AmSp* 8.1.47 **Ozarks,** *Antigoddle* . . . To pursue a zig-zag course. **1938** *AmSp* 13.4 **seAR,** Several decades ago the word was used as a verb . . in such sentences as 'He is anti-godlin' in that saloon.'

2 also *antigogle:* To walk sexily or flirtatiously; hence *antigodling, antigogling* vbl n.

1973 Allen *LAUM* 1.403 **MN, IA, SD, NE,** The action of a woman who enters a room with self-conscious body movements intended to attract attention . . . *antigodling* [reported by 9 Infs]; *antigogling* [reported by 7 Infs].

antigodlin adj, adv Also *annigodlin, antegoddlin', antigadlin* [Var of **antigoglin,** perh infl by folk-etym: see sense **1** quot 1944] **chiefly Sth, S Midl, West** *somewhat old-fash* For varr see *DS* **KK70, MM13, 14, 15** See also **antigod(d)le, antisigodlin**

1 Of an object: lopsided, askew, aslant, out of line.

1917 *DN* 4.417 **wNC,** *Antigodlin', antigadlin'.* **1944** *PADS* 2.17 **sAppalachians,** *Antigodlin, antigoglin, antisigodlin* ['æntɪ͵gɑdlɪn, -gɑg-, -saɪ-] . . . Out of plumb or square, slanting. *Ibid* 53 **MO,** *Anti-godlin* . . Not parallel to something having well-established lines. My grandfather explained the term by saying it referred to the idea of the "four corners of the earth" as created by God; hence anyone who laid the foundation of a new building should make it "square with the world"; otherwise it would be *anti-godlin*—against the wish or example of God. **1949** *PADS* 11.17 **CO.** **1950** *PADS* 14.12 **SC,** *Antigodlin* . . . Awry, askew, irregular. "Your skirt is all antigodlin" (hangs unevenly). Variants are *Sarahgodlin, Sallygodlin,* etc. **1952** Brown *NC Folkl.* 1.515 **wNC,** *Antigodlin* . . . Leaning, not parallel. **1965–70** *DARE* (Qu. KK70, . . *Out of proper shape: "That house is all _____."*) Infs **MT5, SC31, 34, 39,** Antigodlin; (Qu. MM13, *The table was nice and straight until he came along and knocked it _____.*) 9 Infs, **Sth, S Midl, West,** Antigodlin; **GA84, LA28, OK1, TX4,** Annigodlin; (Qu. MM15, . . *At an angle: "He nailed the board on _____."*) Infs **GA72, TX36, VA5,** Antigodlin. **1967** *DARE* File **cwAL,** Antigodlin—out-of-plumb, skeewhoned, cut on the bias, whampus-jawed.

2 Cater-cornered, diagonal(ly), at an angle. See also **antiwalkus**

1905 *DN* 3.69 **nwAR,** *Antigodlin, antigoglin* . . Diagonally. 'We'll have to go across antigodlin.' Common. **1940** *Sun* (Baltimore MD) 21 Sept 10/7 *(Hench Coll.),* I have heard a farmer complain of a plow hand who got drunk, "Why, he couldn't plow a straight furrow; he went antegoddlin' across the field!" The word is not quite synonymous with cater-cornered, nor is it diagonal an exact equivalent; it means, rather, off the true line that should be followed. **1958** McCulloch *Woods Words* 3 **Pacific NW,** *Antigodlin'*—Same as catty-corner; also used to mean any wandering from a straight path. **1962** Atwood *Vocab. TX* 94, Many other words of unknown distribution in the Eastern States are common in all or most of Texas; . . many of them are missing from southern Louisiana. Some of these are . . *antigodlin. Ibid.* 116, Probably the main reason for the decline [among younger speakers] of . . *antigodlin* . . is that they are not sanctioned by dictionaries. **1965–70** *DARE* (Qu. MM14, . . *"The drugstore is _____ the gas station."*) Infs **AR31, CA208, IL96, NC33, OK51, TX18,** Antigodlin; **LA28, MS20,** Antigodlin across from; **OK6,**

Antigodlin across; **OK**1, Annigodlin. **1968** Adams *Western Words*, *Anti-godlin* The cowboy's description of diagonal or roundabout movement. **1970** Tarpley *Blinky* 272 neTX, *To go from one corner of a field to another is to walk . . anti-godlin* [by 19.5% of Infs]. *Ibid* 273, The response heard most frequently among the least educated and the older informants outside the city is *anti-godlin.*

antigogglin(g) See **antigoglin**

antigoggly adv [Var of **antigoglin**]
1967 *DARE* (Qu. MM13, *That table was nice and straight until he came along and knocked it_____*) Inf **SC**32, Antigoggly.

antigogle v [Prob back-formation < **antigoglin**] Cf **antigod(d)le**
1 To move in an erratic fashion.
1949 *PADS* 11.17 **CO**, Antigoglin around all over the road.
2 See **antigod(d)le 2.**

antigoglin adj, adv Also sp *annigoglin, antegogglin', antigogglin(g)* [*anti*- against, counter + *goggling* ppl adj < *goggle* to shake, tremble *(EDD, SND)*] **Sth, S Midl, West** *somewhat old-fash* Now generally replaced by **antigodlin** For addit varr see **antiganglin, antisigodlin**, *DS* KK70, MM13, 14, 15 and headwords. See also **agog, antigogle**
1 Askew, out of plumb; see quots.
1930 *VA Qrly. Rev.* 6.249 sAppalachians, He may affirm . . that . . the line of his barn roof is . . ante-gogglin'. **1944** *PADS* 2.17 sAppalachians, *Antigoglin* . . ['ænti,gɑglɪn] . . . Out of plumb or square, slanting. **1949** *PADS* 11.17 **CO**, *Antigoglin* [ˌænti'gɑglɪn] . . . In a roundabout way, crooked, out of line, confused, out of order, tilted, crosswise. Going every which way. **1967–70** *DARE* (Qu. MM13, *The table was nice and straight until he came and knocked it_____*) Infs **SC**32, **TX**1, 3, 5, 12, Antigoglin; **TX**79, Annigoglin [ˌæni'gɑglən]. **1972** *NYT Article Letters* KY, *Antigoglin* was used to describe a leaning pole or delapidated [sic] building.
2 Slantwise, diagonal(ly). See also **goglin**
1905 *DN* 3.69 nwAR, *Antigodlin, antigoglin* . . . Diagonally. 'We'll have to go across antigoglin.' Common. **1938** *AmSp* 13.4 seAR, *Antigoggling* . . . Still further deterioration from its common meaning of working against God may be seen in the usual use of the word in southeast Arkansas as an adjective meaning located at an angle. For example, 'That cotton-field is certainly anti-gogglin'.' **1950** *Western Folkl.* 9.115 nwOR [Among loggers], *Antigoglin.* Crooked or out of line. **1970** Tarpley *Blinky* 273 neTX, *Anti-goglin* is heard less frequently [than *anti-godlin*], with its greatest occurrence in the city. **c1970** *Halpert Coll.* wKY, Antigogglin = cattycornered, diagonal or leaning diagonally. "The house sits sort of antigogglin' from the road." "We walked antigogglin' from the highway to the pond."

antigoslin adj, adv Also *antigozlin* [Varr of **antigodlin**]
=**antigodlin 1.**
1915 *DN* 4.224 wTX, "The news knocked me all anti-goslin." "Your hat is on antigoslin." **1945** *PADS* 3.9 KY, [ænti'gɑzlɪn] is the form heard here. **1967** *DARE* (Qu. MM15) Inf **WA**30, Antigozlin.

anti-i-over n, exclam Also *Andy-i-over, Annie-i-over, anti-high-over*, folk-etym-sp *aunty-i-over* **chiefly wGt Lakes, Upper MW, West** See Map
=**Antony-over.**
A As noun.
1940 *Sun* (Baltimore MD) 26 Nov 8/3 *(Hench Coll.)*, Robinson gives several variants of the anti-over game, such as Aunty-I-Over and Anthony-Over. **1950** *WELS (Game in which you throw a ball over a low building)* 5 Infs, WI, Anti-i-over; 2 Infs, Anti-high-over; 1 Inf, Anti-anti-high-over; 1 Inf, Andy-Andy-i-over; 2 Infs, Annie(-Annie-Annie)-i-over. **1965–70** *DARE* (Qu. EE22) 97 Infs, **chiefly wGt Lakes, Upper MW, West,** Anti-i-over; **MI**14, 45, **MN**2, 6, 15, **WI**52, Anti-anti-i-over; **MI**75, **UT**3, Annie-i-over; **WI**64, Annie-Annie-i-over. **1970** *DARE* Tape **MI**115, Andy-i-over . . . throw a ball over the schoolhouse. **1980** *DARE* File **WA** (as of 1930s), Anti-i-over.
B As exclamation.
1945 Boyd *Hdbk. Games* 35, Calling "Ante-ante-i-over," an A player throws the ball over the house. **1950** *WELS (What do you shout when you throw the ball?)* 5 Infs, WI, Anti-i-over; 1 Inf, Anti-anti-i-over; 1 Inf, Anti-anti-aye-over; 1 Inf, Anti-high-over; 2 Infs, Andy (-Andy)-i-over; 1 Inf, Annie-Annie-Annie-i-over. **1965–70** *DARE* (Qu. EE23a) 62 Infs, **chiefly wGt Lakes, Upper MW, West,** Anti-i-over; 15 Infs, **chiefly nMI,**

nWI, nMN, Anti-anti-i-over; **MN**28, Anti-i-over-the-cowshed; **UT**10, Anti-i-over, my ball's coming over; **IL**9, Andy-i-over; **MI**75, 114, **OH**23, **UT**3, Annie-i-over; **WI**64, Annie-Annie-i-over.

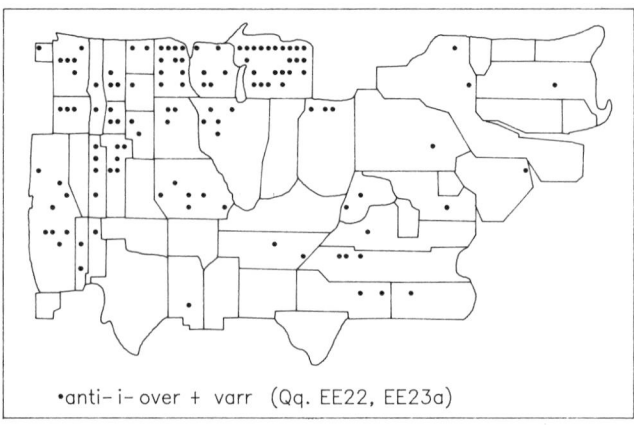

•anti-i-over + varr (Qq. EE22, EE23a)

antimire See **antymire**

an ting See **and thing**

anti-over n, exclam Also simplex *anti*, and spp *ante-over, ant-i-over, anty-over, aunty-over;* for addit varr see quots [Reduced from **Antony-over**] **widespread, but least freq NEast, Gulf States** *now the most common name for the game*
=**Antony-over.**
1895 *DN* 1.395 nIL, IA, KS, MI, MN, NJ, NY, Anty-over. **1897** *KS Univ. Qrly.* 6.85 neKS, Ante over . . children's game, which consists of two players or sides standing on either side of a building and one tossing a ball to the other, at the same time shouting "ante over." **1905** *DN* 3.60 NE, Anti-over. **1905** *DN* 3.69 nwAR, Anty over. **1937** in *1972 Amer. Slave* 2.241 SC. **1940** Marran *Games Outdoors* 97 **MO**, Aunty over. **1946** *PADS* 6.4 VA, NC, Anty over. **1950** *PADS* 14.11 SC, Anti-over. **1950** *WELS (Game in which you throw a ball over a low building to a player or players on the other side)* 18 Infs, **throughout WI,** Anti-over; 11 Infs, Anti-anti-over; *(What do you shout when you throw the ball?)* 11 Infs, **throughout WI,** Anti-anti-over; 10 Infs, Anti-over; 1 Inf, Anti-i-over, or just anti. **1965–70** *DARE* (Qu. EE22) 162 Infs, **widespread, but least freq NEast, Gulf States,** Anti-over; 20 Infs, **chiefly Inland Nth,** Anti-anti-over; **AL**3, Ant-i-over; **CO**21, Anti-come-over; **IN**81, **NC**26, Anti-over-the-house(top); (Qu. EE23a) 114 Infs, **widespread, but least freq NEast, Gulf States,** Anti-over; 23 Infs, **chiefly Inland Nth,** Anti-anti-over; 23 Infs, **scattered but least freq NEast, Sth,** Anti; **NY**75, Anti-Annie-over; **OR**10, Annie-anti-over; **CO**21, Anti-come-over. **1970** *DARE* Tape **KY**75, They'd holler "anti-over" and they'd throw the ball over the house an' if they caught it on the other side then they would come around the house an' try to hit someone with the ball an' when they hit 'im why he would be on their side.

anti-over v phr
1968 *DARE* Tape **MD**12, The one who caught it would have to be the one to anti-over . . . He'd have to throw the ball over.

antiques and horribles n pl [Humorous var of *ancients and honorables*] **NEng** *old-fash* Cf **fantastic, horribles**
See quot 1907.
1907 *DN* 3.180 seNH, *Antiques and horribles* . . . Masked men, dressed in fantastic or ragged clothing, who parade the streets on the Fourth of July. This designation is usually shortened in colloquial language to *horribles.* "The newspaper says there will be *antiques and horribles* in the Fourth of July parade." Formed after the analogy of "Ancients and Honorables," *i.e.,* the Ancient and Honorable Artillery of Boston. **1916** *DN* 4.305 MA, *Antiques and horribles* . . Used in Northampton, Mass., c. 1860. **1940** *AmSp* 15.330 **Boston MA**, On such occasions of state as called for a parade of the . . 'Ancients and Honorables' . . the variegated display of diverse uniforms on unathletic figures looked comic . . . So a time came when it was customary in country villages to burlesque it by a Fourth-of-July parade of 'Antique Horribles' or 'Antiques and Horribles' . . . Nowadays 'Antique' is omitted from the title.

antisigodlin adj Also *antisigogglin* [Varr of **antigodlin, antigoglin**] Cf **si-antigodlin**
=**antigodlin 1.**

1931 *PMLA* 46.1322 **sAppalachians**, *Antisigodlin.* **1941** *AmSp* 16.21 **swIN**, *Anti-si-gogglin.* Crooked, out of proportion. **1944** *PADS* 2.17 **sAppalachians**, *Antisigodlin . . .* Out of plumb or square, slanting.

‡**anti-snakebite** n
=**snakebite remedy.**
    1966 *DARE* (Qu. DD21a, . . *Any kind of liquor*) Inf **WA**11, Anti-snake-bite.

‡**anti-walkus** adv Cf **anti-whampus**
=**antigodlin 2.**
    1970 Tarpley *Blinky* 272 **neTX**, *To go from one corner of a field to another is to walk . .* anti-walkus [in list of "other responses"].

‡**anti-whampus** adj [Blend of **antigodlin** + **catawampus** adj] Cf **anti-walkus, cattygodlin**
Askew; lopsided.
    1967 *DARE* (Qu. KK70) Inf **TX**12, [ˌæntɪˈhwɑmpəs].

ant killers n pl Also *ants-mashers* joc
The feet, esp very large feet.
    1845 in 1930 Meine *Tall Tales* 57 **TN**, Well, let hir keep hir tail clar of my ant killers! **1966** *DARE* (Qu. X38), Inf **SC**26, Ants-mashers.

Antony-over n, exclam Also pronc-spp *Antney-over, Antny-over, atni-over* and simplexes *Antony, Antny* [Prob of Scots origin though earliest quot is US: cf *EDD, SND*] **chiefly sAppalachians** See Map Note: *Antony-over* is a now uncommon form for the game most commonly called **anti-over.** The shouts accompanying this game are generally the same as its name, and they share the same regional distributions. For common forms and varr of both the game and the shouts, see **Andy-over, Annie-over, anti-i-over, anti-over;** for less freq varr see also **Andrew-over, ankety-over,** and *DS* EE22, 23a.

A As noun.
A children's game in which a ball is thrown over a building to a player or players on the other side. The name of the game is usually shouted as the ball is thrown.
    1872 Schele de Vere *Americanisms* 579, *Antony Over,* a game of ball played by two parties of boys, on opposite sides of a schoolhouse, over which the ball is thrown. Used in Pennsylvania. *Antony* is merely a proper name, . . and *Over* requires no explanation. **a1883** (1911) Bagby *VA Gentleman* 15, You don't know how . . to play "Ant'ny over." **1897** *KS Univ. Qrly.* 6.85, *Ante over* or *ant'ny over:* name of a children's game. **1899** (1912) Green *VA Folk-Speech* 67, *Antony over . . .* A game of ball played by two parties of boys on opposite sides of a house, over which the ball is thrown. **1899** (1906) Ade *Doc' Horne* 118 **Chicago IL**, Why, he and the alligator stood out from the wall and began to play 'ant'ny over' with my eye. **1908** Fox *Lonesome Pine* 168 **KY**, The games were new to June, and often Hale would stroll up to the school-house to watch them — Prisoner's Base, Skipping the Rope, Antny Over. **1915** *DN* 4.180 **swVA**. **1952** Brown *NC Folkl.* 1.36, 'Ant'ny Over' . . . game played at several schools in Avery county during the fall of 1917. **1965–70** *DARE* (Qu. EE22) 23 Infs, **chiefly sAppalachians**, Antny-over; **NC**17, 23, Antony-over; **NC**22, Antony; **KY**7, Atni-over. **1969** *DARE* Tape **KY**41, Antny-over — We get on one side with something, usually a yarn ball . . with a little somethin' in the middle [that] would make it bounce and we'd throw it over and when we'd get ready to throw, we'd holler "Antny," the one that had the ball. The other one on the other side'd say "over," and they'd throw the ball over . . . If we caught the ball, then we had a right to run around to the other side . . and . . touch them [and] they had to come to our side.

B As exclamation.
1 In the game of **Antony-over:** the phrase called out when the ball is thrown over the building.
    1946 *PADS* 6.4 **VA, NC**, *Antney over . .* The full expression: "Antney, antney, and over she goes." . . Common among teen-age children. **1952** Brown *NC Folkl.* 1.36 **NC** (as of 1917), A member of the group having the ball calls, "Ant'ny!" someone on the other side then cries, "Over!" The first speaker calls out, "Over she comes!" and throws the ball over the roof. **1965–70** *DARE* (Qu. EE23a) 14 Infs, **chiefly S Midl**, Antny-over; **WV**1, 5, 13, Antny; **NC**22, Antony; **GA**72, "Antny." The other side hollers "Over!"; **GA**77, "Antny." The fellow on the other side says "Over!"; **NC**17, 22, Antony-over. **1966** Wilson *Coll.* **csKY**, [The] thrower shouted "Ant'ny," receiver shouted "over," then threw it [=the ball] back and shouted "Here she comes" or "Here comes." **1969**

DARE Tape **KY**41, When we'd get ready to throw, we'd holler "Antny!" . . The other one on the other side'd say "over," and they'd throw the ball.
2 also *Antny back:* =**pigtail** exclam.
    1967 *DARE* (Qu. EE23b, . . *If you fail to get the ball over the building and it rolls back, what do you call out*) Inf **GA**72, Antny; **GA**77, Antny-back.

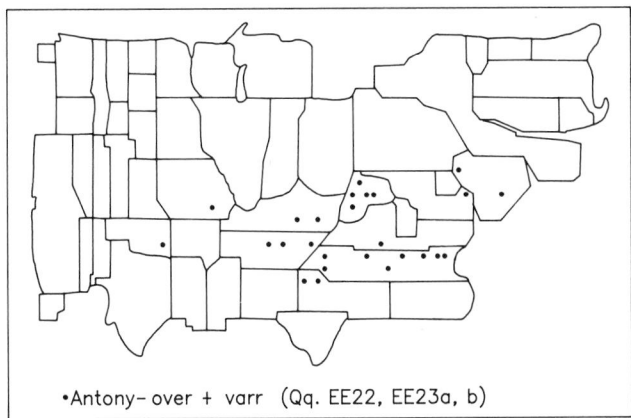

•Antony-over + varr (Qq. EE22, EE23a, b)

ant rice n *?obs*
A **needlegrass 2.**
    1879 McCook *Nat. Hist. Ag. Ant* 34 **TX**, Others were partially covered with a tall, yellowish grass, popularly known as the "needlegrass" . . . This is probably the "ant-rice" . . ; at all events it is an *Aristida*, the plants gathered being identified . . as *A. oligantha*, but some of the seeds as probably *A. stricta*. **1879** Avebury *Scientific Lectures* 109, A Texan ant . . is also a harvesting species, storing up especially the grains of *Aristida oligantha*, the so called "ant-rice." **1885** McCook *Tenants Old Farm* 341 *(DA)*, A sort of grass known as ant-rice, or needle grass.

ant's cow See **ant cow**

antses n pl [Double pl: see **-es 2**] **Sth**
Ants.
    1931 *Scribner's Mag.* 448 **FL**, The antses is bad. I cain't keep the antses out o' Mart's breakfast. **1937** in 1977 *Amer. Slave Suppl. 1* 20 **AL**, She wuz conjured and flying antses come out de pores of her skin. **1942** Rawlings *Cross Creek* 64 **nFL**, Antses in Tim's breakfast. **1966** *DARE* (Qu. R17) Inf **GA**16, Black antses [æntzəz].

ants-mashers See **ant killers**

antsy adj Also earlier sp *ancey* [*ants,* in ref to their constant activity + *-y;* the much later phr *have ants in one's pants,* fidget anxiously, is prob an elaboration of *antsy*] **chiefly Nth**
1 Restless, eager, anxious, annoyed.
    1838 Kemper *Papers* 20G1 **MO**, Minard's talking & Peake's scribbling were enough to drive anyone ancey. **1950** *WELS* (*Eager or anxious:* "He was really _____ to know.") 1 Inf, **cWI**, Antsy — by teenagers; (*When somebody is very eager to do something:* "He was awfully _____ to go.") 2 Infs, **cs, cwWI**, Antsy. **1958** McCulloch *Woods Words* 3 **Pacific NW**, *Antsy* — The condition of having ants in the pants, being over-anxious to get going. **1965–70** *DARE* (Qu. A21, *When someone is in too much of a hurry you might say,* "Now just slow down! Don't _____.") Infs **IL**50, **NY**137, Be so antsy; **WI**58, Get antsy; (Qu. GG11, *To be quite anxious about something, for example, waiting for a letter:* "The letter hasn't come and he's _____.") Infs **CO**21, **IA**46, **MI**26, **MN**35, **NY**42, **WA**33, Antsy; (Qu. GG17, . . "She has been so lonely — She was really _____ (to see him)") Inf **KS**8, Antsy; (Qu. GG2, . . "So many things were going on at the same time that he got completely _____.") Inf **MN**35, Antsy. **1982** *Capital Times* (Madison WI) 12 Feb 29/2, Officials in Wisconsin, however, still can't say when distribution will begin here . . . "People are kind of getting antsy here," said Wilmer Dahl, statewide coordinator of the program.
2 See quot.
    1968–69 *DARE* (Qu. AA4b, *And what expressions about a woman who is very eager to get married:* "She's _____.") Infs **IL**97, **KS**10, Antsy.
‡**3** Lively, spry.
    1973 Allen *LAUM* 1.352 **IA**, Quite lively . . antsy.

anttic n

An attic.

1905 *DN* 3.58 **eNE,** Intrusive *n,* the "nasal infix," occurs in . . *a(n)ttic* . . but it is rare.

‡anty-iron n, usu pl Var of **Andy-iron** Cf *DS* D32

c1970 Pederson *Dial. Survey Rural GA* **seGA,** Anty irons.

antymire n |'ænti'maɪɚ| Also sp *antimire, antymar, antypissmire* [Euphem blend of *ant* + **pismire**] **chiefly N Atl, C Atl, sAppalachians**

An ant.

1899 Bergen *Animal Lore* 62 **cME, OH,** Anty-mire, ants. **1903** *DN* 2.295 **Cape Cod MA** (as of 1850s), *Antimire* . . from *ant* and *pismire.* **1930s** in **1944** *ADD* **eWV,** Antymire. Also *antypissmire.* **1931** *PMLA* 46.1321 **sAppalachians,** Them antymars (pissmires), the little hatefuls. **1942** Warnick *Garrett Co. MD* (as of 1900–1918) **wMD.** **1950** *WELS* 1 Inf, **cwWI,** Antimire. **1967** *DARE* (Qu. R18) Inf **NJ2,** [A] red ant = antymire ['ænti'maɪɚ].

anty-over See **anti-over**

anty up See **ante up**

anud(d)er, anurr(er), anuther See **another**

anvil n, also attrib **esp TX**

A type of primitive firework: see quots.

1939 FWP *Guide NE* 234, The anvil salute consisted of ramming the hole in the top of the anvil with powder, inserting a fuse, turning the anvil upside down and lighting the fuse. **1967–70** *DARE* (Qu. FF14) Inf **TX35,** Anvils—pour powder on an anvil and light it; (Qu. FF15) Inf **TX91,** Shooting an anvil—powder was exploded in a hole in an anvil. Done at Christmas; (Qu. FF28) Inf **TX1,** Anvil.

anvil v

Of a galloping horse: to create sparks by striking the shoes of the hind feet against those of the forefeet.

1968 Adams *Western Words.*

anvil dust n

Iron filings: occas used as an ingredient in folk-medications and conjure preparations: see quots.

1947 (1964) Randolph *Ozark Superstitions* 105 **swMO, nwAR,** Some yarb doctors fortify their choctaw-root with wild-cherry bark and "anvil dust," whatever that may be. **1970** Hyatt *Hoodoo* 521 **Memphis TN,** Git chew some lodestone an' some of dis *anvil dust* an' a little *sugah* in there, an' yo' jis' sew that up together in dat little *red cloth* . . . *Dat anvil dust is jis' lak lodestone. Well, it'll draw dem craps an' make it fall on 'leben or any point dey's trying tuh git.*

anvil head n [From its shape; cf *OEDS* anvil, anvil cloud 1894 →]

The anvil-shaped top of a cumulo-nimbus cloud. Cf **thunderhead**

1967 *DARE* (Qu. B11, . . *Other kinds of clouds*) Inf **OH20,** Anvil head.

anxious adj Usu |'æŋ(k)šəs|; rarely |'æŋkɪš| Pronc-spp *anchus, ankish*

A Forms.

1851 in **1956** Eliason *Tarheel Talk* 306 **NC,** Anchus. **1966** *DARE* (Qu. AA4a, . . *A man who is very eager to get married*) Inf **SC10,** ['æŋkɪš fə mærɪ] Ankish for [to] marry. [Gullah speaker.]

B Sense.

Wonderful, excellent. *among Black speakers*

1958 Hughes–Bontemps *Negro Folkl.* 479 **NYC** [Black], Anxious— Wonderful, excellent. **1970** Major *Afro-Amer. Slang* 20, Anxious: (1940's) a fine state of affairs; anything good.

anxious bench n Also ~*seat* [*anxious* troubled, worried + *bench*] **chiefly N Atl, Sth, S Midl** Cf **amen corner 2, mourners' bench, trailers' row**

1 At revival meetings or in church, a seat in the front for people concerned about their spiritual well-being. Also fig.

1832 Trollope *Domestic Manners* 79 **Sth,** As the poor creatures approached the rail their sobs and groans became audible. They seated themselves on the 'anxious benches'; the hymn ceased, and two or three priests walked down from the tribune. **1839** Marryat *Diary* 1.180 **Cincinnati OH,** In front of the pulpit there was a space railed off, and

strewed with straw, which I was told was the *Anxious seat,* and on which sat those who were touched by their consciences or the discourse of the preacher. **1894** *DN* 1.327 **NJ,** *Anxious seat, anxious bench:* the seat or bench near the altar where persons concerned for their spiritual welfare may sit during revivals. Preserved by the Methodist and Baptist communities . . . Fast falling out of use. [Author: Common in N.E. in figurative sense.] **1905** *DN* 3.2 **cCT,** *Anxious seat* . . . Seats occupied by 'seekers' at a revival. **1949** *PADS* 11.3 **wTX.** **c1960** Wilson *Coll.* **csKY,** *Anxious seat* . . . Mourners' bench at a protracted meeting. "Sammy is sitting in the anxious seat now." **1960** Bailey *Resp. to PADS 20* **KS,** [Anxious seats] were not, and . . are not, much in use. A person who used them would feel on the defensive. **1966–70** *DARE* (Qu. CC5) Infs **AZ2, SC24, VA46,** Anxious seat.

2 usu in phr *(sitting) on the anxious bench:* In a state of anxiety or uneasiness. Cf **anxious seater**

1839 *Knickerbocker* 13.345, He did look as if he had been on 'the anxious seat,' as he used to say, when things puzzled him. **1899** (1912) Green *VA Folk-Speech,* Anxious bench . . . "He has long been on the anxious bench." Uncertainty. **1904** *DN* 2.423 **Cape Cod MA,** Anxious seat . . A situation of suspense or expectancy. **1907** *DN* 3.205 **nwAR.** **1908** *DN* 3.287 **eAL, wGA,** Anxious bench . . . State of uneasiness . . . Also *anxious seat. Ibid* 354, His gal keeps him on the anxious bench half the time. **1950** *WELS* (Expressions about a woman who is very anxious to get married) 1 Inf, **cWI,** On the anxious seat. **1965–70** *DARE* (Qu. GG11, . . *"The letter hasn't come and he's _____."*) Infs **GA15, NJ20, NY206, PA42, SC2, TX65, WI13,** On the anxious bench; **AL6, MI44, NY42, PA223,** On the anxious seat; **SC5,** Sitting on the anxious bench; (Qu. AA4, . . *A man who is very eager to get married:* "He's _____.") Inf **CT16,** On the anxious bench. [11 of 13 Infs are old]

anxioused up ppl phr

Made anxious, excited.

1905 *DN* 3.69 **nwAR,** "He was right smartly anxioused up." Rare.

anxious seat See **anxious bench**

anxious seater n

One who is on the **anxious bench 2.**

1943 *Sun* (Baltimore MD) 5 Oct 13/3 (Hench *Coll.*), Class C members [of Brushoff Clubs] and "anxious seaters" are last in line and get no priorities whatever, without further proof . . . They are not eligible to attend any sympathy sessions—yet.

any pron, adj, adv Usu |'eni|, also |'ini, ini| Pronc-sp *eeny;* eye-dial *enny,* hence also *ennyhow, ennywhar,* etc.

A Forms.

1815 Humphreys *Yankey in England* 105 **NEng,** Enny, any. *Ennywheres,* any where. **1851** Hooper *Widow Rugby's Husband* 47 **AL,** Ef thar's enny strength in cussin', I'll make 'em ashamed! **1884** Murfree *TN Mts.* 249 **TN,** It's the onluckiest place ennywhar nigh about . . . My cow . . hed strayed off through not hevin' enny calf ter our house. **1908** *DN* 3.287 **eAL, wGA,** Any . . Pronounced [ɪnɪ]. **1911** *DN* 3.543 **NE,** Eeny . . Occasional pronunciation of *any.* **1915** *DN* 4.177 **Scott Co VA,** Any, pronounced . . [ɪnɪ]. **1922** Gonzales *Black Border* 86 **sSC, GA coasts,** [Gullah] Well, ennyhow I git all wuh I shoot at. **1928** *AmSp* 3.402 **Ozarks,** In words like *any* and *many* the *a* sounds pretty much like short *i.* **1936** *AmSp* 11.147 **eTX,** At any rate is frequently ['tĩnɪ reɪt]. **1937** *AmSp* 12.287 **nwVA,** The [ɛ] sounds move upward towards [ɪ], in . . *any, many.*

B As pron.

All, everything.

1902 *DN* 2.228 **sIL,** *Any* . . . 'Put in leaves, rotten and any.' 'The ice broke and in I went, bucket and any.'

C As adj.

Every; hence also *anybody* everybody, etc. [See quot] **HI**

1972 Carr *Da Kine Talk* 121, "Anybody go church today!" (the Type II speaker's way of saying that the church was full of people). "Man, get any kind candy in dat box!" In both cases, *any* covers the semantic range of *every.* There is no distinction between *anybody* and *everybody* in the Hawaiian language . . . The failure of Hawaii's dialect to make this distinction has received reinforcement from the speech habits of many Asian immigrants.

‡any-bit n Cf *DS* K73

1968 *DARE* (Qu. K73, . . *The rump of a cooked chicken*) Inf **GA28,** The any-bit.

any God's amount, any God's immense, any God's quantity
See **God's amount, any**

‡any-go-flum-bums n pl [Fanciful formation]
Diarrhea.
   1969 *DARE* (Qu. BB19) Inf **MO**19, The any-go-flum-bums.

any how you (can) fix it See **fix it, any how you (can)**

anymore adv Also *any more* [*EDD, OEDS,* 1898 → with earliest ex from nIreland, but see also 1946 *AmSp* 21.301–2; addit discussion and bibliography in 1959 *AmSp* 34.157, 1975 *AmSp* 50.305–310] **scattered, but least freq NEng** (in use by speakers of all educ levels: see quot 1965–70) See Map
In positive constructions: nowadays, now.
   1859 [see **all anymore**]. **1931** *AmSp* 6.460 **WV**, People used to shop a lot in the morning, but any more the crowd comes in about three o'clock . . . Any more the high school pupils are such babies nobody goes to their entertainments . . . My customers have to see me by appointment any more. **1931** *AmSp* 7.19 **swPA**. **1932** *AmSp* 7.233, 235, 236 **MI, IL, WV**. **1935** *AmSp* 10.160 **NY**. **1939** *AmSp* 14.156, 304 **WV, SC**. **1943** *AmSp* 18.141, 152 **NE, IL**. **1944** *AmSp* 19.39, 204 **Philadelphia PA, IN**. **1946** Stuart *Tales Plum Grove* 228 **KY**, Got so any more there isn't enough good timber for a board tree. **1949** *PADS* 11.17 **CO**. **1950** *PADS* 14.12 **SC**. **1959** *AmSp* 34.157 **IL**. **1965–70** *DARE* (Qu. A26, . . *"People used to walk a lot, but everybody drives a car _____."*) 110 Infs, **scattered, but least freq NEng**, Anymore; **TX**26, Anymore now; **IL**7, Anymores [Of all Infs responding to the question, 31% have grade-school or less educ, 38% hs, 31% coll; of those giving these responses, 45% have grade-school or less, 25% hs, 31% coll.]; (QR p108) Inf **IA**12, We all use night-crawlers anymore; (QR p77) Inf **NC**54, I meet so many people anymore; (QR p20) Inf **PA**70, Anymore it's the living room. **1966–69** *DARE* Tape **NC**29, Most of the work anymore is done by power; **IL**12, Of course, we have two or three coal mines around this part of the country anymore; **CA**145, That's the way I got it figured anymore; **FL**32, We put up quite a bit of hay here anymore. **1966–68** *DARE* FW Addits **GA**33, Anymore—in conversation very common for *nowadays;* **TN**17A, Used in conversation by country people, as in "He's hard of hearing anymore;" **neOK**, "We use a gas stove anymore." "My aunt makes hats all the time anymore." **1976** Wolfram–Christian *Appalachian Speech* 105, While speakers who come from regions where *anymore* is only used in negative contexts may find the positive *anymore* rather obtrusive, native speakers of varieties where positive *anymore* is current tend not to view it as a socially diagnostic linguistic feature. *Ibid* 106, While it has been noted . . that this form is used frequently in parts of "western Pennsylvania, Ohio, Indiana, and parts of Illinois, Kansas, Missouri, Utah and other western states, and is apparently spreading to other parts of the United States," it is apparent that its use in A[ppalachian] E[nglish] is fairly stable and has been for some time. **1980** *DARE* File **Madison WI**, Anymore we aren't following terms as precisely as we used to.

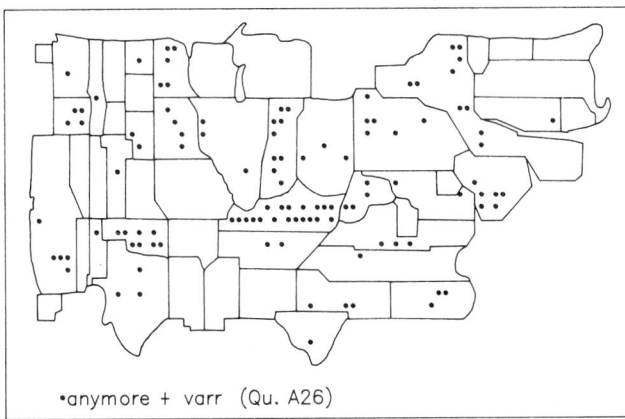
•anymore + varr (Qu. A26)

any much adj phr
Very much.
   1939 *Hall Coll.* **eTN**, Me and my brother went . . a-coon-huntin', but we never done any much good. *Ibid* **wNC**, We had to help them at home and we didn't look out to ever need any much education.

any old See **old**

‡anyothuhbody pron Pronc-sp for *any other body*
Anyone else.

   1946 in 1958 Brewer *Dog Ghosts* 53 **TX** [Black], He ship mo' cattle outen Palacios dan anyothuhbody 'roun' heah.

anyplace adv Also *anywhere*
Someplace, somewhere.
   1968–69 *DARE* (Qu. MM11, *When you're trying to find something— you don't know where it is—you might say, "I must have left it _____."*) Inf **PA**71, Anyplace; **MA**18, Anywhere.

anys exclam Also pronc-sp *ennies*
In marble play: =**anythings**.
   1958 *PADS* 29.29 **OK**, *Anys (ennies)* . . . A call which, if said before an opponent said *vents*, entitles the player to any (whence the name) of a number of advantages: he may "tee up the objective, remove an obstruction in the surface of the ground, fill in a depression, exercise roundance, etc." **1963** *KY Folkl. Rec.* 9.3.65 **eKY**, *(To ask for permission to clean path of shooter to marble being shot at)* Ennies [reported from three counties]; *(To ask for permission to move shooter to a better position)* Ennies [reported from one other county].

anything pron Usu |ˈɛniˌθɪŋ|, occas |ɛn(ə)–, ɪnɪ–; –θæŋ, –θɛŋ, –θɪŋk| See Pronc Intro 3.I.4.a, 3.I.6.d, 3.I.23 Pronc-sp *anythink*
Std senses, var forms.
   1884 Murfree *TN Mts.* 260, Anythink mought happen thar! **1891** *DN* 1.159 **Ithaca NY**, [ɛnθɪn] 'anything'. **1934** in 1944 *ADD* **VA**, [ɛnəθɪn]. **c1960** *Wilson Coll.* **csKY**, *Anything* . . is [pronounced] [ˈɛnɪˌθɛn] or [–θæn]. **1966** *DARE* File **Baltimore Co MD**, Anythink. **1968** *DARE* FW Addit **MD**20, People in Baltimore claimed that some Baltimoreans use [ɛnɪθɪŋk], but I never heard it there.

anything else pron phr
In emphatic negative constructions: see quot 1859.
   1859 (1968) Bartlett *Americanisms, Any thing else.* A hyperbolical phrase, denoting a strong affirmation, which has recently sprung up and become quite common, is given in the following quotation:—*Loco Foco.* Didn't Gen. Cass get mad at Hull's cowardice, and break his sword? *Whig.* He *didn't do any thing else.*—*Newspaper.* **1905** *DN* 3.2 **cCT**, 'He didn't do anything else,' meaning he did just that. **1931–33** *LANE* Worksheets **Boston MA**, I can't pronounce it anything else.

anythings exclam [**anything** + -*s* commonly used in marbles calls and other games] See also **anys, evers 1**
In marble play: see quots.
   1958 *PADS* 29.29 **WI**, *Anything(s)* . . . A call (the opposite of *nothings*) which, if said first, entitles the player to any of several advantages. **1963** *KY Folkl. Rec.* 9.3.63 **ceKY**, Demand for possession of all marbles knocked off squares or out of ring when a shot is taken . . . anythings.

anythink See **anything**

anyway adv Usu |ˈɛniˌweɪ| freq |ˈɪnɪ–, ɛnə–| See Pronc Intro 3.I.4.a
Std senses, var forms.
   1905 *DN* 3.103 **nwAR**, [ɛnəweɪ]. **1942** Hall *Smoky Mt. Speech* 19, Words . . in which [ɛ] is often raised to or toward [ɪ]: . . anyway. **1943** in 1944 *ADD* **WV**, I'll get [ɛnəwé]—2 pound o' that.

anyways adv [*anyway* + -*s* adv-forming suff]
1 To any degree at all. **now chiefly Sth, S Midl**
   1638 in 1898 Springfield MA *First Century* 1.164, It is ordered . . not to sell or any ways pass away any Cannoe . . untill it be five years old. **1842** Kirkland *Forest Life* 1.94 **West**, We can't make them any ways comfortable here. **1884** Jewett *Mate of Daylight* 193 **ME**, Not that I mean that they are any ways contented. **1916** *DN* 4.288 **sAppalachians**, Is he *any ways* hurt? **1928** Peterkin *Scarlet Sister Mary* 230 **SC**, Some women are silly like children, and get spoiled to death if you pet them or treat them anyways soft and easy. **1959** Lomax *Rainbow Sign* 111 **AL** [Black], But if she had talked anyways back, he would have hit her.

2 In any case, anyway. [*OED:* "dialect or illiterate."] **chiefly Sth, S Midl**
   1899 (1912) Green *VA Folk-Speech, Anyways* . . . In any case, at any rate. **1905** *DN* 3.57 **eNE**, The adverbial -*s* is added very commonly in the familiar *somewheres, anywheres, leastways, anyways,* etc. **1905** *DN* 3.287 **eAL, wGA**. **1915** *DN* 4.15 **VA**. **1927** *AmSp* 3.7 **Ozarks**, Another common error is the addition of a terminal *s* sound to such adverbs as *somewhere, anywhere, anyway.* **1936** *AmSp* 11.352 **eTX**, *Anyway* and *noway,* . . appear in the speech of the uneducated both with and without the -*s* ending . . . Trained speakers usually omit the -*s* from all these

words. **1953** Brewer *Word Brazos* 10 **eTX** [Black], Wid dey las' load dat Friday, what was de thirteenth of de mont'—dat's a bad luck day, you know—anyways, dey spy sump'n or 'nothuh swimmin' to'a'ds 'em from de Gulf. **1954** *Harder Coll.* **cwTN**, But we had a nice ride anyways. **c1960** *Wilson Coll.* **csKY**. **1968** *DARE* (Qu. U40, *Somebody who is temporarily out of money: you might say "At the moment he's _____."*) Inf **VT8**, Broke—badly bent, anyways [laughter].

3 At any time. [Perh infl by **anywheres**]
1928 *Ruppenthal Coll.* **KS**, If you get to Taos anyways soon, go and see the ruins. **1965** *DARE* Tape **FL22**, Anyways from May until October.

anywhere See **anyplace**

anywheres adv [*anywhere* + *-s* adv-forming suff]
Anywhere.
1775 in 1877 *Essex Inst. Coll.* 13.171, Your house will be as safe as anywheres to put the Candles in. **1815** Humphreys *Yankey in England* 105 [Glossary], Enny-wheres, any where. **1856** *Knickerbocker* 47.45 **sNJ**, Have you seen him anywheres hereabout? **1891** (1967) Freeman *New Engl. Nun* 145, I can't keep it anywheres. **1891** *DN* 1.168 **cnNY**, [ɛnɪwɔrz]. **1905** *DN* 3.57 **eNE**. **1907** *DN* 3.180 **seNH**. **1908** *DN* 3.287 **eAL, wGA**. **1915** *DN* 4.178 **swVA**. **1926** Kephart *Highlanders* 122 **sAppalachians**, The law wunt let us have liquor shipped to us from anywhars in the State. **1927** [see **anyways 2**]. **1936** *AmSp* 11.352 **eTX**. **1981** *DARE* File **Madison WI**, I couldn't find it anywheres.

aole adv |aˀole, aˀɑle| Pronc-sp *aale* [Haw] **HI**
No, not.
1833 in 1934 Frear *Lowell & Abigail* 78 **HI**, I said to the woman "do you know how to make a bed?" "Aole—(no)." **1938** Reinecke *Hawaiian Loanwords*, Aole [aˈole], often corrupted to *aale* [aˈɑle] . . . Not; not at all . . . No. **1951** *AmSp* 26.22 **HI**, Other common Hawaiian words are *ae* (yes) and *aole* (no). **1955** Day *HI People* 310 [Glossary], Aole: no. **1972** Carr *Da Kine Talk* 86, Hawaiian words commonly heard in Hawaii's English . . . 'a'ole. No, not.

a-one-side See **a** prep[1] **1b**

aout See **out**

A.P. See **apee**

apache n
A type of men's haircut: =**mohawk**.
1950 *WELS* (Kinds of men's haircuts) 1 Inf, **csWI**, Apache. **1966–67** *DARE* (Qu. X5) Infs **OR**1, **WA**9, Apache.

Apache plume n **West esp SW**
1 A much-branched western shrub (*Fallugia paradoxa*) with white roselike flowers and heads of achenes with feathery "tails." [See quot 1941] Also called **ponil**
1889 *Century Dict.*, Apache-plume . . . A name given in New Mexico to the *Fallucia paradoxa*. **1932** Estabrook *Givers of Life* 53 **NM**, And over all, waved the fairy white blossoms and the feathery winged seeds of the Apache plume. **1941** Jaeger *Wildflowers* 89, Because of some fancied resemblance of the reddish, feathery-tailed seed clusters to the plumed war bonnets of the Apache Indians, the common name "Apache-plume" was applied. **1959** Munz–Keck *CA Flora* 746, Apache-Plume. Low deciduous shrubs with flaky bark . . . to Nev., Tex., Mex. May–June. **1966** *DARE* (Qq. S26E, T16) Inf **NM13**, Apache plume.
2 =**mountain mahogany**.
1920 *Torreya* 20.21 **sAZ**, *Cercocarpus* . . rabbit brush, quail brush, Apache plume.
3 =**prairie smoke 1**.
1959 Carleton *Index Herb. Plants* 4, Apache Plume: . . Geum ciliatum.

Apache tears n
Small roughly spherical bits of volcanic glass found in the obsidian formations of the West.
1953 Pough *Rocks & Minerals* 15, Sometimes a network of cracks develops in the obsidian, . . leaving a series of rounded, fresh glassy cores . . . When such lava is . . eroded, . . rounded glassy pebbles are freed. The pebbles are often translucent and a light smoky color. They are locally collected by amateurs for cutting and are called "Apache Tears." **1980** *DARE* File, A geologist friend in Utah showed us his collections of geodes and "Apache tears" when we visited in 1972.

apaloochy, apaloose, apalousa, apalucy See **appaloosa** n[1]

apanchion n Also *apansion* [*a* ?indef art + *pancheon* shallow earthenware bowl]
A small pan in which dishes are washed.
1936 *AmSp* 11.191 **swWY**, Apanchion or Apansion . . . 'Get the apanchion while I siden the table.'

apapane n [Haw]
A common Hawaiian honeycreeper (*Himatione sanguinea*) distinguished by its black wings and tail and chiefly red body plumage.
1930 Degener *Ferns of HI* 232, The *apapane* . . . can be recognized by its scarlet body, black wings and tail, and peculiar whirring noise made by its wings when in flight. **1968** *DARE* (QR p 119) Inf **HI14**, Apapane [apaˈpane]. Native Hawaiian bird—honey eater. **1971** Pukui–Elbert *Hawaiian Dict.* 'Apapane . . . found on all the main Hawaiian Islands. Its feathers occasionally were used for featherwork. **1972** Berger *Hawaiian Birdlife* 169, The very attractive Apapane is the most common of the existing species of honeycreepers.

aparejo n |æpəˈre(h)o| For pronc-spp see quots [Span] **West, esp SW** See also **arapajo**
A packsaddle.
1844 (1954) Gregg *Commerce* 127, It is necessary too for the aparejo to be firmly bound on to prevent its slipping and chafing the mule's back. **1859** Jackson *MS. Diary* 6 (*DAE*), Will start for trappers camp in a few days to bring up my mule and apparaho. **1873** Miller *Modocs* 3, A little narrow pack trail . . barely wide enough to admit of . . little Mexican mules with their apparajos. **1878** Hart *Sazerac Lying Club* 51 (*DA*), We got an aparayho and put it on the burro. **1895** King *Story of Ft. Frayne* 22 **WY**, Ten days' rations were always set aside in readiness to be packaged on the aparejos the moment word should come. **1931** *AmSp* 6.241 **NE**. **1955** Harris *Look of Old West* 233, Aparejo just means "rigging," or "harness," and an aparejo was a clumsy, padded affair, to hitch things to.

aparejo grass n Also *aparejo muhly* **chiefly SW**
A **muhly grass**, usu *Muhlenbergia utilis* but also *M. richardsonis*, formerly used for stuffing **aparejos**.
1894 Coulter *Botany W. TX* 519, *S[porobolus] depauperatus* . . Aparejos [sic] grass. **1912** NM Ag. Exper. Station *Bulletin* 69, Aparejo Grass (*Muhlenbergia utilis*) . . receives its common name because it is used to stuff the pads (*aparejos*) used in certain parts of Mexico in lieu of pack saddles. **1950** Hitchcock *Manual Grasses* 381 **SW**. **1970** Correll *Plants TX* 227, Aparejo muhly . . . Tex. and n.e. Mex.; also Calif. and Nev.

apart prep [*OED apart* adv 7: "*From* is rarely omitted, leaving *apart* to act as a preposition"] ?obs
Beyond, away from.
1902 *DN* 2.228 **sIL**, I got apart the place before I thought about it.

apast adj
Completed, finished.
1941 Stuart *Men of Mts.* 176 **neKY**, It [=winter] is something apast.

apast prep [*a* inert vowel **3** + *past;* also in Engl dial—see *EDD*] **chiefly Midl**
Past, beyond.
1894 *Century Illustr. Mag.* 48.869 **sIN**, A man . . from the hill country . . might have said thirty years ago: "I . . wuz a-cumin' . . apast the woods paster." **1895** *DN* 1.371 **eTN Mts**, I don't pass that shootin' any apast him. **1903** *DN* 2.305 **seMO**, Turn to the right just apast the school-house. **1906** *DN* 3.115 **sIN**. *Ibid* 124 **nwAR**. **1908** *DN* 3.287 **eAL, wGA**. **1926** *DN* 5.398 **Ozarks**. **1927** *Ruppenthal Coll.* **KS**, Old man Hutcher came apast here. **1940** Stuart *Trees of Heaven* 132 **neKY**, I came down the hollow a-past Tussie's. **1952** Brown *NC Folkl.* 1.515, It's a little apast meal's time. **1967** *Hall Coll.* **eTN**, Tell Lena I can't visit her. I'm now apast of travelin' [Hall: that is, I'm too old to travel now.].

ape n
1 also *African ape, Black ape:* A Black person. **chiefly Sth derog**
1884 Harrison *Negro Engl.* 257 **S Atl**, Black ape! **1941** *LANE* Map 252 (*Nicknames for a Negro*) **Long Island NY**, Ape—derogatory. **1960** Wentworth–Flexner *Slang* 7. **1966–68** *DARE* (Qu. HH28) Inf **GA7**, Ape; **LA46**, Ape, African ape; **MS71, SC34**, Black ape.
2 also *tame ape:* Among loggers: see quots. **Pacific NW** *joc*
1930 Williams *Logger-Talk* 15 **Pacific NW**, Ape: Applied generally to

homo sapiens but more particularly to a wage-earner. *Ape, tame:* A wage-earner who likes wage-earning. **1958** McCulloch *Woods Words* 3 **Pacific NW,** *Ape*—A rigging man (often called tame ape).

ape v [Ext of *ape* imitate, mimic]
To pretend.
  1968 *DARE* (Qu. JJ46, . . "*Let's* _____ *we don't know a thing about it.*") Inf **CA**53, Ape that.

ape-ape n |'ɑpe'ɑpe| Also *ape* [Haw: see quot 1940]
Any of the endemic Hawaiian spp of *Gunnera:* perennial forest plants with thick prostrate stems rising to 6 feet at the tip and crowned with huge, more-or-less kidney-shaped leaves.
  1928 Pan-Pacific Research Inst. *Jrl.* 3.8, Gunnera, apè; largest leaved plant in the islands. **1930** Degener *Ferns of HI* 239, One will see in some of the ravines a giant herb . . the *apéapé* of the Hawaiians . . . [The leaf] is so large that it can be made to serve as an umbrella. **1940** Von Tempski *Paradise* 234 **HI** (as of 1900–25), Ape-ape leaves six feet in diameter fringed the forest pools . . . meant "The Flying Away of the Fowls." **1948** (1965) Neal *Gardens HI* 651, 'Ape'ape . . . is a unique-looking plant, characterized by huge, rhubarb-like leaves. **1980** Bushnell *Water of Kane* 395 **HI,** Ulukou, finding a moment's shelter from heavy rains under the enormous leaves of the ape-ape, each as round and broad as an umbrella.

apee n, also attrib Also sp *A.P.,* pl *eepies* [Back-formation from Fr *épice,* understood as pl; for folk-etym see quot 1830] **PA**
Also called **Dutch cake**
A kind of gingerbread.
  1830 Watson *Annals Philadelphia* 716, Philadelphia has long enjoyed the reputation of a peculiar cake called the apee . . . Ann Page . . first made them, many years ago, when the common name of cakes . . . On her cakes she impressed the letters A.P., the letters of her name, and from this cause, ever since the initials have been disused on them, the cakes have continued to be called *apees.* **1924** Lambert *PA Ger. Dict.* 47, *Eepies* . . cooky, Christmas cooky (frequently cut in the shape of animals). F[rench] épice; pain d'épice = gingerbread. **1951** *AmSp* 26.205, Apee . . is clearly from the French *épice,* the full form of the French being *pain d'épice,* meaning gingerbread. Some of the Huguenots who fled for sanctuary to this country, having been for a time in Germany, settled in . . Pennsylvania, not far from Reading. Apee is an interesting linguistic trace of these people. **1954** *AmSp* 29.46, Apee . . is usually combined with cake. Apee cake . . . in Pennsylvania seems to be largely limited to those regions where Huguenot names abound. **1964** Amer. Heritage *Cookbook* 608, *Apees.* These cookies [are] especially popular at Christmastide in Pennsylvania. **1967** *DARE* (Qu. H63) Inf **PA**41, A.P. cookies.

apelousa See **appaloosa** n²

ape oil n
Liquor.
  1940 *AmSp* 15.446 **eTN,** Sallie's man likes his ape oil.

apern See **apron** n A

ape wagon n *joc* Cf **animal car**
Among railroad workers: a caboose.
  1946 in **1953** Botkin *Treas. Railroad Folkl.* 350, If you ever have occasion to locate the caboose on a freight train, don't ask the ORC . . to show you the way to the ape wagon. **1977** Adams *Lang. Railroader* 7.

apex n
In mining: see quots.
  1881 Raymond *Gloss. Mining* 4, *Apex.* In the U.S. Revenue Statutes, the end or edge of a vein nearest the surface. **1968** Adams *Western Words, Apex*—In mining, the top of a vein of ore.

apex v
Of mineral deposits: To present an **apex** at the surface of the ground.
  1914 Atherton *Perch of the Devil* 79 **CA,** It dips towards the ranch . . . It's pretty close. That would be a kettle of fish—if it apexed on your land! **1943** Writers' Program MT *Copper Camp* 43, Through his Rarus Mine, Heinze complacently moved into the Michael Davitt, an adjoining Amalgamated property, which he claimed "apexed" on the Rarus.

aphid wolf n
A larva of the brown lacewing (Hemerobiidae).

  1949 Swain *Insect Guide* 72, The larvae [of brown lacewings], called "aphidwolves," are rather important predators. **1972** Swan–Papp *Insects* 183, [Brown lacewing] larvae . . are sometimes referred to as "aphidwolves," and are valuable enemies of aphids and mealybugs.

apichment See **apishamore**

apint See **appoint**

apishamore n Also sp *apichment, appichimoe, apishiamore,* pl *appishimous* [Ojibwa *apishamon* something to lie down on] **West** *hist*
A saddleblanket, usu of buffalo hide.
  1831 (1940) Ferris *Rocky Mts.* 126 **NM,** We purchased all the dried meat the Indians could spare, together with robes, and "*appishimous*" (square pieces of robes, used under our saddles in travelling, or under our beds in camp). **1846** Stewart *Altowan* 1.36 *(DAE),* The fire was extinguished, and the saddles and appichimoes laid down for a bed. **1848** (1855) Ruxton *Life Far West* 66 **SW,** La Bonté picked up three excellent mules for a mere song, with their accompanying pack-saddles [and] *apishamores.* [Footnote: Saddle-blanket made of buffalo-calf skin] *Ibid* 77, The ravenous animals are a constant source of annoyance to him, creeping to the camp-fire at night, and gnawing his saddles and *apishamores.* **1850** Garrard *Wah-to-yah* 12 **cKS,** Mr. St. Vrain and I; Folger and Chadwick; . . each pair taking an *apishiamore* (saddle blanket), would collect our blankets full of the fuel. **1851** Kelly *Excursion* 1.159, And our packsaddles rigged, with cruppers, britchings, lash-ropes, and apichments. **1968** Adams *Western Words.*

a-plague See **a** prep¹ 4

aplenty adv
Usu after a verb or adj: plentifully, enough.
  1846 *Knickerbocker* 27.412 **N Atl,** Look a-plenty, but when you *have* got enough . . give others an opportunity. **1966–67** *DARE* (Qu. DD9a) Inf **LA**6, He smokes aplenty; (Qu. GG22b, . . *The end of your patience*) Inf **OK**28, That's far aplenty!

aplenty n chiefly **S Atl, Midl**
Abundance, plenty.
  1865 Crockett *Life* 74 **TN,** Having had . . hard times and a plenty of them. **1933** Rawlings *South Moon* 30 **FL,** You had a plenty this evenin'. **1939** McGuire *FL Cracker Dial.* 74, The noun *a-plenty,* sometimes used adverbially or adjectivally, represents fusion with the indefinite article. **1958** Humphrey *Home from the Hill* 267 **TX,** Not me . . . I've had a-plenty. **1965–70** *DARE* (Qu. LL9a, . . "*We've got _____ of apples.*") 13 Infs, chiefly **S Atl, Midl,** Aplenty.

ap'n See **apron** n A

apola See **appola**

aporn See **apron** n A

apostle n Usu |ə'pɑsl|, occas sp-pronc |ə'pɑstl| Pronc-sp *apostul* Cf **epistle**
Std senses, var forms.
  1843 (1916) Hall *New Purchase* 172 **IN,** This apostul of ourn what spoke the text, never rubbed his back agin a collige. **1891** *PMLA* 6.166 **WV,** The *t* between *s* and *l* of words like *apostle* . . is sounded.

apostle's pinch n
?A pinch on the buttocks: see quot.
  1947 Adams *Banner* 62 **NY** (as of 1817–1847), "He pinched me." "Eh? What? Where? The apostle's pinch?" Mrs. Blair snapped. Durie flushed. "No. Just my shoulder."

appalachian See **appaloosa** n¹

Appalachian tea n [See quots]
1 Either of two hollies: **yaupon** (here: *Ilex vomitoria*) or **inkberry 1** (here: *Ilex glabra*).
  1876 Hobbs *Bot. Hdbk.* 4, Appalachian tea, Leaves used as tea, Prinos glaber. **1900** Lyons *Plant Names* 199, I[lex] vomitoria . . . Appalachian . . Tea . . . *Leaves* contain caffeine and were formerly used by Indians to make their "black drink." **1960** Vines *Trees SW* 646, *Ilex vomitoria* . . . A medicinal tea was formerly prepared . . from the leaves, which contain caffeine . . . Local names . . are . . Carolina-tea, Appalachian-tea. *Ibid* 652, *Ilex* . . *glabra* . . . Also known as Appalachian Tea . . . The plant contains no caffeine.
2 =**withe rod** (here: *Viburnum cassinoides*).
  1900 Lyons *Plant Names* 392, V[iburnum] cassinoides . . . Withe-

rod . . Appalachian Tea, False Paraguay Tea. *Leaves* used as tea. **1910** Shreve et al *MD Plant Life* 485, *Viburnum cassinoides*. Appalachian Tea. Rare in the Midland Zone, common in the Mountain Zone; in swamps and bogs. **1966** Gibbons *Stalking Healthful Herbs* 184, Witherod *(Viburnum cassinoides)* . . or Appalachian tea.

appaleeshan See **appaloosa** n[1]

appalo See **appola**

appaloochey See **appaloosa** n[2]

appaloosa n[1], also attrib Usu |ˌæpəˈlusə| occas |ˌæpəˈlusi, ˌæpəˈlus|; also stress shift to first syll, aphet, and rarely |ˌæpəˈlušən, ˌæpəˈlušəs, ˌæpəˈlučə|; |ˌæpəˈlišn̩| and pronc-sp *appalachian* may be infl by folk-etym.   For addit proncs and pronc-spp, see quots [Perh from Louisiana Indian tribal name *Opelousa*, though the horse is freq associated with Nez Percé Indians and the name with the Palouse R. of western Idaho, eastern Washington] **still chiefly West, though recognized throughout US**
A horse of a breed most frequently identified by a "blanket" of white with dark spots over the rump, sparse mane and tail, mottled skin, vertically striated hooves, white-rimmed eyes, and a pink nose.

1849 Bracht *Texas* 85, Nach diesen kommt das sogenannte Kreolenpferdchen, auch Opelousas poney genannt, ein ganz ausgezeichnetes Damenpferd. [=Following these is the so-called Creole pony, also called Opelousas pony, an excellent women's horse.] **1924** Davies *Skyline Trail* 49 *(DA)*, They find death in a dramatic flare: Trying to ride the apaloochy mare. **1938** *Wranglin' Notes (Hench Coll.)* WY, A corral full of brown, gruya, black, apaloose, bay, . . horses. **1946** *NYT Mag.* 20 Oct 35/2 ["Waddies' Lingo"], *Appalucy:* piebald horse with "glass eyes" (white-rimmed). **1947** De Voto *Wide Missouri* 77, The Nez Perces had learned selective breeding . . and had developed a distinctive stock called the Pelouse [sic] horse, the 'Appaloosa' of a later date. **1952** Dobie *Mustangs* 55 **West,** Their [=Nez Percé Indians] outstanding strain of horses, known now as Appaloosas, took their name from the Palouse River of Western Idaho and eastern Washington, which was within their original range. The name has been spelled and pronounced Palousy, Apalousa, Apalucy, Appaluchi . . . If horses were dogs, the Appaloosa would be called a Dalmatian. **1965–70** *DARE* (Qu. K37, . . *A horse of mixed colors*) 40 Infs, **throughout US,** Appaloosa; Infs **CA152, 205, IL134, MN40, OH53,** Appaloosy [ˌæpəˈlusi]; **DE1,** Appaleeshan [ˌæpəˈlišn̩]; **OH89,** Appaloochy; **AR55,** Appaloosious [ˌæpəˈlušəs]; (Qu. K38) Inf **IN32,** Appaloosa; (Qu. K39) 55 Infs, **throughout US but esp West of Missip R,** Appaloosa; **IN44,** Appalachian; **CA124,** Appaloocha—spots and white rump; **OK27,** Appaloosa blue; **IL70,** Appaloosian [ˌæpəˈlušən]; **CT9,** Appaloose [ˈæpəlus]; (Qu. FF16) Inf **CA65,** Appaloosian horse show. **1971** Bright *Word Geog. CA & NV* 169, Appaloosa . . Usually pronounced [æpəˈlusɪ˞].

appaloosa n[2] Also ~*cat* |ˌæpəˈlusə, ˌɑpəˈlusə(s)|, occas |ˌɑpoˈlusi, ˌæpəˈlučə| Also sp *apelousa, appeloosas, appaluchian, appaloochey,* and perh by association with the southern Louisana Indian tribe and place name, *Opelousas* [Prob fr Choctaw *apolusa* 'to be daubed,' referring to the mottled appearance of the fish] **chiefly Gulf States, AR, OK**
=flathead catfish 1.

1845 Hooper *Advent. Simon Suggs* 194 **AL,** Right round *that* was whar I'd ketch the monstrousest, most oudaciousest Appeloosas cat, the week before, that ever come outen the Tallapoosy. **1857** *Porter's Spirit of Times* 17 Jan 319/3, He at length agreed to it, if we would say nothing about his "catching the Apelousa." **1911** *Century Dict. Suppl., Cat . . . Opelousas cat,* the long-jawed catfish, *Leptos olivaris.* **1948** *Dly. Ardmoreite* (Ardmore, Okla.) 23 April 7/1 *(DA),* Some of the larger, like Sand creek and Caney river, yield big blues and tackle-busting river cats, or Appaluchians. **1949** *PADS* 11.3 **OK,** Appaloochey [æpəˈluči] . . . A spotted catfish . . . Rare. **1966** *WI Conserv. Bulletin* July–Aug 14, Many know the fish by such local names as yellow cat, mudcat, morgan cat, opelousa, or just plain bullhead. **1966–69** *DARE* (Qu. P1) Infs **LA12, 14** [ˌɑpəˈlusəs]; **AR51** [æpəˈlusɪ]—spotted cat; **LA2,** [ˌɑpəˈlusə]; **TX37,** [ˌɑpoˈlusi]; **OK23,** Appalushie cat; **OK52,** Appaloosie; **AL56,** Appaloosa—big yellow cat. **1967–69** *DARE* Tape **GA86,** [ˌæpəˈlučə kjæt]; **LA5,** What we call a "yellow cat" . . in the western part of the state they call it a [ˌɑpəˈlusəs kæt] . . . [FW:] That same catfish, the spotted one, is called [ˌæpəˈlusə] in Arkansas. [Inf:] We call it a [ˈɑpəˈlusəs kæt]. **1968** *DARE* FW Addit **sLA,** Opelousas cat [ˌɑpəˈlusəs]—spotted cat: alternate names for the same fish.

apparaho, apparajo, apparejo See **aparejo**

appearance n *obs*
Spoor or other **sign** that wild animals have been present.
1805 (1904) Lewis *Orig. Jrls. Lewis & Clark Exped.* 2.10, Great appearance of beaver on this river. **1806** *Ibid* 4.219, I saw 4 deer in the course of my walk and much appearance of both Elk and deer. **1810** (1895) Pike *Expeditions* 1.94, Much appearance of elk and deer.

appearanced adj *?obs*
Having the appearance named (by a modifier, as *good*).
1895 *DN* 1.370 **TN Mts,** She is very good appearanced. **1934** *W2, Appearanced . . .* Having (such) an appearance. *Colloq. U.S.* **1942** Berrey–Van den Bark *Amer. Slang* 36.2.

appearent adj Also *appearant* |əˈp(j)irənt| Pronc-spp for *apparent* See also next
1908 *DN* 3.287 **eAL, wGA,** Appeerent. **1912** *DN* 3.570 **wIN.** **1930s** in 1944 *ADD* **NY, WV,** Appearant(ly). Common in MSS. **1952** Brown *NC Folkl.* 1.515. **c1960** *Wilson Coll.* **csKY,** Apparent [-pjir-]. **1972** Cooper *NC Mt. Folkl.,* Appearant—apparent.

appearently adv Also *appearantly,* aphet '*pearently* Pronc-spp for *apparently* **chiefly Midl** See also preceding
1884 Lanier *Poems* 169 **GA,** And he was a-wurken' appearently / A 'rethmetic sum that wouldn't gee. **1894** Riley *Armazindy* 7 **IN,** Palsied aunt . . / And still likely, 'pearantly, / To live out the century! *Ibid* 68 **IN,** Wuz jes "a common drunkard"—And he *wuz,* appearantly. **1912** *DN* 3.570 **wIN,** Appearently . . . Very common. **1915** *DN* 4.180 **swVA,** Appearantly. **1919** *DN* 5.32 **seKY.** **1923** *DN* 5.242 **KY.** **1927** in 1952 Brown *NC Folkl.* 1.515, I never planned it—or, I gonnies, I'd feel a sight more responsible for it than Him that did appearantly does. **1952** Brown *NC Folkl.* 1.515. **1976** Garber *Mountain-ese* 3 **sAppalachians,** The totals ain't in yet, but appearantly he won the election.

appearing-out clothes n pl Cf *DS* W39
1967 Cerello *Dakota Co. MN* 43, "Our appearing-out clothes were what we wore when going to church, for parties or for funerals." Heard in six communities.

appearment n [*appear* + *-ment*]
Appearance.
1898 Lloyd *Country Life* 15 **AL,** That was the general appearment to me. *Ibid* 33, I could tell from the general appearment of things that it was most night.

appeloosas See **appaloosa** n[2]

‡**appendic** n [Sg back-formation from *appendix* taken as pl]
The appendix.
1911 *DN* 3.549 **NE.**

appendicitis n Usu |(ə)ˌpɛndɪˈsaɪtəs| also, *somewhat old-fash,* |-sitəs| See also **penny-ciders**
A Forms.
1911 *DN* 3.499 **Sth,** In *appendicitis* . . the learned pronunciation [=|i|] of the penultimate vowel is apparently becoming less popular than that which follows the spelling [=|aɪ|]. **c1960** *Wilson Coll.* **csKY,** Appendicitis [əˌpɪndəˈsitəs] often among the older people. **1966–68** *DARE* (Qu. BB3c) Inf **NC33,** [ˌpɛndəˈsitəs]; **NY69,** [ˌpɛndəˈsaɪtəs]; (Qu. BB49) Inf **MO38,** [ˌpɛndəˈsɑɪtɪs].
B Sense.
Sometimes constr as pl: The appendix. Cf **appendic**
1931–33 *LANE Worksheets* **csCT,** My son had to have his appendicitis took out. **1941** in 1944 *ADD* **sWV,** 'They said it was appendicitis. He had 'em out the next day.' Pl. Pronoun *'em* said repeatedly as if having a pl. antecedent.

‡**appendix** n [Prob malaprop for *appendage*] *joc* Cf *DS* X14
1950 *WELS* (Joking words for the nose) 1 Inf, **cWI,** Appendix, snout.

appernt, appernntment See **appoint**

appichimoe See **apishamore**

appint See **appoint**

appintedly See **pointedly**

appintment See **appoint**

appishimou See **apishamore**

apple n
1 A saddlehorn: see quot 1968. **SW**

1933 *AmSp* 8.1.28 **nwTX.** **1968** Adams *Western Words, Apple—* Small horn whose top was round like an apple. **1977** Watts *Dict. Old West* 11, A real disgrace to *grab the apple* or *pull leather* when trying to stay on a wild one.

2 The Adam's apple.
1942 Berrey–Van den Bark *Amer. Slang* 121.75. **1968** *DARE* (Qu. X7) Inf **PA76,** Apple.

3 also *Christ-apple:* A woman's breast.
1942 Berrey–Van den Bark *Amer. Slang* 121.17, *Breasts.* Apples. **1967–70** *DARE* (Qu. X31) Inf **MO23,** Apples; **MN1,** Apples—if young girl; **TX106,** Christ-apples.

4 One's head. *joc* Cf *DS* X28
1950 *WELS (Joking names for a person's head)* 1 Inf, **cWI,** Apple.

5 also *apple bomb:* A firecracker resembling an apple in its shape and color. Cf **cherry bomb**
1966 *DARE* File **Fitchburg MA,** Apple. **1968** *DARE* (Qu. FF14) Inf **MI89A,** Apple bombs, cherry bombs.

‡**6** in pl: =**Adam 1.** See also **Adam's apple 2,** and cf *DS* II26
1968 *DARE* FW Addit **NY92,** I didn't know who he was from apples.

7 In var compounds referring to one who curries favor: see quots. [Alter of *apple-polisher*] Cf **apple-knock 2, apple up**
1935 *Word Study* Sept. 2 **nwPA,** Dean J.R. Schultz of Allegheny College states that in his section of Pennsylvania *apple shiner,* not *apple polisher,* is the term invariably used to designate a person who curries favor. **1965–70** *DARE* (Qu. JJ3b) Infs **MO14, NJ19,** Apple-shiner; **PA234,** Apple-pusher; **NJ25,** Apple-washer; **NJ54,** Apple-knocker.

apple adj [Prob from *apple-pie order*] See also **apple-pie 1**
1934 *AmSp* 9.313, North Brooklyn says "Everything is Apple!" when ninety-nine percent of the rest of the country would say "It's O.K."

apple banana n [From its flavor; name prob adopted with the fruit from the Caribbean: cf *DJE*]
A small, sweet, thin-skinned banana *(Musa sapientum cubensis).*
1929 Neal *Honolulu Gardens* 78, *Brazilian or common banana (Musa sapientum . .) . . .* Many varieties are known, among them the locally popular apple banana, the fruit of which has a whiter, more acid, and stiffer pulp than the Chinese banana. **1966** *DARE* Tape **FL23,** Apple bananas, locally grown . . small and yellow with flavor of an apple.

apple bee n [bee n[2]] **chiefly NEng** Also called **apple cut (frolic), apple paring, apple peeling (social), schnitz-in**
A social gathering at which apples are prepared for drying.
1827 *Harvard Reg.* Nov. 273, Once Ebenezer Hodge invited me, / To help his Dolly at an apple bee. **1878** (1977) Stowe *Poganuc People* 242 **CT,** Young men, maids, and matrons were taking their places to assist in the apple-bee. **1934** *Hanley Disks* **neVT,** A party at which apples are cut up, strung and dried, that's what they call an apple bee. *Ibid* **neVT,** We used to have apple bees . . . They'd all bring their knife with them and . . pared apples by hand. **1941** Lee *Stage Coach* 27 **VT,** At an apple bee enough greenings were pared and strung for drying to last the winter.

apple betty See **apple (brown) betty**

apple bird n [From its frequenting of orchards and/or its fondness for fruit]
1 =**Lewis's woodpecker. West**
1917 *Wilson Bulletin* 29.82, *Asyndesmus lewisi.* —Apple bird. Bitterroot Valley, Montana. **1969** *DARE* (Qu. Q17) Inf **CA136,** Apple bird.
2 Either of two birds, the **cedar waxwing** or the **hermit thrush.**
1956 *MA Audubon* 40.128, Hermit Thrush. Apple Bird (Maine. From its being observed in orchards.). *Ibid* 129, Cedar Waxwing. Apple Bird (Maine. From feeding among apple blossoms.).

‡**apple-blossom two-step** n Var of **green-apple quickstep** *joc*
1969 *DARE* (Qu. BB19, *Joking names for looseness of the bowels)* Inf **IL61,** Apple-blossom two-step.

apple bomb See **apple n 5**

apple (brown) betty n **NEng and settlement area** Also called **apple crisp, apple crust** =**brown betty 1.**
1939 Wolcott *Yankee Cook Book* 178, Apple Brown Betty . . . 1½ cups bread crumbs combined with ½ cup sugar are sprinkled in layers on top of the sweetened apples. Dot crumbs with bits of butter. Bake in a

moderate oven. **1941** *LANE* Map 292, 2 Infs, **csRI, csNH,** Apple betty. **1968** *DARE* FW Addit **VA4,** Apple betty . . apples, sugar, cinnamon with biscuit or shortcake dough on top. Same as brown betty. **1970** *DARE* (Qu. H63) **NY230,** Apple betty—same as brown betty. **1973** Allen *LAUM* 1.297, *Apple Betty . .* is used by one U[pper] M[idwest] inf., a Nebraskan whose mother came from Ohio.

apple bug n Also ~ *smeller* n [From the apple-like odor of the fluid it exudes when handled]
=**whirligig beetle.**
c**1830** Godman in *Waldie's Library* 2.85/1 *(DA),* Their distant relatives, called by the boys the water-witches and apple smellers, . . [have] a delightful smell, exactly similar to that of the richest, mellowest apple. **1832** Kennedy *Swallow Barn* 1.129 **VA,** The apple-bugs (as schoolboys call that glossy black insect which frequents the summer pools, and is distinguished for the perfume of the apple) danced in busy myriads over the surface of the still water. **1940** Teale *Insects* 150, If you hold . . [whirligigs] in your hand for a time they will exude a milky white fluid which has a faint odor sometimes suggesting apples. Hence, in the Southwest, the beetles are called "apple bugs." **1941** *Nature Mag.* 34.138, Apple bugs (New Jersey, Maryland, Indiana).

apple cabbage n *obs*
Rhubarb.
1896 *DN* 1.411 **ME,** *Apple-cabbage . .* rhubarb, pie-plant.

apple crisp n
=**brown betty 1.**
1932 (1946) Hibben *Amer. Regional Cookery* 267 **GA,** *Apple crisp . . .* Serve warm with whipped cream. **1966–68** *DARE* (Qu. H63) Infs **IA32, MA10, NY41,** Apple crisp; **ND2,** Apple crisp—like apple pie minus the crust, [has a] crumbly crust with crackers and brown sugar; **WA31,** Apple crisp—apples with just a crust of rolled oats and sugar. **1973** Allen *LAUM* 1.297, *Apple crisp . .* appears in south central Iowa.

apple critter n [Folk-etym] Var of **elbedritsch**
1968 *DARE* (Qu. CC17, *Imaginary animals or monsters that people around here tell tales about—especially to tease greenhorns)* Inf **VA33,** Apple critter—hunting for him [is] like snipe hunting; old-fashioned; (Qu. HH14) Inf **VA33,** Apple critter.

‡**apple crust** n
=**brown betty 1.**
1973 Allen *LAUM* 1.297, *Apple crust* is the term of a supplementary inf. in central Nebraska.

apple cut (frolic) n Also ~ *cutting (bee)*
=**apple bee.**
1845 *Lowell Offering* 87 **MA,** My mind involuntarily reverted to the merrymaking scenes, the tea parties, the quilting matches, the apple-cut frolics, and kindred associations. **1859** Cary *Country Life* 246 *(DAE),* He had called to ask her to an 'apple-cutting' at his mother's house. **1876** Burroughs *Winter Sunshine* 125, Then those rural gatherings . . known as 'apple cuts,' now, alas! nearly obsolete. **1878** (1977) Stowe *Poganuc People* 168 **CT,** Mis' Hawkins . . says they're goin' to hev an apple-cuttin' there to-morrow night. **1894** (1934) Robinson *Danvis Folks* 85, 'A apple cut? A parin'-bee? . . You jest try it an' see. **1968** *DARE* (Qu. FF2) Inf **IN10,** Apple-cutting bee: old-fashioned.

apple dowdy See **apple pandowdy**

apple duff See **duff n[1] 1**

apple float n Also called **apple snow**
A frothy dessert made primarily of apples, sugar and beaten egg whites.
1932 (1946) Hibben *Amer. Regional Cookery* 268 **KY,** *Apple Float . . .* Beat the egg whites well and add . . sugar . . . Add the applesauce . . . Grate in a little of the nutmeg . . . Put the float in a glass bowl . . and serve with a jug of rich cream. **1968** *DARE* (Qu. H63) Inf **MD14,** Apple float. Egg custard with canned apples and lemon juice, white of egg beaten in.

‡**apple gray** adj [See *OED dapple gray* note, though this is prob an historically unrelated form]
Of horses: dapple gray.
1967 *DARE* (Qu. K39) Inf **MO21,** Apple gray.

apple grunt n [grunt] **chiefly eMA and settlement areas**
=**apple pandowdy.**

1896 *DN* 1.411 **ncNY**, *Apple-grunt:* a kind of apple dumpling. **1903** *DN* 2.295 **Cape Cod MA** (as of 1850s), *Apple grunt,* or *apple slump* . . . A kind of apple dumplings. **1934** *Hanley Disks* **nwMA**, Apple grunt. **1941** *LANE* Map 292, 15 Infs, **chiefly eMA**, Apple grunt. **1973** Allen *LAUM* 1.297, One Nebraskan of New York parentage offers *apple grunt,* a localism in the Plymouth and Cape Cod area of Massachusetts.

apple haw n Also *apple hawthorn, haw apple* **chiefly Sth**
A large, red-fruited haw, usu a **may haw** (esp *Crataegus aestivalis*).
  1861 Wood *Class-Book* 331, Apple haw . . . [grows] in the edges of ponds and rivers, S. Car. to Fla. and La. **1892** IN Dept. Geol. & Nat. Resources *Rept. for 1891* 271, *Crataegus tomentosa* . . . Apple Haw. Our largest fruited haw, the fruit often attaining a diameter of more than one inch. **1893** *Bot. Gaz.* 18.426, *Crataegus aestivalis,* apple haw. Ala. **1897** Sudworth *Arborescent Flora* 235, Apple Haw (Fla.) **1933** Small *Manual SE Flora* 641, A tree often 9 m. tall, . . fruit . . red . . . Mayhaw. Apple-haw. **1965–68** *DARE* (Qu. I46) Inf **MD30**, Hawapples— small red apples, not very good to eat, grown on hawthorn bush; **FL17**, Haw apples; (Qu. I44) Inf **SC43**, Apple haws. **1970** Correll *Plants TX* 737, *Crataegus opaca* . . . Western mayhaw, apple haw . . . Common in depressions that are filled with water part of the year, . . fruiting May–July. **1979** Little *Checklist U.S. Trees* 108, Apple hawthorn.

applehorn n **West** *obs* Cf **apple** n 1
A type of saddle with a small round horn: see quots.
  1944 Adams *Western Words.* **1961** Adams *Old-Time Cowhand* 106, In the early [eighteen] eighties a new saddle came out and was called the "applehorn." It took this name because of the small horn whose top was round like an apple as compared with the flat ones it replaced. **1977** Watts *Dict. Old West,* Apple-horn . . . The horn was more like an apple cut in half—usually of wood and screwed down into the metal plate or base and covered with leather—and . . it was actually not too small, but often measured three to four inches at the base . . . It was developed in the early 1860s and was common on cattle-drives out of Texas in the post-Civil War period.

applejack n, also attrib
1 Apple brandy; brandy distilled from apple cider. Also called **apple John 1, jack** Cf **blackjack 8**
  1816 Scene Painter *Emigrant's Guide* 30 *(DA),* A partial distillation is also made from apples . . called Apple-Jack. **1838** *Bentley's Misc.* 4.134 **PA**, There was nothing to be had that day but potatoes, bread, and applejack. [Footnote:] A description of brandy made from apples. **1905** *DN* 3.2 **cCT**. **1907** *DN* 3.208 **nwAR**. **1908** Fox *Lonesome Pine* 141 **KY**, They drank apple-jack and hard cider. **1934** *Hanley Disks* **neCT**, They make cider brandy. I suppose you call that applejack. **1950** *WELS (Mixed fermented drinks)* 1 Inf, **seWI**, Applejack. **1952** in 1977 *Pissing in the Snow* 62 **nwAR**, When the fellow sobered up . . Doc advised him to go easy on the applejack. **1965–70** *DARE* (Qu. DD28b, . . *Fermented drinks . . made at home)* 55 Infs, **chiefly east of Missip R**, Applejack.
2 An alcoholic beverage which consists of the unfrozen portion of a container (such as a keg or barrel) of frozen hard cider.
  1934 *Hanley Disks* **nwMA**, Applejack—Alcoholic drink made by freezing hard cider. The boys in college always call it applejack. **1966–68** *DARE* (Qu. DD28b) Inf **CT3**, Applejack—fermented cider which has been frozen; applejack = part left unfrozen; Inf **DC8**, Applejack—Freeze a barrel of cider, then tap. [Applejack is] the alcohol that didn't freeze, flavored with apple, a delicious drink.
3 See quot.
  1968 *DARE* (Qu. H66b, *The sweet liquid that you pour over ice cream)* Inf **VT8**, Applejack, an apple syrup made of sweet cider boiled down.
4 An apple turnover. [Engl dial: see *OED, EDD*] **chiefly NC** Cf **apple John 2, doughboy**
  1852 (1854) Kennedy *Horse-Shoe Robinson* 18 **VA**, Besides these, I can throw in two apple-jacks, a half dozen of rolls. **1937** Johnson *Ante-Bellum NC* 90, A dinner . . entailed heavy burdens on the housekeeper . . and [she] spent long hours at apple jacks, sweet potato pies and jelly cakes. **1940** *Hench Coll.* 13 Dec, A person from Pitt County, NC, told me [Hench] that there a small individual turnover apple-pie is called an "apple-jack." **1968–69** *DARE* (Qu. H32) Inf **NC79**, Applejack, an apple turnover; **NC60**, Applejacks.
5 A recent dance step.
  1977 Smitherman *Talkin* 256 [Black], The names of most popular dances, from roughly 1950 to the present: *applejack.*

apple John n
1 =**applejack 1. NEng** *obs*
  1856 *Spirit of Times* 6 Dec 226/1, In the first place, get extremely 'how-came-you-so?' over night, on bad applejohn or worse rye-whiskey. **1872** Schele de Vere *Americanisms* 415, Known even in the pretentious form of *Apple-John* in New England, it has the terrible name of *Jersey Lightning* farther south, and in Virginia rules supreme as *Apple-Brandy* although here a few peach-kernels are generally added to give it the flavor of peach-brandy.
2 also *apple Johnny, ~ Jonathan:* =**apple pandowdy. chiefly sNEng and settlement areas**
  1931–33 *LANE Worksheets* **sRI**, An apple Jonathan is [made in] an iron basin, crust of biscuit dough on bottom; hole in middle; apple, sugar, spice; crust on top; hole in center for steam; heat on stone then bake in oven. **1934** *Hanley Disks* **nwMA**. **1939** Wolcott *Yankee Cook Book* 180 **ME**, Yankee Apple John . . . Grease shallow baking dish and fill with sliced apples. Mix sugar, spices and salt and sprinkle over apples . . . Roll [dough] to fit over pan . . . Bake in a hot oven . . . Serve with Nutmeg Sauce. **1941** *LANE* Map 292, 6 Infs, **CT, RI**, Apple Jonathan; 2 Infs, **csCT, swMA**, Apple Johnny; 1 Inf, **nwMA**, Apple John. **1967** *DARE* (Qu. H63) Inf **PA49**, Apple John—apples, upside-down cake. **1973** Allen *LAUM* 1.297, *Apple John* and *apple Jonathan,* restricted in *LANE* to Long Island Sound and secondary settlements in the Berkshires, is the usage of one North Dakotan of European parentage and of a South Dakotan whose mother came from New York state.

appleknock v [Back-formation < **appleknocker**]
1 To act the yokel.
  1942 Berrey–Van den Bark *Amer. Slang* 147.4, *Be plebeian; boorish; unpolished* . . . apple-knock.
2 also *apple-shine:* To curry favor. See also **apple** n 7, **apple up** Cf *DS* JJ3a, b
  1969 *DARE* (Qu. JJ3a) Inf **NJ54**, Appleknock [æpḷ nak]; **PA234**, Apple-shine.

appleknocker n *often derog*
1 A fruit picker. [*DAS:* "from the mistaken urban belief that fruit is harvested by being knocked from the trees with long sticks"]
  1927 *DN* 5.437 **NC**, *Apple knocker* . . . An apple picker, and by extension any fruit picker who gathers fruit from trees. **1949** Brown *Amer. Cooks* 590 **NY**.
2 Transf: an itinerant farm laborer.
  1941 FWP *Guide WA* 300, Transient fruit workers, "apple knockers" (packers) . . labor at terrific speed.
3 A rustic. **chiefly Nth**
  1941 *Time* 16 June 71, I don't think every appleknocker in the country will be able to tip the plot. **1949** Hynd *Public Enemies* 81 *(DAS),* Even in good clothes, Floyd looked like an apple knocker. **1950** *WELS (Nicknames for a country person)* 1 Inf, **ceWI**, Apple knocker. **1965–70** *DARE* (Qu. HH1, . . *A rustic or countrified person)* 12 Infs, **chiefly Nth**, Appleknocker. **1973** Allen *LAUM* 1.349 **ceIA**, 1 Inf, Apple knocker.
4 Any outsider.
  1949 Emrich *Wild West Custom* 164 **MT, ID**, This half-and-half work was frowned upon by the year round miner, who coined a variety of expressions for the outsider . . *punkin rollers, alfalfa pickers,* and *apple knockers.* **1969** *DARE* (Qu. HH31, *Somebody who is not from your community, and doesn't belong)* Inf **MI26**, Appleknocker—esp those from Indiana who come up here hunting.
5 Among loggers: see quots. **Pacific NW**
  1950 *Western Folkl.* 115 **Pacific NW** [Among loggers], *Appleknocker.* A farmer. *Ibid* 380 **nCA**, *Appleknocker.* Usually refers to a man who has not worked in the woods and who is attempting to convince people that he is an old-timer in logging work. **1958** McCulloch *Woods Words,* *Apple-knocker*—A part-time logger, usually not very skilled at woods jobs.
6 A stupid person—used as a general term of abuse.
  1939 *New Yorker* 4 Nov 26/1 *(Hench Coll.),* I had a reform-school technique, whereas them other sailors was apple-knockers. They were so dumb they couldn't find their nose with both hands.
7 ~~See **apple** n 7.~~
8 See quot.
  1975 Gould *ME Lingo* 36, *Apple knocker*—One of Maine's many names for a privy. This one means an outhouse so situated that apples

dropping from a tree onto the roof make an obbligato to the business at hand.

apple-kuchen See **kuchen**

apple melon n MD

A small, sweet, round variety of watermelon *(Citrullus vulgaris)* characterized by yellowish flesh.

1968 *DARE* (Qu. I26) Inf **MD**19, Apple melon, like watermelon but smaller, size of dew melon; **MD**28, Apple melon, like watermelon, but cream colored inside; **MD**30, Apple melon, like watermelon but small and round—greenish flesh, black seeds.

apple (of) Peru n

1 A tall, coarse, branching plant *(Nicandra physalodes)* with alternate leaves and pale blue flowers which produces a dry, inedible berry. **chiefly eUS** Also called **fly poison plant 3, globe**

1705 Beverley *Hist. VA* 2.24, The *James-Town* weed . . resembles the Thorny Apple of *Peru.* **1848** Gray *Manual of Botany* 354, Apple of Peru . . . *N[icandra] physaloides* . . . Sparingly naturalized near dwellings; a homely plant, native of Peru. August. **1901** Mohr *Plant Life AL* 708, Apple of Peru . . . Adventive and naturalized from southern Ontario to Pennsylvania, Ohio, and Missouri, and along the mountains to North Carolina. **1941** Walker *Lookout* 52, In some of the oldest gardens on Lookout Mountain is still found a plant that for more than two centuries had followed the old settlers and filled an important niche in their economic lives. This is fly-poison plant, or the Apple-of-Peru.

2 =**jimson weed.** [See 1705 quot above]

1784 in 1785 *Amer. Acad. Arts & Sci. Memoirs* 1.419, *Appleperu.* Stramonium. Thornapple. **1795** Winterbotham *Amer. U.S.* 3.397, Among the native and uncultivated plants of New-England, the following have been employed for medicinal purposes: . . . Appleperu, Datura Strammonium. **1813** *Henderson's N.C. Almanach* 23 *(DAE),* Strammonium is known in some parts of the country by the name of Apple peru and in others by that of James-Town weed. **1850** (1852) Hawthorne *Scarlet Letter* 54, A grassplot, much overgrown with burdock, pigweed, apple-peru, and such unsightly vegetation. **1889** (1971) Farmer *Americanisms* 20, Apple of Peru.—The Northern name for the Thorn Apple *(Datura stramonium)* or Jamestown Weed . . . also called the Devil's Trumpet. A coarse-growing troublesome weed; the seeds and stems are powerful narcotic poisons, sparingly used in medicine. **1960** Williams *Walk Egypt* 258 **GA**, If it [a heifer] had been poisoned, you could tell that easily enough; grab a handful of hide and hair, and if it stood in a peak when you let go, why it had eaten apple-of-Peru. **1971** Krochmal *Appalachia Med. Plants* 108, *Datura stramonium* . . . apple of Peru, apple Peru.

3 See quot. [Editor questions identification]

1895 *DN* 1.384 **sME,** Apple-peru: garden rhubarb, or pie-plant.

apple of Sodom n [After the Apple of Sodom described by Josephus: a fruit which dissolved into smoke and ashes when grasped] **SE** See also **Sodom berry**

=**horse nettle** (here: *Solanum carolinense*).

1892 (1974) Millspaugh *Amer. Med. Plants* 488, This order furnishes our Materia Medica with twenty drugs which [include] . . the Southern and West Indian Apple of Sodom, or Nipple Nightshade (*S. mammosum,* Linn.). **1930** Sievers *Amer. Med. Plants* 36, Horse Nettle . . . Apple of Sodom . . . This plant is easily recognized in late summer and fall by its round, smooth, orange-yellow berries . . . Part used.—The ripe berries, carefully dried. **1951** Teale *North Spring* 222 **NC,** Horse nettle—apple of Sodom or tread-softly—grows in a sandy place. **1960** Williams *Walk Egypt* 55 **GA**, Apple of Sodom thrust up prickly leaves and hung orange fruit everywhere between the rows of turnips, yams, and catnip. Sodom berries dried on the screen frames on the porch. There was nothing better for making a woman "come 'round."

apple palsy n [Prob from **applejack 1**] **NJ**

Drunkenness.

1894 *DN* 1.327 **cwNJ,** Apple palsy: "plain drunk" caused by too much "jack." **1945** Beck *Jersey Genesis* 156, A Jerseyism as strange as apple-palsy and blickey. **1968** McPhee *Pine Barrens* 59 **NJ**, Applejack is the laureate liquid of the pines. It is known as jack, and its effects are known as apple palsy.

apple pandowdy n Also ~ *dowdy* [*apple* + **pandowdy, dowdy**] **chiefly NEng** See *LANE* Map 292. Also called **apple grunt,** ~

John 2, ~ pot-pie, ~ slump, bald-headed pie, deep dish pie

A deep-dish apple dessert, usu with a rich biscuit crust.

1880 in 1939 Wolcott *Yankee Cook Book* 178, *Apple Pandowdy . . .* "Fill a heavy pot heaping full of pleasant apples, sliced. Add 1 cup molasses, 1 cup sugar, 1 cup water, 1 teaspoon cloves, 1 teaspoon cinnamon. Cover with baking powder biscuit crust, sloping it over the sides. Bake overnight. In the morning cut the hard crust into the apple. Eat with yellow cream or plain." **1913** *DN* 4.55 **ME,** *Apple-dowdy.* A kind of pudding made of apples with bread or batter, baked in a deep dish for a long time, and cut so that the crust comes in the middle. It is eaten with sugar and cream. **1923** Nutting *MA Beautiful* 241, Did ever a dish of apple dowdy go to the spot like that? **1932** (1946) Hibben *Amer. Regional Cookery* 269 **RI,** *Apple Pan Dowdy . . .* Toss sugar, spices and salt through the apples and arrange in a buttered baking dish . . . Bake . . . Roll out dough . . and lay on top of apples . . . Turn onto a serving platter apple side up. **1933** *Hanley Disks* ceMA, That's a dowdy, apple dowdy . . apple . . sugar . . nutmeg . . thick crust, either biscuit dough or pie crust . . no bottom. **1951** *AmSp* 26.251 **NY,** *Apple-dowdy.* **1964** *Amer. Heritage Cookbook* 569, *Apple Pandowdy . . .* Place in a preheated 400° oven for 10 minutes, then reduce heat to 325°. At this point, "dowdy" the dessert by cutting the crust into the apples with a sharp, sturdy knife. Return to oven and bake for 1 hour. Serve hot with thick cream or ice cream.

apple paring n, also attrib **chiefly Nth**

=**apple bee.**

1815 in 1895 *Moravian Hist. Soc. Trans.* 4.131, A sociable apple paring was started in which some neighbors joined, besides the numerous family. **1819** Noah *She Would Be Soldier* 19, I'm the boy for a race, for an apple-paring or quilting frolic. **1857** Riley *Puddleford Papers* 93, In the winter, husking-bees, apple-parings, and house-warmings were held every week at some of the farmhouses. **1892** Eggleston *Hoosier Schoolmaster* 6 **IN,** Apple-parin' bees. **1934** *Hanley Disks* ceCT, Huskin's and apple parin's . . . they used to dry apples. **1968** *DARE* Tape **IN**30, Apple parings . . [at which] the women would peel and core and get the apples ready, either to dry or to make into apple butter . . . [There would be] square dancing or a party after the paring.

apple peeling (social) n **chiefly Midl**

=**apple bee.**

1871 Eggleston *Hoosier Schoolmaster* 40 **IN,** One night at an apple-peelin' I tuck a sheet . . to splice out the table-cloth. **1939** (1954) *FWP Guide KY* 105, Barn-raisings, quilting parties, bran-hullings, apple-peelings, log-rollings, and singing parties are a major part of its social life. **1943** *Sun* (Baltimore MD) 29 Nov 6/2 *(Hench Coll.),* The neighbors used to come in for corn shuckin's, apple peelin's and wheat thrashin's. **1949** (1958) Stuart *Thread* 78 **KY,** I went with my pupils, their parents, and neighbors to cornhuskings, apple-peelings, bean-stringings. **1952** Brown *NC Folkl.* 1.243, Apple peelings are quite common social affairs in our section. A crowd of both old and young folks often gather together and peel and cut apples at night for a while. The young folks quit working not later than nine o'clock, and play games. **1967–69** *DARE* (Qu. FF1) Inf **NJ**1, Apple-peeling socials; (Qu. FF2) Infs **IN**30, **KY**40, 45, Apple peelings. **1968** *DARE* Tape **IN**16, Apple peelings . . . social gatherings.

apple Peru See **apple (of) Peru**

apple pickle n, usu pl Also *sweet ~* **chiefly wGt Lakes**

An apple, chopped and pickled in a mixture of vinegar, sugar, cinnamon and other spices.

1960 *Julian Apple Day* [24] **sCA,** *Apple pickle*—Put into a saucepan . . vinegar, . . salt, . . cinnamon and ginger. Pare, core and chop 1 pound of apples, and finely slice 1 pound red Spanish onions . . . pack into jars with a few red chilis. **1966–70** *DARE* (Qu. H56) Infs **IL**9, **MI**68, **MN**14, **SD**3, **WI**20, 66, Apple pickles; **IL**27, Sweet apple pickles.

apple-pie adj

1 Excellent; perfect. [Abbr for *apple-pie order* (see *DAE*)] Cf **apple** adj

1960 Wentworth–Flexner *Slang, Apple-pie . . .* Neat; perfect; orderly. **1968–69** *DARE* (Qu. KK1a, b) Inf **GA**31, Apple-pie—anything good is called apple-pie; **CA**39, Apple-pie, in apple-pie order; **NY**206, Apple-pie.

2 Easy. [Cf *DS* KK42a, b, and the common phr *easy as pie*] See also **applesauce** n 4

1960 Wentworth–Flexner *Slang.* **1967–70** *DARE* (Qu. KK42a) Infs **IL**96, **NY**230, **PA**11, 55, 104, 185, Apple-pie.

apple-pie bed See **apple turnover**

apple pot-pie n chiefly sNEng   See also **apple stew pie, pot apple pie**
=**apple pandowdy.**

   1848 Bartlett *Americanisms* 311, A favorite dish in New England, called an *apple slump*, is . . . called in other parts of the country an *apple pot-pie.* **1939** Wolcott *Yankee Cook Book* 178, Pandowdy is also called "Apple Jonathan" and "Apple Pot-Pie." **1941** *LANE* Map 292, 9 Infs, chiefly CT, RI, Apple pot-pie. **1965** *PADS* 43.24 seMA.

apple pummy See **pomace**

apple-pusher See **apple** n 7

apple sarse, apple sass See **sauce**

applesauce n, exclam [Perh orig in journalistic use: see 1929 *AmSp* 4.430]
1 Nonsense.   Cf *DS* NN13

   1921 *Collier's* 1 Jan 18/4, "Ssh!" interrupted the dealer wearily, as one who hears an old story. "That's all apple sauce." **1927** *AmSp* 2.275 CA. **1937** *Harper's Mag.* Feb 302, Karl Marx . . . called these loose-floating ideas *ideologies,* . . which freely translated into American means "applesauce." **1966–69** *DARE* (Qu. NN13) Infs CT22, NC35, OK31, WI59, WY5, Applesauce. **1979** *WI State Jrl.* (Madison) 15 Sep 4/3, You suggested there might be something organically wrong when the wife said her husband couldn't tie a bow . . . I say, "Applesauce!"

2 Flattery, suave talk.   Cf **applesauce** v
   1929 *Century Mag.* Autumn 70, 'Applesauce' means a camouflage of flattery, and is derived from the boarding-house trick of serving a plenty of this cheap comestible when richer fare is scanty. **1942** Berrey–Van den Bark *Amer. Slang* 188.3. *Ibid* 291.1.

‡**3** Something said to put off a child who asks too many questions.   Cf **layovers to catch meddlers**
   1967 *DARE* (Qu. NN12b) Inf OH8, If I'm making a dress, I say I'm making applesauce.

‡**4** =**apple pie 2.**
   1967 *DARE* (Qu. KK42a, *Expressions about a person who does something very easily: "For him that would be _____."*) Inf PA50, Applesauce.

‡**5** =**Adam's off-ox 1.**
   1968 *DARE* (Qu. II26, . . *"I wouldn't know him from _____."*) Inf OH81, Applesauce.

applesauce v   Cf **applesauce** n **1, 2**
   To take advantage of: see quot.
   1968 *DARE* (Qu. II33, . . *"I don't trust him; he's always trying to _____."*) Inf MD24, Applesauce you.

apple-seed fortune n   Also called *counting apple-seeds*
   A children's counting game and rhyme: see quot 1908.
   1883 Newell *Games & Songs* 109, *Counting Apple-seeds.* The following rhyme, used in New England at the beginning of the present century, remains unchanged in a single word . . . The apple, having been properly named, with a fillip of the finger was divided, to decide the fate of the person concerned according to its number of seeds. **1908** *DN* 3.287 eAL, wGA, *Apple-seed fortune* . . . A game, or rime on the number of seeds found in an apple. "One I love, two I love, / Three I love I say; . . Eleven he courts; twelve he marries." After the seeds are counted, they are placed in the palm of the hand and slapped upon the forehead. The seeds that stick indicate the number of children one will have.

apples from oranges, not to know v phr   Cf *DS* JJ15b
   To be ignorant of the most rudimentary forms of knowledge.
   1969 *DARE* (Qu. JJ15b, *Sayings about a person who seems to you very stupid: "He doesn't know _____."*) Inf RI13, Apples from oranges.

apple shaker n NEng   Cf *DS* B25
   A storm.
   1905 Wasson in 1962 *AmSp* 37.250 ME, We're liable to catch a reg'lar old "apple-shaker" most any day now. **1965** *PADS* 43.25 seMA.

apple-shine See **appleknock 2**

apple-shiner See **apple** n 7

apple shrub n [From the fragrance]
=**Carolina allspice.**
   [**1832** Hale *Flora's Interp.* 30, Carolina Allspice . . . [has] flowers

. . scented like ripe apples.] **1964** Batson *Wild Flowers SC* 48, *Apple-Shrub: Calycanthus floridus* . . . Flowers brownish-purple, . . numerous and fragrant.

appleskiver n, also attrib   Also sp *aebleskive(r)* [Dan *æble-skive(r) < æble* apple + *skive* disk, slice; dial] **Scandinavian settlement areas**
   A round batter cake, usu baked with apples in a special kind of pan.
   1940 Tufford *Scandinavian Recipes* 39, *Buttermilk Æble-skiver* . . . Beat eggs well, add sugar, lemon rind and buttermilk, then flour, salt, baking powder and soda sifted together. Heat Aebleskive pan, put 1 teaspoon melted butter in each hole, then fill half full of the batter. If apples are desired in the cakes, put a slice of cooked apple on top of the batter before turning to bake the second side. **1968–69** *DARE* (Qu. H63) Inf MI108, Appleskiver ['ɑpəlskivɚ]—a Scandinavian dessert made in a pan with round holes; (Qu. H65) Inf MN39, ['ɑbʊlskivɚ]—Danish.

apple slump n [*apple* + *slump*]   chiefly NEng, esp sNEng
=**apple pandowdy.**
   1831 Finn *Amer. Comic Annual* 140, The pumpkin pies and apple slump . . were smoking on the table. **1848** Bartlett *Americanisms* 311, A favorite dish in New England, called an *apple slump*, is made by placing raised bread or dough around the sides of an iron pot, which is then filled with apples and sweetened with molasses. **1903** *DN* 2.295 Cape Cod MA. **1941** *LANE* Map 292, **throughout eMA, CT, RI, and less freq in ME, VT, NH**, Apple slump. **1949** *AmSp* 24.106 SC, *Apple slump* . . . Deep apple pie ('old name'). **1951** *AmSp* 26.251 nNY. **1964** Amer. Heritage *Cookbook* 568, Louisa May Alcott's Apple Slump. The author of *Little Women* was so fond of this New England dessert that she named her house in Concord, Massachusetts, Apple Slump. **1967** *DARE* File scMA (as of 1950s), Apple slump . . . apple-sauce-filled spirals of biscuit dough laid side-by-side in brown sugar syrup and cooked into a pudding.

apple-smeller See **apple bug**

apple-snitzen See **schnitz**

apple snow n
=**apple float.**
   1939 Wolcott *Yankee Cook Book* 183 MA, *Apple Snow* . . . Peel and grate a large sour apple, sprinkling . . sugar over it. Break into this the whites of 2 eggs and beat all constantly until pudding is light and frothy . . . Heap into a glass dish and pour a custard around it and serve cold.

‡**apple sore** n
   Impetigo.
   1967 *DARE* (Qu. BB25) NY27, ['ɪnfɪn,tego]—it's an apple sore.

apple stew pie n   Var of **apple pot-pie**
   1941 *LANE* Map 292, 1 Inf, **seMA**, *Apple stew pie = apple grunt,* with dumplings on top.

appletree-er n   Also sp *appletreer* NAtl coast
   A coaster: a ship, or its passengers, which only travels near the shore. Hence also *appletree fleet,* a group of such coasters.   Also fig.
   1924 *DN* 5.287 Cape Cod MA, The old coasters which plied the coast were referred to as the 'Appletree fleet,' and the saying was they never got out of sight of the orchards along the shore. **1942** ME Univ. *Studies* 56.67, They were looked down upon by deep water sailors who called their crews . . *appletreers* because they never got beyond the range of their apple trees ashore. **1945** Colcord *Sea Language* ME, Cape Cod MA, Long Island NY, *Appletree-er.* **1975** Gould *ME Lingo* 36, *Apple-tree-er*—A coasting vessel that doesn't get out of sight of land, or a skipper who sails one. Also applied scornfully to passengers who are seasick, and particularly those who make a big thing out of fearing they will be. The word is used for timidity and extra caution. Cap'n Hosea Bibber wrote home that he was an *appletree-er* about the funicular at Vesuvius (afraid of height).

apple turnover n   Also *apple-pie bed* joc
   A short-sheeted bed.
   [**1904** Drury *Legends Apple* 47, A bed made up as a practical joke, with one sheet doubled upward in the middle, so that while the bed appears as usual from the outside, it prevents one from getting his limbs down. It is so called from the *apple-turn-over,* a pie folded over in the middle.] **1905**

Jrl. Amer. Folkl. 18.168, Apple-turn-over. As applied to a bed made in a certain way. **1950** *WELS (A bed that is made up the wrong way as a joke)* 1 Inf, **cwWI**, Apple-pie bed; 1 Inf, **cWI**, Apple-pie bed — the sheet is folded half way to make it look like two sheets, but when a person gets in they can't straighten out.

apple up v phr
To curry favor: apple-polish (someone).
    1968 *DARE* (Qu. JJ3a, . . *"He's trying to _____ again."*) Inf **MD41**, Apple her up.

apple-washer See **apple** n 7

applicate v [Back-formation from *application*, perh infl by *supplicate*]
    1929 *AmSp* 5.16 **Ozarks**, Applicate . . . To insist, to pester one with unwelcome requests. A mountain girl said of an undesirable suitor: "That feller jes' applicated me mornin' noon an' night till fin'ly I jes' tol' Paw t' run him off'n th' place."

appoint v Usu |ə'pɔɪnt|, also |ə'paɪnt| *old-fash* or *relic*; in **NYC** occas |ə'pɑnt| See Pronc Intro 3.I.11 Also aphet *'pint* Proncspp *appernt, ap(p)int;* similarly *appernt ment, appintment, 'pintment*
Std senses, var forms.
    1801 in 1956 Eliason *Tarheel Talk* 307 **NC**, Apint. **1803** *Ibid*, Appintment. **1841** (1952) Cooper *Deerslayer* 128 **NY**, The Deleware and I rendezvous'd an app'intment. **1856** in 1956 Eliason *Tarheel Talk* 307 **NC**, Pinted. **1871** Eggleston *Hoosier Schoolmaster* 39 **IN**, I 'low they'll appint the Squire. **a1883** (1911) Bagby *VA Gentleman* 56, Keepin' a appintment. **1891** *DN* 1.152 **cNY**, [əpaɪnt]. **1908** *DN* 3.287 **eAL, wGA**, Appint, appointment. **1916** Howells *Leatherwood God* 71 **OH**, There was 3 'p'intments. **1930s** in 1944 *ADD* **NYC**, Appoint . . . Freq. spelt *appernt* & heard by some as [əpɑnt]. **1942** *New Yorker* 11 July 17/3 **NYC**, Has she got an appernntment?

appola n Also *apola, appalo* [Cf *DCan appalat* in similar sense, from French *apala* titbit; the US use, occas considered an Indian loan, is prob infl by Span *a palo* on a stick] **West** *obs*
Skewered meat; also, the skewers upon which meat was cooked.
    1845 Frémont *Rept. Rocky Mts.* 113, To-night the camp fires, girdled with *appolas* of fine venison, looked cheerful in spite of the stormy weather. [**1850** Garrard *Wah-to-yah* 25 **KS**, At every mess fire, pieces of meat were cooking *en appolas;* that is, on a stick sharpened, with alternate fat and lean meat, making a delicious roast.] **1902** (1968) Clapin *Americanisms, Apola* . . . An Indian word, frequently met in the relations of the old French traders and "voyageurs" of Canada, and designating a certain variety of stew made with larks. **1948** *NE Hist.* 6 Mar, *Appolas*, the sharpened sticks upon which meat was hung over the fire to cook. **1968** Adams *Western Words, Appalos* — A trapper's term for alternate cuts of fat and lean meat skewered on a sharpened stick and roasted.

appreciate v Pronc-spp *'preciate, 'preshate*
A Forms.
    1927 Kennedy *Gritny* 210 **sLA** [Black], 'Tain no use try'n to sattafy some people, w'en dey ain' never learnt how to 'preshate li'l favors.
B Senses.

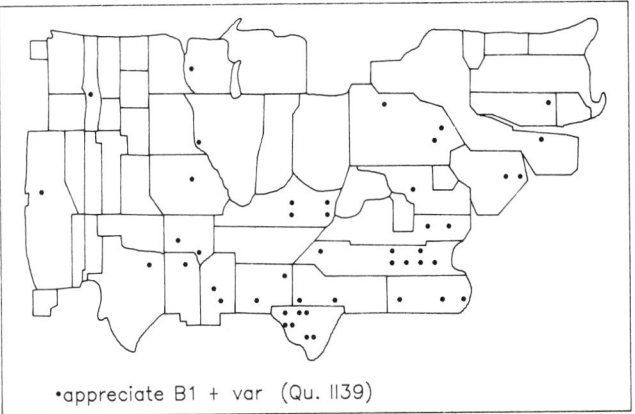

•appreciate B1 + var (Qu. II39)

1 in phr *(ap)preciate it:* Thank you. **chiefly Sth, Midl** *informal* See Map For non-regional varr, see *DS* II39

1965–70 *DARE* (Qu. II39, . . *Other ways . . of saying "thank you"*) 48 Infs, **chiefly Sth, Midl**, (Ap)preciate it.
2 refl: To enjoy oneself.
    1936 *AmSp* 11.368 **nLA**, Appreciate. To enjoy oneself; as, 'I want to appreciate myself very much tonight.'

‡approacher n [From *approach* make overtures to a person in the attempt to corrupt him (*DA* 1857 →)]
One who curries favor.
    1970 *DARE* (Qu. II20a, . . *"He's an awful _____."*) Inf **CA209**, Approacher.

apricot n
A Forms.
    1965–70 *DARE* (Qu. I53, *Other fruits grown around here*) 138 Infs, **widespread exc Nth**, ['eprɪˌkat, 'eprɪkɔt, 'epɚkat, 'epɚˌkɔt]; 53 Infs, **chiefly Nth**, ['æprɪkat, 'æprɪkɔt].
B Sense.
Also *apricot vine, wild apricot:* =The **maypop** vine; also its fruit. [From the resemblance of the fruit to an apricot] **chiefly S Midl**
    1888 Branner *Plants AR* 250, *Passiflora incarnata*, which is here called 'apricot,' is a straggling, careless vine with triple-lobed leaves. **1913** Morley *Carolina Mts.* 68, In some parts of the mountains the people call the maypops "apricots" and eat them. **1916** Muir *1000 Mile Walk* 56 (as of 1867), A species of passion flower is common, reaching back into Tennessee. It is here [Georgia] called 'apricot vine,' has a superb flower, and the most delicious fruit I have ever eaten. **1956** McAtee *Some Dialect NC* 3, Apricot . . the maypop or passion-flower. **c1960** Wilson *Coll.* **csKY**, Apricot vine . . . The maypop or passion-flower *(Passiflora incarnata)* and its fruit. **1964** Campbell *Great Smoky Wildflowers* 46, Passion-Flower . . . Also known as *Wild Apricot* and *Maypop*.

April n Usu |'eprəl|, occas |'eprɪl|; in **Midl**, occas |'epra(ɪ)l|; also |'epəl, 'epʊl, 'epɚl| Pronc-spp *Apriel, Aprile* See also 1939 *LANE* Map 36, 1976 Allen *LAUM* 3.22
Std senses, var forms.
    1855 in 1956 Eliason *Tarheel Talk* 307 **NC**, Apriel. **1890** *DN* 1.38 **ME**, April: [eɪprɪl], not [eɪprəl]. The [ɪ] is distinct. **1894** Riley *Armazindy* 2 **IN**, Nex' Aprile. **1903** *DN* 2.305 **seMO**, April . . ['eprail]. **1908** *DN* 3.287 **eAL, wGA**, April . . . ['epʊl]. **1922** *DN* 5.134 **NE**, Students and others often make these words oxytones . . favorite . . Aprile [aɪ]. *Ibid* 200 **swMO**, Aprĭle. **1936** *AmSp* 11.244 **eTX**, April . . *Hill-Type* ['epɚl] . . *Negro* ['epəl]. **1942** Hall *Smoky Mt. Speech* 72 **eTN, wNC**, April was ['eɪˌpraɪl] in the speech of a young man of Emerts Cove; a high-school girl of Cosby said that this is her grandmother's pronunciation. **1949** *AmSp* 24.106 **GA**, ['eɪˌpra:əl].

April fools n Also *April fool*
=**pasqueflower** (here: *Anemone patens*).
    1893 *Bot. Gaz.* 18.421 **IL**, April fools . . Perhaps because they blossom about April 1, and are afterwards sometimes snowed under. Rockford. **1900** Lyons *Plant Names* 311, American . . Pasque-flower, April-fool, . . or Wild Crocus. **1937** U.S. Forest Serv. *Range Plant Hdbk.* W159 (leaf 2), Although pasqueflower is the common name most widely used, such other appellations as April-fools . . have variously designated this species.

apron n Usu |'e(ɪ)prən|; also, **chiefly Nth, Midl**, |'e(ɪ)pɚn|; occas |'e(ɪ)pən|; rarely |'e(ɪ)mp(r)ən| Pronc-spp *ampron, apern, ap'n, aporn, apun, apurn*
A Forms.
    1805 (1905) Lewis *Orig. Jrls. Lewis & Clark Exped.* 3.166, Canoes . . with aperns, and heads of animals carved on the bow. **1891** *DN* 1.163 **cNY**, ['epən]. **1899** (1912) Green *VA Folk-Speech, Apron strings* . . . Apun. **1905** *DN* 3.58 **eNE**, Intrusive *n*, the "nasal infix," occurs in . . *a(m)pron*, . . but it is rare. **1908** *DN* 3.287 **eAL, wGA**, Apern. **1910** *DN* 3.436 **wNY**, Apurn. **1936** *AmSp* 11.245 **eTX**, Apron . . *Plantation-Type* ['eprən], ['epən] . . *Hill-Type* ['epɚn] . . *Negro* ['epən]. **1941** *LANE* Map 364, **throughout NEng**, Pronunciations of the type of [eɪpən] are described as natural or most common by . . [11 Infs]; and as older though still in use by . . [14 Infs]; **chiefly CT, RI, MA**, [e(ɪ)prn]; 1 Inf, **csNH**, [eːɪmpɚn]. **1942** Hall *Smoky Mt. Speech* 71 **eTN, wNC**, ['eɪpɚn]. **1944** *PADS* 2.17 **sAppalachians**, *Aporn* ['epɚn]. **1966–70** *DARE* (Qu. F12) Infs **AR47, GA1, KY41, MS1**, ['e(ɪ)pɚn]; **MS85**, ['epən]; (QR p 200) Inf **MI75A**, ['ɛmprən]. **1975** Gould *ME Lingo* 36, Ap'n. Correct Maine pronunciation of apron. **1976** Allen *LAUM* 3.296, The majority in each of the three groups have

|ˈepən|. The records also suggest a possible regional weighting . . , since |ˈepən| is more frequent in the Northern speech areas.

B Senses.

1 The infolded abdomen of a crab. **MD, VA**

1877 *Field & Forest* 2.73 **coastal MD, VA,** This mass is very conspicuous, even in the rapidly swimming crab, and causes the abdominal flap (called apron by the fisherman) to be opened almost to its fullest extent. **1899** (1912) Green *VA Folk-Speech.* **1968** *DARE* Tape MD39. **1970** *DARE* FW Addit VA47, Apron—underside of body shell of a crab. **1976** Warner *Beautiful Swimmers* 16 **eMD,** All males have abdominal aprons in the shape of an inverted T. A young female or "she-crab" has a V-shaped apron. When she becomes sexually mature . . the apron changes to a semicircular bell shape with only the point of the V on top.

2 The skirt of a saddle. **?West** See also **apron strap**

1893 Sanborn *Truthful Woman* 177 **sCA,** The corners of the aprons [on a saddle] are tipped with silver. **1977** Watts *Dict. Old West, Apron . . .* Possibly not solely a Westernism.

3 A thin flexible sheet hanging or standing away from a solid body; e.g. in evaporating maple syrup: see quot. See also **apron** v

1965 Teale *Wandering Through Winter* 297 **VT,** Pour some of the syrup from a ladle; if it tends to thicken and form an "apron" along the edge [of the ladle], it is ready to remove from the pan.

4 The flat piece, usu of metal or stone, which protects the floor beneath a wood-burning stove or fireplace. **chiefly Sth, Midl**

1965–70 *DARE* (Qu. F12, *The flat metal piece below a wood-burning stove, to catch the ashes*) 20 Infs, **chiefly Sth, Midl,** Apron; (Qu. D31, *In front of a fireplace . . stonework on the floor*) Infs IA47, NJ28, VT12, Apron.

5 The shoulder of a road. Cf *DS* N25

1966 *DARE* FW Addit eNC, [Highway sign] Do not drive on aprons. **1967–69** *DARE* (Qu. N25, *The unpaved part of a graded road along the edge of the pavement*) Infs CA111, CO7, Apron.

apron v Also with *off* [apron n B3] **VT**

1959 *VT Hist.* ns 27.124 **neVT,** Apron . . . To coat the spoon. Jelly is ready when it *aprons.* Common . . . Apron off . . . In maple sugaring, the liquid aprons off when it is thick enough for syrup. Common.

apron child n Cf **arm baby, breast baby, floor baby, knee baby, lap child, pallet baby, waist baby**

A child old enough to stand by holding on to its mother's apron.

1958 Randolph *Sticks* 111 **Ozarks,** There was one creeper, one walker, two pallet babies, one suckling, and an apron child. The census taker says, "Do all these children belong to you and Jim?"

apron-faced adj **West**

Of a horse: having a large white patch on the forehead.

1942 Berrey–Van den Bark *Amer. Slang* 120.48, *Apron-faced horse,* a horse with a large white streak on the forehead. **1944** Adams *Western Words.* **1977** Watts *Dict. Old West.*

apron strap n, usu pl Also ~ *string* [apron B2] **West**

See quot 1977.

1910 Hart *Vigilante Girl* 137 **CA,** The express messenger, his gun across his knees, had hitched the apron-strap around his leg, thereby keeping himself anchored. **1977** Watts *Dict. Old West, Apron-straps.* Also *apron-strings.* Straps attached to the leather skirt of a saddle, for securing bedroll, slicker, and all manner of things to a saddle.

apron string n

1 A noodle.

1936 Carmer *Listen Drum* 328 **seNY,** Still other delicacies include summer sausage . . "apron strings" (noodles), Training Day gingerbread.

2 See **apron strap.**

apun, apurn See **apron**

apurpose adv [a prep[1] 3 + *purpose;* cf *EDD*] **chiefly NEng, Midl** *somewhat old-fash*

On purpose, intentionally.

1816 in 1947 *AmSp* 22.285, A-purpose. 'he did it apurpose.' is not this an Americanism? **1835** Bird *Hawks* 1.130 **PA, DE,** We're all keeping awake, just a-purpose to be ready and handy. **1899** (1912) Green *VA Folk-Speech.* **1903** *DN* 2.300 eMA (as of 1850s). **1908** *DN* 3.285 **eAL, wGA.** **1915** *DN* 4.180 **swVA.** **1939** *Hall Coll.* **eTN,** He came down

a-purpose to kill him. **1943** *LANE* Map 719 *(On Purpose)* **throughout NEng,** A-purpose. [Commentary:] *A-purpose* is described as the usual or more common expression by . . [5 Infs]; as less common by . . [3 Infs]; and as older though still in use by . . [3 Infs]. **c1960** *Wilson Coll.* **csKY.** **1969** *DARE* FW Addit MA14, Used to walk apurpose to hear him. **1970** *DARE* (Qu. X43b, *If you sleep later than usual*) Inf **LA2,** Stayed in bed apurpose.

aquadiente, aquadinte, aquedent See **aguardiente**

ar See **there**

ar' See **be A1**

a'r See **air** n

Arab n Usu |ˈærəb, ˈɛrəb|, freq, esp in humorous use and non-std senses, |ˈeɪˌræb| Pronc-spp *A-rab, Ayrab, Urb*

A Forms.

1903 *DN* 2.292 **eMA** (as of 1850s), Vowels were pronounced long in . . Ārab. **1966–69** *DARE* FW Addits swNC, Arab [ˈɛrəb]; MA56, Arabs [ˈɛræbz]. **1978** *New Yorker* 6 Feb 59 **GA,** Until lately, nobody in Georgia had thought much about Arabs from anywhere; today, people searching for differences between various parts of the state cite as one of them that whereas north Georgians call Arabs "*Ay*-rabs," south Georgians call them "Urbs."

B Senses.

1 A homeless child, street urchin. [*OED arab* 3, 1848 →; *street Arab,* 1865 →]

1911 Shute *Plupy* 179 **seNH** (as of 1860s), She hated boys and no wonder, and at the approach of a street Arab, the whites of her rolling eyes showed like those of a vicious broncho. **1927** Kennedy *Gritny* 160 **sLA** [Black], He steal off evvy chance he git; an' go yonder in de swamp, wid Mahaley chillun an' some dem yuther hongry li'l A-rabs from down de street.

2 An unkempt or wild-looking person, esp a child. See also **sheik of Araby**

1903 *DN* 2.295 **Cape Cod MA** (as of 1850s), *Arab . . .* A wild looking or acting person. **1945** Colcord *Sea Language* 24 **Long Island NY, Cape Cod MA, eME,** A reproof to a naughty child: "You little Ay-rab, you!" From the Barbary corsairs, reports of whose savagery were widely current in seafaring communities . . . This is no doubt the origin of the landsman's street Arab. **c1960** *Wilson Coll.* **csKY,** [ˈeˌræb] Sometimes a term for a wild-looking or unkempt person. "Who's that Arab a-coming into church?" Still the more common pronc.

3 A huckster; a street peddler of vegetables and fruits. **Baltimore MD** See also **arab** v 1, **arabber**

1935 *Sun* (Baltimore MD) 15 July 4/5 (*AmSp* 26.72), These alien fruits of summer [watermelons from Texas and Georgia] are mighty good when we get them in our markets or from the Arabs that peddle them around. **1940** FWP *Guide MD* 8, The huckster himself is probably called an a-rab. **1940** Mencken *Happy Days* 57, **Baltimore MD,** All Spring the streets swarmed with hucksters selling such things: they called themselves, not hucksters, but Arabs (with the first *a* as in Day), and announced their wares with loud, raucous, unintelligible cries, much worn down by phonetic decay. **1956** *AmSp* 31.311 **Baltimore MD,** My grandmother . . would at times buy from a regular huckster, . . but she would never buy anything from an "ay-rab." This was around 1900. **1968** *DARE* (Qu. U6) Infs MD9, 31, [ˈɛræb]. **1980** *Capital Times* (Madison WI) 9 Apr 53/2 **Baltimore MD,** The traditional fruit and produce vendors of downtown Baltimore—known to locals as street Arabs, ay'rabbers for short—believe they are a dying breed . . . Arabber Larry Crapper says he wants to preserve his only trade.

4 Transf: A street-roaming taker of horse-racing bets. **Baltimore MD** Cf **arab** v 3

1955 *Sun* (Baltimore MD) 27 May B 38/4 *(Hench Coll.),* If you pick up the A-rab all you find is money and a scratch sheet.

5 A Jew.

1927 *Vanity Fair* Nov 67/2, Among some of Conway's more famous expressions are: "Bimbo" (for a dumb girl); . . "Arab" (A Jew). **1936** Mencken *Amer. Lang.* 560, Jack Conway . . of the staff of *Variety* . . is credited with the invention of . . *Arab* (for Jew). **1939** in 1944 *ADD* **NYC.**

6 A people of mixed breed, partially Indian: see quots. **ceNY**

1937 Gardner *Folkl. Schoharie* 43 **ceNY,** "Arabs" is another class name applied in the town of Summit to shiftless people who, as it is often said, are at home wherever night overtakes them. **1963** Berry *Almost White*

23, In Schoharie County [NY] there are several groups of supposedly Indian ancestry—the Honies, the Slaughters of Slaughter Hill, the Clappers of Clapper Hollow, and the "Arabs" of Summit.

7 Among loggers: one who shirks work.

1958 McCulloch *Woods Words* 3 **Pacific NW**, *Arab*—A workman . . always managing to be away when there's dirty or heavy work to be done.

arab v |'eˌræb| **Baltimore MD**

1 To huckster. [**Arab** n **B3**]

1948 Mencken *Amer. Lang. Suppl. 2* 162 **Baltimore MD**, *Arab,* to go huckstering. **1951** *AmSp* 26.71 **Baltimore MD**, 'And what do you do for a living?' His Honor asks. 'I arabs,' replies the defendant. **1980** *Capital Times* (Madison WI) 9 Apr 53/4 **Baltimore MD**, I always arabbed, you were your own boss, you got to take it easy, you met all types of people.

2 To search about.

1949 *Sun* (Baltimore MD) 11 Aug 9/1 (1951 *AmSp* 26.72), Wallace said that the investigators (of a murder) had 'nothing concrete' to go on . . 'We are just "arabing," ' Wallace said. He explained he meant 'canvassing around for clues.'

3 To take a horse-racing bet on the street. [From **Arab** n **B4**]

1952 *Sun* (Baltimore MD) 15 Dec B28/1 (1956 *AmSp* 31.311), 'Arabing' is the word police use to describe present-day bookmaking operations on the streets of Baltimore . . . The 'arabing' bookie will take bets—including the money—from a very few customers at one time, because he writes nothing down and must remember the horses, the bettors and the amounts. **1955** *Sun* (Baltimore MD) 27 May B38/4 (Hench Coll.), The vice squad head described the . . bookmaking operation as "A-rabing bets."

arabber n |'eˌræbə(r)| Also *araber,* pronc-sp *ayraba* **Baltimore MD**

=**Arab** n **B3**.

1942 Footner *MD Main* 8, Every "ayraba" (huckster) dreams of the day when he can purchase a diminutive wagon and a pony to pull it. **1948** Mencken *Amer. Lang. Suppl. 2* 162 **Baltimore MD**, *Araber,* a street huckster. **1951** *AmSp* 26.71 **Baltimore MD**, Our receptionist tells me that in her early youth in South Baltimore, hucksters were called *arabbers* as well as *arabs.* **1968** *DARE* (Qu. U6) Inf **MD9**, ['eˌræbɚ]. Arabber.

arapajo n Also *arapaho* [Metath; perh by false association with the *Arapaho* Indians] **SW**

=**aparejo.**

1854 Delano *Life on Plains* 334 **CA**, We purchased twelve beautiful Peruvian mules, with necessary arapahoes, (Mexican pack saddles). **1903** White *Forest* 24, One hears strange, suggestive words and phrases —arapajo, capote, . . and a dozen others coined into the tender of daily use. **1977** Watts *Dict. Old West*, *Arapaho*—A corruption of *aparejo.* Somebody sometime must have confused the term with the Arapaho Indians.

arastra See **arrastra**

arb See **herb**

arbeauties, arbeauty See **arbutus**

arbor n Usu |'ɑrbɚ|, occas |'hɑrbə(r)| Also sp *arbour,* pronc-spp *harbor, harbour*

A Forms.

1917 in 1944 *ADD* **sWV**, Harbour. **1941** *Ibid* **eWV**, Grape harbor. **1966** *DARE* (QR p61) Inf **SC4**, Scuppernongs grow on ['hɑ·bəz].

B Senses.

1 =**brush arbor**. **Sth Midl**

1823 J. Thacher *Jrnl. Amer. Revol.* 244 (*OED*), We erected a large arbor, with the boughs of trees. **1899** (1912) Green *VA Folk-Speech* 68, *Arbour* . . . A bower formed by trees, shrubs, or vines . . trained over a lattice work, so as to make a leafy roof, usually provided with seats; where meetings are held. **c1937** in 1970 Yetman *Voices* 75, Us niggers didn't have no secret meetin's. All us had was church meetin's in arbors out in de woods. **1938** (1955) FWP *Guide DE* 508, The fire was protected by "harbors" of brush, made windproof and fireproof by a covering of pine "shats" and clay. **c1960** Wilson Coll. **csKY**, *Arbor* . . . A frame of poles over an outdoor meeting place, covered with small boughs cut from trees.

2 Transf: a revival meeting.

1915 *DN* 4.224 **wTX**, *Arbor* . . . Used by metonymy for "revival meeting."

arbor-away n Also *~ down*

A children's game played with a stick: see quot.

1967 *DARE* (QR p 231) Inf **CO3**, Arbor-away: [a game] like free base games. A stick was thrown and the "it" had to get it and get back to base before anyone else touched base. Same as *arbor-down.*

arbuckle n[1] See **carbuncle**

arbuckle n[2] [Trade name of a popular coffee, c1900] **West**

1 also *Arbuckle's:* Any coffee.

1944 Adams *Western Words, Arbuckle's*—The brand of coffee so common on the range that most cowmen never knew there was any other kind. **1966** *Good Old Days* Feb 6 **St. Louis MO**, Remember the saucered coffee days? Nobody could endure their Arbuckles if it was hot. It had to be poured into a saucer. **1977** Watts *Dict. Old West, Arbuckle* . . . A generic term for coffee.

2 A greenhorn cowhand; tenderfoot. [See quot 1941]

1933 *AmSp* 8.1.29 **TX**, *Arbuckle,* Tenderfoot. **1941** FWP *Guide WY* 459, *Arbuckle* . . applied to a cowboy, implying that the boss must have got him by mail order with Arbuckle premium stamps. **1944** Adams *Western Words.* **1977** Watts *Dict. Old West.*

arbutus n Also *trailing arbutus* Pronc-spp and folk-etyms *arbeauties (-y), our beauties, habutus* Cf **madrone**

A creeping evergreen plant (*Epigaea repens*) with hairy oval leaves and clusters of usu pink flowers, native to much of the eastern half of the US. Also called **crocus** n[1] **2c, gravel plant, gravelweed 5, groundhog's forehead, groundlaurel, groundsweet, mayflower, maypink 3, mountain pink 2, shadflower 1, terrapin's foot, winter pink**

1822 Eaton *Botany* 271, *Epigaea* . . trailing arbutus. **1895** *DN* 1.398 **csNY**, *Our beauties.* **1911** NJ State Museum *Annual Rept.* 619, *Epigaea repens* . . Arbutus. **1965–70** *DARE* (Qu. S26c) 45 Infs, **chiefly Atlantic, also Gt Lakes,** (Trailing) arbutus; (Qu. S2) 27 Infs, **chiefly Atlantic, also Gt Lakes,** (Trailing) arbutus; **CT31**, Trailing habutus; (Qu. S26e) Infs **CT12, IL50, MA14, 25, 58, MI31, PA49,** Arbutus; **CT2, MD18, MI76, 82, PA105, TN6, VT16,** Trailing arbutus; **MD20,** ['ɑrˌbjutiz]; **WI78,** Trailing arbeauties [ɑr'bjutiz]; One arbeauty—sg form; (Qu. S26a) Infs **CT11, MA5, MI15, NJ4,** Arbutus; **PA60,** Trailing arbutus; (Qu. S26b) Infs **MA6, MI34, PA74, WI64,** Arbutus; **GA70, MI9, NY1,** Trailing arbutus; (Qu. S26d) Infs **MI2, 17, NJ16, 58,** Trailing arbutus; (Qu. S23) Inf **CT6,** Arbutus; **MA74,** Trailing arbutus; (Qu. S4) Inf **MI26,** Trailing arbutus; (Qu. S21) Inf **IL98,** Trailing arbutus.

arce-up See **ass-up**

arch n

1 also *arch cellar:* A curved area in the basement foundation of a fireplace, used for storage of vegetables; later transf to similar outdoor structures.

1786 (1903) Patten *Diary* 528 **NH**, David began to build the wall of the Arch for our Chimney. **1845** *Lowell Offering* 5.256 **neMA**, We . . descend into her cellar . . . Here is a nice arch for potatoes and all other freezeable commodities. **1967** *DARE* (Qu. M19, *A place for keeping carrots, turnips, potatoes, and so on over the winter*) Inf **PA29,** Arch—in ground, everything covered over.

2 also *boiling arch:* A fireplace or furnace used for boiling down maple sap. **chiefly NEng** Cf **evaporator 1**

1867 *Harper's Weekly* 4 May 286/2, The fluid thus extracted, without further effort is then put in barrels, and drawn to "the arch" or "fireplace," which is built of a few stones laid upon each other to hold the "pans" or "kettles," where it is boiled down to a sirup. **1874** VT State Bd. Ag. *Report* 2.728, Boiling arches should be of good depth, not filled up at back end. **1917** *DN* 4.387 **neOH, VT,** *Arch* . . . Furnace (of brick, stone, or the like) for boiling maple sap. **1923** Frost *New Hampshire* 102, Outside the sugar-house one night for choice, / I called the fireman with a careful voice / And bade him leave the pan and stoke the arch. **1947** *PADS* 8.4 **VT,** *Arch* . . . A long and narrow iron (sometimes brick) furnace. In the earlier days it was made of brick. **1966** *DARE* Tape **MA5,** Almost all of that old sugar that they boiled down in an arch [ɑč] was quite dark-colored . . . There was one pan or pot on each arch and the sap was dipped from one to another or boiled in one till it was syrup; **NH5,** All he had was a big pan, two of 'em . . on brick arches.

3 A curved iron or steel bar supporting the bricks over the opening of a fireplace and hooks to hold cooking utensils.

1954 Harder Coll. **cwTN,** *Arch* . . . A bar of iron or steel that holds up the stones or bricks above the opening of the fireplace. **1968** *DARE* Tape **IN51,** What we called an arch, you built up over your fireplace inside. Made out of steel, about a half-moon circle. Had hooks on it. We took these old-fashioned pots . . and we hooked 'em up there and that's what my grandmother cooked her beans and boiled her ham and all that.

4 =**tournament pole. MD, VA, WV**

1963 *Chr. Sci. Monitor* (Boston MA) 25 March 17 **nwMD, nwVA, neWV,** Newcomers to this beautiful section of West Virginia often slow down and wonder when they notice in fields close to the highways, three high wooden arches in a row, sixty feet apart, with a stiff wire suspended from the center of each crossbar, and a narrow, well-worn path running beneath the arches . . . Each wire holds a cord-wrapped ring . . . Riders on galloping horses, armed with long metal-tipped spears thunder under the arches, picking off the tiny rings. **1968** *DARE* Tape **WV8,** You take an' put up these three arches, then you put a ring on each arch, . . then they take three rides at those rings, . . then those lances should be nine feet long, . . then those rings are iron wrapped, crocheted.

5 also attrib: In logging: a derrick-like device attached to a tractor and used to hold up one end of a log that is being skidded. **West, esp Pacific NW**

1950 *Western Folkl.* 9.115 **nwOR,** *Arch.* A short, curved derrick mounted on a crawler trailer that is pulled by a cat equipped with drums. It is used in cat logging to skid the logs to the landing. **1956** *AmSp* 31.149 **nwCA,** *Arch* . . . A piece of equipment used to hold up one end of the logs being logged by a tractor. **1958** McCulloch *Woods Words* **Pacific NW,** *Arch*—A trailer to be pulled behind a tractor . . . *Arch cat*—A tractor used to yard logs with an arch. *Arch hook*—A two-or three-hole hook permitting several chokers to be attached on one line. *Arch line*—A wire rope which is run over the arch and to which the chokers from the logs are attached. **1968** Adams *Western Words, Arch*—In logging, a piece of equipment used to hold up one end of the logs. A sled, often the fork of a tree, used in skidding logs.

6 In mining: the curved area left between the top and side of a mine when an automatic coal-mining machine is used.

1973 *PADS* 59.25 **sIL.**

archangel n

1 =**angelica 1a** (here: *Angelica atropurpurea*).

1873 in 1976 Miller *Shaker Herbs* 127, *Angelica atropurpurea* . . Archangel. **1900** Lyons *Plant Names* 35. **1971** Krochmal *Appalachia Med. Plants* 46.

2 A **water horehound** (esp *Lycopus virginicus*).

1874 *Shaker Med. Preparations,* Archangel . . Lycopus Sinuatus. **1900** Lyons *Plant Names* 233, *L[ycopus] Virginicus* . . Green Archangel. **1930** Sievers *Amer. Med. Plants* 17, *Lycopus virginicus* . . Other common names . . . green archangel . . purple archangel.

3 =**dead nettle 1.**

1901 Lounsberry *S. Wild Flowers* 448, *Lamium purpureum,* sweet archangel. **1974** (1977) Coon *Useful Plants* 158, *Lamium amplexicaule* . . white archangel. **1982** *Wayside Gardens* 78, *Lamium Galeobdolon 'Variegatum'* Known as Yellow Archangel or Silver Nettle Vine.

4 =**butterfly weed 1.**

1894 *Jrl. Amer. Folkl.* 7.94, *Asclepias tuberosa,* . . Archangel, (near) Providence, R.I.

arch cellar See **arch 1**

arch kettle n [arch 3]

A kettle built into a fireplace for heating water.

1939 *LANE* Map 131 (*kettle; pot*) 2 Infs, **neNH, cwME,** Arch kettle. **1965** Needham – Mussey *Country Things* 130 **seVT** (as of c1850), Places like the old Liberty Pole Tavern . . had to heat a lot of water, so there would be an arch kettle built right in on one side of the fireplace. The arch was generally fired from inside the house, and you had a door that opened out into the shed; you could reach out and bail hot water from outside the partition. The kettle would hold maybe forty gallons.

arch nose n

A hooked nose.

1967–68 *DARE* (Qu. X15, . . *Different kinds of noses, according to shape*) Infs **KS5, PA70,** Arch nose.

arch one's back v phr **West**

Literally of a horse: to start to buck. Also fig, of humans: to show anger.

1944 Adams *Western Words, Arches his back*—Said of an angry person, of a horse preparing to buck. **1961** Adams *Old-Time Cowhand* 295 **West,** When a hoss started to buck there were a lot of slang expressions the cowhand used . . . The hoss "arches his back," "boils over," . . "wrinkles his spine."

‡**archy grass** n Var of **orchard grass**

1970 *DARE* (Qu. L9a, . . *Grass . . grown for hay*) Inf **KY93,** Archy grass. [FW: orchard grass is pronounced "archy grass."]

arctic n[1], also attrib |ˈɑrktɪk, ˈɑrtɪk| Pronc-spp *artic, ar'tic* chiefly **Nth**

A warm waterproof overshoe, freq fur-lined and usu fastened by four buckles; a galosh.

1867 *Territorial Enterprise* (Virginia, Nev.) 1 Mar 1/1 *(DA),* The 'arctic' boots are taking the place of rubber overshoes . . . and are more serviceable. **1878** *Atlantic Mth.* 41.327/2 **ME,** He . . shook the snow of his native city from his arctics, and went forth into the world. **1890** *Harper's Mag.* 81.69 **NYC,** To see Mr. Fox pacing the platform . . with mittens and arctic overshoes. **1909** *DN* 3.292 **nwAR,** *Ar'tics* . . . Overshoes that fasten with one or more buckles. **1911** *DN* 3.541 **NE.** **1937** *FWP Guide MA* 267, In 1800 the State Legislature passed an act to encourage the manufacture of shoes, boots, and 'arctics' (galoshes). **1950** *WELS (Kinds of rubber footwear)* 10 Infs, **throughout WI,** Ar(c)tics. **1954** *Harder Coll.* **cwTN.** **1965–66** *DARE* (Qu. W13; total Infs questioned, 75) Inf **DC4,** Arctics; **OK47,** Four-buckle arctics; **OK18,** Four-buckle artics [ɑrɖɪks]; **OK18A,** "Artic" is a catalogue name, not used much. **1967** *DARE* FW Addit **nwMI,** Arctics [ˈɑrtɪks] meaning overshoes or galoshes—that's the term. I don't think I heard "overshoes" or "galoshes" once.

arctic n[2]

A playing marble: ? =**arnick.**

1969 *DARE* Tape **MI103,** Set-ups [included] arctics, agates, snotties, steelies.

Arctic owl n chiefly **NEast, Gt Lakes**

=**snowy owl 1.**

1839 *MA Zool. & Bot. Surv. Fishes Reptiles* 276, The Arctic, or White-horned Owl, *Strix arctica,* is a rare and beautiful bird. **1951** Graham *My Window* 45 **ME,** I swung round and I seen this big white thing swoopin' down on the lower field. It wuz an ar'tic owl. **1955** *U.S. Arctic Info. Center Gloss., Arctic owl.* A common misnomer for the snowy owl. **1965–70** *DARE* (Qu. Q2, *Other kinds of owls*) 12 Infs, **chiefly NEast, Gt Lakes,** Arctic owl; Infs **ME6, 8, NY227,** [ˈɑrtɪk] owl; **MA78,** Snowy arctic owls; **MA30,** White arctic owls; (Qu. Q10) Inf **WI78,** Arctic owl.

Arctic trout n **AK**

A fish of the trout family, such as the grayling or the **coho salmon,** but in Alaska often the **Dolly Varden** trout.

1935 *Alaska Sportsman* Jan 8 (Tabbert *Alaskan Engl.*), One of my earliest fishing trips was . . . to establish connections with a huge fish known locally as "Arctic Trout." *Ibid* 9, When the first "Arctic Trout" was landed, . . it was revealed to be but a brilliant colored subspecies of the familiar Dolly Varden. **1946** *Alaska Sportsman* May 36 (Tabbert *Alaskan Engl.*), Dolly Vardens really get around. Way back . . some of them wandered up into the rivers of the Bering Sea and Arctic Ocean, where they . . stayed and developed into huge, beautiful fish glorified by the name of Arctic trout. **1946** LaMonte *N. Amer. Game Fishes* 107, *Oncorhynchus kisutch* . . *Names:* Coho Salmon, . . Arctic Trout. **1955** U.S. *Arctic Info. Center Gloss.* 6, *Arctic trout.* A general term for any trout or grayling found in the Arctic. **1972** Sparano *Outdoors Encycl.* 354, *Arctic Char . . . Common Names: . .* Arctic trout.

arctic wine n **AK**

1939 *FWP Guide AK* xxxii, Patrons of bars sometimes attempt to violate the law by demanding a drink of "ar'tic wine"—Alaskan for straight whiskey.

are adv[1] See **there**

are adv[2] See **here**

area n Usu |ˈæri(j)ə, ˈɛr-, ˈer|, rarely |ˈɛərə, ˈæri(ɚ)| Pronc-spp *airy, aree* Cf **airy-way**

A Forms.

1848 Lowell *Biglow* 6 "Upcountry" **MA,** They may talk o' Freedom's airy / Tell they're pupple in the face. *Ibid* 143 [Glossary], *Airy, . . . Aree,* area. **1890** Farmer–Henley *Slang, Airy . . .* A corruption of 'area,' *e.g.,* 'Down the *airy* steps.' **1920s** in 1944 *ADD* **cNY,** *Area . .* [ˈɛriə]. **1942** *Ibid* **seIN,** *Area . .* [ˈæriə]. Radio. **1965–68** *DARE* Tape **FL43,** Area [ˈæri]; **GA77,** Area [ˈɛərə]; **MD1,** The children in our [ˈæriɚ]. **1968** *DARE* FW Addit **LA14,** *Area* [ˈɛriə] . . is Inf's only pronunciation . . ; it seems to compete with [ˈɛriə] in this area; **MA40,** *Area* [ˈerijə].

B Sense.
See **airy-way.**

a'ready See **already**

areally See **a** inert vowel **2**

aree See **area**

arfter See **after**

arg v [Cf *SND arg* to talk ill-temperedly and hot-headedly]
To argue.
1914 *DN* 4.141, Back-formations from words with initial accent . . . *Arg,* from *argue.* To *argue,* grumble. **1941** in **1944** *ADD* **nWV,** *Argue . . .* [ɒrg]. "Don't arg!" By one speaker.

‡**arg** n [**arg** v]
A fault-finder.
1968 *DARE* (Qu. HH12) Inf **PA**114, An arg [ɑrg]—short for *arguing.*

argadent See **aguardiente**

argefy See **argufy**

arger See **argue**

argerfy, argify See **argufy**

argimint See **argument**

argue v Usu |ˈɑrgju, –jə|; also chiefly **Sth, Midl** |ˈɑrg(j)ɪ, ˈɑrgɚ|
Pronc-spp *arger, argy* See also **arg** v, **augur** v[1]
A Forms.
1899 Chesnutt *Conjure Woman* 155 **NC** [Black], Her marster lafft at her en argyed wid her. **1921** Thorp *Songs Cowboys* 171 **AZ,** A stranger . . stopped to arger some. **1923** *DN* 5.200 **swMO,** *Argy.* **1936** *AmSp* 11.163 **eTX,** *Argue . .* [ˈɒrgjə]. **1941** *AmSp* 16.9 **eTX** [Black], [ˈɑːgjɪ]. **1949** *VT Hist.* ns 27.124, [ˈɑrgɚ] . . . Occasional. Rural areas. **c1960** *Wilson Coll.* **csKY,** *Argue* is often [ˈɑrgɪ].
B Sense.
To annoy, verbally abuse (someone). Cf **augur** v[1] **2**
1968–70 *DARE* (Qu. Y7) Inf **VA**73, She keeps |ˈɑrgən| me all the time; **WI**13, He keeps |ˈɑrgɚ-ɪŋ| me.

argufier n [**argufy** 2, 4]
A convincing or argumentative speaker.
1805 Fessenden *Democracy Unveiled* 203, His honour might have pass'd . . . For quite a decent country Squire, / And no bad Jury–*argufier.* **1966** *DARE* (Qu. II36A, *Somebody who talks back or gives rude answers: "Did you ever see such a _____?"*) Inf **MA**6, [ˈɑrgəfɑɪjə] . . [my] father's term.

argufy v, also vbl n *argufying* Pronc-spp *aa'gyfy, argefy, argerfy, argify, arguefy, argyfy* [**argue** + **-ify;** *OED* 1751 → "An illiterate formation on *argue.*"] now chiefly **Sth, S Midl** *esp among speakers with little educ*
1 To be evidence of (something); to signify.
1789 (1918) Low *Politician Outwitted* 366 **NYC,** What argufies your signifies, or your magnifies? **1899** (1912) Green *VA Folk-Speech,* *Argufy . . .* To argue; signify.
2 To contend, wrangle.
1812 Paulding *Diverting Hist.* 123 **NY,** They stopt in the fields from their work to arguefy. **1848** Bartlett *Americanisms, To argufy . . .* To argue. This vile word has a place in several of the English glossaries. In this country it is only heard among the most illiterate. **1867** Lowell *Biglow* 15 "Upcountry" **MA,** It ain't no use to argerfy. **1905** *DN* 3.2 **cCT.** **1908** *DN* 3.287 **eAL, wGA.** **1916** *DN* 4.294 **sAppalachians,** Right*ify,* argy*fy.* **1922** Gonzales *Black Border* 287 **sSC, GA coasts** [Gullah glossary], *Aa'gyfy.* **1930** *AmSp* 5.424 **Ozarks,** The Ozarker very often says *argufy* instead of argue, and the "furrin" schoolmarms laugh at him for it. **1942** Whipple *Joshua* 363 **UT,** But the argufying was what she liked best. David and Mr. Nelson . . argufying on every subject under the sun. **1950** *PADS* 14.12 **SC,** *Argufy, arfigy* [sic]. To argue, with a connotation of aimlessness. **c1960** *Wilson Coll.* **csKY,** *Argufy.* To argue, usually offensively. "He likes to argufy too much." **1967** *DARE* (Qu. KK13) Inf **MI**44, Argufying [ˈɑrgjuˌfɑɪŋ]. That's more just idle talk.
3 To dispute or debate (a point or topic).
1812 *Niles' Natl. Reg.* 3.206/1 **MD,** But general Armstrong is well prepared to *"argufy"* this point. **1817** *N. Amer. Rev.* 4.183 **NY,** After dinner [we] smoked a dirty pipe, 'argufied the topick,' whether the crops were likely to be spoilt. **1843** (1916) Hall *New Purchase* 134 **IN,** And so

I argefied the pint agin this way; sez I, kin a feller go spang up the round of a big punkin? **1933** *Sun* (Baltimore MD) 4 July 6/3 *(Hench Coll.),* Jim talks a great deal and does much glad-handing; but as was said of the colored preacher, the job seekers still complain that he "argifies and argifies but don't pint out and say whar'in."
4 To persuade by argument.
1853 Simms *Sword & Distaff* 474 **VA,** We must, both on us, argufy him into the sense of this needcessity. **1945** Langley *Lion in Streets* 155 **LA,** I never knowed he was so good as to argufy a judge into somethin' so diffrunt as a trial liken t' that. **1966** *Manchester Union Leader* (NH) 28 July 10/4, Futile as argufying may be, I cannot refrain from illustrating by example how these people think, the sort of junk they sell.

argufyingest adj
Of persons: most contentious.
c1960 *Wilson Coll.* **csKY,** *Argufyingest person*—a hard one to get along with.

argument n Usu |ˈɑ(r)gjumənt, ˈɑ(r)gjəmənt|, occas |ˈɑrgəmənt|
Pronc-spp *aa'gyment, argimint, argyment, yargyment*
Std senses, var forms.
1884 Lanier *Poems* 175 **GA** [title:], Jones's Private Argyment. **1891** *DN* 1.118 **cNY,** [ˈɑrgəmənt]. **1894** in 1941 Warfel–Orians *Local-Color Stories* 741 **sAR,** A new set o' argimints. **1901** *DN* 2.181 **neKY** [Black], *Argument . . .* argument, yargyment. **1922** Gonzales *Black Border* 287 **sSC, GA coasts** [Gullah glossary], *Aa'gyment*—argument, arguments. **1936** *AmSp* 11.159 **eTX,** In another group, the medial *u* is pronounced both [jə] and [ə] . . *accumulate, . . argument.* **1955** Adams *Grandfather* 40 **NY,** I don't have no argyment.

argy, argyfy, argyment See **argue, argufy, argument**

arichtocrat n, also aphet *richtocrat;* hence also adj *arichtocratic*
Cf **rusticrat**
An aristocrat.
1942 *Hench Coll.* **cVA,** In a class discussion of popular etymologies, a student said that he had heard Negroes use arichtocrat instead of aristocrat. **1942** Berrey–Van den Bark *Amer. Slang* 450.2, *A richtocrat,* a wealthy aristocrat. *Ibid* 146.4, Arichtocratic.

arigato intj [Japanese] **HI**
Thank you.
1947 *AmSp* 22.54 [Pacific War Language], *Arigato.* Thank you. **1954–60** Hance *Hawaiian Sugar* 1, Arigato [ɑˈriˈgɑto] . . Thank you. **1967** *DARE* (Qu. II39, . . *Ways . . of saying 'thank you'*) Inf **HI**6, Arigato [ɑriˈgɑto]. **1970** *Time* 3 Aug 69 **NYC,** The show's many dance numbers are mesmeric revels . . In midsummer New York, *Golden Bat* is a surprising tonic for which one can only say *arigato.* **1972** Carr *Da Kine Talk* 92 **HI,** Many of the simple and basic [Japanese] expressions are still in use . . : *arigatō* 'thank you.'

aristocratic adj *rural, old-fash*
Stylish; culturally superior.
1846 Cooper *Redskins* 1.159, Ravensnest . . [was] termed an "aristocratic residence." This word "aristocratic," I find since my return home, has got to be a term of expansive signification, its meaning depending on the particular habits and opinions of the person who happens to use it. **1859** (1968) Bartlett *Americanisms* 12, *Aristocratic.* Strangely misapplied in those parts of the country where the population is not dense. The city, in the surrounding country towns, is deemed "aristocratic." The people in the villages consider the inhabitants of the towns "aristocratic," and so on. The term is . . very common in small country newspapers and in political speeches in out of the way places. **1892** Twain *Amer. Claimant* 53, Rowena–Ivanhoe College is the selectest and most aristocratic seat of learning for young ladies in our country. **1905** *DN* 3.2 **cCT,** *Aristocratic . . .* Following the city style of living.

ariv See **arrive**

arivipa n [Prob *Arivaipa* the San Carlos Indian people]
See quot 1969.
1969 O'Connor *Horse & Buggy West* 167 **AZ** (as of early 1900s), In a dry arroyo . . he could have struck cool plentiful water by digging down a few feet. These places where the water runs close to the surface beneath the sands are known as *arivipas.* [**1979** *Nature Conserv. News* 29.6.16 **AZ,** To the north of Ramsey Canyon . . lies another "canyon–oasis"— Aravaipa. Also a permanent stream, Aravaipa Creek cuts through the dry desert slopes of paloverde . . . Its waters originate from distant pine-forested mountains, retreat underground, and resurface within the canyon.]

Arizona cloudburst n *joc* Cf **Idaho brainstorm, Mormon rainstorm**

　　1966 *Western Folkl.* 25.37 **OR,** *Arizona cloudburst.* A sandstorm.

Arizona nightingale n chiefly **SW** *joc*

A donkey or mule.

　　1940 (1966) FWP *Guide AZ* 57, Because of his extraordinary bray, [the burro] is sometimes called the "Arizona Nightingale." **1965** *Western Folkl.* 24.197. **1968** Adams *Western Words* 8, *Arizona nightingale*—A prospector's burro. **1969** *DARE* (Qu. K50, *Joking nicknames for mules*) Inf **AZ**15, Arizona nightingale.

Arizona paint job n *joc*

No paint at all.

　　1962 *Western Folkl.* 21.29 **sCA,** Arizona paint job—used to describe an unpainted, weathered pine building.

Arizona peacock n

=**roadrunner.**

　　1956 *AmSp* 31.181 **CA,** Arizona peacock . . Roadrunner.

Arizona ruby n

A pyrope garnet found in igneous rocks of the Southwest. Also called **Navajo ruby**

　　1893 U.S. Census Office *Moqui Pueblo Indians* 16 **AZ,** The Moqui Indians have quantities of garnets, Arizona rubies, and pieces of turquoise.

Arizona strawberry See **strawberry**

Arizona tenor n [See quot 1977] **SW** *joc*

A coughing tubercular.

　　1942 Berrey–Van den Bark *Amer. Slang* 431.2, *Consumptive Person.* Arizona tenor. **1944** Adams *Western Words.* **1945** *Everybody's Digest* Aug 87 *(DA),* Among his own kind, the waddy calls a coughing tubercular an 'Arizona tenor.' **1977** Watts *Dict. Old West, Arizona tenor*—a man suffering from tuberculosis. The dry desert air was considered beneficial for such sufferers.

Arizony n Pronc-sp for *Arizona* Cf **-y**

　　1931 *N. Amer. Rev.* 231.432/1 **NYC,** A few more past-age pronunciations . . . *Floridy, Arizony, asafoetidy.*

ark n, also attrib

1 A large, flat-bottomed boat, usu used to transport goods to market along the Mississippi, Ohio, and other eastern rivers. *now hist* Also called **broadhorn, flatboat** n **1**

　　1759 *New Amer. Mag.* 2.627, Our great boat called the ark, being near 80 foot long and 30 wide, landed this day from Fort William Henry. **1808** U.S. Congress *Debates & Proc.* 10th Cong 2d Sess 52 **DE,** Our dismantled, ark-roofed vessels . . are indeed decaying in safety at our wharves. **1821** (1927) Rodman *Diary* [5] **MA,** Visited the Lehigh coal yards and observed the coal arks . . . They are linked together in descending the river by two single planks. **1872** Schele de Vere *Americanisms* 337, These *arks,* as they are familiarly called, are now-a-days but rarely seen on the Mississippi, the steamboat having almost entirely superseded them. **1939** (1954) FWP *Guide KY* 111, In November [1815] they started on their 400 mile journey in a flatbottomed boat known in that day as an "ark" or a "Kentucky broadhorn." **1947** *Sun* (Baltimore MD) 30 Oct 16/1 **cPA,** The white settlers used "arks" and "keelboats" to bring flour, timber and other commodities to the markets in Philadelphia and Baltimore.

2 See quot.

　　1895 *Std. Dict. Engl. Lang.* (Funk) 114/1, *Ark* . . . [Eastern U.S.] A moored scow covered by a house in which a business is done, as in oysters, etc.

3 In logging: a houseboat used as bunkhouse, kitchen, or storage area, esp in floating camps. **Nth** Also called **shanty boat, van, wanigan**

　　1905 U.S. Forest Serv. *Bulletin* 61.52, *Wanigan* . . . A houseboat used as sleeping quarters or as kitchen and dining room by river drivers . . . Syn.: ark. **1930** Shoemaker *1300 Words* **cPA Mts** (as of c1900), *Ark*—A house built on a raft, the floating boarding house of the crew of a log drive. **1958** McCulloch *Woods Words* 3 **Pacific NW,** *Ark*—A bunkhouse, particularly one on a raft in a floating camp. **1969** Sorden *Lumberjack Lingo* **NEng, Gt Lakes,** *Ark*—1. Where the camp stores are kept. 2. The boat or raft that followed the logs down the river on a drive.

4 Any old, clumsy boat. *joc*

　　1965–70 *DARE* (Qu. O2) 12 Infs, **chiefly east of Missip R,** Ark; **NC**12, **NY**41, Old ark.

5 In humorous phrr alluding to the era of Noah's ark (Gen 6:14–16): See quots. Cf **arky**

　　1899 (1912) Green *VA Folk-Speech* 68, *Arky* . . archaic. "Came out of the ark." **1949** *PADS* 11.14 **wTX,** As *old* as Noah's ark. **1951** *PADS* 15.58 **sIN,** *Noah had that one in the ark: saying,* of a time-worn joke. **1966–68** *DARE* (Qu. FF21a, *A joke that is so old it doesn't seem funny any more*) Inf **FL**28, Out of the ark; **GA**66, Came in with the ark; **GA**86, Old enough to have come out of the ark; (Qu. FF21b) Inf **HI**1, Was when Noah came out of the ark; **MI**28, It come over on the ark; **NY**66, That was told in the ark; **PA**215, Was on Noah's ark. **c1970** *Halpert Coll.* **wKY,** It's so old it came out of the ark (on crutches).

Arkansas n Usu |ˈɑrkənˌsɔ|; infreq sp-pronc |ɑrˈkænˌsəs| Pronc-sp *Arkansaw* (see **arkansaw**)

Std sense (the state name), var forms.

　　1940 in **1944** *ADD* **swPA, nWV,** [ɑrˈkænsəs] Old illit speaker. **1941** *AmSp* 16.15 **eTX** [Black], [ˈɑ:kjĩnˌsɔ:]. **1941** in **1944** *ADD,* [ˈɑrkɪnˌsɔ]. **1968** *DARE* (Qu. N37) Inf **MO**10, Slow train through [ˈɑrkɛnˌsɒ]; (Qu. HH1) Inf **MO**9, [ˈɑrkɪnˌsɒ] hoosier.

Arkansas asphalt n *joc*

　　1966 *Western Folkl.* 25.37 **TX,** *Arkansas asphalt.* Logs laid side by side to form a "corduroy" road . . . Texas oilmen found conditions in Arkansas particularly primitive.

Arkansas banana See **banana B1**

Arkansas chicken n *joc* Cf *DS* H38, **Arkansas T-bone, Georgia chicken**

=**salt pork.**

　　1905 *DN* 3.69 **nwAR,** *Arkansas chicken* . . . Salt pork; 'salt side meat.' 'We've got plenty of *Arkansas chicken.*' Rare.

‡Arkansas dew n *joc*

A sudden heavy rain.

　　1969 *DARE* (Qu. B47) Inf **TX**62, Arkansas dew.

Arkansas fire extinguisher n *joc*

　　1962 *Western Folkl.* 21.29 **sCA,** Arkansas fire extinguisher—a chamberpot.

Arkansas lizard n *joc*

A louse.

　　1933 *AmSp* 8.3.24 **KS** [Prison dictionary], *Arkansas lizard.* Louse. **1960** Wentworth–Flexner *Slang, Arkansas lizard* . . . Some army and hobo use; archaic.

Arkansas special See **Arkansas traveler**

Arkansas strawberry See **strawberry**

Arkansas T-bone n *joc* Cf **Arkansas chicken**

Bacon.

　　1967 *DARE* (Qu. H38) Inf **NE**7, Arkansas T-bone.

Arkansas toothpick n *joc*

A large bowie knife, or similar knife with a long blade.

　　1837 (1955) *Crockett Almanacks* 112 **TN,** [Woodcut caption:] An Arkansas Toothpick. **1882** *Nation* 7 Dec 485, Things supposed to be required by 'honor' will coarsen as they descend among the vulgar . . the . . duel will develop into a street or bar-room fight, with "Arkansas toothpicks" as the weapons. **1944** Adams *Western Words, Arkansas toothpick*—A large sheath knife; a dagger. **1962** *Western Folkl.* 21.29 **sCA,** Arkansas toothpick—any knife with a blade exceeding the legal limit . . . Los Angeles, 1950. **1978** *Natl. Geog. Mag.* Mar 420 **AR,** At his home in Russellville, Jimmy Lile makes knives: dropped-point hunters and skinners, Arkansas toothpicks, Bowies.

Arkansas traveler n

1 also *Arkansas special:* An unimportant branch railroad. *joc* Cf *DS* N37

　　1950 WELS (*Joking names for a branch railroad that is not very important or does not give the best of service*) 1 Inf, **cwWI,** Arkansas special. **1969** *DARE* (Qu. N37) Inf **OH**89, Arkansas traveler.

2 A fast-growing plant, perh kudzu.

　　1966 *DARE* Tape AL1, [FW:] A type of ivy that . . might cover all the trees. [Inf:] My mama always called it foot-a-night. Arkansas traveler and foot-a-night.

Arkansas travels n *joc*
Diarrhea.
   1965 *DARE* (Qu. BB19) Inf **OK**11, Arkansas travels.

Arkansas water n *joc*
A picnic drink: see quot.
   1951 *AmSp* 26.74 **sIL**, *Arkansas water*. A term of contempt for a drink served at a picnic . . . The picknicker was evidently classing the beverage with pink lemonade or with other ersatz concoctions. His usage perpetuates the old connotation of *Arkansas* with the crude and the humorous.

Arkansas wedding cake n *joc*
   1958 McCulloch *Woods Words* 3 **Pacific NW**, *Arkansas wedding cake*—Corn bread.

arkansaw v Pronc-sp for *Arkansas* **Ozarks**
  1 To kill in an unsportsman-like manner; by ext: to cheat, take advantage of. Cf **ozark**
   1927 *DN* 5.472 **nwAR, swMO**, When a hunter shoots a sitting rabbit with a shotgun at close range the rabbit is said to be *arkansawed*. **1953** Randolph *Down in Holler* 224 **Ozarks**, When a hunter shoots a quail on the ground, the bird is said to be *arkansawed* . . . My neighbor told me that a banker was trying to *arkansaw* him out of his farm.
  2 To sweep with a **brush broom** n¹ or a bunch of green branches.
   1936 *AmSp* 11.314 **Ozarks**, Jest wait till I *Arkansaw* th' kitchen, afore ye set down.
  3 To exhaust, wear down. [Cf *DA Arkansas stone*, whetstone]
   1953 Randolph *Down in Holler* 224 **Ozarks**, No wonder Billy looks young. He never done no hard work to *arkansaw* himself down.

arkansaw adv Cf *DS* II8, 9
=**Dutch** adv.
   1953 Randolph *Down in Holler* 224 **Ozarks**, Postmaster McQuary, of Galena, Mo., ate lunch with me in a little restaurant, I reached for the check. "No," said he positively, "we'll go *arkansaw*," meaning that each man pays for his own food.

Arkansawyan adj [Blend of **Arkansawyer** and *Arkansan*]
Arkansan.
   1906 *DN* 3.124 **nwAR**, *Arkansawyan* . . . Rare.

Arkansawyer n **chiefly AR and adjacent states** Cf **Arkansawyan**
An Arkansan.
   1904 *DN* 2.416 **nwAR**, *Arkansawyer* . . . is general among the uneducated. 'I knew it was dangerous to hurt an Arkansawyer's dog.' **1906** *DN* 3.124 **nwAR**, *Arkansawyer* . . . occurs even among the educated. The adjective and the noun *Arkansan* are in disrepute among the uneducated because the word suggests *Kansan*. Kansas and the Kansans are very unpopular in Arkansas. **1918** *DN* 5.37 **OK**, *Arkansawyer* . . . A derisive term applied to the people of Arkansas by Oklahomans. **1947** *AmSp* 22.255 **AR**, The semiaffectionate, semi-teasing *Arkansawyer*, derived from Arkansas, the local pronunciation of the state name, is still in use, especially on the lower levels, and there is a daily in the town of Stuttgart called the *Leader and Arkansawyer*. **1953** Randolph *Down in Holler* 224 **Ozarks**, John Gould Fletcher, a native of Little Rock and a distinguished literary figure, spells the name *Arkansawyer*.

arked adj [Cf *DA ark* v] See also **ark 1, 3**
Of lumber: having been floated downriver, the planks being fastened together in boat-shaped groups.
   1941 *Sun* (Baltimore MD) 25 Aug 4/3 *(Hench Coll.)*, The great logs of which the tavern was built . . "arked" lumber it was called in the old days, because of the custom of fastening the great planks together by driving wooden pegs through them so they could be floated down the river to their point of destination . . "arked" as in the days of Noah of old.

Arkie n Also sp *Arky* **chiefly West, esp Pacific** Cf **Okie**
  1 A native of Arkansas or neighboring states, esp a migrant from Arkansas. *often derog*
   1958 McCulloch *Woods Words* 3 **Pacific NW**, *Arkie*—Native of Arkansas or neighboring states, green to the West Coast Woods. Generally a traveler, less skilled than native loggers, but not always so. **1959** *AmSp* 34.76, *Arkie* . . . A worker from Arkansas. Also, a term of disparagement. **1968** Fulbright *Cow-Country Counselor* 118, Another time six people from Arkansas, called Arkies, as all natives of Arkansas were called, lived in a small two-room wooden cabin. **1971** Bright *Word*

Geog. CA & NV 194, *Migratory worker* . . . Of 5 *Arkie* responses, 1 was urban, 2 rural, and 2 Nevada.
  2 A rustic person or one considered insignificant. *derog*
   1942 Berrey–Van den Bark *Amer. Slang* 391.3, Arky. **1965–70** *DARE* (Qu. HH1) Infs **CA**61, 83, 94, **TX**72, Arkie; (Qu. HH18) Inf **CA**169, Arkies. **1971** Bright *Word Geog. CA & NV* 194, *A rustic* . . derogatory and neutral terms . . *Arkie.*

arky adj Cf **ark 5**
Old-fashioned, quite out of style.
   1899 (1912) Green *VA Folk-Speech*, Arky . . . archaic. "Came out of the ark." "She had on a very *arky* bonnet." **1942** Berrey–Van den Bark *Amer. Slang* 1.12.

arly, arliest See **early**

armas n pl [Span *arma* weapon] **SW** Cf **armitas**
Leather flaps attached to a saddle to protect the rider's legs.
   1936 McCarthy *Lang. Mosshorn*, [Caption:] *Armas.* cowhide hanging from saddle. **1955** Harris *Look of Old West* 208, The cowboy variety [of leather breeches] really started, down in Mexico away back when, with a sort of skirt or apron. These were big flaps of tough leather called *armas* that fastened over the front of the saddle and hung down on each side. When you climbed aboard you tucked them over your legs like a robe. And when you got down they stayed on the saddle. **1977** Watts *Dict. Old West*, Armas . . . A forerunner of chaps which were little more than two large flaps of hide fastened to the saddle and protecting a rider's legs against brush and thorns.

arm baby n esp **NC** See also **apron child, teeniney**
A baby small enough to be held in the arms; by ext, the youngest and smallest child in a family.
   1939 FWP *Guide NC* 98, The boy, or "chap" may be called a little "shirttailed boy" to distinguish him from her "arm baby and her knee baby." **1952** Brown *NC Folkl.* 1.516 **c,eNC**. **1972** Cooper *NC Mt. Folkl.* 89, Arm baby—child small enough to be carried in the arms.

armchair back See **chairback**

armed up adj phr [Cf *OED arm* v² 2]
Arm-in-arm.
   1935 *Atlantic Mth.* 156.303 **AL**, [We] walked along armed up goin' to get married.

armful n Also sp *armfull* **formerly chiefly Nth; now widespread, but esp common in Nth** See Map Addit map in 1949 Kurath *Word Geog.* Fig. 73 See also **armload, arm of wood, turn**
Usu of firewood: the amount a person can carry at one time.
   1899 (1912) Green *VA Folk-Speech*, Armfull . . . As much as can be carried with the two hands together. A large woman is called an armfull. **1949** Kurath *Word Geog.* 57, *Armful* is the regular expression in the North. In the North Midland *armful* is now more common than the old Midland *arm load* and *load*, but in the South Midland it is less common. **1950** *WELS* ("Go bring in _____ of wood.") 45 Infs, **throughout WI**, An armful. **1962** *AmSp* 37.173 **eNC**, An armful (of wood) [is] a Northern and North Midland usage which does not occur in North Carolina except sporadically in the west . . . [Yet] Ocracokers seem to prefer *armful*. **1965–70** *DARE* (Qu. L56) 522 Infs, **throughout US but esp common in Nth**, Armful; **NC**8, **SC**3, Double armful; **NC**54, Piece of a armful; **IL**31, Whole armful, **NY**69, Couple of armfuls. **1967** Le-

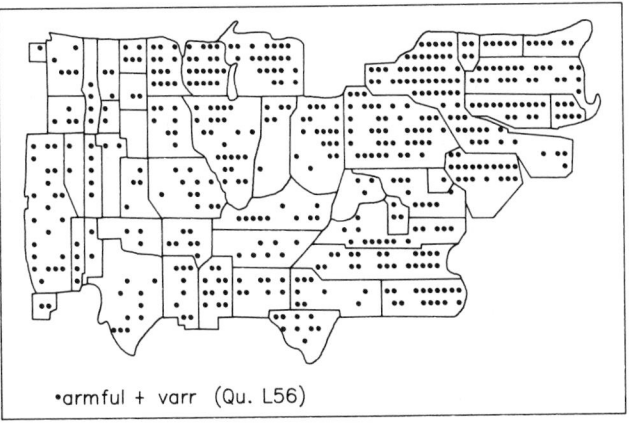

•armful + varr (Qu. L56)

Compte *Word Atlas* 157 **seLA**, *Amount of wood you can carry at one time in both arms* . . . armful 42.9% . . armload 9.5%. **1973** Allen *LAUM* 1.211, Although *armful* prevails in all five states, it is distinctly Northern in its orientation.

arminette n [Fr *arme* weapon] **eLA**
=**foot adz.**

1956 Knipmeyer *Settlement Succession* 155 **eLA**, The *arminette* is the regular long-handled adze with a straight blade . . . The inside [of the pirogue] is hewn out with a hatchet or *arminette* about two inches inside the lines which mark the outline of the dugout.

armitas n pl, rarely sg [**armas** + *-ita* dimin suff] **SW** Also called **chigaderos**
A kind of primitive leather **chaps.**

1942 Berrey–Van den Bark *Amer. Slang* 915.20 **West**, *Armita* . . . a leather riding apron tied around the waist and knees, sometimes used in the summer instead of chaparajos. **1946** Mora *Trail Dust* 90 **SW**, Chinks, or Armitas, are a kind of skeleton chap, and were worn quite a bit on some coast ranges and in Nevada. They are generally made of buckskin, the sides and bottoms often fringed. **1955** Harris *Look of Old West* 209, The armitas were leather aprons, two of them, hanging from a belt around your middle and coming down to your boot tops, and provided with thongs along the sides so you could tie them around your legs. **1977** Watts *Dict. Old West*.

armload n **widespread, but least freq in Nth** See Map Addit maps in 1949 Kurath *Word Geog.* Fig 73, 1973 Allen *LAUM* 1.211 Fig 16.5a
=**armful.**

1906 Casey *Parson's Boy* 22 (*AmSp* 58.249) **sIL** (as of c1860), Bring mother an armload of stove-wood. **1949** Kurath *Word Geog.* 29, *Arm load* and *load* are distinctive Midland expressions for an armful of wood. *Arm load* predominates in the North Midland, *load* in the South Midland. The term *armful* stands by the side of *arm load* in the North Midland and has nearly eliminated it in the Great Valley of Pennsylvania and in the Pittsburgh area; on Delaware Bay, however, *arm load* is well established. **1950** *WELS* ("Go bring in ———— of wood") 5 Infs, **s,cWI**, An armload. **1965–70** *DARE* (Qu. L56) 304 Infs, **widespread, but least freq in Nth,** Armload; **OH**90, Armload full; **VA**24, Armload of wood. **1973** Allen *LAUM* 1.211, *Armload,* which appears once in Minnesota and once in Manitoba but not at all in North Dakota, is clearly linked to the Midland distribution pattern.

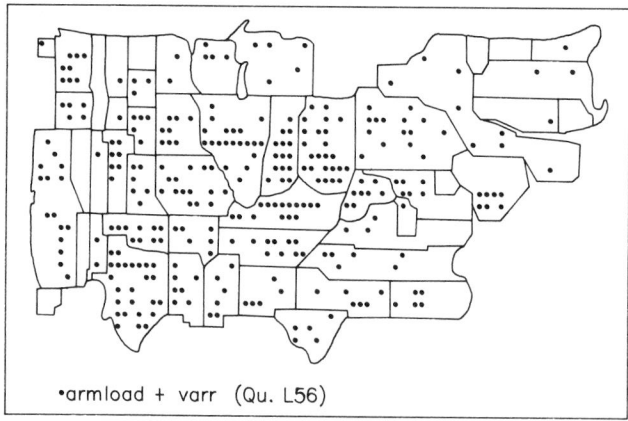

•armload + varr (Qu. L56)

arm of wood n
=**armful.**

1950 *WELS* ("Go bring in ———— of wood.") 2 Infs, **sw, cWI**, An arm. **1966–67** *DARE* (Qu. L56) Infs **GA**5, 14, **LA**7, Arm of wood.

armoire n |'ɑ(r)mə(r), 'ɑrmor, 'ɑ(r)mwɑr| Pronc-spp *armor, armour* [Fr] **chiefly LA, MS** See Map *now more widespread through commercialization* See also **armory**
A large, often ornate, wardrobe or **clothespress 1.**

1834 Brackenridge *Recollections* 24 **LA**, The furniture . . was of the most common kind, consisting of an armoire, a rough table or two, and some coarse chairs. **1855** Thorpe *Master's House* 118 **Sth**, The armoire, of massive proportions, is always composed of the richest of materials, and is very often inlaid with costly and different tinted woods, the panels are composed of costly mirrors that reach almost from the

floor to the ceiling. **1916** *DN* 4.268 **New Orleans LA, NC**, *Armoir* [ɑrmɚ] . . . Wardrobe. **1923** *DN* 5.243 **LA**, *Armour* . . . An armoire, or wardrobe. **1931** Read *LA French* 2, *Armoire* . . . Wardrobe for wearing apparel. Those who do not speak French pronounce the word like English *armor.* **1958** Grau *Hard Blue Sky* 131 **LA**, She'd put whole flowering strands [of jasmine vine] in the armoire with her clothes. **1961** *PADS* 36.13 **LA**, The universal anglicizing of *armoire* is ['ɑ(r)mə(r)]. **1965–70** *DARE* (Qu. E1, *. . Furniture that stands against the wall, and you hang clothes in it*) 24 Infs, **chiefly LA, MS**, Armoire ['ɑrmə(r), 'ɑrmor]; (Qu. E3, *. . Furniture in which you lay clothes flat*) Inf **LA**33, Armoire ['ɑrmə]. **1967** *DARE* FW Addit **swAR**, Armoire ['ɑ:m,wɑr]—closet; [usage among] the rich; **neCO**, Armoire—used . . esp in antique catalogues. **1982** *WI State Jrl.* (Madison) 7 Mar 5.5/3, [Advt:] Sale Priced . . . Includes: 2 armoires, 2 mirrors, and . . island bed.

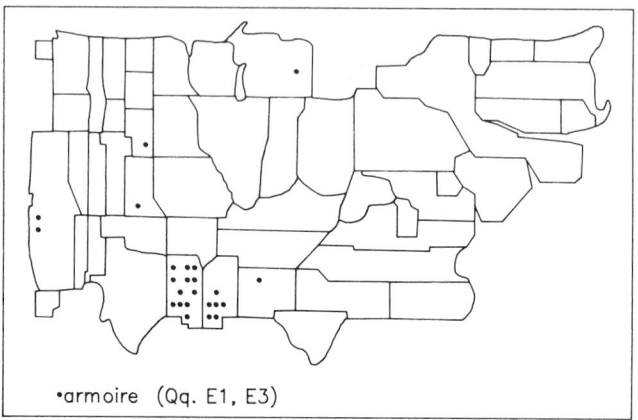

•armoire (Qq. E1, E3)

armored pine n
=**shortleaf pine 1.**

1951 *PADS* 15.7, *Pinus echinata* . . . Armored pine, from the plate-like scales of its bark, Traumfest, N.C.

‡**armory** n [Prob folk-etym, but cf *OED ambry* fr Fr *armarie, aumoire*]
=**armoire.**

1968 *DARE* (Qu. E3, *. . Furniture in which you lay clothes flat*) Inf **WI**47, Armory—two little doors with drawers behind.

armour See **armoire**

arm pull n, also attrib Also *arm pulling* **AK**
An Eskimo game of strength, in which two seated players interlock their arms and each attempts to pull the other over.

1973 *Theata* (Fairbanks AK) Spring 1.9, The old games, such as . . arm pulling . . have been passed down to the people of today and are still kept . . . An arm pulling contest . . . has to do with pulling the opponent's arm to the side where his opponent is sitting. It is almost like . . tug-of-war, but the player isn't standing up pulling a rope. He is sitting on the floor and only pulling with his arm in order to win the game. **1977** *Tundra Times* (Fairbanks AK) 3 Aug 6/1, *Arm Pull Contest* First Place: Pat Tingmiak, N.W.T. *Ibid* 7 [Caption], Freddie Titus, his face showing the strain of competition, in the arm pull event.

armstrong adj, also used absol [Cf *Captain Armstrong* dishonest jockey, "A play upon words, *i.e.,* 'to pull with strong arm' " (Farmer–Henley *Slang*)] *joc* See also **Armstrong heater**
Operated by hand rather than by mechanical means—used as if a trademark for machines and tools.

1914 *DN* 4.102 **KS**, *Armstrong* . . . Operated by the arm as opposed to machinery; used jocosely of scythes, sickles or saws, etc. **1923** *DN* 5.200 **swMO**, *Armstrong* . . . A grain cradle. Applicable also to any primitive form of tool used by hand. **1926** Kephart *Highlanders* 365 **sAppalachian Mts**, In some places to-day we still find the ancient quern or hand-mill, jocularly called an armstrong-machine. **1945** Hubbard *Railroad Ave.* 331, *Armstrong*—Old-style equipment operated by muscular effort, such as hand-brakes, some turntables, engines without automatic stokers, etc. **1950** *Western Folkl.* 9.115 **nwOR** [Logger Talk], *Armstrong plow.* A shovel. **1953** Randolph *Down in Holler* 225 **Ozarks**, Some old-timers call any outmoded tool an *armstrong,* I heard a barber . . refer to his old-fashioned razor in this way: "Most men over fifty would rather shave with an *armstrong,* if they could keep it honed an' stropped." **1958** McCulloch *Woods Words* 3 **Pacific NW,** *Armstrong method*—Any work done by hand, not machine. **1969** *DARE* (Qu. O2, . . *An old, clumsy boat*) Inf **NY**207, Armstrong boats—you row 'em.

Armstrong heater n [**armstrong**] *joc*
One's arms (when used to embrace another).

1920s in **1944** *ADD* **cNY,** *Armstrong heater.* The arms of one's sweetheart . . . 'Are you cold? Where is your Armstrong heater?' Humorous. **1932** *AmSp* 7.329 **Baltimore MD** [Johns Hopkins Jargon], Armstrong heaters—arms when used to hold a girl.

army bean n [Cf common *navy bean*]
A small white bush bean (*Phaseolus* spp.).

1950 *WELS* (*The smaller beans that are white when they are dry*) 1 Inf, **seWI,** Navy beans—common; army beans—occasional usage. **1965–70** *DARE* (Qu. I18, *The smaller beans that are white when they are dry*) Infs **CT**17, **MD**14, **NJ**50, **NM**12, **NC**55, **PA**102, Army beans.

army bug n
Perh a soldier beetle (Cantharidae).

1968–69 *DARE* (Qu. R30, . . *Other kinds of beetles*) Infs **KY**11, Army bug; **TN**26, Army bug—they just go in droves, look sorta like lightning bugs. They crawl on the ground, . . don't fly, . . [and] eat tomatoes.

‡army grass n
1968 *DARE* (Qu. S8, *A common kind of wild grass that grows in fields: it spreads by sending out long underground roots, and it's hard to get rid of*) Inf **MD**26, Army grass.

armyworm bird n
=**bobolink.**

1923 U.S. Dept. Ag. *Misc. Circular* 13.75, Bobolink (*Dolichonyx oryzivorus*) . . . In local use.—Army worm bird (Mo.). **1970** *DARE* FW Addit **KY**86, Armyworm bird: a grey-brown yellow-breasted bird whose appearance portends the coming of army worms which the birds eat. The grey-brown is more solid than speckled. It is long-bodied . . . Common usage.

arn n, v[1], adj See **iron A**

arn v[2] See **earn**

arnarougen See **amarugian**

archy n Cf **airish 2, astorperious**
1926 Van Vechten *Nigger Heaven* 194 **NYC** [Black], They seem to think I'm putting on airs. My clothes or my English are too good. One of 'em called me an archy. *Ibid* 285 [Glossary of Negro Words and Phrases], *Archy:* a person who puts on airs.

arnest See **earnest**

arnica n Usu |ˈɑrnɪkə|, also |ˈɑrnɪki| (cf **-y**); also in r-less areas |ˈɑnɪkə, ˈɑnɪki, ˈɑnɛki|
A Forms.
1936 *AmSp* 11.160 **eTX,** Among older or less well educated people in rural districts, *algebra, Arnica* . . are pronounced . . [ˈældʒɪbrɪ], [ˈɑrnɪkɪ]. **1943** *LANE* Map 516, 3 Infs, **cwMA,** [aˑnɪkiˑ, aˑˑnɪkə, ɑrnɪki]. **1966–68** *DARE* (Qu. S20) Inf **ME**14, [ˈɑnɛki].
B Senses.
1 Std: a plant of the genus *Arnica.* Also called **leopard's bane**
2 Any of several plants which resemble *Arnica* spp., as:
a also *arnica bud:* =**fall dandelion. NEng**
1892 *Jrl. Amer. Folkl.* 5.99, *Leontodon autumnalis,* arnica. E. Mass. **1894** *Bot. Gaz.* 19.432 **MA,** Arnica bud. **1900** Lyons *Plant Names* 219, L[*eontodon*] *autumnalis* . . . Arnica-bud. **1910** Graves *Flowering Plants* 409 **CT,** Fall Dandelion. Arnica. **1916** *Torreya* 16.240, *Leontodon antumnalis* [sic] . . . Arnica, Matinicus I[slan]d., M[ain]e. **1959** Carleton *Index Herb. Plants* 4.
b =**dandelion.**
1900 Lyons *Plant Names* 364, T[*araxacum*] *Taraxacum* . . . Arnica.
c =**gum plant.**
1966 Barnes–Jensen *Dict. UT Slang* 4A, Arnica . . a local name for the gum plant.

arnick n Also *arnie* [Prob back-formation from *onyx* as if it were pl] See also **arctic** n[2]
A clear glass playing marble.

1969 *DARE* (Qu. EE6d) Inf **MI**103, Arnies [ˈɑrnɪs]. **c1970** Wiersma

Marbles Terms **Grand Rapids MI** (as of 1922), Arnick. *Ibid* **wMI** (as of 1924), [ˈɑrnɪk], A large glass marble; it was set up in the V formed by the legs of a player sitting on the pavement for opponents to shoot at; marbles that failed to hit it were his to keep. *Ibid* [Wiersma student list], Arnie(s) [ˈɑrˈniz], Largest size marble; one inch in diameter.

-aroo See **-eroo**

around one's elbow See **go around one's elbow to get to one's thumb**

around the horn exclam
Among loggers: Watch out!

1958 McCulloch *Woods Words* 3 **Pacific NW,** *Around the Horn!*—A cry used by hoisters and hookers to warn knot-bumpers and other men around the landing that a log is being turned end for end in the air while being loaded.

around-the-world n
1 A circular motion of the hand in the game of jacks: see quots.
1953 Brewster *Amer. Nonsinging Games* 138 **AR,** The seventh phase is called 'Round-the-World'. This time the player tosses up the ball, picks up a jack, (with the hand in which the jack is held) makes a circular motion around the ball while it is still in the air, and then catches it. **1968** *DARE* FW Addit **Reno NV,** Around-the-world: Throw up ball. Hand makes a circular motion all the way around the ball. Pick up jack.
2 A marbles game: see quot. Also called **follow-up**
1963 *KY Folkl. Rec.* 9.3.60 **neKY,** *Game played by shooting at opponent's marble, his shooter, no boundaries:* Around-the-world.
3 A game similar to **mumblety-peg,** in which a knife is thrown at different places advancing around the circumference of a circle.
1966 *DARE* (Qu. EE5, *Games where you try to make a jackknife stick in the ground*), Inf **AR**18, Mumble-peg, stretch, around-the-world.

aroya See **arroyo**

arpent n Also *arpen* [Fr] **chiefly LA and other French settlement areas**
A unit of linear or square measure: see quot 1941 McDermott.

1750 (1751) Bartram *Observations* 92, The breadth of the island at its lower end is two thirds of an Arpent, or thereabouts. **1800** in 1910 Commons *Doc. Hist. Amer. Industrial Soc.* 1.253 **LA,** The proprietor of several thousand arpents of land. **1878** *Appletons' Jrl.* new ser 5.413/1, In St. Louis they measure land not by *acres* but by *arpens.* **1931** Read *LA French* 3, *Arpent* is still in common use among the French of South Louisiana. **1941** McDermott *Gloss. Missip. Valley French,* Arpen. Common spelling for *arpent* . . . The exact figure is 191.838 English feet . . . As a unit of measure the *arpent* of Paris equaled .8449 English acre. **1941** O'Donnell *Great Big Doorstep* 225 **LA,** A big sink or a bawg, like, that makes the property not valuable because it uses up two arpents of land. **1968** *DARE* (Qu. L6a, . . *A piece of land under cultivation: less than an acre*) Inf **MO**25, Arpen [ˈɑˑrpɛn].

arr' See **arrow**

arragate See **irrigate**

arrand, arrant See **errand**

arrastra n Also sp *arastra, arrastre,* rarely *arrasta* [Span, from *arrastrar* to trail along the ground] **SW** *now hist* See also **raster**
An early Mexican device used to crush ore: a heavy stone dragged around a circular stone bed by mules or horses.

1835 Parker *Trip to TX* 266 [sic *DA*—quot not found], Upstream you catch the growl of the arrastra. **1867** Richardson *Beyond the Mississippi* 307, The arastra is the most primitive invention for crushing quartz. **1888** Wallace *Land of Pueblos* 163 **NM,** Quartz was ground in rude *arrastres,* or mills to which men and women were yoked like cattle. **1965** *Silver City Daily Press* (NM) 73/3 (as of c1870), They built two arrastras (a rude dragstone mill for pulverizing ores) and with two barrels realized as high as $100 per day. **1969** *DARE* Tape **CA**120, Arrasta [sic]—a round thing that they used to have a water wheel on, . . and they had big rocks that the water wheel turned . . and that's how they crushed the rock.

arre n [Perh a form of *error* reduced to a monosyllable]
In phr *throw one an arre:* to misinform, mislead.
1938 *AmSp* 13.5 **seAR,** 'He threw me an arre.' That is he misinformed me.

arrer See **arrow**

arriero n [Span] **SW** Also called **packer**
A muleteer.
1824 Poinsett *Notes on Mexico* 27, The "arriero," mule owner. **1844** (1954) Gregg *Commerce* 128 **SW,** It is truly remarkable to observe with what dexterity and skill the *Arrieros,* or muleteers, harness and adjust the packs of merchandise upon their beasts. **1897** Inman *Santa Fé Trail* 58, On the march the arriero is kept busy nearly all the time. **1968** Adams *Western Words, Arriero*— A muleteer or packer; a man who packs loads on mules.

arrish adj[1] See **airish**

Arrish adj[2] See **Irish A**

arrive v
Std senses, var forms.
Past tense: usu *arrived,* occas *ariv, arriv, arrove.*
1872 (1973) Thompson *Major Jones's Courtship* 55 **GA,** I ariv here last night. **1893** Shands *MS Speech* 17, *Arrove* . . Used even by educated people for *arrived.* This past being formed upon the analogy of such words as *drive, drove.* **1914** *DN* 4.102 **KS,** *Arrive* . . . Jocose use of *arrove,* . . *arriv* (past tense). **1916** *DN* 4.312 [Dialect of the Folk-songs], "The stage just arrove there." — There Was a Rich Old Farmer.

arrnd See **errand**

arro See **ary**

arroba n [Span] **SW**
A measure of twenty-five pounds or thirty-two pints.
1824 Poinsett *Notes on Mexico* 149, At seventy-five dollars the arroba of 25 lbs. **1891** *DN* 1.187 **TX.** **1909** Porter *Options* 112, They wash the gold . . and then they pack it in buck skin sacks of one arroba each. **1930** Lyman *John Marsh* 205, A cowhide represented two dollars, and tallow fifty cents the *arroba.* **1932** Bentley *Spanish Terms, Arroba* . . . Its chief use is in connection with dealings of flour or other produce in communities where the Mexican units of measure are or have been used and understood. It is not uncommon to hear an American in such communities speak of "an *arroba* of flour."

arrove See **arrive**

arrow n Usu |'æro, 'ærə, 'ero, 'erə|; in **Sth, Midl,** occas |'ɑro, 'ɑrə, ɑr| Pronc-spp *arr', arrer*
Std senses, var forms.
1890 *DN* 1.71 **LA,** *Arrow* . . . *a* as in *father.* **1891** (1967) Freeman *New Engl. Nun* 94, He was jest as straight as an arrer. **1928** *AmSp* 3.401 **Ozarks,** In *narrow, arrow,* . . the accented vowel has exactly the same sound as the *a* in *father;* such words are often reduced to monosyllables —*narr', arr'.* **1942** Hall *Smoky Mt. Speech* 25 **eNC, wTN,** A distinct [ɑ] does appear. A number of old people, and a few others, still say [ðɑɚ] *there* . . . This sound, moreover, is frequent in one group of words: *arrow, harrow, marrow. Ibid* 80, Words of the type of *arrow.* When -r- precedes *ow* or *-o,* the treatment is not with [ɚ], but usually with [ə].

arrow arum n **eastern half US**
A genus of aquatic plants (*Peltandra* spp) distinguished by broad arrow-shaped leaves, a white or green flower resembling a calla lily, and edible rootstocks. Also called **arrowweed 3, breadroot, hog wampee, Indian bread, poison arum, spoonflower, tuckahoe, Virginia wake-robin, wampee, wild calla**
1848 Gray *Manual of Botany* 446, *Peltandra,* Raf. Arrow Arum. **1891** Jesup *Plants Hanover NH* 47, Arrow Arum. **1931** Clute *Common Plants* 22, The thick, starchy rootstocks of the arrow-arum (*Peltandra Virginica*) . . were boiled and thus supplied a nourishing, if not especially palatable dish. **1972** Brown *Wildflowers LA* 10, Arrow-arum . . . Leaves broadly triangular with sharp divergent basal lobes.

arrowbrush n Also *arrowbush* [From the use of the branches as arrow shafts] **SW**
=**arrowweed 1.**
1930 Chalfant *Death Valley* 85 **CA,** *Juncus cooperi* and *Juncus mexicanus,* grow in moist alkaline swales, as does also *Pluchea sericea,* the arrow bush. **1933** Harrington *Gypsum Cave NV* 9, There is a growth of arrow-brush about the nearest spring. **1968** *DARE* (Qu. T16) Inf **NM13,** Arrowbrush.

arrow chase n Also ~ *hunt*
A city version of *hare and hounds:* see quot 1891.

1891 *Jrl. Amer. Folkl.* 4.223 **Brooklyn NY,** On a cold morning, when boys wish to play some game in order to keep warm, "arrow chase" is proposed. Sides are equally chosen, and a large boundary agreed upon. The side that starts first is provided with chalk, with which the players mark arrows upon the pavement, pointing the direction of their course. The others follow when five minutes have elapsed, tracking the pursued by the arrow-marks until all are caught. **1937** (1947) Bancroft *Games* 59, *Arrow Chase* . . . is especially adapted to surroundings where a very devious chase may be given . . . Every ten feet the runners must chalk a small arrow somewhere along their path . . . The runners will use all possible finesse in making it difficult to find their arrows. **1969** *DARE* (Qu. EE33, *Outdoor Games*) Infs **AL26, DC2,** Arrow hunt.

arrowfeather n [From the appearance of the panicle]
A **needlegrass 2** (here: *Aristida purpurascens*).
1946 Reeves–Bain *Flora TX* 51, *A. purpurascens* . . . Arrowfeather. **1950** Hitchcock *Manual Grasses* 478, *Arrowfeather* . . . Panicle . . one-third to half the entire length of the plant.

arrow hawk n
=**dragonfly.**
1935 Sandoz *Jules* 42 **wNE,** An arrow hawk fell noisily upon the fall's last mosquito.

arrowhead n
1 also rarely *arrowhead lily:* An aquatic plant of the genus (*Sagittaria*) characterized by arrow-shaped leaves, white flowers, and edible starchy tubers. Also called **arrowleaf, bull tongue, duck potato, swamp potato, swan potato, wapato.** For other names of the common sp *Sagittaria latifolia* see **Chinese onion, muskrat potato, swan root, tule potato, wampee, water lily, waxflower.** For other names of var spp see **arrowweed 2, dog tongue wampee, goose grass, langue de boeuf, sweet grass, white potato, wild onion, wild potato.**
1793 Amer. Philos. Soc. *Trans. for 1791* 3.180 **PA,** Sagittaria, Arrowhead. **1824** Bigelow *Florula Bostoniensis* 344, *Sagittaria sagittifolia* . . Arrow Head. **1911** Porter *Harvester* 229, Tall and slender, graceful, pearl white and pearl pure—those are the arrowhead lilies. **1968–69** *DARE* (Qu. S26b) Infs **GA35, NJ58, PA89, WI17,** Arrowhead(s).
2 =**highbush cranberry.**
1974 (1977) Coon *Useful Plants* 91, *Viburnum edule*—squashberry, mooseberry, arrowhead, viburnum.

arrow hunt See **arrow chase**

arrowleaf n
=**arrowhead 1,** usu *Sagittaria latifolia.*
1828 Rafinesque *Med. Flora* 259, *Sagittaria* . . . Arrowleaf. **1880** *Harper's Mag.* June 70, The frog pond with lush growth of arrow leaves and pickerel weed. **1931** Clute *Common Plants* 22, The starchy tubers of the arrow-leaf (*Sagittaria latifolia*) . . are now more frequently known as duck potatoes. **1946** Reeves–Bain *Flora TX* 20 Arrowleaf . . Petals imbricated in the bud.

arrowvine n [From the shape of the leaves]
=**tearthumb** (here: *Polygonum sagittatum*).
1950 Gray–Fernald *Manual of Botany* 587, *P[olygonum] sagittatum* . . Arrow-vine. **1961** Smith *MI Wildflowers* 101, Arrow-vine. **1970** Correll *Plants TX* 522, Tearthumb, arrow-vine. **1975** Duncan–Foote *Wildflowers SE* 26, Arrow-vine.

arrowweed n
1 A composite shrub (*Pluchea sericea*), 3–12 ft, with numerous willow-like branches. [See quot 1911] **SW** Also called **arrowbrush, arrowwood e, cachimilla**
1871 Browne *Adventures* 51 **SW,** Thickets of arrow-weed lined the way, and forests of cotton-wood loomed up ahead. **1911** *Century Dict. Suppl., Cachimilla* . . . is used by the Indians in making arrows . . . Also called *arrow-weed.* **1944** (1967) McNichols *Crazy Weather* 37 **AZ,** Here he built the Sacred House of logs and thatched it with arrowweeds and covered it over with sand—setting the pattern for every Mojave's winter house for all time to come. **1965** Teale *Wandering Through Winter* 51 **CA,** Mounds of earth crowned with arrowweed lifted higher than our heads . . . The wands of its stiff stems provided Indians of the valley with arrow shafts. **1970** Correll *Plants TX* 1619, Arrow-weed . . . Locally abundant near streams . . . Reported to be a good honey plant.

2 =**arrowhead 1.** *obs*

1846 J.W. Abert in Emory *Mil. Reconn.* 434 *(OEDS),* Some brackish pools . . bordered with the arrow weed *(sagittaria sagittifolia).* **1886** Mitchell *Roland Blake* 263 **sNJ,** Those pools close by with purpled arrow-weed.

3 =**arrow arum.**

1913 *Torreya* 13.228, Arrow-weed, New Richmond, Mich.

arrowwood n Cf **Indian arrowwood**

Any of various plants with straight, tough shoots formerly used to make arrow shafts as:

a Any of several viburnums, but esp **dockmackie** and *Viburnum dentatum.* **chiefly eastern half US**

1709 (1967) Lawson *New Voyage* 107 **S Atl,** Arrow-wood, growing on the Banks, is used, by the Indians, for Arrows and Gun-Sticks. **1832** Kennedy *Swallow Barn* 1.131 **VA,** Morasses . . now, over-grown with thickets of arrow-wood, nine-bark, and various other shrubs. **1892** Apgar *Trees N. U.S.* 114, Arrowwood . . . a shrub or small tree. **1935** Davis *Honey* 148, A morning fog that clouded low in the wet arrowwood and wild-lilac bush made it seem earlier. [Note: This quot may refer instead to **arrowwood g.**] **1967** *DARE* (Qu. T15, . . *Kinds of swamp trees)* Inf **WA**30, Arrowwood. **1979** Little *Checklist U.S. Trees* 293, *Viburnum . . . Other common name*—arrowwood.

b Flowering **dogwood 1** (here: *Cornus florida*).

[**1828** Rafinesque *Med. Flora* 132, The *C. florida* is a handsome tree . . . In Louisiana, where it is called *Bois bouton* or *Bois de fleche,* (Budwood and Arrowwood) it blossoms in February.] **1850** *New Engl. Farmer* 2.60, The first [=dogwood] . . is the Arrowwood; so called from the use once made of its straight shoots, by the Indians, for their arrows. **1889** *Century Dict., Arrow-wood . . .* A name given in the United States to several species of shrubs or small trees used by the Indians for making their arrows, as . . *Cornus florida,* and in the western territories *Tessaria borealis.*

c Either of two related shrubs: usu **wahoo** (here: *Euonymus atropurpureus*), but also **strawberry bush 1** (here: *Euonymus americanus*). **chiefly Sth**

1884 Sargent *Forests of N. Amer.* 38, *Euonymus atropurpureus . .* Burning Bush. Wahoo. Spindle Tree. Arrow Wood. **1897** Sudworth *Arborescent Flora* 281, *Euonymus atropurpureus . . . Common Names . . .* Arrow-wood (Miss., La., Ill., Mo.). **1933** Small *Manual SE Flora* 818, Arrow-wood . . . The bark of the root is used medicinally. **1972** GA Dept. Ag. *Farmers Market Bulletin* 11 Oct 8, Hearts-a-bustin is only one of many common names for Euonymus americanus. Others include "Puppy Toes," . . "Spindle Bush," . . "Arrowwood."

d =**sourwood.**

1897 Sudworth *Arborescent Flora* 314, *Oxydendrum arboreum . . .* Arrow-wood (W. Va.). **1921** Deam *Trees IN* 265, When coppiced it [sourwood] grows long slender shoots which the boys of the pioneers used for arrows. A pioneer . . called the tree "arrow wood." **1950** Peattie *Nat. Hist. Trees* 529, *Sourwood . . . Other Names:* Sorreltree. Sour Gum. Arrowwood.

e =**arrowweed 1.** **chiefly SW**

1889 [see **arrowwood b**]. **1931** U.S. Dept. Ag. *Misc. Pub.* 101.164, *Arrowweed . .* also known by the vernacular names arrowbush, arrow-wood, . . and osikakamuk, is probably the only western shrub of this group. **1960** Vines *Trees SW* 999, It *[Pluchea sericea]* is also known under the vernacular names of Arrow-wood [etc.].

f =**Carolina buckthorn.**

1951 *PADS* 15.36 **TX,** *Rhamnus caroliniana . . .* Yellow buckthorn; arrow-wood.

g =**ocean spray** (here: *Holodiscus discolor*). **Pacific**

1934 Haskin *Wild Flowers Pacific Coast* 165, Arrow-Wood *Holodiscus discolor . . .* This is one of the Indian arrow-woods, for the straight young shoots made almost perfect arrow shafts.

h =**serviceberry** (here: *Amelanchier alnifolia*).

1951 *PADS* 15.13, *Amelanchier alnifolia . . .* Arrow-wood, Okanagon River [Washington] region.

arroyo n Also *aroya, arroya, royo,* dimin *arroyito, arroyullo* [Span] **chiefly SW** See Map

A brook or creek; also, a gully or water-carved channel. (Note: it is often unclear whether a writer refers to the stream or its bed)

[**1806** U.S. Congress *Debates & Proc.* 1.571 **nwTX,** The country east of the Sabine to the Arroyo Hondo.] **1872** Tice *Over Plains* 49 **nwKS,**

There are many *'aroyas,'* that is beds of temporary streams with pools of water, which answer for stock purposes. **1892** *DN* 1.244 **TX,** *Arroyito, arroyúllo:* diminutives of *arroyo.* **1914** *DN* 4.162 **NW,** *Arroya.* **1915** (1922) Clark *Sun & Saddle* 147 **AZ,** Have you heard the 'royos singin'? **1932** *DN* 6.223 **SW,** *Arroyo . . .* is often used for any small canyon, generally a dry ravine, but its especial meaning seems to be a ravine cut by the water through the earth, so that the sides are not as steep as is often the case with a canyon. **1941** Dobie *Longhorns* 135 **SW,** The light shows me we're in a 'royo with the cattle comin' over the edge. **1962** Atwood *Vocab. TX* 40, The Spanish loanword *arroyo . .* is well established in West and Southwest Texas [for dry creek (bed)], and extends to a limited extent into adjoining parts of the state, but it is unknown in East Texas. **1965–70** *DARE* (Qu. C21, *A deep place cut in sloping ground by running water)* 23 Infs, **chiefly SW,** Arroyo; **NJ**30, Arroyo—not local; from reading; **TX**28, Arroyullo; (Qu. C1) Infs **CA**55, **CO**11, 26, **NM**6, **TX**1, 11, Arroyo; (Qu. D22) Inf **TX**26, Deep arroyo.

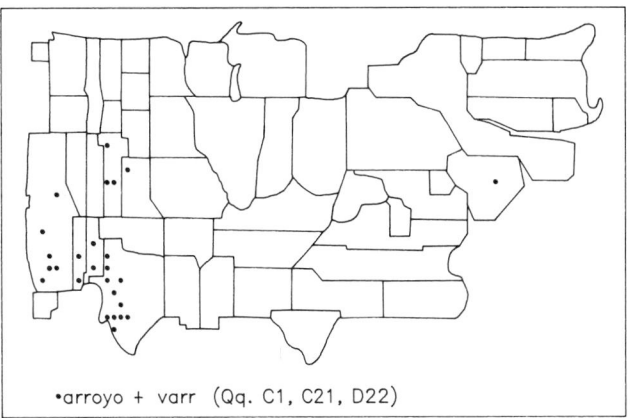

•arroyo + varr (Qq. C1, C21, D22)

arroyo grape n

=**frost grape.**

1886 Havard *Flora W. & S. TX for 1885* 511, Arroyo grape . . . [is a] thrifty climber, the small but excellent berries maturing in October. **1891** Coulter *Botany W. TX* 63, *V. riparia* Michx (Riverside grape.) . . Also known as 'arroyo grape.' **1900** Lyons *Plant Names* 395, *V[itis] vulpina . . .* Aroyo [sic] Grape.

arroz con pollo n [Span] **chiefly SW and other Spanish settlement areas**

Rice cooked with chicken and seasoned with garlic, saffron, and other condiments.

1939 Berolzheimer *U.S. Cookbook* 590 **SW,** Arroz con Pollo . . . Chicken . . paprika . . saffron . . rice . . pimientos . . peas. **1966** *DARE* Tape FL23, Arroz con pollo—Spanish chicken and rice dish which is a specialty of the area. **1967–70** *DARE* (Qu. H45, *Dishes . . that everybody around here would know)* Infs **AZ**12, Arroz con pollo [ros kon ˈpɔɪjo]; **CA**54, Arroz con pollo—rice with chicken sauce; **CO**27, Arroz con pollo.

arry See **ary**

arse-end-to See **ass-end-to**

arse from one's elbow, not to know one's See **ass from one's elbow, not to know one's**

arsemart See **ass-smart**

arsenicker n

=**great white heron 1.**

1945 McAtee *Nomina Abitera* 26, Great White Heron . . Arsenicker Florida east coast.

arsesmart See **ass-smart**

arse-up See **ass-up**

arsh adj See **airish**

arsk See **ask** v **A1d**

arsle v Also sp *assle, azzle* [Du *aarzelen* to move backward, hesitate; recent *assle* is prob due to folk-etym]

1 To back out (of a place or situation). [*EDD* **arsle 1**]

1899 (1912) Green *VA Folk-Speech, Arsle . . .* To arsle, to move backwards; to back out. **1903** *DN* 2.305 **seMO**, *Azzle* or *azzle out* . . . 'We made a fair trade but he azzled out of it the next day and wouldn't deliver the property.'

2 To move when in a sitting position; to fidget. [*EDD arsle* 2]

1930 Shoemaker *1300 Words* 2 **cPA Mts** (as of c1900), *Arsle*—To sit unquietly.

3 To loaf; to idle about restlessly. See also **ass around**

c1960 *Wilson Coll.* **csKY**, *Assle* . . . Fool around, be obviously idle or in the way of those who are trying to work. *Assing around* is apparently the more common local variant. **1967** Wilson *Folkways Mammoth Cave No. 2* 27, *Assle*. To be lazy and aimless. **1970** *DARE* (Qu. KK31, *To go about aimlessly looking for distraction: "He doesn't have anything to do so he's just _____ around.")* Inf **AR56**, Assling; **FL52**, Assling around—[used by] the old folks.

arsmart See **ass-smart**

arsneau n [Etym unknown] Also called **jammer**

In logging: a derrick for loading logs onto a sleigh or railroad car.

1956 Sorden – Ebert *Logger's Words* **Gt Lakes**.

arster See **oyster**

arter prep, adv See **after A1**

arter n [Cf *OED artery* for early exx of this form in Engl]

An artery.

1929 *AmSp* 5.128 **ME coast**, So mad I thought he'd bust an arter. **1974** *AmSp* 49.59 **swME** (as of 1900s), Apocopation occurs in *arter'* 'artery' [in notebooks of George Savary Wasson].

artetu n, also attrib [*arter* pronc-sp for **after** toward the rear + *tu* two] *obs* or *arch*

The fifth **thwart**, or rower's seat, in a six-handed boat.

1945 *Amer. Neptune* 5.87 **Cape Cod MA**, [Question:] I found that in Provincetown the old men . . still call the tub-oar-thwart the 'Artetu' thwart. In fact this thwart was called artetu for a long time . . . [Response:] When the whalers used the 5 handed boat with 4 thwarts the 4 was the after thwart[;] when the 6 handed boat was used, 5 thwarts were used adding one more after thwart which made two after thwarts.

'arth See **earth**

arther, arthur See **author**

‡**arthuratics** n [Blend of **arthuritis + rheumatics**]

Arthritis, rheumatism.

1967 *DARE* (Qu. BB8) Inf **LA8**, [ˈɑθəˌrætɪks].

arthuritis n Usu |ˌɑrθəˈaɪtɪs, –dɪs|; see quots for varr. Pronc-spp *artheritis, arthureetis* [Folk-etym] **esp Sth, Midl** See also **arthuratics, Old Arthur**

Arthritis; rheumatism.

1954 *Harder Coll.* **cwTN**, Arthuritis [ˌɑrðəˈætəs]: Same as . . rheumatism. **c1960** *Wilson Coll.* **csKY**, *Artheritis* . . . Very modern substitute for rheumatis(m). **1965–70** *DARE* (Qu. BB8) 18 Infs, chiefly **Sth, Midl**, Arthuritis [ˌɑrðəˈaɪdɪs, –tɪs]; **AZ2, MI93, WV8**, Arthureetis [ˌɑrðəˈitɪs, –ɪz]; (Qu. BB5) Infs **MO16, 35**, Arthuritis. **1965–66** *DARE* Tape **DC10**, [ɔðəˈraɪtɪs]; **MS56**, [ˌɑrθəˈraɪtɪs].

‡**Arthur's office** n *joc* Cf *DS* W1a–c

An outdoor toilet.

1941 *LANE* Map 354, 1 Inf, **cRI**, Arthur's office.

artic, ar'tic See **arctic** n[1]

artichoke pickle n **S Atl, esp SC**

A Jerusalem artichoke which has been pickled in vinegar with sugar, spices and hot peppers.

[**1847** (1979) Rutledge *Carolina Housewife* 183 **SC**, *To pickle artichokes*. Scrape the artichokes, and throw them into water until all are scraped . . . and put them into fresh vinegar to remain.] **1965** *Colonial Kitchens* 60 **GA**, Artichoke Pickle . . . Soak artichokes and onions in brine . . . Sauce—mix sugar, mustard and tumeric [sic]. Add vinegar. **1965–70** *DARE* (Qu. H56, . . *Kinds of pickles favored around here*) Infs **GA12, 15, NC14, 23, SC1, 4, 7, 22, 43, 56**, Artichoke pickle(s); [**NC16, 79**, Artichokes]; (Qu. H57, *Tasty or spicy side-dishes*) 9 Infs, **all SC**, Artichoke pickle(s). **1976** *DARE* File **SC**, Back to the artichokes of my childhood. Artichoke pickle . . the recipe I have . . says vinegar, sugar, salt, and a string of hot peppers, and some peppercorns.

artichoke potato n

The tuber of the Jerusalem artichoke.

1969 *SC Market Bulletin* 9 Jan 3/3, Artichoke potatoes for pickles.

artichoke relish n Also *Jerusalem ~* **S Atl, esp SC** See also **artichoke pickle**

A condiment consisting of chopped Jerusalem artichokes, onions, and peppers in a spiced vinegar sauce.

1964 *Favorite Recipes Virginias* 9 **seVA**, *Hors D'Oeuvres* . . . *Jerusalem Artichoke Relish* . . . Grind peppers and onions; mix with artichokes, paste, vinegar and 3 cups of sugar. **1965–70** *DARE* (Qu. H57, *Tasty or spicy side-dishes served with meat*) 10 Infs, **all SC**, Artichoke relish; (Qu. H56) Inf **SC56**, Artichoke relish. **1976** *DARE* File **SC**, Artichoke relish . . is chopped artichokes in a "sauce" made with mustard and flour . . . It is eaten with pilau chicken and with pork ham.

article n Usu |ˈɑrtəkəl|; in **Sth, S Midl**, occas stress shift |ɑrˈtɪkl, ˈɑrˌtɪkl| Pronc-sp *ar-tickle*

Std senses, var forms.

1891 *PMLA* 6.175 **TN**, *Article* is accented on the second syllable. **1893** Shands *MS Speech* 17, *Article* . . . is pronounced by illiterate whites with a strong accent on the second syllable. **1940** Stuart *Trees of Heaven* 48 **neKY**, He might make a good renter, . . but a man would have to bind him up mighty tight with a ar-tickle. *Ibid* 172, Git that ar-tickle and bring it in here. **c1960** *Wilson Coll.* **csKY**, *Article* is sometimes |ˈɑrˌtɪkl|.

artificial n *?obs*

An artificial flower.

1842 *Amer. Pioneer* 1.274, After they have passed the lines of silks, laces and artificials. **1856** Whitcher *Bedott Papers* 26.316 **NY**, She had on a yaller bunnit with a great pink artificial on it. **1874** (1895) Eggleston *Circuit Rider* 213 **IN**, He has taken pains to buy her jewelry and "artificials" in abundance. **1935** Sandoz *Jules* 99 **wNE** (as of 1890s), Them plagued Methodist preachers . . . go against dancing and artificials.

artillery n

1 Personal weapons; also occas, personal belongings. **orig West, now more widespread** *joc*

1903 (1965) Adams *Log Cowboy* 198 **NM**, We were in the office of the livery, surrendering our artillery. **1930** Dobie *Coronado* 361 **SW**, *Artillery*, pistols, personal weapons. **1944** Adams *Western Words* 6, *Artillery* . . . I heard one cowhand say of a heavily armed man, "He's packin' so much artillery it makes his hoss swaybacked." **1950** *Western Folkl.* 9.138 **West**, Familiar epithets for the revolver were *equalizer, shootin' iron, . . artillery*. **c1960** *Wilson Coll.* **csKY**, *Artillery* . . . Baggage, belongings. "Here he comes, bringing all his artillery." Rarely used now . . . A gun, esp. a pistol. Normally used as a humorous expression.

2 Beans. *joc*

1930 Irwin *Amer. Tramp*, *Artillery*.—Beans, or any other food likely to ferment. **1946** *AmSp* 21.31 **ceTX**, *Artillery* . . . Beans. **1946** *AmSp* 21.89, The virile language of the culinary workers of the old logging and construction camps or the recent war-time service camps, such as . . *light artillery* (beans).

artistic purposes n pl Also *mechanical and ~*

Devious or illicit intentions: see quot.

1975 Gould *ME Lingo* 37, *Artistic purposes*—The full phrase is "mechanical and artistic purposes" . . . Booze was outlawed except as prescribed by a . . physician, or when it was to be used for "mechanical and artistic purposes." . . In Maine conversations, *artistic purposes* means little more than devious intentions, a high-sounding substitute for something less than noble. Hank Woodbury . . used to go down to Boston on the *steamcars* for what he called *artistic purposes*.

ary adj Usu |ˈeri|, also |ˈæ(ə)ri, ˈɛri, ˈæro| Pronc-spp *air, aire, airy, arro, arry;* old-fash sp *e'er a, ere a* [Alter of *e'er a* ever a] **throughout US, but esp Sth, Midl** Addit quots in *ADD, DAE* See also **airn, arything, nary**

1 Any, either; a single.

1818 Fessenden *Ladies Monitor* 171 **VT** [In list of "Provincialisms" to be avoided], *Ary* for any or either. **1836** (1955) Crockett *Almanacks* 51 **wTN**, Ary one of us could double up two such fellows any minute. **1887** (1967) Harris *Free Joe* 121 **GA**, They hain't arry livin' man . . what's ever seed arrybody wi' them kind er eyes settled down an' married. **1895** *DN* 1.376 **eTN**, *Ary other* shows how completely the old sense has been lost. **1903** *DN* 2.295 **Cape Cod MA**. **1905** *DN* 3.2 **cCT**. *Ibid* 60 **NE**.

1907 *DN* 3.208 **nwAR,** *Ary* or *airy.* **1908** *DN* 3.285 **eAL, wGA.** **1909** *DN* 3.408 **nME.** **1914** *DN* 4.158 **cVA.** **1926** Roberts *Time of Man* 18 **cKY,** I didn't say e'er a word. **1929** Sale *Tree Named John* 24 **MS,** Ah been han'lin babies since 'fo' you er Miss Betty aire one wuz bawn. **1931–33** *LANE Worksheets* **seMA,** *Ary* ['ɛrɨ] Either. Ary one, they're both the same. **1940** *Sat. Eve. Post* 23 Nov 101/2 **sGA,** "You catch air fox?" "You know we caught air fox." **1952** Brown *NC Folkl.* 1.516, *Airy* ['ærɪ] . . . Have you got *ary* cow you can sell me? *Ibid,* *Arro* ['æro] . . . *E'er a,* any . . . Illiterate. **c1960** *Wilson Coll.* **csKY,** *E'er a one* . . still common. |'ær,wən| emphatic; otherwise |ærn|. **1964** Faulkner *Hamlet* 12 **MS,** Go on record as saying he set ere a one of them afire. *Ibid* 33, Careful as ere a horse and mule ever moved in this world. **1967** *DARE* (Qu. LL14) Inf **SC44,** Hain't ary a one—joking only. **1968** *DARE* Tape **GA61,** [æəri].

2 =nary.
    1965–69 *DARE* (Qu. LL14, . . *"This pond used to be full of fish but now there's _____ left."*) Inf **GA18,** Ary one, nary one—used interchangeably by country people; **IN32,** Ary one; **MS30,** Ary ['ærɪ] one; **NH16,** Ary a one.

ary'n See **airn**

arything pron
Something.
    1938 Matschat *Suwannee R.* 152 **nFL, sGA,** Everybody used to feast an' frolic . . like we-uns be goin' to do, provided we git arythin' to feast on.

as conj, pron, prep, adv Usu |æz, əz|; also occas |ɛz, ɪz| Pronc-spp *ez, is, iz, uz*

A Std senses, var forms.
    1848 Lowell *Biglow* 4 **'Upcountry' MA,** It would du ez slick ez grease. **1858** (1892) Holmes *One Hoss Shay* 15 **NEng,** "'N' the way t' fix it, uz I maintain, / Is only jest / T' make that place uz strong uz the rest." **1887** *Scribner's Mag.* 2.475 **AR,** Iz ter dat, . . I ain't no jedge. **1888** Jones *Negro Myths* 3 **GA coast,** Eh jis is bex wid um is eh kin be. **1922** Gonzales *Black Border* 248 **sSC, GA coasts** [Gullah], Soon ez I lef' de 'ooman 'e leddown flat 'puntop 'e back en' gone 'sleep. *Ibid, passim.* **1941** *AmSp* 16.5 **eTX** [Black], *As* [ɛz]. **1942** in 1944 *ADD* **AR,** *As* . . . [jɪst ɪz mʌč] jist iz much. Radio.

B As conj.
1 usu after a neg phr with *know, see,* or *say:* That; if. [*OED as* 28, 1483 →: "*Obs.* and replaced by *that;* but still common in southern [English] dialect speech, where often expanded to *as how.*"] See also **as how**
    1782 in 1859 *Essex Inst. Coll.* 1.13/2 **MA,** I Don't no as I shall [have a dollar] for six months to come. **1843** (1916) Hall *New Purchase* 404 **IN,** "Have the gentlemen given up the bargain?" "Well, I don't know as they has." **1846** (1934) Boynton *Jrl.* 362 **VT,** I am not quite certain as I had better run the risk of this place. **1891** (1967) Freeman *New Engl. Nun* 187, I don't see as he looked a mite different. **1906** *DN* 3.125 **nwAR,** *As* . . . "We visited Brother Joe Spear . . and he tells as he and others around him has a fine prospect for a crop of berries this spring."—Arkansas newspaper. **1908** *DN* 3.287 **eAL, wGA.** **1909** *DN* 3.419 **Cape Cod MA.** **1952** Brown *NC Folkl.* 1.516, *As* . . . "I don't know as I can go today."—Illiterate. **1958** Humphrey *Home from the Hill* 210 **TX,** I don't know as I'd go quite that far myself, but it sure shows he ain't worth much. **1967–68** *DARE* Tape **MI60,** I can't say as I know; **GA25,** I don't know as anybody was ever pestered with warts; **ME6,** I don't know as I can tell you.

2 used to introduce an adv clause: In so far as; that.
    1676 (1878) S. Sewall *Diary* 1.16 **MA,** He gave no answer, as I remember. **1881** *Harper's Mag.* June 63.89/2, She handed back no words, as I could hear. **1947** Dadswell *Hey There Sucker* 47 **FL,** One man . . had all his horses stolen and never found them as we know of. **1966–69** *DARE* (Qu. JJ29) Infs **MO19, NY75,** Not as I can remember; **MD19, 36, 41,** Not as I know of; **SC19,** Not as I recollect.

3 in comparisons: Than. [*OED as* 4 →1824: "*Obs.* exc. in dialects."] **chiefly Midl, Sth** Cf **than** conj
    1891 *PMLA* 6.169 **WV,** Would you rather have this as that? **1893** Shands *MS Speech, As* . . . Used after comparatives . . by illiterate whites . . . "This is better as that." **1895** *DN* 1.376 **eTN,** *As:* for *than.* "I would rather see you as him." **1902** *DN* 2.228 **sIL,** *As* . . . 'I'd rather do this as that.' 'I love this better as that.' **1907** *DN* 3.220 **nwAR.** **1910** *DN* 3.456 **seKY.** **1937** *Hall Coll.* **eTN,** I'd rather work as go to school. **1971** *Foxfire* 5.84 **cwGA,** She wouldn't pay me a bit more 'tention as if I'uz th' wind a'blowin'.

C As prep.
Like; such as. [*OED as* 26 →1705] *relic*
    1941 Stuart *Grandpa Birdwell* **neKY** *(ADD),* I'll never let a little thing as a copperhead crawl into my house.

D As pron.
Who, whom, which, that. [*OED as* 24, "*Obs.* in standard English, but common *dial.* in England and the United States."] **formerly widespread, now chiefly Midl, Sth** See also **all's**
    1630 in 1869 Winthrop *Life & Letters* 2.40 **MA,** I found that love and respect from Capt. Milburne our master, as I may not forget. **1852** Stowe *Uncle Tom's Cabin* 19 **KY,** I've seen 'em as would pull a woman's child out of her arms. **1871** Eggleston *Hoosier Schoolmaster* 118 **sIN,** There's one as'll help me. **1895** (1969) Crane *Red Badge* 8, They like nothing better than the job of leading off a young feller like you, as ain't never been away from home. **1905** *DN* 3.2 **cCT.** **1931** *PMLA* 46.1320 **sAppalachians,** The man as you saw. **1944** *PADS* 2.39 **wNC, LA,** *As* . . . "Them as thinks they can whup me jest come ahead." **1952** Brown *NC Folkl.* 1.516, *As* . . . "These folks as go around meddling with other folks' business ought to be shot." . . Illiterate. **c1960** *Wilson Coll.* **csKY,** *As* . . . "This feller is one as owns this farm." **1967** Cerello *Dakota Co. MN* 48, The only disadvantage of chair-buying as I can see is that you don't get a chance to inspect what you're buying.

asabecca See **asarabacca**

asafetida n, also attrib Usu |ˌæsə'fɛtɪdə|; also |ˌæsə'fɪtədə, –fɪtɪtɪ, ˌæzə–|; often in **Sth, Midl, and less frequently elsewhere,** metath |ˌæs(ə)'fɪdɪtɪ, –fɛdɪtɪ| and aphet |'fɪdɪtɪ| Pronc-spp *asafoetida, asafoetidy, asfedity, as(a)fidity, assafedity, fidity* See also **fetty**
Std sense, var forms.
    1844 Thompson *Major Jones's Courtship* 169 **GA,** I had to take her rite back to the hotel and stay with her all the evenin, and give her assafedity and hold the hartshorn to her nose. **1929** Sale *Tree Named John* 89 **MS,** Put in a few draps uv te'pentime, a little asfedity, en de juice out'n a red ingon, you's got a liniment den dat'll cyore any kin' uv mis'ry er rheumatiz dar is in de worl'. **1931** *N. Amer. Rev.* May 432 **NYC** (as of c1850), My mother told me her own grandparents and . . doctors of that day spoke always of *asafoetidy.* **1936** *AmSp* 11.250 **eTX,** *Asafoetida* Shows interchange of [t] and [d]. It is pronounced [æs'fɪdɪtɪ], [æ⸳s'fɪdɪtɪ], by all. **1940** Harris *Folk Plays* 55 **NC,** Give me my as-fidity pills, honey, . . and a little water in a glass. **c1960** *Wilson Coll.* **csKY,** *Asafetida* . . often |æsə'fɪtədə| or |–'fɪtɪt|. *Ibid, Fidity* ['fɪdɪtɪ]. **1965–70** *DARE* (Qu. BB50) Inf **KS5,** Asafidity [æzə'fɪdɪtɪ]—in a sack 'round the neck; **MI89,** Asfedity [æs'fɛdɪtɪ]; **IL14,** Asafidity [æsəfɪdɪtɪ]—a kind of herb that used to be tied around the neck; (Qu. HH14, *Ways of teasing a beginner . . . "Go get me _____."*) Inf **TX95,** Asfidity [æsfɪdəti]—if you send someone to a newspaper or sawmill to get it (i.e., the wrong place).

asafetida bag n Also ~ *sack old-fash*
A small sack containing asafetida, worn around the neck as a protection from contagious diseases.
    1937 Sandoz *Slogum* 40 **NE,** She cared for all the sick, even if it was typhoid or smallpox, wearing a greasy asafetida sack on a string that lay in the folds of her thickening neck to ward off disease. **1946** *PADS* 6.4 **eNC** (as of 1900–05). **1951** *PADS* 15.52 **neIN.** **c1960** *Wilson Coll.* **csKY.** **1967** *DARE* FW Addit **neLA,** Asafetida [ˌæs'fɪtɪdɪ] bag—prevention for measles. "You never would catch nothing with that around your neck, because nobody never would get that close to you."—old-fashioned. **1967** *DARE* Tape **IA2,** I have relatives that carried an [æsə'fɪdəti] bag around their neck. **1968–69** *DARE* (Qu. BB50a) Inf **PA147,** Asafidity [æsɪ'fɪdɪtɪ] bag—worn around neck to ward away colds; (Qu. BB50d) Inf **KY54,** Asafetida bag—old-fashioned, to ward off disease; **IL35,** Asafidity [æsə'fɪdɪtɪ] bag. [All Infs Old]

asarabacca n Also pronc-spp *asabecca, asarabocca, azabecker, sarabacca* [*OED* 1551 →] **formerly eUS** *now prob relic in Appalachians or obs*
=wild ginger 1.
    1828 Rafinesque *Med. Flora* 71, *Asarum canadense . . . Broadleaf Asarabacca. Ibid* 73, Henry . . . calls it Swamp Asarabocca, although never growing in swamps. **1847** Wood *Class-Book* 465, *A[sarum] Canadense. Wild Ginger. Asarabacca . . . The root . . has been considered useful in whooping-cough . . . A. Virginicum [=Hexastylis virginica] . . . Sweet-scented Asarabacca.* **1942** *Hench Coll.* **cVA,** A fellowteacher who has his home in the country tells me that *asabecca* or *azabecker* is a local . . name for one form of wild ginger. **1971** Kroch-

mal *Appalachia Med. Plants* 66, *Asarum canadense* . . . Common
names: Canada wild ginger, . . broad-leaved sarabacca.

asatoria See **azoturia**

ascarce See **a** inert vowel **6**

ascared *adj* Pronc-spp *ascaid, ascairt, askeared, askeerd, a-
skeered* [**a** inert vowel **1** + *scared*] **chiefly Midl, Sth**
Scared, afraid.
  1926 Vollmer *Sun-Up* 53 **wNC,** I ain't askeered of no Yankee nohow.
1942 Hall *Smoky Mt. Speech* 52 **eTN, wNC,** I never was a-scared so
bad. **1950** *PADS* 14.12 **SC,** Askeared. **c1960** *Wilson Coll.* **csKY,**
Askeared . . . Afraid . . . [əˈskjɪrd, –ˈɛrd]. **1963** Owens *Look to River*
93 **TX,** You ain't got no need to be a-scaid o' me. **1965–70** *DARE* (Qu.
GG25, . . *Frightened: "The children were _____ he was going to hurt
them."*) Infs **CA**15, 107, **IL**97, **MD**2, **MI**26, 33 **TX**28, Ascared; **TN**13,
Ascared to death; **GA**30, A-skeered. **1972** *Atlanta Letters* **Macon GA,**
Have you ever been a-scairt? **1976** Garber *Mountain-ese* 4 **sAppala-
chians,** Most girls are askeerd uv mice.

as 'cording to *prep* [*as* + *'cording* var of *according* + *to*]
According to, depending upon.
  1966 *DARE* Tape **MS**14, Those things do make a big difference as
'cording [əzˈkɔrdɪn] to business in Hattiesburg; **MS**77, Some time it'll
head up an' sometimes it won't as 'cordin' to what kind of season you
have.

ascrew *adv* [Alter of *askew,* infl by *screw* twist]
Askew, out of kilter; awry.
  1966–70 *DARE* (Qu. MM13, *The table was nice and straight until he
came along and knocked it _____*) Infs **CA**99, **NY**230, **WA**1, **WI**21,
Ascrew; (Qu. KK10, . . *"He didn't work it out carefully enough, and his
plan _____."*) Inf **WI**52, Went ascrew.

asement See **easement**

aseria See **azoturia**

as far as *prep* Also *so far as* [Ellip for *as far as (something) is
concerned,* perh infl by *as for*]
As for; regarding.
  [**1927** Fowler *Dict. Mod. Engl. Usage* 170/1, *As* or *so f[ar] as x* cannot be
used as short for *as far as x goes* or *so far as concerns x.*] **1939** Canby
Thoreau 217, The cabin . . was in perfect condition so far as frame and
covering until 1868. **1960** J.F. Kennedy in *U.S. News & World Rept.* 26
Sept 76/1, As for whether I could attend this sort of a function in your
church . . then I could attend. **1975** Newell *If Nothin' Don't Happen* 57
FL, And as far as makin' my brother stumble, eatin' meat ain't got
nothin' to do with it. **1977** *DARE* File **Madison WI** [Radio], They will
know what to do as far as the Oregon School for Girls.

asfedity See **asafetida**

asfelt See **asphalt**

asfidity See **asafetida**

as good as *adv phr* [*OED as* C2c, 1523 →] *old-fash* Cf **good**
adv
As well as not; just as soon.
  1859 (1968) Bartlett *Americanisms,* As good as. In the phrase, I'd as
good's go to New York, instead of "I might as well go to New York."
Only heard among the illiterate. **1871** (1882) Stowe *Fireside Stories* 112
NEng, She said ef there was any thing under that 'are rock, they'd as
good's have it as the Devil. **1905** *DN* 3.2 **cCT,** As good as . . . As well.
'I'd as good's go.'

ash See **ash maple, prickly ash**

ashamed *adj* **chiefly Midl**
Esp of children: bashful, timid.
  1916 *DN* 4.337 **csPA, LA, KS,** Ashamed . . . "The child's always
ashamed before company." **1924** Raine *Land of Saddle-Bags* 104
sAppalachians, "The littl'un's *ashamed* (bashful). She hain't much
manners." **1933** *AmSp* 8.1.47 **Ozarks,** Ashamed . . . When used in
speaking of a child or a young girl, this word does not mean ashamed in
the ordinary sense, but merely timid or bashful. **1946** *PADS* 6.4 **eNC,**
Ashamed . . . Bashful. Said of timid children. **1954** *Harder Coll.*
cwTN. c1960 *Wilson Coll.* **csKY.**

ash-barrel baby *n* Cf *DS* Z11b
An illegitimate child.
  1949 *AmSp* 24.106 **neGA,** Ash-barrel baby . . . Bastard.

‡ash bomb *n*
=**ash can 2.**
  1969 *DARE* (Qu. FF14, . . *Kinds of firecrackers . . around here*) Inf
NY211, Ash bomb.

ash-box *n* Also *ashes box* **chiefly Sth, Midl, West** See Map
=**ashpan.**
  1847 U.S. Patent Office *Annual Rept. for 1846: Arts & Mfgr.* 261, The
chamber of combustion and its grate and ash-box. **1855** Thomson
Doesticks 287 **NYC,** [I] was knocked bodily into an ash-box by the
foreman of engine 73. **1965–70** *DARE* (Qu. F12, *The flat metal piece
below a woodburning stove, to catch the ashes*) 58 Infs, **chiefly Sth, Midl,
West,** Ash-box; **SC**26, Ashes box.

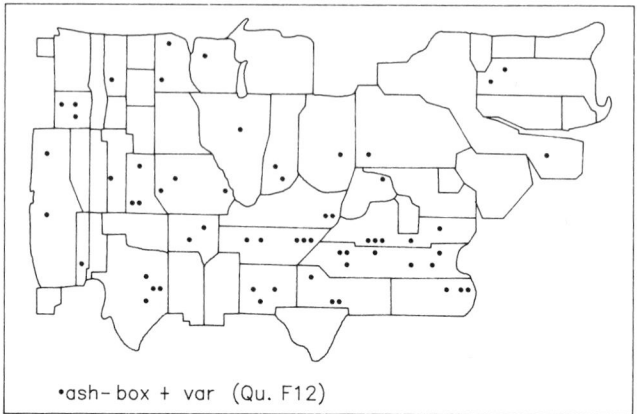

•ash-box + var (Qu. F12)

ash bread *n* **chiefly Sth, Midl**
=**ashcake 1.**
  c1950 *Atlas Checklists* **seWI,** Ashbread—cornbread made in
ashes. **1966** *DARE* FW Addit **SC,** Ash bread—make dough, . . wrap
in paper, rake back the coals—cover with ashes. It's made in the chimbly
[ˈčɪmblɪ]. **1966** *DARE* (Qq. H15, 18) Inf **SC**9, Ash bread. **1967** *PADS*
47.5 **SC.** **1971** Wood *Vocab. Change* 305 **Sth,** 129 [Infs] . . . Ash bread.

ash breeze *n* Also *white-ash breeze* **chiefly Nth, esp NEast**
  1 An oar or oars (as made of ash wood) used instead of a sail and
wind to propel a boat; rowing.
  1834 *Visit to TX* 105 **Nth,** We laid in provisions . . but were disappointed in having no wind. We, however, took advantage of what is
sometimes called the "ash breeze:" that is, our oars, and proceeded down
the bay. **1851** (1976) Melville *Moby-Dick* 351, There she slides, now!
Hurrah for the white-ash breeze! **1883** in 1962 Sears *Adirondack Letters*
157 **nNY,** There came from the outlet a swift, double-ended blue boat
with only a guide in her, and the guide was giving her an ash breeze for all
she was worth. **1919** Kyne *Capt. Scraggs* 92 **CA,** Well, you've lost a
good skiff worth at least twenty-five dollars not to mention the two ash
breezes that went with her. **1950** Moore *Candlemas Bay* 13 **ME,**
"Which you rather have, Pa? A hundred hosspower engine or an ash
breeze?" That last crack was at Grampie's old boat, Jeb knew, because an
"ash breeze" was a pair of oars. **1957** Beck *Folkl.* **ME** 115, If things were
too hard the "ash breeze" (oars) replaced worn-out sails.
  2 Transf: a temporary substitute device or appliance.
  1975 Gould *ME Lingo,* Ash breeze. If the crew of a becalmed sailing
vessel breaks out the sweeps and begins to row, the effort is called
"making an ash breeze." Ash was the favored wood for oars. Hence, any
make-do contrivance can be an ash breeze.

ashbucket apprentice *n obs*
A low-level worker on a canal boat, given the menial task of
emptying ashes.
  1955 Adams *Grandfather* **NY** (as of c1830), The designation of the
vagrant bands that had formerly ranged canalside was familiar to us:
gyppos, pinkies, tenkers, swingkettles, . . and ashbucket apprentices.

ashcake *n*
  1 A cornmeal bread baked in hot ashes. **chiefly Sth, S Midl**
See map in 1949 Kurath *Word-Geog.* Fig 119. Also called **ash
bread, ~ dog, ~ nan, ~ pone, fire cake** See also *DS* H 14, 15, 18
  1816 Ker *Travels* 111, The kind host regaled us with a good supper, or
good for a wilderness country; it consisted of ash cake, venison, and
bear's meat, besides coffee. **a1883** (1911) Bagby *VA Gentleman* 232,

Fish of the very best, both salt and fresh, chicken, eggs, milk and the invincible, never-satisfying ash-cake and fried bacon. **1899** (1912) Green *VA Folk-Speech*, *Ashcake* . . . A loaf of corn bread baked in ashes. **1903** *DN* 2.305 **seMO. 1906** *DN* 3.125 **nwAR. 1908** *DN* 3.287 **eAL,** **wGA. 1947** Bowles–Towle *New Engl. Cooking* 4, Crisp hot ashcakes, baked Indian fashion among the hearth ashes of the kitchen fireplace, were a popular breakfast bread in New England. **1952** Brown *NC Folkl.* 1.270, *Ashcake.*— Sift one pint of cornmeal, add a pinch of salt . . . Cover the cake with ashes and put a few coals on top. Bake for twenty minutes. **1966** *DARE* Tape **MS75**, Ashcakes is corn bread. You make it up . . just soft and warm . . and you cook that in the ashes. **1966–70** *DARE* (Qu. H14, *Bread that's made with cornmeal*) Inf **VA35**, Ashcake—baked in the fireplace—old-fashioned; **TX4**, Ashcakes; (Qu. H18) Infs **FL49, SC1, VA69**, Ashcake; (Qu. H15) Inf **SC26**, Ashcake— lard, flour, milk, salt—roll it, wrap in heavy paper, heat the paper, cook it in the hot ashes—also of cornmeal. **1967** *DARE* FW Addit **ceTN,** Ashcake—take cornmeal, fix it like bread, wrap it in paper, cover with ashes and bake. Eat with sweet milk.

2 Transf: see quot.

1912 Green *VA Folk-Speech*, *Ashcake* . . . Lumps of clay formed on the ends of tobacco hogsheads on the "rolling roads."

ash can n

1 =ash-cat **3.**

1932 *Santa Fe Mag.* 26.2.34/1, A locomotive fireman may be called a tallow pot, ash can.

2 A small but relatively powerful firecracker, cylindrically shaped and covered with tinfoil. [Prob transf from military use of *ash can*, a high-explosive depth charge: cf *DAS, OEDS*] **chiefly NEast** Also called **ash bomb**

1966–70 *DARE* (Qu. FF14, . . *Kinds of firecrackers . . around here*) Infs **NY87, 118, 241, TN65**, Ash cans; **ME15**, Ash cans [drawing in text]; **MA1**, Ash can—bigger than [a] cherry bomb, has tin foil on outside; **PA113**, Ash can—blockbuster.

3 A type of floating buoy resembling an ashcan.

1966 *DARE* (Qu. O14a) Inf **SC21**, Ash cans—a nickname.

‡4 The buttocks. *joc* Cf **can** n **3c**

1966 *DARE* (Qu. X34, *Joking words for the part of the body you sit on*) Inf **FL39**, Ash can.

ash-cat n

1 also *ash-cat-Sam:* A dirty or disheveled person, esp a child. [*EDD* 1808 → in similar sense] Also called **singed cat**

1869 Twain *Innocents* 262, They [=Italian women] sit in the alleys and nurse their cubs. They nurse one ash-cat at a time, and the others scratch their backs against the door-post and are happy. **1899** (1912) Green *VA Folk-Speech* 69, *Ashcat* . . . A child that plays in the ashes, dirtying its hands, face and clothes. **1910** C. Harris *Eve's Husband* 120 *(DA)*, He came home late at night looking like an ash-cat-Sam.

2 A gaunt Black person. Cf **ash-faced**

1909 *S. Atl. Qrly.* 8.47 *Gullah*, The description . . is graphic; so is . . the description of an ill-stead, ill-fed, thin and ragged negro, outcast, a creature of the streets and byways, as an *ash-cat*. [Footnote:] Ill-fed, ill-conditioned negroes were so-called in derision of their grayish-hued, gaunt and dingy faces . . . Masters and owners of such "ash-cats" were held in great contempt.

3 In railroading: a locomotive fireman. Also called **ash can 1, ash-eater**

1945 *Sun* (Baltimore MD) 29 Aug 2–0/6 *(Hench Coll.)*, It's everyday conversation among the men who operate the railroads . . . Ashcat— locomotive fireman. **1945** Hubbard *Railroad Ave.* 331. **1947** Beebe *Mixed Train* 353.

ashdog n Cf **dogbread, hushpuppy**

=ashcake **1.**

1914 *DN* 4.153 **CT, NH,** *Ashdogs* . . . Indian meal [corn meal] with water stirred up until soft, rolled up in cotton paper, put in cold ashes, then in hot ashes.

ash-eater n *joc*

=ash-cat **3.**

1977 Adams *Lang. Railroader*, *Ash eater:* A fireman.

asher n

=ashpan.

1968 *DARE* (Qu. F12) Inf **CT11**, Asher ['æʃɚ]. Empty the asher [FW: conv].

ashes n pl, freq attrib

1 used where sg is expected: Ash.

1836 *Franklin Repository* (Chambersburg, Pa.) 4 Oct 1/3 *(DA)*, Ever since these black stones [=coal] were brought to town, the wood-sawyers and pilers, and then soap-fat and hickory ashes-men, has been going down. **1846** Corcoran *Pickings* 61 **LA,** Knocking over the ashes barrels, shying stones at the lamps. **1902** *DN* 2.228 **sIL,** *Ashes* . . . Used in singular as 'This ashes.' **1966** *DARE* (Qu. F12) Inf **SC9**, Ashes tray; **SC26**, Ashes box.

2 In phrr *haul one's ashes, get one's ashes hauled:* To be sexually satisfied. *chiefly among Black speakers*

a1939 in 1958 Silverman *Folk Blues* 245 **LA** [Black], Well, you see that spider climbin up the wall, / Goin' up there to get her ashes hauled. **1951** Longstreet *Pedlocks* 93 **MT,** We'll get a box at the Comique, then go get our ashes hauled . . . Never had an Indian girl myself. **1963** Wright *Lawd Today* 176 **Chicago IL** [Black], He hauls my ashes / He strokes my fiddle . . / Lawd, he's a damn good man to have around.

ashes box See **ash-box**

ash-faced adj Cf **ash-cat 2, ash-spots, ashy 2, high yellow**

Of Blacks: having an ashen complexion; light-skinned.

1902 *DN* 2.305 **seMO,** *Ash-faced* . . . Applied to mulattoes or light negroes in contempt.

ashfork maple See **ash maple**

ash-gum n Cf **gum** n

A receptacle for ashes, usu made from a section of a hollow gum-tree and kept outside the house.

1851 Hooper *Widow Rugby's Husband* 42 **AL,** A dozen fowls clustered on top of the *ash-gum.* **1923** *DN* 5.233 **swWI,** *Ash-gum* . . . A piece of a tree, generally of the trunk . . hollowed out [and] used to collect ashes for soap. A barrel thus employed is often so called.

ash hominy n

Corn grains hulled by soaking in lye obtained from wood ashes.

1942 Perry *Texas* 122, A few of our rural citizens still make their own ash hominy in their own wash pots.

ash-hopper n, also attrib **chiefly Sth, Midl**

1a A funnel-shaped receptacle for ashes being kept for soap-making. *obsolescent* (Illustr in *DA*) Also called **ash-leach**

1804 in 1814 *Amer. Mineralogical Jrl.* 1.105 **KY,** Cubic Salts . . . thrown upon the ash-hoppers, . . are supposed to assist in precipitating the lime. **1864** (1922) Jackson *Col.'s Diary* 122 **cwPA,** Mr. Hooker . . upset her ash hopper. **1929** in 1977 *Pissing in the Snow* 53 **seMO,** That old man could make the prettiest buckskin you ever seen. He took the hair off with ash-hopper lye. **c1960** *Wilson Coll.* **csKY,** *Ash-hopper* . . . Container for wood ashes, from which lye is obtained to make soft soap. Only a memory now. "We tore down our old ash-hopper last spring and built a new one." **1968** *DARE* Tape **IN3**, Ash-hopper . . . built out of boards, kind of triangle shape and the big part was up and it come down to a point . . open at the bottom . . . And all through the winter they would put their ashes in there. **1972** *Foxfire Book* 157 **neGA** (as of c1920), We'd wet th' ashes and put'em in a ash hopper and save'em . . . And then we'd . . carry th' water . . and throw over th' ashes and drip th' lye.

b in phr *work one's own ash-hopper:* Do one's own work.

1843 (1916) Hall *New Purchase* 54 **IN,** Most time, mam, you'll have to work your own ash-hopper.

2 Transf: =ashpan.

1967–70 *DARE* (Qu. F12, *The flat metal piece below a wood-burning stove, to catch the ashes*) Infs **AL52, IL124, TN30, TX43, VA28, 42,** Ash-hopper.

ash-house n

An outbuilding for ashes and other refuse.

1807 Irving *Salmagundi* 4.53, He once shook down the ash-house by an artificial earthquake, and nearly blew his sister Barbara and her cat, out of the window with thundering power. **1922** (1926) Cady *Rhymes VT* 38, Our ashhouse got to smoking. **1969** *DARE* (Qu. M22, . . *Other kinds of buildings . . on farms around here*) Inf **PA230**, Ash-house.

ash-leach n

=ash-hopper **1a.**

1906 *Pocumtuc Housewife* 47, In the spring when the ash hole is cleared have five or six bushels of ashes put in the ash leach.

ash maple n Also freq *ash-leafed maple, ashleaf ~, ash-leaved ~;* occas *ash, maple ash, maple;* rarely *ashfork maple, ashwood* **chiefly east of the Missip R**
=**box elder.**

1765 (1942) Bartram *Diary of a Journey* 28, Below ye falls is very rich low land produceing . . Ash hicory ash leaved maple. **1834** *S. Lit. Messenger* 1.98 **VA, MD,** On emerging from the wilderness, the customary variety of oak, ash maple and hickory presents itself. **1868** IL State Ag. Soc. *Trans. of 1866* 6.390, The Box Elder of our river bottoms comes back to us under the name of . . Ash Leaf Maple. **1897** Sudworth *Arborescent Flora* 292, *Common Names . . . Maple* (Cal.). **1900** Lyons *Plant Names* 11, *A[cer] Negundo . . .* Ash-leaved Maple, . . Maple Ash. **1950** *WELS* 1 Inf, **cWI,** Box elder—Ash maple; 1 Inf, **ceWI,** Ash-leafed maple. **1965–70** *DARE* (Qu. T13, . . *Other names . . for . . box elder*) 45 Infs, Ash maple; **ME8, MA78, VT4,** Ashleaf maple; **NY227,** Ash-leaved maple—breaks in storms; **IL66, IN35, KS7, ME8, MD13, MS47, WI62,** Ash; **KY94, NC38, PA89,** Maple; **OH98,** Ashfork maple; **MS47,** Ashwood; (Qu. T14) Infs **MA78, VT4,** Ashleaf maple; **ME8,** Ash-leaved maple; **SC7,** Ash; **CT6,** Maple ash. **1968** Pochmann *Triple Ridge* 81 **cWI,** The ash-leaved maple, or box elder, has no spicy fragrance like the red.

ash nan n Also *ash nanny* **SC**
An **ashcake** made with biscuit dough.

1954 *PADS* 21.20 **cnSC,** *Ash Nanny . . .* Biscuit dough cooked on a board before the open fire. **1966** *DARE* Tape SC14, Mix the flour in this paper and open the ashes and put 'im in and cover 'im up with the ashes and take 'im out and wash 'im in water and they come a nice bread as they ever want to eat, . . a ash nan ['ɑsh næn]. **1966** *DARE* FW Addit SC, Ash nan [ɑɪš næn]—ashy bread.

ash oak n, also attrib
Perh =**gray oak 1.**

1771 *NH Gaz. & Hist. Chron.* 30 Aug 1/3, Such persons as are desirous of contracting for White Pine *Masts,* Yards and Bowsprits, . . Lathwood, Ash Oak Rafters, &c. **1968** *DARE* (Qu. T10, . . *Kinds of oak trees*) Inf **CT2,** Ash oak.

ash oven n
a1890 (1944) Robinson *Hist. Morrill* 32 **csME,** The houses . . contained three fireplaces, an oven, and an ash oven, with flues large enough for a boy to go up through.

as how conj phr **chiefly Sth, Midl Cf all how**
=**as B1.**

1781 *PA Jrl. & Weekly Advt.* (Philadelphia PA) 16 May 1, He said *as how* it was his opinion. This absurd pleonasm is more common in Britain than in America. **1843** (1916) Hall *New Purchase* 116 **sIN,** I think if he'd a fired his *own* gun as how he mought a come out even. **1870** Harte *Luck Roaring Camp* 50 **CA,** The doctors came and said as how it was caused all along of his way of life. **1911** *DN* 3.537 **eKY,** *As how . . .* "I heard as how there was a quarrel." **1916** *DN* 4.286 **sAppalachians,** Dock tuck it ez how Flim had slandered him. **1918** *DN* 5.20 **NC. 1949** Dean *Diamond Bess* 14, Just across the border here into Texas, the folks figured as how it was the thing to do to join the Union. **1952** Brown *NC Folkl.* 1.516, *As how . . .* That, whether . . . Illiterate.

ashpan n **widespread, but esp Nth, Midl See Map See also ash-box, asher, ash-hopper 2, ashpit**

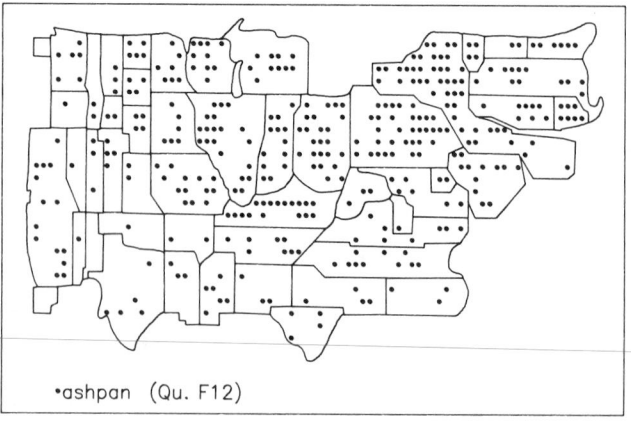

ashpan (Qu. F12)

A pan under a grate for collecting ashes, esp one in a wood-burning stove.

1925 in 1953 Botkin *Treas. Railroad Folkl.* 307, Had no ash pan on the engine, no pilot, no smokestack. **1965–70** *DARE* (Qu. F12, *The flat metal piece below a wood-burning stove, to catch the ashes*) 372 Infs, **widespread, but esp Nth, Midl,** Ashpan.

ashpit n **chiefly Nth**
A hole or receptacle used for the collection of ashes. Cf **ashpan**
1923 U.S. Dept. Ag. *Farmers' Bulletins* No. 1371, In the front grate bars may be provided and an excavation made for an ash pit where the ashes accumulate [in maple sugar production]. **1947** *PADS* 8.4 **VT** [Maple Sugar Language], *Ash pit . . .* A part of the furnace where the ashes accumulate. **1947** *Washington Post* (DC) 13 Jan B1/6 *(Hench Coll.),* When it [=the fire in a locomotive] is "cleaned," it is about the same as cleaning your own furnace. All this goes on over what is called the "ash pits." **1965–70** *DARE* (Qu. F12) 16 Infs, **chiefly Nth,** Ashpit.

ashpit engineer n
Among railroad workers: see quot.
1977 Adams *Lang. Railroader* 8, *Ash-pit engineer:* Any workman (usually the fireman) who services engines, especially at division points and terminals.

ash pone n [*ash* + **pone** cake of cornmeal batter] **chiefly Sth, Midl, esp VA**
=**ashcake 1.**

1816 in 1824 Knight *Letters* 78 **VA,** What slaves I have seen, have fared coarsely upon their hoe-cakes and ash-pone. **1946** *PADS* 5.9 **VA. 1949** Kurath *Word Geog.* Fig 119, [Of 10 instances of *ash pone,* 1 is from SC, 3 from NC, 6 from VA]. **c1950** *LANCS Checklists* seWI, cnIL, Ash *pone*—corn bread made in ashes. **1970** *DARE* (Qu. H14, *Bread that's made with cornmeal*) Inf **VA74,** Ash pone—cooked in ashes—old-fashioned. **1971** Wood *Vocab. Change* 44 **Sth,** A special kind of corn bread baked in the ashes is known in descending order of preferences as *ash cake, ash pone,* and *ash bread.*

ash potato See **Irish A**

ash snake n
=**blue racer** (here: *Coluber constrictor flaviventris*).
1930 *Copeia* 85, *The White-spotted Phase of the Racer (Coluber constrictor flaviventris . .) in Louisiana . . .* This phase is known locally as the ash snake . . . The . . name refers to its appearance . . . The markings may consist of white scales sparsely and irregularly interspersed among the normally colored scales . . or white scales may be very numerous and intermixed with variously mottled scales.

ash-spots n pl **Cf ashy 2**
=**goose pimples.**
1970 *DARE* (Qu. X58) Inf **TN52,** Ash-spots . . because they leave her [=Inf] looking ashy. [Inf Black]

ashwood n See **ash maple**

ashy adj
1 Very angry. **chiefly Sth, S Midl See also dusty**
1846 Porter *Quarter Race* 45 **AL,** An the feller got rite ashy 'bout it, but I didn't mind him. **1891** *PMLA* 6.172 **TN,** *Ashy* is used as a synonym for *angry.* **1899** (1912) Green *VA Folk-Speech, Ashy . . .* Angry. **1941** *LANE* Map 472 *(Angry)* 1 Inf, **cRI,** Ashy = 'angry,' heard. **1946** *PADS* 6.4 **eNC** (as of 1900–1910), *Ashy . . .* Ill-tempered, ill-humored . . . Common. **1970** *DARE* (Qu. GG4, *Stirred up, angry*) Inf **VA69,** Ashy —old-fashioned word. **1971** Wood *Vocab. Change* 40 **Sth,** *Ashy, het up, owly,* and *wrathy* have a limited occurrence.

2 also *ashy-pale:* usu of Blacks: Pale as ashes. Cf **ash-faced, ash-spots**
1952 Brown *NC Folkl.* 1.516, *Ashy (pale) . . .* The greyish color of the Negro's skin when he is sick or frightened.—Rare. **1970** *DARE* (Qu. X58, *When you are cold, and little points of skin begin to come on your arms and legs*) Inf **TN52,** Ash-spots . . leave her [=Inf] looking ashy. **1977** Smitherman *Talkin* 67 [Black], *Ashy* refers to the whitish coloration of black skin due to exposure to the *Hawk* (cold and wind). Whites get ashy too, but the whiteness shows up more pronounced on blacks due to their darker skin pigmentation.

aside adj **Cf side up**
Settled; arranged; in order.
1894 *DN* 1.328 **cNJ,** *Aside:* used in an expression "Are you aside?"

meaning, "Have you your household goods in order after moving?" **1932** Smiley *Gloss. New Paltz* seNY, "Put a house or room *aside*" means to put it in order, straighten it up . . . Mr. Beebe has heard those of Dutch ancestry use it in New Paltz.

aside adv
Side-saddle.
1976 Garber *Mountain-ese* 4 sAppalachians, In the early days the ladies allers rode aside.

aside (of) prep [a prep[1] **1a** + *side; OED* 1615 →"Still in *Sc*.": see also *EDD, SND*]
Beside.
1838 (1925) Kemper *Trip WI* 437 **NY,** The Stockbridges . . have a reservation aside of the Brothertowns. **1855** (1856) Kane *Arctic Explor.* 2.24, We . . are mere carpet-knights aside of these indomitable savages. **1928** Peterkin *Scarlet Sister Mary* 325 **SC,** Does you want me to lay aside you on de bed an' warm you, son? **1968** *DARE* (QR, near Qu. MM17) Inf **PA150,** Sit aside of each other. **1970** Bullins *Electronic* 109 **NEast** [Black], All he's doin' is peein' aside the pole. **1976** Garber *Mountain-ese* 4 sAppalachians, In the classroom the boys were often seated aside the girls.

ask v
A Forms.
1 pres: usu *ask* [æsk]; also:
a [æks]. Pronc-spp *ax, axe* [OE *ascian, acsian:* see *OED ask,* etym note] formerly esp NEng, now chiefly Sth, Midl
1789 Webster *Dissertations Engl. Lang.* 386, This word to *ax* is still frequent in New England. **1815** Humphreys *Yankey in England* 103 [Glossary of Provincialisms] NEng, *Ax,* ask. **1836** (1955) Crockett *Almanacks* 51 wTN, He went all around to the parents of the children to ax them for their custom. **1893** Shands *MS Speech* 18, *Ax* [æks]. Negro for *ask.* **1901** *DN* 2.181 **KY** [Black], *Ask* . . ax. **1930** Shoemaker *1300 Words* 1 cPA **Mts** (as of c1900), *Axe*—to ask. **1942** Faulkner *Go Down* 148 **MS,** Dat's all she axes: just leff her look at you. **1953** Atwood *Survey of Verb Forms* 5, The present form *ax* /æks/ does not occur north of the Pa.–Md. boundary, and is found only at a few isolated points in W. Va., Md., and Va . . . In N.C. this form becomes much more common, reaching considerable concentration in the western one fourth of the state, where nearly all of the Type I informants use it. **1974** Fink *Mountain Speech* 1 wNC, eTN, You *ax* him.

b [æst]. Pronc-sp *ast* chiefly Sth, Midl *esp among speakers with less than coll educ*
1890 *DN* 1.67 **KY,** Many do not say *ask,* but *ast* [æst]; as "Ast me nothing about it." **1893** Shands *MS Speech* 18, The form *ast* . . is very common. **1894** Riley *Armazindy* 31 **IN,** Gran'pap 'ud allus haf to ast— / "How did you rest, last night?" **1905** *DN* 3.69 nwAR. **1953** Atwood *Survey of Verb Forms* 5, The present *ast* /æst/ is scattered through the M[iddle] A[tlantic] S[tates] (except N.Y. and n.N.J.) and the S[outh] A[tlantic] S[tates], reaching something like concentration in s.N.J. and n.e.N.C. Nearly one sixth of the Eastern informants use this form. **1958** Humphrey *Home from the Hill* 40 **TX,** Good snipe day today if you ast me. **1968** *DARE* Tape VA2, They was ['æstɪn] me.

c [ask, ɑsk]. chiefly East *occas considered an affected pronc*
1891 *PMLA* 6.163 **WV,** The sound of *a* in *father* (mid-back-wide) is also very common in words like *ask, demand, pass.* **1892** *DN* 1.226 **NEng,** While usually in New England words like *ask, pass* are pronounced with [ɑ], . . nearly all the children in the Boston schools now say [æsk], [pæs]. **1926** *AmSp* 2.129 **GA** [Alteration of pronunciation among language-conscious students], *Ask,* from [æsk] to [ɑsk]. **1930** *AmSp* 5.325, [a] . . is used by some speakers in America, chiefly in the East, as a substitute for either [æ] or [ɑ] in such words as *ask, last, path.* *Ibid* 340 **eMA,** Speakers educated in Newburyport schools, at Tufts, Harvard, and Boston University . . . There is an extremely front, clear [a] . . in *asked, aunt, can't.* **1931** *AmSp* 6.166 seVA, [ɑ] or [a] occurs also in *answer, last,* . . *ask.* **1943** *LANE* Maps 3.559–561 **NEng,** [Maps show [æsk] to be most common pronc throughout NEng; occas [ask, ɑsk], esp eNEng; less freq [æst]; rarely [æks].]
d Other forms.
1937 *AmSp* 12.288 nwVA, [ɑrsk] for *ask.* **1941** *AmSp* 16.13 **eTX** [Black], [k] is usually omitted from *ask* . . [æˑs]. **1943** *LANE* Map 3.561 nwMA, What do you ask [hwə dɨ jə 'æs]?

2 past, past pple (note: with few exceptions, attested instances of past pple forms are identical to past forms for the same speaker): usu *asked* [æskt]; also:

a [ækst]. Pronc-spp *ax'd, axed, axt* now chiefly Sth, Midl (where [æks] survives in pres)
1818 Fessenden *Ladies Monitor* 171 **VT** [In list of provincialisms to be avoided], *Ax'd* for asked. **1829** Kirkham *Engl. Grammar* 192 **NEng,** I axt him for't, and he sade no. **1837** Sherwood *Gaz. GA* 69 [In list of Provincialisms to be avoided], *Axd,* for asked. **1901** *DN* 2.181 **KY** [Black], *Asked* . . axt. **1953** Atwood *Survey of Verb Forms* 5, Those who use the present *ax* nearly always inflect it regularly (i.e., /ækst/). *Ibid* 6, *Ax* and *axed* are almost exclusively Type I forms. **1966** *DARE* (Qq. OO9a, b; total Infs questioned, 75) Inf **MS44,** Axed.

b Pronc [æst]. Pronc-sp *ast* [*OED* "Already in 15th c . . still current dialectally."] now chiefly Sth, Midl *esp among speakers with less than coll educ* (where [æst] survives in pres)
1890 *DN* 1.6 cNY, [æst] . . asked. **1892** *DN* 1.237 **MI,** Asked . . . [æst] . . is almost universal . . but [æst] = 'ask' is rare . . . *ast* = 'asked' is common in New England. **1903** *DN* 2.290 **Cape Cod MA** (as of 1850s). *Ibid* 2.305 seMO. **1905** *DN* 3.69 nwAR. **1906** *DN* 3.115 sIN. **1908** *DN* 3.287 eAL, wGA. **1952** Brown *NC Folkl.* 1.516, *Ast* [æst] . . . Present, past tense, and past participle . . . General. Older persons; educated and uneducated. **1953** Atwood *Survey of Verb Forms* 5, Those who use the present *ast* . . almost invariably use the same form as a preterite. **1965–66** *DARE* (Qq. OO9a, b; total Infs questioned, 75) Infs **FL4, 10, 11, 22, 28, 30, 36, MS69, NM11, OK6, 20, 52, UT3,** Ast. [Of 14 Infs, 13 have less than coll educ.] **1975** Allen *LAUM* 2.79 ceMN, seIA, sw, scNE, The preterite . . appears as *ast* /æst/ in the speech of . . four in Type I [=oldest informants], one in Type II, and one in type III.

c [æsk]. chiefly Midl *esp among speakers with less than coll educ*
1905 *DN* 3.69 nwAR, *Ask* . . . 'I ask him yesterday about it.' **1930** *AmSp* 5.349 csOH, *Asked* is [æsk]. **1939** *AmSp* 14.126 neTN. **1953** Atwood *Survey of Verb Forms* 5, The leveled combination *ask: ask* occurs in a very scattered way in Pa. and Md., and becomes fairly common in Va., where more than one fourth of the noncultured informants use it. It is also in use, though less commonly, in N.C. and S.C. c1960 *Wilson Coll.* csKY. **1965–66** *DARE* (Qu. OO9a, . . "He won't tell me even though I've _____ him many times."; total Infs questioned, 75) 14 Infs, Ask; (Qu. OO9b . . "Today I'm going to ask him the same question I _____ him yesterday.") 16 Infs, Ask. [15 Infs have less than coll educ.]
d Other forms.
1941 *AmSp* 16.13 eTX [Black], *Asked,* [æɹs]. **1952** Brown *NC Folkl.* 1.516 c,eNC, *Asted* . . . Past tense and past participle of *ask* . . . Rare. Illiterate. **1953** Atwood *Survey of Verb Forms* 5, There are four instances of the leveled combination *ax: ax.*

B Senses.
1 To say, speak, or tell; in phr *ask a blessing* and varr, to pray for.
1884 Harrison *Negro Engl.* 270 **Sth,** To ax one howdy an' spon' howdy = to exchange salutations. **1893** Shands *MS Speech* 18, Ask a blessing . . used by illiterate whites requesting one to ask the blessing, or say grace. **1940** in 1944 *ADD* 37 seWV, I axt him I wouldn't go. **1941** *Hall Coll.* wNC, 'Ask the blessing.'
2 foll by prep, as *into, out of:* To wheedle, cajole.
1938 Rawlings *Yearling* 27 **FL,** She turned on him. "Meat now, and none this winter." "I'll ask the Forresters out of a sow," Penny said. *Ibid* 102, "Do you ever ask your Ma into leavin' you have sich as that [a bear cub]," Penny told him, "you belong to git one young enough to train easy."

askeared, askeerd, askeered See ascared

asleep adj [Transf from naut use: *OED asleep* 5, 1867]
Of inanimate things: motionless, inactive.
1899 (1912) Green *VA Folk-Speech,* Asleep . . Sails are asleep when filled with wind so as not to move . . . A top is asleep when turning rapidly on the peg without wabbling.

asleep at the switch adj
Inattentive; not mindful of one's duties or surroundings.
1914 *DN* 4.219, The net player was asleep at the switch and never saw the return. **1927** *AmSp* 2.255 [Baseball Slang], To be "caught asleep" . . or caught "asleep at the switch" . . have reference to a runner retired from a base by a quick throw. **1939** Gardner *D.A. Draws* 205 *(DAS),* [He] wasn't asleep at the switch. **1950** *WELS* (Very tired) 1 Inf, ceWI, Asleep at the switch. **1965–70** *DARE* (Qu. HH13, . . *Not very*

alert or not aware of things: "He's certainly _____.") 11 Infs, **chiefly Nth, West,** Asleep at the switch; (Qu. JJ30a, . . *Expressions for forgetting something*) Inf **MD**16, Guess I was asleep at the switch. **1966** Barnes–Jensen *Dict. UT Slang* 4, We nearly caught those melon stealers but Jake was asleep at the switch.

aslew adv [**a** prep¹ **1a** + *slew,* turn, twist (*OED slew* sb.²); *EDD* 1873 →] Cf *DS* MM13
  1899 (1912) Green *VA Folk-Speech, Aslew* . . . Askew; diagonally; one-sided.

asmart See **ass-smart**

asp n Also ~ *worm* **TX**
A caterpillar with stinging hairs: see quot 1982.
  1967–70 *DARE* (Qu. R21, . . *Stinging insects*) Infs **TX**12, 73, Asp; **TX**9, Asp [æsp]; **TX**27, Asp—furry, stings many times, raises large lump—very dangerous to children—found on ash trees; **TX**40, Asp—a woolly worm, gets on trees, very poisonous; **TX**33, Aspworm; (Qu. R9a) Inf **TX**17, Asp—poisonous sting; **TX**91, [æsp]; (Qu. R27) Inf **TX**39, Asp—a hairy, poisonous caterpillar [FW: this is a central Texas usage, not common to High Plains; Inf must have got it from his family.]; **TX**62, Asps; **TX**52A, Asp here is a kind of stinging poisonous caterpillar. **1982** *NADS Letters* **TX,** Your *asp,* according to our biology department [Sam Houston State University], is the caterpillar of the *puss moth,* the hairs of which make a really bad sting.

asparagus n Usu |ə'spærəgəs, ə'spɛrəgəs| also, **esp NYC, nNJ,** |ə'spær(ə)græs, –grəs| *occas joc;* also |'spargəs, ə'spægərəs| Pronc-spp infl by folk-etym *asparagrass, asparagrus, aspareguts, aspargus, asper-grass, aspirin grass, spar'gus* [See *OED asparagus* etym note: aphet forms were the earliest in English and are still current] See also **sparrow grass** and *DS* I29
A Forms.
  1931–33 *LANE Worksheets* **Providence RI,** Asparagus [ə'spærə'græs]. **1950** *WELS,* 1 Inf, **csWI,** Asper-grass, . . aspirin grass, . . asparagrus [əspærgrəs]; 1 Inf, **ceWI,** [ə'spærəgræs]—[used by] most everyone around here. **1966** *Wilson Coll.* **csKY,** Asparagus ['spargəs]. We had spar'gus. **1967–69** *DARE* (Qu. I29, *Names or nicknames for asparagus*) Infs **CO**27, **NY**45, 57, 61, 65, Asparagrass [ə'spærəgræs]; **MD**14, **NJ**37, 46, Asparagrus [ə'spærəgrəs]; **GA**75, Aspargus; **IA**32, Aspareguts. **1983** *DARE* File **csWI** (as of c1940), Asparagus was often pronounced [ə'spægərəs].
B Sense.
In logging: see quot.
  1958 McCulloch *Woods Words* **Pacific NW,** *Asparagus*—A bundle of small logs strapped together to make easier handling between woods and pulp mill. Especially useful when logs are towed, keeps them from spreading all over the river.

aspayed See **a** inert vowel **1**

aspen poplar n **chiefly West**
=**quaking aspen.**
  a**1817** (1821) Dwight *Travels* 1.41, Varieties [of] poplar [are]: White, Aspen, Balsam or Black. **1846** (1848) Bryant *What I Saw in CA* 147, Groves of small aspen poplars . . are a great relief to the eye. **1875** *Amer. Naturalist* 9.203 **UT,** The prevalent timber growth was made up of interrupted groves of Aspen poplar. **1946** Stanwell–Fletcher *Driftwood* 33 **West,** On drier, more open ridges, lodge pole pines and aspen poplars are the chief trees.

asper-grass See **asparagus A**

aspersify v [*asperse* (*W3:* arch) + *-ify*]
To sprinkle upon anybody or anything.
  1931 *AmSp* 6.269 **KY,** Redundant or curiously assorted suffixes occur in the . . verbs argufy . . , temptify, . . aspersifyin'.

asphalt n Usu |'æsfɔlt|; also |'ɛæs–, 'æɪs–, 'æz–, 'æš–, 'æž–, –fɛlt, –fɔt, –vɔlt| Pronc-sp *asfelt*
Std senses, var forms.
  1892 *DN* 1.237 **cwMO, MI,** Asphalt . . . ['æsfɛlt]. **1920–40** in 1944 *ADD* **cNY,** Asphalt . . . ['æsfɛlt, –ɔlt]. c**1928** *Ruppenthal Coll.* **KS,** Asfelt . . a common pronunciation, by the near-illiterate. **1967–70** *DARE* (Qu. N21) Inf **NY**57, ['ɛæs,fɔlt]; **TN**58, 61, ['æɪs'fɔlt]—[FW: equal stress]; **AL**39, **GA**91, **MA**36, ['æzfɔlt]; **CT**17, **NJ**3, ['æs,fɛlt]; **TN**47, ['æsfɔt]; **AL**10, 12, ['æsvɔlt]; **AL**26, **MA**42, ['æšfɔlt]; **NY**92, ['æžfɔlt].

asphalt arab n *humorous or derog* Cf *DS* HH2 and **asphalt logger**
A citified person.
  1950 *WELS (A country person's names and nicknames for a city person)* 1 Inf, **cWI,** Asphalt arab.

asphalt logger n Cf **asphalt arab**
Among loggers: see quot.
  1958 McCulloch *Woods Words* 4 **Pacific NW,** *Asphalt logger*—a. One who prefers town to the woods. b. One who makes big talk in town, small work on the job.

aspirin grass See **asparagus A**

aspite prep
Despite; in spite of.
  1943 Writers' Program NC *Bundle of Troubles* 54, "Feller better git on his way," I 'lows along about this time aspite the rain.

aspoil See **a** inert vowel **5**

asp worm See **asp**

assafedity See **asafetida**

ass around v phr Also ~ *about* [Cf *assle* var of **arsle 3**] See also **assen around**
To fool around, loiter, waste time.
  1942 Berrey–Van den Bark *Amer. Slang* 62.8, Gad; wander. Ass about or around. **1954** *Harder Coll.* **cwTN,** Ass around: To wander aimlessly. c**1960** *Wilson Coll.* **csKY,** Assle . . . Fool around, be obviously idle . . . Assing around is apparently the more common local variant. **1969** *DARE* (Qu. KK31, . . "He doesn't have anything to do, so he's just _____.") Inf **CT**29, Assin' around.

assassin bug n
A medium to large-sized, usu black predatory bug of the family Reduviidae. Also called **bedbug hunter, big bedbug, cannibal bug, conenose, devil's riding horse, kissing bug, pirate bug, wheel bug.**
  1895 Comstock *Manual Insects* 137, Family *Reduviidae* . . . There are many bugs which destroy their fellows, but the members of this family are so pre-eminently predaceous that we call them the Assassin-bugs. **1937** *Discovery* Dec 368/2, A . . cheerful brute occurs in North America, where it is known as . . the "assassin bug." **1968** Wigglesworth *Insects* 172, Like all bugs the large assassin bug . . has a powerful salivary pump . . by means of which it can spit out the saliva as a jet that will carry some 30 cm. **1972** *Living Museum* 34.116 **IL,** The assassin bugs (Order Hemiptera, Family Reduviidae) are a large group which generally feed on the blood of mammals, including man.

ass-backward(s) adv See also **ass-end-to, ass-frontwards, assy-fussy, back-asswards, bass-ackward(s), half-assed backwards,** and *DS* MM2, 3
Backwards; in reversed position or confused order.
  1937 *Hench Coll.* **VA,** I have heard for years in the speech of less polished persons the word *assbackwards* as in "He put on his pants assbackwards" or "You're doing that job assbackwards." **1943** McAtee *Dial. Grant Co. IN Suppl. 2, Ass-backwards* . . Extravagance for backwards. **1950** *WELS ("The truck was coming down the road _____.")* **cwWI,** 1 Inf, Ass-backwards. **1965–70** *DARE* (Qq. MM2, 3) 181 Infs, **throughout US,** Ass-backwards; **CO**39, **MA**128, **NV**3, **NY**1, 241, **PA**163, **WI**77, Ass-backward. **1972** *Dict. Contemp. & Colloq. Usage, Ass backwards* . . . Vulgar. Reversed; in a confused order or state, as: to have the questions and answers all *ass backwards.*

ass-breaker n
  1966 *DARE* (Qu. EE29, *When swimmers are diving and one comes down flat onto the water, that's a _____.*) Inf **MA**6, Ass-breaker.

ass-buster n
=**ass-ripper.**
  1954 *Harder Coll.* **cwTN,** Ass-buster: A dive in which the diver holds his nose, jumps, and hits the water arse-first.

ass deep adj phr
In var humorous phrr: exceptionally deep.
  1960 Leckie *March to Glory* 217 [American soldiers as of 1950], The snow is ass-deep to a man in a jeep. **1967** *DARE* FW Addit **WA,** Snow was ass deep to a tall Indian. **1974** Widener *N.U.K.E.E.* 153, Drake was

now floundering around the Alaskan wilderness in snow, ass-deep to a tall moose.

assed up adj　Cf *DS* GG2

Confused; mixed up.

1932 *AmSp* 7.329 **MD** [Johns Hopkins Jargon], Assed up—mixed up. **1942** Berrey–Van den Bark *Amer. Slang* 5.5, *Disorderly; In Confusion* . . . (all) assed up.

assembly n　*somewhat old-fash*

A gathering of persons for purposes of social entertainment, spec a dance party.

1767 *(title)* An Address to Persons of Fashion, concerning frequenting of Plays, Balls, Assemblies, Card-Tables, &c. *(DAE).* **1891** Welch *Recoll. Buffalo* 381 **nwNY**, The leading young men in society during these later years of the decade of the thirties, inaugurated a series of "Assemblies" (dancing parties) of six, sometimes seven each winter, which continued far into the forties. **1899** (1912) Green *VA Folk-Speech, Assembly* . . . A subscription ball. **1926** *AmSp* 1.391 **IA**, The name is laudatory, facetious, or critical rather than definitive. *Ball* for the ceremonious, *hop* for the informal . . an *assembly* for a dancing school, a *shindig* for rowdies. **1966–69** *DARE* (Qu. FF4, . . *Different kinds of dancing parties*) Inf **MA**73, Assemblies; **ME**11, Assemblies—in a hired hall. [Both Infs are old] **1967** LeCompte *Word Atlas* 277 **seLA**, *Large country dance which all the members of the family attend* . . . assembly.

assemblyman n　Also *'semblymen* [Perh from the coloration suggestive of an assemblyman's formal dress]

=**white-winged scoter.**

1888 Trumbull *Names of Birds* 99, At Crisfield, Md., *Assemblyman* (though known as White-wing also), the species being commonly referred to, singly or collectively, as *'Semblymen.* **1917** (1923) *Birds Amer.* 1.150, *White-winged Scoter . . . Other Names* . . . Eastern White-wing; Assemblyman.

assen around v phr [Prob *ass* v + *-en* var of *-ing* + *around:* cf *DJE fishening, icening;* see also *-en* suff[5]]

=**ass around.**

1966 *DARE* (Qu. A9, . . *Wasting time by not working on the job*) Inf **SC**19, Loafing and assening around.

ass end n　*chiefly Nth*

The back end; the buttocks.

1942 McAtee *Dial Grant Co. IN Suppl. 1, Ass end foremost* . . . backwards. **1954** *Harder Coll.* **cwTN**, Ye ass end's a-draggin. **1965–70** *DARE* (Qu. K73, . . *The rump of a cooked chicken*) Infs **MA**6, **MI**8, **OR**13, **WI**40, Ass end (of a chicken); (Qu. A18, . . *A very slow person*) Inf **CT**7, Ass-end looping; (Qu. W24b) Inf **NY**10, Ass-end upward; (Qu. X50) Inf **WI**12, Four feet across the ass end.

ass-end-backwards adv phr [Blend of **ass-end-to** and **ass-backward(s)**]

1967 *DARE* (Qu. MM3, . . *"This is the front, you've got the whole thing turned _____."*) Inf **NY**7, Ass-end-backwards.

ass-end-to adv phr　Also *arse-end-to*　**chiefly Nth**　*rural*　See Map　Cf **back-end-to, hindside-to**

Backwards; in reversed position or confused order.

1943 McAtee *Dial. Grant Co. IN Suppl. 2, Ass end to* . . , with the

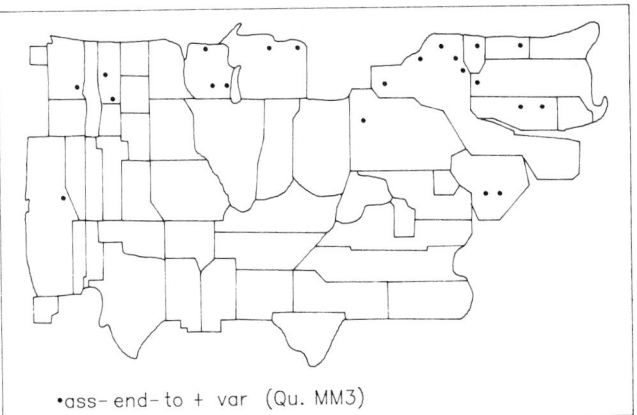
•ass-end-to + var (Qu. MM3)

breech advanced; backwards. **1950** *WELS* ("She had her dress on _____.") 1 Inf, **cwWI**, Ass-end-to. **1965–70** *DARE* (Qu. MM3, . . *"This is the front, you've got the whole thing turned _____."*) 21 Infs, **chiefly Nth**, Ass-end-to; **CT**36, Arse-end-to. [Of all Infs responding to the question, 69% were comm-types 4 and 5; of those giving this response, 90% were comm-types 4 and 5.]

assessment work n　*chiefly West*

Work done on a mining claim to maintain a possessory title.

1877 U.S. Treas. Dept. *Mines* 193 **NV**, Most holders having contented themselves with doing the "assessment-work." **1901** White *Claim Jumpers* 23 *(DAE),* He did not see why they even did the assessment work. **1947** Peattie *Sierra Nevada* 263 **SW**, Preferably it [=his claim] was along the creek, not too far away, and under an oak to shade him while he did the "assessment work" on it that would renew his title for another year. **1968** Adams *Western Words, Assessment work*—In mining, the annual labor required to hold a claim; the work necessary to maintain title to an unpatented mining claim in the public domain.

ass from one's elbow, not to know one's v phr　Also *arse ~,* *asshole ~*　**chiefly N Atl**　*urban*　See Map　For non-regional varr see *DS* JJ15b

To be ignorant; not to possess the most rudimentary knowledge.

1965–70 *DARE* (Qu. JJ15b, . . *Very stupid: "He doesn't know _____."*) 22 Infs, **N Atl**, His ass from his elbow. [Of all Infs responding to the question, 7% were comm-type 1; of those giving this response, 50% were comm-type 1.]; Inf **RI**17, His arse from his elbow; **SC**10, He asshole from he elbow.

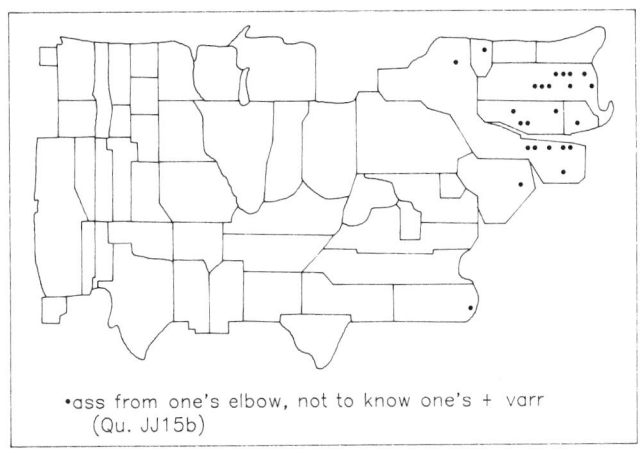
•ass from one's elbow, not to know one's + varr (Qu. JJ15b)

‡**ass-frontwards** adv

=**ass-backward(s).**

1967 *DARE* (Qu. MM3) Inf **MA**71, Ass-frontwards.

asshole n　*West*

In logging: a kink in the logging cable.

1959 *AmSp* 34.77 **nCA**, Asshole . . . A kink in a line. **1968** Adams *Western Words.*

asshole for a hobby-horse n　For varr see quot　Cf *DS* NN12a,b

A non-existent item—in phrr used to distract a bothersome or inquisitive child.

1966–68 *DARE* (Qu. NN12b, *Things that people say to put off a child when he asks, "What are you making?"*) Inf **WI**48, Assholes for hobby-horses; **IN**45, A wooden asshole for a hobby-horse; **ND**1, Whittlin' a wooden asshole for merry-go-round horses.

asshole from one's elbow, not to know one's See **ass from one's elbow, not to know one's**

asshorance Pronc-sp for *assurance*　Cf **insurance A, B**

1908 *DN* 3.287 **eAL, wGA**, *Assurance* . . . [æ'šorəns]. "He's got the asshorance of a brass monkey."

assign v　[*OED assign* v IV →1633]　**Sth**　*obs*

To sign.

1837 Sherwood *Gaz.* **GA** 69 [In list of provincialisms to be avoided], *Assign,* for sign; *assign* is to convey away property; *sign* is merely to write the name. **1872** Schele de Vere *Americanisms* 580, *Assign* . . is in the South used by illiterate persons and by an astounding number of men who ought to know better, instead of *sign.* "I will assign the paper, sir, as soon as you bring it to me . . . " (*Southern Literary messenger,* September, 1849 [sic — quot not found].)

assimilate v Usu |ə'sɪmələ(ɪ)t|, occas |ə'sɪmjulə(ɪ)t| Pronc-sp *assimulate* See Pronc Intro 3.I.23
Std senses, var forms.
1911 *DN* 3.541 **NE,** *Assimulate* . . . Frequent for assimilate. **1914** *DN* 4.166 **NE,** A change of medial unaccented [ə] to [ju] . . . is sometimes heard in *assimulate* for *assimilate.* **1944** in 1944 *ADD* **sWV,** *Assimulate* . . . Usual with 1 educated speaker.

ass-kicker n, also attrib *joc* Cf *DS* W42a, b
A shoe, esp a man's sharply pointed shoe.
1968–70 *DARE* (Qu. W42a, . . *Nicknames . . for men's sharp-pointed shoes*) Infs **PA244, TX54,** Ass-kickers; **PA237,** Ass-kicker shoes [laughter]; (Qu. W42b, . . *Men's square-toed shoes*) Inf **OK57,** Ass-kicker shoes.

‡**ass-kiss** n [*ass-kisser*] See also **ass-licker, ass-sucker, ass-wiper**
One who curries favor; a toady.
1966 *DARE* (Qu. II20a, *A person who tries too hard to gain somebody else's favor: "He's an awful _____."*) Inf **GA6,** Ass-kiss [laughter].

assle See **arsle**

ass-licker n [By analogy with common *ass-kisser*] Cf **ass-wiper**
1 One who curries favor; a toady. **chiefly Sth, Midl**
1939 Miller *Tropic of Capricorn* 18 **NYC,** Besides, I wasn't a good ass-licker. **1954** *Harder Coll.* **cwTN,** Ass-licker. **1965–70** *DARE* (Qu. II20a, *A person who tries too hard to gain somebody else's favor*) 16 Infs, **chiefly Sth, Midl,** Ass-licker; (Qu. II19, . . *"I'd rather quit than _____."*) Inf **PA39,** Be an ass-licker.
2 A homosexual man.
1969 *DARE* (Qu. HH39) Inf **GA84,** Ass-licker.

association n Usu |ə,sosi'eʃən, ə,soʃi'eʃən| Pronc-spp *as-so-sa-shun, sosation* Cf **'sociate**
A Forms.
1874 Taylor *World on Wheels* 141 **NY,** But Elder Peck never *could* say "Association." You can shut your eyes and hear him: "the brethren of the *As-so-sa-shun* will please to give their attention." **1891** *PMLA* 6.167 **WV,** *Gradjate* and *sosation* are vulgarisms. **1942** Hall *Smoky Mt. Speech* 66 **eTN, wNC,** Association [ə,so'seɪʃən] . . transcribed on the speech-record of an aged man.
B Sense.
An annual religious gathering: see quots. [Cf *DAE* association 1a, society of clergymen]
1824 *Baptist Missionary Mag.* 4.242/2 **NEng,** Our present system of annual Associations, is capable . . of being made to answer all the purposes which ought to be attempted by any system of ecclesiastical polity. **1948** *Times–Dispatch* (Richmond VA) 31 Mar 7/4 *(Hench Coll.)* **neMS,** There used to be a Primitive Baptist Church beside the cemetery and each year the congregation held an "association." The meeting would last from Friday through Sunday. On the final day . . "they held a foot-washing."

ass-over-teakettle adv phr For varr see quots See also **ace-over-apex, ass up to teacup, dolly-over-teakettles**
1 Arsy-versy, head-over-heels, topsy turvy.
1899 (1912) Green *VA Folk-Speech* 69, *Ass over head.* Head over heels; topsy-turvy. **1943** McAtee *Dial. Grant Co. IN Suppl. 2, Ass over appetite* (*applecart* or *endways*) . . head over heels. **1958** Humphrey *Home from the Hill* 127 **TX,** Miz Missouri staggers back and the little boy goes ass-over-teakittle. **1967** *DARE* FW Addit **neNY,** *Ass-over-applecart* or *ass-over-tin cup* — when you fall over or get knocked over. **1968–69** *DARE* (Qu. EE9a) Inf **MD29,** Summersault, ass-over-tin cup [laughter]; (Qu. Y1, . . *A person suddenly falling down*) Inf **CA120,** Ass-over-appetite. **1979** Stegner *Recapitulation* 21 **UT,** The sidewalks . . had been encumbered with planters, fountains, flower urns . . . God pity the woman who window-shopped as she walked. Ass over teacup into a fountain or a bed of golardias [sic].
2 In all directions, confusedly.
1969 *DARE* (Qu. MM12a, . . *"He shot into a flock of birds and they went _____."*) Inf **PA209,** Every whichaway, ass-over-tin cups.

ass-poots n pl [*ass* buttocks + **poot**]
Beans.
1968 *DARE* (Qu. I18) Inf **MD37,** Navy beans, white beans, soup beans — same thing; ass-poots ['æs,puts] — the slang term.

ass-ripper n See also **ass-breaker, ass-buster**
A dive in which the diver strikes the water buttocks-first.
1965–68 *DARE* (Qu. EE29) Infs **AL41, MS1,** Ass-ripper.

ass-side-before adv phr Var of **hind-side-before**
1969 *DARE* (Qu. MM2, . . *"Look, you've got your dress on _____."*) Inf **IN61,** Ass-side-before.

ass-smart n Also *arse(s)mart, arsmart, asmart* [*ass* + *smart* smarting pain *OED arsesmart* 1551 →]
A **smartweed:** usu a **water pepper** but also **lady's thumb.**
1640 Parkinson *Theatrum Botanicum* 857 **VA,** Sharpe Arsmart of Virginia . . . Shrub Spotted Arsmart of Virginia with white flowers. **1792** Imlay *Western Terr.* 208 **KY,** Of herbs, . . we have of the wild sort, . . dock, asmart, glass-wort, hellebore. **1805** (1905) Lewis *Orig. Jrls. Lewis & Clark Exped.* 6.122 **Upper MW,** The Ass smart is also found in the Same neighborhood. **1830** Rafinesque *Med. Flora* 66, The *Polygonum persicaria* . . (called Asmart, Smartweed, and Water-pepper). **1876** Hobbs *Bot. Hdbk.* 5, Arsmart, Smartweed, Polygonum hydropiperoides. **1900** Lyons *Plant Names* 300, *P[olygonum] Hydropiper* . . Arse-smart. **1968** *Yankee* April 20, Arsemart has defied me. This most expressive name could not have referred to either nettles or smartweed as neither was used as a medicinal. **1969** *DARE* (Qu. S21) Inf **NJ56,** Ass-smart. Same as smartweed. Pull up that to wipe your backside — you'll jump and holler after a bit. **1971** Krochmal *Appalachia Med. Plants* 204, *Polygonum hydropiper* . . . Common names Marshpepper, smartweed, arsmart . . . Herb . . . A diuretic and has been used in certain uterine disorders.

ass-sucker n
One who curries favor; a toady.
1943 McAtee *Dial. Grant Co. IN Suppl. 2, Ass-sucker* . . bootlicker, toady. **1967** *DARE* (Qu. II20a) Inf **MO2,** Ass-sucker.

assumacy n
Presumption.
1940 *Sun* (Baltimore MD) 4 Apr 10/7 *(Hench Coll.),* Turning away from the Civil War, however, I call it what the Tarheels term "assumacy" for a North Carolinian to raise the question of Maryland's status.

ass-up n Also *ass-up-a-tree* Also sp *arce-up, arse-up*
A nuthatch.
a1870 Chipman *Notes on Bartlett* 12 *(DA), Arse-up.* Small slate-colored woodpecker; so named from its facility and habit of running upward upon a tree's trunk while its head is lower than its tail. Local in Connecticut. **1945** McAtee *Nomina Abitera* 42, I have a term variously spelled arce-up, arse-up, the application of which to these upside-down birds [nuthatches *(Sitta)*] is obvious. **1950** *WELS* (*Insect-eating bird that goes head first down a tree*) 1 Inf, **cWI,** Ass-up. **1967–70** *DARE* (Qu. Q23) Infs **IN18, 80, MI42, NJ39, WV14,** Ass-up; **MI116,** Ass-up-a-tree.

ass up to v phr [Perh from *kiss ass*] Cf *DS* II20a, b, **A.K.** v
To curry favor with.
1970 *DARE* (Qu. II20b, . . *"He's always trying to _____ the boss."*) Inf **IL139,** Ass up to.

‡**ass up to teacup** adv phr Cf **ass-over-teakettle**
Completely, thoroughly, "from head to toe."
1967 *DARE* FW Addit **sIA,** He was soaked ass up to teacup.

ass-wiper n Also *ass-wipe* **NEast** Cf **ass-licker, A-wiper**
One who curries favor; a toady.
1967–69 *DARE* (Qu. II20a, *A person who tries too hard to gain somebody else's favor*) Infs **MA53, NY1, VT16,** Ass-wiper; (Qu. II20b) Inf **NY70,** Boss's ass-wipe; (Qu. II19, . . *"I'd rather quit than _____."*) Inf **MA35,** Be an ass-wiper; (Qu. HH43b) Inf **MA35,** Ass-wiper.

‡**assy-fussy** adv [Alter of *arsy-versy* (*OED, OEDS,* 1539 →)] Cf **ass-backward(s)**
Backside foremost; in reverse position.
1967 *DARE* (Qu. MM3, . . *"This is the front, you've got the whole thing turned _____."*) Inf **OH29,** Assy-fussy.

ast See **ask** v **A1b, 2b**

astamagootis n [Du *als het maar goed is!:* see quots]
A restless person, worrywart.
1980 *DARE* File **Grand Rapids MI,** A restless astamagootis? Of course!.. The term no doubt stems from the Dutch clause "Als het maar goed is," literally translated "If it only good is," or—more freely, "If only everything is all right." **1980** *DARE* File **CT, IA,** A few years ago I was in the midst of an X-raying process when the technician said, "Don't be a restless astamagootis."..."What did you say?"..."Don't be a restless astamagootis," she repeated. "The only person I ever heard use that expression was my mother, from Iowa."—"I have it from *my* mother, in Connecticut." [**1980** *NADS* Letters **IA,** My one remaining aunt.. remembers the word "astamagootis" well, but also has no associations with it.]

asted See **ask** A2d

asteria See **azoturia**

astern adv [Transf from naut use] **NEng**
1 Behind.
1916 Macy–Hussey *Nantucket Scrap Basket* 124, "Astern"—In the rear of, or behind. **1942** ME Univ. *Studies* 56.24, *Astern* meant in the direction of the stern but outside the vessel, even at a considerable distance. [Footnote:] Fig. Behind.
2 in phrr *to go, drop,* or *fall astern:* To lose ground, fail.
[**1911** *Century Dict.* 2126/3, *To fall astern (naut.),* to drop behind.] **1945** Colcord *Sea Language* 25 **NEng,** To drift, drop, fall, go, or run, astern means in coastal dialect to fail of success. "I run astern pretty bad last year when the price of potatoes went down." **1974** *AmSp* 49.62 **ME,** *Go astern* . . . Regress. "People go astern when things is too easy." **1975** Gould *ME Lingo* 112, A business that drops below last year's earnings has gone astern.

astern the lighter adj phr Also *astern of* ~ [See quot 1916] **coastal NEng, esp Nantucket** *derog* See also **behind the lighter**
Tardy, behind, laggardly.
1891 Maitland *Amer. Slang Dict., Astern of the lighter,* behind hand. **1916** Macy–Hussey *Nantucket Scrap Basket* 124, "Astern the Lighter" —Tardy, lagging behind; a lighter being a slow-moving craft used for transferring cargo, to be "astern the lighter" is to be rather a laggard, and the term is used in a contemptuous sense, as "Oh, he's always astern the lighter!" **1942** ME Univ. *Studies* 56.24, A local Nantucket expression, *astern the lighter,* meant literally to be too late for the lighter, or boat that went off to a ship anchored in the harbor. [Footnote:] Fig. Tardy, belated. **1945** Colcord *Sea Language* 118, Nantucket has a rather incomprehensible term meaning belated—astern the lighter. "You're astern the lighter a'ready with all your garden chores."

a-stew See **a** prep¹ 4

as the feller says adv phr For varr see quots **chiefly NEng, S Midl**
As they say—used as a formula to introduce proverbial wisdom or lore, or to apologize for a cliché.
1885 Cable *Dr. Sevier* 400 **TN,** "That's a trick!" said the man. "Thanks, as the felleh says." He looked to Mary for her appreciation of his humor. *Ibid* 411, She wants some more buttermilk . . . If she don't drink it the pigs'll git it, as the ole woman says. **1926** Kephart *Highlanders* 360 **sAppalachians,** These ridges is might' nigh straight up and down, and, as the feller said, perpendic'lar. **1932** Smiley *Gloss. New Paltz* **NY,** Like the fellow says . . . Used in quoting an imaginary person or really an expression of your own which you do not wish to claim credit for as it may be a little beneath you—an apology to cover the identity of the author. **1935** Wolfe *Of Time* 340 **NC,** "A little breath of fresh air is just the thing we need—as the feller says," she said, turning to Eugene now and beginning to laugh slyly. **1949** *Hall Coll.* **eTN. 1951** *PADS* 15.67 **NH. 1975** Gould *ME Lingo* 37, *As the feller says*—An expression of disclaimer. The feller has never been identified, but he gets the blame and credit for a great many remarks: "It may rain but, *as the feller says,* it may not."

asthma n Usu |'æzmə|, also |'æzmɪ| Pronc-sp *asthmy* Cf **-y**
Std senses, var forms.
1938 Liebling *Back Where* 37 **seNY,** Now there's a tug, puffing like she had the asthmy. **1968** *DARE* FW Addit **TN17A,** Asthma ['æzmɪ].

asthma dog n [See quots]
A chihuahua.
[**1953** *Tennessean* (Nashville TN) 18 Jan 6–7 *(Hand Coll.),* In Mex-

ico, the chihuahua is known as the 'asthma dog' or the medicinal dog.] **1966** *Wilson Coll.* **csKY,** Asthma dog—A Mexican hairless or other dog that one sleeps with as a cure for asthma. [**1968** *DARE* FW Addit **TN17, 17A,** Buy a chihuahua and let it sleep with an asthmatic. The dog will breathe the "asthmy" out of the person. Infs know three children who have been cured this way.]

asthma weed n [From its use as an antiasthmatic] **eUS**
=**Indian tobacco 1.**
1819 *Western Rev.* 1.183, The *Lobelia inflata* or Asthma weed, a.. plant with alternate hairy leaves, blue flowers, and swelled seed vessels. **1900** Lyons *Plant Names* 228, Asthma-weed . . . *Leaves* and *tops* . . . Emetic, nauseant, expectorant, anti-spasmodic. **1971** Krochmal *Appalachia Med. Plants* 164, Asthma weed . . . The herb yields lobeline sulfate, which is used in anti-tobacco therapy.

astinemia See **acetonemia**

astink See **a** prep¹ 4

Astorbilt n [Blend of *Astor* + *Vanderbilt,* names of wealthy American families] *joc* See also **Miss Astor, Mr. Astorbilt, Mrs. Astor's pet horse**
1 A member of the "best society" of a community.
1965–70 *DARE* (Qu. II23, *Joking names for people who are, or think they are, the best society of a community)* 14 Infs, **chiefly Sth, SW, Midl,** Astorbilts.
2 By ext: a person who overdresses.
1969 *DARE* (Qu. W37) Inf **RI1,** All Astorbilt.

astoria See **azoturia**

astorperious adj [Blend of *Astor,* wealthy American family + *imperious*] Cf **Astorbilt, Astor's pet horse 2**
Haughty.
1935 Hurston *Mules & Men* 151 **FL** [Black], Aw, gran'pa, don't be so astorperious! **1942** Hurston in *Amer. Mercury* 90 **NYC** [Black], Too blamed astorperious. I just don't pay you no mind. *Ibid* 94 [Glossary of Harlem Slang], Astorperious—haughty, biggity.

Astor's pet horse n Also ~ *pet cow,* ~ *pet pony,* ~ *plush horse*
Varr of **Mrs. Astor's pet horse** **chiefly Nth** Cf **Astorbilt**
1 usu in compar phrr, esp of women: An overly dressed-up or made-up person.
1950 *WELS (When a woman puts on her good clothes and tries to look her best)* 1 Inf, **cWI,** Dressed like Astor's plush horse. **1967–69** *DARE* (Qu. W37, *When a woman puts on her good clothes and tries to look her best)* Infs **DE2, NY22,** (Looks) like Astor's pet horse; **MN6,** Dressed up like Astor's plush horse; **MA14,** Thinks she's Astor's pet horse; (Qu. W36, . . *A woman who uses a lot of cosmetics)* Inf **NY206,** Looks like Astor's pet cow; (Qu. W38, *When a man dresses up in his best clothes)* Inf **MA14,** Astor's pet horse; **NJ2,** Like the Astor's pet pony; (Qu. W40, . . *A woman who overdresses)* Inf **MA14,** Astor's pet horse.
2 A self-important person. Cf **astorperious**
1967–69 *DARE* (Qu. GG19b, *When you can see from the way a person acts that he's feeling important or independent: "He seems to think he's _____.")* Inf **MA14,** Astor's pet horse; **NY12,** Astor's pet pony.

astringent root n
=**cranesbill** (here: *Geranium maculatum).*
[**1828** Rafinesque *Med. Flora* 218, The root is the officinal part, and is a pure, pleasant and valuable astringent.] **1876** Hobbs *Bot. Hdbk.* 6, Astringent root, Cranesbill, Geranium maculatum. **1971** Krochmal *Appalachia Med. Plants* 134.

‡as was adj phr [By analogy with *as is*]
As it was; without alteration or improvement.
1968 *DARE* (Qu. LL25, . . *"He sold out the whole place _____.")* Inf **PA175,** As was.

at prep
1 with nouns of place, direction, or time: In. *?old-fash*
1636 in 1863 MA Hist. Soc. *Coll.* 4th ser 6.515, If Mr. Mayhew hath bought the provisions at the east. **1721** *Journals H. Repr. Mass.* III 94 *(DAE),* The forces at the eastward are without coverings, and scant of cloathing. **1837** (1924) Higbee *Diary* 21 **NJ,** Another traveller enlightened us by saying Mrs. Siddons had died at the eastward. **1840** (1934) Boynton *Jrl.* 347 **VT,** I have always been well treated as yet wherever I have been at the North. **1871** Eggleston *Hoosier Schoolmaster* 28 **IN,**

As they say at the East. **1905** *DN* 3.2 **cCT**, At the south. **1907** *DN* 3.208 **nwAR, cCT**. **1976** Wolfram–Christian *Appalachian Speech* 128, At the wintertime.

2 In phr *sick at one's stomach* and varr: in the area of. **widespread exc in Nth, though gaining currency throughout US** See Map and quots 1949, 1975 See also **on, to**

1731 in 1906 Essex Inst. *Coll.* 42.224 **MA**, I am something better to day than yesterday at my Stomack. **1882** Sweet & Knox *Texas Siftings* 80 *(DAE)*, When he is sick at his stomach . . he goes to Col. Andrews for advice. **1949** Kurath *Word Geog.* 78, *At the stomach* is usual in all of the South and the Midland and is not uncommon in Greater New York City, Connecticut, and Rhode Island. In the greater part of New England and the rest of the Northern area it is exceedingly rare . . . In southern New England and in Greater New York City *at* is now fairly common among younger and cultured persons. **1965–70** *DARE* (Qu. BB16a, *If something a person ate didn't agree with him, he might be sick _____ his stomach*) 408 Infs, **widespread exc in Nth**, At; **DC**1, **DE**6, **GA**59, **LA**18, 25, 31, 40, At the; **NV**8, At the belly; **LA**2, At the craw; **MO**20, At the tummy; (Qu. BB16b) Infs **IN**54, **LA**8, **OK**18, Sick at his stomach; **MO**39, **OH**43, Sick at the stomach; **CA**212, Upset at the stomach; (Qu. BB17, Infs **CA**209, **CO**33, **DE**6, **GA**59, **MI**62, **MO**29, **NJ**9, **VA**42, (Be) sick at his (or the, your) stomach; (Qu. H69) Inf **TX**91, Makes me sick at my stomach; (Qu. II29b) Infs **IN**45, **VA**58, Makes me sick at my (or the) stomach; **1975** Allen *LAUM* 2.64, Data in the U[pper] M[idwest] rather clearly point to the continuing western extension of *to*, . . rather than of *at*, which is a feeble minor variant in Minnesota and the Dakotas and even in Midland Iowa and Nebraska barely scrapes up a 50% frequency—and that only because of its higher proportion among the less-educated infs.

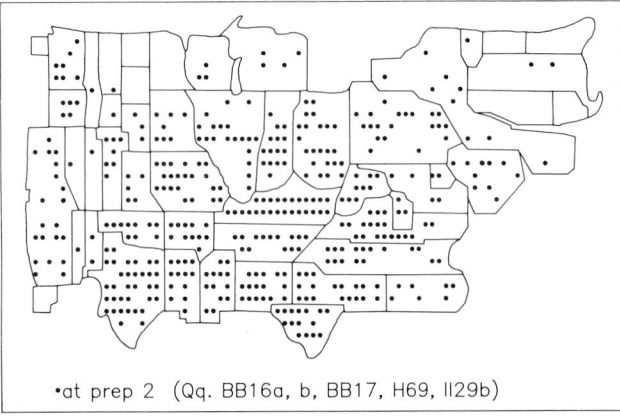

•at prep 2 (Qq. BB16a, b, BB17, H69, II29b)

3 esp after *listen*: To. [Engl dial: *EDD at* IV 3] **chiefly Sth, Midl**

1884 Harrison *Negro Engl.* 275, To lissen at de racket = to hear the noise. **1903** *DN* 2.305 **seMO**, Listen at the bird. **1914** *DN* 4.158 **VA**, Listen at the pop crackers. **1927** Kennedy *Gritny* 17 **sLA** [Black], My head feel feev'ish lis'nin' at her. **c1960** *Wilson Coll.* **csKY**, "Just listen at that mule a-braying." Fairly common. **1966–68** *DARE* Tape **NC**37, I will usually listen at what you say; **IN**14, I listen at the news. **1968** *DARE* (Qu. HH7a) **GA**19, Listen at that bird run off at the mouth. **1976** Wolfram–Christian *Appalachian Speech* 128, I just go at my uncles and fool around. **1976** *DARE* File **ceIN**, Heard from a fortyish white male: "I'll talk at you later." From a twentyish white male: "I'll be talking at you tomorrow."

4 Used redundantly, usu at the end of a *where* clause. [*EDD at* II 1, from nwEngl] **chiefly Sth, Midl** *informal, occas joc or for emphasis*

1859 (1968) Bartlett *Americanisms*, At is often used superfluously in the South and West, as in the question, "Where is he *at*?" **1896** *DN* 1.411 **NYC**, Where at you goin'? **1902** *DN* 2.228 **sIL**, Where is he at? **1903** *DN* 2.305 **seMO**. **1906** *DN* 3.115 **sIN**. **1908** *DN* 3.287 **eAL**. **1910** *DN* 3.456 **KY**. **1935** Horwill *Mod. Amer. Usage*, The Am. jocose use of a superfluous *at* is illustrated in . . 'The business world wants rest. It wants to know where it is at.' **1957** Wyman–Kroeber *Frontier* 186, Mencken was nothing if not bold; he had an ax to grind; he enjoyed telling the English where to get off *at*. **1965–70** *DARE* (Qu. EE3) Inf **KY**62, Guess where it's at; (Qu. HH13) Inf **MA**59, Don't know where he's at; (Qu. JJ15b) Inf **MN**10, Which end his ass is at; (Qu. JJ17) Inf

NY241, Know where he's at; (Qu. KK66) Inf **NY**241, This is where it's at; (Qu. MM22) Inf **CA**177, Where you're at; (Qu. NN10a) Inf **LA**37, Where ya at dere? **LA**45, Where you at?

5 Following a verb of action and usu said with extra emphasis to indicate that the action is somewhat ineffective. [*OED at* prep 17]

1949 *PADS* 11.17 **CO**, "To ride at a horse." To try to ride a horse but get thrown. **1951** *PADS* 15.52 **cnIN**, *At: adv*. Ineffectively. "He washed *at* the windows." **1954** *Harder Coll.* **cwTN**. **c1960** *Wilson Coll.* **csKY**, He's working at his books but don't seem to learn much. **1965–70** *DARE* (Qu. H12, *If somebody eating a meal takes little bits of food and leaves most of it on his plate, you say he _____*) Inf **CA**174, Minces at his food; **MI**68, Kinda munches at it; **OK**44, Minces at it; (Qu. K8, *Joking terms for milking a cow*) Inf **IL**16, Tug at the cows.

6 With; against.

1933 Miller *Lamb in His Bosom* 96 **GA**, She had blamed pore little Cean who had enough to worry over without being quarreled at. **1940** Stuart *Trees of Heaven* 25 **KY**, Stop quarrelin at 'im, Ma.

7 In the direction of; to, toward. [*OED at* 13]

1940 *Sat. Eve. Post* 23 Nov 101/2 **sGA**, My dog ain't back. I'm going at him.

8 Near, close to. See also **right at**

1907 *DN* 3.228 **nwAR, seMO**, At . . . Near. **1969** *DARE* (Qq. X48a, b, *Expressions meaning that a person is not so young anymore . . . "She must be _____ sixty." Or, . . "He's _____."*) Inf **KY**42, Pushing at; Pushing at seventy.

9 From, of, through. [*OED at* prep 10]

1966–67 *DARE* (Qu. MM8, *A bad housekeeper sweeps the dirt either under the rug or _____ the door.*) Inf **AR**31, Out at; (Qu. MM18, *"Going from the kitchen to the back steps he walked _____ the door."*) Inf **AR**51, Out at.

at v [Reduced from *to go at* or similar phr] *obs*

To urge repeatedly.

1837 Smith *Col. Crockett's Exploits* 33 **TN**, I soon saw . . that I must get up and make them a speech. I had no sooner elongated my outward Adam, than they at it again, with renewed vigour. **1873** (1891) Holley *My Opinions* 206 **NY**, I atted Josiah to sell the pork and get the money for that.

'at pron, conj See **that**

atajo n Also sp *hatajo* [Span *hatajo* small herd or flock] **SW** A string of pack animals.

1844 (1954) Gregg *Commerce* 128 **NM**, Indeed it is apt to occasion much trouble to stop a heavily laden *atajo*; for, if allowed a moment's rest, the mules are inclined to lie down, when it is with much difficulty they can rise again with their loads. **1892** *DN* 1.187 **TX**, *Atájo*: a drove of mules. *Ibid* 244, *Atájo* . . Also a "bunch" of horses, tame or wild, though more generally the latter. **1897** Inman *Santa Fé Trail* 57, An old-time *atajo* or caravan of pack-mules generally numbered from fifty to two hundred. **1932** Bentley *Spanish Terms*, The typical *atajo* consists of from fifteen to forty animals . . . It is particularly useful in mountainous districts and in fact was long the only practical mode of transporting merchandise to and from mining, cattle, and other camps. The word is used commonly in the Southwest. **1968** Adams *Western Words, Hatajo* . . . A train of pack animals.

atalked See **a** inert vowel **1**

a-tall adv Usu |ə'tɑl, ə'tɔl| infreq |'e'tɔl| Pronc-spp *a tall, atall, 'tall* [By metanalysis from *at all*]

At all.

1908 *DN* 3.287 **eAL, wGA**, A-tall . . . At all. Sometimes *'tall* is heard. **1927** Shewmake *Engl. Pronc. VA* 44 **eVA**, In . . *at all* the stressed word *all* often attracts *t* to itself, the result being *a tall*. **1930s** in 1944 *ADD* **nWV**, No time atall. **1936** *AmSp* 11.145 **eTX**, The unstressed vowel spelled with *a* is usually pronounced [ə] . . . at all (a-tall). **1941** *AmSp* 16.8 **eTX** [Black], *At all*, [ə'tɔːl]. **1942** McAtee *Dial. Grant Co. IN* (as of 1890s), *A-tall* (first "a" long), . . used intentionally for emphasis, as well as in normal colloquialism; "That don't worry me _____." **1942** Warnick *Garrett Co. MD* (as of 1900–18), *A-tall*. **1954** *Harder Coll.* **cwTN**, Them chillern ain't a'tall good. **c1960** *Wilson Coll.* **csKY**, A-tall—often heard for at all. **1965** *DARE* FW Addit **wOK**, At all [ə'tɔl]. **1976** Brown *Gloss. Faulkner, A-tall* . . . The *a* is pronounced like the name of the first letter of the alphabet, and both syllables are stressed.

at all adv [*OED, OEDS all* 9b; *EDD at* IV (1)] **chiefly Sth, Midl**
In affirmative constrr: of all; only.
   1916 *DN* 4.302 **VA, LA,** He is the greatest man at all. **1936** *AmSp*
11.63 **WV,** Common use of *at all* without a negative (We had the best
time at all). **1942** *AmSp* 17.130 **IN,** She's the finest girl at all. **1945**
AmSp 20.15, This affirmative use [of *at all*] . . lives on in Irish dialect
and in colloquial speech in certain parts of America, especially after a
superlative, as in . . 'We had the best time at all.' . . Of my informants,
[seven, from GA, KY, NC, OK] said that this idiom occurs in their home
speech areas . . and [seven] had heard it outside their home speech areas
[3 in the South, 1 in the Midwest, and 3 uncertain of area]. **1976** *DARE*
File **Madison WI** (as of 1957), Use one statement at all.

atamasco (lily) n [Amer Ind *attamusco* prob related to Algonquian *misk* red: see 1907 Hodge *Hdbk. Amer. Indians* 1.106]
   1 =**zephyr lily,** but esp *Zephyranthes atamasco* which has white
flowers often tinged with red on the outside. Besides those
names given under **zephyr lily,** this species is also called **cullowhee** and **daffodil lily Sth**
   1629 Parkinson *Paradisi* 87, *Narcissus Virgineus.* The Virginia Daffodill . . . The Indians in Virginia do call it Attamusco. Attamusco, some
among us do call it *Lilionarcissus Virginianus,* of the likenesse of the
flower to a Lilly and the leaves and roote to a Daffodill. Wee for brevity
doe call it *Narcissus Virginius,* that is, The Daffodill of Virginia, or else
you may call it according to the former Latine name, The Lilly Daffodill
of Virginia. **1748** (1754) Catesby *Nat. Hist. Carolina* App 1.12, The
Attamusco Lily . . . is a native of *Virginia* and *Carolina,* where in
particular places the pastures are . . thick sprinkled with them and
Martagons. **1848** Gray *Manual of Botany* 479, *Atamasco Lily* . . . Perianth funnel-shaped, white and pink. **1901** Mohr *Plant Life AL* 123, On
the shady borders of the hammock are found, flowering early in the
spring, . . the Atamasco lily . . and hoary lupine. **1933** Small *Manual
SE Flora* 320, *Atamasco-lilies* . . . are gathered about Easter time and
sold especially in southern cities. **1961** Wills–Irwin *Flowers TX* 98,
Bulbs of nearly all the Rain-lilies and Atamascos are marketed by
seedsmen. **1975** Duncan–Foote *Wildflowers SE* 262, *Atamasco-
lily* . . . Leaves and especially the bulbs of this species are known to be
poisonous when eaten.
   2 =**copper lily. TX**
   1946 Reeves–Bain *Flora TX* 56, *H[abranthus] texanus* . . . Yellow
Rain Lily, Atamosco [sic] Lily . . . Perianth copper-brown, with stripes
of purple.

atarnal, atarnity See **eternal, eternity**

ataunto adv, adj Also sp *all tanto, atanto* [Ult Fr *autant* as
much (as possible)] **chiefly N Atl** *old-fash*
Naut, usu in phr *all ~:* fully rigged, with all sails set. By ext: well
equipped, in readiness.
   1838 Cooper *Homeward Bound* 2.170, The fore and fore-top-sail-yards
were in their places, the top-gallant-mast was fitted and, with the
exception of the sails, the ship was what is called a-tanto, forward. **1840**
Crockett Almanac 10/2 (*DAE*), I was rigged all-a-tanto. **1845** *Knickerbocker* 25.424 **nwFL,** The Boston . . lay in the stream, with everything
'ataunto,' ready for sea. **1849** (1855) Melville *Redburn* 210, Some
[=ships] had just arrived from the most distant ports, worn, battered,
and disabled; others were all a-taunt-o—spruce, gay, and brilliant, in
readiness for sea. **1905** Wasson in 1962 *AmSp* 37.254 **ME,** He let her go
right under foot, took and snugged up things on deck all tanto, and went
below and turned in. **1945** Colcord *Sea Language* **ME, Cape Cod MA,
Long Island NY,** A-taunto (Pronounced a-tanto). From the French
autant, to the full. This originally meant, with masts and spars aloft and
fully rigged; by extension, in first-class order, but it is rarely heard
nowadays.

ate, aten See **eat** v A3c, d

a'ter See **after** A2

a-thaut See **athwart**

athere See **a** inert vowel **4**

athirst See **a** prep¹ **4**

athlete n, also attrib Usu |'æθ,lit|, freq |'æθə,lit|, occas |'æt,lit|;
'ɛθə'lɹik| Pronc-sp *athelete* See also **athletic** See Pronc Intro
3.I.14, 3.I.17, 3.I.23
Std senses, var forms.
   1965–70 *DARE* (Qu. BB25) Infs **FL**15, **IL**97, 98, 135, **MO**18, Athe-

lete's foot; **MO**4, 5A, 10, ['æθə,lit(s)] foot (or feet); **MO**16 ['æt,lit] feet.
c**1970** Pederson *Dial. Survey Rural GA* **seGA,** 1 Inf, ['æθə,læz 'fiit]; 2
Infs, ['æθə,li(i)ts 'fiit]; 1 Inf, [ɛθə'lɹik fʊt].

athlete('s) feet n sg See also **athletic foot**
Athlete's foot.
   1968 *DARE* (Qu. BB25) Infs **MO**4, 16, **NY**109, **PA**94, Athlete('s) feet.
c**1970** Pederson *Dial. Survey Rural GA* **seGA,** 5 Infs, Athlete('s) feet; 1
Inf, [æθələæ·z fiit].

athletic adj Usu |,æθ'lɛtɪk| freq |,æθə'lɛtɪk| rarely |,æð–, ,æfə–,
ɛθ–| Pronc-spp *athaletic, atheletic, athuletic* Cf **elm A** Addit
quots in *ADD* See Pronc Intro 3.I.17, 3.I.23
Std sense, var forms.
   1916 *DN* 4.271 **NE, MA, WV, IA, PA,** Atheletic . . widespread for
athletic. **1927** *AmSp* 2.347 **wcWV,** Atheletic . . commonly used for
athletic. **1927** in 1944 *ADD* **NYC,** Athaletic Goods. (sign). **1933** *AmSp*
8.2.44 **neNY,** In the word . . *athletic,* [ə] is sometimes present, giving . . ['æθələtɪk]. **1947** *AmSp* 22.76, 'Athuletic' is certainly modern
and all-American. **1968–70** *DARE* (Qu. BB25) Inf **MO**9, ['æθə,lɛtɪk];
(Qu. BB49) **PA**247, [,æð'lɛtiks]; (Qu. DD22) **VA**73, ['æfə'lɛdɪk]. c**1970**
Pederson *Dial. Survey Rural GA* **seGA,** 1 Inf [æ·θəlɛtɪks]; 1 Inf [æθəlɛtɪk
fiit]; 1 Inf [æθələdɪk fʊət]; 1 Inf [ɛθlɛtɪk fʊt].

athletic fits n pl
Delirium tremens.
   1970 *DARE* (Qu. DD22) Inf **VA**73, D.T.'s, athletic fits.

athletic foot n Also *athletic(s) feet* See also **athlete('s) feet**
Athlete's foot.
   1967–70 *DARE* (Qu. BB25) Inf **MO**5, Athletic foot; **MO**9, Athletic
feet; **PA**247, Athletics feet.

athwart prep Pronc-spp *a-thaut* [Transf from naut use] **N Atl**
   1 Across.
   1942 *ME Univ. Studies* 56.50, Beam ends . . run *athwart* the ship, at
right angles to her keel. [Footnote] Fig . . . "There was a big truck right
a-thaut the garage door." **1945** Colcord *Sea Language* 26 **ME, Cape
Cod MA, Long Island NY,** Athwart (Pronounced athought). Across;
used in the same sense alongshore. **1955** Adams *Grandfather* 242 **NY,** A
local obstructionist, whose sheep-run lay athwart the Adams contract for
a hundred yards or more.
   2 in phr *athwart one's hawse:* Across one's path, in one's way.
   1827 Cooper *Red Rover* 1.132 **RI,** I am often luffing athwart your
hawse, or getting foul in some fashion or other, on one of your quarters.
1945 Colcord *Sea Language* 96 **ME, Cape Cod MA, Long Island NY,**
Athwart the hawse means across, or even resting against, the
bows . . . Alongshore, "Don't you come athwart my hawse!" means
don't interfere.

athwartships (of) adv Also aphet *'thwartships* [Transf from
naut use] **N Atl** See also **athwart**
Crosswise.
   1916 Macy–Hussey *Nantucket Scrap Basket* 124, Athwartships (or
'thwartships) . . . Crosswise, as "'thwartships of the bench." Speaking of
an operation, a Nantucketer said: "they cut him 'thwartships." **1945**
Colcord *Sea Language* 26 **ME, Cape Cod MA, Long Island NY,**
Athwartships means at right angles to the keel; alongshore, it means
crosswise. "This piece wants to go right 'thwartships of the crate, so-fash-
ion!"

atilt See **a** prep¹ **4**

atired See **a** inert vowel **1**

at-it n Cf **at-me**
=**ante** n.
   1963 *KY Folkl. Rec.* 61 **seKY,** The marbles of an individual being
played for in a game . . at-it.

Atlantic yam n [Perh so called in contrast to **Chinese yam**]
=**wild yam** (here: *Dioscorea villosa*).
   1948 Stevens *KS Wild Flowers* 54, *Dioscorea villosa—Atlantic
Yam* . . . The fleshy rootstocks . ., called 'yams', are cooked as potatoes. **1968** Barkley *Plants KS* 101, *Dioscorea villosa* . . . Wild Yam.
Atlantic Yam. Thickets.

at liquor pred adj Pronc-sp ~ *licker* [*OED at* 15, as *at meat,
eating*]
Drinking.

1936 Morehouse *Rain on Just* 79 **NC,** Not one of us ought to be at licker . . . Rease just now buried. Dead along of that same poison.

at-me n Cf **at-it**
A marbles game: see quot.
1963 *KY Folkl. Rec.* 60 **seKY,** *Game played by shooting at opponent's marble, his shooter, no boundaries . .* at-me.

atni-over See **Antony-over**

atole n Also sp *atol, atolle, atolli* [MexSpan] **chiefly SW**
A gruel or mush made usu of Indian corn.
1672 Hughes *American Physitian* 156 (*AmSp* 34.27), *Atolle.* Flour of Indian Wheat, and water mixed together, to put into *Chocolate.* **1824** Poinsett *Notes on Mexico* 145, They are very fond of a gruel *(atolli)* made of the flour [of Indian corn] and sweetened with honey. **1844** (1954) Gregg *Commerce* 109 **NM,** A sort of thin mush, called *atole,* made of Indian meal, is another article of diet . . that in the North . . is called . . the coffee of the Mexicans. **1859** (1968) Bartlett *Americanisms.* **1892** *DN* 1.187 **TX.** **1946** Peattie *Pacific Coast* 41 **CA** (as of 1814), All partook of a morning meal of atole (a whole-wheat gruel). **1968** Adams *Western Words, Atol*—A kind of corn meal, or gruel or porridge made of corn meal.

atoll v See **a inert vowel 5**

at on adv phr
1893 Shands *MS Speech,* At [æt]. Used by negroes as equivalent to *right* . . . "Come at on"; i.e. Come right on, come at once.

at oneself adj phr [EDD *at* VI (11) 1768 →] **chiefly Sth, Midl** *somewhat old-fash*
At one's best; in full possession of one's physical or mental powers.
1872 (1973) Thompson *Major Jones's Courtship* 189 **GA,** I do b'lieve if they hadn't brung little Henry Clay to her, . . she never would got her senses again. She aint more'n half at herself yit. **1895** Twain in *Harper's Mag.* 91.93/2, [Joan] was always at herself. **1896** *Ibid* 93.345/1 **MO,** Tom Sawyer was . . the levelest head I ever see, and always *at* himself and ready for anything you might spring on him. **1902** *DN* 2.228 **sIL,** 'To be at one's self.' To be in a condition equal to the performance of a task. **1903** *DN* 2.305 **seMO.** **1904** *DN* 2.416 **nwAR,** 'When he's at himself, he's a clever man.' This sentence was used of a man periodically insane. **1907** *DN* 3.228 **nwAR, seMO.** **1908** *DN* 3.287 **eAL, wGA,** I can easily pick 300 pounds of cotton when I am at myself. **1915** *DN* 4.180 **swVA.** **1942** (1971) Campbell *Cloud-Walking* 248 **seKY,** Times when she was too plumb bad off to be right at herself. **1944** *PADS* 2.53 **MO,** He was at himself when he made that trade. **c1960** *Wilson Coll.* **csKY,** He certainly was at himself when he married that girl of his. **1966** *DARE* (Qu. HH6, *Someone who is out of his mind*) Inf **GA**7, Not at hisself.

atowards See **a inert vowel 3**

atsui adj [Japanese] **HI**
Hot.
1972 Carr *Da Kine Talk* 92 **HI,** Many of the simple and basic expressions are still in use, particularly . . *atsui* 'hot.'

‡**atsy** adj [Perh from **antsy 3**]
Confused.
1970 *DARE* (Qu. GG2, . . *"So many things were going on at the same time that he got completely _____."*) Inf **CA**174, Atsy.

attackt n [*attack* + excr -*t*] **widespread**
An attack.
1706 in 1875 VA *Calendar State Papers* 1.107, It is most probable that ye first Attackt will be made upon ye shipps in York River. **1891** *DN* 1.165 **cNY.** **1935** in 1944 *ADD* **neNY,** A sudden [ǝtækt]. **1936** *AmSp* 11.239 **eTX.** **1943** *LANE* Map 509, 2 Infs, **swME,** An attackt of 'pendicitis. **1968** *DARE* FW Addit **PA**90, I had a heart attackt in February. **1978** *DARE* File **nwKS,** He had a heart [ǝtækt] and was gone just like that.

attackt v Also sp *attact;* past and past pple *attackted* [*attack* + excr -*t; cf* -**ed** pret suff **1**] **widespread**
To attack.
1689 in 1889 ME *Hist. Soc. Doc. Hist.* 4.463, The enemy Attacted mr ffoxwells Garison att Blwu pwinte. **1756** in 1898 Hamilton *Letters to Washington* 1.220, There was . . four hundred to attact me, and also four hundred to attact the upper fort Cocks. **1781** *PA Jrl. & Weekly*

Advt. (Philadelphia PA) 16 May 2, This is the weapon with which he defends himself when he is *attacted.* **1891** *DN* 1.165 **cNY,** [ǝ'tækt] and [ǝ'tæktɪd]. **1905** *DN* 3.59 **NE.** **1907** *DN* 3.180 **seNH.** **1908** *DN* 3.288 **eAL, wGA,** *Attackted, pret.* and *pp.* of attack. **1910** *DN* 3.436 **wNY.** **1922** Gonzales *Black Border* 288 **sSC, GA coast** [Gullah], Attactid. **1930** *AmSp* 5.265 **Ozarks,** The hillman almost invariably says *attackted* instead of *attacked.* **1936** *AmSp* 11.239 **eTX.** *Ibid* 312 **seNY.** **1966–69** *DARE* Tape **GA**30, That alligator [ǝ'tækdǝd] him; **IL**7, I didn't feel that I was going to be [ǝ'tæktɪd] by anyone when I had this dog with me; **KY**28, That'n what [ǝ'tæktɪd] that man named Andy; **MI**2, Anybody who could prove that he was [ǝ'tæktɪd] by a wolf . . . They would never [ǝ'tækt] a person. **1968** *DARE* FW Addit **PA**142, The bear attacted him.

attend v [OED *attend* 4, *"Obs.",* but this is perh **a** prep¹ **5** + *tend*]
To tend, look after, manage.
1963 Edwards *Gravel* 131 **eTN** (as of 1920s), So happened I wuz attendin about ten acres of that bottom land on the thirds. Usilly got half for upland.

atter See **after A2**

attic n
The upper balcony in a theater.
1966–70 *DARE* (Qu. D40) Infs **MS**45, **VA**13, 75, Attic.

attic fly n [See quot 1975]
=**cluster fly 1.**
1965–70 *DARE* (Qu. R12) Infs **OH**61, **PA**76, Attic flies. **1975** *DARE* File **Madison WI,** Attic flies—some call them cluster flies—are a little bigger than house flies . . . In the fall, the flies go to dark places like attics, and when it gets too warm they come out of the attic (sometimes down the chimney) and fly to the light. At windows they sometimes cluster in balls the size of a football.

attitude n
1 Of the wind: direction, disposition.
1950 *PADS* 14.12 **SC** [Black], Boss, I bu'n off one side de road lak you beena tell me, an' I gwi bu'n off turrer side fus time I ketch de win' in de right attitude.
2 Of persons: a haughty manner.
1970 *DARE* (Qu. Y4, . . *A very uncomplimentary remark*) Inf **NY**249, Don't be getting no attitude—a negative remark. [Black Inf]

attle n [Cornish] **West** Cf **tailings**
In mining: waste rock.
1945 *CA Folkl. Qrly.* 4.320 **CO,** Attle: Waste rock. **1946** *Ibid* 5.167 **MT.** **1968** Adams *Western Words.*

attuh See **after A2**

atween prep [OED →1842, *"arch. and dial."*] *old-fash*
Between.
1834 *Life Andrew Jackson* 103 **TN,** He therefore retired tu a narrow pass atween the swamp and the Missipi. **1841** (1952) Cooper *Deerslayer* 217 **nNY,** The difference atween an Indian gentleman and a white gentleman. *Ibid* 244, The rifle will settle the p'int atween us. **1843** (1916) Hall *New Purchase* 116 **IN,** Made up the little matter of diff'runce atween us. **1926** Kephart *Highlanders* 299 **sAppalachians,** Right sensibly atween the shoulders I've got a pain. **1940** in 1969 Stuart *Come Gentle Spring* 131 **neKY,** A fair fight atween you two.

atwixt prep [OED →1870, *"arch. or dial."*] **now chiefly S Midl** *old-fash*
Between.
1823 Cooper *Pioneers* 2.223 **nNY,** There's been more peace than love atwixt us. **1884** Murfree *TN Mts.* 222, Her brother . . tried ter keep the peace atwixt 'em. **1926** Kephart *Highlanders* 362 **sAppalachians,** Afore, atwixt, . . [are] everyday expressions of the backwoods. **1934** (1970) Wilson *Backwoods Amer.* 64 **Ozarks.** **1944** *PADS* 2.17 **sAppalachians.** **c1960** *Wilson Coll.* **csKY,** I'll be there atwixt two and four.

au n |ɑˀu| [Haw] **HI**
A billfish, esp a sailfish, swordfish, or marlin.
1960 Gosline–Brock *Hawaiian Fishes* 261, *Family Istiophoridae (Sailfishes and Marlins or A'us)* . . a family of large pelagic fishes of the tropical and subtropical oceans. **1967** *Honolulu Star-Bulletin* (HI) 31 May F1/4, A'u—swordfish or marlin. **1967** *DARE* (Qu. P2) Inf **HI**14, Au [ɑˀu]—swordfish or marlin.

auau v [Haw *'au'au* to bathe] **HI**
To swim.
   1938 Reinecke *Hawaiian Loanwords* 8, Auau . . . To swim; to bathe in the sea or a stream.

auau n [auau v] **HI**
   1938 Reinecke *Hawaiian Loanwords* 8, Auau . . . Swimming; bathing.

auctioneer n Usu |ˌɔkšən'ir| occas |ˌɔksən'ir|
Std senses, var form.
   1967 Key *Tobacco Vocab.* **MD, NC,** Auctioneer [ɔksənir].

audacious(ly) adj, adv Usu |ɔ'dešəs(lı)|; in **Sth, Midl** freq |aʊ'dešəs(lı)|, occas folk-etym |aʊt'dešəs| Pronc-spp *oudacious, outdacious, owdacious(lee)*
   A Forms.
   1847 (1962) Robb *Squatter Life* 106 **MO,** Old Alic had a darter Molly, that war the most enticin', heart-distressin' feline creatur that ever made a fellar get owdacious. **1859** (1968) Bartlett *Americanisms, Owdacious,* for audacious. Southern and Western. **1884** Lanier *Poems* 179 **Sth** [Black], She do grow owdaciouslee. **1890** *DN* 1.68 **KY,** Outdacious [aʊtdešəs]. **1891** Page *Elsket* 134 **VA** [Black], It wuz p'intedly ouda-cious for her . . to come to my own house an' rob me. **1899** (1912) Green *VA Folk-Speech, Outdacious.* **1903** *DN* 2.305 **seMO,** *Auda-cious* . . . oudacious. **1907** *DN* 3.228 **nwAR.** **1909** *DN* 3.355 **eAL, wGA,** Outdacious. **1950** *PADS* 14.50 **SC,** *Owdacious* [aʊ'dešəs], *outda-cious* . . . Bold, audacious; unrestrained; outrageous.
   B As adv.
   Extremely, very. [*EDD* 1875 →] Cf **bodaciously**
   1941 *Sat. Eve. Post* 22 Mar 24/1 **NC,** Twenty dollars was outdacious high for three hours' work.

auf See **off** adv

auger See **augur** n, v¹

auger (around) v Also sp *augur* [*auger* to turn or twist, as with an *auger*] **Ozarks**
   1 To look surreptitiously.
   1923 *DN* 5.200 **swMO,** *Augur* . . . To plan, to scheme. To 'augur 'roun'', to investigate surreptitiously.
   2 To go about aimlessly.
   1966 *DARE* (Qu. Y27, *To go about aimlessly . . "He's always _____ around the drugstore."*) Inf **AR**40, Augerin' ['ɔgɚın]; (Qu. KK31, . . *"He doesn't have anything to do, so he's just _____ around."*) Inf **AR**41, Augerin' ['ɔgɚn].

auger-eyed adj **S Midl**
Having sharp or piercing eyes.
   1927 *DN* 5.472 **Ozarks,** *Auger-eyed* . . . Sharp eyed, gimlet eyed. **1931** *PMLA* 46.1309 **sAppalachians,** Other expressions: "heller," "hel-lion," . . "auger-eyed." **1952** Brown *NC Folkl.* 1.517 **swNC,** *Auger-eyed* . . . Having sharp eyes. **1972** Cooper *NC Mt. Folkl.* 89.

augerino n **West** joc
An imaginary creature responsible for boring holes in irrigation ditches.
   1941 *Jrl. Amer. Folkl.* 54.29 **CO,** Where irrigation is practiced, ranchers are humorously angry about the activities of the "Augerino," a malevo-lent subterranean creature whose sole mission in life is to let the water out of irrigation ditches.

augur n Also *auger* [Prob **augur** v¹, perh also infl by *auger* tool for boring holes: see quot 1936] **chiefly West**
   1 An excessive talker; a bore.
   1890 Farmer–Henley *Slang, Augur* . . . (American thieves').—A per-son given to prosiness . . ; a bore. **1936** Adams *Cowboy Lingo* 220 **West,** An 'auger' was a man with unusual 'talkin' talents,' a great and inveterate talker; one who could 'bore you'; 'get his auger into you,' as the cowboy expressed it. **1961** Adams *Old-Time Cowhand* 17 **West,** Augur is a word commonly used in the cattle country to mean . . "a big talker." **1977** Watts *Dict. Old West.*
   2 See **big auger.**

augur v¹ Also sp *auger* [Metath form of **argue**] **West** See also **augur** n, **auguring**
   1 To talk, converse, chat (with).
   1908 in 1975 White *Git Along* 148 **West,** A stranger dropped in and stopped to augur some. **1921** Thorp *Songs Cowboys* 13 **AZ,** Brown

augered me most all the way / Told me cow-punching was just child's play / It was no work at all. **1944** Adams *Western Words, Augur* . . to talk. **1945** Thorp *Pardner* 26 **SW,** We "augered" a bit. I asked where he was bound for.
   2 To argue.
   1961 Adams *Old-Time Cowhand* 26 **West,** They looked to Brimstone to help 'em out, but he declared 'imself hogtied when it come to augurin' with his old woman, and it was jes' as useless as barkin' at a knot.

augur v² See **auger (around)**

auguring vbl n, also attrib [**augur** v¹] **West**
Talking, conversation; arguing.
   1942 Henry *High Border* 292 **nRocky Mts,** There is fighting [at rodeos], liquor-inspired arguing—"augurin' " as an old-timer would say—name-calling, dancing. **1944** Adams *Western Words, Augurin' match* . . . At the start they talk fast and furious, but after an hour or so they slow down to a trot to be savin' of both words and wind.

August bug, August cricket See **August fly**

August flower n **CA**
=**gum plant.**
   1897 Parsons *Wild Flowers CA* 176, Gum-Plant. Resin-Weed. August-Flower. Grindelia cuneifolia. **1898** *Jrl. Amer. Folkl.* 11.229, Grindelia (sp.), gum plant, rosin weed, August flower, Cal.

August fly n Also *August bug,* ~ *cricket*
A cicada.
   1966–70 *DARE* (Qu. R7, *Insects that sit in trees or bushes in hot weather and make a sharp, buzzing sound*) Inf **IL**45, August bug or heat bug—you never see it. It's a twenty-year aphid or something. They make noise in hot weather; **NH**5, Cicada—also called August fly; **NY**83, **PA**70, August fly; (Qu. R8, . . *Creatures that make a clicking or shrilling or chirping kind of sound*) Inf **MA**68, August cricket; (Qu. R10) Infs **IN**45, **KY**80, August fly.

August grape n
=**frost grape** (here: *Vitis vulpina*).
   1960 Vines *Trees SW* 731, *Vitis vulpina* . . . Vernacular names are Fox Grape . . and August Grape.

August ham n joc
A watermelon.
   1926 Van Vechten *Nigger Heaven* 279 **NYC** [Black], Ah hates duh spring; Ah sighs fo' August ham. **1942** Berrey–Van den Bark *Amer. Slang* 91.35.

auhuhu n [Haw *'auhuhu*]
A shrubby legume, *Tephrosia purpurea.*
   1948 (1965) Neal *Gardens HI* 448, *'Auhuhu* . . . Formerly, Hawaiians caught fish by poisoning them with this plant . . fish rose to the surface in a drugged condition and were easily caught for food. **1967** *DARE* (Qq. S16, 21) Inf **HI**4, Auhuhu—horses won't eat it. [People] pound [and] throw [it] in water and kill fish. Hawaiian gunpowder (no explosion). [Laughter]

ault n Pronc-sp for *aught* esp **AR** Cf **nault**
   1966 *DARE* (Qu. LL15, *To write ten, what figure do you put after 1?*) Infs **AR**18, **AR**22, **MS**71, Ault; **AR**31, Zero, aught, ault. [All Infs have less than coll educ.]

aunt n Usu |ænt| **throughout US** For varr see below See also 1941 *LANE* Maps 384, 385 and 1961 Kurath–McDavid *Pronc. of English* Map 67 Cf **ant** n
   A Forms.
   1 [ant, ɑnt]. **esp eNEng, eVA,** and elsewhere among better-educ speakers; sometimes considered affected, esp when over-corrected to [ɔnt].
   1847 Hurd *Grammatical Corrector* 78, *Aunt* . . Incorrectly pro-nounced . . awnt. Correctly pronounced . . ant [with a as in *far*]. **1890** *PMLA* 5.196 **ceVA,** The educated make a distinction between *ant* [ænt] and *aunt* [ɑnt], but the commoner people pronounce both [ænt]. **1891** *PMLA* 6.163 **WV,** *Aunt* . . is often pronounced [ɑnt]. **1908** *DN* 3.288 **eAL, wGA,** *Aunt* . . . Sometimes . . [ant] or [ɔnt] by the partially edu-cated. **1930** *AmSp* 5.340 **eMA,** Clearly [a] in *asked, aunt. Ibid* 348 **Boston MA,** [ɑ] in *aunt, grass. Ibid* 348 **ME,** [a] in *aunt, half.* **1936** *AmSp* 11.21 **eTX,** [ɑːnt] and [aːnt] for *aunt* are never heard except as consciously cultivated pronunciations. **1961** Kurath–McDavid *Pronc. Engl.* 135, In two areas, Eastern New England and Tidewater Virginia,

aunt has predominantly the vowel occurring in *car, garden* . . . : that is, low front [a] in New England, low-back to low-central /ɑ/ in Virginia. **1976** Allen *LAUM* 3.274, Most U[pper] M[idwest] infs . . . pronounce *aunt* as /ænt/ . . . But two out of 10 UM infs. have in *aunt* a vowel ranging in quality from [a] to [ɔ].

2 [e(ɪ)n(t), ẽ(t), ẽ(t)]. Pronc-spp *ai', aint* **chiefly S Midl, less freq Sth**

1903 *DN* 2.290 **Cape Cod MA** (as of 1850s), My grandfather's *Aint Massy* became my father's *Aunt Mercy*. **1928** *AmSp* 3.404 **Ozarks**, The vowel of *aunt* is usually pronounced like short *a*, but many of the older people give it something like a long *a* sound, so that the word can hardly be distinguished from *ain't*. **1929** Sale *Tree Named John* 4 **MS** [Black], Aunt Betsey was slightly above medium height . . Her skin held just enough of brown to escape being black . . . Among the servants the usual solution to a knotty problem was—"Ax Ai' Betsey. She knows." *Ibid passim.* **1933** Miller *Lamb in His Bosom* 112 **GA**, Old Aint Viney's high-voiced cackling. **1934** *AmSp* 9.209 **VA**, In one community in Virginia I have heard at least ten different ways of pronouncing *aunt* . . . [æɪnt], [æɪn], [ent], [en], [eɪnt], [eɪn], [ẽt], [ẽ], [ẽt], [ẽ]. **1936** *AmSp* 11.21 **eTX**, *Aunt* . . . is pronounced [ænt], [æ̃ʌnt], [ẽnt], [ẽɪnt] . . . Frequently, in rapid utterance, it is merely [ẽ?]. **1942** Hall *Smoky Mt. Speech* 24 **wNC, eTN**, *Aunt* . . is usually [ænt], once [ɑnt], but also [ent]. c**1960** *Wilson Coll.* **csKY**, Here comes Aint Mary. *Ibid*, Aunt [ent]. **1961** Kurath–McDavid *Pronc. Engl.* 135, *Aunt* with the vowel /e/ of *paint* occurs in the folk speech of parts of the South and the South Midland. It is not very common, except in eastern North Carolina and southern West Virginia. Only a fraction of those who have /e/ in *can't* use it also in *aunt*. **1967** *DARE* Tape TX49, Aunt [ent].

3 Other forms.

1899 (1912) Green *VA Folk-Speech, An'* . . . For aunt. "It belongs to an' Fanny." **1926** *DN* 5.385 **ME**, *Aunt* [arnt], never [ɔnt]. **1959** *VT Hist.* ns 27.124 **csVT**, Aunt [arnt] . . Occasional.

B Senses. Also *auntie, aunty*

1 An elderly woman unrelated to the speaker—used as a term of respectful address. **chiefly NEng**

1801 *Historical Review* (Cork) 2.189 *(DAE)* **eMA**, People of Nantucket . . always call each other cousin, uncle or aunt, which are become . . common appellations. **1862** (1882) Stowe *Pearl of Orr's Is.* 20 **eME**, These universally useful persons receive among us the title of "aunt" by a sort of general consent, showing the strong ties of relationship which bind them to the whole human family. **1903** *DN* 2.302 **Cape Cod MA** (as of 1850s), Most elderly people were called *uncle* or *aunt. Ibid* 305 **seMO**, *Aunt* . . . Used in speaking of an aged woman. No relationship implied. **1905** *DN* 3.2 **cCT**. c**1960** *Wilson Coll.* **csKY**.

2 usu *aunt* when followed by the woman's name, *auntie* when the name is unknown: An elderly black woman—used as a term of respectful address. **Sth, Midl**

1835 Hoffman *Winter in West* (NY) 2.121 **nKY**, Half a dozen negroes made their appearance from the log-cabin . . . "Aunty," cried my companion . . , "has your master got any apples in the house?" **1893** Shands *MS Speech* 18, *Aunt* or *Aunty* . . . applied by all classes to old colored women . . . It is customary to say *aunty* if her name is not known, and *aunt* with her name expressed if it is known. **1899** (1912) Green *VA Folk-Speech.* **1903** *DN* 2.305 **seMO**, *Auntie* . . . An old negress. A term of respect or affection. **1907** *DN* 3.228 **nwAR**. **1908** *DN* 3.288 **eAL, wGA**, *Aunt* . . . Used as a respectful prefix to the given name of a grown-up or an elderly negro woman . . . *Auntie* . . . when the given name is not known. c**1960** *Wilson Coll.* **csKY**. **1967** *DARE* Tape AL20, I say Aunt Lotti and Uncle Archie . . . It was kind of respect for them. **1967–69** *DARE* FW Addit **SC**, *Auntie*—Title applied to older Negroes, also without the name if you didn't know it; **KY65**, *Aunt*—used to address an adult Negro woman; becoming old-fashioned, but is still used. **1970** Tarpley *Blinky* 263 **neTX**, *Auntie* and *uncle* are given as terms of respect for elderly Negroes.

3 In Mormon polygamous families: the term of address used by children to refer to wives of their father other than their mother.

1965–67 *DARE* Tape UT1, [Question:] Did any of these wives live on, so that you knew them when you were older? . . What did you call them? [Answer:] Aunt; **ID14**, They [=my father's two wives] didn't live in the same house . . . Aunt Anna lived upstairs in the little house; **ID11**, Aunt.

4 A midwife.

1968–69 *DARE* (Qu. AA30, *An older woman who comes in . . to help when a baby is going to be born*) Inf **CA114**, Auntie [ænti]—probably not an aunt at all, midwife—technical term; **MI81**, Midwife, Auntie (first name); **VA34**, Midwife, Aunt so-and-so.

5 usu in comb and in var phrr, as *Aunt Flo is coming* or *visiting:* Menstruation. *euphem, esp among female speakers* Cf *DS* AA27

1948 *Word* 4.183, Female anthropomorphisms . . are numerous: . . *little sister's here, Aunt Jane, my country cousin, I expect a visit from my Aunt Susie,* are some of the more typical phrases. **1954** *AmSp* 29.298 **TX, OK, FL** ["Vernacular of Menstruation"], *Aunt Flo has come* (W[omen], collegiate). **1967–70** *DARE* (Qu. AA27) Inf **MD9**, Aunt Suzie's visiting; **NE3**, An aunt came to see me; **TX95**, Her redheaded aunt is visiting her. **1971** *AmSp* 46.82 **Chicago IL**, Menstrual period . . *Aunt Jody's come with her suitcase*. **1978** *MJLF* 4.1.38 **cTX**, Some women personify the event: "Mother Nature," "Granny's coming," "Aunt Minnie is visiting."

6 In var mild oaths: an exclamation of disbelief or excitement. [*OEDS Aunt Fanny* 1945 →] *euphem*

1965–68 *DARE* (Qu. NN27a, *Weakened substitutes for "God"*) Inf **NY66**, My Aunt Nellie!; (Qu. NN29a) Inf **SC44**, Great Aunt Hattie!

‡**Aunt Arushy** n Cf *DS* W1a–c

1941 *LANE* Map 367 **eMA**, [ænt ə'rʊušɪ], 'Nickname' for an umbrella.

Aunt Dinah's dead n [Prob Scots: reported from wScotl in 1906 *Folk-Lore* (London) 16.343]

A children's ring game in which, after a brief introductory rhyme, each player imitates the successive actions of the leader.

1953 Brewster *Amer. Nonsinging Games* 32, Old Mother Hobble-Gobble . . is known also as . . Aunt Dinah's Dead . . . Each of the other players must imitate the action of the leader. On the second round he sets a new task, but the players must keep on doing the first also . . . For failure to perform any or all of the actions called for by the leader, penalties are imposed. **1970** *DARE* (Qu. EE1, . . *Games . . in which they form a ring, and either sing or recite a rhyme*) Inf **MO30**, Aunt Dinah's dead.

‡**Aunt Dinah's picking her geese** phr

It's snowing: see quot.

1969 *DARE* FW Addit **KY50**, Aunt Dinah's picking her geese—said when huge feathery snowflakes are falling, especially in early winter and first snow falls.—Old-fashioned.

Aunt Hagar's children n pl Also *Aunt Hagar, Hagar's* ~ [Hagar, wife of Abraham and mother of Ishmael: Gen 21:9] *among Black speakers*

The Black race.

1935 Hurston *Mules & Men* 162 **FL**, You fool wid Aunt Hagar's chillun and they'll sho distriminate you and put yo' name in de streets. [Footnote: Negroes are in similie [sic] children of Hagar; white folks, of Sarah.] **1942** Hurston in *Amer. Mercury* 55.94 **NYC** [Black; Glossary of Harlem Slang], Aunt Hagar—Negro race (also Aunt Hagar's chillun). **1954** *PADS* 21.20 **SC**, *Aunt Hagar's chillun, Hagar's chillun* . . . used by Negroes to designate themselves. Not frequently heard. [**1976** Murray *Stomping the Blues* 95, W.C. Handy, 1873–1958, . . is remembered mainly as the composer of *The St. Louis Blues*, . . *Beale Street Blues*, *Aunt Hagar's Children*, . . and *Chantez les Bas*.]

auntie-broke-her-leg exclam Cf **aunty**

In the children's game of **Antony over**: =**anti-come-back**.

1968 *DARE* (Qu. EE23b) Inf **WI66**, Auntie-broke-her-leg.

Aunt Jane n *among Black speakers*

1 =**Aunt Thomasina 1.** *derog*

1970 Major *Afro–Amer. Slang*, Aunt Jane: female Uncle Tom. **1972** Claerbaut *Black Jargon*, Aunt Jane . . . 1. a black female who is a traitor to her race. 2. a black woman who tries to live a white life style. **1977** [see **Aunt Thomasina 1**].

2 A female member of a Black church.

1970 *Time* 6 Apr 71 **NYC**, Black Christians must relearn the wholehearted involvement with religion that typifies the churches' "Aunt Janes." [Footnote:] Affectionate black-church term for the amen-saying, clapping, lustily singing black-church "sister."

Aunt Jane's room n Also with other feminine names, occas abbr, as in *Aunt Jane's* or *Aunt Susie* **chiefly Nth, N Midl** *joc, euphem*

An outdoor toilet, a privy.

1939 *AmSp* 14.268 **IN**, An outdoor toilet is sometimes called 'Aunt Jane's room.' **1941** *LANE* Map 354 *(Privy)* **cCT**, 1 Inf, Aunt Jerusha's. **1950** *WELS*, 1 Inf, Auntie Jones; 1 Inf, Aunt Susie; 1 Inf, Aunt Mary.

1957 Beck *Folkl. ME* 168, To "go see Aunt Sally" is to visit the privy and "Aunt Sally spoke to me" indicates the trip there was a success. **c1960** *Wilson Coll.* **csKY,** Aunt Jane's . . . Outdoor toilet; used largely inside the family, humorous. **1966–68** *DARE* (Qu. M21b) Inf **ID1,** Aunt Jenny's; **NY113,** Aunt Sarah's. **1971** *Today Show Letters* **rural IN,** Aunt Susie—a privy.

Aunt Jemima n
=**Aunt Thomasina.**
    1980 Folb *Runnin' Down* 228 [Black], *Aunt Jemima*—Female counterpart of *Uncle Tom.*

Aunt Jericho n [Folk-etym]
=**angelica 1a,** esp *Angelica atropurpurea.*
    1894 *Jrl. Amer. Folkl.* 7.89, *Angelica,* sp., Aunt Jerichos, N[ew] E[ngland]. **1931** Clute *Common Plants* 48, On the tongues of such folk, *Angelica* becomes Aunt Jericho. **1949** Moldenke *Amer. Wild Flowers* 150, Its name *[Angelica (atropurpurea)]* is often corrupted to *"auntjerichos."* **1971** Krochmal *Appalachia Med. Plants* 46.

Aunt Lucy n [Prob folk-etym alter of *Ellisia*]
    1 A small delicate annual plant *(Ellisia nyctelea)* of the waterleaf family which has deeply-cut tomatolike leaves and small white to lavender flowers followed by globose fruits. Also called **waterpod, wild tomato**
    1940 Steyermark *Flora MO* 440, *Ellisia, Aunt-Lucy (Ellisia Nyctelea) . . .* Moist woods, thickets, and cultivated or waste ground. Throughout M[issour]i. **1970** Correll *Plants TX* 1273, *Ellisia . . . Aunt Lucy.*
    2 =**miami mist.**
    1959 Carleton *Index Herb. Plants* 5, Aunt Lucy: Phacelia purshi [sic].

Aunt Thomasina n Also ~ *Thomasine*
    1 A black woman with a servile attitude toward whites; a female **Uncle Tom.** *derog* Also called **Aunt Jane 1, Aunt Jemima**
    1970 *DARE* (Qu. II20a, *A person who tries too hard to gain somebody else's favor*) Inf **PA239,** Uncle Tom, Aunt Thomasine [ænt ˈtoʊmæsɪn]. **1977** Smitherman *Talkin* 252 [Black], *Aunt Thomasina, Aunt Jane,* highly negative references to black . . female sell-outs, those abandoning black culture for whiteness, as well as those who shuffle before The Man.
    2 Transf: A woman considered untrue to her cause.
    1970 *Atlantic Mth.* 225.112/2, Accommodators and temporizers within the Women's Lib movement were spoken of as Aunt Thomasinas.

aunty n
    1 The ball used in the children's game of **Antony-over.**
    1940 Marran *Games Outdoors* 97 **MO,** The ball used in this game is known as "Aunty," and it may be an indoor baseball, a tennis ball, or a bean bag.
    2 See **aunt B.**

aunty-i-over See **anti-i-over**

aunty-over See **anti-over** n, exclam

ausenburg See **osnaburg**

ausgespielt adj [Past pple of Ger *ausspielen* to play out, play to the end]
Tired out; finished, broken. Also fig.
    1907 Porter *Heart of West* 317, We will now pass you the time of day, as it is up to us to depart. Ausgespielt—nixcumrous, Dutchy. **1950** *WELS (Very tired)* 1 Inf, ce**WI,** Ausgespielt. *Ibid (If a man loses interest in a girl and stops seeing her)* 1 Inf, cw**WI,** Ausgespielt. **1965–70** *DARE* (Qu. KK19, *. . Temporarily out of order:* "My sewing machine is _____.") Inf **MI68,** Ausgespielt; (Qu. LL17, *. . There's no more . . "The potatoes are _____."*) Infs **IL130, PA135, TX1, WA28,** Ausgespielt.

author n Usu |ˈɔθə(r)|, also |ˈɑ(r)θə(r), ˈɔrθər| Pronc-spp *arther, arthur, orther, orthor*
    A Forms.
    1863 in 1973 *AmSp* 48.94 **GA,** Yours truly and immensely The Orthor. **1915** *DN* 4.180 sw**VA,** Arthurs . . . Authors:—the card game. **1943** in 1944 *ADD* n**WV,** Author . . . [ɔrθr]. 'The orther of the book.' Boy age 10. **c1960** *Wilson Coll.* **csKY,** Authors . . . A card game formerly popular. Sometimes [ˈɑrθəz, ˈɑθəz]. **1966** *Ibid,* [ˈɑrθɚ] of a book. **1976** Garber *Mountain-ese* 4 s**Appalachians,** Garber is the arther uv this book.

B Sense.
An authority. [*OED author* sb. 4 →1784] *arch*
    1899 (1912) Green *VA Folk-Speech, Author . . .* A person on whose authority a statement is made, "Brown is my *author* for what I tell you."

automobile n Pronc-spp *autymobile, ottymobile*
Std sense, var forms.
    1934 (1970) Wilson *Backwoods Amer.* 126 **Ozarks,** Autymobile. **1942** Rawlings *Cross Creek* 45 **FL,** We bought us an ottymobile.

automobile weed n Also ~ *plant*
=**puncture vine.**
    1931 Clute *Common Plants* 55, Our caltrop is fond of growing along desert roadsides and other waste places where the fruits may come in contact with the tires of automobiles, greatly to their detriment. It has now become puncture-vine and automobile-weed with every indication that these manufactured names, like the fruits, will stick. **1959** Carleton *Index Herb. Plants* 6, *Automobile Plant:* Tribulus terrestris.

autumn bells n [From the shape of the calyx]
=**gerardia** (here: *Gerardia purpurea*).
    1964 Batson *Wild Flowers SC* 104, Autumn Bells: *Gerardia purpurea . . .* Calyx very short and bell-shaped . . . Summer and fall. New England to Florida.

autumn summer n Cf *OED autumn spring*
=**Indian summer.**
    1968–69 *DARE* (Qu. B32) Infs **KY52, OH48,** Autumn summer.

auwaha n Also sp *awa'a, awaha* [Haw ʻauwaha] **HI**
A trench or furrow.
    1938 Reinecke *Hawaiian Loanwords,* Auwaha . . . A trench, ditch, or furrow. *Ibid,* Awa'a . . . Same as *auwaha.* **1954–60** Hance *Hawaiian Sugar, Awaha . . .* Trench, furrow; cane line.

auwaha v [auwaha n] **HI**
    1938 Reinecke *Hawaiian Loanwords,* Auwaha . . . To cut furrows.

auwai n [Haw ʻauwai] **HI**
An irrigation ditch.
    1865 (1965) Andrews *Dict. Hawaiian* 5/2, *Auwai . . .* The general name for streams used in artificial irrigation. **1934** Frear *Lowell & Abigail* 251 **HI,** A little green garden surrounded by white palings and cherishing both flowers and . . a singing *auwai.* **1938** Reinecke *Hawaiian Loanwords,* Auwai . . . A small ditch for irrigation purposes. **1967** *DARE* (Qu. C1) Inf **HI4,** Auwai.

auwana v [Haw ʻauwana] **HI**
To wander about aimlessly; to go by walking.
    1938 Reinecke *Hawaiian Loanwords,* Auwana . . . To wander; to go from place to place, idling . . . 2. To journey by walking, as to school (used among schoolchildren on Kawai). **1968** *DARE* (Qu. Y29a, *To "go out" a great deal*) Inf **HI4,** Auwana.

auwana n [auwana v] **HI**
    1938 Reinecke *Hawaiian Loanwords,* Auwana . . . Gadabout; wanderer.

auwe intj |ˈɑwe| [Haw *auwē*] **HI**
Oh! An exclamation of surprise or other emotions: see quot 1938.
    1938 Reinecke *Hawaiian Loanwords,* Auwe . . . An exclamation of pleasurable excitement, wonder, surprise, grief, pain, or condolence—indeed, almost any emotion . . . F[requent]. **1955** Day *HI People* 310. **1969** *DARE* File **HI** Auwe [ˈɑwe]. Exclamation of disappointed surprise. Common. **1972** Carr *Da Kine Talk* 86 **HI,** Hawaiian words commonly heard in Hawaii's English . . . Auwē. Oh! Alas!

avalanche n [See quot 1859]
    1 A spring wagon. **TX** *old-fash* Cf **ambulance B1**
    1859 (1968) Bartlett *Americanisms, Avalanche.* A Texan corruption of the French *Ambulance.* A spring waggon. **1872** Schele de Vere *Americanisms* 580, *Avalanche,* a corruption of ambulance, was already before the late Civil War much used in Texas and the outlying territories, but is said to have caused no small merriment in the Confederate Camp, when Prince Polignac . . once showed very great excitement upon being informed by a sergeant that the "*avalanche* was just coming down the hill as fast as fury." **c1937** Yetman *Voices* 336 **TX** (as of c1860), A yellow man drove her down in a two-horse avalanche.
    2 An ambulance.

1968 *DARE* (Qu. N1) Inf **MO**17A, I've heard colored people call it [ævlænč].

avalanche lily n [From its snowline habitat] **Pacific NW** =**dogtooth violet** (here: esp *Erythronium montanum*).

1915 (1926) Armstrong *Western Wild Flowers* 28, Around Mt. Rainier these beautiful plants often grow in large patches at the edge of the snow, alongside the Avalanche Lily. **1934** Haskin *Wild Flowers Pacific Coast* 29, Avalanche lily. This species of dog-tooth violet . . covers large areas in the alpine meadows of the Cascade Mountains. **1949** Peattie *Cascades* 252, Most of the slopes and swales are soon white again . . with lovely, fragile avalanche lilies. **1950** FWP *Guide ID* 67, Horrendously named avalanche lily by some, lamb's tongue by others. **c1960** Chambers *Wild Flowers OR* 5, Wild flowers of the Cascade forest include . . avalanche lily (*Erythronium*).

avast v, usu imper, often aphet *vast* [Transf from naut use; prob orig Du *hou' vast, houd vast* "hold fast"] **chiefly coastal NEng** *somewhat old-fash*
Hold it! Stop!

1942 ME Univ. *Studies* 56.75, The order to start up the capstan was *heave ahead;* to stop, was *avast heaving* or simply *avast* or *'vast.* [Footnote:] Fig . . . Stop talking or exerting an effort. **1945** Colcord *Sea Language* 26 **ME, Cape Cod, Long Island,** *Avast* . . . An old term, only occasionally heard, and then in abbreviated form: "'Vast!"

avenue n Usu |'ævə,nu, –nju, –nɪu| occas |'ævənjə| Pronc-spp *avenoo, avenyuh* See Pronc Intro 3.I.10
Std senses, var forms.

1930s in 1944 *ADD* **NYC,** ['ævenjə]. **1942** *Time* 1 June 58 **NYC,** I bunked into a friend of mine on Moitle Avenoo. **1943** *New Yorker* 11 Dec 31/2 **NYC,** Those cop-shooters and wild men used to be around the West Side, Tenth Avenyuh and around there . . . I come across McElroy, from Eighth Avenyuh, behind one tree.

average n, adj Usu |'ævrɪj|, occas |'ɛvrɪj| Pronc-spp *adverage, evrage*
Std senses, var forms.

1867 Lowell *Biglow* 32 "Upcountry" **MA,** All thet you've gut to know is jes' beyund an evrage darky. **1891** *DN* 1.128 **cNY,** [ɛvrɪdz] 'average'. **1911** *DN* 3.541 **NE,** *Adverage* . . occasional for *average*.

-aw See **-a**

aw adv **sSC, GA coast** *Gullah*
Indeed, to be sure.

1867 Allen *Slave Songs* xxv **eSC,** *Aw,* a kind of expletive, equivalent to "to be sure," as, "Dat clot' cheap." "Cheap aw." "Dat Monday one lazy boy." "Lazy aw—I 'bleege to lick 'em." **1922** Gonzales *Black Border* 288 **sSC, GA coasts** [Gullah glossary], *Aw*—a queer word, sometimes used instead of "fuh true;" meaning, it is true, in truth.

awa n[1] [Haw *'awa* kava] **HI**

1 A medium-sized shrub (*Piper methysticum*) with green jointed stems and heart-shaped leaves, the root of which was used in a drink and as medicine.

1930 Degener *Ferns of HI* 122, *Piper* is represented locally by *Piper methysticum* Forst., the awa of the natives. **1938** Reinecke *Hawaiian Loanwords,* Awa . . . A shrub of the pepper family (*Piper methysticum*). **1948** (1965) Neal *Gardens HI* 291, 'Awa is a native of Pacific islands, and in early times it was distributed eastward through tropical islands by migrating people, who valued the root as the source of a drink and of medicine.

2 An intoxicating drink made from the root of the plant.

1843 in 1934 Frear *Lowell & Abigail* 164 **HI,** We have suspended about twenty persons for rum and awa drinking. **1930** Degener *Ferns of HI* 98, When Kamehameha forsook drinking *awa* . . for alcoholic liquors, many of the Hawaiians followed suit. **1955** Day *HI People* 9, A skinny, ancient priest . . , red-eyed from drinking too much awa, led him . . to mount the . . temple platform. **1967** Reinecke–Tsuzaki *Hawaiian Loanwords,* Ava, awa; /'awa/; n. A stimulating and intoxicating drink made from the root of the kava (*Piper methysticum*), formerly much used by the native Hawaiians, but now used little or not at all.

awa n[2] [Haw] **HI**
The milkfish (*Chanos chanos*) common throughout the tropical Pacific.

1960 Gosline–Brock *Hawaiian Fishes* 97, The awa attains a length of

at least 3 feet—the largest for any Hawaiian herring-like fish. **1967** *Honolulu Star-Bulletin* (HI) 31 May F1/4, Awa—Milk fish. Good for baking. Steam. And for making fishcakes. **1971** Pukui–Elbert *Hawaiian Dict.,* Awa . . . Milkfish . . Stages of growth are *pua awa* (*puawa*), young; *awa-'aua,* medium size; *awa,* commercial size; *awa-kalamoho,* very large.

awa'a See **auwaha** n

awa-awa adj [Haw *'awa'awa,* sour, brackish] **HI**

1967 *DARE* (Qu. H58, *Milk that's just beginning to become sour is* _____.) Inf **HI**6, [ɑʊaʔɑʊa].

awaha See **auwaha** n

awake v (Note: Because *awake, awaken, wake* and *woken* are now used interchangeably, determination of the underlying root of var past and past pple forms is difficult; for discussion, see *OED* awake etym note and *AHD* wake usage note.) See also **wake**
Std senses, var forms.

1 past: usu *awoke, awaked;* also *awakened, esp freq among better-educated speakers;* rarely *awoken, awokened.*

1953 Atwood *Survey of Verb Forms* 25, The preterite is recorded in the context "I (woke) up." . . *Awoke* /əwok/ is fairly common in s.N.Eng. and adjacent parts of N.Y., rare in the North Midland, and does not occur farther south. Seven cultured infs use this form . . . *Awakened* /əwekənd/ is used by 10 informants (nearly all in N.Y. and N.J.), two of whom are cultured. **1960** *PADS* 34.61 **CO,** The prefixed forms *awoke* and *awakened* are typically older popular . . speech. **1965–70** *DARE* (Qu. X42, *What other way do you have to say, "I stopped sleeping at six o'clock"?*) 67 Infs, **throughout US,** Awakened. [Of all Infs responding to the question, 72% were hs- and coll-educ; of those giving this response, 86% were hs- and coll-educ]; **NY**166, "Awokened." I used to say this; **WA**24, "Awokened." **1971** Bright *Word Geog. CA & NV* 206, *I woke up early* . . . *woke up* 73% . . *awakened* 14% . . *awoke* 13%. **1975** Allen *LAUM* 2.31, [Preterite] *awakened,* not found at all among Type I infs, is . . more likely to appear in educated speech. It is scattered in four UM states but not found in North Dakota.

2 past pple: usu *awaked, awakened, awoken;* also *awoke, perh most freq among less educ speakers;* rarely *awokened.*

1816 (1936) Mercer *Baltimore to Louisville* 397 **MD,** We were awoke. **1965–70** *DARE* (Qu. OO32, . . *"Every night this week I've* _____.") 21 Infs, **scattered,** Awoke. [Of all Infs responding to the question, 31% were coll-educ; of those giving this response, none was coll-educ.]; **MN**34, Awokened. **1969** *Amer. Heritage Dict.* 1441/1, The preferred past participle of *awake* is *awaked,* not *awoke: He had awaked several times earlier in the night.* **1975** *DARE* File **Chicago IL,** The woman was awokened (by hearing a would-be assailant).

awar adj [Scots: see *SND* awaur, awaar, awar]
Aware.

1926 Kephart *Highlanders* 362 **sAppalachians,** Afore, atwixt, awar, . . everyday expressions of the backwoods.

away adv

1 Far in time or space from the speaker—used as an intensifier.

1882 Sweet & Knox *Texas Siftings* 45 (*DA*), Lawler . . shot a deer, away back in 1840, on the spot where the capitol now stands. **1906** *DN* 3.125 **nwAR,** It happened some time away back yonder. **1908** *DN* 3.288 **eAL, wGA.** **1939** Hall *Coll.* **wNC,** Away years back. **1958** Blasingame *Dakota Cowboy* 82 **SD,** He's a rough-gaited old sonovabuck, but he'll take you away over yonder and bring you back again! **c1960** Wilson *Coll.* **csKY,** Away . . . Intensifier, meaning much, somewhat, a lot . . . Away back, away below, away down, away up. **1969** *DARE* (Qu. A24, . . *"He's been hot-tempered from* _____.") Inf **NC**67, Away back.

2 In or from a location other than that of the speaker. Cf **away** n

1966 *DARE* Tape **NC**60, We'd buy our corn an' our hominy an' our cow feed away; it would be ground and sent here.

away n [From *away* adv]
Any place other than the place considered home. Cf **away** adv 2

1888 *Boston Journal* 6 Nov 1/4 (*DA*), It is rumored that capitalists from away are making an effort to establish an industry in Rockland. **c1960** Wilson *Coll.* **csKY,** Folks from away. **c1970** Pederson *Dial. Survey Rural GA* **seGA,** "He's from away" can refer to someone who lives either a few miles or hundreds of miles distant. **1975** Gould *ME Lingo, Away*—Any other place. To be *from away* is to be non-native . . . A man who has lived fifty years in your town and paid his taxes faithfully would hardly be called a *furriner,* and certainly not a *pilgrim,* but he will retain his non-Maine status of being *from away.*

aways adv [*OED* →1652, *"Obs."*] Cf **ways** n
Away.
  1934 in 1944 *ADD* **cPA**, *Right aways* . . . By those who speak no German. **1968** *DARE* (Qu. MM4, . . *"The mail box is just _____ the pine tree."*) Inf **IN5**, A piece aways from.

away yonder adv Pronc-spp *way yander, way yonder*
Far; by a considerable margin.
  1895 *DN* 1.375 **eTN**, I reckon if we know'd all we know now, . . we'd be ahead of 'em *way yander.* **1908** *DN* 3.288 **eAL, wGA**, He's away yonder ahead of me. **1909** *DN* 3.406 **nwAR**, *Way yonder.* **1951** *PADS* 15.52 **IN**, He's away yonder bigger'n me. **c1960** *Wilson Coll.* **csKY**.

awda See **ought**

awe See **ewe**

aweary adj [**a** inert vowel **6** + *weary*]
Weary.
  1941 *LANE* Map 479 *(Tired)* **cME**, Aweary [əwi˄ərɨ]. **1968** *DARE* (Qu. X47, . . *"I'm very tired, at the end of my strength."*) Inf **GA33**, I'm [əwɪrɪ].

awendaw n, also attrib |ˈo-ɪnˌdɔ, əˈwɛndə| Also sp *owenda(w),* [Prob AmInd; *Awendaw,* town in seSC] **SE, esp SC** *old-fash*
A spoonbread generally made from hominy as well as corn meal.
  1847 (1979) Rutledge *Carolina Housewife* 20, *Owendaw Corn Bread.* Take about two tea-cups of hommony, and while hot mix with it a very large spoonful of butter . . and lastly, half pint of corn meal . . . It has the appearance, when cooked, of a baked batter pudding, and when rich, and well mixed, it has almost the delicacy of a baked custard. **1932** (1946) Hibben *Amer. Regional Cookery* 16 **MD**, Owenda Bread. **1949** Brown *Amer. Cooks* 754 **SC**, Owendaw bread [made from hominy grits, corn meal, eggs, and milk]. **1955** *PADS* 23.46 **Charleston SC**, [In a list of relic forms] *Awendaw* 'spoonbread.' **1958** Francis *Structure of Amer. Engl.* 524 **seSC**, *Awendaw* [ˈo-ɨnˌdɔ] 'spoonbread, soft cornbread'. **1966** *DARE* (Qu. H14, *Bread that's made with cornmeal*) Inf **SC4**, Awendaw [ˈo-ɨnˌdɔ] is spoonbread, one made with a lot of milk and eggs. It's soft and baked. **1971** Wood *Vocab. Change* 44 **AL, TN**, The soft, mushy forms of this bread are first *spoon bread* and second *batter bread.* *Awendaw bread* may have a wider actual usage than the questionnaire discovered simply because informants did not recognize their pronunciation [əwɛndə] in that spelling. [Author corrects this to [əˈwɛndə] in personal communication, Dec 1977.] **1983** Neuffer–Neuffer *Correct Mispronc.* 7 **seSC**, Awendaw is the corn capital of Christ Church Parish, though the yield is not always used for the famed Awendaw cornbread (some even report their crop yield as so many gallons per acre).

awerdenty See **aguardiente**

awful adj
1 Ugly. [Prob absol, from *awful ugly*] **NEng** *somewhat old-fash*
  1815 Humphreys *Yankey in England* 103 **NEng** [Glossary], *Awful,* ugly. **1816** Pickering *Vocab.* 42, In New England many people would call a disagreeable medicine, *awful;* an ugly woman, an *awful*-looking woman; . . This word, however, is never used except in conversation, and is far from being so common in the *sea-ports* now, as it was some years ago. **1905** *DN* 3.2 **cCT**, *Awful* . . ugly, disagreeable. **1926** *DN* 5.376 **CT**.
2 Excellent, good. Hence superl *awful(l)est,* best. (Cf **-est**) [Absol, from *awful good*] **sAppalachians**
  1931 Hannum *Thursday April* 82 **WV Mts**, "Son," she said, "efn you'll l'arn to pick that banjo proper and sing, I'll buy you a silk handercher'," knowing well that a silk handkerchief was the awfulest thing on earth to a child. He did not say anything, but his black eyes flashed with delight at the promise. **1939** *Hall Coll.* **eTN**, *Awfullest* . . . Best. "He was the awfullest singer ever I heard." **1956** *Hall Coll.* **wNC**, His gran'-daddy was an awful hunter; he hunted bear a lot.
3 foll by infin: Very much inclined, very likely or prone. [Perh from *awful bad:* see **bad** adj **B4** quots 1960, 1968] **Sth, S Midl** See also **easy** adj **3**
  1939 *Hall Coll.* **wNC**, Be awful to. To have a habit (of doing some-

thing) . . "Had an old dog . . and he was awful to find snakes." **1956** *Ibid,* He's awful to tell stories. **1965–69** *DARE* (Qu. GG8, *When a person is very easily offended: "Be careful what you say to him, he's _____."*) Infs **MS63, TN30**, Awful to take exception.

awfulitis See **-itis**

awfully lot n [Hyperurbanism; see quot 1945]
A great deal, a large amount.
  1945 *AmSp* 20.73, The curious idiom, *an awfully lot* . . seems to be growing more common. One hears it from both educated and uneducated speakers . . . I have happened to observe it only in Kansas, but among those using it there has been at least one Texan. Evidently we have here an example of 'genteel false grammar.' Some one, having been instructed to say *awfully good* . . pushed that supposed elegance a step farther. **1980** *DARE* File **scWI**, There's an awfully lot of them goin' around.

awhile now adv phr [PaGer *alleweil* just now]
At once, immediately.
  1935 *AmSp* 10.167 **sePA**, Shall we go awhile now . . ?

a-widowed See **a** inert vowel **1**

aw'inge See **orange**

A-wiper n *euphem*
=**ass-wiper**.
  1968 *DARE* (Qu. II34, *If you think somebody is trying to use you to his advantage: "I'm not going to be his _____."*) Inf **VA11**, A-wiper.

awkward adj Usu |ˈɔkwəd, ˈɑk-| occas |ˈɔkəd|, and, in r-less areas, |ˈɔkwəd| Pronc-spp *awk'ard, ocred*
Std senses, var forms.
  1813 (1939) Hartsell *Memora* 115 **PA**, Some five in a platoon which made the motions quite ocred. **1894** Riley *Armazindy* 54 **IN**, He's jes' a great, big, awk'ard, hulkin / Feller. **1903** *DN* 2.291 **Cape Cod MA** (as of 1850s), *Awkard = awkward.* **1931** *PMLA* 46.1318 **sAppalachians**, *W,* is elided in several words: "awkard," "Edard," "backards." **1941** *LANE* Maps 462, 463, throughout **NEng**, [ɔkwəd]. **1942** Hall *Smoky Mt. Speech* 88, [ˈɔkəd]. **1966** *Wilson Coll.* **csKY**, [ˈɔkəd]. **1970** *DARE* (Qu. HH21) Inf **NJ69**, [ˈɔkəd].

awluz See **always**

awn n, v
(To) yawn.
  1950 *WELS (Opening your mouth when sleepy)* 6 Infs, **WI**, Awn.

awoke, awoken, awokened See **awake**

‡**awomen corner** n [By facetious analogy with **amen corner**]
  c1960 *Wilson Coll.* **csKY**, *Awomen corner* . . . A humorous creation to match the amen corner in the church; men and women, except courting couples, sat on opposite sides of the church.

awork adj
Aswarm, filled or covered with small creatures in a state of restless activity.
  1899 (1912) Green *VA Folk-Speech* 70, The seine was awork with fish . . . The bacon was all awork with the skippers.

ax n [ME *eax;* EDD *ax* sb.[1]] **Nth** Also called **ex** n
An axle.
  1939 *LANE* Map 188 **nwMA**, Names for the *wagon axle* were incidentally recorded in connection with the verb *grease* . . . [æks]. *Ibid* **nwVT**, [wægən æks]. **1939** FWP *Guide MT* 249 (as of 1894), A "dead ax" wagon was sent 10 miles to borrow a small . . organ. **1950** *WELS* 3 Infs, **WI**, Ax. **1965–70** *DARE* (Qu. L48, *The part of a wagon that goes crosswise underneath and has a wheel at each end*) 11 Infs, **Nth**, Ax; **CA87**, Wagon ax.

ax v, *ax'd, axe, axed* See **ask** A

axel-tree See **axle-tree**

ax-handle n
1 Orig among loggers: a unit of measurement, esp of width. *often facetious*
  [**1843** (1916) Hall *New Purchase* 94 **IN**, The entire structure was . . twenty feet square, as measured by an axe-handle.] **1947** Felton *Paul Bunyan* 95, *The Great Blue Ox* . . . Babe . . . His size is rather a matter of doubt, some people holding that he was twenty-four ax-han-

dles and a plug of tobacco wide between the eyes. **1958** McCulloch *Woods Words* 4 **Pacific NW,** Ax handle—a. The width of the back of a school marm's lap. b. A unit of measure shorter than a whoop and a holler. **1967–68** *DARE* (Qu. X50, . . *A person who is very fat*) Inf **WA**30, Four ax-handles across; **WI**47, Five ax-handles acrost. **1975** Newell *If Nothin' Don't Happen* 126 **nwFL,** Goin Henry were, I do believe, the strongest man I ever seen . . . Goin were about two ax handles long and must of weighed close to two fifty.

2 usu in pl, also *wild ~, flying ~:* Diarrhea. **Nth** *joc*

1965–70 *DARE* (Qu. BB19, *Joking names for looseness of the bowels*) Inf **NH**14, Ax-handles [laughter]; **CO**33, The wild ax-handle ("you can't control"); **NY**92, Flying ax-handles; **NY**219, Flying ax-handles—lumberjacks used to say. **1976** *Yankee* Oct 56, I found a letter from an uncle who was mate on a ship out of Boston in August 1869. While on shore leave he wrote . . . "We are all pretty well, only troubled with 'The Flying Axehandle' some." What was that? G.M. *Answer: Same as logus of the bogus, or backyard trot, griping of the gizzard.*

ax-handle party n Cf *DS* Y12b, 13

Among loggers: a brawl.

1958 McCulloch *Woods Words* **Pacific NW,** Ax handle party—A fight using ax handles, clubs, or any other wooden weapon.

ax-held n [Folk-etym, prob infl by *ax helve* + *held* past tense of *hold*] *old-fash*

An ax-handle.

1966 *DARE* FW Addit **cNC,** Ax-held . . . Used by countryman, very old-fashioned.

ax-helm n [Prob alter of *ax-helve*]

An ax-handle.

1939 *Hench Coll.* **VA,** Two fellow teachers, both Virginians, said today that their customary name for an ax-handle is "ax helm." They added that they might consider "ax helve" more correct but that it was not their natural word.

axle-dope See **dope** n

axle-grease n *joc*

1 Butter or margarine.

[**?1883** Peck in 1980 Lighter *Hist. Dict. Amer. Slang,* Pa says that last oleomargarine I got here is nothing but axle grease.] **1928** Ruppenthal *Coll.* **KS,** Axle grease . . . (army) butter. **1930** Irwin *Amer. Tramp,* Axle grease.—One of the many slang terms for butter. **1944** Adams *Western Words.* **1950** *Sun* (Baltimore MD) 3 Jul 7/1 *(Hench Coll.),* Millions of dollars were wasted on such nontested foods as the "axle grease" butter which sent soldiers choking and cussing from Guam to Great Britian. **1958** McCulloch *Woods Words* **Pacific NW,** [Among loggers].

2 Hairdressing. See also **axle-grease** v

1969 *DARE* (Qu. KK38, *To put preparations on the hair to hold it close to the head and make it shiny*) Inf **CA**114, Put axle-grease on. **1970** Major *Afro–Amer. Slang,* Axle grease: any stiff pomade for the hair.

axle-grease v [**axle-grease** n 2]

1968 *DARE* (Qu. KK38, . . *"I wish he wouldn't _____ his hair down so."*) Inf **PA**118, Axle-grease.

axle-tree n Also sp *axel-tree, axl-tree* [*OED* →1862] *somewhat old-fash*

An axle; also fig.

1634 in 1867 NH *Prov. & State Papers* 1.94, One grind-stone with iron handle and axltree. **1770** in 1917 *MD Hist. Mag.* 12.353, I shall send thm . . with a Carriage, that is upon an Axel tree. **1844** Thompson *Major Jones's Courtship* 80 **GA,** It seemed to me that the axeltree of the world wanted greasin or something or other was out o' fix. **1899** (1912) Green *VA Folk-Speech,* Axletree . . . A wooden beam on which cartwheels turn. **1929** (1951) Faulkner *Sartoris* 312 **MS,** We never got to town . . . Axle tree broke just this side of Vernon. **1950** *WELS* 2 Infs, **WI,** Axle-tree. **1967–68** *DARE* (Qu. L48) Inf **AL**34, Axle-tree; **GA**22, Axle, some calls it "axle-tree."

axt v See **ask** A2a

axt n [*ax* + excr *t,* perh infl by Ger *Axt* ax]

1916 *DN* 4.319 **KS, MI,** Axt . . . Ax.

ay chihuahua See **chihuahua** intj

aye, aye god, aye gonnies, aye jallus See **i** prep

aye, yes or no n Also *aye, yes nor no, ay ~* **chiefly Nth, esp NEng**

Usu in negative contexts: a single word, a straight answer, a statement of one's position.

1898 Westcott *Harum* 363 **nNY,** "Yes, I do," declared Mr. Harum, "an' my notion's this, an' don't you say aye, yes, nor no till I git through." **1910** *DN* 3.458 **Chicago IL** [Among "People of New England Antecedents"], *Ay, yes or no, . .* "He wouldn't answer, *ay, yes, or no.*" **1914** *DN* 4.102 **KS,** You can't get *aye, yes or no* out of them about the matter. **1929** *AmSp* 2.129 **ME,** He never said aye, yes or no. **1957** *Eaton Coll.* **cIL,** I never said aye, yes, or no. **1975** Gould *ME Lingo* 38, I asked him how he stood on the matter, and he didn't give me an *aye, yes, nor no!*

ayfter See **after** A3

ay-la intj [*EDD* 1877] *old-fash*

1952 Brown *NC Folkl.* 1.517 **wNC,** *Ay-la* [aɪ-lɑ, -læ] . . . Exclamation of assent (yes), surprise, grief . . . Old persons. Rare.

ayond prep [*EDD* ayont, "Sc. Irel. and all the n. counties to Yks."] *obs*

Beyond.

1843 (1916) Hall *New Purchase* 433 **IN,** Strate ayond is near about whare Bill fust seed the wolf or fox.

ayonder See **a** inert vowel **4**

Ayrab See **Arab** n

ayraba See **arabber**

ayuh adv, intj Usu |'e(j)ə|, also |'æjə, aɪ(j)ə| Pronc-spp *aaay-yuh, aiah, ay-a(h), a-yeh, ayup, ea, eyah* [Prob *aye* yes + *yes* or *yea;* cf *OED yea* etym note] **chiefly NEng, nNY** See Map *somewhat old-fash* See also 1943 *LANE* Map 588

Yes.

1894 *DN* 1.341 **wCT,** Ea: the word *yes* (pron. [jɪs]) is used, but much oftener is heard [ɛɑ, ɛə, eə] (dissyllabic and barytone) very rarely with a final *p.* **1917** *DN* 4.387 **neOH,** Aiah [eə] . . . Yes. **1920** *DN* 5.76, Aiah. Common in Massachusetts about ten years ago; not heard recently. **1944** Adams *Canal Town* 22 **nNY,** "Plenty of night-mist rising?" "Ay-ah. All through the valley." **1945** Partridge *January Thaw* 64 **CT,** Ayuh-ayuh, that's just the way I heard it before. **1948** *AmSp* 23.310, The word *ayuh* . . is found primarily in the state of Maine. The most common pronunciation of it is ['e:jə] or ['æjə], but there are many variations. One extreme is ['e:jə] . . [another] is ['jə]. **1957** Beck *Folkl. ME* 134, "Frankie, I got news foah yew." "Eyah?" "Frankie; we're aground." **1965–70** *DARE* (Qu. NN1, *Other words like "yes"*) 40 Infs, **chiefly NEng, nNY,** Ayuh; **NY**108, Ayup; **NY**163, A-yeh; (Qu. X18) Inf **CT**27, [e'jʌ]; **KS**2, [eə]—I don't say that, though. [Of all Infs responding to Qu. NN1, 62% were old; of those giving these responses, 79% were old.] **1973** Allen *LAUM* 1.387 **ceSD,** Ay-a ['ejɑ] . . is preserved in the speech of a . . speaker whose parents were born in Vermont and Massachusetts. **1975** Gould *ME Lingo* 38, Ayeh—Or, Eyah, Ayuh . . . The one word upon the entire face of the globe only true Mainers can say and use properly. It means "yes" or some variant thereof, and substitutes for the affirmative in a great variety of inflections. **1975** *DARE* File **nME,** Aiah [aɪ(j)ə(ʔ)]. **1977** *UpCountry* July 7/1 **Martha's Vineyard MA,** The islanders themselves are not guiltless in this promotional put-on [concerning "secession"] . . . I have witnessed

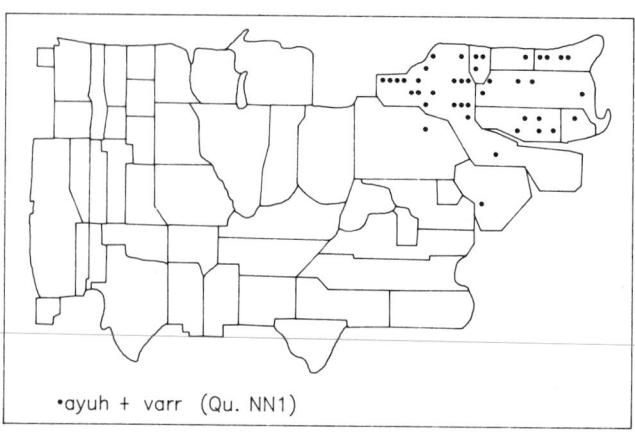

•ayuh + varr (Qu. NN1)

several scenes like this: Islander A (To a fellow islander in exaggerated Old Salt accent . .): "Walp, goin' over to America Thursday to get my damn teeth fixed agin' " Islander B: "Ayup." **1979** *Capital Times* (Madison WI) 20 July 39, Then there's the odd-sounding reply made by a "chummy" after you have made a statement that calls for some response: "Aaay-yuh." This, of course, means yes or "I understand," and probably derives from the nautical term aye, which was used by seamen to show compliance to a command.

ayuntamiento n [Span] **SW** *now hist*

A town council; an administrative body formed by an **alcalde** and counsellors.

1833 (1847) Lundy *Life & Travels* 45 **TX,** It [=Gonzales TX] has its regular ayuntamiento, alcalde &c. **1852** in 1858 Dewees *Letters TX* 140, If after two years from the date of concession, the colonists should not have cultivated his land . . . the respective Ayuntamientos can grant it to another. **1899** *Land of Sunshine* Apr 241, The Ayuntamiento (town council) had appropriated $500 for the school. **1932** Bentley *Spanish Terms* 96, Ayuntamiento . . . occurs frequently in writings concerned with the settlement and government of the early Southwest and was fairly well naturalized at one time. Its use in current spoken English is diminishing.

ay, yes or no See aye, yes or no

azabecker See asarabacca

azetonemia See acetonemia

azituri See azoturia

aznaburgh See osnaburg

azote n [Span] **SW**

A switch, or whip; see also quot 1934.

1892 *DN* 1.244 **TX,** *Azóte:* a switch, or anything used as a whip. **1934** (1975) Mawson *Dict. Foreign Terms, Azote* . . a switch; whip; in Texas, anything used as a whip; *Fig.,* calamity.

azotea n [Span] **chiefly SW**

A flat roof of a house or other building, esp of one built in the Mexican–Spanish style.

1844 (1954) Gregg *Commerce* 291 **TX,** I perceived the *azotea* of the parochial church occupied by armed men. *Ibid* 294, The houses are sometimes built in successive tiers, one above another; the *azoteas* of the lower ones forming the yard of those above. **1850** Garrard *Wah-to-yah* 227, The spectators on the *azoteas* seemed scarcely to move. **1899** *Harper's Weekly* 27 May 523 **NYC,** Above all is an *azotea* . . commanding such a superb view [of New York] that it is in imminent danger of being called the 'Roof Garden.' **1932** Bentley *Spanish Terms* 96 **SW,** The *azotea* is used as an open-air retreat . . particularly for coolness in the evenings . . . In the absence of a suitable English word *azotea* will doubtless maintain a place in the English of the Southwest where it is widely used at present. **1968** Adams *Western Words.*

azoturia n Usu |ezə'turiə| For varr see quots Pronc-spp *aciteria, acituria, asatoria, aseria, asteria, astoria, azituri*

Std sense, var forms.

1950 *WELS (Some common diseases of horses)* 2 Infs, **WI,** Astoria; 1 Inf, Asatoria; 1 Inf, Asteria. **1967–70** *DARE* (Qu. K47, *What diseases do horses or mules commonly get around here?*) Inf **IN80,** Asteria—comes from a bump like a boil, horse usually gets bumps from lifting limb of a tree; **NY230,** Asteria—from feeding them too much; **MI87,** Aciteria [æstə'rijə]—something to do with the kidneys; **IL11,** Aciteria [æsə'tiriə]—kidney infection; **MI83,** Aciteria [æsıtə'rijə]; **NY163,** Aseria [ˌæzə'ijə]—indigestion; **OH95,** [ˌæstə'riə]—from too much protein feed; **PA201,** Azituri [æzı'turi]; **PA141,** Acituria; **VA68,** [ˌæstə'riə].

Aztec two-step n *joc* Cf **two-step** and *DS* BB19

Upset stomach and diarrhea.

1953 Sherman *Aztec Two-Step* [Title]. **1962** Shepard *Forgive Us* 6, There was kaopectate, seconal, . . tablets to discourage the Aztec two-step. **1972** *Des Moines Register* (IA) 18 June, Montezuma's revenge . . . It's also known as . . Aztec two-step . . . In simpler terms it is the traveler's upset stomach. Three government doctors warn about the use of a widely recommended remedy.

azzle See arsle

B

'b See **brother A2**

baa-baa n, also attrib Also *baa-a-ah* [Imit] **West** *sometimes derisive*

A sheep.

   1924 Marks *Plastic Age* 87, Nine tenths of them [=male students at a college] wore "baa-baa coats," gray jackets lined with sheep's wool. *Ibid* 196, They pulled on their baa-baa coats and left the room chattering. **1931** *AmSp* 6.357 **West,** An efficient shepherd not only knows the exact amount of wages coming to him, but also the approximate number of his "woollies" or "baa-baas." **1944** Adams *Western Words,* Baa-a-ah— The cowboy's contemptuous name for sheep. If you want to start a fight, just blat this at a cowboy.

baachie See **backsie**

B-A-Ba See **A-B-Ab**

baba n [*OED baba¹* "an infantile variant of *papa*"]

1 A grandfather. See also **bapa**

   1967–68 *DARE* (Qu. Z3) Inf **OH2,** Baba; **GA28,** Baba [babə]—[FW: Used by Inf's grandchildren].

2 A grandmother.

   1969 *DARE* (Qu. Z4) Inf **CT34,** Baba, nanna.

babai n [Tagalog]

   1972 Carr *Da Kine Talk* 103 **HI,** *Babai:* "girl" or "woman".

baban n

A grandmother.

   1972 McCormick *Vocab.* **HI** 71, *Baban:* mother's or father's mother.

babble v See also **babbler, bawl** v¹ **1, boo** v

Of hunting dogs: to bark confusedly while running in a pack.

   1967 *DARE* Tape **LA3,** You don't want 'em barking out of place or just babbling down the road, as they call it; you know, barking behind [other] dogs.

babbler n [babble + *-er; OED* →1735]

A hound that bays before picking up the scent.

   1937 *Sun* (Baltimore MD) 9 Nov 17/5 **TN** *(Hench Coll.),* "Babblers", exasperating hounds that voice their deep throated cries even when they smell nothing. **1958** Hull *Amer. Fox-Hunting* 190, Babbler—A hound that cries "fox!" when there is no fox. **1966** *DARE* Tape **DC9,** In fox hunting . . when a hound speaks, they only speak when they're on a fox. If they do [speak when they are not on a fox] you get rid of 'em because that's what you call a babbler that just throws his tongue around, you know, without actually being on a scent.

Babdist See **Baptist**

babe n **Sth** *somewhat old-fash*

A pet name for a boy, often carried into adult life.

   1915 *DN* 4.180 **VA,** Babe . . . Used as a pet name for a lad. The youngest son, though grown, is often called the baby. **1976** *DARE* File **wNC** (as of c1918), *Babe*—a pet name for a boy. In the South it often precedes the family name, as in Babe Johnson, Babe Brown, etc.

babeesh See **babiche**

babes in their blankets n pl Cf **pigs in blankets**

?Clams that have been breaded and deep fried.

   1946 Peattie *Pacific Coast* 240, For the less gregarious there were clams at home—raw clams, stewed clams, baked clams, and "babes in their blankets."

babiche n Pronc-spp *babeesh, babish* [CanFr, from Algonquian *apapish* cord, thread; *DCan* 1806 →] **Nth, esp AK**

Thong material, or thread made of raw hide.

   1887 (1895) Robinson *Uncle Lisha* 31 **wVT,** You git ye some babeesh an' I'll give ye tew sides o' sole luther. **1948** *Sat. Eve. Post* 21 Aug 72/4 **AK,** No screws or nails are used at the joints, but *babiche* instead—rawhide thongs. **1974** Osip *Tanning Moosehide and Making Babish and Rawmane* 31 (Tabbert Coll.) **AK,** The lighter softer line is the true babish. It is usually made from caribou skin . . . Babish is used for the lacing and netting of snowshoes, the lashings on small sleds, making bow strings. **1981** *Tabbert Coll.* **AK,** *Babish* is French Canadian *babiche,* but usually pronounced here /bæbɪš/.

babies' breath See **baby's breath**

babies' feet n Also *baby('s) feet, babies' toes, baby('s) toes* [From the shape and color of the blossoms] **NEng**

=**fringed polygala.**

   1891 *Jrl. Amer. Folkl.* 4.148 **NH,** Baby-feet . . . Polygala pauciflora. **1892** *Jrl. Amer. Folkl.* 5.94, *Polygala pauciflora,* babies' feet. N.H. Babies' toes, Hubbardston, Mass. **1959** Carleton *Index Herb. Plants* 6, *Baby Toes . . . Baby's Feet . . . Baby's Toes:* Polygala pauciflora. **1966** *DARE* (Qu. S26e) Inf **MA6,** Fringed polygala—baby-toes—magenta and white (rare). **1967** *DARE* FW Addit **MA5,** Baby toes—fringed polygala. **1983** *DARE* File **c, cnMA,** Baby-toes.

babies' slippers n Also *baby('s) slippers*

1 =**fringed polygala.** [From the shape of the flower]

   1893 *Jrl. Amer. Folkl.* 6.140, *Polygala pauciflora . .* baby's slippers. W. Mass. **1900** Lyons *Plant Names* 298, Babies'-slippers. **1959** Carleton *Index Herb. Plants* 6, *Baby's Slippers:* Polygala pauciflora.

2 =**bird's-foot trefoil** (here: *Lotus corniculatus*).

   1961 *W3,* Babies'-slippers. **1965** Teale *Wandering Through Winter* 150, All across Texas, a host of names have been bestowed on the wild plants. They run from angel's trumpet . . to . . baby slippers.

babies' toes See **babies' feet**

babine See **baboune**

babish See **babiche**

baboon owl n

=**barn owl 1.**

   1891 Goss *Hist. Birds KS* 293, These birds, from their peculiar facial disk, are known as the "Baboon" or "Monkey-faced" Owl. **1955** *AmSp* 30.180 **KS,** With a facial disk distinctive both in color and shape . . , the barn owl is very generally called *monkey-faced owl,* . . often shortened to *monkey-face,* and varied to . . *baboon owl.*

baboune n Also *babine* [Fr *babine* lip] **Fr settlement areas**

1 usu pl *babounes:* Lips.

   1969 Cagnon *Franco–Amer. Terms* 223 **RI,** *Baboune . . .* [baboun] Lips . . . "Did you hurt your little *babounes?*"

2 A pouting expression. (Cf *DCan*)

   1967 LeCompte *Word Atlas* 341 **seLA,** *A look of displeasure . . babine.* [Footnote:] *Babine* (pout) . . standard French. **1969** Cagnon *Franco–Amer. Terms* 223 **RI,** "Don't make a *baboune* like that" = don't pout that way.

babowa n [Minorcan]

A dullard.

   1950 *PADS* 14.81 **neFL,** Many of their descendants . . employ certain expressions peculiar to their own group . . . *babowa* [bə'bauwə] . . . A dull-witted, stupid person.

Babtiss, Babtist See **Baptist**

babushka n Also *bambushka, busha, bushka* [Russ "grand-mother"] **chiefly Nth** See Map Also called **immigrant shawl**
A head-scarf, esp a triangular one tied under the chin.

1945 *New Leader* (Richmond VA) 2 Aug 14/3 *(Hench Coll.)* **Hollywood CA,** This headpiece [shapka] is a cross between a "babushka" and a snood. **1950** *WELS (A square cloth that women fold and tie over their heads)* 23 Infs, **WI,** Babushka; 1 Inf, Babushka — [by] country kids, my daughters tell me; 1 Inf, Babushka — within last ten or twelve years; 1 Inf, Babushka and satka by older people in [the] community; 1 Inf, Bambushka; 1 Inf, Bushka or headscarf. **1965–70** *DARE* (Qu. W3) 139 Infs, **chiefly sNEng, Inland Nth,** Babushka; **MI**108, Babushka, busha [bə'buškə, 'bušə].

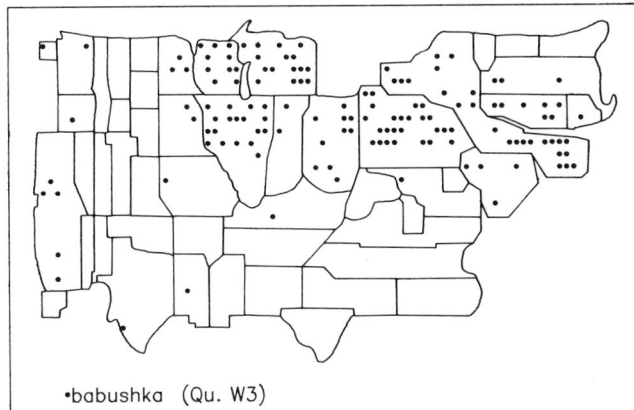
•babushka (Qu. W3)

baby n

1 A term of address used by a man to another man or to a woman, indicating friendship or a sense of community. *chiefly among Black speakers*

1965 Brown *Manchild* 164 **NYC,** I can say 'baby' to another cat, and he can say 'baby' to me. *Ibid* 165, The real hip thing about the "baby" term was that it was something that only colored cats could say the way it was supposed to be said . . . Only colored cats could give it the meaning that we all knew it had without ever mentioning it — the meaning of black masculinity. **1971** Roberts *Third Ear* [Black], *Baby* . . . male form of address to another male who is considered to be an intimate friend. **1972** Claerbaut *Black Jargon, Baby* . . often used in conversation with another person to refer to him: *You got it, baby* . . . friend; pal. **1977** Smitherman *Talkin* 62, In the Black Semantic sense . . it [=baby] can be used between men.

2 A cougar.

1946 Peattie *Pacific Coast* 89, Several frequenters of the outdoors swear that this varmint [=the cougar] at night may shriek, or cry like a baby — in fact, a slang name for the cougar *is* "baby."

3 in phr *not to buy clothes for the baby* and varr: Not to be accomplishing one's task or getting one's work done. **esp Sth**

1898 Lloyd *Country Life* 90 **AL,** Patriotism is a good thing, I reckon, in its right and proper place, but it wont pay the store account nor buy a new frock for the baby. **1929** *AmSp* 4.465 **Nth,** This won't buy the baby's shoes . . . This won't buy a dress for the baby or pay for the one it has on. **1937** *S. Folkl. Qrly.* 1.91 **SC,** This isn't buying shoes for the baby . . . Said when one turns from idling to work. **1946** *PADS* 6.34 **neNC,** Well, this ain't buying the *baby* any clothes (shoes). (Well, I must be going; I have a little work to do.) **1950** *PADS* 13.20 **cTX,** This ain't making the baby any clothes. **1952** Brown *NC Folkl.* 1.364, This isn't making the baby's coat or twiging [sic] the kiln. **1969** *DARE* (Qu. Y19, *To begin to go away from a place)* Inf **MI**103, This isn't buying the baby any shoes.

baby blue-eyes n pl, but sg or pl in constr **chiefly Pacific**
A plant of the genus *Nemophila*, but esp the western *N. menziesii* which is also called **baby eyes, bluebell 1d, California bluebell.** For names of other spp see **five-spot** and **flannel breeches**.

1887 *Overland Mth.* Aug 152/1 **CA,** Then if we could have been there, we should have seen the . . "baby blue eyes" (nemophila). **1932** Austin *Earth Horizon* 215 **CA,** Baby-blue-eyes for nemophila was tourist [=a tourist word]. **1946** Peattie *Pacific Coast* 52 **CA,** There it may be that baby blue-eyes cover the ground. **1967–70** *DARE* (Qq. S11, 23, 26b,

d, e) Infs **CA**12, 101, 115, 140, 144, 150, 162, Baby blue-eye(s); **CA**20, Baby blue-eyes — a five-petal, pale, tiny blue flower; **CA**31, Baby blue-eyes — pale blue and white, black speckling; **CA**79, Baby blue-eyes — in hillsides; **IL**135, Baby blue-eyes has small blue flowers; **WA**30, Baby blue-eyes — doesn't grow here. **1967** *DARE* Wildfl QR Pl.28a Inf **TX**34, Baby blue-eyes; Pl.209b Inf **WA**30, Baby blue-eyes.

baby breath See **baby's breath**

baby buggy n **chiefly west of Appalachians** See Map Cf **baby cab, baby coach**

1 also *buggy:* =**baby carriage 1.**
1896 *DN* 1.411 **WA,** *Baby-buggy.* **1904** *DN* 2.416 **nwAR,** Put Willie in the baby-buggy. **1947** *NYT Mag.* 12 Oct 26/3 **NYC,** A bunch of baby buggies are parked in front. **1949** Kurath *Word Geog.* 77, West of the Alleghenies, *baby buggy* [predominates]. *Baby buggy* is current also in Ohio and on the lower Kanawha in West Virginia. **1950** *WELS* 20 Infs, **WI,** Baby buggy. **1965–70** *DARE* (Qu. N42, *Vehicles . . a baby . . can lie down in)* 442 Infs, **throughout US, but chiefly west of Appalachians,** Baby buggy; 43 Infs, **throughout US, but chiefly west of Appalachians,** Buggy. **1970** Tarpley *Blinky* 107 **neTX,** For 64% of the informants, a vehicle used to push the baby in is a *buggy;* for 24% of them, it is a *carriage.*

2 also *buggy:* =**baby carriage 2.**
1950 *WELS* 1 Inf, **seWI,** Baby buggy. **1965–70** *DARE* (Qu. N43, *Vehicles . . a small child . . has to sit up in)* 20 Infs, Baby buggy; Infs **AL**32, **GA**28, **IL**89, **MO**35, **NY**156, **OH**67, **OK**13, **WV**2, Buggy.

3 See quot.
1942 Henry *High Border* 326 **nRocky Mts,** The expectant ewe throws up her head twice, whereupon the men on watch push a "baby buggy" toward her — an arrangement on wheels, into which the ewe and her lamb, or twin lambs, are placed, to be wheeled to shelter.

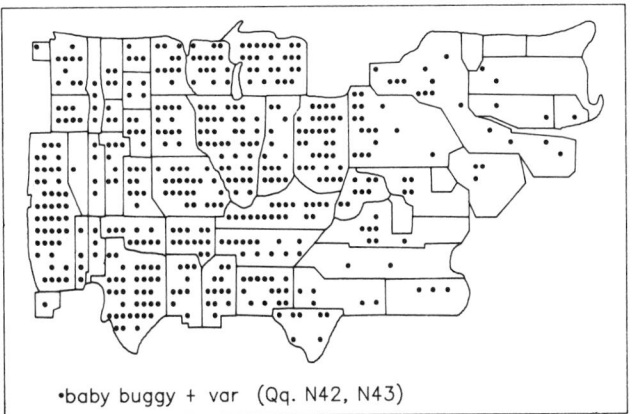
•baby buggy + var (Qq. N42, N43)

baby bumpers n pl *joc*
A woman's breasts.
1968 *DARE* (Qu. X31) Inf **OH**82, Baby bumpers.

baby button n *joc*
The navel.
1968 *DARE* (Qu. X34) Inf **CT**6, Baby button.

baby cab n Also *cab* **chiefly N Cent**

1 =**baby carriage 1.**
1901 *DN* 2.137 **MI,** *Cab* . . . Baby carriage. **1949** Kurath *Word Geog.* 77, In the southeastern counties of Ohio *baby cab* stands for *baby buggy* and *baby carriage.* **1950** *WELS* 1 Inf, **seWI,** Baby cab; 3 Infs, Cab. **1962** *PADS* 38.59, Words receding in the Midland dialect area of northern Illinois . . . *baby cab.* **1962** Salisbury *Quoth the Raven* 113 **AK,** The long plank walk makes use of the baby cabs possible. **1967–69** *DARE* (Qu. N42, *Vehicles . . a baby . . can lie down in)* Infs **IA**11, **IL**32, **IN**69, 73, 83, **MI**81, 106, **OH**56, Baby cab. **1973** Allen *LAUM* 1.341, *Baby cab* . . survived the Midland migration westward, but its low vitality outside Iowa hints at a current decline.

2 =**baby carriage 2.**
1969 *DARE* (Qu. N43, *Vehicles . . a small child . . has to sit up in)* Inf **IL**32, Baby cab.

baby carriage n Also *carriage* **widespread, but least freq in West** See Map Also called **baby buggy, ~ cab, ~ cart, ~ coach, ~ wagon**

1 A vehicle for an infant or small child in which it lies down.

1870 Alcott *Old-Fashioned Girl* 260 **MA,** A young girl pushing a baby-carriage looked round. **1882** Howells *Modern Instance* 277 **MA,** Bartley pushed Flavia about the sunny pavements in a baby carriage. **1896** *DN* 1.411 **NY,** *Baby-carriage.* **1949** Kurath *Word Geog.* 77, *Baby carriage* is the regular term (1) in the New England settlement area from Maine to Lake Erie and (2) in the Southern states. **1950** *WELS* 15 Infs, (Baby) carriage. **1965–70** *DARE* (Qu. N42, *Vehicles . . a baby . . can lie down in*) 503 Infs, **widespread, but least freq in West,** Baby carriage; 87 Infs, **widespread, but least freq in West,** Carriage.

2 A vehicle for an infant or a small child in which it sits up; a stroller.

1965–70 *DARE* (Qu. N43, *Vehicles . . a small child . . has to sit up in*) 16 Infs, **scattered,** Baby-carriage; Infs **AR47, MO4, 35, NY1, 88, SC9, 63, VA59,** Carriage. **1967** *DARE* FW Addit **sLA,** Baby carriage—infant vehicle with three wheels, in which the child must sit up.

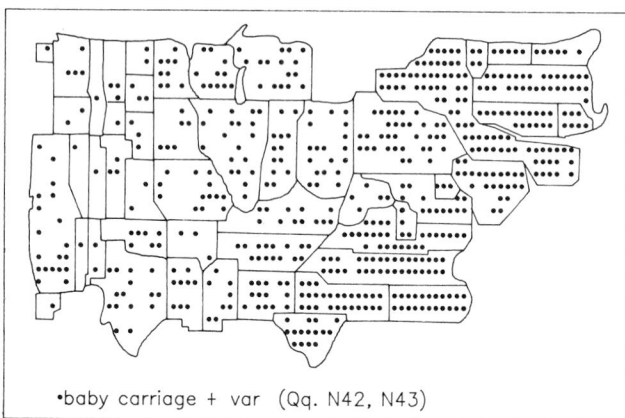

•baby carriage + var (Qq. N42, N43)

baby cart n

1 =**baby carriage 1.**
1940–41 Cassidy *WI Atlas,* 3 Infs, Baby cart. **1967–69** *DARE* (Qu. N42) Infs **GA74, IN22, MD25, TX35, WI18,** Baby cart. **1973** Allen *LAUM* 1.341, *Baby cart . .* exists in the U[pper] M[idwest] with three scattered instances.

2 =**baby carriage 2.**
1965–70 *DARE* (Qu. N43) 15 Infs, **scattered,** Baby cart.

baby catcher n **chiefly Sth**

1 A midwife.
1937 Sandoz *Slogum* 40 **wNE,** Soon Gulla Slogum was baby catcher for all the settlers, going from soddy to dugout, in any weather. **1965–70** *DARE* (Qu. AA30) Infs **SC19, 26, 55,** Baby catcher. [2 of 3 Infs Black]

2 A doctor. Cf **baby-snatcher**
1965–70 *DARE* (Qu. BB53a, *. . Joking names—for a doctor*) Infs **AL61, LA8, OK11, SC70,** Baby catcher. [3 of 4 Infs Black]

baby-catching apron n Cf **baby-catcher 1**
An apron worn by a midwife.
1949 Arnow *Hunter's Horn* 237 **ceKY,** Her big white baby-catching apron had been put on so hastily the bib flapped unpinned on her stomach.

baby chair n Also *baby seat,* ~ *settee*
1966–68 *DARE* (Qu. N42, *Vehicles . . a baby . . can lie down in*) Inf **VA1,** Baby seat; (Qu. N43, *Vehicles . . a small child . . has to sit up in*) Inf **NC44,** Baby chair, stroller; **NC48,** Baby settee.

baby-child n Pronc-sp *baby-chile*

1 A baby.
1927 Kennedy *Gritny* 14 **sLA** [Black], I'm knowin' Miss Mimi ever since she was a baby-chile.

2 Transf: see quot.
1980 *DARE* File **swTN** (as of 1944), Babychild (all one word, not two) is the youngest child in the family even if he or she is 50 years old.

baby-clout n, usu pl [*baby* small child, doll + **clout** n[1] **1**; *EDD babby-clouts*] Cf **baby-rags, breechclout**

1 See quot.
1899 (1912) Green *VA Folk-Speech, Baby-clouts.* Baby-clothes. Pieces of stuff of different colours given to children to dress their dolls with.

2 See quot.

1899 (1912) Green *VA Folk-Speech, Baby-clouts . . .* The clothes used for swaddling babies.

baby coach n Also *coach* **chiefly ePA, sNJ, DE, MD** See Map

1 =**baby carriage 1.**
1896 *DN* 1.411 **NJ,** *Baby-coach.* **1903** *NY Times* (NY) 1 Oct 3 **NYC,** *English Baby Coaches . . .* The carriages are a distinctly English idea—they dub them "Perambulators." We've just imported a hundred from one of the foremost makers. **1949** Kurath *Word Geog.* 77, Within the Philadelphia trade area, that is, in Delaware, in southern New Jersey, and in southeastern Pennsylvania as far west as the Alleghenies, *baby coach* predominates. **1950** *WELS* 1 Inf, **seWI,** Baby coach. **1965–70** *DARE* (Qu. N42) 20 Infs, **chiefly DE, MD, NJ, PA,** Baby coach; **CA147,** Baby coach—heard; **PA27, 88,** Coach. **1977–78** Foster *Lexical Variation* 32 **NJ,** *Baby coach* is used by seven of one hundred informants and recognized by two more; it is more common among older informants . . . four of the *baby coach* responses users are from Mercer [County], one from Cape May, and two, surprisingly, from Hudson; the two recognition responses are from the Philadelphia Suburbs.

2 =**baby carriage 2.**
1969 *DARE* (Qu. N43) Inf **NC72,** Baby coach; **PA242,** Coach.

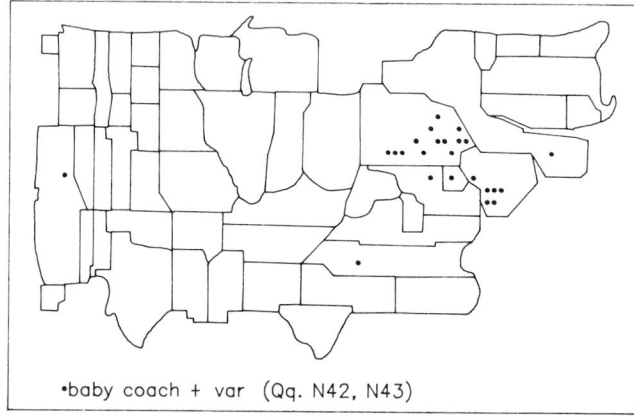

•baby coach + var (Qq. N42, N43)

baby coaster n Also *coaster*
=**baby carriage 2.**
1967 *DARE* (Qu. N43, *Vehicles . . a small child . . has to sit up in*) Inf **MO5,** Baby coaster; **ND1,** Coaster.

baby-cradle n
A cradle.
1906 *DN* 3.125 **nwAR,** God knows there are more baby-cradles in Arkansas than in any other state. **1908** *DN* 3.288 **eAL, wGA.** **1952** Brown *NC Folkl.* 1.517 **wNC.**

baby elephant See **elephant 2**

baby eyes n
A **baby blue-eyes** (here: *Nemophila menziesii*).
1897 Parsons *Wild Flowers CA* 290, When skies are smiling . . we find . . that the baby-eyes have opened in gentle surprise upon the lovely world. **1934** Haskin *Wild Flowers Pacific Coast* 291, *Nemophila. Baby-eyes . . . Nemophila menziesii.*

baby face n
A **woodland star** (here: *Lithophragma bulbifera*).
1956 St. John *Flora SE WA* 183, *Baby Face . . .* Dainty, beloved flower of early spring.

baby feet See **babies' feet**

baby fingers exclam Cf **baby up**
In marble play: see quot 1950.
1950 *WELS* (*Calls used in playing marbles to stop another player from doing something, or to get the right to do something*) 1 Inf, **seWI,** Yell out "Baby fingers!" **1963** *KY Folkl. Rec.* 9.64 **eKY,** The command to push or clip the shooter with one finger: Baby fingers.

baby giant n Cf **giant cracker**
A kind of medium-sized firecracker.
1965–70 *DARE* (Qu. FF14) Infs **AR41, TX26, 38, 54, 98,** Baby giants.

baby go-cart See **go-cart 4**

baby hole See **baby-in-the-hole**

baby house n Nth

A doll's house.

1772 (1894) Winslow *Diary* 63 **MA**, My Papa has promised me, he will bring up my baby house with him. **1843** (1916) Hall *New Purchase* 52 **PA**, As neat as a little girl's baby house. **1847** Lanman *Summer in Wilderness* 156 **nMI**, You happen to see a little girl arranging some rocky specimens in her baby-house. **1870** Alcott *Little Women* 2.14 **MA**, Do you know I like this room best of all in my baby-house. **1970** *DARE* (QR, near Qu. EE33) Inf **MA**100, [A] doll house [is] called a baby house.

baby-in-the-air n

A children's game played with a ball.

1968–70 *DARE* (Qu. EE1) Inf **PA**247, Baby-in-the-air. People have numbers: when you hear your number, you have to run out and catch the ball; (Qu. EE33) Inf **PA**126, Baby-in-the-air: ball in the air, try to hit it. Also spud.

baby in the bushes n Also *child ~* Cf *DS* Z11a, b

An illegitimate child.

1970 Tarpley *Blinky* 220 **neTX**, [2 infs:] Baby in the bushes . . . [1 inf:] Child in the bushes.

baby-in-the-hat n Also *baby-in-the-cap*

A children's game: =**hat ball**.

1967 *DARE* (Qu. EE33) Inf **DC**2, Baby-in-the-hat. Everybody put cap down on ground in a row. "It" standing by now with ball—walk up and down and tease—then drops it in one hat. Owner would grab ball—all [players now] run—and try to hit any player. If he missed he remained "it"; if he hit [a] player, that one became "it"; **PA**28, Baby-in-the-cap.

baby-in-the-hole n Also *baby hole* Cf **bunny-in-the-hole**

A children's game in which marbles (or the like) are rolled into one or more holes dug in the ground.

1896 *DN* 1.411 **csNY**, *Baby-in-the-hole:* The game of roly-poly [played with a ball and small holes in the ground]. **1940** *Recreation* (NY) 34.110, A list of the many games of marbles played throughout the country [includes] . . Baby in the hole. **1950** *WELS* (Outdoor games) 1 Inf, **ceWI**, Baby hole. **1971** *AmSp* 46.84 **Chicago IL**, Ball, puck, and tin-can games [include] . . *baby in the hole.*

baby-lifter n

Among railroad workers: a brakeman on a passenger train.

1931 *Writer's Digest* 11.41, Baby Lifter—Passenger brakeman. **1932** *Santa Fe Mag.* Jan 34/1, A passenger brakeman is a *dude* or a *baby lifter.* **1946** in 1953 Botkin *Treas. Railroad Folkl.* 350, The shack was . . blowing smoke to the Big-O of the time he was a baby-lifter on the varnish.

baby morning-glory n Also *dwarf white morning-glory*

A **heliotrope 1** (here: *Heliotropium convolvulaceum*).

1951 *PADS* 15.39 **TX**, *Heliotropium convovulaceum* . . . Baby or dwarf white, morning-glory.

baby-pepper n [Perh from the red berries] **chiefly Gulf States** =**rouge plant**.

1933 Small *Manual SE Flora* 484, *R[ivina] humilis* . . . Rouge-plant. Baby-pepper . . . Sometimes known as bloodberry. **1953** Greene–Blomquist *Flowers South* 30, Baby-Pepper . . . [is] seen all year throughout its range from Fla. to Tex. and Ark. Sometimes grown as an ornamental in northern greenhouses. **1960** Vines *Trees SW* 253, Vernacular names are Baby-pepper [etc]. It can be planted as a summer annual and propagated by seeds or cuttings in spring over heat, or by root divisions.

baby-rags n pl [Cf *EDD, SND* babby-rags small bits, *EDD* Suppl. bab-rags clothes for a doll] Cf **baby-clout**

1899 (1912) Green *VA Folk-Speech,* Baby-rags . . . Small pieces of various kinds of cloth collected by children for their baby-clothes. Dolls' clothes.

baby's breath n Also *baby breath, babies' breath*

1 A plant of the genus *Gypsophila,* but esp *G. paniculata,* a much-branched perennial with panicles of small white or pinkish flowers which is often grown as an ornamental. Also called **chalk weed, mist**

1895 Gray–Bailey *Field Botany* 75, *G[ypsophila] paniculata* . . . Baby's Breath . . . Innumerable very small and delicate white flowers. **1959** Carleton *Index Herb. Plants* 6, Baby's breath: Galium molluga [sic]; Gypsophila (v); Houstonia angustifolia; Muscari botryoides. **1968** *DARE* (Qu. S26e) Inf **IL**80, Baby's breath.

2 Any of var other plants as:

a A **grape hyacinth** (here: *Muscari botryoides*).

1892 *Jrl. Amer. Folkl.* 5.104, *Muscari botryoides,* baby's breath. E. Mass. **1910** Graves *Flowering Plants* 121 **CT**, Grape Hyacinth. Babies' Breath.

b also *infant's-breath:* A **bedstraw**, esp *Galium mollugo*.

1894 *Jrl. Amer. Folkl.* 7.90, *Galium Mollugo* . . (and other sp.), mist, babies' breath, E. Mass. **1900** Lyons *Plant Names* 167, *G. Mollugo* . . . Babies'-breath, Infant's-breath. **1949** Moldenke *Amer. Wild Flowers* 173, The wildmadder [*Gallium mollugo*] is often called *babiesbreath* because of its resemblance to the garden flower of that name. **1961** Smith *MI Wildflowers* 357, The cultivated Scotch-mist or Baby's-breath, *G[alium] sylvaticum* . . has the lower leaves in whorls of 8.

c =**ground smoke**.

1932 Rydberg *Flora Prairies* 570, *Gayophytum* . . . Baby's Breath. **1953** Nelson *Plants Rocky Mt. Park* 110, Babysbreath . . . A much-branched plant with . . tiny white flowers which turn to red as they wither . . . Our two species are *Gayophytum ramosissimum* . . and *Gayophytum nuttalii*.

d A **woodland star** (here: *Lithophragma parviflorum*).

1956 St. John *Flora SE WA* 184, *Lithophragma parviflora* . . . Baby's Breath.

e =**bluet 2** (here: *Houstonia* spp).

1959 Carleton *Index Herb. Plants* 6, Baby's breath: . . Houstonia angustifolia. **1969** *DARE* (Qu. S11, . . *Other names . . for . . bluets*) Inf **KY**47, Baby breath.

f A **fameflower**.

1968 *DARE* (Qu. S26e) Inf **LA**17, Baby's breath—shrub with small flowers growing along the limb. **1970** Correll *Plants TX* 608, *Talinum paniculatum* . . . Pink baby-breath, rama del sapo.

3 A kind of cloud formation.

1967 *DARE* (Qu. B11) Inf **NY**34, Baby's breath. **1978** *DARE* File **swAR** (as of c1940), Baby's breath. I remember that my mother or one of her sisters used it to refer to the puffy fog-like clouds that occur in the Oachita mountains of southwestern Arkansas.

‡**baby school** n

1967 *DARE* Tape **MA**100, When my brother started going to baby school, public school, every day he brought home a whole collection of things I'd never heard about before.

baby seat, baby settee See **baby chair**

baby's feet See **babies' feet**

baby skull n [Cf *OEDS* baby's head a steak (and kidney) pudding]

1900 *DN* 2.21 **CT** [College words], *Baby-skull* . . . Apple dumpling.

baby slippers See **babies' slippers**

baby-snatcher n Cf **baby catcher 2** joc

A physician; spec an obstetrician.

1925 Lewis *Arrowsmith* 115, He was going to be an obstetrician—or, as the medical students called it technically, a "baby-snatcher." **1968** *DARE* (Qu. BB53a) Inf **OH**47, Baby snatcher.

baby's slippers See **babies' slippers**

baby's toes See **babies' feet**

baby stroller n esp S Atl

=**baby carriage 2**.

1966–69 *DARE* (Qu. N43, *Vehicles . . a small child . . has to sit up in*) Infs **GA**77, 82, **NC**79, **SC**3, **VA**1, Baby stroller.

baby tear n

=**bluet 2**.

1956 Stuart *Year Rebirth* 100 **KY**, They were picking the wild flowers that are so often called *babytears* here, though many call them bluets. **1967–68** *DARE* (Qu. S11, . . *Other names . . for . . bluets*) Inf **OH**38, Baby tears; (Qu. S21) Inf **MN**2, Baby tear—grows along ground.

baby teeth, shed one's v phr

=**eyeteeth, cut one's.**

1894 *Advertiser* (Montgomery AL) 2 Dec 2 (*PADS* 13.11), I've done shed my baby teeth. **1950** *PADS* 13.11 **AL, GA**, To shed one's *baby teeth* . . . To be sophisticated; not easily deceived.

baby toes See **babies' feet**

baby-trough n [From the shape of a cradle]

A children's cradle or playpen.

    1953 Randolph *Down in Holler* 225 **Ozarks,** *Baby-trough* . . . A cradle, or a play-pen. At Zinc, Ark., the *baby-trough* was a sizable enclosure, in which women parked their babies while they worked in the tomato cannery. **1954** *Harder Coll.* **cwTN,** Baby-trough.

baby up v phr Cf **baby fingers, easies**

In marble play: to place one's shooting marble in a more favorable position.

    1942 Berrey – Van den Bark *Amer. Slang* 665.4, Baby up, *to get closer to the ring to shoot.* **1955** *PADS* 23.11 **TN,** *Baby up* . . . To slily approach the ring in order to place the taw or shooter in a more favorable position. Perh. fr. nursery baby-talk or nursery slang. **1958** *PADS* 29.30 **MO,** *Baby up* . . . To approach a *pink* [a circular ring] cautiously for a close shot.

baby wagon n *somewhat old-fash*

A **baby carriage 1** or other vehicle to carry a child.

    1853 McConnel *Western Characters* 282, A steam-engine would have been clogged [even] by the weight of a baby-wagon. **1894** Twain *Pudd'nhead Wilson* 14 **MO,** In front of Wilson's porch stood Roxy, with a local hand-made baby-wagon. **1903** (1965) Adams *Log Cowboy* 354 **West,** At this church fair there was to be voted a prize of a nice baby wagon . . to the prettiest baby under a year old. **1965–68** *DARE* (Qu. N42, *Vehicles . . a baby . . can lie down in*) Infs **MD**18, **MS**63, **NJ**2, **NY**70, Baby wagon. [All Infs old] **1973** Allen *LAUM* 1.341, One instance of *baby wagon* was written by a North Dakotan.

baby-waker n **VA, NC**

A firecracker.

    1947 *Hench Coll.* **VA,** A local judge . . spoke of the tiny harmless firecrackers—baby-wakers—that he and other boys used to use. **1966–70** *DARE* (Qu. FF14, . . *Different kinds of firecrackers*) Infs **NC**16, 41, 42, 44, Baby-wakers; **NC**88, Baby-waker—six or eight inches long, bigger around than an adult thumb; **VA**37, Baby-wakers—old-fashioned; **VA**75, Baby-wakers—small ones; **VA**71, Baby-wakers—little and large, regular firecrackers.

‡**baby woman** n

A midwife. Cf **granny woman 1**

    1968 *DARE* (Qu. AA30) Inf **IN**13, Baby woman.

bacca See **tobacco** n

baccaro See **buckaroo**

bacce, bacco See **tobacco** n

bach button n [Abbr]

    1970 *DARE* (Qu. S11, [Wildflowers] . . *other names . . for bachelor's button*) Inf **FL**48, Bach button.

bachelder n Also sp *batchelder* [*bachelor*, with intrusive *d*] ?**NEng** *old-fash*

A bachelor.

    1725 in 1833 Peirce *Harvard Univ.* 147 **MA,** The President . . called for the Salutatory Oration, and moderated one of the Batchelder's questions. **1739** in 1878 Southampton **NY** *Records* 3.13, Lying between Coopers neck lane and Bachelders hall. **1795** Dearborn *Columbian Grammar* 134, *Improprieties,* commonly called *Vulgarisms* . . . Batchelder for Batchelor. **1907** *DN* 3.181 **seNH,** Bachelder.

bachelor n Also *bachelor perch*

The white **crappie** (*Pomoxis annularis*).

    1877 U.S. Natl. Museum *Bulletin* 9.21, This fish is now, as in Rafinesque's time, abundant at the Falls of the Ohio, where it is now called "Bachelor." **1887** Goode *Amer. Fishes* 71, *Pomoxys* [sic] *annularis* is also known by such names as "Bachelor" in the Ohio Valley. **1933** LA Dept. of Conserv. *Fishes* 332, Known throughout Louisiana as Sac-a-lait, . . its many popular names . . . are as follows: Crappie, Bachelor, . . Bachelor Perch. **1947** Dalrymple *Panfish* 84 *(DA),* Here, my friend, are the various names by which you would address that little gamester, the Crappie, depending on where you happened to be at the moment: Bachelor, Bachelor Perch, . . Lamplighter, . . White Perch. **1972** Sparano *Outdoors Encycl.* 361, *White Crappie . . . Common Names:* . . bachelor perch.

bachelor man n [*EDD* 1874] Cf **widow woman**

An unmarried man.

    1951 Craig *Singing Hills* 110 **swVA, NC,** The old man and me are powerful glad Ikey's made up his mind to talk to a woman. We've been scared he'd be an old bachelor-man.

bachelor needles n

=**beggar ticks 1.**

    1968 *DARE* (Qu. S14, . . *Prickly seeds . . that cling to clothing*) Inf **DE**2, Bachelor needles. [Inf queries resp]

bachelor perch See **bachelor**

bachelor's breeches n

=**Dutchman's breeches 1.**

    1959 Carleton *Index Herb. Plants* 6, *Bachelor's breeches:* Dicentra cucullaria.

bachelor's button n Also *bachelor button*

1 A substitute for a button: see quots.

    1908 *DN* 3.288 **eAL, wGA,** *Bachelor's button* . . . A wooden peg or pin improvised as an attachment for the suspenders. **1915** *DN* 4.180 **swVA,** *Bachelor's button* . . . A wooden peg used as a button. **1967** *DARE* (QR, near Qu. S11) Inf **CO**4, Bachelor button. A two-piece clamp, gripper, or fastener.

2 See quot.

    1969 *DARE* FW Addit **ceNY,** Bachelor's buttons—cookies [with] pink sugar frosting and raisins.

bachelor's lantern n

    1959 Martin *Gunbarrel* 166 **sCO** (as of 1920s), Hanging on the wall was an odd contraption made from a tin can. "It's a bachelor's lantern," Tex replied . . . About midway on the rounded side of an open No. 10 tin can, he cut a cross three quarters of an inch long, punching the four points to the inside. From the outside, he poked a kitchen candle through the hole about three inches, leaving the rest sticking out. Then, on the side of the can opposite the candle, he punched two small holes, one near the rim and one near the bottom, and fastened a piece of wire from one to the other for a bail. For years we used lanterns made that way and found them very useful on camping trips.

bachelor's wife n *?joc*

A metal plunger with a long wooden handle, used in washing clothes in a kitchen tub.

    1959 Martin *Gunbarrel* 82 **cCO,** In the morning we [=men "baching it"] reheated the water until it was a little too warm for the hands and washed the clothes with a "bachelor's wife"—a tin plunger. [Drawing in text.]

bachelor wort n

=**orange milkwort.**

    1966 *DARE* Wildfl QR Pl. 123a Inf **SC**41, Bachelor wort.

back v

1 To mount (a horse). [*OED* back v 10, →1801]

    1821 in 1860 Claiborne *Life Quitman* 1.64 **NY,** Nobody but myself has dared to back him. Perhaps I may get this nag for the journey. **1874** (1895) Eggleston *Circuit Rider* 48 **IN,** As for ridin' Dolly, you know I can back any critter with four legs. **1889** *Century Illustr. Mag.* 37.899/2 **NY,** I . . had not backed a horse for the year past. **1903** *DN* 2.305 **seMO. 1911** *DN* 3.537 **eKY. 1912** Green *VA Folk-Speech* 71, The first time I backed that horse he threw me off. **1930** *VA Qrly. Rev.* 6.244, The Southern backwoodsman . . . would likely straddle or back a horse rather than mount a horse.

2 To carry (on the back). ?**Nth**

    1840 (1841) Dana *Two Years* 202 **MA,** We started off every morning . . and cut wood until the sun was over the point, . . and after dinner, started off again with our hand-cart and ropes, and carted and "backed" it down, until sunset. **1844** Lee – Frost *10 Yrs. OR* 202 **OR,** The Indians back heavy loads, confined by a strap over their foreheads. **1939** *LANE* Map 165 *(Lugged)* 1 Inf, **csRI,** Backed. **1949** Graham *Niagara Country* 222 **nwNY,** Artists depict her as a little woman with her head held forward. This posture was the result of carrying endless burdens on her back with the weight borne on a head-strap across her forehead in the Indian custom. It was in this way that she "backed" all of the boards for her house on Gardow the distance of five miles from a sawmiill on Silver Lake.

3 To endorse a document; esp, to address an envelope or letter. [Scots: cf *DSL, OEDS*] chiefly **Sth, S Midl** See Map See also **backing**

    1834 Sands *Writings* 2.136 **NY,** By-the-way, you may as well back [=endorse] the paper, and send what loose cash you may have, besides.

1859 (1968) Bartlett *Americanisms* 2, *Back* . . . To back a letter, is Western for to "direct" it. **1895** *DN* 1.384 **wFL**. *Ibid* 396 **neIL, IA**. **1899** (1912) Green *VA Folk-Speech*. **1902** *DN* 2.228 **sIL**. **1903** *DN* 2.305 **seMO**. **1907** *DN* 3.220 **nwAR**. **1908** *DN* 3.288 **eAL, wGA**. **1910** *DN* 3.437 **cwNY**. **1915** *DN* 4.180 **swVA**. **1917** *DN* 4.407 **wNC**. **1926** *DN* 5.398 **Ozarks**. **1959** *VT Hist.* ns 27.124, Back a letter . . . Before envelopes were common, letters were folded and the address written on the back. Obsolete. **c1960** *Wilson Coll.* **csKY**. **1965–70** *DARE* (Qu. JJ14, *To write a person's name and where he lives on a letter . . . "I'll mail this letter as soon as I* _____ *it."*) 94 Infs, **chiefly Sth, S Midl**, Back.

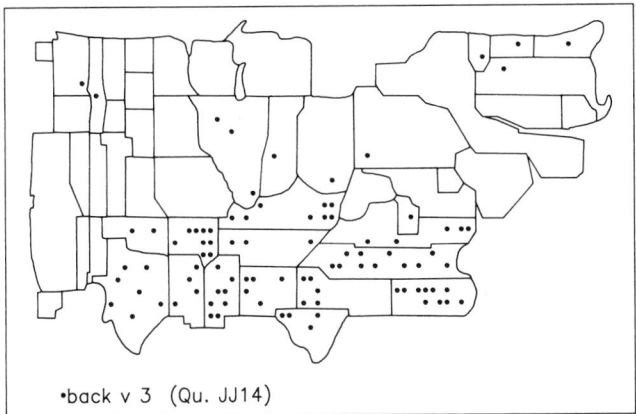

•back v 3 (Qu. JJ14)

‡**4** To reply promptly to a letter received.
   1968 *DARE* Tape **SC54A**, Back me a letter just as soon as you can . . . To back one means [to] answer [a] letter right away.

5 In logging: to make a **back cut.**
   1859 Perry *Turpentine Farming* 52 **GA**, Some persons have entertained an opinion that pines are not worth backing. **1958** McCulloch *Woods Words* **Pacific NW**, *Back 'er up* — To cut the back side of a tree after the undercut has been put in.

6 usu with an adv: Of the wind: to shift in a counterclockwise direction. **Atlantic, esp coastal NEng** Cf **backen**
   1871 Lowell *Study Windows* 5 **MA**, Did the Wind back round, or go about with the sun? **1951** Hough *Singing in Morning* 229 **seMA**, "Backing in" is a phrase that signifies [that the wind is] shifting by a counter-clockwise route. **1965–70** *DARE* (Qu. B15, *When the wind suddenly begins to blow in a different direction, you say it* _____) Infs **CT17, MA23, 40, 100, NC62, NJ22, VA44**, Backed around; **NH5**, Backed; **NC60**, Backed up. **1966** *DARE* FW Addit **ceME**, When wind backs in from south to east to north, it's a sign of bad weather. **1975** Gould *ME Lingo* 2, *Back in* . . . Most of Maine's bad weather comes from the northeast, and if a northeast storm clears by backing in it will usually bring one fair day . . and then it will likely storm again.

7 also with *up* and in phrr *back your foot, back a* (or *your*) *leg*: Of an animal: to stand still in a designated position — often used as a command. **esp S Midl** Cf **back back**
   1912 Green *VA Folk-Speech*, "Back your leg!" said to a milch cow to make her take the right position for milking. **c1950** *Atlas Checklists* **csWI**, Back — call to make cow stand still at milking time. **1965–70** *DARE* (Qu. K81, *To make a cow stand still — for example, when milking her — you say "*_____*."*) Infs **MO24, OK20**, Back up; **SC57**, Say "back" — she'll step back and hold still for milking; **AL34, AR52, MO24, OK49**, Back your leg; **NJ67**, Back a leg — She'll back a leg and stand there [Inf lived for 12 yrs in VA]; **GA19**, Back your foot. **1973** Allen *LAUM* 1.264 **MN**, Calls to horses to stop them . . . back, [back] up [reported by 2 infs].

8 To mend temporarily. [Perh from *backing* piece of cloth used as a foundation or for stiffening]
   1968 *DARE* (Qu. W28, *When a woman is in a hurry to sew up a torn place quickly, she might say, "I'll just* _____*."*) Inf **AK8**, Back it together.

back n, also attrib
   In mining:
1 The ceiling or overhead portion of a mine.
   1843 *Geol. NY* 1.361, The *"back,"* in mining phraseology, means the mass of a vein that has not been removed, and lying above the galleries that have been opened. **1945** *CA Folkl. Qrly.* 4.321 **CO**, The holes

drilled into the face of the rock . . are called from top to bottom "back-holes," "breasters," "relievers," [etc]. **1950** *Western Folkl.* 9.37 **MT** [Song lyrics], Oh, my blond hair has turned to green, Maggie, / From the water that drips from the back. **1960** Climax Molybdenum Co. *Manual* 46, *Back* — Any rock or concrete overhead. **1966** *DARE* Tape **SD4**, Heavy steel posts from the floor to the back, we called it. Some would probably call it the roof or the ceiling, but we always called it the back.
2 in pl: Material from the **back** of a mine.
   1968 *DARE* Tape **NV**, The only chance they've got is . . if they get down what you call "backs." You go into the tunnel . . and everything funny is called "backs."

back adj Cf **front** adj, **backhouse, back kitchen**
   Of living quarters: of secondary importance (and not necessarily at the rear of a home).
   1916 Lincoln *Mary-'Gusta* 18 **MA**, Mrs. Hobbs led her into the little room off the parlor, the "back settin'-room." **1941** *LANE* Map 343 *(Kitchen)* 4 Infs, **NH, MA**, Back room; [Commentary by 1 Inf:] Back room = summer kitchen, a rudely finished structure built on to the house. *Ibid* Map 352 *(Ell)* 2 Infs, **seNH, seMA**, Back room, (if) built on (to the house). **1970** *DARE* (QR, near Qu. D16) Inf **FL49**, The main bedroom is the 'front bedroom.' The other, unless specified as the 'guest room,' is called the 'back bedroom,' even if it's on the front of the house.

back adv
   =**back East 2.**
   1966 *DARE* FW Addit **OK27**, Generally people say, "I'm going back" for "I'm going East."

backache brake n [Perh once used as a backache remedy]
   A lady fern (here: *Athyrium filix-femina*).
   1873 in 1976 Miller *Shaker Herbs* 130 **NY**, Backache Brake . . . *Athyrium filix-femina*. **1876** Hobbs *Bot. Hdbk.* 7, Backache brake, Female fern, Aspidium Filix Fœmina. **1889** *Century Dict.*, Backache-brake . . . A name of the lady-fern.

backache root n
1 =**blazing star 3** (esp *Liatris spicata*). [See quot 1901]
   1828 Rafinesque *Med. Flora* 237, *Liatris* . . . Many vulgar names, *Backache root*, . . *Rough root*, &c. **1876** Hobbs *Bot. Hdbk.* 7, Backache root, Button snake root, Liatris spicata. **1901** Lounsberry *S. Wild Flowers* 501, Backache-root, or also called Devil's-bite . . . When the rattlesnakes are less vicious than their wont, it seems that the decoction made from this plant is held in reserve to cure backache. **1931** Clute *Common Plants* 124, Others [of these plants] are mildly tonic or possess some faint medicinal value . . . Familiar examples are . . backache-root (*Liatris spicata*). **1974** (1977) Coon *Useful Plants* 113.
2 =**colicroot 2** (here: *Aletris farinosa*).
   1971 Krochmal *Appalachia Med. Plants* 40, *Aletris farinosa* . . . Common Names: . . backache root. **1974** (1977) Coon *Useful Plants* 171.
3 A **spleenwort 1.**
   1959 Carleton *Index Herb. Plants* 6, Backache root: Asplenium (v).

back-actually adv Also *black-actually* **Ozarks**
   Truly, absolutely.
   1928 *AmSp* 4.118 **Ozarks**, Well, sir, black actu'lly an' candidly, thet 'ar's the masterest catfish I ever seed! **1930** *VA Qrly. Rev.* 6.249, He [= a Southern Highlander] may affirm candidly and black-actually . . . that the line of his barn roof is hip-skeltered, antegogglin', catawampus or waupajawed. **1934** (1970) Wilson *Backwoods Amer.* 70 **Ozarks**, He may affirm *candid* and *back-actually* that Tola Summerlin's was the best hawg meat he ever et. **1953** Randolph *Down in Holler* 67 **Ozarks**, Wilson . . reports *really and back-actually, candid and back-actually, and candidly and back-actually,* but the hillfolk that I know always say *candidly an' black-actually,* pronouncing the *black* very plainly.

back-a-licks See **back-licks**

back-alley bridge n Also *backyard bridge, ~ garbage*
   1968 *DARE* (Qu. DD35, . . *Card games* . . *around here*) Inf **OH46**, Bridge, poker, hearts, gin rummy, back-alley bridge; **MI103**, Backyard bridge, backyard garbage, little skill, mostly luck.

back along adv phr [*back* + **along 1**; *EDD* back-along 1, 1880 →] **NEng**
   Some time ago; in the past.
   1923 R. Frost in *Century Illustr. Mag.* 106.684 **NEng**, Some sympathy was wasted on the house, / A good old-timer dating back along. **1951** Graham *My Window* 133 **ME**, But just why "the old ones back-along" placed the schoolhouse on a hill . . is a mystery to everyone.

back and fill v phr, hence *backing and filling* vbl n [Transf from naut use: see quots] **chiefly NEng**

1 To move backward and forward repeatedly without making actual progress.

1777 in 1906 Essex Inst. *Coll.* 42.315 **MA,** He was then order'd . . to Stillwarter, then ordered from Stillwarter to Benington . . . This in the Salers Frase is Back[in]g & filling, makes but poor way a head. **1858** *Knickerbocker* 51.152 **Philadelphia PA,** He wound up his wondrous performance [i.e., of dancing] by *reeling* gracefully up to the youthful countess . . and 'backing and filling' twice around her. **1975** Gould *ME Lingo* 1, *Back and fill* . . . is used by farmers for turning a cart in a small area, by repeatedly backing and going ahead in short takes.

2 To vacillate or waver with respect to a position.

1854 *Herald* (NY, NY) 15 June (1859 Bartlett *Americanisms*), There has been so much backing and filling not only upon the Cuba question, but upon every other, that no confidence may be placed in the declaration which either Gen. Pierce or his cabinet may make. **1927** *AmSp* 3.136 **ME,** A man who changed his mind was said to "whop over" . . . If he hesitated, he was said to "back and fill." **1942** ME Univ. *Studies* 4, A vacillating, unreliable person was said to *back and fill.* This was a handy expression and was adopted by people who had no notion that the figure was that of a ship now making progress with sails full and now aimlessly drifting with sails aback. **c1960** *Wilson Coll.* **csKY,** You should have seen him backing and filling when I accused him of cheating me in a horse trade. **1968** *DARE* (Qu. A11, *When somebody takes too long about coming to a decision, . . "I wish he'd quit _____."*) Inf **AK1,** Backing and filling; (Qu. II31, *. . "He saw that he was wrong, so he started to _____."*) Inf **NY123,** Back and fill. **1975** Gould *ME Lingo, Back and fill*—To handle sails so they repeatedly catch and then spill the wind, a maneuver to tack or work a vessel to windward in a narrow channel with a favoring tide. Thus, to *back and fill* is to *fuddy-dud* about without great accomplishment . . . A politician who won't state his position, but talks around it, is *backing and filling.*

back and forth v phr, hence *backing and forthing* vbl n **S Midl**

1 To go from and return to the same place repeatedly, esp with little result.

1916 *DN* 4.294 **sAppalachians,** Numerous . . anomalous compounds and semi-hybrids are found, for example: *backing-and-forthing.* **1931** *PMLA* 46.1307 **sAppalachians,** He kep' a backin' an' a-forthin' all day. **1940** in 1968 Haun *Hawk's Done Gone* 158 **eTN,** She had him backing and forthing to the post office with a pack of letters.

2 By ext: to work ineffectively with much moving about.

1936 *AmSp* 11.314 **Ozarks,** *Backing and forthing* . . . Engaging in some futile enterprise. 'Them CCC boys jest kept a-backin' an' a-forthin' all day.' **1953** Randolph *Down in Holler* 225 **Ozarks,** Back and forth . . . To work in an aimless or futile manner.

back-and-forth n

Talk between two persons.

1941 Percy *Lanterns* 293 **nwMS** [Black], En they had a lot of back-and-forth.

back and to adv phr [*EDD* 1886] **now chiefly S Atl**

To and fro, back and forth.

1856 Holmes *Lena Rivers* 72 **NEng,** Causing grandma to wonder "how the poor critters managed to carry victuals back and to when it was cold and slippery." **1931–33** *LANE Worksheets* **ceCT,** Back an' to. **1936** *Scribner's Mag.* 100.29 **cFL,** I cain't traipse back and to, waiting and waiting all the time. **1952** Brown *NC Folkl.* 1.517 **cnNC,** He goes back and to Altamahaw–Ossipee every day. **1965** *DARE* File **OK,** Back and to: back and forth. Used in the "deep South." **1966–68** *DARE* Tape **FL32,** We use . . trailers to move back and to from one ranch to the other; **GA30,** Just wash 'im, rench 'im in the water, back and to, 'til he comes out o' the hull; **GA51,** Close to her work, back an' to. **1976** *DARE* File **sGA,** Back and to—reported by a south Georgia man to have been "heard all his life."

back'ard(s) See **backward(s)**

back-around n

In logging: see quot.

1958 McCulloch *Woods Words* 5 **Pacific NW,** *Back-around*—A Y for turning trailers in the early days of truck logging before trailers were carried to the woods on the truck.

back-asswards adv For varr see quots **chiefly Inland Nth, West** See also **bass-ackward(s)**
=**ass-backward(s).**

1951 Salinger *Catcher* 53 **PA,** You always do everything backasswards . . . No wonder you're flunking the hell out of here . . . You don't do *one damn thing* the way you're supposed to. **1965–70** *DARE* (Qu. MM2, *. . "You've got your dress on _____."*) Infs **MI24, 63, NY94, PA94,** Back-asswards; **CA136, IL30,** Back-ackwards; (Qu. MM3, *. . "This is the front; you've got the whole thing turned _____."*) 11 Infs, **chiefly Inland Nth, West,** Back-asswards; **MS73, NC14,** Backassards; **NC88,** Back-ackards; **MI118,** Back-ass-backwards; **NC36,** Back-assed.

back back v phr **esp Sth, S Midl** See also **back** v 7 Cf *DJE*

To move backward—usu used in a command to a draft animal.

1907 *DN* 3.240 **eME,** Back back . . . To back (usually, a horse). "*Back back,* wo'n't you, so I can get out of here?" "He *backed* the horse *back.*" **1938** Stuart *Dark Hills* 18 **eKY,** Once they carried him [=Pap] on past the station and Old Buck Stump made them back-back the train two miles and put them off. **1954** *Harder Coll.* **cwTN,** *Back back:* A command to mules or horses. **1966** *DARE* (Qu. K36b, *What do you say to make a horse go backwards?*) Infs **FL6, 9, 27,** Back back!

back-ball exclam

In the game of **Antony-over:** =**pigtail** exclam.

1950 *WELS (What do you call if the ball does not go over the building, but comes back?)* 5 Infs, **WI,** Back-ball. **1965–70** *DARE* (Qu. EE23b) 23 Infs, **scattered,** Back-ball.

backband n Also *backstrap* [*OED*→1848; see also *EDD*] **now chiefly Sth**

A belt which binds a saddle or work harness to a horse's back.

1909 *DN* 3.408 **ME,** *Backstrap* . . . In harness the turnback or strap which runs from the saddle along the horse's back. **1965–70** *DARE* (Qq. LL53a, b) Infs **FL18, GA22, VA105,** Back band; **MS81,** Back band—goes across horse's back; **MO24,** Backband—used with trace chains; **DC3,** Surcingle—[same as] backband.

backbone n, also attrib

Pork meat from near the backbone.

1938 Hertzler *Horse & Buggy Dr.* 80 **cwKS,** She never could eat backbone and sauerkraut without getting stomach distress from it, she explained. **1951** Brown *Southern Cook Book* 100 **NC,** *Backbone with Dumplings* . . . The backbone of the pig is one of the most succulent parts of the meat, and may be boiled plain, stewed with dumplings or baked as spareribs. **1966** *DARE* (QR, near Qu. H55) Inf **MS72,** Backbone dumplings. Stew made with pork backbone for flavor and dumplings, which are dough hunks cooked in the pot. Same as *pork stew.*

backbone fence n [Because it resembles the backbone of a fish] Also called **shadback fence**

A stake-and-rail fence.

1939 *LANE* Map 117, 1 Inf, **cwCT,** We had rail f[ences], backbone f[ences], and post-and-rail f[ences].

backbreaker n, also attrib

A tree stump cut close to the ground.

1931 *AmSp* 7.52 **Sth, SW,** Fourteen inch stumps, because they are low, are called "back breakers." **1950** *WELS (What kinds of saws are commonly used on the farm?)* 1 Inf, **seWI,** Backbreaker saw. **1968** Adams *Western Words, Backbreakers*—In logging, tree stumps.

‡**backbrush** n attrib

Backwoods.

1934 (1970) Wilson *Backwoods Amer.* 17 **Ozarks,** Backbrush humor hangs upon pegs that are unashamedly obvious. *Ibid* 204, The countryside school . . is kept by . . Sherman Ham, who teaches a roomful of backbrush scholars, ranging in age from five to twenty-five years.

back-buster n **Sth, Midl** Cf **belly-buster 2**

A dive in which one lands flat on the water.

1965–70 *DARE* (Qu. EE29) 12 Infs, **Sth, Midl,** Back-buster.

back cant n **Nth**

In logging: a rearward pull with a cant hook.

1968 *DARE* Tape **NH14,** [In a sawmill:] Using a cant dog to stop a log that's rolling away, had to take a back cant on that. **1969** Sorden *Lumberjack Lingo* **NEng, Gt Lakes,** *Back cant*—Reverse use of cant hook to hold log back instead of the usual use to roll it forward.

backcap n

A verbal insult based upon the insulted person's background.

1883 Twain *Life on Missip.* (Boston) 514, I told him all about my being in prison . . . & now I did n't fear no one giving me a back cap *(exposing his past life)* & running me off the job. **1970** Major *Afro–Amer. Slang* 22, *Backcap:* (1940s) a sharp reply—associated with *The Dozens.*

backcap v [backcap n] *somewhat old-fash* Cf **cap** v **1d**

See quot 1889.

1889 *Century Dict., Backcap* . . . To depreciate or disparage. [U.S. slang]. **1891** *Boston Sunday Herald* 20 Sept. 4/5 *(DAE),* Do you think you wouldn't say something that would backcap me? **1896** (1898) Ade *Artie* 7 **Chicago IL,** Mrs. Morton got me a good seat and then back-capped the show a little before it opened up. *Ibid* 99, I don't want to back-cap her. **1928** *Hearst's International* 85.34/2 **SW,** Fine specimen, you are—backcappin' your own neighbors to town trash!

back corner n Cf **back forty, the 1**

Among loggers: see quot.

1958 McCulloch *Woods Words* 5 **Pacific NW,** *Back corner* . . . The far end of a logging operation; similar to "back forty" but not so far away.

back countryman n Cf *DS* HH1

A rustic.

[**1796** *Gaz. U.S.* 19 Nov 2/1 **Philadelphia PA** [Advt]:, A new Ballet Dance, . . called the *Back Countryman, Or, the New Settlers.*] **1845** (1968) Simms *Wigwam & Cabin* (1st ser) 29 **Sth,** The boatman . . knew by his dialect and dress that he was a back-countryman. **1941** *LANE* Map 450 *(A Rustic),* Back countryman [occurs occasionally].

back cut n Also called **after cut** Cf **back** v **5**

In logging: see quot 1958.

1958 McCulloch *Woods Words* **Pacific NW,** *Back cut*—In falling timber, the final cut put in a tree after the undercut has been completed. **1969** Sorden *Lumberjack Lingo* **NEng, Gt Lakes.**

back door n

1 See quot. See also **backdoor trot**

1952 Brown *NC Folkl.* 1.517, *Back door* . . . The anus.

2 in phr *one's back door is open:* See quot.

1968–70 *DARE* (Qu. W24b, *Sayings to warn a man that his pants are torn or split*) Infs **CA212, MN15,** (Your) back door's open.

3 also quasi-adv: A movement in the children's game of jump-rope: see quots. Cf **front door 1**

1943 *TX Folkl. Soc. Pub.* 18.198 **seTX,** The proficient jumper learns not only to keep her feet clear of both ropes, but to enter and run out at will, either "front door" or "back door." **1961** *Western Folkl.* 20.179, *Back door*—Running in when the rope is being turned away from the jumper, very forbidding. **1968** *DARE* File **seID,** *Back door*—Turning the rope away from the jumper so she must jump over the rope when she goes in instead of under the rope. More difficult than Front Door. **1979** [see **front door 1**].

4 See **backdoor treatment.**

backdoor treatment n Also *back door, backdoor chute*

A snub; a "cold shoulder".

1966–68 *DARE* (Qu. II5b, *When you don't want to have anything to do with a certain person . . , "I'd like to give him the _____."*) Inf **NJ1,** Backdoor treatment; **NJ36,** Back door; **MA6,** Backdoor chute. [All Infs old]

backdoor trot n, usu pl but sg in constr For varr see quots [back door 1 + trots; *EDD, OEDS* 1789 →] **widespread** *joc*

1 Diarrhea. See also **barnyard trots, B.D.T.**

1899 (1912) Green *VA Folk-Speech, Back-door-trots* . . . The diarrhoea. **1908** *DN* 3.288 **eAL, wGA,** *Back-do(or) trots.* **1912** *DN* 3.570 **wIN,** Back door trots. **1944** *PADS* 2.39 **sVA,** *Back-door-trots.* **1950** *WELS (Joking or nicknames for diarrhea)* 22 Infs, **WI,** Backdoor trot(s); 1 Inf, Backhouse trots—old-fashioned. **c1960** *Wilson Coll.* **csKY,** I've had a bad spell of back-door trots lately. **1965–70** *DARE* (Qu. BB19, *Joking names for looseness of the bowels*) 131 Infs, **widespread,** Back-door trots; **MA65, NY84,** 121, **WI66,** Backdoor trot; **IN3, MN15, WA28,** Backhouse trots; **CA36, OH98, PA179, SC40,** Backyard trots; **PA162,** Backdoor quicksteps; **CA127,** Backdoor scoots; (Qu. K28) Inf **MA6,** Cows get backdoor trots from milk.

2 Transf: overactive kidneys. **chiefly Sth, Midl**

1950 *WELS (Joking or nicknames for over-active kidneys)* 1 Inf, **csWI,** Backdoor trots. **1965–70** *DARE* (Qu. BB20) 16 Infs, **chiefly Sth, Midl,** Backdoor trots.

back-drawing n

Reluctance, objection, hesitation.

1934 (1970) Wilson *Backwoods Amer.* 170 **AR, MO,** If you-all wanted hit for your own pussonal use, I wouldn't have no back-drawin's about sellin' hit [=moonshine whiskey] to you.

back East adv phr Cf **East** n[1]

1 In the eastern part of the U.S.; in or to a place east of the West Coast (but not necessarily in the Atlantic states). **West**

1876 *S.F. Dly. Examiner* 10 Oct 1/3 *(DA),* O! you ought to see them administer justice back East. **1940** in 1944 *ADD* **OR,** Back East. **1948** *S. Sierran* Mar 3/1 **sCA,** The whole trip had the delightful aspects of a snow trip in winter 'up north' or 'back east.' **1981** *DARE* File **swCA,** Since I can remember (b.1940), people commonly spoke of traveling in the general direction of the Atlantic seaboard as going *back east.* Such places as Wisconsin, for example, were *back east.* Likewise, the people themselves were, to my mind at least, "easterners." *Ibid* **nCA** (as of 1950s), When I was growing up, to go "back East" meant, roughly, to go anywhere east of the Mississippi River and north of the Ohio River. South of the Ohio was "down South."

2 spec: Eastward for a short distance. See also **back** adv

1915 *DN* 4.224 **wTX,** *Back East* . . . Indefinite phrase referring to any part of Texas east of the speaker, to any of the Southern states (Georgia, Alabama, etc.), but never to the Eastern [i.e. Atlantic] states. "I'm a-going back East" usually means to some point in Texas. **1951** Porter *Ragged Roads* 59 **wOK,** Every able-bodied nester was mending his gears and greasing his wagon to go back East to the harvest fields [in central Oklahoma].

backed up adj phr S Midl Cf **balled up**

Constipated.

1969 *DARE* (Qu. BB21) Infs **KY10, TN36,** Backed up. **1978** *NADS Letters* **swAR,** Backed up—I have heard my parents and older relatives use the term . . . My mother's family had been in southwestern Arkansas . . for two or three generations. *Ibid,* I recall *[backed up]* from rural South Carolina and, I think, from eastern Kentucky. I suspect it's pretty archaic—I don't think I've ever heard it at home.

backen v [back v 6 + -en]

1 usu with *(a)round, in,* or *up:* Of the wind: to shift in a counterclockwise direction. **NEng** Cf **back** v **6**

1903 *DN* 2.294 **Cape Cod MA** (as of 1850s), It blowed fresh from the northeast all day, then moderated and backened round to the northard and into the norwest. **1907** *DN* 3.240 **eME,** "The wind is backenin' around." **1909** *DN* 3.422 **Cape Cod MA.** **1945** Colcord *Sea Language* 45 **ME, Cape Cod, Long Island,** *Back(en)* round. Of the wind, to change counterclockwise, a sign of bad weather on the coast. **1967** *DARE* (Qu. B15) Inf **ME10,** The wind changing from northwest to northeast is *comin' around* (good weather); wind from the northwest to the west or southwest is *backenin' in* or *backenin' up* (storm to come).

2 To retard or delay (a process).

1942 Whipple *Joshua* 40 **UT** (as of c1860), "Sister Tuckett's having a pain or two," she said, "but I taken her some peppermint and horehound and made her a toddy." "That ought to backen 'em [=labor pains]." **1950** *WELS Suppl.,* "The bread was rising too fast so I set it in a cool place to backen it"—used by a woman (college graduate) from Maine [who] says it is common there.

back-ended adj Cf **back-end-to, half-assed**

Arsy-versy, perverse.

1904 Day *Kin o' Ktaadn* 59 **ME,** The heedlessest critter that I ever saw . . . We people 'round town kind o' thought he was "out." He always was doin' some back-ended trick.

back end of bad luck n

The worst part of something unfortunate.

1938 Rawlings *Yearling* 119 **cFL,** "Now don't he look like the back end o' bad luck?" Jody thought that Easy looked like a sick gray crane, with feathers draggled by the rain.

back-end-to adv phr For varr see quots [*EDD* back-end-fore 1886 →] **chiefly Nth** Cf **ass-end-to, hindside-to** =**backside-to.**

1926 *DN* 5.385 **ME,** *Back-end-too* [sic] . . . Reversed. "He turned back-end-too." Common. **1959** *VT Hist.* ns 27.124, Back end to: with the rear of something facing one. Common. **1965–70** *DARE* (Qu. MM2, . . *"You've got your dress on _____."*) Infs **AL3, CT25, NY155, WI13, WY5,** Back-end-to; **NJ16,** Back-end-before; **AL51, IL84,** 85, **NY9, PA72, TN36, TX54, WV21,** Back-end-front; (Qu. MM3, . . *"This is the front; you've got the whole thing turned _____."*) Infs **CT19,**

MA61, 73, **NY**136, 155, **PA**190, Back-end-to; **MA**5, Back-end-foremost.

back entry n [back + entry 2]

In bituminous coal mining: =**air course**.

1920 Fay *Gloss. Mining* 55/2, *Back entry.* The air course parallel to and below an entry. **1947** Natl. Coal Assoc. *Gloss., Back entry or back heading*— The entry used for secondary purposes in two-entry system of mining, often used only for ventilation purposes. Locally, any entry not having track in it. **1973** *PADS* 59.25 **AL, sIL, eKY,** *Back entry.*

backer n¹

=**backlog 1.**

1940–41 Cassidy *WI Atlas* **swWI,** Backer. **1969** *DARE* (Qu. D33, *When you build a fire in the fireplace, what do you call the big log that goes behind the others*) Inf **MI**110, Backer.

backer n² See tobacco

backfall See fallback n 2b

back family n Also back stock

A line of descent: one's parents or relatives of an earlier generation.

1966 *DARE* Tape **ME**2, You mean my back family, my father and mother. **1969** *DARE* FW Addit **swNJ,** All my back stock— my ancestors.

back fat n

=**fatback 1.**

1969 *DARE* (Qu. H38, *Other words for bacon*) Inf **NY**226, Back fat.

backfill n

=**flowage 1.**

1967 *DARE* FW Addit **swOR,** Backfill— the water rising from a river fills in low land.

back fin n, also attrib Chesapeake Bay area

The breast meat of the blue crab.

1946 *Sun* (Baltimore MD) 10 Aug 5/3 **eMD** *(Hench Coll.),* August is the real season . . for the old blue crab of the Chesapeake . . with lots of fat and plenty of breast meat, which is commercially called back-fin meat. **1976** Warner *Beautiful Swimmers* 189 **Chesapeake Bay,** Pierce, probe and ream out the posterior bony chambers of the [blue] crab's body section . . . Do it right and out pop nice round lumps of meat, the prized "back fin" or "jumbo lump" of commerce.

‡backfire v

To back down in an argument.

1968 *DARE* (Qu. II31) Inf **MD**24, Backfire.

backfire exclam Cf DS EE23b

In the game of **Antony-over:** =**pigtail** exclam.

1950 *WELS (What do you call if the ball does not go over the building, but comes back?)* 1 Inf, **ceWI,** Backfire!

back fly n Cf face fly, nose fly

Prob a blow fly (Calliphoridae).

1968–70 *DARE* (Qu. R12, *. . Kinds of flies . . around here*) Inf **KY**80, Back fly, face fly, heel fly; **WI**43, Back fly— it lays an egg in the hide of the back of the cow.

back forty, the n [back + forty n B1] Nth, West Cf DCan

1 A remote, large, but often arid or barren piece of land. Also fig: see quot 1958.

1950 *WELS (A large piece of land under cultivation)* 1 Inf, **ceWI,** The back forty. **1956** Ker *Vocab. W. TX* 89, Waste-land . . . "The back forty" [reported by 1 Inf]. **1958** McCulloch *Woods Words* **Pacific NW,** *Back forty*—a. The back end of an operation and beyond. b. Any distant place. c. The ideal logging show you'll never find. **1967–68** *DARE* (Qu. C33, *. . Joking names . . for an out-of-the-way place*) Infs **MN**34, **WI**47, (The) back forty; (Qu. L6b) Inf **MI**67, Back forty— derogatory— never very good land. **1969** Sorden *Lumberjack Lingo* **NEng, Gt Lakes,** *Back forty*—Way back in the brush— a long haul.

2 in phr *plow the back forty:* See quot.

1967 *DARE* (QR, near Qu. L6b) Inf **MI**67, If somebody's wasting his time: "He's been plowing the back forty."

back-front See backwards-front

back-gap n

See quot 1963.

1948 Hurston *Seraph* 95 **wFL** (as of c1920), Jim began to talk about buying an automobile. That back-gap was going to be widened into a driveway. **1963** *PADS* 40.3, *Back-gap . . .* An alley [in ref to quot 1948].

back help n Cf change work

Assistance given reciprocally, as among farmers.

1940 Yoder *Rosanna* 241 **ePA,** This threshing outfit was owned jointly [by several individual farmers] . . They helped each other thresh, and this co-operation was called "back help." **1968** *DARE* (Qu. L5) Inf **PA**75, Back help.

backhouse n Cf back adj

1954 *Harder Coll.* **cwTN,** The *bighouse* is the living room, *backhouse* is the parlor, *doghouse* is the dormer.

backhouse lily n

A day lily (*Hemerocallis* spp).

1980 *Greenfield Recorder* (MA) 21 June B3/2, And don't forget the common, inelegantly named flower, the "backhouse lily" which so often grew beside the path to the privy or backhouse. That's the one that has spread all along roadsides and makes quite a showing.

backhouse trots See backdoor trot 1

backie-horse n Also backie-ride [Scots backie a hoist onto one's back (SND, EDD)]

A ride on an adult's back; a piggyback ride.

1966–68 *DARE* (Qu. Y31) Inf **MN**12, Backie-horse; **ND**2, Backie-ride.

backing vbl n [back v 3]

The address or return address on an envelope or letter.

1928 Chapman *Happy Mt.* 292 **eTN,** 'Taint nought but a advertising letter from a mail-order [company] . . I seen that from the backing. **1954** *Harder Coll.* **cwTN,** I done went 'n put the wrong backing on 'at [=that] letter.

backings n [Cf SND, W3 backings refuse of wool, etc] S Midl

See also **backward(s)** C Cf **tailings**

Weak liquor left after distillation of whiskey.

1867 U.S. Congress *Congressional Globe* 21 Jan App 60/1 **KY,** What run now [in distilling, after the doubling tub is removed] are called "backings." . . These backings are too valuable to be lost, and are placed back into the still, run through again, and come out doublings or proof whiskey. **1911** *DN* 3.537 **eKY,** *Backings . . .* A grade of whiskey intermediate in strength between "first-shot" . . and "singlings." **1917** *DN* 4.407 **wNC, KY.** **1952** Brown *NC Folkl.* 1.517 **wNC.** **1968–69** *DARE* Tape **NC**54, After your whiskey runs out, your first shot, I'd say 220 proof [sic] . . then you can use the rest when it comes out. It comes out . . what you call backins, that's weak. Then you put so many backins in that to make it how you want to drink it, 90 proof, or 100 proof; **GA**72, When it breaks at the worm, it don't keep runnin'— but in different sections of the countries it's called different names. Here the most popular name for it is backins. **1972** *Foxfire Book* 316 **nGA,** *Backings . .* what results after beer [=fermented mash] is run through a thumperless operation once. **1974** Maurer *KY Moonshine* 113 [Glossary], *Backings or backins . . .* Low-proof liquor, not containing enough alcohol to be considered whiskey. Usually low-proof distillate near the end of a run. " . . . about a gallon backins left in the thumper."

back in the saddle (again) pred adj Cf saddle

Menstruating.

1954 *AmSp* 29.298 **TX, OK, FL** [Vernacular of menstruation], *Back in the saddle* [in use by men and women]. **1978** *MJLF* 4.1.38 **cTX,** They also used terms suggestive of feminine hygiene products: . . . "back in the saddle again" (complete with melody).

back in the woods adj phr

Unsophisticated; out of step with the times.

1965 Brown *Manchild* 278 **NYC,** Everybody was far away, way back in the woods. *Ibid* 279, The way I felt about it, I should have been their parents, because I had been out there on the streets, and I wasn't as far back in the woods as they were.

back-jaw v, n [Cf SND, EDD]

A As verb.

To answer in an insolent or hostile manner.

1928 Peterkin *Scarlet Sister Mary* 98 **eSC** [Gullah], "Yuh duh back-jaw me?" [="Are you talking back to me?"] . . "I'll back-jaw you much as I please."

B As noun.
1952 Brown *NC Folkl.* 1.517 **c,eNC**, *Back-jaw* . . . Back-talk, insolent reply. "Don't give me no back-jaw, big boy!" . . Mainly Negroes.

back jockey See **jockey**

back-kill v, hence *back-killing* vbl n, *back-killin(s)* exclam See also **back-lick**
In marble play: to strike one marble with another as it rebounds from a wall.
1922 *DN* 5.186 **KY**, *Back-kill* . . . To hit an opponent's taw while rebounding . . . A case of 'back-killing.' The owner of the taw which hits must cry out "Back-killin'(s)." If the owner of the taw "back-killed" is quicker and cries out "Vence ye back-killins," his taw is not "dead" and he may continue in the game. **1955** *PADS* 23.11 **cwTN**, *Back-kill* . . . *Back-killing.*

back kitchen n [*back* adj] **chiefly NEng** Cf **summer kitchen**
1 See quot 1966.
1849 in 1894 Lowell *Letters* 1.153 **MA**, A skunk was shot in our back-kitchen this morning. **1966** *DARE* (Qu. D10a) Inf **ME20**, Back kitchen—a room (unheated) connected to the kitchen, used for storing, deep freeze, etc.
2 in phr *hotter than hell's back-kitchen:* Extremely hot.
1949 *NY Folkl. Qrly.* 5.234 **VT**, Hotter'n hell's back-kitchen. **1958** *VT Hist.* ns 26.274 **VT**.

back-lick v
In marble play: =**back-kill.**
1955 *PADS* 2.3.11 **cwTN**, *Back-lick* . . . Heard.

back-licks n, exclam Also *back-a-licks*
In marble play: the striking of one marble by another as it rebounds from a wall.
1888 *Century Illustr. Mag.* 36.78/1 **sIL**, Their cries of 'rounses,' 'taw,' 'dubs,' 'back licks,' and 'vent' might often be heard. **1892** *DN* 1.219 **DC**, *Back-a-licks:* used in "back-a-licks takes over"; that is, if a marble hit another by rebounding from a wall, that shot shall not be counted, but another one shall be allowed. **1955** *PADS* 23.11 **cwTN**, Back-licks; no back-licks.

back line n
1 In logging: =**haulback.**
1958 McCulloch *Woods Words* **Pacific NW**, *Back line*—A haulback. **1968** *DARE* Tape **CA100**, Back line . . . A line extending from a bull donkey engine, over pulleys, into the woods to haul logs . . . sometimes two miles long.
2 In marble play: =**taw line.**
1969 *DARE* (Qu. EE8, *The line toward which the players roll their marbles before beginning a game, to determine the order of shooting*) Inf **MI101**, Back line.

backlog n
1 A large log at the rear of a wood-burning fire. **widespread** See also **backpiece, backstick** Cf **forelog**
1684 (1977) Mather *Essay Providences* 162 **RI**, The Spit was carried up Chimney, and came down with the point forward, and stuck in the Back-log. **1845** Judd *Margaret* 158 **NEng**, In the cavernous fire-place burns a great fire, composed of a huge green back-log, a large green forestick, and a high cob-work of crooked and knotty refuse-wood, ivy, hornbeam and beech. **1941** *LANE* Map 2.330, [The map shows *backlog* to be current throughout NEng]. **1952** in 1958 Brewer *Dog Ghosts* 28 **TX** [Black], Tecks his ax an' staa'ts to whackin' down a few trees so's he kin cut 'im a few backlogs for his fiahplace. **1962** *PADS* 38.66, On the basis of the interview response alone, *back log* seems to be a fairly strong Midland word. The checklists, however, point out that the term is also used widely in the Northern area. **1965–70** *DARE* (Qu. D33, . . *The big log that goes behind the others*) 516 Infs, **widespread**, Backlog.
2 Transf: a wife. *joc*
1970 *DARE* (Qu. AA15b, . . *Of the man getting married, "He _____."*) Inf **VA69**, Got a backlog—means somebody to keep his back warm.

‡back man n
A children's game similar to musical chairs: see quot.
1969 *DARE* (Qu. EE2, *Games that have one extra player: when a signal is given, the players change places, and the extra one tries to get a place*) Inf **MO20**, Back man.

back number n, also attrib; also *back-numberish* adj [*back number* an earlier copy or issue of a periodical]
A person, place or thing thought to be out of date.
1882 Peck *Peck's Sunshine* 153 **WI**, There is always some old back number of a girl who has no fellow who wants to go. **1897** *KS Univ. Qrly.* 6.51 **KS**, *Back-number* . . anything out of date or antiquated, as of a stale story or a conservative person = "has-been." **1911** Quick *Yellowstone Nights* 286 **DC**, When there's anything to be done . . repugnant to some back-number criminal law. **1913** Wharton *Custom of Country* 572 **NY**, Well, I did look like a back number, and no blame to you for thinking so. **1939** Brownell *Horse & Buggy Philos.* 199 **swMI**, They say there isn't a single [hitching] post on State Street and so why should we be back numberish and cluttered up with 'em. **1941** *LANE* Map 450 1 inf, **sNH**, Back number, a farmer who is 'behind the times.' **1969** *DARE* Tape **PA198**, It's kind of a back number, but it used to be a pretty well-to-do town.

back of nowhere See **backside of nowhere**

back of the lap n Also *backside of one's lap* *joc or euphem*
The buttocks.
1950 *WELS* 2 Infs, **WI**, Back of the lap. **1969** *DARE* (Qu. X35) Inf **GA72**, "Backside of your lap"—in the presence of ladies.

back of the rip See **rip**

back one out v phr
To challenge (one), to dare.
1840 (1847) Longstreet *GA Scenes* 28, I didn't care about trading; but you cut such high shines, that I thought I'd like to back you out, and I've done it. Gentlemen, you see I've brought him to a hack. **1911** *DN* 3.537 **eKY**, *Back out.* To dare or challenge; e.g., "I'll back you out to do it."

back one's play v phr
To support or defend a person or statement.
1930 Williams *Logger-Talk* 19 **Pacific NW**, *Backed his play:* Stood behind his statement or act. **1958** McCulloch *Woods Words* **Pacific NW**, *Back his play*—To back up a man.

back-out n **Midl** *old-fash or arch*
Cowardice; a disposition to retreat from an opponent.
1828 *Western Souvenir* 314 **KY**, There's no back out in none of my breed. **1832** Paulding *Westward Ho* 2.136 **MO**, He could whip his weight in wild cats, there being no back out in him or any of his breed. **1841** *Knickerbocker* 17.27 **WV**, There is no back out in the captain, no how. **1953** *Hall Coll.* **wNC**, There's hardly any back-out on one of them [=the Plott breed of bear dogs], for he'll fight anything from a woods mouse to a grizzly bear.

back people n pl
People who live in the back country.
1770 in 1918 *MD Hist. Mag.* 13.67, I shall write to the Back People by Mr. Roberts. **1941** *LANE* Map 450 1 inf, **cVT**, Back people, collective term for those living 'in the back country.'

backpiece n
=**backlog 1.**
1949 *AmSp* 24.106 **nwSC**, *Back-piece.*

back porch n *joc* Cf *DS* X35 Cf **front porch 1**
The buttocks.
1950 *WELS* (*Joking words for the part of the body you sit on*) 4 Infs, **WI**, Back porch.

back-porch yardmaster n
Among railroad workers: see quot.
1977 Adams *Lang. Railroader* 9, *Back-porch yardmaster:* The foreman of the yard switchmen.

back reading room See **reading room**

backroom-stretcher See **stretcher**

‡backs adv
Backward.
1967 *DARE* (Qu. JJ15, . . "*He hasn't enough sense to _____.*") Inf **AL16**, Know if he's going forwards or backs.

back-sass n, v [*DAE sass back*, 1884 →]
Impertinent talk; to speak impertinently or discourteously; hence *back-sasser* one who speaks rudely, a "smart aleck."
1950 Stuart *Hie Hunters* 213 **eKY**, "I didn't mean to backsass . . ," Arn

apologized. **1968** Kellner *Aunt Serena* 94 **sIN** (as of c1910), [The problem in arithmetic] read: "Tom's uncle gave him 10 quarts of oats. He said 'Feed the white horse 2 quarts more than the red horse, and the black horse 2 quarts more than the white horse', What do you think Tom should do?" . . "I think he should hit his uncle over the head with the feed bucket, myself." Wilbur said this wasn't arithmetic, it was backsass. **1969** *DARE* (Qu. II36a, *Somebody who talks back or gives rude answers: "Did you ever see such a _____?"*) Inf **IN**79, Back-sasser.

backset n

1 A setback; a check or reverse. [*SND* 1721 →] **chiefly Sth, S Midl**

a A reversal in one's personal or political affairs.

1816 in 1853 Calhoun *Works* 2.170 **SC,** It would give a back set, and might . . endanger their ultimate success. **1878** *Congressional Record* 7 Feb 823/1 **VA,** We cannot afford that there shall be another financial backset. **1904** (1972) Harben *Georgians* 37, Darley was a growing place. It was gradually recovering from the serious back-set given it by the war.

b usu in phr *take a backset:* A relapse during convalescence. **esp Appalachians**

1880 Cable *Grandissimes* 17 **LA,** If you don't mind her you'll have a back-set, and the devil himself wouldn't engage to cure you. **1939** *Hall Coll.* **eTN,** I like to took a back-set when I got to knockin' about. **1942** (1971) Campbell *Cloud-Walking* 248 **seKY,** She said Marthy better get back to her younguns before they et up creation and took a back-set and died off. **1944** *PADS* 2.32 **NC, nSC, cTN, VA. 1946** Stuart *Tales Plum Grove* 196 **seKY,** I feel weak as water. I'll tell you that flu is bad stuff. I got up too soon and took a back-set. **1969** *WV Hist.* 30.464 **Appalachians,** I was getting better, but now I've took a backset with this flu. **1970** *DARE* FW Addit **KY** 89. **1979** *DARE* File **SC** [Black], "He left the hospital too soon and had a backset."

2 An eddy or countercurrent of water.

a A slow or negligible current.

1860 Greeley *Overland Journey* 274 **wNV,** We contrived . . to get stuck in a bayou or back-set of the Humboldt sink. **1882** *Harper's Mag.* 65.612/1 **Missip Valley,** Much of this was slack water, or the backset caused by the overflow. **1968** *DARE* (Qu. C14) Inf **NY**92, Backset.

b A strong countercurrent.

1903 White *Forest* 94 **MI,** Jimmy . . was incontinently swept over a dam and into the boiling back-set of the eddy below.

backset v, hence *back-setting* vbl n **Upper MW** *somewhat old-fash*

To replow prairie land in autumn (thereby restoring its ridges to their original position).

1880 *Harper's Mag.* 60.531/2 **ND,** In the fall the decayed furrow is reversed, which is termed "back-setting", and then the harrow is applied to tear the turf to tatters . . . The cost of breaking, back-setting, and harrowing is about four dollars per acre. **1894** *Congressional Record* 31 July 8047/2 **MN,** In some cases it will pay to "break and back-set" the roadway to kill out the weeds. **1935** Sandoz *Jules* 60 **wNE** (as of 1880–1930), He located new settlers; in return they backset his old land and broke out more.

backside n

1 The backyard of a house. *arch*

1634 in 1896 Cambridge MA Proprietors *Records* 1, The Constable . . shall make a surueyinge of the Houses backsids . . and other lands. **1890** in 1919 Hale *Letters* 246 **RI,** Only this stirs the back side to any activity. **1899** (1912) Green *VA Folk-Speech,* Backside . . . Backyard; the yard behind the house.

2 The side of a road next to rising ground.

1949 Hornsby *Lonesome Valley* 279 **VA, NC,** Anything wide as a wagon would have to hug the backside of the road and practically graze the trees to keep from slipping over the bank.

backside of nowhere n Also *back of nowhere* *joc*

=end of nowhere.

1967–70 *DARE* (Qu. C33, . . *An out-of-the-way place, or a very unimportant place*) Infs **GA**84, 89, **KY**88, **TN**26, **TX**32, Backside of nowhere; **MI**67, Back of nowhere.

backside of one's lap See back of the lap

backside outwards adv phr

Backwards, or inside out.

1937 *Hall Coll.* **eTN,** "I put on my dress that mornin' backside

out'ards." . . A figurative expression meaning that she had bad luck all day.

backside-to adv phr Also *backside-front* For varr see quots **chiefly Nth** *somewhat old-fash* See Map See also **back-end-to, back-to** adv phr, **backwards-front, hindside-to**

Backwards; in reversed position; inside out.

1920s in 1944 *ADD* **cNY,** Backside front. **1950** *WELS* ("She had her dress on _____.") 3 Infs, **WI,** Backside to; 1 Inf, Backside foremost; 1 Inf, Backside front; 1 Inf, Backside fore. **1959** *VT Hist.* ns 27.124, Back side to . . . Inside out. **1965–70** *DARE* (Qu. MM2, . . *"You've got your dress on _____."*) 23 Infs, **chiefly Nth,** Backside-to; 11 Infs, **chiefly Nth,** Backside-front; **DC**3, **IL**34, **MD**32, **MO**13, **NJ**2, 7, 64, **PA**181, Backside-forward(s); **IL**106, **IA**8, **NY**242, Backside-before; **IL**63, **MD**30, **VT**10, Backside-foremost; (Qu. MM3, . . *This is the front; you've got the whole thing turned _____."*) Infs **AK**8, **CT**8, **MA**2, 61, 98, **NY**67, 88, 205, Backside-to; **KS**7, **TN**12, **VT**6, **WI**52, Backside-front; **NJ**19, **VT**10, Backside foremost.

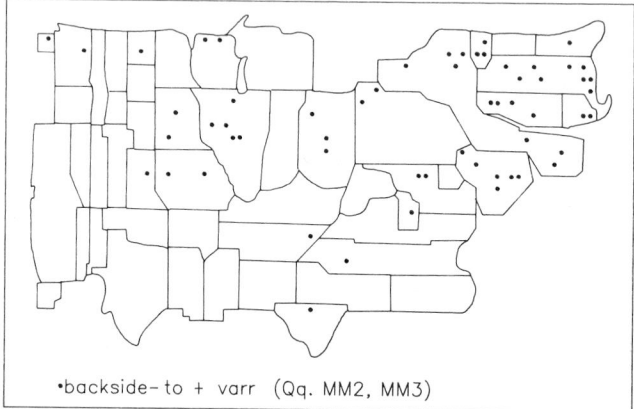

•backside-to + varr (Qq. MM2, MM3)

backsie adj, usu used as exclam Also sp *baachie, baxy* [Prob rel to Scots *bach* cow-dung] **?chiefly PA** Cf *DS* NN23 See also **bakkes**

Dirty! Filthy!

1930 Shoemaker *1300 Words* 3 **cPA Mts** (as of c1900), Baachie—Nasty tasting, filthy. **1939** Aurand *Quaint Idioms* 22 **sePA,** When youngsters in diapers get their hands in any kind of dirt, it is common to hear some adult say: "Baxy, baxy; pooh bah." (Baby talk for "dirty, dirty" . .). **1981** *DARE* File **nePA** (as of c1920), ['bæksi] was used by Pennsylvania Germans as an exclamation of warning to a child, meaning "Don't [do that]". A similar form, ['bæki], was heard in Iowa in 1979, with the same meaning.

back slap exclam Cf *DS* EE23b

In the game of **Antony-over:** =pigtail exclam.

1950 *WELS* (*What do you call if the ball does not go over the building, but comes back?*) 1 Inf, **cnWI,** Back slap.

back slaps n

A marbles game: see quot.

1950 *WELS* (*Different kinds of marble games*) 1 Inf, **ceWI,** Back slaps—played between railroad tracks; have to hit rail and come back to strike marbles.

backslider exclam Also *backslide* Nth

In the game of **Antony-over:** =pigtail exclam.

1905 *DN* 3.60 **NE,** Backslider. **1950** *WELS* 1 Inf, **cwWI,** Back slider. **1967–68** *DARE* (Qu. EE23b, . . *If you fail to get the ball over the building and it rolls back, what do you call out?*) Infs **IA**11, **WI**24, Backslider; **OR**6, Backslide.

backsliders' bench n Cf *DS* CC5

1954 *Harder Coll.* **cwTN,** Backsliders' bench(es)—Seats toward the back of the church.

‡backslode ppl adj

Backslidden; reprobate.

1949 Webber *Backwoods Teacher* 129 **sAppalachians,** Wanted to be baptized, but I never was in a backslode condition, livin' with them two ladies.

back (something) off the boards v phr

To surpass.

1922 *DN* 5.155 **eNE,** This radiator's got the one in my apartment backed off the boards.

backstaff n Cf **backstay**

A support; also fig.

1953 Randolph *Down in Holler* 225 **Ozarks,** Back-staff . . . A support. When a mountain man says that a certain tale "has got a *back-staff* behind it," he means that it is supported by substantial evidence.

backstall v

1952 Brown *NC Folkl.* 1.517, Backstall . . . To hold back; "to stall back." . . Rare.

backstand v [Transf from hunting: *backstand* to point when another hound points]

To support or stand behind another.

1938 *Sun* (Baltimore MD) 28 Mar 7/4 *(Hench Coll.),* He has a right to be uppity—and from Matchitank on the south, to Clam on the north—folks will backstand Amos [a coon dog]. **1940** *Hench Coll.* **VA,** A native Virginian (on the Univ Va faculty) said of someone standing up for the position taken by another man, "He'll backstand you every time."

backstay n Cf **backstaff**

The background of a story or event.

1953 Randolph *Down in Holler* 225 **Ozarks,** Back-stay . . . The background, history, or antecedents that explain an occurrence. A story or anecdote is much more interesting after some old-timer tells you the *back-stay.* Judge Tom Moore . . says that the word was common at the turn of the century, but is seldom heard now.

back-step n **S Midl** *old-fash*

A dance-step: see quots.

1899 (1912) Green *VA Folk-Speech,* Back-step . . . A step in dancing; by placing one foot behind the other, alternately. **1966–69** *DARE* (Qu. FF5a, . . *Dance steps . . in past years*) Infs **AR**18, **KY**19, Back-step; **IN**13, Back-step—a comical, backward "two-step"; **KY**5, Square dance steps—double-shuffle, back-step; **KY**45, Back-step—old fashioned; [**MO**37, Back-stepped].

backstick n **chiefly sAppalachians, Gulf States** See Map Cf **forestick**

=**backlog 1.**

1852 *Harper's Mag.* 6.132, What cared we for that, as we sat by the old-fashioned fire? Log, back-stick, fore-stick, top-stick, and superstructure, all in their place. **1877** *VT State Bd. Ag. Report* 4.92, The boy would . . return to the wood-yard for the back stick and fore stick. **1941** *LANE* Map 330 *(Log)* 1 inf, **seMA,** Backstick. **c1960** *Wilson Coll.* **csKY. 1962** Atwood *Vocab. TX* 45 **c,eTX,** There are nine Texas occurrences of *back stick,* a term that shows somewhat more currency in southern Arkansas. **1963** Edwards *Gravel* 92 **eTN** (as of 1920s), The dull glow on the back-stick played on his spectacles. **1965–70** *DARE* (Qu. D33) 29 Infs, **chiefly sAppalachians, Gulf States,** Backstick; **LA**6, Backstick of wood.

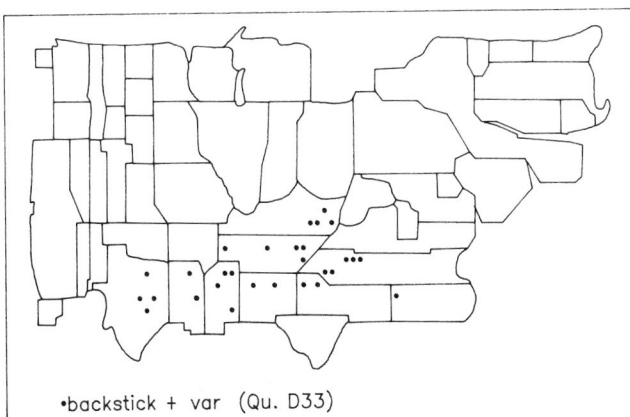

•backstick + var (Qu. D33)

back stock See **back family**

backstrap n

1 See **backband.**

2 also sp *backstrop:* Venison sliced from the back of a deer. [Cf

DA backstrap v (under *back* 3), "to remove a back strip from pork"]

1904 White *Mountains* 185 **SW,** Next in order is the "back strap" and tenderloin . . . Deer-steak, to my notion, is best broiled. **1926** *AmSp* 1.414 **seGA,** I ain't eat a piece er venison since the Lord knows when . . . In them days I hardly ever eat a mess in there . . without a good piece er back-strop. **1938** Rawlings *Yearling* 250 **FL,** Penny cut out the backstraps from the fattest buck and sliced them for frying for supper . . . "I'll leave you fry that backstrap when I'm done with the pan."

back street n

1 A poor, usu residential, district.

1967–68 *DARE* (Qu. C35, . . *Different parts of your town or city*) Inf **CO**47, Back street—where the cribs [=brothels] were; **NY**92, Back street—one part [of town]; (Qu. II25, . . *The part of town where the poorer people . . live*) Inf **LA**32, The back street; **NY**92, Back street, tobacco road.

2 A predominantly Black neighborhood. **MD** Cf **black belt 2**

1968 *DARE* (Qu. C35) Inf **MD**32, Back street—Negro section in Elton; **MD**48, Back street—Negro area of Bel Air; (Qu. II25) Inf **MD**36, Back street—where colored people live—means any street, as opposed to main street.

3 See quot.

1967–68 *DARE* (Qu. FF5b, *More recent dance steps*) Infs **LA**6, 37, (The) back street.

backstrop See **backstrap 2**

backswath v [*backswath* n]

To turn around a mower or reaper and cut in the opposite direction.

1917 *DN* 4.387 **neOH, VT, IL, NY,** Backswath . . . To reverse a mower or reaper and drive the horses back in the swath just cut, so as to cut the hay or grain just passed over by the machine and horses without being cut. Done in beginning a field of hay or grain. **1927** *AmSp* 2.348 **wcWV,** *Back swath* . . , to cut around the field in the opposite direction from that used in mowing the grass, in order to cut the grass driven over when the driver enters the field.

backswitch n [Reversed compound: see Intro "Language Changes" I.1]

1939 *Hall Coll.* **eTN,** Backswitch . . . Switchback on a trail or railroad [used by two speakers]. This word illustrates the mountain tendency to reverse the order of elements in compounds.

backtalking vbl n

Gossiping conversation.

1968 *DARE* (Qu. V1, *When you suspect . . that something is going on behind your back, you say, "There's _____."*) Inf **MI**97, Backtalking.

back teeth are floating phr For varr see quots *joc* Cf **backwater** n **2**

1 One's bladder is very full.

1914 *DN* 4.102 **KS,** Back teeth under water . . . Descriptive of distress from fullness of the bladder. **1923** *DN* 5.200 **swMO,** Back teeth's a-floatin' . . . To express painful fullness of the bladder. **1950** *WELS* 1 Inf, **cWI,** Back teeth are floating. **1967–69** *DARE* (Qu. BB20, *Joking . . expressions for overactive kidneys*) Infs **NY**34, **PA**202, (My) back teeth are floating; **CT**3, **NC**72, **OH**4, (My, your) teeth are floating; **IN**13, Jaw teeth's a-floatin'.

2 One has imbibed to excess.

1888 *Missouri Republican* Jan 25 (Farmer–Henley *Slang* 90), On Friday night . . in company with . . other gentlemen, his honour once more drank until, as an onlooker put it, his back teeth were well afloat.

back the breeze v phr Cf **back** v **6**

To talk excessively.

1958 McCulloch *Woods Words* **Pacific NW,** Backin' the breeze—A man so gabby he makes the wind blow backwards.

back-tick exclam Cf *DS* EE23b

In the game of **Antony-over:** =**pigtail** exclam.

1950 *WELS* (What do you call if the ball does not go over the building, but comes back?) 1 Inf, **cnWI,** Back-tick.

back-to adv phr See also **back-to** adj Cf **backside-to**

With one's back toward (someone or something).

1950 Moore *Candlemas Bay* 207 **ME,** Evelyn had stayed back-to at the drain board, hoping she might be able, in some way, to avoid facing a stranger.

back-to adj

Of a church: see quot.

1971 *Courier-Gaz.* (Rockland ME) 15 Aug 20/1 **eME,** In the late 1840s . . . the building was changed from the typical meeting house to what is colloquially known as a "back-to" church . . . Bench pews were made to face the pulpit and entrance doors. Thus the designation "back-to"; in most churches the pews face away from the entrance.

‡back-tooth hog n

1966 DARE (Qu. K55, *A pig that doesn't grow well and is not worth keeping*) Inf **DC8,** Back-tooth hog—can't eat corn.

back to taw adv phr [Cf *OED taw* sb[2] c for similar phrr]

In marble play: see quot.

1955 *PADS* 23.11 **TN,** *Back to taw* . . . In certain situations a player must return to the point from which he rolled or shot his marble.

back to the farm adj phr

Among railroad workers: laid off; fired.

1945 Hubbard *Railroad Ave.* 331 [Glossary], *Back to the farm*—Laid off on account of slack business. When a man is discharged he is given *six months twice a year.* **1977** Adams *Lang. Railroader.*

back up a car length v phr

1897 *KS Univ. Qrly.* 6.85 **MO,** *Back up a car length:* to be thus addressed signifies that your tale is improbable and should be modified. From the R[ail] R[oad].

backward-front See backwards-front

backward in coming forward adj phr Also *backward in going forward* [*OEDS* 1830 →]

Reluctant, shy.

1899 (1912) Green *VA Folk-Speech* 24, Backward in coming forward. **1927** *AmSp* 3.136 **ME,** A pushing individual was "not backward in going forward." **1969** DARE (Qu. AA11, *If a man asks a woman to marry him and she refuses*) Inf **MA42,** She'd be backward in comin' forward.

backward(s) adj, adv, n Usu |'bækwǝ(r)d(z)| also, esp **Sth, Midl** |'bækǝ-d(z)|; in r-less areas, occas |'bækwʊd(z)| Pronc-spp *back'ard(s), backwoods*

A Forms.

1841 Cooper in 1944 *ADD,* Back'ard. **1887** *Scribner's Mag.* 2.479 **AR,** Gwine back'ards and for'ards on the river. **1891** *DN* 1.162 **cNY,** ['bækǝ-dz], 'backwards.' **1908** *DN* 3.281 **eAL, wGA. 1915** *DN* 4.178 **swVA. 1929** Sale *Tree Named John* 85 **MS,** Ah fus' step over dem tracks en had a step back ove'm ag'in back'ards. **1933** *AmSp* 8.1.51 **Ozarks,** He's jest a-fixin' t' fall over back'ards. **1936** *AmSp* 11.235 **eTX,** The loss of [w] is usual in . . backwards . . ['bækǝ-dz]. **1942** Hall *Smoky Mt. Speech* 93 **eTN, wNC,** ['bækǝ-dz]. **1954** *Harder Coll.* **cwTN,** Backwards ['bækǝ-dz] . . . She had her dress on backards. **1965–68** DARE (Qq. MM2, 3) Infs **AR22, LA7, MS61, NC37,** Back'ards; **MA4,** ['bækwʊdz]. **1966** *Wilson Coll.* **csKY,** Backwards ['bækǝ-dz]. **1966** DARE Tape **NC29,** The woof is the thread that goes in the bobbin that goes back'ards ['bækǝ-dz] and for'ards. **1975** DARE File **MA,** My brother wrote to tell me he could "skate backwoods."

B As adv.

In phr *to get up backwards:* to be irritable; to get up "on the wrong side of the bed." See also **hindside to**

1941 *Hall Coll.* **wNC,** Me and Blondie got up backwards this morning. **1952** Brown *NC Folkl.* 1.364, He got up backward.

C As noun.

=backings.

1938 *Hench Coll.* **cVA,** A resident native of Blackwell's Hollow . . commented . . . that the new liquor was weak in contrast to moonshine: "It's as poor as back'ards." He explained, when asked, that back'ards is wine made from mash that has already been used once.

backwards-front adv phr Also *back-front, backward-front* For addit varr see quots See also **backside-to**

Backwards; inside out.

1950 *WELS* ("She had her dress on _____.") 1 Inf, **cWI,** Back-front. **1967–69** DARE (Qu. MM2, . . "*Look, you've got your dress on _____.*") Infs **HI13, IL52,** Backward(s)-front; **KY19,** Backwards-behind; **OR4,** Backwards-way-before; (Qu. MM3) Inf **WI6,** Backwards-in.

backwater n

Std senses, in var fig phrr:

1 in phr *take backwater,* occas *take water:* To change course, reverse one's position, retreat. **chiefly Midl** Cf **back water** v phr

1902 Harben *Abner Daniel* 136 **GA,** I didn't honestly think there was a man in Georgia that could give me any tips about investments, but I had to take back water, and for a woman. **1909** *DN* 3.379 **eAL, wGA. 1939** *AmSp* 14.92 **cTN,** He took back water on what he said about the preacher. *Ibid* 262 **IN,** A quiet, easygoing man . . , when threatened with a fight, 'crawfishes' or 'takes backwater.' **1965–70** DARE (Qu. II31, . . *"He saw that he was wrong, so he started to _____."*) 17 Infs, **chiefly Midl,** Take backwater; **IL14, NC33, NJ2, VA31, 91,** Take water; (Qu. JJ40) Inf **GA72,** Take backwater.

2 See quot. *joc* Cf **back teeth are floating**

1950 *WELS* (*Joking or nicknames for over-active kidneys*) 1 Inf, **cWI,** The backwater is standing in my eyes.

back water v phr [Transf from naut use: see quots 1859, 1945] **chiefly Nth, Atlantic** *esp among male speakers* Cf **backwater** n 1

To retreat, withdraw, as from an argument or position.

1844 *Times-Picayune* (New Orleans LA) 17 Mar 1/6, Day before yesterday Boston waked up under a new coverlid of snow, dropped from the clouds over-night. This makes business *back water.* **1859** (1968) Bartlett *Americanisms, To back water* . . . To retreat, or withdraw; a Western metaphor, derived from steamboat language. **1905** *DN* 3.2 **cCT. 1907** *DN* 3.208 **nwAR. 1919** Kyne *Capt. Scraggs* 150 **CA,** In order to earn that fifty dollars, I got to back water. It wouldn't be playin' fair if I didn't. **1945** Colcord *Sea Language* 28 **ME, Cape Cod, and Long Island,** *Back water.* To row a boat backwards. In shore speech it means to retract or hedge. **1950** *PADS* 14.12 **SC. 1952** Brown *NC Folkl.* 1.517 c, **eNC. 1954** *Harder Coll.* **cwTN. c1960** *Wilson Coll.* **csKY,** When I began to tell him off, he began to back water. **1965–70** DARE (Qu. II31, . . *"He saw that he was wrong, so he started to _____."*) 28 Infs, **chiefly Nth, Atlantic,** Back water. [Of all Infs responding to the question, 47% were men; of those giving this response, 82% were men]; **ME5,** Backwatered; (Qu. JJ25, . . *"He thought he could take the place over, but I made him _____."*) 9 Infs, **NEast,** Back water.

backwater exclam

In the game of **Antony-over:** =**pigtail** exclam.

1969 DARE (Qu. EE23b) Inf **MI92,** Backwater.

backway n [Engl dial in same sense; see *EDD backway* sb.[1]] *?obs*

1899 (1912) Green *VA Folk-Speech,* Backway . . . The yard or space at the back of a house.

backways adv [*EDD backway* wrongly, awkwardly] See also **hindside-backways** Cf *DJE*

Backward.

1968 DARE (Qq. MM2, 3) Inf **LA45,** Backways.

backwooder See backwoodser

backwoods See backward(s)

backwoodser n Also *backwooder, backwoodster* **?chiefly Midl** *often joc* See also **backwoods jockey, backwoodsey**

A countrified person; a rustic.

c1935 in 1944 *ADD* **nWV,** Backwoodster . . . A rustic. **1940** in 1944 *ADD* **PA, WV, OH,** Backwoodser . . . A backwoodsman . . Reported by one person. **1941** *LANE* Map 450 (*A Rustic*) 1 inf, **swNH,** Backwooder. **1965–68** DARE (Qu. HH1, *Names and nicknames for a rustic or countrified person*) Infs **DE1, GA44, MS56, NJ3,** Backwooder. **1967** *IN Engl. Jrl.* 2.2–3.1 **IN,** Expressions for people from the country who look awkward and out of place in town . . . include *backwooder, backwoodsman, clod.* **1968** DARE Tape **MO25,** He ran into a lot of hardship because lots of these backwooders . . could speak no English. **1973** Allen *LAUM* 1.349 **IA,** Backwooder [1 inf].

‡backwoodsey n

1970 Tarpley *Blinky* 266 **neTX,** *A poor white from the back country* . . 8.5% [of 200 infs gave the responses] backwoodsman, backwoodsey.

backwoods gawky See gawky n

‡**backwoods jockey** n *joc*

A farmer.

1954 *Milwaukee Jrl.* (WI) 20 July green sheet 4, [Cartoon caption:] Here comes a backwoods jockey—Let's ask him or his mule!

backy n¹ Also *backy-house* **?Sth** Cf **bakkie**

A backhouse; a privy.

1908 *DN* 3.288 eAL, wGA, Backhouse . . . also called *backy.* **1949** *AmSp* 24.109 e,neGA, Backy . . . Privy. *Ibid* neGA, Backy-house. **1967–70** *DARE* (Qu. M21b) Infs KY90, LA12, Backy.

backy n² See **tobacco**

backyard n

Std sense, in var fig phrr: see quots.

c1970 *Halpert Coll.* wKY, First clean up your own backyard—don't talk about other people if there is anything you do wrong. [Also:] Clean up your own backyard before you look into others' yards. *Ibid*, Stay in your own backyard—mind your own business.

backyard bridge See **back-alley bridge**

backyard cousin n Cf **backyard relation**

1983 *DARE* File cwMA, Backyard cousin—Heard from an 81-year-old woman who didn't specify illegitimacy. She said, "A backyard cousin is somebody you're not especially proud to own."

backyard garbage See **back-alley bridge**

backyard relation n Cf **yard child** and *DS* Z11a, b

A relative by illegitimate birth.

1939 (1962) Thompson *Body & Britches* 498 **NY**, He's a backyard relation: (their cat came over into our yard once).

backyard telephone booth See **telephone booth**

backyard trots See **backdoor trot 1**

back yonder adv, sometimes quasi-noun **chiefly S Midl** See also **away** adv **1**

In former days, many years ago; a time in the remote past.

1899 (1912) Green *VA Folk-Speech*, Back yonder . . . A long time ago. "Away back yonder." **1906** *DN* 3.125 nwAR, It happened some time away back yonder. **1925** *DN* 5.356 sSC, eGA [Black]. **1938** Stuart *Dark Hills* 30 **KY**, I don't know what this world is a-comin' to. Back yander in my day it was different. **1963** Edwards *Gravel* 8 eTN (as of 1920s), Renewal of association with Speedwell folks made me know again that "there ain't no differents now from back yonder." **1966** *DARE* (Qu. A24, . . *"He's been hot-tempered from _____."*) InfSC6, Way back yonder. **1967–70** *DARE* Tapes SC46, TN51, (Way) back yonder. **1967–69** *DARE* FW Addit ceNC, Back yonder—old days— old fashioned; seTN, Back yonder—a long time ago—heard in conversation with country people, reminiscing about when they were young.

bacon n, v Usu |ˈbekən|, rarely |ˈbekŋ|, beˈkin, ˈbikən| Pronc-spp *bakin, bakun*

A Forms.

1843 (1916) Hall *New Purchase* 459 **IN**, King's tuk the bakun with him. **1922** Gonzales *Black Border* 288 sSC, GA coast [Gullah glossary], Bakin—bacon. **1941** *AmSp* 16.10 eTX [Black], Bacon, [ˈbekŋ]. **1968** [see **bacon B**]. c1970 Pederson *Dial. Survey Rural GA* seGA [Black], 1 inf, [ˈbɪˣkən].

B As noun.

Pork cured in salt or brine. **chiefly Sth, S Midl** Also called **salt pork, white bacon**

1740 (1942) Byrd *Another Secret Diary* 82 **VA**, Several gentlemen came . . and dined and I ate bacon and greens. **1877** Bartlett *Americanisms* 132, In the South . . . "bacon and *collards*" are a universal dish. **1899** (1912) Green *VA Folk-Speech* 72, Bacon . . . Pork. **1904** *DN* 2.416 nwAR, Bacon . . . Pork. Cured hog meat is bacon; fresh hog meat, pork. c1960 *Wilson Coll.* csKY. **1962** Atwood *Vocab.* TX 62, For the sides of pork preserved in salt, usually at home, *salt pork* is most frequent . . . Other terms in occasional use in Texas include *bacon, side bacon*. **1968** *DARE* (Qu. H38) Inf LA33, Bakeen [,beˈkɪn]—salt meat, unsmoked salted pork [FW: Inf's spelling]. **1971** Wood *Vocab.* Change 43 **Sth**, Blocks of meat cut from the sides of a hog and salted . . . *Middlin(g)s* and *bacon* range in choice from one-tenth to nearly one-third everywhere. **1973** Allen *LAUM* 1.290, [Ten] scattered infs., mostly in North Dakota, use *bacon* to designate salt pork.

C As verb.

Also *bacon up:* To convert into bacon.

1821 (1909) Thomas *Diary* 2.76 **MA**, Sent Legs of Pork to be baconed. **1829–30** Dunglison in *Va. Lit. Mus.* 102 *(DA)*, In Virginia, we hear of a man intending to 'bacon his pork.' **1890** *Congressional Record* 20 Aug 8887/1 **MS**, We consumed or sold our own pork, and we baconed it ourselves. **1917** *DN* 4.407 wNC, Reckon I'll haffter kill that hog and bacon it up.

bacon beetle n Also *bacon bug*

The larder beetle *(Dermestes lardarius).*

1832 Williamson *Hist. ME* 1.171, Dermestes Lardarius; *Bacon Beetle.* **1837** (1962) Williams *Territory FL* 68, The Insects of Florida are numerous . . . Those most common, are . . Bacon Bug.—Dermestes. **1854** Emmons *Agriculture NY* 5.60, The *Dermestes lardarius* commits the depredations in houses, usually in furs, meat, pork, bacon (whence it is sometimes called *bacon bug*). **1889** *Century Dict.* 1553/2, Dermestes . . . One species, *D. lardarius,* is known by the name of bacon-beetle.

bacon meat n Cf Intro "Language Changes" I.4

1952 Brown *NC Folkl.* 1.517 wNC, Bacon-meat . . . Bacon.

‡**bacon sprout** n [Cf *OED bacon hog* 1709 →]

A young pig.

1970 *DARE* (Qu. K51) Inf KY86, Bacon sprout.

bacon-stretcher See **stretcher**

bacon up See **bacon C**

bacquero See **buckaroo**

bactize v Pronc-sp for *baptize* See Pronc Intro 3.I.14 **SC, GA coasts** *Gullah*

Baptize.

1888 Jones *Negro Myths* 54 **GA coast**, Me prommus fuh bactize er chile dis berry hour. **1922** Gonzales *Black Border* 288 sSC, GA coasts [Gullah glossary], Bactize—baptize, baptizes, baptized, baptizing.

bad adj

A Gram forms.

Compar *badder;* superl *baddest.* *chiefly among less educ speakers* Cf **-er** compar suff, **-est**

1908 *DN* 3.284 eAL, wGA, Badder, baddest. **1940** *AmSp* 15.52 sAppalachians, Baddest. **1953** Brewer *Word Brazos* 81 seTX [Black], Anytime a Texas Nigguh git bad de peoples say, "Dat Nigguh mus' be from de Brazos Bottoms," 'case dey hab de record for bein' de baddes' Nigguhs in de whole state. **1967** *DARE* (Qu. X52, . . *A person . . who had been sick was looking*) Inf OH12, Badder. **1980** Folb *Runnin' Down* 125 sCA [Black], My cousin, Titus Hanes, is badder. He taught Dawson everythang he know.

B Senses.

1 Seriously ill or injured. [*OED bad* 8, 1748 →; *EDD bad* 2] See also **bad sick**

1716 (1901) Hempstead *Diary* (*AmSp* 15.226) **CT**, Joshua was taken Extream bad about Midnight. **1737** (1974) Parkman *Diary* 1.42 **MA**, I was called away . . to see old Captain Byles, who was very bad with his Throat. **1840** (1841) Dana *Two Years* 405, One of our watch was laid up for two or three days by a bad hand, (for in cold weather the least cut or bruise ripens into a sore). **1889** Nelson *50 Yrs.* 339 **West**, Frank . . was now very bad, and we did not know what to do with him. I went again up the hill and dug some roots, which I cut up and placed on the wound. **1963** Edwards *Gravel* 105 eTN (as of 1920s), Hey, Doc, git up as soon as ye can and go to Mark Lane's. His wife is awful bad. **1965–70** *DARE* (Qu. BB42, *If a person is very sick, you say he's _____*) 15 Infs, **scattered**, Bad; CA17, CO20, FL39, IL123, IN76, MD28, PA133, Real bad; CT9, FL17, MO14, PA70, Very bad; MD35, NY126, 213, Pretty bad; KY10, VA1, Awful bad; MO16, PA199, Really bad.

2 Not well; out of sorts; enervated. **chiefly Sth, S Midl** See Map on p. 126

1954 Harder *Coll.* cwTN, Dog if I ain't feelin' bad dis mornin'; ain't hardly able [to] drag one foot fore othern. **1965–70** *DARE* (Qu. BB39, *On a day when you don't feel right, though not actually sick . . "I'll be all right tomorrow—I'm just feeling _____ today."*) 68 Infs, **chiefly Sth, S Midl**, Bad; (Qu. KK30, *Feeling slowed up or without energy*) 10 Infs, **Sth, S Midl**, Bad.

3 Sorrowful; depressed. [See *EDD bad* 3]

1839 Marryat *Diary* 2.33, *Bad* is used in an odd sense; it is employed for

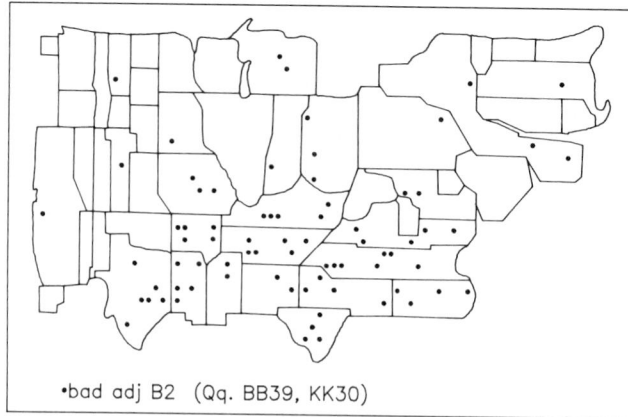

•bad adj B2 (Qq. BB39, KK30)

awkward, uncomfortable, sorry . . . "Se [sic] was so *bad,* I thought she would cry," sorry. **1871** Eggleston *Hoosier Schoolmaster* 83 **IN,** "Why, how do you feel?" "Kind o' bad and lonesome, and like as if I wanted to die." **1887** Freeman *Humble Romance* 138 **NEng,** I felt too bad to cry. **1954** *Harder Coll.* **cwTN,** *Bad* . . . depressed.

4 foll by infin or *for:* Very much inclined, very likely or prone. **chiefly Appalachians, esp wNC, eTN** See also **awful 3, easy adj 3**

1918 *DN* 5.20 **NC,** He is bad to fight. **1939** *Hall Coll.* **wNC, eTN,** "He was bad to hunt coon." "She is awful bad to talk." "Old Sam McGaha was a bad man to drink." "Little John Cable was perty bad to cuss." **1942** Warnick *Garrett Co. MD* 3 (as of 1900–1918), *Bad for that* . . . prone to. "John is so bad for that." **1960** Hall *Smoky Mt. Folks* 24 **eTN, wNC,** Zeke was the meanest of the lot. He burned Creek George's barn an' cut the years (ears) off a man named Miles. Zeke was awful bad to drink. **1967** Green *Horse Tradin'* 4 **West,** He was hard to saddle, hard to mount . . hard to ride—although he was not bad to buck. **1967** *DARE* FW Addit **swNC,** *I'm bad to*—I do it often, unfortunately. "I'm bad to talk like that." **1968** *Foxfire* 2.3-4.23 **cwNC,** "Bad" often indicates excessive interest . . . "He was awful bad to pay attention to the signs," means that he was very interested in the use of the signs of the zodiac for planting his crops and the like. **1968–70** *DARE* (Qu. DD9a, . . *"He's _____."*) Inf **NC49,** Bad for smoking; (Qu. GG8, . . *"Be careful what you say to him, he's _____."*) Inf **TN66,** Bad to take exception. **1976** Wolfram–Christian *Appalachian Speech* 173, Well, now my folks never was bad to use whiskey for anything like that [=toothache].

5 with *after:* Intensely desirous. See also **bad off 3**

1941 Stuart *Men of Mts.* 252 **neKY,** How would you like to . . see your dream-wife in the arms of a man bad after women.

6 Good, excellent, worthy of esteem or value; hence *baddest* best. *chiefly among Black speakers* See also **bad-doing, bad hair, bad nigger, bad rags**

1958 *PADS* 30.43 [Language of jazz musicians], *Bad* . . . Good . . . The listener must determine meaning fr[om] context, tone of voice, facial expression . . . Occ., older. **1965** Brown *Manchild* 281 **NYC** [Black], The slang had changed. In this day when somebody would say something about a bad cat, they meant that he was good. **1970** *DARE* (Qq. KK1a, b . . , *Very good, for example, . . "That pie was _____"; "His farm is _____."*) Inf **MO30,** Bad; (Qu. W38, *When a man dresses himself in his best clothes, you say he's _____*) Inf **VA39,** Bad—younger slang usage. [Both Infs Black] **1970** *DARE* Tape **OH100** [White], You might describe someone's clothes, as being bad, or sharp, or something like that. Or cool, or groovy. **1977** Smitherman *Talkin* 59 [Black], *He is a bad dude* would suggest to whites the idea of an undesirable character, whereas to blacks it would indicate a highly desirable person. *Ibid* 225, You ever hear of the Titanic? . . . Now this here ship was the biggest and baddest ship ever to sail the sea. **1980** Folb *Runnin' Down* 35 [Black], Like if you have a buncha friends, he the baddest. Real tight partner.

7 in var combs: Malicious, devilish, noxious. (Note: whereas *bad* is most commonly employed in a privative sense, "not good," *DARE* evidence sugg several regional combinations in which *bad* has retained absolute force, "evil") [See *OED bad* a.5-8] **chiefly Sth, Midl** See also **bad child, bad man 2, bad place, bad religion, bad sick**

[**1912** Green *VA Folk-Speech, Bad* . . . Leading an evil life. "He's been pretty bad in his time."] **1981** *AmSp* 56.40, In the South and Midland, the formative *bad* enters into several combinations with meanings that are not employed elsewhere. Thus *bad man* is a euphemism for the 'devil,' and *bad place* for 'hell' . . , with geographical distributions strikingly similar to that for *bad child.*

8 Of an animal: bad-tempered, mean. **chiefly Sth, Midl**

1965–70 *DARE* (Qu. K16, *A cow with a bad temper*) Infs **GA16, MO8, NC79, 81, SC26, TX16, 37,** Bad cow; **DC5, OH65,** Bad; (Qu. K42, *A horse that is rough, wild or dangerous*) Infs **AL11, GA3, KY58, NC26, PA1, VA68, WI6,** Bad horse; **DC1, IN69,** Bad actor; **PA10,** Bad one; (Qu. K68, . . *A goat that habitually strikes people*) Infs **MS60, MO3,** Bad goat; **MS1,** Bad billy; **MD38,** Bad buck.

bad *adv*

1 In a bad or faulty manner; poorly, wrongly.

1816 in 1915 *MD Hist. Mag.* 10.273 **MD,** Land of not much Account farm'd bad. **1831** (1940) Motte *Charleston to Harvard* 93 **SC,** It is not quite so certain that some light-fingered rogue may not behave bad by paying his devotions to my chattels in my absence. **1891** (1905) Ryan *Told in Hills* 333 **WA,** I was just mean enough to treat her pretty bad—flung her on the floor when she tried to stop me.

2 Very; very much; severely. Note: in post-verbal position, as *I want to go so bad,* this usage is **widespread;** in other, esp pre-adj positions, this usage is **appar Sth, Midl.** Cf **bad sick**

1845 Hooper *Advent. Simon Suggs* 24 **AL,** Bob kin do it, it's reasonable to s'pose that old Jed'diah Suggs won't be bothered *bad. Ibid* 94, "Pshaw!" said Suggs, "you aint bad hurt." **1859** (1922) Jackson *Col.'s Diary* 21 **PA,** Some of them appeared bad scared. **1905** *DN* 3.3 **CT.** **1907** *DN* 3.209 **nwAR.** **1926** Roberts *Time of Man* 266 **KY,** I was bad cut up over that and throwed away all the money ever I had saved up. **1939** *Hall Coll.* **wNC,** This water's not bad cold. **1967** Green *Horse Tradin'* 152 **West,** The next morning it was a bad cold morning. **1969** *DARE* (Qu. BB27) Inf **KY19,** Struck bad awful fast.

bad-ass(ed) *adj, n chiefly among Black speakers*

Mean-tempered; a belligerent person; see also quot 1980.

1956 *AmSp* 31.191, A marine who postures toughness is sarcastically labeled a *badass* or a *hairy-assed marine.* **1970** Abrahams *Deep Down* 79 **Philadelphia PA** [Black], I'm that bad-ass so-and-so they call 'Stacko-lee' . . . I'ma . . . reach in my cashmere and pull out my bad-ass gun. **1970** *DARE* (Qu. HH17) Inf **CA177,** Bad-ass, hard guy, heavy dude. **1972** *Intellectual Digest* Aug 6, Melvin Van Peebles, the . . Chicago-born black militant whose *Sweet Sweetback's Baadasssss Song* is the most violently successful independent movie ever made . . has no place of his own. **1980** Folb *Runnin' Down* 228 [Black], *Bad-ass(ed)* . . . Mean . . . Belligerent . . . Worthless . . . Shiftless (negative intensifier).

bad child *n* [**bad** *adj* **B7**] **chiefly Sth, Midl** See Map *esp freq among Blacks*

A malicious or devilish child.

1965–70 *DARE* (Qu. Z16, *A small child who is rough, misbehaves, and doesn't obey*) 50 Infs, **chiefly Sth, Midl,** Bad child. [16 Infs Black]

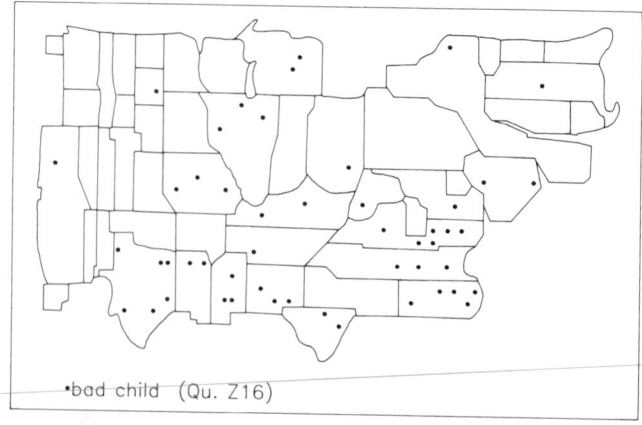

•bad child (Qu. Z16)

bad clothes See **bad rags**

bad day See **bad time**

bad disease n Also *bad disorder* chiefly *sAppalachians*

A venereal disease.

1899 (1912) Green *VA Folk-Speech, Bad disorder* . . . Venereal disease. **1930** Shoemaker *1300 Words* cPA Mts (as of c1900), *Bad disorder.* **1949** Nelson *Backwoods Teacher* 247 *(Hench Coll.)* sAppalachians, Hi Slocum carried an extra large "seed-hog's tush" in his pocket when he went "a visitin'," because . . it was the surest way to keep from getting "ary bad disease." **1958** *PADS* 29.7 **TN,** Syphilis is always referred to as the bad disease. c1960 *Wilson Coll.* csKY, *Bad disease* . . . Any venereal disease. "I'm afraid that boy's got a bad disease."

baddo See **bateau** A

bad-doing adj [**bad** adj B6]

First-rate, superior.

1965 Brown *Manchild* 304 **NYC,** Any decent, self-respecting whore could pull at least two hundred dollars on Saturday night in some of the bad-doing bars on 125th Street. *Ibid* 281, Somebody would . . see Sidney Poitier in a film, and they'd say, "Man, that's a bad-doin' nigger."

baddy-bread See **batter bread** 1

bad eye n *chiefly among Black speakers* Cf **bad mouth** n 1

The evil eye: a curse or threatening glance.

1887 (1967) Harris *Free Joe* 231 ceGA, Den de Miss Stucky won't git atter you wid de kyards en cunjur you. Dat de 'oman got er mighty bad eye, mon. **1970** Major *Afro-Amer. Slang, Bad eye:* a threatening glance. **1970** *DARE* (Qu. CC14, . . *Where one person supposedly casts a spell over another*) Inf OH95, Gave him the bad eye.

bad-feeling days See **bad time**

badger n

1 A lead miner. [See quot 1937]

1834 in 1941 *AmSp* 16.105 **MO,** Badgers von den Blei minen Missouris [=Badgers from the lead mines of Missouri]. **1835** Hoffman *Winter in West* (NY) 1.176, There was . . a keen-eyed leather-belted "badger" from the mines of Ouisconsin. **1937** Shankle *Nicknames* 588, *Badger* . . . was applied to the early lead miners, who on first coming to a new location dug in the side of a hill and lived under ground much as the badger digs in his burrow.

2 also attrib: A native or resident of Wisconsin—a nickname first applied to lead miners in southwestern Wisconsin.

1835 [see **1** above]. **1844** *Knickerbocker* 24.286 **WI,** Do you know that there is such a country as Wisconsin? . . . that the inhabitants are called 'badgers'? and that the forests they clear and the houses they rear fully attest their right to that title? **1955** Shankle *Nicknames, Badger State* . . Wisconsin.

3 An old man—used as a general epithet, usu of disparagement. Cf **codger** 1

1834 *Life Andrew Jackson* 92 **TN,** The gineral . . compelled every . . lolly-poop, sea-crab, caper merchant, Badger . . he cou'd lay hands upon . . tu muster in his army. **1944** Wellman *Bowl* 267 **KS,** Knew an old, tough, ornery cowman . . without an iota of education, culture, or cleanness—just an old plains badger. **1968** *DARE* FW Addit nePA, Dirty old badger. An old man with a dirty mind. Common, rural. **1970** *DARE* (Qu. HH40, *Uncomplimentary words for an old man*) Inf VA67, Badger.

4 A chamber pot. *joc* See also **badger fight**

1968 *DARE* FW Addit swVA, Badger—same as thunder mug.

5 also *badgerweed:* =**pasqueflower.**

1896 *Jrl. Amer. Folkl.* 9.179, *Anemone patens* . . badger, general in Wis. **1900** Lyons *Plant Names* 311, Badger-weed. **1950** *WELS* (*Pale blue flowers with downy leaves and petals that bloom on hillsides in March or early April*) 1 Inf, csWI, Badgers, windflowers, pasque flowers.

badger bird n

=**marbled godwit.**

1888 Trumbull *Names of Birds* 206, Maynard, in Birds of Eastern Massachusetts, 1870, records *Badger-Bird*. **1923** U.S. Dept. Ag. *Misc. Circular* 13.58, *Marbled Godwit . . . Vernacular Names . . . In local use.*—Badger-bird, brant-bird (Mass.). **1955** Forbush–May *Birds* 205.

badgerbrush n

A **coralberry** (here: *Symphoricarpos occidentalis*).

1920 *Torreya* 20.25 **ND,** *Symphoricarpos occidentalis* . . badgerbrush.

badger fight n Also called *pulling the badger* Hence also *badger season* **SW, esp TX** Cf **badger 4,** *DS* CC17

A practical joke in which an inexperienced person plays referee in a fake fight between a badger and a dog: see quot 1961.

1929 Dobie *Vaquero* 180, We stopped at Las Animas long enough to see a badger fight, but as this institution of practical Western jokers is, like the song, too "technical" to be expounded in polite print, we'll let it pass. **1961** Adams *Old-Time Cowhand* 320 **TX,** The loafin' months in the winter came to be knowed as "snipe-huntin' season" and "badger season." *Ibid* 321, "Pullin' the badger" got to be a standard joke . . . it had to be pulled on an Easterner who knowed absolutely nothin' 'bout the West . . . they'd gather 'round 'im . . and begin talkin' excitedly 'bout the comin' badger fight . . . Declarin' they'd have to have some disinterested party, they'd begin lookin' 'round and suddenly discover the greener . . . some cowhand would give the new referee some advice as to how to pull the badger . . . When they got to the place of the fight, there was the dog . . . Nearby was the tub the badger was supposed to be under, and there was a rope runnin' out some distance from beneath the tub . . . When he [the "referee"] was ordered to "pull" he gave the rope a hard yank jes' as one cowhand tipped up the tub from the rear . . . There was no badger on the end of the rope at all, . . but . . one of them vessels usually found under the bed at night. **1967** *DARE* Tape TX43, Badger fight . . . The tenderhorn pulls on a rope which he thinks attaches to the badger—to pull him out for the fight—but which actually attaches to a piss-pot.

badgerweed See **badger** 5

bad hair n *among Black speakers* Cf **bad** adj B6

1942 *Amer. Mercury* 55.94 **NYC** [Black], Bad hair—Negro type hair.

badly adj [*EDD* "Sc. and n. counties"] Cf **poorly**

Sick, unwell.

1899 (1912) Green *VA Folk-Speech, Badly* . . . Sickly . . . "He looks badly."

badly off See **bad off** 2, 3a

bad man n

1 A desperado, outlaw, or professional killer; see also quot 1977. **chiefly West** *now hist*

1855 *Santa Barbara* (Calif.) *Gaz.* 28 June 1/4 *(OEDS),* The 'bad man' was floored by the weight of a walking stick that the quaker had been known to carry. **1907** White *AZ Nights* 72, There's a good deal of romance been written about the "bad man," and there's about the same amount of nonsense. The bad man is just a plain murderer, neither more nor less. He never does get into a real, good, plain, stand-up gun fight if he can possibly help it. **1922** Rollins *Cowboy* 54 **West,** All actual 'bad men' were wholly untrustworthy, were natural killers, moral and mental degenerates, inhuman brutes who would slay for personal gain or merely to gratify a whim. **1977** Watts *Dict. Old West* 17, The word *badman* could have any number of meanings read into it. It was used with both admiration and distaste: decent men had "misunderstandings," killed a man, . . and bore the title; so did men who had their own way simply through ruthlessness or skill with a gun.

2 usu preceded by *the* or *old,* and often cap: The Devil. **chiefly Sth, S Midl** See Map *euphem* Cf **bad place, boogerman** 2

1884 Harrison *Negro Engl.* 277 **Sth,** De Bad Man = the devil. **1915** *DN* 4.180 swVA. **1952** Brown *NC Folkl.* 1.517, *Bad man* . . . The devil. Usually to children to induce good behavior. "If you don't stop crying the (old) *bad man* will get you."—General. Obsolescent. **1954** *Harder Coll.* cwTN, Old Bad Man . . . The devil. c1960 *Wilson Coll.* csKY,

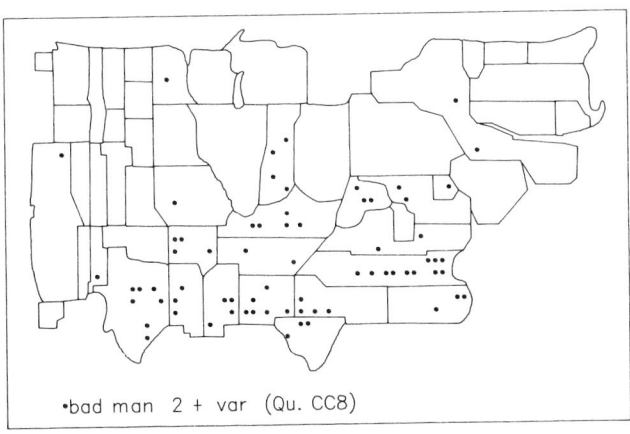

•bad man 2 + var (Qu. CC8)

The bad man will get you if you talk like that. **1962** Atwood *Vocab. TX* 71, *The Bad Man* (15 [infs]) is in restricted use, and appears to be archaic. **1965–70** *DARE* (Qu. CC8) 69 Infs, **chiefly Sth, S Midl,** (The) bad man [Among Infs of all age groups]; MN33, Bad man with the pitchfork. **1973** Allen *LAUM* 1.384, *Devil* . . . bad man [is reported by 27 infs throughout the Upper Midwest].

badman's oatmeal n [**bad man 2** + *oatmeal*] Cf *OED, EDD devil's oatmeal*

=poison hemlock 1.

1900 Lyons *Plant Names* 113, *C[onium] maculatum* . . . Bad-man's-oatmeal. **1930** Sievers *Amer. Med. Plants* 46, *Poison Hemlock* . . . *Other common names* . . . Bad-man's-oatmeal. **1951** Teale *North Spring* 218 **NC,** The harvest of an American plant hunter may include badman's oatmeal, truelove, tread softly.

bad mouth n [**badmouth** v] *chiefly among Black speakers* Cf **bad eye**

1 esp in phr *put (the) bad mouth on:* A curse, a spell.

1853 (1890) Simms *Partisan* 182 **SC** [Black], Maybe he would have a love charm . . or he has an enemy, and would have a bad mouth put upon him, shall make him shrivel up and die by inches, without any disease. **1922** Gonzales *Black Border* 288 **sSC, GA coasts** [Gullah glossary], *Bad mout'*—a spell, a form of curse. **1927** Kennedy *Gritny* 112 **sLA** [Black], She . . assured him that she would be the "las' person in dis worl' to put bad mouth on him an' roll any stone in his way." **1930** *DN* 6.79 **cSC,** *Bad mouth* . . . To suggest an evil contingency is supposed to bring it about. Such a suggestion is referred to in the expression, "Don't put bad mouth on me." Fairly general. **1965** Brown *Manchild* 26 **NYC** [Black], If one of these ole people put the bad mouth on you, maybe you'll be satisfied. **1966–67** *DARE* (Qu. CC14) Infs **SC**19, 54, Put the bad mouth on; SC26, Put bad mouth on [Black Inf]; **SC**44, Bad mouth—used jokingly by Whites. **1970** Hyatt *Hoodoo* 255 **NYC** [Black], I have known people that have had the record of saying that they could put a bad mouth on you. They would say, "so-and-so will happen to you," and you will not go very far before something will happen to you.

2 Transf: see quots.

1966–67 *DARE* (Qu. Y3, *To say uncomplimentary things about someone*) Infs **SC**7, **TX**37, Put the bad mouth on ('em). **1970** Major *Afro–Amer. Slang* 22, *Bad mouth:* malicious gossip.

3 Transf: a person who speaks rudely to others.

1968 *DARE* (Qu. II36a) Inf **PA**94, A bad mouth. **1980** Folb *Runnin' Down* 228 [Black], *Bad mouth*—One who talks in a provocative, belligerent, or argumentative manner . . . One who talks badly about others.

badmouth v [See quots 1949, 1977 Smitherman] *esp among Black and young White speakers* Cf **fat-mouth, sweet-mouth**
To speak ill of someone; see also quot 1949.

1941 *Sat. Eve. Post* 5 Apr 9/2 **sOH,** He bad-mouthed everybody. **1949** Turner *Africanisms* 233, [bɑd mʊt] 'to curse,' 'to put a spell on,' i.e., 'to bad mouth.' Cf. the Vai expression [dɑ ŋɑmɑ] 'a curse,' lit. 'a bad mouth.' **1965–70** *DARE* (Qu. Y3, *To say uncomplimentary things about someone*) 10 Infs, **scattered,** Badmouth; (Qu. Y4) Inf **CA**184, To badmouth. [2 of 11 Infs Black, 6 young] **1972** Claerbaut *Black Jargon, Bad mouth* . . to slander, to verbally attempt to destroy another's reputation. **1977** Smitherman *Talkin* 45, *Bad mouth,* to talk about somebody negatively, from Mandingo *dajugu,* literally "bad mouth." **1977** Adams *Bad Mouth* 1, "Bad mouth" in its pure original is an active transitive verb with the odor of the ghetto upon it, and a meaning akin to "denigrate." . . "Bad mouth" is a black term primarily. *Ibid* 2, Bad-mouthing . . amounts to nothing more than vocal hostility . . directed immediately against the victim. **1979** *WI State Jrl.* (Madison) 20 Oct 3/3 **csNY,** [A judge had sentenced a man to wash out his mouth with soap for shouting obscenities to a policeman. The judge said later:] "I use it [=such a sentence] just if somebody bad-mouths a police officer who really has no comeback."

badness n
Pus.

1943 *LANE* Map 513 (*Pus*) 1 inf, **nwCT,** Badness [bædnɪs], also used: The badness is coming out of that boil.

bad nigger n Also *bad-doing nigger* [**bad** adj **B6**] *among Black speakers*
A Black person who commands the respect of other Blacks.

1965 Brown *Manchild* 281 **NYC** [Black], Somebody would . . see Sidney Poitier in a film, and they'd say, "Man, that's a bad-doin' nigger." They didn't mean that he was running out in the street cutting somebody's throat . . . But this was all that a bad nigger meant to Mama and Dad and the people their age. It was the bad-nigger concept from the South, but it didn't mean that any more. **1969** Hannerz *Soulside* 115 **DC** [Black], The "gorilla" type of ghetto man is idealized in long elaborate rhymes (known as "toasts") about legendary "bad niggers." **1970** Major *Afro–Amer. Slang, Bad nigger:* a black person who refuses to be meek or who rejects the social terms of poverty and oppression the culture designs for him. **1977** Adams *Bad Mouth* 1 [Black], A "bad nigger" is a good brother.

bad off adj phr

1 In poor circumstances or condition.

1815 Humphreys *Yankey in England* 77, Bad as I am off, I wouldn't swop conditions. **1891** (1967) Freeman *New Engl. Nun* 221, Eph couldn't be so dreadful bad off. **1915** *DN* 4.180 **swVA,** *Bad off* . . . Poor. **1917** *DN* 4.387 **neOH.** **1927** *AmSp* 2.348 **WV,** *Bad off* . . . used to denote a time when one's business affairs are not in good condition. **1966–68** *DARE* (Qu. U41a, *Somebody who has lost everything and is very poor: "He's _____."*) Infs **MT**5, **LA**37, **NY**109, Bad off.

2 also rarely *badly off:* In a poor state of health, very ill. **widespread, but esp Sth, S Midl** See Map Cf **bad sick**

1863 Gilmore *S. Friends* 13 **NYC,** She's very bad off, very bad indeed. **1893** Shands *MS Speech, Bad off* . . . Used by all classes to mean *unwell, sick.* **1903** Burnham *Jewel* 125 **NY,** "She's very badly off, very badly off, I'm afraid." "I hope not, sir. Children are always flighty if they have a little fever." **1908** *DN* 3.288 **eAL, wGA,** *Bad off* . . . Seriously ill. **1915** *DN* 4.180 **swVA.** **1917** *DN* 4.387 **neOH.** *Ibid* 407 **wNC.** **1919** *DN* 5.76 **NEng.** **1941** *Harder Coll.* **cwTN,** If she gets Bad off you call us. **1965–70** *DARE* (Qu. BB42, *If a person is very sick you say he's _____*) 98 Infs, **chiefly Sth, S Midl,** Bad off; NY73, Pretty bad off; FL10, Real bad off; (Qu. BB38) Inf **WI**18, Bad off; (Qu. BB44, . . *"He _____ pneumonia."*) Inf **KY**19, Got bad off with.

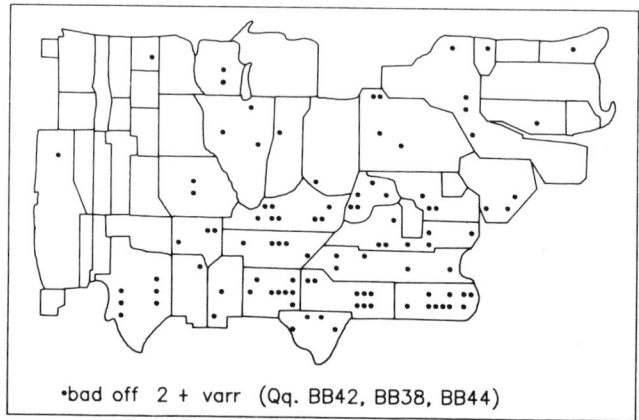

•bad off 2 + varr (Qq. BB42, BB38, BB44)

3 with *for* or *to:*

a also *badly off:* Wanting; in need of (something). [*EDD bad* 8(3), 1863]

1794 (1936) Parry *Jrl.* 383 **PA,** He told me when he 1st settled this place, he feared he sho'd be bad off for water. **1821** (1898) Fowler *Jrl.* 15 **KY,** Haveing left two be Hind and three more unfitt for survice makes us bad of [sic] for horses. **1852** (1854) Bartlett *Personal Narr.* 2.490 **RI,** We should have been badly off for fodder. **1893** Shands *MS Speech, Bad off* . . . sometimes means poorly provided with; as, This country is *bad off* for horses.

b Desirous (to do something). **Sth** See also **bad** adj **B5**

1845 Hooper *Advent. Simon Suggs* 152 **AL,** Yes, send for your marshal . . if you're bad off to. **1893** Shands *MS Speech, Bad off* . . . also means *anxious for* or *desirous of;* as, "He is *bad off* for a gun." **1942** Faulkner *Go Down* 89 **nMS,** I needs to go to bed . . . I'm bad off to sleep. **1967** Green *Horse Tradin'* 168 **swTX,** He didn't know how bad off I was to sell these little mules.

bad order n
Chiefly among railroad workers:
1 A defective locomotive or railroad car.

[**1940** Cottrell *Railroader* 118, When a defective car is found by the car inspector, he tacks a small card with 'Bad Order' in bold lettering on it.] **1945** Hubbard *Railroad Ave.* 331, *Bad order*—Crippled car or locomotive. [**1977** Adams *Lang. Railroader, Bad order:* A command placed on a card and tacked to a defective car . . . The car is not to be moved, except to the *rip track* . . if the repairs are too extensive to be made on the siding where it stands.]
2 Transf: see quots.
    1947 Beebe *Mixed Train* 353, *Bad order:* Equipment in disrepair. **1958** McCulloch *Woods Words* 6 **Pacific NW,** *Bad order* . . . now used to mean anything in the camp which is broken or not in shape to work, either men or machines. **1962** *AmSp* 37.131 **nCA,** *Bad-order* . . . A term originally applied to a railroad car in need of repairs; now used to refer to anything defective. **1969** *AmSp* 44.254 **Chicago IL,** *Bad order* — 1: Defective material or equipment 2: Incompetent employee.

bad pay n Also *bad paymaster* **Sth, S Midl**
    1965–70 *DARE* (Qu. U17, . . *A person who doesn't pay his bills*) Infs **AL17, DE3, MD42, NC6, TN24, TX26,** Bad pay; **LA28,** He's bad pay; **AL60, LA8, MS60,** Bad paymaster.

bad place n **chiefly Sth, Midl** See Map *euphem* Cf **bad man 2**
Hell.
    1884 Harrison *Negro Engl.* 277 **Sth,** De Bad Place = hell. **1899** (1912) Green *VA Folk-Speech* 73. **1913** Porter *Laddie* 146, He exploded in a kind of a snarl that meant, I'll see you in the Bad Place first. **1915** *DN* 4.180 **swVA,** Bad-place . . . Hell. **1943** Caldwell *GA Boy* 51, I thought when I come to that I was in the bad place. I sure thought I had been knocked all the way down to there. **1950** *WELS (Other words for hell)* 2 Infs, **swWI,** Bad place. **1954** *Harder Coll.* **cwTN,** Old bad place . . . Hell. **c1960** *Wilson Coll.* **csKY,** He's not afraid of the bad place or he wouldn't talk thata-way. **1965–70** *DARE* (Qu. CC9, . . *"That man is headed straight for _____."*) 69 Infs, **chiefly Sth, Midl,** (The) bad place. **1968** Kellner *Aunt Serena* 2 **sIN** (as of c1930), On the way home in the surrey, Aunt Serena was very sharp . . . I was a careless, thoughtless girl, and if I did not mend my ways, I would certainly go to The Bad Place. (This term covered all references to eternal torment. The word "hell" was never used except by ministers, by Lawnie our hired man, and occasionally by my Grandfather.)

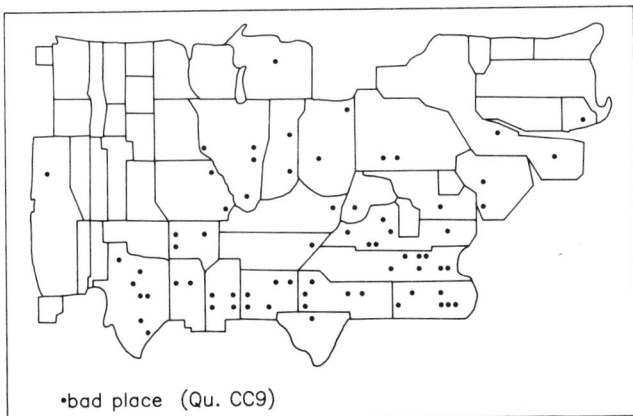
•bad place (Qu. CC9)

bad place in the road n Also *bad spot in the road*
A small, unimportant, or out-of-the-way settlement.
    1967–68 *DARE* (Qu. C33) Inf **TX45,** A bad place in the road; **LA27,** A bad spot in the road.

bad rags n pl Also *bad clothes, bad weave* [**bad** adj **B6**] *among Black speakers*
Stylish clothes.
    1968 *DARE* (Qu. W39, *Joking ways of referring to a person's best clothes*), Inf **PA66,** Bad clothes—clothes in the latest fashion; bad rags. [Inf Black] **1972** Claerbaut *Black Jargon, Bad* . . . Stylish; in vogue: a *bad weave* . . . *bad rags* . . . nice clothes; handsome or attractive attire: *The cat's got some bad rags.*

bad religion n [**bad** adj **B7**]
Reprehensible or hypocritical behavior on the part of a person purporting to be religious.
    1953 Brewer *Word Brazos* xiii **seTX** [Black], *Bad Religion . . . Good Religion* [Headings for groups of stories]. *Ibid* 52, She sho'-fire proof

dat Bad Religion am still foot loose in de country. Sistuh Mariah speshly hab a habit of complainin' all de time; she hab a mean habit an' a haa'd haa't [=hard heart] an' she allus sayin' mean things 'bout de preachuhs an' de membuhship . . . She 'speshly don' hab no good blood for anothuh sistuh in de chu'ch.

bad sick adj phr [*EDD* 1679 →] **chiefly Sth, S Midl, but esp Inland Sth** See Map
Seriously ill.
    1928 Peterkin *Scarlet Sister Mary* 321 **SC,** Unex was sick, bad sick . . . If he died he could not . . bear it. **1929** Sale *Tree Named John* 100 **MS,** Ah jes kep' feelin' dat baby callin me, en Ah knowed hit wuz bad sick. **1939** *Folk-Lore* (London) 50.314 **nWV,** If a person is bad sick, he will die when the moon changes. **1942** in 1944 *ADD* **nKS,** '[My brother is] bad sick.' Rural. **1965–70** *DARE* (Qu. BB42, . . *Very sick*) 30 Infs, **scattered Sth, S Midl, but esp Inland Sth,** Bad sick. **1966** *DARE* Tape **NC54,** The kid got bad sick an' the closest doctor was fourteen miles. **1969** *DARE* File **ceKY,** Had a bad-sick spell . . . To be very sick for quite a while. **1979** *Verbatim* 6.3.14 **MO,** *Bad sick* meant it was time to call the undertaker.

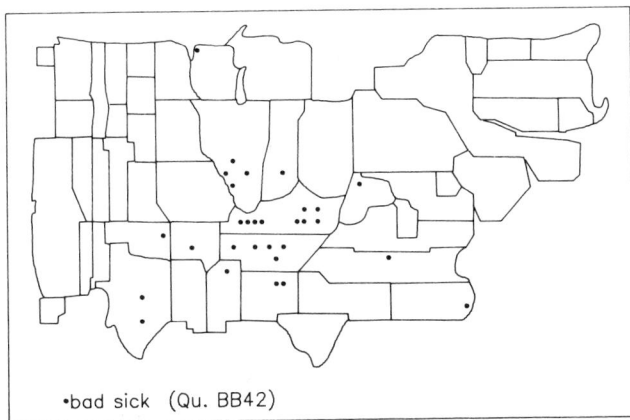
•bad sick (Qu. BB42)

bad spot in the road See **bad place in the road**

bad time n Similarly *bad day, bad-feeling days, bad week*
Menstruation.
    1954 *AmSp* 29.298 **TX, OK, FL** [Vernacular of menstruation], *Bad time* [in use among women]. **1967–70** *DARE* (Qu. AA27) Infs **MA29, NJ13, NY234,** (Her) bad time; **MO32,** Her bad time, her bad week; **MI87,** Bad time of the month; **CA134, PA221,** My bad day; **AR47,** Bad-feeling days.

bad weave See **bad rags**

bad-weed milk n
=bitterweed milk.
    1966 *DARE* (Qu. K14, *Milk that has a taste from something the cow ate in the pasture*) Inf **MS21,** Bad-weed milk.

bad week See **bad time**

baffle around v phr
    1970 *DARE* (Qu. A10, *When somebody takes too long about coming to a decision, you might say, "I wish he'd quit _____."*) Inf **FL51,** Baffling around.

‡**baft** n *?obs* Cf *DS* LL8b
A quantity or large number (of something).
    1896 *DN* 1.411 **neTX,** "There was a great *baft* of people."

bag n Usu |bæg|, also |bæɪg, bɛɪg|, occas |bag|
A Forms.
    1939 *LANE* Map 149, [*Bag* is usu [bæg], freq [bæɪg], occas [bæəg, bæeg]]. **c1970** Pederson *Dial. Survey Rural GA* **seGA,** *Bag* is usu [bɛɪg], often [bæg], occas [bɛɪg, bag]. **1980** *DARE* File **csWI,** Bag is widely pronounced [bɛɪg].
B Senses. In fig phrr *in the bag, put the bag on* and varr:
1 To be or become drunk. **chiefly NY, CT** See also **bagged**
    1951 Spillane *Big Kill* 51 **NYC,** He had half a bag on and looked it. **1967–69** *DARE* (Qu. DD13, . . *Just beginning to show the effects of the liquor*) Infs **CT7, NY10,** (Half) in the bag; (Qu. DD14, . . *Partly drunk*) Infs **CT9, 29, NY10, 211,** Half in the bag; (Qu. DD15, . . *Thoroughly*

drunk) Infs **CT**35, 37, In the bag; (Qu. DD16, *To have a drinking bout and get drunk*) Inf **NY**76, Putting the bag on.

2 Transf: to participate in a raucous party.

1969 *DARE* (Qu. FF18, . . *A noisy or boisterous celebration or party:* *"They certainly _____ last night."*) Inf **NY**213, Put the bag on.

bag v

1 usu in phrr *bag school, bag it:* To play truant. **chiefly PA, esp Philadelphia area, and sNJ** (See maps in Kurath *Word Geog.* Figs 22, 158)

1889 *AN&Q* 2.297/2, The expression for playing truant by school boys in Camden, New Jersey, is to "bag it." **1892** *DN* 1.216 **swNJ**, *Hookey . . .* In Camden, N.J., the boys 'bag it.' **1934** (1947) O'Hara *Appointment* 203 **PA**, She had taught him in Sunday School, and did not report him on Sunday afternoons when he "bagged it" to go to a ball game. **1949** Kurath *Word Geog.* 35, *Bag school . . .* is common in Philadelphia and in Chester, less so in northern Delaware and in West Jersey. **1950** *New Yorker* 11 Nov 60/2 **Philadelphia PA**, [After my mother's death] I took to baggin' school. **1957** *DE Folkl. Bulletin* 1.28 **DE**, Bagged school (played hookey). **1965–70** *DARE* (Qu. JJ6, *To stay away from school without excuse*) 10 Infs, **PA, sNJ, CT**, Bag school. **1971** Wood *Vocab. Change* 284, 298, **GA, TN**, 2 infs, Bag school.

2 Transf: to feign illness in order to avoid one's responsibilities.

1967 *DARE* (Qu. BB27) Inf **PA**36, Bagging something.

baga n Usu |'bɛgi, 'be(ɪ)gə|, less freq |'bægi|, occas |'begɚ| Also sp *baggie, bagie, beggie* [Abbr for *rutabaga;* cf Engl dial *bagaroot, baggie* a type of Swedish turnip (*EDD*)] **chiefly MI, WI, MN** See Map

A rutabaga or Swedish turnip.

1854 MI State Ag. Soc. *Trans. of 1853* 597, In the month of November half an acre was accurately set off by the chain, and the bagas taken up. **1936** Lutes *Country Kitchen* 211 **sMI** (?as of c1890), Between Christmas and the first "greens" of spring our only vegetables were Hubbard squash, cabbage, "beggies," and such others as could be kept in the cold cellar or root house. **1950** *WELS* (Names or nicknames . . for large yellow turnips) 15 Infs, **WI**, Beggies ['bɛgiz]; 7 Infs, Baga(s) ['begəz]; 3 Infs, Baggies ['bægiz]; **1965–70** *DARE* (Qu. I3) 19 Infs, **chiefly MI, MN, WI**, Beggies ['bɛgiz]; Infs **MI**116, 119, Bagies ['bɛgiz]; **TN**34, Bagas ['beɪgəz]; **MI**108, Baggies ['bægiz]; **FL**30, ['begɚ] [Inf's father from **WI**]. **1966** *DARE* Tape **MI**28, ['begi].

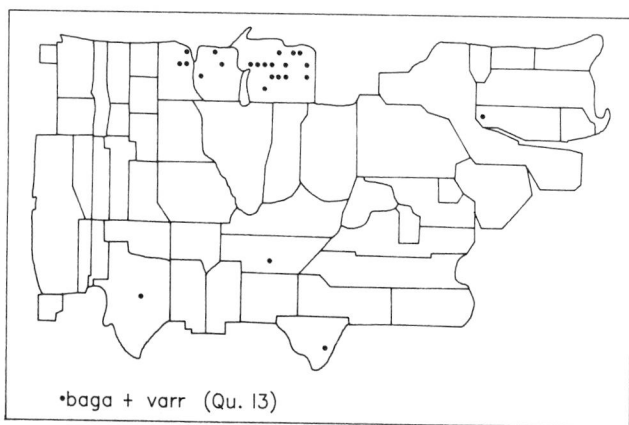

•baga + varr (Qu. I3)

bag fever n See also **udder fever**

Milk fever, a disease in a cow's udder.

1966–69 *DARE* (Qu. K7, *What sickness can a cow get in her udder— for example, if she's left unmilked too long?*) Infs **CA**63, **KY**62, **NE**7, **NM**3, **SC**7, 40, **TX**6, 33, Bag fever.

bagged adj Cf **bag** n **B1**

Drunk.

1968 *DARE* (Qu. DD15) Inf **NY**76, Bagged.

baggie See **baga**

bagging (sack) n **Sth**

A sack, as for feed or for packing cotton.

1830 in 1938 Gardiner *Chron. Old Berkeley* 303 **KY**, This town has . . 3 factorys turned by horse power (to wit) Cotton, Woolen & Bagging, Ropeworks. **1872** Schele de Vere *Americanisms* 438, *Bagging*, in the

majority of cases, does not mean the material for making bags generally, but the hempen bags made specially for packing cotton. **1966–69** *DARE* (Qq. F19, 20, *A cloth container for grain* [or] *feed*) Inf **TX**26, Bagging; **MS**45, Bagging sack; **NC**50, Tow sack, tow bag, baggin's; **TX**62, Bagging sack—chicken; cowfeed sacks are still sold in bags which are fine enough to make cup towels and dresses out of. They wear like linen, come in nice prints.

baggonet See **bagonet**

‡baggy n *joc*

An outdoor toilet.

1970 *DARE* (Qu. M21b) Inf **TX**89, The baggy, the crapper.

bagie See **baga**

bag leaves n [So called because the leaves can be inflated to form a sort of bag] **NEng** Cf **bag plant, frog plant, pudding bag, witches' moneybags**

An *orpine* (here: *Sedum telephium*).

1900 Lyons *Plant Names* 340, *S[edum] Telephium . . .* Bag-leaves. **1910** Graves *Flowering Plants* 214 **CT**, Bag-leaves. **1959** Carleton *Index Herb. Plants* 7, *Bag leaves:* Sedum purpureum.

bagnet, bagnit See **bagonet**

bagodbajees exclam Also *bagodbagee, bagodbejingoes* [See quot] *euphem* Cf **DS NN7–9b**

1970 *DARE* (QR, near p. 1) Inf **MA**78, "Bagodbejees." By-God-by-Jesus . . . Sometimes soft-pedaled to "Bagodbagee," "Bagodbejingoes." . . Exclamations of impatience and exasperation. Old Yankee "soft profanity."

bag of meal n For varr see quots **NEast**

A person one does not know and cannot identify.

1904 *DN* 2.395 **cNY**, "I didn't know him from a bundle of brooms" . . . Similarly used [is] *bag of meal.* **1967–68** *DARE* (Qu. II26, . . *"I wouldn't know him from _____."*) Inf **NJ**16, Bag of beans; **PA**15, Bag of beets; **VT**10, Bag of potatoes.

bag one's bowline v phr

To tie a bowline knot incorrectly; fig, to perform or talk about a task unskillfully or ignorantly.

1975 Gould *ME Lingo* 2, *Baggin' the bowline*—Not unlike *makin' a granny;* tying a knot the wrong way; botching the job . . . The reef, or square knot, can be mis-tied into a *granny,* and the bowline can be *bagged.* Neither comes apart smoothly, if improperly made. Another explanation . . is that the bowline holding the weather edge of a sail must be rightly set or the sail will bag, making for sloppy sailing. Thus, a man who doesn't know what he's talking about, or tries to do something he can't, is *baggin' his bowlines.* The expression can be a way of calling somebody a liar.

bag one's head v phr

1914 *DN* 4.68 **ME, nNH**, Bag yer head. Retire; pull in one's horns; be more modest. "I cal'late he better bag his head!"

bagonet n Also sp *baggonet, bagnet, bagnit* [*OED* "obs. or vulgar form"; cf *EDD*] *?obs*

A bayonet.

1808 in 1810 Lambert *Travels* 2.436 **SC**, How can we charge bagonet without our guns? **1843** (1916) Hall *New Purchase* 355 **IN**, The bagnit had silenced the rifle and avenged the fall of our . . comrades. **1848** Cooper *Oak-Openings* 1.161 **nNY**, You, sir, with preachin' and prayin', and I with gun and baggonet. **1871** Eggleston *Hoosier Schoolmaster* 195 **IN**, A old soldier what fit the Britishers, and lost his leg by one of the blamed critters a punchin' his bagonet through it. **1878** in 1929 Summers *Annals* 1599 **swVA**, That bad man was riding behind him sticking a bagnit in him to keep up with their hosses. **1899** (1912) Green *VA Folk-Speech*, Bagonet . . . Bayonet.

bagonet plant See **Spanish bayonet**

bagoong n [Tagalog] **HI**

A condiment made from fermented fish or shrimp.

1940 Bazore *Hawaiian Foods* 77 **HI**, But the most widely used fish product is a fermented salty fish paste called bagoong. It flavors pork; is added to vegetable dishes; is eaten raw. **1967** *DARE* (Qu. H50) Inf **HI**6, Bagoong ['baga'ʊŋ] . . slightly rotten small fish. **1972** Carr *Da Kine Talk* 104 **HI**, *Bagoong,* a hot sauce or paste, is as powerful as its name suggests. To prepare it, shrimp or small fish are mixed with salt and allowed to ferment for several days, after which they are pressed and the liquid is drained off.

bag plant n [See quots] **NEng** Cf **bag leaves, witches' money-bags**

1 also *pudding-bag plant:* An **orpine** (here: *Sedum telephium*).
1892 *Jrl. Amer. Folkl.* 5.96, *Sedum Telephium* . . pudding-bag plant. Mass. . . Because of a children's custom of blowing up a leaf. **1898** *Jrl. Amer. Folkl.* 11.227, *Sedum Telephium* . . bag plant, Holyoke Mass. . . Because the epidermis of the leaves is blown out into bags. **1899** (1909) Earle *Child Life* 389, From the live-for-ever, or orpine [leaves] . . we made . . a bladder which, when blown up, would burst with a delightful pop. The New England folk-names by which this plant is called, such as frog-plant, blow-leaf, pudding-bag-plant, show the wide-spread prevalence of this custom.
2 =**houseleek 1.**
1929 *Torreya* 29.150 **ME,** *Sempervivum tectorum, "Live Forever," "Bag-plant"* (because the children blew up the leaves), and *"Aaron's Rod."*

bagpod n
A tall annual rather woody legume *(Glottidium vesicaria)* found chiefly in the Gulf States which has pinnately compound leaves, yellowish flowers, and bladdery elliptic pods. Also called **bladderpod, castle bean, coffee bean 2, devilweed, mole bean 1, snake bean 1**
1942 *Amer. Joint Comm. Horticult. Nomenclature Std. Plant Names* 275, *Glottidium vesicarium* [sic] . . Bagpod. **1960** Vines *Trees SW* 544, Bagpod . . . Although not truly a woody plant it has superficial resemblance to the Rattlebox. **1970** Correll *Plants TX* 836, Bag-pod, bladderpod . . . Legume body . . valves separating at maturity into 2 layers (the outer thicker, the inner thin and papery-membranous).

bag school See **bag v 1**

bague See **beg**

ba'gum See **bargum**

bagworm n
A larva of the bagworm moth (family Psychidae), which spins a silk case for its protection.
1862 *U.S. Congress Congressional Globe* 8 Jan 232/1 **PA,** On the avenue and in the parks you will find the evergreen trees . . being destroyed by the bag-worm. **1871** (1882) Stowe *Fireside Stories* 68 **MA,** There was pig-weed, and pusley, and Canady thistles, cut-worms, and bag-worms, and canker-worms, to say nothin' of rattlesnakes. **1876** VT State Bd. Ag. *Report* 3.585, The Bagworm, *Thyridopterix ephemerae formis, Haw.,* sometimes attacks the leaves of apple trees in other States. **1933** *East Liberty Tribune* (Pittsburgh PA) 28 July 6/5 *(Hench Coll.),* The bagworm, an injurious insect, has almost completely defoliated the Evergreen trees in some sections of the East End . . . This caterpillar or larva may be readily recognized by its curious habit of crawling about on the infested trees in a baglike case about three-quarters of an inch in length. **1965–70** *DARE* (Qu. R27, . . *Kinds of caterpillars*) 12 Infs, **chiefly Midl,** Bagworm; (Qu. P6) Inf **TN26,** Bagworms—make a tough sack to live in; they hang on cedars and ornamental evergreens.

bah See **bakkes**

bahada See **bajada**

bah-ma See **bamma**

bahskit See **basket**

baid
1 See **bed** n.
2 See **beard.**

baidar(ka) See **bidar**

baig See **beg**

baignet See **beignet**

bail n[1] See **bale** n[1]

bail n[2] Also *bail net*
A brail: see quot 1976.
1969 *DARE* (Qu. P13, . . *Other ways of fishing*) Inf **RI15,** Bail net. **1976** Warner *Beautiful Swimmers* 129 **VA,** The brail or "bail," as the

Virginia watermen prefer to call it, is no more than a giant-sized version of the little dip nets used in home aquaria.

baile n, also attrib |'baɪˌle| Also sp *bayle* [Span] **SW**
1 A dance or ball, esp one at which Spanish or Mexican folk dances are performed.
1844 (1954) Gregg *Commerce* 170 **NM,** *Fandangos* . . is the usual designation for those ordinary assemblies where dancing and frolicking are carried on; *baile* (or ball) being generally applied to those of a higher grade. **1856** (1928) Jaeger *Diary Fort Yuma* 103 **NM,** In the evening the boys got up a fine baile—also kept it up till 2 o'clock. **1892** in 1894 *DN* 1.324 **seTX,** A woman of Matamoras attended the *baile,* and got up to dance. **1967** *DARE* (Qu. FF4) Inf **CA4,** Baile ['baɪˌle].
2 Transf: a dance hall.
1880 *Cimmaron News* 15 Apr 1/7 *(AmSp* 17.65) **NM,** Charles Fernandez, a buckboard driver on the Santa Fe and Alamosa line, was killed in a baile near Chama. **1907** White *AZ Nights* 166, We . . built a *baile* and saloon houses out of adobe.

baile chango n [baile + Span *chango* monkey: see quot]
1932 Bentley *Spanish Terms* 97, Boys use the term to describe any queer or fantastic dancing motions or contortions as in "He went through a regular *baile chango*" or "He did a *baile chango* on his head." . . It may have been acquired from travelling entertainers . . who usually have as a main feature a monkey trained to do tricks and dance.

bailer n
1916 *DN* 4.340 **seOH,** *Bailer* . . . One who asks questions.

bailey-wax See **belly-wax**

bail net See **bail** n[2]

baily-ole n Cf **haily-over** n and *DS* EE22, 23a
=**Antony-over** n.
1934 *Hanley Disks* **seNY,** Baley ole ['belɪ'olɪ] was a game played by teams with a ball.

baird See **beard**

baird-splitter See **beard-splitter**

baire See **bar** n[3]

baister See **baster**

bait n
1 Food; a meal. [*OED* 1570 →] See also **baiting**
a Feed for a horse; pasturage. See also **bait v 1, bait and board**
1896 *DN* 1.412 **nNY,** Bait . . the grass eaten by a horse when he is "baited." **1903** *DN* 2.349 **neOH,** Bait . . . Pasturage.
b A meal, often a light one. [*OED* "Still dial."] **chiefly S Midl, West**
1905 *DN* 3.69 **nwAR,** Bait . . . A meal. **1944** Adams *Western Words, Bait*—Food, a meal. **1953** Randolph *Down in Holler* 157 **Ozarks,** A *bait* is usually a meal, sometimes a light lunch or a snack. **1953** *PADS* 19.8 **sAppalachians,** Bait . . . Light lunch, "I'll get me a bait to eat before I meet you." **1958** *AmSp* 33.268 **eWA** [Ranching terms], Bait . . . A small feed or lunch; a meal.
c One serving of food.
1940 McCullers *Lonely Hunter* 248 **GA,** She helped herself to white meat and gravy and grits and a few raisins and mixed them up together on her plate. She ate three baits of them. **1967** *DARE* FW Addit **SC,** *Bait*—one serving of food.
d A large amount, an ample portion (of food). **chiefly Sth, S Midl** See also **dog bait**
1926 Kephart *Highlanders* 367 **wNC,** "I et me a bait" literally means a mere snack, but jocosely it may admit a hearty meal. **1944** *PADS* 2.6 **MS,** Bait . . . A large amount (of food) . . . "He ate himself a plumb bait of pie." *Ibid* 2.53 **MO.** **1950** *PADS* 14.12 **SC,** Bait . . . All that one can eat. A *bait* of plums, watermelon, oysters, etc. **1958** McCulloch *Woods Words* 6 **Pacific NW,** Bait . . . A good meal. To put away a bait means to eat a good meal. **c1960** Wilson *Coll.* **csKY,** Bait . . . All the food one can hold, a big meal or snack. "I sure got a bait at his house." **1964** Will *Hist. Okeechobee* xi **FL,** Bait . . . an ample portion. **1966–69** *DARE* (Qu. LL4, *Very large . . helping of potatoes*) Infs **AL51, SC19, TN12, 23,** A bait. **1967** *DARE* FW Addit **SC,** People could serve a bait . . of fish, collards; **TN,** Bait [beɪt]—a large helping of food. (Joking.) "Give me a bait of them potatoes." . . Heard in restaurants. **1972** *Atlanta Letters* **GA,** "I have et a bait," . . the speaker has eaten a sufficiency. **1976**

Garber *Mountain-ese* **sAppalachians,** *Bait . . .* Huge meal. "Clem got sick after eatin' a bait uv cabbage fer supper last night."

2 A sufficient or excessive quantity or amount. **Sth, S Midl**

1851 in 1956 Eliason *Tarheel Talk* 258 **wNC,** Cousin Sophia has been taking a bait of kine pox. **1935** Hench Coll. **cVA,** A local woman reported of someone who had grown weary of her in-laws, "She's finally had a bait of them." **1938** *Ibid,* A native . . , in speaking of the enormous amount of time that certain of her nephews spend at her farm, said, "We've had a bait of those boys." **1938** Rawlings *Yearling* 11 **nFL,** You carry your Ma a good bait o' wood now. *Ibid* 99, I'd love some rale coffee. I've had a bait o' them wild coffee beans. **1966–70** *DARE* (Qu. AA12, *If a man loses interest in a girl and stops seeing her, you'd say he* _____) Inf **MS6,** Got a bait of her; (Qu. LL8a, . . "*He's got* _____ *of time.*") Inf **AL51,** A bait; (Qu. LL9a, *As much as you need or more . . :* "*We've got* _____ *of apples.*") Inf **TN43,** A bait.

3 An earthworm. [*OED* →1799] **chiefly Sth** *esp among Black speakers* See also **baitworm** Cf *DS* P5

1908 *DN* 3.288 **eAL, wGA,** I saw a bait crawlin' in the dirt. **1929** Sale *Tree Named John* 89 **MS** [Black], Take some uv dem baits, de red uns de bes', en rend' de grease out uv'm. *Ibid* 109, Fer de nex' two times dey go fishin', he 'uz gwi dig all de baits hisse'f. **1966–70** *DARE* (Qu. P5, . . *The common worm used as bait*) Infs **FL48, GA47, NY236, SC11, 26, 34, 40,** Bait(s). [4 of 7 Infs Black] **1971** Wood *Vocab. Change* 374 **Sth,** *Bait(s) . . .* worm used for bait.

4 In marble play: =**ante** n.

1934 *AmSp* 9.75 **ND,** *Baits.* The marbles which a player puts in the game as his *ante.* **1955** *PADS* 23.11 **AL, TN,** *Bait . . . ante. Ibid* 20 **TN,** *I got my . . bait . . .* Stated when the player has finished playing with the same number with which he began. **1963** *KY Folkl. Rec.* 9.61 **neKY,** *The marbles of an individual being played for in a game . . .* bait . . . baits.

5 A fulcrum. **Nth, esp NEng**

1889 (1971) Farmer *Americanisms* 33, In New England a *bait* is the means by which a leverage is obtained; a fulcrum. **1931–33** *LANE Worksheets* **seMA,** *Bait* /beɪt/ . . A piece of wood used for a fulcrum. **1958** McCulloch *Woods Words* 6 **Pacific NW,** *Bait . . .* A block used for leverage in prying something. **1975** Gould *ME Lingo* 3, *Bait* is also the Maine term for the fulcrum in leverage, meaning a block of wood or a rock placed under a crowbar or pole in lifting: "Give me a little more *bait* and we'll h'ist this still into place."

bait v

1 To feed (an animal); to pause in a journey in order to feed animals. [*OED* 1375 →]

1856 (1862) Colt *Went to KS* 40 **NY,** A very large drove of cattle passed us this forenoon . . We come up to them now—they have stopped to bait. **1859** (1931) Tuttle *CA Diary* 69 **WI,** We stopped for to bait after which we continued. **1887** (1895) Robinson *Uncle Lisha* 182 **wVT,** At noon they stopped to bait their teams and eat their lunch. **1891** *Jrl. Amer. Folkl.* 4.317 **cTN,** The horse is brought around, baited and resaddled. **1930** Shoemaker *1300 Words* 3 **cPA Mts** (as of c1900), *Bait*—To feed horses or oxen. **1954** Harder Coll. **cwTN,** Bait 'em mules. **1958** *AmSp* 33.268 **eWA** [Ranching terms], *Bait . . .* To feed. **1959** *VT Hist.* ns 27.124 **VT,** Bait the cows . . . To let the cows graze at the roadside. Common. **1969** *DARE* (QR, near Qu. J10) Inf **MA58,** Bait—to feed (animals).

2 To gather bait, spec small crabs, for fishing.

1899 (1912) Green *VA Folk-Speech, Bait . . .* Soft crabs are used for bait in fishing; the act of catching the crabs is *to bait.* "*I baited* all the tide and caught two dozen crabs."

3 To entice, lure, provoke. See also **bay** v

1903 (1965) Adams *Log Cowboy* 19 **NM,** Our men held the cattle as they came out, in order to bait the next bunch. **1940** Richter *Trees* 254 **OH,** She was the one who had baited him to run off with his own woman's sister. **1966** *DARE* Tape **GA3,** You can bait wild hogs . . , bait 'em regular in one place and get 'em to coming there; **NC24,** [FW:] "I imagine you could bring 'em in a little closer to where you wanted to go get 'em if you . . put some [food] out for 'em." [Inf:] "Well, that's strictly against the law—to bait 'em." **1967–68** *DARE* (QR, near Qu. P39) Inf **CA32,** Boys came in to Luis to get some overripe fruit to use as bait for wild pig hunting—they wanted to go "bait some hogs in"; (Qu. Y5, . . "*Johnny wouldn't have tried that if the other boys hadn't* _____.") Inf **NJ18, NE6,** Baited him (on). **1970** *DARE* FW Addit **VA47,** They'll [=nesting ducks] bait—sneak along, get you after 'em, get you away from the nest."

4 To curry favor.

1968 *DARE* (Qu. JJ3a, *When a school-child makes a special effort to "get in good" with the teacher in hopes of getting a better grade:* "*He's trying to* _____ *again*") Inf **IL29,** Bait her on.

bait and board n [**bait** n 1] Also *boarding and baiting*

Food and shelter for a horse.

1903 *DN* 2.349, *Baiting . . .* The more common use for the single meal of a horse is still preserved in the sign 'boarding and baiting' of a public stable. **1954** Forbes *Rainbow* 88 **CT, NH** (as of c1850), As for where we put up for the night, it was like this—anybody who employed a craftsman . . by custom gave him meals, lodging, bait and board for his horse if he had one. **1962** Morison *One Boy's Boston* 20 **MA** (as of 1890s), Boarding and baiting stables, where gentlemen who drove in from the suburbs behind fast trotters left their rigs during the day.

bait can n [**bait** n 1b: cf *EDD* bait-bag, *OED* bait-poke in similar sense]

Esp among loggers: a lunch bucket.

1926 *AmSp* 5.398 **Ozarks,** *Bait can . . .* A dinner pail or lunch basket. **1956** *AmSp* 31.149 **nwCA** [Logger lingo], *Bait can . . .* Lunch pail. **1958** McCulloch *Woods Words* 6 **Pacific NW.** **1968** Adams *Western Words.*

baited for widow adj phr Cf *DS* W37, 38

Spruced up; dressed to catch the attention of widows or other women.

1960 Williams *Walk Egypt* 20 **GA,** He come by my house last night, baited for widow, blue tie and yellow shirt.

baitfish n **chiefly Atl, esp C Atl, N Atl**

Any small fish used as bait.

1820 Rafinesque *Ohio R. Fishes* 51 **Allegheny Mts,** *Rutillus compressus . . .* A small fish from two to four inches long, called Fall-fish Bait-fish, Minny, &c. **1931–33** *LANE Worksheets* **csCT,** Baitfish—a minnow, same as redfin. **1939** *LANE Map* 234 (*Minnow*), The inclusive terms *bait fish, fish bait,* and *live bait* are widely used. **1965–70** *DARE* (Qu. P7, *Small fish used as bait*) 20 Infs, **chiefly Atl, esp N Atl, C Atl,** Baitfish.

bait hook See **bait iron** n

baiting vbl n, also attrib [**bait** v 1] **chiefly NEng** *somewhat old-fash* See also **bait** n 1, **bait and board**

A meal, or feed for an animal, esp as given on a journey or during a respite from work.

1825 Neal *Brother Jonathan* 2.95 **CT,** When we come nigh the taverns; or baitin' places, or post offices. **1843** *Knickerbocker* 22.430 **NH,** The country tavern, whose long shed and sanded hall give surety to the stranger and his beast of a comfortable noontide baiting. **1868** Brackett *Farm Talk* 99 **ME,** "Got your fodder all fed out?" "Nearly. There's a hundred or two more of fodder corn, which I keep for baitings." **1941** *LANE Map* 314 (*A bite [between meals]*) 9 infs, **c,nNEng,** Baiting. [Of these] *Baiting* is described as older though still in use by [6 infs]. **1968** *DARE* FW Addit, *Baiting* pasture—pasture for refreshing a horse . . . [From a] curator, Shaker museum. Old-fash. **1969** *DARE* Tape **MA58,** Then you went out there an' mowed till 9, 10 . . then you'd bring out the baitin': sandwich, cookies, fruit.

bait iron n, v Also *bait hook, ~ needle, ~ spear* **ME**

In lobstering: a needle-like tool used to insert small fish as lures in lobster traps; to prod with such a tool.

1975 Gould *ME Lingo* 3, *Bait Iron . . .* It is not unlike a chef's larding needle; a steel rod with a sharpened point and an eye, and a wooden handle. The imagery has come ashore: "He jumped's though somebody *bait-ironed* him!" **1978** Merriam *Illustr. Lobstering* 8 **ME,** *Bait iron*— A device for threading the bait bag, or whole bait, onto the bait string. It consists of a handle, often a piece of an old oar, and a long metal spike which has a hole near the end. The fisherman sticks the iron through the bait bag, then threads the bait string through the hole in the iron, and pulls the bait string through the bag. Also called bait hook, bait needle, bait spear.

bait-stealer n

1 =**cunner** n[1] 1.

1884 Goode *Fisheries U.S.* 1.273 **N Atl,** At Salem they are called "Nippers," and occasionally here and elsewhere "Bait-stealers."

2 See quot.

1968 DARE (Qu. P3, *Freshwater fish that are not good to eat*) Inf **IL**29, Mollies or bait-stealers—look like a real small catfish, yellowish color.

bait tree n Also called **fish-bait tree**
=**catalpa B1.**
   1941 FWP *Guide SC* 293, Descendants of the Scotch-Irish and Hugue-not settlers are still inveterate hunters and anglers, prizing catalpas as "bait trees" for their burden of caterpillars. **1965** *McDavid Coll.* **sSC,** Bait tree.

baitworm n **chiefly Midl, Sth** (See map in Kurath *Word Geog.* fig 139) See also **bait n 3**
The common worm used for bait; an earthworm.
   1949 Kurath *Word Geog.* 74, *Fish bait* and *bait worm* occupy smaller areas within the extensive *fishworm* and *fishing worm* areas of the Midland and South, namely, . . south-central Pennsylvania and adjoin-ing parts of Maryland and . . the western piedmont of Virginia and adjoining parts of Virginia. **1958** *PADS* 29.7 **cnTN,** Bait worm . . . Earthworm. **c1960** *Wilson Coll.* **csKY,** Baitworm . . . Worm used in fishing; heard occasionally. **1965–70** *DARE* (Qu. P5) 19 Infs, **chiefly Midl, Sth,** Baitworm; (Qu. P6) Inf **PA**240, Baitworm. [7 of 20 Infs Black] **1977–78** Foster *Lexical Variation* 66 **NJ,** *Bait worm . .* 2 [responses].

bajada n |bə'hɑdə| Also *baja,* pronc-sp *bahada* [Span] **SW**
A steep descent, road, or trail; also, an alluvial fan.
   1866 *Wkly. N. Mex.* 17 Nov 2/3 *(DA),* The road from here to Algodones by way of the Bajada is being worked. **1919** Chase *CA Desert* 259 **sCA,** I came up with him just as we emerged upon the sloping *bajada,* which is the feature of almost every desert cañon mouth. **1932** Bentley *Spanish Terms* 97, *Bajada . . .* A downgrade in the road or trail; a dugway; a sharp descent. The term is commonly used in New Mexico, Arizona and parts of Texas and California. **1933** *AmSp* 8.3.8 **SW,** A word which has been in use as a place name, but has only recently become generally descriptive is *bajada,* descent. This is quite explicitly applied to the abrupt break-off of a lava flow . . . Special types of plant life find their footing there which can best be described as bahada inhabiting. **1942** Kearney *Flowering Plants* 16 **AZ,** The bajadas are smooth, with gravelly surface, and are dominated by nearly pure stands of *Colegyne ramosis-sima.* **1968** Adams *Western Words,* Baja—A descent, usually severe, as at Raton Pass.

bake n Cf **clambake**
1 A meal or food usu prepared by baking. **chiefly NEng**
   1939 Wolcott *Yankee Cook Book* 26 **RI,** After the hot clams come more hot clams—and all the other good things that were in the bake. **1967–68** *DARE* (Qu. H48) Inf **MA**5, Bake—a bake of meat, a bake of roast; **NC**52, Potato bake; (Qu. H50) Inf **KS**20, Sweet-sour bean bake. **1969** *DARE* Tape **RI**8, A layer of wood and a layer of stone . . enough to make a bake. **1979** Flagg *Cape Cod Cooking* 213 **eMA,** It is rather strange that this most delicious of meals has always been called a "bake," since the food is not baked but steamed. *Ibid* 214, Kitchen bake—Fol-low the same directions as for the barrel bake, but do the cooking in a large kettle on the kitchen stove [rather than in the metal barrel out-doors].
2 A social gathering at which a meal, esp of baked food, is served. **?chiefly N Atl**
   1846 *Spirit of the Times* 6 June 174/3 **NY** *(DA),* In search of that five pound pickerel which he was bound to pull in every year, for the grand 'bake' at the village hotel. **1948** *Natl. Geog. Mag.* 94.170/2, If Rhode Island had never produced anything but a bake like that . . it would have been enough. **1967–68** *DARE* (Qu. FF1) Inf **NY**83, Cake sale, pizza bakes; (Qu. FF16) Inf **PA**7, Bakes—give food to raise money; **CT**19, Shad bake.

bake v **West** Cf **baked**
See quot 1944.
   1944 Adams *Western Words,* Bake—To ride in such a way as to overheat a horse. **1971** Jennings *Cowboys* 44 **West,** Bake just one of them horses, and you'll be sorry you ever laid eyes on him. I'm like a horse. I ain't no good when I get heated up.

bake a cake v phr Cf **bakehead**
Among railroad workers: to build up steam in a locomotive.
   1958 McCulloch *Woods Words* 6 **Pacific NW,** *Bake a cake*—To get a good fire going in a locie or donkey engine. **1977** Adams *Lang. Railroader.*

bake closet n
   1967 *DARE* (Qu. D8, *The small room next to the kitchen . . where dishes and sometimes food are kept*) Inf **NY**34, Pantry—no longer found in houses. Use [a] "bake closet"—of Dutch origin—to store baking things, [as] flour.

baked ppl adj Also called **beefsteak** v, **nigger-branded** Cf **bake** v
Of a horse: bruised or scraped by an ill-fitting saddle.
   1961 Adams *Old-Time Cowhand* 113 **SW,** Some saddles don't fit the hoss they're on, and cause sores, . . and the hoss is "baked."

baked-apple berry n Also *baked-apple* [Prob from the flavor and the wrinkled skin; *DCan* 1775 →]
=**cloudberry.**
   [**1889** *Century Dict.* Baked-apple . . . A name given in Labrador to the dried fruit of the *Rubus Chamaemorus,* or cloudberry.] **1900** Lyons *Plant Names* 325, *R. Chamaemorus . . .* Baked-apple-berry. **1947** Bowles–Towle *New Engl. Cooking* 159, Blueberries, huckleberries, raspberries, and the less known amber-colored baked-apple berries and salmon berries were all used for pies. **1950** Gray–Fernald *Manual of Botany* 819, *Baked-apple-berry, Baked-apple.* **1981** Tabbert *Alaskan Engl.* 277, *Rubus chamaemorus . . .* is also said to be called frequently baked-apple berry.

baked-apples-and-pears n [Perh from the flavor]
=**bunchberry 1.**
   1940 Clute *Amer. Plant Names* 256, *Cornus Canadensis.* Baked-apples-and-pears.

bakehead n Cf **bake a cake**
Among railroad workers: a locomotive fireman.
   1929 *Bookman* 69.525, The fireman has many names, some of which will not bear repeating. He is a . . Clinker-boy or a Bakehead. **1943** *AmSp* 18.162. **1947** Beebe *Mixed Train* 353. **1958** McCulloch *Woods Words* 6 **Pacific NW,** Bakehead—A railroad fireman . . . "After a man has fired so long he's baked all his brains out, they promote him to engineer." **1962** *AmSp* 37.131 **nCA,** Bakehead . . . A fireman on a steam locomotive.

bake-oven n [Du *bakoven;* cf Pa-Ger *back offe, bock offe*]
1 An oven used for baking. **somewhat old-fash**
   1859 (1968) Bartlett *Americanisms,* Bake-Oven. This term is often used in the West for the simple word *oven* in a bakery. It is also applied to the iron bake-pan. **1940** Yoder *Rosanna* 138 **cePA,** Large pieces of home-made bread baked in a bake oven. **1967** *DARE* Tape **PA**14, We had what they called a bake-oven . . big enough for eight loaves of bread and twelve to fifteen pies.
2 A Dutch oven, a heavy covered pot used esp for baking over an open fire. **somewhat old-fash**
   1809 in 1924 Austin *Papers* 1.164 **LA,** Also of Kitchen Utensils one table two Iron Pots one Bake Oven. **1883** *Harper's Mag.* 66.504/2 **AZ,** A few old men trudge about their bake-ovens. **1891** (1905) Ryan *Told in Hills* 100 **MT,** Without looking up from the eggs she was scrambling in the bake-oven of a few minutes before. **1902** (1969) Sears *Catalogue* 582/2, *Bake oven,* deep pattern . . . can be set in center of wood fire without injury to contents; cover fits down snug, so that nothing can get inside.
3 also attrib: An outdoor oven, or a farm building used princi-pally for baking.
   1777 in 1901 *Documents Revol. Hist. NJ* 1.335, A Good two story Brick-House, . . [with] bake-oven, a cedar log barn, and stables. **1848** Bryant *What I Saw in Cal.* 464 *(DAE),* The furnaces are of the simplest construction exactly like a common bake-oven. **1968–69** *DARE* (Qu. M22, *What other kinds of buildings would there be on farms around here?*) Inf **PA**141, Woodshed, bake-oven, wagonshed—old-fashioned; (Qu. H18, . . *Special kinds of bread*) Inf **MI**93, Bake-oven bread—made with pastry flour . . in an outside brick oven.
4 Among loggers: see quot. [Cf *DA* baker n[2], tent constructed to capture heat from a campfire]
   1969 Sorden *Lumberjack Lingo* 4 **NEng, Gt Lakes,** *Bake oven*—A cruiser's tent with one sloping side and two ends.

baker n[1]
1 A covered metal container used for baking; a Dutch oven.
   1841 *Lowell Offering* 1.227 **MA,** A peep into the baker told that the potatoes were cooked. **1897** *Outing* 29.489/1 **MT,** The cooking uten-

sils, consisting of three dripping pans, one patented baker and one large coffee-pot. **1952** Callahan *Smoky Mt.* 87 **NC,** When mealtime approached, the housewife would rake out on the hearth a glowing mass of embers, and place over them the covered cast-iron oven known as a "baker." **1956** *Hall Coll.* **eTN,** "The witch doctor told the folks to put the baker lid in the fire." *Baker lid* . . . The lid of a Dutch oven, which is placed in the coals of the fire place. **1960** Hall *Smoky Mt.* Folks 59 **wNC, eTN,** *Baker* . . a cast iron pan with three legs and a cover set in the coals of the fireplace. **1967** *DARE* FW Addit **TN16,** Corn dodgers used to be cooked in "baker and led [lɛd]" . . "led" means "lid."

2 A griddle; a shallow frying pan or skillet. Cf *DS* F1

1958 *PADS* 29.7 **cTN,** Baker . . . Informants describe it as "a small rimless skillet," "made of iron . . . used for baking biscuit and corn bread; it is too shallow for frying." **1965–70** *DARE* FW Addit **OK13,** Baker—shallow "frying pan" with long handle—used for quick frying; **KY85,** Baker—a rectangular griddle for hoecakes or flitters. **1970** Tarpley *Blinky* 94 **neTX,** *Heavy iron pan used for frying* . . . other responses[:] baker, . . Dutch oven, iron skillet.

3 also *bakie:* Any item of food which is suitable for baking. [*EDD* 1859 →]

1948 *Sun* (Baltimore MD) 5 Jan 10/2 *(Hench Coll.),* The term "fowl" is not always understood by housewives . . . In some retail markets fowls are called "bakers." **1967** *DARE* (Qu. I9) Inf **CA32,** Bakers—good baking ones. "Do you have any bakers?" **1968** *ID State Jrl.* (Pocatello) 20 Feb C26/5, The potato inside the strip retains the mealy texture and white color of Idaho bakers. **1976** Garber *Mountain-ese* **sAppalachians,** *Bakie* . . . Baking squash . . . We raised ten bushels uv *bakies* in our garden this year.

4 The rear room of an addition to a home. Cf **bake-oven 3, ell** n¹ 1

1941 *LANE* Map 352 **ceME,** *Lean-to* or [beɪkə], the rear part of the ell.

baker n² See **tobacco**

baker bread See **baker's bread**

baker flying See **flying baker**

baker's bread n Also *baker bread, bakers'* ~ [*OEDS* 1813 →] **throughout US, but esp Nth, N Midl, West** *old-fash* See Map Section

Bread baked by a baker (as opposed to home-baked bread).

1802 in 1929 Weems *Mason Locke Weems* 2.225 **NJ,** Some of those [books] . . look . . like sixpenny loaves of Baker's bread and feel to the full as light and spungy. **1895** U.S. Dept. Ag. *Yearbook for 1894* 41, Very few accurate weighings and analyses of bakers' bread have been made in this country. **1899** (1912) Green *VA Folk-Speech.* **c1960** *Wilson Coll.* **csKY,** *Baker's bread* . . . Bread in loaves bought from a bakery. Rarely heard now: it is just *bread* or a *loaf of bread.* **1965–70** *DARE* (Qu. H13, *Bread that is not made at home*) 283 Infs, **chiefly Nth, N Midl, West,** Baker's bread; 22 Infs, **chiefly Inland Nth,** Baker bread. [Of all Infs responding to the question, 70% were old; of those giving these responses, 93% were old.] **1983** *DARE* File **csWI** (as of 1930s), *Baker's* bread was what we called it; kids did too.

baker-sheet n **ME**
=**dripping pan.**

1907 *DN* 3.240 **eME,** *Baker sheet* . . . A shallow tin pan for baking cake. **1926** *DN* 5.385 **ME,** *Baker-sheet* . . . Dripping pan. "Biscuits are baked in a baker-sheet." Common. **1926** *AmSp* 2.79, She baked her biscuits in a dripping-pan, . . while my mother in Maine still uses a "baker-sheet," . . the same utensil called by a different name. **1934** *Hanley Disks* **swME,** What they called the baker sheet.

bakery n

1 also *bake wagon:* See quot. *obs*

1896 *DN* 1.412 **cNY,** *Bakery* . . . *bake wagon:* a travelling baker's cart.

2 Baked goods, esp sweet baked goods. **chiefly Ger settlement areas**

1949 *WELS Suppl.* **csWI,** Bakery—for the baked goods themselves. At the bakery you buy bakery. **1967** *DARE* FW Addit **Cleveland OH,** Bakery—one or several of various kinds of sweet baked goods. "I went to the doughnut shop and got some bakery." Some bakery could mean one cream puff or a dozen sweet rolls other than doughnuts. **1975** Morris *Usage* 62, The use of the word *bakery* to refer to baked goods is fairly widely heard in Dialect and folk speech, particularly among people of German descent. **1978** *Milwaukee Sentinel* (WI) 22 Dec sec 3 1/3, Fresh bakery is so rare in our house that my men get giddy over

brown'n'serve rolls. **1979–81** *DARE* File **Cleveland OH** (as of c1940), I heard it fairly often . . . "would you pick up some bakery on your way home?"; **Madison WI** [Sign in coffee shop], Fresh, fresh, fresh . . bakery; [Sign in supermarket], Order your Christmas bakery now.

bake-stuff n
Baked goods.

1903 *DN* 2.349 **neOH,** *Bake-stuff* . . . The baker's product in general.

‡bake up (someone) v phr
To prepare baked goods for (a number of people).

1939 Coffin *Capt. Abby* 19 **ME** (as of 1859–70), These hamlets had strawberry beds . . cucumber frames, a Dutch oven, big enough to bake up a whole family for a week.

bake wagon See **bakery 1**

bakie See **baker** n¹ 3

bakin See **bacon**

baking bread vbl n
A maneuver in the game of jump rope: see quot 1909.

1888 *Amer. Anthropologist* 266 **DC,** *Baking Bread* requires a rope with two to turn it. The performer holds in one hand a stone (representing a loaf of bread, I suppose) while she jumps three times. **1909** (1923) Bancroft *Games* 120, "Baking Bread." A player runs in with a stone in his hand, and while jumping places it on the ground, straightens up, picks up the stone again, and runs out.

baking powders n **chiefly sAppalachians, Ozarks** Cf **powders** Baking powder.

1905 *DN* 3.69 **nwAR,** *Baking powders* . . . "We don't make our biscuits with cream of tartar; we use Price's baking-powders." **1924** Raine *Land of Saddle-Bags* 165 **eKY,** [Caption:] When she's "clean out o' bakin' powders . . ," the "woman" takes her baby and a basket of eggs and rides to the little store five miles away to barter for groceries and "fixin's." **1926** Kephart *Highlanders* 371 **sAppalachians,** Tomato, cabbage, molasses and baking powder are always used as plural nouns . . . "How many bakin'-powders has you got?" **1928** Ruppenthal Coll. **KS.** **1967–68** *DARE* (Qu. H16, *What do people use to raise the bread before it's baked?*) Infs **AR47, TN27,** Baking powders.

bakkels n [Norw *bakkels(e)* cookie] Cf **fattigmanns bakkels**

1950 *WELS* (Other foods made with dough and cooked in deep fat) 1 Inf, **cWI,** Crullers, bakkels (Norwegian); (Foreign foods) 1 Inf, **cWI,** Bakkels—Scandinavian pastry.

bakkes adj, exclam |ˈbɑkəs, bækəs| Also *bakkie, baks, bax, bah; akkes, akkie, akkes bakkes* [Du] *in Dutch communities* See also **backsie**

Characterized by foulness or filth; repulsive. Dirty! Filthy!— often used as a warning to children.

1982 *DARE* File, My students confirm that *bakkes* ['bɑkəs], *bah* [bɑx], and *akkes* ['ɑkəs] are all used to describe filth. The forms *akkie* and *bakkie* are also very common, as is the combination *akkes bakkes.* The students who know and use these words are from Dutch backgrounds in Lynden, WA; Bellflower, CA; Denver, CO; Sioux Co., IA; Pella, IA; Grand Rapids, MI; Whitinsville, MA; and Paterson, NJ. *Ibid* **seWI,** *Bakkes* ['bækəs] is used as an adjective or as an expression of disgust or revulsion. I use *bakkie* in the same way—so do my kids. Not too long ago, Joel came into the house and said, "I just stepped in something bakkie." A shorter form, *baks* or *bax* ([bɑx] or [bɑks]), is used only as an exclamation. My German grandfather always used it, but I assumed that it was a form of our Dutch word. He'd say "Baks!" to warn a child away from something the kid was messing in, but he'd also use it to warn his dog. *Ibid* **swMI,** I recently caught myself warning my daughter that something was "bakkie" ['bɑkɪ]. Since then I've talked to a lot of Dutch people back in Holland and Grand Rapids about it; most of them know "bakkie" as an adjective and "bakkes" as an exclamation for something unpleasantly dirty or repulsive. The words are used most often in referring to food or excrement, and usually they're spoken to children. *Ibid* [see **bakkie**].

bakkie n See also **bakkes**

1982 *DARE* File **swMI,** When the first vowel in *bakkie* is long [bɑːkɪ], the word is specifically a noun meaning excrement: "I want to take a bakkie." When the vowel is shorter [bɑkɪ], the word is an adjective. Then it doesn't necessarily refer to biological elimination but can refer to anything filthy or distasteful, including spoiled soup or rancid butter.

bakont ppl adj Pronc-sp [Ger *bekannt* known]
Known, acquainted.
 1939 Aurand *Quaint Idioms* 11 **sePA,** Come here once . . and make yourself *bakont.*

baks See **bakkes**

bakun See **bacon**

bal' See **bald** n

balahack See **ballyhack**

balanced wall n Also *balance wall* **NEng** Cf **double stone wall, face wall**
A stone wall or fence.
 1931–33 *LANE Worksheets* **ceMA,** Balanced ['bælənst] wall . . . those stones were balanced on each other. **1934** *Hanley Disks* **seCT,** The balance wall, you can use anything. You don't have to have . . any particular shape stone. **1966–69** *DARE* (Qu. L60, *A fence made of stone or rock without mortar*) Inf **RI**12, Stone wall or balanced wall; **NH**3, Balanced wall.

balao n Also sp *ballaho, ballyhoo* [AmSpan *balajú*]
Either of two halfbeaks (*Hemiramphus balao* or *Hemiramphus brasiliensis*) found in waters off the Florida coast.
 1867 De Voe *Market Asst.* 199, There are likewise to be caught in the winter season, fish, by towing over this bank, if a person has suitable bait, such as the *ballaho*, which they have generally in the West Indies. **1902** Jordan–Evermann *Amer. Fishes* 242, The balaos (genus *Hemiramphus*) have the body compressed . . . There are 2 species in our waters. **1922** *Outing* 79.253/1, For sail and other large fish they use a sardine-sized, sword-nosed minnow called a ballyhoo. **1949** *Esquire* Mar 81, Bait—mullet, squid, balao. **1975** Evanoff *Catch More Fish* 140, Most offshore trolling is done with various . . fish such as mullet, balao or ballyhoo, eels, mackerel, . . and similar fish.

balcony n Usu |'bælkənɪ|; in **Sth,** freq |bæ-kənɪ| Cf Pronc Intro 3.I.22
A Form.
 1940 *AmSp* 15.259 **Sth,** In the South the *l* is frequently lost before *-k* when it is preceded by any vowel . . . Thus . . *balcony* . . [bæ-kənɪ].
B Sense.
A porch constructed at the ground level of a home.
 1860 Holmes *Professor* 197 **NEng,** On such a balcony or "stoop," one evening, I walked with Iris. **1950** *PADS* 14.12 **SC,** Balcony . . . A small side porch with an iron railing, usually ornate. **c1960** *Wilson Coll.* **csKY,** Balcony. Porch. Rare.

bald n Pronc-sp **bal'** chiefly **S Midl, esp sAppalachians, Ozarks** See also **baldhead 2, slick**
A bare or treeless mountain top.
 1838 *S. Lit. Messenger* 4.231/2 **AL,** At length . . we came to the top of the near Bald; from this we had an extensive and delightful prospect . . . After a short pause, we went on to the far Bald, which we found a good deal higher than the near. **1907** Wright *Shepherd* 18 **Ozarks,** Reckon you know 'bout Colonel Dewey, him the Bal' up thar's named fer? **1939** *Hall Coll.* **wNC, eTN,** We took our dogs, took out to the top, . . and down in under the bald we went. **1939** *FWP Guide TN* 514, Treeless areas or "balds"—called slicks by the natives because of their deceptive appearance of smoothness—are found on some of the ridge tops. **1960** Williams *Walk Egypt* 7 **nGA,** On Ellie Bald . . no trees had grown since time began . . . Folks said it was not the only bald in the mountains, that there were half a dozen more, some a quarter of an acre wide, one a thousand acres. **1961** Douglas *My Wilderness* 164 **NC,** Some of the ridges in the Smokies, particularly in the western part, have no trees. They are the "balds" found on or near summits. Some slopes that are covered with rhododendron, laurel, blueberry, and minniebush (all of the heath family) are called "heath balds" by botanists.

bald adv [Ger *bald* almost, nearly]
 1914 *DN* 4.103 **KS,** Bald . . . About. "It's bald half mile up there."

bald brant n Also *bald-headed brant*
=**blue goose** n **1.**
 1874 Long *Wild-Fowl* 243 *(DA)*, The younger [blue geese] . . are further characteristically distinguished as bald-brant or white-heads. **1888** Trumbull *Names of Birds* 9, Names of *Chen cærulescens*, as follows: . . Bald-headed Brant or Bald Brant. **1917** (1923) *Birds Amer.*

1.156, *Blue Goose* . . Other Names . . . Bald-headed Brant. **1932** Bennitt *Check-list* 18 **MO,** *Blue goose* . . . bald brant.

bald coot n
1 also pronc-sp **ball coot:** =**coot** n[1] **1.** *?obs*
 1709 (1967) Lawson *New Voyage* 153 **S Atl,** Black Flusterers . . . Some call these the great bald Coot. **a1782** (1788) Jefferson *Notes VA* 77, Besides these [birds], we have The Royston crow . . . Black head. Ballcoot. Sprigtail. **1859** Willis *Convalescent* 387 **VA,** He said there were thirty [kinds], naming, among others, the blue-wing, . . the ball-coot [etc.].
2 =**Florida gallinule.**
 1923 U.S. Dept. Ag. *Misc. Circular* 13.44, *Florida Gallinule* . . Vernacular Names . . . *In local use* . . Bald coot (S.C.).

bald cow See **baldhead** n **3**

baldcrown n
=**baldpate 1.**
 1888 Trumbull *Names of Birds* 21, *Anas americana* . . At Crisfield, Md. (east shore of Chesapeake), and Wilmington, N.C., *Bald-crown.* **1917** (1923) *Birds Amer.* 1.120, *Baldpate* . . Other Names . . . Bald-crown. **1932** Bennitt *Check-list* 18 **MO,** *Baldpate* . . bald crown. **1968–70** *DARE* (Qu. Q5, *Kinds of wild ducks*) Inf **MD**36, Baldcrown—real name is baldpate; **MD**45, **VA**52, Baldcrown—(same as) baldpate.

bald cypress n
A timber tree of the genus *Taxodium*, esp *T. distichum*, a deciduous conifer which in wet areas produces woody projections or "knees" from the roots; found throughout the South and as far north as southern Illinois. Also called **cypress 2a, red cypress, sabino, swamp cedar, swamp cypress, white cypress, yellow cypress** See also **pond cypress**
 1709 (1967) Lawson *New Voyage* 103 **S Atl,** Cypress is not an Evergreen with us, and is therefore call'd the bald Cypress. **1832** Browne *Sylva* 143, It is called . . in the ancient Southern States *Cypress*, and sometimes *Bald Cypress*. **1901** Mohr *Plant Life AL* 110, On the . . banks of both of these rivers a fine timber growth of bald cypress frequently forms brakes of considerable extent. **1967–70** *DARE* (Qq. T15, 16) Infs **MO**12, **MA**78, Bald cypress; **CT**4, Bald cypress—found rarely, imported. **1969** *DARE* FW Addit **eNC,** Bald cypress—plant common on Hatteras Island.

bald eagle n
1 also *bald-headed eagle, baldhead:* A large North American eagle (*Haliæetus leucocephalus*) which has dark juvenile plumage, but develops a white head and tail with maturity. Also called **black eagle 2, brown eagle, Washington eagle**
 1688 in 1694 Royal Soc. London *Philos. Trans. for 1693* 17.989 **VA,** The Second is the Bald Eagle, for the Body and part of the Neck being of a dark brown, the upper part of the Neck and Head is covered with a white sort of Down, whereby it looks very bald, whence it is so named. **1705** Beverley *Hist. VA* 2.34, In the Air you see a Fishing-Hawk flying away with a Fish, and a Bald-Eagle pursuing, to take it from him. **1836** (1935) Holley *Texas* 100, The bald-headed eagle, and the Mexican eagle . . are among the birds of prey, and are very common. **1850** Garrard *Wah-to-yah* 175 **NM,** The magnificent "bald head" unfolded his wings slowly. **1878** Beadle *Western Wilds* 483 **CO,** Small is the pleasure one can take . . in the sweep of the bald eagle, where the next occupation of that eagle may be in picking the meat from his bones. **1965–70** *DARE* (Qq. Q4, 10, 13) Infs **AK**1, **CA**137, **FL**13, **GA**28, 35, **NJ**39, **OK**25, **SC**4, **VA**47, Bald eagle; (Qu. Q4) Inf **WI**43, Bald-headed eagle.
2 A kind of caterpillar.
 1967 *DARE* (Qu. R27, *What kinds of caterpillars or similar worms do you have around here?*) Inf **PA**44, Bald eagle.

baldface n
1 also *bald-faced widgeon* and pronc-sp *ballface:* =**baldpate 1.**
 1709 (1967) Lawson *New Voyage* 155 **S Atl,** The bald, or white Faces are a good Fowl. They cannot dive. *Ibid* 141, Water fowl are . . Sheldrakes, Bald Faces, [etc.]. **1768** (1925) Washington *Diaries* 1.253 **VA,** Went a ducking between breakfast and dinner and killd 2 Mallards and 5 bald faces. **1888** Trumbull *Names of Birds* 20, *Anas americana* . . . At Washington, D.C., Alexandria, Va., and Morehead, N.C., *Bald-face* (not recognized in latter locality by any other name) . . . At St. Augustine, Fla., *Bald-faced widgeon.* **1889** *Century Dict.* 6921/1, American widgeon . . . Also called locally *bald-faced widgeon.* **1917** (1923) *Birds*

Amer. 1.120, *Baldpate . . Other Names . . .* Ballface. **1925** Bailey *Birds FL* 21, Ballface.

2 A horse having a white face or a conspicuous white mark on the face—often used as a nickname. Cf **bald-faced, baldy** n[1]

1785 (1925) Washington *Diaries* 2.436 **VA,** Completed the Acct. of my Stock . . which stands thus . . Black bald face. **1894** *Outing* 24.216/2 **CT,** I jest had time to hitch old Bald Face into the cart and git here. **1927** *Ruppenthal Coll.* **KS. 1968–70** *DARE* (Qu. K39, . . *Names . . for horses according to their color*) Infs **TX8**, 16, Baldface; **CA63**, Baldface —white all the way down front of head; **TX102**, Baldface—lot of white in front.

3 also *bald-faced whisk(e)y,* pronc-spp *ball-face, ball-faced whiskey:* Unaged whiskey. [*W3 "obs. slang"*] **chiefly Sth, Midl**

1836 *Wkly. Advertiser* (Russellville, Ky.) 21 Jan 1/5 *(DA),* He has refused to keep anything to drink but ball-[sic] faced whiskey. **1845** Hooper *Advent. Simon Suggs* 90 **AL,** The Captain and "Lewtenant Snipes" sat down, with a bottle of bald-face between them. **1851** (1969) Burke *Polly Peablossom* 60 **IN,** If you've got any more of that baldface, pour it out! *Ibid* 150 **MS,** Mat Cain . . drunk up my last bottle of "ball-face." **1953** Randolph *Down in Holler* 225 **Ozarks,** Bald face . . . Raw corn whiskey. Said to be a reference to *bald-face hornets;* they're hot, too. **1954** *Harder Coll.* **cwTN,** Bald face . . . Whiskey. **1969** Sorden *Lumberjack Lingo* 4 **NEng, Gt Lakes,** *Bald-faced whisky* —A potent, cheap grade of whisky. **1972** Cooper *NC Mt. Folkl.* 89, Bald faced whiskey—whiskey fresh from the still.

4 See **baldhead 3.**

baldface v

Among loggers and railroad workers: to push head-on with a locomotive; see quots.

1950 *Western Folkl.* 9.116 **OR,** *Baldfacing logs.* Shoving a train of logs ahead of the engine. **1977** Adams *Lang. Railroader, Baldfacing logs:* Loaded log cars being pushed by a locomotive from the rear.

bald-faced adj See also **baldface** n 1, 2, **bald-faced hornet**

1 Of an animal, esp of a horse: having a white face, or a white mark on the face. See also **baldy** n[1]

1648 in 1887 *Archives of MD* 4.425, Making a private conueyance betweene themselues of a Bawld-facd heighfer. **1899** (1912) Green *VA Folk-Speech, Baldfaced . . .* Having a white face. Said of animals. **1930** *AmSp* 6.97 **cnNY,** *Baldfaced:* white-faced (as applied to horses). "Dan's baldfaced nag was a fast walker." **1944** Adams *Western Words, Bald-faced . . .* [is] also applied to a horse when the white on its head includes one or both eyes. Sometimes white-faced cattle are called *baldfaced.* **1967** *DARE* (Qu. K39) Inf **KS1**, Bald-faced horse.

2 Transf: see quot.

1969 *DARE* (Qu. X29, *Joking or uncomplimentary words for a person's face*) Inf **MA15**, Bald-faced.

bald-faced hornet n Also *baldface hornet, bald hornet*

A **paper wasp** *(Vespula maculata)* which is largely black with yellowish-white markings. Also called **white-assed hornet, white-faced hornet**

1796 (1905) Latrobe *Jrl. of Latrobe* 104 **VA,** The bald-face hornet. This dangerous fly is proverbially fierce. **1859** Taliaferro *Fisher's R.* 194 **nwNC** (as of 1820s), It was as if you had assaulted a ball-hornet's nest. **1861** IL Dept. Ag. *Trans. for 1859–60* 4.341, The nest of our American bald-faced hornet is occasionally suspended in a house to kill off the house-flies. **1899** (1912) Green *VA Folk-Speech, Baldface hornet . . .* A hornet so called because it has a whitish head. **1953** [see **baldface** n 3]. **1966–70** *DARE* (Qu. R21) Inf **MI2**, Bald-faced hornet—the biggest hornet, has a white face; **MI65**, Bald-faced hornet—the ones that make the paper nests; he is striped brown and white; **MI116, WI43**, Bald-faced hornet; **CA197**, Bald hornet; **KY5**, Bald hornet—black with gray abdomen, white face.

baldface dish n Cf **bald-faced shirt**

A white china plate.

1968 Adams *Western Words, Baldface dishes*—A cowboy's term for china dishes. He is used to eating out of granite or tin plates or bowls.

bald-faced shirt n Also *bally-faced shirt* **West** See also **boiled shirt, hereford**

A men's white dress shirt.

1889 (1971) Farmer *Americanisms* 33, *Bald-faced shirt.*—The name

by which a Western cowboy knows a white shirt. It is thought to come from the fact of Hereford cattle having white faces. **1941** FWP *Guide WY* 213, These occasions filled the inn to capacity: women in evening gowns, men in 'bally-faced, board shirts' and tails. **1944** Adams *Western Words, Baldfaced*—A stiff-bosomed shirt, sometimes called *boiled.*

bald-faced whisk(e)y See **baldface** n 3

bald-faced widgeon See **baldface** 1

baldface hornet See **bald-faced hornet**

baldhead n

1 =**wood ibis.**

1913 *Auk* 30.491, *Mycteria americana . . .* 'Baldhead'. **1936** *Oriole* 1.3, *Wood Ibis.*—Bald-head.

2 The bare, rounded top of a plateau, mesa or mountain. **SW** Cf **bald** n

1923 *Natl. Geog. Mag.* 43.205 **AZ,** The purple sage . . found in the crevices of these "baldheads." **1941** FWP *Guide UT* 509, The tops of plateaus, mesas, and mountains in the area are rounded—natives call them whalebacks and baldheads.

3 also *bald cow, baldface, bald-headed cow:* A naturally hornless cow. [Cf *EDD bald* 5 in similar sense] **chiefly VA, NC**

1969–70 *DARE* (Qu. K12, *A cow that has never had horns*) Infs **NC68, OK56, VA77**, Baldhead; **VA40, 75**, Bald-headed; **NC63**, Bald; **MS81**, Bal'head or bal'face.

4 See **bald eagle 1.**

bald-headed adj

1 pronc-sp *ball-headed:* Foolish.

1884 Harrison *Negro Engl.* 277 **Sth,** To be de ball-headest creetur . . to be the biggest fool.

2 also as exclam, in var mild oaths: See quots. **?Nth**

1939 FWP *ID Lore* 242, Some Mild Profanity . . . By the bald-headed Jews—the more emphatic variants substitute . . members of the Trinity. **1965–66** *DARE* FW Addit **neME,** Bald-headed—a mild cuss word, as in "Oh, bald-headed!" or "Why you bald-headed so-and-so!" **1966** *DARE* (Qu. NN29c, *Exclamations . . . : "Holy _____!"*) Inf **MI10**, Old bald-headed . . . [phrase] can be continued.

bald-headed adv

1 Precipitately; hurriedly, without caution. [See quot 1872] **chiefly Nth, West**

1848 Lowell *Biglow* 79 **NEng,** I scent wich pays the best, an' then / Go into it baldheaded. **1872** Schele de Vere *Americanisms* 581, *Bald-headed,* to go it, is a very peculiar but not unfrequent phrase in New England, suggestive of the eagerness with which men rush to do a thing without taking time to cover their head. **1888** *Pall Mall Gaz.* 22 June 4/2, The Chicago Republicans, to use an Americanism, have gone "baldheaded" for Protection. If shouting could win a Presidential contest, Blaine and Protection would be certain. **1958** McCulloch *Woods Words* 6 **Pacific NW,** *Bald-headed . . .* To go at a job by main strength and ignorance, having no real savvy of how to do it. **1967** *DARE* (Qu. KK52, . . *In an indirect and complicated way: "I don't know why he had to go _____ to do that."*) Inf **WY3**, At it bald-headed.

2 in phr *snatch* or *jerk (one)* ~: To manhandle; to treat roughly.

1869 *Overland Mth.* 2.190/2, None but a wild and savage animal, of course, would "snatch a gentleman bald-headed," as the old man expressed it. **1909** Twain *Is Shakespeare Dead* 6 **Missip Valley,** Can't you keep away from that greasy water? pull her down! snatch her! snatch her baldheaded! **1928** *Ruppenthal Coll.* **KS,** If you do not mind her she'll snatch you baldheaded. **1945** *Jefferson Co. Republican* (Golden Colo.) 28 Feb 2/2 *(DA),* Just let me get hold of em, I'll jerk 'em bald-headed!

bald-headed brant See **bald brant**

bald-headed buzzard n

=**turkey vulture.**

1969 *DARE* (Qu. Q13) Inf **GA80**, Bald-headed buzzard—a kind [of] vulture.

bald-headed cow See **baldhead 3**

bald-headed eagle See **bald eagle 1**

bald-headed gannet n

=**wood ibis.**

1955 *Oriole* 20.3, *Wood Ibis . . . Bald-headed Gannet* (the head is unfeathered; gannet, perhaps by transfer from the large sea fowl, ordinarily so called, probably from resemblance in color pattern — mostly white with black wing tips).

bald-headed pie n
=apple pandowdy.

1941 *LANE* Map 292 *(Apple Dumpling)* 1 inf, **cMA,** Bald-headed pie.

bald-headed row n Also *bald-head row* *joc*
1 The front row of a theater (proverbially occupied by bald-headed men).

1887 *Courier-Jrl.* (Louisville KY) 16 Jan 10/1, The arts and wiles of the occupant of the bald-head row were of no avail, the proud Italian girl treating them with scorn. **1889** (1971) Farmer *Americanisms, Bald-headed Row.* — The first row of stalls at theatres, especially those which make a feature of ballets . . . the innuendo is obvious. **1944** Pyle *Brave Men* 120 **IN,** One night I went to a USO show given in a rest area and was put in the bald-headed row up front. **1968** *DARE* (QR, near Qu. CC5) Bald-headed row — front seats in a burlesque.

2 Transf: a row of seats within a church, usu near the front.

1965–70 *DARE* (Qu. CC5, . . *Seats in a church, especially near the front)* Infs **IA3, NY145, UT4, WI19,** Bald-headed row; **CA7,** Bald-headed rows — first two rows; **CT12A,** Bald-headed row — in back; **NC13,** Bald-headed row [laughter]; **SC11,** Bald-headed row — for people who can't hear well, near the front; **SC21,** Bald-head row — front row — old men sat there — from the front row in a burlesque show. All the old men went up front.

bald hornet See bald-faced hornet

baldpate n
1 A medium-sized, reddish-brown duck (*Mareca americana,* also known as *Anas americana*) distinguished by a prominent white crown. Also called **baldcrown, baldface** n 1, **bald widgeon, ballie, bluebill** 3, **brown widgeon, gray duck, green-headed widgeon, poacher, robber duck, smoking duck, specklebelly, summer duck, wheat duck, whistler, whistling dick, whistling duck, white-belly, white-face, widgeon, zin-zin**

1814 Wilson *Amer. Ornith.* 8.86 **Chesapeake Bay,** The . . Widgeons, or as they are called round the bay, *Bald pates.* **1838** Audubon *Ornith. Biog.* 4.337, *Anas Americana* . . In the Western Country, and in most parts of the Eastern and Middle States, it is called the *Bald Pate.* **1917** *DN* 4.422 **LA, NEng. 1950** *WELS* 1 Inf, **ceWI,** Baldpate. **1967–70** *DARE* (Qu. Q5) Infs **GA18, MD45, PA180, VA47,** Baldpate (duck); **IA3,** Baldpate — American widgeon; **MD34,** Baldpate — half the size of [a] mallard, usually fat; **PA155,** Widgeon or bal'pate.

2 =surf scoter.

1888 Trumbull *Names of Birds* 103, *Surf Scoter* . . . to some at Eastport [ME], *Bald-pate.* **1917** (1923) *Birds Amer.* 1.151, *Surf scoter* . . *Other Names* . . . Baldpate.

3 =bufflehead 2.

1955 *MA Audubon* 39.316, *Buffle-head.* Baldpate (Mass. In allusion to the white crown, which, however, is far from bald.).

bald widgeon n
=baldpate 1.

1917 (1923) *Birds Amer.* 1.120, *Baldpate . . Other Names:* . . Bald Widgeon. **1932** Bennitt *Check-list* 18 **MO,** Baldpate . . . bald widgeon. **1947** *Sun* (Baltimore MD) 29 Jan 12/3 *(Hench Coll.),* Baldpate — Mareca Americana (Gmelin). Also known as . . bald widgeon.

baldy n[1] Also *bally, bawsie* See also **baldface** n 2 and *SND bawsey*
A **bald-faced** horse or cow — often used as a nickname.

1894 *Outing* 24.216/2 **CT,** Well, I tried to wear it [=a whip] out on Baldy coming down. **1904** (1932) Rice *Sandy* 94 **KY,** I d-drove dad's buggy . ., so he would come to the r-rescue, and he swung on to old B-Baldy's neck like he had been a racehorse. **1913** (1979) Barnes *Western Grazing* 380 **West,** *Baldy* . . . Horse with a white face. **1930** Shoemaker *1300 Words* 8 **cPA Mts** (as of c1900), *Bawsie* — A white faced horse or bovine animal. **1941** FWP *Guide WY* 395, Breeds [of cattle] are mixed on the average farm, producing roans, 'black ballies,' and spotted reds.

baldy n[2] Also called **steelie**
A ball bearing used as a playing marble.

1966 *DARE* (Qu. EE6d, *Special marbles)* Inf **ME15,** Baldies — ball bearings.

bale n[1] Also sp *bail* [*bale* large bundle of merchandise]
A small package.

1940 *AmSp* 15.446 **eTN,** *Bale.* A package. 'I focht [=fetched] a bale of soda from the crossroads store.' **1954** *Harder Coll.* **cwTN,** Bale . . . Box of baking soda. **1980** *DARE* File **wNC** (as of c1918), Bail of snuff — a very small quantity in a paper package, price then five cents.

bale n[2] [?*bail* hoop-handle of a pot or similar vessel]
In a homemade distillery: see quot.

1972 *Foxfire Book* 315 **neGA,** *Bale* — wire or chain strapped across top of cap to keep it from blowing off during the cooking process.

bale of hay n
1 See quot.

1948 *Collier's* 14 Feb 23 **Boston MA,** In the summer the demands for blueberry cake, strawberry shortcake and, for some mysterious reason, "bale of hay" — a combination of peas, string beans and potatoes — reach enormous proportions.

2 In phr *not to know one from a bale of hay* (or *crap*): A person one does not know or cannot identify. *joc*

1965–70 *DARE* (Qu. II26, . . *"I wouldn't know him from _____."*) Infs **IL80, MI44, NE4, NY1,** 32, 199, 219, **OH95, PA175,** Bale of hay; **NY131,** Bale of crap.

3 Among loggers: see quot.

1958 McCulloch *Woods Words* 6 **Pacific NW,** *Bale of hay* — A very crude splice in wire rope made by a green logger; has jaggers sticking out on all sides.

balfouder n [See quot]
1940 *Hench Coll.* **neKY,** A member of the English faculty of the Univ. of Va. said that once when he was in Maysville, Ky . . he heard children dressed up for Christmas, Thanksgiving, etc., called "balfouders." He said the word was originally "bal poudré," a powdered ball, or by extension, a person who goes to a powdered ball. A powdered ball was a high-class social function, with dancing, etc. "Powder" presumably refers to powder on wigs.

balk n
1 See quot.

1940 *Hench Coll.* **cnVA,** A native Virginian . . said that a *balk* can be a pile of leaves, or brush piled up around a tree or bush.

2 See quot.

1959 *VT Hist.* ns 27.124, *Balk* . . . The unploughed section in the middle of the road, left when roads were "broken out" by a two-horse team and heavy farm sled . . obsolescent.

3 See quot.

1894 *DN* 1.340 **seNY,** *Balk* . . . an iron stake used to "stake out" an animal to graze.

4 in phr *the balks:* Fits of stubbornness.

1941 Percy *Lanterns* 76 **nwMS,** I was a sickly youngster who never had illnesses, . . who was . . docile but given to the balks.

balkenbry n Also sp *balken brie, balkenbrij* [Du *balk* beam, rafter (from which the meat mixture is hung to cure) + **bry**]
swMI and other Dutch settlement areas
See quot 1940.

1940 *AmSp* 15.83 **swMI,** *Balkenbry* ['bɑlkənbraɪ]. A loaf made of pork liver and lean pork, cooked, and later sliced and fried. **1950** *WELS* *(Foreign foods favored in your neighborhood)* 1 Inf, **seWI,** Balken brie. **1964** (1971) *Eet Smakelijk* 307 **swMI,** *Balkenbrij.* Ibid 567, *Balken Brij* — Dutch Breakfast Mush . . Slice as needed and fry slices brown . . . Serve as a breakfast dish in place of bacon or sausage. **1969** *DARE* (Qu. H43, *Foods made from parts of the head and inner organs of an animal)* Inf **MI102,** Balkenbry ['bɔlkən,braɪ] — mainly liver and pork; mixture is cooked, stuffed into a cloth bag, spices added, then recooked; the slices are cut off and fried . . . similar to liver sausage. **1981** [see **bry**].

ball n[1]
‡**1** The yolk of an egg. Cf *DS* H34

1941 *LANE* Map 296 *(Yolk)* 1 inf, **neMA,** [bɔl], 'I call it.'

2 See quot.

1954 *PADS* 21.20 **SC,** *Ball* . . . One of the two bulging sides of a bale of cotton, i.e., the two sides which were subjected to pressure in baling.

3 also *French ball:* Hair coiled at the back of a woman's head; a bun. **chiefly Sth** See Map See also **ball** v[1]

1965–70 *DARE* (Qu. X3, *When a woman puts her hair up on her head in a bunch you call this a _____*.) 73 Infs, **chiefly Sth,** Ball; **VA**73, French ball.

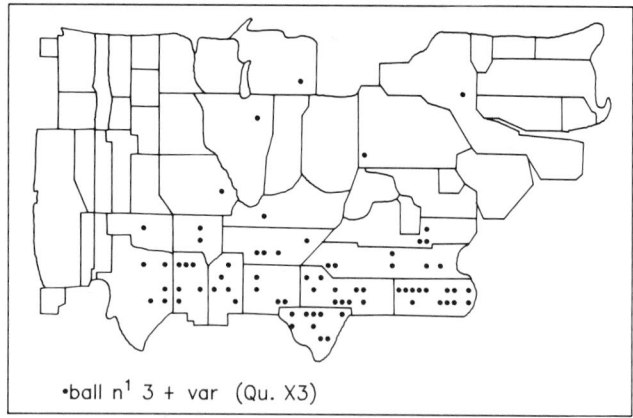

•ball n¹ 3 + var (Qu. X3)

4 The rounded back part of the head.

1982 *Foxfire* 7 250 **nGA,** She'd lay her hand on me and kiss the ball of my head.

ball n² [Fr *bal* dance] *esp among Black speakers* See also **ball** v²

An uninhibited, noisy drinking party. (Note: this is the origin of the widespread phr *have a ball* to enjoy oneself; see *DS* FF17)

1934 *AmSp* 9.287 **PA** [Black], *Ball.* Any riotous or hilarious party or pre-arranged gathering. 1960 Wentworth–Flexner *Slang, Ball . . .* a party, esp. a wild, unrestrained, uninhibited, boisterous, or noisy party . . . *some early c1935 Negro jive use. Orig. pop. by bop and cool use, and assoc. with jazz . . . Now common student and teenage use.* 1967–70 *DARE* (Qu. DD34, *A party at which there is considerable drinking*) Infs **FL**52, **MI**115, **PA**164, **SC**68, 69, **TN**50, Ball; **GA**82, Drunken ball; (Qu. FF18) Infs **AL**60, Ball; **MO**35, Made a ball—young kids like "ball"; **SC**40, Put on a ball. [5 of 10 Infs Black]

ball v¹ Also *ball up* [**ball** n¹ 3] **Sth**

To put up one's hair in a bun.

1966–68 *DARE* (Qu. X3) Inf **TX**36, Balling her hair; **NC**49, Balling it; **GA**9, Balled up; **NC**40, Ball up; **GA**33, She balls it up. 1967 *DARE* FW Addit **cnNC,** Ball up—to put your hair up on your head in a ball (bun). 1967 *DARE* Tape **SC**46, You get a certain age, you were eligible to have your hair balled up. As long as you were in your teenage, you wore your hair hangin' down, plaited.

ball v² Hence *balling* vbl n [**ball** n²] *chiefly among Black speakers* See also **ball the jack** 4

To have a good or exciting time.

1942 *Amer. Mercury* 55.94 **NYC** [Black], Balling—having fun. 1958 Hughes–Bontemps *Negro Folkl.* 481 **NYC,** Ball: To have riotous fun. *On Saturday we ball!* 1968–70 *DARE* (Qu. FF18, *. . About a noisy or boisterous celebration or party: "They certainly _____ last night."*) Infs **DC**12, **IL**140, **MO**23, **MA**128, **NY**55, 235, **OH**103, Balled. [All Infs Black] 1970 Major *Afro–Amer. Slang, Ball:* to have social or sexual fun or both. 1970 *DARE* (QR, near Qu. DD34) Inf **FL**52, We're going balling tonight. [Inf Black]

ballad n Usu |'bæləd|; **chiefly in S Midl,** freq |'bælɪt| Pronc-spp *ballet, ballit, ballot, valet* [*OED ballet, -ette,* "obs. forms of *ballad*"]

A Forms.

1896 *DN* 1.425 **swNC,** Song-valet. 1899 (1912) Green *VA Folk-Speech, Ballet . . .* Ballad. 1917 *DN* 4.407 **wNC,** Ballet. Variant of *ballad.* 1926 Kephart *Highlanders* 352 **sAppalachians,** Most hillsmen say . . ballet (ballad). 1927 *DN* 5.472 **Ozarks,** My boy he written out th' ballot o' thet 'ar song. 1927 Kennedy *Gritny* 39 **sLA** [Black], All the "ballets" and "sinful songs" disseminated by "backsliders" and "evil-workers." 1930 Shoemaker *1300 Words* **cPA Mts** (as of c1900), *Ballet* —An old time poem, or folk song. 1931 *PMLA* 46.1317 **sAppalachians,** Ballet. 1934 Carmer *Stars Fell on AL* 69, Pick a ballit . . and sing it. Pick *Barbary Allen.* 1937 *AmSp* 12.231 **NJ** [Black], *Ballet.* 1952 Brown *NC Folk.* 1.518 **wNC,** ['bælɪt]. c1960 *Wilson Coll.* **csKY,** *Ballad* /'bæləd, bælɪt/.

B Sense.

The words or the written manuscript for a song. **chiefly S Midl** [*EDD ballet* 1] Also called **song-ballad**

1927 [see *DN* quot at **A** above]. 1927 *AmSp* 2.348 **WV,** She has promised to write me the ballet of that song. 1929 *AmSp* 5.87 **sAppalachians,** None of the singers whom I visited . . possessed any printed song-sheets, but some of them produced written copies, usually made by children, which they call "ballets." *Ibid* 88 **MS,** Those among whom ballads were current applied the term "ballet" to the manuscript copy of a ballad or song without reference to the maker of it. c1960 *Wilson Coll.* **csKY,** *Ballad . . .* Used for the written words of a song, whether a ballad in the usual sense or not.

ballaho See **balao**

ball and (the) jack See **ball the jack** 2

ballast n [Transf from nautical use, material placed aboard ship to stabilize it when empty of cargo]

1 in phr *have ballast on board:* To be drunk.

1891 Maitland *Amer. Slang Dict.* 24, A drunken man has too much ballast on board. 1912 Green *VA Folk-Speech, Ballast . . .* "With their ballast on board;" that is, drunk.

2 Esp among railroad workers: heavy food, as turkey stuffing. *joc*

1945 Hubbard *Railroad Ave.* 332, *Ballast*—Turkey or chicken dressing. 1958 McCulloch *Woods Words* 6 **Pacific NW,** *Ballast . . .* Heavy bread (but never mentioned in the hearing of the camp cook). 1977 Adams *Lang. Railroader* 10.

ballawhang v Cf **ballyhack** v 3, **whang**

To beat or handle roughly.

1908 *DN* 3.288 **eAL, wGA,** He was ballawhanged all over the head.

ball-back See **ball-come-back**

ball bug n

=**sowbug.**

1967 *DARE* (QR, near p121) Inf **CO**31, Ball bug—sow bug—will roll up in a round ball if they are touched.

ball cheese n Cf **hand cheese**

1970 *DARE* (Qu. H60, *The lumpy white cheese that is made from sour milk*) Inf **PA**242, Ball cheese.

ball-come-back exclam Also *ball-back* See also **back-ball, anti-come-back,** and *DS* EE23b

In the game of **Antony-over:** =**pigtail** exclam.

1967 *DARE* (Qu. EE23b) Inf **OH**8, Ball-come-back; **IL**9, Ball-back.

ball coot See **bald coot** 1

balled up adj phr Cf **backed up**

Constipated.

1968 *DARE* (Qu. BB21) Inf **MD**24, Balled up. 1983 *NADS Letters* **TX,** My father, who died at age 86 in 1974, always used the expression "balled up". He grew up in East Texas but lived in Houston more than 50 years.

ballet See **ballad**

ballface See **baldface** n 1, 3

ball-faced whiskey See **baldface** n 3

ball fish n [From its shape when distended]

=**porcupine fish.**

1884 Goode *Fisheries U.S.* 1.170, The Porcupine Fishes . . . are commonly known by such names as 'Burr Fish,' 'Ball Fish,' [etc].

ballhead n, also attrib Also *bullhead*

See quot 1962.

1955 Adams *Grandfather* 20 **cNY** (as of 1870s), We could have told a ballhead from a needleboat a mile away. 1962 Wyld *Low Bridge* 84 **nNY,** One type of canal boat was rounded rather than blunt-ended. Nicknamed ball-head boats at first, they later became known as bull-heads. 1978 *Pioneer Amer.* June 92, The first important water craft of the mountain people was the dugout . . . This boat is commonly called a *Tennessee River busthead* or *bullhead,* but other names are used.

ball-headed See **bald-headed** adj 1

ballhoot v, hence *ballhooting* vbl n, *ballhooter* n [Cf **scallyhoot**]
In logging: to roll logs down a steep incline.

 1926 Kephart *Highlanders* 269 **wNC,** I have had a drunken "ball-hooter" (log-roller) from the lumber camps fire five shots around my head as a *feu-de-joie* **1929** *WV Review* 7.1.28, Anyone who has fre-quented logging operations has heard . . *ball-hootin'* logs . . . shooting logs down over a steep incline to a lower level. **1930** *DN* 6.86 **cWV,** *Ballhoot.* **1956** *AmSp* 31.149 **nwCA,** *Ball Hooting* . . . Rolling logs free down an incline. **1966** *DARE* Tape **NC31,** And that word was ball-hooting. Ball-hooting logs. The tree was sawed down . . and then you took a . . hook and turned it over to where it would go down the hill of its own momentum. **1968** Adams *Western Words.* **1969** Sorden *Lum-berjack Lingo* 5 **NEng, Gt Lakes,** *Ball Hooter*—One who rolls logs down a hillside.

ballie n
=**baldpate 1.**

 1955 *MA Audubon* 39.314, *Baldpate* . . . Ballie (Mass. Nickname for Baldpate.).

ballie-callie n Also called **call-ball**
A children's game: see quot 1883.

 1883 Newell *Games & Songs* 181, Ballie-callie . . was formerly a com-mon sport of school-boys in New England. The ball was thrown against the house, and . . a name called. The lad named must strike back the ball on its rebound. **1966** *DARE* (Qu. EE33) Inf **SC19,** Ballie-callie.

ballin' the jack See **ball the jack 2**

ballit See **ballad**

ballix See **bollix** v, n

ball moss n [See quot 1970]
Either of two clump-forming epiphytes native to the southern U.S.: *Tillandsia recurvata,* also called **bunch moss, fence moss,** and **wire moss,** or *Tillandsia baileyi,* also called **bunch moss** and **cigarette moss.**

 1939 Tharp *Vegetation TX* 47, Ball Moss (*Tillandsia recurvata*) is common on oaks and mesquite in the uplands . . . Bailey's Ball Moss (*Tillandsia baileyi*) . . . is much larger than the former and has large, deep rose-colored flowers an inch across. **1951** *PADS* 15.28 **TX,** *Til-landsia baileyi* . . . Big or Mexican, bunch or ball, moss. **1970** Correll *Plants TX* 356, *Tillandsia recurvata* . . . *Ball moss* . . . Plants typically in dense ball-like clumps.

ball naked adj [Cf *OEDS* ballock-naked] Cf **bollicky**
Completely naked.

 1970 *DARE* (Qu. W20) Inf **NC87,** Ball naked.

ball nettle n
=**horse nettle.**

 1950 Gray–Fernald *Manual of Botany* 1254, *S. carolense* . . . Horse-nettle, Ball-nettle. **1971** Krochmal *Appalachia Med. Plants* 236, *So-lanum Carolinense* . . Common Names: Horse nettle, . . ball nettle.

ballo See **bayo 2**

ballocks See **bollix** v

ball off v phr *arch* Cf *DS* U15

 1896 *DN* 1.412 **seNY,** *Ball off:* to treat. "He balled off his customers."

balloon n
1 Now esp among loggers: a bedroll. See also **balloon it**

 1930 Irwin *Amer. Tramp, Balloon.* — Bedding, especially when carried over the shoulder in a roll, which when loosely tied does resemble a balloon in some degree. **1958** McCulloch *Woods Words* 7 **Pacific NW. 1968** Adams *Western Words.* **1969** Sorden *Lumberjack Lingo* 5 **NEng, Gt Lakes,** *Balloon*—A pack; a bedroll.
2 also *balloon Y:* See quots.

 1958 McCulloch *Woods Words* **Pacific NW,** *Balloon Y*—A balloon shaped track for turning engines. **1962** *AmSp* 37.131 **nCA,** *Bal-loon* . . . A balloon-shaped track for turning the [logging railroad] en-gines.

balloon bread n
See quot 1965.

 1965 *Britannica Book of Yr.* 868, *Balloon bread.* A one-pound loaf of bread shaped and puffed to look like a standard 1½-lb. loaf. **1967** *DARE*

(Qu. H18, . . *Special kinds of bread*) Inf **OR3,** Balloon bread—puffs up, but not as heavy as loaf.

balloonfish n [From its ability to inflate its body]
1 A fish of the family Diodontidae (see **porcupine fish**). [*OED* 1834 →]

 1906 NJ State Museum *Annual Rept. for 1905* 366, *Trichodiodon pilosus* . . . Balloon Fish . . . *Chilomycterus schoepfi* . . . Spotted Bal-loon Fish. Balloon Fish . . . It . . has less power of inflating than our puffers. **1960** Amer. Fisheries Soc. *List Fishes* 49, Balloonfish . . *Dio-don holacanthus.*
2 A fish of the family Tetraodontidae (see **puffer**).

 1889 *Century Dict., Balloon-fish* . . . A fish of the . . suborder *Gymno-dontes,* as the tropical *Tetraodon lineatus* . . , or a species of one of the genera *Triodon* and *Diodon.* So called because it has the power of swallowing air, which is retained in a dilatation of the esophagus, and thus of blowing itself up into a nearly spherical shape like a balloon. **1926** Pan-Pacific Research Inst. *Jrl.* 1.13 **HI,** *Tetraodon hispidus* . . . Oopuhue. Balloonfish; Gourd fish. **1960** Gosline–Brock *Hawaiian Fishes* 298, *Family Tetraodontidae (Puffers or Balloon-fishes)* . . . They . . not only have the power of inflating themselves like a balloon but have the reputation of being poisonous when eaten. **1967** *DARE* (Qu. P4, *Saltwater fish that are not good to eat*) Infs **HI4,** 14, Balloonfish.

balloon it v phr [**balloon 1**]

 1958 McCulloch *Woods Words* **Pacific NW,** Balloon it—To pack up and leave camp.

balloon net n Cf **flat net**
A shrimp net with a large belly or catching area.

 1966–69 *DARE* Tape **SC18,** Balloon nets and flat nets are the two main types; **TX14,** There's different ways of making the nets . . . They got what they call the balloon net, . . they got the flat net . . . [FW:] Which one do you use mostly around here? [Inf:] Well, a balloon net offshore . . . It's just a lot more webbing. If you're very skimpy when you're building your net, you can't get much in the bag or tail of the net.

balloon plant n Also *balloon (-pod) milkvetch*
A western **milkvetch** (*Astragalus whitneyi*) with greatly inflated, bladdery pods.

 1925 Jepson *Manual Plants CA* 564, *Balloon Plant* . . . Pods strongly inflated, . . balloon-shaped. **1961** Peck *Manual OR* 483, *A. Whit-neyi* . . . *Balloon-pod Milk Vetch.* **1973** Hitchcock–Cronquist *Flora Pacific NW* 236, Balloon m[ilkvetch].

balloon roof n
A barn roof having rounded or arched sides.

 1950 *WELS (Shapes of roofs on barns)* 3 Infs, **ce,cwWI,** Balloon roof. [2 Infs drew pictures.]

balloon vine n
An herbaceous vine (*Cardiospermum halicacabum*) with in-flated, bladdery seed capsules, each containing three black seeds marked with a white heart-shaped scar. Also called **heartseed, Indian heart, puffball, winter cherry**

 1840 Phelps *Lectures on Botany* App 84, Balloon vine. [Native of] East Indies . . . Flowers white and green. **1847** Wood *Class-Book* 215, *Heart-seed, Balloon-vine* . . . Native on the Missouri and its branches. **1901** Mohr *Plant Life AL* 608, *Balloon Vine* . . . [grows in] Louisianan area. South Carolina, Florida, and Texas. **1932** Rydberg *Flora Prairies* 531, *Balloon Vine* . . . Capsule inflated, 3-angled, membranous, veiny. **1968** Barkley *Plants KS* 229, *Cardiospermum halicacabum* . . . Bal-loonvine . . . Escaped from cultivation.

balloon weed n
A **ground cherry** (here: *Physalis mollis*).

 1951 *PADS* 15.38 **TX,** *Physalis mollis* . . . Cowslip vines; paper hearts; balloon weed.

balloon Y See **balloon 2**

ballot See **ballad**

ballow v [*EDD* ballow v 1] Cf **aikie(s)** and *DS* V5b, II8
Among children: to lay claim to (something).

 1956 *AmSp* 31.37 **eMA,** There is the pattern *I hosie*—or *hoosie* . . or *ballow* . . *that.* All these assert 'This is mine.'

ball shoe n ?chiefly S Midl

A sneaker.

1954 *Harder Coll.* **cwTN,** Ball shoes: Same as tennis shoes. "'Em old ball shoes make ye stank worsern a mad polecat." **1966–69** *DARE* (Qu. W8, . . *Low canvas-top shoes with rubber soles*) Infs **AR**23, **KY**23, 42, Ball shoes.

ball the jack v phr [See quot 1968 at **2**]

1 Esp of a locomotive or train: to move rapidly; transf, to work swiftly or energetically.

c1925 in 1944 *ADD* **nWV,** The car certainly did ball the jack. **1931** *AmSp* 7.53 **Sth, SW,** "Ballin' the jack" and "railroadin' without steam" mean going fast. **1935** in 1953 Botkin *Treas. Railroad Folkl.* 232, I can make out the sparks from the two engines. That is why she is balling the jack so much . . . She won't lose any time going where she is going. **c1960** *Wilson Coll.* **csKY,** Ball the jack — move swiftly, a term often used for a train that goes fast. **1962** *AmSp* 37.131 **nCA,** 'Ballin' the Jack . . . A logging train that is highballing or making a fast run. **1970** *DARE* (Qu. KK29) Inf **IL**116, Ballin' the jack. **1970** Major *Afro–Amer. Slang, Balling the Jack* . . . To work swiftly.

2 To perform an energetic dance accompanied by vigorous handclapping; also n *ballin' the jack,* occas *ball and (the) jack.* chiefly among Blacks

1934 *Natl. Geog. Mag.* 65.253 **GA coast,** Nine-year-old Isaac rolled up his long trouser legs and began "balling the jack," while one of his sisters provided the cadence by clapping her hands. **1959** Lomax *Rainbow Sign* 35 **AL** [Black], Meanwhile some old boy be just ballin-the-jack and cuttin up dancin. **1963** Wright *Lawd Today* 93 **Chicago IL** [Black], Suddenly she stopped, cut a few steps from the Charleston, Balled the Jack, crooned snatches from a popular blues song, and tripped off softly in perfect time to the music. **1968** Stearns *Jazz Dance* 98, *Jack* is the name given to the locomotive by the Negro folk, on the analogy of the indestructible donkey or jackass, while *ballin'* comes from *high balling,* the trainman's hand signal to start rolling. Hence, "ballin' the jack" means traveling fast and having a good time. The Negro folk had been dancing the various steps incorporated in "Ballin' the Jack" for many years . . before the song [by Cris Smith] was published [in 1914]. **1968–70** *DARE* (Qu. FF5a) Infs **SC**10, 26, Ball the jack; **KY**23, 92, **MS**86, Ball and (the) jack; **NC**49, Balling the jack. [4 of 6 Infs Black.] **1970** Major *Afro–Amer. Slang, Balling the Jack:* Negro dance accompanied by lusty handclapping and chants.

3 To move in a conspicuous manner.

1970 *DARE* (Qu. Y22, *To move around in a way to make people take notice of you: "Look at him _____."*) Inf **IL**116, Ball the jack.

4 =**ball** v².

1968 *DARE* (Qu. FF18, . . *"They certainly _____ last night."*) Inf **PA**175, Balled the jack.

5 See quot.

1927 *AmSp* 2.348 **wcWV,** Ball the jack . . . To risk everything on one attempt. "The team balled the jack on that play."

6 To be the last straw.

1968 *DARE* (Qu. GG22b, *When you come to the end of your patience, you might say, "Well, that certainly _____."*) Inf **PA**175, Balls the jack.

ball up See **ball** v¹

ballup n [Scots; prob alter of *bag* + *lap* flap (cf **earlapper**); *OED* "Obs. exc. dial."]

1952 Brown *NC Folkl.* 1.518 **cnNC,** Ballup ['bæləp] . . The front or flap of the breeches; the codpiece.

ball willow n

1895 *Outing* 29.538/1 **nIL,** A low swale filled with grass and a species of willow called locally "ball" willow.

ballwood tree n

=**sycamore.**

1941 *LANE* Map 244 (*Sycamore*) 1 Inf, **swCT,** Ballwood tree, the buttonball, used to make butchers' blocks.

bally n¹ [Perh alter of *belly*] Also called **lemon-belly, punk**

A mature female crab laden with eggs.

1976 Warner *Beautiful Swimmers* 143 **eMD,** The sooks . . begin to open their abdominal aprons . . . The egg mass is ponderously large, with a texture resembling a torn rubber ball . . . In addition to sponges, the egg-heavy females are . . known as . . "ballies."

bally n² See **baldy** n¹

bally-faced shirt See **bald-faced shirt**

ballyhack n Also *balahack, ballwhack, ballywack, belhack* [Etym uncert; perh Ir *baile* town, village + *hack, heck* hell] chiefly NEng *euphem*

Hell.

1844 Thompson *Major Jones's Courtship* 57 **GA,** Thunderation, how the steem did fly! enuff to blow all creation to Ballyhack. **1845** Judd *Margaret* 55 **NEng,** "Yes, and Obed is here too." "Let Obed go to Ballyhack. Come along out." **1859** (1968) Bartlett *Americanisms, Ballyhack* — "*Go to Ballyhack!*" a common expression in New England. I know not its origin. It savors in sound, however, of the Emerald Isle. **1895** *DN* 1.396 **cNY,** Ballyhack [bælɪhæk]: To knock anything to *ballyhack* is utterly to ruin it. "He knocked the plate all to ballyhack." **1901** *Nation* 73.413/3 **NEng** (as of c1850), The phrase "Go to Ballyhack" (or "to Balahack") was in use among the young, as a general rejoinder. **1903** *DN* 2.295 **Cape Cod MA** (as of 1850s), Belhack . . . In expression 'go way to Belhack.' **1905** *DN* 3.3 **cCT,** Ballyhack or *ballywack* . . . To go to Ballyhack is to go to hell. **1908** *DN* 3.288 **eAL, wGA.** **1967–70** *DARE* (Qu. NN26b, . . *Substitutes for 'hell': "Go to _____!"*) Inf **MA**71, Bally-hack; **MA**98, Ballwhack.

ballyhack v Also sp *balahack, bollyhock* [**ballyhack** n] Cf **malahack**

1 To confuse (something); to blunder.

1901 *Nation* 73.413/3 **NEng** (as of c1850), The expression "Don't Balahack it now," seems familiar too.

2 See quot.

1952 Brown *NC Folkl.* 1.518 **c,wNC,** Ballyhack . . . To impose on.

3 To beat thoroughly.

1966 *DARE* (Qu. Y15, . . *"John really _____ that fellow."*) Inf **ME**13, Bollyhocked.

ballyhoo See **balao**

balm n Usu |bɑm|; in **Sth, Midl** freq |bæm|; occas |bɔm| Similarly adj *balmy* |bæmɪ| Pronc-spp *ba'm, ba'my, bammy* Cf **calm, palm**

A Forms.

1908 *DN* 3.288 **eAL, wGA,** Balm . . . Commonly . . [bæm]. So also *balmy* [bæmɪ]. **1921** Thorp *Songs Cowboys* 36 **NM,** Where the air is soft and bammy and dry and full of health. **1923** *DN* 5.200 **swMO,** Ba'm . . . Balm. Ba'my . . . Balmy. **1928** *AmSp* 3.401 **Ozarks,** Calm and *balmy* are regularly pronounced *cam* and *bammy.* **1942** Hall *Smoky Mt. Speech* 104 **eTN, wNC,** Older speakers say [bæm] . . others say [bɔm]. **c1960** *Wilson Coll.* **csKY,** Balm [bæm]. **1969** *WV Hist.* 30.468 **Appalachians,** Pronunciation of many words has changed . . . *bammy* for *balmy.*

B Senses.

1 Any of var aromatic plants, esp of the mint family, as here:

a =**lemon balm.**

1637 (1972) Morton *New Engl. Canaan* 67, Hunnisuckles, balme, and divers other good herbes are there, that grow without the industry of man. **1709** Lawson *Carolina* 77 *(DAE),* Our Pot-herbs and others of use, which we already possess, are Angelica wild and tame, Balm, Buglos. **1813** Muhlenberg *Catalogus Plantarum* 56, *Melissa:* balm, . . common. Pens. fl. Aug. Georg. **1840** MA Zool. & Bot. Surv. *Herb. Plants & Quadrupeds* 183, *M. officinalis* . . . The true Balm . . . Formerly used as a tonic, diuretic, and stomachic. **1894** *Jrl. Amer. Folkl.* 7.96, Lemon-balm, common balm, . . N[ew] E[ngland]. **1930** Sievers *Amer. Med. Plants* 8, Balm is found sparingly in waste places, thickets, and woods. **1975** Hamel–Chiltoskey *Cherokee Plants* 24, Balm . . . Stimulant and tonic; for old colds.

b =**horsemint 1.**

1828 Rafinesque *Med. Flora* 35, *Monarda coccinea* . . . *Names* . . . *Vulgar* . . Mountain Balm, Red Balm. **1840** MA Zool. & Bot. Surv. *Herb. Plants & Quadrupeds* 175, *M. didyma* . . . Commonly called *balm* or *bee-balm.* **1895** Gray–Bailey *Field Botany* 352, *Monarda, Horsemint* or *Balm.* **1915** (1926) Armstrong *Western Wild Flowers* 456, There are several kinds of Monarda, all . . aromatic herbs . . . These plants are called Balm, Bergamot, and Horse-mint. **1971** Krochmal *Appalachia Med. Plants* 178, *Monarda didyma* . . . *Common Names:* . . low balm, . . red balm, rose balm, scarlet balm.

c A **pennyroyal 3** (here: *Monardella odoratissima*).

1961 Peck *Manual OR* 678, *M[onardella] odoratissima . . . Western Balm.*

2 See **balm tree.**

balm buds See **balm tree**

balm for Gilead See **balm of Gilead 4**

balm gily See **balm of Gilead 2a**

balm lemon See **lemon balm**

balm of Gilead n For pronc and sp varr see quots

1 also *herb of Gilead:* A fragrant garden plant *(Cedronella canariensis)* of the mint family, naturalized to some extent in California.

    1822 Eaton *Botany* 269, *Dracocephalum . . . canariense* (balm of gilead herb.). **1961** Thomas *Flora Santa Cruz* 299 **CA,** *Cedronella . . . canariensis . . .* Herb-of-Gilead, Balm-of-Gilead. Occasional as an escape from cultivation in San Francisco.

2 A balsam-yielding tree, here:

a A poplar, esp the **balsam poplar,** or a clone or hybrid thereof.

    1784 in 1785 *Amer. Acad. Arts & Sci. Memoirs* 1.491, *Populus . . .* The *Black Poplar,* commonly called, in the northern states, the *Balm of Gilead.* **1844** Lee–Frost *10 Yrs. OR* 116, It is a kind of rolling prairie, . . along its rivulets, fringed with the cotton-wood or balm of Gilead. **1916** Seton *Woodcraft Manual Girls* 273, Balsam Poplar, Balm of Gilead, or Tacamahac *(Populus balsamifera).* **1941** FWP *Guide WI* 322, Adjacent Woodlots are crowded with . . a fast-growing, sweet-smelling, soft popple, which lumberjacks called bumgillian, said to be a garbled form of Balm of Gilead. **1944** *PADS* 2.53 **MO, VA,** *Bammy-gilly-um* ['bamɪ'ɡɪlɪəm]. **1946** *PADS* 6.5 **eNC,** *Bamly Gillyard tree* ['bæmlɪ 'ɡɪljɚd, -əd] . . . The *balm of Gilead tree.* **c1960** *Wilson Coll.* **csKY,** Balm [bæm] of Gilead . . . Also ['ɡɪlɪ], ['ɡɪləm], ['ɡɪljəm]. **1965–70** *DARE* (Qu. T12) 44 Infs, **chiefly Nth,** Balm o' Gilead; **ME21, MA5, MI45, 53, 108,** Balm of Gilead; **AR24,** Balm o' gilyum; **KY47, NV8, NY219, NC72, OH72, VA46,** Balm o' gilyum; **MN16,** Balm gily; **KY16,** Balm o' gilya; **NY10,** Balm o' galea; (Qu. T13) Inf **ID5,** Balm of Gilead; (Qu. T16) Inf **WV5,** Balm of gillian. **1982** *Smithsonian Letters* **WV,** When they were laying out the house old timers cautioned them that they had several stands of *bammagilla* trees on their land. "Ain't hardly none of them left no more." And they took pains to save a couple of *bammagillas* by the front porch . . . The name floored my daughter who was a botany major in college. She remembered nothing in textbooks or labs about *bammagillas.* Eventually, after the trees leafed out, she determined that they are *Balm of Gilead,* a poplar.

b also *balm of Gilead fir, balm of Gilead tree:* =**balsam fir;** also the resin obtained from this tree.

    1785 Marshall *Arbustrum* 102, *Pinus-Abies Balsamea. Balm of Gilead Fir-Tree.* **1803** Lambert *Descr. Pinus* 1.48, *Balm of Gilead Fir. Pinus Balsamea . . .* Habitat in Virginia, Canada. **1832** Browne *Sylva* 96, This resin [of the silver fir] is sold in Europe and the United States under the name of *Balm of Gilead.* **1902** (1968) Clapin *Americanisms* 35, *Balsam Fir . . .* The tree itself is also known as *Balm of Gilead,* in imitation of the Eastern terebinth. **1945** (1946) MacDonald *Egg & I* 264, We parked the truck under a large Balm of Gilead tree near the restaurant.

3 A salve made from the buds of the **balm of Gilead 2.**

    1946 *PADS* 6.5 **eNC,** *Bamly Gillyard salve . . .* A salve made from the exudation of the balm of Gilead tree . . . Mainly among Negroes. **c1960** *Wilson Coll.* **csKY,** Balm of Gilead . . . A salve made from the buds of the tree. **1968** *DARE* File **seMA,** Balm of gilead—from buds off the myrrh tree or American balsam; put with rum, it forms jelly, and is used for cuts and bruises. **1969** *DARE* (Qu. BB50c) Inf **KY19,** [bæmbə'ɡɪliə] —a black salve. **1975** *Mountain Eagle* (Whitesburg KY) 26 June B3, She recommended some of her "bam-of-Gilly" salve.

4 also *balm for Gilead:* Money.

    1895 *DN* 1.384 **TN** [Black], *Balm of Gilead:* slangy [sic] for money. **c1970** *Halpert Coll.* **wKY,** *Balm for Gilead*—money. Negro, illiterate.

5 See quot.

    1906 *DN* 3.125 **nwAR,** *Balm of Gilead . . .* Illicitly distilled whiskey. "You can get Balm of Gilead over in Newton County."

balm of heaven n

=**California laurel.**

    1897 Parsons *Wild Flowers CA* 373, This tree is known in different localities by a variety of names, such as "balm of heaven," . . and "California laurel." **1900** Lyons *Plant Names* 383, *U. Califor-*

nica . . . Balm-of-heaven . . . *Leaves* stimulant, anodyne, used as a condiment.

balmony n [Etym unknown]

1 =**turtlehead.**

    1848 Gray *Manual of Botany* 298, *C[helone] glabra . .* Called also . . *Balmony.* **1901** Lounsberry *S. Wild Flowers* 461, *C[helone] glabra,* turtle-head, shell-flower, or balmony. **c1937** in 1970 Yetman *Voices* 214 **OK,** Balmony and queen's delight boiled and mixed would make good blood medicine. **1971** Krochmal *Appalachia Med. Plants* 84.

2 A **beardtongue** (here: *Penstemon laxiflorus*).

    1970 *DARE* (Qu. S26a) Inf **TX84,** Penstemon—balmony—used as remedy for diseases, used as tea. **c1979** TX Dept. Highways *Flowers,* Early settlers called the plant "balmony," and brewed a laxative tea from the leaves. *Penstemon laxiflorus.*

balm tree n Also *balm, balm buds*

A poplar, esp the **balsam poplar.**

    1825 (1933) Sibley *Santa Fe Diary* 141, There is some scattering willows and balm trees. **1873** Miller *Modocs* 387 **CA,** A stream . . is foaming among the mossy rocks in a cañon below the house, with balm and madroño on its banks. **1930** Sievers *Amer. Med. Plants* 9, *Balm-of-Gilead Poplar . . . Other common names.*—Balsam poplar, balm buds. **1940** (1951) FWP *Guide OR* 413, Deception Creek bridge is near a beautiful cascade in the river shadowed by balm trees. **1950** Peattie *Nat. Hist. Trees* 100, To the pulp loggers of the North Woods it is Balm-of-Gilead . . . Sometimes the loggers call it Balsam, . . or, again, they may designate it simply as Bam—a corruption, presumably, of Balm. **1958** McCulloch *Woods Words* 7 **Pacific NW,** *Balm*—A cottonwood tree. **1966–67** *DARE* (Qu. T12) Infs **MI10, 27,** Balm; **OR5,** Balm tree. **1980** *DARE* File **cwOR,** We don't say [bɑm] but ['bæm,trɪ] here.

balmy See **balm**

baloney See **bologna**

balooey n [Blend of *baloney* + *hooey*]

Nonsense.

    1967–69 *DARE* (Qu. NN13, *When you think that the thing somebody has just said is silly or untrue: "Oh, that's a lot of _____."*) Infs **MO18, TX74,** Balooey [bə'luɪ].

‡**balore** adj Cf **aglore** and DS LL9a, b

Galore; in abundance.

    1968 *DARE* (Qu. LL9b, . . *"She's got clothes _____."*) Inf **NC55,** Balore [bə'lor].

balsam n

1 =**balsam poplar. chiefly Nth**

    1785 Marshall *Arbustrum* 107, *Populus balsamifera. Balsam.* **1927** Keeler *Our Native Trees* 422, Balsam . . *Populus balsamifera.* **1931** Otis *MI Trees* 87, Balsam. **1965–70** *DARE* (Qu. T12) 23 Infs, **chiefly Nth,** Balsam; (Qu. T13) **WI22,** Balsam; (Qu. T15) 11 Infs, **MI, NY, WI,** Balsam.

2 sometimes with a qualifier: =**jewelweed.**

    1840 MA Zool. & Bot. Surv. *Herb. Plants & Quadrupeds* 76, *I[mpatiens] Balsamina . .* Balsam. **1848** Gray *Manual of Botany* 76, *Impatiens . .* Balsam. **1891** Jesup *Plants Hanover NH* 8, *Impatiens . .* Balsam. **1900** Lyons *Plant Names* 200, *I. aurea . .* Wild balsam, Pale Balsam-weed. *Ibid* 201, *I. biflora . .* Balsam-weed, Wild Balsam. **1936** IL Nat. Hist. Surv. *Wildflowers* 191, *Impatiens biflora . .* also called Wild Balsam. **1968** *DARE* (Qu. S26b) Inf **VA11,** Touch-me-not = balsam. **1970** Correll *Plants TX* 1008, *Impatiens . .* Balsam. **1973** Hitchcock–Cronquist *Flora Pacific NW* 290, Orange balsam . . *I[mpatiens] capensis.*

3 often with a qualifier: A **cudweed 1,** usu *Gnaphalium obtusifolium* (formerly *G. polycephalum*).

    1873 in 1976 Miller *Shaker Herbs* 132, Balsam, Sweet—*Gnaphalium polycephalum . .* White Balsam . . . Old Field Balsam. **1892** *Jrl. Amer. Folkl.* 5.98 **NEng,** *Gnaphalium polycephalum . .* old field balsam. **1894** *Jrl. Amer. Folkl.* 7.92 **NY,** Balsam. **1900** Lyons *Plant Names* 176, *Gnaphalium obtusifolium . .* Sweet Balsam, Field or White Balsam, Old-field Balsam . . Balsam-weed. **1916** *Torreya* 16.240 **VA,** *Gnaphalium* sp.—Field balsam. **1968** *DARE* (Qu. S26d) Inf **DE3,** Old-field balsam—white, something like ageratum.

4 =**cypress spurge.**

    1894 *Jrl. Amer. Folkl.* 7.98 **NY,** *Euphorbia Cyparissias* [sic] . . balsam.

5 Any of several firs, as **alpine fir, balsam fir, she-balsam,** or **white fir.**

1897 Sudworth *Arborescent Flora* 50, *Abies fraseri* . . Balsam (N.C., S.C.) . . *Abies balsamea* . . Balsam (Vt., N.H., N.Y.). *Ibid* 53, *Abies lasiocarpa* . . Balsam (N. Mex., Colo., Utah, Idaho, Oreg.). *Ibid* 55, *Abies concolor* . . *Balsam* (Cal.). **1916** Sudworth *Spruce & Balsam Fir* 17, It seems probable that trees of this group [*Abies* spp.] were given the popular names "balsam" and "balsam fir" because of the liquid resin which is obtained from the pockets of some species for medicinal and mechanical purposes. **1965–70** *DARE* (Qu. T5) 65 Infs, **chiefly NEng, Gt Lakes,** Balsam; (Qu. T17) 9 Infs, **Gt Lakes, S Midl,** Balsam. **1979** Little *Checklist U.S. Trees* 34, *Abies balsamea* . . Other Common Names—balsam. *Ibid* 35, *Abies fraseri* . . balsam . . *Abies lasiocarpa* . . balsam.

balsam bell n [From the bell-like shape of the blossom]
A **bead lily** (here: *Clintonia borealis*).

1933 Small *Manual SE Flora* 296, *C. borealis* . . . *Balsam-bell.* **1949** Moldenke *Amer. Wild Flowers* 333, A great favorite in the northeastern part of our area is the *balsambell* or *blue beadlily.*

balsam fir n Also *balsam pine,* ~ *spruce* Cf **fir balsam 1**
Any of var firs of the genus *Abies,* but esp *A. balsamea* which is also called **balm of Gilead 2b, balsam 5, balsam tree c, blister pine, Canada balsam, fir balsam 1, silver fir, single spruce.**

1804 (1905) Lewis *Orig. Jrls. Lewis & Clark Exped.* 3.279, We Continue to put up the Streight butifull balsam pine on our houses. **1805** in 1916 WI State Hist. Soc. *Coll.* 22.274, Saw pitch pine and balsom [sic] fer [sic] which grow verry tall on the Spring runs and Sides of the mountains. **1847** Wood *Class-Book* 516, *A[bies] balsamea* . . Balsam spruce. **1897** Sudworth *Arborescent Flora* 50, *Abies fraseri* . . . Common Names . . . Balsam Fir (N.C., S.C.). *Ibid* 51, *Abies balsamea* . . Balsam Fir (N.H., Vt., Mass., R.I., N.Y., Pa., W.Va., Mich., Minn., Nebr., Ohio, . .). *Ibid* 55, *Abies concolor* . . . Balsam Fir (Cal., Idaho, Colo.). **1916** [see **balsam 5**]. **1965–70** *DARE* (Qu. T5) Infs **MN14, NC48,** Balsam fir; (Qu. T12) Inf **OH52,** Balsam pine; (Qu. T17) Inf **IA13,** Balsam fir; **MN38,** Balsam pine. **1979** Little *Checklist U.S. Trees* 33, *Abies balsamea* . . . Balsam fir. *Ibid* 34, *Abies concolor* . . . Balsam fir . . . *Abies fraseri* . . . Balsam fir. *Ibid* 35, *Abies lasiocarpa* . . . Balsam fir.

balsam gourd n [Prob from the fragrance and the shape of the fruit]
=**wild balsam** (here: *Ibervillea lindheimeri*).

1961 Wills–Irwin *Flowers TX* 218, Balsam Gourd is found in thickets, open woods, and on fences.

balsam hickory n *obs*
=**pignut.**

1785 Marshall *Arbustrum* 68, *Juglans alba odorata. Balsam Hickery* [sic]. **1815** Drake *Natural View Cincinnati* 2.80, Forest trees . . of the Miami country . . [include] Balsam hickory.

balsam pine See **balsam fir**

balsam poplar n Also *balsam popple, poplar balsam*
An American poplar (*Populus balsamifera*) with fragrant, resin-covered buds. Also called **balm of Gilead 2a, balm tree, balsam 1, Carolina poplar 2, cottonwood, hackmatack, popple, sweet balsam 2, sweet bud, sweet poplar, tacamahac**

[**1786** J. Abercrombie *Arrangem. in Gard. Assist.* 32/1 *(DA),* Tacamahacca, or great balsam poplar.] **1819** D. Thomas *Travels* 93 *(DA),* The true balsam poplar differs greatly in the leaf [from *Populus angulata*]. **1847** Wood *Class-Book* 506, The balsam poplar, though nowhere abundant, is found in woods and fields, disseminated throughout N[ew] England and Canada. **1897** Sudworth *Arborescent Flora* 130, *Populus balsamifera* . . . *Common Names* . . . Balsam Poplar (N.H., Vt., Nebr., Minn.). **1946** Stanwell–Fletcher *Driftwood* 178, It's [=dugout canoe] thirty feet long and is made . . from the trunk of a huge balsam poplar. **1966–69** *DARE* (Qu. T12) Inf **ME8,** Balsam poplar; **NY209,** Balsam popple. **1971** Krochmal *Appalachia Med. Plants* 206, *Populus balsamifera* . . . *Common Names:* . . poplar balsam, tacamahac poplar, tacamahac.

balsamroot n
A plant of the western genus *Balsamorhiza.* For other names of var spp see **big root 2, breadroot 3, graydock, sunflower**

1889 *Century Dict., Balsam-root* . . . A name given in California to

species of *Balsamorhiza* [sic], a genus of low, coarse, perennial composite plants, allied to the sunflower. **1940** Writers' Program OR *Mt. Hood* 439, West of Beatty are sagebrush hills on which the black and yellow balsam root blooms in early spring. **1967** *DARE* (Qu. S26a) Inf **WY1,** Balsamroot. **1973** Hitchcock–Cronquist *Flora Pacific NW* 495, *Balsamorhiza* . . . Balsamroot.

balsam spruce See **balsam fir**

balsam steak n *joc*
Venison having a very gamey taste.

1969 *DARE* Tape **WI77,** We used to shoot 'em [=deer] in the woods, they had a stronger taste . . sometimes you used to call 'em balsam steaks . . they'd be so strong. [FW:] So that's from eating balsam? [Inf:] Yeah.

balsam tree n
Any of var trees which produce balsam as:

a See quot.

1769 Stork *Descr. East FL* 15, Balsam-tree, of the same size and with leaves like the sycamore tree in England, yields the true balsam of Tolu.

b A **balsam poplar,** or similar poplar.

1785 Marshall *Arbustrum* 107, *Populus balsamifera. Balsam, or Tacamahac-Tree. Ibid* 108, *Populus balsamifera lanceolata. Lance-leaved Balsam Tree.*

c Any of various firs: see quots.

1822 Eaton *Botany* 391, *Pinus* . . . *balsamea* . . fir tree, balsam tree. **1832** (1899) Wyeth *Corresp. & Jrls.* 159 **OR,** On the highest point we had snow accompanied with heavy thunder and being out of meat fed upon the inner bark of the Balsam trees. **1874** Glisan *Jrl. Army Life* 480, Thus the Coast Range [of Oregon] . . is covered with evergreen forests . . intermixed at places with . . Oregon alder, balsam tree, rhododendron, . . Oregon ash. **1897** Sudworth *Arborescent Flora* 53, *Abies lasiocarpa* . . . Oregon Balsam Tree (Cal.). *Ibid* 55, *Abies concolor* . . . Balsam Tree (Idaho). **1900** Lyons *Plant Names* 7, *A. balsamea* . . . Balsam tree . . . *A. Fraseri* . . . Mountain Balsam-tree.

balsamweed n

1 =**jewelweed.**

1822 Eaton *Botany* 317, *Impatiens balsamina* (balsam weed. . .). **1876** Hobbs *Bot. Hdbk.* 7, Balsam weed, Jewel weed, Impatiens pallida. *Ibid* 182, Impatiens balsamifera, Balsam weed. **1900** Lyons *Plant Names* 200, *I[mpatiens] aurea* . . Pale Balsam-weed; . . *I. biflora* . . Balsam-weed.

2 A **cudweed 1.**

1889 *Century Dict., Balsam-weed,* a name of the common everlastings. **1900** Lyons *Plant Names* 176, *G[naphalium] obtusifolium* . . Balsam Weed.

Baltimore, Baltimore bird See **Baltimore oriole**

Baltimore buckeye See **bugeye n²**

Baltimore hangnest See **Baltimore oriole**

Baltimore minnow n
See quot 1956.

1956 *Progress* (Charlottesville VA) 14 Jun 9/5 *(Hench Coll.),* Baltimore minnows (German carp fry) as bait are prohibited. **1969** *DARE* (Qu. P7) Inf **GA72,** Baltimore minners [sic].

Baltimore oriole n Also *Baltimore,* ~ *bird,* ~ *hangnest*
A common oriole (*Icterus galbula*), colored chiefly black and orange in the male and chiefly olive and yellow in the female, which builds a hanging nest. Also called **basket bird, English robin, firebird, golden oriole, golden robin, goldfinch, hammock-bird, hangbird, hangnest, pea-bird, redbird, weaver bird**

1808 Wilson *Amer. Ornith.* 1.25, Orioles . . with a few exceptions build pensile nests. Few of them, however, equal the Baltimore in the construction of these receptacles for their young. **1844** Giraud *Birds Long Is.* 142, *Icterus Baltimore* . . Baltimore hang-nest. **1917** (1923) *Birds Amer.* 2.258, Baltimore oriole *Icterus galbula* . . Baltimore Bird. **1946** Hausman *Eastern Birds* 556, Baltimore oriole *Icterus galbula* . . Baltimore bird. **1966–68** *DARE* (Qu. Q11) Inf **MD26,** Baltimore oriole; (Qu. Q14) Infs **NH5, PA**121, 128, 147, 155, **WI8,** Baltimore oriole.

balunst v Pronc-sp for *balance* + excr *t*
1940 *Sat. Eve. Post* 23 Nov 101/2 **sGA,** Never had to balunst on no gatepost to sing before.

'Bam See **Alabama A**

ba'm See **balm**

'Bama See **Alabama A**

'Bama chukker See **Alabama B2**

bambache n Also sp *bamboche* [Fr *bamboche* spree]
A social gathering at which there is considerable drinking; a
drinking spree.
1944 Kane *Deep Delta Country* 247 **LA,** Sometimes he was to be
found . . at the "bamboches," gatherings of the men for gay evenings of
yarn-spinning. These were meetings about large tables, on which sat
pitchers of wine. **1945** Saxon *Gumbo Ya-Ya* 203 **sLA,** Occasionally a
Cajun will go on 'one beeg Bambache,' a drinking spree. *Ibid* 204, 'We
stay in town maybe Friday, maybe Saturday, maybe Sunday. Those
bambache is bad. Me, I always have head like one big barrel.'

bamberry n [Prob folk-etym alter of Fr *bain-marie,* double
boiler]
1971 *Today Show Letters* **seNY** (as of 1930s), Bamberry . . . device for
keeping food warm in the kitchen.

bamboche See **bambache**

bamboo n Cf **wild bamboo**
Usu with a qualifier: any of various **greenbriers.**
1709 (1967) Lawson *Carolina* 101 *(DA),* The small Bamboo is . . a
certain Vine, . . growing in low Land. **1901** Mohr *Plant Life AL* 446,
Smilax laurifolia . . Bay-Leaf Bamboo. **1927** Boston Soc. Nat. Hist.
Proc. 230, *Smilax laurifolia* 'Black bamboo' . . *Smilax Walteri* 'Red
bamboo'. **1934** *Natl. Geog. Mag.* 65.602/1 **seGA,** The . . "hoorah
bushes," . . and other shrubs are interlaced with the thorny vines of
"bamboo" or smilax. **1950** Gray–Fernald *Manual of Botany* 450,
S[milax] laurifolia . . "Bamboo".

bamboo brier n Pronc-sp *bramboo* ~
Any of various **greenbriers.**
1728 (1922) Byrd *Descr. Dismal* 18 **VA, NC,** The skirts of the Dismal
towards the east were overgrown with reeds ten or 12 feet high, interlaced
everywhere with strong bamboe-bryers, in which the men's feet were
perpetually intangled. **1840** (1847) Longstreet *GA Scenes* 74, This
came . . over me like a rake of bamboo briers. **1872** (1973) Thompson
Major Jones's Courtship 165 **GA,** They would be left hangin by ther
whiskers in the bamboo briars, like so many Absaloms of old. **1945**
Democrat 4 Jan 2/2 *(DA)* **AL,** His progress was slowed up by a multitude
of bamboo briers. **1950** *PADS* 14.16 **SC,** *Bramboo briar* . . . The
bamboo briar. **1975** Newell *If Nothin' Don't Happen* 100 **nwFL,** Unless
a feller has been through the middle of that swamp, he just don't know
what a real rough, bad place is like . . . Every tree is hung with bamboo
briar.

bamboodle See **bamfoozle**

bamboo vine n
Any of several **greenbriers** (*Smilax* spp). Also called **bamboo,
bamboo brier, blaspheme vine, China brier**
1853 Hammett *Stray Yankee in TX* 22, [I aided] his rude attempts at
road-making whenever a mass of bullbrier or bamboo-vines . . called for
action. **1897** *Jrl. Amer. Folkl.* 10.145, *Smilax Bona-nox* . . bamboo
vine. **1950** *PADS* 14.74 **FL,** *Bamboo vine* . . . The smilax, the tender
tips of which are cooked and eaten for greens. **c1960** *Wilson Coll.* **csKY,**
Bamboo-vine (or *brier*): Sawbrier, wild smilax, cat brier. "I tore my pants
on a bamboo vine." **1960** Vines *Trees SW* 76, *Smilax lanceolata* . . Also known under the vernacular names of . . Bamboo-vine.
Ibid 77, *Smilax auriculata* . . Vernacular names are Bamboo-vine.

‡**bamboozle** v [Perh by confusion with **vamoose** v]
To make a hasty departure.
1969 *DARE* (Qu. Y18, . . *"Before they find this out, we'd better*
_____.") Inf **NC76,** Take off, bamboozle, get outa here.

bambushka See **babushka**

bamfoozle v Also *bamboodle, bamfuzzle;* also *bamfoozling*
vbl n, *bamfoozled, bamfuzzled* ppl adj [Varr of *bamboozle*
(*OED* 1703 →)] Cf **bumfuzzle** and *DS* KK36
1 To deceive, confuse.
[**1842** in 1947 *AmSp* 22.127, "The American Dialect of Charles
Dickens" [includes] *Bamfoozling.*] **1911** Porter *Harvester* 470 **IN,**
Bamfoozle all the rest of them as much as you please, lad, but I stand to

you in the place of your ma. **1916** *DN* 4.340 **OH,** *Bamfoozle . . bamboozle,* which is not heard. **1950** *WELS* ("*It's easy enough to* _____
him.") 1 Inf, **swWI,** Bamfuzzle. **1950** (1965) Richter *Town* 152 **OH,**
Sayward might be bamfoozled a little but not beat our. **1966–68** *DARE*
(Qu. KK36, . . *A person who is easily fooled: "It's easy to* _____.")
Infs **CO7, FL38, IA9, MT2,** Bamfoozle him; **NY93,** Bamboodle him;
(Qu. GG2, . . *Confused, mixed up*) Inf **FL2,** Bamfuzzled.
2 To damn—used as a mild oath.
1967 *DARE* (Qu. NN25, . . *"Well, I'll be* _____.") Inf **CA8,** Bamfoozled.

bamly Gillyard See **balm of Gilead 2a, 3**

bamma n Also sp *bah-ma* See also **bampa, bapa**
A grandmother.
1968–69 *DARE* (Qu. Z4) Inf **PA220,** Gramma, bamma ['bɑmə];
GA57A, Bah-ma.

bammagilla See **balm of Gilead 2a**

bammy adj See **balm**

'Bammy n See **Alabama A**

bammy-gilly-um See **balm of Gilead 2a**

bam-of-Gilly See **balm of Gilead 3**

bamoose See **vamoose** n

bampa n Also sp *bampaw, bampi* Cf **bapa**
A grandfather.
1969 *DARE* (Qu. Z3) Inf **CA170,** Bampi, grampa; **MO32,** Bampaw—
some say this. **1982** *DARE* File, My husband has always referred to his
Missouri grandfather as *bampa* ['bæm,pɑ].

'Bamy See **Alabama A**

ba'my See **balm**

banana n Usu |bə'nænə|, occas |bə'næni, bə'nænɚ| and aphet
|'nænɚ, 'nænə|, less freq |pɚ'nænə| Pronc-spp *bannanner, 'nan-
ner*
A Forms.
1867 Twain *Jumping Frog* 19 **CA,** A yaller one-eyed cow that didn't
have no tail, only jest a short stump like a bannanner. **1891** *DN* 1.121
cNY, [bə'næni]. **1929** *Sat. Eve. Post* 17 Aug 136/2 **Missip Valley,** I
b'lieve I'm gonter go up and git me a dozen 'nanners and set down and
eat myse'f a bait. **1941** *AmSp* 16.8 **eTX** [Black], Banana, ['nænə]. **1942**
Hall *Smoky Mt. Speech* 77 **wNC, eTN,** Banana [bə'nænɚ], ['nænɚ].
1966–67 *DARE* FW Addit **swNC,** Bananas [pɚ'nænəz]—common
among older folks. **1967** *DARE* (Qu. I53) Inf **HI11,** [bə'nænəɚz].
B Senses. [From the fruit, which resembles a stubby banana]
1 also *American banana, Arkansas* ~, *custard* ~, *dog* ~, *false* ~,
Hoosier ~, *Kansas* ~, *Missouri* ~, *wild* ~: A **pawpaw 1.** chiefly
mid **Missip Valley**
1897 Sudworth *Arborescent Flora* 200, *Common Names* . . . Pawpaw . . . Banana (Ark.). False Banana (Ill.). **1901** Morris *Life on Stage*
13 **swIL,** But never could I acquire a taste for the 'paw-paw,' that inane
custard-like fruit, often called the American banana. **1917** (1923)
Rogers *Trees Worth Knowing* 169, This "wild banana tree" is the
favorite fruit tree of the negroes in the Black Belt. **1921** Deam *Trees IN*
161, *Pawpaw* . . . Recently some enthusiasts have christened it the
"Hoosier Banana". **1931** *K.C. Star* 9 Oct. *(DA),* Pawpaws, known also
as the Kansas banana, and persimmons are ripening already, before the
first frost. **1931** *K.C. Times* 16 Oct. *(DA),* Coming from Kansas, Mr.
Garvin is not expected to have a taste for the Missouri bananas. **1950**
Moore *Trees AR* 73, Pawpaw . . Local Names: Custard Apple, Arkansas
Banana. **1950** Peattie *Nat. Hist. Trees* 287, Pawpaw . . . Other Names:
Wild Banana. **1955** *S. Folkl. Qrly.* 19.235, Small animals devour the
fruit of the *Dog Banana* (Asimina augustifolia). **1960** Vines *Trees SW*
291, *Asimina parviflora* . . . Vernacular names are Small-fruited Pawpaw, Small Custard-apple, and Custard-banana. **1967** *DARE* (Qu. I46)
Inf **MO7,** Pawpaw—same as Missouri banana.
2 The fruit of a **yucca** (here: *Yucca aloifolia*). Cf **Mexican
banana**
1900 Lyons *Plant Names* 401, *Y. aloifolia* . . . Fruit succulent, edible,
locally called *banana.* **1901** Lounsberry *S. Wild Flowers* 56, By the
negroes and many whites as well, the sweet, fleshy fruits of the yucca are
eaten and which, from a similarity in their shape, they call bananas.
3 See **banana fish.**
4 See **banana melon.**

banana belt n NW, esp AK

1 The warmer parts of a region which is regarded as severely cold.

1898 *Century Illustr. Mag.* 56.840/1, The glittering prospectuses that used to invite the world to come to the 'banana belt' of the Dakotas are not now . . circulated by the millions. **1959** Hart *McKay's AK* 29, *Banana belt:* Words used to describe the "tropical" areas of Alaska, notably the warmer southeastern region with its lush forests, heavy undergrowth, rapid-growing vegetation, and moist climate. **1973** *Tabbert Coll.* AK, Banana belt . . . I've seen it applied both to the Anchorage area and to southeastern Alaska.

2 Transf: see quot.

1958 McCulloch *Woods Words* Pacific NW, *Banana belt* . . . An easy show . . . An open winter, softer weather than usual.

banana cantaloupe See **banana melon**

banana fish n Also *banana* [See quot 1979]
=**bonefish 1.**

1896 U.S. Natl. Museum *Bulletin* 47.411, *Albula vulpes* . . . *Banana-fish* . . . A beautiful and active fish, in most places little valued as food. **1902** Jordan–Evermann *Amer. Fishes* 88, *Banana-fish* . . . As a game-fish it is highly appreciated by those familiar with it. **1968** *DARE* (Qu. P4) Inf **LA**37, Banana fish. This is the same fish called skipjack in south Texas, horse mackerel farther north and east in Texas. (May be the same as ladyfish in Florida.) **1972** Sparano *Outdoors Encycl.* 379, *Bone-fish* . . . *Common Names:* Bonefish, ratfish, banana. **1979** Hallowell *People Bayou* 139 s**LA**, There were dead, leathery banana fish shaped uncannily like banana peels.

banana lily See **banana waterlily**

banana melon n Also *banana*, *~ cantaloupe*, *~ muskmelon*

A long slender muskmelon with pale orange flesh and a slightly ribbed rind.

1941 Faherty *Big Old Sun* 54 (Hench Coll.), She brought from the house . . a scrawny dried banana melon, long and yellow. **1949** *Natl. Geog. Mag.* 96.198/1, Such odd varieties as the elongated Banana should not be called "cantaloupes." **1950** *WELS* 1 Inf, sw**WI**, Banana melons grow long and slender . . and taste much like a mushmelon except they have a flavor of bananas. **1954** *Harder Coll.* cw**TN**, Banana melon— hardly a foot long, favors a banana. **1965–70** *DARE* (Qu. I26) 14 Infs, **chiefly Sth**, Banana melons; **IN**35, Banana mushmelons; **FL**23, **MO**32, Banana cantaloupes.

banana peddler n Also *banana pusher* [Ref to the stereotype of Italian immigrants as fruit peddlers] *derog*
An Italian.

1969 *DARE* (Qu. HH28) Inf **CA**166, Dago, wop, banana pushers. **1970** Tarpley *Blinky* 250 ne**TX**, Nicknames for Italian people . . . other responses [include] banana peddlers, . . spaghetti eaters.

banana peel n Also *banana peeling*

Std sense, in phr *have one foot on a banana peel* and varr:

1 To be severely ill or very old, slipping toward death.

1965–70 *DARE* (Qu. BB54, *When a sick person is past hope of recovery*) Inf **TX**98, Got one foot on a banana peelin' and the other one in the grave; **UT**7, He's on a banana peeling; **WI**47, One foot in the grave and the other on a banana peel; (Qu. HH40, *Uncomplimentary words for an old man*) Inf **OK**48, He's got one foot on a banana peel and the other in a grave; (Qu. X48b, . . *Not so young any more*) Inf **MI**120, Got one foot in the grave, the other on a banana peeling; **LA**37, One foot on a banana peel and the other in the grave.

2 Transf: to fall on hard times, experience bad luck.

1967 *DARE* (Qu. CC12a, . . *Bad luck*) Inf **CA**7, One foot on [a] banana peel, the other in the grave.

banana pepper n widely scattered exc NEast, West See Map
A banana-shaped pepper, usu yellow.

1965–70 *DARE* (Qu. I22a, . . *Different kinds of peppers—small hot*) 14 Infs, **esp Sth, S Midl**, Banana pepper; **AL**6, Banana pepper—shaped like a banana and red; (Qu. I22b, . . *Large hot*) 37 Infs, **widely scattered exc NEast, West**, Banana peppers; **CT**2, Banana peppers—built like a banana; hot, long ones; **GA**85, Banana peppers—thicker than a finger; **IL**41, Banana peppers—long, yellow, not too hot; **IL**117, Hot banana peppers; **KY**28, Banana—hots; **OK**43, Banana peppers are sometimes sweet; long but pretty thin, fairly small; (Qu. I22c, . . *Small sweet*) 15 Infs, **esp Sth**, Banana peppers; **AL**11, Banana peppers—green and

yellow; **MS**59, White banana pepper; (Qu. I22d, . . *Large sweet*) 19 Infs, **chiefly Missip Valley**, Banana peppers; **LA**2, Called banana pepper in the store—same as wax pepper; **NC**81, Banana peppers—yellow and long, a little hot; **TN**26, Banana peppers—tolerable long yellow pepper.

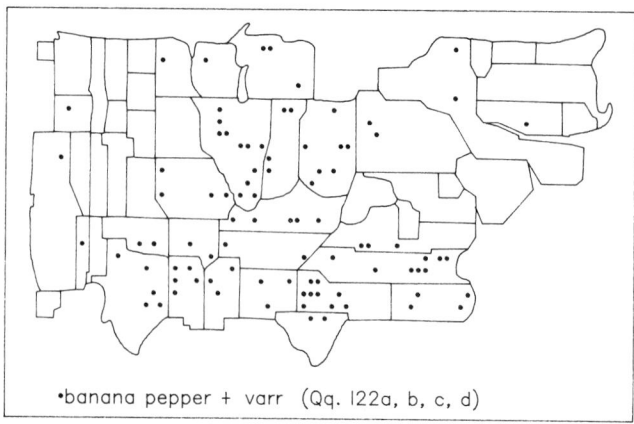

•banana pepper + varr (Qq. I22a, b, c, d)

banana pusher See **banana peddler**

banana ring n Also *banana split*
A marbles game: see second quot.

1968 *DARE* (Qu. EE7) Inf **LA**43, Banana split. **1968** *DARE* Tape **LA**46, Banana ring . . . A marble game in which each player places one marble in the mud; collectively, the marbles form a banana shape. Each player has a turn to shoot at the marbles in the banana ring, and keeps any which he knocks out.

banana shrub n [From the fragrance]
An evergreen shrub *(Michelia figo)* planted as an ornamental in the southern US.

1968 *Patriot–Tribune* (Glenmora–Lecompte LA) 15 Feb 5/4, I have in mind some more pretty ornamentals, which have been growing well in our area . . . The Magnolia family— Banana shrub (Michelia Fuscata) —is a pretty evergreen, large shrub with brownish yellow flowers, inconspicuous but with a delicious banana fragrance. **1976** Bailey– Bailey *Hortus Third* 731, *[Michelia] Figo . . . Banana shrub . . . Fl[ower]s . .* with banana fragrance to 1½ in. across. China.

banana slug n [From the shape and color]
A relatively large, bright yellow or orange slug *(Ariolimax columbianus).*

1964 *Natl. Geog. Mag.* 126.20 CA, I was . . photographing an oxalis cluster when I spotted . . a so-called banana slug, bright-orange and as long but not quite as thick as its namesake. Common in the humid redwood forest, this creature . . . feeds on plant tissue, leaving a path of glistening slime as it inches along. **1977** Hanify–Blencowe *Guide to Hoh* [27] w**WA**, Banana Slugs are double-sexed, having both male and female reproductive parts. **1982** Heat Moon *Blue Highways* 219 cs**OR**, I poked about the woods and turned up a piece of crawling yellow jelly nearly the length of my hand. It was a banana slug, so named because the mollusk looks like a wet, squirming banana. **1982** *DARE* File n**CA**, In the woods of Marin County, banana slugs are often found under damp leaves and forest duff. They vary in color from dull to bright yellow.

banana split See **banana ring**

banana squash n
An elongated, cultivated squash.

1950 *WELS* (*Kinds of squash*) 10 Infs, **WI**, Banana squash. **1965–70** *DARE* (Qu. I23) 100 Infs, **chiefly West, Upper MW, N Cent**, Banana squash.

banana tree n [From the appearance of the beans]
=**catalpa B1.**

1968–69 *DARE* (Qu. T9) Infs **IL**41, **PA**111, Banana tree.

banana waterlily n Also *banana lily* [From its banana-like tubers]

A yellow-flowered **water lily 1** (here: *Nymphaea mexicana*) found from eastern Texas to Florida. Also called **duckpond lily, Florida waterlily, herbe au coeur, sun lotus**

1926 *La. Dept. of Conservation Rep. 1924–26* 144 *(DA),* Duckweeds, leafy pondweed and banana waterlily are most important. **1933** *Torreya* 33.83, *Castalia mexicana* . . . Banana, Florida, or yellow waterlily. **1951** Martin *Amer. Wildlife & Plants* 451, Banana waterlily . . has demonstrated much value for ducks . . . Its rootstocks, banana-like tubers, and seeds have been eaten extensively. **1954** Sprunt *FL Bird Life* 77, Other vegetable foods, of course, constitute its [=the canvasback's] diet, among them . . . the banana water lily *(Castalia flava).* **1961** Wills–Irwin *Flowers TX* 115, The Banana Water-lily . . has yellow flowers and occurs in scattered localities in the eastern half of Texas. **1972** Brown *Wildflowers LA* 49, Yellow Water-lily, Banana-lily . . . Flowers . . 3 to 5 inches wide . . . Ponds and lakes.

banana wiggler n [From its appearance]
A worm used as bait in fishing.
    1969 *DARE* (Qu. P6) Inf **GA**77.

banana yucca n
A southwestern **yucca** *(Yucca baccata)* which produces edible, somewhat bananalike fruits. Also called **amole 1b, datil, Mexican banana, soap plant, Spanish bayonet**
    1937 U.S. Forest Serv. *Range Plant Hdbk.* B157, The datil, . . often called banana yucca, is similar . . . Its somewhat banana-like fruits have a sweet, edible pulp surrounding the seeds. **1960** Vines *Trees SW* 53, Vernacular names are Banana Yucca [etc.] . . . The fruit is eaten raw, dried, or roasted. **1976** Dodge *Roadside Wildflowers* 2, *Banana Yucca* . . . is widespread throughout the Southwest and elevations from 3,000 to 8,000 feet.

banco n [Span] **SW**
An area of land in a river cut off by changes in the river's course.
    1888 *Congressional Record* 23 Sept 8937/1 **TX**, Sometimes the stream will suddenly cut a new channel, . . and . . a tract or "banco" of a hundred acres will be found to be on the other side of the river. *Ibid*, Some bancos increase by deposit; some wear away till they are entirely swept off. **1940** Fergusson *Our Southwest* 64 **TX**, The erratic habits of the Rio Grande and the Colorado, which are always cutting *bancos* off one country and delivering them to the other, necessitate constant adjustments.

band n[1]
A swaddling band.
    1981 *High Coll.* **ceKY** (as of c1930), When I started having children, ever old woman around fussed at me for not putting bands on my babies.

band n[2] *chiefly West* See also **band** v[2], **drop band**
A herd or flock of range animals, spec a flock of about two thousand sheep.
    1824 Keating *Narrative* 395 *(DA)*, The term *band,* as applied to a herd of buffalo, has almost become technical, being the only one in use in the west. **1903** (1965) Adams *Log Cowboy* 49 **NM**, After following this trail about three miles, I sighted the band of cattle. **1929** *AmSp* 5.67 **NE**, He also speaks . . of a number of grouped horses as a "band." **1967** *DARE* (QR, near p74) Inf **NV**1, Ten thousand head of sheep divided into "bands" of twenty-five hundred. **1967** *DARE* Tape **OR**18, Band . . of 2000–2200 sheep; **OR**11, Band . . of about 2200 sheep. **1970** *DARE* File **nIA**, Band (of sheep)—a flock. **1977** Watts *Dict. Old West,* Band . . . While the word usually referred to horses, it was sometimes applied to other animals and to men.

band n[3] [Etym uncertain, but see quot 1960] *among Black speakers*
A woman.
    1934 *AmSp* 9.26 **MD** [Prison parlance; Black], *Band.* A woman. **1960** Wentworth–Flexner *Slang, Band* . . . A woman. *Some Negro use. Prob from "bantam."* **1970** Major *Afro–Amer. Slang, Band:* a woman.

band v[1]
1 with *up:* To bandage.
    1917 *DN* 4.407 **wNC**, *Banded up* . . . Bandaged. "I was banded up for about three weeks." **1934** *W2, Band* . . . To bandage,—often with *up. Local, U.S.*
2 To castrate an animal by means of a rubber band.
    1966–70 *DARE* (Qu. K70) Inf **AL**2, Band—new term—use rubber band when they [=the animals] are small; **MN**2, Banding, give 'em the elastic (what most of the farmers use); **TN**58, Castrate (with a knife), band (with a rubber band).

band v[2] Also *band up* [**band** n[2]] **West**
To form into a herd or flock.
    1878 Taylor *Between the Gates* 266 **CA**, I leave him to "band" his sheep and herd his bees as he pleases. **1902** (1968) Clapin *Americanisms* 36, In prairie parlance, *to band* means . . to assemble cattle, sheep, into vast flocks. **1961** Adams *Old-Time Cowhand* 160 **West**, The single animal or a small bunch were referred to as "strays"; but when a large number were . . "banded up," . . as long as they stayed together the group was said to be a "drift." **1977** Watts *Dict. Old West, To band,* to herd together.

bandanna daisy n [From the mixed colors of the flower]
=**gaillardia.**
    1933 Small *Manual SE Flora* 1461, *Gaillardia* . . . Blanket-flowers. Fire-wheels. Bandana-daisies.

banded See **-ed** pret suff **1**

banded rattlesnake n Also *banded rattler*
=**timber rattlesnake.**
    1823 James *Acct. of Exped.* 1.267, *Crotalus horridus* . . Banded rattlesnake. **1944** *MA Audubon Soc. Bulletin* 8.262 **NC**, The eight species of poisonous snakes found in the region under discussion are coral snake, copperhead, water moccasin, and five rattlers—massasauga, pigmy, diamond-back, banded, and canebrake rattlesnakes. **1949** Dickinson *Lizards & Snakes WI* 60, Timber or Banded Rattler . . . Still fairly common west of the Wisconsin River.

bander-shank See **bandy-shanked**

bandge, bandgeing place See **bange**

bandido n [Span] **SW**
An outlaw, esp one of Mexican origin.
    [**1898** Lummis *Awakening* 4 **Mexico**, By every country road—even into the very heart of cities—the bandido robbed and murdered.] **1929** Dobie *Vaquero* 60 **TX**, One issue . . reported the following items from the lower country, all pertaining to *bandidos.* **1968** Adams *Western Words, Bandido* . . . Used near the Mexican border to refer to a Mexican outlaw. *Bandit* is the more common word for an American outlaw.

bandit n [From the mask-like facial markings]
=**raccoon.**
    1967–68 *DARE* (Qu. P31) Infs **IL**27, **TX**32, Bandit.

‡**band rubber** n [Reversed compound; see Intro "Language Changes" I.1]
A rubber band.
    1968 *DARE* (Qu. F49) Inf **IL**29, Band rubber.

band-tailed pigeon n Also *band-tail pigeon*
A wild western pigeon *(Columba fasciata)* marked with a dark band on the tail. Also called **blue pigeon, blue rock, mountain pigeon, passenger pigeon, white-collared pigeon, wild pigeon**
    1823 James *Acct. of Exped.* 2.10, This species . . may be distinguished by the name of band-tailed pigeon. **1917** (1923) *Birds Amer.* 2.38, Band-tailed pigeon. **1969–70** *DARE* (Qu. Q7) Inf **CA**130, Band-tail pigeon; **CA**78, Band-tailed pigeon.

bandudelums n pl |ˌbæn'dudələmz| For varr see quots **RI** Cf **bending ice**
Large pieces of broken ice in salt water.
    1968 *DARE* File **seRI** [in a 1957 news clipping], Bandadudeums . . large pieces of floating ice in salt water . . . It was used by youngsters about 50 years ago. In the winter, when the ice was thin between Long Wharf and the Newport Yacht Club, those who dared run across it, with the ice quaking under their feet, were said to be running "bandadudeums." **1968** *DARE* File **seRI**, Bandudelums [ˌbæn'duːdələmz], also bendudelums—I use to use that word 45 years ago and use to run bandudelums near shore where they would touch bottom—also I tried to push one down under the next one with a stick. **1969** *DARE* (Qu. B35, *Ice that will bend when you step on it, but not break*) Inf **RI**1A, The ice has bendudelums.

band up v phr[1] See **band** v[1] **1**

band up v phr[2] See **band** v[2]

bandy n[1] [Prob alter of **banter** n **1**] *chiefly KS*
A stunt or feat; in phr *do (one) bandies:* to perform or out-perform another at such a feat.
    1914 *DN* 4.105 **KS**, Do bandies . . . "You can't do me any bandies; I'll climb the tower that you clum." **1916** *DN* 4.319 **KS, Philadelphia PA**, *Bandies* . . . Feats of agility or strength: used by children. **1928** *Rup-*

penthal Coll. **KS**, *Bandies* . . to do bandies, to do (one) bandies . . . children's term. To do something regarded as a physical feat; to do such and dare others to do the same or to excel.

bandy n² See **banty** n

bandy-shanked adj Pronc-sp *bander-shank* **prob Sth, S Midl**
See also **banty** adj, **gander-shanked**
Bandy-legged; having crooked shanks or legs; also *banjer-shanks*—used as a nickname: see quot 1930.
1908 *DN* 3.289 **eAL, wGA**, *Bandy-shanked* . . . Having thin crooked shanks, bowlegged. **1930** *Herald–Advt.* (Huntington WV) 30 Nov **KY, WV**, A lad is usually "old man Jones' boy" instead of being his son. When he grows up, . . if very slender, [he] may bear the happy sobriquet "Banjer-Shanks." **c1960** *Wilson Coll.* **csKY**, Bandy-shanked. **1966–69** *DARE* (Qu. X37, . . *Peoples' legs, if they're noticeably bent, or uneven, or not right*) Inf **SC24**, Bander-shank—don't walk exactly right; **KY24**, Bandy-shanked—could be anything wrong with a leg or legs.

baneberry n [*bane* poison + *berry*; *OED* 1755 →]
1 A poisonous plant of the genus *Actaea;* also its poisonous berries. Also called **cohosh 1a, snakeberry, toadroot.** For other names see **red baneberry, white baneberry**
1785 *Amer. Acad. Arts & Sci. Memoirs for 1784* 1.454, *Actaea . . . Baneberries* . . . The root is useful in some nervous cases. **1821** *Amer. Jrl. Science* 3.276, [Plainfield, Mass . . .] June . . . 6. The redberried actea or baneberry . . [is] in flower. **1847** Wood *Class-Book* 146, *A. rubra* . . . Red Bane-berry . . . *A. alba* . . . White Bane-berry. **1887** *Harper's Mag.* 75.303/2, I jumped out to secure some tall stalk of baneberry flowers. **1966** *DARE* Wildfl QR Pl.62 Inf **OH14**, Baneberry; Pl.63b Inf **NY91**, Baneberry. **1969** *DARE* (Qu. S26c) Inf **NY134**, Baneberry. **1973** Hitchcock–Cronquist *Flora Pacific NW* 125.
2 =**black snakeroot 1.**
1873 in 1976 Miller *Shaker Herbs* 157, *Cimicifuga racemosa* . . . Baneberry.

bang v *?obs*
To beat, surpass.
1817 *Niles' Natl. Reg.* 18 Jan 337/1 **MD**, We were not prepared for this—to use a sheer Yankee phrase, "it bangs every thing." **1848** Bartlett *Americanisms* 22 **OH**, This bangs all things. **1855** (1940) Chambers *Jrl.* 104 **MT**, Of all the fools I have ever seen Faillant bangs all. **1872** Twain *Roughing It* 328 **MO**, If this don't bang anything that ever I saw, I'm an Injun! **1884** Harrison *Negro Engl.* 263, Ef dis don't bang my times! = to pass belief. **1978** *AP Letters* c**GA**, My mother, born in 1859 . . would hear of something quite unusual and say: "Well if that don't bang bob-tail!" Perhaps it was the equivalent of . . "Well, if that's not the limit!"

bang n¹ [Aphet form of *shebang*]
A group or crowd.
1966–68 *DARE* (Qu. LL10, *A whole group of people: "They made too much noise, so he sent the whole _____ home."*) Inf **FL33**, Bang; **WI6**, Shootin' bang.

bang n² See **beignet**

bange v |bænj| Also sp *bandge* [Cf *W3 bang* vi 3 "to . . frequent a place without definite . . purpose"] **NEng, esp ME**
To idle about; to take advantage of another's hospitality; hence also vbl n *bandgeing place, banging place.*
1886 Jewett *White Heron* 9 **ME**, Squer'ls she'll tame to come an' feed right out o' her hands . . . Last winter she got the jay-birds to bangeing here. **1890** *DN* 1.21 c**ME**, *Bange* [bænj] . . . "a pair of boots to bange round in." **1897** Howells *Landlord* 187 **MA**, It'll interest him to go out there; and we can make him believe it's just to bange around for the winter. **1914** *DN* 4.68 **ME, nNH**, *Bandge* . . . To idle, loaf. *Bandgeing-place* . . . A lounging place, *e.g.* a country store. **1927** *AmSp* 3.137 **ME**, "Bange" was employed in speaking of those who would come visiting and remain till their unwilling host was to be pitied. It was said that certain relatives or visitors would "bange" or make a "banging place" all summer, "sponging" idly, neither paying nor working.

bang ears v phr Cf **ear banger** and *DS* JJ3a
To curry favor.
1957 Battaglia *Resp. to PADS 20* (*When a student tries to be extra nice to the teacher in hopes of getting a better grade*) e**MD**, He's trying to bang ears again.

banged See **bangy** adj

banger See **banjo** A

banging place See **bange**

bangleberry n [Prob alter of **dangleberry**]
A large **huckleberry.**
1932 *Hanley Disks* ce**MA**, Bangleberry.

bango n [Japanese *bango* number] **HI**
An identification tag.
1951 *AmSp* 26.26 **HI**, Only the mainland visitor is startled to see this sign in a Honolulu pineapple cannery: 'Show Your Bango Here.' *Bango* . . is the localism for a job identification disk. **1954–60** Hance *Hawaiian Sugar*, Bango . . . Ban-go . . . Number, hence a number ticket or identification tag. **1972** Carr *Da Kine Talk* 92 **HI**, Many of the simple and basic expressions are still in use . . *bangō* 'number', hence 'identification tag'.

Bangor rule n
Orig a device used in scaling logs; now fig: see quot.
1975 Gould *ME Lingo* 167, The first such rule [=log rule, used by sawyers to determine the number of board feet in a log] is said to be the *Bangor Rule,* figured out in Maine for old-growth stumpage, and in popular speech it has become a gauge of probity: if a man goes by the Bangor Rule in his daily affairs, he will be just and upright and can be trusted.

bang-spang See **spang**

‡bangy n
1967 *DARE* (Qu. N41c, *Horse-drawn vehicles to carry light loads*) Inf **PA34**, Bangy [bæni]—a buggy without any top.

bangy adj Also *banged*
Of cattle: having Bang's disease.
1966–68 *DARE* (Qu. K28, . . *Diseases that cows have around here*) Inf **OK43**, We've got bangy cows here; (Qu. K47) Inf **WV8**, Fistula—get [it] from banged cattle.

banical n
A broken-down horse or mule.
1958 *AmSp* 33.268 e**WA**, Horse. Here I bring together all the current terms . . . hay baler, bangtail, banical ['bænəkl], mustang. **1967** *DARE* Tape IA8, They hollered and said "get the mules down below" . . . Old Smokey left his outfit up on top of this knob, a bunch of old banicals ['bænɪkəlz], hide and hair was about all there was to 'em.

banio See **banya**

banjer-shanks See **bandy-shanked**

banjo n Usu |'bænjo|; in **Sth, Midl** freq |'bænjɚ, 'bænjə| Pronc-spp *banger, banja, banjer, banjor, bunger* [Intro from W. Africa in var forms prob ult < Port *banza* guitar] For hist development and addit spp see *DA, DAE, DJE, Ethnomusicology* 19.359–360
A Forms.
c1770 in 1833 Boucher *Glossary* xlix **MD, VA**, A *Bandore* (pronounced *banjor*); a rude musical instrument, made of the shell of a large gourd . . much used by negroes. **1905** Culbertson *Banjo Talks* 1 **SE**, W'en a picker gits ter pickin' / An' de banjer talks. **1936** *AmSp* 11.159 e**TX**, The vowel in the final syllable . . is usually [ə] . . . [in] banjo. **1941** in 1944 *ADD* e**WV**, Banja. **1942** Hall *Smoky Mt. Speech* 23 e**TN, wNC**, Banjo ['bænjɚ]. **1951** Porter *Ragged Roads* 2 **OK**, I was not ready for I had to fetch my valise and "bunger." *Ibid* 43, I stored my things in town, which just about meant my banger. **c1960** *Wilson Coll.* cs**KY**, Banjo ['bænjə]—almost universal. ['bænjɚ] . . older people's pronunciation. **1963** Edwards *Gravel* 7 e**TN** (as of 1920s), You could sing it with a git-tar or a banjer.
B Senses.
1 In railroading: a banjo-shaped railroad signal.
1895 *Searcher* 1.244/2, The block signal on our railways, conspicuous by reason of its height and color, is known among railway men, I am told, as "the banjo." The signal-master of one of the way stations on the Consolidated New York and Boston, *via.* Springfield—proffered this bit of information. **1945** Hubbard *Railroad Ave.* 332, Banjo . . old-style banjo-shaped signal. 1977 Adams *Lang. Railroader.*
2 A rounded scoop or shovel. **chiefly Nth, West** Also called **idiot stick 1, Irish banjo**
1930 Irwin *Amer. Tramp*, Banjo.—A short-handled scoop shovel, especially one used for coal. **1945** Hubbard *Railroad Ave.* 332, Banjo—Fireman's shovel. **1954** *AmSp* 29.273 **NY**, Banjo . . . a kind of

shovel vaguely resembling a banjo. **1966** *DARE* Tape **SD4A**. **1967** *DARE* FW Addit **ID**, Banjo—miner's term for a shovel. I have also used this term myself when working in the mines of Idaho. **1969** Sorden *Lumberjack Lingo* **NEng, Gt Lakes**, Banjo—A number two shovel.

banjo frog n

1969 *DARE* (Qu. P21, *Small frogs that sing or chirp loudly in spring*) Inf **GA77**, Banjo frog—good-sized frog, rust color.

bank n[1]

1 A heap of potatoes or other vegetables covered with mulch and earth, and over this sometimes a shed, to preserve them during winter. **chiefly Sth** See Map See also **bank v 2, cave n 1**

1837 Wheeler *Practical Treatise* 202 **SC**, It appeared the slave was stealing potatoes from a bank near the defendant's house. **1856** Davis *Farm Bk.* 12 **AL** *(DA)*, The Bank of cut potatoes was first used up but the cook failed to get all a few were left covered up in dirt. **1965–70** *DARE* (Qu. M19, *A place for keeping carrots, turnips, potatoes and so on over the winter*) 44 Infs, **chiefly Sth**, Potato bank; 10 Infs, **chiefly Sth**, Bank; **MS46, SC32, TX40**, Turnip bank; **AL52**, Cabbage bank; **NC10**, Sweet potato bank; (Qu. M22, *. . Other kinds of buildings . . on farms*) Inf **AR52**, Potato shed or potato bank—potatoes were banked in dirt, covered with hay and then the shed over that; **TX32**, Tool shed, potato bank, cotton house; **GA16**, Tater bank. **1969** *DARE* FW Addit **GA**51, Bank—a construction of mulch and earth for preserving sweet potatoes over winter. Pyramidal heap in back yard.

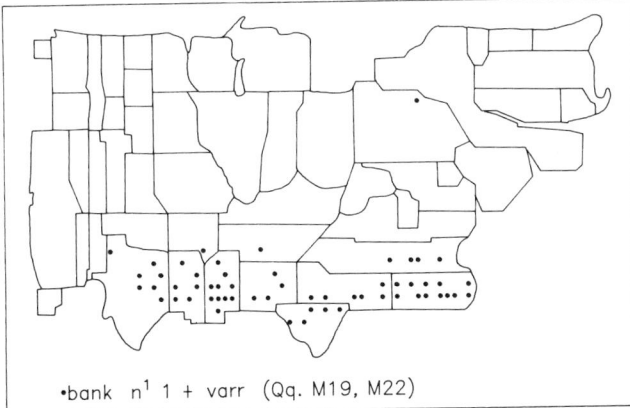

•bank n[1] 1 + varr (Qq. M19, M22)

2 also attrib, also *coal bank*: A coal mine and its immediate surroundings; the surface of a mine.

1804 (1904) Clark *Orig. Jrls. Lewis & Clark Exped.* 1.58, At 3 Miles [we] passed a Coal-Mine, or Bank of stone Coal, . . this bank appears to Contain great quantity of fine Coal. **1946** Stuart *Tales Plum Grove* 122 **seKY**, "You didn't have any business goin' in that coal mine on Bill Sexton," Grandma answered. "You went in that coal bank to whop him." **1968** Adams *Western Words*, Bank . . . In mining, the surface of the mouth of a mine pit. **1969** *DARE* Tape **KY**28, He loaded coal in the cars, in the bank cars what brought the coal outside. **1973** *PADS* 59.42 **WV, wVA**, All the buildings, grounds, and underground passages associated with a particular coal mining operation . . . bank. *Ibid* **WV, wVA**, Coal haulage vehicle . . . bank car.

3 See **banking ground(s)**.

4 See **tree bank**.

bank n[2]

In marble play: see quot.

1906 Lovett *Old Boston Boys* 42, He, among many others, used to run a "bank," as we called it,—which consisted of a strip of wood, perhaps twelve or fifteen inches long, with six or eight little arches cut in it, each somewhat wider than a marble, and numbered from one up. This row of arches was held upright upon the ground, and the marksman, a few feet away, would shoot his marble with the object of entering one of the arches; if he succeeded, he was given the number of marbles which corresponded with the number over the arch, while, if he failed, the marble was appropriated by the banker.

bank v

1 also with *up:* To insulate a building against winter cold by piling earth or branches against its base. **chiefly NEng** See also **banking 1**

1720 in 1896 Canton MA *Records* 6, Ten Pounds granted . . To Repaire The Roof of ye meeting Hovse and To Bank ye out side of ye scils of sd hovse. **c1853** (1860) Taylor *January & June* 143 **Chicago IL**, They 'banked up' the house, yesterday; put the cabbages in the cellar, the day before. **1929** *AmSp* 5.125, A Maine house . . . was "banked up" in winter to keep the cellar from freezing, pine and hemlock boughs being used and sometimes sawdust. **1951** Graham *My Window* 101 **ME**, The neighbors are beginning to bank their houses with evergreens. **1952** Caldwell *Lamp for Nightfall* 156 **ME**, Thede and Howard had already banked the house for the winter and now the leaves were covering the unsightly sawdust until none of it could be seen. *Ibid* 191, He had finished banking the house with sawdust and fir boughs.

2 To store potatoes or other vegetables beneath a pile of earth and mulch; hence vbl n *banking*. [**bank n**[1] **1**] **chiefly Sth**

1851 in 1927 Jones *FL Plantation Rec.* 418, 2 [slaves] Banking Potatoes and soforth. **1966** *DARE* (Qu. M19) Inf **GA9**, Banked up—buried in dirt. **1966–70** *DARE* Tape **AL1**, He would bank these potatoes in the smoke house . . . You pile these potatoes in there on the ground, then you put a lot o' hay on top of 'em, then you put dirt on top of them to keep 'em warm, and those potatoes would keep then; **TX104**, Bank the potatoes in wintertime; **FL41**, You bank the leaves and limbs of peanuts. **1972** Hilliard *Hog Meat* 275, "Banking" is a term used to describe a method of food preservation . . . Since sweet potatoes are susceptible to frosts, southerners piled the tubers on a bed of straw or pine needles and then covered them with another layer of bedding.

3 also with *out:* To stack logs, usu at a river bank or landing to await transportation. **chiefly Nth** See also **banking ground(s)**

1856 MI State Ag. Soc. *Trans. for 1855* 7.828, There will be logs enough cut and "banked" for 100,000,000 feet of lumber. We are informed that the amount now banked daily, will amount to 2,500,000 feet. **1958** McCulloch *Woods Words* **Pacific NW**, Bank—To deck logs on a river bank, to be moved downstream on the spring freshet. **1959** Robertson *Ram* 93 **sID** (as of 1875), Father used to "bank out" cordwood on top of a ridge at the edge of our place. Sometimes there would be ricks containing forty or fifty cords. **1968** Adams *Western Words*, Bank—In logging, to pile logs along a railroad track. **1969** Sorden *Lumberjack Lingo* **NEng, Gt Lakes**, Bank—To pile up logs on a landing for transporting to the mill.

bank barn n chiefly PA, OH, MD, VA, IN See Map Also called **basement barn**

A barn built into the side of a hill, affording entrance on at least two levels.

1894 *Congressional Record* 18 Jan 1036/1 **PA**, On my father's farm . . there stood a big bank barn. **1903** *DN* 2.349 **neOH**, Bank-barn . . . A barn built on the hill side so that three sides of the lower story are surrounded by earth, the fourth being open. **1940** Mencken *Happy Days* 85, By the time they got to the barnyard he was disappearing through the door of the old bank-barn. **1940** Yoder *Rosanna* 79 **sePA**, Besides a large bank barn, there were all the necessary out-buildings. **1942** Warnick *Garrett Co. MD* (as of 1900–1918). **1946** *PADS* 5.10 **nwVA**. **1947** *PADS* 8.30 **swOH**. **1950** *WELS* (*A barn built on a hillside with entrances on two levels*) 1 Inf, **cwWI**, Bank barn. **1965–70** *DARE* (Qu. M1, *. . Different or special kinds of barns*) 58 Infs, **chiefly PA, OH, MD, VA, IN**, Bank barn. **1968** *DARE* Tape **MD20**, We have a bank barn over there to store away feed and keep cows in the wintertime and we have a cow barn to do the same thing.

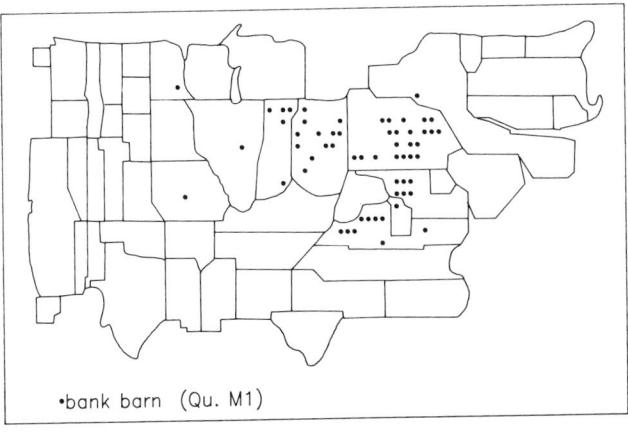

•bank barn (Qu. M1)

bank beaver n

1969 Sorden *Lumberjack Lingo* **NEng, Gt Lakes,** *Bank beavers* — Rivermen or river rats driving the rear on a log drive.

banker n

1 An inhabitant of the outer banks of the North Carolina seacoast. **chiefly NC**

1750 in 1886 NC *Colonial Rec.* 4.1306, The Bankers . . a set of People who live on certain sandy Islands lying between the Sound and the Ocean. **1849** Cooper *Sea Lions* 1.136, This term of 'Banker' applies to a scattering population of wreckers and fishermen, who dwell on the long, low, narrow beaches . . from Cape Fear to near Cape Henry. **1939** FWP *Guide NC* 97, The coast people, the "bankers" in particular have lived so long isolated that their ways have a distinct flavor of their own. **1969** *DARE* FW Addit **neNC,** Banker — someone from the outer banks of North Carolina.

2 A vessel or person engaged in fishing for cod off the banks of Newfoundland. [*DCan* 1777 →] **NEng** See also **banking dory**

1704 *Boston News – Letter* (MA) 13 Nov 2/2, The Advice Man of War took a *French* Banker on the Banks of *Newfoundland.* **1848** Bartlett *Americanisms.* **1904** *DN* 2.394 **MA,** Banker . . . A codder, cod fisherman. **1933** *Hanley Disks* **Cape Cod MA,** They used to send out the bankers out of Provincetown, lots of vessels — and they cured the fish there. **1975** Gould *ME Lingo,* Banker — A fishing vessel that went to the Grand or Georges Bank, or a crewman aboard.

3 See **mossbanker.**

banket n |baŋ'kɛt| [Du] *in Dutch communities* Also called letter

A rolled pastry filled with almond paste.

1969 *DARE* (Qu. H63) Inf **MI**102, Banket — almond filling in a flaky butter pastry. **1982** *Christian Renewal* 11 Oct 21 **swMI,** [Advt:] This month we will be mailing a special Christmas catalog for chocolate initials, gingerbreads, banket, Christmas banket wreaths, marzepan, fancy tins with cookies and/or rusk. **1982** *DARE* File, The original Dutch is *banket letters,* almond filling in puff pastry baked in the shape of your initial for your birthday . . . In Dutch communities in America everybody recognizes the word *banket,* though sometimes it is not the most common word . . . The Polish bakers on the West Side of Grand Rapids make *banket* and do not know it is Dutch. *Ibid* **cCA,** I make banket in pieces about 12 inches long and about 2 inches in circumference. It can also be shaped into letters, like if you want to give it as a Christmas gift. Then you might shape it into the form of someone's initial. *Ibid* **swMI,** Banket [bɛŋ'kɛt] is especially popular around the holidays when the kids get special treats.

‡bank fence n

A type of log fence; see quot.

1966 *DARE* (Qq. L61, 62) Inf **ME**12, Bank fence: logs laid horizontally, spaced by rocks, held [in place] by vertical poles.

bankfish v

To fish from the shore.

1966 *DARE* Tape **SC**7, I bankfish. I have fished from a boat but I rather be on the dirt.

bank frog n

1968 *DARE* (Qu. P21, *Small frogs that sing or chirp loudly in spring*) Inf **IA**29, Bank frog.

bank hook See **bank line**

banking n

1 Earth or other material placed around the base of a building as protection against the cold. [**bank** v 1] **chiefly NEng**

1872 VT State Bd. Ag. *Report for 1872* 1.309, The exclusion of cold air should be possible without the annual banking that is put around most farm houses in the fall. **1900** Day *Up in ME* 35, Good double winders and bankin' are mighty good friends. **1926** *AmSp* 2.79 **ME,** Pine, hemlock, and spruce boughs . . had served as a "bankin'" around the foundation of the house through the winter to keep out the cold. **1951** Graham *My Window* 39 **ME,** They cut the thatch for winter banking.

2 See **bank** v 2.

banking dory n Also called **banker 2, nesting dory**

A flat-bottomed boat used for cod fishing off the banks of Newfoundland.

1957 Beck *Folkl. ME* 119, Dories were an improvement of the onshore fishing boats, with certain modifications to allow for easy stowage aboard the schooners . . . Eventually they became known as "banking" or "nesting" dories.

banking ground(s) n Also *bank* **chiefly Nth** Also called **rollway** See also **bank** v 3

In logging: a place along a river where logs are stacked while awaiting further transportation.

1880 *Lumberman's Gaz.* Jan 728 *(DA),* The banking ground is about 125 feet above the bed of the river. **1902** White *Blazed Trail* 91 **MI,** It is necessary to follow briefly an outline of the process after the logs have been piled on the banks. **1958** McCulloch *Woods Words* **Pacific NW,** *Banking ground* — More or less level ground beside a lake or river on which logs were banked or decked, to be floated out later on the drive. **1964** Hargreaves *Story of Logging* 30 **MI,** [Caption:] The rollway or banking grounds. This is where the shanty boys' job ended and where the river-drive started in the springtime — when the ice melted and the driving streams ran high. **1969** Sorden *Lumberjack Lingo* **NEng, Gt Lakes.**

banking log n Also *bank log* [*bank* to maintain a slow and even rate of a fire's burning]

=**backlog 1.**

1966 – 70 *DARE* (Qu. D33, . . *In the fireplace . . the big log that goes behind the others*) Infs **PA**165, **IL**141, Banking log; **ME**23, Bank log.

bankit See **banquette**

banklick bass n *prob obs*

The black **crappie** (*Pomoxis nigromaculatus*).

1887 Goode *Amer. Fishes* 69, The names "Bitter Head" and "Lamplighter" are also ascribed to it . . , and "Bank Lick Bass". **1902** Jordan – Evermann *Amer. Fishes* 336, Banklick bass.

bank line n Also *bank hook,* ~ *pole*

A baited fishing line attached to the shore and left unattended.

1955 *Sun* (Baltimore MD) 1 Apr B12/5 *(Hench Coll.)* **MD,** [Legislation] Removing Montgomery County from provisions legalizing use of bush bobs and bank poles for fishing. **1965 – 70** *DARE* (Qu. P13, . . *Other ways of fishing*) Infs **AL**62, **IL**7, 108, 115, **KS**12, **KY**11, **MO**6, **NE**9, **OK**52, **SC**11, Bank line; **IL**11, 119, Bank pole(s); **KS**15, Bank pole — cut willows, put hook and line on it, no weights or floats; **NC**53, Set bank hooks; **OK**25, Bank hooks — line tied to pole stuck in bank and left for a while.

bank log See **banking log**

bank martin n [*OED* 1774 →]

=**bank swallow 1.**

1806 (1904) Lewis *Orig. Jrls. Lewis & Clark Exped.* 5.279, [We] saw several herds of buffalow, . . also . . bank martins. **1917** (1923) *Birds Amer.* 3.91, Bank Swallow . . . Other Names . . . Bank Martin. **1946** Goodrich *Birds in KS* 317.

bank pole See **bank line**

bank rat n

A **muskrat** or similar animal.

1939 *Sun* (Baltimore MD) 16 Mar 6/3 *(Hench Coll.),* Maryland's ten-week muskrat-trapping season ends at midnight . . The fur of bank rats, which live in holes in stream banks, is not as good as that of marsh rats, although it brings the same price. **1968** *DARE* (Qu. P31) Inf **MN**42, Bank rat — a small one — not the same [as a muskrat].

‡bankrupture adj [Folk-etym]

Bankrupt.

1954 *Harder Coll.* **cwTN,** He's gone bankrupture.

bank swallow n

1 Std: a swallow (*Riparia riparia*) which makes a nesting hole in a bank. Also called **bank martin, bee martin 2, ground swallow, sand bird, sand martin, sand swallow**

2 =**rough-winged swallow.**

1903 in 1951 Kumlien – Hollister *Birds WI* 93, Rough-winged Swallow. From our observation this is the common breeding "bank swallow" which is found scattered over the most [sic] of the state [Wisconsin]. **1962** Imhof *AL Birds* 364, Rough-winged Swallow . . . Other Names: . . Bank Swallow.

bannanner See **banana**

banner v See **banter** v 2

banner n See **banter** n

bannock n |'bænək, 'bænɪk| [Scots and nEngl dial] **chiefly Nth, esp eNEng** See also **Indian bannock**

A thin bread, usu made from cornmeal and cooked on a griddle.

1848 Bartlett *Americanisms* 23, In New England, cakes of Indian meal, fried in lard, are called *bannocks.* **1907** *DN* 3.240 **eME,** *Bannock . . .* Corn bread. Woodmen's term. **1934** Harwich Port Lib. Assoc. *From Cape Cod* 140 **eMA,** *Bannock . .* a muffin made of cornmeal, eggs, and milk. **1941** *LANE* Map 287, [*Bannock,* usu ['bænək, 'bænɪk], is widespread in northern and eastern New England]. **1958** McCulloch *Woods Words* **Pacific NW,** *Bannock*—A flat cake of breadstuff made in a frying pan in a woods camp. Usually so tough it is easier to eat the pan. **1966–68** *DARE* (Qu. H18, . . *Special kinds of bread*) Inf **MD**12, Bannock ['bænək]—white bread dough cooked on a griddle, about an inch thick; **ME**7, Bannock—made of cornmeal flour, salt, soda, sour milk, baked thin in [an] oven; **WA**31, Bannock ['bænɪk]—sourdough bread with soda and water and flour and baked in a skillet; (Qu. H19) Inf **SD**8, Bannocks—sourdough biscuits baked in [a] frying pan; (Qu. H25) Inf **ID**4, Bannock—early Indian preparation with cornmeal; (Qu. H24) Inf **NH**16, Bannock. **1973** Allen *LAUM* 1.279 **neMN,** 1 inf, *Bannock:* Baking-powder bread made in a frying pan over an open fire in the woods. **1975** Gould *ME Lingo,* *Bannock . . .* In Maine it means a coarse meal cake intended for a dog—before patent dog foods . . . If somebody says, "She fed me *bannock!*" it means the food wasn't that good.

banquette n Usu |'bæŋkɛt| Pronc-sp *bankit* [Fr *banquette* foot-path] **sLA, occas eTX**

A raised sidewalk or footpath.

1841 *Daily Picayune* (New Orleans LA) 28 Jan 2/3, Bill Posey, the flower of loafers, was found stretched on the banquette on Tuesday night, like a turtle in a market cart. **1886** Amer. Philol. Assoc. *Trans.* 17.45, *Banquette* or *bankit . .* sidewalk in New Orleans. **1927** Kennedy *Gritny* 152 **sLA** [Black], W'en dey see Cindy comin' long de banquette, dey crosses over to de yuther side de street. **1958** Grau *Hard Blue Sky* 64 **sLA,** The saddle horses and the carts were tied two deep to the hitchingstands along the banquettes. **1962** Atwood *Vocab. TX* Map 44, [The map shows one instance of *banquette* in **eTX,** 23 instances in **sLA**]. **1968** *DARE* (Qu. N44) Inf **LA**40, Banquette ['bæŋkɪt]—this included the whole thing from the fence to the curb, including the sidewalk.

ban't See **be** C1a

ban-tailed hawk n Also *ban-tail hawk* [Perh for *band-tailed;* cf *band-tailed buzzard,* former name of the *zone-tailed hawk*]

1966–69 *DARE* (Qu. Q4) Inf **FL**4, Ban-tail hawks; **CA**117, Ban-tailed hawk.

banter v [Engl dial] See also **banter** n

1 To haggle. *old-fash*

1793 *Thomas' MA Spy or Worcester Gaz.* (MA) 4 Apr 1/2 **NY,** The husband . . , after a few minutes bantering, accepted, in exchange for his wife, an old horse, with nine dollars in cash to boot. **1895** *DN* 1.396, *Banter:* to haggle at a price. **1946** Greer–Petrie *Angeline Steppin'* 36 **csKY,** Lum *bantered* him fur a trade, and even offered the feller his Barlow knife and six bits. **1968** *DARE* (Qu. U12, *If you were buying something and you argued with the person selling it till you made him lower the price, you might say, "I _____."*) Infs **NY**75, 96, Bantered him down; **GA**44, Bantered with him [laughter]. [All Infs old]

2 also *banner:* To challenge, dare; goad. **chiefly Sth, Midl**

1810 Cuming *Sketches* 135 **OH,** Two hunters sat down with us . . . At last they bantered each other to go out and kill a deer. **1872** Eggleston *End of the World* 177 **IN,** He grew excited, and bantered the whole crowd. Was there no *gentleman* in the crowd who would lay a wager of wine for the company on this interesting little trick? **1892** *DN* 1.235 **wMO,** A boy will say, "I'll *banter* you to dive from that bank." **1902** *DN* 2.228 **sIL.** **1903** *DN* 3.305 **seMO.** **1906** *DN* 3.125 **nwAR.** **1908** *DN* 3.289 **eAL, wGA.** **1948** *WELS Suppl.* **csWI,** When children dared each other to jump a stream, they said, "Banner you to jump the branch." **1950** Stuart *Hie Hunters* 167 **eKY,** He just ran up and fronted a man, stuck his face out like he was bannering the man to strike it, and squirt! It was all over. He always got one eye. **c1960** *Wilson Coll.* **csKY.** **1967** *DARE* (QR p26) Inf **CO**8, Bannered me to go [FW: Inf's spelling—I misheard . . as "bantered," but it's "bannered"]; (Qu. Y5, . . *"Johnny wouldn't have tried that if the other boys hadn't _____."*) Inf **CO**7, Bannered him.

banter n Pronc-sp *banner* **chiefly Sth, Midl** See also **banter** v

1 A challenge, dare.

1840 (1847) Longstreet *GA Scenes* 28, "Well," said Blossom, "make a pass at me." "No," said Peter; "you made the banter, now make your pass." **1872** *Harper's Mag.* 45.28/2 **PA,** But, having a mind to try the mare a little stretch, I took up his banter. **1892** *DN* 1.235 **wMO.** **1950** *Jrl. Amer. Folkl.* 63.432 **MO,** Children about to perform some hazardous "banner," such as jumping from a high place, often chant.

2 A match or contest.

1859 (1968) Bartlett *Americanisms, Banter . . .* Southern and Western. "There will be a banter on the bare ground," meaning a shootingmatch. **1906** *DN* 3.125 **nwAR.**

3 in phr *whet a banter:* See quots.

1927 *AmSp* 2.366 **wcWV,** *Whet a banter . .* to challenge for a contest in mowing by the manner of whetting the scythe. "John whet a banter just then." **1936** *AmSp* 11.318 **Ozarks,** *Whet a banner . .* To make a loud rattle with a whetstone, scraping it on a scythe or cradle. A sort of challenge to other reapers at harvest-time.

bantling n [*OED* →1864 in lit use]

A small child, an infant.

1809 W. Irving *Knickerb.* (1861) 48 (*OED*), A tender virgin, accidentally and unaccountably enriched with a bantling. **1936** *AmSp* 11.275 **cTN Mts,** The bantling is in the cradle. **1939** (1962) Thompson *Body & Britches* 210 **NY** [In lyrics to a ballad], A woman tall, who, on each arm, / A little, pale-faced bantling bore. **1944** *PADS* 2.40 **sVA, wNC,** *Bantling . . .* A child. **1952** Brown *NC Folkl.* 1.518 **wNC,** *Bantlin'.*

banty n, often attrib Pronc-sp *bandy* **widespread, esp east of Missip R**

A bantam; also fig.

1890 *DN* 1.76 **NJ, MD,** *Banty:* for bantam. **1892** *DN* 1.214 **NEng.** *Ibid* 234 **KY.** **1912** *DN* 3.571 **wIN.** **1936** *AmSp* 11.161 **eTX,** ['bæ·ntɪ] is almost as widely used as the standard form in the phrase 'bantam rooster.' **1942** *AmSp* 17.100 **ePA,** [bændɪ] *. . bantam.* **1954** *PADS* 21.20 **SC, wMD.** **c1960** *Wilson Coll.* **csKY,** Be sure to feed the old banty hen. **1960** Williams *Walk Egypt* 225 **GA,** She giggled. "Better men in Bugtown. Don't need a banty, I can get me a rooster." *Ibid* 255, "Mama says we can hunt banty eggs." **1965–70** *DARE* (Qu. K76, . . *Other kinds of poultry*) 20 Infs, **widespread, esp east of Missip R,** Banties; **NY**92, Buff cochin banties; **MN**34, **NV**8, **NY**230, **TX**33, **VT**16, Banty hen(s); **KY**23, **MN**33, **PA**10, Banty chickens; **PA**80, **VA**7, Banty rooster; **WI**14, Banty; **OH**10, Bandies.

banty adj Also *banty-legged* [Alter of *bandy-legged* perh infl by **banty** n] Cf **bandy-shanked**

Bowlegged.

1927 in 1944 *ADD* **WV,** *Banty-legged . . .* Bowlegged. **1930** Shoemaker *1300 Words* **cPA Mts** (as of c1900), *Banty*—Bow-legged.

banya n Also sp *banio* [Russ] **AK**

A bath house.

1882 Elliot *Seal Islands* 173 **AK,** *Banio . . .* A steamy bath-house. **1941** *Alaska Sportsman* July 22 (Tabbert *Alaskan Engl.*), Old Russian banyas or detached bath-houses, such as were once to be found in the yard of every Russian family, are still being used by some Kodiak families. **1973** *AK Mag.* Nov 17, Many . . have large communal banyas that house as many as 30 to 40 people.

‡bap v [Var of **bat** v[2] 1]

1970 *DARE* (Qu. X24, *When a person opens and closes his eyes quickly, he _____*) Inf **NC**88, Baps.

bapa n Also sp *baw-pa* [Varr of **baba** 1] Cf **bamma**

A grandfather.

1966–69 *DARE* (Qu. Z3, . . *Grandfather*) Inf **MO**32, Bapa [bæpɚ]; **WA**17, Baw-pa [bɔpə]. **1983** *DARE* File **cnCT,** [bɑpə] is used by a family from near Hartford, Conn. The kids are ca. 12–16 years old; [bɑpə] is 77.

bapsouse v, hence *bapsouzing* vbl n [Blend of *baptize* + *souse* immerse] *joc*

To baptize.

1906 *DN* 3.125 **nwAR,** There's going to be a bapsouzin at the creek next Sunday. **1926** Roberts *Time of Man* 119 **cKY,** "I baptize you . . ." "Quit, I already been bapsoused."

Baptist n Usu |'bæp‚tɪst, 'bæptɪs|; **esp Sth, Midl** |'bæb‚tɪs(t), 'bæb‚dɪs(t)| Pronc-spp *Babdist, Babtiss, Babtist,* pl *Babtises,*

Baptises, Baptisis (cf -**es 1**) Thus also *baptism* |ˈbæbˌtɪzm̩|, *baptize* |ˈbæbˌtɑɪz|

A Forms.

1837 Sherwood *Gaz. GA* 69 [In list of provincialisms to be avoided], *Babtises*, for Baptists. **1843** (1916) Hall *New Purchase* 147 **IN**, History of the Baptisis. **1892** *DN* 1.238 **cwMO**, *Babdist.* **1895** *DN* 1.375 **seKY, eTN, wNC**, *Babtist.* **1903** *DN* 2.305 **seMO**, *Babtiss.* **1905** *DN* 3.228 **nwAR**, *Babtis'.* **1911** *DN* 3.503 **Sth**, [Of 239 Infs, 85 report medial *p*, 154 report medial *b* in *Baptist*]. **1934** Carmer *Stars Fell on AL* 23, I belongs to the Babtists and we don't dance. *Ibid* 25, The babtizin was before us. **1936** *AmSp* 11.237 **eTX**, The tendency in illiterate speech . . is toward full voicing of the medial *p* . . . [ˈbæbˌtɑɪz], [ˈbæbˌtɪzm], [ˈbæbˌtɪs]. **1942** Hall *Smoky Mt. Speech* 97 **eTN, wNC**, [ˈbæbdɪs]. **1966** *Wilson Coll.* **csKY**, Baptist [ˈbæbtɪs] church. **1967** *DARE* FW Addit **LA**12, [ˈbæbˌtɑɪz]. **1967–68** *DARE* Tape **TX**49, [ˈbæbˌtɪs]; **IN**10, [ˈbæbˌtɪst].

B Sense.

=pond slider. [See quot]

1952 Carr *Turtle* 248, Yellow-bellied Turtle *Pseudemys scripta scripta* . . . In west Florida, where turtles are commonly speared in deep, clear springs, it is regularly recognized and is called "Baptist," with reference to the thick, hard shell.

Baptist cake n Also *Baptist bread* [See quot 1956] **NEng** Also called **fried bread 1, holy poke, huffjuff**

Raised bread-dough fried in deep fat.

1931–33 *LANE Worksheets* **csMA**, Baptist cake. A sweet roll made of breadflour, sweetened, twisted, dropped in hot fat. **1939** Wolcott *Yankee Cook Book* 368 **NEng**, *Baptist bread:* small irregular pieces of raised bread-dough fried in deep fat; served with maple syrup. **1941** *LANE* Map 285 3 Infs, **ceCT, csMA**, Baptist cake(s). **1956** Culinary Arts Inst. *New Engl. Cook Book* 17, Baptist Cakes. These crisp, tempting morsels got their name, so legend says, "because they were immersed" — in deep fat, that is.

Baptist dam-breaker See **dam-buster**

Baptist pallet n [See quot 1970] **chiefly Sth** Also called **Methodist pallet** Cf **pallet**

A temporary bed or shakedown used in connection with protracted religious meetings.

1962 Atwood *Vocab. TX* 47, *Bed on the floor* . . . Four informants give *Baptist pallet*, probably in allusion to large religious gatherings and their attendant discomforts. **1965–66** *DARE* (Qu. E18) Infs **AL**11, **MS**1, Baptist pallet; **AR**47, Free-will Baptist pallet. **1970** Tarpley *Blinky* 105 **neTX**, Informants who recall the use of *pallets* for the children at summertime evangelist services (usually held outdoors) still refer to the home variety as *Baptist . . pallets.*

baptist plant n

Perh an agapanthus.

1970 *DARE* Tape **TN**52, A baptist plant is a beautiful plant, it blooms in the summer . . . It doesn't stay bloomed long, but it's pretty . . . I keep it [inside] through the winter . . . [and] put them outdoors in spring . . . [The blossoms are a] pretty blue . . . It's a bud [sic; = bulb?] . . . They multiply a lot; they grow and bloom and one year they're naked and the pot is so thick you have to thin it out.

baquero See **buckaroo**

bar n¹

1 A horizontal line in a cattle brand, often used in the names of ranches. **West**

1890 *Stock Grower* 29 Mar 6/4 (*DA*), Circle Bar Ranch. *Ibid* 15 Mar 6/3, The G-bar-outfit. **1911** *Outing* Mar 736/1, With the beginning of Bonanza's espionage the Bar Cross cattle ceased to disappear. **1951** Grant *Cowboy Encycl.* 29, A dash was a Bar. Capital letters were known as Big. **1961** Adams *Old-Time Cowhand* 261 **West**, A straight line's a "bar" if it rests in a horizontal position.

2 freq attrib: A surface deposit of gold ore. **West** *hist*

1852 Coke *A Ride to Oregon and California* 358 (*Perrin Coll.*), By the law of mutual agreement each miner is entitled to a certain portion of this "bar" as it is called, in which gold is found. **1867** Hollister *Mines CO* 60, Langley lighted upon some placer or bar-diggings in a gulch on South Boulder Creek. *Ibid* 46, The Foot-hills furnished many gulch, placer, and bar-mines, that is, surface deposits containing gold which could be got out by washing. **1871** U.S. Treas. Dept. *Mines* 199 **ID**, It is not practical to carry on bar-mining in the Snake while the stream is

high. **1896** *Land of Sunshine* July 62 **sCA**, Some of the bar claims were quite rich — as high as $8 to the pan being obtained in some places. **1968** Adams *Western Words, Bar diggings* — Gold washing on river bars. Bars are worked when the water is low or with the aid of cofferdams.

3 also attrib: An oblong cookie or pastry. **chiefly Nth, NW** Cf **maple bar**

1966–69 *DARE* (Qu. H30, *An oblong cake, cooked in deep fat*) Infs **CA**162, **ID**1, **OR**1, **WA**19, Bar(s); **VA**1, Bar cake; (Qu. H28) Inf **IA**17, Bars; **IL**91, Bar doughnuts. **1981** *DARE* File **csMN**, Cub Scouts are asked to bring bars to bake sales. Bars are any cookies like brownies, date bars, etc. that are baked in a shallow pan and cut into squares or rectangles. Sometimes bars are frosted. **1982** *Sunshine* (Madison WI) 16 June 3/3 **csWI**, A collection of favorite bread and bar recipes will also be for sale.

4 See **water bar.**

‡**5** In marble play: see quot. Cf *DS* EE8

1933 *Hanley Disks* **swCT**, Bar. Lag-line in marble play.

bar n² See **bear** n¹ A

bar n³ Also sp *baire, bear, bère, bier* [LaFr *boire* mosquito net, rel to Fr *barre* cross-bar] **Sth, esp sLA and other Fr settlement areas**

A mosquito net.

1775 (1962) Romans *Nat. Hist. FL* 189, Where musketoes are plenty, have a close covering, called in this country a *Bère*, and made in form of a musketo net, to put up over your bed. *Ibid* 228, [Footnote:] *Baires* are a kind of tent made of light coarse cloth, like canvas gauze. **1797** (1856) Baily *Jrl.* 309 **sLA**, The bedrooms . . are furnished with nothing but a *hard-stuffed* bed . . covered with a clean, white sheet; and over the whole there is a large gauze net (called a *bear*), which is intended as a defence against the mosquitos. **1805** (1965) Lewis–Clark *Hist. Lewis–Clark Exped.* 2.417, [Footnote:] I had left my bier, of course suffered considerably. **1894** Twain *Pudd'nhead Wilson* 415, Get their bed ready . . and see that you drive all the mosquitoes out of their bar. **1916** *DN* 4.268 **New Orleans LA**, *Bar.* **1945** Saxon *Gumbo Ya-Ya* 273 **LA**, She journeys from bedchamber to bedchamber, raising mosquito *baires* and peering hopefully into the face of each sleeper. **1955** Warren *Angels* 80 **LA**, After a while, I rose, took off only my dress and shoes, then lay down on the bed. But I had no intention of going to sleep. I arranged the *baire.* **1965–70** *DARE* (Qu. R16, . . *The fine, thin cloth that lets air in but keeps mosquitoes and other insects out;* total Infs questioned, 75) 24 Infs, **chiefly MS, OK, FL**, Mosquito bar; **AR**28, 41, Skeet bar. **1967** LeCompte *Word Atlas* 144 **seLA**, *Fine thin cloth that lets air in and keeps mosquitoes and other insects out . . . baire* [given by 6 of 21 infs].

bar n⁴ Also *bar hog, ~ pig* |bɑ(r), bɑɹ| [Reduced form of **barrow** n²] **chiefly Sth, Midl, nNY**

A gelded hog.

1915 *DN* 4.180 **swVA**, *Bar* . . . Short for *barrow.* **1931–33** *LANE Worksheets* **swVT**, Bar pig . . . castrated hog. **1941** Stuart *Men of Mts.* 345 **neKY**, We see crates of chickens, geese . . bar hogs . . and bulls. **1946** *PADS* 6.5 **eNC** (as of c1900), *Bar* [bɑr, bɑː] . . A *barrow*, a castrated hog . . . The usual word. **c1960** *Wilson Coll.* **csKY**, [ˈbɑrˌhɑg] — The male, castrated hog. **1965–70** *DARE* (Qu. K58) 15 Infs, **Sth, Midl**, Bar; **NY**13, 109, 233, Bar [bɑr, bɑɹ]; **NY**92, Bar [bɑr] — "Inf's spelling is barr" [FW]; **KY**62, Bar-hog; **NC**3, **NY**209, Bar pig. [Of all Infs responding to the question, 48% were from comm-type 5; of those giving these responses, 86% were from comm-type 5.]

bar adj See **bare**

barabara n Usu |bəˈrɑbərə| Also sp *barabarra, barabba, barrabara,* and dim *barrabkie* [Russ] **AK**

A simple hut, usu built partially underground, used in the Aleutian Islands.

1868 Whymper *Travel AK* 162, We came to a small and very dilapidated Indian shanty, not much better than an open camp, known by the Russians as 'Ivan's barabba' (house). **1882** Elliot *Seal Islands* 173 **AK**, *Barrabkie* . . . A hut. *Barrabara* . . . A large hut. **1903** *Jrl. Amer. Folkl.* 17 **AK**, He preceded them, and cleared out of the barrabara all of the straw and bedding. **1943** *Alaska Sportsman* Jan 28 (Tabbert *Alaskan Engl.*), In its correct interpretation a barabarra is a primitive native Aleut home which . . . is a crude framework of driftwood shaped over a hole in the ground and covered with sods and earth. **1951** Winchell *Home Bering Sea* 60 **AK**, But Feodor liked it, for he had always lived in a house just like that. It was a barabara (ba rabʹ ɑrə) by the river. **1981** Tabbert *Alaskan Engl.*, Barabara . . . Several quotations . . indicate main stress on the second syllable.

baraboo See **barbaree**

barb n [See quot 1906] **NJ**

A **kingfish 1** (either *Menticirrhus americanus* or *M. saxatilis*). **1873** in 1878 Smithsonian Inst. *Misc. Coll.* 14.2.27, *Menticirrus* [sic] *nebulosus* . . . Barb *(New Jersey).* **1887** Goode *Amer. Fishes* 123, The *King*-fish, . . also known as . . the "Barb" about Barnegat [New Jersey]. **1906** NJ State Museum *Annual Rept. for 1905* 336, *Menticirrhus saxatilis* . . . Barb . . . A single short thick fleshy barbel at symphysis of mandible below.

Barbara's-buttons n

A perennial plant of the chiefly southeastern genus *Marshallia* which has alternate leaves, no ray flowers, and a white to purplish corolla. Also called **false scabish, puffballs**

1933 Small *Manual SE Flora* 1455, *Marshallia* . . . Barbara's buttons. **1964** Batson *Wild Flowers SC* 122, *Barbara's-buttons* . . . Moist pinelands and clearings in the Coastal Plains. **1975** Duncan–Foote *Wildflowers SE* 220, *Barbara's-buttons* . . . *Marshallia trinerva* . . . *Marshallia tenuifolia.*

barbaree n, exclam Also *baraboo, barbaroot, (high) barbary* **Nth** Cf **blankie-lie-low**

A hiding game usu played with teams; also the call yelled or whispered by the hiders as a hint of their location.

1901 *DN* 2.136 **cNY**, *Barbaree* . . . A game similar to black-a-li-lo . . , both cries in this case being "barbaree." **1945** Boyd *Hdbk. Games* 67, *Baraboo*—One player blinds while the other players hide . . . When a player is touched, he becomes a hunter . . . When the hunters have exhausted their power to find the hiders, the original hunter may call "Baraboo," whereupon all those hiders who hear his voice must answer "Hilow." **1950** *WELS (Games in which one captain hides his team and the other team tries to find it)* 1 Inf, **cWI**, Barb-a-ree—old-fashioned [but] being revived by teenagers. **1966–70** *DARE* (Qu. EE12, *Games in which one captain hides his team*) Infs IL135, PA194, Barbary; **SD8**, Barbaroot ['bɑrbə'rut]; (Qu. EE13a) Inf NY82, Barbary; (Qu. EE16) Inf PA194, Barbary; NJ39, Barbary—"it" counts, hider yells "Barbary"; "it" calls, "[I've] lost track"; hider must yell or whisper "Barbary"; (Qu. EE33) Inf MI109, High barbary ['bɑbəri]—divide into groups, one group would hide and call out "high barbary."

bar bass n [From its habit of staying over gravel bars in river channels]

=**red drum.**

1946 LaMonte *N. Amer. Game Fishes* 79, *Channel Bass Sciænops ocellatus* . . Names: . . Bar Bass.

barb-d'espanole See **barbe espagnole**

barbeau n

=**cornflower 1.**

1896 *Jrl. Amer. Folkl.* 9.191, *Centaurea Cyanus* . . barbeau, Louisiana . . . A name common along the Mississippi a generation and more ago, from a M. Barbeau, who brought it from France.

barbed-wire pie n Cf **barb wire deal**

Fig: something utterly disagreeable.

1942 Hurston *Dust Tracks* 103 **sFL** [Black], I just had to talk back at established authority and that established authority hated backtalk worse than barbed-wire pie.

barbe espagnole n Also *barb-d'espanole* [See quot 1931] **chiefly LA**

=**Spanish moss 1.**

1931 Read *LA French* 4, *Barbe Espagnole* . . . Spanish moss . . . Pénicaut, writing in 1699 . . , says: " . . . This moss is an herb of a long, fine fiber, growing upon the trees, which the French of this part of the country call *Spanish-beard* . . ." Barbe à l'Espagnole . . [is] the exact [term] . . that Pénicaut uses for "Spanish moss". **1937** *Torreya* 37.96, *Dendropogon usneoides* . . . Barbe espagnole, Louisiana and Missouri. **1972** Brown *Wildflowers LA* 12 *Spanish-moss, Barb-D'Espanole.*

barber n [See quot 1889]

A winter storm in which frozen ice crystals are driven by fierce winds.

1832 McGregor *Brit. Amer.* 1.133, [Footnote:] The keen north-west wind, during winter, is often called the "Barber" in America. [**1889** (1971) Farmer *Americanisms*, Barber . . . The cold wind . . comes down across the track of a warm wind . . the moisture is instantly

condensed to powdery snow, in some instances as sharp as fragments of steel . . . When the vapour is so suddenly condensed as to form sharp spicules, the Canadian voyageurs call it the *barber,* as it cuts the face like a razor.] **1889** (1968) Reddall *Fact* 57, Barber . . . A severe storm, accompanied by intense cold, peculiar to the Gulf of St. Lawrence . . . The name is also applied to a phase of cold along the coasts of Nova Scotia and New England. **1982** *TWA Ambassador* July 47, *Barber.* A term used in some sections of the United States and Canada to describe a strong wind that carries precipitation that freezes upon contact with objects, especially the beard and hair.

barber chair n, v **Nth** Cf **goose pen, tombstone**

In logging: a chair-shaped stump usu resulting from improper felling of a tree; to fell a tree so as to produce such a stump.

1950 *Western Folkl.* 9.380 **cnCA**, *Barber chair.* A long slab hanging on a stump. This oversized splinter is caused by a tree not being sufficiently undercut. **1956** Sorden–Ebert *Logger's Words* **Gt Lakes**, *Barber-chair,* A stump with part of the tree still on it due to the tree splitting when falling. **1958** McCulloch *Woods Words* **Pacific NW**, *Barber chair* . . . a. A tree which is split up the trunk in falling, leaving the split portion on the stump, instead of breaking through cleanly to the undercut. b. The act of making a tree into a barber chair. **1959** *AmSp* 34.76 **nCA**, *Barber chair* . . A . . tree . . with a hole in the base caused by fire burning out the rotted center . . . Also, a stump on which a slab is left standing that splintered off the tree as it fell. **1966** *DARE* Tape **MI10**, If you were out there felling timber and caused a tree to split when you knocked it down, . . and leave part of the trunk attached to the stump, it was said that you had barber-chaired that tree.

barber pole n Also *barber's pole*

1 also attrib: A stick of spirally striped candy.

1944 Howard *Walkin' Preacher* 19 **IA**, "You boys help me out trading here for your mother so I'll give you a barber pole." Then he would hand each of us a large stick of red-striped candy. **1968–69** *DARE* (Qu. H82b) Inf **CA105**, Barber pole candy; **IL98**, Barber poles.

2 In logging: see quot.

1969 Sorden *Lumberjack Lingo* **NEng, Gt Lakes**, *Barber pole*—A sawed tree fallen on another, bending it over.

3 =**sugarstick.**

1934 Haskin *Wild Flowers Pacific Coast* 245, One of the most showy of the saprophytes found growing in our deep forests is . . barber's pole . . . The whole stem is splashed and striped with scarlet, on pure white. **1949** Peattie *Cascades* 233 **Pacific NW**, The most striking member of this group is the barber's pole or sugar-stick, *Allotropa virgata.* Numerous scale-like leaves clothe the bottom of a distinctive red-and-white striped stalk.

4 See quot.

1968 *DARE* (Qu. P2, . . *Saltwater fish . . [that] are good to eat*) Inf **CA65**, Barber pole, a cod.

barber-pole paint n *joc*

=**striped paint.**

1967–68 *DARE* (Qu. HH14, *Ways of teasing a beginner or inexperienced person—for example, by sending him for a "left-handed monkey wrench": "Go get me _____.")* Infs **IA30, SC40**, (A can of) barber-pole paint.

barberry n [Folk-etym]

Std: a plant of the genus *Berberis;* also the berries thereof. Also called **agarita, agrillo 1, hollygrape, mountain grape, Oregon grape**

barbeshela See **bobbasheely**

bar-bill n

=**ring-necked duck.**

1953 Jewett *Birds WA* 134, Bar-bill . . . Bill . . black, crossed by blue band near end.

barbood, barbooth See **barbudi**

barboquejo n Also sp *barbiquejo* [Span] **SW** Also called **bonnet string**

The chin strap of a cowboy hat.

1945 Thorp *Pardner* 298 **SW**, *Barboquejo*—chin-strap on a cowboy's hat, used especially in brushy country to keep the hat on the wearer's head. **1955** Harris *Look of Old West* 105, The hats many of them wore were Mexican sombreros, with high curved edges . . and a *barbiquejo* . . dangling long and loose under the wearer's jaw. **1977**

Watts *Dict. Old West*, *Barboquejo* . . . The chin strap of a hat . . . I have seen this term used only in the brush-country of southwest Texas, but it was possibly more widely used.

barbot n [Var of **burbot**]
=**burbot.**
    1968 *DARE* (Qu. P1) Inf **AK**9, Barbot ['bɑr,bɑt] —ling cod.

barbudi n Pronc-spp *barbood, barbooth, barbute, barbuti* [CanFr *barbote* from Turkish *barbut*] **?esp West**
A gambling game played with dice.
    1967 *DARE* (Qu. DD35) Inf **IA**5, Barbudi [bɑr'bʊt,di] —a Greek gambling game; (Qu. DD37) Inf **OR**10, [bɑr'bʊt] —dice, a Basque game, but played all around here. **c1971** Hall *Snake River Valley* **swID,** 1 inf, Barbooth; 1 inf, Barbute. **1982** *Contract Bridge Letters* **swCA,** Barbuti . . is played between two players; each arrived with a minature dice-cup containing two very small dies. They cast the dice in turn . . . It is the only "even-break" dice game known! i.e., 1-1, 1-2 loses; 6-5/5-6 wins by whoever is shooting. *Ibid* **swCA,** Barbudi, barbood and barbooth . . . a 2-dice game also called even-up craps. It is played where Greek immigrants, or Jewish ones gather.

barb wire deal n Cf **barbed-wire pie**
    1958 McCulloch *Woods Words* **Pacific NW,** *Barb wire deal* —A tough situation to handle.

bar cat n[1] [*bar* perh from *sand bar* + *cat*]
=**crab scraper.**
    1976 Warner *Beautiful Swimmers* 204 **Chesapeake Bay,** The boat was small . . . Its freeboard amidships . . [was] not more than eighteen inches . . . "Funny looking things, ain't they?" . . "They're crab scrapers . . . over on Tangier [Sound] they call them 'bar cats.' "

bar cat n[2] [Prob pronc var of *bear cat*]
=**lynx.**
    1967 *DARE* (Qu. P31) Inf **KY**34, Bar cat ['bɑr,kæt] —has short tail.

bardacious See **bodacious**

bardaciously See **bodaciously**

barda grease See **bardy grease**

bar ditch n [Pronc var of **barrow ditch;** for folk-etym, see quot 1963 at **1**]
1 =**barrow pit 1.** **chiefly OK, TX** See Map and Map Section Cf **bar pit 1**
    1949 *PADS* 11.17 **CO.** **1950** [see **barrow pit 1**]. **1963** *AmSp* 38.157 **TX,** Several [students] pointed out that a *bar ditch* is a ditch that runs parallel to a roadway and *bars* cattle or sheep from the roadway. **1965–70** *DARE* (Qu. N24, *A ditch along the side of a graded road*) 31 Infs, **chiefly OK, TX,** Bar ditch. **1971** Wood *Vocab. Change* 53, In Oklahoma . . the first preference is for *bar ditch.*

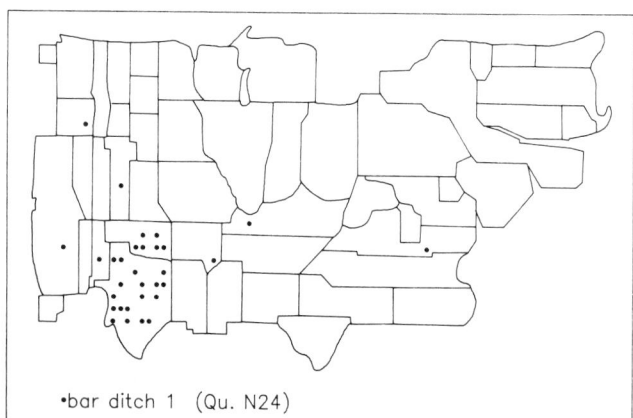

•bar ditch 1 (Qu. N24)

2 =**barrow pit 2.**
    1982 *Smithsonian Letters* **TX,** Bar ditch —These are long narrow ponds alongside a roadway constructed across a lowland area. Fill for the roadway was "borrowed" (excavated) from the right-of-way and thus caused the pond. Our supposition is that *bar* is a contraction of *borrow.*
3 See quot.
    1966 *DARE* (Qu. N44, *In a town, the strip of grass and trees between the*

sidewalk and the curb) Inf **OK**20, Bar ditch —that's what the old men who mow it for me call it.

bar-dog n **West** *joc*
A bartender.   Hence vbl n *bar-dogging* tending bar.
    1944 Adams *Western Words*, *Bar-dog* —A bartender. Many were former cowboys too stove-up for riding. **1971** Jennings *Cowboys* 182 **West,** He'd settle down somewhere and learn a nice trade, maybe, like bar-dogging . . . Drinkers always seemed to like bartenders.

bardy grease n Also sp *barda grease* [Pronc-sp or folk-etym for *verdigris*] **sAppalachians**
Fusel oil.
    1962 *Mt. Life* Winter 12 **sAppalachians,** From the end of the worm is suspended an old sock filled with charred hardwood to "cut out the bardy grease" from the singing liquid before it rings into the glass jar below. **1972** *Foxfire Book* 324 **nGA,** The alcohol which flows out here is usually strained through hickory coals to remove the fusel oils (barda grease). *Ibid* 339, The coals remove the "bardy grease" (it shows up as an oil slick on top of the whiskey if not drained off) which can make one very ill.

bare adj Usu |bɛr, bɛə, beə|; also, **esp S Midl,** |bɑr, bær, ba| Pronc-sp *bar*
A Forms.
    1677 in 1965 *AmSp* 40.236 **VA,** "He hoped that Coll. Swan would be pulked [=plucked] bar." **1893** Shands *MS Speech* 6, [ba] for *bare.* **1899** (1912) Green *VA Folk-Speech*, *Bar* . . . *Bare*, "On his bar back." **1927** Shewmake *Engl. Pronc. VA* 17, *Bare* [bæ:r]. **1934** Carmer *Stars Fell on AL* 182, Brer B'ar tu'n 'roun' an' look, he scratch his head, he say: 'Dat 'ar rabbit done left me bar.' **c1960** *Wilson Coll.* **csKY,** *Bare* . . rarely /bɑr/ among the elderly.
B Sense.
See **barefooted 1.**

bare-ass(ed) adj, adv Also abbr *B.A.;* for addit varr see quots **chiefly NEast** See Map *esp among male speakers* See also **bare-naked**
Naked.
    1936 Kingsley *Dead End* 24 **NYC,** *Philip:* Besides, I haven't got my suit. *Tommy:* Well, go in bareass. **1965–70** *DARE* (Qu. W20, *. . No clothes on at all . . "They went in swimming _____."*) 19 Infs, **chiefly NEast,** Bare-assed; **CT**9, **NJ**54, **NY**80, 81, 201, **NC**76, Bare-ass;**MA**7, 72, **VT**16, Bollicky bare-ass(ed); **MA**1, B.A.; **ME**21, Bare-arse; **MO**27, Bare-ass naked; **CA**59, Bare-assed naked. [Of all Infs responding to the question, 60% were male; of those giving these responses, 86% were male.]

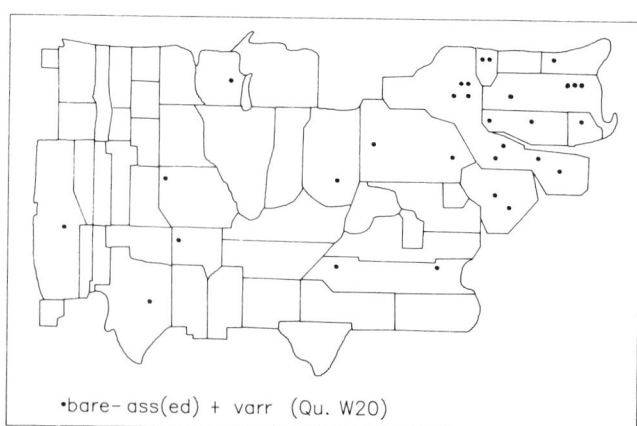

•bare-ass(ed) + varr (Qu. W20)

‡**barebones** adv
Bareback; without a saddle.
    1940 (1978) Still *River of Earth* 66 **KY,** A pony went by, shoeless, feet whispering on rocky ground. A man rode barebones.

bared adj Pronc-sp for *barred*
    1953 Randolph *Down in Holler* 10 **Ozarks,** The noun bar is correctly sounded, but the adjective barred is generally *bared;* a boy . . told me that the windows of the jail-house were *bared all round.* A woman . . described a dried-apple pie as *cross-bared.*

barefeeted adj

Without shoes, barefoot.

1928 Peterkin *Scarlet Sister Mary* 245 **SC,** E got such a awful splinter in e heel de last time e danced barefeeted. **1967** *DARE* Tape **AL**14, We didn' have shoes . . . We would go barefeeted.

barefooted adj Also *barefoot* [Cf *SND barefoot(ed) broth* broth made without meat]

1 also *bare,* rarely *bare-handed:* Of coffee, tea, or liquor: undiluted. **chiefly Mid and C Atl, Ohio Valley** See Map Also called **naked B1** Cf **socks**

1847 Paulding *Amer. Comedies* 194 **Philadelphia PA,** I thought even a Yankee knew that 'stone fence barefooted' is the polite English for whisky uncontaminated—pure, sir! **1867** Lowell *Biglow* lxii **NEng,** "I take my tea *barfoot,*" said a backwoodsman when asked if he would have cream and sugar. **1888** Whitman *November Boughs* 406, "Barefoot whiskey" is the Tennessee name for the undiluted stimulant. **1954** *PADS* 21.20 **eSC,** Barefoot. **c1960** *Wilson Coll.* **csKY,** *Barefoot(ed)* . . . Straight, as coffee without cream and sugar, or whiskey, undiluted. **1965–70** *DARE* (Qu. KK61, . . *"Would you like milk or lemon in your tea?" "No thanks, I'll take it _____."*) 19 Infs, **chiefly Mid and C Atl, Ohio Valley,** Barefooted (coffee); **NC**7, Barefooted (coffee); **TX**11, Barefooted; **GA**67, **IN**32, **NJ**1, 39, **PA**234, **TN**13, **VA**15, Barefoot; **PA**35, Branch water and barefoot; 11 Infs, **chiefly Mid and C Atl, Ohio Valley,** Bare; **KY**47, Bare-handed. **1967–68** *DARE* FW Addit **ceIA,** Barefoot—coffee with neither cream nor sugar—heard from waitress in Iowa City; **swOR,** Barefooted coffee—straight.

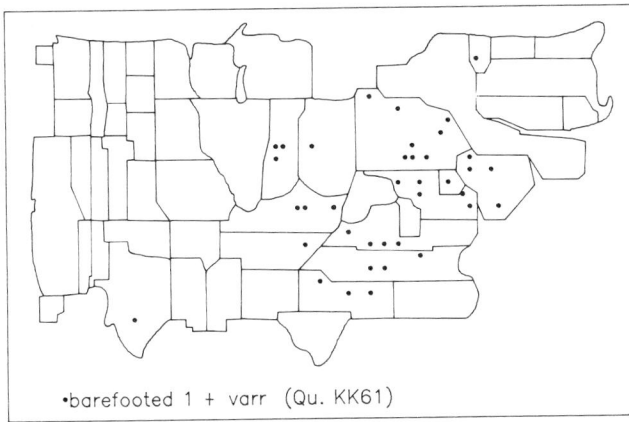

•barefooted 1 + varr (Qu. KK61)

2 Of bread: plain, without anything added.

1933 *AmSp* 8.1.47 **Ozarks,** Barefoot bread . . Hard cornbread made without shortening. **1954** *Harder Coll.* **cwTN,** Barefoot bread . . Hard bread without ingredients such as eggs or lard.

3 Of horses: unshod. **West**

1805 (1905) Lewis *Orig. Jrls. Lewis & Clark Exped.* 3.15 **MT,** Yet notwithstanding our horsed[s] [sic] traveled barefoot . . over them . . fast . . and did not detain us. **1927** (1944) Russell *Trails Plowed Under* 142 **MT,** Barefoot ponies on well-grassed sod travel mighty silent, an' the savages ain't doin' no talkin' except with their hands. **1941** FWP *Guide WY* 459, Barefooted. **1968** Adams *Western Words,* Barefoot.

bare-naked adj [Redund] **scattered, but chiefly Nth** See Map See also **bare-ass(ed)**

Naked.

1914 *DN* 4.69 **ME, nNH,** Barenaked . . . Usually "All barenaked." **1923** *DN* 5.201 **swMO,** He come a-runnin' out jist plumb bare naked. **1942** *AmSp* 17.130 **IN.** **1944** *PADS* 2.24 **cwOH, cwNC.** **1954** *Harder Coll.* **cwTN.** **c1960** *Wilson Coll.* **csKY,** Bare-naked. Redundant for *naked.* Not common. **1965–70** *DARE* (Qu. W20, . . *No clothes on at all . . "They went in swimming _____."*) 40 Infs, **chiefly Nth,** Barenaked.

barf v, n [Perh imit] **chiefly Nth, West** *esp among young speakers*

To vomit; vomit.

1964 *AmSp* 39.117 [Campus slang], *Barf,* a verb meaning 'to vomit,' assignable on the basis of my own observation and that of an independent observer to . . the fall of 1957 or the summer of 1958. **1965–70**

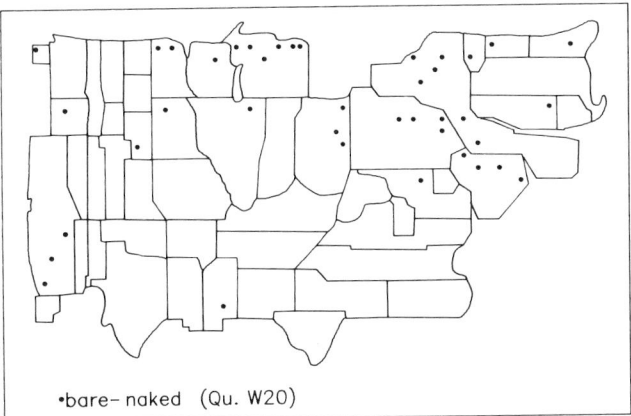

•bare-naked (Qu. W20)

DARE (Qu. BB17, *Other words . . for vomiting*) 19 Infs, **chiefly Nth, West,** Barf. [Of all Infs responding to the question, 10% were young; of those giving this response, 68% were young.] **1965** *DARE* File **IL** (as of 1957), The history department won't let you drink milk . . because they claim it will make you barf. **1966** *DARE* FW Addit, *Barf bag*—one of those "discreet" little bags tucked into a pouch on the back of an airplane seat. Used in case of air sickness. **1967** Stegner *Little Live Things* 143 **CA,** This kid comes out into the view of the crass materialist world to exercise his spiritual rectum. I'm *not* interested. I want to barf.

barfish n [From its being striped or barred]

1 The black **crappie.**

1882 U.S. Natl. Museum *Bulletin* 16.465, *P[omoxis] sparoides . . . Calico Bass . . Barfish.* **1887** Goode *Amer. Fishes* 69, In Lake Erie, and in Ohio generally, it is the "Strawberry Bass," . . . and it is also called "Bar-fish" . . . In Lake Michigan the name "Bar-fish" is in general use. **1902** Jordan–Evermann *Amer. Fishes* 336, Grass bass, barfish, . . and lamplighter are names which have been applied to this fish [black crappie].

2 =**yellow bass.**

1887 Goode *Amer. Fishes* 33, Another species . . is . . generally known as the Yellow Bass, but sometimes called Bar-fish in the South. *Ibid* 34, In Louisiana this species is called "Bar-fish" probably on account of its stripes. **1972** Sparano *Outdoors Encycl.* 362, *Yellow Bass . . . Common Names:* . . barfish.

3 =**white bass.**

1933 LA Dept. of Conserv. *Fishes* 361, The White Bass appears in Louisiana to be known almost exclusively by the name of Barfish. **1967** *DARE* Tape **LA**5, Catch a good many barfish at times . . . To me, something like a striped bass, only they're a lot bigger 'round here than what striped bass gets. **1968** *DARE* (Qu. P1) Inf **LA**15, Barfish. [FW: Same as white bass.] **1972** Sparano *Outdoors Encycl.* 362.

barge n

1 See **header barge.**

2 Orig a horse-drawn wagon or sleigh used for transporting a large number of people; now also a bus, esp a school bus. **NEng** *somewhat old-fash*

1882 Howells *Modern Instance* 328 **NEng,** Marcia watched him drive off toward the station in the hotel barge. **1888** in 1960 *AmSp* 35.267, Barge. In New England, a name given to an omnibus on wheels. **1907** *DN* 3.181 **seNH.** **1939** *LANE* Map 185 **seMA,** 1 inf, Barge, a bus for transporting school children. **1959** *VT Hist.* ns 27 **swVT,** Barge . . . A bus. The school *barge.* Occasional. **1967–69** *DARE* (Qu. N40b) Inf **MA**72, Barge—on runners in winter, before the trolley came in, would hold 15 to 20 people; **MA**74, School barge—a pung, really; (Qq. N41a, b) Inf **MA**40, Barge; **CT**32, Barge—wagon, [has] 4 horses, carries kids to school; **NH**16, Barge—holds 20 to 30 people. [All Infs old] **1976** *Yankee* Sept 106 **seMA** (as of 1902), [The] barge line to and from all sections of Provincetown leaves . . hourly.

3 See quot. [Perh transf from naut *barge* container for food storage aboard ship]

1979 Lewis *How to Talk Yankee* **NEng,** Barge . . . One of many names for the receptacle into which clams are placed as they are dug out of the mudflats.

4 A big foot. *joc* Cf **canal boat**

c1960 *Wilson Coll.* **csKY,** Barges . . . Big feet; barges on the river suggested the figure. **1967–68** *DARE* (Qu. X38) Infs **LA**37, **PA**76, 94, **SC**40, Barges.

bar-geist n [Cf Engl dial *barghest* ghost, Ger *Berggeist* gnome]
 1930 Shoemaker *1300 Words* 6 **cPA Mts** (as of c1900), "Bar-Geist," a ghost which frequents bars [=gates] or fields.

bargum n Also *ba'gum* Pronc-spp for *bargain*
 1905 Culbertson *Banjo Talks* 145 **SE** [Black], Dey kin have hit at a ba'gum. **1917** Torrence *Granny Maumee* 63 **Sth** [Black], Does you know when we mek de bargum about you buyin' dis heah house?

‡bar-head n [Etym unknown]
 1950 *PADS* 14.74 **FL**, Bar-head . . . A horse that cannot be trained to work or to be ridden. Cowboy speech.

barick n [Prob Engl dial *bargh* a long low ridge or hill] Cf *DS* C17
 1916 *DN* 4.337 **csPA**, Barick . . . A hill. "There's a high barick back of the town."

bario n
 See quot 1955.
 [**1894** Gomme *Traditional Games* 1.364, Different kinds of marbles are alleys, barios, . . stonies.] **1955** *PADS* 23.11 **cwTN**, Bario . . . A toy marble made from barium; hence the name.

bark v[1]

 1 To participate in a **barking exercise**. **S Midl** *now hist*
 1807 McNemar *KY Revival* 69 **OH, KY, TN, VA, wPA**, About the latter end of the year 1804, there were regular societies of these people . . praying, shouting, jerking, barking, or rolling.
 2 Of a dog: to bark with a sound indicating that a pursued animal is at bay or has been treed.
 1908 Roosevelt *Outdoor Pastimes* 7, He was not a very noisy dog, and when "barking treed" he had a meditative way of giving single barks separated by intervals of several seconds. **1939** *Hall Coll.* **wNC**, They fought right down to the . . butt of the ridge into the flat laurel and commenced barkin'. I thought was treed. **1947** Guthrie *Big Sky* 12 **KY** (as of c1830), He's just barkin' a coon. **1970** *DARE* Tape AR56, He'd begin to bark bay like he had something treed.

bark n[1] See **barking exercise**

bark n[2]

 1 A scalp. *obs* See also **bark** v[2] 2
 1848 (1855) Ruxton *Life Far West* 18, They say he took the bark off the Shians when he cleared out of the village with old Beaver Tail's squaw.
 2 A container made of bark.
 1853 Barry *Hist. Sketch Hanover MA* 37, Children . . may be seen daily . . [going berrying] with *baskets*, or tin *kettles*, or *barks* on their arms. **1957** McMeekin *Old KY Country* 204, The pole he carries is called a "bark" and is a container for . . berries . . . A bark is made of a poplar trunk about eight inches thick.
 3 also *bark sack:* Transf: a cloth bag of bark-like texture.
 1967–68 *DARE* (Qu. F23) Inf **TN**11, Bark sack—very coarse; **VA**13, Bark.
 4 Among loggers: any outer layer, as a potato peel or pie crust.
 1925 *AmSp* 1.137 **Pacific NW** [Logger talk], "Chase us some of them spuds with the bark on (unpeeled potatoes)." . . For dessert he "takes on" "open-face pie" or "pie with the bark on." **1958** McCulloch *Woods Words* **Pacific NW**, Bark . . . The outside of anything.
 5 The hull of a walnut. **chiefly NEast**
 1941 *LANE* Map 277 *(Walnut shell)* **CT, swME**, 3 infs, Bark. **1965–70** *DARE* (Qu. I39) Infs **CT**21, 39, **MA**5, **NJ**31, 50, **NY**206, **OH**45, **OK**17, **PA**100, 128, Bark. **1973** Allen *LAUM* 1.307 **seMN**, 1 inf, Bark.

bark v[2]

 1 To kill a squirrel by shooting a bullet into the limb on which it is sitting. **chiefly S Midl**
 1831 Audubon *Ornith. Biog.* 1.293 **KY**, [Kentuckians] will *bark* off squirrels one after another, until satisfied with the number procured . . . The concussion . . killed the animal, and sent it whirling through the air. **1899** (1912) Green *VA Folk-Speech*. **1940** (1978) Still *River of Earth* 5 **KY**, Father was so angry he took his rifle-gun and went off into the woods for the day, bringing in four squirrels for supper. He had barked them, firing at the tree trunk beside the animal's heads, and bringing them down without a wound. **1941** *FWP Guide AR* 327, He

killed 47 gunners as fast as they peeped from behind parapets, picking them off as accurately as he had "barked" squirrels back home in Big Lake. **c1960** *Wilson Coll.* **csKY**.
 2 To scalp; hence ppl adj *barked* bald. See also **bark** n[2] 1
 1958 McCulloch *Woods Words* **Pacific NW**, Barked—A man who has lost his hair. **1968** Adams *Western Words*, Bark—An old trapper's word meaning *to scalp*.

bark a ride v phr
 In logging: see quot.
 1950 *Western Folkl.* 9.123 **Pacific NW**, Barking a ride. Peeling a lengthwise strip of bark off a log so that the log will "ride" easily over a skidroad.

bark-eater n
 1 Among loggers: see quot 1958.
 1958 McCulloch *Woods Words* 7 **Pacific NW**, Bark eater—a. a logger. b. A sawmill hand. **1969** Sorden *Lumberjack Lingo* **NEng, Gt Lakes.**
 2 =**porcupine**.
 1969 *DARE* (Qu. P31) Inf **NY**183, Bark-eater.

barker n
 1 ?One who makes a living by stripping bark from trees.
 1896 *DN* 1.412, Barker: "Poor Barkers," poor whites. Southern.
 2 also *bark horn:* A noise-making device consisting of a tin can (orig a cone of bark) and resin-smeared thread, and attached to a doorknob. See also **devil's fiddle, horse fiddle**
 1905 *DN* 3.69 **nwAR**, Barker . . . A horse-fiddle . . attached to a doorknob and pulled at a safe distance. **1946** *TN Folk Lore Soc. Bulletin* 12.1.21, The noise that can be made only by the blaring of bark horns.

barkie n
 See quot 1958.
 1958 McCulloch *Woods Words* 8 **Pacific NW**, Barkie—A small pole sold with the bark on. **1968** *Times–Std.* (Eureka CA) 7 Sept 9/5, Fir barkie poles are ranging from 29 cents to 55 cents per lineal foot.

barking bird n
 =**black-crowned night heron**.
 1955 *MA Audubon* 39.312, Black-crowned Night Heron. Barking Bird (Vt. In allusion to its *quok, quok* cries.)

barking dogs n pl *joc* Cf *DS* X38
 Tired or aching feet.
 1939 *AmSp* 14.89 **cTN**, Barking dogs. Aching feet. **1939** *Sun* (Baltimore MD) 12 Sept 3/6 (Hench Coll.), "Warden's feet," the first occupational ailment to result from the war—known in the United States as "barking dogs" was dignified with official recognition today by the British Association of Chriopodists [sic]. **1960** Wentworth–Flexner *Slang* 20, Barking dogs—Tired or sore feet.

barking exercise n Also *bark* [*bark* to emit a noise resembling the bark of a dog + **exercise B**] **chiefly S Midl, esp KY** *now hist* See also **bark** v[1] 1
 The spasmodic movements of hyperventilation producing animal-like noises, practiced at certain religious meetings.
 1807 McNemar *KY Revival* 63, The quickest method to find releasement from the jerks and barks, was to engage in the voluntary dance. **1834** *Biblical Repertory* 6.350, A lady from Tennessee, who brought into a certain part of Virginia the barking exercise, immediately was imitated by certain of those affected with the jerks. **1848** Collins *Hist. Sketches KY* 109, Those extraordinary and disgraceful scenes [of 1799] produced by the *jerks*, the *rolling* and the *barking exercises* . . which extensively obtained among some . . persuasions of those days. **1926** Kephart *Highlanders* 344 **KY**, Thousands of men and women at the camp-meetings [in 1800] fell victims to "the jerks," "barking exercises," erotic vagaries, physical wreckage, or insanity.

barking owl n Cf **laughing owl**
 An unidentified owl.
 1969 *DARE* Tape KY16, Back then we had all kind of owl. We had . . barking owl and laughing owl.

barking squirrel n
 =**prairie dog**.
 1814 Brackenridge *Views of LA* 239, In the course of my ramble, I happened on a village of barking squirrels, or prairie dogs, as they have been called. **1928** Anthony *N. Amer. Mammals* 218, *Cynomys ludovicianus* and related forms. Names.—Prairie-dog; Barking Squirrel.

barking wolf n obs

=**coyote** n **B1.**

> **1867** Amer. Naturalist 1.289, The Prairie or Barking Wolf (Canis latrans Say) is by far the most abundant carnivorous animal . . in almost every part of the West.

bark ooze n

Tree sap used as a cough remedy.

> **1966** DARE (Qu. BB50) Inf **AL4,** Bark ooze they call it—same as red oak police [=poultice].

bark sack See **bark** n² **3**

barl See **barrel A**

barley exclam Also barley out, barley's out [Prob alter of parley: OED "Sc. and north. dial." See also SND] Cf **barley me, borrows**

In children's games: time out!

> **1890** DN 1.60, Barley: a child's word, common in Pennsylvania, meaning to intermit play (for a rest). The opposite is "barley's out." **1917** DN 4.387 neOH, Barley out . . . Call for a truce in children's games. **1967–68** DARE (Qu. EE20, When two boys are fighting, and the one who is losing wants to stop, he calls out, "_____.") Infs **OH8, 18, WI66,** Barley out!; (Qu. EE17) Infs **OH18, VA30,** Barley (out)!

barley bright n [Blend of barley break, the older English name for the game (OED), and marlow bright or **Molly Bright**]

A children's game of chase.

> **1966** Peden Land 41 **IN,** Exciting games going on outside . . . Andy Over, Barley Bright, Hide-and-Go-Seek. **1966** DARE File swIN, Barley-bright—A type of children's game.

barleycorn sprints n [(John) barleycorn any alcoholic beverage + sprints hasty visits to the toilet] joc Cf DS BB19

Among loggers: see quot.

> **1958** McCulloch Woods Words **Pacific NW,** Barleycorn sprints—Dysentery following a drunk.

barley knife See **barlow knife**

barley me exclam [Perh rel to **barley**] Cf DS V5b, II8

In children's games: that's mine!

> **1956** AmSp 31.37 eMA, First there is the pattern I hosie . . . 'This is mine.' . . There are the Bags I and Barley me patterns, with colloquial inversion in the first and the old dative in the second.

barley out, barley's out See **barley**

barlow knife n Also barlow penknife, Russell Barlow knife, absol barlow; pronc var barley knife [After Russell Barlow, 18th-cent Engl knifemaker] **chiefly Sth, Midl** See Map

A single-bladed pocket knife.

> **1779** in 1906 Documents Revol. Hist. NJ 3.676, To be sold by Stephenson and Canfield, In Morris Town, . . Barlow penknives, Knives and forks. **1845** Judd Margaret 36 **NEng,** On the left were cuttoes, Barlow knives, iron candlesticks. **1903** DN 2.305 seMO, 'How will you swap barlows?' is a very common proposition among schoolboys. **1907** DN 3.228 nwAR. **1908** DN 3.289 eAL, wGA. **1915** DN 4.224 wTX, Barlow . . . Now used for any large pocket-knife. **c1937** in 1972 Amer. Slave 2.1.207 **SC,** They give us Christmas Day. Every woman got a handkerchief to tie up her hair. Every girl got a ribbon, every boy a

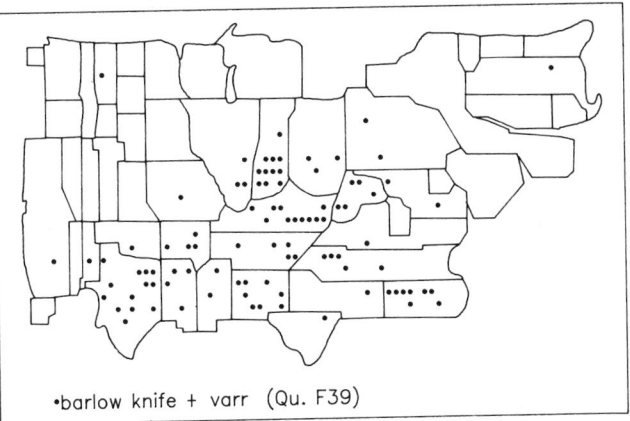

•barlow knife + varr (Qu. F39)

barlow knife, and every man a shin plaster. **1939** Hall Coll. **wNC, eTN. 1950** WELS (Large pocket knife) 1 Inf, **cnWI,** Barlow knife. **c1960** Wilson Coll. **csKY,** Barlow . . . Any knife, but esp. one made by Russell Barlow. **1965–70** DARE (Qu. F39) 47 Infs, **chiefly Sth, Midl,** Barlow; 47 Infs, **chiefly Sth, Midl,** Barlow knife; **AL14, OK51, WV14,** Barley knife; **IN52, VA9,** Russell Barlow knife.

barm n¹ Hist sp barme [OE beorma, preserved also in Engl dial] Yeast.

> **1859** Elwyn Glossary, Barme, yeast . . . is in common use, in New England. **1975** Gould ME Lingo 5, The barm was carefully kept alive and was handed mother to daughter at weddings. Mainers never used the word sourdough too much, although they knew what it was, but their barm-bread was essentially the sourdough of the western prospectors.

barm n² [Perh from barm bosom, lap; see EDD sb.²]

A large quantity.

> **1924** DN 5.288 **Cape Cod MA,** If a boat returns with a load of fish, it has a 'barm of fish.'

barmy adj [barm n¹; cf EDD barmy]

Light-headed; foolish.

> **1915** DN 4.213, It makes me tired to listen to such barmy folks. **1975** Gould ME Lingo 5, Although some think barmy (not just right in the head) derives from this barm, more likely the term is balmy . . . Mainers . . pronounce barm and balm alike.

barn n See **barren**

barn v See **burn** v **A**

barnacle n

A **slipper shell.**

> **1881** Ingersoll Oyster-Industry 241, Barnacle.—The slipper-limpet, Crepidula sp . . . At Cape May limpets are called "barnacles", and confounded by many with the true barnacles. **1894** DN 1.328 eNJ, Barnacle: in Cape May used incorrectly for limpet found on oysters.

barnacle grass n

=**eelgrass 1.**

> **1900** Lyons Plant Names 404, Z. marina . . . Barnacle-grass. **1940** Clute Amer. Plant Names 154, Eel-grass . . . Barnacle-grass. **1958** Progress (Charlottesville VA) 21 Oct 10/3 (Hench Coll.), Zostera Marina is variously known as eelgrass, tape grass, barnacle grass, wild celery, and water celery. It flowers underwater . . . The short stem of each new plant bears a tuft of slender, grass-like green leaves that may stretch 6 feet.

barnacle mushroom n Also tree barnacle

Perh a bracket fungus.

> **1966–69** DARE (Qu. S19) Inf **ME14,** Barnacle mushrooms; **CA111,** Tree barnacles.

barn ball n Also barn tick, barnyard ball **chiefly NEast**

A children's game in which a ball is thrown against a barn or other building and caught on the rebound.

> **1841** Daily Picayune (New Orleans LA) 25 May 2/2 neOH, Who has not played "barn ball" in his boyhood? **1850** Knickerbocker 35.84 **NYC,** As we . . never indulged in a game of chance . . save the 'bass-ball' . . and 'barn-ball' of our boyhood. **1879** Taylor Summer-Savory 122 **NY,** The writer knew a boy who . . never got farther than "barn-ball," which means throwing a ball at the gable and catching it when it returns. **1895** DN 1.384 cNY, Barn ball: a schoolboy's game. **1909** DN 3.408 nME, Barn ball . . . A game which consisted of bounding a ball against a barn and catching it. **1969** DARE (Qu. EE11) Inf **MA73,** Barn tick—boys threw a ball against the barn and hit it or caught it when it came back—usually played by one person; **KY66,** Barnyard ball.

barn boss n

1 The person in charge of a stable. **Nth**

> **1902** White Blazed Trail 201 **MI,** So Shearer had picked out a barn-boss of his own. **1958** McCulloch Woods Words **Pacific NW. 1967** DARE Tape MI42, [The] barn boss was supposed to take care of all the horses at [the] livery stable. **1969** Sorden Lumberjack Lingo **NEng, Gt Lakes,** Barn boss—A man whose duty was to care for the horses and stables in a logging camp.

2 Transf: a dominating wife. joc

> **1969** DARE (Qu. AA21) Inf **NY86,** She's the barn boss.

barn burn n Also barn rot, barn scald

Of tobacco: see quots.

1944 *PADS* 2.64 **KY**, *Barn-rot* . . . The decay of tobacco while in the barn, caused by too much moisture and too little ventilation among the stalks. **1967** Key *Tobacco Vocab.* 33 **TN**, A general darkening of the curing leaf caused by excessive moisture in the barn . . . barn burn . . barn scald.

barn burner n

1 also *barn lighter, barn match*: A kitchen match; a wooden match which can be struck on any friction surface. **chiefly PA, sNJ, MD** See Map

1965–70 *DARE* (Qu. F46, . . *The kind of matches you can strike anywhere*) 27 Infs, **PA, sNJ, MD**, Barn burners; **IA22, PA**194, 213, Barn matches; **PA**63, Barn lighter. **1966** *DARE* File **sePA**, Barn burners— wooden matches with a tip that strikes anywhere.

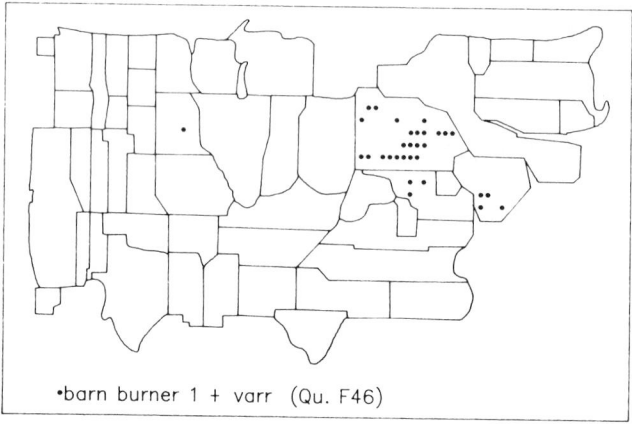

•barn burner 1 + varr (Qu. F46)

2 A highly successful or enjoyable occasion.

1968 *DARE* (Qu. FF17, . . *"We all had a _____ last night."*) Inf **MN38**, Barn burner. **1979** *Verbatim Letters* **IL** (as of 1940), Barn burner—My wife went back stage at the intermission of one of Jean Kerr's plays to congratulate her on the excellence of her play and used this term to describe its resounding success. Ms Kerr was puzzled and asked what it meant. Apparently it is midwest in origin. I don't know how it got to mean "huge and resounding success."

barn chamber n [*barn* + *chamber* B2] **chiefly NEng, esp ME, NH**

A barn loft.

1838 *MA Ag. Surv. Report for 1837* 16, The best method of curing it [=herd's-grass] . . is to . . tie it in bundles; and set it upright in a barn chamber. **1871** (1882) Stowe *Fireside Stories* 28 **NEng**, If you'll come up in the barn-chamber this arternoon . . I'll tell ye all about it. **1926** *AmSp* 2.79 **ME**, The barn loft is likewise the "barn-chamber," even when it consists of mere planking without walls. **1939** *LANE* Map 102 (*Loft; scaffold*) 25 infs, **chiefly ME, NH**, Barn chamber. **1971** Wood *Vocab. Change* 299 **Sth**, 6 infs, Barn chamber.

barn door n

1 also attrib: A triangular tear in a piece of cloth. **Nth** Also called **trapdoor, winklehawk**

1865 (1889) Whitney *Gayworthys* 256, Skirts were trodden on, and came out at the gathers; and there was more than one "barn-door" rent. **1895** *DN* 1.383 **MA**, Triangular tear in cloth . . . *Barn-door*. **1967–69** *DARE* (Qu. W27, . . *A three-cornered tear in a piece of clothing*) Infs **CT**8, 30, **IA**13, **MI**51, 110, **NY**53, **PA**74, Barn-door (tear).

2 A wide front flap on trousers, buttoned at the sides.

a usu attrib, as *barn-door britches, barn-door pants.* **chiefly Nth** *somewhat old-fash*

1885 Cable *Dr. Sevier* 297 **LA**, The bulky contents of his high-waisted, barn-door trowsers now bulged out. **1940** FWP *Guide OH* 519, Dunkard couples are often met wearing the traditional dress: the man in a long black coat, flat-brimmed hat, 'barn door pants' that button up the side, and plain-toed shoes. **1942** Whipple *Joshua* 17 **UT** (as of c1860), Abijah, as befitted his superior dignity, clung to his black barn-door trousers (he considered the front closing immodest) and cloth frock coat. **1945** *AmSp* 20.231 **MA**, A friend of a generation gone (1840– 1916) told me about trousers, the front of which had an oblique row of buttonholes on each side, by means of which a large flap could be let down. This was the 'barn door,' giving origin to . . . 'barn-door' trousers. **1947** *AmSp* 22.72 **ceIA**, 'Barn-door britches' was in common

use in my home community. **1967** *DARE* Tape **PA29**, Their pants are all pulled across . . they call that the barn door, they open the barn doors. They button at the side instead of down the front.

b in phr *your barn door is open* and varr: See quots. (Note: any association with **barn door 2a** is now generally lost; for additional varr see *DS* W24c) *joc* Cf **cow barn is open**

1928 *Ruppenthal Coll.* **KS**, Barn door open—said of little children. To have the rear of lower garments hanging down as if unbuttoned, etc. **1950** *WELS* (*Sly words of warning for . . a trouser fly open*) 30 Infs, **throughout WI**, (Your) barn door('s) open. **c1960** *Wilson Coll.* **csKY**, *Barn door open!* Signal to a man or boy that his trousers fly is undone or a button unhooked. **1965–70** *DARE* (Qu. W24c) 230 Infs, **throughout US**, (Your) barn door('s) open; **TX27**, Barn door open and the owls are coming out; **VT12**, Barn door open, horse might get out; **WA6**, Shut the barn door or the sheep will get out.

3 in pl: A marble game: see quot.

1968 *DARE* (Qu. EE7) Inf **NY98**, Barn doors = put two marbles together and try to "open the barn doors"—hit between and spread them apart.

barned owl n

Prob a **barn owl.**

1967–69 *DARE* (Qu. Q2) Infs **KY21, TN13**, Barned owl.

Barnegat turkey n [*Barnegat* town in southeastern New Jersey] =**coot** n[1] 1.

1956 *AmSp* 30.181, Barnegat turkey—American coot—N[ew] J[ersey].

barney clapper n [Var of **bonnyclabber**]

1 See **bonnyclabber.**

2 =**lily of the valley 1.**

1904 *DN* 2.424 **Cape Cod MA** (as of 1850s), *Barney-clapper* . . . The lily of the valley.

Barney's brig, like adj phr

In a thoroughly disorderly state.

1942 *ME Univ. Studies* 56.80, "Like Barney's brig; both main tacks over the foreyard." Used to express a ridiculous state of disorder. **1975** Gould *ME Lingo, Barney's brig*—Whoever Barney was, he was not a shipshape sailor. The complete expression is: " . . . like *Barney's brig,* both main tacks over the foreyard." It means such complete disorder as to be ridiculous.

barn-filler n Also called **hanger**

In tobacco farming: a person who hangs tobacco in a curing barn.

1966 *PADS* 45.7 **KY**, We don't have any one person to be a barn filler; we just use everybody.

barn fly n

1 =**stable fly.**

1960 Bailey *Resp. to PADS* 20 **KS**, Barn flies . . . The house fly looks like the barn fly but the barn fly can bite and the house fly can not. **1965–70** *DARE* (Qu. R12) 17 Infs, **chiefly Nth**, Barn fly (*or* flies); (Qu. R13) Inf **MO19**, Barn fly.

2 A gnat or midge.

1968–69 *DARE* (Qu. R10) Inf **CA127**, Barn flies; (Qu. R11) Inf **VA34**, Barn fly.

3 Transf: a rustic, a rube. Cf *DS* HH1

1970 *DARE* FW Addit **cwOH**, Barn fly—meaning one from rural area.

barn grass See **barnyard grass**

barn hawk n

1970 *DARE* (Qu. Q4) Inf **NJ69**, Barn hawk—very near the same as chicken hawk.

barnitis See **-itis**

barn lighter See **barn burner 1**

barn-loft swallow n

=**barn swallow 1.**

~~**1917** (1923)~~ *Birds Amer.* 3.86, *Barn Swallow . . . Other Names.*— American Barn Swallow; Barn-loft Swallow. **1944** Hausman *Amer. Birds* 527.

barn lot n **chiefly Midl, Sth** See Map and Map Section See also 1949 Kurath *Word Geog.* fig 62

=**barnyard 1.**

1724 in 1914 NH *Prov. & State Papers* 32.250, I Give to my Daughters . . the other half part of my afores[aid] Barn Lott in Salsbury. **1867** Crawford *Mosby* 78 **VA**, His men . . were feeding their horses in the barn-lot of a farm. **1905** *DN* 3.69 nwAR. **1949** Hornsby *Lonesome Valley* 56 **KY**, Johnny watched two bluebirds build a nest in a knothole in the gatepost over at the barn lot. **1949** Kurath *Word Geog.* 40 From the Rappahannock southward *lot, barn lot, stable lot* . . are the usual terms for the barnyard, and these expressions are current in all of the South Midland as well as in parts of northern West Virginia, but not in the Shenandoah Valley. **c1960** *Wilson Coll.* csKY. **1965–70** *DARE* (Qu. M13) 102 Infs, **chiefly Midl, Sth**, Barn lot; (Qu. M14) 92 Infs, **chiefly Midl, Sth**, Barn lot. **1973** Allen *LAUM* 1.189, *Barnlot* [is] almost limited to the South Midland speech area of southern Iowa.

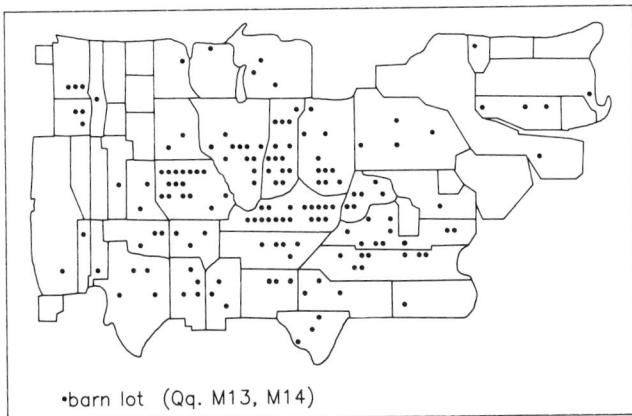

•barn lot (Qq. M13, M14)

barn martin n esp **KY, MO, TN**

=**barn swallow 1.**

1932 Bennitt *Check-list* 44 **MO**, *Barn swallow. Hirundo erythrogaster* . . . Barn martin. **1967–70** *DARE* (Qu. Q14) Infs **CA105, KY11, 65, MO3, TN1**, Barn martin; (Qu. Q20) Infs **KY5, 53, 75**, Barn martin.

barn match See **barn burner 1**

barn owl n

1 Std: a long-legged owl *(Tyto alba)* distinguished by a white, heart-shaped face, reddish-brown to buffy upper plumage, and white or buffy under plumage; native to most of the United States. Also called **baboon owl, church owl, degati owl, golden owl, hoot owl, man-faced owl, monkey-faced owl, poker face, rat owl, snake owl, snowy owl 2, tawny owl, white-faced owl, white owl 2**

2 =**saw-whet owl.**

1888 (1890) Warren *Birds PA* 152, This pigmy mass of owl-life is, I suppose, the species which was regarded as not destructive to poultry and game, by the author of the "Scalp Act," when he introduced therein a clause exempting "The Arcadian Screech or Barn Owl."

3 also *barred barn owl:* The barred owl.

1927 Forbush *Birds MA* 2.202, Barred Owl. Other names: Barn Owl (Maine). **1955** *MA Audubon* 39.81, *Barred Owl.* Barn Owl (Maine. From its occasionally taking shelter in barns.). **1968** *DARE* (Qu. Q2) Inf **VA8**, Barred barn owl—eats chickens.

4 Any of var other owls which sometimes frequent barns: see quots.

1966–69 *DARE* (Qu. Q1) Inf **CA130**, Barn owl or screech owl—I believe they're the same animal; (Qu. Q2) Inf **AR10**, Barn owl, horned owl [are] same; **CA120**, Hoot owl—same as barn owl; **IA8**, Barn owl—same as a screech owl; **IL38**, Barn owl—same thing as hoot owl; **NJ52**, Cat owl [same as] barn owl; **NY52**, Hoot owl or barn owl; **OH61**, Barn owl and hoot owl are same thing; **VA8**, Barn owl = hoot owl.

barn pewee n [See quot 1956]

The eastern **phoebe** *(Sayornis phoebe).*

1917 (1923) *Birds Amer.* 2.198, *Phoebe* . . . *Other Names* . . Barn Pewee. **1932** Bennitt *Check-list* 43, *Eastern phoebe* . . . Barn pewee. **1956** *MA Audubon* 40.83, *Eastern Phoebe.* Barn Pewee (Maine, Mass. It sometimes nests on beams in barns; "pewee" sonic.).

barn preacher See **barnyard preacher**

barn raising n

1 also attrib: A social gathering for the purpose of erecting a barn. **chiefly Nth, N Midl** *old-fash*

1856 T.D. Price *MS. Diary* 28 April *(DAE),* Went to D.D. Keller's barn raising. **1872** Eggleston *End of the World* 51 **IN**, I never went . . to a barn-raising, nor indeed to any of our rustic feasts. **1907** *DN* 4.387 **IA, KY, NH, NY, neOH, VT**, *Barn-raising* . . . A bee for the purpose of setting in place the bents . . of a barn already framed. **1965–70** *DARE* (Qu. FF2, . . *Kinds of parties*) 17 Infs, **chiefly Nth**, Barn raisings; **IN45, MI106**, Barn raising bees; **NY36**, Barn raising parties [18 of 20 Infs old]; (Qu. FF1) Infs **IN32, TX33**, Barn raising; (Qu. L5) Infs **NY92, 213**, Barn raising(s); **NY1**, Barn raising bee. **1971** *Foxfire* Spring–Summer 100 neGA, We had a house raisin' t' raise this house, and we had a barn raisin' t' raise th' barn.

2 A quilt pattern: see quots. Cf **log cabin**

1967 *DARE* FW Addit swOR, Barn raising—quilt pattern [illustr in text shows a pattern of concentric squares, the sides of which are different colored stripes]. **1979** *WI Then & Now* July 7, Patterns of folded narrow strips set in rectangles usually are made of wool and usually have red wool squares in the center of the blocks, some say to represent the red brick chimney of a cabin. Variations, created by different color layouts . . [include] "Barn Raising." . . A large "Barn Raising" in wool was made about 1886 by Cynthia Dorcas Case.

barn rot, barn scald See **barn burn**

barn snake n

Prob =**milk snake 1.**

[**1958** Conant *Reptiles & Amphibians* 170, *Eastern Milk Snake* . . . Sometimes called "house snake," but "barn snake" would be more descriptive, for it would reflect the frequency with which farm buildings are entered in search of rodents.] **1969** *DARE* (Qu. P25) Inf **IL81**, Barn snakes—eat insects, brown like garter snake, not too large.

barn sparrow n Also *barnyard sparrow*

Prob an English sparrow.

1965–70 *DARE* (Qu. Q21) 18 Infs, **esp N Cent, Upper MW**, Barn sparrow; **FL7**, Barnyard sparrow; **NE8**, Common barn sparrow; (Qu. Q22) **KY65, NE4**, Barn sparrow.

barn swallow n

1 Std: a common swallow *(Hirundo erythrogaster)* which nests in barns and similar structures. Also called **barn-loft swallow, barn martin, field swallow, fork-tailed swallow, meadow swallow**

2 =**cliff swallow.** [From its nesting on the outside of barns and similar structures]

1917 (1923) *Birds Amer.* 3.84, *Cliff Swallow* . . . *Other Names.* —Eave Swallow; Jug Swallow; Barn Swallow. **1944** Hausman *Amer. Birds* 527, Swallow, Barn —See Swallow, Cliff. **1953** Jewett *Birds WA* 449, *Petrochelidon pyrrhonota aprophata* . . . Other names: . . Barn Swallow.

barn-tender n

In tobacco farming: see quot 1944.

1944 *PADS* 2.64 **KY**, *Barn-tender* . . . A person who takes care of the barn while the tobacco is being cured. **1966** *PADS* 45.7 **KY**.

barn tick See **barn ball**

barny adj

Of milk: see quot.

1968–69 *DARE* (Qu. K14, *Milk that has a taste from something the cow ate in the pasture* . . *"That milk is ____."*) Inf **NY109**, Barny —from ensilage; **MA68**, Barny |'bɑni| —if [the] farmer wasn't too fussy about the way he handles the milk.

barnyard n

1 The area adjacent to a barn. **widespread, but chiefly Nth, N Midl, West** See Map and Map Section Cf **barn lot**

1663 in 1887 Huntington NY *Town Rec.* 1.54 seNY, All my right and titell of house, house lott, barn yards, garden. **1789** in 1835 MA Hist. Soc. *Coll.* 4.145, As this will always be a grazing country, the manure from the barn yard will be a fruitful source. **1852** Stowe *Uncle Tom's Cabin* 1.92, The whole party made a . . descent into a barn-yard belonging to a large farming establishment. **1949** Kurath *Word Geog.* 55, The yard adjoining or surrounding the barn is regularly called *barn yard* north of the Potomac . . . It seems that *barn yard* is on the way to nation-wide currency. **c1960** *Wilson Coll.* csKY, *Barn-yard* . . . Somewhat literary in the area. **1960** *PADS* 34.64 **CO**, Barnyard [is most common among younger speakers]. **1965–70** *DARE* (Qu. M13) 362 Infs, **chiefly Nth, N Midl, esp NEast**, Barnyard; (Qu. M14) 338 Infs, **chiefly Nth, Midl, West**, Barnyard. **1973** Allen *LAUM* 1.189, The New England and North Midland term *barnyard* is common in the eastern half of the U[pper] M[idwest], although some distinctions of meaning appear . . . with *barnyard* then referring to open area . . and *barn lot* to a fenced-in enclosure, or with the two terms referring simply to different parts of the land near a barn.

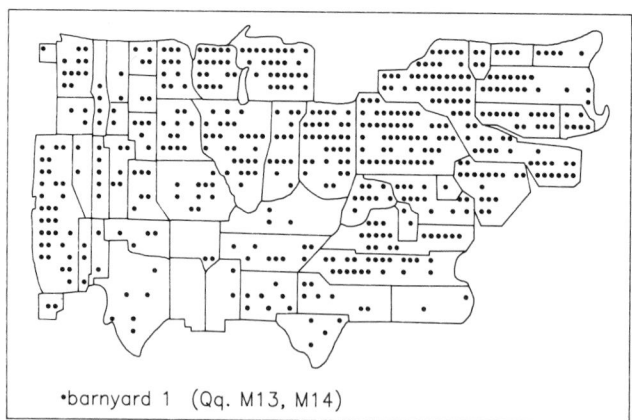

•barnyard 1 (Qq. M13, M14)

2 Manure from a barn, used as fertilizer. **?Gulf States**
1965–70 *DARE* (Qu. L17) Infs **AL31, TX105,** Barnyard; **MS1,** Fertilizer, cow shit, barnyard; **MS58,** Manure, barnyard, dung.

barnyard ball See **barn ball**

‡barnyard bed n
1950 *WELS (A bed that is made up the wrong way as a joke)* 1 Inf, **cWI,** Barnyard bed—beans and rice [are concealed] under [the] lower sheet.

barnyard expression n Also *barnyard language, ~ talk*
Coarse or vulgar language.
1968 *DARE* FW Addit **seNY,** Barnyard expression—language not considered proper in the best circles; or slang. **1982** *DARE* File **cwCA,** Barnyard language—dirty language; **swMI,** Barnyard talk—off-color or coarse language.

barnyard golf n chiefly **Nth** *joc*
The game of quoits or horseshoes.
1929 *AmSp* 5.71 **NE,** Their "pitching horseshoes," sometimes called "barnyard golf," is a common pastime. **1938** FWP *Guide IA* 383, Horseshoe pitching has been a favorite recreation, mainly for older men, since pioneer days. "Barnyard golf" old timers renamed it when golf was becoming popular. **1939** *LANE* Map 199, **CT, MA, VT,** 15 infs, *Barnyard golf* . . offered as jocular or 'newfangled' names for the game of quoits. **1965–68** *DARE* (Qu. EE37) Infs **NC38, PA104, UT3,** Barnyard golf. **1968** *DARE* FW Addit **swVA,** Barnyard golf—horseshoes. **1973** Allen *LAUM* 1.248 **MN, IA,** 4 infs, Barnyard golf.

barnyard grass n Also *barn grass*
A common annual grass (*Echinochloa crusgalli*). Also called **blue duck food, cattail, cocksfoot grass 2, cockspur 2, corn grass 3, duck millet, goose grass, redshank, rice cousin, shank grass, watergrass, whiteshank, wild millet, wild rice**
1822 Eaton *Botany* 372, *Panicum . . . crus-calli* [sic] . . . Barn grass. **1843** Torrey *Flora NY* 2.424, *Barnyard Grass* . . . [grows in] wet places, and about barnyards: common; the rough-sheathed variety along ditches near the salt water. **1895** U.S. Dept. Ag. *Farmers' Bulletins* 28.24, Barn grass, barnyard grass, cocksfoot. Panicum crus-galli. **1966–70** *DARE* (Qu. S9) Infs **IL19, PA104, VA59, WA6,** Barnyard grass; **NY148,** Barn grass; **VT4,** Barn grass—grows up about a foot high, has large brown seed pod, grows fast; **VT13,** Barn grass.

barnyard owl n
=**barn owl.**
1967 *DARE* (Qu. Q2) Inf **IA14,** Barnyard owl.

barnyard pipe n
1970 *DARE* FW Addit **TX99,** Barnyard pipe—old-fashioned but still common term for "corncob pipe."

barnyard preacher n Also *barn preacher*
An unprofessional or part-time lay preacher.
1805 Fessenden *Democracy Unveiled* 184 **MA,** We always possessed a violent antipathy to your bawling, itinerant, field and barn preachers. **1970** *DARE* (Qu. CC10) Inf **TN66,** Barnyard preacher.

barnyard relation n
A distant relation.

1967 *DARE* FW Addit **WA,** Barnyard relation—Same as shirttail relation; **swOR,** Barnyard relation . . . seventy-second cousin, or so.

‡barnyard salad n *joc*
Manure.
1968 *DARE* (Qu. L17) Inf **PA71,** Barnyard salad.

barnyard sparrow See **barn sparrow**

barnyard trots n
=**backdoor trot 1.**
1970 *DARE* (Qu. BB19, *Joking names for looseness of the bowels*) Inf **AR56,** Barnyard trots.

bar off v phr chiefly **Sth, S Midl** Cf **side** v
To plow or hoe soil away from the sides of crop plants, leaving the roots in a narrow ridge.
1835 Ingraham *South-West* 2.283 **MS,** If there are many hoe-hands there are several ploughs "barring off" as it is called. **1887** *Century Illustr. Mag.* 13.111/1 **LA,** In the stubble-fields the first spring, work consists in "barring off," or moving the dirt away from the roots of the cane with plows and hoes. **1893** Shands *MS Speech* 19, When nearly all of the dirt is ploughed away from the cotton, so that the cotton-plant stands on a narrow ridge of ground, the *cotton* is said to be *barred off.* **1902** *DN* 2.228 **sIL,** Bar off. **1907** *DN* 3.220 **nwAR,** Bar off. **1954** *Harder Coll.* **cwTN,** Bar off corn . . . To turn the cultivator disks outward away from the row of corn . . . It is said that a boy is a man when he can "bar off corn"; the task is rather exacting. **1966** *DARE* Tape **GA1,** Take a Hammond plow and bar it off. That's to pull your dirt away from it. **1970** *DARE* FW Addit **KY84,** *Barring off*—"throw dirt away" from the rows of tobacco plants in the middle of the row to cover and kill weeds—old-fashioned.

barometer bush n
A **silverleaf** (here: *Leucophyllum frutescens*).
1936 Whitehouse *TX Flowers* 131, *Leucophyllum texanum* . . . It is a startling and lovely sight to see a hillside . . transformed overnight into a delicate hue of lavender. This happens shortly after heavy rains, and for this reason the plant is sometimes called barometer bush. **1965** Teale *Wandering Through Winter* 150, All across Texas, a host of other picturesque names have been bestowed on the wild plants of the state. They run from angel's trumpet . . to shame vine, barometer bush . . and kiss-me-and-I'll-tell-you.

bar pin n Cf **beauty pin**
A kind of brooch.
1966–67 *DARE* (Qu. W35) Infs **AL30, AR52, MS70, TX42,** Bar pin. [All Infs old]

bar pit n [Pronc var of **barrow pit**] See also **bar ditch, barrow ditch**

1 =**barrow pit 1.** chiefly **West** See Map and Map Section
1949 *PADS* 11.17 **CO,** Bar ditch, bar pit . . . The ditch by the side of an upgraded road. **1950** *AmSp* 25.85 **OR,** Barrow-pit . . frequently . . shortens to *bar-pit.* **1958** *PADS* 30.11, Bar-pit and its variants . . . are clearly a feature of the southwestern quarter of the Upper Midwest. **1965–70** *DARE* (Qu. N24, *A ditch along the side of a graded road*) 18 Infs, chiefly **West,** Bar pit; (Qu. N25) Inf **CO3,** Bar pit [17 of 19 Infs old]. **1966** *Silver City Enterprise* (NM) 17 Mar 4/3, The drive through the Burro Mountains was very pretty, most of the snow is gone and clear water is trickling down the bar pits. **1971** Wood *Vocab.*

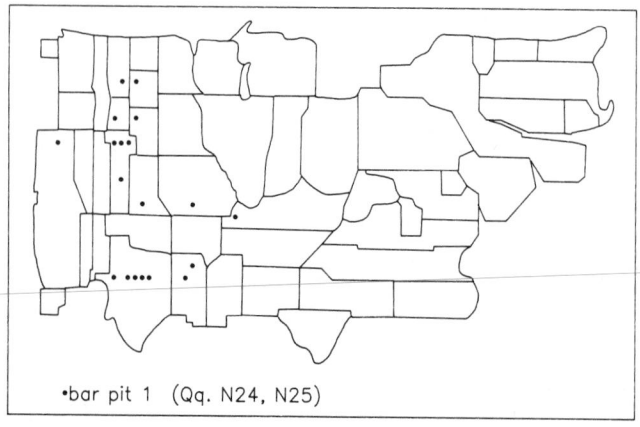

•bar pit 1 (Qq. N24, N25)

Change 53, A ditch provided in the course of such grading . . . in Mississippi, Louisiana, and Arkansas it is *bar pit.*

2 =**barrow pit 2.**

1950 *AmSp* 25.85 **OR.** **1958** *PADS* 30.11 **IA,** Railroad construction workers use . . *bar-pit* to refer to an excavation from which gravel is taken to build up the roadbed. This excavation is not necessarily near to the roadbed. **1965–68** *DARE* (Qu. C4a, . . *Fairly large body of fresh water*) Inf **LA**20, Bar pits [ˈbɔˌpɪts] back of the levee; (Qu. C14, *A stretch of still water going off to the side from a river or lake*) Inf **AR**55, Bar pit [bɑːpɪt]—where they dug the levee; (Qu. C27, *A hillside or deep hole where stone is taken out*) Inf **FL**21, [bar] pit—gravel and clay taken from it; **FL**27, Bar pit—[for] sand. **1967** *DARE* FW Addit **AR**52, Bar pits—where they took out material to make a levee.

barrabara, barrabkie See **barabara**

barrack n [Abbr for **hay barrack**] **chiefly NY, C Atl**

A roofed structure supported by poles, used for storage of hay (and occas other crops); a large stack of hay.

1697 in 1852 Munsell *Annals Albany* 3.27 **NY,** Desyred yt his Estate of Lands, houses, Barns, Berghs, &c., should be apprized by indifferent good men. **1756** in 1941 Woodward *Ploughs & Politicks* 371 **NJ,** A Barrack of 10 ft. Plate 5 posted contains 166 superficial square feet & 1 ft. & 2/10 high will hold a load of hay Settled or being 15 ft. high will hold 12 and 1/2 load. **1854** *Harper's Mag.* 9.849/2, We crept slyly around a 'barrack,' as it is called, of standing hay, and by the pegs at a corner-post we climbed up to the top of the hay-mow. **1949** Kurath *Word Geog.* 54, The Dutch settlement area (western Long Island and the Hudson and Mohawk valleys) has *barrack,* a term of Dutch origin. **1966–68** *DARE* (Qu. L14, *A large pile of hay stored outdoors*) Inf **PA**127, Barracks; (Qu. M1, . . *Special kinds of barns*) Inf **NJ**10, Barrack; (Qu. M22, . . *Buildings . . on farms*) Inf **DC**8, Barracks = tobacco barn; can be used for hay; boards are vertical; **VA**33, Barracks—used to store hay, apples, and fodder; old-fashioned. **1973** Allen *LAUM* 1.185, *Barrack* appears, once in the speech of a Duluth [Minnesota] woman of European parentage, who identifies its meaning as a haypile surmounted by a protective sliding roof supported on four poles.

barracuda n

Std: a fish of the family Sphyraenidae, esp of the genus *Sphyraena.* For names of var spp see **cuda, saltwater muskellunge, saltwater pike, scooter, sea tiger**

barranca n Also sp *barranco* [Span] **SW**

A deep gully or ravine.

[**1836** Latrobe *Rambler in Mexico* 182, Cuernavaca is most nobly situated, on a tongue of land, girdled on three sides by tremendous barrancas.] **1892** *DN* 1.187 **TX,** *Barránca:* a deep ravine with very steep banks and without water at the bottom except in the rainy season . . . The form *barranco* is applied to a bluff or to the steep bank of a river. **1907** White *AZ Nights* 87, So we went along, me on the rim-rock and around the barrancas, and Larry in the bottom carryin' of the kid. **1932** *DN* 6.223 **AZ, CA, NM.** **1968–70** *DARE* (Qu. N24, *A ditch along the side of a graded road*) Inf **CA**176, Barranca [bəˈrɛnkə]—if large; (Qu. C21) Inf **CA**36, Barranca. **1971** Bright *Word Geog.* CA & NV 102.

barranca bush n

A California shrub (*Ceanothus verrucosus*).

1938 Van Dersal *Native Woody Plants* 91, *Ceanothus verrucosus* . . . Barranca bush . . . A small to large, wide-spreading shrub; flowers January–April.

barred barn owl See **barn owl 3**

barrel n Usu |ˈbærəl, ˈbɛrəl|; also *somewhat old-fash* |bɑrl|; occas |baːl| Pronc-spp *barl, berril, bor'l*

A Forms.

c1820 W.C. Bryant in 1941 *AmSp* 16.157 **NYC,** Barl—barrel. **1861** Holmes *Venner* 379 **wMA,** Not if he's got a double-berril gun. **1891** *DN* 1.118 **cNY** [bɑrl]. **1893** Shands *MS Speech, Barl* [barl]. Illiterate white for *barrel.* Negroes generally call *barrel . .* [bæl]. Immigrants from North Carolina nearly always say *barl.* **1906** *DN* 3.115 **sIN,** *Barrel,* pronounced *barl.* **1909** *DN* 3.392 **nwAR,** Barl. **1935** *AmSp* 10.295 **Upstate NY,** Barrel . . . 106 [instances of [ɛ] as against] 135 [instances of [æ]]. **1940** Richter *Trees* 225 **OH,** I got to keep takin' my bor'l off. **1940** *AmSp* 15.85 **neTN,** [kræʊdɪd wɪð barəlz]. **1941** *AmSp* 16.10 **eTX** [Black], *Barrel . .* [baːl].

B Senses.

1 A measure for corn, usu one or five bushels. (See *DA barrel* 1b for related senses) **chiefly Midl, Sth**

1641 in 1883 *Archives of MD* 1.108, The Barrell to contein five of the said Bushell & no more or lesse. **1788** in 1793 Amer. Philos. Soc. *Trans.* 3.226, A barrel is a measure of five bushels, much used in Virginia. **1899** (1912) Green *VA Folk-Speech* 75, A barrel of corn is five bushels of corn in the ears, or unshelled. **1903** *DN* 3.306 **seMO.** **1917** *DN* 4.421 **eLA,** Barrel . . . In measuring maize, a bushel. "Three shakes and a heap" make a barrel. **1955** *AmSp* 30.76 **cwTN,** A *barrel* of corn is the standard measurement. Corn always goes by the barrel, instead of by the bushel. **c1960** *Wilson Coll.* **csKY,** Barrel . . . A measure, usually five bushels.

2 Barrels. (Sg for plural; cf Intro "Language Changes" II.7)

1909 *DN* 3.392 **nwAR,** We made nine barl of soggum (sorghum). **1958** *PADS* 29.7 **TN,** That field made 40 barrel of corn. **c1960** *Wilson Coll.* **csKY,** We made ten barrel of corn to the acre.

barrel cactus n [From the shape]

A succulent spiny plant of the genera *Echinocactus* or *Ferocactus;* native to the desert Southwest. Also called **bisnaga, compass cactus, fishhook cactus, Indian melon, pincushion cactus, traveller's friend.** For other names of var spp see **beehive cactus, cottontop cactus, devil's head, devil's pincushion, eagle claws, fishhawk cactus, hedgehog cactus, horse crippler, Mexican fireball, niggerhead cactus, pineapple cactus, strawberry cactus, turban cactus, turk's head**

1896 *Jrl. Amer. Folkl.* 9.188, *Echinocactus Wislizeni* . . barrel cactus. **1915** (1926) Armstrong *Western Wild Flowers* 306, Barrel Cactus . . *Echinocactus Wislizèni.* **1924** Austin *Land of Journeys' Ending* 126 **AZ,** Ocotillo and sahuaro are to be found growing together . . , and with them the bisnaga or barrel-cactus, which the stranger frequently mistakes for a young sahuaro. **1970** Correll *Plants TX* 1103, *Ferocactus Wislizenii* . . . Southwestern Barrel Cactus. *Ibid, Echinocactus . .* Barrel Cactus. **1973** *AZ Highways* March 33, Because the Barrel more than any other cactus inclines toward the southwest, it makes a foolproof compass.

barrel-dogging vbl n Cf **bulldog** v², **sweat** v

In moonshining: heating used whiskey barrels to extract whiskey which has been absorbed by the wood; hence *barrel-dogger, barrel-sweater* one who heats barrels in such a way.

1954 *Courier–Jrl.* (Louisville KY) 25 Apr mag sec 7/2 **eKY,** It only takes a second for the barrel doggers to recover from their surprise at the sudden appearance of the revenue agents. *Ibid* 8/1, Barrel dogging . . . was tried on a small scale back in 1940 . . but it died out until just last October. Then, when the distilleries . . started their Christmas bottling, a real rash of barrel dogging broke out. **1957** McMeekin *Old KY Country* 131 **eKY,** Now and again a big ring or conspiracy of "barrel sweaters" is rounded up [by officers of the law]. (Barrels recently drained of bonded bourbon are bought up and steamed to coax about a gallon of "spirits" per barrel which had been absorbed by the wood.) **1963** Carson *Social Hist. Bourbon* 109 **KY,** "Barrel dogging" . . . involves "sweating" bourbon out of tightly closed barrels by steaming the barrel. After three or four hours of heating, the whiskey is tapped out and filtered . . . The proof is often quite high, the color likewise, and the whiskey is good.

barrel-maker n [See quot 1955]

=**bittern.**

1917 *Wilson Bulletin* 29.2, In order to have in one place a fairly complete catalog of nicknames for the bittern, I have gathered the following from various sources: barrel-maker, Michigan. **1925** (1928) Forbush *Birds MA* 1.315, *Botaurus lentiginosus . .* Other names: . . Barrel-maker. **1955** *MA Audubon* 39.313, American bittern . . . Barrel-maker (Mass. The notes suggest resonant hammering.).

barrel of snakes n

In var proverbial phrr: see quots.

1967–69 *DARE* (Qu. V2b, . . *"I wouldn't trust him _____."*) Inf **LA**15, On a barrel of snakes; (Qu. V7, . . *A person who sets out to cheat others while pretending to be honest*) Inf **GA**89, He is as crooked as a barrel of snakes; (Qu. II26, . . *"I wouldn't know him from _____."*) Inf **AR**51, A barrel of snakes.

barrel pipe n Cf *DS* D29

A pipe carrying rainwater from the roof to a barrel.

1966 *Wilson Coll.* **csKY,** Barrel pipe . . . downspout.

barrel-sweater n See **barrel-dogging**

barren n Usu |ˈbærən, ˈbɛrən|, occas |bɑrn| Pronc-sp *barn*

Std senses, var form.

1903 *DN* 2.306 **seMO**, *Barrens* . . often pronounced barns. **c1960** *Wilson Coll.* **csKY**, Barren County is sometimes, among the older ones, /barn/.

barren heath n

=**beach heather.**

1951 Hough *Singing in Morning* 39, Beach heather—also known popularly as barren heath, ground cedar, poverty plant and false heather.

barren hen n [See quot 1895]

A **heath hen 1** or **prairie chicken 1.**

1888 Trumbull *Names of Birds* 136, Other old names are *Barren Hen* [etc.]. [**1895** Minot *Land-Birds New Engl.* 405, The Pinnated Grouse . . choose dry, wooded soils for their haunts, such as are called "barrens."] **1953** *AmSp* 28.281 **NJ, PA, KY**, Barren hen. Pinnated grouse.

barren oak n [See quot 1927]

1 also *barrens oak:* =**blackjack oak.**

1785 Marshall *Arbustrum* 120, *Quercus alba minor.* Barren White Oak. **1897** Sudworth *Arborescent Flora* 174, *Quercus marilandica* . . Barren Oak (Kans., Tenn.) . . Barrens Oak (Fla.). **1927** Keeler *Our Native Trees* 370, Barren Oak—*Quercus marilandica* . . . Grows on sandy barrens. **1960** Vines *Trees SW* 183, *Quercus marilandica* . . Also known by the vernacular names of . . Barren Oak.

2 =**bear oak.**

1908 Britton *N. Amer. Trees* 297, Bear Oak—*Quercus ilicifolia* . . It is also known as Barren oak.

barrens oak See barren oak 1

barren strawberry n [Prob from its similarity to *Waldsteinia,* also known as *barren strawberry*]

=**cinquefoil** (here: esp *Potentilla canadensis* and *P. norvegica*).

1837 Darlington *Flora Cestrica* 303, *P[otentilla] canadensis* . . Barren Strawberry. **1896** *Jrl. Amer. Folkl.* 9.187 **ME, MA**, *Potentilla Norvegica* . . barren strawberry. **1900** Lyons *Plant Names* 303, *Potentilla,* . . Barren Strawberry. *Ibid* 304, *P. Norvegica* . . Barren Strawberry. **1966** *DARE* Wildfl QR Pl.92a Inf **NY91**, Barren strawberry.

barrer, barrey See barrow n²

barrier n Also *barrier pillar* [N Engl dial] Also called **entry pillar, entry stump**

In coal mining: see quots.

1881 Raymond *Gloss. Mining* 7, *Barrier-pillars.* Pillars of coal, larger than ordinary, left at intervals to prevent too extensive crushing when the ground comes to be *robbed.* **1973** *PADS* 59.25 **OH, PA, MD, nWV**, *Barrier (pillar)* . . a particularly large *pillar* of coal left at the crossing or opening of *entries* . . for extra roof support.

barrio n [Span] chiefly SW

A Spanish-speaking community or neighborhood in an American city; a Latino or Chicano district.

1939 *Time* 13 Mar 78/2 **NYC**, At 110th Street, Manhattan's sveltly starched Fifth Avenue passes the extreme northeast tip of Central Park, plunges into a new world—the teeming, Spanish-speaking slums, or barrio, of Lower Harlem. [**1945** *AN&Q* 5.85 **Puerto Rico**, The *barrio* is a region of indefinite size—as much as a hundred square miles in the country, as little as a few blocks in the city.] **1954** Burma *Spanish-Speaking Groups* 88, Always in the Southwest and commonly throughout the rest of the United States, the Mexican lives in a segregated section of town. He calls it the *barrio* or the *colonia;* Anglos call it "Mextown," "Spiktown," "Little Mexico," or some such term. **1955** *Holiday* Oct 117 **AZ**, The other day I happened to go to North Meyer Street [in Tucson]. It lies in a *barrio* of narrow streets marked with little corner grocery stores and flanked with ragged palms and old adobe houses. **1966** *Time* 24 June 30/3 **Chicago IL**, On Division Street, main stem of the barrio that holds the majority of Chicago's Puerto Rican population, people drooped languidly from tenement windows and crowded the front stoops. **1978** Moore *Homeboys* 12 **SW**, It is equally necessary that the concept of urban ghetto expand to include the shacktowns, enclaves and barrios of the Sunbelt cities. These "new" ghettos have a historical origin and ecological linkage quite different from the older, decayed central city slums of the Chicago type. **1980** Folb *Runnin' Down* 100 **sCA**, I was conducting a communication workshop with some community people from . . the East Los Angeles barrio.

barroom n chiefly NEng

Among loggers: see quot 1914.

1914 *DN* 4.68 **ME, nNH**, *Bar-room* . . . Bunk-room in a logging camp. **1938** (1939) Holbrook *Holy Mackinaw* 258, Barroom. That part of a New England camp where the loggers sleep. **1942** Rich *We Took to Woods* 198 **ME**, *"Barroom?* . . *"* "Oh, not that kind of a barroom. It's where the men [=loggers] sleep." **1969** Sorden *Lumberjack Lingo, Bar room* . . . Term used occasionally in lake states, more often in New England.

barroom man n chiefly NEng

Among loggers: a chore boy, **flunky 1.**

1938 (1939) Holbrook *Holy Mackinaw* 258 **NEng**, Barroom man. Common name for a bullcook. **1969** Sorden *Lumberjack Lingo* 7 **NEng, Gt Lakes**, Bar room man—A chore boy, bull cook, flunky.

barrow n¹ See barrow ditch

barrow n², also attrib Usu |'bæro, 'bɛro|; also |'barɚ| Pronc-spp *barrer, barrey, barruh, borrow* See also **bar n⁴**

Std senses, var forms.

1899 (1912) Green *VA Folk-Speech, Borrow* . . . A gelt hog. **1908** *DN* 3.289 **eAL, wGA**, *Barrow* . . . ['barə]. **1922** Gonzales *Black Border* 289 **sSC, GA coasts** [Gullah glossary], *Barruh* . . a bacon hog. **1927** *AmSp* 2.348 **cWV**, *Barrey hog* . . . A castrated hog. "That barrey hog will weigh two hundred pounds." **1929** *AmSp* 5.127 **coastal ME**, "Barrer" . . pigs.

barrow ditch n Also, by folk-etym, *borrow ditch;* rarely *barrow* [*EDD* 1752–c1900, "Obs."; see also **barrow pit**] Cf **bar ditch 1** and see Map Section

=**barrow pit 1.**

1927 *Ruppenthal Coll.* **KS**, Often along the railroad right of way we see hollows where earth was dug up . . to raise the grade or level of tracks . . . These are "barrows" in railroad parlance. **1950** [see **barrow pit 1**]. **1963** Owens *Look to River* 73 **nTX**, Jed went down through the borrow ditch. **1966–69** *DARE* (Qu. N24, *A ditch along the side of a graded road*) Infs **TN36, UT15**, Barrow ditch; **AR51**, Borrow ditch, pit [FW: [bar] or ['barə], depending on context]; **CO16, OK18**, Barrow ditch; **OK52**, Some newspapers say bar ditch or barrow, but that's wrong; it's *borrow*—where they borrow dirt to make the road; **TN34**, ['barə] ditch.

barrow pit n Also, by folk-etym, *borrow pit* [Prob from *barrow* a mound of earth; for folk-etym see quot 1950] See also **barrow ditch, bar ditch, bar pit**

1 rarely *burrow pit:* A roadside drainage ditch. **chiefly West, esp Rocky Mts** See Map and Map Section

1931 *AmSp* 7.120 **eID**, A *barrow pit* is a ditch along the road. **1949** *PADS* 11.17 **CO**, *Barrow pit* . . . A few people say it is a ditch edged with a mound or barrow of dirt. **1950** *AmSp* 25.85 **OR**, *Barrow-pit* is common in road-making, to mean the ditch or excavation beside a roadway. *Ibid* 165 **CO**, The ditch by the side of an upgraded road is called 'bar pit,' 'borrow pit,' 'barrow pit,' 'bar ditch,' 'borrow ditch,' 'barrow ditch,' 'grader ditch,' and 'gutter.' . . One informant . . explained that *barrow* meant the mound of earth formed when the pit was dug. A few informants connect *barrow* with the wheelbarrow probably used to carry away the dirt. Informants who use *borrow pit* explain that the dirt is borrowed from one place to be used in another. The word *pit* is

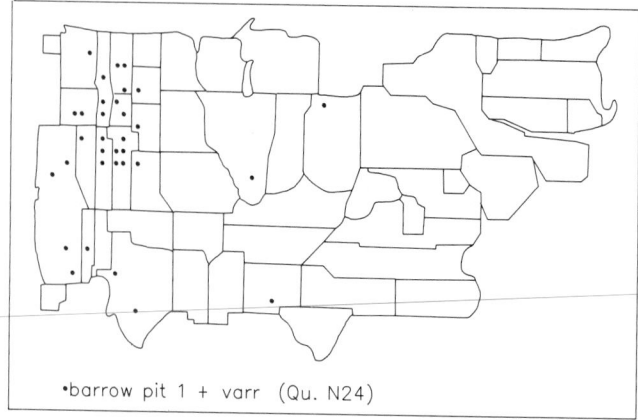

•barrow pit 1 + varr (Qu. N24)

much more frequent than *ditch* or *gutter*. **c1960** *Wilson Coll.* **csKY,** *Borrow pit* . . . A ditch or hole by the roadside from which dirt has been removed to build the road. Very modern and rare in use. **1965–70** *DARE* (Qu. N24, *A ditch along the side of a graded road*) 25 Infs, **chiefly West, esp Rocky Mts,** Barrow pit [21 Infs old]; **CA91, CO33, 35, NV2, OR**1, Borrow pit; **CA36,** Borrow pit—in Montana it's called that; ditch in California; **CO7,** Bar pit [Inf: occas], barrow pit [Inf: I always use], borrow pit [Inf: old-fash]; **CO20,** [ˈbaro] pit; **CO47,** Burrow [bɝˑo] pit. **1968** *Hungry Horse News* (Columbia Falls MT) 20 Dec 10/5, Brown tried to avoid contact and ended up in the borrow pit. **1973** Allen *LAUM* 1.272, *Ditch* . . the man-made depression for drainage along a graded road. For some inf[ormant]s in the western sector of the U[pper] M[idwest] . . especially in Nebraska . . the equivalent term is *borrow pit.*

2 A place from which material for construction has been excavated and which, esp in the Gulf States, often fills with water.
c1940 Newman *Conserv. Notes* 5 **neLA,** The barrow-pits at the base of the nearby levee harbored large flocks of ducks. **1940** *Sun* (Baltimore MD) 6 Apr 22/1 *(Hench Coll.),* Dry fill from a nearby borrow pit is placed in the holes to bring the surface up to grade. **1950** *AmSp* 25.85 **OR,** Occasionally the meaning is extended, evidently through Western folk-etymology, to include any excavation made for the purpose of securing fill material. So *barrow-pit* is used to describe the sources of material for an earth-fill dam. **1958** *PADS* 30.11 **IA,** *Barrow pit* . . *borrow pit.* **1962** Faulkner *Reivers* 65 **MS,** Grandfather had added . . the tin bucket to fill the radiator when we passed creeks or barrow pits. **1966–67** *DARE* (Qu. C14, *A stretch of still water going off to the side from a river or lake*) Inf **MS**45, [ˈbarə] pit; (Qu. N24) Inf **OH**27, Borrow pit—a lake formed by fill taken out to raise the road; [the fill is] borrowed, [hence] "borrow pit." **1968** *DARE* FW Addit **Providence LA,** *Borrow pit.*—A place from which dirt has been removed for a levee. "The old river beds and borrow pits along the Mississippi River."

barruh See **barrow** n[2]

barsdown n Also *bar up and bar down* *?obs*
A children's game similar to hi-spy: =**sic-a-nine-ten.**
1895 *DN* 1.396 **cNY,** *Barsdown . . . sic-a-nine-ten.* **1907** *DN* 3.181 **seNH,** *Bar up and bar down* . . . A boys' outdoor game.

barse-ackwards See **bass-ackward(s)**

barshare plow n Also *barshare;* pronc-sp *barshear (~)* **esp Mid Atl** *old-fash*
A type of plow: see quots 1912, 1948.
1785 (1925) Washington *Diaries* 2.438 **VA,** Tools and Implemts: . . Bar Shear Plows 9. **1799** in 1956 Eliason *Tarheel Talk* 259 **NC,** Barshear plow. **1820** *Hillsborough* (N.C.) *Recorder* 12 July *(DA),* When my corn is up, I run a barshear one round in each corn row. **1912** Green *VA Folk-Speech,* *Bar-shear plough* . . . A plough with a wooden mould-board on which thin bars of iron were nailed to save the board from wear. **1944** Duncan *Mentor Graham* 115 **IL,** Only a brief pageant was to be theirs, of oxcart and bar-share plow, spinning-wheel and gritter. **1948** Dick *Dixie Frontier* 99 **Sth,** An improved plow was known as the "bar-share" plow, which has been described as a profanity-provoking mechanism with a long iron share and a wooden moldboard which, when it struck a root or stump, brought the handles up with a vigorous jerk, stopping the team. The operator, unable to stop so quickly, was thrown onto the handles, knocking the wind out of him. **1968** *DARE* (Qu. L18) Inf **MD**26, Barshear [ˈbarˌšɪr] plow—wooden beam, bar share to cut ground, moldboard turned ground over; **MD**29, Barshear [ˈbarˌšɪr] plow—one furrow, three horses, man walked behind; **VA**33, Barshear plow—turns the soil over.

bar-stretcher See **stretcher**

‡bart-all n [Perh rel to Scots *bardy* insolent, quarrelsome] *?*A bully.
1950 Moore *Candlemas Bay* 65 **ME,** Neal . . . was prodding at Maggie with the pine dagger . . . Mertis got up, walked over and kicked Neal hard with her sneaker . . . "Let her go, you big bart-all," she said.

bar thorn fence n
1970 *DARE* (Qu. L65, . . *Kinds of fences*) Inf **VA**43, Bar thorn—a small hedge fence with sharp thorns.

bar toad n Cf *DS* DD12
Among loggers: see quot.
1958 McCulloch *Woods Words* **Pacific NW,** *Bar toad*—Same as bar fly; a man who goes into a saloon and squats there like a toad on a rock.

bar up and bar down See **barsdown**

barvel n [Prob ME *barmfell* lap-skin] **NEng, esp coastal ME**
1 A fisherman's apron made of leather or oilcloth.
1629 in 1853 MA (Colony) *Rec. of Gov.* 1.404, We have now sent by these 3 shipps . . lynes, hookes, knives, bootes, & barvells, necessary for ffishinge. **1896** *DN* 1.412 **neMA,** *Barvel:* large leather apron worn by fishermen. **1950** Moore *Candlemas Bay* 7 **ME,** The little boat would be jumping like a flea, and Grampie standing there in his rubber boots and oilskin barvel, steering her as easy as if he were sitting at home in the parlor. **1975** Gould *ME Lingo.* **1978** Merriam *Illustr. Lobstering* 11 **ME.** **1979** *Yankee* Jan 233 **ME,** To a boy who grew up in Maine, barvels, poverty boxes, and hair touchers are familiar items.
2 in phr *barvel and boots:* See quot. Cf *DS* U15
1975 Gould *ME Lingo* 7, Other men in the crew had to provide (or find) their own gear, but the skipper provided *barvel* and boots to the one on salt duty. Today, occasional reference to "barvel and boots" means a little frosting on the cake; a special consideration.

barway n **chiefly NEng**
A driveway or gateway closed by bars; the bars themselves.
1863 (1864) Mitchell *My Farm* 207 **NEng,** Broken bar-ways have been replaced by new ones. **1884** *Century Illustr. Mag.* 7.218/1 **NY,** Lines and boundaries are disregarded; gates and bar-ways are unclosed. **1904** *DN* 2.424 **Cape Cod MA** (as of 1850s), *Barway . . .* A driveway closed by bars. **1910** *DN* 3.452 **seVT,** Drive in at the second barway. **1967** Borland *Hill Country* 271 **nwCT,** When we first came to this lower Berkshire country . . my neighbor . . spoke of a barway. It baffled me, until I saw that what he meant was what I had always called a gate. But his word for it was logical. Most of the gates, as I called them, were closed by long cedar poles, bars, slipped into slots on each side. I had half a dozen barways on my place.

Basco n Also *bascal* **NW**
A member of the Basque community—used as an affectionate nickname.
1931 *AmSp* 6.230 **neOR,** The 'chinook' is a mild winter wind, . . and 'bascals' are herdsmen from a certain province in Spain. **1967** *DARE* Tape **OR**18, My folks are Bascos [ˈbæskoz]; **OR**11, Basco [ˈbæsko]. **1967** *DARE* (Qu. HH28) Inf **WY**3, Basco—Basque. **1980** *DARE* File **sID** (as of 1960s), There were quite a few Basque people in the Boise Valley. They were a highly respected minority, and were often affectionately called Bascos. **1981** *KS Qrly.* 13.2.64 **nNV,** *Basco* . . a Spanish or French Basque or person of Basque background; the term of preference for many Basques themselves.

base n, exclam, v, adj Usu |bes|, occas |best| Pronc-sp *bast(e)* Cf Pronc Intro 3.I.23
A Forms.
1895 *DN* 1.384 **sOH,** *Base* . . generally [best] . . in schoolboy game "prisoner's base." **1905** *DN* 3.77 **nwAR,** *Dare-base(t)* . . . Prisoner's base. **1954** *Harder Coll.* **cwTN,** He ain't gonna make it to home bast [best]. **1976** Garber *Mountain-ese* 6 **sAppalachians,** The runner slud into second baste.
B As noun.
1 A children's game of ball or tag, sometimes equivalent to **dare-base** or **prisoner's base.** [*OED base* sb.[2] 1558 →]
1845 *Knickerbocker* 26.427 **NYC,** The motion very much resembles that of one who, in playing 'base,' screws his ball. **1866** Smith *Bill Arp* 129 **GA,** Sherman was playin base around about Atlanta. **1952** Brown *NC Folkl.* 1.73, *Base* . . . Two bases are selected as far apart as possible . . . One side goes over and dares the other . . . The others chase their opponents home, catching as many as they can. **1966** *DARE* Tape **AL**2, Base . . . designate a base; if you're tagged when off base, you're out; the side with players left last, won. **1967–69** *DARE* (Qu. EE33) Inf **KY**41, Base (prisoner's base); **LA**6, Base—a kind of tag in which the players have bases where they can't be caught; **PA**210, Base—a form of tag. **1980** *Foxfire 6* 274 **nGA,** Base . . . Any number of people can play. They are divided into two equal teams and each team is assigned to a base. The two bases face each other twenty to thirty feet apart . . . The object of the game is to circle the opponent's base and return "home" without being caught and tagged out by one of the opponents.
2 The starting place for "it," or the place to be safely reached in tag, hide-and-seek, and other children's games. **widespread, but esp Sth, Midl, West** See Map See also **goal, home, baseman** and *DS* EE14–17
1943 *LANE* Map 585 *(Goal),* 2 infs, **wMA,** Base. **c1960** *Wilson Coll.* **csKY,** Base . . . The head spot where It was when a game like I Spy was

being played. **1965–70** *DARE* (Qu. EE14) 315 Infs, **chiefly Sth, Midl, West,** Base. **1973** Allen *LAUM* 1.396, *Base* . . is clearly Midland, with acceptance greatest in Nebraska, Iowa, and South Dakota.

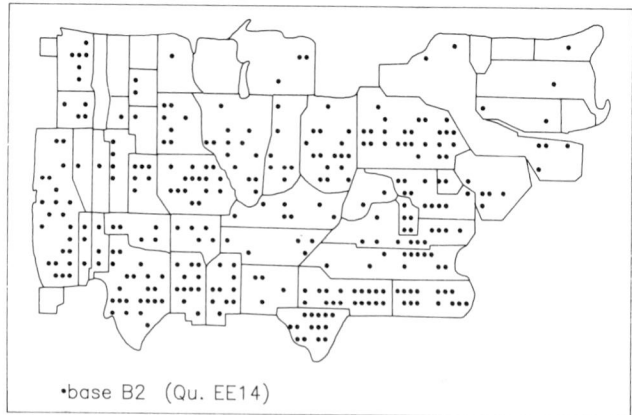

•base B2 (Qu. EE14)

3 also *base line, home base:* The starting line in marble games.

1967–70 *DARE* (Qu. EE8) Infs **CA**165, **DE**3, **GA**33, **MO**36, **PA**71, Base; **AR**51, **PA**245, Base line; **GA**72, Home base. **1969** *DARE* Tape **CA**172, Base . . place from which first shot is made in a marble game.

4 Lines sung by the chorus in gospel singing. See also **base** v (at **D** below), **baser**

1863 Allen *Family Papers* 69 **SC**, Tony, Taffy and Ishmael sat or stood about and joined in the "base." **1867** Allen *Slave Songs* v **SC coast**, When the "base" begins, the leader often stops, leaving the rest of his words to be guessed at, or it may be that they are taken up by one of the other singers.

C As exclam.

Also *base on* (name): In var children's games: =**all (in) free.**

1966 *DARE* Tape **GA**13 [In the game of hide-and-seek], He'd run around and holler, "Base!" **1970** *DARE* (Qu. EE15, *When he has caught the first of those that were hiding, what does the player who is "it" call out to the others?*) Inf **VA**39, Base on so-and-so.

D As verb.

1 In gospel singing: see quot 1867. [**base** n **B4** above] See also **baser**

1863 Allen *Family Papers* 69 **SC**, Billy sang or rather chanted, and the others "based" him as they say. *Ibid* 163, "Edward come base me" cried Gibb in the midst of his delirium. *Ibid* 201, Dido sang the "Lonesome Valley" . . in a very rich contralto voice, the others "basing" her. **1867** Allen *Slave Songs* v **SC coast**, The leading singer starts the words of each verse, often improvising, and the others, who "base" him, as it is called, strike in with the refrain, or even join in the solo, when the words are familiar.

2 Transf: to disparage or ridicule; to confront (someone). *among Black speakers*

1970 *DARE* (Qu. Y4, . . *Uncomplimentary remark*) Inf **NY**249, Basing at me—has to do with one. **1980** Folb *Runnin' Down* 95 Los Angeles **CA** [Black], An' he squared up and he said, "Man, you wants to *base*? You get to basin' more or less put a man or woman in dey place. *Ibid* 48, I went to the principal office an' I went in dere and I base. " . . Now, if you don' wan' me to commence to turnin' dis school out, you git me my transfer!"

E As adj.

See **baseborn.**

baseball n Also *baseball jackknife* **?Inland Nth**

A children's knife game similar to **mumblety-peg.**

1950 *WELS* (*Games where you try to make a jackknife stick in the ground*) 1 Inf, **csWI**, Baseball; 1 Inf, **ceWI**, Baseball—recent [name]; 1 Inf, **ceWI**, Baseball jackknife. **1966–69** *DARE* (Qu. EE5) **MN**1, **MT**1, **PA**196, Baseball; **MN**21, Baseball—[a two-bladed knife at right angles]; **PA**167, Baseball—two blades. "Knife"—both blades out. Depending on how it lands the batter scores a base. If it lays flat, you're out.

base-begotten See **baseborn**

baseboarding n See **basing**

baseborn adj, also absol Also *base,* earlier *base-begotten* [*OED base-born* 3, 1645 →] **chiefly Delmarva, wNC** (See map in 1949 Kurath *Word Geog.* fig 36)

Born out of wedlock.

1793 in 1956 Eliason *Tarheel Talk* 259 **cnNC**, The sum of Ten Pounds for the support of a Base begotten child. **1946** *PADS* 5.10 **eVA**, *Base-born* . . . Illegitimate child. **1949** Kurath *Word Geog.* 77, On Chesapeake Bay, especially on the Eastern Shore, we find *base-born (child)*, and this term appears also here and there in the Appalachians (but not in the intervening Virginia Piedmont). **1952** Brown *NC Folkl.* 1.518, *Baseborn* . . A bastard; illegitimate. **1956** Hall Coll. **wNC**, Baseborn. **1956** Eliason *Tarheel Talk* 162 **NC**, *Base-begotten child* . . is not reported as current today, though in the western part of the state . . base-born child is occasionally still used. **1968** *DARE* (Qu. Z11a, b) Inf **NC**55, Base child; **WV**8, Baseborn.

basekeeper See **baseman**

base line See **base B3**

baseman n Also *basekeeper* [**base B2**]

In var children's games: "it," the person who must chase or catch the other players.

1966 *DARE* Tape **GA**13 [Describing the game of hide-and-seek], Selecting a baseman. **1966–67** *DARE* (Qu. EE13b) Infs **MO**8, **TN**14, Baseman; **SC**32, Basekeeper; (QR, near Qu. EE13b) Inf **OK**18, Baseman.

basement n

1 also attrib: The part of a building which is wholly or partly below ground level. **widespread, but least common in NEast** See Map Cf **cellar** n[1] **B2**

1833 in 1837 NH Hist. Soc. Coll. 5.68, *In the basement, or cellar,* three rooms on the south side were filled with boxes. **1834** (1898) Kemper *Jrl.* 408 **NY**, The 2 school rooms are in the basement story of the Ch[urch]. **1855** Simms *Forayers* 274 **SC**, This building, a comfortable frame-work of two stories on a basement . . faced south and west. **1950** *AmSp* 25.165 **CO**, *Cellar* . . . is competing with *basement* and tends to be supplanted by *basement* especially when the underground room has cement floors. **c1960** Wilson Coll. **csKY**, Basement . . . Space under a house. *Cellar* is rarely so used, as most cellars were separate from houses. **1965–70** *DARE* (Qu. D18) 671 Infs, **widespread, but least common in NEast**, Basement; (Qu. D19) 361 Infs, **widespread, but least common in NEast**, (Down) to the basement; 102 Infs, (Down) in(to) the basement; 32 Infs, Down (the) basement; **NJ**21, **SC**19, Down in (that) basement; **MI**1, **WI**35, Downstairs to the basement; **CA**182, **GA**89, **NY**45, (Into) basement.

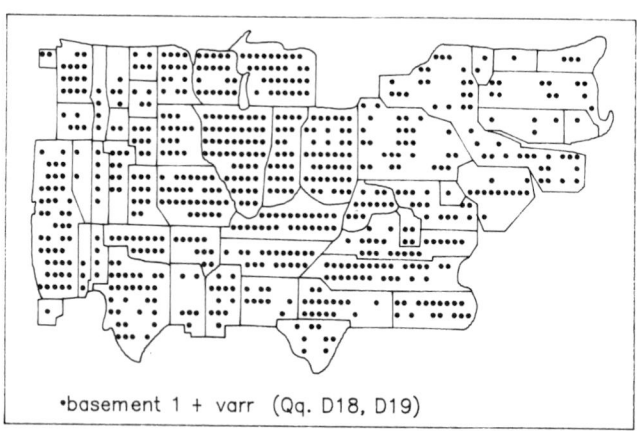

•basement 1 + varr (Qq. D18, D19)

2 A toilet room in a public school. *euphem*

1966 *DARE* FW Addit **MA**6, Basement—school toilet . . because toilets always used to be in the basement. **1970** Tarpley *Blinky* 149 **neTX**, His son had been corrected by the first grade teacher when he asked if he might go to the *toilet.* "You must say *basement*," the teacher scolded. Now the child has convinced his entire family that the path behind the house leads to the *basement.* **1982** *DARE* File **NH**, *The basement* = the bathroom of a public school, regardless of its location.

basement barn n **Inland Nth** =**bank barn.**

1950 *WELS* (*A barn built on a hillside with entrances on two levels*) 27 Infs, **WI**, Basement barn. **1965–70** *DARE* (Qu. M1), Inf **IA**14, Basement barn—has a rock foundation part way up, about eight feet; **IL**15, Basement barn—partially underground; **NY**75, Basement barn—cows are stabled below; **MI**116, **NY**206, Basement barn. **1973** Allen *LAUM* 1.187 **seMN**, 1 Inf, Basement barn.

baser n [base B4]

In gospel singing: a member of the chorus; also, lines sung by the chorus.

1867 Allen *Slave Songs* v **SC coast,** The "basers" themselves seem to follow their own whims, beginning when they please and leaving off when they please, striking an octave above or below . . so as to produce the effect of a marvellous complication and variety, and yet with the most perfect time, and rarely with any discord. **1942** (1965) Parrish *Slave Songs* xvi **GA coast,** The effect of an inexhaustible supply of breath is achieved through the simple expedient of the "basers" — as members of the chorus are called . . . In the old days . . the basers played as important a part in group singing as the one who sang the leading lines. **1970** Major *Afro–Amer. Slang, Basers:* responding line sung by a gospel group.

bases-out exclam Also called **kicks**

In marble play: see quot.

1963 *KY Folkl. Rec.* 9.65 **seKY,** Bases-out: [A call for] permission to kick [one's] shooter away from an undesirable position such as being by a tree or a wall.

base steer See **bay steer**

bashaw n Also *basha, bashaw cat* [Etym unknown, but perh related to Choctaw *basha* "marked, a mark" in reference to the mottled skin; cf **appaloosa** n[2]]

=**flathead catfish 1.**

1882 U.S. Natl. Museum *Bulletin* 16.102, *P[ylodictis] olivaris* . . . Bashaw; Goujon . . . A fish of unprepossessing appearance, although much used as food. **1884** Goode *Fisheries U.S.* 628, The "Mud Cat," "Yellow Cat," "Goujon," or "Bashaw" is found in all the large rivers of the West and South. **1911** *Century Dict., Bashaw* . . . The mud cat, *Leptos olivaris.* [Louisiana.] — Bashaw cat. **1923** *Public Opinion* 12 Oct. 357/3 *(DA),* A good-sized fish, itself Carnivorous, called a basha. **1933** LA Dept. of Conserv. *Fishes* 424, The Yellow Cat, . . or Bashaw, is the fourth of the big Mississippi Cats.

basil balm n

Either of two plants of the mint family:

a A savory (here: *Satureja acinos*).

1900 Lyons *Plant Names* 107, *C. acinos* . . . Basil balm.

b A **horsemint 1** (here: *Monarda clinopodioides*).

1910 Graves *Flowering Plants* 388 **CT,** Basil Balm . . . Waste ground and roadsides. **1931** Harned *Wild Flowers Alleghanies* 429, *Basil Balm* . . . Characterized by its yellowish-pink flowers. **1959** Carleton *Index Herb. Plants* 8.

basing n Also *baseboarding* **Sth**

A baseboard.

1965–70 *DARE* (Qu. D37, *The strip of wood about eight inches high along the bottom of the wall*) Infs **LA6, MS85,** Basing; **GA78,** Baseboardin'; (Qu. D38) Inf **MS63,** Basing.

basket n Pronc-sp *bahskit*

1 A leaky vessel; also fig. **ME**

1903 Wasson *Cap'n Simeon's Store* 39 **ME,** Why . . don't you folks turn to and condemn the tormented ole basket? **1975** Gould *ME Lingo, Basket* . . . A leaky boat, or a kettle with a hole in it; hence, a person who can't keep a secret. "Tell it to that *bahskit* and it's all over town!"

‡**2** in phr *give one the basket:* To jilt. Cf *DS* AA11

1940–41 Cassidy *WI Atlas* **seWI,** She gave him the basket. [Laughter]

3 See quot.

1943 *LANE* Map 585 *(Goal),* 1 inf, **nwMA,** Basket, the goal in run-sheep-run.

4 also *black basket,* in phr *son of a ~:* See quots. **Nth** euphem Cf **biscuit B5**

1950 *WELS (Humorous substitutes for stronger exclamations: "Why the son of a _____.")* 1 Inf, **seWI,** Basket. **1966–68** *DARE* (Qu. NN24, . . "*Son of a _____!*") Infs **PA167, WI48,** Basket; **NH1,** Black basket — used by one individual.

5 See **fish basket.**

6 in phrr alluding to pregnancy:

a *have one in the basket* and varr: To be pregnant. Cf **oven**

1967–70 *DARE* (Qu. AA28) Infs **NH18, VT3, WI47,** Got one in the basket; **CA106,** Has one in the basket; **TX5,** One in the basket; **MA123,** Something in the basket.

b *carry a basket:* To prepare for imminent childbirth.

1966–69 *DARE* (Qu. AA28) Infs **IN3, PA177,** Better start carrying a basket; **PA134,** Better carry a basket; **OK42,** Better start carrying a basket with her.

basket ash n [See quot 1958]

=**black ash 1.**

1897 Sudworth *Arborescent Flora* 325, *Fraxinus nigra* . . . Basket Ash (Mass.). **1911** *Century Dict. Suppl., Ash* . . . *Basket-ash,* the black ash . . so called because it affords basket splints. **1958** Petrides *Trees & Shrubs* 34, Black Ash . . . Known also as . . Basket Ash. Short logs or planks when hammered repeatedly on the ends split along the annual growth rings into thin sheets that can be cut into strips for weaving pack baskets. **1979** Little *Checklist U.S. Trees* 136.

basket bird n [From its hanging woven nest]

Either the **Baltimore oriole** or the **orchard oriole.**

1913 Bailey *Birds VA* 209, *Icterus galbula* . . . Weaver Bird. Basket Bird. Golden Robin. **1917** (1923) *Birds Amer.* 2.256, *Icterus spurius* . . . Basket-bird. **1946** Hausman *Eastern Birds* 555, Orchard oriole *Icterus spurius* . . Basket bird.

basket buggy, basket carriage See **basket wagon**

basket dinner n Also *basket lunch, ~ meal* **chiefly Midl, occas Sth** Cf **dinner on the ground**

A social gathering to which participants bring food to be shared by all; also the food itself.

1892 *Ill. Kentuckian* (Lexington) Dec. 88/3 *(DA),* This is a noted place for picnics where pies and cake and basket dinners prevail. **1915** *DN* 4.180 **swVA,** *Basket dinner* . . . Lunch brought in baskets to an "all-day meetin'," a religious service lasting through the day. **1940** Stong *Hawkeyes* 134 **IA,** Basket dinners made a good reason for getting together. **1950** *WELS (When people bring hot dishes to a meeting place and share them together, you call that a _____ meal)* 1 Inf, **swWI,** Pot-luck or basket. **1965–70** *DARE* (Qu. H70, *When people bring baked dishes, salads, and so forth to a meeting place and share them together, that's a _____ meal.)* Infs **IL113, IN48, MS23, MO3, 16, OH4,** 57, 98, Basket dinner; **SC70,** Basket; (Qu. FF1) Inf **MO34,** Basket dinners. **1967** *DARE* Tape IL23, They had a hanging here once and women took their children and took a basket dinner and spent the day and watched the hanging. **1968** *Tuscaloosa News* (AL) 1 Aug 26/6, The Rev. H.B. Holt, former pastor, conducting the morning worship service. A basket lunch will be served at noon with afternoon singing to follow.

basket elm n

=**cedar elm.**

1851 *DeBow's Rev.* 11.46, Basket Elm and Water Elm. **1897** Sudworth *Arborescent Flora* 180, *Ulmus crassifolia* . . . Basket Elm (Ark.). **1979** Little *Checklist U.S. Trees* 290, *Cedar elm* . . . *Other common names* — basket elm.

basket-fish n **NEng coast**

A brittle star (*Astrophyton agassizii*).

1670 in 1671 Royal Soc. London *Philos. Trans.* 6.2223, Until a fitter *English* name be found for it, why may it not be called . . a *Basket-Fish,* or a *Net Fish,* or a *Purs-net Fish?* **1753** Chambers *Cyclopedia Suppl., Basket-fish* . . a name given by the English in North America to a very remarkable fish, sometimes caught in the seas thereabout. **1881** Ingersoll *Oyster-Industry* 241, *Basket-fish.* — *Astrophyton Agassizii,* a kind of many-armed starfish. **1901** Arnold *Sea-Beach* 215, This very singular ophiuran is commonly called the basket-fish, from its resemblance to a basket when the tentacles are rolled up . . . It is found off the northern New England coast. **1911** *Century Dict., Basket-fish* . . . So named by Governor John Winthrop of Connecticut, about 1670.

basket flower n [From fancied resemblance of the flower bracts to a basket]

A **star thistle** (here: *Centaurea americana*).

1942 Hylander *Plant Life* 496, Our native Basket Flower has . . rose or flesh-colored flowers with narrow fringe-like lobes often an inch in length; it ranges from Missouri and Louisiana to Kansas and Arizona. **1968** Barkley *Plants KS* 375, Basketflower. Prairies and plains. Scattered central and southeast. **1972** Brown *Wildflowers LA* 195, *Basket Flower, Star-thistle* . . . Flower heads . . 2 to 3 inches wide, bell-shaped.

basketful of chips See **basket of chips**

‡**basketful of possum-heads** n Cf **basket of chips c**

1906 *DN* 3.151 **nwAR,** *Pleased as a basketful of possum-heads* . . . Exceedingly well pleased. The possum's grin is proverbial. Rare.

basket grass n

1 =squaw grass.

1898 *Jrl. Amer. Folkl.* 11.282, *Xerophyllum tenax* . . basket grass . . Pierce Co., Wash. **1963** Craighead *Rocky Mt. Wildflowers* 31, *Beargrass* . . . *Other names:* Basket-grass . . . The leaves when dried and bleached were used by the Indians of the Northwest for making clothing and fine baskets.

2 =bear grass 1b.

1951 *PADS* 15.29 **TX,** *Nolina* spp. . . Basket grass. These are employed to weave mats for household use or for burial purposes.

basket lunch, basket meal See **basket dinner**

basket meeting n, also attrib **Sth, S Midl**

A social gathering, usu for religious purposes, frequently accompanied by a **basket dinner.**

1859 (1968) Bartlett *Americanisms,* Basket meeting. In the West a sort of pic-nic, generally with some religious "exercises." **1874** (1895) Eggleston *Circuit Rider* 215 **IN,** He had ben to Jinkinsville t'other day to what the Methodis' called a "basket meetin'." **1890** *DN* 1.65 **KY,** A "basket-meetin'" is a two or three days' *meetin',* when they have "dinner on the ground." **1892** *AN&Q* 8.309/1 **FL,** "Basket meetings" are not confined to the Southern negroes. On the contrary they are more common among the white people. Neither are they always religious. Quite frequently they are political, sometimes educational. When purely social they are called picnics. **1966** *Lexington Herald & Leader* (KY) 27 Aug 14/3, Sunday will be Homecomin and Basket-meetink [sic] Day at the Avon Baptist Church.

basket name n **sSC, GA coast** *Gullah*

A nickname given to a child at birth: see quots.

1949 Turner *Africanisms* 40 **sSC, GA coast,** Most of the Gullah people use two kinds of given names. One is English, and they call it their real or true name . . . The other is the nickname, known also as the . . basket name . . . The nickname is nearly always a word of African origin . . [or] something regarding the nature of the weather at the time of the child's birth . . or health of the child . . or the time of birth. **1950** *PADS* 14.13 **SC,** Basket name . . . A pet name given by Negro nurses to their helpless infant charges. Used before the rites of christening, lest some evil spirit, hearing the true name before it is ritually bound to the child, should call the child's spirit from the body and enter into the child, thus making it a changeling. They also give basket names to their children, which sometimes usurp the place of the real name, which is thus completely lost.

basket oak n [See quot 1967 at **3**]

1 An oak *(Quercus michauxii)* with silver-white bark and rather beechlike tomentose leaves, native chiefly to the South and the lower Mississippi Valley. Also called **cow oak, swamp chestnut oak 2, white oak**

1876 Dodge *Black Hills* 103, The oak is a white oak, of sometimes a straight fiber, like the basket oak of the Eastern States. **1940** (1978) Still *River of Earth* 240 **KY,** I never figure spring's in for shore till the basket oaks sprout buds. **1969** *DARE* (Qu. T10) Infs **KY**29, 30, Basket oak.

2 =**Durand oak** or a var thereof.

1897 Sudworth *Arborescent Flora* 159, *Quercus breviloba* . . . Durand Oak . . . Syn. . . *Quercus Durandii* . . . Common Names . . . Basket Oak (Ala., La., Tex.). **1960** Vines *Trees SW* 157, *Durand Oak—Quercus durandii* . . . Also known by the vernacular names of . . Basket Oak. Wood used for making splint cotton baskets in early times.

3 =**swamp chestnut oak 1.**

1930 OK Univ. Biol. Surv. Pub. 2.2.58, *Quercus prinus* . . Basket Oak. **1960** Vines *Trees SW* 153, Swamp Chestnut Oak. *Quercus prinus* . . . Basket Oak. **1967** Borland *Hill Country* 161 **nwCT,** Among the oaks there is one sometimes called basket oak . . . The "basket" name . . has a clear reason—its wood, when split into splints and soaked to make it pliable, was once used extensively to make durable baskets.

basket of chips n Also *basketful of chips*

In allusive use and compar phrr, as:

a *as smiling as a basket of chips:* Showing great happiness.

[*OEDS* 1788 "He grins like a basket of chips" (Grose) *?obs*

[**1800** *The Nightingale, or Rural Songster* 77 (DAE), She smiled like a basket of chips.] **1834** in 1956 Eliason *Tarheel Talk* 104 **NC,** Little Tom looks as smiling as a basket of chips. **1907** Obenchain *Aunt Jane* 45 **KY,** There he was as smilin' as a basket o' chips.

b *polite as a basket of chips:* Extremely or obsequiously polite.

1905 *DN* 3.16 **cCT,** *Polite as a basket of chips* . . . Very polite and smiling. **1907** *DN* 3.216 **nwAR.** **1927** *AmSp* 2.362 **WV,** He was as polite as a basket of chips to the ladies. **1929** *AmSp* 5.123 **ME.** **1952** Brown *NC Folkl.* 1.366.

c other phrr: See quots. Cf **basketful of possum-heads**

1827 *MA Spy & Worcester Co. Advt.* (Worcester MA) 28 Nov 2/1, The Yankee . . . will say of a . . young lady, "she is a real *pretty* girl, but she is as *homely as a basket of chips.*" **1904** *DN* 2.395 **NYC,** I didn't know him from a . . basket of chips. **1906** *DN* 3.151 **nwAR,** *Pleased as a basketful of chips* . . . Delighted. **1946** *CA Folkl. Qrly.* 5.242 **OR,** Busy as a basket of chips going to a bonfire. **1950** *PADS* 14.80 **cwFL,** *Pleasant* as a basket of chips.

basket phaeton See **basket wagon**

basket sleigh n *old-fash* Cf **basket wagon**

A cutter sleigh with a wicker body.

1968 *DARE* (Qu. N40b) Inf **MD**31, Basket sleigh—cutter type, made of woven basket material; **MD**48, Basket sleigh—like cutter sleigh, but vehicle part made of woven basket material.

basket social n Also *basket sociable* **chiefly Upper MW, NW** =**box social.**

1895 *Denver Times* 5 Mar 5/4 (*AmSp* 17.124), The Prohibitionists will give a basket social (cake only) at the Women's Exchange. **1965–70** *DARE* (Qu. FF1) Infs **ND**1, 2, 10, **PA**40, **SD**2, 3, 5, 8, Basket social; **CO**9, Basket social—old-fashioned; **ID**1, 4, Basket social—bid on lunches; **IL**35, Basket social—women bring food in baskets, men buy baskets and get to eat with the girl who brought it; **MN**28, Basket social—auction off a basket of food, eat with person who made it; **MT**3, Basket social—boys bid on girls' lunches; **MN**12, Basket sociable.

basket spider n

A kind of spider.

1968 *DARE* (Qu. R28) Inf **UT**6, Basket spiders.

‡**basket upset** n

=**fruit basket upset.**

1968 *DARE* (Qu. EE2, *Games that have one extra player—when a signal is given the players change places, and the extra one tries to get a place*) Inf **PA**104, Basket upset.

basket wagon n Also *basket buggy,* ~ *carriage,* ~ *phaeton* **Nth** *old-fash* Cf **basket sleigh**

A horse-drawn vehicle with a wicker body.

1863 (1889) Whitney *Faith Gartney* 25 **NEast,** One happy, little child . . was riding over the lawn in her basket-wagon. **1941** FWP *Guide MI* 616, Brightly painted basket buggies . . stand ready to take the visitors on leisurely sight-seeing tours [of Mackinac Island]. **1948** Rittenhouse *Amer. Horse-Drawn Vehicles* 17 (as of 1870), Basket phaetons frequently had a single rumble seat. They did not have the heavy appearance of phaetons with painted wood panels. **1967** *DARE* (Qu. L13, . . *Wagon used for carrying hay*) Inf **NY**160, Basket wagon, kicker, in current use. Hay rack—formerly used. **1968** *DARE* Tape NJ30, The carriages were gone except for an occasional straw carriage pulled by a pony, a basket carriage, when I was a little girl. [Inf born 1911]

basket worm n [From the silk case it spins]

=**bagworm.**

1889 *Century Dict.,* Bag-worm . . . *Thyridopteryx ephemeræformis* . . . The larva . . has also received the names *basket-worm, drop-worm,* etc.

bass See **basswood 1**

bass-ackward(s) adv, adj Also pronc-spp *barse-ackwards, bass-ackard(s)* [By metath] **widespread** *esp among men; joc or euphem* See also **back-asswards**

=**ass-backward(s).**

1930 Shoemaker *1300 Words* **cPA Mts** (as of c1900), *Bass-ackwards*—head over heels, a tumble. **1931** *PMLA* 46.1322 **sAppalachians,** Bass ack'ard. **1937** Hench Coll. **cVA,** My note . . on "assbackwards" reminds me that for years I have heard . . *bass-ackwards* meaning the same thing. **1949** *PADS* 11.3 **wTX,** Bassackwards . . . Totally backwards. A euphemistic Spoonerism. **c1960** Wilson Coll. **cwKY,** *Bass-ackwards.* Humorous transposition "for men only." "He put on his pants bassackwards." **1965–70** *DARE* (Qu. MM3, . . *"This is the front, you've got the whole thing turned _____."*) 119 Infs, **widespread,** Bass-ackwards; **CA**3, **CT**25, **VA**5, Bass-ackward; **AL**51, **MS**71, Bass-ackards; (Qu. MM2, . . *"Look, you've got your dress on _____."*) 15 Infs, **scattered,** Bass-ackwards; **MA**61, **OH**18, Bass-ackward; **TX**51,

Bass-ackards; (Qu. KK52) Inf **WA**1, Bass-ackwards; (Qu. JJ42) Inf **SC**44, Got it bass-ackwards. [Of all Infs responding to Qq. MM2 and 3, 48% were men; of those giving these responses, 70% for MM3 were men, and 80% for MM2 were men.] **1968** *DARE* FW Addit **csLA**, Bass-ackwards [ˌbæs'ækwɚdz] . . . confused, mixed up, said of mental state. **1975** Gould *ME Lingo, Barse-ackwards.*

‡bassalon n

1952 Brown *NC Folkl.* 1.518 **wNC**, Bassalon . . . A ragged man.

bass fly n

1967 *DARE* (QR, near Qu. R4) Inf **NY**10, Bass fly: flat; comes out of the water; bass eat them.

bass gull n

The common **tern** *(Sterna hirundo hirundo).*

1903 Dawson *Birds OH* 2.559, Common Tern . . . Synonyms . . . "Bass-gull." **1917** (1923) *Birds Amer.* 1.60. **1968** *DARE* (Qu. Q10) Inf **OH**67, Bass gull.

basswood n

1 also *bass:* **=linden.**

1670 *Rowley Rec.* 210 (DA), The Northwest Angle is a basswood tree. **1728** in 1882 Boston Registry Dept. *Records* 8.222, We are of the opinion that no popler, chestnut, pine, henlock [sic], sassifax, black ash, basswood, or cedar shall be corded up. **1907** *DN* 3.181 **seNH,** Basswood. American linden. **1926** *West Virginia Legislative Handbook* 508 *(Hench Coll.),* And "he calls him basswood," was another complaint. [The West Virginian's term for basswood is *linn.*] **1950** Moore *Trees AR* 99, *Tilia americana . . Local Names . . . Bass.* **1965** Needham–Mussey *Country Things* 138 **sVT,** The pitch from off of logs or lumber would look like the nicest basswood honey you ever saw. **1967–70** *DARE* (Qu. T13, *Names for [linden] trees)* 162 Infs, **scattered, but esp NEast, W Midl, Gt Lakes, Upper MW,** Basswood; (Qu. T9) Infs **CT**30, **NY**191, **NC**48, Basswood; (Qu. T12) Inf **WV**2, Basswood.

2 **=tulip tree.**

1897 Sudworth *Arborescent Flora* 198 **OH,** *Liriodendron tulipifera . .* Basswood.

bast See base A

bastard n

1 A volunteer crop.

1966–68 *DARE* (Qu. L24, *A crop or part of a crop that springs up and grows by itself from old seed)* Infs **MN**2, **NY**79, 102, 107, **PA**1, **WV**3, Bastard; **IN**35, Bastard—applies to wild stuff [such as] wild millet.

2 attrib: An animal, plant, or mineral that resembles and is sometimes mistaken for the "true" form; a hybrid. See also separate entries below Cf **false** adj

1709 Lawson *Carolina* 92 (DA), Bastard-Spanish is an Oak betwixt the Spanish and Red-Oak. **1851** *S. Lit. Messenger* 17.374/2 **Plains States, I** am convinced that it is the Mezquite; which is not known to exist in our prairies; their frequenters have no name for it that I have heard, except perhaps, 'bastard locust.' **1859** (1968) Bartlett *Americanisms* 37, Blue curls . . . A common plant resembling pennyroyal, and hence called bastard pennyroyal. **1952** *AmSp* 27.294, 'Bastard,' meaning hybrid, in the names of American birds . . . [Bastard] Loon (gray-cheeked grebe, Long Island, N.Y.) . . . Gannet (white ibis, Ga.) . . . Goose (snow goose, N.J.) . . . Mallard (gadwall, Calif.) . . . Widgeon (European widgeon, Va., N.C.) . . also *bastard redhead* . . . Teal (hooded merganser, Wash.) . . . Robin (blue bird, La.) . . . Blackbird (yellow-headed blackbird, Texas). **1968** Adams *Western Words* 14, Bastard quartz. Valueless quartz with no accessory minerals.

3 attrib: See quot.

1967 *DARE* Tape **WA**29, I cut my grape stake material two different ways; I cut it vertical grain like the shakes are made, and what they call bastard grain—that's more or less of a logger's expression. [FW:] What does it mean? [Inf:] It's opposite the grain.

4 See **bastard dowitcher.**

bastard ash n

1 **=green ash.**

1897 Sudworth *Arborescent Flora* 329, *Fraxinus pennsylvanica . . .* Bastard Ash (Vt.).

2 **=box elder.**

1968 *DARE* (Qu. T13, *. . Other names . . for . . box elder)* Inf **NH**14, Bastard ash.

bastard Baltimore n

=orchard oriole.

1731 (1754) Catesby *Nat. Hist. Carolina* 1.49 *Icterus minor. The Bastard Baltimore.* Weighs thirteen Penny-Weight. **1808** Wilson *Amer. Ornith.* 1.24, Buffon, and Latham, have both described the male of the bastard Baltimore *(Oriolus Spurius),* as the female Baltimore. **1946** Hausman *Eastern Birds* 555, *Orchard Oriole . . . Other Names . .* Bastard Baltimore.

bastard berry n

1967 *DARE* (Qu. I44) Inf **LA**11, Bastard berries—come between black [berries] and dewberries in old fields on low vines.

bastard bread n

Bread made with a mixture of meal and flour.

1965 *DARE* (Qu. H18) Inf **FL**21, Bastard bread—half meal and half flour.

bastard broadbill n esp NY, RI Cf broadbill

=ring-necked duck.

1844 Giraud *Birds Long Is.* 324, *Ring-necked . . Duck . . .* By our gunners generally, it is considered a hybrid, and familiar to them by the name of "Bastard Broad-bill." **1899** Howe *Birds RI* 38, *Aythya collaris . . . Bastard Broad-bill.* **1910** Eaton *Birds NY* 1.208, This species, called also . . Bastard broadbill, is a rare migrant in eastern New York. **1944** Hausman *Amer. Birds* 507, Broad-bill, Bastard—see Duck, Ring-necked.

bastard dowitcher n Also bastard, bastard dowitch

=stilt sandpiper.

1889 *Century Dict.* 1749/2, *Bastard dowitcher* or *dowitch,* the stilt-sandpiper, *Micropalama himantopus.* **1923** U.S. Dept. Ag. *Misc. Circular* 13.52, Stilt Sandpiper . . . Vernacular Names . . . In local use.—Bastard, bastard-dowitcher (Long Id., N.Y.). **1952** *AmSp* 27.294, Stilt sandpiper . . . is called also *bastard dowitch* and simply, *bastard,* on Long Island, N.Y.

bastard indigo n [See quot 1900]

1 **=false indigo 1** (here: *Amorpha fructicosa).*

1900 Lyons *Plant Names* 29, *A. fructicosa . . .* False or Bastard Indigo . . . Formerly a source of *indigo.* **1901** Lounsberry *S. Wild Flowers* 271, Bastard, or false indigo, grows as a shrub to often the height of twenty feet. **1960** Vines *Trees SW* 521, Also known under the vernacular names of False Indigo and Bastard Indigo. **1970** Correll *Plants TX* 818.

2 **=deervetch.**

1950 Gray–Fernald *Manual of Botany* 896, *Lotus* L. Birdsfoot-Trefoil. *Bastard Indigo.*

bastard oak n

1 also *bastard white oak:* **= Durand oak** or its var Bigelow oak. **chiefly Sth**

1897 Sudworth *Arborescent Flora* 159, *Quercus breviloba . . .* Bastard Oak (Ala., La., Tex.). **1901** Mohr *Plant Life AL* 470, *Quercus brevilobata . . .* Texan White Oak. Pin Oak. Bastard Oak . . . Of some value for its timber and for fuel. **1908** Britton *N. Amer. Trees* 325, *Quercus austrina . . .* is also called Pin oak and Bastard oak. **1933** Small *Manual SE Flora* 426, *Q. Durandii . . . Bastard White-oak.* **1969** *DARE* (Qu. T10) Inf **MO**39, Bastard oak. **1970** Correll *Plants TX* 481, *Quercus sinuata . . . Bastard oak.*

2 **=Lacey oak.**

1903 Small *Flora SE U.S.* 353, *Quercus Laceyi . . .* South-central Texas. *Bastard Oak. Mountain Oak.* **1960** Vines *Trees SW* 160, *Lacey Oak . . .* Vernacular names are . . Mountain Oak, Smoky Oak, and Bastard Oak.

3 **=water oak** (here: *Quercus nigra).*

1913 *Torreya* 13.229, *Quercus nigra* L.—Bastard oak, Santee Club, S.C.

4 **=scarlet oak.**

1938 Van Dersal *Native Woody Plants* 324, Bastard, . . oak *(Quercus coccinea . .).*

bastard pine n

1 Any of various pines as:

a **=shortleaf pine 1** (here: *Pinus echinata).*

1785 Marshall *Arbustrum* 100, *Pinus echinata . . .* Bastard Pine.

b =slash pine 1 (here: *Pinus elliottii*).

1884 Sargent *Forests of N. Amer.* 202, *Pinus Cubensis* . . Bastard Pine.

c =loblolly pine 1 (here: *Pinus tæda*).

1897 Sudworth *Arborescent Flora* 26, *Pinus tæda* . . Bastard Pine (Va., N.C.).   **1900** Lyons *Plant Names* 292, *P[inus] tæda* . . called also . . Bastard . . Pine.   **1960** Vines *Trees SW* 23, *Pinus tæda* . . Other vernacular names are . . Bastard Pine.

2 =white fir.

1897 Sudworth *Arborescent Flora* 55, *Abies concolor* . . Bastard Pine (Utah).

bastard teal n

=hooded merganser.

1923 U.S. Dept. Ag. *Misc. Circular* 13.7, *Hooded Merganser . . . Vernacular Names . . . In local use.*—Bastard teal (Wash.).   **1952** *AmSp* 27.294, *Bastard . . . Teal* (hooded merganser, Wash.). Any small duck may be called a teal, but this one, with a conspicuous white and black crest, is no ordinary teal, hence is deemed probably the result of hybridization.

bastard white oak See **bastard oak 1**

bastard yellowleg(s) n [See quots]

=stilt sandpiper.

1899 Howe *Birds RI* 49, *Micropalama himantopus . . . Bastard Yellow-leg.*—An uncommon spring, but not uncommon fall migrant. **1917** (1923) *Birds Amer.* 1.231, The Stilt Sandpiper . . is frequently mistaken for the Yellowlegs . . . The similarity of the two species is acknowledged by the popular name, "Bastard Yellow-legs," which the sportsmen of Long Island have given to the Stilt Sandpiper. **1952** *AmSp* 27.294 **MA, NY, RI, VA,** *Bastard . . Yellowleg.* **1962** Imhof *AL Birds* 253, Bastard Yellowlegs. The Stilt Sandpiper looks like a cross between a dowitcher and a yellowlegs. **1970** *DARE* (Qu. Q10) Inf **VA47,** Bastard yellowlegs.

baste n See **base A**

‡**baste** v

1931–33 *LANE Worksheets* **ceMA,** In connection with a fire in a fireplace: the only thing that would go with the back log would be the kindling. When you put that in you call it basting it.

baster n |ˈbestɚ| Pronc-sp *baister* [Etym unknown, but see quots 1940, 1975] **ME** See also **basting big**

Something remarkably large for its type; see quot 1975.

c1900 Wasson in 1974 *AmSp* 49.61 **swME,** It was a baster of a rat. **1940** *Harper's Mag.* 182.107/1 **ME,** Baster (pronounced bayster) is a popular word with boys . . . He's an old baster, they say, when they pull an eel out of an eel trap. It probably derives from bastard, but it sounds quite proper and innocent when you hear it, and rather descriptive. **1975** Gould *ME Lingo* 3, *Baister*—Possibly *baster* . . . Indicating large size . . . Often with the adjective "old": "He hooked an old *baister* of a togue." . . . The word is apt for a storm: "An old *baister* blew up." A high swell which jolts a lobster boat may be described as an old *baister*. The word comes from a big rooster or roast which requires much basting in the oven.

basting big adj phr [Pple of *baste*, back-form from **baster** + **big**] **chiefly ME** See also **baster**

Exceptionally large.

1900 Day *Up in Maine* 103 (*AmSp* 41.21), In the shark's insides was a bastin' big tape worm. **1914** *DN* 4.69 **ME, nNH,** *Bastin' big* . . . Very big.

basto n, often pl [Span] **SW**

The skirt of a saddle; also, the leather lining of a saddle.

1881 Farrow *Mt. Scouting* 138, The Mexican or California saddles . . . [are] usually furnished with wool-lined bastos. **1907** White *AZ Nights* 119, The pony I was riding did his best, but even then could not avoid a sharp prod that would have ripped him up had not my leather bastos intervened. **1932** Bentley *Spanish Terms* 101 **SW,** *Basto* . . . is a technical term restricted to those engaged in the saddle industry and to cattlemen.

bast-tree n

A linden (here: *Tilia americana*).

1900 Lyons *Plant Names* 371, *T[ilia] Americana* . . Bast-tree. **1930** Sievers *Amer. Med. Plants* 6, American Linden—*Tilia americana* . . Other common names . . . bast tree. **1960** Vines *Trees SW* 733, It *[=T. americana]* has many vernacular names such as Bast-tree.

bas ufft v phr [Ger *aufpassen*, PaGer *uffbasse* to pay attention, watch out]

1967 *DARE* (Qu. JJ26, *If somebody has been doing poor work or not enough, the boss might say, "If he wants to keep his job he'd better _____."*) Inf **PA11,** Bas ufft [bɑs ʊft]—expression used about a guy laying on the job and not producing.

bat n[1] Cf **chimney bat, great bat, Virginia bat**

1 =nighthawk. Cf **bullbat**

1709 (1967) Lawson *New Voyage* 148, East-India Bats or Musqueto Hawks, are the Bigness of a Cuckoo, and much of the same Colour. **1812** Wilson *Amer. Ornith.* 5.65, *Night-Hawk* . . . This bird, in Virginia and some of the southern districts, is called a bat. **1899** (1912) Green *VA Folk-Speech*, *Bat* . . . The night hawk. **1923** *WV State Ornith. Birds WV* 33, His [=nighthawk's] bat-like stunts while he is taking insects on the wing give him the name of "bat." **1955** *Oriole* 20.1.9 **GA,** *Night-hawk.*—Bat (from its nocturnal habits).

2 =chimney swift.

1955 *AmSp* 30.179, Simply *bat* has been recorded for it [=chimney swift] in Florida, Missouri, and Kansas.

bat n[2] [**bat** v[2]]

A blink.

1932 (1974) Caldwell *Tobacco Road* 32 **GA,** Jeeter suddenly broke into a terrific plunge that landed him upon the sack of turnips almost as quickly as the bat of an eye. **1966–70** *DARE* (Qu. A14, . . *"It won't take any longer than _____."*) Inf **NC83,** A bat of your eye; (Qu. KK42b, . . *"He could do that _____."*) Inf **FL33,** In the bat of an eye.

bat n[3] Also sp *batt* Also *batboard* See also **bat** v[3], **batting**

=batten n.

1929 *AmSp* 4.69, The side parts [of a stage backdrop] are fastened to strips or battens, called *bats*. **1940–41** Cassidy *WI Atlas*, Bat—a strip of wood with beveled edges, applied outside a board wall to seal the cracks between boards. **1965–70** *DARE* (Qu. D27, *Strips of wood used to cover the outside of a frame house*) 11 Infs, **scattered,** Bats; **AZ8,** Batboard. **1981** *DARE* File **CA,** Board and batten [is] frequently shortened to board and batt.

bat n[4] See **batoon**

bat v[1] Usu with an adv or prep, as *along, around, through*

To move or go about erratically.

1907 in 1960 Howells *Twain–Howells Letters* 2.826, [She] was in England . . batting round with two other girls, and having a great time. **1911** *DN* 3.541 **NE,** *Batting* . . . Going about in an aimless, or harum-scarum manner. "She went batting along the street." **1930** Irwin *Amer. Tramp, Batting.*—Travelling aimlessly and without purpose, much as a bat flits from place to place. **1931** *PMLA* 46.1309 **sAppalachians,** Whenever he is hailed concerning his health, . . . [his] replies usually run something like these . . . Jist a-battin' about (or aroun'). **1940** *Sat. Eve. Post* 6 Jan 32/1 **MS,** Saw Buck [=a boy] battin' through the woods.

bat v[2] [Alter of *bate* to flutter (as a hawk)]

1 To wink or blink (one's eyes). **widespread, but chiefly Sth, Midl** See Map See also **bap, bat** n[2]

1845 Hooper *Advent. Simon Suggs* 143 **AL,** I didn't say nuthin, but jist batted my eye at old Chamblin, and he laffed. **1892** *DN* 1.235 **KS, OH,** *Bat the eyes*, used of the quick action of the lids when one tastes sharp vinegar. **1899** (1912) Green *VA Folk-Speech*, *Bat* . . . to wink, or move

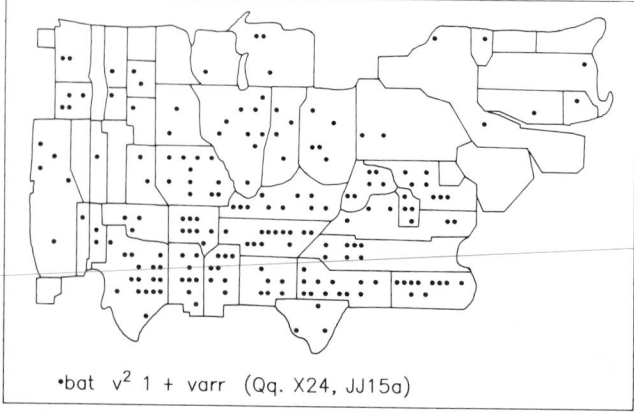

•bat v[2] 1 + varr (Qq. X24, JJ15a)

the eyelids up and down. **1903** *DN* 2.306 **seMO.** **1905** *DN* 3.69 **nwAR.** **1906** *DN* 3.115 **sIN.** **1908** *DN* 3.28 **eAL, wGA.** **1915** *DN* 4.180 **swVA.** **1923** *DN* 5.201 **swMO.** **1939** *Hall Coll.* **wTN,** The bear was battin' his eyes when the master-hunter found him. **1954** *Harder Coll.* **cwTN.** **1965–70** *DARE* (Qu. X24) 116 Infs, **chiefly Sth, Midl,** Bats his eyes; 61 Infs, **chiefly Sth, Midl,** Bats; **GA7, 9, OK11,** Bats them (*or* 'em); **IL99,** Bats his eyelashes; **OK7, WA30,** Bats his eyes like a toad (-frog) in a hailstorm; **FL39, IN77, MO17, 19, 39, NC55,** Batting his eyes; **CA128, TN50,** Bat; **LA6, SC26,** Bat his eye(s); (Qu. JJ15a) Inf **TN46,** Bat his eye.

a in neg phrr *not to bat an eye* (or *eyelash*): To betray no emotion; to show no sign of wavering.

    1958 Humphrey *Home from the Hill* 54 **TX,** Cap'm stand there lookin him over an never bat a eyelash. **1968–70** *DARE* (Qu. Y2) Inf **CT12,** Didn't bat an eyelash; (Qu. II6) Inf **PA220,** Didn't bat an eyelash; (Qu. JJ23, *To refuse to give in or yield: "He tried to scare me off but I _____."*) Inf **IL141,** Didn't bat an eye.

b in neg phrr suggesting the ease with which a task is accomplished: See quot.

    1965–70 *DARE* (Qu. KK42b, .. *"He could do that _____."*) Infs **CA8, DE1, LA17, MN16, NY64, PA126, TX65, VA66,** Without batting an eye; **IL50, NJ55, NY238,** Without batting an eyelash.

c in phrr suggestive of a very short period of time: See quot.

    1966–67 *DARE* (Qu. A14, .. *"It won't take any longer than _____."*) Inf **AR47,** Quick as a cat can bat its eye; **AR13,** Time you can bat an eye.

2 Transf: to open and close rapidly (one's mouth, hand, etc.).

    1914 *DN* 4.103 **KS,** *Bat . . .* To open and close; "He stood there *batting his fists."* **1950** *WELS* (*To talk for the sake of talking . . . "Don't mind him, he's always _____."*) 1 Inf, **cnWI,** Batting his gums. **1970** *DARE* (Qu. HH8, *A person who likes to brag*) Inf **PA242,** Battin' his gums.

‡3 See quot.

    1892 *DN* 1.235 **cwMO,** *Bat . . .* "To bat the ears" is said of the action of a rabbit or other animal when it lays its ears close to the body.

bat v[3] Also with *up* [Alter of *batten* v] **sAppalachians** See also **bat** n[3], **batting**

To cover cracks between boards with narrow strips of wood.

    1943 Stuart *Taps* 257 **KY,** We had to bat the cracks between the boxin with narrow planks. *Ibid* 261, We . . nailed a plank roof on the sheetin and batted the cracks. **1949** Webber *Backwoods Teacher* 213 (*Hench Coll.*) **sAppalachians,** I had thoughts of slipping back to watch, but I had "batted" up the cracks until I wasn't certain I could find a peeping place.

bat v[4] [*bat* or *batt* continuous sheet of cotton]

To prepare cotton sheeting for use in quilt-making.

    1939 *Hall Coll.* **wNC,** I can bat enough cotton in a day to quilt a quilt. **1970** *DARE* Tape **VA38,** I've seen her bat cotton, make home-made bed quilts.

bata n [Tagalog] **HI**

    1972 Carr *Da Kine Talk* 103 **HI,** Bata 'child' (boy or girl).

batawfel n [Alter of **catalpa**]

=catalpa B1.

    1967 *DARE* (Qu. T9) Inf **IL4,** Batawfel [bəˈtɔfəl].

batawga n [Alter of **catawba**]

=catalpa B1.

    1966 *DARE* (Qu. T9) Inf **NC1,** [bəˈtɔgə].

batboard See **bat** n[3]

batch and caboodle See **caboodle**

‡batched up adj phr [*batch* (or *bach*) live as a bachelor]

    1970 *DARE* (Qu. AA19, *Words or expressions about a man and woman who are not married but live together as if they were*) Inf **TX87,** Batched up.

batchelder n See **bachelder**

batch up v phr [Alter of *botch,* perh infl by *patch*]

To mend hastily or unskillfully.

    1966–69 *DARE* (Qu. W29, .. *Things that are sewn together carelessly . . "They're _____."*) Inf **IN55,** Batched [bæčt] up; **TN27,** Batched up; (Qu. KK63, *To do a clumsy or hurried job of repairing something: "It never will last—he just _____."*) Inf **NC9,** Batched it up.

bat crab n

An unidentified crustacean.

    1968 *DARE* Tape **MD25,** Bat crab .. gets its name from the design of a bat on its back.

bate v[1] [Engl dial from *abate*]

Of the wind: to diminish, fall off.

    1939 *LANE* Map 92 (*The wind is going down*) 1 Inf, **swME,** Bating.

bate n, v[2] See **bet** n[1], v

batea n Also sp *batella* [Span] **SW**

A large shallow pan, freq used in mining for gold.

    [**1759** Venegas *Hist. CA* 1.81, The manner of negociating their marriages .. was to present the bride by way of earnest with a batea or jug .. made of mezcale thread.] **1844** (1954) Gregg *Commerce* 120 **SW,** A round wooden bowl called *batea,* about eighteen inches in diameter, is the washing vessel. **1862** in 1948 *Western Folkl.* 7.5 **sCA,** They [=independent miners] came with nothing but a little pinole [=corn flour] and a batella, desirous of stopping at the first place where they could dry wash four bits or a dollar a day. **1951** Fergusson *New Mexico* 405, Batea—a large shallow pan used for washing sand to recover gold or other valuable minerals. **1969** *DARE* FW Addit **CA114,** Batea [bəˈteə]—a gold pan, from the Indian bowl used as a model for the gold pan.

bateau n, v Also sp *batteau* Usu |ˌbæˈto|, often |ˈbæˌto|, also |bæti, bætu, ˈbado| Pronc-spp *baddo, batoe, batto(e), batty* [Fr]

A Forms.

    1759 (1886) Putnam *Jrl.* 84 **NY,** This day a detachment .. marched up the Mohawk River in order to Battoe up that River. **1773** [see C below]. **1891** *DN* 1.121 **cNY,** [bætu] .. *bateau.* **1901** *DN* 2.136 **eVA** [Black], Batto [bæto], for *bateau.* **1941** *Sat. Eve. Post* 13 Sept 15/2 **Sth,** Take your baddo and your rahfle . . . A lady don't feel like baddo rides. **1968** *DARE* (Qu. O1) Inf **NJ21,** Bateau [bæto] or batty [bæti]—12 to 14 feet long; (Qu. O10) Inf **ME1,** [ˈbado]. **c1970** Pederson *Dial. Survey Rural GA* 5 infs, Batteaus [ˈbæˌto(z)].

B As noun. (Cf *DCan* for these and other distinctions)

1 A large flat-bottomed cargo and passenger boat, with sharply pointed bow and stern, used esp by loggers. **Nth, esp NEng**

    1711 in 1940 *AmSp* 15.226 **NEng,** Finding their battoes very leaky, [the troops] were obliged to pitch them again. **1907** *DN* 3.241 **eME.** **1914** *DN* 3.69 **ME, nNH,** Bateau . . . Lumberman's boat. **1938** (1939) Holbrook *Holy Mackinaw* **MI,** *Batteau.* Type of boat used on Eastern river drives. **1942** ME Univ. *Studies* 57.131 **NEng.** **1966–68** *DARE* Tape **MN19,** Bateau . . . pointed at both ends, used by river pegs [=loggers] as sort of taxi service; **ME26,** They used bateaus and like that on the [log] drive. A bateau's a big boat and it's built peaked on both ends . . . It's awful good in rough water. **1968** *DARE* (Qu. O10) Inf **VT4,** Bateaus—long boat used on the Connecticut River, held 15 to 20 men, not used any more. **1969** Sorden *Lumberjack Lingo* **NEng, Gt Lakes,** *Bateau . . .* was a French boat used first in fur trading, built to stand heavy work, especially hard to tip over. Flat-bottomed, tapering toward the ends, it was sometimes forty feet long.

2 A small, flat-bottomed rowboat. **chiefly C and S Atl, Gulf States** See Map

    1894 *DN* 1.328 **NJ,** *Bateau:* used only by oystermen. A small, flat-bottomed boat. **1930** *DN* 6.79 **cSC,** *Bateau . . .* A small home-made flat-bottomed boat, used by fishermen. **1946** *PADS* 5.10 **eVA.** **1946**

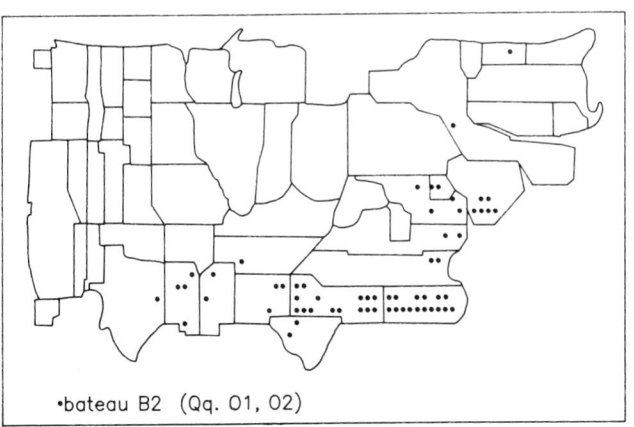

•bateau B2 (Qq. O1, O2)

PADS 6.5 **eNC**, Bateau ['bæˌto]. **1949** *AmSp* 24.250, *Bateau,* 'flat-bottomed rowboat,' is practically universal in South Carolina and Georgia but is rare in the Middle West. **1950** *PADS* 14.13 **eSC**. **1965–70** *DARE* (Qu. O1, . . *A small rowboat, not big enough to hold more than two people*) 55 Infs, **chiefly C and S Atl, Gulf States,** Bateau; (Qu. O2, . . *An old, clumsy boat*) Infs **FL**13, **GA**22, **LA**15, **NH**14, **TN**24, **TX**35, Bateau; **GA**77, Old bateau.

3 in var localized and restricted senses: See quots.
1827 (1936) Bolling *Diary* 127 **VA**, Put 412 bushels Wheat on board J. Pierce's large Batteaux. **1930** Shoemaker *1300 Words* **cPA Mts** (as of c1900), *Batteau*—A round bottom boat propelled by poles or paddles to carry 20 to 30 river drivers across the river. **1947** *PADS* 8.34 **sVA**, *Bateau* . . is not a small boat but a flat-bottomed freight boat . . . The bateau had to be poled up the river and through the canal. It was similar to the more common *barge* of today. **1956** Knipmeyer *Settlement Succession* 170 **LA**, *Bateau* as now used in Louisiana has a very restricted meaning which applies to only one kind of boat . . . The *bateau* is a large flat-bottomed boat with a blunt bow and stern. The length is usually over fifteen feet, and the width is between four and five feet . . . Most *bateaux* are so large that they must have an inboard motor. The largest have cabins over the well . . . On the other end of the scale they become indistinguishable from flatboats. **1968** *DARE* (Qu. O9, . . *Kinds of sailboats*) Inf **MD**36, Bateau ['bæˌto]—one mast, one sail; **MD**45, Bateau ['bæˌto]—square stern, one mast, same as a skipjack or dredge. **1968** *DARE* FW Addit **csLA**, Bateau ['bæˌto]—flat-bottomed boat with square ends.

C As verb.
To travel or convey by **bateau B1.** *?obs*
1759 [see **A** above]. **1773** (1922) Walden *Narrative* 21.86 **MI**, The army went forward to Detroit, and left about sixty men to batoe provisions up from the Great Falls. **1854** in 1905 *Superior Telegram* (WI) 16 Dec 13/2 **wWI**, We batteauxed up the St. Croix River with the goods and traveled on foot the barrens along side, up to the crossing of the river.

batella See **batea**

‡bat-eye n Cf *DS* X20
A bruise near the eye.
1954 *Harder Coll.* **cwTN**, "Git a bat-eye when ye['re] hit with a bat or sumpin." "'E shore went'n giv ye a bat-eye, din't 'e?"

batfish n [From the more-or-less winglike processes]
1 A fish of the family Ogcocephalidae found chiefly in warm South Atlantic waters and the Gulf of Mexico. Also called **sea bat 2**
1873 in 1878 Smithsonian Inst. *Misc. Coll.* 14.2.14, *Malthe vespertilio* . . . Bat-fish; nose-fish. Newfoundland to Florida. **1898** U.S. Natl. Museum *Bulletin* 47.2735, *Ogcocephalidae.* (The Bat-Fishes.) . . . Pectoral fin well developed, its base strongly angled, with long pseudobrachia and 3 actinosts. **1933** LA Dept. of Conserv. *Fishes* 292, The Batfish . . seems much more like a grotesque medieval fancy than an actual fish. **1960** Amer. Fisheries Soc. *List Fishes* 50, Ogcocephalidae—batfishes.

2 =**flying gurnard. Atl coast**
1873 in 1878 Smithsonian Inst. *Misc. Coll.* 14.2.21, *Dactylopterus volitans* . . . Bat-fish . . . Newfoundland to Florida. **1898** U.S. Natl. Museum *Bulletin* 47.2183, *Flying Robin; Bat-fish* . . . Atlantic Ocean, . . very abundant on South Atlantic and Gulf coasts; a handsome and singular fish. **1911** *Century Dict.,* Bat-fish . . . A name of the flying-fish or flying-robin, *Cephalacanthus volitans.*

3 =**bat ray. CA**
1882 U.S. Natl. Museum *Bulletin* 16.51, *M[yliobatis] californicus* . . . *California Sting Ray; Batfish* . . . The wings anteriorly convex . . . San Francisco southward; very common on the Pacific coast. **1896** U.S. Natl. Museum *Bulletin* 47.89, *Batfish* . . . California from Cape Mendocino southward; very common along mud flats. Destructive to oysters.

bath n See **bath flower**

bath v [*W3:* "Brit"] *?*chiefly **Sth, S Midl**
To bathe; to give a bath to (a person or an animal).
1931–33 *LANE Worksheets* **swCT**, Have to bath [bæθ] them young'uns. **1962** Faulkner *Reivers* 185 **MS** (as of 1905), "Walk him back to the barn," he said to me. "Cool him out. Then we'll bath him." **1968** *DARE* FW Addit **MD**21, I have to bath [bæθ] the dog. **1970** Hyatt *Hoodoo* 2508 **csLA**, Bath [not bathe] yoreself wit runnin' watah an'

ammonia fo' nine mawnin's. **1976** Garber *Mountain-ese* 6 **sAppalachians**, I'll be ready to go with you jist as soon as I bath the baby.

bathcloth n **Sth**
A washcloth.
1965–70 *DARE* (Qu. G17, . . *Kinds of towels*) Infs **FL**49, 51, **NC**82, Bathcloth(s); **FL**18, Bathcloth = facecloth. **1970** Tarpley *Blinky* 92 **neTX**, *Cloth used for washing face or bathing* . . . 9% [of infs] bath cloth.

bath flower n Also *bath, bathroot, bathwort* [Alter of *birth:* cf **birthroot**]
A **trillium** (here: either *Trillium erectum* or *T. grandiflorum*).
1847 Wood *Class-Book* 546, *T[rillium] erectum* . . . Bath Flower. [**1891** *Jrl. Amer. Folkl.* 4.149 **NH**, Trillium erectum . . my grandmother would sometimes call it Bä-ä-th Root, as nearly as I can represent it, unquestionably a broad pronunciation for Birth Root.] **1900** Lyons *Plant Names* 378, *T. erectum* . . . Bath-wort, Bath-flower . . . *T. grandiflorum* . . . Bath-flower, White Bath. **1911** *Century Dict. Suppl.,* Bath . . . Same as *bath-flower* . . . *Bath-flower* . . . The birth-root, *Trillium,* especially *T. grandiflorum.* **1940** Clute *Amer. Plant Names* 14, Bath-root. **1949** Moldenke *Amer. Wild Flowers* 338, Bathflower. **1971** Krochmal *Appalachia Med. Plants* 256, Bath flower, bathwort.

bat hide n Also *bat wing* **chiefly SW** *old-fash*
Paper money, esp a dollar bill.
1929 *AmSp* 4.357, Will Rogers, in a recent magazine article used . . the term *bat hides,* meaning money. **1966–68** *DARE* (Qu. U26, . . *Nicknames for a paper dollar*) Infs **CO**33, **OK**42, 51, **TX**3, 35, 51, Bat hide; **TX**1, 4, Bat wing; **GA**44, Bat wing [laughter]. [All Infs old]

bathroomitis See **-itis**

bathroot, bathwort See **bath flower**

batler, batlet See **battle** n[1]

‡bat naked adj Cf *DS* W20
Completely naked.
1966 *DARE* (Qu. W20, . . *No clothes on at all* . . "*They went in swimming _____.*") Inf **SC**3, Bat naked.

bat-nosed ray See **bat ray**

batoe See **bateau**

batoon n Also sp *battoon* Also *bat* [*batoon,* arch var of *baton*] *old-fash*
A short, straight stick; spec, a pool cue.
1806 (1970) Webster *Compendious Dict.,* Batoon . . a club, truncheon, staff. **1899** (1912) Green *VA Folk-Speech,* Battoon . . . A stick; a club. **1970** Thompson *Coll.* **AL** (as of 1920's), Bat . . . a cue stick, in pool, billiards. Batoon is an equivalent.

batra See **battle** v 1

bat ray n Also *bat-nosed ray, bat stingray*
An eagle ray (*Myliobatis californicus*) of the California coast. Also called **batfish 3, California stingray**
1933 John G. Shedd Aquarium *Guide* 25, *Bat-nosed Ray.* This ray is found on the southern California Coast. **1960** Amer. Fisheries Soc. *List Fishes* 9, Bat stingray . . *Myliobatis californicus.* **1970** *DARE* (Qu. P4) Inf **CA**191, Bat ray.

batselboom n |'bɑtsʊlˌbum| [PaGer *bottzelbawm,* Ger *Purzelbaum*]
A somersault.
1968 *DARE* (Qu. EE9a) Inf **PA**162, Batselboom ['bɑtsʊlˌbum]—bottoms up—a translation.

bat stingray See **bat ray**

batt See **bat** n[3]

batteau See **bateau**

batten n, also attrib **scattered, but esp Pacific** See Map See also **bat** n[3], **batting**
A strip of wood, esp one nailed lengthwise over two adjacent boards to cover the crack or space between them.
1891 *Scribner's Mag.* 10.318/1 **NY**, The cracks between the boards are covered with battens. **1950** *WELS* 2 Infs, **WI**, Boards and batten(s). **1965–70** *DARE* (Qu. D27, *Strips of wood used to cover the outside of a frame house*) 34 Infs, **scattered, but esp Pacific,** Batten(s); **CA**4, 19, 210, **IL**3, **KY**8, **OR**1, **PA**74, **VA**94, Board and batten(s); **AZ**15, **CA**41, Batten

board(s); **RI**1, Batten board strips; **NY**23, Batten strips. **1971** *Bright Word Geog. CA & NV* 84, [Map shows the distribution of *batten, board 'n' batten,* and *batten board siding* to be current chiefly in southern California.]. **1981** *DARE* File **CA**, *Battens*— Thin wood strips used to cover joints between plain boards. When battens are used, siding is applied vertically to the walls and the combination is called board and batten, frequently shortened to board and batt. (Often used on barns and rustic farm buildings.)

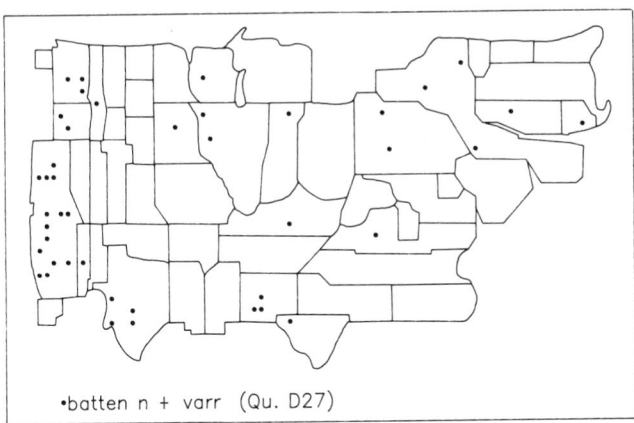

•batten n + varr (Qu. D27)

batten v See **battle** v **1**

batter n[1] [Abbr of **battercake**] **SC**

A pancake.

1966–67 *DARE* (Qu. H20b, *. . Other names . . for pancakes*) Infs **SC**9, 26, 43, Batters; **SC**22, Batters [FW sugg].

batter n[2] [*OED batter* sb.[2], slope of a wall, terrace, or bank from the perpendicular]

See quot c1975.

[**a1828** in **1911** Buchanan *Works* 12.289 **cwPA**, My father, James Buchanan, was a native of the county of Donegal, in the kingdom of Ireland . . . Immediately after his arrival in Philadelphia [in 1783] . . . he became an assistant in the store of Mr. John Tom, at Stony Batter, a country place at the foot of the North Mountain, then in Cumberland now in Franklin county, Pa.] **c1975** *DARE* File **cPA**, *Batter* is used as a generic term, for any street running up a hillside (rather narrow). **1982** *NADS Letters* **cwPA**, The road leading out of Cove Gap about 1/2 mile to [President] Buchanan's birthplace is today posted "Stony Batter," though no town or even buildings presently exist at this site . . . Stony Batter is indeed a steep narrow hillside slope at the foot of a gap between two Allegheny ridges.

‡**batter board** n

A baseboard.

1966 *DARE* (Qu. D37, *The strip of wood . . along the bottom of the wall . . joining to the floor*) Inf **ME**1, Batter board.

batter bread n

1 pronc-sp *baddy-bread:* Cornbread made with eggs and milk. **chiefly VA** See Map Also called **egg bread, spoon bread** See also **battercake 2**

1897 Terhune *Old-Field School* 87 *(DA)*, Batter-bread is a mixture of

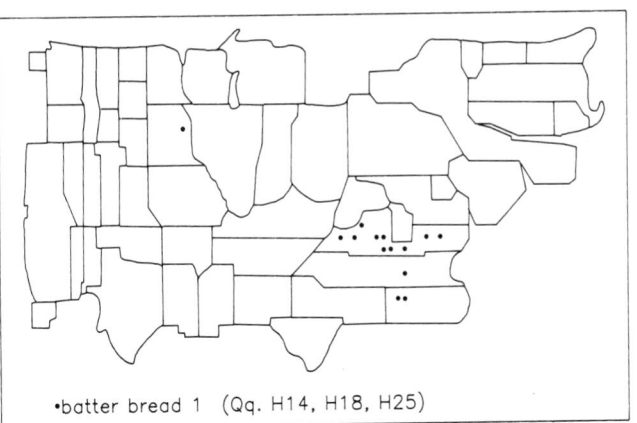

•batter bread 1 (Qq. H14, H18, H25)

Indian meal, milk and eggs, beaten light and baked in a mould. When hot and fresh, it is puffy and delicious. In cooling, it becomes heavy and sticky. **1899** (1912) Green *VA Folk-Speech, Batter-bread . . .* Bread made of corn meal, eggs and milk, and baked in a deep earthenware dish or tin pan. **1906** *DN* 3.125 **nwAR**, *Batter-bread . . .* Soft corn bread containing lard or butter, and served with a spoon. **1916** *Scribner's Mag.* 57.358/2 **VA**, A big plate o' baddy-bread. **c1960** *Wilson Coll.* **csKY**, *Batter bread . . .* Cornbread, with milk and eggs. **1962** Atwood *Vocab. TX* 84, Words from Eastern Virginia include *batter bread . .* and *corn house.* **1965–70** *DARE* (Qu. H14, *Bread that's made with corn-meal*) 11 Infs, **chiefly VA**, Batter bread; (Qu. H18) Inf **IA**17, Batter bread; **NC**10, Batter bread—like spoon bread; (Qu. H25) Inf **SC**34, Batter bread. **1967** *DARE* Tape **SC**46, Batter bread . . made from cornmeal, milk, soda, shortening and eggs, baked in square pan and cut into squares.

2 also *batty-bread:* See quots. Cf **battercake 1**

1906 *DN* 3.125 **nwAR**, *Batter-bread . . .* Thick griddle-cakes made of flour and meal. **1969** *DARE* (Qu. H20b, *. . Other names . . for pancakes*) Inf **KY**5, Batty-breads = cornbread pancakes. **1972** Hilliard *Hog Meat* 55 **VA**, Breakfast was made up of "coffee, small hot wheaten rolls [probably biscuits] batter bread, and hoe-cake."

battercake n

1 also attrib: A pancake. **chiefly Sth, S Midl** See Map See also **batter bread 2**

1840 (1847) Longstreet *GA Scenes* 37, Waffles were handed to Ned, and he took one: batter-cakes were handed, and he took one; and so on. **1899** (1912) Green *VA Folk-Speech, Batter-cake . . .* A thin cake made of corn meal, milk and eggs and baked on a hot iron. **1930** *DN* 6.79 **cSC**, *Batter cakes . . .* The only term for any kind of hot cake, wheat cake or flap jack. **1950** *WELS* 2 Infs, **WI**, Batter cakes. **1960** *PADS* 34.12 **CO**, 1 inf, Batter cake 'pancake.' **c1960** *Wilson Coll.* **csKY**. **1965–70** *DARE* (Qu. H20b, *. . Other names . . for pancakes*) 72 Infs, **chiefly Sth, S Midl**, Battercakes; (Qu. F3, *When you're frying things—for example, eggs—you turn them over with a _____*) Infs **AL**43, **LA**2, 9, 11, **SC**46, **TN**57, Battercake turner.

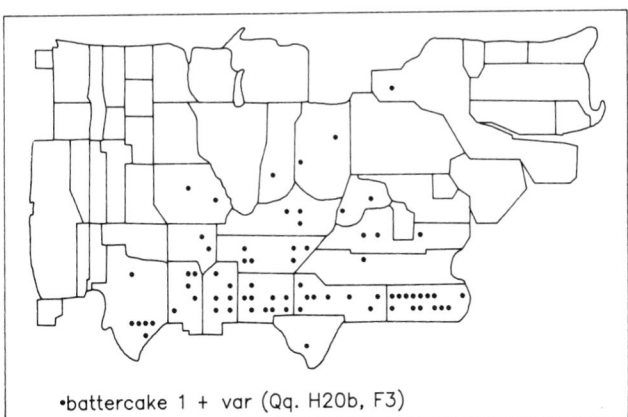

•battercake 1 + var (Qq. H20b, F3)

2 Fried cornmeal. See also **batter bread 1**

1833 in **1918** *MD Hist. Mag.* 13.319, Hot muffins and corn batter cakes. **1966–70** *DARE* (Qu. H25) Infs **GA**79, **NC**55, **TN**24, **VA**104, 69, Battercakes; **KY**63, Battercakes . . can be made from cornmeal; **MS**54, Hush puppies, battercakes; (Qu. H14) Inf **KY**79, Battercakes— cornbread mixture fried in a little grease; **VA**23, Battercakes = corn-cakes; (Qu. H18) Inf **GA**1, Battercakes—fried batter.

batterfang v [*OED* "*obs.* or *dial.*"] *obs*

To assail violently.

1836 (1955) *Crockett Almanacks* 49 **wTN**, What should he see but his landlady with a big knotted club in her hand batterfanging a dozen rattle snakes.

battern n [Alter of *OED* **batten** sb.[2], movable arm on a silk-loom]

1917 *DN* 4.408 **wNC**, *Battern . . .* In weaving, the arm that knocks in the thread.

battery n

1 A deep coffin-shaped boat which allows hunters to shoot fowl from below the level of the water; also, a device attached to such a boat. **chiefly Delmarva** Also called **coffin-boat, sink**

1842 Hawes *Sporting Scenes* 1.198 **seNY,** A machine, or battery, is a wooden box of the necessary dimensions to let a man lie down upon his back, just tightly fitting enough to let him rise again. **1872** Schele de Vere *Americanisms* 334 **Chesapeake Bay,** A *battery* is . . not unlike a coffin in shape . . . Its peculiar build enables the hunter to float gently down upon his unsuspecting game, lying below the surface of the water, while the heavy calibre of his gun, and the fact that he fires it from a kind of miniature embrasure, have . . led to the use of the word *battery.* **1897** *Outing* Sept 544/1 *(DAE),* A stick . . to which pieces of flat cedar are fixed . . effectively hides his movements from any ducks in front of the boat. This in the local parlance is called a 'battery.' **1969–70** *DARE* Tape **VA55,** He had a battery, three barrels welded in one, and one hammer fired all three barrels, and he had that mounted on a sneak boat; **NC76,** A lay-down battery just helt one man, an' it consisted of a thing 'bout the size of a coffin, 'bout the same depth, an' it would stick up 'bout 3 to 4 inches above the water . . . A set-up battery . . would hold 2 to 3 men.

2 The smallest pan of the set used in sugar boiling. [Fr *batterie* large kettle in which sugar is made]

1833 Silliman *Man. Sugar Cane* 33 *(DA),* The names appropriated to the different kettles are as follows: the largest is called the *grande,* . . . and the last the *battery.* **1888** Cable *Bonaventure* 14 **LA,** She was as sweet as the last dip of cane-juice from the boiling battery. **1941** FWP *Guide UT* 353, Sliced [sugar] beets are dumped into diffusion tanks or "batteries" where hot water is added.

3 See **floating battery.**

batting n [**bat** n[3] or **bat** v[3]; perh sometimes a hypercorrection for **batten:** cf **-ing**]
=**batten** n.

1950 *WELS (Strips of wood used to cover the outside of a frame house)* 1 Inf, **seWI,** Batting. **1965–70** *DARE* (Qu. D27) Infs **CA**21, 144, 194, **MO**21, **MA**40, **OR**5, **WA**18, Batting(s); **AZ**8, Batting ['bætɪŋ]; **IN**58, ['bætɪn, bætənz]; **LA**11, Batting—used on cabins to cover cracks, thin strips; **OK**18, Batting—covers cracks between foot-wide strips running up and down; **CA**139, Board and batting ['bætɪn] — batting is the strip of wood between the boards; **NC**48, Board and batting.

batting stick See **battling stick**

battle v

1 also *batra, batten:* To clean soiled clothes by beating them with a paddle (or **battle** n[1]) after removing them from boiling water. [*OED* battle v[4], 1570 "*obs.*"; see also *EDD*] **chiefly Sth, S Midl** See also **battling block, battling stick**

1883 Harris *Nights with Remus* 2 **GA,** En Brer Rabbit, he say, sezee, dat she battlin' cloze. **1895** *DN* 1.370 **seKY, eTN, wNC,** Battle: to beat. **1903** *DN* 2.306 **seMO.** **1908** *DN* 3.289 **eAL, wGA,** Battle . . . Almost obsolete. "We don't battle clothes these days." **1917** *DN* 4.408 **wNC.** **1950** *PADS* 14.13 **seSC,** Batra ['bætrə] . . . To beat clothes on a wooden block in washing them. *Ibid* **SC,** Battle . . To beat, as clothes, with a *battling stick. Ibid* **cSC,** Batten . . . Same as *batra.* **1956** *Hall Coll.* **eTN,** We'd battle the clothes with the battlin' stick. **1966** *DARE* Tape **AL**1, We battled our clothes . . . [We] had a great big old stump . . . and . . . overalls and shirts and things that be real dirty, we'd put 'em up on this thing and take a stick and we'd whup 'em, [slapping on table] whup the dirt out of 'em.

2 Transf, and with *out:*
a To wash thoroughly.

1949 Hornsby *Lonesome Valley* 162 **VA, NC Mts** *(Hench Coll.),* [He] dipped out some water and handed the pan to Fred. "Better battle out your face and eyes," he said.

b See quot.

1981 *Broaddus Coll.* **ceKY,** Battle it out — to beat the grain off the stalks of wheat.

battle n[1] Also *batler, batlet, battler* [**battle** v **1**] **S Midl**
=**battling stick.**

1915 *DN* 4.180 **swVA,** Battle . . . A beetle (for battling clothes). "The washwoman broke the battle handle." **1924** Raine *Land of Saddle-Bags* 11 **sAppalachians,** Upon it [=the battling bench] lies the batler or batlet. **1933** *AmSp* 8.2.29 **KY,** He had no call to pelt my piedy heifer with the battler.

battle n[2] [Calque from Fr *bataille* battle, a card game] **sLA, TX**
The children's card game more commonly known as *war.*

1967 *DARE* Tape **TX**28, In battle, you played it with cards. **1968**

DARE (Qu. DD35) Inf **LA**37, Battle or bataille; **LA**45, Fish, knucks, battle — children's card games. **1982** *Contract Bridge Letters* **cTX,** As children in central Texas in the 1940's my sister and I used to play a card game called Battle. *Ibid* **LA,** *Battle.* To determine who is to win the "Battle," the players who played the "high cards" must go to "War." *Ibid* **ceTX,** We played "Battle" from about 1938–3 through 1943 (most of us were 8 – 12 years old): Two players each with one deck of 52 cards. Each player simultaneously turns the top card face up. The player who turns over the higher denomination wins both cards. *Ibid* **cs,seLA,** [Two additional letters identify the card game of battle].

battle-hammed adj *chiefly among Black speakers; relic*
Having thick or deformed hips.

1727 *N. Engl. Wkly Journal* 11 Sept *(DA),* Ran-away from his Master . . . a young Negro Man-Servant, . . speaks pretty good English, has thick Lips, battle-ham'd, and goes something waddling. **1942** Hurston *Dust Tracks* 143 **FL,** It is an everyday affair to hear somebody called a mullet-headed, mule-eared, wall-eyed, . . butt-sprung, battle-hammed, knock-kneed, . . unmated so-and-so! **1942** Hurston in *Amer. Mercury* 55.94 **NYC** [Glossary of Harlem slang], Battle-hammed — badly formed about the hips. **1968** *DARE* (Qu. X38) Inf **NC**49, Battle-hammed [hæmdɪd] — knocks ankles.

battler See **battle** n **1**

battleship n *chiefly Nth, N Midl* See Map Note: the trademark *Battleship,* for a board game, was registered in 1968.
A game in which players try to discover the position of ships on grids drawn by the other players.

1950 *WELS (Games played on paper . . by two people)* 2 Infs, **WI,** Battleship; 1 Inf, **WI,** Battleship — sometimes called Trafalgar. **1965–70** *DARE* (Qu. EE39) 33 Infs, **chiefly Nth, N Midl,** Battleship; **CO**14, Battleship — on graph paper; battleship took 4 spaces, cruiser took 3, destroyers took 2. Called letter and number; took turns; all [spaces covered by the ship had to be] hit to be sunk [diagram in text]; **NY**81, Battleship — sea battle game played on a graph; **PA**126, Battleship — new game. **1982** *DARE* File **seWI** (as of c1960), We played *battleship* with grid squares drawn on a piece of paper. Each square was numbered and you had to find where your opponent had hidden his ships.

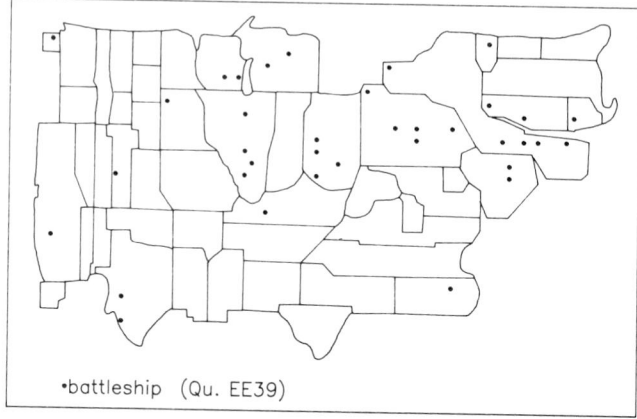

•battleship (Qu. EE39)

battle stick See **battling stick**

battleweed n
=**bugbane** 1 (here: *Cimicifuga racemosa*).

1971 Krochmal *Appalachia Med. Plants* 96, *Cimicifuga racemosa . . . Common Names:* Cohosh bugbane, battle weed [etc].

battling block n Also *battling bench, ~ board* [**battle** v **1**] **chiefly S Midl** *old-fash*
A bench-like wooden stand with a flat surface on which clothes are beaten in washing.

1845 Hooper *Advent. Simon Suggs* 183 **AL,** John Green's sister . . goes to her battlin bench. **1887** *Harper's Mag.* July 272/1 **LA,** The splay-legged battling-boards fastened themselves firmer and firmer into the earth under the blows of the bats. **1913** Kephart *Highlanders* 246 **sAppalachians,** Alongside . . is the "battlin' block" on which the family wash is hammered with a beetle ("battlin' stick") if the woman has no washboard. **1917** *DN* 4.408 **wNC,** Battlin' block. **1924** Raine *Land of Saddle-Bags* 10 **sAppalachians,** At the edge of the branch . . is the big iron wash kettle and the "battling" bench for the family.

battling stick n Also *batting stick, battle ~* [battle v 1] **Sth, S Midl** *old-fash* Also called **battle** n¹, **washing paddle**

A paddle-shaped piece of wood used to beat dirt out of soiled clothes after removing them from boiling water.

1851 Hooper *Widow Rugby's Husband* 96 **AL**, What a devil of a paddlin' the old woman gin him with the battlin'-stick. **1895** *DN* 1.370 **seKY, eTN, wNC**, *Battling-stick.* **1902** Harben *Abner Daniel* 192 **eTN**, A negro woman at the wash-place . . was using a batting-stick on some clothing. **1903** *DN* 2.306 **seMO**, Instead of using a washboard the clothes are laid on an inclined smooth board and beaten with the battling-stick. **1908** *DN* 3.289 **eAL, wGA**. **1917** *DN* 4.408 **wNC**. **1952** Brown *NC Folkl.* 1.518, *Battling-stick.* **c1960** *Wilson Coll.* **csKY**, *Battling-stick* . . . Now exceedingly rare, so much so that only the elder people know the word and cannot recall having seen the actual object. **1966** *DARE* (Qu. F5) Inf **GA8**, Battling stick. **1966** *DARE* Tape **AL1**, Mama . . had a battlin' stick. **1975** McDonough *Garden Sass* 92 **AR**, While it was cooking it was stirred with the battlin' stick. [Footnote:] This was the long paddle to beat the clothes clean on washday. **1981** *Broaddus Coll.* **ceKY**, Battle stick.

batto(e) See **bateau** A, C

battoon See **batoon**

bat tree n
=southern magnolia.
1897 Sudworth *Arborescent Flora* 193 **TN**, Bat Tree.

batture n, also attrib |ba'tʊr, 'bæčɚ, 'bæčə| [Fr "waterside bank"] **lower Missip Valley, esp sLA**

Orig a sandbar or gravel deposit thrown up by the current on the inner turn of a river bend; now more generally the land between the levee and a river.

[**1784** (1968) Hutchins *Hist. Narr. LA & W. FL* 66, Behind it, there is a large bay called L'ance de la Grand [sic] Bature, 8 miles East of Pascagoula bluff.] **1823** (1878) Aime *Plantation Diary* 8 **sLA**, Ice was thick enough on the "batture" to bear the weight of a person. **1842** *Ibid*, Dug a pond on batture pasture. One hundred and twenty feet long, twenty feet wide, and eight feet deep. **1914** *DN* 4.162 *Batture* . . . Along the Mississippi River, the space between the levee and the water. **1941** *FWP Guide LA* 411 **sLA**, The houseboats and makeshift shacks of the batture dwellers (squatters who live between the levee and the river and eke out an existence by fishing and selling firewood made from driftwood) stand against the river banks. **1955** Grau *Black Prince* 257 **LA**, The river is high. The trees that grow out on the *batture*—on the land between the river's usual bed and the levee, on the land that all summer and fall has been dry and fertile—are half-covered with water. **1967** LeCompte *Word Atlas* 222 **seLA**, *Batture* . . . All informants in Lafourche pronounced this response as /ba'tür/, but in the New Orleans area, this word has come into English as /bæčə/. **1968** *DARE* FW Addit **LA23**, Batture ['bæčɚ]—land between levee and river.

batty See **bateau** A

batty-bread See **batter bread** 2

bat wing n
1 See **bat hide**.
2 also *batwing chaps*: Exceptionally wide, usu snap-on, **chaps**; hence adj *batwing-chapped*. **West**
1935 Sandoz *Jules* 409 **wNE** (as of 1880–1930), The corral was lined with young people watching the wild horses push into a far corner, away from the batwing-chapped boys in gaudy shirts. **1955** Harris *Look of Old West* 209, Those with a big, flaring wing are called bat-wing chaps. And you could, if you wished, have wings on closed-leg chaps as well. **1961** Adams *Old-Time Cowhand* 82 **West**, The most pop'lar chaps were the heavy, bullhide bat wings. They have wide flappin' legs that're fastened with snaps. **1981** *KS Qrly.* 13.2.64 **nNV**, Batwings were popular . . in the 1920s and replaced the older style "shotgun" and Angora "hair chaps"; they were popularized by movie cowboys . . and today are confined in use largely to rodeos, parades, and special events.
3 See quot.
1950 *PADS* 14.49 **SC**, A . . half-pint flask, especially of bootleg liquor, is called a *bat wing*.

baubee See **bawbee**

bauch n [PaGer]
The belly, stomach.

1939 Aurand *Quaint Idioms* 11 **sePA**, It hurts me so much in the *bauch* . . . maybe I ate too many green apples.

bauchgot n |'baˌgat, 'baˌkat| [PaGer, Ger *bauchgurt*] **sePA**
A bellyband.
1967–68 *DARE* (Qu. L53a, b, *The band that goes under a horse's middle to hold a saddle on*) Inf **PA158**, Bauchgot ['baˌgat]; **PA63**, Bauchgot ['baˌkat].

baum v
1903 *DN* 2.295 **Cape Cod MA** (as of c1850), *Baum (=balm?)* . . . To rub the nose over, particularly of a calf.

baw See **bawl** v¹ 2

bawbee n Also sp *baubee, bobee* [Scots *bawbee* halfpenny]
A trifle; anything of little value.
1866 Smith *Bill Arp* 115 **GA**, I don't care a bobee about his being free, if I can subjugate him. **1906** *DN* 3.126 **nwAR**, *Baubee* . . . A trifle. "It isn't worth a baubee." **1908** *DN* 3.289 **eAL, wGA**, "I don't care a baubee for that." **1953** Randolph *Down in Holler* 225 **Ozarks**, Of a young ruffian it was said, "He'd kill you for a *bawbee*, an' eat you for two." **1955** Adams *Grandfather* 246 **NY**, Either way I don't see as it puts an extra bawbee into my chicken account.

bawdacious See **bodacious**

bawl v¹
1 also with *out*: Of a hunting dog: to bay. [*OED bawl* v. 1, to bark or howl as a dog] See also **babble, bawling-hound**
1926 Hunnicutt *Twenty Years* 47 (Hall Coll.) **eTN, wNC**, Old Muse had gone on ahead and by the time we got in hearing of Little Cove, I heard Old Muse "bawl out" very shrilly. **1968** *DARE* Tape **IN36**, He's barking and a-bawling.
2 pronc-sp *baw*: Usu of cows: to utter loud noises, usu of distress. Hence n *bawl*, vbl n *bawling*. **widespread but chiefly Midl, West** See Map and Map Section Cf **bellow** See also **bawley**
1903 *DN* 2.306 **seMO**, *Bawl* . . . Bellow (of cattle), to low. **1906** *DN* 3.126 **nwAR**. **1922** Rollins *Cowboy* 287 **West**, The average pitching bronco emitted grunts and snorts, and usually loud "bawls" of rage. **1939** *Hall Coll.* **eTN**, And that bear [after being stabbed with a knife] sunk down and bawled . . like a calf. **1949** Kurath *Word Geog.* 30, Cows whose calves are being weaned are said to *bawl* . . . This expression is current throughout the Midland, including West Jersey, except only the Pennsylvania German settlements of Eastern Pennsylvania. It occurs sporadically in New York state, but nowhere else. **1951** *AmSp* 26.253 **Upstate NY**. **c1960** *Wilson Coll.* **csKY**. **1962** Atwood *Vocab. TX* 55, *Bawl* . . is also scattered through the state, with the exception of East Texas, where there is but one occurrence. **1965–70** *DARE* (Qu. K19, *Noise made by a calf that's taken away from its mother*) 475 Infs, **widespread but chiefly Midl, West**, Bawl; 34 Infs, **chiefly Midl**, Bawling; **TX10**, Baw [bɔ:]; **OK33**, A-bawlin'; (Qu. K21, *The noise a cow makes, calling for her calf*) 310 Infs, **chiefly Midl**, Bawl; 24 Infs, **chiefly Midl**, Bawling; **OK33**, A-bawlin'; **WA5**, Bawing; (Qu. K66, *The noise made by a sheep*) Infs **MO8, VA27**, Bawl; (Qu. K40) Inf **MS58**, Bawl; (Qu. K83) Inf **MN31**, Bawl at them like a cow; (Qu. X45) Inf **OK18**, Sounds like a bull a-bawlin'. **1967** *DARE* (QR, near Qu. K13) Inf **CA10**, If you cut them [=the horns of a cow] off by the dark of the moon, she won't bawl, she will in the light of the moon. **1973** Allen *LAUM* 1.251, For the noise

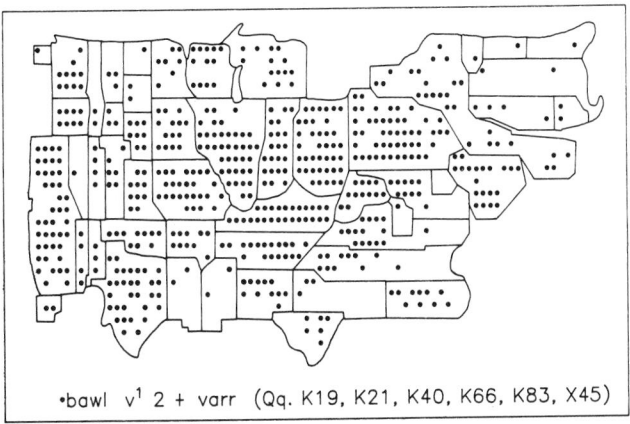

•bawl v¹ 2 + varr (Qq. K19, K21, K40, K66, K83, X45)

made by a hungry calf during the weaning period the most common U[pper] M[idwest] word is *bawl* . . . Although in the East this term is sharply Midland, it has spread widely in the UM.

bawl n[1] See **bawl** v[1] 2

bawl n[2], v[2] See **boil** n[1], v

bawlbaby n [*bawl* cry as does a child]
A crybaby; a tattletale.
    1937 Sandoz *Slogum* 63 **NE**, "Poor child," she whispered . . . "Poor, poor child." "Oh—poor fiddlesticks—" Gulla snorted, shaking the boy to consciousness. "Make a bawl baby out of him! Anybody can get a hand cut." **1938** Farrell *No Star* 237 **Chicago IL**, Bill might laugh at him, and he would be showing himself off like a bawl baby. He sniffled. He didn't know what it was that made him cry and feel like this. **1965** *DARE* (Qu. Y9, . . *"His brother is an awful _____."*) Inf **OK**1, Bawl-baby—he just wants to go along. **1973** Allen *LAUM* 1.398 *(Children's nickname for one who "tattles")* 1 inf, **cwMN**, Bawl baby.

bawley n Also *bawly* [**bawl** v[1] 2]
    1954 *Harder Coll.* **cwTN**, Bawly [bɔːlɪ] . . . Name given to a calf that has been taken away to be weaned. *Ibid*, Bawley . . . usual name for a male calf. Call to calf: "Sook bawley," if it's a boy calf.

bawling-hound n [**bawl** v[1] 1]
A hunting dog: see quot 1929.
    1929 *AmSp* 5.16 **Ozarks**, Bawlin'-hound . . . A dog which bays when trailing coons, possums or foxes. A "ginooine red-bone bawlin'-hound" is a big red dog with drooping ears, very highly prized by the mountain hunters. **1954** *Harder Coll.* **cwTN**, Bawlin' hound . . . baying dog.

bawly See **bawley**

‡**bawly-ike** n [Prob *bawly* prone to bawl or complain + **Ike** n[1] impudent person]
A complaining person; a nuisance.
    1935 Davis *Honey* 309 **OR**, Of course that could only be the horse-trader. The helpless old bawly-ike had reached her at last.

baw-pa See **bapa**

bawsie See **baldy** n[1]

bax See **bakkes**

baxy See **backsie**

bay n[1] [*bay* inlet of the sea or other body of water]
    1 Std sense, in phrr *over the bay, half the bay over*: Somewhat intoxicated. **chiefly NEast**
    1833 Greene *Life Dr. Dodimus* 2.176 **NEng**, He was seldom downright drunk; but was often . . a little over the bay. **1844** Stephens *High Life in NY* 1.167 (Taylor–Whiting *Dict. Amer. Proverbs*), Some on 'em were pretty well over the bay. **1864** *Harper's Mag.* 29.679 **NH**, On one occasion, when about two-thirds "over the bay," he reeled into the tavern stable. **1896** *DN* 1.398 **seMN, NYC**, *Ibid* 418 **seNY**, Half the bay over. **1916** *DN* 4.335 **eMA**. **1968–69** *DARE* (Qu. DD14) Inf **CT**16, Half seas over, over the bay; **VT**7, Over the bay; (Qu. KK30) Inf **RI**15, Three sheets in the wind—for drinking—or over the bay. **1975** Gould *ME Lingo* 8, *Over the bay* means one has had more than enough to drink and is temporarily out of *contact*.
    2 A part of the prairie extending into a forest.
    1820 Gilleland *Ohio & Miss. Pilot* 205 *(DA)*, Several long lines of prairie, which are called *Bays*, extend from the main Opelousas prairie. **1849** (1850) Colton *3 Yrs.* 370 **cCA**, Still, in some of its bays [=of the San Joaquin Valley], the evidences of fertility exist. **1905** *DN* 3.3 **cCT**, *Bay* . . . A piece of land surrounded by woods. **1907** *DN* 3.209 **neAR**.
    3 See quot 1934. **SC, NC** See also **pocosin, savanna**
    1934 *Sun* (Baltimore MD) 16 Feb 10/6 *(Hench Coll.)*, The latest of these discoveries . . . presents the hypothesis that an enormous comet . . once struck the earth in the region . . . For in the Carolinas there are 3,000 shallow pits, unique features of the landscape which the Carolinians call . . "bays." Each is surrounded by a circular wall. Some of the pits are several miles long and more than a mile wide. **1950** *PADS* 14.13 **SC**, *Bay* . . . A low place or depression, whether containing water or not, and usually covered with undergrowth or thicket. **1967** *DARE* FW Addit **SC**19, Bay—a small swamp of cold water confined to an area, also [called] *savannah*.

bay n[2] [*bay* compartment within a building] **chiefly NEng** For map see 1939 *LANE* Map 103

A compartment in a barn, usu extending from floor to ceiling and used for storing hay.
    1693 in 1880 Groton MA *Early Rec.* 107, Euery barn with one baye [shall be taxed] at one peney in the single. **1844** *Knickerbocker* 23.440 **NY**, There goes Jim from the highest scaffold into the straw at the bottom of the 'deep bay.' **1903** *DN* 2.295 **Cape Cod MA** (as of 1850s), *Bay* . . . recess in a barn. **1914** *DN* 4.153 **NH**. **1917** *DN* 4.387 **neOH**, *Bay* . . . Compartment in a barn for hay or unthresht grain . . . this compartment is not under the scaffold, but at one side of it. The typical barn had a barn floor in the center, one or two scaffolds above, and a bay on each side of the barn floor, one at each end of the barn. **1931–33** *LANE Worksheets* **cwMA**, Bay . . . The whole upper part of a barn. **1949** Kurath *Word Geog.* 54, Many New England barns have compartments for storing hay that run from the barn floor to the roof. These are known as *bays* throughout the New England settlement area except for Cape Cod, Narragansett Bay, and the Maine Coast. **1950** *WELS (Place where grain is kept in a barn)* 1 Inf, **cWI**, Bay. **1965–70** *DARE* (Qu. M3, *The place inside a barn for storing hay*) 9 Infs, **NEng, NY**, Bay; **MI**116, **NY**109, **OH**6, **TN**19, Hay bay; (Qu. M5, . . *The hole for throwing hay down below*) Inf **VT**16, Bay; (Qu. M12) Inf **MA**74, Bays of hay. **1966–67** *DARE* Tape **NH**5, Filled the bay right up full [with hay]; **MA**5, Take a whole forkful off and throw it over into the bay at one time. **1973** Allen *LAUM* 1.184 *(Place for hay in the barn)* 8 infs, **chiefly IA**, (Hay) bay. [Commentary:] *Hay bay:* Extends from ground floor to roof: a mow covers only the second floor.

bay n[3]
    1 A low marshy area where bay trees are abundant. **chiefly S Atl** [Prob abbr for **baygall** or **bayhead**; prob also infl by **bay** n[1]]
    1795 (1821) Asbury *Jrl.* 2.239 **SC**, This country abounds with bays, swamps, and drains. **1802** Drayton *View of SC* 7, [Footnote:] They are called *bays*, from the quantities of *bay trees* which grow therein. And which are so tall and closely connected with each other, as to throw a continual shade over the lands below. **1855** Simms *Forayers* 354 **SC** (as of 1780s), The bay was the abiding place only of the reptile and the wild cat. **1969** *DARE* (Qu. C7, . . *Land that usually has some standing water with trees or bushes growing in it*) Inf **NC**67, Bay—where water stands. **1971** Detro *Generic Terms* 188 **LA**, [In 1816] Darby . . encountered the term "bay" applied to "dilatations" of full sluggish streams in the Atchafalaya Basin . . . [Recent] Field interviews with residents . . confirmed that this connotation persisted and that the term "bay" also signified small impounded lakes surrounded by swamp as well as small wetland areas in which bay trees and thickets occurred.
    2 A thicket in a swamp—used esp of cypress stands or water-grass meadows in Okefenokee Swamp. **S Atl, esp seGA, neFL**
    1884 *Harper's Mag.* 68.601/1, Swamp and "bay" (the word applied in Florida to slough and water-grass meadows) amplify the area. **1918** *DN* 5.18 **NC**, *Bay*. A small thicket. **1926** *AmSp* 1.407 **seGA**, Okefinokee Swamp . . . consists largely of so called 'prairies' . . and dense 'bays' of cypress timber growing in water. **1937** Heyward *Madagascar* 121 **SC**, Back of the field lay an impenetrable jungle, generally known as a bay, through which it was practically impossible for one to make his way. **1938** Matschat *Suwannee R.* 79 **nFL, sGA**, Beyond the fence was the prairie, flanked on both sides by dense bays of stately cypresses. **1968** *DARE* Tape **GA**51, Thick places in the swamp, now, we call that a bay. Lower ground than hammock. A bay is the thick jungle. **1972** *DARE* File **nwFL**, Cypress head: A bay is about the same.

‡**bay** v [Perh back-form of **bait** v 3 understood as past tense]
To entice or lure.
    1970 Green *Ely* 101 **eTN**, Grandpa had call him a hog rustler. He had found this sow and six pigs. He had bayed the sow by feeding her corn.

bayao n Also sp *bayaw* [Tagalog and related Philippine languages] **HI**
    1 See quot.
    1972 Carr *Da Kine Talk* 103 **HI**, Bayao or bayaw 'brother-in-law' . . or 'sister-in-law.'
    2 also attrib: A Filipino. [Because commonly used in sense **1** among Filipinos] *joc, but sometimes taken as derog*
    1954–60 Hance *Hawaiian Sugar*, Bayao . . . Synonymous with "Filipino." A widely used word but resented by the intelligent Filipinos. **1972** Carr *Da Kine Talk* 103 **HI**, Bayaw . . has long been taken as a humorous nickname for the Filipinos in Hawaii. The term *bayaw style* . . refers to their supposed habit of segregating at gatherings, with the men on one side of the room and the women on the other. It is applied in jest to any situation where people tend to divide in this way.

bay bed n [bay n²]

1981 *Broaddus Coll.* **ceKY** (as of 1958), Bay bed—a one post bed built into a corner of a room, using the two walls as supports.

bayberry n

1 =**wax myrtle.**

1690 in 1913 *Colonial Soc. MA Pub.* 14.152 **RI,** One thing I would annexe of a rare sort of Candle found out last y. 1689 wch is made of a gumous matter gatherd by boiling of ye berries of a little bush or shrub wch they here call bay berries but I take it to be a sort of myrtle but ye leaves are deciduous in sharp winters. **1709** (1967) Lawson *New Voyage* 97 **NC, SC,** The Bay-Berries yield a Wax, which besides its Use in Chirurgery, makes Candles that, in burning, give a fragrant Smell. **1792** Belknap *Hist. NH* 3.123, The *bayberry* . . the leaves of which yield an agreeable perfume, and the fruit a delicate green wax, which is made into candles. **1868** (1870) Gray *Field Botany* 306, *Myrica, Bayberry, Sweet Gale.* **1966–69** *DARE* (Qu. I44) Infs **CT**6, 11, **DE**1, **GA**17, **MA**72, **RI**12, Bayberries; (Qu. S26e) Infs **CT**37, **NC**37, Bayberries. **1971** Craighead *Trees S. FL* 199, Bayberries, *Myrica* spp.

2 =**coffeeberry 2a(1).**

1897 Sudworth *Arborescent Flora* 299, *Rhamnus purshiana* . . . Common Names . . . Bayberry (Oreg., Cal.).

baybush n [From the resemblance of the leaves to those of the European bay tree]

A **sweet gale** (here: *Myrica gale*).

1688 in 1887 Huntington NY *Town Rec.* 1.517, Ye east bounds is a hamake of bay bushes and a rocke. **1845** (1968) Simms *Wigwam & Cabin* (1st ser) 26 **SC** (as of late 1790s), He heard something like a sudden breeze that rustled through the bay bushes at his feet. **1913** Eaton *Barn Doors* 170 *(DA),* The shores of the ponds are broken by small promontories crowned with oak, bay bushes and huckleberries. **1969** *DARE* (Qu. T5) Inf **NC**76, Baybush.

bay chicken n Cf **dry-land fish**

An edible mushroom: perh an oyster mushroom.

1967 *DARE* (Qu. I37) Inf **LA**3, Bay chicken—in umbrella shape but grows on wood, not on the ground.

bayeta n Also sp *bayjeta, vayeta* [Span *bayeta* baize] **SW**

See quot 1977.

1852 in 1893 U.S. Census Office *Moqui Pueblo Indians* 25 **AZ,** This evening we bought enough corn for the mules at $5 per faneja (2.5 bushels), paying in bayjeta, or red cloth. **1902** *Everybody's Mag.* 6.33/2 **NM,** The loom-sticks he either borrowed or copied from the Pueblos, and then, by ravelling a very hard-twist Spanish cloth, known as "vayeta," he rewove it and made the "Serape Navaho" of the old traders and explorers. **1912** *Out West Mag.* 35.114/1 **SW,** The most highly prized of Navajo blankets are known as bayeta blankets. **1951** Fergusson *New Mexico* 405, *Bayeta* . . . a kind of baize. **1977** Watts *Dict. Old West, Bayeta* . . . A wool-fiber yarn, extremely hard-wearing, apparently spun by the Pueblo Indians; also, the cloth made from it. The word could also be applied to the material from which the Navaho made blankets, some of which were known as *bayeta blankets.*

bay fly n Cf **Green Bay fly**

=**mayfly.**

1834 (1898) Kemper *Jrl.* 418 **Green Bay WI,** Lieut. Clary thinks that the bay flies wh[ich] are yet very numerous arise from what I consider their carcasses, not those from which they creep, but their own dead bodies. **1950** *WELS* 5 Infs, **WI,** Bay fly. **1967–70** *DARE* (Qu. R4) Infs **NJ**21, **NY**6, **SC**69, **WI**50, 58, Bay fly.

baygall n Also sp *baygoll* [*bay* (tree) + **gall**] **Gulf States** See also **bay n³, bayhead**

An area of low-lying boggy land, overgrown with the sweet bay or other trees.

1773 in 1953 McMullen *Topog. Terms FL* 70/2, Crossed a cypress bay gall [sic] issuing out of . . ponds. **1775** (1962) Romans *Nat. Hist. FL* 31, The bay galls are properly water courses, covered with spungy earth mixed with a kind of matted vegetable fibres . . . their natural produce is a stately tree called loblolly bay, and many different vines, briars, thorny withs, and on their edges a species of red or summer cane. **1829** U.S. Congress *Serial Set* 187 Doc 147.10 **FL,** In the upper parts of Santa Fé, numerous bay-golls, ponds, and extensive palmetto flats, are met with in every direction. **1851** Burke *Polly Peablossom* 18 **GA,** Old Snip *seed* something white over in the bay-gall, and shy'd *clean* out o' the road. **1941** O'Donnell *Great Big Doorstep* 78 **LA,** There were no more

smell-melons by our bay-gall. **1966** *DARE* Tape **FL**16, The cows . . would have their calves down in the baygall. **1967–68** *DARE* (Qu. C7) Inf **TX**9, Baygall—smaller [than a swamp]; (Qu. C28, *A place where underbrush, weeds, vines and small trees grow together so that it's nearly impossible to get through)* Inf **TX**37, Baygall.

baygall bush n

A **gallberry** (here: *Ilex coriacea*).

1960 Vines *Trees SW* 652, *Ilex coriacea* . . . Vernacular names are Shining Inkberry, Large Gallberry, Baygall-bush. **1979** Little *Checklist U.S. Trees* 148, *Large gallberry* . . . Other common names—sweet gallberry, bay-gallbush.

baygalls n [Perh from **baygall**]

=**red bay 1.**

1861 Wood *Class-Book* 620, Red Bay. Bay Galls . . . P[ersea] Caroliniensis . . . Wood of a fine rose-color, once used in cabinet-work. **1897** Sudworth *Arborescent Flora* 201, Red Bay . . . Common Names . . . Bay Galls (Tenn.). **1940** Clute *Amer. Plant Names* 118.

bayhead n **FL**

=**baygall.**

1773 in 1953 McMullen *Topog. Terms FL,* Passed 2 ponds a bay gall or head, running in a big swp. **1938** Rawlings *Yearling* 99 **nFL,** Jody laughed out. The picture of his mother's great frame pushing through the bay-heads made him shout in spite of himself. **1966** *DARE* (Qq. C6, 7) Inf **FL**15, Cypress swamp, bayhead; (Qu. C9) Inf **FL**34, A bayhead—with sawgrass; (Qu. T1) Inf **FL**27, Bayhead—in swampy land. **1966** *DARE* FW Addit **sFL,** Bayheads—slightly elevated clumps of trees in [the] Everglades. **1975** Newell *If Nothin' Don't Happen* 9 **nwFL,** A bay head is a low, swampy place with bay trees a-growin' real thick. There ain't no worse place to try to go through.

bayjeta See **bayeta**

bayle See **baile**

bay lynx n **NEast**

The bobcat.

1784 Pennant *Arctic Zool.* 1.51, *Bay Lynx* . . . This species is found in the internal parts of the province of *New York.* **1838** MA Zool. & Bot. Surv. *Repts. Zool.* 27, *Felis rufa.* Bay Lynx. Wild Cat . . . Three times the size of the domestic cat . . . Stands high on its legs, has a short tail curved upwards. **1890** *Century Dict., Lynx* . . . The common wildcat of North America is the bay lynx, . . which runs into several varieties. **1928** Anthony *N. Amer. Mammals* 166. **1969** *DARE* (Qu. P31) Inf **VT**12, Bay lynx.

bay mule See **bay steer**

bayo n [Span]

1 also *bayo bean:* See quots. **chiefly CA**

1855 *NY Herald* (NY) 12 Dec 2/4, Beans.—Sales of 175 sacks California bayos at 6½c., and 20 do. do. red at 4½c. per lb. **1875** in 1877 Phillips *Letters CA* 92, Then, and finally, came a sort of purple-colored bean, called "bayo," and the desert [sic], in the shape of a pie. **1947** *AmSp* 22.90, Considering the poor repute in which they [Chile beans] were held, they may well have been *Bayos,* . . for this name has been found in many contemporary [c1900] advertisements of foodstuffs. **1965** *DARE* File, Bayo beans ['beɪoˌbinz]—beans used to make chili; from the Spanish word meaning "bay-colored." . . used in Oklahoma. **1968–69** *DARE* (Qu. I17, *Beans (not pods) that are dark red when they are dry)* Inf **CA**99, Bayo beans—not grown here any more; **CA**139, Bayo beans—not the same as red beans; (Qu. I20, *Kinds of beans that are grown around here)* Inf **CA**105, Bayos—most popular locally; **CA**126, Bayo ['beo] beans; **CA**138, Bayo ['bejo] beans; **CA**162, Bayo beans. **1971** Bright *Word Geog. CA & NV* 64, [The map shows that *bayo(s)* and *bayo bean* occur chiefly in northern California]. **1976** *Wanigan Catalog* 3, *Bayo* . . . A very old California baking bean. Said to be of Chilean origin. The seed [sic] are light chestnut. Midseason.

2 hist sp *ballo:* A bay or dun horse. **SW** Cf **coyote n B4**

1857 in 1948 *Western Folkl.* 7.5 **sCA,** There were three entries: Moro, by Mr. Brady; a Tordillo, by Don Jose Sepulveda; and a Ballo. **1944** Adams *Western Words, Bayo coyote* . . . The Southwest's name for a dun horse with a black stripe down its back. **1952** Dobie *Mustangs* 297 **SW,** The dark line running down the horse's back gave him his name: *bayo coyote* (coyote dun), also *bayo lobo* (lobo dun), the fur of both coyote and gray wolf being shaded along the spine. **1977** Watts *Dict. Old West* 25, *Bayo* . . . In Mexican-Spanish, the word came to mean a *dun* rather than a *bay* horse. It was in fact a faded bay. While some varieties had other markings, most had black points (such as ears, muzzle, and lower legs).

bayonet top n

In logging: see quot.

1958 McCulloch *Woods Words* 8 **Pacific NW,** *Bayonet top*—A tree whose top was once broken out by snow or ice. A branch turning up sharply to make a new leader often looks like a bayonet attached to a rifle barrel.

bayou n Usu |'baɪˌ(j)u|; also, **esp Sth, Midl,** |'baɪˌ(j)o, 'bajə| Pronc-spp *bayo, bay-you, bio, byo;* hist spp *bayoo, bayoue* [LaFr from Choctaw *bayuk* creek, river]

A Forms.

1766 [see **bayou B1**]. **1804** [see **bayou B3**]. **1834** Crockett *Narrative* 53 **TN,** He was closely pursued by several Indians, until he came to a small byo, across which there was a log. **1834** *Life Andrew Jackson* 94, Encamp'd on the Bay-you St. John. **1843** (1916) Hall *New Purchase* 79 **IN,** Keep rite strate along the bottim till you come to the bio. **1916** *DN* 4.346, *Bayo* [baɪːo] . . . Same as *bayou*. Texas pronunciation. *Ibid* 268 **New Orleans LA** [among the non-French, White population], *Bayou* ['bajə]. **1950** *WELS* 1 Inf, **cWI,** Bayou ['baɪʊˑ]—body of water to the side, from a river; connected to the river by a channel; 1 Inf, **ceWI,** ['baɪo]. **1967** *DARE* FW Addit **seAR,** Bayou ['baɪjou]. **1968–70** *DARE* Tape **TX**87, Bayou ['ba.o, 'baɪ.u]; **IN**36, ['baɪ.o].

B Senses.

1 A creek or small river, esp one characterized by a sluggish current. **chiefly LA** See Map

1766 in **1916** Mereness *Travels* 484 **sLA,** We left New Orleans . . and lay that night at the Bayoue. **1826** Flint *Recollections* 330 **LA,** The term "*Bayou*" . . is understood here to mean an alluvial stream with but little current, and sometimes running from the main river, and connected with it again, as a lateral canal. **1916** *DN* 4.268 **New Orleans LA,** *Bayou* . . . Any natural narrow body of water, except a river. **1962** Atwood *Vocab. TX* 39, *Running stream* . . . *Bayou* . . is concentrated in southeastern Texas (Map 53), yet there are two contiguous occurrences in . . West Texas. **1965–70** *DARE* (Qu. C1, . . *A small stream of water not big enough to be a river*) 21 Infs, **chiefly LA,** Bayou. **1967** LeCompte *Word Atlas* 221 **seLA** (*Stream of sluggish water*), Bayou [given as the only response of all infs].

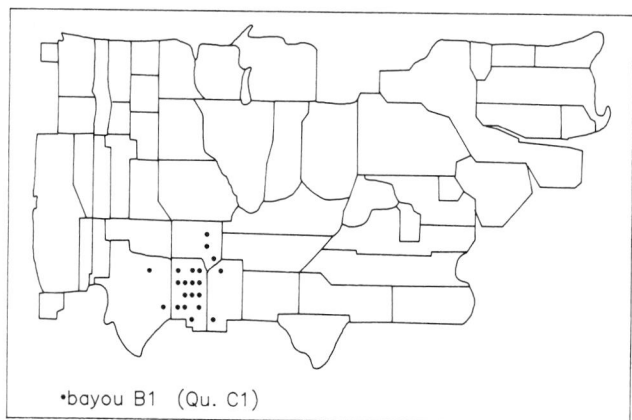

•bayou B1 (Qu. C1)

2 A deep ravine or usu dry watercourse. **West**

1823 James *Acct. of Exped.* 2.229 **NE,** The fertile but narrow eastern margin of the ravine, or as it would be called in the settlements of the Arkansa, *bayou*. *Ibid* 120, The Bayous, as they are named in this country, . . are large and often very profound ravines or watercourses. **1841** Kennedy *Texas* 1.25, The word *bayou* . . is rather loosely applied in the topography of Texas and the West. In strictness, I believe it means a deep inlet, which affords a channel for the water in time of flood, and remains dry, or nearly so, at other seasons. **1853** Hammett *Stray Yankee in TX* 29, Poke, so full of the chase that he had not noticed the dry bayou before him, pitched headlong down the precipitous bank. **1944** *AmSp* 19.309 **NE,** Bayous, used in the plural, is the name applied by residents of Emmett, in Polk County, Nebraska, near the Sandhills, to former river beds of the Niobrara River.

3 A lagoon or slough; a body of still water off to the side of a river or lake. **chiefly west of Appalachians** See Map

1804 (1930) Dunbar *Jrl.* 221 **MS,** Green matter floating on the river, supposed to come from the Catahoola and other lakes and bayoos of stagnant water. **1822** J. Woods *English Prairie* 234 *(DAE)* **IL,** A slue, or bayou (that is, where the water breaks out over a low place). **1862** *Cornhill Mag.* 6.476 **LA,** Immense bayous, as they are termed—wide wastes of water and of marsh, covered with rushes. **1877** Wright *Big Bonanza* 410, We had not traveled half a mile before we came to a bayou or slough, half as large as the river itself, of which it was a sort of a cut-off. **1944** *AmSp* 19.309 **eNE,** The use of the term *[bayou]* reported to me was from Douglas County, near Omaha, where it was applied to "a small armlet of a lake." **1965–70** *DARE* (Qu. C14, *A stretch of still water going off to the side from a river or lake*) 60 Infs, **chiefly west of Appalachians,** Bayou; (Qu. C7) Infs **AR**39, **IA**22, **IN**42, **SD**5, Bayou; (Qu. C9) Inf **IA**33, Bayou.

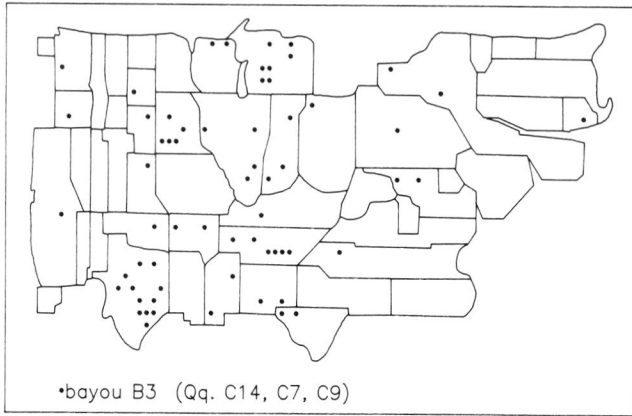

•bayou B3 (Qq. C14, C7, C9)

4 An inlet on the Gulf of Mexico. **Gulf States**

1823 in **1908** *FL Hist. Qrly.* 1.1.38, A large bayou at the southwest penetrates within five rods of the Gulf. **1844** Houstoun *TX & Gulf* 123 **seTX,** [Galveston] island is intersected with several inlets of the sea, or Bayons [sic], as they are called. **1953** McMullen *Topog. Terms FL* 71, *Bayou* . . . It is probable that at least the second meaning (bay, inlet) is peculiar to the Gulf coast region of Florida.

5 A small lake or pond.

1935 *AmSp* 10.316 **NE,** In certain parts of northeastern Nebraska, as Boone county, a pond or small lake in pasture land is called a bayou. **1941** *AmSp* 16.238 **cCA,** A swimming hole in the San Joaquin valley . . though not an inlet from the Gulf of Mexico or from a large river or lake, was called in his boyhood days 'The Bayou.' **1966–69** *DARE* (Qu. C4a, . . *A fairly large body of fresh water*) Inf **MS**73, Bayou, pond; **OK**51, Bayou [baɪjo]—in inner country, a natural lake; **IN**55, Bayou [baɪjo], lake.

bayou bass n

=largemouth bass.

1902 Jordan–Evermann *Amer. Fishes* 358, The fish *[Micropterus salmoides]* has received many vernacular names, among which . . bayou bass. **1946** LaMonte *N. Amer. Game Fishes* 135, Large-mouth Black Bass . . *Huro salmoide* . . Names: . . Bayou Bass. **1978** *Outdoor Life* Sep 56, Scientists call the large-mouth bass Micropterus salmoides . . . But there are many lesser-known names too. Some of them are . . bayou bass, welchman [etc.].

bay ox See **bay steer**

bay poplar n

1 **=tupelo gum.**

1960 Vines *Trees SW* 800, *Nyssa aquatica* . . Vernacular names are . . Bay Poplar.

2 **=balsam poplar.**

1967 *DARE* (Qu. T12) Inf **AL**30, Bay poplar.

bay star vine n

A woody vine *(Schisandra coccinea)* native to the southeastern United States which has crimson flowers followed by orange-red berries. Also called **magnolia vine, wild sarsaparilla**

1903 Small *Flora SE U.S.* 450, *Bay-star Vine* . . . In woods, South Carolina to Florida and Louisiana. Spring and summer. **1960** Vines *Trees SW* 287, *Carolina Magnolia-vine* . . . Also known under the vernacular names of Bay Star-vine and Wild Sarsaparilla. **1976** Bailey–Bailey *Hortus Third* 1016.

bay steer n Also *base steer, bay mule, bay ox* [See quot 1951] **chiefly West**

Std sense, used in var fig phrr (esp *kick like a bay steer*) to indicate vigorous protest or exertion: see quots.

1906 *DN* 3.143 **nwAR,** *Kick worse than a bay steer (down hill backwards)* . . . To resist with might and main. **1931** *K.C. Times* 28 Sept (DA), The next morning he came down town kicking like a bay steer. **1933** *AmSp* 8.1.28 **TX,** *Kick like a bay steer.* To kick vigorously—applied to animals and figuratively to persons. **1939** FWP *ID Lore* 243, You're as crazy as a bay steer in a cornfield. **1946** *CA Folkl. Qrly.* 5.231 **wOR,** He kicks like a bay steer. He makes a strenuous objection . . . I have often heard this saying as "a base steer," modified, I suppose, by popular etymology. *Ibid* 338 **CA,** To sweat like a bay steer. [**1951** Fergusson *New Mexico* 405, Bay steer—a reddish-brown steer. Cowmen think the Hereford steer of that color is especially vicious.] **1966–67** *DARE* (Qu. X56b) Inf **SD3,** Sweat like a bay steer; **LA2,** Sweating like a bay ox—I said that the other day, but a ox don't sweat; (Qu. KK11) Inf **IL5,** Bucked like a bay steer. **1970** *DARE* Tape **TX89,** They kick like a bay mule.

bay-top palmetto n
=**silver palm.**

1908 Britton *N. Amer. Trees* 134, *Cocothrinax argentea,* sometimes called Silver-top or Bay-top palmetto, attains a height of 10 meters.

bay truck n *?obs*
Seafood caught off the New Jersey coast and sold nearby.

1895 *DN* 1.382 **NJ,** *Bay truck:* used "along shore" for food from the bays which indent the coast; in distinction from "garden truck."

bay-you See **bayou** A

bazoo n [Perh Du *bazuin* trumpet]

1 also *bazook:* A person's mouth; by ext, idle, loud, or boastful talk. **now chiefly West** *joc* or *derog*

1904 (1972) Harben *Georgians* 43 **GA,** I shot off my bazoo about what I thought was Scriptur. **1906** *DN* 3.126 **nwAR,** *Bazoo* . . . Mouth, talk. "Shut up your bazoo." "We've had enough of your bazoo." **1908** *DN* 3.289 **eAL, wGA.** **1948** *Sat. Eve. Post* 24 Apr 173/2 **WA,** Shut yer big bazoo! **1950** *WELS (Joking or uncomplimentary words for a person's mouth)* 2 Infs, **WI,** Bazoo; 1 Inf, **cnWI,** Bazook; 1 Inf, **swWI,** Close your bazoo. **1965–70** *DARE* (Qu. X9) 11 Infs, **chiefly West,** Bazoo; **MT2,** Bazook.

2 in phr *blow one's bazoo* and varr: To boast.

1877 Bartlett *Americanisms* **TN,** *Blowin' his Bazoo.* Gasconade; braggadocio. **1903** *DN* 2.306 **seMO,** *Bazoo* . . . An imaginary trumpet. 'He blows his own bazoo,' meaning that he is boastful and obtrusive. **1932** Farrell *Young Lonigan* 113 **Chicago IL,** His mother was always blowing off her bazoo about him being her blue-eyed baby.

3 also *bazoon, bazookas:* Buttocks.

1950 *WELS (Joking words for the part of the body that you sit on)* 1 Inf, **ceWI,** Bazookas. **1969–70** *DARE* (Qu. X35) Inf **CA184,** Bazoo [bə'zu]; **PA182,** Bazoon [bə'zun].

bazoo wagon n [**bazoo 1** + *wagon;* prob also infl by **zoo,** and in sound by *caboose*]

1977 Adams *Lang. Railroader* 12, *Bazoo wagon:* A caboose.

bazzy See **buzzy** n[2]

B.D.T. n [Abbr of **backdoor trot**] Cf *DS* BB19

1915 *DN* 4.246, *B.d.t.* . . . explanatory of an insistent 'call of nature.'

be v

A Pronc varr.

1 *are:* usu |ɑr|; also |ɑː|; **formerly widespread, now chiefly Sth, S Midl,** |ær, æə|; occas |ɔr|. Pronc-sp *air;* eye-dial *ar'.* Addit quots in *ADD, DAE*

1777 in 1911 *MD Hist. Mag.* 6.144 **cnMD,** You must divide this . . as i think it may serve you both if you air moderate. **1848** Lowell *Biglow* 143 "Upcountry" **MA** [Glossary], *Air, are.* **1889** Edwards *Runaways* 99 **GA,** I ar' er-goin' ter tell yuh suthin'. **1890** *DN* 1.67 **KY,** *Are* [ɑː]. Pronounced like *air* [æə] by a few who have not forgotten their 'old field school' training. *Ibid* 71 **LA,** *Are* . . rhyming with *pare.* **1893** Shands *MS Speech,* *Air* [æə]. Negroes and illiterate whites nearly always use this pronunciation for *are.* **1927** Shewmake *Engl. Pronc. VA* 17 **eVA,** There are Virginians still living who have often heard *are* called [ær], or, rather, [æə]. **1929** (1931) Faulkner *Sound & Fury* 142 **MS,** Air you satisfied the gal ain't took any hurt? **1937** *AmSp* 12.287 **nwVA,** In the speech of

uneducated [Shenandoah] Valley people . . . [ə] appears in both *are* and *or,* in both *farmer* and *former.* **c1960** *Wilson Coll.* **csKY,** *Are* [ær] . . very old people. **1968** *DARE* (Qu. Y24) Inf **CA59,** Air you going my way? **1974** Maurer *KY Moonshine* 54, "The main thing," he concluded, "is the people. Air they fur hit or air they agin hit?"

2 *been:* usu |bɪn|; also, **widespread, esp NEng, S Midl,** *somewhat old-fash,* |bɛn|; occas, **esp sAppalachians,** |bin|. Pronc-spp *ben, be'n, bean, bin*

1622 *Mourt's Relation* *Iournall Plimoth* 4 **MA,** Having bin forced to cut her downe in bestowing her betwixt the decks. **1778** in 1886 *MA Hist. Soc. Proc. for 1885–86* 2d ser 2.447, Mr. Aaron Thompson likd to ben killd breaking a colt. **1829** Kirkham *Engl. Grammar* 192, *Provincialisms . . . New England . .* [bɛn]. **1884** Jewett *Mate of Daylight* 203 **ME,** There'd be'n trouble about the property. **1890** *DN* 1.38 **NEng,** [bɪn]. **1892** *DN* 1.238 **MO, NY, NEng,** [bɛn]. **1894** *DN* 1.340 **wCT,** [bɛn]. **1895** *DN* 1.370 **TN, KY, wNC,** Ef you'd a ben thar. **1906** *DN* 3.115 **sIN,** *Been,* pronounced *ben.* *Ibid* 126 **nwAR,** *Ben . . .* Common. **1917** in 1944 *ADD* **s,cwWV,** It's bean [bin] a long time. **1928** *AmSp* 3.403 **Ozarks,** *Been* is nearly always given the short *e* sound, and is best written *ben.* Alice French, better known as Octave Thanet, says that in Arkansas the people pronounce *been* in the old way . . to rhyme with *seen,* but the present writers have not heard this pronunciation in the Ozarks. **1933** *AmSp* 8.1.24 **c,sAppalachians,** Sometimes *been* is *bean.* This pronunciation . . seems to be fairly well distributed through the southern and central Appalachians, although it is not heard on the tongues of many persons in any one place.

3 *is:* usu |ɪz|. Pronc-spp *yis, yiz (Gullah);* eye-dial *iz*

1888 Jones *Negro Myths* 7 **GA coast,** Buh Rabbit say: "Me yent." Buh Wolf say: "You yis." *Ibid* 157, Me could pint dem out an tell you who dem yiz. **1922** Gonzales *Black Border* 283 **sSC, GA coasts** [Gullah], "Enty," "ent," "yent," sometimes "ain'," serve for isn't, aren't, didn't, don't, doesn't . . . Preceded by a soft vowel sound, "iz" and "ent" are changed to "yiz" and "yent;" as: "him iz," "him ent," become, by the substitution of "'e" for him, "'e yiz," "'e yent."

4 *was:* usu |wəz, wʌz|; occas, esp in stressed position, |wɑz|. Eye-dial *wuz, 'uz*

1867 Lowell *Biglow* 241 "Upcountry" **MA,** Puzzlin' which side wuz preudentest to pin to. **1887** (1967) Harris *Free Joe* 104 **GA,** That's who I 'lowed hit wuz. **1890** *DN* 1.71 **LA,** Such sentences as this may be heard: "You *wuz* (emphatic) there, for I saw you." **1942** Hall *Smoky Mt. Speech* 29 **eTN, wNC,** *Was* and *what* stressed have [ɑ], [ɒ], [ʌ]; unstressed [ə]. **1958** Humphrey *Home from the Hill* 80 **TX,** "Hit's a wile hawg, sho nuff, Cap," he said. "I mean, one that never wuz nothin but wile . . . Hit uz Monday a week when I uz runnin mah line. I skeered im up f'om whur he uz bedded down." **1972** *Foxfire Book* 279 **nGA,** So I went back up th' ridge sort'a opposite to where he'uz at.

5 *were:* usu |wɚ, wɝ, wɜ|; also, **formerly widespread, now chiefly S Midl,** *old-fash,* |wɑr|; occas |wær, wɛr|. Pronc-spp *wahr, war, ware;* eye-dial *wur*

1795 Dearborn *Columbian Grammar* 139 ["List of Improprieties"], War for Were. **1829** Kirkham *Engl. Grammar* 193 **KY, VA, MD, MS,** I war than. **1837** in 1956 Eliason *Tarheel Talk* 320 **NC,** *Were . .* ware. **1884** Baldwin *Yankee School-Teacher* 177 **VA,** Dat eber I wur 'flicted to own. **1890** *DN* 1.71 **LA,** *Were . .* rhyming with *there . . .* used to a considerable extent by persons of respectable education. **1917** *DN* 4.419 **wNC, IL, KY,** *War.* **1926** Kephart *Highlanders* 358 **sAppalachians,** *War . .* was or were—the *a* as in far. **1931** *PMLA* 46.1319 **sAppalachians,** "It useter [war] (were)" means "It used to be." **1942** in 1944 *ADD* **cWV,** /wɛr/ or /wær/. **1956** Eliason *Tarheel Talk* 206 **NC,** The vowel of *ware* for *were* was formerly a standard pronunciation. **c1960** *Wilson Coll.* **csKY,** *Weren't* /wɑrnt/ among the very old people. **1976** Garber *Mountain-ese* 48 **sAppalachians,** Thar wahr jest two choices to make.

B Gram forms. (For evidence of contemporary British use, see *Ling. Atlas England* M1–M30.)

1 *be.* Note: some of the senses are difficult to distinguish. For use in negative constructions, see **C1.**

a as indic. Note: some authorities consider this form to be tenseless, with the tense of the sentence instead indicated by adverbs or other markers.

(1) pres: Am, are, is. [*OED:* "*Be* continued in concurrent use [with *are* and its varr] till the end of the [16th] century (see Shakspere, and Bible of 1611), and still occurs as a poetic archaism, as well as in certain traditional expressions and familiar quotations of 16th c. origin, as 'the powers that be.' . . Southern and eastern [British] dialect speech retains *be* both in singular and plural, as 'I be a going,' 'we be ready.' "] **chiefly NEast, Sth** *somewhat old-fash*

1789 Webster *Dissertations Engl. Lang.* 385 **NEng,** The verb *be* . . is still used after the ancient manner, I *be,* you *be,* we *be, they* be. **1829** Tenney *Female Quixotism* 2.41 **Philadelphia PA** [Black], Spose he want to know how old you be first. **1894** *DN* 1.340 **wCT,** Be: . . The regular forms of the present indicative are all used, but there is a secondary inflection as follows:—I be / you be / he is / we be / you be / they be. **1914** *DN* 4.69 **nNH, ME,** Be . . . Am; are. **1936** Morehouse *Rain on Just* 128 **NC,** "Young uns," said Least Dolly, . . "We be saved, I reckon." **1938** Matschat *Suwannee R.* 69 **sGA,** Cannibals, they be. **1968** *DARE* (Qu. EE33, . . *Outdoor games*) Inf **IN39,** "Squat where you be"—similar to "Statues." **1972** *Orbis* (Louvain) 21.26 **TN** [White], That be a flat tire. **1982** *DARE* File **sIN,** As long as that be all they are [in price], I could get a lot of them.

(2) past: Was, were.

1953 Brewer *Word Brazos* 4 **eTX** [Black], We was all listenin' to de preachuh . . . Evuhbody wonder what de trouble be an' staa't lookin' outen de windows. **1974** *PADS* 61–62.24 **cnGA,** The frequency with which invariant *be* is used to indicate past events makes the adjective "deviant" seem questionable for this usage: "It was one time when she *be* cold, cause my dad [now dead] he would always keep my mother warm when she *be* cold in the wintertime." [Beryl] Bailey cites examples such as . . "He *be* there yesterday" to illustrate the point that the element of time is optional in the verb when time is expressed adverbially or contextually in nonstandard black dialect. Thus the invariant form is used not only for repetitive action and for future or conditional occurrences (with *will* or *would* omitted) as Fasold states, but also for the present moment and for a past occurrence. **1975** Allen *LAUM* 2.33 **nMN,** "They be coming home about midnight": in past context. **1981** Bailey–Bassett *Invariant "Be"* 10 **Sth,** In the data used here only two examples of "distributive *be*" clearly refer to actions in the past . . . "I never was called a bad man. I never did *be* out very much in the public." . . The other refers to an action that took place the preceding day: "I was telling Mr. — yesterday you *be* here, and he was telling me about he locate some of his people." . . In spite of these examples, "distributive *be*" seems to be rarely used in past contexts. "Distributive *be*" is usually tenseless, but the few examples in past contexts deserve further consideration.

(3) future: Will be. esp Sth

1942 Rawlings *Cross Creek* 89 **FL** [Black], I'll go with him . . . I be back Tuesday mornin' on the nine o'clock train. **1954** *Harder Coll.* **cwTN** [White], I be so glad when Ray come home. **1972** *Orbis* (Louvain) 21.25 **Sth** [White], I think it be close . . . Mr. Nixon be our nex' president. *Ibid* [White], I be seventy-six my nex' birthday. **1977** Smitherman *Talkin* 20, The Black English speaker can use *be* to convey a sense of future time, as in *The boy be here soon* and *They family be gone Friday.*

b in emphatic uses: See quots.

1894 *DN* 1.340 **wCT,** A restatement with emphasis of a previous remark after a contradiction would usually take *be.* "Now, Hiram, you aint agoin' t' the store to-night!" "I say I be agoin' tew!" **1903** *DN* 2.292 **Cape Cod MA** (as of 1850s), *Emphatic* . . I be / you be / he is / we be / you be / they be. **1938** Matschat *Suwannee R.* 123 **nFL, sGA,** What for the gov'ment need more trees? Hain't no use for all the trees thar be! **1945** *PADS* 3.9 **nVT,** One of my farmer friends . . uses "I be" in statements, possibly more emphatic than "I am."

c in interrog contexts: See quots. esp NEng & settlement areas; also Sth

1816 Pickering *Vocab.* 46, This was formerly much used in *New England* instead of *am* and *are,* in phrases of this kind: *Be* you ready? *Be* you going? I *be,* &c. **1843** (1916) Hall *New Purchase* 310 **swIN,** Well—who be you? **1894** *DN* 1.340 **wCT,** I be / you be / he is / we be / you be / they be . . . It is used in dependent sentences generally, . . especially indirect questions, and the second part of the favorite Yankee form of inquiring if the contrary of a stated negative is true. "You ain't goin' up town, be ye?" "The cattle aint yourn, be they?" **1899** Garland *Boy Life* 143 **nwIA,** "They're plannin' to lick us like shucks, that's all." "Oh, they be?" **1903** *DN* 2.292 **Cape Cod MA** (as of 1850s), *Emphat. Inter* . . . be I? be yi? is he? be wi? be yi? be they? **1938** Matschat *Suwannee R.* 17 **nFL, sGA,** Fowkses must live in bunches! How be it they get aroun'? *Ibid* 262, "Look," Cella whispered, "what be that bird a-doin'?" **1944** *PADS* 2.40 **VA, NC,** Be . . . Present tense, all persons, singular or plural; generally employed in questions. "You *be* that fellow that's staying at Jink's?" "What *be* your name?" Rare and obsolescent.

1947 Guthrie *Big Sky* 19 **KY** (as of 1830s), I reckon there ain't much that skeers you, be there, Zeb? **1953** Atwood *Survey of Verb Forms* 27, *Be* occurs most frequently [as a variant of *are*] in the phrase "How are you?," where it is particularly common in n.e. N. Eng. Of the 56 spontaneous occurrences . . in N. Eng., 40 are in the northeast. *Be* is very characteristically an older form, both in N. Eng. and in those areas of N.Y. and Pa. where it occurs. **c1960** *Wilson Coll.* **csKY,** "Be you going?" Said by a few elderly folks. **1966–69** *DARE* (Qu. NN10a) Infs **MA68, NY94, WA11,** How be ya (*or* you)?; **MS35,** How you be? **1975** Allen *LAUM* 2.32 **nIA,** As a finite form, *be* has only a ghostly existence in the UM. Actually, only two bona fide instances appear in the field records, both from the free conversation of Type I speakers . . . "Be I on the right road?": inf frequently uses *be* in this way.

d in compar constrs: See quots. chiefly NEast *old-fash*

1833 in 1834 Smith *Letters Jack Downing* 155 **ME,** Your Aut [sic] tells me she dont think Brother Joshua can be so strong of his Age as I be. **1932–34** *Hanley Disks* **cnCT,** He ain't as old as I be; **csCT,** He wasn't quite as old as I be; **cwMA,** In some towns they're more so than they be in others. **1953** Brewer *Word Brazos* 16 **seTX** [Black], His pappy Tom jes' ez 'sponsibul as li'l Bill be. **1953** Atwood *Survey of Verb Forms* 27 **NEng, NY, nNJ, nPA,** In "tall as I am," *be* . . is even more characteristically an older feature; of 28 N. Eng. informants who use it, 21 fall in Type IA and four in IIA [=old, with little or moderate educ]. **1968** *DARE* FW Addit **NY72,** Heck of a lot older 'n I be.

e as aux:

(1) in progressive constrs: Am, are, is.

1829 Kirkham *Engl. Grammar* 192, *Provincialisms . . . New England.* I be goin. **1894** *DN* 1.328 **NJ,** Be: used for both *am* and *are;* as "I be going," "we be going." **1936** Morehouse *Rain on Just* 129 **NC,** You be working them young uns . . almighty hard. **1938** Matschat *Suwannee R.* 15 **nFL, sGA,** She be a-huntin' weeds an' flowers. **c1960** *Wilson Coll.* **csKY,** Be you going? Said by a few elderly folks. **1969** *DARE* Tape **RI1,** Now we be sewing for the lawn party so we wouldn't be doing sewing for the hospital . . . On the right-hand side as you going out.

(2) conditional: Would be. See also if so be

1972 *Orbis* (Louvain) 21.26 **TN** [White], If this was a communist country—we just be talkin' about the weather. **1981** Bailey–Bassett *Invariant "Be"* **LA, MS** [White], If we'd get out working and *be* dirty . . , we'd wash . . . [Black] It'd be a one-by-twelve . . or whatever it *be.*

(3) with done: Will have.

1977 Smitherman *Talkin* 25, Here's how Black English speakers render this future perfect: *be* plus *done* plus verb. ["]He *be* done left by the time we get there. I *be* done finish before anyone arrive.["]

f to signify habitual or repeated action, or to refer to continuous actions or usual conditions. *esp freq among Blacks; occas among Whites in the Sth* See also **B1a** above

1887 (1967) Harris *Free Joe* 95 **nwGA** [Black], He holler dat out eve'yday, en den, wiles he be talkin', he'd stop en look roun'. **1935** Hurston *Mules & Men* 241 **nFL** [Black], It is Midsummer Eve, and the Sun give special benefits then and need great honor. The special drum be played then. It is a cowhide stretched over a half-barrel. **1966–70** *DARE* Tape **LA7** [Black], The cane grow so late here; it be so green and the frost catch it; **SC10** [Black], Summer be a long time 'fore it get out, the hotness; **SC11** [White], They don't be much pulled off the floor now; **VA55** [White], If you keep in the channel . . it be all right, but if it's going to shove water you go to pieces if the sea's heavy. **1974** *PADS* 61.23 **Atlanta GA** [Black], The invariant *be* form is not limited to the single function of indicating repetitive action, but may also indicate a constant state: "Cause that one be a old one, and I want the one with two sticks." "They [waffles] be already cooked, but they be frozen." "All those old snakes and alligators and things be over there." **1977** Smitherman *Talkin* 231 [Black], I be lonely all the time . . . Sometimes I . . cry because I'm lonely. **1979** Ellsworth *Effect of Kindergarten* 139 **csWI** [Black children], We be 'it', you hide your eyes. *Ibid* 141, They hafta find us and tag us and we be it . . . Whoever git caught and they be caught, they hafta be It. **1980** Folb *Runnin' Down* 37 **Los Angeles CA** [Black], They *mean* mothas. Don't be *messin'* wid 'em. *Ibid* 100, See, Chicanos they be real quiet, don' say a lot . . . Black folks, they be righteously talkin' all d' time. Yeh, but lots of time, don' be sayin' anything, really. **1981** Bailey–Bassett *Invariant "Be"* 11 **LA, MS,** Invariant *be,* including "distributive *be* [used for actions and states across the time spectrum]", is clearly not unique to black speech. In fact, the form has a similar pattern of distribution for both races, with education, age, and sex all influencing the pattern. However, among blacks the form is much more common and is used by a larger segment of the population. *Ibid*, Unlike Fasold, we found more examples of *be* used for continuous actions and general conditions than for intermittent actions. In addition, the use of invariant *be* for actions which occur at a definite point in time cannot be ignored. *Ibid* 18, Examples of Invariant *Be* . . . [Among] Whites . . . [That land] don't *be* [sandy] . . . When people *be* together, they soon understand one another . . . My biscuits . . don't *be* spongy like hers . . . [Among] Blacks . . . We don't *be* bothered with them . . . The horse *be* in the barn to hisself . . . The land *be* blue.

g *be* + (-s, -d) — often to signify habitual action or usual condition: See quots. [Cf *DNE* xx "*Am, is,* and *are* are employed for an assertion about an event at the present moment, while *be's,* for all persons, indicates continuous or repeated activity." See also *EDD be* I.1. But the forms *be(e)s* and *beed* may also represent analogical formations with present and past tense forms of other verbs.] **chiefly Sth** *esp among Black speakers* See also **B1f** above

1917 *DN* 4.420 **csLA,** Bes [bis] . . . Second person present indicative of *to be* . . . "You bes on the ferry," meaning 'You are employed in some capacity on the ferry.' **1937** *AmSp* 12.268 **cnVA,** Which ever one they bes. **1941** Percy *Lanterns* 297 **nwMS** [Black], It don't make no difference how hard I tries or how good I bees. **1942** Rawlings *Cross Creek* 83 **FL,** Name be's Beatrice. I be's 'Geechee. Folks jes' calls me 'Geechee. **1944** *PADS* 2.40 **sVA,** Bes [biz] . . . Present tense of *be,* singular or plural . . . Obsolescent. **1966** *DARE* Tape **SC17** [Black], It kinda draws and bes hot under there. It sweats and it'll just scald 'em. **1969** *Black World* 17.11.16, Black Poetry is becoming what it has always been but has not quite *beed.* **1972** Claerbaut *Black Jargon* 57, It be's that way sometimes. **1972** *Atlanta Letters* **cGA,** I bet it bees cold in the morning. **1974** *PADS* 61–62.61 **cnGA,** "No one *bees* at the company" [so that the child's carpenter father might call in to the office on rainy days to inquire about reporting for work]. **1977** Smitherman *Talkin* 3 [Black], "It bees dat way sometime." Here the language aspect is the use of the verb *be* to indicate a recurring event or habitual condition, rather than a one-time-only occurrence. *Ibid* 19, *The coffee bees cold* means *Every day the coffee's cold* . . . if you the cook and *The coffee cold,* you might only just get talked about that day, but if *The coffee bees cold,* pretty soon you ain't gon have no job! **1981** Bailey–Bassett *Invariant "Be"* 18 **eLA** [Black], It ain't too much of a river, but it rain like it rain now and water gets up, it bees pretty bad. *Ibid* 19 [Black], Now, soot bees down here at the bottom. *Ibid* **MS** [Black], It bees trees all on the other side.

2 *am.*

a for finite forms of *be.*

(1) pres: Is, are. *chiefly among Black speakers with little formal educ*

1893 Shands *MS Speech* 17, Negroes . . . say: "I is," "You am," . . "We am," etc. **1901** *DN* 1.182 **KY** [Black], Am yo' de' man? [=Are you the man?]. **1903** *DN* 2.292 **Cape Cod MA** (as of 1850s), The verb *to be* is inflected . . Pres. Indic. I'm, you'm, he's, we'm, you'm, they'm . . . Interrog. em I? em yi? is he? em we? em yi? em they? **1944** *PADS* 2.6 **AL** [Black], *Am* is frequently used as third person singular as well as first person. **1945** FWP *Lay My Burden Down* 36 **TX** [Black], Three months am the total time I's spent going to school. *Ibid,* There am . . folks . . what says we-uns believes in superstition. **1977** Smitherman *Talkin* 15, As a former slave said, "Everything I tells you am the truth, but they's plenty I can't tell you."

(2) past: Was.

1884 Baldwin *Yankee School-Teacher* 177 **VA,** She [=a mule] am de catty-corneres' sort of beast dat eber I wur 'flicted ter own, dat she am. **1945** FWP *Lay My Burden Down* 37 **TX** [Black], It am 40 years ago now when I's first fully realize that I has the power. **1949** Gipson *Hound-Dog Man* 113 **csTX,** It were way back yonder when I'm a shirttail kid. **1969** *DARE* FW Addit **cwNJ,** Alfalfa didn't come to our country when I'm a boy.

(3) past perf: Have been. [Loan transl from Ger *Ich bin*] **chiefly C Atl**

1934 *Language* 10.3 **cPA,** The Pennsylvania Dutch . . . often follow the German usage: *the first time since I'm here,* instead of *since I've been here.* **1935** *AmSp* 10.167 **sePA,** Such expressions . . to the great mass of people of this region . . are the accepted currency of daily speech . . . This is the first time it's happened since I'm here.

b as aux: Are, have.

1843 (1916) Hall *New Purchase* 268 **IN,** I heerd, sir, you wanted somebody to teach the State school, and I'm come to let you know I'm willing to take the place. [Ed: archaic formal usage] **1887** (1967) Harris

Free Joe 107 **ceGA,** This yer one what I'm already got don't amount to shucks. **1927** Kennedy *Gritny* 86 **sLA** [Black], I'm bin gone from yonder a good w'ile. **1953** Atwood *Survey of Verb Forms* 26 **PA, C Atl,** [20 infs] use the form *I'm* /aim/ . . "I'm been thinking." . . Nearly all of these informants are in or near the Chesapeake Bay area, and all but two fall in Type I [=old, with little educ]. **1953** Brewer *Word Brazos* 50 **eTX** [Black], Young man, are you lookin' for Soul's salvation? **1968** *DARE* (Qu. X47, . . *Other ways . . of saying, "I'm very tired, at the end of my strength"*) Inf **NC49,** I feel like I'm had it today.

c in contr *I'm* — used redund: See quots.

1908 *DN* 3.322 **eAL, wGA,** I'm am. A common reduplication. **1914** *DN* 4.158 **cVA,** Am is . . . "I'm is the man!" **1927** Kennedy *Gritny* 171 **sLA** [Black], You begrudge me a li'l bit o' licker to keep me from ketchin' col', wet as I'm is? **1959** Lomax *Rainbow Sign* 82 **AL** [Black], While I'm is got this trip, I'm gonna see what I can see. **1967** *DARE* (Qu. NN9a, *Exclamations showing great annoyance*) Inf **AL25,** I'm be damned.

3 *is.*

a also in contr *I's(e):* Am. **chiefly Sth** *esp freq among Blacks*

1837 Sherwood *Gaz. GA* 70 [Provincialisms to be avoided], *I is . .* for I am. **1875** *Scribner's Mth.* 10.240 **AL** [Black], I'se pow'ful skeered; but neversomeless I ain't gwine run away. **1893** Shands *MS Speech* 17, Negroes . . . say: "I is." **1907** *DN* 3.233 **nwAR, seMO,** I'se monstrous hungry. **1929** (1951) Faulkner *Sartoris* 51 **MS** [Black], "Ise gwine, Ise gwine," Simon answered pettishly. **1932** (1974) Caldwell *Tobacco Road* 101 **GA** [White], "Ain't you going to get a preacher to finish doing it [=marrying a couple]?" "I is not! Ain't I a preacher of the gospel?" c**1937** in 1972 *Amer. Slave* 2.15 **SC,** I's black as a crow. **1953** Atwood *Survey of Verb Forms* Fig 21, [The Map shows occurrences of *Is I going* to be concentrated in Virginia and North Carolina, with scattered examples in neighboring states]. *Ibid* 27, In the South *is* has considerable currency in this phrase among Type I informants [=old, with little educ] . . . more than half of the Southern Negro informants [use this expression]. **1966** *DARE* Tape **GA4** [Black], He had three girls older than I is. **1973** Himes *Black on Black* 133 **NYC** [Black], I'se tired as you are. *Ibid* 136, Ise already free.

b Are. **chiefly Sth, S Midl**

1837 Sherwood *Gaz. GA* 70 [Provincialisms to be avoided], *I is . . you is,* for I am . . you are. **1894** *DN* 1.340 **wCT,** *Is* is sometimes used as a plural, especially with demonstrative pronouns, or with two personal pronouns . . . "Them's the kind I want." "Him and me's good friends." **1903** *DN* 2.292 **Cape Cod MA** (as of 1850s), For the 3d pers. pl. *is* is used with any other subject than the pronoun *they: His folks is away, who is them folks? Them's the new neighbors.* **1932** (1974) Caldwell *Tobacco Road* 83 **GA** [White], When is you and Dude going to do all this riding around . . ? **1944** *PADS* 2.6 **Sth,** The forms *is* and *are* are used interchangeably for any person or number by Negroes over much of the South. **1953** Brewer *Word Brazos* 9 **eTX** [Black], Ah wants to see yo' fawm, Sid. Le's see what kinda fawmuh you is. **c1960** *Wilson Coll.* **csKY,** *Is . .* is often used with plural subjects. **1965–70** *DARE* (Qu. B8) Inf **SC32,** Clouds is moving; (Qu. P9) Inf **TX24,** Things is slow; **NC87,** Fish is not biting today; (Qu. H12) Infs **OK26, TN13,** Eyes is bigger than his stomach; (Qu. W24a) Inf **AR51,** Your dry goods is showing; (Qu. Y17, . . *"I hear they_____"*) Inf **SC26,** Is friends now; (Qu. BB19) Inf **FL26,** Screws is loose; (Qu. BB21) Infs **MD24, SC10, 58,** Bowels is tight; (Qu. EE1) Inf **FL48,** The henchies is walking; (Qu. GG8) Inf **NC55,** [His] feelings is easy hurt; (Qu. HH5) Inf **GA30,** [His] wits is off; (QR, near Qq. N20, T10) Inf **SC24,** The signs is up all along; those long pods is there. [11 of 15 Infs White; 11 Infs have grade school educ or less] **1967** *DARE* Tape **AZ7,** The Navahos is good people. **1975** Allen *LAUM* 2.33, The only U[pper] M[idwest] deviation from standard *am* and *are* is that of Minnesota Type I [=old, with little educ] inf. 44, who asks "Is they?" in conversation.

c as aux: Have, has. **chiefly Sth, S Midl** Cf **ain't v¹ 2**

1817 in 1830 Royall *Letters AL* 39 **VA,** My witnesses *is* come and I *ar* ready for trial. **1844** Thompson *Major Jones's Courtship* 30 **GA,** I spose you all know as how my friends is fotched me out to represent this county in the next Legislater. **1851** Burke *Polly Peablossom* 96 **GA,** "Now you is done it," ses Bill. Tom know'd he had. **1893** Shands *MS Speech* **MS,** The verb *to be* is largely used, by negroes, in the place of the auxiliary *to have;* as, "He is got a store"; "I is had it." *Is* is much more frequently used in this sense than any other form of the verb *to be,* and generally takes the place of *has.* **1929** Sale *Tree Named John* 90 **MS** [Black], Baby is you seed dat ole black tormcat . . ? **1966–70** *DARE* (Qu. H11a, . . *He_____*) Inf **KY44,** Is got no manners; (Qu. K11, . . *She_____*) Infs **CA136, IA36, KY90,** Is calved; **KY39,** Is come in; (Qu. AA10) Inf **GA77,** He is fell for her; (Qu. CC12a) Inf **PA237,** Snake eyes is got him; (Qu.

BB54) Inf **FL**19, Doctors is given him up. [All Infs White; 6 of 8 Infs have grade school educ or less]

d Do, did.   *esp Gullah*   Note: the verb, uninflected in basilectal Gullah, may be the equivalent here of the infinitive or participle in English, so that in quot 1928 "have known" and "have called" might be equally possible translations.   Cf **ain't** v¹ 3

1888 Jones *Negro Myths* 170 **seGA coast** [Gullah glossary], *Yiz,* am, is, to be, did. **1928** Peterkin *Scarlet Sister Mary* 161 **sSC coast** [Black], Mary asked if she knew what love is . . . "Is I know love? Honey, I knew em fo-true." *Ibid* 100, Is you call me, July? **1945** FWP *Lay My Burden Down* 37 **TX** [Black], It am 40 years ago now when I's first fully realize that I has the power.

4 *are.*

a **Am, is.**   **chiefly S Midl**

1817 in 1830 Royall *Letters AL* 39 **VA**, I *ar* ready. **1843** (1846) Haliburton *Attaché* (1st ser) 2.147 **TN**, I'm whipped, that are a fact; and thar is no denyin' of it. **1848** (1855) Ruxton *Life Far West* 90, Thar arn't a devil as hisses thar, as can 'shine' with this child, I tell you. **1887** *Scribner's Mag.* 474/2 **AR**, She are mighty fair-minded. *Ibid* 484/2, I are plum' surprised. **1891** Page *Elsket* 137 **VA** [Black], 'Whar air P'laski?' I tell him I don' know whar P'laski air. **1901** *DN* 2.181 **neKY** [Black], *Are* is, am. **1928** Aldrich *Lantern* 11 **NE** (as of 1854), She aren't going to give 'em to us until our wedding days. **1974** *PADS* 61.66 **Atlanta GA** [Black], She are too crazy.

b **Have.**

1918 *DN* 5.36 **GA, NC, TN**, "You-uns ain't got ary auger, air [=are] ye?" The word is common among most of the hillsmen of the South.

c with mass noun treated as count noun.

1954 Roberts *I Bought Dog* [13] **KY**, There are enough wood in that tree to last a whole year.

5 *was.*

a in contrs *I's(e), ize.*   **esp Midl, Sth**   See also **B3a** above

1829 Kirkham *Engl. Grammar* 192 **NEng**, He sade no; and then ize up a stump. **1834** *Life Andrew Jackson* 228 **eTN**, We had the snigger at their expense; tho' I'se a while in a twitter when that are [=that there] wicket feller Strong . . com'd out upon us. **1941** *AmSp* 16.14 **eTX** [Black], I was born . . . (aez bɔ:n]. *Ibid* 15, (aɪz bɔ:n]. **1941** Stuart *Men of Mts.* 95 **neKY**, I'll never forget how I felt when I's shot. **1966** *AmSp* 41.77, In the "common speech" . . in Pennsylvania and the rural South, . . a form *I's* is very frequently heard in contexts which seem to require the past tense . . . *I's* (past) is evidently a contraction of *I was* . . . I have occasionally heard corresponding interrogative forms, such as *'s I?* and *'s you?* [for *was I?, was you?*]. **1972** *Foxfire Book* 21 **nGA**, "If I's stout enough I could pull it out *(struggling)* but I ain't." *Ibid* 23, "I don't know where my oven is. I's studyin' about it th' other day."

b **Were.**   **chiefly Midl, Sth**   *esp among speakers with little formal educ*

1892 *DN* 1.242 **MO**, *Was.* Almost the only form of the verb in the past tense, which runs: *I was, you was, he was, we was,* etc. **1894** *DN* 1.340 **wCT.** **1953** Atwood *Survey of Verb Forms* 29, *You were* . . . In NEng . . . No cultured informant uses only *was,* though three give this form alongside *were.* In the M[iddle] A[tlantic] S[tates] *was* is practically universal in Types I and II [=those with little or average educ] (more than nine tenths of both groups use it), but is rare in cultured speech . . . In the S[outh] A[tlantic] S[tates], also, *was* is practically universal in Type I . . and it is strongly predominant . . in Type II. Only four cultured informants (Va. and N.C.) give the form *was.* [The same general patterns hold for *we was.*] **1965–70** *DARE* (Qu. A16) Infs **SC**34, **VA**36, Since the woods was afire *(or* on fire); (Qu. A21) Inf **KY**7, You wasn't born in a minute; (Qu. P9) Infs **OH**12, 58, **SC**7, (We just said) they wasn't biting *(or* bitin', a-biting); (Qu. W29) Inf **MO**10, They wasn't done very neatly; (Qu. BB18) Inf **VA**2, Vomit till I thought my insides was a-coming out; (Qu. EE21b, . . *"For a while those fellows really ___.")* Infs **FL**14, **KY**29, **MO**5, **SC**3, 32, **TN**59, Was fighting *(or* knocking, slinging it out, etc.); (Qu. FF18, . . *"They certainly ___ last night.")* Inf **KY**40, Was rude; **MD**18, Was wild; **VA**25, Was noisy; (Qu. II21) Inf **NH**14, Where was you brought up?; (Qu. KK54) Inf **NC**55, They was good matches; (Qu. NN2) Inf **NY**68, You was right. [All Infs have high school educ or less] **1966** *AmSp* 41.77 **PA, rural Sth**, In the plural *we's, you's,* and *they's* are dependent on the prior substitution of *was* for Standard English *were* (which I believe is itself less usual, even among the semi-illiterate, than it was a couple of generations ago). **1966–69** *DARE* Tape **CA**134, You was all by yourself; **KY**6, They was several companies buying ties; **ME**18, There was sledge straps on them harnesses; **VA**2, Some of 'em was called back and some wasn't. **1975**

Allen *LAUM* 2.34 **Upper MW**, Not much more than one-half of the Type I's [=old, with little educ] use *was,* and none of the college graduates.

c for contrary-to-fact subjunc forms.   Note: once frowned upon by grammarians, subjunc *was* is now widespread among all classes of speakers, *were* having become primarily a formal usage.   See also **if so be**

(1) prec a subject, without conditional *if.*   *old-fash* or *arch*

1938 Rawlings *Yearling* 10 **FL**, What would I do this fine spring day, was I a boy? **1949** Gipson *Hound-Dog Man* 213 **csTX**, Watch me'n Grizzly here. Was we to take us a notion to grab up a young filly apiece and rattle our old bones some, you young bloods'd see some caper cutting like it was meant to be done.

(2) usu with conditional *if* or compar *like.*

1892 *DN* 1.237 **wMO**, I wouldn't go along thet-a-way, if I was you. **1927** *AmSp* 3.3 **Ozarks**, One always hears *ef I was you,* never *if I were you.* **1950** Stuart *Hie Hunters* 85 **eKY**, If ye's to live here a while, ye might like it! **1965–70** *DARE* (Qu. A22) Inf **NC**48, She worked like the house was on fire; (Qu. V2b, . . *"I wouldn't trust him ___.")* Infs **IN**45, **MD**40, **MI**10, **TX**41, If he was God himself *(or* the last man in the world, etc); (Qu. W41) Infs **CT**30, **OK**47, Looks like she was thrown *(or* throwed) together; (Qu. X52) Infs **MI**55, 107, Like he was drawn through a knothole; **AR**28, Like he was playing hookey from the graveyard; (Qu. Y21) Inf **TX**32, Get around like dead lice was falling off of them; **AL**3, Moves like the dead lice was dropping off of him; (Qu. GG2) Inf **ME**5, Didn't know if they was comin' or goin'; (Qu. JJ30a) Inf **LA**3, I'd forget my head if it wasn't hung on my shoulders; **IA**22, I'd lose my head if it wasn't tied to me; (Qu. KK34, . . *"Her house always looks ___.")* Inf **TX**33, Like the preacher was coming. [See also *DS* A11, 18, N12, CC12a, KK42b, 55c, 62, NN4, 13] [**1975** Morris *Usage* 582, As Porter Perrin remarked: "Today the subjunctive is a trait of style rather than of grammar and is used by writers chiefly to set their language a little apart from everyday usage."]

d in phr of greeting *How you was?*: How are you?

1950 *WELS* (Expressions used when you meet somebody you know quite well) 1 Inf, **ceWI**, Hi! Hey, there! How you was! **1967** *DARE* (Qu. NN10a) Infs **AR**55, **TX**1, How you *(or* ya) was?

6 *were*: Was.   **chiefly Sth, S Midl**

1829 Kirkham *Engl. Grammar* 193 **KY, VA, MD, MS**, I war thar . . . I *was there.* **1884** Baldwin *Yankee School-Teacher* 177 **VA**, De catty-corneres' sort of beast dat eber I wur 'flicted ter own. **1889** Edwards *Runaways* 99 **GA**, Th' parson war erlong ter-day. **1928** Aldrich *Lantern* 8 **NE** (as of 1854), Father were what they call an aristocrat. **1931** *PMLA* 46.1318 **Appalachians**, Use of plural for singular forms is not common, but it is sometimes heard in primitive Baptist sermons: "He were said to be," etc. **1933** Rawlings *South Moon* 77 **FL**, I were jest crossin' the river from the outfit . . when a raft o' logs passed me. **1952** *Hall Coll.* **wNC, eTN**, *Were* . . . often used in the sing[ular] . . "He were so little and he were so brave" [song lyrics]. **1966** *DARE* Tape **SC**24A, We weren't supposed to sell his meat but a certain amount. **1975** Newell *If Nothin' Don't Happen* 3 **nwFL**, There is no set pattern for . . "to be." Billy might say, "It were a right cold day and I was a long way from home," using the different forms in the same sentence—whatever came easiest off his tongue and flowed the smoothest. *Ibid* 40, I remember a Canadian feller named Jack Mayer who were a great duck hunter and knowed just about all there were to know about ducks.

7 *been.*

a **Have been, has been, had been.**

1802 in 1924 Steele *Papers* 1.250 **NC**, I have had but one bushel & half of Sault Sence I been under your Dirrection for the Stock. **1952** Brown *NC Folkl.* 1.519, *Been* . . . Used even by educated persons who would never use *taken* and *seen* in the same way. "Where you *been* all day, Henry?"—General. Common. **1954** *Harder Coll.* **cwTN**, I been choppin' down trees. **c1960** *Wilson Coll.* **csKY**, *Been,* often used for *have been;* "Where you been lately?" **1966–69** *DARE* (Qu. W41) Inf **TX**11, Clothes look like they been slept in; **IL**96, Looks like their clothes been throwed at them; (Qu. X42) Inf **FL**26, I been awake ever since six o'clock; (Qu. BB47, . . *In the best of health)* Inf **AR**47, Like I just been let out of a cage; (Qu. II39) Inf **CO**38, You been a dear; (Qu. NN10a) Inf **OK**11, How you been?; **MN**10, Where ya been keepin' yourself?; (Qu. NN10b) Inf **WA**24, Been a long time since I saw you. **1972** *Foxfire Book* 22 **nGA**, I been awful little all my life. **1977** Smitherman *Talkin* 22, Generally where Black English speakers use *been,* White English speakers would use *have, has,* or *had* plus *been.* Black English: He been there before. White English: He has been there before . . . Black English:

She been there and left before I even got there. White English: She had been there and left before I even got there. **1978** *Parade* 16 Apr 21/2 **FL**, It's possible I been hurt. It's possible I been bad hurt.

b followed by a particle (here spelled *a, er,* or *uh*) which functions as auxiliary to a following uninflected verb. Note: the constr is creole *(Gullah),* its prob basilectal components being *been* |bɪn| + **da** aux verb + verb. When decreolized, **a** prep¹ 5 takes the place of **da,** and later, *-ing* is added to the verb. Ex: |bɪn da kʌm| > |bɪn a kʌm| spelled *binnuh come* (see quot 1922) > *been a-coming am* (or was, have been) coming.

1888 Jones *Negro Myths* 65 **seGA,** Two fren, dem bin a mek one journey togerruh [=Two friends were making a journey together]. *Ibid* 103, Es de ole man bin er pass long eh notus um [=As the old man passed along he noticed him]. **1922** Gonzales *Black Border* 36 **sSC, GA coasts** [Gullah], One buckruh binnuh talk 'puntop de flatfawm [=A white man was talking on the platform]. *Ibid* 62, Uh binnuh walk duh paat' [=I been a-walking the path]. **1949** Turner *Africanisms* 225, In Gullah also, [bɪnə] 'been' placed before a verb may be expressed in English by the past, perfect, or pluperfect tense and the action may or may not be continuous: [wɒt unə bɪnə du] means 'What did you do?' or 'What were you doing?' or 'What have you done?' or 'What have you been doing?' or 'What had you done?' or 'What had you been doing?'

c prec a pres pple: equivalent to *have* + past pple, used to indicate continuity over time.

1898 Westcott *Harum* 340 **cNY,** I ben losin' him over an' agin all these years. **1967–68** *DARE* FW Addit **LA7,** Yeah, I been knowing Mister Joe for forty years now; **csLA,** I been knowing Flossie since she was sixteen. **1970** *DARE* Tape **VA38,** I've been owning my farm ever since I bought it in thirty-six.

d in var other constrs: See quots.

1922 Gonzales *Black Border* 63 **sSC, GA coasts** [Gullah], Uh Tengk Gawd uh did'n' bin hab on uh new *britchiz!* [=I thank God I didn't have on a new (pair of) breeches!]. **1942** Faulkner *Go Down* 74 **MS** [Black], We been had it [=a marriage license] since I sold my cotton last fall. **1966** *DARE* Tape **SC10** [Black], One time we used to have a short summer. And i' been a long winter. I' been cold . . . But one time it use' to been so cold right first of the winter; **SC16** [Black], But no tobacco been here then. **1982** *Parade* 19 Dec 5/4 **VA** [White], Then come all the pretty Christmas cards. It was the happiest time of my life. It *still* been the happiest time.

8 Forms of *be* omitted.

a absence of *are.*

(1) following interrog pron.

1829 Kirkham *Engl. Grammar* 193 **MD, VA, KY, MS,** Whar you gwine? . . . *Where are* you *going?* **1903** *DN* 2.293 **Cape Cod MA** (as of 1850s), After *where, are* is omitted: "Where you from?" "Where you going?" **1932** (1974) Caldwell *Tobacco Road* 83 **GA,** When you going to buy a new automobile? **1965–70** *DARE* (Qu. W38) Infs **IN15, MI78, OK18, 42, WI27,** Where you going to preach (today, tonight, this evening)?; **MO5, 27,** Where you (*or* ya) gonna preach?; (Qu. II15) Infs **CO47, MI55,** Where you going (in such a hurry)?; (Qu. MM22) Inf **MO27,** Where you from?; (Qu. NN10a) Inf **LA37,** Where ya at dere?; **LA45,** Where you at?

(2) following noun or personal pron.

1938 Rawlings *Yearling* 398 **FL,** You mighty biggety now. **1952** O'Connor *Wise Blood* 57 **GA,** You the first familer face I seen in two months. **1966** *DARE* Tape **SC17,** Seems like some days they off and some days they on. **1972** *Orbis* (Louvain) 21.26 **TX,** Colleges just like business. *Ibid* 27 **TN,** They right over here. **1976** Warner *Beautiful Swimmers* 151 **eMD,** They so dumb they can't see where the start of it is.

b absence of *is* or *was*—often to signify the non-habitualness of the action or event described. *esp freq among Blacks* Note: this constr was prob reinforced in Black usage by substrate infl from W Afr languages in which absence of copula is structurally normal.

1776 in 1977 Smitherman *Talkin* 9 [Black], Me massa name Cunney Tomsee. **1872** (1973) Thompson *Major Jones's Courtship* 103 **GA,** I hadn't no sort of a idee how she gwine to do it. **1887** (1967) Harris *Free Joe* 95 **nwGA** [Black], He'd stop en look roun' en say, 'Whar Trunion?' **1953** Brewer *Word Brazos* 16 **seTX** [Black], His pappy Tom jes' ez 'sponsibul as li'l Bill be. **1972** *Orbis* (Louvain) 21.22 **Sth,** *Be* finite and the absence of *be,* two features which social dialectologists have persistently called features of "Black speech", are structures which I have found in the speech of the alltime defenders of white supremacy—the

Klu [sic] Klux Klan. *Ibid* 24, He our mean and ugly bastard . . . He runnin' a cripple third . . . He not gonna to carry anything. *Ibid* 27, He mad . . . He over there . . . He always comin' by my place. **1977** Smitherman *Talkin* 5, [West African languages allow for the construction of sentences without a form of the verb *to be*. Thus we get a typical African–English Pidgin sentence such as "He tell me he God," used by . . a slave . . at the Salem witch trial in 1692]. *Ibid* 21, The Black English speaker omits *be* when referring to conditions that are fixed in time and to events or realities that do not repeat themselves . . . *He a hippie now . . . He too tall for me.*

C Neg constrs. See also **ain't** v¹ and v², **hain't, tain't, twan't**

1 present.

a *beant,* also sp *ban't, beent, beint, ben't, beunt:* Am not, is not, are not. **chiefly NEng** *old-fash* Cf *EDD*

1702 (1972) Mather *Magnalia* 3.182/1 **MA,** *I been't afraid, I thank God, I been't afraid to die!* **1810** (1912) Bell *Journey to OH* 2 **CT,** "Well! Gals where are you going?" . . "You bant though—to New Connecticut? Why what a long journey!" **1815** Humphreys *Yankey in England, Ban't, Ben't* . . am, or as [sic], or are not. **1818** Fessenden *Ladies Monitor* 171 **VT,** Provincial words and phrases . . . *ban't* for are not or be not. **1836** (1838) Haliburton *Clockmaker* (1st ser) 64, They beant good saddle horses, and they beant good draft beasts. **1894** *DN* 1.328 **NJ,** *Beant:* negative form of . . *[be];* used for both *am not* and *are not.* **1905** *DN* 3.3 **cCT,** *Beunt.* **1938** Matschat *Suwannee R.* 197 **nFL, sGA,** Beint ye a-comin back, Cella? **1971** *Down East* Nov 25 **ME,** Beant— still exists in Maine for "are not" and "is not."

b *isn't:* usu pronc |'ɪznt|; also occas |'ɪdn(t), 'ɪtnt|.

1949 *PADS* 11.7 **wTX,** Id'nt ['ɪdnt] . . . Isn't. Occasional. Not limited to the uneducated. **c1960** *Wilson Coll.* **csKY,** Isn't, esp among children, is often ['ɪdnt] or ['ɪtnt]. **1965–68** *DARE* (Qu. NN3) Infs **OK14, PA69,** ['ɪdnt ɪt]. **1966–67** *DARE* Tape **CO**1, I'm right on that, idn't ['ɪdnt] I?; **MS**15, Id'n ['ɪdn] that sump'm?

2 past: usu *wasn't* |'wʌznt, wɑznt|, *weren't* |'wɝ-(ə)nt|; also:

a |'wɑtn̩, 'wɑdn̩(t), 'wʌdn̩t|. Pronc-sp *wadn't.* **?chiefly Sth, Midl**

1949 *PADS* 11.12 **wTX,** Wadn't ['wɑdnt] . . . Common. **1953** Atwood *Survey of Verb Forms* 32, The assimilation of /z/ to /d/ before /n/—/wadənt/, /wʌdənt/—is recorded a number of times in the South Midland and in S.C.—and it shows up a few times in n. and w. N.Y. . . . mainly in rapid conversation. **1960** (1962) Lee *Mockingbird* 101 **sAL,** Maybe he wadn't mad, maybe he was just crazy. **1967** *DARE* FW Addit **nwAR,** Wasn't [watn] or [waʔn]. The young man who used this pronunciation was from the Ozarks . . . I have heard it from the younger people here, too, and from a middle-aged Florida cracker. It is more commonly pronounced [wadn] through the Ozarks. **1968** *DARE* (Qu. P9) Inf **LA29,** Fish wad'n bitin'. **1972** *Foxfire Book* 30 **nGA,** Ulysses said they wadn't no use. **1975** Allen *LAUM* 2.43, The assimilated form /wʌdənt/ appears in the speech of four scattered Type I [=older, less educated] infs.

b |wɑnt, wɔnt, wont|. Pronc-spp *wan't, won't.* **chiefly NEng, NY, nPA; also Sth, esp eVA, eNC** For map see 1953 Atwood *Survey of Verb Forms* Figs 24, 30

1795 Dearborn *Columbian Grammar* 139 ["List of Improprieties"], Want for Was not. **1843** (1916) Hall *New Purchase* 135 **IN,** He wan't nere so stuck up a feller as folks said. **1891** *DN* 1.69 **LA, NEng,** Wa'n't [wɔnt]: wasn't. "He said he wa'n't goin' to do it." **1892** *DN* 1.234 **KY, MI,** Wa'n't. **1893** Shands *MS Speech* 67, Want [wɔnt]. Negro and illiterate white for *was not* or *were not.* **1894** *DN* 1.340 **wCT,** The past tense is *was* (neg. *wa'n't*—pron [wɔnt]) in all cases. **1898** Lloyd *Country Life* 19 **AL,** We think the plan of the government would go all to smash and smithereens if we want runnin the machinery. **1905** *DN* 3.23 **cCT,** *Wan't.* **1907** *DN* 3.203 **seNH,** *Wa'n't.* *Ibid* 219 **nwAR,** *Wa'n't.* **1909** *DN* 3.386 **eAL, wGA,** *Wa'n't.* **1910** *DN* 3.451 **cwNY,** *Won't.* **1939** FWP *These are Our Lives* 6 **ceNC,** He found out that they won't going to be a cent left after the bills was paid. **1944** *PADS* 2.51 **nLA, eNC, SC, cTN, sVA,** Wa'n't . . . Was + not, were + not. **1950** *PADS* 14.72 **SC,** Won't . . . "We *won't* there when it happened." **1952** Brown *NC Folkl.* 1.604 **c,eNC,** Wa'n't [wont, wɔnt] . . . "He *wa'n't* there yesterday." **1953** Atwood *Survey of Verb Forms* 32, Was not . . . The form *wan't* . . /wɔnt/, /wɔnt/, and sometimes /wont/ . . shows a striking geographic distribution. Throughout N. Eng., except for R.I., parts of c. and w. Mass., and s. Vt., this form is extremely common . . . It appears among all types of informants, including one fourth of the cultured group. In N.Y. and n. Pa. it also appears in a good many communities, usually among Type I informants [=old, with little educ] only. In the

Southern area *wan't* is very solid in e. Va., extending inland to the Blue Ridge, and almost as common in e. N.C... It is used .. by half the cultured group in this area.

c |wɑrnt, wɔrnt|. Pronc-spp *wahrn't, warn't.* old-fash or arch **1843** (1916) Hall *New Purchase* 145 **IN**, I'll be doggd if thare warn't a wild cat jist goin to spring. **1942** Whipple *Joshua* 14 **UT** (as of c1860), I'd forget my head if it warn't fastened on. **1953** Atwood *Survey of Verb Forms* 32/1, *Warn't* /wɑrnt/ or /wɔrnt/ is not very common anywhere, being found only in scattered communities, mainly along the Southern coast and in w. N.C. and w. Va. **1975** Allen *LAUM* 2.43, *Warn't* occurs in the conversation of a Type I [=older, less educated] Minnesota housewife . . . "I warn't /wɑrnt/ through." **1976** Garber *Mountain-ese* 99 **sAppalachians**, There wahrn't no water in the well.

d other forms of *weren't:* See quot. **1953** Atwood *Survey of Verb Forms* 32/1, The preterite negative form of *to be* is recorded in the context "It (wasn't) me." . . *Weren't* /wʌnt/ is found in several communities in coastal N.C., and there are a few scattered occurrences elsewhere . . . The unusual form *werdn't* /wʌdnt/ or /wɔtnt/ occurs five times in Delmarva and once on the lower Susquehanna.

3 as a tag question: See *DS* NN3, and **ainna, ain't** v², **ain't it** interrog exclam², **enty, inso.**

beach aster n
=**seaside daisy.**
1897 Parsons *Wild Flowers CA* 304, Beach-Aster. *Erigeron glaucus.* **1915** (1926) Armstrong *Western Wild Flowers* 534, Beach Aster—*Erigeron glaucus.* **1934** Haskin *Wild Flowers Pacific Coast* 367, Beach Aster . . *Erigeron glaucus.* **1954** CA Div. Beaches & Parks *Pt. Lobos Wild Flowers* 19, Seaside Daisies, also called beach asters, begin to bloom by the middle of April and continue their great display until late fall.

beachberry n
A succulent shrub *(Scaevola plumeri)* with white or pinkish flowers followed by black, juicy berries native to the Gulf coast and Florida Keys. Also called **inkberry**
1971 Craighead *Trees S. FL* 94, Some of the more characteristic trees and shrubs of the beaches and coastal ridges are .. bay cedar, beachberry, .. and saffron plum. **1982** *Naples Now* May 36 **sFL**, Walking along stretches of beach, one might notice the *inkberry* or *beach berry,* a succulent plant that can reach four feet. It has sprawling stems that spread under the sand to form extensive colonies.

beach burr n Also *beach clotbur, ~ cocklebur*
A **cockleburr 1** (here: *Xanthium strumarium*).
1936 Winter *Plants NE* 137, Beach Cocklebur. On river and lake banks inland as far west as N.D. **1961** House *Wild Flowers* 287, Beach Clotbur . . . An annual, coarse, rough herb of seashores and river beaches. **1966** *DARE* Wildfl QR Pl.213 Inf **NC28**, Beach burr.

beach clam n
A **surf clam,** esp *Spisula solidissima.*
1793 in 1889 Huntington NY *Town Rec.* 3.170, That no Beach Clams on the south side of the Islands .. be catched by any Person Whatsoever to Sell to Boatmen. **1881** Ingersoll *Oyster-Industry* 242, Clam . . . Many kinds are distinguished by an additional definitive word, prefixed, as beach-clam *(Mactra),* etc. **1931–33** *LANE* Worksheets **seRI**, Beach clam: a large clam.

beach clotbur See **beach burr**

beach cloud n
1967–68 *DARE* (Qu. B10, . . *Long trailing clouds high in the sky*) Inf **PA26**, Beach clouds; (Qu. B11) Inf **SC11**, Beach clouds—high, thin, moving, wispy.

beach cocklebur See **beach burr**

beachcomber n
Perh the **piping plover** or the semipalmated plover.
1970 *DARE* (Qu. Q10, . . *Water birds and marsh birds*) Inf **SC69**, Beachcomber.

beach crow n
=**northwestern crow.**
1968 *DARE* (Qu. Q11, . . *Kinds of blackbirds*) Inf **AK1**, Beach crow, fish crow.

beach daisy n Also *beach red-daisy*
=**gaillardia.**
1951 *PADS* 15.42 **TX**, *Gaillardia pulchella* . . . Beach red-daisy. **1967** *DARE* (Qu. S26e, . . *Other wildflowers*) Inf **TX12**, Beach daisy—brownish and yellowish streaks; **TX15**, Beach daisy—also called sand dollars; red and yellow, grow on beach.

beach flea n
=**piping plover.**
1951 Pough *Audubon Water Bird* 319, Beach flea. See Piping plover. **1956** *AmSp* 31.183 **NY**, Beach flea—Piping plover.

beach fly n
1965–70 *DARE* (Qu. R12, *Other kinds of flies*) Infs **FL22, HI14, NH18, NY34, PA246**, Beach fly; **MI37**, Some call 'em beach flies, others call 'em fish flies, and one person I know calls 'em stable flies; [it's the] size of a house fly, stings terribly; speckled.

beach grass n
Either of two sand-binding grasses: *Ammophila arenaria,* which is also called **sea sand reed** and **sea matweed,** or *A. breviligulata.*
1681 in 1887 East Hampton NY *Records* 2.102, Thomas Bee doth .. maintaine a .. fence one the beach .. down soe low as any Beach grass groues. **1782** Crèvecoeur *Letters* 128 **seMA**, Those declining grounds which lead to the sea-shores abound with *beach grass,* a light fodder when cut and cured, but very good when fed green. **a1862** (1865) [see **beach pea**]. **1947** *Atlantic Mth.* Sept 35/2 **Cape Cod MA**, We made headquarters on a small beach-grass rise opposite Fish Hog Eddy. **1968–69** *DARE* (Qu. L34, . . *Important crops*) Inf **NC76**, American beach grass; (Qu. S8, . . *Wild grass . . it spreads by sending out long underground roots . . hard to get rid of*) Inf **AK1**, Beach grass—grows along seashores; (Qu. S9, . . *Kinds of grass*) Inf **NC76**, American beach grass; **WI32**, Beach grass.

beach heather n
A heathlike plant of the genus *Hudsonia.* Also called **barren heath, dog's dinner, false heather, gold heather, ground cedar, poverty grass** For other names of var spp see **bear grass 4, cloth-of-gold 1, field pine, ground moss**
1900 Lyons *Plant Names* 194, *H. tomentosa* . . . Beach Heather. **1913** *Torreya* 13.251, Many herbaceous plants cover the ground .. dense tufts of beach heather, *Hudsonia tomentosa.* **1931** Clute *Common Plants* 69, The heather is rare or missing with us, but a little heather-like plant of sandy regions is a good substitute as the beach heather *(Hudsonia tomentosa).* **1951** Hough *Singing in Morning* 39, New England cushions (and mattresses) have been stuffed with everything first and last, and dried beach heather .. can be no worse than corn husks or seaweed. **1976** Bruce *How to Grow Wildflowers* 215, Another matformer dots the white dunes behind the head of the beach—*Hudsonia tomentosa,* called Beach-heather though not a true heather at all.

beach lavender n
=**sea lavender.**
1943 Pratt *Barefoot Mailman* 4 **FL**, On the other was a tangled vegetation of sea grapes, beach lavender, flowering Spanish bayonet, and half a dozen kinds of palms.

beach morning glory n
1 =**railroad vine.** chiefly **HI**
1929 Pope *HI Wayside Plants* 173, Beach Morning-glory . . . *Ipomoea pes-caprae* . . . seems to prefer the coral sands above high tide. **1948** (1965) Neal *Gardens HI* 709, Beach morning-glory . . . is a vigorous vine commonly seen creeping on sandy beaches just above high-water mark. **1979** Bushnell *Stone of Kannon* 271 **HI**, The only relief for the eyes in this bleakness is a thin verge of green along the shore, where coarse grass and pohuehue, the beach morning glory, cling to the wet sand.
2 A white-flowered **morning glory** *(Ipomoea stolonifera)* found along the Gulf coast.
1961 Wills–Irwin *Flowers TX* 175, The Goat-foot-creeper is .. often in the company of the Beach Morning-glory, *I. stolonifera* . . . , a white-flowered species. **1972** Brown *Wildflowers LA* 149, Beach Morning-glory . . . Confined to the sandy beach along the Gulf above high tide level . . . Also Texas and Mississippi.

beach pea n Also *beach sweet pea*
A leguminous, usu purple-flowered plant *(Lathyrus maritimus)* found on beaches and seashores. Also called **sea pea**
1802 MA Hist. Soc. *Coll.* 1st ser 8.145 **seMA**, Beach grass, the beach

pea, beach ivy, . . grow here luxuriantly. **a1862** (1865) Thoreau *Cape Cod* 124, Here and there were tracts of Beach-grass mingled with the Sea-side Golden-rod and Beach-pea. **1967–70** *DARE* (Qu. S26e, . . *Wildflowers*) Inf **MA**100, Beach pea—purple and magenta; **MA**57, Beach sweet pea—grows in beach sand, bush a foot high; several purple flowers on one stem.

beach plum n *chiefly NEast, esp NEng*
A seacoast shrub (*Prunus maritima*).
1784 in 1785 Amer. Acad. Arts & Sci. *Memoirs* 1.449 **eMA**, *Prunus, . . . Beach,* or *Sea-Side Plumb . . .* The fruit of some of them, when fully ripe, is well-tasted. **1810** in 1889 East Hampton NY *Records* 4.365, No person . . . shall be permitted to pick or gather any cranberries, beach plums or bayberries on any of the common lands. **1856** Whittier *Panorama* 138 **ME**, Where the purple beach-plum mellows / On the bluffs. **1892** B. Torrey *Foot-path Way* 78 (*DAE*), The beach-plum crop was a failure. **1910** Graves *Flowering Plants* 244 **CT**, Beach Plum . . . The fruit is sometimes gathered for preserves. **1939** Wolcott *Yankee Cook Book* 308, The beach plum is found rooted in the dunes along the beaches of Cape Cod and Martha's Vineyard where excavations bring nothing to light but coarse beach sand. **1946** *Sat. Eve. Post* 3 Aug 70/1 **Long Island NY**, We . . descended toward the marsh, . . keeping in the concealment of the trees, and later, . . of the sumacs and bayberries and beach plums. **1965–70** *DARE* (Qu. I46) Infs **CT**16, **DE**1, **ME**1, 5, **MA**40, 50, 55, 72, 98, **NJ**39, 55, Beach plum(s); (Qu. I53) Inf **NJ**39, Beach plums.

beach quail n
=**knot** n².
1923 U.S. Dept. Ag. *Misc. Circular* 13.52, *Knot . . . Vernacular Names . . . In local use.*—Beach quail (Tex.).

beach red-daisy See **beach daisy**

beach robin n *esp NC*
=**knot** n².
1888 Trumbull *Names of Birds* 179, *[Knot]* Again at Moriches, L[ong] I[sland], and at Morehead, N[orth] C[arolina], *Beach-Robin.* **1923** U.S. Dept. Ag. *Misc. Circular* 13.52, *Knot . . . Vernacular Names . . . In local use . . .* Beach-robin (N.C.). **1955** *AmSp* 30.181 **NY, NC**, The knot is . . . also known . . as *beach robin.* **1966** *DARE* (Qu. Q10, . . *Water birds and marsh birds*) Inf **NC**1, 12, Beach robin.

beach sweet pea See **beach pea**

beachwood n
1965 *DARE* File, *Beachwood*—driftwood. Heard in eastern U.S.

bead n
1 In marble play: a cheap marble. Cf **bead line**
1958 *PADS* 29.30 **WI**, Bead.
2 A squirt of tobacco juice.
1968 *DARE* (Qu. DD4) Inf **SC**54, To spit a bead is to rid oneself of the brown juice.
3 In moonshining: the bubbles that form when whiskey is shaken and that are an indicator of quality.
1917 *DN* 4.408 **wNC, KY**, *Bead . . .* In moonshine whiskey, iridescent bubbles that form when the liquor is shaken up. **1964** Faulkner *Hamlet* 49 **MS**, He shook the bottle and raised it to the light as though testing the bead. **1969** *DARE* Tape **GA**72, The bead—which is the bubble, when you shake it—if the bead flies up there coarse it's high proof; if it's very fine, it's low proof. **1972** *Foxfire Book* 337 **nGA**, This helps . . the mixture begin working, and helps the final product hold a good bead. **1974** Maurer *KY Moonshine* 113, *Bead . . .* The little bubbles that form along the meniscus of liquor when shaken in a bottle, allowing an experienced moonshiner to judge the proof and quality of the liquor with great accuracy. "This stuff holds a good bead."
4 In phr **put the bead on:** see quot. Cf **bee** n¹ **2**
1968 *DARE* (Qu. Y6, *Words meaning to put pressure on somebody to do something he ought to have done but hasn't: "He's a whole week late. I'm going to _____."*) Inf **MN**15, Put the bead on him.

bead v [**bead** n **3**]
In moonshining: see quot 1974.
1969 [see **break** v C7]. **1972** *Foxfire Book* 333 **nGA**, We use what we call 'mule feed' for malt, and we add beading oil to make it bead good. **1974** Maurer *KY Moonshine* 113, *Bead . . .* To form bubbles and hold them around the surface periphery, as liquor tends to do. "This don't bead so good."

be-addled ppl adj Also sp *be-attled* [*be-* prefix (*OED* 7) + *addled*]
Confused, addled.
1917 in 1944 *ADD* **sWV**. **1939** *Ibid* **nWV**, I'm beattled (|bi'ætld|). **1966–70** *DARE* (Qu. GG2, *Expressions meaning "confused, mixed up"*) Inf **OK**18, [bijædld]; **OH**95, [bi'jædəld]; (Qu. HH5, *Someone who is queer but harmless*) Inf **CA**66, Be-addled but nice.

beadle n, also attrib [Alter of *beagle*]
A beagle.
1930s in 1944 *ADD* **IN, eWV**, Beadle. **1938** (1955) FWP *Guide DE* 386, Dogs trot along in gangs under the leadership of a setter or a beadle dog (rabbit hound).

bead lily n [From the beadlike berries]
A plant of the genus *Clintonia*. Also called **bluebead**. For other names of var spp see **amber bell, balsam bell, bearberry 5, bear corn 1, bear plum, bear tongue, bride's bonnet, calf corn, cornflower 2, corn lily, cowtongue 1, dogberry, dog plum, globe amorette, hatpin plant, hound's tongue, northern lily, queen cup, wild corn, wild lily of the valley, wood lily**
1948 Wherry *Wild Flower Guide* 19, *White Beadlily (Clintonia umbellulata). Ibid* 20, Yellow Beadlily (*Clintonia borealis*). **1961** Douglas *My Wilderness* 231 **White Mts NH**, The bead lily (*Clintonia borealis*), with greenish-yellow flowers, appears in unexpected places. With it grows the painted trillium. **1964** Campbell *Great Smoky Wildflowers* 38, *Clintonia umbellulata . . . Clintonia borealis . . .* Both species are also called *bead lily.* **1966** *DARE* Wildfl QR Pl.17 Inf **MI**31, Bead lily. **1973** Hitchcock–Cronquist *Flora Pacific NW* 689, *Clintonia . . .* Bead-lily; Clintonia.

bead line n Cf **bead** n **1**
The starting line in a game of marbles.
1966 *DARE* (Qu. EE8) Inf **FL**37, Bead line.

be a-doing v phr Also *be doing*
To do something merely to have something to do.
1902 *DN* 2.229 **sIL**, *Be a doin' . . .* To pass the time; 'Whatche comin' around here for? O, jes to be a doin'.' **1906** *DN* 3.115 **sIN**. **1907** *DN* 3.220 **nwAR**. **1937–39** Hall Coll. **eTN, wNC**, "Got drunk just to be a-doin'." "Pap asks you what you done that for—you say 'just to be a-doin'." **1968** *DARE* (Qu. NN12a, *Things that people say to put a child off when he asks too many questions: "What's that for?"*) Inf **MO**16, Oh, just to be doin'.

bead-puller n [In ref to rosary beads] *derog* Cf *DS* CC4
A Roman Catholic.
1964 *PADS* 42.34 **Chicago IL**, The Catholic is identified by multiple responses . . . *Roman* is found only among Protestants . . as are *bead-puller* and . . *statue-lover.*

bead ruby n Also *ruby bead*
=**false lily of the valley**.
1894 *Jrl. Amer. Folkl.* 7.102, *Maianthemum Canadense . .* bead ruby, N.Y. . . . Probably from the beauty of the berries. **1940** Clute *Amer. Plant Names* 13, *M. Canadense . . .* Mayflower, ruby-bead. **1954** Sharpe *101 Wildflowers* 11, *Beadruby . . . Maianthemum dilatatum . . .* Fruit a reddish-speckled, green berry, lasting from July till September. **1961** Douglas *My Wilderness* 231 **NH**, On shady trails the Canada bead-ruby (*Maianthemum canadense*) grows, showing a delicate raceme of white flowers above two bright waxy leaves.

bead tree n, also attrib Also *beadwood* [From the former use of the fruits as beads; *OED* 1668 →] **Sth**
=**Chinaberry 1.**
1847 Darlington *Ag. Botany* 21, Pride of India. Bead-tree . . . This tree has been introduced into the Southern States, as an ornamental shade tree,—and is now, . . perfectly naturalized. **1911** *Century Dict.*, *Melia . . .* Variously known as pride-of-India, bead-tree, false sycamore, etc. **1937** Hall Coll. **wNC, eTN**, To cure blood poison, use catnip and beadwood bark boiled together and made into a poultice. **1952** Taylor *Plants Colonial Days* 24, The chinaberry has other common names, among them . . bead tree. **1966** *DARE* (Qu. BB50d, . . *A spring tonic.*) Inf **NC**30, Bead-wood tea.

beady See **biddy** n³

beaft prep [Perh from *by + aft;* but cf ME *baft* and **abaft**] **NEng coast**

Behind, in back of.

1945 Colcord *Sea Language* 31 **ME, Cape Cod, Long Island,** *Beaft.* Same as abaft [=behind], and more common in later years, both at sea and alongshore. Perhaps a manufactured word, on the analogy of before. **1974** *AmSp* 49.61 **swME** (as of c1900), *Be-aft . . .* In back of.

beak v

To talk excessively or maliciously; to "peck" at someone.

1947 Ballowe *The Lawd* 183 **LA** [Black], They [=hussies] beaked an' clawed me, comin' an' gwine. **1968** *DARE* (Qu. HH7b, *Someone who talks too much, or too loud: "He's always _____."*) Inf **PA**66, Beaking. [Inf Black] **1969** *DARE* Tape **OH**100, Who've you been beaking with?

beal n Also sp *beel* [Alter of *boil* a pustule; *OED* c1400 →, "*Obs.* or *dial.*"]

=**bealing.**

1942 *Hench Coll.* **swVA,** All sores were 'beels.' At first I thought that meant boils, but a doctor told me that they meant any kind of infection. **1967** *DARE* (Qu. BB37, *When yellowish stuff comes out of a person's ear, he has . . _____*) Inf **OH**15, Beals.

beal v [**beal** n] **chiefly Appalachians**

To fester or suppurate.

1895 *DN* 1.384 **swPA,** *Beal:* to suppurate. **1916** *DN* 4.337 **cs,wPA, SC. 1917** *DN* 4.408 **wNC, SC. 1939** *AmSp* 14.155 **WV. 1942** *Hench Coll.* **swVA,** A doctor told me that they meant [by the word 'beel'] any kind of infection, and they would say 'my arm is beeling' or 'my foot has beeled.' **1944** *PADS* 2.26 **cwOH, cwNC,** *Beal* [bil]. **1965–70** *DARE* (Qu. BB36, *When there's an open sore and . . yellowish stuff is coming out of it, you say it's _____*) Infs **MI**27, 55, **NY**105, **PA**237, **SC**11, Bealing; (Qu. BB37, *When yellowish stuff comes out of a person's ear, he has a _____*) Inf **MI**55, Bealing ear.

bealed ppl adj Also sp *beeled* [**beal** v] **chiefly Appalachians, esp wPA** See Map

Usu of an ear: infected, abscessed.

1903 *DN* 2.349 **MN,** *Bealed . . .* Sore and suppurating, as a 'bealed ear.' **1965** Weller *Yesterday's People* 119 **sAppalachians,** Other common complaints are "beeled head," "low blood," and "nerves." **1965–70** *DARE* (Qu. BB37) 41 Infs, **chiefly Appalachians,** Bealed ear. **1979** Stegner *Recapitulation* 96 **UT,** "Maybe you could go swimming." "Where? There's only Warm Springs, and last time I was out there I got a bealed ear." **1982** *Barrick Coll.* **sePA,** Bealed — infected . . . Related to *boil,* n.

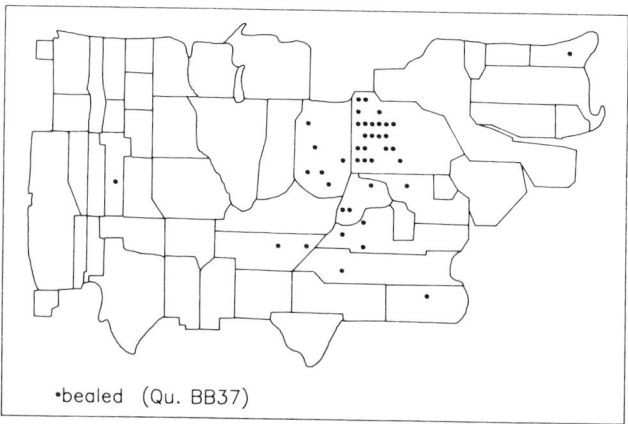

•bealed (Qu. BB37)

bealing n **formerly more widespread, now chiefly Appalachians** See Map

An abscess or boil, esp in the ear.

1824 in 1956 Eliason *Tarheel Talk* 259 **swNC,** Your negro woman Easther has been verry bad with a bealing on her brest. **1886** Amer. Philol. Assoc. *Trans.* 17.37 **Sth,** *Bealing,* a 'boil *or* sore.' Very common in East Tennessee, and known also in the West. **1902** *DN* 2.229 **sIL. 1912** *DN* 3.571 **wIN. 1914** *DN* 4.103 **KS. 1927** *AmSp* 2.348 **WV,** He has a bad bealing on his hand. **1959** *Hench Coll.* **VA Mts,** A Ch[ar-lottes]ville V[irgini]a doctor said that "a bealing [is] an infection of the ear." **1965–70** *DARE* (Qu. BB37, *When yellowish stuff comes out of a person's ear, he has a _____*) 15 Infs, **chiefly Appalachians,** Bealin';

VA1, Bealin' in his head; **OH**66, **PA**142, Bealing [15 of 18 Infs old]; (Qu. BB30, *. . A hard, painful swelling . . under the skin*) Infs **OH**50, **PA**74, Bealing; (Qu. BB33a, *. . A swelling under the skin, bigger than a pimple, that comes to a head*) Infs **TN**12, **WV**13, Bealing.

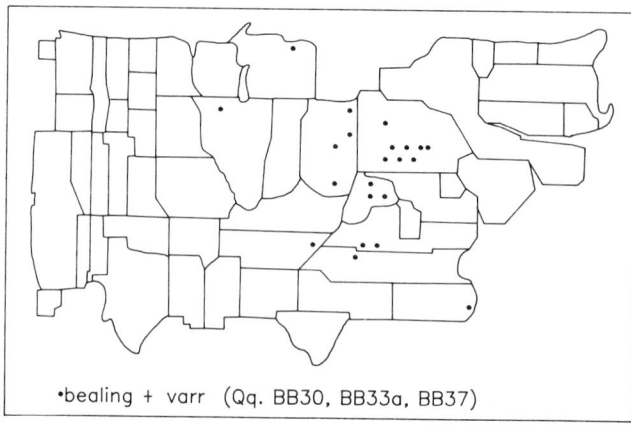

•bealing + varr (Qq. BB30, BB33a, BB37)

beamy adj [See quot 1975; cf the naut phr *broad in the beam* used in same sense]

Usu of a person: broad, wide.

1974 *AmSp* 49.61 **swME** (as of c1900), *Beamy . . . Physically broad (of a person).* **1975** Gould *ME Lingo* 9, *Beamy* — Wide. The width of a vessel is her beam, and a *beamy* boat is traditionally a comfortable one with *room for name and hail . . . Beamy* is a favorite Maine adjective for a lady with steatopygous accumulation.

bean n See **beaner 2**

bean v See **be A2**

bean aphid n

Std: An aphid (esp *Aphis fabae* or *A. rumicis*) which feeds on various plants, esp beans. Also called **black dolphin, black fly, collier** n[1]**, dolphin fly**

bean bird n

The eastern **phoebe** *(Sayornis phoebe).*

1917 (1923) *Birds Amer.* 198, *Phoebe . . . Other Names.*—Phoebe Bird; . . Bean Bird. **1946** Hausman *Eastern Birds* 401.

bean day n

1 See quot. Cf *DJE* **Banian Day**

1918 *DN* 5.15 **Martha's Vineyard MA,** *Bean day.* A day when fishermen catch no fish and must eat beans as a substitute. "We can't get out to the trap, so I guess it'll be a bean-day."

2 Saturday. [From the practice of serving baked beans on Saturday]

1926 *AmSp* 2.78 **ME,** It may be near enough "bean day," which is Saturday, so that you will be regaled with cold or "warmed-up" beans.

bean eater See **beaner 2**

beaner n

1 See quots.

1911 *DN* 3.541 **NE,** *Beaner . . .* Term of appreciation, or compliment; equivalent to fine or excellent. "That new dress is a beaner," "That story is a beaner." **1942** Berrey–Van den Bark *Amer. Slang* 29.2, *Something excellent . . .* Beaner.

2 also attrib, also *bean, bean eater, beano:* A person of Mexican origin. **chiefly SW** *derog*

1919 *DN* 5.63 **NM,** *Bean-eater,* a name given to the low class Mexicans. "That row of adobes is filled with bean-eaters." **1944** Adams *Western Words, Bean-eater* — A nickname for a Mexican. **1965–70** *DARE* (Qu. HH28) Inf **CA**14, Beans; **CA**169, 183, 190, Beaner; **CA**8, Beano; (Qu. II25) Inf **CA**161, Bean eaters. A newspaper columnist of our town [=Red Bluff] once referred to the division of the artichoke eaters and [the] bean eaters; (Qu. W42a) Inf **CA**183, Beaner shoes — Mexican; (Qu. N5) Inf **CA**177, Beaner wagon — because beaners, i.e., Mexicans, drive them. **c1971** Hall *Snake River Valley* 1 inf, **swID,** Beano. **1974** *DARE* File **cWI** [Among students], Beaner: Mexican migrant worker. Beaner wagon: The kind of car the Mexican migrant workers drive.

beanery n, also attrib

1 A cheap restaurant.   **chiefly Nth, N Midl**   See Map

1888 *Texas Siftings* 7 Jan 4/2 *(OEDS),* In a beanery you get biscuit fresh from the nest, Canada grouse from New Jersey and immigrant waiters. **1915** *DN* 4.243 **MT. 1918** *DN* 5.10 **KS. 1919** *DN* 5.22 **NW. 1925** *AmSp* 1.38 **CA, eMA. 1926** (1939) Hemingway *Torrents* 27 **MI,** Inside the door of the beanery Scripps O'Neil looked around him. **1932** *Santa Fe Employes' Mag.* Jan 35, A railroad eating house is called a *beanery . .* ; a waitress is a *beanery queen.* **1940** Cottrell *Railroader* 119, *Beanery queen*—A waitress in a Beanery. **1950** *WELS (A small eating place)* 6 Infs, **WI,** Beanery. **c1960** *Wilson Coll.* **csKY,** *Beanery . .* A cheap eating place . . . Very modern. **1965–70** *DARE* (Qu. D39, . . *A small eating place where the food is not especially good)* 44 Infs, **chiefly Nth, N Midl,** Beanery.

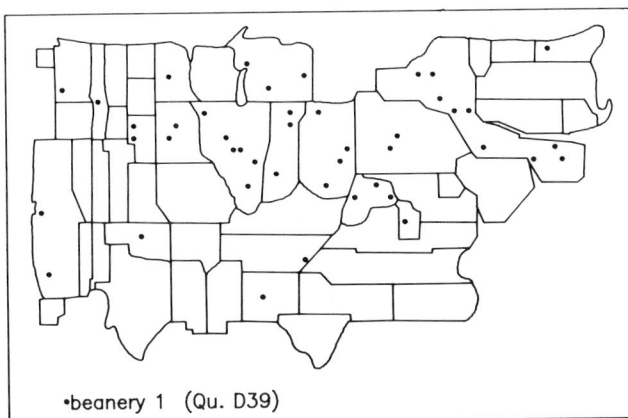

•beanery 1   (Qu. D39)

2 See quots.

1932 *AmSp* 7.400 **WA** [Orphans' Home argot], *Beanery . . .* The disciplinary farm, named from the principal food there. **1940** *AmSp* 15.446 **eTN,** *Beanery.* Jail. 'Sol's in the beanery.'

bean-flip(per) See **bean-shooter**

bean-head n   Cf *DS* HH3

See quots.

1919 *DN* 5.61 **NM,** *Bean-head,* a dull, stupid person. "John is such a bean-head." **1942** Berrey–Van den Bark *Amer. Slang* 433.3, *Stupid person . . .* Bean-head.

bean hole n, also attrib   **chiefly ME, Gt Lakes**

See quot 1969.

1907 *DN* 3.241 **eME,** *Bean-hole . . .* A hole in the ground in which beans are baked in live coals and over which there is usually a log shed or other rude shelter. A feature of logging camps. **1909** *DN* 3.408 **nME. 1913** *DN* 4.2 **ME, Gt Lakes. 1923** *Outing* 81.252/2, A bean hole can be made by digging a hole some larger than the largest kettle and a foot deep. **1966** *DARE* (Qu. H50) Inf **ME2,** Baked beans or bean hole beans—some make it in a bean-hole, in a pot covered with live coals and buried in [the] ground over night; (Qu. HH14, *Ways of teasing a beginner . . "Go get me a _____."*) Inf **MI26,** Bean hole. **1969** Sorden *Lumberjack Lingo* **NEng, Gt Lakes,** *Bean hole*—A hole in the ground in which beans were baked . . . Hardwood coals were raked into it and on top of the bean kettle which had a tight lid; then it was covered with dirt. **1975** Gould *ME Lingo* 9, In lumber camps, and particularly on drives, Cook liked a cast-iron pot for his *bean*-hole. Baking *beans* in a *bean*-hole uses the retained heat principle of the *clambake.* **1977** *Yankee* Nov 57 **ME,** The crew [in a hunting camp] could always count on steak on Friday and beanhole beans on Saturday.

bean hulling n   Also *bean shelling, ~ thrashing*   [hull v]

A social gathering or **bee** at which beans are shelled.

c1960 *Wilson Coll.* **csKY,** *Bean-hulling . . .* A community "working" or "bee" once common. **1965–70** *DARE* (Qu. FF1, . . *A "social" or "sociable")* Inf **IN32,** Bean thrashing; (Qu. FF2, . . *Kinds of parties)* Inf **KY23,** Bean shellings; **MD18,** Bean hulling.

beanie n

In marble play:

1 A small or cheap marble.

1955 *Progress* (Charlottesville VA) 10 Mar 24/1–3 *(Hench Coll.),* A circle was drawn on the ground and cheaper marbles, sometimes called

"beanies" or "clays", were placed in the center to be shot at from the edge of the circle. **1966–68** *DARE* (Qu. EE6b, c) Infs **DC8, MD39, NY104,** Beanie.

2 A shooter.

1970 *DARE* (Qu. EE6a) Inf **TN55,** Beanie.

bean master n

See quots.

1944 Adams *Western Words, Bean-master*—A slang name for the cook. **c1965** *DARE* File [Unidentified newspaper clipping], The range cook is often a target for the jibes of the cowhand. A cook is biscuit roller, . . cookie, bean-master.

beano See **beaner 2**

‡bean-rabbit n

1981 *High Coll.* **ceKY** (as of c1930), Bean-rabbit: . . A piece of meat (rabbit) used numerous times to season food (related to me as part of a humorous story). "Sam used the same bean-rabbit all winter, he was so low on meat."

beans n

=**dibs.**

1956 *AmSp* 31.36, "I have beans on your seat." or "I have ducks on your pie."

beans bird See **pork-and-beans**

bean shelling See **bean hulling**

bean-shooter n   Also *bean-flip(per), ~ snapper*   Cf **beany** n

A slingshot.

1890 *Congressional Record* 4 Mar 1920/1 **AR,** I have not excused this rudeness or shooting with a bean-shooter. *Ibid* 5 Sept 9744/2 **AR,** Judge Benjamin . . . was . . shot in the forehead with a leaden bullet from a weapon known as a "bean-shooter." **1948** *Sat. Eve. Post* 29 May 4/3, We boys in the Midwest 50 years ago called it a beanshooter. **1950** *WELS (Weapon used by children)* 1 Inf, **cwWI,** Bean-snapper. **1962** Atwood *Vocab. TX* 68, The familiar piece of boys' artillery made of a forked stick and rubber strips . . . *Bean shooter* and *bean flip,* which are very rare in Texas, appear fairly often in southern Arkansas and eastern Oklahoma. **1970** Tarpley *Blinky* 230 **neTX,** *Boy's weapon made of rubber strips on a forked stick . .* [2 infs:] bean-shooter . . [1 inf:] bean-flipper.

beans, not to know v phr   For addit var phrr, see *DS* JJ15b

(Note: the basic phr is widespread and std.)

To be very stupid—used in var expanded phrr, as:

a *not to know beans when the bag's open* and varr.   **chiefly Nth, N Midl**   See Map

1876 Nash *Century* 27 (Taylor–Whiting *Dict. Amer. Proverbs)* **NEng,** I told him he was a moonshiny calf . . and didn't know beans, when the bag's open. **1905** *DN* 3.85 **nwAR,** *Know beans when the bag's opened . . .* Negatively, to know little, to be stupid. **1907** *DN* 3.246 **eME,** *Know beans when the bag's untied . . .* To be sophisticated. "I guess I know beans when the bag's untied."] **1912** *DN* 3.581 **wIN,** He doesn't know beans when the bag's open, does he? **1917** *DN* 4.395 **neOH,** *Know beans . . .* To know anything. The full phrase in the '80's was, *He don't know beans when the bag's untied* [in Ill., *when the bag's full;* in Vt., *with the bag open*]; i.e. "doesn't recognize beans." **1950** *WELS (The most basic thing: "He doesn't know _____ . . .")* 1 Inf,

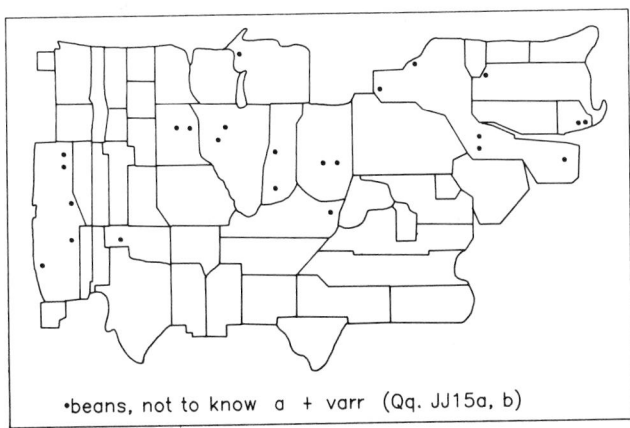

•beans, not to know a + varr   (Qq. JJ15a, b)

cwWI, Beans when the bag's open. **1965** [see **d** below]. **1965–70** *DARE* (Qu. JJ15a, . . *"He hasn't sense enough to _____."*) Inf **CA21**, Know beans when the bag's open; (Qu. JJ15b, . . *"He doesn't know _____."*) 13 Infs, **scattered Nth, N Midl**, Beans with the bags open; 12 Infs, **Nth, N Midl**, Beans (even) when the (bag is *or* bags are) open; **KY44**, Beans with the sack open. [20 of 23 total Infs old]

b *not to know beans from (apple) butter.* **chiefly Missip-Ohio Valleys**

1965–70 *DARE* (Qu. JJ15b, . . *"He doesn't know _____."*) Infs **IL126, 141, IN76, MO27, OH40, 61, 97**, Beans from apple butter; **IA22, TN65**, Beans from butter.

c *not to know beans from bull's foot* and varr. **esp Sth, S Midl**

1965–70 *DARE* (Qu. JJ15b, . . *"He doesn't know _____."*) Infs **AR28, KY78, MS1, TX1**, Beans from (a) bull's foot; **GA12**, Beans from bull foot; **MO25**, Beans from bull; **FL15**, Beans from bullfrogs. **1982** Claiborne *Feast Made* 26 **cMS** (as of c1930), "Dora, you don't know beans from bullfoot about biscuits," Mother said. [Speaker born in AL]

d *not to know beans from barley.*

1954 *Harder Coll.* **cwTN**, Not to know beans from barley—lacks common sense. "He don't know beans from barley." **1965** *DARE* File **csWI** (as of 1940s), He wouldn't know beans from barley if the bags were open. **1966–69** *DARE* (Qu. JJ15b, . . *"He doesn't know _____."*) Infs **IL48, MS65, NY228, WI13**, Beans from barley.

e *not to know beans from peas.*

1966–68 *DARE* (Qu. JJ15b, . . *"He doesn't know _____."*) Inf **MN6**, Beans from peas; **SD3**, Beans from peas when the pods are open; [**OH78**, Beans when the pod's open].

f *not to know beans from buttons.*

1965–68 *DARE* (Qu. JJ15b, . . *"He doesn't know _____."*) Infs **UT3, 6**, Beans from buttons.

bean stringing n **chiefly sAppalachians, esp eKY** Cf **bean hulling, leather britches (beans)**

A social gathering at which beans are strung together to be hung up for drying.

1908 Fox *Lonesome Pine* 289 **KY**, There was a "bean-stringing" at the house that day. **1942** (1971) Campbell *Cloud-Walking* 181 **seKY**, Ever last funeral meeting or bean-stringing or lasses stir-off or other gathering had its crowd of candidates misputting theirselves to be sociable. **1959** Roberts *Up Cutshin* 30 **KY**, When the crops come in, we'd have to start gathering 'em and putting 'em up. When our beans come in, we'd have bean strings. **1960** Hall *Smoky Mt. Folks* 59 **eTN, wNC**, *Bean-stringin'*: a group of women, or of girls with their sweethearts, putting beans on strings to make "leather britches" (also called "shuck beans," that is, dried beans). **1969** *DARE* (Qu. FF2, . . *Kinds of parties*) Infs **KY40, 41, 45**, Bean stringing. **1981** *Broaddus Coll.* **ceKY**.

beans up one's nose n

1 in phr *put beans up one's nose* (or *in one's ear*): To do something stupid after being warned not to.

1936 Sandburg *People* 82, Why did the children / put beans in their ears / when the one thing we told the children / they must not do / was put beans in their ears? **1966** *Dangerous Songs* (Phonodisc), My mama said not to put beans in my ears . . . Now why should I want to put beans in my ears . . . You can't hear your teacher with beans in your ears . . . Hey maybe it's fun to put beans in our ears. **1979** *DARE* File **csWI**, Nobody would tell a kid to put "Beans up his nose" anymore than you'd tell him to put "Fingers in the Meatgrinder . . ." "Beans up his nose" meant another person egging on the "his" to do some dumb thing. **1982** *DARE* File **seMN** (as of 1920s), One cannot help recalling the story of the mother who had to go out and leave her children at home. "Do not put beans up your noses," she cautioned, and left. Since this trick had never occurred to them, they of course tried it at once. *Ibid* **csWI** (as of 1950s), I remember the expression "beans up your nose" from when I was a little girl in Madison. The meaning it had for me was that if you tell children not to do something, they will be sure to do it. This came to light because a neighbor girl of ours did, in fact, put beans up her nose.

2 in phr *have beans up one's nose* and varr: To have ulterior motives or dishonest intentions.

1950 *WELS* (If somebody has dishonest intentions, or is up to no good: "I think he's got _____.") 1 Inf, **csWI**, Beans up his nose—there's more up his sleeve than his arm. **1966–69** *DARE* (Qu. JJ19, *If somebody has dishonest intentions, or is up to no good, you might say, "I think he's got _____."*) Inf **IL106**, Beans in his hat; **VA15**, Something up his sleeve; beans in his head; **WA33**, Beans up his nose. **1982** *DARE* File

NYC (as of c1920), He has beans up his nose—ulterior motives. *Ibid* **csWI** (as of 1950), She has beans up her nose. I don't trust her. [Inf has NEng background]

bean supper n Cf **pie supper**

1968–69 *DARE* (Qu. FF1, . . *A kind of group meeting called a "social" or "sociable"*) Inf **MA73**, We have bean suppers at church; **IN45**, Bean supper.

beant See **be C1a**

bean thrashing See **bean hulling**

Bean Town n Also *Bean Row*

See quots.

1927 *DN* 5.438 [Underworld argot], *Bean-town* . . . Boston. **1967–68** *DARE* (Qu. C34, *Nicknames for nearby settlements*) Inf **CT6**, Danbury is Bean Town; **NJ25**, Bean Town—raised string beans in a part of the town; (Qu. C35, *Nicknames for . . parts of . . town*) Infs **CT2, OH31**, Bean Town; **OH38**, Bean Row; (Qu. II25, . . *Where poor people or foreigners live*) Inf **OH33**, Bean Town.

bean tree n [Because the pod resembles a bean]

=catalpa B1.

1847 Darlington *Weeds & Plants* 222 (*DAE*), Bignonia-like Catalpa. Catawba. Bean-tree . . . Cultivated as a shade tree, but indigenous in the Southwest. **1897** Sudworth *Arborescent Flora* 335, Common Catalpa . . . Common names [include] . . Beantree (N.J., Del., Pa., Va., La., Nebr.). **1907** Hodge *Hdbk. Amer. Indians* 1.213, Catalpa . . . The two species native in the United States are the common catalpa, bean-tree, Indian bean, or candle-tree (*Catalpa catalpa*); and the western catalpa, larger Indian bean, or Shawnee wood (*C. speciosa*). **1966–70** *DARE* (Qu. T9) 9 Infs, **scattered**, Bean tree. **1968** McPhee *Pine Barrens* 63 **NJ**, Standing under the old catalpa trees, with their long-podded seeds hanging down above us, Fred said, " . . . Aunt Katie Gunner was the last person to live here . . under these bean trees." **1968** *DARE* FW Addit **ceOK**, Bean tree—A children's name for catalpa.

beanwater, be on one's v phr **NEng** *old-fash*

To feel lively or animated; to be in high spirits.

1907 *DN* 3.241 **eME**, *Beanwater* . . . In the expression, "to be right on one's bean-water," to be overflowing with animal spirits. **1914** *DN* 4.69 **ME, nNH**, *Bean-water, up on one's* . . . Feeling very lively, strong, frisky. "Gosh! I'm right up on my bean-water this mornin'!" **1980** *DARE* File **cnMA** (as of c1920), As a child I knew the expression "to be up on one's beanwater" which meant to feel frisky or lively. I thought it had something to do with the vile-smelling water in which beans were soaked preparatory to baking for Saturday night supper.

beany n Also sp *beaney*

A bean-shooter.

1949 *PADS* 11.17 **CO**, *Beany* . . . A small sling-shot. **1950** *WELS* (*Weapon used by children*) 1 Inf, **swWI**, Beany. **1963** Burroughs *Head-First* 107 **CO**, From time to time I have mentioned a "beany," a piece of equipment that no boy of my generation in his right mind ever ventured abroad without. Succinctly, a beany consisted of a willow crotch in the shape of a V with a handle on it.

beany adj [*bean* the head]

1 See quot 1914.

1914 *DN* 4.103 **KS**, *Beany* . . . Mentally defective, whether feeble-minded or insane. **1950** *WELS* 1 Inf, **seWI**, You're beany! You're crazy as a louse!

2 Infatuated: see quot.

1919 *DN* 5.71 **NM**, *Beany*, crazy. "She's gone beany about him."

bear n¹

A Pronc forms.

Usu |bɛ(ə)r, bɛə|; also, **chiefly Sth, Midl**, *old-fash* |bæ(r), bæə, ba(r)| Pronc-spp *baar, b'ar, bar(r)*

1790 D. Boone in 1926 *AmSp* 1.314 **KY**, Taking fur and Baar Skines. **1827** (1939) Sherwood *Gaz.* **GA** 139 [In list of provincialisms to be avoided], *Bar*, for bear. **1843** (1916) Hall *New Purchase* 438 **IN**, We wouldn't a cooked ba'r meat down here. *Ibid* 154, Tarrifying the barr. **1859** (1968) Bartlett *Americanisms*, *Bar*, for bear. The common pronunciation in certain parts of the Southern and Western States. **1905** *DN* 3.3 **cCT**, *Bear* . . . Pronounced bar. **1917** *DN* 4.408 **wNC**, *Bar*. Variant of *bear*, n. and v. **1927** *DN* 5.470 **Appalachians**, Bear [is pronounced] bar. **1927** Shewmake *Engl. Pronc.* **VA** 17, *Bear* . . . as a noun it was . . sometimes [bæɚ . . bæə]. **1938** Matschat *Suwannee R.* 137

nFL, sGA, Hants of b'ar an' dur an' gators. **1942** Hall *Smoky Mt. Speech* 24 eTN, wNC, [æ] occurs in . . bear. Old timers of a former day may have said [bɑɚ] . . but I have never heard it. **1946** *AmSp* 21.97 sIL, *B'ar*, bear. **c1960** *Wilson Coll.* csKY, Bear [bɑr] rare among the very old people.

B Gram form.
Used as pl: bears.   **?chiefly Sth, Midl**
   1843 (1916) Hall *New Purchase* 129 cIN, A missionary . . saw in the edge of our clearing "three barr" —i.e., three bears. **1905** *DN* 3.69 nwAR, There are no bear left in Washington County. **1966–68** *DARE* Tapes **FL**16, 36, 47, **TX**24, Bear [used as plural]; **AZ**4, He had some good dogs that he used for trailin' bear with; **GA**30, Unless you fool with them young bear; **MI**2, We had four bear tied up in our yard at one time. **1967** *DARE* FW Addit ceTN, Ya seen any bear up in Cade's cove?

C Senses.
1 See quot.
   1950 *PADS* 14.13 SC, *Bear* . . In the phrase: "The bear got him," he was overcome by the heat, had a sunstroke.
2 See quots.
   1972 Claerbaut *Black Jargon* 57, *Bear* . . A physically repulsive man or woman. **1977** Smitherman *Talkin* 258 [Black], *Bear, booger bear*, . . ugly female.

bear v
Std senses, var forms.
1 Past usu *bore,* occas *beared;* pple usu *borne,* occas *beared.*
   1927 *AmSp* 3.2 Ozarks, Principal parts of some common Ozark verbs: *Present*—bear . . *Preterite*—beared . . *Past Participle*—beared. **1966** *DARE* Tape OK24, It [=a road] beared to the right and crossed the creek up above. **1967–68** *DARE* (Qu. A22, . . *"She had only ten minutes to clean the room, but she* ——— *[and had it done in no time]."*) Inf IL8, Beared down; (Qu. OO35b, . . *"That land is poor—nothing has ever* ——— *there."*) Inf CA77, Beared.
2 In passive constr indicating the fact of birth: usu *born;* also, **chiefly Sth, S Midl** *(esp among speakers with little formal educ), borned,* occas *bornded;* pronc-sp *barned.*
   1892 *DN* 1.233 KY, *Borned:* born. Used by illiterate persons. **1902** *DN* 2.229 sIL. **1903** *DN* 2.307 seMO. **1904** *DN* 2.417 nwAR. **1906** *DN* 3.115 sIN. **1908** *DN* 3.293 eAL, wGA. **1923** *DN* 5.202 swMO. **1935** (1944) Rawlings *Golden Apples* 260 FL, How the young uns gits bornded. **1938** Rawlings *Yearling* 126 FL, Grandma, was Oliver borned good-lookin'? **1965–70** *DARE* (Qu. A24) Inf MO2, Day he's borned; KY44, Time he was borned; (Qq. Z11a, b) Infs KY21, LA28, NC24, Borned out of wedlock; (Qu. Z17) GA33, Bred and borned; (Qu. II21) Inf TN26, Borned in a barn. [4 Infs grade school, 3 Infs high school educ] **1965–70** *DARE* Tapes **AR**56, **CA**156, **GA**8, **IN**21, **MO**8, **VA**9, Borned. [All Infs grade school educ] **1966** *DARE* FW Addit SC, He was barned in May. **1975** Newell *If Nothin' Don't Happen* 8 nwFL, Us folks had moved up to the Hammock from the little settlement out from Fort Myers where my daddy was borned.

bear n² See **bar** n³

bear a hand v phr [Orig naut; *OED* 1769 →]
To assist, "lend a hand"; to hurry, make haste (esp in assisting someone).
   1872 Schele de Vere *Americanisms* 343, To *bear a hand* is a similar term borrowed from the sea-phrase, and means, even in the Far West, to be active and not to delay. **1899** (1912) Green *VA Folk-Speech, Bear a hand* . . To lend a hand; take hold; give aid or assistance. To work quickly. **1905** *DN* 3.3 cCT, *Bear* . . In the expression to 'bear a hand,' to assist. **1939** *AmSp* 14.77 [Naval Academy slang], *Bear a hand.* Shake a leg. **1942** ME Univ. *Studies* 56.41, A sailor must always *look alive*. When anything was doing, he must be ready . . to *bear a hand*. [Footnote:] Fig. Lend assistance.

bearberry n
1 A cranberry (here: *Vaccinium macrocarpon*).
   1672 Josselyn *New-Englands Rarities* 65, Cran Berry, or Bear Berry, because Bears use much to feed upon them, is a small trayling Plant that grows in Salt Marshes. **1940** Clute *Amer. Plant Names* 42, *O. macrocarpus.* Large Cranberry . . Bear-berry.
2 A plant of the genus *Arctostaphylos.* [*OED* 1625 →] Also called **kinnikinnick, manzanita** For other names of the most common sp, *A. uva-ursi*, see **bear's bilberry, bear's grape, bear's weed 2, checkerberry 2, chipmunk's apple, crowberry 2, devil's**

tobacco, foxberry, hog cranberry, Indian tobacco, larb, meal-berry, mealy-plum vine, mountain box, mountain cranberry, mountain laurel, rapper dandies, redberry, rockberry, sand-berry, universe vine, upland cranberry, uvursy, whortleberry, wild cranberry
   1785 Marshall *Arbustrum* 12, *Arbutus* Uva ursi. *The Bearberry* . . The flowers are produced in small bunches, near the ends of the branches, and are succeeded by red berries. **1861** Wood *Class-Book* 485, *Arctostaphilos* [sic] . . . *Bear-berry.* **1897** Parsons *Wild Flowers CA* 12, Manzanita. Bearberry. *Arctostaphylos manzanita.* **1960** Teale *Journey into Summer* 18, We wandered over the wiry mountain grass and the mats of the bearberry. **1961** Douglas *My Wilderness* 104 neMN, Blueberries and bearberries had found footing in cracks. **1967** *DARE* Wildfl QR Inf CO7, Bearberry—*Arctostaphylos uva-ursi.*
3 =**bear huckleberry 1.** *?obs*
   1860 Curtis *Cat. Plants NC* 86, *Bear Huckleberry. Bearberry* . . . The flowers are . . in the Bearberry cup-shaped. **1883** Hale *Woods NC* 140, *Bearberry* . . . The berry is purplish or dark red, insipid and dry, ripening in July and August.
4 Either of two western buckthorns: **coffeeberry 2a(1)** or *Rhamnus purshiana*, the latter also called *bearberry tree.*
   1884 Sargent *Forests of N. Amer.* 41, *Rhamnus Purshiana* . . . *Bear-berry. Bear Wood. Shittim Wood.* **1893** *Jrl. Amer. Folkl.* 6.139, *Rhamnus Californica,* wild coffee; bearberry. S. Barbara Co., Cal. **1898** *Ibid* 11.225, *Rhamnus Purshiana* . . bear berry, Pierce Co., Wash. **1900** Lyons *Plant Names* 318, *R. purshiana* . . . Bearberry tree. **1979** Little *Checklist U.S. Trees* 248, *Rhamnus purshiana* . . . *Other common names* . . bearberry, chittam, coffeetree.
5 =**bead lily** (here: *Clintonia borealis*).
   1898 *Jrl. Amer. Folkl.* 11.281, *Clintonia borealis* . . bear berry, Farmington, Me.
6 A possum haw (here: *Ilex decidua*).
   1897 Sudworth *Arborescent Flora* 280, *Ilex decidua* . . . *Common Names* . . . Bearberry (Miss.). **1933** Small *Manual SE Flora* 815, *Deciduous-holly. Bear-berry. Possum-haw. Welk-holly.* **1960** Vines *Trees SW* 655, Local names are . . Welk Holly, Bearberry, and Winterberry.
7 A low trailing blackberry (here: *Rubus canadensis*).
   1916 *Torreya* 16.238, *Rubus canadensis* L.—Bear berry, October berry, North Carolina. **1941** *Ibid* 41.48, *Rubus canadensis* . . . Bear berry . . North Carolina.
8 See **bearberry honeysuckle.**
9 A silk tassel (here: *Garrya wrightii*).
   1937 U.S. Forest Serv. *Range Plant Hdbk.* B81, Wright silktassel, known by a variety of local names—bearberry, chaparral, . . and quinine-bush—is a shrub from 1½ to 10 feet high.
10 =**bunchberry 1.**
   1940 Clute *Amer. Plant Names* 97, *C[ornus] Canadensis. Bunchberry* . . . Bear-berry.

bearberry honeysuckle n Also *bearberry* **chiefly West**
A shrub **honeysuckle** (*Lonicera involucrata*) which produces paired black berries. Also called **fly honeysuckle, inkberry, pigeonberry, skunkberry**
   1931 U.S. Dept. Ag. *Misc. Pub.* 101.146, *Bearberry honeysuckle* . . known also as bearberry, fly honeysuckle, . . and skunkberry, . . is probably the commonest and best known of the western honeysuckles. **1940** Clute *Amer. Plant Names* 263, *Lonicera involucrata.* Bear-berry. **1961** Douglas *My Wilderness* 17 cnCO, Swamp or bearberry honeysuckle is a coarse shrub with yellow flowers. **1967** *DARE* Wildfl QR Inf OR12, Bearberry (honeysuckle family). **1972** Viereck *AK Trees* 250, *Bearberry Honeysuckle* . . . The bitter fruits are said to be poisonous.

bearberry tree See **bearberry 4**

bear brush n
A silktassel (here: *Garrya fremontii*).
   1911 Jepson *Flora CA* 304, *G. fremontii* . . . Bear Brush . . . High Coast Range ridges and slopes. **1961** Peck *Manual OR* 582, *Bear Brush.* A shrub 1–3 m. high . . . West of the Cascade divide, to Wash. and Calif.

bear bush n Also *bear's bush*
An **inkberry 1** (here: *Ilex glabra*).
   1787 in 1888 Cutler *Life* 1.201 MA, Brought home Bear's-Bush and two species of Sumach. **1920** *Torreya* 20.22, *Ilex glabra* . . . Bear-bush,

Brown's Mills, N.J. **1952** Taylor *Plants Colonial Days* 51 **VA**, Ink-berry . . . Other names are gallberry, winterberry . . , and bear bush. **1966** *DARE* (Qu. S11) Inf **SC10**, Bear bush.

bear cabbage n Also *bear's cabbage* Cf **squaw lettuce**
=**cat's-breeches.**

1915 (1926) Armstrong *Western Wild Flowers* 418, Waterleaf . . . is sometimes called Bear's Cabbage, but this name is far fetched, both as regards bears and cabbages! **1937** U.S. Forest Serv. *Range Plant Hdbk.* W98, Ballhead waterleaf is also known as . . bear-cabbage . . . The young, tender shoots of this plant . . are often eaten by both Indians and white men. They provide excellent greens. **1967** *DARE* (Qu. I28b, . . *Greens that are cooked*) Inf **CO45**, Bear cabbage—a wild plant —green leaf with purple flower—a strong tasting plant.

bear cat n

Something extraordinary in some way—as good, powerful, dangerous, etc.

1942 Berrey–Van den Bark *Amer. Slang* 29.2, *Something excellent* . . . bearcat. **1951** Porter *Ragged Roads* 93 **wOK**, To the south . . was sprawled that endless sweep of moving, blinding sand bars—that bear cat, the South Canadian River. **1967** *DARE* File **neOR**, A bear cat—something that is tops [=of superior quality].

bear caterpillar n

=**woolly bear.**

1935 *AmSp* 10.202, The *bear caterpillar* (a larva of the tiger moth, so named from its hairiness). **1968** *DARE* (Qu. R27, . . *Kinds of caterpillars*) Inf **WI23**, Bear.

bear claw n Also *bear's claw, bear paw* **chiefly West, esp Pacific** See Map
A large sweet pastry shaped like a bear's paw.

1942 *AN&Q* 2.55 **San Francisco CA**, Another variety [of "snail" pastry], with raisin filling, is (from its shape) known as a "bear-claw." **1946** *AmSp* 21.87 **CA**, *Bearclaw*—a sweet bread shaped something like its name implies. **1965**–**70** *DARE* (Qu. H32, . . *Fancy rolls and pastries*) 60 Infs, **chiefly West**, Bear claws; **IA13, MT5, WA3**, Bear paws; **CA87, NY94**, Bear's claws; (Qu. H28) Inf **UT8**, Bear claw. **1965** *DARE* File **csWI**, Bear claw—a type of sweet-roll, paw-shaped, with indentations along one side. Sold by bakeries. **1968** *ID Enterprise* (Malad City) 1 Feb 8/1, Hostess Bear Claws . . . 2 for 95¢. **1971** Bright *Word Geog. CA & NV* 177, *Sweet roll* . . [84 infs:] bear claw.

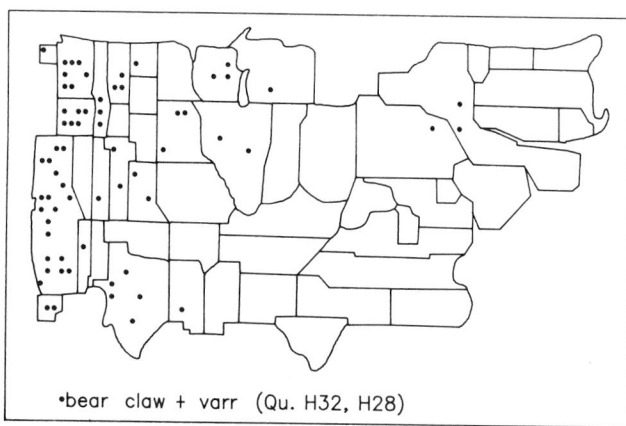

•bear claw + varr (Qu. H32, H28)

bear-climb See **bear-hug**

bear-clover n

=**mountain misery.**

1897 Parsons *Wild Flowers CA* 92, Mrs. Brandegee writes of it: "Along the line of the railroad in Placer County, it is often called 'bear-clover,' perhaps in accordance with our felicitous custom of giving names, because it bears not the least resemblance to clover, and the bear will have nothing to do with it." **1911** Jepson *Flora CA* 205, Mountain Misery . . . Also called . . Bear-clover and Tarweed. **1923** Davidson–Moxley *Flora S. CA* 180, *Chamaebatia. Mountain Misery. Tar-bush. Bear-clover.* **1968** *DARE* (Qu. L9b, . . *Kinds of plants*) Inf **CA105**, Bear-clover.

bear corn n Also *bear's corn*

1 A bead lily (here: *Clintonia borealis*).

1886 Burroughs *Signs & Seasons* 137, Another very abundant plant in these woods was the *Clintonia borealis*. Uncle Nathan said it was called "bear's corn," though he did not know why. **1942** *Torreya* 42.6.158, *Clintonia borealis* . . Bear's corn, Maine.

2 =**Indian poke 1.**

1900 Lyons *Plant Names* 389, *V[eratrum] viride* . . . Bear-corn. **1930** Sievers *Amer. Med. Plants* 6, Bear corn . . . The large bright-green leaves of this plant make their way through the ground early in spring, followed later in the season by a stout, erect leafy stem, sometimes growing as tall as 6 feet. **1971** Krochmal *Appalachia Med. Plants* 262, Bearcorn . . . Its dried roots and rhizomes . . are a strong cardiac stimulant drug.

3 =**squawroot 1.**

1931 Harned *Wild Flowers Alleghanies* 455, Squaw Root (*Conopholis americana* . .) . . . Often called Bear Corn.

beard n Pronc-spp *baid, baird, by'ud*
A Forms.

Pronc varr: see quot 1961.

1891 *DN* 1.138 **cNY**, [bɪəd, bæɚd], *beard*. **1903** *DN* 3.290 **Cape Cod MA** (as of 1850s), Men shaved off their *bairds*. **1905** Culbertson *Banjo Talks* 124 **LA** [Black], You teck my hy'ar an' my by'ud erway. **1922** Gonzales *Black Border* 288 **sSC, GA coasts** [Gullah glossary], *Baid*—beard, beards. **1931** *N. Amer. Rev.* 231.428 **NYC** (as of 1826–1900), Why, if you ain't shaven off your baird! I abhor a baird. **1961** Kurath–McDavid *Pronc. Engl.* 117, [*Beard* is usu pronounced /bɪrd, bɪrd/ in the Nth and N Midl; occas when stressed, it is /bijəd/ in eNEng and other areas that lack post-vocalic /r/; it is usually /bed, bɛd/in SC and GA; it is commonly /bjɛd/ in NC, VA, sWV, MD.]

B Senses.

1 A hair, or patch of hairs, on the face. Cf **hair** n[1]

1937 J. Stuart in *Esquire* Jan **neKY** (*ADD*), Ah, them old beards Bill. They don't become you one bit. You look awful in them. **1937**–**39** *Hall Coll.* **eTN, wNC**, "I wanted to shave off my beards." "Dan Mars ez got lots of beards (a big beard)." **1966** *DARE* Tape **MS75**, A false-face with white beards hanging way down there.

2 A corn tassel. [Note: *tassel*, the male inflorescence at the top of the stalk, is also often used of the "silks" at the top of the ear—see *LANE* Map 262, and cf *DJE corn-mouth*]

1966 *DARE* (Qu. I31, *When a corn stalk is well grown, what comes out at the top?*) Inf **MS73**, Beard.

Bear Day n Note: this is no doubt a borrowing from Ger folklore, in which the bear, not the groundhog, was the animal observed.

Groundhog Day.

[**1932** Smiley *Gloss. New Paltz* **seNY**, Nipper tells me that in the back country the Groundhog superstition is applied not to the Woodchuck but to the Black Bear. If or when he comes out, if he sees his shadow winter is nearly over. Nipper does not believe in any of the Feb. 2nd superstitions.] **1953** *Ibid*, 2 Feb. Bear Day. The Black Bear, not the groundhog, looks for his shadow here.

bearded adj

Of an animal: see quot.

1958 *AmSp* 33.268 **eWA**, *Bearded*. Having an abcessed sore in the mouth, caused by cheat-grass beards, grain beards, etc. This condition often requires surgery.

bearded tongue See **beardtongue**

beardgrass n [From the thick bunch of awns]

A grass of the genus *Andropogon*. Also called **bluejoint, bluestem, broom grass, broom sedge, bunchgrass, sage grass, turkey foot.** For other names of var spp see **beargrass 3c, big feathergrass, broom, broomrape, feather bluestem, poverty grass, purple-fingered grass, wheatgrass, wire grass** See also **big bluestem, little bluestem**

beard-splitter n Pronc-sp *baird-splitter*

1930 Shoemaker *1300 Words* 4 **cPA Mts** (as of c1900), *Baird-splitter* —A libertine.

beardtongue n Also *bearded tongue, beardstongue* [See quot 1961]

A plant of the genus *Penstemon*. Also called **foxglove 2b, honeysuckle.** For other names of var spp see **balmony 2, dead**

men's bells, fairy bell 1, firecracker, pride of the mountains, scarlet bugler 1

1821 in 1900 *MA Hist. Soc. Coll.* 2d ser 9.153, *Pentstemon pubescens,* Beard tongue. **1891** Jesup *Plants Hanover NH* 30, *Pentstemon . . Beard-tongue.* **1937** Sandoz *Slogum* 96 **wNE,** This horse pasture, where tall spikes of blue beardtongue bloomed. **1949** Peattie *Cascades* 241, They are called beardtongue in the eastern part of America and in Europe, but here in the Northwest we usually call them penstemon. **1961** Smith *MI Wildflowers* 341, The name Beard-tongue refers to the 5th, sterile, bearded stamen, which is found in all members of this genus. **1966** *DARE* Wildfl QR Pl.198 Inf **WA**10, Beardtongue. **1967-68** *DARE* (Qu. S1) Inf **MD**39, Bearded tongue; (Qu. S26b) Inf **CO**7, Beardtongues. **1967** *DARE* FW Addit **CO,** *Beardstongue* or *beardtongue—Penstemon.*

beardy man *n arch*

A Dunkard.

1888 Gossler *Turnpike-Road* 28 **PA,** The most notable . . sect is that of the Dunkards (they were called "Beardy Men" when I was a boy, because they never clipped their hair or beard.)

bear fighter *n Cf* **fight the bear**

1968 Adams *Western Words, Bear fighter*—In lumbering, the man who separates strips from boards in a sawmill.

bear foot *n* Also *bear's foot* [From the shape of the leaf] **chiefly SE**

A **leafcup** (here: *Polymnia uvedalia*) or its root.

1900 Lyons *Plant Names* 300, *P. Uvedália . . .* Eastern U.S. . . Bear's-foot, Yellow Bear's-foot. **1901** Mohr *Plant Life AL* 792, *Bear Foot . . .* Economic uses: The root, called "bear foot," is used in domestic medicine. **1933** Small *Manual SE Flora* 1406. **1969** *DARE* FW Addit **wKY,** Bear foot roots and whiskey—the roots are soaked in whiskey and resulting solution is used for rheumatism. **1975** Duncan–Foote *Wildflowers SE* 210, Yellow Leafcup . . . Leaves opposite, palmately lobed or cut, . . their shape promoting the name "Bears-foot."

bear-garden *n* [Orig, in England, a place for baiting bears; fig, a tumultuous scene (*OED* 1687 →)]

1930 Shoemaker *1300 Words* **cPA Mts** (as of c1900), *Bear-garden*—A noisy domestic bickering.

bear grass *n*

1 Any of var somewhat similar plants of the family Agavaceae as:

a =**yucca.**

1750 (1888) Walker *Jrl.* 12 Apr, On the Banks is some Bear-Grass. **1848** U.S. Patent Office *Annual Rept. for 1847: Ag.* 162, Some interesting statements have recently been made respecting the *bear grass* or Florida hemp. **1949** *PADS* 11.3 **wTX,** *Bear grass . . .* A type of yucca. Common. **1960** Wilson *Coll.* **csKY,** *Bear grass . . .* Yucca. **1966–69** *DARE* (Qu. S20) Infs **FL**7, **TN**31, Bear grass; (Qu. S26c, *Wildflowers that grow in woods*) Inf **VA**24, Bear grass [FW: =silk grass]; (Qu. S26e) Inf **TN**24, Bear grass [FW: =yucca]. **1967** *DARE* Tape **AL**15, We . . hung it [=meat to be cured] with bear grass . . Bear grass has a blade about . . foot or foot an' a half long, an' you pull those off an' just one blade for each piece of meat an' it'll just hold, no tellin' how much, an' you just tie it in a knot and then you have poles that go across your smokehouse . . you lay these poles up there with these pieces of meat tied with the bear grass, they hang down, then you build your fire with hickory wood underneath it. **1967** *DARE* FW Addit **LA**2, *Bear grass*—local word for yucca. **1967** *DARE* Wildfl QR (Wills–Irwin) Pl.3c Inf **TX**34, Bear grass.

b A plant of the genus *Nolina.* Also called **basket grass 2, bunchgrass, devil's shoestring, ribbon grass, sacahuista, thread grass**

1854 (1932) Bell *Log TX–CA Trail* 301 **NM,** The Bear Grass stem grows to a considerable size here, about four inches through at the base. [Note: this quot may refer instead to **bear grass 1a** above.] **1913** Wooton *Trees NM* 36, *Bear Grass (Nolina microcarpa).* This vernacular name is applied in the southwestern part of the State to a plant somewhat closely resembling the last *[Dasylirion wheeleri].* **1951** *PADS* 15.29 **TX,** *Nolina* spp.—Bear . . grass. These are employed to weave mats for household use or for burial purposes. **1961** Douglas *My Wilderness* 82 **AZ,** The lower slopes of Baboquivari show the bear grass, the lowbush cat's-claw, and many, many yuccas whose tall stalk is now dry and brittle. This plant, whose flaming plume makes Baboquivari gay in May and whose dry husks make good fires for cowboys, is related to the lily,

not the cactus, family. Yet it thrives in this desiccated land. **1965** Teale *Wandering Through Winter* 79 **sAZ,** For here the beargrass, *Nolina,* grew in unparalleled profusion. **1967** *DARE* (Qu. S26e) Inf **CA**4, *Nolina* = Bear grass. **1981** Benson–Darrow *Trees SW Deserts* 60, Even though the plant is reputed to be poisonous under certain growth conditions, bear grass is used for emergency feeding of livestock when forage is exceedingly scarce.

c =**sotol.**

1886 Havard *Flora W. & S. TX for 1885* 517, *Dasylirion Texanum . . .* (Bear Grass; the Sotol of the Mexicans) . . . Abundant west of the Pecos . . , the most striking botanical feature of the country. **1897** *Jrl. Amer. Folkl.* 10.145, *Dasylirion Wheeleri . .* bear grass, Ariz. **1976** Bailey–Bailey *Hortus Third* 364, *Dasylirion* Zucc. *Sotol, Bear Grass . . .* The leaves are used for thatching and baskets; the fiber is used for cordage.

2 Any of several plants of the family Liliaceae as:

a =**squaw grass. chiefly NW**

1805 (1808) Gass *Jrl.* 242 **WA,** One of them had a hat made of the bark of white cedar and bear-grass, very handsomely wrought and waterproof. **1806** (1965) Lewis–Clark *Hist. Lewis–Clark Exped.* 2.769 **Pacific NW,** It is for the construction of these baskets that the bear-grass forms an article of considerable traffic. It grows only near the snowy region of the high mountains; the blade, which is two feet long and about three-eighths of an inch wide, is smooth, strong, and pliant. **1836** Irving *Astoria* 1.166, Hither also, the tribes from the Rocky Mountains brought down horses, bear grass, quamash, and other commodities of the interior. *Ibid* 2.284, Some [=Indians] wore a corslet, formed of pieces of hard wood, laced together with bear grass. **1911** Jepson *Flora CA* 107, *X. tenax . . . Bear Grass . . .* The fibers of the leaves were employed . . for decorative work in baskets. **1949** Peattie *Cascades* 248, In days gone by the Indians used its tough leaves in making their baskets, which accounts for its common names of squaw-grass and Indian basket-grass. It is so conspicuous and attractive that it has a number of other popular names, some of which are bear-grass, elk-grass, pine grass, pine lily, and mountain lily. **1950** FWP *Guide ID* 71, Called variously soap grass, squaw grass, and elk grass, the gorgeous plant, more commonly known as bear grass, is a thorough rebuke to the unimaginativeness of the human mind. **1973** Hitchcock–Cronquist *Flora Pacific NW* 696, *Xerophyllum* Michx. Beargrass.

b A **camas 1** (here: *Camassia quamash*).

1830 Rafinesque *Med. Flora* 255, *Quamasia esculenta . . .* Quamash, *Bear grass, Wild Hyacinth . . .* Kentucky to Oregon. **1911** *Century Dict., Bear-grass . . .* A name given to the camass . . of Oregon; also, in Texas, to *Dasylirion Texanum,* the young pulpy stems of which are much eaten by bears; and to species of the genus *Yucca,* for the same reason. **1959** Carleton *Index Herb. Plants* 9, *Bear Grass:* Camassia esculenta (C. fraseri or C. quamasia).

c A **colicroot 2** (here: *Aletris farinosa*).

1966 *DARE* Wildfl QR Pl.16 Inf **NC**28, Bear grass—*Aletris farinosa.*

3 Any of several grasses as:

a A **burr grass** (here: esp *Cenchrus pauciflorus*).

1894 *Jrl. Amer. Folkl.* 7.104, *Cenchrus tribuloides . .* bear-grass, Iowa. **1966–68** *DARE* (Qu. L9a, . . *Grass . . grown for hay*) Inf **AL**26, Bear grass; (Qu. S8, . . *Wild grass that . . spreads by sending out long underground roots*) Inf **NC**41, Bear grass; (Qu. S9, . . *Kinds of grass that are hard to get rid of*) Inf **GA**38, Bear grass; (Qu. S21, . . *Weeds that are a trouble in gardens and fields*) Infs **GA**38, **SC**7, Bear grass.

b A **needlegrass** (here: *Stipa pulchra*).

1911 *Century Dict. Suppl., Bear-grass . . .* A bunch-grass, *Stipa setigera,* ranging from the mountains of California, where it is considered valuable, to Oregon and Texas. **1937** U.S. Forest Serv. *Range Plant Hdbk.* G118, California needlegrass, a conspicuously awned grass, is sometimes called . . beargrass.

c Either of two **beardgrasses:** *Andropogon barbinodis* or *A. saccharoides.*

1937 U.S. Forest Serv. *Range Plant Hdbk.* G14, Cane beardgrass differs from silver beardgrass chiefly because its head is shorter, fan-shaped, rather than elongated . . . Other local names such as . . feather bluestem, and beargrass, are applied indiscriminately to these species.

4 =**beach heather** (here: *Hudsonia tomentosa*).

1900 Lyons *Plant Names* 194, *H. tomentosa . . .* Canada and northeastern U.S. Woolly Hudsonia, . . Bear-grass. **1959** Carleton *Index Herb. Plants* 9, *Bear grass: . .* Hudsonia tomentosa.

bear huckleberry n

1 A **huckleberry 1** (here: *Gaylussacia ursina*).

1897 *Jrl. Amer. Folkl.* 10.49 **NEng,** *Gaylussacia ursina*, . . bear huckle-berry. **1901** Lounsberry *S. Wild Flowers* 396, Bear huckleberry. **1938** Van Dersal *Native Woody Plants* 136, Bear huckleberry.

2 A **huckleberry 2** (here: *Vaccinium hirsutum*).

1894 *Jrl. Amer. Folkl.* 7.94 **NC,** *Vaccinium hirsutum* . . bear-huckle-berry.

bear-hug v, hence *bear-hugging* vbl n Also *bear-climb,* ~ *lift,* ~ *walk* **chiefly S Midl**

To shinny up a tree.

1965–70 *DARE* (Qu. EE36, *To climb the trunk of a tree by holding on with your legs while you pull yourself up with your hands*) Infs **AR**51, **KY**84, 85, **LA**11, **NM**9, **TX**37, **VA**27, Bear-hugging; **CA**105, **NJ**53, Bear-hug; **KY**44, 80, 89, Bear-climbing; **AR**47, Bear-climb; **IN**32, Bear-lift; **NC**53, Bear-walking.

bearing tree n [*bearing* the position of one point with respect to another]

=**witness tree.**

1817 *Niles' Natl. Reg.* 12.98/2, At each corner the courses are taken to two trees, in opposite directions as nearly as may be, and their distance from the post measured. These trees are called "bearing trees," and are blazed on the side next the post. **1878** *Harper's Mag.* 56.210/2 **AR,** A "bearing" tree has been blocked to get at a "blaze" made in the spring of '38. **1958** McCulloch *Woods Words* **Pacific NW,** *Bearing tree*—A tree marked to identify a survey corner. **1969** Sorden *Lumberjack Lingo* **NEng, Gt Lakes.**

bear-lift See **bear-hug**

bear lily n [See quot 1963]

=**squaw grass.**

1923 in **1925** Jepson *Manual Plants CA* 210, *X[erophyllum] tenax* . . Also called . . Turkey-beard, Bear-lily, and Pine-lily. **1963** Craighead *Rocky Mt. Wildflowers* 31, Bearlily . . . Bears reportedly eat the white succulent leaf base in spring.

‡**bearm** n [Perh transf from **barm** n[1]; cf **barmy**]

Excitement, agitation.

1928 Chapman *Happy Mt.* 118 **eTN,** "Such bearm I never see!" Waits quarreled at them. *Ibid* 132, Old Homer's voice came nirly from his bed: "Let be, girls, let be! Leave your bearm and lay you down, and a man might maybe help himself to a dose of sleep."

bear mat n [From its low, thick growth]

=**mountain misery.**

1911 Jepson *Flora CA* 205, *Chamaebatia foliolosa* . . . Odorous low shrub . . . often covering extensive tracts. Also called Bear-mat, Bear-clover and Tarweed. **1915** (**1926**) Armstrong *Western Wild Flowers* 222, The shrub has many names, such as Bear-mat and Kittikit.

bear moss n Cf **bear's bed**

A **haircap moss** (here: *Polytrichum juniperinum*).

1935 *AmSp* 10.201, Many other plants named from the bear are to be found, such as . . *bear moss*.

bear mouse n

A field mouse (*Microtus* spp.).

1857 U.S. Patent Office *Annual Rept. for 1856: Ag.* 84 **nIL,** Where several species [of meadow mice] are found in one locality, they are commonly considered by farmers as one animal, known under various names, as "Short-tailed Field Rats or Mice," "Bear Mice," "Bull-headed Mice," "Ground Mice," "Bog Mice," &c. **1935** *AmSp* 10.202, Very few animals are named from the bear. They include the *bear mouse* (as the field mouse is sometimes called in the Middle West).

bear oak n [See quots 1847, 1900]

Either of two shrubby oaks, *Quercus ilicifolia* or *Q. pumila*. Also called **barren oak 2, bitterbush, bitter oak, scrub oak, shrub oak**

1810 Michaux *Arbres* I.24 *(DAE),* Bear' oak (Chêne d'ours), connu sous ce nom dans les Etats de New-Jersey et de New-York [=(Bear oak), known under this name in the States of New Jersey and New York]. **1847** Wood *Class-Book* 495, Q[uercus] *ilicifolia* . . Bear Oak . . . Acorns small and abundant, and said to be greedily eaten by bears, deer and swine. **1927** Keeler *Our Native Trees* 368, The early settlers of

New England called it [=*Quercus pumila*] Bear Oak . . because the bears loved its bitter little acorns.

bear over the river n

A children's outdoor game.

1968 *DARE* (Qu. EE33) Inf **IN**14, Bear over the river.

bear paw See **bear claw**

bear pen n

1960 Hall *Smoky Mt. Folks* 61, Bear pen: a dead-fall bear trap.

bear plum n

A **bead lily** (here: *Clintonia borealis*).

1894 *Jrl. Amer. Folkl.* 7.101, *Clintonia borealis* . . . Bear-plum, Franconia, N.H. **1935** *AmSp* 10.201, Many other plants named from the bear are to be found, such as . . *bear plum*.

bear's ass exclam

1942 Stegner *Mormon Country* 143 **UT,** I have never found . . [outside the Mormon area] the characteristic "Bear's ass!" with which a native of Cache Valley expresses disgust.

bear's bed n

1 A **haircap moss.**

1876 Hobbs *Bot. Hdbk.* 9, Bears' bed, Haircap moss, Polytrichum juniperum [sic]. **1935** *AmSp* 10.201, Many other plants named from the bear are to be found, such as . . bear's bed.

2 =**Christmas fern.**

1975 Hamel–Chiltoskey *Cherokee Plants* 33 **TN,** Bear's bed—*Polystichum acrostichoides*.

bear's-berry weed See **bear's weed 2**

bear's bilberry n

A **bearberry 2** (here: *Arctostaphylos uva-ursi*).

1900 Lyons *Plant Names* 44, *A. Uva Ursi* . . . Bear's Bilberry. **1935** *AmSp* 10.201, Many other plants named from the bear are to be found, such as . . *bear's-bilberry*. **1974** (**1977**) Coon *Useful Plants* 133, Bear's bilberry . . . The lovely red berries are listed in some books as being edible when cooked.

bear's bush See **bear bush**

bear's cabbage See **bear cabbage**

bear's claw See **bear claw**

bear's corn See **bear corn**

bear's foot See **bear foot**

bear's grape n

A **bearberry 2** (here: *Arctostaphylos uva-ursi*).

1842 Buckingham *E. & W. States* 1.161 **ME,** The bear's grape, which trails on the ground, is effective in dysentery. **1876** Hobbs *Bot. Hdbk.* 9, Bears' grape, The fruit of Uva Ursi, Arctostaphylos Uva Ursi. **1930** Sievers *Amer. Med. Plants* 10, Bearberry . . . *Other common names* . . . Bear's grape, . . sagachomi, rapper dandies (fruit).

bear's head n Also *boar's head*

An edible fungus (*Hydnum caput-medusae*), the surface of which is covered with long soft spines.

1908 Hard *Mushroom Edible* 437, *Hydnum caput-ursi* . . . The Bear's Head Hydnum. Edible . . . It has a wide distribution through the states. **1967** *DARE* FW Addit **cOR,** Bear's Head—Corral-like cluster of mushrooms. Also called Boar's Head.

bear sign n [**sign**]

1 Bear droppings or tracks.

1839 *S. Lit. Messenger* 5.377/1 **GA,** To be sure I did see a powerful sight of bear signs. **1938** Rawlings *Yearling* 13 **nFL,** "When kin we go, Pa?" "Soon as we git the hoein' done. And see bear-sign." **1939** *Hall Coll.* **eTN, wNC,** "We went out that evenin' lookin' fer bear sign." "And they found no bear signs to turn the bear hounds loose on." **1946** Peattie *Pacific Coast* 84, You may note "bear sign" from the Gualala River to the Siskiyous and beyond. **1953** *Hall Coll.* **eTN, wNC,** "We had quite a time to getting our dogs through the bear sign in the orchard."

2 Transf: doughnuts. **West**

1903 (**1965**) Adams *Log Cowboy* 280 **NM,** She asked me to make the bear sign—doughnuts, she called them. **1942** Berrey–Van den Bark *Amer. Slang* 926.5 **West,** Bear sign, doughnuts. **1944** Adams *Western Words*, Bear-sign—The cowboy's name for doughnuts.

3 Transf; among loggers: berry jam. **West**

1942 Berrey – Van den Bark *Amer. Slang* 513, *Logging terms.* bear sign, *berry jam.* **1958** McCulloch *Woods Words* **Pacific NW,** Bear sign— Blackberry jam, particularly if very seedy.

bear's-paw root n Also *bear's paw*
=**male fern.**

1876 Hobbs *Bot. Hdbk.* 9, Bears' paw root, Male fern root, Aspidium Filix Mas. **1900** Lyons *Plant Names* 141, *D[ryopteris] Filix-Mas* . . Bear's-paw root. **1941** FWP *Guide WV* 140, Bear's-paw root tea is considered good to cure a cold or a fever, although the remark is made that 'it takes a good nerve' to drink it because of its 'dark bitterness.' **1974** (1977) Coon *Useful Plants* 198, Bear's paw . . . has a value as an anthelmintic, and taenicide.

bear's thread n [See quot 1949]
=**Adam's needle (and thread)** (here: *Yucca filamentosa*).

1861 Wood *Class-Book* 709, *Y. filamentosa* . . . Bear's-Thread . . . The margin [of the leaf] filamentous, that is, bearing long, thread-like fibers. **1900** Lyons *Plant Names* 401. **1949** Moldenke *Amer. Wild Flowers* 368, The leaves produce long and tough threads along their margins, with which the inrolled sharp tip of the leaf may be "threaded" to form a crude needle—hence the common names of *bearsthread* and *evesdarningneedle*.

bear story n Also *bear tale*
An exaggerated account, a "tall tale."

1856 *Spirit of Times* 25 Oct 129/1, Whether the forty-bear-in-a-day story . . was founded on fact, or was merely a *bear-story,* we are unable to decide. **1871** *Atlantic Mth.* 28.564/2, A company of hunters . . went on in their old eternal way of making bear-stories out of whole cloth. **1939** *Hall Coll.* **eTN, wNC,** A fellow would come in and tell a little extra story, a little out of line, like he'd had a extra drink or somethin'; we'd call that a bear tale. It meant his story was a little exaggerated in places. **1958** McCulloch *Woods Words* **Pacific NW,** *Bear story*—Any kind of a tall story. Once the bear story was an important part of daily life in the woods, but bears, and bear hunters, and bear stories are all much scarcer nowadays.

bear's weed n
1 also *bearweed:* A **yerba santa** (here: *Eriodictyon californicum*).

1887 *Century Illustr. Mag.* 34.325 **NEng,** The stem [is] two feet high, very leafy, and coarser than bear-weed. **1900** Lyons *Plant Names* 149, *E. Californicum* . . . Bear's-weed. **1974** (1977) Coon *Useful Plants* 152, Bear's weed . . . is a plant which is to be found growing on the dry hillsides of California.

2 also *bear's-berry weed:* A **bearberry 2** (here: *Arctostaphylos uva-ursi*).

1951 *PADS* 15.18, *Arctostaphylos uva-ursi* L.—Bear's-berry weed, bear's weed.

bear tale See bear story

bear tick n
A hard tick (family Ixodidae).

1968 *DARE* (Qu. R23a, *Insects . . that fasten themselves to the skin and suck blood*) Inf **NC80,** Bear tick (the big kind).

bear tongue n
A **bead lily** (here: *Clintonia borealis*).

1900 Lyons *Plant Names* 108, *C[lintonia] borealis* . . . Bear-tongue. **1940** Clute *Amer. Plant Names* 11, *C. borealis* . . . Dog-berry, bear-tongue, heal-all. **1959** Carleton *Index Herb. Plants* 9.

bear trap n
1 A difficult or undesirable situation.

1835 Bird *Hawks* 1.269 **PA,** Look you, boy, you are in a bear-trap, and the log will soon be on your back. **1958** McCulloch *Woods Words* **Pacific NW,** *Bear Trap* . . . A tricky situation . . . A tangle of logs such that when the bucker makes a cut, one or more logs may roll and mash him.

2 A type of horse's bit.

1942 Berrey – Van den Bark *Amer. Slang* 915.3 **West,** Bear trap, *a very severe bit.* **1944** Adams *Western Words,* Bear trap . . . A severe bit.

3 also attrib: See quot 1977.

1944 Adams *Western Words,* Bear-trap—The name for a certain style of saddle. **c1965** *DARE* File [Unidentified newspaper clipping], They

[=saddles] were designed by the old Cowboys Turtle Assn. and are used so nobody has an advantage by riding a bear trap—an extra deep saddle. **1977** Watts *Dict. Old West* 26, The term *bear trap saddle* was given to a saddle developed in the first quarter of the twentieth century . . which had a small seat and cantle close to the fork, making it a major achievement to fall out of it. Shame on the man who used one.

bear trout n
=**lake trout.**

1887 Goode *Amer. Fishes* 467, Mr. George Barnston . . claims that there is a third species of Lake Trout, different from the Siscowet, on the south shore of Lake Superior, called the "Mucqua" or "Bear Trout." **1911** *Century Dict., Trout* . . . Bear-trout, the great lake-trout. [Lake Superior.] **1935** *AmSp* 10.202, Very few animals are named from the bear. They include the . . *bear trout* (the lake trout, so known in Lake Superior).

bear-walk See bear-hug

bearweed See bear's weed 1

bearwood n [Perh because the berries are favored by bears]
Cascara sagrada.

1869 *Amer. Naturalist* 3.407, *Oregon Bearwood (Frangula Purshiana).* This species of Buckthorn occurs on both slopes of the Coeur d' Aleñe [sic] Mountains. **1897** Parsons *Wild Flowers CA* 68, As we go northward . . the prevailing type . . is . . *R[hamnus] purshiana* . . . In Oregon it is known as . . "bear-wood." **1930** Sievers *Amer. Med. Plants* 21.

be-ashamed See be-shame' bush

beaslings n pl Also sp *beaslins, beazlings, beeslings, beezlins, beslings, bislings* Pronc-spp *beastling, beestlings* [Alter of *beestings, OED* c1000 →] *old-fash*
The first milk given by a cow after calving.

1723 *New-Engl. Courant* (Boston MA) 18–25 Nov 2/1, She does not know . . how to boil a Skillet of Beaslings without letting it turn. **1809** (1814) Weems *F. Marion* 130, Unless they are well worked and scoured of their mother milk, or beastling partiality to the English, they are lost. **1896** *DN* 1.412 **sME,** *Bislings* (=beestings): first milk after a cow has calved. **1899** (1912) Green *VA Folk-Speech, Beestlings* . . . Beeslings, Beaslins, Beslings. First milk of a cow with her first calf. Generally poured on her rump to make her gentle and a good milch cow. **1924** *DN* 5.295 **csNH,** *Beezlin's* . . . First milk given after calving. **1927** *AmSp* 2.348 **cwWV,** Do not milk the beaslings on the ground or the cow will grow dry. **1929** Ellis *Ordinary Woman* 97 **CO,** Sometimes, when the cow is dry, we can hardly wait for her to 'come in'; then there is the three days' wait for the 'beeslings' to get good. **1936** Morehouse *Rain on Just* 37 **NC,** Sukey's calf still born; Sukey herself with a corruption in her tit, and her milk still partly beazlings.

beast n
A Forms.

Pl: usu *beasts;* also, **chiefly S Midl,** *beastes, beasties, beastis,* and double pl *beastes(s)es, beastises.*

1884 Harrison *Negro Engl.* 245 **Sth,** *Beastesses* (beas's). **1888** Jones *Negro Myths* 49 **GA coast,** Buh Rabbit an de tarruh [=other] beastises. **1895** *DN* 1.374 **eTN,** I got a *right smart little bit* of roughness [=coarse fodder] for the beastis. **1903** *DN* 2.306 **seMO,** *Beasties* . . . Pl. of beast. Commonly applied to horses and mules. **1908** *DN* 3.284 **eAL, wGA,** Nouns. Abnormal plurals: . . beastes, beastesses. **1911** *DN* 3.537 **eKY,** *Beastie* . . . Horse; especially common in the plural. **1926** Kephart *Highlanders* 359 **wNC, eTN,** The ancient syllabic plural is preserved in beasties (horses), nesties, posties . . (these are not diminutives). **1940** *AmSp* 15.45 **sAppalachians, Ozarks,** 'Chaucerian' syllabic plurals survive in *nestes, beastes, postes, ghostes* and *jiste-es* (joists). **c1960** Wilson *Coll.* **csKY,** Beasts ['bistɪz].

B Senses.

1 A horse. **Sth, S Midl, NEng**

1684 (1977) Mather *Essay Providences* **NEng,** They had a horse near by, . . but . . the beast was slow and dull. **1820** *Amer. Farmer* I.369 **nVA,** The frequent custom of husband and wife going a junketing on the same horse or 'beast,' as in those days it was more commonly called. **1840** (1847) Longstreet *GA Scenes* 22, Do you want to swap hosses? . . I believe I've got a beast I'd trade with you. **1859** (1968) Bartlett *Americanisms, Beast.* A common name for a horse in the Southern and Western States. It is quite common to see in villages the invitation to travellers, "Entertainment for man and beast." **1930** *AmSp* 5.425 **Ozarks,** A horse, in the Ozarks, is very often called a beast, a usage formerly very common in England. **1969–70** *DARE* (Qu. II15, *When somebody is passing by and you want him or her to stop and talk a while, you might say: "_____."*) Infs **MA58, WV16**, Alight and look to your beast.

2 also *cow beast, male ~, stock ~:* A male domestic animal used for breeding, esp a bull. **chiefly Sth, S Midl, occas NEng** *euphem* Cf **brute**

1890 *DN* 1.69 **LA**, *Beast:* euphemism for *bull.* Common among the women-folk on farms. **1909** *DN* 3.392 **nwAR**, *Beast* . . . Bull. Common among the women on farms. **1939** *LANE* Map 190 **scattered throughout NEng**, Euphemisms used when a direct reference to the bull is avoided on ground of delicacy . . *the animal, the beast, the brute.* **1949** Kurath *Word Geog.* 62, Expressions for the bull are . . . *beast, stock beast, male beast* in the coastal section of the Carolinas. **1950** *PADS* 14.13 **SC**, *Beast* . . . An uncastrated domestic animal, as a bull, boar, or stallion. **c1960** *Wilson Coll.* **csKY**, *Beast* . . . Male, usually uncastrated, animal. "That old beast chased Pappy across the pasture field." **1960** *PADS* 34.63 **CO**, *Older Speech . . beast 'bull.'* **1965–70** *DARE* (Qu. K22, . . *A bull*) Infs **AR4, GA3, MS4, SC7**, Beast; **GA3, NC49**, Male beast; (Qu. K23, *Words used by women or in mixed company for a bull*) Infs **GA7, 46, IN8, SC43, TN44**, Beast; **GA3, NC10**, Male beast; **WV2**, Cow beast.

beast-back *adv* Cf **critter-back** [beast B1]
On horseback.

1890 *DN* 1.63 **KY**, *Beastback* . . . Horseback. "I went *beast-back* to town."

beast, bird, or fish See **bird, beast, or fish 1**

beastling See **beaslings**

beat *n*

1 Something that surpasses. **chiefly NEng, Midl**

1827 in 1941 Bird *Cowled Lover* 147 **KY**, Did you ever see the beat o' that? **1833** in 1834 Smith *Letters Jack Downing* 129 **ME**, Such a sight of folks, and fine ladies . . and fire works a whisking about, I never see the beat of it. **1878** (1977) Stowe *Poganuc People* 110 **CT**, That Bill is saassy enough to physic a hornbug. I never see the beat of him! **1902** Richards *Mrs. Tree* 70, "There! you hear her!" murmured Direxia. "Oh, she is the beat of all!" **1905** *DN* 3.3 **cCT**, *Beat* . . . Superior. 'I never saw the beat of him.' **1907** *DN* 3.209 **nwAR**. **1911** Porter *Harvester* 343 **IN**, Did you ever see his beat to go swimmin'? He's always in splashin'! **1914** *DN* 4.69 **ME, nNH**, She never seen the *beat on't.* **1937** Sandoz *Slogum* 209 **wNE** (as of 1900–20), "There ain't your beat in the country when it comes to cookin'," she said. **c1960** *Wilson Coll.* **csKY**, *Beat* . . . The equal or better. "I never saw the beat of that horse."

2 A shiftless, unreliable person; one who regularly fails to pay his debts. [Abbr for *deadbeat*] **formerly widespread, now esp Mid Atl** See Map *derog* Cf **beater 2**

1865 *Canteen Songster* (1868) 26 *(DA)*, Before 'this cruel war' broke out he was what's termed 'a beat.' **1888** Whitman *November Boughs* 71, Among the crowd were . . three Virginia beats. **1902** Riis *Making of Amer.* 139 **NYC**, When the grocer on my corner complained that he was being ruined by "beats" who did not pay their bills . . I started in at once to make those beats pay up. **1948** *Chicago Daily Tribune* (IL) 4 Apr comic sec, Well, you can't get money out of a turnip!! You're no turnip—you're a *beat!* **1965–70** *DARE* (Qu. U17, . . *A person who doesn't pay his bills*) 18 Infs, **scattered Sth, S Midl**, Beat; (Qu.

U36a, . . *A person who saves in a mean way or is greedy in money matters*) Inf **SC69**, Beat; (Qu. V2a, . . *A deceiving person, or somebody that you can't trust*) Infs **KY18, MD19, 43, MO8, SC3**, Beat; (Qu. V7, *A person who sets out to cheat others while pretending to be honest*) Infs **MD19, 43, NC50, 85**, Beat; (Qu. HH20a, *An idle, worthless person: "He's a _____."*) Inf **MS45**, Beat.

beat *adj* [Abbr for **beat out**] *esp among young, urban, and Black speakers*
Tired, exhausted.

1905 *DN* 3.3 **cCT**, *Beat* . . . Tired. 'I was quite beat.' **1938** *AmSp* 13.317 **NE** [Black], *Beat* means bedraggled, fagged out. **1957** *AmSp* 32.277 [Jazz argot], *Beat.* Tired. **1965–70** *DARE* (Qu. X47, . . *Other ways . . of saying, "I'm very tired, at the end of my strength."*) 132 Infs, **throughout US**, Beat. [Of all Infs responding to the question, 12% were comm types 1 and 2, 11% young, 6% Black; of those giving this response, 29% were comm types 1 and 2, 32% young, 22% Black.]

beat a hen a-flying *v phr* Also *beat a hen a-routing*
=beat the Dutch.

1966–68 *DARE* (Qu. GG22b, *When you come to the end of your patience, you might say, "Well, that certainly _____."*) Inf **TN26**, Don't that beat a hen a-flyin'; **NC37**, Beats a hen a-routin'.

beat around *v phr*
To putter, trifle, loaf; to gad about.

1960 Wentworth–Flexner *Slang* 25, *Beat around*—To wander aimlessly, as a pastime or in search of fun; to loaf or idle. **1966–69** *DARE* (Qu. A10, . . *Doing little unimportant things*) Inf **KY28**, Beating around; (Qu. Y29b, *About a man who doesn't stay home much: "He's always _____."*) Inf **SC10**, Beating around; (Qu. KK31, *To go about aimlessly looking for distractions: "He doesn't have anything to do, so he's just _____ around."*) Inf **SC19**, Beatin' around.

beat bobtail *v phr* [Prob allusion to horse racing, perh to Stephen Foster's *Camptown Races*] **?Sth**
To surpass (one's) expectation or comprehension; also as adv phr *to beat bobtail* to an extreme degree, "to beat the band."

1898 Lloyd *Country Life* 47 **AL**, Blev Scroggins was mixin' around among the various delegates . . to beat bobtail. **1945** *Hench Coll.*, A fellow-teacher and friend, raised in eastern North Carolina, told me of the proverb *That beats bobtail* meaning *that beats the devil.* Sometimes the proverb has a longer form: *That beats bobtail and everybody knows what bobtail beats.* When I asked my informant what bobtail meant, he said that he did not know. **1954** *Ibid*, A native Virginian (raised in Norfolk) was speaking of something that surprised him a great deal, something that he could not comprehend. Summing up his impression, he said, "Doesn't it beat bobtail—for him to do that!"

beat down See **beat one down**

beaten biscuit *n* Also *beat biscuit* **chiefly Sth, S Midl, esp KY, MD, VA** See Map Also called **Maryland beaten biscuit**
A biscuit made with dough lightened by beating and folding.

1877 Henderson *Practical Cooking* 69, Beat the dough well with a rolling-pin for half an hour or more, or until the dough will *break* when pulled. Little machines come for the purpose of making beaten biscuit, which facilitate the operation. **1881** *Georgians* 123 *(DA)*, This is regular old-fashioned hoe-cake; . . and this is beat-biscuit, I'm sure. **1912** Green *VA Folk-Speech*, *Beat-biscuit* . . . An unrisen biscuit. **1929**

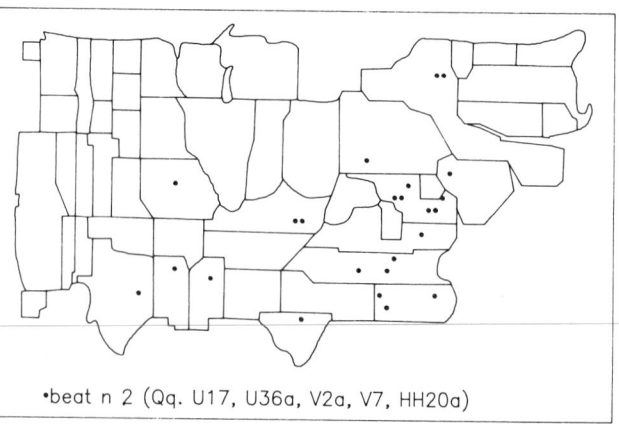

•beat n 2 (Qq. U17, U36a, V2a, V7, HH20a)

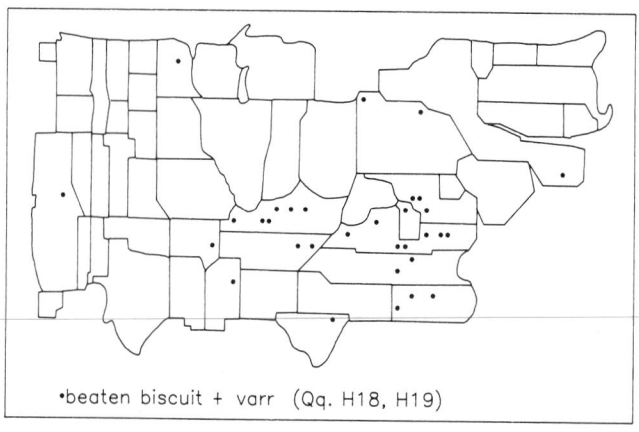

•beaten biscuit + varr (Qq. H18, H19)

(1951) Faulkner *Sartoris* 26 **MS,** A thin woman in a funereal purple turban, poising a beaten biscuit heaped with mayonnaise. **1931** *Sun* (Baltimore MD) 1 May 12/7 *(Hench Coll.),* Maryland biscuits? I *object* to that description. *Beaten* biscuits. They make them *just* as good in *Virginia!* **c1937** in 1977 *Amer. Slave Suppl. 1* 1.67 **AL,** My mammy made de best beaten biscuit and de best pound cake. **1965–70** *DARE* (Qu. H19, *What do you mean by a biscuit?*) 28 Infs, **chiefly Sth, S Midl,** Beaten biscuit(s); **MD**19, Beat biscuit—dough beaten with an ax for hours; (Qu. H18, . . *Special kinds of bread*) Infs **AR**8, **KY**94, **MD**7, 27, **MS**54, Beaten biscuit(s). **1968** *DARE* Tape **MD**27, Beaten biscuits have to be beaten before they are baked.

beatenest adj Also sp *beatenist, beatin(g)est;* formerly *beate-mest, beatomest* [*beating* ppl of *beat* to surpass + *-est;* for early forms, prob *beat* + *'em* them + *-est;* cf Engl dial *beatem* victor] **chiefly Sth, S Midl**

Most remarkable or unusual.

1831 *Daily Eve. Transcript* (Boston MA) 9 Aug 2/3, He . . sees old Susap . . stan' there with his gun pyntin' right into the door—beatemest feller with a gun ever you seed. **1845** Judd *Margaret* 245 **ME,** The Parson [=a cow] . . is the worst pair of horns I ever druv,—and I have had the business now rising of sixty year, and take it by and large fifty head a season, and she is the beatomest. **1860** *Harper's Mag.* 22.135/2, A countryman . . attracted by the white slab . . exclaimed, "Well, if this ain't the beatenest town I ever saw!" **1885** Twain *Huck. Finn* 106 **MO,** It's the beatenest thing I ever struck. **1892** *DN* 1.229 **KY. 1893** Shands *MS Speech* 70, *Beatenest.* This word is used in Mississippi with exactly the same sense as in Kentucky; i.e. *not to be beaten, not to be surpassed.* **1895** *DN* 1.370 **eTN. 1902** *DN* 2.229 **sIL. 1903** *DN* 2.306 **seMO,** *Beatingest* or *beatinest.* **1905** *DN* 3.89 **nwAR. 1908** *DN* 3.289 **eAL, wGA,** *Beatin(g)est.* **1909** *DN* 3.408 **nME. 1912** *DN* 3.571 **wIN. 1915** *DN* 4.181 **swVA. 1916** *DN* 4.319 **KS,** Beatinest. **1927** *AmSp* 2.348 **WV,** Beatenist. **1929** (1951) Faulkner *Sartoris* 27 **MS,** Ef you ain't de beatin'es' man! **1941** Faulkner *Men Working* 24 **MS,** I declare, he's the beatin'est child I ever saw. **c1960** *Wilson Coll.* **cwKY,** *Beatenest . . .* Unusual. "He made the beatenest speech you ever heard."

beatenest n

One's best; one's utmost effort.

1907 Wright *Shepherd* 12 **Ozarks,** 'Taint no wonder 't all, God rested when he made these here hills; he jes naturally *had* t' quit, fer he done his beatenest an' was plumb gin [=given] out.

beater n

1 A heavy hammer or maul; also a wedge used in splitting wood.

1950 *AmSp* 25.236 [City surveying argot], *Beater . . .* A sledge hammer. **1954** *Harder Coll.* **cwTN,** Beater—a wooden wedge used to split boards or slats. **1958** McCulloch *Woods Words* **Pacific NW,** *Beater*— A name used for a sledge or a maul.

2 =beat n **2. chiefly Sth** *esp among Black speakers*

1965–70 *DARE* (Qu. U17, . . *A person who doesn't pay his bills*) Infs **LA**8, 20, **NC**85, **VA**70, Beater; (Qu. V7, *A person who sets out to cheat others while pretending to be honest*) Infs **FL**51, **LA**8, **MS**15, **SC**26, Beater; (Qu. HH19, . . *A tramp*) Inf **FL**52, Beater. [6 of 8 Infs Black].

3 See quot.

1969–70 *DARE* (Qu. X13b, . . *False teeth*) Inf **MO**19, Gum beaters; **TX**106, Beaters.

beatermost adj [Var of **beatenest** adj] *obs*

=beatenest adj.

1843 Stephens *High Life N.Y.* 2.28 *(DAE),* Aint I the beatermost feller for losing things? **1845** Kirkland *Western Clearings* 98, The Maine-man . . will declare [his cow] to be the "beatermost critter under the canopy."

beat her on the back v phr

In railroading: see quot 1945.

1929 *Bookman* 69.525, I give the old boiler the prod and take up the slack in the train, then I begin beatin' her on the back. We're goin' so fast I can look back and see the door in the hack [=caboose]. **1943** *AmSp* 18.162, *Beat her on the back.* To maintain a high rate of speed, using the full power of the engine. **1945** Hubbard *Railroad Ave.* 332, *Beat 'er on the back*—Make fast time; work an engine at full stroke.

beatinest, beatingest See **beatenest** adj

beating stick n

=battling stick.

1952 Brown *NC Folkl.* 1.519, *Beating-stick . . .* A stick used to beat clothes while washing them.

beatin's vbl n pl [*beat* to get the better of, win, surpass]

1896 *DN* 1.412 **NY,** *Beatin's . .* the advantage. "I got the beatin's of him then."

beat in time v phr Also *beat time* **chiefly Midl**

To waste time; to busy oneself with unimportant things.

1965–70 *DARE* (Qu. A9, . . *Wasting time by not working on the job*) Infs **AR**53, **NC**31, 41, **SC**46, **VA**28, 87, Beating time; (Qu. A10, . . *Doing little unimportant things: somebody asks, "What are you doing?" And you answer, "Nothing in particular—I'm just _____."*) Infs **IL**113, 134, Beating in time; (Qu. A11, *When somebody takes too long . . "I wish he'd quit _____."*) Inf **VA**36, Beating time; (Qu. Y29b, *About a man who doesn't stay home much: "He's always _____."*) Inf **VA**5, Beating in time; (Qu. KK31, *To go about aimlessly looking for distractions: "He doesn't have anything to do, so he's just _____."*) Infs **IL**126, 136, **KY**47, Beating in time.

beat it v phr **widespread, but most freq in Nth, N Midl, West** See Map

To leave in a hurry, to rush away—freq used in imper: Clear out! Scram!

1906 H. Green *Actors' Boarding House* 108 *(OEDS),* I told 'em to beat it. **1914** *DN* 4.103 **KS,** *Beat it . . .* To depart in haste. "It's dinner time and I guess I'll beat it to the house." **1915** *DN* 4.243 **eMA, MT,** *Beat it . . .* Go. "Beat it while going is good." **1916** *DN* 4.271 **IA, IL, LA, MA, MI, NE, NY, NC, PA, TN,** *Beat it . . .* Depart. "What became of all you people all of a sudden?" "O, we decided to beat it." **1923** *DN* 5.201 **swMO,** *Beat it . . .* To hurry away. **1927** *AmSp* 2.348 **WV. 1950** *WELS* (To leave in a hurry) 26 Infs, **WI,** Beat it; (Expressions used to drive away people or animals) 15 Infs, **WI,** Beat it. **1965–70** *DARE* (Qu. A19, *Other ways of saying . . to hurry: "I'm late, I'll have to _____."*) 10 Infs, **Nth,** Beat it; (Qu. Y18, *To leave in a hurry: " . . We'd better _____."*) 188 Infs, **esp Nth, N Midl, West,** Beat it; (Qu. Y19, . . *To go away from a place*) 19 Infs, **esp Nth, N Midl, West,** Beat it; (Qu. Y20, *To run fast: "You should have seen him _____!"*) 32 Infs, **chiefly Nth, N Midl,** Beat it; (Qu. II22, *Expressions to tell somebody to . . mind his own business*) 10 Infs, **Nth, NW,** Beat it; (Qq. NN12a,b) Infs **NY**250, **UT**8, Beat it (kid); (Qq. NN22a,b,c,d) 199 total Infs, **chiefly Nth, N Midl, scattered West,** Beat it (kitty, you kids).

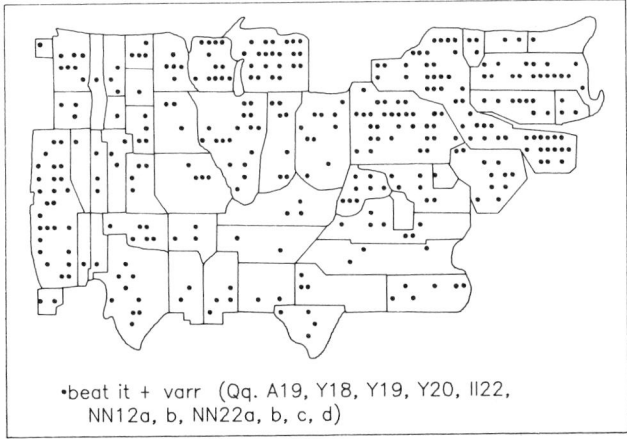

•beat it + varr (Qq. A19, Y18, Y19, Y20, II22, NN12a, b, NN22a, b, c, d)

beat one down v phr Also *beat down* **chiefly east of Missip R, but esp NEast** See Map on p. 192

To get a lower price (on something) by haggling aggressively.

1942 Berrey–Van den Bark *Amer. Slang* 545.6, *Beat down . . to secure a lower price by haggling.* **1950** *WELS* (If you were buying something and you argued with the seller till you made him lower the price, you might say, "I _____.") 3 Infs, **WI,** Beat him down; [1 Inf, **csWI,** Beat down his price]. **1965–70** *DARE* (Qu. U12) 60 Infs, **chiefly east of Missip R, but esp NEast,** Beat him down; [**AL**50, **ME**22, **NH**10, Beat him; **CT**6, 7, **NY**181, **TX**86, **VT**13, Beat down the price].

beat out adj phr

1 Tired, exhausted. **scattered, but esp NEng**

1746 in 1895 Sheldon *Hist. Deerfield* 1.548 **MA,** I . . ordered him to put on faster. He told me his horse was about beat out. **1860** Holmes *Professor* 239 **NEng,** The landlady insisted that she'd . . haf to give up, if

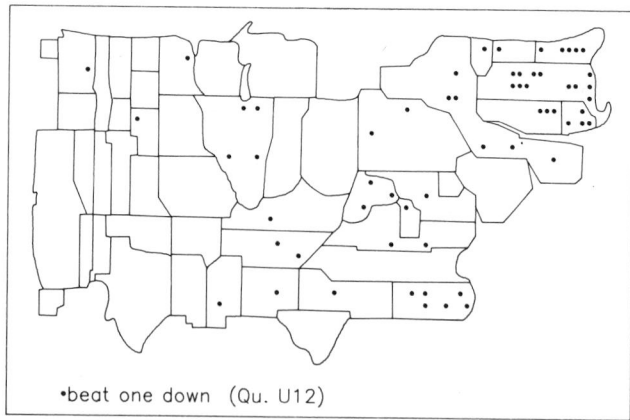

•beat one down (Qu. U12)

she didn't want to be clean beat out in less 'n a week. **1899** (1960) Norris *McTeague* 169 **San Francisco CA,** I'm beat out. I've walked the city over—ten miles, I guess—an' I'm going to bed. **1905** *DN* 3.3 **cCT.** **1907** Lincoln *Cape Cod* 286 **MA,** I went off by myself . . and laid down to rest, being beat out. **1907** *DN* 3.209 **nwAR, cCT.** **1909** *DN* 3.408 **nME.** **1914** *DN* 4.69 **ME, nNH.** **1935** Safford *Bennington Mob* 105 **VT,** "Been travelin' far?" "So-so." "Ye don't look much beat out." "No." **1935** Davis *Honey* 15 **OR,** He'll be all beat out when he gets here. **1941** *LANE* Map 481 **throughoutNEng,** The map shows the adjectival phrases *tuckered out, fagged ~, beat ~.* **1950** *WELS (Very tired)* 2 Infs, **WI,** Beat out. c**1960** Wilson *Coll.* **csKY.** **1965–70** *DARE* (Qu. X47, . . *Ways of saying, "I'm very tired, at the end of my strength."*) Infs **ME22, MA5, NY197, SC40, VA69,** Beat out; (Qu. Y21, *To move about slowly and without energy*) Inf **CA32,** Beat out. **1971** Wood *Vocab. Change* 40 **Sth,** Expressions for the state of exhaustion . . . Least widely distributed are *beat out* (not reported in Florida), *done out* . . and *used up.*

2 Mentally or nervously exhausted; at one's wits' end.

1943 Peattie *Great Smokies* 128 **eTN,** The North Carolina woman . . "got so plumb beat out with the no-account ways of her fam-il-ee, that she just tuk to the bed and stayed thar, year in and year out." **1950** (1965) Richter *Town* 200 **OH,** Sayward was beat out about Chancey.

beat the cars v phr

To be the last straw; also used adverbially in *to beat the cars:* to an extreme degree.

1922 *DN* 5.156 **AR,** *Beat the cars, to* . . . To the skies, highly. "He is boosting that country to beat the cars." **1968** *DARE* (Qu. B26, *When it's raining very heavily, you say, "It's raining_____."*) Inf **MN38,** To beat the cars; (Qu. GG22b, *When you come to the end of your patience, you might say, "Well, that certainly_____."*) Inf **MD33,** Beats the cars.

beat the cats v phr

1909 *DN* 3.392 **nwAR,** *Beat the cats* . . . Be surprising. "That does beat the cats."

beat the Dutch v phr

To be surprising or astonishing; to be exasperating.

1775 in 1857 *New Engl. Hist. & Geneal. Register* 6.191, Our cargoes of meat, drink and cloaths beat the Dutch. **1859** (1968) Bartlett *Americanisms* 134, *It beats the Dutch* is an expression often applied, in New York and New England, to any thing astonishing. **1902** Harben *Abner Daniel* 279 **GA,** "Well, that beats the Dutch!" laughed Abner. **1907** *DN* 3.211 **nwAR, cCT,** *Dutch, beat the* . . . To be astonishing. **1939** *AmSp* 14.267 **sIN,** If it is startling news, it 'beats the Jews' or 'beats the Dutch.' **1965–70** *DARE* (Qu. GG22b, *When you come to the end of your patience, you might say, "Well, that certainly_____."*) Infs **GA15, MA58, MI17, MN36, NY69, OH56, WI29,** Beats the Dutch. [6 of 7 Infs old] **1968** *DARE* FW Addit **MN32,** Don't it beat the Dutch—a parallel expression to "don't that beat all." c**1970** Halpert *Coll.* **wKY,** Beat. Said about something unusual. "If that don't beat the Dutch!"

beat the hound out of v phr esp SC

To thrash or beat soundly.

1966–67 *DARE* (Qu. Y15, *To beat somebody thoroughly: "John really_____that fellow."*) Infs **SC19, 29, 34, 42, 46,** Beat the hound out of. **1967** *DARE* FW Addit **ceTN,** Heard in conversation: "I beat the hound out of him," meaning "I gave him a bad beating."

beat the throttle with a stick v phr Cf beat her on the back

See quot 1958.

1958 McCulloch *Woods Words* **Pacific NW,** *Beat the throttle with a stick*—An attempt to get more steam out of an engine. **1962** *AmSp* 37.131 **NW** [Logging railroad argot].

beat time See beat in time

be-attled See be-addled

beat up v phr

1967 *DARE* (Qu. B12, *When the wind begins to increase, you say it's_____*) Inf **NY34,** Beating up.

beau v [beau (*OED* 1720 →) sweetheart, suitor, lover < Fr *beau* fine, beautiful] chiefly NEng old-fash

To escort; to act as suitor to; to date.

1859 (1968) Bartlett *Americanisms, To Beau.* To act in the capacity of a gallant or beau. ["]Well, I got to *beauin'* Miss Patience about a spell; and kept my eye on Nance, to see how the cat was jumpin'.["]— *Yankee Hill's Stories.* **1891** Maitland *Amer. Slang Dict.* 29, *Beau* . . . "To beau" is to court or gallant a girl. **1904** Day *Kin o' Ktaadn* 94 **ME,** You were running your legs off beauing girls. *Ibid* 97, And vowed to beau no maidens home; you see, I was a youngster then. **1941** *LANE* Map 402 **scattered throughout NEng,** The map shows the expressions recorded in the context *May I escort you home?* as addressed by a young man to a girl after a dance or on some similar occasion: *escort you home, see ~, take ~, bring ~, beau ~. Ibid* Map 405, The map shows the expressions *keeping company with her, going (out, around) with her, . . beauing her around, ~ out.* **1942** Hale *Prodigal Women* 400 **MA** (as of 1905–40), Good old Sam, who was now beauing Jane. **1965–70** *DARE* (Qu. AA1, *When a man goes to see a girl often and seems to want to marry her, he's_____her*) Inf **PA234,** Beauin' her around; (Qu. AA2, . . *"John is going to_____Mary to the dance."*) Infs **CA36, MA5, 48, 69,** Beau; **CT1,** Beauing. [All Infs old]

beau n [Transf from *beau* a male escort, sweetheart]

1899 (1912) Green *VA Folk-Speech, Beau* . . . A piece of thorn or briar which becomes attached to a woman's dress and drags along after her.

beau-catcher n, also attrib

See quots.

1923 *DN* 5.239 **swWI,** *Beau-catcher* . . . Fluffed-out hair on a girl's temples. (Obs.) **1942** Berrey–Van den Bark *Amer. Slang* 121.48, *Curls. Spec.* beau catcher, . . *a ringlet on the forehead or cheek, a lovelock.* **1955** *Hand Coll.* **neOH,** Girls used to soap the hair to make beau catchers. These was sometimes one by each ear. Some all along the edge of one's hair. It was like bangs, only laid in a flat curl tight to the head. **1956** McAtee *Some Dialect NC* 4, Beau-catcher: . . a spit curl, used as a beauty spot. c**1960** Wilson *Coll.* **csKY,** *Beau-catcher curl* . . . A "fetching" curl on the forehead. "She had a beau-catcher curl that sure attracted the boys." **1978** *DARE* File **cnMA,** Beau catcher—I knew this word as a child, and in the 1920's I think. Something like spit curls. *Ibid* **nOH** (as of 1920s).

beaucoup adj, n, adv Freq beaucoups Pronc-spp bogoobs, boo-coo(s), bookoo(s) [Fr beaucoup much, a great deal] chiefly Sth See Map Cf boocoodles

Many, much; an abundance, a lot; in abundance, galore.

1929 *AmSp* 4.357, If you wish to boast of having a great deal of money, you may speak of . . being *filthy* or *lousy* with money. *Beaucoup jack* is a survival of the war. **1930** *AmSp* 5.382 [Armed forces in Europe],

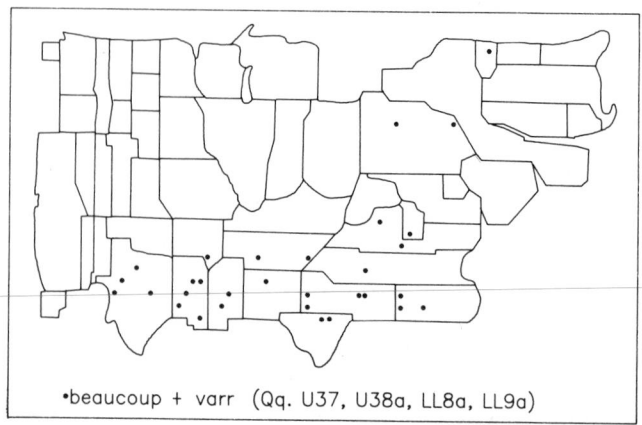

•beaucoup + varr (Qq. U37, U38a, LL8a, LL9a)

Bookoo (beaucoup). Abundance. **1958** *AmSp* 33.225 [Jazz musicians' argot], A considerable amount of anything is *bogoobs* (e.g., 'It's a mickey band, but there's bogoobs bread'), quite obviously from *beaucoup.* **1965–70** *DARE* (Qu. U37, . . *Plenty of money*) Inf **VT**16, Money beaucoup; (Qu. U38a, . . *A great deal of money:* "He's got _____ [*of money].*") Infs **AL**27, **DC**11, **LA**3, **NC**68, **PA**199, 228, **TX**72, 89, Beaucoup; **FL**8, **GA**1, 9, **VA**42, Beaucoups; **GA**9, 89, **SC**43, Boocoos; (Qu. LL8a, *A large amount or number: more than enough—for example, of time:* "*He's got _____ of time.*") Infs **AR**52, **LA**35, **VA**34, Beaucoup (time); 10 Infs, **chiefly Sth,** Boocoos; **TX**72, Boocoo; (Qu. LL9a, *As much as you need or more—for example, of apples:* "*We've got _____ of apples.*") Infs **LA**35, 37, **TX**81, Beaucoup; **LA**11, Boocoo; **GA**84, 89, **LA**3, 32, **TX**33, **VT**16, Boocoos. **1967** *DARE* FW Addit **cLA,** Boocoo ['buˌku] "She's got money boocoo." **1970** Major *Afro–Amer. Slang, Boo koos:* a large quantity of anything. **1980** *DARE* File **Madison WI,** Heard in conversation with a native of Madison: "It's obvious he has boocoo money." **1982** *Ibid* **neLA,** *Boo coo's*—lots of . . . I use it regularly.

beau dollar n Also sp *bo dollar, Boer ~, bow ~* [Prob through assoc with *beau* a dandy; *Boer dollar* appears to be folk-etym] **chiefly Sth, S Midl** See Map and Map Section *esp freq among Black speakers*
A silver dollar.

1944 TN Folk Lore Soc. *Bulletin* 10.9, A reader inquired about the origin of the term "bo-dollar" . . . The expression is widely used by negroes in the Mid-South, particularly at lumber camps along the Mississippi River . . . Several explanations . . were sent in . . . One suggested that "bo-dollar" is a corruption of "boat-dollar" . . . Another reader said the term was a corruption of . . "hobo dollar" . . . Another . . suggested that "bo-dollar" was a corruption of the expression "boar dollar," so-called after the male hog . . . because the negroes considered the boar to be an animal that always achieved what it wanted. **1950** *PADS* 14.15 **SC,** *Boer dollar* . . . A silver dollar, carried as a lucky piece. Said to have originated among British soldiers during the *Boer* War. **1953** *PADS* 19.9 **NC,** *Bo dollar* . . . Silver dollar. Used by Negroes of Pilot Mountain, who customarily go to a local bank to have paper dollars exchanged for silver ones. **1965–70** *DARE* (Qu. U27, . . *A silver dollar*) 34 Infs, **chiefly Sth, S Midl,** Beau dollar. [27 Infs Black] **1972** *Atlanta Letters* **nGA,** Beau dollar. Bow dollar—silver dollar. **1973** *Patrick Coll.* **Sth,** *Bo dollar* . . . Silver dollar. **1973** *DARE* File **cAL,** Bo dollar . . . Silver dollar.

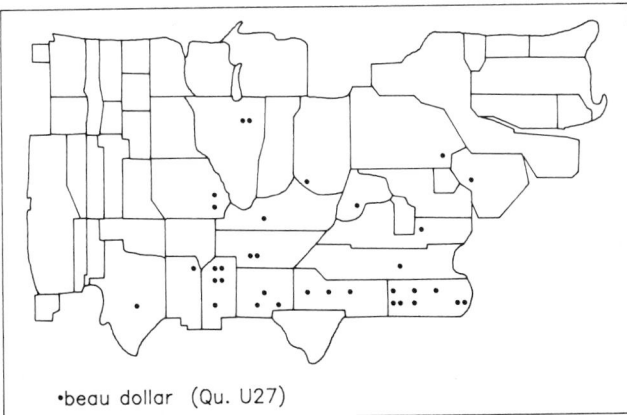

•beau dollar (Qu. U27)

beautyberry n **chiefly Sth**
A plant of the genus *Callicarpa,* esp **French mulberry.**

1923 Amer. Joint Comm. Horticult. Nomenclature *Std. Plant Names* 61/1, Callicarpa . . . White Beautyberry (*C. americana alba*). **1933** Small *Manual SE Flora* 1143, Callicarpa . . . Shrubs or trees . . . *Beauty-berries.* **1941** Walker *Lookout* 60 **TN,** It is doubtful if there is any shrub . . more beautiful than beauty-berry, which is listed by botanists under the very ill-fitting name of French mulberry. It is not a mulberry and is American and not French. **1952** Taylor *Plants Colonial Days* 41 **VA,** French mulberry . . . Ranging from Virginia to Texas, [it] is neither French nor a mulberry . . . Other common names include . . beautyberry. **1972** Brown *Wildflowers LA* 155, *American Beauty Berry* . . . A large shrub . . . Widely distributed, more abundant in but not confined to cutover pine-oak-hickory woods along streams.

beauty pin n Also *beauty bar*
A brooch.

1967–69 *DARE* (Qu. W35, *A piece of jewelry that a woman wears fastened at the neck of her dress*) Infs **CT**23, **KY**44, **TN**23, Beauty pin; **MA**6, Beauty bar.

beautysome adj [*beauty* + *-some*]
1908 Wasson *Home from the Sea* 37 **ME** (*AmSp* 37.251), Ef it didn't sound beautysome to hear them old chanties acrosst the river.

beaver n
1 A man's silk hat.
1870 Alcott *Little Women* 2.144 **MA,** Two of the young men were settling their beavers before the hall mirror. **1885** Twain *Huck. Finn* 204 **MO,** He'd take off his new white beaver and make a bow. **1889** *Century Dict.* 1.496/1, The modern stiff silk hat was commonly called a *beaver* until recently. **1903** *DN* 2.295 **Cape Cod MA,** *Beaver* . . . Silk hat. **1905** *DN* 3.3 **cCT.** **1907** *DN* 3.181 **seNH.** **1909** *DN* 3.408 **cnME.**
2 Money. [In ref to the use of pelts as a medium of exchange] *arch*
1848 (1855) Ruxton *Life Far West* 64, With a pack of cards in his hand, and a handful of dollars in his hat . . [he] cries out—"Ho, boys, hyar's a deck, and hyar's the beaver (rattling the coin)." **1949** Guthrie *Way West* 35 (as of 1847), He would saw open the big log where he had cached his beaver, beaver being what they were. **1968** Adams *Western Words, Beaver*—A fur trapper's name not only for the animal he trapped but also for money.
3 Among loggers: see quots. Cf **beaver** v
1958 McCulloch *Woods Words* **Pacific NW,** *Beaver* . . . A clumsy axman. **1969** Sorden *Lumberjack Lingo* **NEng, Gt Lakes,** *Beaver*—A poor chopper. Same as wood pecker.

beaver v Also *beaver down* Cf **beaver** n 3
Among loggers: see quot 1958.
1942 Berrey–Van den Bark *Amer. Slang* 512.14, *Logging* . . . Beaver down, *to hack a tree down.* **1958** McCulloch *Woods Words* **Pacific NW,** *Beaver* . . . To chop or saw a rough uneven cut, as would be done by a green hand in the woods.

beaver duck n Also *beaver*
=ruddy duck.
1955 *AmSp* 30.178, *Beaver,* an old-time market designation of the ruddy duck in Chicago, and the folk name *beaver duck* (Wis.) were given because of the resemblance to beaver fur of the thick down remaining on the bird's body after the ordinary feathers are plucked.

beaver lily n
=spatterdock.
1892 *Jrl. Amer. Folkl.* 5.91, *Nuphar advena* . . . Beaver-lily. M[ain]e. **1911** *Century Dict. Suppl., Lily* . . . *Beaver-lily,* the yellow pond-lily, *Nymphaea advena.* Also called *beaver-root.* **1959** Carleton *Index Herb. Plants* 9, Beaver lily: Nymphozanthus advena (Nuphar).

beaver meadow n **chiefly Nth, esp NEng**
A grassy open area formed when an abandoned beaver dam no longer blocks off the stream.
1644 in 1857 New Haven (Colony) *Records* 1.126, A proposi[on] . . thatt they may have the Bever meadowes granted to them. **1809** Kendall *Travels* 3.176 **NH,** The dams being in the end abandoned by the beaver, and broken through by the water, large tracts of meadowland are formed, which, from their origin, are described as beavermeadows. **1968** *DARE* FW Addit **ceNY,** Beaver meadow—a meadow that originated when beavers dammed a creek and killed the timber with water and other activities; when the water went down after the dam went out, it left rich land good for hay. **1969** Sorden *Lumberjack Lingo* **NEng, Gt Lakes.**

beaver poison n
=poison hemlock 1.
1857 Gray *Manual of Botany* 157, C[icuta] maculata, Spotted Cowbane, Musquash-Root, Beaver-Poison . . . Root a *deadly poison.* **1930** Sievers *Amer. Med. Plants* 46, Poison Hemlock . . . Other common names . . . Beaver poison. **1970** Correll *Plants TX* 1145, Cicuta maculata . . Beaver-poison.

beaver root n
=spatterdock.
1832 Williamson *Hist.* **ME** 1.126, Of the *Lily* tribe, we have several species, . . Such as the yellow water-lily, or dog-lily, or beaver-root. **1876** Hobbs *Bot. Hdbk.* 9, Beaver root, Yellow pond lily, Nuphar advena. **1911** [see **beaver lily**]. **1959** Carleton *Index Herb. Plants* 9.

beavertail grass n [Prob from the shape and hairiness of the petals] **CA**

A **mariposa lily** (here: *Calochortus coeruleus*).

1925 Jepson *Manual Plants CA* 238, *C. caeruleus . . . Beavertail Grass.* **1949** Moldenke *Amer. Wild Flowers* 320, The *beavertailgrass . .* produces lovely umbels of 2 to 10 small flowers. **1959** Munz–Keck *CA Flora* 1347.

beaver tree n [See quot 1901] Cf **castorwood**

Usu =**sweet bay 2.**

1801 in 1966 Brown *Beverages* 91, Beaver tree seldom grows further north than Pennsylvania and the Jerseys . . . its red berries are steeped in rum or brandy, (to) cure coughs, consumptions, and other disorders. **1822** Eaton *Botany* 347, *Magnolia glauca . .* beaver tree. **1828** Rafinesque *Med. Flora* 31, *Magnolia macrophylla . . .* Beaver Tree. **1901** Lounsberry *S. Wild Flowers* 167, *M. Virginiana . . .* In early days the people of Pennsylvania observed that beavers ate greedily of the tree's fleshy roots, . . to which the common name of beaver tree is in allusion. **1933** Small *Manual SE Flora* 536, *Magnolia virginiana . .* Beaver-tree. **1960** Vines *Trees SW* 286, *Magnolia virginiana . . Beaver-tree.*

beaverwood n Cf **beaver tree**

1 =**magnolia.**

1828 Rafinesque *Med. Flora* 32, The genus *Magnolia . . .* includes about ten American species . . . They are promiscuously called Laurels, Beaver-wood, . . &c. **1941** *Torreya* 41.47, *Magnolia virginiana . . .* Beaver-wood.

2 A **hackberry** (here: *Celtis occidentalis*).

1894 *Jrl. Amer. Folkl.* 7.98, *Celtis occidentalis . .* beaver-wood, N.Y. **1960** Vines *Trees SW* 206, *Vernacular names* are . . Beaverwood . . and Oneberry. **1970** Correll *Plants TX* 494, *Beaver-wood.*

beazlestone n [From an arch pronc of *bezoar stone*, e.g. *beazer stone* (*OED* at *bezoar* 2)]

A hard object found in the entrails of an animal, used as a charm or amulet. Cf **madstone**

1981 Harper–Presley *Okefinokee* 97 **sGA** (as of a1952), Uncle Ben [a conjure doctor] had a beazlestone, just a little rock he had in his pocket. Lay it on you and make it sweat. *Ibid* 99, Local tradition has it that this special deer [a white one] carries a "beazlestone" in its throat . . . Allen Chesser spoke of seeing them. He said they "grow in the deer's runnet, right where his swaller . . goes into his maw." . . Other residents of Billys Island have maintained that many deer . . have "beazlestones" in or near the heart.

beazlings See **beaslings**

becaise See **because** conj

bec-a-lance n Also *bec à lancette* [Fr *bec à lancette* lancet-bill] **LA**

=**anhinga.**

[**1768** in 1931 Read *LA French* 158, Il y a un autre oiseau nommé bec à lancette, qui a effectivement le bec fait de même [=There is another bird called the bec à lancette which actually has a beak of the same sort]]. **1916** *DN* 4.422 **LA**, *Anhinga (Anhinga anhinga) . .* Bec-a-laucet [sic]. **1917** *Wilson Bulletin* 29.2.74 **LA**, *Anhinga anhinga.*—Bec-a-lance. **1931** Read *LA French* 7, *Bec à lancette . .* American Snakebird.

because conj Usu |ˌbɪ-, ˌbə-; -ˈkɔz, -ˈkʌz|; occas |-ˈkɑz|; also, **in Sth, S Midl,** |bɪˈke(ɪ)z, -ˈke(ɪ)s| Pronc-spp *becaise, becase, becaze, becuz, bekase,* and aphet forms *case, caze, cos, cose, coz, kase* Also *becassin, causen, kasin* (see **-en** suff[3]) See also **acause**

Std senses, var forms.

1815 Humphreys *Yankey in England* 103 **NEng**, *Becaise,* because. **1837** Sherwood *Gaz. GA* 69 [In a list of provincialisms to be avoided], *Becase,* for because. **1843** (1916) Hall *New Purchase* 79 **IN**, Turn to the left, but not quite—'cos the path goes to the rite like. **1848** Lowell *Biglow* 52 "Upcountry" **MA**, But he mus'n't be hard on partickler sins, / Coz then he'll be kickin' the people's own shins. **1871** Eggleston *Hoosier Schoolmaster* 39 **IN**, I 'low they'll appint the Squire . . . kase he's the peartest *ole* man in this deestrick. *Ibid* 40, She . . turned up her nose one night at a apple-peelin' bekase I tuck a sheet off the bed. **1883** (1971) Harris *Nights with Remus* 4 **GA** [Black], Dey [=geese] don't cross der legs . . kase dey sets down right flat-footed. **1884** Murfree *TN Mts.* 253, I knowed it war the track o' Jeremiah Stubbs, . . 'kase his old shoe jes' fit the track. **1888** Jones *Negro Myths* 124 **GA coast**, Buh Rab-

bit . . gie way caze Buh Wolf bague um so bad. **1899** Chesnutt *Conjure Woman* 136 **ceNC** [Black], "How do you know it brings good luck?" I asked. "'Ca'se I ain' had no bad luck sence I had it, suh." **1899** (1912) Green *VA Folk-Speech, Cos . . .* Because; by reason of. **1901** *DN* 2.181 **KY** [Black], *Because*—'case. **1906** *DN* 3.116 **sIN**, *Cause,* pronounced [kez]. Because. "I won't go case it's cold." **1908** *DN* 3.290 **eAL, wGA**, *(Be)kase* /kes, keɪs/ . . . Because. Sometimes *kasin.* **1909** *DN* 3.392 **nwAR**, *Becaze . . .* Because. *Ibid* 393, *Caze.* **1916** Howells *Leatherwood God* 216 **sOH**, They had n't brung much money; even Mr. Hingston had n't, becuz they expected the Good Old Man to work miracles. **1922** Gonzales *Black Border* 289 **sSC, GA coasts** [Gullah glossary], *Bekase . .* because. **1926** Vollmer *Sun-Up* 34 **wNC**, This here country is ourn, 'cose God let us be born here. **1928** McKay *Home to Harlem* 33 **NYC** [Black], Git off'n her. 'Causen she's down. *Ibid* 66, You thinks I only hangs out with low-down trash becassin Ise in a place like this, eh? **1934** Carmer *Stars Fell on AL* 270 [Black], Can't nothin' hurt me 'caze I'se a chile o' God. **1943** *LANE* Map 729 **NEng**, *Because* [Usu [bɪkɒz], freq [bɪkɔz]; also [bɪ-, bə-], [-kʌz], infreq [-kɑz]; and aphet forms [kʌz, kəz, kɔz]]. c**1960** *Wilson Coll.* **csKY**, *Because* [bɪˈkez]. Old, rare . . . Rarely [əˈkɔz] or [kɔz]. **1961** Kurath–McDavid *Pronc. Engl.* 162, The vowels /ɔ~ɒ/ are fairly generally used in *because* throughout the Eastern States. However, one other pronunciation, the /ʌ/ of *sun,* is rather widely current . . . *Because* with the vowel /e/ of *eight* occurs in the folk speech of the South and South Midland; it is sharply recessive. Scattered instances of the /ɑ/ of *lot* appear in various places, but especially in the New England settlements. **1976** Allen *LAUM* 3.259, As in the East, a back rounded vowel /ɔ - ɒ/ occurs in the stressed syllable of *because* throughout the U[pper] M[idwest]. A corresponding unround vowel /ɑ - ɑ/ is less usual, with occurrences in western Iowa and Nebraska not quite consistent with its heavier frequency in New England and derivative western settlement areas. Unlike other words in this class, *because* has also a pronunciation with /ʌ/ that lacks regional or social differentiation.

because adv

Why.

1970 *Thompson Coll.* **cwGA**, You done give me six reasons why not. Now give me at least one reason because!

becaze See **because** conj

bec-croche n Also sp *becroche* [See quot 1931] esp **LA** Cf **black bec-croche**

=**white ibis.**

1828 in 1868 McCall *Letters Frontiers* 178 **FL**, I saw a large flock of the white ibis or, as it is called here, *Becroche,* settle down at the water's edge near by. **1917** *DN* 4.422 **LA**, *Beccroche.* The white ibis (Guara alba). **1931** Read *LA French* 7, The *bec-croche,* "crooked bill," . . . for which the technical name is "white ibis" . . , inhabits the swampy regions of lower Louisiana. **1962** Imhof *AL Birds* 106, *White Ibis . . . Other Names: . .* bec-croche (Hookbill). **1968** *DARE* (Qu. Q8) Inf **LA**31, Bec-croche [ˌbɛkˈrouč]; (Qu. Q10, . . *Water birds*) Inf **LA**26, Bec-croche [ˌbɛkˈrɔš]—this has a curved bill. The Anglicized pronunciation is [ˈbeˌkrɔs].

becket n [Naut; *OED* 1769 →] chiefly **ME**

See quots.

1942 *ME Univ. Studies* 56.28, Various forms of rope handles or fastenings were called *beckets.* [Footnote:] A general term for handle, esp. of rope; jestingly, a trouser pocket. **1945** Colcord *Sea Language* 32 **ME, Cape Cod, Long Island.** **1975** Gould *ME Lingo* 10, *Beckets*— Rope handles on sea chests . . . Somehow the word came to mean a man's pockets. "He was amblin' along with his hands in his *beckets.*"

beckon n

A children's outdoor hiding game; see quots.

1945 Boyd *Hdbk. Games* 69, *Beckon,* or *Sheep in My Pen . . .* One player . . blinds while all the other players hide . . . The hunter . . must call the name of any player whom he sees . . . When discovered, the hider must come into goal. This hider then calls "Give me a beckon." One of the other hiders . . may . . beckon to him, which gives him the right to slip away and hide again. **1965–68** *DARE* (Qu. EE12, *Games in which one captain hides his team and the other team tries to find it*) Inf **WA**25, Beckon [bɛkɪn]. One side goes and hides in different places and other side hunts them. When hunters call the hiding time, [a hider] has to wave at hunter; (Qu. EE13a, *Games in which every player hides except one, and that one must try to find the others*), Inf **IN**39, Beckon; (Qu. EE16, *Hiding games that start with a special, elaborate method of sending the players out to hide*) Inf **KS**15, Beckon—go out and hide;

when "it" finds you he puts you in a circle. Then "it" goes out to find others and the person in the circle can leave the circle if another player beckons to him.

beckon back v phr [Prob alter of backen 1 + back]
Of the wind: to change direction.

1931–33 *LANE Worksheets* **MA,** The wind sometimes beckons back from northeast to southwest.

Becky See Betsy 1

‡become v
To resemble.

1969 *DARE* (Qu. Z10, *If a child looks very much like his father, you might say "He _____ his father."*) Inf **GA**72, Becomes.

become to be v phr
To come about, come to be.

1970 Green *Ely* 155 **TN,** Most colored people don't work on this day. How this day became to be is this . . . This became to be [held] annually . . . When he later became to be Judge . . everything about it was a part of him. **1970** *DARE* Tape **MI**121, When the Western states became to be settled.

becount n [Perh blend of because + account]
1966 *DARE* Tape **MS**72, On becount of the way that man talked.

bec-scie n Also sp bexie [See quot 1931] Gulf States, esp LA
Any of three ducks: the common **merganser,** the **hooded merganser,** or the **red-breasted merganser.**

1888 Trumbull *Names of Birds* 75, The captain adds that the present species [*Lophodytes cucullatus*] is known to all about Mobile, as *Bec-scie;* this (the French for "Sawbill") distinguishing it from the Sea Bec-scie. **1917** *DN* 4.422 **LA,** *American merganser* . . . Bec-scie. *Ibid* 426, *Hooded merganser* . . . Bec-scie. *Ibid* 429, *Red-breasted merganser* . . . Bec-scie de mer. **1923** U.S. Dept. Ag. *Misc. Circular* 13.4, *Mergansers . . . Vernacular Names . . . In local use.* —Bec-scie (sawbill, sometimes misspelled "bexie") (. . Ala., Miss., La.). **1931** Read *LA French* 8, *Bec-scie* . . . American Merganser . . . This duck owes its name to the fact that the teeth in its bill resemble the edge of a saw . . . *Bec-scie de Mer,* "sea saw-bill," is the name of the Red-breasted Merganser . . . *Bec-scie du Lac,* "lake saw-bill," or *Bec-scie de Cyprière,* "Cypress-swamp saw-bill," distinguishes the Hooded Merganser. **1962** Imhof *AL Birds* 160, *Hooded Merganser . . . Other Names: . .* Bec-scie, Bexie. *Ibid* 161, *Common Merganser . . . Other Names: . .* Bec-scie, Bexie. **1968** *DARE* (Qu. Q5) Inf **LA**44, Bec-scie [ˌbɛkˈsi] —they got a sort of pointy mouth, like. More like a chicken; **LA**37, Bec-scie mer [ˌbɝgˌsiˈmɛr], grand bec-scie, petit bec-scie; (Qu. Q9) Inf **LA**44, Bec-scie [ˌbɛkˈsi].

becuz See because conj

bed n Usu |bɛd|; also, chiefly Sth, |beɪd| Pronc-sp baid
A Forms.
1 Pronc varr.

1905 Culbertson *Banjo Talks* 165 *(ADD)* **Sth,** I tucken hit inter baid. **1917** Torrence *Granny Maumee* 51 **Sth** [Black], I goin' to baid. **1925** *DN* 5.358 **seGA,** [beɪd].

2 with the: One's bed. chiefly Sth, S Midl

1946 *AmSp* 21.270 **neKY,** Phrase, 'In the bed.' 'He's been sick in the bed all week.' 'I was so tired (tard) I was in the bed before eight o'clock.' This use of the definite article may derive from a time when one house normally contained one bed. **1965–70** *DARE* (Qu. X43b) Inf **MS**63, Stayed on the bed; (Qu. BB41) Infs **AR**21, **VA**74, (Sick) in the bed; (Qu. BB42) Inf **MA**5, In the bed; (Qu. BB43) Inf **GA**42, On the bed; **GA**72, Homesteaded in the bed; (Qu. II3) Infs **AR**3, 18, 33, Thick as six in the bed; **KY**44, Like two in the bed. **1973** Patrick Coll. **Sth,** In the bed . . . Sick in bed. "She is in the bed."

B Senses.
1 The place where an animal sleeps. Sth, S Midl

1938 Rawlings *Yearling* 373 **FL,** Wherever the bed, it was hollowed out in a trench, over the edge of which the bear would rest his forequarters. **1939** *Hall Coll.* **eTN,** So we found his sign and found where he was a-layin'. His bed was warm yet, so we knowed he was close. **1966–70** *DARE* Tape **AR**56, The pigs too little to follow, they stayed in the bed; **GA**3, There was a bed with some pigs in it; **NC**30, By the time you get the last dog turned loose, this first dog has got to where the bear is layin' in his bed.

2 In tobacco growing: a plot of ground in which tobacco seedlings are grown prior to transplanting.

1965–70 *DARE* (Qu. L22, . . *About a crop he intends to plant . . . a farmer might say, "This year, I'm going to _____."*) Inf **KY**49, Sow the beds; **KY**58, Sow a bed; **NC**24, Plant tobacco beds; **SC**1, Sow tobacco seed bed. **1966** *PADS* 45.7 **cnKY,** *Bed . .* =tobacco bed . . . "I use chemicals for sterilizing my beds." **1966–70** *DARE* Tapes **IN**45, **KY**9, **NC**7, **VA**38, 40, Bed [with ref to tobacco growing]. **1967** Key *Tobacco Vocab.* **GA,** Bed leaves: lowest leaves on a tobacco plant.

3 In logging: a pile of small trees used to cushion the fall of a large tree; hence *bedding* the trees or any piece of ground so used. **chiefly Pacific NW** Also called **layout** n Cf **bed v 1**

1936 in 1949 Powers *Redwood Country* 116 **nCA, sOR,** After determining the direction of the fall [of a redwood tree], smaller trees, called 'bedding,' are felled into the layout to build up the low spots. **1941** Williams *Strange Woman* 430 **ME,** Dan saw the first tree come down. Bed pieces had been laid to break its fall . . . It . . crashed down upon the bed pieces with a tremendous, ground-shaking impact. **1949** Powers *Redwood Country* 115 **nCA, sOR,** A tree several yards through and from two to three hundred feet high . . was likely to break up and be made worthless unless there was prepared for it a soft bed, which upon uneven ground might require enough wood to suffice a householder for a year. **1959** *AmSp* 34.76 **nCA,** *Bedding* . . . A bed into which large trees are felled to prevent breakage, made by leveling the ground surface either through excavation or filling or both. **1968** *DARE* Tape **CA**103, When they chop 'em down they have to have a bed for 'em to drop on.

4 See quot. Cf **bed v 4, bank n¹ 1**

1967–70 *DARE* (Qu. M19, *A place for keeping carrots, turnips, potatoes, and so on over the winter*) Inf **AL**31, Potato or carrot bed; **NJ**67, Turnip bed.

5 =**stoneboat;** see quot.

1967–69 *DARE* (Qu. L57, *A low wooden platform used for bringing stones or heavy things out of the fields*) Infs **KY**64, **PA**141, Stone (*or* rock) bed; **MO**25, Gravel bed; **OH**90, Bed.

6 A place where fish congregate and may be caught.

1968 *DARE* (Qu. P9) Inf **GA**47, A bed of fish or a school of fish is a spot where they catch 'em.

bed v
1 occas with *up:* In logging: to furnish with a **bed** n B3. **now chiefly Pacific NW**

1792 Belknap *Hist. NH* 3.103, When a mast tree is to be felled, . . the workmen have a contrivance which they call *bedding* the tree; . . they cut down a number of smaller trees . . and place them so that the falling tree may lodge on their branches. **1905** U.S. Forest Serv. *Bulletin* 61.30 **Pacific NW,** *Bed a tree, to.* To level up the path in which a tree is to fall, so that it may not be shattered. **1968** *DARE* Tape **CA**100, They had a big tree . . laying along the hillside and they'd fell him [=the tree] and . . they had him bedded up so it didn't break.

2 usu with *up:* To plow (land) into broad ridges in preparation for planting. **chiefly Sth**

1830 W. Edwards *MS Diary* 13 April **NC** *(DA),* Bedding low grounds. **1858** *TX Almanac for 1859* 81, The ploughs . . should be started to bed up the ground. **1938** Rawlings *Yearling* 373 **FL,** He planned to have the ground in good condition, bedded up and ready to plant in early March. **1942** Faulkner *Go Down* 42 **MS,** If it had not been for George Wilkins, he would have had it [=a cotton field] all broken and bedded and ready now. **1946** *PADS* 6.5 **swVA, eNC,** c**1960** *Wilson Coll.* **csKY,** *Bed up ground . . .* To form rows with four furrows turned together. Also called *listing.* Rarely found now. **1967** Key *Tobacco Vocab.* **GA,** They bed up the rows.

3 freq with *out:* To place (esp sweet potatoes) in specially prepared ground for sprouting.

1854 Davis *Farm Bk.* 19 *(DA)* **AL,** Bedded it & planted it in spanish & yam Potatoes—then bedded about 35 or 40 bushels of Potatoes for slips. **1858** *TX Almanac for 1859* 82, If he has bedded his sweet potatoes early . . . the ground should be sufficiently moist . . . he will have slips to set for early use. **1967** *DARE* (Qu. L22, *When talking about a crop he intends to plant . . a farmer might say*) Inf **LA**10, Bed it out, bed sugar cane; **LA**7, Bed out sweet potatoes.

4 To store vegetables in a **bed** n B4.

1938 Rawlings *Yearling* 278 **FL,** "Now you take down that tipply-tumbly pen, and build a coop to kiver the 'taters." . . With the potatoes bedded and covered, there was no more serious trouble. **1967** *DARE*

(Qu. M19, *A place for keeping carrots, turnips, potatoes, and so on over the winter*) Inf **AL**15, Bed them; **AL**31, Potatoes are piled in a cave on straw, with straw around and then dirt packed around—called it "bedding" the item.

5a To cause to be in bed.

1944 *PADS* 2.40 **wNC**, Bed . . . To cause to go to bed . . . "If you fool with me, I'll bed you." **1969** *DARE* (Qu. BB41, *Not seriously ill, but sick enough to be in bed: "He's been _____ for a week."*) Inf **MA**69, Bedded.

b often with *it*: To lie in bed.

1917 *DN* 4.408 **wNC**, Bed it . . . To lie abed. "I ain't goin' to bed it no longer." **1931** *PMLA* 46.1320 **Appalachians**, I won't bed it (lie in bed) no longer. **1944** *PADS* 2.40 **wNC**, Bed . . . To lie in bed. "He's bedding late today."

6 To stack, put in a pile.

1970 *DARE* (Qu. LL24, *To keep firewood neat you have to cut it, split it, and _____ it up*) Inf **NC**88, Bed.

bed baby n Cf apron child

1954 *Harder Coll.* **cwTN**, Bed-baby . . . A baby too small to crawl.

bed blanket n [Redund; cf Intro "Language Changes" I.4]

A blanket.

1770 in 1918 *MD Hist. Mag.* 13.68, 6 pr of the Best Bed Blankets. **1850** Judd *Richard Edney* 28 **MA**, She went half a mile, with a bed-blanket, before tea. **1904** *DN* 2.424 **Cape Cod MA**. **1949** Webber *Backwoods Teacher* 262 **Ozarks**, A shiny milk bucket, pans and lids, a pair of "bed blankets," and what not. **1952** Brown *NC Folkl.* 1.519. **c1960** *Wilson Coll.* **csKY**, Bed blanket . . . Just blanket, with no intention of distinguishing kinds of blankets: dog, baby, horse, etc. "Ma always made us take a bed blanket to wrap up with, even when it was hot weather."

bedbound adj

=bedfast.

1968 *DARE* (Qu. BB43, *A person who has to stay in bed all the time: "For two years now he's been _____."*) Inf **AK**1, Bedbound.

bedbug hunter n Also masked (bedbug) hunter [See quots]

An **assassin bug** (here: *Reduvius personatus*).

1895 Comstock *Manual Insects* 137, In the Atlantic States one sometimes finds . . a bug . . having its body and legs completely covered with dust . . . This is the Masked Bed-bug Hunter. **1911** *Century Dict. Suppl.*, Bedbug-hunter . . . It preys upon bedbugs, flies, and other household pests. When young it disguises its appearance by covering itself with dust and fibers . . . Called the *masked bedbug-hunter*. **1964** Borror–DeLong *Intro. Insects* 229, The masked hunter . . is a brownish-black bug that is often found in houses.

bedbug row n Also bedbug alley

A squalid and run-down building or area of a town.

1968–69 *DARE* (Qu. C35, *Nicknames for . . parts of a city*) Inf **PA**88, Bedbug Row; (Qu. V11, . . *Joking names . . for a . . jail*) Inf **CA**147, Bedbug Alley; (Qu. II25, *Nicknames for the part of a town where the poorer people . . live*) Inf **NJ**33, Bedbug Row.

bed clothes n

1972 Carr *Da Kine Talk* 122 **HI**, "No can go show in bed clothes!" In American speech, *bed clothes* refers ordinarily to blankets and sheets, *night clothes* to pajamas and gowns. In Hawaii, *bed clothes* seems to cover both meanings.

bedcord strong adj phr

1953 Randolph *Down in Holler* 226 **Ozarks**, Bedcord strong . . . Very strong indeed. A reference to the stout cords which serve as slats and springs in the old-fashioned bedsteads. "Jim he's bedcord strong when it comes to book-learnin'."

bedded ppl adj

1944 Adams *Western Words*, Bedded—In the cowman's language, this means that a roped animal has been thrown full length with such force as to cause it to lie still.

bedder n [bed v 2]

A type of plow used to **bed** land.

1968–70 *DARE* (Qu. L18, *Kinds of plows*) Inf **TX**51, Bedder—2 and 4 row, modern; **TX**89, Bedder—puts land up in rows.

bedding See bed n B3

bedding ground, bedding place See bed-ground

beddle v, hence beddlar n [Ger betteln, Bettler] PaGer

To beg; a beggar.

1939 Aurand *Quaint Idioms* 11 **sePA**, That old *beddlar* (beggar) don't come around no more; guess he *beddled* himself enough money to quit *beddling*.

bedfast adj Also, by folk-etym, bed-fastened, ~ fasting [bed + fast fixed, immovable; OED "north. dial. and Sc.," a1639 →] chiefly Midl, West See Map

Confined to bed because of illness, infirmity or injury; bedridden.

1890 *DN* 1.69, Bed-fast: confined to bed. I have heard this word but once, and in the parish of East Baton Rouge [LA] . . . An Illinois friend tells me that it is common in that state. **1892** *DN* 1.234 **KY**. **1907** *DN* 3.229 **nwAR, seMO**, Bedfast . . . Bedridden. "He is old and bedfast now." **1927** *DN* 5.468 **Appalachians**, Bed-fast . . . Confined to bed; bed-ridden. **1935** *Advertiser* (Huntington WV) 24 Jan (*AmSp* 14.155), His father had been bedfast since the accident. **1939** *AmSp* 14.155 **neKY, csOH, cwWV**. **c1960** *Wilson Coll.* **csKY**, Bedfast—Confined to his bed or bedrid. **1965–70** *DARE* (Qu. BB43) 243 Infs, **chiefly Midl, West**, Bedfast; **GA**8, Bed-fasting; **GA**77, Bed-fastened; (Qu. BB41) 66 Infs, **chiefly N Midl, KY**, Bedfast; (Qu. BB42) 9 Infs, Bedfast. **1967** *Independence Enterprise* (OR) 12 Jan 3/3, [He] is recovering from a heart attack he had the week before Christmas. He will be bedfast for about three weeks.

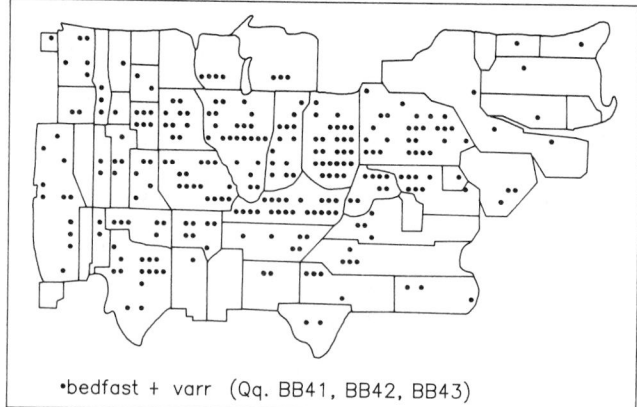

•bedfast + varr (Qq. BB41, BB42, BB43)

bed-ground n Also bedding ground, ~ place West

An area where cattle or sheep are bedded down for the night, esp on a drive; also transf.

1874 McCoy *Cattle Trade* 99 **West**, When all is still, and the herd well over its scare, they are returned to their bed-ground, or held where stopped until daylight. **1903** (1965) Adams *Log Cowboy* 24 **sTX**, The only fault I ever found with Priest was that he could use the poorest judgment in selecting a bed ground for our blankets. **1929** *AmSp* 5.55 **NE**, The more particular ranchers have "bed grounds" or a "bedding place" for their cattle, a piece of ground, often within the corral, covered thinly with hay and near the "feed place," a mound of hay. **1938** (1952) FWP *Guide SD* 85. **1939** FWP *Guide MT* 413, Bedding ground—Sheltered place where stock beds down at night, usually in a ravine or a clump of brush. **1941** FWP *Guide WY* 459. **1942** Dale *Cow Country* 53 **West**, Toward sundown the herd was moved out away from the stream to a stretch of level land which would furnish a suitable 'bed ground.' **1959** Robertson *Ram* 204 **cID** (as of c1908), The life of a sheepherder is full of ups and downs. He may . . sit up half the night to keep his flock from leaving the bedground. **1966** *DARE* Tape **NM**14, They'd [=cattle] leave the bed-ground and walk from three to five miles.

bed house n

A caboose.

1945 in 1953 Botkin *Treas. Railroad Folkl.* 344 [In a list of terms for the caboose], It is a . . crummy, way car, van . . bedhouse. **1977** Adams *Lang. Railroader* 12, Bed house: A caboose.

bedide intj [Euphem for be damned or bedad by God]

Used as a mild oath.

1903 Wasson *Cap'n Simeon's Store* 114 **ME**, Then, thinks I, bedide ef I don't try a trip or two into one o' them timber ships they was all telling about so much.

bed line n
1967 *DARE* (Qu. P13, . . *Ways of fishing . . besides the ordinary hook and line*) Inf **SC43**, Bed line — six-inch lines with baited hooks hanging from the longer line which is strung from bank to bank [across a stream].

bed log n
=**backlog 1.**
1967 *DARE* (Qu. D33, *When you build a fire in the fireplace, what do you call the big log that goes behind the others?*) Inf **NY4**, Bed log.

bed louse n
1965–70 *DARE* (Qu. R24, . . *Other names . . for a bedbug*) 21 Infs, scattered, Bed louse; **MN28, NY52, OK11, VT16**, Bed lice.

bed moth n [Perh for *bed moss:* cf **house moss**]
1967 *DARE* (Qu. E20, *Soft rolls of dust that collect on the floor under beds or other furniture*) Inf **MO8**, Bed moth.

be doing See **be a-doing**

bedpost v **S Midl**
See quot 1953.
1943 Bauersfeld *Breezes from Persimmon Holler* 115 (Randolph *Down in Holler* 226) **Ozarks.** 1953 Randolph *Down in Holler* 226 **Ozarks,** Bed-post . . . To confine a small child by placing a bedpost on his dress or other garment. In Stone County, Mo., the county nurse and I entered a cabin where two children were sitting on the floor. They smiled but didn't get up. Their mother was out picking greens. "She's got us bed-posted down," said one, "so we cain't mess with the fire." Then I noticed that each child's shirt-tail was put under the bedpost, so that he couldn't move. Mary . . of Mincy, Mo. . . told me that this was a common practice in the backwoods. 1954 *Harder Coll.* **cwTN,** *Bed-post* . . . To confine a child by placing a bedpost on his dress. [1981 *New Yorker* 9 Feb 38 **KY,** "We'll never go anywhere. We've got our dress tail on a bedpost." [sic] "What does that mean?" . . "Use to, if a storm was coming, people would put a bedpost on a child's dress tail, to keep him from blowing away. In other words, we're tied down."]

bed pot n **scattered, but esp cent Missip Valley**
A chamber pot.
1965–70 *DARE* (Qu. F38, *Utensil kept under the bed for use at night*) 12 Infs, Bed pot.

bedrid adj
Bedridden.
c1960 *Wilson Coll.* **csKY,** Bed rid. Confined to bed for a long time. 1964 Faulkner *As I Lay Dying* 84 **MS,** He might have hurt himself bed-rid. How far'd you fall, Cash? 1965–70 *DARE* (Qu. BB43) Inf **GA19, NJ21, NY27, PA4, 8,** Bedrid.

bedroom shoe n Also *bed shoe* **chiefly Sth, esp S Atl** See Map
A house slipper.
c1960 *Wilson Coll.* **csKY,** Bedroom shoes . . . Unknown in older days. 1965–70 *DARE* (Qu. W21) 55 Infs, **chiefly Sth, esp S Atl,** Bedroom shoes; **VA48,** Bed shoes. 1970 *DARE* File **wNC,** I can't go outside — I have my bedroom shoes on. 1982 *DARE* File **eVA,** I went upstairs to change out of my bedroom shoes, forgot what I was doing, and came down with them on.

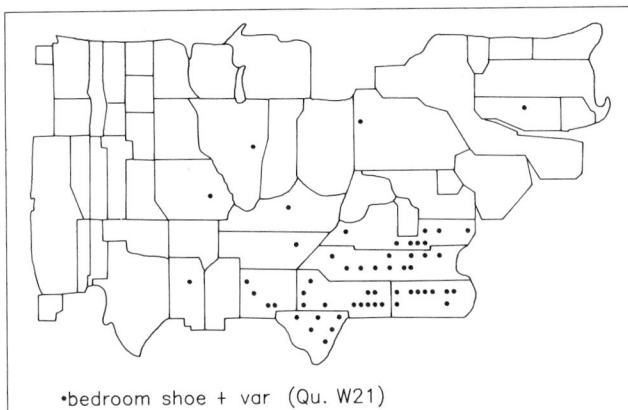

•bedroom shoe + var (Qu. W21)

bed rug n [Engl dial] *arch*
1899 (1912) Green *VA Folk-Speech, Bed-rug* . . . A counterpane; a coverlid.

bed shoe See **bedroom shoe**

bedsink n [Prob blend of *bedroom* and **sinkroom** a room with a sink, usu near a kitchen]
See quots.
1973 Allen *LAUM* 1.166, An inf. in Marshall, Minnesota, offered *bedsink*, a New York state word for a small alcove off a kitchen where older people could sleep warmly in winter. 1982 *McDavid Coll.* **nNY** (as of 1940s), *Bed sink* wasn't recorded in *LANE* . . but I have found it often in Upstate NY, especially from the Finger Lakes west. As defined by my informants, it was a windowless alcove off the kitchen, with a curtain rather than a door, just large enough for a bed and dresser . . ; my informants said that it was designed as a place where grandpa and grandma could sleep warm on the cold nights that were so common Upstate.

bed-slat rib n
A protruding rib of an emaciated animal; hence *bed slat* the animal itself.
1944 Adams *Western Words, Bed-slat ribs* — Said of an animal in poor condition. A cowhand in New Mexico told me of a drought when "them bed-slats got so poor their shadows developed holes in 'em." 1961 Adams *Old-Time Cowhand* 155, Poor calves were said to . . have "bed-slat ribs."

bed slipper n [Abbr for *bedroom slipper*] **?Nth** Cf **bedroom shoe, house shoe**
1965 *DARE* (Qu. W21, *Soft shoes that people wear only inside the house*) Infs **CT23, 34, MI81, NY49, VT8,** Bed slippers.

bed spell, set a v phr
1933 *AmSp* 8.1.52 **Ozarks,** Set a bed spell . . . To stay until bedtime. "You-all come over, an' set a bed spell with me an' Mary."

bedstead n Usu |ˈbɛdˌstɛd|; also, **chiefly Sth, S Midl,** |(ˈbɛd)ˌstɪd| Also abbr *stead;* pronc-spp *bedstid, stid*
Std sense, var forms.
1751 in 1956 Eliason *Tarheel Talk* 307 **NC,** Bedstids. 1820 *Ibid,* Bedstids. 1899 (1912) Green *VA Folk-Speech, Bedstid* . . . A bedstead. 1908 *DN* 3.289 **eAL, wGA,** *Bed-stid* . . . Bedstead. 1914 Furman *Sight* 42 **KY,** Take the women's bonnets, Evy, and lay 'em on my 'stead. 1936 *AmSp* 11.317 **Ozarks,** Stid . . . A bedstead. A young bride told us: 'Maw gimme two stids an' th' makin's for 'em,' that is, shuck mattresses, featherbeds, and coverlets. 1954 *Harder Coll.* **cwTN,** Stid . . . A bedstead. 1959 *VT Hist.* ns 27.125, Bedstead [ˈbɛdˌstɪd] . . . Occasional. Rural areas. c1960 *Wilson Coll.* **csKY,** Bedstead /ˈbɛdˌstɪd/ "This is an old bedstid that belonged to Grandma."

bedstead relation n
An in-law.
1967 *DARE* (Qu. Z9) Inf **WA20,** Bedstead relations — the ones you get in marriage.

bedstick n
See quots.
1899 (1912) Green *VA Folk-Speech, Bedstick* . . . Bedstaff. A long stick used for smoothing the bedclothes when bedsteads were too high and broad to be reached with the hand. 1952 Brown *NC Folkl.* 1.519, *Bed-stick* . . . A smooth stick about three feet long used to level a feather bed when making it up. 1967 LeCompte *Word Atlas* 143 **seLA.**

bedstraw n
Std: a plant of the genus *Galium* formerly used to fill mattresses. Also called **beggar's lice 5, chickenweed, cleavers, goose grass, gull grass, robin-run-ahead, stickleback, wild licorice.** For other names of var spp see **baby's breath 2b, cross cleavers, glue leaf, kidney vine, lady's bedstraw, Scotch mist, stickygrass, whip-tongue, wild madder**

bedstraw milkweed n
A **milkweed** (here: *Asclepias subverticillata*).
1937 U.S. Forest Serv. *Range Plant Hdbk.* W29, Horsetail milkweed [*Asclepias galioides*], also known as bedstraw milkweed and whorled milkweed . . ranks among those plants most deadly to range livestock.

bed-stretcher See **stretcher**

bed swell n
A ground swell.

1966 *DARE* (Qu. O15, . . *Different kinds of waves*) Inf **MI**14, Bed swell—quite big, don't break.

bed wagon n, also attrib **West**

In cattle ranching: a wagon used to carry bedding and supplies.

1869 in 1948 *Colorado Mag.* 25.71 **CO,** He, upon seeing my condition, very kindly asked me to ride in his bed wagon, one that carries the bedding. **1909** *Sat. Eve. Post* 2 Jan 8/2 **OK,** I've got to shoe that lil' ol' bedwagon mule. **1935** Sandoz *Jules* 83 **nwNE** (as of 1880–1930), Irwin . . sent twelve good cow hands equipped with grub and bed wagons into the hills. **1945** Thorp *Pardner* 240 **SW,** If the outfit was of medium size, and it was not expected that very many stray men would work with them, the bedrolls were all piled into the one wagon. If a good many extra hands were expected, the ranch would furnish a second wagon, known as the bed wagon. **1967** *DARE* Tape **CO**5, In Wyoming . . they always have a chuckwagon and a bedwagon, two wagons.

bee n[1]

1 A small lump of yeast cells in mycelium, used in making wine, vinegar, and beer. [From its appearance of busy activity as it rises and sinks in the fermenting liquid]

1914 *Hartford Times* (CT) 17 Apr 8, My acquaintance with Australian bees, the "California bees" of your correspondent . . dates back some two years. In another guise they were, so I found, very old acquaintances . . . [A patient speaks:] "Doctor, do you know anything about these here Australian bees?" *Ibid* 29 Apr 2, Suspended in the liquid are the "bees", varying in size from that of a number four shot to that of a kidney bean, and looking like lumps of dough as much as anything. If one looks closely they will observe quantities of bubbles arising and mounting to the surface, which furnishes a clue as to what is going on within. After coming to rest in a suitable place where the temperature is maintained at about 68 or 70 degrees, the bees will be seen to leave the bottom and ascend to the top where after remaining an instant they will turn and descend again to the bottom. *Ibid,* Not many yeasts aggregate themselves into masses such as we see here . . . The one we are studying here has been propagated for generations in some of the counties of southern New Jersey and eastern Pennsylvania, where they are known as "beer bees." They are valued because of the comparatively high percentage of alcohol that they are able to produce . . . In other words, *they make a strong beer.*

2 Pressure exerted on someone, often to make or repay a loan —usu in phr *put the bee on (someone).* [In allusion to a bee's stinging and to *sting* to cheat, defraud]

1918 Witwer *Baseball to Boches* 131 **NYC,** It's always open season for Americans over here [=France]. They sure know how to put the bee on you too. **1929** *AmSp* 4.338 [Vagabond argot], *Bee*—"To put the bee on," means to beg. **1930** Irwin *Amer. Tramp, Bee.* —"To put the bee on" is to beg or borrow, usually with a hard luck story. To say, "I put the bee on him," usually means that the donor has been "stung" when he gives up the loan, since seldom is it repaid. **1938** *AmSp* 13.5 **seAR,** *Bee* . . . 'I'll put the bee on him.' That is, I'll plague him. This use is probably a variant from the usual one of 'bee in one's bonnet.' **1958** Blasingame *Dakota Cowboy* 124, We figured we had fixed things up just dandy for "Uncle Frank" and that the bee wouldn't be on him any more. **1965–70** *DARE* (Qu. U16, *If somebody was caught short of money and went to a friend to get some*) Inf **CA**197, Putting the bee on him; **TX**5, I'd like to put the bee on you for five dollars; (Qu. U18, *If you force somebody to pay money that he owes you, but that he did not want to pay*) Infs **GA**44, **WA**30, Put the bee on him; (Qu. Y6, *Words meaning to put pressure on somebody to do something he ought to have done but hasn't: "He's a whole week late. I'm going to _____."*) 11 Infs, **scattered,** Put the bee on him; (Qu. GG24, *Other words meaning to frighten: "Now don't let those fellows _____ you."*) Inf **IN**5, Put the bee on; (Qu. AA5, *If a woman seems to be going after one certain man that she wants to marry: "She's _____ him."*) Inf **KY**94, Put the bee on.

bee n[2], freq in comb [Orig uncertain; perh alter of *been, bean* varr of Engl dial *boon: EDD boon* sb.[2] *2,* "Voluntary help, given to a farmer by his neighbours, in time of harvest, haymaking, etc." Prob also in allusion to the social behavior of the insect.] **chiefly Nth, N Midl** (exc in combs *quilting ~, sewing ~, spelling ~,* which are widespread) See Map

A meeting or social gathering to accomplish cooperatively a particular task or to engage in some group activity.

1769 *Boston Gaz. & Country Jrl.* (Boston MA) 16 Oct 1/3 **seMA,** Last Thursday about Twenty young Ladies met at the House of Ms. Nehemiah Liscome, here, on purpose for a Spinning Match: (or what is call'd

in the Country a Bee. **1816** in 1924 Kittredge *Old Farmer* 169 **NEng,** Husking is now a business for us all. If you make what some call a *Bee,* it will be necessary to keep an eye on the boys, or you may have to husk over again the whole heap. **1890** Custer *Following* 257 **West,** If one of us was plunged into difficulties . . the rest came in for a "bee," and made light work about the sewing-machine. **1905** *DN* 3.3 **eCT. 1909** *DN* 3.408 **nME,** *Bee* . . . A neighborhood gathering for special work. Various kinds of bees are distinguished, as quilting bee, chopping bee, plowing bee, piling bee, husking bee, sewing bee, paring bee, spelling bee. **1910** *DN* 3.437 **cwNY. 1938** *AmSp* 13.21 **NE** (as of 19th cent), [Footnote:] *Bees* were an important part of the social life. I have collected accounts of 'breaking (sod plowing) bees,' 'husking bees,' 'painting bees,' 'stone bees,' 'paring bees,' 'apple bees,' 'knitting bees,' 'quilting bees,' 'spelling bees,' 'kissing bees' in the early days of Nebraska. **1950** *WELS* (*When a farmer gets help on a job from his neighbors*) 2 Infs, **WI,** A bee. **1953** *Sun* (Baltimore MD) 31 Aug ed. B 3/4 *(Hench Coll.)* **MI,** Homes mushroomed throughout the tornado-made wilderness of Flint's Beecher district as 5,000 "good neighbors" turned out . . in "the nation's biggest building bee." **1965–70** *DARE* (Qu. FF2, . . *Kinds of parties*) 53 Infs, **chiefly Nth, N Midl,** Bees; 22 Infs, **chiefly Nth, N Midl,** (Corn-) husking bees; **MI**18, 28, 66, **MA**24, **VT**3, Work bees; **IN**45, **MI**106, Barn raising bees; **IN**10, Apple-cutting bee; **MI**9, Painting bee, roofing bee; **SD**8, Shingling bee; **NY**115, Cancer-dressing bees; **IA**9, Carpet-rag bees; **IN**19, Carpeting bees; **SD**8, Chicken-picking bees; **VA**42, Singing bees; **IL**58, Thrashing bees; **IL**4, Wood-chopping bees; (Qu. FF1, . . *A "social" or "sociable"*) Inf **NJ**1, Husking bee; **CO**27, Bees; (Qu. FF4, . . *Joking names for . . dancing parties*) Inf **NY**59, Bees; (Qu. FF9, *A Christmas gathering . . where there are songs and presents*) Inf **OH**72, Singing bee; (Qu. FF16, . . *Local contests or celebrations*) Infs **CT**6, **NJ**33, Corn-husking bees; (Qu. W32, . . *A group of women that meet to sew together*) Inf **NY**107, Bee; **NY**109, Women's bee; **NY**165, Mending bee; (Qu. DD34, *A party at which there is considerable drinking*) Inf **WA**3, Drinking bee.

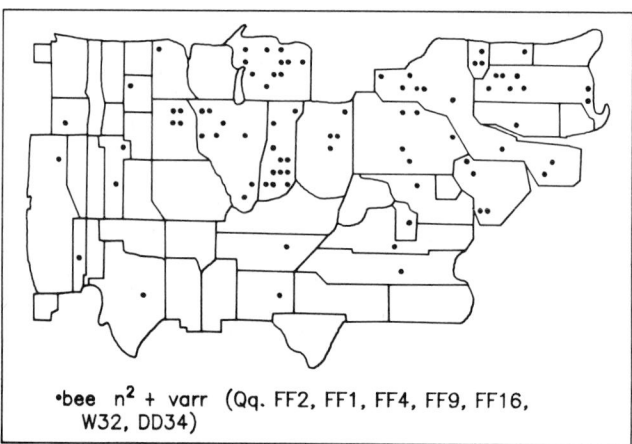

•bee n[2] + varr (Qq. FF2, FF1, FF4, FF9, FF16, W32, DD34)

bee v Also sp *bie* [See quot 1924] **chiefly Ger settlement areas, esp PA**

Come!—used as a call to chickens.

1924 Lambert *PA Ger. Dict.* 28, Bie! bie! . . call for chickens. d[ialect] G[erman] bieb. **1949** Kurath *Word Geog.* 65, Calls to Chickens . . . The German *bee!* is still common in the Pennsylvania German area. **1967–68** *DARE* (Qu. K79, *How do you call the chickens to you at feeding time?*) Infs **PA**3, 21, 158, Bee (bee bee, etc.). **1971** Wood *Vocab. Change* 183 **TN, GA,** A call to chickens . . [2 infs] bee. **1973** Allen *LAUM* 1.267, Calls to chickens at feeding . . . *Bee,* in the east a typical Pennsylvania German call, seems to be common among the German Russians in southeastern North Dakota.

beebalm n [From its sweet fragrance that attracts bees]

1 =**horsemint 1.**

1840 MA Zool. & Bot. Surv. *Herb. Plants & Quadrupeds* 175, M[onarda] didyma . . . Commonly called *balm* or *bee-balm.* **1887** *Century Illustr. Mag.* 34.328, I have never found it [=cardinal flower] with its only rival color, the monarda or bee-balm, a species of mint. **1904** Waller *Wood-carver* 264 **VT,** Some stalks of the bee-balm stand in my pitcher on the bench. **1937** U.S. Forest Serv. *Range Plant Hdbk.* W132, The beebalms are widely distributed within their range, and are common and often locally abundant. **1966** *DARE* Wildfl QR Pl.189 Infs **NC**28, **WI**34, Beebalm. **1966–69** *DARE* (Qu. S26a) Infs **CT**11, **NJ**29, **NY**199,

Beebalm; (Qu. S26d) Infs **KY**24, **MA**6, Beebalm. **1976** Dodge *Road-side Wildflowers* 61 **SW**, Also known as wild bergamot, beebalm . . . is readily recognized as a mint because of its square stem.

2 =lemon balm.

  1869 U.S. Dept. Ag. *Rept. of Secy. for 1868* 281, Plants from which bees gather honey and pollen . . [include] bee-balm, *(Melissa officinalis).* **1903** Porter *Flora PA* 270, *Melissa officinalis* . . . Bee-balm. **1931** Harned *Wild Flowers Alleghanies* 432, *Bee-Balm* . . . A lemon-scented plant naturalized from Europe. **1973** Hitchcock–Cronquist *Flora Pacific NW* 404, *M. officinalis* . . . Garden, lemon, or bee balm.

bee basswood See **bee tree**

beebee n [Alter of *baby*]

  1930 Shoemaker *1300 Words cPA Mts* (as of c1900), *Beebee*—The youngest member of a family or brood.

bee bee bumblebee exclam

  In the game of hide and seek: see quot.

  1966 *DARE* (Qu. EE15, *When he has caught the first of those that were hiding what does the player who is "it" call out to the others?*) Inf **NC**30, Bee bee bumblebee, all come in free.

bee bird n

1 =kingbird. [See quot 1862]

  1862 in 1865 IL State Ag. Soc. *Trans.* 5.734, The Bee bird will eat bees, and working bees even, when he cannot get drones. **1917** (1923) *Birds Amer.* 2.192, *Tyrannus tyrannus* . . Other Names . . . Beebird. **1936** *Oriole* 1.10, Eastern Kingbird.—Bee-bird . . (from its feeding on honey-bees). **1965–70** *DARE* (Qu. Q14) 10 Infs, **chiefly S Atl**, Bee bird.

2 also *red bee bird:* **=summer tanager.**

  1911 Howell *Birds AR* 70, This tanager has received the name of "bee bird" on account of its habits of feeding on honeybees. **1917** *Wilson Bulletin* 29.2.83, *Piranga rubra.*—Rose tanager, beebird, Hickman, Ky. **1946** Hausman *Eastern Birds* 566, *Summer Tanager* . . . Other Names . . Red Bee Bird . . . Often is seen darting about in the open after flying insects. **1969** *DARE* FW Addit **KY**31, Bee bird (summer tanager)—the kingbird is rare in the Southern mountains; **KY**39, Bee bird or dogwood winter bird. Bee bird is common . . . (Summer tanager).

3 =ruby-throated hummingbird.

  1955 *AmSp* 30.184, Another insect term gets into a bird name to indicate small size (and perhaps similarity in flight) in *bee bird* (Ohio) for the ruby-throated hummingbird.

bee-blossom n

1 A **butterfly weed 2** (here: *Gaura suffulta).*

  1961 Wills–Irwin *Flowers TX* 165, *Gaura suffulta* . . . Known as Bee-blossom and Kisses, grows mainly in limestone soils. **1970** Correll *Plants TX* 1126.

2 =bee brush.

  1960 Vines *Trees SW* 888, Vernacular names are Bee-brush, White-brush, Bee-blossom.

3 A **senna** *(Cassia* spp.).

  1933 Small *Manual SE Flora* 662, *Chamaecrista . . . Honey-cups. Bee-blossoms. Partridge-peas.*

bee bread n [See quot 1889]

=red clover.

  1889 *Century Dict.,* Bee-bread . . . A plant much visited by bees or cultivated for their use, as red clover, *Trifolium pratense,* or borage. **1900** Lyons *Plant Names* 377, *T[rifolium] pratense* . . . Bee-bread. **1959** Carleton *Index Herb. Plants* 9, *Bee bread:* Trifolium pratense.

bee brush n [See quot 1951]

  Any of var southwestern shrubs of the genera *Aloysia* and *Lippia,* but esp *A. lycioides* which is also called **bee blossom 2, hierba dulce, hummingbird brush, Mexican heliotrope, palo amarillo, vara dulce, whitebrush.** For other names of var spp see **high-mass, redbrush, sweet-stem** See also **bee myrtle**

  1951 *PADS* 15.39 **TX**, *Aloysia ligustrina* . . . Bee, or hummingbird, brush. One of the loveliest to see, or to smell, of all the Texas wild shrubs, and beloved of bees and hummingbirds. **1960** Vines *Trees SW* 888, *Aloysia ligustrina* . . . Vernacular names are Bee-brush, White-brush [etc.] . . . Plant . . is considered good bee food. **1970** Correll *Plants TX* 1334, *Aloysia macrostachya . . . Woolly bee-brush. Ibid* 1335, *Aloysia gratissima . . . Common Bee-brush.* **1981** Benson–Darrow *Trees SW Deserts* 202, *Lippia Wrightii . . . Bee Brush . . . Lippia gratissima . . . Bee Brush.*

bee-butcher n

  A **dragonfly** of the family Aeshnidae.

  1965 *DARE* File **FL**, *Coryphaeschina ingens* (possibly other large aeshnids also) is known as bee-butcher from its habit of preying on honey bees.

bee catcher n

1 also *bee killer:* **=robber fly.**

  1859 Gosse *Letters from AL* 211, I have since observed this powerful and predaceous fly carrying insects heavier than itself, on several occasions, and so well are its instincts recognised, that it has obtained the common name of the "Bee-catcher." **1901** Howard *Insect Book* 141, Persons engaged in bee culture especially fear these robber-flies, which are known rather generally in this country as bee-killers.

2 =kingbird.

  1967–70 *DARE* (Qu. Q14) Inf **IL**143, Bee catcher—a small gray bird with colored feathers on the head to attract insects; **MO**11, Martin—a bee catcher.

beechdrops n Cf **Albany beechdrops, Carolina beechdrops, false beechdrops**

1 A slender-stemmed plant *(Epifagus virginiana)* parasitic on the roots of beech trees. Also called **broomrape, cancer drops, cancerroot 1, fir-rape**

  1815 Drake *Natural View Cincinnati* 86, Plants useful in medicine [include] . . beech-drops, *the root.* **1822** Eaton *Botany* 272, *Epiphegus* [sic] . . . virginianus [sic] . . beech drops, cancer-root . . . The whole plant is yellowish-white and of a naked appearance. **1861** Wood *Class-Book* 511, *Beechdrops* . . . Parasite on the roots of the beech. **1901** Lounsberry *S. Wild Flowers* 470, Beech drops, more showy in its purple-and-white striped bloom than the squaw-root, chooses to grow on the beech. **1931** Harned *Wild Flowers Alleghanies* 454, *Beech Drops* . . . If you are not familiar with these curious little naked parasites you may pass over them. **1969** *DARE* (Qu. S26c, *Wildflowers that grow in woods*) Inf **RI**15, Beechdrops.

2 =squawroot.

  1900 Lyons *Plant Names* 114, *C[onopholis] Americana* . . . Improperly called Beech-drops, as it grows in Oak woods.

3 =sweet pinesap.

  1911 *Century Dict. Suppl.,* Beech-drops . . . The sweet pine-sap, *Monotropsis odorata.*

4 A **pinesap** (here: *Monotropa hypopithys*).

  1959 Carleton *Index Herb. Plants* 9, *Beech drop:* Epifagus virginiana; Monotropa hypopitys [sic].

bee clover n

=white sweetclover.

  1937 U.S. Forest Serv. *Range Plant Hdbk.* W123, White sweetclover, known also as bee-clover, honeyclover . . is a robust biennial herb.

beed See **be B1g**

beedie See **biddy** n[3]

beef n

  A Forms.

1 sg: usu *beef;* rarely, by back-formation from pl, *beeve.*

  1859 (1965) Marcy *Prairie Traveler* 38, They covered the entire shoe with green beeve or mule hide, drawn together and sewed upon the top, with the hair inside.

2 pl: usu *beef, beefs;* also, **esp in Plains States, TX,** *beeves.*

  1859 (1968) Bartlett *Americanisms, Beef.* In Louisiana, Texas, and some other parts of the South-west, an ox is called a *beef,* and oxen, *beeves.* **1872** Burnham *Memoirs U.S. Secret Service* 234, This last comer was a cattle-dealer from New Jersey, and had come all the way north in search of beeves and a few Canadian or Vermont horses. **1899** (1912) Green *VA Folk-Speech, Beef* . . . Beeves. **1920** Hunter *Trail Drivers TX* 267, We gathered fed beeves that year. **1921** Thorp *Songs Cowboys* 84 **TX**, We had no little herd—two thousand head or more—And some as wild brush beeves as you ever saw before. **1929** *AmSp* 5.68 **NE**, The "spring round-up" . . is for the purpose of branding—not for yielding "beeves" for the market. **1961** Sackett–Koch *KS Folkl.* 202, To many it was a day of joy and high speculation. There were fresh-killed beeves hanging in the chill granaries usually on both farmsteads, with rings of pork sausages, smoked and otherwise. **1969** *DARE* Tape **TX**75, Beeves [bivz].

  B Sense.

See quot.

1953 *Hall Coll.* **wNC,** *Beef* . . . A piece of bear meat. "He cut [the bear] open and had him a piece of beef cut out and was going to broil and eat it."

beef v

1 To kill (a beef animal) for food; hence vbl n *beefing.*

1869 *Harper's Mag.* 38.159/1 **West,** Then, as he expressed it, they [=buffalo] were to be *beefed* and sent East, or put into cattle-cars, and killed after they had arrived in the Eastern cities. **1922** Cady *Rhymes of Vt.* (1923) 43 *(DA),* Well; I shan't call it no disgrace / To beef that critter on the place. **1929** *AmSp* 5.122 **ME,** If a cow were unproductive it was said, "better beef her," or she is a "beef cow." **1944** Adams *Western Words, Beef* . . . To kill an animal for food . . . *Beefing*—Slaughtering. **1958** *AmSp* 33.268 **eWA,** *Beef* . . . To butcher (an animal). **1964** Faulkner *Hamlet* 158 **MS,** Houston just kept the yearling up . . . Then last week for some reason he decided to go and get it. I reckon he figured to beef it.

2 To strike or knock (someone) down.

1926 (1927) Black *You Can't Win* 185 **cwCA,** When one of them got peeved . . . some hard-fisted miner beefed him like an ox with a fast one to the jaw. **1938** Stuart *Dark Hills* 66 **KY,** They said he shore beefed him. Hit him right under the eye. **1958** *AmSp* 33.268 **eWA,** *Beef* . . . Metaphorically, to knock (a man) down. **1968** Adams *Western Words, Beef* . . . To knock a man down.

beef club n

In days before refrigeration was widespread, a group formed to provide its members with fresh beef on a regular basis; a gathering of such a group to slaughter a beef.

1941 FWP *Guide LA* 641, Hog butcherings and "beef clubs" are events in the community life. **1978** Mayer *Beef Club* 1 (as of 1830s), A type of cooperative effort known as the beef club [developed]. Its membership consisted of those individuals in the neighborhood or countryside who acquired shares by supplying beeves to the club for butchering. Apparently this type of organization could be found scattered throughout the South, including areas of such diverse heritage as French-settled Louisiana and the Dutch Fork of South Carolina. *Ibid* 2, Most clubs consisted of eight or sixteen shareholders, making up what were known as eight- and sixteen-hand clubs . . . By the end of the eight or sixteen weeks each [member] would have received the equivalent of what he had contributed . . . The beef club continued with very little modification until approximately 1940 . . . With a ready means of preservation available, it was no longer necessary to divide beef up for quick consumption.

beef creature n Also *beef critter* chiefly NEng Cf cow critter

A full grown bull, cow or ox intended as a source of beef.

1782 *N.H. Comm. Safety Rec.* 299 *(DA),* Authorized Col. Badger to dispose of one beef creature towards his own Expenses. **1837** (1940) Arnold *Diaries* 134 **VT,** Killed a beef-creature weight 540 [lbs.]. **1858** *Harper's Mag.* 16.854/2 **cMA,** Here in the country, when one of the neighbors kills a 'beef creature,' he is expected to send a piece 'to each one of the families near by.' **1905** *DN* 3.3 **cCT,** *Beef* . . . An ox. Sometimes *beef critter.* **1941** *LANE* Map 303 **cnCT,** [1 inf:] *Dried beef* was taken out of the thigh part of the beef creature. *Ibid* **csCT,** Kill a beef critter, i.e. kill an ox for meat, father's expression. **1966** *DARE* Tape **ME5,** They'd bring in a quarter or a half of beef-critter. **1967** *DARE* (Qu. K22, . . *A bull*) Inf **AZ2,** Beef critter. **1978** *UpCountry* Jan 19/2 **ME,** He has also had sheep and a steer or two (called "beef creatures" around here) grazing in his pasture.

beefeater n [In ref to Engl yeomen of the guard]

1 A person of English origin.

1965–70 *DARE* (Qu. HH28, *Names and nicknames around here for people of foreign background . . English*) Infs **CA87, MA30, PA202,** 223, 234, Beefeaters.

2 A cattle poacher.

1958 Blasingame *Dakota Cowboy* 183 **SD** (as of 1900–10), The more I thought of it, the more I wanted to look inside it [=a house]—for a Matador [Ranch] man was always on the lookout for "beefeaters."

bee feed n

A **buckwheat** (here: *Eriogonum fasciculatum*).

1959 Carleton *Index Herb. Plants* 9, Bee Feed: *Eriogonum fasciculatum.*

beefer, beef-eye See beefsteak eye

beef from bull's foot, not to know v phr Also *beef from butter, ~; beef from the bull's tail, ~* [Prob alter of **B from (a) bull's foot,**

not to know by assim of *f*] Cf **beans, not to know**

To be very stupid.

1965–70 *DARE* (Qu. JJ15b, . . *A person who seems to you very stupid: "He doesn't know _____.")* Infs **IN79, OK1, VA15,** Beef from bull's foot; **NJ28,** Beef from butter, **NM12,** Beef from the bull's tail. **c1970** *Halpert Coll.* **wKY,** He is so dumb he doesn't know beef from bull's foot.

beef-head n

A Texan.

1872 *Harper's Mag.* 44.318/1, Texas, Beef-Heads; Vermont, Green Mountain Boys. **1937** Shankle *Nicknames* 521, The Texans are called *Beef-heads.* **1968** Adams *Western Words, Beef head*—A Texan.

beefheart mushroom See beefsteak fungus

bee flower n

1 The New England aster.

1840 MA *Zool. & Bot. Surv. Herb. Plants & Quadrupeds* 134, New England aster. The most beautiful of our species . . . [is] called by the people, *bee-flower,* because it is in September so sought for by the honey-bee.

2 A **spider flower,** esp the **Rocky Mountain bee plant.**

1932 Rydberg *Flora Prairies* 385, *Peritoma* . . . Bee Flower, Indian Pink, Stink Flower. **1936** McDougall *Plants of Yellowstone* 69, Several members of the family are quite important as honey plants [but are] . . . represented here only by the bee-flower. **1968** Barkley *Plants KS* 170, *Cleome serrulata* . . . Bee Flower . . . Sandy areas, plains, prairies.

3 An orchid (here: *Ophrys apifera*).

1959 Carleton *Index Herb. Plants* 9, Bee flower: *Ophrys apifera.*

beef on weck n Also *beef on wick* [Abbr for Ger *Kümmelweck* caraway roll] chiefly cwNY

A sandwich made of beef in a hard roll covered with grains of salt and caraway seed.

1969 *DARE* (Qu. H45, *Dishes made with meat*) Inf **NY135,** Beef on wick. **1975–77** *DARE* File **wNY,** I have seen beef on wick on a menu. The beef was on a soft bun with three caraway seeds. *Ibid* **Rochester NY,** I saw "beef on wick" on a menu. **1980** *New Yorker* 25 Aug 82/3 **cwNY,** The tour . . also included . . a couple of places that serve beef-on-weck—a beef sandwich on a salty roll—which happens to be the local specialty that was replaced in the hearts of true Buffalonians by chicken wings. **1982** *Smithsonian Letters* **wNY,** Beef on weck. Weck is short for the German Kummelweck (pronounced "kimmelwick") . . . Kummelweck is a crusty roll topped with a sprinkling of *caraway* seeds and coarse salt.

bee from a bull's foot, not to know (a) v phr Also *beeswax from bull foot, ~* [Var of **B from (a) bull's foot, not to know**]

To be ignorant or stupid.

1812 in 1957 Knopf *Doc. War 1812* 2.207, I belong to the Artillery Company their is not an officer belonging to it that knows a Bee from a Bulls foot. **1896** *DN* 1.413 **wNY,** "He don't know a bee from a bull's foot." **1966–67** *DARE* (Qu. JJ15b, . . *A person who seems to you very stupid: "He doesn't know _____.")* Inf **TX11,** Beeswax from bull foot; (Qu. LL16, . . *"He doesn't know _____ . . about plumbing.")* Inf **MS1,** Bees from a bull's foot.

beefsteak n

1 In marble play: see quot.

1935 *AmSp* 10.158 **seNE,** *Beefsteak.* Any game [of marbles] in which it is agreed that any type of illegal play may be used which the players can 'get away with.'

2 A children's outdoor game: see quot.

1967 *DARE* (Qu. EE33) Inf **IL20,** Beefsteak—player hides eyes, others have to hide but must freeze when the person who is "it" opens his eyes (after counting to one hundred) and shouts "beefsteak"; **CA4,** Beefsteak.

3 A mistake, blunder. [Prob joc alter of *mistake*]

1950 *WELS* (*An embarrassing mistake: "Last night she made an awful _____.")* 1 Inf, **ceWI,** Beefsteak. **1968** *DARE* (Qu. JJ41) Inf **IN19,** Beefsteak.

4 See **beefsteak plant 3.**

5 A trillium (here: *T. recurvatum*).

1940 Clute *Amer. Plant Names* 15, *T[rillium] reflexum* . . . beafsteak [sic]. **1959** Carleton *Index Herb. Plants* 9, Beefsteak: *Trillium reflexum.*

beefsteak v, hence *beefsteaked* ppl adj **West** See also **baked**
See quots.
   1927 *AmSp* 3.168 **SW**, *Cowboy Speech* . . . To ride so that the horse's
back becomes sore is to "gimlet" or "beefsteak" him. **1929** *AmSp* 5.64
NE, If he is a "light rider" or "rides light," he does not "gimlet" or
"beefsteak" the horse, make its back sore, as does the "hard rider." **1961**
Adams *Old-Time Cowhand* 113, Some saddles don't fit the hoss they're
on, and cause sores, . . and the hoss is . . "beefsteaked."

beefsteak eye n Also *beefer, beef-eye* [From the practice of
putting a raw beefsteak on a black eye]
A black eye.
   1950 *WELS (A black eye)* 2 Infs, **c,csWI**, Beefsteak eye. **1954** *Harder
Coll.* **cwTN**, Beef-eye—a black eye. **1967–70** *DARE* (Qu. X20, . . *A
black eye)* Infs **KS5, OH72**, Beefsteak eye; **KY89**, Beefer.

beefsteak fungus n Also *beefheart mushroom, beefsteak ~,
beeftongue* [See quot 1972; *OEDS* 1886 →]
An edible fungus *(Fistulina hepatica).*
   1908 Hard *Mushroom Edible* 387, It *[Fistulina hepatica]* is known
as . . Beefsteak Fungus. **1948** Boyce *Forest Pathology* 426, *Fistulina
hepatica* . . , the beefsteak fungus, causes a brown cubical rot. [*Ibid* 427,
The soft red juicy flesh, which is variegated with brighter streaks, exudes
a red bloodlike juice when broken.] **1961** *W3*, *Beeftongue* . . beefsteak
fungus. **1965–70** *DARE* (Qu. I37) Inf **OK18**, Beefsteak mushroom,
large, safe to eat; (Qu. S18) Inf **IN31**, Beefsteak; **MI92**, Beefsteak, [pick]
while still firm; **MI120**, Beefsteak, fluffy, large, red; **OH33**, Beefheart
mushroom; (Qu. S19) Inf **NJ58**, Beefsteak mushroom. **1972** Miller
Mushrooms 180, *Fistulina hepatica* . . . "Beefsteak Fungus" . . . The
texture of beef and the oozing red juice give it its name. It is a good edible
and sought by many mushroom hunters.

beefsteak geranium See **beefsteak plant 3**

beefsteak leaf See **beefsteak plant 1**

beefsteak mushroom See **beefsteak fungus**

beefsteak plant n

1 also *beefsteak leaf:* An introduced, coarse, often weedy, annual plant *(Perilla frutescens)* now found in much of the eastern
half of the U.S. [See quot 1948]
   1933 Small *Manual SE Flora* 1180, *P[erilla] frutescens* . . Beefsteak-
plant. **1940** Clute *Amer. Plant Names* 227, *Perilla frutescens.* Beefsteak
plant. **1948** Wherry *Wild Flower Guide* 168, *Beefsteak-leaf (Perilla
frutescens)* . . The name of this old-fashioned garden plant refers to the
resemblance of the leaf color to raw beefsteak. **1970** Correll *Plants TX*
1376, *Perilla frutescens* . . Beefsteak plant.

2 A lousewort (here: *Pedicularis canadensis).*
   1900 Lyons *Plant Names* 278, *P[edicularis] Canadensis* . . Beefsteak
plant. **1912** Mathews *Amer. Wild Flowers* 432, *Beefsteak Plant . . Pedicularis Canadensis.* **1940** Clute *Amer. Plant Names* 31.

3 also *beefsteak, beefsteak geranium:* A saxifrage (here: *Saxifraga sarmentosa).*
   1822 Eaton *Botany* 449, *Saxifraga sarmentosa* (beef-steak . .). **1900**
Lyons *Plant Names* 336, *S[axifraga] sarmentosa* . . Beefsteak Geranium. **1959** Carleton *Index Herb. Plants* 9, *Beefsteak Plant:* . . Saxifraga sarmentosa.

beef-suet tree n [See quot 1942]
A **buffalo berry** (here: *Shepherdia argentea).*
   1889 *Century Dict.*, *Beefsuet-tree* . . The buffalo-berry, *Lepargyrea
argentea.* **1942** Torreya 42.163, *Lepargyraea argentea* . . Wied
. . wrote "Graines de boeuf," considering "graisse de boeuf" an error; he
was mistaken, however, as the name "beef-suet tree" indicates. **1949**
Brown *Amer. Cooks* 502 **MT**, There's a buffalo berry . . also called
rabbitberry and bullberry and picked from what's sometimes called a
beef-suet tree.

beef tea n
   1944 Adams *Western Words*, *Beef-tea*—The old-timer's name for
shallow water in which cattle had stood—usually green, stagnant, and
full of urine.

beeftongue See **beefsteak fungus**

beef to the heel(s) adj phr
Of a person: massive, bulky.
   1958 *VT Hist.* ns 26.274, Built like a Mulinger heifer, beef to the heels.
1967 *DARE* (Qu. X37, . . *Words . . to describe people's legs)* Infs **NY1,
33**, Beef to the heel.

beefwood n Also *beeftree*
A **blolly** (here: *Guapira discolor).*
   1897 Sudworth *Arborescent Flora* 192, *Pisonia obtusata . . . Common
Names . . .* Beef Wood (Fla.). **1900** Lyons *Plant Names* 293. **1979**
Little *Checklist U.S. Trees* 141, *Guapira discolor . . . Other common
names* . . beeftree, beefwood, porkwood, pigeonwood . . . Coast of s.
Fla. incl. Fla. Keys, n. on e. coast to Cape Canaveral.

bee gum n **chiefly Sth, S Midl**

1a A hollow tree or log used as a beehive. See Map
   1817 in 1929 Weems *Mason Locke Weems* 3.215 **MD**, To be
run . . round & round the circumference of a Bee-gum like a Dog in
chase of his tail, is enough to try the patience of ten Jobs. **1888** Warner
On Horseback 92 **NC**, Big Tom was always on the alert to discover and
mark a bee-gum. **1923** *DN* 5.233 **swWI**, Bee-gum . . . A piece of a tree,
generally of the trunk, hollowed out and set up to serve as a bee-hive.
1926 Roberts *Time of Man* 130 **KY**, Erastus found a bee-gum tree and
robbed the wild bees of their fruit. **1941** Stuart *Men of Mts.* 230 **neKY**,
"You ain't no man," says Big Aaron, "if you can't carry a bee gum
loaded with honey and bees." My bee gum is a cut of a hollow log with
boards nailed on the top and bottom. It is black gum and it is
heavy . . . "I've got the heaviest bee gum of all you. I got a cut from a
hollow beech-log." **1944** *PADS* 2.26 **cwOH, wNC**, Bee-gum . . . A
sawed-off portion of the hollow trunk of a tree (frequently the gum) used
as a beehive. **1965–70** *DARE* (Qu. R19b, *The place where wild bees live
and store their honey)* 37 Infs, **chiefly Sth, S Midl**, Bee gum; **MS6**, Bee
gum on tree.

b Any beehive. See Map
   1859 (1968) Bartlett *Americanisms*, *Bee-gum.* In the South and West, a
term originally applied to a species of the gum-tree from which beehives
were made; and now to beehives made of any kind of boards. **1903** *DN*
2.306 **seMO**, *Bee-gum* . . . Bee hive. This name is derived from the
custom of using the section of a hollow gum tree, but is applied to other
kinds of hives, as 'patent gum,' that is a modern, patented hive. **1904**
DN 2.416 **nwAR**. **1908** *DN* 3.289 **eAL, wGA**, *Bee-gum* . . . Bee hive:
used originally of a hollow gum tree, but now of any bee hive. "I got half a
dozen pattent [sic] bee-gums when I was in Opelika." **1911** *DN* 3.537
eKY. **1912** *DN* 3.571 **wIN**, *Bee-gum* . . . A plain, box-like bee-hive.
The term is not generally applied to the more pretentious, manufactured
hives. **1965–70** *DARE* (Qu. R19a, *The place where bees live and store
their honey—tame bees)* 44 Infs, **chiefly Sth, S Midl**, Bee gum.

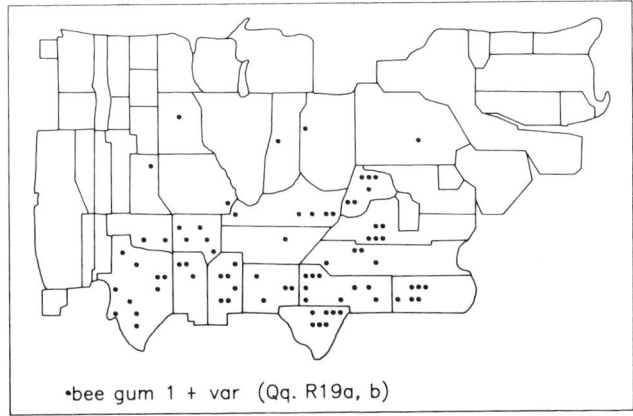

•bee gum 1 + var (Qq. R19a, b)

2 Transf: a man's hat with a high crown.
   1880 Harris *Uncle Remus Songs* 230 **GA**, One er deze yer slick-lookin'
niggers, wid a bee-gum hat an' a brass watch ez big ez de head uv a beer
bar'l, come 'long an' bresh up agin me. **1904** *DN* 2.416 **nwAR**, *Bee-gum
hat* . . . Silk hat. 'You must wear a bee-gum hat at the laying of the
corner-stone' (addressed to the worshipful master of a Masonic blue
lodge). **1929** Dobie *Vaquero* 185, Over in England, Buffalo Bill said,
Tom would retire to his dressing room after the performance was over,
take off his cowboy clothes, emerge in attire of the latest fashion,
including a beegum hat, and then mingle with admiring nobility. **1939**
FWP Guide NC 505 **cwNC**, In this section any high hat is called a
"beaver," or, in derision, a "bee gum."

3 See quot.
   1967 *DARE* (Qu. X3, *When a woman puts her hair up on her head in a
bunch, you call this a _____*) Inf **TN1**, Bee gum.

4 A **black gum** (here: *Nyssa sylvatica).*

1960 Vines *Trees SW* 802, *Nyssa . . . sylvatica . . .* Vernacular names are . . Pepperridge [sic], Bee Gum, and Sour Gum . . . The flowers serve as bee food.

beehive cactus n [From the shape]

A **barrel cactus** (here: *Echinocactus johnsonii*).

1941 Jaeger *Wildflowers* 168 **Desert SW,** *Beehive Cactus . . . Echinocactus Johnsonii octocentrus.*

bee killer See **bee catcher 1**

beeler n [Prob var of **beater 1**] **S Midl**

See quots.

1953 Randolph *Down in Holler* 226 **Ozarks,** Beeler . . . A wooden maul used in splitting rails. The *beeler* is just a big mallet, distinguished from the *mankiller* maul which is made in one piece like a huge club. **1954** *Harder Coll.* **cwTN,** Beeler . . . A wooden wedge used to split up boards or slats. **1981** *Broaddus Coll.* **ceKY** (as of 1958), Beeler—a wooden maul for splitting rails.

bee linden See **bee tree**

Beelzebub n Pronc-sp *Belzibub*

1 The devil; a devil or hobgoblin. **chiefly Gt Lakes** See Map

1943 *LANE* Map 532 **scattered throughout NEng,** *The Devil . . .* ['bɛlzəbʌb], [,bi'ɛlzɨbʌb]. **1965–70** *DARE* (Qu. CC8, *Other names for the devil*) 33 Infs, **chiefly Gt Lakes,** Beelzebub; (Qu. EE41, *A hobgoblin that is used to threaten children and make them behave*) Inf **OH82,** Beelzebub; (Qu. HH22b, . . *"He's meaner than _____."*) Inf **MA58,** Beelzebub. **1973** Allen *LAUM* 1.384 **ceNE, cSD,** *Devil . . .* [2 infs:] Beelzebub.

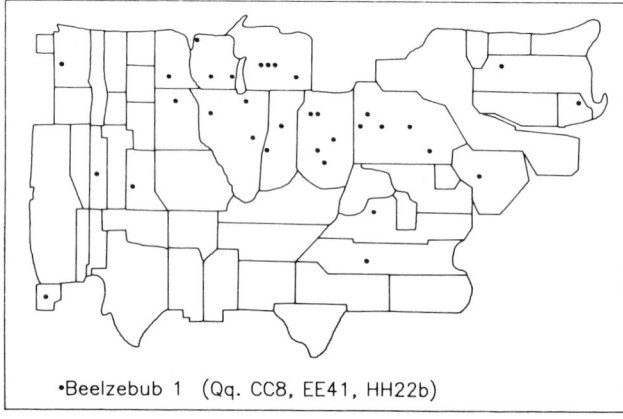

•Beelzebub 1 (Qq. CC8, EE41, HH22b)

2 See quot.

1940–41 Cassidy *WI Atlas* **swWI,** Belzibub—Child born out of wedlock.

bee martin n

1 also *betty (bee) martin:* =**kingbird. chiefly Sth, S Midl** See Map Cf **bee bird 1, billy martin, buddy bee martin**

1805 (1904) Lewis *Orig. Jrls. Lewis & Clark Exped.* 2.141, The bee martin or kingbird is common to this country. **1908** *DN* 3.290 **eAL, wGA,** Bee-martin . . . King-bird. **1913** Bailey *Birds VA* 176, *Tyrannus*

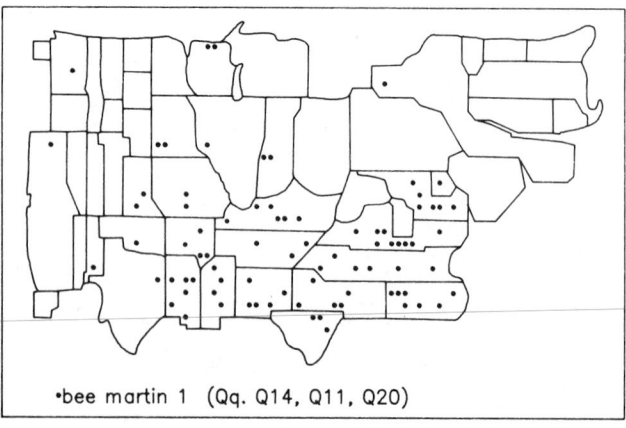

•bee martin 1 (Qq. Q14, Q11, Q20)

tyrannus, . . Betty Bee Martin, Bee Martin, Billy Bee . . . This bird, better known to the local inhabitants as the Bee Martin, arrives about April 11. **1917** *Wilson Bulletin* 29.282, *Tyrannus tyrannus.*—Betty martin [VA]. **1965–70** *DARE* (Qu. Q14) 79 Infs, **chiefly Sth, S Midl,** Bee martin; (Qu. Q11) Inf **GA72,** Bee martin; (Qu. Q20) Infs **AR56, GA89, KY86, VA40,** Bee martin.

2 =**bank swallow 1.**

1917 *Wilson Bulletin* 29.2.84, *Riparia riparia.*—Sand swallow or martin, bee-martin, Hickman K[entuck]y.

3 =**purple martin.**

1940 in 1968 Haun *Hawk's Done Gone* 75 **eTN,** He said he was sure Pairlee's spirit flew as straight to heaven as a bee martin to its gourd. **1956** *MA Audubon Soc. Bulletin* 40.84, *Purple Martin.* Bee Martin (Maine. It occasionally eats honeybees).

bee myrtle n

Prob =**bee brush.**

1956 Gipson *Old Yeller* 76 **TX,** I finally came across her, holed up in a dense thicket of bee myrtle.

been See **be A2**

beent See **be C1a**

bee plant n

1 A **spider flower,** esp the **Rocky Mountain bee plant. West**

1898 *Jrl. Amer. Folkl.* 11.223, *Cleome integrifolia . . .* Bee-plant, Colo[rado]. **1963** Craighead *Rocky Mt. Wildflowers* 69, Yellow Bee-plant *(C. lutea . .) . .* has yellow instead of pink flowers. **1976** Dodge *Roadside Wildflowers* 15, Beeplant is also called stinkweed . . in some localities.

2 Either of two **figworts,** esp *Scrophularia californica* but also *S. marilandica.* Cf **California bee plant**

1911 *Century Dict. Suppl.,* Bee-plant . . . The name has been applied specifically to *Scrophularia Marylandica* and to *S. Californica.* **1954** CA Div. Beaches & Parks *Pt. Lobos Wild Flowers* 35, *Scrophularia californica . . .* Coast Figwort (Bee Plant).

3 =**butterfly weed 2.**

1951 *PADS* 15.37 **TX,** *Gaura* spp.—Wild honeysuckles; bee plants.

beer n **chiefly sAppalachians**

1 Fermented mash used as an alcoholic drink or put through a still to make moonshine. Cf **buck n[4]**

1887 (1967) Harris *Free Joe* 105 **GA,** The way I do my countin', one tub of beer is natchally wuth two revenue chaps. **1917** *DN* 4.408 **wNC, KY.** **1933** Rawlings *South Moon* 92 **cFL,** Zeke dipped a gourd in one of the barrels of seething mash. "You want some o' the beer, Lulu?" **1940** Hall *Coll.* **wNC, eTN,** Beer—that's fermented cooked meal—still beer, corn beer. **1956** *Ibid,* Jake was makin' liquor. Zeke was stealin' it, carryin' his beer off and all such stuff. Zeke was drunk. **1968** *DARE* Tape **NC54,** Then you take and pour your beer in there . . . that there's what you make your whiskey out of, the beer is. You take that corn and your sugar, and it works off and makes a beer. And then you put the beer in your still; **GA21A,** It's a beer before you make the whiskey out of it. **1972** *Foxfire Book* 316 **nGA,** Beer—the fermented liquid made from corn meal bases which, when cooked in the still, produces the moonshine. **1974** Maurer *KY Moonshine* 114 **KY,** Beer . . . Fermented mash, either grain or sugar. "That beer's working off good." Also called "still-beer."

2 See quot.

1972 Hilliard *Hog Meat* 90 **Sth,** Occasionally used for persimmon wine, locally called "beer."

beer blast See **blast n 3**

beer keg See **keg B**

beer seed n, also attrib See also **California beer**

See quot 1969.

1969 *DARE* File **eKY,** Beer seed—an effervescent, nonalcoholic drink; used to be made out of beer seed, molasses, and other stuff. **1970** *DARE* (Qu. DD28b, . . *Fermented drinks . . made at home*) Inf **KY84,** Beer-seed beer, nonalcoholic.

beer yeast n Pronc-sp *beer east*

1967–69 *DARE* (Qu. H17, . . *Kinds of yeast*) Inf **IN23,** Beer east—made with cornmeal and hops; **IN54,** Used to use beer east; **MI95,** Beer [yeast]—same as yeast starter; **MA1,** Beer yeast.

bees See **be B1g**

bee sage n [From its use as a honey plant]
1 =**desert lavender.**
   1925 Jepson *Manual Plants CA* 879, *H[yptis] emoryi . . . Bee-Sage.*
   1938 Van Dersal *Native Woody Plants* 325, Bee-sage *(Hyptis emoryi).*
   1981 Benson–Darrow *Trees SW Deserts* 212, Desert lavender often is
   called bee sage because of its value as a honey plant.
2 also *white bee sage:* A **white sage** (here: *Salvia apiana*).
   1931 U.S. Dept. Ag. *Misc. Pub.* 101.141, *White sage . .* known as bee
   sage, greasewood, and white bee sage, is a white-leaved, white-flowered
   shrub . . common and widespread at low elevations in southern California. **1981** Benson–Darrow *Trees SW Deserts* 209, *Bee Sage, White
   Sage . . .* This is one of the most important honey plants of southern
   California.

beeslings See **beaslings**

bee's nest plant n Also *bee's nest (seed)*
A **wild carrot** (here: *Daucus carota*).
   1873 in 1976 Miller *Shaker Herbs* 148, *Daucus carota.* Bee's Nest Seed.
   Queen Anne's Lace. **1876** Hobbs *Bot. Hdbk.* 10, Beesnest plant, Wild
   carrot, Daucus carota. **1940** Clute *Amer. Plant Names* 257, *Daucus
   carota.* Bee's-nest plant. **1959** Carleton *Index Herb. Plants* 9, *Bee's
   Nest:* Daucus carota.

bee spiderflower n
=**Rocky Mountain bee plant.**
   1948 Stevens *KS Wild Flowers* 121, *Cleome serrulata . . . Bee Spider-*
   flower . . . The first part of the common name is appropriate because the
   flowers are noted for their yield of honey . . . 'Spiderflower' seems to
   come from a resemblance between the spreading slender stamens and
   sprawling spider legs. **1976** Dodge *Roadside Wildflowers* 15 **SW**, *Bee*
   spiderflower . . . is . . . considered a valuable source of nectar by bee-
   keepers.

bees swarm phr For varr, see quots **S Midl** *euphem*
A baby is born; see quots 1953, 1960 (Hall).
   1953 Randolph *Down in Holler* 114 **Ozarks**, At Granby, Missouri,
   when a man's wife was about to be delivered of a child, a friend said to the
   husband, "Well, Tom, it looks like *your bees are a-swarmin'.*" **1960**
   Campbell *Birth of Natl. Park* 99 **eTN**, Well, the bees swarmed ten times
   at my house, and your pappy [=a well-known doctor] was there every
   time. **1960** Hall *Smoky Mt. Folks* 65, "Watchin' his bees" or "waitin'
   for his bees to swarm" are euphemisms for expecting a baby: "John,
   when are your bees going to swarm?" **1972** *Courier-Jrl.* (Louisville KY)
   4 May A12, Hit was February, and I was afeared that the bees would
   swarm of a night [i.e., that his wife would deliver a child] . . and sure
   enough the bees swarmed about nine o'clock.

bee stand n chiefly **S Midl** Cf **bee gum 1**
A hive of bees.
   1882 *Harper's Mag.* 65.968/1, He ran right over a bee stand . . and was
   stung in thirty places. **1949** *AmSp* 24.106 **nGA**, *Bee-stand . . .* Beehive. **1967–69** DARE (Qu. R19a, *The place where bees live and store*
   their honey—tame bees) Infs **GA**72, **KY**9, **TN**1, 11, Bee stand. **1976**
   Garber *Mountain-ese* 87 **sAppalachians**, Pappy went out and robbed his
   bee stand and got a gallon uv honey.

beestlings See **beaslings**

bee swallow n Cf **bee martin 3**
Prob =**purple martin.**
   1967 DARE (Qu. Q20) Inf **NY**32, Bee swallow.

beeswax n
1 One's own concerns or responsibilities. [Joc alter of *busi-*
ness]
   1942 Berrey–Van den Bark *Amer. Slang* 253.9, *None of your busi-*
   ness! . . None of your biz! *or* beeswax! **1950** *WELS* 1 Inf, **cwWI**, None
   of your beeswax. **1965–70** DARE (Qu. II22, *Expressions to tell some-*
   body to keep to himself and mind his own business) 29 Infs, **scattered,**
   Mind your own beeswax; **NC**37, Keep your nose out of my beeswax;
   IA34, Tend to your own beeswax; (Qu. NN12b, *Things that people say to*
   put off a child when he asks, "What are you making?") Inf **PA**93, None of
   your beeswax.
2 See quot.
   1960 Hall *Smoky Mt. Folks* 52 **eTN, wNC**, If a widower said "beeswax"
   to a widow whom he had been "sparkin'," he was proposing marriage. If
   she wished to marry him, she answered, "sticks."

beeswax from bull foot, not to know See **bee from bull's foot, ∼**

beet bird n [See quots 1931, 1956]
=**goldfinch.**
   1917 (1923) *Birds Amer.* 3.13, *Astragalinus tristis tristis . .* Other
   Names . . . Beet Bird. **1931** *Randolph Enterprise* (Elkins, W. Va.) 24
   Sep. 5/4 *(DA),* We used to wonder why old folks of early days called the
   wild canary the 'beet bird' until this summer they eat our beet tops.
   1956 *MA Audubon* 40.254, *Goldfinch.* Beet Bird (N.H. From feeding on
   the seeds of that plant.).

beet greens n pl chiefly **Nth, scattered West** See Map
The edible leaves and stems of garden beets usu served boiled.
   1896 (c1973) Farmer *Orig. Cook Book* 263 **Boston MA,** Hothouse beet
   greens and dandelions appear in market the first of March, when they
   command a high price. Those grown out of doors are in season from
   middle of May to first of July. *Boiled Beet Greens.* **1938** Damon
   Grandma 277 **NEng,** I found in the buttery a platter of cold beet greens.
   1965–70 DARE (Qu. I28b, . . *Greens that are cooked*) 123 Infs, **chiefly**
   Nth, scattered West, Beet greens; (Qu. I28a, . . *Kinds of . .*
   "greens" . . eaten raw) 14 Infs, **chiefly Nth,** Beet greens.

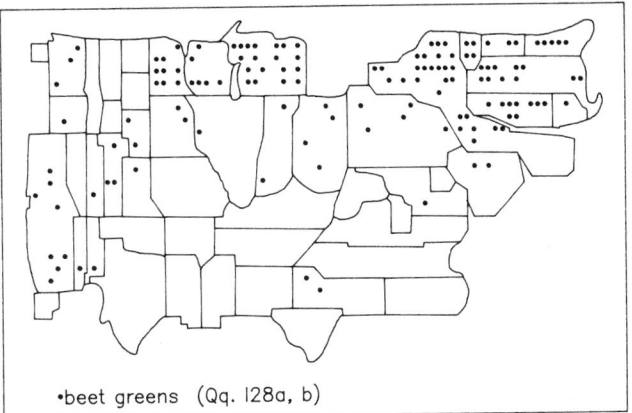

•beet greens (Qq. I28a, b)

bee thistle n
A **coyote thistle** (here: *Eryngium articulatum*).
   1925 Jepson *Manual Plants CA* 694, *E. articulatum . . . Bee-*
   thistle . . . Herbage with a strong disagreeable odor. **1949** Moldenke
   Amer. Wild Flowers 148, The *beethistle . . .* may be looked for in river
   marshes and wet meadows from Idaho and Oregon south into California. **1973** Hitchcock–Cronquist *Flora Pacific NW* 325.

beetle See **beetlehead 1**

beetlebung n [Etym unknown]
A **black gum 1** (here: *Nyssa sylvatica*).
   1900 Lyons *Plant Names* 262, *N. sylvatica . . .* Tupelo, . . Black
   Gum, . . Beetle-bung. **1960** Vines *Trees SW* 802, Vernacular names
   are Swamp-hornbeam, Yellow Gum, Snag-tree, Beetle-bung.

beetlehead n [*beetle* a mallet]
1 also *beetlehead(ed) plover, beetle:* =**black-bellied plover.**
   1828 in 1877 Ticknor *Life & Letters* 1.386 **Cape Cod MA**, Mr. Webster
   has been out shooting all day, and brought home a fine quantity of
   beetle-heads, curlews, and other things whose names I do not remember. **1839** MA Zool. & Bot. Surv. *Fishes Reptiles* 361, The
   beetle-headed plovers . . Toward the last of September . . collect in great
   flocks, preparatory to their migration. **1844** Giraud *Birds Long Is.* 212,
   The Black-bellied Plover . . . In the month of August it returns with its
   young, which is so different in plumage that by many it is considered a
   distinct species, being called "Bull or Beatle-headed [sic] Plover." **1888**
   Trumbull *Names of Birds* 191, [*Black-bellied Plover*] In Maine at Bath,
   Portland, and Pine Point, at Portsmouth, N.H., in Massachusetts at
   Ipswich, Salem, North Scituate, Provincetown, West Barnstable,
   Chatham, and New Bedford, at Stratford, Conn., and Shinnecock Bay,
   L.I., *Beetle-head;* at Eastville, Va., *Beetle* simply. **1892** *Auk* 9.144, The
   young birds, commonly called Beetle-heads, Chuckle-heads, or Bull-
   heads, have the entire upper parts brownish gray-black covered with
   irregular spots of white and pale yellow. **1918** Grinnell *Game Birds CA*
   454, In California and elsewhere it is known as . . Beetle-head by reason
   of the large size of its head. **1955** *MA Audubon* 39.445, *Black-bellied*
   Plover. Beetle (Maine); Beetle-head (Maine, N.H., Mass., Conn., R.I.);
   Beetle-head Plover (Mass. Large head.). **1969** DARE (Qu.
   Q10, . . *Water birds and marsh birds*) Inf **MA**57, Beetlehead.

2 =scoter.

1923 U.S. Dept. Ag. *Misc. Circular* 13.28, American Scoter . . . Vernacular Names . . . In local use. —Beetlehead (N.Y.).

beetlehead(ed) plover See **beetlehead 1**

beetleweed n Also *beetle plant* **chiefly S Midl**
=galax.

1861 Wood *Class-Book* 495, Galax . . . Beetle-weed . . . Damp, mountain woods, Md. . . to Tenn. . . and S. Car. **1901** Lounsberry *S. Wild Flowers* 402, Beetle-Weed . . . Galax aphylla . . . In the mountainous parts of North Carolina I saw them . . spreading over acres. **1915** *Torreya* 15.18 **GA,** One of the popular names of the species, "beetle plant" suggests the inquiry whether its odor may not possess attractions for some . . beetle . . whose visits might be in some way beneficial to the plant. **1931** Harned *Wild Flowers Alleghanies* 378, Beetle Weed . . . The leaves are broadly heart-shaped. **1952** Taylor *Plants Colonial Days* 43 **VA,** Known also as beetleweed and colt's foot . . galax flowers in May.

beetling block n Also sp *beteling ~* [*beetle* to beat (fabric) with a heavy wooden bat or pestle] Cf **battle v 1, battling stick** old-fash

A block of wood on which to beat clothes while washing.

1966 *Good Old Days* Jan 34 **wNC** (as of c1900), She had a big block of wood settin' on its end about two feet high she called her beteling block. She'd wet the clothes and lay them over on the block and beat them with a blatching stick. It was sorta like a baseball bat.

bee tree n Also *bee basswood, bee (tree) linden* [See quot 1950]
=linden (esp *Tilia americana* and *T. heterophylla*).

1890 Newhall *Trees NEast Amer.* 22, Bee Tree. T[ilia] Americana. **1897** Sudworth *Arborescent Flora* 301, Tilia americana . . Common Names . . . Beetree (Vt., W. Va., Wis.). **1903** Small *Flora SE U.S.* 760, Tilia . . Bee-tree. **1941** FWP *Guide WV* 18, The . . linden . . is called the 'bee tree' because of the swarms of bees that seek its nectar. **1950** Peattie *Nat. Hist. Trees* 488, Other Names: . . Beetree . . . Yet, if you happen to be tramping abroad at that season, the haunting odor may waft down wind to you, or you may hear the roar of the nectar-mad bees at its flowers. **1960** Vines *Trees SW* 733, Tilia americana . . It has many vernacular names such as . . Bee-tree . . . The flowers are valuable for bee pasture. *Ibid* 734, Tilia caroliniana . . Vernacular names . . Bee Basswood . . . Tilia floridiana . . Other names are Bee Linden . . . Bee-tree Linden Tilia heterophylla.

beetroot n [From the red stem]

A **pigweed 1** (here: *Amaranthus retroflexus*).

1898 *Jrl. Amer. Folkl.* 11.277, Amaranthus retroflexus, . . red-root, beet-root, careless weed, Kans. **1910** Graves *Flowering Plants* 169 **CT,** Beet-root . . . A bad weed in cultivated ground.

beet tops n pl **widespread, but least freq Sth, S Midl** See Map
=beet greens.

1960 *PADS* 34.48 **CO,** Beet tops, beet greens 'greens, salad.' **c1960** *Wilson Coll.* **csKY,** Beet tops . . used for greens; also to wilt and put on sprains, bruises, and boils. **1965–70** *DARE* (Qu. I28b, . . Greens that are cooked) 174 Infs, **widespread, but least freq Sth, S Midl,** Beet tops; (Qu. I28a, . . Kinds of . . "greens" . . eaten raw) Infs **AL6, FL19, MI69, NJ21, NY83, TX17,** Beet tops.

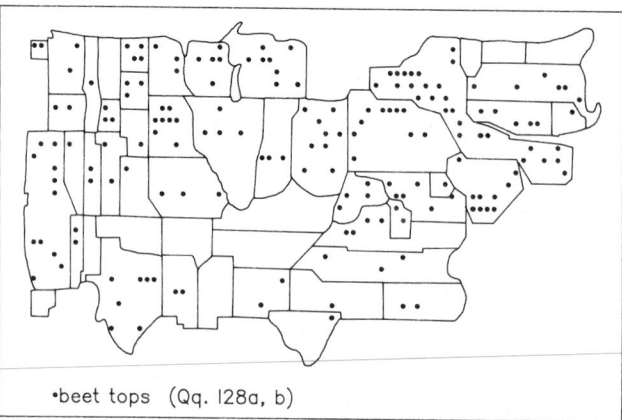

•beet tops (Qq. I28a, b)

beeve(s) See **beef A**

bee weed n

1 The blue wood aster (*Aster cordifolius*). **eUS**

1894 *Jrl. Amer. Folkl.* 7.91, Aster cordifolius . . Blue Devil, stick-weed, bee-weed, Fall Aster, West Va. **1931** Clute *Common Plants* 95, The bee-weed (Aster cordifolius), and the bee balms . . derive their names from the fact that bees favor them. **1940** Clute *Amer. Plant Names* 75, Heart-leaved aster . . . Bee-weed.

2 Any of var other bee plants as:

a =Rocky Mountain bee plant.

1911 *Century Dict. Suppl.,* The Rocky Mountain bee-plant (also called bee-weed) is one of the spider-flowers, Cleome serrulata.

b A **milkweed** (here: *Asclepias subverticillata*).

1937 U.S. Forest Serv. *Range Plant Hdbk.* W29, Horsetail milkweed [Asclepias subverticillata], also known . . locally as beeweed, a poisonous perennial herb, ranks among those plants most deadly to range livestock.

c =wild carrot.

1966 *DARE* (Qu. S6, Other names around here for Queen Anne's lace) Inf **NM13A,** Beeweed.

d =white sweetclover.

1967 *DARE* (QR p57) Inf **CO11,** Beeweed—sweet clover or a large white flower.

bee wine n [**bee** n[1] **1**]

See quots.

1914 *Hartford Times* (CT) 17 Apr 8/6, I would like to ask . . readers of your paper if they have ever heard of the California bee. These bees are of a very peculiar species, being somewhat like a soft white sponge, and if put into a common ordinary Mason jar with sugar, water and molasses will in the course of a week make bee wine. **1968** *DARE* (Qu. DD28b, What fermented drinks are made at home around here?) Inf **NJ35,** Bee wine: rice and sugar and water.

beewort n [*bee,* because it is attractive to bees, + *wort* plant]
=sweet flag.

1900 Lyons *Plant Names* 13, A. Calamus . . . Beewort . . . Aromatic. **1974** (1977) Coon *Useful Plants* 65, Beewort . . . The part most used is the rhizome . . as well as the sweet and fragrant stem of young leaves.

beezer n [Perh blend of *beak* and *sneezer*]

1 One's nose.

1915 C.E. Van Loan in Grayson *New Stories for Men* (1941) 550 (*OEDS*), Perhaps it should be explained that, in the patois of the [boxing] profession . . the nose becomes a beezer. **1920** Ade *Handmade Fables* 12 **IN,** One brilliant Man about Town, with a Beezer that never could have been coloured by the use of Malted Milk. **1929** *AmSp* 4.338 [Hobo jargon], Beezer—The nose. **1932** *AmSp* 7.329 [Johns Hopkins University jargon], Beezer—nose. **1956** *Sun* (Baltimore MD) 30 Nov ed. B 28/2 (Hench Coll.), These are the main differences between Archie Moore and Floyd Patterson as they start poking each other in the beezer tonight [in a professional boxing match]. **1965–70** *DARE* (Qu. X14, . . The nose) Infs **CA201, CT27, FL15, IN39, WI47,** Beezer. **1980** in 1982 *Barrick Coll.* **sePA,** Beezer—nose; slang.

2 Transf: the head, the mouth.

1932 *AmSp* 7.400 **WA,** Beezer . . . Head, forehead. A visiting psychologist [in an orphans' home] with a peculiar growth on his forehead was known as "The brainy old bozo with a bump on his beezer." **1968–69** *DARE* (Qu. X9, Joking or uncomplimentary words for a person's mouth) Inf **MA58,** Beezer; (Qu. X28, Joking words . . for a person's head) Inf **MO10,** Beezer.

beezer-weezer n

Prob a **cicada**.

1970 *DARE* (Qu. R7, Insects that sit in trees or bushes in hot weather and make a sharp, buzzing sound) Inf **IL143,** Beezer-weezers ['bizɚ'wizɚ].

beezlings See **beaslings**

beezlums n pl [Alter of **beaslings**]

1897 *KS Univ. Qrly.* 6.51 **KS,** Beezlums: cake from first milk of fresh cow.

before-dark n Cf **before-day**

Dusk, twilight.

1965–70 *DARE* (Qu. A4, The time of day when the sun goes out of *sight*) Inf **PA**220, Before-dark; (Qu. A5, *The time right after the sun goes out of sight, before it becomes all dark*) Infs **AR**6, **GA**30, **IA**8, **KY**26, **LA**43, **NC**37, Before-dark.

before-day n, also attrib Pronc-sp *afore-day,* aphet forms *fo'- day, fore-day* **chiefly Sth, S Midl** See Map *esp freq among Black speakers* Cf *DJE*

The time just prior to sunrise.

1896 *DN* 1.417, *Fore-day* . . the period of time immediately before sunrise. **1902** *DN* 2.233 **sIL,** For early morning . . 'long before day' and 'just before day' (i.e. dawn) are commonly employed . . . Morning is the time 'before day,' or early rising time. **1927** Adams *Congaree* 76 **cSC** [Black], "You up soon, Bubber," . . "Yes, Aunt Rhody, I been up since fo' day." **1942** (1965) Parrish *Slave Songs* 62 **eGA,** I am told that this shout was once a favorite at "foreday meetin'," held on Sunday in the neighborhood of five o'clock. **1965–70** *DARE* (Qu. A1, . . *The time in the early morning before the sun comes into sight*) 30 Infs, **chiefly Sth, S Midl,** *11 Black,* Before-day; **TN**11, Afore-day [əˈfɔrˌdeɪ]; (Qu. L4b, . . *The time early in the morning and at night when you have to feed livestock, clean stalls, and so on*) Inf **OK**52, Before-day. **1975** McDonough *Garden Sass* 297 **AR,** They went to church 'fore day in the morning—they had a 'fore-day service. They'd leave home about four o'clock in the morning and they'd go to church and stay till day.

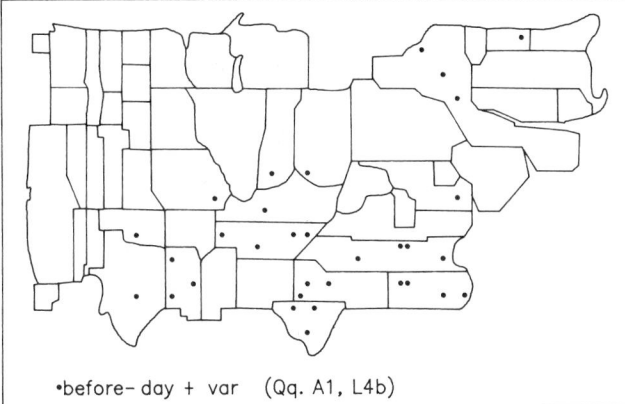

•before- day + var   (Qq. A1, L4b)

beforetimes adv

Early.

1960 Williams *Walk Egypt* 107 **GA,** Yet it was before-times for such to bloom; they came along in April.

beg v Usu [bɛg]; often, **chiefly in Sth,** *esp among Black speakers,* [be(ɪ)g]; occas [bæg] Pronc-spp *bague, baig* Cf **egg** n A

Std sense, var forms.

1888 Jones *Negro Myths* 36 **GA coast,** Wen eh bin er eat de bread, Buh Tiger come long an bague um fuh some. **1894** Chopin *Bayou Folk* 295 **LA** [Black], An' he say he baig my pardon fo' his intrudement. **1922** Gonzales *Black Border* 288 **sSC, GA coasts** [Gullah glossary], Baig. **1934** *AmSp* 9.211 **Sth,** Some words with standard [ɛ] before [g] or [k] change [ɛ] to [eɪ] or [e]. This pronunciation is decidedly vulgar . . . *Beg, egg* [etc.]. **1936** *AmSp* 11.15 **eTX,** *Beg* and *dregs* . . have [ɛ] consistently. **1941** *AmSp* 16.5 **eTX** [Black], *Beg, peg,* are [bɛːg], [beɪg], [pɛːg], [peɪg]. **1942** Hall *Smoky Mt. Speech* 20, [æ] is common also in *beg, keg, leg* [etc.].

beggar n

1 A toady, apple-polisher.

1968–69 *DARE* (Qu. II20a, *A person who tries too hard to gain somebody else's favor: "He's an awful _____."*) Infs **IN**49, **MO**37, Beggar; (Qu. JJ3b, *When a school child makes a special effort to "get in good" with the teacher in hopes of getting a better grade: "She's an awful _____."*) Inf **IL**48, Beggar.

2 See quot.

1969 *DARE* (Qu. H71, . . *The last piece of food left on a plate*) Inf **PA**221, The beggar.

beggar burr n

=**beggar ticks 1.**

1969 *DARE* (Qu. S15, . . *Weed seeds that cling to clothing*) Inf **KY**40, Beggar burrs—flat, three-cornered.

beggar lice (weed), beggar louse See **beggar's lice**

beggarly adj

Stingy.

1967 *DARE* (Qu. U33, . . *A stingy person*) Inf **WA**20, Beggarly; (Qu. U35, *Words meaning thrifty but not in a complimentary way: "She's not a bad housekeeper, but very _____."*) Inf **WA**20, Beggarly.

beggarman's lice See **beggar's lice**

beggar patches n Cf **poor man's patches**

=**tick trefoil** or the loments thereof.

1966 *DARE* (Qu. S15, . . *Weed seeds that cling to clothing*) Inf **NC**1, Beggar lice or beggar patches—little round, flat, green seeds.

beggar's basket n [Prob from the shape of the flower head]

A **wild carrot** (here: *Daucus carota*).

1959 Carleton *Index Herb. Plants* 9, *Beggar's Basket:* Daucus carota.

beggar's blanket n [From the furry leaves] Cf **blanket leaf**

=**mullein.**

1959 Carleton *Index Herb. Plants* 9, *Beggar's Blanket:* Verbascum thapsus.

beggar's button n

1 =**burdock 1.** [Prob from the shape]

1900 Lyons *Plant Names* 43, *A[rctium] Lappa* . . Beggar's buttons. **1930** Sievers *Amer. Med. Plants* 17, *Burdock Arctium minus* . . beggar's-buttons. **1931** Harned *Wild Flowers Alleghanies* 601, Other names locally applied to Burdock *[Arctium lappa]* are Cockle-bur, Stick-button, and Beggar's-button. **1933** Small *Manual SE Flora* 1480, *A[rctium] minus* . . Beggar's-buttons. **1971** Krochmal *Appalachia Med. Plants* 58, *Arctium lappa* . . Common names: . . beggar's button.

2 =**buttercup.**

1959 Carleton *Index Herb. Plants* 10, *Beggar's Buttons:* Arctium lappa . . ; Ranunculus (v).

beggar's lice n Also *beggar('s) louse, beggar lice (weed), beggarman's lice, beggy lice*

1 =**stickseed 1,** esp *Hackelia virginiana.*

1837 Darlington *Flora Cestrica* 121, *Virginian Echinospermum. Vulgo* —Beggar's Lice . . . Nuts covered with hooked prickles. **1897** IN Dept. Geol. & Nat. Resources *Rept. for 1896* 670, Beggar's Lice. Stickseed. Sticktight . . . Open woods, borders of thickets and fence-rows; common. **1950** Stevens *ND Plants* 235, *Hackelia* and *Lappula* . . . The burs are often called sticktights or beggar's lice, names applied to various other burs. **1966** *DARE* Wildfl QR Inf **CO**7, Beggar's lice (*Hackelia floribunda*). **1976** Bailey–Bailey *Hortus Third* 535, *Hackelia* . . . Stickseed, Beggar's-lice . . . Nutlets armed with barbed bristles on the margins and angles.

2 =**tick trefoil.**

1859 (1968) Bartlett *Americanisms* 27, *Desmodium* . . is sometimes called Beggar-Lice. **1885** in 1944 Harper *Weeds AL* 136, There is a forage plant now rapidly coming into . . popularity . . and known as Beggars Lice. It belongs to the genus Desmodium. **1893** *Jrl. Amer. Folkl.* 6.149, *Desmodium Canadense,* beggar's lice. Concord, Mass. **1953** Greene–Blomquist *Flowers South* 62, *Beggar's-Ticks, Beggar-Louse, Tick-Trefoils (Desmodium)* Among the assortment of various fruits that stick to your clothing . . the most common are the joints of the fruits (loments) of *Desmodium.* **c1960** *Wilson Coll.* **csKY,** Beggar lice . . . The sticky seeds on a common weed, a member of the bean family. **1965–70** *DARE* (Qu. S13, . . *A common wild bush with bunches of round, prickly seeds . . [that] stick to your clothing*) 22 Infs, **scattered, but esp N Midl,** Beggar('s) lice; **AR**55, Beggy lice—flat, fuzzy bean-like seeds. **1966** *DARE* Wildfl QR Pl.111 Inf **AR**46, Beggar louse; Pl.112 Inf **LA**21, Beggar's lice.

3 =**beggar ticks 1.**

1873 in 1976 Miller *Shaker Herbs* 163, *Cuckold* . . . *Bidens frondosa* . . . Beggar Lice . . . Seeds are also used as an expectorant in throat irritation. **1900** Lyons *Plant Names* 63. **1909** *DN* 3.421 **Cape Cod MA,** *Beggar-lice* . . . Fork-shaped seeds of a weed that sticks to clothes. **1913** *DN* 4.3 **ME,** *Beggar lice* . . . The seeds of an annoying weed that clings to clothing. These are elsewhere called *sticktights* or *pitchforks.* **1965–70** *DARE* (Qu. S14, . . *Prickly seeds, small and flat, with two prongs at one end, that cling to clothing*) 260 Infs, **widespread exc Inland Nth, West,** Beggar('s) lice; **FL**48, Beggar lice weed; **MS**86, Beggar's louse; **NY**211, Beggarman's lice; **SC**36A, Beggar lice. **1971** GA Dept. Ag. *Farmers Market Bulletin* 20 Jan 8/1, Beggar-tick (often called bur-marigold, stick-tight, beggar-lice, boot-jack, or Spanish needles) is of the large genus Bidens, somewhat weedy herbs.

4 =hound's tongue 1.

1897 *Jrl. Amer. Folkl.* 10.51, Cynoglossum (all species), beggar lice, Sulphur Grove, Ohio. **1940** Clute *Amer. Plant Names* 66, C[ynoglossum] officinale . . . Beggar-lice. **1966** DARE Wildfl QR Inf **CO7**, Beggar's lice (Cynoglossum officinale). **1975** Hamel–Chiltoskey *Cherokee Plants* 30, Beggar lice Gynoglossum [sic] virginianum . . take this and other "stick-on" plants, drink decoction every four days for bad memory.

5 =bedstraw, esp *Galium aparine.*

1896 *Jrl. Amer. Folkl.* 9.190, Galium (various species), beggar lice, S.W. Mo. **1919** DN 5.37 **OK,** Beggar-lice . . . The snatch-burr of Kentucky. **1936** Winter *Plants NE* 133, G. aparine . . . Cleavers. Bedstraw. Beggar-lice. A common weed . . . Has over 70 English common names. **1959** Carleton *Index Herb. Plants* 9, Beggar Lice: Galium aparine.

6 The common agrimony *(Agrimonia eupatoria).*

1940 Clute *Amer. Plant Names* 5, A. Eupatoria. Agrimony . . Beggar-lice. **1959** Carleton *Index Herb. Plants* 10, Beggar's Lice: Agrimonia eupatoria; Cynoglossum officinalia [sic]; Desmodium canadense; Lappula (v).

7 =wild carrot.

1965–66 DARE (Qu. S6, *Other names . . for Queen Anne's lace*) Inf **MS31,** Beggar lice; **AR41,** Beggar's lice.

beggar's needles n, usu pl esp **NJ**
=beggar ticks 1.

1898 *Jrl. Amer. Folkl.* 11.229 **NJ,** Bidens (sp.), beggars' needles. **1966–69** DARE (Qu. S14, . . *Prickly seeds, small and flat, with two prongs at one end, that cling to clothing*) Inf **NJ21, 39, 52, 55,** Beggar's needle(s); **NJ16,** Beggar's needle—one point; (QR, near Qu. S15) Inf **SC2,** Beggar's needles.

beggars' night n

The night when children dress up as beggars and go door to door asking for candy and other sweets.

a Halloween eve: see quots.

1949 *Natl. Geog. Mag.* 96.24/1 **Appalachians,** The custom [of going from house to house] is similar to beggars' night, before Hallowe'en, because handouts are expected. **1968** DARE Tape **WI13,** Beggars' night . . . Trick or treat. **1969** DARE FW Addit **OH,** "Beggars' Night, how 'bout a bite?"—said on Beggars' Night (night before Halloween) to people by children who are "begging."

b Thanksgiving eve or day: see quots.

1938 FWP *Guide NH* 117, In Portsmouth . . on Thanksgiving eve children go from door to door with bags and carts crying "Give us something—this is beggar's night"—and are seldom refused. **1944** AN&Q 4.87/2 **Newbury MA,** I should like some information on the custom of Beggars' Night, which in this region takes place on the eve of Thanksgiving. Children dress up in old clothes and, armed with large paper bags, they tour the neighborhoods, begging for candy, cookies, and other delicacies. Apparently this is not a nation-wide custom. In fact, within a few miles of Newburyport it is not observed; and in other parts Beggars' night comes at Halloween. *Ibid* 4.109/2 **NYC,** Beggar's Night. On Thanksgiving Day (not Eve) children in New York City still beg for food and money. They are masked and rigged out in "grown-ups" clothing, and they plant themselves at strategic spots, often at some of the busiest street corners.

beggar's nits n Cf **beggar's lice**
=beggar ticks 1.

1970 DARE (Qu. S13) Inf **MO22,** Beggar's nits.

beggar ticks n Also *beggar tick, beggar's tick(s)*

1 A plant of the genus *Bidens.* Also called **bachelor needles, beggar's lice 3, beggar's needles, bootjacks 1, boy lice, bube lice, bullhead 4, burr marigold, chigger 4, chiggerweed 6, cockle 2, cowcatcher 4, cuckold 1, devil's beggarticks, devil's bootjacks, devil's pitchforks, harvest lice, hitchhikers, pitchforks, Spanish needles, stickseed, sticktights, tickseed, tickseed sunflower, water agrimony.** For other names of var spp see **brook sunflower, cow lice, doubletooth, niggerhead, old ladies' clothespins, shepherd's needles, wild goldenglow**

1822 Eaton *Botany* 204, Bidens . . cernua (water beggar-ticks . .). *Ibid* 205, [Bidens] bipinnata (hemlock beggar-ticks . .). **1840** MA Zool. & Bot. Surv. *Herb. Plants & Quadrupeds* 137, B. frondosa . . . Common Beggar Ticks or Cuckold, or, more elegantly, Burr Marygold [sic] . . . As the seeds have 2 barbed awns, they fasten

themselves to the clothes. **1859** [see **beggar ticks 2**]. **1896** *Jrl. Amer. Folkl.* 9.191, Bidens frondosa, . . cernua, . . and connata, . . beggars' ticks, Paris, M[ain]e. **1931** Harned *Wild Flowers Alleghanies* 585, Moreover, the common name Beggar-ticks is perhaps equally appropriate for the reason that the curiously formed seed are [sic] constantly and most persistently begging a ride and are willing to be dropped in almost any near or distant port. **1961** Douglas *My Wilderness* 251 **nME,** Beggar-ticks are present in abundance. **1965–70** DARE (Qu. S14) Infs **CT37, IL119, MA68, MI31, PA89, 234, 242, VA101,** Beggar's ticks; **VT10,** Beggar's tick; **MD29, MA5,** Beggar tick; **MA78, WI61,** Beggar ticks. **1966** DARE Wildfl QR Inf **CO7,** Beggar's tick (Bidens cernua); **WA10,** Beggar ticks (bur marigold). **1971** [see **beggar's lice 3**].

2 =tick trefoil.

1859 (1968) Bartlett *Americanisms* 27, Beggar-ticks. A species of Bidens whose seeds (fruit) adhere to the clothes. The term is also applied to a species of Desmodium whose pods break at the joints. **1889** Vasey *Ag. Grasses* 94, Desmodium . . . These are often called beggar-tick, beggar-lice, beggar-weed, or tick-weed. **1912** Blatchley *IN Weed Book* 91, Of them Thoreau has written: " . . . I have often found myself covered, as it were, with an imbricated coat of the brown seeds or a bristling chevaux-de-frise of beggars' ticks". **1940** Gates *Flora KS* 205, Desmodium acuminatum . . . Beggar's Ticks . . . Rocky woods, and hillsides . . . Hemicryptophyte. **1961** Smith *MI Wildflowers* 201, Canada Beggar's-tick, Tick-trefoil, Tick-clover . . . Everyone who has hiked . . is familiar with the fruits of this and related species, which cling so tenaciously to clothing, especially to wool socks. **1968** DARE (Qu. S13) Inf **PA89,** Beggar's tick. **1975** Duncan–Foote *Wildflowers SE* 78, Beggar's-ticks . . . Stout erect perennial to 1.5 m tall.

3 An agrimony, esp *Agrimonia eupatoria*

1893 *Jrl. Amer. Folkl.* 6.141, Agrimonia Eupatoria . . beggar's ticks. West Va. **1900** Lyons *Plant Names* 19, A[grimonia] hirsuta . . . Beggarticks, Stick-seed, Stick-weed . . . These names . . are applied also to other indigenous species. **1910** Graves *Flowering Plants* 240 **CT,** Beggar-ticks . . . Frequent. Roadsides, thickets and borders of woods. **1959** Carleton *Index Herb. Plants* 10, Beggar's ticks: Agrimonia eupatoria; Bidens (v); Desmodium canadense.

4 =stickseed 1.

1897 *Jrl. Amer. Folkl.* 10.51, Echinospermum Virginicum . . beggar ticks, Southwestern Mo. **1932** Rydberg *Flora Prairies* 666, Lappula . . . Stick-tight, Beggar-ticks. **1937** U.S. Forest Serv. *Range Plant Hdbk.* W101, Stickseeds, also known as burseeds, sticktights, and beggarticks, thus named because the burlike nutlets cling to clothing and the fur of animals, compose a genus of about 40 species. **1940** Clute *Amer. Plant Names* 67, L. Virginiana . . . Beggar-ticks.

5 A hound's tongue 1 (here: *Cynoglossum officinale*).

1940 Clute *Amer. Plant Names* 66, C. officinale . . . Beggar-lice, beggar-ticks.

6 =wild carrot.

1947 in 1951 PADS 15.17 **TX,** Daucus carota . . . Beggars'-ticks, bird's-nest. **1966** DARE Wildfl QR Pl.31 Inf **TX34,** Beggar tick.

beggar-trash n

Someone thought to be low-class or worthless.

1939 FWP *Guide TN* 135, "When it comes to farming," they will tell you, "I'd sink down to beggar-trash in no time if I didn't know the things I learnt from my daddy and he learnt from his daddy about farming." **1969** DARE (Qu. HH18, *Very insignificant or low-grade people*) Infs **TN31, 36,** Beggar-trash.

beggarweed n [OED 1878 →]

1 =tick trefoil, esp *Desmodium tortuosum* in the South.

1889 Vasey *Ag. Grasses* 94, Desmodium . . . There are about forty species native in the United States . . . These are often called beggar-tick, beggar-lice, beggar-weed, or tick-weed. **1933** Torreya 33.83, Meibomia purpurea . . . Florida beggarweed. **1944** Harper *Weeds AL* 136, Desmodium . . . They are commonly called beggar-lice in the South, and sometimes beggar-ticks and beggar-weed. **1965–70** DARE (Qu. L9a) Inf **GA33,** Beggarweeds; (Qu. S13) Inf **FL20,** Beggarweeds; (Qu. S15) Infs **FL6, 9, 27, GA20, 35, SC70, VA52,** Beggarweed(s). **1976** Bailey–Bailey *Hortus Third* 375, [Desmodium] tortuosum . . . Beggarweed . . . Grown as an ann[ual] forage and cover crop in s. U.S. **1978** *New Yorker* 6 Feb 46 **GA,** Even more evident are billboards that stress the agricultural nature of the state: "Nail Beggarweed in Peanuts," "Brake Nematode Losses in Soybeans."

2 Any of var other plants such as corn spurry, dodder, knotweed (esp *Polygonum aviculare*), or **stickseed 1: see quots.**

1900 Lyons *Plant Names* 126, *Cuscuta* . . . Names applied to the various species are Beggar-weed, Bind [etc.]. *Ibid* 300, *P[olygonum] aviculare* . . . Beggar-weed, Bird's-tongue. *Ibid* 353, *S[pergula] arvensis* . . . Corn Spurry, Beggar-weed. **1910** Graves *Flowering Plants* 173 CT, Corn . . Spurrey [sic] . . . Beggar-weed . . . Roadsides, waste places and cultivated ground throughout. **1940** Clute *Amer. Plant Names* 221, *Cuscuta epilinum.* Devil's guts, beggar-weed. **1959** Carleton *Index Herb. Plants* 10, *Beggar Weed:* Polygonum aviculare; Lappula (v).

beggie See **baga**

beggy lice See **beggar's lice**

begin v

A Forms.

1 Past: usu *began;* freq, *esp among speakers with little formal educ, begun;* occas, **chiefly Sth, S Midl,** *begin;* infreq *beginned, begint.*

1689 (1878) S. Sewall *Diary* 1.268 MA, I begun on Tuesday to drink. **1863** in 1973 *AmSp* 48.89 nGA, Then begun the ovashun. **1884** Harrison *Negro Engl.* 251 Sth, Begin—*Past.* begin, beginned, begint. **1891** (1967) Freeman *New Engl. Nun* 154 eMA, Then he begun to chirp. **1893** Shands *MS Speech,* Begun. Used by educated people for *began.* **1895** (1969) Crane *Red Badge* 102, When we was a-fightin' this afternoon, all-of-a-sudden he begin t' rip up an' cuss an' beller at me. **1903** *DN* 2.293 Cape Cod MA, Many strong verbs use the same form for the past and past participle . . . *begin—begun.* **1924** Lardner *How to Write* 225, It would be a few holes at lease before they begun to turn sour. **1926** Kephart *Highlanders* 357 wNC, eTN, In mountain vernacular the Old English strong past tense still lives in begun, drunk, . . rung, shrunk. *Ibid* 362, I don't know how the fraction [=fracas] begun. **1935** Hurston *Mules & Men* 41 nFL [Black], And they beginned to bow all over dat church. **1953** Atwood *Survey of Verb Forms* 6, *Begin* . . Preterite . . in the context "He (began) to talk." . . The form *begun* /bɪ'gʌn/ occurs in about half the communities in N. Eng. and in something less than half in most other areas. It is slightly more common in Type I [=old infs, with little educ] than in Type II [=old infs, with moderate educ]. The uninflected *begin* /bɪ'gɪn/ occurs in only seven N. Eng. communities . . . In most of the M[iddle] A[tlantic] S[tates] this form is also quite rare, but it becomes more common in the S[outh] A[tlantic] S[tates], occurring more often than *begun* in e. Va. **c1960** *Wilson Coll.* csKY, Begun . . . Almost universal for *began.* **1965–70** *DARE* (Qu. OO39b, *Talking about a meeting beginning: "Yes, it _____ [an hour ago]."*) 843 Infs, **widespread,** Began; 105 Infs, **scattered,** Begun; 15 Infs, **Sth, S Midl,** Begin; MO16, Beginned. [Of all Infs responding to the question, 22% were grade school educ; 38% of those responding with *begun,* 38% were grade school educ.] **1965–70** *DARE* Tapes CA172, FL35, GA77, IN3, 16, 30, 41, MI56, 96, TX13, 100, VA52A, Begin; FL3, IN17, Begun.

2 Past pple: usu *begun;* freq, *esp among speakers with little formal educ, began;* occas, **chiefly Sth, S Midl,** *begin;* rarely *beginned, begint.*

1675 in 1871 MA Hist. Soc. *Coll.* 5th ser 1.428, We had began. **1830** (1930) Phelps *Diary* 209 cwIL, I have concluded to keep a journal of my life as I have began with rather bad prospects—today is my wedding day. **1884** Harrison *Negro Engl.* 251 Sth, Begin . . *Pass. Part.* beginned, begint. **1893** *DN* 1.276 nwCT, No verb in their [=the rural population's] speech, with the single exception of *see,* has more than two forms . . begin [present], begun [past and past pple]. **c1960** *Wilson Coll.* csKY, Begin . . . [pple] begun. **1965–70** *DARE* (Qu. OO39a, . . *"Has the meeting _____ [yet]?"*) 799 Infs, **widespread,** Begun; 160 Infs, **scattered,** Began; 20 Infs, **Sth, S Midl,** Begin; KY75A, Beginned. [Of all Infs responding to the question, 22% were grade school educ; of those responding with *began,* 37% were grade school educ.] **1965–66** *DARE* Tape FL22, Begin; MI20, Many of our small towns . . were began as small sawmill towns.

B Sense.

Usu with *with:* to compare (with). [Ellip for *begin to compare (with)*] *old-fash*

1862 in 1903 Norton *Army Letters* 47 PA, There is no other man whom I would be so much pleased to have taken as . . Floyd. Jeff Davis wouldn't begin. **1877** Twain in *Atlantic Mth.* 40.589/2 MO, There ain't a book that begins with it. It lays over 'em all. **1893** *KS Univ. Qrly.* 1.137 KS, NY, *Begin with:* compare with, as, 'He doesn't begin with Jones.'

beg on v phr [*beg* + redund *on* prep]

To implore, urge.

1942 (1971) Campbell *Cloud-Walking* 76 seKY, Squire and the Little Teacher begged on her to sing again. *Ibid* 84, They begged on the teacher women to let them learn to sing school song ballets.

begone v, often imper [*OED* c1370 →] **chiefly S Midl**
=beat it.

1927 *DN* 5.471 sAppalachians, Begone . . . Used as a scolding word in the sense "be off." **1953** *PADS* 19.8 sAppalachians, Begone! . . Away! Used in speaking to dogs only. **1965–70** *DARE* (Qu. Y18, *To leave in a hurry*) Infs MS86, TN53, Begone; (Qu. Y19, . . *To go away from a place*) Infs NC16, SC24, Begone; (Qu. NN22b, c, *Expressions used to drive away children; . . a dog*) Infs CA9, 105, GA72, IN49, KY24, 30, 77, NC35, OH49, SC44, TN1, TX18, WV3, Begone.

begorra See **gorry**

begouge v [*be-* pref, thoroughly + *gouge*]

1953 Randolph *Down in Holler* 226 Ozarks, Begouge . . . To stab, to pierce. I heard of a woman who "*begouged* herself accidental" with an ice pick.

begrudge v Usu |bɪ'grʌj|; also, **chiefly in NEng,** |bɪ'grɛj|, –'grɛč, –'grʌč| Pronc-spp *begredge, begretch, begrutch* Cf Pronc Intro 3.I.5.d, 3.I.15

Std senses, var forms.

1861 Holmes *Venner* 1.139 wMA, If she'd ha' known that folks would begrutch cravin' a blessin' over sech a heap o' provisions, she'd rather ha' staid t' home. **1891** (1967) Freeman *New Engl. Nun* 52, I s'pose I kinder begretched you that black silk. **1895** *DN* 1.384 cNY, *Begretch:* for *begrudge* . . . *Begrutch* is known in W[estern] Conn. **1904** Day *Kin o' Ktaadn* 22 ME, But I'm never begretchin' the gruntin's. **1909** *DN* 3.419 Cape Cod MA, *Begretched* . . . Begrudged. "It was said of thin porridge that it was *water bewitched and meal begretched.*" **1952** Brown *NC Folkl.* 1.519, *Begredge* [bɪ'grɛdʒ] . . . Begrudge.—General. Illiterate. **1959** *VT Hist.* ns 27.125, *Begrudge* [bɪ'grɛč] . . . Rare.

‡**beg-take** v phr

To receive something without paying for it.

1942 (1971) Campbell *Cloud-Walking* 150 seKY, Lize was packing two jugs of buttermilk in her saddle bags to trade for papers, not wanting to beg-take nothing.

behavishness n

Bad behavior.

1928 Peterkin *Scarlet Sister Mary* 286 SC [Gullah], You got to stop dis behavishness or I'm gwine to tell evybody on you.

behind prep Pronc-spp *behin(e), behint, b'hin';* **chiefly Sth, among Black speakers,** also *behime*

A Forms.

1895 (1969) Crane *Red Badge* 2, We're goin' way up the river, cut across, an' come around in behint 'em. **1901** *DN* 2.181 KY [Black], *Behind—b'hin'.* **1905** Culbertson *Banjo Talks* 8 Sth [Black], W'en the moon scrouch down behime de hill. *Ibid* 72, I crope up behime de rock. **1922** Gonzales *Black Border* 140 sSC, GA coasts [Gullah], 'E roll 'up behine'um. *Ibid* 289, *Behime, behin', behine*—behind. **1929** Sale *Tree Named John* 49 MS [Black], Dat's behime us now. **1942** Thomas *Blue Ridge Country* 285 sAppalachians, I'm a-feared of that 'mobile. I'd druther ride behint old Nell in the jolt wagon. **1967** Faulkner *Wishing Tree* 44 MS [Black], That thing jes' jumped behime that tree: I seen him! **1977** in 1982 Barrick *Coll.* sePA, Behint—*behind.* "The sun's went behint that big cloud."

B Senses.

1 Before.

1942 Greene *Papa is All* 105 sePA, Good luck, if I don't see you behind your wedding day.

2 Following, after; in pursuit of. **chiefly Sth**

1965–70 *DARE* (Qu. KK33, . . *"In succession":* "He had a cold, then the measles, then chicken pox _____.") Infs FL48, 52, GA7, 61, 84, LA3, 25, 28, 32, NC76, 79, SC11, 26, One (right) behind (the other, another, each other); SC65, One in behind the other; (Qu. U36, . . *A person who saves in a mean way or is greedy in money matters*) Inf SC26, He's a hawk behind money. [5 of 14 total Infs Black] **1970** Major *Afro-Amer. Slang, Behind:* afterward.

3 Concerning, with regard to, about.

1965 Brown *Manchild* 308 NYC [Black], I was supposed to act as old as he had treated me. One of the things had been to treat the lady like she was just a friend of Dad's and to be cool behind it. *Ibid* 371, "No, that ain't none of her stepfather. That's just her natural daddy, just a doggish old nigger, that's all." I just didn't know what to say behind that.

4 By reason of, because of.

1965 Brown *Manchild* 210 **NYC** [Black], It looked as though he were in pain, as though he were hurt behind leaving so early. *Ibid* 290, You'll never want to leave there, and behind some of this good cocaine, you might decide to stop workin' altogether. **1968** *DARE* FW Addit **PA**172 [Black], Behind them tearing up the street, we couldn't drive to his house.

behind adj Pronc-sp *behime*

Hind, back.

1916 *Scribner's Mag.* 59.356/1 **VA** [Black], Ef dis here house was ter git up on its behime-legs. **1934** Carmer *Stars Fell on AL* 182 [Black], Brer B'ar he lif' Brer Fox by de behime legs.

behind a dime adv phr Also *behind a broomstraw, ~ knife, ~ pin* For addit varr, see quot **chiefly Sth, S Midl, esp Mid Atl See Map** *chiefly among Black speakers*

At all, in the least.

1965–70 *DARE* (Qu. V2b, *About a deceiving person, or somebody that you can't trust, you might say: "I wouldn't trust him _____."*) Infs **DC**12, **MS**88, **NC**6, 24, 87, **SC**68, 69, **VA**39, 70, Behind a (thin) dime; **MA**124, **SC**26, Behind a dime edgeways (*or* turned edgewise); **PA**202, The other side of a dime (*or* nickel); **KY**94, **MO**8, 29, **VA**35, 39, 42, Behind a (*or* the) broomstraw; **MS**16, **PA**248, **TN**24, 53, Behind a (*or* the) straw; **VA**73, Around a broomstraw; **FL**2, Behind a knife, and it turned sideways; **NY**55, Behind a pin; **NC**11, Behind a hat pin; **NY**61, Behind a needle; **DC**4, Behind a corkscrew; **NC**24, Behind a dust of flour. [20 of 27 total Infs Black]

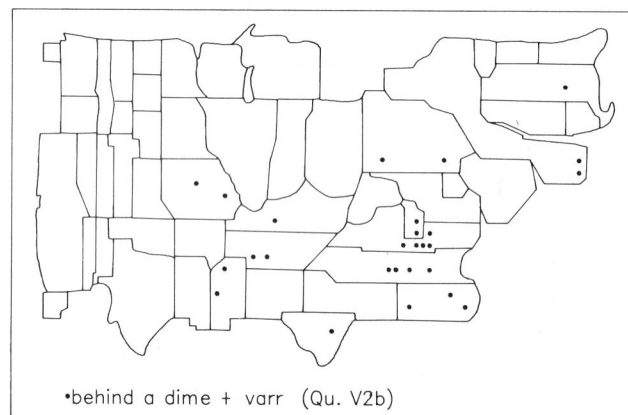

•behind a dime + varr (Qu. V2b)

behindest adj, n Pronc-sp *behin'est* [*behind* slow + *-est* superl]

1952 Brown *NC Folkl.* 1.519, *Behin'est:* adj. Behindest; the one behind, late: sometimes used as a noun. "He's the behin'est one in the field."— Occasional.

behind of prep phr Cf *of* prep

Behind.

1967–70 *DARE* (Qu. MM8, *A bad housekeeper sweeps the dirt either under the rug or_____ the door*) Infs **AZ**12, **TX**28, 81, 104, Behind of.

behind the lighter adj phr [*lighter* a barge used to transfer cargo from ship to shore]

=astern the lighter.

1929 *AmSp* 5.119 **ME**, A late man was "always behind the lighter."

behine, behint See **behind** prep

behinten n [Ger *Hintern* buttocks, perh infl by *behind*]

The buttocks.

1950 *WELS* (*Joking words for the part of the body that you sit on*) 1 Inf, **ceWI**, Behinten [Inf of German background]. **1968** *DARE* (Qu. X35, *. . "He slipped and came down hard on his _____."*) Inf **WI**47, Behinten [bi'hɪntn̩].

beholden adj Also (perh by hypercorrection) *beholdin(g)* now **chiefly Sth, S Midl**

Obliged, indebted.

1835 Kennedy *Horse Shoe Robinson* 2.222 (*DAE*), I am much beholden to your lordship's generosity. **1887** Cooke *Happy Dodd* 203 **NEng**,

I'm a livin' woman this day, beholden to nobody. **1903** *DN* 2.295 **Cape Cod MA**, Beholden. **1907** *DN* 3.205 **nwAR**. **1927** *DN* 5.472 **Ozarks.** **1937** (1963) Hyatt *Kiverlid* 10 **KY**, They live on what they have and are "beholdin'" to no man. **1938** Rawlings *Yearling* 300 **FL**, I'll be beholden to you to look out for my share and do my tradin' for me. **1946** *PADS* 5.11 **VA**, Beholden. **1958** Humphrey *Home from the Hill* 14 **TX**, They make a man feel beholden. **1959** *VT Hist.* ns 27.125, Beholden . . . Under obligation . . . Old fashioned. Occasional. Chittenden. c**1960** Wilson *Coll.* **csKY**, Beholding to—Indebted to, under obligation to. **1965–70** *DARE* (Qu. II38, *To be indebted to somebody for a favor or kindness [not money]: "I'm very much _____ to him";* total Infs questioned, 75) Infs **GA**1, **MS**6, 30, 37, 49, 71, Beholden; (Qu. II39, *. . Other ways . . of saying "thank you"*) Infs **FL**48, **GA**73, I'm beholden (to you).

behoodle v [Prob alter of **ferhoodle**]

To annoy, harass.

1967 *DARE* (Qu. GG13a, *When something keeps bothering a person and makes him nervous . . "It _____ me."*) Inf **PA**24, [ˌbi'hudəlz].

beignet n Also sp *baignet, beigné;* pronc-sp *bang* [Fr] **sLA**

A fritter or doughnut.

1835 Irving *Crayon Misc.* 1.251, We . . supped heartily upon stewed buffalo meat, roasted venison, beignets, or fritters of flour fried in bear's lard, and tea made of a species of the golden rod. **1941** McDermott *Gloss. Missip. Valley French* 22 (as of 1673–1850), *Beigne* . . . A fried cake, a kind of doughnut . . . Sometimes written *beigné, beignet,* and, by Americans, *bang.* **1962** Atwood *Vocab.* TX 63 **sLA**, Doughnut . . . Some five informants of German-speaking background use *krebbel,* while a few of French origin in southern Louisiana give *baignet.* **1967** LeCompte *Word Atlas* 297 **seLA**, Fried bread dough . . . beignets. **1968** *DARE* FW Addit **LA**23, Beignet ['bɪn,jeɪ]— means doughnut.

beijo See **byo** n[1]

being conj **chiefly Sth, S Midl, NEng**

1 also with *as* or *that*: Because, since.

1658 in 1856 **RI** (Colony) *Records* 1.396, The collonies . . seeme to be ofended with us, beinge the sayd people [=Quakers] have theire liberty amongst us. *Ibid* 398, And beinge a barrill of furrs was returned in that shippe . . the collony hath taken order for the recruitinge of that loss. **1707** in 1836 Archdale *New Descr.* 2.94 **SC**, It is a Pity they should be farther thined with Civil Quarrels, being their Service is in all Respects so necessary. **1879** (1880) Tourgée *Fool's Errand* 44 **Sth**, I thought it would be no more than neighborly, being as you were strangers as I may say. **1892** *DN* 1.229 **KY**, *Bein' as* [bins]. "Bein's it's you, I will take a dollar for it." [*DN* note:] Also in New England; but the pronunciation is *binz* . . . In Michigan *bɪən əz.* **1905** *DN* 3.3 **cCT**. *Ibid* 69 **nwAR**, *Bein's* [binz], *adv. conj.* Because . . . Common among the uneducated. **1907** *DN* 3.209 **nwAR**, *cCT*, Because—usually *bein' 's* (*being as*). **1908** *DN* 3.290 **eAL, wGA**. **1942** Faulkner *Go Down* 125 **MS**, "I'll tote her," George said. "Bein as she's Nat's." **1944** *PADS* 2.26 **wNC, cwOH**, Being I can't go with him, I won't wait. **1946** *PADS* 6.5 **eNC, swVA**, *Being; being that* . . . Since. **1952** Brown *NC Folkl.* 1.519, *Being (as)* . . . Since, because . . . General. Illiterate. **1966–68** *DARE* FW Addit **ceME**, "Bein' as you're here" means since you are here; **IA**29, Being as how you're ready, let's go.

2 If. *obs*

1845 Judd *Margaret* 141 **NEng**, I got two of um, and should have got the rest bein Dr. Spoor hadn't a come in.

beint See **be** C1a

beisich adj [Ger *beissig* biting, pungent] *PaGer*

1939 Aurand *Quaint Idioms* 22 **sePA**, Gosh, that stuff's *beisich* (bitter, pungent).

bekase See **because** conj

belated ppl adj [*OED* 1670 →] *arch*

1899 (1912) Green *VA Folk-Speech, Belated* . . . Hindered; behind the time. "Hurry up, don't be *belated.*"

belay v, usu imper [*OED* "Sailor's slang," 1796 →; ult from OE *be-* + *lecgan* to lay] **chiefly NEast coast**

To stop, wait; to cancel, disregard.

1931–33 *LANE Worksheets* **neMA**, Belay there. Wait. "Belay there a minute." Used by sailor. **1942** Berrey–Van den Bark *Amer. Slang* 11.6, *Stop; cease.* Belay, break off. *Ibid* 11.10, *Interj . . . Cease!, Stop!* Avast!, belay that *or* there! *Ibid* 141.5, *Interj* . . . *Silence!; Be quiet!* . . Belay that! *or* there! **1942** ME Univ. *Studies* 56.15, To make fast halyards, clewlines, etc., without tying a knot was to *belay* which was used only as a command. [Footnote to *belay:*] Stop, discontinue, especially talking. **1945** Colcord *Sea Language* 33 **NEast coast,** "Belay your jaw!" means "Shut up!" *Ibid* 145, "I thought I heard our chief mate say, 'Give one more pull and then belay.' " **1948** *Western Folkl.* 7.72 [U.S. Naval Academy], Belay that: Disregard the last order.

belcher-squelcher n [Fanciful allusion to the bird's booming cry; cf **thunder pumper**]
=**bittern.**
    1955 *MA Audubon* 39.313, *American bittern* . . . Belcher-squelcher (Mass.).

belduque n Pronc-spp *berduque, verduque* [AmSpan] **TX** *old-fash*
See quot 1892.
    1838 Texian *Mexico v. Texas* 218 *(DA),* Away went the quarteroon, armed with a large knife, or *beldúque,* to dig up the roots. **1892** *DN* 1.188 **TX,** *Beldúque* (or Spanish *verdúgo*): a sheath knife, smaller than the *machete* and larger than the *cuchillo* . . . The forms used in Texas and Mexico are *verduque, berduque, belduque.* This word is in very common use in Western Texas. **1894** *Scribner's Mag.* 15.606/2 **TX,** The smuggler . . . quickly drew his terrible "belduque," and slashing right and left he made his escape.

belge See **bulge** A

Belgian adj Also *Belgium* **NY, esp NYC**
Denoting a type of paving stone with a rectangular surface.
    1855 *NY Herald* (NY) 26 Dec 6/4, In addition, the small cobble stone is used to some extent, and the small square stone, or Belgian pavement—as it is here called—in many of the chief thoroughfares. **1897** Haswell *Reminiscences* 273 **NYC,** It was about this year [=1832–33] that the first block, or Belgian, pavement was laid in a street of this city or country. **1904** *Brooklyn D. Eagle* 5 June *(DA),* It ought also to be possible to leave well-defined routes of belgian blocks over which heavy loads may be drawn to every part of the city. **1966–69** *DARE* (Qu. N23, . . *Kinds of paved roads*) Infs **NY34,** 76, Belgium block.

belhack See **ballyhack** n

belike adv [*be-* + *like* adj; *OED* 1533 →] **?Sth**
Perhaps.
    1932 Faulkner *Light in August* 154 **MS,** You gave it to your foster-mother to keep for you, belike? **1938** Matschat *Suwannee R.* 62 **nFL, sGA,** Belike Manthy'll be clean bereft, we-uns havin' stayed so long on our ventures. *Ibid* 122, Belike come cane grindin', ye-all will have invites to Cella's pledge-troth to Pompano.

belike v [*be-* + *like* v; *OED* 1557 →] *arch*
To like, be pleased with; hence ppl adj *beliked.*
    1843 (1916) Hall *New Purchase* 147 **IN,** I do believe me and Nancy was beliked by them. **1899** (1912) Green *VA Folk-Speech,* Beliked . . . Liked; beloved. "Much beliked."

belix n
=**blixen.**
    1955 *AmSp* 30.233 **cIN,** *Belix.* In similes: cold, or hot, as belix—a coined word not seen in dictionaries.

bell n See **bell pepper**

bell v[1], hence vbl n *belling* [OE *bellan* to roar, bark, bellow]
Of a dog: to bay.
    1942 Faulkner *Go Down* 176 **MS,** After a while they would hear the dogs. Sometimes the chase would sweep up and past quite close, belling and invisible. **1951** Giles *Harbin's Ridge* 56 **eKY,** There was something about the stilly night, and the belling of the hounds . . that excited and quickened him.

bell v[2] [See quot] Cf **belling** vbl n[2]
    1952 Brown *NC Folkl.* 1.238, The first night in their home they are "belled." A large crowd of friends get together and have bells, tin pans, guns—in fact, anything that will make a noise—and then proceed after dark to the house. Quite often the crowd is invited in by the bride and groom, and games are played. I have helped with a number of "bellings" myself.

bell a buzzard v phr Also *bell a bull* (or *buzzer, cat, cow, goose*) [*bell* to attach a bell to] **chiefly Mid and S Atl** See Map

To do the most rudimentary task.
    1965–70 *DARE* (Qu. JJ15a, *Sayings about a person who seems to you very stupid: "He hasn't enough sense to _____."*) 39 Infs, **chiefly Mid and S Atl,** Bell a buzzard; **FL33, VA51,** Bell a bull; **VA65,** 102, Bell a buzzer; **FL26, GA7,** Bell a cow; **NC7,** 84, Bell a (*or* the) cat; **FL31,** Bell a goose.

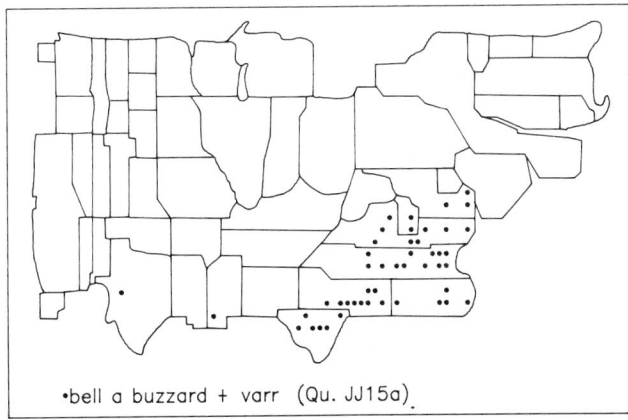

•bell a buzzard + varr (Qu. JJ15a)

bellbind n [*bell* in ref to the shape of the flower + *bind*]
Either of two **bindweeds:** *Convolvulus arvensis* or *C. sepium.*
    1900 Lyons *Plant Names* 115, *C[onvolvulus] arvensis* . . Bell-bind . . . *C. Sepium* . . Bell-bind. **1949** Moldenke *Amer. Wild Flowers* 270, It [*Convolvulus arvensis*] possesses scores of common names including such picturesque ones as . . *bellbind.* **1973** Hitchcock–Cronquist *Flora Pacific NW* 364, Bell-bind . . *C[onvolvulus] sepium.*

bell bird n
1 =**wood thrush 1.**
    1917 *DN* 4.388 **neOH,** Bell-bird . . . Wood thrush. **1917** (1923) *Birds Amer.* 3.226, Wood Thrush . . . Other Names . . . Bell Bird; Swamp Robin. **1968** *DARE* (Qu. Q14, *Other names around here for* . . *thrush*) Inf **NY106,** Bell bird; vesper bird.
2 =**hermit thrush.**
    1956 *MA Audubon* 40.128, Hermit Thrush . . . Bell Bird (Maine. In allusion to its ringing song.). **1970** *DARE* (Qu. Q14) Inf **PA242,** Hermit thrush: bell bird.

bell bonnet n [From the shape]
    1970 *DARE* (Qu. W2, . . *A cloth bonnet worn by women for protection from the sun*) Inf **TX106,** Bell bonnet—old-fashioned.

bell cow n Also *bell ox*
1 A cow or ox wearing a bell and serving as the leader of a herd. **esp Sth, S Midl**
    c1860 (1927) Hancock *Narrative* 3 **Ozarks,** The Indians finding it impossible to get near this "bell cow" endeavored to kill her. **1878** (1887) Jackson *Bits of Travel* 313 **MA,** It is the faint and distant tinkle of the bell-cow's bell. **1905** Watson *Bethany* 20 **GA,** I hear the "toll, tolang, toll, tolong," of the bell-cow down in the meadow by the creek. **1952** [see **2** below]. **c1960** *Wilson Coll.* **csKY,** Bell-cow—One that wore the bell and thus led the herd. Old Brindle, our bell-cow. **1967–70** *DARE* (Qu. K18) Inf **VA40,** Bell cow—leader; old-fash; (QR, near Qu. K18) Inf **AL29,** Bell cow—leader who wears the bell in a group of cows. **1969** [see **2** below]. **1982** *Barrick Coll.* **sePA,** Bell cow—lead cow (wearing a cowbell).
2 Transf: a leader; a big shot.
    1896 (1898) Ade *Artie* 103 **Chicago IL,** If you can't travel with the bell-cow, why stick to the gang? **1947** *Sun* (Baltimore MD) 9 Aug 8/4 *(Hench Coll.),* Phil Marchildon, bell cow of a mound corps rated one of the best in the American League, joined the conversation. **1952** Brown *NC Folkl.* 1.519 **wNC,** Bell-cow . . . The lead cow of a herd, the one that wears the bell; figuratively a leader. **1966** *DARE* (Qu. HH17, *A person who tries to appear important, or who tries to lay down the law in his community: "He'd like to be the _____ around here."*) Inf **MS71,** Bell cow. **1969** Sorden *Lumberjack Lingo* **NEng, Gt Lakes,** Bell ox—Foreman. A nickname given to the camp foreman because he was to the crew what the leader or bell ox was to the herd when it was turned out to pasture.

belled snake See **belltail**

beller See **bellow**

bellerses See **bellows**

Bellesnoggle See **Belsnickel**

bell ewe See **bell sheep 1**

bellflower n [From the shape]
Std: a plant of the family Campanulaceæ. Also called **bluebell, harebell**

bell frog n Also *cowbell frog*
A **tree frog** (here: *Hyla cinerea*).
[**1688** in 1846 Force *Tracts* 3.12.38 **VA,** Another small sort of Frog, . . makes a Noise like Pack-horse Bells all the Spring long.] **1791** (1958) Bartram *Travels* 277, The bell frog, so called because their [sic] voice is fancied to be exactly like the sound of a loud cow bell. **1942** A.A. & A.H. Wright *Handbook of Frogs* 136 *(DA),* Bell Frog . . . Cow-bell Frog . . . The voice is loud and at a distance sounds like a cow-bell. The individual call is quonk, quonk. **1958** Conant *Reptiles & Amphibians* 279, Green Treefrog . . . Voice: Bell-like, and the origin of the local names of "bell-frog" and "cowbell frog."

bell horse n Also *bell mare, ~ mule* **chiefly West**
A horse or mule wearing a bell and usu serving as leader of a pack train or herd.
1775 Adair *Amer. Indians* 337 **Gulf States,** But they used an artful strategem, . . for they stole one of the bell horses. **1844** (1954) Gregg *Commerce* 129 **NM,** The mules at night . . are all turned loose without tether or hopple, with the *mulera* or bell-mare, to prevent them from straying abroad . . . It is the office of the *madre* . . to lead the mulera ahead, during the journey, after which the whole pack follows in orderly procession. **1853** in 1930 Brewerton *Overland* 41 **CA,** The wily Californians . . . are in the habit of employing a steady old white mare . . . to act as a kind of mother and guide to each drove of unruly mules. This animal is sometimes called the "bell-mare" from a large bell which they attach to her neck. **1859** Marcy *Prairie Traveler* 70 **West,** As soon as it is discovered that the animals [=horses and mules] have taken fright, the herdsmen should use their utmost endeavors to turn them in the direction of the camp, and this can generally be accomplished by riding the bell mare in front of the herd and gradually turning her toward it. **1922** *Outing* 82.124/3 **eCA,** Old Mose, the Bell-mule. **1959** Martin *Gunbarrel* 36 **WY** (as of 1920s), "A bell horse. What's that?" I interrupt. "We strap bells around the necks of the horses that stray away from the herd so they can be traced by the jingle." **1970** *DARE* Tape **CA201,** They had big long pack trains of horses to carry the groceries up to these camp tents . . . they'd pack a couple of hundred horses . . and they'd have one called the bell mare that they'd lead out, and all the rest of the mules and horses would follow her. **1973** Allen *LAUM* 1.408 **swSD,** Bell horse. In a string or cavy, the most amenable horse, belled, and used to guide the cavy when on the move.

bell house n
See quot c1960.
1839 in 1934 Frear *Lowell & Abigail* 137 **MA,** Our meeting house is nearly finished . . . Bell house is up and the bell hung. **c1960** Wilson *Coll.* **csKY,** Bell-house . . . The small house on a church or school roof in which the large bell is housed, a belfry. **1969** *DARE* (Qu. CC1, *On a church building . . the part that sticks up high*) Inf **KY40,** Bell house.

belling vbl n[1] See **bell v[1]**

belling vbl n[2], also attrib [**bell v[2]**] **now chiefly wPA, WV, OH, IN, MI** See Map
A noisy celebration or mock serenade for newlyweds; a **shivaree.**
1862 G.W. Wilder *MS Diary* 18 July *(DA),* E. thought we would probably get a belling. **1878** *Dly. State Jrnl.* (Lincoln, Neb.) 1 Jan. 1/3 *(DA),* A number of uninvited guests gave the couple a belling. **1896** *DN* 1.412 **nNY, nOH. 1942** McAtee *Dial. Grant Co.* **IN NY, OH,** *Bellin'* . . doubtless from the lavish use of cow-bells. **1946** *PADS* 5.11 **VA,** *Belling:* Serenade after a wedding; in the northern part of the Blue Ridge and the central part of the Piedmont. **1949** Kurath *Word Geog.* 79, *Belling* [is used] in large parts of the Midland . . . Pennsylvania is doubtless the original home of *belling* in the New World. **1949** (1958) Stuart *Thread* 78 **cKY,** I went with my pupils, their parents, and neighbors . . to the belling of the bride when there was a wedding. **1960** *PADS* 34.58 **CO,** Older Folk Speech . . . belling 'chivaree'. **1965–70** *DARE* (Qu. AA18, . . *A noisy celebration after a wedding, where the married couple is expected to give a treat*) 63 Infs, **chiefly wPA, WV, OH, IN, MI,** Belling; **NC62,** Belling bee — newlyweds are serenaded to annoy

them; **WV10,** Belling party. **1966** *DARE* File **WV,** A "bellin' " or a "shivaree" was a noisy serenade given a newly married couple. Bells, shotguns or any noise-making device was used. One device was a circular saw, hung from a fence rail and carried by 2 men. The noise was made by beating the saw with a hammer. **1971** Wood *Vocab. Change* 39 **Sth,** The local custom of greeting newly wedded persons with a noisy mock celebration . . . [12 infs:] *Belling.* [1 inf:] *Belling bee.*

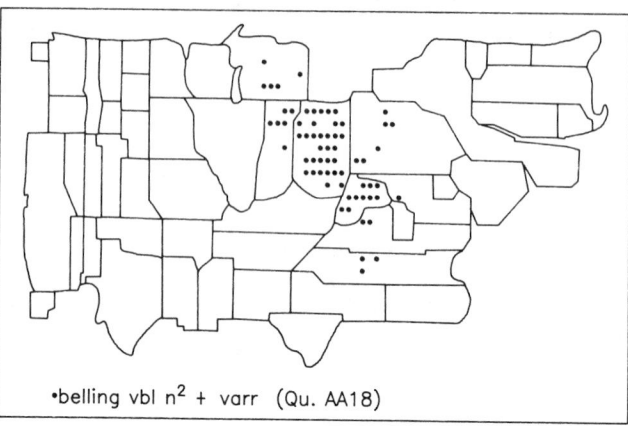

•belling vbl n[2] + varr (Qu. AA18)

bellity-bump n, adv Also *bellity bumper*
=**belly-flop 1.**
1943 *LANE* Map 576, 1 inf, **ceMA,** [bɪˑlɪ tɪbʌˑmp]; 1 inf, **nME,** [bɛlɪ tɪbʌnt]; 1 inf, **cwVT,** [bɛɬɚ tɪˑbʌnt]. **1973** Allen *LAUM* 1.391 **ceIA,** The act of a boy's throwing himself face down as he starts to coast downhill on a sled . . . bellity bumper [1 inf].

bellity-split adv [Cf *belly-* as in **belly-buster,** and *split* as in *lickety-split*]
At top speed.
1935 Davis *Honey* 284 **OR,** The dogs cocked their tails and went whooping across it bellity-split.

bell mare, bell mule See **bell horse**

bellnose (pepper) See **bullnose pepper**

bellow n, v Usu |'bɛlɚ|; also |'bɛlo, 'bɛlə|; occas |'bælo, 'bælɚ| Pronc-spp *beller, belluh* **widespread, but least freq in Midl** See Map and Map Section Cf **bawl v[1] 2**
The sound a cow or calf makes, esp when distressed; to make such a sound.
1939 *LANE* Map 194 **throughout NEng,** The map shows the verbs *moo (mew),* . . *bellow* . . used to designate the sound made by a cow . . . [Usu [bɛlo, bɛlə], occas [bɛlr].] **1949** Kurath *Word Geog.* 62, For the loud noise cows make, especially when their calves are taken from them, New England says *bellow, beller,* the Midland *bawl.* **1960** *PADS* 34.70 **CO,** The probable importation of Northern terms along the South Platte is amply illustrated by the spread of the expressions *Dutch cheese,* . . and *bellow, beller.* **c1960** Wilson *Coll.* **csKY,** Bellow /'bɛlə/: v. and n. To give the sound of a bull or, rarely, of a cow, esp. when she smells blood and "bellers." **1965–70** *DARE* (Qu. K19, *Noise made by a calf that's taken away from its mother*) 91 Infs, **widespread but least freq in Midl,** Beller; 11 Infs, **scattered but esp Nth,** Bellow; **MN3,** Bellowing; **WA18,**

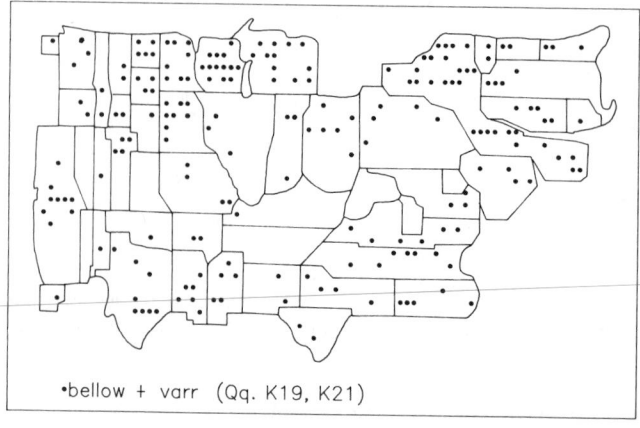

•bellow + varr (Qq. K19, K21)

['bælo]; (Qu. K21, *The noise a cow makes, calling for her calf*) 111 Infs, **widespread but least freq in Midl**, Beller; 7 Infs, **esp Nth**, Bellering; 22 Infs, **esp Nth**, Bellow; **MN**3, **OH**44, **WI**66, Bellowing; **WA**18, ['bælo]. **1973** Allen *LAUM* 1.251, *Bawl* (of a calf being weaned) . . . *Bawl* . . has spread widely in the U[pper] M[idwest], where it competes on even terms with *bellow/beller* in Minnesota and North Dakota . . . *Bellow* and *beller*, of New England origin, exhibit a slight Northern orientation . . . *Beller:* Pronounced /bælⱶ/ [by 2 infs]. *Ibid* 252, *Low* (during feeding time) . . . Both *bawl* and the Northern-oriented *bellow* and *beller* are less favored by younger speakers than is the Northern and North Midland *moo*.

bellows n, v Usu |'bɛloz|; also, **esp in Sth, S Midl**, |'bɛləs| Pronc-sp *bellus*
A Forms.
1 Pronc varr.
    1908 *DN* 3.290 **eAL, wGA**, *Bellows* . . . Pronounced *bellus.* **1922** Gonzales *Black Border* 289 **sSC**, **GA coast** [Gullah glossary], *Bellus*— bellows (blacksmith's). **c1960** *Wilson Coll.* **csKY**, *Bellows* /'bɛləs/ common. **1967** *DARE* FW Addit **nwWA**, Bellows ['bɛləs]—heard in conversation.
    2 Pl: usu *bellows;* also, **esp S Midl (formerly also NEng)**, *bellowses.* Pronc-spp *bellerses, bellowsis, bellus(s)es* Cf **-es 2**
    1805 (1905) Whitehouse *Jrl.* 99 **KY**, We put in the carsh [=cache] or hole . . the bellowses & tools augur plains Saw &c. **1848** Lowell *Biglow* 143 "Upcountry" **MA**, Bellowses, *lungs.* **1861** Holmes *Venner* 152 **MA**, We blowed with the belluses . . but nothin' could make that fire burn. **1867** Lowell *Biglow* 60 "Upcountry" **MA**, I ha'n't no patience with sech swellin' fellers ez / Think God can't forge 'thout them to blow the bellerses. **1871** (1882) Stowe *Fireside Stories* 234 **NEng**, Come to drive him as a body wants to drive, why, he [=horse] blows like my bellowsis. **1897** [see **B** below]. **1899** (1912) Green *VA Folk-Speech*, *Bellowses* . . . For *bellows.* **1942** Hall *Smoky Mt. Speech* 82 **wNC, eTN**, *Belluses* . . ['bɛləsəz]. **c1960** *Wilson Coll.* **csKY**, *Bellows* . . /'bɛləsɪz/, rare.
B As noun.
Shortness of breath—used in ref to a horse. [Transf from *bellows* lungs (*OED* 1615 →)]
    1897 Barrère–Leland *Slang* 1.98/2, *Bellows, bellowses* (American), the heaves in a horse. ["]And when old Tom Jefferson sent for me to go to Washington, I was still here with fifteen children and as a good a hoss as any man ever sid, only she was blind and had the *bellusses*["]—*Uncle Steve's Stump Speech.* **1968** *DARE* (Qu. K40, *The sound that a horse makes*) Inf **NC**49, Bellows [bɛləs]—breath's heavy; (Qu. K48, *When a horse is short of breath, you say it's _____*) Inf **SC**57, Got the bellows.
C As verb.
To become winded or short of breath; to be tired or exhausted— used esp of a horse; hence ppl adj *bellowsed.* Pronc-sp *bellust* [Engl dial] **chiefly S Atl, Gulf States** See Map
    1898 Lloyd *Country Life* 88 **AL**, A third-class farmer, and a bellused and broke down politician. **1908** *DN* 3.290 **eAL, wGA**, *Bellows, v.i.* and *tr.* To become or cause to become winded: said of a horse. Pronounced *bellus, bellust*, etc. **1954** *PADS* 21.20 **SC**, *Bellowsed* . . . Affected with the heaves, said of a horse. **1965–70** *DARE* (Qu. K48, *When a horse is short of breath, you say it's _____*) 25 Infs, **chiefly S Atl**, Bellowsed; **GA**1, Bellust; **GA**9, Bellust ['bɛləst]. **1966–68** *DARE* FW Addit **SC**, Bellowed [bɛləst]—when a horse gets too winded and has trouble

breathing; **GA**22, "I'm bellowsed" ['bɛləst] meaning "I'm tired." Heard in conversation.

bellows fish n
1 A **snipefish** (here: *Macrorhamphosus scolopax*). [*OED* 1684 →]
    1882 U.S. Natl. Museum *Bulletin* 16.388, *C. scolopax* . . . Snipe-fish; Trumpet-fish; Bellows-fish. **1896** U.S. Natl. Museum *Bulletin* 47.759, *Macrorhamphosus scolopax* . . . Bellows-fish . . . North Atlantic Coast. **1911** [see **2** below].
2 A fish of the family Tetraodontidae. See also **puffer**
    1807 in 1846 MA Hist. Soc. *Coll.* 2d ser 3.55, The puff fish, or swell fish, or bellows fish, is a cartilaginous fish. It is seven inches long; and . . its proportions are those of a sculpion nearly. **1911** *Century Dict.*, *Bellows-fish* . . . 1. A local name of the trumpet-fish, *Macrorhamphosus scolopax.*—2. A name of sundry plectognath fishes, of the . . family *Tetrodontidae* [sic].—3. A local name in Rhode Island of the angler, *Lophius piscatorius.*
3 =**goosefish.**
    1814 in 1825 Lit. & Philos. Soc. NY *Trans.* 465, *Bellows-fish,* or common *Angler. Ibid* 466, He is called by some the *bellows-fish,* from some resemblance his figure bears to a bellows, and from a power to inflate or swell himself immediately after being taken out of water. **1842** DeKay *Zool. NY* 3.163, Its monstrous form has given rise to many popular names, such as . . *Bellows-fish, Angler, Goose-fish, Monk-fish.* **1905** (1906) NJ State Museum *Annual Rept.* 425, Bellows Fish . . . This large fish is abundant on our coast. **1933** LA Dept. of Conserv. *Fishes* 294, References to its lack of beauty are expressed in such popular names for it as Bellowsfish and Allmouth.

bell ox See **bell cow**

bell pepper n Rarely **bell** **widespread, but chiefly Sth, S Midl, West** See Map Cf **green pepper 1**
A large sweet pepper.
    1876 Hobbs *Bot. Hdbk.* 10, Bell pepper, Capsicum grossum. **1941** O'Donnell *Great Big Doorstep* 72 **LA**, I'd show you how to set out tomato plants growed in a tray . . , and lovely bell peppers. Them bell peppers is only the thing to stuff and bake on a Sunday. **1965–70** *DARE* (Qu. 122d, . . *Peppers—large sweet*) 328 Infs, **widespread but chiefly Sth, S Midl, West**, Bell peppers; **FL**19, Bells; **OK**32, Red bell peppers; **NC**18, Sweet bell peppers.

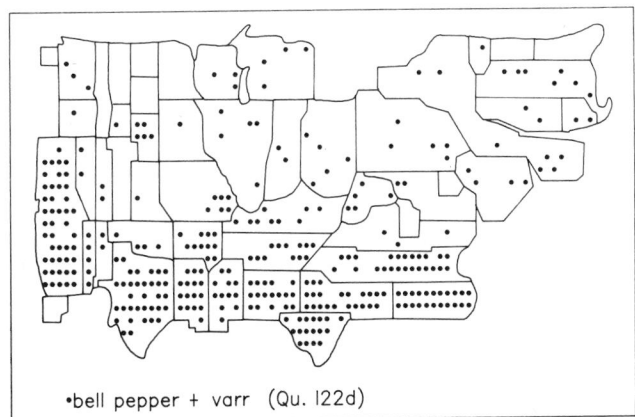

•bell pepper + varr (Qu. 122d)

Bellschnickel See **Belsnickel**

bell sharp adj phr [*bell* abbr of **bell horse** + *sharp* specially attentive]
    1968 Adams *Western Words, Bell sharp*—Said of a mule that becomes especially attached to the *bell horse.*

bell sheep n
1 also *bell ewe:* A sheep wearing a bell and serving as the lead animal of a flock; a bellwether.
    1939 *LANE* Map 200 **sRI**, Terms for a castrated male sheep were incidentally recorded in a few cases . . *bell sheep* [1 inf]. **1973** Allen *LAUM* 1.407 **Upper MW**, The male sheep that leads a flock, usually with a bell on his neck, is known by historical *bellwether* in all five states. *Bell sheep,* perhaps an Americanism, is found principally in Iowa and Nebraska . . . One South Dakota inf. reports that a female sheep used as a flock leader is the *bell ewe.*

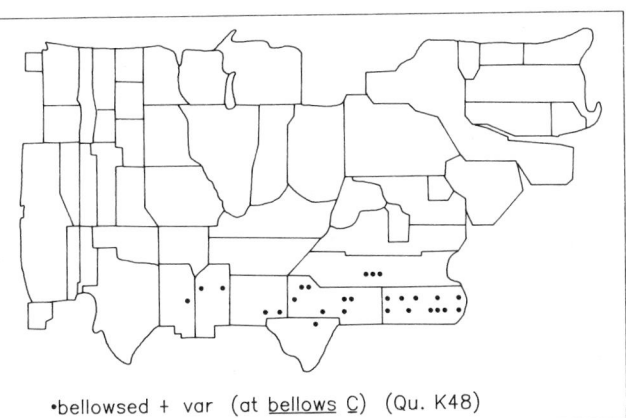

•bellowsed + var (at bellows C) (Qu. K48)

2 Transf: a leader; a big shot.

1969 *DARE* (Qu. HH17, *A person who tries to appear important, or who tries to lay down the law in his community: "He'd like to be the ——— around here."*) Infs **KY**19, **MO**39, Bell sheep.

Bellsnickel, Bellsnickle See **Belsnickel**

bells, wear the v phr Cf **caps and bells, play**

To act the fool.

1931 Hannum *Thursday April* 225 **WV Mts,** You cain't fault me jest 'cause Joe in his old age tuk the notion to wear the bells.

belltail n Also *belled snake*

A rattlesnake.

1917 *DN* 4.408 **wNC,** Bell-tail . . . Rattlesnake. **1968** Adams *Western Words,* Belled snake—A rattle snake.

bell-tongue coot n

=**white-winged scoter.**

1888 Trumbull *Names of Birds* 99, Oidemia deglandi . . . In Connecticut at Milford (to the older gunners) Bell-Tongue Coot. **1917** (1923) *Birds Amer.* 1.150, White-winged scoter—Oidemia deglandi . . Other Names . . . Bell-tongue Coot.

belltree n Also *bellwood* [From the bell-shaped flowers]

=**silverbell.**

1897 Sudworth *Arborescent Flora* 323, M[ohrodendron] carolinum . . Syn.—Halesia Carolina . . Common Names . . . Bell-tree (Tenn.). **1900** Lyons *Plant Names* 250, Bell tree. **1950** Peattie *Nat. Hist. Trees* 545, Halesia carolina . . Other Names: Belltree. Bellwood. **1960** Vines *Trees SW* 842, Bell-tree.

belluh See **bellow**

bellus(t) See **bellows**

bellwort n

A plant of the genus *Uvularia* with bell-shaped yellow flowers. Also called **hay-bells, merrybells, strawflower, wild oats.** For other names of var spp see **cornflower 4, Mohawk weed, straw bell, strawlily, yellow bells**

1784 in 1785 Amer. Acad. Arts & Sci. *Memoirs* 1.434, Uvularia, . . Bellwort. Sweet-smelling Solomon's Seal. Jacob's *Ladder.* **1830** Rafinesque *Med. Flora* 272, Uvularia . . . Bellwort . . . Shoots edible like Asparagus, roots edible when dry and cooked. **1910** Graves *Flowering Plants* 119 **CT,** Uvularia sessifolia . . . Bellwort. Frequent to common. **1964** Batson *Wild Flowers SC* 31, Bellwort . . . Flowers yellowish or straw-colored, ¾ in. long and drooping . . . Rich woods and bluffs.

bellyache root n [For its use against indigestion]

=**angelica 1a.**

1828 Rafinesque *Med. Flora* 192, Angelica lucida . . Belly-ache root. **1876** Hobbs *Bot. Hdbk.* 10. **1900** Lyons *Plant Names* 35. **1971** Krochmal *Appalachia Med. Plants* 46, Angelica atropurpurea . . Common Names: . . bellyache root.

bellyache weed n Cf **bellyache root, belly weed**

A goldenrod.

1896 Jrl. Amer. Folkl. 9.193, Solidago bicolor . . belly-ache weed, Paris, Me. **1900** Lyons *Plant Names* 350, S[olidago] bicolor . . Belly-acheweed.

belly-bacon n

Bacon from the belly of a hog.

c1770 in 1833 Boucher *Glossary* 1 **MD, VA,** At dinner, let me that best *buck-skin* dish, Broth . . and *belly bacon* see. **1938** Rawlings *Yearling* 274 **nFL,** The meat itself was dressed out into hams and shoulders, side-meat and belly-bacon.

bellyband n **Sth**

A band of cloth wrapped around the abdomen of an infant or a newly delivered mother.

1899 (1912) Green *VA Folk-Speech,* Belly-band . . . An infant's binder. **1931** VA Qrly. Rev. 7.96 **LA** [Black], The twins were naked, save for the flannel "bellybands" about their stomachs to ward off the colic. **1959** Lomax *Rainbow Sign* 90 **AL** [Black], The granny woman washed me and sewed on a bellyband and gave me some catnip tea.

belly-bare adv

=**belly-flop 1.**

1940–41 Cassidy *WI Atlas* **seWI,** Belly-bare—manner of sliding face-down on a sled.

belly-bender n [*belly* + **bender 1**] Cf **bendy-bow** and *DS* B35

1877 Bartlett *Americanisms* 39, Belly-Bender. Floating pieces of ice, or weak ice, which bend under one, as he passes from one cake to another. Boys take great pleasure in this precarious amusement.

belly-bluster See **belly-buster 2**

belly-board adv

=**belly-flop 1.**

1943 *LANE* Map 576 **swNH,** The map shows adverbial expressions recorded in the phrase . . meaning 'to coast down-hill lying prone on the sled' . . . [1 inf:] belly-board, 'very common.'

belly-booster See **belly-buster 1**

belly-bounce n Also *belly-bouncer*

=**belly-flop 1.**

1969–70 *DARE* (Qu. EE25) Inf **MI**118, Belly-bounce; **PA**221, Belly-bouncer.

belly-breaker n

1950 *PADS* 14.74 **FL,** Belly-breakers . . . The large biscuits served by cooks in cow camps.

belly-bumber, belly-bumbo See **belly-bumper 1**

belly-bump n, adv, v

1 =**belly-flop 1.** chiefly **NEng** See Map Cf **belly-bunt 1**

1888 in 1971 Farmer *Americanisms* 51 **?Chicago IL,** Barney had his sled out yesterday, belly-bumping on a little patch of ice and snow. **1890** [see **belly-bunt 1**]. **1912** *DN* 3.566 **cVT,** Belly-bump. **1949** Kurath *Word Geog.* 80, Belly-bump, belly-bumper(s), belly-bumping are characteristic (1) of coastal New England and (2) of Eastern Pennsylvania to the Alleghanies. **1950** *WELS Suppl.,* 1 Inf, **swWI,** Belly-bump—child throws himself on a sled. **c1960** Wilson *Coll.* **csKY,** Belly-bump . . . A sudden falling down on a sled and starting down the hill. **1962** Morison *One Boy's Boston* 34 (as of 1890s), At the top of the hill you . . hurled yourself and sled on the snow, to coast down "belly-bump." **1965–70** *DARE* (Qu. EE25) 22 Infs, chiefly **NEng,** Belly-bump; **MA**82, Belly-bumps. **1971** Wood *Vocab. Change* 292 **Sth,** To coast lying down flat . . [20 infs:] belly bump. **1973** Allen *LAUM* 1.390, Coast lying down . . . *Belly-bump,* found in coastal and northern New England, is offered only by infs. in Minnesota and Dubuque, Iowa.

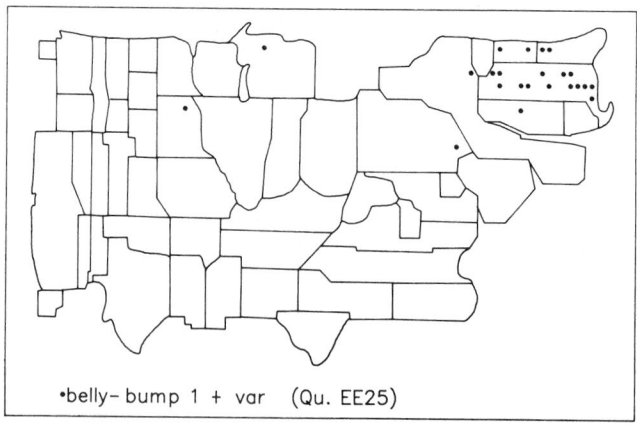

•belly- bump 1 + var   (Qu. EE25)

2 =**belly flop 2.**

1966 *DARE* (Qu. EE29) Inf **MI**24, Belly-bump.

belly-bumper n, adv, v

1 also *belly-bumber,* ~ *bumbo,* ~ *bumpers,* ~ *bumpits,* ~ *bumpo,* ~ *bumpus:* =**belly flop 1.** chiefly **sNEng, PA** See Map

1877 Bartlett *Americanisms,* Belly-Bumbo. A mode of sliding down hills by boys on their sleds, when lying on their bellies. **1912** *DN* 3.566 **sePA, IL,** Belly-bumper. **1912** *DN* 3.571 **wIN,** I'm not afraid to ride down that hill belly-bumper. **1919** *DN* 5.76, In Warren, Mass., about 1890, the term was *belly-bumper* or *belly-flopper.* **1943** *LANE* Map 576 **chiefly sNEng,** [Belly-bumper(s)—occas; belly-bumpits, belly-bumpo, belly-bumpus—rare.] **1950** *WELS* 2 Infs, **WI,** Belly bumper. **1965–70** *DARE* (Qu. EE25) 41 Infs, chiefly **sNEng, PA,** Belly-bumper; **RI**6, Belly-bumber. **1971** Wood *Vocab. Change* 292 **Sth,** To coast lying down flat . . [58 infs:] belly bumper.

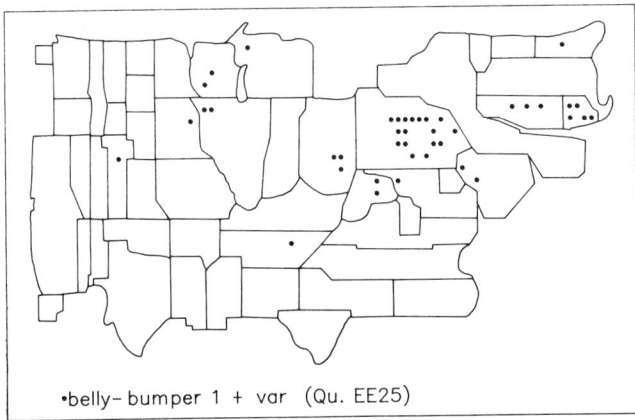

•belly-bumper 1 + var (Qu. EE25)

2 =belly-flop 2.

1868 Channing *Recollections* 33 **RI** (as of late 1790s), The boy who happened to make the "belly-bumper" movement, as it was termed, was ejected from the circle [of divers]. Jumping was not allowed. **1890** *DN* 1.60 **sePA**, *Belly-bumper:* an awkward dive, when the boy, instead of cleaving the water with his hands and head, falls flat on his stomach with a splash. Common in Philadelphia. **1965–70** *DARE* (Qu. EE29) Infs **PA**35, 190, **RI**12, Belly-bumper.

belly-bunk *n, adv* Also *belly-bung* **NEast** Cf **bunk** v[1]
=belly-flop 1.

1866 *Harper's Mag.* 32.355/2 **NYC**, Running at full speed [with the sled], he tumbled "belly-bung" upon it. **1896** *DN* 1.412 **c,swNY**, *Belly-bunk* . . used by boys for coasting on sleds face downwards. **1943** *LANE* Map 576 *(Belly-bump),* 3 infs, **nwVT**, **sME**, Belly-bunk. **1967** *DARE* (Qu. EE25) Inf **MA**50, Belly-bunk.

belly-bunker *v phr*
=belly-flop 1.

1971 Wood *Vocab. Change* 290 **wTN, nMS, sLA, nAR,** To coast lying down flat . . [6 infs:] belly bunker.

belly-bunt *n, adv*

1 =belly-flop 1. esp NEng Cf **belly-bump 1**

1890 *DN* 1.60 **ME, MA,** To coast lying on the stomach . . "to go belly-bump" and "to go belly-bunt." **1910** *DN* 3.452 **seVT,** *Belly-bunt* . . Used very frequently by children. "I'll slide down hill belly-bunt." **1949** Kurath *Word Geog.* 80, *Belly-bunt* predominates in the upper Connecticut Valley, in Worcester County, Massachusetts, and in parts of Maine. **1950** *WELS Suppl.,* 1 Inf, **swWI,** Belly-bunt—child throws himself on a sled; 1 Inf, **csWI** (formerly of Bangor ME), Belly-bunt—coasting on a sled. **1965–70** *DARE* (Qu. EE25) Infs **ME**9, **MA**5, 6, 38, **NH**5, **NY**23, 75, **OH**8, **VT**12, **WI**52, Belly-bunt. **1973** Allen *LAUM* 1.390, Coast lying down . . . Belly-bunt is recorded only as attributed to the local Irish in Winona, Minnesota.

2 =belly-flop 2.

1966 *DARE* (Qu. EE29) Inf **ME**9, Belly-bunt.

belly burglar See **belly robber**

belly-buster *n, adv* Also *belly-bust,* ~ *busting*

1 also *belly-booster:* **=belly-flop 1. chiefly W Midl, Rocky Mts, NW** See Map

1889 (1971) Farmer *Americanisms* 50, *To take a belly-buster* . . to ride down a hill in a sled lying on one's stomach. **1892** *DN* 1.235 **cwMO,** *Belly-buster.* **1906** *DN* 3.126 **nwAR,** *Belly buster, adv. phr.* . . . "I like to coast belly buster." **1912** *DN* 3.571 **wIN,** *Belly-booster.* **1918** *DN* 5.22 **NW,** *Belly-buster* . . . The manner of coasting by lying on the sled on one's belly. Especially by children, but general. **1944** *PADS* 2.53 **nwAR, swNC, nwSC,** Belly-buster. **1949** Kurath *Word Geog.* 80, Adverbial expressions for coasting 'face-down' on a sled . . *belly-bust, belly-buster* occur in the South Midland and in parts of Virginia. **1950** *WELS Suppl.,* 1 Inf, **swWI,** Belly-buster—belly-flop, coasting; 1 Inf, **swWI,** Let's take a belly-buster, let's go belly-buster—sleigh ride on one's tummy; 1 Inf, **seWI,** Belly booster—throwing yourself on a sled. **1965–70** *DARE* (Qu. EE25) 125 Infs, **chiefly W Midl, Rocky Mts, NW,** Belly-buster; **IL**140, **IN**16, 19, **IA**34, **NM**9, **UT**12, **WV**14, **WY**4, Belly-booster; **MO**38, **TN**36, **WA**9, Belly-bust; **CO**14, **MO**36, **OH**77, Belly-busting; (Qu. EE24b) Inf **PA**234, Belly-busting. **1971** Wood *Vocab. Change* 40 **Sth,** When someone . . (during brief periods of snow in the

South) coasts lying down flat . . . The common choices are *belly buster, belly bust, belly booster.* **1973** Allen *LAUM* 1.390, Coast lying down . . . *Belly-buster,* which spread west from Virginia, West Virginia, and southern Ohio, is the expression used by one-half of the Iowa and South Dakota speakers and by three-fourths of those in Nebraska. One rare variant, *belly-bust,* is scattered; another, *belly-booster,* is only in Iowa.

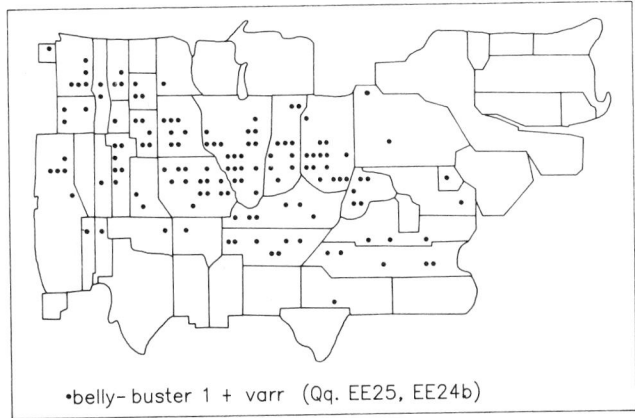

•belly-buster 1 + varr (Qq. EE25, EE24b)

2 also rarely *belly-bluster:* **=belly-flop 2. chiefly Sth, W Midl, Cent** See Map and Map Section

1892 *DN* 1.214 **NC, VA,** Lieutenant H.J. Darnall writes that *belly-buster* is the word he has always heard in this sense [i.e., "an awkward dive, when the boy . . falls flat on his stomach"]. **1899** (1912) Green *VA Folk-Speech* 80, To jump from a height into the water, falling on the belly, is to make a *belly-buster.* **1906** *DN* 3.126 **nwAR,** *Belly-buster.* **1908** *DN* 3.290 **eAL, wGA,** *Belly-buster.* **1954** Harder *Coll.* **cwTN,** Belly-buster—a dive in which the water is hit "flat" with the abdomen. **c1960** Wilson *Coll.* **csKY,** *Belly-buster.* **1965–70** *DARE* (Qu. EE29) 307 Infs, **chiefly Sth, W Midl, West,** Belly-buster; 22 Infs, **scattered Sth, Midl,** Belly-bust; **KS**5, Belly-busting; **SC**5, Belly-bluster. **1971** Wood *Vocab. Change* 40 **Sth,** When someone who is diving hits the water face down . . . It is *belly buster* in three-fourths of the choices or more. *Belly bust* is next.

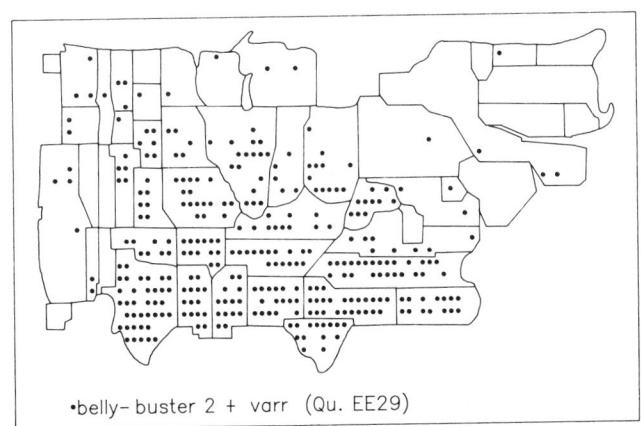

•belly-buster 2 + varr (Qu. EE29)

3 See **buster 6.**

belly-butting *n, adv* Also *belly-butt;* perh by folk-etym, *belly-button* **esp NEng**
=belly-flop 1.

1943 *LANE* Map 576 1 inf, **seMA,** [bɛˑɫɪ bʌˑt]; 1 inf, **sVT,** [bɛlɪ bʌt]; 1 inf, **nME,** [bɛlɪ 'bʌt]; 1 inf, **seMA,** [bɛlɪˑ bʌtn]; 1 inf, **cnMA,** [bɛlɪ bʌtn]. **1965** *PADS* 43.27 **seMA,** *Belly-bump* . . 1 [inf] *belly button.* **1973** Allen *LAUM* 1.391 **swND,** The act of a boy's throwing himself face down as he starts to coast downhill on a sled . . . belly butting [1 inf].

belly-cabump *n, adv* Also *belly-cachunk,* ~ *cahoot* (cf **cahot**), ~ *kabonk,* ~ *kachug,* ~ *kachunk* [*ca-* var of **ker-** + *bump* or other onomatopoeic element]
=belly-flop 1.

1943 *LANE* Map 576 **seCT,** Adverbial expressions recorded in the phrase *to coast (slide, go) belly-bump* . . . *Belly-cachunk,* ~ *cabump. Ibid* **sNH,** *Belly-cahoot.* **1970** *DARE* (Qu. EE25) Inf **NY**232, Belly-kabonk. **1971** Wood *Vocab. Change* 293 **Sth,** To coast lying down flat . . [3 infs:] belly kachug . . [3 infs:] belly kachunk. **1973** Allen *LAUM* 1.391, Coast lying down . . . *Belly-kachug* . . is checked by two Midland respondents, one in Iowa of Illinois and English parentage and one in Nebraska of Swedish parentage.

belly cheater See **belly robber**

belly-clapper n
1 =**belly-flop 1.**
    1968 *DARE* (Qu. EE25) Inf **OH72,** Belly-clapper.
2 =**belly-flop 2.**
    1968 *DARE* (Qu. EE29) Inf **OH72,** Belly-clapper.

belly-coast n Also *belly-coaster, ~ coasting*
=**belly-flop 1.**
    1965–70 *DARE* (Qu. EE25) Infs **NE6, OH77,** Belly-coasting; **NY88,** Belly-coast; **OH23,** Belly-coaster. **1973** Allen *LAUM* 1.391 **neNE,** Respondents voluntarily wrote in several expressions, presumably their natural ones: . . *belly-coaster* [1 respondent]. *Ibid* 392, *Belly coaster:* Inf. says he used this as a boy when he lived near Madison, Wi.

belly-cutter See **belly-gut 1**

belly-deep n [Echoic]
=**bullfrog 1.**
    1968 *DARE* (Qu. P22) Inf **IN42,** Belly-deep.

belly-dive n
=**belly-flop 2.**
    1965–70 *DARE* (Qu. EE29) Infs **AZ15, CA22, 51, IN23, LA12, NM9, NV55, NC16, OK28, 31, SD1, TX12,** Belly-dive.

belly-down v phr
=**belly-flop 1.**
    1971 Wood *Vocab. Change* 290 **Sth,** To coast lying down flat . . [28 infs:] belly down.

belly-fashion adv
=**belly-flop 1.**
    1973 Allen *LAUM* 1.391 **MN, ND,** A boy's throwing himself face down as he starts to coast downhill on a sled . . . belly fashion [4 infs].

belly fleece n
    1968 Adams *Western Words* 17, *Belly fleece*—The thin layer of flesh on the belly of an animal.

belly-flop n; also v, adv Also *belly-flapper, ~ flip, ~ flopper* **chiefly Nth, N Midl, West**

1 also rarely *belly-flat:* The act of coasting on a sled face down, usu after running and throwing oneself onto the sled; hence v, to perform such an action; hence adv, with such an action. See Map
    1896 *DN* 1.412 **IL,** Used by boys for coasting on sleds face downwards . . . *Belly-flop.* **1912** *DN* 3.566, "Ride belly gut" . . *Belly-flapper* is reported from Northern Vermont. **1943** *LANE* Map 576 **wCT, wMA,** Adverbial expressions . . *to coast (slide, go) belly-flop,* ~ *flop,* ~ *flopper.* **1947** *Denver Post* (CO) 5 Mar 1/2 **CO** [Caption:], *Taking no chance of missing the fun* of sliding on the snow, Tommy . . took what he feared might be one of his last "belly-flops." **1949** Kurath *Word Geog.* 80, Adverbial expressions for coasting 'face-down' on a sled . . *belly-flop,*

belly-flopper, in Western New England and on Delaware Bay. **1951** *PADS* 15.65 **cwNH,** *Belly-flop* or *flopper* . . . A plunge, belly down, on a sled. **1965** *PADS* 43.27 **seMA,** *Belly-bump* . . 5 [infs] *belly-flopper,* 2 [infs] *belly flapper,* 1 [inf] *belly flat.* **1965–70** *DARE* (Qu. EE25, *When a child picks up his sled, runs with it, and then throws himself down on it, that's a _____*) 143 Infs, **chiefly Nth, N Midl, West,** Belly-flop; 60 Infs, **chiefly Nth, N Midl, West,** Belly-flopper; **RI3,** Belly-flapper; **VA9,** Belly-flip; (Qu. EE24b, *When children go down hill on a sled . . they're _____*) Inf **NJ58,** Belly-flopping. **1973** Allen *LAUM* 1.390, Coast lying down . . . *Belly-flop,* common in western New England, dominates the Northern speech territory of the U[pper] M[idwest].

2 also *belly-flap:* A dive in which the front of the body strikes flat against the water; to do such a dive. See Map and Map Section
    1895 *DN* 1.396 **nwIL, csNY,** *Belly-flop, belly-flopper:* an attempt at diving which results in striking the water on the stomach. **1965–70** *DARE* (Qu. EE29, *When swimmers are diving and one comes down flat onto the water, that's a _____*) 289 Infs, **chiefly Nth, N Midl, West,** Belly-flop; 62 Infs **chiefly Nth, N Midl,** Belly-flopper; **CT35, MA57, MO17, NH5,** Belly-flap; **PA190, 245, RI12,** Belly-flapper; **VA9,** Belly-flip.

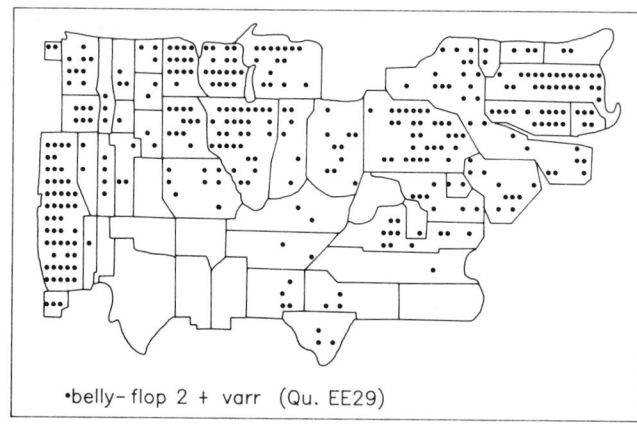
•belly- flop 2 + varr (Qu. EE29)

belly-flouncer n Also *belly-flounders, ~ flumps*
=**belly-flop 1.**
    1859 Willis *Convalescent* 75 **seNY,** The only attitude he patronizes on his sled ("belly-flumps") is slightly apoplectic. **1860** *Marysville Appeal* 30 Mar 4/1 *(DA)* **CA,** None of your belly-flounders! This lying down on a sled [is] not the thing. **1943** *LANE* Map 576 **Nantucket MA,** Belly-bump . . ~ flouncer.

belly-gert n, adv [Prob alter of **belly-gut;** perh infl by **belly girt**]
=**belly-flop 1.**
    1943 *LANE* Map 576 **MA,** Adverbial expression . . *to coast (slide, go) belly-bump,* . . [2 infs:] ~ *gert(s).* **1969** *DARE* (Qu. EE25) Inf **MA21,** Belly-gert.

belly girt n Also *belly girth* **chiefly NEng, S Atl** See Map Cf **girt**
A band that goes around the belly of a horse and holds the saddle or harness in place; a bellyband.
    1965–70 *DARE* (Qu. L53a, *The band that goes under a horse's middle*

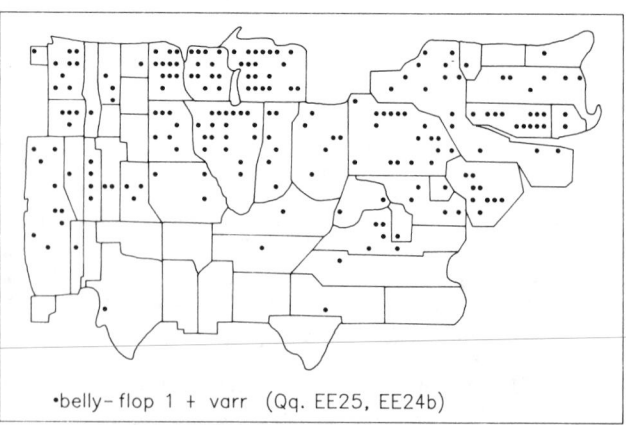
•belly- flop 1 + varr (Qq. EE25, EE24b)

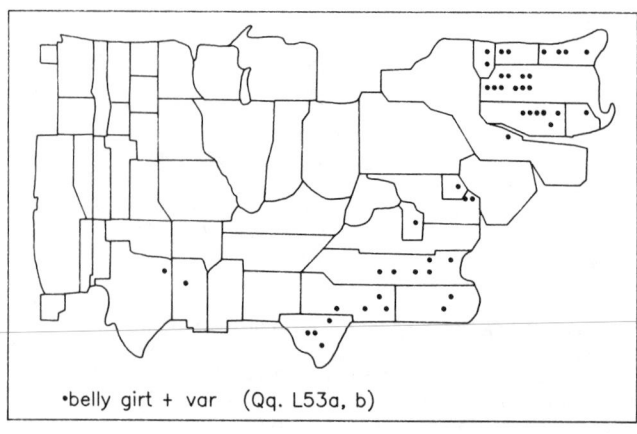
•belly girt + var (Qq. L53a, b)

to hold a saddle on) 28 Infs, **chiefly NEng, S Atl,** Belly girt; **CT**24, 26, 29, 32, **FL**34, **LA**15, **MA**5, 6, **RI**8, **SC**19, Belly girth; (Qu. L53b, *The band that goes under a horse's middle . . if it's a part of a work harness*) 32 Infs, **chiefly NEng, S Atl,** Belly girt; **CT**24, **LA**15, **MD**34, **MA**6, **RI**8, **SC**19, **VT**16, Belly girth.

belly-grinder v, adv
=**belly-flop 1.**
   1890 *DN* 1.60 **swOH, wPA,** *Belly-grinder:* to coast lying on the stomach.   **1949** Kurath *Word Geog.* 80 **WV,** Adverbial expressions for coasting 'face-down' on a sled are numerous . . . *belly-grinder,* in the Wheeling area.   **1971** Wood *Vocab. Change* 291 **Sth,** To coast lying down flat . . [6 infs:] belly grinder.

belly-gut n, v, adv Also *belly-gutter*
1 also *belly-cutter,* ~ *guts,* ~ *gutter(s);* rarely ~ *gutsies:* =**belly-flop 1. chiefly NEast, esp NY, PA   See Map**
   1845 Judd *Margaret* 173 **ME,** "I shall take it knee-bump, next time." . . "Try bellygut, you'll like that better."   **1859** (1968) Bartlett *Americanisms,* Belly-guts. More commonly Belly cutter or gutter . . . A term applied by boys to the manner of sliding down hill on their sleds, when lying on their bellies.   **1890** *DN* 1.60 **NJ,** Belly-gutter.   **1894** *DN* 1.340 **wCT,** *Belly-gut:* manner of coasting—face downward on sled.   **1912** *DN* 3.566 **cNY, eMA,** *Belly-gut* . . . To slide down hill lying face downward on the sled . . . *Belly gut* and *gutsies* from vicinity of Boston.   **1943** *LANE* Map 576 **wNEng,** Belly-bump, . . ~ gut(s), . . ~ gutter(s).   **1949** Kurath *Word Geog.* 80, Adverbial expressions for coasting 'face-down' on a sled . . . *Belly-gut, belly-gutter* are found from the lower Connecticut to the Great Lakes and on the Allegheny River in Pennsylvania.   **1950** *WELS Suppl.,* 2 Infs, **WI,** Belly-gut, belly-gutter.   **1965–70** *DARE* (Qu. EE25) 12 Infs, **9 in NY,** Belly-gut; **CT**6, **NJ**8, **NY**52, 206, **PA**4, 71, Belly-gutter; (Qu. EE24b) Inf **PA**174, Belly-gutting.   **1971** Wood *Vocab. Change* 291 **FL, TN,** To coast lying down flat . . [2 infs:] belly gut . . [1 inf:] belly gutter.   **1973** Allen *LAUM* 1.390, Coast lying down . . . *Belly-gut,* found from western Connecticut to the Great Lakes, survives with two infs. in Minnesota and one each in northeastern Iowa and in North Dakota.

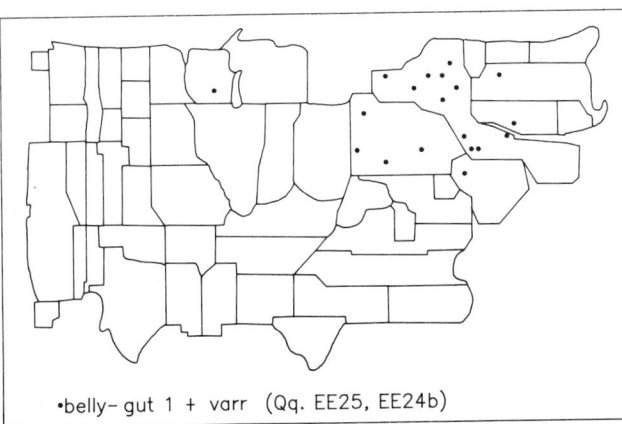

•belly- gut 1 + varr (Qq. EE25, EE24b)

2 =**belly-flop 2.**
   1965–69 *DARE* (Qu. EE29) Infs **NY**206, **UT**4, Belly-gutter; **WI**18, Belly-gut.

belly-guts n
1 See quots.   *?obs   *Cf **belly-wax**
   1859 (1968) Bartlett *Americanisms* 29, Belly-guts . . . In Pennsylvania, molasses candy so called.   **1870** *Nation* 11.56/2 **PA,** The molasses candy which had been "worked" till it became white went by another name . . . "Belly-guts" was the name it bore.
2 See **belly-gut 1.**

belly-gutsies, belly-gutter(s) See **belly-gut**

belly hole n
   1965–70 *DARE* (Qu. X34, . . *The navel*) Infs **KY**19, **MD**19, 27, **MO**19, **PA**44, 164, **TX**51, Belly hole.

belly-hoocher n
=**belly-flop 1.**
   1968 *DARE* (Qu. EE25) Inf **IN**5, Belly-hoocher.

belly-hump v
=**belly-flop 1.**

1892 *Jrl. Amer. Folkl.* 5.145 **MA,** Bellygut, Bellyhump. —Terms used in "coasting." To lie on a sled with the face down.

belly-jumper n
=**belly-flop 1.**
   1968 *DARE* (Qu. EE25) Inf **IN**10, Belly-jumper.

belly-kabonk, belly-kachug, belly-kachunk See **belly-cabump**

belly-landing n Also *belly-land*
=**belly-flop 2.**
   1965–70 *DARE* (Qu. EE29) Infs **CA**1, **IN**41, **KS**20, **NC**88, **VA**42, Belly-landing; **IN**16, **KS**7, **MS**30, **NC**1, Belly-land.

‡belly member n
   1967 *DARE* (Qu. CC7, . . *A person who goes to church very seldom*) Inf **IL**21, Belly member—because he only comes when there's a church supper.

belly pad n NW joc Cf **blanket 3**
A pancake.
   1958 McCulloch *Woods Words* **Pacific NW,** Belly pads—Hotcakes.   **1977** Churchill *Don't Call* 58 **nwOR** (as of c1918), "A belly pad," sighed Mrs. Johnson with a resigned look, "is a hot cake. Now don't tell me they don't have hotcakes in Boston!" Mother said they did but they called them hot cakes.

belly-plumper adv
=**belly-flop 1.**
   1877 Bartlett *Americanisms,* Belly-Plumper . . . The same as *Belly-Guts* ["A term applied by boys to the manner of sliding down hill on their sleds, when lying on their bellies."] . . . Sometimes when the slide is without the sled. Eastern Massachusetts.

belly-ride n Also *belly-riding*
=**belly-flop 1.**
   1950 *WELS Suppl.,* 1 Inf, **csWI,** Belly-riding.   **1965–70** *DARE* (Qu. EE25) Infs **IN**41, **KS**15, **MN**23, **MO**20, **NY**70, 200, Belly-ride; **KY**5, Belly-riding.

belly robber n Also *belly burglar,* ~ *cheater joc*
A steward or cook.
   1914 *DN* 4.150 [Navy slang], Bellyrobber . . . Commissary steward.   **1942** *AmSp* 17.68 [Army slang], 'Belly robber (mess sergeant).' Rather rare, and used only by old regulars.   **1944** *AmSp* 19.104 [Sailors' argot], A ship is a *workhouse* . . . Her steward is the belly-robber.   **1944** Adams *Western Words* 17, Belly-cheater—A slang name for the cook. Many cooks were merely cooks and not cowmen. One cowhand informed me that the cook with his outfit "didn't savvy *cow* unless it was dished up in a stew."   **1956** Sorden–Ebert *Logger's Words* **Gt Lakes,** Belly-burglar . . . Belly-robber, A name often given to the cook, especially if he was a poor one.   **1958** McCulloch *Woods Words* **Pacific NW.**

belly-rub n, v chiefly S Midl
A dance; to dance closely (with someone).
   1938 Stuart *Dark Hills* 295 **eKY,** People can't dance like that nowadays. They just dance and belly-rub a little.   **1938** *AmSp* 13.316 **NE** [Black], A dance is a *struggle* or a *bellyrub.* 'Bellyrub' is original in Lincoln.   **1941** *AmSp* 16.21 **sIN.**   **1944** *PADS* 2.53 **AR, NC, SC, TN,** *Belly-rub* . . . Almost any dance.   **1954** *Harder Coll.* **cwTN,** Belly-rub—a "round" dance. To "round" dance.   **1964** Baraka *Dutchman & Slave* 34 **NYC** [Black], That ol' dipty-dip shit you do, rolling your ass like an elephant. That's not my kind of belly rub. Belly rub is not Queens. Belly rub is dark places, with big hats and overcoats held up with one arm.   **1967–68** *DARE* (Qu. FF4, . . *Kinds of dancing parties*) Infs **OH**47, **TX**5, Belly-rub; **NY**73, **TX**51, Belly-rubbing.

belly-shot adj arch
See quots.
   1688 in 1844 Force *Tracts* 3.12.26 **VA,** After that sweet Food they are not so prompt to brouze on the Trees, and the coarse Grass which the Country affords; so that thus their Guts shrink up, and they become Belly-shot as they call it.   **1899** (1912) Green *VA Folk-Speech,* Belly-shot . . . Cattle that have become lean and pinched from lack of food in the winter.

belly-slam n, v Also *belly-slammer* chiefly eGt Lakes
1 =**belly-flop 1.**
   1948 *WELS Suppl.* 1 Inf, **cWI,** Belly-slam; 1 Inf, **cWI,** Throwing yourself on a sled—go belly-slamming.   **1950** *Ibid* **nwPA,** Belly-slam [used in an advertisement for sleds made in Titusville, PA].   **1950**

WELS (When a child picks up his sled, runs with it, and then throws himself down on it) 2 Infs, **cWI,** Belly slam. **1965–70** *DARE* (Qu. EE25) Infs **NY99, OH1,** 15, 29, 68, **PA130,** 185, **WV13,** Belly-slam; **NY30, OH5, PA152,** Belly-slammer. **1971** Wood *Vocab. Change* 291 **Sth,** To coast lying down flat . . [9 infs:] belly slam.

2 =belly-flop 2.

1965–70 *DARE* (Qu. EE29) Infs **OH1,** 15, 29, **PA76,** 130, Belly-slam; **NY30, OH5,** Belly-slammer.

belly-slap n Also *belly-slapper*

=belly-flop 2.

1968–70 *DARE* (Qu. EE29) Inf **NJ69,** Belly-slap; **OH74,** Belly-slap-per.

belly-slider n Also *belly-slide, ∼ sliding, ∼ sledding*

=belly-flop 1.

1950 *WELS Suppl.,* 1 Inf, **seWI,** Belly-sledding—a child throws himself on a sled. **1969–70** *DARE* (Qu. EE25) Inf **MO6,** Belly-slider; **TN66,** Belly-sledding. **1971** Wood *Vocab. Change* 40 **Sth,** For the act of coasting while lying down flat . . some informants added *belly slide.* **1973** Allen *LAUM* 1.391 **IA, MN, NE,** The act of a boy's throwing himself face down as he starts to coast downhill on a sled . . . belly slide [1 inf], ∼ sliding [3 infs].

belly-smacker n chiefly eGt Lakes

1 =belly-flop 1.

1917 *DN* 4.388 **neOH,** *Belly-smacker* . . . Same as *belly-gut,* the usual term. **1919** *DN* 5.76, *Belly-smacker.* **1965–70** *DARE* (Qu. EE25) Infs **MI114, NY144,** 145, 184, **OH70,** 88, 97, **PA130,** 133, 134, 165, 167, 177, 196, **WV10,** Belly-smacker.

2 also *belly-smack:* =belly-flop 2. See Map and Map Section

1965–70 *DARE* (Qu. EE29) 50 Infs, **chiefly eGt Lakes,** Belly-smacker; **MI69,** 118, **OH88, PA185,** Belly-smack.

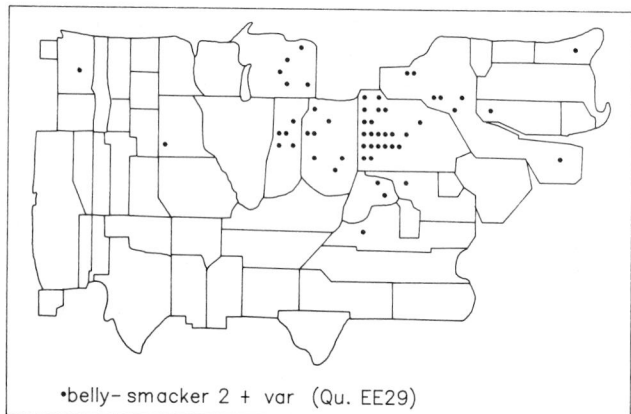

•belly- smacker 2 + var (Qu. EE29)

belly-smasher n

1=belly-flop 1.

1967–68 *DARE* (Qu. EE25) Infs **MI49,** 78, Belly-smasher.

2 also *belly-smash:* =belly-flop 2.

1965–70 *DARE* (Qu. EE29) Infs **MI65,** 75, 78, 81, **MA58, NM12, PA194, OH23, WA6,** Belly-smasher; **OH68,** Belly-smash.

belly-splash n Also *belly-splasher*

=belly-flop 2.

1965–70 *DARE* (Qu. EE29) Infs **IL4,** 92, **MI61,** 105, **NY59,** 99, 232, **SC21,** 65, 68, Belly-splash; **GA72, IN69, MI8,** 49, 101, **NY75, TX71, VA13,** Belly-splasher.

belly through the brush v phr

1968 Adams *Western Words* 18, *Belly through the brush*—A cowboy's expression meaning to hide and dodge the law.

belly-thumper n

=belly-flop 2.

1975 Gould *ME Lingo* 11, The "*belly*-flopper" taken in the ol' swimmin' hole often comes out in Maine as *belly*-thumper and *belly*-whacker.

belly tickler n [From the sensation in the stomach caused by the sudden drop in elevation]

=thank-you-ma'am.

1950 *WELS (Sudden, short dip in the road)* 1 Inf, **seWI,** Belly tickler. **1968** *DARE* (Qu. N30) Inf **OH82,** Belly tickler.

belly timber n [Engl dial]

Food.

1899 (1912) Green *VA Folk-Speech, Belly-timber* . . . Food; that which supplies the belly. **1969** *DARE* (Qu. H6, . . "*He certainly enjoys his _____.*") Inf **GA79,** Belly timber. **1981** *AmSp* 56.157 **nwNC,** My father, . . a man of seventy with under seven years of formal education who has spent less than one year of his life outside northwestern North Carolina, declared: "Old Mr. _____ could top them all. He could really put away the belly-timber."

belly-to-butt v

=belly-flop 1.

1967 *DARE* FW Addit **ME,** Belly to butt down the mountainside on slats—what Inf's grandfather used to do as a child when it snowed in Maine.

belly-tunk n

=belly-flop 1.

1975 Gould *ME Lingo* 11, The *belly*-bumper that means a face-down flop onto a child's sled is often, in Maine, a *belly*-bunt or a *belly*-tunk.

belly up v phr

1979 in 1982 *Barrick Coll.* **sePA,** Belly up—Show signs of pregnancy. "She bellied up." . . Only occurrence.

belly-wallop n

=belly-flop 1.

1968 *DARE* (Qu. EE25) Inf **MD15,** Belly-wallop.

belly wash n

1 A soft drink.

1900 *DN* 2.22 [College jargon], *Belly-wash* . . . Any soft drink. **1931** *AmSp* 7.50 [Loggers' argot], Water, soda water, and other "soft" drinks are known as "belly-wash." **1964** *Jrl. Amer. Folkl.* 77.79 **cPA,** In our community . . it [=belly-wash] always referred to bottled soft drinks "pop," and was never used for any other potable. We had a plant in our town which bottled pop, and we boys would go to the "belly-wash factory." **1965–70** *DARE* (Qu. H78, *Ordinary soft drinks, usually carbonated*) Infs **AR55, CT2,** 29, **MT5, NJ1, NY209, NC52, OR3, SC43,** Belly wash. **1968** *DARE* FW Addit **DE1,** Belly-wash—joking name for a large Pepsi-cola. **1970** Tarpley *Blinky* 194 **neTX,** *Carbonated beverage in a bottle* . . [1 inf:] belly-wash.

2 A weak or bad drink, usu alcoholic.

1889 *Century Dict., Belly-wash* . . . Any kind of drink of poor quality. [Vulgar.] **1926** *DN* 5.385 **ME,** *Belly-wash* . . . A wretched drink, "For coffee they give (past tense) us belly-wash." Common. **1932** *Progress* (Charlottesville VA) 7 Sept 2/3 *(Hench Coll.),* I am told many "beer places," . . are really entirely within the law . . . It is only the weak concoction scoffers call "belly wash." **1932** *AmSp* 7.329 [Student jargon at Johns Hopkins Univ.], Belly-wash . . bad liquor. **1950** *WELS (Bad liquor)* 1 Inf, **cwWI,** Belly wash. **1965–70** *DARE* (Qu. DD21a, . . *Liquor*) Infs **AK8, PA230,** Belly wash; (Qu. DD21b, . . *Bad liquor*) Inf **PA148,** Belly wash; (Qu. DD21c, . . *Whiskey, especially illegally made*) Inf **ID5,** Belly wash; (Qu. DD25, . . *Beer*) Infs **AK8, CA137,** 141, **MA33, MN21, NY209, OK42, PA230, UT4, VT16,** Belly wash; (Qu. DD27, . . *Wine*) Inf **NJ1,** Belly wash; (Qu. DD28b, . . *Fermented drinks made at home*) Inf **MD36,** Belly wash. **1968** Adams *Western Words, Belly wash*—What the cowboy calls weak coffee. **1969** *DARE* Tape **GA72,** If it's very bad liquor, it's usually called belly wash or neighbor liquor.

3 Nonsense, "hog wash."

1958 McCulloch *Woods Words* **Pacific NW,** *Belly wash* . . . Another word for baloney.

belly washer n

1 =belly wash 1. ?Sth, S Midl

1909 Ware *Passing Engl., Belly-washer (Amer. Saloon).* Lemonade or aerated water. **1966–70** *DARE* (Qu. H78, *Ordinary soft drinks, usually carbonated*) Infs **FL19, KY84, LA40, SC32,** Belly washer(s). **1970** *DARE* FW Addit **TN,** Belly washer—soda pop. Overheard in conversation.

2 See quot. Cf **belly wash 2**

1966 *DARE* (Qu. DD27, . . *Nicknames . . for wine*) Inf **GA9,** Belly washer.

3 See quot. Cf **gully washer**

1967–70 *DARE* (Qu. B25, . . *A very heavy rain*) Infs **CA181, IL15, IN15,** 69, Belly washer.

4 =**belly-flop 2.**
1969–70 *DARE* (Qu. EE29) Infs **NC**72, **TN**46, Belly-washer.

belly-wax n Pronc-sp *bailey-wax* *?obs* Cf **belly-guts 1**
1894 *DN* 1.328 **sNJ**, *Belly-wax:* molasses candy . . . Often pron[ounced] *Bailey-wax.*

belly weed n Cf **bellyache root, bellyache weed**
1970 *NC Folkl.* 18.16, Roots of what the old backwoodsmen called "belly weed" are good for colic and stomachache.

belly-whacker n, adv Also *belly-whack,* ~ *whacky* **chiefly NEast, esp NY**

1 also *belly-whacking,* ~ *wocker:* =**belly-flop 1.**
1896 *DN* 1.412 **cwNY**, Coasting on sleds face downwards . . . *Bellywhack.* **1943** *LANE* Map 576 **scattered sNEng,** [Belly-whack; belly-whacker; belly-whacky]. **1949** Kurath *Word Geog.* 80, Adverbial expressions for coasting 'face-down' on a sled . . occur in scattered fashion: *belly-whack,* sporadically throughout the North [i.e., sNEng, NY, PA, neOH]. **1950** *WELS* 1 Inf, **cwWI**, Belly Whacker. **1950** *WELS Suppl.,* 1 Inf, **cwWI**, Belly-whacking. **1965–70** *DARE* (Qu. EE25) Infs **MI**67, **NY**28, 154, 162, 172, 213, 223, **PA**94, 181, Belly-whacker; **MA**14, Belly-whack; **NY**190, Belly-wocker [-wakɚ]. **1971** Wood *Vocab. Change* 291 **Sth,** To coast lying down flat . . [1 inf:] belly whack.

2 =**belly-flop 2.**
1965–70 *DARE* (Qu. EE29) Infs **MI**67, **MA**14, 100, **NY**113, 123, 154, 162, 200, 213, 234, Belly-whacker; **CT**9, **NY**107, Belly-whack.

belly whistle n
See quot 1894.
1894 *DN* 1.328 **NJ,** *Belly-whistle:* a drink made of molasses, vinegar, water, and nutmeg used by harvesters at the daily nooning. **1912** *DN* 3.569, *Switchel* . . . A drink made of water, vinegar, molasses, and ginger. In Connecticut and Vermont called *ginger water;* in New Jersey, *belly whistle.*

belly-whopper n, v, adv Also *belly-whomper,* ~ *whop* Pronc-spp *belly-womper,* ~ *wop,* ~ *wopper(s)* **chiefly Nth, N Midl, esp NY, NJ**

1 =**belly-flop 1.** See Map
1890 *DN* 1.60 **cNJ,** *Belly-whopper:* to coast lying on the stomach. **1934** *Sun* (Baltimore MD) 1 Feb 10/7 *(Hench Coll.),* Sledding is not so popular with those who went belly-whopper twenty or thirty years ago. **1943** *LANE* Map 576 **CT,** *Belly-bump, . . ~ whopper, . . ~ whop.* **1949** Kurath *Word Geog.* 80, *Belly-wop, belly-wopper(s)* dominates (1) the lower Hudson, Long Island and East Jersey, and (2) Maryland. **1950** *WELS Suppl.,* 2 Infs, **WI**, Belly-whopper; 1 Inf, **seWI**, Belly-whopping — sledding, as children in New England. **1951** Graham *My Window* 148 **ME,** There is an icy crust, and Lani and I go belly-whopper down the hill into the pasture. **c1960** *Wilson Coll.* **csKY,** *Belly-whopper* . . When a child throws himself face downward on his sled. **1965–70** *DARE* (Qu. EE25) 96 Infs, **scattered Nth, N Midl, esp NY, NJ,** Belly-whopper; 9 Infs, Belly-whomper; 19 Infs, **chiefly NY, NJ, MD,** Belly-wop; **CT**8, Belly-whopping; **PA**242, Belly-womper; (Qu. EE24b, *When children go down hill on a sled . . they say they're ——*) Infs **NY**45, 57, **PA**81, Belly-whopping; **DC**2, **NY**51, Belly-wopping. **1971** Wood *Vocab. Change* 291 **Sth,** To coast lying down flat . . [7 infs:] belly wop . . [29 infs] belly wopper.

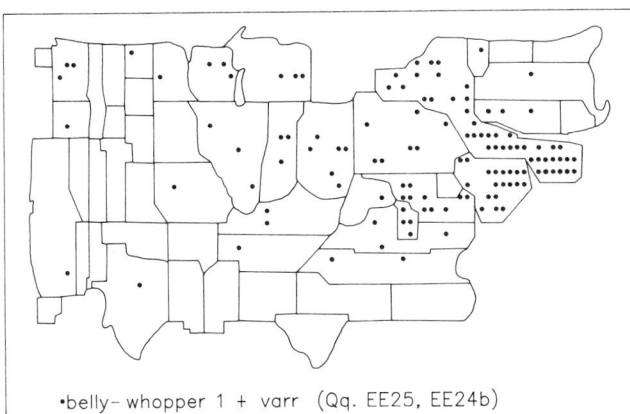

•belly- whopper 1 + varr (Qq. EE25, EE24b)

2 =**belly-flop 2. chiefly Nth, N Midl, esp NY, C Atl** See Map and Map Section

1940 *New Yorker* 15 June 37/2, We passed canals in which boys were taking bellywhoppers. **1965–70** *DARE* (Qu. EE29) 71 Infs, **scattered, but esp NY, C Atl,** Belly-wopper; 10 Infs, Belly-whopper; 13 Infs, Belly-wop; **OH**80, Belly-whomper.

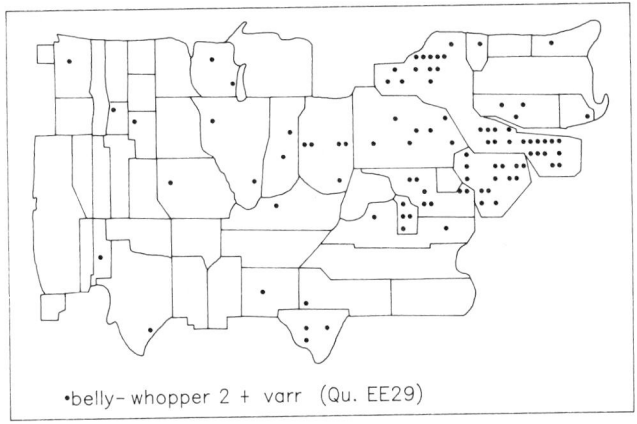

•belly- whopper 2 + varr (Qu. EE29)

belong v
A Forms.

1 pres, pres pple: usu *belong, belongs, belonging;* rarely *belongen* (cf **-en** suff[5]); also, *esp in representations of Gullah speech,* pronc-spp *blan, blanks, blants, b'long, blongst, blonx.*
1888 Jones *Negro Myths* 59 **GA coast,** One er de hen wuh blanks ter Buh Chanticleer fambly. *Ibid* 163, Eh blants ter you. **1891** Page *Elsket* 124 **VA** [Black], Mr. P'laski Greener, whar Lucindy use' to b'longst to. **1908** *S. Atl. Qrly.* 7.343 **SC** [Gullah], *Disha kounou blanks tuh we!* . . in English: . . this canoe (a cypress dugout) belongs to us. **1922** Gonzales *Black Border* 70 **sSC, GA coasts** [Gullah], Cap'n, all dese 'yuh mans blonx to quality. *Ibid* 290 [Gullah Glossary], *Blan*—belong, belongs, belonged, belonging . . . *B'long, Blonx*—belong, belongs, belonged, belonging. **1928** Peterkin *Scarlet Sister Mary* 129 **SC** [Gullah], You can' nebber blongst to nobody, honey, an' nobody can' blongst to you. **1953** Randolph *Down in Holler* 46 **Ozarks,** *Belongen* is a form of belong, as in the sentence, "Them dogs *belongen* to Ab Landers."

2 past, past pple: usu *belonged;* occas *b'longded* (cf **-ed** pret suff **1**); also, *in representations of Gullah speech,* pronc-spp *blan, blong, blongst, blonx.*
1891 Harris *Balaam* 140 **GA** [Black], It b'longded in de . . fambly. **1908** *S. Atl. Qrly.* 7.341 **SC** [Gullah], Me yerre dem; dem blan fuh yerre we. [=I heard them; they were obliged to hear us.] **1922** [see A1 above]. **1928** Peterkin *Scarlet Sister Mary* 292 **SC** [Gullah], I ain' never blongst to nobody but you since de day you marked me in de ear wid dat knife.

B Sense.
Preceding infin: to be obliged, need, ought; to be accustomed. [Engl dial] **Sth, S Midl**
1888 Jones *Negro Myths* 1 **GA coast,** Eh know Buh Alligatur blan come out de ribber an sun isself in de broom-grass fiel. *Ibid* 12, Eh mek fur de spot way de Sun blan sleep. **1911** *DN* 3.537 **eKY,** *Belong* . . . An auxiliary indicating duty or obligation; e.g., "Do I belong to chop the wood?" = "Must (shall I) chop the wood?" **1913** *DN* 4.58 **eTN,** *Belong* . . . Used as auxiliary in the sense of "should," "ought to" . . . "It belongs to be here." **1914** *DN* 4.158 **cVA,** John Henry belongs to folla afteh Sayrah. **1917** *DN* 4.408 **KY, wNC**. **1918** *DN* 5.20 **NC**. **1930** *DN* 6.86 **sWV**. **1933** Rawlings *South Moon* 37 **FL,** You kin make it, but you belong to git a license and pay a tax. **1941** *AN&Q* 138/1 **VA**. **1944** *PADS* 2.40, **neLA, NC, SC, TN, VA,** *Belong* . . . Should, ought, to be supposed, to be accustomed. "He belongs to come to work at eight o'clock." **1946** *PADS* 6.5 **eNC** (as of 1900–10). **1950** *PADS* 14.13 **SC,** "If a drink belongs to be hot, I want it hot." **1967–70** *DARE* FW Addit **seGA,** You belong to find 'em—meaning you must find them; **LA**29, That meal come out of there just like it belonged to; **GA**22, He belong to come when you call him. He belongs to catch fish; **VA**51, That house belongs to be painted white. **1968** *DARE* Tape **NC**58, Please paint that boat like it b'longs to be.

below the ford adj phr
Under the weather.
1966 *DARE* (Qu. BB39, *On a day when you don't feel just right, though not actually sick, you might say, ". . I'm feeling —— today."*) Inf **NC**33, Below the ford.

Belsnickel n Also *Pelznickel;* for addit spp, see quots [Ger *Pelz* fur + *Nickel* dim of *Nicholas*] **Ger settlement areas**

1 St. Nicholas, Santa Claus, or St. Nicholas' servant whose duty it was to punish naughty children or reward good ones.

1823 James *Acct. of Exped.* 1.188 **PA** (as of 1819), Several Canadians . . came this evening to dance and sing before us . . in celebration of the termination of the year . . This dance . . may have had its origin in the same cause that produced our *Belshnickles,* who make their appearance on Christmas Eve. **1830** Watson *Annals Philadelphia* 242 **PA,** "Belsh Nichel," in high German, expresses "Nicholas in his fur" . . . He is always supposed to bring good things at night to good children, and a rod for those who are bad. **1869** *Atlantic Mth.* 24.485/1 **sePA,** This was the real Bell-schnickel, personated by the farmer. I presume that he ought to throw down his store of nice things for the good children, and strike the bad ones with his whip. Pelznickel is a bearded Nicholas, who punishes bad ones. **1872** Haldeman *PA Dutch* 58 [German words in English], *Bellsnickle,* PGr. beltsnickkl . . . A masked and hideously disguised person, who goes from house to house on christmas eve, beating (or pretending to beat) the children and servants, and throwing down nuts and cakes before leaving. A noisy party accompanies him, often with a *bell,* which has influenced the English name. **1890** *DN* 1.72 **ePA,** *Bell-snickle.* **1890** Howells *Boy's Town* 17 **OH,** His mother had told him how the Peltsnickel used to come with a bundle of rods for the bad children when the Chriskingle brought presents for the good ones. **1935** *AmSp* 10.170 **sePA,** Other German words used in English are . . *Belsnik'l.* **1940** Wright *Pioneer Life* 90 **wPA,** Among the Germans the Beltznickel Man, a member of the community disguised in a panther skin with trailing tail, black bearskin cap, and mask, romped with the children and filled their stockings with apples and nuts. **1945** *AmSp* 20.254 **sPA,** *Belschnickel.* **1948** *AmSp* 23.108 **swIL,** Santa Claus is widely known as *Bensnickel* or *Belsnickel.* **1959** *Progress* (Charlottesville VA) 10 Dec 14/1–2 **sePA** (*Hench Coll.*), Belsnickel is the Pennsylvania Dutch Santa Claus, the patron saint, the grandfather image of Christmas Eve . . . Belsnickel wears the livery of the Santa everybody knows . . . He comes openly to the front door . . . The presents he gives—and receives, according to custom—are sturdy, practical, down-to-earth . . . With him often goes a little German band. Young and old join the march, stopping to serenade persons especially chosen for the honor. **1967** *Lake Mills Leader* (WI) 21 Dec, Pelsnickle . . . accompanied St. Nicholas as his servant and . . had the unwelcome task of punishing naughty boys and girls with "gifts" of lumps of coal and switches. **1968** *DARE* FW Addit **VA,** Due to an old German custom in our family, New Year was also celebrated with the arrival of Bellesnoggle, a jolly old fellow who would drop candy and nuts over the bannister into the lower hall and it was a mad scramble to see who would get the most. **1968–69** *DARE* (Qu. EE41) Inf **MI93,** Pelznickel; **PA162,** Belsnickel ['bɛl,snıkl]—he came on Christmas Eve before Santa Claus would come; he brought coal and onions and gave them to the naughty children, brought out a switch and spanked them.

2 also *Belsnickler:* A person in disguise who visits friends or relatives at Christmas time to play pranks or beg for gifts or refreshments. Cf **Christmas fool**

1869 *Atlantic Mth.* 24.484/2 **sePA,** I was sitting alone, one Christmas time, when . . there entered some half-dozen youths or men . . . These, I suppose, were Christmas mummers, though I heard them called "Bellschnickel." **1953** *AmSp* 28.245 **nwPA,** [Footnote:] *Bellsnickels* in the Bedford subarea beg for gifts, they do not bring them . . . In the Bedford subarea the word and the verbal phrase I have given *[to go bellsnickling]* are both used, and the association in the popular mind is with bells, not with Saint Nicholas, furry or other. **1958** *Jrl. Amer. Folkl.* 71.164, I wish to record a folk custom of the Christmas and New Year's season, now extinct, which formerly existed in the Shenandoah Valley of Virginia. During the period between Christmas and New Year's, bands of young people, about 15 to 20 years of age, went about in disguises visiting neighbors. Those going about in the evening, dressed in various kinds of makeshift disguise were known as "belsnickles," and those going about in the daytime, frequently dressed like clowns, were called "shanghais." **1964** Smith *PA Germans* 123, Today some belsnicklers still visit homes in some neighborhoods of Page, Rockingham, Shenandoah, and Augusta Counties in Virginia and in Pendleton County, West Virginia, but most of them travel in automobiles rather than by foot. They wear commercial masks and even commercial costumes at times, but they are as boisterous and fun-loving as were their grandparents before them . . . The custom is rapidly fading from the contemporary scene. **1967** *DARE* Tape **PA9,** Did you ever hear of the Belsnickles? . . It was done out in the country areas, in Lancaster County, a great

deal . . . They would go around . . the night before Christmas and the young fellas . . would . . play tricks and things like that. Sometimes they'd unhitch his horse and put the wagon, his buggy or carriage, up on top of the roof, straddle the peak of a roof of a shed . . . Sometimes, long ago, they would dress up maybe or wear masks. **1982** *Barrick Coll.* **sePA,** Belsneakles—Costumed pranksters who came door to door between Xmas and Near Years Day . . . Also *belsninckles.*

belsnickeling pres pple, vbl n Also sp *bellsnick(e)lin(g), -sniggling* [**Belsnickel** 2] **Ger settlement areas, esp PA**

A Christmas-season celebration; to engage in such: see quots.

1881 *Scribner's Mth.* 22.350 **PA,** He broke it [=an accordion] last New-Year's Night "out bell snicklin'." This custom is known in other parts of the Neck as "New-Year's Shooting." On New-Year's Eve, crowds of men and boys dress themselves in fantastic costumes, and roam through the Neck and lower part of the city all night. This custom . . grows year by year in Philadelphia. **1940** FWP *Guide PA* 61, [The mummers' parade's] immediate ancestor is the old German tradition of 'bell-snickeling.' As early as 1800 scattered groups of mummers from South Philadelphia paraded the streets and rang bells to receive the award of cakes and candy if their identity was not guessed. **1949** *Natl. Geog. Mag.* 96.23/2 **VA, ePA,** Bellsniggling. About a week before Christmas the men, wearing women's clothes, and the women, dressed in men's clothes, all wearing home-made masks, come to her door, she told me. "I'm supposed to guess who they are." . . handouts are expected. **1953** *AmSp* 28.245 **csPA,** To go bellsnickling, which describes the Christmas custom of dressing in grotesque costumes to go from house to house begging treats of cookies and candy. **1964** Smith *PA Germans* 119 **VA,** An amazing number of elderly residents of the dialect-speaking neighborhoods of the [Shenandoah] Valley remember when "belsnickeling" was common throughout the Christmas season. **1967** *DARE* File **scPA,** Bell [snıkəlıŋ]—farmers get in sleighs and go around caroling. Also, [at] New Holland, these people play pranks at Christmas time, [e.g.] put a wagon on a roof top.

Belsnickler See **Belsnickel 2**

Belsnik'l, Belsninckle See **Belsnickel**

Beltashazur's off-ox n [Cf Daniel 4:18f, where Daniel, also called Belteshazzar, foretells the degeneration of Nebuchadnezzar into an ox-like condition]

=Adam's off-ox 1.

1867 Harris *Sut Lovingood Yarns* 79, I didn't know hit frum Beltashazur's off ox.

Beltznickel See **Belsnickel**

Belzibub See **Beelzebub**

ben n[1] [Scots *ben* < OE *be-innan*] *relic* See also **but-and-ben**

One room, traditionally the inner room, of a two-room house.

1950 *WELS Suppl.* 1 Inf, **cwWI,** But and ben. Of a house: front and back parts [=rooms]. **1959** *VT Hist.* ns 27.125, Ben . . . Parlor. Occasional among the Scotch in Orleans Co. **1973** Allen *LAUM* 1.158 **MN,** Sitting room . . . ben [offered by 1 inf who had heard it used by her Scottish grandmother].

ben n[2] Pronc-sp *bend* [Alter of *bin*] See Pronc Intro 3.I.4.a Cf **bent** n[2] 2

A storage bin.

1965–70 *DARE* (Qu. M6, *The place where grain is kept in a barn*) 36 Infs, **scattered,** Ben; 9 Infs, Grain ben; **AR21, 40, GA5, MS4, NE5, OR4,** Bend; **LA18,** Corn bend; **MS21, TN53,** Grain bend; (Qu. M1) Inf **TN53,** Storage bens; (Qu. M3) Inf **GA19,** Ben; **NC49,** Grain ben; (Qu. M7) Inf **OK72,** Ben; (Qu. M8) Infs **NY66, OK52,** Ben; **NH14,** Corn ben; (Qu. M12) Inf **AR29,** Bend; **AR40,** Bens; (Qu. M22) Inf **NY70,** Coal ben; **KY72,** Grainery ben; **TN53,** Storage ben.

ben n[3] See **bent** n[2] 2

ben, be'n v See **be** A2

ben exclam [Var of **ven**] See also **nudges**

=fen.

1896 *DN* 1.412 **cwNY,** Ben nuggins [nʌjınz]: A term in marbles.

benasty v esp **S Midl**

To soil, make dirty.

1917 *DN* 4.408 **wNC,** Benasty . . . To befoul; besmear. "The little feller tumbled down and benastied himself to beat the devil." **1931** Randolph *Ozarks* 86, On another occasion she remarked to a total stranger that her husband had done got drunk ag'in an' plum benastied hisse'f! **1960** Williams *Walk Egypt* 143 **GA,** You think I be-nasty folks' minds with my jokes and songs and such. **1972** Cooper *NC Mt. Folkl.* 89 **wNC,** Benasty—degrade.

benaut adj |bə'naʊt, bə'nɔt| [Du *benauwd*] *in Dutch communities*

1 Of the atmosphere: close, oppressive.

1969 *DARE* (Qu. B4, *A day when the air is very still, moist, and warm—it's _____*) Inf **MI**102, Benaut [bə'nɔt]—a local expression used by the Dutch. **1982** *DARE* File **seWI,** The weather is benaut—not threatening, but overcast, dullish; it's lowering, and you know something's coming, though you're not sure what. *Ibid* **swMI,** *Benaut* [bə'naʊt] can also refer to external elements: the weather or atmosphere can be benaut.

2 Uncomfortable, esp as the result of anxiety; hard pressed.

1969 *DARE* (Qu. BB7, *A feeling that lasts for a short while, with difficult breathing and heart beating fast*) Inf **MI**102, Benaut [bə'nɔt]—a Dutch term meaning uncomfortable. **1982** *DARE* File **swMI,** *Benaut* [bə'naʊt]—describes a person struck with discomfort-producing anxiety. A person can be benaut from anything that produces a panicky feeling, including heat, but central is a feeling of anxiety and pain. *Ibid* **cCA,** To be benaut is to have a feeling of oppression. It's typically caused by heat, humidity, or too many people around. *Ibid* **seWI,** If you're benaut [bə'nɔt], you're uncomfortable and anxious. You feel aggrieved, even though that's not necessarily with reason. There's a sense that something external is going to get you, but it isn't anything specific.

‡ben box n [*Prob ben* within] Cf **rough-box**

A casket.

1966 *DARE* Tape **AL**1, We called em ben box . . . That's a ben [bɛn] box, the casket.

bench n Usu |bɛnč|; also |bɪnč|; less freq |binč, bеnč, bænč| See Pronc Intro 3.I.4.a

A Forms.

1936 *AmSp* 11.16 **eTX,** *Bench* . . . [bĩntʃ], [bĩntʃ] . . . [bẽntʃ], [bẽĩntʃ]. **1941** *AmSp* 16.5 **eTX** [Black], *Bench* . . sometimes . . [bĩntʃ], [bẽĩntʃ]. **1942** Hall *Smoky Mt. Speech* 19, *Bench-legged* often occurs in the expression ['bæntʃˌlegəd 'fɑɪst], a dog of mixed breed. *Ibid* 24, *Bench* . . ['bæntʃ]. **1969** *DARE* (Qu. C17) Inf **KY**28, [bænč].

B Sense.

A raised plateau, esp one in foothills. **chiefly Midl, West**

1795 in 1940 *AmSp* 15.155 **VA,** Two poplars and a red oak on the Bench of a ridge. **1803** (1965) Lewis *Jrls.* 34 **wPA,** What is called the third bottom is more properly the high benches of the large range of hills. **1859** (1942) Patterson *Travel Diary* 103 **ceNE,** Fronting the town is a low flat bench of land . . . The second bench—upon which the town is built—rises abruptly some forty or fifty feet, and spreads out into a broad, level plateau. **1916** *DN* 4.319 **KS,** *Bench* . . . Land that rises terrace-like above other land. **1932** *DN* 6.224 **West,** Bench. This is commonly used all over the West for the levels above a plain, or more commonly between a river and the bounding hills. **1934** Vines *Green Thicket* 9 **cnAL,** That's what we call the foothills or benches to the big bluff. **1960** Hall *Smoky Mt. Folks* 57 **wNC, eTN,** Bench: a level area, sometimes cultivated, on the side of a mountain. **1965** Guthrie *Blue Hen's Chick* 2 **MT,** Benches climbed from the valley of the Teton River and to the east leveled into flatlands that ran out of sight. **1968** *DARE* File **swID,** Bench[es]—Small foothills that are similar to buttes. Houses can be built on benches. **1969** *DARE* (Qu. C17) Inf **KY**28, Bench—a round, flat-topped hill.

bench-fice n [*bench* from **bench-legged** + *fice* alter of **feist** n]

1912 Green *VA Folk-Speech,* Bench-fice . . . A cur-dog with long body and short legs like a bench.

benching exclam [Var of **vents**]

In marble play: =**fen.**

1966 *DARE* Tape **GA**13, If he [=another player] started to draw back a little, you'd holler "benching," "no fudging." . . Benching meant that you couldn't shoot a slinging shot or a fudge shot. You had to put your tighten-ups on the ground . . you couldn't move your hand.

bench-jumper n

1 See quot.

1969 *DARE* (Qu. CC4, . . *Various religions*) Inf **GA**74, Bench-jumpers = Holy Rollers.

2 See quot.

1982 *DARE* File **Ozarks** (as of c1920), We always referred to people who constantly changed churches as "bench-jumpers".

bench-legged adj Also *bench-kneed* **chiefly Sth, S Midl**

Esp of dogs: bowlegged; hence n *bench(ed) legs.*

1859 Taliaferro *Fisher's R.* 125 **nwNC,** His stout, well-compacted body stood firmly upon, and was carried with great ease and facility by, a short, stubbed pair of benched legs and little feet, after the Chinese fashion. **1866** Smith *Bill Arp* 159 **GA,** He'd have his soul transmigrated to a bench-leg'd fice. **1898** Lloyd *Country Life* 12 **AL,** Old Jack [=a dog] got into a rough and tumble fight with a big bench-legged coon. **1902** *DN* 2.229 **sIL,** *Bench-legged* . . . With legs set wide apart, as in a 'bench-legged fiste.' **1905** *DN* 3.70 **Ozarks.** **1906** *DN* 3.126 **nwAR,** *Bench-kneed* . . . Having legs far apart and crooked. "He's as ugly as a bench-kneed dog." **1908** *DN* 3.290 **eAL, wGA,** *Bench-legged* . . . Having sprawling or crooked legs: used of dogs, and in derogation, of persons. **1937–39** *Hall Coll.* **wNC, eTN,** *Bench-legged* . . like legs of bulldogs, short and spread apart . . . A beagle is a bench-legged fiste. **1965–70** *DARE* (Qu. X37, . . *People's legs if they're noticeably bent, or uneven, or not right*) Infs **IL**7, **KY**59, **MS**16, **MO**29, **NC**18, Bench-legged.

bench man n

A judge.

1965 Brown *Manchild* 398 **NYC** [Black], If I go to court and the bench man throws a dime [=a ten-year jail sentence] on me, I'll walk with that too, Sonny.

bend n¹ **chiefly S Midl**

Used in place-names to represent a small or unimportant community.

1964 Faulkner *Hamlet* 325 **MS,** Likely that Texas man wouldn't have knowed where Frenchman's Bend was if Mr. Snopes hadn't showed him. **1965–70** *DARE* (Qu. C34, . . *Nearby settlements, villages, or districts*) Inf **DC**12, Hell's Bend; **AR**55, Nigger Bend; **MS**23, Possum Bend; **LA**2, Sharely's Bend; **NY**20, Shirttail Bend; (Qu. C35, . . *Different parts of your town or city*) Inf **IL**130, Bumblebee Bend; **KY**21, The Bend; Salt Lick Bend, Turkey Neck Bend.

bend n²

1 A drinking spree. [Scots] Cf **bend one's elbow** and std *bender*

1887 F. Francis, Jr. *Saddle & Moccasin* 84 (*DAE*), They do say as he was 'customed to go on a scoop—on a bend, occasionally, as it were. **1942** Berrey–Van den Bark *Amer. Slang* 103.1, *Spree* . . bend. **1968** *DARE* (Qu. DD16, *To have a drinking bout and get drunk is to go on a _____*) Inf **CT**6, Bend.

2 See **bender 1.**

bend n³ See **bent** n² 2

bend n⁴ See **ben** n²

bend-a-bow See **bendy-bow 1**

bend doughnut n Also *ben doughnut, bendy ~* **sNEng**

=**bender 1.**

1943 *LANE* Map 575, *Sliding on thin ice* . . . 1 inf, **seRI,** To run ['bɛn 'donəts]; 1 inf, **seMA,** Run ['bɛn 'donəts]; 1 inf, **seMA,** Having ['bɛn 'donəts]. **1969** *DARE* (Qu. B35, *Ice that will bend when you step on it, but not break*) Infs **MA**74, **RI**3, 5, Bendy doughnuts; **CT**25, **RI**15, Bend doughnuts.

bender n

1 also *bend, benders:* =**rubber ice,** thin, flexible ice that will bear one's weight; a sliding maneuver performed on such ice. **esp NEast** Cf **bending ice, bendy-bow, cracky benders**

1894 *DN* 1.328 **NJ,** *Bender.* **1943** *LANE* Map 575, 3 infs, **RI,** *Sliding on thin ice* . . . Run(ning) benders; 1 inf, **seMA,** Run bends. **1965–70** *DARE* (Qu. B35, *Ice that will bend when you step on it, but not break*) Infs **CT**13, **MI**115, **NJ**39, **NY**2, 80, Bender; **CT**29, 39, **NH**16, Benders.

2 See quot.

1916 *DN* 4.344 **seSC,** *Bender* . . . A type of kite.

3 pl *benders,* also *bends:* Delirium tremens. Cf std *go on a bender*

1966–70 *DARE* (Qu. DD22) Inf **NJ**68, Benders, (the) bends; **NC**23, Benders.

benders See **bender 1, 3**

bendified adj [*bend* + *-ified*]

Bent.

1919 *DN* 5.36 **wNC**, *Masterest . . .* "Zeke . . dremp of drappin' down on his bendified knees . . and a-makin' the masterest moanin' you ever hear." **1942** Berrey – Van den Bark *Amer. Slang* 43.4, *Curved . .* bendified, bent. *Ibid* 121.61, Bendified knees, *bended knees.*

bending ice n Also *bendy ice* **chiefly Nth, N Midl** Cf **bandudelums**

=**bender 1.**

1950 *WELS (Soft ice that will bend when you step on it, but will not break)* 1 Inf, **ceWI**, Bending ice. **1965 – 70** *DARE* (Qu. B35, *Ice that will bend when you step on it, but not break)* 16 Infs, **chiefly N Midl, esp IL, sIN**, Bending ice; **CT6, PA18, WI71**, Bendy ice; **MA68**, Bending [ice].

‡**bending rod** n

A divining rod.

1968 *DARE* (Qu. CC13a, . . *A forked stick that's used to show where there's water)* Inf **MN28**, Bending rod—made of willow.

bend one's elbow v phr Cf **elbow bending**

To drink liquor.

1937 *Hench Coll.* [Hench: Heard over the radio in an imitation Ozark Mountain skit], Uncle Zeke bent his elbow too much last Saturday night. **1943** *Progress* (Charlottesville VA) 30 Sep 1/7 *(Hench Coll.)*, If you quit bending the elbow and put that money in War Bonds, you will be in shape to come to work next day. **1960** Wentworth – Flexner *Slang*, *Bend . . [one's] [the] elbow.* **1968** Adams *Western Words*, *Bendin' an elbow*—Drinking whisky.

ben doughnut See **bend doughnut**

bends See **bender 3**

bend the crab v phr

To do a somersault.

1968 *DARE* (Qu. EE9a, *The children's trick of turning over rapidly straight forward close to the ground)* Inf **MD8**, Bend the crab.

bendudelums See **bandudelums**

bendy adj

Pliable, limber.

1965 – 70 *DARE* (Qu. KK25, *Something that bends or yields easily: "That willow branch is very _____.")* 25 Infs, **scattered**, Bendy.

bendy-bow n

1 also attrib, also *bend-a-bow, bendy, bendy-go:* =**bender 1.** **esp sNEng**

1896 *DN* 1.412 **NH**, *Bend-a-bow:* thin ice that bends when skated upon . . . bendy, Conn[ecticut]. **1950** *WELS (Soft ice that will bend when you step on it, but will not break)* 1 Inf, **swWI**, Bendy bow ice. **1965 – 70** *DARE* (Qu. B35) Infs **CT32, MI65**, Bendy-bows; **CT4, 17**, Bendy-bow; **MA17, 55**, Bendy-go; **CT36**, Bendies; **CT6**, We used to run bendies. **1968** *DARE* (QR, near Qu. B33) Inf **CT2**, Did ya' ever run bendy-bows on ice? You run out and it bends and bounces back repeatedly.

2 also *bow:* See quots.

1903 *DN* 2.349 **MA**, *Bendy bow . . .* An elastic or springy place in a clay road due to moisture chiefly in spring time. Children make bendy bows where the conditions seem favorable and jump on them till they break through. **1966 – 68** *DARE* (Qu. N30, . . *A sudden short dip in a road)* Infs **AL14, PA104**, Bendy-bow; **ME22**, Bow.

bendy doughnut See **bend doughnut**

bendy-go See **bendy-bow 1**

bendy ice See **bending ice**

bendy leather n [*EDD bendy leather* (at *bend* sb.[1]), "A boy's name for ice in a half-thawed condition, yet elastic and capable of bearing a weight."]

=**rubber ice.**

1967 *DARE* (Qu. B35) Inf **PA29**, Bendy leather.

bene See **benne**

beneath prep Pronc-spp *beneaf, beneth* Cf Pronc Intro 3.I.17
Std senses, var forms.

~~**1837** Sherwood *Gaz.* GA 69 [In a list of provincialisms to be avoided], *Beneath,* for beneath.~~ **1899** Dunbar *Lyrics Hearthside* 167, Lay me down beneaf de willers in de grass.

bengal See **bergall**

benighted ppl adj **formerly widespread, now chiefly S Midl**
Overtaken by darkness.

1805 (1904) White *Jrl.* 26 **MA**, The sun was setting then and I did not know what to do about going for fear of being benighted. **1838** (1925) Kemper *Trip WI* 431 **NY**, Were benighted but finely [=finally] arrived. **1915** *DN* 4.224 **TX**, *Benighted . . .* Overtaken by night. "Before he reached home he was benighted." **1950** *Western Folkl.* 9.158 **CA**, *Benighted.* Caught on a climb after nightfall. **1953** Randolph *Down in Holler* 226 **Ozarks**, We figured on gittin' to Joplin, but we was *benighted* just south of Tipton Ford. **1974** Fink *Mountain Speech* 2 **wNC, eTN**, John figured he'd be home by sundown, but he was benighted. **1976** Garber *Mountain-ese* **Appalachians**, *Benighted . .* stranded overnight. The travelin' salesman got benighted and had to stay at the farm house.

benjamin n Also *benjamins, benjamin white* [By folk-etym from Middle Fr *benjoin* benzoin, in ref to its aromatic fragrance] **chiefly NEng** Cf **stinking Benjamin**

=**trillium.**

1887 *Harper's Mag.* 75.303/1 **NEng**, In the woods the painted trilliums —the "Benjamins" of the country folk—were unfolding their delicate pink and white flowers. **1891** *Jrl. Amer. Folkl.* 4.149 **NH**, Trillium erectum . . . My father used to gather the early plants for greens, and called them *Benjamins.* **1892** *Jrl. Amer. Folkl.* 5.104, *Trillium erectum . . .* Benjamins. S[outhern] V[ermon]t . . . *Trillium erythrocarpum,* Benjamins. New England. **1897** *Jrl. Amer. Folkl.* 10.145, *Trillium erectum . .* red Benjamin, Woodstock and Paris, M[ain]e . . . *Trillium erythrocarpum . .* white Benjamin, Woodstock and Paris, M[ain]e. **1900** Lyons *Plant Names* 378, *T. cernuum . . .* White Benjamin . . . *T. erectum . . .* Red Benjamin . . . *T. grandiflorum . . .* White Benjamin. **1968 – 69** *DARE* (Qu. S2) Inf **VT13**, Benjamin; **MO35**, Benjamin white [FW sugg]; **NY39**, Benjamin white [heard]; **NH14**, Red benjamin, white benjamin.

benne n, also attrib |'bɛni| Also sp *bene, bhene* [See quot 1949] **Sth, esp SC**
Sesame.

1769 in 1789 *Amer. Philos. Soc. Trans.* 1.309 **seGA**, I send you a small keg of Bene or Bene Seed, which you will please to present to your Society for their inspection. **1818** Darby *Emigrant's Guide* 185 **LA**, That species of sesamum, called oriental bhené. **1867** De Voe *Market Asst.* 358 **Sth**, Bene Plant. This plant is much used in the South for culinary purposes. **1932** (1946) Hibben *Amer. Regional Cookery* 316, *Charleston Benné Wafers.* **1941** FWP *Guide SC* 155, Peach leather and benne-seed [sesame seed] brittle are Charleston specialties in the way of confectionery. **1949** Turner *Africanisms* 191, *West African Words in Gullah . . .* ['bɛne] 'benne, the sesame'—W[olof], [bene] . . B[ambara] [bene]. **1966 – 68** *DARE* FW Addit **SC**, Sesame seeds are benne seeds —(Informant has never heard of sesame); **ceSC**, Benne seed—sesame seed. **1966 – 70** *DARE* (Qu. H80, *Kinds of candy often made at home around here)* Inf **SC62**, Benne brittle; **SC4**, Benne candy; **SC19**, Benne wafers; (Qu. H82b, . . *Cheap candy . . sold years ago)* Inf **SC70**, Benne ['bɛni] candy.

bennie bush n

A usu small California shrub (*Ceanothus papillosus*).

1938 Van Dersal *Native Woody Plants* 89, *Ceanothus papillosus . . .* Bennie bush . . . Flowers May – June; inflammable.

benny n

1 A man's straw hat. **old-fash**

1922 Lewis *Babbitt* 121, I tip my benny to him. [In the "Fourth Printing, November, 1922" *benny* was changed to *kelly.*] **1926** *Textile World* 12 June 43 *(W3 File)*, One of the tragic features of the game was the irrevocable step taken by catcher Harding when he stepped through a new straw "benny," when doing all and more than a catcher should really attempt in going after a high foul ball. **1927** *Republican* (Springfield MA) 15 Sep *(W3 File)*, [Headline:] Men Say Goodby to Straw Hats For Another Season: Tradition Has it That All Summer Bennies Are Discarded on the 15th So Panamas, Sailors and Leghorns Sing Their Swan Song.

2 also sp *binny:* A man's overcoat. [Abbr for *benjamin*]

1924 Henderson *Keys to Crookdom* 397, *Benjamin.* An overcoat. Also called a binny. *Ibid, Binny.* Overcoat. Especially one with big pockets for concealing loot. **1927** *DN* 5.438 [Underworld jargon], *Benny . . .* An overcoat. **1929** *AmSp* 4.338 [Among hoboes], *Benny*— An overcoat. **1931** *AmSp* 6.329 [Carnival cant], *Benny . . .* An overcoat. **1932** *Santa Fe Mag.* Jan 34/2 *(Hench Coll.)*, A short overcoat is called a Benny. **1957** *AmSp* 32.277 [Among jazz musicians], *Benny.* Overcoat. **1966** *DARE* (Qu. W4, . . *Men's coats or jackets for work or outdoor wear*) Inf **WA**11, Benny. **1969** *DARE* (QR, near Qu. W43) Inf **CA**107, A benny is an overcoat.

3 also sp *bennie:* See quot.

1977–78 Foster *Lexical Variation* 28 **NJ**, *Bennie,* referring to tourists from New York City and North Jersey, is universal in Monmouth County and is the only specific term in northern Ocean (Point Pleasant, Bricktown, and Toms River) . . . Probably *bennie* comes from *Benny* 'Jew,' well-known in working-class New York City.

Bensnickel See **Belsnickel**

Benson's turkey n
=**great blue heron.**

1956 *AmSp* 31.181, A name . . embodying that of an individual . . is *Benson's turkey* . . . This appellation for the great blue heron has persisted in the Puget Sound country since 1898. The tideland farm of a man named Benson was a good heron habitat, the birds were often seen on his dikes and became known as Benson's turkeys.

bent adj Cf **bend** n² **1**
Partially or thoroughly drunk.

1833 Greene *Life Dr. Dodimus* 2.176, He was seldom downright drunk; but was often . . confoundedly bent. **1927** *New Republic* 9 Mar 1 [Words denoting drunkenness], Bent. **1968–70** *DARE* (Qu. DD15, *A person who is thoroughly drunk*) Infs **NY**241, **OH**102, Bent; [(Qu. DD14, *When a person is partly drunk, "He's _____."*) Inf **WI**40, Half bent out of shape].

bent n¹ See **bentgrass 1**

bent n²
1 A section of the supporting framework of a building: see quots.

1815 *Niles' Natl. Reg.* 9.200/2 **PA**, The floats were placed at proper distances, with their ends to the shore, and on each of them were raised two bents or frames. **1892** *DN* 1.229 **KY**, *Bent:* the timbers of one side of a barn as they stand framed together. **1910** Burroughs *Catskills* 57 **NY**, Slowly the great timbers go up; louder grows the word of command, till the bent is up. **1934** Hanley *Disks* se**CT**, And when they raised this east bent of the church . . they had forty yoke of oxen; ne**CT**, They put it [=a barn] together in bents. **1957** *Springfield Union* (MA) 5 Aug, This frame was made in sections, or bents extending the width of the barn. **1966** *PADS* 45.7 **KY**, *Bent* . . . A subdivision of the framework of a tobacco barn framed by the intersection of the rails and the vertical supporting members of the barn. **1967** Key *Tobacco Vocab.* **CT, MO,** *Bent.*

2 also *ben, bend:* The space between the supporting timbers of a barn, often used for hay storage; a space reaching from floor to ceiling used for hay storage. **chiefly Nth** Cf **ben** n²

1939 *LANE* Map 103 **scattered NEng,** *Bent* or *ben(d),* a section of the mow or bay formed by the framework of the barn [10 infs, *Bent;* 2 infs *Bend;* 1 inf *Ben*]; 1 inf, *Bent,* a ten-foot section for hay, from the floor up. **1950** *WELS* (*The spaces between the joists in a barn or shed*) 10 Infs, **WI**, Bents; 1 Inf, Handle-bents; (*The place for storing hay in a barn*) 1 Inf, Bent. **1968–69** *DARE* (Qu. M3, *The place inside a barn for storing hay*) Infs **IN**45, **KY**49, **NY**189, Hay bent; **KY**49, Storage bent; **IL**26, Hay ben; (Qu. M5, . . *Hole for throwing hay down below*) Inf **CA**145, Bent. **1973** Allen *LAUM* 1.184, The same meaning [a second floor with a large open space reaching from the ground floor to the roof] is represented by *bent,* used by a North Dakota farmer of New York background; but *hay bent,* reported in northern Iowa, refers to an unpartitioned division made by vertical studdings. Although unrecorded in the east, *hay bent* was also recorded in Kenosha, Wisconsin, with this sense.

ben't See **be** C1a

bentgrass n
1 also *bent:* A grass of the genus *Agrostis,* often important as forage. [*OED* 1778 →]

1791 in 1793 *Amer. Philos. Soc. Trans.* 3.160, *Agrostis,* Bentgrass. **1843** Torrey *Flora NY* 2.442, *Agrostis stricta . . . Upright-flowered Bent-grass . . .* Sandy field near the outlet of Oneida Lake. **1889** Vasey *Ag. Grasses* 46, Herd's grass [of Pennsylvania], Bent Grass, . . . is extensively cultivated. **1966–69** *DARE* (Qu. L9a) Inf **RI**16, Rhode Island bent; **WI**21, Bentgrass; (Qu. S9) Inf **WA**12, Creeping bent.

2 The common reed (*Phragmites communis*).

1871 *U.S. Dept. Ag. Rept. of Secy. for 1870* 423, *Bent grass . . .* This species of reed, which grows abundantly around St. Thomas, in Southern Utah, during the summer months, produces a kind of white, sweet gum.

bequilla n [AmSpan] **SW**
=**Colorado River hemp.**

1960 Vines *Trees SW* 547, Hemp Sesbania . . . Other vernacular names are Zacate de Agua, Bequilla [etc.]. **1970** Correll *Plants TX* 836, Bequilla. Robust annual . . . infrequent or locally abundant, e. third of Tex.

‡berantled adj [*berattled* + intrusive *n*]
Confused, "shook up."

1969 *DARE* (Qu. GG2, . . *"Confused, mixed up": "So many things were going on at the same time that he got completely _____."*) Inf **KY**6, Berantled [ˌbɪˈræntld].

berbenia n Also sp *berbena, berdena* Pronc-spp for *verbena*
1966–70 *DARE* (Qu. S26e) Infs **AL**15, **IL**26, **IA**34, **MD**36, **MA**25, **NC**40, **OH**5, Berbenia; **NC**87, Berbena; **TX**64, Wild berdena.

berberry n [Var of **barberry;** *OED* 1725 →]
1843 Torrey *Flora NY* 1.33, *Berberis vulgaris, . . . Common Berberry . . .* [grows in] hedges, field and road sides. **1863** *U.S. Dept. Ag. Rept. of Secy. for 1862* 157, The May apple . . belongs to this class, as does the red berried plant well known as Berberry. **1911** *Century Dict.* **1965** *DARE* (Qu. S26a) Inf **OK**1, Berberries.

berdena See **berbenia**

berduque See **belduque**

bère See **bar** n³

bereft adj [Abbr for *bereft of reason* (or *sense*)]
Crazy.

1926 Kephart *Highlanders* 371 s**Appalachians,** Air ye plumb bereft? **1938** Matschat *Suwannee R.* 62 n**FL,** s**GA,** Belike Manthy'll be clean bereft, we-uns havin' stayed so long on our ventures. **1944** *PADS* 2.17 s**Appalachians,** *Bereft . . .* Crazy, "touched." "Air ye plum' bereft, ye fool!"

berg See **burg**

bergall n Also *bengal, berg-gylt, burgall, gall* [Scots *bergel(l);* cf *SND*]
=**cunner** n¹ **1.**

1815 *Lit. & Philos. Soc. NY Trans.* 402, *Bergall of New-York . . .* is very troublesome to fishermen by nibbling away their bait . . . It is a large bergall that weighs ten ounces. **1859** (1968) Bartlett *Americanisms* 58, *Burgall . . .* A small fish, very common in New York; also found on the coast of New England, and as far south as Delaware Bay. **1887** Goode *Amer. Fishes* 296, The Chogset, or Cunner, or Bergall . . . In New York, the name "Burgall" has continued in use since the revolutionary times. **1898** *U.S. Natl. Museum Bulletin* 14.1577, *Cunner; Chogset; Blue Perch; Bergall; Berg-gylt . . .* A pest to the fishermen from their habit of nibbling the bait from their hooks. **1906** *NJ State Museum Annual Rept. for 1905* 343, *Tautogolabrus adspersus . . .* Bengal. Gall. Bergall. **1933** John G. Shedd Aquarium *Guide* 142, *Bergall . . .* is extremely variable in coloration.

bergamot n Also sp *burgamot,* pronc-sp *bergamont*
=**horsemint 1.**

1838 Flagg *Far West* 2.29, The *orchis,* the balmy thyme, the burgamot, and the asters of every tint, . . then prevail. **1900** Lyons *Plant Names* 11, *Monarda . . .* Bergamot. **1915** (1926) Armstrong *Western Wild Flowers* 456, There are several kinds of Monarda . . . These plants are called Balm, Bergamot, and Horse-mint. **1968–70** *DARE* (Qu. S21) Inf **NY**75, Bergamont; (Qu. S26a) Infs **NJ**29, **PA**200, Bergamont; (Qu. S26b) Inf **MD**18, Bergamot; (Qu. S26e) Inf **OH**98, Bergamot. **1972** Brown *Wildflowers LA* 158, *Bergamont, Beebalm . . .* Widespread in variety of habitats from dry sand to moist pinelands.

berg-gylt See **bergall**

berl See **boil** n¹, v A

berlaskin n [Etym unknown]
1952 Brown *NC Folkl.* 1.519, *Berlaskin . . .* A hurting, an annoyance.

Berliner n Also *Berlin, Berliner pfannkuchen* [Ger *Berliner* of Berlin + *Pfannkuchen* pancake] **esp WI** Cf **bismarck**
A doughnut with jelly inside.

1950 *WELS* (*A round cake, deep fried with jelly inside*) 4 Infs, **WI**, Berliner. **1950** *WELS Suppl.* **csWI**, Berliner—a kind of filled doughnut. **1967–68** *DARE* (Qu. H29, *A round cake cooked in deep fat, with jelly inside*) Inf **WI62**, Berliner pfannkuchen; (Qu. H32, . . *Fancy rolls and pastries*) Inf **NY9**, Berlin—like a lady finger.

Berliner kranzer n Also sp *Berliner kranser* [Ger *Berliner* of Berlin + *Kranz* wreath, garland]   **Ger, Scan settlement areas**
A pastry shaped into a wreath.

1951 Tufford *Scandinavian Recipes* 22, Berliner-kranser . . . Roll each piece of dough into about 7 inch lengths, form into a wreath and cross ends. **1952** Tracy *Coast Cookery* 175 **ND**, Berliner-Kranser . . . Mix beaten egg yolks with sugar and hard-boiled egg yolks . . . work in the flour and butter . . . Chill the dough . . . Form into wreaths. **1967** *DARE* Tape **MN6**, And then there are Berliner kranzer ['krɑntsɚ] which you make with the yolks of hard boiled eggs, and sugar, and raw egg yolk, and flour, and butter . . . They're a harder cookie than the others. **1983** *Capital Times* (Madison WI) 11 May 19/2, On the menu for the smorgasbord will be . . Norwegian meatballs, . . rommegrot, . . and Norwegian pastries. Pastries include . . rosettes, krumkake, . . and berlinerkranser.

‡**berlin kettle** n   [?*boiling kettle;* cf **boil** n[1], v **A**]

1968 *DARE* (Qu. F4, . . *The deep metal container used to boil foods*) Inf **IA18**, Berlin ['bɝlɪn] kettle—the large one to boil a ham in.

berlot n |'bɝlo| [CanFr] Cf *DCan*
A sleigh resembling a cutter: see quot.

1967–69 *DARE* (Qu. N40b, *Different kinds of sleighs for carrying people*) Inf **VT17**, Berlot—a kind of sleigh; it isn't a pung; usually painted red. It had a rounded dashboard and back. It was on low runners and was very low. You'd say "Low as a berlot" ['bɝlo]; (Qu. N40c, . . *For carrying other things*) Inf **NY24**, Berlot ['bɝlo]—cutter box on wooden runners, built down low.

berm n Also sp *berme, birm, burm*

1 orig *berm-bank,* pronc-sp *burn-bank:* The bank of a canal opposite the tow path; transf: the bank of a road cut.

1854 *N&Q* 1st ser 9.12/2 **PA**, The bank of a canal opposite to the towing-path is called the *birm-bank.* **1883** *Williamsport* (Pa.) *Gazette* March 30 (1912 Thornton), The horse plunged over the bank into the bed of the canal. **1930** Shoemaker *1300 Words* 7 **cPA Mts** (as of c1900), *Burn-bank*—The opposite side of the canal from the tow path. **1943** Powell *I Can Go Home* 54 **swGA**, It tilted the car into the air and pitched the passengers off on to the berm of a cut through which the train was passing. **1955** Adams *Grandfather* 17 **NY** (as of 1830s), He swam across to the berm opposite. **1962** Wyld *Low Bridge* 17 **wNY** (as of 1825–60), The canal itself consisted of a *berm* side (berm-bank . .) and a towpath side.

2 A long mound or bank, spec:

a A levee or dike; a supporting ridge.

1937 *Sun* (Baltimore MD) 22 July 9/4 *(Hench Coll.),* Along with the regular fill now being put in place on the site of the new airport, loose rock is being deposited on the berm against the outside bulkhead, for additional strength. **1941** Percy *Lanterns* 246 **LA**, A boil is a small geyser at the base of or on the berm of the levee, on the land side, of course. **1968** *DARE* File **nDE**, Berm—A raised bank of dirt to impound water in a marsh. **1970** *DARE* File **seNE**, Berm—The base of a government levee along the Missouri River, 100 ft. wide at base, tapering to 15 ft. at top. In this region, non-government banks of the same type to restrain rivers are called *dykes.* **1973** *News-Miner* (Fairbanks AK) 14 Dec (Tabbert *Alaskan Engl.*), In marginal areas a berm or bank of gravel can be spread on the surface for supporting the pipeline without upsetting the balance of the active thawing layer and the permafrost table, he said. **1976** *Alaska Business and Development* (Winter Issue) 8 (Tabbert *Alaskan Engl.*), As one facet of his contract, Green has built a depression in the dam foundation near the Chena River. This is a rectangular pit, around the edge of which is a large berm or dike extending 500 by 700 feet across. **1977** *News-Miner* (Fairbanks AK) 24 Dec B3/3 (Tabbert *Alaskan Engl.*), By Friday, the fuel had spread over about 2,000 square feet, including 1,500 square feet outside the dike berm which is intended to contain spills within the tank farm.

b A bank of snow or earth, usu at the side of a road.

1940 *Hall Coll.* **wNC**, Berme—A ridge at the side of a road; used by loggers and road-builders. **1968** *DARE* (QR, near Qu. N24) Inf **CA62**, Berm—The pile of dirt at the side of the shoulder. **1972** *News-Miner* (Fairbanks AK) 21 Apr (Tabbert *Alaskan Engl.*), There is no license required for road sign hunting, but a driver's license is recommended,

since few sign hunters are physically fit enough to venture onto the berm on foot. **1976** *Ibid* 12 Feb, Bruce released the brake and the dogs took off . . . I watched as the team sprinted across the road, headed directly toward the icy berm created by the snowplows. The berm was about three feet high. **1979** *Ibid* 1 Sep 3, The suit charged that in late July or early August Gavora, Inc. or its agents blocked Pennsylvania Street by excavating two ditches and placing two dirt berms across it with the specific purpose of denying the use of the street to the public.

c freq attrib: A bank of debris formed in clearing land.

1953 *Jessen's Weekly* (Fairbanks AK) 30 Apr (Tabbert *Alaskan Engl.*), Forest fire fighters received a call at 4 p.m. Sunday that a burm pile was burning at 33 mile on the Richardson highway. **1962** *AK Sportsman* Oct 33/1 **AK**, That first summer we spent picking up the endless quantity of roots and sticks that lay deep on our field, and burning the many piles of debris left by the bulldozer. When deep snow interrupted this project in early November, the berm piles looked as large as ever. **1973** *News-Miner* (Fairbanks AK) 30 June (Tabbert *Alaskan Engl.*), The fire escaped into a berm pile and Beistline was unable to control it. **1979** *Agroborealis* Jan 33 (Tabbert *Alaskan Engl.*), The vegetation was sheared with an angled blade and dozed into tightly packed, large berm rows by long pushes with a tractor. **1979** *News-Miner* (Fairbanks AK) 22 March 1 (Tabbert *Alaskan Engl.*), A warm wind blew across berms of piled brush on Dennis Green's 3,000-acre farm in the Delta agricultural project.

d By ext: see quot.

1981 Tabbert *Alaskan Engl.* 383, From several long-time Alaskans I have heard *berm* applied to the forest vegetation mat itself—the moss, low plants, brush, leaf mold, etc. and the entwined roots and clinging soil if a piece is dug up. In none of these instances was the mat piled up in a berm. Perhaps this use has developed from folk analysis of the compound *berm pile.* That is, just as a rock pile is made up of rocks . . , so a berm pile is made up of berm.

3 rarely *bern:* The shoulder of a road.   **chiefly PA, OH, IN, WV** See Map

1935–42 in 1944 *ADD* **nWV**, *Berm* . . . Usu. unknown to visitors . . but known to about 1 of 4 natives. **1943** Morgantown *Post* 23 Feb 2/7 *(ADD)* **WV**, The trailer traveled along the berm for about 78 feet, knocking down the guard rails, before plunging over the hill. **1944** *Ibid* 17 Jan 1/5 **nWV**, The fog was so heavy in some sections that motorists had to 'feel' their way along the berm or, where possible, painted lines in the center of the road. **1965–70** *DARE* (Qu. N25, *The unpaved part of a graded road along the edge of the pavement*) 120 Infs, **esp PA, OH, IN, WV**, Berm; **OH15, 56**, Bern.

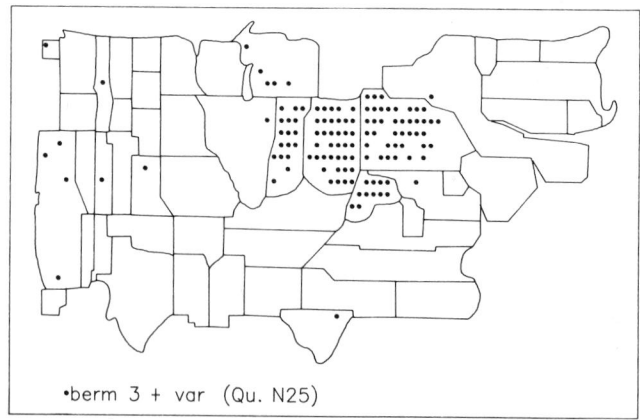

•berm 3 + var (Qu. N25)

4 The strip of grass between the sidewalk and the curb.   **esp Gt Lakes**

1965–70 *DARE* (Qu. N44) Infs **IN69, MI47, OH70, PA128, 234, 246, WI19**, Berm. **1968** *E. Liverpool Rev.* (OH) 19 June 11/3 **OH**, [Ref to an auto–pedestrian ramp], The blacktop surface has been applied to the bridge floor, virtually all of the sidewalk has been poured and guardrails are in place. Workers are slated to shape up and seed the berms and remove the concrete forms from the under side of the span. **1973** Allen *LAUM* 1.382 **MN, ND**, [4 infs, *berm;* 1 inf has heard *berm* in Iowa].

5 The median strip of a four-lane highway.

1967–68 *DARE* (Qu. N17, . . *The separating area in the middle of a four-lane road*) Infs **CA35, IN13, 34**, Berm.

6 See quot.

1940 *Hall Coll.* **wNC**, A berme is a bulge in a tree.

Bermuda mulberry n

=**French mulberry.**

1900 Lyons *Plant Names* 75, C[allicarpa] Americana L. Virginia to Florida and Texas. French Mulberry, Bermuda Mulberry. Sour-bush. **1952** Taylor *Plants Colonial Days* 41 **VA**, This native species . . is neither French nor a mulberry . . . Common names include Bermuda mulberry. **1970** Correll *Plants TX* 1339, *Bermuda-mulberry* . . . Fruit showy, rose-pink or lilac to violet or red-purple.

bern See **berm 3**

‡**bernie ball** n

1969 *DARE* Tape NY199, We played at what you call bernie ball out in the middle of the road . . . That's just an ordinary game of ball but they used to let the girls run the bases.

berries, the n

1 Something or someone thought to be very good, excellent.

1920 in 1954 Weingarten *Amer. Dict. Slang.* **1922** *DN* 5.140 [Bryn Mawr students], *Berries, quite the* . . . signifying approval. **1926** Van Vechten *Nigger Heaven* 285, *Berries, the:* an expression of approbation. **1932** *AmSp* 7.329 [Johns Hopkins jargon], The berries—splendid; perfect (used to indicate intense pleasure or superlative quality). **1965–70** *DARE* (Qu. GG19b, . . *A person acts . . important: "He seems to think he's _____."*) Infs FL14, KY74, NY66, OH65, PA109, 175, The berries; (Qu. II23, . . *The best society of a community*) Infs IN76, MD23, Berries; [(Qu. II24, . . *Where the well-off people live*) Inf NY234, The berries]; (Qu. KK1a, . . *Words meaning very good*) Inf NY234, The berries; (Qu. NN6a, *Exclamations of joy*) Inf MS64, This is the berries; (Qu. KK2, . . *"Very likable or popular"*) Inf MS14, The berries.

2 The limit; the last straw.

1960 Partridge *Slang* 424, *Berries, the.* The extreme, whether of good or of bad; the limit: from ca. 1900. E.g. "It's the berries!" **1966–70** *DARE* (Qu. GG22a, *When you have come to the end of your patience, you might say, "Well, that's the _____."*) Infs MT2, WI72, Berries; (Qu. GG22b, . . *"Well, that certainly _____."*) Inf IN60, Is the berries; IN76, That's the berries; WI34, Ain't that the berries; [KY74, Takes the berries].

berril See **barrel**

berrin See **burying**

berry n

A dollar.

1922 Lewis *Babbitt* 103, A fellow . . pulls down fifteen thousand berries a year. **1924** Marks *Plastic Age* 231, I'm nearly a hundred berries to the good. **1932** *AmSp* 7.329 [Johns Hopkins jargon], Berry—a dollar. **1942** Berrey–Van den Bark *Amer. Slang* 559, *Money* . . berries. *Ibid*, 559.16, *Silver Dollar* . . berry. **1967–69** *DARE* (Qu. U19a, . . *Money in general: "He's certainly got the _____."*) Inf MO19, Berries; (Qu. U20, . . *Dollars . . "It cost a hundred _____."*) Inf TN11, Berries.

berrying See **burying**

berry picker n

1968 *DARE* (Qu. HH1, . . *A rustic or countrified person*) Inf MI78, Berry picker.

‡**berumpus** n [*be-* as in *behind* n + **rumpus**] *joc*

The buttocks.

1970 *DARE* (Qu. X35, *Joking words for the part of the body . . you sit on*) Inf MS86, Berumpus.

bes See **be B1g**

bes' See **best**

bescrow and bescrew v [Alter of *beshrew*]

1952 Brown *NC Folkl.* 1.519, *Bescrow and bescrew* . . . To curse.

‡**besetter** n [*be-* as in *behind* n + **setter**] *joc*

The buttocks.

1967 *DARE* (Qu. X35, *Joking words for the part of the body . . you sit on*) Inf WA28, Besetter [bəˈsɛtɚ].

be-shame' bush n Also *be-ashamed* [From its habit of closing its leaves when touched; cf **shame briar** and *DJE shamer*] Cf **sensitive plant**

A mimosa.

1914 *Jrl. Amer. Folkl.* 27.247 **SC** [Black], The sensitive-plant is the "be-shame'-bush." **1966** *DARE* (Qu. S26) Inf MS47, "Be-ashamed" —a weed.

beshow n Cf **bashaw**

=**sablefish.**

1884 Goode *Fisheries U.S.* I.268 *(DA)*, Black Candle-fish . . in the Straits of Fuca . . is called by the Indians 'Beshow.' **1887** Goode *Amer. Fishes* 271, The Beshow . . is generally known in Puget Sound by the name of "Horse-mackerel." **1902** Jordan–Evermann *Amer. Fishes* 498, It *[Anoplopoma fimbria]* is the beshow.

beslings See **beastlings**

besom n |ˈbizəm| [Prob from *besom* broom]

Energy; zest.

1969 *DARE* (Qu. KK28, *Feeling ambitious and eager to work*) Inf NY199, Full of besom [ˈbizəm]. **1975** *DARE* File **c,cnNY**, A lackadaisical worker wasn't using enough besom; an over-exuberant small child was told "You have too much besom."

bespoke adj

1 See quot. [Engl dial; *EDD* "Obsol."]

1899 (1912) Green *VA Folk-Speech*, Bespoke . . . Bewitched; conjured.

2 also *bespoken*: Engaged (usu to be married). *old-fash*

1929 *AmSp* 5.124 **ME**, A girl who was engaged was "be-spoken." **1931–33** *LANE Worksheets* **ceMA**, Bespoke—Engaged to be married. "They're bespoke." **1933** *AmSp* 8.1.47 **Ozarks**, *Bespoke*, adj. Asked for, engaged. When a girl is described as *bespoke* it usually means that she is engaged to be married, but sometimes only that she has a date for a particular party or dance.

bespritzed adj [Ger *bespritzen* to squirt at, spray]

1935 *AmSp* 10.169 [Among PaGer speakers], Spritz is in common use for 'sprinkle.' The man with the garden hose is spritzing his lawn, and if you go too close you are likely to get bespritzed.

bess adj, adv See **best**

bess beetle, bess bug, besse bug See **betsy bug**

Bessie n

1 See **Betsy 1.**

2 also *Bess, Betsy*: Used as a name for a cow or calf. Cf **boss** n¹

1942 *Sat. Eve. Post* 7 Feb 14/1, The menfolks couldn't leave the Bessie cow. *Ibid* 15/1, The new calf, lying on the clean straw beside the Bessie cow. **1965–70** *DARE* (Qu. K80) Infs NY66, Come Bess; OK56, PA242, Come, Bessie; (Qu. K81) Inf WA27, Ho, Bessie; GA33, So, Bessie, so; NJ35, Wo, Bessie; NJ25, Quiet, Betsy!; (Qu. K83) OK56, Come, Bessie; NY72, Come here, Bessie; FL20, Soo, Bess!; (Qu. K8) Inf MO16, Milk old Betsy.

3 also *(old) Betsy;* Transf: used as a name for an automobile.

1967–69 *DARE* (Qu. N5) Infs OR1, Bessie; IL108, NC55, Betsy; CO7, Old Betsy.

bessie bug See **betsy bug**

bessroot See **bethroot**

best adj, adv Pronc-spp *bes', bess* See **Pronc Intro 3.I.22**

Std senses, var forms.

1837 Sherwood *Gaz. GA* 69 [In a list of provincialisms to be avoided], *Bess*, for best. **1905** Culbertson *Banjo Talks* 25 [Black], De linsey-woolsey for ow' dress, / De cas'net clof fer Marster's bes'. **1922** Gonzales *Black Border* 289 **sSC, GA coasts** [Gullah glossary], Bes'—best.

be standing v phr [Prob infl by imper *be seated*]

To stand up.

1906 *DN* 3.126 **nwAR**, *Be standing* . . . To stand up, to get up (from a sitting posture). "And now shall we all be standing while we pray." "If you will be standing, I will now read the charge to you."

bestest adj, adv [*best* + *-est*]

1893 Shands *MS Speech* 19, *Bestest* [bestəs]. Double superlative, formed from *best*. Used by negroes. **1953** Brewer *Word Brazos* 9 **eTX** [Black], Of occasion in De Bottoms . . you kin fin' some of de bestes' preachuhs dat done evuh de grace a pulpit. **1965** *DARE* Tape FL21 [Inf White], I like 'em raw bestest of all.

best girl See **best woman**

best-goodest n [Redund; cf *-est*]

A favorite.

1948 Hurston *Seraph* 30 **wFL**, You wouldn't take and kill you [=your] best-goodest would you?

best lady, best maid See **best woman**

bestmost n [Redund *best* + *-most*] Cf **bettermost**
    One's best, utmost.
        1887 *Scribner's Mag.* 2.474 **AR,** But w'en she seen doctor war doin' his bestmost, she never said nary nuther word.

best room n Also *best parlor* old-fash
    The parlor (of a house).
        1907 *DN* 3.181 **seNH,** Best room . . . Old-fashioned front parlor, used only on formal occasions, such as the visit of the minister. **1941** *LANE* Map 323, Most New England houses built more than a generation ago have one 'best' room set aside for use on special occasions only . . *best room* [occurs infrequently]. **1950** *WELS* 1 Inf, **ceWI,** Best parlor . . . Passed [out of use] with plush-covered furniture. **c1960** *Wilson Coll.* **csKY,** Best room . . . Sometimes used instead of *front room* or *parlor.* **1968–69** *DARE* (Qu. D13, *The room where you entertain company*) Infs **MA59, WV13,** Best room. [Both Infs old] **1973** Allen *LAUM* 1.159, Three respondents in Minnesota and Iowa, of Ohio and Connecticut background, reported the use of *best room,* a minor variant in New England.

best woman n Also *best girl,* ~ *lady,* ~ *maid* esp **Midl**
    A maid or matron of honor at a wedding.
        1965–70 *DARE* (Qu. AA17, . . *Other people beside the bride and groom . . in a wedding party*) Infs **KY40, NC49, PA57, TX26,** Best woman; **KS5, PA70,** Best lady; **IN26, VA27,** Best girl; **GA28,** Best maid (*changed to* best woman).

bet n¹, v Usu |bɛt|; in **NEng, esp ME,** also |beɪt, bɛɪt| Pronc-sp *bate*
    Std senses, var forms.
        1861 Holmes *Venner* 2.181 **wMA,** The' won't be much iron on that hoss's huffs an haour after daylight, I'll bate ye a quarter. **1909** *DN* 3.408 **neME,** Bate . . . To bet. **1914** *DN* 4.69 **ME, nNH,** Bate, n. and v. Bet. **1943** *LANE* Map 590, 14 infs, **chiefly ME, less freq sNH, eMA,** Bet [beɪt, bě‧ɪt].

‡bet n² [Short for *alphabet*]
    A letter of the alphabet.
        1969 *DARE* Tape **KY23,** [With just one teacher for 60 or 70 pupils, we] done mighty well to ever learn to read our bets, you know.

beteling block See **beetling block**

bethroot n Also *beth, bettroot, bessroot* [Var of **birthroot**]
    Any of several **trilliums,** but esp *Trillium erectum.*
        1828 Rafinesque *Med. Flora* 96, *Trillium latifolium . . . Names . . . Vulgar.* Bethroot. **1876** Hobbs *Bot. Hdbk.* 10, Beth root, Trillium, Trillium pendulum. **1903** Small *Flora SE U.S.* 276, *Trillium . . . Wake-robin. Birth-root. Bess-root. Ibid* 278, *Trillium erectum . . . Beth.* **1949** Moldenke *Amer. Wild Flowers* 339, Next in popularity . . is the *purple wakerobin* or *bethroot . . T. erectum.* **1968** *DARE* (Qu. S2) Inf **NY69,** Beth. **1971** Krochmal *Appalachia Med. Plants* 256, *Trillium erectum . . . Common Names: . .* bethroot, bettroot.

betimes adv [Alter of *by times;* cf *EDD* betimes adv.², Scots, Ir, nEngl dial]
    Occasionally.
        1926 Kephart *Highlanders* 289 **wNC, eTN,** They glance betimes with "a slow, long look of mild inquiry." **1930** *AmSp* 5.389 **N Atl,** Betimes . . now and then. **1941** *Time* 16 June 71/1, For the past ten years, Dolan has toiled in Hollywood, worked betimes on radio scripts for the *Big Town* series.

bet-piyan n [Fr *bête puante* stinking animal]
    A polecat or skunk.
        1968 *DARE* (Qu. P26) Inf **LA26,** [ˌbɛtˌpiˈjã]; **LA34,** [ˌbɛtˌpiˈjõ].

Betsey See **Betsy**

bet straightening ppl
    Kibitzing.
        1935 Hurston *Mules & Men* 23 **nFL** [Black], All of those who were not actually playing [Florida flip] were giving advice — "bet straightening" they call it.

Betsy n
    1 also *Becky, Bessie, Betsey,* freq prec by *old:* A shotgun or rifle.
        1837 Smith *Col. Crockett's Exploits* 29, Well, I shouldered my Betsey, and she is just about as beautiful a piece as ever came out of Philadelphia,

and I went out to the shooting ground. **1856** *Spirit of Age* (Sacramento) 4 Nov 3/1 *(DA)* **CA,** Jest let them raise that check agin me, and if I don't shoot why old Betsy won't blizzard. **1869** *New No. West* (Deer Lodge, Mont.) 20 Aug. 2/7 *(DA),* Mr. Fredericks proceeded immediately on the horse, loaded 'Betsey,' (his shot gun). **1946** *Outdoors* June 82/2 *(DA),* I'll just bet you old Betsy here against that machine-gun of yours that I can get off 25 shots faster'n you can! **c1960** *Wilson Coll.* **csKY,** Betsy (or Old Betsey) . . . One's gun; echo of pioneer times. **1965–70** *DARE* (Qu. P37b, . . *A shotgun*) 48 Infs, **scattered,** Old Betsy, **AZ2, CA15,** Betsy; **NC41,** Old Bessie, **NJ16,** Old Becky; (Qu. P37a, . . *A rifle*) Infs **IA8, MN36, MO10, TX29,** Betsy. **1971** *WI Conserv. Bulletin* Sept–Oct 8, Partridge are still with us. In fact, if you haven't shouldered old Betsy for a while, get her ready. It looks like a good season ahead!
    2 A tool: see quot.
        1927 *DN* 5.472 **Ozarks,** Betsey . . . This term is applied to various tools and utensils, but applies chiefly to the big mallet used in driving fence-posts. "I'll take ol' betsey and jes' bust hell out o' thet 'ar [=that there] feller!"
    3 See **Bessie 2, 3.**
    4 See quot.
        1966 *DARE* (Qu. S11, . . *Other names . . for . . bachelor's button*) Inf **NM9,** Some call them Betsies.

betsy-beetle See **betsy bug**

‡Betsy bread n [*Betsy* famil form of *Elizabeth,* used to suggest domesticity, + *bread*]
    A type of corn bread.
        1970 *DARE* (Qu. H14, *Bread that's made with cornmeal*) Inf **TN66,** Betsy bread — has baking powder and milk in it; baked in oven.

betsy bug n Also *betsey bug, betsy beetle, bess* ~, *bess bug, bess(i)e* ~, *betty* ~ Often in phr *crazy as a* ~ chiefly **Sth, S Midl, esp AR, KY**
    A rather large black beetle of the family Passalidae. Also called **horn beetle, patent-leather beetle, pinch bug**
        1910 Blatchley *Coleoptera* 908 *(DA),* This well-known species, commonly known as the 'horn' or 'bess-beetle,' occurs abundantly throughout the state [Indiana]. **1910** Harris *Eve's Husband* 234 *(DA),* A young congressman has to . . encourage them [his constituents] to ask for little things like sample betty-bugs to eat other bugs, garden seed [etc.] . . . The Government furnishes the betty-bugs. **1931** Randolph *Ozarks* 101, The approved treatment for earache is to prick a "betsy-bug" with a pin, and put a drop of its blood in the ear. **1944** *Harper's Mag.* 188.373/2 **IA,** He always lived over the crick from us . . . Crazy as a betsey bug most of the time. **1946** *PADS* 6.5 **eNC** (as of 1900–10), Bessie bug . . . A handsome black bug whose habitat is rotten wood. It is about one inch long. To children it seems to say "Bessie" when touched with a blade of grass . . . Common among children. **c1960** *Wilson Coll.* **csKY,** Betty (or Betsy) bug — any large beetle. "Jimmy caught a Betsy bug and put it down my back." **1964** Borror–DeLong *Intro. Insects* 382, These beetles are called by a variety of names — bessbugs, betsy-beetles [etc.]. **1965–70** *DARE* (Qu. R5) Inf **AR42,** Betsy bug; (Qu. R30) Infs **KY28, 47,** Bess bug; **AR5, 48, 51, KY34,** Bessie bug; **AR48, 52, GA84, KY28, LA2, 10, 15, SC46, TN6,** Betsy bug. **1967** *DARE* FW Addit **wNC,** Crazy as a bess bug. **c1974** Jones *Ozark Hill Boy* 42 **AR** (as of c1930), I personally have been subjected to . . May apple root and senna tea for biliousness, besse bug blood for earache, sorghum molasses for sore eyes. **1981** *Broaddus Coll.* **ceKY,** Bess bug.

better adj, n [Infl by adv use, as in "It is better than a mile to town"]
    In ref to time:
    a More; a longer period.
        1914 *DN* 4.103 **KS,** Better . . . More, as, when we have better time. **1931** *PMLA* 46.1306 **Appalachians,** He's been a-livin' here these six weeks an' better.
    b Later.
        1967 Green *Horse Tradin'* 127 **swTX,** When I walked out onto the street it was better than dark and getting pretty chilly.

bettermost adj Cf **bestmost**
        1905 *DN* 3.3 **cCT,** Bettermost . . . Best.

bettersome adj [*better* + *-some*] *obs*
    Better.
        1843 (1916) Hall *New Purchase* 136 **IN,** There's a speretil [=spiritual] and bettersome idee.

better-to-do adj [Compar of *well-to-do*]
Well-off.
    1970 Wilhelm *Last Rig* 195 **NV** (as of c1865), There were no middle-class Chinese in the very early days. There were the very poor and the better-to-do.

bettie grass See **betty grass**

bettie wood See **bettywood**

bettroot See **bethroot**

betty n [*Betty* famil form of *Elizabeth,* used to suggest domesticity]
    1 See quot.
    1912 Green *VA Folk-Speech, Betty* . . . A chamber-pot.
    2 See quot.
    1967 *DARE* (Qu. JJ1a, . . *A schoolteacher* . . *a woman*) Inf **MA**71, The Betty — when I was in school. [Inf old]
    3 See **bettywood**.

betty bee martin n See **bee martin**

betty bug See **betsy bug**

bettyfuss n [Cf *OED betty sb.*[2] "Given in contempt to a man who occupies himself with a woman's household duties" and **fuss** n **B1**]
    1967 *DARE* FW Addit **MA**5, *Bettyfuss* — A fussbudget.

betty grass n Also sp *bettie grass*
A **colicroot 2** (here: *Aletris farinosa*).
    1892 (1974) Millspaugh *Amer. Med. Plants* 172, *Aletris farinosa* . . . Com[mon] Names . . . *Bettie Grass.* **1940** Clute *Amer. Plant Names* 250, *Betty-grass.*

betty martin See **bee martin**

betty stick n [Etym unknown, but cf **bettywood**]
    1982 *Smithsonian Letters* **ID,** My grandfather was a transplanted Kentuckian. I remember when he staked out plots for certain vegetables or in preparation of building pens or erecting a fence, he called the stakes he used Betty Sticks.

bettywood n Also *bettie wood, betty (tree), bitty wood* [Prob varr of *buttonwood,* infl by *betty* a word commonly sugg familiar things. Note: *Betula,* birch, has been considered, but evidence in its favor is weak.] **esp KY**
Prob the sycamore *(Platanus occidentalis),* but the tree, once well known by this name, has not been conclusively identified.
    1786–1804 Bourbon Co. KY *Surveys Book A,* [Letter of Edna T. Whitley: In pages 24–525, bettywood trees are so named 20 times (*bettie wood* once) as corner trees. No alternative name is given.]. **1798** Bourbon Co. KY *Rept. Processioners,* Beginning at the corner of the settlement . . a buckeye which we marked with the letters B.B. [for B. Bedford, processioner] thence with the line of the patent N 353 60 poles to a sycamore and elm in the edge of Stoner, thence crossing Stoner's fork . . at the end of such distance we marked a corner four Bettywoods and sugartree and Buckeye, 1 Bettytree and sugar tree we marked with the letters S.C. [for Saml. Clay] thence North 54 East 157 poles to a hickory and buckeye, thence . . to the beginning corner, given under our hand this 2nd of April 1798. [Signed] **1958** *KY Folkl. Rec.* 4.1.176, The Bettywood . . was often named as a corner tree in early surveys. Some in Bourbon County were dated "July 1779" and were still standing when the tract was resurveyed in 1808. In one instance some sycamores were marked to indicate the corner where only the Bettywood stump remained. **1980** *DARE* File **neKY,** In 1807 one of two bettywoods in this county [Bourbon Co. KY] . . "dated July 1779" was still standing and the stump of the other was there, so a nearby sycamore was chosen as a corner tree for that survey in its place. Between 1798 and 1817 the county surveyor used these trees as corners in local surveys — ash 114 times, . . beech 8, bettywood 13, box elder 60, buckeye 222, cherry 17, . . sugar trees 277, sycamores 13, thorns 48, white thorns 5, white walnut and black walnut 76 . . . As to its widespread use I tabulated the names of surveyors, pilots, markers, chain carriers etc. who knew the tree by that name [=*bettywood*] . . . It was more than sixty, possibly eighty. **1981** *Ibid* **Boone NC** (as of c1920), When I was a small chap, an old lady by the name of Miss Bennett lived part of the time with a great uncle and aunt [of mine]. She made yearly trips to Kentucky . . and she is the one I remember using the word bettywood. Now I am thinking, could she and others have used the bitter wood for bettywood. But I can still hear her

say, what I think was bettywood . . . She dipped snuff and used a birch toothbrush while doing so. This is the time white birch was needed to make a new tooth brush. It should have been called a snuff brush. I am positive Miss Bennett picked up the bettywood while in Kentucky . . . The only two birches that I am familiar with is the white and black. I am almost sure the bitterwood is a white birch or a spicewood bush when spoken of around here . . . Recently I talked with a friend who remembers visiting his grandmother [about 1900] and the old lady asking someone to bring her a small limb from a bettywood tree. What she used the limb for, he does not know but he is positive of the bettywood being used as a name for some kind of birch. **1982** *Ibid* **neKY** (as of c1960), One of the nurses had heard a cousin speak of the "bitty-wood" tree. She lived in a nearby county to Bourbon I think Bath county. The tree had a nobby, rough bark, was never cut for lumber so might have been left for staking out fields. **1982** *Ibid* **cwWV** (as of c1920), Not most, but a considerable number of people in Roane County, W. Va., called sycamores "buttonwoods." I cannot remember a time when I did not know what they were, and I knew Aunt Catherine's old house, with two in the yard. She said "bettywood" in referring to them.

betwattled adj Also sp *betwaddled* [Cf *EDD betwattled* "confused, distressed, bewildered, stupid" and std *twaddle, twat*]
Infatuated.
    1927 *AmSp* 3.135 **ME,** An excellent and common term was "betwaddled" or "betwattled after" someone, when a person was so in love as to be unable to use good judgement. **1968** *DARE* (Qu. AA10, *A very special liking that a boy may have for a girl*) Inf **PA**118, Betwaddled [bɪ'twɑdld].

between daylight and daylight adv phr
During the night. Cf **can't see**
    1969 *DARE* FW Addit **cnNC,** *Between daylight and daylight:* Night. *Mildly humorous.*

between hawk and buzzard adv phr, adj phr
    1 At twilight. *old-fash*
    1832 Kennedy *Swallow Barn* 1.6, I [=a Yankee] entered Richmond [Virginia] between hawk and buzzard — the very best hour, I maintain, out of the twenty-four, for a picturesque tourist. **1912** Green *VA Folk-Speech* 24, *Between hawk and buzzard.* The twilight hour. When it is too dark to tell a hawk from a buzzard.
    2 In a difficult or uncomfortable position. *?obs*
    1856 in 1958 Taylor–Whiting *Dict. Amer. Proverbs,* I declare, a body who has young ones, has no peace of her life. She's just between hawk and buzzard, as a body may say. **1866** Smith *Bill Arp* 48 **GA,** What satisfaction is there in living between hawk and buzzard?

between hay and grass adj phr Also *between grass and hay*
    1 Between youth and adulthood; not fully mature.
    1848 Mitchell *Nantucketisms* 40 (*AmSp* 10.40), Betwixt hay & grass, between Boyhood & Manhood. **1857** *Knickerbocker* 49.38, Mace was a young shaver of fifteen and sixteen, just getting under way and learning the ropes . . a youth just between hay and grass. **1872** Schele de Vere *Americanisms* 208, The great importance which a crop of grass has for all stock-raisers and the Indians, whose very life depends on the buffaloes finding food and their horses pasture, has led to the use of the peculiar phrase in which the youth, who is no longer a boy and not yet a man is picturesquely said to be between grass and hay. **1891** Bunner *Zadoc Pine* 17 **NY,** He . . got a couple of eggs cooked for his private supper . . . The eggs were, as he told Mr. Bryan, "kinder 'twixt grass and hay." **1905** *DN* 3.3 **cCT,** *Between hay and grass.* **1933** Williamson *Woods Colt* 177 **Ozarks,** Jest a kid, but at the same time she's growin' up, too. Them legs o' her'n is as big as a woman's. She's between hay an' grass, an' maybe more grass than hay, but grass cures fast, this time o' year. **1968** Adams *Western Words.*
    2 Between seasons of plenty, hence, in a difficult or uncomfortable position.
    1939 FWP *Guide MT* 413, *Between hay and grass* — In difficult times, as in early spring, when hay is gone and grass has not come up. **1968** Adams *Western Words, Between hay and grass* — The time between winter and spring, when hay has gone and grass has not yet come up. Difficult times. Also *between grass and hay,* between summer and winter.
    3 See quot.
    1928 Ruppenthal Coll. **KS,** *Between hay and grass* . . . Vague; indefinite; inconclusive; colorless.

between jobs n [Prob by analogy with trademark *Between the Acts* a small cigar, 1948 →]

1967 *DARE* (Qu. DD7, . . *Cigars*) Inf **SC**34, Between Jobs—a short cigar; about like a cigarette—traveling salesmen used to smoke them between calls on stores.

betweenst adv, prep [*between* + *-st,* prob infl by *betwixt*]
Between.

1887 (1967) Harris *Free Joe* 154 **ceGA,** Yonder's the Yankees on one side, and here's the blamed niggers on t'other, and betwixt and betweenst 'em a white man's got mighty little chance. **1942** Rawlings *Cross Creek* 223 **nFL,** Now you let 'em stand three to seven days. I cain't tell you which, nor what day in betweenst.

between you and me and the post adv phr Also *between you and me and the gatepost, ~ lamp post*
Secretly; in confidence.

1796 in 1972 Tyler *Prose* 209 **VT,** I heard Ben Burgler whisper . . "That was a cursed treaty—Between you and I, *and the post.*" **1833** Neal *Down-Easters* 1.23 **ME,** Between you' an' me an' the post. **1871** Eggleston *Hoosier Schoolmaster* 119 **IN,** But *I* say, atwixt you and me and the gate-post, don't you never believe nothing that Mirandy Means says. **1887** (1967) Harris *Free Joe* 156 **ceGA,** And I tell you what, gener'l, betwixt you and me and the gate-post, it's done come to that pass where a man can't afford to be too plegged particular. **1941** *AmSp* 16.21 **sIN, MO,** Between you and me and the gatepost (lamp post). **1966** Barnes–Jensen *Dict. UT Slang* 5, Between you and me and the gate post . . . confidentially. **1982** *DARE* File **cwMA** (as of 1915), Between you and me and the gatepost was used to mean "in confidence."

betwixt prep Also *twix(t)* **scattered, but chiefly Sth, S Midl** See Map
Between.

1871 (1892) Johnston *Dukesborough Tales* 70 **GA,** No difficulties betwixt you and me, nor betwixt me and Miss Larrabee . . not even betwixt me and Rum. **1887** (1967) Harris *Free Joe* 113 **ceGA** [Black], You can't spat a man harder betwixt the eyes than to set back an' not break bread wi' 'im. *Ibid* 151, It look like I run inter all de gullies . . 'twix' dis en Marse Tip's. **1940** *Esquire* 14.44/1 **neKY,** I'll let 'im have it betwixt the eyes. **1942** *Sat. Eve. Post* 22 Aug 42/2 **NC,** Thar wuz an enjoyment betwixt 'em that gimme grief. **1946** *AmSp* 21.96 **sIL,** Words . . that we have in common with Appalachia . . *betwixt.* **1953** *PADS* 19.14, 'Twixt . . . Still in use in extremely isolated sections of the mountains of Kentucky. **c1960** *Wilson Coll.* **csKY,** Just betwixt you and me. [Used by very old people.] **1965–70** *DARE* (Qu. MM7, *If there's a house on each side of the school . . you'd say, "The school is _____ the houses.")* 42 Infs, **esp Sth, S Midl,** Betwixt; **FL**48, **MA**61, **NY**209, **TN**14, 20, **TX**97, Twixt; **AR**47, **DC**3, **DE**1, **IN**38, **MA**5, Betwixt and between; **TN**46, 'Twixt and between; **GA**31, Twix; (Qu B8, *When clouds come and go all day, you say it's _____)* Inf **WV**5, Betwixt and between.

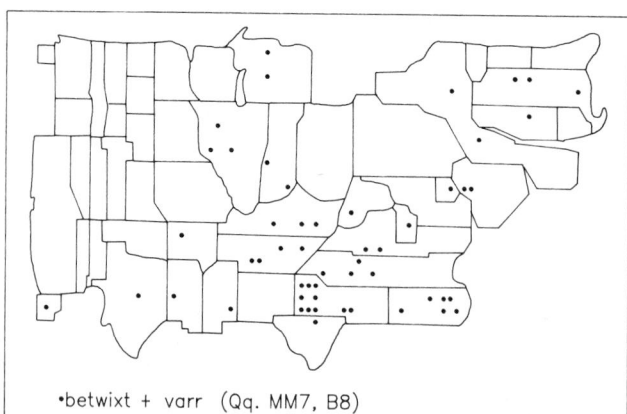

•betwixt + varr (Qq. MM7, B8)

betwixt a balk and a breakdown adj phr
=fair to middling.

1884 Harrison *Negro Engl.* 269 **Sth,** 'Twix er bauk en' er breakdown—so-so (of health).

betwixt and between n
A temporary or insignificant task between more important jobs.

1968 *DARE* FW Addit **nePA,** "I'm doing betwixt and betweens" means "I'm doing jobs of little importance."

betwixt and betweentimes adv For var see quot
Meanwhile.

1954 *Harder Coll.* **cwTN,** Betwixt-an'-betweentimes . . . Also 'twixt-an'-'tweentimes . . . Meanwhile.

Beulah land n Also *Beulah shore* [See Isaiah 62:4]
As a synonym for heaven or the Promised Land: a place of perfection or happiness; also used ironically.

1939 Coffin *Capt. Abby* 129 **ME** (as of c1860), They got to Venice next day, September 20, and came to anchor at noon in Beulah Land . . . If you had asked any Yankee wife in the middle of the nineteenth century what her idea of heaven was—after Saturday night, baked beans, and the whole family gathered around them—she would have answered Venice. **1955** Warren *Angels* 49 **VA** (as of c1855), You gentlemen know how a will begins—you all being the kind of gentlemen having estates to set in order before taking out for the Beulah shore. **1970** *DARE* Settle *O Beulah Land* [title] **WV.** **1967** *DARE* (Qu. C35, *Nicknames for the different parts of your town or city*) Inf **TN**11, Beulah land—old fashioned for colored section of Jonesboro TN. **1982** *Milwaukee Jrl.* (WI) 26 Sept mag sec 22, What a Beulah Land of single-class plutocracy this country would be!

beunt See **be** C1a

‡bewhisker n
A whisker.

1967 *DARE* (Qu. GG13b, *When something keeps bothering a person and makes him nervous, he may say, "It _____ me."*) Inf **CO**34, Scares your bewhiskers up.

bewitchness n
Witchcraft.

1951 Craig *Singing Hills* 169 **WV,** The legs of Josiah Smith's calf had been frozen and it had died, but Josiah said it was bewitchness.

bex v, hence *bex(ed)* ppl adj [Alter of *vex*] *among Black speakers* Cf Pronc Intro 3.I.17
Std senses, var forms.

1888 Jones *Negro Myths* 44 **GA coast,** Buh Snake . . gone to him house in de swamp berry bex case de man . . gone back on eh prommus. **1922** Gonzales *Black Border* 289 **sSC, GA coasts** [Gullah glossary], Bex—vex, vexes, vexing; angry, anger, angers, angered, angering. **1970** *DARE* (Qu. GG3, . . *"See those big boys trying to _____ (that little one)."*) Inf **SC**68, Bex—It's vex, but we say bex; (Qu. GG4, *Stirred up . . "When he saw them coming he got _____."*) Inf **SC**68, Bexed.

bexie See **bec-scie**

beyond prep, adv Pronc-spp *beyend* and, **chiefly Sth, S Midl,** *beyant, beyent, beyon, beyonst, beyont*
Std senses, var forms.

1818 Fessenden *Ladies Monitor* 171 **NEng** [In a list of provincialisms to be avoided], *Beyend* for beyond. **1837** Sherwood *Gaz. GA* 69 [In a list of provincialisms to be avoided], *Beyant,* for beyond. **1866** in 1944 *ADD* **MA,** Beyend. **1891** in 1944 *ADD* **WV,** Beyent. **1893** Shands *MS Speech, Beyant* . . . A common form used by illiterate whites for *beyond.* **1898** Deland *Old Chester* 166 **PA,** My wife wants to see you. She's in beyont. **1916** *DN* 4.347 **nTX** (as of 1896), *Beyonst* . . . Beyond. **1931** *Scribner's Mag.* 89.453/2 **FL,** Iffen they do float, they'll dreeft on beyant where we could ketch 'em at. **1933** in 1944 *ADD* **KY, s,c,nWV,** Beyon. Usual. **1945** *Hench Coll.* **cVA,** Just beyant this hill was Mr. Shiflett's farm. **1965–70** *DARE* (Qu. MM4, . . *"The mail box is just _____ the pine tree."*) Infs **MD**17, **NC**41, [bɪ'jænt]; **MA**5, Beyant—Irish Molly; **TN**12, Beyont—country people; **VA**15, Beyont; **TX**97, Beyonst.

bezabor n [Perh for *gazabo* guy, fellow]
See quots.

1930 *AmSp* 6.97 **cNY** (as of c1830), Bezabor: a peculiar character. "He's a queer old bezabor." **1940** *Sat. Eve. Post* 10 Feb 88/1 (as of 1836), [A circus clown speaking to a lion:] "Lay down, you big bezabor, here I come."

bezzler n [*EDD* "anything very large of its kind"]
1903 *DN* 2.349, Bezzler . . . A 'big-gun'; one who thinks himself, or is a person of importance.

B from (a) bull's foot, not to know v phr For varr see quots [See quot 1908; cf *OED B* I.2 quot 1401, "I know not an A from the wyndmylne, ne a B from a bole foot"] **now chiefly Sth, Midl** See Map Cf **A from B, not to know** and *DS* JJ15b
To be ignorant or illiterate.

  1792 Brackenridge *Mod. Chivalry* 49 **Philadelphia PA,** For there were persons there who scarcely knew a B from a bull's foot. **1832** Paulding *Westward Ho* 1.101 **VA,** You don't know a B from a buffalo's foot. **1834** *Life Andrew Jackson* 114, They begin'd with confidence 'sposen the gineral didn't know B from broomstick in the science of war. [**1843** (1916) Hall *New Purchase* 321, Big and little colleges were erected by persons who, . . in all matters pertaining to "high larnin," had not sufficient discrimination to know the second letter of an alphabet from a buffalo's foot.] **1856** Whitcher *Bedott Papers* 308 **cNY,** He don't know B from a broomstick, nor bran when the bag's open. **1908** *DN* 3.327 **eAL, wGA,** *Know B from bull('s) foot* . . . Used in negative expressions to indicate one's ignorance or illiteracy . . . The foot- or track-print of a bull is somewhat like the letter B. **1912** *DN* 3.581 **wIN.** **1915** *DN* 4.184 **swVA.** **1923** *DN* 5.243 **LA.** **1927** *AmSp* 2.359 **WV,** That driver doesn't know B from bull's bag about loading his wagon. **1942** *AmSp* 17.130 **sIN,** Don't know B from bull's foot. *Ibid* 172 **sIL,** He doesn't know B from a bull's foot. **1965–70** *DARE* (Qu. JJ15b, . . *A person who seems to you very stupid: "He doesn't know _____."*) 35 Infs, **chiefly Sth, Midl,** B from (a) bull('s) foot; **FL22, 26, NC2,** B from bully; **IL96, SC32,** B from bull; **TX40,** B from bat's foot; **TX19,** B from bull's ass; **AL5,** B from bullfrog; **AR55,** B from bullshit.

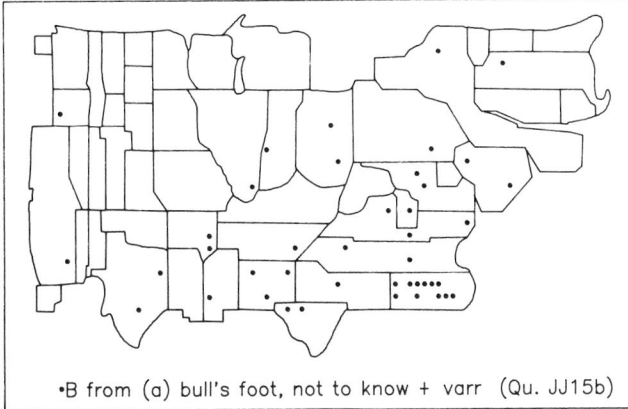

•B from (a) bull's foot, not to know + varr   (Qu. JJ15b)

bhene See **benne**

b'hin' See **behind** prep

b'hoy n [Representing Irish pronc of *boy*]
  1 also *bo-hoy:* A rowdy young man.
  1846 *Knickerbocker* 27.467 **MD,** A smile on his lips peculiar to one of the bo-hoys. **1859** (1922) Jackson *Col.'s Diary* 21 **cwPA,** The former teacher they turned off, or rather the "bhoys" were too many for him. **1866** *Atlantic Mth.* 18.727/1 **NYC,** "I want," said the stranger, "to see a b'hoy,—a real b'hoy." **1942** Berrey–Van den Bark *Amer. Slang* 461.7, *Desperado; thug . .* b'hoy.
  2 A political henchman.
  1938 *Sun* (Baltimore MD) 10 Sept 3/4–5 *(Hench Coll.),* City Hall B'hoys [on a sign used in a political campaign]. **1953** *Sun* (Baltimore MD) 20 July 28/6 *(Hench Coll.),* [Headline] *All is confusion for the b'hoys.*

bialy n |bi'ali| [From *Bialystok* Poland] **chiefly in Jewish settlement areas**
  See quot 1970.
  1968 *New Yorker* 24 Aug 63, [Allen] Ginsberg's stepmother, Edith, was in the kitchen fixing a big breakfast of bagels, bialy, lox, cream cheese, and scrambled eggs. **1968** *DARE* (Qu. H18, . . *Kinds of bread*) Inf **NY119,** Bialies. [Inf Jewish] **1970** Feinsilver *Yiddish* 357, Bialys . . a short bilingual plural for *bialystoker beygel,* the type of bagels made in Bialystok . . . The dough is softer and chewier than that of the authentic bagel . . and has a floury finish. Also, the center is a depression rather than a hole and is filled with onion flakes.

bias adv, adj [*OED* "Obs. exc. of dress"] Cf **catabias**
  1 Diagonally; catercornered.

  1965–70 *DARE* (Qu. MM15, *If a carpenter nails a board crossing another board at an angle, you might say, "He nailed the board on _____."*) Infs **CO4, IL126, MD26,** Bias; (Qu. MM16, *If you're walking with somebody to the other corner of a square . . you might say, "It'll be shorter if we _____."*) Inf **MD26,** Walk bias acrost.
  2 Askew, awry.
  1970 *DARE* (Qu. MM13, *The table was nice and straight until he came along and knocked it _____*) Inf **VA46,** Bias.

bias road n
  See quot 1950.
  1950 *PADS* 14.13 **SC,** *Bias road,* a road leading off at an acute angle from the main road. **c1960** *Wilson Coll.* **csKY,** You turn at a bias road and go left.

bias-ways adv
  =**bias 1.**
  1968 *DARE* (Qu. MM15, . . *"He nailed the board on _____."*) Inf **MD17,** Bias-ways.

bibbed overalls See **bib overall(s)**

bibble v [Cf *OED bib* v, *bibble* v] *arch*
  To drink as ducks drink.
  1683 in 1960 Taylor *Poems* 13 **MA,** Let Conscience bibble in it with her Bill. **1899** (1912) Green *VA Folk-Speech, Bibble* . . . To drink like a duck. "Ducks bibbling in the water."

Bible n
  Biblical injunction or authority.
  1898 Westcott *Harum* 162 **nNY,** Peleg Hopkins grumbled audibly when he was requested to build the fires on Christmas day, and expressed his opinion that, "if there warn't Bible agin workin' on Chris'mus, the' 'd ort ter be."

bible-back n
  1 also adj *bible-backed:* See quot 1903. *old-fash*
  1857 in 1912 Thornton *Amer. Gloss.* 60, We might, in consequence [of lack of funds], become somewhat round-shouldered and *"bible-backed."* **1894** Frederic *Marsena* 103 **nNY,** He was a man of more than fifty, I should think, tall, lean, and what Marcellus called "bible-backed." **1903** *DN* 2.349 **seNY, neNJ,** *Bible-back* . . . A round-shouldered, hump-backed person.
  2 See quot.
  1938 *AmSp* 13.160, I myself am hunting for a word other than 'bible-back' to describe an uncomfortable, stiff or straight-back chair.
  3 A pious or sanctimonious person. *often derog*
  1942 Berrey–Van den Bark *Amer. Slang* 327.2, *Sanctimonious person.* Bible back. **1964** *PADS* 42.35 **Chicago IL,** More specific epithets [for a Protestant] include *bigoted Protestant . . , bible-back . . ,* and *anti-Catholic . . ,* all of which were given by Irish Catholics. **1967** *DARE* (Qu. CC4) Inf **WA20,** Bible backs—good religious people.

bible-backed See **bible-back 1**

Bible banger n Also *Bible beater, ~ pounder, ~ puncher, ~ ranter, ~ reader, ~ spouter, ~ thumper, ~ toter often derog*
  A fanatical or zealous religious person or lay preacher.
  1897 Barrère–Leland *Slang* 1.105/1, *Bible-pounder* (popular), a parson. **1927** *DN* 5.438 [Underworld jargon], *Bible-ranter* . . . a preacher, the most despised person on earth from the tramp's viewpoint. **1931** *PMLA* 46.1311 **Appalachians,** Bible-reader (preacher). **1940** *Sun* (Baltimore MD) 13 Feb 11/3 **wNC** *(Hench Coll.),* O'Connell said the judge was "a Bible-toter that . . wants to make a speech." **1942** Berrey–Van den Bark *Amer. Slang* 327.7, *Preacher* . . . Bible pounder, -puncher *or* thumper, Bible ranter, Bible reader. **1955** Stong *Blizzard* 119 **IA,** More of these Bible-spouters like Abe Jamieson ought to read that book [=Gibbon's *The Decline and Fall of the Roman Empire*]. **1965–70** *DARE* (Qu. CC10, . . *An unprofessional, part-time lay preacher*) Infs **CA209, IL78, IN13,** Bible banger; **AL41,** Bible beater; **NY10,** Bible puncher; **PA209,** Bible thumper. **1969** Sorden *Lumberjack Lingo* **NEng, Gt Lakes,** Bible pounder—A street corner preacher; reformer.

Bible-book n [Pleonastic formation]
  1952 Brown *NC Folk.* 1.520, *Bible-book* . . . *Bible.*—West[ern NC]. Illiterate.

Bible bug n [Cf Exod 10:12–19] See also **ferro**
  1969 *DARE* (Qu. R8, *Other kinds of creatures that make a chirping or*

shrilling or clicking sound) Inf **KY**21, Bible bug—billions of 'em every 8–10 years, holler "Pharaoh" over and over.

biblical measure n [Cf Deut 25:15, Micah 6:10]
An equitable amount.
1969 *DARE* (Qu. LL28, . . *Entirely full*) Inf **MA**58, Biblical measure.

bib overall(s) n Also *bibbed overalls, bib pants, bibs* Pronc-sp *bib overhauls* **chiefly Inland Nth, N Midl, West** See Map
Work trousers which have shoulder straps and a bib-like piece covering the chest.
1902 (1969) Sears *Catalogue* 1154, *Conductors' or Mail Agents' Bib Overalls.* **1935** Sandoz *Jules* 346 **wNE** (as of 1880–1930), He bought a pair of bib overalls that never quite hid his innate elegance. **1965–70** *DARE* (Qu. W9, *A work garment, usually of blue cloth, covering the legs and sometimes the chest, worn by farmers*) 64 Infs, **chiefly Inland Nth, N Midl, West,** Bib overall(s); 19 Infs, Bib overhauls; **CA**87, 94, **KY**44, Bibbed overalls; **DE**2, Bib pants; **CA**94, **OR**13, **WA**18, Bibs. **1976** Garber *Mountain-ese* 8 **Appalachians,** *Bibs . . .* High-front overalls. "Zack wears his bibs to cut the corn."

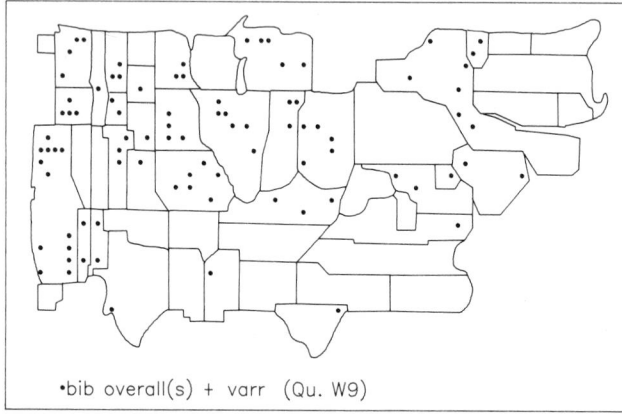

•bib overall(s) + varr (Qu. W9)

bicker v [Ext of *bicker* to argue, wrangle, prob infl by *dicker*]
To haggle, bargain.
1967–70 *DARE* (Qu. U12, *If you were buying something and you argued with the person selling it till you made him lower the price, you might say, "I_____."*) Infs **CA**32, 163, **IL**126, **NY**163, 201, Bickered; **MN**28, Bickered with him; **PA**27, Bickering.

bicycling n
Among rodeo cowboys: see quots.
1941 FWP *Guide WY* 459, *Bicycling*—Holding one foot down or under surcingle, while 'scratching' with the spur on the other foot, and then alternating. **1944** Adams *Western Words, Bicycling*—The act, when riding a bucking horse, of scratching with first one foot and then the other in the manner of riding a bicycle.

bid n
1 See **bid whist.**
‡**2** A trade-last.
1968 *DARE* (Qu. KK35, *When someone wants to pass on a compliment to you, in exchange for one about himself, he says, "I have a_____for you."*) Inf **PA**126, Bid.

bidaciously See **bodaciously**

bidar n Also sp *baidar(ka), bidari* (pl), *bidarrah* [Russ *baidara,* dimin *baidarka*] **AK**
A boat with a wood, or sometimes bone, frame covered with seal skin or canvas and having one or more openings in which the rowers sit.
1802 Sauer *Acct. Exped.* 176 **AK,** The customs of these savages are nearly allied to those of the Oonalashkans. They have the same kind of instruments, darts, and boats, or baidars; but much worse made; nor are they so active upon the water. **1867** *The Esquimaux* (Libbysville, Port Clarence AK) 7 Apr 31 (Tabbert *Alaskan Engl.*), Mr. Sergie Stepanoff . . accompanied the Major thus far in his three hole baidarka (skin canoe). **1886** Turner *Contribs. AK* 96, The natives of the present day cross pretty well to the north side of the pass until they get under Amlia Island and then run near the shore of Amlia with their small *bidari* or open boats. **1939** FWP *Guide AK* 336, The baidars or boats of

Oonalashka are infinitely superior to those of any other island. *Ibid* 378, He got about . . on sea in a seal-skin kayak or baidarka. **1965** Chevigny *Russian America* 33, The Aleuts were as amphibious as human beings can be. Their canoe, to which the Russians gave the name *baidarka . . ,* was a wonderfully unsinkable contraption. **1965** *Alaska Sportsman* Nov 81 (Tabbert *Alaskan Engl.*), The traditional boat of the Aleutian Islands is the bidarrah. The frame is tied together for flexibility in rough water, but oil-treated canvas has replaced sealion skins for covering. **1975** *AK Mag.* Jan 37 (Tabbert *Alaskan Engl.*), My favorite discovery, though, was the big company-built *bidars* used to transport freight from supply boats through the shallow water to the dock.

biddable adj [*bid* to command, enjoin + *-able;* orig Scots] **chiefly Sth, S Midl**
Obedient, tractable, docile; hence *biddableness* tractability.
1859 (1968) Bartlett *Americanisms, Biddable.* This Irish word is in use in the West. "White servants are not biddable," that is, manageable, obedient to order. **1886** Amer. Philol. Assoc. *Trans.* 17.36, *Biddable,* "obedient, tractable." . . *Biddableness,* disposition to obey . . . I have been familiar with the word in this sense in South Carolina all my life, and it is so used in East Tennessee, Georgia, and no doubt elsewhere (Ohio). **1890** *DN* 1.69 **LA.** **1914** Furman *Sight* 71 **KY,** I hain't only got these fine store-teeth and a tamed and biddable stummick. **1923** *DN* 5.201 **swMO.** **1935** (1944) Rawlings *Golden Apples* 333 **FL,** You'll have to bless her out now and agin, but on the whole she's biddable. **1951** West *Witch Diggers* 7 **sIN,** Pretty girl. Clever and biddable too.

biddy n[1] [Orig uncertain: perh imit; perh rel to **biddy** n[2]]
1 A mature chicken; a hen—often used as a call. **chiefly NEng, S Atl**
1844 *Spirit of the Times* 9 Sept (1912 Thornton), The way that factory at the Masonic Hall turns out the chickens [by steam heat] is a caution to "biddies." **1857** (1862) Colt *Went to KS* 228 **KS,** The fence . . . to keep the "biddies" from roaming, is being built. **1894** VT State Bd. Ag. *Report* 14.175, Hang up a head of cabbage and let the hens pick it, or throw in a few apples to supply biddy with green food. **1907** *DN* 3.181 **seNH.** **1939** *LANE* Map 213 **neMA,** [bɪdɨz], affectionate term for hens. *Ibid* Map 214 **csCT,** [Biddy] 'a mother hen.' *Ibid* Map 227 **throughout NEng,** Bid(die) is used in calling both hens and chickens, but some informants limit it to hens. **1949** Kurath *Word Geog.* 65, Calls to Chickens . . . Biddie! (widdie!) occurs in three separate areas: (1) from the Connecticut Valley eastward to Cape Cod and Maine, (2) from southern Delaware southward to Cape Charles, and (3) in North Carolina and on the Peedee. **1965–70** *DARE* (Qu. K72, *When the hen stops laying and begins to sit on the eggs to hatch them, she's a_____*) Inf **NV**8, Cranky biddy; (Qu. K79, *How do you call the chickens to you at feeding time*) 16 Infs, **chiefly S Atl, NEng,** Biddy (biddy) (biddy). **1973** Allen *LAUM* 1.255 **csMN,** Setting hen . . . [1 inf:] setting biddy. *Ibid* 1.267, *Calls to chickens at feeding . . .* Biddy and *come biddy, . .* 3 southern Iowans use it, as does one southern Minnesotan.
2 Any of var wild birds.
1953 *AmSp* 28.277, The familiar term *biddy* is applied with some reason to the henlike, ruffed grouse (Cape Cod, Mass.), but rather wildly to such species as the ruddy duck (Wis.) and the least sandpiper (*beach biddy,* Fla.). **1955** *AmSp* 30.181, *Biddy duck* (ruddy duck, Minn.).

biddy n[2] [Dimin of *Bridget,* infl by **biddy** n[1]] **chiefly Nth, N Midl, West**
1 A woman—freq used disparagingly, esp of an elderly, gossipy, or dissolute woman.
1867 Holmes *Guardian Angel* 233 **NEng,** Don't trouble yourself about Kitty Fagan . . . The Biddies are all alike, and they're all as stupid as owls, except when you tell 'em just what to do, and how to do it. A pack of priest-ridden fools! **1950** *WELS* (*Uncomplimentary names and nicknames for a woman*) 3 Infs, **WI,** (Old) biddy; (*Joking names that a man may use to refer to his wife*) 1 Inf, **csWI,** Biddy. **1951** *Collier's* 10 Feb 22/1, Charley had met an old biddy named Zoe Winthrop. **1965–70** *DARE* (Qu. AA7b, . . *A woman . . fond of men . . not respectable about it*) Inf **NY**241, Bad biddy; (Qu. AA22, *Joking names that a man may use to refer to his wife*) Infs **NE**11, **NY**96, (Old) biddy; (Qu. GG14, . . *Someone who fusses or worries a lot*) Inf **RI**15, Old biddy; (Qu. GG36a, . . *Person . . always poking into other people's affairs "She's an awful_____."*) Infs **LA**32, **NH**15, **NY**18, **OR**6, (Nosy) old biddy; (Qu. HH11b, *Someone who is too particular or fussy—if it's a woman*) Infs **MN**15, **SC**40, Old biddy; (Qu. HH34, . . *Words . . for a woman, not necessarily uncomplimentary*) Infs **CA**107, **WA**3, Biddy; **NM**4, Old biddy; (Qu. HH36, *A careless, slovenly woman: "She's just an old*

_____. ") Infs **MI88, MA68,** Biddy; (Qu. JJ1a, . . *A schoolteacher — a woman*) Infs **CA110, NH10, NY211,** Old biddy; **ME19,** Biddy.
2 See quots.
  1939 FWP *Guide MT* 413, *Biddy*—[An] aged and toothless ewe. **1968** Adams *Western Words, Biddy*—A sheepman's name for an old ewe.
3 See quot. *derog*
  1970 *DARE* (Qu. HH40, . . *An old man*) Inf **CA190,** Biddy.

biddy n[3] Pronc-spp *beady, beedie* [Prob coalescence of **biddy** n[1] and *beedie* of Afr origin, akin to Kongo *bidibidi* a bird] **chiefly Sth, esp S Atl**
A young or newly hatched chicken.
  1908 *DN* 3.290 **eAL, wGA. 1928** Peterkin *Scarlet Sister Mary* 111 **SC** [Gullah], My lil blue hen stole a nest in de chimney corner and hatched dese beedies. **1930** *DN* 6.84 **cSC. 1949** Turner *Africanisms* 237, The following are a few of the many onomatopoetic expressions heard in Gullah: . . 'bidi'bidi 'a small bird'; 'a small chicken.' Cf. the Kongo word *bidibidi* 'a bird.' **1952** in 1958 Brewer *Dog Ghosts* 29 **TX** [Black], Unkuh Aaron hab to 'ten' to de chickens hisse'f, ebun down to settin' de hens an' lookin' out attuh de li'l' biddies dey done hatched. **c1960** *Wilson Coll.* **csKY. 1966–69** *DARE* Tapes **GA25, NC6,** Biddy [=baby chicken]. **1967–69** *DARE* (Qu. K79) Inf **GA77,** Beady-beady-beady; (Qu. HH22c, . . *"He's mean enough to _____."*) Inf **NC38,** Push little biddies in the creek. **1968** *DARE* FW Addit **LA32,** Biddy = a baby chick.

biddy bridle n [**biddy** n[2]]
See quot 1939.
  1939 FWP *Guide MT* 413, *Biddy bridle*—Old-fashioned bridle with "blinders." **1961** Adams *Old-Time Cowhand* 117, 'Bout the only bridle a cowhand was shy of was a "biddy bridle," what he called a bridle with blinders as sometimes used by a nester who couldn't afford a ridin' bridle, but used the same one on hossback that he used on his plow hoss.

biddy-hen n [**biddy** n[1] **1**] Cf **broody**
=**biddy** n[1] **1.**
  1907 *DN* 3.181 **seNH,** *Biddy-hen* . . . In children's language, a hen. **1942** *Sun* (Baltimore MD) 3 Nov 12/3, On my part of the "[Eastern] Shore" a "biddy" was an old hen that all the folk spoke of as "that biddy hen." **1968** *DARE* (Qu. K72, *When the hen stops laying and begins to sit on the eggs to hatch them, she's a _____*) Inf **MD29,** Biddy-hen.

biddykin n [**biddy** n[1] + *-kin* dimin suff]
  1952 Brown *NC Folkl.* 1.520, *Biddykin* . . . A little person; a little chicken. Suffix *kin* = "little." *Biddy* may be related to Gaelic *bîdeach,* "very small"; thus *biddykin* would be a double diminutive.—Harnett county.

biddy-peck v, hence *biddy-pecked* ppl adj
To nag, hen-peck.
  1970 *DARE* (Qu. AA21, . . *A wife who gives the orders and a husband who takes them from her*) Inf **NC86,** Biddy-pecked. **1972** Cooper *NC Mt. Folkl.* 90, Biddy-peck—to nag mildly.

biddy pen n Also *biddy coop* [**biddy** n[1]]
A chicken coop.
  1968 *DARE* (Qu. M16, *The small shelter for a hen that can be moved about from place to place*) Infs **GA22, NC49,** Biddy pen; **GA22,** Biddy coop.

biddy's eyes n
A Johnny-jump-up (here: *Viola tricolor*).
  1900 Lyons *Plant Names* 394, *V. tricolor* . . . Biddy's-eyes. **1931** Harned *Wild Flowers Alleghanies* 326, *Pansy* . . . This species has a multitude of common names, among which are . . Biddy's Eyes, Cat's Faces, Garden Gate, etc . . . This species is common in waste places.

bide v [Aphet form of *abide*]
To tolerate or endure.
  1914 *DN* 4.158 **cVA** (as of 1901–07), *Bide* . . . To endure. "Ah can't bide cats." **1923** *DN* 5.201 **swMO,** *Bide* . . . To bear, to endure. "I caint bide a squallin' young-un." **1968–70** *DARE* (Qu. II29a, *An unexplainable dislike . . [for] a person: "I don't know why, but I just can't _____ him."*) Infs **MO4, NY234,** Bide.

bideable adj [**bide** + *-able*]
  1923 *DN* 5.201 **swMO,** *Bideable* . . . Bearable, tolerable.

bide a wee v phr [Scots] *old-fash*
  1918 *DN* 5.20 **seNC,** *Bide a wee,* stay a while.

bid whist n Also *bid* **chiefly Sth, S Midl** *chiefly among Blacks* See Map
A variation of the card game whist in which players bid to name trump.
  1952 Culbertson *Card Games* 184, Whist Variants—Bid Whist . . . Setback Bid Whist. **1965–70** *DARE* (Qu. DD35, . . *Card games*) 29 Infs, **chiefly Sth, S Midl,** Bid whist. [24 of 29 Infs Black] **1981** *DARE* File **Chicago IL** [Black], We always used to play Bid, Gin, and Spades in High School. Bid Whist is like bridge, except you only bid once and there isn't a dummy. **1982** Walker *Color Purple* 213 **GA** (as of c1930s) [Black], Us sit by the fire with Harpo and Sofia and play a hand or two of bid whist, while Suzie Q and Henrietta listen to the radio.

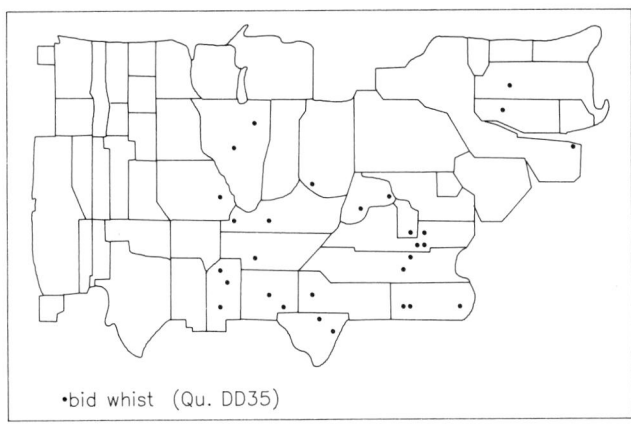
•bid whist (Qu. DD35)

bie See **bee** v

bier See **bar** n[3]

biff adv [Echoic] See also **biff** n[1], v
With a short, sharp blow.
  1847 (1962) Robb *Squatter Life* 137 **MO,** I hit him, *biff,* alongside his smeller. **1924** *DN* 5.263, *Exclamations* . . . *Biff* (sound of blow with fist).

biff v Also sp *bif* [**biff** adv, echoism] **scattered, but esp Sth, S Midl**
To strike or hit (someone or something).
  1890 *DN* 1.72 **Boston MA. 1892** *DN* 1.214, *Bif* . . or *biff.* "Current among students in the South, meaning 'to strike.' It is used oftenest in the game of marbles." **1895** *DN* 1.396 **seNY. 1905** *DN* 3.60 **NE. 1906** *DN* 3.115 **sIN. 1908** *DN* 3.290 **eAL, wGA. 1909** *DN* 3.392 **nwAR. 1910** McCutcheon *Rose* 337 **NY,** Jimmie Parsons . . tried to stop him after he biffed me. Jimmie's got two wonderful black eyes as a result. **1955** *PADS* 23.11 **Sth,** *Bif(f)* . . . To hit or strike a marble with a taw. **1956** *Hall Coll.* **eTN, wNC,** *Biff* . . . To strike a blow, hit. **1966–70** *DARE* (Qu. Y11, . . *A very hard blow*) Infs **GA44, NC18,** Biffed him one; (Qu. Y14a, *To hit somebody hard with the fist*) Infs **MD29, VA90, WI43,** Biff.

biff n[1] Also sp *bif* [**biff** adv] **scattered, but esp Sth, S Midl**
1 A sharp or quick blow.
  1890 *DN* 1.72, *Bif:* usually a noun, meaning 'a quick blow.' Philadelphia. Common in Boston . . . "To give one a biff in the ear." **1897** *KS Univ. Qrly.* 6.85 **MO,** *Biff:* a blow. **1904** (1968) Lynde *Grafters* 368, But Hawk's next biff was more to the purpose. **1905** *DN* 3.60 **NE. 1908** *DN* 3.290 **eAL, wGA. 1909** *DN* 3.392 **nwAR. 1947** *Sat. Eve. Post* 15 Mar 146/3 **TN,** Giving her a good biff on the nose . . might . . create the erroneous idea that he was a bully. **1969** *DARE* (Qu. Y11, . . *A very hard blow*) Inf **MI108,** Biff.
‡2 By ext: a black eye.
  1968 *DARE* (Qu. X20, . . *A black eye*) Inf **OH70,** Biff.

biff n[2] See **biffy**

biffy n Also *biff* [Etym unknown] **chiefly Upper MW and WI** See Map *euphem*
A toilet, spec:
a An outdoor toilet, outhouse.
  1950 *WELS* (*An outside toilet building*) 6 Infs, **WI,** Biffy; 1 Inf, **cwWI,** Biff. **1965–70** *DARE* (Qu. M21b, . . *An outside toilet building*) 14 Infs, **chiefly Upper MW and WI,** Biffy; **MN42,** Biff. **1968** *DARE* FW Addit

swVA, Biffy—an outhouse. Old-fashioned. **1973** Allen *LAUM* 1.181 **MN, cwND, SD,** *Privy* . . . [7 infs:] Biffy.

b An indoor toilet.

1942 Berrey–Van den Bark *Amer. Slang* 84.11, *Parts of houses* . . . *Toilet* . . . Biffy. **1950** *WELS* (*An indoor toilet*) 7 Infs, **WI,** Biffy; 1 Inf, **csWI,** Biff. **1965–70** *DARE* (Qu. F37, . . *An indoor toilet*) Infs **AK3, MN33, 42, PA74, WI29, 47,** Biffy; **MN34, 42,** Biff. **1973** Allen *LAUM* 1.181 **nwMN, ceIA,** *Privy* . . . [2 infs:] Biff. **1975** Bellow *Humboldt's Gift* 239 **Chicago IL,** I leaned against the partition of the biffy in the county building trying to get light from above on her letter.

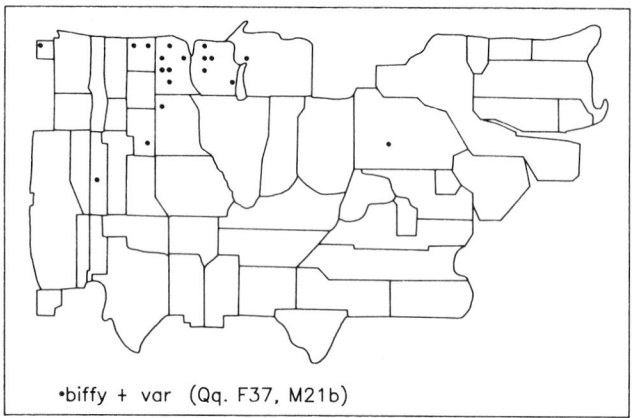

•biffy + var (Qq. F37, M21b)

big adj

1 Pregnant. [*OED* 1535 →] **chiefly Sth, S Midl** See Map Cf **big** v

c1960 *Wilson Coll.* **csKY,** *Big* . . . Pregnant. **1963** Wright *Lawd Today* 18 **Chicago IL** [Black], If you hadn't lied and said you was big, I wouldn't've never married you, neither. **1965–70** *DARE* (Qu. AA28, . . *Expressions . . women use to say that another is going to have a baby:* "*She('s)* _____.") 22 Infs, **chiefly Sth, S Midl,** Big; **NJ67, SC26,** Big again; **KY44,** Getting big; [**IL5,** In the big league].

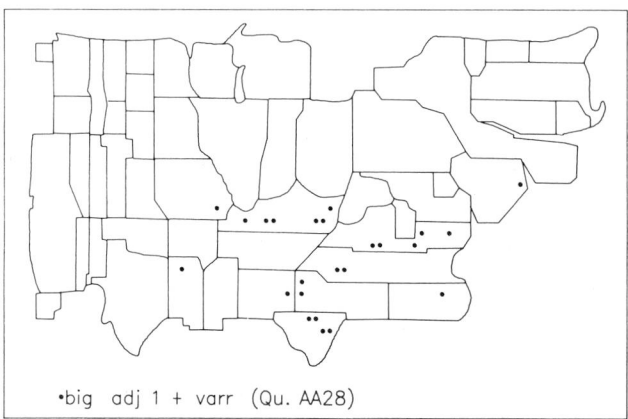

•big adj 1 + varr (Qu. AA28)

2 as superl, often in phrr *the biggest part* (or *half*): Most. **chiefly S Midl**

1899 (1912) Green *VA Folk-Speech,* Biggest . . . Most. "I was there the biggest part of the day." **1942** Warnick *Garrett Co. MD* (as of 1900–18), *Biggest,* . . most. "He slept the biggest part of the day." **1944** *PADS* 2.34 **NC, SC, TN, VA,** *Half, the biggest* . . . The majority, most. "The biggest half of the people does it." **c1960** *Wilson Coll.* **csKY,** *Biggest* . . . The most, the largest portion. "He just sets around the biggest part of the time and does nothing." *The biggest half* . . . The most or the majority, not exactly half by any means. **1970** *DARE* Tape **VA**70, The ladies would do biggest of the work on the chitterlins.

3 Of an amount or quantity: considerable, great.

1946 *AmSp* 21.54, A refusal of a second helping of food . . , 'No, thank you. I have had a big plenty.' **1965–68** *DARE* (Qu. BB18) Inf **OH44,** Puked a big lot; (Qu. LL9a, *As much as you need or more—for example . . "We've got* _____ *of apples."*) Inf **OK6,** A big plenty.

4 Of a frost: severe. **Cf black frost 1**

1967–70 *DARE* (Qu. B30, *A frost that kills plants*) Infs **AL48, AR1, 19, GA31, LA2, NJ28,** Big frost.

big adv

1 Very, exceedingly.

1890 in 1950 *PADS* 13.4 **GA,** Well, my brother Ben lives over there and he's got big rich. **1898** Lloyd *Country Life* 195 **AL,** It aint much probable that I will ever git big rich or run for congress. *Ibid* 204, Sometimes I would get good tired and big lazy and swear eternal disgust for the farm. **1906** *DN* 3.126 **nwAR,** *Big rich* . . . Wealthy. "He's big rich."

2 To a high degree.

1939–41 *Hall Coll.* **eTN, wNC,** "I'll divide with you big." "She smiled real big at me." "Sing big this time!" **1970** *DARE* Tape **IL**115, I have a . . pointer that's a big goin' dog; he goes real big. He'll go a mile, but he'll check in on ya an' if he gets on a point, he will stay there.

big v, hence *bigged* ppl adj

1 To make pregnant. [**big** adj 1] **chiefly Sth, S Midl**

1917 *DN* 4.408 **wNC, SC.** **1932** (1974) Caldwell *Tobacco Road* 27 **GA,** "Lov's going to big her," Dude said. "He's getting ready to do it right now, too . . . He acts like an old stud-horse." **1936** Morehouse *Rain on Just* 303 **NC,** What a way to be in—bigged, and no pappy. Bigged and no woman to stay with her. **1937** *Hall Coll.* **eTN, wNC,** [A poor woman] is a woman that's bigged, in a family way, in other words pregnant. **1942** Hurston *Dust Tracks* 70 **cFL,** It did not take me long to know what was meant when a girl was spoken of as "ruint" or "bigged." **1950** *PADS* 14.14 **SC.** **1952** Brown *NC Folkl.* 1.520, *Big* . . . To make pregnant.—General. **1967** *DARE* File **FL, NC,** Big—to make pregnant. Common. **1968** *DARE* (Qu. GG14) Inf **GA67,** He bigged her—He impregnated her.

2 To exaggerate.

1972 Cooper *NC Mt. Folkl.* 90, Bigging and bigging it—exaggerating.

big auger n [*auger* tool for boring holes] **chiefly West**

An important person, **big bug**; a foreman.

1903 (1965) Adams *Log Cowboy* 125 **NM,** I reckon he's some big auger—a senator or governor, maybe. **1936** Adams *Cowboy Lingo* 21 **West,** The [ranch] owner . . had divers titles, such as 'presidente,' 'ramrod' or . . 'big auger.'

big bag n

A fish used as lobster bait, perh a porgy.

1966 *DARE* Tape **ME**22, To string 'em [=lobsters] on sometime we use mostly porkies, "big bags" we call 'em.

big bedbug n

=**assassin bug** (here: *Triatoma* spp esp *T. sanguisuga*).

1895 Comstock *Manual Insects* 137, A closely allied species . . insinuates itself into beds . . [and] sucks human blood . . . This insect occurs in the Southern and Western states; it is the Big Bed-bug. **1937** *Discovery* Dec 368/2, A . . cheerful brute occurs in North America, where it is known as the "big bed bug" and the "assassin bug."

big blue crane, big blue shitepoke See **big crane**

big bluestem n

Any of several **beardgrasses,** esp *Andropogon furcatus, A. gerardi,* and *A. scoparius.*

1894 *Jrl. Amer. Folkl.* 7.103 **NE,** *Andropogon scoparius* . . big blue stem. **1910** Graves *Flowering Plants* 48 **CT,** *Andropogon furcatus* . . Big Blue-stem. **1912** Baker *Book of Grasses* 55, Big Blue-stem. **1950** Hitchcock *Manual Grasses* 757, *Andropogon gerardi* . . Big Bluestem. **1950** Stevens *ND Plants* 84, *Andropogon furcatus* . . Big Bluestem.

big boy n

1 See quot.

1942 *Amer. Mercury* 55.94 **Harlem NY,** Big boy—stout fellow. But in the South, it means fool and is a prime insult.

‡**2** also *big toter:* See quot.

1970 *DARE* (Qu. P37b, . . *A shotgun*) Inf **TN**53, Big boy, big toter. [Inf Black]

‡**big boy** v

To take advantage of (someone); to bully or tease.

1967 *DARE* (Qq. GG3, II33) Inf **PA**35, Big boy (someone).

big buck(s) See **buck** n[1] 3a

big bug n [Cf Engl dial *bug* conceited, pompous] Cf **big auger, big-butt, big dog, big dude**

An important, often self-important, person; a bigwig; hence *bigbuggery* n, *big-buggish* adj (both rare).

1827 *Harvard Reg.* Oct 247 **MA**, He who desires to be a *big / Bug*, rattling in a *natty* gig, / *No-top*, or chaise, or tandem. **1843** (1916) Hall *New Purchase* 55 **IN**, I allow the stranger and his woman-body thinks themselves mighty big-bugs. *Ibid* 199, No one would have become popular in the New Purchase, but for mistaken opinions in the neighbours about "Mr. Carlton's bigbuggery and stuckupness." *Ibid* 407, Big-buggish, aristocratic yankee notions! **1894** Frederic *Marsena* 46 **nNY**, These big bugs with plenty o'money always have to be waited on. **1905** *DN* 3.3 **cCT**. **1905** *DN* 3.60 **NE**. **1907** *DN* 3.181 **seNH**. **1907** *DN* 3.209 **nwAR, CT**. **1908** *DN* 3.290 **eAL, wGA**. **1909** *DN* 3.408 **nME**. **1910** *DN* 3.437 **wNY**. **1927** *AmSp* 2.348 **WV**. **1937** Sandoz *Slogum* 264 **NE**, Then why did he get the fences torn down—get all the big bugs of the country against him? **1965–70** *DARE* (Qu. II23) 15 Infs, **esp west of Appalachians**, Big bugs; (Qq. U37, HH2, 8, 17, II35) 8 Infs, **scattered**, Big bug; (Qu. II24) Inf **IA**30, Big-bug hill; **GA**19, **OK**1, Where the big bugs (are) (live). **1970** *DARE* Tape **MA**73, The man who built it never lived there . . he was the big bug in town at that time.

big-butt n Cf big bug
1952 Brown *NC Folkl.* 1.520, Big-butt . . . An aristocrat, a "bigwig," "bigbug."

‡big chested adj
Conceited, **biggity** adj.
1968 *DARE* (Qu. GG19a, . . *A person [who] acts . . important or independent: "He surely is _____ these days."*) Inf **TX**51, Big chested.

big church n ironic
See quots.
1897 *KS Univ. Qrly.* 6.51 **sKS**, Big church . . no church, as, "He belongs to the big church." **1908** *DN* 3.290 **eAL, wGA**, Big church, the . . . No church: used facetiously to indicate that one is not a member of any church or denomination. "I belong to the big church." **1912** Green *VA Folk-Speech*, Big church . . . The devil's church. **1952** Brown *NC Folkl.* 1.527 **cnNC**, Church, the big . . . No church at all.

big circle See big ring 1

bigcone pine n
The Coulter pine *(Pinus coulteri)*.
1897 Sudworth *Arborescent Flora* 24, *Pinus coulteri* . . Bigcone Pine (Cal.). **1911** Jepson *Flora CA* 18, *P[inus] coulteri* . . Big-cone Pine.

big crane n Also big blue crane, ~ shitepoke
=**great blue heron**.
1888 (1890) Warren *Birds PA* 57, *Ardea herodias* . . . Great Blue Heron; "Big Crane." **1913** Bailey *Birds VA* 38, Great Blue Heron [Big Blue Crane. Cranky]. **1945** McAtee *Nomina Abitera* 26, Great blue heron . . . Big blue shitepoke, Chester County, Pennsylvania. **1955** *MA Audubon* 39.312, Great Big Heron. Big Crane (Maine. Herons are frequently miscalled cranes.). **1962** Imhof *AL Birds* 81, Other Names . . . Big Blue Crane.

big cranky See cranky n

big daddy n Also big dad, big pa(pa) chiefly Sth See Map esp common among Black speakers Cf big mamma
One's grandfather.
1955 Williams *Cat Tin Roof* 2 **LA**, Big Daddy . . threw down his fork. **1962** Atwood *Vocab. TX* 65, Grandfather . . . Miscellaneous nicknames

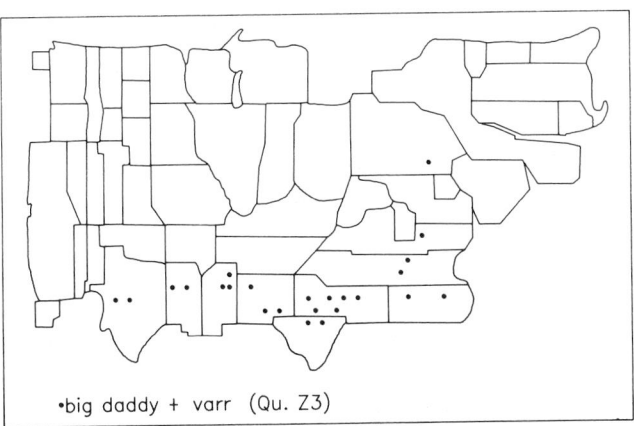
•big daddy + varr (Qu. Z3)

recorded for this item include: *Big Papa, Gompy, Grandpap.* **1965–70** *DARE* (Qu. Z3, . . *Grandfather*) 21 Infs, **chiefly Sth**, Big daddy; **AL**4, Big dad; **AL**6, **MS**47, Big papa; **LA**14, Big pa. [10 of 25 Infs Black] **1970** Tarpley *Blinky* 210 **neTX**, *Usual term of affection for grandfather* . . . Big daddy. **1971** *Today Show Letters* **cAL** (as of 1930's), Big daddy . . . Grandfather. **1982** Walker *Color Purple* 227 **GA** [Black], They have two kids . . . He say he thought something was funny bout his mama (my mama) cause she and big daddy was so old and strict and set in they ways.

big day n Also big daylight Sth among Black speakers
Broad daylight.
1927 Kennedy *Gritny* 81 **sLA** [Black], Somebody ain' use' to muskeeters, an' gotta ride in big daylight, settin' up und' a muskeeter net. **1927** Adams *Congaree* 85 **NC** [Black], *Paul:* . . I ain't visit there . . 'cep' in de day-time. *Tad:* My Brother, dat what I talk 'bout. I visit there in de Big Day, 'en dem white folks was standin' on de front piazza shooten' peoples cows. **1947** Ballowe *The Lawd* 124 **LA**, She . . came home stark naked, . . beat up one judge, and is hot behind another in the cane field, and, big day, hasn't a stitch on her back.

big dealer n
=**big dog**.
c1960 *Wilson Coll.* **csKY**, Big dealer . . . Name for self-important person. **1970** *DARE* (Qu. GG19a, . . *A person [who] acts . . important or independent*) Inf **IL**126, Big dealer; (Qu. HH17, *A person who tries to appear important*) Inf **IL**122, Big dealer.

big dog n chiefly Sth, S Midl, esp SC See Map and Map Section
An important, sometimes self-important, person; a **big bug**.
1847 in 1956 Eliason *Tarheel Talk* 260 **NC**, Dick . . . pretends to be the biggest dogg in the meat house. **1859** (1968) Bartlett *Americanisms*, *Big Dog.* In some parts of the country the principal man of a place or in an undertaking is called the *big dog with a brass collar*, as opposed to the little curs not thought worthy of a collar. **1950** *PADS* 14.14 **SC**. **1953** Brewer *Word Brazos* 45 **eTX** [Black], De Baptis' moderatuh's a big dawg in de Baptis' Chu'ch. **c1960** *Wilson Coll.* **csKY**, Big dog . . . A VIP, or one who pretends to be. **1965–70** *DARE* (Qu. HH17) 17 Infs, **chiefly Sth, S Midl**, Big dog; **IN**45, Big dog in the meathouse; (Qu. II23) 19 Infs, **scattered Sth, S Midl**, Big dogs; (Qq. GG19b, HH2, 43a) 5 Infs, Big dog.

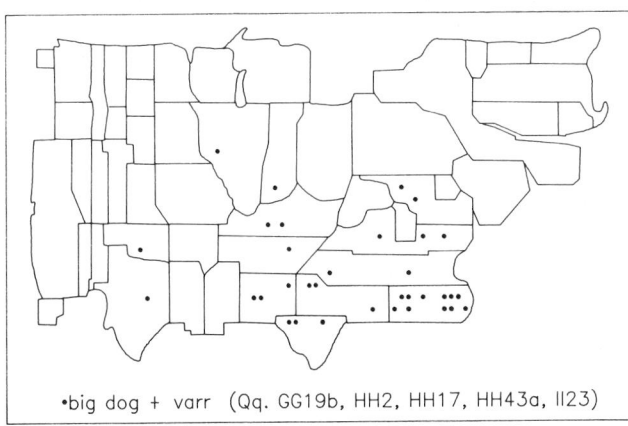
•big dog + varr (Qq. GG19b, HH2, HH17, HH43a, II23)

big doings n [doing]
1 A celebration, party; a formal social ceremony or gathering. Cf **big time**
1932 *Durant* (Okla.) *D. Democrat* 12 Nov 4/2 *(DA)*, Come to town and tell your neighbor to come, for there'll be big doings for all. **1935** Hurston *Mules & Men* 27 **FL**, There was going to be big doin's in Glory. **1938** Matschat *Suwannee R.* 248 **GA**, The party was to be big doin's, and the Plant Woman looked forward to it with keen anticipation. **1951** West *Witch Diggers* 6 **IN** (as of 1899), Looks like big doings at the Dumphys' tonight. **c1960** *Wilson Coll.* **csKY**, Big-doin's . . . Great occasion of some sort, like a party, a reunion, a marriage, or even a funeral. **1968** *DARE* Tape **KS**18, We always have a big doins on Decoration Day.

2 A braggart. Cf **big doings** adj
1970 *DARE* (Qu. HH8, *A person who likes to brag*) Inf **SC**68, Big doings.

big doings adj [big doings n]

Haughty, conceited, high-and-mighty.

1928 Peterkin *Scarlet Sister Mary* 98 **SC** [Gullah], Sho, I'll back-jaw you much as I please. Who is you to be so big-doins anyhow? *Ibid* 287, Walk off proudful. Strut. Dat is de way to treat big-doins town men. Let em see you ain' noways down-hearted. **1930** *DN* 6.79 **ceSC**, *Big doin's* . . . Conceited, haughty. General.

big-drunk bean n [From the narcotic properties of the seeds] =**frijollilo 1.**

1960 Vines *Trees SW* 569, *Sophora secundiflora* . . . Other vernacular names are . . Coral Bean, Big-drunk Bean, and Colorín. **1965** Teale *Wandering Through Winter* 150, All across Texas, a host of . . names have been bestowed on the wild plants . . . Big-drunk bean, nimble Kate [etc.].

big dude n Cf **big bug**

See quots.

c1960 Wilson Coll. **csKY**, *Big dude* . . . A self-important person, a VIP. "He's the Big Dude of that town." **1969** *DARE* (Qu. HH17, *A person who tries to appear important, or who tries to lay down the law in his community*) Inf **KY**19, Big dude.

big end n

The most important part.

1968 *DARE* Tape **MD**18, That was the big end of it [after explaining how to play a game].

big eye n

1 in phr *to have a* (or *the*) *big eye:* Greed, covetousness.

1903 *DN* 2.306 **seMO**, *Big-eye* (to have the) . . . To overestimate. 'He has the big-eye on that horse.' **1950** *PADS* 14.14 **SC**, *Big eye* . . . A child is said to have a big eye when he helps himself to more food than he can eat. Also applied to older persons. "His eye is bigger than his belly," is an often-heard expression of the same idea. *Big eye* expresses also greed in general. "He got de big eye," he wants more than his share. **1953** Randolph *Down in Holler* 205 **Ozarks**, Mary . . of Mincy, Missouri, once tried to buy some household relics from her neighbors. "They *had* the big eye," she told me, meaning that they regarded the stuff as more important and valuable than it really was.

2 Insomnia.

1967 *DARE* (Qu. OO32b, *If a person can't sleep steadily but keeps on waking, he might say, "Every night this week I've _____."*) Inf **TN**1, Had the big eye. **1976** Garber *Mountain-ese* **Appalachians**, *Big-eye* . . insomnia . . . The chillurn allers git the big-eye on Christmas night.

3 A television.

1965–70 *DARE* (Qu. FF27, . . *Television*) Infs **KY**73, **MN**2, **OH**47, **OR**1, **TX**95, **VA**109, Big eye.

4 See **big-eyed herring.**

big-eye adj Also *big-eyed*

1 Greedy, covetous. [See quot 1949] **Sth** *among Black speakers* Cf *DJE*

1947 Ballowe *The Lawd* 135 **LA** [Black], Aun' Big Eye was a character. As a child she cried for everything she saw; that is how she got the name. *Ibid* 195, Mollie, his wife, was big-eyed when it came to putting things on her back, and he was hard put to pay for them. **1949** Turner *Africanisms* 233 [Gullah], [bɪg ɒɪ] 'covetous,' i.e., 'big eye,' being a translation of the Ibo expression [aɲa uku] 'covetous,' lit. 'eye big.' **1972** [see **big I, little you**].

‡2 Self-important.

1969 *DARE* (Qu. GG19a, *When you can see from the way a person acts that he's feeling important or independent: "He surely is _____ these days."*) Inf **MA**35, Big-eyed.

big-eyed herring n Also *big eye*

=**alewife.**

1896 U.S. Natl. Museum *Bulletin* 47.426, *Alewife;* . . *Big-eyed Herring; Ellwife.* **1946** LaMonte *N. Amer. Game Fishes* 150, *Alewife* . . . Names: Branch Herring, Big-eyed Herring [etc.]. **1976** Warner *Beautiful Swimmers* 127 **Chesapeake Bay**, There is *Alosa pseudoharengus,* most commonly known as the alewife. Watermen prefer to call it the big eye.

big-eyed scad n Also *bigeye scad*

A small food fish (*Selar crumenophthalmus*) with prominent eyes. Also called **akule, goggle-eye, goggle-eye jack, goggler**

1873 in 1878 Smithsonian Inst. *Misc. Coll.* 14.2.25, *Trachurops crumenophthalmus* . . . Big-eyed scad; . . goggler. **1902** Jordan–Evermann *Amer. Fishes* 303, Its common names in American waters are goggler, big-eyed scad, and goggle-eyed jack. **1960** Gosline–Brock *Hawaiian Fishes*, Bigeye scad . . . may be easily identified by its large eyes, the diameter of which goes about 3 times into the length of the head.

big feathergrass n Cf **feathergrass** *chiefly SW* =**beardgrass** (here either *Andropogon barbinodis* or *A. saccharoides*).

1937 U.S. Forest Serv. *Range Plant Hdbk.* G14, *A. saccharoides* and *A. barbinodis* . . . Other local names, such as . . big feathergrass . . are applied . . to these species . . . Cane beardgrass . . is less widely distributed and more distinctly western than silver beardgrass.

big feeler n [big-feeling]

An arrogant or haughty person.

1967–69 *DARE* (Qu. GG19a, . . *A person [who] acts . . important or independent: "He surely is _____ these days."*) Infs **KY**24, **MO**3, A big feeler. **1976** *DARE* File **KS**, Big feeler—A person who thinks he's important and behaves accordingly.

big-feeling adj *chiefly Nth, N Midl*

Haughty, proud, **biggity** adj.

1887 Eggleston *Graysons* 253 **sIL**, Markham had got too big-feeling for his place. **1940** Yoder *Rosanna* 37 **PA**, It looks a little big feelin' for us, I'm afraid, but it is not against the rules of the church to drive two horses, and everybody knows that we did need a new carriage. **1942** Warnick *Garrett Co. MD* (as of 1900–1918), *Big feeling,* . . conceited. "She's so big feelin'." **1967–70** *DARE* (Qu. GG19a, . . *A person [who] acts . . important or independent: "He surely is _____ these days."*) Infs **MA**33, **MI**63, Big-feeling (guy); (Qu. HH35, *A woman who puts on a lot of airs: "She's too _____ for me."*) Infs **KY**84, **MA**75, **WV**3, Big-feeling.

bigfin bass n

The black **crappie** (*Pomoxis nigromaculatus*).

1887 Goode *Amer. Fishes* 69, It is also called . . "Big Fin Bass."

Bigfoot n, also attrib *chiefly CA* Cf **Sasquatch**

A large, hairy, man-like creature reported as living in the forests and mountains of California.

[**1958** *Washington Post* (DC) 7 Oct B2/3–4 *(Hench Coll.),* A plaster cast of a footprint 16 inches long and 7 inches wide is held by Jerry Crew, who said he made the cast in a forest 50 miles north of Eureka, Calif. A taxidermist said the footprint was not made by any known animal and Crew and his logging associates have simply dubbed it "Bigfoot."] **1965–70** *DARE* (Qu. CC17, . . *Monsters that people . . tell tales about —especially to tease greenhorns*) Inf **CA**30, Bigfoot—in Mount Shasta; one sees his footprints; **CA**32, Bigfoot in the Klamath area, half-ape, half-man, foot seventeen inches long; he hasn't done anything but some say he's real; **CA**118, Bigfoot—at Oakhurst—a big footprint found; many tales told about Bigfoot—nine feet tall with hair; supposed to be an abominal [sic] snowman like in the Himalayans [sic]; the Indians call him Bigfoot; **CA**137, The Bigfoot—our abdominal [sic] snowman; started seven to eight years ago. Some loggers claimed their fifty-gallon barrels were thrown down into a gully; saw big tracks, made casts. Now it's a big money scheme.—Some claimed they got up close enough to it to see that it had a woman's breasts. Tracks are about sixteen inches long, look sort of human; **CA**144, Bigfoot, of Trinity and Humboldt County; **CA**161, Bigfoot—same one up in Trinity County; **CA**163, Hairy giants, similar to Bigfoot of Trinity County; **CA**80, 213, Bigfoot. **1969** *DARE* Tapes **CA**138, 213, Bigfoot. **1974** *New Scientist & Sci. Jrl.* 3 Jan 26/3, A recent book had listed 800 sightings of Bigfoot . . the bear/ape/man whose existence has been persisted in by Californians for a century at least.

bigger n

1901 *DN* 2.136 **cNY**, *Bigger* . . . In phrase 'one's *biggers*'—one's betters.

biggin n [Brit dial *bigging*]

1952 Brown *NC Folkl.* 1.520, *Biggin* . . . A house, a dwelling.— Chapel Hill.

biggity adj Also sp *biggedy, big(g)ety, biggoty* [Prob *big* + *-ity* quality, state; cf **uppity**] *chiefly Sth, S Midl* See Map Cf **briggity**

Conceited, vain, self-important; impudent, boastful.

1880 Harris *Uncle Remus Songs* 80 **GA**, Like po'in' spring water on one er deze yer biggity fices. **1902** *DN* 2.229 s**IL**. **1903** *DN* 2.306 se**MO**. **1905** *DN* 3.70 nw**AR**. **1906** *DN* 3.115 s**IN**. **1918** *DN* 5.18 **NC**. **1933** Rawlings *South Moon* 81 **FL**, You'd better not to go to gittin' biggety nor lookin' for a fuss. **1943** Writers' Program NC *Bundle of Troubles* 25, And biggoty—he [=Mr. Bullfrog] was 'bout the biggotiest and high-steppinest critter I ever seed—and seem like all he think 'bout was his fine clothes. **1944** *PADS* 2.54 **MO, VA, NC, SC, TN,** Biggety. **1948** Faulkner *Intruder* 19 **MS,** You goddamn biggity stiffnecked stinking burrheaded Edmonds sonofabitch. **1952** Brown *NC Folkl.* 1.520, *Biggity, biggedy, bigety, biggoty . . .* Self-important.—General. **1965–70** *DARE* (Qu. GG19a, *When . . a person acts . . important or independent: "He surely is _____ these days."*) 14 Infs, **chiefly Sth, S Midl,** Biggity; (Qu. HH8, *A person who likes to brag*) Infs **SC**10, 11, Biggity; (Qu. HH35, *A woman who puts on a lot of airs: "She's too _____ for me."*) Infs **GA**74, **KY**26, **NJ**15, **VA**15, Biggity; (Qu. II23, *. . People who are, or think they are, the best society of a community*) Infs **FL**48, **KY**44, 85, Biggity; (Qu. II36b, *If somebody who talks back or gives rude answers you might say, "She certainly is _____!"*) Inf **FL**52, Biggity; (Qu. U37, *. . Expressions about somebody who has plenty of money*) Inf **NC**85, Biggety.

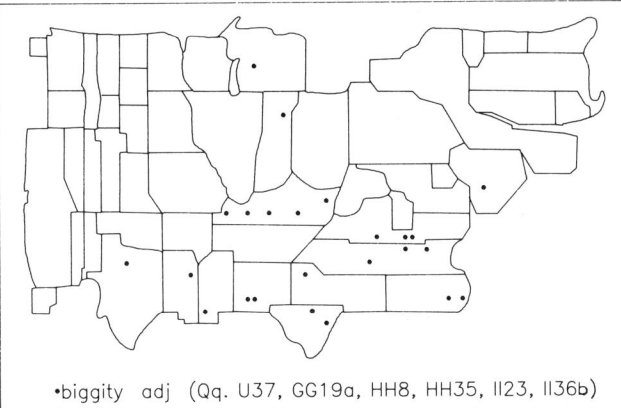

•biggity adj (Qq. U37, GG19a, HH8, HH35, II23, II36b)

biggity adv Pronc-sp *biggidy* [**biggity** adj]
Presumptuously, conceitedly.
    1927 Kennedy *Gritny* 52 s**LA** [Black], You gotta study yo' lesson a heap mo', befo' you go 'roun' hyuh preachin' to people so biggidy.

biggyhead n
A fish of the family Cottidae, esp **cabezon.**
    1887 Goode *Amer. Fishes* 302, The Cottidæ . . are . . known by such names as . . . "Biggyhead," and "Cabezon."

big hat n
1 A law enforcement officer.
    1967–70 *DARE* (Qu. V9, *. . A policeman*) Inf **LA**8, Big-hat man [laughter]; (Qu. V10a, *. . A sheriff*) Inf **VA**70, Big hat. [Both Infs Black] **1969** *AmSp* 44.202 [Truck drivers' jargon], *Big hat*—State trooper, state patrolman, or state policeman, especially one whose uniform includes a large hat.
2 A self-important person, a **big bug.**
    1966–67 *DARE* (Qu. GG19b, *When . . a person acts . . important or independent: "He seems to think he's _____."*) Inf **FL**33, The big hat; (Qu. HH17, *A person who tries to appear important . . "He'd like to be the _____ around here."*) Inf **TN**12, Big hat.
3 A person of Mexican heritage.
    1970 *DARE* (Qu. HH28, *. . People of foreign background . . Mexicans*) Inf **NY**234, Big hats.

bighead n
1 =**black-bellied plover.**
    1923 U.S. Dept. Ag. *Misc. Circular* 13.68, *Black-bellied Plover . . Vernacular Names . . In local use . . .* Big-head (Miss.).
2 A tadpole.
    1966 *DARE* (Qu. P20, *Very young frogs—when they still have tails but no legs*) Inf **FL**7, Bigheads.
‡3 A kind of cigar.
    1967 *DARE* (Qu. DD7) Inf **IA**4, Bighead.

big Herb n
    c**1905** in **1974** *AmSp* 49.61 sw**ME,** *Big herb . . .* Important person (used sarcastically).

big hole n [See quot 1968] **chiefly West**
1 In railroading: an emergency stop.
    1930 Irwin *Amer. Tramp, Big hole.*—A quick stop; an emergency application of the air brakes, so called since the brake valve permits an immediate and heavy flow of air to the brake mechanism when placed in the emergency position or on the "big hole." Boomers [=migratory railroad workers] carried the term to the tramps . . and it is now widely used to indicate an immediate cessation of any activity. **1931** *Writer's Digest* 11.41 [Railroad lingo], Big Hole—Emergency position of the air brake valve; the act of applying brakes abruptly to the full reduction. **1945** Hubbard *Railroad Ave.* 332, *Big hole*—Emergency application of air-brake valve, causing a quick stop.
2 By ext: the lowest gear of a truck or other vehicle.
    1947 Berrey–Van den Bark *Amer. Slang Suppl.* 25.2, *Gearshift Positions . . .* Big hole, . . low gear. **1958** McCulloch *Woods Words* **Pacific NW,** *Big hole . . .* The low gear on a truck or donkey. **1959** *AmSp* 34.76 n**CA** [Logger lingo], *Big hole . . .* The lowest gear on a logging truck.

big hole v phr Also *big hole it, ~ the air* **chiefly West**
In railroading, logging, and trucking: see quots.
    1930 Irwin *Amer. Tramp, Big hole.*—To stop quickly. **1958** McCulloch *Woods Words* **Pacific NW,** Big hole the air. **1962** *AmSp* 37.132 n**CA** [Logging railroad language], *Big-hole the air . . .* To let the air escape from the biggest hole in the valve which applies the brakes sharply in an emergency. **1969** *AmSp* 44.202 [Truck drivers' jargon], Apply brakes for an emergency stop . . . Big hole it. **1970** *Current Slang* 5.1.4 **CA,** *Bighole . . .* "We were about to hit a car, so the engineer bigholed the train."

big hominy n **Sth, S Midl** Cf **hominy, little hominy, lye hominy**
See quot 1908.
    1908 *DN* 3.291 e**AL**, w**GA**, *Big hominy . . .* Whole grains of Indian corn hulled and boiled. Same as *lye-hominy.* **1918** *DN* 5.18 **NC**. **1938** Rawlings *Yearling* 56 **FL,** She ladled food into pans . . . There were . . swamp cabbage, big hominy, biscuits, cornbread, syrup and coffee. **1950** *PADS* 14.14 **SC**. c**1960** *Wilson Coll.* cs**KY,** Big hominy (usually just *hominy*) . . . Whole-grain, home-made hominy. **1966** *DARE* FW Addit **SC,** Big hominy.

big hook n **chiefly West**
In railroading: see quots.
    1931 *Writer's Digest* 11.41 [Railroad lingo], Big Hook—Wrecking crane. **1932** *Santa Fe Mag.* Jan 34/1, A wrecking crane is the *big hook.* **1945** Hubbard *Railroad Ave.* 332, *Big hook*—Wrecking crane. **1967** *DARE* Tape **ID**9, A big crane on wheels that picks up cars that are upset, locomotives, things like this—it's commonly called "the wrecker" or "the big hook." **1970** *Current Slang* 5.1.4 **CA,** *Big hook . . .* The steam-driven mobile crane (railway) used to pick up derailed cars and engines.

big house n
1 A manor or the main house on a plantation. **chiefly Sth**
    1811 in **1956** Eliason *Tarheel Talk* 260 **NC,** Work on the big house. **1894** Twain *Pudd'nhead Wilson* 186 **MO,** I had a pow'ful good start, 'ca'se de big house 'uz three mile back fum de river. **1928** Peterkin *Scarlet Sister Mary* 13 **SC,** A great empty Big House, once the proud home of the plantation masters, is now an old crumbling shell. **1953** Brewer *Word Brazos* 67 e**TX** [Black], She keep li'l' Milly rat in de Big House an' she come to be de house girl. **1954** *Holiday* Apr 46 **MS,** She began to spend more and more time in the house, not her cabin but the big house. **1967** LeCompte *Word Atlas* 169 se**LA,** Main plantation house . . big house.
2 The principal room of a house; the living room. **chiefly S Midl** Cf **big room, main house** Cf *EDD* house sb.[1] 7 "The kitchen or general living-room in a farm-house or cottage"
    1903 *DN* 2.306 se**MO,** *Big-house . . .* The parlor or principal room of a house. This term is, perhaps, derived from the old custom of having separate log houses covered by one roof. **1915** *DN* 4.181 sw**VA**. **1918** *DN* 5.32 **KY,** *Big house . . .* In a house of two or more rooms, the largest one is thus designated. **1949** Kurath *Word Geog.* 51, In the simple homes of the piedmont and the mountains of North Carolina (also on the Peedee in South Carolina, rarely in West Virginia) the living room is called the *big-house* or the *great-house.* **1954** Harder Coll. cw**TN,** *Big house . . .* The room where company is entertained; occasionally *living room* is heard. The room where members of the family spend most of their time together. **1956** Hall Coll. e**TN,** w**NC,** *Big house . . .* The main, or living room of the house. In the old log houses the rooms were often built separately (and detached) as the family needed more room,

but were covered usually with a common roof. Often an open hallway . . separated two such linked log houses. **c1960** *Wilson Coll.* **csKY.** **1963** Edwards *Gravel* 20 **eTN** (as of 1920s), After supper Uncle Jeems walked into the big house and stood in the middle of the floor and stretched.

3 A jail or penitentiary.

1916 *Lit. Digest* 52.424/3 **NY,** Then comes . . the final curtain of the piece, when the malefactor is sent away to the "big house." **1940** in 1963 Fitzgerald *Letters* 68, I feel like a criminal who has been in a hideout, been caught, and has to go back to the Big House. **1967–70** *DARE* (Qu. V11, . . *A county or city jail*) Infs **CO5, 47, MD19, PA240,** Big house. **1970** Tarpley *Blinky* 270 **neTX,** *Other names for jail* . . . Big house.

bight n Also sp *bite* [OE *byht* a bend, curve]

1 A shoreline cove or bay. **chiefly Atl States**

1640 in 1911 *MD Hist. Mag.* 6.68, A line drawn from the head of Prior's Creek East into a bite called Adam's bite. **1827** Cooper *Red Rover* 1.44, This is a pretty bight of a basin. **1899** (1912) Green *VA Folk-Speech,* *Bight* . . . A small, circular sheet of water between two points of land. "We put the boat in the bight, out of the way of the ice." **1935** *AmSp* 10.154 **eMD,** *Bight.* Very rare; Eastern Shore. **1966** *DARE* FW Addit **FL,** Bight—cove or bay (salt-water). **1968** *DARE* (QR p15) Inf **AK2,** Bight—small indentation along shore. **1968** *DARE* Tape **NC57,** We had a three-mast schooner came in the bight of Cape Lookout; that's a small basin-like an' inside of it was smooth water.

2 Esp in logging: a loop or bend in a slack rope or wire; also fig (see quot 1967). **chiefly Pacific NW**

1920 *DN* 5.80 **NW,** *Bite.* For bight, the angle of the rope which is drawn through a pulley. "A man was killed yesterday—standing in the bite when a block and cable broke." *Seattle Post Intelligencer.* **1950** *Western Folkl.* 9.116 **OR** [Logger speech], *Bight of the line.* The "belly" of a line when it is hanging slack or lying on the ground. Anyone standing within this area may suffer serious injury or death when the line is suddenly jerked tight. Hence, "to step into the bight of the line" is to get into trouble. **1967** *DARE* FW Addit **cwWA,** *Caught in the bight of the line.* In logging or sailing, to get caught in a loop of slack when a line tightens. Also used to mean caught between two sides of an argument, for instance the possible negative result of playing both ends against the middle.

3 See quot.

1952 Brown *NC Folkl.* 1.520, Bight [baɪt] . . . a suction current.—Edenton.

big I See **big I, little you**

big I-am See **I am**

bigified adj [*big* + *-ified*]

=**biggity** adj.

c1960 *Wilson Coll.* **csKY,** *Bigified* . . . Egotistic. "He's always acting bigified when company comes." **1962** Wilson *Folkways Mammoth Cave* 40, *Bigified.* Another term for being *stuck-up* or *smart-alec.*

big Ike n, also attrib [*big* + *Ike* n[1]] **chiefly Sth, S Midl**

=**big bug.**

1902 Harben *Abner Daniel* 72 **GA,** He's a big Ike in some church in Atlanta. **1908** *DN* 3.291 **eAL, wGA,** *Big Ike* . . . A person of much importance, especially in his own opinion. **1915** *DN* 4.181 **swVA.** **c1937** in 1972 *Amer. Slave* 2.1.77 **SC,** Every Yankee I see had de stamp of poor white trash on them. They strutted 'round, big Ike fashion, a bustin' in rooms widout knockin'. **1954** Harder *Coll.* **cwTN,** *Big Ike* . . . A loud, self-assertive person. **1969–70** *DARE* (Qu. HH17, *A person who tries to appear important, or who tries to lay down the law in his community: "He'd like to be the _____ around here."*) Infs **KY42, 53, 91,** Big Ike; (Qu. GG19b, *When you can see from the way a person acts that he's feeling important or independent: "He seems to think he's _____."*) Inf **MS39,** Big Ike.

big I, little you n Also abbr *big I* [Perh folk-etym of **big-eye** adj (see quot 1972 below) punningly with the letters *i* and *u*] Cf **big bug, big Ike**

An important or self-important person.

1967–69 *DARE* (Qu. HH8, *A person who likes to brag*) Infs **MI101,** Big I and little you [laughter]; **TX18,** Big I, little you; (Qu. HH17, *A person who tries to appear important* . . . "*He'd like to be the _____ around here.*") Inf **MA35,** Big I and little you; (Qu. II23, . . *People who are, or think they are, the best society of a community: The _____*) Inf **IN41,**

Big I's. **1972** Kochman *Rappin'* 178, *Probable Africanisms in American English* . . . Big eye—"greedy." [Footnote:] Dr. J.L. Dillard has informed me that this term was rationalized by white Texans as "big I" (in the phrase "big I, little you").

big indigo n

The blue grosbeak (*Guiraca caerulea*).

1949 Sprunt–Chamberlain *SC Bird Life* 512, *Eastern blue grosbeak* . . *Local Names: Big Indigo.* **1955** *Oriole* 20.13, *Blue Grosbeak.* —*Big Indigo* (that is, indigo bird; "big" in contrast to the smaller Indigo Bunting of the same general coloration).

‡big injun n Cf **big Ike**

1907 *DN* 3.181 **seNH,** *Big Injun* . . . Nickname for a coarse, boastful man. "Big Injun says he has seen the world."

‡bigite n [*big* adj + nominalizing suff *-ite*]

A conceited person.

1967 *DARE* (Qu. II35, *A person who is disliked because he seems to think he knows everything*) Inf **LA11,** Bigite ['bɪg,aɪt].

big John the Conqueror See **conquer John**

big jump, the n *euphem*

Death.

1942 Berrey–Van den Bark *Amer. Slang* 117.1, *Death* . . . The big jump. **1968** Adams *Western Words,* *Big jump*—A cowman's reference to death. When a person died, he was said to have taken the *big jump.*

big laurel n

1 The southern **magnolia** (*Magnolia grandiflora*).

1810 Michaux *Arbres* 1.32 (DA), The large magnolia, . . . [or] Big laurel. **1883** Hale *Woods NC* 110, Magnolia grandiflora . . . Farther south it is often called *Big Laurel.* **1961** *W3.*

2 also *big-leaf laurel*: A **rosebay** (here: *Rhododendron maximum*).

1853 Kennedy *Blackwater Chron.* 89 **WV,** This dale is girt round . . by a broad belt of the *Rhododendron*—commonly called the *big laurel* out here. **1897** Sudworth *Arborescent Flora* 315, *Rhododendron maximum* . . . *Common Names* . . . Bigleaf Laurel (Pa.). Big Laurel (W. Va.). **1931** *Randolph Enterprise* (Elkins, W. Va.) 12 March 1/2 (DA), The shrubbery should not be cut down along the banks, but more planted, 'Big Laurel,' rose-bushes [etc.]. **1944** *PADS* 2.32 **wNC,** Big laurel (when white) . . . The rhododendron . . . Reported. **1950** Peattie *Nat. Hist. Trees* 517, *Big Rhododendron* . . . *Other Names:* . . . Big-leaf . . Laurel. Rose Bay.

‡big lazies, the n pl

Laziness; a strong inclination to idleness.

1898 Lloyd *Country Life* 21 **AL,** He want worth his weight in sap saw dust, and the general wonderment was that he could have the big lazies continually all the time and still keep out of the poor house.

big-leaf elm n

Perh the **cedar elm.**

1966–69 *DARE* (Qu. T11) Infs **AL11, 19, IL76, OK52,** Big-leaf elm.

big-leaf laurel See **big laurel 2**

big-leaf maple n

Std: a large-leaved maple (*Acer macrophyllum*) native to the Pacific coast. Also called **California maple 1, canyon maple, Oregon maple, white maple**

big-leaved magnolia n

=**southern magnolia.**

1971 GA Dept. Ag. *Farmers Market Bulletin* 7 July 8, The southern magnolia also known as the evergreen magnolia, bull-bay and big-leaved magnolia . . . is of the family Magnoliaceae and the species Magnolia grandiflora L.

big leg n [From the swelling of the legs]

=**milk leg 2.**

1952 Brown *NC Folkl.* 1.520, *Big-leg* . . . Common name for "milk-leg."—Durham and Duplin counties. **1967** *DARE* (Qu. K47, . . *Diseases [of] horses or mules*) Inf **TN2,** Big leg.

big loon n **chiefly NEng** Cf **little loon**

=**loon.**

1844 DeKay *Zool. NY* 2.285, The *Great Diver,* or *Big Loon,* may be regarded as a perpetual resident in this State. **1899** Howe *Birds RI* 26,

Gavia immer . . . Big Loon.—A common winter resident along the ocean beaches and cliffs. **1932** Bennitt *Check-List* 11 **MO,** *Common loon . . . Big loon; walloon.* **1955** *MA Audubon* 39.309, *Common Loon. Big Loon . . . (New England).*

big loop n **West**
See quots.
    1940 FWP *Guide NM* 110, *Big loop . . . The lasso of a cattle-thief.* **1968** Adams *Western Words, Big loop*—A cattle thief's rope. When a man is suspected of stealing cattle, it is said that he "throws a big loop."

bigly adv
In a haughty manner.
    1942 Perry *Texas* 134, When a negro acts superior to his fellows, he is accused of "acting bigly."

big mamma n Also *big mother, big nana* **chiefly Sth** See Map *esp among Black speakers* Cf **big daddy**
One's grandmother.
    1946 McCullers *Member* 35 **GA,** When Berenice said *we,* she meant Honey and Big Mama. **1965–70** *DARE* (Qu. Z4, . . *Grandmother*) 31 Infs, Big mamma; Inf **TX**61, Big mother; **GA**28, Big nana. [Of all Infs responding to the question, 6% were Black; of those giving this response, 40% were Black] **1970** Tarpley *Blinky* 208 **neTX,** *Usual term of affection for grandmother . . . Big mama.* **1971** *Today Show Letters* **cAL** (as of 1930s), Big mamma . . . Grandmother.

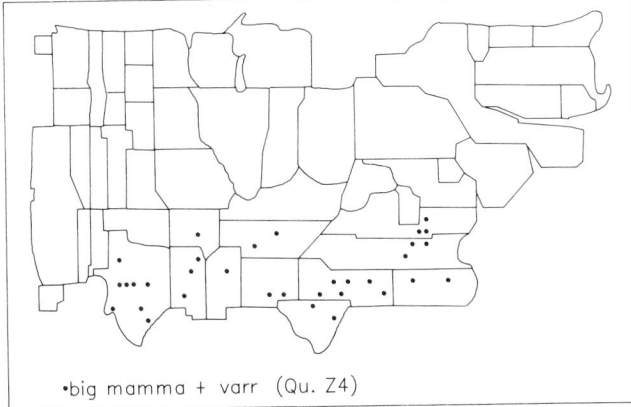

•big mamma + varr (Qu. Z4)

‡**big man** n
A gallon of wine.
    1970 Bullins *Electronic* 163 [Black], *Clark:* Let's go on up to the store and get us a big man. *Ray:* A big man? *Clark:* That's right . . . a whole gallon.

‡**big me** n
=**big I, little you.**
    1968 *DARE* (Qu. HH8, *A person who likes to brag*) Inf **IN**5, Big me.

big meeting n **chiefly Sth, S Midl** Cf **protracted meeting**
A series of revival meetings lasting several days.
    1805 in 1943 Fries *Rec. Moravians* 6.2814 **NC,** There was a Methodist *big meeting* in the neighborhood. **1859** (1968) Bartlett *Americanisms, Big meeting.* Common in the West for "protracted meeting." In country towns where there are no churches and where preachers are seldom seen, the arrival of one is a matter of importance to the whole surrounding region. The people . . having come so far, one sermon will not suffice; so for several days together religious services are held. **1890** *DN* 1.65 **KY.** **1899** (1912) Green *VA Folk-Speech, Big-meeting . . .* A meeting at country churches kept up for several days, the preachers and congregation coming from a distance. "Protracted meeting." **1907** *DN* 3.229 **nwAR, seMO.** **1942** Warnick *Garrett Co. MD* (as of 1900–1918). **1950** *PADS* 14.14 **SC.** **1954** *Harder Coll.* **cwTN.** **c1960** *Wilson Coll.* **csKY,** *Big-meeting . . .* Protracted meeting, revival.

bigmouth n
1 also *bigmouth(ed) perch:* =**warmouth.**
    1887 Goode *Amer. Fishes* 67, The Black Warmouth, *Chaenobryttus antistius,* a species also called . . "Big-mouth." **1933** LA Dept. of Conserv. *Fishes* 342, The Warmouth Bass has come to bear many confusing popular names. These [include] . . Bigmouth. **1946** La-Monte *N. Amer. Game Fishes* 142, *Warmouth—Chaenobryttus coron-*

arius Names: . . Bigmouth. **1966** *DARE* (Qu. P1) Inf **OK**52, Goggle eye (bigmouthed perch). **1968** *DARE* File **LA,** Bigmouth perch—an alternate name for "warmouth."
2 =**squawfish.**
    1902 Jordan–Evermann *Amer. Fishes* 69, *Ptychocheilus oregonensis . .* Other names by which it is known are . . big-mouth. **1946** LaMonte *N. Amer. Game Fishes* 156, *Squawfish—Ptychocheilus oregonensis . .* Names: . . Big-mouth.
3 also *bigmouth bass:* =**largemouth bass.**
    1966 *DARE* Tape **FL**37, Every now and then we'd catch what they call a bigmouth bass. **1972** Sparano *Outdoors Encycl.* 359, Largemouth Bass—Common Names: . . bigmouth bass . . . Scientific Name: *Micropterus salmoides.*

bigmouth buffalo n
Std: a **buffalo fish** *(Ictiobus cyprinellus)* which is usu olive-bronze dorsally and yellowish-white ventrally.   Also called **blue buffalo, bullhead ~, chubnose ~, gourdhead ~, gourdseed ~, lake ~, mud ~, pugnose ~, redmouth(ed) ~, roundhead ~, slough ~, stubnose ~, white ~**

bigmouthed perch See **bigmouth 1**

bigmouthed sunfish n
=**warmouth.**
    1933 LA Dept. of Conserv. *Fishes* 342, The Warmouth Bass has come to bear many confusing popular names. These [include] . . Bigmouthed Sunfish. **1946** LaMonte *N. Amer. Game Fishes* 142, *Warmouth—Chaenobryttus coronarius* Names: . . Big-mouthed Sunfish.

bigmouth perch See **bigmouth 1**

bigmouth trout n
=**largemouth bass.**
    1967–69 *DARE* (Qu. P1) Infs **NJ**60, **SC**43, Bigmouth trout.

big nana See **big mamma**

bigness n **chiefly NEng** *old-fash*
Size.
    1871 (1882) Stowe *Fireside Stories* 7 **NEng,** This 'ere's what Cap'n Eb Sawin told me when I was a boy about your bigness, I reckon. **1899** (1912) Green *VA Folk-Speech, Bigness . . .* Size, large or small. "They are about of the same bigness." **c1905** in 1974 *AmSp* 49.61 **swME,** He was the bigness of a trawl-kag. **1914** *DN* 4.69 **ME, nNH,** *Bigness . . .* Size. He fell into the lake, clear up his hull bigness.

big O n Also *big ox* [See quot 1930]
In railroading: the conductor.
    1930 Irwin *Amer. Tramp, Big O.*—A railroad conductor; from the Labour Union, The Order of Railroad Conductors, or "Big O," to which practically every conductor belongs. **1943** *AmSp* 18.162 [Railroad terms], . . . *Big ox, . . big O,* brains. Some of the titles given the conductor. **1946** in 1953 Botkin *Treas. Railroad Folkl.* 350, The shack was in the angel's seat of the ape wagon, blowing smoke to the Big-O of the time he was a baby lifter on the varnish. Or, to say it in another way: The brakeman was in the cupola of the caboose, boasting to the conductor of the time he was a brakeman on a passenger train.

big one n
See quot 1915.
    1915 *DN* 4.181 **swVA,** *Big one . . .* An incredible story; whopper. "Now tell us a big un, the biggest 'n you know." **1939** *Hall Coll.* **eTN,** "He told 'em great big ones /bɪgənz/." (i.e., he told people big stories.)

bigoted adj [Perh hypercorrection for **biggity** adj, infl by *bigoted* intolerant]
=**biggity** adj.
    1902 *DN* 2.229 **sIL,** *Bigoted* or *bigoty . . .* Conceited; proud; haughty. **1968** *DARE* (Qu. GG19a, . . *A person [who] acts . . important or independent: "He surely is ＿＿＿ these days."*) Inf **UT**5, Bigoted.

big ox See **big O**

big papa See **big daddy**

big pasture n Cf **big house 3**
    1968 Adams *Western Words, Big pasture*—What the cowboy sometimes calls the penitentiary.

big pine n
Either of two pines, **sugar pine** or **ponderosa pine.**

1897 Sudworth *Arborescent Flora* 15, *Pinus lambertiana* . . big pine. *Ibid* 20, *Pinus ponderosa* . . big pine.

‡big place n
=**big house 3.**
1970 *DARE* (Qu. V11, . . *A county or city jail*) Inf **NY**249, Big place.

big ring n
1 also *big circle:* In marble play: a large circle drawn on the ground; a marble game using such a circle; see quots 1958, 1973.
1934 *AmSp* 9.75 **ND**, Big rings. A large marble ring, usually over ten feet in diameter. 1958 *PADS* 29.30 **MA, WI,** Big ring: . . A marble game using a ring from 6 to 8 feet in diameter with 13 to 17 agates at the exact center in form of a cross. Players *lag* for first play, *knuckle down tight* and shoot from outside the ring attempting to knock the agates out, thus winning them. Upon knocking out an agate, the shooter remains in the ring or pays to get out. If a shooter is knocked out of the ring, its owner is out of the game. 1965–70 *DARE* (Qu. EE7) Infs **CA**65, **IL**57, **MD**8, **MI**14, **OR**15, **PA**167, **TX**9, Big ring; **IL**47, Big circle. 1966–68 *DARE* Tape **MD**51, Big ring; **MI**14, Big ring . . . A ring about maybe eight feet in diameter . . and each fellow put in three or four marbles and then you had a shooter which was about three quarter inch in diameter and you had to shoot the marbles in the center and knock 'em out of the ring; **NM**6, Big ring. 1973 Ferretti *Marble Book* 39, *Big ring.* Game similar to Ring Taw and Ringer. *Ibid* 50, *Ringer* . . . Played by placing 13 marbles in the form of a cross in the middle of a 10-foot-diameter ring. Shooters shoot from the ring's edge and knock marbles out of the ring. The first player scoring seven hits wins.
2 A square dance.
1969 *DARE* (Qu. FF2) Inf **GA**70, "Let's have a big ring" — same as [a] square dance.

big road n **chiefly Sth, Midl**
A main road or highway.
1818 (1821) Harris *Tour U.S.A.* 104 **csOH**, Oh, *I guess* you can't miss it, stranger; only keep the Big Road. 1871 Eggleston *Hoosier Schoolmaster* 41 **IN**, The "big road" (Hoosier for *highway*) ran along the north-west side. 1902 *DN* 2.229 **sIL**. 1906 *DN* 3.115 **sIN**. 1907 *DN* 3.229 **nwAR, seMO**. 1908 *DN* 3.291 **eAL, wGA**. 1915 *DN* 4.181 **swVA**. 1923 *DN* 5.201 **swMO**, Big road . . . A main thoroughfare, a highway. 1927 Kennedy *Gritny* 245 **sLA** [Black], The two of them comin' up the big road. 1937 in 1977 *Amer. Slave Suppl. 1* 1.97 **AL**, I went on down de big road tell I come to a oman's house what de yankees didn't burn. 1941 Stuart *Men of Mts.* 229 **neKY**, I walk down the hollow to the big road. 1967–68 *DARE* (Qu. N16a, . . *A highway*) Inf **GA**40, Big road; (Qu. U41b) Inf **MO**8, A big road.

big rock n Cf **big house 3**
A jail or penitentiary.
1967–69 *DARE* (Qu. V11, . . *A county or city jail*) Infs **GA**82, **SC**32, Big rock.

big room n
=**big house 2.**
a1883 (1911) Bagby *VA Gentleman* 79 **VA**, The glory of the new house is the "big room," upstairs. This spacious chamber boasts four great windows. 1949 Kurath *Word Geog.* 51, The living room is called . . on the Eastern Shore of Virginia the *big-room.* 1960 *PADS* 34.57 **CO**, *Older Folk Speech* . . big room 'living room.' 1972 Cooper *NC Mt. Folkl.* 90, Big room — family room.

bigroot n
1 A climbing or trailing plant of the genus *Marah* with a much enlarged, woody, intensely bitter root and bladdery, often spiny fruits; native to the Pacific coast. Also called **bitterroot 4, chilicothe, man-in-the-ground, manroot, old man, wild cucumber**
1897 Parsons *Wild Flowers CA* 26, Seeing its rather delicate ivy-like habit above ground, one would never dream that it came from a root as large as a man's body . . From this root, it has received two of its common names, "big-root" and "man-in-the-ground." 1925 Jepson *Manual Plants CA* 661, *Big Root* . . . Fusiform or globose roots, sometimes as large as and not unlike the shape of a man's body. 1973 Hitchcock–Cronquist *Flora Pacific NW* 457, Bigroot, Manroot.
2 A **balsamroot** (here: *Balsamorrhiza sagittata*).
1915 (1926) Armstrong *Western Wild Flowers* 558, *Arrow-leaf Balsam-root, Big Root* . . . A very handsome plant. 1963 Craighead *Rocky Mt. Wildflowers* 197, Bigroot . . . Clumps of large leaves and naked stems arising from thick taproot.

3 also *bigroot morning glory:* =**man-of-the-earth.**
1932 Rydberg *Flora Prairies* 648, *I[pomoea] leptophylla* . . . Bush Morning Glory, Big Root. 1949 Moldenke *Amer. Wild Flowers* 268, *I. leptophylla* . . . grows from an enormous, deep-seated fleshy root . . . Because of this root the plant is often called *bigroot* or *manroot.* 1968 Barkley *Plants KS* 280, Ipomoea pandurata . . . Man-of-the-Earth. Bigroot Morning-glory.

big savage n
In logging: see quots.
1942 Berrey–Van den Bark *Amer. Slang* 511.4, *Logging . . . Foreman.* Big bull, big savage. 1968 Adams *Western Words*, Big savage — A logger's name for the general superintendent.

big shoat n [*shoat* a young hog of either sex]
1954 Harder *Coll.* **cwTN**, Big shoat . . . Euphemism for boar.

big show n
=**big bug.**
1966–68 *DARE* (Qu. GG19a, . . *A person [who] acts . . important or independent*) Inf **MI**3, Big show; (Qu. HH17, *A person who tries to appear important*) Inf **AK**5, Big show.

big squeeze n Cf **main squeeze**
=**big bug.**
1942 Berrey–Van den Bark *Amer. Slang* 388.2, *Person of importance or self-importance* . . . Big squeeze. 1967–68 *DARE* (Qu. HH17, *A person who tries to appear important, or who tries to lay down the law in his community*) Infs **OR**1, **WI**27, Big squeeze.

‡big star n [From the star-shaped badge]
=**big hat 1.**
1967 *DARE* (Qu. V10a, . . *A sheriff*) Inf **MN**2, Big star.

big stick n [Prob from *big stick* coercive force]
1 A person of authority, as a police officer or foreman.
1966–67 *DARE* (Qu. V10b, . . *A marshal*) Inf **KS**5, Big stick; (Qu. HH43a, *The top person in charge of a group of workmen, the _____*) Inf **GA**13, Big stick.
2 =**big bug.**
1968–69 *DARE* (Qu. GG19a, . . *A person [who] acts . . important or independent*) Inf **VT**12, Thinks he's a big stick; (Qu. HH17, *A person who tries to appear important*) Inf **AK**5, Big stick.

big sticks n pl
In logging: the woods.
1942 Berrey–Van den Bark *Amer. Slang* 512.5, *Logging . . . Woods.* The big sticks. 1968 Adams *Western Words*. 1969 Sorden *Lumberjack Lingo* **NEng, Gt Lakes**.

big sugar n
See quots.
1942 Berrey–Van den Bark *Amer. Slang* 913.6, *Rancher; cattleman . . . Spec.* big sugar, . . *the owner.* 1968 Adams *Western Words*, Big sugar — A cowboy's name for the owner of the ranch.

big sunflower n
A **balsamroot** (here: *Balsamorrhiza sagittata*).
1963 Craighead *Rocky Mt. Wildflowers* 197, Big Sunflower . . . can be confused with the true sunflowers (*Helianthus*) and other closely related plants.

big-talk adj
Boastful, blustering.
1935 Sandoz *Jules* 234 **wNE** (as of 1880–1930), She knew what a shock it would be — after Jules's big-talk letters.

big tide See **big water**

big time n **widespread, but esp Sth, S Midl**
A convivial party or celebration; an enjoyable time.
1863 in 1903 Norton *Army Letters* 183 **PA**, The brigade was flying round, getting into line, drums beating and a big time generally. 1937 in 1972 *Amer. Slave* 2.1.222 **SC**, Dem cornshuckings wuz big times, dat dey wuz. 1941 *LANE* Map 414 **throughout NEng**, The map shows . . general terms for a social gathering or party, usually private: . . big time. 1942 Warnick *Garrett Co. MD* (as of 1900–1918), *Big time*, . . lots of fun, also used ironically as "They had a big time at Smiths when he came home drunk." 1956 Hall *Coll.* **eTN, wNC.** c1960 Wilson *Coll.* **csKY.** 1965–70 *DARE* (Qu. FF17, . . *A very good or enjoyable time:* "We all had a _____ last night.") 23 Infs, **esp Sth, S**

Midl, Big time; (Qu. FF18, . . *A noisy or boisterous celebration or party:* "*They certainly* _____ *last night.*") Infs **MD**26, **MN**30, **NC**45, **RI**17, **VA**29, 92, 69, Had a big time; (Qu. KK12, *A meeting where there's a lot of talking:* "*They got together yesterday and had a real* _____.") Infs **GA**28, **LA**32, **MO**34, Big time; (Qu. AA18, . . *A noisy neighborhood celebration after a wedding*) Inf **KY**44, Big time. **1968–69** *DARE* Tapes **IN**9, **MI**49, 115, Big time.

big toter See **big boy** n 2

big water n Also *big tide*
A flood.
1969 *DARE* Tape **KY**16, A big log washed up in big tide. **1970** *DARE* FW Addit **swKY,** Big water—a very high flood. Common.

big way, in a adj phr
Excited, agitated, vociferous.
1903 *DN* 2.306 **seMO,** The preacher got in a big way and you could hear him a mile. **1906** *DN* 3.115 **sIN,** *Big-way* . . . A noisy manner. "He's in a big-way." **1907** *DN* 3.229 **nwAR, seMO.**

big wheels n pl Also *big-wheel rig* **chiefly Nth**
In logging: see quot 1968.
1941 FWP *Guide WA* 73, A high-wheeled carriage or "big-wheel rig" was chained to a log and rolled away—the whole looking like an underslung siege gun. **1958** McCulloch *Woods Words* **Pacific NW.** **1967** *DARE* Tape **MI**47. **1968** Adams *Western Words,* *Big-wheel rigs*—In logging, the huge carts that carried logs suspended beneath their 15-foot-high wheels. **1969** Sorden *Lumberjack Lingo* **NEng, Gt Lakes.** **1970** *DARE* FW Addit **MI**121, Big wheels . . . Used for hauling logs out of the forest in summer.

big winnebago n
=**greater scaup.**
1963 Gromme *Birds WI* 218, Winnebago, Big (Greater Scaup).

bile See **boil** n¹, v

bilge n [Perh punning alter of *binge*]
A drinking spree; a binge.
1968–69 *DARE* (Qu. DD16, *To have a drinking bout and get drunk is to go on a* _____) Infs **DE**3, **MA**40, **NY**226, Bilge.

bilin' See **boiling** n

bilious, (the) n *old-fash*
Yellow or bilious fever.
[**1819** Thomas *Travels W. Country* 213, The prevailing diseases of this country are *bilious,* which sometimes terminate in malignant typhus.] **1834** (1928) Underwood *Jrl.* 127 **MA,** After having partially recovered from the billious I was atacked with the fever and ague. **1858** in 1956 Eliason *Tarheel Talk* 260 **NC,** Leiza has had a smart atact of the Bilyows but is on the mend. **1970** *DARE* (Qu. BB13, . . *Chills and fever*) Inf **TX**103, Bilious.

bill n¹
1 The proboscis of an insect (as a mosquito or tick).
1939 (1962) Thompson *Body & Britches* 133 **NY,** A swarm of mosquitoes had hit that pan so hard that they drove their bills into it. **1967** *DARE* (QR p124) **CO**22, Black tick will put his bill into you—goes clean in. **1981** *Broaddus Coll.* **ceKY,** This spring, in Rockcastle County, Ky. a man used "bill" to describe whatever it is a tick sticks into one, or bites with.

2 freq in combs: A person's nose. **chiefly Sth, S Midl** *derog*
1942 Berrey–Van den Bark *Amer. Slang* 121.69, *Nose* . . . Beezer, bill. **1952** in 1960 Wentworth–Flexner *Slang* 37, The GI Bill of Rights allowed a lot of impoverished [ex-soldiers] to get educated instead of getting their bills busted. **1965–70** *DARE* (Qu. X14, . . *The nose*) Infs **FL**8, **NC**41, **PA**231, **TN**67, Bill; **VA**2, Hog bill; **KY**40, Knocker bill; (Qu. X15, . . *Different kinds of noses*) Infs **NC**36, 76, **TN**23, 65, **TX**32, Hawk-bill; **KY**40, **MS**16, **VA**24, Hawk-bill nose; **GA**12, Bill nose; **OR**3, Hook bill.

bill n² [Short for *bill of divorce*]
A divorce; see quots. **NEast** Cf **bill** v²
1894 *DN* 1.340 **wCT,** *Bill:* to get a bill = to get a divorce. **1901** *DN* 2.136 **NY.** **1907** *DN* 3.241 **eME.** **1912** *DN* 3.566 **NY.** **1926** *DN* 5.385 **ME,** *Bill* . . . Divorce. "Mrs. Jones has got a bill from her husband." Universal. **1926** *AmSp* 2.81 **ME,** A woman who obtains a divorce is said to have got a "bill." **1975** Gould *ME Lingo* 12, *Bill*—Maine word for a divorce action started by the wife: "Myra's sending Harry her *bill.*"

bill v¹ [*OED* and *W3* "*obs*"]
To strike with the beak.
1969 *DARE* FW Addit **seGA,** "They'd bill him and bill him . . . " Said of vultures attacking a small pig.

bill v² [**bill** n²]
To divorce (one's spouse).
1885 Jackson *Zeph* 42 **CO,** He's a blamed fool he don't bill her.

billbook n
A pocketbook; a billfold.
1895 *Montgomery Ward Catal.* 101/1 *(OEDS),* Seal grain leather bill book, size 3½ x 8 inches. **1905** *New York Times* (NY) 3 Feb 3/4, In a billbook in an inside pocket were many checks for various sums on Plainfield banks. **1906** *DN* 3.126 **nwAR,** *Bill-book* . . . Pocket-book. "He lost a bill-book between here and Pleasant Plains."

Bill Brown's big black hog n
1905 *DN* 3.70 **nwAR,** *Bill Brown's big black hog* . . . The name of a game played by children.

billbug n
A snout beetle of the subfamily Calendrinae, esp of the genus *Sphenophorus.*
1861 *Harper's Mag.* 23.319/1, The next . . belongs to the family of *Rhyncophorus,* or "Weevils;" . . It is familiarly called at the South and West, "Bill-bug," "Corn-borer," and "Cane-piercer." **1911** *Century Dict. Suppl., Bill-bug* . . . Any calandrid beetle of the genus *Sphenophorus,* as the *corn bill-bug.* **1960** Williams *Walk Egypt* 261 **GA,** Corn had fewer rotten ears from billbugs. **1966** *DARE* Tape **SC**12, Something ate them [rice] seeds up before they matured . . what gets in the rice is a big old bug they call bill bugs.

billet n¹ [*OED billet* a short written document, "*Obs.*"; a short informal letter, "*arch.*"]
A note, letter, or document.
1847 McCallum *ME Letters,* One day Charles Hi found a billet in the road. On opening it, found it to be a permit for a negro to be married. **1968** *DARE* Tape **IN**19, Sometimes you'd get a message [at a spiritualist meeting]. They'd take up billets, they called 'em, and you write questions and they'd take up those billets ['bɪləts] and if you happened to be called you got a message.

billet n², also attrib Also sp *billett* Cf **billy** n²
A chunk of wood; a small log, often used for firewood.
1837 Peck *Gaz. IL* 77, A billet of charred wood [is] buried [to mark a survey corner], if no rock is near. **1899** (1912) Green *VA Folk-Speech, Billett* . . . A stick of wood, such as cut for firewood. **1902** White *Blazed Trail* 14 **MI,** Mike cut a short thick block, and all three stirred the heavy timber sufficiently to admit of the billet's insertion. **1938** FWP *Guide MS* 472 **cnMS,** Farmers in this area cut a few pines, sell the "billets," and plant a crop of corn where the trees formerly stood. **1966** *DARE* Tape **ME**26, Billets. **1967** *DARE* (Qu. L65, . . *Kinds of fences*) Inf **LA**10, Billet fence—stretch two wires and staple cypress blocks to them. **1967** *DARE* FW Addit **swAR,** Billet—a 5′ 5″ piece of wood to be used for pulp. **1968** Coatsworth *ME Memories* 2, In the big kitchen range the billets are snapping and sighing in the firebox and the coffee is already boiling.

billfish n
1 Any of var "beaked" saltwater fishes of the families Istiophoridae and Xiphiidae.
1793 in 1794 *MA Hist. Soc. Coll.* 1st ser 3.119, We also have the bill-fish in great plenty in the month of October. **1955** *Times-Dispatch* (Richmond VA) 2 Sept 34 *(Hench Coll.),* The Ocean City white marlin fleet had landed a total of 488 of these fast bill fish [a fish with a long narrow beak].

2 =**longnose gar** *(Lepisosteus osseus).*
1820 Rafinesque *Ohio R. Fishes* 88, Common in the Wabash, called Gar or Billfish, two feet long and quite slim; bill six inches and pointed. **1884** in 1887 Goode *Fisheries U.S.* 1.458, 'Bill-fish' . . is also applied by our fishermen to the slender species [of silver garfishes] of the swordfish family. *Ibid* 663, The Long-nosed Gar-pike, *Lepidosteus osseus,* . . is known as . . 'Bill-fish.'

billfold n **widespread, but least freq in NEast, Pacific** See Map Cf **wallet**
A pocketbook to carry folded paper money; a wallet.
1950 *WELS (What do you keep money in when you carry it around with*

you?) 46 Infs, **WI,** Billfold. **1965–70** *DARE* (Qu. U30) 557 Infs, Billfold.

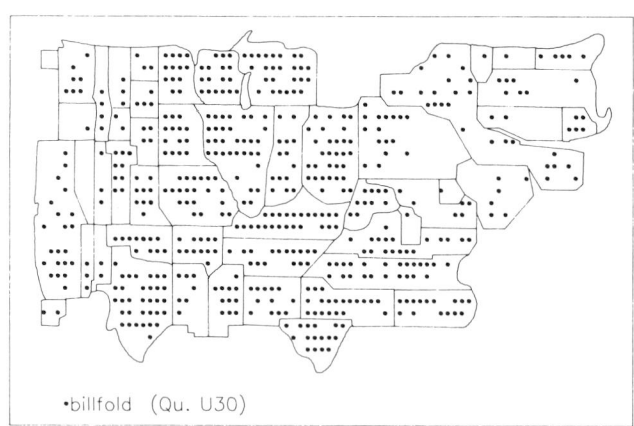

•billfold (Qu. U30)

billfolder n [billfold + -er affix] **chiefly Sth, S Midl** *esp among Black speakers*
=**billfold.**

1909 Porter *Options* 35 **NYC,** When he drew out his bill-folder to pay the cabman you couldn't help seeing hundreds and thousands of dollars in it. **1965–70** *DARE* (Qu. U30, *What do you keep money in when you carry it around with you?*) Infs **KY94, MS60, MO23, NC50, NJ22, SC26,** 55, 63, Billfolder. [5 of 8 Infs Black]

billies n pl
1905 *DN* 3.70 **nwAR,** *Billies* . . . Overalls and blouse. 'You'll have to wear billies to do that dirty job.' Rare.

‡**bill-jump** n
1968 *DARE* (Qu. U17, . . *A person who doesn't pay his bills*) Inf **PA135,** Bill-jump.

Bill-show n, also attrib
1944 Adams *Western Words, Bill-show*—A wild west show such as Buffalo Bill's and Pawnee Bill's. *Bill-show cowboy*—A show-off cowboy of the Buffalo Bill show type. **1967** *DARE* FW Addit **cnNY,** The Bill Show = the Buffalo Bill Show.

billy n[1]
1 also attrib in combs *billy boy, ~ man:* A law enforcement officer. [*billy* a policeman's club]
1968 *DARE* (Qu. V9, . . *A policeman*) Inf **PA70,** Billy; **WI21,** Billy boy; (Qu. V10a, . . *A sheriff*) Inf **NC55,** Billy man.
‡**2** A binge. Cf **bilge.**
1966 *DARE* (Qu. DD16, *To have a drinking bout and get drunk is to go on a* _____) Inf **AL4,** Billy.
3 A grasshopper. [Cf *EDD billy sb.[1],* used in compounds in names of animals, birds, and insects]
1968 *DARE* (Qu. R6) Inf **SC57,** Billy—a black and yellow grasshopper.

billy n[2], also attrib [Alter of **billet** n[2]]
1968 *DARE* (Qu. HH1) Inf **SC59,** Billy—a 5 foot section of wood; billy wood—pulp wood, "He cuts billy wood."

billy apple n
=**mayapple.**
1970 *DARE* (Qu. S4) Inf **GA91,** Billy apple.

billy barlow See **billy knife**

billy bean n
1957 Battaglia *Resp. to PADS 20* **e shore MD** (*The smaller beans that are white when they are dry*) Billy beans.

billy-be-damned n Also euphem sp *Billy Bedam* **chiefly Nth** Cf **billy hell**
In compar phrr used as an intensive: an extreme extent.
1914 *DN* 4.71 **ME, nNH,** *Dead as Billy-be-damned* . . . Very dead. **1938** *AmSp* 13.74 **cwOH,** 'It was as cold as Billy Bedam' (accent on the dam). **1958** *VT Hist.* ns 26.260, Colder than Billy be damned. (Billy hell, Billy Thunder.) Hotter than Billy be damned. **1968** *DARE* (Qu. U41b, . . *"He's poor as* _____") Inf **ND3,** Billy-be-damned; (Qu. HH22b, . . *"He's meaner than* _____*"*) Inf **OH77,** Billy-be-damned.

billy bee (martin) See **billy martin**

‡**billy blue** n Cf **blue blazes**
=**billy hell.**
1969 *DARE* (Qu. B3) Inf **IN71,** Hotter than Billy Blue.

billy boy See **billy** n[1] **1**

billy buster n [Perh Scots *billy* fellow, comrade + *buster* one who strikes, beats, or breaks]
1950 *WELS* (*Substitutes for stronger exclamations: "Why the son of a* _____.*"*) 1 Inf, **cwWI,** Billy buster.

billycock hat n
1906 *DN* 3.126 **nwAR,** *Billycock hat* . . . A Derby hat.

‡**Billy Devil** n Cf **billy hell**
1969 *DARE* (Qu. CC8, *Other names for the devil*) Inf **KY21,** Billy Devil.

‡**billy goat** n
1 Effrontery, nerve, pushiness.
1968 *DARE* (Qu. GG5, *When someone does something unexpectedly bold or forward, you might say: "Well, she certainly has a lot of* _____.*"*) Inf **NY42,** Billy goat.
2 =**sawbuck.**
1973 Allen *LAUM* 1.221 **csMN,** *Sawbuck* (for firewood) . . . Billy goat.

billy-goat beard n
=**goatsbeard.**
1968 *DARE* (Qu. S26a, . . *Other wildflowers*) Inf **VA11,** Billy-goat beard.

billy-goat hill n Also *billy-goat alley*
The run-down or poor section of a town.
1935 *AmSp* 10.80 **seMO,** Closely allied to the Toonerville concept is the satirical reference made to that nondescript neighborhood on the outskirts of a town. In this part of the state such a straggling settlement may be referred to as *Billy-Goat Hill.* **1969–70** *DARE* (Qu. C35) Inf **KY68,** Billy-goat alley—a slummy place, prostitution; (Qu. II25, . . *Part of a town where poorer people live*) Inf **MI108,** Billy-goat hill.

billy hawk n Cf **killy hawk**
Perh the **sparrow hawk 1.**
1967 *DARE* (Qu. Q4, . . *Kinds of hawks*) Inf **SC46,** Billy hawk.

billy hell n Also euphem pronc-sp *Billy Hal* Cf **billy-be-damned**
A desolate place, hell; havoc—freq used in compar phrr as an intensive.
1903 (1965) Adams *Log Cowboy* 64 **NM,** It was no vague statement of the man who said if he owned hell and Texas, he'd rent Texas and live in hell, for if this isn't Billy hell, I'd like to know what you call it. **1958** *Hench Coll.,* Today a Univ[ersity of] V[irgini]a fellow-teacher said: "The University President raised all sorts of billy hell about the schedule of courses of the Education Department." (The fellow-teacher was raised in Texas.) **1965–70** *DARE* (Qu. B3) Inf **IN30,** Hot as Billy Hal; (Qu. U41b, . . *"He's poor as* _____.*"*) Inf **ND3,** Billy hell; (Qu. HH22b, . . *"He's meaner than* _____.*"*) Inf **KY11,** Old billy hell; (Qu. KK11, *To make . . a big fuss . . "He* _____.*"*) Inf **NM9,** Raised all billy hell.

billy knife n Also *billy barlow*
A pocket knife or **barlow knife.**
1916 *DN* 4.345 **TN,** *Billy Barlow.* = Barlow, a knife. **1951** Johnson *Resp. to PADS 20* **DE** (*A large pocketknife with blades that fold in and out*) Barlow; billyknife. **1966** *DARE* (Qu. F39) Inf **SC19,** Billy knife.

billy man See **billy** n[1] **1**

‡**billy-maria** n
1908 *DN* 3.291 **eAL, wGA,** *Billy-maria* . . . A populite, a country cracker . . . hill-billy.

billy martin n Also *billy bee (martin)* Cf **bee martin**
=**kingbird.**
1913 Bailey *Birds VA* 176, *Tyrannus tyrannus* . . Billy Bee. **1969–70** *DARE* (Qu. Q14) Inf **KY21,** Billy martin; **VA57,** Billy bee martin.

billy owl n esp **CA**
=**burrowing owl.**
1913 *Pacific Coast Avifauna* 9.51 **CA,** "Billy owl" is the name by which this, our smallest owl, is known to everyone. **1923** Dawson *Birds CA*

1122, *"Billy Owl"* is the humorous and half affectionate name bestowed by all good Californians upon this familiar sprite of the roadside. **1946** Goodrich *Birds in KS* 317. **1951** Teale *North Spring* 44 **FL,** We are looking at the burrowing owl, the billy owl of the Florida prairies. **1967–69** *DARE* (Qu. Q2) Infs **CA**22, 31, 115, 163, Billy owl.

billy whicker n [Cf *EDD billy sb.¹,* used in Scots and n Engl dial names of animals, birds, insects; + *whicker,* in ref to the sound made by the bird]
    1970 *DARE* (Qu. Q18, . . *Woodpeckers*) Inf **VA**38, Billy-whickers; **VA**43, Billy whicker ['hwɪkə]—big as a crow; [FW:] probably pileated woodpecker.

bilou n
    In nursery use: see quot.
    1969 Cagnon *Franco–Amer. Terms* 223 **NEng,** *Bilou* . . [bilu]; [belu] Nasal mucus. "Let me clean your bilous."

bim adv [Echoic; perh of Afr origin]
    With a sharp blow.
    1888 Jones *Negro Myths* 9 **GA coast,** Buh Rabbit hit um, bim, wid eh tarruh han.

bimbo n Also *bim*
    A girl or woman—sometimes used disparagingly.
    1929 *AmSp* 4.338, *Vocabulary of Bums* . . . *Bimbo*—A woman. **1932** *AmSp* 7.329, *Johns Hopkins Jargon* . . . *Bim; bimbo*—a girl. **1950** *WELS* (*An immoral woman*) 1 Inf, **csWI,** A bimbo. **1969** *DARE* (Qu. AA22, *Joking names a man may use to refer to his wife: "I have to go down and pick up my _____.")* Inf **CT**23, Bimbo.

bimeby adv Also sp *bimebye, bumby(e), by-am-by, bymby* [Alter of *by-and-by* (see *EDD, OEDS bimeby(e)*); prob reinforced in Sth by slave use since it was widespread in pidgin and creole English of 17th cent and after]
    Presently, soon, before long.
    1722 in 1930 Winslow *Amer. Broadside* 115/2 **MA,** Indian bimeby take Captain Westbrook's fort. **1844** Stephens *High Life in NY* 2.61 **CT,** By-am-by, they all give out. **1844** Thompson *Major Jones's Courtship* 114 **GA,** Bimeby Bill Byers called out the names of all the lords and ladys what belonged to the court. **1867** Lowell *Biglow* 61 "**Upcountry**" **MA,** Your "You'll see *nex'* time!" an' "Look out bumby!" / Most ollers ends in eatin' umble-pie. **1893** Shands *MS Speech, Bimeby* . . . Negro for *by and by.* **1899** (1912) Green *VA Folk-Speech.* **1907** *DN* 3.181 se**NH.** **1908** *DN* 3.291 e**AL,** w**GA.** **1922** Gonzales *Black Border* 290 s**SC, GA coasts** [Gullah glossary], *Bimebye, bumbye*—bye and bye. **1925** *DN* 5.358 [Gullah], An bymby [bɑimbɑi] ah hyeah de wahtah come splashin an nex de hollow soun when he fill up he pitchah. **1934** *Hanley Disks* se**MA,** He'd start to run, and bumbye the other'n 'd start run. **1950** *PADS* 14.17 **SC** [Black], *Bumbye* . . . Bye and bye. **1951** *AmSp* 26.26, Common expressions in the pidgin of Hawaii are . . *bimeby* (by-and-by), *wasamatta* (what's the matter). **1967** *DARE* Tape **HI**4, Bumby you ask some people. **1972** Carr *Da Kine Talk* 126 **HI,** *Bumbye, bymby* . . . Mean 'later', 'some other time'.

bin v See **be** A2

binacle See **binnacle**

bind v
    Std senses, var forms.
    Past: usu *bound;* also *binded,* infreq *bount.*
    1842 Walker in 1940 Drury *Pioneers Spokanes* 171 **ME,** Stitched, pressed, and binded one and one half dozen of the first book in Flathead. **1954** *Harder Coll.* cw**TN,** They binded him over to court. **1962** *Mt. Life* Spring 17 s**Appalachians,** The *-d* and *-ed* endings of past forms of verbs are frequently pronounced *-t,* particularly when the ending is preceded by *l, m, n,* or *r.* A few such verbs are *bound, bount; held, helt.* **1966** *DARE* (Qu. BB21) Inf **OK**25, Binded. **1967** *DARE* (QR p86) Inf **HI**3, Chains are binded so as not to hurt horses.

bind n [**bind** v]
    A sheaf or bundle (of grain, corn leaves, etc).
    1902 *DN* 2.229 s**IL,** *Bind* . . . Sheaf, as:—'A bind of wheat.' **1903** *DN* 2.307 se**MO.** **1906** *DN* 3.126 nw**AR,** Bind. **1939** *LANE* Map 126 ne**MA,** The map presents synonyms of *sheaf* . . . [a bundle of wheat; a bind of corn]. **1967–70** *DARE* (Qu. L30a, *When grain is cut it is (or used to be) tied up in _____*) Infs **IA**33, **IL**66, **OK**53, Binds. **1968** *DARE* FW Addit se**KY,** A local for-sale ad: "for sale, three hundred binds of blade-fodder." **1973** Allen *LAUM* 1.274, The name for a tied

bundle of cereal grain, as of wheat or oats . . . Relic *bind* is the form checked by one Iowan . . and by 2 North Dakotans.

binder n
    1 In the tobacco industry: see quots.
    1940 *AmSp* 15.133, *Binders.* Leaves used as inside wrappers of cigars. **1966** *DARE* Tape **FL**24, Then it [=cigar tobacco] had what we call a binder. Then you'd tuck that binder and you'd roll that binder over this filler; **FL**26, Binder. **1967** Key *Tobacco Vocab.* **CT, PA,** *Binder* . . . Tobacco leaf used as inside wrapper of cigar filler.
    2 usu pl: A brake, esp a hand brake. [Orig railroad jargon]
    1943 *AmSp* 18.162 [Railroad terms], *Binder.* Hand brake. **1953** Botkin *Treas. Railroad Folkl.* 326, The foreman [=conductor] . . told this student to set a binder [=hand brake] on the first car in. **1954** *AmSp* 29.93 ["Hot Rod" terms], 'Hit those binders quick!'; i.e., put on the brakes fast. **1962** *AmSp* 37.267 [Language of traffic police], *Binders* . . . Brakes. Most often used in referring to emergency stops. 'Hit the binders!' **1969** *AmSp* 44.202 [Truck drivers' jargon], *Binders* —Brakes (does not exist as singular).
    3 =cap n¹ 1.
    1966–68 *DARE* (Qu. L31, . . *The top bundle of a shock*) Infs **NC**30, **OH**50, **WA**8, Binder.
    4 See **rubber binder.**

bindle n [Prob alter of *bundle,* or perh from Ger *Bündel;* Engl dial *bindle* is rare and differs in sense] *esp among loggers and hoboes*
    A bedroll in which one's belongings are wrapped.
    1916 *Lit. Digest* 53.425/1, A package is a "bindle," derived from "bundle." **1937** Steinbeck *Of Mice* 10 **CA,** George unslung his bindle and dropped it gently on the bank. **1942** *AmSp* 17.219 [Logger talk], *Bindle.* A blanket roll. **1954** *AmSp* 29.47, *Bindle* is homophonous with P[ennsylvani]a G[erman] /bindəl/ G[erman] *Bündel* 'package, bundle.' I have several times heard this word used in English by bilingual speakers, but always jocosely as a deliberate and obvious borrowing from the dialect. **1956** Sorden–Ebert *Logger's Words, Bindle,* A blanket roll. A lumber-jack sometimes brought his belongings wrapped in his own blanket when he came to camp. Used in the East and in early logging in the Middle West. **1969** O'Connor *Horse & Buggy West* 45 c**AZ,** [He] strode up to the front gate carrying a tight neatly rolled "bindle," or bedroll.

bindle stiff n Also rarely *bindle man* [**bindle** + *stiff* vagabond, laborer] **scattered, but esp Pacific States** Also called **blanket stiff**
    A tramp; an itinerant worker.
    1900 Willard *Itinerant Policeman* 167, Among the "Bindle Men," "Mush Fakirs," and "Turnpikers," of the middle West, the East, and Canada, there exists a crude system of marking "good" houses. **1901** in 1965 London *Letters* 126 **CA,** Wyckoff only knows the workingman, the stake-man, and the bindle-stiff. **1931** *AmSp* 7.104 [Underworld argot], *Bindle-stiff* . . . A bum who carries a bundle of belongings, usually tied in a handkerchief, or wrapped in paper. "Hard times bring back the bindle-stiffs." **1946** Peattie *Pacific Coast* 233 [Logger talk], The bindle stiff who got gay with the boss was a lucky boy if he lived with the wish to fight another day. **1952** Steinbeck *East of Eden* 46 **CA,** Before he knew it he was a bindlestiff himself. **1965–70** *DARE* (Qu. HH19, . . *A tramp*) Infs **CA**4, 66, 107, 110, **MA**58, **VT**12, **VA**25, Bindle stiff. **1967** *DARE* Tape **ID**6, Bindle stiff.

bindweed n
    1 Any of various species of *Convolvulus,* a perennial plant with trailing, twining, or erect stems and pink, purple, or white flowers. Also called **devil's shoestring, glorybind, morning glory, tie-vine.** For other names of various species see **bellbind, California rose, cornbind 1, corn lily, creeping Jennie, hedge bindweed, lap-love, moonflower, possession vine, sheepbine, wild hollyhock, wild potato**
    1731 (1754) Catesby *Nat. Hist. Carolina* 1.35, The Purple Bindweed of Carolina. The Flower of this *Convolvulus* [sic] is of a reddish purple, and of the size and shape of common white Bindweed. **1822** Eaton *Botany* 248, *Convolvulus* . . bindweed. **1903** Small *Flora SE U.S.* 965, *Convolvulus* . . Bindweed. **1961** Thomas *Flora Santa Cruz* 275 **CA,** *Convolvulus* . . Bindweed. **1965–70** *DARE* (Qu. S5, . . *Wild morning glory*) 121 Infs, **widespread,** Bindweed; **VA**24, Field bindweed; **MI**31, Upright bindweed; (Qu. S21) 11 Infs, **scattered West,** Bindweed.

2 =**greenbrier** (here: esp *Smilax rotundifolia*). *?obs*
1737(1911) Brickell *Nat. Hist. NC* 96, *Prickley Bind-weed*, or *Sarsaparilla*, is a kind of *Prickley Vine*, not unlike the former *[Small Bamboo]*. **1837** Darlington *Flora Cestrica* 566, *S[milax] rotundifolia* . . Rough Bind-weed.

3 Any of various species of *Polygonum;* also *Bilderdykia scandens.* Cf **smartweed**
1840 MA Zool. & Bot. Surv. *Herb. Plants & Quadrupeds* 1.102, *P[olygonum] convolvulus* . . Bindweed. **1891** Jesup *Plants Hanover NH* 35, *Polygonum*, . . Bindweed. **1903** Porter *Flora PA* 117, *Polygonum cilinode* . . Fringed Black Bindweed. **1910** Graves *Flowering Plants* 163, *Polygonum scandens* . . Hedge, Bush, or Thicket Bindweed . . *Polygonum clumetorum* . . Bush or Thicket . . Bindweed. **1966** *DARE* Wildfl QR Pl.15b, Inf **WA**30, Bindweed.

4 A **heliotrope 1** (here: *Heliotropium convolvulaceum*).
1951 *PADS* 15.39 **TX**, *Heliotropium convolvulaceum* . . . Bind-weed or tie-vine.

5 =**morning glory** (here: *Ipomæa* spp).
1959 Carleton *Index Herb. Plants* 11, Bindweed: . . Ipomæa.

bing v [Echoic]
1952 Brown *NC Folkl.* 1.520, *Bing* . . To slap or hit.

bingle n chiefly AK
A coin of little value; see quots.
1921 *DN* 5.110 **CA**, *Bingle* . . . A coin of base metal, value ten cents, used for gambling. Sierra County. **1936** *Fairbanks Daily News-Miner* 28 Jan 1 (Tabbert *Alaskan Engl.*), Tokens minted by the federal government will be used as money among the colonists on the federal government's agricultural project in the Matanuska Valley . . . They already have been termed "bingles." **1959** Hart *McKay's AK* 29, The $5 and $10 bingles were gold in color and all lesser denominations were silver in color. **1972** National Bank of Alaska advertisement *Alaska Magazine* A3 (Tabbert *Alaskan Engl.*), Way back when, you could do a lot of dealing with a bagful of beads and bingles.

‡**bing, on the** n [Cf *on the beam*]
Energetic, on the ball.
1967 *DARE* (Qu. KK29, *To start working very hard: "He was slow at first but now he's really _____."*) Inf **LA**11, On the bing.

‡**binky** n
1 See quot.
1912 *DN* 3.571 **wIN**, *Binky* . . . Any little mechanical contrivance.
2 The buttocks. [Cf Scots *bink* a bench to sit on]
1968 *DARE* (Qu. X35, . . *The part of the body that you sit on*) Inf **MN**39, Binky.

binnacle n Also sp *binacle, binnekill, binocle* [Du *binnen* within, inner + *kil* watercourse, channel] **NY** *old-fash* Cf **binnewater**
A side branch of a river; a millrace.
1860 in 1901 *DN* 2.132 **cNY**, Running thence down along the shore of said river at low water mark to a point at the mouth of the binacle, thence up along the western side of said binacle at low water mark. **1881** Burroughs *Pepacton* 27 **NY**, There was a whirlpool, a rock eddy, and a binocle within a mile. **1896** *DN* 1.412 **cNY**, *Binnacle:* the flume of a mill stream, a mill race. **1901** *DN* 2.132 **cNY**, Along the course of the Susquehanna River, between Otsego, N.Y., and Afton, N.Y., the word binnacle is known. It has also been reported from Ithaca, N.Y., and Kinderhook, N.Y. . . In Ulster County, N.Y., . . binnekill. **1902** (1968) Clapin *Americanisms, Binnacle.* In parts of New York, the flume of a mill stream, a mill race.

binnewater n [Du *binnen* within, inner + *water*] **NY** *old-fash* Cf **binnacle**
A small lake.
1901 *DN* 2.133, In Ulster County, N.Y., in the vicinity of Kingston, two words exist side by side, *binnewater* and *binnekill* . . . A *binnewater* is a lake. **1929** *AmSp* 5.154 **eNY**, For a time *binnewater* and *cripplebush* were current. [**1968** *DARE* (Qu. C34) Inf **NY**87, Binnewaters—a settlement of Protestants.]

binny n
1 See quot.
1908 *DN* 3.291 **eAL, wGA**, *Binny* . . . A nursery euphemism for belly. "The baby has the binny-ache."
2 See **benny 2.**

binocle See **binnacle**

bio See **bayou A**

biorque n [See quot 1931]
=**bittern.**
1916 *DN* 4.422 **LA**, *Biorque.* The American bittern (*Botaurus lentiginosus).* [**1931** Read *LA French* 11, *Biorque* . . . American Bittern . . . This novel word seems to be connected with dialectal French *bior, bihor*, "bittern," whence has come French *bihoreau*, a species of night heron.]

bip into v phr [*bip* echoism for "to strike, hit"]
1893 Shands *MS Speech* 20, *Bip into* . . . Used by illiterate whites to mean to attack with either words or blows. Two speakers are said to *bip into* each other, when they attack each other in a lively or severe manner; so also of pugilists.

birch n [Alter of *bitch*] *euphem, joc*
In phr *son of a birch:* used as an exclam.
1965–70 *DARE* (Qu. NN24, *Humorous substitutes for stronger exclamations: "Why the son of a _____!"*) Infs **IL**54, 66, **MI**55, **NY**214, **WI**71, **WV**4, Birch.

birch beer n **NEast** Cf **spruce beer**
A drink, usu carbonated, made with oil of birch.
1883 *Wheelman* 1.392/2 **nePA**, We [bicyclers] reached Bushkill at 12.30 P.M., stopping—for birch beer—at odd places. **1931–33** *LANE Worksheets* **csCT**, Birch beer . . . A soft drink, [it] is either light or dark. **1954** Forbes *Rainbow* 120 **NH**, We bought us birch beer and gingerbread and hunks of molasses candy as soon as the selling of such was authorized. **1968** *DARE* Tape **NJ**11, During the summer we always made . . . birch beer. **1969** *DARE* (Qu. H78, . . *Ordinary soft drinks, usually carbonated*) Inf **NJ**56, Birch beer.

bird n
A Forms.
1 Pronc: usu |bɜ˞d| and in r-less areas |bɜd|; also, esp coastal Sth, NYC, eNEng, |bɜɪd, bʌ(ɪ)d|.
1927 Shewmake *Engl. Pronc. VA* 41, *Bird* . . . To give the prevailing Virginia pronunciation . . omit *r* altogether. **1937** *AmSp* 12.169, The pronunciation of *girl* and *bird* in New York City, which is popularly represented as *goil* and *boid*, is one in which a diphthong somewhat like [əɪ] has developed. **1939** *LANE* Map 213 ce,neMA, [bɜ˞·dz, bɜ·dz, bɜ˞·dz]. **1941** *Ibid* Map 292 neMA, [bɜ·dz]; sw,c,cwVT, [bɜˑ·dz, bɜ˞dz, bɜ˞dz, bɜɪdz]. **1941** *AmSp* 16.7 eTX [Black], *Bird, burn, churn, . .* occur with both [ʌ:], as the typical, and [ʌɪ˞], as the occasional sound. **1942** *AmSp* 17.150 seNY, *Bird . .* [ɜ˞] . . 6 [informants] . . . [ɜ] . . 8 [informants] . . . [ɜɪ] . . 6 [informants]. **1966** [see **curl n A**]. c**1970** Pederson *Dial. Survey Rural GA*, [In southeast Georgia *bird* is most often pronounced [bɜ˞d], also (especially in coastal communities) [bɜɪd], and occasionally [bɜ˞·d].]

2 used attrib in combs where possessive often occurs: See quots. **chiefly Sth, S Midl** Cf **hen egg**
1906 *DN* 3.126 **nwAR**, *Bird-egg* . . . Bird's egg. "I've got a big collection of bird-eggs." **1908** *DN* 3.291 **eAL, wGA.** **1933** Miller *Lamb in His Bosom* 13 **GA**, Her mother had brought her three settings of eggs—one of geese, long and white; one of guineas, small, speckled, cunning-looking, like bird eggs; and one of chickens. **1955** *PADS* 23.22 **cwTN**, *Knuckle down and bird eggs* . . . [In marble play] A call. c**1960** *Wilson Coll.* **csKY**, *Bird egg* is regular; *bird's egg* sounds foreign. **1965–70** *DARE* (Qu. W19) Inf **MS**72, Bird-eye cloth; (Qu. X21b) Inf **MO**2, Bird eyes; (Qu. X37) Infs **GA**59, **IN**30, **TX**68, Bird legs; (Qu. EE6b) Inf **MO**16, Bird eyes; (Qu. LL2) Inf **OK**31, Bird egg.

B Senses.
1 In hunting: a quail. **chiefly Sth**
1929 (1951) Faulkner *Sartoris* 330 **MS**, He and Buddy tried for birds in the skeletoned fields in the rain in which the guns made a flat, mournful sound . . or tried the stagnant backwaters . . for duck and geese. **1966** *DARE* Tape **NC**36, I only have bird hunted. **1967** *DARE* FW Addit **SC**, Bird hunting—specifically after quail; bird means quail to the hunter. **1968** *DARE* (Qu. Q7) Inf **AL**38, Local hunters use *bird hunting* to mean quail hunting; latter term is a sign of inexperience.

2 Std sense, but used redundantly. ~~**chiefly Sth, S Midl**~~
1931 *AmSp* 7.94 **eKY**, *Quail-bird*, a bird similar to the bob-white with a very short tail. **1944** *PADS* 2.18 **sAppalachians**, *–Bird* . . . Redundantly used after the names of birds: *spar'-bird, wren-bird*, etc. c**1960** *Wilson Coll.* **csKY**. **1965–70** *DARE* (Qu. Q3) Inf **FL**7, Kite bird; (Qu.

Q8) Inf **WA**2, Loon bird; (Qu. Q10) Inf **IA**29, Kingfisher bird; (Qu. Q11) Infs **LA**29, **MD**34, Crow bird; (Qu. Q14) Infs **LA**7, **SD**3, **VA**7, Canary bird; **MD**20, **MS**63, Martin bird; (Qu. Q20) Inf **LA**8, Martin bird; (Qu. Q21) Infs **LA**22, **NC**30, Sparrow bird; **KY**39, Spar' bird.

3 See quot. [In ref to the eagle on the coin]
  1950 *WELS (Nicknames for $.25)* 1 Inf, **csWI**, A bird.

‡4 A point of contention or disagreement.
  1969 *DARE* (Qu. KK14, *Something that people disagree about: "I have a _____ to pick with you."*) Inf **KY**28, Bird.

bird v
  To scare up or flush (game birds).
  1968 *DARE* (Qu. P39b, *If the dog makes a bird or covey fly, you'd say he _____*) Inf **WI**52, Birds it.

bird bath n Cf **cat bath**
  1953 *AmSp* 28.144, *Bird bath, Dutch bath, . .* and *wipe-off* are baths requiring a minimum of water . . . All these terms apparently have fairly wide usage.

bird battling See **bird knocking**

bird, beast, or fish n
  1 also *beast, bird, or fish:* A children's guessing game (method of play varies locally): see quots. Cf **colors**
  1883 Newell *Games & Songs* 140, *Beast, Bird, or Fish . . .* A member of the party throws to another a knotted handkerchief, saying one of the above words, and counting up to ten. The catcher must answer in the given time the name of some animal of the kind required, not already cited by some other player. Whoever fails to reply while the counting is going on, is out of the game. **1953** Brewster *Amer. Nonsinging Games* 34 **IN**, Bird, Beast, or Fish . . . The leader points suddenly to one of the other players and says one of the above words. If, for example, the word is "fish," the player must name a fish before the leader can count to ten aloud. **1969** *DARE* (Qu. EE33) Inf **NY**126, Beast, bird, or fish—same as "colors" but you'd have to guess whether the person who was "it" was thinking of a beast, bird, or fish.
  2 A game similar to musical chairs. See *DS* EE2
  1950 *WELS (Games with an extra player: at a signal the other players change places, and the extra tries to get a place)* 1 Inf, **cnWI**, Bird, beast or fowl [sic]. **1968** *DARE* (Qu. EE2, *Games that have an extra player*) Inf **NY**123, Bird, beast, or fish.
  3 A children's game; see quot.
  1967 *DARE* (Qu. EE3, *Games in which you hide an object and then look for it*) Inf **IA**7, Bird, beast, or fish.

bird berry See **bird cherry 2**

bird bill n
  1 also *bird's bill:* =**shooting star**. chiefly NW and AK
  1932 Rydberg *Flora Prairies* 626, *Dodecatheon . .* Bird-bills. **1936** *Nature Mag.* 27.354, Shooting star, or "bird bill", *Dodecatheon frigidum,* is a northern representative of this group of lovely plants, members of the Primrose family, that boasts one or more species in most localities in temperate North America. Whether in eastern woodlands, on the sagebrush plains of the West, or in the mountain meadow, this perky flower is always a welcome sight. **1938** (1958) Sharples *AK Wild Flowers* 45, *Dodecatheon . . .* The sharp dart, poised for striking, suggests another common name, "Bird's Bill." **1959** Anderson *Flora AK* 375, *Dodecatheon . .* The various species of this genus are known as . . Bird Bills. **1963** Craighead *Rocky Mt. Wildflowers* 143, *Shooting-star . . . Other names:* American Cowslip, Birdbills. **1969** *DARE* (Qu. S26d) Inf **MO**15, Bird's bills.
  2 =**Johnny-jump-up**.
  1967 *DARE* (Qu. S3) Inf **OR**3, Birdbill, same as Johnny-jump-up; **OR**13, Birdbill or Johnny-jump-up.

bird cage n
  In railroading: see quots.
  1945 Hubbard *Railroad Ave.* 333, *Bird cage*—Brakeman's or switchman's lantern. **1968** *AmSp* 43.285, *Bird cage.* Switchtender's kerosene lantern, so named for the wire frame that surrounds and protects the glass shade.

bird cherry n
  1 Any of var small-fruited cherry trees as:
  a Std: either of two trees—the mazzard cherry (*Prunus avium*) or the European bird-cherry (*P. padus*)—cultivated and sometimes naturalized locally in the United States.

b =**pin cherry**. chiefly Nth, esp NEng
  1785 Marshall *Arbustrum* 113, *Prunus-Cerasus* montana. *Mountain Bird-Cherry-Tree . . .* The fruit . . . is smaller, of a red colour, and an extremely acid taste. **1843** Torrey *Flora NY* 1.196, *Cerasus Pennsylvanica . . . Bird Cherry . . .* Fruit the size of a large pea, red, austere, scarcely eatable. **1897** Sudworth *Arborescent Flora* 240, *Wild Red Cherry . . . Common Names . . .* Bird Cherry (Me., N.H., N.Y., Pa., Minn., Iowa). **1917** (1923) Rogers *Trees Worth Knowing* 153, The . . bird . . cherry grows in rocky woods . . . The birds enjoy the ruddy little fruits . . . and in many burnt-over districts, the bird-sown pits strike root. **1969** *DARE* (Qu. I46) Inf **MA**25, Bird cherries. **1979** Little *Checklist U.S. Trees* 215.
  2 also *bird berry:* =**pepper vine**.
  1916 *Torreya* 16.238, *Ampelopsis arborea . . .* Bird berry, Waccamaw Plantation, S[outh] C[arolin]a. **1940** Clute *Amer. Plant Names* 131, *C. arborea.* Pepper-vine. Bird cherry, snow-vine.

bird dock n [Folk-etym]
  =**burdock 1**.
  1968 *DARE* (Qu. S13) Inf **IN**14, Bird dock.

bird dog n [Perh joc alter of *buttock*]
  The buttocks.
  c1970 *Halpert Coll.* **wKY**, Knocked on your bird dog = knocked down, landing on the buttocks.

bird dog v
  1967 *DARE* (Qu. Y29b, *About a man who doesn't stay home much: "He's always _____."*) Inf **WA**22, Bird dogging.

‡bird-dogger n
  1967 *DARE* (Qu. II20a, *A person who tries too hard to gain somebody else's favor: "He's an awful _____."*) Inf **SC**40, Bird-dogger.

bird eater n [From *eat like a bird* to be a fussy or light eater]
  A person who eats little or is finicky about food.
  1968–70 *DARE* (Qu. H12, *If somebody eating a meal takes little bits of food and leaves most of it on his plate*) Infs **CA**77, **IL**131, Bird eater.

bird egg See **bird-egg bean 3**

bird-egg bean n
  1 A dark red bean.
  1968 *DARE* (Qu. I17) Inf **MD**24, Bird-egg beans.
  2 =**black-eyed pea**.
  1969 *DARE* (Qu. I19) Inf **PA**210, Bird-egg beans.
  3 also *bird egg:* See quots.
  1954 *Harder Coll.*, Bird-egg beans—round, sort of look like a bird egg with little red specks. **1968–69** *DARE* (Qu. I20, *Other kinds of beans that are grown around here*) Infs **PA**213, **VA**24, **WI**49, Bird-egg beans. **1976** *Wanigan Catalog* 4 **MA**, Bird Egg Bean . . . A buff hort type, blunt oval, . . lavender bloom. Late here. *Ibid* 4, Bird Egg . . . Not like a bird's egg or the others with the name. It is a black seed, . . round to oval with tan specks. Early.

bird-egg pea n Also *bird's-egg pea* [See quot 1950]
  A western **milkvetch** (*Astragalus ceramicus*) which has inflated ovoid pods mottled with purple. Also called **painted pod, rattlepod 1** See also **rattleweed 1**
  1930 *OK Univ. Biol. Surv. Pub.* 2.66, *Astragalus pictus . . .* Bird-egg Pea. Long-leaved Astragalus. **1936** Winter *Plants NE* 102, Long-leaved Painted Pod. Bird-egg Pea. In sandy soil in western Nebr. **1950** Stevens *ND Plants* 184, Long-leaved Milkvetch . . . The papery pods are very striking and their spotted appearance has given rise to the name "Birdsegg Pea."

bird eye n
  1968 *DARE* (Qu. EE6b, *Small marbles*) Inf **MO**16, Bird eyes.

bird-eye bean n
  1 also *bird's-eye bean,* ~ *pea:* =**black-eyed pea**.
  1966–69 *DARE* (Qu. I19) Infs **MD**24, **ND**1, Bird-eye beans; **NY**75, **OH**63, **VA**2, Bird's-eye beans; **KY**62, Bird's-eye pea.
  2 also *bird-eye:* Any of var other beans: see quots.
  1966–68 *DARE* (QR near Qu. I19) Inf **ND**1, Birdeye beans—the yellow string beans; (Qu. I20) Infs **MD**21, Bird-eye beans—brown, white speckles; **VA**13, Bird-eye bean—brown with yellow eye; **VA**9, Bird-eyes—like a black-eyed pea, halfway between a black-eyed pea and a bean.

bird-eye maple See **bird's-eye maple**

bird-eye pepper n Also *bird-eye, bird's-eye pepper* **S Atl, Gulf States** Cf **bird pepper**

A small hot red pepper.

1966–68 *DARE* (Qu. I22a) Infs **AL15, FL37, LA11**, Bird-eye peppers; **LA28**, Bird-eye pepper or cayenne pepper; **LA43**, Bird-eye peppers— small—that's what they make Louisiana red-hot sauce out of; **GA3, 28, LA2, 15**, Bird-eye peppers; **NC79**, Bird-eyes—put in vinegar to make sauce; **NC81**, Bird-eyes; **LA3, MS2, 16, 73, SC43, TX36**, Bird's-eye peppers; **FL31, GA11, SC22**, Bird's-eye peppers; **SC4**, Bird's-eye peppers—round, pea-size.

bird-eye pine n [Prob from the knots in the wood] Cf **bird's-eye maple**

=**lodgepole pine.**

1967 *DARE* (Qu. T17, . . *Kinds of pine trees*) Inf **WY1**, Lodgepole— bird-eye.

bird-foot (trefoil) See **bird's-foot trefoil**

bird-foot (violet) See **bird's-foot violet**

bird grape n

1 A vine *(Vitis munsoniana),* native to Florida and Georgia, which produces small, nearly black grapes. Also called **bullace 2, everbearing grape, little muscadine grape, mustang grape**

1920 *Torreya* 20.23, *Vitis munsoniana* . . . Everbearing, bird or mustang grape. **1942** *Amer. Joint Comm. Horticult. Nomenclature Std. Plant Names* 278.

2 Perh =**catbird grape.**

1968 *DARE* (Qu. I46) Inf **MD12**, Bird grapes—small, dark blue or black, with seeds.

bird hawk n

1 A small hawk, such as the **pigeon hawk 1** or the **sparrow hawk 1,** or a similar bird.

1832 Williamson *Hist. ME* 1.141, The *Whetsaw* . . . frequents logging camps; and is thought to be the same as the *Bird-hawk,* though as to this naturalists differ. **1967–68** *DARE* (Qu. Q4) Inf **KY31**, Bird hawk (a falcon); **MD36**, Bird hawk—only in marsh, looks like big owl; **MD48**, Bird hawk—various sizes; **MN12**, Swallow hawk or bird hawk—will take bird; a smaller hawk; **NJ22**, Bird hawk (merlin) or pigeon hawk; **NJ39**, Bird hawk (merlin).

2 =**sharp-shinned hawk.**

1917 (1923) *Birds Amer.* 2.66, *Sharp-shinned Hawk . . . Other Names.*—Pigeon Hawk; Sparrow Hawk; Bird Hawk. **1923** Dawson *Birds CA* 1657, *Sharp-shinned Hawk . . . "Sparrow" Hawk. Bird Hawk.* **1953** Jewett *Birds WA* 163, *Accipiter striatus velox* . . . Bird Hawk. **1954** Sprunt *FL Bird Life* 103, The Sharp-shin is one of the "bird hawks." **1966–70** *DARE* (Qu. Q4) 19 Infs, **scattered, but chiefly east of Missip R**, Bird hawk; **FL51**, Chicken hawk—bird hawk . . same hawk; **MD13**, Bird hawk—small, catches birds and baby chickens; **MD22**, Bird hawk—small, eats birds; **MD32, 42**, Bird hawk—small, catches birds; **NC80**, Bird hawk (may be the chicken hawk); **UT5, VA46, 75**, Bird hawk—a small one; **VT10**, Bird hawk—smaller than chicken hawk. [Note: some of these Infs may refer instead to **bird hawk 1.**]

birdie n Cf *DS* E20

See quot 1969.

1950 *WELS Suppl.,* 1 Inf, **seWI**, Birdies—dust rolls. **1969** *DARE* (Qu. E20, *Soft rolls of dust that collect on the floor under beds or other furniture*) Inf **CA126**, Little birdies.

birding vbl n [Perh folk-etym for *burden* chorus, refrain]

1944 *PADS* 2.32 **NC**, *Birding* . . . Singing a part in a song such as "Oh come, come, come, come . . . " which accompanies the lead tune in "The Church in the Wildwood." . . Rare.

bird-in-the-bush n

A **prickly poppy** (here: *Argemone mexicana*).

1892 *Garden and Forest* 5.614, In Massachusetts the Argemone Mexicana is Bird-in-the-bush. **1900** Lyons *Plant Names* 44, *A[rgemone] Mexicana* . . . Bird-in-the-bush. **1936** Whitehouse *TX Flowers* 34, Mexican Poppy . . . is also called bird-in-the-bush.

bird-in-the-cup n

A children's game: see quot.

1966 *DARE* (Qu. EE3) Inf **FL14**, Bird-in-the-cup—They say this to

someone; he guesses the bird, and if it's the one in the cup, they throw the water (in the thimble) in your face.

bird knocking vbl n Also *bird battling*

Bat fowling: see quots.

1950 *PADS* 14.14 **SC**, *Bird-battling* . . . Bat-fowling; beating the bushes or trees where birds are roosting at night, dazzling them with lights, and striking them down with sticks or brushes. **c1974** Jones *Ozark Hill Boy* 9 **AR** (as of c1920), Bird knocking was a common sport . . . Every new ground had huge brush piles being dried in preparation for burning. These piles made excellent roosting shelters for all types of birds . . . The brush heap was surrounded with boys each of whom had a torch . . held high over the head in one hand and a small thorn bush in the other. Someone would kick the brush heap and the birds would flutter above the heap, having been blinded by the lights. The thorn bush frails went into action and the dead birds were gathered up to be cleaned, salted, and roasted.

bird-minder n **SC**

One who frightens birds away from a crop; also *bird-minding* the act of so doing.

1936 Smith–Sass *Carolina Rice* 27 **SC**, The work of bird-minding commenced. Men with muskets and cracking whips, women and children with whoops and clapping shingles kept the birds from "settling" and incidentally from eating seed-rice. *Ibid* 67, They [=muskets] were used by the bird-minders, who in the planting season patrolled the fields. **1937** Heyward *Madagascar* 32 **SC**, Some planters thought that by putting "bird-minders" in their fields . . they would decrease the damage. **1941** FWP *Guide SC* 389, Plantation 'bird-minders,' armed with muskets, tin pans, and rawhide whips, were stationed on the banks to scare the marauders away.

bird of death See **death bird**

bird of Washington See **Washington eagle**

bird-on-the-wing n Also *bird-wings* [From the shape of the flower]

=**fringed polygala.**

1896 *Jrl. Amer. Folkl.* 9.182, *Polygala paucifolia* . . bird-on-the-wing, M[ain]e. **1931** Harned *Wild Flowers Alleghanies* 270, Fringed Milkwort . . . This species, often called by the children "Bird-wings," is an exceedingly dainty and delicate perennial. **1949** Moldenke *Amer. Wild Flowers* 50, Best known in the north is . . the fringed milkwort . . or bird-on-the-wing. **1951** Graham *My Window* 176 (*Hench Coll.*), Most of our spring flowers appear in the bogs and marshes: . . bird-on-the-wing!

bird o' Satan n

=**blue jay.**

1959 *Names* 7.112, Very generally associated with Hell and the Devil in southeastern folk-lore is the blue jay . . and it is called bird o' Satan by some Virginia negroes.

bird owl n

1966–69 *DARE* (Qu. Q2) Infs **ME22**, Bird owl (catches birds); **MA15**, Bird owl.

bird-peck n Also *chicken-peck*

1966 *DARE* (Qu. X34, . . *The navel*) Inf **NC22**, Bird-peck; **SC32**, Chicken-peck; [**GA75**, Where the chicken pecked you; **GA59**, Where the goose pecked; **NC6**, Where the hen pecked you].

bird pepper n

A small hot red pepper (*Capsicum annuum* or *C. frutescens* or a var thereof). See also **bird-eye pepper, chilipitin**

1785 (1925) Washington *Diaries* 2.383 **VA**, Next to this are two rows of the Bird pepper. **1890** *Harper's Mag.* July 230/2 **TX**, The tiny bird-peppers, brilliant in hue, small as a pea, hot as fire. **1906** Low *Some Recoll.* 9 (as of 1830s), The men used to work for me except when we had a thousand or more bags of bird peppers (small red peppers). **1913** *Torreya* 13.234, *Capsicum baccatum* . . . Bird peppers, Cameron, L[ouisian]a. **1953** Greene–Blomquist *Flowers South* 106. **1966–69** *DARE* (Qu. I22a) Infs **FL8**, Bird peppers; **FL23**, Bird peppers—small red ones; **NJ56**, Bird peppers; **TX11**, Chilipitin—also called bird peppers. **1976** Bailey–Bailey *Hortus Third* 219, *Capsicum . . . annuum . . .* Var. *glabriusculum . . .* Bird p[epper]. Includes the wild or spontaneous forms, ranging from s. U.S. and Mex. to Colombia.

bird's bill See **bird bill 1**

bird's-egging n *arch*

One's affairs, business.

1854 Smith *'Way Down East* 32 **NEng,** So now go on with your birds'-egging, and make your Christmas as fast as you please. **1896** *DN* 1.412 **se,cNY,** "That's none of my *bird's-egging*," that's none of my affair. "Go on with your *bird's-egging*," go on with your story.

bird's-egg pea See **bird-egg pea**

bird's eye n

1 also *bird's-eye primrose:* Any of var primroses (*Primula* spp). [*OED* 1597 →]

1822 Eaton *Botany* 409, *Primula . . . farinosa* (bird's eye primrose . .). **1938** FWP *Guide MN* 288, Also growing among damp, decaying leaves on the steep slopes facing the lake is the dainty little blue birdseye or wild primrose. **1950** Gray–Fernald *Manual of Botany* 1137, *P. laurentiana . . . Bird's-eye-Primrose.* Ibid 1138, *P. mistassinica . . . Bird's-eye-Primrose.* **1961** Smith *MI Wildflowers* 285, *Bird's-eye Primrose . . . Primula mistassinica . . . Bird's-eye Primrose . . . Primula intercedens.*

2 also *birdseyes:* An annual California plant (*Gilia tricolor*) which has pale to deep blue-violet flowers with purple-spotted yellow throats. Also called **pink eyes**

1897 Parsons *Wild Flowers CA* 288, *Bird's-eyes. Gilia tricolor.* **1915** (1926) Armstrong *Western Wild Flowers* 394, *Bird's Eyes . . .* The flowers are in clusters, . . [with] two dark purple spots in the throat below each of the blue or whitish corolla-lobes, forming an "eye." **1949** Moldenke *Amer. Wild Flowers* 250, The *birdseyes, G. tricolor,* has similar leaves. **1961** Thomas *Flora Santa Cruz* 282, *G. tricolor . . .* Birds Eyes, Tricolor Gilia. **1968–69** *DARE* (Qu. S26e) Infs **CA**60, 115, Bird's eye.

bird's-eye bean See **bird-eye bean**

‡**bird's-eye gravy** n

Prob =**frog-eye gravy.**

1967 *DARE* (Qu. H37) Inf **NC**48, Bird's-eye gravy.

bird's-eye maple n Also *bird-eye maple*

A **sugar maple** (here: *Acer saccharum*) or the wood of such a tree distinguished by eyelike markings prob caused by a virus.

1807 J. Mease *Geol. Account of U.S.* 259 *(DA),* A species of maple abounds in Nova Scotia, and no doubt, farther south, called bird-eye maple . . very beautiful. **1847** (1853) Thompson *Locke Amsden* 20, A small, neatly-made, oblong box, holding, perhaps, about a pint, which he had chiseled and cut out from a solid billet of the beautiful bird's-eye maple. **1904** (1916) Porter *Freckles* 59, They tak', . . for instance, a burl maple—bird's-eye they call it in the factory. **1967** *DARE* FW Addit **ncNY,** Bird's-eye maple—describing a speckled surface quality of decorative finished maple. **1968–69** *DARE* (Qu. T3) Inf **MI**107, Bird's-eye maple; (Qu. T14) Infs **KY**6, **NY**97, 211, **OH**42, **WV**7, Bird's-eye maple; (Qu. T16) Inf **WV**7, Bird's-eye maple.

bird's-eye pea See **bird-eye bean**

bird's-eye pepper See **bird-eye pepper**

bird's-eye primrose See **bird's eye 1**

birdseyes See **bird's eye 2**

birds fly See **feathers, feathers, animal's feathers**

bird's foot See **bird's-foot trefoil, bird's-foot violet**

bird's-foot bramble n

=**strawberry bramble.**

1949 Peattie *Cascades* 238, *Rubus pedatus,* with three to five leaflets . . . is sometimes called bird's-foot bramble.

bird's-foot trefoil n Also *bird-foot (trefoil),* *bird's-foot (deervetch)* [See quot 1899; *OED* 1833 →]

Any of several **deervetches,** but esp the cultivated *Lotus corniculatus* widely grown for hay and forage; the latter is also called **babies' slippers 2, ground honeysuckle.**

1889 *Century Dict.* 561, *Bird's-foot trefoil,* the popular name of *Lotus corniculatus:* so called because its legumes spread like a crow's foot. **1900** Lyons *Plant Names* 230, *Lotus . . . Bird's-foot Trefoil.* **1934** Haskin *Wild Flowers Pacific Coast* 201, The umbels of the pink bird's-foot are raised on slender stems. **1937** U.S. Forest Serv. *Range Plant Hdbk.* W110, The deervetches . . . are distributed throughout the West . . . examples being birdsfoot deervetch, . . (L. ameri-

canus), . . and foothill deervetch (L. humistratus). **1956** St. John *Flora SE WA* 224, *Lotus Douglasii . . . Trailing Bird-foot.* **1965–70** *DARE* (Qu. L9a) Infs **NY**164, 200, 226, Bird's-foot; **PA**103, 132, Bird's-foot trefoil; (Qu. L9b) Infs **NY**109, 113, 171, 187, 216, **PA**207, 212, 222, 230, Bird's-foot trefoil; **IA**6, **PA**218, Bird's-foot; **CT**24, **IL**116, **NY**93, Bird-foot trefoil; (Qu. S26a) Inf **VT**13, Bird's-foot trefoil.

bird's-foot violet n Also *bird-foot (violet),* *bird's-foot* [From the shape of the leaves]

1 A perennial violet (*Viola pedata*), native chiefly to the eastern half of the US, with pedate leaves and large, most often light purple flowers. Also called **crowfoot violet, horseshoe violet, horse violet, Johnny-jump-up, pansy violet, piney-woods violet, sand violet, snake violet, velvet violet, wood violet**

1822 Eaton *Botany* 512, *Viola . . . pedata* (birdfoot violet . .) leaves many-parted pedate. **1839** *Columbian Reg.* (New Haven, Conn.) 19 Feb 4/5 *(DA),* The pedate violet . . is sometimes called, bird's foot, or parsley violet. **1965–70** *DARE* (Qu. S3) 15 Infs, *scattered,* Bird-foot violet; **LA**17, **RI**15, **WI**8, Bird's-foot violet; **KY**43, **MA**5, Bird's-foot; **AL**42, **IL**50, **MA**78, **NY**213, **PA**89, **VA**96, **WI**64, Bird-foot; (Qu. S11) Inf **GA**18, Bird's-foot; **GA**70, Bird's-foot violet.

2 =**prairie violet.**

1940 Clute *Amer. Plant Names* 275, *Viola pedatifida.* Bird-foot violet. **1965–66** *DARE* (Qu. S3) Infs **NM**9, **OK**1, Bird-foot violet.

3 A western violet such as *Viola beckwithii* or *V. hallii.*

1934 Haskin *Wild Flowers Pacific Coast* 221, *Bird-foot Violet.* Hall's *Violet . . .* Petals, five; . . two upper ones violet; three lower ones yellow . . . Not found north of the Willamette Valley. **1966** Barnes–Jensen *Dict. UT Slang, Bird-foot violet . . .* The reference is to the Western Pansy Violet (*Violet* [sic] *beckwithii*). **1967** *DARE* (Qu. S3) Inf **WA**22, Bird-foot.

bird's nest n

1 also *bird's-nest pudding:* A pudding usu made of apples and often having a dough crust and a sauce. **chiefly NEast, esp NEng** Cf **crow's nest 2**

1833 Child *Amer. Frugal Housewife* 63 *(DAE),* If you wish to make what is called 'bird's nest puddings,' prepare your custard [etc.]. **1896** *DN* 1.412 **seNY, nOH,** *Bird's-nest:* a fruit pudding, in which any kind of pudding fruit may be used. Also called *apfel-kuchen.* **1922** *DN* 5.156 **NY,** *Bird's nest . . .* a fruit pudding. **1934** Hanley *Disks* **seMA,** We always called them bird's nest puddings, but it wasn't a whole dish. It was made and the dough was filled with the apples and then baked. *Ibid* **swVT,** That's what they call a bird's nest . . . They used to melt up some sugar to put on it. **1939** Wolcott *Yankee Cook Book* 191 **NEng,** Yankees differ widely as to what a Bird's Nest Pudding should taste like. The only ingredient on which all agree is apples. In Connecticut they pour a baked custard mixture over apples . . . In Vermont, where maple sugar is widely used, they serve a sour sauce over the pudding. In Massachusetts, where there are comparatively few maple trees, they serve it with shaved maple sugar. **1941** *LANE* Map 292 **scattered throughout NEng,** An old-fashioned dish made of apples and biscuit dough . . . *Bird's nest (pudding).*

2 See quot.

1969 *DARE* (Qu. H29, *A round cake, cooked in deep fat, with jelly inside*) Inf **NH**16, Bird's nest.

3 See quot. Cf **bird-peck**

1968–70 *DARE* (Qu. X34, *. . The navel*) Infs **NC**82, **VA**35, Bird's nest.

4 also *bird's-nest plant:* =**wild carrot.** [See quot 1902; *OED* 1597 →]

1802 Drayton *View of SC* 65, Wild carrot, or bird's nest. (*Daucus.*) **1876** Hobbs *Bot. Hdbk.* 11, Birds' nest, . . Wild carrot, Daucus carota. **1894** *Jrl. Amer. Folkl.* 7.89, *Daucus Carota . .* bird's nest, N.J. **1912** Mathews *Amer. Wild Flowers* 306, The aged flower-cluster curls up and resembles a bird's nest, from which circumstance the plant *[Daucus carota]* derives that name. **1931** Harned *Wild Flowers Alleghanies* 344, Wild carrot . . . curls gracefully into the semblance of a bird's nest, by which name it is frequently called. **1950** *WELS* (*Other names in your locality for Queen Anne's Lace*) 4 Infs, Bird's nest. **1965–70** *DARE* (Qu. S6, *Other names around here for Queen Anne's Lace*) 11 Infs, **7 in Upper Missip Valley,** Bird's nest; **FL**27, Bird's nest plant.

5 also *bird's-nest plant:* =**Indian pipe 1.** [From the tangled mass of roots] Cf **giant bird's nest**

1784 in 1785 Amer. Acad. Arts & Sci. *Memoirs* 1.442, Birdsnest. Blossoms yellow. About Great Ossapy pond, in . . New-Hampshire.

1847 Wood *Class-Book* 380, Bird's nest . . . [is] a small, succulent plant . . . common in woods, near the base of trees, on whose roots it is said to be parasitic. **1889** *Century Dict.,* Bird's-nest . . [is] a parasitic ericaceous plant . . the leafless stalks of which resemble a nest of sticks. **1900** Lyons *Plant Names* 252, Indian-pipe . . Nest-root, Bird's-nest plant.

6 =pinesap.

1900 Lyons *Plant Names* 198, *M[onotropa] hypopitys* . . . Bird's-nest, Yellow Bird's-nest.

bird's-nest fern n [*OED* 1858 →]

An epiphytic fern (*Asplenium nidum*).

1873 in 1966 Bishop *Sandwich Is.* 81/2, There were some superb plants of the glossy tropical-looking bird's-nest fern, or *Asplenium Nidus*. **1948** (1965) Neal *Gardens HI* 21, In the lower forests of Hawaii, the birds-nest fern perches as a large, dark green rosette of fronds on tree trunks and branches.

bird's-nest weed n

=snake cotton.

1951 *PADS* 15.30, *Froelichia drummondii* . . . Cotton weed; bird's nest weed (a nesting material, used both for walls and lining, by many birds in its range).

bird snow n Cf blackberry winter

1946 *PADS* 6.6 **swVA,** *Bird snow* . . . Late spring snow . . . Occasional.

bird's toe n

1969 *DARE* (Qu. I28b, *Kinds of greens*) Infs **KY40,** Bird's toe—not synonymous with crowsfoot; **KY42,** Bird's toe—small white root, pink blossom, grows in rocky places.

bird's-tongue n

1 =knotweed. [See quot 1889]

1899 *Century Dict.,* Bird's-tongue . . . The name . . is . . from the shape of its leaves. **1900** Lyons *Plant Names* 300, *P[olygonum] avicu-lare* . . Bird's-tongue. **1910** Graves *Flowering Plants* 160 **CT.**

2 A bindweed 1.

1969 *DARE* (Qu. S5) Inf **MI93,** Bird's-tongue.

‡bird tongue n joc

1940 *AmSp* 15.446 **eTN,** *Bird tongues.* An extra dish of food. 'We had bird tongues for supper.' [Reported by at least five Infs]

birdweed n

1 =knotweed.

1828 Rafinesque *Med. Flora* 65, *Polygonum Aviculare* . . *Vulgar* . . . Birdweed. **1876** Hobbs *Bot. Hdbk.* 11. **1900** Lyons *Plant Names* 300. **1959** Carleton *Index Herb. Plants* 12, Bird Weed: Polygonum arviculare [sic].

2 =smartweed.

1951 *PADS* 15.30 **TX,** *Persicaria longistyla* . . birdweed.

bird wheat n [From the resemblance of the capsules to grains of wheat]

=haircap moss.

1909 *DN* 3.408 **nME,** *Bird wheat* . . . A kind of moss on old and barren pastures. **1947** Grout–Howe *Mosses & Liverworts* 39, The Hair-Cap Mosses, called Bird Wheat or Pigeon Wheat in many localities, are the largest . . of all our mosses. **1951** Dunham *How to Know Mosses* 163, In some localities known as "bird wheat."

bird-wings See bird-on-the-wing

bird wire n

1927 *DN* 5.473 **Ozarks,** *Bird wire* . . . A four-foot piece of thin wire, with a weight at one end. Cast into a covey of quails or other birds this primitive weapon is quite effective, and is widely used among the boys in the Ozarks.

bird-work v

See quots.

1923 (1946) Greer–Petrie *Angeline Doin' Society* 1 **csKY,** Ruther than git in *trouble,* me and Lum decided to bird-work, so . . we tore out'n a side door, and kept a-runnin' atter we hit the street. **1933** *AmSp* 8.47 **Ozarks,** *Bird-work* . . . To leap, to hop, to progress by a series of high jumps. "Last I seen o' Lem, he was a-bird-workin' down th' road like th' yaller-jackets was atter him."

birdy adv

Of a bird-dog: in a manner indicating the nearby presence of game birds.

1970 *WI Conserv. Bulletin* Sept–Oct 20/1, The hunters were halfway around the hill when the dog began to act "birdy." The men were right up by the dog when most of the birds flushed.

birk n [Scots, nEngl dial]

See quot.

1932 *Sun* (Baltimore MD) 12 Sept 7/3 *(Hench Coll.)* **Hatteras Island NC,** Sept 10—[In the vocabulary here] . . birk means birch.

birl v |bɜ-l| Nth

In logging: to stand on a floating log and rotate it with one's feet; hence *birler* n, *birling* vbl n.

1904 White *Blazed Trail Stories* 4 **MI,** "Birling match," he explained briefly. *Ibid* 7, They commenced to birl the log from left to right. *Ibid* 10, Darrell still trod the quarter-deck as champion birler for the year. **1933** *Natl. Geog. Mag.* 63.166, From the lumber camps throughout the Northwest come sawyers, axmen, "tree toppers," . . and "birlers." **1938** (1939) Holbrook *Holy Mackinaw, Birling.* The loggers' game of logrolling. **1958** McCulloch *Woods Words* **Pacific NW.** **1969** Sorden *Lumberjack Lingo* **NEng, Gt Lakes,** *Birl*—To rotate a floating log by treading upon it to find the water mark. *Birling*—The logger's game of rolling often played on log drives. Two players wearing calked shoes spun a log to see how long their opponent could stay on without being thrown into the water.

birm See berm

birth v chiefly Sth, S Midl Cf born v

To give birth (to).

1928 Peterkin *Scarlet Sister Mary* 209 **SC,** "Do Jedus," she cried out in alarm, "don' le me fall an' broke my leg today. I got some birthin to do my own sef before long." [She is pregnant and near term.] **1938** Rawlings *Yearling* 405 **FL,** Heap o' good it do a woman to birth a mess o' young uns and raise 'em and then have 'em all go off to oncet. **1967–68** *DARE* (Qu. K11, *When a cow has a calf, you say she _____*) Inf **MN33,** Birthed a calf; (Qu. K45, *When a mare has had a young horse, you say she just _____*) Infs **CA6, MI67,** Birthed her colt (*or* foal); (Qu. W20, *If somebody has no clothes on*) Inf **GA32,** Has a birthday dress on—'cuz you ain't got nothing when you're birthed. **1969** Emmons *Deep Rivers* 6 **eTX** [Black], But Mary Willis was an old midwife and had helped lots o' women in birthin' their babies. **1972** Cooper *NC Mt. Folkl.* 90, Birthed.

‡birthdame n

A midwife.

1947 Adams *Banner* 149 **NY** (as of 1817–1847), "With a couple of birthdames." Noting the incomprehension in the other's face, she explained: "Midwives."

birthday clothes See birthday suit

birthday party n

1906 *DN* 3.126 **nwAR,** *Birthday-party* . . . A party to which one pays an admission fee based upon the number of birthdays one has had.

birthday suit n Also birthday clothes

Usu in phr *in one's birthday suit:* Bare skin, nakedness.

1752 in 1897 *Documents Colonial & Post-Revol. Hist. NJ* 19.165, She . . was married to her Spouse (if not in a Wedding Suit) in her Birth Day Suit. **a1783** (1969) Williams *Mr. Penrose* 84, As to dress he was compleatly to be seen in his birthday suit without any manner of a disguise by art. **1933** *Sun* (Baltimore MD) 17 Aug 1/2 *(Hench Coll.),* "You are an optimist," Judge F . . today told counsel . . The attorney sought to attach costumes of Sally R . . , fan dancer at the Century of Progress Exposition, for an alleged unpaid bill. Sally's costume, for the most part, consists of her birthday suit. The motion for attachment was quashed. **c1960** Wilson *Coll.* **csKY,** In one's birthday suit . . . naked. **1965–70** *DARE* (Qu. W20, *If somebody has no clothes on at all*) 229 Infs, **widespread,** (In his) birthday suit; 19 Infs, **scattered,** In his (or their) birthday clothes.

birth hole See birthmark 2

birthing vbl n [birth] chiefly Sth, S Midl

The act of giving birth; birth.

1928 Peterkin *Scarlet Sister Mary* 72 **SC,** The whole earth was full of birthing and growing. **1942** Rawlings *Cross Creek* 261 **FL,** Unfortunately, the spring birthings also mean pigs. **1942** Whipple *Joshua* 210 **UT,** Birthin's the same whether y're rich or poor. **1949** Arnow *Hunter's Horn* 111 **KY,** She had borne her first lamb; King Devil had stolen that . . and scared her in the birthing of the second. **1960** Williams *Walk Egypt* 203 **GA,** More sorry women from being half-tended at birthing.

birthmark n

1 also verb: A phobia or other defect supposedly induced in a fetus by the mother's (usu traumatic) experience; to mark in such a way.   See also **mark v¹ 3**   Cf **birthscald**

1935 *Sun* (Baltimore MD) 14 May 1/3–4 swIA *(Hench Coll.),* Her father . . explains her apparent inability to talk . . as a "birth-mark." . . Mr. Wall told of the incident he believes "birthmarked" his daughter.

2 also *birth hole, birthspot:* See quot.

1966–70 *DARE* (Qu. X34, . . *The navel*) Infs **MO**39, **SC**32, **WA**18, Birthmark; **PA**237, Birth hole; **AL**26, Birthspot.

birthnight supper n

A social gathering to celebrate someone's birthday.

1928 Peterkin *Scarlet Sister Mary* 157 **SC,** The Quarter people came . . to dances and birth-night suppers.

birthroot n Also birthspot [See quot 1974]

=**trillium.**

1822 *Jrnl. Science* IV.62 *(DA),* Plants collected by Professor B. Douglass . . around the Great Lakes . . [include] Birth root: Black Rock, May 3d. **1857** Gray *Manual of Botany* 464, *T. erectum* . . . *Purple Trillium. Birthroot.* **1900** Lyons *Plant Names* 378, *Trillium* . . . Wake-robin, Birthroot . . . *T. erectum* . . . Birthroot . . . *T. grandiflorum* . . . White Birth-root. **1915** (1926) Armstrong *Western Wild Flowers* 42, *Birthroot . . . Trillium ovatum.* **1960** Hall *Smoky Mt. Folks* 44, Birth-root's good medicine. **1974** (1977) Coon *Useful Plants* 177, *Trillium erectum*—Trillium, wake robin, birth-spot, etc. . . The Indians used one species to aid parturition, and an herbal medicine was made of it by the Shakers.

birthscald n See also mark v¹ 3

=**birthmark 1.**

1939 FWP *Guide TN* 136, She maybe goes to town and sees a scary movie show. Then what? The baby's born with a birth-scald on his face.

birthspot n

1 See **birthmark 2.**
2 See **birthroot.**

birth suit n [Alter of birthday suit]

Nakedness.

1965–70 *DARE* (Qu. W20) Infs **DC**13, **FL**17, **TN**53, **TX**64, (In his) birth suit.

birthwort n

1 A plant of the genus *Aristolochia.* [*OED* 1551 →] For other names of var spp see **Dutchman's pipe 1, pelican flower, pipe-vine, snagrel, snakeweed, swan flower, Virginia snakeroot, wild ginger**

1785 Marshall *Arbustrum* 12 swPA, *Aristolochia frutescens. Pennsylvanian Shrubby Birthwort.* This grows naturally near Pittsburg. **1797** Morse *Amer. Gaz.,* Pennsylvania . . . The shrubby bithwort [sic] grows near Fort Pitt . . in the shade, in a rich soil; grows about 30 feet high, and sends off many twining branches. The roots have a lively aromatic taste, and are thought to have equal medicinal virtue to the small Virginia snake-root. **1847** Wood *Class-Book* 465, Birthworts . . . are successfully employed in medicine. **1950** Gray–Fernald *Manual of Botany* 564, *Aristolochia* L. Birthwort. **1971** Krochmal *Appalachia Med. Plants* 64, *Aristolochia serpentaria . . . Common Names:* . . birthwort, . . thick birthwort.

2 A trillium, esp *Trillium erectum.* [See quot 1971]

1900 Lyons *Plant Names* 378, *T. erectum* . . . Birthwort. **1930** Sievers *Amer. Med. Plants* 48, *Purple Trillium . . . Other common names* . . . Birthwort. **1964** Batson *Wild Flowers SC* 33, *Birthwort, Wake Robin:* Trillium catesbaei. **1971** Krochmal *Appalachia Med. Plants* 256, *Trillium erectum* . . . birthwort . . . The plant has been used as an . . uterine astringent.

birtle v

To behave boisterously.

1952 Brown *NC Folkl.* 1.520, *Birtle* . . . To cut up. "Aye, *birtle* a bit, lad, a wee bit."—Chapel Hill. Rare.

bisagre See bisnaga

bisbirinda n [MexSpan bizbirinda]

=**goatbush.**

[**1942** Santamaría *Dicc. Americanismos,* Bizbirinda (*Castela texana*) . . . Planta rutácea que crece en . . Tejas, donde también le dicen *amargoso* y *chaparro amargoso* [=Bizbirinda (*Castela texana*) . . . Rutaceous plant which grows in . . Texas, where it is also called *amargoso* and *chaparro amargoso*]]. **1960** Vines *Trees SW* 600, *Castela texana* . . . Vernacular names are Bisbirinda, Amargosa, and Goat-bush. **1970** Correll *Plants TX* 911, *Castela texana* . . . Allthorn, bisbirinda, chaparro amargoso . . . The young branches with grayish-white intensely bitter bark . . . Flowers . . red to salmon-pink or orange-color . . . On gravelly hills and bluffs in thickets and in mesquite prairies.

Biscayne-palm n

=**silver palm.**

1933 Small *Manual SE Flora* 241, *C[occothrinax] argentea* . . Biscayne-palm. **1979** Little *Checklist U.S. Trees* 93, *Coccothrinax argentata* . . Other common names—Biscayne-palm.

biscuit n

A Form.

Used as a mass noun or pl: Biscuits. **chiefly Sth, S Midl, NEng**

1888 [see **beanery 1**]. **1891** Garland *Main-Travelled Roads* 207 **WI,** He has red hair, and is death on b'iled corn and hot biscuit. **1902** (1904) Rowe *Maid of Bar Harbor* 50 **ME,** A moment later she was scolding Tabby for her shiftlessness in allowing the biscuit to scorch. **1907** *DN* 3.220 nwAR, sIL. **1908** *DN* 3.291 eAL, wGA. **1941** *LANE* Map 282 **throughout NEng,** *Biscuit* is felt either as a mass noun or as an uninflected plural. **1942** Faulkner *Go Down* 113 **MS,** Molly stood at the stove drawing the biscuit out. **1954** *Harder Coll.* cwTN, Boy you should taste the biscuit I cook. **1965–70** *DARE* (Qu. H15, *Bread made with wheat flour*) 31 Infs, **Sth, S Midl,** Biscuit. **1968** *DARE* FW Addit LA11, We had no money to buy flour, so we had no biscuit.

B Senses.

1 See quot. **chiefly Sth, S Midl** See Map Note: it is impossible to determine from this evidence whether the geographical distribution of this response reflects a difference in the Informants' understanding of the terms *bread* and *biscuit* or simply a greater preference for biscuits in the Sth and S Midl.

1965–70 *DARE* (Qu. H15, *Bread made with wheat flour*) 107 Infs, **Sth, S Midl,** Biscuit(s).

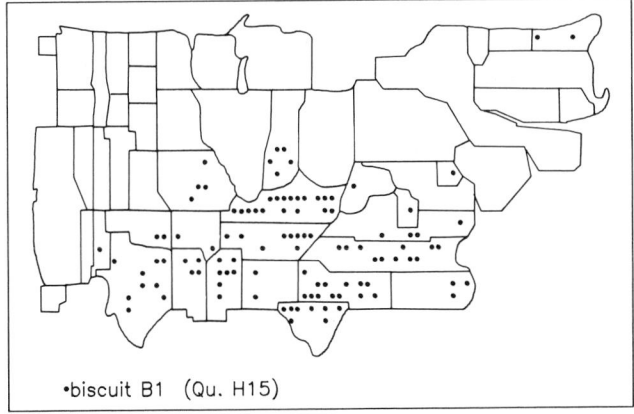

•biscuit B1 (Qu. H15)

2 A watch. *joc*

1905 *DN* 3.70 nwAR, Biscuit . . . A watch. 'My biscuit is too slow.' Common slang. **1908** *DN* 3.291 eAL, wGA. **1915** *DN* 4.224 wTX.

3 See quots. **West**

1940 FWP *Guide NV* 75, Biscuit . . . Nevada cowboy's term for the horn of the saddle. **1968** Adams *Western Words,* Biscuit . . . The saddle horn.

4 One's head.

1942 Berrey–Van den Bark *Amer. Slang* 121.56, *Head* . . biscuit. **1969** Gordone *No Place* 39 **NYC** [Black], Way we was raised, husslin' an' usin' yo' biscuit to pull quickies was the only way we could feel like we was men.

5 =**biscuit-eater 2.** **chiefly Nth** See Map *euphem* Cf **sea biscuit**

1950 *WELS* (Substitutes for stronger exclamations: "Why the son of a _____.") 6 Infs, **WI**, Biscuit. **1965–70** *DARE* (Qu. NN24, *Humorous substitutes for stronger exclamations:* "Why the son of a _____!") 23 Infs, Biscuit.

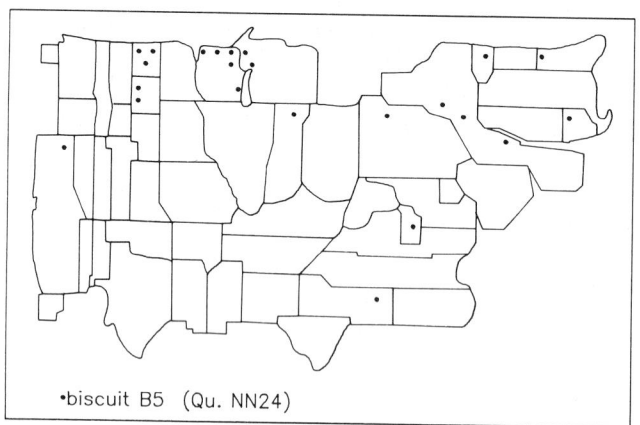

•biscuit B5 (Qu. NN24)

6 A woman's hairdo: see quots.

c1960 *Wilson Coll.* **csKY,** *Biscuit* . . . Hair done up in a small knot; a bun. Usually said of some elderly woman who has very little hair—or style. **1965–70** *DARE* (Qu. X3, *When a woman puts her hair up on her head in a bunch, you call this a* _____) Infs **CA2, CO7, IL96, KY28, 74, PA130,** Biscuit; (Qu. X2, *When a woman divides her hair into three strands and twists them together*) Inf **MO9,** They used to call it wearin' biscuits. **1981** *Broaddus Coll.* **ceKY,** Biscuit—a small bun or roll of hair. When a woman wears two or more buns, they are called "biscuits."

7 The buttocks. *joc*

1965–70 *DARE* (Qu. X35, . . *The part of the body that you sit on*) Inf **KS5,** Biscuit; **CA36, IL143, MA25, OH22,** Biscuits.

biscuit beggar n *derog*

1966 *DARE* (Qu. HH28, . . *People of foreign background . . Indian*) Inf **ID1,** Biscuit beggar.

biscuit bread n **chiefly S Midl**

Biscuits (distinguished from **bread** n **1** or **light bread**).

1917 *DN* 4.408 **wNC,** *Bread* . . . Corn bread. Biscuit are [sic] called *biscuit bread.* **1935** Hurston *Mules & Men* 93 **FL,** Nearly every skillet is full of corn-bread. But some like biscuit-bread better. **1938** Stuart *Dark Hills* 329 **KY,** Here is a plate of cold biscuit bread. **1946** *AmSp* 21.99 **sIL.** **1952** Brown *NC Folkl.* 1.520. **1954** *Harder Coll.* **cwTN.** **c1960** *Wilson Coll.* **csKY.** **1965–70** *DARE* (Qu. H15, *Bread made with wheat flour*) Infs **GA70, IL119, KY5, 28, MO8, NC44, NJ67,** Biscuit bread; (Qu. H18, . . *Special kinds of bread*) Inf **OK56,** Biscuit bread.

biscuit bush n Cf **flitter tree**

An imaginary object used in teasing a naive person.

1967 *DARE* (Qu. HH14, *Ways of teasing a beginner or inexperienced person—for example, by sending him for a "left-handed monkey wrench"*) Inf **WA28,** Biscuit bush.

‡**biscuit doughnut** n

1970 *DARE* (Qu. H28, . . *Types of doughnuts*) Inf **SC70,** Biscuit doughnut or ball doughnut.

biscuit-eater n [Euphem for *bitch*]

1 See quots.

1970 Tarpley *Blinky* 168 **neTX,** *A worthless dog* . . . Biscuit eater. **1971** Wood *Vocab. Change* 369 n62 **Sth,** [A dog of mixed and uncertain breed] . . . *Biscuit eater.*

2 in phr *son of a biscuit-eater:* See quots. **chiefly Sth, S Midl** See Map Cf **biscuit 5**

1950 *WELS* (Substitutes for stronger exclamations: "Why the son of a _____") 1 Inf, **ceWI,** Biscuit eater. **1965–70** *DARE* (Qu. NN24, *Humorous substitutes for stronger exclamations:* "Why the son of a _____!") 42 Infs, **chiefly Sth, S Midl,** Biscuit-eater.

‡**biscuit getter** n *joc* Cf **meal ticket 1**

A breadwinner.

1966 *DARE* (Qu. AA23, *Joking names a woman may use to refer to her husband*) Inf **NM9,** Biscuit getter.

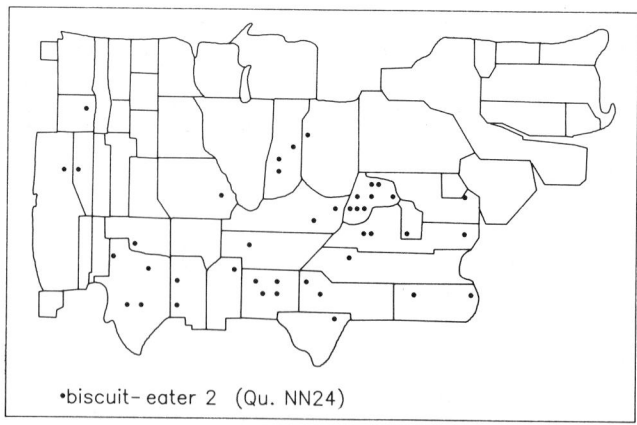

•biscuit-eater 2 (Qu. NN24)

biscuit hooks n pl *joc* Cf **bread hooks**

One's hands.

1932 *AmSp* 7.329 [Johns Hopkins jargon], Biscuit hooks—hands. **1966** *DARE* (Qu. X32, . . *Hands* . . "Those are mine. You keep your _____ [out of them].") Inf **WA33,** Biscuit hooks.

biscuit hound n Cf **biscuit eater 1**

1968 *DARE* (Qu. J2, . . *Uncomplimentary words . . for dogs*) Infs **WV4, 5,** Biscuit hound [laughter].

biscuit-leaves n pl Also *biscuit plant*

A greenbrier (here: *Smilax rotundifolia*).

1892 *Jrl. Amer. Folkl.* 5.104 **MA,** *Smilax rotundifolia,* biscuit-leaves. **1894** *Jrl. Amer. Folkl.* 7.102 **MA,** *Smilax rotundifolia* . . biscuit-plant. **1960** Vines *Trees SW* 75, *Smilax rotundifolia* . . Vernacular names for the plant are Biscuit-leaves.

biscuit pudding n

See quot 1954.

1938 Rawlings *Yearling* 216 **FL,** He butted a feather pillow . . until it burst, so that feathers drifted for days . . and appeared from nowhere in a dish of biscuit pudding. **1954** *Harder Coll.* **cwTN,** Biscuit pudding . . . A dessert made from left-over biscuits, milk, and sugar.

biscuit roll n

1968–70 *DARE* (Qu. H32, . . *Fancy rolls and pastries*) Inf **MS79,** Biscuit rolls; **NV7,** Biscuit rolls—fixed in the shape of a biscuit.

biscuit roller See **biscuit shooter 1**

biscuit root n

1 A plant, or the edible root of a plant, of the chiefly western genus *Lomatium.* Also called **carrotleaf, cous, desert parsley, hog fennel, prairie fennel, whiskbroom parsley, wild carrot, wild parsley.** For other names of var spp see **bladder parsnip, chuchupate, Indian balsam, Indian biscuit, lace parsnip, pepper and salt, pestle parsnip, sheep parsnip, wild parsnip**

1837 Irving *Rocky Mts.* 2.99, The cowish, also, or biscuit root, about the size of a walnut; . . they reduce to a very palatable flour. **1847** (1978) Smet *OR Missions* 116, The bitter root . . grows in light, dry, sandy soil, as also the caious or biscuit root. **1889** [see **2** below]. **1947** De Voto *Wide Missouri* 432, Some of these were very important sources of food, notably the camas . ., the biscuitroot . ., and many species of lilies. **1966** *DARE* Wildfl QR Inf **CO7,** Biscuit-root: Indians dug them, powdered root, made cakes; **OR12,** Biscuit root: *kouse* ['kaʊs] (also Indian food; mentioned as *kouse* by Meriwether Lewis). **1973** Hitchcock-Cronquist *Flora Pacific NW* 327, *Lomatium* Raf. Biscuit-root.

2 A **camas 1,** its root, or a similar plant or root.

1889 *Century Dict.,* Biscuit-root . . . A name given to several kinds of wild esculent roots which are extensively used for food by the Indians of the Columbia river region, especially to species of *Quamasia* and *Lomatium.*

biscuits n [See quot 1936 for possible origin] **Sth** =**trumpetleaf.**

1900 Lyons *Plant Names* 334, *S. flava* . . . Southeastern U.S. . . Biscuits. **1936** Whitehouse *TX Flowers* 39, *Trumpet-Leaf (Sarracenia sledgei)* is also called . . watches and biscuits. The . . names are suggestive of the broad, umbrella-shaped structure bearing the stigmas and occupying the center of the flower. **1959** Carleton *Index Herb. Plants* 12, *Biscuits: Sarracenia flava.*

biscuit shooter n

1 also *biscuit roller:* A cook at a camp or ranch. **West** Also called **cookee**

1893 *Harper's Mag.* 88.57/2 **West,** His helpmeet in her night-gown and the biscuit-shooter each seized a broom. **1911** *DN* 3.550 **WY,** *Biscuit shooter,* cook, at camps, ranches, etc. **1941** FWP *Guide WY* 459, *Biscuit shooter . . .* Cook. **1968** Adams *Western Words, Biscuit roller . . . Biscuit shooter . . .* The ranch cook.

2 A waiter or waitress. Also called **cookie pusher**

1913 *DN* 4.2 **Nth,** *Biscuit shooter . . .* A waiter in a logging camp. **1919** *DN* 5.63 **NM. 1927** *Collier's* 12 Nov 11/1, The former biscuit shooter's photo begin [*sic*] hitting the rotogravures and fan magazines regularly. **1927** *AmSp* 2.275 [Stanford University slang], *Biscuit shooter*—waiter at a table. **1931** *AmSp* 7.104 [Underworld argot], *Biscuit shooter . . .* A waitress. **1950** *WELS (Waiters or waitresses in restaurants)* 2 Infs, **WI,** Biscuit shooter. **1961** Adams *Old-Time Cowhand* 338, Brazos Joe . . used to ride twenty miles to town ever' chance he got to spend his wages for pies and such throat-ticklin' truck . . all because there was a biscuit shooter workin' there that was easy on the eyes.

bishop pine n

Std: a California pine *[Pinus muricata].* Also called **bull pine 1a, obispo pine, pricklecone pine, swamp pine**

bishop's cap n [From the shape of the seed pods]

=**miterwort 1.**

1839 Longfellow *Voices of Night* Prelude xi, When . . bishop's caps have golden rings. **1869** Fuller *Uncle John* 45, The flowers of the 'Bishop's Cap' are small and white, and grow usually upon wet rocks. **1900** Higginson *Outdoor Studies* 37, One may still find, usually close together, the Hobble-bush and the Painted Trillium, the Mitella, or Bishop's Cap, and the snowy Tiarella. **1966** *DARE* Wildfl QR Pl.90 Inf MI57, Bishop's cap; Pl.90b Inf OH14, Bishop's cap. **1971** GA Dept. Ag. *Farmers Market Bulletin* 57.35.8, The leaves . . show great similarity to its near relatives, Foam-flower and Bishop's cap.

bishop's nose n

=**pope's nose.**

1965–70 *DARE* (Qu. K73, . . *The rump of a cooked chicken*) Infs AL24, AR4, DE1, MS66, NJ69, OR7, TX22, 69, 102, VA82, Bishop's nose.

bishop's weed n

1 A plant of the genus *Ammi:* in the US either *A. majus,* which is also called **Queen Anne's lace,** or *A. visnaga.* [*OED* 1614 →]

1900 Lyons *Plant Names* 28, *Ammi . . .* Bishop's-weed. **1901** Mohr *Plant Life AL* 649, *Ammi visnaga . . .* Toothpick Bishop's Weed . . . Adventive on ballast . . . *Ammi majus . . .* Greater Bishop's Weed . . . Introduced at Mobile, and here and there escaped from gardens. **1970** Correll *Plants TX* 1150, *Ammi* L. Bishop's-weed.

2 also *bishop weed, mock bishop('s) weed:* A plant of the genus *Ptilimnium.*

1822 Eaton *Botany* 171, Bishop-weed . . . Pursh says it grows in sandy fields. But at N. Haven and N. York it grows in salt-marshes. **1848** Gray *Manual of Botany* 162, *Discopleura . . . Mock Bishop-weed.* **1876** Hobbs *Bot. Hdbk.* 11, Bishop's weed, American, Discopleura capillacea. **1901** Mohr *Plant Life AL* 648, *Ptilimnium capillaceum . . . Mock Bishop's Weed.* **1968** Barkley *Plants KS* 262, Ptilimnium nuttallii . . . Mock Bishop Weed. **1972** Brown *Wildflowers LA* 125, *Mock Bishop's-weed, Ptilimnium costatum . . .* Wet sites in prairie, margins of swamps, and fresh marshes.

3 =**goutweed.** [*OED* 1861 →]

1900 Lyons *Plant Names* 17, *A[egopodium] podagraria . . .* Bishop's weed. **1967** *DARE* Tape NY30, Bishop's weed—snow-on-the-mountain.

bislings See beaslings

bismarck n chiefly Upper MW, wGt Lakes

1 An oblong cake, cooked in deep fat; a **long-john.**

1930s in 1944 *ADD* St. Paul MN, If a solid oblong, called *bismarck.* **1965–70** *DARE* (Qu. H30) Infs IL17, 45, 50, IN1, IA32, 41, 47, **ME16, MA122, MI13,** 46, 96, **VT8,** Bismarck. **1976** *LaCrosse Tribune* (WI) 8 Apr 17/4, The resulting fry bread is similar to bakery bismarcks, but less sweet and more airy.

2 A deep-fried cake with a filling, usu of jelly. See Map

1950 *WELS Suppl.,* 1 Inf, **csWI,** Bismarck—round doughnut with

jelly or prune center. **1965–70** *DARE* (Qu. H29, *A round cake, cooked in deep fat, with jelly inside*) 125 Infs, **chiefly Upper MW, wGt Lakes,** Bismarck; **ND1,** Chicago bismarck. **1971** *AmSp* 46.79 **Chicago IL,** Jelly-filled doughnut: bismarck. **1973** Allen *LAUM* 1.282 **ceMN, csND,** Doughnut . . . Bismarck: With jelly in the center. **1976** Winsor *3 Motives* 96, She placed the tray of cups . . and a plate of sugared jelly doughnuts on the coffee table. "We still call them bismarcks, don't know why." I said, "I remember that's what they called them in Milwaukee."

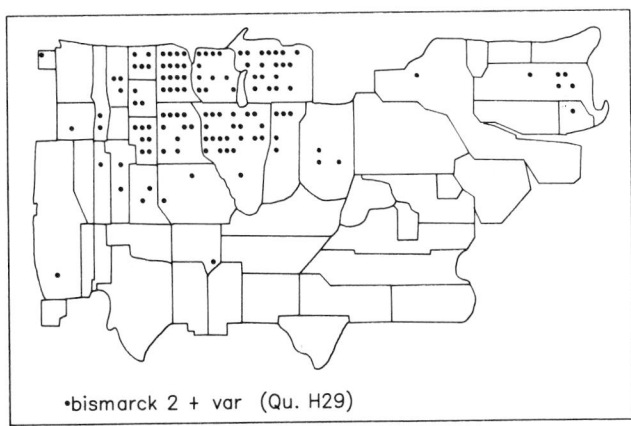

·bismarck 2 + var (Qu. H29)

bismaroon See bizmaroon

bisnaga n Also *bisagre, biznacha, visnada, visnaga,* dimin *bisnagita* [MexSpan *biznaga*]

Any of var spiny cacti of the genera *Echinocactus* or *Ferocactus.*

[**1845** Frémont *Rept. Rocky Mts.* 264, Fuentes pointed out one [cactus] called by the Spaniards *bisnada* [*sic*], which has a juicy pulp, slightly acid, and is eaten by the traveller to allay thirst.] **1892** *DN* 1.188 **TX,** *Biságre:* a plant of the cactus family, sometimes sliced and candied in Mexican sugar *(Echinocactus horizonthalonius).* **1892** in 1941 *Torreya* 41.50, *Echinocactus horizonthalonius . . .* Bisagre, Texas. **1915** (1926) Armstrong *Western Wild Flowers* 306, Bisnaga—*Echinocactus Wislizeni.* **1940** AZ Univ. *Biol. Sci. Bulletin* 4.108, *Echinocactus Johnsonii . . .* Johnson bisnagita. *Ibid* 112, *Echinocactus polyancistrus . . .* Fishhook bisnagita. **1941** Jaeger *Wildflowers* 168, *Bisnaga . . Echinocactus acanthodes.* **1969** O'Connor *Horse & Buggy West* 167 (as of early 1900s), Many a greenhorn who did not know the desert has died of thirst when he was surrounded by plump bisnagas filled with cool green water. **1974** (1977) Coon *Useful Plants* 83, *Echinocactus wislizeni* or *Ferocactus wislizeni*—Visnada, biznacha. **1976** Bailey–Bailey *Hortus Third* 411, *Echinocactus . . .* Visnaga. *Ibid* 474, *Ferocactus . . .* Visnaga.

-bit suff In var combs, esp *dog-bit, flea-bit, snake-bit* (see quots, esp 1954, for other combs) **chiefly Sth, S Midl** See Map

Bitten by (a dog, flea, snake, etc.).

1904 *DN* 2.418 **nwAR,** He said the lady told him she never knew the dogs to bite anyone; he said if that was true, he would hate to be dogbit. **1906** *DN* 3.136 **nwAR,** I sure got fleabit bad. **1940** *Sat. Eve. Post* 23 Nov 104/4 **sGA,** He was dying mighty easy for a man that had been cottonmouth bit . . . "I bet I been cottonmouth bit a dozen times." **1944** Wellman *Bowl* 189 **KS,** He was snake-bit. The rattler had found him on

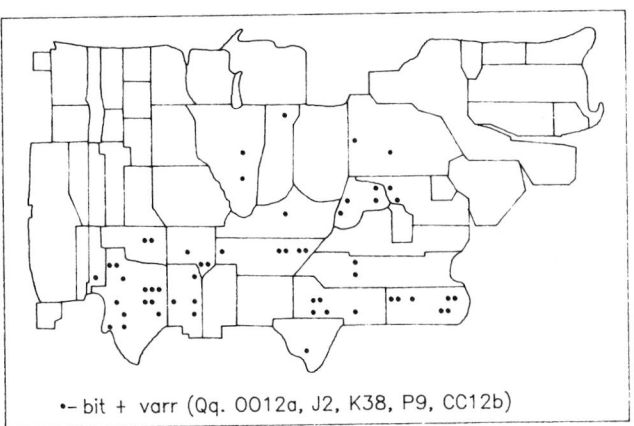

·– bit + varr (Qq. OO12a, J2, K38, P9, CC12b)

the right ankle. **1949** *PADS* 11.6 **wTX,** *Fleabit gray.* **1953** Atwood
Survey of Verb Forms 6, An interesting geographical phenomenon is the
compound *dogbit* ("he was dogbit," or "he got dogbit"), which covers
the South Midland and adjoining parts of the South . . . In W. Va. the
distribution is south of the Kanawha and in s.w. Va. it is practically universal; it reaches north
to s.w. Pa. and southeast to the Atlantic in the Peedee and Cape Fear
valleys. It is fairly common in the inland portions of S.C. and e. Ga.
1954 *Harder Coll.* **cwTN,** -*Bit* . . . Bitten. In combinations: squirrelbit,
snakebit, mulebit, hogbit, bugbit, chiggerbit, mosquito-bit, dogbit.
c1960 *Wilson Coll.* **csKY,** *Dog bit.* **1965–70** *DARE* (Qu. OO12a,
. . "*Last week the mailman was* _____.") 47 Infs, **chiefly Sth, S Midl,**
Dog-bit; **NM11, SC1,** 23, Snake-bit; (Qu. J2) Inf **IL78,** Flea-bit; (Qu.
K38) Inf **TN14,** Flea-bit; (Qu. P9) Inf **FL4,** Been snakebit; (Qu. CC12b)
Infs **GA82, LA46, PA185,** 209, **TX37,** 73, Snake-bit. **1968** *DARE* Tape
VA25, I got snakebit on my finger once.

bit and grain See **every bit and grain**

bitawby n [Alter of **catawba**]
=**catalpa B1.**
   1967 *DARE* (Qu. T9) Inf **LA7,** [bɪ'tɔbɪ].

bitch n

1 also attrib: An improvised lamp consisting of a twisted rag
wick in a container of grease. [Cf *OED slut* sb.⁴] See also
grease lamp
   1904 (1969) Robins *Magnetic North* 155 **AK,** 'I'll light a piece of fat
pine,' shouted the Boy . . . 'Where's your bitch?' said Dillon. **1927**
(1944) Russell *Trails Plowed Under* 159 **West,** In the long winter nights
their light was coal oil lamps or candles — sometimes they were forced to
use a 'bitch,' which was a tin cup with bacon grease and a twisted rag
wick. **1942** Whipple *Joshua* 33 **UT** (as of c1860), Hit be too hot here in
the summers fer candlemakin'; agin I git a new batch done, we gits along
with a "bitch." **1953** Randolph *Down in Holler* 285 **Ozarks,** Slut . . . A
primitive lamp, made by attaching a rag wick to a pebble and setting it in
a vessel of grease . . . An old man told me that such a lamp was properly
called a *bitch,* but that folks nowadays thought *slut* was more refined!
c1957 *Hand Coll.* **UT,** A midwife of Moab, Utah said that all she needed
to ease the pains of delivery was a "bitch-light." **1968** *DARE* FW Addit
NY72, Bitch — take a button, put a wick through it and set it in a dish of
melted tallow; an emergency lamp.

2 See quot. Cf **caboose** n¹ **4, cuna 2**
   1944 Adams *Western Words, Bitch* . . . A cowhide stretched under a
wagon from axle to axle for carrying wood.

3 also attrib: An argument or fight. Cf **bitch v**
   1967 *DARE* (Qu. Y12a, *A fight between two people, mostly with words;*
Qu. Y12b, *A real fight in which blows are struck*) Inf **WA22,** A bitch; (Qu.
KK15, *A disagreement or quarrel*) Inf **OR1,** Bitch. **1970** *DARE* File
AR, TX, Bitch fight — a fight between two people, mostly with words.

4 Something regarded as outstanding of its kind, esp in unpleasantness. **?chiefly Nth, N Midl**
   1964 *AmSp* 39.190 [College slang], *Bitch* 'something difficult or formidable.' **1965–70** *DARE* (Qu. B25, . . *A very heavy rain:* . . "*It's a
regular* _____.") Infs **PA94,** 170, Bitch; (Qu. KK41, *Something that is
very difficult to do: "I managed to get through with it, but it was*
_____.") Infs **IL98, NY119, PA76,** 94, **TX72, WA28,** 33, Bitch. **1966**
DARE Tape **MI26,** Bitch of a day.

bitch v **chiefly Nth, N Midl, West** See Map *esp among young
and mid-aged speakers and among males* Cf **bitch n 3**
To complain or gripe; hence *bitcher* one who complains or
grouses.
   1937 *Hench Coll.* **cePA** [Fraternity newsletter], Biggest Eater . . . Biggest Bitcher. **1941** Schulberg *What Makes* 127 **sCA,** What the hell have
you got to bitch about? **c1960** *Wilson Coll.* **csKY,** *Bitcher* . . . A complainer, a belly-acher. Not too common in use. **1965–70** *DARE* (Qu.
GG16, *Words for finding fault, or complaining: "You just can't please
him — he's always* _____.") 91 Infs, **chiefly Nth, N Midl, West,**
Bitching; **NY10,** Bitcher [Of all Infs responding to Qu. GG16, 11% were
young, 25% mid-aged, 46% male; of those giving these responses, 23%
were young, 41% mid-aged, 65% male.]; (Qu. GG35a, *To sulk or pout:
"It won't do any good to* _____ *about it."*) 8 Infs, Bitch; (Qu. GG35b,
Of a person who acts annoyed or disappointed . . "She's been _____
all day.") 10 Infs, Bitching; (Qu. GG39, *Somebody who seems to be
looking for reasons to be angry*) Infs **PA219,** 227, **SC40,** (Habitual,
perpetual, *or* professional) bitcher; (Qu. HH12, *A person who is always
finding fault about unimportant things*) Inf **CA83,** Bitching; **NY9,**

Always bitching; **KY84, NY93, PA69,** 94, Bitcher; **MN35, WA33,**
(Chronic, professional) bitcher; (Qu. KK13, . . *Arguing: "They stood
there for an hour* _____.") Infs **CA9, GA19, MA45, MO30, NY86,
PA236,** Bitching.

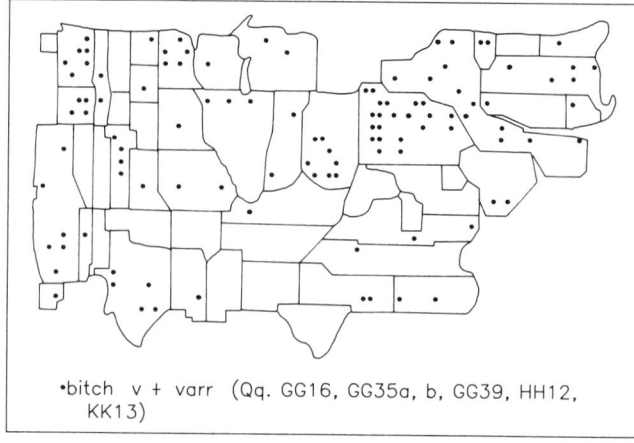

•*bitch* v + varr (Qq. GG16, GG35a, b, GG39, HH12,
KK13)

bitch bath n
See quots.
   1953 *AmSp* 28.145, Then there are the so-called baths without
water: . . a *bitch bath* requires talcum powder, deodorant, and perfume. **1965** *AmSp* 40.264, *Bitch-bath.* One that a soldier takes in his
helmet.

bitcher v With *about* or *after* [*bitch* to act like, or seek out, a
female (dog) + -*er* frequentative *(OED suffix⁵)*]
To pursue members of the opposite sex, spec for sexual pleasure.
   1967 Cerello *Dakota Co. MN* 44, Bitchering about town was all he ever
thought about . . . She was always bitchering after the married men of
our town . . . His wife lifted her skirts and bitchered about like a high-
stepping woman . . . All young men do a certain bitchering about before
they settle down.

bitcher n See **bitch v**

bitch's wool n Also *bitch wool* Cf **slut's wool**
   1967–69 *DARE* (Qu. E20, *Soft rolls of dust that collect on the floor
under beds or other furniture*) Inf **NY220,** Bitch's wool; **NC48,** Bitch
wool.

bitchwood n
A **spindle tree** (here: *Euonymus europaeus*).
   1963 *AmSp* 38.38, *Bitchwood* . . . The spindle tree, *Euonymus europaeus.*

bite v

A Forms.
Past pple: usu *bitten;* esp among males and lesser educ speakers,
often *bit;* also *bite;* rarely *bited.*
   1704 (1935) Knight *Jrl.* 63 **NEng,** They . . . were once Bitt by a
sharper. **1834** [see **B1** below]. **1863** in 1965 *DARE* File **cNY,** I was bit
by a musquetoe [sic] to day. **1898** Westcott *Harum* 105 **nNY,** He'll find
he's bit off a dum sight more'n he c'n chaw. **1953** Atwood *Survey of
Verb Forms* 6, The past participle is recorded in the context "He was
(bitten) by a dog." The form *bitten* . . is strongly favored by cultured
informants everywhere . . . *Bit* . . is used by a slight majority of Type IA
informants [=old, with little educ] in N.Eng., and by from one fourth to
one third of the other noncultured types . . . Elsewhere in the Eastern
States . . *bit* predominates very heavily in Type I [=infs with little educ],
and a little less heavily in Type II [=infs with moderate educ]. Most
Southern Negroes use this form, though two use bite . . : "got bite."
1965–70 *DARE* (Qu. OO12a, *Talking about dogs biting: "Some dogs
will bite — last week the mailman was* _____.") 262 Infs, **widespread,**
Bit [Of all Infs responding to the question, 28% had grade school educ,
50% were male; of those giving this response, 37% had grade school educ,
60% were male]. **1966** *DARE* Tape **FL19,** He was bit. **1971** Bright
Word Geog. CA & NV 168, [In the context "He was bitten by a dog,"]
bitten [was said by] 67% [of 300 informants] . . *bit* [was said by] 33%.

B Senses.

1 usu in constr *get bit:* To be cheated. **chiefly Sth, S Midl**
   1834 *Life Andrew Jackson* 101, The gineral, who was never . . squad-

dled in a fite, or bited in a bargin, .. wasn't backward, when his country needed him. **1892** *DN* 1.229 **KY, MI, NEng,** *Bit.* "To get bit": to be cheated in making a purchase. **1893** Shands *MS Speech* 70, *Bit.* *To get bit* is used in Mississippi to mean *to be cheated.* **1903** *DN* 2.306 **seMO,** *Bit* . . . Cheated. 'If you trade with him you are likely to get bit.' **1906** *DN* 3.115 **sIN,** *Bit* . . . Cheated. **1907** *DN* 3.229 **nwAR, seMO,** *Bit* . . . Cheated. **1908** *DN* 3.291 **eAL, wGA,** *Bite* . . . To cheat. Chiefly in the pret[erite]. and p[ast] p[articiple]. "He got bit in that trade." **1965–70** *DARE* (Qu. LL23, *Cheated, treated dishonestly:* "*These apples are wormy, I think you got _____.*") 18 Infs, **chiefly Sth, S Midl,** Bit.

2 Of frost: to damage vegetation. Cf **biting frost**

1970 *DARE* (Qu. B29) Inf **KY**83, Sometimes a light frost won't bite.

bite n See **bight**

bite a punkin See **eat a pumpkin through a knothole, be able to**

bite one's bait v phr

1970 *DARE* FW Addit **MI**116, Bite your bait—to hold off on a decision to see what develops, not to push a point too fast.

biter n

1 The claw of a crab. **Chesapeake Bay**

1952 *Sun* (Baltimore MD) 23 June ed B 14/6 **cMD,** Language peculiar only to soft-crabbing . . . With the right thumb push downward and in on the top "biter" of the crab until the hard shell cracks away. **1968–70** *DARE* Tape **MD**18, Biters; **VA**47, Break one half of each biter off so they [=crabs] can't bite one another and kill one another. **1976** Warner *Beautiful Swimmers* 61 **Chesapeake Bay,** The crew members will tell you to take a close look at the color of the females' claws. "Look at them biters," one will say.

2 A tooth. *joc*

1965–70 *DARE* (Qu. X12, . . *Large front teeth that stick out*) Inf **NY**144, Biters; (Qu. X13a, . . *Joking names . . for teeth*) Infs **IL**50, **MD**15, 41, **MN**33, 37, **MT**4, **NE**3, **NJ**67, **OH**44, **PA**76, 243, Biters.

‡**bites** n

Pliers.

1970 *DARE* (Qu. F33, *A small tool that you hold in one hand, with "jaws" for gripping things*) Inf **MA**124, Bites.

bite-tongue n Also *biting tongue* [From the acrid juice]

=**water pepper.**

1900 Lyons *Plant Names* 300, *P[olygonum] Hydropiper* . . Bite-tongue. **1910** Graves *Flowering Plants* 162 **CT. 1971** Krochmal *Appalachia Med. Plants* 204, *Polygonum Hydropiper* . . *Common Names:* . . biting tongue.

bitey root n [From the peppery taste of the cooked root]

=**jack-in-the-pulpit 1.**

1969 *DARE* (Qu. S1) Inf **VT**17, Bitey root.

biting ppl adj **S Midl**

Of an animal: likely to bite.

1921 (1923) Greer–Petrie *Angeline Seelbach* 2 **KY,** He was afeard Miss Seelback might have some bad bitin' dogs that would resh out and grab aholt of us. **1941** Stuart *Men of Mts.* 230 **neKY,** "Don't be afraid, boys," says Big Aaron. "He ain't no bitin' dog. He's one of them barkin' dogs that never bites." **1954** *Harder Coll.* **cwTN,** *Biting dog* . . . A dog likely to bite. "'At's nold bitin' dog. Better leave'm 'lone." **1966** *Wilson Coll.* **csKY,** *Biting sow* . . . Dangerously angry sow. "There's a biting sow in that 'ere field." Often used in phr "mad as a biting sow."

biting frost n

A severe frost.

1912 Green *VA Folk-Speech, Biting-frost* . . . A heavy frost that kills young plants: "We had a biting-frost last night." **1965–70** *DARE* (Qu. B29, *A frost that does not kill plants*) Infs **MI**1, **SC**1, Biting frost; (Qu. B30, *A frost that kills plants*) Infs **IN**29, **KY**76, **TX**2, **VA**87, Biting frost. **1981** *Broaddus Coll.* **ceKY,** Biting frost—a killing frost.

biting knotweed n [From the acrid juice and jointed stems]

=**water pepper.**

1876 Hobbs *Bot. Hdbk.* 11, Biting knot weed .. Polygonum hydropiper. **1900** Lyons *Plant Names* 300, *P[olygonum] Hydropiper* . . Biting Knotweed. **1971** Krochmal *Appalachia Med. Plants* 204, *Polygonum Hydropiper* . . biting knotweed.

‡**bit-player** n *euphem* Cf **biscuit-eater 2**

1968 *DARE* (Qu. NN24, *Substitutes for stronger exclamations:* "*Why the son of a _____!*") Inf **PA**74, Bit-player.

bitter adj

Of milk:

1 Tainted; see quot. **scattered, but chiefly Sth, S Midl** See Map Cf **bitterweed milk**

1965–70 *DARE* (Qu. K14, *Milk that has a taste from something the cow ate in the pasture—you say,* "*That milk is _____.*") 73 Infs, Bitter; 9 Infs, Bitter milk; **CA**79, Bitter from eating weeds; **SC**26, Bitter with weeds.

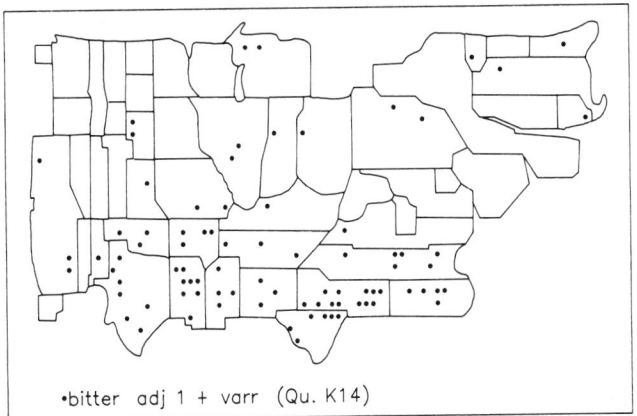

•bitter adj 1 + varr (Qu. K14)

2 =**blinky** adj **1a.**

1970 Tarpley *Blinky* 192 **neTX,** *Milk that is beginning to sour* . . bitter milk.

bitter n [From *bitters* a tonic made of crushed or distilled herbs or plant matter]

A medicinal tea.

1956 *Hall Coll.* **wNC, eTN,** Asked if she prepared teas of the different herbs and used them for different illnesses, . . Mollie . . replied, "I fix a bitter of it all and use it for everything."

bitter apple n

=**mayapple.**

1965 *DARE* (Qu. S4) Inf **MS**60, Bitter apple.

bitter ash n

A **wahoo** (here: *Euonymus atropurpureus*).

1876 Hobbs *Bot. Hdbk.* 11, Bitter ash, Wahoo, Euonymus atropurpureus. **1900** Lyons *Plant Names* 155, *E. atropurpureus* . . . Bitter Ash. **1930** Sievers *Amer. Med. Plants* 59, *Wahoo* . . . Other common names . . . Bitter ash, pegwood. **1971** Krochmal *Appalachia Med. Plants* 116, Bitter ash . . . The bark is reported to be of value as a drastic purgative.

bitterbark n

1 also *bitterbark tree:* =**fever tree;** also the bark of such a tree.

1828 Rafinesque *Med. Flora* 57, *Pinckneya pubens. Names* . . . *Vulgar.* Bitter Bark, . . Fever-tree. **1884** Miller *Dict. Engl. Names of Plants* 231/1, *Pinckneya pubens. Bitter-bark-tree, Fever-tree* of Georgia. **1892** (1974) Millspaugh *Amer. Med. Plants* 299, The important medicinal plants of this family are: The cinchonas or Peruvian barks, . . bitter bark *(Pinckneya pubens, Mich.),* . . and others of minor import. **1900** Lyons *Plant Names* 290, *Fever-tree. Bark* . . Bitter bark; tonic, febrifuge. **1911** *Century Dict.,* Georgia, bitter, Carolina or Florida bark, the bark of *Pinckneya pubens,* a small rubiaceous tree of the southern United States, having the same properties as French Guiana bark.

2 =**cascara 1.**

1897 Parsons *Wild Flowers CA* 62, In Oregon it [*Rhamnus purshiana*] is known as "chittemwood" and "bitter bark," and also as "wahoo" and "bear-wood." **1914** in **1950** *Western Folkl.* 9.344, Bitter bark . . of the American pioneers, or *cascara sagrada* of the Spanish Californians.

bitterberry n

1960 Williams *Walk Egypt* 95, Half a dozen children played Squat Tag . . . One squatted and bit her nails. Another yelled, "You better quit that. Your ma'll sop 'em in bitter-berry."

bitterbrush n

1 Either of two western browse plants (*Purshia tridentata* or *P. glandulosa*), both of which are much-branched shrubs with tridentate leaves, yellow flowers, and spindle-shaped achenes.

Also called **antelope brush 1, black sage, buckbrush, deer brush, greasewood, quinine bush**

1925 Jepson *Manual Plants CA* 504, *P[urshia] tridentata* . . . Also called Bitter-Brush. **1931** U.S. Dept. Ag. *Misc. Pub.* 101.53, Despite the characteristic taste of its herbage, alluded to in the common name "bitterbrush," . . Purshia is one of the most important . . browse plants occurring on western ranges. **1951** Martin *Amer. Wildlife & Plants* 327, There are two species of bitterbrush in the world—both of them confined to arid slopes and valleys of the Mountain–Desert region. **1966** *DARE* Wildfl. QR Inf **OR**12, Bitterbrush—also buck brush 'cause bucks eat it. **1969–70** *DARE* (Qu. T5) Infs **CA**136, 208, Bitterbrush.
2 A **cliffrose** (here: *Cowania mexicana*).
1931 U.S. Dept. Ag. *Misc. Pub.* 101.49, *Cliffrose* . . is known also by a variety of local names, including . . bitterbrush.

bitterbush n
=**bear oak.**
1900 Lyons *Plant Names* 314, *Q[uercus] nana [Q. pumila],* Bitter-bush.

bitter buttons n [From the bitter-tasting flower heads]
A **tansy** (here: *Tanacetum vulgare*).
1900 Lyons *Plant Names* 364, *T. vulgare* . . . Bitter-buttons. **1955** *Moosehead Gazette* (Dexter ME) Feb 17/4 *(Hench Coll.),* Tansy is better known as Bitter Buttons. **1971** Krochmal *Appalachia Med. Plants* 246, *Tanacetum vulgare* . . . Bitter buttons.

bitter coco n Cf **coco grass, sweet coco grass**
A **nut grass 1** (here: *Cyperus rotundus*).
1941 *Torreya* 41.46, *Cyperus rotundus* . . . Bitter coco, Catahoula, L[ouisian]a.

bitter dock n
Usu the broad-leaved dock (*Rumex obtusifolius*), but also **curled dock.**
1837 Darlington *Flora Cestrica* 236, Bitter Dock . . . Grass-lots, gardens, and meadows: frequent. **1848** Gray *Manual of Botany* 391. **1892** (1974) Millspaugh *Amer. Med. Plants* 144/1, The Bitter Dock . . . is much harder to exterminate than *R. crispus.* **1937** Stemen *OK Flora* 109, *Broad-leaved* or *Bitter Dock.* **1971** Krochmal *Appalachia Med. Plants* 218, *Rumex crispus* . . . *Common Names:* . . bitter dock.

bitter dogbane n Also *bitter dogsbane*
=**spreading dogbane.**
1828 Rafinesque *Med. Flora* 49, *Apocynum androsemifolium* . . . *Bitter Dogsbane.* **1900** Lyons *Plant Names* 40. **1963** *AmSp* 38.34. **1971** Krochmal *Appalachia Med. Plants* 50, Bitter dogbane . . . is extremely poisonous.

bitter grass n Also *bitter plant*
=**colicroot 2** (here: *Aletris farinosa*).
1828 Rafinesque *Med. Flora* 37, *Aletris farinosa* . . . *Vulgar Names—* Star-Grass, . . Bitter Grass, . . Devil's-bit. **1892** (1974) Millspaugh *Amer. Med. Plants* 172, *Bitter Grass* . . . The fresh root is chopped and pounded to a pulp . . . The resulting tincture has . . a very bitter taste. **1949** Moldenke *Amer. Wild Flowers* 318, *A. farinosa* . . . is often called *agueroot, huskroot,* and *bittergrass.* **1959** Carleton *Index Herb. Plants* 12, *Bitter grass:* Aletris farinosa. *Ibid* 13, *Bitter plant:* Aletris farinosa.

bitter half n [Alter of *better half* one's spouse] *joc*
A spouse.
1950 *WELS (Wife)* 1 Inf, **cwWI,** Bitter half. **1966–68** *DARE* (Qu. AA22, . . *Wife;* Qu. AA23, . . *Husband*) Infs **CO**42, **IL**11, **NY**109, **WA**17, Bitter half.

bitterhead n
1 The black **crappie** (*Pomoxis nigromaculatus*).
1887 Goode *Amer. Fishes* 69, The names "Bitter Head" and "Lamplighter" are also ascribed to it. **1902** Jordan–Evermann *Amer. Fishes* 336, Grass bass, . . bitterhead, . . and lamplighter are names which have been applied to this fish.
2 =**golden shiner.**
1933 LA Dept. of Conserv. *Fishes* 445, Known by a wide variety of popular names, such as Bitterhead, . . and Windfish, the Golden Shiner can be successfully reared. **1946** LaMonte *N. Amer. Game Fishes* 158, *Golden Shiner* . . *Names:* . . Bitterhead, Chub, Gudgeon, Windfish.

bitter herb n Cf **bitterweed**
A **turtlehead** (here: *Chelone glabra*).

1873 in 1976 Miller *Shaker Herbs* 132, *Chelone glabra* . . . Bitter Herb. **1971** Krochmal *Appalachia Med. Plants* 84, Bitter herb . . . The leaves have been used . . as an anthelmintic and tonic.

bitter hickory n
=**bitternut 1.**
1813 Muhlenberg *Catalogus Plantarum* 88 **PA,** *Juglans* . . . sulcata, amara[:] bitter hickory, white. **1897** Sudworth *Arborescent Flora* 111, *Hicoria minima* . . . *Common Names* . . . Bitter Hickory (N.H.). **1967** *DARE* (Qu. T16) Inf **MI**71, Bitter hickory.

bitter melon n
The **balsam pear** (*Momordica charantia*).
1948 (1965) Neal *Gardens HI* 808, *Bitter melon* . . . Common in Oriental vegetable gardens of Hawaii is an annual, high-climbing vine, 8 to 12 feet long. *Ibid* 809, A smaller . . form . . differs from the bitter melon in the size of the vine and in the fruit. **1967** *DARE* (Qu. I23, . . *Kinds of squash*) Inf **HI**3, Bitter melon—from China; a squash; (Qu. I25, . . *Nicknames for cucumbers*) Inf **HI**11, Bumpy—similar shape and size to cucumber—"bitter melon"—cook—very bitter—more like squash.

bittern n
Std: a marsh bird (*Botaurus lentiginosus*). Also called **barrelmaker, belcher-squelcher, biorque, bog bull, bog crane, bog hen, bog-pumper, bogtrotter, boomer, boompike, bottle-kachunk, bum cluck, butterbump, buttermunk, conk-onk, dunkadoo, flying fox, fly-up-the-creek, fool fowl, garde-soleil, grass hen, green-legged crane, Indian hen, Indian pullet, jack grindle, Johnny Gongle, jumper, look-up, marsh hen, meadow hen, mire drum, night hen, plum puddin', plunket, poke, postdriver, pumper, quock, shagpoke, shitepoke, sibitron, skygazer, slough-pumper, slough pup, slugtoot, snake eater, stake-driver, stargazer, stump-driver, sungazer, thunder pumper, vision-la, wollerkertoot, wop**

bitternut n
1 also *bitternut hickory:* A hickory (*Carya cordiformis*) which has compound leaves with 7–11 leaflets and thin-shelled, beaked nuts enclosing a bittertasting kernel. Also called **bitter hickory, bitter pecan, bitter walnut, pig hickory, pignut, pig walnut, red hickory, swamp hickory, white hickory, yellowbud hickory**
1810 Michaux *Arbres* 1.19 *(DA),* Bitter nut hickery [sic] . . , seul nom en usage dans N.Y. [=only name in use in N.Y.]. **1814** Pursh *Flora Americae* 2.638, *Juglans* . . . *amara* . . . This is known by the name of *Bitter Nut, White* or *Swamp Hickory.* **1947** *Amer. Midland Naturalist* 38.39, Bitternut . . [is] occasional in bottomland forest and wood margins. **1967–70** *DARE* (Qu. I43) Infs **IL**35, **LA**11, **PA**234, **WI**10, Bitternut(s); **MI**64, Bitternut hickory; (Qu. T16) Infs **MN**29, **WI**22, Bitternut.
2 =**pignut** (here: *Carya glabra*).
1897 Sudworth *Arborescent Flora* 115, *Hicoria glabra* . . . *Common Names* . . . Bitternut (Ark., Ill., Iowa, Wis.). **1908** Britton *N. Amer. Trees* 237, *Pignut Hickory* . . . is also called Pignut, Bitternut [etc.]. **1940** Clute *Amer. Plant Names* 254.

bitternut hickory See **bitternut 1**

bitter oak n
1 =**wahoo** (here: *Euonymus atropurpureus*).
1960 Vines *Trees SW* 661, *Eastern Wahoo* . . . Vernacular names are . . Bitter-oak, and Strawberry-tree.
2 =**bear oak.**
1900 Lyons *Plant Names* 314, *Q[uercus] nana [=Q. pumila]* Bitter Oak.

bitter pecan n **Gulf States**
Usu the **water hickory,** but also other hickories such as the **bitternut** (here: *Carya cordiformis*) or the **pecan.**
1884 Sargent *Forests of N. Amer.* 136, Water Hickory. Swamp Hickory. Bitter Pecan. **1897** Sudworth *Arborescent Flora* 110, *Juglans cordiformis* . . . *Common Names* . . . Bitter Pecan Tree (La.). *Ibid* 112, *Hicoria aquatica* . . . *Common Names* . . . Bitter Pecan (Miss., La., Tex.). **1922** Sargent *Manual Trees* 179, *Carya texana Schn[ecke]. Bitter Pecan.* **1967–68** *DARE* (Qu. I43) Infs **LA**2, 15, 28, Bitter pecan(s); (Qu. T15) Inf **LA**2, Bitter pecan; (Qu. T16) Inf **LA**10, Bitter pecan.

bitter pepper root n

=**sweet flag.**

1971 Krochmal *Appalachia Med. Plants* 32, *Acorus calamus* . . . Bitter pepper root.

bitter plant See **bitter grass**

bitterroot n

1 =**spreading dogbane.**

1828 Rafinesque *Med. Flora* 49, *Apocynum androsemifolium* . . . *Vulgar Names* . . Bitter-root . . . Root perennial, large, bitter and milky like the whole plant. **1876** Hobbs *Bot. Hdbk.* 12, Bitter root, Apocynum androsaemifolium. **1940** Clute *Amer. Plant Names* 89, *Spreading Dogbane* . . . Bitter-root. **1973** Hitchcock–Cronquist *Flora Pacific NW* 362, Spreading d[ogbane], flytrap d[ogbane], bitter-root.

2 also *bitterroot daisy:* A plant with thick, starchy roots of the western genus *Lewisia,* esp *L. rediviva* which is also called **mountain rose, redhead Louise, resurrection flower, rock rose, sand rose, tobaccoroot.**

1838 Parker *Jrl. Rocky Mts.* 204, To these may be added the racine amère, or bitter root, which grows on dry ground, fusiform, and though not pleasant to the taste, yet it is very conducive to health. **1885** *Century Illustr. Mag.* 29.447 **MT,** It was too late to find the exquisite camellia-like flower of the bitter-root, which in May stars the ground. **1939** FWP *Guide MT* 16, The State flower is the bitterroot. **1941** FWP *Guide WA* 21, The low rose-red bitterroot, often called the rockrose. **1945** (1946) Macdonald *Egg & I* 20, The bitterroot daisies, the Montana State flower, had little foliage and no stems and lay flat and pink and exquisite on the brown hard earth. **1966** DARE Wildfl QR Inf **WA**10, Bitterroot. **1976** Bailey–Bailey *Hortus Third* 654, *Bitter root* . . . The thick root shaped like a forked radish or short carrot was a much-used food plant by Indian tribes.

3 =**buckbean 1.**

1828 Rafinesque *Med. Flora* 33, *Names.* American Buckbean . . . *Vulgar.* Marsh Trefoil, . . Bitter Root. **1974** (1977) Coon *Useful Plants* 144, *Menyanthes trifoliata* . . . Bitter root . . . At times in the past the bitter roots have been used for flavoring beer.

4 =**bigroot 1.**

1889 *Century Dict.,* Bitter-root . . . The big-root, *Megarrhiza Californica.* **1900** Lyons *Plant Names* 248, *M. fabacea* . . and *M. Marah* . . , both of California, are called . . Bitter-root.

bitterroot daisy See **bitterroot 2**

bitterstem n

Prob =**bitterweed.**

1966 DARE Tape **NC**10, A weed, if eaten by cows in the spring, causes bitter milk; bitterstem is what we call that weed.

bittersweet n chiefly Nth, N Midl

Any of three plants: 1) a **nightshade** (*Solanum dulcamara: OED* 1568 →), which is also called **dwale, fever twig, felonwort, matrimony vine, morel, poisonberry, poisonflower, pushion-berry, scarlet berry, skawcoo, snakeberry, terrididdle, tether-devil, violet bloom,** and **wolf grape,** or 2) *Celastrus scandens,* which is also called **climbing bittersweet, climbing orangeroot, false bittersweet, fever twig, fever-twitch, gnome's gold, Jacob's ladder, Roxbury waxwork, staff tree, staff vine, waxwork, yellowroot,** or 3) =**pipsissewa.**

1766 (1942) Bartram *Diary of a Journey* 41 *(DAE),* Bitter sweets . . are next in goodness to the china. **1813** Muhlenberg *Catalogus Plantarum* 25 **PA,** *Stafftree* climbing, (bitter-sweet). **1832** Williamson *Hist. ME* 1.120, *Bitter-sweet,* . . a hardy climbing plant of five feet high and shrubby, is good for the rheumatism, asthma, and jaundice, and in diet-drink. **1870** *Amer. Naturalist* June 215, Bittersweet (*Celastrus scandens),* also called Roxbury Waxwork, . . is a hardy climber. **1892** *Jrl. Amer. Folkl.* 5.100, *Chimaphila umbellata,* . . bittersweet. N[ew] H[ampshire]. **1930** Sievers *Amer. Med. Plants* 4, *American Bittersweet Celastrus scandens. Ibid* 11, *Bitter Nightshade* . . . Other common names. **1965–70** DARE (Qu. I44) Inf **IL**31, Bittersweet — not edible; **MN**29, Bittersweet — edible; **OH**3, Bittersweet — Chinese red outside, breaks off and curls up, small, decorative; (Qu. S17) Inf **MD**29, Bittersweet — climbs tree, gets red berry in fall; (Qu. S21) Inf **RI**12, Bittersweet — a vine; (Qu. S26a) Infs **IA**3, 47, **MI**69, **OH**2, 78, Bittersweet; **NJ**66, Bittersweet — vine with red berries; (Qu. S26c) Infs **KS**16, **NY**12, Bittersweet; (Qu. S26d) Inf **IL**55, Bittersweet; (Qu. S26e) Inf **MI**106, Bittersweet — a vine with an orange flower; **NJ**29, Bitter-

sweet — lives anywhere; **OH**41, Bittersweet — a viny thing with berries along the road; (Qu. T16) Infs **IA**22, **MA**5, Bittersweet — a vine; **KY**47, 76, Bittersweet. **1966** DARE Wildfl QR Pl.194a Inf **OR**12, Bittersweet.

bitter thistle n

A blessed thistle (*Cnicus benedictus).*

1876 Hobbs *Bot. Hdbk.* 118, Thistle, Bitter, Blessed thistle, Centaurea benedicta. **1900** Lyons *Plant Names* 108. **1971** Krochmal *Appalachia Med. Plants* 98, Bitter thistle . . . has been used to treat worms.

bitter walnut n

A **bitternut.**

1897 Sudworth *Arborescent Flora* 111, *Hicoria minima* . . . *Common Names* . . . Bitter Walnut (Vt.). **1950** Peattie *Nat. Hist. Trees* 146, *Bitternut Hickory* . . . Bitter Walnut. **1967** DARE (Qu. I43) Inf **NY**2, Bitter walnuts.

bitter water hickory n

Either of two hickories: **nutmeg hickory** or **water hickory.**

1979 Little *Checklist U.S. Trees* 72, *Carya aquatica* . . . *Other common names* — bitter pecan, . . bitter water hickory. *Ibid* 74, *Carya myristiciformis* . . . *Other common names* — swamp hickory, bitter water hickory.

bitter waternut n Cf **water bitternut**

=**nutmeg hickory.**

1897 Sudworth *Arborescent Flora* 112, *Hicoria myristicæformis* . . . *Common Names* . . . Bitter Waternut (La.). **1933** Small *Manual SE Flora* 405, *Bitter-Waternut* . . . Woods, hillsides, and low grounds. **1950** Moore *Trees AR* 30, Local Names: Bitter Water Nut, Blasted Pecan . . . Nut egg-shaped, pointed at ends, not flattened; kernel sweet. **1960** Vines *Trees SW* 135.

bitterweed n scattered, but chiefly Sth, TX See Map

Any of var plants containing a bitter principle.

1819 Thomas *Travels W. Country* 222 *(DA),* Ambrosia artimisifolia hog or bitter weed. **1900** Lyons *Plant Names* 221, *L[eptilon] Canadense* . . . Canada Fleabane, Horseweed, . . Bitter-weed. **1908** DN 3.291 **eAL, wGA,** *Bitter-weed* . . . Dog fennel . . : so called because when eaten by cows it makes the milk bitter. **1940** Clute *Amer. Plant Names* 29, *C[helone] glabra.* Turtle-head . . . Bitter-weed. **1944** *Clarke Co. Democrat* (Grove Hill AL) 18 May 3/5 *(DA),* Bitterweed, a serious pasture pest which causes unpalatable milk, can be controlled by proper management of the pasture. **1960** Williams *Walk Egypt* 5 **GA,** They were lost among the brighter fall flowers, maypop and yarrow, bitterweed and goldenrod. **1965–70** DARE (Qu. S21) 90 Infs, **scattered, but chiefly Sth, TX,** Bitterweed(s); (Qu. S7) Inf **MS**82, Bitterweed; (Qu. S17) Inf **TX**68, Bitterweed; (Qu. S20) Inf **AL**6, Bitterweed — yellow top; (Qu. S26a) Infs **GA**2, 5, Bitterweed; (Qu. K14) Infs **FL**1, 17, 34, **GA**68, **LA**23, **MS**74, (Ate, been eating, eating, *or* tainted with) bitterweed(s).

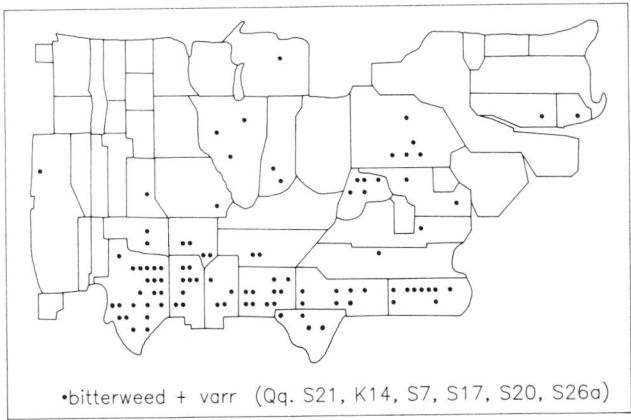

•bitterweed + varr (Qq. S21, K14, S7, S17, S20, S26a)

bitterweed milk n [bitterweed + *milk*] chiefly Sth, S Midl See Map on p. 252 Cf **bad-weed milk, bitter** adj **1**

Milk tainted by plants which the cows have grazed on.

1965–70 DARE (Qu. K14, *Milk that has a taste from something the cow ate in the pasture*) 46 Infs, Bitterweed milk; 10 Infs, Bitterweed.

bitter wintergreen n

A **pipsissewa** (here: *Chimaphila umbellata*).

1822 Eaton *Botany* 236, *Chimaphila . . . umbellata* (prince's pine,

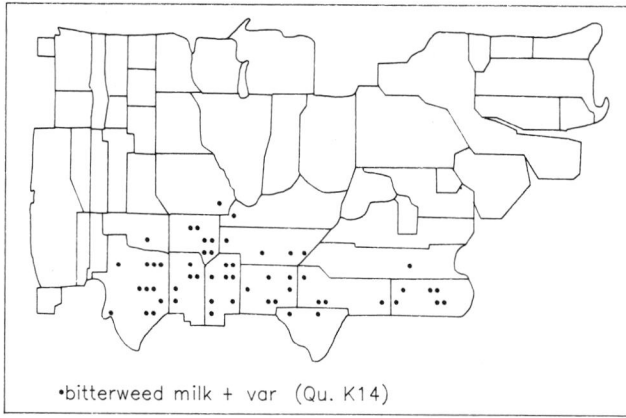

•bitterweed milk + var (Qu. K14)

bitter wintergreen . . .) . . . Tonics and diuretics. **1900** Lyons *Plant Names* 96. **1971** Krochmal *Appalachia Med. Plants* 90, Bitter wintergreen . . . An evergreen perennial that grows to 10 inches in height. **1974** (1977) Coon *Useful Plants* 217, Bitter wintergreen . . . has also been used to give its pleasant taste to root beer.

bitterworm n
=**buckbean 1.**

1873 in 1976 Miller *Shaker Herbs* 142, Buckbean . . . Bitterworm. Marsh Trefoil. Bog Myrtle. Used in the treatment of scurvy, . . hepatics, and worms. **1900** Lyons *Plant Names* 245, *M. trifoliata* . . . Bitterworm, Bog Hop . . . *Leaves*, . . bitter tonic. **1974** (1977) Coon *Useful Plants* 144, Buckbean, . . bitter-worm, . . bog hop . . . One writer claims that "it is the most serviceable of all known herbal tonics."

bittle See **victual**

bittrun n [Metath of **bittern**]
=**black-crowned night heron.**

1932 Bennitt *Check-List* 15, Black-crowned night heron. *Nycticorax nycticorax hoactli* . . bittrun. **1955** Forbush–May *Birds* 35, *Black-Crowned Night Heron* . . *Other Names:* . . Bittrun. **1955** *MA Audubon* 39.312, *Black-Crowned Night Heron* . . . Bittrun (Mass. That is, bittern, through confusion with the American Bittern.)

bitty wood See **bettywood**

biver, all of a adj phr [*all of a* + *biver* alter of Scots and Engl dial *bever* a shiver, tremor]
1914 *DN* 4.68 **ME, nNH,** *All of a biver* . . . Excited.

bizmaroon n, also attrib Also *bismaroon* [Prob imit] Cf *DS* P22
A **bullfrog 1.**

1950 *WELS* (*A very large frog that makes a deep, loud sound*) 1 Inf, **ceWI,** Bismaroon; 1 Inf, **cwWI,** Bizmaroon—FW: Inf has heard or read of, not used around here. **1950** *WELS Suppl.*, 2 Infs, **WI,** Bismaroon—a bull frog; 1 Inf, **csWI,** Bismaroon—large frog; "an old Frenchman called at Joe's parents at Green Bay selling bismaroon legs;" 1 Inf, **seWI,** Bizmaroon—a bull frog, used 40 years ago in Chippewa Co.

biznacha See **bisnaga**

bizzing vbl n
=**bum-riding.**

1969 *DARE* File **cnUT,** [Brigham Young Univ. brochure about traffic regulations:] Penalties for Registration, Parking and Moving Violations . . . Miscellaneous: (1) Bizzing—$5.00. **1984** *Ibid* **cnUT,** Bizzing —hanging on the back bumper of a car and skiing on one's shoes on slippery pavement; the term is especially common in the Utah Valley; **cwCO,** Bizzing.

bla n Also *blala* [See quot 1972] **HI**
A brother, friend, pal.

1972 Carr *Da Kine Talk* 124 **HI,** *Bla, blala* vs. *brother*—"Look at that *blala!*" uttered by a *haole* [=a white person] who is unsympathetic may be insulting. "Ey, bla!" uttered by a member of the peer group may be a warm and affectionate greeting. Reductions of the word *brother*, these are terms of address used by, and for, Island-born men and boys, whether relatives or friends. **1983** *Des Moines Register* (IA) 28 Jan sec T1 **HI,** "Rest da body; cool head maintain, blala," said Lagorio. "Blala means brother."

blaa n, v |blæ:,blɑ:| [Imit] chiefly **Nth**
The bawl or bleat of a calf or sheep; to make such a noise.

1939 *LANE* Map 195 **scattered throughout NEng,** The map shows the verbs . . *blare, blaa,* . . used to designate the cry of a calf. **1967–69** *DARE* (Qu. K19, *Noise made by a calf that's taken away from its mother*) Infs **MA55, NY163,** [blæ:]; (Qu. K66, *The noise made by a sheep*) Infs **CA145, IN69, MA1, 25,** [blæ:]; **MN23,** [blæ]; **PA132,** Blaa; **TX33,** [blɑ:].

blab n [Transf from *blab* one who chatters; idle talk; *OED* c1374 →]

1 also *blabber:* The mouth. *joc, sometimes derog*
1942 Berrey–Van den Bark *Amer. Slang* 121.66, Mouth . . . blab, blabber. **1967–70** *DARE* (Qu. X9, *Joking or uncomplimentary words for a person's mouth—for example, you might say, "I wish he'd shut his _____."*) Infs **LA6, MN12, 23, VA69, WI13,** Blab; **FL17, SC26, 34,** Blabber.

2 A device attached to a calf's nose to prevent suckling; see quot 1884. chiefly **West** See also **blab-board (weaner)**
1884 (1966) Aldridge *Life on a Ranch* 183 **KS,** A 'blab' is a piece of thin board, six inches by four inches, which has a piece cut out of the middle of one of the longer sides, so shaped that you can just force it on to the membrane that divides the nostrils of a calf. When put on it hangs down over the mouth of the animal so that it cannot suck, but is able to graze without difficulty. **1922** Rollins *Cowboy* 193 **West,** The calf and his mater had to be chased so far apart as to permit the cowboy to rope and throw the calf, attach the blab, and remount his horse. **1934** Charlottesville *Dly Prog* 7 July 1/1 (*Hench Coll.*), Will Rogers Says . . . You know what a blab is? It's a thing you put over a calf's mouth to keep it from eating between meals. **1967** *DARE* FW Addit **CO,** Blabs—a weaner for calves. Some have prongs or sharp points; momma objects [to it]. Others just keep the calf from sucking.

blab v, hence vbl n *blabbing* [**blab** n 2] chiefly **West**
To attach a device to keep a calf from suckling.
1884 (1966) Aldridge *Life on a Ranch* 183 **KS,** One of our occupations, as winter advanced, consisted in 'blabbing' calves. **1922** Rollins *Cowboy* 193 **West,** There were inspection trips . . on such ranches as "blabbed" their calves . . . Blabbing was not always easy of accomplishment. **1937** Sandoz *Slogum* 92 **NE,** "We'll have to blab the kid," the brother sneered under his moustache, "like a damned sucking calf."

blabber See **blab** n 1

blabber-fest See **blab-fest**

blabberskite n [Blend of *blabber* + *blatherskite* a foolish person] *joc, sometimes derog*
A talkative, blustering person.
1968–70 *DARE* (Qu. HH7a, *Someone who talks too much, or too loud: "He's an awful _____."*) Inf **MD31,** ['blæbɚ‚skaɪt]; **PA245,** Blabberskite.

blab-blab n [Redup form of *blab* one who gossips or chatters]
c1960 *Wilson Coll.* **csKY,** Blab-blab . . . A too-ready talker, a gossip, a blabmouth.

blab-board (weaner) n [**blab** n 2] chiefly **West** Cf **blab** v
=**blab** n 2.
1961 Adams *Old-Time Cowhand* 154, Them boards were called "blab-boards," or "blab-board weaners."

blab-fest n Also *blabber-fest* [*blab, blabber* idle or excessive talk + *fest*] *joc*
A gathering of people for talking or gossip; a gabfest.
1942 Berrey–Van den Bark *Amer. Slang* 191.1, *Conversation; discussion* . . . Blabfest. **1968** *DARE* (Qu. KK12, *A meeting where there's a lot of talking: "They got together yesterday and had a real _____."*) Infs **CT9, IN22,** Blab-fest; **NJ61,** Blabber-fest.

black adj Cf **black man 1**
In var phrr referring to imaginary animals or beings: fearsome, evil, terrible.
1965–70 *DARE* (Qu. EE41, *A hobgoblin that is used to threaten children and make them behave:*) Infs **IN76, TN8, VA35,** (Big) black dog; **MN15,** Big black bear; **WI24,** Black goblin; **IN14,** Black lady; **AR3,** Black witch; **NY89,** Old black Joe.

black n Cf **blackie**

1 A **black duck** (here: *Anas rubripes*).

1923 U.S. Dept. Ag. *Misc. Circular* 13.9, *Vernacular Names . . . In general use.*—Black duck, black mallard, often shortened to blacks. **1943** Musgrove *Waterfowl IA* 19, *Black Ducks . . .* Other names: dusky duck, black, black mallard. **1955** *MA Audubon* 39.314, *Black Duck . . .* Black (Maine. Mass. Prevailing color dusky or blackish brown). **1982** Elman *Hunter's Field Guide* 143, While in formation they fly a straight course, but a black flying alone . . may abruptly rise . . . Blacks are large, almost 2 feet long.

2 =**wood duck.**

1923 U.S. Dept. Ag. *Misc. Circular* 13.16, *Wood Duck . . . Vernacular Names . . . In local use . . .* Black (Ill.). **1932** Bennitt *Check-list* 19 **MO,** *Wood Duck . . .* Squealer; black; plumer.

black v [Abbr for *blackball*]

1906 *DN* 3.126 **nwAR,** *Black . . .* To blackball. "He blacked 'em." Used by members of lodges.

black-actually See **back-actually**

black adder n

=**hognose snake** (here: *Heterodon platyrhinos*).

1966–68 *DARE* (Qu. P25) Infs **GA**25, **SC**19, Black adder.

black alder n

1 An alder (here: the introduced and locally naturalized *Alnus glutinosa,* or the native spp *A. rugosa* and *A. serrulata*). [Note: the latter two spp are combined by some authors under *Alnus rugosa* (Du Roi) Spreng.]

1805 (1905) Lewis *Orig. Jrls. Lewis & Clark Exped.* 3.261, The large black alder. **1889** *Century Dict.* 1.134/1, In the eastern United States the common species are the smooth alder, *A. serrulata,* and the speckled alder, *A. incana.* Both are also known as black alder. **1967** *DARE* Tape **TX**1, And he used black alder [for home remedies]. **1979** Little *Check-list U.S. Trees* 48, *Alnus glutinosa . . . Other common names*—black alder. *Ibid* 49, *Alnus serrulata . . .* Other common names—common alder, . . black alder.

2 A **winterberry** (here: *Ilex verticillata*).

1824 Bigelow *Florula Bostoniensis* 129, *Prinos Verticillatus. Black Alder . . .* Berries of a bright scarlet, . . . bitter and unpleasant to the taste, with a little sweetness and some acrimony. **1868** (1870) Gray *Field Botany* 219, *Common Winterberry* or *Black Alder.* Common in low grounds. **1913** *Torreya* 33 **NY,** The berries of the black alder (*Ilex verticillata*) make the swamps gay after the leaves have fallen. **1942** Peattie *Friendly Mts.* 206 **VT,** At the border of the bog among the tall cinnamon ferns grows the black alder or winterberry. **1968** *DARE* (Qu. T15) Inf **WI**8, Black alder—scrub; some call it Wisconsin holly. **1976** Bailey–Bailey *Hortus Third* 593, *Black Alder . . .* The most widespread of the N. Amer. hollies, a variable sp. with many intergrading forms.

3 The alder buckthorn (*Rhamnus frangula*).

1974 (1977) Coon *Useful Plants* 235, *Rhamnus frangula*—Black-alder . . . is . . now widely naturalized, as the new plants are distributed by birds.

black-a-li-lo See **blankie-lie-low**

black-and-tan n, also attrib Also *black tan* **chiefly Sth, S Midl**

A dog, esp a hound, with black and tan coloring.

1856 *Porter's Spirit of Times* 1 Nov 140/2 **AR,** Dan brought home two of the finest *black tans* you ever laid your eyes on. **1884** *Harper's Mag.* 69.464/2 **MA,** A jealous little black-and-tan stood by. **1939** Hall Coll. **wNC,** It was one of the bear hounds, a black and tan hound, and he was just cut up, bloody all over. **1948** Faulkner *Intruder* 5 **MS,** The boy . . was waiting at the house with the dog—a true rabbit dog, some hound, . . maybe mostly hound, redbone and black-and-tan with maybe a little pointer somewhere once. **1967** *DARE* Tape **LA**1, Them boys got an old black-and-tan they say'll tree a coon; **LA**2, She was a black-and-tan; **LA**3, The black-and-tan and bluetick and redbone, they're slower, they're more used for coon dogs.

black and white n

A children's tag game; see quots.

1909 (1923) Bancroft *Games* 52, *Black and White . . .* The leader is provided with a flat disk which is white on one side and black on the other . . . He . . twirls this disk, stopping it with one side only visible to the players. If the white side should be visible, the party known as the Whites may tag any of their opponents who are standing upright. The Blacks should therefore drop instantly to the floor, as in Stoop Tag . . . Any player tagged drops out of the game. The party wins which puts out in this way all of its opponents. **1968** *DARE* (Qu. EE33, *Other*

outdoor games . . that children play) Inf **PA**133, Black and white—a stick, black on one side, white on the other, indicates which team chases the other.

black-and-white creeper n

=**black-and-white warbler.**

1858 Baird *Birds* 235, *Mniotilta varia . .* Black and White Creeper. **1917** *DN* 4.422 **LA,** Black and white creeper. The black and white warbler (*Miniotilta varia*) [sic]. **1946** Hausman *Eastern Birds* 497, *Mniotilta varia . .* Other Names . . Black and White Creeper. **1967** *DARE* (Qu. Q23) Inf **PA**44, Black-and-white creeper—looks like a warbler.

black-and-white creeping warbler See **creeping warbler**

black-and-white warbler n

Std: a small woodland bird (*Mniotilta varia*) with black and white plumage. Also called **black-and-white creeper, blue-and-white pied creeper, creeping warbler, striped warbler, whitepoll warbler**

black ankle n, also attrib [Prob var of **brass ankle**] **chiefly S Atl**

A person of mixed race, usu Black, Indian and White.

1966–68 *DARE* (Qu. C35, *Nicknames for the different parts of your town or city*) Infs **NC**49, 67, Black ankle (settlement); (Qu. HH29b, *Names for people of mixed blood—part Negro*) Inf **GA**15, Black ankle —light mulatto.

black Annie n Also *black Betsy* [By analogy with *black Maria*]

A police vehicle.

1967 *DARE* FW Addit **neIL,** Black Annie, same as black Maria. **1969–70** *DARE* (Qu. N3, *The car or wagon that takes arrested people to the police station or to jail*) Infs **KY**6, 94. Black Annie; **WV**21, Black Betsy.

black ape See **ape** n **1**

black ash n

1 An American ash (*Fraxinus nigra*). **chiefly NEast, Gt Lakes** Also called **basket ash, brown ash, hoop ash, swamp ash, water ash**

1673 in 1864 *Essex Inst. Coll.* 6.178/2 **MA,** From the heap of stones on the No East Corner . . to a forked black ash. **1737** (1901) Hempstead *Diary* 316 *(DA)* **CT,** I cut a black ash ladder pole. **1872** VT State Bd. Ag. *Report* 154, An experiment had been tried by a Cornwall farmer, packing butter in spruce, oak and black ash tubs. **1916** Seton *Woodcraft Manual Girls* 295, *Black Ash, Hoop Ash,* or *Water Ash* (*Fraxinus nigra*)—A tall forest tree of swampy places; 70, 80, or rarely 100 feet high. **1965** Needham–Mussey *Country Things* 85 **sVT,** Black ash or swamp ash was what he used to make baskets. **1965–70** *DARE* (Qu. T15) 10 Infs, **chiefly NY, MN, WI,** Black ash; (Qu. T16) Infs **MI**64, 76, 116, **NY**227, **WI**58, Black ash.

2 =**green ash.**

1897 Sudworth *Arborescent Flora* 328, *Fraxinus pennsylvanica . . .* Black Ash (N.J.). **1936** Winter *Plants NE* 179, *F. pennsylvanica . . .* Green, Red or Black Ash.

3 =**box elder.**

1897 Sudworth *Arborescent Flora* 291, *Acer negundo . . .* Black Ash (Tenn.). **1940** Clute *Amer. Plant Names* 128, *A[cer] negundo . . .* Black ash, water ash.

blackassed pea n *joc*

1979 *DARE* File **sMS** [Black speaker], Blackeyed peas are called blackassed peas.

blackback See **blackback flounder, black-backed woodpecker, great black-backed gull**

black-backed gull See **great black-backed gull**

black-backed woodpecker n Also *blackback*

A woodpecker (*Picoides tridactylus*) distinguished by its dark color and three toes. Also called **three-toed woodpecker**

1872 Coues *Key to N. Amer. Birds* 194, *Black-backed Woodpecker . . . Picoides tridactylus . . arcticus.* **1927** Forbush *Birds MA* 2.270, *Picoides arcticus . . .* Other names: Black-backed woodpecker. **1946** Hausman *Eastern Birds* 391, *Picoides arcticus . .* Other Names . . Blackback. **1953** Jewett *Birds WA* 414, Black-backed Woodpecker. *Picoides arcticus.* **1968** *DARE* (Qu. Q17) Inf **MN**15, Black-backed woodpecker.

blackback flounder n Also *blackback, black flounder*
=**winter flounder.**

 1966 *DARE* Tape **ME**17, Gray sole, lemon sole, blackbacks, dabs. **1969** *DARE* (Qu. P2, . . *Saltwater fish . . good to eat*) Inf **MA**40, Black-back; **RI**4, Blackback flounder. **1972** Sparano *Outdoors Encycl.* 384, *Common Names:* Winter flounder, . . blackback, black flounder.

blackback pine See **black pine 2b**

blackback sucker See **black sucker 2**

black balsam n

1 Prob =**black spruce.**

 1883 Zeigler *Heart of Alleghanies* 57, Every grove is composed of both black and white balsams, and no single tree is widely separated from its opposite sex.

2 =**white fir** (here: *Abies concolor*).

 1941 FWP *Guide UT* 20, The white fir, bearing the contradictory local name of "black balsam," is found at lower elevation.

blackbark pine See **black pine 2b**

black basket See **basket 4**

black bass n

1 Any of several freshwater fish of the genus *Micropterus,* esp **largemouth bass, smallmouth bass, spotted bass.**

 1815 Lit. & Philos. Soc. NY *Trans.* 1.146, *Basse;* is a Dutch word, signifying perch. *Black, or Oswego, basse,* a fine fish, like our black fish. **1859** (1968) Bartlett *Americanisms, Black Bass* . . . A favorite game fish, found in abundance in most of our Northern lakes and Western rivers. **1896** U.S. Natl. Museum *Bulletin* 47.1011, *Micropterus* . . (Black Bass.) **1905** *DN* 3.3 **cCT. 1907** *DN* 3.209 nwAR, *Black bass* . . . A lake fish. **1920** Forbes–Richardson *Fishes of IL* 268, The black-bass fisheries of Illinois, practically consisting altogether of the present species, amounted in 1894 to nearly 9,000 lb. **1933** LA Dept. of Conserv. *Fishes* 313, None of our other fresh water fishes has been given so many popular names as our Black Bass. **1965–70** *DARE* (Qu. P1, . . *Freshwater fish . . good to eat*) 65 Infs, **scattered,** Black bass.

2 See **black sea bass.**

3 =**black rockfish.**

 1887 Goode *Amer. Fishes* 268, *Sebastichthys mystinus,* is most generally called the "Black Rockfish," but in Puget Sound is known, with its more abundant relative, *Sebastichthys melanops,* as the "Black Bass." **1898** U.S. Natl. Museum *Bulletin* 47.1783, Monterey to Kadiak [sic], most abundant northward; very abundant at Sitka, where it is called "Black Bass." **1965–70** *DARE* (Qu. P2, . . *Saltwater fish . . good to eat*) Infs **AK**1, **CA**65, Black bass; **CA**176, 191, Black sea bass. [Note: CA Infs may refer instead to sense 4.]

4 =**red roncador.**

 1946 LaMonte *N. Amer. Game Fishes* 82, *Sciæna saturna* . . Names: . . Black Bass.

black bean n

1 =**hyacinth bean.**

 1868 (1870) Gray *Field Botany* 109, *D[olichos] Lablab* . . Black Bean. **1900** Lyons *Plant Names* 212, *L[ablab] Lablab* . . Black Bean.

2 also *black wax bean:* =**black-eyed pea.**

 1965–70 *DARE* (Qu. I19) Infs **GA**88, **LA**33, **MA**68, **NY**70, **OH**87, Black beans; **PA**119, Black wax beans.

black bec-croche n Cf **bec-croche**
Either of two similar birds: the **glossy ibis 1** or the **white-faced ibis.**

 1917 *DN* 4.423 **LA,** Black beccroche. The white-faced glossy ibis (Flegadis [sic] guarauna). **1931** Read *LA French* 7, The term "Black Bec-croche" is given to the Glossy *(Plegadis autumnalis . .),* as well as to the White-faced Glossy Ibis *(Plegadis guarauna . .),* two species that inhabit principally the thick woods along the swamps and rivers in the southwestern parishes of Cameron and Calcasieu.

black beech n [?From the similarity of the leaves to beech leaves]
A **hornbeam** (here: *Carpinus caroliniana*).

 1920 *Torreya* 20.20, *Carpinus caroliniana* . . . Black beech, Admiral, M[aryland]d. **1970** *DARE* (Qu. T16) Inf **MA**100, Black beech.

black-bellied darter See **darter**

black-bellied killdeer n
=**black-bellied plover.**

 1888 Trumbull *Names of Birds* 190 **NEng,** *[Squatarola squatarola]* called by many gunners along the coast the *Black-bellied Killdeer.* **1923** U.S. Dept. Ag. *Misc. Circular* 13.68, *Squatarola squatarola* . . black-bellied kildeer [sic] (Long I[slan]d, NY). **1955** *MA Audubon* 39.445, In full, this name is Black-bellied Killdeer, . . "Black-bellied" also is a misnomer, as the black of the under parts extends only to the thighs and it is precisely the belly that is not black.

black-bellied plover n
Std: a plover *(Squatarola squatarola)* with black ventral plumage. Also called **beetlehead, bighead, black-bellied killdeer, blackbelly, black-breasted plover, blackhead, blackheart n**[1] **2, blacksnipe, bottlehead, brownie, bullhead 2a, bull plover, Christmas ~, chucklehead 1, four-toed plover, frost bird, gray lapwing, gray plover, gray sandpiper, gump, hollowhead, killdeer, May cock, mud plover, old-field plover, owlhead, oxeye, palebelly, pilot, specklebelly, whistling plover**

black-bellied sandpiper n
=**red-backed sandpiper.**

 1874 Coues *Birds NW* 489, *Tringa alpina* . . Black-bellied Sandpiper. **1888** Trumbull *Names of Birds* 181, *Black-bellied sandpiper [Pelidna alpina].* **1917** (1923) *Birds Amer.* 1.237, *Red-backed Sandpiper — Pelidna alpina* . . Other Names . . . Black-bellied Sandpiper. **1946** Hausman *Eastern Birds* 282, *Red-backed Sandpiper Pelidna alpina* . . Some twenty-five or more local names, among which are . . Black-bellied Sandpiper.

black-bellied tree duck n Also *black-bellied whistling duck*
A **tree duck 2** (here: *Dendrocygna autumnalis*).

 1898 (1900) Davie *Nests N. Amer. Birds* 103, *Black-bellied Tree-duck* . . . The eggs are deposited in hollow trees and branches, often at a considerable distance from water. **1923** U.S. Dept. Ag. *Misc. Circular* 13.38, *Black-bellied Tree-duck.* **1938** Oberholser *Bird Life LA* 680, The Black-bellied Treeduck, although several times accredited to Louisiana, has apparently no definite record. **1951** Pough *Audubon Water Bird* 74, Black-bellied Whistling Duck . . . *Voice:* A peculiar and characteristic shrill, chattering whistle, which it utters constantly on the wing. **1969** *SC Market Bulletin* 9 Jan 2, 1 pair black-bellied tree ducks.

blackbelly n

1 =**glut herring.**

 1896 U.S. Natl. Museum *Bulletin* 47.426, *Pomolobus æstivalis* . . Black-belly.

2 =**black-bellied plover.**

 1925 (1928) Forbush *Birds MA* 1.463, [The gold plover is] generally more yellowish above and below than Black-belly in autumn. **1944** Hausman *Amer. Birds* 263, Black-bellies *[Squatarola squatarola]* frequent the sand bars and flats exposed by the falling tide. **1954** Sprunt *FL Bird Life* 165, Flying out over the surf on one's approach, the Black-belly *[Squatarola squatarola]* will circle and alight again on the sands behind.

black belt n

1 A region where **black tobacco** is grown. Cf **black patch**

 1944 *PADS* 2.64, The *black-belt* is a district where the soil and climate are suitable for this type of tobacco [i.e. black-tobacco].

2 The section of a city which is populated predominantly by Blacks; the poor section of a city; a ghetto. Cf **back street 2**

 1970 *DARE* (Qu. II25), Inf **DC**11, Inner city—used to be called the black belt or the ghetto—the poor section; **NC**88, Black belt—all Negro section of town. [Both Infs Black]

blackberry iris n

 1970 *DARE* (Qu. S24, *A wild flower that grows in swamps and marshes and looks like a small blue iris*) Inf **KY**89, Blackberry iris.

blackberry lily n
An introduced, now naturalized, lilylike plant *(Belamcanda chinensis)* of the family Iridaceae, which in fruit has a blackberry-like cluster of shiny black seeds. Also called **dwarf tiger-lily, flag, leopard flower, pardelle**

 1824 Eaton *Botany* 334, Blackberry lily . . . Corol[la] about 6-petalled: stem flexuose: leaves ensiform. **1895** Gray–Bailey *Field Botany* 420, *Blackberry Lily* . . . Orange-colored flower . . mottled above with crimson spots, the fruit, when the valves fall and expose the berry-like seeds, imitating a blackberry, whence the common names. **1946** Tatnall *Flora DE* 88, Blackberry Lily. Escaped to roadsides . . . July. Nat. from Asia. **1967** *DARE* (Qu. S24) Inf **PA**99, Blackberry lily. **1967** *DARE* Wildfl QR Pl.13 Infs **AR**44, 45, Blackberry lily.

blackberry storm n Also *blackberry rain, ~ squall* [Ref to the time of the year when blackberries bloom] **chiefly Sth, S Midl** Cf **blackberry winter**
A spring storm or cold snap.
1906 *DN* 3.126 **nwAR**, Blackberry storm . . . A storm said to occur when blackberries are in blossom. "The Easter snap has passed; we now await the blackberry storm." **1947** *Sun* (Baltimore MD) 27 May 18/3 (*Hench Coll.*), The rains of the past week in Maryland were of the kind we used to refer to as the blackberry rains; and, sure enough, in keeping with this tradition, the blackberry bloom all over the State has come forth. **1952** Brown *NC Folkl.* 1.520, Blackberry storm . . . The cold season that sometimes comes when blackberries are in bloom. **1953** Randolph *Down in Holler* 227 **Ozarks**, Blackberry winter . . . A late cold spell in May or early June . . . *Blackberry squall* is used in the same meaning. **1956** *Hand Coll.* swOH.

blackberry summer n *infreq* Cf **blackberry winter** Cf *EDD*
1946 *PADS* 6.6 **NC, VA**, Blackberry summer . . . The season when blackberry vines are in bloom. Rainy weather is said to prevail.

blackberry vinegar n
A drink made with blackberries, sugar and vinegar: see quot 1939.
1818 (1920) Clark *Diary* 2319 **CT**, Had some blackberry vinegar to prepare. **1939** Wolcott *Yankee Cook Book* 326, Blackberry Vinegar— 2 quarts blackberries—sugar—2 quarts cider vinegar—Combine and let stand . . . Mash and strain through cloth. For every 3 quarts of juice add 5 pounds sugar. Boil . . . When cool, bottle and seal. To serve, add one tablespoon to a glass of water. **1941** Percy *Lanterns* 42 **MS**, Aunt Nana might rustle in with glasses of blackberry vinegar, which apparently went out when cocktails came in.

blackberry winter n Also *blackberry weather* [Ref to the time of year, usu May and early June, when blackberries bloom] **chiefly Sth, S Midl** Cf **blackberry storm, blackberry summer, blackbird storm, bloom winter, dogwood winter, fox-grape winter**
A period of cold weather in the spring; see quots.
1904 (1913) Johnson *Highways South* 162 **cKY**, Then, later, when the blackberries are in blossom, we have another cold spell what we call the blackberry winter. **1906** *DN* 3.126 **nwAR**. **1918** *DN* 5.18 **NC**. **1932** *AmSp* 7.233 **MO**. **1933** *AmSp* 8.1.47 **Ozarks**. **1949** Hornsby *Lonesome Valley* 53 **KY**, March stayed well on into April . . . The weather turned cold. Uncle Lihugh said it was blackberry winter, but Aunt Rhody argued that it was dogwood winter. **1950** *PADS* 14.14 **SC**. **1954** *Harder Coll.* cwTN. **c1960** *Wilson Coll.* csKY. **1960** Williams *Walk Egypt* 202 **GA**, It crept along during the fall and winter and next spring, a blackberry winter with the air so clear that she could hear from a mile away. **1966** *DARE* FW Addits **GA, sIL, MS, TN, VA**, Blackberry winter. **1967–70** *DARE* (QR p13) Inf **AL**21, Blackberry weather—a cold spell after Easter; (QR p12) Inf **VA**44, Blackberry winter. **1972** Mead *Blackberry Winter* (title).

black Betsy See **black Annie**

black betty n Also *black betts* [Cf *OED betty* sb.3] **chiefly Midl** *old-fash*
Liquor, spec a bottle of liquor passed among the guests at a wedding.
1823 Doddridge *Logan* 42 **VA**, He that got first to the bride's house, got black betty, which was the name they called the bottle. *Ibid* 43, Every boy and gal, old and young . . must kiss black betty; that is to take a good slug of a dram. **1846** Crawford *Hist. White Mts.* 45 **NH**, There I was loaded . . with a plenty of what some call "Black Betts," or "O be joyful," as it was the fashion in those days, to make use of this kind of stuff. **1859** (1922) Jackson *Col.'s Diary* 13 **PA**, Black Betty having gone dry, a man was started to town for some more—what? Why, liquor, of course. **1904** Greve *Centennial Hist. Cincinnati* 1.463, They did not forget to pass the 'old black Betty,' filled with good old peach brandy, among the old pioneers. **1956** Settle *Beulah Land* 162 **WV** (as of 1760s), They say marriages are made in heaven, but I reckon up here they're made in Black Betty. These Presbyterians have to get drunker to face a

marriage than they do to face a hangin. **1957** McMeekin *Old KY Country* 64, Pretty late in the night someone would remind the company that the new couple must stand in need of some refreshments: 'Black Betty,' which was the name of the bottle, did not go alone.

black bill n
=**black-billed cuckoo**.
1969 *DARE* (Qu. Q14) Inf **NY**134, Black bills.

black-bill buzzard n
=**black vulture**.
1967 *DARE* (Qu. Q13) Inf **SC**43, Black-bill buzzard.

black-billed cuckoo n
Std: a grayish-brown common North American cuckoo (*Coccyzus erythropthalmus*) distinguished by a red circle around the eye and a black bill. Also called **black bill, brush hen, chowchow 1, cowbird, cow-cow 2, egg-sucker, milk-sourer, rain crow, storm crow**

black-billed logcock n
=**pileated woodpecker**.
1953 Jewett *Birds WA* 399, Western Pileated Woodpecker. *Dryocopus pileatus picinus* . . Other names: . . Black-billed Logcock.

black-billed raincrow n
=**black-billed cuckoo**.
1969 *DARE* (Qu. Q14) Inf **CT**29, Black-billed raincrow.

black bindweed n
An annual species of *Polygonum* (*P. convolvulus*) which is a troublesome weed, esp in cultivated areas throughout the U.S. Also called **blackbird bindweed, climbing buckwheat, cornbind, corn bindweed, devil's tether, ivy bindweed, knot bindweed, nimble-will, sow bindweed, wild bean, wild buckwheat**
1824 Bigelow *Florula Bostoniensis* 158, *Polygonum convolvulus* . . Black Bindweed. **1891** Jesup *Plants Hanover NH*. **1910** Graves *Flowering Plants* 163 **CT**. **1974** Munz *Flora S. CA* 703.

blackbird n
1 A Black person. **chiefly SC**
1965–70 *DARE* (Qu. HH28, . . *People of foreign background* . . *Negro*) Infs **GA**7, **PA**130, **SC**3, 11, 19, 21, 26, 40, 44, 54, Blackbird.
2 See quot. [Perh by analogy with *black sheep*]
1966 Barnes–Jensen *Dict. UT Slang*, Black bird: . . one whose family looks down upon his activities.

blackbird bindweed n
=**black bindweed**.
1900 Lyons *Plant Names* 300, *P[olygonum Convolvulus]* . . Blackbird Bindweed. **1910** Graves *Flowering Plants* 163 **CT**.

blackbird storm n Cf **blackberry storm, buzzard storm**
1953 Randolph *Down in Holler* 227 **Ozarks**, Blackbird storm . . . A short cold spell in late spring, after the appearance of the blackbirds.

black blizzard n, also attrib Also *black wind* [From the dark color of soil particles suspended in air; orig coined to describe the dust storms of KS and OK in the 1930s] **chiefly Plains States** Cf **black duster, ~ roller, ~ snow**
A dust storm.
1934 *Hench Coll.* **VA**, The black blizzards of dust from the vast plains of Canada had spent their force, sweeping to sea on the Eastern seaboard, dropping tons of fertile farm soil en route. **1936** in **1938** *AmSp* 13.72 **CO, OK**, [Newspaper citations], 'Black Blizzard' Reaches Central Part Of Oklahoma . . . A vast cloud of dust rolled over Oklahoma today paralyzing traffic on highways, ravaging wheat-fields, and blotting out the sun. *Ibid*, [It was] one of the worst 'black-blizzard' duststorms ever to strike this area. **1938** (1952) FWP *Guide SD* 53, Ushered in by the famous and devastating "black blizzard" of November 1933, the dust storm scourge . . was something new to Dakota prairies. **1952** Peattie *Black Hills* 86 **SD**, Despite drought and depression and the "black blizzards" of the thirties, these rugged ranchers hung on. **1967** *DARE* (Qu. B18, *Are there any special kinds of wind that you get around here?*) Inf **CO**24, Black wind—dust storm from Kansas. [Inf old] **1967** *DARE* Tape **CO**19, And ever' time you'd get a little wind why it was just a reg'lar black blizzard you might call it; **KS**1, When these black blizzards

came . . . you couldn't see where the windows were . . . for this terrific dust storm.

blackboard eraser n [From the practice of pupils to ingratiate themselves with the teacher by cleaning the blackboard]

1967 *DARE* (Qu. JJ3b, *When a school child makes a special effort to "get in good" with the teacher in hopes of getting a better grade: "She's an awful _____."*) Inf **NJ1**, Blackboard eraser.

black bonito See **bonito 2**

black bottle n Also *black draught* [From the association of "black" with death; orig hobo and underworld jargon] **widespread, but esp Sth**

A poisonous drink.

1927 *DN* 5.439 [Underworld jargon], *Black bottle* . . . (1) Knock-out drops. (2) An opiate. Tramps believe that doctors in charity hospitals administer a poisonous opiate to a sick man to save the trouble of curing him. 1935 *AmSp* 10.78 [Sailors' slang], *The black draught.* A death potion supposed to be given to undesirable patients in charity wards. Also referred to as *the black bottle.* 1945 Saxon *Gumbo Ya-Ya* 76 **LA**, The black bottle is reputed to be a potent dose administered to the innocent and unknowing on entry to the charity hospital. Instant death is certain to follow, the body then to be rendered up to the students for carving. 1950 *PADS* 14.14 **SC**, *Black bottle* . . . Poison. To give one the *black bottle* was supposed to have been a method of getting rid of a patient in a hospital. Charleston. 1970 *DARE* (Qu. II5b) Inf **FL52**, Black bottle or needle if they want to kill him.

black bottle fly See **bottle fly 1**

Black Bottom n [*Black* Negro + **bottom** n 2] **esp SC**

The part of a town where Black people live.

1915 *Lit. Digest* 51.500/2 **Sth**, Uncle Mose aspired to the elective office of justice of the peace in the "black bottom" part of town. 1967–68 *DARE* (Qu. C35, *Nicknames for the different parts of your town or city*) Inf **GA19**, Black Bottom—colored section; **SC32**, Black Bottom—mostly Negro inhabitants; **SC51**, Black Bottom—Negro area; (Qu. II25, *Names or nicknames for the part of town where the poorer people, special groups, or foreign groups live*) Infs **GA19, SC32, 54**, Black Bottom [where Black people live].

black-bottom pie n **chiefly Sth**

A pie which has chocolate custard as the bottom layer of the filling.

1951 Brown *Southern Cook Book* 308, Black Bottom Pie. 1952 Tracy *Coast Cookery* 122 **MS**, *Black-Bottom Pie* . . . Bittersweet chocolate, 4 egg whites, . . 1 cup whipped cream . . . Pour the chocolate custard into the piecrust, then cover with plain custard. 1968 *DARE* (Qu. H63, *Kinds of desserts especially favored by people around here*) Inf **LA40**, Black-bottom pie.

black-bottom road n

=**black road.**

c1970 Pederson *Dial. Survey Rural GA* **seGA**, Black bottom road [=one paved with a black surface].

black bream n

Prob =**pumpkinseed 1.**

1966 *DARE* (Qu. P1, . . *Freshwater fish . . good to eat*) Inf **GA25**, Black bream.

blackbreast n

1 also *blackbreasted sandpiper:* =**red-backed sandpiper.**

1844 DeKay *Zool. N.Y.* 2.240, The Black-Breasted Sandpiper—*Tringa cinclus* . . . This species is common on the coast of New York, which it reaches in April, and is then called Black-breast. 1888 Trumbull *Names of Birds* 182, At Seaford, L.I., in New Jersey at Tuckerton, Pleasantville, above mentioned, Atlantic City, Cape May C.H., Cape May City, and Cobb's Island, Va., *Black-Breast.* 1904 Wheelock *Birds CA* 66, Red-Backed Sandpiper, . . Common names: . . Black Breast. 1917 (1923) *Birds Amer.* I.237, *Red-backed Sandpiper—Pelidna alpina* . . Other Names . . . Little Blackbreast. 1932 Howell *FL Bird Life* 241, *Red-backed Sandpiper* . . Other Names: . . Blackbreast. 1955 *MA Audubon* 39.19, *Red-backed Sandpiper.* Black-breast (Maine).

2 See **black-breasted plover.**

black-breasted plover n Also *blackbreast (plover), blackbreaster*

Usu the **black-bellied plover;** sometimes the **golden plover.**

1888 Trumbull *Names of Birds* 191, At Pine Point, Me., Portsmouth, N.H., in Massachusetts at Provincetown, West Barnstable, Chatham, New Bedford, and Falmouth, and at Stratford, Conn., *Black-Breast [Squatarola squatarola]* . . . On Long Island at Moriches, Bellport, and Seaford, and in New Jersey at Barnegat, Tuckerton, and Cape May City, *Black-Breast Plover.* Ibid 195, Black-breast [*Charadrius dominicus*]. 1923 U.S. Dept. Ag. *Misc. Circular* 13.68, Black-bellied Plover (*Squatarola squatarola*) . . black-breaster. 1946 Hausman *Eastern Birds* 258, Black-bellied Plover *Squatarola squatarola* . . . Some twenty-five or more local names, among which are: Blackbreast. 1954 Sprunt *FL Bird Life* 164, *Black-bellied Plover: Squatarola squatarola* . . Local Names: Black-breasted Plover. 1955 *MA Audubon* 39.444, *American Golden Plover [Charadrius dominicus].* Black-breast (Maine, Mass.); Black-breasted Plover (Maine. The under parts of both sexes in breeding plumage are largely black.). 1967–70 *DARE* (Qu. Q10) Inf **MI53**, Black-breasted plover; **VA47**, Black-breasted plover—plentiful.

blackbrush n **chiefly SW**

1 A tar bush (here: *Flourensia cernua*).

1913 Wooton *Trees NM* 151, Blackbrush. Almost glabrous resiniferous much branched shrub . . . *F[lourensia] cernua.* 1944 AZ Univ. *Biol. Sci. Bulletin* 6.349, Tar Bush; Black Brush; Hojase . . . An indicator of the Chihuahuan Desert flora, . . it occurs in isolated areas in southeastern Arizona. 1981 Benson–Darrow *Trees SW Deserts* 295, Blackbrush . . . Shrubs usually less than 1 m. high.

2 also *blackbush, Dixie blackb(r)ush:* A desert shrub (*Coleogyne ramosissima*). Also called **burrobrush**

1923 Davidson–Moxley *Flora S. CA* 179, Black Bush. A diffusely branched somewhat spinescent shrub. 1937 U.S. Forest Serv. *Range Plant Hdbk.* B61, Blackbrush, also called Dixie blackb(r)ush . . . The common name, blackbrush, is appropriate, since this bush, when abundant, lends a dark gray or blackish appearance to the landscape. 1957 *Plateau* (Flagstaff AZ) 30.33 **AZ**, In some of the side canyons . . . will also be found black bush (*Coleogyne ramosissima*). 1968 Abbey *Desert Solitaire* 33 **seUT**, Blackbrush, I observe, the common variety, sprinkled with tightly rolled little green buds, ready to burst into bloom on short notice.

3 =**mountain mahogany.**

1931 U.S. Dept. Ag. *Misc. Pub.* 101.43, Mountain-mahoganies (*Cercocarpus Spp.*) . . . Local names for these shrubs include . . blackbrush . . and tallow bush. 1937 U.S. Forest Serv. *Range Plant Hdbk.* B51, True mountain mahogany . . . bears a number of local names, . . including alder, blackbrush [etc].

4 A chaparro prieto (here: *Acacia rigidula*).

1938 Van Dersal *Native Woody Plants* 37, *Acacia amentacea . . . Blackbrush* . . . A large shrub to small trees, bearing spines. 1954 *True* June 68 **TX**, The Palo Duro is filled with dense cedar brakes, mesquite jungles and blackbrush thickets. 1967 *DARE* (Qu. T5) Inf **TX43**, Blackbrush. 1967 *DARE* Tape **TX29**, Blackbrush.

black buggy See **black wagon**

black-bumper n, also attrib [From the practice of painting car bumpers black; see quot 1967] **chiefly eOH, wPA Cf hook-and-eye Dutch**

A member of an Amish or Mennonite sect which allows the use of cars and other motor-driven vehicles.

1967 *DARE* Tape **PA30**, Then in that group you also have the black-bumper Mennonites . . . The black-bumper is . . an off-fall [=off-shoot] of the original horse-and-wagon Mennonites. . . . They decided that they wished to use machines or automobiles and farm-tractors and more modern equipment of this nature . . . They painted their bumpers black so they could be spotted. If a black-bumper was going to drive to an ungodly place of some sort [like a tavern or movie theater], another member of the church would see him park there. They'd be able to recognize his car. 1968 *DARE* FW Addit **OH81**, [Inf] belongs to conservative Mennonites . . . Knows black-bumper Amish as well as old order.

blackbush See **blackbrush 2**

black butterbill n

=**scoter.**

1888 Trumbull *Names of Birds* 107 **MA**, *Oidemia americana* . . To some at Cohasset, Black Butter-bill. 1917 (1923) *Birds Amer.* 1.148, *Scoter Oidemia americana* . . Black Butter-bill.

black buzzard n

1 =**rough-legged hawk.**

1889 *Century Dict.* 2742, *Black hawk,* the American rough-legged hawk or black buzzard, *Archibuteo lagopus sancti-johannis.*

2 =black vulture.

1917 (1923) *Birds Amer.* 2.57, *Black Vulture . . . Other names.* — Black Buzzard. **1932** Bennitt *Check-list* 21 **MO,** *Black vulture . . .* Black buzzard . . . Southern Missouri. **1962** Imhof *AL Birds* 165, Black Buzzard . . . Except for the *large, white areas* near the *tip of each wing,* this vulture is black, even to the skin on the bare head. **1968–70** *DARE* (Qu. Q13) Inf **GA**18, Black buzzard — same as carrion crow; **MS**87, Black buzzard.

black cahash See **black cohosh**

black cake n Also *black fruitcake*

A kind of fruit cake.

1883 in 1958 Dickinson *Letters* 3.783 **MA,** Black Cake — 2 pounds Flour[ᵢ] 2 Sugar[ᵢ] 2 Butter[ᵢ] 19 Eggs . . Raisins . . Currants . . Citron [etc]. **1885** Hearn *Cuisine* 144 **LA,** Rich Wedding Cake, or Black Cake . . . Flour, . . eggs, . . butter, . . currents [sic], . . raisins, . . citron. **1964** Amer. Heritage *Cookbook* 603, This recipe is of English origin and is known variously as Dark Fruitcake, English Fruitcake, Black Fruitcake, and Merry Christmas Cake. **1969** *DARE* FW Addit **KY**25, Black cake — a fruit cake made around Christmas time by informant's mother. It was made in a wood stove, in a dishpan two feet in diameter and ten inches deep. It was baked slowly, one stick of wood at a time in the stove. It was for guests only and was supposed to last all year.

blackcap n

1 A black raspberry. **chiefly Nth, esp NEast** *somewhat old-fash*

1817 in 1959 *AmSp* 34.27 **NY,** Black Caps. **1895** *DN* 1.399 **cNY. 1932** *DN* 6.283 **CT. 1941** *LANE* Map 276 **throughout NEng,** These terms refer to black (or purple) raspberries only, especially the large cultivated variety . . . Black caps. **1950** *WELS* (*What kinds of berries grow wild in your neighborhood*) 3 Infs, **WI,** Black caps. **1953** Hench *Coll.* **wVA,** We picked a mixture of blackberries, black caps and blueberries. **1965–70** *DARE* (Qu. I44) 43 Infs, Blackcaps. [42 of 43 Infs **Nth;** of all Infs responding to the question, 71% were old; of those giving this response, 81% were old.]

2 A wave resulting from strong wind. [By analogy with *white-cap*]

1968 *DARE* (Qu. O15, . . *Kinds of waves*) Inf **WI**12, Blackcaps — wind stronger than whitecaps.

black-cape sparrow n

Prob Harris's sparrow *(Zonotrichia querula).*

1966 *DARE* (Qu. Q21) Inf **MI**36, Black-cape sparrow.

black-capped night heron See **black-crowned night heron**

black-capped nuthatch n

=white-breasted nuthatch.

1828 Bonaparte in NY Acad. Sci. *Annals Lyceum Nat. Hist.* 2.96, White-breasted black-capped Nuthatch, *Sitta carolinensis,* . . . Inhabits throughout North America. **1967** *DARE* (Qu. Q23) Inf **OH**16, Black-capped nuthatch.

black cat n

1 =fisher 1. NEast

1791 *Mass. Laws* (1801) 1.509 *(DA),* No person . . . shall hereafter, in either of the months of June, July, August or September, . . . kill, any Otter, Beaver, . . . Black-Cat, [etc.]. **1882** *Century Illustr. Mag.* 23.719/2 **ME,** The black cat is the most successful cub slayer. **1930** Shoemaker *1300 Words* 3 **cPA Mts,** *Black cat* — The fisher fox, (Pennant's Marten). **1966** *DARE* Tape **ME**26, Black cat and the fisher, and they're the same animal. **1968** *DARE* (Qu. P32) Inf **NY**71, Black cat — same as fisher. **1968** *DARE* FW Addit **ceNY,** Black cat — alternate name for fisher, a tree-dwelling member of the weasel family.

2 A children's game played with a bat and ball. Cf **cat n 3a**

1968 *DARE* (Qu. EE11, *Bat-and-ball games for just a few players*) Inf **OH**42, Black cat — batter has to make it to first base and back.

black catfish n Also *black cat*

1 =brown bullhead 1.

1805 Harris *Jrl. Alleghany Mts.* 116 **OH,** The *Black Cat-Fish* are caught weighing from six to one hundred and ten pounds. **1842** DeKay *Zool. NY* 4.185, The Black Catfish, *Pimelodus atrarius,* . . occurs commonly in Wappinger's creek. **1905** (1906) NJ State Museum *Annual Rept.* 169, *Ameiurus nebulosus* . . Black Cat Fish. **1946** LaMonte *N. Amer. Game*

Fishes 164, *Ameiurus nebulosus* . . Black Catfish. **1966–70** *DARE* (Qu. P1, . . *Freshwater fish . . good to eat*) Infs **GA**25, **LA**8, **SC**32, **VA**79, Black cat.

2 A black **bullhead 1b.**

1960 Amer. Fisheries Soc. *List Fishes* 53, Black catfish — see bullhead, black *[Ictalurus melas].*

black cat on a line n Var of **dead cat on the line**

1981 *NADS Letters* **Atlanta GA** [Black], "[If] dey promise you somethin' and don't do it — specially if dey promises it sev'ral times and don't do it: dat's de black cat on a line." "You said 'black cat' — I thought it was 'dead cat'." "It don't make no diffunce . . . It's when somebody do somethin' *contrary* to what dey say dey gonna do dat's de cat on a line." "Kinda like 'double-crossing' somebody?" "Yeah — dat's exactly it."

black cats, rain v phr

1969 *DARE* (Qu. B26, *When it's raining very heavily, you say, "It's raining _____.")* Inf **AL**54, Black cats.

black cattle n pl

1899 (1912) Green *VA Folk-Speech,* Black cattle . . . Cattle for slaughter, not work cattle, or for breeding.

black chaparral n [*black* + **chaparral;** see also quot 1953] **chiefly SW**

A chaparro prieto (here: *Acacia rigidula).*

1944 Adams *Western Words* 12, Black chaparral — A very thorny kind of brush peculiar to the Southwest. **1951** *PADS* 15.33 **TX,** *Acacia amentacea* . . . Black chaparral. **1953** *AmSp* 28.100 **SW,** *Black chaparral* . . . *Acacia amentacea* . . . *Black chaparral* might be considered a partial loan-translation of *chaparro prieta,* another name for this plant. **1967** *DARE* (Qu. T5) Inf **TX**22, Black chaparral.

black-cheek n Also *black-jaw*

=Maryland yellowthroat.

1955 *Oriole* 20.12 **GA,** *Black-cheek; Black-jaw* (the male has a black mask-like marking).

black cherry n Also *mountain black cherry, wild black cherry*

A large, wild cherry *(Prunus serotina).* Also called **cabinet cherry, chokecherry, rum cherry, Virginia prune bark, whiskey cherry, wild cherry**

1720 (1882) S. Sewall *Diary* 3.272 **MA,** She gave me a Dram of Black-Cherry Brandy, and gave me a lump of the Sugar that was in it. **1784** in 1785 Amer. Acad. Arts & Sci. *Memoirs* 1.449 **PA,** *Prunus* . . . The *Small Black Cherry.* The tree is small and shrubby. **1844** *Knickerbocker* 23.442 **NY,** The canal . . leads to the old mills down to the right yonder, where you see that grove of black-cherry trees. **1905** U.S. Forest Serv. *Bulletin* 60.20 **wNC,** About fifteen years ago some fine black cherry was lumbered on . . Grandfather Mountain. **1965–70** *DARE* (Qu. I44) Infs **MA**58, **NC**76, Black cherries; (Qu. I46) 28 Infs, **chiefly Atl,** Black cherries; **NJ**16, **NY**79, Wild black cherries; **AR**39, Black cherry; (Qu. I53) Infs **IL**31, **MN**42, **OH**35, **PA**18, Black cherries; (Qu. T16) 8 Infs, **chiefly NEast,** Black cherry tree; **PA**188, **VA**47, Black cherry; **PA**231, Wild black cherry. **1979** Little *Checklist U.S. Trees* 215, *Prunus serotina* . . . *Other common names* — wild black cherry, . . mountain black cherry.

black Christmas n [By analogy with *white Christmas*]

A snowless period in late December.

1938 Stuart *Dark Hills* 337 **KY,** It was a black Christmas last year. It takes a white Christmas for a good crop year. **1950** *WELS* (*Sayings about the weather in connection with holidays*) 3 Infs, **WI,** Black Christmas. **1968** *DARE* Tape **AK**6, Sometimes we have a black Christmas — we don't have snow.

black cloud See **cloud** n¹

blackcoat n, also attrib

A man that is not wearing a mask at a costume ball.

1916 *DN* 4.268 **New Orleans LA,** Blackcoats . . . At a carnival ball, the men who are not masked. "It's time they let the blackcoats dance." **1934** Carmer *Stars Fell on AL* 238, The younger men and the male visitors in town importantly make engagements for the "black-coat" dances that the maskers unselfishly allow them [at the Strikers' Ball on New Year's Eve in Mobile, Alabama].

black cod n

=sablefish.

1887 Goode *Amer. Fishes* 271, The Beshow, *Anoplopoma fimbria,* . . is the "Black-cod." **1968** *DARE* (Qu. P1, . . *Freshwater fish . . good to eat*) Inf **AK1**, Black cod.

black cohosh n Also *black cahash* Cf **cohosh**

1 =**bugbane 1**, esp *Cimicifuga racemosa.*

1828 Rafinesque *Med. Flora* 85, *Botrophis serpentaria . . . Vulgar Names*—Squaw root, . . Black Cohosh &c. **1830** *Huntington* (Penna.) *Courier* 15 Sep 4/5 (*DA*), American Remedies Wanted . . Rattle Weed or Black Cahash. **1859** (1968) Bartlett *Americanisms* 91, *Cohosh,* sometimes called Black Cohosh or Black Snake-root (*Cimicifuga racemosa*), a well-known medicinal plant. **1910** Graves *Flowering Plants* 192 **CT. 1964** Campbell *Great Smoky Wildflowers* 62, *Black Cohosh . . . Cimicifuga americana.* **1976** Bruce *How to Grow Wildflowers* 167, Bugbane . . . Other names for this plant are Black Cohosh and Black Snakeroot.

2 =**baneberry 1.**

1896 *Jrl. Amer. Folkl.* 9.179, *Actaea spicata . .* var. *rubra . .* black cohosh, Paris, M[aine]. **1936** Winter *Plants NE* 52, *Actaea* L. Baneberry. Black Cohosh. **1974** (1977) Coon *Useful Plants* 219, *Actaea* (various species)—Baneberry, black cohosh . . . All with pretty berries which are highly poisonous.

black coot n Also *black sea coot, black coot butterbill* =**scoter.**

1888 Trumbull *Names of Birds* 107, *Oidemia americana . .* In Massachusetts at Salem and Cohasset, at Stonington, Conn., and on Long Island at Shinnecock Bay and Bellport, *Black Coot.* **1917** (1923) *Birds Amer.* 1.148, *Scoter Oidemia americana . .* Black Coot; Black Sea Coot. **1925** (1928) Forbush *Birds MA* 271, *Oidemia americana . .* Black Coot Butterbill. **1968** *DARE* (Qu. Q9) Inf **MD45**, Black coot.

black crane n

1970 *DARE* (Qu. Q10) Inf **VA47**, Black crane . . probably the black-crowned night heron.

black crappie See **crappie**

black-crested night heron See **black-crowned night heron**

black croaker n

Either of two Pacific **croakers 1a(2)**: esp the **red roncador 1** but also the **roncador.**

1898 U.S. Natl. Museum *Bulletin* 47.1456, *Sciæna saturna . . . Red Roncador; Black Croaker.* **1946** LaMonte *N. Amer. Game Fishes* 82, *Black Croaker . . . Sciaena saturna . . . Spotfin Croaker . . . Names: . .* Black Croaker. **1960** Amer. Fisheries Soc. *List Fishes* 31, Black Croaker . . *Cleilotrema saturnum.*

black-crowned night heron n Also *black-capped ~, black-crested ~*

A North American **night heron** (*Nycticorax nycticorax*). Also called **barking bird, bittrun, bumcutter, buttermunk, fox bird, frog catcher, gobly-gossit, grosbec, Indian hen, Indian pullet, little crane, marsh hen, meadow hen, night bird, night crane, nighthawk, night hen, night heron, night raven, night skoggins, plunket, quack, quark, quaw bird, quawk, red-eye, shitepoke, squalker, squaw bird, squawk, wagin**

1844 DeKay *Zool. NY* 2.227, The *Black-crowned Night Heron,* or *Quawk, . .* derives its popular name from the deep guttural cry. **1965**–**70** *DARE* (Qu. Q3) Inf **ME8**, Black-crested night heron; **CT5**, Black-crowned night heron; (Qu. Q8) Inf **CA140**, Black-crowned night heron; (Qu. Q10) Infs **GA25, IA3, MA78**, Black-crown(ed) (night) heron; **CO7, GA35**, Black-capped night heron.

black curlew n prob chiefly Sth

Either the **glossy ibis 1** or the **white-faced ibis.**

1917 (1923) *Birds Amer.* 1.177, *Glossy Ibis—Plegadis autumnalis . .* Other Names . . . Black Curlew. **1928** Bailey *Birds NM* 101, At a distance they [=the white-faced glossy ibis] looked black enough to justify their common local name Black Curlew. **1932** Howell *FL Bird Life* 115, Eastern Glossy Ibis: *Plegadis falcinellus . .* Other Name: Black Curlew. *Ibid* 117, White-faced Glossy Ibis: *Plegadis guarauna . .* Other Name: Black Curlew. **1951** Teale *North Spring* 34 **FL**, To natives of the region the glossy ibis, with its dark plumage and downcurving bill, is the "black curlew." **1954** Sprunt *FL Bird Life* 43, *Eastern Glossy Ibis: Plegadis falcinellus . .* Local Names: Black Curlew. **1962** Imhof *AL Birds* 105, *White-faced Ibis—Plegadis chihi . .* Other Names: Black Curlew.

black dark n prob Sth, S Midl̲ Cf **black night, full dark**

Nighttime at its darkest.

1939 Hall *Coll.* eTN, wNC, *Black dark . . .* "When it's so dark you can't see nothin'." . . The informant contrasted "black dark" with "dusky-dark." **1942** Hurston *Dust Tracks* 32 **FL**, About an hour later . . it was almost black dark. **1967** *DARE* FW Addit **LA7**, Black dark—completely dark, in the evening. "He wants us to stay around here till it's black dark."

black darter See **darter**

black diamond n

1 freq pl: Coal. **chiefly in coal mining areas**

1916 *DN* 4.320 **KS, NE, PA**, *Black diamonds . . .* Coal. **1926** *AmSp* 1.265 [Railroad jargon], The diamond thrower was cracking the black diamonds. **1929** *AmSp* 4.368 swPA. **1943** *AmSp* 18.162 [Railroad terms], *Black diamonds.* Company coal. **1970** *DARE* (Qu. C26, . . *Kinds of stone or rock . . in this part of the state*) Inf **PA245**, Black diamond—coal.

2 pl: Dense black hematite.

1959 Hart *McKay's AK* 29, *Black diamonds:* Local iron ore which is brilliant jet when cut and polished, and is popularly used as settings for rings, bracelets, and other types of jewelry.

3 See quots.

1926 *AmSp* 1.660, Paul sent me after two wagon loads of pole holes and strung the wires to forty miles of Western Union "Black Diamonds" (poles dipped in creosote). **1968** Adams *Western Words, Black diamonds*—A logger's term for poles dipped in creosote.

black-diamond rattler n Also *black diamond* [From the dorsal markings] =**diamondback rattlesnake.**

1967–**70** *DARE* (Qu. P25) Infs **CA191, LA8, TX74, WV3**, Black-diamond rattler; **CA7**, Black-diamond.

black diphtheria n [From the association of "black" with death] **chiefly Nth** *old-fash*

An extreme form of diphtheria.

1943 *LANE* Map 508 swNH, *Diphtheria, white ~,* a mild form of the disease; *black ~,* fatal. **1967**–**69** *DARE* (Qu. BB49, . . *Kinds of diseases*) Inf **MI105**, FW: Inf recalls years ago the "black diphtheria," when victims were buried at night; **MN10, NY8**, Black diphtheria—old-fash. [All Infs old]

black dish n

1914 *DN* 4.103 **KS**, *Black dishes . . .* Cooking utensils,—by contrast with glass and china. "I will leave the black dishes for her to clean up."

black-dogged ppl adj [*black* + **dog** v] *euphem*

Damned, darned.

1943 Hench *Coll.* **VA**, I'll be black-dogged if I'll keep on doing for some people what I've been doing.

black dolphin n ?*obs*

=**bean aphid** (here: *Aphis fabae; A. rumicis*).

1849 U.S. Patent Office *Annual Rept.: Ag.* 339, Another species, which, from their sooty color, are called the . . black dolphins, or colliers.

black draught See **black bottle**

‡**black drops, the** n [*drop* in ref to falling]

A state of mild physical discomfort.

1966 *DARE* (Qu. BB39, *On a day when you don't feel just right, though not actually sick you might say*) Inf **FL10**, I have the black drops [laughter].

black drum n **chiefly C and S Atl**

A saltwater **drum** (here: *Pogonias cromis*).

1709 (1967) Lawson *New Voyage* 159 **NC**, Black Drums are . . shap'd like a fat pig; they are . . not so common with us as to the Northward. **1887** Goode *Amer. Fishes* 137, The adult is known as the 'Black Drum,' the young as the 'Striped Drum.' **1968** *Atlantic Co. Rec.* (Mays Landing NJ) 25 July 2/2, A 109-lb. black drum, 10½ pounds above the recognized world all-tackle record for this species, was reported caught in mid-June off Highland Beach in Delaware Bay. **1968**–**70** *DARE* (Qu. P2, . . *Salt-water fish . . good to eat*) Infs **MD36, SC63, VA41**, Black drum; (Qu. P4) **FL13**, Black drum. **1969** *DARE* FW Addit **NC**, Black drum—a fish.

black duck n

1 Any of var ducks dark in color as the **Florida duck**, the **mallard**

1, the **ring-necked duck,** or the **scoters** but esp *Anas rubripes.* chiefly **NEast, Mid and C Atl** See Map *A. rubripes* is also called **black, black English duck, blackie, blackjack, black mallard, brown duck, brown mallard, clam duck, dusky duck, dusky mallard, English duck, Labrador duck, mallard, marsh duck, nigger duck, October duck, puddle duck, puttylegs, red-legged black duck, redleg, red paddle, spring black duck, summer black duck, summer duck, velvet duck, winter black duck, winter duck**

    1637 (1972) Morton *New Engl. Canaan* 68, Ducks there are of three kindes, pide Ducks, gray Ducks, and black Ducks in great abundance. **1844** DeKay *Zool. NY* 2.344, The *Black Duck [Anas rubripes],* as it is universally called except in the books, is very abundant in this State. **1888** Trumbull *Names of Birds* 17, *Anas obscura . . .* Very generally known in New England and Middle States as *Black Duck. Ibid* 98, *White-winged Scoter . . .* In the neighborhood of Niagara Falls *Black Duck. Ibid* 103, *Surf Scoter: Surf Duck: Black Duck.* **1917** *Wilson Bulletin* 29.2.77, *Anas platyrhynchos.* — Black duck, Cape Hatteras, N.C. **1923** U.S. Dept. Ag. *Misc. Circular* 13.8, *Mallard . . . Vernacular Names . . . In local use.* — Black duck (N.C.). *Ibid* 9, *Black Duck (Anas rubripes). Ibid* 10, *Southern Black Duck (Anas fulvigula). Ibid* 21, *Ring-necked Duck . . . Vernacular Names . . . In local use . . .* Black duck (Minn., Wis., Ala., Miss., La., Tex., Oreg.). *Ibid* 27, *Scoters . . . Collective Vernacular Names . . . In local use . . .* Black ducks (Alaska). *Ibid* 29, *White-winged Scoter . . . Vernacular Names . . . In local use . . .* Black duck (N.Y.). *Ibid* 30, *Surf Scoter . . . Vernacular Names . . . In local use . . .* Black Duck. **1946** Hausman *Eastern Birds* 167, American Scoter [has] . . some twenty-five or thirty local names, among which are: Black Scoter, Black Sea Duck, Black Coot, Black Duck. **c1960** *Wilson Coll.* **csKY,** Black duck — One of the species known to most natives. **1965–70** *DARE* (Qu. Q5) 112 Infs, **chiefly NEast, Mid and C Atl,** Black duck.

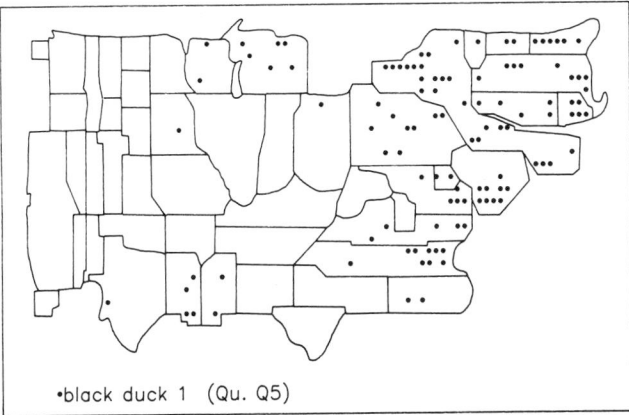

•black duck 1 (Qu. Q5)

2 An Indian. *obs*
    1768 Hutchinson *Hist. MA Bay* 2.295, From this or a like action, probably took rise a common expression among English soldiers and sometimes English hunters who, when they have killed an Indian, make their boast of having killed a black duck. **1889** Nelson *50 Yrs.* 336 **West,** We selected a high hill, and . . I laid on the ground with my glass, watching for "black ducks."

black duster n
=**black blizzard.**
    1962 Atwood *Vocab. TX* 77, *Black duster.* A heavy sandstorm. Recorded in the Panhandle.

black Dutch n Also *black Dutchman* **esp common Sth, S Midl**
A dark-complexioned people of uncertain origin: see quots.
    1854 (1932) Bell *Log TX–CA Trail* 35.224, Along down the center of my breast is a brown stripe like the stripe on a black Duchmans [sic] back. **1867** Crawford *Mosby* 115 **VA,** Mosby moved us some three miles . . with the view of surprising a camp of black Dutch cavalry. **1920** Hunter *Trail Drivers TX* 41, We passed some two or three times a big black Dutchman rolling a wheelbarrow. **1930** Shoemaker *1300 Words* 8 **cPA Mts** (as of c1900), *Black Dutch* — Dark Pennsylvania Mountain people, probably near Eastern or aboriginal stock. **1939** *Hall Coll.* **eTN, wNC,** *Black Dutch . . .* A local type of people of Germanic (?) extraction. The Foxes are known as "black Dutch. Pennsylvania is as far back as we can trace them. They are low, not tall, small and have black features." **1960** Hall *Smoky Mt. Folks* 27 **TN,** "One of my

grandpaws was part Black Dutch and part Irish." . . Just who the Black Dutch were originally seems to be a mystery, though the term is well-known in the mountains. **1965–69** *DARE* (Qu. HH28, *Names and nicknames around here for people of foreign background . . . Hollanders*) Infs **IN10, OK6, VA11, 29,** Black Dutch; **NC55,** Black Dutch — dark skinned, long hair, from England; (Qu. HH29a, *Names around here for people of mixed blood — part Indian*) Inf **GA77,** Black Dutchman [FW: Inf is not able to explain the term].

black eagle n

1 =**golden eagle.** [From the color of the immature plumage]
    1693 Royal Soc. London *Philos. Trans.* 17.989, The Third is the Black Eagle, resembling most the *English* Eagle; they build their Nests . . generally at the top of some tall old Tree. **1917** (1923) *Birds Amer.* 2.82, *Golden eagle — Aquila chrysaëtos . . Other Names . . .* Black Eagle.

2 =**bald eagle 1.**
    1888 (1890) Warren *Birds PA* 135, The "Black," "Gray" and "Washington" Eagles are all young of the Bald Eagle. **1955** *MA Audubon* 39.442, *Bald Eagle . .* Black Eagle (Maine. For birds in immature plumage . .).

3 =**rough-legged hawk.** [From the size and color]
    1968 *DARE* (Qu. Q4) Inf **WI43,** Black hawk — big, some call black eagles.

black-eared bream n

1 =**bluegill 1.**
    1935 Caine *Game Fish* 11, *Bluegill — Lepomis pallidus . . . Synonyms: . .* Black-eared Bream. *Ibid* 26, *Redbreasted sunfish — Lepomis auritus . . . Synonyms: . .* Black-eared Bream.

2 also *black-eared pondfish:* =**red-breasted sunfish.**
    1935 [see **1** above]. **1946** LaMonte *N. Amer. Game Fishes* 139, *Lepomis auritus . . . Names: . .* Black-eared Pondfish.

blackears n
=**longear sunfish.**
    1820 *Western Rev.* 2.49, Big-ear Sunfish, *Icthelis megalotis, . .* a fine species, called . . Black-ears. **1946** LaMonte *N. Amer. Game Fishes* 139, *Lepomis megalotis . . Names: . .* Blackears.

blacked road See **black road**

black English duck n Cf **English duck**
A **black duck** (here: *Anas rubripes*).
    1888 Trumbull *Names of Birds* 17, *Black Duck . . .* We hear . . reaching South Carolina or Georgia, *Black English Duck,* the . . title continuing into Florida. **1932** Howell *FL Bird Life* 131, *Red-legged Black Duck . . . Other Names: . .* Black English Duck.

blackeye See **black-eyed pea**

black-eyed bean n Also *blackeye bean* **chiefly Nth, Midl** See Map
=**black-eyed pea.**
    1868 (1870) Gray *Field Botany* 109, *Black-eyed Bean.* [*Vigna sinensis*]. **1965–70** *DARE* (Qu. I19) 135 Infs, **chiefly Nth, Midl,** Black-eyed beans; **CA77, MO10, NJ5, NY87, 200, OR3,** Blackeye beans.

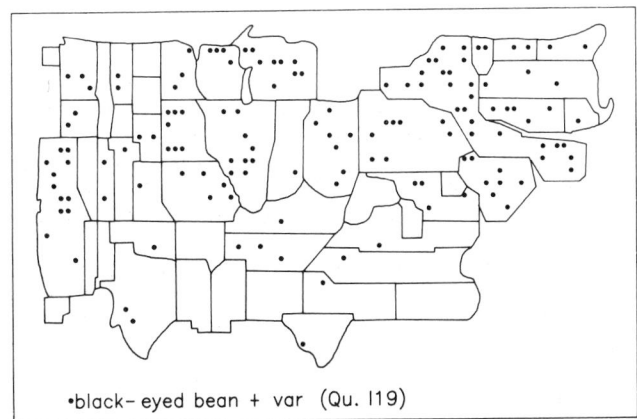

•black-eyed bean + var (Qu. I19)

black-eyed clockvine See **black-eyed Susan 1**

black-eyed cowpea See **cowpea**

black-eyed daisy n
=black-eyed Susan 2.
  1920 *Torreya* 20.25, *Rudbeckia hirta* L.—Black-eyed daisy, Baltimore, Md. **1965–70** *DARE* (Qu. S7, *A kind of daisy, bright yellow with a dark center, that grows along roadsides in late summer*) Infs **KY**28, 35, **LA**43, **NY**60, **SC**4, Black-eyed daisy.

black-eyed flirt n
=black-eyed Susan 2.
  1921 *DN* 5.113 **CA**, *Blackeyed flirt* . . . Brown-eyed Susan.

black-eyed mollie n
=black-eyed pea.
  1968 *DARE* (Qu. I19) Inf **DE**3, Black-eyed mollies.

black-eyed owl n
A barred owl.
  1927 Forbush *Birds MA* 2.202, *Barred Owl.* Other names: . . *Black-eyed Owl* . . . Iris brownish-black or bluish-black, always nearly black. **1955** Forbush–May *Birds* 272.

black-eyed pea n Also *blackeye (pea)*, rarely *black pea* [From the black hilum] widespread, but esp freq in Sth, Midl
A frequently cultivated white bean of the genus *Vigna*, esp *V. sinensis.* Also called black bean, black-eyed bean, black-eyed Susan, blue-eyed bean, bung belly, chain-gang pea, China bean, cow bean, cowpea, cream pea, crowder
  1728 (1841) Byrd *Westover Mss.* 27, Each cell [of a N.C. pine cone] contains a seed of the size and figure of a black-eye pea. **1855** Davis *Farm Bk.* 183 **AL** *(DA)*, We thrashed 24 Bushels black peas. **1856** *TX Almanac for 1857* 13, Plant Black-Eyed . . Peas. **1895** Gray–Bailey *Field Botany* 135, *V[igna] Sinensis* . . Black Pea. **1965–70** *DARE* (Qu. I19) 594 Infs, **esp common Sth, Midl**, Black-eyed peas; 31 Infs, **chiefly Sth**, Blackeye peas; 14 Infs, **scattered**, Blackeye(s); (Qu. I20) Infs **CA**36, **MD**14, Black-eyed peas; **NC**81, Blackeye peas; **GA**17, Blackeye; **NC**15, 81, **TN**52, Black peas. **1970** Correll *Plants TX* 889, *Vigna unguiculata* . . Black-eyed pea. **1972** Hilliard *Hog Meat* 275, There were several varieties of peas grown in the southeastern states. Known locally by such names as "crowders," or "blackeyes," they were much more commonly grown than green peas or any of the beans. The species was *Vigna sinensis.*

black-eyed Sue See black-eyed Susan 2, 4

black-eyed Susan n Cf purple black-eyed Susan
1 also *black-eyed Susan vine, black-eyed clockvine:* A twining ornamental plant *(Thunbergia alata)* with dark-centered flowers. Also called **bright eyes 3**
  1891 *Century Dict.* 22.6320/1, *Thunbergia* . . . the hardy annual *T. alata,* known locally by the name *black-eyed-Susan* from its buff, orange, or white flowers with a purplish-black center. **1933** Small *Manual SE Flora* 1226, *T. alata* . . . *Black-eyed Susan* . . . Prairies, roadsides, and wasteplaces, Fla. **1949** Moldenke *Amer. Wild Flowers* 287, The *black-eyed clockvine* or *black-eyed-susan, Thunbergia alata,* is an immigrant from Africa. It has . . trumpet-shaped flowers with a conspicuous deep purple "eye." **1976** Bailey–Bailey *Hortus Third* 1232, Popular ornamentals . . in the southern U.S. for covering porches, trellises, and arbors . . . *Black-eyed Susan Vine.*
2 also *blackeye Susan, black-eyed Sue, ~ Susanna:* A coneflower 1, esp *Rudbeckia hirta.* Also called **black-eyed daisy, black-eyed flirt, black-eyed Susie, black Susie, brown betty 2, brown daisy, brown-eyed daisy, brown-eyed Susan 1, brown Susan, bull's-eye daisy 1, button daisy, chiggerweed 3, coneflower 1, cow daisy, daisy, dark-eyed daisy, lane daisy, lazy daisy, lazy Susan, nigger daisy, niggerhead, nigger hill, nigger navel, niggernose, nigger tits, niggertoe, oxeye, oxeyed daisy, oxeyed Susan, sheepnose, suwanee daisy, wild-eyed Susan, yellow daisy, yellow Susan.** For other names of *R. hirta* see **bull daisy 1, English bullseye, golden Jerusalem, meadow coneflower, poor man's daisy, Susan, yellow oxeye daisy.** For other names of var spp see **blackhead 6, darkey head, deer-eye daisy, goldenglow, green-headed coneflower, nigger thumb, prairie coneflower, sweet coneflower, thimble flower, thimbleweed**
  1892 *Jrl. Amer. Folkl.* 5.98, *Rudbeckia hirta,* . . black-eyed Susans. N. V[ermon]t; Cape Cod. **1896** *Ibid* 9.193, *Rudbeckia hirta,* . . black-eyed Susan, Sulphur Grove, Ohio. **1907** *DN* 3.181 **seNH**, *Black-eyed*

Susan . . . Daisy with dark brown centre and orange-colored rays. **1965–70** *DARE* (Qu. S7) 590 Infs, **widespread**, Black-eyed Susan; 10 Infs, **scattered**, Blackeye Susan; **MI**53, Black-eyed Sue; **NC**44, Black-eyed Susanna; (Qu. S26a) Infs **CT**15, **IL**26, **NY**67, **NC**52, **TX**59, Black-eyed Susan; (Qu. S26c) Inf **FL**1, Black-eyed Susans; (Qu. S26d) Infs **CT**9, **KY**49, **MI**80, Black-eyed Susans.
3 =flower-of-an-hour.
  1892 *Jrl. Amer. Folkl.* 5.93, *Hibiscus trionum,* black-eyed Susan. N[ew] H[ampshire]. **1949** Moldenke *Amer. Wild Flowers* 111, The dark-centered blossoms have inspired the name *black-eyed susan.* **1959** Carleton *Index Herb. Plants* 13, *Black Eyed Susan: Hibiscus trionum.*
4 also *black-eyed Sue, ~ Susie:* =black-eyed pea.
  1965–70 *DARE* (Qu. I19) 16 Infs, **scattered**, Black-eyed Susans; **NJ**53, Black-eyed Sues; **IL**41, **KY**44, **PA**159, Black-eyed Susies.
5 =Johnny-jump-up.
  1966–69 *DARE* (Qu. S3, *A flower like a large violet with a yellow center and small ragged leaves*) Infs **AL**2, **GA**25, **IN**62, Black-eyed Susan.
6 See quot.
  1968–69 *DARE* (Qu. P6, . . *Worms* . . *used for bait*) Infs **IL**32, Black-eyed Susan—half inch wide and as long as an old-fashioned match—golden beige color; **WI**38, Black-eyed Susans.

black-eyed Susanna See black-eyed Susan 2

black-eyed Susan vine See black-eyed Susan 1

black-eyed Susie n chiefly Sth, S Midl
1 also *blackeye Susie:* =black-eyed Susan 2.
  1965–70 *DARE* (Qu. S7) 21 Infs, **chiefly Sth, S Midl**, Black-eyed Susie; **FL**48, **MD**20, **OH**69, **SC**10, 67, Black-eye Susie; (Qu. S21) Inf **IN**26, Black-eyed Susie; (Qu. S26a) Infs **SC**7, **VA**43, Black-eyed Susies.
2 See black-eyed Susan 4.

black-eye gravy n Cf brown-eye gravy, frog-eye gravy, red-eye gravy
See quot 1966.
  1966 *DARE* FW Addit **SC**, Black-eye gravy—a ham or cured ham gravy used on grits, rice, etc. **1966–67** *DARE* (Qu. H37) Infs **NC**41, **SC**3, Black-eye gravy.

blackeye pea See black-eyed pea

blackeye sunfish n Also *blackeyes*
=green sunfish.
  1819 *Western Rev.* 1.376, Blackeye Sunfish, *Icthelis melanops.* Vulgar names, blue-fish, black-eyes. **1946** LaMonte *N. Amer. Game Fishes* 138, *Green Sunfish—Lepomis cyanellus* . . . Names: . . Blackeye Sunfish.

black fay n [*black + fay*]
A Black who is deferential or subservient toward Whites.
  1964 *PADS* 42.29 **Chicago IL** [Black], Most of the terms collected exclusively from Negro informants are rare within the Caucasian social dialects of Chicago, e.g., . . *black fay.* *Ibid* 44, *Black fay* is applied to the modern counterparts of Uncle Tom.

blackfin cisco n Also *blackfin*
A herring-like foodfish found esp in the Great Lakes. Also called **bluefin**
  1875 *Amer. Naturalist* 9.135, This Indiana *Argyrosomus* appears to be quite distinct from the species found in Lake Michigan; i.e., the shallow-water 'herring' . . and 'black fin' (*A. nigripennis*). **1960** Amer. Fisheries Soc. *List Fishes* 11, Blackfin cisco . . *Coregonus nigripinnis.* **1976** *DARE* File **Isle Royale MI**, Some fishermen called deep-water bluefin "blackfin."

blackfish n
1 also *smooth blackfish:* =tautog. chiefly N and C Atl
  1765 Rogers *N. Amer.* 68, In the sea adjacent to this island [=Long Island, N.Y.] are sea-bass and black-fish in great plenty. **1842** DeKay *Zool. NY* 4.176, The Common Black-fish, or *Tautog,* . . is a well known and savory fish, affording equal pleasure to the angler and the epicure. **1887** Goode *Amer. Fishes* 288, On the coast of New York it [*Tautoga onitis*] is usually called "Black-fish"; in New Jersey also "Black-fish" and "Smooth Black-fish." **1905** *DN* 3.3 **ceCT**, *Blackfish* . . . Tautaug. **1931–33** *LANE Worksheets* **cCT**. **1939** Natl. Geog. Soc. *Fishes* 66, The tautog has several names . . . In New York and New Jersey it is known as the blackfish. In Chesapeake Bay it occasionally is called blackfish. **1947** *Hunting & Fishing* Feb 32/2 *(DA)*, Blackfish (Tautog): from May to

November you will find them on their runs in the salty waters, and it is said that around "apple blossom" time is one of the best early runs. **1949** *Richmond (VA) Times-Disp.* 30 Aug 20/1 *(Hench Coll.),* A fish which is abundant in the [Chesapeake] Bay, especially in the Fall, and which is sometimes neglected by the fisherman, is the blackfish or tautog. **1968–70** *DARE* (Qu. P2) Infs **CT**13, 14, 17, 31, 42, **NY**47, 66, 236, Blackfish; **RI**4, Tautog or blackfish; **RI**17, Tautog = blackfish; (Qu. P4) Inf **MA**40, Blackfish. **1975** Evanoff *Catch More Fish* 105, Another popular bottom fish . . is the blackfish or tautog. They are most plentiful from Massachusetts to Virginia.

2 =black sea bass. **chiefly Mid and C Atl**

   1882 U.S. Natl. Museum *Bulletin* 16.533, *S[erranus] atrarius . . Black Fish; Black Sea Bass.* **1887** Goode *Amer. Fishes* 39, The Sea Bass is also known south of Cape Hatteras as the "Blackfish." **1896** U.S. Natl. Museum *Bulletin* 47.1199, *Centropristes striatus* . . Blackfish. **1906** NJ State Museum *Annual Rept. for 1905* 308, *Centropristes striatus* . . Black Fish. **1939** Natl. Geog. Soc. *Fishes* 84, The common sea bass, which is . . known . . almost always as blackfish in the southern states, ranges from Massachusetts to the Atlantic coast of Florida. **1966–70** *DARE* (Qu. P2) Infs **NC**12, Blackfish or black bass; **SC**4, 21, 63, 66, 69, Blackfish. **1970** *DARE* Tape **VA**112. **1976** Warner *Beautiful Swimmers* 134 **Chesapeake Bay,** He diversifies, making strong rectangular pots for the ocean capture of "blackfish" or sea bass, as practiced in the Carolinas.

3 The Alaska blackfish *(Dallia pectoralis).*

   1870 Dall *Alaska* 579, Blackfish. **1933** John G. Shedd Aquarium *Guide* 56, *Dallia pectoralis* . . The Blackfish is the sole representative of its family. **1981** Tabbert *Alaskan Engl.* 321, *Blackfish—(Dallia pectoralis).*

4 =cobia.

   1966–70 *DARE* (Qu. P14) Inf **NC**27, Covia ['koʊvijə] or blackfish—no commercial market now.

5 =bowfin.

   1949 Caine *N. Amer. Sport Fish* 132, Mudfish . . . *Colloquial Names.* Blackfish, Bowfin. **1965–68** *DARE* (Qu. P1, . . *Freshwater fish . . good to eat)* Inf **GA**19, Blackfish; **GA**34, Blackfish—we call 'em mudfish; **NC**24, **SC**26, Blackfish; (Qu. P3, . . *Freshwater fish . . not good to eat)* Infs **AL**17, **FL**18, **GA**65, **NC**15, 49, Blackfish.

black flounder See **blackback flounder**

black fly n **chiefly NEast**

An insect of the family Simuliidae. Also called **black gnat, buffalo gnat, midge, stinging gnat, turkey gnat**

   1776 in 1932 *MD Hist. Mag.* 27.258, Bit very much with black flies, face in lumps. **1875** *Fur, Fin & Feather* Sept 139 *(OEDS),* At Calais, Maine, last fall rugged grouse were thick as black flies in August. **1937** *Torreya* 37.79 **NY,** We recommend . . an ample supply of "fly dope," to keep off black flies . . and mosquitoes. **1946** *Outdoors* June 23/2 *(DA),* There is no place under God's heavens where the black flies are so numerous and so enthusiastic, and so hungry, as round-about a beaver bog. **1965–70** *DARE* (Qu. R10) 8 Infs, **chiefly NEast,** Black fly; (Qu. R11) 32 Infs, **chiefly NEast,** Black fly (*or* flies); (Qu. R12) 20 Infs, **chiefly NEast,** Black fly; (Qu. R13) 15 Infs, **east of Missip R,** Black fly; (Qu. R21) Infs **NY**30, 92, 97, Black fly. **1966** *DARE* Tape **FL**32, These little old black flies, . . they get 'em [cattle] by the millions and they'll sting 'em day and night.

black French See **frenching**

black Friday n

Good Friday.

   1967 Schilla *Prairies* 105 **ND,** Two church holidays stand out . . . These were Good Friday, or Black Friday—"Karf[r]eitag," in German—and Ascension Day.

black frost n [*black* ref to the absence of snow or frost (Cf **black Christmas**); see quot 1890]

1 A frost or cold that kills vegetation and is usu unaccompanied by hoarfrost. **chiefly NEast, Gt Lakes, C and S Atl, CA** See Map *somewhat old-fash*

   1709 (1967) Lawson *New Voyage* 159 **NC,** The Blue-Fish . . come (in the Fall of the Year) generally after there has been one black Frost. **1792** Imlay *Western Terr.* 467 **NY,** The severe weather generally sets in about the beginning of December, with sharp cold, black frosts, and falls of snow. **1842** *S. Lit. Messenger* 8.467/1 **nTX,** The weather was very cold, and we had generally black frosts. **1890** *DN* 1.69 **LA,** *Black frost:* a

"freeze." Popularly supposed to be so called because the wilted vegetation turns black. A friend suggests that a black frost is so called because of the absence of any white frost (rime). **1939** *LANE* Map 98 **throughout NEng,** *Black frost* is sometimes defined as less severe than a freeze . . , sometimes as the same thing. **1940** Richter *Trees* 122 **OH,** It had black frost early in October that the axe couldn't chop the ground. **1965–70** *DARE* (Qu. B30, *A frost that kills plants)* 98 Infs, **chiefly NEast, Gt Lakes, C and S Atl, CA,** Black frost. [Of all Infs responding to the question, 71% were old; of those giving this response, 83% were old.]

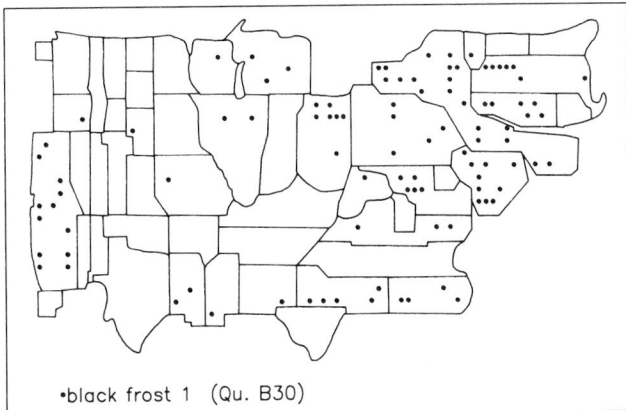

•black frost 1 (Qu. B30)

2 By ext: freezing weather not cold enough to kill vegetation. **chiefly Sth**

   1965–70 *DARE* (Qu. B29, *A frost that does not kill plants)* 10 Infs, Black frost. [9 of 10 Infs from comm types 4 and 5; 4 of 10 Infs Black]

black fruitcake See **black cake**

black gnat n Also *black stinging gnat*

Either the **punkie** or the **black fly.**

   c**1960** *Wilson Coll.* **csKY,** Black gnats—very small, vicious gnats, no-see-ums. **1965–70** *DARE* (Qu. R11) 81 Infs, **scattered,** Black gnat; **CA**105, Black stinging gnat; (Qu. R10) Infs **MI**37, **NY**28, **TN**26, Black gnat.

black goose n

Perh the American **brant** *(Branta bernicla),* but cf **niggergoose.**

   1967–69 *DARE* (Qu. Q6, . . *Wild geese)* Infs **IL**6, **MD**45, **TX**62, Black geese; (Qu. Q10, . . *Water birds and marsh birds)* Inf **VA**79, Black geese.

black grama n

1 A **grama grass:** usu *Bouteloua eriopoda* or *B. hirsuta,* but also *B. gracilis.*

   1886 Havard *Flora W. & S. TX for 1885* 528, Black Grama *(B. hirsuta);* hardly distinguishable from the last in appearance, and equally good. **1889** Vasey *Ag. Grasses* Pl.62, *Bouteloua oligostachya,* Gramma [sic] grass. Black gramma [sic]. **1894** *Jrl. Amer. Folkl.* 7.104, *Bouteloua hirsuta* . . . Black grama grass. Neb. **1912** Wooton *Grasses NM* 100, In southeastern New Mexico "Black Grama" is *Bouteloua hirsuta. Ibid* 101, In south central and southwestern New Mexico *Bouteloua eriopoda* . . is known as Black Grama. **1933** Small *Manual SE Flora* 117, *B. hirsuta* . . . *Black-grama.* **1960** Correll *Plants TX* 247, *Black grama* . . . Second glume . . often a dark-dull-purple. **1970** in 1983 *Carleton Coll.,* Black grama—*Bouteloua eriopoda.* SW USA.

2 A **galleta grass** (here: *Hilaria jamesii).*

   1906 Rydberg *Flora CO* 20, Black Grama . . . *Hilaria Jamesii* . . . Hillsides and gulches of the mesas. **1912** Wooton *Grasses NM* 100, In several of the earlier bulletins relating to the Western range grasses, *Hilaria jamesii* is referred to as "Black Grama." **1937** U.S. Forest Serv. *Range Plant Hdbk.* G70, Galleta, sometimes . . referred to . . as black grama, is an erect perennial.

3 A **muhly grass** (here: *Muhlenbergia porteri).*

   1912 Wooton *Grasses NM* 100, In a recent bulletin on The Grazing Ranges of Arizona Professor Thornber refers to *Muhlenbergia porteri* as "Black Grama." **1937** U.S. Forest Serv. *Range Plant Hdbk.* G82, Bush muhly . . . is frequently called black grama in grazing literature, although it is neither a grama nor a close relative of the grama grasses. **1950** Hitchcock *Manual Grasses* 401, Bush muhly . . . Known also as mesquite grass and black grama.

black grass n, also attrib

The black rush *(Juncus gerardii).*

1782 Crèvecoeur *Letters* 159 **seMA,** The best mowing grounds in the island, yielding four tons of black grass per acre. **1872** Schele de Vere *Americanisms* 408, *Salt-Hay,* a very important product of salt-marshes, is of two principal sorts, called *salt-grass* and *black-grass*. **1912** Baker *Book of Grasses* 332, Black-grass *(Juncus Gerardi),* easily recognized by its characteristic dark-green colour, blooms in midsummer and is common along the Atlantic coast and by tidal waters of rivers from Canada to Florida. **1945** Beck *Jersey Genesis* 112, Black grass, called *juncus gerardi,* is an in-between, neither salt nor upland hay, and always finds a market for fodder. **1968** *DARE* (Qu. L9b) Inf **NJ53,** Black grass hay.

black grasset n
=**kingbird.**

1917 *DN* 4.427 **LA,** *Kingbird (Tyrannus tyrannus)* . . . Black Grasset.

black ground n Cf blackland
Loose, dark soil.

1966–70 *DARE* (Qu. C30) Infs **DE1, IL126, OH31, SD2,** Black ground. **1970** *DARE* Tape **IL126,** This soil here is primarily black ground.

black grouper n

1 A grouper (here: *Myctoperca bonaci*). Also called **black rockfish, gray grouper, jewfish, long-boned rockfish, warsaw**

1882 U.S. Natl. Museum *Proc.* 5.273, *Trisotropis stomias* . . . *Black grouper.* **1946** LaMonte *N. Amer. Game Fishes* 49, Black Grouper . . *Myctoperca bonaci.* **1966** *DARE* (Qu. P2, . . *Saltwater fish . . good to eat*) Inf **FL24,** Black grouper.

2 Either of two fish of the genus *Epinephelus:* the **warsaw grouper** or the **spotted jewfish.**

1879 U.S. Natl. Museum *Proc. for 1878* 1.182 **FL, SC,** The Black Grouper *(Epinephelus nigritus)* . . of the Southern Coast. **1887** Goode *Amer. Fishes* 49, The Black Grouper, *Epinephelus nigritus*. **1933** LA Dept. of Conserv. *Fishes* 206, The giants among our Louisiana food fishes are the Jewfishes, also called Black Groupers . . the Spotted Jewfish, *Promicrops itaiara.* **1946** LaMonte *N. Amer. Game Fishes* 45, Spotted Jewfish—*Promicrops itaiara* . . *Names:* . . Black Grouper. *Ibid* 57, *Garrupa nigrita* . . Black Grouper.

black grunt n

1 =**tripletail.**

1815 Lit. & Philos. Soc. NY *Trans.* 1.419, Some of the fishermen call him *[Bodianus triouras]* black grunts. **1906** NJ State Museum *Annual Rept. for 1905* 313, *Lobotes surinamensis* . . . Black Grunt. **1933** LA Dept. of Conserv. *Fishes* 206, Elsewhere this species *[Lobotes surinamensis]* has been called . . Black Grunt.

2 Any of several **grunts,** esp *Hæmulon plumieri, H. macrostomum,* and *H. bonariense.*

1882 U.S. Natl. Museum *Proc.* 5.603, *Diabasis plumieri* . . Black Grunt. **1933** John G. Shedd Aquarium *Guide* 108, *Hæmulon bonariense*—Black Grunt. **1946** LaMonte *N. Amer. Game Fishes* 64, *Hæmulon macrostomum* . . Black Grunt. *Ibid* 66, *Hæmulon plumieri* . . Black Grunt.

blackguard n, v, adj, adv |ˈblægə(r)d, ˈblæ(k)gard, ˈblaɪgard|; in Midl also |ˈblæ(k)gjə(r)d| Pronc-spp blackyard, blaggard

A Forms.

1902 *DN* 2.229 **sIL,** *Blaggard* [blægard or blægeard]. **1917** *DN* 4.408 **wNC, KY,** *Blackgyard* . . . Variant of *blackguard*. **1923** *DN* 5.201 **swMO,** *Blaggard.* **1949** *AmSp* 24.106 **neGA,** *Blackguard drunk* [ˈblæk.gjaːəd]. **c1960** *Wilson Coll.* **csKY,** *Blackguard* [ˈblægə·d]. **1968–70** *DARE* (Qu. Y3) Inf **IL135,** Blackguard; **NJ9,** [ˈblaɪgard]; **NY96,** [ˈblægard]; **PA214,** [ˈblaɪgard]; **NJ3,** [ˈblæk.gardɪn].

B As noun.

See quots.

1930 *DN* 6.86 **cWV,** *Blackguard,* a foul-mouthed person; an excessive user of profanity. **1954** *Harder Coll.* **cwTN,** *Blackguard* . . . A person who talks obscenely, especially in the presence of women.

C As verb.

1 To slander or abuse verbally; to talk in scurrilous terms about (someone or something).

1950 (1965) Richter *Town* 30 **OH,** The new Moonshine Church Weekly Centinel blackguarded Tateville and the Western Repository Gazette of Tateville ran down Moonshine Church. **1968–70** *DARE* (Qu. Y3, *To say uncomplimentary things about somebody*) Infs **IL135, NJ9, NY96, PA214,** Blackguard; **NJ3,** Blackguarding.

2 To talk obscenely; to curse or swear (at). **chiefly S Midl**

1902 *DN* 2.229 **sIL,** *Blaggard* . . . To use obscene language, to talk obscenely. **1907** *DN* 3.220 **nwAR, sIL.** **1927** *DN* 5.473 **Ozarks.** **1949** Hornsby *Lonesome Valley* 82 **KY,** When he's full of moonshine he cusses and blackguards something scandalous. **1954** *Harder Coll.* **cwTN,** *Blackguard* . . . To talk obscenely. "I ain't a-goin' set there and let that ol' son-of-a-bitch blackguard 'fore ye." **1966** *DARE* (Qu. NN16, *Swearing or using obscene language: "He's always_____."*) Infs **GA3, 7, MS71,** Blackguarding. **1976** Garber *Mountain-ese* 9, He wuz expelled from school fer blackgardin' the teacher.

3 See quot. *?obs*

1893 Shands *MS Speech,* *Blackguard* . . . Used by illiterate whites as a verb meaning to laugh and talk in a gay, frivolous manner, even though the conversation be perfectly chaste. This class of people speaks of the ordinary small talk of a sociable or reception as *blackguarding*.

D As adj.

Characterized by abusive or obscene language. **chiefly S Midl**

1806 (1905) Clark *Orig. Jrls. Lewis & Clark Exped.* 3.344, The Indians inform us that they Speak the Same language with ourselves, and gave us proofs of their varacity by repeating . . maney blackguard phrasses. **1855** (1968) Whitman *Leaves of Grass* 36, At he-festivals with blackguard jibes and ironical license and bull-dances and drinking and laughter. **1927** *DN* 5.473 **Ozarks,** *Blackguard talk* . . . Obscene language, smutty anecdote. "I'm agin this hyar blackguard talk right in th' church-house." **1939** *Jrl. Amer. Folkl.* 52.63 **cNJ,** Broad songs such as most singers give only after a few drinks are called 'blackguard' songs. **1953** Randolph *Down in Holler* 227 **Ozarks,** *Blackguard* . . . The adjective is common.

E As adv.

See quot.

1949 *AmSp* 24.106 **neGA,** *Blackguard drunk* . . . Drunk to the point of viciousness.

blackguarding vbl n, also attrib [blackguard C2] chiefly S Midl
Vulgar or coarse talk; cursing.

1935 *Yale Rev.* 25.183 **KY,** That church out there is about the worst place I know of to go—so much blackguardin' out around it and boys lookin' in at the winders. **1954** *Harder Coll.* **cwTN,** Blackguardin' is talking ugly. **1966** *Wilson Coll.* **csKY,** Blackguarding . . . Using nasty words.

blackguarding ppl adj chiefly S Midl

1 Obscene.

1953 Randolph *Down in Holler* 227 **Ozarks,** One of my foul-mouthed visitors was described as "the *blackguardin'est* feller that ever set foot in this town." **1969** *DARE* FW Addit **cwNC,** Blackguardin' tales—dirty stories.

2 See quot.

1966 *Wilson Coll.* **csKY,** Blackguarding . . . Dishonest.

black gull n
=**black tern.**

1932 Bennitt *Check-list* 34, Black tern . . . Black gull . . . Formerly, and probably still, U[ncommon] S[ummer] R[esident] in central and northern Missouri.

black gum n

1 also *swamp blackgum:* A **tupelo** (*Nyssa sylvatica*). **chiefly**

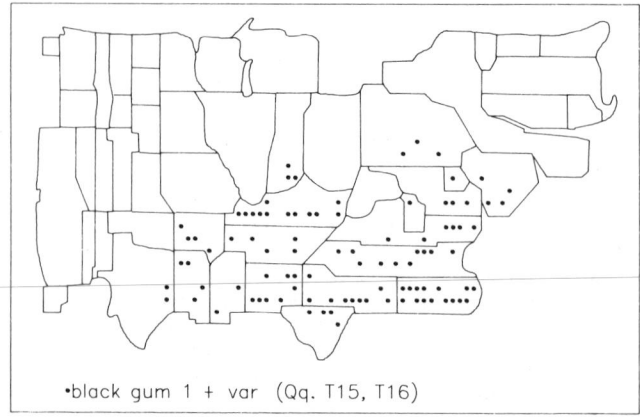

•black gum 1 + var (Qq. T15, T16)

Sth, S Midl See Map   Also called **bee gum, beetlebung, gum-tree, hornbeam, pepperidge, snag tree, sourgum, swamp tupelo, water tupelo, yellow gum**

1709 (1967) Lawson *New Voyage* 102 **NC**, Of the Black Gum there grows, with us, two sorts . . . The one bears a black, well-tasted Berry . . . The Bears crop these Trees for the Berries, which they mightily covet.   **1785** (1925) Washington *Diaries* 2.346 **VA**, Planted all the . . Blackgums in my Serpentine Walks.   **1835** Ingraham *South-West* 2.79, A fine though dusty road . . bordered with noble forests of oak, black gum.   **1869** *Amer. Naturalist* 2.122, When mast is not plenty, they [=bears] lap black-gum berries.   **1901** Mohr *Plant Life AL* 32, Chestnut . . and black gum (*Nyssa sylvatica*) are common.   **1941** Walker *Lookout* 66 **TN**, The blackgum or tupelo, is a common tree . . . In pioneer days, the fruit of the larger kind was employed as a substitute for olives.   **c1945** Hopkins *Okefenokee* 50 *(DA)*, This fire killed forty to fifty million feet of Swamp black gum.   **1965–70** *DARE* (Qu. T15) 93 Infs, **chiefly Sth, S Midl**, Black gum; (Qu. T16) Infs **AR**41, **DC**2, **PA**169, Black gum tree.

2 =**white fir.**

1897 Sudworth *Arborescent Flora* 55, *Abies concolor* . . Black Gum (Utah).

black hand n [*black* + *hand* n **B**]

A witchcraft spell, a charm.

1928 Peterkin *Scarlet Sister Mary* 101 **SC** [Gullah], Maybe she could get Daddy Cudjoe to put a black hand on Cinder that would get the wicked slut out of July's way. *Ibid* 122, I got to make a charm to fight a charm. Black hand is got to squeeze black hand.

black hare n

=**marsh rabbit.**

1927 Boston Soc. Nat. Hist. *Proc.* 38.373 **Okefinokee**, *Sylvilagus palustris palustris* . . . Sam Mizell's only name for it is 'Black Hare.'

black harry n

=**black sea bass.**

1814 in 1825 Lit. & Philos. Soc. NY *Trans.* 416, *Black harry, hanna-hills,* and *blue-fish,* are some of the names by which he [the black sea bass] is known.   **1887** Goode *Amer. Fishes* 39, In the Middle [Atlantic] States the Sea Bass is called "Black Will," "Black Harry," and "Hanna-hills."   **1946** LaMonte *N. Amer. Game Fishes* 48, *Centropristes striatus* . . Black Harry.

black haw n Pronc-sp *black haul*

1 A viburnum, such as *Viburnum lentago* or *V. rufidulum,* but esp *V. prunifolium.* **esp Sth, S Midl** *V. prunifolium* is also called **alisier, arrowwood a, boots, cramp bark, nannyberry, sheepberry, shonny, sloe, stagbush, sweet haw**

1709 (1967) Lawson *New Voyage* 112 **NC**, A slender tree . . bears the black Haw, which People eat, and the Birds covet also.   **1818** in 1821 Schoolcraft *Jrl.* 21 **MO**, Our approach to a warmer climate is further indicated by several green plants . . and particularly by the black haw, which we have this day found in great perfection.   **1899** Garland *Boy Life* 123 **nwIA**, All things not positively poisonous were eaten or at least tasted. The roots of ferns, black haws, choke-berries, . . May-apples.   **1901** Mohr *Plant Life AL* 743, The bark . . is used in medicine [as] "black-haw bark."   **1945** Saxon *Gumbo Ya-Ya* 547 **LA**, Water-finding rods are either willow or forked sticks of peach, black haw, . . or witch-hazel.   **1965–70** *DARE* (Qu. T16) 10 Infs, **chiefly Sth, S Midl**, Black haw; (Qu. I43) Inf **MO**9, Black haws; (Qu. I44) Infs **AR**52, **IN**3, **KY**5, **PA**234, **SC**57, Black haws; **TX**26, Black hauls; (Qu. I46) Infs **LA**2, **MO**38, **VA**42, Black haw.   **1976** Bruce *How to Grow Wildflowers* 130, Five species comprise the purely American section *Lentago:* Nanny-berry, *V. lentago;* Black-haw, *V. prunifolium;* Southern Black-haw, *V. rufidulum;* Withe-rod, *V. cassinoides;* Smooth Withe-rod, *V. nudum.*

2 A buckthorn, usu *Bumelia lanuginosa* or *B. tenax.*

1897 Sudworth *Arborescent Flora* 318, *Bumelia tenax* . . . *Common Names.* Black Haw (Fla.) . . . *Bumelia lanuginosa* . . . *Common Names* . . . Black Haw (Fla.).   **1913** *Torreya* 13.233, *Bumelia lanugin-osa* . . Black haw, Cameron, La.   **1933** Small *Manual SE Flora* 1034, *B. lanuginosa* . . . *Black-haw* . . . The yellow or light-brown heart-wood is close-grained, but rather soft . . . *B. tenax* . . . *Black-haw* . . . The light-brown and white-streaked heart-wood is hard and close-grained.   **1960** Vines *Trees SW* 833, *B. lanuginosa* . . . Vernacular names are . . Chittamwood, False-buckthorn, and Blackhaw. The black fruit is edible, but not tasty.   **1976** Bailey–Bailey *Hortus Third* 190, *Black haw.* Deciduous tree, to 45 ft. . . . Va. to Fla., w. to Kans., Tex., n. Mex.

3 also *black hawthorn:* A blackfruited **hawthorn** (*Crataegus*

douglasii) most prevalent in the western US.   Also called **black thorn, river hawthorn**

1897 Sudworth *Arborescent Flora* 215, *Crataegus douglasii* . . . *Common Names* . . . Black Haw (Mont.).   **1917** (1923) Rogers *Trees Worth Knowing* 158, In the West the black haw is a round-headed native tree found from Puget Sound southward through California and eastward to Colorado and New Mexico.   **1956** St. John *Flora SE WA* 195, *Black Hawthorn.* Erect, compact shrub, occasionally a tree up to 12 m. tall.   **1972** Viereck *AK Trees* 172, *Black Hawthorn* . . . *Fruits* like small apple [sic] . . , shiny black . . , thick light yellow flesh.

black hawk n

1 =**rough-legged hawk.**

1812 Wilson *Amer. Ornith.* 6.82, Black Hawk. *Falco Sancti Jo-hannis?* . . . is found most frequently along the marshy shores of our large rivers . . . The Black Hawk . . is a native of North America alone.   **1870** *Amer. Naturalist* 3.228, The Black-hawk, by some supposed to be only a darker race of this species [=rough-legged buzzard], and once occasionally to be met with, is now unknown [in New England].   **1965–70** *DARE* (Qu. Q4) 12 Infs, **scattered**, Black hawk.

2 Any of several other dark-colored hawks, such as Harris's hawk, **Mexican black hawk,** Swainson's hawk, or a subsp of **red-tailed hawk,** all native chiefly to the West and Southwest.

1858 Baird *Birds* 22, *Buteo calurus* . . . *Red-tailed Black Hawk* . . . To a casual observer this bird would present somewhat the appearance of the black hawk of the United States, *Archibuteo sanctijohannis,* with the tail attached of the common red-tailed buzzard, *Buteo borealis.*   **1944** Hausman *Amer. Birds* 516, Hawk, Black—see Hawk, Rough-legged; see also Hawk, Swainson's.   **1946** Goodrich *Birds in KS* 316, Colloquial Name . . Hawk, black . . . Common name . . Hawk, American rough-legged; hawk, Harris's; hawk, western red-tailed.   **1961** Ligon *NM Birds* 71, *Buteogallus anthracinus* . . . The Black Hawk . . is one of the two . . nesting Hawks with distribution confined to the southwest part of the state.

black hawthorn See black haw 3

blackhead n

1 also *blackhead duck:* Any of var **scaups: lesser scaup, greater scaup, ring-necked duck.**

a1782 (1788) Jefferson *Notes VA* 77, Black head.   **1848** *Knickerbocker* 32.331 **MD**, Good enough duck, for the matter of that, seeing it be but a black-head.   **1852** Stansbury *Expedition* 324, Little Black-head; Shuffler. Found across the continent; very common throughout the interior.   **1874** Coues *Birds NW* 573, I frequently saw Black heads in Dakota and Montana, especially during the migrations.   **1888** Trumbull *Names of Birds* 55, *Aythya marila* . . At the mouth of the Susquehanna, very commonly on the Chesapeake, by some at Cape May C.H., at Eastville and Cobb's Island, Va., and at Charleston, S.C., *Black-head* . . I have heard the term "black-head" as far south as St. Augus-tine.   **1933** *Sun* (Baltimore MD) 12 Dec 22/2–3 *(Hench Coll.),* He killed a ring-necked or black-head duck yesterday.   **1954** Sprunt *FL Bird Life* 75, *Ring-necked Duck: Aythya collaris* . . . Local Names: Blackhead. *Ibid* 78, *Greater Scaup Duck: Aythya marila* . . Local Names: Black-head. *Ibid* 79, *Lesser Scaup Duck: Aythya affinis* . . Local Names: . . Blackhead.   **1955** *MA Audubon* 39.315, *Ring-necked Duck.* Blackhead (Mass. Lumped with the scaups under this name, the Ring-neck justifies the application by the adult male's black head with metallic reflections.). *Ibid* 316, *Lesser Scaup Duck.* Blackhead (All along the coast . . .).   **1965–70** *DARE* (Qu. Q5) 14 Infs, **chiefly C and Mid Atl,** Black-head duck; **VA**70, Black-headed duck.

2 =**black-bellied plover.**

1955 *MA Audubon* 39.445, Blackhead (Mass. The lower surface of the head is black in adults, but the crown and nape are not black in any normal plumage.)

3 See **black vulture.**

4 A sedge (here: *Carex sitchensis*).

1923 in 1925 Jepson *Manual Plants CA* 187, *C[arex] sitchensis* . . Blackheads.

5 A **cattail 1** (here: *Typha latifolia*).

1959 Carleton *Index Herb. Plants* 13, Black Heads: Typha latifolia.

6 A **coneflower** (here: *Rudbeckia occidentalis*).

1973 Hitchcock–Cronquist *Flora Pacific NW* 543, Black head . . . *R[udbeckia] occidentalis.*

7 See **black-headed gull.**

8 See quot.   [Prob infl by *thunderhead*]

1954 *Harder Coll.* **cwTN**, Blackhead . . . Black raincloud.

blackhead duck See **blackhead 1**

black-headed buzzard n

=**black vulture**.

1955 Forbush–May *Birds* 95, *Black Vulture . . . Other names: . .* Black-headed buzzard.

black-headed gull n Also *blackhead, black-headed mackerel gull*

=**laughing gull** *(Larus atricilla)*.

1814 Wilson *Amer. Ornith.* 9.90, The Black-headed Gull is the most beautiful and most sociable of its genus. **1870** *Amer. Naturalist* 3.234, The Black-headed Gull, a Southern and somewhat rare species. **1925** (1928) Forbush *Birds MA* 1.82, *Larus atricilla . . Other names:* Black-headed gull; Black-head; Black-headed mackerel gull. **1966–70** *DARE* (Qu. Q10) Infs **NC**1, **VA**47, Black-headed gull.

black-headed vulture See **black vulture**

black-headed woodpecker n

Prob the **red-cockaded woodpecker**.

1966–67 *DARE* (Qu. Q17) Infs **FL**39, **NJ**3, **NC**15, Black-headed woodpecker.

blackhead minnow n

=**fathead minnow**.

1967 *DARE* (Qu. P7) Inf **SC**45, Blackhead minnows.

blackheart n

1 =**red-backed sandpiper**.

1888 Trumbull *Names of Birds* 181, *Black-heart [Pelidna alpina].* **1955** *MA Audubon* 39.19, *Red-backed Sandpiper . . .* Black-heart (Mass. From the large black spots on the lower sides of the male in breeding plumage.).

2 =**black-bellied plover**.

1923 U.S. Dept. Ag. *Misc. Circular* 13.68, Black-bellied Plover *(Squatarola squatarola) . .* Vernacular Names *. . . In local use . . .* blackheart (Mass.). **1925** (1928) Forbush *Birds MA* 1.459, *Squatarola squatarola . . . Other names: . .* Black-heart. **1955** *MA Audubon* 39.445, *Black-bellied Plover . .* Black-heart (Mass. All of the under surface, except the belly, is black in adults.).

3 =**whortleberry**.

1900 Lyons *Plant Names* 386, *V[accinium] Myrtillus . .* Black-heart.

4 Any of var **smartweeds**.

1894 *Jrl. Amer. Folkl.* 7.97, *Polygonum Persicaria . .* black heart, So. Vt. **1898** *Ibid* 11.278, *Polygonum Pennsylvanicum . .* black heart, Kans. **1900** Lyons *Plant Names* 300, *P[olygonum] Persicaria . .* Black-heart. **1966** *DARE* Wildfl QR Pl.47a Inf **NC**28, Blackheart.

5 A mean or ill-tempered person.

1968 *DARE* (Qu. GG38, . . *"He's an awful _____."*) Inf **VA**31, Blackheart.

blackheart cherry n

Perh the **sweet cherry** *(Prunus avium)*.

a1883 (1911) Bagby *VA Gentleman* 258, He dare not shave both ways, for if he does he leaves my face as bloody as a black-heart cherry, just skinned.

Black Hills spruce n Also *Black Hill spruce*

A **white spruce** (here: *Picea glauca*).

1966–68 *DARE* (Qu. T5) Infs **CT**2, **MN**7, 38, **SD**2, 3, Black Hill spruce. **1973** Stephens *Woody Plants* 2, *Picea glauca . . .* White spruce, Canadian spruce, Black Hills spruce . . . This is an attractive tree and often covers a hillside in the Black Hills, the conical tops forming a geometric pattern.

blackhood n

Harris's sparrow.

1917 (1923) *Birds Amer.* 333, Harris's sparrow—*Zonotrichia querula . .* Other Names.—Blackhood.

black hornet n chiefly **N Cent**, esp **MI**

A large, dark-colored wasp such as the **bald-faced hornet** or the **mud dauber 1**.

1965–70 *DARE* (Qu. R21) 16 Infs, **chiefly N Cent, esp MI**, Black hornet(s); (Qu. R20) Infs **IL**4, **MI**36, 47, Black hornet.

black horse n

A dark-colored sucker *(Catostomus elongatus).* Also called

gourdseed sucker, Missouri sucker, shoenaher, suckerel, sweet sucker

1842 DeKay *Zool. NY* 4.203, *Catostomus elongatus. The Missouri Sucker, Black Horse* and *Black Buffalo.* **1920** Forbes–Richardson *Fishes of IL* 65, *Cycleptus elongatus . . .* Black-horse. **1934** Vines *Green Thicket* 4 **cnAL**, He told her of the many red horses and black horses and salmon trout, red suckers and black suckers, buffaloes and drums, blue cats and yellow cats, he had caught. **1969** *DARE* (Qu. P1, . . *Freshwater fish . . good to eat)* Inf **AR**56, Black horse.

black ice n Cf *OEDS*

1 A smooth layer of ice which forms on still water and which is transparent, giving it a dark appearance. chiefly **NEast**, esp **NEng**

1944 *AN&Q* 4.152/1 **nNEng**, "Black ice," coming in the late fall with early freezes when the ice has not been defaced by snow, is a much more delightful phenomenon [than "slush"]. **1955** Adams *Grandfather* 174 **NY** (as of 1830s), That was the iron-hard winter of 1826, when the black ice held on all waters from Lake Ontario to Chesapeake Bay. **1968–69** *DARE* (Qu. B34, *When a pond or lake becomes entirely covered with ice, you say it is _____*) Inf **CT**6, Black ice—good for skating; **CT**25, Black ice. **1979** *DARE* File, [23 letters received chiefly from the Northeastern U.S. in response to the published query "What is 'black ice'?" typically said: "A smooth, transparent layer of ice that forms on a lake or pond."] *Ibid* **seNY**, Black ice is what forms on ponds or lakes when the temperature drops very low very fast and there is no wind. This forms ice that is clear rather than white. It is a marvelous sensation to skate on it because you can look down into the depths of the water (which appears very dark, if not black) and even see fish swimming beneath your feet!

2 By ext: smooth, clear ice that forms on pavement allowing the dark road-surface to show through, making the ice virtually invisible and very dangerous for driving. chiefly **NEast, Rocky Mts and Pacific**, esp **WA, OR**

1967 *DARE* (Qu. N22, *When a road that is surfaced with smooth pavement gets wet so that cars slip or skid on it, you say it's _____*) Inf **OR**1, Black ice—frozen. **1973** *Inyo Reg.* (Bishop CA) 18 Jan 1, Residents again faced hazardous driving when crystal-clear Wednesday morning skies and colder temperatures froze sheets of black ice on streets and highways. **1979** *DARE* File **Pacific NW**, "Black ice" is a hazardous road condition which develops when the temperatures drop into the 28°–32° range accompanied by a heavy fog, *light* mist or *light* drizzle. This causes the pores of the asphalt pavement to fill with ice. I've always assumed it was called black ice because you can't see it. The term is used in TV and radio weather forecasts, which I guess puts a sort of an official stamp of approval on it. **1979–80** *DARE* File, [78 letters received chiefly from the Northeast, Rocky Mountain, and Pacific states in response to the published query: "What is 'black ice'?" typically said: "A thin, transparent sheet of ice that forms on a hard-surfaced road."]

3 Among mountain climbers: see quot.

1979 *DARE* File **NY**, As an old mountaineer, I would like to explain that in mountain climbing we refer to "black ice" when we may encounter ice attached to the rock which has not melted for years and has actually acquired a black color. It is so hard that it sometimes cannot be chipped with an icepick and extremely slippery and hence, dangerous. Black ice is anathema to the mountain climber.

blackie n

1 A **black duck** (here: *Anas rubripes*).

1923 U.S. Dept. Ag. *Misc. Circular* 13.9, *Vernacular Names . . . In general use.*—Black duck, black mallard, often shortened to . . blackie. **1932** Bennitt *Check-list* 18 **MO**, *Anas rubripes . . .* Black mallard; dusky duck; blackie. **1951** Pough *Audubon Water Bird* 320, Blackie. See Black duck. **1982** Elman *Hunter's Field Guide* 143, *Black Duck . . . Common & Regional Names:* black, blackie.

2 =**ring-necked duck**.

1923 U.S. Dept. Ag. *Misc. Circular* 13.21, *Ring-necked Duck . . . Vernacular Names . . . In local use . . .* Blackie (Tex.).

3 The black bear *(Ursus americanus)*.

1982 Elman *Hunter's Field Guide* 557, *Black Bear . . . Common & Regional Names:* bruin, blackie.

black iron n chiefly **Sth**

A simple heavy-metal device which is heated and used to press clothes; a flatiron.

1965–67 *DARE* (Qu. F29, *Different kinds of irons—not electric— used around here for smoothing clothes after they're washed)* Infs **MS**55,

SC42, Black iron.   **1967** LeCompte *Word Atlas* 134 **LA,** Device, not electric, to smooth clothes after washing . . . [3 of 21 informants said] black iron.

blackjack n

1 Any of three similar ducks:

a The **ring-necked duck** and the **lesser scaup** which prefer freshwater areas, and the **greater scaup** which prefers saltwater areas.

   1888 Trumbull *Names of Birds* 60, *Ring-necked Duck* . . . In Putnam Co., Ill., *Black-jack;* this being heard also at Chicago, though less commonly; and Mr. J.P. Leach, of Rushville, Ill., writes that this name is "generally applied along the Illinois River."   **1923** U.S. Dept. Ag. *Misc. Circular* 13.18, *Scaup Ducks* . . . *Collective Vernacular Names* . . . *In local use.* — . . blackjacks (Calif.). *Ibid* 21, *Ring-necked Duck* . . . *Vernacular Names* . . . *In local use.* — . . blackjack (Ill., Iowa, Mo., Ky., Ark., La., Tex., Calif.).   **1940** Gabrielson *Birds OR* 154, *Ring-necked Duck* . . . More discriminating sportsmen, particularly those who have shot in the Midwest, use the name "Black-jack" for this species, the name commonly given it along the Mississippi.   **1966–69** *DARE* (Qu. Q5) Infs **CA**136, **IA**22, 29, **LA**22, **MS**53, **MO**17, **NY**219, **SC**40, Blackjack; (Qu. Q9) Inf **CA**140, Blackjack.   **1967** *DARE* FW Addit **cwLA,** Blackjack—a kind of duck with black head and feet.

b =**ruddy duck.**

   1925 (1928) Forbush *Birds MA* 1.280, *Ruddy Duck. Other names: Butter-ball; Black-jack* [etc.].   **1966** *DARE* (Qu. Q5) Inf **OK**18, Butter duck—small, black, might also be called blackjacks.

c A **black duck** (here: *Anas rubripes*).

   1917 *Wilson Bulletin* 29.2.77, *Anas rubripes.*—Black-jack, Hickman, Ky.   **1982** Elman *Hunter's Field Guide* 143, *Black Duck . . . Common & Regional Names:* black, blackie, blackjack.

2 See **blackjack oak.**

3 usu pl: A usu level, open, sometimes grassy region with scattered blackjack oaks. [By ext of *blackjack* (oak) which is indigenous to the Sthn US]

   1843 in 1961 *AmSp* 36.293 **cnSC,** It is the natural outlet for most of the water that sometimes covers those vast plains, known in the up country as the *Blackjack,* from the tree that constitutes their chief natural production . . . Except the comparatively level land, called the Blackjacks, our section of country is very broken.   **1962** Atwood *Vocab. TX* 41, *Land where scrubby oak grows* . . . The term *blackjacks* occurs a few times in Oklahoma.   **1969** *DARE* (Qu. C33) Inf **NC**62, The blackjacks—a poor soil area named after the blackjack oak tree.

4 A hard candy made with molasses.

   1886 Bates *Old Salem* 63 **MA,** A Black-jack is a generous stick of a dark and saccharine compound which combines a variety of flavors. In tasting Black-jack you imagine that you detect a hint of maple syrup, a trace of butter, a trifle of brown sugar and molasses, and a tiny fancy of the whole mixture's having been burnt on to the kettle . . . This burnt flavor is . . intentional.   **1977** *Yankee* Feb 21 **NEng,** Blackjacks are a close second in popularity [to Gibraltars]. These are slender round candy sticks flavored with blackstrap molasses.

5 also attrib: A heavy dark soil.   **chiefly Sth**

   1967 LeCompte *Word Atlas* 242 **LA,** *Heavy black soil which tends to clod when wet and is very hard when dry* . . . [12 of 21 informants said] Blackjack.   **1967–70** *DARE* (Qu. C30, . . *Loose, dark soil*) Inf **LA**20, Blackjack; **SC**29, Blackjack soil; (Qu. C31, . . *Heavy, sticky soil*) Infs **VA**59, 64, Blackjack.

6 In marble play: see quot.

   1969 *DARE* (Qu. EE6a, *Names for different kinds of marbles—the big one that's used to knock others out of the ring*) Inf **GA**77, Blackjack—the name of the head taw man when no marbles went out of the ring at the first shot.

7 See quot.   Cf **mumblety-peg**

   1967 *DARE* (Qu. EE5, *Games where you try to make a jackknife stick in the ground*) Inf **MN**3, Blackjack.

8 Illegal liquor; moonshine.   Cf **applejack 1**

   1968 *DARE* (Qu. DD21c, *Nicknames for whiskey, especially illegally made whiskey*) Inf **IL**67, Blackjack.

9 Very strong coffee without cream or milk.   Cf *DS* H74a

   1950 *WELS* (*Different words for coffee*) 1 Inf, **seWI,** Blackjack (very strong).   **1969** Sorden *Lumberjack Lingo* **NEng and Gt Lakes,** *Blackjack*—Coffee.

10 See quots.

   1975 Gould *ME Lingo* 14, *Blackjack*—Gingerbread.   **1977** *Yankee* Jan 73 **csME,** Black jack is another name for gingerbread.

blackjack bean n

   1970 Anderson *TX Folk Med.* 60, Rheumatism—Carry three blackjack beans in your pocket. *Colorado.*

black jacket n   Cf **blue jacket 2, yellow jacket**

A dark-colored wasp of the family Sphecidae such as the **mud dauber 1.**

   1966–68 *DARE* (Qu. R21) Infs **MS**47, **NC**35, **OK**31, **VA**15, Black jacket.

blackjack oak n   Also *blackjack*   **chiefly Sth, S Midl**   See Map

An oak, esp *Quercus marilandica,* but also freq **water oak** (here: *Q. nigra*) or Emory oak *(Q. emoryi).*

   1765 (1942) Bartram *Diary of a Journey* 31 July 17/1, Ye oaks black which is reconed ye best fire wood they have they call them black Jacks seldom grow above A foot diameter very scruby & of good use for timber for boats.   **1879** (1880) Tourgée *Fool's Errand* 75, The wide fireplace, in which the dry hickory and black-jack was blazing brightly.   **1903** *Cosmopolitan* 34.633, A little town five miles off the railroad down in the black-jack country of Arkansas.   **1904** *DN* 2.416 **nwAR,** *Black jack* . . . Black oak. 'Bring me a rick of black jack.'   **1941** Walker *Lookout* 64 **TN,** The lowest in commercial value, known as the common black jack, . . finds a use for fuel.   **1946** *Reader's Digest* 48.93/1, He started off through Texas blackjack oaks.   **c1960** *Wilson Coll.* **csKY,** *Blackjack* . . . Scrub Oak *(Quercus marilandica)* a very common tree on the thin-soiled ridges, and worthless except for wood. "Why, that land won't grow nothing but blackjacks."   **1965–70** *DARE* (Qu. T10) 83 Infs, **chiefly S Midl, Sth,** Blackjack oak.   **1975** Newell *If Nothin' Don't Happen* 8 **nwFL,** Most of the trees was second-growth pine and scrub oaks—what we call blackjacks and turkey oaks.

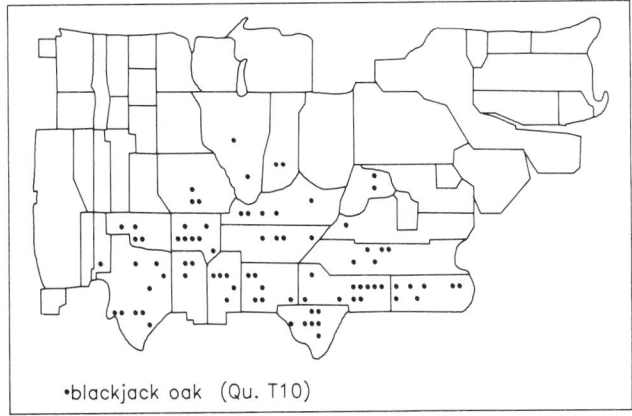

•blackjack oak (Qu. T10)

blackjack pine n

1 =**jack pine 1.**

   1897 Sudworth *Arborescent Flora* 30, *Pinus divaricata* . . . Black Jack Pine (Wis.).   **1908** Britton *N. Amer. Trees* 44, It [=*Pinus banksiana*] is also known as . . Jack pine, . . Black pine, Black Jack pine.

2 =**ponderosa pine.**

   1960 Vines *Trees SW* 18, Ponderosa Pine . . . Other vernacular names are . . Yellow Pine, Bull Pine, Blackjack Pine [etc.].   **1973** Hitchcock–Cronquist *Flora Pacific NW* 62, Large tree up to 70 m, with bark at first dark brown or blackish but becoming very thick and changing to cinnamon red in old trees . . blackjack, or bull p[ine] . . *P[inus] ponderosa.*

3 Prob =**loblolly pine 1.**

   1968–70 *DARE* (Qu. T17) Infs **VA**8, 43, Blackjack pine.

blackjack possum n

   1965–66 *DARE* (Qu. P31) Infs **GA**1, **MS**60, Blackjack possum—possum with dark coloring.

blackjack steer n   [**blackjack 3**]

   1944 Adams *Western Words, Blackjack steer*—A scrawny steer from the timbered country.

black jaundice n   [From the association of "black" with death]   Cf **black diphtheria**

An extreme case of jaundice.

1960 Taber *Med. Dict., Jaundice . . . j., black.* J. to an extreme degree; icterus melas. **1969** *DARE* (Qu. BB49, . . *Kinds of diseases*) Inf **TX**62, Black jaundice.

black-jaw See **black-cheek**

black jewfish n
=**warsaw grouper.**

    1902 Jordan–Evermann *Amer. Fishes* 386, The only known species is *Garrupa nigrita,* known as the black jewfish. **1946** LaMonte *N. Amer. Game Fishes* 49, Black Jewfish—*Garrupa nigrita.*

blackland n, also attrib **chiefly TX, OK, AR, LA** See Map Cf **black ground**

A heavy, loose, or sometimes sticky dark soil; also countryside which has such soil.

    1803 MA Hist. Soc. *Coll.* 1st ser 9.140, On the low, or, what is commonly called, black land, the timber is chiefly white and Norway pine, spruce, and hemlock. **1860** *Charleston* (S.C.) *Mercury* 27 Nov 4/2 *(DA),* I hear from the 'black-land' counties that nearly every man is for Secession. **1910** *Sat. Eve. Post* 8 Oct 10/3 **MO,** John Simmons lived on a black-land farm in central Missouri. **1939** *Sun* (Baltimore MD) 26 June 14/2 **cMS** *(Hench Coll.),* That motorists might drive through the delta country, engineers had to subexcavate along the right-of-way and import sandy loam material for insulation against the soft, rich blacklands. **1965–70** *DARE* (Qu. C30, . . *Loose, dark soil*) 16 Infs, Blackland [11 Infs **TX**]; (Qu. C31, . . *Heavy, sticky soil*) Infs **AR**53, 55, **LA**11, 20, **OK**21, 25, **TX**2, 40, Blackland. **1971** Green *Last Trail Drive* 52 **ncTX,** We were in the blackland.

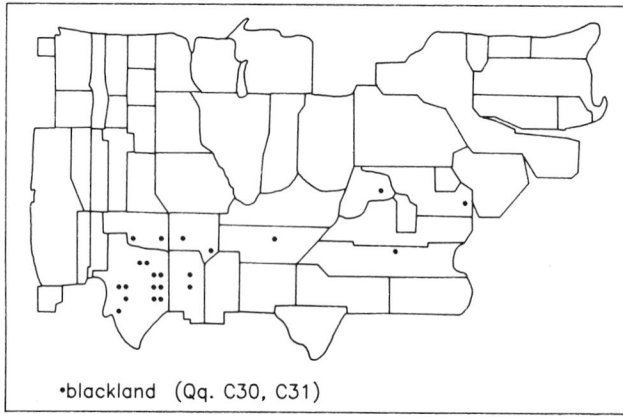

•blackland (Qq. C30, C31)

black lark n Cf **brown lark**
Perh the American **pipit.**

    1970 *DARE* (Qu. Q15, . . *Different kinds of larks*) Inf **NJ**67, Black lark.

black laurel n
1 =**loblolly bay 1.**

    1897 Sudworth *Arborescent Flora* 273, *Gordonia lasianthus . . .* Black Laurel (N.C.). **1933** Small *Manual SE Flora* 877, *Black-laurel . . .* Non-alluvial swamps and bays, often in acid soil, Coastal Plain, Fla. to La. and N.C. **1953** Greene–Blomquist *Flowers South* 74, *Black-Laurel . . .* A small to fairly good-sized tree growing in borders of swamps and bays. **1976** Bruce *How to Grow Wildflowers* 144, *Gordonia lasianthus,* the Loblolly-bay (also called Tan-bay, Black-laurel, and, erroneously, Red-bay).

2 An evergreen shrub *(Leucothoe davisiae)* found chiefly in California. Also called **Sierra laurel**

    1931 U.S. Dept. Ag. *Misc. Pub.* 101.131, *Black laurel . .* occurs in the Sierra Nevada of California; while sometimes both local and rare, it is plentiful and abundant in other places . . . Very small quantities will poison sheep. **1937** U.S. Forest Serv. *Range Plant Hdbk.* B92, The origin of the common name, blacklaurel, is somewhat obscure . . . The name blacklaurel probably originated because of the black stems or possibly the dark green leaves of this species, which are a decided contrast to the rather paler stems and the light-colored leaves of western azalea *(Azalea occidentalis),* also frequently called laurel.

blacklegs n
=**coot** n[1] **1.**

    1966 *DARE* (Qu. Q9) Inf **DC**8, Blacklegs.

black lime tree n
A **linden** (here: *Tilia americana*).

    1897 Sudworth *Arborescent Flora* 301, *Tilia americana . .* Common Names . . . Black Limetree (Tenn.). **1930** Sievers *Amer. Med. Plants* 6, *American Linden . . Other common names . . .* black lime tree. **1960** Vines *Trees SW* 733, It *[Tilia americana]* has many vernacular names such as . . Blacklime-tree.

black locust n
Either of two trees: the **honey locust 1** (here: *Gleditsia triacanthos*) or *Robinia pseudoacacia,* the latter also called **green locust, honey locust 2, post locust, red locust, silver chain, silver locust, sweet locust 2, white locust, yellow locust 1.** See also **shipmast locust**

    1787 Amer. Acad. Arts & Sci. *Memoirs* 2.157, The Black Locust . . grows from six inches to two feet and a half in diameter. **1901** Mohr *Plant Life AL* 77, On its flanks [=Lookout Mt.] the black locust *(Robinia pseudacacia)* is found, one of the few localities in Alabama where it can be considered to be indigenous. **1945** *Prairie Farmer* 22 Dec. 4/1 *(DA),* Honey locusts are harmless but the common or black locust tree is responsible for many cases of animal poisoning. **1967–70** *DARE* (Qu. T16) 39 Infs, **scattered,** Black locust; (Qu. T9) Infs **AR**41, **MO**22, **NE**6, **NH**5, **OK**52, Black locust; (Qu. I53) Inf **LA**2, Black locust pods.

black mallard n Also *black mallard duck*
A **black duck** (here: *Anas rubripes*).

    1888 Trumbull *Names of Birds* 17, *Black Duck . . .* As we move westward, and farther south, we hear *Black Mallard.* **1903** in 1951 Kumlien–Hollister *Birds WI* 12, *Anas obscura rubripes . . .* This is the common form of the "black mallard" which is shot in Wisconsin during the fall flight. **1913** Bailey *Birds VA* 22, *Black Duck.* [Black Mallard. Dusky Duck]. **1954** Sprunt *FL Bird Life* 61, Sportsmen and others insist on calling it "Black Mallard." It is definitely not a mallard . . . Certainly, it bears no resemblance to that species. Nor, indeed, is it a *black* bird. **1962** Imhof *AL Birds* 125, *Black Duck . . . Other Name:* Black Mallard. **1965–70** *DARE* (Qu. Q5) Infs **DE**3, **GA**25, **LA**31, **MI**10, 42, **VA**75, **WI**12, Black mallard; **VA**43, Black mallard duck.

black-mammy n [Prob *black* + *mammy* folk-etym for *mummy* a brown bituminous pigment; see *OED* **mummy** sb.[1] 2d]
A tar-like substance used to repair small leaks in a boat.

    1968 *DARE* (Qu. O6, *If a wooden boat is leaking, what do you have to do to stop the leaks?*) Inf **NC**54, Put black-mammy on it—sort of a tar you can buy.

black man n
1 An evil spirit, boogeyman, devil. **esp common Sth, S Midl** Cf **black** adj and *EDD*

    1692 in 1914 Burr *Narr. Witchcraft* 159 **MA,** The afflicted persons said, the Black Man whispered to her in the Assembly. **1915** *DN* 4.180 **swVA,** Bad-man . . . The devil. Also, *black-man.* **1939** *AmSp* 14.268 **IN,** Terms referring to the Devil: . . 'the Black Man,' and 'old Ned.' **1943** *LANE* Map 533 **scattered throughout NEng,** Names for a particular demon invoked to frighten children, in most cases more or less clearly identified with the devil . . *the bad man, the black man.* **c1960** Wilson Coll. **csKY,** Black Man . . . The Devil. **1966–68** *DARE* (Qu. EE41, *A hobgoblin that is used to threaten children and make them behave*) Infs **AL**6, 10, **CA**105, **IN**14, Black man. **1971** Wood *Vocab. Change* 38 **Sth,** Some parents threaten a child with a supernatural creature who will get him if he does not mind. The common word is *booger man* . . . Scattered instances occur of *black man.*

2 also *black man's base:* A children's outdoor game: see quot 1953. **chiefly N Cent, Cent** See Map Cf **black Tom**

    1895 *DN* 1.398 **IL, IA, PA,** A common game among boys is known variously as *king* and . . *blackman.* **1915** *DN* 4.181 **swVA,** Black-man . . . A kind of game among boys. **1953** Brewster *Amer. Nonsinging Games* 56 **IN,** Black Man . . . This game is played by six or more youngsters, two of whom are "black men." The others have two safety bases, on which they cannot be caught. If they run between the bases, however, they can be caught and then they too become "black men." The "black man" must pat each captive three times on the back. The first two players caught are "black men" for the next game. **1964** Wallace *Frontier Life* 47 **OK,** Each day at school brought new adventures, . . catching my opponents in a strenuous game of "Black-man." **1965–70** *DARE* (Qu. EE26) Infs **CA**105, **IL**11, 126, **OK**1, **PA**221, Black man; (Qu. EE33) 26 Infs, **chiefly N Cent, Cent,** Black man;

Inf **OH**66, Black man's base. **1969** Kantor *MO Bittersweet* 142 **nwMO,** There used to be a game children played, in . . these-here parts . . . They called it Black Man . . . It, the Black Man, would try to catch as many as he could. Once caught, a player became a Black Man. He joined the Its.

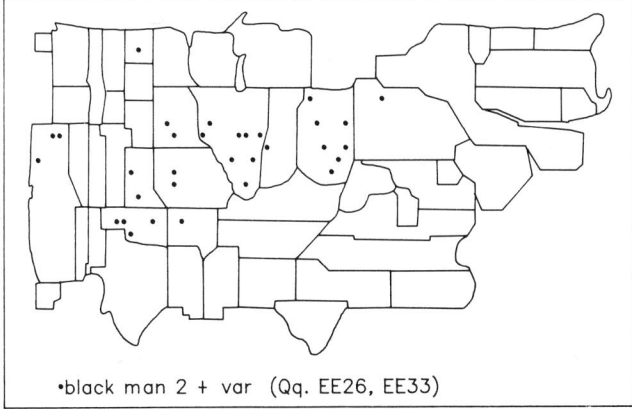

•black man 2 + var (Qq. EE26, EE33)

3 also *black man's buff:* A children's game similar to blindman's buff.

1968 *DARE* (Qu. EE4, *Games in which one player's eyes are bandaged and he has to catch the others and guess who they are*) Inf **OH**74, Black man; **MI**81, Black man's buff—touch each other on the face.

black mangrove n Also *black mango, black tree, blackwood* [*OED* 1697 →]

A large evergreen shrub or tree (*Avicennia germinans*) found in Florida and on the Gulf coast. Also called **honey mangrove, white mangrove**

1775 (1962) Romans *Nat. Hist. FL* App xxvii, There are some mangrove and blackwood bushes on them. *Ibid* lxxx, The chief growth on the keys are [sic] mangrove and blackwood bushes. **1884** Sargent *Forests of N. Amer.* 117, *Black Mangrove. Black Tree. Blackwood* . . . Wood very heavy, hard, . . color dark brown or nearly black. **1939** Tharp *Vegetation TX* 67, Black Mango (*Avicennia*) . . (saline marshes). **1967** Will *Dredgeman* 66 **FL,** Then there also was the black mangrove, a different tree entirely [from red mangrove]. Instead of standing on spidery legs, its trunk, tall and straight, springs directly from the ground. Since it normally grows in flooded areas, its roots, like those of a cypress, come above the surface to get their air. Yet instead of a few knees such as the cypress has, the black mangrove sends up hundreds, yes, thousands of what look like asparagus tips above the ground. **1976** Fleming *Wild Flowers FL* 41, Black mangrove is one of the most common trees in the coastal swamps of southern Florida. **1979** Little *Checklist U.S. Trees* 59, *Black-mangrove* . . . Other common names— blackwood.

black maple n Also *black sugar (maple)*

A dark-barked subsp of the **sugar maple** (*Acer saccharum* subsp *nigrum*) with dark green foliage. Also called **hard maple, rock maple, sugar maple, sweet tree**

a1817 (1821) Dwight *Travels* 1.40, The *Hard Maple*, sometimes called the *Black*, is extensively called the *Sugar Maple.* **1884** Sargent *Forests of N. Amer.* 49, *Black Sugar Maple* . . . A large tree along streams and river bottoms, in lower ground than the species with which it is connected. **1921** Deam *Trees IN* 246, *Black Maple. Black Sugar* . . . Medium to large sized trees with dark furrowed bark on old trees. **1947** *AmSp* 22.152, *Black maple* (saccharum nigrum). One of the two varieties of maples from which sirup is made. **1965–70** *DARE* (Qu. T14) 11 Infs, **scattered,** Black maple; (Qu. T3) Inf **KY**68, Black maple is the same as sugar maple; **MA**47, Black sugar maple won't produce but a little sap, and not very sweet.

black Maria n Also sp *black mariah* [Transf from *black Maria* a patrol wagon] Cf **black wagon**

1 A hearse.

1965–70 *DARE* (Qu. N2, *The car used to carry a dead body for burial*) 18 Infs, **esp common NEast and CA,** Black Maria.

2 An ambulance.

1965–70 *DARE* (Qu. N1, *Other names for an ambulance*) 12 Infs, **esp NEast,** Black Maria.

3 A fishing net.

1969 Lyons *My Florida* 69, Helping to haul in the huge "black mariahs" which encircled the fish of the river.

black martin n

=**purple martin.**

1895 Minot *Land-Birds New Engl.* 150, *Purple Martin. "Black Martin."* . . "Lustrous blue black; no purple anywhere." **1917** *Wilson Bulletin* 29.2.84, *Progne subis.*—Big, black, house, or large martin, Hickman, Ky. **1965–70** *DARE* (Qu. Q14) Infs **GA**1, 65, **IA**29, **KY**9, **LA**29, **MD**42, 45, **OH**49, **VA**57, Black martin; (Qu. Q11) Inf **NC**54, Black martin. **1969** Longstreet *Birds FL* 102, *Purple Martin. Other names:* Black Martin . . . The entire body of the male is covered with blue-black feathers that have a purple tint when rays of light shine on them.

black mason n

=**mason wasp.**

1968 *DARE* (Qu. R20) Inf **SC**57, Black mason.

black mike n

1968 Adams *Western Words, Black Mike*—A logger's term for stew.

black minister n Cf **minister, white minister**

=**great black-backed gull.**

1956 *MA Audubon* 40.22, *Great Black-backed Gull* . . . Black Minister . . (Mass. From its black mantle and white vest.).

black moccasin n

Prob =**cottonmouth.**

1966–67 *DARE* (Qu. P25) Inf **OK**32, Black moccasin ['mɔsɪkæn] [sic]; **TX**14, Black moccasin.

black moke See **moke**

black-monster tea n

A kind of herb tea.

1970 *DARE* (Qu. BB50d, *Favorite spring tonics around here*) Inf **VA**69, Black-monster tea—made by boiling a certain herb from the woods.

black mosquito n

Perh a **black fly** or **punkie.**

1966–67 *DARE* (Qu. R15a, . . *Nicknames . . for mosquitoes*) Inf **NC**10, Black mosquito; **OK**52, Black mosquito—after windy spells; **LA**8, Black skeeter.

black moss n [See quot 1911]

=**Spanish moss 1.**

1775 (1922) Schaw *Jrl. of a Lady* 152, The trees that keep clear from this black moss (as it is called) are crowned with the Mistletoe. **1857** Gray *Manual of Botany* 458, *T[illandsia] usneoides* . . . Black Moss . . . A characteristic plant of the Southern States. **1894** Coulter *Botany W. TX* 2.426, *Common Long-moss. Black moss* . . . Hanging on trees, forming long tufts, southern Texas. **1911** *Century Dict., Black-moss* . . . The Spanish moss . . of the southern United States: so called from the black fiber that remains after the outer covering of the stem is removed. It is used as a substitute for horsehair in mattresses, etc. **1950** Gray–Fernald *Manual of Botany* 392.

black mountain trout n

Prob a **cutthroat trout** or a **rainbow trout.**

1967 *DARE* (Qu. P1, . . *Freshwater fish . . good to eat*) Inf **OR**13, Black mountain trout.

blackmouth See **blackmouth salmon**

black-mouthed bass n

=**black bass 1.**

1966 *DARE* (Qu. P1, . . *Freshwater fish . . good to eat*) Inf **FL**29, Black-mouthed bass.

blackmouth salmon n Also *blackmouth*

=**chinook salmon,** esp the immature fish.

1946 LaMonte *N. Amer. Game Fishes* 106, *Chinook Salmon . . . Names: . .* Blackmouth Salmon. **1961** *W3, Blackmouth . . blackmouth salmon . .* a king salmon esp. when immature. **1972** Sparano *Outdoors Encycl.* 352, *Chinook Salmon . . . Common Names: . .* blackmouth (immature stage).

black mullet n

1 =**kingfish 1.**

1887 Goode *Amer. Fishes* 123, The King-fish, *Menticirrus nebulosus,* also known as . . the "Black Mullet" in the Chesapeake. **1911** *Century Dict., Kingfish* . . . Also called *whiting, tomcod, hake, black mullet* and *mink,* names properly belonging to different animals.

2 =striped mullet.

1960 Amer. Fisheries Soc. *List Fishes* 46, Striped mullet . . *Mugil cephalus* . . Known as black mullet in Florida. **1968** *DARE* (Qu. P2, . . *Saltwater fish . . good to eat*) Inf **LA26,** Black mullet.

blackneck n [See b quot 1911]

Any of three similar ducks:

a =greater scaup.

1888 Trumbull *Names of Birds* 54, This, the larger scaup, is distinguished . . as *Lake blue-bill,* . . . and certain gunners about Detroit prefer *Black-neck* to the more common Western term "blue-bill." **1917** (1923) *Birds Amer.* 1.135, *Scaup Duck* . . . *Other Names* . . Black-neck. **1944** Hausman *Amer. Birds* 506, Black-neck — see Duck, Scaup.

b =lesser scaup.

1911 *Century Dict. Suppl., Blackneck* . . . Either one of the scaup-ducks . . which have the head and upper part of the neck black. **1923** U.S. Dept. Ag. *Misc. Circular* 13.18, *Scaup Ducks* . . . *Collective Vernacular Names* . . . *In local use* . . . Blacknecks (Mich., Wis., Nebr.).

c =ring-necked duck.

1923 U.S. Dept. Ag. *Misc. Circular* 13.21, *Ring-necked Duck* . . . *Vernacular Names* . . . *In local use* . . . Blackneck (Wis., Ky.).

black-necked stilt n

A stilt *(Himantopus mexicanus).* Also called **daddy-long-legs, humility, jack snipe, lawyer, long-legs, longshanks, Mormon elder, tilt**

1839 MA Zool. & Bot. Surv. *Fishes Reptiles* 358, The Black Necked Hilt [sic], *Himantopus nigricollis.* **1970** *DARE* (Qu. Q10) Inf **VA52,** Black-necked stilt — new to the area.

black night n Cf black dark, full night

Nighttime at its darkest.

1953 *PADS* 19.9 sAppalachians, *Black night* . . . "I'll need a lantern as it's black night outside." **c1960** *Wilson Coll.* csKY, *Black night* . . . Dark rather than dusky. "He didn't get home till black night."

black Norway pine See black pine 1c

black oak n, also attrib

Any of several oaks with dark-colored bark or foliage, but most frequently *Quercus velutina,* which is also called **dyer's oak, spotted oak, tanbark oak, yellowbark oak, yellow oak.**

1634 Wood *New Engl. Prospect* 1.16, Of Oakes there be three kindes, the red Oake, white, and blacke. **1773** in 1963 *AmSp* 31.185 **Ohio Valley,** In five miles we crossed the Cantucky [sic] river to the east side along the path; five miles in a piece of black oak timber land. **1799** *Ibid* 181 **Ohio Valley,** The country was chiefly black-oak and white-oak land, which appeared generally to be good wheat land. **1906** *DN* 3.127 nwAR, *Black oak, red oak, scrub oak, white oak* . . . Various kinds of oak. **1947** *Amer. Midland Naturalist* July 40, Black Oak . . [is] common in upland oak forest; occasional in terrace forest. **1965–70** *DARE* (Qu. T10) 284 Infs, **widespread,** Black oak; (Qu. T15) Infs **CT6, SC10,** Black oak; (Qu. T16) Inf **KY84,** Black oak.

black oat grass n [From the color of the lemma]

A **needlegrass 1** (here: *Stipa avenacea*).

1848 Gray *Manual of Botany* 584, *S. avenacea* . . . *Black Oat-Grass.* **1894** Coulter *Botany W. TX* 516, *Black oat-grass* . . . Floret . . brown or nearly black, with a prominent brown hairy stipe. **1941** Walker *Lookout* 49 **TN,** Black oat grass, thrives in the open woodlands on the mountain. Its seed when ripe clings to the clothing and by a cork-screw-like device . . works its way through until it strikes the flesh. **1967** Braun *Monocotyledoneae* 129, *Black Oat Grass* . . . Woods, eastern United States to Michigan and Texas.

blackout spell n Also *black spell* [*blackout* loss of consciousness + *spell* a brief period]

1966–68 *DARE* (Qu. BB6, *A sudden feeling of weakness, when sometimes the person loses consciousness*) Infs **AR15, MS6, SC40, TN27,** Blackout spell; **WY4,** Black spell.

black patch n

=black belt 1.

1960 Heimann *Tobacco* 228, The most troubled area was the so-called Black Patch of western Kentucky and Tennessee, this dark tobacco area being the last to go over to loose-leaf selling.

black pea See black-eyed pea

black pepper tree n

Prob a **prickly ash 1** (here: *Zanthoxylum clava-herculis*).

1968 *DARE* (Qu. I35) Inf **LA33,** Black pepper tree.

black perch n

1 Any of var freshwater fish as:

a =largemouth bass or smallmouth bass.

1706 in 1907 *Amer. Hist. Rev.* 12.335 **SC,** There are . . Pearch of severall sorts. the white Bellied Pearch, the Red Bellied Pearch the Black Pearch and the Yellow Bellied Pearch. **1780** (1916) Fleming *Travels KY* 646, The Inhabitants of this place [in Kentucky] catched numbers of fish yesterday and today, all cat fish except a black pearch such as in Roanoke. **1820** Rafinesque *Ohio R. Fishes* 31, Brown River-Bass . . . Vulgar names, Black Bass, Brown Bass, Black Pearch; &c. *Ibid* 32, Trout River-bass . . . Vulgar names . . Black Bass, Black Pearch, &c. **1883** *Century Illustr. Mag.* 26.376/2 **KY,** I have heard them [=black bass] called black perch, yellow perch, and jumping perch up the Rockcastle and Cumberland rivers. **1887** Goode *Amer. Fishes* 56, Black Perch [is another name] applied to one or both species [*Micropterus salmoides; M. dolomiei*]. **1946** LaMonte *N. Amer. Game Fishes* 134, *Micropterus dolomieu* . . Black Perch. **1968** *DARE* (Qu. P1, . . *Freshwater fish . . good to eat*) Inf **MD36,** Black perch. **1972** *DARE* File nwFL, Black perch — a type of panfish, similar to bream. Common.

b =warmouth.

1968 *DARE* FW Addit swMO, Black perch — warmouth bass, a brown-spotted, thickset sunfish with red eyes.

2 Any of var saltwater fish as:

a =tripletail.

1882 U.S. Natl. Museum *Proc.* 5.604, *Lobotes surinamensis* . . . Black Perch. **1887** Goode *Amer. Fishes* 148, *Lobotes surinamensis* . . [is] known in South Carolina as the "Black Perch." **1906** NJ State Museum *Annual Rept. for 1905* 313, *Lobotes surinamensis* . . Black Perch. **1933** LA Dept. of Conserv. *Fishes* 206, Elsewhere this species [*Lobotes surinamensis*] has been called . . Black Perch.

b Std: The fish *Embiotica jacksoni* which is also called **blue perch 2, croaker 1c, surf-fish.**

c =red roncador 1.

1946 LaMonte *N. Amer. Game Fishes* 82, *Sciæna saturna* . . *Names:* . . Black Perch.

d =white perch.

1953 Md. State Dept Educ *Our Underwater Farm* 15 (Hench Coll.), Fish have different names in different parts of our [=Chesapeake] Bay . . . on the Western Shore the common white perch is called a black perch. **1968** *DARE* (Qu. P2, . . *Saltwater fish . . good to eat*) Inf **MD40,** Black perch.

black persimmon n

A **persimmon** tree *(Diospyros texana)* native to southern Texas which produces black, dark-fleshed fruits. Also called **chapote, Mexican persimmon, mustang persimmon, possum plum**

1846 (1941) Gregg *Diary* 1.239 **TX,** Among other wild fruits of this vicinity, [is] that called by Mexicans *chapote* and generally by Americans, black persimmon. **1897** Sudworth *Arborescent Flora* 321, *Diospyros texana,* Mexican Persimmon . . . Common names [include] . . Black Persimmon (Tex.), Chapote (Tex.). **1967** *DARE* (Qu. T16) Inf **TX13,** Black persimmon.

black-pied curlew n Also *black-pieded curlew*

=white ibis.

1913 *Auk* 30.491 sGA, They [=natives of Okefenokee] also designate some brown and white ones [*Gaura alba* (White Ibis)] as . . 'Black-pieded Curlews,' which roost with the other two. **1955** *Oriole* 20.3, White Ibis. — Black-pied Curlew (black-pied refers to the black wing tips).

black pine n

1 Any of several pines native chiefly east of the Mississippi River as:

a also *black slash pine:* **=loblolly pine 1.**

a1782 (1788) Jefferson *Notes VA* 39, Black, or pitch-pine, *Pinus taeda.* **1809** Kendall *Travels* 3.146 **ME,** The black pine or pitch pine *(pinus taeda)* grows in sands. **1897** Sudworth *Arborescent Flora* 26, *P[inus] taeda* . . . Black Slash Pine (S.C.) . . . Black Pine (Va.). **1960** Vines *Trees SW* 23, *Pinus taeda* . . . Other vernacular names are . . . Black Pine. **1968–70** *DARE* (Qu. T17) Inf **GA20,** Black pine — same as loblolly; **VA**75, Black pine—long tag. Note: In addition to those listed here and at **1c**, 40 Infs responded with *black pine* to Qq. T15, T16, and T17. These responses cannot be differentiated further for **black pine 1.**

b =**jack pine 1.**

1897 Sudworth *Arborescent Flora* 30, *Pinus divaricata* . . . Black Pine (Minn.). **1908** Britton *N. Amer. Trees* 44, It [=*Pinus banksiana*] is also known as . . . Jack pine, . . . Black pine. **1968–69** *DARE* (Qu. T17) Infs **MI**93, 102, **WI**23, 64, Black pine.

c also *black Norway pine:* =**pitch pine 1.**

1897 Sudworth *Arborescent Flora* 27, *Pinus rigida* . . . Black Pine (N.C.) . . . Black Norway Pine (N.Y.). **1900** Lyons *Plant Names* 292, *P[inus] rigida* . . . Black Norway Pine. **1967–69** *DARE* (Qu. T17) Infs **CT**2, **RI**15, **TN**14, Black pine.

d A **pond pine** (here: *Pinus serotina*).

1903 Small *Flora SE U.S.* 28, *Pinus serotina* . . . Black Pine. **1927** Boston Soc. Nat. Hist. *Proc.* 38.213 **Okefenokee GA**, *Pinus serotina* Black pine.

2 Any of three western pines:

a =**lodgepole pine.**

1884 Sargent *Forests of N. Amer.* 195, *Black Pine. Lodge-pole Pine* . . . A tree 18 to 24 meters in height. **1897** Sudworth *Arborescent Flora* 23, *Pinus murrayana* . . . Black Pine (Wyo.). **1973** Hitchcock–Cronquist *Flora Pacific NW* 62, Black pine . . . *P[inus] contorta.*

b also *blackbark pine, blackback* ∼: =**Jeffrey pine.**

1897 Sudworth *Arborescent Flora* 22, *Pinus jeffreyi* . . . Black Pine (Cal.) . . . Blackbark Pine . . . (Cal. lit.). **1970** *DARE* (Qu. T17) Inf **VA**43, Blackback pine.

c =**ponderosa pine.**

1910 Jepson *Silva CA* 79, The bark of *Pinus ponderosa* is exceedingly variable. Black-barked or brown-barked trees . . are very common . . , all of which indicates the significance of their local names, "Black Pine," . . and "Yellow Pine." **1967** *DARE* (Qu. T17) Inf **ID**5, Black pine—ponderosa. Note: In addition to the above Inf, 12 Infs (**CA, OR, WA**) responded with *black pine* to Qu. T17. These responses cannot be differentiated further for **black pine 2.**

black plantain n [Perh from the blackish appearance of the heads]

A **buckhorn plantain** (here: *Plantago lanceolata*).

1969 *DARE* FW Addit **seNY**, Black plantain—black dock; a narrow leaf plantain; cook into tea and rub on poison ivy. **1969** *DARE* (Qu. S9) Inf **NY**207, Black plantain.

black plaster n

1968 *DARE* FW Addit **neWV**, In dealing with injuries of horses and cows, locally they use "black plaster," the principal ingredient of which is tar, with medicine added.

black porgy n

=**tautog.**

1939 Natl. Geog. Soc. *Fishes* 66, In Chesapeake Bay it *[Tautoga onitis]* occasionally is called blackfish, other names being . . black porgy.

black Portuguese n Also *black Portagee*

=**brava.**

1941 *LANE* Map 452a **seMA**, *Negro . . . Colored man*, used also of a [blæk ˈpɔrtəgi]. **1969** *DARE* (Qu. HH28, . . *People of foreign background . . . Portuguese*) Inf **RI**13, Black Portuguese.

black potato bug n Cf **old-fashioned potato bug**

Prob a **blister bug.**

1966 *DARE* (Qu. R30) Inf **MI**37, Black potato bug—about an inch long, they fly.

black pox See **black smallpox**

black Protestant n [*black* hostile + *Protestant*] **chiefly NEast** *usu derog*

A Protestant who is felt to be intolerant of or prejudiced against Catholics; a non-practicing Protestant.

1968–69 *DARE* (Qu. CC4, . . *Nicknames . . for various religions or religious groups*) Inf **NY**78, Black Protestant—old-fash, not practicing; **NY**213, Black Protestants—What Catholics call Protestants; **RI**13, Black Protestant. **1969** *DARE* Tape **PA**225, There was a strong line drawn between Catholics and Protestants . . . They'd call them Black Protestants. **1980** *DARE* File **Boston MA**, Among Irish Catholics, especially of my grandmother's generation, black Protestants are those

who are bigoted in their opposition to Catholics. The term is definitely derogatory.

black racer n

1 also *blacksnake racer, black runner:* Either of two common black subspp (*Coluber constrictor constrictor* and *C.c. priapus*) of the **racer 1** which range throughout much of the eastern third of the US. Note: despite the wider distribution of the snake, *DARE* Infs who used the term 'black racer' were **chiefly S Midl**; *DARE* Infs using 'black runner' were **chiefly Sth.** See Map Section

1788 Schöpf *Reise Staaten* 2.214 **FL**, Eine Schlange, der schwarze Läufer (Black Runner) genannt, wurde vor einiger Zeit getödet, und 12 Fuss lang gefunden. [A snake, called the black runner, was killed some time ago and found [to be] 12 feet long.] **1836** Latrobe *Rambler in N. Amer.* 2.46 **FL**, He would tell us . . of the powers of the black-runner in destroying the rattle-snake, by the inconceivable swiftness of its motions. **1849** Lanman *Letters Alleghany Mts.* 22 **GA**, I saw one [snake fight], Monday was a week, between a black-racer and a rattlesnake. **1869** (1970) Jones *Wild Western* 246 **MO**, Dod, they ain't pisen! . . . They're nearly all black racers, and they don't bite. **1908** *DN* 3.291 **eAL, wGA**, *Black-runner* . . . A black snake noted for fleetness. Also called *black racer*, or simply *racer.* **1928** Pope *Amphibians* 53 **WI**, *Black Snake* . . . Also may be called Black Racer. **1965–70** *DARE* (Qu. P25) 28 Infs, **chiefly S Midl**, Black racer; 17 Infs **chiefly Sth**, Black runner; Infs **WV**13, 16, Blacksnake racer. **1969** *DARE* FW Addit **NC Coast**, *Black racer* . . . Snake common on Hatteras Island.

2 A black phase of the **coachwhip snake** (esp of *Masticophis flagellum piceus*). **SW**

1947 Pickwell *Amphibians* 43 **SW**, Coloration and markings of this Snake vary greatly, and . . . until recently the Black Racer was classified as a separate species. **1964** Lowe *Vertebrates* 168 **AZ**, Coachwhip . . . Color phases . . in Arizona and elsewhere are called red racer and black racer. **1970** *DARE* (Qu. P25) Inf **CA**211, Black racer; **TX**81, Black racer—[same as] coachwhip. **1974** Shaw–Campbell *Snakes West* 88, The second phase of the same subspecies *[Masticophis flagellum piceus]* is entirely black on its back. (It is often called the western black racer in this region.)

black rattlesnake n Also *black rattler*

A dark-colored rattlesnake such as the **massasauga** or the **timber rattlesnake.**

1778 Carver *Travels N. Amer.* 479 **N Cent**, The *Rattle Snake.* There appears to be two species of this reptile; one of which is commonly termed the Black, and the other the Yellow. **1928** Pope *Amphibians* 71 **WI**, *Banded Rattlesnake. Crotalus horridus* . . . Other common names for this snake are Common Rattlesnake, Timber Rattlesnake, Rock Rattlesnake, Yellow Rattlesnake and Black Rattlesnake . . . Varies from sulphur-yellow to velvety-black . . . Common in the western part of the state. **1967–68** *DARE* (Qu. P25) Infs **TN**1, **WV**2, 5, 7, Black rattler; **FL**34, **VA**1, Black rattlesnake; **DC**2, Black rattlesnake—twenty years ago; a rare case.

black road n Also *blacked road*

A road paved with blacktop.

1931–33 *LANE Worksheets* **ceMA**, Some years ago a black road (a tar-bound macadam) was built which was called a concrete road; **swME**, Blacked road . . . Tarred road. **1936** *Sun* (Baltimore MD) 15 Sept 11/2 *(Hench Coll.)*, In appearance there will be little difference between the cotton roads and th[e] so-called "black roads" of bitumonous [sic] macadam. **1974** *DARE* File **cwMA** (as of 1920–30), Prescott never had any black roads.

black rock n

1962 Wyld *Low Bridge* 98 **cwNY**, The canaller's diet included at times a commodity known as "Black Rock" pork, a canal equivalent to the western cowboy's "jerky."

black rockfish n

1 also *spotted* ∼: Either of two fish of the genus *Sebastichthys*: *S. mystinus* or *S. melanops.* Also called **blue rockfish, pêche prêtre, priestfish, rockfish**

1887 Goode *Amer. Fishes* 268, *Sebastichthys mystinus*, is most generally called the "Black Rockfish." . . The Spotted Black Rockfish, *Sebastichthys melanops*, is founded with *S. mystinus* by the fishermen, under the name of "Black Bass" in Puget Sound, "Black Rockfish" in San Francisco. **1902** Jordan–Evermann *Amer. Fishes* 497, *S. mystinus*, the black rockfish, is the most abundant species in rather shallow water about San Francisco. **1939** Natl. Geog. Soc. *Fishes* 228, Black rockfish

(Sebastodes mystinus). **1960** Amer. Fisheries Soc. *List Fishes* 37, Black rockfish . . . *Sebastodes melanops.*

2 =black grouper 1.

1933 John G. Shedd Aquarium *Guide* 100, *Trisotropis bonaci — Black Rockfish.* **1946** LaMonte *N. Amer. Game Fishes* 49, *Mycteroperca bonaci . . . Names:* . . . Black Rockfish.

black roller n, also attrib

=black blizzard.

1936 *The Daily Oklahoman* 17 Mar **nwCO** *(AmSp* 13.72), He disappeared just before a 'black roller' dust cloud made midnight of mid-day Sunday. **1938** *AmSp* 13.71 **OK,** *Black roller,* also applying to the severest sandstorms.

black roncador n

=red roncador 1.

1887 Goode *Amer. Fishes* 134, *Corvina saturna,* is known wherever found as the "Red Roncador," less commonly as "Black Roncador" or "Croaker."

blackroot n, also attrib

1 =culver's root.

1709 (1941) Byrd *Secret Diary* 4 **VA,** I sent him some blackroot . . for the gripes. **1876** Hobbs *Bot. Hdbk.* 13, Black root — *Leptandra Virginica.* **1965–68** *DARE* (Qu. BB22, . . *Home remedies . . for constipation)* Infs IL83, IN13, MS1, TN31, 34, 36, Blackroot; (Qu. BB50d, *Favorite spring tonics around here)* Inf MS60, Blackroot tea. **1971** Krochmal *Appalachia Med. Plants* 268, *Veronicastrum Virginicum* . . . Common names: Culver's physic, Beaumont root, blackroot . . . Uses: The rhizome is reputed to be a laxative, emetic, cholagogue, and tonic.

2 A plant of the genus *Pterocaulon,* native to the South.

1892 Coulter *Botany W. TX* 201, *Pterocaulon* . . . (Black-root.) . . Perennial herbs. **1933** Small *Manual SE Flora* 1400, *Pterocaulon* . . . Black-root . . . The thick black root gives this plant its common name. **1975** Duncan–Foote *Wildflowers SE* 206, Black-root . . . Perennial from large dark roots. Leaf undersides and stem with feel of kid leather because of short, densely felted, and light-colored hairs.

3 =colicroot 2 (here: *Aletris farinosa).*

1892 (1974) Millspaugh *Amer. Med. Plants* 172, *Aletris farinosa* . . . *Com. Names* . . . Black Root . . . When used in the fresh state, emetic, cathartic, and somewhat narcotic. **1959** Carleton *Index Herb. Plants* 13, Blackroot: Aletris farinosa.

black runner See black racer 1

black sage n West

1 also *black sagebrush:* A **sagebrush** (here either *Artemisia arbuscula* or *A. tridentata).*

1876 Bourke *Journal* 12 Mar *(DA),* Across the Southern boundary of Montana, in a region well grassed with gramma and the 'black sage,' a plant almost as nutritious as oats. **1924** Amer. Botanist 30.33, *A[rtemisia] tridentata* is called "black sage" about as often as "sage-brush." **1931** U.S. Dept. Ag. *Misc. Pub.* 101.167, *Big sagebrush (Artemisia tridentata)* . . . Other vernacular names include black sage, a name derived from the dark bark color of the older stem. *Ibid* 173, *Low sagebrush (A. arbuscula),* locally known as black sage, is a dwarf bush. **1940** *Jrl. Mammalogy* 21.168 **NV,** The bark of black sagebrush *(Artemisia tridentata)* was often used. **1960** Vines *Trees SW* 969, *Artemisia tridentata* . . . is also known as Black Sage.

2 A blue-flowered **sage 1** *(Salvia mellifera)* native to California and noted as a honey plant. Also called **blue sage**

1897 Parsons *Wild Flowers CA* 294, *Black Sage. Ball Sage* . . . Particularly abundant in the south, . . often covering whole hill-slopes. **1940** *Jrl. Mammalogy* 21.388 **CA,** This farm was originally covered with such plants as . . black sage *(Salvia mellifera).* **1946** Peattie *Pacific Coast* 53, White sage, black sage, and purple sage all yield fine honeys. **1967–68** *DARE* (Qu. S26a) Inf CA4, Black sage; (Qu. S26e) Inf CA60, Black sage — desert; CA79, Black sage — hill sides.

3 A **blue curls 1** (here: *Trichostema lanatum).*

1900 Lyons *Plant Names* 376, *T. lanatum* . ., California, is called Black Sage. **1916** Parsons *Wild Flowers CA* 323, *Woolly Blue-Curls* . . . This plant is also sometimes called "black sage."

4 A **bitterbrush 1** (here: *Purshia tridentata).*

1931 U.S. Dept. Ag. *Misc. Pub.* 101.52, *Bitterbrush (Purshia tridentata)* . . . Other English names often applied to it are . . black sage, deer brush, and quinine brush. **1937** U.S. Forest Serv. *Range Plant Hdbk.*

B116, Other common names often applied to this plant are . . black sage and deerbrush.

black sagebrush See black sage 1

black salmon n

1 Prob an Atlantic salmon *(Salmo salar).*

1832 Williamson *Hist. ME* 1.160, There are three varieties; the *black* Salmon, which is the smallest; the *hawkbill* . . ; and the *smoothnosed.* **1966** *DARE* Tape ME10, Some stay in all winter and go back in the spring and then they call them black salmon.

2 =cobia.

1935 Caine *Game Fish* 57, *Rachycentron canadus . . . Synonyms:* Black Bonito, Black Salmon, . . Cobio, Crab-eater [etc.]. **1972** Sparano *Outdoors Encycl.* 376, *Cobia . . . Common Names:* . . coalfish, black salmon, black bonito.

black sampson n

A **purple coneflower,** usu *Echinacea purpurea.*

1848 Gray *Manual of Botany* 223, *E. purpurea* . . . Root thick, black, very pungent to the taste, used in popular medicine under the name of *Black Sampson.* **1901** Lounsberry *S. Wild Flowers* 520, *Black Sampson* . . . More gorgeous than any Rudbeckia and infinitely more charming are these great, heavy heads of crimson blossoms. **1930** OK Univ. Biol. Surv. *Pub.* 83, *Echinacea purpurea* . . . Black Sampson. **1961** Wills–Irwin *Flowers TX* 234, *Echinacea angustifolia* . . . Purple Coneflower, or Black-sampson as it is sometimes called, . . . was applied to burns and superficial wounds. **1974** (1977) Coon *Useful Plants* 107, Black sampson . . . is a tallish growing perennial widely found in the Midwest . . . The roots are the part used.

black Saturday n

1938 (1955) FWP *Guide DE* 402, "Black Saturday" . . at Bowers Beach . . was set aside by the landowners in 1852 or soon afterwards as a holiday for slaves and free Negroes who also wanted to celebrate the opening of the oyster season. Like Big Thursday, Black Saturday survives as a day of rest and amusement, with much eating, sleeping, and promenading in fine clothes.

black scavenger n

=black vulture.

1917 (1923) *Birds Amer.* 2.57, *Black Vulture . . . Other Names* . . . Black Scavenger.

black scoter See scoter

black sea bass n

1 also *black bass:* A dark-blue, black-banded food fish *(Centropristes striatus)* of the Atlantic coast. Also called **blackfish, black harry, black perch 2, black will, hannahill, humpback, tallywag, rock bass, sea bass**

1842 DeKay *Zool. NY* 4.25, The Black Sea Bass, *Centropristes nigricans,* . . [is] sometimes called Blue-Fish, Black Harry. **1855** U.S. Natl. Museum *Annual Rept. for 1854* 323, *Black Bass — Sea-Bass, Centropristes nigricans* . . . The black fish, as an article of food, may be reckoned among the best of the fishes of the coast. **1859** (1968) Bartlett *Americanisms, Black Bass* . . . On the Jersey coast, this name is also given to the Sea Bass *(Centopristes nigricans).* **1906** NJ State Museum *Annual Rept. for 1905* 308, *Centropristes striatus* . . . Black Sea Bass. **1966–68** *DARE* (Qu. P2, . . *Saltwater fish . . good to eat)* Infs MD36, NC12, Black bass.

2 also *California ~, giant ~:* **=giant sea bass 1.**

1882 U.S. Natl. Museum *Bulletin* 16.531, *S[tereolepis] gigas* . . . Black Sea Bass. **1902** Jordan–Evermann *Amer. Fishes* 380, Imagine this, and you have the jewfish, black sea-bass, or *Stereolepis gigas* of the Pacific coast. **1946** LaMonte *N. Amer. Game Fishes* 45, California Black Sea Bass — *Stereolepis gigas* . . . *Names:* . . Black Sea Bass. **1972** Sparano *Outdoors Encycl.* 382, *Common Names:* California black sea bass, giant black sea bass. *Scientific Name: Stereolepis gigas.*

black sea coot See black coot

black sea duck See sea duck

blacks, give one the v phr

To snub or ignore someone.

1966 *DARE* (Qu. II6, *If you meet somebody who used to be a friend, and he pretends not to know you: "When I met him on the street he _____."*) Inf **SC26,** Give me the blacks.

black sheep n

1 A children's game: see quot.

1968 *DARE* (Qu. EE12, *Games in which one captain hides his team and the other team tries to find it*) Infs **NJ27, PA148,** Black sheep; (Qu. EE15) Inf **MO**17, Black sheep—part of run-sheep-run.

2 A call used in blindman's buff; see quot. Cf **blacksnake** n **4**

1966 *DARE* Tape **AL3,** If blindfolded person went where he shouldn't, the others shouted "black sheep."

black sheep v

1927 *AmSp* 2.348 **WV,** *Black sheep one* . . to obtain another person's job. "Will Henry blacksheeped me while my father was sick and they needed me at home."

black-sheep cloud n Cf **sheep cloud, sheepshead**

A storm cloud.

1967 *DARE* (Qu. B11, *Are there any other kinds of clouds that come often around here?*) Inf **LA**11, Black-sheep clouds—come in one behind the other before a storm.

black slash pine See **black pine 1a**

black smallpox n Also *black pox* [From the association of black with death]

An esp lethal form of smallpox.

1957 Beck *Folkl. ME* 45, The most commonly recognized diseases— black pox (smallpox), spotted fever. **1965** *Dorland's Med. Dict.* 1397, *Black s[mallpox],* hemorrhagic s[mallpox]. **1967** *DARE* (Qu. BB49, . . *Kinds of diseases*) Inf **CO20,** Black smallpox.

black snake n

1 A **racer 1**—esp the **black racer 1** in the East and Southeast— or a similar snake.

1634 Wood *New Engl. Prospect* 46, A great long blacke snake, two yards in length which will glide through the woods very swiftly. **1900** U.S. Natl. Museum *Annual Rept. for 1898* 794, The *Zamenis constrictor* is the "black snake" of the East and the "blue" and "green racer" of the West. **1945** Mathews *Talking Moon* 150 **OK,** The blacksnakes, having no young rabbits to prey on, are a greater menace to the birds. **1965–70** *DARE* (Qu. P25) 487 Infs, **widespread,** Black snake. Note: some of these Infs may be referring instead to **black snake 2.**

2 =**pilot blacksnake.**

1892 IN Dept. Geol. & Nat. Resources *Rept. for 1891* 501, *Alleghany Black-snake . . . Coluber alleghaniensis . . .* Our indistinctly spotted and almost jet black form is not distinguished by most people from the Black-racer, although it is a very different snake. [**1935** *Copeia* 1.42, The pilot blacksnake . . has several times been noted on the islands of the St. Lawrence River . . . Two live ones from Gananoque Lake were sent . . . Farmers in the vicinity have told me that they have seen as many as 15 or 20 blacksnakes in the spring.] **1967** *DARE* (Qu. P25) Inf **AR**51, Blacksnake or chicken snake; **LA**3, Blacksnake—same as chicken snake.

3 also attrib: A long, leather whip.

1914 *DN* 4.162 **NW,** *Black snake* . . . A short-handled whip with a long lash; used on stages and dog-teams. **1928** in 1977 *Pissing in the Snow* 202 **Ozarks,** "If you-uns ever come back," says old lady Mosely, "it will be a regular blacksnake next time, instead of these little switches." **1929** *AmSp* 5.62 **NE.** c**1960** *Wilson Coll.* cs**KY,** *Blacksnake whip* . . . A leather whip of four strands, plaited round. **1967–69** *DARE* Tape **CA**160, A blacksnake . . was a leather tube sort of thing with a buckskin popper on it that tapered . . . They [=muleskinners and teamsters] used to always carry them around their neck; **MI**56, A blacksnake . . . The stock was two and a half, maybe three foot long; it was all braided leather, eight foot long to the tip; **WV**2, That was the height in your career when you got so you could drive six mules to a wagon and use a big blacksnake wagon whip. **1967–70** *DARE* (Qu. K27) Infs **LA**12, **VA**10, Blacksnake; **IN**3, **VA**38, Blacksnake whip.

4 A call used in blindman's buff to warn the blindfolded player of an obstacle. Cf **black sheep** n **2**

1968 *DARE* (Qu. EE4) Inf **GA**58, Call "black snake" if you're going to run into anything.

5 Among railroad workers: see quot.

1945 Hubbard *Railroad Ave.* 333, *Black snake*—Solid train of loaded coal cars.

blacksnake v

1 To whip or punish (someone). [**black snake** n **3**]

1935 Davis *Honey* 173 **OR,** His uncle blacksnaked him for coming home late.

2 To crawl on one's belly.

1923 *DN* 5.233 sw**WI,** *Blacksnake; blacksnake it* . . . To crawl as a blacksnake would crawl. "He blacksnaked it up to git within gunshot."

blacksnake racer See **black racer 1**

black snakeroot n

1 A **bugbane 1,** usu *Cimicifuga racemosa.*

1698 (1848) Thomas *Hist. & Geog. Acct.* 19, There grows also in great plenty the *Black Snake-Root,* (fam'd for its sometimes preserving, but often curing the *Plague,* being infused only in Wine, Brandy or Rumm.). **1782** (1788) Jefferson *Notes VA* 36, Black snake-root, Actaea racemosa. **1840** MA Zool. & Bot. Surv. *Herb. Plants & Quadrupeds* 21, Cohosh. Black Snakeroot . . . Strong medicinal properties; cultivated in the gardens of the Shakers. **1941** Walker *Lookout* 48 **TN,** Among the wild plants once employed as antidotes for the bites of poisonous reptiles, are rattlesnake master, blacksnake root, rattlesnake-weed, Samson snakeroot, or scurfy. **1976** Bruce *How to Grow Wildflowers* 167, Bugbane, *Cimicifuga racemosa* . . . Other names for this plant are Black Cohosh and Black Snakeroot.

2 =**sanicle 1,** usu the more easterly spp.

1837 Darlington *Flora Cestrica* 184, *S[anicula] marilandica . . . Vulgo* —Black Snake-root . . . Woodlands and thickets: common. **1848** Gray *Manual of Botany* 156, *Sanicula . . . Sanicle. Black Snake-root.* **1891** Coulter *Botany W. TX* 145, *Black snakeroot . . .* Fruit densely covered with hooked prickles. **1916** Keeler *Early Wildflowers* 169, *Black Snakeroot . . .* blooms about the middle of May, ripening its fruit in July. **1963** Zimmerman–Olson *Forest* 151, *Black Snakeroot . . .* Sometimes solitary, sometimes in colonies but present in almost all Oak stands.

3 also *black snakeweed:* A **wild ginger 1** (here: *Asarum canadense*).

1876 Hobbs *Bot. Hdbk.* 13, Black snakeweed, Wild ginger, Asarum Virginicum. **1900** Lyons *Plant Names* 49, *A. Canadense . . .* Black or Coltsfoot Snakeroot. **1971** Krochmal *Appalachia Med. Plants* 66, Black snakeroot, black snakeweed . . . The rhizome has value as an expectorant, antiseptic, and tonic.

4 Either of two other plants considered medicinal: see quot.

1975 Hamel–Chiltoskey *Cherokee Plants* 55, Snakeroot, black; . . white baneberry . . *Actaea pachypoda . . .* Tea to relieve and rally a patient at point of death . . . Snakeroot—black, virginia . . *Aristolochia serpentaria . . .* Chew root and spit on snakebite.

black snap n chiefly **NEng**

A black **huckleberry 1** (here: *Gaylussacia baccata*).

1894 *Jrl. Amer. Folkl.* 7.93, *Gaylusaccia resinosa* . . black snaps, Wells, M[ain]e. **1907** *DN* 3.181 se**NH,** *Black-snaps . . .* Gaylussaccia; huckleberries. The seeds snap when eaten. **1931** Clute *Common Plants* 42, One might be puzzled to know why one species of huckleberry (*Gaylussacia baccata*) is called crackers, cracker berry, and black-snaps, until in eating the fruit he finds the seeds cracking between his teeth. **1960** Vines *Trees SW* 815, *Gaylussacia baccata . . .* Also known as the . . Black Snap. **1966** *DARE* (Qu. S26a) Inf **ME**7, Black snaps—similar to blueberries.

black snapper n

1 Either of two **snappers:** esp the **schoolmaster,** but also *Apsilus dentatus.*

1882 U.S. Natl. Museum *Proc.* 5.275, *Lutjanus caxis . . . Black Snapper.* **1887** Goode *Amer. Fishes* 79, It [*Lutjanus caxis*] is called . . the "Black Snapper" at Pensacola. **1946** LaMonte *N. Amer. Game Fishes* 59, *Lutianus apodus . . . Names: . .* Black Snapper. **1960** Amer. Fisheries Soc. *List Fishes* 26, Black snapper . . *Apsilus dentatus.*

2 =**jewfish** (here: *Epinephelus itajara*).

1946 LaMonte *N. Amer. Game Fishes* 45, Spotted Jewfish—*Promicrops itaiara . . . Names: . .* Black Snapper.

3 =**massasauga.**

1951 Conant *Reptiles OH* 112, *Sistrurus catenatus catenatus . . . Massasauga; Swamp Rattler; Black Snapper.* **1958** Conant *Reptiles & Amphibians* 188.

blacksnipe n

1 =**solitary sandpiper.**

1925 (1928) Forbush *Birds MA* 1.440, *Tringa solitaria . . .* Solitary Sandpiper. *Other names: . . .* Black Snipe. **1946** Hausman *Eastern*

Birds 271, *Eastern Solitary Sandpiper Tringa solitaria* . . . Other Names . . . Black Snipe. **1955** *MA Audubon* 39.18, *Solitary Sandpiper.* Black Snipe (Mass., R.I. Dark grayish brown above, the wings appearing very dark . .).

2 =**black-bellied plover.**

1923 U.S. Dept. Ag. *Misc. Circular* 13.68, *Black-bellied Plover (Squatarola squatarola) . . . In local use:* . . black spine (Ala.). **1962** Imhof *AL Birds* 229, *Black-bellied Plover—Squatarola squatarola* . . . Other Names: Beetlehead, Blacksnipe.

black snow n Cf **black blizzard**

1941 FWP *Guide CO* 5, These weather-beaten plainsmen . . continue to grow crops . . in spite of . . the now lessening menace of dust—"black snow"—to their fields.

black socks n

A religious group that shuns the use of church buildings.

1967 *DARE* (Qu. CC4, . . *Nicknames . . for various . . religious groups*) Inf **NE8**, Black socks—for people without church buildings, who don't believe in being frivolous; **NE10**, Black socks—they don't believe in church buildings and go about two by two. They call themselves undenominational.

black sop n [*black* + *sop*] Cf **white sop**

1906 *DN* 3.127 nwAR, *Black sop* . . . Ham gravy. "Us children used to like black sop on our bread."

black spell See **blackout spell**

black spot n

An area shaded from the sun.

1936 *AmSp* 11.275 cTN, *Black spots.* Shade. "You don't have any black spots in your yard." **1944** Adams *Western Words, Black spot*—What the cowboy calls a piece of shade.

black-spotted trout n Also *black trout*

=**cutthroat trout.**

1882 U.S. Natl. Museum *Bulletin* 16.316, *S[almo] purpuratus* . . Black Trout. **1887** Goode *Amer. Fishes* 457, The Black Spotted Trout, the *Salmo purpuratus.* **1911** *Century Dict.* 6503, *Black trout,* the Lake Tahoe trout: specified as *Salmo henshawi.* **1946** LaMonte *N. Amer. Game Fishes* 115, *Salmo clarkii* . . . Names: . . Black-spotted Trout. **1972** Sparano *Outdoors Encycl.* 356, Black-spotted trout . . . Scientific Name: *Salmo clarki.*

black spruce n

1 also *black spruce fir:* An evergreen resinous conifer *(Picea mariana).* Also called **bog spruce, cat spruce, double spruce, he-balsam, juniper, spruce pine, swamp spruce, tamarack, white spruce, yew pine**

1765 Rogers *N. Amer.* 48 NH, You will find beach, hemlock, and some white pines; higher up the growth is chiefly black spruce. **1803** Lambert *Descr. Pinus* 1.41, Black Spruce Fir . . . *P. nigra,* grows wild only in New England, Canada, Nova Scotia. **1965–70** *DARE* (Qu. T5) 10 Infs, Nth, Black spruce; (Qu. T15) Infs **CT**13, **ME**8, **MI**53, **MN**14, Black spruce; (Qu. T16) Inf **NH**4, Black spruce.

2 =**white spruce** (here: *Picea glauca).*

1897 Sudworth *Arborescent Flora* 37, *Picea canadensis* . . . *Common Names* . . . Black Spruce (Pa. . .).

black stinging gnat See **black gnat**

black story n [*black* wicked, dishonorable + *story* lie, falsehood]

1952 Brown *NC Folkl.* 1.521, *Black story* . . . A decidedly bad lie.—General.

black striker n

=**black tern.**

1917 *Wilson Bulletin* 29.2.76, *Hydrochelidon nigra surinamensis.*—Adult is black striker, young, pigeon gull, Wallops Id., Va.

black sucker n

Any of several **suckers,** esp:

1 =**spotted sucker.** *obs*

1820 Rafinesque *Ohio R. Fishes* 58, A singular species seen at the falls. It is rare and called Spotted Sucker or Black Sucker.

2 also *blackback sucker, black suckrel:* =**Missouri sucker.**

1820 Rafinesque *Ohio R. Fishes* 58, Black-back Sucker . . . Vulgar names Black Sucker and Blue Sucker. **1820** *Western Rev.* 2.355, Black Suckrel. *Cycleptus nigrescens* . . . A rare fish, whose flesh is very much

esteemed. It is also found in the Missouri, whence it is sometimes called the Missouri Sucker. Length two feet. **1839** MA Zool. & Bot. Surv. *Fishes Reptiles* 86, *Cyprinus nigricans* . . . The black Sucker . . . Color of the back, black; sides reddish yellow. **1871** *Amer. Naturalist* 4.386, Mud-loving species . . common to the Delaware and its tributaries . . . [include] Black Sucker. **1967** *DARE* (Qu. P3, *Freshwater fish . . not good to eat*) Inf **IA**11, Black sucker.

3 =**white sucker.**

1949 Caine *N. Amer. Sport Fish* 159, *White Sucker—Catostomus commersonii—Colloquial Names*—Black Sucker.

4 =**hog sucker.**

1960 Amer. Fisheries Soc. *List Fishes* Z3, Black sucker [*Hypentelium nigricans*].

black sugar See **black maple**

black sugar bread n

1967 *DARE* (Qu. H18, . . *Special kinds of bread*) Inf **HI**6, Black sugar bread—azuke beans mashed up, bean curd, and sweetened with brown sugar, then steamed in a bun.

black sugar maple See **black maple**

black sunfish n

=**warmouth.**

1933 LA Dept. of Conserv. *Fishes* 342, The Warmouth Bass has come to bear many confusing popular names. These are: . . Black Sunfish.

black Susie n

=**black-eyed Susan 2.**

1968 *DARE* (Qu. S7) Inf **IN**14, Black Susie; (Qu. S11) Inf **NC**80, Black Susie.

black swallow n

Perh the **purple martin.**

1966–69 *DARE* (Qu. Q20) Infs **GA**3, **IL**85, **LA**37, **MI**101, Black swallow.

black-tailed deer n Also *black-tail (deer), black-tail mule deer*

A **mule deer** or a subsp thereof.

1806 (1905) Lewis *Orig. Jrls. Lewis & Clark Exped.* 4.87, The Black tailed fallow deer. **1825** (1929) *Atkinson–O'Fallon Exped.* 24 **ND**, A black tail deer was killed on this river by one of the hunters. **1826** Godman *Amer. Nat. Hist.* 2.304, *The Black-tail Deer.* Cervus Macrolis. **1848** (1962) U.S. Army *Abert's NM Rept.* 33, Of the latter there are two varieties, the common deer, and the black tail. **1965–70** *DARE* (Qu. P32) 10 Infs, chiefly **West**, Black-tail deer; **HI**14, Black-tail mule deer. **1968** Adams *Western Words, Blacktail*—Black-tailed deer. **1969** O'Connor *Horse & Buggy West* 162, He would even tell you about the canyon where he'd seen a big desert mule deer buck (which he always called a "blacktail").

blacktail sunfish n

=**longear sunfish.**

1820 Rafinesque *Ohio R. Fishes* 29, Big-Ear Sunfish . . . tail black, slightly forked: . . . A fine species, called . . Black-tail Sunfish &c. **1946** LaMonte *N. Amer. Game Fishes* 139.

black tern n

A small dark short-tailed tern *(Chlidonias nigra surinamensis).* Also called **black gull, black striker, marsh tern, mosquito gull, pigeon gull, sea pigeon, short-tailed tern, slough gull, water swallow**

1844 Giraud *Birds Long Is.* 352, The Black Tern, like the rest of its tribe, has great powers of wing, and though apparently delicately formed, it is strong and muscular. **1967–70** *DARE* (Qu. Q10) Infs **MI**53, **VA**47, Black tern.

black thorn n

1 =**black haw 3.**

1897 Sudworth *Arborescent Flora* 215, *Crataegus douglasii* . . . *Common Names* . . . Black Thorn (Idaho, Utah, Wash.).

2 A **nannyberry** (here: *Viburnum lentago*).

1900 Lyons *Plant Names* 392, *V. Lentago* . . . Black Haw, Black Thorn.

blackthorn locust n

1951 *PADS* 15.34 **TX**, *Gleditsia aquatica* . . . Black-thorn, swamp, or water locust.

black timber ant n

Prob =**carpenter ant.**

1967 *DARE* (Qu. R18) Inf **CO**37, Black timber ant, in timber, ¾ inches long.

black titi n |'blæk 'taɪˌtaɪ| Cf **red titi, white titi**

1 =**buckwheat tree.**

1897 Sudworth *Arborescent Flora* 277, *Cliftonia monophylla . . . Common Names . . .* Black Titi (Fla.). **1933** Small *Manual SE Flora* 812, *Black-titi . . .* The flowers are an important source of honey. **1972** Brown *Wildflowers LA* 104, *Black Titi . . .* Common in the acid pinelands, bogs, and wet sites in southeastern Louisiana.

2 =**he-huckleberry 1.**

1901 Mohr *Plant Life AL* 601, *Cyrilla racemiflora . . . Black Ti-ti . . .* Sandy swamps, borders of pine-barren streams. **1953** Greene–Blomquist *Flowers South* 68, *Black Titi . . .* This small tree of swamps, pocosins, bays, and stream banks . . is easily spotted . . by its sprays . . of white flowers. **1976** Bruce *How to Grow Wildflowers* 149, *Gray's Manual of Botany* (which lists its common names as He-huckleberry and Black Ti-ti as well as those already given) says the following about the plant: "Autumnal foliage scarlet or orange, gorgeous when mingled with the bright yellow fruit."

black tobacco n

1 See quot. Also called **dark tobacco**

1944 *PADS* 2.64, *Black-tobacco, dark-tobacco . . .* A variety of tobacco grown especially in western Kentucky; it is also grown in other parts of the country.

2 also *export tobacco:* See quot. Also called **dark-faced tobacco** Cf **African black fats**

1944 *PADS* 2.64, *Black-tobacco . . .* A shade of color of the cured leaf affecting the price on the market . . . Formerly the term *export-tobacco* was often used. This kind of tobacco has a stronger, more marked flavor which was preferred in certain foreign countries.

black Tom n chiefly **NYC** *old-fash* Cf **black man 2**

A children's tag game: see quots.

1891 *Jrl. Amer. Folkl.* 4.224 **Brooklyn NY**, *Black Tom*—The boy who is "it" stands in the middle of the street, and the others on the pavement on one side. When "it" cries, "Black Tom" three times, the other players run across, and may be caught, in which case they must join the one who is "it" in capturing their comrades. **1901** *DN* 2.136, *Black-Tom . . .* A game. Brooklyn. The cry used is pron[ounced] [blæk tɔm]. **1909** (1923) Bancroft *Games* 54 **NYC**, *Black Tom . . .* Two parallel lines are drawn on the ground with a space of from thirty to fifty feet between them. All of the players except one stand beyond one of these lines. In the middle territory between the lines the one player who is chosen to be It takes his place . . . The other players must all rush across to the opposite line, being chased by the center player . . . Any one . . caught joins him thereafter in chasing the others . . . The game as here given is played in Brooklyn, N.Y. **1965** Dundes *Folklore* 331, The games . . Black Tom, and Dodge the Skunk . . are similar to Pom-Pom-Pullaway . . . *It* was required to tag pack members as they ran from one home area to the other . . . The Black Tom *It* called a series of names the last one of which (Black Tom) was the signal that required the pack members to run to the opposite home.

blacktongue n chiefly **Sth, S Midl** See Map

Any of various diseases (including anthrax and pellagra) of humans and animals in which darkening of the tongue is symptomatic.

1834 *Amer. Railroad Jrl.* 3.120/3, A disease in horses and cattle called the *Black Tongue* or the *Burnt Tongue.* **1845** in 1956 Eliason *Tarheel Talk* 260 **NC**, A very fatal disease has been ravaging the counties of Edgecomb & Northampton, it is called the "black tongue," the patient dies in six hours after he is taken & very few cures are effected. **1919** Dunn *Indiana* 2.804 **sIN**, In 1842–3 epidemic erysipelas prevailed in a number of counties in southern Indiana, and was known by a number of popular names, as "black tongue," "sore throat." **1937** *Hall Coll.* **wNC**, I allowed they [=deer] might a tuck the black tongue and died, just like it tuck the cattle. There was no cure. **1938** Rawlings *Yearling* 267 **FL**, A plague has hit the wild creeturs. Hit's the black tongue. **1954** *Harder Coll.* **cwTN**, *Black tongue . . .* A disease of cows. **1965–70** *DARE* (Qu. K28, . . *Diseases that cows have around here*) 24 Infs, **chiefly Sth, S Midl**, Blacktongue; (Qu. K47, . . *Diseases . . horses or mules commonly get around here*) Inf **MI**67, Blacktongue.

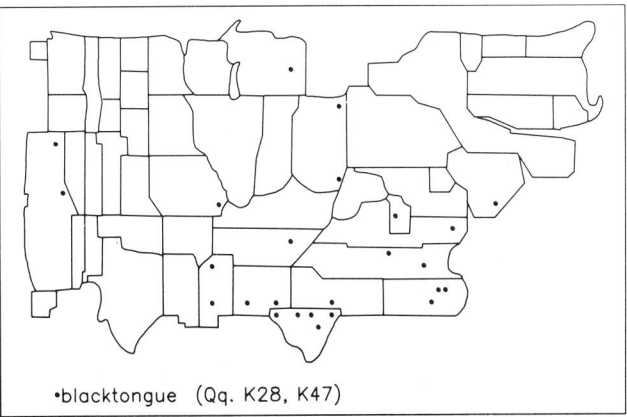

•blacktongue (Qq. K28, K47)

black-top mushroom n

=**inky cap.**

1970 *DARE* (Qu. I37) Inf **OH**95, Black-top mushroom.

black tree See **black mangrove**

black tripletail See **tripletail**

black trout n

1 =**largemouth black bass.**

1849 Lanman *Letters Alleghany Mts.* 9.65, On inquiring of a homespun angler what fish the river did produce, he replied: "Salmon, black-trout, red horse, hog-fish, suckers and cat-fish." **1882** *U.S. Natl. Museum Bulletin* 11.75, *Micropterus salmoides . . .* The "Black Trout" occurs . . and is still more abundant.

2 See **black-spotted trout.**

3 A black-and-white, cultivated bush bean. Also called **coachdog bean, polka dot**

1976 *Wanigan Catalog* 4, *Black Trout* A strain of Trout [bean], with the red color replaced with black. Growth similar to Trout.

black tupelo n

=**black gum 1.**

1950 Moore *Trees AR* 102, *Nyssa sylvatica . . .* Local Names: Black Tupelo. **1960** Vines *Trees SW* 801, *Black Tupelo—Nyssa sylvatica.*

black turtle n

=**alligator snapper.**

1968 *DARE* (Qu. P24) Inf **LA**34A.

black valentine bean n

An early-maturing bush bean (*Phaseolus* spp.).

1966–69 *DARE* (Qu. I20) Infs **GA**72, **NC**37, Black valentine (beans). **1978** *Wanigan Catalog* 4, *Black Valentine* Syn[onym]s: French String, May Queen, King of the Earlies . . . A flat light green snap bean. Seed thin, black.

black velvet spider n

1967 *DARE* (Qu. R28) Inf **TX**17, Black velvet spider—supposed to be poisonous.

black viper n

=**hognose snake.**

1969 *DARE* (Qu. P25) Inf **KY**11, Spread heads—includes two species: black vipers and spotted vipers.

black vulture n Also *black-headed vulture, blackhead*

A large scavenger bird (*Coragyps atratus*). Also called **black buzzard 2, black scavenger, carrion crow, Charleston buzzard, corn crow, Jim Crow, zopilote** Cf **turkey vulture**

1791 (1958) Bartram *Travels* 289, These breed and continue the year round in Pennsylvania: . . Vultur atratus, black vulture. **1814** Wilson *Amer. Ornith.* 9.105, It is said that the Black Vultures sometimes attack young pigs, and eat off their ears and tails. **1858** Baird *Birds* 5, *Cathartes Atratus . . .* The Black Vulture. **1917** (1923) *Birds Amer.* 1.57, Black vulture. **1938** Oberholser *Bird Life LA* 152, *Black Vulture Coragyps atratus atratus* (Meyer) . . . It may be distinguished by its black head and its rather square instead of rounded tail which is very conspicuous when the bird is in flight. **1966–70** *DARE* (Qu. Q13) Inf **FL**51, Blackhead; **DC**8, Black-headed vulture.

black wagon n Also *black buggy* [*black* (from the association with death and because usu painted black) + *wagon*]

1 =**black Maria 1.**

1967–68 *DARE* (Qu. N2, *The car used to carry a dead body for burial*) Infs **NJ**1, 16, **WI**12, Black wagon; **VA**38, Black buggy.

2 =**black Maria 2.**

1967–70 *DARE* (Qu. N1, *Other names for an ambulance*) Infs **KY**49, **MI**108, **NJ**1, **PA**44, Black wagon.

black warmouth See **warmouth**

black warrior n [Prob from the large size and usu dark coloration]

1 =**Harlan's hawk.**

1831 Audubon *Ornith. Biog.* 1.442, The Black Warrior has been seen to pounce on a fowl, kill it almost instantly, and . . conceal it. 1839 MA *Zool. & Bot. Surv. Fishes Reptiles* 269, The *Black Warrior* . . subsists on poultry, partridges and other birds. 1858 Baird *Birds* 24, Harlan's Buzzard; The Black Warrior . . . In the collection . . are two specimens of the bird which . . . were obtained near Fort Thorne, New Mexico. 1874 Coues *Birds NW* 352, Harlan's Buzzard; Black Warrior . . . I regard the claims of this species to validity as not yet established. 1932 Bennitt *Check-list* 22, Harlan's hawk . . . Black warrior. 1946 Goodrich *Birds in KS* 320, Colloquial Name . . . Warrior, black. 1951 Pough *Audubon Water Bird* 320, Black warrior. See Harlan's hawk.

2 =**channel catfish.**

1957 Trautman *Fishes* 415 **OH,** Largest adults (colloquially called . . black warriors and loggerheads) are dark steel-blue with whitish bellies.

black wasp n

Any of var dark-colored wasps such as the **mud dauber 1.**

1789 Morse *Amer. Geog.* 62, INSECTS found in America . . [include the] Black Wasp. 1902 Harben *Abner Daniel* 52 **nGA,** "You look fer the world like a dirt-dauber." This comparison to a kind of black wasp came from Pole Baker. 1965–70 *DARE* (Qu. R21) 106 Infs, **chiefly east of Missip R,** Black wasp; (Qu. R20) 9 Infs, **scattered,** Black wasp.

black water n

1 Coffee, esp weak coffee.

1850 Garrard *Wah-to-Yah* (*AmSp* 16.185), **SW,** Though coffee, sugar, tobacco, and other luxuries are high-priced, and often purchased with a whole season's trapping, the "black water" is offered with genuine free-heartedness. 1968 Adams *Western Words, Black water*—A freighter's term for weak coffee.

2 Ink.

1939 *AmSp* 14.89 **cTN,** Black water. Ink. 'School children write their lessons with black water.'

3 See **black waterite.**

black waterite n Also *black water* [See quot 1963] **chiefly eKY** Cf **melungeon**

A person of mixed race, usu Black, Indian and White.

1947 *AmSp* 22.82, [Tri-racial mixed-blood groups] *Black Waterites,* or *The Black Waters.* (A division of the *Melungeons.*) 1963 Berry *Almost White* 35, In Eastern Kentucky the mixed-bloods are called Black Waterites, because they live along the Black Water Creek.

black watermelon n [See quot 1981]

See quots.

1954 *Harder Coll.* **cwTN,** Black watermelon . . . Big, dark green watermelon with black seeds. 1981 *NADS Letters* **NC,** The term *black watermelon* is most likely to be a more generic term for a particular variety of watermelon, the "black diamond" watermelon . . . The melon itself is an extremely large, slightly elongated round melon with a skin of such a dark shade of green that it is (or appears to be) almost black.

black watersnake n

=**water moccasin.**

1952 Ditmars *N. Amer. Snakes* 218, Common Water Snake, Water "Moccasin," *Natrix sipedon sipedon* . . . Occasional specimens are very dark brown and called "black" water snakes. 1965–70 *DARE* (Qu. P25) Infs **CT**17, **MD**45, **NY**155, 212, 233, **RI**15, Black watersnake.

black wax n, also attrib Also *black waxy* **chiefly AR, sOK and esp nTX** Cf **waxy**

A dark soil which is sticky or wax-like.

1893–5 *Stand. Dict.* 2042/1 (*DA*), Black wax . . . A tenacious black mud found in Texas. 1903 (1965) Adams *Log Cowboy* 357 **cnTX,** If any of you know anything about that black-waxy, hog-wallow land in Ellis County, you know that when it gets muddy in the spring a wagon wheel will fill solid with waxy mud. 1927 *My Okla.* Apr 24/1 (*DA*), The crop may be grown on about any type of soil except the 'black-waxy' and extremely heavy clays. 1941 FWP *Guide AR* 237, In the "black wax" soil of the delta are great plantations, farmed principally by Negro sharecroppers or day laborers. 1970 *DARE* (Qu. C31, . . *Heavy, sticky soil*) Inf **TX**84, Black waxy.

black wax bean See **black bean 2**

black will n **C Atl**

=**black sea bass.**

1887 Goode *Amer. Fishes* 39, In the Middle [Atlantic] States the Sea Bass is called "Black Will," "Black Harry," and "Hannahills." 1936 *Hench Coll.* **VA,** On a guided fishing trip we heard a guide call a fish a "black will." It is a fish with large black and white spots. It is usually called "sea bass." 1939 Natl. Geog. Soc. *Fishes* 84, The common sea bass, which is often known as black will, in the Chesapeake region, . . ranges from Massachusetts to the Atlantic coast of Florida. 1968 *DARE* (Qu. P2, . . *Saltwater fish . . good to eat*) Infs **DE**1, **MD**36, Black wills. 1970 *DARE* Tape **VA**112, They catch . . black will, they call 'em; black bass is the proper name for 'em.

black willow n

1 Any of var dark-barked willows, but esp *Salix nigra* which is also called **pussy willow** and **swamp willow.**

1802 (1803) Ellicott *Jrl.* 284 **LA,** Black-willow . . [is] not in great abundance, and becomes more scarce as you descend the river. 1947 *Amer. Midland Naturalist* July 38, Black Willow . . [is] occasional (locally common) in river swamps. 1965–70 *DARE* (Qu. T15) Infs **NM**13, **TX**5, 22, **UT**3, 4, 13, **WI**12, 17, Black willow; (Qu. T16) Inf **OR**10, Black willow.

2 =**mule fat.**

1894 *Jrl. Amer. Folkl.* 7.91, *Baccharis viminea,* . . black willow, Santa Barbara Co., Cal.

black wind See **black blizzard**

blackwood See **black mangrove**

black woodcock n

=**pileated woodpecker.**

1811 Wilson *Amer. Ornith.* 4.27, In Pennsylvania and the northern states he is called the Black Woodcock; in the southern states, the Log-cock. 1858 Baird *Birds* 107, Black Wood Cock. 1932 Bennitt *Check-list* 41 **MO,** *Northern pileated woodpecker. Ceophloenus pileatus abieticola* . . black woodcock. 1953 Jewett *Birds WA* 399, Western Pileated Woodpecker. *Dryocopus pileatus picinus* . . . Other names: . . Black Woodcock. 1962 Imhof *AL Birds* 331, *Pileated Woodpecker . . . Other Names:* . . Black Woodcock.

black woodpecker n

1 =**pileated woodpecker. East**

1917 (1923) *Birds Amer.* 154, Pileated Woodpecker . . . *Other Names* . . . Great Black Woodpecker. 1946 Hausman *Eastern Birds* 382, Black Woodpecker . . . *Field Marks*—A large black woodpecker almost as large as a crow. 1955 Forbush–May *Birds* 294.

2 =**Lewis's woodpecker. West**

1917 (1923) *Birds Amer.* 2.158, *Lewis's Woodpecker . . . Other Names.*—Black Woodpecker. 1923 Dawson *Birds CA* 1033, For all the Black Woodpecker keeps largely to the tops of trees, it is not averse to . . fallen acorns. 1953 Jewett *Birds WA* 400. 1966 *DARE* (Qu. Q17) Inf **ID**1, Black woodpecker.

black word n [*black* hostile, dishonorable]

1966 *DARE* (Qu. Y4, . . *A very uncomplimentary remark*) Inf **MI**18, Black word.

blackworm n

1 An earthworm.

1949 *AmSp* 24.106 **seGA, ceSC,** Blackworm . . . Earthworm. 1970 *DARE* (Qu. P6) Inf **VA**41, Blackworm.

2 Perh a sawfly larva. *obs*

1859 Perry *Turpentine Farming* 106 **NC,** Black Worm.—This insect is to be found on green pines in the latter part of spring, from which time, during the remainder of the season, they may be seen wherever scars reach the wood. They commence working on the tender skin, which passes out with the turpentine, and cakes, getting their growth, which is about the size of a common garden worm, and of the same shape, while at work.

bladder bush See **bladder sage**

bladder campion n
Std: a **catchfly 1,** usu *Silene vulgaris* which is also called **bull rattle, cottonweed 7, cowbell, devil's rattlebox, fairy potatoes, maiden's tears, rattlebags, rattlebox, snappers, white bottle**

bladder parsnip n
A **biscuit root 1** (here: *Lomatium utriculatum*).
    1911 Jepson *Flora CA* 303, *Bladder Parsnip* . . . Many stems and leaves from a thick taproot. **1961** Thomas *Flora Santa Cruz* 261, Bladder Parsnip. Open grassy slopes and ridges.

bladderpod n
1 A plant of the genus *Lesquerella.* Also called **popweed**
    1857 Gray *Manual of Botany* 37, *Vesicaria . . . Bladder-pod.* **1901** Lounsberry *S. Wild Flowers* 203, *Bladder-pod. Lesquerella Lescurii . . . Pods:* inflated; round; two-valved. **1915** (1926) Armstrong *Western Wild Flowers* 184, There are a good many kinds of Lesquerella . . . Pods roundish, more or less inflated, and giving the common name, Bladder-pod. **1973** Hitchcock–Cronquist *Flora Pacific NW* 171.
2 also *bladder-podded lobelia:* =**Indian tobacco** (here: *Lobelia inflata*).
    1876 Hobbs *Bot. Hdbk.* 2, Bladder podded lobelia, . . Lobelia inflata. **1900** Lyons *Plant Names* 228, *L. inflata* . . . Bladder-pod. **1911** Henkel *Amer. Med. Leaves* 35, *Lobelia inflata . . . Other common names.—*Indian tobacco, . . bladder pod, low belia, eyebright. **1971** Krochmal *Appalachia Med. Plants* 164, *Common Names:* . . bladder pod, bladder-podded lobelia . . . Flowers situated in axils of alternate leaves, the bottom of which greatly inflate in the fruiting stage.
3 A shrub *(Cleome isomeris)* native to California and the Desert Southwest which produces inflated pods. Also called **burro fat**
    1897 Parsons *Wild Flowers CA* 144, *Bladderpod* . . . Its yellow flowers attract one to it, only to be repulsed by the dreadful odor of its foliage. **1923** Davidson–Moxley *Flora S. CA* 161, *Bladderpod* . . . Pod oval, inflated, coriaceous, tardily 2-valved. **1957** Jaeger *N. Amer. Deserts* 254, *Bladder Pod* . . . Common much-branched shrub with yellow wood, ill-scented leaves, handsome yellow flowers, and inflated green fruits . . . A favorite source of nectar for bees and hummingbirds.
4 =**bagpod**.
    1933 Small *Manual SE Flora* 703, *Sesbania vesicaria* . . . *Bladderpod.* **1948** Miami (Okla.) D. *News-Record* 30 June 8/2 *(DA),* Farmers call it bladderpod, coffeebean and castle-bean. **1970** Correll *Plants TX* 836, *Bag-pod, bladder pod* . . . Coastal States, N.C. to Tex.
5 =**double bladderpod.**
    1961 Peck *Manual OR* 373, *P[hysaria] Chambersii . . . Chambers' Bladder-pod* . . . Silicles densely stellate, strongly inflated.

bladder sage n Also *bladder bush* [From the inflated mature calyx]
A desert shrub *(Salazaria mexicana)* of the southwestern US. Also called **paper-bag bush**
    1915 (1926) Armstrong *Western Wild Flowers* 448, *Bladderbush . . . Salazaria Mexicana* . . . The calyxes become inflated and form very curious papery globes, over half an inch in diameter. **1925** Jepson *Manual Plants CA* 865, *Bladder Sage* . . . Stems several in a cluster, . . forming a clumpy bush 2 to 4 ft. high. **1981** Benson–Darrow *Trees SW Deserts* 204, *Bladder Sage* . . . is a common shrub in the Mojave Desert, and sometimes it forms nearly pure stands.

bladderscat n [Alter of *blatherskite* a blustering incompetent person]
    1969 *DARE* (Qu. V2a, . . *A deceiving person, or somebody that you can't trust*) Inf TX72, A ['blædə,skat].

bladderstem n [From the inflated hollow flowering stem] =**desert trumpet.**
    1975 Zwinger *Run River* 249 UT, The weird bladderstems seem appropriate to this other world, plants so far apart that each seems a glorious invention.

blade n chiefly **Sth, S Midl**
1 also attrib: A leaf of a corn plant.

1688 in 1693 Royal Soc. London *Philos. Trans.* 17.986 **VA,** I advised her likewise to save, and carefully gather her *Indian* Corn-tops, and blades, . . and whatever could be made Fodder. **1724** (1865) Jones *Present State VA* 40, *Indian Corn* is the best Food for *Cattle* . . and the *Blades* and *Tops* are excellent *Fodder.* **1865** *Nation* 1.333 **NC,** Later in the day they could be seen coming up out of the fields, carrying on their heads great stacks of the dried fodder, which is at once stowed away in blade-houses. These are small buildings with walls of logs, between which are left wide apertures for the admission of air, as the fodder is apt to grow musty. **1899** (1912) Green *VA Folk-Speech, Blades* . . . The leaves of corn pulled and dried for fodder. **1966–69** *DARE* Tape **GA1,** Fodder, that's the blades off'n the corn for feed; **KY28,** Some just pull the blade off. **1968–70** *DARE* (Qu. L9b, *Hay from other kinds of plants [not grass]*) Inf **FL50,** Used to make hay from blades offa that corn; **VA14,** Blades and tops. Made from corn: the blades from the ear down, the tops from the ear up. It was cured, bundled, and stacked in the barn to be used like hay.
2 The stalk of a green onion.
    1966–67 *DARE* (Qu. I7, *The small plants like onions with hollow green leaves that are cut up in salad*) Infs **GA8, OK27,** Onion blades; **TX37,** Blades.
3 usu as second element in var combs: A tool used to cut vegetation (as grass, weeds, grain). See Map
    1954 *Harder Coll.* cwTN, *Briar blade* . . . Tool used for cutting briars, weeds, small bushes, and often grain. **1965–70** *DARE* (Qq. L28, L35, L37) 187 Infs, **chiefly Sth, S Midl,** (Briar, bush, ditch, grass, mowing, sling) blade [see further in DS]; 2 Infs, Blade.

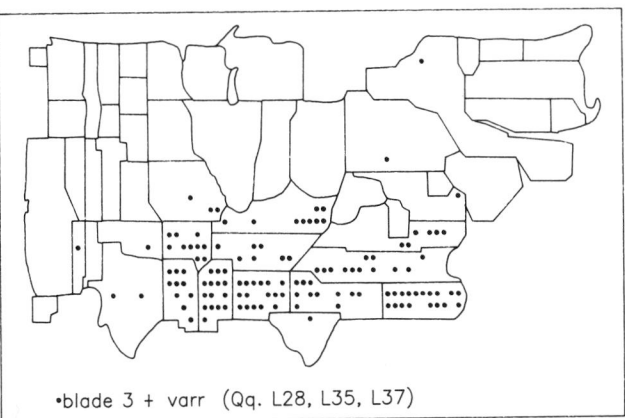

•blade 3 + varr (Qq. L28, L35, L37)

4 usu *old ~:* One's wife. [By ext of *blade* a woman] *joc*
    1915 *DN* 4.181 swVA, *Blade* . . . Wife. "My old blade's been sick now goin' on a week." **1967–69** *DARE* (Qu. AA22, *Joking names that a man may use to refer to his wife*) Infs **GA77, TN15,** Old blade—old-fashioned.

blade fodder n [blade 1 + fodder n 2] chiefly **S Midl**
Corn leaves (and sometimes tops) dried and used as feed for cattle and horses.
    1823 in 1910 Commons *Doc. Hist. Amer. Industrial Soc.* 1.256 ceTN, For example, the tops are not cut from the corn. The blade fodder only is pulled, and that not always. **1904** (1913) Johnson *Highways South* 321 seVA, In a few days the "blade fodder" was ready for storage. **1917** *DN* 4.408 wNC, KY, *Blade fodder.* Tops of corn stalks. **1945** *Richmond Times Dispatch* 26 May 6/7 (Hench Coll.), After the War between the states . . . Corn played the dual role of grain and fodder. When it was ripe, the leaves were stripped off and tied in bunches and hung on the stalk to dry. This was known as blade fodder, and considered fine horse feed. **1969** *DARE* FW Addit **KY,** Blade fodder is cattle feed made from the blades or leaves of a corn plant.

blade-knife n
    1970 *DARE* (Qu. F39, *A large pocket knife with blades that fold in and out*) Infs **CA205,** Snap blade-knife; **MA124,** Blade-knife; **VA36,** Folding blade-knife; **VA42,** Long blade-knife.

blaggard See **blackguard**

blala See **bla**

blan See **belong A1, 2**

blanc-bec n Also sp *blan-bec* [Fr *blanc* white + *bec* beak, nose, mouth] **West** *rare* or *obs*

See quots.

1846 in 1938 *AmSp* 13.87, A Missouri voyageur who had never passed the Platte was called a *Blan-bec;* and upon his first passing he was subjected to an initiation.   **1968** Adams *Western Words,* Blanc-bec — Greenhorn; from the French, meaning *white-face.*

blanket n

1 also attrib in *blanket-piece:* Among whalers: a large strip of whale blubber.   **chiefly N Atl**   *hist*

1851 (1976) Melville *Moby-Dick* 304, The long upper strip, called a blanket-piece, swings clear.   **1938** Tripp *Flukes* 202 **New Bedford MA,** The big blubber-hook came steadily up the side of the schooner bringing with it the long strip of blubber, termed the "blanket piece."   **1942** Berrey–Van den Bark *Amer. Slang* 789.4, Blanket, *a whale's coating of blubber.*

2 also attrib: A beaver pelt, esp a large one.

1954 White *Adirondack Country* 249 **nNY,** They tell of the "blankets" — the big ones — they did get, and how the biggest beaver of all slipped away.   **1969** *DARE* Tape **NY183,** They added the length and width . . and everything over 72 inches they considered a blanket beaver . . . It's extra large.

3 also in combs *horse blanket, monkey ~, saddle ~:* A pancake. *joc*

1927 *DN* 5.439 [Underworld jargon], *Blankets . . .* Griddle cakes.   **1942** Berrey–Van den Bark *Amer. Slang* 91.14, *Griddle cakes.* Blankets, . . monkey blankets, . . saddle blankets.   **1967–68** *DARE* (Qu. H20b, *What other names do you have for pancakes?*) Inf **OR1,** Horse blankets; **WA30,** Monkey blankets or saddle blankets.   **1969** Sorden *Lumberjack Lingo* **NEng and Gt Lakes,** *Blankets* — Pancakes.

4 also *saddle blanket:* A dollar bill.   *joc*

1967–68 *DARE* (Qu. U26, *Names or nicknames around here for a paper dollar*) Inf **IN45,** Blanket; **TX29,** Saddle blanket.

blanket-buck n   Also *blanket-ass*   *derog*

An American Indian.

1967–69 *DARE* (Qu. HH28, *Names and nicknames around here for . . Indians*) Inf **AZ6,** Blanket-bucks; **TX72,** Blanket-ass.

blanket busted adj

Among loggers: see quot.

1958 McCulloch *Woods Words* **Pacific NW,** *Blanket busted* — A man who has lost everything on a bet, including his bedroll.

blanket chest n   **chiefly Nth, esp NEng**

A large case with a hinged lid and drawers underneath, used to store bedding, linen, dishes, etc.

1941 *LANE* Map 340, The map shows the terms *chest of drawers,* . . *blanket chest . . .* **cwCT,** *Blanket chest,* low and long . . . **swME,** *Blanket chest,* a low chest with a hinged lid.   **1951** Ormsbee *Early Amer. Furniture* 175, At the same time, its [=the chest of drawers'] ancestor with drawer beneath was not discarded as obsolete. Known as a blanket chest, it too continued to be made.   *Ibid* 185, *Early Blanket Chest . . .* Made all of maple or pine from Massachusetts to Pennsylvania.   **1967–68** *DARE* (Qu. E3, E5) Infs **MA5, MI68, OH36, VT8,** Blanket chest.

blanket drawers n

Among loggers: see quot.

1958 McCulloch *Woods Words* **Pacific NW,** *Blanket drawers* — Long handled underwear about the same itchiness and same thickness as a horse blanket.

blanket fever n

1969 Sorden *Lumberjack Lingo* **NEng and Gt Lakes,** *Blanket fever* — Referring to condition of lumberjack who stays in bed in the morning after the other men are up. Generally a lazy lumberjack.

blanket flower n [From the similarity of its coloration, often red-and-yellow, to that of an Indian blanket]
=gaillardia.

1879 Meehan *Native Flowers* 1st ser 2.182, In the settled parts of Texas, where some of the species are found wild, the *Gaillardia* is known as the "Blanketflower."   **1900** Lyons *Plant Names* 166, *Gaillardia . . .* Blanket-flower . . . Herbs with large flower heads, the rays occasionally wanting.   **1933** Small *Manual SE Flora* 1461, *Gaillardia . . .* About 20 species, all except one North American. — Blanket-flowers.   **1963** Craighead *Rocky Mt. Wildflowers* 212, Blanketflower . . . First appears

when Bitterroot is in bloom and elk are calving.   **1969** *DARE* (Qu. S26a, c) Inf **NC76,** Blanket flowers.

blanket hoist n

1969 Sorden *Lumberjack Lingo* **NEng and Gt Lakes,** *Blanket hoist* — A punishment as well as a game. If a jack got out of place, other jacks would put him in a blanket, get hold of the sides of the blanket, and hoist him in the air a few times.

blanket leaf n   Also *blanketweed*   [*EDD* 1882 →]
=mullein.

1900 Lyons *Plant Names* 389, *V[erbascum] thapsus* [sic] . . . Adam's flannel, Blanket-leaf.   **1930** Sievers *Amer. Med. Plants* 42, *Mullein . . .* Other common names . . . Old-man's-flannel, blanket-leaf.   **1951** Teale *North Spring* 222, Mullein, that plant of many names — . . blanket leaf, Adam's-flannel . . — was beginning the production of the thick, felty leaves of a new year.   **1976** Dodge *Roadside Wildflowers* 63 **SW,** *Blanketweed . . .* Merely a rosette of woolly leaves the first year, each plant produces, the second summer, a flower-dotted stalk 2 to 6 feet tall.

blanket man See **blanket stiff**

blanket, on the wrong side of the adv phr

Out of wedlock.

1968 *DARE* (Qu. Z11b, . . *A child of unwed parents*) Infs **IN39,** Wrong side of the blanket; **OH80,** Born on the wrong side of the blanket.

blanket-piece See **blanket 1**

blanket squad n

Among loggers: see quot.

1958 McCulloch *Woods Words* **Pacific NW,** *Blanket squad* — A new crew coming in to camp in the old days, each man carrying his blankets.

blanket stiff n   Also *blanket man*   [*blanket* (from the freq hobo practice of carrying a bed-roll) + *stiff* tramp, laborer]   **chiefly West**
=bindle stiff.

1872 Powers *Afoot* 309 **CA,** One of the notable phenomena of California is the multitude of its tramps, the so-called "blanket-men."   **1891** *AN&Q* 7.187/2, The 'blanket man' is known only in California. In the East he would probably be called a tramp . . . But he is not really a tramp. He is one of those hard-working fellows that the conditions of agricultural life in California have called into existence . . . When they have finished the work . . , they pack their blankets and seek occupation elsewhere.   **1900** Willard *Itinerant Policeman* 167 **West,** Among the "Blanket Stiffs" in the far West . . there exists a crude system of marking "good" houses.   **1935** *AmSp* 10.12, *Blanket stiff.* A hobo or migratory worker who carries a blanket roll . . . Persists only in hobo lingo.   **1945** Service *Ploughman* 191 **CA,** I hardly think they would have wanted to know a blanket-stiff, idly dreaming, while his few dollars melted away.   **1968** *DARE* (Qu. HH19, *Other words or nicknames for a tramp*) Inf **CA87,** Blanket stiff — carries blankets and change of clothes; can be trusted to do some work.

blanketweed See **blanket leaf**

blankie-lie-low exclam, n   See quots for var proncs   Also *black-a-li-lo* [*blankie, blacka* perh from *blackie* ref to *black sheep* + *lie low* a warning to hiding players]   **chiefly Nth**   *old-fash*   Cf **black sheep** n 1

A call used in a children's hiding game; the game itself; see quots 1901, 1953.

1901 *DN* 2.136 **NY,** *Black-a-li-lo . . .* "In this game the one who is *it* must find the others by calling out 'holler or I won't foller,' which they must answer by 'black-a-li-lo.' Through the dark and tangled garden the timid hunter must follow that fleeting cry." Marion, Wayne Co., N.Y. In Steuben Co., N.Y., the first cry is "hoop hoop holler or I shan't foller."   **1950** *WELS* (Games in which one captain hides his team and the other *team tries to find it*) 1 Inf, **cWI,** ['blæŋk o ˌlaɪlo].   **1953** Brewster *Amer. Nonsinging Games* 50 **VT,** *Blankie Lie Low . . .* This game is similar to Run, Sheep, Run in that one group of players hides from the other. In the former, however, *all* the players of a group hide, and the warning cry "Blankie lie low!" is uttered not by the leader only but by any member of the hiding group.   **1966** *DARE* FW Addit **PA,** Blankie-lie-low: a hide and seek game. [Inf 67 years old]   **1968–70** *DARE* (Qu. EE16, *Hiding games*) Inf **PA234,** Kids run and hide — call out ['blænč ə laɪlo], all after dark; **WI24,** [blæŋk šə laɪlo]. [Both Infs old]

blanks See **belong A1**

blanny n [From *blarney* n by r-loss]
Ingratiating or flattering speech.
  1926 *DN* 5.398 **Ozarks,** *Blanny* . . . Cajolery. [*DN:* Blarney?] "Ab
Lee's blanny shore did gravel th' school-marm."

blanny v [**blanny** n]
To ingratiate oneself; to apple-polish, esp by using flattering
speech.
  1968 *DARE* (Qu. JJ3a, *When a schoolchild makes a special effort to 'get
in good' with the teacher in hopes of getting a better grade: "He's trying to
_____ again."*) Inf **IN8,** Blanny ['blæni].

blants See **belong A1**

blare v
  1 Of cows and occas sheep: to low or bleat; hence vbl n *blaring.*
chiefly Nth, esp NEng Cf **blate**
  1903 *DN* 2.295 **Cape Cod MA** (as of 1850s), *Blare* . . . Bellow, of a cow
or calf. **1907** *DN* 3.181 **seNH.** **1939** *LANE* Map 194 **throughout
NEng,** The map shows the verbs *moo,* . . *blare,* . . used to designate the
sound made by a cow. **1949** Kurath *Word Geog.* 23, **MA, NH,** The
Merrimack Valley . . has retained some striking localisms: . . *blare* for
the loud cry of a calf. **1967–68** *DARE* (Qq. K19, K21) Inf **NV1,** Blare;
(Qu. K66) Infs **MO36, NV1,** Blare. **1973** Allen *LAUM* 1.252, *Bawl* (of a
calf being weaned) . . . *Blare,* a New England equivalent not reported by
fieldworkers, seems to be the term used by 14 respondents [to a mailed
checklist], 8 in Minnesota, 2 in northern Iowa, and 2 in South Dakota. A
Northern bias is evident.
  2 To distort the mouth as if bleating.
  1970 *Foxfire* Spring–Summer 16 **nGA,** When they [=raccoons] first
come out an' hit th' fresh air, they'll just blare their mouth like a possum
grinnin' an' they'll fall over.
  3 also *blare out:* See quot. [By ext of *blare* to sound loudly]
  1908 *DN* 3.291 **eAL,** *Blare (out)* . . . To break forth in vituperation.
"What did you blare out on me for?"
  4 To open (the eyes) widely; to stare wildly. [By ext of *blare* to
shine forth brilliantly, to glare] **chiefly Sth** Cf **blared, blare-
eyed**
  1930 Faulkner *As I Lay Dying* 179 **MS,** "You won't help me?" Jewel
says, them white eyes of hisn kind of blaring and his face shaking like he
had a aguer. **1964** Faulkner *Hamlet* 309 **MS,** That varmint in the door
behind me blaring its eyes at me. **1981** *NADS Letters* **neLA,** Horses eyes
often blare, in fear, and sometimes in anger.
  5 See quot.
  1912 Green *VA Folk-Speech,* *Blare* . . . To open wide: "The door was
blared wide open."

blared ppl adj [**blare 4**] **chiefly Sth** Cf **blare-eyed**
Of an eye: wide-open, bulging.
  1966 *DARE* (Qu. X21a, *What words are used to describe people
according to their eyes—for example, if they stick out?*) Inf **FL26,** Blared
eyes. **1973** *Foxfire 2* 304 **nGA,** Aunt Arie told us . . of a neighbor who
was shot during a fight and died with his eyes open — "blared," she called
it. "And you could see th'devil in 'em — them fightin', y'know."

blare-eyed ppl adj [**blare 4**] **chiefly Sth** Cf **blarey-eyed**
Having wide-open, bulging eyes.
  1964 Faulkner *Hamlet* 288 **MS,** Whoa you blare-eyed jack rabbit,
whoa! **1966** *DARE* (Qu. X21a, *What words are used to describe people
according to their eyes—for example, if they stick out?*) Inf **MS23,**
Blare-eyed. **1981** *NADS Letters* **neLA,** I have experienced an angry
blare-eyed man with a rifle, because I did not survey to suit him.

blarey-eyed adj [Prob alter of **blare-eyed** perh infl by *bleary-
eyed*]
Having eyes which turn outward; walleyed.
  1970 *DARE* (Qu. X26b, *If a person's eyes look in different directions,
looking outward, he's _____*) Inf **NY236,** [blærɪ]–eyed. [Inf Black]

blarsted See **blasted**

blask n [Alter of *blast*]
  1896 *DN* 1.412 **csSC,** *Blasks:* for *blasts.*

blaspheme vine n [From its thorny, virtually impenetrable
vines which invite blasphemy]
A **greenbrier** (here: *Smilax laurifolia*).
  1933 Small *Manual SE Flora* 314, *S[milax] laurifolia* . . Blaspheme-

vine. **1950** Gray–Fernald *Manual of Botany* 450. **1966** Grimm *Recognizing Native Shrubs* 75, *Smilax laurifolia* . . Also known as
the . . Blaspheme-vine. **1970** Correll *Plants TX* 411, *Smilax laurifolia* . . Blaspheme-vine.

blasphemious adj Pronc-sp for *blasphemous* Cf **mischievious**
  1908 *DN* 3.291 **eAL, wGA,** *Blasphemious* . . . Blasphemous. **1914**
DN 4.69 **ME, nNH,** *Blasphemious* . . . Blasphemous.

blast n
  1 A severe reprimand, a verbal attack. Cf **blast** v
  1874 in 1917 Twain *Letters* 1.226, I gave the P.O. Department a blast in
the papers. **1935** *Time* 11 Mar 23/3, Despite blast and counter-blast
between President Roosevelt and Soviet Foreign Minister Litvinoff.
1965–70 *DARE* (Qu. Y4, . . *A very uncomplimentary remark*) Inf
CA59, Blast; (Qu. II27, . . *A very sharp scolding* . . "*I certainly got a
_____ for that.*") Infs **CA15, IL30, MD24, MI81, MA45, 71, PA162,
WI73,** Blast.
  2 See quot.
  1899 (1912) Green *VA Folk-Speech,* *Blast* . . . A small wood-fire in a
fireplace: "Make a small blast, it is chilly this morning."
  3 freq in phr *beer blast:* A raucous party, spec one at which
much liquor or beer is consumed; a drinking bout or binge.
chiefly among younger, educ speakers; casual
  1963 *AmSp* 38.171 **FL, MI, KS** [College jargon], A particularly rough
and noisy party: *blast* . . *beer blast.* **1965–70** *DARE* (Qu. AA18, . . *A
noisy neighborhood celebration after a wedding*) Infs **IL97, 126,** Blast;
(Qu. DD16, *To have a drinking bout and get drunk is to go on a _____*)
Infs **FL39, MN28, VA79,** Blast; (Qu. DD34, *A party at which there is
considerable drinking*) 22 Infs, **scattered,** Blast; **IL97, IN1, NY7, 123,
198, OH46, PA223,** Beer blast; (Qu. FF2, . . *Kinds of parties*) Infs **IL98,
TX28,** Beer blast; (Qu. FF4, . . *Dancing parties*) Inf **PA202,** Blast. [Of 34
total Infs, 14 were young, 14 mid-aged, 6 old; 18 were coll educ, 15
high-school educ, 1 grade-school educ.] **1968** *New York Times* (NY) 6
Sept 46/4 **NJ,** The girls were looking for campus clothes and the first
item on their list was pants to wear to "beer blasts and dances."
  4 usu in phr *have a blast:* Fun, a good time. **chiefly Nth, N
Midl, West, scattered Sth** See Map *chiefly among younger,
educ speakers; casual*
  1967–70 *DARE* (Qu. FF17, *Words meaning that people had a very
good or enjoyable time: "We all had a _____ last night."*) 93 Infs,
Blast; Inf **TX33,** Real blast; **NY7,** First-class blast; (Qu. FF18, . . *A noisy
or boisterous celebration or party: "They certainly _____ last night."*)
34 Infs, Had a (big) blast. [Of all Infs responding to these Qq., 11% were
young, 25% mid-aged, 76% coll or high-school educ; of those giving this
response, 36% were young, 32% mid-aged, 92% coll or high-school educ.]

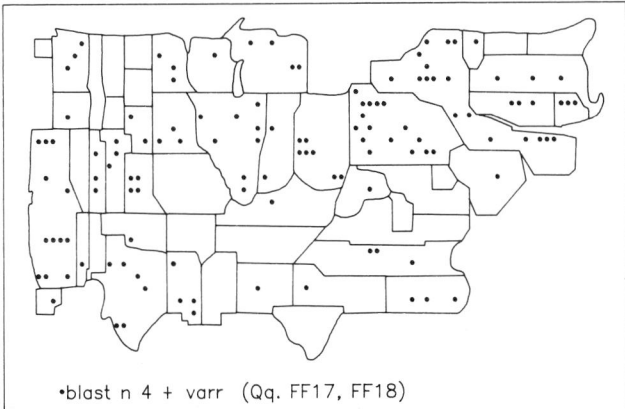

·blast n 4 + varr   (Qq. FF17, FF18)

blast v [**blast** n 1]
To scold, slander or attack verbally.
  1965–70 *DARE* (Qu. Y3, *To say uncomplimentary things about somebody*) Infs **CA15, TN48,** Blast; **MA72,** Blast him out; (Qu. II27, . . *A very
sharp scolding*) Inf **VA25,** Blasted right out.

blast intj
Damn!
  1943 *LANE* Map 599 **scattered throughout NEng,** Expressions . . used
as curses or imprecations . . . *Damn,* . . *blast.* **1965–70** *DARE* (Qu.
NN8a) Infs **IL135, NE10, OH71, VA99,** Blast; **MI13,** Blast it; (Qu.

NN8b) 25 Infs, **scattered,** Blast; (Qu.NN9a) 9 Infs, **Nth, N Midl,** Blast it; **NJ**57, **OH**92, Blast; (Qu. NN9b) 26 Infs, **scattered,** Blast him; **LA**32, **NC**36, **NY**92, **PA**196, Blast it; **HI**13, Blast his hide; **IN**83, Blast the luck; (Qu. NN20b) Inf **NY**230, Blast it; (Qu. NN25a) 15 Infs, **scattered,** Blast; (Qu. NN26a) Infs **MO**21, **NY**241, Blast it.

blasted adj, adv Pronc-sp *blarsted* Also *blasting esp common among younger speakers*

Confounded; damned; awfully.

1854 (1923) Holmes *Tempest & Sunshine* 145 **KY,** Lord's sake be spry, for I'm blasted hungry! **1938** Rawlings *Yearling* 98 **FL,** Yes, and fatten the blasted fawn and you grow up puny. **1955** Stong *Blizzard* 12 **IA,** You expect us to shoo 'em back in this blasted blizzard. **1965–70** *DARE* (Qu. NN17, . . *"That _____ fly won't go away."*) 76 Infs, Blasted; (Qu. LL37, . . *"I could have wrung her neck, I was so _____ mad."*) 20 Infs, Blasted; (Qu. MO18, Blasting; (Qu. LL36, . . *"I think it's a _____ shame."*) Infs **CA**22, **IL**126, **OR**1, **TX**33, **WA**1, Blasted. [Of all Infs responding to Qu. NN17, 38% were young or mid-aged; of those giving this response, 55% were young or mid-aged.]

blasting root n

A **colicroot 2** (here: *Aletris farinosa*).

1959 Carleton *Index Herb. Plants* 14, *Blasting root: Aletris farinosa.*

blat n, v |blæt| [Imit] Cf **blate**

1 The cry of a calf (occas a cow); to make such a sound. **chiefly NEast, Gt Lakes** See Map and Map Section

1850 Northall *Life Yankee Hill* 102 **MA,** Your fellow-country-men . . are not allowed to emigrate north of the Columbia River, on account of a raging he-calf who is bla-ting on the other side. **1892** *DN* 1.238 **MO,** *Bleating.* Generally [blætɪŋ] in Kansas City. **1907** White *AZ Nights* 149, Perhaps the calf blatted a little as the heat scorched. **1939** *LANE* Map 194 **throughout NEng,** The word *blat* was recorded four times . . . This word is generally used only of the sound made by calves. *Ibid* Map 195, The map shows the verbs *blat,* . . *bellow,* . . used to designate the cry of a calf. **1965–70** *DARE* (Qu. K19, *Noise made by a calf that's taken away from its mother*) 123 Infs, **chiefly NEast, Gt Lakes,** Blat; **MA**68, [blætɪn]; [Of all Infs responding to the question, 73% were old; of those giving this resp, 82% were old.] (Qu. K21, *The noise a cow makes, calling for her calf*) Inf **ME**12, 14, **MA**5, 11, **PA**158, 226, Blat. **1973** Allen *LAUM* 1.251, The noise made by a hungry calf . . . *Blat.*

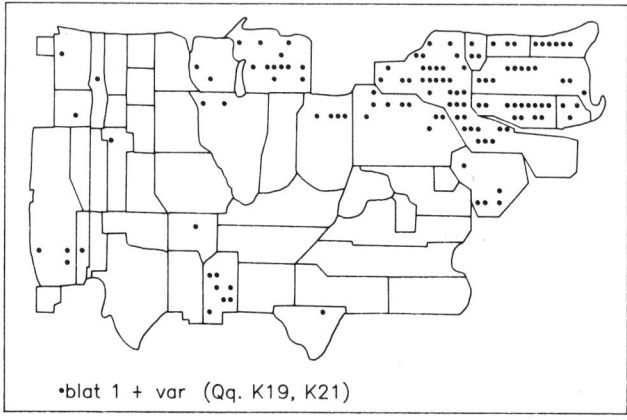

•blat 1 + var (Qq. K19, K21)

2 The cry of a sheep (rarely a deer); to make such a sound. **chiefly Nth and West** See Map and Map Section

1914 *DN* 4.153 **NH,** *Blat* . . . A sheep blats. **1935** Davis *Honey* 22 **OR,** He looked so much like a sheep himself that when he opened his mouth you half expected him to blat. **1939** *LANE* Map 195 **scattered throughout NEng,** *Blat* is used by five informants . . to denote the cry of both calves and sheep. **1965–70** *DARE* (Qu. K66, *The noise made by a sheep*) 133 Infs, **chiefly Nth and West,** Blat; Inf **WA**2, Blatting [blætɪŋ]; (Qu. K85) Inf **MN**40, Blat; **MI**98, Blatting. [Of all Infs responding to Qu. K66, 73% were old; of those giving this resp, 80% were old.] **1966** *DARE* Tape **MI**2, They'd hear the deer blat.

blate n, v |bleɪt|, infreq |blek| Also *blayt* [ME *blete*] Cf **blat**

A As noun and verb.

1 The cry of a sheep (rarely a deer); to make such a sound. **chiefly Sth, S Midl** See Map and Map Section

1859 Taliaferro *Fisher's R.* 92 **nwNC** (as of 1820s), I kep' blatin' away,

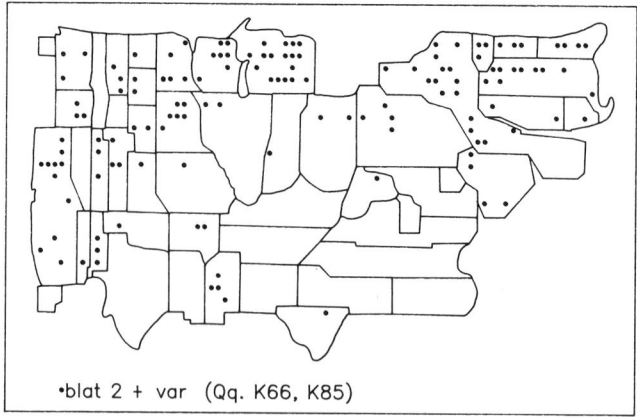

•blat 2 + var (Qq. K66, K85)

and uvery time I'd blate it [=a fawn] would answer me. [**1870** in 1884 Lanier *Poems* 169 **cGA,** I heerd him bleat / To hisself, like a lamb: "Hauh? nine from eight / Leaves nuthin'."] **1890** *DN* 1.72 **LA,** *Bleat* (with the vowel [e]). **1903** *DN* 2.306 **seMO,** *Blate.* **1908** *DN* 3.291 **eAL, wGA,** *Blate.* **1923** *DN* 5.201 **swMO,** *Blate.* **1938** Rawlings *Yearling* 98 **FL,** Yes, and fatten the blasted fawn and you grow up puny. Much as we all got to do, what on earth do you want with one o' them things, blayting around here day and night. **1950** *PADS* 14.14 **SC,** *Blate* . . . To bleat. An upcountry pronunciation. **1965–70** *DARE* (Qu. K66, *The noise made by a sheep*) 160 Infs, **chiefly Sth, S Midl,** Blate; **AR**29, **IN**32, **LA**40, **VA**20, Blating. [Of all Infs responding to the question, 73% were old; of those giving this response, 83% were old.]

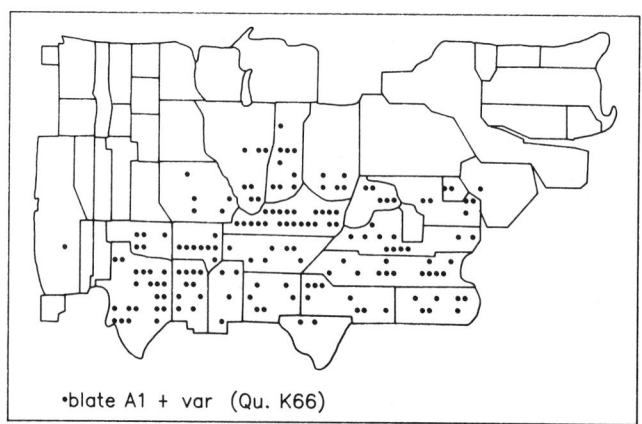

•blate A1 + var (Qu. K66)

2 The cry of a calf (occas a cow); to make such a sound. **chiefly Sth** See Map and Map Section Cf **bleat**

1949 *AmSp* 24.106 **GA,** *Blate* . . . The noise made by a cow. **1965–70** *DARE* (Qu. K19, *Noise made by a calf*) 85 Infs, **chiefly Sth,** Blate; **FL**26, **KY**90, **LA**40, **VA**20, Blating; (Qu. K21, *The noise a cow makes*) Infs **SC**40, 43, **TN**17, **TX**8, **VA**49, 95, Blate; **TN**53, Blating; **SC**9, [blekɪn]. [Of all Infs responding to these Qq., 73% were old; of those giving this response, 79% were old.]

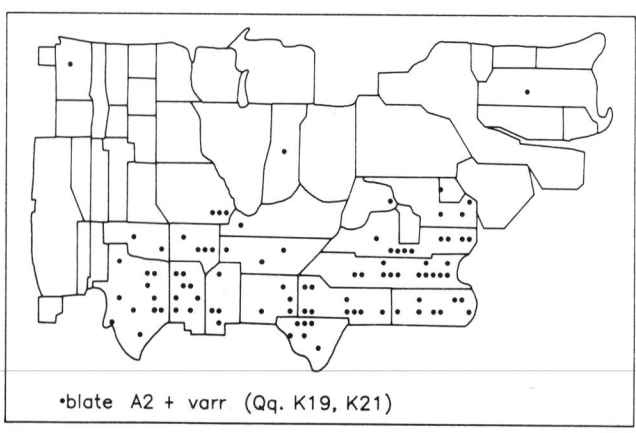

•blate A2 + varr (Qq. K19, K21)

B As verb.

1 By ext, freq with *out:* see quots. **chiefly Sth, S Midl**

1903 *DN* 2.307 **seMO,** *Blate out* . . . Speak out; out with it! **1908** *DN* 3.291 **eAL, wGA,** *Blate.* **1909** *DN* 3.392 **nwAR,** *Blate out* . . . To blurt out, especially a secret. "Jim had to blate out and tell." **1970** *DARE* (Qu. JJ43, *To give away a secret or tell a piece of news too soon: "He wasn't supposed to know. Somebody must have _____."*) Inf **TX**99, Blated. [Inf old]

2 By ext: see quot.

1905 *DN* 3.70 **nwAR,** *Bleat* [bleɪt] . . . To tattle. 'He bleated on me.' Common.

‡blathergab n [*blather* foolish talk + *gab* idle talk]

A gossip, chatterer.

1942 Whipple *Joshua* 100 **UT,** The old blathergabs, she thought. It ain't *Clory's* fault!

‡blatherskite intj [*blatherskite* nonsense, blather]

1970 *DARE* (Qu. NN8a, *Exclamations of annoyance or disgust:*) Inf **PA**234, Blatherskite.

blating duck n Pronc-sp *blaten duck*

=gadwall.

1888 Trumbull *Names of Birds* 24, On the coast of New Jersey, at Barnegat, Tuckerton, and Atlantic City, it [=gadwall duck] has long been known as the blaten duck (blatant, or bleating, like *"strepera"*, from its obstreperousness). **1970** *DARE* (Qu. Q5) Inf **VA**52, Blating ['bleɪtn] duck [=gadwall], because it "blate like a sheep."

blatting cart n [*blat 1*]

A wagon used to carry newborn calves.

1954 Gard *Chisholm Trail* 109, Many of the cows bore calves while on the trail . . . Usually the trail boss had them shot [because the] . . calves couldn't keep up . . . In later days some drovers hauled them in a calf wagon or "blattin' cart" for the first day or two. **1961** Adams *Old-Time Cowhand* 276.

blaze v, hence ppl adj *blazed*

=box v[1].

1966–68 *DARE* Tape **FL**19, Blazin' the tree [=cutting a box into a tree to gather turpentine; this finally leads to the death of the tree] . . . Blazed face [the part of the tree which has been cut for turpentine]; **GA**23, You have to go out and blaze a tree and put a tins [sic] and cup and a nail on it.

blaze-face n Also *blazed-face*

1 A face (usu of a horse) with a white spot or streak on it. [*blaze* a white spot on the face of an animal; *OED* 1639 →] **chiefly Sth, W Midl**

1787 (1925) Washington *Diaries* 3.155 **VA,** A sorrell Stallion, a blaze face, 2 hind feet and off fore foot white. **1856** *Spirit of Times* 25 Oct 131/1 **Long Island NY,** The three came down the quarter-stretch at a great flight of speed, . . each having a blaze-face, or a stripe and snip. **1954** *Harder Coll.* **cwTN,** *Blazed-face* . . . In horses and mules: a distinctively marked face.

2 By ext: a horse which has a white mark on its face.

1937 Sandoz *Slogum* 252 **wNE,** Dodie was told to unhitch the matched team of blaze-faces and turn them into the horse pasture to rest and fatten a little. **1967–70** *DARE* (Qu. K37, *What do you call a horse of mixed colors?*) Infs **MS**81, 87, **MO**24, **OH**95, Blaze-face; (Qu. K39, . . *Names . . for horses according to their colors?*) Infs **GA**14, **KY**75, **LA**10, **MO**37, **VA**77, Blaze-face.

blaze-faced adj Also *blazed* [**blaze-face**]

Of a horse or cow: see quot 1950.

1870 Eggleston *Queer Stories* 65 (*DAE*), If she were rich, she would buy an omnibus with four 'blaze-faced,' sorrel horses. **1939** *Hench Coll.* **csVA,** Blaze-faced. **1950** *PADS* 14.15 **SC,** *Blaze-faced* . . . Of a horse or cow, having a blaze, or white stripe running down the face; also, of a cow, having the entire head white. **1954** *PADS* 21.20 **SC,** *Blazed* . . . Blaze-faced. **c1960** *Wilson Coll.* **csKY,** Blaze(d)-faced. **1966** *DARE* FW Addit **SC**19, Blaze-faced.

blaze-faced shirt n *rare*

1909 *DN* 3.392 **nwAR,** *Blaze-faced shirt* . . . A starched white shirt.

blazer n **chiefly West**

An error or lie; often in phr *run a blazer:* to deceive or bluff.

1903 (1965) Adams *Log Cowboy* 81, Are you sure you was n't running a blazer yourself, or is the wind merely rising? **1906** *Springfield* [MA] *W.*

Republican 19 Apr 1 (*DA*), The Kaiser's telegram to Count Goluchowski recalls some of his blazers in the past. **1907** White *AZ Nights* 11, It was just a cold, raw blazer; and if it didn't go through I could see me as an Apache parlour ornament. **1940** White *Wild Geese* 265 **WA, AK** (as of c1895), The real reason was that they had run a blazer on Ashley in getting this job . . . They wanted mightily to make that bluff good.

blazes n, intj **widespread, but chiefly Nth, N Midl** See Map *euphem* Cf **blue blazes**

Hell.

1838 Neal *Charcoal Sketches* 134 **Philadelphia PA,** Here I've been serving my country . . these ten years, like a patriot . . hurraing my daylights out, and getting as blue as blazes. **1876** Twain *Old Times* 53, Look sharp, I tell you! Oh blazes, there you go! **1907** *DN* 3.209 **nwAR, cCT.** **1922** Brown *Old Crow* 504 **MA,** You went by 'fore light, drivin' like blazes. **1941** *LANE* Map 473 **CT,** *Mad as blazes.* **1943** *Ibid* Map 716, **scattered throughout NEng,** *Cold as blazes . .; colder than blazes.* **1965–70** *DARE* (Qu. NN26b, . . *"Go to _____!"*) 87 Infs, **widespread, but chiefly Nth, N Midl,** Blazes; (Qu. NN26c, . . *"What the _____!"*) 21 Infs, Blazes; (Qu. NN26a, *Weakened substitutes for "hell"*) Infs **AL**22, **OH**71, **PA**130, Blazes.

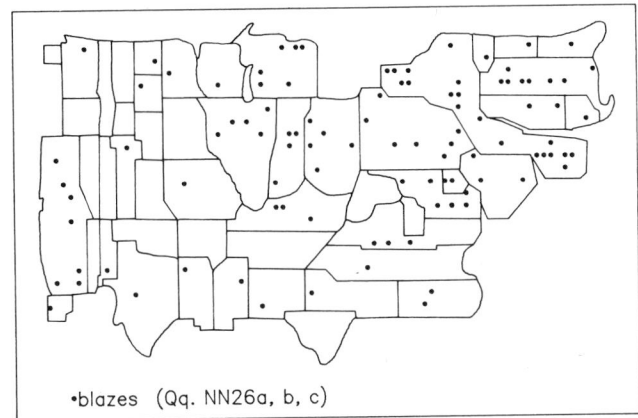

•blazes (Qq. NN26a, b, c)

blazing star n

1 A **colicroot 2** (here: *Aletris farinosa*).

1789 in 1793 Amer. Philos. Soc. *Trans.* 3.xx, The root of Aletris *farinosa* is taken in powder, or bruised and steeped in liquor: this root is called star-root, blazing star, devil's bit. **1828** Rafinesque *Med. Flora* 37, *Aletris farinosa* . . . *Vulgar Names*—Star-Grass, Blazing Star. **1892** (1974) Millspaugh *Amer. Med. Plants* 172, *Blazing Star* . . . furnishes one of the many examples of the uncertainty attending the use of vulgarisms in reference to plants. **1930** Sievers *Amer. Med. Plants* 4, *Aletris . . . Other common names.*—Stargrass, blazing star [etc.]. **1971** Krochmal *Appalachia Med. Plants* 40, Blazing star . . . has been used to treat colic, and . . rheumatism.

2 A perennial plant (*Chamaelirium luteum*) native chiefly in the Midland and South. Also called **angel's wand, colicroot 6, devil's bit, devil's root, fairy wand, false unicorn, false unicorn root, grub root, lamb's tail, rattlesnake root, red-seed, squirrel tails, star root, starwort, unicorn plant, unicorn root, unicorn's horn**

1822 Eaton *Botany* 303, *Helonias . . . dioica . .* blazing star, false unicorn root. **1830** *Huntingdon* (Penna.) *Courier* 15 Sep. 4/5 (*DA*), American Remedies Wanted . . . Angelica, Wild, Devil's Bit or Blazing Star, (*Helonias Dioica*). **1869** Fuller *Flower Gatherers* 170 (*DAE*), The country people usually know it as 'The Blazing Star,' or 'Unicorn Plant.' **1903** Porter *Flora PA* 80, *Chamaelirium luteum* . . . Blazing-star . . . In moist meadows and thickets. **1931** Harned *Wild Flowers Alleghanies* 102, *Blazing Star* . . . is said to possess some medicinal value. **1976** Bruce *How to Grow Wildflowers* 172, *Chamaelirium luteum* . . hardly lives up to some of the dramatic common names applied to it—Devil's Bit, Blazing Star, Fairy Wand, Rattlesnake Root.

3 Any of the perennial composite plants of the genus *Liatris* which grow from underground corms and have alternate elongate leaves and heads of white to purple flowers in spikes or racemes. Also called **backache root 1, button snakeroot, colicroot 4, devil's bite, gayfeather, prairie pines, rattlesnake master, rough root, sawwort, throatwort** For other names of var spp see **devil's bit, snakeroot**

1828 Rafinesque *Med. Flora* 237, *Liatris*. . . Many vulgar names, *Backache root*, . . *Blazing Star*, . . *Rough root*, &c. **1861** Wood *Class-Book* 413, *Liatris squarrosa* . . *Blazing Star* . . A splendid plant, . . . with large brilliant purple florets. **1904** (1916) Porter *Freckles* 274, These [vases] she filled with fringed gentians, blazing-star, asters, golden-rod, and ferns. **1939** FWP *Guide FL* 21, Among the most showy native species are the Liatris, commonly called the Blazing Star, whose nodding purple spikes decorate the landscape in late summer and fall. **1966** *Badgerland* (Stoughton WI) 15 Oct 6/2, Those who planned it [the arboretum prairie] managed to not only propagate the grasses, but also most of the prairie flowers—cornflowers, blazing star, . . golden-rod, etc. **1966–70** *DARE* (Qu. S25) Inf **MI**31, Blazing star; (Qu. S26e) Inf **FL**48, Blazing star—spreads wider, pale red. **1966** *DARE* Wildfl QR Inf **WI**34, Blazing star *(Liatris pycnostachya)*—also called prairie gayfeather. **1976** Bruce *How to Grow Wildflowers* xiv, "Blazing Star," for example, can be a *Liatris*, a *Chamaelirium*, or a *Mentzelia.*

4 =stickleaf, esp *Mentzelia laevicaulis.* **West**

1897 Parsons *Wild Flowers CA* 168, *Blazing-Star. Mentzelia laevicaulis* . . . waited for the firmament to be clear of other stars before bursting upon the sight. **1925** Jepson *Manual Plants CA* 649, *Blazing Star* . . . Shining white nearly smooth stems; . . flowers in clusters of 2 or 3 at the ends of the branches, 3 to 4 in. broad, light yellow. **1947** *Desert Mag.* May 28/3 *(DA)*, Until the middle of June visitors will find . . mimulus, chia, blazing star, . . and ground cherry in the Valley of Fire and other rocky areas. **1966–68** *DARE* FW Addit **CO**7, Blazing star—7:30 opening, teacup size *(Mentzelia decapetala);* **OR**12, Blazing star—Loasa family; stickleaf. **1976** Dodge *Roadside Wildflowers* 43, *Blazing-star* . . . The attractive star-shaped flowers make the plants eligible for inclusion in the backyard wildflower garden.

bleach v

1 To blanch (celery).

1950 *WELS* (When you cover celery to keep it white, you are _____ it) 35 Infs, **WI,** Bleaching. **1981** Broaddus Coll. **ceKY,** Bleach—to keep growing celery white by covering it.

2 To treat with sulfur as a method of preservation.

1969 *Foxfire* Winter 26 **nGA,** Several people in the area still remember the days when fruit was "bleached" with sulfur for preservation . . . "Everybody nearly bleached fruits. And it was the sulfur whited the apples, and they had a little sulfur flavor."

bleat n |blit|, infreq |blik| **scattered, but least freq in Midl** See Map Cf **blate A2**
=blat 1.

1965–70 *DARE* (Qu. K19, *Noise made by a calf that's taken away from its mother*) 72 Infs, Bleat; Infs **DC**8, **SC**23, Bleating; **MA**25, [blik].

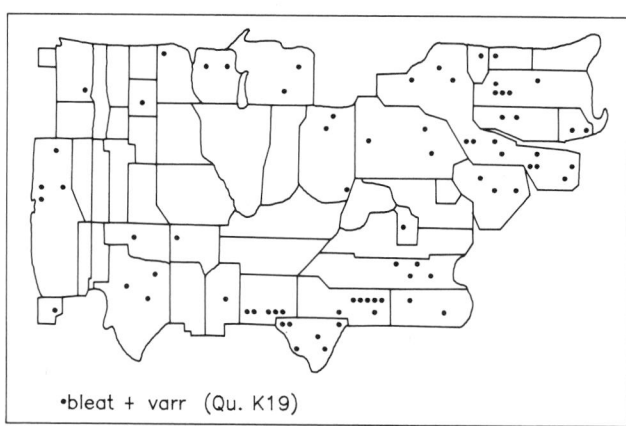

•bleat + varr (Qu. K19)

bleebe v Pronc-sp for *believe* Gullah
Std sense, var form.

1888 Jones *Negro Myths* 124 **GA Coast,** Buh Wolf now, him yent hab no better sense den fuh bleebe wuh Buh Rabbit duh talk. **1922** Gonzales *Black Border* 290 **sSC, GA coasts** [Gullah glossary], *B'leebe*—believe, believes, believed, believing.

bleed v, hence *bleeding* vbl n **chiefly Sth, S Midl**
To sweat heavily.

1965–70 *DARE* (Qu. X56a, *Other words for sweat*) Inf **TX**61, Bleeding; (Qu. X56b, *Expressions about sweating very heavily*) Infs **OK**7, 42, **SC**19, **TX**26, Bleeding; **KY**65, Bleeding to death; **GA**9, Bleeding it out.

bleeding heart n

1 A plant of the genus *Dicentra,* such as the cultivated *D. spectabilis* which has heart-shaped pink and white flowers. For other names of var spp see **Dutchman's breeches, eardrop 3, golden eardrops, lady's eardrops 2, squirrel corn, steershead**

1887 *Century Illustr. Mag.* 34.325 **NEast,** I have an eye out for the white-hearts (related to the bleeding-hearts of the gardens, and absurdly called "Dutchman's breeches") the last week in April. **1923** Wyatt *Invisible God* 16 *(DAE),* An aster bed in the center of its lawn surrounded by the rosy foam of peonies, the sprays of bleeding hearts. **1965–70** *DARE* (Qu. S2) Inf **IL**110, Bleeding heart; (Qu. S3) Infs **MD**24, **WA**24, Bleeding heart; (Qu. S26c) Infs **IL**67, **MI**80, **MN**33, **OH**57, 98, **OR**4, **PA**216, **WI**12, Bleeding heart(s); (Qu. S26e) Infs **CA**60, 105, **MI**93, 120, **OH**68, **TN**33, Bleeding heart(s); **HI**4, Bleeding heart seed.

2 A **wahoo** (here: either *Euonymus americanus* or *E. atropurpureus*). [From the shape and color of the seed capsule]

1897 Sudworth *Arborescent Flora* 281 **NC,** *Evonymus atropurpureus* . . . Bleeding heart. **1933** Small *Manual SE Flora* 818, *E. atropurpureus* . . . Bleeding-heart . . . The dangling fruits are pinkish-purple. **1960** Vines *Trees SW* 661, *Eastern Wahoo* . . . Vernacular names are . . Bleeding-heart . . and Strawberry-tree. The tree is sometimes used as an ornament because of its beautiful scarlet fruit in autumn.

3 A plant of the genus *Corydalis.*

1938 (1958) Sharples *AK Wild Flowers* 41, *Corydalis* . . . Hardy plants allied to the Dutchman's Breeches . . . "Wild Bleeding Heart."

4 =redbud.

1967 *DARE* (Qu. T16) Inf **AR**52, Bleeding heart—same as redbud or Judas tree.

bleeding tooth n [See quots 1901, 1937]
A marine shell (*Nerita* spp., usu *N. peloronta*) found in waters off southern Florida. Also called **cat's tooth**

1881 *Jrl. Conchology* 3.165, I did not find the "Bleeding Tooth" very common at Key West. **1901** Arnold *Sea-Beach* 363, *N. peloronta.* This shell has two teeth on the wide, flat columellar lip, and about them a blotch of red, suggesting blood. The common name of this shell, "bleeding-tooth," is very appropriate. **1937** *Natl. Geog. Mag.* 71.210 **FL,** The third *(Nerita peleronta)* is the well-known "bleeding tooth." Turning it over, we find that the mouth opening bears two flat teeth on its white inner margin, one or both of which are blotched with yellowish red resembling a bloody stain. **1974** Abbott *Seashells* 63, Bleeding Tooth . . . is a popular souvenir.

‡**bleenie** n [Perh blend of *baloney* + *weenie* sausage]
A frankfurter.

1942 *AmSp* 17.29 **IA,** Whether the word exists elsewhere, I do not know, but in Dubuque, Iowa, one occasionally hears *bleenie* used for 'frankfurter.'

‡**bleep** n

1974 Betts–Walser *NC Folkl., Bleep:* a small amount (Raleigh).

blemage n [Alter of *blemish*]

1927 *DN* 5.473 **Ozarks,** *Blemage* . . . Blemish. "She's a plum purty critter, 'thout nary spot nor blemage."

‡**blemish** n

1899 (1912) Green *VA Folk-Speech, Blemish* . . . A motion as if to strike. "He made a blemish at him."

blend v
To marry.

1942 Berrey–Van den Bark *Amer. Slang* 359.4, *Marry; be married* . . . Blend. *Ibid* 359.7, *Married* . . . Blended. **1967** *DARE* (Qu. AA15a, . . *Ways . . of saying that people got married . .* "They _____.") Inf **NY**35, Get blended.

blessing n **chiefly S Atl, Inland Sth** See Map
Usu in phr *blessing-out:* A scolding, tongue-lashing.

1863 (1922) Jackson *Col.'s Diary* 95 **PA,** The major gave the steamboat man a regular blessing. **1899** (1912) Green *VA Folk-Speech, Blessing* . . . A fierce scolding. "You'll get a blessing when you go home." **1965–70** *DARE* (Qu. II27, *If somebody gives you a very sharp scolding, you might say, "I certainly got a _____ for that.*") 53 Infs, **chiefly S Atl, Inland Sth,** Blessing-out; **MD**47, **MO**20, **SC**19, Blessing.

bless out v **chiefly Sth, S Midl** See also **blessing**
To scold or rebuke.

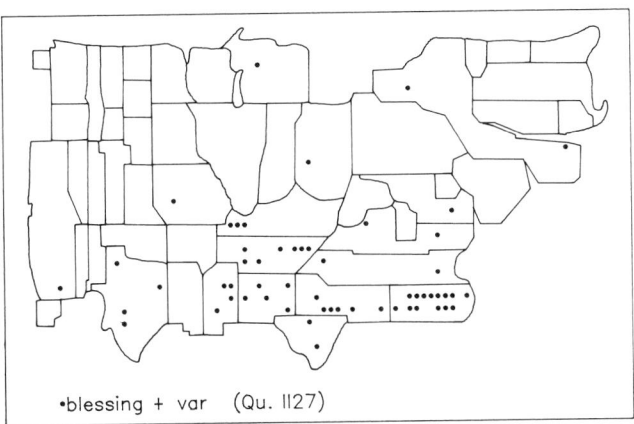

•blessing + var (Qu. II27)

88, **NY**72, **SC**22, **TN**57, **TX**21, Window blinds; **LA**18, Lattice-work blinds; **NC**82, Outside blinds; **OH**36, Slat blinds; **MO**14, Type of blinds; **MO**16, Ventilation blinds.

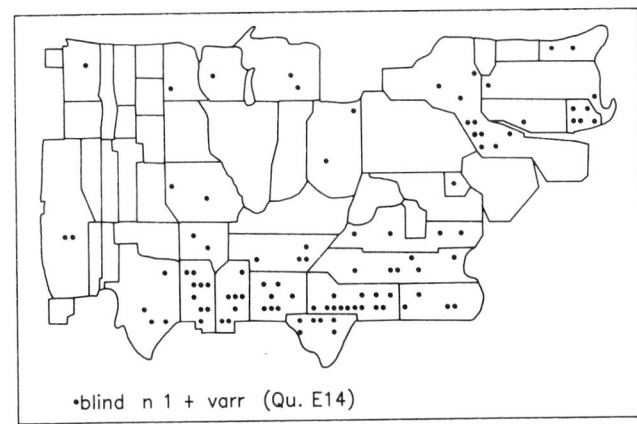

•blind n 1 + varr (Qu. E14)

1935 [see **biddable**]. **1937** in 1977 *Amer. Slave Suppl. 1* 1.97 **AL**, Ole Mistis, en all of us cried whilst de yankees whippin Unker Luke, en she sho did bless em out. **1944** *PADS* 2.32 **Sth**. **1946** *PADS* 6.6 **VA, NC**. **1954** *PADS* 21.20 **SC**. **1956** Gipson *Old Yeller* 27 **TX**, Then she blessed me out good and proper for being so bossy with him. **1958** *PADS* 29.7 **TN**. **1965–70** *DARE* (Qu. Y3, *To say uncomplimentary things about somebody*) Inf **GA**63, Bless out; (Qu. Y4, . . *Uncomplimentary remark*) Inf **FL**15, Blessed him out; (Qu. Y6, . . *"He's a whole week late. I'm going to _____."*) Inf **TN**24, Bless him out; (Qu. Y12a, *A fight between two people, mostly with words*) Inf **LA**3, Blessed each other out; **AR**11, Blessed him out; (Qu. II27, . . *A very sharp scolding*) Infs **MO**20, **MA**127, **VA**41, Blessed out; (Qu. LL27) Inf **FL**26, Blessed him out. **1976** Wolfram–Christian *Appalachian Speech* 97.

blickey n[1] |ˈblɪki| Also sp *blickie, blicky* [From Du *blikje* dimin of *blik* tin, a pail] **chiefly seNY, NYC, and NJ**
A pail or bucket; a lunch pail.
   1859 (1968) Bartlett *Americanisms, Blickey* . . . In New York, a tin pail. **1881** Vanderbilt *Social Flatbush* 56 **NYC**, The tin dipper that hung at the well curb was a "blikke," from the Dutch word "blik," for tin. **1894** *DN* 1.328 **NJ**, *Blicky (blickie, blickey):* a small bucket or pail. Said to be Dutch in its origin, but used extensively in S[outh] J[ersey], where there are no Dutch. **1945** Beck *Jersey Genesis* 49, "A blickey," he said, "is a small bucket or pail. It's a Dutch word." **1967** *DARE* FW Addit **nwNJ**, *Blicky* [ˈblɪki]—a pail, usually about four quarts. A woman might use one of these to gather berries.

blickey n[2]
A short coat or jacket.
   1895 *DN* 1.382 **NJ**, *Blickey* . . . In Vincentown and vicinity this word is used for a coat or "jumper," such as workmen wear with overalls—a Garibaldi jacket of jean. **1969** *DARE* (Qu. W4, . . *Men's coats or jackets for work and outdoor wear*) Inf **NJ**56, Blickey [ˈblɪki].

blige n [Aphet form of *oblige*]
   1903 *DN* 2.307 **seMO**, *Blige* . . . Obligation. 'I had a blige to go.'

‡**blimey** n [Ext of Brit intj *blimey* prob infl by *limey* an Englishman]
A British person.
   1969 *DARE* (Qu. HH28, . . *People of foreign background . . English*) Inf **NJ**55, Blimey.

blind n

1 usu pl: A window shutter usu having adjustable horizontal slats that let in light and air but keep out sun and rain. **chiefly Sth, NEast** See Map Cf **jalousie**
   1771 in 1914 Copley–Pelham *Letters* 142 **NY**, Those Windows having new fassioned Blinds such as you see in Mr. Clarke's Keeping Room. **1840** *Knickerbocker* 16.245 **NYC**, To add to his gloomy feelings, it was a dark, dull day, and the wind moaned sadly through the blinds of his windows. **1892** VT State Bd. Ag. *Report* 12.114, Vergennes . . is largely engaged in the manufacture of horse nails, curtain rollers, doors, sash, blinds, and furniture. **1926** *AmSp* 2.79 **ME**, If you mentioned "blinds," you would of course mean those slatted shutters without which no Maine house seems modestly attired. **1941** *LANE* Map 327 **throughout NEng**, Board shutters on the outside of the window . . [blɘindz], . . [blaɪnz]. **1965–70** *DARE* (Qu. E14, *Wooden slats built into a window frame that shut out the sun but let in light and air*) 80 Infs, **chiefly Sth and NY**, Blinds; **CA**6, **GA**4, **ME**20, 23, **NC**52, **RI**14, **TX**15, Blind; **AR**47, **GA**63,

2 usu pl: A roller window shade. **widespread, but least freq NEast, Sth** See Map
   1875 Stowe *We & Neighbors* 49 **NYC**, I . . sometimes wish I could go right into some . . dark church, and pull down all the blinds, and shut all the doors. **1902** Twain in *Harper's Mag.* 104.429/2, Mr. Holmes's blinds were down; but by-and-by he raised them. **1949** Kurath *Word Geog.* 28 **Midl**, The roller shades inside the windows are called the *blinds*. **1949** *PADS* 11.16 **CO**. **1953** *AmSp* 28.248 **csPA**. **1965–70** *DARE* (Qu. E12, *Pieces of stiff material that you pull down on the inside of a window to keep the sun out*) 234 Infs, **widespread, but least freq NEast, Sth**, (Window) blinds; (Qu. E13, . . *To pull the shades . . "When the sun is too bright, you go to the window and _____."*) 112 Infs, **widespread, but least freq NEast, Sth**, Pull (down) the blinds [and varr—see DS]; 54 Infs, **scattered Midl and West**, (Lower, draw, close, let down, *or* shut) the blind(s). [Ed note: Because of the ambiguity of these questions, it is not always clear whether the Infs were referring to roller shades or to venetian blinds.] **1973** Allen *LAUM* 1.167, The Midland *blind*, which two generations ago was making inroads upon Northern territory in Minnesota and North Dakota—although not in South Dakota—apparently is declining in the face of the growing popularity of the slatted window-covering and its designation Venetian blind(s), often ambiguously shortened to blind(s). **1977–78** Foster *Lexical Variation* 27 **NJ**, Within this transition area may be found numerous Midland . . terms . . *blinds* 'roller shades.'

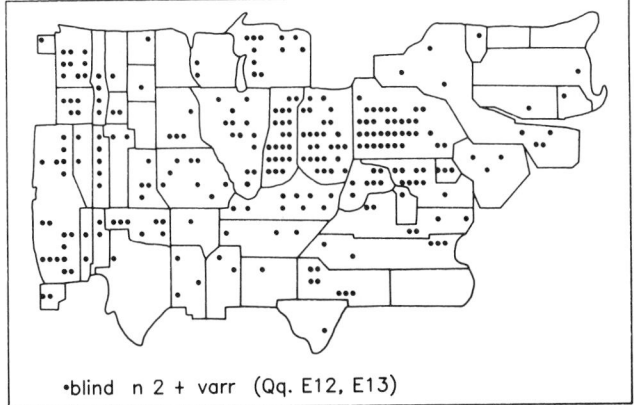

•blind n 2 + varr (Qq. E12, E13)

3 =**blind tiger 1**.
   1967–68 *DARE* (Qu. DD30, *A place where liquor is [or was] sold and consumed illegally*) Infs **NY**36, **OR**13, **PA**98, Blind.

4 also *blind post:* In the game of hide-and-seek, the place where the seeker waits while the other players hide. Cf **blind** v 2
   1967–69 *DARE* (Qu. EE14, *The place where the player who is 'it' has to wait and count while the others hide*) Infs **IL**9, **MA**24, (The) blind; **MA**14, Blind post.

5 See quot.
   1980 *Greenfield Recorder* (MA) 8 Nov [Ruby Hemenway column], Cows wore "blinds" to prevent them from jumping fences—that was a

board, held by the cow's horns over its eyes so it could see only down to feed, but not to jump.

blind v

1 Among college students: to confound or stump (someone); see quots. **NC**

1916 *DN* 4.343 **NC** [Student jargon], *Blind* . . . To expose (one's) ignorance. "Professor _____ blinded me to-day on Latin." **1946** *PADS* 6.6 **NC**, *Blind* . . . To ask questions that students are unprepared to answer. "The professor blinded me today." University of N.C., 1912. Common. **1952** Brown *NC Folkl.* 521, *Blind* . . . To confuse or fool; to surprise a teacher by knowing the correct answer (used at University of N.C.).—Central and east.

2 used imperatively in the game of hide-and-seek: To go to the **blind** n 4 and close one's eyes.

1982 *DARE* File **csWI** (as of 1930s), We used to use the verb *blind* [in hide-and-seek], instructing "it" to "blind and count to 100 by ones."

blind alley n

=**blind tiger 1.**

1966–69 *DARE* (Qu. DD30, . . *A place where liquor is [or was] sold and consumed illegally:*) Infs **KY**10, **MI**19, **WA**3, Blind alley.

‡blind bat n

A bat-and-ball game: =**one cat out.**

1970 *DARE* (Qu. EE11, *Bat-and-ball games for just a few players*) Inf **VA**69, Blind bat—same as one-cat-out.

‡blind Billy n

Blindman's buff.

1968 *DARE* (Qu. EE4, *Games in which one player's eyes are bandaged and he has to catch the others and guess who they are*) Inf **NY**82, Blind Billy.

‡blind bogie n

An exchange of things unseen; a blind trade.

1968 *DARE* (Qu. U14, *When you're exchanging with somebody when neither one has seen what the other has . . you'd call that a* _____) Inf **WI**8, Blind bogey ['bogi].

blind breaker n [*blind* difficult to discern + *breaker* wave]

A tidal wave: see quot.

1938 Tripp *Flukes* 127 **N Atl**, They ran into what we call a "blind breaker," probably caused by a berg breaking off a glacier and making a sudden tidal wave.

blind bridle n **scattered, but esp common Sth, S Midl Cf bridle blind**

A bridle fitted with blinders.

1833 Hall *Harpe's Head* 30 **KY**, Some rode with blind-bridles. **1899** (1912) Green *VA Folk-Speech*, *Blind* . . . Anything which obstructs the sight. A *blind* bridle. **1944** Clark *Pills* 142 **neSC** (as of c1870), For the first six months of that year he bought . . fifty-six plugs of tobacco, . . a blind bridle, . . and a bottle of Hoyt's cologne. **1946** *PADS* 6.6 **NC**. **1950** *PADS* 13.16 **cTX**, *Blind-bridle* . . . A bridle having blinders. Always used on work horses; never used on saddle horses; used on buggy horses only when their skittishness will not permit the use of an *open-bri-dle*. **1965–70** *DARE* (Qu. L52, *Pieces of leather used to cover the sides of a horse's eyes:*) 15 Infs, **scattered**, Blind bridle(s).

‡blind-buck and Davy n **Cf duck on davy**

1930 Shoemaker *1300 Words* 6 **cPA Mts** (as of c1900), *Blind-buck and Davy*—A clumsy, weak-sighted, stumbling person.

blind buff See **blindman's buff**

blind cat n

A bat-and-ball game similar to **cat** n 3c.

1939 Hall *Coll.* **eTN**, *Blind cat*—a ball game, something like baseball. "The ball was th'owed from one point here to another across there. A fellow would bat."

blind entry n **Cf air course**

In coal mining: see quot.

1973 *PADS* 59.24 **all bituminous coal mining areas exc wKY**, *Blind entry* . . a passage which does not connect with any other passage or ultimately lead to the shaft *bottom* or surface, a dead-end.

‡blind-eye n attrib

An opal, whose milky color is like a sightless eye.

1933 Miller *Lamb in His Bosom* 128 **GA**, Secretly Margot had felt a little guilty when she gave Cean the gold finger ring with the opal setting, for an opal is a curse . . . Cean would never wear the blind-eye ring, because it was too precious.

‡blind fence n

A high fence which provides privacy.

1967 *DARE* (Qu. L65, . . *Other kinds of fences*) Inf **SC**39, Blind fence—any sort of fence that you can't see through, used to protect one's privacy—several feet high.

blindfold n **chiefly Sth, Midl See Map**

Blindman's buff.

1905 *DN* 3.70 **nwAR**, *Blindfold* . . . Blindman's buff . . . General. **1908** *DN* 3.292 **eAL, wGA**. **1939** Hall *Coll.* **eTN, wNC**, *Blindfold* . . . The game 'blind man's buff.' In general use. **1963** Edwards *Gravel* 22 **eTN** (as of 1920s), We're gonna play blind fold and Uncle Jeems is gonna play too. **1965–70** *DARE* (Qu. EE4, *Games in which one player's eyes are bandaged and he has to catch the others and guess who they are*) 172 Infs, **chiefly Sth, Midl**, Blindfold.

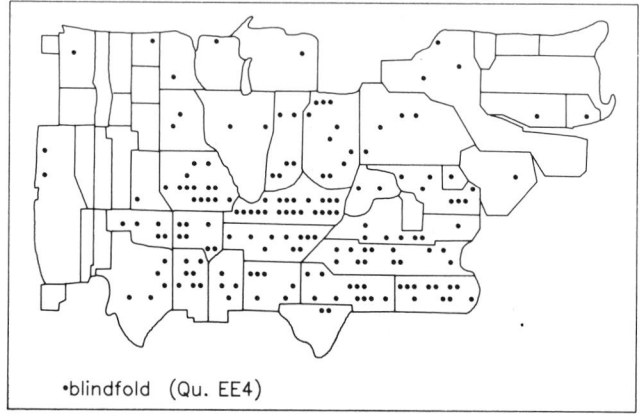

•blindfold (Qu. EE4)

blindfold buff n **Also** *blindfold bluff* **Cf blindfold**

Blindman's buff.

1967–70 *DARE* (Qu. EE4) Infs **IN**39, **VA**90, Blindfold buff; **IL**9, **MD**34, **WA**20, Blindfold bluff.

‡blindfolder n

A deceiver, fraud, cheater.

1966 *DARE* (Qu. V7, *A person who sets out to cheat others while pretending to be honest*) Inf **GA**7, Blindfolder.

blindfold party n

A party at which **blindfold** is played.

1856 in 1956 Eliason *Tarheel Talk* 260 **NC**, Sis wrote to the gentlemen of town in quite a hifalutin style inviting them to attend a *"blindfold"* party that night. **1966** Wilson *Coll.* **csKY**, *Blindfold party* . . . Party where blindman's buff was played; or boys hidden and shoes auctioned to girls.

blind gentian n [See quot 1966]

=**closed gentian.**

1894 *Jrl. Amer. Folkl.* 7.94 **NEng**, *Gentiana Andrewsii*, . . blind-gentian. **1900** Lyons *Plant Names* 171, Blind gentian. **1966** *DARE* Tape **NC**36, The blind gentian is a very tight, closed blossom. **1976** Bruce *How to Grow Wildflowers* 265, These are tightly closed ovals in *G. andrewsii* and slightly open at the mouth in *G. saponaria*. Both species are often called Blind or Bottle Gentian, though the flowers are not really bottle-shaped at all. They look more like little eggs or footballs than bottles.

blind God n, also attrib **Pronc-sp** *bline Gawd* **Gullah**

See quot 1922.

1922 Gonzales *Black Border* 290 **sSC, GA coasts** [Gullah glossary], *Bline Gawd*—blind God—personal idol or fetish of African suggestiveness whose aid is invoked to further the desires of its owner. **1925** *DN* 5.366 **seGA**, "Yoall come to Sam place, Sam e blind-gawd niggah." [Footnote:] blind God nigger, i.e. a Catholic nigger, a rarity and much avoided by the other niggers.

‡blind grandma n

Blindman's buff.

1968 *DARE* (Qu. EE4, *Games in which one player's eyes are bandaged and he has to catch the others and guess who they are*) Inf **NC53**, Blind gran'maw.

‡blind hook n

An unbaited hook used in tuna fishing.

1967 *DARE* Tape **HI9**, [Inf:] They t'row de live bait, den . . dey . . t'row . . de blin' hook . . . Bamboo, get a line on dat, den a hook on a line. [FW:] Well, that means there's no bait on the hook? [Inf:] No, no bait on a hook.

‡blind horse n

=off-horse.

1968 *DARE* (Qu. K32a, *With a team of horses, what do you call the horse on the driver's right hand?*) Inf **MD9**, Blind horse [Inf queries response].

‡blinding lights n pl

The high beams of a car's headlights.

1968 *DARE* (Qu. N10, . . *Words . . for the bright and dim lights on a car*) Inf **CA91**, Blinding lights and dim lights.

blind lead n Also *blind lode*

In mining: a lode not visible on the surface.

1872 Twain *Roughing It* 280, A "blind lead" is a lead or ledge that does not "crop out" above the surface. 1880 in 1942 *AmSp* 17.65 **NM,** A blind lode cut within the first 20 feet assayed 98½ oz. of silver. 1968 Adams *Western Words*, Blind lead—In mining, a lead, or lode, that has no visible outcrop and cannot be detected from the surface. Also called *blind lode.*

blindman's buff n Also *blindman (buff), blindman('s) bluff;* rarely *blind buff;* for other varr see quots [*blindman's + buff* abbr for *buffet* a blow, stroke; *OED* 1590 →] Cf **blindfold**

Std sense, var forms.

a *blindman('s) buff.* **widespread but esp common Nth, N Midl** *somewhat old-fash*

1965–70 *DARE* (Qu. EE4, *Games in which one player's eyes are bandaged and he has to catch the others and guess who they are*) 371 Infs, Blindman's buff; 18 Infs, Blindman buff. [Of all Infs responding to the question, 64% were old; of those giving these responses, 74% were old.]

b *blindman('s) bluff.* *esp common among younger speakers*

1965–70 *DARE* (Qu. EE4) 342 Infs, Blindman's bluff; 58 Infs, Blindman bluff. [Of all Infs responding to the question, 11% were young and 25% were mid-aged; of those giving these responses, 20% were young and 31% were mid-aged.]

c *blindman.* **chiefly Sth, Midl**

1908 *DN* 3.292 **eAL,** Blindman . . . Blindman's buff . . . Rarely used. 1915 *DN* 4.181 **swVA,** Blindman . . . Blindman's buff. 1965–70 *DARE* (Qu. EE4) 14 Infs, **chiefly Sth, Midl,** Blindman.

d other less freq forms: See quot.

1966–69 *DARE* (Qu. EE4) Inf **TX26**, Blind buff; **OK52**, Blindman catch; **IL70**, Blindman seek; **NC14, OH46**, Blindsman('s) bluff; **IA43**, Blindsman buff.

blind mosquito n [*blind* stingless, as in *blind nettle*] **FL** Cf **chizzywink**

A non-stinging insect (Chironomidae) resembling a mosquito.

1964 Will *Hist. Okeechobee* 96 **FL,** There was another insect called a chizzy-wink . . . Since he looked like a mosquito only a little larger, but with a light gray body and fuzzy legs, folks mostly called him a "blind mosquito." Now this was no reflection on his eyesight, it simply meant that he couldn't bite. 1966 *DARE* (Qu. R4) Inf **FL34**, Blind mosquitoes; (Qu. R10, *Very small flies that don't sting*) Inf **FL32**, Blind mosquitoes; (Qu. R15a, . . *Nicknames . . for mosquitoes*) Inf **FL39**, Blind mosquitoes or no-see-ums. They don't bite. 1971 *DARE* FW Addit **cwFL**, I heard a man complaining today about "blind mosquitoes" on the Sarasota golf course. He said they didn't bite but flew in swarms, into your face, around your head and ears. 1978 *NADS Letters* **FL,** There was an insect that swarmed in and near the grass at the edge of the lake where we lived near Gainesville . . that fit the description "similar to a mosquito, but stingless." If I recall right, it even whined like a mosquito. We were told the name was blind mosquito. 1978 FL Coop. Extension Serv. *Extension Entomol. Rept.* 62.1, The Chironomidae are often referred to as aquatic midges since the larvae live in fresh water. Blind mosquito is a layman's term which may refer to several species of aquatic midges. Blind mosquitoes do not bite, suck blood, or carry

disease. They are important to man only when they emerge in such large numbers that they are a nuisance. 1981 *DARE* File **FL,** These mosquitos . . hatch by the millions . . along the beach of the river . . . These tiny insects, on hatching, leave behind shells or casings about the size of oat hulls, which can cover a large surface of the river. Meanwhile, the newly hatched "blind mosquitos" fly off, partly driven by the wind. They see only black and white—distinguish night and day—and head for our [white] building . . . They easily become attached to the wood surface and die right there. The sun bakes them on, more of their species land and the layers become cumulative.

blind path See **blind trail**

blind pig n [See **blind tiger**] *somewhat old-fash*

1 =blind tiger 1. **chiefly w Inland Nth, CA** See Map and Map Section

[1870 Macrae *Americans* 2.315 **MA,** In desperate cases it has to betake itself to the exhibition of Greenland pigs and other curious animals, charging 25 cents for a sight of the pig and throwing in a gin cocktail gratuitously.] 1887 MN Laws *Genl. Statutes* 2.248, Whoever shall attempt to evade or violate any of the laws of this state . . by means of the artifice or contrivance known as the "Blind Pig," or "Hole in the Wall" . . shall . . be punished. 1901 *DN* 2.136 **ND, PA,** *Blind pig* . . . A speak-easy; saloon without a license. 1912 *DN* 3.571 **wIN.** 1950 *WELS (A place where liquor is [or was] sold and consumed illegally)* 29 Infs, **WI,** Blind pig. 1965–70 *DARE* (Qu. DD30, *Joking names for a place where liquor is [or was] sold and consumed illegally*) 111 Infs, Blind pig; **CA14**, Blind peg [sic]. [Of all Infs responding to the question, 67% were old; of those giving this resp, 78% were old.]

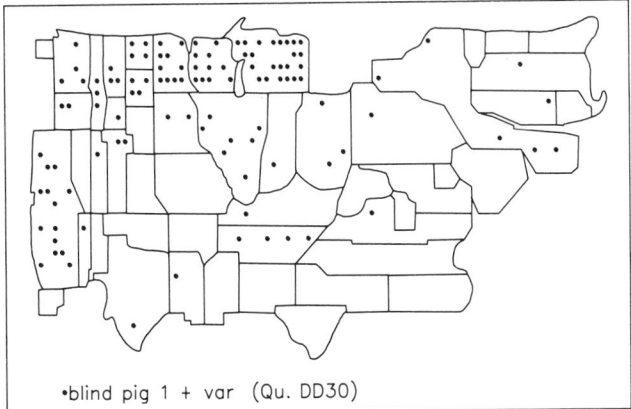

•blind pig 1 + var (Qu. DD30)

2 =blind tiger 3.

1966 *DARE* (Qu. DD21c, *Nicknames for whiskey, especially illegally made whiskey*) Inf **WA18**, Blind pig.

blind-pigger n [From **blind pig**] *somewhat old-fash*

One who sells liquor illegally, a bootlegger.

1894 *Voice* (NY) 6 Dec 1/5 *(OEDS),* Headed by one of the blind-piggers who was under arrest. 1918 *DN* 5.54 **NW,** Blind-pigger. "Two Kelso blind-piggers arrested and fined." 1967 *DARE* (Qu. DD32, *A person who sells illegal liquor*) Inf **MN5**, Blind-pigger.

blind post See **blind** n 4

blind shot n

In logging: see quot.

1958 McCulloch *Woods Words* **Pacific NW,** Blind shot—a dynamite shot which fails to go off.

blind side n **chiefly Midl**

A point where one is vulnerable; freq used in phr *get on one's blind side:* to take advantage of someone.

1903 *DN* 2.307 **seMO,** Blind side . . . In expression 'to get on the blind side of,' to take advantage of. 1907 *DN* 3.229 **nwAR,** Blind side . . . In the expression, "to get on the blind side of," i.e. to take advantage of. 1942 McAtee *Dial. Grant Co. IN* (as of 1890s), Blind side, . . in both factual and figurative senses; "I'll try to get on his ———", i.e. take advantage of him. (Ark., Mo., Va.) c1960 Wilson Coll. **csKY,** Blind side . . . An unsuspecting approach. "You'll have to slip up on his blind side if you want to collect any money."

blindsight n

Guesswork.

1969 *DARE* (Qu. KK48, *When you work something out as you go, without having a plan or pattern to follow: "I didn't have anything to go by, so I just did it _____."*) Inf **NJ**57, By blindsight.

blind snake See **blind worm**

blind tag n
Blindman's buff.
1970 *DARE* (Qu. EE4, *Games in which one player's eyes are bandaged and he has to catch the others and guess who they are*) Inf **MI**114, Blind tag.

blind the trail v phr
1968 Adams *Western Words, Blind the trail*—To conceal tracks or give them the appearance of going in a different direction.

blind tiger n, also attrib [Perh from an establishment's disguise as an exhibition hall of natural curiosities to conceal its illegal selling of liquor (see quot 1857); or perh ref to the one-eyed peep-hole through which the proprietor of such an establishment inspected customers before admitting them] *somewhat old-fash* Cf **blind pig**

1 A place that sells liquor illegally; a speakeasy. **chiefly Sth, W Midl** See Map and Map Section Cf **blind** n 3, **blind alley**
1857 *Spirit of the Times* 23 May 182/1 *(DA)*, I sees a kinder pigeon-hole cut in the side of a house, and over the hole, in big writin', 'Blind Tiger, ten cents a sight.' . . Says I to the feller inside, 'here's your ten cents, walk out your wild-cat.' Stranger, instead of showin' me a wild varmint without eyes, I'll be dod-busted if he didn't shove out a glass of whiskey. You see, that 'blind tiger' was an arrangement to evade the law, which won't let 'em sell licker there, except by the gallon. **1897** (1952) McGill *Narrative* 268 **SC**, We countrymen readily consume a fifty cent dinner and more so when a "blind tiger" has been found, . . the accommodating attendants . . accept a wink as we rise, which being interpreted means a drink the first chance we get. **1905** *DN* 3.70 **nwAR**. **1908** *DN* 3.292 **eAL, wGA**. **1916** *DN* 4.320 **KS**. **1922** *DN* 5.156 **AR, NE**. **1941** Daniels *Tar Heels* 9 **NC**, An old Negress let us watch her put the corks in blind tiger liquor bottles. **1950** *WELS* 5 Infs, **WI**, Blind tiger. **1962** Faulkner *Reivers* 290 **MS**, Ned . . entered the first blind tiger he came to and found Bobo trying to outface his doom through the bottom of a whiskey bottle. **1965–70** *DARE* (Qu. DD30, *Joking names for a place where liquor is [or was] sold and consumed illegally*) 84 Infs, **chiefly Sth, W Midl**, Blind tiger; **TX**1, Blind tiger joint. [Of all Infs responding to the question, 67% were old; of those giving these responses, 82% were old.]

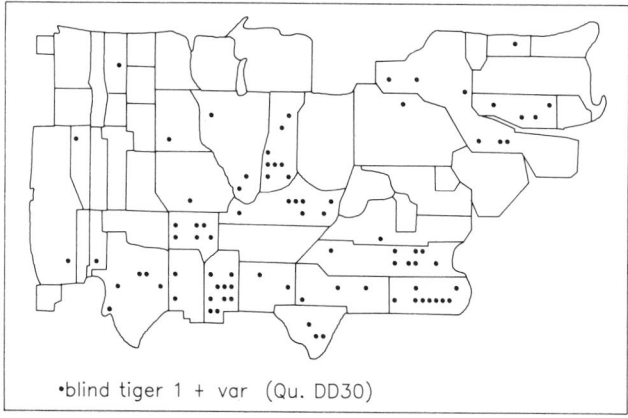

•blind tiger 1 + var (Qu. DD30)

‡**2** =**blind pigger.**
1966 *DARE* (Qu. DD32, *A person who sells illegal liquor is called a _____*) Infs **GA**13, **NC**2, Blind tiger. [Both Infs old]

‡**3** Illegally made whiskey. Cf **blind pig 2**
1968 *DARE* (Qu. DD21c, *Nicknames for whiskey, especially illegally made whiskey*) Inf **LA**34, Blind tiger.

blind trail n Also *blind path*
See quot 1968.
1843 (1916) Hall *New Purchase* 352 **sIN**, A blind path has that name because it tries the eyes and often requires spectacles to find it; or because one is in constant jeopardy of having the eyes blinded or struck out by unceremonious limbs, bushes, branches, and sprays. **1968** Adams *Western Words, Blind trail*—A trail with indistinct markings, or signs.

blind worm n Also *blind snake*
The Florida worm lizard *(Rhineura floridana)*.
1894 US Natl. Museum *Proc.* 17.321 **FL**, *Rhineura floridana* . . . The "blind worm" or "blind snake," as it is called, is not scarce in sandy places in Orange county. It is often found by people digging or grubbing in the gardens or plowing in the orange groves. **1960** Williams *Walk Egypt* 110 **GA**, He had gotten bit by a blind worm and died. [Note: author is native of FL.]

bline Gawd See **blind God**

blinger n |ˈblɪŋɚ|, occas |ˈblɪŋgɚ| [Perh echoic suggesting resonance of something struck, by analogy with *zinger* and *humdinger*] **chiefly NEast** Cf **sockdolager**
An extreme example of its kind.
1949 *Reader's Digest* Dec 18/1, 241 [persons] caught one or more colds . . . One hundred seventy-nine of them developed real blingers going through the phase of secondary infections. **1966–69** *DARE* (Qu. B3, *If a day is very hot, you say it's [a] _____*) Infs **NY**93, **PA**115, 216, [ˈblɪŋɚ]; (Qu. Y11, *Other words for a very hard blow . . "Joe really hit him a _____."*) Inf **MI**9, [ˈblɪŋɚ]—anything hard, not just a blow; **NY**145, [ˈblɪŋgɚ]; (Qu. LL5, *Something impressively big: "That cabbage is really a _____."*) Inf **PA**216, Blinger. **1968** *DARE* FW Addit **cnNY**, Blinger—a very hard rain.

blink v
1 Of milk: to turn sour. [From *blink* to exercise an evil influence, bewitch, hence to sour (souring of milk being formerly ascribed to witchcraft); see *EDD*] **chiefly Midl** Cf **blink** n[1] and adj, **blinked, blinky**
1905 *DN* 3.70 **nwAR**, Blink . . . To turn sour. Used of milk only. 'The milk's blinked.' 'It was so warm that the milk blinked.' Rare. **1941** *Hench Coll.* **VA**, A woman from Richmond . . says that her name for souring milk is "blinking milk." **1953** Randolph *Down in Holler* 227 **Ozarks**, Blink . . . To sour. "That milk'll blink sure if you leave it settin' out in the sun that-a-way." **c1960** Wilson *Coll.* **csKY**, Blink . . . To turn sour. "That milk is beginning to blink." **1968–69** *DARE* (Qu. H58, *Milk that's just beginning to become sour is _____*) Infs **IN**54, **VA**1, 23, Blinking.

2 See quot. [*SND* 1768 →]
1899 (1912) Green *VA Folk-Speech, Blink* . . . To smile, to look kindly, but with a modest eye, the word being generally applied to females.

blink adj [From **blink** v] **chiefly Midl** Cf **blinked** =**blinky.**
1883 *Amer. Philol. Assoc. Trans.* 14.45 **WV**, Blink milk, 'milk somewhat soured.' **1916** *DN* 4.271 **NE, KS**. **1927** *AmSp* 2.348 **WV**. **1941** *Hench Coll.* **swVA**. **1953** *AmSp* 28.248 **csPA**, Blink milk . . . Milk that is 'turning'; that is, slightly sour. Popular speech. Older residents. **1958** *PADS* 29.7 **TN**. **1967–70** *DARE* (Qu. H58, *Milk that's just beginning to become sour is _____*) Infs **AL**27, **KY**22, **VA**1, 28, Blink milk; **TN**66, Going blink.

blink n[1] [**blink** v] **chiefly S Midl** *somewhat old-fash* Cf **blinky, blue john** n 2
Slightly sour milk.
1895 *DN* 1.384 **swVA**, Blink: sour milk. So *blinky* . . (of milk), sour. **1950** *PADS* 14.15 **SC**, Blink . . . Milk that has turned or begun to turn sour. **1965–70** *DARE* (Qu. H58, *Milk that's just beginning to become sour is _____*) 14 Infs, **scattered S Midl**, Blink. [All Infs old]

blink n[2] **chiefly N Atl coast**
In fishing: a young or small mackerel.
1856 in 1884 Goode *Fisheries U.S.* 298 **NEng**, The mackerel . . are not sold by weight, but are culled, and are denominated as follows: Large ones, second-size, 'tinkers,' and 'blinks.' **1887** Goode *Amer. Fishes* 174 **N Atl coast**, Fish of this size are sometimes called 'Spikes' . . . The next year I think they are the 'Blinks,' being one year old. **1930** *AmSp* 5.389 **N Atl coast**, Blinks . . . Undersized or culled mackerel.

‡**blink** n[3] [Perh from *blink, ice-blink* a shining whiteness at the horizon caused by reflection from ice; a mass or field of ice] A thin layer (of ice).
1968 *DARE* (Qu. B33a, *The first thin ice that forms over the surface of a pond or pool: "There's just a _____ of ice."*) Inf **MO**34, Thin blink of ice.

blinked ppl adj [**blink** v] **chiefly S Midl** Cf **blink** n[1] and adj =**blinky.**

1916 *DN* 4.337 **cwPA,** *Blinked* . . . Slightly soured: of milk. **1944** *PADS* 2.40 **wNC,** *Blinked* . . . Said of milk that is slightly sour . . . Common. **1958** *PADS* 29.7 **TN,** *Blinked* . . . Sour, said of milk. **1965–70** *DARE* (Qu. H58, *Milk that's just beginning to become sour is* _____) 10 Infs, **scattered S Midl,** Blinked.

blinked out adj phr [Prob from *on the blink* "out of order," perh ult from **blink, on the**]
Out of order, broken down.
    1970 *DARE* (Qu. KK20b, *Something that looks as if it might collapse any minute: "Our old washing machine is* _____.") Inf **NJ68,** Blinked out.

blinker n [*blink* look with half-closed eyes + *er*]
    1972 *Atlanta Letters* **nwGA,** *Blinker* . . . a horse with poor eyesight. Also called "moon eyed."

blink-eye n
A very small community (one that one can pass through in the blink of an eye or a very short time).
    1969 *DARE* (Qu. C33, . . *An out-of-the-way place, or a very unimportant place*) Inf **IL41,** Blink-eye.

blink-eyed adj Also *blink-eye*
Cross-eyed.
    1966–69 *DARE* (Qu. X26a, *If a person's eyes look in different directions, looking inward, he's* _____) Infs **MA40,** Blink-eyed; **SC10,** Blink-eye.

blink, on the adj phr [**blink** v]
=**blinky.**
    1967–68 *DARE* (Qu. H58, *Milk that's just beginning to become sour is* _____) Infs **IL7, IA33, KS16, LA28,** On the blink.

blinky adj [**blink** v] Cf **blink** n[1] and adj, **blinked, blue john** n and adj
1a Of milk: beginning to go sour. **chiefly W Midl, Plains States, SW** See Map
    1902 *DN* 2.229 **sIL. 1905** *DN* 3.70 **nwAR. 1915** *DN* 4.181 **swVA.** *Ibid* 227 **wTX. 1917** *DN* 4.408 **wNC. 1936** *AmSp* 11.275 **cTN,** *Blinky.* Slightly sour or curdled. 'This milk is blinky.' **c1960** *Wilson Coll.* **csKY,** *Blinky* . . . Turning sour. "Ma, this sweet milk is blinky." **1965–70** *DARE* (Qu. H58, *Milk that's just beginning to become sour is* _____) 147 Infs, Blinky; **KY44,** Blinky milk; **OH72,** Turning blinky. **1970** Tarpley *Blinky* 193 **neTX,** In the days before improvements in refrigeration and dairy processing, milk would often become *blinky* or turn into *blue-john* after a few days. Almost one-half of the informants give *blinky* as the only synonym they know; this term is least common in the city.

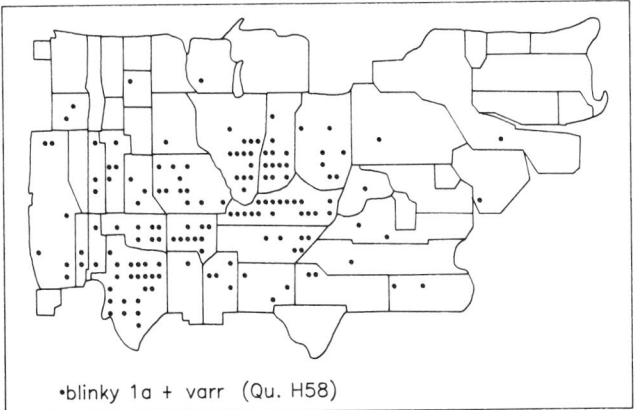

•blinky 1a + varr (Qu. H58)

b Of things other than milk: sour. *infreq*
    1895 *DN* 1.370 **eTN, wNC,** *Blinky:* sour. "The vinegar is blinky." [*DN:* Elsewhere apparently used only of things spoiled by souring, as milk.] **1928** Chapman *Happy Mt.* 91 **seTN,** I just took me a swallow out of both bottles . . and my in'ards has turned blinky.
2 By ext; of milk: bad tasting, flavored by plants that the cows have grazed on. Cf **marshy milk**
    1967–68 *DARE* (Qu. K14, *Milk that has a taste from something the cow ate in the pasture—you say, "That milk is* _____.") Infs **IN8, MO17, NE11, TX11, 51, VA7,** Blinky.

blinky-blue n [Perh blend of **blinky** + **blue john** n] Cf **blink** n[1], **blinky-john**
=**blue john** n.
    1944 *PADS* 2.40 **wNC,** *Blinky-blue:* sour skimmed milk.

blinky-john n [Blend of **blinky** + **blue john** n]
=**blink** n[1].
    1902 *DN* 2.229 **sIL,** *Blinky-john* . . . Milk just beginning to sour. **1970** Tarpley *Blinky* 193 **neTX,** For milk that is beginning to sour . . . Two informants in Upshur County say *blinky-john*.

blip n, intj [Echoic] **prob Sth, S Midl** *old-fash*
A sudden, brisk blow; pop!
    1880 Harris *Uncle Remus Songs* 24 **GA** [Black], Brer Rabbit draw back wid his fis', he did, en blip he tuck 'er side er de head. **1894** Twain *Tom Sawyer Abroad* 187 **MO,** We took him a blip in the back and knocked him off. **1899** Edwards *Defense* 110 **GA** [Black], Mas' Ramsey say somep'n' 'bout de young lady . . an' fus' t'ing you know—blip! an' Dr. Bailey's stick come down on es head.

blister n
1 A person in some way disapproved. *derog*
    1854 *Yale Lit. Mag.* 20.29 (*DAE*), Here's Mrs. Grind now,—rooms to let,—good rooms, but the dowager's a blister. **1885** Twain *Huck. Finn* 256 **MO,** Well, I never see such a blister for clean out-and-out cheek. **1930** Shoemaker *1300 Words* 8 **cPA Mts** (as of c1900), *Blister*—A tottering, disgusting, old drunkard. **1941** *LANE* Map 465 **seNH,** Derogatory names applied to a stupid person . . . [blɪstə].
2 Spec: an immoral woman; a whore.
    1905 *DN* 3.70 **nwAR,** *Blister* . . . An immoral woman. 'She's a blister.' Not uncommon. **1942** Berrey–Van den Bark *Amer. Slang* 439.2, *Slut* . . . Blister. **1968–69** *DARE* (Qu. HH37, *An immoral woman*) Inf **MA68,** Blister [ˈblɪstə]; (Qu. NN24, *Humorous substitutes for stronger exclamations: "Why the son of a* _____!") Inf **OH47,** Blister.
3 A young or immature kernel of corn; an ear with such kernels. Cf **blistered corn**
    1969–70 *DARE* (Qu. I33, . . *Ears of corn that are just right for eating*) Inf **IN69,** In the blisters; (Qu. I34, *If you don't have sweet corn, you can always eat young* _____) Inf **KY94,** Blisters.
4 A small oyster; see quots.
    1894 *DN* 1.328 **NJ,** *Blister:* an oyster smaller than a quarter dollar. Used from Barnegat south to Cape May. **1948** *AmSp* 23.297 **Puget Sound WA,** *Blisters* are small seeds [=young oysters] less than half an inch long.

blister balsam n Cf **blister pine**
=**Fraser fir.**
    1851 in 1956 Eliason *Tarheel Talk* 259 **NC,** The balsam is of two kinds, the He and She (or Blister). The latter has blisters in the bark, which alone contain the balsam.

blister bug n Less freq *blister beetle* [From the skin blisters caused by contact with the insect; *OED* 1816 →] **chiefly TX, Cent** See Map
A beetle of the family Meloidae.
    1868 *Amer. Entomologist* 1.24/1, The blister-beetles . . are . . poisonous when taken internally in large doses. *Ibid* 1.24/2, The Ash-gray

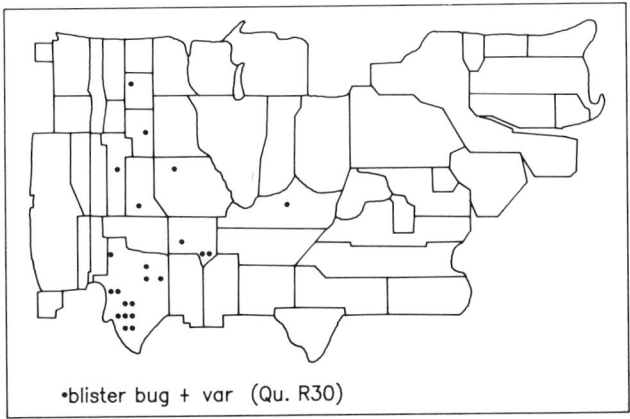

•blister bug + var (Qu. R30)

Blister-beetle (Lytta cinerea, Fabr.) . . . attacks not only potato vines, but also honey-locusts. **1881** *Amer. Naturalist* 15.143, Others, as the true blister-beetles, *(Lyttini)*, feed on locust eggs. **1909** Smith *Insect Friends* 99, But there can be no doubt . . that in regions where grasshoppers are very abundant, . . blister beetles are a most important check. **1965–70** *DARE* (Qu. R30) 15 Infs, **esp TX**, Blister bug; 8 Infs, **esp Cent**, Blister beetle. **1967** *DARE* Tape TX1, Blister bugs. **1967** *DARE* FW Addit **TX**, Blister bug—a small, greyish beetle often found on tree bark, contact with which causes blisters to appear on the skin. About ¾ inch long, ⅜ inch wide. General.

blistered corn n Cf **blister 3**

Young corn, just ripe enough to eat.

　1966 *DARE* (Qu. I33, . . *Ears of corn that are just right for eating*) Inf MS16, Blistered corn.

blister end n

In logging: see quot.

　1958 McCulloch *Woods Words* **Pacific NW**, *Blister end*—the handle of a shovel, ax, or other hand tool.

blister pine n [From the resin vesicles] **esp WV**
=**balsam fir.**

　1894 *Jrl. Amer. Folkl.* 7.99, *Abies balsamea* . . blister pine, balm of Gilead fir, West Va. **1897** Sudworth *Arborescent Flora* 51, *Abies balsamea* . . . Blister Pine (W. Va.). **1933** Small *Manual SE Flora* 8, *A[bies] Fraseri* . . . The bark with balsam-yielding blisters . . . Blister-pine. **1952** Strausbaugh–Core *Flora WV* 44, Balsam Fir . . . Bark warty with resin blisters . . . The resin blisters account for the name "Blister Pine" commonly used in the Alleghenies.

blister plaster n

See quot 1975; also fig.

　1937 Johnson *Ante-Bellum NC* 345, At least one man applied a *'blister-plaster'* to his wife to cure her of Methodism. **1975** Gould *ME Lingo* 15, Blister plaster—A mustard plaster; a remedy for aches and pains in the bygone. Their efficacy was presumed to lie in the "heat" of the mustard, and when a child got one applied for the croup it could blister.

blister the air v phr

To curse or swear violently.

　1941 FWP *Guide AL* 127, A slave . . wanted to "cuss out" his master. He went to the conjure doctor and explained his desire; then, charm in pocket, he "purely blistered de air."

blitz adj [Ger *Blitz* flash, lightning] **chiefly in Ger settlement areas**

Of food, esp pastry: easy or quick (to prepare).

　1946 Rombauer *Joy of Cooking* 580, *Blitztorte*—This is the German mother of the preceding Cream Tart. A little more frugal, a little less flossy—mighty good. **1948** *AmSp* 23.107 **swIL**, German names having to do with foods and cooking are . . numerous in the local vocabulary . . . Blitz kuchen, blitz cake, . . blitz tart. **1956** Crocker *Picture Cook Book* 232, Blitz Torte (Lightning Cake) *Beautiful . . . the meringue top encrusted with sugar and toasted almonds.*

blitzen See **blixen**

‡**blitz, the** n [*The Blitz* WWII air attack, from *Blitzkrieg*] Menstruation.

　1970 *DARE* (Qu. AA27, *What other names or expressions are used for a woman's menstruation?*) Inf PA245, The blitz.

blixen n Also *blitzen, blixens, blixes, blixian, blixum* [Prob from Ger *Blitz* lightning, *blitzen* to lighten, flash] **chiefly Midl** Cf *dickens*, **flugens** n

Usu in phr *cold (or hot) as blixen:* hell, tarnation, **blazes.**

　1876 in 1969 *PADS* 52.43 **seIL**, It froze last night as hard as blixum . . . Fearful cold in the morning froze like blixian. **1906** *DN* 3.131 **nwAR**, *Cold as blixum* . . . Extremely cold. **1908** *DN* 3.299 **eAL, wGA**, *Cold as blixes* . . . Very cold. **1911** *DN* 3.541 **NE**, *Blixen* . . . Used only in phrase, "cold as blixen," meaning extremely cold. **1912** *DN* 3.573 **wIN**, *Cold as blixum* (or *blixen*) . . . Very cold. "It was as cold as blixum this morning." **1927** *AmSp* 2.351 **WV**, *Colder 'n blixens* . . very cold. "This weather is colder 'n blixens this month." **1942** Warnick *Garrett Co. MD* (as of 1900–1918), *Cold as blixen,* . . very cold weather. **1942** McAtee *Dial. Grant Co. IN* (as of 1890s), *Cold as blixen,* . . very cold, said of weather. **1966** *Wilson Coll.*

csKY, *Cold as blitzen* . . Very cold. **1968** *DARE* (Qu. B3, *If a day is very hot, you say it's _____*) Inf MI94, Hotter than blixen.

blixen-bus n *old-fash*

An automobile.

　1916 *DN* 4.271 **NE**, *Blixen-bus* . . . Automobile. "There comes a blixen-bus over the hill." Reported from Nebraska sandhill region. **1928** *AmSp* 4.132 **NE**, An automobile is a "blunderbus" or a "blixen bus."

blizzard n [Origin unknown but prob related to Ger *blitzen* to flash; perh also to *blasen* to blow] **chiefly Sth, S Midl**

A spell of very cold weather, not necessarily accompanied by snow or strong wind.

　1954 *Harder Coll.* **cwTN**, *Blizzard* . . . A period of extremely cold weather. **c1960** *Wilson Coll.* **csKY**, *Blizzard* . . . Common name for a severe cold spell, especially with snow. **1967–68** *DARE* FW Addits **GA**19, 22, 45, Blizzard—a strong cold wind with no snow.

bloater n

1 also *bloat, bloater chub, bloater whitefish:* A **cisco**, usu *Coregonus hoyi.* **chiefly Gt Lakes**

　1896 U.S. Natl. Museum *Bulletin* 47.471, *Argyrosomus prognathus* . . . Long Jaw; Bloater. **1902** Jordan–Evermann *Amer. Fishes* 138, *Bloater Whitefish . . . Argyrosomus prognathus* . . . The bloater is known also as bloat, longjaw [etc]. **1947** Hubbs–Lagler *Fishes Gt. Lakes* 42, Great Lakes bloater—*Leucichthys hoyi.* **1966** *DARE* Tape MI21, They're like a small chub, a bloater grows into a chub after it gets bigger. **1974** WI Univ. *Fish Lake MI* 18, *Bloater . . . Coregonus hoyi* . . . Common names: bloater chub, bloat . . . Lake Michigan's catch of bloater has dropped almost 16% a year since 1969. In addition, female bloaters now make up about 90% of the population and biologists hold out little hope that the bloater chub will survive.

2 See quot.

　1966 *DARE* Tape ME17, The big fish they use for bloaters most of 'em . . . [FW:] What's a bloater? [Inf:] A big sardine, sardine which is around ten–twelve inches long. [FW:] What do they do with them? [Inf:] They smoke 'em.

3 A **bonito 1** (here: *Sarda sarda*).

　1935 Caine *Game Fish* 53, Bonito . . . Synonyms: Bloater, Blue Bonito, Bone-eater [etc.]. **1946** LaMonte *N. Amer. Game Fishes* 20, *Sarda sarda* . . . Names: Bonito, . . Little Tunny, Bloater.

bloater chub, bloater whitefish See **bloater 1**

blob n

1 =**mottled sculpin.**

　1881 *Amer. Naturalist* Nov 879, These [fish] were the common blob, *Potamocottus meridionalis.* **1882** U.S. Natl. Museum *Bulletin* 16.696, *U[ranidia] richardsoni* . . *Blob.* **1887** Goode *Amer. Fishes* 302, In the lakes and streams of the Northern States are numerous species of *Uranidea* and allied genera, . . also called . . "Blobs." **1911** *Century Dict.* 590/2, *Blob* . . . A cottoid fish, *Cottus ictalops,* a kind of miller's-thumb. **1933** John G. Shedd Aquarium *Guide* 131, *Cottus ictalops* . . Blob.

2 A **pitcher plant 1** (here: *Sarracenia purpurea*).

　1936 Eaton *Wild Gardens New Engl.* 26 **ceMA**, We visited the blobs (*sarracenia purpurea* to you) every season, and we children . . did not have to sit on a bed of them to discover that the leaves were partially filled with water.

3 See quot 1900. Cf **blob** v²

　1900 *DN* 2.23 [College words], *Blob* . . . A mistake. **1934** *Hench Coll.* **Baltimore MD**, An unfortunate blob in Saturday's column made Hercules a five-tyne fork man in the "Aegean," instead of the Augean, Stables. **1942** Berrey–Van den Bark *Amer. Slang* 170.2, *Error; mistake; blunder* . . . Blob.

blob v¹ [Prob alter of *blab* to chatter]

To talk indiscreetly or excessively.

　1899 (1912) Green *VA Folk-Speech*, *Blob out* . . . To blab out. "He blobs everything right out." **1941** *LANE* Map 419 **sME**, Chat . . . [blob, gab, jawp, glab, buzz], very old slang terms. **1954** *Harder Coll.* **cwTN**, *Blob* . . . Blab . . . "Well I better hush before I blob too much."

blob v² [From *blob* a small drop, globule] See **blob** n **3**

To spill; by ext, to make a mistake.

　1900 *DN* 2.23 [College words], *Blob* . . . To make a mistake. **1912** *DN* 3.566 **cNY**, *Blob* . . . To spill.

blobber-lipped adj [Alter of *blubber* fat, infl by *blob* globule]
See quot 1946.
    1946 *PADS* 6.6 **NC**, *Blobber-lipped* . . . Thick-lipped; voluptuous-looking. The term usually applied to a negro man having such lips . . . Occasional. **c1960** *Wilson Coll.* **csKY**, "That blobber-lipped boy of Jim Smith's."

blobbermouth n Also *blob-mouth* [Alter of *blabbermouth*] Cf **blob** v¹
See quots.
    1949 *PADS* 11.3 **wTX**, *Blobber-mouth* . . . A talkative person; one who will not keep secrets. Occasional. **1954** *Harder Coll.* **cwTN**, *Blobber-mouth* . . . A person who talks too much. **1969** *DARE* (Qu. HH7a, *Someone who talks too much, or too loud: "He's an awful_____.")* Inf **GA74**, Blob-mouth.

block n

1 also attrib: A connected or compacted group of houses or other buildings. [Prob from Du *blok*]
    1796 *Aurora. Genl. Advert.* (Philadelphia PA) 13 Dec 2/4, A fire broke out . . and raged with such fury as to baffle all human exertion, till it had laid in ashes the whole block of buildings. **1801** in 1888 Cutler *Life* 2.50 **DC**, The buildings [in Washington] are brick, and erected in what are called large blocks, that is, from two to five or six houses joined together, and appear like one long building. **1881** *Harper's Mag.* 62.712/2, In the case of Milwaukee . . solid blocks of houses flush with the sidewalk are very few. **1905** *DN* 3.4 **cCT**, *Block* . . . Any mass of houses or apartment buildings. **1967** *DARE* FW Addit **sePA**, Block houses—a row of houses that fill the block.

2 A large single building.
a A commercial building.
    1874 in 1923 Adams *Pioneer Hist. Ingham Co.* 149 **MI**, A little old "corner grocery" building occupied the corner where Pratt & Millspaugh's block now stands. **1905** *DN* 3.4 **cCT**, *Block* . . . A single building in the business part of a city. **1907** *DN* 3.209 **nwAR**, *Block*. **1917** *DN* 4.388 **neOH**, *Block* . . . A single building with one or more stores or offices, etc . . . Most W[estern] R[eserve] towns have one or more principal buildings called "_____ Block;" as "Phoenix Block." General. **1966** *Daily Kennebec Jrl.* (Augusta ME) 13 Apr 21/7, *Block For Sale* . . . A grocery store has been operated here for over 80 years. **1966** *DARE* FW Addit **cMA**, Block—a business building, such as the Starrett Block.
b An apartment building.
    1941 *LANE* Map 355 **scattered throughout NEng**, Terms for a house or a large building divided into separate dwellings for two or more families . . . *Block*. **1965–70** *DARE* (Qu. D23, *A house that is divided in two through the middle so that two families can live in it)* Infs **MD21, PA245**, Block.

3 A writing pad or tablet. **esp common MA**
    1965–70 *DARE* (Qu. F48, *What do you call pages of writing paper glued together at the top with a cardboard back?)* 9 Infs, **6 in MA**, Block. **1966** *DARE* FW Addit **cwIN**, Block—a pad of writing paper.

4 A package (of chewing gum).
    1968 *DARE* FW Addit **cNC**, Block—used for "pack" in a "block of chewing gum."

5 In the children's game **foot-and-a-half**: see quot. *old-fash*
    1901 *DN* 2.140 **NH**, *Foot-and-a-half* . . . The name of a game like Spanish fly . . . The player over whom the others leap is called the block.

6 also *blockie*: A men's square-toed shoe.
    1969 *DARE* (Qu. W42b) Inf **KY70**, Blocks or blockies.

7 A quarter-pound stick (of butter).
    1968 *DARE* Tape **MD44**, You take a half a block of butter or margarine.

block v

1 =**blockade** v.
    1917 *DN* 4.408 **wNC**, *Block* . . . *Blockade* [=to make moonshine whiskey]. "He's blockin' over in Hell's Holler."

2 To clear of trees and brush.
    1935 *Yale Rev.* 25.171 **KY**, I blocked a road through the woods for the oxen, so a body could see some daylight.

3 Among sugar-beet farmers: see quot 1930; hence vbl n *blocking*.
    1930 *AmSp* 6.11 **CO**, When the beet plants are a few inches high,

blocking or *bunching* is done with a hoe and then *thinning* is completed by hand. The former process eliminates whole blocks of plants at regular intervals. **1942** *Sun* (Baltimore MD) 3 July 13/6 **ID** *(Hench Coll.),* High school boys and girls, reported by J.B. Newport, Idaho Commissioner of Agriculture, were able to block and thin more beets than the average city grownup.

blockade n, also attrib [See quot 1968] **chiefly S Midl**
Illicit liquor, moonshine.
    1867 Scott *Partisan Life* 195 **ncVA**, The truth is, the parson had taken about a half a pint of "blockade," and did not care the snap of a finger for the reproachful looks. **1896** *Congressional Record* 31 Mar 3408/2 **NC**, I ask . . if it is not infinitely better that we should have a little blockade whisky occasionally. **1913** Morley *Carolina Mts.* 66, Corn . . supplies as well that important beverage . . known as . . "blockade". **1917** *DN* 4.408 **wNC**. **1924** Raine *Land of Saddle-Bags* 132 **Appalachians**, There is no shame, no sense of guilt in making or selling this "blockade" whiskey. **1965–70** *DARE* (Qu. DD21c, . . *Illegally made whiskey)* Infs **NC35, SC32**, Blockade; **GA72**, Blockade juice; **TN16**, Blockade liquor; **NC45**, Blockade whiskey. **1968** *Foxfire* Fall-Winter 100 **nGA**, The name [blockaders] is a hold-over from the days when blockades were common . . . Also gave rise to the expression "blockade whiskey."

blockade v, hence *blockading* vbl n **chiefly S Midl** Cf **block** v **1, blockader**
To make illicit liquor.
    1883 Zeigler *Heart of Alleghanies* 141 **wNC**, Blockading, or "moonshining" . . is not as prevalent in these mountains as is generally supposed. **1917** *DN* 4.408 **wNC**, *Blockade* . . . To make moonshine whiskey. **1926** Vollmer *Sun-Up* 3 **wNC**, Moonshining? . . Yes, blockadin'. Why not? **1939** *FWP Guide NC* 467, The making of illicit liquor, locally called "blockading," contributed to the feuds that have given this region its old name of "Bloody Madison." **1943** *Natl. Geog. Mag.* 84.766/1 **seKY**, Naturally Henderson in his 'blockading' (moonshining) . . had made many enemies.

blockader n [blockade v] **chiefly S Midl**
One who makes illicit liquor; a moonshiner.
    1883 Zeigler *Heart of Alleghanies* 141 **wNC**, In the wilderness, we would be taken for revenue officers, and, as such, shot on sight by blockaders. **1926** Kephart *Highlanders* 126 **sAppalachians**, The big blockader makes unlicensed whiskey on a fairly large scale. **1943** Writer's Program NC *Bundle of Troubles* 114, The revenooers got fifty dollars for every still they took, and they didn't get nothing for catching a blockader. **1951** Craig *Singing Hills* 3 **swVA**, I'm not a blockader, and don't make illicit liquor. **1969** *DARE* Tape **GA72**, A moonshiner is also known as a blockader.

block and fall n
Block and tackle.
    1953 Randolph *Down in Holler* 227 **Ozarks**, *Block-and-fall* . . . Block and tackle. **1958** McCulloch *Woods Words* **Pacific NW**, *Block and fall*—A block and the line leading from it to which the power is applied. **1968** *DARE* Tape **NY79**, We'd pull it up with the block and fall. **1976** *PA Folklife* Spring 30, *Block and fall*, block and tackle.

block and tackle n, also attrib *joc*
Whiskey.
    1951 *Western Folkl.* 10.81 **NM**, Block and Tackle Whiskey (take a drink, walk a block, and you'll tackle Joe Louis, a lion, or a tiger). **1967** *DARE* FW Addit **IL**, Block and tackle whiskey. **1967** Will *Dredgeman* 28 **FL**, Piney woods champagne! That real old block and tackle—makes you run a block and tackle anything! **c1970** *Thompson Coll.* **GA** (as of 1920s), Block-and-tackle whiskey.

block and tickle n Also *block and teckle* [Alter of *block and tackle*] **chiefly Sth, S Midl**
Pulley blocks with ropes for hoisting or hauling; block and tackle.
    1893 Shands *MS Speech, Block and tickle* . . . Almost universally used by workmen for *block and tackle.* **1909** *DN* 3.381 **eAL, wGA**, *Tickle* . . . Tackle. Heard only in 'block and tickle.' Sometimes *teckle* is heard. **1933** *AmSp* 8.1.30 **nTX**, Block and tackle (pronounced *tickle*). **1954** *PADS* 21.20 **SC**, *Block and tickle* . . . Block and tackle. **1954** *Harder Coll.* **cwTN**, *Block and tickle* . . . Block and tackle. **c1960** *Wilson Coll.* **csKY**, We'd better git a block and tickle to raise this tree off of the road.

block boy n

1954 *Harder Coll.* **cwTN,** *Block boy . . .* In hay-baling, the person, usually a boy, who ties the bales.

blockbuster n Also *blockburster* [By ext from *blockbuster* a large bomb used in WWII]

A large firecracker or cherry bomb.

1954 *Sun* (Baltimore MD) 20 May 40/6 **nwMD,** An exploding fireworks bomb burned two boys . . . when a lighted "cherry bomb" or "blockbuster" was tossed at them. **1968** *DARE* (Qu. FF28, . . *Kinds of fireworks*) Inf **WI66,** Blockbursters.

block dance n **chiefly NY, NJ** Cf **block party**

A public dance held outdoors (as in a street closed to traffic) commonly featuring folk or ethnic dancing; hence *block dancing,* the dances performed at such a gathering.

1932 *Daily Progress* (Charlottesville VA) 12 Aug 1/5 (Hench Coll.), Taking advantage of the laxity of police and traffic regulations during the convention, visiting firefighters have nightly turned Alexandria's main business section into a tumultuous carnival with their sirens, automobile parades and block dances. **1965–70** *DARE* (Qu. FF4, . . *Kinds of dancing parties*) Infs **NJ4, 27, 29, NY28, 111, 121, 175, 190, PA202,** Block dance; (Qu. FF5a, *Names for different steps and figures in dancing*) Inf **NJ54,** Block dancing. **1968** *Catskill Mt. News* (Margaretville NY) 4 July 1/8, Thursday activities include a block dance during the evening on the A&P parking lot.

blocked adj

=**blocky.**

1970 *DARE* FW Addit **cMI,** Blocked (cow)—a squarish-hipped cow. Usually a good milker.

blocked ppl adj

In tobacco production: see quot.

1967 *Key Tobacco Vocab.* **GA, KY, MO, NC,** Blocked . . . Of a tobacco warehouse: containing more piles than can be sold in the allotted time, overfull.

blocker n[1] Also *blocker loop* [See quot 1961] **West**

A large loop used in roping cattle.

1921 Thorp *Songs Cowboys* 163, Building big loops we called "blockers,"/ Spinning the rope in the air. **1933** *AmSp* 8.1.29 **nwTX,** *Blocker loop.* As long a loop as can be made, used for *fore-footin'*— named for a prominent cattle man of South Texas, who had a reputation as a roper. **1961** Adams *Old-Time Cowhand* 232, The "Blocker loop" was a large loop, takin' this name from John Blocker, a well-known roper and trail driver of Texas, who originated and made this loop famous. It was started like a straight overhead loop, bein' taken 'round the head to the left. When throwed it turned over and went over the animal's shoulders and picked up both front feet.

‡blocker n[2]

A hanger-on.

1970 *DARE* (Qu. II18, *Someone who joins himself on to you and your group without being asked and won't leave*) Inf **FL52,** Blocker—[the word is] kind of slangy, a bit vulgar.

blockey See **blocky**

block-house n Also *block-home* **S Atl**

A house raised off the ground on supports to keep it dry and cool.

1966 *Plant City Courier* (FL) 31 Mar 19/1, *For Rent:* Small furnished block house. *Ibid* 19/2, 3 B[ed]R[oom] block house, garage. *Ibid* 19/6, 1 acre and 3 bedroom 2 bath block home. **1969** *DARE* FW Addit **seGA,** Block-house—the type of house that is set on house-blocks or low pillars of brick or stone.

blocking n

A method of fishing: see quot.

1970 *DARE* (Qu. P13) Inf **KY86,** Blocking—2 one-quart oil cans attached to each other, free floating [from which baited lines are dropped]. For catfish.

block-on-block n

A children's game: see quot.

1970 *DARE* Tape **KY75,** Block-on-block was a boys' game. One player guarded a block of wood set on another block; the rest had clubs and hid, then watched for a chance to run in and knock off the top block. If the guard caught a player sneaking in, that player stayed with the block, along with other caught players. If a player knocked off the block while others were caught, the caught ones were free to hide again while the guard went after the block. The game continued until all were caught. The last one caught was guard in the next game.

block out v phr

Of tobacco plants: see quot.

1967 *Key Tobacco Vocab.* **CT,** Block out . . . Of growing tobacco: to reach the stage where the leaves spread.

block party n [*block* a group of city buildings between cross-streets] **chiefly Nth, N Midl** Cf **block dance**

An outdoor public party commonly sponsored by an organization and usu held in a street temporarily barred to traffic.

1941 *Sun* (Baltimore MD) 18 July 12/1 (Hench Coll.), That "block party" for service men which the hospitable residents of North Montford avenue staged night before last proved something rather special and perhaps important. **1958** Golden *For 2¢ Plain* 118 **NYC,** I remember going to an Italian block party and watching twenty or thirty little Italian girls dance the tarantella. **1967–69** *DARE* (Qu. FF1) Inf **PA245,** Block party; (Qu. FF2) Inf **PA66,** Block parties; **MD8,** Block party—participants all share food, have music, games, firecrackers; (Qu. FF4) Inf **NY81,** Block party—people on the block get together and have a party; **PA4,** Block parties—kids dancing on a lot; **PA113, 205,** Block party. **1981** *DARE* File **csWI,** During the 60's in Madison the block party became spread to colleges as a resistance activity with political overtones. Today it is still a common summertime activity, though it is less politically oriented.

block sleigh n Also *block sled* *old-fash*

A kind of sleigh used to haul loads.

1967–68 *DARE* (Qu. N40a, . . *Kinds of sleighs . . for hauling loads*) Inf **PA136,** Block sled; **MI56,** Block sleigh; (Qu. N40b) Inf **PA3,** Block sleigh. [All Infs old]

blocky adj Also sp *blockey* Cf **blocked** adj

Of an animal: sturdily built, stocky.

1904 *New York Tribune* (NY) 15 May mag sec 15/3, A blocky pair of forty-seven inch ponies. **1967** Fetterman *Stinking Creek* 70 **seKY,** I got a good cow. She's a four-year-old blocky cow. **1969** *DARE* Tape **CA163,** A beef animal, they're supposed to be blocky and deep-bodied. **1969** *SC Market Bulletin* 9 Jan 4, 900 pound mare mule, will ride or walk to one horse wagon, runs with cattle, plows good, gentle, blockey.

blonde bound adj phr

Among loggers: see quot.

1958 McCulloch *Woods Words* **Pacific NW,** *Blonde bound*—Held up by a woman; an excuse for being late on the job.

blond Swede n

Among loggers: see quot.

1968 Adams *Western Words, Blond Swede*—What the loggers call an elderly man.

blong See **belong** A2

blongst, blonx See **belong** A1, 2

blood n

1 A fellow Black person. *among Black speakers*

1967 *DARE* Tape **LA3,** I wish you would go by my crib [=house] and get my blood to raise me [=free me on bond]. [Convict speech of Blacks in Louisiana State Penitentiary heard by Inf.] **1970** Major *Afro-Amer. Slang, Blood:* one black person to another. **1971** Roberts *Third Ear, Blood . . .* a fellow black; friend. **1977** Smitherman *Talkin* 225 [Black], They say that the one dude who got away was a Blood . . . He was a big, Black, strong brother by the name of Shine. *Ibid* 251, *Blood,* highly positive term, for males and females; obvious reference to genetic kinship of blacks who all share the same racial blood line.

2 Wine. *chiefly among Black speakers*

1966–70 *DARE* (Qu. DD27, . . *Nicknames . . for wine*) Infs **DC11, FL52, MA8, NY249, SC68, 69, VA73,** Blood [All Infs Black]; [**NC33,** Blood of the fruit; **WA11,** Blood of the grape]. **1970** Major *Afro-Amer. Slang, Blood: . .* wine. **1981** Pederson *LAGS Urban Material* **swTN,** *Wine: . .* [1 Inf] blood.

‡3 In gambling: a bet.

1967 *DARE* FW Addit **NYC,** *Get your blood in*—in a dice game means to "get your bet in."

4 in phr *son of a blood:* See quot. *euphem*

1969 *DARE* (Qu. NN24, *Humorous substitutes for stronger exclamations: "Why the son of a _____!"*) Inf **GA77,** Blood.

blood adv *esp among Black speakers* Cf Brit *bloody*

Used as an intensifier—see quot 1960.

1945 Saxon *Gumbo Ya-Ya* 504 **LA** [Black], Man, Buster gets blood mad when I talks to him. I just let him be. **1960** Wentworth–Flexner *Slang, Blood* . . . Very; blooming, blasted, goddamn(ed). **1970** *DARE* (Qu. LL37, *To make a statement as strong as you can: "I could have wrung her neck, I was so _____ mad."*) Inf **DC**13, Blood.

blood v, hence vbl n *blooding*

To put blood on a hunter's face as a mark of initiation.

1966 *DARE* Tape **DC**9, [In fox hunting] there's a ceremony which is known as blooding . . . If this is the first kill a person has been on, . . we blood him . . . We take a pad and dip where it's nice and bloody and paint it on their face; **SC**19, They blood him, . . blood his face [when he kills his first deer].

blood agate n [From its color]

1969 *DARE* (Qu. EE6d, *Special marbles*) Inf **PA**167, Blood agates.

blood alley n[1]

1967 *DARE* FW Addit **CA**, *Blood alley*—a strip of road when a four lane highway becomes a two lane highway. Applied to specific places in California where the road so narrows. There's one between Monterey and San Luis Obispo, for instance.

blood alley n[2] [alley n[2]; *EDD* blood-alley "In *gen.* dial. use"]

In marble play: see quot 1955.

1890 *DN* 1.76, "Agates" and "blood-alleys" were used in Boston fifteen years ago. **1890** Howells *Boy's Town* 81 **sOH**, As my boy was skilful at marbles, he was able to . . come home at night with a pocketful of white-alleys and blood-alleys, striped plasters and bull's-eyes. **1955** *PADS* 23.10 **cwTN**, *Alley, blood* . . . A highly valued marble made of red painted alabaster or clay, or painted with red streaks or circles.

blood and butcher n See **bloody butcher 1**

blood-an'-ound See **bloodynoun**

blood bay n

1944 Adams *Western Words, Blood bay*—A horse of darker red color than the bay.

blood beet n Also *blood turnip*

A garden beet.

1829 *Free Press* (Tarboro NC) 20 Feb *(DA)*, Blood Beets. **1859** IL State Ag. Soc. *Trans. for 1857–58* 3.503, The early blood turnip is a standard sort [of beet], turnip shaped, blood red, very tender and good for early use and late keeping. **1868** MI State Bd. Ag. *Annual Rept.* 7.349, John Ford, Detroit . . [exhibited] 12 blood beets. **1941** Lee *Stage Coach* 29 **VT**, Great Great Grandmother took as much pride in the display of marrow fat peas, parsnips, blood beets, and limas as she did in her china roses. **1950** *WELS (Other names in your neighborhood for beets)* 1 Inf, **cWI**, Blood beet; 1 Inf, **cWI**, Blood turnip.

blood boil n chiefly **Sth, S Midl**

A localized, infected skin swelling that discharges blood and pus.

1965–70 *DARE* (Qu. BB33a, *. . A swelling under the skin, bigger than a pimple, that comes to a head*) Infs **AL**34, **AR**51, **KY**34, Blood boil; **KY**77, Blood boil—blood comes out; **LA**28, The blood boil runs a thick bloody fluid; **SC**58, Blood boil—smaller than ordinary; a bloody pus; (Qu. BB33b, *. . A swelling under the skin*) Inf **MO**4, Blood boil.

blood bread n

A bread made with blood.

1968 *DARE* (Qu. H18, *. . Special kinds of bread*) Inf **MI**34, Blood bread—they [=Finnish people] call it lumpa ['lumpɑ]. It's made with rye flour, white flour and blood.

blood drawing n chiefly **NW**

A community project organized to collect blood donations.

1967 *Arlington Times* (WA) 5 Jan 1/5, A date for the next public blood drawing has been set for Feb. 2. **1967** *Burns Times–Herald* (OR) 23 Mar 8/1, [Headline:] *Blood drawing nets 230 pints* [Text:] A final total of 230 pints of blood was donated to the Bloodmobile during its two-day draw in Burns this week. **1968** *Power Co. Press* (Amer. Falls ID) 25 Jan 5/2, Each member is asked to donate two dozen cookies to be used at the blood drawing here on Thursday. **1973** *DARE* FW Addit **cwNH**, Mrs. Janet Kimball, Blood Program chairman . . announces that a blood drawing will be held next week . . in the Baptist Church. **1980** *DARE* File **sID** (as of 1960s), At our College the sororities and fraternities competed to see which could muster the greatest participation in blood drawings.

blooddrops n pl, but sg or pl in constr Also *blooddrop, blood-flower* [See quot 1897]

=**wind poppy**.

1897 Parsons *Wild Flowers CA* 129, The wind-poppy is an exceedingly variable flower . . . In the south it is usually very small, making tiny flecks of red in the grass, for which reason it is there called "blood-drop." **1911** *Century Dict. Suppl., Blood-drops* . . . A variety of the wind-poppy, . . bearing many small red flowers: found in California. **1968** *DARE* (Qu. S26a) Inf **CA**87, Bloodflower—a gray-green stem; alternate buds, four-petalled small flower.

bloodenhound See **bloodynoun**

bloodflower See **blooddrops**

bloodick n Also *bloody* [Perh imit] chiefly **MD** Cf **bloodynoun**

A bullfrog **1**.

1937 *Sun* (Baltimore MD) 16 Jun 10/8, For the first time this season I heard . . the voice of a big bullfrog, the kind we kids used to call "bloodies." **1939** *Hench Coll.*, A resident of Charlottesville, Va., spoke today of his boyhood (around 1880's) in Cumberland, Maryland, and about playing in the water . . . The boys played with frogs that they called *bloodicks*. The frogs were good-sized normal ones, with green back and white chest. **1951** *MD Hist. Mag.* 46.127, In the eastern part of the Eleventh District of Baltimore County country boys who hunted bull-frogs, called them *bloodies*. **1968** *DARE* (Qu. P22, *. . A very large frog that makes a deep loud sound*) Inf **MD**22, Bloodick ['blʌdɪk].

blooding See **blood** v

blood kin n chiefly **Sth, S Midl**

=**blood relative**.

1880 Twain *Tramp Abroad* 173 **MO**, The seven hundred inhabitants are all blood-kin to each other. **1897** *KS Univ. Qrly.* 6.85, *Blood kin:* kin.—New Eng. **1965–70** *DARE* (Qu. Z9, *General word for others related to you by blood*) 13 Infs, chiefly **Sth, S Midl**, Blood kin.

bloodleaf n [See quot 1969]

A plant of the genus *Iresine*.

1900 Lyons *Plant Names* 203, *Iresine,* . . Blood-leaf, . . *I. paniculata* . . Blood-leaf. **1937** Stemen *OK Flora* 123, *Iresine panicu-lata* . . . Blood-leaf. **1938** Madison *Wild Flowers OH* 54, *Bloodleaf. Iresine paniculata* . . . Calyx and bracts silvery and woolly. **1969** *Capital Times* (Madison WI) 31 May "Green" section 1/6 **WI**, Iresine berbstii, a showy plant with wine-red, rounded leaves and light red veins . . . is known as Chicken-gizzard or Bloodleaf. **1970** Correll *Plants TX* 563, *Iresine* . . . Bloodleaf.

blood medicine n *joc*

1897 *KS Univ. Qrly.* 6.86, *Blood medicine:* liquor.—Western.

bloodnoun See **bloodynoun**

blood on the moon n

A foreboding, menacing, or suspicious situation or set of events.

1933 *Sun* (Baltimore MD) 19 Apr 8/1 *(Hench Coll.)*, [Title:] *Blood on the Moon* [Text:] When we read charges that "public officials shake down" the bootleg gentry . . . the fair name of Cobb Island is badly smirched. **1950** Reeves *Man from SD* 207, As spring came again, and Hitler swept into Holland, it was perfectly apparent that there was blood on the moon.

blood pie n

1968 *DARE* FW Addit **New Orleans LA**, *Blood pie*—a pie made with hog's blood.

blood poison n

Blood poisoning, septicemia.

1920 *DN* 5.80 **NW**, *Blood poison.* Frequently found in rural papers and heard in conversation. **1921** *DN* 5.109 **CA**, *Blood-poison* . . . Blood-poisoning. 'He died of blood-poison.'

blood relative n Also *blood relation* esp **Nth, N Midl, West** Cf **blood kin**

A member of one's family by birth.

c1960 Wilson *Coll.* **csKY**, *Blood-relatives* (or *relations*) . . . Persons who are actually related rather than in-laws. "I've sure got a sight of blood relatives." **1965–70** *DARE* (Qu. Z9, *General word for others related to you by blood*) 18 Infs, scattered **Nth, N Midl, West**, Blood relatives; 15 Infs, **Nth, N Midl, West**, Blood relation(s).

bloodroot n

1 also *bloodwort:* A perennial white-flowered plant *(Sanguinaria canadensis)* native in much of the US east of the Mississippi River which produces thick roots containing red acrid juice. Also called **coon root, Indian paint, pauson, puccoon, red Indian paint, redroot, she-root, snakebite, sweet-slumber, tetterwort, tobaccoroot, turmeric**

1722 in 1724 Royal Soc. London *Philos. Trans.* 32.295 **NEng**, Remedies for the Sting of a Rattlesnake; among others, . . is a Root they call Blood-root. **1778** Carver *Travels N. Amer.* 515, *Blood Root.* A sort of plantain that springs out of the ground in six or seven long rough leaves, the veins of which are red. **1824** Doddridge *Notes Indian Wars* 148, Indian physick . . was frequently used for a vomit and sometimes the pocoon or blood root. **1828** Rafinesque *Med. Flora* 78, *Names.* Common Bloodroot . . . *Vulgar.* Red Puccoon, Bloodwort, Redroot. **1898** *Atlantic Mth.* 81.460/1 **VA**, Day by day the sun's heat did its work, melting the snow of the shadbushes and the bloodroot. **1941** Stuart *Men of Mts.* 164 **KY**, The wind is blowin among the green grass and the windflowers and the bloodroots. **1965–70** *DARE* (Qq. S26a–e) 46 Infs, **chiefly Nth**, Bloodroot; (Qu. S11) Inf **IL**29, Bloodroot; (Qu. S21) Infs **NY**94, **PA**163, Bloodroot.

2 =**redroot** *(Lachnanthes tinctoria).*

1951 Teale *North Spring* 41 **FL**, The Kissimmee cranes are specialists at finding the underground tubers of Gepotheca tinctoria, the pinkroot, bloodroot, Indian root, or painroot of the prairie.

blood rush, have a v phr

To get angry.

1945 Saxon *Gumbo Ya-Ya* 559 **LA**, He's havin' a blood rush (getting angry).

bloodshotten adj [*shotten* obs past pple of *shoot*] **chiefly S Midl, Sth**

Bloodshot.

1899 (1912) Green *VA Folk-Speech*, *Blood-shotten* . . . Red and inflamed, said of the eye, from a blow, or other cause. **1903** *DN* 2.307 **seMO**. **1906** *DN* 3.127 **nwAR**. **1927** *AmSp* 3.9 **Ozarks**, A final *n* sound is sometimes added to certain adjective forms—the mountaineer's eyes are always *blood-shotten* rather than *blood-shot.* **1954** Harder Coll. **cwTN**, *Bloodshotten.* **c1960** Wilson Coll. **csKY**, *Blood-shot* (or *-shotten*). **1966–69** *DARE* (Qu. X20) Inf **SC**7, Bloodshotten eye; (Qu. X39) Inf **VA**2, Bloodshotten; (Qu. AA29) Inf **GA**77, Bloodshotten veins.

blood soup See **duck's blood soup**

blood staunch n Also *blood stanch* [See quot 1911]

=**horseweed 1.**

1876 Hobbs *Bot. Hdbk.* 14, Blood staunch, Canada fleabane, Erigeron Canadense. **1911** *Century Dict.*, *Blood-stanch* . . . One of the various names given to the common fleabane, *Leptilon Canadense,* from its use in arresting hemorrhages. **1959** Carleton *Index Herb. Plants* 14, *Blood stanch:* Erigeron canadensis.

bloodstone n

In marble play: see quot.

1980 *NADS Letters* **Birmingham AL**, There probably were few marbles made of real agate. Some were beautiful ruby red with swirling interior coloring; these were called bloodstones.

bloodsucker n [*OED* 1387 →] **chiefly Nth** See Map

A leech.

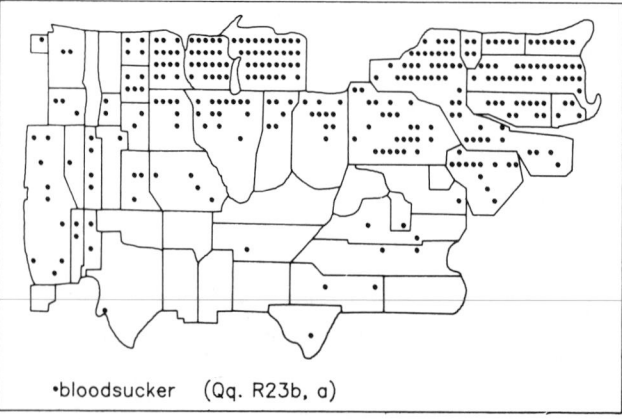

•bloodsucker (Qq. R23b, a)

1889 *Century Dict., Bloodsucker* . . . Any animal that sucks blood, as a leech, a mosquito, etc. **1935** Pratt *Manual Animals* 367, *Macrobdella . . . decora* . . . Very common in fresh water, a fierce blood sucker, attacking men, cattle, fish, frogs, etc., but also eating other animals. **1965–70** *DARE* (Qq. R23a, b) 311 Infs, **chiefly Nth**, Bloodsuckers.

blood turnip See **blood beet**

bloodweed n [See quot 1951] **chiefly Sth, esp TX**

The giant **ragweed** *(Ambrosia trifida).*

1898 *Jrl. Amer. Folkl.* 11.229, *Ambrosia trifida,* . . blood-weed, Tex. **1926** *Torreya* 26.6, *Ambrosia trifida* . . . Bloodweed, Natchez, Miss. **1933** Hanley *Disks* **seMA**, You go out to the vegetable garden and pick . . blood weed. **1946** Reeves–Bain *Flora TX* 246, Bloodweed . . . Coarse annual; usually 1–3 m. tall. **1951** *PADS* 15.41 **TX**, The giant ragweed or bloodweed reaches a height of fifteen or more feet on the Texas coast . . . The stems are easily snapped without breaking the strong outer skin, under which a fluid strikingly similar in coloring to blood gathers, to stain the skin, and exude in a "bloody" seepage when the skin is really broken. **1967–69** *DARE* (Qu. S21) Infs **TX**11, 51, **VA**69, Bloodweed(s); **LA**20, Bloodweed—tall weed with three-pronged leaves—has green stalks but when you squeeze a leaf or break the stalk you get like a bloodstain on your finger [FW—sounds like giant ragweed].

bloodworm n

1 A worm used for bait. **chiefly C and Mid Atl** See Map

1965–70 *DARE* (Qu. P6) 64 Infs, Bloodworm; (Qu. P5) 18 Infs, Bloodworm.

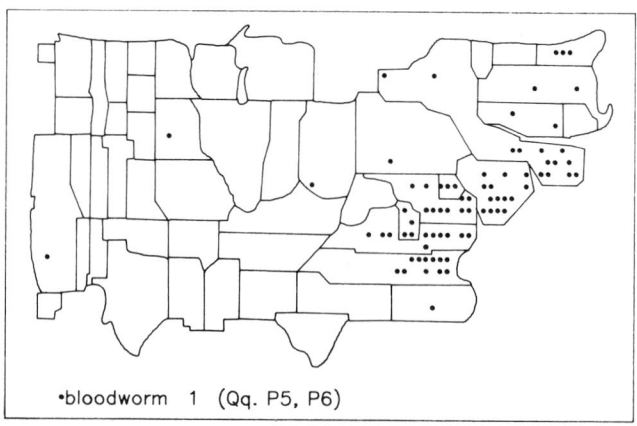

•bloodworm 1 (Qq. P5, P6)

2 The larva of a midge (family Chironomidae).

1905 Kellogg *Amer. Insects* 310, Looking not unlike mosquitoes are the larger species of the family Chironomidae . . . The name bloodworm . . [is] applied to the reddish aquatic larvae of certain species. **1949** Swain *Insect Guide* 191, Some are red from the hemoglobin they contain and are called "bloodworms." **1964** Borror–DeLong *Intro. Insects* 591, The larvae of some species are red in color, and are known as bloodworms.

bloodwort See **bloodroot 1**

bloody adj

Of a section of a city, spec a political district: disputatious, dissentient, embattled.

1920 Clark *Quarter Century* 1.164 **MO**, When I first reached Congress the district was popularly called "The Bloody Ninth." **1926** Odland *Knute Nelson* 111 **MN**, The most vivid and lurid story was that of the St. Paul Globe, written by H.P. Hall. The heading was "The Bloody Fifth," and from that time on the district bore that sensational name. **1967–70** *DARE* (Qu. C35, *Nicknames for different parts of your town or city*) Inf **IL**7, Bloody seventh ward; **PA**29, Bloody third ward; **TX**86, Bloody fifth ward; **WI**19, Bloody fourth ward.

bloody n See **bloodick**

bloodybones n **Sth**

=**rawhead and bloodybones.**

1970 Tarpley *Blinky* 278 **neTX**, Who is supposed to "get" little children who aren't good? . . . *Bloody bones.* **1971** Wood *Vocab. Change* 368 **Sth**, *Bloody bones.*

bloody bucket See **bucket of blood**

bloody butcher n, also attrib

1 also *blood and butcher*: An ear of corn having red kernels.
1937 *DN* 6.594 cwIL, "Bloody butcher" corn, for red corn. **1968** *DARE* Tape IN30, There was a type of red corn and they called it bloody butcher . . . They would hide a few ears of bloody butcher corn in these corn piles and whoever found the red ear would get to kiss the girl of his choice. **1983** Montell *Don't Go Up* 49 csKY, Some farmers grew . . blood and butcher corn, named for the red kernels ("blood") among the white ("butcher") on the ear.

2 See **bloody nose.**

Bloody Mary n

A menstruating woman.
1948 *Word* 4.183, Female anthropomorphisms . . are numerous: . . others make direct reference to blood, like *I'm Bloody Mary today.*

bloodymenoun See **bloodynoun**

bloody monthlies n *euphem*

A woman's menstrual period.
1948 *Word* 4.183, The use of red or blood in speaking of menstruation is more often found in male speech than in female: *the Red Sea's out, she's got the bloody monthlies,* and *blood and sand,* are or were common euphemisms in the speech of men.

bloody nose n Also *bloody butcher*

A purple **trillium.**
1931 Clute *Common Plants* 44, The red trillium *(T. erectum)* is bloody nose. **1940** Clute *Amer. Plant Names* 15, *T. reflexum* . . . Bloody noses, . . bloody butchers . . . *T. sessile* . . . Bloody butchers. **1951** Voss *IL Wild Flowers* 43, *Bloody Noses* . . . *Trillium recurvatum.* **1959** Carleton *Index Herb. Plants* 14, *Bloody nose:* Trillium erectum.

bloodynoun n |ˈblʌdɪnɑun| Also *blood-an'-ound, bloodenhound, bloodnoun, bloodymenoun* [Prob imit, perh of Afr orig] **chiefly SC, esp Charleston area** *prob orig Gullah* Cf **bloodick**

=**bullfrog 1.**
1872 *Harper's Mag.* 44.901/1 SC, Monstrous frogs, named 'blood-an'-'ounds', from the sounds they utter, called in loud, deep bass for 'blood and wounds.' **1911** *Century Dict. Suppl., Bloodnoun* . . . A local name of the bullfrog, *Rana catesbiana.* [Southern U.S.] **1949** Turner *Africanisms* 237, The following are a few of the many onomatopoetic expressions heard in Gullah: . . 'blʌdɪnɒŋ 'a large frog.' **1950** *PADS* 14.15 SC, *Blood and 'ounds, blooden hound* . . . A bullfrog. Onomatopeia. **1951** *AmSp* 26.15 [Black], *Bloody-noun,* 'large bullfrog' (cf. Gullah [ˈblʌdɪnɒŋ]) has been recorded in the Santee and Savannah valleys, and along the coast from Georgetown to the Florida line. **1954** *PADS* 21.20 SC, *Bloodymenoun* [ˈblʌdɪ mɪ ˈnɑun] . . . A bullfrog. **1966–67** *DARE* (Qu. P22, . . *A very large frog that makes a deep loud sound)* Infs SC4, [ˈbludɪnɑun]; SC43, [blʌdɪˈnɑun]—[Inf:] Negro word. **1967** *PADS* 47.15, *Bloody-noun* 'bullfrog,' and *cooter* 'turtle' are characteristic Charleston [SC] terms, unknown in the Midland.

bloom n¹

1 A blossom; collectively: blossoms, flowers. **chiefly Sth, S Midl**
1902 *DN* 2.229 sIL. **1903** *DN* 2.307 seMO. **1906** *DN* 3.127 nwAR, *Bloom* . . . Blossom, blossoms. "I never saw so many blooms on peach trees as this year." "With the farmers all busy with their spring crops, the fruit trees opening their bloom, . . prosperity had settled at War Eagle." "Blossom" is unusual. **1908** *DN* 3.292 eAL, wGA, *Bloom.* **1949** Hornsby *Lonesome Valley* 53 KY, Blooms covered the peach trees and leaves broke out all over the sassafras sprouts. **1959** *Hall Coll.* eTN, wNC, *Bloom* . . . A blossom . . chiefly used collectively. "And he had a lot of bees. They was plenty of bloom up there for 'em to make honey on." c**1960** *Wilson Coll.* csKY, *Bloom* . . . Blossom, flower. "There are lots of blooms on our peach tree." Blossom known, but literary.

2 A corn tassel.
1941 *LANE* Map 262 **scattered in NEng,** The map shows the terms . . *blossom, bloom, blow* . . denoting the blossoming top of a corn stalk.

bloom n², v

1981 *DARE* File cwTN, *Bloom* n. The turning outward of the anus of a mule or horse after it defecates, apparently for cleaning purposes. "That mule sure has a pretty bloom," usually jocularly said. *Bloom* v. To turn

the anus outward after defecating. "That mule's a-bloomin'." I never heard other forms, such as present tense, past tense, or past participle, only in name form and in present participle.

bloomer n [Orig Austr slang: abbr for *blooming error*]

A great mistake, blooper.
1935 *Scribner's Mag.* 98.378/2, I made a gorgeous bloomer in my list of one hundred Best Books. **1949** in 1960 Wentworth–Flexner *Slang* 44, A 'bloomer' by [President Harry S.] Truman and [General George C.] Marshall, about a grave that was not there. **1968–69** *DARE* (Qu. JJ41, *An embarrassing mistake: "Last night she made an awful _____."*) Infs CA74, 107, 110, IL53, Bloomer; (Qu. JJ42, *To make an error in judgment and get something quite wrong: ". . He certainly _____."*) Inf OH44, Made a bloomer.

blooming sally n [*blooming* + *sally* alter of *sallow* willow]

A **willow herb** (here: *Epilobium angustifolium*).
1889 *Century Dict., Blooming-sally* . . The willow-herb, *Epilobium angustifolium.* **1959** Carleton *Index Herb. Plants* 14. **1973** Hitchcock–Cronquist *Flora Pacific NW* 306, [*Epilobium angustifolium*] blooming Sally.

blooming willow n

A forsythia.
c**1960** *Wilson Coll.* csKY, Forsythia—a shrub that is very common in the area, called golden bell, blooming willow, etc.

bloom-sock n Also *blumpsack* [From Ger *Plumpsack* a twisted kerchief; a clumsy fellow] **PaGer area** *old-fash*

See quots.
1882 (1971) Gibbons *PA Dutch* 29, The bloom-sock (*oo* short) . . is a handkerchief twisted long, from the two opposite corners. When it is twisted, you double it, and tie the ends with a knot. One in front hunts the handkerchief, and those on the bench are passing it behind them. If they get a chance, they'll hit him with it, and if he sees it he tears it away. Then he goes into the row, and the other goes out to hunt it. **1924** Lambert *PA Ger. Dict., Blumpsack,* . . game played with a knotted handkerchief with which blows are dealt.

‡**bloom winter** n

=**blackberry winter.**
1941 *Sat. Eve. Post* 10 May 113/2 KY, Father would come home that day, bringing the [window] frames to set against robbers and bloom winters.

bloomy adj

Of hair: gray.
1940 *AmSp* 15.446 TN, *Bloomy.* Gray hair. 'Lillie's hair is bloomy.'

blossom n

1 A corn tassel or inflorescence. **chiefly Nth**
1941 *LANE* Map 262 RI, The map shows the terms *tassel (tossel), corn ~,* . . *blossom, bloom.* **1967–68** *DARE* (Qu. I31, *When a corn stalk is well grown, what comes out at the top?)* Infs CA167, NY43, Blossom. **1973** Allen *LAUM* 1.313, For the inflorescence at the top of a corn stalk . . two Minnesota instances of *blossom* [occur].

2 A pimple, acne spot or other localized, usu facial, blemish. [Perh infl by Ger *Bläschen* pustule, pimple] **chiefly Inland Nth, esp in Ger settlement areas**
1942 Berrey–Van den Bark *Amer. Slang* 107.4, "Grog blossom." (An eruption on the face or nose caused by drinking.) Blossom, . . rum blossom or bud, toddy blossom. **1968–70** *DARE* (Qu. X59, . . *The small infected pimples that form, usually on the face)* Infs MI108, 120, PA131, 165, WI13, 71, Blossoms; WI52, Acne blossoms; PA223, Rum blossoms; FL39, Whiskey blossoms.

3 See quot.
1950 *WELS (A black eye)* 1 Inf, cnWI, Blossom.

blossom bush n

1917 *DN* 4.408 NEng, Blossom bushes. Garden flowers.

blossom rock n **chiefly West, esp CO** Cf **gossan, iron hat**

In mining: see quot 1968.
1870 Pine *Beyond the West* 102 CO, Gold before breakfast, at breakfast and after breakfast, together with a good show of blossom rock all day and specimens in the evening. **1878** Beadle *Western Wilds* 479 CO, Men were let down from above to "prospect," a crevice was found with "blossom" rock. **1941** FWP *Guide CO* 74, An *arastra,* a primitive ore crusher of Spanish origin, was at work in Gregory Gulch early in the

summer of 1859, pulverizing "blossom rock" and other soft ores from decomposed surface veins. **1968** Adams *Western Words, Blossom Rock*—In mining, quartz stained with metallic oxides that indicate the proximity of mineral deposits, differing but little in gold and silver lodes.

blotch n [Prob alter of *botch* swelling] **chiefly Nth** See Map
Std sense: a skin blemish.

1965–70 *DARE* (Qu. X59, . . *The small infected pimples that form, usually on the face*) 11 Infs, Blotches; (Qu. BB24, . . *A rash that comes out suddenly*) 11 Infs, Blotch(es); **NY7**, Red blotches; (Qu. BB25, . . *Common skin diseases*) Inf **WA6**, Blotches.

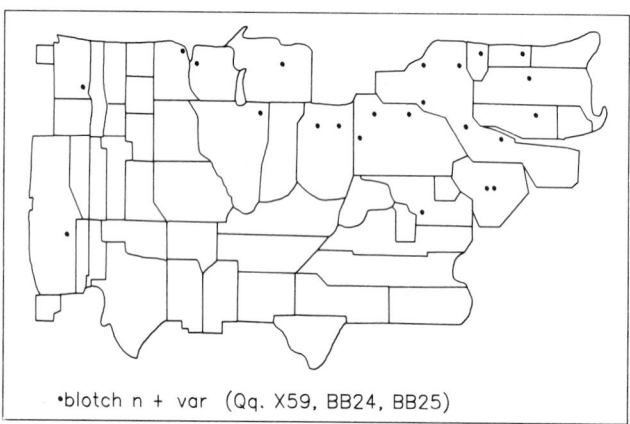

•blotch n + var (Qq. X59, BB24, BB25)

blotch v [Ext of *blotch* to mar with blotches, infl by *botch* to bungle]
To spoil or ruin because of ineptness or stupidity; to botch.

1965–69 *DARE* (Qu. KK63, *To do a clumsy or hurried job of repairing something: "It will never last—he just _____."*) Infs **CA101, MS56, SC2, WA11**, Blotched it (up); **KY16**, Blotched her up.

blotz v, n Also *blutz* [See quot 1968] **PaGer area**
See quots.

1937 *AmSp* 12.205 **PaGer**, 'Blutz' (verb or noun meaning *bounce* or *bump*) . . . 'Blutz' and 'outen the light' are confined to speech. **1967** *DARE* FW Addit **cePA**, We blutz along on a bumpy road. **1968** *Helen Adolph Festschrift* 35, *Blotz*—This verb, derived from Pennsylvania German *blotze*, is used, as in the dialect, in the sense of 'bounce' or 'bump'; for example, "Don't blotz me around so." **1978** *DARE* File **sePA**, Blutzes = bumpy places.

blouse n Usu |blaʊs|; also, esp in **Sth, S Midl** |blaʊz| Cf **greasy** adj
Std sense, var forms.

c1960 *Wilson Coll.* **csKY**, Blouse, always with the z-sound. **1967** *DARE* Tape **TX32**, Blouse [blaʊz]. **1969** *DARE* (Qu. W6) Inf **KY30**, [blaʊz].

‡blouse v
To strike or hit (someone).

1966 *DARE* (Qu. Y14a, *To hit somebody hard with the fist*) Inf **MI32**, Shut your mouth or I'll blouse you between the eyes.

blow v[1]
A Forms.

1 pres 3rd pers sg: usu *blows;* rarely *blow.*
1901 *DN* 2.136 **cnNY**, Blow . . . Pres[ent tense] for blows. "The wind blow don't it."

2 past: usu *blew;* often *blowed* (**chiefly Sth, S Midl, and scattered Nth,** *esp among less educ male speakers*); occas *blow* (for *blowed,* See Map and cf **-ed** pret suff **2**).
1775 in 1867 RI Hist. Soc. *Coll.* 6.3, The weather, accompanied by a fog and heavy rain, blowed very fresh. **1833** in 1934 Frear *Lowell & Abigail* 45 **MA**, This afternoon a large finbacked whale came right along side and blowed a number of times. **1860** (1936) Hawley *Diary* 332 **WI**, The wind blowed very hard. **1904** *DN* 2.417 **nwAR**, Blow . . (with weak preterit *blowed*). 'The wind blowed hard yesterday.' **1943** *LANE* Map 637 **scattered throughout NEng**, The map shows the preterite of the verb *blow* . . *Blowed* is described as older though still in use by . . [13 informants]. **1953** Atwood *Survey of Verb Forms* 6, Southward from c.Pa., *blowed* becomes more and more frequent until in N.C. it is used by

more than nine tenths of Type I and by about four fifths of Type II.
1965–70 *DARE* (Qu. OO14a, . . *"Last night the wind _____ [very hard]."*) 875 Infs, Blew; 108 Infs, Blowed; **KY5, 84**, Blowed a gale; **KY5**, Blowed awful hard; **OK6**, Blowed over; Infs **NC78, SC9, 19, 26, VA55**, Blow. [Of all Infs responding to the question, 30% grade school educ, 50% male; of those giving the resp *blowed,* 62% grade school educ, 65% male.] **1965–70** *DARE* Tapes **CA137, GA30, IL69, ME26, MI125, OK18, TX49, 104**, Blowed [past tense]. **1968** *DARE* FW Addit **IA31**, "The storm blowed over."

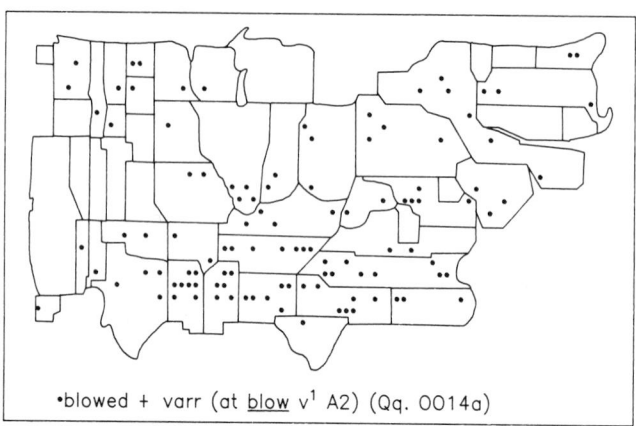

•blowed + varr (at <u>blow</u> v[1] A2) (Qq. OO14a)

3 past pple: usu *blown;* often *blowed* (same distrib as for past); occas *blow;* rarely *blew.*
1843 (1916) Hall *New Purchase* 150 **sIN**, Providence seemed to have blow'd it down jist for me! **1865** (1922) Jackson *Col.'s Diary* 215 **PA**, Sherman's first treaty with Johnson at Raleigh . . was blowed considerably by some home guard soldiers as a terrible bad affair. **1908** *DN* 3.292 **eAL, wGA**, *Blowed*, pret[erite] and p[ast] p[article] of *blow.* **c1960** *Wilson Coll.* **csKY**, Blowed . . . Past and past participle of *blow.* **1965–70** *DARE* (Qu. OO14b, . . *"One of my apple trees was _____ [down]."*) 802 Infs, Blown; **CA11, IL23, MO8, SC51**, Blow; 134 Infs, Blowed. [Of all Infs responding to the question, 30% grade school educ, 50% male; of those giving the resp *blowed,* 63% grade school educ, 68% male]. **1966** *DARE* Tape **MI34**, The wind had blew several big trees over; **NC1**, That was all blowed to pieces.

B Senses.

1 Usu of a horse, sometimes of a person: to (allow to) pause for breath. **esp West and Midl** Cf **blow** n[2] **1**
a Intr.
1774 (1900) Fithian *Jrl.* 1.211 **NJ**, In the mean Time tho', (as Workman [sic] say) I must blow a little, to be sure I am fatigued. **1843** (1916) Hall *New Purchase* 227 **sIN**, He stops for the furst [sic] time to blow and takes a look back. **1939** *AmSp* 14.267 **IN**, The average farmer is not averse to stopping work a while for a rest and to let his horses 'blow.' **1961** Adams *Old-Time Cowhand* 73, A cowhand was mighty careful of his feet, and never passed up a chance to soak 'em in some shaded water hole while he let his hoss blow. **1963** Edwards *Gravel* 171 **eTN**, "Light, boys; light and rest yer nags," said Doc . . . "Light and blow awhile."
b Tr.
1941 FWP *Guide WY* 460, Blow . . . To let a horse stop for breath in high altitudes. **1942** Faulkner *Go Down* 18 **MS**, Uncle Buck rode for Mr. Hubert's, stopping on the hills to blow the horses.

2 also *blow off:* To brag, boast. Cf **blow** n[2] **2**
1859 (1968) Bartlett *Americanisms*, To blow. To boast, brag; to "talk big." "You blow behind my back, but dare not say any thing to my face." **1905** *DN* 3.4 **cCT**. **1907** *DN* 3.209 **nwAR, cCT**. **1932** *AmSp* 7.329 **MD**, Blow—to brag. **1950** *WELS (Someone who talks too much or too loud . . "He _____.")* 1 Inf, **cwWI**, Blows. **c1960** *Wilson Coll.* **csKY**, Blow . . . To brag. "Don't go to blowing about your big-bug folks." **1963** in 1982 *Barrick Coll.* **sePA**, Blow—brag; boast. "She always blows about that property." [Also] blow off.

3 To treat, regale (someone).
1896 *DN* 1.412 **NY, nOH**, Blow . . : "To blow oneself," to spend money freely. **1903** Burnham *Jewel* 97 **NEng**, "Father took me to the horse show." "He did, eh?" "Yes, he told mother he was going to blow me to it." **1932** *AmSp* 7.329 **MD**, Blow . . to treat. **c1960** *Wilson Coll.* **csKY**, Blow . . . To treat. "He blowed us all to a bottle of pop."

4 To disclose (a secret), inform against (someone).

1942 Perry *Texas* 98, It's agin' my profession to blow on my pals. **1956** *AmSp* 31.146 **cnIN**, Blow . . to tell a secret. **c1960** *Wilson Coll.* **csKY**, Blow . . . To tell a secret. "I'd tell Jim, but he always blows everything he hears." **1968–69** *DARE* (Qu. JJ43, *To give away a secret . . "He wasn't supposed to know. Somebody must have _____."*) Inf **KY**53, Blowed it; **MD**26, Blowed on him; **NC**53, Blowed the works; **RI**1, Blown it.

5 See quot 1955.

1948 Feather *Inside Be-Bop* 72 *(OEDS)*, Nobody ever gave Diz or Bird a lesson in the art of blowing a jazz chorus. **1955** *Encycl. Jazz* 345, Blow . . . Play (used of all instruments, including those that are not actually blown, such as piano, bass, drums). **1958** *PADS* 30.44, *Blow* . . . Orig. to play a wind instrument. Generalized to performing upon any instrument (thus, one can "blow guitar"). Probably fr. fact that all solo instruments in traditional jazz are wind instr[uments]. **1965** Brown *Manchild* 220 **NYC** [Black], He asked me to come down . . and hear Sonny Rollins blow . . . This gave me a stronger urge to blow piano, or blow a box, as they used to say.

6 To smoke (tobacco, marijuana, etc). *chiefly among Black speakers* Cf **blow gage**

1946 (1972) Mezzrow *Really Blues* 330, Blow: *smoke marihuana.* **1947** *AmSp* 22.121 **OH** ["Language of Delinquent Boys"], *Blow.* To smoke. **1970** Major *Afro–Amer. Slang*, Blow . . . One "blows" grass [=marijuana]. **1970** *DARE* (Qu. DD9a, . . *Expressions . . about a person who smokes a great deal . . "He . . _____."*) Inf **NY**249, Blows two packs a day. [Inf Black]

7 See **blow one's stirrup.**

blow v² , hence ppl adj *blowed old-fash* Cf *DJE*

To blossom.

1884 Baldwin *Yankee School-Teacher* 190 **VA**, [Black] De peach trees hob blowed out mighty peart. **1899** (1912) Green *VA Folk-Speech*, Blow . . . To bloom; blossom; flower. **1902** *DN* 2.229 **sIL**, Blow . . . To blossom or flower, the latter not used. **1929** [See **blow** n¹]. **1941** *LANE* Map 249 **csCT**, The laurel blows in June. **1959** *VT Hist.* new ser 27.126, Blowed out . . . Said of potatoes in bloom. Rare.

blow n¹ *chiefly NEng old-fash*

A flower blossom; collectively, bloom.

1744 in 1940 *AmSp* 15.226 **MA**, The ap[p]le trees are full in the blow. **1832** Williamson *Hist. ME* 1.126, *May-weed*, a low plant with white blows. **1887** Cooke *Happy Dodd* 122 **CT**, Feelin's ain't worth a red cent without they come to facts, no more'n flowers that ain't fruit-blows. **1902** *DN* 2.229 **sIL**, Blow . . . Always used for a blossom or flower. **1929** *AmSp* 5.129 **ME**, The archaic "blow" as in the "lilacs are blowing" or in "apple-blow" was still in use, both as a verb or a noun. **1941** *LANE* Map 262, The map shows the terms . . *blossom, bloom, blow,* . . denoting the blossoming top of a corn stalk; 1 inf, **csCT**, The blows come at the same time as the silk.

blow n²

1 A pause to catch one's breath; a brief stop (of a horse) for rest; a breathing spell. [**blow** v¹ **B1**]

1855 *Knickerbocker* 46.146 **RI**, I seized her bridle, and brought the whole party to a stand. I determined that the horses should now have a good 'blow,' . . and resolutely held on. **1947** Ballowe *The Lawd* 99 **LA**, With everything finished and the shoat browning in the oven, Patsy stood up, taking a blow. **1948** *Sat. Eve. Post* 11 Sept 19/3 **OR**, He stopped to give the horses a blow.

2 freq attrib or in comb (see quot 1965–70): A braggart, loud-

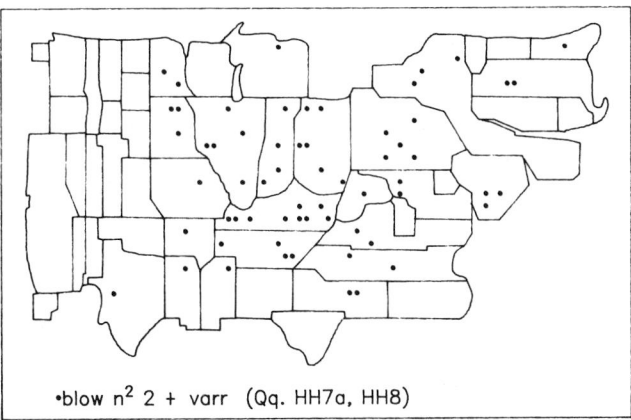

•blow n² 2 + varr (Qq. HH7a, HH8)

mouth. **scattered, but esp common in Midl** See Map (Note: *blowhard* in same sense is used throughout U.S.) Cf **blow** v¹ **B2**, **blowfly, blowgun, blow-off**

1915 *DN* 4.181 **swVA**, Blow . . . Boaster. "That feller is nothing but a big blow." **1950** *WELS* (*Someone who talks too much or too loud:* "He's a _____.") 5 Infs, **WI**, (Big) blow; 1 Inf, Blow bag; 1 Inf, Blow top; *(A person who likes to brag)* 3 Infs, A (big) blow; 1 Inf, Blow bag; 1 Inf, Blow belly. **1965–70** *DARE* (Qq. HH7a, HH8) 35 Infs, (A big) blow; 30 Infs, Blow gut *(or* bag, boy, George, hammer, heels, hole, horn, hot, house, pipe). **1968** Kellner *Aunt Serena* 105 **sIN** (as of c1910), Willadene, whose father was the biggest Blow in Henry County, and whose mother was the biggest Blab-Mouth.

3 in pl: A long period of time. **chiefly Sth, S Midl**

1940 *AmSp* 15.446 **TN**, 'I've knowed him fur blows.' **1965–70** *DARE* (Qu. A16, *A very long period of time:* "I haven't seen him _____.") Inf **MO**29, Scores and blows; (Qu. FF21b, . . *About old jokes people say*) Inf **MS**63, I [haven't] heard it in blows.

blow adder See **blowing adder**

blow around v phr

1921 *DN* 5.109 **CA**, *To blow around* . . . To come to see or visit, or to go to see or visit.

blowdown n

An uprooted tree, or an area where trees have been blown down; a windfall.

1895 *Outing* 26.448/2 **NH**, After that a line of blazes wanders erratically back and forth up the side of the mountain, dodging "blow-downs" and ledges. **1937** *FWP Guide ME* 415, There is a sudden crash as the startled animal attempts to flee, and the white flag of its tail shows over the 'blow-downs.' **1942** Faulkner *Go Down* 238 **MS**, The bear . . which he had seen . . crossing the blow-down. **1949** Peattie *Cascades* 154 **NW**, On down the rough, swamped road that twists among stumps, brush, and blowdowns. **1951** Giles *Harbin's Ridge* 74 **KY**, By the light we could tell we were in a blowdown, with tree laps all around us. **1970** *WI Conserv. Bulletin* Sept–Oct 18, The male grouse . . had chosen the upturned roots of a blowdown for his nightly roost. **1975** Newell *If Nothin' Don't Happen* 100 **nwFL**, Every tree is hung with bamboo briar and there are a lot of blow-downs so that it's near 'bout impossible to get through.

blowed v See **blow** v¹ **A2, 3**

blowed ppl adj

1 in phr *I('ll) be blowed:* Darned, damned. *euphem*

1865 (1868) Trowbridge *3 Scouts* 4, I be blowed if I'd throw it back again. **1905** *DN* 3.60 **NE**, *Blowed* . . . Confounded. "Well, I'll be blowed."

2 See quot.

1970 *DARE* (Qu. GG2, . . *"Confused, mixed up":* "So many things were going on at the same time that he got completely _____.") Inf **OH**103, Blowed.

blower n

1 See **blowfish 1.**

2 See **blow snake.**

3 =**blow** n² **2.**

1859 (1968) Bartlett *Americanisms*, Blower . . . A braggart; a teller of incredible anecdotes, feats, and hairbreadth escapes. **1899** (1912) Green *VA Folk-Speech*, Blower . . . Braggart. "Blow-hard." **1907** *DN* 3.209 **nwAR, cCT**, Blower . . . A braggart. **1950** *WELS* (*A person who likes to brag*) 1 Inf, **csWI**, A blower. **1968–70** *DARE* (Qu. HH7a, *Someone who talks too much, or too loud*) Inf **TN**53, Blower; (Qu. HH8, *A person who likes to brag*) Inf **WI**29, Blower.

4 See quot.

1970 *DARE* (Qu. P37b, . . *A shotgun*) Inf **TX**88, Blower.

blower fly See **blowing fly**

blow fire (out) v phr Also *blow out fire* **Sth, S Midl** *old-fash*

To heal a burn magically: see quot 1956.

c1937 in 1970 Yetman *Voices* 286 **MO** [Black], In "blowing fire," my grandfather simply blew on de burn and de fire and pain was gone. It was a secret charm, handed down from generation to generation. He said only one could be told. He told my Aunt Harriet and she could "blow fire" same as my grandfather. **1956** *Hall Coll.* **eTN, wNC**, *Blow fire out* . . . To cure a burn on the body by blowing on it, using a certain incantation. "Kitty Grooms used to blow fire out." "My uncle Wes can blow out fire and it won't blister." **1967** *DARE* FW Addit **SC**, Blow out fire — to heal people who have been burned by blowing "the fire" out of them, or out of the burned part. An art passed on to the opposite sex; the power was lost if imparted to one of the same sex.

blowfish n

1 also *blower:* A **puffer** (here: *Sphaeroides* spp) or similar fish.

1842 DeKay *Zool. NY* 4.327, *The Common Puffer. Tetraodon turgidus* . . . This curious fish receives its popular names of *Puffer* and *Blower,* from its being enabled to inflate itself when taken from the water. **1898** U.S. Natl. Museum *Bulletin* 47.1733, *Spheroides* [sic] *marmoratus . . . Spiny-back Blow-fish.* **1965–70** *DARE* (Qu. P2) Infs **CT**13, **NJ**21, 27, 30, 50, **NY**40, 54, **VA**47, Blowfish; (Qu. P4) 29 Infs, **chiefly Atlantic,** Blowfish.

2 =**walleye.**

1902 Jordan–Evermann *Amer. Fishes* 361, *Wall-eyed Pike* . . . In different parts of its range it is known by different names . . . Southward in the Mississippi Valley it is the jack. Elsewhere it is called okow, blowfish, or green pike. **1935** Caine *Game Fish* 31 **Sth,** *Wall-eyed Pike* . . . *Synonyms:* Blowfish, Blue Pike [etc].

blowfly n [*blow* n[2] **2** + *fly* (punningly with *blowfly* the insect)] Cf **blowgun**

A loudmouth, braggart.

1965–68 *DARE* (Qu. HH7a, *Someone who talks too much, or too loud: "He's an awful_____."*) Inf **WV**3, Blowfly; (Qu. HH8, *A person who likes to brag*) Infs **MS**30, **SC**32, Blowfly.

blow frog n

1950 *WELS* (*Names or nicknames for a very large frog that makes a deep, loud sound*) 1 Inf, **csWI,** Blow frog.

blow gage v phr Also *blow gauge* [**blow** v[1] **B6** + *gage* perh alter of *ganja* cannabis] *chiefly among Black speakers*

To smoke marijuana.

1965 Little *Autobiog. Malcolm X* 57, Shorty would take me to groovy, frantic scenes in different chicks' and cats' pads, where with the lights and the juke down mellow, everybody blew gage and juiced back and jumped. **1970** Major *Afro–Amer. Slang, Blow gage (gauge):* to smoke pot.

blow gum n

Bubble gum.

1959 Sanders *Echoes* 34 **swAR** (as of c1910), I had blow gum that all the kids at school wanted to chew until recess. **1967** *DARE* FW Addit **seGA,** Blow-gum = bubble gum. **1968** *DARE* (Qu. H82b) Inf **NC**52, Blow gum — gum used for blowing bubbles.

blowgun n [*blow* n[2] **2** + *gun*] Cf **blowfly**

A loudmouth, braggart.

1968 *DARE* (Qu. HH7a, *Someone who talks too much, or too loud: "He's an awful_____."*) Inf **PA**71, Blowgun; (Qu. II35, *A person who is disliked because he seems to think he knows everything*) Inf **PA**126, Blowgun.

blow horn n Also *blowin' horn* **chiefly S Midl** Cf **fox horn** n **2**

See quots.

1933 *AmSp* 8.1.47 **Ozarks,** *Blowin' horn* . . . A polished cow horn which the fox hunter blows to call his hounds. **1954** *Harder Coll.* **cwTN,** *Blow-horn* . . . A cow horn used by foxhunters.

blowie See **blow weed**

blow in v phr

To spend (money) recklessly.

1889 *Century Illustr. Mag.* 37.784/1, His story was that the brother sold out his share and 'blew it all in' in about a week. **1929** *AmSp* 5.75 **NE,** The custom was to "blow in" one's "stake," one's salary, "pay," or "winnings," at the end of the round-up. **1946** *AmSp* 21.56, Americans 'blow in' their cash, but if you are English you 'blue' it or 'blew' it.

blow-in n

A stranger, outsider.

1967 *DARE* (Qu. HH31, *Somebody who is not from your community, and doesn't belong*) Inf **MA**71, Blow-in.

blowing adder n Also *blow adder* [From its habit of puffing itself up when disturbed]

A **hognose snake** (here: *Heterodon platyrhinos*).

1882 *Amer. Naturalist* 16.566 **West,** Of all strange habits in snakes, none equals that observed in the blowing adder (*Heterodon simus*).

1901 *Everybody's Mag.* 4.384/1 **NY,** We may sometimes find a milk snake, garter snake, or blowing adder (hognosed snake) sunning himself upon a rock. **1928** Pope *Amphibians* 50, This snake *[Heterodon contortrix]* is also known under various names in different localities, such as, . . Blowing Adder. **1967–68** *DARE* (Qu. P25) Infs **MI**76, **NJ**1, 6, Blow adder; **NJ**8, **TN**14, Blowing adder.

blowing fly n Also *blower fly* [From its blowing or depositing its eggs under animals' skins] **esp NC, VA**

Any of var flies of the family Calliphoridae.

1805 (1904) Lewis *Orig. Jrls. Lewis & Clark Exped.* 2.51 **VA,** This stream we named *Blowing Fly Creek,* from the immence quantities of these insects found in this neighbourhood. **1823** James *Acct. of an Expedition* 1.116, The blowing flies swarmed in inconceivable numbers, attacking . . the provision of the party. **1946** *PADS* 6.6 **eNC,** *Blowing fly* . . . A large green fly that lights on freshly killed meat. *(Calliphora erythrocephala.)* . . . Common. **1954** *Harder Coll.* **cwTN,** *Blowing fly* . . . A large fly, a horse fly. **1966–70** *DARE* (Qu. R12, *What other kinds of flies are common around here — for example, those that fly around animals*) Inf **FL**20, Blowing fly; **CA**119, Blower fly; (Qu. R13, *Flies that come to meat or fruit*) Infs **DC**8, **NC**8, 10, 13, 27, 80, 85, **VA**38, Blowing fly.

blowing snake See **blow snake**

blowing viper n Also *blow viper* [See **blowing adder**] **chiefly Appalachians** See Map

A **hognose snake** (here: *Heterodon platyrhinos*).

1869 *Amer. Naturalist* 3.555 **sePA,** A female snake, *Heterodon platyrhinus,* commonly known in this locality as the "Blower," or "Blowing Viper," was killed in Martic Township. **1941** Stuart *Men of Mts.* 164 **KY,** Never saw nothin but a blowin viper snake and a couple of crows. **1958** Conant *Reptiles & Amphibians* 138, As a result of their behavior these harmless snakes [=hognose snakes] have earned such dangerous-sounding names as "hissing adder," "blow viper." **1965–70** *DARE* (Qu. P25) 15 Infs, **chiefly Appalachians,** Blowing viper.

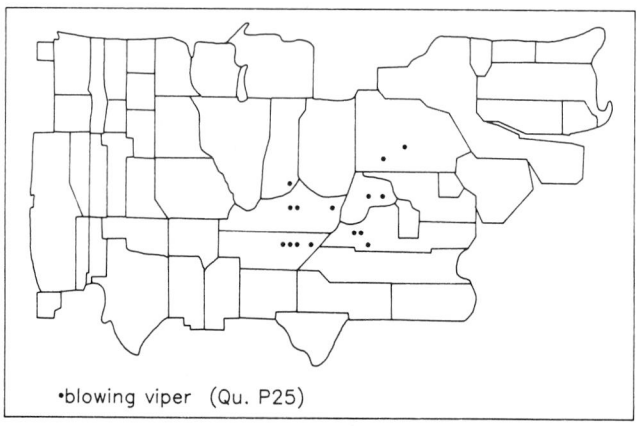

•blowing viper (Qu. P25)

blow-leaf n [See quot 1899] **NEng**

An **orpine** (here: *Sedum telephium*).

1891 *Jrl. Amer. Folkl.* 4.148, Sedum telephium we knew correctly as *Houseleek;* but in other places in New Hampshire I have found it called *Blow-leaf.* **1899** (1909) Earle *Child Life* 389, From the live-for-ever, or orpine . . we made frogs, or purses, by gently pinching the fleshy leaves between thumb and forefinger, thus loosening the epidermis on the lower side of the leaf and making a bladder which, when blown up, would burst with a delightful pop. The New England folk-names by which this plant is called, such as frog-plant, blow-leaf, pudding-bag-plant, show the wide-spread prevalence of this custom.

blown ppl adj Also *blown up* [**blow** v[1] **B1**] Cf **blow** n[2] **1**

Of a horse: out of breath, winded.

1967–69 *DARE* (Qu. K48, *When a horse is short of breath, you say it's_____*) Infs **IL**31, **RI**12, **WA**23, Blown; **MO**26, Blown up.

blown up ppl adj

Drunk.

1940 *AmSp* 15.446 **TN,** *Blown up.* Intoxicated. 'Lee's blown up tonight.' **c1970** *Halpert Coll.* **wKY, TN,** To be blown up = to be intoxicated.

blow off v phr See **blow** v[1] **B2**

blow-off n
=**blow** n² **2.**

1950 *WELS (Someone who talks too much or too loud: "He's a
_____.")* 2 Infs, **WI**, Blow-off.   **1954** *Harder Coll.* **cwTN**, *Blow-
off*. . . One who jokes, or talks loudly and angrily.   **c1960** *Wilson Coll.*
csKY, *Blow-off*. . . A boaster, braggart.   **1965–70** *DARE* (Qq. HH7a,
HH8) 15 Infs, **chiefly Sth, Midl**, Blow-off.

blow one's bone v phr *Gullah*

1954 *PADS* 21.21 **SC**, *Blow one's bone*. . . To drool as an infant
beginning to teethe. "Dat chile blowin' 'e bone."

blow one's head and horns off v phr

1906 *DN* 3.127 **nwAR**, *Blow one's head and horns off* . . . To talk too
much. "He blowed his head and horns off."

blow one's shoes v phr Cf **cool** n

To lose one's composure, to become over-excited.

1969 *DARE* (Qu. GG15, *Talking about a person who became over-excited and lost control, "At that point he really _____.")* Inf **KY**65, Blew
his shoes.

blow one's stirrup v phr Also *blow* **chiefly West**

Among cowboys: see quot 1968.

1937 *DN* 6.619 **swTX**, If the bronco-buster retains his seat but loses his
foothold on the stirrup, he simply *blows his stirrup*.   **1941** *FWP Guide
WY* 460, *Blow* . . . To lose a stirrup while riding.   **1968** Adams *Western
Words, Blow a stirrup*—To lose a stirrup, which in a rodeo contest,
disqualifies the rider.

blowout n **orig NE, now more widespread**

A hollowed out area of bare ground caused by wind erosion.

1892 Smith–Pound *Bot. Survey Neb.* 2.8 *(DAE)*, If a spot on a dry hill
becomes bare, the loose sand is blown away, a small hollow is made, the
surrounding grass dies from drought . . . Such blow outs were seen 100
meters in diameter and 15 . . meters deep.   **1928** *AmSp* 4.125 **cnNE**,
The wind . . scoops "blow-outs," great yellow hollows that splotch the
landscape.   **1937** Sandoz *Slogum* 374 **NE** (as of 1900–20), The boundary between grassland and shifting desert, [was] pockmarked into deep
blowouts and moving dunes by the wind.   **1944** Quaife *Lake Michigan*
304 **nIN**, On occasion the air currents are reversed, and instead of
building up hills, conical amphitheaters are hollowed out . . known by
the expressive name of 'blowouts'.   **1967** *DARE* Tape **NE**10, We still
have huge blowouts, but the soil conservation office is working to heal
those old fields over.   **1969** *DARE* FW Addit **sTX**, Blowout—an area
where sand (in sandhills) has blown away exposing the layer of clay
underneath.

blowout grass n

1 A **muhly grass** (here: *Muhlenbergia pungens*).

1906 Rydberg *Flora CO* 27, *Muhlenbergia pungens* . . . *Blow-out
Grass*. On sand-hills and "bad-lands" from Neb. to Utah.   **1936** Winter
Plants NE 32, Purple Hair-grass. Blow-out-grass . . . Frequent in blow-
outs.

2 A sand-binding grass (*Redfieldia flexuosa*). Also called **sand
grass**

1932 Rydberg *Flora Prairies* 108, *Blow-out Grass* . . . *R[edfieldia] flexuosa* . . . Sand hills.   **1940** Gates *Flora KS* 136, Blowout Grass . . . Hemicryptophyte.   **1950** Stevens *ND Plants* 61, *Blowout Grass* . . . is the
first grass to invade bare sand and is useful to check blowing, though too
tough and wiry to be of much value as forage.   **1960** Correll *Plants TX*
213, *Blowout grass* . . . is of great economic importance as a soil-binder
in the states north and west of Texas.   **1970** in 1983 *Carleton Coll.*,
Blowout grass = Redfieldia flexuosa. Great Plains.

blow out one's lamp v phr Also *blow out one's light*

To kill someone.

1916 *DN* 4.320 **KS, PA, LA**, *Blow out one's light* . . . To kill (a
person).   **1944** Adams *Western Words, Blow out his lamp*—A slang
expression for *kill*.

blowpipe n **West**

A rifle.

1921 *DN* 5.111 **CA**, *Blow-pipe* . . . A rifle.   **1944** Adams *Western
Words, Blow-pipe*—A slang name for a rifle.

‡blow sand n

Wind-driven or drifted sand.

1967 *TX Observer* (Austin) 7 July 3/3, Most of the drive-in movies are
piled high with tumble-weeds and blow sand.

‡blow smoke up one's leg v phr

To tease (someone) good-naturedly.

1967 *DARE* FW Addit **TX**, Blowing smoke up his leg—joshing him.

blow snake n Also *blower, blowing snake* [See **blowing adder**]
chiefly Inland Nth, West
=**hognose snake.**

1688 in 1695 Royal Soc. London *Philos. Trans.* 18.134 **VA**, The
Blowing-Snake [is] an absolute Species of a Viper, but larger than any I
have seen in *Europe*.   **1806** (1905) Clark *Orig. Jrls. Lewis & Clark
Exped.* 6.224 **MT**, [We] saw a blowing snake.   **1857** (1923) Beadle *To
Nebraska* 115, We found a snake called here a blower. this one was as
much as five feet long. they are spotted like a milk snake and perfectly
harmless.   **1928** Pope *Amphibians* 50, This snake *[Heterodon contortrix]*
is also known under various names in different localities, such
as . . Blow Snake.   **1953** Schmidt *N. Amer. Amphibians* 179, *Heterodon
platyrhinos* . . *Common name* . . . blow snake.   **1965–70** *DARE* (Qu.
P25) 21 Infs, **Inland Nth, West**, Blow snake.

blow-snow n

1944 *PADS* 2.32 **wNC**, *Blow-snow* . . . A combination of wind and
snow.

blow-toad n [*blow* to puff up + *toad* (from the resemblance of
the fish to a toad)] **eVA**

A **puffer** (here: *Sphaeroides* spp).   Also called **blowfish 1**

1946 *Times Dispatch* (Richmond VA) 4 Aug sec IV 4–D/2 *(Hench
Coll.),* Among the general nuisances [caught in bottom fishing] are the
oyster toad and the blow toad, the latter, however, having a little chunk
of meat in his body which is about as good to eat as anything that comes
out of the water.   **1970** *DARE* (Qu. P2, *What kinds of saltwater fish
caught around here are good to eat?*) Infs **VA**41, 79, Blow-toads.   **1970**
DARE Tape **VA**112, [FW:] What kind of a fish is a sugar toad? [Inf.] It's
that one with all them little bristles on 'im, real white an' sort of yellowish
on top an' he's got teeth almost, well, like a turtle an' he's got a little teeny
mouth an' he swells up, he keeps puffin' until it blows up. In other words,
you call 'em blow-toads, the old people did. But now they call 'em
chicken of the sea, an' sell 'em in the market, forty cents a pound.

blow up v phr, hence ppl adj *blowed up* (cf **blow** v¹ A2)

1 To make pregnant.   *obs*

1803 in 1956 Eliason *Tarheel Talk* 260 **NC**, There has Been A talk that
Betsey . . . was Blowed up.

2 To be out of order; to fail, collapse.

1923 *DN* 5.245 **KS**, *Blow up* . . . To end in failure; play out. "He was
going with Alta for awhile, but that blew up."   **1950** Reeves *Man from
SD* 123, The herder complained about the grass on the south section.
"It's blowing up," he said. "The sheep won't do nothing but run, and
they ain't doing any good on it." . . "The water holes are blowing up," he
said to me next. "The first sheep there muddies the water and the rest
won't drink."   **c1960** *Wilson Coll.* **csKY**, *All blowed up* . . . Out of kilter
or order or humor.   **1967** *DARE* Tape **CA**137, After I left, they [=a gold
mining operation] just all blowed up.

3 To overpraise.

1916 *DN* 4.343 **KS, MD**, *Blow up* . . . To praise unduly. "That man has
been blowed up a great deal, but I can't see anything in him."   **1939** *Hall
Coll.* **eTN, wNC**, *Blow someone up* . . . To flatter (a person).

4 See quot.

1966 *Wilson Coll.* **csKY**, *Blow up* . . . To be disgusted. "He's blowed up
at the world"—He's mad at everybody.

blow-up n

1 A massive deposit of mineral (as distinct from a lode).

1870 Pine *Beyond the West* 369 **NV**, One very unusual deposit of ore,
the celebrated Comstock Ledge, . . more a wonderful blow-up or deposit, than a lead.

2 See quot.

1940 *FWP Guide GA* 367, The houses [or clumps of bushes and trees]
are formed and bogs extended by a phenomenon known locally as a
"blow-up." This occurs when gases, formed beneath the water by decaying vegetable matter, force masses of vegetation, some a hundred feet
square, from the bottom of the water.

3 In logging: see quot.

1958 McCulloch *Woods Words* **Pacific NW**, *Blow up*—A fire which
suddenly blazes up, jumps control lines, takes off across country.

4 A billowy cloud.

1967 *DARE* (Qu. B11, . . *Kinds of clouds*) Inf **CO**7, Blow-ups—white ones piled high.

5 See quot.

1973 Allen *LAUM* 1.400, For a hole or depression in a street or road . . . Infrequent are *blowout, blowup*, . . and *washout*.

blow viper See **blowing viper**

blow-way n Cf **breezeway**

An open porch.

1933 Rawlings *South Moon* 15 **FL,** " 'Hain't nothin' like a kivered blow-way for comfort." . . "Yes, . . but the men-folks keeps 'em so littered with their contraptions, . . they ain't no room hardly to set and shell peas."

blow weed n Also *blowie*

=**dandelion.**

1968 *DARE* (Qu. S11b) Inf **IL**27, Blow weed; **DE**4, Blowies.

blow-wives n [blow v²]

A low-growing composite plant (*Achyrachaena mollis*) with narrow leaves and yellow to reddish-brown ray-flowers which is native to California and Oregon.

1911 Jepson *Flora CA* 450, Blow-wives . . . Abundant in adobe soil of the plains and valleys . . . Readily recognized in fruit by its expanded heads of black achenes with their silvery pappus. **1961** Peck *Manual OR* 808, Blow-wives. Plant very villous throughout.

blowy adj

Windy.

1871 (1882) Stowe *Fireside Stories* 14 **NEng,** It was such an awful blowy night. **1899** (1912) Green *VA Folk-Speech,* Blowy . . . Windy; blustering. "It's a blowy day." **1967** *DARE* (Qu. B12, *When the wind begins to increase, you say it's* _____) Inf **NC**38, Blowy. **1970** *DARE* Tape **VA**52, There come up a blowy day.

blow your horn if you don't sell a fish phr Cf **fish horn 1**

1904 *DN* 2.424 **Cape Cod MA,** Blow your horn if you don't sell a fish. Said to anyone who blows his nose vigorously.

blow Z's v phr joc Cf **Z's**

To sleep or snore.

1968 *DARE* (Qu. X45, . . *Joking expressions . . about snoring*) Inf **PA**126, Blowing Z's. **1972** Claerbaut *Black Jargon,* Blowing Z's . . to sleep; nap: *He's been blowing Z's all day.*

blub n [Prob alter of *blob*]

A small amount, blob.

1953 Johnson *Sullivan* 53 **csME,** A little blub of foam showed against the silver. **1970** *DARE* File **KY,** Blub . . . In a recipe: 10 blubs of molasses.

blubber v Also *blubber up* [ME *blubren, blobren; OED* "Obs."] chiefly Sth, S Midl

To bubble.

1806 (1905) Clark *Orig. Jrls. Lewis & Clark Exped.* 5.252, This Spring . . contains a very considerable quantity of water, and actually blubbers with heat for 20 paces below where it rises. **1887** (1967) Harris *Free Joe* 217 **GA** [Black], I sot up dar en b'iled de 'lasses [=molasses]. De 'lasses 'u'd blubber en I'd nod, en I'd nod en de 'lasses 'u'd blubber, en fus news I know de 'lasses 'u'd done be scorched. **1906** *DN* 3.127 **nwAR,** Blubber . . . To bubble. "There must be natural gas there because you can see where it blubbers up through the water." **1971** *Foxfire* Spring–Summer 95 **nGA,** It will "blubber up"—or bubble, and then the bubbles will settle.

blubber n [ME *bluber, blober* bubble, foam; *OED* "Obs. exc dial."] chiefly Sth, S Midl

A bubble; collectively, foam.

1899 (1912) Green *VA Folk-Speech,* Blubber . . . For bubble. **1906** *DN* 3.127 **nwAR,** Blubber . . . Bubble, soap bubble. "Let's blow blubbers." **1943** Chase *Jack Tales* 24 **wNC** (as of 1880s), One day the bull put his head down to drink out of a spring and a lot of blue blubbers came up in the water. **1956** *AmSp* 31.146 **cnIN,** Blubber (bubble). **1968** *Foxfire* Fall–Winter 100 **nGA,** Blubber—the bubbles which result when moonshine in the proof vial is shaken violently.

blue adj

1 Drunk. Cf *DS* DD14, 15

1818 Weems *Drunkard's Looking Glass* 4, At this stage of the disease,

the patient goes by a variety of nicknames . . such as *boozy—groggy—blue.* **1851** (1969) Burke *Polly Peablossom* 105 **LA,** The blue tickets he sold out to some upper-country flatboatmen who were pretty *blue.* **1930** Parker *Laments for Living* 181, When you were blue you got the howling horrors. **1942** Berrey–Van den Bark *Amer. Slang* 106.7, *Drunk . . .* Blowzy, blue.

2 Of an animal: drab, mouse-colored. *old-fash*

1895 *DN* 1.384, *Blue pony:* mouse-colored pony. West. **1905** *DN* 3.70 **nwAR,** *Blue chicken, blue hen, blue horse, blue mule* . . . In each of these cases 'blue' means 'drab,' 'mouse-colored.' 'Blue horse' is rare, the other expressions being common.

3 Extreme—freq used as an intensifier.

1958 McCulloch *Woods Words* **Pacific NW,** Blue one—A big anything. **1967–68** *DARE* (Qu. B3, *If a day is very hot, you say it's [a]* _____ *day*) Inf **NV**1, Hotter than blue hell; (Qu. B30, *A frost that kills plants is a* _____) Inf **TN**11, Blue frost—very heavy; (Qu. X56b) Inf **VA**24, Sweat like blue heaven; (Qu. BB12, . . *"He has a* _____ *cough."*) Infs **MS**60, **PA**147, **TN**43, **WV**14, Blue.

4 Of milk: =**blinky.** chiefly Sth, S Midl Cf **blue john**

1966–67 *DARE* (Qu. H58, *Milk that's just beginning to become sour is* _____) Infs **AL**21, **SC**9, **TX**11, Blue; **KY**41, Blue milk.

blue n

1 An esp dark-skinned Black person. *chiefly among Black speakers*

1926 Van Vechten *Nigger Heaven* 285, Blue: a very black Negro. **1964** *PADS* 42.29 **Chicago IL,** Most of the terms collected exclusively from Negro informants are rare within the Caucasian social dialects of Chicago, e.g., *Cuff, Ned,* blue. **1970** *DARE* (Qu. HH29b, *Names for people of mixed blood—part Negro*) Inf **FL**48, Blue—if he's super black; **FL**52, Dark-skinned are called "blue." [Both Infs Black]

2 See quot.

1967 LeCompte *Word Atlas* 254 **LA,** A mixture of Indian, Negro, and white . . . "Blue" translated from *les blues* [sic] is a dialectal term found only in Lockport.

3 See **blue butt.**

4 also *snapper blue:* =**bluefish 1.**

1942 Kennedy *Palmetto Country* 255 **sFL,** The Conchs is God-fearin honest people . . . When the blues [bluefish] is runnin they give handsome contributions to the church. **1968–70** *DARE* (Qu. P14, . . *Commercial fishing . . What do the fishermen go out after?*) Inf **NY**235, Blue; **NY**80, Cod, tuna, blue; **CT**39, **NY**89, **VA**79, Blues; **NY**40, **RI**4, Snapper Blues; (Qu. P2) 8 Infs, **Atlantic,** Blues. **1975** Evanoff *Catch More Fish* 180, Both the jumbo blues and the smaller "snapper" blues can be caught on many of the same flies used for stripers.

5 A bachelor's button.

1967 *DARE* (Qu. S11, . . *Other names . . for . . bachelor's button*) Inf **NC**41, Blue.

6 See **blue goose 1.**

blue v

1 To turn blue when bruised.

1967 *DARE* FW Addit **wNC,** Blue—to bruise. "My skin blues easily."

‡**2** In logging: see quot. [Cf *blow* to misplay, blunder]

1958 McCulloch *Woods Words* **Pacific NW,** Blue it—To spoil anything.

‡blue adv Cf **blue adj 3**

Extremely, damned.

1968 *DARE* (Qu. LL37, *To make a statement as strong as you can: "I could have wrung her neck, I was so* _____ *mad."*) Inf **VA**29, Blue.

blue-and-white pied creeper n Also *blue-and-white striped creeper*

=**black-and-white warbler.**

1917 (1923) *Birds Amer.* 3.112, *Mniotilta varia . . . Other Names . .* Blue and White Striped Creeper; Blue and White . . Pied Creeper.

blue angel n

=**pasqueflower.**

1969 *DARE* (Qu. S23, *Pale blue flowers with downy leaves and cups that come up on open, stony hillsides in March or early April*) Inf **NY**183, Blue angels.

blue as a whetstone adj phr Also *bluer than a whetstone* [With pun on *blue* melancholy] chiefly NEast *old-fash*

Depressed, melancholy, dejected.

[**1812** Henry *Campaign Against Quebec* 36 **ME,** Johnny, you look like a blue leather whet stone.] **1857** (1930) DeLong *Jrls.* 156 **NY,** At home during the day feeling blue as a whetstone owing to a crisis in financial affairs. **1914** *DN* 4.69 **ME, nNH,** *Bluer'n a whetstone* . . . Extremely dejected. **1922** *DN* 5.157 **ME, NH, NE. 1950** Moore *Candlemas Bay* 149 **ME,** By God, Jen, you better fix that up with him. Fast. He's as blue as a whetstone over it.

blue ash n

1 An American tree *(Fraxinus quadrangulata),* the bark of which was formerly used in the production of a blue dye.

1783 (1916) Fleming *Travels KY* 667, Blue Ash a spieces [sic] of the White Ash and called so from the bark tinging water of that colour, grows to be a large tree. **1804** (1904) Lewis *Orig. Jrls. Lewis & Clark Exped.* 1.54, Such as Oake of different kinds Blue ash. **1968** *DARE* (Qu. T16) Inf **LA15,** Blue ash. Hard to split — grayish wood, finegrained. **1973** Stephens *Woody Plants* 448, Blue ash . . . New York, west to Ontario and Michigan, southwest to Kansas, south to Oklahoma, east to Alabama, and north to Ohio . . . [A] dye was formerly made [by soaking the inner bark] and used a great deal, but this is no longer a common practice.

2 =**green ash.**

1897 Sudworth *Arborescent Flora* 329, Green Ash . . . Syn. — Blue Ash (Ark., Iowa). **1900** Lyons *Plant Names* 164, *F[raxinus] lanceolata* . . . Green Ash, Blue or Swamp Ash. **1911** *Century Dict.*

blue-assed hornet See blue hornet

blue-backed swallow See blue swallow 1

blueback herring n Also *blueback, blue herring*

Any of several herrings, here esp **alewife, glut herring, skipjack herring.**

1814 in 1825 *Lit. & Philos. Soc. NY Trans.* 457, *Blue Herring. (Clupea cœrulea).* **1873** in 1878 Smithsonian Inst. *Misc. Coll.* 14.2.33, *Pomolobus pseudoharengus* . . blueback . . (Portland, Me.). **1882** U.S. Natl. Museum *Proc.* 5.247, *Clupea chrysochloris . . . Blue herring.* **1896** U.S. Natl. Museum *Bulletin* 47.426, *Pomolobus oestivalis* . . . Blue-back. **1960** Amer. Fisheries Soc. *List Fishes* 10, Blueback herring . . . *Alosa æstivalis.* **1969** *DARE* (Qu. P14) Inf **MI101,** Blue herring.

blueback salmon n Also *blueback*

=**sockeye salmon.**

1882 U.S. Natl. Museum *Bulletin* 16.308, *O[ncorhynchus] nerka . . . Blue-back Salmon.* **1887** Goode *Amer. Fishes* 481, The Nerka or Blue-back Salmon, *Oncorhynchus nerka* . . . In the Lower Columbia it is known by the appropriate name of "Blue-back." **1960** Amer. Fisheries Soc. *List Fishes* 66, Blueback — see salmon, sockeye. **1966** *DARE* (Qu. P1) Infs **ID4, WA3,** Blueback; (Qu. P14) Inf **ID4,** Blueback. **1968** *Caribou Co. Sun* (Soda Springs ID) 25 Jan 12/6, Thus there is much angling now for steelhead, whitefish, kokanee or blueback salmon, perch, trout — and soon for Bear Lake cisco with dipnets.

blueback trout n

Any of var trout, here esp **oquassa** and **rainbow trout.**

1882 U.S. Natl. Museum *Bulletin* 16.318, *S. oquassa . . . Blueback Trout.* **1904** *Salmon & Trout* 211, The Blue-back trout of Lake Crescent, Wash., — *Salmo gairdneri. Ibid* 286, The Oquassa trout or blueback, — *Salvelinus oquassa.* **1950** Everhart *Fishes ME* 27, Blueback Trout — *Salvelinus oquassa.*

bluebait n Also *blueworm* [*blue* + **bait** n 3] **SC**

An earthworm used for bait.

1949 *AmSp* 24.106 **SC,** *Blue-bait* . . . Earthworm. **1966–70** *DARE* (Qu. P5, . . *The common worm used as bait*) Inf **SC19,** Earthworm — also blueworm or bluebait; **SC26,** Bluebait [FW: among bait sellers]; **SC43,** Blueworm = earthworm; **SC66,** Bluebait — a bluish-brown earthworm; (Qu. P6) Inf **SC19,** Bluebait; **SC40,** Bluebait — short, stumpy, found in swamp; **SC53,** Bluebait — not so common; **SC21, 63,** Blueworm.

blue-ball n [Folk-etym from *bubo*]

A bubo.

1935 Hurston *Mules & Men* 341 **LA,** When there are blue-balls (buboes), smear the swellings with mashed up granddaddies (daddy-long-legs) and it will bring them to a head.

‡blue bar, bet one's v phr

To be certain (of something).

1970 *DARE* (Qu. JJ20, . . "*I'm so sure, I'd* _____ *it.*") Inf **TX90,** Bet my blue bar on.

blue bass n

=**green sunfish.**

1820 Rafinesque *Ohio R. Fishes* 29, Blackeye Sunfish . . . Vulgar names, Blue-fish, . . Blue-bass &c. **1946** LaMonte *N. Amer. Game Fishes* 138, *Green Sunfish — Lepomis cyanellus . . . Names:* . . Blue Bass. **1968–70** *DARE* (Qu. P1) Infs **IA46, KY82,** Blue bass.

bluebead n Also *bluebead lily* [From the blue beadlike fruit]

=**bead lily.**

1933 Small *Manual SE Flora* 296, C*[lintonia] borealis . . . Balsambell. Blue-bead lily. Yellow wood-lily.* **1943** Peattie *Great Smokies* 265, Clintonia . . the "bluebead lily" of the north woods; the "amber bell" of the southern highlands. **1967** *DARE* Wildfl QR Pl.17 Inf **MI57,** Clintonia — people call it blue-beads. **1973** Hitchcock–Cronquist *Flora Pacific NW* 689, *C. uniflora . . .* Queen's cup, bride's bonnet, blue-bead.

blue bean n Also *blue hull bean, blue pole bean* **Sth**

A garden bean.

1956 Rayford *Whistlin' Woman* 33 **csAL,** And in the gardens, they raised calico beans and blue pole beans. People would not eat white beans, they boiled even the colored beans in iron pots to make them a deeper blue. **1965–69** *DARE* (Qu. I20, *Other kinds of beans*) Inf **MS63,** Blue beans; **TX62,** Blue hull.

blue beech n [From the resemblance, esp of the leaves, to the beech] chiefly Midl

=**hornbeam** (here: *Carpinus caroliniana*).

1882 U.S. Natl. Museum *Proc.* 5.85 **IL, IN,** "Blue Beech" . . . Very common in rich bottom lands. **1916** Seton *Woodcraft Manual Girls* 280, Blue Beech, Water Beech, or American Hornbeam (*Carpinus caroliniana*) A small tree, 10 to 25, rarely 40, feet high; bark smooth. Wood hard, close-grained, very strong; much like Ironwood . . . United States east of Missouri River. **1926** West Virginia Legislative Hand Book 452 *(Hench Coll.),* It is pleasant to see the untouched forest . . . They are all there from the Blue Beech to the Hemlock. **1950** Moore *Trees AR* 37, American Hornbeam . . . Local Names: . . Blue and Water Beech. **1973** Wharton–Barbour *Trees KY* 436, *Blue Beech* . . . Bark gray, smooth, and fluted.

bluebell n

1 Any of var plants with blue, bell-shaped flowers as:

a =**bellflower.**

1900 Lyons *Plant Names* 77, C*[ampanula] rotundifolia . . .* Bluebell. **1967** *DARE* Wildfl QR (Craighead) Pl 19.7 Inf **CO29,** Bluebell.

b also *bluebell valerian:* =**Jacob's ladder.**

1873 in 1976 Miller *Shaker Herbs* 125, *Polemonium reptans . . .* Blue Bells. **1892** *Jrl. Amer. Folkl.* 5.101 **OH,** *Polemonium reptans,* bluebell. **1898** *Ibid* 11.275 **WI. 1900** Lyons *Plant Names* 298. **1933** Small *Manual SE Flora* 1100, *P[olemonium] reptans . . .* Blue-bell Valerian. **1951** Voss–Eifert *IL Wild Flowers* 58, Bluebells.

c =**grape hyacinth.**

1892 *Jrl. Amer. Folkl.* 5.104, *Muscari botryoides* . . bluebell. Chestertown, Md. **1900** Lyons *Plant Names* 254, *M[uscari] botryoides . . .* Blue-bell.

d =**baby blue-eyes.**

1894 *Jrl. Amer. Folkl.* 7.94, *Nemophila insignis,* . . blue-bells.

e A speedwell (here: *Veronica americana*).

1894 *Jrl. Amer. Folkl.* 7.96 **ME,** *Veronica Americana* . . bluebells. **1900** Lyons *Plant Names* 391, *V[eronica] Americana . . .* Bluebell.

f also *bluebell vine:* A plant of the genus *Clematis.*

1900 Lyons *Plant Names* 106, *C[lematis] crispa . . .* Bluebell vine. **1951** *PADS* 15.31 **TX,** *Clematis pitcheri . . .* Bluebell; bell flower; wild blue or purple clematis.

g A plant of the genus *Mertensia.* Also called **chiming bells, languid ladies, lungwort.** For other names of var spp see **cowslip, Virginia bluebells, wild forget-me-not**

1936 McDougall *Plants of Yellowstone* 106, Bluebells (*Mertensia*). **1937** U.S. Forest Serv. *Range Plant Hdbk.* W126, Bluebells — *Mertensia.* **1966** *DARE* Wildfl QR Pl.181 Infs **CO29, NC28, WA10,** Bluebells. **1976** Bruce *How to Grow Wildflowers* xiv, "Bluebell" can be a squill, a bellflower, or a borage (*Mertensia*).

h =**catchfly gentian. TX**

1951 *PADS* 15.37 **TX,** *Eustoma russellianum . . .* Texas bluebell; big

bluebell. **1961** Wills–Irwin *Flowers TX* 171, Blue-bell—*Eustoma grandiflorum.* **c1979** TX Dept. Highways *Flowers #46*, Bluebells . . . *Eustoma grandiflorum.*

i See quot.

1969 *DARE* FW Addit **KY**40, Bluebells, also called four-o-clocks. A yard flower. Common.

2 See quot.

1942 *Sun* (Baltimore MD) 18 Jul 12/1 *(Hench Coll.)*, Lower Delaware farmers and their families . . will realize hundreds of dollars from a crop which they have not cultivated. The huckleberry crop especially "bluebells," are maturing.

3 See quot.

1967 *DARE* (Qu. T16, *What kind of trees are "special" around here*) Inf **TN**14, Bluebell—same as peablossom. Blue, looks like a peablossom, gets plumb full of little bells, real purty.

blue-bellied adj Freq in phr *blue-bellied Yankee* [**blue-belly** n] *often derog* Addit exx in *DA*
From the northern states, esp New England.

1852 *S. Lit. Messenger* 18.681/1 **GA** (as of 1836), I'd disgrace the party—and am no better than a dratted, blue-bellied, federal whig! **1914** *DN* 4.103 **KS**, Blue-bellied Yankee . . . An out and out New Englander. "My mother was a German from North Carolina, but my father was a blue-bellied Yankee." **1968** *DARE* (QR p114) Inf **WI**38, Blue-bellied Yankees—people from the East, Maine, etc.

bluebells-of-Scotland n

1 =**bellflower.**

1949 Moldenke *Amer. Wild Flowers* 238, Famous in song and story are the *bluebells of Scotland, Campanula rotundifolia.* **1973** Hitchcock–Cronquist *Flora Pacific NW* 458, *Campanula* . . . Bluebells-of-Scotland.

2 The rose-of-Sharon *(Hibiscus syriacus).*

1970 *DARE* (Qu. T16, *What kinds of trees are "special" around here*) Inf **NC**87, Bluebells-of-Scotland, Rose of Sharon, cotton blossom—names for one bush, has lavender flowers.

bluebelly n, also attrib

1 A Northerner, particularly a New Englander; a Yankee. [From the color of the U.S. Army uniform] *often derog*

1827 (1832) Pickering *Inquiries* 138, The inhabitants are chiefly Americans . . . In short "blue bellies" of all sorts and conditions, equal to any of the frontier towns on both sides of the "lines." **1857** Gladstone *Englishman* 43 **KS**, No highfalutin' airs here, you know. Keep that for them Yankee Blue-bellies down East. **1944** Adams *Western Words*, Blue-belly—The southern cowman's name for any Yankee. **1967** Cerello *Dakota Co. MN* 7, My family was purebred, blue-belly Yankee. **1968** *DARE* (Qu. HH28, *. . People of foreign background*) Inf **LA**28, Northerners—Yankees, bluebellies.

2 By ext: see quot.

1950 *PADS* 14.15 **SC**, Bluebelly . . . A proud, pretentious person. Term of reproach.

3 A wild rabbit. Cf **blue dick**

1967–68 *DARE* (Qu. P30, *. . Wild rabbits around here*) Inf **CA**31, Bluebellies; **PA**73, 147, Bluebelly.

blueberry n

1 Std: a plant of the genus *Vaccinium;* also the fruit of such a plant. Cf **huckleberry**

2 =**blue cohosh 1.** [See quot 1951]

1873 in 1976 Miller *Shaker Herbs* 157, Blue Berry . . . The seeds, which ripen in August, make a decoction which closely resembles coffee. **1876** Hobbs *Bot. Hdbk.* 14, Blue berry, Blue cohosh, Caulophyllum thalictroides. **1910** Graves *Flowering Plants* 195 **CT**, Blueberry Root. Blueberry. Rich rocky woods, especially in moist situations. **1951** Voss *IL Wild Flowers* 67, Blue cohosh . . . The bright blue fruits easily gave it the name of blueberry.

3 =**black snakeroot 1.**

1971 Krochmal *Appalachia Med. Plants* 96, *Cimicifuga racemosa* . . . Common Names: . . black cohosh, black snakeroot, blueberry.

blueberry plain n Also *blueberry barren, ~ burn*
An area of land burned or cleared of vegetation and used for blueberry cultivation.

1937 FWP *Guide ME* 232, The blueberry industry has grown up in the

wake of lumbering . . . The land is burned over every third year to stimulate new growth . . . 'Blueberry plains' or 'barrens' as they are locally called, are privately owned and protected by the state. **1953** Johnson *Sullivan* 97 **csME**, As these large tracts of land were cleared of wood, both pulp and lumber, they became plains, which have been cleared of stumps and underbrush and cultivated into blueberry plains. **1969** *DARE* FW Addit **Upper Peninsula MI**, *Blueberry burn*—A place where blueberries grow in the wake of a fire. (Indians burned parts of the forest to produce these areas.)

blueberry root n, also attrib [From the blue, berrylike seeds and the medicinal use of the root]

=**blue cohosh 1.**

1830 in 1976 Miller *Shaker Herbs* 212 **ceNY**, Blueberry Root . . . A favorite remedy in chronic uterine diseases, and as a parturient it has proved invaluable. **1910** Graves *Flowering Plants* 195 **CT**, Blueberry Root . . . The rhizome and roots are of some value medicinally and were formerly officinal. **1930** Sievers *Amer. Med. Plants* 14. **1960** Williams *Walk Egypt* 77, Old Man Willing wavered around on his blueberry-root cane. **1968** *Foxfire* Summer 48, Blue cohosh . . . is sometimes collected as "blue-berry root."

blueberry special n Cf *DS* N37

1950 *WELS* (A branch railroad that is not very important or does not give the best of service) 2 Infs, **cwWI**, Blueberry special.

bluebill n

1 A scaup, esp *Aythya affinis* or *Aythya marila.*

1813 Wilson *Amer. Ornith.* 8.84, Scaup Duck . . . This Duck is better known among us by the name of the Blue Bill. **1858** Baird *Birds* 791, *Fulix marila* . . . Bluebill. *Ibid, Fulix affinis* . . . Bluebill. **1911** Howell *Birds AR* 21, The scaup, or "blue-bill," as it is frequently called, occurs regularly in moderate numbers as a winter resident. **1961** Ligon *NM Birds* 53, The Lesser Scaup [*Aythya affinis*] . . is also known to hunters as the Bluebill. **1966–68** *DARE* (Qu. Q5) Infs **NY**10, Bluebill—lesser broad bill, greater broad bill; **PA**155, Bluebill—lesser scaup, greater scaup; **MN**29, Bluebill—a medium-sized duck; most numerous—bill has bluish tint; **MI**14, Bluebill—scaup I think is the technical name; **MI**53, Bluebill—same as greater scaup or lesser scaup. **1975** Newell *If Nothin' Don't Happen* 32 **nwFL**, "And what in the horrible hell is a scaup?" Uncle Winton asked her. "It's a broadbill," she told him. "You got plenty of 'em down at the mouth of the river." "She means bluebills, Uncle Wint," Tarley said.

2 =**ruddy duck.**

1888 Trumbull *Names of Birds* 110, Ruddy duck . . . At Machiasport, Me., *Blue-bill.* **1917** (1923) *Birds Amer.* 1.152, *Ruddy Duck . . . Other Names* . . . Blue-bill. **1943** Musgrove *Waterfowl IA* 71, *Ruddy Duck* . . . Other names: . . bluebill. **1951** Pough *Audubon Water Bird* 506, Bluebill . . . Ruddy duck.

3 also *bluebilled widgeon:* =**baldpate 1.**

1955 *MA Audubon* 39.314, *Baldpate* . . . Bluebill (Mass. The bill is grayish blue); Blue-billed Widgeon (Maine, Mass. . .).

4 =**ring-necked duck.**

1923 U.S. Dept. Ag. *Misc. Circular* 13.21, Ring-necked Duck . . . *Vernacular Names . . . In local use* . . . Bluebill (Va., Wash.). **1940** Gabrielson *Birds OR* 154, Some gunners group all three [=greater scaup, lesser scaup, ring-necked duck] under the name "Bluebill." **1968** *DARE* (Qu. Q5) Inf **MD**15, Bluebill—another name for blackhead.

5 =**goldeneye.**

1968 *DARE* (Qu. Q5) Inf **IA**22, Bluebill—has a golden eye.

bluebird weather n chiefly **MD, eVA** Cf **Indian summer**
A brief period of warm weather in autumn.

1943 *Sun* (Baltimore MD) 22 Nov 5/2 *(Hench Coll.)*, "Bluebird" weather prevailed Saturday. **1949** *Sun* (Baltimore MD) 16 Nov 21/2 *(Hench Coll.)*, "Just now we're having what we call 'blue bird' weather," said Malcolm E. King, of the Game and Inland Fish Department. "It's so warm, the birds are not very active." **1976** Warner *Beautiful Swimmers* 34 **MD, eVA**, To be sure, sparkling days may yet come. But there will be no more "bluebird weather" during which the yachtsman sails in his shirtsleeves or the hunter sweats uncomfortably in his blind. Autumn, a charmingly indecisive time on the Chesapeake, has given way to winter.

blue blazes n [**blue** adj **3** + **blazes**]

=**blazes.**

a in phrr *hot as* or *hotter than blue blazes:* Used as an intensive with ref to the weather. **chiefly Sth, esp SC** Cf **blixen**

1908 *DN* 3.292 **eAL, wGA,** *Blue-blazes* . . . Used in the expression, "As hot as blue blazes," i.e., extremely hot. **1937** *Hench Coll.* **VA,** "Blue blazes" is an expression that I hear often, as in "It's been as hot as blue blazes today, hasn't it?" or "Go to blue blazes!" **1965–70** *DARE* (Qu. B3, *If a day is very hot, you say it's (a)* _____) Infs **GA**84, 89, **LA**14, **MO**21, **SC**22, 29, 38, 43, 46, 56, 62, Hot as (*or* hotter than) blue blazes.
b in var other phrr: Hell, hellfire — often used in imprecations or interjections; also used adverbially.
   1818 Weems *Drunkard's Looking Glass* 49, Ye steep down gulphs of liquid fire! Ye blue blazes of damnation! **1840** (1847) Longstreet *GA Scenes* 57, Dod etarnally darn my soul . . if I wouldn't drive blue blazes through him in less than no time. **1885** *Harper's Mag.* 71.397/2 **GA,** Hannah–Maria–Jemimy! goldarn an' blue blazes! **1911** Saunders *Col. Todhunter* 123 **MO,** What in blue blazes and Sam Hill is that man a-doin' there? **1939** FWP *ID Lore* 243, *Some Mild Profanity* . . . *Jumpun blue blazes!* — a meaningless expletive. **1941** *LANE* Map 473 **cCT, swVT,** When a person is very angry he is said to be *as mad as* . . . [Blue blazes]. **1965–70** *DARE* (Qu. NN26c, . . "*What the* _____!") 18 Infs, **scattered,** Blue blazes; (Qu. HH22b, . . "*He's meaner than* _____.") Inf **IN**76, Blue blazes; (Qu. KK29, . . "*He was slow at first but now he's really* _____.") Inf **MI**18, Going blue blazes; (Qu. NN26b, *Weakened substitutes for "hell"*: "*Go to* _____!") Inf **LA**14, Blue blazes.

blue blizzard n [**blue** adj **3** + *blizzard,* perh infl by **blue norther**]
   =**blue norther.**
   1909 in 1914 Stewart *Letters* 47 **WY,** It was in November, and one night when they had reached the plains a real blue blizzard struck them. **1956** Ker *Vocab. W. TX* 66, Strong wind from north . . . The response *blue blizzard,* [was] offered by three informants.

blueblossom n Pacific, esp CA
   Usu **California lilac** (here: *Ceanothus thyrsiflorus*) but also **deer brush** (here: *C. integerrimus*).
   1897 Parsons *Wild Flowers CA* 274, *Ceanothus thyrsiflorus* . . . is known in some localities as "blue myrtle," and in others as "blue-blossom." **1911** Jepson *Flora CA* 253, *Blue Blossom.* Shrub 5 to 8 ft. high or becoming a small ungainly . . tree up to 15 or 25 ft. high. **1931** U.S. Dept. Ag. *Misc. Pub.* 101.105, Bluebrush . . . Other local names include blue blossom, blue bush, and deer brush. **1961** Peck *Manual OR* 513, *Blue Blossom* . . . Flowers blue, in large panicles up to 15 cm. long. **1968** *DARE* (Qu. T16) Inf **CA**105, Tick brush or blueblossom — full of wood ticks in spring; **CA**36, White blossom in [the] Sierras, like blueblossom of coast.

blue boneset n
   A **boneset 1** (here: *Eupatorium coelestinum*).
   1894 *Jrl. Amer. Folkl.* 7.92, *Eupatorium cælestinum* . . mist-flower, blue boneset, West Va. **1939** *Natl. Geog. Mag.* 76.258/2 **Upper MW,** *Mistflower* . . . the misty blue which gives rise to the name for this species, also called "blue boneset." **1976** Bailey–Bailey *Hortus Third* 460, *Blue B[oneset]* . . . Flowers bright blue to violet.

bluebonnet n
1 also *Texas bluebonnet*: =**lupine.** chiefly TX
   1928 *Natl. Geog. Mag.* June 681, Chosen by the [Texas] Legislature as the State flower, the bluebonnet rules a region more limited than do most State flowers. **1951** *PADS* 15.34 **TX,** *Lupinus texensis* . . . Bluebonnet (state flower of Texas). **1965–70** *DARE* (Qu. S26a, . . *Roadside flowers*) 24 Infs, **TX,** Bluebonnet(s); **CA**31, Lupine — the bluebonnet; **NJ**58, Texas bluebonnets; **NY**205, Maid's bonnets (bluebonnets); (Qq. S26c, d, e) Infs **KY**28, **SC**24, **TX**17, 66, 87, **VA**7, Bluebonnets; (Qu. S11) Inf **SC**36, Texas bluebonnet — came in horse's hay brought from Texas by soldiers during the Confederate War; (Qu. S21) Inf **NC**49, Bluebonnet; (Qu. S23) Infs **AR**42, **KS**5, 6, **OK**9, **TX**54, Bluebonnet(s); **MO**9, Texas bluebonnet; (Qu. S25) Inf **NC**49, Bluebonnet. **1967** *DARE* Wildfl QR Pl.106 Infs **CO**7, **TX**44, Bluebonnet; **TX**34, If that's bluebonnet, it'll need some doctoring.
2 =**cornflower 1.**
   1900 Lyons *Plant Names* 89, *C[entaurea] Cyanus* . . . Blue-bonnets, Blue-caps. **1952** Taylor *Plants Colonial Days* 29, Cornflower — *Centaurea cyanus* . . . It is also known as . . bluebonnet. **1970** *DARE* (Qu. S11, . . *Other names . . for . . bachelor's button*) Inf **MA**78, Bluebonnet.

bluebonnet bird n
   =**blue jay 1.**

1955 *AmSp* 30.184 **TX,** *Bluebonnet bird* . . blue jay, . . from a legend connecting this species with the state flower of Texas, a lupine.

blue bottle n
   A children's game similar to blindman's buff.
   1966 *DARE* Tape **AL**4, Blue bottle . . put people in a ring an' one of 'em puts on a blindfold, y' see, . . an' if he's goin' the wrong way they'd holler "blue bottle" . . an' as long as he's about to catch a person then he's all right.

bluebottle n
1 =**cornflower 1.**
   1822 Eaton *Botany* 230, *Centaurea cyanus* . . blue-bottle. **1925** Jepson *Manual Plants CA* 1169, *C[entaurea] cyanus* . . . Bluebottle. **1936** Winter *Plants NE* 164, *C[entaurea] cyanus* . . . Blue-bottle. **1966** *DARE* Wildfl QR Inf **WA**10, Centaurea cyanus — bachelor's button, bluebottle. **1970** *DARE* (Qu. S26a) Infs **IL**143, **VA**89, Bluebottle.
2 =**grape hyacinth.** esp PA
   1892 *Jrl. Amer. Folkl.* 5.104, *Muscari botryoides* . . bluebottle. Mansfield, O[hio]. **1946** Tatnall *Flora DE* 48, *M[uscari] botryoides* . . . Blue Bottle . . . *M. racemosum* . . . Blue Bottle. **1950** Klees *PA Dutch* 398, Oddly enough, the Pennsylvania Dutch have a wild flower of their own unrecognized as wild by the rest of the country. This is the grape hyacinth, known locally as bluebottle, or to give it its Dutch name, *wei glessli* (little wine glass) . . . A little boy or girl with a tight bunch of bluebottles in his or her hand is a common springtime sight in the Dutch country. **1967–70** *DARE* (Qq. S26a, b, c, d, e) Infs **PA**1, 40, 169, 176, 242, **SC**31, Bluebottle(s).
3 =**bluebell.**
   1970 *DARE* (Qu. S26a) Inf **VA**34, Bluebottle [=bluebell].
4 =**bluet 2.**
   1945 Saxon *Gumbo Ya-Ya* 564 **sLA,** Bluets, *Houstonia* (springers, bluebottles).
5 A Portuguese man-of-war.
   1971 Gantz *Naturalist in S. FL* 21, Entangled in it [=seaweed] are hundreds of physalia, the Portuguese man-of-war (called locally "blue bottles.").

bluebottle fly n Also *bluebottle*
   A large blowfly, usu brilliant blue in color.
   1822 Irving *Bracebridge* 2.229 **NY,** The buzzing of a stout blue-bottle fly. **1885** Murfree *Prophet of Smoky Mts.* 179 **eTN,** The drone of a blue-bottle, fluttering in and out of the window. **1901** Howard *Insect Book* 164, The large blue-bottle fly of rather dull color with black spines on the thorax is known as *Calliphora erythrocephala.* **1949** Swain *Insect Guide* 211, *Blow Flies — Family Calliphoridæ* . . . The brilliant species are called bluebottle . . flies. **c1960** *Wilson Coll.* **csKY,** *Bluebottle flies* . . . A large blow-fly. **1965–70** *DARE* (Qu. R13) 56 Infs, **scattered,** Bluebottle fly; (Qu. R12) 19 Infs, **chiefly Nth,** Bluebottle (fly).

blue brant See **blue goose 1**

blue bream n Cf **bream** n B3
   =**bluegill 1.**
   1887 Goode *Amer. Fishes* 67, The Blue Sun-fish, *Lepomis pallidus,* is also known as the "Blue Bream." **1902** Jordan–Evermann *Amer. Fishes* 349, *Bluegill — Lepomis pallidus* . . . It is known also as blue bream, . . and doubtless by many other vernacular names. **1946** LaMonte *N. Amer. Game Fishes* 138, *Bluegill Sunfish — Lepomis macrochirus* . . . Names: . . Blue Bream. **1966–68** *DARE* (Qu. P1, . . *Freshwater fish . . that are good to eat*) Infs **GA**25, **NC**24, **SC**40, Blue bream. **1975** Evanoff *Catch More Fish* 88, The bluegill (*Lepomis macrochirus*) is . . also called the bream, blue bream, etc.

bluebrush n Also *bluebush*
   Any of var chiefly Pacific, usu blue-flowered woody plants of the genus *Ceanothus,* such as **deer brush** or **California lilac** (here: *C. thyrsiflorus*). For other names of var bluebrushes see **pine mat, plumas brush, squaw carpet**
   1931 U.S. Dept. Ag. *Misc. Pub.* 101.105, Bluebrush (*Ceanothus integerrimus . .*) . . . Other local names include . . blue bush, and deer brush. *Ibid* 107, *Trailing bluebrush (C. diversifolius)* . . . Lemmon bluebrush (C. lemmoni). **1935** Davis *Honey* 61 **OR,** The road ahead of them pitched down through scrub-oak and blue-brush into a flat valley. **1937** U.S. Forest Serv. *Range Plant Hdbk.* B39, Many species of *Ceanothus* have individual names as . . . bluebush (or bluebrush), buckbrush, lilac, and myrtle. **1961** Thomas *Flora Santa Cruz* 235 **CA,** *C. thyrsi-*

florus . . . Blue Brush, Blue Blossom. **1979** Little *Checklist U.S. Trees* 80, *Other common names* . . blue-brush, California-lilac.

blue buffalo n

=**bigmouth buffalo.**

1956 Harlan *IA Fish* 72, *Ictiobus cyprinellus* . . . Other Names . . blue buffalo.

blue bug n

1968 *DARE* (Qu. K78, *What diseases do chickens commonly get around here?*) Inf **CA**90, Blue bugs—a tick.

blue bullet n [From the color and speed]

1 =**pigeon hawk 1.** Cf **bullet hawk**

1946 Hausman *Eastern Birds* 204, *Eastern Pigeon Hawk* . . . *Other Names*—Pigeon Falcon, . . Blue Bullet . . . Upper parts bluish-slate . . . The bird is very adroit, pursuing and capturing dragonflies on the wing! **1955** Forbush–May *Birds* 129.

2 =**ring-necked duck.**

1955 *Oriole* 20.4 **GA,** Ring-necked Duck . . . Blue Bullet (in allusion to its speed in flight).

blue bullsnake n [From its color and its resemblance to the **bull snake**]

=**indigo snake.**

1952 Ditmars *N. Amer. Snakes* 151, *Blue Bull Snake* . . . *Drymarchon corais couperi* . . . *Blue Bull Snake* . . . *Drymarchon corais melanurus.* **1958** Conant *Reptiles & Amphibians* 153, *Eastern Indigo Snake* . . . This is the "blue bullsnake" . . of the snake charmer and carnival "pit" show.

bluebush See **bluebrush**

blue butt n Also *blue* [**blue** adj 3]

In logging: see quots.

1958 McCulloch *Woods Words* **Pacific NW,** *Blue butt*—A large pine butt, usually a sinker. Sometimes also applied to other trees, fir or redwood particularly. **1969** Sorden *Lumberjack Lingo* **NEng, Gt Lakes,** *Blue butt*—A log larger at one end than at the other; prone to roll faster on the large end. Same as big blue, blue.

blue buttercup n

A blue-flowered **flax.**

1951 *PADS* 15.35 **TX,** *Linus* [sic, for *Linum*] *lewisii* . . . Blue buttercup.

blue button n

A bachelor's button.

1950 *WELS (Other names for . . bachelor's button)* 1 Inf, **cWI,** Blue button. **1967–69** *DARE* (Qu. S11, . . *Other names . . for . . bachelor's button*) Inf **MI**69, Blue button; (Qu. S23) Inf **IN**62, Blue buttons.

blue cane n

A type of sugarcane (*Saccharum officinarum*).

1949 *AmSp* 24.106 **GA,** *Blue cane* . . . Ribbon cane: the large but easily infected sugar cane. **1973** *News & Courier* (Charleston SC) 25 Nov E1, "Years ago all we had was blue cane," says the elder Reeves. "This white cane makes a better tasting, lighter colored syrup."

blue catfish n

1 also *blue cat,* ~ *channel cat(fish):* A large freshwater catfish (*Ictalurus furcatus*). **chiefly Sth, S Midl, esp lower Missip Valley** See Map Also called **chuckleheaded catfish, flannelmouth cat, forktail cat 1, fulton cat 1, humpback cat, Mississippi cat 1, poisson bleu, silver catfish, white cat, white fulton, willow cat 2**

1882 U.S. Natl. Museum *Proc.* 5.245, *Arius felis* . . . Blue cat. **1906** *DN* 3.127 **nwAR,** *Blue cat* . . . A kind of cat-fish of a bluish hue. **1908** *DN* 3.292 **eAL, wGA,** *Blue-cat.* **1920** Forbes–Richardson *Fishes of IL* 178, *Ictalurus furcatus*—Blue cat. **1963** *Progress* (Charlottesville VA) 6 Jul 13/3 *(Hench Coll.),* Everyone knows the channel cat fish when he looks like himself, slate gray back lighter and spotted below . . but sometimes when very old and big he loses his spots and is sometimes called a blue cat or a flat head. **1965–70** *DARE* (Qu. P1) 54 Infs, **chiefly Sth, S Midl, esp lower Missip Valley,** Blue cat; **AR**28, **IN**13, **NC**44, **SC**43, **TX**52, 88, Blue catfish; **KY**86, **LA**15, Blue channel cat; **MI**101, **TX**37, Blue channel catfish; (Qu. P3) Infs **KS**10, **LA**34, **NC**53, Blue cat; (Qu. P14) Inf **KY**11, Blue cats; **KY**86, Blue channel cat. **1967** Cross *Hdbk. Fishes KS* 211, This fish . . was a blue channel cat and weighed

315 pounds. *Ibid* 212, A blue cat weighing 79 pounds was taken near Malta Bend [Missouri].

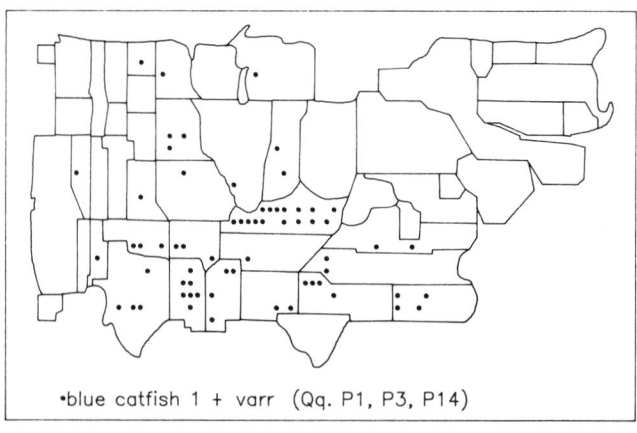

•blue catfish 1 + varr (Qq. P1, P3, P14)

2 =**channel catfish.**

1887 Goode *Amer. Fishes* 377, The . . Blue Cat, *Ictalurus punctatus,* abounds in all the larger Western and Southern streams, living in the river channels. **1957** Trautman *Fishes* 414, I follow the American Fisheries Society recommendation in calling it Blue Catfish, which to Ohio fishermen is the Channel Catfish. *Ibid* 415, Adults *[Ictalurus punctatus]* . . (colloquially called . . blue cats) . . . Largest adults (colloquially called . . blue cats).

3 =**gafftopsail catfish.**

1968 *DARE* (Qu. P2, . . *Saltwater fish . . good to eat*) Inf **LA**37, Blue catfish—[same as] gafftops'l catfish.

blue channel cat(fish) See **blue catfish 1**

blue chickweed n

A **blue-eyed Mary 1** (here: *Collinsia parviflora*).

1959 Anderson *Flora AK* 414, *C. parviflora* . . . Blue Chickweed . . . Corolla . . blue or whitish.

blue-clawed crab n Also *blue-claw (crab)*

A blue crab (*Callinectes sapidus*).

1807 (1846) MA Hist. Soc. *Coll.* 2 ser 3.58 **seMA,** There is the large crab, called here the blue claw. **1947** Ballowe *The Lawd* 154 **LA,** "Whar us gwine?" Unc' Jasper asked. "They's blue-claws in the bayou back o' the dreenin machine," Cricket informed them. **1968** *DARE* (Qu. P18) Inf **NY**89, Blue-claw crab; **NY**40, Blue-clawed crab.

bluecoat n

1 A policeman. **esp Nth, N Midl**

1875 *Chicago Daily Tribune* (IL) 29 Aug 5/4 *(DAE),* Occasionally one of the blue coats would attempt to put back the crowd, but they would not be put back. **1903** Lewis *Boss* 15 **NYC,** With that, the bluecoat seized Sheeny Joe, and there we were, one in each of his hands. **1932** Farrell *Young Lonigan* 153 **Chicago IL,** And he told the damn bluecoat that if he would take off the star, he'd punch him all over the corner. **1965–70** *DARE* (Qu. V9, . . *A policeman*) Infs **CA**36, **GA**77, **MN**2, **NJ**4, 25, **NY**36, 37, **SC**32, **TX**88, Bluecoat. **1969** *Rockford Labor News* (IL) 7 Feb 16, The bluecoats said they heard scrambling sounds inside the room and then the fellow opened the door.

2 =**blue jay 1.**

1917 (1923) *Birds Amer.* 2.217, Blue Jay *Cyanocitta cristata cristata* . . . *Other Names* . . . Blue Coat. **1946** Hausman *Eastern Birds* 420, Northern Blue Jay . . . Other Names . . Bluecoat.

blue cod n

1 =**lingcod 1.**

1882 U.S. Natl. Museum *Bulletin* 16.646, *O[phiodon] elongatus* . . . Blue Cod. **1887** Goode *Amer. Fishes* 270, The name "Blue Cod" is also given to it *[Ophiodon elongatus]* from the color of its flesh. **1933** John G. Shedd Aquarium *Guide* 130, *Ophiodon elongatus* . . . Blue Cod . . . It has a superficial resemblance to the true Cod but is not related to that splendid food fish. Like the Cabezon . . both the flesh and the bones have a bluish green tinge.

2 =**cabezon.**

1939 Natl. Geog. Soc. *Fishes* 240, *Marbled Sculpins [Scorpænichthys marmoratus]* . . also known as *Cabezone* or *Blue Cod,* have flaps of skin somewhat resembling feathers above their eyes. **1946** LaMonte *N. Amer. Game Fishes* 87, *Cabezone Scorpænichthys marmoratus . . . Names: . . Blue Cod.*

blue-cod possum n

1968 *DARE* (Qu. P31) Inf **NC53**, Blue-cod possum [FW: Refers to the bluish scrotum].

blue cohosh n Also *blue cohash* Cf **cohosh**

1 A perennial woodland plant *(Caulophyllum thalictroides)* having small flowers and blue berrylike seeds. Also called **blueberry, blueberry root, blue ginseng, cohosh 1c, electric light-bulb plant, false cohosh, green vivian, papoose root, squawroot, toothache berries, umbrella leaf, yellow ginseng**

1821 Mass. *H.S. Coll.* 2 Ser. IX.148 *(DA)*, Plants, which are indigenous in the township of Middlebury, [Vermont, include] . . . *Caulophyllum thalictroides,* Blue cohosh. **1859** (1968) Bartlett *Americanisms* 91, There are also White and Blue Cohosh, other allied plants. **1901** Mohr *Plant Life AL* 517, *Blue Cohosh . . .* The rhizoma [sic] and roots are the blue cohosh of medicine. **1931** Clute *Common Plants* 27, It is difficult to decide which was the original cohosh. Circumstances, however, point to the blue cohosh. **1968** *DARE* (Qu. S26c, *Wildflowers that grow in woods)* Inf **PA99,** Blue cohosh. **1975** Duncan–Foote *Wildflowers SE* 48.

2 =**white baneberry.**

1896 *Jrl. Amer. Folkl.* 9.179, *Actaea alba . .* blue cohosh, Paris, M[aine]. **1900** Lyons *Plant Names* 14.

blue corporal See **little blue corporal**

blue crane n

1 Either the **great blue heron** or the **little blue heron. chiefly Sth**

1806 (1905) Clark *Orig. Jrls. Lewis & Clark Exped.* 4.139, The large Blue . . . *Herons* or crains as they are usialy [sic] called in the U. States. **1917** *DN* 4.423 **LA,** *Blue crane.* 1. The great blue heron (Ardea herodias): also called *poor Joe.* 2. Ward's blue Heron (Ardea herodias wardii). It is darker than the 'poor Joe', and breeds mostly in the southwestern parts of the state. **1962** Imhof *AL Birds* 84, *Little Blue Heron . . . Other names:* Blue Crane, White Crane. **1965–70** *DARE* (Qu. Q10) 24 Infs, **esp Sth, West,** Blue crane; (Qu. Q8) Inf **LA29,** Blue crane. **c1965** *DARE* FW Addit **neTX,** Blue crane—great blue heron.

2 =**Louisiana heron.**

1917 *DN* 4.423 **LA,** *Blue crane . . .* The Louisiana heron (Hydranassa tricolor ruficollis).

3 =**sandhill crane.**

1923 U.S. Dept. Ag. *Misc. Circular* 13.40, *Sandhill Crane . . . Vernacular names . . . In local use:* Blue crane (Man., Nebr.). **1955** Forbush–May *Birds* 156, *Sandhill Crane . . . Other names:* Brown Crane; Blue Crane; Turkey.

blue curls n

1 A plant of the genus *Trichostema.* Also called **camphor weed 1, vinegar weed 1.** For other names of var spp see **black sage, heart's angel, romero, tarweed, turpentine weed**

1822 Eaton *Botany* 490, *Trichostema . . . dichotoma . .* blue curls . . stamens very long, blue, curved. **1859** (1968) Bartlett *Americanisms* 37, *Blue curls. (Trichostema dichotomum.)* From the shape and color of its flowers. A common plant resembling pennyroyal, and hence called bastard pennyroyal. **1901** Lounsberry *S. Wild Flowers* 449, To many the personality of blue-curls appeals as with a subtle magnetism. **1931** Harned *Wild Flowers Alleghanies* 420, At first the flower is nearly erect, but very early curves inward forming a lovely blue curl, whence the name, Blue Curls. **1966–69** *DARE* (Qq. S26b, d) Infs **MI31, NJ58,** Blue curls. **1967** *DARE* Wildfl QR Pl.182b Inf **TX44,** Blue curls. **1975** Duncan–Foote *Wildflowers SE* 152.

2 =**self-heal** (here: *Prunella vulgaris).*

1847 Wood *Class-Book* 424, *P[runella] vulgaris. Self-heal. Blue-curls.* **1894** *Jrl. Amer. Folkl.* 7.96, *Brunella vulgaris . .* blue curls, somewhat general. **1933** Small *Manual SE Flora* 1155, *Prunella . . . Self-heals. Heal-alls. Blue-curls.* **1971** Krochmal *Appalachia Med. Plants* 208, Blue curls . . . is used as an aromatic and carminative.

3 A **scorpionweed,** esp *Phacelia congesta.* **TX**

1939 Tharp *Vegetation TX* 66, Blue Curls (Phacelia). **1961** Wills–Irwin *Flowers TX* 177, *Blue-curls . . . Phacelia congesta . . .* Of the dozen or more species in Texas, Blue-curls is the most widely distributed.

blue daisy n

Any of several plants with blue, daisy-like flowers: see quots.

1896 *Jrl. Amer. Folkl.* 9.191, *Cichorium Intybus . .* blue daisies, Southold, L[ong] I[sland]. **1951** *PADS* 15.31 **TX,** *Anemone decapetala . . .* Blue daisy. **1954** Harder *Coll.* **cwTN,** Blue daisy . . . Swamp lily. **1968** *DARE* (Qu. S25, . . *Small wild chrysanthemum-like flowers . . that bloom in fields late in the fall)* Inf **OH41,** Blue daisy—at the time of the goldenrod; (Qu. S26e) Inf **CT12,** Blue daisy—also called wild aster.

blue dandelion n

=**chicory.**

1891 *Jrl. Amer. Folkl.* 4.149, I cannot tell the exact locality where Cichorium Intybus was called *Blue Dandelions,* but think it was in the southern part of New Hampshire. **1892** *Jrl. Amer. Folkl.* 5.99, *Cichorium Intybus,* blue dandelion. N[ew] H[ampshire]. **1959** Carleton *Index Herb. Plants* 15. **1971** GA Dept. Ag. *Farmers Market Bulletin* 10 Feb 8/1, Chicory—Cichorium Intybus, or succory, blueweed, blue dandelion or coffeeweed.

blue dangler n Also *blue dangles*

A **dangleberry 1** (here: *Gaylussacia frondosa).*

1861 Wood *Class-Book* 481, *Gaylussacia frondosa . . .* Blue Dangles. Grows in open woods, N. Eng. to Fla. and La. **1937** *Sun* (Baltimore MD) 6 Jul 13/6 *(Hench Coll.),* Although the botanical textbooks recognize only three species of American whortle or huckleberries, the [Eastern] Shore [of Maryland] trademarks at least five varieties. They are two kinds of "high-bush blues," . . and the "blue dangler." The danglers are picked until the first frost.

blue darter n

1 also *blue dorter:* =**blue norther.**

1966 *DARE* (Qu. B18, . . *Special kinds of wind)* Inf **OK25,** Blue darter—a strong ice-cold wind that cuts through you; same as a norther. **1970** Tarpley *Blinky* 58 **neTX,** A strong cold wind from the north . . . Blue dorter.

2 also *blue darter hawk, blue dart hawk, bluewing darter;* pronc-sp *blue dotter hawk:* Any of three somewhat similar birds—the **sharp-shinned hawk** (also called *little blue darter),* the **Cooper's hawk,** or the **goshawk 1** (the latter two also called *big blue darter).* **chiefly Sth**

1892 Harris *Uncle Remus & Friends* 5 **GA,** Dey er done broke in ter ketchin' chickens—de goshawk, de swamphawk en de bluedarter. **1908** *DN* 3.292 **eAL, wGA,** *Blue-darter . . .* A small species of hawk. **1917** *DN* 4.423 **LA,** *Blue darter.* Cooper's hawk. **1917** (1923) *Birds Amer.* 2.68, *Goshawk—Astur atricapillus atricapillus . . . Other Names . . .* Blue Darter. **1950** *PADS* 14.14 **SC,** *Big blue darter . . .* Cooper's hawk. *Ibid* 45, Little blue darter . . . The sharp-shinned hawk. **1954** Harder *Coll.* **cwTN,** Blue-darter hawk. **c1960** Wilson *Coll.* **csKY,** *Blue-darter . . .* The Cooper's or the sharp-shinned hawk. **1965–70** *DARE* (Qu. Q4, . . *Kinds of hawks . . found around here)* 54 Infs, **chiefly Sth,** Blue darter; **AL22, IL93, SC43, TX52,** Blue darter hawk; **MS6, 63,** Blue dotter hawk; **MS60,** Blue dotter hawk—catches chickens in the day; **CO11,** Blue dart hawk; **FL32,** Blue-wing darter.

3 Perh an **indigo snake.**

1966 *DARE* (Qu. P25, . . *Snakes . . found around here)* Inf **FL16,** Blue darter.

blue day n

1981 *Broaddus Coll.* **ceKY,** Blue day—a clear, cold, wintry day.

blue devil n

1 also attrib, usu pl: Melancholy, low spirits, the blues.

1810 (1854) Jefferson *Writings* 5.511 **VA,** We have something of the blue devils at times. **1849** (1948) Melville *Jrl. London & Continent* 8, A regular blue devil day. A gale of wind, & every one sick. **1899** (1912) Green *VA Folk-Speech, Blue-devils . . .* Low spirits; depression of mind. **1930** Shoemaker *1300 Words* 4 **cPA Mts** (as of c1900), *Blue-devils*—Despondency after a spree. **1970** *DARE* (Qu. GG34a, *To feel depressed or in a gloomy mood: "He has the _____ today.")* Infs **TN43, WV14,** Blue devils.

2 pl: See quot. [Engl dial]

1899 (1912) Green *VA Folk-Speech, Blue devils . . .* Delirium tremens.

3 In logging: see quot. Also called **blue goose** n **5**

1969 Sorden *Lumberjack Lingo* **NEng, Gt Lakes,** *Blue devil*—A rutter used in cutting ruts for the ice road. They were generally painted blue.

4 pl: =**viper's bugloss.**

1837 Darlington *Flora Cestrica* 119, Blue weed . . . Blue

Devils . . . This vile foreign weed is extremely troublesome in some portions of our Country. **1931** Clute *Common Plants* 111, As a prickly weed in cultivated fields, it [=*Echium vulgare*] is more commonly known, to the farmer at least, as blue devils. **1976** Bruce *How to Grow Wildflowers* 165, It is attractive as a garden plant, but must be watched, as one of its colloquial names, "Blue-devils," implies.

5 also pl: An aster.

1894 *Jrl. Amer. Folkl.* 7.91 **WV,** *Aster cordifolius* . . . Blue Devil, stick-weed, bee-weed, Fall Aster. **1959** Carleton *Index Herb. Plants* 15, *Blue devils:* Aster azureus.

6 =**chicory 1.**

1969 *DARE* (Qu. S26a) Inf **NY**227, Chicory—a lot of them—also called blue devil.

7 =**blue jay 1.**

1959 *Names* 7.112, In Pennsylvania, the jay has been stigmatized as blue devil by hunters because of its cries warning game of their approach.

blue devil v [blue devil n 1] *obs*

To make (one) melancholy or depressed.

1836 in 1941 *AmSp* 16.235 **VA,** To be hemmed up in a strange place without acquaintance and anything to interest you . . . is enough to *Blue Devil* one who has not even heard from home for nearly two months.

blue dick n Cf **bluebelly 3**

1969 *DARE* (Qu. P30, . . *Wild rabbits around here*) Inf **CA**141, Blue dick.

blue dicks n

A **brodiaea** such as *Brodiaea douglasii,* but usu *B. pulchella,* a sp with hyacinth-like flowers, common esp in California, which is also called **cluster lily, covena, grass nut, hog onion, Indian potato, ookow, papago bluebells, Spanish lily, wild hyacinth.**

1911 Jepson *Flora CA* 101, *B[rodiaea] capitata* . . . Blue Dicks. **1915** (1926) Armstrong *Western Wild Flowers* 16, *Blue Dicks* . . . *Brodiaea capitata.* **1949** Moldenke *Amer. Wild Flowers* 355, Differing from all the species previously mentioned in having very dense, headlike, flower clusters is the *bluedicks, Dichelostemma capitatum.* **1961** Thomas *Flora Santa Cruz* 125, *B[rodiaea] pulchella* . . . Blue Dicks. **1963** Craighead *Rocky Mt. Wildflowers* 17, *Brodiæa douglasii* . . . Other names: . . Bluedicks.

blue dogbane n

=**blue star 1.**

1933 Small *Manual SE Flora* 1059, *Amsonia* . . . Corolla mainly salverform, blue or purple-blue . . . *Blue-dogbanes.* **1953** Greene–Blomquist *Flowers South* 101, The blue-dogbane is an attractive plant with panicles of blue flowers.

blue dorter See **blue darter 1**

blue dotter hawk See **blue darter 2**

blue dragon n

=**dragonfly.**

1968 *DARE* (Qu. R2, . . *Other names . . for the dragonfly*) Inf **OH**56, Blue dragon.

blue duck food n

=**barnyard grass.**

1913 *Torreya* 13.227, *Echinochloa crus-galli* . . . Blue duck food, Mississippi Delta, La.

blue duck millet See **duck millet**

blue eye n chiefly Sth

1 The darkened area around an eye caused by bruising; a black eye.

1965–70 *DARE* (Qu. X20, *What other words do you have for a black eye?*) 11 Infs, **chiefly Sth,** Blue eye. [5 of 11 Infs Black]

2 A kind of playing marble.

1970 *DARE* (Qu. EE6b, *Small marbles or marbles in general*) Inf **GA**93, Blue eye.

blue-eyed babies n

A **bluet 2** (here: *Houstonia caerulea*).

1892 *Jrl. Amer. Folkl.* 5.97, *Houstonia cærulea,* blue-eyed babies. Springfield, Mass. **1940** Clute *Amer. Plant Names* 53, *H. cerulea* . . . Blue-eyed babies.

blue-eyed bean n

=**black-eyed pea.**

1968 *DARE* (Qu. I19) Inf **WI**29, Blue-eyed beans.

blue-eyed grass n

1 A plant of the genus *Sisyrinchium.* Also called **bluegrass 2, fever grass, irisette, star grass.** For other names of var spp see **blue-eyed Mary 2, blue star 2, eyebright, forget-me-not, golden-eyed grass, grass flower, grass widow, nigger baby, pepper grass, rush lily**

1783 in 1785 *Amer. Acad. Arts & Sci. Memoirs* 1.487 **PA,** *Sisyrinchium* . . . *Blue-Eyed Grass.* Blossoms blue. In grass land . . . It makes very pretty edging for borders in gardens. **1939** *Natl. Geog. Mag.* 76.219/2 **Upper MW,** Marsh marigolds . . and blue-eyed grass enliven meadows. **1949** Marshall *Little Squire Jim* 89 **KY,** They'll be sweet and longin in spring night time, with the blue-eyed grass and trillies in bloom. **1967–69** *DARE* (Qu. S9) Inf **PA**99, Blue-eyed grass; (Qu. S24) Inf **CA**87, Blue-eyed grass—on the order of an iris; (Qq. S26a, d) Infs **CA**40, 41, 79, **MA**5, **NC**47, **RI**15, **VA**21, Blue-eyed grass.

2 =**bluet 2.**

1896 *Jrl. Amer. Folkl.* 9.190, *Houstonia cærulea* . . blue-eyed grass, Brodhead, Wis. **1966–67** *DARE* (Qu. S11, . . *Other names . . for . . bluets*) Infs **IA**3, **MI**17, Blue-eyed grass.

blue-eyed Mary n

1 also *blue-eyes:* A plant of the genus *Collinsia.* Also called **Chinese houses, innocence.** For other names of var spp see **blue chickweed, blue lips 1, sunbonnet babies**

1894 *Jrl. Amer. Folkl.* 7.96 **IN,** *Collinsia verna,* . . blue-eyed Marys. **1906** Rydberg *Flora CO* 305, *Collinsia* . . . *Blue-eyed-Mary.* **1945** *Sat. Review* 5 May 12/3 **AR,** The author has an artist's eye and ear for . . the "blue-eyed Mary" that closes at night and opens with the sun. **1963** Craighead *Rocky Mt. Wildflowers* 170, *Blue-eyed Mary* . . . *Other names:* . . Blue-eyes. **1973** Hitchcock–Cronquist *Flora Pacific NW* 422.

2 =**blue-eyed grass 1** (usu *Sisyrinchium angustifolium*).

1900 Lyons *Plant Names* 347, *S. angustifolium* . . . Blue-eyed Mary. **1936** Winter *Plants NE* 15, *S. angustifolium* . . . Called also Blue-eyed Mary or Star-eye Grass. **1959** Carleton *Index Herb. Plants* 15, *Blue-eyed Mary:* . . Sisyrinchium (v).

blue-eyes See **blue-eyed Mary 1**

blue-faced booby n

A **booby** n[1] **1** (here: *Sula dactylatra*) which has black-edged wings, a black tail, and a blue area around the base of the bill and is occasional on the Gulf coast.

1911 *Century Dict.* 623, The common booby of the United States is *Sula leucogastra* . . . Others are the red-footed booby, . . and the blue-faced booby. **1917** *DN* 4.423 **LA,** *Blue-faced booby* (Sula cyanops). One specimen only in La. **1954** Sprunt *FL Bird Life* 15, *Atlantic Blue-faced Booby* . . . This booby is a very tame bird . . . They frequent the waters between Garden and Loggerhead Keys almost entirely . . . The food is composed entirely of fish.

bluefin n

1 Any of var **ciscos,** esp the **blackfin cisco.**

1884 Goode *Fisheries U.S.* 1.541, The "Blue-fin" or "Black-fin" . . . has . . been taken only in the deeper waters of Lake Michigan. **1896** *U.S. Natl. Museum Bulletin* 47.472, *Argyrosomus nigripinnis* . . . Bluefin. **1911** *Century Dict., Blue-fin.* A local name in the United States of the lake-herring or whitefish of Lake Michigan, *Coregonus nigripinnis.* **1920** Forbes–Richardson *Fishes of IL* 55, *A. nigripinnis,* the bluefin. **1966** *DARE* Tape **MI**21, The first really money-making fish that was around here in the early days was the bluefin . . . I haven't seen a bluefin for many years. They were a fat fish, . . they were one of the best smoker fish that was ever caught. **1972** Sparano *Outdoors Encycl.* 359, *Cisco*—Common Names: . . bluefin, . . Scientific Name: Coregonus artedii (and others).

2 in full, **bluefin tuna:** A large tuna, *Thunnus thynnus.* Also called **great albacore, horse mackerel, tunny**

1946 *Sun* (Baltimore MD) 19 Dec 10/2 (Hench Coll.), Only recently considered of commercial value, the Atlantic tuna, or bluefin, is light red in appearance. ~~1958 *Washington Post* (DC) 27 Jul C12/4–5 (Hench Coll.),~~ Also offshore now are school bluefin tuna. **1972** Sparano *Outdoors Encycl.* 374, *Bluefin Tuna*—Common Names: . . bluefin, horse mackerel. Scientific Name: *Thunnus thynnus.* **1975** Evanoff *Catch*

More Fish 212, The bluefin tuna *(Thunnus thynnus)* is also known as the horse mackerel, great albacore, and tunney. Small ones are called "school tuna," while the bigger ones are called "giant tuna."

bluefish n

1 Std: an important foodfish *(Pomatomus saltatrix)* esp prevalent on the Atlantic coast. Also called **blue** n 4, **chopper** 6, **fatback, greenfish, horse mackerel, jumbo, skipjack, snapper, snapping mackerel, tailor, whitefish**

2 Any of var fish, but esp the **weakfish** (as, *Cynoscion parvipinnis, C. regalis*), the **black sea bass**, and the *wrasse* (as, *Halichoeres radiatus, Tautogolabrus adspersus*).

1814 in 1825 *Lit. & Philos. Soc. NY Trans.* 424, *Horse Mackerel.* *(Scomber plumbeus.)* . . Colour of the head and body such that they often call him *blue-fish. Ibid* 402, *Bergall of New-York. (Labrus chogset.)* Chogset of the Mohegans. Blue-fish. **1819** in 1821 *Western Rev.* 1.376, *Ichthelis cyanella,* . . a small species hardly three inches, called Blue-fish or Sunfish. **1871** *Amer. Naturalist* 5.398, At Great Egg Harbor [NJ] . . . Weak-fish *(Cynoscion regalis)* [is] called 'Blue-fish.' **1882** U.S. Natl. Museum *Bulletin* 16.560, *G[irella] nigricans* . . . Blue-fish. *Ibid* 580, *C[ynoscion] parvipinnis* . . bluefish. *Ibid* 603, *P[latyglossus] radiatus* . . . Blue-fish. **1887** Goode *Amer. Fishes* 39, The Sea Bass *[Centropristis striatus]* is also known . . about Newport and New Bedford, [as] "Bluefish." *Ibid* 296, The . . Cunner . ., *Ctenolabrus adspersus* . . has numerous common names . . . In Mitchill's time, it was also called "Bluefish." **1889** U.S. Natl. Museum *Bulletin* 47.1410, *C[ynoscion] parvipinnis* . . . California "bluefish". **1967** *DARE* (Qu. P2) Inf **CA**13, Bluefish; **CA**25, Bluefish—out at sea.

3 =**green sunfish.**

1820 Rafinesque *Ohio R. Fishes* 28, A small species *[Lepomis cyanellus]* . . called Bluefish . . . Appearing entirely blue at a distance.

blue flag n Also *blue flag iris* **chiefly NEast, N Cent**

A blue-flowered iris.

1783 in 1785 Amer. Acad. Arts & Sci. *Memoirs* 1.406 **PA**, *Iris . . . Blue Flag . . . A* decoction of the fresh roots is a powerful cathartic. **1874** *Shaker Med. Preparations* **NY**. **c1960** *Wilson Coll.* **csKY**, Blue flag . . . Wild iris (Iris versicolor). **1965–70** *DARE* (Qu. S24, *A wild flower that grows in swamps and marshes and looks like a small blue iris*) 119 Infs, **widespread, but esp NEast, N Cent**, Blue flag(s); **MI**53, Dwarf blue flag; (Qu. S11, . . *Iris*) Inf **OK**52, Blue flag; (Qq. S26b, d) Infs **CT**21, **MA**6, **PA**89, Blue flag(s). **1967–68** *DARE* Wildfl QR Pl.27 Infs **OH**14, **TX**34, **WI**35, Blue flag.

blue flax n Also *blue prairie-flax*

A blue-flowered **flax**, usu *Linum lewisii* in the western United States.

1951 *PADS* 15.35 **TX**, *Linus* [sic] *lewisii* . . . Blue prairie-flax. **1966** *DARE* Wildfl QR Inf **WA**10, Linum—blue flax of North Dakota. **1976** Dodge *Roadside Wildflowers* 38, Blue flax, when eaten by livestock, is said to cause drowsiness.

blue fly n Also *blue horsefly* **esp Nth**

=**bluebottle fly.**

1836 *Knickerbocker* 8.395, You might hear the blue-flies, with their droning hum, all day in the air. **1856** Stowe *Dred* 1.160 **NC**, He just puts me in mind of one of these blue-flies, whirring and whisking about. **1965–70** *DARE* (Qu. R13, *Flies that come to meat or fruit*) 16 Infs, **scattered, but esp Nth**, Blue fly; (Qu. R12, . . *Other kinds of flies*) Infs **NE**1, **NM**6, **NY**134, **OH**2, **PA**235, **VA**8, **WA**33, Blue fly; **OH**17, Blue horsefly.

blue fulton n Cf **fulton cat, white fulton**

=**channel catfish.**

1920 Forbes–Richardson *Fishes of IL* 181, This fish is often known by fishermen as the . . "blue Fulton," but anglers on the upper Illinois and the Fox usually refer to it as the "channel-cat."

blue gentian n

1 =**false pennyroyal.**

1822 Eaton *Botany* 320, *Isanthus . . . cæruleus,* . . (blue gentian, false pennyroyal . . .) Along the Hudson . . . Odour resembles the spikenard. **1940** Clute *Amer. Plant Names* 225, *Isanthus brachiatus.* Blue gentian, flux-weed.

2 A bachelor's button.

1968–70 *DARE* (Qu. S11, . . *Other names . . for . . bachelor's button*) Infs **NY**99, **PA**248, Blue gentian.

bluegill n **widespread, but least freq in Atl and Gulf States**

1 also *bluegill bream,* ~ *sunfish:* A **sunfish** *(Lepomis macrochirus)* native and common to much of the eastern half of the U.S. but widely introduced elsewhere. Also called **black-eared bream** 1, **blue bream, blue-mouthed sunfish, blue perch** 5, **blue sunfish** 2, **bream** B3, **coppernose** 2, **copperhead** 5, **dollardee, perch, pumpkinseed, red-breasted sunfish, sunfish, sun perch**

1881 in 1930 *Forest & Stream* 31.3, The Blue Gills. **1946** LaMonte *N. Amer. Game Fishes* 138, Bluegill Sunfish—*Lepomis macrochirus.* **1965–70** *DARE* (Qu. P1) 266 Infs, **widespread, but least freq in Atl and Gulf States**, Bluegill(s); **GA**89, Bluegill bream; (Qu. P3) Infs **MA**47, 72, Bluegill(s); (Qu. P7) Infs **IL**115, **KY**65, **MD**22, 26, Bluegill(s); **IL**4, Little bluegills; (Qu. P14) Inf **IN**51, Bluegill. **1975** Evanoff *Catch More Fish* 88, The bluegill *(Lepomis macrochirus)* is . . also called the bream, blue bream, blue-mouthed sunfish, blue sunfish, copper-nosed bream, sun perch, and dollardee . . . The bluegill . . is now common in most of our warm waters.

2 See quot.

1966–67 *DARE* (Qu. Q5, . . *Kinds of wild ducks*) Inf **FL**29, River duck or bluegills; **WA**30, Bluegill.

3 A poultry disease.

1966 *DARE* (Qu. K78, *What diseases do chickens commonly get around here?*) Inf **OK**43, Bluegill—bad for turkeys, too.

blue ginseng n [Prob from the color of its fruit + its similarity to ginseng]

1 =**blue cohosh** 1.

1876 Hobbs *Bot. Hdbk.* 14, Blue ginseng . . Caulophyllum thalictroides. **1900** Lyons *Plant Names* 87. **1930** Sievers *Amer. Med. Plants* 14, Blue ginseng . . . is found in the deep rich loam of shady woods from New Brunswick to South Carolina and westward to Nebraska, being abundant especially throughout the Allegheny Mountain region. **1968** *Foxfire* Summer 48, Blue cohosh . . . is sometimes collected as . . "blue ginseng."

2 =**black snakeroot** 1.

1971 Krochmal *Appalachia Med. Plants* 96, *Cimicifuga racemosa* . . . blue ginseng.

blue goose n

1 also *blue, blue brant, blue snow goose, blue wavey, bluewinged goose:* A slaty blue goose *(Chen caerulescens)* with a white head and neck. Also called **bald brant, brant, California goose, eaglehead goose, gray brant, outlaw, silver brant, skillethead, wavey, white-headed goose**

1874 Coues *Birds NW* 553, *Anser cærulescens . . . Blue Goose . . . Hab[itat].*—North America generally. **1888** Trumbull *Names of Birds* 9, Names of *Chen cærulescens,* as follows: *Blue Goose: Blue Snow Goose: Blue Wavey: Blue-winged Goose.* **1917** *DN* 4.423 **LA**, *Blue goose* . . *Blue Brant; Gray Brant;* . *Skillet Head.* **1943** Musgrove *Waterfowl IA* 14, *Blue Goose . . .* Other names: . . blue wavey, . . blue, . . blue brant. *Ibid* 16, The blue goose is the most abundant goose migrating through Iowa in the spring of the year . . . Young blues in small flocks often remain around streams, ponds, and marshes as late as the middle of May. **1965–70** *DARE* (Qu. Q6, . . *Kinds of wild geese . . around here*) 34 Infs, **scattered, but esp Missip Valley**, Blue geese; **MI**101, **NE**11, Canadian blue geese; **MO**10, Big blue geese. **1982** Elman *Hunter's Field Guide* 292, *Blue Goose . . . Common & Regional Names:* blue wavey, . . blue brant, . . blue snow goose, blue-winged goose. *Ibid* 293, On the western fringe of their range, where a few blues are often included in a large flight of snows, some or all of the blues may be white-bellied or piebald.

2 See quots.

1927 *DN* 5.439, *Blue goose . . .* The convict cage at a prison camp. **1930** Irwin *Amer. Tramp, Blue goose.*—The general cage or cell, shared by all the prisoners, in a convict road camp or on a chain gang. Also, the general room in a prison or jail from which access is had to the cells.

3 Perh by ext: a cheap or shabby restaurant, bar, or other public establishment.

1966–68 *DARE* (Qu. C35) Inf **SC**38, Blue goose—a junction, bus stop, filling station; (Qu. D39, . . *A small eating place where the food is not especially good*) Inf **IA**8, The blue goose; **UT**13, Blue goose—we used to call it; (Qu. DD30, . . *A place where liquor is [or was] sold and consumed illegally*) Inf **MS**71, Blue goose.

4 In marble play: see quot.

1963 *KY Folkl. Rec.* 9.60 **neKY,** Blue goose: when another steals or grabs the marbles and will not give them back to the owner.

5 In logging: see quot. Also called **blue devil n 3**

1969 Sorden *Lumberjack Lingo* **NEng, Gt Lakes,** *Blue goose*—A type of rutter used to cut ruts in the ice so sleigh runners could follow.

blue-goose v [Perh punningly with *goose* to poke someone in the buttocks]

Of a man: to chase after women, to be involved in sexual affairs.

1970 *DARE* (Qu. Y29b, . . *About a man who doesn't stay home much: "He's always _____."*) Inf **NC86,** Blue-goosing; **NC88,** Blue-goosing —getting into affairs; **VA69,** Blue-goosing—they say it a lot about men. [All Infs Black]

blue gopher snake n Also *blue gopher*

=**indigo snake.**

1952 Ditmars *N. Amer. Snakes* 151, *Blue* Gopher Snake, *Drymarchon corais couperi.* **1958** Conant *Reptiles & Amphibians* 153, *Eastern Indigo Snake . . .* This is the "blue bullsnake" or "blue gopher" of the snake charmer and carnival "pit" show.

bluegrass n

1 Std: any of var grasses of the genus *Poa.*

2 =**blue-eyed grass 1. chiefly NEast**

1894 *Jrl. Amer. Folkl.* 7.101, *Sisyrinchium angustifolium,* . . blue-grass, . . Concord, Mass. (children). **1929** *Torreya* 29.149 **ME,** Sisyrinchium [was] *"Blue Grass,"* (not "Blue-eyed"). **1966** *DARE* Wildfl QR Pl.28a Inf **NH4,** Bluegrass. **1967–70** *DARE* (Qu. S24, *A wild flower that grows in swamps and marshes and looks like a small blue iris*) Inf **RI1,** Bluegrass [Inf questions response]; (Qu. S26d, *Wildflowers that grow in meadows*) Infs **MA49, NJ45, NY233,** Bluegrass; **NY205,** Bluegrass—tall weed, one blue flower; (Qu. S26a) Inf **CA24,** Bluegrass—a star-shaped blue flower that grows along the road.

3 A **spiderwort** (here: *Tradescantia virginiana*).

1933 Small *Manual SE Flora* 261, *T. brevicaulis . . .* Blue-grass.

4 A **bulrush** (here: *Scirpus californicus*).

1942 *Torreya* 42.158, *Scirpus californicus . . .* Blue grass, Louisiana.

blue grouse n

1 =**dusky grouse. NW, Rocky Mts**

1860 in 1874 Coues *Birds NW* 397, This bird, called generally in Oregon the *Blue* Grouse, and also known as the Pine Grouse, Dusky Grouse, [etc.]. **1966–67** *DARE* (Qu. Q7, . . *Other kinds of game birds*) Infs **MT3, 4, OR15, WA11, 24, WY1, 5,** Blue grouse; **CO37,** Mountain blue-grouse.

2 =**spruce grouse.**

1913 *DN* 4.2 **ME,** *Blue hooter . . .* the blue grouse.

blue gum n[1] **chiefly Sth, S Midl**

1 also attrib: A Black person who has bluish gums and whose bite, according to superstition, is poisonous. *freq derog*

1927 *DN* 5.473 **Ozarks,** *Blue-gum moke . . .* A negro whose gums are bluish instead of red. It is said that the bite of one of these fellows is deadly poison. **1929** (1931) Faulkner *Sound & Fury* 67 **MS** [Black], They making a bluegum out of you . . . And you know who et him. Them bluegum chillen did. **c1937** in 1972 *Amer. Slave* 2.31 **SC,** White ladies do dat 'kalkilating' trick sometime but you take a blue-gum nigger gal, all wool on de top of her head and lak to dance and jig wid her foots . . her ain't gonna have money in de back of her head when her pick out a man to marry. **1960** Williams *Walk Egypt* 186 **GA,** When an ordinary bad nigger die, he turn to a mule, gots to keep on working thu eternity. But when a blue-gum die, he turn to maggot, gots to eat dead corpses. **1967** *DARE* FW Addit **neLA,** *Blue gum*—a Negro.

2 A person of mixed Indian, White, and Black ancestry.

1970 *DARE* (Qu. HH28, . . *People of foreign background*) Inf **TX95,** Blue gum—Creole; **TX98,** Blue gum—Cajun.

3 See quot.

1972 *Atlanta Letters* **cnGA,** Moonshine, shine, blue-gum, or stump water—home made whiskey, bootleg.

blue gum n[2]

1 An introduced eucalyptus *(Eucalyptus globulus).* [*OED* 1802 →] **CA**

1967–68 *DARE* (Qu. T5) Inf **CA22,** Blue gum—the eucalyptus—stays green all year; (Qu. T16) Inf **CA79,** Eucalyptus or blue gum (a variety); **CA87,** Blue gum, or eucalyptus, lower down toward San Diego;

CA36, Eucalyptus—especially the red gum, blue gum, flowering eucalyptus; (QR, near p79) Inf **CA23,** Blue gum used for windbreak in early days.

2 =**black gum 1** (here: *Nyssa sylvatica*).

1968 *DARE* (Qu. T15) Inf **CT13,** Blue gum—called a pepperidge here; **LA15,** Blue gum—hard to split.

blue-gummed adj [**blue gum** n[1]] **chiefly Sth, S Midl** *derog*

Of a Black person: having bluish gums; see quot 1908.

1908 *DN* 3.292 **eAL, wGA,** *Blue-gum(med) nigger . . .* A negro whose gums are blue or black. The bite of such a negro is supposed to be poisonous. **1947** Ballowe *The Lawd* 171 **LA,** "'Fo' the man choked me, Ah bit him in the laig." . . The Sheriff . . told the cowering man that, if Go-Easy had been a blue-gummed nigger, he would have been a goner. **c1960** *Wilson Coll.* **csKY,** *Blue-gummed Negro . . .* Supposedly one such is cursed from birth; his bite is poisonous. Not widely known.

blue hawk n

1 =**marsh hawk.**

1874 Coues *Birds NW* 331, *Marsh Hawk . . .* The old male is also sometimes called "Blue Hawk." **1895** (1907) Wright *Birdcraft* 215, *Circus hudsonius. Harrier. Blue Hawk . . . Male:* Above bluish gray; below white mottled with brown. **1917** (1923) *Birds Amer.* 2.64, *Marsh Hawk . . . Other Names.*—Harrier; Marsh Harrier; Blue Hawk (adult). **1955** *MA Audubon Soc. Bulletin* 39.442, *Marsh Hawk.* Blue Hawk (Maine, Mass. The fully plumaged male is chiefly light bluish gray). **1965–70** *DARE* (Qu. Q4, . . *Kinds of hawks . . around here*) 16 Infs, **west of Appalachians,** Blue hawk; **MO38,** Little blue hawk. [Note: Some of these Infs may refer instead to **2** or **3** below.]

2 =**goshawk 1.**

1888 (1890) Warren *Birds PA* 124, *American Goshawk; Blue Hawk . . .* Above dark lead color, black on top of head. **1923** Dawson *Birds CA* 1670, Fortunately for our game and poultry, the "Blue Hawk" is comparatively rare in California. **1955** Forbush–May *Birds* 100, *Eastern Goshawk . . . Other names:* Blue Hawk; Partridge Hawk.

3 =**Cooper's hawk.**

1932 Bennitt *Check-list* 22, *Cooper's hawk . . .* Big blue darter; blue hawk . . . U[ncommon] P[ermanent] R[esident] throughout the state [of Missouri].

bluehearts n

A plant of the genus *Buchnera.*

1822 Eaton *Botany* 213, *B[uchnera] americana,* blue hearts. **1901** Mohr *Plant Life AL* 728, *Buchnera . . . Blue-hearts . . .* Flowers . . May to July. **1975** Duncan–Foote *Wildflowers SE* 178, *Blue-hearts . . .* Perennial . . probably root-parasitic . . . Corolla purple or white . . . Fruits many-seeded.

blue hen See **blue marsh-hen**

blue hen hawk n

1 =**goshawk 1.**

1903 Dawson *Birds OH* 401, *American Goshawk . . . Synonym.*—*Blue Hen Hawk . . .* The bird . . appears at times among the poultry . . , carrying off the choicest of the flock before the farmer's face and eyes. **1946** Goodrich *Birds in KS* 316, Colloquial Name . . hawk, blue hen . . . Common name, A.O.U. Check-List . . goshawk, eastern. **1953** Jewett *Birds WA* 161, *Eastern Goshawk . . .* Other names: Blue Hen Hawk; Blue Darter.

2 =**Cooper's hawk.**

1907 Anderson *Birds IA* 245, The Cooper Hawk or "Blue Hen-hawk" is a common summer resident in all parts of the state.

blue hen's chicken n Also *blue hen's chick* [From *blue hen* a kind of hen reputed to breed good gamecocks] **chiefly Sth, S Midl**

1 A good fighter; a person with spirit or pluck.

1799 in 1956 *AmSp* 31.223 **NC,** We were the bravest of the brave; we were a formidable flock of blue hen's chickens of the game blood, of indomitable courage, and strangers to fear. **1818** in 1830 Royall *Letters AL* 69, He [=Andrew Jackson] was dressed in a blue frock coat . . . and loves a jest. He told one of our party, he was "one of the blue hen's chickens." **1927** *DN* 5.473 **Ozarks,** *Blue hen's chicken . . .* A formidable fighter. "You-uns git Hank rousted up now, an' he shore is one o' th' ol' blue hen's chickens." **1932** Stribling *Store* 463 **AL,** You're up agin one of the blue hen's chickens this time. **1965** Guthrie *Blue Hen's Chick* 86 **KY,** Here's to you, Buddy—the blue hen's chick. *Ibid* 9, Without apology she told them in so many words that I was the blue hen's chick.

2 A resident of Delaware. [See quot 1840]

1840 *Niles' Natl. Reg.* 58. 154/3, In the revolutionary war . . . Captain Caldwell [of Delaware], had a company [of men] . . called by the rest "Caldwell's game cocks," and the regiment after a time in Carolina was nicknamed from this "the blue hen's chickens" and "the blue chickens." . . But after they had been distinguished in the south the name of the *Blue Hen* was applied to the state. **1949** *AmSp* 24.26, Almost every American has heard . . *Blue Hen's Chicken* for a Delawarean.

3 A dominant, aggressive, or quick-tempered person (usu a woman).

1951 *AmSp* 26.196, In Henry County, Tennessee, the phrase 'she's one of the blue hen's chicks' is used to describe 'a high-tempered woman'; in Johnson County, Illinois, someone who 'flies off the handle easily' is called 'one of the old blue hen's chicks.' **c1960** *Wilson Coll.* **csKY,** *Blue hen's chicken* . . . A dominant chicken; hence a dominant person, usually a woman. "She's one of the blue hen's chickens."

4 An important or high-class person, or one who pretends to be.

1946 *PADS* 6.6 **VA,** *Blue hen's chickens* . . . Local aristocracy. **1951** *AmSp* 26.196 **csIL, cnKY, neTX,** Blue hen's chicks . . . is also used about 'high-toned' people who 'think they are just a little better than someone else.' **1970** *DARE* (Qu. II23, *. . People who are, or think they are, the best society of a community*) Inf TX98, She's the old blue-hen chicken.

5 Of weather: see quot.

1951 *AmSp* 26.197 **wKY,** 'This is one of the blue hen's chickens (chicks)' . . . usually meant 'a cold, brisk day.'

blue heron See **great blue heron, little blue heron**

blue herring n[1] See **blueback herring**

blue herring n[2] [Alter of *blue heron*] Cf **-ing**

=**great blue heron.**

1966–67 *DARE* (Qu. Q10, *. . Water birds*) Inf MI36, Blue herring [FW: heron]; NY32, Blue herring.

bluehill crane n

Prob =**great blue heron.**

1968 *DARE* (Qu. Q10) Inf IA29, Crane—the bluehill crane (blue) and the sandhill crane (white).

blue hole n [**blue** adj **3** + *hole*] Cf *DJE*

A deep hole in a river or stream.

1951 Craig *Singing Hills* 89 **wVA,** Then he deliberately rowed out of his way and informed me we were directly over the blue hole which had no bottom. **c1955** *Hench Coll.*, In Albemarle County, Virginia, blue hole is the regular name for an unusually deep hole in a stream.

blue hooter n

=**spruce grouse.**

1913 *DN* 4.2 **ME,** Blue hooter . . . the blue grouse. "The blue hooters called from the top of the hills."

blue hornet n Also *blue-assed hornet*

A large bluish wasp of the family Sphecidae.

1931–33 *LANE Worksheets*, 1 Inf, **ceVT,** Blue-assed hornet . . . A kind of hornet, nest in trees. Smaller ones are called yellow-assed wasps. **1967** *DARE* (Qu. R21) Inf MA1, Blue hornet.

blue horsefly See **blue fly**

blue hubbard squash n Also *blue hubbard, blue squash* **esp NEast**

A hubbard squash *(Cucurbita maxima)* or similar cultivar.

1814 (1914) Bentley *Diary* 4.280 **MA,** This squash is commonly known by the name of the Blue Squash . . & is also called the African squash. **1965–70** *DARE* (Qu. I23) 12 Infs, **chiefly NY, NEng,** Blue hubbard squash; NY99, Blue squash; MN36, Blue squash—alternative name for Hubbard. **1968** *DARE* Tape IN36, Blue hubbard squash. **1974** *Burpee Seeds* 115, *Blue Hubbard* . . . Attractive, blue-gray, slightly ridged fruits, larger than True Hubbard. Flesh is bright yellow orange. **1976** Bailey-Bailey *Hortus Third* 928, 'Queensland Blue' *(C. maxima)* is called a pumpkin in Australia, . . but in the United States it would be considered a typical winter squash, somewhat like 'Blue Hubbard'.

blue huckleberry n

1 =**blueberry 1.**

1848 Gray *Manual of Botany* 261, *V[accinium] Pennsylvanicum* . . . Berries abundant, large and sweet, ripening early in July: the

earliest *blueberry* or *blue huckleberry* in the market. **1942** *Torreya* 42.164, *Vaccinium ovalifolium* . . . Tall blue huckleberry, Oregon. **1968** *DARE* (Qu. I44) Inf CA105, Blueberries = blue huckleberries here.

2 =**huckleberry 1.**

1860 Curtis *Cat. Plants NC* 85, *Blue Huckleberry* (Gaylussacia frondosa . .). The berries are . . perhaps the finest flavored we have, ripening in June.

blue hull bean See **blue bean**

blue jack See **blue john** n **2**

bluejack n

1 also *bluejack oak:* A deciduous low oak tree *(Quercus incana)* native to the southeastern US. Also called **cinnamon oak, high-ground willow oak, sandjack, shin oak, turkey oak, upland willow oak.**

1860 *Southern Cultivator* 18.384 *(DA),* As the traveller journeys westward [in Texas] he passes through what are called 'bluejack' lands, the soil being very loose and the growth stunted and gnarled. **1901** Lounsberry *S. Wild Flowers* 130, Blue Jack, is a small and shapely species of oak which thrives in sandy places from North Carolina to Florida and westward. **1979** Little *Checklist U.S. Trees* 233, *Bluejack oak . . . Other common trees*—cinnamon oak, sandjack, bluejack.

2 See **blue jacket 2.**

blue jacket n

1 See quot.

1969 Sorden *Lumberjack Lingo* **NEng, Gt Lakes,** *Blue jackets*—Body lice. Same as crumbs.

2 also *blue jack:* A wasp of the family Sphecidae. Cf **black jacket, yellow jacket**

1911 *Century Dict.,* Blue-jacket . . . A name given in the United States to hymenopterous insects of the family *Sphegidæ* [sic]. The predominant color is blue. The best-known are the *Pelopæus cæruleus,* a northern species, and the *Chlorion cyaneum,* whose range is more to the south. Both are known under the collective name of *mud-daubers.* **1968–70** *DARE* (Qu. R20, *Wasps that build their nests of mud*) Inf MN29, Blue jackets—¾ inch long, bluish-black; (Qu. R21) Inf IA21, Blue jacket—a purplish-black wasp; VA73, Blue jack—look [sic] like a bee, but it's blue.

3 =**spiderwort.**

1933 Small *Manual SE Flora* 260, *Tradescantia . . . Spiderworts.* Blue-jackets. **1949** Moldenke *Amer. Wild Flowers* 306, The true spiderworts or bluejackets, *Tradescantia,* were named by Linnaeus.

bluejack oak n

1 See **bluejack 1.**

2 =**water oak** (here: *Quercus nigra*).

1960 Vines *Trees SW* 181, *Quercus . . nigra* . . . Vernacular names are Bluejack Oak, Duck Oak, . . and Possum Oak.

blue jay n

1 Std: the common jay *(Cyanocitta* spp). Also called **bird o' Satan, bluebonnet bird, bluecoat 2, blue devil 7, blue jaybird, blue Jesus, corn bird, corn thief 2, jaybird, nest robber**

2 See quot.

1969 Sorden *Lumberjack Lingo* **NEng, Gt Lakes,** *Blue jay*—A man who keeps the sleigh road in good condition. Same as road monkey, hay man on the hill.

blue jaybird n

=**blue jay 1.**

1966–68 *DARE* (Qu. Q16, *. . Kinds of jays*) Infs FL32, NC49, Blue jaybird.

‡**blue Jesus** n

=**blue jay 1.**

1968 *DARE* (Qu. Q16, *. . Kinds of jays*) Inf NH14, Blue jay or blue Jesus.

blue Jimmy n

=**bluestem 1.**

1968 *DARE* (Qu. S9, *Other kinds of grass that are hard to get rid of*) Inf LA15, Blue Jimmy—also called bluestem.

blue jingler n

1939 *FWP Guide NJ* 525, Locally the mineral [argilite] is called "blue jingler" because, when fresh, it rings if struck sharply.

blue john n, also attrib **chiefly Sth, S Midl**

1 Skim milk.

1869 *Overland Mth.* 3.129/2, North Carolinians call skim-milk "blue John." 1908 *DN* 3.292 eAL, wGA. 1916 *DN* 4.320 KS, LA. 1937 (1963) Hyatt *Riverlid* 110 KY, Milk that ever drap o' cream has been scum off'n, you might say jist the puore [=pure] blue-john. 1949 Brown *Amer. Cooks* 37 AR, On the eastern border, along the Mississippi, a very monotonous diet of sweet taters, turnips, corn pone, and thin "Blue-John Gravy" is relieved by an occasional feed of "cat." c1960 *Wilson Coll.* csKY, Blue john . . . Skimmed milk, which often has a bluish appearance. "This milk is nothing but blue john." 1966–70 *DARE* (QR p47) Infs SC1, VA30, Blue john same as skim milk; (QR p65) Inf KY72, Blue john is skim milk. 1967–68 *DARE* FW Addits GA, SC, Blue john—skimmed milk.

2 also *blue jack, blue johnny:* Milk, usu skimmed, which is sour or just beginning to turn sour. See Map Cf **blink** n[1], **blinky 1a**

1929 *AmSp* 5.16 Ozarks, Blue john . . . Sweet milk which is just becoming *blinky*—just on the point of turning sour. 1944 *PADS* 2.6 AL, KY, cTN, SC, Blue-John, less often *blue-Johnny* . . . Milk skimmed (hence blue) and slightly sour. 1944 *PADS* 2.54 MO. 1950 *PADS* 14.15 SC. 1958 *PADS* 29.7 TN, Blue john. 1965–70 *DARE* (Qu. H58, *Milk that's just beginning to become sour is* _____) 53 Infs, **chiefly Sth, esp Gulf States,** Blue john; AL15, Blue jack.

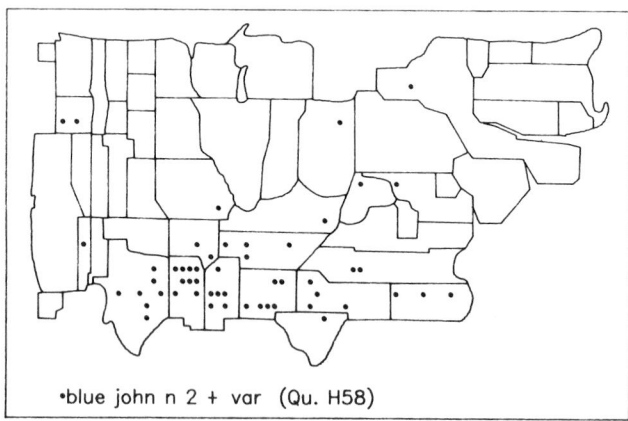

•blue john n 2 + var (Qu. H58)

3 A blue heron. Cf **blue peter**

1933 Rawlings *South Moon* 303 FL, You do favour a Blue-john somethin' turrible.

4 =**bluet 2.**

1968 *DARE* (Qu. S11, . . *Other names . . for . . bluets*) Inf TN24, Blue johns.

blue john adj

1905 *DN* 3.70 nwAR, Blue John . . . Sour. 'That milk's blue John.' Common.

blue johnny See **blue john** n 2

bluejoint n

1 also *bluejoint grass, ~ reedgrass:* A **reedgrass** (here: *Calamagrostis canadensis*). Also called **marsh pinegrass, meadow pinegrass**

1832 NH Hist. Soc. *Coll.* 3.205, Hay of good quality is cut upon the upland; . . in the intervals and meadows . . bluejoint and several other kinds of grasses. 1906 Rydberg *Flora CO* 31, *Calamagrostis* . . . Bluejoint. 1937 U.S. Forest Serv. *Range Plant Hdbk.* G41, Bluejoint *[Calamagrostis canadensis],* also known in some localities as bluejoint reedgrass, . . is the most common and widespread species of *Calamagrostis* in North America. 1952 Strausbaugh–Core *Flora WV* 116, *C[alamagrostis] canadensis* . . . Bluejoint grass. 1966–69 *DARE* (Qu. L8) Infs ME5, 12, 19, Bluejoint; MA74, Bluejoint—ordinary swamp grass; NY219, Bluejoint—hay; (Qu. L9a) Inf MI107, Bluejoint. 1973 Hitchcock–Cronquist *Flora Pacific NW* 630, Bluejoint reedgrass . . . *C[alamagrostis] canadensis.*

2 A **wheatgrass** (here: *Agropyron smithii*).

1889 Vasey *Ag. Grasses* 48, *Agropyrum* [sic] *glaucum* (Blue Stem, Bluejoint) . . occurs nearly everywhere, but sparsely, on the plains. 1937 U.S. Forest Serv. *Range Plant Hdbk.* G5, Bluestem *[Agropyron smithii],* known as bluejoint in the Montana region and sometimes called . . . Smith bluejoint . . is one of the commonest . . of the western wheatgrasses.

3 also *bluejoint turkeyfoot:* A **beardgrass** (here: *Andropogon furcatus, A. gerardi,* and *A. scoparius*).

1894 *Jrl. Amer. Folkl.* 7.103, *Andropogon furcatus* . . blue joint, Minn. . . . *Andropogon scoparius* . . big blue joint, Central Neb. 1939 FWP *Guide KS* 11, Bluestem has the greatest forage value, and both species—big and little bluestem, also known as bluejoint turkeyfoot and prairie beardgrass—grow in almost all parts of the state. 1940 Gates *Flora KS* 121, *Andropogon furcatus* . . . Bluejoint Turkeyfoot. 1968 Barkley *Plants KS* 36, Andropogon gerardi . . . Bluejoint Turkeyfoot.

blue kite n

=**Mississippi kite.**

1873 *Amer. Naturalist* 7.202 sIL, Soaring gracefully above them [=swallow-tailed kites] with a similar flight were smaller numbers of the "blue kite" *(Ictinia Mississippiensis).* 1917 (1923) *Birds Amer.* 2.62, *Mississippi Kite . . . Other Name.*—Blue Kite . . . Plumage, bluish-gray. 1955 Forbush–May *Birds* 98, Blue Kite . . . A very dull-appearing bird, with its generally bluish plumage.

blue laurel n

Catawba rhododendron *(Rhododendron catawbiense).*

1932 *Country Life* 62.65, The natives call it the Blue Laurel; others, more sensitive to color discrimination, have chosen for its name Purple Rhododendron.

bluelegs See **bluestocking 2**

blue leopard n Also *blue lip* Cf **bluetick**

A type of spotted hound.

1952 *Argosy* (NY) June 99 LA, The dark spotting and blotching of its coat, which in the "blue leopard" strain resembles that of the blue-tick hound, but with a difference that is as subtle as it is definite. 1967 *DARE* Tape LA2, That's what they call all leopard dogs . . . blue lip . . . blue leopard.

blue light n Cf **mother may I, red light, stealing steps**

A children's game: see quot.

1966 *DARE* (Qu. EE33, . . *Outdoor games . . that children play*) Inf NC22, Stealing steps or blue light—one person was "it"; he said take so many giant steps, monkey jumps, scissor steps, etc. You had to say "may I?" or else had to go back. [The object was to] see who could get home first.

blue lightning n **West**

See quot 1889.

1889 (1971) Farmer *Americanisms, Blue lightning.*—One of the grimly facetious names with which Texans have christened revolvers. 1922 Rollins *Cowboy* 148 TX, The affronted citizen would be justified, if he 'dug for' his own 'blue lightning.' 1944 Adams *Western Words, Blue lightnin'*—A slang name for a six gun. 1950 *Western Folkl.* 9.138 (as of late 1800s), Familiar epithets for the revolver were *equalizer, . . blue lightning.*

blue lily n Also *blue swamp-lily*

=**blue flag.**

1897 *Jrl. Amer. Folkl.* 10.145, *Iris versicolor* . . blue lily, Madison, Wis. 1951 *PADS* 15.29 TX, *Iris* spp.—Blue swamp-lilies. 1966–69 *DARE* (Qu. S24) Infs ME7, 12, 20, NY205, Blue lily.

blue lily of the Nile n

A cultivated lilylike plant *(Agapanthus africanus).*

1959 Carleton *Index Herb. Plants* 16, *Blue lily of the Nile:* Agapanthus africanus. 1966 *Wichita Eagle* (KS) 9 Apr 8B/6, A marvelous area for planting blue lily of the Nile, gloxinias and African violets (in summer). 1968 *DARE* Tape WV11, It's a beautiful lily—one name is the blue lily of the Nile.

blue lip See **blue leopard**

blue lips n

1 A **blue-eyed Mary 1,** esp *Collinsia grandiflora* or *C. parviflora* **West**

1915 (1926) Armstrong *Western Wild Flowers* 488, *Blue-lips . . . Collinsia multiflora . . .* This grows in the woods around Mt. Shasta. 1934 Haskin *Wild Flowers Pacific Coast* 321, *Collinsia grandiflora . . .* The name blue lips it shares with other species of *Collinsia,* as also that of innocence. 1963 Craighead *Rocky Mt. Wildflowers* 170, *Collinsia parviflora . . . Other names:* Blue-lips . . . Flowers grow on very slender stalks.

2 See quot. Cf **blue gum 1**

1968 *DARE* (Qu. HH28) Inf LA46, Blue lips—Negro; old-fashioned.

blue-liz n Cf **lizzy, white lizard**
    1918 *DN* 5.23 **NW**, *Blue-liz* . . . Patrol wagon.

blue lobelia n
    =**lobelia**.
    1873 in 1976 Miller *Shaker Herbs* 147, *Lobelia syphilitica* . . . Blue
    Lobelia. **1900** Lyons *Plant Names* 228, *L. syphilitica* . . . Blue Lobe-
    lia. **1940** Gates *Flora KS* 231, *Lobelia siphilitica* . . . Blue Lobelia.
    1968 *DARE* (Qu. S26c) Inf **PA**99, Big blue lobelia; (Qu. S24) Inf **PA**70,
    Blue lobelia.

blue Lucy n
    1 A **self-heal** (here: *Prunella vulgaris*).
    1916 *Torreya* 16.239, *Prunella vulgaris* . . . Blue lucy, Matinicus Id.,
    Me. **1959** Carleton *Index Herb. Plants* 16, *Blue lucy:* Prunella vulgaris.
    2 =**blue flag**.
    1966 *DARE* Wildfl QR Pl.26 Inf **NC**28, Blue Lucy or wild iris.

blue magnolia n [Prob from the color of the leaves]
    =**cucumber tree 1**.
    1920 *Torreya* 20.21, *Magnolia acuminata* . . . Blue magnolia.

blue marsh-hen n Also *blue hen, blue pond-hen*
    A **coot** n[1] **1** or similar bird.
    1888 Trumbull *Names of Birds* 117, Mr. Everett Smith speaks of
    hearing it *[Fulica americana]* called the *Blue Marsh-Hen* in Maine.
    1955 Forbush–May *Birds* 168, *American coot—Fulica americana
    americana* . . . *Other names:* . . Blue Marsh-hen. **1955** *MA Audubon*
    39.443, *American Coot.* Blue Hen (Mass. General color bluish slaty;
    form somewhat henlike); . . Blue Pond Hen (Mass.). **1966** *DARE* (Qu.
    Q10, . . *Water Birds*) Inf **GA**7, Blue hen—small, a crane.

blue martin n esp **Sth, Missip Valley**
    Prob =**purple martin**.
    1965–70 *DARE* (Qu. Q14, . . *Other names* . . *for* . . *[the] martin*) 17
    Infs, **esp Sth, Missip Valley**, Blue martin; (Qu. Q20) Infs **MI**23, **NY**100,
    VA43, Blue martin.

blue mayflower n Cf **mayflower**
    =**liverwort** (here: *Hepatica* spp).
    1970 *DARE* (Qu. S23) Inf **MI**116, Blue mayflower—hepatica.

blue meat n
    1944 Adams *Western Words, Blue meat*—The flesh of an unweaned
    calf.

blue-mouthed sunfish n
    =**bluegill 1**.
    1935 Caine *Game Fish* 11 **Sth**, *Bluegill—Lepomis pallidus* . . . Blue-
    mouthed Sunfish. **1975** Evanoff *Catch More Fish* 88, The bluegill
    (Lepomis macrochirus) is . . also called the . . blue-mouthed sunfish.

blue mud dauber n
    A **mud dauber** (here: *Chalybion californicum*).
    1949 Palmer *Natural Hist.* 433, Blue mud dauber, *Chalybion californi-
    cum,* is steel-blue throughout and usually smaller than yellow wasp.

blue mud wasp See **blue wasp**

blue mustard n **West**
    A purple-flowered plant *(Chorispora tenella)* of the mustard
    family.
    1937 Stemen *OK Flora* 181, *Blue Mustard.* Annual . . . Flowers small
    purplish . . . Waste places. **1968** *ID Enterprise* (Malad City) 1 Feb 5/4,
    Other weeds creating problems are white top, blue mustard, fan weed,
    burdock, larkspur, wild oats and rye. **1973** Hitchcock–Cronquist *Flora
    Pacific NW* 160, Chorispora; Blue Mustard . . . Eurasian weed widely
    estab in dry areas, but rare w Cas. [=west of the Cascades]

blue myrtle n Cf **myrtle**
    1 A **California lilac** (here: *Ceanothus thyrsiflorus*). **chiefly CA**
    1884 Sargent *Forests of N. Amer.* 41, *Ceanothus thyrsiflorus,* . . Blue
    Myrtle. **1897** Parsons *Wild Flowers CA* 274, *California Lilac* . . . is
    known in some localities as "blue myrtle," and in others as "blue-blos-
    som." **1937** U.S. Forest Serv. *Range Plant Hdbk.* B39, Several spe-
    cies . . including . . blue myrtle . . become small trees under favorable
    conditions. **1979** Little *Checklist U.S. Trees* 80, *Other common names*
    —blueblossom ceanothus, blue-myrtle.
    2 A **periwinkle** n[1] (here: *Vinca minor*). **prob NEng**
    1898 *Jrl. Amer. Folkl.* 11.275, *Vinca minor* . . , blue myrtle, Cam-

bridge, Mass. **1910** Graves *Flowering Plants* 321 **CT**, Common Periwinkle. Blue Myrtle . . . Roadsides near dwellings . . escaped from cultivation.

blue nettle n
    A **nightshade**.
    1951 *PADS* 15.39, *Solanum* spp.—All the prickly-leaved nightshades
    are either blue, purple, white, or yellow nettles. **1968** *DARE* (Qu.
    S17, . . *Other kinds of plants* . . *that will cause itching and swelling*) Inf
    TX40, Blue nettles, bull nettle—ruin milk if cow gets them.

blue norther n Also infreq *blue Texas norther, blue-tailed
norther* [**blue** adj **3** + *norther* a northerly wind] **TX** See **Map**
See also **norther** Cf **blue blizzard, blue darter 1, blue whistler 2**
    A cold wind from the north that brings rapidly falling tempera-
    tures.
    c1856 in 1947 *AN&Q* 7.144 **TX**, On page 187 of the second volume of
    Ordeal of the Union, Allan Nevins, treating of the cattle country of
    Texas, refers to a record (from the University of Texas Archives) written
    by an early cattle driver. The driver speaks of a "blew-tailed norther,"
    which he encountered on a cattle drive sometime around 1856. Such
    winds, he says, were "very common in Texas 40 to 60 years ago." **1873**
    Morrell *Flowers & Fruits* 234 **TX**, A blue Texas norther whistled around
    my ears. **1942** Perry *Texas* 90, Even more Texan are the blue northers
    that sweep out of the Panhandle under a blue-black sky and sometimes
    slam the temperature down thirty or forty degrees in a single night. **1965**
    Teale *Wandering Through Winter* 160 **TX**, During one of our last days at
    Rockport, a blue norther struck. **1967**–70 *DARE* (Qu. B18, . . *Special
    kinds of wind*) 16 Infs, **TX**, Blue norther. **1970** Tarpley *Blinky* 58 **neTX**,
    A strong cold wind from the north . . . Blue norther. **1980** *AZ Highways*
    Feb 2, Missing too [from the cowboy legend] are references to . . the icy
    grip of a "blue norther."

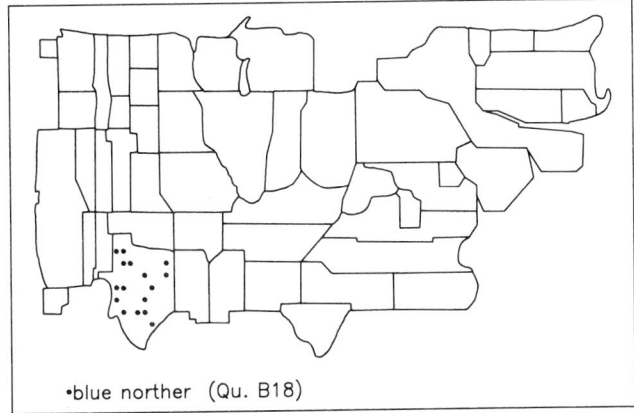

•blue norther (Qu. B18)

bluenose n, also attrib Occas *bluenoser*
    1 A native of eastern Canada, particularly Nova Scotia, and
    sometimes New Brunswick or Prince Edward Island. **chiefly
    NEng** *sometimes derog* Cf *DCan*
    1830 in 1912 Thornton *Amer. Gloss.* 79 **ceNY**, A real *"blue-nose,"* fresh
    from the land of steady habits. **1840** Haliburton *Clockmaker* (3d ser)
    152 **NEng**, I broke my leg a-ridin' a cussed Blue-nose hoss. **1873** Beadle
    Undeveloped West 711, The Yankee shudders as he thinks of the hard
    fate of the "Canucks" and "Blue-noses" of British America. **1905**
    Nation 80.105/1 **MA**, The Blue-nose fishermen would doubtless be glad
    to sell the herring direct. **1907** *DN* 3.182 **seNH**. *Ibid* 241 **eME**,
    Bluenose . . uncomplimentary. **1909** *DN* 3.408 **nME**. **1914** *DN* 4.69
    ME, nNH. **1926** *DN* 5.385 **ME**. **1931**–33 *LANE* Worksheets **MA**,
    Blue-nose . . . Nickname for a Nova Scotian. **1954** Forbes *Rainbow*
    185, **NEng**, They came from everywhere and from nowhere—Frenchies
    from Canada, Herringchokers and Bluenoses from down East.
    1966–69 *DARE* (Qu. HH28, *Names and nicknames around here for
    people of foreign background*) Infs **CA**110, **ME**13, Bluenose; **ME**1,
    Bluenose—from part of Canada; **MA**35, Bluenoses—Nova Scotians;
    MA68, Bluenose or bluenoser.
    2 A variety of potato. **chiefly NEng** *old-fash*
    1836 in 1957 Old *Farmer's Almanac Sampler* 98 **NEng**, A good, buxom
    country lass, who knows how to boil a potato, and can tell a mealy
    chenango from a bluenose. **1848** Lowell *Biglow* 21 **MA**, I'd give a year's
    pay fer a smell o' one good bluenose tater. **1872** *VT State Bd. Ag. Report*
    1.232, He . . sighs for a potato that will yield as much and cook as well as

the old Blue Noses used to do forty years ago. **1909** *DN* 3.408 **nME,** *Bluenose . . .* A kind of potato.

3 A person who is excessively puritanical; now esp one who advocates abstinence from alcoholic drinks; a teetotaler. **chiefly Nth, Pacific**

1928 Brown *In Golden Nineties* 187 **NYC,** With a lot of blue noses on the Board, . . this concession was not secured without great diplomacy. **1929** *Variety* 3 Apr 11/4 **NYC,** That this picture may aggravate blue nose censors is not beyond the bounds of possibility. **1937** *Sun* (Baltimore MD) 18 Feb 8/5 *(Hench Coll.),* He declared the attorney offered him a drink and called him a "blue nose" when he declined. **1950** *PADS* 14.15 **SC,** *Blue nose . . .* An overstrict Sabbatarian. **1965–70** *DARE* (Qu. DD33a, *A person who drinks no liquor at all)* Infs **CA**154, 168, 197, **MN**36, **WA**11, Bluenose; (Qu. DD33b, *A person who is actively against drinking)* Infs **AK**1, **CO**39, **MD**4, **NM**11, **OR**1, **SC**5, Bluenose; **NY**1, Bluenoser.

4 A toady, apple-polisher. [By assoc with **brownnose** n]

1967–70 *DARE* (Qu. II20a, *A person who tries too hard to gain somebody else's favor: "He's an awful _____."*) Infs **IL**5, 141, Bluenoser.

5 See quot.

1970 *DARE* (Qu. II23, . . *People who are, or think they are, the best society of a community: the _____)* Infs **IL**141, **MI**118, Bluenoses.

6 A variety of clam.

1883 *Leisure Hour* 252/1 *(DA),* The coarsest is the mud-clam, or blue nose, which is dug out of the mud with tongs.

blue oak n

1 =**burr oak.**

1817 Brown *Western Gaz.* 25 **IL,** Sugar maple, blue and white oak, black locust. **1966–67** *DARE* (Qu. T10) Infs **IL**11, **ND**3, Blue oak. **1979** Little *Checklist U.S. Trees* 236, *Quercus macrocarpa . . . Other common names*—blue oak, mossycup oak, mossy-overcup oak, scrub oak.

2 also *California blue oak:* A deciduous oak *(Quercus douglasii)* native to California with bluish-green foliage. Also called **hill oak, iron oak, mountain white oak, rock oak, white oak**

1869 in 1911 Muir *First Summer* 10 **sCA,** The trees, mostly the blue oak *(Quercus Douglasii),* are about thirty to forty feet high, with pale blue-green leaves and white bark. **1884** Sargent *Forests of N. Amer.* 143, *Mountain white oak. Blue oak . . .* Common on the low foot-hills of the sierras. **1908** Sudworth *Forest Trees Pacific* 285, Appropriately called blue oak on account of the blue-green color of its foliage. **1969** *DARE* (Qu. T10) Infs **CA**150, 161, Blue oak. **1979** Little *Checklist U.S. Trees* 228, *Quercus douglasii . . . Other common names*—California blue oak, iron oak, mountain white oak.

3 also *Mexican blue oak:* An evergreen oak *(Quercus oblongifolia)* native to Arizona and New Mexico. Also called **white oak**

1908 Britton *N. Amer. Trees* 320, *Blue Oak—Quercus oblongifolia . . .* The leaves are . . firm, bright bluish and shining. **1960** Vines *Trees SW* 160, *Mexican Blue Oak . . .* Tree attaining a height of 35 ft . . . *Leaves . . .* Mature ones bluish green and shiny above.

blue palm See blue palmetto 2

blue palmetto n

1 A low, clump-forming palm *(Rhapidophyllum hystrix)* native from South Carolina to Florida and Mississippi. Also called **creeping palmetto, dwarf palmetto 2, needle palmetto, porcupine palmetto, vegetable porcupine**

1861 Wood *Class-Book* 667, *Blue Palmetto . . . C[hamærops] Hystrix . . .* In clayey soils around Savannah, to Fla. **1901** Lounsberry *S. Wild Flowers* 31, Through its range many natives know this palm and familiarly speak of it as the blue palmetto. **1976** Bailey–Bailey *Hortus Third* 946, *Blue palmetto . . .* The hardiest of palms, withstanding temperature to -6° F.

2 also *blue palm:* =**dwarf palmetto 1.**

1901 Mohr *Plant Life AL* 96, The appearance of the dwarf or blue palmetto *(Sabal adansonii)* . . indicates that the subtropical region of the State has been entered. **1960** Vines *Trees SW* 48, *Sabal . . . minor . . .* Also known locally under the names of Dwarf Palmetto, Blue Palm, . . and Swamp Palm.

3 =**cabbage palm.**

1976 Bailey–Bailey *Hortus Third* 991, *Cabbage palmetto . . blue palmetto.* Trunk to 90 ft., . . lvs. green, to 6 ft. long.

blue peep See peep

blue perch n

1 =**cunner.**

1839 *MA Zool. & Bot. Surv. Fishes Reptiles* 78, *Crenilabrus* [sic] . . . *burgall . . .* Blue Perch. **1859** (1968) Bartlett *Americanisms* 58, *Burgall . . .* Other names . . are Nibbler, . . Chogset, . . and in New England, those of Blue Perch and Conner. **1887** Goode *Amer. Fishes* 297, At Provincetown they *[Ctenolabrus adspersus]* are called "Sea-perch," and at the Isle of Shoals and occasionally on the adjoining mainland, "Blue-perch." **1902** Jordan–Evermann *Amer. Fishes* 476, Other names which have been applied to it *[Tautogolabrus adspersus]* are blue perch, bergall and bergylt.

2 Usu *Embiotica lateralis* which is also called **rainbow perch, squawfish, striped perch, striped surf fish, surf fish;** but also the **black perch** (here: *Embiotica jacksoni*).

1882 U.S. Natl. Museum *Bulletin* 16.594, *D[itrema] laterale . . .* Blue Perch. **1902** Jordan–Evermann *Amer. Fishes* 472, *T[æniotoca] lateralis,* the blue perch. **1939** Natl. Geog. Soc. *Fishes* 255, Among the 22 species of viviparous perch in the family, the blue perch, *Tæniotoca lateralis,* is nearest like this species *[Embiotoca jacksoni].* **1960** Amer. Fisheries Soc. *List Fishes* 63, Blue [perch]—see . . perch, black.

3 =**black rockfish.**

1930 *Copeia* 11, They were to be seen on any clear day while fishing for blue perch *(Sebastodes mystinus).*

4 A demoiselle (here: *Chromis punctipinnis*).

1960 Amer. Fisheries Soc. *List Fishes* 63, Blue [perch]—see black-smith.

5 =**bluegill 1.**

1885 Thompson *By-Ways* 126, Speaking of bream, as the Southerners call the blue-perch, it is a royal fish. **1935** Caine *Game Fish* 11, *Bluegill Lepomis pallidus . . . Synonyms: . .* Blue Perch. **1946** LaMonte *N. Amer. Game Fishes* 138, *Lepomis macrochirus . . . Names: . .* Blue Perch.

blue Peter n Also blue Pete

1 The **purple gallinule** or **Florida gallinule. chiefly Sth, esp FL**

1709 (1967) Lawson *New Voyage* 154 **NC,** *Blue-Peters.* The same as you call Water-Hens in *England,* are here very numerous, and not regarded for eating. **1923** U.S. Dept. Ag. *Misc. Circular* 13.44, *Purple Gallinule . . . In local use.*—Blue-Peter (Mo., La.) **1954** Sprunt *FL Bird Life* 150, *Purple Gallinule: Porphyrula martinica . . .* Local Names: . . Blue Peter. *Ibid* 152, *Florida Gallinule: Gallinula chloropus cachinnens . .* Local Names: . . Blue Peter. **1955** *Oriole* 20.6, *Purple Gallinule.—Blue Peter* (latter term for its walking over water plants at the surface and thus apparently on the water). **1969** Longstreet *Birds FL* 56, *Purple Gallinule Other names:* Blue Pete.

2 =**coot** n[1] **1. Atlantic**

1888 Trumbull *Names of Birds* 118, *[Fulica americana* is] known very generally in Virginia, and southward to Florida, and less commonly in latter state at Jacksonville, St. Augustine, and Enterprise, as *Blue-Peter* (quite familiar to the older Floridians by this name). **1917** (1923) *Birds Amer.* 1.214, *Coot—Fulica americana . . . Other Names . . .* Blue Peter. **1932** Howell *FL Bird Life* 212, *American Coot: Fulica americana americana . .* Other Names: . . Blue-pete. **1950** *PADS* 14.15 **SC,** *Blue peter: . .* The American coot. **1954** Sprunt *FL Bird Life* 153, *American Coot: . . Local Names: . .* Blue-pete. **1956** *AmSp* 31.123, *Blue peter* is a name used along the Atlantic coast from Maine to Florida for the ivory-billed coot . . . The fact is that when this bird is in high plumage, the elongated feathers on the back are bluish. As it treads on floating stalks . . and splatters along on its take-off, it appears to be walking on the water. Hence *blue peter* in allusion to its color and to Peter's experience told of in Matthew 14:24–33. **1968–70** *DARE* (Qu. Q5) Infs **NC**80, 85, Blue Peter; **NY**47, Blue Peter—same as blue-head; **VA**47, Coot = chicken duck = blue Peter; **GA**20, Blue Pete—same as coot. **1969** Longstreet *Birds FL* 57, *American Coot Other names:* . . Blue-pete.

blue pickerel See blue pike 1

blue pig n [Prob erron for **blind pig**]
=**blind pig.**

1953 *AmSp* 28.12, A *blue pig* is an establishment for the sale of illicit liquor.

blue pigeon n
=**band-tailed pigeon.**

1918 Grinnell *Game Birds CA* 575, *Columba fasciata fasciata* . . . Other names—Blue Pigeon. **1923** U.S. Dept. Ag. *Misc. Circular* 13.73, *Columba fasciata* . . . *Vernacular names.*—Blue pigeon (Calif.).

blue pike n

1 also *blue pickerel, blue pikeperch:* =**walleye** or a subsp thereof. **esp eGt Lakes**
    1842 DeKay *Zool. NY* 4.19, Fishermen enumerate . . . three species or kinds. The Blue Pike . . I . . consider as an aged individual of the present species. **1947** *Detroit News* 31 Dec 3/1–2 *(Hench Coll.)*, Your fish dealer . . has fillets of perch, blue pike, yellow pike, . . and herring. **1960** Amer. Fisheries Soc. *List Fishes* 64, Pickerel . . blue—see pike, blue . . pikeperch, blue—see pike, blue. **1967–69** *DARE* (Qu. P1) Inf **NY**227, Blue pike; (Qu. P14) Infs **NY**103, 132, 227, Blue pike; **OH**16, At Fairport they go for blue pike, and perch, carp. **1967** *DARE* Tape **OH**16, Blue pike disappeared. Blue pike came back this last year or so.

2 =**muskellunge.**
    1949 Caine *N. Amer. Sport Fish* 98, Muskellunge . . . Colloquial Names . . Blue Pike. **1972** Sparano *Outdoors Encycl.* 366, *Muskellunge. Common Names:* . . pike, blue pike, . . tiger muskellunge.

blue pikeperch See **blue pike 1**

blue pill n Also *blue plum* Cf **blue lightning, blue whistler 1**
    Transf (from pill containing mercury): a bullet.
    1834 *Life Andrew Jackson* 27, They bravely pop'd their blue pills at one another at six feet distance. **1861** *NY Daily Tribune* (NY) 19 Nov 6/1 **MO**, Between blue pills, halters, and the penitentiary, we shall soon work off this element of rascaldom from the body politic. **1889** (1971) Farmer *Americanisms*, Blue pill.—A bullet; also called *blue plum.* **1942** Berrey–Van den Bark *Amer. Slang* 78.3, *Bullet.* Blue pill.

blue pimples n pl
    =**goose pimples.**
    1968 *DARE* (Qu. X58, *When you are cold, and little points of skin begin to come on your arms and legs, you have* _____) Inf **TX**40, Blue pimples.

blue plover n esp **MA**
    =**knot** n².
    1888 Trumbull *Names of Birds* 179, *[Knot]:* At Ipswich, Mass., *Buff-Breast, Blue Plover,* and *Silver-back.* **1925** (1928) Forbush *Birds MA* 1.402, *Knot . . . Other names:* . . *Gray-back; Silver-back;* . . *Blue Plover . . . Adult male in breeding plumage:* Above mainly light gray. **1956** *MA Audubon Soc. Bulletin* 40.18, *American Knot.* Blue Plover (Maine, Mass. In winter plumage, the wings and back are brownish-gray, the feathers edged with white; nothing calling for the adjective "blue."). **1969** *DARE* (Qu. Q14, . . *Other names . . for . . killdeer*) Inf **MA**57, Plover; father mentioned a blue plover ['plʌvə]—not common.

blue plum See **blue pill**

bluepoint n, also attrib Also *blue-pointer*

1 An oyster: see quot 1881.
    1789 in 1869 MA Hist. Soc. *Proc.* 11.24 **NY**, Judge Hobart . . treated us with Blue Point oysters from the shell. **1844** *Knickerbocker* 23.500 **NY**, Here we are with our Prince's Bays, . . and Blue pointers, a shilling's worth of either worth all the shell-fish that ever grew on the French coast. **1880** Twain *Tramp Abroad* 574, I have selected a few dishes, . . as follows: . . Blue points, on the half shell. **1881** Ingersoll *Oyster-Industry* 242, *Blue Points.*—Oysters originally found off Blue Point, eastern end of Great South bay [sic], Long Island, but now applied to all oysters from any part of the south shore of Long Island, whether native or transplanted, eastward of Babylon.

2 =**three-ridge.**
    1966 *WI Conserv. Bulletin* May–June 27/1, By far the most important mussel is the three-ridge or bluepoint. **1969** *DARE* (Qu. P18) Inf **RI**4, Bluepoint mussel. **1982** U.S. Fish & Wildlife Serv. *Fresh-Water Mussels* II, Threeridge. Bluepoint . . . One of the two most abundant Upper Mississippi River mussels . . in spite of commercial harvest.

blue pole bean See **blue bean**

blue pond-hen See **blue marsh-hen**

blue pop n [Fr *pape bleu*]

1 =**indigo bunting.**
    1917 *DN* 4.423 **LA**, *Blue pop.* The indigo bunting (Passerina cyanea): also called . . *pape bleu.* **1938** Oberholser *Bird Life LA* 626, *Indigo Bunting* . . . In Louisiana it is called 'blue pop', and by the French 'aveque' [sic].

2 The blue grosbeak.
    1917 (1923) *Birds Amer.* 3.69, *Blue Grosbeak . . . Other Name.*—Blue Pop. **1946** Hausman *Eastern Birds* 573, *Eastern Blue Grosbeak* . . . *Other Names*—Blue Pop.

blue poplar n Also *blue popple*
    =**tulip tree.**
    1897 Sudworth *Arborescent Flora* 198 **DE, WV,** *Liriodendron tulipifera* . . . Blue Poplar. **1900** Lyons *Plant Names* 227, L[iriodendron] Tulipifera . . . Blue Poplar. **1960** Vines *Trees SW* 280, *Liriodendron . . tulipifera . . .* Blue-poplar. **1966** *DARE* (Qu. T13, . . *Other names . . for . . tulip tree*) Inf **MS**38, Tulip poplar, blue poplar; **MA**4, Blue popple.

blue prairie-flax See **blue flax**

blue quail n **SW**
    =**scaled quail.**
    1848 Emory *Notes Reconnoissance* 62 **NM**, We saw here also, in great numbers, the blue quail. **1928** Bailey *Birds NM* 217, The . . Scaled or Blue Quail . . . whose life is spent in . . the arid cactus, mesquite, and greasewood valleys . . , is the palest of its family, its bluish gray tones presenting a striking contrast to the dark tones of . . quail living in humid, forested regions. **1939** FWP *Guide CA* 410, The Pomos dwelt here undisturbed . . weaving the plumes of the blue quail into their baskets, until white men came, trappers and cattle herders, in the 1840's. **1961** Ligon *NM Birds* 96, The Scaled Quail [is] also widely known as Blue Quail, Cottontop, Blue Racer, and Cactus Quail. **1966–69** *DARE* (Qu. Q7, . . *Other kinds of game birds*) Infs **OK**25, **TX**1, 71, Blue quail.

blue racer n

1 also *blue runner:* Either of two snakes which are subspp (and/or their intergrade) of the **racer 1:** *Coluber constrictor mormon,* found chiefly west of the Rocky Mts, but esp the "blue" *C.c. flaviventris* which ranges east of the Rocky Mts through Ohio. See *racer* in Map Section. Also called **ash snake, blue snake 1, cowsucker 1, milk snake 2, green racer, whiteoak racer**
    1886 Ebbutt *Emigrant Life* 66 **KS**, The "blue-racer" snake . . is a quick traveller; in fact, it is no sooner seen than gone, like a flash of greased lightning with the brake off. **1900** U.S. Natl. Museum *Annual Rept. for 1898* 793, Thus in Michigan the species is generally of a bluish green or greenish blue tint above, and is known as the "blue racer." **1928** Ortenburger *Whip Snakes* 213, *Coluber constrictor mormon . . . Western Yellow-bellied Racer, Green Racer, Blue Racer.* **1947** *Reader's Digest* Oct 143/2 **IN**, A blue racer came looping through the grass at me. **1965–70** *DARE* (Qu. P25) 129 Infs, **chiefly between Appalachians and Rocky Mts,** Blue racer; **LA**2, 8, 10, 15, 31, 34, **MA**26, **TN**44, **TX**9, 14, Blue runner.

2 =**scaled quail.**
    1961 Ligon *NM Birds* 96, The Scaled Quail, also widely known as . . . Blue Racer, and Cactus Quail, is listed in most bird publications as the Arizona Scaled Quail.

blue rail n
    The **purple gallinule** or **Florida gallinule.**
    1888 (1890) Warren *Birds PA* 73, All of my informants mention this Gallinule—called by sportsmen Blue Rail—as a straggler or very rare migrant. **1895** (1907) Wright *Birdcraft* 249, This Gallinule [=*Gallinula chloropus*] . . . is called Blue Rail by sportsmen because, at a little distance, the various tints of its plumage merge in a grayish blue. **1917** *DN* 4.423 **LA**, *Blue rail.* The purple gallinule (Ionornis martinicus). **1923** U.S. Dept. Ag. *Misc. Circular* 13.44, *Purple Gallinule . . . In local use . . .* blue rail (La.).

blue rice bird n
    The blue grosbeak.
    1917 *DN* 4.423 **LA**, *Blue rice bird.* The blue grosbeak (Guiraca caerulea).

blue rock n [*blue* + *rock* abbr for *rock pigeon*]
    Any of three common pigeons with bluish plumage: **band-tailed pigeon** (*Columba fasciata*), **red-billed pigeon** (*C. flavirostris*), and a color variation of *C. domestica.*
    1923 U.S. Dept. Ag. *Misc. Circular* 13.73, *Columba fasciata . . . Vernacular names* . . blue rock (Calif., Ariz., N. Mex.). **1927** Forbush *Birds MA* 2.51, *Columba domestica . . . Other names:* . . Blue Rock. **1961** Ligon *NM Birds* 131, *Columba fasciata . . .* It resembles the

domestic Pigeon, but can be distinguished by the white crescent neck stripe and uniform bluish color which gives it the designation "Blue Rock."

blue rockfish n

A **black rockfish 1** (here: *Sebastodes mystinus*).

1960 Amer. Fisheries Soc. *List Fishes* 37, Blue rockfish . . . *Sebastodes mystinus.*

‡blue room n *joc*

1950 *WELS* (An indoor toilet) 1 Inf, **cWI,** The blue room.

blue rooster See **rooster**

blue runner See **blue racer**

blue sage n

1 A blue-flowered **sage 1** (*Salvia* spp).

1791 (1958) Bartram *Travels* 261 **AL,** Observed abundance of the tall blue Sage; it grows six or seven feet high .. and .. the branches .. terminate with spikes of large flowers of a celestial blue colour. **1967** *Ozark Visitor* (Point Lookout MO) Feb 6/2, A patch of blue sage gave contrast to the white of New Jersey tea.

2 A **sagebrush** (here: *Artemisia tridentata*).

1937 U.S. Forest Serv. *Range Plant Hdbk.* B24, Big sagebrush, known locally as black sage or blue sage, . . is a large deciduous shrub with silvery green leaves.

blue sailors n

1 also *blue sailor:* =**chicory 1.** [See quot 1949]

1892 *Jrl. Amer. Folkl.* 5.99, *Cichorium Intybus* . . blue sailors. Brooklyn, N.Y. **1931** Harned *Wild Flowers Alleghanies* 485, Chicory, also commonly known as "Blue Sailor," . . came to the shores of this country like many an immigrant. **1949** Moldenke *Amer. Wild Flowers* 177, The name of *bluesailors* alludes to a . . legend of a beautiful girl who fell in love with a sailor. Her lover left her for the sea and so she sat day after day along the side of the highway looking for his return. Eventually the gods took pity on her and turned her into a chicory plant which wears sailor blue in its blossoms and still haunts roadsides in the hope of meeting the returning lover. **1967–70** *DARE* (Qu. S11) Inf **NJ4,** Blue sailor; (Qu. S26a) Inf **VA101,** Blue sailors—same as chicory. **1975** Duncan–Foote *Wildflowers SE* 226, *Blue-sailors* . . . The ground roots are roasted and used as a substitute for or to flavor coffee.

2 =**cornflower 1.**

1959 Carleton *Index Herb. Plants* 16, *Blue sailors:* Centaurea cyanus.

blue scorpion n Cf **scorpion, stinging lizard**

Either a lizard of the genus *Sceloporus,* such as the **fence lizard,** or a **blue-tailed skink.**

1969 *DARE* (Qu. R21) Inf **KY28,** Blue scorpion.

blueshanks See **bluestocking 2**

blueskin See **bluestocking 1**

blueskin oak n

=**water oak.**

1969 *DARE* (Qu. T10) Inf **KY9,** Blueskin oak—water oak.

blue snake n

1 =**blue racer 1.**

1967–68 *DARE* (Qu. P25) Inf **MO17,** Blue snake; **MO26,** Blue snake —blue racer is another name used; **OR15, TX51,** Blue snake.

2 The Texas **indigo snake** (*Drymarchon corais erebennus*).

1967 *DARE* (Qu. P25) Infs **TX1,** 13, Blue snake.

blue snapper See **snapper**

blue snow n

A light snowfall.

1967–68 *DARE* (Qu. B39) Inf **KY67,** Blue snow—when the wind's a-blowing a few flakes; **NC53,** Blue snow.

blue snowbird n

=**slate-colored junco.**

1895 Minot *Land-birds New Engl.* 230, Junco . . . Often called the Black or Blue Snow-bird, in distinction from the Snow Bunting, or "White Snow-bird." **1951** *AmSp* 26.276, The slate-colored junco, widely known as *snowbird,* has attracted additional specifying adjectives. These are . . *blue snowbird* (Maine, N.H., Vt., Mass., Mich., Iowa) . . ; *little blue snowbird* (Maine). **1962** Imhof *AL Birds* 554, Junco, Blue Snowbird, White-tailed Sparrow.

blue snow goose See **blue goose 1**

blue spiderweed n

A **scorpionweed** (here: *Phacelia congesta*).

1951 *PADS* 15.38 **TX,** *Phacelia congesta* . . . Blue spiderweed.

blue-spotted sunfish See **blue sunfish 1**

blue spruce n

Std: a spruce (*Picea pungens*) with bluish-green foliage which is native to the western US, but widely planted elsewhere in the country. Also called **Colorado spruce, silver spruce, white spruce**

blue squash See **blue hubbard squash**

blue star n

1 A plant of the chiefly southern genus *Amsonia.* Also called **blue dogbane**

1933 Small *Manual SE Flora* 1059, *Amsonia* . . . Corolla mainly salverform, blue or purple-blue . . . *Blue-stars.* **1964** Batson *Wild Flowers SC* 94, *Blue Star* . . . Flowers ½ in. wide, blue and in terminal cluster. **1972** Brown *Wildflowers LA* 142, *Blue-star* . . . Common and widespread, wet sites in alluvial pineland and prairie soils.

2 A **blue-eyed grass 1** (here: *Sisyrinchium angustifolium*).

1973 Hitchcock–Cronquist *Flora Pacific NW* 698, Blue-eyed grass, blue star, eye-bright . . . *S. angustifolium.*

blue stargrass See **star grass**

bluestem n

1 =**beardgrass.**

1906 Rydberg *Flora CO* 20, *Andropogon* . . . Beard-grass, Blue-stem. **1929** Dickson *Covered Wagon Days* 191 **MT** (as of 1864), I was not a little proud of my skill as the lush bluestem and redtop, waist high, fell in neat windrows at the swing of my scythe. **1939** FWP *Guide KS* 11, Bluestem has the greatest forage value, and both species—big and little bluestem, also known as bluejoint turkeyfoot and prairie beardgrass— grow in almost all parts of the State. **1965–70** *DARE* (Qu. L7, *A piece of land with a hay crop planted on it*) Inf **OK49,** Bluestem meadow; (Qu. L9a) Infs **KS20, LA15, OK1,** 10, 18, Bluestem. **1966** *DARE* File **csWI,** The most beautiful sight of all is the Curtis prairie which lies between shrub clusters that border Arboretum Drive and the Leopold pines. Prairie grasses (big bluestem, little bluestem, and Indian grass) change color in the fall. **1970** Correll *Plants TX* 192, *Andropogon* . . . Bluestem.

2 also *bluestem wheatgrass, Colorado bluestem:* A **wheatgrass** (here: *Agropyron smithii*).

1912 Wooton–Standley *Grasses NM* 153, *Agropyron smithii.* Colorado Blue-stem. **1937** U.S. Forest Serv. *Range Plant Hdbk.* G5, Bluestem [*Agropyron smithii*], . . sometimes called Colorado bluestem, . . and western wheatgrass, is one of the commonest and most abundant of the western wheatgrasses. **1973** Hitchcock–Cronquist *Flora Pacific NW* 616, Bluestem w[heatgrass] . . . *A. smithii*

3 See **blueweed 1.**

4 A dwarf palmetto (here: *Sabal minor*).

1933 Small *Manual SE Flora* 240, *S. minor* . . . Dwarf-palmetto. *Blue-stem.* **1960** Vines *Trees SW* 48, *Sabal . . . minor* . . . Also known locally under the names of Dwarf Palmetto, . . Blue Stem, and Swamp Palm.

bluestem wheatgrass See **bluestem 2**

bluestocking n, also attrib

1 also *blueskin,* freq attrib: A Christian, esp a Presbyterian, who adheres to a strict moral code. [See quot 1848] *sometimes derog*

1790 Tyler *Contrast* 30 **NYC,** It is no shame, my dear Blueskin, for a man to amuse himself with a little gallantry. **1829** Royall *Pennsylvania* 1.152, The sole and all-weighing cause of my partiality for the Germans, is their aversion to the grey coats, or, as they are called in Pennsylvania, *blue stockings.* [Footnote:] They have a number of names here, as in other States, "Grey-backs, Round-heads, etc." **1848** Bartlett *Americanisms* 38, [On the restoration of Charles II . . . The epithet *blue* was applied to any one who looked with disapprobation on the licentiousness of the times. The Presbyterians, under which name all dissenters were often included, as they still dared to be the advocates of decency, were more particularly designated by this term.] *Ibid* 39, *Blue-Skins.* A nickname applied to the Presbyterians, from their alleged grave deportment. **1868** *Harper's Mag.* 36.267/1 **NYC,** A Presbyterian minister of the genuine old "blue stocking" school.   **1967** *N. Chester Co. Herald* (Honey Brook PA) 31 May 2/1, Mattie J. was . . a "blue stocking" Presbyterian who wouldn't comb her hair or wash her face on Sunday. **1967–68** *DARE* (Qu. CC14, . . *Nicknames . . for various . . religious groups*) Inf **KS**13, Bluestocking Catholics—Episcopalians; **PA**27, Bluestocking Presbyterians; **VA**5, Bluestocking—a Presbyterian.

2 also *bluelegs, blueshanks:* The American avocet *(Recurvirostra americana).*   Also called **English curlew, Irish snipe, lawyer bird, never-sweat, sicklebill, tilter, white curlew, white snipe**

1844 DeKay *Zool. NY* 2.267, The American Avoset, or Blue-stocking as it is called in New Jersey, is a scarce bird on the shores of this State. **1892** *Outing* 20.457/1 **CT**, A lonely blue-stocking, the first of its kind I had seen in many a year, stood motionless by a bed of rock-weed. **1917** *DN* 4.423 **LA**. **1951** Pough *Audubon Water Bird* 320, Blue-legs . . . Blueshanks . . . Bluestocking. See Avocet. **1953** Jewett *Birds WA* 283, *American Avocet . . .* Other names: . . Blue-stocking . . . Feet and legs bluish.

blue sucker n
=**Missouri sucker.**
1820 Rafinesque *Ohio R. Fishes* 58, The blue sucker *(Cycleptus elongatus).* **1957** Trautman *Fishes* 221, *Blue Sucker—Cycleptus elongatus.* **1960** Amer. Fisheries Soc. *List Fishes* 17, Blue sucker . . . *Cycleptus elongatus.* **1966** *DARE* (Qu. P14) Inf **AR**36, Fish on snag lines for blue sucker, buffalo, catfish, croppie.

blue sunfish n
1 also *blue-spotted sunfish:* =**green sunfish.**
1820 Rafinesque *Ohio R. Fishes* 28, Blue Sunfish . . . Appearing entirely blue at a distance. **1896** U.S. Natl. Museum *Bulletin* 47.996, *Apomotis Cyanellus . . .* Blue-spotted Sunfish. **1946** LaMonte *N. Amer. Game Fishes* 138, *Green Sunfish—Lepomis cyanellus . . .* Names: . . Blue-spotted Sunfish . . Blue Sunfish.

2 =**bluegill 1.**
1975 Evanoff *Catch More Fish* 88, The bluegill *(Lepomis macrochirus)* is . . also called the . . blue sunfish.

blue swallow n
1 also *blue-backed swallow:* A **tree swallow, cliff swallow,** or similar bird.
1946 Hausman *Eastern Birds* 412, *Tree Swallow . . . Other Names . .* Blue-backed Swallow, Stump Swallow. **1968–70** *DARE* (Qu. Q20, . . *Kinds of swallows*) Inf **TN**53, Blue swallow; **AK**9, Blue swallow—in banks of rivers; **MD**15, Blue swallow—small, bluish.

2 =**purple martin.**
1968–70 *DARE* (Qu. Q20, . . *Kinds of swallows*) Inf **LA**26, Blue swallow = purple martin; **VA**46, Blue swallow (martin).

blue swamp-lily See blue lily

bluet n
1 =**farkleberry.**
a1718 (1864) Perrot *Mémoire* 52, On y ramasse cependant des bluets dans les mois d'aout et de septembre. [However, one collects bluets there in the months of August and September.] **1897** Sudworth *Arborescent Flora* 312 **LA**, *Vaccinium arboreum . . .* Tree Huckleberry . . Bluet.

2 A plant of the genus *Houstonia.* Also called **baby's breath 2e, baby tear, blue john 4, chickweed 4, diamond flower, innocence, Quaker ladies, skybloom, star violet, Venus' pride, wild forget-me-not.** For other names of the common *H. cærulea* see **angel-eyes, blue-eyed babies, blue-eyed grass 2, bright-eyes, eye-bright, little washerwomen, mayflower, nuns, Quaker bonnets, skyflower, starflower, starlights, star-of-Bethlehem**
1821 Barton *Flora* 1.119, Fairy-flax. Bluett. Innocence. Venus' Pride. **1843** Torrey *Flora NY* 1.315, *Hedyotis caerulea . . .* Common Bluets. Dwarf Risk. **1905** *DN* 3.4 c**CT**, *Bluet . . . Oldenlandia caerulea.* **1907** *DN* 3.241, *Bluet . . .* Houstonia caerulea; innocence. **1941** Walker *Lookout* 50 **TN**, Bluets . . persist on the sides and top of the mountain. **1965–70** *DARE* (Qu. S11) 88 Infs, scattered, but esp NEast, Bluet(s); (Qu. S23) Infs **MA**39, **NH**4, 14, **NY**21, 30, **OH**5, 72, Bluets; (Qu. S26a, d) Infs **MA**5, 71, Bluets. **1966–68** *DARE* Wildfl QR Pl.209b Inf **NH**4, Bluets; **NY**91, Bluets or Quaker ladies. **1967** Borland *Hill Country* 120 nw**CT**, In the meadow that sloped down to the bog were a few patches of bluets, *Houstonia caerulea,* which some call Quaker Ladies and some call Innocence.

3 A bachelor's button.
1950 *WELS* (Other names for . . bachelor's button) 1 Inf, cs**WI**, Bluet.

bluetail See bluetail hawk, bluetail fly 1

blue-tailed skink n Also *blue-tail(ed) lizard*
Any of several lizards of the genus *Eumeces.* See also **scorpion**
1743 (1754) Catesby *Nat. Hist. Carolina* 2.67, *Lacertus cauda caerulea. The Blue-Tail Lizard . . .* They are seen often on the Ground, and frequent hollow Trees . . . They are found in *Virginia* and *Carolina.* **1842** DeKay *Zool. NY* 3.29, *Blue-tailed Skink . . .* This harmless little animal, miscalled the *Blue-tailed Lizard* and *Striped Lizard,* is not uncommon in the Southern Counties of the State. **c1940** Newman *Conserv. Notes* 5 **LA**, There are . . alligators, blue-tailed lizards, chameleons. **1967** *Ozark Visitor* (Point Lookout MO) Feb 6/3, A blue tailed skink slithered under a decaying log.

bluetail fly n
1 also *bluetail, blue-tailed fly:* See quots. Cf **bluebottle fly**
1849 Howe *Glee Book* 165 (DA), De 'skeeters bites ye through your close, De gallinipper sweeten high, But wusser yet de blue tail fly. **1965** *AN&Q* 3.105 s**IL**, In short, the blue-tail fly is the good, old-fashioned horse-fly of eastern America. **1966–69** *DARE* (Qu. R12) Inf **CT**31, Bluetail fly—they're green; **MD**9, Bluetail fly—smaller than horsefly, larger than housefly, bluish in color; it bites, hangs around animals and near water; **MA**6, Horsefly—similar to bluetail; **VA**15, Bluetail; (Qu. R13) Inf **CA**87, Blue-tailed fly.

2 =**dragonfly.**
1968 *DARE* (Qu. R2, . . *Other names . . for the dragonfly*) Inf **IA**32, Bluetail fly.

bluetail hawk n Also *bluetail, blue-tailed hawk* esp KY, sIN, NC
Usu **Cooper's hawk,** but also the **sharp-shinned hawk.**
1859 Taliaferro *Fisher's R.* 117 nw**NC**, 'Gius had his eye on her like a blue-tailed hawk watchin' a chicken. **1867** Harris *Sut Lovingood Yarns* 250 **TN**, Yere's the blue-tail hawk, an' he's a-flyin low. **1954** Harder *Coll.* cw**TN**, Blue-tail hawk. **c1960** *Wilson Coll.* cs**KY**, Blue-tailed hawk . . . Either the Sharp-shinned or the Cooper's persecuted endlessly for its actual or imagined depredations on poultry. **1965–70** *DARE* (Qu. Q4, . . *Kinds of hawks . . around here*) 13 Infs, esp **KY**, s**IN**, **NC**, Bluetail hawk; **IN**33, Blue-tailed hawk. **1969** Longstreet *Birds FL* 41, *Cooper's Hawk. Other names . . .* Bluetail.

bluetail lizard See blue-tailed skink

bluetail wasp See blue wasp

blue tangle n Cf **tangleberry**
=**dangleberry 1.**
1848 Gray *Manual of Botany* 259, *G[aultheria] frondosa . . .* Blue Tangle. **1903** Small *Flora SE U.S.* 892, *Gaylussacia frondosa . . .* Blue Tangle. **1960** Vines *Trees SW* 814, Blue Tangle.

blue thistle n
=**viper's bugloss.**
1822 Eaton *Botany* 270, *Echium . . . vulgare* (viper's bugloss, blue thistle . .). **1843** Torrey *Flora NY* 2.84, Blue-weed, Viper's Bugloss, [or] Blue Thistle. **1937** (1963) Hyatt *Kiverlid* 79 **KY**, We picked wild mustard an' . . blue-thistle. **1968–70** *DARE* (Qu. S21) Infs **WV**17, **VA**43, Blue thistle(s); (Qu. S26e) Infs **NY**213, **VA**26, Blue thistle.

bluetick n, also attrib [*blue + tick* a dot, speck] Sth, Midl
An American hound having a white coat with bluish gray flecks or blotches.
1959 Faulkner *Mansion* 7 **MS**, That big Bluetick hound running like a greyhound or another horse along beside it. **1966–70** *DARE* Tape **KY**75, Some of 'em they call bluetick, which is a kind of a blue hound with dark spots in 'em; **LA**2, The catahoula cur, that's a cur and this bluetick is a hound; **LA**3, The black-and-tan and bluetick and redbone, they're slower. They're more used for coon dogs; **NC**30, Bluetick; **PA**35, Bluetick coon dog. **1967** *Northwest Signal* (Napoleon OH) 15 Nov 10/7, Blue tick male dog lost west of Napoleon.

bluetip hawk See bluewing hawk

blue toadflax n
A blue-flowered **toadflax** (here: *Linaria canadensis*). Also called **harebell, old-field toadflax**
1931 Harned *Wild Flowers Alleghanies* 443, Blue Toad Flax *(L. canadensis . .).* is . . a near relative of the commoner "Butter and Eggs." **1951** *PADS* 15.40 **TX**, *Linaria texana . . .* blue toad-flax. **1972** Brown *Wildflowers LA* 167, *Blue Toadflax . . .* A common weed in disturbed soils, flower beds, and idle areas.

blue tulip n

=**pasqueflower.**

1932 Rydberg *Flora Prairies* 333, *Pulsatilla [Anemone]* . . Blue Tulip. **1963** Craighead *Rocky Mt. Wildflowers* 54, *Pasqueflower—Anemone patens* . . Other names: . . Blue Tulip.

blue vein n

A varicose vein.

1967–68 *DARE* (Qu. AA29, . . *The blue, swollen veins that a woman often gets on her legs while expecting a baby*) Infs **CA**106, **LA**12, **OH**43, **WV**2, Blue veins.

blue wasp n Also *blue mud wasp, bluetail wasp* **esp Nth**

A **mud dauber** (here: esp *Chalybion californicum*).

1939 *LANE* Map 239 *(Wasp)* 6 Infs, **CT, MA, VT**, Blue wasp . . . some regard it as distinct from the *mud wasp.* **1949** Palmer *Nat. Hist.* 433, *Chalybion californicum* . . . Pupa of blue wasp, silk-covered. **1949** Swain *Insect Guide* 178, Blue Mud Wasp *Chalybion caeruleum* Widely distributed in our region. **1966–69** *DARE* (Qu. R20, *Wasps that build their nests of mud*) Inf **NY**71, Mud wasp or blue wasp; They are black, make a roundish mud nest; **NY**133, Blue wasp—very thin wings; **PA**70, There is a blue wasp around here; (Qu. R21) Infs **IL**7, **NY**71, 83, **OH**84, **WI**12, Blue wasp; **MA**6, Bluetail wasp—a blue wasp.

blue wavey See **blue goose 1**

blueweed n

1 also *bluestem:* =**viper's bugloss.** [*EDD* 1750 →]

1837 Darlington *Flora Cestrica* 119, *Echium* . . . *vulgare* . . . Vulgo—Blue weed. Viper's Bugloss. Blue Devils . . . This vile foreign weed is extremely troublesome in some portions of our Country. **1843** Torrey *Flora NY* 2.84, Blue-weed, Viper's Bugloss, [or] Blue Thistle . . ; rare: introduced from Europe. A very ornamental plant when in full flower, but sometimes a troublesome weed. **1894** *Jrl. Amer. Folkl.* 7.95, *Echium vulgare* . . blue weed, blue stem, West Va. . . blue weed, Iowa. **1897** *Ibid* 10.51, *Echium vulgare* . . blue weed, Jackson County, Mo. **1912** Mathews *Amer. Wild Flowers* 382, Sometimes called blueweed, and in fact a flower sufficiently approaching a blue tone to justify the name. **1949** Moldenke *Amer. Wild Flowers* 258, One of the worst pests to farmers in some sections between Nova Scotia and Ontario in the North and Georgia and Nebraska in the South and West is the *vipersbugloss,* . . usually just spoken of as *blueweed.* **1969** *DARE* (Qu. S26a) Inf **NY**209, Blueweed—blue flowers on it, long straight root; **NY**213, Blueweed [FW sugg].

2 =**chicory 1.**

1877 Bartlett *Americanisms* 53, *Blue Weed (Chicorium).* Wild endive, bearing a large dark-blue flower. New England. **1925** Jepson *Manual Plants CA* 990, Chicory . . . Also called Blueweed. **1968–70** *DARE* (Qu. S21, . . *Other weeds* . . *that are a trouble in gardens and fields*) Inf **MD**30, Blueweed—chicory; (Qu. S25) Inf **MD**20, Blueweeds; (Qu. S26a) Inf **NJ**69, Blueweed [FW: chicory]. **1971** GA Dept. Ag. *Farmers Market Bulletin* 10 Feb 8/1, Chicory . . . succory, blueweed, blue dandelion.

3 A plant of the genus *Aconitum.*

1897 Parsons *Wild Flowers CA* 328, Aconite . . Our own species is also poisonous, and among the mountaineers it is called "blueweed," and remembered only for its disastrous effect upon their sheep. **1915** (1926) Armstrong *Western Wild Flowers* 136, Aconite is the ancient Greek name and other common names are Blueweed and Friar's-cap.

4 also *Texas blueweed:* A sunflower (here: *Helianthus ciliaris*) native to the Southwest.

1935 Muenscher *Weeds* 498, *Helianthus ciliaris* . . , Blue-weed, a native perennial of the grasslands of the Southwest, causes considerable trouble in cultivated land in western Texas. **1967–70** *DARE* (Qu. S21) Infs **TX**43, 78, Blueweed. **1968** Barkley *Plants KS* 358, Blueweed. Texas Blueweed. Cultivated fields, scattered, north central. **1970** Correll *Plants TX* 1651, *Blue-weed* . . Locally abundant near streams or canals, often in subalkaline desert soil.

5 A sea oxeye (here: *Borrichia frutescens*).

1971 Craighead *Trees S. FL* 199, Blueweed (sea daisy), *Borrichia frutescens.*

blue whistler n

1 A bullet. Cf **blue pill**

1843 (1969) Lewis *Odd Leaves* 44 **MS**, I determined to go this time for the "antlered monarch," by loading one barrel with fifteen "blue whistlers," reserving the other for small game. **1894** *Outing* 23.439/1

Sth, Didn't they all watch me count the blue-whistlers for my gun? **1944** Adams *Western Words, Blue whistler*—A bullet, so called because of the blue frame of the pistol. [Ed. questions explan; ref is prob to lead of bullets.]

2 =**blue norther.** **chiefly OK, TX**

1929 Dobie *Vaquero* 278 **TX**, No one who has not experienced a blue whistler on the open prairies of West Texas really knows what a cold north wind is like. **1932** *Durant Daily Democrat* (OK) (*AmSp* 8.1.80), The blue whistler that come [sic] up Friday night sure came from the north pole Saturday and Sunday. **1933** *AmSp* 8.1.80 **OK**, A *blue whistler* is a bitter norther. The people at large think the term refers to the peculiar blue of the atmosphere which accompanies the cold, and to the whistling of the wind around the houses, trees, and telephone poles. **1944** Adams *Western Words, Blue whistler* . . . A norther. **1967** *DARE* (Qu. B18, . . *Special kinds of wind*) Inf **TX**37, Norther—a bad one is a blue whistler.

3 By ext, among oil-field workers: see quot.

1949 *AmSp* 24.34 **OK, TX**, Producing [oil] wells may be *blue whistlers,* . . *gushers,* . . or *wild wells.*

4 See quot.

1981 Harper–Presley *Okefinokee* 136 (as of a1951), Referring to turpentine barrels with a sixty-gallon capacity, Uncle Lone Thrift said, "We call 'em blue whistlers."

blue wine n

Homemade wine from concord grapes.

1967 *DARE* Tape IL5, The blue wine is pressed real hard and tight.

bluewing n

The blue-winged teal.

1714 (1860) Lawson *Hist. Carolina* 243, The blue-wings are less than a duck, but fine meat. **1768** (1925) Washington *Diaries* 1.294 **VA**, Went into the Neck and up the Creek after Blew Wings. **1874** J.W. Long *Amer. Wild-fowl Shooting* xv.192 (*OEDS*), They are a trifle smaller than the blue-wings. **1982** Elman *Hunter's Field Guide* 163, *Blue-winged Teal* . . . *Common & Regional Names:* bluewing, summer teal, fall teal, autumn teal, southern teal, white-faced teal, breakfast duck . . . Blue-wings often fly in moderately large flocks, and a group numbering more than a score can remain tightly massed.

bluewing darter See **blue darter 2**

blue-winged blackbird n Also *bluewing ~*

Prob Brewer's blackbird (*Euphagus cyanocephalus*).

1968 *DARE* (Qu. Q11, . . *Kinds of blackbirds*) Inf **MN**34, Blue-winged; **KS**15, Blue-winged blackbird; **NV**6, Bluewing—old-fashioned, . . by the color spot on the wing.

blue-winged goose See **blue goose 1**

bluewing hawk n Also *bluetip hawk*

Prob =**blue darter 2.**

1967–70 *DARE* (Qu. Q4) Inf **MO**3, Bluewing hawk; **VA**38, Bluewing hawk—small; **LA**15, Bluewing hawk—wingspread about eighteen inches [FW: I believe this is comparable with the blue darter]; **MS**66, Bluetip hawk.

bluewood n [See quot 1960]

A thicket-forming, black-fruited shrub or tree (*Condalia hookeri*) native to Texas. Also called **brasil, chaparral, logwood, purple haw**

1884 Sargent *Forests of N. Amer.* 4, *Condalia obovata,* . . Blue Wood, Log Wood, Purple Haw. **1897** Sudworth *Arborescent Flora* 297, *Condalia obovata* . . . *Bluewood* . . . *Common Names.* Bluewood (Tex.). **1939** Tharp *Vegetation TX* 61, Bluewood; Purple Haw (*Condalia*). **1960** Vines *Trees SW* 697, Other vernacular names are . . Bluewood . . and Chaparral. The wood yields a blue dye and is sometimes used as fuel.

blueworm See **bluebait**

bluff n[1]

A clump or grove of trees growing in open country. [The shift in meaning from *bluff,* a high steep usu wooded bank, prob occurred independently in the two regions.]

a chiefly Sth

1796 in 1953 McMullen *Topog. Terms FL* 74, Seven miles to the eastward of Boca Chica there is a *Small Island* with a remarkable high bluff of trees, which in most views appear *in the shape of a saddle.* **1874** *Ibid* 75, We soon passed Long Bluff, a grove of palmettoes half a mile in length . . . Possum Bluff is a charming island, alive with opossums and alligators. **1971** Wood *Vocab. Change* 34 **Sth,** An isolated group of trees growing in open country . . . *Bluff* in this sense is more frequent east of the Mississippi than west of it.

b chiefly ND, WI [See quots 1958 and 1967; cf *DCan*]

[**1938** *Jrl. Amer. Folkl.* 51.67 **swOntario Canada,** 'Bluffs'—clumps of trees.] **1958** *PADS* 30.9, *Bluff,* peculiar only to the extreme northern border area [of the Upper Midwest], is a Canadian immigrant. Reported by correspondents as common in Saskatchewan and Alberta with reference to a clump of trees on the level open prairie, this term has understandably eased itself into North Dakota over the easily crossed boundary. **1966–68** *DARE* (Qu. T1, *. . A bunch of trees growing together in open country, especially on a hill*) Infs **WI**22, 54, Bluff; (Qu. T2a, *. . A piece of land with trees—if it's only a few acres*) Inf **ND**3, Bluff. [**1967** *Engl. Lang. Notes* 5.49, The shift of meaning from land formation to trees appears to have taken place during the 1860's and in the area of southern Manitoba then known as the Red River Settlement. The process would appear to be one of synecdoche . . . That is, the term for the land elevation seems to have become associated with the trees that grew upon it and was finally attached to the trees alone.]

‡**bluff** n² [Prob blend of *bluster* or *blast* and *puff*]

A gust (of wind).

1942 (1960) Robertson *Red Hills* 250 **SC,** "I heard the first bluff," Mary said, "for if there's anything that wakes me it is a wind."

bluff v

1 To feign (illness). **chiefly Nth** See Map

1965–70 *DARE* (Qu. BB27, *When somebody pretends to be sick . . you'd say he's _____*) 21 Infs, **scattered,** Bluffing; **IL**28, Bluffing off.

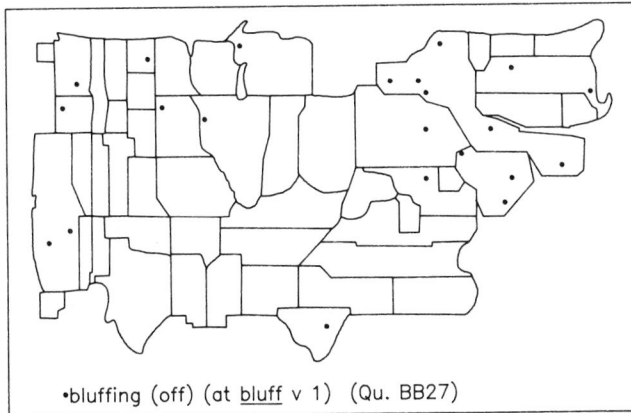

•bluffing (off) (at <u>bluff</u> v 1) (Qu. BB27)

2 To faze, disconcert (someone).

1967–68 *DARE* (Qu. Y2, *Other words for upsetting or disturbing somebody: "Losing all that money didn't seem to _____ him a bit."*) Inf **IN**9, Bluff; (Qu. GG9, *To suddenly embarrass somebody and throw him off balance: "When they told him what she had said about him, it certainly did _____ him."*) Infs **MO**36, **TX**40, Bluff.

bluff lettuce n

A succulent plant (*Dudleya farinosa*) of the stonecrop family native from coastal central California to southern Oregon. Also called **hen-and-chickens, live-forever, stonecrop**

1925 Jepson *Manual Plants CA* 452, *C. farinosa . . . Bluff lettuce . . .* Flowers cream-white, on very short stout pedicels . . . Bluffs along the ocean. **1954** *CA Div. Beaches & Parks Pt. Lobos Wild Flowers* 19, *Bluff Lettuce . . .* Thick, angular, basal leaves are covered with a white, sticky, powder-like substance. **1982** *Modern Maturity* June–July 53 **cwCA,** Atop less buffeted ridges, tawny bluff lettuce clings to crevices and flowers in meadows.

blugeons n [Prob blend of *blue* + **flugens** n] *rare*

=**flugens** n.

1969 *PADS* 52.43 **Olney IL** (as of 1876), "It was cold as blugeons." . . Another citation of *flugens . .* suggests a possible source of *blugens* as a portmanteau formation: "cold as blue flugins" (Winchester, Kentucky).

blum adj

=**blasted.**

1901 *DN* 2.136 **c,nNY,** *Blum* [blʌm] . . . Variant of blame in same use, "not a blum thing."

blumpsack See **bloom-sock**

blunderbus n [From *blunder* to move unsteadily, an error or mistake, with pun on *blunderbuss* a gun] *joc*

A vehicle: see quots.

1928 *AmSp* 4.132 **NE,** An automobile is a "blunderbus" or a "blixen bus." **1966** *DARE* (Qu. N42, *Vehicles for a baby or small child*) Inf **NH**10, Blunderbus.

blundershoot See **bumbershoot**

blunt n¹

1913 *DN* 4.55 **Cape Cod MA,** *Blunts . . .* The older quahogs, which are worn round by tidal scour. "Good rakin' out in the channel?" "No, nothin' but blunts."

blunt n² Freq in phr *bear the blunt* [Alter of *brunt*] **chiefly S Midl**

Blame; consequences.

1939 *Hall Coll.* **eTN,** The poor old driver . . always bore the blunt. **1966–69** *DARE* (Qu. JJ40, *When you admit that you did something wrong and are willing to take the consequences, you might say: "It was my fault and I'm willing to _____."*) Infs **AR**35, **KY**41, **NC**61, Bear the blunt; **IN**83, Stand the blunt.

blur-eyed adj

1899 (1912) Green *VA Folk-Speech, Blur-eyed . . .* Blear eyed.

blursh See **brush** n, v¹ **A4**

‡**blurt** n [Perh from *blurt* an abrupt outburst]

1974 Peden *Speak to Earth* 23 **IN,** Grace Mitchell's grandfather used to say, "Maybe it won't work, but anyway I'm going to hit it a blurt."

‡**blusteriner** adj Cf **-er** compar suff

More blustering.

1898 Westcott *Harum* 163 **cNY,** It don't appear to me 's if I ever see a blusteriner day, 'n I ain't as strong as I used to be.

bluster up v phr

1946 *PADS* 5.11 **VA,** *(Be) blustering up . . .* Of the weather, look stormy; used among older people, rare.

blutter adj [Prob alter of obs *bluter* dirty, but cf Scots *bluiter, blutter* filth in a liquid state] *relic*

1952 Brown *NC Folkl.* 1.521, *Blutter . . .* Dirty, unclean.

blutz See **blotz**

blutz wagon n [Alter of **blotz** + *wagon*] **PaGer area**

See quots.

1950 Klees *PA Dutch* 281, *Blutz-wagon,* a farm wagon without springs. **1967** *DARE* FW Addit **Kutztown PA,** A "blutz wagon" is a spring wagon.

bo n Also sp *boh* [Uncert: perh abbr of **bozo** or *hobo;* perh an independent word, the base of *hobo* and **bozo;** cf *beau,* and *bro* at **brother A1**]

A fellow, buddy—usu used as a term of address.

1893 *Chicago Record* 14 July 11/3 (*OEDS*), An' den w'en ye meets one uv yer own kind ye feels like old pals, 'cause he calls ye 'Ho' an' ye call him 'Bo'. See? **1916** *DN* 4.272 **NE, MA, PA,** *Bo . . .* Used to men or boys, in direct address. "The swaggerest rag you can put on, bo, is one of the new non-skid, full-dress shirt bosoms." . . "Keep the change, bo." **1928** McKay *Home to Harlem* 22 **seNY** [Black], I ain't told no nigger but you, boh. **1966–68** *DARE* (Qu. II10a, *Asking directions of somebody on the street when you don't know his name—what you'd say to a boy: "Say, _____, where's the post office?"*) Inf **GA**7, Bo; (Qu. II10b, *. . To a man: "Say, _____, how far is it to the next town?"*) Infs **GA**7, 30, Bo.

B.O. adj [Acronym for *bad order*]

In iron mining, of a piece of machinery: malfunctioning.

1978 Kalibabky *Hawdaw* **neMN,** B.O.: bad order . . . "Go up to da warehouse up dere an' go get a new junction box. Dis one's B.O."

boag See **bogue** v

boal n [Alter of Scots *bole*]

1930 Shoemaker *1300 Words* 5 **cPA Mts** (as of c1900), *Boal*—A small press, or cupboard in the wall.

boar n attrib **chiefly Sth, S Midl** Cf **buck** n¹ **1**

A male animal.

a in *boar cat:* A male cat.

 1899 (1912) Green *VA Folk-Speech,* Boar-cat . . . A he-cat; a male cat. **1915** *DN* 4.181 **swVA,** Boar-cat . . . Tom-cat. **1951** Porter *Ragged Roads* 6 **wNC, eTN,** The din . . sounded like boar cats fightin' in garbage cans.

b in *boar hog, ~ pig:* A male pig; boar. See Map

 1908 *DN* 3.292 **eAL, wGA,** Bo(ar)-hog. **1915** *DN* 4.181 **swVA,** Boar-hog. **1928** Peterkin *Scarlet Sister Mary* 270 **SC,** Grinning tusks like a boar hog. **1939** *LANE* Map 206 **scattered throughout NEng,** The map shows the terms *boar, boar hog, boar pig.* **1942** Rawlings *Cross Creek* 106 **FL,** Now I'm carrying that sow there to Mr. Martin's boar hog. **1965–70** *DARE* (Qu. K52, *A male pig kept for breeding is a _____*) 31 Infs, **chiefly C Atl, Sth,** Boar hog; **MD38, MO26, OH81, SC43, WI14,** Boar pig. **1973** Allen *LAUM* 1.241 **SD,** [1 informant] Boar hog. *Ibid* 249 **scattered throughout Upper MW,** Boar pig.

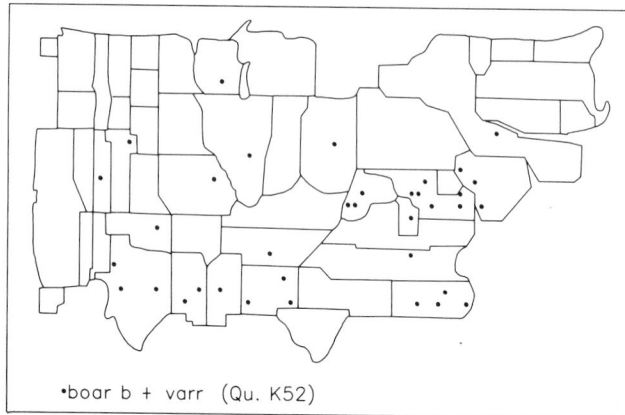

•boar b + varr (Qu. K52)

c in var combs: The male of any of numerous other, usu small, animals; see quots.

 1899 Edwards *Defense* 211 **GA,** Peter, bless goodness, dat sho' big bo' possum. **1902** *DN* 2.229 **sIL,** Boar . . . The male of any small animals. The male fox, however, is called *dog fox.* **1907** *DN* 3.220 **nwAR,** Boar. **1929** Dobie *Vaquero* 260 **TX,** We jumped a big boar panther out in the shinnery and the whole outfit, eighteen or twenty of us, spurred in after it. **1941** Faherty *Big Old Sun* 54 *(Hench Coll.),* Run down the road loud and fast as number-six shot whistling sideways across a boar possum's arse. **1947** Ballowe *The Lawd* 222 **LA,** Handy's leg began to hurt. He hoped that the coon was a she one. The teeth of boar coons are rank poison. **1951** Porter *Ragged Roads* 101 **wOK,** One little fellow, scarcely bigger than a boar coon. **1958** Humphrey *Home from the Hill* 58 **TX,** One big old boar squirrel was hopping up and down. **1975** Newell *If Nothin' Don't Happen* 120 **nwFL,** One time the catch dogs bayed up a big old boar panther back in sort of a cave in the riverbank.

board n, also attrib **chiefly Sth, S Midl** Cf **board tree**

 A riven piece of wood, usu about three feet long, used for siding and roofing; a shingle.

 1650 (1923) Bland *New Brittaine* 7 **VA,** Which will make twenty Cuts of Board timber. **1853** Hammett *Stray Yankee in TX* 65, This same camp was . . formed by setting up a few crotches to sustain a rude roof of undressed shingles, . . there known as "boards." **1902** *DN* 2.229 **sIL.** **1903** *DN* 2.307 **seMO,** Board . . . A long shingle split out but not shaved . . . Generally used in covering log houses, stables, etc. Sawed lumber is always 'plank.' **1907** *DN* 3.220 **nwAR, sIL.** **1917** *DN* 4.408 **wNC, KY.** **1923** *DN* 5.201 **swMO.** **1941** FWP *Guide AR* 104, The farmer would set his shingle block, take his frow, and split "boards," as the hand-rived shingles are called. **1950** *PADS* 14.15 **SC,** Board . . . A shake, a quarter to a half inch in thickness, from four to five inches wide and three to four feet long, split from an oak block (not sawed), and used for roofing barns, sheds, and other outhouses. **c1960** *Wilson Coll.* **csKY.**

board v

 See quots.

 1941 FWP *Guide MI* 395, A man found guilty of stealing a cow bell was sentenced to "bend over a huge log and let each person present give him a severe blow on the rotundity of the body with a piece of board four feet long and six inches wide." Apparently the whole town turned out, and the culprit was boarded almost to death. **1950** *PADS* 14.15 **SC,** Board . . . To beat with a board. Only of persons.

boardcast v, hence agentive n *boardcaster* [Alter by metath of *broadcast* to scatter (seed)]

 To broadcast or sow (seed).

 1969 *DARE* (Qu. L22) Inf **KY39,** Boardcast oats; (Qu. L23) Inf **KY9,** Boardcaster. [Both Infs old with grade-school educ]

boarder n, also attrib **esp Nth, N Midl**

 An unproductive farm animal not worth its keep.

 1932 *Sun* (Baltimore MD) 27 Feb 4/6 *(Hench Coll.),* Death bells are tolling for lazy, shiftless "boarder" hens in scores of Queen Anne's county farm flocks. The ultimatum has gone forth to clear hen roosts . . of all fowls that fail to "pay their keep." **1936** Barnard *Rider* 226 **cnOK,** He possesses the information that enables him to determine a money-making dairy cow from a 'boarder.' **1950** *WELS* (A bony or poor-looking cow) 1 Inf, **cwWI;** (A pig that is poor or no good) 1 Inf, **csWI,** Boarder; (When a cow stops giving milk . . you call her a _____) 5 Infs, **WI,** Boarder. **1965–70** *DARE* (Qu. K3b, *When a cow stops giving milk, you say she's a _____*) Infs **NY32, OH87,** Boarder; (Qu. K44, *A bony or poor-looking horse*) Inf **OH87,** Boarder; (Qu. K55, *A pig that doesn't grow well and is not worth keeping*) Infs **IN35, KS18, NY227, WI21, 70,** Boarder; **OR13,** Boarder pig.

boarding and baiting See **bait and board**

boarding car n [*board* to provide meals]

 In logging: see quot.

 1958 McCulloch *Woods Words* **Pacific NW,** Boarding car—A cook-shack on wheels, the original mulligan.

boarding house n *joc*

 A jail.

 1942 Berrey–Van den Bark *Amer. Slang* 466.11 *Jail* . . . Boarding house or school. **1965–70** *DARE* (Qu. V11, . . *A county or city jail*) Infs **CA36, GA72, MI78, 97, 105,** (County) boarding house; **NJ53,** Free boarding house; **MI76,** McBride's boarding house (McBride is the sheriff); **VA6,** Sheriff's boarding house.

boardinghouse man n

 In logging: a cook.

 1968 Adams *Western Words,* Boardinghouse man—A logger's name for the cook. **1969** Sorden *Lumberjack Lingo* **NEng, Gt Lakes,** Boarding house man—A cook.

‡**boardinghouse potatoes** n pl

 Panfried potatoes.

 1966 *DARE* (Qu. H47, . . *Fried potatoes*) Inf **MS2,** Boardinghouse potatoes—fried, but not in deep fat.

board is board phr

 1950 *WELS* (Expressions . . *from card games*) 1 Inf, **ceWI,** Board is board—once a thing is on the board, it's O.K.—you've accepted it tacitly; object beforehand if you're going to.

board light n *old-fash* Cf **lightwood**

 A burning pine knot used for light.

 1971 *Foxfire* Spring–Summer 46 **nGA,** "I'll make you a board light." There wadn't such a thing as a lantern or a light or a flashlight . . . That 'uz just a big ol' pine knot, y'know, and they just keep a'burnin' and a'goin'.

board out v phr

1 intr: To sleep and eat at someone else's expense.

 1928 *AmSp* 4.128 **NE,** A "grub line rider" . . "makes" a good cook's home just before mealtime, to get a free meal. If he is fortunate enough to have several such homes on his calling list, he may be said to "board out."

2 tr: To spend time in jail.

 1935 Sandoz *Jules* 255 **wNE** (as of 1880–1930), Jules was found guilty . . and fined one hundred dollars. William came forward to pay it. "Hell, no," Jules told him. "I'll board it out." . . . Jules was having a comfortable time in jail. Three meals a day, with all the company he wanted.

board-stretcher n [*board* + *stretcher*] **chiefly Nth, N Mid**

 An imaginary tool which is the basis of a practical joke.

 1965–70 *DARE* (Qu. HH14, *Ways of teasing a beginner or inexperienced person* . . "*Go get me _____*") 18 Infs, Board-stretcher.

board tree n [*board* n] **chiefly S Midl**

 A straight-grained tree, usu oak or pine, which can be readily split into shingles or boards.

1878 Guild *Old Times in TN* 117 **cnTN,** The first was interrogated very closely as to the cutting of some rail-timber and its value; the second, as to the cutting of five board trees. **1923** *DN* 5.201 **swMO,** *Board tree . . .* Any straight grained tree that may be split easily. Ordinarily the term has reference only to oak or pine timber. **1946** Stuart *Tales Plum Grove* 228 **KY,** Got so anymore there isn't enough good timber for a board tree. **1950** Faulkner *Stories* 27 **MS,** We went on to the board tree. **c1960** *Wilson Coll.* **csKY,** *Board tree . . .* A good oak tree suitable for making boards.

board with Aunt Polly v phr
In logging: see quots.
    1931 *AmSp* 7.53 **Sth** [Lumberjack lingo], "Boarding with Aunt Polly" means to be drawing accident or sick insurance. **1969** Sorden *Lumberjack Lingo* **NEng, Gt Lakes,** *Boarding with Aunt Polly*—To draw insurance for sickness or accident.

boar's head See **bear's head**

boar's nest n scattered but esp **West**
    1 A camp of only male workers; a place where only men reside.
    1927 *AmSp* 2.349 **WV,** *Boar's nest . .* , a camp of laborers where there are no women. "We are all staying at the boar's nest this winter." **1934** *Cattleman* 21.2.5 **TX,** These [smaller camps] are usually one- or two-roomed affairs with small corral and storage for saddle horse feed. In the cow country they are called "Boar's Nests" because . . they are occupied for the most part by one man who is more interested in his duties as a [sic] cowhand than in culinary or housekeeping arts. **1951** *Western Folkl.* 10.80 **sCO, NM,** *Barroom Slang from the Upper Rio Grande.*— The setting: . . boar's nest (strictly man's place). **1969** Lyons *My Florida* 35, The most interesting people I know are hermits who live in boar's nests . . . A proper boar's nest should not cost more than a dime, if you don't count the nails and baling wire that it takes to hold it together.
    2 also *boar's room:* An untidy or messy room or house.
    1950 *WELS* (*If a house is untidy and everything is upset, you say it looks like _____*) 1 Inf, **cWI,** A boar's nest. **1958** McCulloch *Woods Words* **Pacific NW,** *Boar's nest . . .* An untidy bunkhouse. **1966–70** *DARE* (Qu. D7, *A small space anywhere in a house where you can hide things or get them out of the way*) Inf **CA163,** Boar's nest—not tidy; (Qu. E22, *If a house is untidy and everything is upset, you might say, "It's a _____!"*) Infs **CA205, MT5, ND5, SD5, TX11,** Boar's nest; **WA1,** Boar's room; (Qu. Y38, *Mixed together, confused*) Inf **WI43,** Boar's nest.

boary-eyed drunk adj phr
Thoroughly drunk.
    1980 *DARE* File **WI,** Said to be common around Chippewa Falls: "boary-eyed drunk."

boasterous adj [Alter of *boisterous* infl by *boast*]
Boisterous.
    1968–70 *DARE* (Qu. HH7a, *Someone who talks too much, or too loud*) Inf **MN12,** Boasterous [bostə˞əs]; **MO15,** Boasterous [boustrɪs].

boat n
    1 =**stoneboat.** chiefly **Nth, N Midl** *old-fash, rural* Also called **log boat, mud boat, rock boat**
    1965–70 *DARE* (Qu. L57, *A low wooden platform used for bringing stones or heavy things out of the fields*) Infs **CA87, IN72, MD48, MA16, MI78, OH70, PA218, WI30,** Boat. **1968** *DARE* Tape **IN23,** The roads weren't open . . . Everybody went in boats, bobsleds. And when they had funerals they couldn't take the horse-drawn hearses and they would take the corpse to the cemetery in the boats.
    2 =**submarine sandwich.**
    1968 *DARE* (Qu. H42, *The kind [of sandwich] in a much larger, longer bun, that's a meal in itself*) Inf **IN41,** Boats.
    3 See **boat shell.**

boatfin n
=**bowfin.**
    1968 *DARE* Tape **GA20,** Mudfish, he's known as a grinny, boatfin.

boating stage n
    1904 *DN* 2.376, *Boating-stage . . .* Depth of water which will permit the movement of boats . . . "The Alleghany River is nearly free from ice, with a good boating stage." . . Common among rivermen.

boat road n
    1968 *DARE* FW Addit **nwLA,** Boat road—passage in large shallow lake or swamp where trees and brush have been cleared for boats.

boat shell n Also *boat* [See quot 1978]
=**slipper shell,** esp *Crepidula fornicata.*
    1881 Ingersoll *Oyster-Industry* 242, *Boat.* — The little mollusk, *Crepidula fornicata. Ibid* 248, *Slipper-limpet.* — Mollusks of the genus *Crepidula* (three species). Also known as *Deckhead, Boat.* **1949** Palmer *Nat. Hist.* 362, *Boat Shell. Crepidula fornicata . . .* Has commercial value as base for oyster beds. Common in shallow water. **1978** Whipple *Vintage Nantucket* 243 **MA,** The only shells that competed with the scallops in number, as we walked along the beach, were those of the slipper snail, or as some call it because of the slot that looks like a thwart, the boat shell.

boat sled n [*boat 1 + sled*]
A runnerless sled for hauling loads.
    1943 *LANE* Map 573–574 scattered in **NEng,** A flat-bottomed sled . . *boat sled.* **1967** *DARE* (Qu. N40c) Inf **OH12,** Boat sled—"for loads."

boat-tailed grackle n Also *boat-tail, boat-tailed blackbird, boat-tailed crow blackbird*
A large grackle *(Cassidix mexicanus)* with a long, keel-shaped tail, native to the South and Southwest. Also called **chock, cowbird 3, crow blackbird, crow-jack, fan-tailed grackle, jackdaw, saltwater blackbird**
    1839 Audubon *Ornith. Biog.* 5.480 **Gulf States,** Boat-tailed Grakle has been of late given to our Common Crow Blackbird, *Quiscalus versicolor.* **1898** (1900) Davie *Nests N. Amer. Birds* 353, From the Carolinas to the Rio Grande, the Boat-tailed Crow Blackbird is an abundant species. **1938** Oberholser *Bird Life LA* 598, It is called 'Boat-tailed Grackle,' or 'boat-tailed blackbird', because of the shape of its long tail, which, when the bird is in flight, resembles very much the keel of a boat. **1946** Hausman *Eastern Birds* 559, *Boat-tailed Grackle . . . Other Names*— Boat-Tail. **1969** Longstreet *Birds FL* 143, The boat-tailed grackle is the largest blackbird in Florida.

boat-tide n Cf **boating stage**
    1915 *DN* 4.181 **swVA,** *Boat-tide . . .* A freshet sufficient to float laden boats.

‡bob n¹ [Perh from *bob* to move up and down]
    1916 *DN* 4.340 **seOH,** *Bobs . . .* Window shades.

bob n² [ME *bobbe*]
    1 An earring. Cf **earbob**
    1793 (1890) Lindley *Exped. Detroit* 589 **PA,** The bodies of some [Indians] almost covered over with silver, tin and other plates, broaches, bobs, etc. **1968–70** *DARE* (Qu. W34, *Jewelry that a woman wears on her ears*) Infs **MD26, TN50,** Bobs.
    2 See quot. [Abbr for *bobtail*]
    1967 *DARE* FW Addit **MA6,** *Bob*—a bobtail cat. "Mother had five kittens, one bob in each litter."

bob n³ [Abbr for *bobsled*]
    1 A bobsled. chiefly **Nth,** esp **NEast** Cf **bob** v
    1856 (1939) Loehr *MN Farmers' Diaries* 145, Went to Kinnik-kinnik . . yesterday with the bobs. Had to stay over night & return to day with part of a load of lumber. **1906** *Eve. Post* (NY NY) 19 May 9/3 **seNY,** The same spruce and hemlock logs drawn on bobs. **1945** Pearson *Country Flavor* 109 **NH,** A one-horse bob with its four tall, sturdy oak stakes is a good vehicle to handle. **1965–70** *DARE* (Qu. N40a, . . *Sleighs . . for hauling loads*) Infs **NJ1, NY75, 82, 105, 233, OR10, WA1, WI77,** Bob; **MN19,** Big bob; (Qu. N40b, . . *Sleighs for carrying people*) Infs **IA14, NY226,** Light bob; **NY231,** Two-seater bob; (Qu. N40c) Infs **NY195, 201,** (Log) bob. **1969** Sorden *Lumberjack Lingo* **NEng, Gt Lakes,** *Bob*—A two-runner sled for hauling logs out of the woods. A drag sled, dray, lizard, skidding sled, yarding sled.
    2 In logging: see quot.
    1958 McCulloch *Woods Words* **Pacific NW,** *Bob . . .* A detached railroad truck, just four wheels and a bunk, used for hauling long logs.

bob v [*bob* n³ 1] chiefly **Gt Lakes** and **NEng**
    1 To ride or coast on a sled.
    1880 *Wisconsin Rep.* 254 *(DA),* For injuries suffered . . by collision with persons 'bobbing' or 'coasting' on such street, the city is not liable. **1893** *Outing* Mar 125/1, Grown men and women took to "bobbing" as they liked the sensation of school-boyishness and girlishness it recalled. **1901** *DN* 2.136 **sME,** *Bob . . .* To coast. **1906** *DN* 3.127 **nwAR,** *Bob . . .* To coast. "We used to go bobbing down the mountain."
    2 In logging: see quots.

1959 *VT Hist.* new ser 27.126, *Bob* . . . In logging, to haul the logs with a bobsled with one end of the logs fastened to the sled . . . Common among lumbermen. **1969** Sorden *Lumberjack Lingo* **NEng, Gt Lakes,** *Bob logs* — To transport logs on a bob or dray.

bob n⁴ See **bob calf**

bob n⁵

1 =**bob-white.**

1883 *Century Illustr. Mag.* 4.483/2, The European partridge . . . weighs twice as much as Bob White, but he has not Bob's sturdy, rapid . . flight.

2 =**bobolink.**

[**1912** *Outing* 61.228/2, Numbers of gay bobolinks drifted over, and sang as they traveled. Like the Lapland longspur, Bob does not believe in keeping his music till he reaches his summer home.] **1956** *MA Audubon Soc. Bulletin* 40.130, *Bobolink.* Bob (Mass. Short for Bobolink, a sonic term.).

bob-a-link, bob-a-linkum See **bobolink** A

Bob Andy pie n

See quots.

c1965 Randle *Cookbooks* (Plain Cookery) 3.14 **Cleveland OH,** *Bob Andy Pie* . . brown sugar . . butter . . milk . . eggs. . . . Bake at 375 until set like a custard pie. **1972** *DARE* File **sIL,** Bob Andy pie . . . A sweet, rich one-crust pie containing eggs, sugar, and butter.

bobashela, bobashilly See **bobbasheely** n

bob-ass See **bobtail** 4

bob-back n

A toy: see quot.

1960 Williams *Walk Egypt* 158 **GA,** He resembled a bob-back, one of those toys mounted on a round base which, hands folded over tummies and wide smile under plaster of black hair, bob back no matter how hard they are pushed.

bobbasheely n Also sp *barbeshela, bobashela, bobashilly* [Alter of Choctaw *itibapishili* my brother] **esp Gulf States** Cf **bobbasheely** v

A very close friend.

1829 Maury *Letter* (1984 *DARE* File), My dear Sir [=Silas Dinsmoor]. My nephew . . will inform you that we are at home, and shall expect you and your friends to spend the day with us. Bobashela — Th.W. Maury. [Note: Maury and Dinsmoor had met while Dinsmoor was U.S. Agent to the Choctaws in Mississippi and Alabama.] **1893** Shands *MS Speech, Barbeshela* . . . A word borrowed from the Choctaw Indian language, and used in the southern central portion of the State, by negroes and illiterate whites, to signify a *friend.* **1906** *DN* 3.127 **nwAR,** *Bobashillies, n. pl.* Chums. "We're big bobashillies." **1967** *DARE* (Qu. II3, *Expressions to say that people are very friendly toward each other: "They're _____."*) Inf **TX35,** Big bobbasheelies |ˌbabiˈšiliz|, (Indian word for friend).

bobbasheely v Also sp *bobbashiel(y)* [**bobbasheely** n] **Gulf States**

To saunter, sashay, move in a friendly fashion; to associate with socially.

1932 Stribling *Store* 16 **AL,** It's social suicide even to vote the Republican ticket here in Florence, much less bobbashiely with niggers! *Ibid* 107, My gracious, boy, as much as I bobbashieled with Sheriff Dalrymple, not to remember him! **1962** Faulkner *Reivers* 177 **MS,** You and Sweet Thing bobbasheely on back to the hotel now, and me and Uncle Remus and Lord Fauntleroy will mosey along.

bobbed calf See **bob calf**

bobbely bird See **bobolink** A

bobbe mayse See **bubbe-mayse**

bobber n chiefly **Nth**

In logging: see quots.

1958 McCulloch *Woods Words* **Pacific NW,** *Bobber* — A deadhead, a log sunk on one end, the other bobbing up and down in the water. **1969** Sorden *Lumberjack Lingo* **NEng, Gt Lakes,** *Bobber* — A water-soaked log lying on the bottom of a river or lake or a partly sunken log. Same as dead head or sinker.

‡**bobbered** adj [Perh from **conbobberated;** cf **bobble** v] Confused, mixed up.

1969 *DARE* (Qu. GG2, . . "Confused, mixed up": "So many things were going on at the same time that he got completely _____.") Inf **MO15,** Bobbered ['babərd].

bobble v

1 To bungle, botch, spoil.

1968 *DARE* (Qu. JJ42, *To make an error in judgment and get something quite wrong: "He usually handles things well, but this time he certainly _____."*) Inf **MN35,** Bobbled it up; (Qu. KK63, *To do a clumsy or hurried job of repairing something: "It will never last — he just _____."*) Inf **IA22,** Bobbled it up.

2 See quot 1908.

1908 *DN* 3.292 **eAL, wGA,** *Bobble* . . . To make a slight turn or twist from a direct or straight line, wabble; hence, to make a break or mistake. "He can't plow a furrow without bobbling from one side of the row to the other." **1942** Faulkner *Go Down* 19 **MS,** Tomey's Turl ran right clean over him. He never even bobbled.

bobble n¹ [From **bobble** v]

1 A mistake, error. **chiefly Sth, S Midl** Cf **misbobble**

1887 (1967) Harris *Free Joe* 155 **ceGA,** She jess reads right straight along from cover to cover without a bobble. **1905** *DN* 3.70 **nwAR. 1912** *DN* 3.565 **MO. 1915** *DN* 4.181 **swVA. 1928** Chapman *Happy Mt.* 67 **seTN,** He'll play any piece you can think to set a name to, and never will make a bobble. **1943** Chase *Jack Tales* 52 **wNC** (as of 1880s), Hit's a failure, Jack. You made a bobble this time, too. **1965–70** *DARE* (Qu. JJ41, *An embarrassing mistake: "Last night she made an awful _____."*) Infs **AL30, AZ1, AR22, GA77, 80, IL71, KY47, MS65, MT3, TN30, TX10,** Bobble. **1967–69** *DARE* Tape **AZ1,** Bobble [=an embarrassing mistake]; **KY9,** I tore it up three different times; I'd make a bobble on it.

2 An unsuccessful undertaking, a failure.

1920 *Cosmopolitan* Aug 101/2 **NYC,** The Committee on Arrangements had made it impossible for the Dinner to be a Bobble. **1970** *DARE* (Qu. W29, . . *Expressions . . for things that are sewn carelessly*) Inf **TX98,** She made a bobble out of that.

bobble n²

In fishing: see quot.

1966 *DARE* (Qu. W4) Inf **ME23,** Bobble — oilcloth or rubber apron, like a skirt; worn by fishermen.

‡**bobble-ass** n [**bobble** bounce rapidly + *ass* rump] =**killdeer.**

1967 *DARE* (Qu. Q14, . . *Killdeer*) Inf **KY31,** Bobble-ass.

‡**bobblehead** n

=**bufflehead.**

1970 *DARE* (Qu. Q5) Inf **VA47,** Bobblehead [same as] bufflehead, little dippers.

bobbler n

=**ruddy duck.**

1982 Elman *Hunter's Field Guide* 192, *Ruddy Duck:* (. . . *Erismatura jamaicensis*) . . . Common & Regional Names: . . bobbler.

bobby n¹ [Transf from Brit *bobby* policeman] *sometimes derog* An Englishman.

1966–69 *DARE* (Qu. HH28, . . *People of foreign background . . . English*) Infs **MA6, NV7, NY204,** Bobbies.

bobby n² See **bubbe**

‡**bobby-bomb** n

1966 *DARE* (Qu. FF14, . . *Kinds of firecrackers*) Inf **GA8,** Bobby-bomb — pull string on each end and it explodes.

bob calf n Occas *bob, bobbed calf* [Engl dial *bob* a very young calf] **NEast** See Map See also **bob veal**

A very young calf slaughtered for veal.

1959 *VT Hist.* new ser 27.126, *Bob* . . . A calf to be sold as veal. Common among farmers. **1965–70** *DARE* (Qu. K20, *A calf that is sold for meat*) 14 Infs, **NEast,** Bob calf; **NJ1,** Bobbed calf — two or three days old. **1967** *DARE* FW Addit **neNY,** Bob calf — 2 or 3 weeks old. The next stage is veal; **cnNY,** Bob calf is a calf sold for veal as soon as it is born — no older than two weeks.

bobee See **bawbee**

bob house n

A small hut used for fishing through ice.

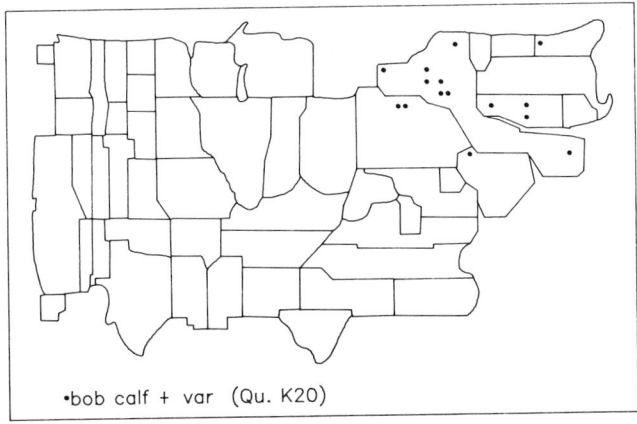

•bob calf + var (Qu. K20)

1954 *People and Places* 11.9.21 *(Hench Coll.),* There's a whole cult of anglers, up in New Hampshire, who never wet their lines until the ice on Lake Winnipesaukee is thick enough to hold their "bob houses." A bob house is about five by seven feet in size, usually has a wooden floor with a hole or two in it, where the fisherman drops his line and where he pulls up his catch . . . Some fishermen have wire springs that bob up and down, whence the name "bob house.". . Some bob houses are elaborate affairs, with efficient stoves to keep one warm or on which to cook your fish. **1974** *Yankee* Jan [np] **NH,** For days I snowshoed from one bobhouse (these are little huts and cabins put on the lake for ice fishing) to another asking about the man.

bob jack n chiefly **NC**
A playing piece used in the game of jacks; in pl: the game of jacks.
1946 *PADS* 6.6 **NC,** *Bob jack* . . . A right-angled metal crisscross used in the game of bob jacks. Four jacks are used. They are tossed a few inches in the air, and caught, if possible, on the back of the hand. They are swept up with one hand (one or more at a time) from the floor or ground while a bounced rubber ball is in the air . . . Common. **1966** *DARE* Tape **NC22,** *Bob jacks* . . . When I first started a-playin', we jist throwed a bob jack in the air an' pick 'em up, but later on they began to play with little balls an' let the ball bounce before they'd catch it. **1969–70** *DARE* (Qu. EE7) Inf **NC77,** Played bob jacks all the time; (Qu. EE33) Inf **NC84,** Bob jacks. **1970** *DARE* Tape **NJ67,** Bob jacks . . . Th'o' 'em up an' catch 'em in your han' like that.

boblincoln, boblincon, boblink See **bobolink A**

bobo n [Fr]
A hurt or sore.
1969 Cagnon *Franco–Amer. Terms* 223 **NEng,** *Bobo* . . [bobo] Hurt. *Faire bobo* = to hurt, hurt oneself. "You'll make (a) bobo if you do that." "Do you have a bobo?" **1983** *Reinecke Coll.* **New Orleans LA,** *Bobo* ['bobo]—nursery word for sore, abrasion, cut, "hurt." Very general in New Orleans.

bobolink n Also chiefly hist forms *bob-a-link, bob-a-linkum, bobbely bird, boblincon, boblink, bob-o-Lincoln, bob-o-linkhorn*
A Forms.
1774 in 1850 Adams *Works* 2.401 **MA,** Young Ned Rutledge is a perfect Bob-o-Lincoln,—a swallow, a sparrow, a peacock. **1804** Fessenden *Poems* 146 **NH,** In strains as sad as you can think on, / In unison with bob-o-linkhorn. **1810** Wilson *Amer. Ornith.* 2.48, Rice Bunting. *Emberiza Oryzivora.* This is the *Boblink* of the eastern and northern states, and the *Rice* and *Reed-bird* of Pennsylvania and the southern states. **1826** Flint *Recollections* 243 **MO,** I saw early in the spring a flock of those merry and chattering birds, that we call bob-a-link, or French black-bird. **1840** Hoffman *Greyslaer* 2.104 **NEast,** There he goes . . singing for all the world like a Bob-a-linkum on the wing. **1855** Irving *Wolfert's Roost* 33 **NY,** The happiest bird of our spring, however, and one that rivals the European lark in my estimation, is the Boblincon, or Boblink, as he is commonly called. **1966** *DARE* (Qu. Q14, . . *Bobolink*) Inf **DC4,** Bobbely ['baba,li] bird.
B Sense.
Std: a small songbird *(Dolichonyx oryzivorus)* freq in grain fields, grasslands, and meadows. Also called **armyworm bird, bob n[5] 2, butterbird 1, conquedle, fatty, French blackbird, maybird, meadow bird, meadowwink, oat bird, ortolan, reedbird, ricebird, Robert of Lincoln, skunk blackbird, strawberry bird, sucker, towhee, wheat bird, white-winged blackbird**

bobora head n
1972 Carr *Da Kine Talk* 113 **HI,** *Bôbora head* (Portuguese via Japanese + English). A Japanese citizen as distinguished from a Japanese American. *Bôbora* is used by the local Japanese to mean 'pumpkin', although it derived from the Portuguese *abóbora* meaning 'gourd'.

bob sawyer n Cf **bobber**
1968 Adams *Western Words, Bob sawyer*—A tree rooted to the river bottom, its broken top bobbing and sawing with the undulations of the current; a trap for careless boatmen.

bobsleigh n chiefly **Nth** See Map
A bobsled, usu used to haul loads.
1889 *Century Dict.* 3.607/2, *Bob-sleigh* . . . A sleigh constructed upon the same principle as a bob-sled. **1896** *DN* 1.413, *Bob-sled:* a *short, heavy* sled for hauling logs . . . In N.Y.w[estern]. also *bob-sleigh.* **1965–70** *DARE* (Qu. N40a, . . *Sleighs . . for hauling loads*) 102 Infs, chiefly **Nth,** Bobsleigh; **MN12,** Kind of bobsleigh; (Qu. N40b, . . *Sleighs for carrying people*) 9 Infs, Bobsleigh; **MN12, WI51,** Light bobsleigh; **MI27,** Little bobsleigh; **NH16,** Horse bobsleigh; **MI47,** Small bobsleigh; **NY206,** Two-seated bobsleigh.

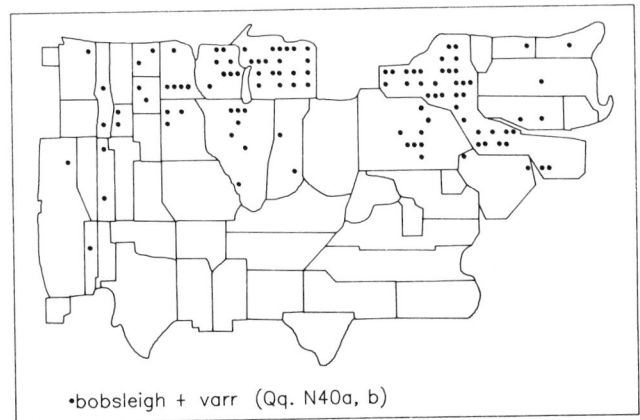

•bobsleigh + varr (Qq. N40a, b)

bob sumach n
A sumac *(Rhus* spp).
1941 *LANE* Map 250 *(Sumach),* The non poisonous variety of sumach is occasionally distinguished by a special term, such as . . *bob sumach* . . . 1 Inf, **ceRI,** *Swamp sumach,* common here, very poisonous; *bob sumach,* a smaller variety; 1 Inf, **ceRI,** *Bob sumach,* formerly used to dye cloth brown.

bobtail n
1 See quot.
1899 (1912) Green *VA Folk-Speech, Bobtail* . . . A contemptible fellow; a cur.
2 See quot.
1901 *DN* 2.136 **cnNY,** *Bob-tail* . . . A very small sled.
3 =**red-necked grebe.**
1917 *Wilson Bulletin* 29.2.74, *Colymbus holboelli.*—Bobtail, Shitepoke . . Matinicus Id., Me. **1955** *MA Audubon Soc. Bulletin* 39.309, *Holboell's Grebe.* Bobtail (Maine. All grebes have a rudimentary tail.).
4 also *bob-ass:* =**spotted sandpiper.**
1841 *S. Lit. Messenger* 7.77 Innumerable species of the snipe are every where to be met with, from the little Bobtail of the sandbar, up to the Beccasse of the plain. **1945** McAtee *Nomina Abitera* 34, Spotted Sandpiper *(Actitis macularia)*—All of the names here cited have references to the constant tail-bobbing in which this species indulges. Bobass, Springfield, Massachusetts.
5 A shortened form (of a name).
1949 Guthrie *Way West* 19, "Name's Hig," the figure announced. "Or that's what they call me. It's bobtail for Higgins."
6 in phr *no siree bobtail*—used for emphasis.
1966–68 *DARE* (Qu. KK55c, *Other expressions of strong denial*) Infs **MS14, SC40, 44, 54, 59,** No siree bobtail.

bobtail buzzard n [From the short square tail]
=**black vulture.**
1970 *DARE* (Qu. Q13) Inf **VA61,** Bobtail buzzard, Carolina eagle—different kinds of buzzards.

bobtailed flush n Also *bobtail flush, bobtail(ed) straight* [From *bobtail* shortened, deficient] **scattered, but more common Sth and West**

In card play: see quot 1944; also fig.

1873 *Courier* (Winfield KS) 15 Feb 1/5 *(DA)*, For a little man Senator Allen could play a pretty large game. The clerical part of the House was also well up in all the mysteries of a 'pair' or a 'bobtailed flush.' **1875** *Enquirer* (Cincinnati OH) 2 July 2/3 *(DA)*, The gentlemen have shown their hand a little too soon, and, in our opinion, can not 'bluff' to any success on their 'bob-tail flush.' **1894** Chopin *Bayou Folk* 2 **LA**, Mr. Wallace Offdean hurried to the bank in order to replenish his portemon-naie, which had been materially lightened at the club through the medium of unpropitious jack-pots and bobtail flushes. **1897** *KS Univ. Qrly.* 6.86, *Bob tailed flush:* poker term.—General. **1944** *AN&Q* 4.85/1, *Bobtailed Straight or Flush:* a three-card (and therefore worth-less) straight or flush in a five-card poker hand; a term hitherto confined to the South but apparently in general use at present in the Army. **1968** Adams *Western Words, Bobtail flush*—In five-card poker, a worthless three-card flush. *Ibid, Bobtail straight . . .* A worthless three-card straight.

bobtailed squid n

1968 Mercer *Systemics Sepiolid Squids,* Squids of this genus *[Rossia palpebrosa]* are small . . and have a bursiform configuration, leading to such names as "bottleass squid" and "purse squid" in Newfoundland and "bob-tailed squid" in New England.

bobtail guard n

1944 Adams *Western Words, Bob-tail guard*—The first guard at night herding.

bob veal n, also attrib [Engl dial *bob* a young calf]

1 The meat of a newly born calf, the youngest salable as veal. **chiefly NEast, esp NY** See also **bob calf** Cf **deacon veal**

1855 in 1867 De Voe *Market Asst.* 421 **NYC**, He saw nine quarters of plated veal hanging up in a meat-shop in Grandstreet . . . Butchers call this *bob-veal.* **1911** *Eve. Post* (NY NY) 13 Oct 1/4 **NYC**, A former butcher was sentenced . . for . . shipping . . the carcasses of five bob veal calves to this city. **1945** Webster *Town Meeting* 232 **NEng**, Sellin' much bob veal these days? **1968–69** *DARE* (Qu. K20, *A calf that is sold for meat*) Infs **MA68, NY27,** 75, 92, 99, 219, Bob veal.

2 See quot.

1935 *AmSp* 10.270 **NE**, *Bob veal.* Flesh of an unborn calf from a slaughtered cow—unmarketable.

bob-white n

Std: A ground-dwelling, somewhat chickenlike brown bird *(Colinus virginianus).* Also called **bob** n⁵ **1, partridge, quail**

bocce n |'bačǐ| [From Ital *boccia* ball]

Lawn bowling.

1953 *Sun* (Baltimore MD) 1 Apr B12/2, He reminded his listeners of the joys of such simple pleasures as a game of quoits in the back yard, of neigh[bor]hood games like *bocce.* **1969** *DARE* (Qu. EE33, . . *Outdoor games*) Inf **RI15,** ['bačǐ]—lawn bowling.

boche n |baš| [Fr *boche* a German]

1918 Witwer *Baseball to Boches* 154 **NY**, The whole outfit is crazy to go to the mat with these here *boches* [=Germans], as they call 'em here. **1967–69** *DARE* (Qu. HH28, . . *People of foreign background . . German*) Inf **MI67,** Boche [baš]; **NJ30,** Boche; **OH27,** Low Boche.

bock n¹ See **bock beer**

‡**bock** n²

1944 *PADS* 2.40, *Bock . . .* The string bean. Mountain woman, near Blowing Rock, N.C.: "Do you want some yaller, greasy bocks." . . Probably rare.

bock n³ [Prob from Ger *bock* he-goat] *derog* Cf **bohunk**

1967 *DARE* (Qu. HH28, *Names . . for people of foreign background . . Bohemian*) Inf **IL11,** Bocks.

‡**bock** n⁴ [Perh echoic, or perh back-formation of *box* a blow, buffet]

1968 *DARE* (Qu. Y11, . . *A very hard blow: "You should have seen Bill go down. Joe really hit him a _____."*) Inf **PA164,** Bock.

bock beer n Also *bock* [Ger *bockbier*] **chiefly Nth**

A relatively sweet dark beer brewed in winter for consumption in spring.

1856 *Ill. State Reg.* 26 June 4/3 *(DA)*, There is a Bavarian lager beer which is called 'bock'—in English buck or goat—and is so called because of its great strength making its consumers prance and tumble about like these animals. **1897** in 1970 Norris *Norris of Wave* 65 **San Francisco CA**, An open car had appeared on the cross-town cable line and Bock beer was on draught at the "Wein Stube," and Polk Street knew that Spring was at hand. **1932** *K.C. Times* 5 Mar 26 *(DA)*, That causes the Mail to recall that it is almost the season of the year when bock beer signs appeared. **1965–70** *DARE* (Qu. BB50a) Infs **IL9, MN10,** Bock beer; (Qu. BB50d) Infs **IL21, MI19, MN10, NY2,** Bock beer; (Qu. DD25) Inf **WI51,** Bock beer.

bodacious adj, adv Also infreq pronc-spp *bardacious, bawda-cious, bowdacious* [Prob blend of *bold + audacious;* cf *EDD boldacious*] **chiefly Sth, S Midl**

1 Thorough, remarkable; completely, extremely.

1845 Thompson *Pineville* 178 **GA**, She's so bowdacious unreasonable when she's raised. **1888** Murfree *Keedon Bluffs* 153 **TN**, Air ye turned a bodacious idjit, Skimp? **1896** Pool *In Buncombe County* 239 *(DAE)* **NC**, I'm er bawdacious fool. **1926** Van Vechten *Nigger Heaven* 285 **NYC** [Black], *Bardacious:* marvellous. **1937** *Lit. Digest* 4 Dec 30/3 **NYC** [Black], *New York slang*—Here are some of the more engaging vulgarisms and their sources: . . Harlemites—"bardacious" (marvelous). **1964** Will *Hist. Okeechobee* 27 **sFL**, I'm a-fixing for to spin you the most fantastic, the most bodacious tale of hidden treasure that you've scarcely ever heard. *Ibid* 232, A most bodacious, torrential rain scat-tered the multitude.

2 Audacious, unceremonious(ly).

1908 *DN* 3.292 **eAL, wGA**, *Bodacious . . .* Bold, unceremonious, outright. Also *bardacious.* **1929** *AmSp* 4.204 **Ozarks**, He . . jes' plum bodacious hipped an' ruinated her. **1940** Stong *Hawkeyes* 214 **IA**, The seizure of a carload of near-beer by a bodacious chief of police in Des Moines. **1951** *Sun* (Baltimore MD) 17 Mar 5/2, [Picture caption:] Quack-Quack, a bodacious duck, plays roughhouse with two dogs in East Point, Ga. **1964** Will *Hist. Okeechobee* 253 **FL**, It had a most bodacious promoter. **1966** *DARE* (Qu. GG5, *When someone does something unexpectedly bold or forward*) Inf **GA15,** Bodacious.

bodaciously adv Also rare or obs pronc-spp *bardaciously, bida-ciously, bodiaciously, bodyaciously* [**bodacious** adj] **chiefly Sth, S Midl**

1 Thoroughly, completely, extremely.

1832 Hall *Legends West* 82 **KY**, It seems like it would *jist* use me up *bodyaciously.* **1843** (1916) Hall *New Purchase* 149 **IN**, Then I gits bodaciously sker'd. **1901** *Century Illustr. Mag.* 62.904/2 **TN** [Black], I des bardaciously wants ter see what dey done wid 'em. **1915** *DN* 4.181 **swVA**, *Bidaciously . . =*bodaciously. **1951** Craig *Singing Hills* 204 **nwNC**, After a lot of folks go tramping through it, a snow is bodaciously ruined. **1968** *DARE* (Qu. KK22, *Other ways of saying completely shattered: "The jug fell out of the window and was _____."*) Inf **IN32,** Bodaciously smashed. **1972** Cooper *NC Mt. Folkl.* 90, Bodaciously ruint—seriously injured.

2 Unceremoniously, boldly.

1884 Harrison *Negro Engl.* 263 **Sth**, To slip bodiaciously inter de callerboose = to get into jail. **1896** *DN* 1.413 **swNC, eKY**, *Bodaciously.* **1898** Harris *Tales Home Folks* 164 **GA**, I 'lowed may be you'd have been took prisoner an' carried bodaciously off. **1908** *DN* 3.292 **eAL, wGA**, *Bodaciously.* **1951** Hench Coll. **VA**, The student was bodaciously fired then and there. **1967** *DARE* FW Addit **cLA**, The roustabouts just bodaciously [ˌboʊˈdeɪšəslɪ] packed all that stuff into the boats.

bodark, bodock, bodok See **bois d'arc**

bo dollar See **beau dollar**

body n

1 A person—freq used by a speaker in ref to himself. **wide-spread, but esp Midl**

1800 (1907) Thornton *Diary* 134 **DC**, A strange kind of mad body his name is Wilcox. **1843** (1916) Hall *New Purchase* 68 **IN**, How in creation is a body to have dinner if a body aint time cook it? **1872** Eggleston *End of the World* 170 **sIN**, A body'd have more sense than to do such a soft thing. **1895** *DN* 1.370 **eTN**. **1902** *DN* 2.228 **sIL**. **1940** Richter *Trees* 6 **sOH**, What's a body to do if the game's left the country? **1950** *WELS* (Other words meaning "a person": "What's _____ to do in a case like that?") 14 Infs, **WI**, A body. **1965–70** *DARE* (Qu. HH32, *Other words meaning a person;* total Infs questioned, 75) 11 Infs, Body. **1966** *PADS* 46.24 **cnAR**.

2 attrib: Straight-grained wood without knots; wood cut from the trunk of a tree.   **chiefly Nth**

1941 FWP *Guide WI* 310, The timber chap who lives like an Indian and can cut seven cords of body maple in a day.   **1958** McCulloch *Woods Words Pacific NW, Body wood*—Clear, straight-grained wood cut between clumps of knots on the main stem of a tree.   **1967** *Tupper Lake Free Press & Herald* (NY) 3 Aug 8, Body wood for sale.   **1967** *Bulletin* (Bend OR) 13 Mar 13/4, Dry body pine and jackpine. Any length.   **1969** Sorden *Lumberjack Lingo* **NEng, Gt Lakes,** *Body wood*—Cordwood cut from whole trees or limbs as distinguished from slab wood.

3 See **body waist.**

bodyaciously See **bodaciously**

body, boots, and britches n Also *body and breeches*

Everything—freq used adverbially by analogy with *lock, stock, and barrel:* entirely, completely.

1878 *Congressional Record* 12 Apr 2492/1 **NY,** The Yankee notions produced by Newark every year will buy out, body and breeches, any thoroughly democratic State in the Union.   **1901** *McClure's Mag.* 18.151/2 **NY,** Platt . . got nearly to the door; then turned back, and surrendered, body and breeches.   **1939** (1962) Thompson *Body & Britches* 19 **NY,** *Body, boots, and britches* is a proverbial expression collected in Dutchess County; it means "the whole thing."   **c1960** *Wilson Coll.* **csKY,** *Body, boots, and britches.*

bodyfied adj [*body* + *-ified*]

Incarnated, embodied.

1942 Hurston *Dust Tracks* 89 **FL,** Something rushed across Blue Sink like a body-fied wind.

body linen n

Underclothing.

a1883 (1911) Bagby *VA Gentleman* 96, The Virginia ant, as you are well aware, has a choice knack of getting under the "body-linen," as old folks call it, which sets wristbands and collar-buttons at defiance.

body-naked adj

1933 *AmSp* 8.1.48 **Ozarks,** *Body-naked* . . . Naked.

body waist n Also *body* **chiefly Sth, S Midl** *old-fash*

See quots.

1908 *DN* 3.292 **eAL, wGA,** *Body* . . . A child's garment worn about the body and fitted with buttons or supports for the lower garment, a waist, an underbody.   **1952** Brown *NC Folkl.* 1.521, *Body-waist* . . . A child's underwaist.—Alexander county.   **c1960** *Wilson Coll.* **csKY,** *Body* (or *body-waist*) . . . A child's under-waist, to which was buttoned his drawers. "Mammy bought me a new body yesterday."

Boer dollar See **beau dollar**

boerenjongens n [Du "peasant boy"]   **in Dutch settlement areas**

A drink usu made with whiskey and raisins usu served around Christmas time.

1940 *AmSp* 15.83 **Holland MI,** *Boerenjongens* [ˈbuːrənˈjɔŋgəns]. A popular drink of brandy and raisins.   **1969** *DARE* Tape MI103, [ˌbudiˈʊŋgəs] . . that's raisins and whiskey that they soak for a few weeks before Christmas.   **1976** *Eet Smakelijk* 35 **swMI,** *Boerenjongens* cocktail . . . Served especially during the Christmas season in Dutch homes . . . Cook raisins, water and cinnamon . . . Add sugar and whiskey . . . Seal. Let stand 3 months.

bofe adj, pron Also sp *bof* Pronc-spp for *both* See Pronc Intro 3.I.17   **chiefly Sth** *esp among Black speakers*

Both.

1922 Gonzales *Black Border* 290 **sSC, GA coasts** [Gullah glossary], *Bofe*—both.   **1929** (1931) Faulkner *Sound & Fury* 314 **MS** [Black], You bofe get pneumonia down here on dis wet flo.   **1950** *PADS* 14.15 **SC,** *Bofe* . . . Both. Prevailingly but not exclusively a Negro usage.   **1953** Brewer *Word Brazos* 55 **eTX** [Black], Sebun hunnud Town Nigguhs, Pos'-oak Nigguhs, an' Bottom Nigguhs conjugates on bof sides of de Big Brazos.

bog n Usu as second element in var phrr, as *chicken bog, squirrel ~* **SC**

A dish made with meat and rice.

1941 FWP *Guide SC* 153, In the Pee Dee region, chicken bog, a variety of chicken pilau, is favored for midday or moonlight picnics.   **1950** *PADS* 14.15 **SC,** *Bog* . . . Rice cooked with poultry or game; pilau.

Usually only in compounds: *chicken bog, squirrel bog.*   **1966** *DARE* (Qu. H45) Inf **SC7,** Chicken bog—rice and chicken cooked together.   **1966** *DARE* FW Addit **SC,** *Chicken bog*—chicken perleau.   **1981** *Playboy* Apr 201/2 **SC,** I didn't want to make my debut as a Washington [D.C.] hostess ladling plates of chicken bog, a stewlike concoction of rice, sausage and chicken.

bog v[1], hence vbl n *bogging*

1 To work in a bog or wet field.

1854 [see **bog hoe**].   **1934** *Hanley Disks* **seMA,** "My work has been mostly bogging." "In the cranberry bog?" "Yes."

2 To dig in the mud in order to catch crabs.

1968 *DARE* Tape **SC64,** Go down and bog in the mud . . . You can really catch crabs that way . . . You have your string attached to you, and you pull it in gently and the crabs come in and you scoop them up with a net . . . That's what's called bogging; **SC65,** Bogging, that's when you have low tide and you have to go in the mud to dig them [= crabs] out.

bog v[2] See **bogue** v

bog a buzzard's shadow See **bog the shadow of a buzzard**

‡bogalosha n [Alter of *tuberculosis,* infl by place-name *Bogalusa,* Louisiana] Cf **bug** n[1] **5b**

1967 *DARE* (Qu. BB10, . . Names . . for tuberculosis) Inf **LA6,** Bogalosha [ˈboʊgələʊʃə]—if you didn't want to say T.B.

bogan n |ˈbogən| [Prob Algonquian]   **chiefly nME** Cf **logan, pokelogan**

A section of still water extending from a stream or lake.

1903 *Jrl. Amer. Folkl.* 16.128 **nME,** A word very much used by guides and others who go into the New Brunswick woods is *bogan*—a still creek or bay branching from a stream.   **1939** *LANE* Map 40 **ME,** Attention is called to [boʊgən], used of a fresh backwater in northern Maine and N[ew]. B[runswick].   **1966** *DARE* (Qu. C14, *A stretch of still water going off to the side from a river or lake*) Infs **ME1, 9,** Bogan [bogən].   **1966** *DARE* FW Addit **nME,** Bogan [ˈbogən]—a stretch of still water on a river, generally at a wide spot.   **1971** *Down East* Nov 54 **nME,** I came to a bogan—a mudhole with a couple of feet of water extending into the swamp for several hundred feet before coming to a dead end, but always connected to the river.

bogart n[1] Also sp *boggard* [Engl dial *boggart* hobgoblin, specter]

=**hellgrammite.**

1901 Howard *Insect Book* 212, In 1889 Professor W.W. Bailey . . collected the names in use in Rhode Island alone for this insect, and they are . . . goggle goy, bogart, crock [etc].   **1911** *Century Dict. Suppl., Boggard*[1] . . . The hellgrammite. [Local, U.S.]

bogart n[2] Pronc-sp *bogard* [Prob from (Humphrey) *Bogart,* a movie actor who often played the role of a bullying tough-guy] *chiefly among Blacks*

An aggressive or bullying person.

1970 *DARE* (Qu. V6, . . *A thief*) Inf **TN50,** Bogard—just takes something boldly [Inf young, Black].   **1972** Claerbaut *Black Jargon* 58, *Bogart* . . a brawler; a bully . . a strong, physically aggressive person.

bogart v Also pronc-spp *bogard, boguard* [**bogart** n[2]] *chiefly among Blacks*

To act in a bold, aggressive way; to tease or bully.

1970 Major *Afro–Amer. Slang, Bogard (Bogart):* . . to act in a forceful manner; black people growing up during the 50's identified easily with tough-guys like Humphrey Bogart.   **1970** *DARE* (Qu. GG3, *To tease:* "See those big boys trying to _____ [that little one].") Inf **PA236,** Bogart. [Inf young, Black]   **1971** Roberts *Third Ear, Bogart (boguard)* . . to take advantage of; to bully.   **1972** Claerbaut *Black Jargon* 58, *Bogart* . . . to throw an elbow in a fight.   **1980** Folb *Runnin' Down* 102 **Los Angeles CA** [Black], The expression to *bogart/bogard* is one of the commonly used terms to describe muscling into someone's personal space. The act and the expression are associated with Humphrey Bogart.

bogbean n [From its habitat]

=**buckbean 1.**

1876 Hobbs *Bot. Hdbk.* 14, Bog bean, Buckbean, Menyanthes trifoliata.   **1910** Graves *Flowering Plants* 320 **CT,** Bog Bean . . . Bogs, borders of ponds and in wet meadows . . . The leaves and rootstock are used medicinally.   **1967** *DARE* Wildfl QR Pl.169 Inf **MI7,** Bogbean; another common name is "buckbean."   **1973** Hitchcock–Cronquist *Flora Pacific NW* 361.

bog birch n

1 =**Carolina buckthorn.**

1897 Sudworth *Arborescent Flora* 298, *Rhamnus caroliniana*. . . Common names [are] . . Stinkwood (La.), Bog Birch (Minn.). **1960** Vines *Trees SW* 702, Other vernacular names are Yellow Buckthorn, Indian-cherry, Bog-birch.

2 also *mountain bog birch*: =**scrub birch.**

1931 U.S. Dept. Ag. *Misc. Pub.* 101.18, *Resin birch (B. glandulosa)*, often called mountain bog birch . . does not exceed 6 or 7 feet in height . . . Its palatability is generally considered to be good . . but it is often inaccessible because of the boggy sites it inhabits. **1932** Rydberg *Flora Prairies* 260, Twigs brown and densely glandular-resiniferous . . . *Bog Birch.* **1972** Viereck *AK Trees* 130, *Resin Birch* . . . Other names: . . bog birch . . . Moist soils, especially in muskegs or boggy areas.

bog blueberry n

A **blueberry 1** (here: *Vaccinium uliginosum*).

1900 Lyons *Plant Names* 386, *V. uliginosum* . . . Bog Blueberry . . . *Fruit* edible. **1959** Anderson *Flora AK* 372, Bog Blueberry . . . This is the common blueberry of interior Alaska and used in large quantities. In southeast Alaska it is largely an alpine or alpine dweller and not much used. **1977** *New Yorker* 9 May 94/1 **AK**, The trails would go along, well cut and stamped out through moss campion, reindeer moss, sedge tussocks, crowberries, prostrate willows, dwarf birch, bog blueberries, white mountain avens, low-bush cranberries, lichens, Labrador tea; then, abruptly, and for no apparent reason, the trails would disappear.

bog bugle n [From the habitat and the trumpet-shaped leaf]

A southern sp of **pitcher plant 1.**

1933 Small *Manual SE Flora* 580, *Sarracenia* . . . Eve's-cups. Frog-bonnets. Bog-bugles. **1980** *DARE* File **seGA** [Okefenokee Swamp guide], Pitcher plants—some call 'em bog bugles.

bog bull n [In ref to its habitat and booming call]

=**bittern.**

1898 (1900) Davie *Nests N. Amer. Birds* 111, This noted bird (*Botaurus lentiginosus*) is known by various names, such as . . Bog-bull. **1917** (1923) *Birds Amer.* 1.181, *Bittern* . . . Other Names . . . Bog Bull. **1937** FWP *Guide ID* 140, The racket it [=the American bittern] makes has been variously compared with that of bellowing cattle, with the gurgle of an old wooden pump, and with the driving of a peg into a bog; and it has passed in folklore under such names as thunder-pumper, stake-driver, butter-bump, and bog-bull. **1953** Jewett *Birds WA* 94, *Western American Bittern* . . . Other names: . . Bog-bull.

bog candle n Cf bog torch 2

A **fringed orchid** (here: *Habenaria dilatata*).

1950 Gray–Fernald *Manual of Botany* 472, *H. dilatata* . . . Leafy White Orchis, Bog-candle . . . Swales, meadows, bogs and wet woods. **1966** Heller *Wild Flowers AK* 43, Bog Candle . . . An orchid with stout stems up to 3 feet high. **1973** Hitchcock–Cronquist *Flora Pacific NW* 703.

bog cotton n

=**cotton grass 1.**

1950 Gray–Fernald *Manual of Botany* 276, Cotton-grass. Bog-cotton. **1967** Braun *Monocotyledoneae* 211, *Eriophorum* L. Cotton-grass. Bog-Cotton.

bog crane n [From its habitat and shape]

=**bittern.**

1955 *MA Audubon* 39.313, *American bittern* . . . Bog Crane (Maine. Herons are often miscalled cranes.).

bogey lice See boogey lice

boggard See bogart n[1]

bogger n [bog v[1] 1]

One who harvests cranberries.

1934 *Hanley Disks* **seMA**, These boggers, you know, men work for fifty cents an hour and he can pick quite a number of barrels [of cranberries] in an hour with them [scoops].

boggie See boggy 1

boggin n [Aphet form of *toboggan* abbr for *toboggan cap* a stocking cap]

See quots.

1954 *Harder Coll.* **cwTN**, Boggin . . . A hat or cap. From 'toboggan.' **1969** *DARE* FW Addit **ceKY**, Boggin ['bagɪn]—a woolen stocking cap, knit for winter wear.

bogging See bog v[1]

boggle v, hence ppl adj boggled

To bungle; to do something badly.

1870 in 1872 Schele de Vere *Americanisms* 585 **NY**, His affairs were found to be woefully boggled, and his creditors have little chance to recover anything. **1905** *DN* 3.60 **NE**, Boggle . . . Bungle, make a poor job of. "He boggled the whole thing." **1953** Randolph *Down in Holler* 228 **Ozarks**, Boggle . . . To bungle, to blunder. "Bill set up for a horse-doctor, but he boggled everything, an' killed more'n he cured." **c1960** *Wilson Coll.* **csKY**, Boggle . . . To blunder, bungle. **1967–69** *DARE* (Qu. W29, . . *Things that are sewn carelessly* . . "They're _____.") Inf **MA5**, Boggle it up; **MA58**, Boggled; (Qu. KK63, *To do a clumsy or hurried job of repairing something:* "It will never last—He just _____.") Inf **MA5**, Boggled it.

boggling vbl n [Prob from boggle]

1815 Humphreys *Yankey in England* 103, Boggling, difficulty, delaying, unnecessarily hesitating.

bog grass n Also bog hay chiefly NEast

Any of several grasses (esp of the genus *Spartina*) that grow in a bog or marshy area and are used for hay.

1821 *MA Hist. Soc. Coll.* 2d ser 9.149, Plants, which are indigenous in the township of Middlebury, [VT] . . Bog grass. **1860** *Harper's Mag.* 20.583/2 **NJ**, The bogs . . were covered with a dense growth of bog grass. **1965–70** *DARE* (Qu. L8, *Hay that grows naturally in damp places*) Infs **CT22, IL31, MA42, NJ3, 29, RI4**, Bog hay; **MA15, NJ3, NY52**, Bog grass.

boggy adj [*OED boggy* b "Of a soft, spongy consistency; flabby" 1664, 1852]

1 also sp *boggie*; Of meat: soft, in bad condition.

1935 *AmSp* 10.270 **NE** [Stockyard language], Boggy ham. A soft, flabby ham. **1981** Stratton *Pioneer Women* 114 **KS** (as of 1860s), Mother . . never turned them [=Indians] away quite empty handed when they came begging for her cornmeal or 'boggie meat.'

2 Fig: see quot.

1927 *DN* 5.473 **Ozarks**, Boggy . . . Semi-delirious, as under the influence of drugs.

boggy-top (pie) n

See quots.

1933 *AmSp* 8.1.27 **nwTX**, Boggy-top pie. Pie with one crust; pie with meringue. **1968** Adams *Western Words*, Boggy top—The cowboy's name for a pie with no top crust.

bog hawk n

=**marsh hawk.**

1927 Forbush *Birds MA* 2.99, *Circus hudsonius* . . . Other names: bog hawk; mouse hawk. **1932** Bennitt *Check-list* 24 **MO**, Bog hawk . . . Throughout the state. **1955** *MA Audubon Soc. Bulletin* 39.442, *Marsh Hawk* . . . Bog Hawk . . (Mass. "Bog" used in the sense of marsh . . .).

bog hay See bog grass

bog hen n

=**bittern.**

1932 Bennitt *Check-list* 15 **MO**, American Bittern . . . Bog-hen; shite-poke; long-necked fly-up-the-creek. **1953** *AmSp* 28.281, Name . . . Bog Hen . . . Bird . . . American bittern . . . *Known Distribution of the Name* . . . Maine, Mass. **1955** Forbush–May *Birds* 38.

bog hoe n NEng rural

A hoe used to turn up or cut the turf in a **bog meadow.**

[**1748** in 1934 Eliot *Field Husbandry* 10 **CT**, The Bog Meadow [will be] the next in Charge, because the Bogs must be cut up with a Bog Plough or with the Hoe.] **1854** (1969) Thoreau *Walden* 221 **MA**, My host . . worked "bogging" for a neighboring farmer, turning up a meadow with a spade or bog hoe. **1874** *VT State Bd. Ag. Report* 2.551, Then with axes, potato hooks, and bog hoes, the turf was all peeled off. **1966–69** *DARE* (Qu. L35, *Hand tools used for cutting underbrush and digging out roots*) Infs **MA25, 58, NH3, 12, VT2**, Bog hoe.

boghopper n derog

A hick, hillbilly.

1970 *DARE* (Qu. HH1, . . *A rustic or countrified person*) Inf **NJ64**, Boghopper.

bog hornet n

A **yellowjacket** or similar wasp.

1939 *LANE* Map 240–241 *(Hornet),* The *yellowjacket* (vespa vulgaris) . . . The following terms are used for 'hornets' of this type, as well as for wasps of similar appearance . . . *bog h[ornet]* [1 inf, **seNH**].

bogie n[1] [Brit *bogie* a low sturdy cart or truck]

In logging: see quot.

1968 *DARE* Tape **GA**22, Bogie [boʊgi] . . . I've heard 'em [small steam-engine used in logging operation] called that; **GA**50, This bogie [boʊgi], this logging train, brings them out.

bogie n[2]

In marble play: a taw.

1970 *DARE* (Qu. EE6a, . . *Kinds of marbles—the big one that's used to knock others out of the ring*) Inf **MO**30, Bogie.

bogish See **boguish**

boglander n

=**bogtrotter 3.**

1834 *Life Andrew Jackson* 125, It wou'd 've made your hart sick tu've seen so many of the brave boglanders in the dust.

bog lily n

Prob a **blue flag** or a **spiderwort.**

1967 *DARE* (Qu. S24, *A wildflower that grows in swamps and marshes and looks like a small blue iris*) Inf **NE**11, What we call a "bog lily" is similar to that.

bog meadow n chiefly NEng, esp CT

A marshy or swampy meadow.

1748 [see **bog hoe**]. **1843** *Geol. NY* 371, The argillite portion of the county of Orange embraces an unusual *number . . * of swamps, or, as they are called, *bog meadows.* **1857** Stone *Life Howland* 247 **RI**, They had no grass for winter fodder, but bog or salt meadow or thatch. **1860** *Harper's Mag.* 20.583/2 **NJ**, They . . found themselves in an open space of bog meadow. **1939** *LANE* Map 29 **throughout sNEng, esp CT**, *Bog meadow* . . . Low-lying grass land. **1968–69** *DARE* (Qu. C6, . . *A piece of land that's often wet, and has grass and weeds growing on it*) Infs **CT**21, 25, 26, Bog meadow; (Qu. C7, . . *Land that usually has some standing water with trees or bushes growing on it*) Inf **CT**17, Bog meadow.

bog onion n [Prob from the shape of the rootstock or corm]

1 The royal fern *(Osmunda regalis)* or its root.

1889 *Century Dict.* 4167/3, Six species are known, of which three are found in North America, *O. regalis* being the royal fern or osmund royal, also called *bog-onion, buckhorn-brake, ditch-fern,* and *king-fern.* **1959** Carleton *Index Herb. Plants* 17, *Bog Onion:* Arisaema triphyllum; Osmunda regalis.

2 =**jack-in-the-pulpit 1** (here: *Arisaema triphyllum*).

1892 *Jrl. Amer. Folkl.* 5.104, *Arisæma triphyllum,* bog onion. Worcester Co., Mass. **1898** *Bot. Gaz.* 26.256, *Arisaema triphyllum . .* bog onion, Rumford, M[ain]e. **1930** Sievers *Amer. Med. Plants* 37. **1945** Pickard–Buley *Midwest Pioneer* 42 (as of c1820), Jimson-leaf salve was recommended for infection, Indian turnip or bog onion for carbuncles. **1974** (1977) Coon *Useful Plants* 67, *Arisaema triphyllum . .* bog-onions . . . The raw corm (bulb) is poisonous . . and yet the Indians in many parts used the corms boiled as a main item of their diet.

bogoobs See **beaucoup**

bog orchid n Also *bog orchis*

Any of var **fringed orchids** of the genus *Habenaria.*

1903 Porter *Flora PA* 93, *Limnorchis dilatata . . . Tall White Bog Orchis . . .* In bogs and wet woods. **1949** Peattie *Cascades* 240, Out there in the middle of the bog that very handsome one is a fine rein-orchid, Habenaria leucostachys, generally called white bog orchid. **1967** *DARE* Wildfl QR Plates 38, 41b Inf **OR**12, Bog orchid.

bog-pumper n Also *bog-pump* [See quot 1959]

=**bittern.**

1936 Roberts *MN Birds* 1.188, *American Bittern . . . Other names:* Thunder-pumper, Slough-pumper, Bog-pumper. **1959** *Names* 7.119, Likening the bittern's vocalization to the sounds made by the operation of an old-fashioned suction-pump has also been a fruitful source of folk-names. Among these allusions are: bog-pump (Minn., Sask.), bog-pumper (Minn.).

bog rider n West

In cattle raising: see quot 1913.

1913 (1979) Barnes *Western Grazing* 380, *Bog Riders.—*Men whose

duties are to ride the ranges in the spring and look out for weak cows that get into mud holes and have not sufficient strength to get out again. **1920** Hunter *Trail Drivers TX* 299, A "bog rider" is the cowboy who "tails" up the poor cows which get stuck in the mud.

bog shoe n

1940–41 Cassidy *WI Atlas* **seWI**, *Bog shoe*—A block of wood ten inches square and two inches thick, fastened in sets to a horse's hooves to enable it to walk through a bog without sinking.

bog spruce n

=**black spruce 1.**

1910 Graves *Flowering Plants* 36 **CT**, *Picea mariana . . .* Black Spruce. Bog Spruce. Swamps and sphagnum bogs. **1972** Viereck *AK Trees* 51, *Black Spruce . . .* Other names: bog spruce, swamp spruce. Evergreen resinous tree of interior forests . . . Characteristic of cold wet flats, muskegs, . . and lake margins.

bog strawberry n

=**cinquefoil** (here: *Potentilla palustris*).

1910 Graves *Flowering Plants* 233 **CT**, Bog strawberry.

bog the shadow of a buzzard v phr Also *bog a buzzard's shadow* **Sth**

To mire down even the lightest thing.

1898 Lloyd *Country Life* 285 **AL**, The roads was sloppy and soft enough to bog the shadow of a buzzard. **1938** Rawlings *Yearling* 361 **FL**, We got into mud Pa said would bog a buzzard's shadow.

bog torch n

1 =**golden club.** [See quot 1911]

1903 Small *Flora SE U.S.* 228, *Orontium aquaticum . . . Golden-club. Bog Torches.* **1911** *Century Dict. Suppl., Bog-torches . . .* The golden-club, *Orontium aquaticum:* so called from the shape and color of its flower-stalk and flowers. **1934** *Natl. Geog. Mag.* 65.599 **GA**, The swamp boatman amuses himself by pushing the dark-green blades of the bog torch beneath the water and watching them emerge to justify their local name of "never-wets." **1951** Teale *North Spring* 113 **LA**, From time to time we would slow down in little openings, wild water gardens in the marsh, brilliant with the spiked blooms of the golden club. In masses these "bog torches" lifted above the dark water.

2 A **fringed orchid** (here: *Habenaria nivea*).

1933 Small *Manual SE Flora* 373, *G. nivea . . . Bog-torches. Frog-spear. White rein-orchid.* **1953** Greene–Blomquist *Flowers South* 26, *White Rein-Orchid . . .* It is sometimes called "bog-torches." **1976** Bailey–Bailey *Hortus Third* 534, *[Habenaria] nivea . . . Snowy orchid, . . bog-torch . . .* Pine barrens, N.J., s. to Fla., Ala., and Tex.

bogtrotter n

1 =**marsh hawk.**

1874 Coues *Birds NW* 331, The Marsh Harrier . . . often courses very low over the ground, and rather swiftly, turning, passing and repassing, "quartering" the ground like a well-broken dog. This is the habit that has given it the name . . of "Bog-trotter." **1917** (1923) *Birds Amer.* 2.64. **1955** *MA Audubon Soc. Bulletin* 39.442, Marsh Hawk . . . Bog Trotter (Mass. "Bog" used in the sense of marsh; "Trotter" as a patroller thereof.).

2 =**bittern.** [From its habitat]

1917 *Wilson Bulletin* 29.2.78, *Botaurus lentiginosus . . .* bog trotter, Michigan.

3 An Irish person. [From the assoc of peat bogs with Ireland] **chiefly NEast, esp NEng** *joc, sometimes derog*

1930 Shoemaker *1300 Words* 5 **cPA Mts** (as of c1900), *Bog-trotter*— An Irish railroad or canal laborer. **1931–33** *LANE Worksheets* **ceMA, cwCT**, Bog trotters—nickname for Irishmen. **1939** (1962) Thompson *Body & Britches* 222 **NY** (as of c1850), Wild Irish bog trotters from West Ireland . . were set to work knee deep in the wet muck. **1941** *LANE* Map 454 **throughout NEng**, The map shows the nicknames, jocular and derogatory, applied to an Irishman: . . *Bogtrotter.* **1966–69** *DARE* (Qu. CC4, . . *Nicknames . . for various religions or religious groups*) Inf **CT**9, "Bogtrotters" for Irish Catholics; (Qu. HH28, *Names and nicknames around here for . . . Irish*) Infs **VT**12, **WA**6, Bogtrotter.

boguard See **bogart** v

bogue v, hence vbl n *boguing* |bog| Also sp *boag, bog* [Origin unknown] **chiefly Sth, S Midl** Cf **brogue**

Freq with *about, along,* or *around:* To wander or walk aimlessly; to trudge; to grope.

1775 in 1901 Ranck *Boonesboro* 179 **KY,** [We] were four days bogning [sic] in the woods seeking the way.   **1828** (1936) McCoy *Jrl. Exped.* 368 **PA,** On reaching the creek we bogued along its banks by moonshine.   **1870** (1935) Duval *Advent. Big Foot* 132 **TX,** The first thing he knows he will have his 'hair lifted,' 'boging' about alone, with nothing but that 'pop-gun' of his to fight with.   **1899** (1912) Green *VA Folk-Speech, Bogue* . . . To grope, or wander uncertainly about: as, "Bogueing about in the dark."   **1929** *AmSp* 5.17 *Ozarks, Bog* . . . To move slowly; pronounced so as to rhyme with rogue. "I ben a-feelin' so dang dauncy-like I cain't bog scarcely."   **1934** Hurston *Jonah's Gourd Vine* 33 **FL,** John shifted from one foot to another a time or two, then started off with the long stride known as boaging.   **1944** *PADS* 2.40 c**VA,** *Bogue around.*   **1950** *PADS* 14.15 **SC,** *Bogue* . . . To trudge slowly. Usually with adv. *along.*   **1955** Adams *Grandfather* 242 **NY,** Otherwise sensible people went bogueing about the country . . cracking open stones with sledges.   **1967** Will *Dredgeman* 110 **FL,** The men weren't pleasured no great heap to have to slosh and bog in shoe-top water and mud to get to work.   **1967** *DARE* (Qu. Y21, *To move about slowly and without energy*) Inf **TX**1, Bogue ['boug] around; (Qu. Y25, *To walk heavily, making a lot of noise: "He came _____ into the house."*) Infs **KY**5, **OK**1, ['bogɪn]; **MS**16, ['bogɲ].

bogue n [From Choctaw *bog, bok* creek, stream]   **chiefly Gulf States**

1 A stream or waterway—freq used in place names (see quot 1931).   **esp LA**

1814 (1922) Tatum *Jrl.* 67 **NC,** Proceeded to Chicasaw Bogue (a creek so called).   [**1826** Flint *Recollections* 317 **LA,** The rivers that run through these level and swampy pine forests, are called, in the Indian language, "Bogue," with some attribute denoting the character of the stream.]   **1916** *DN* 4.268 **New Orleans LA,** *Bogue* . . . Bayou: in proper names, as Bogue Chitto, Bogue Falaya.   **1923** *Arrow Points* 5 Jan 4 **AL,** Many of the streams in the Choctaw country carry the affix 'Bogue,' in designating their present name.   **1927** (1955) Faulkner *Mosquitoes* 278 **MS,** They'd only see their heads swimming across the bogues and sloughs.   **1931** Read *LA French* 157, Bogue Chitto, "Big Creek or River,"—Choctaw *bog,* "creek," etc., and *chitto,* "big." *Bogue Falaya,* "Long River,"—Choctaw *bog,* "creek," etc., and *falaia,* "long."

2 A native or resident of Florida.

1826 Flint *Recollections* 319 **"West FL"** [now s**MS**], They are a wild race, with but little order or morals among them; they are generally denominated "Bogues," and call themselves "rosin heels."   **1949** *AmSp* 24.26, *Bogue,* and *Rosin-heel* for a Floridian.

bogue adj [Prob abbr for *bogus*]   Cf **boguish**
Phony, fake, bogus.

1953 Randolph *Down in Holler* 228 **Ozarks,** *Bogue-sang* . . . False ginseng.   **1977** Smitherman *Talkin* 45, *Bogue,* adjective used in a derogatory sense (as in *He a bogue dude*), from Hausa *boko,* literally "deceit" or "fake."

bogue-sang n [From **bogue** adj + **sang**]
The root of **pokeweed 1.**

1953 Randolph *Down in Holler* 228 **Ozarks,** *Bogue-sang* . . . False ginseng.   A two-year-old root of the pokeweed *(Phytolacca americana),* properly dried, looks very much like a genuine sang root.

boguish adj |'bogɪš| Also sp *bogish* [Alter of *bogus*]   **chiefly Sth, S Midl** *among Black speakers*   Cf **bogue** adj
Bogus, fake.

1935 Hurston *Mules & Men* 56 **FL** [Black], Dat's bogish [Footnote: Bogus].   **1970** *DARE* (Qu. V7, *A person who sets out to cheat others while pretending to be honest*) Inf **TN**50, Boguish [bogɪš].   **1977** Dillard *Lexicon* 153 [Black], Bogish—"bogus."

bog willow n
The balsam willow *(Salix pyrifolia)* or a **pussy willow** (here: *Salix discolor*) or a hybrid of the two.

1833 Eaton *Botany* 319, *S. discolor,* bog willow, red-root willow, basket willow.   **1938** FWP *Guide MN* 285 **nMN,** Swamp laurel, bog- and autumn-willow, and black currant are only a few of the plants characteristic of this region.   **1979** Little *Checklist U.S. Trees* 266, *Salix pyrifolia* . . . Other common name—bog willow.

bog wintergreen n
A **wintergreen 1,** such as *Pyrola asarifolia.*
1966 *DARE* (Qu. S26c, *Wildflowers that grow in woods*) Inf **MI**31, Bog wintergreen.

boh See **bo**

bohak, bohawk See **bohunk 1**

Bohemian waxwing n   Also *Bohemian chatterer*
A brownish passerine bird *(Bombycilla garrula)* with prominent crest and secondaries with red waxlike tips.   Also called **Canada robin, chinook bird, silktail, winter waxwing**

1828 Bonaparte *Amer. Ornith.* 3.10, Whence does the Bohemian Wax-wing come at the long and irregular periods of its migrations?   **1858** Baird *Birds* 317, Wax-wing [or] Bohemian Chatterer . . [is] seen in the United States only in severe winters, except along the great lakes.   **1968** *Caribou Co. Sun* (Soda Springs ID) 25 Jan 3/1, We saw a huge flock of stray birds and Grace says they are Bohemian Wax Wings or more familiarly known as the Canadian Robin.

Bohemie n [Alter of *Bohemian*]   Cf **bohunk**
1968 *DARE* (Qu. HH28, . . *People of foreign background . . Bohemian*) Infs **IA**32, 46, Bohemies [bohimɪz]

bohind n [Prob blend of **bohunkus** + *behind*]
The buttocks.
1967 *DARE* (Qu. X35, *Joking words for the part of the body that you sit on*) Inf **TX**9, Bohind.

bo-hog n   Pronc-sp for *boar hog*
=**boar b.**
1966 Wilson *Coll.* c**sKY,** Bo-hog . . . Boar.

bo-hoy See **b'hoy 1**

bohunk n [*bo* from *Bohemian* + *hunk* shortening and alter of *Hungarian*]

1 also *bohak, bohawk, bohunkus:* An eastern or southeastern European, esp of the working class.   **chiefly Inland Nth and West** See Map   *often derog*

1903 *Enquirer* (Cincinnati OH) 9 May 13/1 *(DA),* Bohunk—A Bohemian; a foreigner.   **1918** *DN* 5.23 **ID,** Bohunk.   **1924** Holliday *Mining-Camp Melodies* 15 **MT,** He's just a poor Bohunkus, / And his name he can't pronounce.   **1926** *AmSp* 2.88 **NW,** Bohunk.   **1935** Sandoz *Jules* 271 w**NE** (as of 1880–1930), "A Bohemian, forty years old." . . "Cold as the devil up there—freeze the poor Bohunk stiff."   **1946** Thompson *Amer. Daughter* 112 **ND,** Knudt called them flat-headed Polacks or square-headed bohunks.   **1950** *WELS* (People of foreign background: Bohemian) 28 Infs, **WI,** Bohunk.   **1964** *PADS* 42.40 **Chicago IL,** Terms for Czecholovakian [sic] include ten responses of *bohunk,* four of *bohak* /'bohak/.   **1965–70** *DARE* (Qu. HH28, *Names and nicknames . . for people of foreign background . . Bohemian*) 115 Infs, **chiefly Inland Nth and West,** Bohunk.   **1971** *AmSp* 46.81 **Chicago IL,** Czechoslovakian: *bohunk* . . . Lithuanian: . . *bohawk* . . . Polish: . . *bohunk.*

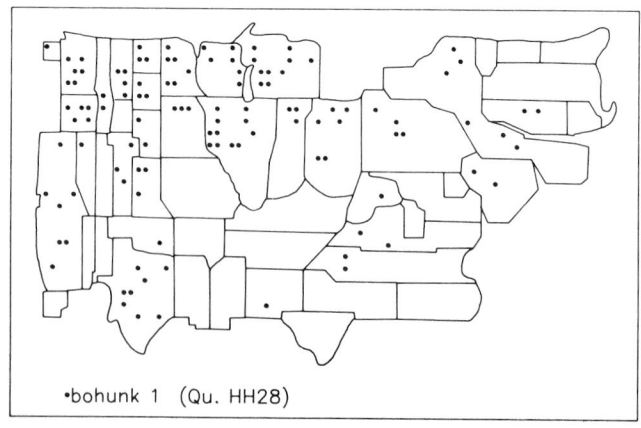

•bohunk 1 (Qu. HH28)

2 See quot.
1930 *DN* 6.86 c**WV,** Bohunk, a heavy, short-handled hammer carried at the hames of a horse.

3 In marble play: a taw, shooter.
1969 *DARE* (Qu. EE6a, . . *Kinds of marbles—the big one that's used to knock others out of the ring*) Inf **NC**63, Bohunk.

4 See **bohunkus 1.**

bohunkus n

1 also *bohunk(y):* The buttocks, haunches. [Perh alter of **bohunk**] **chiefly Sth, esp TX** *joc, euphem*

1962 Atwood *Vocab. TX* 70, *Haunches* . . . Other words are very scattered, and include *ass, bohunkus, butt.* **1965–70** *DARE* (Qu. X35, *Joking words for the part of the body that you sit on*) Infs DC11, LA11, TX51, Bohunkus; TX83, Bohunk; CT9, Bohunky.
2 See **bohunk 1.**

bohunky See **bohunkus 1**

boi n Pronc-sp for *pie PaGer*
1953 *PADS* 19.4 *PaGer*, The pronunciation of [ɔɪ] for standard English [aɪ] in *groier* "crier" and *boi* "pie." . . The word *boi* is also used in a number of compounds, e.g., *bot-boi* "pot pie," *boi-graut* "pie plant" (a regional variant for "rhubarb"), *ebel-boi* "apple pie," and *shnits-boi* "dried apple pie."

boil n¹, v Usu |bɔɪl|; also |baɪl| esp in **Sth, Midl, NEng**; |bɔl| esp in **S Midl**; occas |baɪl|, |bɝl| See Pronc Intro 3.I.11 Pronc-spp *bawl, berl, bile, burl*
A Forms.
1759 in **1882** *Essex Inst. Coll.* 19.67 **MA**, Roberson and I Bilid ris for the Lewtn [boiled rice for the Lieutenant]. **1818** (1920) Clark *Diary* 2322 **CT**, The only hope I have that he is still alive was a bile that was just appearing on his foot as he started. **1893** Shands *MS Speech, Bile* . . . This word is used by both negroes and illiterate whites for the verb *to boil* and for the noun *boil*, a running sore. It is heard also in Louisiana, and may be said to be common throughout the South. **1904** Day *Kin o' Ktaadn* 91 **ME**, Ye can bile a pot of potaters but you can't unbile 'em! **1922** (1926) Cady *Rhymes VT* 254, Your appetite for biled dish calls / For mother's biggest nappy. **1940** *AmSp* 15.374 **NYC**, In the second group is found a diphthong . . [ɔɪ] . . This group includes: *boil, toil, broil.* **1941** *AmSp* 16.230 **Baltimore MD**, Bawled aig [boiled egg]. **1941** *Time* 30 June 52/2 **NYC**, But there is still a problem: how to yell for her [a girl working as "copy boy"]. One faction shouts "Boil" (a portmanteau for "boy" and "girl")—Brooklynite staffmen pronounce it "Burl." **1943** *Sat. Eve. Post* 22 May 37/3 **NYC**, They [=editors] are very hard berled and want glamour in their murder pictures. **1950** (1965) Richter *Town* 226 **OH**, He hadn't heard . . any "b'iling" water. **1961** Kurath–McDavid *Pronc. Engl.* 167, *Boiled, spoiled, oil,* and *boil* . . . Before the velarized /l/ in these words, the earlier /ɔi/ has . . developed into the sequence /ɔr/ . . in scattered instances in the Midland. **1966** *Wilson Coll.* **csKY**, *Boiled* [baɪld]. **1969–70** *DARE* (Qu. BB33a, . . *A swelling under the skin . . that comes to a head*) Infs IL96, KY94, Bile; (Qu. LL10) Infs MD30, MA58, NC38, Kit and bilin'.
B As verb.
1 To prepare or make (coffee).
1931–33 *LANE Worksheets* **cCT**, Boil a pot of coffee. **c1960** *Wilson Coll.* **csKY**, Boil *coffee* rare, "make" more common. **1966** *DARE* Tape AL1, Boil coffee. **1973** Allen *LAUM* 1.296, Expressions for preparing coffee . . . [11 informants] Boil.
2 Of clouds: to grow, increase in size.
1937–40 *Hall Coll.* **eTN, wNC**, "Look at them thunderheads a-bilin' up." "The clouds are a-bilin' up on those mountains." **1966–69** *DARE* (Qu. B6, *When clouds begin to increase, you say it's_____*) Infs AR14, MA17, Boiling up; MO4, Boiling over; AR17, GA80, Clouds are boiling (up).
C As noun.
1 A turbulent swirl or eddy in a stream.
1805 (1905) Clark *Orig. Jrls. Lewis & Clark Exped.* 3.151, In those narrows the water was agitated in a most shocking manner boils swells & whorlpools. **1826** Flint *Recollections* 87, The Mississippi . . is full of singular boils, where the water . . rises with a strong circular motion. **1876** Twain *Old Times* 59 **MO**, Those tumbling "boils" show a dissolving bar and a changing channel there. **1948** *Oklahoman* (Okla. City OK) 4 June 8/1 *(DA)*, The water churned through in boils, and seeped up on the inner side. **1967** *DARE* (Qu. C3, *A place in a swift stream, where the surface of the water is broken*) Inf OR14, A boil (the water is boiling). **1969** *DARE* FW Addit **csKY**, When the river is flooded the current may force itself into an eddy and cause a whirlpool or "boil."
2 Water gushing from a break in a levee.
1938 Burman *Blow for a Landing* 277 **MS**, Occasionally there would come a shout as the earth somewhere inside the levee gave way under the terrific pressure of the water above to form that curious break known to engineers as a boil. **1941** Percy *Lanterns* 246 **MS**, A boil is a small geyser at the base or on the berm of the levee . . . It is caused by the river's pressure fingering out some soft stratum in the soil of the levee or by a crawfish hole.

boil n² [Hypercorrection of *bile* the fluid secreted by the liver; cf **boil** n¹, v **A**]
See quots.
1890 *DN* 1.67 **KY**, Boil. Used sometimes for *bile*, by persons when trying to be exceedingly 'proper'; as, "I took some calomel to work off the boil." **1893** Shands *MS Speech, Boil* . . . Illiterate white for *bile*, used also in Kentucky. "He vomited boil."

boil adj **chiefly Sth, NEng** Cf Pronc Intro 3.I.22
Boiled, cooked by boiling.
1907 *DN* 3.182 **seNH**, *Boil-dinner . . . Boil-dish.* **1932** *DN* 6.283 **swCT**, *Boil cakes.* **1966–67** *DARE* (Qu. H45) Inf PA22, Boil beef; (Qu. H49) Inf SC11, Boil potatoes; (Qu. H51) Inf MS46, Boil cabbage; (Qu. H52) Inf AL6, Boil cabbage. **1967** LeCompte *Word Atlas* 372, [14 of 21 Infs] We had boil shrimp for supper.

boil a few wallops v phr
1975 Gould *ME Lingo* 17, *Boil a few wallops*—To bring to a hard, rolling boil for a short time, as water for a pot of tea.

boil cabbage See **cook turnips**

boil cake See **boiled cake**

boil dinner See **boiled dinner**

boil dish See **boiled dish**

boiled cake n Also *boil cake* **chiefly sNEng** *old-fash* Cf **fried-cake 1**
A doughnut.
1895 *DN* 1.387, *Doughnut . . was biled-cakes* if in twisted form . . . On Cape Cod, and generally in Eastern Mass. **1932** *DN* 6.283 **swCT**, *Boil cakes.* Doughnuts. **1947** Bowles–Towle *New Engl. Cooking* 202, In Connecticut, sweet twisted doughnuts were "biled cakes"; in Massachusetts they were fried cakes.

boiled cider n, also attrib **chiefly NEng**
Cider concentrated by boiling to the consistency of syrup.
1705 in **1884** Lancaster MA *Early Rec.* 153, They drank a barell of boyled Cyder & a barell of strong bear. **1832** *Louisville Public Advt.* 13 Mar *(DA)*, 25 bbls. boiled cider, for sale. **1907** *DN* 3.182 **seNH**, *Boiled-cider apple sauce* . . . Defined by its name. "Apple butter" not used. **1966** *DARE* (Qu. H63) Inf NH6, Boiled-cider dried apple sauce—made of boiled cider and dried apples. **1966–67** *DARE* Tapes NH6, What I was most familiar with was what we called boiled cider drink. We boiled the cider down until it was . . about as thick as maple syrup. And a tablespoon or two . . of the boiled cider and just a pinch of ginger and one-quarter cup of sugar, and that would be mixed with say a quart of water; MA6, They used to make boiled cider there. You've probably heard of boiled cider applesauce and all that.

boiled-cider applesauce See **cider applesauce**

boiled collar n
=**boiled shirt.**
1969 Sorden *Lumberjack Lingo* **NEng, Gt Lakes**, *Boiled collar*—A white dress shirt.

boiled cookie n
A kind of cookie.
1968 *DARE* (Qu. H63) Inf NJ5, Boiled cookie—no flour, no baking; shortening, oatmeal, peanut butter, nuts.

boiled corn See **boiling corn**

boiled custard n **chiefly Sth, S Midl**
A kind of custard; see quot 1932.
1932 (1946) Hibben *Amer. Regional Cookery* 247, *Boiled Custard* (Mississippi) . . eggs . . sugar . . milk, scalded . . vanilla . . cream . . blanched almonds. **1967–68** *DARE* (Qu. H63) Infs CT5, MD50, NC5, 16, TN24, TX38, Boiled custard.

boiled dinner n, also attrib Also rarely *boil dinner* **chiefly Nth, N Midl** See Map See also **New England boiled dinner**
A dish made of meat and vegetables boiled or simmered together; see quot 1979.
1882 Howells *Modern Instance* 120 **MA**, I'm goin' to give 'em potatoes and cabbage to-day,—kind of a boiled-dinner day. **1906** *Pocumtuc Housewife* 9, Directions for a Boiled Dinner may seem unnecessary. **1907** *DN* 3.182 **seNH**, *Boil-dinner . . .* New England boiled dinner; domestic corned beef boiled with vegetables. **1926** *AmSp* 2.78 **ME**.

1936 Lutes *Country Kitchen* 39 **sMI,** A boiled dinner in Southern Michigan differed from its counterpart in New England by the absence of beets. **1950** *WELS (Dishes made with cooked cabbage)* 13 Infs, **WI,** Boiled dinner. **1965–70** *DARE* (Qu. H49, *Dishes made by boiling potatoes with other foods*) 184 Infs, **chiefly Nth, N Midl,** Boiled dinner. **1979** Flagg *Cape Cod Cooking* 13, *Boiled Dinner . . corned beef . . carrots . . parsnips . . turnips . . onions . . potatoes . . cabbage . . . Bring to boil and simmer for about 4 hours.*

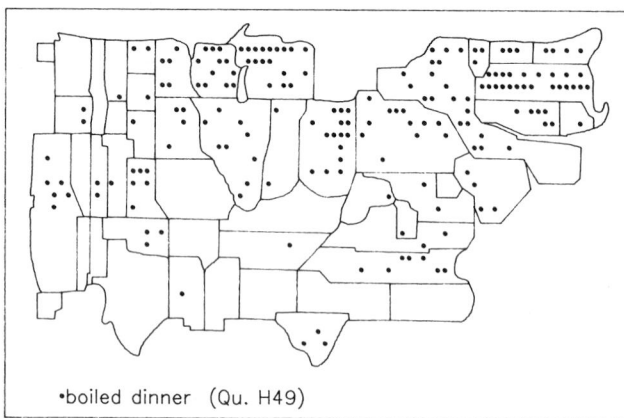

•boiled dinner (Qu. H49)

boiled dish n Also *boil dish*

=**boiled dinner.**

1907 *DN* 3.182 **seNH,** *Boil-dish . . .* New England boiled dinner. **1967** *DARE* (Qu. H49, *Dishes made by boiling potatoes with other foods*) Inf **NY21,** Boiled dish.

boiled dough n

Dumplings.

1960 Korson *Black Rock* 200 **PA,** Dutch mining families went in heavily for dumplings, or "boiled dough," as it was commonly called.

boiled New England dinner See **New England boiled dinner**

boiled owl n Usu in compar phrr *humorous*

1 in v phr *to feel like a boiled owl:* To be physically uncomfortable or nervously exhausted; to be hung over.

1857 *Harper's Mag.* 15.367/1 **NYC,** I felt, to use a certain figurative expression, "like a boiled owl." **1892** *Jrl. Amer. Folkl.* 5.60 **MA,** To feel like a stewed owl, or like a stewed monkey. More idiomatically, like a biled owl. **1907** *DN* 3.187 **seNH,** *Feel like a boiled owl . . .* To be nervously exhausted, as from loss of sleep. "I feel like a boiled owl this morning." **1909** *DN* 3.375 **eAL, wGA,** *Stewed witch . . .* Used to indicate a very uncomfortable bodily condition or state of feeling . . . Similar expressions are *boiled owl, grated potato,* etc. **1951** West *Witch Diggers* 36 **sIN,** I'll feel like a biled owl tomorrow if I don't get to bed.

2 in adj phr *(drunk as, drunker than,* or *full as) a boiled owl:* Extremely drunk.

1862 (1864) Browne *Artemus Ward Book* 114 **NY,** Mike gits as drunk as a biled owl. **1899** (1912) Green *VA Folk-Speech* 27, Drunk as boiled owl. **1907** Porter *Trimmed Lamp* 33 **NYC,** Babbitt was in last night as full as a boiled owl. **1946** *Western Folkl.* 5.335 **CA,** As drunk as a boiled owl. **1967** *DARE* (Qu. DD15, *A person who is thoroughly drunk*) Inf **OH16,** Drunker than a boiled owl.

3 Used as a symbol of a tough or inedible meal.

1929 *AmSp* 5.130 **ME,** It's tough as a b'iled owl. **1975** Gould *ME Lingo* 17, *Boiled owl*—A presumptive, last ditch meal than which, in Maine cookery, there is nothing tougher: "I'm hungry enough to eat a boiled owl!"

boiled pie n Cf **fried pie 1**

A fruit-filled dumpling.

1970 *DARE* (Qu. H63) Inf **NC88,** Boiled pies—dumplings. Make biscuit dough; roll it out like pie crust. Put fruit or berries in center of dough. Pinch sides together in a ball. Drop ball in boiling water.

boiled pot pie n

A stew made with dumplings.

1967–68 *DARE* (Qu. H45) Inf **PA18,** Boiled pot pie—with beef, put dough into the beef stock; (Qu. H49) Inf **MD27,** Boiled pot pie—boiled beef and potatoes, dough dumplings dropped in.

boiled shirt n Also called **fried shirt** Cf **hard-boiled**

A man's starched dress shirt.

1853 in 1954 *AmSp* 29.7 **CA,** I don't look much older, or at least I think I won't, when I get shaved and get a 'boiled shirt' on, which I have not had on since I left home, for we don't boil our shirts here, for we think cold water quite enough in a country where there is no female society. **1872** Twain *Roughing It* 416 **CA,** They [=miners] had a particular and malignant animosity toward what they called a "biled shirt." **1908** *DN* 3.291 **eAL, wGA.** **1912** *DN* 3.571 **wIN.** **1913** *DN* 4.10 **MN.** **1948** *Time* 17 May 73/1, Socialites in boiled shirts or mink coats and plainer citizens in their Sunday best swarmed in. **1950** *PADS* 14.14 **SC.** **c1960** *Wilson Coll.* **csKY,** Boiled shirt . . . A dress-up shirt and all the trimmings. "He's got on his biled shirt today."

boiled yarn n

1909 *DN* 3.419 **Cape Cod MA,** *Boiled yarn . . .* A dish made of brown bread crusts boiled in sweetened milk and water.

boiler n[1]

1 A metal vessel for cooking food. **chiefly Sth** See Map

1903 *DN* 2.295 **Cape Cod MA,** *Boiler . . .* An iron kettle. **1965** *DARE* File **MS** (as of 1956), *Boiler*—the usual word for an ordinary cooking pot or kettle. **1965–70** *DARE* (Qu. F4, *. . The deep metal container used to boil foods*) 65 Infs, **esp Sth,** Boiler.

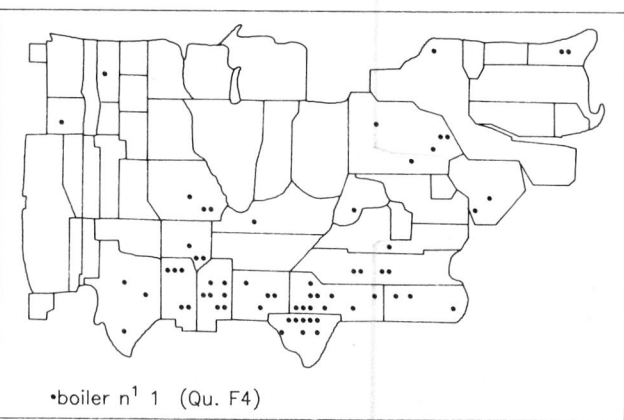

•boiler n[1] 1 (Qu. F4)

2 In the production of illegal whisky: see quot 1974. Also called **evaporator 2**

1934 *AmSp* 9.26, *Boiler.* Whiskey still. **1968** *Foxfire* Fall–Winter 49 **nGA,** *Still*—the container into which the beer is placed for boiling. Also called the *Evaporator* or *Boiler.* **1974** Maurer *KY Moonshine* 114, *Boiler . . .* An enclosed vessel in which water is boiled to generate steam for a steam still. It may be anything from an old oil drum, with crude fittings, to a standard upright, factory-made steam boiler with gauges . . . "Boiler blowed up and kilt three of 'em."

3 Among loggers: a poor cook. **chiefly Nth, Pacific NW**

1927 *DN* 5.439, *Boiler . . .* The cook at a construction or lumber camp. **1938** (1939) Holbrook *Holy Mackinaw* 258, *Boiler.* A bum cook. **1958** McCulloch *Woods Words* **Pacific NW,** *Boiler . . .* A poor cook. **1969** Sorden *Lumberjack Lingo* **NEng, Gt. Lakes.** **1975** Gould *ME Lingo* 17, *Boiler*—Uncomplimentary terms for a woods cook whose talents are limited to boiled foods. Life in camp is bad enough without having a cussid boiler in the cookshack.

4 A tobacco pipe.

1950 *WELS (A tobacco pipe)* 2 Infs, **WI,** Boiler. **1966** *DARE* (Qu. DD6c, *. . A pipe*) Inf **FL28,** Boiler.

5 in phr *smoke like a boiler:* To smoke (tobacco) excessively.

1968 *DARE* (Qu. DD9b, *Of a person who smokes a great deal you might say, "He smokes like a _____."*) Infs **IN35, MO16,** Boiler.

6 The stomach.

1886 in 1950 *AmSp* 25.30 **New Orleans LA,** Getting his biler loaded on free beer and booze. **c1960** *Wilson Coll.* **csKY,** *Boiler . . .* Stomach. "You'll bust your biler if you eat one more bite."

7 See quot. [Transf from *boiling mad*]

1950 *WELS (A bad-tempered, quarrelsome man)* 1 Inf, **seWI,** Boiler.

boiler n[2]

A furuncle, boil.

c1960 *Wilson Coll.* **csKY,** *Boiler . . .* "He's got a boiler on his leg."

boiler compound n [Cf **boiler** n¹ 6]
Among loggers: see quot.
1958 McCulloch *Woods Words* **Pacific NW**, *Boiler compound*—Any medicine taken inside.

boiling n Freq pronc-sp *bilin'*, also *bylin'* [*boiling* a mass of material boiled together at one time; cf *OED boiling* vbl. sb. 4] **chiefly Sth, S Midl, NEng** Cf **kit and biling**
Everyone, the whole lot; a crowd; rabble.
1833 Neal *Down-Easters* 1.61 **NEng**, Gage was the biggest gentleman ever you see, an' so's the whole bylin' of 'em. **1885** Twain *Huck. Finn* 257 **MO**, The whole *bilin'* of 'm 's frauds! **1907** *DN* 3.229 **nwAR, seMO**, *Bilin'* . . . All of a number. **1917** *DN* 4.408 **IL, KY, NE, wNC, NEng**, *Bilin'*. **1941** *LANE* Map 415 **scattered NEng**, The map shows the collective terms applied to a group of persons whom the speaker dislikes or of whom he disapproves: . . *boiling*. **1944** *PADS* 2.17 **sAppalachians**, *Bilin'* ['baɪlɪn] . . . Common in the South. **1957** Faulkner *Town* 333 **MS**, Unless your father really does get shut of the whole damned boiling of you. **1969** *DARE* (Qu. LL10, *A whole group of people: "They made too much noise, so he sent the whole _____ home."*) Inf **IL53**, Boiling of them.

boiling ppl adj
Of meat: fit only for boiling; tough.
1966–69 *DARE* (Qu. H38, *Other words for bacon*) Inf **SC11**, Boiling bacon; (Qu. H49, *Dishes made by boiling potatoes with other foods*) Inf **CA107**, Boiling beef; **IN60**, Boiling beef and potatoes or noodles.

boiling arch See **arch 2**

boiling corn n Also *boiled corn, boiling ear* Cf **roasting ear**
Young or sweet corn.
1941 *LANE* Map 261 **MA**, The map shows the terms *sweet corn, green corn* . . [boɪld kɔən]. **1949** *AmSp* 24.106 **ceGA**, *Boiling-corn* . . . Green corn. **1950** *WELS* (*When ears of corn are just ripe enough for eating, you call them _____*) 1 Inf, **csWI**, Boiling ears. **1968** *DARE* (Qu. I33, *What do you call ears of corn that are just right for eating?*) Inf **NJ21**, Boiling corn.

boiling down n *?obs*
1884 Harrison *Negro Engl.* 262, To need bilin' down = to need correction or rebuke.

boiling ear See **boiling corn**

boiling out n
A scolding, tongue-lashing.
1969 *DARE* (Qu. II27, . . *A very sharp scolding . . "I certainly got a _____ for that."*) Inf **RI4**, Boiling out.

boiling water n **chiefly Sth**
A boat's wake.
1965–70 *DARE* (Qu. O16, . . *The stirred-up water following a boat*) 12 Infs, Boiling water. [6 Infs Black]

boil me down exclam [Cf *blow me down*]
1954 Harder *Coll.* **cwTN**, *Boil me down* . . . Exclamation expressing surprise or incredulity.

boil off the stomach v phr
1970 *DARE* (Qu. BB18, *To vomit a great deal at once*) Inf **DC13**, Boil off the stomach.

boil one's cabbage twice See **chew one's cabbage twice**

boil out See **boil up**

boil over v phr **West**
Of a horse: to start to buck.
1937 *DN* 6.619 **swTX**, When the bronco commences to buck, he *wrinkles his spine*, . . or *boils over*. **1961** Adams *Old-Time Cowhand* 295, When a hoss started to buck there were a lot of slang expressions the cowhand used for a description of this act. The hoss "arches his back," "boils over," . . or was said to be "slattin' his sails."

boil pot n Cf **boiled dinner, boil the pot**
1968 *DARE* (Qu. H49, *Dishes made by boiling potatoes with other foods*) Inf **CT2**, Boil pot—boiled potatoes and usually turnips; old-fashioned.

boil pricker n Also *boil picker* joc
A man's shoe with a pointed toe.

1968–70 *DARE* (Qu. W42a, . . *Men's sharp-pointed shoes*) Inf **NY105**, Boil prickers; **PA234**, Boil pickers [laughter]. [Both Infs old]

boil the pot v phr *old-fash* Cf **boil pot**
See quots.
1908 *DN* 3.292 **eAL, wGA**, *Boil the pot* . . . To cook a vegetable dinner, boil vegetables. "Mrs. Blackstone boils the pot nearly every day." **1912** Green *VA Folk-Speech* 89, Country folks "boiled the pot," that is boiled ham, corned beef, or chine, with vegetables, nearly every day in the week.

boil-thickened adj
1914 *DN* 4.69 **ME, nNH**, *Boil-thickened* . . . Referring to a kind of gravy, thickened, while boiling, by flour stirred in.

boil up v phr Also *boil out* [From the practice of boiling clothes to delouse them] **chiefly Nth, Pacific NW** *esp among loggers*
To wash one's clothes (or oneself); by ext, *boil up* n attrib.
1919 *DN* 5.41 [Hobo argot], *Boil up* . . . To wash oneself and boil one's clothes. **1929** *AmSp* 4.338 [Hobo argot], *Boil up*—To wash your clothes. **1938** (1939) Holbrook *Holy Mackinaw* 258, *Boiling-up*. Washing one's clothes. **1958** McCulloch *Woods Words* **Pacific NW**, *Boil up* . . . To wash clothes by boiling them. **1968** Adams *Western Words*, *Boil out*—A logger's expression meaning to *wash one's clothes.* Also *boil up.* **1969** Sorden *Lumberjack Lingo* **NEng, Gt Lakes**, *Boiling up, boiling out*, or *boil up*—Washing one's clothes; sometimes to delouse one's clothes by boiling them. Early camps were often infested with body lice and bedbugs. The lumberjacks tried to kill them by boiling their clothes when the clothes were washed. Boil up day was always Sunday.

boil water v phr
To waste time.
1950 *WELS* (*Wasting time by doing unimportant or useless things*) 1 Inf, **cnWI**, Boiling water.

bo-ink-um n Cf **spizzerinctum**
Stamina, grit.
1903 Wasson *Cap'n Simeon's Store* 200 **ME** (as of c1850), You got the bo-ink-um right into ye, yit, hain't ye, Cap'n?

bois d'arc n, also attrib Usu |'bo₁dɑ(r)k|, occas |'bwɑ₁dɑrk|, rarely |'bɔr–| Pronc-spp *bodark, bowdark, bodock, bodok* [Fr *bois d'arc* bow wood] **chiefly TX, LA, OK, AR, TN, KY** See Map
=**Osage orange.**
1805 U.S. Congress *Debates & Proc.* 9th Cong 2d Sess 1138 **LA**, At this place Mr. Dunbar obtained one or two slips of the *"bois d'arc,"* (bow wood, or yellow wood,) from the Missouri. **1844** (1954) Gregg *Commerce* 360, In many of the rich bottoms from the Canadian to Red River . . is found the celebrated *bois-d'arc* . ., usually corrupted in pronunciation to *bowdark*. **1872** Schele de Vere *Americanisms* 110, *Bois d'arc* . . became in the hands of English hunters *Bowdark*, in which form it was long familiar along the whole Western frontier, and finally it settled down into the still shorter *Bodok*, which is now the common designation. **1885** Thompson *By-Ways* 158, The cat-bird . . is . . the musical deity of our blackberry jungles and *bois d'arc* hedges. **1933** *AmSp* 8.1.48 **Ozarks**, *Bodark* . . . The Osage orange or *bois d'arc*, a tree which is very common in the prairie country north and west of the Ozark hills. **1949** Dean *Diamond Bess* 115 **TX**, I want to thank you for handling the bois d'arc apples for us . . . those settlers out on the prairies are buying them for seeds to sow along the lines of their land to grow hedges and make fences, and they call them Osage oranges. **1950** *PADS* 14.15 **SC**,

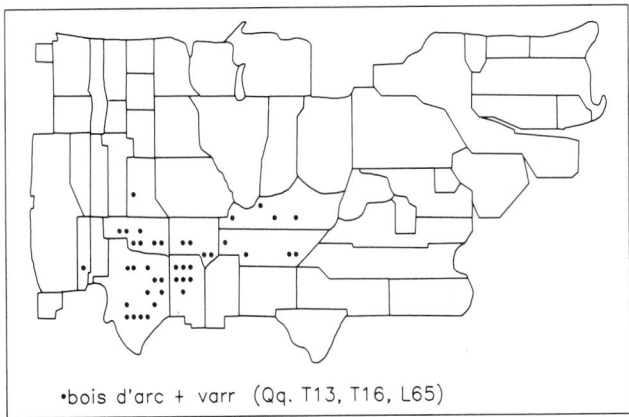

•bois d'arc + varr (Qq. T13, T16, L65)

Bodock . . . The *bois-d'arc* or Osage orange. Sporadic and obsolescent in S.C. **c1960** *Wilson Coll.* **csKY,** *Bois-d'ark* . . . /ˈboˌdak, ˈboˌdark/. **1965–70** *DARE* (Qu. T13) 28 Infs, **chiefly TX, AR, LA,** Bodark; KS2, Bois d'arc; LA18, [ˈbouˌdark]; LA33, [ˈbwaˌdark]; TN26, Bodock [ˈbouˌdak]; (Qu. L65) Inf MS58, Bodock [ˈboˌdak] fence . . a hedge fence—a tree full of thorns; TX75, [ˈbɔr dark] fence; TX89, [ˈbo dark] fence; TX42, 51, [ˈbouˌdɔrk] hedge; (Qu. T16) Infs OK7, 11, 18, 20, 25, 42, 52, Bodark. **1979** Little *Checklist U.S. Trees* 165, *Osage-orange* . . . Other common names—bodark, bodock.

boist n
A rough shelter.
1939 *LANE* Map 110 **CT, RI,** *Pig Pen; Hog House* . . . *Hog boist,* used as a boy; cf. [dɔg bɐɪst], a dog house.

bo-jack n [bo + *jack*] Cf **man jack**
A fellow, person.
1970 *DARE* (Qu. CC11, *When somebody has had a lot of good luck, you say he _____*) Inf TN53, Is a lucky bo-jack.

bold adj, adv
Of running water: swift; swiftly, abundantly.
1805 (1904) Lewis *Orig. Jrls. Lewis & Clark Exped.* 1.298, The little Missouri . . is 134 yards wide at it's mouth and sets in with a bould current. *Ibid* 362, A beautifull bold runing stream. **1821** (1898) Fowler *Jrl.* 28 **swKS,** A streem of Bold Running Water one Hundred and fifty feet Wid. **1837** in 1926 *AmSp* 2.28 **IL,** A fine mill stream, with a bold current. **1895** *DN* 1.370 **eTN, wNC,** *Bold:* freely, plentifully. "The spring don't flow as bold as it did." **1943** Chase *Jack Tales* 91 **wNC** (as of 1880s), So Jack took that walkin' stick and went on to where there was a very bold spring comin' out the ground. **1969** *SC Market Bulletin* 11 Sept 1/2, 51 Acres in heart of mountains, large log home, guest house, bold streams.

bolden v, adj Also *boulden* [Scots *boldin, boulden* to swell; see 1840 Jamieson *Etym. Dict.*] *relic*
1953 Randolph *Down in Holler* 229 **Ozarks,** *Bolden* . . . To swell . . . *Boulden* . . . Swollen.

bold hives n
1 Croup. *now hist*
1824 Doddridge *Notes Indian Wars* 148 **WV, PA,** The croup, or what was then [c1775] called the "Bold hives" was a common disease among the children, many of whom died of it. **1945** Pickard–Buley *Midwest Pioneer* 22, Quite a few children died from the croup, or "bold hives."
2 also *boll hives, bone hives:* A supposedly fatal skin disease; see quot 1947. **chiefly S Midl**
1947 (1964) Randolph *Ozark Superstitions* 111, Nearly every hillman has heard of the strange disease called *bold* hives or *boll* hives, supposed to be invariably fatal. Ozark M.D.'s tell me there is no such thing . . . "When I get there," said Dr. J.H. Young, "I generally find a case of ordinary hives, and they always get well." **1949** Arnow *Hunter's Horn* 241 **KY,** At mention of the boll hives Milly's eyes widened with terror; they could kill a young baby, and even plain hives could be dangerous if they worked in. **1968** *DARE* (Qu. BB25, . . *Common skin diseases*) Inf OH45, Boll hives is the worst. **1971** *Foxfire* Winter 252 **nGA,** Mrs. Andy Webb told us . . . "It looks sort'a like th'measles, but it ain't measles. Them's bold hives. . . . Th'bold hives works around th'heart." . . Ethel Corn told us . . . "If them hives don't break out on 'em—if it's th'bone hives—it'll kill 'em." **1981** *Broaddus Coll.* **ceKY,** Bold hives—a severe variety of hives. Should they "go in," they are fatal, according to informant.

bolichi roast n [CubanSpan *boliche* round of beef + *roast*]
1939 FWP *Guide FL* 196 **Key West FL,** Bolichi roast . . . Beef stuffed with hard boiled eggs.

bolita n [AmSpan *bolita* dimin of *bola* ball]
Prob a puffball.
1967 *DARE* (Qu. S18, . . *Mushroom that grows like a globe*) Inf CO31, Bolita. [FW: three people know this term].

boll-evil n [Perh folk-etym]
1928 Peterkin *Scarlet Sister Mary* 188 **SC,** Some people called the creatures boll-weevils, others called them boll-evils.

boll hives See **bold hives 2**

bollicky adj, adv Also in phr *bollicky bare-ass(ed)* |ˈbɒlɪki, ˈba‑| [Prob orig Ir Engl from *ballock* testicle + *-y*] **NEng** Cf **bollix**
Naked; nakedly.
[**1922** Joyce *Ulysses* 610 **Ireland,** See them there stark ballock-naked.] [**1936** in 1943 Hone *W.B. Yeats* 480 **Ireland,** I went in and there she was saving your presence, bollicky naked.] **1967–69** *DARE* (Qu. W20, *If somebody has no clothes on at all—for example, "There was Johnny, _____," or, "They went in swimming _____."*) Inf CT9, [ˈbalɪki]; MA27, Bollicky; MA7, 33, 72, [ˈbɒlɪki] bare-ass(ed); VT16, Bollicky bare-assed.

bolliwog n Cf **bolly wash**
=belly wash 3.
1950 *Sun* (Baltimore MD) 20 Jan 21/3, This propaganda campaign is a lot of bolliwog.

bollix v, hence ppl adj *bollixed* Usu with *up* Also sp *ballix, ballocks, bullox* [From *ballocks* testicles] **chiefly Nth, N Midl**
1 To throw into disorder or confusion, mix up. See Map
1937 (1959) Weidman *I Can Get It* 47 **NY,** Watch your script . . . You're getting your cues all bollixed up. **1940** *New Yorker* 7 Dec 23/1 **NYC,** All papers were kept together, and finding any one of them was a task. "It was bollixed up then," Patrolman McQuillan told us reflectively. **1949** *AmSp* 24.152 (as of c1890), *Bullox* . . . It means to confuse, mess, or disarrange things . . . A Nebraska man who knew and used the word in the later part of the nineteenth century has reported the same meaning, but he rhymed it with *frolics.* **1959** Faulkner *Mansion* 52 **MS,** Likely what bollixed Montgomery Ward at first . . was exactly why Flem wanted him specially in Parchman. *Ibid* 131, God was anyhow a gentleman and wouldn't bollix up the same feller twice with the same trick. **c1960** *Wilson Coll.* **csKY,** All ballixed up—Mixed up, confused, out of fix. **1965–70** *DARE* (Qu. GG2, *Expressions meaning "confused, mixed up": "So many things were going on at the same time that he got completely _____."*) 20 Infs, **chiefly Nth, N Midl,** Bollixed (up).

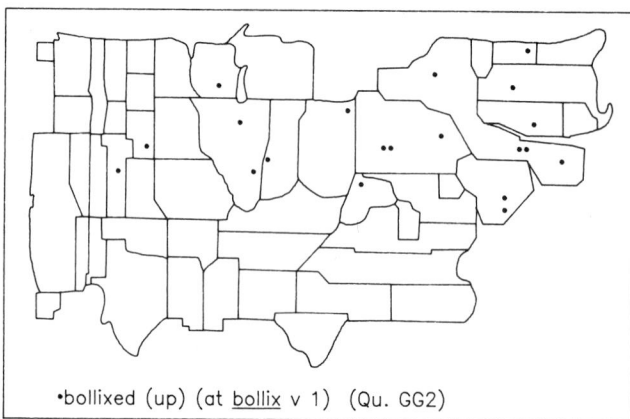

•bollixed (up) (at <u>bollix</u> v 1) (Qu. GG2)

2 To perform badly, do a poor job; botch, bungle.
1946 *New Yorker* 17 Aug 14/3 **NYC,** I bollixed the plot by deliberately playing the wrong number at the wrong time. **1949** *PADS* 11.3 **wTX,** *Ballocks* [ˈbalɔks] . . . To do a job improperly, particularly to do it so that it is harder to finish than it was originally. "He ballocksed the job." Rare. **1952** Steinbeck *East of Eden* 550 **nCA,** He'd made a mess of things. He wondered if he'd bollixed up the breaks. **1967–69** *DARE* (Qu. JJ42, *To make an error*) Inf NY60, Bollixed it up; (Qu. KK63, *To do a clumsy or hurried job . . "It will never last—He just _____."*) Infs IN32, MI9, Bollixed it (up); WI27, Bollixed up the job.

3 with *around:* To fool around: see quot.
c1960 *Wilson Coll.* **csKY,** *Ballocksing around* . . . Spreeing around, not necessarily in a sexual way. "He's always ballocksing around when he ought to be at work."

bollix n Also sp *ballix* [**bollix** v]
1958 McCulloch *Woods Words* 7 **Pacific NW,** *Ballix*—Any kind of a messed-up situation. **1967** *DARE* (Qu. JJ41, *An embarassing mistake: "Last night she made an awful _____."*) Inf PA39, Bollix.

bollo n [AmSpan, from Span *bollo* small loaf or roll]
A fritter made of black-eyed peas.
1966 *DARE* Tape FL23, Bollo [ˈbɔɪjə] . . a little fritter . . . served often at parties. They're quite spiced. The basis for the fritter is a meal or a batter made from black-eye peas and they're fried in deep fat.

boll weaver n Also sp *bowl weever* [Folk-etym for *boll weevil*]
1 A period of severe infestation by the boll weevil.

1947 *True* 32.105 **New Orleans LA** [Black], Even with those hard times during the Bowlweever I'd be willing to live them all over again.

2 The larva of the boll weevil *(Anthonomus grandis).*

1969 *DARE* (Qu. R27) Inf **GA**89, Bollworm, on cotton—also called boll weaver.

boll weevil n Pronc-sp *boweevil* **esp TX, OK** *chiefly among oil-field workers*

A novice, tenderfoot; a worthless or contemptible person.

1932 *AmSp* 7.264 **CA,** [Oil field language:] *Boll-weevil* . . . A Texan. 1941 FWP *Guide OK* 121, Oil-field workers use . . the following expressions . . . Boweevil—(Boll Weevil) A worthless fellow, or a novice at oil-field work. 1967 *DARE* (Qu. HH15, *A very inexperienced person, one who is just learning how to do a new thing*) Infs **TX**11, 18, 19, Boll weevil—among oil men. 1967 *DARE* Tape **TX**19, When they get an inexperienced man on there, he's a boll weevil ['bɔ,wivəl]. 1969 *AmSp* 44.202, [Truck drivers' jargon] *Boll weevil*—Novice truck driver. 1971 *Today Show Letters* **Birmingham AL** (as of 1930s), Boll weevil . . . A mean, despised person.

boll weevil weather n

Cold, wet weather.

1966 *DARE* Tape **NC**15, The boll weevil thrives in cold, damp, wet weather, like we're having this spring. This is boll weevil weather.

bollworm n, also attrib Also *cotton bollworm* **Sth**

Any of var noctuid moth larvae, but esp the **earworm** when feeding on cotton.

1848 U.S. Patent Office *Annual Rept. for 1847: Ag.* 171 **AL,** In view then of . . the destruction caused by the boll worm . . the receipts at Mobile will show another short crop. 1856 U.S. Patent Office *Annual Report for 1855: Ag.* 67, Mocking-birds and bee-martins catch and destroy the boll-worm moth. 1870 *Amer. Naturalist* 3.168, Will our Southern friends, as the season opens, remember that we want specimens of the Cotton Ball [sic] Worm and Army Worm, in all their stages. 1899 U.S. Dept. Ag. *Yearbook for 1898* 256, The habit of the boll worm larva of feeding in concealment renders it practically impossible to kill it with poisons . . . Late fall plowing is of value in ridding infested fields of the boll worm. 1900 Bailey *Cyclop. Horticulture* 1.376, The corn worm is also known south as the cotton-boll worm. It is destructive to sweet corn especially. 1909 Smith *Insect Friends* 264, In the southern states the cotton at this time begins to offer an attraction . . and . . the "boll-worm" makes its appearance. 1965–70 *DARE* (Qu. R27) Infs **GA**89, **SC**40, 43, 49, 53, 57, Bollworm.

bolly n

A cotton boll pulled off with the dry or green cover still on it.

1929 Vance *Human Factors* 132 **Sth,** Frost bitten bolls harvested whole are called "bollies." 1949 *PADS* 11.3 **wTX,** *Bollies* . . . Cotton that is pulled off with the burr, not picked. Common rural.

bollyhock See **ballyhack** v

bolly wash n Cf **bolliwog, bottlewash**

=**belly wash 3.**

1967 *DARE* (Qu. NN13, *When you think that the thing somebody has just said is silly or untrue: "Oh, that's a lot of _____."*) Inf **AL**25, Bolly wash.

bologna n, also attrib Also sp *baloney* **chiefly NEast and West**

A poor quality beef animal fit only to make sausage.

1899 *Chicago Daily News* (IL) 7 June 11/5, Choice fat light bulls went at stronger prices, but the heavy bologna stock was still dragging at the bottom. 1935 *AmSp* 10.270 **NE,** *Bolognas.* Bulls of low grade, suitable for bologna [sausage]. 1965–70 *DARE* (Qu. K15, *A thin, bony, or poor-looking cow*) 27 Infs, **chiefly NEast,** Baloney (cow); **KY**35, Baloney-type; (Qu. K20, *A calf that is sold for meat*) Inf **NJ**8, Baloney cow. [27 of 29 Infs old] 1968 *Blackfoot News* (ID) 23 Jan 6/4, Farm to Market Report . . . Bologna bulls. 1968 Adams *Western Words, Bologna bulls*—Animals of inferior quality whose meat is used to make Bologna sausage.

bolson n, also attrib [MexSpan *bolsón*] **chiefly SW**

A flat desert basin surrounded by mountains or higher ground.

1905 Bray *Vegetation* 20, Covillaea forms a characteristic feature of the bolson desert vegetation in West Texas. 1951 Fergusson *New Mexico* 405, Bolson—A flat-floored desert valley.

bolt-stretcher See **stretcher**

bomb n Cf **bomber**

1 See quot.

c1970 Wiersma *Marbles Terms* **cwMI,** *Bomb* . . . A sharp downward throw, performed from the standing position; the object is to hit the other player's marble.

2 See **bombsie(s).**

bombardment n

1 A children's group game; see quot 1909.

1909 (1923) Bancroft *Games* 334, *Bombardment* . . . This game . . consists in trying to overturn Indian clubs or tenpins set up in the opponents' court . . . The players are divided into two teams . . . Each player will . . serve both as a guard to protect his clubs, and as a thrower . . . Each club overturned scores one point for the side which knocked it down. 1969 *DARE* (Qu. EE33, . . *Outdoor games . . that children play*) Inf **IL**97, Elimination—also called bombardment.

2 See quot.

1981 Pederson *LAGS Urban Material* **Dallas TX,** *Rough games:* . . bombardment [1 inf]. Six or seven people stand against a wall. Someone else stands about 20 feet away and tries to hit them with a volleyball. Whoever gets hit is "out"; the last one left at the wall is the winner.

Bombay n

1901 *DN* 2.136 **St. Louis MO,** *Bombay* . . . Same as Spanish fly. *Ibid* 148, *Spanish fly* . . . A kind of leap-frog, played at St. Paul's School, Concord, N.H.

bombazine n [Transf from *bombazine* a twilled fabric of silk and wool; perh also infl by **bumbershoot**] *joc*

An umbrella.

1943 *Sun* (Baltimore MD) 24 Aug 10/7, Bombazine . . was also the chief fabric . . of umbrellas. Hence those useful implements were occasionally called "bombazines." The word was almost always used humorously, probably because it has such a formidable sound. 1970 *DARE* (Qu. W1c, *Joking names . . for an umbrella*) Inf **NJ**69, Bombazine ['bʌmbə,zin].

bomber n

1 In marble play: a large marble dropped or thrown to knock other marbles out of a ring. Cf **bomb, bombsie(s), boulder**

1967 *DARE* (Qu. EE6d, *Special marbles*) Inf **SC**44, Bomber—a large one. c1970 Wiersma *Marbles Terms* **seMI,** *Bomber*—Marble used in bomb shot. *Ibid* **neIL,** *Bombers*—Marbles dropped from chest height.

2 See quot.

1973 Ferretti *Marble Book* 67, In *boss-out* . . the player who hits or spans to his opponent's marble takes that marble . . . If the distance between the marbles is less than a step but more than a span, the shooter has the option . . of picking his marble up and dropping it straight down from face level in an attempt to hit his opponent's marble. This is called *bomber.*

3 =**submarine sandwich.**

1969 *DARE* (Qu. H42, *The kind [of sandwich] in a much larger, longer bun, that's a meal in itself*) Inf **IL**45, A bomber.

bombersoll See **bumbersol**

bomb fly n

The northern cattle grub *(Hypoderma bovis).*

1928 Metcalf–Flint *Destructive & Useful Insects* 791, Two different botflies attack cattle in America: one is known as the striped ox-warble fly . . the other has been called the . . northern cattle grub and recently the fanciful name "bomb fly" has been proposed for it. 1969 WI *Statist. Reporting Serv. Report* 2 June, H.V. of Barron County says: Bomb flies causing cattle to run.

bombosity n Also *bumbosity* [Cf *OED bombous* convexly rounded] *joc* Cf **bum** n[1]

The buttocks.

1932 *AmSp* 7.329 **MD,** [Johns Hopkins University Jargon] Bombosity —the buttocks. 1950 *WELS (Joking words for the part of the body that you sit on)* 1 Inf, **seWI,** Bumbosity. 1965–70 *DARE* (Qu. X35) Infs **CA**2, **MI**2, **VA**39, Bombosity; **CA**59, Bumbosity.

bombsie(s) n Also *bomb* Cf **bomb**

In marble play: see quots.

1968 *DARE* (Qu. EE7, . . *Marble games*) Inf **PA**163, Bombsies—drop a marble on others. c1970 Wiersma *Marbles Terms* **cwMI,** *Bomb*—Shot in which the marble is thrown into the playing area. *Bombsie*—A type of dropping shot. **1973** Ferretti *Marble Book* 40, *Bombsie.* A rather unsophisticated arching, dropping shot.

bonanza farm n **chiefly Upper MW, scattered West**

A very large and productive farm; hence *bonanza farmer, ~ farming.*

1878 Conklin *Picturesque AZ* 32, One can get an extended and . . at least a flattering idea of a bonanza farm of Southern California. **1909** *Sat. Eve. Post* 30 Jan 30/2, What bonanza-farming is in any way equal to that? **1937** Woodward *Checkered Years* 10 **eND, wMN,** One bonanza farmer alone had, at one time, 600,000 bushels of No. 1 hard in the elevators which he was holding for better prices. **1938** FWP *Guide MN* 93, The invention of farm machinery made possible the "bonanza" wheat farms, the like of which the world had never seen before. One farm alone boasted 30,000 acres. **1943** Howard *Montana* 175, As a matter of fact, up to this time the few 'bonanza' farms in Montana were primarily livestock operations. **1946** Gray *Pine* 17 **MN, WI,** The soil is rich and deep; great dramas of bonanza farming have been enacted on it. **1966** *DARE* Tape ND2, Bonanza farm . . . A very large farm.

bonaparte n

1 A custard-filled pastry. [Cf *napoleon* a filled pastry]
1968 *DARE* (Qu. H32, . . *Fancy rolls and pastries*) Inf **NY88,** Bonapartes—flaky crust with custard filling.

2 See quot. [Punning *bony + part*] *joc*
1967–70 *DARE* (Qu. K15, *A thin, bony, or poor-looking cow*) Inf **TN58,** Bonaparte; **CO7,** Bonaparte ['bonɪˌpɑrt].

bonas See **boners**

bonce n [Engl dial]
1955 *PADS* 23.11 **cwTN,** Bonce . . . A large marble . . . A game played with large marbles.

bon dance n [See quot]
1972 Carr *Da Kine Talk* 113, Bon dance (Japanese + English). A Japanese folk dance performed in mid-July in Hawaii as a part of the *O-bon* 'festival of the dead.'

bond boy n Cf **bound** adj **1**
1959 *VT Hist.* ns 27.126, Bond boy . . . A boy sent to work for another family, if his own family could not support him. Rare.

bondfire n [?Folk-etym]
A bonfire.
1979 *DARE* File **IA** (as of c1910), I [Allen Walker Read] said *bondfire* as a boy in Iowa, and learned *bonfire* in school.

bondy-bun n
1954 *Harder Coll.* **cwTN,** Bondy-bun . . . Sweetheart.

bone n

1 A dollar. *old-fash*
1896 *DN* 1.413 **seNY,** Bones: "Cold bones," dollars. **1896** (1898) Ade *Artie* 10 **Chicago IL,** I guess I saw as much as two bones change hands. **1909** *DN* 3.393 **nwAR. 1912** *DN* 3.571 **wIN. 1916** *DN* 4.272 **IL, IA, KS, MA, NE, PA. 1919** *DN* 5.66 **CA, NM. 1927** *AmSp* 2.349 **WV. 1950** *WELS (A silver dollar)* 1 Inf, **csWI,** Bone. [Inf old] **1970** *DARE* (Qu. U20, . . *Dollars*) Inf **IL117,** Bones. [Inf old] **1981** Pederson *LAGS Urban Material* **swAL,** Money: . . [1 inf] Bones.

2 in var combs: A dog. *joc*
1916 *DN* 4.340 **seOH,** Bone eater. A dog. **1926** *AmSp* 1.650, [Hobo argot] *Bone polisher*—a bad dog. **1966–69** *DARE* (Qu. J2, . . *Words . . for dogs*) Infs **PA226, TN34,** Bone hound; **NH12,** Bone head.

3 also *bones* and in var combs: A medical doctor. *joc*
1965–70 *DARE* (Qu. BB53a, . . *Joking names . . for a doctor*) Infs **CA80, 164, MD5, MI10,** Bone-crusher; **ID5, MO20,** Bone-breaker; **MS15,** Bone-butcher; **CA209,** Bone doctor; **CT23,** Bone-setter; **OH71,** Bones.

4 A cherry seed.
1968 *DARE* (Qu. I48, *The hard center of a cherry: you call that a cherry _____*) Inf **CA87,** Bone—common.

5 A person of mixed racial heritage. [Cf **red bone**]
1945 *Amer. Jrl. Sociol.* 51.34 **SC,** These outcastes [people of White, Indian and Black ancestry], whom I call "mestizos," are designated by a wide variety of names, none of them flattering . . . In some localities they are given the most common surname in the group and are called . . "Creels," . . or "Bones," the last being an impudent corruption of the family name Boone.

6 =**bone coal.**
1973 *PADS* 59.27 **coal mining areas of PA, sWV, VA,** Bone . . . = *bone coal.*

7 A woman.
1970 *DARE* (Qu. HH34, *General words around here for a woman, not necessarily uncomplimentary*) Inf **OH103,** Bone. [Inf Black]

8 The penis; an erection.
1954 *Harder Coll.* **cwTN,** Bone . . . An erection, esp in phr "get or have a bone on." **1972** (1974) Wilson *Playboy's Words* 45, Bone—The penis; a *bone-on* is an erection.

9 See **bonefish 1.**

bone v [Engl dial *bone* to annoy by constant solicitation; see *EDD bone* v.¹] *old-fash*

1 To beg, request demandingly, importune.
1858 *Harper's Mag.* 16.566/1 **NJ,** You had better go to the head-waiter, and he will give you some [raisins] . . . And if he dont give you some, *bone* him. **1896** *DN* 1.413 **seNY. 1902** *DN* 2.229 **sIL,** Bone . . . To solicit, to importune. This word seems to convey, slightly, the idea of peremptory demand; and the act of *boning* to involve a test of a person's liberality or generosity . . . To dun. **1903** *DN* 2.307 **seMO. 1906** *DN* 3.115 **sIN. 1909** *DN* 3.393 **nwAR. 1930** Shoemaker *1300 Words* 5 **cPA Mts** (as of c1900), Bone—To beg or wheedle. **1950** *WELS (To ask somebody for a donation in a situation where it would embarrass him to refuse)* 1 Inf, **cnWI,** Boned him. [Inf old, coll educ]

2 To chide, reprove; to pester.
1858 (1930) DeLong *Jrls.* 375 **NY,** On the way [home] she boned us about getting married, and we both denied it. **1884** Murfree *Where the Battle* 292 **TN,** He was a trifle confused to be boned on a point like this. **1912** Green *VA Folk-Speech,* Bone . . . To call a person to account for something: "As soon as I saw him I boned him about it."

bone, carry a v phr Also *bring a bone* [Cf *bone of contention* and *to have a bone to pick*]

To spread a rumor or story; hence *bone carrier* a gossip.
1912 *DN* 3.573 **wIN,** Carry a bone . . . To pack a tale about. **1939** FWP *Guide TN* 134, A gossip is a "bone carrier." **c1965** *DARE* File **cnMA,** I had declined to respond to a question she asked with a tidbit of gossip she knew I had. She professed respect for my reluctance, saying "A dog that will bring a bone will carry one away." **1967** DeVries *Vale Laughter* 128 **Chicago IL,** You've got to be careful what you say and do, because she's a terrible gossip, and as they say, a dog that'll bring a bone will take one away.

bone coal n Also *bony coal* Also called **bone** n **6**
See quot 1973.
1857 *Harper's Mag.* 463/1 **PA,** Much of the slate and 'bony coal' that occurs in the vein is separated . . and thrown around the slope. **1884** in 1904 *DN* 2.376, Bone-coal . . . "A hard, black slate, about a foot thick, which is always piled in masses about the mouth of the mine." **1973** *PADS* 59.27, Bone coal . . ["bone" probably from its brittleness] . . a coal particularly high in slate or shale content, not marketable.

bone-dust sack n [*bone dust* bone meal]
A coarse cloth sack.
1968 *DARE* (Qu. F23, *A container made of rough, loosely woven, brown cloth; commonly used for potatoes, etc*) Infs **IN12, 19,** Bone-dust sack.

bone-eater n [Folk-etym for *bonito*]
=**bonito 1.**
1935 Caine *Game Fish* 53, Bonito—*Sarda sarda* . . . Bone-eater.

bone felon n Pronc-spp *bone fellern, ~ felling, ~ fellum* [Redund *bone + felon, fellum*] **chiefly Sth, S Midl** See Map and Map Section
See quot 1908.
1908 *DN* 3.292 **eAL, wGA,** Bone-felon . . . An inflammatory tumor, a whitlow, a felon. **1934** Carmer *Stars Fell on AL* 281, To cure bone felon, catch a live frog, split open its back, . . and place the space over the affected part. **1946** *PADS* 6.7 **eNC,** Bone felon . . . Whitlow. (Paronychia.) . . . Somewhat rare. **1954** *Harder Coll.* **cwTN,** Bone felon . . . "I'm a-gonna git t'at bone fellern lanched [lanced] today." **c1960** Wilson *Coll.* **csKY,** Bone felon . . . Paronychia or whitlow, an inflammation, often said to be sore to the bone. "Aunt Sally's got a bone felon on her finger." **1965–70** *DARE* (Qu. BB30, . . *A hard, painful swelling [often on a finger] that seems to come from deep under the skin*) 219 Infs, **chiefly Sth, S Midl,** Bone felon; 12 Infs, **chiefly S Atl,** Bone fellum; **KY51, MD24,** Bone felling.

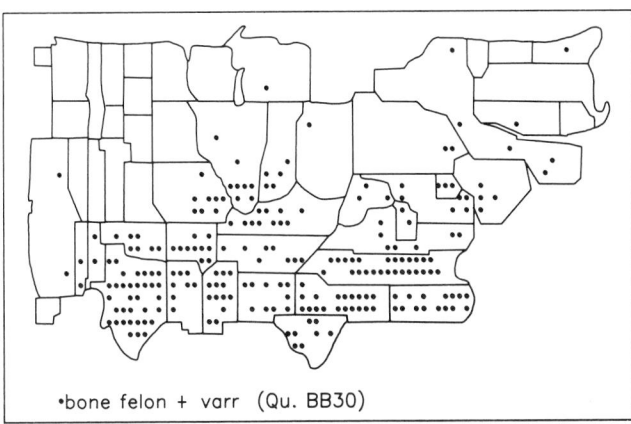

•bone felon + varr (Qu. BB30)

bone fever n
Prob=**breakbone fever.**
    1941 O'Donnell *Great Big Doorstep* 187 **LA,** They got the bone-fever
from the dampness and the shade, they say.

bone-fire n [From *bone-fire* (the orig form of *bonfire*) a fire of
bones (*OED* 1483–1674)]
A bonfire.
    1926 *AmSp* 2.79 **ME,** Everything which a housewife thinks may safely
be discarded is . . carried out to the "bone-fire." I think you hear
"bon-fire" nearly everywhere now, but in my boyhood the pronunciation was distinctly indicative of the word's etymology.

bonefish n
1 also *bone:* Any of several similar fish, but esp *Albula vulpes.*
Also called **banana fish, gray ghost, ladyfish, ratfish, skipjack,
white fox, white ghost**
    1734 Royal Soc. London *Philos. Trans.* 38.317, *Mormyrus, ex cinereo
nigricans.* The *Bone-Fish.* **1897** *Outing* 29.331/1 **FL,** The bone-fish . . .
somewhat resembles a whiting in shape, with the mouth of a sucker and
no teeth. **1967–68** *DARE* (Qu. P4) Infs **LA37, MA1,** Bonefish. **1975**
Evanoff *Catch More Fish* 216, The bonefish (*Albula vulpes*) is also
known as . . bone.
2 =**menhaden.** Cf **bonyfish 1**
    1931–33 *LANE Worksheets* **seCT,** Bonefish—nickname for moss-
bunkers.
3 =**ten-pounder.** Cf **bonyfish 2**
    1935 Caine *Game Fish* 98, *Elops saurus . . . Synonyms:* . . Bonefish,
Bonyfish. **1944** *Times-Dispatch* (Richmond VA) 20 Oct 18/1 *(Hench
Coll.),* I wish you could see those ladyfish . . . They are shaped something
like a pike, look a lot like a bonefish, and must be kin to a tarpon. **1975**
Newell *If Nothin' Don't Happen* 84 **nwFL,** Some people call a ladyfish a
bonefish, but that's wrong. A bonefish is something plumb different. He
don't *need* to jump! He just takes off.
4 A baleen whale of the suborder *Mysticeti.* *obs*
    1809 Kendall *Travels* 2.204 **MA,** The . . whale . . was . . called the
bone-fish, . . valued for . . *whale-bone.*

bonehead n
1 A stubborn person; hence *boneheaded* stubborn.
    1912 *DN* 3.571 **wIN,** Bone-headed . . . Stubborn. **c1970** *Halpert Coll.*
wKY, Bonehead . . . To be a bonehead = to be stubborn or unruly. "He's
a bonehead." Evidently not the same as a numbskull.
2 See quot.
    1918 *DN* 5.23 **NW,** Bonehead . . . A stupid error. Often with the vb. *to
pull.* "He pulled a bonehead, all right."
3 Perh the **wood ibis.**
    1967 *DARE* (Qu. Q7, . . *Other kinds of game birds*) Inf **LA8,** Bonehead
—favors a turkey, a water bird.

bone heap See **heap of bones**

bone hives See **bold hives 2**

bone hunter See **bone picker**

bone idle adj Also *bone lazy* [*bone* (i.e., *to the bone, bone tired*)
extremely, utterly + *idle*] **chiefly S Midl** Cf **bone loafer**
See quot 1933.

1928 Chapman *Happy Mt.* 13 **seTN,** Hit's idle you are—bone idle, 'n'
slack-twisted. **1931** Hannum *Thursday April* 81 **WV Mts,** Joe would
have been content to let the boy sit about the house bone idle. **1933**
AmSp 8.1.48 **Ozarks,** Bone idle . . . Wilfully and incurably idle. *Bone
lazy* is common, too. **1982** *Smithsonian Letters* **cwWV** (as of c1850),
He sat in the dense shade far too much to suit her. "He done passable till
them bettywoods growed big enough to shade him," she said. "After that
a bone-lazier old cuss you never seen."

bone in its teeth n Also *bone in her teeth,* ~ *mouth*
The white water that splashes up around the bow of a fast-moving ship; also transf.
    1919 Kyne *Capt. Scraggs* 271 **CA,** He dreamed that the *Maggie II* came
into view around the headland, a bone in her teeth and every stitch of
canvas flying. **1939** Faulkner *Wild Palms* 65 **MS,** Moving faster now . .
the truck even had a slight bone in its teeth, its bow-wave spreading
beyond the submerged sidewalks and across the adjacent lawns. **1945**
U.S. Bur. Naval Personnel *Seamanship* 413, Bone: the white foam
created at the bow of the ship by its onward motion. She is said to carry a
"bone in her mouth" or "teeth." **1967** *DARE* FW Addit **swWA,** Bone
in its teeth—a description of a ship cutting through waves, creating
white water, teeth-like waves. Common.

bonejack n
=**bonito 1.**
    1935 Caine *Game Fish* 53, Bonito—*Sarda sarda* . . . Bonejack. **1946**
LaMonte *N. Amer. Game Fishes* 20, *Common Bonito—Sarda sarda* . . .
Bonejack.

bone lazy See **bone idle**

bone loafer n [*bone* (i.e. *to the bone*) utterly + *loafer*] Cf **bone
idle**
A lazy person, an idler.
    1933 *AmSp* 8.1.48 **Ozarks,** Bone idle . . . Wilfully and incurably idle
. . . I once knew a man who was described as a *bone loafer.*

bone orchard n esp **Nth, Midl** *humorous* Cf **marble orchard**
A cemetery.
    1872 Burnham *Memoirs U.S. Secret Service* 415 **NY,** You're makin
good time towards the bone-orchard—*you* ar. **1925** *AmSp* 1.151, With
all his feeling for simplicity, the true Westerner has a penchant for the
picturesque that is unmistakable, as when he says "bone-orchard" for
graveyard. **1943** *LANE* Map 525 **wCT,** The map shows the word
cemetery, and . . synonymous and related terms . . . *Bone orchard* . . is a
jocular term. **c1960** *Wilson Coll.* **csKY,** Bone orchard . . . Humorous
name for graveyard. **1965–70** *DARE* (Qu. BB61b, . . *A cemetery*) Infs
IL47, IN28, KS10, NY75, OK20, PA4, WV2, 4, 7, Bone orchard.

bone picker n Also *bone hunter,* ~ *pilgrim* **chiefly West** *hist*
See quots.
    1884 (1966) Aldridge *Life on a Ranch* 169, The bone-pilgrim used to be
quite an institution in Western Kansas, gathering up the remnants of
defunct bisons and hauling them to the railway, to be sent east for
manufacturing into artificial manure. **1939** FWP *Guide KS* 367, The
buffalo hunters, bone pickers, and cowboys who made up a considerable
part of the population of Wallace were a care-free, fun-loving bunch of
fellows. **1968** Adams *Western Words,* Bone hunter.

boner n
1 A hard blow or stroke (as with the fist or a blunt instrument).
[**1890** Farmer–Henley *Slang Engl,* Boner . . (Winchester College).—A
sharp blow on the spine.] **1950** *WELS* (*A very hard blow:* . . "*Joe really
hit him* _____.") 1 Inf, **seWI,** A boner. **1968–70** *DARE* (Qu. Y11, . .
A very hard blow: "*You should have seen Bill go down. Joe really hit him
a* _____.") Infs **PA234, WI72,** Boner.
2 A conclusive stroke, the "last straw."
    1969 *DARE* (Qu. GG22b, *When you have come to the end of your
patience, you might say, "Well, that certainly* _____.") Inf **MO15,** Is a
boner.

boners v Also *bonas* [Prob Brit dial *bunce* n, a share, profit, and
bunce intj, used to claim possession (*SND* 1825 →); perh infl by
bonus]
= **boney.**
    1895 *DN* 1.384 **eMA,** Bonas [bɒnəs]; in phrase "I bonas it"="I claim
it," or "I take possession of it." **1966** *DARE* (Qu. II8, *When one person
wants to share or divide something with another person, he might say
"Let's* _____.") Inf **NM6,** Divvy; halvers; boners.

bones See **bone** n 3

bone-seasoned adj

1968 Adams *Western Words,* Bone-seasoned—A cowman's term meaning *experienced.*

boneset n, freq attrib in *boneset tea* [See quot 1889]

1 A plant of the genus *Eupatorium.* Also called **Joe-Pye weed, thoroughwort, white snakeroot.** For other names of var spp see **agueweed 1, blue boneset, Christmas bush 2, cypress-weed, dog fennel, false hoarhound, feverwort, Indian gravelweed, Indian sage, justice weed, king-of-the-meadow, marsh milkweed, mist-flower, motherwort, niggerweed, queen of the meadow, quill-wort, sweating plant, teagel, thoroughgrow, thoroughwax, trum-pet weed, vegetable antimony, wild Isaac, wild sage, woolly head, yankee weed**

1822 Eaton *Botany* 278, Boneset, thoroughwort. **1839** (1969) Briggs *Advent. Franco* 2.153, "Dear soul," said the good woman, "let me warm your bed, and give you some boneset tea." **1874** *Shaker Med. Preparations.* **1889** (1971) Farmer *Americanisms,* Boneset (Eupatorium perfoliatum) . . . It owes its popular American name to the fact that it is generally regarded as a specific for the so-called *break-bone fever.* **1905** *DN* 3.4 cCT. **1965–70** *DARE* (Qu. I35) Inf **KY**17, Boneset—made tea of it, for colds; (Qq. S26a–c, e) Infs **MA**78, 100, **NY**232, 233, **OH**82, **PA**234, **VT**13, Boneset; **GA**38, Boneset—similar to rabbit tobacco; (Qq. BB22, 50a, d) 19 Infs, **scattered, but esp MD, PA,** Boneset (tea). **1968** *DARE* FW Addit **VA**1, Boneset—used for flu; **WV,** Boneset—when someone is ill, you make tea and drench them with it; **neNY,** Boneset or thoroughwort—medicinal herb. **1976** Bruce *How to Grow Wildflowers* 259, The true Boneset, *E. perfoliatum,* is a tall (to about five feet), comparatively coarse plant . . . of historical interest as an old-time remedy for broken bones, hence the common name. It grows anywhere, but is most common in wet meadows. *Ibid* 272, A wet meadow overlay the same sort of soil, producing the same sort of conditions. It was bright all summer long with hardhack and meadowsweet, milkweed, asters, ironweed, boneset, Joe-pye weed, bur-marigolds, vervains, and a dozen others.

2 See **climbing boneset.**

‡**bone stiff** adj

1970 *Eaton Coll.* **neWI,** Bone-stiff . . . Rigid. Said of a dead cat.

bone-top n

A bonehead.

1919 *DN* 5.62 **CA,** Bone-top, a dull fellow; one who makes blunders. "The old bone-top forgot to close the windows of the chapel last night."

bone, to the adv phr

To perfection; to the last detail.

1967–68 *DARE* (Qu. KK3a, . . *The perfect condition—for example, in cooking: "It's done to _____."*) Infs **LA**8, **TN**46, The bone; (Qu. KK50, *When something is planned out carefully, down to the last detail: "He had it all worked out _____."*) Inf **OH**80, To the bone.

‡**bone wagon** n

One's body.

1937 (1963) Hyatt *Riverlid* 106 **KY,** "A leetle more meat on yore frame wouldn't hurt none." "They ha'n't nothin' ails me . . . I can tote as big a grist now," said the girl proudly, "an' pack as much wood on my bone-wagon as Pappy can."

boney v Also *boney-eye, bonny* Cf **boners**

To claim possession of (something).

1944 *AmSp* 19.39, Yakers on it!'I claim it'; also, *Goods (on it)!*'I claim a share.' These idioms . . belong to schoolboys' jargon . . . When I went to school (near New York), we used to say 'I boney it.' **1950** *WELS Suppl.,* 1 Inf, **cwWI,** I *bonny* that one—for *dibs* or *druthers:* "I bonny *that* piece of candy." "I bonny that dress when you outgrow it." Used by children at school, especially by girls. **1968** *DARE* FW Addit **nwWI** (as of c1925), I boney-eye ['boniaɪ] the red one. When you want something among a choice of articles. For instance, several children . . looking at several trucks. If a child likes the red truck he might say "I boney-eye the red one." Then none of the other children can choose the red truck.

boneyard n

1 An emaciated horse or cow; a very thin person.

1905 *DN* 3.70 **nwAR,** Boneyard . . . An emaciated horse. "That old boneyard ought to be killed." Common. **1944** Adams *Western Words,* Bone yard . . . An emaciated horse. **1965–70** *DARE* (Qu. K15, *A thin,*

bony, or poor-looking cow) Infs **GA**72, **PA**147, Boneyard; **NY**72, Regular boneyard; (Qu. K44, *A bony or poor-looking horse)* Infs **CO**38, **KY**35, **NJ**31, **NY**142, Boneyard; **NC**12, Walking boneyard; (Qu. X49, *Expressions used about a person who is very thin)* Inf **MD**9, Boneyard.

‡**2** An area where horses and mules are traded.

1960 Williams *Walk Egypt* 91 **GA,** There were strings of horses and mules tied in "the boneyard," a few ponies thrown in.

bonhomme n |ˈbʌnəm| [Fr *bonhomme* good fellow]

A type of pastry: see quot.

1980 *DARE* File **csMA,** In my hometown [Southbridge], which was largely populated by French-Canadians, bread dough fried in deep fat was known as bonhommes (pronounced by us non-French people as bunnums). For folks as poor as we were they would make a whole supper. We would buy a pound of bread dough from the bakery, fry the bonhommes (which would expand to the size of tennis balls), poke a hole in the side of one and put in a little butter and maple syrup . . and eat them hot in our fingers.

bonita See **bonito** 2

bonito n [Prob Span]

1 Std: any of var scombrid fishes, esp of the genus *Sarda.* Also called **bloater 3, bone-eater, bonejack, Boston mackerel, false albacore, frigate mackerel, horse mackerel, little tunny, skip-jack, Spanish mackerel**

2 also *bonita, black bonito:* =**cobia.**

1884 Goode *Fisheries U.S.* 444, The cobia or crab-eater—*Elacate canada.* This fish, known in the Chesapeake Bay as the 'Bonito' . . is considered one of the most important food fishes of Maryland and Virginia. **1933** LA Dept. of Conserv. *Fishes* 197, The Cobia, *Rachycentron canadus* . . is invariably known . . on the Atlantic Coast as the Black Bonito. **1935** Caine *Game Fish* 57, *Rachycentron canadus* . . . Black Bonito . . . Bonito. **1946** *Times-Dispatch* (Richmond VA) 4 Aug 4.4–D/4 *(Hench Coll.),* While [bottom] fishing for cobia, or bonita, as these fish are locally called, big channel bass are also frequently landed. **1976** Warner *Beautiful Swimmers* 35, The huge cobias, also called "northern bonita."

bonk n [Prob echoic]

A small swelling on the head caused by a sharp blow.

1966 *DARE* (Qu. X60) Infs **DC**8, **FL**31, **NJ**63, **SD**3, Bonk.

bonnet n Pronc-spp *bunnet, bunnit*

A Forms.

1857 *Putnam's Mag.* 10.347 **CT,** An' so I slipt on my Shaker bunnet jist as quick's I could. **1891** (1967) Freeman *New Engl. Nun* 90, I remember you had a real handsome blue bunnit once. **1895** in 1944 *ADD* **seKY, eTN, wNC,** I can't go outen my sunbunnit. **1905** *DN* 3.56 **NE,** In . . bonnet . . [ʌ] is likely to appear; if not, the vowel is [ɑ]. **1918** *DN* 5.15 **seMA,** Bonnet (pron. bunnet).

B Senses.

1 also *bonnet leaf, bonnet lily:* A **water lily 1** of the family Nymphaeaceae. **chiefly Gulf States** See also **alligator bonnet, egg ~, mulefoot ~, purple ~**

a =**spatterdock** (esp *Nuphar luteum*), so called from the in-folded leaf.

1822 Simmons *Notices of E. Fla.* 29 *(DA),* The bonnet leaf, a species of lotus, abounds in the dead water formed by the meeting currents. **1836** *Knickerbocker* 8.283, The banks of the river [near Rolls Town FL] are . . lined with 'bonnets,' as they are called there. **1883** *Century Illustr. Mag.* 4.383/1, The boatman rows the boat . . along the edges of the saw-grass, water-lettuce, bonnets, or other aquatic plants which border the . . lakes of Florida. **1913** *Auk* 30.490 **Okefenokee GA,** A bird . . sailing across a bit of bonnet-strewn prairie . . presents a striking and beautiful spectacle. **1937** *Natl. Geog. Mag.* 71.216, Its (the purple gallinule's) brilliant plumage and bright yellow legs present an attractive picture among the deep-green "bonnets" or lily pads. **1938** Rawlings *Yearling* 93 **nFL,** Penny called . . . "Don't let him [fish] git under them bonnets. Keep the tip o' your pole up." **1966–68** *DARE* (Qu. S26b) Infs **GA**7, 20, Bonnet(s); **GA**35, Bonnet lily. **1969** *DARE* Tape **GA**51, There's two kinds o' that [waterlily]—the west side has got a bigger brand of the bonnet than the east side; **GA**48, Bonnet [waterlily leaf, and golden club blossom].

b =**water chinquapin.**

1920 *Torreya* 20.21, *Nelumbo lutea* . . . Bonnet, yonkapin bonnet, Reelfoot Lake, Tenn. **1942** *Ibid* 42.159, *Nelumbo lutea* . . . Big bonnet, Mississippi.

c A white water lily (here: *Nymphaea odorata*).

1927 Boston Soc. Nat. Hist. *Proc.* 286 **Okefenokee GA,** When either a boat or a Bear passes over a watery prairie, the 'bonnet' *(Castalia)* leaves in the trail remain upturned on one side for several hours afterwards. *Ibid* 386, 'Bonnet' *(Castalia)*. **1940** FWP *Guide GA* 367 **Okefenokee,** White and golden water lilies, locally called "bonnets," . . form bright splashes against the silvery, gently swaying screen of Spanish moss. **1974** (1977) Coon *Useful Plants* 193, *Nymphaea odorata*—Fragrant waterlily, pond-lily, bonnets, water cabbage.

d =**water shield 1.**

1942 *Torreya* 42.160, *Brasenia schreberi* . . . Small bonnet, Mississippi. **1966** *DARE* (Qu. S24) Inf **GA3,** Bonnet.

2 The cap or leafy top of a strawberry.

1967–68 *DARE* (Qu. I47, *When you pull the stem out of a strawberry, what do you call the green part that comes off with the stem?*) Infs **AL33, VA24,** Bonnets.

3 See quot.

1968 *DARE* (Qu. L31, . . *The top bundle of a shock [of grain]*) Inf **VA24,** Bonnet.

4 See quot.

1954 *Harder Coll.* **cwTN,** Bonnet . . . The "rib" part of the back of a chicken.

bonnet leaf, bonnet lily See **bonnet B1**

‡bonnet pleaser n

1970 *DARE* (Qu. W1c, . . *Joking names . . for an umbrella*) Inf **OK57,** Bonnet pleaser.

bonnet squash n

=**vegetable sponge.**

1834 (1900) Harris *Reminiscences* 100 **TX,** The women . . made bonnets out of a plant called a bonnet squash. **1892** Harris *On Plantation* 124 **GA,** The girls made their hats of rye and wheat straw, and some very pretty bonnets were made of the fibrous substance that grows in the vegetable known as the bonnet squash.

bonnet string n Also called **barboquejo**

The chin-strap of a cowboy hat.

1934 Weseen *Dict. Amer. Slang, Bonnet strings*—Leather thongs in a western hat with which to tighten it. **1951** Grant *Cowboy Encycl.* 70/1, Some hats have "bonnet strings," which come down from beneath the brim and in back of the head to hold the hat on in windy weather. **1955** Harris *Look of Old West* 202, The hat . . . had a . . bonnet string, meaning a chin strap, which had better not be too tight.

bonnet walker n Also *pad walker* [See quots] **esp FL, GA**

Either of two water birds: the **Florida gallinule** or the **purple gallinule.**

1955 *Oriole* 20.6 **GA,** Purple Gallinule . . . Bonnet Walker (as walking on the floating leaves of waterlilies or "bonnets"). **1955** Forbush–May *Birds* 166, *Florida Gallinule* . . . *Other names:* . . Bonnet-walker; Pad-walker; Rice Hen . . . Like the Purple Gallinule, its large, long-toed feet serve like snowshoes to support it as it walks or runs over the surface of the water from one lily pad to another. **1966** *DARE* (Qu. Q10) Inf **FL27,** Bonnet walker. **1969** Longstreet *Birds FL* 56, *Purple Gallinule* . . . *Other names: Bonnet-walker* . . . Nearly always found where the fragile pads of yellow pond lilies, or "bonnets," cover the surface of the water, they move from pad to pad with amazing lightness and ease. *Ibid* 57, *Common Gallinule* . . . *Other names:* . . Bonnet-walker.

bonnet worm n Also *water-bonnet worm* **esp FL**

The larva of the long-horned leaf beetle (*Donacia* spp.) which feeds on the submerged parts of "**bonnets**" or water lilies and is used as bait.

1887 Goode *Amer. Fishes* 58, In Florida . . [black bass] feed on a grub called the "bonnet worm," which burrows in the flower-buds of the "bonnets" or yellow water lilies. **1938** Rawlings *Yearling* 93 **nFL,** He began fishing for Ma Baxter's bream with a hand-line and bonnet worms. **1970** *DARE* (Qu. P6) Inf **FL48,** Water-bonnet worm. **1975** Evanoff *Catch More Fish* 3, If worms don't work too well [for bluegills], try "bonnet worms," which are found in the upper stalks of "bonnets" or lily pads.

bonny adj [Scots *bonny* beautiful, attractive, great, considerable] Pleasant.

1968–69 *DARE* (Qu. B1, *If a day is very pleasant, you say it's a _____ day*) Infs **AZ15, MI81,** Bonny.

bonny v See **boney**

bonnyclabber n Also *barney clapper* (rare), *bonnyclabbered milk, bonnyclapper* (**esp eNEng;** see quot 1949), *bonnyclobber* (infreq), *bonyclabber, ~ clapper* [Ir *bainne clabair* thick sour milk] **chiefly N Atl** *somewhat old-fash* Cf **loppered milk** =**clabber** n[1] **1.**

1731 in 1906 Essex Inst. *Coll.* 42.233 **neMA,** To day wee din'd . . upon roast Mutton, & for Sauce a Sallet, mix'd with Bonyclabber Sweetned with Molasses. **1807** (1935) Janson *Stranger in Amer.* 187 **Philadelphia PA,** The morning's milk turns to curd in the evening. This they call *'bonny clabber,'* and eat it with honey, sugar, or molasses. **1883** *Harper's Mag.* 66.603/2 **NJ,** I had so much bonny-clabber, or curdled milk. **1903** *DN* 2.295 **Cape Cod MA** (as of 1850s), *Barney clapper* . . . thick soured milk. **1904** Conway *Autobiog.* 1.18 **VA** (as of 1830s), We had our supper in summer under the apple-trees,—griddle-cake and molasses, bonnyclabber, preserves. **1925** Parrish *Perennial Bachelor* 50 **MD,** Lunch on Sundays was cold . . . There was Saturday's roast-beef, and bread and butter, and then a great tin pan of solidified sour milk . . called "bonny-clabber," and eaten unenthusiastically with cream and sugar. **1941** *LANE* Map 298 throughout **NEng,** The map presents the words for naturally soured and curdled milk: . . *bonny-clapper, bony ~, bonny-clabber, bony ~, . . loppered milk, . . bonny-clabbered ~.* **1949** Kurath *Word Geog.* 70, *Bonny-clabber* is still common in the Philadelphia area, *bonny-clapper* (less often *bonny-clabber*) in Eastern New England (except for Rhode Island, the New London area, and the greater part of Maine). *Bonny-clabber* appears in scattered fashion in central and western Pennsylvania and from there southward to North Carolina, an area in which it has been largely replaced by other terms. **1965–70** *DARE* (Qu. H59, *Milk that becomes thick as it turns sour*) Infs **ME7,** 16, 19, **MA34,** 57, **NJ18,** 21, 32, 40, 53, **PA163, RI1,** 9, Bonnyclabber; **MA83, NJ56,** Bonnyclapper; **NJ15,** Bonnyclobber. [15 of 16 Infs old] **1973** Kluger *Wild Flavor* 102 **IN,** Clabbered milk, or bonnyclabber, is thick sour milk which has separated into curds and whey. The curds are the bonnyclabber and they are used in the shortcakes.

bonnyclabber cheese n Also *bonnyclapper cheese* **scattered NEast** *somewhat old-fash* Cf **clabber cheese**

Cottage cheese.

1941 *LANE* Map 299 **scattered in NEng,** The map shows the terms *cottage cheese, . . bonnyclapper* ch[eese]. **1949** Kurath *Word Geog.* Fig 126, Cottage cheese . . [2 infs **eVA,** 2 infs **sNJ**] Bonny-clabber cheese.

bony n

A marble.

1968 *DARE* (Qu. EE6c, *Cheap marbles*) Inf **WV7,** Bonies—home-made of clay. **1971** Bright *Word Geog. CA & NV* 115, Marbles: . . Bony . . . Diminutive of *bone.* "Obsolete now."

bony coal See **bone coal**

bonyfish n

1 =**menhaden.** Cf **bonefish 2**

1815 Lit. & Philos. Soc. NY *Trans.* 1.453 **NY,** *Bony-fish, Hard-heads,* or *Marsbankers . . . [are]* about fourteen inches long. **1894** *DN* 1.332 **sNJ,** Menhaden: called "moss bunkers," . . "green tails," . . and "bony fish." **1904** *DN* 3.4 **cCT. 1905** (1906) NJ State Museum *Annual Rept.* 103, *Brevoortia tyrannus . . .* Bony Fish. **1939** *LANE* Map 233 *(Porgy; Pogy)*, *Brevoortia tyrannus* (a clupeoid), a commercially important fish found from Maine to Florida . . . This fish is called *pogy* . . from Maine to Narragansett Bay; *menhaden* from Cape Cod west-ward . . ; *bony-fish* from Narragansett Bay westward. **1945** Beck *Jersey Genesis* 148 **NJ,** "Sometimes," said Jack, "we just called 'em bony-fish and mud-shad, but greentails was always the fav'rite. Maybe they got a name like that because they always left a slick behind 'em in the water."

2 =**ten-pounder.** Cf **bonefish 3**

1896 U.S. Natl. Museum *Bulletin* 47.410, *Elops saurus . . .* Bony-fish. **1946** LaMonte *N. Amer. Game Fishes* 14, *Ten-Pounder—Elops saurus . . . Names: . . .* Bonyfish . . . (The name "Bonefish" for this fish . . would be better forgotten, as they are the causes of much confusion.)

bony pike n

The longnose **gar** (*Lepisosteus osseus*).

1842 DeKay *Zool. NY* 4.271, The Buffalo Bony Pike, *Lepisosteus bison* . . . was obtained at Buffalo, Lake Erie, where it is called the *Bony Pike, Alligator* and *Alligator Gar.* **1889** *Century Dict.*, *Bony pike.* Same as *garpike.*

bony pile n

A rubbish heap.

   1981 *DARE* File **nwPA,** They throw it on the bony pile.

bonytail n

The Colorado chub *(Gila robusta).*

   1896 U.S. Natl. Museum *Bulletin* 47.227, *Gila elegans . . . Bony-tail.* **1963** Sigler – Miller *Fishes UT* 72, *Colorado Chub — Gila robusta . . . Common Names: . .* bonytail. **1967** *DARE* (Qu. P3, *Freshwater fish that are not good to eat)* Inf **AZ**7, Bonytail.

boo n¹ Also *boo boo* [Prob abbr for **booger** n¹ **3**] **scattered, but esp Nth**

Mucus in the nose; see quots.

   1892 *KS Univ. Qrly.* 1.95, *Boo:* dried mucous. **1901** *DN* 2.136 **cnNY,** *Boo . . . Usually in pl.* Mucus in nose . . . "There are boos in your nose." Also, but more rarely, in sing., "there's a big boo." **1968** *DARE* (Qu. X16, *Sticky mucus that forms in the nose — children's words for this)* Infs **CT**11, **NY**48, **WI**68, Boo boo.

boo n² Also *boobie, boo boo* [Hypocoristic form of *brother*]

   1967 – 68 *DARE* (Qu. Z5, . . *"Brother")* Inf **MN**33, Boo; **CA**6, Boo boo; **IN**16, Boobie.

boo v

=**babble.**

   1934 (1970) Wilson *Backwoods Amer.* 108 **AR, MO,** Native foxes never run in pell-mell confusion. You may see them at times, now jumping high in the air to look behind, now pausing to listen for the hounds that may likely be booing and yapping at a cold trail, miles and miles behind.

boob n Also *boo boo* [Abbr for **booby** n²] *esp among young and coll educ speakers* Cf **bubby** n¹ **1**

A woman's breast.

   1949 Miller *Sexus* 2.57, I felt her sloshy boobs joggling me but I was too intent on pursuing the ramifications of Coleridge's amazing mind to let her vegetable appendages disturb me. **1955** Williams *Cat Tin Roof* 7, He always drops his eyes down my body when I'm talkin' to him, drops his eyes to my boobs an' licks his old chops! **1965 – 70** *DARE* (Qu. X31, . . *A woman's breasts)* 78 Infs, **widespread in US,** Boobs [Of all Infs responding to the question, 12% were young, 31% were coll educ; of those giving this response, 40% were young, 50% were coll educ]; **OH**76, Boo boos.

boobee See **bubeleh**

boober n [Alter of *boo-boo* perh infl by *boob* a stupid fellow; cf **bugger** v **2**]

   1968 *DARE* (Qu. JJ41, *An embarrassing mistake: "Last night she made an awful _____")* Infs **NJ**9, **WI**34, Boober.

boo boo n¹ [Prob from an Afr word (cf Fon *būbŭ* insect), perh infl by **booger** n¹ **2** or **bugaboo;** cf *DJE bubu*]

   1966 *DARE* (Qu. R25, . . *A head louse, or body louse)* Inf **SC**9, Boo boo.

boo boo n² See **boo** n¹

boo boo n³ See **boo** n²

boo boo n⁴ See **boob**

booby n¹

1 Std: a bird of the family Sulidae.

2 also *booby coot, booby duck, broadbill booby:* =**ruddy duck.**

   1888 Trumbull *Names of Birds* 111, At Newport, R.I., Stratford, Conn., very generally on Long Island, and at Norfolk, Va., *Booby . . ;* and sometimes on the south side of Long Island, *Booby Coot.* **1917** (1923) *Birds Amer.* 1.152, *Ruddy Duck — Erismatura jamaicensis . . . Other Names . . .* Booby Coot. **1954** Sprunt *FL Bird Life* 85, *Ruddy Duck: Oxyura jamaicensis . . . Local Names: . .* Broadbill Booby. **1968 – 70** *DARE* (Qu. Q5, . . *Kinds of wild ducks)* Inf **NC**80, Booby duck; **VA**47, Booby duck — "ruddy duck" — considered stupid because it doesn't fly away when shot at. **1982** Elman *Hunter's Field Guide* 192, *Ruddy Duck . . . Common & Regional Names:* booby.

3 Any of several ducks of the genus *Oidemia,* esp the **scoter,** the **surf scoter,** and the **white-winged scoter.**

   1888 (1890) Warren *Birds PA* 47, *Oidemia americana . . .* Booby. **1895** (1907) Wright *Birdcraft* 265, *American Scoter: Oidemia americana.* Booby. **1917** (1923) *Birds Amer.* 1.148, *Scoter — Oidemia ameri-*

cana . . . Booby. **1982** Elman *Hunter's Field Guide* 237, *American Scoter . . . Common & Regional Names: . .* booby. *Ibid* 240, *Surf scoter . .* booby. *Ibid* 250, *White-winged scoter . .* booby.

booby n² [Alter of **bubby** n¹ **1**] **chiefly Nth, N Midl** See Map Cf **boob**

A woman's breast.

   1916 in 1944 *ADD* 79 **cNY,** Boobies /'bubiz/. Common. **1934** Miller *Tropic of Cancer* 120 **NY,** She was lying on the divan with her boobies in her hands. **1965 – 70** *DARE* (Qu. X31, . . *A woman's breasts)* 59 Infs, **chiefly Nth, N Midl,** Boobies. [Of all Infs responding to the question, 12% were young; of those giving this response, 22% were young.]

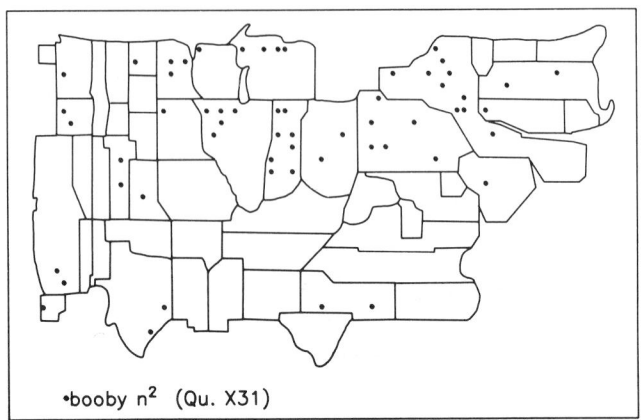

•booby n² (Qu. X31)

booby n³

A hard blow, as with the fist.

   1968 *DARE* (Qu. Y11, . . *A very hard blow: "You should have seen Bill go down. Joe really hit him a _____")* Inf **PA**139, Booby.

booby n⁴ See **booby hut**

booby coot, booby duck See **booby** n¹ **2**

booby hack See **booby hut**

booby hatch n Also *booby house*

A jail.

   1859 Matsell *Vocabulum, Booby-hatch.* Station-house; watch-house. **1927** *DN* 5.439 [Underworld jargon], *Booby hatch . . .* The station house. **1930** Irwin *Amer. Tramp, Booby hatch.* — A police station or village gaol. **1968 – 70** *DARE* (Qu. V11, *Joking names . . for a county or city jail)* Infs **CA**36, **CO**5, **PA**234, **WI**68, Booby hatch; **NJ**19, Booby house.

booby hut n Also *booby, booby hack, booby hutch* [From *booby hutch* (in former Brit use) a small clumsy cart or carriage] **chiefly NEng** *old-fash*

A sleigh with an enclosed carriage body.

   1766 *Boston – Gaz. & Country Jrl.* (Boston MA) 29 Dec 4/3, A Very neat Booby-Hutch, [to] be sold cheap for Cash. **1795** *Columbian Centinel* 24 Jan 3/4 **Boston MA,** Two second hand Booby-Huts. **1839** Mathews *Memoirs* 4.325 **Boston MA,** I induced him on Wednesday to accompany Mrs. Eliot and myself in a 'Booby Hut' (for so a *covered* sleigh is called). **1897** Haswell *Reminiscences* 34, Carts and wheeled vehicles were replaced by sleds and sleighs, even to carriage- and hack-bodies being set upon runners, as is still the case in Boston, for example, when they were termed booby hacks. **1931 – 33** *LANE* Worksheets **Newport RI,** Booby hut . . . A covered sleigh. A booby hut is a hack on runners. **1962** Morison *One Boy's Boston* 33 (as of 1887 – 1901), "Boobys," covered sleighs with coachlike bodies, cozily lined with red plush or silk. [Footnote:] Short for "booby-hutch" or "booby-hut."

booby owl n [Perh alter of *Bubo,* a genus of owls, but cf **booby** n¹] **Chesapeake Bay**

Perh a barred owl or **great horned owl.**

   1966 – 68 *DARE* (Qu. Q1, . . *The kind of owl that makes a shrill, trembling cry)* Inf **DC**4, Hoot owl = booby owl; **MD**20, Booby owl, goes ['huʔ'huʔ]; (Qu. Q2) Infs **DE**3, **MD**42, Booby owl; **MD**15, Booby owl — another term for screech owl; **MD**34, Booby owl — large.

booby trap n

A firework that is set off when the strings at each end are pulled.

1967–68 *DARE* (Qu. FF28, . . *Kinds of fireworks*) Inf **LA35**, Booby trap—a piece of string at each end; you pull the strings, it goes off; **SC65**, Booby trap—tied to a door; goes off when the door is opened; **TX28**, Booby trap.

booby wagon n Cf **booby hatch, booger wagon**
1967 *DARE* (Qu. N3, *The car or wagon that takes arrested people to the police station or to jail*) Infs **NJ2, TX9**, Booby wagon.

booch See **bush** v²

boochren See **butcher**

boock See **book** v²

boocoo See **beaucoup**

boocoodles n [Blend of *boocoo* (see **beaucoup**) + *oodles* abundance, lot] *joc*
A great deal, a large number.
1965–68 *DARE* (Qu. LL8a, *A large amount or number: more than enough—for example, of time: "He's got _____ of time."*) Infs **MS42, 56, SC44**, Boocoodles; (Qu. LL9a, *As much as you need or more—for example, of apples: "We've got _____ of apples."*) Inf **GA23**, Boocoodles.

boocoos See **beaucoup**

boo-daddy n Also *boo-hag*
=**booger** n¹ **1.**
1941 FWP *Guide SC* 287, Negroes say the hill is inhabited by a variety of ghosts . . boo-daddies, boo-hags, and drolls.

boodle n [From Du *boedel* estate, property]
1 usu in phr *the whole boodle:* Collection; crowd. **esp NEng** *sometimes derog* Cf **caboodle**
1833 Neal *Down-Easters* 1.61, I know a feller 'twould whip the whool [sic] boodle of 'em an' give 'em six. **1858** Holmes *Autocrat* 139 **MA**, He would like to have the whole boodle of them, (I remonstrated against this word, but the Professor said it was a diabolish good word, and he would have no other,) . . shipwrecked on a remote island. **1859** (1968) Bartlett *Americanisms, Boodle.* "The whole boodle of them," i.e. all, the whole. New England. **1907** *DN* 3.209 **nwAR, cCT. 1930** *AmSp* 6.159 **NYC,** *Boodle* means a lot of anything. **1941** *LANE* Map 415 **MA,** The map shows the collective terms applied to a group of persons whom the speaker dislikes or of whom he disapproves, usually recorded in some context like this: *All the loafers and hoodlums in town came to the dance; the whole crowd was there.* The following terms were offered by two or more informants each: . . *boodle.* **1969** *DARE* (Qu. LL8b, *A large number . . . "She has a whole _____ of cousins."*) Inf **RI1**, Boodle.
2 In reference to money:
a also attrib: Counterfeit money; money illegally or dishonestly acquired or used. *old-fash*
1858 *Harper's Weekly* 3 Apr 222/1 **OH**, "Boodle" is a flash term used by counterfeiters . . . The leaders [of the gang] were the manufacturers and bankers of the "boodle." **1872** Burnham *Memoirs U.S. Secret Service* 81, But having informed the big dealer that he was "copped" two years previously, as a "boodle carrier," and showed him plainly that he was "up to snuff," the former appoints a time and place to deliver him a bundle of "new stock," at twenty cents on the dollar. **1887** *Nation* 44.307/3, New York is better known all over the . . world for boodle Aldermen and municipal rings than for anything else. **1900** in 1923 Twain *Europe & Elsewhere* xxxiv, The stately nation called Christendom, returning . . from pirate raids . . with her . . pocket full of boodle. **1904** *McClure's Mag.* 22.591/1, "Driftwood" was boodle bills for business men, and some of it was blackmail, but it was all irregular. **1968** Adams *Western Words, Boodle*—What the traders and freighters called graft or illegal fees.
b Money in general.
1905 *DN* 3.4 **cCT,** *Boodle* . . . Slang for money. **1907** *DN* 3.209 **nwAR. 1942** Warnick *Garrett Co. MD* (as of 1900–1918), *Boodle* . . ordinary money, with no implication of graft. **1950** *WELS (Words used for money in general)* 1 Inf, **csWI,** Boodle. **c1960** Wilson *Coll.* **csKY,** *Boodle* . . . Money, not necessarily tainted. "He's made a lot of boodle since I first saw him."
c A great deal of money. **chiefly Nth**
1965–70 *DARE* (Qu. U19b, *Talking of paper money: "He always carries a big _____."*) Infs **NY88, RI6**, Boodle; (Qu. U38a, . . *A great deal of money: "He's got _____ [of money]."*) Infs **ID5, MA49, WI48**, Boodles; (Qu. U38b, . . *A great deal of money: "He made a _____ [of*

money].") 10 Infs, **chiefly Nth**, Boodle; **RI12**, Boodles. **1967** *DARE* Tape **MA6**, I guess Will Newton made quite a boodle out of it.

boodle bag n [**boodle** n **2b** + *bag*]
A money pouch or purse.
1950 *WELS (What do you keep money in when you carry it around with you?)* 1 Inf, **csWI**, Boodle bag.

boo-dock n [Alter of *buttock*] *joc euphem*
The buttocks.
1966 *DARE* (Qu. X35, *Joking words for the part of the body that you sit on—for example, "He slipped and came down hard on his _____."*) Inf **MS16**, Boo-dock.

boody n Pronc-sp *booty* *chiefly among Blacks*
1 The female body or sex organs; sex.
1926 Van Vechten *Nigger Heaven* 285, *Boody* . . hootchie-pap. **1935** Hurston *Mules & Men* 192 **FL**, Oh, go to Ella Wall / If you want good boody. **1970** Major *Afro–Amer. Slang, Booty:* a woman's body. **1977** Dillard *Lexicon* 154 [Black], Boody—"sex." [Footnote:] Again, the term seems to mean, in the inner city and among southern whites, the female sex organs (or "ass") rather than "sex."
2 The buttocks. *joc*
1967 *DARE* (Qu. X35, *Joking words for the part of the body that you sit on*) Infs **LA6, 8**, Booty [laughter]. [Both Infs Black] **1976** *DARE* File Baton Rouge LA [Black], It was on the boody.

boodydunk n [Var of **bloodynoun**]
1951 *AmSp* 26.15, *Bloody-noun*, 'large bullfrog' . . . [Footnote:] An onomatopoetic variant /ˈbudidəŋk, bə-, -ˌduŋk/ seems to be confined to the Georgetown [SC] area.

boof n¹
1896 *DN* 1.413 **cTX,** *Boof* . . scare, fright. "He got a boof."

boof n² [See quot]
1872 Haldeman *PA Dutch* 59, *Boof,* peach brandy. In Westerwaldish, *buff* is water-cider,—cider made by wetting the pomace and pressing it a second time.

boog See **boogerlee 1**

booga See **borga**

boogalee See **boogerlee**

boogaloo n Pronc-sp *bugaloo* **esp Nth, N Midl**
A rock-and-roll dance popular in the 1960s.
1965–70 *DARE* (Qu. FF5a) Inf **MO23**, Bugaloo; (Qu. FF5b) 18 Infs, **chiefly Nth, N Midl**, Boogaloo; 11 Infs, **chiefly Nth, N Midl**, Bugaloo. **1968** Stearns *Jazz Dance* 4, A second wave of dances crashed over American dance floors during and after the Twist: . . Hully-Gully, Jerk, Boogaloo, and so on. **1969** *New Yorker* 1 Mar 39/3 **TN**, You cain't tell—we might go out and do the *Boog*aloo.

boogarman See **boogerman**

booger n¹ Usu |ˈbʊgə(r)|, occas |ˈbugə(r)|, infreq |ˈbʌ–| Also sp *bugger* [Alter of *boggart* < *buggard* < ME *bugge* ghost, hobgoblin] Cf **boogie**
1a A ghost, hobgoblin, haunt—often used to threaten children. **chiefly Sth, S Midl** See Map Cf **boogerman**
1866 Smith *Bill Arp* 78 **GA**, Imagining that . . their bones are . . to rot in some thicket, far, far away, where ghosts and boogers go dodging around. **1902** *DN* 2.230 **sIL**, Bugger [bʌgɚ] . . . Bogie; spectre. **1907** *DN* 3.221 **nwAR**, Bugger [bʊgɚ]. **1910** *DN* 3.438 **cwNY**, Bugger [bʊgɑr]. **1915** *DN* 4.181 **swVA**, Bugger. **1938** Rawlings *Yearling* 220 **FL**, I know there's one o' the boogers'll not harm nobody. **1943** *LANE* Map 533 **scattered throughout NEng**, Names for the imaginary demons invoked to frighten children into obedience, . . goblin, hobgoblin, imp, bugger, booger, bogie, bugaboo. **1944** *PADS* 2.40 **wNC**, Booger [ˈbʊgə, -ɚ] **1948** *AmSp* 23.264 **Ozarks**, Booger. **1949** *PADS* 11.18 **CO**, Booger. **1950** *PADS* 14.16 **SC**, Booger. **1959** Faulkner *Mansion* 378 **MS**, I still think you found a booger where there wasn't one. **c1960** Wilson *Coll.* **csKY**, Booger [ˈbʊgə]. **1962** Atwood *Vocab. TX* 71, Ghost . . . Booger, sperit (or spirit), and goblin . . are characteristic of older informants. **1965–70** *DARE* (Qu. EE41, *A hobgoblin that is used to threaten children and make them behave*) 26 Infs, Booger(s); **GA13, OK48**, Old booger; **GA72**, Bugger; (Qu. CC17, *Imaginary animals or monsters*) Infs **AR52, GA74, KY6, LA2, MD20, NC69, SC24**, Booger; **MO5**, The [ˈbʊgɚz]'ll git you. **1971** *Foxfire* Spring–Summer 28 **nGA,**

My grandmother always used the times to the best advantage by telling ghost stories—or "booger" tales.

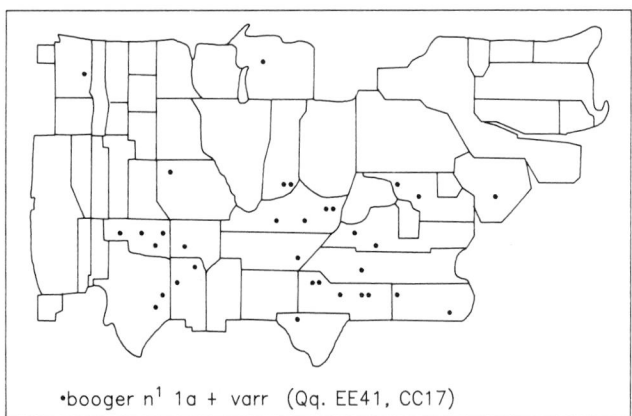

•booger n¹ 1a + varr (Qq. EE41, CC17)

b in phr *no buggers out tonight:* See **no bears out tonight.**

2 A louse, esp a head louse. [Cf Engl dial *bug, buggart* a louse] **chiefly Sth, S Midl** See Map

1893 Shands *MS Speech* 70, It is the unfortunate destiny of a large number of the negro nurses to have lice in their heads, and these are called *boogers* by the children. **1912** *DN* 3.566 **cNY,** *Booger* . . . Now and then used for *lice.* **1915** *DN* 4.181 **swVA,** *Bugger* . . . A louse. **1944** *PADS* 2.40 **wNC, SC,** *Booger* ['bʊgə, -ɚ] . . . A louse. **c1960** *Wilson Coll.* **csKY,** *Booger* . . . Head louse. "Them new kids at school have got boogers." **1965–70** *DARE* (Qu. R25, . . . *A head louse, or body louse*) 28 Infs, **scattered Sth, S Midl,** Booger; **KY21,** Body booger, head booger.

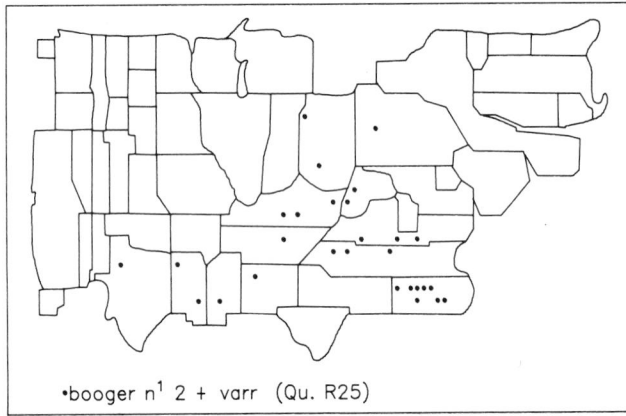

•booger n¹ 2 + varr (Qu. R25)

3 Nasal mucus; occas mucus from the eye.

1891 *DN* 1.214, [A ball of mucus in the nose is] Called *bugger* in the South, the *u* sounded like [ʊ]. **1892** *DN* 1.235 **MI, MO,** Booger. **1908** *DN* 3.292 **eAL, wGA,** Booger. **1914** *DN* 4.153 **NH,** Booger. **1915** *DN* 4.181 **swVA,** Bugger. **1944** *PADS* 2.40 **NC, LA,** Booger. **1950** *WELS* (*Sticky mucus that forms in the nose*) 6 Infs, **WI,** Bugger(s); 2 Infs, Boogers; 1 Inf, Buggers or buggies (used by children). **1956** McAtee *Some Dialect NC* 6, Bugger: . . dried mucus in the corners of the eyes or in the nose; pronounced to rhyme with sugar. **1965–70** *DARE* (Qu. X16, *Sticky mucus that forms in the nose*) 157 Infs, **throughout US,** Booger(s); 25 Infs, **scattered,** Bugger(s).

4 Something distasteful, troublesome, or discomforting, esp a spell of remarkable or unusual weather.

1956 Ker *Vocab. W. TX* 59, Storm with rain and thunder and lightning . . *booger.* *Ibid* 61, *Snorter* and *booger* . . here designate a storm. **1967–70** *DARE* (Qu. B3, *If a day is very hot, you say it's [a]* _____) Inf **IL141,** Booger [bʊgɚ]; (Qu. KK41, *Something that is very difficult to do: "I managed to get through with it, but it was* _____ .") Inf **CA209,** A bugger [bʌgɚ]; **WA28,** A bugger, a burden, a bitch.

5 A dust ball.

1968 *DARE* (Qu. E20, *Soft rolls of dust that collect on the floor under beds or other furniture*) Inf **NY93,** Boogers.

booger n² See **bugger** n¹

booger v¹ [**booger** n¹ 1] **chiefly Sth, S Midl, SW**

1 Of an animal, esp a horse: to shy, be frightened; hence adj *boogered* frightened. Cf **boogery**

1893 Shands *MS Speech* 70, *Booger* . . . The word is used also, by illiterate whites, as a verb, meaning *to shy, to get slightly frightened,* and is said of a horse. **1896** *DN* 1.413 **swNC.** **1902** (1968) Clapin *Americanisms, Booger.* In parts of New York, to shy, be frightened. "That horse boogers a little at dogs." **1905** *DN* 3.71 **nwAR,** *Booger* . . . 'He boogers.' Used of a skittish horse. Rare. **1952** Brown *NC Folkl.* 1.521, *Booger at* . . . To start at from fright(?). "The horse kinda boogered at him."—Central and east. Rare. **1970** *DARE* (Qu. GG24, *Other words meaning to frighten: "Now don't let those fellows* _____ *you.'*) Inf **TX80,** Get you boogered.

2 Of a group of horses or cattle: to get excited and move about nervously; to frighten, make nervous.

1929 Dobie *Vaquero* 253 **TX,** For some time they "boogered" at every chance sight or sound. **1961** Adams *Old-Time Cowhand* 285, No matter how gentle a herd, it was forever on the lookout for somethin' to booger at. **1966** *DARE* FW Addit **swNM,** They "boogered" or "cowboyed"—of cattle; to raise a ruckus when scared. **1969** *DARE* Tape **TX70,** They [=horses] 'd maybe run halfway around the track, and something would booger ['bʊgɚ] 'em, and they'd turn and pitch back the other way.

booger v² See **bugger** v 2

boogerbear n Also sp *buggerbear,* pronc-sp *buggabear* Occas *boogiebear* [By analogy with *bugbear,* infl by **booger** n¹]

1 =**booger** n¹ 1. **chiefly Sth, S Midl** See Map

1939 Hench *Coll.* **AL, VA,** I accidentally got into a talk with two other Univ. Va. people—one a history teacher, the other a secretary—about the word "buggabear." The teacher learned it as a boy in Alabama; and the secretary, a Charlottesville woman, uses it at present here in Charlottesville. Both say they would spell it "buggerbear." The first syllable rimes with "bug." **1965–70** *DARE* (Qu. EE41, *A hobgoblin that is used to threaten children and make them behave*) 19 Infs, **chiefly Sth, S Midl,** Boogerbear; **IN35, KY89, 94, OR1, VT11,** Boogiebear; **GA72,** Bugger [bʊgɹ] bear; **MS8,** Buggerbear; **IN5,** A buggabear ['bʌgə,ber]; (Qu. CC17, *Imaginary animals or monsters*) Infs **KY94, LA3, TN35,** Boogerbear.

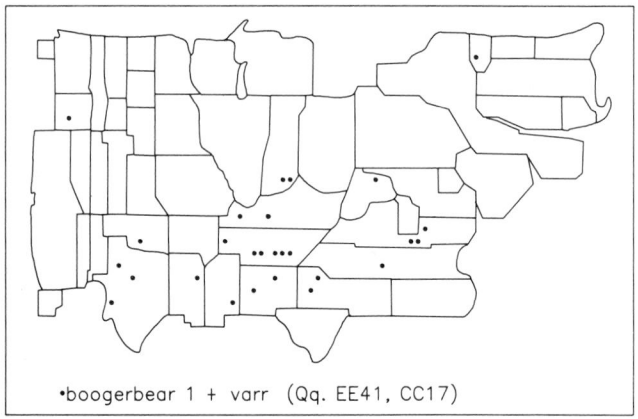

•boogerbear 1 + varr (Qq. EE41, CC17)

2 in phr *no buggerbears out tonight:* See **no bears out tonight.**

boogerboo See **bugaboo**

boogered See **booger** v¹

boogered up See **bugger** v 2

boogerish adj [**booger** n¹ 1 + *-ish*] Cf **booger** v¹

Frightening, eerie.

1907 *DN* 3.182 **seNH,** *Boogerish* . . . Uncanny; suggestive of bogies. **1938** Rawlings *Yearling* 223 **FL,** Hit looks mighty boogerish. **1967** Will *Dredgeman* 18 **FL,** A right boogerish place, this dark swamp looked to be, for sure, plumb creepified!

boogerlee n |ˈbʊgəˈli, ˈbu–| Also sp *boogalee, bougalee* [Perh from **booger** n¹ or **bugger** n¹] **chiefly LA**

1 also *boog:* A Cajun n¹ 1.

1968 *DARE* (Qu. HH28) Inf **LA23,** "Cajun" is a person of French descent in south Louisiana, called *coon-ass* and *boogalee* [ˌbʊgəˈli]; **LA46,** Cajun—['bʊgə,liz], also [bʊgz]. **1968** *DARE* FW Addit **New Orleans LA,** Boogerlee—same as Frenchman. Another person in town spelled it "boogalee." Common. **1983** Reinecke *Coll.* **New Orleans LA,** *Bougalee* ['bʊgə,li]—Not certainly French in origin. Contemptuous or taunting name for a lower-class Cajun. Probably related to "bougre." Now largely supplanted by "coon-ass" which is also controversial.

2 A person of mixed Black and White ancestry.

1966–68 *DARE* (Qu. HH28) Inf **FL4**, ['bʊgəli] — from New Orleans, dark skinned; **LA40**, French mixed with negroes are called boogalees ['bʊgəliz].

boogerman n Also sp *boogarman, buggerman* [**booger** n¹]

1 also *boog man:* =**booger** n¹ **1a.** **chiefly Sth, Midl** See Map (Note: *boogeyman* is the more frequently used term throughout the U.S. except in the Sth where it is slightly less common than *boogerman.*)

1903 *DN* 2.295 **Cape Cod MA,** *Boogarman* . . . A spirit of the dark that carries off children. **1905** *DN* 3.60 **NE.** **1907** *DN* 3.182 **seNH.** *Ibid* 206 **nwAR.** **1908** *DN* 3.292 **eAL, wGA.** **1912** *DN* 3.566 **cNY.** **1950** *PADS* 14.16 **SC.** **c1960** *Wilson Coll.* **csKY,** *Boogerman* . . . An imaginary Nemesis of childhood. "The boogerman will get you if you don't quit crying and go to sleep." **1965–70** *DARE* (Qu. EE41, *A hobgoblin . . used to threaten children and make them behave*) 190 Infs, **chiefly Sth, Midl,** Boogerman; **OK6,** Old boogerman; **OH48,** Boog man; (Qu. CC17, *Imaginary animals or monsters*) Infs **AR37, CA144, IL4, LA11, 35, TN66,** Boogerman; (Qu. DD22, . . *Expressions meaning delirium tremens*) Inf **GA72,** Buggerman's after you.

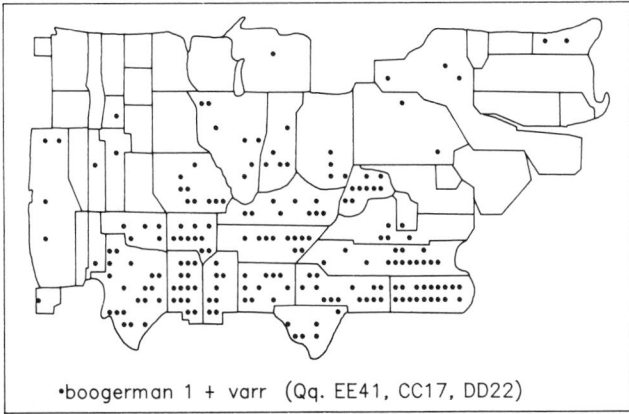

•boogerman 1 + varr (Qq. EE41, CC17, DD22)

2 also *boogeyman, boogieman, buggarman, buggyman:* The devil. **chiefly Sth, S Midl** See Map

1905 *DN* 3.60 **NE,** *Buggyman* [bʌ–] . . . Corruption of *bogyman.* **1915** *DN* 4.180 **swVA,** *Bad-man* . . . The devil. Also, *black-man, buggar-man.* **1926** Kephart *Highlanders* 24 **sAppalachians,** My goddamighty, Mam, thar's the boogerman — I done seed him! **1939** *AmSp* 14.268 **IN,** Terms referring to the Devil: . . 'the booger (bogie) man,' . . 'the Black Man,' and 'old Ned.' **1943** *LANE* Map 533 **scattered throughout NEng,** Several informants use *bugger man* or *booger man* as a veiled term synonymous with devil . . . In some cases, on the other hand, the informants state explicitly that the term . . *bad man, bugger* ~, *booger* ~, or *boogie* ~ is not a name of the devil. **1944** *PADS* 2.32 **wNC, SC, VA,** *Boogey-man.* **1952** Brown *NC Folkl.* 1.521, *Booger man.* **1954** *Harder Coll.* **cwTN,** *Booger man, boogeyman.* **1965–70** *DARE* (Qu. CC8, *Other names for the devil*) 39 Infs, **chiefly Sth, S Midl,** Boogerman; **AL33, KY11, OK18, SC46,** Old boogerman; **KY74, MO2, 20, NC35, SC54, VT12, VA21,** Boogeyman; (Qu. NN26b, *Weakened substitutes for 'hell': "Go to _____!"*) Infs **GA72, 73,** Boogerman.

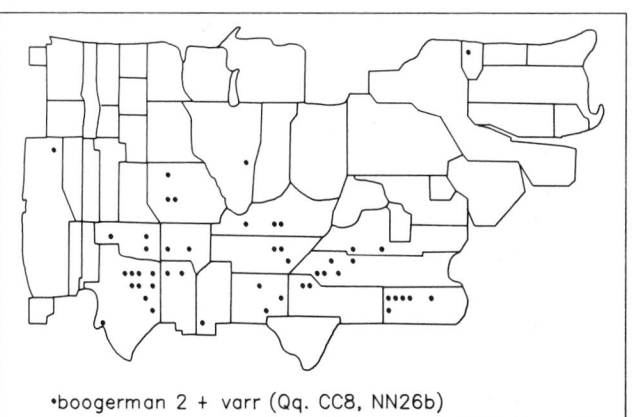

•boogerman 2 + varr (Qq. CC8, NN26b)

1971 Bright *Word Geog. CA & NV* 132, Terms in common with Texas . . . Satan, boogey man. **1973** Allen *LAUM* 1.384, *Devil . . . Booger man* (spelled *bugger* on the checklist) is again clearly Midland. [Response identified by 9% of respondents in ND, 10% in MN, 15% in SD, 17% in IA, 25% in NE.]

3 also *boogeyman:* A policeman. **S Atl**

1967–69 *DARE* (Qu. V9, . . *A policeman*) Inf **GA72,** Buggerman; **SC34,** Boogerman; (Qu. V10a, . . *Joking names . . for a sheriff*) Inf **NC87,** Boogeyman. **1967** *DARE* Tape **SC35,** Not a white man nor nigger in this country don't know what you're talkin about. You call the boogerman ['bʊgɚ,mæn]. They's talkin about the highway patrol. **1967** *DARE* FW Addit **nwSC,** Boogerman — state highway patrolman.

booger up See **bugger** v 2

booger wagon n Also *boogey wagon* [Prob abbr for **boogerman** 3] Cf **booby wagon**

A patrol wagon.

1966–69 *DARE* (Qu. N3, *The car or wagon that takes arrested people to the police station or to jail*) Inf **GA72,** Booger [bʊgɚ] wagon; **KS16,** Boogey wagon — used to call it this; **NC31,** Booger wagon — used to transport prisoners for road work; **NC67,** Boogey wagon.

boogery adj Also *buggery* [**booger** n¹] Cf **booger** v¹

Frightened; frightening.

1941 *AN&Q* 1.86, The use (non-obscene) of this word [=*bugger*] in colloquial American speech seems clear, but some details remain to be worked out. Into this category would go the non-obscene *buggery* . . with its original sense of "Devilish!" or even merely "Spritely!" **1956** McAtee *Some Dialect NC* 6, Buggery-looking: ugly, forbidding or scary-looking. **1967** Green *Horse Tradin'* 4 **TX,** Because he [=a horse] was so snorty, snaky, and boogery, he was hard to ride — although he was not bad to buck.

boogery-eyed adj [**booger** v¹]

Having large round eyes; wide-eyed.

1969 *DARE* (Qu. X21c) Inf **MO15,** Boogery-eyed.

boogey lice n Also *bogey lice, boogley* ~, *boogy* ~ [Prob var of **bube lice,** but cf **boogie** n 4] **sePA**

=**beggar ticks 1.**

1968–70 *DARE* (Qu. S14, . . *Prickly seeds, small and flat, with two prongs at one end, that cling to clothing*) Inf **PA242,** Beggars ticks, boogey lice; **PA152,** Boogley [bʊgli] lice; **PA111,** Bogey [bogi] lice. **1982** *Barrick Coll.* **sePA,** Boogy lice — any of several weed seeds that stick to hair and clothing like Spanish needles.

boogeyman See **boogerman**

boogey wagon See **booger wagon**

boogie n [Prob alter of *bogey* devil, goblin, specter; but cf **booger** n¹]

1 =**booger** n¹ **1a.**

1968–70 *DARE* (Qu. CC17, *Imaginary animals or monsters*) Inf **NY78,** Boogie; (Qu. EE41, *A hobgoblin that is used to threaten children and make them behave*) Inf **VA42,** Boogie.

2 See quots. **chiefly Nth** Cf **booger** n¹ **3**

1890 *DN* 1.18 **NH,** *Boogie* . . ball of mucus in the nose. **1950** *WELS* (*Sticky mucus that forms in the nose*) 3 Infs, **WI,** Boogies. **1960** (1962) Eichenlaub *Minnesota Dr.* 144, Nasal crusts or boogies form just inside the nose. **1965–70** *DARE* (Qu. X16, *Sticky mucus that forms in the nose — children's words for this*) 14 Infs, **scattered Nth,** Boogie.

3 A Black person. [Orig criminal and hobo speech] **esp common Nth** *derivative* Cf **bugger** n¹ **B1**

1923 Anon. *Confessions of a Bank Burglar* (Partridge *Underworld Dict.*), Boogie. **1926** *AmSp* 1.650 [Hobo argot], *Boogie* — a negro. **1930** Irwin *Amer. Tramp, Boogie.* — A negro. **1967–70** *DARE* (Qu. HH28, . . *Negro*) Infs **MD23, MA75, NJ1, NY1, 76,** Boogie.

4 A louse, **booger** n¹ **2.**

1966–69 *DARE* (Qu. R25, . . *A head louse, or body louse*) Infs **FL32, IL97,** Boogie.

boogiebear See **boogerbear**

boogieboo See **bugaboo**

boogied up See **bugger** v 2

boogieman See **boogerman** 2

boogie shot n

In marble play: see quot.

1962 *PADS* 37.1 **cKS,** *Boogie shot.* This occurs when a player drops a marble, picks it up instantly, and shoots from where it fell.

boogie up See **bugger** v 2

boogley lice See **boogey lice**

boog man See **boogerman 1**

boogy lice See **boogey lice**

boo-hag See **boo-daddy**

boo-holey n

1966 *DARE* (Qu. X34, . . *Nicknames for the navel*) Inf **AR3,** Belly button, boo-holey.

boohoo v

To weep loudly.

1843 Field *Drama Pokerville* 91, The little woman "*boo-hoo'd* right out," as the orientals of *Varmount* have it. **1884** *Harper's Mag.* 69.697/1 **MA,** I . . boo-hooed like a baby. **1887** (1967) Harris *Free Joe* 92 **nwGA** [Black], Dey cried. En I ain' tellin' you no lie, suh, I stood dar en cried wid um. Let 'lone dat, I des fa'rly boohooed . . . W'en I git ter cryin' sho' nuff, I bleeze ter boohoo. **1905** *DN* 3.4 **cCT,** *Boo-hoo . . .* To bawl, cry aloud. **1907** *DN* 3.209 **nwAR, cCT,** *Boo-hoo . . .* To bawl, cry aloud. **1919** Kyne *Capt. Scraggs* 25 **CA,** No use boo-hooin' over spilt milk, Scraggsy. **1968** *DARE* (Qu. GG35b, . . *Annoyed or disappointed* . . *"She's been _____ all day.'*) Inf **IA30,** Boohooing.

boo-hoo-owl See **hoo-owl**

boojum n

1976 *Harper's Weekly* 65.18 **TN** [Black], White people in our neighborhood are called "boojums." If you try to become friendly with the "boojums," you are accused of "jeffing."

booji adj [Alter of *bourgeois*] *among Black speakers*

See quots.

1970 Major *Afro–Amer. Slang, Booji:* bourgeois. **1977** Smitherman *Talkin* 251, Terms for Blacks (used only for blacks) . . . *Booji,* an adjective, derived from *bourgeoisie,* referring to elitist blacks whose money and position make them think they're white.

book n[1]

1 A magazine, pamphlet.

1917 *DN* 4.408 **wNC,** *Book . . .* Applied to magazines and pamphlets. **1926** Kephart *Highlanders* 318 **wNC,** A magazine is always called a book in this region.

2 A stack of tobacco leaves. Cf **book** v[1] 2

1969 *DARE* Tape **KY35,** We put it [=tobacco] down in what we speak of as a book, lay it down straight, pile it up an' maybe cover it with a tarpaulin.

book n[2] [By folk-etym from ME or Scots *bouk* belly; cf the other names: *psalterium, manifold, manyplies,* and the *leaves* of the omasum]

The omasum, the third stomach of a cow or other ruminant.

1954 *PADS* 21.21 **SC,** *Bouk* [bʊk] . . . The psalterium . . . The word is widely known and used by butchers and by farmers who slaughter their own cattle. I recall from childhood supposing that it was called "book" because it had so many "leaves" in it.

book v[1]

1 See quot 1923.

1923 *DN* 5.202 **swMO,** *Book . . .* To credit, to charge, to enter as a debit when payment is deferred. **1966–67** *DARE* (Qu. U11, *If you buy something but don't pay cash for it, you might say, "I _____."*) Inf **GA9,** Booked it; **SC43,** Book that to (*or* for) me; booked it.

2 In tobacco production: to lay tobacco leaves in a stack; also vbl n *booking.* Cf **book** n[1] 2

1966 *DARE* Tape **FL26,** Book down . . . Lay tobacco leaves on top of one another for about 3 weeks to allow it to go through a sweat. Done after tobacco has been air or fire cured. Makes it more flexible; **SC17,** You have to book your 'bacco now. **1967** Key *Tobacco Vocab.* 59 **CT,** *Casing* is putting it [=tobacco] into boxes, also called *booking.*

‡**3** To leave (something) unfinished, to lay (something) aside for the time being.

1969 *DARE* (Qu. KK47, *Something that is left undecided or unfinished: "Perhaps we'd better just _____."*) Inf **CA136,** Book it.

book v[2] Also sp *boock* [Prob var of **buck** v[1] **B2a**]

To butt.

1930 Stoney–Shelby *Black Genesis* 143 **seSC,** Billy-Goat . . is sho' goin' to put dat hard head o' he-own to you an' *boock* you till you is change a whole lot mo'! **1954** *PADS* 21.21 **SC,** *Book* [bʊk] . . . To push with the horns; to hook. "Look out, that cow books. She will book you."

book count n **West**

See quot 1968.

1926 Branch *Cowboy* 109 **WY, MT,** But in the fervor of speculation, book counts were the basis of transactions, and were accepted as security by the banks. **1942** Dale *Cow Country* 108 **WY,** They soon discovered that book count in selling cattle was a thing of the past. **1968** Adams *Western Words, Book count*—An estimate of the number of cattle on the ranch, based on the ranch records. Selling cattle by book count was commonly resorted to in the early days, sometimes much to the profit of the seller.

booked ppl adj [Perh from *book* to reserve a space]

Fatally ill, beyond recovery.

1968 *DARE* (Qu. BB54, *When a sick person is past hope of recovery, you'd say he's _____.*) Inf **IN38,** Booked.

bookety-book See **bookity-book**

bookie-sug n Cf **sug**

A sweetheart, lover.

1970 *DARE* (Qu. AA3, *Nicknames or affectionate names for a sweetheart*) Inf **SC68,** Bookie-sug ['bʊkɪ səg] [laughter].

booking n

=**book learning.**

1974 *AmSp* 49.61 **seME** (as of c1900), *Booking . . .* Reading, learning. "He's got too much booking in school."

bookity-book adv, n Also sp *bookety-book* [Echoic] **chiefly Sth, S Midl** *esp among Black speakers*

Quickly, swiftly; used to represent the sound of running feet.

1935 Hurston *Mules & Men* 173 **FL,** Dat de lion give John de book; de bookity book. [Footnote: Sound word meaning running] He hauled de fast mail back into de woods. **1947** Ballowe *The Lawd* 253 **LA,** It seemed that I heard the soft patter of little galloping feet: bookety-book, bookety-book. **1968** *DARE* FW Addit **swAR,** Bookity-book—expression indicating speed. Negro. "Here he comes round the corner bookity-book, bookity-book."

bookity Sam n Cf **boogerman 1**

=**booger** n[1] **1.**

1966 *DARE* (Qu. EE41, *A hobgoblin that is used to threaten children and make them behave*) Inf **MS15,** Bookity Sam.

book-keep v [Back-formation from *bookkeeper*]

1917 *DN* 4.408 **wNC,** *Book-keep . . .* To act as bookkeeper. "He book-kept for the camp."

book learning n Pronc-spp *book larnin(g) old-fash* Cf **book schooling**

Education derived from books or schooling.

1838 (1932) Hawthorne *Amer. Notebooks* 49 **MA,** Intelligent as respects book-learning but much deficient in worldly tact. **1871** Eggleston *Hoosier Schoolmaster* 40 **sIN,** Book-larnin' don't do no good to a woman. **1916** Howells *Leatherwood God* 99 **sOH,** I don't want any book-l'arning to know what *you* are. **1926** Kephart *Highlanders* 345 **sAppalachians,** The mountain clergy, as a general rule, are hostile to "book larnin'." **1943** *LANE* Map 535 **scattered throughout NEng,** *Learning, book learning . .* the old-fashioned term for education. **1951** in 1977 *Pissing in the Snow* 223 **Ozarks,** That must be a lie because everybody knowed he didn't have no book-learning, so how could he read anything out of a newspaper? **1953** Brewer *Word Brazos* 48 **eTX** [Black], He smaa't too, 'caze he hab lots of book learnin' an' he study de bishop lackwise. **c1960** *Wilson Coll.* **csKY.**

bookooing vbl n [*beaucoup*]

1935 Hurston *Mules & Men* 30 **FL,** We could hear the boys in the first car doing what Ellis Jones called bookooing [Footnote: Loud talking, bullying, woofing] before they even hit the ground.

bookoo(s) See **beaucoup**

‡**book pine** n [Etym unknown]

1970 *DARE* (Qu. T17, . . *Different kinds of pine trees*) Inf **TX106,** Book pine—just little bitty kernels.

books n pl constr as sg **chiefly Sth, S Midl**

School or the time spent in school — sometimes used as a call.

1896 DN 3.413 cTX, Books: school, school-time. "Is it books?" "Has books taken up?" = "Has school taken up (i.e. begun)?" **1906** DN 3.127 nwAR. **1908** DN 3.292 eAL, wGA. **1936** AmSp 11.275 TN. **1951** Giles Harbin's Ridge 29 eKY, Books took up at eight o'clock. Ibid 37, He was always the first one out the door when the teacher called, "books away" at the end of the day. **1952** Brown NC Folkl. 1.521, Books . . . A call (in former days) to lessons. "Books, books, come to books!" — Central and east. **c1960** Wilson Coll. csKY. **1964** Wallace Frontier Life 38 swOK (as of 1893–1906), We children regarded lesson periods, referred to as "books," a punishment to be borne with fortitude until the bell rang.

book schooling n
=**book learning.**

1952 Brown NC Folkl. 1.521, Book-schoolin' . . . Education. — Caldwell county.

Book, the n
The Bible.

1916 Howells Leatherwood God 95 sOH, If He was so mighty and terrible, would n't He have ways of showing it in these times just as much as in those old times that we read about in the Book? **1923** DN 5.202 swMO, Book . . . The Bible. **c1960** Wilson Coll. csKY, Book . . . The Bible, often used by very old people, especially preachers. "He preached from the Book."

book-write v

1952 Brown NC Folkl. 1.521, Book-write . . . To write a book. "Mrs. Dargan is always book-writing."

book-writer n
An author or writer of books.

1952 Brown NC Folkl. 1.521, Book-writer . . . One who writes books. "Oh, he's probably another one of them book-writers."

boolge See **bulge A**

boom v

1 Of plants: to grow vigorously, thrive. **chiefly Nth**

1966–70 DARE (Qu. OO35a, Talking about vegetables thriving: "Last year we fertilized the garden, and the plants really _____.") Infs IL31, 37, NH5, NY75, OH82, PA234, Boomed.

2 with around: To move from place to place, wander. [Perh var of bum around; but cf **boomer** n²]

1967 DARE (Qu. Y29b, About a man who doesn't stay home much: "He's always _____.") Inf CA15, Booming around.

boomalally n [Echoic] **SC, esp Charleston** old-fash
See quot 1954.

1952 PADS 17.36 SC, Boomalally, meaning a soldier marching to music, was reported by a lady from Charleston as being used by the nurses when the soldiers marched by. "Here come the Boomalallies," they said. **1954** PADS 21.21 SC, Boomalally ['bʊmə̩læli] . . . Formerly (down to 1900) applied only to a cadet of the South Carolina Military Academy . . . Later applied to any soldier, especially to one on parade marching to music. The name seems to be derived from the sound of the drum. Charleston.

boomble v [Frequentative of boom]

1904 in 1966 AmSp 41.22 ME, Boomble . . . To make a booming noise. "The stones came tumblin' and boomblin' down like thunder."

boomer n¹ [From boom to make a deep hollow sound]

1 =**mountain boomer** or similar animal: see quots. **chiefly sAppalachians, esp eTN, wNC**

1878 (1929) Summers Annals 1544 swVA, The formidable animal proved to be a boomer, a species of mountain squirrel. **1917** DN 4.408 wNC, Boomer . . . The red squirrel. **1936** AmSp 11.275 eTN, Boomer. Gray squirrel. 'I killed a boomer.' **1943** Chase Jack Tales 129 wNC (as of 1880s), Then all kinds of pizen snakes and wildcats and boomers and ground hogs came and tried to get in. **1949** AmSp 24.106 nGA, Boomer; Mountain boomer . . . A small gray squirrel. **1966–69** DARE (Qu. P27, What kinds of squirrels do you have around here?) Infs GA72, LA22, NC30, 36, 37, 44, 48, 72, Boomer; (Qu. P31) Inf OR5, Boomer — like a large chipmunk; not many around.

2 The mountain beaver (Aplodontia ruffa). **chiefly Pacific NW**

1884–85 Kingsley Std. Nat. Hist. 5.121 OR, WA, The 'Showt'l' or

'Sewellel' of the aborigines . . [is] known to more prosaic hunters and trappers as the 'Boomer.' **1947** Cahalane Mammals 391 OR, 'Boomer' is the name applied in Oregon, but it [the mountain beaver] never booms. **1958** McCulloch Woods Words Pacific NW, Boomer . . . The mountain beaver, a rodent about the size of a muskrat, living mostly in the Coast Range. It forages a great deal on freshly planted or other young coniferous trees, and is a real menace to forestry. **1962** Times (Seattle WA) 6 May 38, In parts of Oregon, the mountain beaver is called "boomer," another misnomer because it does not boom.

3 A thunderhead.

1970 DARE (Qu. B9, What do you call the big clouds that roll up high before a rainstorm?) Inf IL117, It looks like a boomer.

boomer n², also attrib [boom a rapid expansion of economic activity] **esp West** Cf **floater**
An itinerant worker: see quots.

1925 Cather Professor's House 181 NM, The crowd was fussing about one fellow, Rodney Blake, who had come in from his [train] engine without cleaning up . . . I asked him who was winning. "Blake. The dirty boomer's been taking everything." **1940** (1966) FWP Guide AZ 369, It was the top of a small glory hole that yielded over $100,000 worth of ore besides what was stolen by the hordes of "boomers" who rushed to the spot. **1947** Harper's Mag. 194.67/2 IN, Then, restless, he became a boomer machinist. **1958** McCulloch Woods Words Pacific NW, Boomer . . . Originally a tramp railroader, moving from job to job; now applied to loggers who shift between camps, in contrast to the homeguards who stay put. **1966** DARE (Qu. HH19, . . A tramp) Inf MI26, Boomer — not so much trampish as wanderlust. **1967** DARE Tapes ID6, 9, Boomer.

boomer n³ [boom chain of floating logs with the logs it encloses]
In logging: =**boom man.**

1941 AmSp 16.232 [Lumberjack lingo], A boom man, who has charge of a boom, is also called a boomer. **1959** AmSp 34.76 nCA [Logger lingo], Boomer . . . A man in charge of a boom.

boomer-peg n
=**cricket** n².

1969 DARE (Qu. EE10, A game in which a short stick lying on the ground is flipped into the air and then hit with a longer stick) Inf GA89, Boomer-peg.

boom man n Cf **boomer** n³
See quots.

1920 DN 5.80 NW, Boom men. Men who tend to a boom of logs. **1955** Seattle Daily Times (WA) 21 Aug 10, The boom men, who collect the logs into booms for towing, must be agile. **1956** AmSp 31.149 nwCA, Boom man . . . A worker who poles floating logs to a sawmill.

boompie See **bumpy** n

boompike n [boom in ref to the bird's cry + pike prob in ref to the long tapering bill]
=**bittern.**

1955 MA Audubon 39.313, Many of the local names of the bittern have reference to, or are in imitation of, the peculiar notes of the male during the mating season . . . Boom-pike (N.H.).

boom pole n

1981 Broaddus Coll. ceKY, Boom pole — a log fastened on top of a load of hay in a wagon to hold the hay down.

boon n¹ [Prob abbr for **ace-boon-coon**, but cf **bone** n 5]
A Black person.

1967–68 DARE (Qu. HH28, . . Negro) Infs MA1, PA94, Boon.

boon n² Arch pronc for bone

1954 PADS 21.17 nwSC, In the same neighborhood occur the pronunciations boon, droon, . . for bone, drone.

boon-coon n [Abbr for **ace-boon-coon**]
A close or intimate friend.

1970 DARE (Qu. II1, Words meaning a close friend . . "He's my _____.") Inf SC68, Boon-coon.

boondock n, usu pl, also attrib Usu |'bundɑk|, occas |'bʌn–| Pronc-spp boondog, bundock [Tagalog bundok mountain] orig military slang, now widespread, esp among urban, young and mid-aged speakers

1 Rough or wild country; rural backcountry, the sticks.

1944 Metcalf *Marine Corps Reader* 139, The sand and boondocks of Parris Island. **1950** *Word Study* Oct 7/1, Today Marines use *boondock* clothes and *boondock* shoes for hikes and maneuvers. **1965–70** *DARE* (Qu. C33, . . *An out-of-the-way place*) 70 Infs, **widespread,** Boondocks; **CA**2, **MO**7, **NE**11, **NH**1, **NC**62, **PA**220, 239, (Out *or* back) in the boondocks; **MN**15, Out in the boondogs; **MD**17, Bundocks ['bʌndɑks]; [Of all Infs responding to the question, 13% were comm types 1–2, 31% young and mid-aged; of those giving these responses, 21% were comm types 1–2, 62% young and mid-aged.] (Qu. C34) Inf **DC**11, Boondocks; (Qu. HH1) Inf **MA**1, Somebody who comes from the boondocks; (Qu. II25) Infs **NY**241, **PA**167, **WA**22, Boondocks. **1969** *DARE* Tape **KY**6, They was bundocks ['bʌndɑks]. They was no road in here.

2 See **boondocker.**

boondock v [**boondock** n]
1950 *Word Study* May 8/1 **TN,** *Boondocks,* a term used in the U.S. Marine Corps to mean "back country" or "isolated outpost," . . in Tennessee college circles has been made into a verb, as an equivalent for "to park" and "to neck."

boondocker n Also *boondock* [**boondock** n]
A heavy work or walking shoe.
1953 Uris *Battle Cry* 127, Andy Hookans was dumping a can of footpowder into his boondockers. **1956** *AmSp* 31.192 [Marine Corps slang], His working shoes are *boondockers.* **1959** Hench Coll. **VA,** While a Univ[ersity] of V[irgini]a teacher and his wife were hiking in the Blue Ridge with us, they both talked about their heavy walking shoes and called them "boondockers." **1967–70** *DARE* (Qu. W11, *Men's low, rough work shoes*) Infs **AR**52, **NY**83, **WA**20, Boondockers; **MO**29, **WI**47, Boondocks.

boonie n¹ [Familiarized form of **boondock** n]
1 pl: The backwoods, the sticks.
1956 *AmSp* 31.190 [Marine Corps slang], The *boonies* (woods, jungles, etc.). **1967–70** *DARE* (Qu. C33, . . *An out-of-the-way place, or a very unimportant place*) Infs **CA**166, 191, **IA**45, **OH**99, Boonies; (Qu. HH1, . . *A rustic or countrified person*) Inf **NV**4, Lives in the boonies. **1977** *UpCountry* Dec 14 **csME,** There I stood before him, with 19 years of schooling, aspiring to be a dirt farmer far in the boonies. **1978** *Capital Times* (Madison WI) 11 Oct 64/1, Now, in the boonies, where I reside, the way you get all this ritzy stuff is by making it with your own little hands.

2 An outdoor toilet.
1944 *Hench Coll.* "Boonie" is widely used in Tidewater Virginia for privy. **1969** *DARE* (Qu. M21b, . . *An outside toilet building*) Inf **CA**163, Boonie.

boonie n² [Prob from *boon* favor, blessing + *-ie*]
1970 *DARE* FW Addit **seKY,** Boonie—Something very good—(a term of enthusiasm). "Say that's a boonie!"

boopety adj [Cf *uppity* arrogant]
Self-important.
1948 Young *Light* 178 **OH,** With the boopety little pipsqueak with them, they couldn't make fun of the performance.

boopsie n
A sweetheart, darling.
1968–70 *DARE* (Qu. AA3, *Nicknames or affectionate names for a sweetheart*) Inf **OH**23, Boopsie; (Qu. AA23, *Joking names a woman may use to refer to her husband*) Inf **PA**234, Boopsie.

boose n [Prob from Scots *boose, buss, bush* mouth]
A snout; a person's mouth.
1968 *DARE* (Qu. K61, *What do you call a pig's nose?*) Inf **NC**49, [bus]; (Qu. X9, *Joking or uncomplimentary words for a person's mouth*) Inf **NC**49, [bus].

boosh See **bush** n¹, v¹ A

booshel See **bushel** A

booshwah See **bushwa** n²

booshway n Also sp *budgeway, bugheway, bushwa* [Alter of CanFr *bourgeois* (pronc ['bu(r)ž'wɛ]) head voyageur] Cf *DCan* **booshway**
Orig the voyageur in charge of a trading post or expedition; by ext, a boss, leader; a big shot.
1850 Garrard *Wah-to-yah* 116 **NM,** Oh! a lot of darned gover'ment men; but as I'm 'bugheway' they do pretty well. [Footnote:] Bugheway

—bourgeoise [sic]—master. **1870** Pine *Beyond the West* 276, After a camp [of fur traders] is organized, and is on the march, a military discipline is observed; a leader is chosen, known as a 'Booshway,' whose business is to take the supervision—look after the condition of the whole camp. **1966** Giles *Great Adventure* 58 **Rocky Mts** (as of 1830s), Jim Bridger's as good a budgeway as ever led a brigade and made beaver come. **1966** *DARE* (Qu. II23, *Joking names for the people who are, or think they are, the best society of a community: the _____*) Inf **ME**16, Bushwa [bušwɑ]. **1967** Guthrie in Lomax *Hard Hitting Songs* 344, *Bourgeois Blues* . . . That just means "bushwa." Bushwa means moneyed folks with a lot of high falooting notions. Think they're just a shade better than you and me, . . or that colored people are all right so long as they "stay in their place."

boost v
1 See quots.
1906 *DN* 3.127 **nwAR,** *Boost* . . . To laud, boast of. "He is a boosting that country to beat the cars." **1908** *DN* 3.293 **eAL, wGA,** *Boost* . . . To laud, boast of, log-roll for. Usually heard with up.
2 See quot.
1970 *DARE* (Qu. Y5, *Words meaning to urge somebody to do something he shouldn't: "Johnny wouldn't have tried that if the other boys hadn't _____."*) Inf **TN**53, Boosted.

booster n [Var of **buster**]
1 Something extraordinary of its kind.
1968 *DARE* (Qu. LL5, *Something impressively big: "That cabbage is really a _____."*) Inf **NY**73, Booster.
2 See quot.
1967 *DARE* (Qu. Z12, . . *A small child: "He's a healthy little _____."*) Inf **TX**9, Booster.

booster v
1966 *DARE* FW Addit **ND,** *Booster*—to boost, to help someone up into a tree.

boot n¹ [*boot* advantage, good; cf *OED* boot sb.¹ c1000 →]
1a also attrib: Something extra given in a sale or exchange to make up the difference in value; a premium, **lagniappe. scattered, but chiefly Sth, Midl** See Map
1811 Graydon *Memoirs* 20 **PA,** He picked up six or eight of my marbles, . . throwing me down three or four times the number of his own, the amount of boot being apparently wholly unworthy of calculation. **1827** in 1957 Old Farmer's Almanac *Sampler* 201 **NH,** Now we don't agree exactly as to the boot; he offers fifteen dollars and I do suppose, to be honest, that is enough. **1859** *Harper's Mag.* 19.137/1 **GA,** Jones Adare was a great swapper of horses . . . Jones kept on trading and having his boot-notes shaved. **1911** *DN* 3.550 **WY.** **1914** *DN* 4.69 **ME, nNH.** **1923** *DN* 5.202 **swMO.** **1929** Sale *Tree Named John* 106 **MS,** Brer Frawg knowed he had 'im dar; so he ax him how much boot he want, en Brer Mole say he want fo' bits. **1954** *Harder Coll.* **cwTN.** **1965–70** *DARE* (Qu. U15, *When you're buying something, if the seller puts in a little extra to make you feel that you're getting a good bargain, you call that _____*) 69 Infs, **chiefly Sth, Midl,** Boot. [Of all Infs responding to the question, 50% were male; of those giving this response, 62% were male.] **1966** *Wilson Coll.* **csKY.** **1967** Green *Horse Tradin'* 65 **TX,** I decided that was the most boot I ever drawed in a trade.

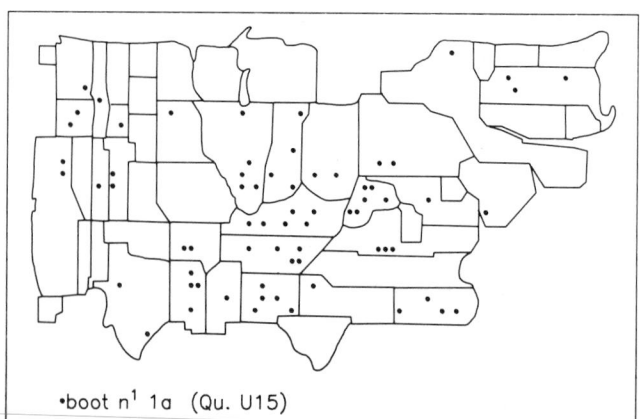

•boot n¹ 1a (Qu. U15)

b in adv phr *to boot:* In addition, besides. **widespread, but esp Atl States, Missip Valley; scattered West**

1667 in 1882 Southold NY *Town Rec.* 1.450, John Swezy exchanged w[i]th Capt John Tooker a gray hors . . for a baye hors . . only John Swazy is to give Cpt. Tooker two peeces of roope to boote. **1713** in 1869 *Essex Inst. Coll.* 10.101 **MA**, I am to give him 3£ 10 shil. to boot. **1898** Westcott *Harum* 229 **cNY**, I . . fin'ly traded him off fer another record-breaker an' fifteen dollars to boot. **1909** *DN* 3.351 **eAL**, Something given as a gratuity to a purchaser . . . *To boot* is the only form of the expression used in east Alabama. **1943** *LANE* Map 561, 8 Infs, **sNEng**, To boot. **1951** West *Witch Diggers* 52 **sIN** (as of 1899), It's hard ground to work in . . . Gravelly and frozen to boot. **c1960** *Wilson Coll.* **csKY**. **1965–70** *DARE* (Qu. U15, *When you're buying something, if the seller puts in a little extra to make you feel that you're getting a good bargain, you call that _____*) 53 Infs, **chiefly Atl States, Missip Valley, West**, (Something) to boot; 9 Infs, [Var phr +] to boot; (Qu. U41b, . . *"He's poor as a _____."*) Inf **SD8**, Church mouse and a Democrat to boot.
2 Fig: the children of a widowed or divorced woman who remarries.
1887 *Scribner's Mag.* 2.474/2 **AR**, He p'intedly swore dat w'en he got married he didn't want no boot. **c1960** *Wilson Coll.* **csKY**, *Boot* . . . Advantage or "extra." . . . Sometimes the word is used about some fellow who has married a widow with children.
3 See quot 1908. *old-fash* Cf **boot** v[1]
1908 *DN* 3.293 **eAL, wGA**, *Boot*. . . A fawning or subservient action or remark, an effort to curry favor . . . "He tried to get in a boot on the professor, but it wouldn't work." **1946** *PADS* 6.7 **NC**, *Boot* . . . A favor . . . "He had a boot on the professor." . . University of N.C., 1912.

boot n[2]
1a The trunk of a car.
1950 *WELS Suppl.*, 1 Inf, **cwWI**, Boot—the trunk compartment of a car. **1969** *DARE* FW Addit **c,seKY**, *Boot* . . . Trunk of a car. **1972** *Atlanta Letters*, As a child around Athens, Georgia, I heard "the boot of a car" which we now know as the trunk. *Ibid* **ncGA**, Boot . . . Car trunk. "Putting something in the boot."
b A luggage rack on a vehicle. [See *OED boot* sb.[3] 4]
1935 *AmSp* 10.75 **nwWY**, *Boot*. Luggage carrier on the back of a bus.
2 also attrib: The enclosing sheath near the top on the stems of grains; hence *in the boot* in the stage of developing the inflorescence.
1858 *TX Almanac for 1859* 70, A severe frost fell in Northern Texas on the 5th of April, 1857, when the wheat was in the boot. **1899** (1912) Green *VA Folk-Speech, Boot* . . . Wheat is in the *boot* when the stalk is swollen near the top, just before the head has come out of the upper leaf or sheath. **1971** WI *Statist. Reporting Serv. Report* 21 June, Jackson [Co]: Oats are looking good, they are just coming into the boot stage so heads will appear soon.
3 A trainee in a military boot camp; a novice, greenhorn.
1915 *Recruiter's Bull.* (U.S.) Apr 11/1 (*OEDS*), One of the 'boots' transferred to the Recruit Depot recently. **1946** *CA Folkl. Qrly.* 5.383 [Navy slang], Recruits are *boots*. **1956** *AmSp* 31.190 [Marine Corps slang], A trainee is a *boot*. **1966** *DARE* Tape **NC26**, With seven of those boots, that was beginners in the [Coast Guard] service. **1970** *DARE* (Qu. HH15, *A very inexperienced person, one who is just learning how to do a new thing*) Inf **SC69**, Boot—from the service, but used around here.
4 See **bootjack 2.**
5 A Black person. *among Black speakers; sometimes derog*
1967–68 *DARE* (Qu. HH28, . . *Negro*) Infs **MI72, PA66**, Boot. [Both Infs Black] **1970** Major *Afro-Amer. Slang, Boot* . . a black person. **1971** Bright *Word Geog. CA & NV* 115 [Black], [A *Negro*] Boot . . . Jocular. "Among ourselves. May come from the color of shoes." **1971** Roberts *Third Ear, Boot* . . a black person, usually male. (Often derogatory, depending upon context.) **1977** Smitherman *Talkin* 251, Terms for Blacks (used only by blacks) . . . *Boot*, neutral to positive term, depending on user; obvious reference to blackness of boots; possible allusion, via whites, to "bootblack," since shoeshine "boys" stereotypically are blacks.

boot v[1] [**boot** n[1] 3]
1946 *PADS* 6.7 **NC**, *Boot* . . . To seek a favor . . . "He booted the professor." University of N.C., 1912.

boot v[2]
1 often in phr *boot it:* To walk; hence vbl n *booting*. *old-fash*
1905 *Superior Telegram* (WI) 16 Dec 13/5, The cavalry boots . . had eighteen notches cut in the top of the leg, signifying 100 miles of booting it to the notch. **1907** *DN* 3.241 **eME**, *Boot*. . . Go afoot. "I booted down town in a hurry." *Boot it* . . . To walk. "I booted it to town."

2 To remove the leaf sheaths from a cabbage palmetto. Cf **bootjack 2**
1966 *DARE* Tape **FL37**, Swamp cabbage is booted, various layers are taken off to get to the tender core.

bootcher See **butcher**

bootchkey n Also sp *butchski, butchsky* [See quot 1945] *derog* Cf **chesky**
A Czechoslovakian.
1945 Mencken *Amer. Lang. Suppl. 1* 602, *Bootchkey* is also sometimes applied to a *Czech*. It comes from the Czech word *počkej*, meaning wait, hold, which is often used by Czech boys in playing games. **1964** *PADS* 42.40 **Chicago IL**, *Czezski, butchski*, . . *Czech* . . . Both of the very old forms *czezski* (or *chesky*) and *butchsky* were offered by an old German who remembered using those terms in her youth on the West Side of Chicago, where many poor European nationality groups begrudgingly shared territory.

bootheels, heave (or **throw**) **up one's** See **boots, throw up one's**

boot hill n [In the frontier West the name for the town cemetery for men who supposedly died with their boots on] *joc*
Orig a cemetery for men who died by violence; now, any cemetery.
1901 *Everybody's Mag.* 4.582/2 **KS**, Occasionally his six-shooter brought order and a new grave or two in Boot Hill Cemetery. **1930** Ferber *Cimarron* 160 **OK**, The body, unclaimed, was interred in Boot Hill, with only the prowling jackals to mourn him, their own kin. **1940** *FWP Guide NM* 110, Boothill—A kind of burial ground. **1940** *FWP Guide TX* 669, *Boot hill:* A cemetery where rest those who died with their boots on. **1965–70** *DARE* (Qu. BB61b, *Joking names for a cemetery*) 40 Infs, **widespread**, Boot hill.

boot hill two-step n [boot hill + *two-step* a dance] *joc*
Diarrhea.
1967 *DARE* (Qu. BB19, *Joking names for looseness of the bowels*) Inf **KS2**, Boot hill two-step.

bootjack n
1 usu pl, also *devil's bootjacks:* =**beggar ticks 1.**
1898 *Jrl. Amer. Folkl.* 11.228, *Bidens frondosa* . . boot-jacks, Western Conn. and Philadelphia, Pa. **1912** Blatchley *IN Weed Book* 160, *Bidens connata* . . . is one of 8 or 10 species of troublesome weeds occurring in the State and known as . . devil's bootjacks. **1950** *WELS (Small flat weed seeds with two prongs that stick to clothing)* 3 Infs, **WI**, Bootjack. **1965–70** *DARE* (Qu. S13) Inf **IL27**, Bootjacks; (Qu. S14) Infs **IA13, IL10, 27, PA60, 78, 245**, Bootjacks. **1971** GA Dept. Ag. *Farmers Market Bulletin* 20 Jan 8/1, Beggar-tick (often called bur-marigold, stick-tight, beggar-lice, boot-jack, or Spanish needles). **1979** *DARE* File **cnOH** (as of c1920), 'Bootjacks' was what we called them [=*Bidens*], from their shape. They stuck to our clothes.
2 also *boot:* The old leaf-stalk of the **cabbage palm.** **chiefly S Atl**
1938 Matschat *Suwannee R.* 211 **GA**, The trunk of the cabbage palm is always studded with the bases of dead leafstalks; the natives call these leafstalks bootjacks. **1950** *PADS* 14.74 **FL**, Cabbage boot . . . The part of the palmetto leaf which is attached to the tree. **1960** McGeachy *Hdbk. FL Palms* 10, Cabbage palm . . In natural state generally found growing in large groups, close together, trunks encased in the plaited-like "bootjacks" of old leaf bases on the younger Palms. An occasional older specimen will have shed the "boots" and have a smooth trunk. **1969** Lyons *My Florida* 105, We used the boots or dry butts of the palm fronds, which protect the young tree from the elements but fall as it starts to grow tall. **1971** Gantz *Naturalist in S. FL* 119, Here is a young cabbage palm, its trunk adorned with ferns that have lodged in the old leaf bases—the so-called boot jacks.

bootkisser n Cf **footkisser**
=**bootlick** n.
1966 *DARE* (Qu. II20a, *A person who tries too hard to gain somebody else's favor: "He's an awful _____."*) Inf **MS49**, Bootkisser.

bootleg n
See quots.
1950 *PADS* 14.15 **SC**, Bootleg . . . A twenty-four pound sack of flour. Dutch Fork. Possibly so called because of its shape. **1954** *PADS* 21.37 **SC**, The twenty-four pound sack is called a *bootleg*, . . and the ninety-six pound sack is called a *sack* of flour.

bootlegger's turn n

A method of reversing a vehicle's direction; see quot.

1967 *DARE* FW Addit **ND,** [To make a] bootlegger's turn [is] to reverse the direction in which a vehicle is going by backing it across the other lane of the road, then going forward.

bootlick v **chiefly Sth** Cf **boot** v[1]

See quot 1908.

1845 Hooper *Advent. Simon Suggs* 58 **AL,** A young man who was inclined to boot-lick any body suspected of having money. **1850** in 1956 Eliason *Tarheel Talk* 261 **NC,** One little fool . . . suspected . . . I was bootlicking [in volunteering to do something for a professor]. **1908** *DN* 3.293 **eAL, wGA,** *Boot-lick . . .* To seek to ingratiate oneself, do subservient things to gain one's favor. **1932** Farrell *Young Lonigan* 98 **Chicago IL,** He bootlicked around until he became a ward committeeman. **1965–70** *DARE* (Qu. II20b, *A person who tries too hard to gain somebody else's favor: "He's always trying to _____ the boss."*) Infs **GA**86, 89, **KY**6, **NY**35, **NC**4, **SC**54, **TX**18, **VA**58, Bootlick.

bootlick n, also attrib [Var of *bootlicker*] **now chiefly Sth** Cf **boot** n[1] **3**

See quot 1908.

1849 *Yale Banger* 6 Nov 6 *(DA),* When Boot-lick hypocrites upraised their might. **1899** (1912) Green *VA Folk-Speech, Bootlick . . .* A person who tries to gain favour by mean behavior. **1905** *DN* 3.4 **cCT,** *Boot-lick . . .* A toady. [Rare]. **1908** *DN* 3.293 **eAL, wGA,** *Boot-lick . . .* One who bootlicks; a flattering, fawning, obsequious person. **1966** *DARE* (Qu. II20a, *A person who tries too hard to gain somebody's favor: "He's an awful _____."*) Infs **GA**1, 9, 12, 15, Bootlick.

boot liquor n [*boot* abbr of *bootleg* illegal liquor]

1969 *DARE* (Qu. DD21b, . . *Bad liquor*) Inf **MO**20, Boot liquor.

bootpack n [From *boot* + *pack*] **esp common West** Cf **shoe-pack**

Orig a high-topped moccasin, now usu a rubber boot; see quot 1926.

1893 *Scribner's Mag.* 13.715 **MI,** Logger's Footgear . . . Old-fashioned boot-pack. Modern rubber-soled boot-pack. **1923** *DN* 5.233 **swWI,** *Boot-pack . . .* A rawhide moccasin having only one lift on the heel, a top like a boot, and no lacing over the instep. A *shoe-pack* is similar, but the top is lower. Both boot-pack and shoe-pack have passed from use and speech with the coming of the rubber boot. "The snow was dry, and I was wearin' my boot-packs." **1926** Rickaby *Ballads* 233 *(DA), Boot-pack.* A heavy and roomy foot-wear, usually of rubber, somewhat higher than a shoe buckled or laced.

boot pants n

Trousers designed to be worn with boots.

1944 Howard *Walkin' Preacher* 192 **Ozarks,** I bought Clayton . . a pair of high laced boots, a shirt and a pair of whipcord boot pants. **1960** Lee *Mockingbird* 102 **AL,** He was long-nosed, wore boots with shiny metal eye-holes, boot pants and a lumber jacket.

boot, pour piss out of a See **pour piss out of a boot**

boots n

A **black haw 1** (here: *Viburnum prunifolium*).

1900 Lyons *Plant Names* 392, *V. prunifolium . . .* Boots.

boots, throw up one's v phr Also *throw up one's bootheels, heave up (one's) boots* (or *bootheels*)

To vomit profusely.

1965–70 *DARE* (Qu. BB18, *To vomit a great deal at once*) Infs **CA**158, 164, **CT**16, Throw (*or* threw) up his (*or* your) bootheels; **MI**2, **WA**1, Throwing (*or* threw up) his boots; **CO**3, **NY**113, **OH**23, **WA**28, Heave up your (*or* heave his) boots; **AK**1, Heave up bootheels.

bootstrapper n [Cf *pull oneself up by one's bootstraps*] Cf **boot** n[2] **3**

A novice, greenhorn.

1969 *DARE* (Qu. HH15, *A very inexperienced person, one who is just learning how to do a new thing*) Inf **CA**169, Bootstrapper.

booty See **boody**

boo up v phr

1953 Randolph *Down in Holler* 229 **Ozarks,** *Boo up . . .* To praise. "Them fellers was a-booin' up the hotel down at Hollister, tryin' to tole folks away from my boardin'-house."

booya n, also attrib |'buja| Also sp *booyah, booyaw, bouja, boulyaw, boyou* [CanFr < Fr *bouillon* broth, soup; see *DCan bouillon*] **MI, WI, MN**

A kind of stew.

1938 FWP *Guide MN* 256, Those of Polish descent, who predominate in the western part of the city [=St. Cloud], delight in colorful church festivals at which they feast on *bouja* (meat and vegetable stew) of their ancestors. **1949** Brown *Amer. Cooks* 414, Hunters in the Michigan woods practically live on a kind of hunter's stew which is called variously, "boulyaw," "boyou" or "booyaw." **1950** *WELS Suppl.* 1 Inf, **csWI,** Booya—A stew, usually made with wild game, especially rabbit or squirrel meat, pieces of the meat left in the broth; 1 Inf, **cnWI,** Booya—stew made for a large gathering at which each one contributes some ingredients. Contains meat and vegetables. **1965** *Bee* (Phillips WI) 19 Aug 1/4, Following the meeting a lunch of chicken booya was served and card games were played. **1968** *DARE* (Qu. H45) Inf **WI**52, Chicken booyah ['buja]—it's like a stew. **1978** *DARE* File **seMN,** [On a flyer announcing a picnic:] American Legion Annual "All Beef" Booya Feed. Bring the whole family. **1983** *Milwaukee Jrl.* (WI) 13 Mar state sec 1 **nwWI,** Booyah, that delicious north-country soup made with chicken, veal, beef and lots of vegetables and things, was the main course as members of the Cozy Corners Snowmobile club of Moose Junction held their annual winter picnic.

booze belly n Also *booze gut, ~ pot* **esp Nth, N Midl**

1965–70 *DARE* (Qu. X53b, *An oversize stomach that results from drinking*) Infs **IN**80, **MA**27, 58, **OH**43, Booze belly; **IN**80, **WI**34, Booze gut; **GA**75, Booze pot.

boozefuddle n

1914 *DN* 4.69 **ME, nNH** [Rural], *Boozefuddle . . .* Liquor.

boozer n **widespread, but chiefly Nth, N Midl** See Map

1965–70 *DARE* (Qu. DD12, . . *A person who drinks steadily or a great deal*) 99 Infs, Boozer; **CT**17, Heavy boozer; **MN**23, Regular boozer; [Of all Infs responding to the question, 35% were young or mid-aged; of those giving these responses, 57% were young or mid-aged.] (Qu. DD13) Inf **IA**32, Boozer; (Qu. DD17) Inf **NY**209, He's a boozer.

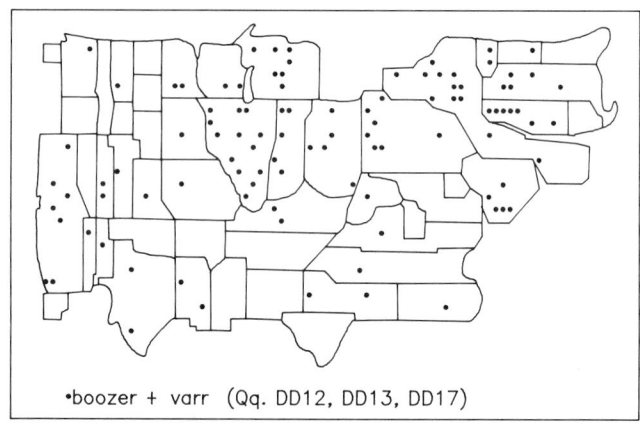

•boozer + varr (Qq. DD12, DD13, DD17)

bop around v phr [Prob assoc with bop music]

To move or go about energetically; to gallivant.

1968–70 *DARE* (Qu. Y29b, *About a man who doesn't stay home much: "He's always _____."*) Inf **NJ**63, Boppin' around; (Qu. KK27, *A very lively, active old person: "For his age, he's _____"*) Inf **PA**94, Bopping around.

bop out v phr [*bop* to strike]

To faint, pass out.

1970 *DARE* (Qu. BB14, *To suddenly become unconscious and fall: "Just as she came to the door she _____."*) Inf **PA**234, Bopped out.

bopper n [*bop* a blow]

1970 *DARE* (Qu. Y11, *Other words for a very hard blow . . "Joe really hit him a _____."*) Inf **KY**94, Bopper.

borasca See **borrasca**

borax n

An **amaranth** (here: *Amaranthus retroflexus*).

1929 *Torreya* 29.150, [In Maine] Amaranthus retroflexus was always "*Borax,*" why I do not know.

Borden's and Elsie's n pl Also *Borden and Bowman* [From names and trademarks of dairy companies] *joc* Cf **milk can**
See quots.
   1970 *DARE* (Qu. X31, . . *A woman's breasts*) Inf **NY237**, Borden's and Elsie's. **1971** *AmSp* 46.82 **Chicago IL**, Breasts . . . *Borden and Bowman* [Chicago dairies].

border n
   1967–69 *DARE* (Qu. N44, *In a town, the strip of grass and trees between the sidewalk and the curb*) Infs **CA121, MI67, 97, NY100,** Border.

border spout n
   =**eaves spout.**
   1968 *DARE* (Qu. D28, *What hangs below the edge of the roof to carry off rain-water?*) Inf **WV8**, Border spout.

bore v[1] [Perh from *bore* to mock, trick, cheat, gull; see *OED* **bore** v.[1] 6 "obs"] **chiefly Midl**
1 To ridicule, humiliate, or embarrass.
   1800 *Aurora* (Philadelphia PA) 12 Sept *(DAE)*, The institution of the Lazy Society was a mere sportive hoax, to bore some of the laziness of the District. **1836** *Knickerbocker* 8.558 **FL**, If he returned without firing a shot, after all his preparations, . . he would be bored for life. **1923** *DN* 5.202 **swMO**, I shore was bored when I foun' out they was a big hole in m' overhauls. **1930** *AmSp* 5.424 **Ozarks**, When a hillman says that someone has *bored* him, he means that he has been ridiculed. **c1960** *Wilson Coll.* **csKY**, Bored . . . Embarrassed rather than tired of things. **1970** *DARE* FW Addit **cwOH**, Bored—commonly used to mean embarrassed. **1971** *Today Show Letters* **csOH**, Bored—embarrassed. 1890's and still current. **1972** *DARE* File **cOH**, Bore—to embarrass. "You bored me to tears." Used by my grandmother when my father had disgraced himself in company.
2 See quot.
   1954 *Harder Coll.* **cwTN**, Bore . . . To cheat. "They bored 'im a new one in that hog tradin'."

bore v[2]
Of a horse: to put weight against the bit by thrusting the head forward and low.
   1938 Faulkner *Unvanquished* 74 **MS**, Jupiter was fine to watch . . boring a little and just beginning to drive. **1959** Faulkner *Mansion* 39 **MS**, The stallion boring, frothing a little, wrenching its arrogant vicious head at the snaffle and curb. **1968** Adams *Western Words*, Boring— Said of a horse that is constantly leaning the weight of his head and neck on the bit.

bore n[1] [Alter of *boor*] **chiefly Nth, N Midl** See Map
See quots.
   1848 Bartlett *Americanisms* 43, Bore. A[n] . . unwelcome visitor, who makes himself obnoxious by his disagreeable manners. **1889** *Century Dict.*, Bore . . . One who or that which . . causes ennui or annoyance; . . [an] uncongenial person who . . annoys by forcing his company or conversation on others. **1899** (1912) Green *VA Folk-Speech*, Bore . . . One who or that which . . causes annoyance. [**1912** Thornton *Amer. Gloss.*, Bore. To annoy . . . The word assumed new life in America, and examples from 1800 to 1827 have been collected.] **1965–70** *DARE* (Qu. AA6b, . . *A man who is fond of being with women and tries to attract their attention—if he's rude or not respectful*) 22 Infs, **chiefly Nth, N**

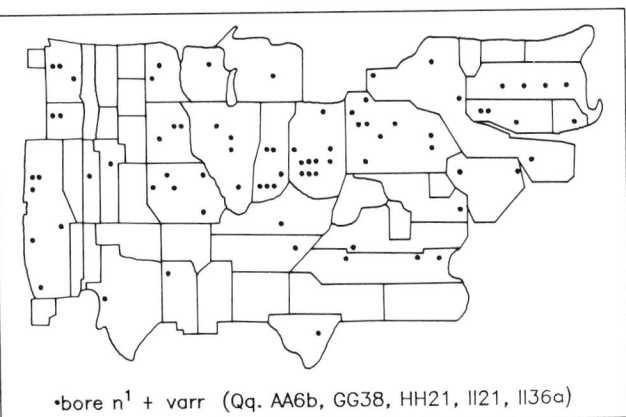

•bore n[1] + varr (Qq. AA6b, GG38, HH21, II21, II36a)

Midl, Bore; **OH34,** Crude bore; (Qu. GG38, *Somebody who is usually mean and bad tempered: "He's an awful _____."*) 30 Infs, **chiefly Nth, N Midl,** Bore; **OH52,** Nasty bore; (Qu. HH21, *A very awkward, clumsy person*) Infs **CA202, CT8, IN82, IA36, KY10, MD40, NY166,** Bore; (Qu. II21, *When someone behaves unpleasantly or without manners: "The way he behaves, you'd think he was _____."*) Infs **MO32, NJ8, NY35, PA181,** (A) bore; (Qu. II36a, *Somebody who talks back or gives rude answers: "Did you ever see such a _____?"*) 17 Infs, **chiefly Nth, N Midl,** Bore.

bore n[2] [Perh from *bore* to pierce by twisting or turning]
A small whirlpool or circular eddy in a stream.
   1972 *Down East* Mar 57, Smart oldtimers seek "bores" or spots where a log or some other obstruction sets up a circular motion in the water.

‡**bore-a-hole** n
A kind of guessing game.
   1967 *DARE* (Qu. EE33) Inf **MA2**, Bore-a-hole. Take fist and say [bore-a-hole] while rubbing a person's back; object—to guess who the person is.

bore for the simples v phr Also *tap for the simples* [*bore* to make a hole in; *simples* foolishness, folly. Prob alter of Engl dial *to have one cut for the simples;* see *EDD* **simple** 7–8] **chiefly Midl** *joc*
See quot 1953.
   1916 *DN* 4.342 **seOH**, *Bore for the simples.* Ironical expression used in asserting any one to be of unsound mind; e.g. "I shall bore him for the simples." **1923** (1946) Greer–Petrie *Angeline Doin' Society* 18 **csKY**, If the Sennater paid sich a outlandish price as that, he orter have his head *bored for the simples.* **1927** *AmSp* 2.34 **WV**. **1951** West *Witch Diggers* 44 **IN**, "You don't care much for Mr. Conboy, I guess." "Conboy ought to have his head bored for the simples," Mr. Korby said. **1953** Randolph *Down in Holler* 229 **Ozarks**, *Bore for the simples* . . . A jocular expression referring to a stupid individual. "The old fool orter be bored for the simples!" One sometimes hears *tapped for the simples,* with the same meaning. The idea is that a hole in the skull might let some of the foolishness out.

boresome adj **chiefly Sth, S Midl**
Tiresome, boring.
   1954 *DE Folkl. Bulletin* 1.16, Boresome (boring). **1965–70** *DARE* (Qu. A25; total Infs questioned, 75) Inf **MS11**, Boresome; (Qu. FF19) Infs **FL22, KY59, 84, MD38, MI115, NC45,** Boresome; **AR18,** Dull and boresome; (Qu. HH3) Inf **TX80,** Boresome; (Qu. HH11a) Inf **MO9,** Boresome. **1969** *DARE* Tape **GA79**, It's quite interestin' sometimes; 'course, when it's more than I can handle, it's kinda boresome.

borga n Also sp *booga* [Etym unknown]
See quot.
   1968 *DARE* File **ceFL, seGA**, Borga ['bɔrgə] . . . Paper sack; **swNC**, Booga ['bugə] . . . Paper sack.

borinki n |boˈriŋki| [Alter of Span *Borinqueño,* from *Borinquén* earlier name for Puerto Rico] **HI**
See quots.
   1961 Judd *Hawaii* 134, In Hawaii one finds a combination of *haoles,* "Portugees," *Pakes* (Chinese), . . *Borinkis* (Puerto Ricans). **1967** *DARE* (Qu. HH28, . . *Nicknames around here for . . Puerto Ricans*) Inf **HI13**, [boˈriŋki]. **1972** Carr *Da Kine Talk* 106 **HI**, The general public occasionally gave them [=Puerto Ricans] the humorous title *Borinki.*

bor'l See **barrel A**

born v tr Past and past pple usu *borned* **chiefly Sth, S Midl**
1 To give birth to.
   1901 *Century Illustr. Mag.* 62.906/2 **TN** [Black], Dis de lan' dat borned him. **1911** *DN* 3.537 **eKY**. **1926** Roberts *Time of Man* 344 **KY**, Who's thought to born a brat of Joe Phillips in your house? **1926** Vollmer *Sun-Up* 78 **wNC**, I reckon these here hills that borned me, and nursed me kin take keer of me fer a little while. **1933** Miller *Lamb in His Bosom* 142 **GA**, No woman could know, 'lessen she had borned one. **1936** (1951) Faulkner *Absalom* 339 **MS**, Two people neither of whom had taken pleasure or found passion in getting him or suffered pain and travail in borning him. **1942** (1971) Campbell *Cloud-Walking* 16 **seKY**, To leave them at Sary's till Marthy was done borning her baby. **1963** Owens *Look to River* 13 **TX**, "Jed's might nigh like one of us, ain't he, Basil?" . . . "Almost like we borned him." **1968** *DARE* (Qu. K11, *When a cow has a calf, you say she _____*) Inf **MO16**, Born her calf.

2 To be delivered of.

1971 *Foxfire* Winter 261 **nGA,** Russ Ander's wife, when she was borned [*Foxfire* editor: gave birth], it was a awful stormy night.

3 To assist at the birth of.

1919 *DN* 5.80 **NW,** "Whenever any children were born she had to born them." In eulogy of a Skagit County nurse. **1949** Faulkner *Knight's Gambit* 101 **MS,** He taken her in and fed her and nursed her and got help to born that child. **1951** Giles *Harbin's Ridge* 6 **KY,** She had been a granny woman most of her days and had borned all the younguns up and down the ridge.

born days n Also *borned days* **chiefly Sth, S Midl** *somewhat old-fash* Cf *EDD*

Usu in phr *all one's born days:* a lifetime; the time elapsed since one's birth.

1859 Taliaferro *Fisher's R.* 55 **nwNC** (as of 1820s), I cum right plum upon one uv the curiousest snakes I uver seen in all my borned days. **1871** Eggleston *Hoosier Schoolmaster* 64 **IN,** An' me a delvin' and a drudgin' fer you all my born days. **1904** *DN* 2.424 **Cape Cod MA. 1907** *DN* 3.206 **nwAR. 1908** *DN* 3.293 **eAL, wGA. 1943** Writers' Program NC *Bundle of Troubles* 163, I never seed a body so happy in my borned days. **1946** *PADS* 6.7 **eNC. 1949** *PADS* 11.18 **CO.** **c1960** *Wilson Coll.* **csKY,** I've never seen the like of that in all my borned days.

born in a barn adj phr For varr, see *DS* **widespread exc in NEast** See Map Cf **brought up in a barn, raised ~**

Lacking manners, uncouth, boorish.

1942 Berrey – Van den Bark *Amer. Slang* 147.7, Rough; unpolished; crude. Born *or* raised in a barn. **1965–70** *DARE* (Qu. II21, *When somebody behaves unpleasantly or without manners: "The way he behaves, you'd think he was _____."*) 170 Infs, **widespread exc in NEast,** Born in a barn.

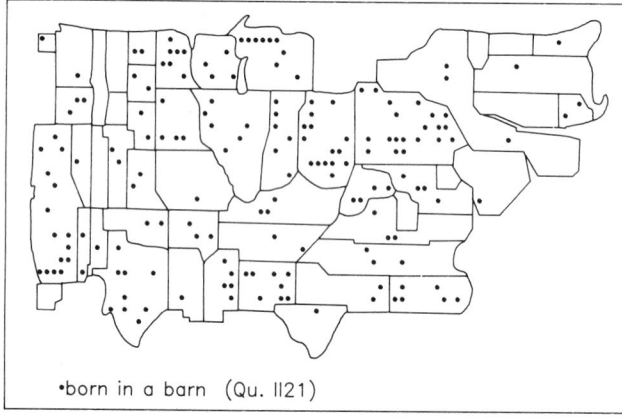

•born in a barn (Qu. II21)

borning vbl n, also attrib [**born v**] **chiefly Sth, S Midl, NEng** *old-fash*

1 Birth.

1889 (1971) Farmer *Americanisms, Borning ground.* — The country of one's birth; the ground upon which one was born; one's native soil. **1949** Marshall *Little Squire Jim* 50 **wNC,** Lucy McVay had been at the borning of him. **1949** Guthrie *Way West* 36 **MO** (as of 1847), It remembered deaths and bornings and the young. **1955** Taber *Still-meadow Daybook* 114 **swCT,** Jill's bedroom is across the landing from the keeping room, up and down steps, and was the "borning room." Here the babies and mothers stayed in the early days. **1967** *DARE* (QR p20) Inf **MA24,** Borning room — used in the South; (QR p26) Inf **MA72,** ['bɒnɪn rum] — regular inside room, no windows, entry from kitchen, stairs going to second floor.

2 Assisting at the birth of a child, midwifing.

1939 (1954) FWP *Guide KY* 429, "Borning" was the job of a woman — usually a grandmother whose qualification was the number of children and grandchildren she had "borned."

born on Wednesday looking both ways for Sunday adj phr For var see quots Cross-eyed.

1906 Low *Some Recoll.* 45 (as of 1840s), Thomas Hunt . . was a very short, stout man and was cross-eyed; you could not tell where he was looking. He said he was "born in the middle of the week, looking both

ways for Sunday." **1916** Macy – Hussey *Nantucket Scrap Basket* 126, "Born in the Middle of the Week and Looking Both Ways for Sunday" —A queer old local expression applied to a very cross-eyed person. **1970** *DARE* (Qu. X26a) Inf **TX98,** Born on Wednesday lookin' both ways for Sunday.

born with burnt feet adj phr [From running too fast] Of a child: illegitimate.

1973 Allen *LAUM* 1.344, *Illegitimate child* . . . Other lively but rare Midland euphemisms are [1 informant, **neIA**] *baby born with burnt feet, child bred in the ditch, early variety.*

borracho n, adj [Span] A drunkard; drunk.

1932 Bentley *Spanish Terms* 102, In the sense of a drunkard one hears it along the [Mexican] border in such expressions as "I was disturbed during the night by two *borrachos.*" **1949** *AmSp* 24.236 **AZ** [Univ. of AZ slang], *Borracho* [buratʃo], meaning *drunk.* This term is used in the sense of *He was borracho last night.* To indicate a person who is thoroughly saturated, the [ɑ] sound is lengthened [burɑ:tʃo]. **1968** Adams *Western Words, Borracho*—A drunkard; from the Spanish. The word is used near the Mexican border.

borrasca n Also sp *borasca, borraska* [MexSpan *borrasca* unproductiveness (of a mine)] **West** A mine or section of a mine that is largely oreless; a state of unproductiveness.

1864 Mowry *AZ & Sonora* 130, When a borasca made its appearance, as it will in every mine once in a while, they . . found themselves . . without the requisite funds to enable them to pierce through the poor ores and dead rock in order to strike rich ores again. **1913** Goodwin *As I Remember* 127 **NV** (as of 1859), It looked as though the whole lode was going into perpetual borasca. **1941** Fisher *Illusion* 357 **NV,** When the end came, when bonanza ran into borrasca, pay-dirt into sand, the crash would be terrific. **1949** Emrich *Wild West Custom* 163, When the vein *pinched out,* they were digging *country rock* and were working in *borra-sca.* **1968** Adams *Western Words, Borraska.*

borrego n [Span *borrego* young lamb] **esp sTX**

1 See quot.

1967 *DARE* (Qu. K63, . . *A male sheep*) Inf **TX6,** Borrego [bɑ'reːgo].

2 Transf: a cloud. [From the fleecy appearance]

1967–70 *DARE* (Qu. B11, . . *Kinds of clouds*) Inf **TX1,** Borregos (=‘sheep'); **TX22,** [,bʌ'rego]—small, white, like a flock of sheep; **TX102,** Sheep clouds or [,bɔ'regoz].

borrer See **borrow** v

borrera n

1968 Adams *Western Words, Borreras*—Sheep; from the Spanish. In New Mexico *borreras* is used almost as commonly as *sheep.*

borrow v Pronc-spp *borrer, borruh, borry* A Pronc varr.

1 |'bɑri, 'bɔri| **chiefly Sth, S Midl and NEng, esp ME** Cf **-y**

1880 (1886) Woolson *Rodman* 258 **SC,** Jim had come "to borry an axe." **1905** Culbertson *Banjo Talks* 171 **Sth** [Black], Kase mommer wanster borry—w'at? **1906** *DN* 3.128 **nwAR. 1908** *DN* 3.293 **eAL, wGA. 1913** *DN* 4.4 **ME. 1931** Hannum *Thursday April* 29 **WV,** And efn we could borry hit outright, why, the hull family would die of doctor's bills starvation! **1943** *LANE* Map 564 **throughout NEng,** Borrow . . . [bɒrɪ]. **c1960** *Wilson Coll.* **csKY,** Borrow /'bɑrɪ/ . . . "Can I borry some far [=fire]; ours went out." **1966** *DARE* (Qu. GG14) Inf **ME5,** He's a-borryin' trouble. **1966** *DARE* FW Addit **ME,** My grandfather took an iron kettle to borry ['bɔri] fire from neighbors.

2 |'bɔrə|

1922 Gonzales *Black Border* 290 **sSC, GA coasts** [Gullah glossary], *Borruh*—borrow. **1936** *AmSp* 11.159 **eTX,** The vowel in the final syllable of all the words listed below is usually [ə] . . . Borrow, borrowed. **1943** *LANE* Map 564 **scattered throughout NEng,** Borrow . . . [bɒrə].

3 |bɑr|

1936 *AmSp* 11.159 **eTX,** In illiterate speech . . borrow, borrowed . . [bɒ:r], [bɒ:rd]. **c1960** *Wilson Coll.* **csKY,** Borrow . . /bar/.

4 |'bɑrɚ| See Pronc Intro 3.I.12.d

1815 Humphreys *Yankey in England* 103, Borrerd, borrowed. **1843** (1916) Hall *New Purchase* 145 **sIN,** That one you're old womin neighbour Ashford borrered last year to bile sugar in. **1908** *DN* 3.293 **eAL, wGA,** Borry . . . Sometimes *borrer.* **1916** Lincoln *Mary-'Gusta* 86 **MA,**

Mr. Bacheldor had appeared at the door with the request that he might "borrer the loan of Cap'n Gould's shotgun."

B Senses.

1 To lend. [Cf Ger *borgen* to borrow, lend] **scattered, but esp wGt Lakes** See Map *esp among young speakers and speakers with grade school educ*

1896 *DN* 1.413 **cwNY**, *Borrow:* to lend. "I'll borrow the book to you." **1917** *DN* 4.408 **IL, KY, wNC**, "Will you borry me some sugar?" **1926** Kephart *Highlanders* 235 **sAppalachians**, They had the book, and they borried it to us to read. **1950** *WELS* ("My friend _____ me $5 till Saturday") 4 Infs, **WI**, Borrowed. [2 Infs of Ger, 2 Infs of Swiss background] **1950** *WELS Suppl.*, 1 Inf, **seWI**, Borrow me your pencil. **1965–70** *DARE* (Qu. U16, . . *"I need five dollars before Saturday, will you _____ it to me?"*) 31 Infs, **scattered, but esp wGt Lakes**, Borrow; **WI**76, Borrow me. [Of all Infs responding to the question, 9% were young, 24% mid-aged, 26% grade school educ or less; of those giving this response, 23% were young, 32% mid-aged, 39% grade school educ or less.] **1982** *Barrick Coll.* **sePA**, Borrow—*lend.* Uneducated use. "Will you borrow me a dollar?"

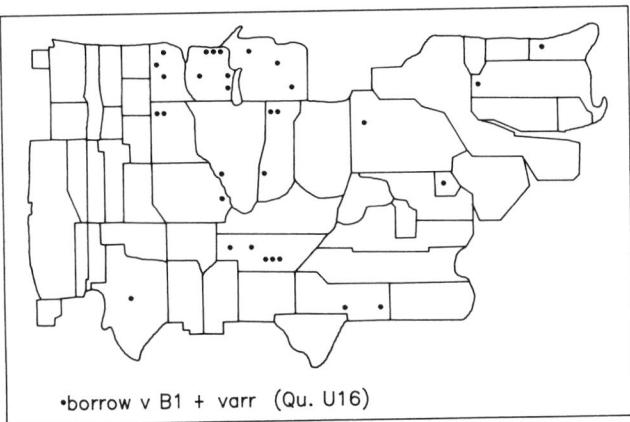

•borrow v B1 + varr (Qu. U16)

2 with *out:* To hire (something) out.

1965 *Bee* (Phillips WI) 19 Aug 6/2, Bulls borrowed out, any color or breed. Helgo Arvidson, Livestock Dealer.

3 See quot.

1949 *PADS* 11.18 **CO**, Borrow . . . To lead with a gun on a moving target, to allow for windage or a crooked sight. "I borrowed about three feet on him and got him dead center."

borrow n See **barrow** n[2]

borrow ditch See **barrow ditch**

borrow fire See **fire, come to borrow**

borrowing-days n pl

1899 (1912) Green *VA Folk-Speech, Borrowing-days* . . . The last three days of March are said to have been borrowed from April, and supposed to be especially stormy.

borrow pit See **barrow pit**

borrows exclam Also *I borrow, I'm borrowed* **esp MI, WI, MN** Cf **barley**

In children's games, esp tag: time out! king's ex!

1950 *WELS* (*In a game of tag, if you want to rest, what do you call out so that "it" can't catch you?*) 2 Infs, **WI**, Borrows! **1966–67** *DARE* (Qu. EE17) Inf **MI**2, I borrow; **MI**44, I'm borrowed; **MI**8, 45, **MN**11, Borrows.

borruh, borry See **borrow** v

borsch n Also pronc-sp *borscht* [From Russ *borshch*] **chiefly Nth**

1 A soup made of red beets and other vegetables.

1950 *AmSp* 25.196, They [=Russian Jews] introduced a few food names, most outstandingly *borsch* (beet soup). **1965–70** *DARE* (Qq. H36, H65) Infs **KS**8, **MA**6, **NJ**30, **NY**105, 119, 181, **SD**2, Borscht; **PA**221, Borsch.

2 =**boche.**

1969 *DARE* (Qu. HH28, . . *People of foreign background . . German*) Inf **PA**197, Borsch.

‡**bory-hole** n [Prob *bore* to pierce]

1967 *DARE* (Qu. X34, . . *The navel*) Inf **AR**51, ['bɔrɪ,houl].

bosal n Also sp *bosaal, bozal* [Span *bozal* muzzle] **chiefly SW**

A halter that fits around a horse's nose: see quot 1961; a rope used for such a halter.

1844 (1954) Gregg *Commerce* 131 **NM**, The head of the animal is turned towards his subduer, who, in order to obtain the mastery over him more completely, seldom fails to throw a *bozal* (or half-hitch, as boatmen would say) around the nose, though at full rope's length. **1853** Hammett *Stray Yankee in TX* 117, A fish spear is to him [the Texan] a *groin; . .* a halter, a *bosaal.* **1917** Morgan *Recoll. Rebel Reefer* 9 **LA** (as of c1854), A bridle without a bit, but with a tight-fitting halter to keep him from biting,—it was called a "bosal"—and prevented the animal from opening his jaws,—was fitted to him. **1961** Adams *Old-Time Cowhand* 121, "Bosal" . . meanin' a muzzle [is] . . . usually a plaited rawhide nose-band placed jes' above the mouth, used in place of a bit. **1962** Atwood *Vocab. TX* 52, *Halter.* For various devices . . used to control an unruly horse . . . A historical Spanish borrowing, *bosal* occasionally appears with this meaning or a similar one.

bosal brand n [bosal] **West**

1961 Adams *Old-Time Cowhand* 261, The "bosal brand" is a stripe burned 'round an animal's nose.

bosh n [From Turkish *bosh* empty, worthless; see *OED*] **chiefly Sth, S Midl, NEast** See Map *old-fash*

Nonsense, foolishness; something worthless.

1872 Burnham *Memoirs U.S. Secret Service* 187, What do you mean by all this bosh? **1887** in 1950 *AmSp* 25.30 **seLA**, It is all bosh. **1929** *AmSp* 4.330, Bosh. **1950** *AmSp* 25.171 **NY** (as of c1870), *Bosh* . . . Mere talk, falsehood. **c1960** *Wilson Coll.* **csKY**, *Bosh* . . . Nonsense. **1965–70** *DARE* (Qu. NN13, *When you think that the thing somebody has just said is silly or untrue: "Oh, that's a lot of _____."*) 27 Infs, **chiefly Sth, S Midl, NEast**, Bosh. [Of all Infs responding to the question, 62% were old; of those giving this response, 93% were old.]

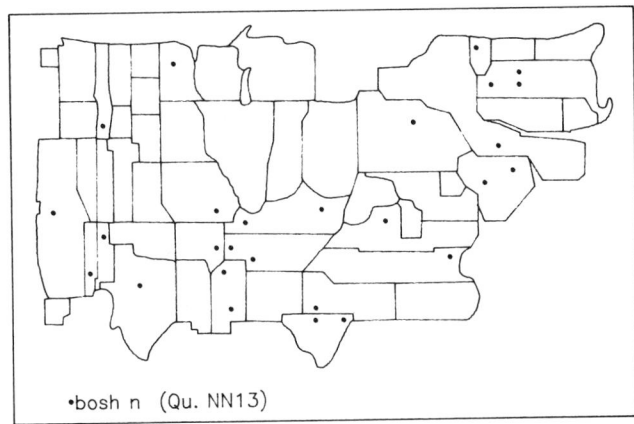

•bosh n (Qu. NN13)

bosh exclam [bosh n] *old-fash*

Nonsense! Darn!

1924 *DN* 5.263, Bosh. **1940** Richter *Trees* 35 **OH**, "Bosh and moonshine!" she flared out at him. **1965–68** *DARE* (Qu. NN8a, *Exclamations of annoyance or disgust: "Oh _____."*) Infs **FL**6, **IA**4, **NY**14, **PA**71, Bosh; (Qu. NN25a) Inf **MS**64, Bosh; (Qu. NN26a, . . *"Hell": "Oh _____!"*) Infs **FL**20, 30, Bosh. [All Infs old]

bosky See **bosque**

bosom friend n

1973 *DARE* File **csWI**, *Bosom friend*—A packet of money kept inside the brassiere by elderly women when traveling. Current.

bosom-hook n

=**bosom-pin.**

1953 *PADS* 19.9 **NC**, *Bosom-hook* . . . Brooch.

bosom-pin n *old-fash*

A breastpin, brooch.

1855 Barnum *Life* 123 **CT**, What a fool I was to give you that finger-ring and bosom-pin. **1887** Custer *Tenting* 213 **MI**, This cambric finery, ornamented with three old-fashioned bosom-pins. **1912** Green *VA Folk-Speech, Bosom-pin* . . . Breast-pin, Broach. **1967–68** *DARE* (Qu. W35) Infs **NC**82, **TN**3, Bosom-pin. [Both Infs old]

bosque n, also attrib |'bɔski, -e| Rarely sp *bosquet* Pronc-sp *bosky* [Span *bosque;* perh also Fr *bosquet* in same sense] **chiefly SW**

A forest; a dense growth of trees and underbrush; a clump of trees.

1771 (1925) Mease *Narr. Journey W.* FL 79 **sMS,** Upon some of the Eminences are Bosquets or Clumps of Pine Trees which seem to have been left expressly both as Shade for Cattle and the Adornment of the Country. **1834** Pike *Prose Sketches* 44 **NM,** The Bosque Redondo is about one hundred and twenty miles from San Miguel. **1902** Garcia *Shade Trees* 17 *(DA),* It is native in our valleys, and many places have dense "bosques" or forests of it. **1930** in 1942 *CA Folkl. Qrly.* 1.270 **CA,** Up from a waller what should appear / But a moss-horned maverick, a bosky steer. **1940** FWP *Guide NM* 110, Bosque ['boske]—Thickly wooded area. **1958** *AmSp* 33.106 **SW,** The term *plaza* is typical of a large cluster of Spanish American words, such as . . *bosque,* . . which have pushed north from Mexico and traveled east and west because of trade and settlement. **1962** Atwood *Vocab. TX* 41, There are six Texas occurrences of *mesquital* and three of *bosque,* the latter having been observed only in El Paso and Hudspeth Counties. **1966–67** *DARE* (Qq. C6, T2a, b) Infs NM6, TX5, 10, Bosque ['bɔski].

boss adj [By ext of *boss* master, principal (quot 1836) < Du *baas* master] **scattered but esp in urban areas of Nth, N Midl, Pacific** *now esp among Black speakers*
Excellent, first-rate.

[**1836** in 1910 Commons *Doc. Hist. Amer. Industrial Soc.* 4.287 **NY,** I am a boss shoemaker.] **1880** in 1956 Eliason *Tarheel Talk* 261 **NC,** If a coast man wants to express the superlative degree he says "That is a 'Boss' log or a 'Boss' suit." **1885** Twain *Huck. Finn* 215 **MO,** It's the most dazzling idea 'at ever a man struck . . . Oh, this is the boss dodge, ther' ain't no mistake 'bout it. **1916** *DN* 4.272 **KS, MA, MI, NE, NY, NC, PA, VA,** Boss. . . Extra good. "The pancakes at that boarding house are boss." **1965** Brown *Manchild* 108 **NYC** [Black], He said it [=heroin] was pretty good. He said he had a real boss feeling. **1966** *AmSp* 41.304, In its modern development *boss* is current in all social classes among both whites and Negroes . . . It is current not only in Chicago but also in the New York area and probably on the West Coast. **1968–70** *DARE* (Qu. W38, *When a man dresses himself up in his best clothes, you say he's* _____) Inf **VA39;** (Qu. W39, *. . A person's best clothes)* Inf **PA66,** Boss clothes or bad clothes—clothes in the latest fashion; (Qu. FF17, *Words meaning that people had a very good or enjoyable time: "We all had a* _____ *last night."*) Infs **PA172, 239, TN46,** Boss time; (Qu. KK1b, *Words meaning "in the very best condition": "His farm is* _____*."*) Infs **NY55, PA94,** Boss; (Qu. NN7, *Exclamations of surprise: "They're getting married next week? Well,* _____*."*) Inf **NY236,** Boss—that's nice. [7 of 8 Infs Black] **1968** *DARE* FW Addit **Oakland CA,** Man, that was real boss. **1969** Keiser *Vice Lords* 16 **Chicago IL** [Black], They was boss humbuggers, Jack! [Keiser: Boss—very good, humbuggers—fighters.] **1970** Bullins *Electronic* 32 **sCA** [Black], Any place is better than L.A. but I heard that Buffalo is really boss. **1971** Roberts *Third Ear* [Black], *Boss*. . excellent; stylish; popular; e.g. There was a boss flick on TV last night.

boss n[1] Also *bossie, bossy* [Engl dial *buss, boss* a young calf; see *EDD buss* sb.[2]]

1 also attrib: A cow or calf.

1863 Dodge *Gala-Days* 95 **NEng,** He is like a calf tied to a tree in the orchard by a long rope. Bossy starts from the post, tail up, in a hand gallop. **1911** Quick *Yellowstone Nights* 314 **MT,** Ever try to feed a young caff? . . Nothin' but actual experience can impart any remote approach to a notion o' what it means to incorporate the fruit of the nest [=eggs] with the bossy. **1927** in 1952 Crane *Letters* 291 **OH,** I had just landed in town after three months with the bossy cows. **1939** *LANE* Map 192 *(Calf)* 11 infs, chiefly **ME,** Bossie; 1 inf, **sME,** Bossie calf. **1966–70** *DARE* (Qu. K1, *A cow that is giving milk is a* _____) Infs **MI98, WA3,** Bossie; (Qu. K8, *Joking terms for milking a cow* . . *"It's time to go out and* _____*."*) Infs **AL38, KY49,** 80, **MO5,** (Strip, pull on, juice the) old bossie; **CA199, FL12,** (Relieve, pail the) bossie; **NY187, WI21,** (Juice, sap) the bossies; **ND1,** Put the bossies in; **MN34,** Milk the boss. **1982** *Capital Times* (Madison WI) 24 Nov 25/1–2 [Headline], Brown County bossy sold for $1 million plus.

2 Used in calls to a cow or calf: see quots. **chiefly Nth and West** See Map See also **co-boss(ie), come boss** (at **come** v A5a), **so-boss**

1848 Bartlett *Americanisms* 44, *Bossy.* A familiar name applied to a calf. **1874** VT State Bd. Ag. *Report for 1873–74* 2.706, So-o-o boss!

There, you've kicked it over—/ All that milk, now, I declare! **1949** Kurath *Word Geog.* 63, Calls to Cows in the Pasture . . . *Boss!, bossie!,* sometimes preceded by *co* or *come,* is used in all of New England and the New England settlements of New York State, northern Pennsylvania, and Ohio, as well as in the Hudson Valley. **1950** *WELS (Call to a calf at feeding time)* 2 Infs **c,cwWI,** Bossie, bossie (bossie); *(Call to cows to come in from the pasture)* 1 Inf, **cwWI,** Come to your mealy, Bossie; *(To make a cow stand still, you say* _____*)* 34 Infs, **WI,** (So, soo, stand still, steady, whoa) Boss(ie); 1 Inf, **cwWI,** Now please let's not move at all, Bossie. **1965–70** *DARE* (Qu. K80, *The call* . . *to get the cows in from the pasture)* 180 Infs, Come boss(ie); 114 Infs, Co-boss(ie); 12 Infs, So-boss(ie); 11 Infs, Boss(ie) [usu repeated]; 72 Infs, (Here, soo, sook, *etc)* boss(ie); (Qu. K81, *To make a cow stand still—for example, when milking her—you say, "*_____*."*) 160 Infs, So-boss(ie); 31 Infs, Soo-boss(ie); 14 Infs, Wo-boss(ie); 9 Infs, Ho-boss; 18 Infs, (Saw, steady, *etc)* boss(ie); (Qu. K83, *To call a calf to you at feeding time)* 61 Infs, Come boss; 11 Infs, Co-boss(ie); 10 Infs, Bossie (bossie); **IL31, NY2,** 216, **OH20, PA**129, **WI5,** Here bossie; **IL5,** 116, **KS15, OK53,** So-boss(ie); **FL20, OH43,** 75, Soo-boss(ie); **MI64,** 71, Come bossie bossie (bossie); **KS18,** So-boss so-boss; **ME14,** Come boss come boss; **VT2,** Boss boss; **WI40,** Um-m-m boss; **ME1,** Bossie bossie come bossie; **MA40,** Come calfy come bossie; **NY187,** Hi bossie; (Qu. NN22d, *Expressions used to drive away animals)* Infs **MA6, SC31,** Go 'long, boss(ie); **ME22,** Come boss(ie); **ME22, MN12, LA35,** (Co, hi, ho) boss; **AZ5, MA14, NY94, OR4, SC31, WI6,** (Get along, git there, go, shoo, so, soo) boss; [(Qu. K82, *The call* . . *to get horses in from the pasture)* Inf **IN82,** Co-boss.] **1973** Allen *LAUM* 1.258, Calls to cows . . . The eastern sharp division between Northern *come boss* and Midland *sook cow* is not as rigidly maintained in the U[pper] M[idwest] . . since the *boss* forms have clearly invaded the Midland speech areas of central Iowa and Nebraska . . . Returns from 1,004 respondents closely support the field data, with *co boss* and *come boss* having an 85% to 90% frequency everywhere but in southern Iowa. [Less freq responses include *boss, bossy, here boss(y), hi boss, huh boss, soo boss(y), sook boss(y).*] *Ibid* 259, Call to cows during milking . . . the most common call in the eastern states, *so,* often followed by *boss* or *bossy,* is also dominant in the U[pper] M[idwest].

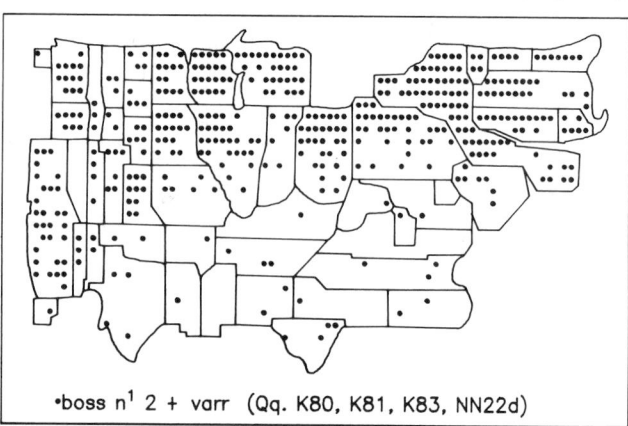

•boss n[1] 2 + varr (Qq. K80, K81, K83, NN22d)

boss n[2] [Engl dial; *EDD boss* sb.[1] 5 "A large round stone or iron ball, used in marble playing."]

1 In marble play: see quots.

1955 *PADS* 23.12 **cwTN,** Boss . . . A large playing marble, of either stone or iron. **1973** Ferretti *Marble Book* 40, Boss. A shooter.

2 =boss-out.

1973 Ferretti *Marble Book* 40, Boss . . . Short for Boss-Out, a chase game.

boss and span See **boss-out**

boss dice n Also *boss, bull dice* **esp CA**
A kind of dice game: see quot 1960.

1960 Giesecke–Fagan *How to Play Bull* 12, Bull dice or boss dice . . . Both players throw simultaneously. Player with highest throw of one pair or better, becomes "boss". He holds his best pair . . three of a kind or four of a kind and shakes the remaining dice . . . If, after second shake, "boss" . . has sufficient strength on the table to believe he can beat his opponent, he calls the other player "up" . . . [Opponent may shake again.] Both hands are then exposed and highest hand wins first leg, or "horse" . . . First player to win two "horses" wins the game. **1967–69** *DARE* (Qu. EE40, . . *Table games* . . *using dice)* Inf **CA32,** Boss dice—a bar game:

two boxes, shake out; highest total points—two 3's beat two 2's; loser of first decides if he will reshake or play the one he's got; **CA**107, Boss dice—same as poker dice; shake five dice; the guy who has the best hand is the boss and he tells the other fellow when to "come up," to shake again to try and beat the boss's hand; shake three times; **CA**142, Boss.

boss dog n
=**big dog.**
    1967–70 *DARE* (Qu. HH17, . . *"He'd like to be the _____ around here."*) Inf **VA**35, Boss dog; **SC**31, Boss dog of the barnyard.

boss, get oneself a v phr **chiefly Sth, sMissip-Ohio Valleys**
See Map
To get married.
    1965–70 *DARE* (Qu. AA15b, . . *Joking ways . . of saying that a man is getting married . . "He _____."*) 10 Infs, Got himself a boss; **FL**15, 19, **IL**84, **SC**32, **TN**15, 31, Got a boss (now); **SC**24, 26, 40, Got him a boss; **TX**87, Got a new boss; (Qu. AA15c, . . *Joking ways . . of saying that a woman is getting married . . "She _____."*) Infs **IL**83, **IN**3, **SC**29, Got (herself) a boss; **SC**7, 34, Got her a boss.

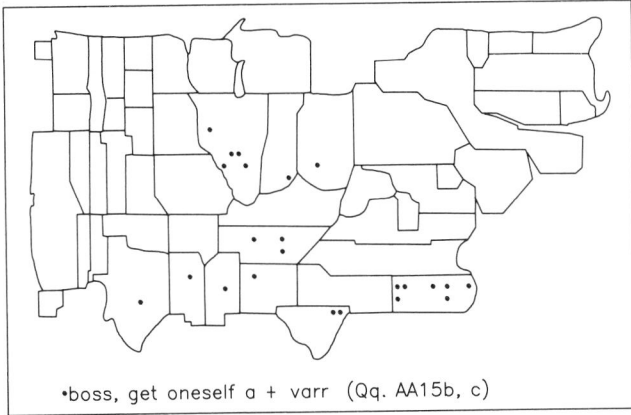

•boss, get oneself a + varr (Qq. AA15b, c)

boss horse n
=**near horse.**
    1968 *DARE* (Qu. K32b, *The horse on the left side in plowing or hauling*) Inf **NJ**25, Boss horse.

bossie See **boss** n[1]

boss-lady See **boss-woman**

boss line n [**boss** n[2]]
In marble play: see quot.
    1967 *DARE* (Qu. EE8, *The line toward which the players roll their marbles before beginning a game, to determine the order of shooting*) Inf **HI**6, Boss line.

boss-man n
    1 An employer, supervisor; a person in authority. **chiefly Sth, sAppalachians** See Map *esp common among Black speakers*
    1908 *DN* 3.293 **eAL, wGA,** *Boss* . . . A term of respect used by the negroes for any white man, especially one who employs them. Also *boss-man.* **1934** Carmer *Stars Fell on AL* 212, Wade came up to the house and stayed night and day, waiting on the old boss-man. **1942**

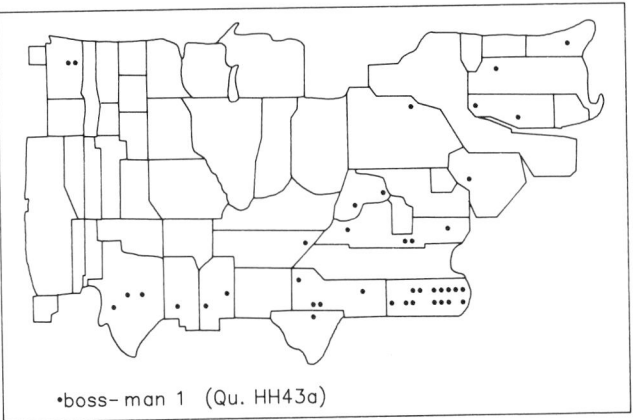

•boss-man 1 (Qu. HH43a)

Faulkner *Go Down* 152 **MS** [Black], Dass awright, boss-man. **1950** *PADS* 14.16 **SC.** **1953** Brewer *Word Brazos* 10 **eTX** [Black], Two han's on de ole Babb plannuhtation . . was cuttin' logs . . to buil' a bawn on de boss-man's premisus. **1954** Armstrong *Satchmo* 217 **LA,** Joe Glaser . . was . . the nicest boss man I've ever worked for. **1965–70** *DARE* (Qu. HH43a, *The top person in charge of a group of workmen, the _____*) 40 Infs, Boss-man. [Of all Infs responding to the question, 6% were Black; of those giving this repsonse, 23% were Black.] **1966** *DARE* Tape **GA**4 [Black], The boss-man what us was staying with.
    2 See quot. Cf **boss-woman**
    1966–70 *DARE* (Qu. AA23, *Joking names that a woman may use to refer to her husband: "It's time to go and get supper for my _____."*) 11 Infs, **scattered,** Boss-man.

boss-out n Also *boss and span* [**boss** n[2]]
In marble play: see quot 1955.
    1955 *PADS* 23.12 **cwTN,** *Boss out* . . . A game of marbles in which two boys alternately shoot at their taws, usually called bonces in this game . . . Also known as *boss and span:* the boss, or taw, is pitched or tossed out and the other boss has to span the distance in order to hit the first one. **1973** Ferretti *Marble Book* 65, *Boss-out* . . . The oldest marbles game as well as the oldest chase game.

boss-woman n Also *boss-lady* Cf **boss-man** 2
    1966–68 *DARE* (Qu. AA21, . . *Joking expressions . . about a wife who gives the orders*) Inf **GA**10, Boss-woman; (Qu. AA22, *Joking names that a man may use to refer to his wife*) Inf **SC**58, Boss-woman; **FL**26, 48, **IL**141, **MN**15, Boss-lady.

bossy See **boss** n[1]

‡**bossy-barefoot** n
    1969 *DARE* FW Addit **MA**14, Bossy-barefoots—people who are always trying to tell others what to do.

Boston n
    1 also attrib, also *Bostonian;* Among Pacific Coast Indians: a White citizen of the U.S. *hist*
    1793 in 1836 Lincoln *Jrl. Treaty* 130, [Spoken by Captain Brandt to the Indians:] We have met to-day our brothers, the Bostonians and English. **1844** Lee–Frost *10 Yrs. OR* 148, He boasted that the "Bostons," as he termed us, "should never make him good." **1909** *Nation* 29 July 104/1, Almost to this day a "Boston man" among the [Pacific Coast] Indians is the more intelligent equivalent for American. **1934** *Natl. Geog. Mag.* 65.178/1 **OR,** In pioneer days the Williamette [sic] Valley was the meeting place of two currents, the border Missourians, who came by the Plains, and the so-called "Boston Men," who arrived by sea. **1946** Peattie *Pacific Coast* 190, The long-lived Indians out on the coast could have heard from their grandparents of the coming of the "King George men," the English, and the "Bostons," the American traders. **1951** Morgan *Skid Road* 21 **nwWA** (as of 1850s), Sealth was, as the settlers put it, "an old Indian," meaning he refused to wear "boston"—that is, American—clothing.
    2 A marble game in which players use their taws to try to knock marbles out of a ring or into a hole.
    1895 *DN* 1.384 **MO,** *Boston:* a game at marbles. **1940** *Recreation* (NY) 34.110, Games of marbles played throughout the country . . . Boston. **1958** *PADS* 29.30, *Boston* . . . A marble game played with a large ring; a player keeps the marbles he has shot out of the ring (Okla.). The player's hand is not obliged to hug the ground (Wash.). (Also Mo.) **1967** *DARE* (Qu. EE7, . . *Marble games*) Inf **NV**3, Boston—with a hole in the ground, had to knuckle down. To play Boston—if taw got in hole, you kept marbles in there at the time. **1970** *DARE* File **ceKS** (as of 1890s and after), Boston—a marbles game. "We kept the marbles that we knocked out of the ring."

Boston baseball n
    1969 *DARE* FW Addit **MA,** *Boston baseball*—Played in the 1940s and early 50s in Southbridge, Worcester and Boston. Two or more players: the player "at bat" (there was no bat) faced someone's front steps and threw a rubber (usually tennis) ball at them so that it rebounded. The other player(s) stood behind him. If the ball got by the other players, it was a home run; if one of them caught it, the batter was out.

Boston bluefish n Also *Boston blue*
=**pollack.**
    1946 LaMonte *N. Amer. Game Fishes* 96, *Pollachius virens* . . . Names: . . Boston Bluefish. **1966–69** *DARE* (Qu. P2) Inf **ME**10, Pollock or bluefish or Boston bluefish; (Qu. P4) Inf **RI**4, Pollock or Boston blue.

1972 Sparano *Outdoors Encycl.* 383, *Pollock*—Common Names: . . Boston bluefish . . . Scientific Name: *Pollachius virens*.

Boston (brown) bread See **brown bread**

Boston chub n

A fish of the family Cyprinidæ.

1969 *DARE* (Qu. P7, *Small fish used as bait for bigger fish*) Inf **KY**43, Branch chubs = Boston chubs.

Boston coffee n

See quots.

1943 *AmSp* 18.307 **wLA, eTX,** *Boston Coffee*. Half coffee and half cream. **1969** *DARE* FW Addit **neIL,** Boston coffee—means half cream and half coffee. [**1980** Safire *On Language* 43, "In the United States," reports Phil Shea, public relations director of Sheraton hotels, "with only one exception, an order for 'regular coffee' would produce plain coffee with sugar and cream on the side. The exception is Boston. An order for 'regular coffee' in the coffee shop would produce coffee with cream already added, and sugar on the side."]

Boston cooler n

1968 *DARE* FW Addit **OH3,** *Boston cooler*—Vanilla ice cream in root-beer; a root-beer float.

Boston cracker n **NEast, esp NEng** Cf **common cracker**

A thick round biscuit, usu unsalted and served split.

1818 Fearon *Sketches* 44 **NYC,** In the evening . . the table is filled with cheese, biscuits (called Boston crackers,) molasses, and slices of raw dried beef. **1907** *DN* 3.185 **NYC,** A round brittle biscuit three inches in diameter, consisting of two separable layers . . . Called in New York City *Boston crackers*. **1922** (1926) Cady *Rhymes VT* 247, Some Boston crackers than [sic] appeared / And passed from vision slow. **1939** Wolcott *Yankee Cook Book* 127, The crackers should be the round "Boston" crackers—they called them "common crackers" when I was a boy. Split them . . and put a few in the chowder. **1944** Holton *Yankees* 239 *(DA),* People used to think chowder should be poured into a tureen lined with Boston crackers.

Boston dollar n **West** *joc*

A penny.

1902 *Out West Mag.* 17.30 **CA,** Where the tradition was to toss at least "four bits" to a beggar, it was revolutionary to see the new-comer carefully hand him a "Boston dollar." [Note:] Cowboy satire for a copper. **1968** Adams *Western Words, Boston dollar*—A cowboy's name for a penny.

Boston exchange n

1969 *DARE* (Qu. EE2, *Games that have one extra player—when a signal is given, the players change places, and the extra one tries to get a place*) Inf **MA**42, Boston exchange—musical chairs.

Boston fir n

1968 *DARE* (Qu. T17, . . *Kinds of pine trees*) Inf **MD**9, Boston fir.

Bostonian See **Boston 1**

Boston mackerel n

1 The Atlantic **mackerel** (*Scomber scombus*).

1975 Evanoff *Catch More Fish* 206, The Atlantic mackerel (*Scomber scombus*) is also called the Boston mackerel and the common mackerel; small ones are called spikes and tinkers . . . The Atlantic mackerel is found from Canada south to the Carolinas. It is very plentiful in Maine and the rest of New England . . . Mackerel bite best during the daytime.

2 =**bonito 1.**

1935 Caine *Game Fish* 53, Bonito—*Sarda sarda* . . . Boston Mackerel. **1939** Natl. Geog. Soc. *Book of Fishes* 86, Bonito (*Sarda sarda*) . . . In the Chesapeake Bay region it is often sold as "Boston mackerel." **1970** *DARE* (Qu. P14) Inf **VA**47, Boston mackerel.

‡**Boston pine** n

1970 *DARE* (Qu. T17 . . *Kinds of pine trees*) Inf **DC**13, Boston pine.

Boston pink n

=**bouncing Bet 1.**

1893 *Jrl. Amer. Folkl.* 6.138, *Saponaria officinalis*, Boston pink. Poland, Me.; Wellfleet, Mass.

Boston screwdriver n *joc*

1969 *DARE* FW Addit **MA,** Boston screwdriver—a hammer. Used by workmen in building trades, Southbridge. "Big-city workmen in Boston do a quick, cheap job by driving a screw all or most of the way in with a hammer instead of using a screwdriver." Thirty or forty years old at least.

Boston strawberry See **strawberry**

Boston tag n

A children's tag game.

1969 *DARE* (Qu. EE33, . . *Outdoor games*) Inf **RI**17, Boston tag.

Boston woodcock n

Pork and beans.

1937 *Hench Coll.* **PA,** In a Philadelphia restaurant he ordered something that seemed good and not expensive—Boston Woodcock, the menu called it. It turned out to be pork and beans.

bot See **bots**

botcher n [*botch* patching material]

1957 *DE Folkl. Bulletin* 1.28, A good botcher (i.e., patcher-up of leaks, etc.).

bother exclam

Used as a mild expletive.

1924 *DN* 5.263, *Bother*: oh— (vex[ation].) **1965–70** *DARE* (Qu. NN8a, *Exclamations of annoyance or disgust*) Infs **CA**97, **FL**38, **GA**72, **MI**67, **MT**2, **NE**11, **NY**211, **PA**175, **WI**52, Bother; (Qu. NN9a) Infs **MD**17, **NY**48, Bother; (Qu. NN9b) Inf **WA**20, Bother.

botherate v [Back-formation from **botheration** n] **esp S Midl**

See quots.

1905 *DN* 3.71 **nwAR,** *Botherate* . . . To bother. 'Don't botherate me.' Negroism. **1953** *PADS* 19.9, *Botherate* . . . To bother, trouble. Cocke Co., Tenn., and Canoe, Ky.

botheration n

Something that bothers; see quot 1927.

1834 Smith *Life Jack Downing* 49 **ME,** The people are growing pretty mad at all this botheration. **1848** Judson *Mysteries NY* 5.32, Och, botheration take 'em all! **1880** Twain *Tramp Abroad* 219, A cozy and delightful human nest, shut away from the world and its botherations. **1927** *AmSp* 2.349 **WV,** *Botheration*, . . an annoyance or a nuisance. "You are such a botheration to me." **1968–70** *DARE* (Qu. Y9, . . *"His little brother is an awful _____."*) Infs **LA**25, 37, Botheration; (Qu. II18, *Someone who joins himself on to you and your group without being asked and won't leave*) Inf **VA**69, Botheration.

botheration exclam **chiefly Nth**

=**bother.**

1903 *DN* 2.295 **Cape Cod MA,** *Botheration* . . . An exclamation of impatience. **1927** *AmSp* 2.349 **WV,** *Botheration* . . . "Botheration! Why don't you let me alone." **1943** *LANE* Map 600 **throughout NEng,** The map shows . . expressions used as exclamations of impatience, irritation, sudden anger and the like . . . Here listed in the order of their frequency: *shucks, botheration, tarnation*. **1950** *WELS* (*Exclamations of annoyance or disgust*) 1 Inf, **cnWI,** Botheration. **1959** *VT Hist.* ns 27.127, Botheration! *interj.* Occasional. **1966** Barnes–Jensen *Dict. UT Slang* 6 **UT,** Botheration! n. A mild oath. Good Mormons are not supposed to take the Lord's name in vain; so when they hit the thumb with a hammer they curse with such words as "botheration," "Thunder and Blixen" and the like. **1967** *DARE* (Qu. NN8a, *Exclamations of annoyance or disgust*) Infs **MI**67, **MA**71, Botheration.

bothered up ppl adj **S Atl**

Apprehensive; agitated.

1951 *Collier's* 24 Nov 64/4 **seGA,** Others acknowledge that there have been times when they've been "bothered up" and they admit to a lot of respect for the [Okefenokee] swamp, but they hate to hear it referred to as a dismal, terrifying place. **1966** *DARE* (Qu. A21, *When someone is in too much of a hurry you might say, "Now just slow down! Don't _____."*) Inf **SC**6, Get all bothered up; (Qu. GG2, *Expressions meaning "confused, mixed up"*) Inf **SC**26, Bothered up.

botherment n [*bother* + *-ment*]

Something troublesome.

1843 Thompson *Major Jones' Courtship* 8 **GA,** Ther aint so much botherment of the brains involved. **1931** Hall *Book of Coverlets* **eKY** *(ADD),* Hit's right smart botherment to put in just one kiverlet.

bother one's time v phr

To matter, be of importance.

1933 Smiley *Gloss. New Paltz*, "It doesn't bother my time any" means "it doesn't make any difference to me." Sometimes with the inference that it may bother someone else.

both two pron Also *both the two* esp S Atl Cf **all both, all two**
The one and the other, both.

1870 in 1931 *AmSp* 6.320 SC [Black], You would have one brought after the other, unless accompanied by the request, 'all at the same time,' or in their own language, *'go fetch 'em come; both two, one time'!* **c1960** *Wilson Coll.* **csKY,** *Both two* — very rarely heard. **1966–69** *DARE* (Qu. LL21, *Two things* — *one and also the other: "Do you want the red one or the blue one?" "I want* ____ *of them.")* Inf **GA**72, Both two; **NC**33, Both the two.

bots n pl Also sp *botts;* rarely *bot* [From *bot* the larva of the botfly]
1 A disease of horses caused by the infestation of botfly larvae in the digestive tract. **chiefly S Midl, Gulf States** See Map

1788 in 1888 Cutler *Life* 1.433 **CT,** I rather thought the symptoms were those of bots. **1884** Nye *Baled Hay* 198, A scientific work upon "The Rise and Fall of Botts in America." **1908** *DN* 3.293 **eAL, wGA,** *Bots . . .* A disease among horses. **1965–70** *DARE* (Qu. K47, *What diseases do horses or mules commonly get around here?)* 60 Infs, **chiefly S Midl, Gulf States,** Bots; **CA**101, Bot.

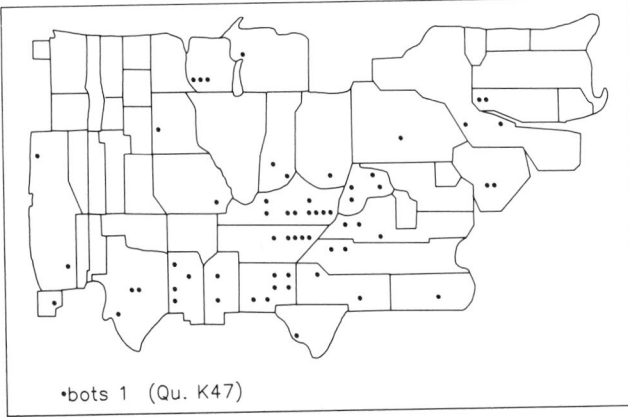

•bots 1 (Qu. K47)

2 Transf: a vague feeling of unwellness in human beings; **mulligrubs.**
1898 Lloyd *Country Life* 120 **AL,** Life is powerful short at best, but yet still it is most too long for a man to have the botts and stay mad with anybody all the time. *Ibid* 131, We didn't change neighborly visits and we didn't swap any family lies. I had the mullygrubs and Sandy he had the botts. But at the same time I want [=wasn't] so mighty mad with Sandy. **1908** *DN* 3.293 **eAL, wGA,** *Bots . . .* The blues. **1968** *DARE* FW Addit **GA**22, "I've got the bots, the scours, and the thumps." You say this when you're not feeling well but are not really sick.

botsel See **butsel**

bottle v
1 To preserve (fruit, vegetables, etc.) by canning in glass jars. **chiefly West**
1967 *DARE* Tape **ID**11, My mother used to bottle a great deal of fruits, vegetables, and meat. **1967–69** *DARE* (Qu. H75, *. . To preserve fruit in jars)* Infs **CA**132, **CO**11, **HI**9, **UT**4, 6, 8, Bottle.
‡**2** See quot.
c1970 *Halpert Coll.* **wKY, wTN,** Bottle — bottlin' — walking in a hurry. "He was just a-bottlin' down the street in a big hurry."

bottle-arsed tupelo n [From the bulging shape of the trunk base]
A **tupelo gum** (here: *Nyssa aquatica*).
1775 (1962) Romans *Nat. Hist. FL* 29, The true back swamps . . bear scarcely any other tree, than a variety of that species of Nyssa distinguished by Botanists by the name of *Nyssa foliis latis acuminatis non dentatis fructu œleagni minore, pedunculis multiflore,* vulgarly called bottle arsed tupelo.

bottle-assed spider n Also *bottle-arse spider* [From its bottle-shaped abdomen]
1966–68 *DARE* (Qu. R28, *. . Kinds of spiders . . you have around here)* Inf **MA**6, Bottle-assed spider — father's term; **ME**12, Bottle-arse spider. [Both Infs old]

bottlebrush n
1 also *bottlebrush grass:* A grass of the genus *Hystrix,* esp *H. patula.*
1843 Torrey *Flora NY* 2.478, Bottle-brush Grass . . . Moist, rocky woods, and along shady ravines: not rare. **1912** Baker *Book of Grasses* 250, Bottle-brush Grass. Hystrix patula. **1950** Hitchcock *Manual Grasses* 266, Hystrix patula . . . Bottlebrush.
2 A **horsetail** (here: *Equisetum arvense*).
1900 Lyons *Plant Names* 147, *Equisetum arvense* . . . Bottle-brush. **1970** Correll *Plants TX* 42, Bottle brush . . . In sandy or clayey soil along streams and about lakes.
3 =**mare's tail 2.**
1900 Lyons *Plant Names* 192, *Hippuris vulgaris* . . . Bottle-brush. **1953** Nelson *Plants Rocky Mt. Park* 111, Bottlebrush, *Hippuris vulgaris* . . occur[s] in the park.
4 An introduced shrub or small tree of the genus *Callistemon,* often planted in warmer regions (esp California) for its showy flower heads.
1967–68 *DARE* (QR, near p90) Inf **CA**23, Bottlebrush — red flower. The blossom looks like a brush you'd use in a bottle; (Qu. S20) Inf **CA**60, Bottlebrush — grows from a rosette, has a fluffy bottle-brush spike.

bottlebrush buckeye n Also *bottlebrush bush* [See quot 1976 Bruce]
A **buckeye** (here: *Aesculus parviflora*).
1933 Small *Manual SE Flora* 822, Aesculus parviflora . . . Bottlebrush-buckeye. **1938** Van Dersal *Native Woody Plants* 44. **1976** Bailey–Bailey *Hortus Third* 33, Aesculus parviflora . . . Bottlebrush bush. **1976** Bruce *How to Grow Wildflowers* 139, Another buckeye native to the Southeast warrants discussion here: *A. parviflora,* Bottle-brush Buckeye . . . The common name derives from the spike's resemblance to a white bottle-brush. **1979** Little *Checklist U.S. Trees* 46.

bottlebrush grass See **bottlebrush 1**

bottlebush n
A **buttonbush 1**(here: *Cephalanthus occidentalis*).
1967 *DARE* Wildfl QR Pl.210 Inf **SC**41, Bottlebush.

bottlebush tree n
Prob **bottlebrush 4.**
1967 *DARE* (Qu. T16) Inf **CA**12, Bottlebush tree.

bottle butt n
In logging: see quot 1958; hence adj *bottle-butted.*
1958 McCulloch *Woods Words* **Pacific NW,** Bottle butt — Swell butt; very rapid taper on a butt log. **1969** Sorden *Lumberjack Lingo* **NEng, Gt Lakes,** Bottle butted — A tree greatly enlarged at the base. Same as churn butted, swell butted.

bottled drink n Also *bottle drink* **chiefly Sth, esp NC** *old-fash* Cf **drink**
A soft drink, soda pop.
1965–70 *DARE* (Qu. H78, *Ordinary soft drinks, usually carbonated)* Infs **AL**33, **NC**82, 84, Bottle drinks; **NC**3, 11, 18, 48, 88, **TX**40, **VA**4, Bottled drink(s). [9 of 10 Infs old] **1970** Tarpley *Blinky* 195 **neTX,** Carbonated beverages in a bottle are more likely to be called *cold drinks* or *soda pop* than any other name . . . *Bottle drink* is limited [in this survey] to men over 50.

bottled earthquake See **earthquake**

bottled in a pepper-patch adj phr
1954 *Harder Coll.* **cwTN,** *Bottled in a pepper-patch . . .* Of whiskey: very strong.

bottled-in-the-barn n [Cf *bottled in bond*]
Moonshine.
1940 *AmSp* 15.446 **eTN,** Bottled in the barn. Liquor. 'Bottled in the barn is hard on the nerves.' **1941** Hall *Coll.* **eTN, wNC,** *Bottled in the barn* . . . Home-made, bootleg whiskey. **1969** *DARE* (Qu. DD21c, *. . Illegally made whiskey)* Inf **IL**81, Bottled-in-a-barn.

bottle fishing n
A method of fishing using a bottle as a float or bobber.
1966–69 *DARE* (Qu. P13, *. . Ways of fishing)* Infs **AR**33, **FL**27, **IL**41, **MO**26, Bottle fishing. [Infs explain that the line is attached to an empty bottle which floats.]

bottle fly n

1 also *black bottle fly, bottle-nose fly, green bottle fly:* A fly of the family Metopiidae.

1849 Holmes *Poems* 259 **Boston MA,** The first was a bottle fly, big and blue. **1966–70** *DARE* (Qu. R12, . . *Other kinds of flies*) Infs **IL**26, **NJ**55, **NY**48, 123, **PA**128, Bottle fly; **NY**165, Bottle fly—green; **OH**12, Greenheaded fly—same as bottle fly; (Qu. R13, *Flies that come to meat or fruit*) Infs **IL**135, **NY**205, 219, **OH**45, 47, 94, Bottle fly; **IL**126, Bottle flies—blue in color; **MN**36, Bottle fly—the bluish ones; **PA**162, Black bottle fly; **DC**11, **NC**16, **NY**34, Green bottle fly; **IN**42, Bottle-nose fly.

2 =**dragonfly.**

1967–68 *DARE* (Qu. R2, . . *Other names . . for the dragonfly*) Inf **AZ**2, Bottle fly; **OH**38, Bottle fly, snake-feeder.

bottle gentian n Also rarely *bottled gentian*

Either of two spp of **gentian:** usu *Gentiana andrewsii* but also *G. saponaria.*

1894 *Jrl. Amer. Folkl.* 7.94, *Gentiana Andrewsii* . . bottle-gentian, barrel-gentian, Concord, Mass. **1966–68** *DARE* Wildfl QR Pl.168 Infs **NC**28, **OH**14, **WI**34, Bottle gentian; **OH**14, Bottle gentian or closed gentian; **OR**12, Closed or bottled gentian. **1967–69** *DARE* (Qq. S26a, c, d) Infs **MI**108, **PA**53, 223, Bottle gentian. **1972** Brown *Wildflowers LA* 137, *Bottle Gentian, Soapwort Gentian. Gentiana saponaria* . . . Flowers usually blue, more or less tubular, . . closed at first and then opening slightly. **1976** Bruce *How to Grow Wildflowers* 265, These are tightly closed ovals in *G. andrewsii* and slightly open at the mouth in *G. saponaria.* Both species are often called Blind or Bottle Gentian, though the flowers are not really bottle-shaped at all. They look more like little eggs or footballs than bottles.

bottle gourd n

A white-flowered gourd (*Lagenaria siceraria*) which produces fruits with hard shells often used as utensils. Also called **calabash gourd, dipper gourd, Hercules'-club gourd, sugar-trough gourd, trumpet gourd**

1834 (1900) Harris *Reminiscences* 101 **TX,** Each man had a knife, a tin cup, a gun, and a bottle gourd. *Ibid* 180, A bottle gourd of whiskey. **1880** Darlington *Amer. Weeds* 138, *Common Lagenaria.* Calabash. Bottle Gourd . . . The thin firm woody shell of the fruit affords a very convenient kitchen utensil. **1933** Small *Manual SE Flora* 1286, *Bottle-gourd. Gourd. Calabash* . . . Fla. to Tex. **1970** Correll *Plants TX* 1507, *Bottle Gourd* . . . Commonly cult. for ornament and for the use of its fruit as containers and decoration.

bottle grass n [Prob from its green color]

=**green foxtail.**

1840 MA Zool. & Bot. Surv. *Herb. Plants & Quadrupeds* 244, *Setaria.* Bottle Grass. **1950** Gray–Fernald *Manual of Botany* 226, *Setaria viridis* . . . Bottle-Grass. **1910** Graves *Flowering Plants* 57 **CT,** *Setaria viridis* . . . Bottle Grass.

bottlehead n **MA**

=**black-bellied plover.**

1877 Bartlett *Americanisms* 777, *Bottle-Head.* (*S. Helvotica* [sic].) The black-bellied plover; also called "beetle-head" and "green-head." **1888** Trumbull *Names of Birds* 191, [*Black-bellied Plover*] At North Plymouth, Mass., *Bottle-head.* **1917** (1923) *Birds Amer.* 1.256, *Squatarola squatarola* . . . *Other Names.*—Bottle-head; Chuckle-head; Hollow-head. **1955** MA Audubon Soc. *Bulletin* 39.445, *Black-bellied Plover* . . . Bottle-head (Mass. Means big-head.).

‡bottle-kachunk n [Imit of its characteristic cry]

=**bittern.**

1967 *DARE* (Qu. Q8, *A water bird that makes a booming sound before rain, and often stands with its beak pointed almost straight up*) Inf **MI**65, Bottle-kachunk ['bɑtl̩kəčʌŋk], stake-driver; bittern I guess their real name is.

bottle lamb n [From its being fed from a bottle] Cf **bucket** n **4, bum** n[2]

1950 *WELS* (*A sheep that is kept as a pet*) 1 Inf, **WI,** Bottle lamb.

bottle lamp n

1953 *PADS* 19.9 **sAppalachians,** *Bottle lamp* . . . A lamp made by putting kerosene into a bottle, with a homemade wick in the opening. Such a lamp is often used when a lantern is not available.

bottle legs n pl

Crooked legs.

1950 *WELS* (*Words . . to describe people's legs . . . Not straight*) 1 Inf, **WI,** Bottle legs.

bottle-nose fly See **bottle fly**

bottle plant n Also *bottle stopper*

=**desert trumpet.**

1875 *Amer. Naturalist* 9.143, The singular fistulous-stemmed species *Eriogonum inflatum* . . from the peculiar bulging appearance of its main stalk and upper branches . . has received the fanciful popular name of "bottle stoppers." **1915** (1926) Armstrong *Western Wild Flowers* 90, *Bottle-plant* . . . This is a most extraordinary looking plant, with queer, inflated, hollow stalks.

‡bottle pocket n

The left side trousers pocket.

1980 *DARE* File **csKY** (as of 1955), One of my informants . . used *pistol pocket* and *bottle pocket,* respectively, for the right and left side pockets of the trousers.

bottle rocket n

A small firework rocket that is launched from a bottle.

1967–69 *DARE* (Qu. FF28, . . *Kinds of fireworks*) Inf **LA**17, Bottle rocket—a small rocket with a stick at the back; you put the stick in a coke bottle for launching; **NC**76, **TX**33, Bottle rocket.

bottle stopper See **bottle plant**

bottle-stretcher See **stretcher**

bottlewash n Cf **bolly wash**

Nonsense, 'hogwash.'

1944 *Richmond Times–Dispatch* 25 May 6/5 (*Hench Coll.*) [In letter to the editor], In answer to _____'s letter . . . I say bottlewash.

bottom n

1a also attrib: Alluvial land, esp low-lying land near a stream; the soil in such an area. **chiefly Sth, W Midl** See Map

1634 in 1883 Boston Registry Dept. *Records* 4.9, The hedgey ground that lies in the bottom betwixt his house and the water. **1696** (1945) Dickinson *Jrl.* 28 **FL,** I espied a place almost a furlong within that beach being a bottom. **1750** (1893) Gist *Jrls.* 34 **OH,** The Land from Shannopin's Town is good along the River, but the Bottoms [are] not broad. **1856** in 1956 Eliason *Tarheel Talk* 261 **NC,** Our bottom-corn we had it to plant the Seckond time. **1909** *DN* 3.393 **nwAR.** **1942** Faulkner *Go Down* 42 **MS,** Messing around up yonder in the bottom all last night! **1949** *PADS* 11.18 **CO.** **1950** *WELS* (*Hay that grows naturally in damp places*) 1 Inf, **WI,** Bottom grass. **1965–70** *DARE* (Qu. C19, . . *Low land running between hills*) 33 Infs, **chiefly Sth, S Midl,** Bottom(s); **KY**84, **LA**11, **MI**65, Creek bottom; (Qu. C6, . . *Land that's often wet*) Infs **GA**77, **IL**3, 8, **LA**33, **MO**27, **TX**90, Bottom(s); **LA**20, Low bottom; **SC**20, Swampy bottom; (Qu. C7, . . *Land that usually has some standing water with trees or bushes growing on it*) Infs **KY**39, **MO**38, **SC**3, 20, Bottom; **AR**47, **IL**19, River bottom; **LA**20, Low bottom; (Qu. C9, *Water from a river that comes up and covers low land when the river is high*) Infs **IL**64, **MS**86, **NC**52, (Flooded) bottom; (Qu. C20; total Infs questioned, 75) Infs **MS**2, 63, Bottom; (Qu. C29, *A good-sized stretch of level land with practically no trees*) Infs **AL**52, **NC**30, 36, **OH**38, **TN**14, Bottom; **GA**84, Bottom—a few acres; high bottom; **cannot** be flooded by stream; (Qu. C30, . . *Loose, dark soil*) Infs **GA**89, **OK**53, Bottom soil; **CO**18, Bottom ground; **MO**35, River bottom or creek bottom dirt; (Qu.

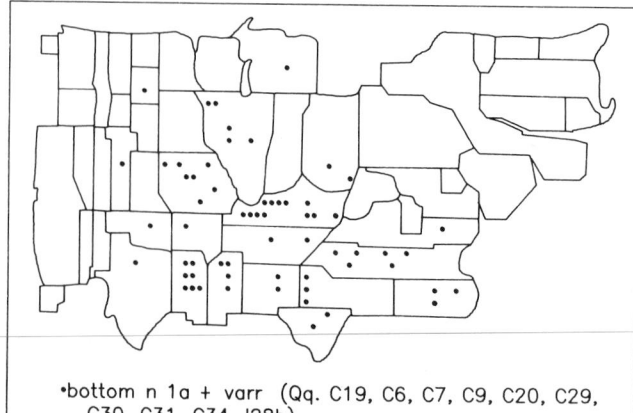

•bottom n 1a + varr (Qq. C19, C6, C7, C9, C20, C29, C30, C31, C34, I28b)

C31, . . *Heavy, sticky soil)* Inf **KY**75, Black bottom—heavy, black soil; **MS**45, Gum bottom; (Qu. C34) Inf **NC**17, Bottom—any low swampy place; (Qu. I28b) Inf **MO**2, Bottom greens—they grow down close to the creek. **1973** Allen *LAUM* 1.231, *Meadow* (low-lying grassland) . . . *Bottom(s),* missing in both Wisconsin and Minnesota, appears in southern Iowa also, with some extension westward.

b in phrr *first bottom, second ~, third ~:* The first and succeedingly higher levels of flatland along a stream.

1788 in 1797 Imlay *Western Territory* 595 **OH**, Next to these are what is called second bottoms, which are elevated plains, and gentle risings of the richest uplands, and as free from stone as the low or first bottom. **1803** (1965) Lewis *Jrls.* 34 **PA**, What is called the third bottom is more properly the high benches of the large range of hills. **1876** in 1940 *AmSp* 15.177 **VA**, In every portion of Tidewater along the streams are 'first' bottoms, composed of mixed materials, the sediment of the waters— these, where above tide or where protected by embankments, have a perpetual fertility. **1948** *Durant* (Okla.) *Dly. Democrat* 4 July 5/4 *(DA),* The first bottom is the red tide lands, the second bottom is the mixed land and the third bench is the sandy lands. **1973** Allen *LAUM* 1.232, [2 Infs] *Second bottom:* Lowland not susceptible to flooding.

2 By ext: a community or district situated in a low-lying area; the poor section of a city or town—freq used as last element in place names. **chiefly Sth, Midl** See Map See also **Black Bottom, Coon Bottom**

1930 Brown *Washington* 163 **DC** (as of 1900), Over in the old First Ward of an earlier day . . . where originally had been the little town of Hamburgh, which existed before Washington was even conceived, was —and still is—Foggy Bottom, lying west of Twenty-third Street and extending to Rock Creek and stretching from the river nearly to Pennsylvania Avenue. In its southern reaches it was formerly a section of swamps and flats, from which arose at night miasmatic vapors which gave to it its colorful cognomen. **1950** *Newsweek* 24 Apr 36/1 **DC**, The section of Washington known as Foggy Bottom. **1965–70** *DARE* (Qu. C34, *Nicknames for nearby settlements, villages, or districts)* Inf **DC**12, Froggy Bottom; **KY**41, Big Bottom; **MS**60, Pigeon-roost Bottom; **NC**17, Liza's Bottom; (Qu. C35, *Nicknames for different parts of your town or city)* Inf **GA**3, The Bottom; **GA**89, **KY**65, **MS**18, The Bottom [=where Black people live]; **IN**22, **OH**76, 99, **PA**167, **TN**66, Bottoms; **IL**122, Cunningham Bottoms; **NC**5, Hayes' Bottom; **AL**6, Sweet Gum Bottom; **KS**16, West Bottom; **VA**44, White's Bottom; (Qu. II24, . . *The part of town where the well-off people live)* Inf **DC**3, Foggy Bottom; (Qu. II25, . . *The part of town where the poorer people, special groups, or foreign groups live)* Infs **GA**89, **OH**99, **PA**167, The Bottom(s); **KY**65, The Bottom—Black ghetto of Burgin; **PA**239, Bottom; **GA**67, Hamp Brown's Bottom; **FL**18, Happy Bottom; **NY**238, Rocky Bottom; **GA**7, Sandy Bottom. **1969** *DARE* Tape **CA**112, There's quite a farming area: Arcata Bottom and Lolita Bottom—farming and cattle.

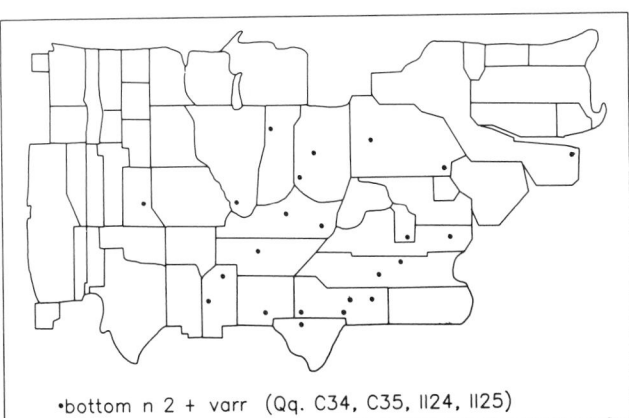

•bottom n 2 + varr (Qq. C34, C35, II24, II25)

3 The bulbous root of certain plants such as onions and turnips. Cf **bottom v 1**

1833 Greene *Life Dr. Dodimus* 1.25 **NEng**, Another of their notions was, that turnips, onions, and all manner of bulbous roots, would be utterly destitute of bottoms, if not sown in the old of the moon.

4 In coal mining: see quots.

1929 *AmSp* 4.369, *Bottom*—The floor of the mine. It begins where the coal stratum stops. **1973** *PADS* 59.27, *Bottom* . . the floor of the mine at any place.

5 pl: See quot. Cf **hay bottom**

1913 *DN* 4.55 **Cape Cod MA**, *Bottoms* . . . (1) Scattered hay left after the bulk of the cock has been loaded on the wagon. "You pitch on, and I'll rake up the bottoms." (2) Cranberries which have been knocked from the vines in picking, and which lie on the ground. "Stop your scalping and pick up your bottoms."

6 Stamina, staying power—used esp of horses and dogs.

1843 Field *Drama Pokerville* 109 **KY**, D. had travelled, on foot, from the Blackbird Hills to Fort Lisa, a distance of ninety miles, in thirteen hours! Mal Boeuf also boasted some astonishing feats of "bottom," and both were stationed at the fort. *Ibid* 110, The pluck of the other was roused in an instant, rightly interpreting the vaunt as a challenge to a trial of speed and bottom. **1877** Dodge *Plains Great West* 126, A buffalo can run only about two-thirds as fast as a good horse; but what he lacks in speed he makes up in bottom or endurance. **1889** (1971) Farmer *Americanisms, Bottom.*—Power of endurance; stamina. English slang which is thoroughly and respectably colloquial in the States. **1929** (1951) Faulkner *Sartoris* 326 **MS**, Jackson . . . Aims to raise a breed of animals with a hound's wind and bottom and a fox's smartness and speed. **1950** Stuart *Hie Hunters* 221 **eKY**, It ain't any fun to have a burnout dog like old Lightnin' and a cheater like old Fleet . . . I love a hound-dog with a good bottom like old Thunderbolt. **1958** *AmSp* 33.268 **eWA**. **1968** Adams *Western Words, Bottom*—Endurance . . . One of the sayings of the cow country is, "Real bottom in a good horse counts for more than his riggin'."

7 See quot.

1912 Green *VA Folk-Speech, Bottom* . . . Cocoon of the silkworm. "Sent over ten bottoms taken from Apple trees."

8 in phrr describing a hard rain: See quots. **Sth, S Midl**

1966–70 *DARE* (Qu. B5, *When the weather looks as if it will become bad, you say it's_____)* Inf **TX**52, Looks like the bottom's going to fall out; (Qu. B24, . . *A sudden, very heavy rain)* Infs **MS**1, **SC**69, The bottom fell out; (Qu. B25, . . *A very heavy rain)* Infs **GA**13, **NC**10, 81, The bottom fell out; **KY**83, The bottom of the bucket fell out; (Qu. B26, *When it's raining very heavily, you say)* Inf **VA**69, The bottom is falling out; **SC**34, Bottom's fell out. **1970** Tarpley *Blinky* 54 **neTX**, *Very heavy rain that doesn't last long* . . . Bottom fell out.

bottom v

1 Of a plant, esp an onion: to form a bulb or similar enlargement. Cf **bottom n 3**

1931–33 *LANE Worksheets* **swCT**, Bottom . . . "Some scallions never will bottom"; **csNH**, *Bottom* . . . To develop a root. "Scallions don't bottom"; **swNH**, "Scallions don't bottom out."

2 in phr *bottom chairs:* To be lazy. *joc*

1926 *DN* 5.386 **ME**, *Bottom* . . . Humorous. A lazy man is said to bottom chairs for a vocation. **1926** *AmSp* 2.83 **ME**, The lazy man is also a joke. Yankee humor describes him as "bottoming chairs" for an occupation.

3 See quot.

1943 *AmSp* 18.75 **swWI**, Apple-picking terms . . . *Bottom* a tree (picking everything he can reach standing on the ground).

‡bottom cat n

=muskrat.

1970 *DARE* (Qu. P31, . . *Other names . . for the muskrat)* Inf **TN**53, Bottom cat.

bottom ground n Cf **bottomland**

=bottom n 1a.

1637 (1972) Morton *New Engl. Canaan* 64, If any man be desirous to finde out in what part of the Country the best Cedars are, he must get into the bottom grounds. **1843** *Amer. Pioneer* 2.253 **OH**, They concluded to leave the bottom grounds. **1967–68** *DARE* (Qu. C6, . . *A piece of land that's often wet)* Inf **CO**18, Bottom ground; (Qu. C19, . . *Low land running between hills)* Inf **MO**2, Bottom ground—has water; (Qu. C29, . . *Level land with practically no trees)* Inf **IN**3, Bottom ground.

bottomland n, also attrib **chiefly Sth, Midl** See Map

=bottom n 1a.

1728 *Weekly News-Letter* (Boston MA) 23 May 2/2, Fifty Acres of . . Meadow and Meadow Bottom Land. **1841** Cist *Cincinnati* 66 **OH**, The larger streams are now found meandering through alluvial plains called "bottom lands." **1923** *DN* 5.202 **swMO**, *Bottom land* . . . Valley land adjacent to a stream. **1949** Kurath *Word Geog.* 61, In the Midland and the South *bottom lands* and *bottoms* are the most common expressions for low-lying flat meadow lands and fields along large and small watercourses. *Bottom lands* is more common in the North Midland, *bottoms* in the South and the South Midland. **1949** *PADS* 11.18 **CO.** **1953** *PADS* 19.9 **sAppalachians. 1965–70** *DARE* (Qu. C19, . . *Low land running between hills*) 34 Infs, **Sth, Midl,** Bottomland; **AR47, KY86,** River bottomland; **AR47,** Creek bottomland; (Qu. C7, . . *Land that usually has some standing water with trees or bushes growing on it*) 31 Infs, **chiefly Sth, Midl,** Bottomland(s); (Qu. C29, *Level land with practically no trees*) 15 Infs, **Sth, Midl,** Bottomland; (Qu. C6, . . *Land that's often wet*) 13 Infs, **Sth, Midl,** Bottomland; (Qu. C30, . . *Loose dark soil*) Infs **CA171, GA89, MO25, TN30, TX54,** Bottomland; **MS45,** Bottomland dirt; (Qu. C9, *Water from a river that comes up and covers low land when the river is high*) Infs **CA153, 181, IN80, TX66,** Bottomland; (Qu. L8, *Hay that grows naturally in damp places*) Inf **TX105,** Bottomland grass. **1968** *DARE* Tapes **IN5, 30, 35,** Bottomland. **1973** Allen *LAUM* 1.231, *Meadow* (low-lying grassland) . . . *Bottomland,* which appeared only three times in Wisconsin and once in Minnesota, is common in the Midland area of southern Iowa and extends into Nebraska and the Dakotas.

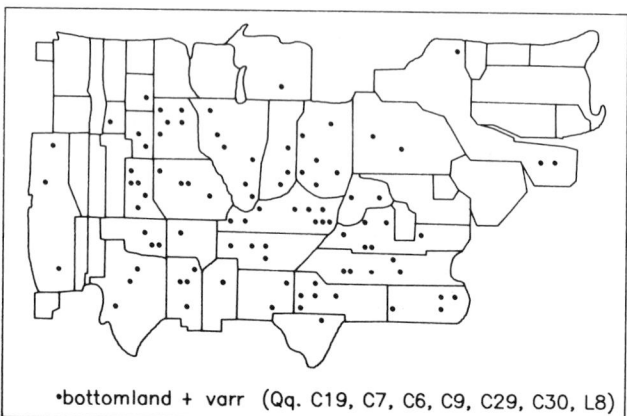

•bottomland + varr (Qq. C19, C7, C6, C9, C29, C30, L8)

bottom oak n [**bottom** n 1a]
1 =**valley oak.**
1910 Jepson *Silva CA* 209, So frequently an inhabitant of the delta lands, it [valley oak — *Quercus lobata*] is called "Water Oak," "Bottom Oak," and "Swamp Oak," while the folk-name "Mush Oak" carries with it a species of contempt and tells a long story of its failure to meet the requirements of a tough, strong wood in a land where good oak is scarce and dear. **1969** *DARE* (Qu. T10, . . *Different kinds of oak trees*) Inf **CA161,** White, bottom, blue.
2 Prob either of two oaks: **cherrybark oak** (*Quercus falcata*) or a **post oak** (*Quercus stellata*).
1970 *DARE* (Qu. T10, . . *Different kinds of oak trees*) Inf **KY75,** Yellow bottom — best lumber for hardwood floors. [**1979** Little *Checklist U.S. Trees* 231, *Quercus falcata* . . bottomland red oak. *Ibid* 242, *Quercus stellata* . . bottomland post oak.]

bottomside up adj Also *bottomsides up, bottomside upwards, bottom up(wards)*
1 Upside down; topsy-turvy.
1858 NH Hist. Soc. *Coll.* 12.362, But, alas for Mormon hopes, we entered the hotel to find it "bottom side upwards," as country folks say. **1954** Harder Coll. **cwTN,** *Bottom upwards* . . . Upside down. "Turn ever'thang bottom up'ards." **1966** *DARE* (Qu. Y48, *To look in every possible place for something you've mislaid . . "I've _____.")* Infs **AR40, OK28,** Turned it (*or* my room) bottomside up. **1968** *DARE* Tape **MI96,** The barrel will turn bottomside up. **1968–70** *DARE* FW Addit **nwPA,** Bottomside up; **csNY,** He allus had a short clay pipe in his mouth and it 'uz allus bottom up.
2 In reverse direction or order; backward.
1969–70 *DARE* (Qu. MM3, *When someone does something the wrong way round you might tell him: "This is the front, you've got the whole thing turned _____.")* Infs **MA46, FL48,** Bottomside(s) up; **LA11,** Bottom upwards.

botts See **bots**

botworm n [*bot* the larva of the botfly]
=**bots 1.**
1967–68 *DARE* (Qu. K28, . . *Diseases that cows have*) Inf **LA31,** Botworms; (Qu. K47, . . *Diseases [of] horses or mules*) Inf **LA7, MD13,** Botworm(s).

boucan n [LaFr, see quot 1931] *not fully naturalized*
See quot 1923.
1923 *DN* 5.243 **LA,** Boucan . . . A smudge to keep off mosquitoes. [**1931** Read *LA French* 82, *Boucane* is the usual La.-Fr. equivalent of French *fumée,* "smoke."]

boucherie n |ˌbuˈšri| [Fr] **LA**
See quots.
1967 LeCompte *Word Atlas* 282 **LA,** A gathering of two or more families to butcher a pig . . . *Boucherie.* **1968** *DARE* (Qu. H43) Inf **LA20,** Boucherie [ˌbuˈšri] — the processing of a hog. **1968** *DARE* FW Addit **LA33,** *To make a boucherie* [ˌbuˈšri] means to kill and butcher a hog or cow.

boucherie v [**boucherie** n] **LA**
1968 *DARE* FW Addit **sLA,** *To boucherie* [ˌbuˈšri] means to butcher an animal and make sausage, headcheese, boudin, etc. "I didn't know y'all boucheried this week."

bouchette n [Fr *bouchette* a small mouth; here a small mouthful]
1945 Saxon *Gumbo Ya-Ya* 202 **LA,** Spaghetti and bouchettes, the latter a kind of meatball made with chopped onion and sweet pepper.

bouchren See **butcher**

bouco n *hist*
See quots.
1939 FWP *Guide KS* 471, The "bouco" or coracle, two hides sewed together, distended like a leather tub with willow rods (used by pioneers to cross streams). **1961** Sackett–Koch *KS Folkl.* 110, Coracle . . . A boat made by stretching hides over a framework of poles. (Also called a *bouco.*)

boudin n |ˈbuˌdæ̃| [Fr]
1 The intestines of buffalo, esp as prepared for food. **West** *hist*
1805 (1904) Lewis *Orig. Jrls. Lewis & Clark Exped.* 2.15, From the [buffalo] cow I killed we saved the necessary materials for making what our wrighthand cook Charbono calls the *boudin (poudingue) blanc,* and immediately set him about preparing them for supper. **1845** Frémont *Rept. Rocky Mts.* 22, The hunters came in with a fat [buffalo] cow; and . . we enjoyed well a supper of roasted ribs and *boudins,* the *chef d'oeuvre* of a prairie cook. **1848** (1855) Ruxton *Life Far West* 16, Lies tumbled out of his mouth like boudins out of a bufler's stomach. **1947** Guthrie *Big Sky* 211 **West,** He wanted . . to kill a buffalo and cook the *boudins* by his own small fire. **1966** Giles *Great Adventure* 57 **West** (as of 1830–40), 'Tain't as good as fat hump or tenderloins or boudins. **1968** Adams *Western Words,* Boudin — A hunters' and trappers' delicacy made from the buffalo intestine containing chyme, cut in lengths, wrapped around a stick, and toasted before a fire until crisp.
2 A kind of pork sausage; see quot 1979. **chiefly LA**
1961 *PADS* 36.11 **LA,** *Boudin* (kind of sausage). **1967** LeCompte *Word Atlas* 292 **LA,** Blood sausage . . . *Boudin.* **1968–69** *DARE* (Qu. H43, *Foods made from parts of the head and inner organs of an animal*) Inf **IL57,** French blood sausage — boudin in French; a great favorite in this area; **LA28,** Boudin [ˈbuˌdæ̃] — pork intestines stuffed with rice, seasoning, lights (i.e., lungs), liver, and then boiled; **LA33,** White boudin — made with rice, some of the insides of hogs; red boudin — made with blood and some of the pork, lots of seasoning and rice; **NY28,** Boudin [butən] — blood sausage; Canadian word. **1977** *Mais Jamais* 31 **LA,** To begin to make boudin, you use the hog's head, ears, heart, liver, and kidneys . . . put the meat to boil. Chop parsley and onion tops. When the meat is through boiling, you take the meat apart from the bone and begin grinding it up . . . Then pour the mixture into a boudin stuffer or stuff the mixture through a cow's horn. This is white boudin. The only difference in making the red boudin is that you add the hog's blood instead of juice. **1979** *New Yorker* 9 Apr 122/2 **LA,** Around noon, the Mamou Mardi Gras riders stopped to eat boudin. Boudin is a sort of meat pudding, with pork and rice and spices, packed like sausage into a casing made of hog intestine. It is not merely a ceremonial dish. Any country store in a Cajun parish is likely to keep a steam pot full of homemade boudin, for immediate consumption.

bougalee See **boogerlee**

bough v
1907 *DN* 3.241 **eME,** *Bough* (a house) . . . To lay branches of evergreen trees against the underpinning of a house as protection against the inclemency of winter and for embellishment during the winter.

bought ppl adj

1 =**boughten 1.**

1939 McGuire *FL Cracker Dial.* 169, *Bought bread* . . . Store bread. **1965–70** *DARE* (Qu. H13, *Bread that is not made at home*) 62 Infs, **scattered, but somewhat more freq Sth, S Midl,** Bought bread; (Qu. O10) Inf **SC43,** Bought boats; (Qu. U2, . . *Clothing not made at home*) Infs **KS7, MA44, MI90, MO18, NC79, OK51, SC19,** Bought (clothes, clothing, garment, material); (Qu. CC5) Inf **SC5,** A bought pew—people owned their pews until recently.

2 =**boughten 2.**

1965–70 *DARE* (Qu. X13b, . . *False teeth*) Infs **IL72, IN19, NC33, 40, NY219, SC7, 24, 26, 42, 55,** Bought teeth.

boughten adj [*bought* pple of *buy* + *-en* adj suff] **chiefly Nth, N Midl** See Map Cf **brought-on**

1 Commercially made; purchased, spec as opposed to home-made.

1801 *Spirit Farmers' Mus.* 235 (*DAE*), Jotham, get your boughten shirt. **1839** *S. Lit. Messenger* 5.431/2 **ME,** For calico, tea . . and other "boughten" articles of use . . he goes . . to Sebec. **1894** *DN* 1.328 **NJ.** **1905** *DN* 3.4 **cCT.** **1907** *DN* 3.182 **seNH.** *Ibid* 209 **nwAR.** **1923** *DN* 5.202 **swMO.** **1926** *DN* 5.386 **ME.** **1941** *LANE* Map 285 **scattered throughout NEng,** *Boughten bread* . . . *Boughten sugar, a boughten dress, boughten ones.* **1944** *PADS* 2.54, *Boughten* . . . That which is purchased, ready-made. N[orth] w[est] Mo. Rural. Becoming rare. **1948** Young *Light* 126 **neOH** (as of 1872), The flowers in Willoughby's rather lavish arrangements were what Matild called "boughten." **1950** *WELS (Bread that is not made at home)* 14 Infs, **WI,** Boughten bread; *(A dress not made at home—one that you buy)* 19 Infs, **WI,** Boughten dress. **1965–70** *DARE* (Qu. H13, *Bread that is not made at home*) 97 Infs, **chiefly Nth, N Midl,** Boughten bread; (Qu. U2, . . *Clothing not made at home*) 48 Infs, **chiefly Nth, N Midl,** Boughten; **CA156, ME21, MO5, VT8,** Boughten clothes (*or* dress, goods); (Qu. H17, . . *Kinds [of yeast]*) Infs **CA22, IN19, MN37, MO39, OH80, TN11,** Boughten (yeast, east); (Qu. H82b) Inf **AZ8,** Boughten candy; (Qu. I25) Inf **NJ8,** Boughten cucumbers; (Qu. EE40, . . *Table games*) Inf **WI40,** Boughten games. **1969** *DARE* Tape **AZ15,** They are boughten. **1975** Allen *LAUM* 2.10, *Boughten bread* . . . In the U[pper] M[idwest] *boughten* is the choice of 56 infs., more than one-fourth of the total . . . *Bought* in this context is the choice of only three infs.

2 Of teeth: artificial, false.

1966–69 *DARE* (Qu. X13b, . . *False teeth*) Infs **MN33, MT4, NE6, OH88, PA60, WA1,** Boughten teeth.

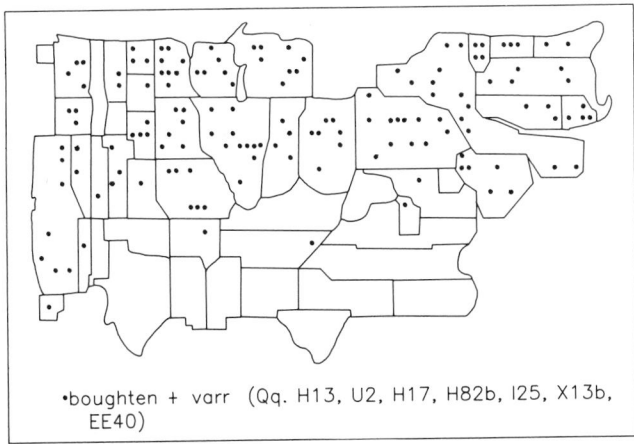

•boughten + varr (Qq. H13, U2, H17, H82b, I25, X13b, EE40)

bought-made adj [By analogy with *homemade*] =**boughten 1.**

1967 *DARE* (Qu. U2, . . *Clothing not made at home*) Inf **TX27,** Bought-made dress.

bouja See **booya**

boulden See **bolden**

boulder n, also attrib Also sp *bowlder* [Alter of **bowler,** infl by *boulder* a large usu smooth rock] **esp wGt Lakes, West** See Map *esp among young speakers*

In marble play: see quots.

1905 *DN* 3.71 **nwAR,** *Boulder* . . . A large marble. 'How many boulders you got.' **1950** *WELS (Marbles . . Large ones)* 6 Infs, **WI,** Boulders.

1958 *PADS* 29.30 **IA, WI,** *Boulder* . . . Same as *bowlder.* **1962** *PADS* 37.1 **cKS,** *Boulder.* Any large marble. **1965–70** *DARE* (Qu. EE6a, . . *Marbles—the big one that's used to knock others out of the ring*) 28 Infs, **scattered, but esp wGt Lakes, West,** Boulder; (Qu. EE6d, *Special marbles*) Infs **MI118, IL85, 86, OR10, WI20,** Boulders. [13 of 33 Infs young] **1968** *DARE* Tapes **IA27, MD51,** Boulder. **c1970** Wiersma *Marbles Terms* **seMI, neIL,** *Boulder* . . . A large glass marble. **1971** Bright *Word Geog. CA & NV* 115, Marbles: . . Boulder purie.

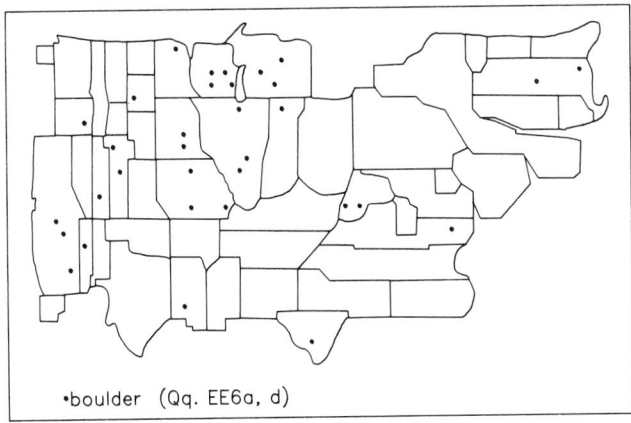

•boulder (Qq. EE6a, d)

boulette n [Fr]

1967 *DARE* FW Addit **sLA,** *Boulettes* [ˌbu'lets]—French term for fish cakes or patties. Used occas by English-speaking cooks.

boulevard n

1 also *boulevard strip:* See quots. **chiefly Upper MW, N Cent** See Map

1945 *AmSp* 20.154 **csMN,** *Boulevard.* The grassed area between curbing and sidewalk, without regard to the width or type of street. **1950** *WELS Suppl.,* 4 Infs, **WI,** Boulevard (strip). **c1950** *Atlas Checklists (Grass strip between sidewalk and street)* 3 Infs, **WI,** Boulevard (strip). **1965–70** *DARE* (Qu. N44, *In a town, the strip of grass and trees between the sidewalk and the curb*) 42 Infs, **chiefly Upper MW, N Cent,** Boulevard; **CA119, NY45, OH92,** Boulevard strip. **1966** *PMLA* 81.2.14, The grass strip between the sidewalk and the curb, . . a *boulevard* in Minneapolis and St. Paul. **1971** Wood *Vocab. Change* 53 **Sth,** A grass strip . . left between the sidewalk and street . . . *Boulevard* occurs everywhere in a second or lesser preference as does *boulevard strip.* **1973** Allen *LAUM* 1.381, The strip of grass between a sidewalk and the street . . . *Boulevard,* the most frequent term, conspicuously characterizes the Northern speech area of the U[pper] M[idwest].

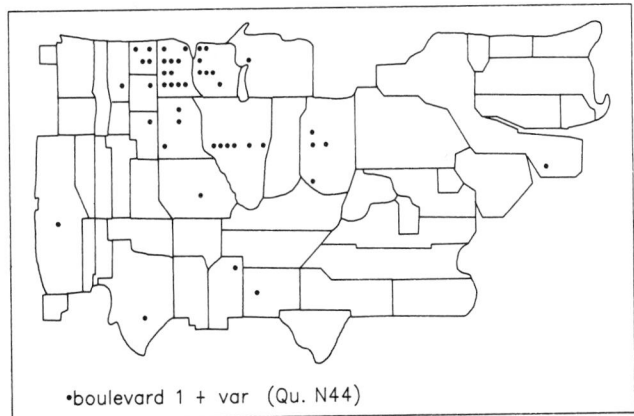

•boulevard 1 + var (Qu. N44)

2 A median strip. **chiefly wGt Lakes, Gulf States** See Map on p. 352

1965–70 *DARE* (Qu. N17, . . *The separating area of a four lane highway*) 21 Infs, Boulevard. **1983** *DARE* File **csWI** (as of 1940s), East Washington Avenue had boulevards running down its middle, . . with handsome plantings of flowering crabs . . . The islands were always called *boulevards.*

boulevard strip See **boulevard 1**

boulyaw See **booya**

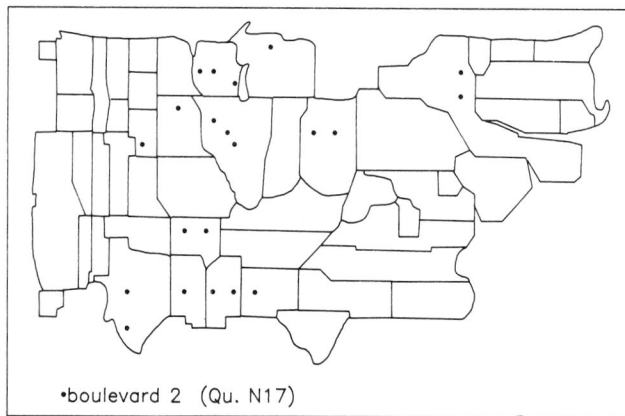

•boulevard 2 (Qu. N17)

bounce v

1 also with *up*: To cause a game animal to start from cover; to flush.

1840 *Crockett Almanac* 11 *(DAE)*, The rest of the time he spent in . . bouncing deer. **1858** *Harper's Mag.* 17.615/2, It is a common thing for still-hunters, when a deer is suddenly "bounced up," . . to bleat, imitating the noise of a fawn. **1968–70** *DARE* (Qu. P39a, *When a hunter or a dog finds a game animal and makes it start running you'd say he _____ it*) Infs **IL**115, **KY**44A, 47, **NJ**17, Bounced. **1968** *DARE* FW Addit se**NJ**, "The dogs bounced a rabbit," i.e., scared it out, flushed it.

2 =**bounce, give one the.**

1893 (1904) French *Stories W. Town* 213 **IA,** You don't suppose it would be any use to offer Esther a cool hundred thousand to promise to bounce this young fellow? **1966–68** *DARE* (Qu. AA11, *If a man asks a girl to marry him and she refuses, you'd say she _____*) Inf **IL**14, **NJ**18, Bounced him; (Qu. AA12) Inf **WA**18, Bounced her.

3 To change the direction of movement (of an animal). **West**

1941 FWP *Guide WY* 460, *Bounce* . . . To turn animals. **1968** Adams *Western Words, Bounce*—A cattle term meaning *to turn animals;* not commonly used.

bounce n Also *bounce about*, ~ *eye* [Prob coalescence of Engl dial *bonce* a large marble, a marble game, and *bounce* v]

A marble game; see quots.

1955 *PADS* 23.12 cw**TN,** *Bounce* . . . A marble game, usually played with large marbles . . . *Bounce about* . . . Prob[ably]. var[iant]. game of *bounce.* **1958** *PADS* 29.30 **WI,** *Bounce eye* . . . A marble game: the player drops his shooter from below his eye to marbles in the center of a small ring, trying to knock them out. **1965–70** *DARE* (Qu. EE7, . . *Marble games*) Infs **NE**11, **NY**59, 139, **PA**190, **TN**30, **WI**52, Bounce. **1967** *DARE* Tape **IA**37, To play bounce, you draw a circle about ten feet acrost, then you drew a circle in the center of this circle about three feet acrost. Marbles were placed in the center circle; you had to stand outside of the outer ring and you had to bounce your marble before it hit the inner ring and knock a marble out.

bounce, give one the v phr Also *give one the grand bounce, give the bounce* [*bounce* expulsion, dismissal] **esp Nth** See Map Cf **mitten, give one the**

To jilt or dismiss (someone).

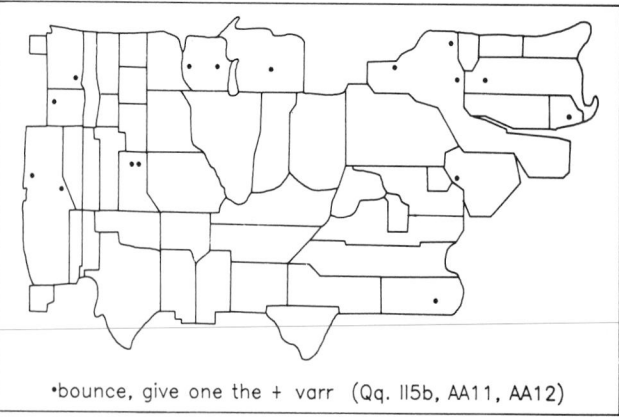

•bounce, give one the + varr (Qq. II5b, AA11, AA12)

1894 Twain *Pudd'nhead Wilson* 313, I finally saw plainly that there was really no way but one—I must simply give her the grand bounce. **1912** Porter *Rolling Stones* 122 **CO,** 'Had you ever thought,' I asks, ' . . of giving her the bounce yourself?' **1951** *PADS* 15.52 n**IN,** Bounce . . . Dismissal . . . To give the bounce was to break a marriage engagement. **1965–70** *DARE* (Qu. II5b, *When you don't want to have anything to do with a certain person . . you might say, "I'd certainly like to give him the _____."*) 13 Infs, **esp Nth,** Bounce; (Qu. AA11, *If a man asks a girl to marry him and she refuses, you'd say she _____*) Infs **CA**127, **MI**115, **WI**49, Gave him the (grand) bounce; (Qu. AA12) Inf **RI**1, Gave her the bounce.

bouncer n

1 Something very large of its kind.

1899 (1912) Green *VA Folk-Speech, Bouncer* . . . A large, strong, vigorous person. **1930** Shoemaker *1300 Words* 2 c**PA Mts** (as of c1900), *Bouncer*—A big, fleshy girl or woman. **1967–69** *DARE* (Qu. LL5, *Something impressively big: "That cabbage is really a _____."*) Infs **MD**17, **MA**25, **NY**43, **RI**3, **TX**37, **VA**11, 24, Bouncer.

2 A brazen lie.

1899 (1912) Green *VA Folk-Speech, Bouncer* . . . A bareface lie. **1942** Warnick *Garrett Co. MD* (as of 1900–1918), *Bouncer,* . . a bare-faced lie.

3 Among railroad workers: a caboose.

1945 Hubbard *Railroad Ave.* 334, *Bouncer*—Caboose. **1977** Adams *Lang. Railroader, Bouncer:* A caboose, especially one of the little early-day four-wheelers.

bounce up See bounce v 1

bouncing adj Cf bouncer 1, 2

1899 (1912) Green *VA Folk-Speech, Bouncing* . . . Exaggerated; excessive; big.

bouncing Bet n [Engl dial *bouncing bess (EDD)*]

1 also *bouncing Bess,* ~ *Betsy,* ~ *Betty:* A **soapwort** (here: *Saponaria officinalis*). Also called **Boston pink, chimney pink, hedge pink, lady-by-the-gate, latherwort, London pride, monthly pink, my lady's washbowl, old-maid's-pink, ragged sailor, sheepweed, soaproot, sweet Betty, wild sweet William, woods phlox, world's wonder**

1822 Eaton *Botany* 447, *Saponaria officinalis* (soapwort, bouncing bet). **1928** Aldrich *Lantern* 27 **NE,** There were flowers in the deep, dark recesses of the Big Woods,—wild honey-suckles and Bouncing-Bets and tall ferns. **1965–70** *DARE* (Qu. S26a) 10 Infs, **chiefly NEast,** Bouncing Bet; **CT**2, **MI**65, Bouncing Bess; **IN**83, **OH**57, Bouncing Betty; **IL**37, Bouncing Bets, Bouncing Betsy; (Qu. S11) Inf **MI**80, Bouncing Betsy; (Qu. S21) Infs **CT**11, **MI**45, Bouncing Bet; (Qu. S25) Inf **NY**30, Bouncing Bet; (Qq. S26d, e) Infs **CT**23, **IA**8, **MI**108, **MA**42, Bouncing Bet(s); **IL**55, Bouncing Bettys. **1966** *DARE* Wildfl QR Inf **WI**34, Bouncing bet—pink flower similar to phlox, flat blossom. **1967** Borland *Hill Country Harvest* 235 nw**CT,** Bouncing Bet is in bloom along the roadsides, great banks of it, pale pink and sometimes almost white. **1968** *DARE* FW Addit **CO**7, Bouncing Bet—smuggled in apron pockets from Europe to East, from East to West; **VA**15, Bouncing Bet.

2 A pink (here: *Dianthus barbatus*).

1893 *Jrl. Amer. Folkl.* 6.138, *Dianthus barbatus,* . . bouncing Bet. Ferrisburgh, Vt.

bouncing Betsy, bouncing Betty See bouncing Bet 1

bound v, hence *bound* ppl adj [*bind* to subject to an obligation]

1 To bet, wager—usu used in assertions or affirmations. **chiefly Sth**

a in constr *I bound (you). esp freq among Black speakers*

1845 Thompson *Pineville* 97 c**GA,** [Black], I bound he never bite nobody, massa. **1887** (1967) Harris *Free Joe* 217 **GA** [Black], I boun' you some er deze yer folks 'll go off en say I'm 'stracted. **1908** *DN* 3.293 e**AL,** w**GA. 1915** *DN* 4.224 w**TX. 1929** Sale *Tree Named John* 39 **MS** [Black], Ah boun' ju he got fever yit, ain't he. **1952** Brown *NC Folkl.* 1.522, *Bound* . . . "I bound he'll come." **1963** Edwards *Gravel* 116 e**TN** (as of 1920s), Many of 'em had a lot of truth in 'em too, I'll bound je.

b in passive constr *I (will) be bound.*

1852 Stowe *Uncle Tom's Cabin* 2.128, You've been stealing something, I'll be bound. **1887** (1967) Harris *Free Joe* 117 **GA,** Tuck didn't say he was comin', but I be boun' he comes, an' more'n that, I be boun' a whole passel er gals an' boys'll foller Babe home. **1899** (1912) Green *VA Folk-Speech.* **1899** Edwards *Defense* 19 **GA,** 'I'll be boun' you picked out this day ter come for that ar sewin'-machine.' I tole her I had. **1916**

Howells *Leatherwood God* 114 **OH,** You'll want your supper, I'll be bound. **1968** *DARE* (Qu. JJ34, *When you decide it would be to your advantage to do something, you might say, "Yes, I_____ I'll be better off that way."*) Inf **VA**15, I'll be bound.

2 in phr *I will be bound:* Darned—used as a mild oath.   *euphem*
1884 Jewett *Mate of Daylight* 205 **ME,** I'll be bound if the . . house hadn't got stuck fast. **1915** *DN* 4.224 **wTX,** *Bound . . .* Exclamatory, as "I'll be bound." **1967** *DARE* (Qu. NN32, *Exclamations like "I swear" or "I vow"*) Inf **IL**26, I'll be bound.

bound adj
1 Of a boy or girl: indentured, apprenticed. [*OED* bind v. 20, c1500 →] *hist* Cf **bound out**
1800 (1907) Thornton *Diary* 10.139 **DC,** Dr T. . . inoculated Joe (a negro-man) William & Betsy bound children and (Bet) Lucy's child. **1843** *Amer. Pioneer* 2.140 **PA,** Our family consisted of my father, mother, and three children, . . and a bound boy of fourteen. **1871** Eggleston *Hoosier Schoolmaster* 27 **sIN,** The bound girl was milking the cows. **1929** *AmSp* 5.121 **ME,** We heard of "bound girls," of boys who were "bound out". **1940** Richter *Trees* 91 **OH** (as of early 19th cent), He saw the trader's bound boy with two Shawnee boys laying for him outside the door. **1963** Owens *Look to River* 3 **TX,** Then he set Jed his bound boy, to drive the blackbirds from the cornfield. **1966** *PADS* 46.24 **cnAR,** *Bound boy . . .* A boy who was "hired out" as a sort of slave to an employer for a flat fee, which was paid to the boy's parents. The practice belongs to the past. It was current in the last half of the nineteenth and perhaps very early twentieth century.

2 See quot. [*OED* bind v. 21, 1530 →]
1903 *DN* 2.307 **seMO,** *Bound . . .* Obliged; beholden. 'If you will help me this time I will be bound to you as long as I live.'

3 See quot.
1930 Shoemaker *1300 Words* 8 **cPA Mts** (as of c1900), *Bound*—Impotent, lacking in manhood.

bound n
An obligation, duty.
1941 in **1944** *ADD* **swWV,** I'd like to go, but I just got a bound to be [somewhere else] tonight. **1942** Thomas *Blue Ridge Country* 155 **sAppalachians,** He's got a-bound to act like a man, now. *Ibid* 325, We've got a-bound . . to put our shoulders to the wheel.

bound and sot pple
Of the spirit of a dead person: prevented by a spell from wandering away from the burial place.
1889 Edwards *Runaways* 7 **cGA** [Black], "Well," said Isam, . . "w'en er sperrit gits out'n de flesh, de only way hit can be boun' en' sot es ter plug er tree."

boundary n chiefly **S Midl**
1 A tract of land, esp one with timber on it.
1881 in **1940** *AmSp* 15.158 **swVA,** In the Clinch Mountain are large boundaries of chestnut, chestnut oak, with hickory, etc. **1917** *DN* 4.408 **wNC,** *Boundary . . .* A farm; a fenced-in field; a large, unfenced estate, such as a tract of timber land. **1941** Alley *Random Thoughts* 482 **NC,** They bought a considerable boundary of timber lands. **1944** Univ. Va. Extension Division Publication *New Dominion Series* No. 51 1 July 1 (Hench Coll.), In the northeastern corner of Georgia . . are eighteen families, each occupying a neat farmhouse . . and each working a "boundary" of approximately forty acres. **1958** *PADS* 29.8 **TN,** *Boundary . . . Stand* is used in the same sense as *boundary,* a tract or area of standing timber. **1967–69** *DARE* (Qu. L6b, *A piece of land under cultivation*) Inf **KY**46, Boundary; (Qu. T2b, . . *A piece of land covered with trees*) Infs **KY**16, 29, 34, Boundary (of timber, of trees).

2 Transf: a collection, group.
1939 *Hall Coll.* **eTN, wNC,** "I never lost a woman in the whole boundary of 'em," i.e., in her practice as a midwife; she had previously stated that she had "handled over two hundred babies."

bound-backs n Cf **back-lick**
1901 *DN* 2.136, *Bound-backs.* Same as bombalics. A game of marbles played at Ithaca [NY].

bounden adj chiefly **S Midl**
Obliged; obligatory.
1899 (1912) Green *VA Folk-Speech, Bounden . . .* Obliged, bound or under obligation. The bounden duty. **1952** Brown *NC Folkl.* 1.522, *Bounden . . .* To be sure; to be obliged . . . "He'll be *bounden* to go see her." **1953** Randolph *Down in Holler* 229 **Ozarks,** *Bounden . . .* Under

legal or moral obligation. "It was my bounden duty to put that feller in jail," said a village constable who could neither read nor write. **c1960** *Wilson Coll.* **csKY,** *Bounden . . .* Owed as an obligation. "This is your bounden duty."

bounder v
1895 *DN* 1.382 **NJ,** *Bounder:* to scrub or wash thoroughly (the person).

bounder n [*EDD* bounder sb.[2] "A heavy blow"]
1966 *DARE* (Qu. Y11, . . *A very hard blow* . . *"Joe really hit him a _____."*) Inf **AR**40, Bounder.

bound out pple Also *bounden out old-fash* Cf **bound** adj 1
Apprenticed; made the ward of (someone).
1929 *AmSp* 5.121 **ME,** Boys . . were "bound out" or "prenticed to" someone. **1931–33** *LANE Worksheets* **swCT,** *Bounden out . . .* The relationship of an orphan to a guardian. **1968** *DARE* Tape **WI**22, At nine years of age he was bound out to a man. He was with him for eleven years. **1969** *DARE* FW Addit **ceCT,** Bound out to a farmer—A county ward from the "poor house" is given to the charge of a farmer till age 16.

bound round n
A swaddling cloth.
1955 *Sun* (Baltimore MD) 9 May ed. B 10/7 *(Hench Coll.),* My colored friend and helper, who was raised near Norfolk, tells me that her grandmother used to use old shirttails and parts of other discarded garments to make "boun' roun's" for the children.

bounky See **bunky**

bounty v
To claim a reward or bounty (on something).
1966 *DARE* Tape **MI**2, I had to kill it [a timber wolf] and bounty it.

bourbon ball n Also *bourbon candy* chiefly **KY**
A confection flavored with bourbon whiskey.
1951 Brown *Southern Cook Book* 282, *Kentucky Bourbon Balls . . .* 30 vanilla wafers, ground—2 tablespoons cocoa—2 tablespoons Karo syrup—⅓ cup crushed pecans—4 tablespoons Bourbon whisky. **1969** *DARE* (Qu. H80, . . *Candy often made at home*) Infs **KY**25, 48, Bourbon candy; **KY**37, 48, Bourbon balls.

bourré n [Fr *bourrer* to stuff] **LA**
A card game played with trump suits and tricks.
1967–68 *DARE* (Qu. DD35, . . *Favorite card games*) Infs **LA**2, 14, 23, 45, ['bu,reɪ]; **LA**20, ['bʊ,re]; **LA**34, [,bu're]; **LA**37, ['bu,re]. **1974** Gibson *Hoyle* 39, *Bourre:* A modern adaptation of Écarté . . with two to seven players using a full pack of fifty-two cards. **1983** *Reinecke Coll.* **New Orleans LA,** *Bourré* [bure]—Card game popular in rural S. La. and known in New Orleans. Characterized by the way in which stakes rise dramatically as game progresses.

'bout See **about**

bow n[1] [*EDD* bow sb.[1] 12]
1899 (1912) Green *VA Folk-Speech, Bow . . .* Handle of scissors; or of a key.

bow n[2]
1930 Shoemaker *1300 Words* 8 **cPA Mts** (as of c1900), *Bow*—A rainbow.

bow n[3] See **bendy-bow** 2

bow v
To strike, as if with the bow of a boat.
1911 *DN* 3.537 **eKY,** *Bōw . . .* To strike; used primarily by rivermen of a raft, as in "The raft bowed a snag." Also with extension of application; e.g., "I was running across a pasture and bowed a post before I knowed it."

bow-and-arrow n chiefly **Nth** *derog*
An American Indian.
1930 Williams *Logger-Talk* 15 **Pacific NW,** *Bow-and-arrow:* An Indian. **1958** McCulloch *Woods Words* **Pacific NW.** **1966–68** *DARE* (Qu. HH28, . . *Nicknames for . . [an] Indian*) Infs **MN**10, **WI**65, Bow-and-arrow; **MI**10, Bow-and-arrow; for French-Canadian-Indian crossbreed: bow-and-arrow French. **c1971** Hall *Snake River Valley, (Terms for Indians)* 1 Inf, **seID,** Bows and arrows.

‡**bow-and-arrow wedding** n [Prob by analogy with *shotgun wedding*]
1967 *DARE* (Qu. AA20, *A marriage that takes place because a baby is on the way*) Inf **NY**1, A bow-and-arrow wedding.

bow-arrow n

1899 (1912) Green *VA Folk-Speech*, Bow-arrow . . . A bow and arrow.

bow backed adj

1981 *Broaddus Coll.* ceKY, Bow backed — sway backed.

bowdacious See **bodacious**

bowdark See **bois d'arc**

bow dollar See **beau dollar**

bowdow, drunk as a adj phr |'bauˈdau| [Prob alter of **boiled owl** n 2]

Very drunk.

1980 *DARE* File MS (as of 1950s), If the people at church were talking about someone who had gotten drunk, they would say he was drunk as a bowdow ['bauˈdau].

boweevil See **boll weevil**

bowel off v phr

1953 Randolph *Down in Holler* 229 **Ozarks**, Bowel off . . . To have a diarrhea. "Tom he was a-pukin' an' a-bowellin' off somethin' turrible, so finally they sent after Doc Holton."

bowel-rack v [*bowel* + *rack* alt sp of *wrack* to ruin, destroy]

1953 Randolph *Down in Holler* 229 **Ozarks**, Bowel-rack . . . To cut or wound so that the intestines are exposed. An acquaintance of mine was bowel-racked in a knife fight.

bowels n pl

See quots.

1929 *AmSp* 5.17 **Ozarks**, Bowels . . . Faeces. "Th' baby's bowels looks mighty black-like an' dismal, Doc." **1954** *Harder Coll.* cwTN, Bowels . . . Feces.

bower n

1966 *DARE* (Qu. FF9, *A Christmas gathering*) Inf **AR3**, A bower — presents hung on ropes covered with cedar.

bowery n¹ [*bower* a dwelling; a place closed in with tree branches or shrubs + *-y;* infl by *bough*] **chiefly Inland Nth**

A large open pavilion with a roof sometimes made of boughs.

1788 (1873) May *Jrl.* 78 OH, Our long bowery is built on the east bank of the Muskingum; a table laid sixty feet long, in plain sight of the garrison. **1830** (1892) McCall *Jrl.* 189 WI, A bowery covered with boards, and seated for 500 people. **1878** Beadle *Western Wilds* 341 **cnUT**, At once the brethren were called together in the bowery — an open shed where they usually worshiped. **1967** Schilla *Prairies* 161 **ND** (as of 1887–1906), There usually was a bowery built for the Fourth of July dances. It consisted of a platform with a wooden floor and studdings to hold up a roof, which was covered with the branches of trees. **1967** *DARE* Tape **ID11**, It's really a pioneer term, I think . . . They would gather . . trees and make poles out of them, make . . uprights to hold a roof, they didn't have walls, and then on the roof they'd place limbs with the leaves on it, to make a covering for meeting places, and they used these in . . Salt Lake Valley before they built any buildings, to assemble great numbers of people. They called 'em a bowery. That's quite commonly used today by people in this area to designate a covering, oh, like in a public park. [FW:] Picnic shelter. [Inf:] Yes. **1968** *DARE* FW Addit seID, Bowery — either an auditorium or an amphitheater. "Next year we will try to have the family reunion at a place where there is a bowery."

bowery n² [The *Bowery*, a district on Manhattan Is. NYC]

The part of a city notorious for low life; skid row.

1967–69 *DARE* (Qu. C35, *Nicknames for different parts of your town or city*) Inf **PA66**, The bowery; **PA220**, The bowery — down on East Main Street where brawling takes place; **TX39**, The bowery — old-fashioned name for part of Amarillo where bars, whorehouses, etc. were.

bowery dance n **chiefly Inland Nth**

A dance held in a **bowery** n¹.

1936 Lutes *Country Kitchen* 159 **sMI**, They would stay for the bowery dance in the evening. **1951** in 1965 *DARE* File cwWI, Bowery dance . . . "Young people of neighborhood lay a board floor out under the trees, erect a roof frame over it and roof it with boughs, and give free dances with beer; collection paid for fiddler and beer, and what was left over paid the cleaner-uppers." **1967** *DARE* (Qu. FF4, . . *Kinds of dancing parties*) Inf **IA9**, Bowery dances — held outdoors on a platform on 4th of July.

bowfin n

A dull green freshwater fish (*Amia calva*) characterized by an

elongated dorsal fin and a black spot at the base of the tail. Also called **blackfish 5, boatfin, brindle cat, bullfin, choupique, cottonfish, cypress trout, dogfish, grindle, grinnel, grinner, jack grindle, John A. Grindle, lake lawyer, lawyer, mudfish, mudjack, poisson de marais, prairie bass, scaled ling, speckled cat, spot-tail**

1845 Storer *Synopsis Fishes N.A.* 213 *(DA)*, Called the 'Bowfin,' at Lake Champlain. **1882** U.S. Natl. Museum *Bulletin* 16.94, A[mia] calva . . . Bow-fin . . . A voracious fish of remarkable tenacity of life. The flesh is peculiarly soft and pasty, and is of no value for food. **1920** Forbes–Richardson *Fishes IL* 38, Bowfin . . . This species is abundant and widely distributed throughout the Great Lake region and the Mississippi Valley, principally in sluggish waters. **1957** Trautman *Fishes* 171, The Bowfin was not adverse to waters made cloudy by the abundance of plankton. **1969** *DARE* (Qu. P3, *Freshwater fish that are not good to eat*) Inf **PA209**, Bowfins.

bow-gun n

1906 Lovett *Old Boston Boys* 21, Then there was the bow-gun . . . This was a homemade article, some of the boys producing beautiful specimens, which those less eagerly purchased; they had finely finished black walnut stocks, polished lancewood bows, strings of catgut, and delicately hung triggers. These guns would throw a buckshot most spitefully and with fair precision. When buckshot ran short, screws and other articles of hardware were used.

bowing blade n

1969 *DARE* (Qu. L37, *A hand tool for cutting weeds and grass*) Inf **NC73**, [bo-ɪn] blade.

bow-jawed adj

1967 *DARE* (Qu. X6, *If a person's lower jaw sticks out prominently, you say he's _____*) Inf **PA3**, Bow-jawed.

bow knot n Also *bow tie*

A pastry (as a doughnut or roll) shaped like a ribbon bow.

1950 *WELS* (*Fancy home-baked rolls*) 1 Inf, ceWI, Bow knots. **1967–68** *DARE* (Qu. H28, *Different shapes or types of doughnuts*) Inf **NY105**, Bow ties; **AZ8**, Figure eight = bow knots.

bowl n¹

A drinking vessel, a cup or mug.

1887 in 1950 *AmSp* 25.30 **New Orleans LA**, While I run over to Mike Fanin's for a bowl of beer. **1935** Hurston *Mules & Men* 93 **FL**, A big bowl of coffee.

bowl n² [Abbr for **bowler**]

1955 *PADS* 23.12 **cwTN**, Bowl . . . A large marble.

bowlder See **boulder**

bowler n [Engl dial *bowl* a marble, *booler* a large marble used for throwing]

=**boulder**.

1905 *DN* 3.71 **nwAR**, Bowler . . . A large marble. **1950** *WELS* (*Marbles . . Large ones*) 3 Infs, Bowlers; (*The marble used to knock the others out of the ring*) 1 Inf, csWI, Bowler. **1958** *PADS* 29.30 **IA, WI**, [Marble terms:] *Bowler*. **1965–70** *DARE* (Qu. EE6a, . . *Marbles — the big one that's used to knock others out of the ring*) Infs **CA190, IL97, MA1, 8, 23, NY10, SC19, TX88, 104**, Bowler. **1973** Ferretti *Marble Book* 40, *Bowlers*. Large shooters, often aggies, often of scrap glass, but just as often reflectors pried out of traffic signs.

bowlhead n [Prob alter of **bullhead 9**] Cf **hardhead, roundhead**

A fieldstone.

1968 *DARE* (Qu. C25, . . *Kinds of stone . . about . . the size of a person's head, smooth and hard*) Inf **MO16**, Bowlhead.

bowling alley n *joc*

1945 Hubbard *Railroad Ave.* 334, Bowling alley — Hand-fired coal-burning locomotive. (A fireman throwing in the lumps of coal goes through motions that resemble bowling.)

bowl weever See **boll weaver**

bowman's root n Also *bowman root* [Folk-etym from *beaumont root*]

1 The flowering **spurge** (*Euphorbia corollata*).

1815 Drake *Natural View Cincinnati* 87, Euphorbia colorata — bowman's root. **1876** Hobbs *Bot. Hdbk.* 15, Bowman's root, Euphorbia corrolata [sic]. **1900** Lyons *Plant Names* 156.

2 =**Indian physic** (here: *Gillenia stipulata* or *G. trifoliata*).

 1822 Eaton *Botany* 291, *Gillenia . . . trifoliata, . .* Indian physic, Bowman's root . . . An emetic and tonic. **1824** Doddridge *Notes Indian Wars* 148 **wVA, PA,** Indian physick, or bowman root, a species of epicacuanha was frequently used for a vomit. **1847** Wood *Class-Book of Botany* 257, *G[illenia] stipulacea . . . Bowman's Root.* **1901** Mohr *Plant Life AL* 539, *Porteranthus trifoliatus . . .* Bowman's Root. *Spiraea trifoliata . . . Gillenia trifoliata . . .* Alleghenian and Carolinian area; . . rare west of the Alleghanies. **1931** Clute *Common Plants* 126, Some plants have been so regularly used by certain individual medical practitioners as to have become indissolubly connected with their names. This is the case with . . . Bowman's root *(Gillenia trifoliata).* **1976** Bailey–Bailey *Hortus Third* 510, *Indian-physic, Bowman's-root.*

3 =**culver's root.**

 1828 Rafinesque *Med. Flora* 20, *Leptandra purpurea . . . Names . . . Vulgar . . .* Bowman-root. *Ibid* 21, The local names of Bowman, Brinton, Culvert, were given from men who used the roots in practice. **1900** Lyons *Plant Names* 221, Beaumont-root, Bowman's-root . . . Emeto-cathartic, reputed cholagogue, alterative. **1933** Small *Manual SE Flora* 1209, *Bowman's-root . . .* Meadows and moist woods. **1971** Krochmal *Appalachia Med. Plants* 268, *Veronicastrum virginicum . . . Common Names: . .* Beaumont root, blackroot, bowman's root . . . The rhizome is reputed to be a laxative, emetic, cholagogue, and tonic.

4 =**Indian hemp 1.**

 1900 Lyons *Plant Names* 40, *A[pocynum] cannabinum . . .* Bowman's-root . . . *Root* emeto-cathartic, diaphoretic, expectorant. **1930** Sievers *Amer. Med. Plants* 34, *Hemp Dogbane . . . Other common names . . .* Bowmans root. **1974** (1977) Coon *Useful Plants* 62, Bowman's root . . . Poisonous to stock as well as man and yet medicinal when used by the knowing.

bow one's back v phr [*bow* to bend into a curve, to arch] Cf **bow up** v phr[2]

 1958 McCulloch *Woods Words* **Pacific NW,** *Bow his back*—To refuse to do a job.

bow the blinds v phr [*bow* to make into a curve + **blind** n **1**]

 1923 *DN* 5.243 **LA,** *Bow the blinds . . .* To close the shutters till they nearly meet.

bow tie See **bow knot**

bowtree See **bowwood**

bow up v phr[1] |baʊ| [As the counterpart to *bow down* to defer, yield]

1 To assert oneself, stand up to (someone).

 1941 Stuart *Men of Mts.* 159 **neKY,** Though he did bow up to Lead the other day when Lead snapped him through the ear and left a tiny hole. **1951** *PADS* 15.69 **nLA,** *Bow up to* [baʊ] . . . To assert oneself. "Bow up to him. Don't let him bluff you."

2 By ext: see quot.

 1939 *AmSp* 14.89 **csTN,** *Bow up.* To improve. 'Mose will have to bow up if he holds his job.'

bow up v phr[2] |boʊ| Cf **bow one's back**

1 See quot.

 1958 McCulloch *Woods Words* **Pacific NW,** *Bow up*—To get mad, turn mean, refuse to do a job.

2 See quot.

 1961 Adams *Old-Time Cowhand* 160, When cattle in winter stopped and humped their backs up they were said to "bow up."

bowwood n Also *bowtree*

=**Osage orange.**

 1806 U.S. Congress *Debates & Proc.* 2 Sess. 1138, One or two slips of the bois d'arc, bow wood, or yellow wood, from the Missouri. **1892** Apgar *Trees Nth. U.S.* 137, Osage Orange. Bow-wood . . . [Has] fruit as large as an orange, golden-yellow when ripe. **1941** FWP *Guide AR* 314, Bois d'arc, known variously as ironwood, . . bowwood, . . is highly prized by makers of archery equipment. **1970** *DARE* (Qu. T13, . . *Other names . . for . . osage orange*) Inf **MA78,** *Bow tree*—[I] have read or heard this out of [this] area, Indians used to make bows from them. **1979** Little *Checklist U.S. Trees* 165, *Osage-orange . . . Other common names . . .* bowwood, hedge-apple, horse-apple.

bowwow n [*bowwow* a dog, in ref to size or something considered inferior]

 See quots.

1935 *AmSp* 10.270 **NE,** *Bowwow.* A stunted, aged steer, unsuited for beef or fattening—same as *tripe* and *canner.* **1942** Kennedy *Palmetto Country* 224 **FL, sGA, sAL,** In cracker cow-jargon, a bow-wow is a runty steer.

box n

1 also attrib: A cavity made in a tree trunk for collecting sap or turpentine. See also **box** v[1]

 1720 Royal Soc. London *Philos. Trans.* 31.27 **NEng,** You box the Tree, as we call it, *i.e.* make a hole with an Axe, or Chizzel, into the Side of the Tree, within a Foot of the Ground; the Box you make may hold about a Pint. **1775** (1962) Romans *Nat. Hist. FL* 150, A hole is cut in the tree on the side most exposed to the solar rays . . . This hole is called a box, and the turpentine is dipped out of it. **1859** Perry *Turpentine Farming* 41 **NC,** Many of the pines had but one box cut in them, and these were found to fill their boxes better, with less chipping, than any others. **1903** *Evening Post* (New York NY) 1 June 7/1, The "box system" of orcharding [in the turpentine industry], which has hitherto been almost exclusively pursued, starts with the cutting of the boxes. These are cavities 14 inches wide, 7 inches deep, and 3½ inches from front to back, hewn into the base of a tree by a long, narrow axe. **1938** Daniels *Southerner* 316 **GA,** But Dr. Herty in those days was already teaching the South to use the less destructive cups in place of the old box system in collecting the crude turpentine from the scarred pine trees. **1968** *DARE* Tape **GA22,** [FW:] Can you tell me how you gathered the turpentine? [Inf:] Well, I chipped the boxes and let the gum run out in the box and then I dipped it out in a bucket.

2 also attrib: A stringed musical instrument, esp a guitar or banjo. **Sth, S Midl**

 1928 Peterkin *Scarlet Sister Mary* 56 **SC,** June's box had gone crazy, its soft wailing had changed into chords that twanged out hot and wild. **1935** Hurston *Mules & Men* 87 **FL,** The guitars cried out . . instrumental hits with no name, that still are played by all good box pickers. **1939** *AmSp* 14.89 **csTN,** *Box knocker.* Banjo player. 'Beesley's a first-rate box knocker.' **1942** (1965) Parrish *Slave Songs* 16 **GA coast,** Now and then a fiddle, "box" (guitar), mouth-organ, or jew's harp is heard in rural districts. **1952** Brown *NC Folkl.* 1.522, *Box . . .* A stringed musical instrument, generally a guitar. c**1960** *Wilson Coll.* **csKY,** *Box . . .* Guitar. "Joe can surely play on his box." **1967** *DARE* FW Addit **nwSC,** *Box*—The name for a musical instrument with a 'box' and strings, such as a guitar, banjo, fiddle.

3 A coffin. **chiefly Sth, S Midl**

 1899 (1912) Green *VA Folk-Speech,* Box . . . A coffin. **1930** Faulkner *As I Lay Dying* 2 **MS,** Addie Bundren could not want a better one, a better box to lie in. **1937** *Hall Coll.* **eTN,** Graves in Cades Cove are four feet deep, or three feet down to the box. **1943** *LANE* Map 524, *Coffin . . .* [1 Inf] [bɒks], jocular term. **1953** Randolph *Down in Holler* 229 **Ozarks,** *Box . . .* Coffin. A washerwoman at Galena, Mo., disapproved of my white shirts. "I'd rather see my box a-comin' as to iron these here shirts!" **1954** *Harder Coll.* **cwTN,** *Box . . .* Coffin. c**1960** *Wilson Coll.* **csKY,** *Box . . .* Coffin. "He'll never do any such thing until he is in his box." **1965–66** *DARE* (Qu. BB59, *The box that a body is put into for burial;* total Infs questioned, 75) Infs **FL36, MS15,** 59, **OK7,** 18, (Rough) box.

4 See quots.

 1950 *PADS* 14.16 **SC,** *Box . . .* A tin or can with its contents. "A box of salmon." . . "Fish box," a can of salmon, etc. c**1960** *Wilson Coll.* **csKY,** *Box . . .* Tin can. "Ed made away with a whole box of salmon."

5 Fig—usu in combs:

a used to represent a person having a particular trait. Cf **budget 3, funbox, fussbox, pot** n

 1871 Eggleston *Hoosier Schoolmaster* 99 **IN,** Yes, I war too, you little sass-box! **1965–70** *DARE* (Qu. HH7a, *Someone who talks too much or too loud*) 87 Infs, **widespread,** Chatterbox; **KS7,** Blabber-box; **NC7,** Brag-box; **GA72,** Clatter-box; **ID5, IL50, MN42,** Jabber-box; **MN2,** Noise-box; **WY3,** Noisy-box; **GA77,** Tattle-box; (Qu. II36a, *Somebody who talks back or gives rude answers*) 51 Infs, **widespread,** Sass-box; 9 Infs, **Sauce-box; AL33,** Sassy-box; (Qu. GG14, . . *Someone who fusses*) 11 Infs, **chiefly Mid, S Atl,** Fuss-box; **MS21, SC3, SD2,** Worry-box; (Qu. GG16) Inf **NC82,** Old fuss-box, grouch-box; (Qu. GG32b, *To . . play . . jokes on people: "He's an awful _____."*) Inf **KY40,** Joke-box; (Qu. GG36a, *The kind of person who is always poking into other people's affairs*) Infs **PA66, VA46,** Nose-box; **NC82, VA46,** Meddle(some)-box; (Qu. GG38, *Somebody . . mean and bad tempered*) Infs **GA3,** 82, Grouch-box; (Qu. HH11a, b, *Someone who is . . fussy*) Infs **GA6,** 84, **MD47, MA30, PA13, SC26, TX74,** Fuss-box.

b used to represent a part of the body characterized as having particular attributes or functions.

1916 *DN* 4.330 **KS**, Think-thank . . . Brain. Also *think tank, think box.* **1942** Berrey–Van den Bark *Amer. Slang* 121.10, Stomach . . . Feed box. *Ibid* 121.38, *Female pudendum* . . . Hot box. *Ibid* 121.56, *Head* . . . Knowledge box, . . phrenology box. *Ibid* 121.57, *Skull* . . . Bone box. *Ibid* 121.66, *Mouth* . . . Bone box, box of ivories, . . gob box, . . grub trap *or* box, . . ivory box, . . prattle box, . . talk box. **1951** *New Yorker* 12 May 32/2, First crack outa Don's box is 'What is with you, Sonny?' **1966–70** *DARE* (Qu. X8, . . *Organs inside the body*) Inf **MA30**, Think box = brain; (Qu. X9, . . *A person's mouth*) Inf **GA72**, Gossip box; **GA77**, Dental box; **IL19**, Box; (Qu. X14, . . *The nose*) Infs **IN56, WI57**, Snot box; (Qu. X28, . . *A person's head*) Inf **DC13**, Box; **GA72**, Think box; (Qu. X35, . . *The part of the body you sit on*) Inf **NC30**, Box; **PA76**, Fart box; **TN50**, Thunder box; (Qu. X53a, . . *An oversize stomach*) Inf **GA17**, Bread box. **1970** Major *Afro–Amer. Slang*, Dream box: the human head. **1976** Hobbs *Tisha* 85 **AK**, "Been goin' around with 'is hat off too long. Froze 'is brain box."

6 See **boxes 1.**

box v[1], hence vbl n *boxing* esp **S Atl** Cf **blaze, box n 1, corner v 1**

To cut a hole in the trunk of a tree usu to obtain turpentine.

1700 *Springfield Rec.* 2.357 **MA** *(DA)*, No Stranger . . shal box any trees or Improve the sam for Turpintine. **1737** (1911) Brickell *Nat. Hist. NC* 265, *Negroes* cut large Cavities on each side of the *Pitch-Pine* Tree (which they term *Boxing* of the Tree) wherein the *Turpentine* runs. **1889** (1971) Farmer *Americanisms*, *Box* . . . A technical term, signifying, in North Carolina, a large bowl-like incision made in gum-bearing or resinous trees for the purpose of collecting the exuding sap. This operation is known as "boxing a tree." **1903** *DN* 2.307 se**MO**, *Box* . . . To cut a block out of a standing tree. This is often done to ascertain the quality of the timber. **1944** Barbour *Vanishing Eden* 79 **FL**, This, of course, is not the case where the trees have been "boxed" for turpentine. **1967** *DARE* Tape **AL20**, [FW:] What do you call it when you tap a tree for turpentine? [Inf:] Boxin'.

box v[2], hence *boxing* vbl n **chiefly Sth, S Midl**

To hit with the hand or fist.

1899 (1912) Green *VA Folk-Speech*, *Box* . . . To strike on the side of the face with the open hand. "Box his jaws." **1965–70** *DARE* (Qu. Y14a, *To hit somebody hard with the fist*) Infs **SC7, 64, 66**, Box; (Qu. Y14b, *To hit somebody with the open hand*) Infs **KY51, NY130, OK28, 42, WV2**, Box. **1980** *DARE* File ne**TX** (as of c1930), Spanking = a good boxing.

box-ankled adj Also *box-ankle, boxed-ankled* **chiefly Sth** *freq derog*

See quot 1950.

1919 *DN* 5.70 **NM**, *Box-ankled* hound, a term of disparagement. "That box-ankled hound has the tickets." **c1937** in 1972 *Amer. Slave* 2.231 **SC**, I see so many knock-knee, box-ankle, spindly-shank, flat nose chillun, when I was growin' up. **1950** *PADS* 14.16 **SC**, *Box-ankled* . . . Having a conformation of legs and feet so that in walking the ankle bones are supposed to strike together. Often used in vituperation, *e.g.*: "You freckle-faced, knock-kneed, box-ankled son of a gun." **c1960** Wilson *Coll.* cs**KY**, *Box-ankled* . . . With ankles striking together; used also as a term of disgust. **1966–70** *DARE* (Qu. X37, . . *Words . . to describe people's legs if they're noticeably bent, or uneven, or not right*) Inf **DC11**, Boxed-ankled; **MS16**, Box-ankled; (Qu. X38, . . *Big or clumsy feet*) Inf **LA6**, Box-ankle—this is used of somebody who has flat arches and large ankles; **SC55**, Box-ankle [laughter]. [3 of 4 Infs Black]

box around v phr [Naut *box about* to sail changing directions often; see *OED* box v.[1] 12, 13]

To play around, move about idly.

1967 Fetterman *Stinking Creek* 133 se**KY**, Some Sundays I got things to do. Run the dogs. Go to the head of the holler and box around with a friend . . . We just cut up and talk.

box back n Also *box (hair) cut*

1965–70 *DARE* (Qu. X5, . . *Kinds of men's haircuts*) Infs **AL6, 19, MS60, PA24, 26, TX106**, Box back; **HI8, PA94**, Box cut; **HI9, NJ21**, Box (haircut).

box ball n **chiefly NYC**

An outdoor ball game; see quot 1937.

1937 (1947) Bancroft *Games* 477, *Box ball* . . differs from Hand Tennis only in the ball used and the absence of net and foul lines . . . The server

stands behind his end line and bounces a handball, driving it with a stroke of the open hand so that it goes over the line into the opponent's court. The receiver . . drives it back with the open hand, either after it has bounced or . . on the fly. **1968** *DARE* (Qu. EE33, . . *Outdoor games*) Inf **NY119**, Box ball. **1968** *DARE* Tape **NY118**, There was also box ball, which was played only with two boxes, sort of like tennis or ping-pong but without a net but with boxes. **1975** *DARE* File **NYC** (as of c1925), *Box ball* . . a form of handball in which the players faced each other in a game similar to tennis—but without a net—and hit a rubber ball back and forth in a "court" formed by the more-or-less standard 4-foot-square concrete pavement outlines, the seam between them serving as the "net" beyond which the player must hit the ball. **1977** *New York Times* (NY) 6 July 29/3 **NYC**, Box ball—street tennis, using the much-loved pink rubber "spaldeen,"—is still box ball and 21 points still win.

box barn n Cf **box house**

1968–69 *DARE* (Qu. M1, . . *Kinds of barns*) Infs **KY39, MO9**, Box barn(s).

boxberry n

1 A **wintergreen 2** (here: *Gaultheria procumbens*).

1706 in 1889 Plymouth **MA** *Records* 1.26, Thirty six acres of land . . bounded by a stake in the range of said Cooks land in boxberry swamp. **1802** *MA Hist. Soc. Coll.* 1st ser 8.197, The bushes are whortleberries, . . bay-berries, and box-berries. **1873** in 1976 Miller *Shaker Herbs* 254, *Gaultheria procumbens* . . Box-Berry. **1951** Hough *Singing in Morning* 241 se**MA**, The checkerberry or wintergreen, more often called boxberry by our own people. **1966–67** *DARE* (Qu. I44) Inf **ME1**, Boxberries; **MA72**, Boxberries—similar to chokeberries. **1971** Krochmal *Appalachia Med. Plants* 128, Boxberry. **1975** Gould *ME Lingo*, Boxberry—Maine term for checkerberry . . . The pulpy red berries would elsewhere be called checkerberries, but a boy brought up on a Maine farm will call them *boxberry* plums.

2 =**partridgeberry 1.**

1895 *Jrl. Amer. Folkl.* 5.98 **MA**, *Mitchella repens* . . boxberry. **1900** Lyons *Plant Names* 249, Boxberry.

box bird n Also *box martin*

=**purple martin.**

1956 MA Audubon Soc. *Bulletin* 40.84, *Purple Martin* . . . Box Martin (R.I. From its nesting in boxes erected by man.). **1969** *DARE* (Qu. Q14, . . *Other names . . for . . martin*) Inf **KY53**, Box bird.

box board n, also attrib Also *boxing-board* Cf **box house 1**

=**boxing 1.**

1941 FWP *Guide OK* 94, Boxing-board shacks became common, but they did not entirely replace log buildings. **1956** Ker *Vocab. W. TX* 104, Overlapping boards on [the] outside of [a] house . . . box-boards—low grade pine . . running perpendicular.

box brush n

1971 *Today Show Letters* c**CT**, Box brush . . . Carpet sweeper. Fairly general in Connecticut among my mother-in-law's friends.

box canyon n **West**

A steep-sided, narrow valley closed off at one end by a rock wall or land mass.

1873 Bourke *Diary* 21 Mar **AZ**, We descended into a box cañon on R. and made camp. **1907** White *AZ Nights* 3, We . . followed it into box cañons between rim-rock carved fantastically. **1932** *DN* 6.225 **West**, *Box-canyon*. A word used everywhere for a canyon that runs up against a dead wall, instead of becoming shallower until one gets out on the level. **1939** FWP *Guide MT* 413. **1940** FWP *Guide NM* 110. **1958** McCulloch *Woods Words* **Pacific NW.**

boxcar n

1 A big or clumsy foot. Cf **flatcar 2**

1950 *WELS (Big feet)* 1 Inf, c**WI**, Boxcars. **1965–70** *DARE* (Qu. X38) 18 Infs, **scattered**, Boxcars.

2 See quot.

1967–70 *DARE* (Qu. W42b, . . *Men's square-toed shoes*) Infs **AZ1, GA75, TX32**, Boxcars; **VA42**, Boxcar toed.

3 A large or clumsy person.

1966–70 *DARE* (Qu. X50, . . *A person who is very fat*) Inf **VA42**, A boxcar; (Qu. HH21, *A very awkward, clumsy person*) Inf **MI4**, Boxcar.

4 In marble play: =**boulder.**

1963 *KY Folkl. Rec.* 9.58 ne**KY**, Large marbles . . . box-car. **1966–68** *DARE* (Qu. EE6a, . . *Kinds of marbles—the big one that's used to knock others out of the ring*) Infs **NC22, VA24**, (The) boxcar.

box chin n Cf **box-jawed**
A square or prominent jaw.
 1967 *DARE* (Qu. X6, *If a person's lower jaw sticks out prominently*) Inf TX106, Box chin.

box cooter n Cf **cooter** n
A box turtle, here prob *Terrapene carolina.*
 1950 *PADS* 14.16 **SC**, *Box cooter* . . . The box tortoise. **1966** *DARE* (Qu. P24) Inf **GA**3, Box cooter.

box cut See **box back**

boxed ppl adj Also *boxed out*
Drunk.
 1947 Williams *Streetcar* 132 **LA,** Are you boxed out of your mind? **1968** *DARE* (Qu. DD15, . . *Thoroughly drunk*) Infs **LA**34, 45, Boxed out.

boxed house See **box house**

box elder n
Std: a widely-distributed maple tree *(Acer negundo).* Also called **ash maple, bastard ash 2, black ash 3, boxwood 4, California maple, Canadian maple, cutleaf maple, false maple, Manitoba maple, maple ash, plane tree, red river maple, split-leaf maple, stinking ash, sugar ash, sugar maple, three-leaved maple, water ash**

box-elder bug n Also *box-elder beetle* **chiefly Upper MW, N Cent** See Map
A common grass bug *(Leptocoris trivattatus),* blackish with red markings, which feeds on box elder. Also called **Canadian soldier 2, democrat bug, McKinley bug, populist bug**
 1892 Kellogg *Common Insects KS* 99, Box-elder Bug *(Leptocoris trivittatus)* . . . In winter the bugs frequent houses, and many appear in sunny places on warm days. **1965** Teale *Wandering Through Winter* 202 **IL,** This was a black-and-red box-elder bug hibernating in luxury. **1965–70** *DARE* (Qu. R30, . . *Other kinds of beetles*) 58 Infs, **chiefly Upper MW, N Cent,** Box-elder bug; **MI**108, **MN**36, **WI**8, Box-elder beetle; (Qu. R21) Inf **MI**104, Box-elder bug; (QR, near Qu. R29) Inf **GA**12, Box-elder bug [in list of "other kinds of beetles"]. **1973** Allen *LAUM* 1.328 **NE,** *Box elder bug* is clearly an error despite the inf.'s claim that it is his usual expression for a firefly.

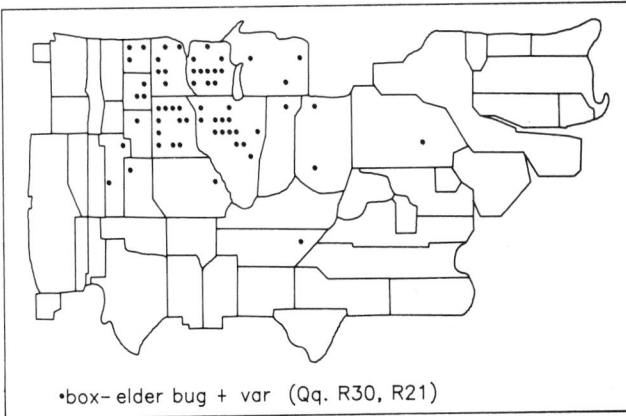

•box- elder bug + var (Qq. R30, R21)

boxes n pl constr as sg
1 also *box, box game:* See quot.
 1965–70 *DARE* (Qu. EE39, . . *Games played on paper by two people*) Infs **DC**12, **MI**114, **NY**89, 107, 144, **TN**55, Boxes; **NC**77, **NY**123, 220, Box; **IL**107, Box game—dots made boxes; **VA**39, Box game—same as dot game.
2 Hopscotch.
 1967 *DARE* (Qu. EE19, *The game in which children mark a "court" on the ground or sidewalk*) Inf **NY**34, Boxes.

box-face n [**box** n 1 + **face** n 4]
A cavity made in a tree trunk for collecting turpentine.
 1969 *DARE* Tape **GA**22, They'd have a face, what they call a box-face.

box fence n
 1968 *DARE* (Qu. L63) Inf **NJ**10, Box fence—a kind of woven fence.

box game See **boxes 1**

box haircut See **box back**

boxhead n
=**squawfish.**
 1902 Jordan–Evermann *Amer. Fishes* 69, *Ptychocheilus oregonensis* . . Other names by which it is known are . . box-head.

box house n
1 also *boxed house:* A small, often poorly constructed house resembling a box; spec a simple frame house whose outer walls are made of vertically placed, unfinished boards or **boxing 1.** **chiefly S Midl, esp Ozarks**
 1881 U.S. Bur. Indian Affairs *Report* 83 **KS,** The school was . . conducted in . . the house formerly used by the agent and some box-houses constructed for the purpose. **1907** *DN* 3.229 **nwAR, seMO,** *Box house.* **1929** *AmSp* 5.17 **Ozarks,** *Box house.* **1936** Barnard *Rider* 161 **OK,** Douthitt had built a house on the west side of the claim, and Sniderwine built a box house on the east side. **1960** Hall *Smoky Mt. Folks* 59, A more modern expression is "boxed house," for a house with outside walls built of vertically set planks, with strips nailed on to cover the cracks between boards. **1966** *DARE* Tape **OK**21, Just a little box house. **1968** *DARE* (Qu. D21, *A small, poorly-built house, or one in rundown condition*) Inf **TX**51, Box house; (Qu. D27, *Strips of wood used to cover the outside of a frame house*) Inf **MO**9, It's a box house.
2 See quots. [*box* a theater box] Cf **box rustler**
 [**1941** FWP *Guide WA* 145 (as of 1876), Washington's first theater . . was of the "box" type: that is, it had a small stage and auditorium and, most important, a row of boxes around the sides, connected with a bar in the rear.] **1951** Morgan *Skid Road* 123 **cwWA,** The box-house was a saloon with a theater attached. The entertainment was rowdy, and the box-houses were restricted to an area where they competed with establishments offering even rougher entertainment.

box huckleberry n Also *box-leaved huckleberry*
A **huckleberry 1** (here: *Gaylussacia brachycera*). Also called **Jerusalem huckleberry, juniper, whortleberry**
 1848 Gray *Manual of Botany* 259, *G. brachycera* . . . *Box-leaved Huckleberry* . . . Leaves in shape and aspect like those of the Box. **1922** *Torreya* 17 **WV,** But when he described it as a blue berry more acid than the common "huckleberry" on pretty green bushes, I suspected that it might be the box huckleberry, *Gaylussacia brachycera.* **1938** (1955) FWP *Guide DE* 12, The site of a single specimen of box huckleberry, for example, was known a dozen years ago . . and a new station has been more recently discovered. **1941** FWP *Guide WV* 19, The box huckleberry, believed to be one of the oldest, if not the oldest, in existence, is found in Summers, Greenbrier, and Monroe Counties. **1966** Grimm *Recognizing Native Shrubs* 235, *Box Huckleberry* . . . *Range.* Delaware and Pennsylvania south to South Carolina and Tennessee.

box hustler See **box rustler**

boxing n **chiefly Sth, S Midl** Cf **box board, box house**
1 Vertical wood siding for houses.
 1941 Smith *Going to God's Country* 105 **MO** (as of 1890), They all got together and put up the fraim [sic] and boxing. For every thing was box houses. **1943** Stuart *Taps* 256 **KY,** In one week we had the framework up, the boxin nailed to the framework, the winders and doors sawed. *Ibid* 257, We had to bat the cracks between the boxin with narrow planks. **1965–70** *DARE* (Qu. D27, *Strips of wood used to cover the outside of a frame house*) Infs **AL**52, **AR**55, **GA**92, **LA**27, **MS**1, 3, **NC**31, 55, **TN**13, 30, **TX**1, 32, **VA**2, Boxing. **1971** Wood *Vocab. Change* 48 **Sth,** Overlapping, milled boards used to form the outer walls of frame houses . . . *Boxing* and *shiplap* are widely volunteered [by informants].
2 See **box** v[1]

boxing vbl n See **box** v[2]

boxing board See **box board**

box iron n *old-fash*
A hollow clothes iron heated inside by a hot piece of iron or live coals.
 1666 in 1888 *Essex Inst. Coll.* 25.147 **MA,** Inventory of Gou[erno]r Endecott household . . . It[em] boxe Iron & heaters. **1720** in 1888 Sewall *Letter-Book* 2.107 **ceMA,** Item a good Box-Iron to Iron with. **1899** (1912) Green *VA Folk-Speech, Box-iron* . . . A hollow smoothing-iron, kept hot by a piece of hot iron put inside called a "heater." Spoken

of as a "box-iron and heater." **1966** *DARE* (Qu. F29, . . *Irons . . for smoothing clothes*) Inf **NC1**, Box iron—use live coals in.

box-jawed adj Cf **box chin**

1967 *DARE* (Qu. X6, *If a person's lower jaw sticks out prominently, you say he's* _____) Inf **AL27**, Box-jawed.

box-leaved huckleberry See **box huckleberry**

box martin See **box bird**

box oak n Also *box white oak*

A **post oak** (here: *Quercus stellata*).

1785 (1925) Washington *Diaries* 2.360 **VA,** These [acorns] grew on a tree resembling the box Oak. **1810** Michaux *Arbres* 1.22 **MD** *(DA),* Post oak, . . Iron Oak, . . Box oak (chêne buis), [ou] Box White-Oak . . dans l'Etat de Maryland. **1897** Sudworth *Arborescent Flora* 154, *Quercus minor* . . . Common Names . . . Box White Oak (R.I.) . . . Box Oak (Md.). **1938** Van Dersal *Native Woody Plants* 346, Box White Oak *(Quercus stellata).* **1968** *DARE* (Qu. T10) Inf **NJ39**, Box oak; **MD13**, Box oak—smaller leaves than white oak.

box, off one's adj phr Also *offen one's box, off of* ~, *out of* ~ [Prob substitution of **box** n 5b in such phrr as *out of one's head* and *off one's rocker* crazy, insane] **chiefly S Midl** *joc, sometimes derog*

Crazy; foolishly mistaken.

1903 *DN* 2.322 **seMO,** *Offen his box* or *off his box* . . . Mistaken. 'If he thinks he can fool me he is offen his box.' **1907** *DN* 3.234 **nwAR,** *Off(en) his box* . . . Mistaken. "Yes, he said so, but he's off his box." **1966–70** *DARE* (Qu. HH6, *Someone who is out of his mind*) Inf **WV12**, Out of his box; (Qu. HH9, *A very silly or light-headed person*) Inf **AR28**, Off her box; (Qu. KK59, . . *To be quite wrong about something: "If he thinks she'll help him, he's* _____ *."*) Infs **AR31, KY85**, Off (of) his box; **IL97**, Out of his box.

box oyster n **CT, NY coast**

See quot 1881.

1881 Ingersoll *Oyster-Industry* 242 **CT, NY,** *Box oyster.* An oyster from seven to ten years old, of round, handsome shape, not less than 3 inches wide and 5 inches long . . . The name is due to the fact that many years ago it was customary to ship oysters of this grade to New York in boxes instead of the ordinary barrel. **1931–33** *LANE Worksheets* **swCT,** *Box oysters* . . . Large oysters; those that are boxed. "A regular oyster basket would hold one hundred and fifty box oysters." **1934** Hanley Disks **swCT,** *Box oyster* . . . Medium-sized oyster. "The next size, the box oysters, would be 150 to a basket." **1941** *LANE* Map 360 **swCT,** The regular oyster basket holds 200 [kʌlɪnz] or 150 [bɑks ɔɪstɹ̩z].

box party n Cf **box supper**

=**box social.**

1939 Harris *Purslane* 257 **NC,** The teacher suggested a box party to raise a little money for baseballs and bats. **1968** *DARE* (Qu. FF1, . . *A kind of group meeting called a "social"*) Infs **PA104, 130**, Box party.

box ravine n Cf **box canyon**

1973 Attwood *Length Maine* 13, *Box ravine*—A rectangular ravine with approximately perpendicular walls of rock.

box rustler n Also *box hustler* [*box* a theater box + *rustler* an energetic, enterprising person] **NW** *hist* See also **box house 2** See quot 1941.

1939 Abbott *We Pointed Them* 95 **ceMT** (as of 1883), In that kind of theaters [sic] they used to have curtained boxes running all around inside, and box rustlers was what they called the girls that worked them. **1941** FWP *Guide WA* 145 (as of 1876), The women did their song and dance on the stage and then, in costumes that . . were considered the extreme of indecency, mingled with the customers in the boxes, encouraging the sale of liquors. The women became known as box-rustlers, and box-rustling theaters sprang up all over the west. **1951** Morgan *Skid Road* 117 **cwWA** (as of c1900), From the curtained box seats in the low balcony came laughter and shouts and giggles and, most important, a steady ringing of bells as the box-hustlers summoned waiters with drinks.

boxshell n

=**box turtle.**

1972 *DARE* File **nwFL,** 2 speakers, Boxshell—land turtle.

box social n Also *box sociable* **chiefly Nth, N Midl, West** See Map Cf **box party, box supper, ice-cream social**

A fund-raising gathering at which boxed meals are auctioned off and then shared by donor and buyer.

1928 *AmSp* 4.130 **NE,** The school house is generally the center for . . "box socials." **1937** Sandoz *Slogum* 236 **NE** (as of 1900–20), There were literaries and box socials and dances among the settlers. **1938** FWP *Guide MN* 6, To raise money for the purchase of books and equipment, they sponsor special programs and "box socials." **1951** *PADS* 15.65 **NH,** *Box sociable* . . . Fund-raising auction at which box lunches prepared by the women were eaten by the donor in company with the man who made the highest bid for her donation. **1965–70** *DARE* (Qu. FF1, . . *A kind of group meeting called a "social"*) 147 Infs, **chiefly Nth, N Midl, West,** Box social; **IA3, IL58, IN13, NY205, 206, 209, PA104, WI5,** Box sociable; (Qu. FF2, . . *Kinds of parties*) Inf **PA71,** Box social. **1967** *East Oregonian* (Pendleton OR) 17 Mar 5/6, Pend-Air Hall; women bring decorated boxes for box social; everyone invited. **1969** *DARE* Tape **CA134,** Box social.

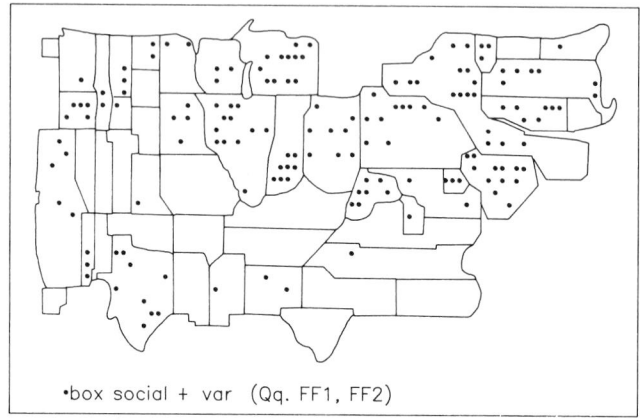

•box social + var (Qq. FF1, FF2)

box steps n pl

1971 *Today Show Letters* **seLA,** Box steps . . . Steps from sidewalk to entrance of a house without a porch.

box stove n **chiefly Nth, N Midl**

A woodburning stove whose shape resembles a box.

1820 *Columbian Centinel. Amer. Federalist* (Boston MA) 1 Jan 3/3 **MA,** Oblong and oval Box Stoves. **1887** (1895) Robinson *Uncle Lisha* 29 **wVT,** The later comers had the choice of seats on a roll of sole leather, the cold box stove, or a board laid across the tub. **1945** *Chicago Daily Tribune* (IL) 18 Nov 7.1/5 **AR,** Low unpainted benches stood in three rows with a woodburning box stove in the middle. **1950** *WELS* (*Stoves used for heating houses*) 1 Inf, **swWI,** Box stove—wood burning. **1967** *DARE* Tape **OR3,** I've sit there many a time 'n' propped my feet up around that old box wood stove there with a railing around it, to warm my feet when I was a kid. **1968** *DARE* FW Addit **cNY,** Box stove . . . Long cast iron, wood stove, rectangular in shape.

box-stretcher See **stretcher**

box supper n **chiefly W Midl, TX** See Map Cf **ice-cream supper**

=**box social.**

1934 *Sun* (Baltimore MD) 15 Feb 19/7 **AL** *(Hench Coll.),* The box suppers are the favorite social affairs of the countryside. Belles of the

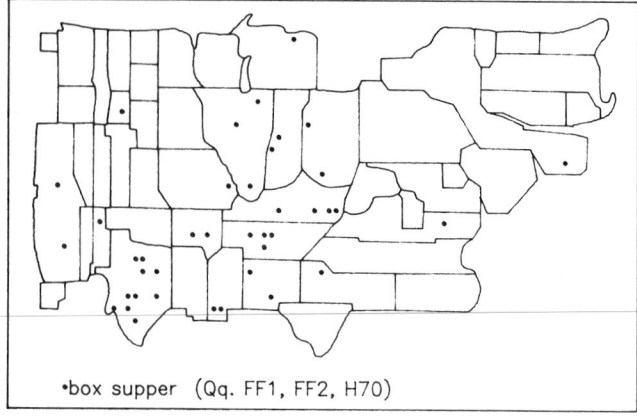

•box supper (Qq. FF1, FF2, H70)

community prepare boxes of choice edibles which are auctioned . . . The highest bidder's reward is eating with the girl of his choice. Churches and schools in need of funds usually sponsor the suppers. **1942** Warnick *Garrett Co. MD* (as of 1900–1918), *Box-supper, . .* an event for raising church or other funds by auctioning box lunches donated by the women of the community. **1942** Perry *Texas* 113, The box suppers by which church funds were raised. **1965–70** *DARE* (Qu. FF1, . . *A kind of group meeting called a "social"*) 37 Infs, **chiefly W Midl, TX**, Box supper; (Qu. FF2, . . *Kinds of parties*) Infs **KY5, MI4**, Box supper; (Qu. H70, *When people bring baked dishes, salads, and so forth to a meeting-place and share them together, that's a _____*) Inf **IL49**, Box supper. **1967** *DARE* Tape IL23, Box suppers . . . we use to have 'em.

box teeth n pl
1967 *DARE* (Qu. X13b, . . *False teeth*) Inf **PA14**, Box teeth.

box terrapin n
=**box turtle.**
1966–68 *DARE* (Qu. P14) Inf **MD45**, Box terrapin; (Qu. P24) Infs **DE3, FL9, GA28, MD36**, Box terrapin; **MD24**, Box terrapin—stays on land, doesn't go in water.

box tortoise n
=**box turtle.**
1839 MA *Zool. & Bot. Surv. Fishes Reptiles* 214, From the circumstance of the sternum being divided into two portions, . . enabling the animal when disturbed, to encase itself entirely within its shell, the species is generally known under the name of *"box tortoise."* **1908** *Biol. Soc. Washington DC Proc.* 21.89 **AR**, *Terrapene carolina triunguis . . .* Box tortoise. **1967** *DARE* (Qu. P24) Inf **TN11**, Box tortoise.

box turtle n
A small terrestrial turtle *(Terrapene carolina)* with a hinged plastron and a keeled, high-domed carapace. Also called **box cooter, boxshell, box terrapin, box tortoise, cooter n 2, cow-dung cooter**
1965–70 *DARE* (Qu. P24) 112 Infs, **widespread, esp east of Rocky Mts**, Box turtle.

box up the dough v phr
Among loggers: to cook.
1907 *DN* 3.241 **eME**, *Box up the dough . . .* To cook. Woodsmen's slang. Not common. **1969** Sorden *Lumberjack Lingo* **NEng, Gt Lakes**, *Box up the dough*—To cook.

box white oak See box oak

box with five nails n Also *box with (two) handles* [Punning *box* a buffet, blow (cf **box** v²) + punning *nails* fingernails] *joc*
A blow with the hand.
1908 *DN* 3.293 **eAL, wGA**, *Box with two (or more) handles (to it) . . .* A facetious way of refusing a request. "Give me some of that candy." "I'll give you a box with four handles to it if you don't go on away from here," i.e., "I'll give you four cuffs or blows over the head." **1912** *DN* 3.571 **wIN**, *Box with five little nails in it . . .* A blow with the hand. A half serious way of refusing a request for a box of something. "Give me the rest of that box of popcorn." "I'll give you a box with five little nails in it, right along the side of the head; that's what I'll give you." **1927** *AmSp* 2.349 **WV**, *Box with five red nails . .* a slap with the open hand. "I will give you a box with five red nails."

boxwood n, also attrib Cf false box 2, Florida boxwood, Oregon boxwood
1 Std: an evergreen plant of the genus *Buxus.*
2 The flowering **dogwood** *(Cornus florida).*
1832 Browne *Sylva* 141, In the United States at large, it is known by the name of *Dogwood*, and in Connecticut it is also called *Box Wood.* **1897** Sudworth *Arborescent Flora* 308, *Cornus florida . . . Common Names . . .* Boxwood (Conn., R.I., N.Y., Miss., Mich., Ky., Ind. . .). **1907** *DN* 3.182 **seNH**, *Box-wood . . . Cornus florida*; known in Arkansas as *dog-wood.* **1979** Little *Checklist U.S. Trees* 97, *Flowering dogwood . . . Other common names*—dogwood, cornel, boxwood.
3 =**Florida boxwood 1.**
1884 Sargent *Forests of N. Amer.* 39, *Schaefferia frutescens, . .* Yellow wood, Box wood. **1933** Small *Manual SE Flora* 820, *S. frutescens . . . Boxwood . . .* It is sometimes used as a substitute for boxwood in engraving. **1971** Craighead *Trees S. FL* 199, Boxwood . . *Schaefferia frutescens.*
4 =**box elder.**

1965–70 *DARE* (Qu. T13, . . *Other names . . for . . box elder*) Infs **AL30, GA70, MI79, NC16, PA202, VA105**, Boxwood; **OR4**, Boxwood?—square-leafed; **CT28**, Boxwood?; **MD26**, Boxwood [FW: Inf unsure if this is [the] same thing—small bush-like tree with small leaves, brown flowers in spring].

‡**5** =**linden.**
1970 *DARE* (Qu. T13, . . *Other names . . for . . linden*) Inf **PA234**, Boxwood.

boy n
1 Formerly a slave or servant; now sometimes used of a Black adult male—usu considered insulting when the speaker is White. **chiefly Sth, S Midl** *decreasing currency*
1764 in 1904 Jefferson *Writings* 4.15 **VA**, You mention one [=letter] which you wrote last Friday, and sent by the Secretary's boy. **1835** (1906) Bradley *Jrl.* 229 **MS**, He informs me . . that every negro, or boy as they call them, will cultivate ten acres of cotton. **1888** *Harper's Mag.* 76.705/2 **GA**, I will defend this boy. I know nothing whatever of the case, but I happen to know something of the negro. **1907** *DN* 3.229 **nwAR, swMO**. **1952** Hughes *Laughing* 12 **MO**, "Don't call me *boy*," said the Negro. "I'm as old as you, if not older." **1969** *DARE* FW Addit **KY65**, Boy plus first name is used to address an adult Negro man. Becoming old-fashioned, but is still used. **1971** Bright *Word Geog. CA & NV* 115 [Black], [A Negro] Boy . . . The informant disliked all such terms of contempt.
2 also *boy bone*: A wishbone.
1949 *AmSp* 24.106 **cnGA**, *Boy-bone . . .* Wishbone. **1971** *Wood Vocab. Change* 375 **Sth**, *(The) boy . .* bone from a chicken breast.
3 One's husband. *joc*
c**1960** Wilson *Coll.* **csKY**, *Boy . . .* Nickname for husband. **1969** *DARE* (Qu. AA23, *Joking names a woman may use to refer to her husband:* "*It's time to go and get supper for my _____.*") Inf **IL78**, Boy.
4 See quot.
1952 Brown *NC Folkl.* 1.522, *Boys . . .* The rebounding raindrops after they hit the surface.—A child's word. Obsolescent(?).

boy and girl's pants n
=**Dutchman's breeches 1.**
1967 *Good Old Days* Feb 29 **MI**, Recall going into the woods in the spring of the year . . . Gathering . . boy and girl's pants, Jack-in-the-pulpit, cow slips, atter [sic] tongues.

‡boy dog n
1968 *DARE* (Qu. R15b, . . *An extra-big mosquito*) Inf **IN42**, Boy dog.

‡boy drownder n
1968 *DARE* (Qu. O2, . . *An old, clumsy boat*) Inf **NJ21**, Boy drownder—an unsafe old boat.

boyfriend n chiefly Nth *somewhat old-fash*
In var phrr: see quots.
1968–69 *DARE* (Qu. W24a, . . *Expressions . . to warn a woman slyly that her slip is showing*) Inf **MI93**, Your boyfriend is thinking of you; **NJ45**, You're losing your boyfriend; **NY111**, You've got a boyfriend. **1969** *DARE* FW Addit **ceNY**, *Got your boyfriend*—When skirt is turned up accidentally just a little, this is said as a sly warning. **1976** *DARE* File **cMA** (as of c1920), I knew the phrase *your beau,* (or *(best) fella, boyfriend) is thinking of you* which meant that your skirt was turned up at some point—"cocked up," we said.

boy lice n [Transl of Ger *Bube* boy; see **bube lice**]
=**beggar ticks 1.**
1967–68 *DARE* (Qu. S13, . . *A common wild bush with . . round, prickly seeds*) Inf **OH82**, Boy lice; (Qu. S14, . . *Prickly seeds, small and flat, with two prongs at one end, that cling to clothing*) Inf **OH82**, Boy lice; **PA44**, Bube lice, boy lice—lice that sticks to boys.

boyou See booya

boys exclam chiefly NEast
Used as an exclam of pleasure or strong feeling.
1965–66 *DARE* FW Addit **cnME**, *Boys*—narrative punctuation, similar to "boy," "man," etc; **ME22**, *Boys*—used like *boy* even when addressing one person. "Boys, was that a trip." **1967–68** *DARE* (Qu. X47) Inf **NY65**, Oh boys, am I tired; (Qu. NN6a, *Exclamations of joy*) Inf **NY14**, Oh boys.

boys-and-girls n Cf girls-and-boys
1 =**Dutchman's breeches 1.**

1859 (1942) Patterson *Travel Diary* 106 **IL,** I saw . . the modest "Boys and Girls" tufting the slopes of a timbered ravine [near Omaha NE]. **1893** *Jrl. Amer. Folkl.* 6.137, *Dicentra cucullaria* . . boys and girls. N.Y. **1951** Voss – Eifert *IL Wild Flowers* 5, Dutchman's Breeches (Boys and Girls. Snowboys). **1968 – 70** *DARE* (Qq. S26c, e) Inf **MI**96, Boys-and-girls; **PA**234, Boys-and-girls—white flower with slim pants and some with skirts. Dutchman's britches [are] like [the] girls in boys-and-girls; **WI**78, Boys-and-girls—looks like orchid—always two on single stem—3″ high or less.

2 A euphorbiaceous plant (*Mercurialis annua*).

1950 Gray – Fernald *Manual of Botany* 961, *Boys-and-Girls*.—Weak erect, leafy-stemmed annual.

3 A **hound's tongue 2.**

1891 Victor *Atlantis Arisen* 225 **NW,** "Boys and girls" (*Cynoglossum*), pink and blue on the same stem.

boy's ax n

1958 McCulloch *Woods Words* **Pacific NW,** *Boy's ax*—A small or light ax; also used as a term of contempt for any tool too small to do a job properly.

boy's britches n

1 The kernel of a walnut.

1940 in 1968 Haun *Hawk's Done Gone* 42 **eTN,** He made us crack walnuts and pick out the kernels for him. One time he got . . mad at Amy because she didn't get the boy's britches out whole.

2 See **little boy's breeches.**

boysie n Also sp *boyzee* Cf **-ie** suff **3**

A boy, brother.

1894 *DN* 1.328 **NJ,** *Boyzee:* boy; as, "when I was a boyzee." **1906** *DN* 3.128 **neAR,** *Boysie* . . . Dear boy. **1950** *WELS* (*Affectionate words meaning brother*) 1 Inf, **seWI,** Boysie.

boy's-love n Also *lad's love* [Engl dial: cf *EDD; OED* 1863 →]

Either of two related plants: absinthe (*Artemisia absinthium*) or **southernwood.**

1876 Hobbs *Bot. Hdbk.* 15, Boys' love, Southernwood, Artemisia abrotanum. *Ibid* 62, Lads' love, Southernwood, Artemisia abrotanum. **1883** *Century Illustr. Mag.* 4.959/1, Whosoe'er I first do meet / With the Boy's-Love in my shoe, / He's the one I'm sure to wed. **1887** Freeman *Humble Romance* 25 **NEng,** Boys'-love, sweet-williams, and pinks were the fashionable and prevailing flowers. **1892** *Jrl. Amer. Folkl.* 5.99, *Artemisia abrotanum,* boy's love; lad's love. Various parts of New England . . . Names apparently given from supposed aphrodisiac qualities, or because used in love divinations. **1894** *Ibid* 7.91, *Artemisia Absinthium,* . . boys' love, Wellfleet, Mass. **1934** Harned *Wild Flowers Alleghanies* 594, *Artemisia Absinthium* . . . is variously known under the . . names . . Mugwort, and Boy's love.

bozal See bosal

bozo n [Etym uncert] esp Nth, N Midl *somewhat derog*

1 A fellow, guy.

1920 *Collier's* 11 Dec 5/3 **NYC,** He picks out the most glarin' weaknesses . . of the other bozo. **1926** *AmSp* 1.293 **NYC,** He lets on he croaks a bozo, when it was actually done by a dancin' hophead. **1929** *AmSp* 4.338 [Hobo lingo], Bozo—A man. **1932** *AmSp* 7.329 **MD,** [Johns Hopkins jargon] *Bozo*—a fellow. **c1960** *Wilson Coll.* **csKY,** *Bozo* . . . Some "feller" whose name you may not know or wish to know. **1978** *Sat. Review* 22 July 51/3 **NYC,** All you've got to do is tell the big bozo [=waiter] standing there what it is you want.

2 A dull-witted person, lout.

1930 *AmSp* 5.239 **NY,** [Colgate University slang] *Bozo:* a large crude individual. "Is that bozo from your school?" **1934** in 1950 Chandler *Art of Murder* 57 **CA,** Drive the heap, bozo. **1966 – 69** *DARE* (Qu. HH1, . . *A rustic or countrified person*) Inf **MI**4, Bozo; (Qu. HH3, *A dull and stupid person*) Inf **PA**214, Bozo.

bra See brother A6

brace v

1 To ask for money or other support, esp in a demanding way.

1889 (1971) Farmer *Americanisms, Brace* . . . To get credit by swagger. **1923** Watts *Luther Nichols* 269 **Chicago IL,** I haven't quite the cheek to brace you for board and lodging both. **1927** *DN* 5.440 [Underworld jargon], *Brace* . . . To request a loan. **1935** *AmSp* 10.12, *To Brace.* To beg.

2 By ext: to lend money.

1966 *DARE* (Qu. U16, . . "*I need five dollars before Saturday, will you _____ it to me?*") Inf **FL**16, Brace.

brace n

1 A metal piece fastened to the bottom of a shoe to prevent slipping or wear. **esp SW** *esp among Black speakers* Cf **brad** n² **1**

1965 – 70 *DARE* (Qu. W12a) Infs **MO**8, **VA**2, Braces; **OK**1, Heel braces; (Qu. W12b) Infs **NM**9, **OK**13, Braces; **TX**106, Toe braces. [3 of 6 Infs Black]

‡**2** See quot.

1950 *WELS Suppl.,* Brace—a coat hanger. Used by inf who grew up in Louisiana and whose family was from Indiana. A regularly used word in the family.

bracero n |ˌbrɑ'sɛro, ˌbrɑ-, -ə| [Span *bracero* one with strong arms, hence, a laborer] chiefly SW

Orig a Mexican admitted to the US for seasonal agricultural work; now more widely, any Mexican laborer in the US.

1959 *Wall St. Jrl.* (NYC) Eastern ed. 13 Feb 9/1 – 2 (*Hench Coll.*), Up for renewal is the Migrant Labor Agreement of 1951 . . . under which nearly 500,000 Mexican braceros ("arm men") enter the U.S. each year for seasonal agricultural work. **1962** Atwood *Vocab. TX* 73, *Person of Mexican origin* . . . Other nouns of less frequency are *Peon,* . . and *Bracero.* **1966** *DARE* File **csWA,** Backbone of hop growing and many others of the Yakima Valley's agricultural industries is the bracero, the Mexican worker. **1967 – 69** *DARE* (Qu. L1, *A man who is employed to help with work on a farm*) Inf **CA**10, [brɑ'sɛrouz]; [they] come from Mexico on a limited visa; **TX**5, Bracero; (Qu. HH18) Inf **CA**169, Bracero; (Qu. HH28) Inf **CA**66, Bracero—a national (came legally from Mexico); **CA**169, **TX**10, Bracero. **1967** *DARE* Tape **TX**10, Since the government has cut off the braceros [brə'sɛrəz] from comin' over from Mexico, we don't have enough labor; **TX**31, Braceros, Mexican laborers. **1970** Tarpley *Blinky* 259 **neTX.** **1971** Bright *Word Geog. CA & NV* 103, Bracero—migratory worker.

braces n pl Also *bracers* chiefly Nth, N Midl See Map Cf gallus 1

Suspenders.

1909 *DN* 3.408 **ME,** Braces . . . Suspenders. **1941** *LANE* Map 363 (*Suspenders*) **chiefly eNEng,** Braces. [Several infs note that braces have more straps than suspenders, usually one across the back and sometimes one under the arms.] **1944** Nute *Lake Superior* 210, Trousers—sustained by what were variously known as braces, suspenders or galluses. **1950** *WELS* (*What does a man wear over his shoulders to hold up his trousers?*) 6 Infs, **WI,** Braces. **c1960** *Wilson Coll.* **csKY,** *Braces* . . . Suspenders. A citified, uppity word; ordinarily *galluses* is used. **1966 – 70** *DARE* (Qu. W7) 30 Infs, **chiefly Nth, N Midl,** Braces; **NY**35, Bracers.

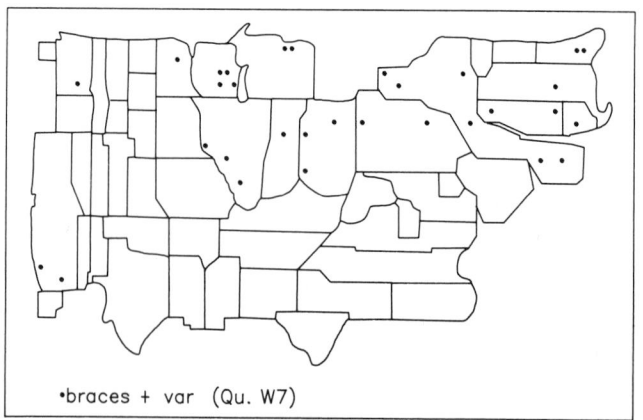

•braces + var (Qu. W7)

brace up v phr [*brace* to form a pair + *up* (*OED* adv 21)]

c1900 in 1974 *AmSp* 49.61 **seME,** Brace up . . . Get married.

brack n [Prob Scots form of *break* n] chiefly NEng *old-fash*

A tear or flaw, usu in fabric.

1816 Pickering *Vocab.* 51, *Brack* . . . This old English word is still used *colloquially* in many parts of *New England,* where it is commonly applied to a breach or flaw in a piece of cloth. **1871** (1882) Stowe *Fireside Stories* 59 **MA,** There warn't a brack in his silk stockin's. **1890**

AN&Q 5.143/1, When I was a child, living in New England, the word "brack" was used to describe a small thin place in wearing apparel . . . Many a time I have been told "there is a 'brack' which must be darned or mended immediately or it will become a hole." **1899** (1912) Green *VA Folk-Speech, Brack* . . . A break; a crack; a flaw. "Without a brack or a crack." **1905** *DN* 3.4 cCT, *Brack* . . . A break or flaw.

bracken fern See **brake** n[1]

bracket n Also *bracket sheldrake*
Either of two ducks: esp the common **merganser** but also the **red-breasted merganser.**
 1888 Trumbull *Names of Birds* 65, [Common Merganser] At Stonington, Conn., *Bracket Sheldrake,* or *Bracket* simply. **1923** U.S. Dept. Ag. *Misc. Circular* 13.4 *American Merganser . . . Vernacular Names . . . In local use* . . . Bracket, bracket sheldrake (Conn.). **1955** *MA Audubon* 39.378, *American Merganser* . . . Bracket (Conn. Meaning unknown.); Bracket Sheldrake (Mass., Conn.). *Ibid* 379, *Red-breasted Merganser.* Bracket (Conn. Meaning unknown.).

brackish adj
 1909 *S. Atl. Qrly.* 8.44 seSC [Gullah], *Brackish* is used to mean slightly flavored, sweetish, sourish; not salty.

‡**bracky wagon** n [Perh from *break* a four-wheeled, straight-bodied wagon]
A horse-drawn carriage.
 1969 *DARE* (Qu. N41a, *. . Horse-drawn vehicles . . used around here . . to carry people*) Inf IN74, Bracky wagon.

brad n[1] See **bread** n A

brad n[2]
1 A metal piece fastened to the bottom of a shoe to prevent wear. S Atl *among Black speakers* Cf **brace** n 1, cap n[1] 10
 1966–70 *DARE* (Qu. W12b) Infs FL48, 51, NC87, SC10, 26, 68, 70, Brads; SC26, Heel brads, toe brads. [All Infs Black]
2 See quot.
 1902 *DN* 2.229 sIL, *Brad* . . . A rivet. Never used for a small nail.
3 See quot.
 1950 *WELS* (*Sharp pointed stick used to get oxen to move*) 3 Infs, seWI, Brad.

brad v [**brad** n[2] 2]
See quot 1902.
 1902 *DN* 2.229 sIL, *Brad* . . . To rivet. **1907** *DN* 3.220 nwAR, *Brad.*

brade See **bread** n A

brad wurst See **bratwurst**

braes n [Fr *braise* charcoal]
 1894 *DN* 1.328 NJ, *Braes:* burned and charred wood in a charcoal pit.

brag adj Also *bragging* **chiefly Sth, Midl** Cf **braggable**
Excellent or superlative; worth bragging about.
 1838 *Jeffersonian* 5 May 1.96/1 OH, Moselle was a new *brag* boat, and had recently made several exceedingly quick trips. **1893** Twain *£1000000* 159 MO, I remember the brag run of a steamer which I traveled in once on the Pacific—it was two hundred and nine miles in twenty-four hours. **1942** Perry *Texas* 64, A ranch of 100,000 acres is by no means from a quantitative standpoint, "a braggin' ranch." A 300,000-acre ranch is a little more respectable. **1952** Brown *NC Folkl.* 1.522, *Brag cotton* (corn, tobacco, etc.) . . . Prize cotton (etc.); that on which the owner brags.—Central and east. **1953** Randolph *Down in Holler* 229 Ozarks, *Brag dog* . . . Favorite, pride, pet. "Jim had lots of hounds, but old Biggy was always his *brag dog*." Used figuratively of children, pupils, and friends. I once heard a fox hunter in Joplin, Mo., refer to his mistress as "the *brag bitch*." **1969** Sorden *Lumberjack Lingo* NEng, Gt Lakes, *Brag load*—An extremely large load or record load of logs on a sleigh. Often loaded especially for a photograph.

‡**brag** v
Std sense, var form. [On analogy of *drug* dragged]
Past: usu *bragged;* also *brug* |brʌg|.
 1968 *DARE* FW Addit seGA, Brug [brʌg]—past tense of *brag.* Heard in conversation.

brag n
1 A boast. Cf **make one's brags**
 c1900 in 1974 *AmSp* 49.61 sME, *Brags* . . . Boasts "He said his brags."

1945 Le Sueur *North Star Country* 248 MN, WI (as of 1850s), The many tough, roaring, hard-working, and fast-living men "cut their brag in the bark": I'm the toughest goldarned alligator [=lumber raft crewman] in the North Woods.
2 often in combs: A braggart. **chiefly east of Missip R** See Map
 1950 *WELS* (*A show-off: "He is such a _____."*) 2 Infs, WI, Brag. **1965–70** *DARE* (Qu. HH8, *A person who likes to brag*) 18 Infs, **scattered east of Missip R,** (Big) Brag; GA28, Brag-pot; MS21, Brag-hard; MO25, Brag-ass; NC1, Brag-about; NC7, Brag-box; PA130, Brag-head; (Qu. HH7a, *Someone who talks too much, or too loud*) Infs IL61, MN2, VA11, Brag; NC7, Brag-box; (Qu. II35, *A person who . . knows everything*) Inf MO25, Brag; NY224, Big brag.

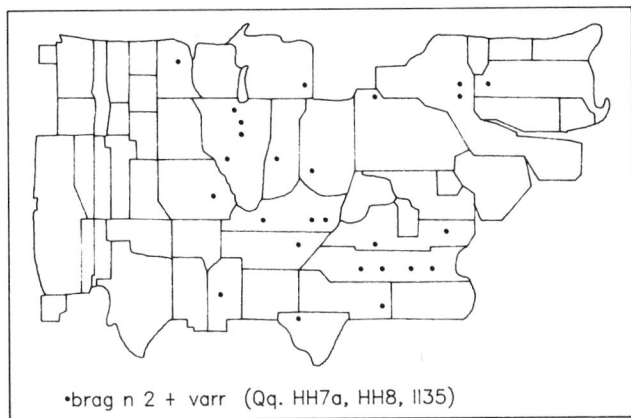
•brag n 2 + varr (Qq. HH7a, HH8, II35)

braggable adj Cf **brag** adj, *EDD* braggable
Fit to be boasted about.
 1960 Williams *Walk Egypt* 202 GA, "How you all making out?" . . . She satisfied them. "Nothing braggable."

braggadocious adj
Boastful.
 1954 *Sun* (Baltimore MD) 26 Feb [Editorial] B3 *(Hench Coll.),* Billy began his sermon . . . I haven't come to tell you in a braggadocious way about the United States. **1966–70** *DARE* (Qu. HH8, *A person who likes to brag*) Infs FL52, GA19, KY78, LA17, NM12, NV7, Braggadocious.

braggadoe n [From **braggadoshe**]
One who brags.
 1967 *DARE* (Qu. HH8, *A person who likes to brag*) Infs OR3, 14, 15, Braggadoe.

braggadoshe n Also *braggadosha, braggadoshoo* [From *braggadocio* braggart, boaster] See also **braggadoe**
One who brags.
 1965–70 *DARE* (Qu. HH8, *A person who likes to brag*) 16 Infs, **scattered, but esp NEast, Cent,** Braggadoshe; AR55, TX31, Braggadosha [ˌbrægəˈdo(ʊ)šə]; MO39, Braggadoshoo [ˌbrægəˈdoʊšuˑu]; (Qu. II35) Inf IA17, Braggadoshe.

bragging See **brag** adj

braggy adj
Boastful.
 1956 Gipson *Old Yeller* 30 TX, We heard the second bull . . . His bellering was just as loud and braggy as the first one's. **1983** *NADS Letters* TX, "Braggy" was common in Houston . . in the 1930's and '40's. I can still remember the expression, "Well! You don't have to be so 'braggy' about it!" *Ibid* cIL, My wife and I . . grew up in central Illinois . . and have heard and used the word [=braggy] for as long as we can remember. We've lived in . . Lower Alabama for about eight years, and I don't think the natives here use it . . [Example:] . . . "She's too braggy for me."

braggy n [**braggy** adj]
A braggart—used as a nickname.
 1934 (1970) Wilson *Backwoods Amer.*67 Ozarks, There are frequent substantives [derived from adjectives] like old *braggy* and little *hatefuls.* **1954** *Harder Coll.* cwTN, *Braggy*—An excessively boastful person. "He's old braggy."

brag on v phr **chiefly Midl**

To praise or boast about someone or something.

1850 (1869) Watson *Camp-Fires* 49 **MA**, It would have been somethin' to brag on, I know. **1898** Westcott *Harum* 191 **cNY**, "You have been very generous all through, Mr. Harum." "Nothin' to brag on," he replied. **1932** *Sun* (Baltimore MD) 3 Oct 8/3 *(Hench Coll.)*, If we had the money, darned if we wouldn't all the time go so people would brag on us more. **1942** (1971) Campbell *Cloud-Walking* 28 **seKY**, Preaching Jim Speaks never done chopping and heaving logs enough to brag on. **1965–70** *DARE* (Qu. HH8) Infs **MO**8, 38, **OH**72, 80, 90, **OK**13, 18, **TN**30, **TX**42, (He) brags on himself. **1967** Green *Horse Tradin'* 208 **TX**, He bragged on how big and how pretty my horses were. **1967** *DARE* Tape **SC**34, Somebody 'ud brag on it; **LA**2, I ain't . . bragging on 'em. **c1974** Jones *Ozark Hill Boy* 53 **AR** (as of c1930), I bragged on all the kids and dogs and he invited me in.

brag the potatoes v phr Also *count one's potatoes*

1928 Ruppenthal *Coll.* **KS**, *Count one's potatoes* . . . To say grace at table. **1949** *PADS* 11.12, *Talk to (one's) plate* . . . To say grace before meals. One of my Oregon friends reports the use of *brag the potatoes* in the same sense.

brag up v phr Cf **brag on**

To praise or commend lavishly.

1885 Howells *Rise Lapham* 13 **NEng**, I ain't a-going to brag up my paint. **1942** (1971) Campbell *Cloud-Walking* 74 **seKY**, The Little Teacher bragged to Sary how good it was to stay in such a pretty house. Sary wished the Biggest Teacher would brag up her house, too. **1950** (1965) Richter *Town* 248 **OH**, Most every time his paper came, it bragged up the railroad. **1952** Bissell *Monongahela* 141 **PA**, This was written about 1870, in one of those volumes bragging up the local industries.

brail n, v [ME *brayle* girdle, strap]

In logging: see quots 1881, 1905.

1879 *Lumberman's Gaz.* 1 Oct *(OED)*, This part of the Slough is wide and deep, and is used for coupling up the strings into brails and rafts. **1881** T.B. Walker *Letter* 4 June *(DA)*, A brail of logs is a crib of loose logs surrounded by a boom of longer ones whose ends are fastened together . . . Three or four brails are put side by side and fastened together to form a raft and towed by steam tugs. **1905** U.S. Forest Serv. *Bulletin* 61.31 **Gt Lakes**, *Brail, v.* To fasten logs in brails. *Brail, n.* A section of a log raft, six of which make an average tow. **1969** Sorden *Lumberjack Lingo* **NEng, Gt Lakes**, *Brail*—A boom filled with logs ready to be towed; a section of a log raft . . . The brail was developed by W.J. Young of Wisconsin in 1875.

brain box n Also *brain cage,* ~ *wagon* [See quot 1953] *joc*

A railroad caboose.

1945 Beebe *Highball* 219, The modern streamlined brain cages of the Lehigh Valley are in reality small mobile apartments with electric iceboxes and sponge rubber mattresses on their berths. [**1953** Botkin *Treas. Railroad Folkl.* 297, A smoke-maker [engineer] and his "brains," as we ironically called the conductor.] **1977** Adams *Lang. Railroader* 19, *Brain box:* A private car. A caboose. *Brain cage:* A caboose, so called because the conductor rides in it . . . *Brain wagon:* A caboose.

brain mushroom n

Perh a cauliflower fungus (*Sparassis radicata*).

1967 *DARE* FW Addit **neOR**, Brain mushroom—convoluted like a brain. Common.

braish See **brush** n, v[1] **A3**

brake v See **break** v **A2, 3**

brake n[1] Also *bracken fern, brake* ~

A tall fern, usu of the genus *Pteridium.* Also called **fiddlehead, fiddleneck, fiddlesticks, pasture brake**

1748 in 1934 Eliot *Field Husbandry* 10 **CT**, The lower part next the Salt Marsh is Rushes, the next are Reeds, then large Brakes and Bushes. **1880** Eastman *Poems* 150 **VT**, Half covered by the wild woodbine / And scented by the brake. **1894** *DN* 1.340 **wCT**, *Brake:* fern of any kind. **1919** *DN* 5.54 **NW**, *Brakes* . . . Bracken. Getting the streets and vacant lots cleared of weeds, thistles and brakes. **1930** Shoemaker *1300 Words* 2 **cPA Mts** (as of c1900), The sweet fern or brake, the young shoots in the spring are eaten as "greens" like asparagus. **1967–70** *DARE* (Qu. S26a, c) Inf **MA**5, Brake; **CT**26, Brake—large fern; **NY**75, Ferns or brakes; (Qu. I28b, *Kinds of greens that are cooked*) Inf **MA**15, Brakes—same as fiddlesticks; (Qu. L8) Inf **MA**74, Brakes—a kind of fern. **1969** *DARE*

Tape **NY**223, We used to call 'em brake . . they're a bright green and quite fine fern. **1974** (1977) Coon *Useful Plants* 199, *Pteridium aquilium*—Bracken fern, brake fern.

brake n[2], also attrib Also sp *break* [ME *-brake,* akin to OE *brecan* to break]

A thicket, esp of a single kind of vegetation; the land, often low and wet, on which such thickets grow. **chiefly Sth, S Midl, TX** Used alone or in combs, as:

a *brake.*

1657 in 1940 *AmSp* 15.158/2 **VA**, About 90 poles to the second marked Tree by the brake. **1757** in 1841 Drake *Tragedies Wilderness* 176 **ceNY**, I threw myself into a break, and lay for some minutes apparently at the last gasp. **1852** Reynolds *Pioneer Hist. IL* 195, The cane grew so thick and strong [along the Ohio River] that man, or beast, could scarcely penetrate it. These were called brakes. **1853** Hammett *Stray Yankee in TX* 55, A wolf skin, or the nearest palmetto brake, furnishes him with a hat. **1933** *AmSp* 8.1.48 **Ozarks**, *Brake* . . . A thicket, usually of cedar trees. **1945** Saxon *Gumbo Ya-Ya* 563 **LA**, Brake cane: wild cane. **1956** Ker *Vocab. W. TX* 89, *Waste land* . . brakes. **1967–68** *DARE* (Qu. C7, . . *Land that usually has some standing water with trees or bushes growing in it*) Infs **LA**15, **TX**37, Brake; (Qq. T1, T2a) Inf **LA**3, Brake. **1971** Detro *Generic Terms* 213, In Louisiana, the term "brake" signifies . . thicket . . primarily when applied to canebrakes. The meaning of the term was extended to signify large trees and . . signified a low wet area with cypress or gum trees, a meaning synonymous with the dominant connotation of swamp.

b *canebrake.*

1770 *SC Gaz. & Country Jrl.* 18 Oct 5, There is a large Neck, or Island, of Swamp or Cane-Brake Land. **1810** Cuming *Sketches* 157 **KY**, He said that the whole country was then an entire cane brake, which sometimes grew to forty feet high. **1836** (1935) Holley *Texas* 62, Indian corn . . is commonly obtained from the prairie cane-brake lands the first year, when there is no time to prepare the land with the plough, by merely making a hole for the seed with the hoe. **1876** *IL Dept. Ag. Trans. for 1875* 13.311, Cane-brakes were found in which buffalo, deer, horses and other animals were completely housed and sheltered, and I may add fed, during the winter storms. **1883** Smith *Report for 1881 & 1882* 472 **AL**, The chief crops in the Canebrake are cotton and corn. **1944** *AmSp* 19.443 **TX**. **1972** Hilliard *Hog Meat* 34, Supplementing this forage were the "canebrakes," dense patches of cane that occurred along many of the rivers and smaller streams of the South, especially in Alabama and Mississippi.

c *cedar brake.*

1830 in 1858 Dewees *Letters TX* 124, The night was very dark, and our course lay over mountains of rock and through cedar brake. **1889** (1971) Farmer *Americanisms* 131, The *cedar swamps* of the South, unlike the mere swampy marshes of the North, are low-lying grounds mainly under water; these are also called *cedar brakes.* **1909** Porter *Options* 137 **TX**, Across the river were a dozen little mountains densely covered by cedar-brakes. **1939** FWP *Guide MT* 413, *Cedar breaks*— Broken land overgrown with scrub cedar. **1954** *True* June 68/1 **nwTX**, The Palo Duro is filled with dense cedar brakes, mesquite jungles and blackbrush thickets.

d *cypress brake* (also abbr *cypress*).

1843 (1969) Lewis *Odd Leaves* 108 **LA**, I . . suddenly awakened and found myself lost—the road having given out in a cypress brake. **1853** Hammett *Stray Yankee in TX* 56, Below us was a *"marais"* or slough, which, according to my friend Joe's account, changed into a "branch:" then after running through a cypress brake or two, ultimately assumed the form of a palmetto swamp, and in that guise joined the river. **1891** (1900) French *Otto* 169 **AR**, They had agreed to meet "an' talk 'bout things" that afternoon, at a lonely spot in the cypress brake. **1901** Mohr *Plant Life AL* 46, In the paludial forest . . the cypress (*Taxodium distichum*) forms in the so-called cypress brakes the most imposing feature. **1903** *DN* 2.311 **seMO**, *Cypress* . . . A group of cypress trees; a cypress brake. 'He lives just beyond the big cypress.' **1907** *DN* 3.230 **nwAR**.

brake n[3] See **break** n[1] **2, 3**

brake n[4] [*OED* brake sb.[6] cage, framework] **Sth**

1 also *cow brake:* A cow pen.

1949 Kurath *Word Geog.* 55/1, In Delamarvia and on Albemarle Sound *(cow) pound* still predominates, and in a belt directly west of the *pound* area on Albemarle Sound one hears *cow brake* (from the James to the Neuse). *Ibid* Fig 61, *Brake* or *cow brake.* **1971** Wood *Vocab.*

Change 47/1 **AL, GA, TN,** *Cow brake, cow pound, cuppin,* and *farm lot* are chosen more often east of the Mississippi than west of it. [5 instances of *cow brake* from approx 1000 infs]

2 A stanchion.

1966–70 *DARE* (Qu. M11, *What do you put the cow's head through when she stands in the barn?*) Infs **AL2, FL20, 37, GA7, MS87, NC15, SC7,** Brake.

brake fern See **brake** n[1]

bramble scythe n Also *bramble blade,* ~ *saw, brambling scythe* **Delmarva** *old-fash*

A tool for cutting underbrush.

1899 (1912) Green *VA Folk-Speech,* Bramble-saw . . . A saw the use of which is undetermined. "Cross-cut bramble-saw." **1933** *Sun* (Baltimore MD) 3 Mar 4/5 *(Hench Coll.),* The complete list as recorded at the sale was as follows: One wagon 50 cents; 1 truck wagon, 25 cents . . . 2 bramble blades, 10 cents. **1968** *DARE* (Qu. L35) Inf **DE3,** Brambling scythe—for small bushes, same shape as mowing scythe but much shorter blade; **MD20,** ['bræml] scythe—stick with sharp blade swung around, used to trim near fence; (Qu. L37) Inf **MD42,** Bramble blade— same as scythe. [All Infs old]

brambling vbl n

The act of clearing an area of brush and undergrowth.

1937 *Sun* (Baltimore MD) 5 May 6/1 *(Hench Coll.),* These men will be used throughout the rural county on different projects . . such as clearing the right of way of bushes and overhanging limbs, brambling and opening side drains. **1966** *DARE* File **ME,** Brambling—a general clean-up of weeds, brush, etc., usually done in August.

‡bramboo brier n

=**greenbrier.**

1950 *PADS* 14.16 **SC,** Bramboo briar . . . The *bamboo* briar.

branch n, also attrib

1 A small stream. **chiefly Sth, S Midl** See Map

[**1624** Smith *Genl. Hist. VA* 23, Here doth the river divide it selfe into 3 or 4 convenient branches.] **1663** in 1886 NC *Colonial Rec.* 1.20, That Parcell of land lying and being on ye same Neck, Begining at a small creek or Branch. **1746** *London Mag. & Mth. Chronologer* 15.327 **GA,** We pass'd several Branches and Savannahs. [Footnote:] A *Branch* is a Stream running across the Road, from some neighbouring Creek or River. **1844** Thompson *Major Jones's Courtship* 46 **GA,** I jest tuck hold of the gentleman and pitched him neck and heels rite into the branch.

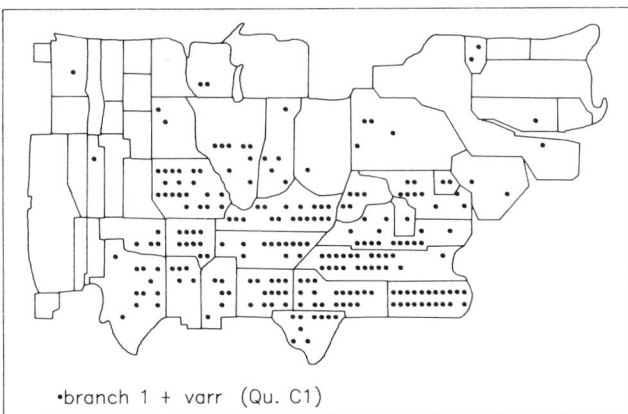

•branch 1 + varr (Qu. C1)

1870 U.S. Dept. Ag. *Rept. of Secy. for 1869* 270 **GA,** The soil was "branch land," (creek bottom,) black mud or muck swamp, five feet deep, containing a mixture of sand. **1902** *DN* 2.229 **sIL. 1903** *DN* 2.307 **seMO. 1905** *DN* 3.71 **nwAR. 1908** *DN* 3.293 **eAL, wGA. 1911** *DN* 3.537 **eKY. 1912** *DN* 3.571 **wIN. 1923** *DN* 5.202 **swMO. 1938** Matschat *Suwannee R.* 141 **nFL, sGA,** Swamp fowkses sing a little rhyme about that branch crick runnin' back of the island. **1946** *Harder Coll.* **cwTN,** I stretched net wire fence from the branch run back to the cow lot fence. **1950** *WELS* (*Name for a small stream of water not big enough to be a river*) 6 Infs, **WI,** Branch. **1965–70** *DARE* (Qu. C1, *. . A small stream of water not big enough to be a river*) 226 Infs, **chiefly Sth, S Midl,** Branch; 8 Infs, **Sth, S Midl,** Spring branch; **GA4,** Branch head; **CT14,** Branch stream; **MO37,** Small branch.

2 See quot.

1942 Footner *MD Main* 36, In Maryland speech "branch" is an inlet from tidewater while "run" is the running stream that empties into it.

3 =**bayou 3.**

1965–70 *DARE* (Qu. C6, *A piece of land that's often wet and has grass and weeds growing on it*) Inf **GA3,** Branch; (Qu. C7, *Land that usually has some standing water with trees or bushes*) Inf **DE4,** Branch; (Qu. C14, *A stretch of still water going off to the side from a river or lake*) 9 Infs, **scattered,** Branch; **NY24,** Branch stream.

branch bird n

=**wood thrush 1.**

1962 Imhof *AL Birds* 402, Wood Thrush. Hylocichla mustelina . . . Other names: Brown Thrush, Swamp Sparrow, Branch Bird.

branch chub n Also *branch minnow*

Prob a creek chub.

1966–69 *DARE* (Qu. P7) Inf **KY43,** Branch chubs; **AL2, KY68,** Branch minnow; **KY43,** Branch [mɪnɚz].

branch herring n

An **alewife** (here: *Alosa pseudoharengus*).

1884 Goode *Fisheries U.S.* 1.580, C[lupea] vernalis is known along the Potomac River as the 'Branch' Herring. **1943** Carson *Food from Sea* 16, The first runs of alewives reach the streams of the Massachusetts Bay area in early April and the Maine streams later in the month or about the first of May. These are the true alewives (Pomolobus pseudoharengus), called also "branch herrings." **1976** Warner *Beautiful Swimmers* 127, The river or branch herring . . will ascend far up the rivers to the smallest creeks or branches, passing from the sea world to the shady forests and tumbling rills of the piedmont.

branch lettuce n

A **golden saxifrage** (here: *Chrysosplenium americanum*).

1951 *PADS* 15.12 **nwNC,** Chrysosplenium americanum Schweinitz.— Branch lettuce. **1953** *PADS* 19.9 **wNC,** Branch lettuce . . . A wild plant that grows in certain areas of the mountains of North Carolina. It is a saxifrage (Chrysosplenium americanus). Some of the natives eat it as one ordinarily eats lettuce, but the majority "wilt" . . it. **1966** *DARE* (Qu. BB50d, *Favorite spring tonics*) Inf **NC30,** Ramps (wild onions), branch lettuce, . . sassafras tea.

branch maple n

Perh =**silver maple.**

1968 *DARE* (Qu. T14) Inf **DE3,** Branch maple—grow down in wet places and have a smooth bark, light in color; **DE5,** Branch maple—they grow down in the swamp, the branch; **MD34,** Branch [maple]; **MD42,** Branch [maple]—smaller leaf than [sugar maple].

branch minnow See **branch chub**

branch oak n

Perh a **pin oak.**

1968 *DARE* (Qu. T10) Inf **MD15,** Branch oak—many knots, many small limbs.

branch pike n

Prob the **redfin pickerel.**

1968 *DARE* FW Addit Inf **DE3,** Branch pike = smaller than regular ones—live in small streams. [FW: From Inf's descriptions, *pike* refers to chain pickerel and *branch pike* to one of its smaller cousins, perhaps the grass pickerel.]

branch rabbit n

Prob a **marsh rabbit.**

1966–70 *DARE* (Qu. P30, *. . Wild rabbits around here*) Inf **GA7,** Branch rabbit—dark brown, white rabbit; **NC87,** Branch rabbit—bigger than a cottontail. Cottontail—highland rabbit, as opposed to branch rabbit, which hangs out down by the low land, or water.

branch sparrow n

Perh **wood thrush 1.**

1968 *DARE* (Qu. Q21) Inf **DE3,** Branch sparrow—lives down on branches (small streams).

branch water n [**branch** n 1] **chiefly Sth, S Midl**

1 Water from a stream (rather than from a well).

1836 (1934) Ford *Summer* 291 **VA,** What a contrast between these dreams of happiness and the reality of sleeping rolled up in a blanket upon a bear-skin at night and eating bull buffalo, drinking warm branch water, and riding a hard trotting horse by day. **1859** (1968) Bartlett

Americanisms, "*Branch*-water" is distinguished from "well-water."
1902 *DN* 2.235 **sIL**. **1905** *DN* 3.71 **nwAR**, *Branch-water* . . . Common. **1934** (1970) Wilson *Backwoods Amer.* 154 **AR, MO,** They were accustomed to wash their clothes in branch water, they made their own soap. **1943** Peattie *Great Smokies* 117 **eTN, wNC,** If it is branch water they drink, it must come from some stream running in laurel and rock. **1947** Guthrie *Big Sky* 368 **KY** (as of 1840s), Just straight meat and branch water, that's what he wants. **1953** Randolph *Down in Holler* 230 **Ozarks,** *Branch water folks* are people who camp anywhere and drink surface water; regularly settled hillfolk live near a well or spring.

2 Transf: any weak beverage, esp coffee.

c**1960** *Wilson Coll.* **csKY,** *Branch-water* . . . Something trifling, or weak, . . e.g. weak coffee. **1966–69** *DARE* (Qu. H74b, . . *Coffee . . very weak*) Infs **GA85, NC3, 11, 20, TX52,** Branch water; [**FL8, KY25, 37, MO15, NC23,** Weak as branch water; **VA9,** I just as soon go to the branch and get me a drink of branch water; **OK9,** Tastes like it swum the branch]; (Qu. KK61) Inf **PA35,** Branch water and barefoot—an old term.

3 Plain water (as opposed to soda water).

1968 *DARE* (Qu. DD21a) Inf **GA59,** Bourbon and branch water. **1977** *Yankee* Nov 58 **ME,** There is the joy of coming in out of the cold to a warm fire, the easing out of boots with the prospect of being revivified with good whiskey and branch water.

bran dance n old-fash

A dance or dancing party on a surface that is sprinkled with bran.

1833 *Sketches D. Crockett* 148 **wTN,** This is the famous bran dance of the west, and derives its name from the fact that the ground is generally sprinkled with the husk of Indian meal. **1883** (1972) McDowell *Dialect Tales* 152 **Sth,** They're goin' to have a bran dance to-morrer over in the settle*ment.* [*Ibid* 155, We found the dancers in a rustic arbor . . . Floor there was none save the smooth earth covered three inches deep with wheat-bran. Slightly dampened, it was pleasant to dance on; but Heaven preserve them when they danced it dry.] c**1960** *Wilson Coll.* **csKY,** *Bran-dance*—An old-fashioned solo dance, done on an open space at the country store or on a barn door [sic] properly sprinkled with bran or sand.

brand artist n West Cf brand blotter

One skilled in altering the brands on stolen cattle.

1934 *Denver Post* (CO) 4 Aug 10/4 *(DA),* Another tradition credits him [Samuel Maverick] with being a 'brand artist' of little scruple. **1968** Adams *Western Words, Brand artist*—A rustler; a man expert at changing brands. **1977** Watts *Dict. Old West* 50, A *brand artist* could create an effective imitation of an established brand with a cinch-ring heated in a fire and held with the tips of two sticks, or he could deftly alter an existing brand to one more to his own liking: a camp cook's pot-hook was used on more than one occasion.

brand blotter n Also brand blotcher and vbl n brand blotting West Cf brand burner

One who illegally alters a cattle brand.

1910 Raine *B. O'Conner* 107 *(DA),* Move, you red-haided son of a brand blotter, and I'll pump holes in you! **1939** FWP *Guide MT* 413, *Brand blotting*—Making a brand indistinct and alterable by applying heat through a wet sack or blanket. **1940** FWP *Guide NM* 110, *Brand-blotter*—A person who illegally alters a brand. **1968** Adams *Western Words, Brand blotter* . . . Also called *brand blotcher.* **1977** Watts *Dict. Old West* 50, In the states in which a man could be arrested for carrying a running-iron tied to his saddle, the brand blotter merely resorted to carrying a short one in his boot-top, slicker, or maybe his *warbag* [sack for personal belongings].

brand burner n Also vbl n brand burning West
=brand blotter.

1926 Branch *Cowboy* 118, Brand-burning was the altering of brands so that owners, if they found their stolen cattle, had no proof by which they could identify them. **1931** (1960) Dobie *Open Range* 304 [Glossary], *Brand burner.* A cow thief who mutilates brands in order to destroy the legitimate owner's claim. **1968** Adams *Western Words, Brand blotter* . . . Also called . . *brand burner.*

branded in the hide adj phr

Uncompromising in principle; dyed-in-the-wool.

1965 Guthrie *Blue Hen's Chick* 240 **MT,** He was a Republican, true-blue, branded-in-the-hide, right-wing Republican, doctrinal fellow of Hoover and Goldwater.

brand-fire-new adj phr Also bran-fire-new, bran(d)-fired-new [Blend of brand-new + fire-new] chiefly S Midl

Completely new and unused.

1825 Neal *Brother Jonathan* 1.151 **CT,** Bran-fire noo, as I'm alive! **1834** Crockett *Narrative* 72 **TN,** I returned, and set out electioneering, which was a bran-fire new business to me. **1911** *DN* 3.537 **eKY,** *Bran-fired* . . . Very; used only before 'new'; e.g., "His hat is bran-fired new." **1915** *DN* 4.181 **swVA,** *Bran fire new* . . . Absolutely new. **1940** Stuart *Trees of Heaven* 246 **neKY,** I might get your old furniture since you's gittin brand-fired new furniture. **1950** *PADS* 13.22 **sKY,** *Brand-new, brand-fire-new* . . are all fairly common. **1966** *Wilson Coll.* **csKY,** That's a bran-fire new one to me. **1968** Haun *Hawk's Done Gone* 349 **eTN,** She was . . all dyked out in a brand-fired new dress—blue silk—bought just for the show off.

brand goose See brant 1

brand-spanking-new adj phr Also bran ~; for addit varr see quots
=brand-fire-new.

1806 *Weekly Inspector* 1.65 **NY,** A *bran-span,* excellent *new* word, as we Yankies would say. **1905** *DN* 3.60 **eNE,** *Bran new*. . . Variants are . . *bran spankin' new, bran span new, bran spandy new, spinking spanking bran new, bran spick span new. Ibid* 71 **nwAR,** *Bran spankin' new* . . . Absolutely new. Common. **1908** *DN* 3.293 **eAL, wGA,** *Bran-spankin(g)-new.* **1939** Hench *Coll.,* The wife of a Univ[ersity of] V[irgini]a colleague (originally from Waterville, N.Y.) spoke of a dress as being "brand span new." She used the word several times, always thus. **1941** *AmSp* 16.21 **sIN,** *Brand-spang new.* **1943** *AmSp* 18.66 **SC,** *Brand-spankin'* (not *spang*) *new.* **1951** *PADS* 15.65 **cwNH,** *Bran spankin' new.* **1952** Brown *NC Folkl.* 1.522, *Brand-spank-firing new* . . . Brand new.

brand-splinter-new adj phr Also bran ~; for addit varr see quots [Blend of brand-new + splinter-new]
=brand-fire-new.

1905 *DN* 3.60 **eNE,** *Bran new* . . . Variants are *bran splinder new, bran splinter-fired new, bran splinter clean new.* **1919** *DN* 5.54 **WA,** *Bran-splinter new.* C.H. Olson of Kelso drove through Kalama on his way home from Portland, Wednesday, in a *bran-splinter new* Studebaker Six. Kalama Bulletin. **1942** McAtee *Dial. Grant Co. IN* (as of 1890s), *Brand-splinter-new.* **1982** Barrick *Coll.* **sePA,** Brand splinter new—common intensifier.

brandy bottle n

A **spatterdock** (here: *Nuphar luteum*).

1910 Graves *Flowering Plants* 183 **CT,** *Nuphar advena* . . . *Spatterdock* . . . Brandy Bottle. **1931** Clute *Common Plants* 43, The . . yellow pond lily . . are spatterdocks. Another name . . is brandy-bottle in allusion to the thick squat seed-vessels.

brandywine cowslip n [Prob ref to Brandywine River]
=Virginia bluebells.

1937 Lincoln *Wilmington DE* 147 (as of early 1800s), In the spring the children went a-Maying on the meadows which then extended from Orange to West streets and between Second and Third. They gathered the wild honey-suckle, the blood-root, May-apple and violet, as well as the . . Brandywine cow-slip (*Mertensia Virginica*). **1946** Tatnall *Flora DE* 217, *Virginia* (or *Brandywine*) *Cowslip.* Common in alluvial soil in the Piedmont area.

brandywine lily n

A **dogtooth violet** (here: *Erythronium albidum*).

1897 *KS Univ. Qrly.* 6.52, *Easter-bells:* Easter-lilies, . . Brandywine lily . . . (Erythronium albidum).

bran-fire(d)-new See brand-fire-new

brang See bring

brank v, adj [?From blink v 1]

To turn sour; sour.

1966 *Wilson Coll.* **csKY,** *Branking* . . . Said of milk. **1983** *DARE* File **csKY,** I recall a cousin from that area using *brank* for milk which was 'blinky,' or 'blue' (though 'blue' milk usually meant milk from which all butterfat had been extracted—today's popular lo-fat beverage). In those days, the late 'forties, blue milk was more likely than other varieties to go blinky or 'brank'; I recall the giggles over her use of the inappropriate term, used in the collocation 'to go _____'.

branle v [*branle* a dance < Fr *branler* to shake, agitate]

1967 Cerello *Dakota Co. MN* 46, *Branle*... To dance vigorously about in pairs. Father always accompanied us to dances to keep us from branling about with the young swains... They branled all over the floor as everyone looked on... We were never allowed to branle about with boys at dances.

branle n [Fr *branler* to swing as a pendulum]

A hammock-like cradle.

1894 Chopin *Bayou Folk* 197 **LA,** So away they [the family] all went. All but Bibine, who was left swinging in his branle... This branle consisted of a strong circular piece of cloth, securely but slackly fastened to a large, stout hoop suspended by three light cords to a hook in a rafter of the gallery.

bran-meal coffee n

A coffee substitute: see quot.

1959 Lomax *Rainbow Sign* 90 **AL,** Mama made me some bran-meal coffee. We didn't have no real coffee, but she sift meal and she parch it dark brown and put it in a bucket and pour boilin' water over it, put the lid on it, let it stand for a while, and that was our coffee.

brannigan n *old-fash*

1 A drinking bout, a bender; a state of drunkenness; a spree.

1927 *New Republic* 9 Mar 72 [List of expressions for *drunk*], On a brannigan. **1928** *Amer. Mercury* 14.100/1, He may seek escape by going on prolonged.. crossword puzzle brannigans. **1940** Mencken *Happy Days* 270 **cnMD,** In the intervals of his washing and polishing Jim took out rigs to the homes of clients of the stable, and thereby sometimes acquired quiet brannigans, for it was the custom to reward him, not with money, but with drinks. **1943** (1945) Smith *Life Putty Knife* 165 **NYC,** This party was a stag dinner and brannigan. **1968** *DARE* FW Addit **nePA,** When you are partly drunk, you have a brannigan. Common.

2 also *bronnigan, Jim Brannigan:* A disagreement or fight.

1941 *AmSp* 16.70, On a brannigan [*AmSp:* I have seen this word used as meaning *in a fight*]. **1951** in 1960 Wentworth–Flexner *Slang,* Wave after wave of ugly vituperation [in Congress]... Republicans and Democrats alike are guilty of this branigan [sic]. **1967–70** *DARE* (Qu. Y12a, *A fight.. mostly with words*) Inf **CA15,** Brannigin; (Qu. Y12b, *A real fight in which blows are struck*) Inf **CA173,** Brannigan; **NY166,** Jim Brannigin; **CA201,** Regular bronnigan. [All Infs old]

bran sack n **NEast** *old-fash* Cf **gunny sack**

A burlap bag.

1967–70 *DARE* (Qu. F19, *A cloth container for grain*) Infs **MA5, NY213,** Bran sack; (Qu. F20, *A cloth container for feed*) Infs **NJ56, NY75, 213, 233,** Bran sack; (Qu. F23, *A container made of rough, loosely woven, brown cloth*) Infs **NJ56, VT8,** Bran sack. [6 of 7 Infs old]

bran-span(dy)-new, bran-spanking-new, bran-spick-span-new See **brand-spanking-new**

bran-splinder-new, bran-splinter(-fired)-new See **brand-splinter-new**

brant n

1 also *brand goose, brant goose, brent goose:* Any of var geese, such as the American brant *(Branta bernicla)* which is also called **clatter goose, light-bellied brant, quink, white-bellied brant.**

1612 Smith *Map VA* 15, In winter there are great plenty of Swans, Craynes.. Herons, Geese, Brants, [etc]. **1672** Josselyn *New-Englands Rarities* 9, There are three kinds; the *Gray Goose,* the *White Goose,* and the *Brant.* **1888** Trumbull *Names of Birds* 6, *Branta bernicla...* Brant: Brent: Brant Goose: Brent Goose: Brand Goose: Common Brant. **1899** Garland *Boy Life* 55 **IA,** Many brant and geese also passed, and it was always a great pleasure to Lincoln to see these noble birds pushing their way boldly into the north. **1950** *WELS (Kinds of wild geese)* 6 Infs, **WI,** Brant. **1967** *Calhoun Times* (St. Matthews SC) 31 Aug 4/4, The goose and brant season will be from November 6 to January 13.

2 also *sea brant:* =**white-winged scoter.**

1888 Trumbull *Names of Birds* 99, *Oidemia deglandi..* to some at Portsmouth, N.H., Sea Brant. **1917** (1923) *Birds Amer.* 1.150, *White-winged scoter—Oidemia deglandi...* Sea Brant. **1955** *MA Audubon* 39.376, *White-winged scoter...* Brant (Mass. This term may allude to the bird's large size, for a duck.).. Sea Brant (N.H....).

brant-bird n

1 also *brant snipe:* =**ruddy turnstone.**

1844 DeKay *Zool. NY* 2.216, *The Turnstone...* It is known among our

gunners (a class of men who earn a livelihood by shooting birds) under the names of *Brant-bird..* and *Beach-bird.* **1888** Trumbull *Names of Birds* 186, *Arenaria interpres...* On Long Island at Shinnecock Bay, Moriches, Bellport, and Seaford, *Brant-Snipe* and *Brant-Bird.* **1917** (1923) *Birds Amer.* 1.268, *Ruddy Turnstone—Arenaria interpres morinella...* Other Names... Brant-bird. **1955** *MA Audubon* 39.446, *Ruddy Turnstone...* Brant Bird (Mass., R.I.).

2 also *brant snipe:* =**red-backed sandpiper.**

1888 Trumbull *Names of Birds* 181, *Tringa alpina pacifica..* in New Jersey at Barnegat and Tuckerton, *Brant-Snipe;* and at Atlantic City, *Brant-Bird.* **1917** (1923) *Birds Amer.* 1.237, *Red-backed Sandpiper—Pelidna alpina sakhalina...* Other Names... Brant-bird. **1955** *MA Audubon* 39.19, *Red-backed Sandpiper...* Brant Bird, Brant Snipe (Mass. From a fancied association with the Brant Goose.).

3 Either the **Hudsonian godwit** or the **marbled godwit.**

1888 Trumbull *Names of Birds* 205, *Limosa fedoa...* Maynard, in Birds of Eastern Massachusetts, 1870, records... *Brant-Bird. Ibid* 208, *Limosa haemastica... Brant-Bird.* **1917** (1923) *Birds Amer.* 1.241, *Hudsonian Godwit—Limosa fedoa...* Other Names... Brant-bird. **1925** (1928) Forbush *Birds MA* 1.427, *Limosa fedoa... Other names:..* Brant-bird. *Ibid* 1.429, *Limosa haemastica... Other names:..* Brant-bird. **1955** *MA Audubon* 39.20, *Hudsonian Godwit...* Brant Bird (Maine, Mass.).

brant coot n

=**white-winged scoter.**

1888 Trumbull *Names of Birds* 99, *Oidemia deglandi...* On Long Island.. at Moriches *Brant Coot.* **1917** (1923) *Birds Amer.* 1.150, *Oidemia deglandi...* Brant Coot. **1955** *AmSp* 30.181, Of bird names given for size, consider.. *brant coot* (white-winged scoter, N.Y.). **1982** Elman *Hunter's Field Guide* 250, *White-winged Scoter...* Common & Regional Names:.. brant coot.

brant goose See **brant 1**

brant snipe See **brant-bird 1, 2**

bran up v phr

To eat.

1929 *AmSp* 5.151 **cNY,** If you are hungry, go out into the kitchen and bran up.

brasada n [Span *brazada* having many arms or branches] **TX**

See quot 1932.

1929 Dobie *Vaquero* 204 **TX,** The Brasada is still a *brasada,..* It is still cow country, and brush hands.. still "kill up" their horses running wild cattle. *Ibid* 229, As has been made clear, the Brasada—the brush country—marked the meeting of the East and the West. **1932** Bentley *Spanish Terms* 103, *Brazada*—English modification *brasada...* A term applied in parts of Texas to a region densely covered with thickets, i.e., brush country. **1968** Adams *Western Words.*

brasero n [Span] **TX**

A container used to hold burning charcoal.

1892 *DN* 1.188, The *braséro,* which takes the place of fireplaces and stoves in Spanish America, is found in every household in Southern Texas, to keep lighted charcoal from one meal to another. *Ibid* 245, *Braséro...* Used also in southwestern Texas for heating purposes during northers. **1930** (1935) Porter *Judas* 24 **TX,** "Light the brasero and cook food for me," he told her... When he returned, she.. was fanning the fire in the charcoal burner.

brash n[1] [Scots, nEngl dial]

1 See quot.

1921 *DN* 5.120 **IL,** Brash... A great or unusual number coming in rapid succession; flood; rush. "We had a regular brash of calls this afternoon."

2 A slight attack of sickness often arising from a digestive disorder such as heartburn. *old-fash*

1830 in 1938 Gardiner *Chron. Old Berkeley* 299 **WV,** Had a sick brash which came on me last night. **1870** *Nation* 11 July 57/1 **sePA,** To have a "brash" was to have a sick turn. **1872** Schele de Vere *Americanisms* 446, In Southern New Jersey and in Pennsylvania, an acid rising taste in the mouth is frequently called *brash.* **1899** (1912) Green *VA Folk-Speech,* Brash, n. Sudden nausea, with acid rising in the mouth, as in heartburn.

brash adj[1] [Etym uncert; perh merges Engl *brash* a heap of fragments (*OED* sb.[2]) with Scots *brash* to bruise, crush, break bones, and *brashy* delicate in constitution *(SND)*, all with underlying implication of brittleness]

1 Brittle, often as a result of drying.

1848 Bartlett *Americanisms*, *Brash*. Brittle. In New England this word is used in speaking of wood or timber that is brittle. In New York it is often heard in the markets applied to vegetables. Ex. "These radishes are brash," i.e. brittle. **1892** Eggleston *Hoosier Schoolmaster* 174 **IN**, [Footnote:] *Brash* in the sense of brittle. **1906** *DN* 3.115 **sIN**. **1927** *DN* 5.424 **NEng**, *Brash*. "Brittle." In this sense the word is American. But it is not difficult to see how it originated. *Brash*, in the North of England, signifies "Twigs or Brush" — slender, fragile branches; and hence it has been used adjectively in the sense of brittle. **1931–33** *LANE Worksheets* **seNH**, *Brash* . . Generally, good for nothing. Specifically, a tree that's not good for lumber; **ceME**, Dry, brittle — used of hair. **1950** *WELS (Dry wood is always more _____ than green wood)* 3 Infs, **WI**, Brash. **1966–70** *DARE* (Qu. KK24, *Something that breaks easily*) Infs **AR**41, **DC**8, **KY**85, **MD**26, **TX**37, Brash; (Qu. KK25, *Something that bends or yields easily*) Inf **MD**30, Brash. [All but one Inf old] **1967** *Key Tobacco Vocab.* **PA**, *Brash* . . . Brittle. The faster it [=tobacco] grows the brasher it is.

2 See quot.

1926 *DN* 5.386 **ME**, *Brash* . . . Coarse, "The meal is too brash." Common.

3 Hasty, rash, self-assertive.

1837 Bird *Nick of Woods* I.viii.120 *(OEDS)* **KY**, Strannger [*sic*] thar's as brash as a new hound in a b'ar fight. **1871** Eggleston *Hoosier Schoolmaster* 136 **IN**, I'd a staid and died right here by the ole cabin. But I reckon 'ta'n't best to be brash. **1889** Murfree *Despot* 27 **eTN**, Ye notice how turrible brash Josiah Preen be, — can't wait fur pa'son ter summons him. **1892** *DN* 1.229 **KY**. **1899** (1912) Green *VA Folk-Speech*, *Brash* . . . Impetuous; rash. **1902** *DN* 2.230 **sIL**. **1905** *DN* 3.71 **nwAR**. **1908** *DN* 3.293 **eAL, wGA**. **1940** Lewis *Bethel Merriday* 268 **CT**, She felt that that brash young man deserved what he got. **1965–70** *DARE* (Qu. AA6b, *. . A man who is fond of being with women and tries to attract their attention — if he's rude or not respectful*) Inf **MI**114, Brash fellow; (Qu. AA7b, *. . A woman who is fond of men and is always trying to know more — if she's not respectable about it*) Inf **VA**13, Brash; (Qu. II36b, *Of somebody who talks back or gives rude answers, . . "She certainly is _____."*) Infs **KS**4, **SC**45, Brash.

4 Eager, lively, forward.

1885 Twain *Huck. Finn* 65 **MO**, When I got to camp I warn't feeling very brash, there warn't much sand in my craw. **1891** Ryan *Pagan* 118 **Allegheny Mts**, I ain't so brash in the timber as I'd like to be. **1904** (1969) Robins *Magnetic North* 126, 'Well,' said O'Flynn [an Irish American from San Francisco] hopefully, 'bide a bit. He ain't lookin' very brash.' **1914** *DN* 4.69 **ME, nNH**.

5 Easily angered.

1903 *DN* 2.307 **seMO**, *Brash* . . . Quick tempered. **1909** *DN* 3.408 **nME**, *Brash* . . . Sharp tempered.

brash adj² [**brash** n¹ **2**] *old-fash* Cf **brashy** adj²

Indisposed; susceptible to illness.

1895 *DN* 1.384 **East**, *Brash*: sickly, in poor health. O[ld-fash]. **1909** *DN* 3.419 **Cape Cod MA**, *Brash*. Uneasy, windy (of the stomach). "I don't like to drink cold water before breakfast, it makes my stomach feel brash."

brash n² See **brush** n, v¹ **A2**

brash n³ [**brash** adj¹ **3**, perh infl by *brass*]

Audacity.

1966 *DARE* (Qu. GG5, *When someone does something unexpectedly bold or forward . . "Well, she certainly has a lot of _____."*) Inf **MS**5, Brash.

brash oak n *?obs*

A **post oak** (here: *Quercus stellata*).

1897 Sudworth *Arborescent Flora* 154, *Quercus minor* . . . Common names [include] . . . Box Oak (Md.), Brash Oak (Md.).

brashy adj¹

=**brash** adj¹ **1**.

1929 *AmSp* 5.128 **ME**, Dry, brittle hair was termed "brashy," easily broken. **1950** *WELS (She broke her arm again; her bones are certainly _____)* 1 Inf, **cwWI**, Brashy. **1967** *Key Tobacco Vocab.* **MD, MO, PA, TN**, *Brashy* . . . Brittle [The tobacco leaf] hasn't wilted right. **1968** *DARE* Tape **NY**96, Your maple made 'bout as poor a turning stock as

we'd get because it was brashy . . . [FW:] Brashy? [Inf:] Well, when you saw it [=maple] off, it's so damned hard, it shines.

brashy adj² *old-fash*

=**brash** adj²

1872 Schele de Vere *Americanisms* 446, In Southern New Jersey . . an indisposed person is said to be *brashy*. **1911** *DN* 3.541 **NE**, *Brashy* . . . Having a tendency to fall sick easily, from some passing ailment. "My little girl is so brashy." Reported from Polk County.

brasil n [Prob Span]

=**bluewood**.

1891 Coulter *Botany W. TX* 58, *C[ondalia] obovata* . . . Known as 'brasil' and 'logwood' . . [is] one of the common 'chaparral' plants of western Texas. **1931** U.S. Dept. Ag. *Misc. Pub.* 101.112, Bluewood, known locally as brasil, capulin, . . and purple haw, . . is limitedly browsed. **1967** *DARE* (Qu. T16, *What kinds of trees are "special" around here*) Inf **TX**22, Brasil [ˌbrɑˈzɪl]; (Qu. T5) Inf **TX**29, Brasil. **1967** *DARE* Tape **TX**29, [braˈziəl].

brass about one, have See **brass on one's face, have**

brass ankle n [See quot 1943] **chiefly coastal SC** *freq derog* Cf **black ankle**

A person of racially mixed ancestry (White, Black, Indian), esp in coastal South Carolina.

1930 *DN* 6.79 **cSC**, *Brass ankle* . . . A person who passes for white, but who is suspected of having "a streak down his back". **1940** *AmSp* 15.446 **eTN**, *Brass ankle*. Mulatto. 'The hotel cook is a brass ankle.' **1943** *AmSp* 18.152 **SC**, *Brass ankle*, for 'mulatto,' is very often used by the older generation, though less often by younger speakers. My father thinks that the term originated in the neighborhood of Monck's Corner, South Carolina, where the descendants of a Portuguese colony who had intermarried with Negroes and afterwards married largely within their own group were noted for their brass bracelets and anklets. To this group the white and Negro settlers in the neighborhood applied the name *brass ankle*, which was later extended to any mulatto. **1950** *PADS* 14.16 **SC**. **1963** Berry *Almost White* 27, The Brass Ankles . . are found in large numbers in the [South Carolina] counties of Dorchester, Berkeley, Charleston, Orangeburg, Colleton, Clarendon, and Williamsburg. **1966–70** *DARE* (Qu. HH28, *People of foreign background*) Inf **SC**26, Brass ankle — not Negro or White; belong to the real social structure of neither race; frequently have their own schools, churches, etc.; (Qu. HH29a, *People of mixed blood — part Indian*) Inf **SC**5, Brass ankle — not Negro or White, and live apart from both races; **SC**19, Brass ankle — not part of White community and don't want to be Black; **SC**44, Brass ankle — don't gee-haw with White or Black community; live apart; racial composition a mystery; **SC**54, Brass ankle — Indian and Negro and White; **SC**68, Brass ankle; (Qu. HH29b, *People of mixed blood — part Negro*) Inf **GA**15, Brass ankle — Negro, White, and Indian; **SC**21, Brass ankle. **1966** *DARE* Tape **SC**25, White and colored refer to them as brass ankles which they don't appreciate at all. **1967** *DARE* FW Addit **SC**, Brass ankle — one who belongs with neither White nor Negro community, quite apart and distinct. White + Indian + Negro in unknown proportion.

brass bass See **brassy bass**

brass buttons n pl

An introduced composite plant (*Cotula coronopifolia*) with bright yellow flower heads; common in states along the Pacific coast. Also called **butterheads, mud disks**

1897 Parsons *Wild Flowers CA* 151, *Brass Buttons* . . . These little weeds are . . now common everywhere . . . and their little flowers, like brass buttons, are very familiar objects along our roadsides. **1925** Jepson *Manual Plants CA* 1143, *Brass Buttons* . . . Most abundant in the salt marshes. **1961** Peck *Manual OR* 824, *Brass Buttons* . . . On beaches, from Wash. to Calif. Introduced from South Africa. **1973** Hitchcock–Cronquist *Flora Pacific NW* 507.

brass-eye n Also *brass-eyed whistler*

=**goldeneye**.

1838 MA Zool. & Bot. Surv. *Repts. Zool.* 393, The Golden Eye . . [has also] the name of Brass-eyed Whistler. **1844** DeKay *Zool. NY* 2.330, *Fuligula clangula*, the Brass-eye, Whistler or Great-head, . . is another northern species. **1946** Hausman *Eastern Birds* 157, *American Goldeneye* . . . Brasseye . . . Brass-eyed Whistler. **1982** Elman *Hunter's Field Guide* 219, *American Goldeneye* . . . Common & Regional Names: . . brass-eye.

brasshead n

A mosquito.

1975 Newell *If Nothin' Don't Happen* 68 **nwFL,** The mosquitoes would have eat a feller up. They was so thick you could make a quick scoop with a pint cup and catch a quart! "Let's get out of here . . before the devilish brassheads walk off with us!"

brass on one's face, have v phr For varr, see quot [*brass impudence*] **chiefly S Atl**

To be forward or over-confident.

1966–69 *DARE* (Qu. GG5, *When someone does something unexpectedly bold or forward, you might say: "Well, she certainly has a lot of ———."*) Infs **NC9, 22, 30, 49, SC7, TX32,** Brass on her face; **GA77,** Brass in her face; **SC19,** Brass about her.

brass-wing blackbird n

=bobolink.

1966 *DARE* (Qu. Q14, . . *Other names . . for . . bobolink*) Inf **FL7,** Brass-wing blackbird.

brass wood n [From the color of the wood]

=Osage orange.

1830 *Monitor* (Newark, N.J.) 7 Sept 2/5 *(DA),* Freemasonry is as gross an imposture on the public as the *wooden nutmegs,* or *horn flints,* . . or *brasswood pumpkin seeds.*

brassy bass n Also *brass bass* [See quot 1889]

=yellow bass.

1884 Goode *Fisheries U.S.* 1.424, The Brassy Bass of the Lower Mississippi Valley, *Roccus interruptus.* **1889** *Century Dict.* 664/1, *Brass-bass,* a percoideous fish, *Morone interrupta:* so called from its bright brassy color, tinged with blue on the back. **1920** Forbes–Richardson *Fishes of IL* 320, Brassy bass *(Morone interrupta).* **1933** John G. Shedd Aquarium *Guide* 96, *Chrysoperca interrupta* . . . Brassy Bass. **1972** Sparano *Outdoors Encycl.* 362, *Yellow Bass*—Common Names: . . brassy bass, . . Scientific Name: *Roccus mississippiensis.*

brat n[1] |bræt| **chiefly Inland Nth, N Midl** *esp among women*

An illegitimate child.

1926 Roberts *Time of Man* 344 **KY,** No brat of Joe Phillips can be borned in my house . . . Joe Phillips, why don't he support you? Cheap, he is. Has he made his plans to bring up his brat? **1962** Atwood *Vocab. TX* 66, *Illegitimate child* . . . Uncommon and perhaps sometimes improvised terms . . include *brat.* **1966–70** *DARE* (Qu. Z11a, . . *A child whose parents were not married*) Infs **IL60, MI51, NJ13, NY179, OH87,** Brat; (Qu. Z11b) Infs **CA21, IA34, IN77, MD24, NY70, 199, PA184, VA69, WA6,** Brat. [All 14 Infs women] **1973** Allen *LAUM* 1.344 **Upper MW,** *Illegitimate child.* For four scattered infs. *brat* has this meaning. [All four are women. Two other infs, one man and one woman, report having heard the term.]

brat n[2], also attrib |brɑt| [Abbr for **bratwurst**] **esp WI**

=bratwurst.

1950 *Sheboygan Press* (WI) 25 May 28/5, Brats Guaranteed Not to Fry Away. **1968** *DARE* (Qu. H41, . . *Roll or bun sandwiches*) Inf **WI13,** Brats. **1977** *Capital Times* (Madison WI) 16 Sept 2, Friday, in downtown [Wisconsin] Dells, there will be Maxwell Street Days, brat and corn roast. **1980** [see **bratwurst**]. **1983** *Milwaukee Jrl.* (WI) 26 Jan Food sec 3, You throw it [=turkey] on the grill and when it's done, you just close off the vents. We slice it and serve it for sandwiches. We think it's nicer than brats or hamburgers, and it's a heck of a lot easier. **1983** *DARE* File **ceWI** [Letter], We [=Johnsonville Sausage Co.] have used the term bratwurst or brats for many years. In fact, I remember when we advertised Brats for sale at \$.49 a pound and that was in the late '40's or early '50's. I suspect that the term Brat has been used in this area a lot longer than that.

brats See **brother A6**

‡**brattlebrained** adj [Alter of *rattlebrained*]

1969 *DARE* (Qu. HH9, *A very silly or light-headed person*) Inf **RI13,** Brattlebrained.

bratwurst n Also sp *brad wurst, broat-warsht* [Ger] **Ger settlement areas, esp WI** See also **brat** n[2]

A type of fresh pork sausage usu grilled or fried and served on a bun with condiments and sauerkraut.

1938 *Amer.–German Rev.* Sept 41 **sePA,** They [=early PaGer settlers] also had a fondness for . . *Brad Wurst,* fried sausage. *Ibid* 53, The

second annual feast of the Pennsylvania dutch was held in April, 1938, at Reading, the menu being selected by mail vote as follows: . . Fried Fresh Sausage or Broat-Warsht. **1950** *WELS (Kinds of sausage)* 7 Infs, **WI,** Bratwurst; *(Kinds of outdoor amusements . . favored in your neighborhood)* 1 Inf, **seWI,** Bratwurst fry. **1965** *Rhinelander Daily News & New North* (WI) 12 Aug 5 [Caption], This shows part of the noon hour rush at the Lions Club bratwurst stand. **1965** *Bee* (Phillips WI) 19 Aug [7] [Advt], Homemade bratwurst lb. 59c. **1967–68** *DARE* (Qu. H41, . . *Roll or bun sandwiches*) Inf **WI13,** Bratwurst; (Qu. H45, *Dishes made with meat*) Inf **WI47,** Bratwurst; (Qu. H65 *Foreign foods favored around here*) Infs **IA47, MO12,** Bratwurst. **1980** *WI State Jrl.* (Madison) 27 July 5th sec 14/1, Brat Day in this Bratwurst Capital of Wisconsin was reason enough to put the kids in the back seat and take off for a day of fun and frolic. **1983** *DARE* File **ceWI** [Letter], Our Company [=Johnsonville Sausage] has been the pioneer in what is known as the Sheboygan style of bratwurst. Bratwurst has been made that way here in Johnsonville since the early 1900's. The term bratwurst in German is actually a generic term, it means "fry sausage."

brauche n, v [Ger *Brauch* custom, habit, practice] Cf **powwow**

Secret rituals, words, and remedies for curing sickness and disease; to use such remedies.

1964 Smith *PA Germans* 156, *Brauche* . . . A sizeable body of cures, rituals and remedies for sickness and disease associated with supernatural causes has been handed down from generation to generation. *Ibid* 157, Some individuals were believed capable of performing both the black and white magic arts, while others were called upon only to heal or *brauche. Ibid* 163, Among the older residents, the term *brauche* was used to refer to a special class of treatment for sickness or injury. Brauche "words" were used in the treatment of high fever, burns, hard breathing, stopping the flow of blood, for curing warts and other problems. Although brauche practices were common, they were not necessarily commonly believed in. Without doubt some residents had complete faith in the brauche cures, others believed in some of them, and still others . . [thought] they might possibly have an influence and at least could do little harm.

braughtus See **broadus**

braunschweiger n [Ger; see quot 1945] **chiefly in Ger settlement areas**

1 Smoked liver sausage.

1934 *Sun* (Baltimore MD) 22 Aug 10/7 *(Hench Coll.),* The conversation changed to liverwurst or braunschweiger. **1945** Mencken *Amer. Lang. Suppl. 1* 429, In 1930 Swift & Company, the Chicago packers, began calling the sausage [=liverwurst] *braunschweiger*—the adjective often prefixed to *leberwurst* by the Germans, for the variety most esteemed in their homeland comes from Braunschweig (Brunswick). **1950** *WELS (Kinds of sausage most eaten in your neighborhood)* 4 Infs, **WI,** Braunschweiger. **1965** *Bee* (Phillips WI) 19 Aug 3, [Advt:] Bologna or Braunschweiger. **1967–68** *DARE* (Qu. H43) Inf **CO27,** Liver sausage—Braunschweiger; **PA134,** ['brɑnzwaɪgɚ]; (Qu. H65) Inf **NE9,** [braʊnswaɪgɚ]. **1973** Allen *LAUM* 1.289 **neMN,** *Braunschweiger.* This smoked liver sausage is widely known, but only one inf. named it.

‡**2** See quot.

1934 *AmSp* 9.318, A *braunschweiger,* in Nebraska usage, is a sandwich made of bread and ground meat.

brava n Also *bravo* [*Brava* one of the Cape Verde Islands] **seMA, RI** Also called **black Portuguese**

A resident of the Cape Cod area whose ancestors were Black and Portuguese immigrants from the Cape Verde Islands.

1931–33 *LANE Worksheets* **seRI,** Bravoes, colored Portuguese. **1933** *Sun* (Baltimore MD) 4 May 1/4 *(Hench Coll.),* During the afternoon a man described as "a brava"—a common Cape Cod name for the dark-skinned natives of the Cape Verde Islands who are numerous along the cape—was taken into custody by the police for questioning. **1948** *Ibid* 19 July 7/1 *(Hench Coll.),* The hardy Bravas, Portuguese-American seafaring men of Cape Verde Islands origin. **1969** *DARE* (Qu. HH28, *People of foreign background*) Inf **RI13,** Bravos.

‡**brave around** v phr

To swagger, perh like an Indian brave.

1949 Guthrie *Way West* 239 **West** (as of c1845), It would be like him to go to Mr. Mack and brave around and settle happy for a horse or ox, as if that was the price of her.

bravish adj [Engl dial *bravish* considerable, pretty fair]

Large, notable.

1967 *DARE* (Qu. H9, *If somebody always eats a considerable amount of food, you say he's a ———*) Inf **PA52**, Bravish eater.

bravo See **brava**

brawdus, brawtus See **broadus**

bray n **chiefly Sth, S Midl** See Map

A neigh.

1965–70 *DARE* (Qu. K40, *The sound that a horse makes*) 30 Infs, **chiefly Sth, S Midl**, Bray; [(Qu. K19, *Noise made by a calf that's taken away from its mother*) Inf **VT2**, Bray]. **1973** Allen *LAUM* 1.253 **Upper MW**, For the noise made by a horse during feeding time [4 infs use the term *bray*].

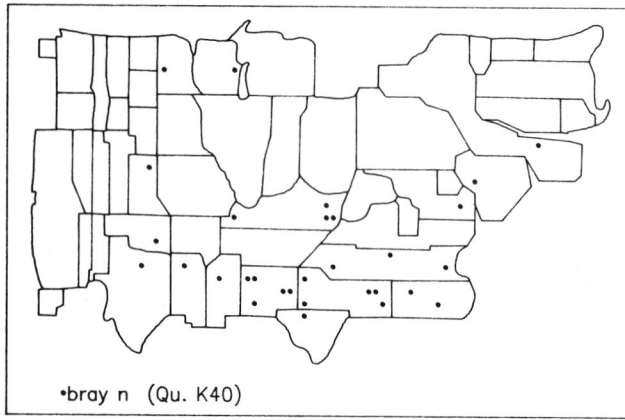

•bray n (Qu. K40)

bray v [*OED bray* v.² 1 to beat, crush; 1382 →]

To pound up or otherwise prepare a medicine or remedy. (Cf Proverbs 27:22 "bray a fool in a mortar with a pestle")

1938 Matschat *Suwannee R.* 86 **GA**, He was took with the water disease, an' swelled until he nigh bust. I brayed him a powder of elderberries an' strawberry leaves. *Ibid* 96, I brayed King nigh a double potion of warm milk for his supper.

braysh See **brush** n, v¹ A3

breach n

1931–33 *LANE Worksheets* **ceVT**, Breach, A rupture or hernia.

breachy adj Also sp *breechy* Pronc-sp *brichy* [*breach* to smash a gap through + -*y*] **chiefly NEng, West**

1 Of livestock: apt to break out of enclosures.

1780 (1899) Parkman *Diary* 275 **MA**, To my sorrow, my Oxen have been breachy at Mr. Isaac Parker's and let in Cattle with ym, into his Cornfield. **1816** Pickering *Vocab.* 52, *Breachy.* This is a common word among the *farmers* of *New England,* in speaking of oxen, &c. that are unruly, and apt to *break* through their enclosures. **1899** Brown *Tiverton Tales* 133 **NEng**, That cussed breachy cow . . hooked it [=a fence] down. **1907** *DN* 3.182 **NH**, *Brichy* . . . Breachy; apt to break out of pasture or any enclosure. **1914** *DN* 4.69 **ME, nNH**. **1933** *AmSp* 8.1.29 **TX**. **1937** Sandoz *Slogum* 314 **NE** (as of 1900–20), Newly bought two-year-olds, blacks, tough-hided, so breachy no fence would hold them. **1940** (1951) *FWP Guide OR* 83, A southern Oregon farmer broke a breachy horse . . by tying an iron nut to the animal's foretop in such a manner that it hit him between the eyes each time he tried to jump. **1965** *DARE* FW Addit **NM6**. **1966–69** *DARE* (Qu. K16, *A cow with a bad temper*) Infs **ID1, MA68, UT6**, Breachy.

2 By ext: inclined to disregard prevailing moral constraints.

1929 *AmSp* 5.123 **ME**, The word "breechy" was sometimes applied to a woman who was immoral and "jumped the pasture fence." **1949** *PADS* 11.18 **CO**, *Breachy* . . . Lecherous.

bread n Pronc-spp *brad, brade*

A Forms.

1894 in 1941 Warfel–Orians *Local-Color Stories* 740 **Sth** [Black], Co'n-brade. **1914** *DN* 4.159 **cVA** (as of 1901–07), *Brade* [breɪd]. **1933** *AmSp* 8.1.23 **WV**, *Brad.*

B Senses.

1 Corn bread. **chiefly Sth, S Midl**

1895 *DN* 1.390 **wFL**, [Bread] means corn bread. **1903** *DN* 2.307 **seMO**, *Bread* . . . Corn-bread. **1905** *DN* 3.71 **sAR**, Corn bread. 'I'll take *bread;* no fodder (raised wheat bread) for me.' **1908** *DN* 3.293 **eAL**,

wGA. **1909** *DN* 3.345. **1917** *DN* 4.408 **wNC**. **1942** Rawlings *Cross Creek* 208 **FL**, If I asked a neighbor for some bread in an emergency, I should receive a pan of cornbread.

2 Biscuits; hardtack. Cf **biscuit bread**

1904 *DN* 2.417 **nwAR**, *Bread* . . . Cream of tartar biscuit. It used to surprise me to be asked to pass the bread when only cream of tartar biscuits were on the table. **1939** Coffin *Capt. Abby* 111 **ME** (as of c1860s), Bread means the sort of unleavened cracker, christened "pilot bread," which, when he bit into it, even a strong man in his prime . . might leave three of his best incisors in. **1960** Hall *Smoky Mt. Folks* 7, Bread (biscuits) drenched in 'lasses (sorghum molasses).

3 Corn. See also **bread corn**

1924 Raine *Land of Saddle-Bags* 105 **sAppalachians**, Bread may mean corn-bread, or simply corn. "I'm clearin' a field to raise my *bread.*" **1933** *AmSp* 8.1.48 **Ozarks**, *Bread* . . often used to designate the growing crop. *Bob he got hisse'f all crippled up, so we-uns jest whirled in an' planted his bread for him.*

4 See quot. *obs*

1824 Doddridge *Notes Indian Wars* 101, The lean venison and the breast of the wild turkies, we were taught to call bread. The flesh of the bear was denominated meat.

bread v **chiefly Midl, esp S Midl**

To supply with bread.

1797 in 1924 Steele *Papers* 1.152 **NC**, I cannot return you corn again this fall as what I have . . . will Scarcely Bread the Negroes and feed the Work Horses. **1877** in 1937 Ruede *Sod-House* 194 **PA**, You need not wait till September before I can tell whether I'll have enough to bread us—I can tell that by 1st of July. **1903** *DN* 2.307 **seMO**. **1917** *DN* 4.408 **KS, KY, wNC**. **1919** *DN* 5.32 **KY**. **1927** *AmSp* 2.349 **WV**, There is enough corn in the crib to bread us for a year. **1944** *PADS* 2.26 **cwOH, cwNC**. **1952** Brown *NC Folkl.* 1.522. **1962** *Mt. Life* Spring 17 **sAppalachians**, The mountain farmer talks of raising enough corn to "bread" his family.

bread-and-butter n

1 A greenbrier (here: *Smilax rotundifolia*).

1892 *Jrl. Amer. Folkl.* 5.104 **MA**, *Smilax rotundifolia* . . bread-and-butter . . . The young leaves eaten by children. **1959** Carleton *Index Herb. Plants* 18, *Bread And Butter:* . . Smilax rotundifolia. **1960** Vines *Trees SW* 75, *Smilax rotundifolia* . . Vernacular names for the plant are . . Bread-and-butter.

2 also *bread-and-butter plant:* =**butter-and-eggs 1.**

1900 Lyons *Plant Names* 226, *L[inaria] Linaria* . . Bread-and-butter. **1959** Carleton *Index Herb. Plants* 18, *Bread And Butter:* Linaria vulgaris. **1967–70** *DARE* (Qu. S11) Infs **KY83, 85, TN6, VA21**, Bread-and-butter; **IA13**, Bread-and-butter plant.

bread and butter exclam Cf **needles and pins**

An exclam used when two people walking together are momentarily separated by someone or something coming between them.

1939 *FWP Guide KS* 104, Beliefs prevalent among Kansas children include . . the ubiquitous "bread and butter" incantation used in passing on opposite sides of a post. **1966** Goldstein–Byington *Two Penny Ballads* 143 **sePA** (as of c1920), If you are separated from the person you are walking with by a pole, say . . "bread and butter." **1980** *DARE* File **nCA** (as of 1950s), If two children were walking together and were separated by a third person, an animal, or any obstruction, they would call out "Bread and butter!" I guess it was supposed to ward off bad luck.

bread and butter, come to supper exclam, n

The call which begins the action in a children's hiding game; the game itself.

1892 *DN* 1.229 **KY**, Bread and butter, come to supper. In the game of "hiding the switch" this is the call to hunt the switch. **1905** *DN* 3.71 **nwAR**. **1908** *DN* 3.294 **eAL, wGA**, Bread and butter, come to supper. Used in the children's game of 'hiding the switch.' Sometimes used as the name of the game. **1970** *DARE* (Qu. EE3, *Games in which you hide an object and then look for it*) Inf **PA247**, Bread and butter, come to supper.

bread-and-butter plant See **bread-and-butter** n 2

bread-and-butter teeth See **butter teeth**

bread and skip n Cf **bread and with it**

A scanty meal.

1976 *Yankee* 56, Dear Oracle: A friend of mine told me that . .

whenever he asked his mother what they were having for dinner, she always answered "bread and skip." He never found out what that meant. Do you know? *Answer: No second course.* **1981** *NADS Letters* **Sth,** Bread and skip: "bread and molasses, and skip the molasses," or whatever the sweet stuff mout be.

bread and with it n
A meal of more than just bread.

1942 Whipple *Joshua* 18 **UT** (as of c1860), But Brother Lee interrupted himself. 'Howsomever, come in an' set a spell . . . We ain't got only "bread-and-with it," but — ' . . . *No, thank you,* she thought; *your bread would be corn pone* and your 'with-it' *salt pork.*

breadcake n
See quot 1907.

1856 (1862) Colt *Went to KS* 137 **NY,** I gave him some of our farina gruel with bread-cakes. **1907** *DN* 3.182 **seNH,** *Bread-cake . . .* A simple breadlike cake containing raisins and baked in a bread-pan.

bread corn n Cf bread n B3
Indian corn used for making bread.

1668 in 1887 East Hampton NY *Records* 1.288, Whosoever shall grind Malte at the mill shall after[wards] . . clear the mill with at least halfe a peck of bread corne. **1775** Adair *Amer. Indians* 407, The third [kind of corn grown by the Indians] is the largest, of a very white and soft grain, termed "bread-corn." **1899** (1912) Green *VA Folk-Speech, Bread-corn* . . . The white, and best corn, was always used for grinding into meal for bread. When a man had a scant crop it was said that he would not make *bread-corn;* that is enough for bread. **1956** Gipson *Old Yeller* 4 **TX,** If you let the varmints eat up the roasting ears, we'll be without bread corn for the winter.

bread cutter n Also *bread cracker,* ~ *grinder joc*
A tooth.

1965–70 *DARE* (Qu. X13a, . . *Teeth*) Infs **NC49, VA46,** Bread cutters; **TN52,** Bread grinders; (Qu. X13b, . . *False teeth*) Inf **KY40,** Bread crackers.

bread-dough biscuit n Also *bread biscuit, dough* ~ **chiefly Nth, AR, MS** See Map
A biscuit made from a small amount of ordinary bread dough.

[**1896** (c1973) Farmer *Orig. Cook Book* 54, To shape bread dough in biscuits, pull or cut off as many small pieces (having them of uniform size) as there are to be biscuits.] **1965–70** *DARE* (Qu. H19, *Kinds of biscuits*) 53 Infs, Bread-dough biscuits; **CT39, MA43, MI34, MN13, 42, NJ1, NY53,** Bread biscuits; **IA2, OH4,** Dough biscuits.

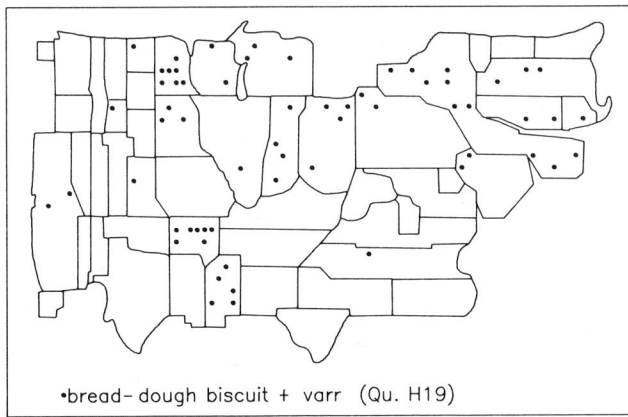

•bread- dough biscuit + varr (Qu. H19)

bread-eatin'est See -est

bread hoe n Cf hoe, hoecake
A griddle.

1967 *DARE* Tape **SC46,** Spread it [=batter] out evenly . . on a griddle —they call it a bread hoe. It was an iron bread hoe. We call 'em bread hoes to this day. **1983** *DARE* File **neGA** (as of 1947), Bread hoe—griddle.

bread hooks n pl Also *bread snatchers joc*
=biscuit hooks.

1966–68 *DARE* (Qu. X32, . . *Hands*) Infs **CA36, MS1,** Bread snatchers; **PA115,** Bread hooks.

bread is not done, one's phr Cf std *half-baked*
See quots.

1940 *AmSp* 15.446 **eTN,** To indicate that a person is mentally dull or feeble-minded. 'Henry's bread is not done.' **1966** *DARE* (Qu. HH6, *Someone who is out of his mind*) Inf **MS35,** His bread ain't done.

bread jar n
A container for storing bread.

1950 *WELS* (To prevent bread and cakes from drying out, you put them in a _____) 1 Inf, **cwWI,** Bread jar. **1968** *DARE* Tape **OH48,** I had a big bread jar . . . about a twelve-gallon jar.

breadroot n
1 =**Indian breadroot. West**

1829 Eaton *Botany* 349, *Psoralea . . . esculenta . . .* Bread root . . . The root affords a staple article of diet to the western Indians. **1846** Sage *Scenes Rocky Mts.* 50, A specimen of the bread-root . . was procured from the creek-bank . . . This . . attains a size from twenty to thirty inches in circumference. **1876** Hobbs *Bot. Hdbk.* 15, Bread root, Prairie turnip, Psoralea esculenta. **1947** De Voto *Wide Missouri* 432, Some of these were very important sources of food, notably the camas, . . the breadroot or prairie turnip, . . and many species of lilies. **1973** Hitchcock–Cronquist *Flora Pacific NW* 272, *Psoralea . . .* Bread-root; Scurfpea; Psoralea.

2 =**cinnamon fern.**

1900 Lyons *Plant Names* 270, *O[smunda] cinnamomea . . .* Canada and eastern U.S. Cinnamon Fern, . . Bread-root.

3 A **balsamroot** (here: *Balsamorrhiza sagittata*).

1937 U.S. Forest Serv. *Range Plant Hdbk.* W43, Arrowleaf balsamroot . . . is locally called sunflower, graydock, and breadroot.

4 An **arrow arum** (here: *Peltandra virginica*).

1961 Smith *MI Wildflowers* 35, *Peltandra virginica . . .* was the "breadroot" of the eastern Indians.

bread snatchers See bread hooks

breadwagon n
1 Std sense, in var phrr: see quots.

1905 *DN* 3.99 **nwAR,** (So) *ugly that he'd stop a bread wagon.* **1908** *DN* 3.294 **eAL, wGA,** *Bread-wagon . . .* Baker's wagon. Often used in the facetious expression 'I couldn't stop a *bread-wagon,*' i.e., 'I haven't a nickel.'

2 Thunder. Cf **potato wagon**

1915 *DN* 4.181 **VA,** *Bread wagon . . .* Thunder clap. **1931** *PMLA* 46.1304 **sAppalachians,** Listen at that bread wagon (thunder). **1972** Hall *Sayings Old Smoky* 44, *Bread Wagon.* "That's the old bread wagon!" Sometimes said when thunder is heard because the rain makes the corn and wheat grow.

break v
A Forms.

1 pres: usu *break(s);* also *broke, bruk* (Gullah).

1888 Jones *Negro Myths* 12 **GA coast** [Gullah], Long befo day duh broke Buh Rooster knock eh wing togarruh an crow. *Ibid* 155, Day dis biggin fuh broke. **1922** Gonzales *Black Border* 188 **sSC, GA coasts** [Gullah], Uh git to de place weh de tide bruk t'ru de beach. *Ibid* 291 [Glossary], *Bruk*—break, breaks. **1928** Peterkin *Scarlet Sister Mary* 209, **sSC coast** [Gullah], Don' le me fall an' broke my leg to-day.

2 past: usu *broke;* sometimes *breaked;* also *brake, break;* occas *bruk, bruck;* rarely *broked, broken.*

1689 (1892) Hammond *Diary* 148 **MA,** Ye Lightning came downe ye Chimney, wth some [sic] bricks just above ye mantletree. **1838** (1955) Crockett *Almanacks* 126 **wTN,** I brake three of his ribs, and he knocked out five of my teeth and one eye. **1884** Murfree *TN Mts.* 249, I . . slipped on a icy rock, an' bruk my ankle-bone. **1904** Day *Kin o' Ktaadn* 165 **ME,** She bruk' loose an' sailed away. **1905** Culbertson *Banjo Talks* 72 **Sth,** Saw him w'en he bruck his line. **1916** Howells *Leatherwood God* 79 **OH,** He bruk through. **1931** *PMLA* 46.1319 **sAppalachians,** "Bruk" (broke). **1966–70** *DARE* (Qu. AA13, *When two people . . stop going together, you might say, "I guess they _____."*) Inf **SC10,** Breaked up; (Qu. OO13a, *About breaking a leg: "He limps ever since he _____ his leg."*) Infs **LA18, NJ67, SC10,** Break; **IL77, MS69, NY10, TX103, 106,** Breaked; **KY81,** Broked; **LA8, VA73,** Broken. **1966** *DARE* Tape **IL77,** I don't know if it [=the wind] broke [brʊ‧k] the root off or what.

3 pple: usu *broken;* freq, *esp among speakers with little formal* *educ, broke;* infreq *breaked, broked;* rarely *brake, break, breke, bruk.*

1690 (1892) Hammond *Diary* 155 **MA,** A Young man's thigh being brake, he dyed soon. **1697** in 1875 VA *Calendar State Papers* 1.53, I have had bread (bred) on the side of my neck, a Verry grate Impost, and it is lately break'd, soe that now is a Hole in my Neck. **1723** *New-Engl. Courant* (Boston MA) 5 Aug 2/2, Several Houses [are] blown down and breke. **1823** Cooper *Pioneers* 2.138 **NY,** You've broke the law. **1883** (1971) Harris *Nights with Remus* 20 **GA** [Black], Dish yer chicken-nabber look lak he dead, but dey aint no bones broked. **1926** Kephart *Highlanders* 106 **sAppalachians,** I fell over a rock clift twenty feet down, and if 'it hadn't been for the laurel I'd a-bruk some bones. **1927** Adams *Congaree* 21 **cSC** [Black], Ellen, I is all broked up. I guh lef' you now. [=I'm going to leave you now]. **1934** Carmer *Stars Fell on AL* 41, It's about the only chance I git tuh say suthin' 'thout bein' broke in on. **1950** *WELS (To feel very sorry about something: "When he got the news he was _____")* 2 Infs, **WI,** All broke up; *(When two people have been going "steady" and stop going together: "I guess they have _____")* 2 Infs, **WI,** Broke up; *(That's the second time he has _____ that leg)* 13 Infs, **WI,** Broke. **1953** Atwood *Survey of Verb Forms* 7, *Break* . . . The past participle is recorded in the context "The glass is (broken)." *Broken* /brokən/ is in use in all areas [of the eastern U.S.]; it is almost universal in cultured speech, and predominates in Type II speech [younger infs, with moderate educ]. *Broke* /brok/ predominates in Type I speech [older infs, with little educ] in all areas except in the New York City area . . . Roughly, two thirds of the Type I informants in the M[iddle] A[tlantic] S[tates] and the S[outh] A[tlantic] S[tates] use this form, as well as about one third of the Type II informants. Only four cultured informants in the East use *broke.* **1965–70** *DARE* (Qu. F32, . . *"A water pipe must have _____.")* 67 Infs, Broke [Of all Infs responding to the question, 25% were grade-school educ; of those giving this response, 37% were grade-school educ]; *(Qu. AA13, When two people . . engaged, stop going together, you might say, "I guess they _____.")* Inf **GA**15, Have broked off; *(Qu. OO13, . . "That's the second time he has _____ [that leg]."*) 247 Infs, Broke [Of all Infs responding to the question, 25% were grade-school educ; of those giving this response, 45% were grade-school educ.]; **SC**10, Break; **IL**77, Breaked. **1965–70** *DARE* Tape **CA**136, It's a wonder one didn't get a leg broke; **CA**156, I have been bucked off of horses that was supposed to be broke; **GA**3, You're gonna have a broke leg; **GA**30, And one leg broke; **IN**18, Broke [past participle]; **MI**19, The stock on it is broke; **MI**101, Boat got broke in two; **TX**70, You'd probably get your arm broke; **VA**2, Until the charm had been broke. **1967** *DARE* FW Addit **swOR,** Did you get that ten dollar bill broke up?

B Transitive senses.

1 also with *out* or *up:* To plow (land), esp for the first time; hence vbl n *breaking.* Cf **breaker 1**

1716 in 1902 Davis *Tracts Mass. Bay* 174, The improving the sowing of *Hemp* and *Flax* . . is much obstructed by the inability to many to break up Land suitable. **1860** Greeley *Overland Journey* 10, Despite the hard times, Illinois is growing. There are new blocks in her cities, . . new breakings on this or that edge of almost every prairie. **1880** *Harper's Mag.* 60.817/2 **MN,** Here and there a great square of black earth was exposed in a new "breaking." **1899** (1912) Green *VA Folk-Speech, Break up* . . . To plough pasture land for cultivation. **1902** *DN* 2.230 **sIL,** *Break . .* To plow ground for a crop with a turning plow. **1909** *DN* 3.393 **nwAR,** He is breaking prairie. **1935** Sandoz *Jules* 92 **wNE** (as of 1880–1930), He saw the broad field of breaking the lean little man had turned up with the slow plough critters. **1942** Faulkner *Go Down* 42 **MS,** You needs to be in bed if you going to get that creek piece broke . . . If it had not been for George Wilkins, he would have had it all broken and bedded and ready now. **1950** *AmSp* 25.230 **ceMS,** *Break the land.* To plow for the first time in the early spring. **1950** *WELS (When you plow land or break sod that has never been plowed before, you are _____)* 43 Infs, **WI,** Breaking (ground, land, new land, sod, etc.) **1965–70** *DARE* (Qu. L19, *When you plow land or sod that has never been plowed before;* total Infs questioned, 75) 14 Infs, **scattered,** Breaking (new) ground; 14 Infs, **scattered,** Breaking (land, sod); **OK**33, 43, Breaking it; **MS**1, 58, Breaking stubble land; **OK**52, Breaking stump land; **FL**1, Breaking the soil; **MS**21, Breaking up turf ground; **AR**40, Break out stumpy land; *(Qu. L36, . . [To] dig out roots and underbrush to make a new field)* 13 Infs, **scattered,** Breaking (up) (new) ground; **CT**10, **UT**7, Breaking up land; **UT**4, Breaking it up; **MN**34, Breaking new land; **MN**40, Breaking the sod; **GA**33, Breaking your ground; **MI**67, Break the sod. **1967** *DARE* Tape **IA**8, That fall dad broke up prairie out there in Nebraska; **CO**1, He broke out ten acres.

2 also with *out:* To clear (deep snow) from a path or road. **Nth**

1779 in 1896 MA Hist. Soc. *Coll.* 2d ser 2.478, The roads [were] very bad this day, and not broke. **1831** (1901) Baldwin *Diary* 92 **MA,** The people are busy in breaking out roads which have been blocked up with snow. **1888** (1889) Howells *Annie Kilburn* 12 **NEng,** The sidewalks . . were promptly broken out in winter by the public snow-plough. **1917** *DN* 4.388 **neOH,** *Break a road* . . . After a deep snow to break a roadway, either in a field or on a highway. "I had to break a road to town this morning . . ." Also N. Eng., Ky., N.Y., Ill., Ia., Neb. **1968–69** *DARE* Tape **CA**165, We'd wear our boots to school in the snow and then carry our shoes. Now of course they break all the trails and you don't have that trouble; **PA**69, Break a path. **1969** Sorden *Lumberjack Lingo* **NEng, Gt Lakes,** *Break out* . . . To open a logging road after heavy snowfall.

3 To open (hogsheads containing tobacco) prior to a public sale. Cf **break** n[1] **1**

1872 Schele de Vere *Americanisms* 447, *Break,* to, is in Virginia, and other Tobacco-raising States, applied to the opening of the hogsheads, as they are sent from the plantations, previous to a public sale.

4 To soften (water); hence vbl n *breaking. old-fash*

1836 (1929) Willson *Journey* 22 June **DC,** We have to break all the water to wash with for we can not catch any rain water. **1848** (1870) Drake *Pioneer Life* 94 **KY,** Much [of the water] had to be brought from the spring and broke with ashes. **1853** *Harper's Mag.* 6.582/2, The water of Lake Superior . . being . . entirely unfit for the laundry without a previous 'breaking,' by soda or other means. **1893** *KS Univ. Qrly.* 1.138, *Break:* to soften (of water). **1968** *DARE* Tape **CA**90, Take and fill a 20 gallon tub full of water and you put 2 tablespoons of lye in it, and you build a fire underneath it and that broke the water.

5 See quot. [*OED* 1753] *?obs*

1899 (1912) Green *VA Folk-Speech, Break* . . . To break wool was to mix the white and black wools, card them together to make gray or mixed colour for cloth or stockings.

6 also with *up;* In whiskey-making: to eliminate the lumps from the cooked meal.

1968–69 *DARE* Tape **NC**54, The first thing you do . . you cook your meal and put it in your barrels or your boxes, and then in about two days you go back and break it . . break it up and put your sugar in it; **GA**72, You've got to thin that down with cold water, an' you call that breaking it up. **1974** Maurer *KY Moonshine* 114, *Break up* . . . To sift the scalded mass of meal through a coarse screen (usually hardware cloth) in order to remove the lumps. Part of the mashing operation.

7 To pick or harvest (ears of corn); hence vbl n *breaking.* **chiefly Sth**

[**1701** Wolley *2 Yrs. Jrl.* 38 **NY** (as of 1678), Their Harvest is in *October,* their Corn grows like clusters of Grapes, which they pluck or break off with their hands.] **1776** in 1930 Dunbar *Life* 32 **MS,** The Other negroes employed in hoeing and breaking down corn. *Ibid* 33, 4 Negroes cutting stave timber . . . Employed all day all hands in breaking down Corn. **1851** (1878) Aime *Plantation Diary* 147 **LA,** Breaking corn with all the hands on the 1st. **1864** in 1945 Easterby *SC Rice Plantation* 313, I have finishd Picking Peas & commencd Breakeing the Corn but have to stop on account of Rain. **1948** *Clarke Co. Democrat* (Grove Hill AL) 24 June 8/3 *(DA),* Farmers should notice especially the highly fertilized hybrid corn from now to breaking season. **1950** *PADS* 14.74 **FL,** *Breaking corn* . . . Taking the ear of corn from the stalk. **1966** *DARE* Tape **GA**1, We called it [picking ears of corn from the stalk] . . "pulling corn." A heap of folks called it "breaking corn."

C Intransitive senses.

1 To plow land, esp for the first time. Cf **B1** above

1719 (1901) Hempstead *Diary* 87 *(DAE),* I was about home fitting my plow & Looking my Steer & getting oxen to break up. **1903** *DN* 2.307 **seMO,** *Break* . . . Always used instead of plow. 'I have just begun breaking for cotton.' **1950** *WELS (When you plow land or break sod that has never been plowed before, you are _____)* 12 Infs, **WI,** Breaking; 1 Inf, New breaking. **1965–70** *DARE* (Qu. L19, *When you plow land or sod that has never been plowed before;* total Infs questioned, 75) Infs **FL**15, 18, 22, 27, 37, **MS**60, **OK**14, **UT**3, Breaking; *(Qu. L36, . . [To] dig out roots and underbrush to make a new field)* Infs **MN**4, **ND**3, **WI**17, 42, 66, Breaking.

2 To clear a path or road through heavy snow. Cf **B2** above

1780 (1903) Patten *Diary* 410 **NH,** We broke out to our wood and I shoveled snow about the door.

3 also with *up:* To cease, come to an end—used esp of school or church services. **chiefly S Midl**

1859 (1864) Browning *Hunter* 23 **wMD,** I done everything I could to get into her favor, until the school broke up. **1881** Pierson *In the Brush* 180 **KY**, At the conclusion of this prayer the benediction was pronounced, and the meeting "broke." In all this region meetings were never said to be "out" or to "close." They were said to "break," or, more frequently, "the meeting is done broke." **1896** *DN* 1.413 **swNC**. **1903** *DN* 2.307 **seMO**. **1933** *AmSp* 8.1.13, *To break meeting*. To bring the Meeting to an end. This happens when the person sitting at the head of the Meeting shakes hands with the person next him. **1948** Dick *Dixie Frontier* 186 **KY** [Black], Finally the handshaking ended, the meeting "broke," and the [church] service was over. **1949** Kurath *Word Geog.* 79, *(School) lets out* . . . The Virginia Piedmont has its own expression, *breaks up* or *breaks,* but *lets out* and *turns out* compete with it. **1952** Brown *NC Folkl.* 1.522, *Break* . . . Of school: to close.—Central and east. **1968** *DARE* FW Addit **eKY**, The meetin's broke—"come to an end."

4 Of weather: =**fair off. chiefly Nth** Cf **break away, break off, break up 1**

1939 *LANE* Map 89 **neCT, MA, sVT**, *Breaking* . . referring to a change in the weather from cloudy to fair. **1965–70** *DARE* (Qu. B7, *When clouds begin to decrease, you say it's* ——) Infs **CT2, 4, IL50, IA17, MS86, MT1, NJ39, NY37, PA96**, Breaking. **1971** Bright *Word Geog. CA & NV* 140, The weather is *clearing up* . . *breaking.* **1973** Allen *LAUM* 1.152, The two common East Coast terms for the ending of a storm, *clearing* and *breaking,* retain their popularity in the U[pper] M[idwest].

5 To grow old; to show signs of aging. **chiefly S Midl**

1800 (1907) Thornton *Diary* 10.174 **PA**, Mrs. Washington is much broke since I saw her last. **1899** (1912) Green *VA Folk-Speech*, *Broke* . . . A young woman who has lost her beauty is said to be "*broke* all to pieces." **1903** *DN* 2.307 **seMO**, *Break* . . . To turn gray or otherwise show the approach of age. 'You have broken a heap since I seed you last, but you're looking mighty well.' **1907** *DN* 3.229 **nwAR**. **1949** Arnow *Hunter's Horn* 51 **KY**, Her proudness and her prettiness were breaking; her face looked gray and pinched for a woman not yet twenty-one. **1952** Brown *NC Folkl.* 1.522. **c1960** Wilson *Coll.* **csKY**, *Break* . . . To grow old or weak. "Uncle Bob is breaking fast." **1969** *DARE* (Qu. X48b, *If a person is not so young any more, you might say, "He's* ——.") Inf **KY**19, Breaking fast.

6 To become bankrupt. *old-fash*

1800 (1907) Thornton *Diary* 10.201 **PA**, In consequence of Chorley's breaking he is brought into difficulties. **1810** (1912) Bell *Journey to OH* 23 **MA**, A bridge was begun over it, but the man broke & was unable to finish it. **1912** Green *VA Folk-Speech*, *Broke* . . . In the sense of bankrupt, or failing in business: "He *broke* twice before."

7 often in phr *break at the worm;* In whiskey making: to drop to a low proof.

1969 *DARE* Tape **GA**72, When it runs till the heavy part of the alkyholic content is in there, we call it—when it stops beadin'—we call it breakin' at the worm [=condenser]. **1972** *Foxfire Book* 316 **nGA**, *Breaks at the worm*—an expression used at the moment when the whiskey coming out of the flake stand turns less than 100 proof, and thus will no longer hold a bead. **1974** Maurer *KY Moonshine* 114, *Break* . . . Used of the distillate. To drop to a low proof, indicating that the beer is becoming exhausted in the still. The moonshiner often says that the liquor "breaks at the worm" or "breaks at the coil" since he becomes aware of the drop of proof at this point.

8 To escape or move out suddenly; hence vbl n *breaking.* (In std usage *break* is instead followed by a prep such as *away, out,* etc.)

1810 Cuming *Sketches* 135 **OH**, A fine dog, led by a string to prevent his breaking (or hunting the game beyond the reach of their rifles). **1846** Stewart *Altowan* I.vi.174 *(DAE)*, He . . looked out, and saw a robe!—broke, leaped into the river. **1967** *DARE* Tape **LA**10, If one [=a hog] breaks the bunch [=herd], he'll [=the owner] just catch him and put him back in there. **1970** TN Folk Lore Soc. *Bulletin* 36.33 **TN**, She broke to run and run to the house and fell at the door dead.

9 also with *open:* To discharge pus. Cf **fester, matterate**

1965–70 *DARE* (Qu. BB36, *When there's an open sore and this yellowish stuff is coming out of it, you say it's* ——) Infs **IL39, OR1**, Breaking; **CA164, ME9, MA29, MO8, OH95, PA115, VA27**, Broke; **PA94, 195**, Broke open; **NY209**, Sore is broke.

break n¹

1 A sale of tobacco from opened hogsheads; occas the assembled hogsheads themselves; see quot 1967. **chiefly VA, NC** Cf **break v B3**

1859 (1968) Bartlett *Americanisms, Break.* A regular sale of tobacco at the "breaking" or opening of the hogsheads. Local in Virginia. **1960** Heimann *Tobacco* 152 **wVA** (as of 19th cent), Buyers were summoned by trumpet to the leaf markets or "breaks," so called because the first item of business was breaking open hogsheads to get samples on which purchasers based bids. **1967** Key *Tobacco Vocab.* **NC, MO**, *Break* . . . Hogshead market. There hasn't been an old-time break in Fayette County in many a year. *Ibid* **TN**, *Break* . . . Mass of tobacco baskets on floor for auction. "We got a big break on the floor."

2 also sp *brake:* A topographical interruption, as:

a in a mountain.

1760 in 1882 *New Engl. Hist. & Geneal. Register* 36.32, On arriving on the Lake, I took the bearing of a Notch or Break in the Mountains. **1781** (1925) Washington *Diaries* 2.251, These hills have very few interstices or Breaks in them. **1836** in 1940 *AmSp* 15.159 **VA**, To a dogwood & white oak under a rocky point then with the Brake of the mountain . . . to the Beginning. **1929** Summers *Annals* 1591 **swVA** (as of 1777), They continued their journey to the "Breaks," where the Russell and Pound forks of Big Sandy pass through the Cumberland mountain. **1967–68** *DARE* (Qu. C15, *A place in the mountains where you can get through without climbing over the top*) Inf **AR**47, Break of the mountain; **PA**66, Break.

b in a stream.

1808 (1892) Summer *Tour OH* 65, The bottom taken together is perhaps freer from breaks than any like quantity on the river. **1897** Brodhead *Bound in Shallows* 238 *(DAE)*, Logs blackened the stream, showing the terrific speed of the current as they dashed over the break. **1930** Shoemaker *1300 Words* **cPA Mts** (as of c1900), *Breaks*—Where a stream changes from still water to swift over a rocky bed.

3 also sp *brake:* A gulch; rough ground. **chiefly West**

1869 Browne *Adventures* 226 **swAZ**, Not far beyond the mesa we entered upon a rugged region, abounding in breaks and arroyas very rocky and difficult for our horses. **1896** *DN* 1.413 **NE**, *Break:* a rough, irregular piece of ground. **1927** Adams *Ranch on Beaver* 163 **West**, A hundred miles distant, lay a vague and indefinite country . . . In its brakes and dips, thankful if a lone tree was the only landmark, an outfit of men were combing its hills and vales in search of their cattle. **1949** Guthrie *Way West* 81, Dick carried a big rag with him and sometimes tore pieces from it and posted little flags across breaks and washes to show the lead teamster where to head. **1958** Blasingame *Dakota Cowboy* 44 **SD** (as of 1904), I had made a long ride out over the river breaks.

4 See quot.

1932 *DN* 6.225 **West**, The usual Western word *breaks* [is] applied to a series of ridges and valleys running down from a bench or any higher country into the plain. In this meaning the word is found in the strip of the Far West between Dakota and Arizona, sometimes as a proper name, like the well known Cedar Breaks, Utah.

5 A blunder or mistake, often in a social situation. **esp Sth, S Midl**

1884 Nye *Baled Hay* 200, Possibly science may be wrong. We have known science to make bad little breaks. **1893** *KS Univ. Qrly.* 1.138, *Break:* blunder, especially in 'a bad break.' **1899** (1977) Norris *McTeague* 96 **CA**, He kept . . [making] cackling imitations of Mc-Teague's words: "That's the best *beer* I ever drank. Oh, Lord, ain't that a break!" **1908** *DN* 3.294 **eAL, wGA**, *Break* . . . Mistake. **1931** *AmSp* 6.203 **MO**, *Break* . . a social mistake. **1950** *WELS (An embarrassing mistake: "Last night she made an awful* ——.") 4 Infs, **WI**, Break. **c1960** Wilson *Coll.* **csKY**, *Break* . . . An inappropriate act or word, a faux pas. **1966–69** *DARE* (Qu. JJ41, *An embarrassing mistake*) Infs **CA**87, **KY**70, **NY**84, **NC**82, **SC**5, **TN**26, **TX**1, Break.

6 See quot. Cf **brake n⁴ 2**

1966 *DARE* FW Addit **SC**, *Break*—a pole in a stall that a cow is required to straddle to keep her from kicking; also the whole stall with such a pole.

7 =**gallows n 1a.**

1862 IL Dept. Ag. *Trans.* 5.160, I selected the gallows stalks, or breaks of my shocks [of sorghum].

8 in combs *corn break, hay ~:* A sled used to transport corn or hay.

1970 *DARE* (Qu. L13, . . *Wagon used for carrying hay*) Inf **VA**77, Corn break—sled-like thing with [two] straight sides; hay break—sled-like, flat-bottom[ed] with [four] wide, slanting sides.

9 =**breakwall.**

1969–70 *DARE* (Qu. O13, *A heavy stone structure, often with masonry* *work, that encloses and protects a harbor)* Inf **MA**26, 35, **MI**108, **NY**241, Break.

10 See **break cart.**

11 See **breaker 4.**

break n² See **brake** n²

break a breath v phr Cf **crack one's teeth**

To speak, say a word.

1935 Hurston *Mules & Men* 147 **FL** [Black], So he raced on home without breakin' another breath wid de dog. *Ibid* 148, Dat goat ain't broke a breath wid you and nobody else. **1942** Hurston *Dust Tracks* 195 **FL** [Black], Dat Cracker Quarters Boss wears two pistols round his waist and goes for bad, but he won't break a breath with Big Sweet lessen he got his pistol in his hand. *Ibid* 26.

‡break-a-loose n

A landslide.

1970 *DARE* (Qu. C16, *When a mass of earth and rock comes loose from a high place and rushes down, you call it a* _____) Inf **TN**52, Break-a-loose.

break a trace-chain v phr

1908 *DN* 3.294 **eAL, wGA,** *Break a trace-chain*. . . To make a supreme effort.

break at the worm See **break v C7**

break away v phr Also *break way* **esp Atl States** Cf **break off, break up 1**

=**break v C4.**

1758 in **1881** *Essex Inst. Coll.* 18.98 **MA,** Cloudy cool Morning wind West Northerly breaks away about Noon. **1816** in **1916** *MD Hist. Mag.* 11.221, This morning rains very much, about Ten o'Clock breaks away. **1859** (1931) Tuttle *CA Diary* 72, Rain until about 10 oclock when it broke away. **1939** *LANE* Map 89 **throughout NEng,** A change in the weather from cloudy to fair. . . *Breaking away*. . is often used with particular reference to the disintegration and disappearance of clouds. **1950** *WELS* (*When fog goes up very fast, you say it's* _____) 1 Inf, **nwWI,** Breaking away. **1965–70** *DARE* (Qu. B7, *When clouds begin to decrease, you say it's* _____) 21 Infs, **chiefly Atl States,** Breaking away; **NC**34, Breaking way; (Qu. B19) Inf **MA**55, There she breaks away. **1973** Allen *LAUM* 1.152, It's *clearing up*. . . For the ending of a storm . . . [6 informants said] breaking away.

breakback n *?obs*

See quots.

1857 Goodrich *Recollections* 1.78 **CT,** The house . . was a low edifice . . two stories in front; the rear being what was called a *breakback,* that is, sloping down to a height of ten feet. **1859** (1968) Bartlett *Americanisms, Break-back.* A term applied to a peculiar roof, common in the country, where the rear portion is extended beyond the line of the opposite side, and at a different angle. The addition thus acquired is used as a washroom, a storehouse, or for farming implements.

break bean n

=**snap bean.**

1906 *DN* 3.128 **nwAR,** *Break-bean*. . . Edible bean-pod so tender that it does not have to be strung. **c1960** *Wilson Coll.* **csKY,** *Break beans*— Snap beans, green beans. **1968** *DARE* (Qu. I14, *Kinds of beans that you eat in the pod before they're dry*) Inf **NJ**53, Break beans.

breakbone n Also *breaking bone*

The wishbone of a chicken.

c1960 *Wilson Coll.* **csKY,** *Breakbone*. . . Pulley-bone, wishbone. **1968–70** *DARE* (Qu. K74, *A bone from the breast of a chicken, shaped like a horseshoe*) Inf **NC**85, Breakbone; **IN**54, **LA**18, Breaking bone. **1971** Wood *Vocab. Change* 45 **Sth,** *Lucky bone* and *breakbone* are reported in scattered instances. **1973** Allen *LAUM* 1.257, *Breakbone,* not found on the Atlantic coast, was checked by 6 respondents, 2 in southern Minnesota, 2 in Iowa, and one each in South Dakota and Nebraska.

breakbone fever n Also *brokebone fever, brokenbone ~*

Dengue fever.

1859 (1968) Bartlett *Americanisms, Break-bone fever.* A term commonly used to denote the "Dengue," a malarious fever of the South. It is so called from the "pain in the bones," of which patients complain. **1872** *Newton Kansan* 22 Aug 4/2 *(DA),* Dengue fever—what is known in South Carolina and Georgia as 'Broken Bone' fever—is still on the

increase in Calcutta and the neighborhood. **1948** *Reader's Digest* May 32/2, He was among the first 16 to be exposed to the virus of dengue fever, the "breakbone fever" which was causing more casualties among our troops in the Pacific than the enemy. **1950** *PADS* 14.17 **SC,** *Broke-bone fever, broken-bone fever* . . . Dengue fever.

break cart n Also *break* [See quot 1948] Cf **break n¹ 8**

1 A small cart or wagon used to train draft animals.

1948 Rittenhouse *Amer. Horse-Drawn Vehicles* 43, *Break.* (Period: 1895 . .) . . . This [picture] is an example of the true "break," a vehicle used in "breaking" horses. **1967** *DARE* FW Addit **SC,** *Break cart*— Used for breaking mules—had extra long shafts to keep the mule from kicking the cart to pieces.

2 A small horse-drawn wagon used to carry light loads.

1966–69 *DARE* (Qu. N41a, . . *Horse-drawn vehicles* . . *to carry people*) Inf **KY**64, Break cart; (Qu. N41c, . . *To carry light loads*) Inf **SC**24, Break—an all purpose thing, same as a one horse wagon.

break daylight v phr

To become light in the early morning.

1939 *Hall Coll.* **wNC,** We just stood there until it went to breakin' daylight and it got to snowin'. *Ibid,* Time we got the tree cut down it was just a-breakin' daylight.

breakdown n, also attrib **chiefly Sth, S Midl, occas NEng**

A boisterous rural dance or dancing party; a hoedown, shindig.

1819 in **1860** Claiborne *Life Quitman* 1.42, Lay at Point Pleasant, where Whiting and I visited a Virginia 'break-down.' **1843** Field *Drama Pokerville* 180, There were river yarns, and boatmen songs, and "nigger break-downs." **1864** Nichols *40 Yrs.* 1.227 **AL,** She . . heard a long impromptu song composed in her honour, with a banjo and breakdown accompaniment. **1899** (1912) Green *VA Folk-Speech.* **1907** *DN* 3.209 **nwAR.** **1908** *DN* 3.294 **eAL, wGA.** **1912** *DN* 3.571 **wIN.** **1937** in **1958** Brewer *Dog Ghosts* 97 **TX** [Black], Habs 'em a rail break-down ball what las' slap-bang up to de time de roosters staa't to crowin' for daytime Sunday mawnin'. **1941** *LANE* Map 410 **throughout NEng,** Terms for the old kitchen dance (a private dance held on the farm or in the village) . . . *(Kitchen) breakdown.* **1942** (1960) Robertson *Red Hills* 125 **SC,** There was . . a whole strain of kinfolks, who spent their time fiddling at breakdown dances. **c1960** *Wilson Coll.* **csKY.** **1965–70** *DARE* (Qu. FF4, *Different kinds of dancing parties*) 13 Infs **chiefly Sth,** Breakdown; (Qu. FF18, *A noisy or boisterous celebration or party: "They certainly* _____ *last night."*) Inf **SC**26, Had a breakdown; **MS**46, Had a regular breakdown; **GA**1, Georgia breakdown.

break down v phr [**breakdown** n]

To dance in a vigorous or boisterous fashion.

1838 *Lexington Observer & Rep* 8 Aug *(DAE),* He got to 'breaking down' so hard toward the end of his dance, that the head [of the barrel] went in. **1873** Twain–Warner *Gilded Age* 157 **MO,** The twang of a banjo became audible as they drew nearer, and they saw a couple of negroes . . "breaking down" a juba.

breaker n

1 also attrib: =**breaking plow. esp Plains States**

1857 *Lawrence (Kansas) Republican* 28 May 3 *(DA),* A large assortment of Breakers of all sizes, especially of my extra Two-Horse Moldboard Breakers. **1937** Sandoz *Slogum* 294 **NE** (as of 1900–20), Sod rolled in a smooth, dark ribbon from his breaker bottom. **1961** Sackett–Koch *KS Folkl.* 109, *Breaker*—A breaking plow, as contrasted with a stirring plow; a plow for breaking the prairie for the first time. **1968** *DARE* (Qu. L18, *Kinds of plows*) Inf **MN**23, Breaker—a strong plow with a ten foot beam, a moldboard plow for breaking sod; (Qu. L36, *What do you call it* . . *when you dig out roots and underbrush to make a new field*) Inf **CT**10, Breaking up land—use a breaker plow.

2 See quot.

1895 *DN* 1.385 **swPA,** *Breaker:* ridge of earth in hilly part of country road, to throw surface water into side ditches . . . (Other names for same thing: *"thank-you-ma'am," cradle (in-the-road).*)

3 also attrib; In coal mining: a tower in which anthracite is broken up and the slate removed.

1901 *Cosmopolitan* 31.629/1, First, the boy of eight or ten is sent to the breaker to pick the slate and other impurities from the coal which has been brought up from the mine. **1905** *Coal Miners' Pocket Book* 574, *Breaker.*—In anthracite mining in which the coal is broken, sized, and cleaned for market. Known also as *Coal Breaker. Breaker Boy.*—A boy who works in a coal breaker. **1948** *Chicago Daily News* (IL) 18 June 1/5

PA, He veered way from a huge anthracite breaker towering 265 feet into the air.

4 also *break* and in var combs: See quots.

1966–68 *DARE* (Qu. N30, . . *A sudden short dip in the road*) Inf **AR**15, Break; **MD**31, **PA**134, Breaker; **AL**31, **MO**29, Speed breaker; **TX**32, Snooze breaker; **AK**9, Spring breaker.

5 A breakwater. Cf **breakwall**

1965–70 *DARE* (Qu. O13, *A heavy stone structure, often with masonry work, that encloses and protects a harbor*) Infs **IL**54, **MD**25, 42, **MA**35, **NY**27, 151, **NC**63, **PA**76, 185, **TN**36, Breaker; **MD**31, Stone breaker; **MD**26, Wind breaker; **NC**49, Wave breaker.

breakfast n Usu |'brɛkfəst|; also |-wəst, -fəs| Pronc-spp *break-fuss*, by metath, *brefkast*, and with intrusive r, *breakferst*, *breck-frust*; in *Gullah*, brekwus, brukwus(s) See Pronc Intro 3.I.22–23 and Intro "Language Changes" I.1
Std senses, var forms.

1888 Jones *Negro Myths* 61 **GA coast**, Ebry mornin, arter brukwus, eh mobe [=he moves] off. **1899** (1912) Green *VA Folk-Speech*, *Break-fusses* . . . For breakfasts. **1905** *DN* 3.58 **NE**, *Brefkast*. **1908** *S. Atl. Qrly.* 7.342 **S Atl coast** [Gullah], *Brukwuss* . . *breakfast*. **1922** Gonzales *Black Border* 291 **sSC, GA coasts** [Gullah glossary], *Brekwus', Brukwus* —breakfast, breakfasts. **1926** *AmSp* 2.78 **ME**, *Breckfrust*. **1941** *AmSp* 16.11 **eTX** [Black], *Breakfast*, ['brɛkfəs]. **1961** *Mt. Life* 1.6 **sAppalachians**, *Breakferst*. **1982** Barrick *Coll.* **sePA**, Breakfast—pronounced /'brɛkwəst/.

breakfast bacon n Also *breakfast meat*, ~ *strip* **chiefly Mid and S Atl** Cf **salt pork, white bacon**
Smoke-cured, usu sliced, bacon, as opposed to **bacon**, which is cured in salt or brine.

1884 Shepherd *Prairie Exper.* 220 **NV**, A slightly better quality is sold in smaller joints, wrapped in yellow waterproof cloth, and styled breakfast bacon. **1942** Rawlings *Cross Creek* 213 **FL**, We call it [=salt pork] white bacon to distinguish it from breakfast bacon, or side meat. **1949** Kurath *Word Geog.* 70, In Virginia and southern West Virginia and adjoining parts of North Carolina *breakfast bacon* is the usual name, and this expression is current also in Maryland and northern West Virginia beside the simple *bacon*. In the Carolinas *breakfast strip* predominates, a term used also in eastern Virginia south of the James River. *Breakfast meat* is used by some of the simpler folk south of the Potomac to whom *meat* means primarily *pork*. **1950** *WELS (Other words for bacon)* 1 Inf, **cnWI**, Breakfast meat. **1965–70** *DARE* (Qu. H38, *Other words for bacon*) 11 Infs, **esp SC**, Breakfast bacon; **GA**24, 32, **SC**43, Breakfast bacon—sliced (in a package); **NC**18, Breakfast bacon—strips; **NC**84, Breakfast bacon—smoked strip meat; **NM**12, Breakfast bacon—bacon other than salt pork; **SC**46, Breakfast bacon—what you buy at the store now; **VA**9, Breakfast bacon—dry-cured the old-fashioned way like country ham; **VA**18, Breakfast strip.

breakfast bread n

1968–69 *DARE* (Qu. H18, . . *Special kinds of bread*) Inf **MI**96, Breakfast bread; (Qu. H32, . . *Fancy rolls and pastries*) Inf **MI**100, Coffee cakes—called breakfast breads.

breakfast meat, breakfast strip See **breakfast bacon**

breakferst See **breakfast**

breakhorn n [Etym unknown]
The common **merganser**.

1888 Trumbull *Names of Birds* 65, [Common Merganser] On Buzzard's Bay [Massachusetts], from New Bedford to Barney's Joy Point, *Breakhorn*. **1923** U.S. Dept. Ag. *Misc. Circular* 13.4, *American Merganser* . . . *Vernacular Names* . . . In local use . . . Breakhorn (Mass.). **1932** Bennitt *Check-list* 21 **MO**, *American merganser* . . . Break-horn. **1955** *MA Audubon* 39.378, *American Merganser* . . . Breakhorn (Mass., R.I.).

breaking n
In butter making: the stage at which the cream curdles.

1965 Needham–Mussey *Country Things* 66 **VT**, In making butter there is three stages to the cream . . . the swell, the breaking, and the gathering.

breaking vbl n See **break** v **B1, 4, 7, C8**

breaking bone See **breakbone**

breaking exercise n [**break** v **C3** + **exercise** B]
1948 Dick *Dixie Frontier* 186 **KY** (as of 19th cent), At the conclusion of the service the Negroes could not separate without the breaking exercises, so called from breaking up the meeting . . . They began to sing and move in a procession by the pulpit, shaking hands with the minister as they passed . . . Finally . . the meeting "broke," and the service was over.

breaking plow n Also ~ *plough, breaking-up plow* [**break** v **B1**] **widespread, exc Atlantic and West** Cf **breaker 1**
A plow used for turning virgin land.

1781 (1903) Patten *Diary* 438 **NH**, Our 4 oxen and breaking up plow helped james Walker break up. **1830** *Cortland Observer* (Homer, N.Y.) 2 July 1/3 (*DA*), They also make . . . a large assortment of plows, heavy and light . . . from the large breaking-up or greensward ploughs, to the small light corn ploughs . . . and side hill ploughs. **1853** *Knickerbocker* 42.593, The great 'breaking-plough,' with its dozen yoke of cattle, in the first place, goes tearing and groaning through the roots and grubs that lie twisted under it. **1935** Sandoz *Jules* 359 **wNE** (as of 1880–1930), With the awkward breaking plough the man turned smooth ribbons of gray earth in a low spot where the grass was densely rooted. **1950** *WELS (Kinds of plows used in your neighborhood)* 5 Infs, **WI**, Breaking plow. **1965–70** *DARE* (Qu. L18, *Kinds of plows used around here*) 94 Infs, **widespread, exc Atlantic and West**, Breaking plow; **ME**12, Breaking-up plow. **1966** *Cynthiana Democrat* (KY) 28 Apr 6, *Public Auction* . . . two-way McCormick Super H breaking plow 14 inch.

breaking-up See **break-up** n **2**

breaking-up plow See **breaking plow**

break in two v phr **SW**
Of a horse trying to unseat a rider: to change tactic suddenly, from running to bucking or from bucking to running.

1936 Adams *Cowboy Lingo* 98, When he [=a horse] started to buck, it was said that he 'boiled over,' 'broke in two,' . . or 'wrinkled his spine.' **1937** *DN* 6.619 **swTX**, When the horse starts pitching from this position [i.e. his head between his knees], he *breaks in two*. **1945** Thorp *Pardner* 258 **SW**, Some horses [being broken] . . would pitch and run both, usually, after a few seconds of pitching—"breaking in two" was the term the cowboys used when a bronc quit pitching and started running. *Ibid* 32. **1951** Grant *Cowboy Encycl.* 33, A horse "breaks in two" when he leaps into the air after a short run.

break it off in v phr **Sth, S Midl**
To wound (someone) with a sarcastic or cutting retort or rebuke.

1906 *DN* 3.128 **nwAR**, *Break it off in* . . . To rebuke sternly. "Bud won't do it any more; the old man *broke it off in him*." **1914** *DN* 4.103 **KS**, *Break off in* . . . To revenge (something) on (one). "The first chance he gets he will *break it off in you*." **1923** *DN* 5.202 **swMO**. **1949** *PADS* 11.4 **wTX**, He broke it off in Joe with that last crack. **1954** *Harder Coll.* **cwTN**. **1970** *Thompson Coll.* **AL** (as of c1920), You broke it off in me that time—and you can start sucking it out just any old time you're ready.

break off v phr **chiefly Sth** Cf **break** v **C4, break away, fair off**
To become less cloudy, clear up; to stop raining.

1966–70 *DARE* (Qu. B7, *When clouds begin to decrease, you say it's _____*) Infs **AL**1, 48, **AR**56, **GA**7, **KY**20, **TX**22, 96, Breaking off; **MS**63, Fixing to break off; **TX**51, Gonna break off; (Qu. B13, *When the wind begins to decrease*) Inf **LA**7, Fixing to break off; **NC**49, Breaking off; (Qu. B19, *When fog begins to go up in the air*) Inf **SC**9, Breaking off. **1966** *DARE* Tape **NM**13, The rain had broke off. **c1970** Pederson *Dial. Survey Rural GA*, (The weather is _____) 3 infs, **seGA**, Breaking off. **1971** Wood *Vocab. Change* 312 **AR, FL, GA, TN**, Breaking off.

break one's arm v phr [In ref to the physical effort required to pat one's own back]
To brag.

1966 *DARE* (Qu. HH8) Inf **FL**38, Breaking your arm and patting yourself on the back. **c1970** *Halpert Coll.* 2 **wKY**, Don't break your arm. [Said to someone bragging.]

break one's leg v phr Also *break one's toe* **chiefly Sth** *euphem*
To become pregnant.

1908 *DN* 3.294 **eAL, wGA**, *Break one's leg* . . . Of a woman, to become with child illegitimately. **1965–70** *DARE* (Qu. AA28, . . *Expressions . . to say [a woman] is going to have a baby: "She['s] _____."*) Infs **FL**51, **LA**6, **NJ**69, **NC**88, **VA**41, Broke her leg; **AL**50, Broke a leg; **AL**56, Got a leg broke; **CA**114, **GA**70, **MS**60, **WV**4, 5, Broke her toe. **1979** *DARE* File **cSC**, There used to be the expression . . meaning pregnant. Mrs. Brown's daughter broke her leg.

break one's neck v phr esp Sth

To get married.

1965–70 *DARE* (Qu. AA15a, . . *Ways . . of saying that people got married: "They _____."*) Infs **NJ**67, **NC**49, **PA**110, Broke their neck; (Qu. AA15b, . . *Ways . . of saying that a man is getting married: "He _____."*) Infs **CA**123, **DC**13, **LA**3, 6, 16, 20, 31, 46, **MD**24, 27, **MO**25, **PA**206, **VA**35, 41, Broke his neck; [**TX**35, Broke his leg;] (Qu. AA15c, . . *A woman . . getting married: "She _____."*) Inf **KY**11, Broke her own neck.

break one's pick v phr

1968 Adams *Western Words*, *Break one's pick*—In mining, to quit, be discharged, or become discouraged.

break one's toe See **break one's leg**

break out v phr

1 To cause to erupt.

1937 *Hall Coll.* **wNC,** Catnip tea is used to break out the hives. **1968–69** *DARE* FW Addit **VA,** Catnip given to babies to break the hives out of 'em; **KY,** Ground ivy tea used to break the hives out in small babies.

2 See quot.

1923 *DN* 5.202 **swMO,** *Break out* . . . To break or train an animal to work. "I broke out that colt m'se'f."

break out at the mouth v phr, hence vbl n *breaking* ~

To talk too much, or too loudly.

1912 *DN* 3.571 **wIN,** A habit of talking too much. ". . George has got a breakin' out at the mouth." **1969** *DARE* (Qu. HH7b) Inf **VT**12, Breaking out at the mouth.

break over v phr

To violate a rule or a resolution.

c1937–43 in **1944** *ADD* **WV,** Once in a while you got to break over & read a whole book . . . I broke over & smoked a cigaret . . . I made a resolution not to smoke, but I'll break over just once.

breaks and keeps n

In marble play: see quot.

1968 *DARE* (Qu. EE7, . . *Marble games*) Inf **CA**105, Breaks and keeps—each takes all his marbles and tries to break the other's with his agate.

break up v phr

1 =**break** v C4.

1939 *LANE* Map 89 **scattered in NEng,** *Breaking, ~ up* . . referring to a change in the weather from cloudy to fair. **1950** *WELS* (*When clouds begin to decrease, you say it's _____*) 3 Infs, **WI,** Breaking up. **1962** Atwood *Vocab.* TX 38, Breaking up. **1965–70** *DARE* (Qu. B7, *When clouds begin to decrease, you say it's _____*) 32 Infs, **widespread, but esp Upper MW, SW,** Breaking up; **MO**26, **WA**3, Beginning to break up. **1971** Wood *Vocab. Change* 312 **AL, AR, LA,** Breaking up. **1973** Allen *LAUM* 1.152, It's *clearing up* . . . For the ending of a storm . . . [8 informants said] breaking up.

2 To burst out laughing.

1895 Twain in *N. Amer. Rev.* 160.61, Well, humour is the great thing, the saving thing, . . so, when M. Bourget said that bright thing about our grandfathers, I broke all up. **1965–70** *DARE* (Qu. GG30, *To suddenly break out laughing: "When he told her that, she just _____."*) 28 Infs, **esp Nth, N Midl,** Broke up; (Qu. GG31, *To laugh very hard: "I thought I'd _____."*) Infs **MA**8, **NY**123, Break up. [Of all Infs responding to the question, 63% were old; of those giving this response, 23% were old.]

break-up n

1 also attrib: The late spring melting of ice and snow. **AK** Cf **freeze-up**

1868 Whymper *Travel AK* 194, First real break-up of the Yukon, the ice coming down in a steady flow. **1904** Schrader *Reconnaissance* 15 **AK,** The party waited at Bergman for the disappearance of the snow and ice—the "break-up," as it is called . . . Owing to the heavy snowfall of the previous winter and the lateness of the spring, the break-up period of 1901 was of unusual length, extending from the middle of May to June 6. **1915** Stuck *10000 Miles* 133 **AK,** A visit to the telegraph station informed us that the warm wave was spread all over interior Alaska and that there was general expectation of an early break-up. **1953** *Jessen's Weekly* 5 Mar *(Tabbert Coll.)* **AK,** No one will ever forget the eggs which Fairbanks had to eat during the winter months, before there was a Richardson highway to bridge the months between freezeup and

breakup. **1980** *New Yorker* 4 Aug 46 **AK,** He wears . . an elbow-patched canvas shirt, bluejeans, and L.L. Bean's shoepacs, which he calls "breakup boots."

2 also *breaking-up:* The American Civil War.

1869 Browne *Adventures* 133, It [Tucson] became during the few years preceding the "break-up" quite a place of resort for traders, speculators [etc]. **1883** Sweet–Knox *Mexican Mustang* 74 **TX,** Before the civil war, or, as a Texan would say, "'fore the break-up." **1945** FWP *Lay My Burden Down* 86, Most the niggers I know, who had their marriage put in the book, did it after the breaking-up.

breakwall n chiefly eGt Lakes

A breakwater.

1965–70 *DARE* (Qu. O13, *A heavy stone structure, often with masonry work, that encloses and protects a harbor*) Infs **AL**26, **NY**5, 100, 103, 105, 133, 151, 183, 226, **NC**72, **OH**16, 29, **PA**128, Breakwall.

break way See **break away**

break western v phr

1982 *Smithsonian Letters* **cVA,** "Breaking western . ." has been used in this area of the Blue Ridge for as long as anyone extant can remember and they all say that their parents used the expression, too. In their definition it means "talking rough." There may be profanity mixed in but not necessarily. I get more than a little inference of loss of temper.

bream n Usu |brim|, **esp in Sth, S Midl;** also |brim|; infreq |brɛm| Pronc-sp *brim*

A Forms.

1634 Wood *New Engl. Prospect* 90, In frostie weater [sic] they [=Indians] cut round holes in the yce, about which they wil sit . . catching of Pikes, Pearches, Breames, and other sorts of fresh water fish. **1772** in 1924 Phillips *Notes B. Romans* 123 **FL,** Those [=river fish] peculiar to America are three Species of the Bream, One of which is here Called Perch, the Striped Rock, and a kind of Fish . . on which there is not a Name yet fixed. **1854** (1969) Thoreau *Walden* 199 **MA,** There have been caught in Walden . . shiners, chivins or roach, . . a very few breams, and a couple of eels, one weighing four pounds. **1887** *Harper's Mag.* 75.270/1 **LA,** If they could slip away . . there would be a diminished number of "brim" and "goggle-eye," in the ditch. **1894** *Outing* 23.403/2 **MA,** Besides these, there was the brim, a small, red fish, which is excellent fried. **1908** *DN* 3.294 **eAL, wGA,** Brim . . . Bream. The latter is not heard. **1936** *AmSp* 11.314 **Ozarks,** Brim . . . Black perch. Commonly used in the White River country of northern Arkansas. Not much heard in Missouri. **1942** Hall *Smoky Mt. Speech* 14, Bream (a kind of sunfish) [brɛm]. **c1960** Wilson *Coll.* **csKY,** Bream . . . Also *brim*. **1965–70** [see quot at B3 below].

B Senses.

1 =**golden shiner.**

1882 U.S. Natl. Museum *Bulletin* 16.250, *N[otemigonus] chrysoleucus* . . Bream. **1946** LaMonte *N. Amer. Game Fishes* 158, *Notemigonus crysoleucus* . . American Bream, Bream.

2 often with a qualifier: Any of various fish of the family Sparidæ.

1873 in 1878 Smithsonian Inst. *Misc. Coll.* 14.2.27, *Stenotomus argyrops* . . bream (Rhode Island . . .). **1882** U.S. Natl. Museum *Bulletin* 16.558, *D[iplodus] rhomboides* . . Bream. *Ibid* 559, *D. holbrooki* . . Bream. **1882** U.S. Natl. Museum *Proc.* 5.605, *Lagodon rhomboides* . . Brim. **1933** John G. Shedd Aquarium *Guide* 110, *Diplodus argenteus* —Bream . . . *Diplodus holbrookii*—Spot-tail Bream. **1946** LaMonte *N. Amer. Game Fishes* 71, Bream *Lagodon rhomboides* . . . Saltwater Bream, . . Sea Bream.

3 Any of various fish of the family Centrarchidæ, here esp **warmouth** and **bluegill.** Sth, S Midl See Map

1885 Thompson *By-Ways* 126, Speaking of bream, as the Southerners call the blue-perch [=bluegill], it is a royal fish. **1933** LA Dept. of Conserv. *Fishes* 342, The Warmouth Bass has come to bear many confusing popular names. These are: . . Bream . . Warmouth Bream. **1965–70** *DARE* (Qu. P1) 83 Infs, **Sth, S Midl,** Brim [brim]; 45 Infs, **Sth,** Brim(s); **GA**89, Bluegill brim, redbreast brim; **NC**49, Brim fish; **SC**40, Blue brim, government brim; 22 Infs, **Sth, S Midl,** Bream(s); **GA**25, Blue bream, black bream, green bream; **NC**24, Blue bream; **LA**15, Yellow bream; (Qu. P2) Inf **GA**3, Sea brim; (Qu. P3) Inf **MA**68, Bream [brim]; **TX**5, Brim; (Qu. P7) Infs **AR**56, **LA**14, Brim; (Qu. P14) Inf **FL**51, Brim. **1966–68** *DARE* Tape **FL**37, There was a lake right there by us, and we'd . . fish and catch the most biggest brim [brim] you ever seen; **GA**35, Our best fishin' is what we call the perch fishin', is the warmouths, brim [brɪm]; **LA5,** Now they have the brim [brɪm], good many brim; **NC36,** We have bass and brim [brɪm], or bluegills. **1975** Evanoff *Catch More Fish* 2, Many still fishermen seek sunfish, of which the bluegill or bream (pronounced "brim" down South) is the most popular.

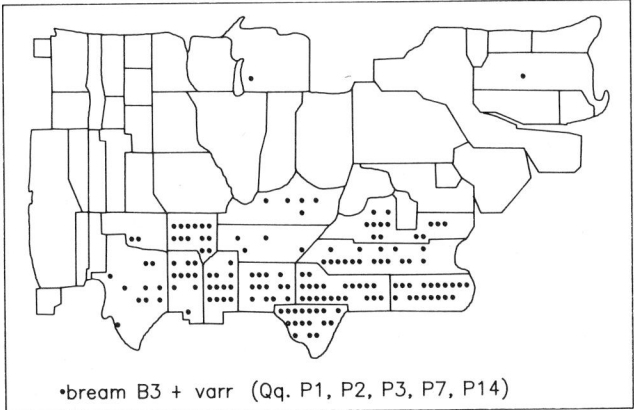

·bream B3 + varr (Qq. P1, P2, P3, P7, P14)

4 =**rosefish.**
1887 Goode *Amer. Fishes* 257, The Rose-fish, *Sebastes marinus . .* is known . . as "Bream" in Gloucester, Mass. **1902** Jordan–Evermann *Amer. Fishes* 495, *Sebastes marinus,* known as the rose-fish . . bream.

breaming adv [Perh from Engl *breme,* Scots *breem* fierce, violent] Cf **brimsy**
Intensely.
1936 Morehouse *Rain on Just* 41 **NC,** So breaming hot the figs were already plumping out.

breast n
1 The chest—used of both human sexes and of animals.
1902 *DN* 2.230 **sIL,** *Breast.* The chest. **1941** *LANE* Map 489 **throughout NEng,** In asking for these terms the fieldworker usually pointed to his own chest and shoulders. Forty-four informants offered the word *breast* as a first response instead of *chest.* **1946** *PADS* 5.13 **VA,** *Breast:* Chest; fairly common. **c1960** *Wilson Coll.* **csKY,** *Breast* . . . Chest, rather indefinite as to location, from neck to navel. "Doc, I've got a pain in my breast." **1967** *Hall Coll.* **eTN,** Hit [=a hog] stood right on his breast, lookin' down on his face. **1969** *DARE* Tape **CA107,** Breast [the chest of a horse].
2 The udder of a cow.
1965–70 *DARE* (Qu. K4, *The cow's udder*) Infs **CT39, MO36, MA2, NY43, 58, SC9,** Breast; (Qu. K7, *What sickness can a cow get in her udder?*) Inf **MA6,** Broken breast; **NY37,** Caked breast; **SC9,** Boil in the breast.
3 A pair of draft animals harnessed side by side.
1965–70 *DARE* (Qu. K26, *If six oxen are hitched together two and two, you have three____*) Infs **CA157, IL90, MO24, SC19,** Breast; **GA77,** A double breast—more than two steers abreast; **OK43,** That's three different breasts.

breast baby n Also *breast child* Cf **apron child**
See quots.
1944 *PADS* 2.41 **NC, SC,** *Breast baby . . .* A nursing baby. **1950** *PADS* 14.16 **SC,** *Breast-child . . .* An unweaned infant. **1954** *Harder Coll.* **cwTN,** *Breast baby*—A nursing baby.

breastbone n scattered, but least freq in Nth and Sth old-fash
A wishbone.
1960 *PADS* 34.57 **CO,** *Older Folk Speech . . . Breast bone* 'wishbone.' **1965–70** *DARE* (Qu. K74, *A bone from the breast of a chicken, shaped like a horse shoe*) 22 Infs, **scattered exc Nth and Sth,** Breastbone [21 of 22 Infs old]. **1966** *PADS* 46.24 **cnAR,** *Breast bone . . .* The clavicles of a fowl.—"Some people call the breast bone the 'pulley bone.'" **c1971** *Hall Snake River Valley* (Bone in the breast of a chicken) 11 Infs, **sID,** Breastbone.

breast child See **breast baby**

breast complaint n Also *breast disease* [**breast 1**]
Pulmonary tuberculosis.
1837 Sherwood *Gaz. GA* 82, Dyspepsy carries off some; consumption, or breast complaint, as it is termed, affects some persons. **1914** Furman

Sight 33 **eKY,** She died of the breast-complaint; some calls it the galloping consumpt'. **1939** *AmSp* 14.89 **eTN,** *Breast disease.* Tuberculosis. 'She died with breast disease.'

breastweed n ?*obs*
=**lizard's tail.**
1829 Eaton *Botany* 381, Lizard's tail, breast weed . . . Rare in New York east of Cayuga Lake—abundant west of it. **1837** Darlington *Flora Cestrica* 237, Lizard's Tail. Breast weed . . . The fresh *roots,* bruised and applied in the form of poultice, are a popular remedy for inflamed breasts. **1900** Lyons *Plant Names* 335.

breath n Usu |brɛθ|; also, *chiefly among Black speakers,* |brɛf| Pronc-spp *bref(f)* See Pronc Intro 3.I.17
A Forms.
1893 Shands *MS Speech* 15 [Black], [brɛf] for breath. **1901** *Century Illustr. Mag.* 62.904 **TN** [Black], Shed plumb lose he bref in dis ole town! **1901** *DN* 2.181 **neKY** [Black], *Breath . .* breff. **1941** *AmSp* 16.13 **eTX** [Black], *Breath . .* [brɛf].
B Senses.
1 A very short time; a moment.
1917 *DN* 4.408 **NC,** *Breath.* A moment. I'll be there in just a breath. Also Me., N.H. **1942** (1971) Campbell *Cloud-Walking* 18 **seKY,** She went on in the house . ., telling him to wait a breath while she found out how bad off Marthy was. **c1960** *Wilson Coll.* **csKY,** We expected to fall down every breath as we run away from the vicious hog. **1966** *DARE* (Qu. A14, . . *"I'll be ready in____."*) Inf **GA15,** [A] breath.
2 See quot.
1952 Brown *NC Folkl.* 1.522, *Breath . . .* The least idea, word, conception. "I didn't think a *breath* of what he said."—Central and east.

breath-and-britches n
A no-account person.
1937 (1977) Hurston *Their Eyes* 27 **FL,** Ah don't want no trashy nigger, no breath-and-britches, lak Johnny Taylor usin' yo' body to wipe his foots on.

breathe v Usu |brið|; also, *chiefly among Black speakers,* |briv| Pronc-sp *breeve* See Pronc Intro 3.I.17
Std senses, var forms.
1893 Shands *MS Speech* 15 [Black], [briv] for breathe. **1901** *DN* 2.181 **neKY** [Black], *Breathing . .* breevin'. **1941** *AmSp* 16.13 **eTX** [Black], *Breathe . . .* [briv].

breath harp n chiefly **Sth, S Midl** Cf **harp** n[1] **1**
1 A harmonica.
1946 *PADS* 6.7 **swVA** (as of 1900–10), *Breath harp . . .* A harmonica, a mouth harp. **1968** *DARE* (Qu. FF7) Infs **NC49, VA13, 18,** Breath harp. **1971** Wood *Vocab. Change* 39 **Sth,** *Breath harp* is barely present in Tennessee and Oklahoma.
2 A Jew's harp.
1971 Wood *Vocab. Change* 40 **Sth,** A harp with a kind of tine which is plucked while one blows against it . . . Instances of *breath harp* in this sense are reported from Tennessee, Alabama, Georgia, and Oklahoma.

breathing image n
A perfect likeness, spitting image.
1966–67 *DARE* (Qu. Z10, *If a child looks very much like his father, you might say "He____ his father."*) Infs **AL6, SC40,** Is a breathing image.

breath of spring n
A honeysuckle (here: *Lonicera fragrantissima*).
1942 *Sun* (Baltimore MD) 1 Apr 10/7 (*Hench Coll.*), *Lonicera fragrantissma . . .* Breath of Spring . . is a variety of honeysuckle. **1970** *DARE* (Qu. S26e) Inf **VA43,** Breath of spring—sweet smell, first to bloom.

breathy adj Cf **bitterweed milk, marshy milk**
Of milk: having the taste of the plants on which the cows have grazed.
1966–68 *DARE* (Qu. K14, *Milk that has a taste from something the cow ate in the pasture*) Inf **ME5,** Breathy milk; **MD43,** Breathy ['brɛθɪ]—tastes like the breath of the cow.

breckfrust See **breakfast**

bred See **breed** v **1**

breddah See **brother A3**

bredduh See **brethren A, brother A3**

bred-in-the-bone adj phr
Native.

1942 McAtee *Dial. Grant Co. IN* (as of 1890s), *Bred in the bone* . . inherent. (Va.)   **1947** Bowles–Towle *New Engl. Cooking* 201, It is difficult for any bred-in-the-bone New Englander to picture a time when doughnuts built around holes did not fill a special stone crock on the butt'ry shelf.

bredren(s) See **brethren**

bree n Also sp *brie* [Prob Scots *bree* broth, gravy, juice; but cf Ger *brei* pap, porridge, and **bry**]
Gravy, juice.

1939 Aurand *Quaint Idioms* 12 *PaGer,* Good *bree* (gravy, or juice) I always like on my bread.   **1951** Danner *PA Dutch Dict.* 58, Juice—*brie* . . juicy—*brieich.*

breechclout n Pronc-sp *britchclout* [**breech** buttocks + **clout** n[1] 1] Cf **britches** 4
A diaper.

1912 Green *VA Folk-Speech,* Breech-clout . . . The cloth put around the buttocks of a child.   **1926** *DN* 5.398 **Ozarks,** To mean *diaper* . . *britch-clout* is heard occasionally.   **1967** *DARE* (Qu. W19) Inf **IL26,** Britchclout [brɪč].

breeches See **britches**

breeches flower n
=**Dutchman's breeches 1.**

1814 Pursh *Flora Americae* 2.462, *Corydalis . . . Cucullaria . . .* This singularly constructed flower is known among the inhabitants by the name of *Breeches-flower* or *Yellow-breeches.*   **1893** *Jrl. Amer. Folk.* 6.137, *Dicentra cucullaria . . .* breeches flower. N[ew] Y[ork].   **1959** Carleton *Index Herb. Plants* 18, *Breeches flower: Dicentra cucullaria.*

breechless adj Also *britchless*
Of a man: not "wearing the breeches" but being dominated by a woman.

1952 Brown *NC Folkl.* 1.523, *Breechless, britchless . . .* Henpecked.— Caldwell county. Rare.

breechman n Also *breechment, britchmans*
=**britchin 1.**

1896 *DN* 1.413 **nwMD,** Breechman [brɪčmən]: breech-band of harness.   **1930** Shoemaker *1300 Words* **cPA Mts** (as of c1900), *Breechment* —Breeching of a horse-harness.   **1930s** in **1944** *ADD* **WV,** Britchmans.

breechy See **breachy**

breed v

1 To be pregnant; to give birth; hence ppl adj *bred* pregnant. [*OED* 1629 →; "Now chiefly *dial.*"]
1912 Green *VA Folk-Speech,* Breeding . . . "His wife is breeding again."   **1917** *DN* 4.408 **wNC, ME.**   **1939** Faulkner *Wild Palms* 217 **MS,** "But women have been bearing children—You have borne two yourself— " "Damn pain too. I take easy and breed hard but damn that, I'm used to that, I don't mind that. I said they hurt too much. Too damned much."   **1966** *DARE* (Qu. AA28, *What joking or sly expressions do women use to say that another is going to have a baby? "She's _____."*) Inf **SC26,** Breeding.   **1967** *DARE* Tape **MI49,** They must have got one of the little twelve-year-old girls bred and they had a little baby.

2 in phr *breed up a storm:* To become cloudy. Cf **weather breeder**
1939 *LANE* Map 90 **sME,** A change in the weather from fair to cloudy . . . [It's] *breedin' up a storm.*

breed n, also attrib **scattered, but esp West**
A person of American Indian and White parentage.
1892 *Harper's Mag.* 84.387/2 **sOK, nTX,** One-quarter of the number of 'breeds' could read and write.   **1895** *DN* 1.385 **West,** Breed: half or quarter breed Indian. (Not used of any other race.)   **1926** (**1927**) Black *You Can't Win* 229 **Pacific NW,** I soon mastered Chinook, practicing on the two "breed" boys.   **1935** Sandoz *Jules* 128 **wNE** (as of 1880–1930), The first squaw men and breeds that slipped into Rushville and Gordon asking protection sent the settlers into a panic.   **1965** Guthrie *Blue Hen's Chick* 20 **MT** (as of c1920), The white-and-Indian hybrids . . [were] known universally as breeds.   **1965–70** *DARE* (Qu. HH29a, *Names around here for people of mixed blood—part Indian*) 34 Infs, **scattered, but esp NW,** Breed.

breed a scab (on one's nose) v phr Also *breed a black eye*
To stir up trouble (for oneself)—often used as a warning.
1941 *AmSp* 16.21 **sIN,** Breeding a scab. Preparing to make serious trouble for oneself. 'You're breeding a scab when you talk to him like that.'   **1942** McAtee *Dial. Grant Co. IN* (as of 1890s), Breed a scab on one's nose, . . act so as to provoke retaliation; "Better stop that, you're breeding a scab on your nose."   **1967** *DARE* (Qu. HH26, *A person who is always ready to stir up trouble*) Infs **PA13, WA30,** Breeding a scab.   **1967** *DARE* FW Addit **seOR,** Breeding a black eye—you're getting on my nerves.   **1981** *NADS Letters* **cIL** (as of 1930s), "Breeding a scab on your nose."   Stirring up trouble so one may get hit in the nose.   **1981** *DARE* File **sID** (as of 1950s), The mother of one of my friends would keep her children from being too obstreperous by warning "You're breeding a scab on your nose." She would never have hit them, but the warning was effective; **MN** (as of c1922), "You're breedin' a scab on (the end of) your nose"—i.e., asking for trouble, a punch on the nose.

breeder n Cf **breed** v 1
One who produces many children.
1899 (**1912**) Green *VA Folk-Speech,* Breeder . . . A woman who has many children. "She is a good-breeder, she has a dozen children."   **1942** Kennedy *Palmetto Country* 74 **FL,** It was customary for slave-owners to encourage or force the marriage or breeding of their slaves . . . The strongest and most intelligent Negroes were selected as "breeders," and some slave-holders saw to it that their strongest Negro man fathered the children of all their women slaves. The women selected as breeders were maintained primarily for that purpose.

breediness n Cf **breedy** adj[1]
1949 *PADS* 11.18 **CO,** Breediness . . . The good breeding of a horse. "The horse showed its breediness."

breeding vein n [Because such veins freq appear during pregnancy; cf **breed** v 1]
A varicose vein.
1966–68 *DARE* (Qu. AA29, . . *The blue, swollen veins that a woman often gets on her legs while expecting a baby*) Infs **IN13, SC10, 26,** Breeding veins.

breed of cat n Also *breed of dog, ~ pup*
Usu prec by *another* or *different:* a kind or sort—freq used of a person thought to be different notably from the usual kind.
1906 *DN* 3.128 **nwAR,** Breed of dogs, breed of purps [sic] . . . "He belongs to a different breed of dogs."   **1927** *AmSp* 2.349 **WV,** Breed of pups . . those having common traits. "They all belong to the same breed of pups."   **1929** *AmSp* 5.119 **ME,** A person inferior or different from the community was characterized as of "another breed of cats."   **1943** *AmSp* 18.238 **neMA,** A white man born at South Groton (now Ayer) Massachusetts, in 1840, and college educated, liked these expressions: *Another breed of cats* . . something different . . . etc.   **1970** *DARE* (Qu. KK68) Inf **PA242,** A different breed of cat.   **1981** *Capital Times* (Madison WI) 27 May 48/3 [Art Buchwald column], It was easy to tell a Commie or fellow traveler in the '50s, because he always carried a "Daily Worker" under his arm, and didn't bother to shine his shoes . . . But a secular humanist is a different breed of cat.

breed up a storm See **breed** v 2

breedy adj[1] [*breed* n] **West**
Of a horse: exhibiting good characteristics worth breeding for.
1949 *PADS* 11.18 **CO,** Breedy . . . Indicating good breed. "A breedy look."   **1967** Green *Horse Tradin'* 58 **West,** There were some breedy-looking riding-type mares in the shipment.

breedy adj[2] [*breed* to engender] Cf **weather breeder**
Of weather conditions: building up for a storm.
1954 Forbes *Rainbow* 243 **NEng,** It had been too hot and breedy a day for good shooting. Mostly he had just sat there and watched the storm cooking up at the head of the valley.

bre'er See **brother** A2

breetherin See **brethren**

breeve See **breathe**

breeze v Usu with *on* or *up;* hence vbl n *breezing on* **chiefly N Atl, C Atl** Cf **breezen 1, breeze of wind**
Of a wind: to increase considerably in strength, often to gale force.
1752 (**1925**) Washington *Diaries* 1.31 **VA,** At noon the Wind breezed

up at So. and clouded. **1899** (1912) Green *VA Folk-Speech,* Breeze up . . . When the wind begins to grow in force from a calm. "The wind began to *breeze up* from the south." **1903** *DN* 2.293 **Cape Cod MA,** Breeze on . . . Gradually blow harder. *Breeze up fresh* . . . Begin to blow hard. **1950** Moore *Candlemas Bay* 57 **ME,** What he'd felt on his skin when he'd come out of the water was *wind.* It was beginning to breeze on. *Ibid* 290, If the wind breezed up, you'd very likely lose your haul. *Ibid* 293, But the real menace was weather—a quick squall or any breezing-on of wind. **1965–70** *DARE* (Qu. B12, *When the wind begins to increase, you say it's* _____) 20 Infs, **NEng and C Atl states,** Breezing up; NC81, TX26, Breezing; VA55, A-breezing. **1966** *DARE* Tape NC25, We'd have one calm day, no wind at all, and it would breeze up that night . . . It's breezed up now. **1973** Allen *LAUM* 1.155 **cMN, cnNE,** The wind is *rising* . . . Breezing up. **1976** Warner *Beautiful Swimmers* 267 **Chesapeake Bay,** Maybe it won't breeze up and we'll get a crab or two.

breeze n Cf **breezen 2**

1899 (1912) Green *VA Folk-Speech,* Breeze . . . A noisy quarrel; a disturbance; a row.

breezen v Also *breezen up* [**breeze** v + -en suff⁵] **chiefly ME**

1 also with *on:* See quots.

1942 *ME Univ. Studies* 56.58, Changes in the wind are indicated in various ways . . . To *breeze* (or *breezen*) on, to *breeze up fresh* . . mean to increase in velocity, often to a gale. **1945** Colcord *Sea Language* 41 **ME, Cape Cod, Long Island,** Breezen . . to blow harder; to increase nearly to the velocity of a gale . . . [also] breezen on. **1975** Gould *ME Lingo,* Breezen—Usually with up. A breeze is good sailing weather, and so is a fresh breeze and a stiff breeze. But if it then *breezens* up, it is too much of a good thing.

2 To become angry.

1975 Gould *ME Lingo,* A person with a short temper may be said to *breezen* up unduly.

breeze of wind n Cf **breeze v, breezen 1**

A wind of moderate gale force.

[**1842** *Jukes* ii 162 *(DNE),* We met a fleet of boats, large and small, with mainsails down, foresails reefed, and every sign of a heavy breeze blowing.] **1945** Colcord *Sea Language* 41 **ME, Cape Cod, Long Island,** A breeze o' wind signifies a moderate *gale.*

‡**breezeport** n [Perh blend of **breezeway** and *carport*]

1968 *DARE* (Qu. D16, . . *Parts added on to the main part of a house*) Inf KS7, Breezeport.

breezeway n **widespread exc West** See Map Also called **dogtrot**

A roofed passage, usu open at the sides, connecting two buildings or parts of a house.

1931 K.N. Burt *Man's Own Country* 39 *(DA),* A small log building attached to the end of his own ranch-house by means of what is known to the Far West as a breeze-way. This construction is a floored and roofed-over passage, open at the sides. **1933** Rawlings *South Moon* 41 **FL,** The trail passed up through . . a gate in the slat fence to the house yard. They crossed the breezeway and lifted the latch into the front room. **1944** *PADS* 2.8 **LA,** Breeze-way . . . A wide, floored passage-way running between two halves of a house, built, except for a common roof and floor level, as two separate structures. Being open at both ends, the passage-way is cool, and many of the household activities are carried out there. This type of structure is common in retired parts of the South where the building was done by the owner and neighbors. **1950** *WELS* (*Parts built*

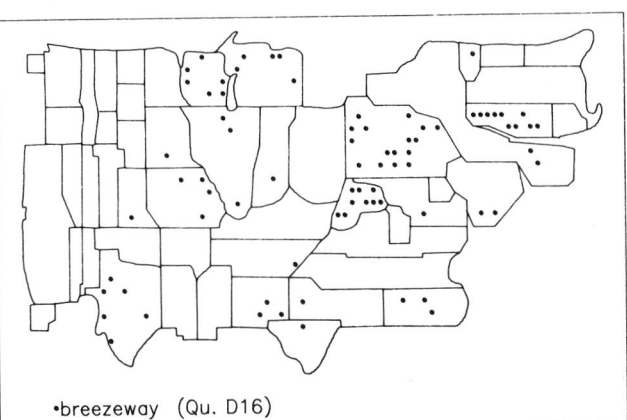

•breezeway (Qu. D16)

on outside the main part of the house) 2 Infs, **WI,** Breezeway. c**1960** *Wilson Coll.* **csKY,** Breezeway . . . Open passage between parts of a house; a modern little-used word for dogtrot. **1965–70** *DARE* (Qu. D16, . . *Parts added on to the main part of a house*) 77 Infs, **widespread exc in West,** Breezeway. **1967** *DARE* FW Addit **swAR,** Breezeway— An open hallway through a house with entrances to rooms on right and left. It led directly from the front porch to the back. **1971** Bright *Word Geog. CA & NV* 148, *Covered walk* . . [78 informants:] *breezeway.*

bref(f) See **breath**

brefkast See **breakfast**

breke See **break** v A3

brekwus See **breakfast**

brella n Also *brelly* [Aphet forms of *umbrella*]

1966–68 *DARE* (Qu. W1c, . . *An umbrella*) Infs **AL8, SC70,** Brella; **OH61,** Brelly.

Bremmer n, also attrib [Alter of *Brahma(n)* any of several breeds of cattle orig imported from India]

A variety of large cattle, usu silvery gray in color.

1962 *Catahoula Hog Dog* 2 **LA,** A small boy in a LaSalle Parish rural section was attacked by a Brahman (colloquially Bremmer) bull. **1967** *DARE* Tape TX8, FW: You raise cattle don't you? What kind? Inf: ['brɛmɚ] . . . They [=local farmers] like the cross better . . . They're going to a Hereford-Bremmer cross.

brennessel n [Ger] **Ger settlement areas** See also **burned hazel**

A stinging nettle.

1967–68 *DARE* (Qu. S16, *A three-leaved plant that grows in woods and countryside and makes people's skin itch and swell*) Inf **PA11,** Brennessel ['brænezəl]; (Qu. S17, *Other kinds of plants . . that will cause itching and swelling*) Inf **PA53,** Nettles, called [brɪnɛzəl].

brent goose See **brant 1**

brenth n [Engl dial; alter of *breadth* infl by *lenth* < *length*]

1927 *SPE Tract* 27.201 [Footnote], Even Mrs. Anne Bradstreet has notable dialect forms at times, disguised by the conventional spellings. Her rhyme of *caught* with *bait* implies a late survival of the old form *keight,* while *breadth* rhyming with *length* is evidence both for the pronunciation *lenth* and for the analogical *brenth,* a form still current in England and the United States. **1963** in **1982** *Barrick Coll.* **sePA,** Brenth—width or breadth. **1970** *Ibid.*

brer See **brother** A2

‡**brer rabbit fence** n

1968 *DARE* (Qu. L62, *A fence made of split logs*) Inf **VA24,** Brer rabbit fence—same as stake-and-rider fence.

bresh See **brush** n, v¹ A1, v²

brethren n pl

A Forms. For pronc and sp varr, see quots.

1837 Sherwood *Gaz. GA* 69, Breethering, for brethren. **1843** (1916) Hall *New Purchase* 152, None of us, my bruthren will live half that long. **1871** Eggleston *Hoosier Schoolmaster* 106 **IN,** My brethering-ah and sistering-ah, the ox knoweth his owner-ah, and the ass-ah his master's crib-ah. **1884** Harrison *Negro Engl.* 245 **Sth,** Bredrens. *Ibid* 257, Bredren. **1890** *DN* 1.67 **KY,** Bredren: for brethren. Sometimes pronounced "britheren" and "brutherin" and "breetherin." "I tell you, breetherin and sisterin." **1893** Shands *MS Speech,* Brotheren or Brudderen [brʌðərn] *or* [brʌdərn]—Negro and illiterate White for brethren. **1908** *DN* 3.294 **eAL, wGA,** Bretherin . . . often in the phrase "bretherin and sisterin," referring to members of the church. **1912** Green *VA Folk-Speech,* Brothren . . . Brethren. **1922** Gonzales *Black Border* 290 **sSC, GA coasts** [Gullah glossary], Bredduh—(also brudduh) . . brethren (formal). **1928** Green *In the Valley* 148 **NC,** All honor to them and their brethering. **1936** *AmSp* 11.245 **eTX,** Brethren ['brɛðrɛn] *Plantation-Type* [speech]; ['brɛðə·n] *Hill-Type;* ['brʌðən] *Negro.* **1941** *AmSp* 16.10 **eTX** [Black], Brethren, ['brɛðn, 'brʌðn]. **1942** Hall *Smoky Mt. Speech* 21, ['brʌðə·ɪn] . . brethren. **1950** *PADS* 13.23 **sKY,** "Brethern and sistern, our text for today is . . . ." (Illiterate minister). c**1960** *Wilson Coll.* **csKY,** Brethren, sometimes /brɛðrɪŋ/.

B Sense.

Also attrib, usu cap: any of several religious sects, differing locally in their affiliations, but simply called "the Brethren": see quots. **chiefly C Atl and Ohio River Valley**

1822 U.S. Congress *Debates & Proc.* 17th Cong 1st Sess 230, The Brethren (for by that name they began to be known) established themselves in the village of Shekomeko, . . some 50 miles west of Hartford [Conn.]. **1883** Schaff–Herzog *Relig. Encycl.* 3.2401/2, The name originally adopted by themselves [i.e. the Dunkers], and . . . now generally used, is simply "The Brethren"; but they frequently use the term "German Baptists," even in their official documents. **1938** FWP *Guide IA* 505, The town [=Dallas Center IA] is the home of the Brethren in Christ, and several other divisions of the religious sect known as the Old Order of River Brethren, whose members are baptised in the river. **1938** Hark *Hex* 101 **PA**, [The] River Brethren . . [are] also called Brethren in Christ. **1967–70** *DARE* (Qu. CC2, . . *Predominant religious denominations around here*) 10 Infs, **chiefly C Atl and Ohio R Valley**, Brethren; **IN22, MD30, PA243, VA23**, Church of the Brethren; **PA18**, Church of Brethren; **PA29**, Reformed River Brethren; (Qu. CC3) Infs **IA3, MD42, PA36, VA42, 93**, Brethren; **VA13**, Brethren Church; **PA205**, Free Church of the Brethren.

brewis n [ME *browes* broth, stew] **NEng** *old-fash*
A pudding-like dish made of bread crusts soaked in liquid.

1859 Elwyn *Glossary* 25, *Brewis* . . . In New England, in our school days, it meant flinty crusts of rye and Indian bread softened with milk and eaten with molasses. **1906** *Pocumtuc Housewife* 7, Get some rice Porridge or brewis and cold meat. **1939** Wolcott *Yankee Cook Book* 187, *Brown Bread Brewis* . . . Take hard crusts from brown bread, put in a pan with a little salt and cold water . . . simmer. Add . . butter and a little cream . . . Cook until mixture is the consistency of thick mush. Serve with cold meats, or as a pudding . . . New England Hard-Scrabble is another name for this dish.

briar See **brier**

briar blackberry See **brierberry**

brichy See **breachy**

brickaty, bricketyest See **briggity**

bricklayer n
=**mud dauber.**

1966 *DARE* (Qu. R20, *Wasps that build their nests of mud*) Inf **SC9**, Bricklayer ['brɪklə]. [Gullah speaker]

brickle adj Also *brickly* [Engl dial; cf *EDD, SND*]
1 Brittle; crisp. **chiefly Sth, Midl** See Map

1837 Sherwood *Gaz. GA* 69, *Brickly*, for brittle. **1890** *DN* 1.70 **LA**, *Brickle, brickly:* brittle. Both *brickle* and *brickly* are somewhat common among settlers of English lineage. **1893** Shands *MS Speech* 21, *Brickle* and *Brickly* . . . Used mostly by negroes and illiterate whites, meaning *brittle, easily broken.* **1899** (1912) Green *VA Folk-Speech, Brickly* . . . Easily broken; brittle. Brickle. **1902** *DN* 2.230 **sIL**, *Brickle.* **1917** *DN* 4.408 **wNC, KS**, *Brickle.* **1926** Kephart *Highlanders* 352 **sAppalachians**, *Brickle.* **1927** *AmSp* 2.349 **WV**, *Brickle.* **1942** McAtee *Dial. Grant Co. IN* (as of 1890s). **1943** Chase *Jack Tales* 65 **wNC** (as of 1880s), Jack never noticed when he set his foot on a brickly snag. Put all his weight on that rotten limb, and hit broke. **1953** Randolph *Down in Holler* 230 **Ozarks**, *Brickle* . . . Brittle, crisp. "If cowcumber pickles ain't *brickle*, they ain't fit to eat." **1965–70** *DARE* (Qu. KK24, *Something that breaks easily*) 22 Infs, **chiefly S Midl**, Brickle; 11 Infs, **chiefly Sth, S Midl**, Brickly. **1967** Key *Tobacco Vocab.* **MO**, *Brickly*—Brittle. My tobacco's too brickly to handle; **NC**, Brickly—too dry; **TN**, *Brickly* is the brittle condition in the field; **KY**, Brickly. **1969** *DARE* FW Addit **seKY**,

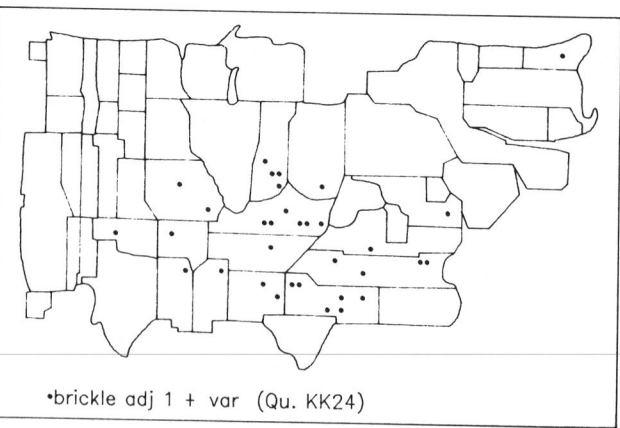

•brickle adj 1 + var (Qu. KK24)

Cabbage buried in the ground over winter stays "brickle as pie crust"; **csKY**, The cutting and bundling were done at night since the corn leaves and stalks were dew-covered since they were "too brickle" to handle during the day. **1981** *Broaddus Coll.* **ceKY**, Brickle—crisp, as cucumbers.

2 Changeable. [Cf *SND* bruckle adj 2a, b]

1872 Schele de Vere *Americanisms* 586, We have had brickle weather of late. **1930** Shoemaker *1300 Words* **cPA Mts** (as of c1900), *Brickle*—Changeable, uncertain. "Maids is brickle."

3 Eager or keen. Cf **work brickle**

1902 *DN* 2.230 **sIL**, *Brickle* . . . industrious; ambitious.

brickle v [brickle adj 1; cf *SND* bruckle v (1)]
To flake or peel because of brittleness.

1936 *AmSp* 11.314 **Ozarks**, *Brickle* . . . To crack off, become brittle, to fall away. 'I shore don't want th' icin' t' *brickle* off'n that 'ar cake.' **1968** *DARE* FW Addit **swPA**, "The paint is brickling." This means that it is peeling.

brickly See **brickle** adj

brick-stretcher See **stretcher**

bricktop n Cf **brickyard blonde**
A person with red hair, or the head of hair itself; hence adj *bricktopped* having red hair.

1856 in 1937 *AmSp* 12.115, A head of hair which the youth of America are accustomed to designate as a 'brick-top.' **1912** *DN* 3.572 **wIN**, *Brick-topped* . . . Red-headed. **1960** Wentworth–Flexner *Slang, Bricktop* . . . A red-haired person;—often used as a nickname.

brickyard blonde n Cf **bricktop**
A woman with red hair.

1970 *Halpert Coll.* **wKY**, She's a brickyard blonde = a redhead.

bridal-veil tree n
=**fringe tree.**

1951 *PADS* 15.37 **TX**, *Chioanthus virginica* L.—Bridal-veil tree; grand-daddy gray-beard.

bridal-wreath n
1 also *bridewort*: A **spirea**, esp *Spiraea prunifolia* and *S. x Vanhouttei.*

1889 *Century Dict., Bridal-wreath* . . . The common name of a cultivated species of *Spiræa, S. hypericifolia*, with long recurved branches and numerous small white double flowers in the axils of the leaves. **1908** Atherton *Californians* 262, Over a high bush on the lawns . . the long "bridal wreaths" tumbled. **1910** Graves *Flowering Plants* 221 **CT**, *Spiraea prunifolia* . . . Bridal Wreath. Local. Roadsides as an escape from gardens . . *Spiraea latifolia* . . . Bridewort . . . Frequent or common. **1968–70** *DARE* (Qu. S26e) Infs **IL58, NC87**, Bridal-wreath; **LA17**, Bridal-wreath—shrub with small cluster of tiny blossoms. **1976** Bailey–Bailey *Hortus Third* 1064, *Spiraea* . . . Spirea or spiraea, bridal-wreath . . . Many spireas are planted as ornamentals.

2 also *wild bridal-wreath*: A **ninebark** (here: *Physocarpus capitatus*). **West**

1897 Parsons *Wild Flowers CA* 85, Another shrub closely resembling the *Spiræas* is *Neillia opulifolia* . . the wild bridal-wreath, or ninebark. **1934** Haskin *Wild Flowers Pacific Coast* 171, Asa Gray, lacking his usual clear discernment calls them—"White flowers of no beauty," but the popular name of bridal-wreath proves that Gray was for once mistaken in his verdict.

3 See quot.

1952 Brown *NC Folkl.* 1.523, *Bridal wreath* . . . A herb bath supposed to restore virginity.—Central and east.

bride v
To marry.

1940 *AmSp* 15.52 **S Midl**, Nouns are freely converted to verbs: . . 'When're ye a-goin' to *bride* her.'

bridemaid n
A bridesmaid.

1857 Hawthorne *Twice-Told* 1.40 **MA**, The window between her fair young bridemaids. **1968** *DARE* (Qu. AA17, . . *Other people besides the bride and groom . . in a wedding party*) Inf **MD19**, Bridemaid ['brad,med].

bride perch n
Prob the white **crappie** *(Pomoxis annularis).*

1819 *Western Rev.* 1.375, *Calliurus, Painted Tail.* Calliure . . . Vulgar names, Painted-tail or Bride-perch. **1820** *Ibid* 2.54, *Ohio Red-eye, Aplocentrus calliops* . . . lives in the lower parts of the Ohio, in Green river, &c. Vulgar names Red-eyes, Bride pearch, Batchelor's pearch, Green bass, &c. **1947** Dalrymple *Panfish* 84 *(DA),* Here, my friend, are the various names by which you would address that little gamester, the Crappie, depending on where you happened to be at the moment: . . . Bride Perch, . . . Grass Bass, . . . Rockfish.

bride's biscuit n

A tough or unpalatable biscuit.

1967–68 *DARE* (Qu. H19) Inf **NJ**29, A bride's biscuit—one made by a bride, not any good; **NY**1, Bride's biscuit—same as baking powder [biscuits] but rather tough and heavy.

bride's bonnet n

A western **bead lily** (here: *Clintonia uniflora*).

1911 Jepson *Flora CA* 108, *C. uniflora* . . . Bride's Bonnet. Flowers 1 or 2, white, ¾ in. long.—Sierra Nevada. **1949** Moldenke *Amer. Wild Flowers* 333, The *bridesbonnet,* of coniferous forests, at elevations of 3500 to 6000 feet, . . has solitary white flowers [sic] on stalks shorter than the leaves. **1973** Hitchcock–Cronquist *Flora Pacific NW* 689, *C. uniflora* . . . Bride's bonnet, blue-bead . . . Alas to Cal, from the coast inl to sw Alta, Mont, Ida, and e Ore.

bridewort See **bridal-wreath 1**

bridge bird See **bridge pewee**

bridge lifter n Cf *DS* B25

A heavy rain.

1940 *Hench Coll.,* In a group conversation at Univ. [of] Va. on synonyms for a "heavy rain storm," a colleague, whose home area was Pitt County, N.C., listed "bridge lifter."

bridge perch n

The white **crappie** *(Poxomis annularis).*

1887 Goode *Amer. Fishes* 71, *Pomoxys* [sic] *annularis* . . . has other names of local application as "Tin Mouth," "Bridge Perch," [etc]. **1933** LA Dept. of Conserv. *Fishes* 332, Known throughout Louisiana as Sac-a-lait, one of its many popular names . . is . . . Bridge Perch. **1947** Dalrymple, Byron W. *Panfish* 84 *(DA),* [Synonyms:] Bridge perch, Calico, . . Sand Perch, Shad.

bridge pewee n Also *bridge bird* [From its nesting under bridges]

=**phoebe.**

1867 *Amer. Naturalist* 1.54 **MA**, Ornithological Calendar for March . . . Meadow Larks, Bridge Pewees or Phoebes . . arrive. **1895** Minot *Land-Birds New Engl.* 286, *Phoebe-bird. Bridge Bird* . . . The nest of the Pewee is most often built on a beam or pillar, or under the eaves of some building, occasionally those of a bridge. **1898** (1900) Davie *Nests N. Amer. Birds* 304 This species is called "Bridge-bird," from its habit of nesting in old wooden bridges. **1917** *DN* 4.428, *Phoebe* . . . The bridge bird of the North. **1962** Imhof *AL Birds* 349, *Eastern Phoebe . . . Other Names:* Bridge Pewee, Tick Bird . . . The bird always places its nest out of the weather—for example, under a bridge, culvert, dam [etc].

bridge swallow n

=**rough-winged swallow.**

1917 (1923) *Birds Amer.* 3.92, *Rough-winged Swallow . . . Other Names.*—Bridge Swallow; Rough-wing . . . Very often, however, their nests are under bridges or railroad trestles or along the under sides of jutting walls. **1968** *DARE* (Qu. Q20, . . *Kinds of swallows)* Inf **DE**3, Bridge swallows—build under bridges.

bridgewall n Cf **forebay**

1982 *Barrick Coll.* **sePA**, Bridgewall—ramp leading to upper level of Penna. barn. Common.

bridle blind n Also *bridle shield* **esp S Midl** Cf **blind bridle**

A blinder on a horse's bridle.

1966–70 *DARE* (Qu. L52, *Pieces of leather used to cover the sides of a horse's eyes)* Infs **GA**14, 72, 77, **KY**43, 49, 75, **MS**60, Bridle blinds; **LA**20, Bridle shields.

bridlewise adj [*bridle* + *wise* knowing, responsive] **chiefly West**

Of a horse: trained to respond to the reins and bridle; by ext, of a human being: obedient.

1840 *Daily Picayune* (New Orleans LA) 6 Oct. 2/5, Phrases in use among the 'natives' [of Ill.]: . . . The horse was not fit for a lady to ride; he was not *bridle wise.* **1843** (1916) Hall *New Purchase* 33 **PA**, A noble-looking young man, mounted on a spirited horse, scarcely broken, and certainly not "bridle-wise." **1895** *Century Illustr. Mag.* 50.626/1 **KY**, Each man dresses usually as he dresses on foot, his seat is the military seat, his bridle has one rein, his horse is bridle-wise, and his hunter is his saddle-horse. **1898** Canfield *Maid of Frontier* 100 **TX**, Just like a woman. You can't never make 'em bridle-wise. **1899** (1912) Green *VA Folk-Speech, Bridle-wise* . . . A horse trained to the use of the bridle; "not *bridle-wise,*" said of an untrained colt, and also of a young person headstrong and undisciplined. **1921** Thorp *Songs Cowboys* 125 **West**, En I could see quite quick en pronto / That she was bridle-wise. **1958** *AmSp* 33.268 **eWA**, *Bridle wise.* Trained to respond to the bridle . . . In Nebraska the term is used to refer to a horse trained to respond to pressure of the reins against his neck. **1969** *DARE* Tape **CA**156, Get him bridlewise.

bridlewise v [bridlewise adj]

1958 *AmSp* 33.268 **eWA**, To *bridle wise* is to break a horse to the bridle.

brie n[1] See **bree**

brie n[2] See **bry**

brief adj[1] [Orig uncert but see *OED brief* adj. 5 and quot 1872] **chiefly NEng** *arch*

1 Esp of a communicable disease: prevalent, widespread.

1722 *New-Engl. Courant* (Boston MA) 9 Apr 2/2, Sundry evil minded Persons have of late industriously reported in the Country Towns, that the Small Pox is again very brief in this Town [=Boston]. **1774** (1900) Fithian *Jrl.* 1.235 **MA**, I hear nothing of the Ague abroad, it seems to go by turns, sometimes brief, then exceedingly scarce. **1816** Pickering *Vocab.* 53, *Brief* . . . is much used in *New England* by the illiterate, in speaking of a rumour or report, as well as of epidemical diseases. **1859** (1968) Bartlett *Americanisms, Brief.* Rife, common, prevalent . . much used by the uneducated in the interior of New England and in Virginia, when speaking of epidemic diseases. **1872** Schele de Vere *Americanisms* 447, *Brief* is used in the South very often . . for prevalent, and has been regarded a corruption of "rife." **1892** *DN* 1.209 **NEng**, "Measles are brief in Westport." **1899** (1912) Green *VA Folk-Speech.*

2 Of wind: strong, prevalent. [Cf *SND brief* adj. 2 (1)] *arch*

1872 Schele de Vere *Americanisms* 447, A traveller in Virginia hearing the driver say "The wind is *brief,*" asked what that meant, and received the answer, "The wind is a sort of peart." **1889** Murfree *Despot* 159 **TN**, This air [=are] a powerful rough kentry, an' the air is brief.

3 See quot.

1893 Shands *MS Speech, Brief* . . . Used by negroes to mean *nice, elegant.* I once heard a negro tell a young man who had dressed up to go to see his sweet-heart: "Boss, you sho looks brief."

brief adj[2] [*brief* short, insufficient]

1952 Brown *NC Folkl.* 1.523, *Brief* . . . Poorly, not well. "I'm feeling pretty brief today."—Central and east.

brier n Also sp *briar*

1 A thorn or spine of certain plants such as blackberry or rose bushes.

1902 *DN* 2.230 **sIL**, *Brier* . . . The small thorn of a shrub or vine. The thorns of a locust, wild apple, etc., are so called. A *brier* or thorn is sometimes called a *sticker.* **1907** *DN* 3.221 **nwAR**, *Brier* . . . The small thorn of a shrub, vine, or tree. **1908** *DN* 3.294 **eAL, wGA**, Brier. **1950** *WELS (Sharp points on the stems of rose bushes, berry bushes, etc.)* 8 Infs, **WI**, Briars. **1954** *Harder Coll.* **cwTN**, *Briar*—a rose thorn, as distinct from thorns found on trees. **c1960** *Wilson Coll.* **csKY**, Briars on blackberry and sawbriar; thorns on honey locust. **1965–70** *DARE* (Qu. S12a–b, . . *The sharp points along the stems of rose bushes, berry bushes, and so on;* total Infs questioned, 75) 12 Infs, Briers.

2 in adj phr *keen* (or *sharp*) *as a briar:* Sly; quick-witted. **esp S Midl**

1834 Davis *Letters Downing* 24 **NY**, As keen as a brier to catch any thing cunnin. **1880** Harris *Uncle Remus Songs* 155 **GA**, Sin's ez sharp ez a bamboo-brier. **1902** Harben *Abner Daniel* 257 **GA**, She's pretty, an' stylish, an' as sharp as a brier. **1954** *Harder Coll.* **cwTN**, "Sharp as a briar." Something very sharp, or someone quickwitted or intelligent. **1966–68** *DARE* (Qu. KK37, *Words to describe a very sly person)* Infs **MD**12, **NC**82, Keen as a briar; **SC**19, 34, Sharp as a briar.

3 See **brier hopper.**

brier baby n See **brierpatch child**

brierberry n Also *briar blackberry* **Sth**
A blackberry, usu *Rubus cuneifolius*.

  1795 Winterbotham *Amer. U.S.* 3.395, Flowering Trees, Shrubs, &c. [include the] . . Briar blackberry. **1938** Rawlings *Yearling* 105 **nFL**, He was abstracted and only the flavor of fresh brierberry jam brought him back to a consciousness of his food. **1965–70** *DARE* (Qu. I44) Infs **FL**1, 36, **NC**8, 10, 50, Brierberries; **FL**19, Brierberries—black; **LA**2, Blackberries—some call 'em "brierberries"; **NC**1, Brierberries or dewberries; **FL**9, **GA**3, 8, 23, **NC**84, **VA**69, Brierberries; (Qu. S26b) Inf **GA**5, Brierberry. **1966** *DARE* Wildfl QR Pl.93b Inf **NC**28, Dewberry, brierberry.

brier blade See **brier hook**

brier heister See **brier hopper**

brier hook n Also *brier blade, ~ knife, ~ scythe, ~ snath, ~ sy* **chiefly Sth, S Midl** See Map
A hand tool for cutting weeds or undergrowth; also fig.

  1813 *Niles' Natl. Reg.* 3.296/1 [List of military supplies], 50 briar scythes. **1819** *Plough Boy* 1.130/2 **SC**, The common red pea . . . should be cut with a small briar-hook. **1843** (1916) Hall *New Purchase* 289 **IN**, I applied, out of a broken blue tea-cup, as much brown soap lather to my face as would stick; and then with a genuine far-east barber's flourish, touched the vile old briar-hook to my cheek. **1946** *PADS* 6.7 **eNC** (as of 1900–10), Briar hook . . . A thin curve-bladed ax used for cutting bushes, etc. **1954** *Harder Coll.* **cwTN**, Briar hook, briar blade—tool used to cut briars, weeds, small bushes, and often grain. **1958** *PADS* 29.8 **TN**, Briar hook: A scythe or sickle . . . Briar blade is also reported. **c1960** *Wilson Coll.* **csKY**, Briar hook—a long-handled, two-handed blade for cutting weeds and briars. **1965–70** *DARE* (Qu. L35, *Hand tools for cutting underbrush*) Infs **KY**6, **LA**3, 10, 20, **MD**32, **NC**13, **OK**20, **PA**29, Brier hook; **PA**6, **TN**1, 44, **VA**61, Brier scythe; **KY**75, Brier sy; **TN**7, Brier snath; (Qu. L37) 13 Infs, **chiefly S Midl**, Brier hook; **GA**74, **KY**80, 86, **TN**26, **VA**75, Brier blade; **KY**84, Brier knife; **IL**90, **MO**4, **NC**73, **PA**71, **TN**1, 16, 44, Brier scythe; **KY**9, Brier sy [saɪ].

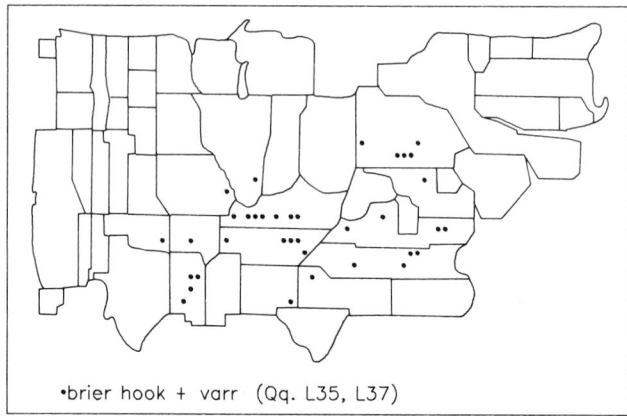

•brier hook + varr (Qq. L35, L37)

brier hopper n, also attrib Also *brier, ~ heister* **OH, TN, KY**
A poor farmer or worker; a rustic.

  1940 *AmSp* 15.447 **eTN**, Briar hopper. Dirt farmer. 'Tilman's jist a plain briar hopper.' **1940** *Time* 7 Oct 84, With a fond ear for briarhopper speech the Tennessee Writers' Project (WPA) gathered 25 well-chawed, well-whittled anecdotes from the Great Smokies to the levees in *God Bless the Devil.* **1966** *DARE* File **swOH**, Brier hoppers. Poor hill folk (hillbillies) who come into Ohio from Kentucky and West Virginia to make money. Usually live on credit. **1967–69** *DARE* (Qu. HH1, *Names and nicknames for a rustic or countrified person*) Infs **KY**53, 70, **OH**2, 57, Brier hopper; **TN**1, Brier heister. **1968** *DARE* FW Addit **seOH**, *Brier hopper:* Lower-class white folk from West Virginia; a ridgerunner. **1981** *DARE* File **seOH** (as of c1910), *Brier . . .* my mother . . grew up in Steubenville . . . I learned to my surprise that she was using it to mean people and not plants . . . She explained that the word was short for *brier-hopper . . .* To my mother . . it meant a specific sort of rustic, an immigrant to southern Ohio from backwoodsy Kentucky.

brier knife See **brier hook**

brierpatch n
  1967 *DARE* (Qu. DD21c, . . *Illegally made whiskey*) Inf **AR**55, Brierpatch—if it's made surreptitiously.

brierpatch child n Also *brierpatch kid, brier baby*
An illegitimate child.

  1950 *PADS* 14.16 **SC**, Briarpatch chillun . . . Illegitimate children. **1967–69** *DARE* (Qu. Z11b, *Nicknames and joking words for a child of unwed parents*) Inf **AR**55, Brierpatch kid; **GA**84, Brier baby.

brier scythe, brier snath, brier sy See **brier hook**

brigaty, brigetty, briggidy See **briggity**

briggit around v phr [Cf **briggity**]
  1981 *Broaddus Coll.* **ceKY**, Briggiting around—acting biggity, or briggity.

briggity adj Also sp *brickaty, brigaty, brigetty, briggidy, brigity;* superl *bricketyest* [Alter of **biggity** adj] **chiefly sAppalachians**
Self-assertive, conceited, headstrong.

  1884 Murfree *TN Mts.* 189, Did you tell Tom to put up your 'beastis'? He is so 'brigaty' that he might not stand. **1895** *DN* 1.385 **ceKY**, *Brigetty:* smart and forward. **1898** Dunbar *Folks from Dixie* 63, My 'Lias done got right brigity an' talk about bein' somep'n'. **1911** *DN* 3.537 **eKY**, *Briggity . . .* Headstrong, stubborn, "bigoted." **1917** *DN* 4.409 **KY**, *Brigaty . . .* Foppish; also overbearing; stuck up . . . Also *brickaty,* and (in negro lingo) *biggety.* **1926** Kephart *Highlanders* 94 **sAppalachians**, When I say that Doc Jones thar is brigaty among women-folks, hit means that he's stuck on hisself and wants to show off. **1934** *WV Review* Dec 79 **cwWV**, I heard a man say that an acquaintance of his was "the *most bricketyest* fellow" he knew. **1968** *DARE* FW Addit **PA**, Briggidy—smart-alecky, comes from my mother. Used only in the phrase "briggidy and overbearing." **1968–69** *DARE* (Qu. II36b, *Of somebody who talks back or gives rude answers you might say, "She certainly is _____!"*) Infs **IN**32, **MD**24, Briggity; (Qu. GG42, *A reckless person, one who takes foolish chances*) Inf **KY**40, Briggity.

briggle v [Prob obs Scots *breeghle* to fiddle, make little progress despite much bustling]
To fuss about ineffectively; see quot 1912.

  1889 *Jrl. Amer. Folkl.* 2.155 **OH**, *Briggle . . .* To be in an uneasy mental condition, to shift attention from one thing to another. "Don't briggle so." **1912** *DN* 3.572 **wIN**, *Briggle . . .* To busy oneself without purpose; to potter. "He never stops brigglin' around." **1930s** in 1944 *ADD* **eWV**, 'Stop brigglin' with that.' Common. **1967** *DARE* (Qu. A10, . . *Somebody asks, "What are you doing?" and you answer, "Nothing in particular, I'm just _____."*) Inf **IA**8, Briggling around. [Inf old]

briggler n [**briggle** v]
  1930 Shoemaker *1300 Words* **cPA Mts** (as of c1900), Briggler—One who attempts but never finishes anything, a trifler.

Brigham tea n Also *Brigham brush, Brigham's tea, Brigham Young weed* [After Mormon leader Brigham Young] **SW**
=Mormon tea.

  1915 Wooton–Standley *Flora NM* 38, The shrubs are variously known as "popotillo," "cañatillo," "Mormon tea," and "Brigham Young weed." **1931** Dayton *Important Browse* 12, All the species are known also as Mormon-tea, canatillo, Brigham tea. **1942** Whipple *Joshua* 29 **UT**, Would you rather have Brigham tea? . . . Clory over at the wagon rummaged for the sack of tiny, yellow-green, jointed stocks of mountain rush, whose brew Brigham Young had so popularized that it retained his name. **1945** McAtee *Nomina Abitera* 7, Such medication and popular opinion as to those in need of it are indicated in the vernacular names: Brigham's tea, . . . Brigham Young weed, . . . clapweed, . . . teamster's tea. **1966** *DARE* (Qu. BB50a, . . *Remedies . . for a cough*) Inf **NM**9, Brigham tea; (Qu. BB50d, *Favorite spring tonics*) Inf **NM**9, Brigham tea. **1967** *DARE* Tape **OR**1, Brigham brush . . looks like rabbit brush only it's taller.

bright adj

1 also absol; Of tobacco: light-colored as a result of **flue-curing**; flue-cured tobacco. **chiefly S Atl, S Midl**
  1765 in 1922 *Amer. Hist. Rev.* 27.71 **VA**, Saw some of the bright couloured [sic] tobaco which sels So Dear in foreign markets. it is of a light yelow Coulour . . . the Inhabitants call it bright tobacco. **1940** *AmSp* 15.133, Bright tobacco. Flue-cured tobacco, mostly yellow in color, grown mainly in Virginia, North Carolina, South Carolina, and Florida. Used mostly for cigarettes. **1944** *PADS* 2.64 **sVA**, *Bright . . .* Having the desired shade of color; a variety of tobacco. **1966** *PADS* 45.8 **cnKY**, *Bright . . .* Of tobacco: Cured leaf of light color . . . "My crop cured bright." . . "I got good prices for my bright last year." *Ibid,* *Bright-crop* . . . Tobacco from the center of the plant (leaf grade) that

cures to a thin body. **1966** *DARE* (Qu. L34, . . *The most important crops grown around here*) Inf **FL**26, Bright leaf tobacco. **1967** *Key Tobacco Vocab.* 135 **MD, MO, TN,** *Bright.* Ibid 136 **NC,** *Bright-crop*—orange or lemon color; **TN,** *Bright lugs.* **1968–70** *DARE* Tapes **KY**56, 93, **OH**57, Bright leaf; **VA**38, Bright leaf tobacco.

2 also *bright-skin(ned);* Of a Black person: having light-colored skin. **Sth** *now chiefly among Black speakers*

1831 *Georgian* (Savannah) 5 April 3/3 *(DA),* For sale, a bright Mulatto Man. **1888** Warner *On Horseback* 116 **NC,** Mary, the "bright" woman (this is the universal designation of the light mulatto), was a pleasing but bold yellow girl. **1911** Harrison *Queed* 211, Now a young bright-skin negro desires to marry Laura. **1927** Kennedy *Gritny* 68 **sLA** [Black], "Dey was'n all dark-skin mens w'at meddled you . . ?" . . "Dey had one de mens sho did look bright-skin to me." **1970** *DARE* (Qu. X57, *A person with light-colored hair and skin*) Infs **FL**51, **GA**90, He's bright; **FL**48, Bright-skinned. [All Infs Black] **1973** Vidal *Burr* 196 (as of 1833), Slaves were everywhere, hard at work. I was surprised to see how "bright" they were. I do not know if that word is still in use at [sic] the south, but in those days [=1806] a slave with a large degree of white blood was known as "bright." **1977** Smitherman *Talkin* 251, Terms for Blacks (used only by blacks) . . . *Bright,* adjective designating a light-skinned black person; a more neutral term than *high-yelluh,* but still with some shading of ambivalence.

bright n

1 Used as a name for one of a pair of oxen. **NEast** *old-fash* Cf **buck** n[1] **1d**

1852 Hawthorne *Blithedale* 120 **eMA,** Mankind . . is but another yoke of oxen, as stubborn, stupid, and sluggish, as our old Brown and Bright. **1907** *DN* 3.241 **eME,** *Buck and Bright* . . . The inevitable names of a yoke of oxen. **1953** Van Wagenen *Golden Age* 42 **ceNY** (as of 1800s), There were certain eccentric or misguided owners who gave their teams unusual or fanciful names . . but the most common names for oxen were just two, Buck and Bright . . . This usage was surely almost universal over New York and New England, and perhaps farther afield . . . The nigh ox was called Buck, while his mate was Bright, and this custom was so set that it had (to quote a phrase of legal jargon) almost "the force and effect of statute law."

2 See quot.

1917 *DN* 4.409 **wNC, NEng,** *Bright* . . . Polish. "The bright sorter wore off."

bright barn n [*bright* adj **1**]

1966 *DARE* (Qu. M1, *Kinds of barns*) Inf **FL**26, Bright barn—smaller than a shade barn, with heaters for [curing "bright"] tobacco.

brighten up v phr

1 Of weather: to become less cloudy. Cf **break** v **C4**

1939 *LANE* Map 89 **MA,** The map shows the terms . . *brightening, ~ up* . . usually recorded in the context the *weather is clearing up* . . and referring to a change in the weather from cloudy to fair.

2 To become more lively or cheerful.

1965–70 *DARE* (Qu. GG27a, *To get somebody out of an unhappy mood, you might say to him, "Everything's going to be all right, so _____."*) Infs **GA**84, **KY**59, **MA**6, **MS**8, 67, **NC**63, **VA**21, Brighten up.

3 To improve in one's work.

1969 *DARE* (Qu. JJ26, *If somebody has been doing poor work or not enough, the boss might say, "If he wants to keep his job he'd better _____."*) Inf **MA**35, Brighten up.

brighteye n

The goldeneye duck (here: *Glaucionetta clangula*).

1923 *U.S. Dept. Ag. Misc. Circular* 13.22, Goldeneye . . . *Vernacular Names . . . In local use* . . . Brighteye (Wash.).

bright eyes n

1 also *bright eye:* A **bluet 2** (here: *Houstonia caerulea*).

1892 *Jrl. Amer. Folkl.* 5.97, *Houstonia caerulea* . . . Bright-eye. Baltimore, M[aryland]d. **1898** Ibid 11.228, Bright-eyes, Boston, Mass. **1940** Clute *Amer. Plant Names* 53, Bright eyes.

2 A violet (*Viola* spp.).

1921 *DN* 5.113 **CA,** Bright-eyes . . . Wild violet. Always in plural.

3 =**black-eyed Susan 1.**

1959 Carleton *Index Herb. Plants* 18, *Bright eyes:* Thunbergia alata.

bright in one's books adj phr [*bright* showing mental quickness]

Good at learning.

1906 *DN* 3.128 **nwAR,** He's right bright in his books.

bright-skin(ned) See **bright** adj **2**

bright sumach n

The smooth **sumac** (here: *Rhus glabra*).

1941 *LANE* Map 250 *(Sumach)* **seCT,** 1 Inf, White sumach, poisonous; bright [sumach], has a brown bark. [Commentary:] The non-poisonous variety of sumach is occasionally distinguished by a special term, such as *bright sumach.*

brigity See **briggity**

brij See **bry**

brim n

1 See **bream.**

2 See quots. [Perh from **bream,** usu pronc *brim,* but deriv is not clear] **ME**

1966 *DARE* Tape **ME**22, [FW:] What'd they use for bait [in lobster traps]? [Inf:] We use herring, redfish trimming, brim [brɪm] we call it, anything we get ahold of. **1975** Gould *ME Lingo, Brim*—Salted bait used by lobstermen. The words *bream* and *brim,* as varieties of non-Maine fish, are probably not the root of this term. But somehow *brim* became a Maine term for trash fish. Specifically, *brim* is the head and skeleton of the ocean perch or redfish, after edible fillets have been cut and packed for market. **1978** Merriam *Illustr. Lobstering* **ME, Brim**—Lobster bait. The head, backbone, and tail of the redfish (Sebastes marinus) from which the fillets have been taken. It is used as bait most of the year when herring and alewives are not available.

brimstone buster n [*brimstone* sulphur, alluding to flames of hell + *buster* one who breaks or smashes]

A ranting preacher who threatens sinners with hellfire.

1939 *FWP Guide MT* 99, This followed a period of preaching in saloons, dance halls, and gambling houses, where roulette wheels, card tables, and other paraphernalia were pushed aside to let the "brimstone busters" hold forth.

brimstone match n Also *brimstone, brimstoner* [*OED* 1594 →] chiefly **NEast** *old-fash*

A kitchen match.

1967–70 *DARE* (Qu. F46, . . *Matches you can strike anywhere*) Infs **CT**12, 39, **NJ**1, 56, **NY**72, **PA**70, Brimstone matches; **MA**57, **NY**230, Brimstone; **PA**77, Brimstoners. [All Infs old] **1973** Allen *LAUM* 1.160 **IA, ND,** Brimstone matches. [2 infs; one labels term archaic or old-fash.]

brimstone snake n Also *brimstone*

=**glass snake.**

1709 (1967) Lawson *New Voyage* 139 **NC, SC,** The Brimstone is so call'd, I believe, because it is almost of a Brimstone Colour. **1946** *Jrl. Amer. Folkl.* 59.175, The brimstone snakes of North Carolina, being brittle as glass, were easily broken.

brimsy adj [Engl dial *breme, brim* fierce + *-sy* familiarizing suff] Cf **breaming, brinjing**

Extreme, intense.

1950 *PADS* 14.17 **SC,** *Brimsy* ['brɪmzɪ] . . . Variant of brinjin'.

brin n [Prob Fr *brin* very small piece, hence of small mesh]

1941 *FWP Guide LA* 687, In Louisiana, *brin* is screen wire.

brindle cat n

=**bowfin.**

1949 Caine *N. Amer. Sport Fish* 132, Mudfish . . . *Colloquial Names.* Blackfish. Bowfin. Brindle Cat.

brindle gravy n

1 =**frog-eye gravy.**

1906 *DN* 3.128 **nwAR,** Brin'le gravy . . . Ham gravy. Rare. **1946** *AmSp* 21.99 **sIL,** In olden times, rarely now, *brindle gravy,* sometimes called *frogeye gravy,* was a popular dish; a dash of water in a little hot ham grease in the skillet did the trick. **1967** *DARE* (Qu. H37) Inf **TX**40, Brindle gravy—same as red-eye gravy.

2 See quot.

1968 *DARE* (Qu. H37) Inf **LA**16, Brindle gravy or poor man's gravy—this is made with flour and shortening when you don't have any meat.

brindly adj [*brindle* having dark streaks or spots]

Brindled.

1949 Arnow *Hunter's Horn* 14 **KY**, She heard Sue Annie Tillers [sic] big brindly Bess high up across the creek, and from up the valley . . two iron-belled Jerseys. **1967** *DARE* (Qu. J5, *A cat with fur of mixed colors*) Inf **SC32**, Brindly cat.

bring v

A Pronc varr.

Usu |brıŋ|; **in Sth, S Midl** often |bre(ı)ŋ, bræŋ|; occas |breŋ|. See Pronc Intro 3.I.6.d.

1934 *AmSp* 9.210 **Sth**, A few words having standard [ı] before [ŋ] change [ı] to [e] or [eı]. The diphthong is perhaps heard more often than the simple vowel . . . *Bring, sing, spring, string, thing.* **1941** *AmSp* 16.4 **eTX** [Black], Before *ng, nk,* [ı] becomes [ẽ], [ẽı] : bring . . [brẽŋ]. **1944** *PADS* 2.29 **eKY, wNC**, Bring [breŋ] . . . Illustrates a pronunciation of *i* in many monosyllabic words ending in -*ing*. Other examples are: *ring, sing, thing, wing*. Rural. Common. **1950** *PADS* 13.22 **sKY**, Brang [bræŋ]: Present tense of *bring*. This pronunciation is common among the uneducated. **c1960** *Wilson Coll.* **csKY**, Bring [bræŋ] or [breŋ]. **1967–68** *DARE* FW Addit **swNC**, Bring [bræŋ]; **cNY**, [breŋ].

B Gram forms.

1 past: usu *brought;* also *brung;* occas *brang;* infreq *bring, bringed, broughten.*

c1820 in 1941 *AmSp* 16.157 **NY**, I brung—I brought. **1884** Bunner *Airs from Arcady* 65, I brung the original pair f'm the States in eighteen-'n'-fifty. **1894** Riley *Armazindy* 136 **IN**, Wunst he bringed us some. **1927** *AmSp* 3.2 **Ozarks**, [Present] bring; [preterite] brang, brung; [past pple] brung. **1950** *WELS* (I _____ *a saw*) 9 Infs, **WI**, Brung; 4 Infs, **WI**, Brang; 1 Inf, **ceWI**, Bringed. **1953** Brewer *Word Brazos* 10 **eTX** [Black], Dey cut de cypress trees down on de wes' side an' brung de logs 'cross to de eas' side on a li'l ole row boat. **1965–70** *DARE* (Qu. OO16b, . . *"I did bring the hammer, and I also _____ a saw."*) 953 Infs, **widespread**, Brought; 32 Infs, **widespread**, Brung; 8 Infs, **scattered**, Brang; **SC9, 26**, Bring; **DC5, MS69**, Broughten; **VA53**, Bringed. **1970** *DARE* Tape FL37, Brung; VA47, Redheads [=ducks] brung the best price; MS86, Police brung him in. **1972** in 1982 *Barrick Coll.* **sePA**, Brung—p[ast]. t[ense]. of *bring.*

2 past pple: usu *brought;* also *brung;* occas *brang;* infreq *bring, bringed, broughten.*

1950 *WELS* (Have you _____ *the hammer and nails*) 9 Infs, **WI**, Brung; 1 Inf, **csWI**, Brang. **1953** Atwood *Survey of Verb Forms* 7, [For] the past participle . . *Brought* . . is very heavily predominant in all major areas among all classes. *Brung* . . occurs in very scattered fashion throughout the Eastern States . . . One N. Eng. informant uses *broughten* . . and a few Southern Negroes say *done bring*. **1965–70** *DARE* (Qu. OO16a, . . *"I was supposed to bring the nails — you should have _____ the hammer."*) 951 Infs, **widespread**, Brought; 39 Infs, **scattered**, Brung; **AL11, NY213**, Brang; **SC26**, Bring; **VA53**, Bringed; **MS69**, Broughten; (Qu. Z17, *To . . bring up a child: "All her children were _____ [on the farm.]"*) Inf **SC10**, Bring up; **IL113, NC33, NJ33, 59, PA108**, Brung up; (Qu. II21) Inf **MA35**, He wasn't brung up — he just grew up. **1975** Allen *LAUM* 2.9, *Brought* is the well-nigh unanimous choice of U[pper] M[idwest] infs. as the participial form of *bring* . . . Only four infs . . have *brung;* and two others report having heard it in their communities. Its frequency is clearly much less than in the eastern states.

C Senses.

1 To take; to escort, accompany.

1901 *DN* 2.136 **seIA**, Bring . . . Used like take. **1967–68** *DARE* (Qu. AA2, *If a man is going to a dance and a girl is going with him, you might say, "John is going to _____ Mary to the dance."*) Infs **IA30, IN35, MN15, MA3, NY81, 89**, Bring. **1968** *DARE* FW Addit **csLA**, I'll tell you what; I'll go bring him home and then I'll come back and get you; **swLA**, Confusion of *bring* and *take* is fairly common here.

2 To cause (curd or butter) to coagulate from milk. *old-fash* Cf **come v B1**

1855 MI State Ag. Soc. *Trans.* 6.183, The milk for cheese is made into curd . . by adding sufficient rennet to "bring" it in about fifteen minutes. **1881** (1939) Mayne *Maud* 8 **sIL**, I got up and churned awhile (Corinne had almost brought the butter before I began) and then worked it.

3 To produce or yield (a crop); to cause (a crop) to mature.

1738 (1901) Byrd *Hist. Dividing Line (DAE)* **VA**, [The Ridge] is so wretchedly poor that it will not bring potatoes. **1831** Peck *Guide for Emigrants* 47, The bottoms . . . will bring three or four crops of corn without manure. **1916** *DN* 4.302 **LA, csVA**, Bring. To yield (produce). "That field *brings* wonderfully." **1927** *AmSp* 2.349 **cwWV**, "That

garden brings fine tomatoes." **1943** *Sun* (Baltimore MD) 25 Jun 6/3 (Hench Coll.), The market crisis, . . . was precipitated by continued excessive heat, which "brought in" the bean crop almost overnight in many localities.

4 To give birth to; to bear, hatch; to assist at the birth of. **chiefly Sth, S Midl**

1843 *Amer. Pioneer* 2.172, The moose is an animal similar to the deer or elk, except vastly larger . . . They usually bring two young at a time. **1909** *DN* 3.419 **Cape Cod MA**, Bring out . . . "I sat one hen, she brought out eleven chickens." **1949** Arnow *Hunter's Horn* 134 **KY**, They's many a woman a sayen now that I'm gitten too old to bring babies any more. **1966–68** *DARE* (Qu. K10, *Words used about a cow that is going to have a calf*) Inf **GA52**, She's supposed to bring a calf; **LA18**, Fixing to bring a calf; **MS1**, Going to bring forth; **NM13, TN17**, Going to bring a calf; (Qu. K11) 21 Infs, **chiefly Sth, S Midl**, Brought a calf; **NM13**, Brought her calf; **KY39**, Brung her a calf; (Qu. K45) 9 Infs, **chiefly Sth, S Midl**, Brought a colt; **GA52**, Bring a small horse. **1967** Fetterman *Stinking Creek* 64 **seKY**, That sow brought seven of the prettiest pigs I ever saw. **1967** Green *Horse Tradin'* 59 **West**, The . . mare brought a colt and lost it.

bring-and-buy social n

1967 *DARE* (Qu. FF1, . . *A [kind of] "social" or "sociable"*) Inf **IL5**, Bring-'n-buy social — a kind of white elephant sale.

bring-and-share n

A potluck dinner.

1970 *DARE* (Qu. H70, *When people bring baked dishes, salads, and so forth to a meeting-place and share them together, that's a _____ meal*) Inf **OH98**, Bring-and-share.

bringer See brinjer

bringing up vbl n Nth, N Midl

Rearing, childhood training.

1965–70 *DARE* (Qu. AA6b, . . *A man who is fond . . of women and tries to attract their attention — if he's rude*) Inf **NY75**, He don't show good bringing up; (Qu. II21, *When somebody behaves unpleasantly or without manners*) Infs **IL16, IA38, MA123, MI81, MN40, NJ33, 55, OH80, PA91, RI15**, (He) had no bringing up; **NY139, OH8, UT4**, Didn't have (or never had) any bringing up; **CT6**, Had no better bringin' up.

brinjer n |'brınjə| Also sp bringer [Prob Scots *breenger* a formidable foe < *breenge* to plunge or rush forward recklessly, to make a violent effort] Sth obsolescent

1 freq in compar phrr with *like* or *as*: An extreme instance of something (such as cold weather, punishment, etc.).

1851 (1969) Burke *Polly Peablossom* 52 **MS**, He 'gin pickin' up rocks an' slinging' um at the dogs like bringer! **1908** *DN* 3.294 **eAL, wGA**, Bringer [brındʒə] . . . Used in several comparative phrases: 'hot as bringer,' 'cold as bringer,' etc. Ibid 3.315 **eAL, wGA**, Give one bringer . . . To give one severe punishment, make it hot for one. "I'll take a cowhide an' *give you bringer* if you don't mind [=obey]." **1950** *PADS* 14.17 **SC**, Brinjer ['brındʒə] . . . Extremely cold weather. "How's the weather outside, Uncle Ned?" "'E brinjer!" Rare except in coastal area of S.C., Rock Hill, Aiken. **1952** *PADS* 17.32 **SC**, A friend of the writer buttonholed him and reported that his mother had often used these two words: "It's *brinjin'* cold today"; "today is a *brinjer*."

2 A name given to an animal, implying fierceness or high spirits. [Cf *DJE* brinjah]

1880 Harris *Uncle Remus Songs* 190 **GA**, Nuthin' never 'sturbs his mine, / Twel he hear ole Bringer bark. **1892** Harris *Uncle Remus & Friends* 60 **GA**, High, my lady! Brinjer, ho.

brinjing adv [brinjer] Cf brimsy

Extremely, intensely.

1950 *PADS* 14.17 **SC**, ['brındʒın] . . . Extremely (cold). "It's *brinjin'* cold today." Sporadic and obsolescent in S.C. except on coast. **1952** [see **brinjer 1**].

brinnie n

=**brownie** n[1] **2**.

1958 *PADS* 29.30 **NY** [Marble terms], Brinnie . . . A brownie.

brisket n, also attrib [Scots]

The human breast or chest.

1942 McAtee *Dial. Grant Co. IN* (as of 1890s), Brisket . . a person's breast; "I've got a stitch in my _____" Chiefly Scot. **c1960** *Wilson Coll.* **csKY**, Brisket . . . Chest, used humorously. "I've gotten a misery in my brisket." **1961** Adams *Old-Time Cowhand* 45, Oh, he's packin' a six-gun for the county and sportin' a tin badge on his brisket that shows up like a patent-medicine sign. *Ibid* 182, We soon learned that he had a yeller streak down his back so wide it lapped plumb 'round his brisket bone.

brisk up v phr
    1939 *LANE* Map 91 **swNH,** An increase in the strength of the wind . . *brisking up.*

bristle burr n
    A **cockleburr.**
    1969 *DARE* (Qu. S13) Inf **CA117,** Bristle burr.

bristlecone pine n
    A moderate to large-sized upland pine *(Pinus aristata)* with dense persistent foliage and cones armed with prominent prickles, found chiefly in the Southwest and Rocky Mts. Also called **foxtail pine 2, hickory pine**
    1893 Coville *Botany Death Valley* 221 **CA,** In none of the other mountains east of the Sierra Nevada . . did the bristle-cone pine occur. **1911** (1912) NM Ag. Exper. Station *Bulletin* 81.13, The commonest trees are the Bristle-cone Pine *(Pinus aristata),* . . the Quaking Aspen *(Populus tremuloides),* and one or two willows of the Transition Zone. **1948** in 1949 *Pacific Discovery* 1.29/1, Thus we find . . "hickory pine" for "bristle-cone" pine. **1969–70** *DARE* (Qu. T17) Infs **CA113, 120, 208,** Bristlecone pine. **1982** Heat Moon *Blue Highways* 175 **AZ,** The bristlecone pine of American Indians, Hopis live where almost nothing else will, thriving long in adverse conditions: poor soil, drought, temperature extremes, high winds. Those give life to the bristlecone and the Hopi.

bristlegrass n
    1 Std: a grass of the genus *Setaria.* Also called **foxtail**
    2 A **squirreltail** (here: *Sitanion hystrix*).
    1937 U.S. Forest Serv. *Range Plant Hdbk.* G107, Bottlebrush squirreltail, sometimes called bristle grass, . . is a bright green, bristly headed, perennial bunch grass.

bristletail n
    1 Std: an insect of the order Thysanura.
    2 =**ruddy duck.** [So called from the stiff tail-feathers]
    1888 Trumbull *Names of Birds* 112, [Ruddy duck] at St. Georges, Del. . . called also *Bristle-tail.* **1911** Howell *Birds AR* 22, The little ruddy duck, sometimes called "bristle-tail" or "booby," occurs in the Mississippi Valley as a common migrant. **1951** Pough *Audubon Water Bird* 321, Bristle-tail. *See* Ruddy duck.

bristle-tip cliff brake *See* **cliff brake**

bristling n [*bristle* v]
    Hackles.
    1969 *DARE* FW Addit **seGA,** "When I see him [a dog] raise his brislin' [brıslın] I knew there was something in the bushes."

bristly foxtail *See* **foxtail**

britch n, often attrib with *loader* [Alter of *breech*]
    The breech of a gun.
    1899 (1912) Green *VA Folk-Speech, Britch* . . . Breech. *Britch* of a gun. **1923** *DN* 5.202 **swMO,** *Britch loader* . . . Breech loading, as a fire arm. **1946** *AmSp* 21.147, The sergeant who taught us the mechanics of the machine-gun called the breech of the gun the 'britch'. **1950** *WELS* (Nicknames for a rifle) 1 Inf, **cWI,** Britch-loader. **1966–70** *DARE* (Qu. P37b, *Nicknames for a shotgun*) Infs **KY47, NC12, VA96,** Britch-loader [brıč].

britchclout *See* **breechclout**

britchen *See* **britchin**

britches n pl [Alter of *breeches*]
    1 Trousers, pants. **chiefly Sth, S Midl** *See Map*
    1867 Lowell *Biglow* xlv **NEng,** The now universal *britches* for *breeches.* **1908** *DN* 3.294 **eAL, wGA,** *Britches* . . . Trousers. **1912** Green *VA Folk-Speech, Britches* . . . Breeches; garment for a man's legs. **1933** Miller *Lamb in His Bosom* 13 **GA,** His long, sweaty shirts and britches. **1950** *WELS* (Trousers rolled up or cut off below the knee) 1 Inf, **cwWI,** Britches. **1965–70** *DARE* (Qu. AA21) 52 Infs, **chiefly Sth, S Midl,** She wears (the) britches; **NV9,** She's got the britches; **VA27,** Wear the britches; (Qu. GG23a) 39 Infs, **chiefly Sth, S Midl,** Britches on;

NC40, Keep on your britches; **CA17,** Shirt in your britches; (Qu. A21) Inf **NY123,** Bust your britches; **KY5,** Tie your britches up; (Qu. U39) Infs **AL6, IL114, MS1, 80, NJ20, NC31, TX94,** Lost his britches; (Qu. W10) Infs **CO6, NY68, NC41, VA16, 42, WI21,** Britches; **MN33,** Riding britches; **TN3,** Work britches; (Qu. W24b) 26 Infs, **chiefly Sth, S Midl,** Your britches are busted [and var phrr: see *DS*]; (Qu. W24c) Infs **MO4, OK7,** Button your britches; **LA18, TX98,** (You) better fasten your britches; **GA23,** You better check, your britches are unzipped; **OK7,** Britches; (Qu. W43) Inf **RI4,** Britches; (Qu. Y6) Inf **NC36,** Warm his britches; (Qu. Y21) Inf **TX51,** Lead in his britches; (Qu. AA7b) Inf **FL26,** She'd go for a breath of britches; (Qu. AA28) Inf **KY84,** Had her britches off; (Qu. GG4) Inf **VA42,** Tore my Sunday britches; (Qu. GG9) Inf **MS5,** Shock the britches off; (Qu. GG11) Inf **MS5,** Ants in his britches; (Qu. GG23b) Infs **MS1, MO18,** Your britches; **VT12,** On boy, before you lose your britches; **IN27,** Onto your britches; (Qu GG23c) Infs **MO3, OH40, VA11,** Keep your britches on; (Qu. GG31) Infs **KY94, MA11, TX104,** Bust my britches; **CT15, PA242, TX27,** Split my britches; **CA134,** Wet my britches; (Qu. JJ21) Infs **KY50, OH29,** Bet your britches; (Qu. JJ42) Inf **AR35,** Tore his britches; (Qu. KK45) Inf **MD30,** Got off by the slack of his britches.

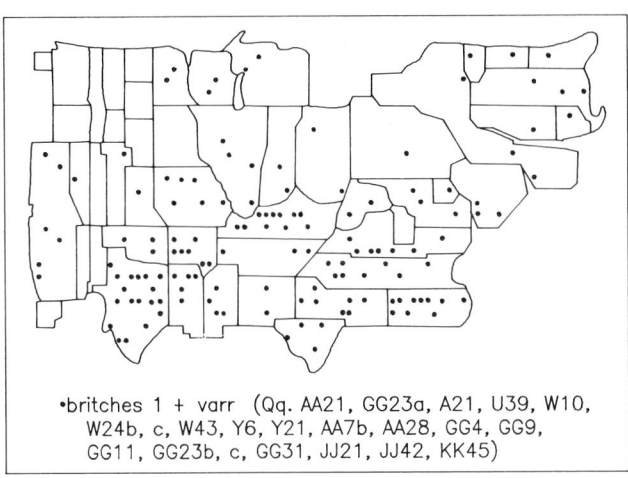

•britches 1 + varr (Qq. AA21, GG23a, A21, U39, W10, W24b, c, W43, Y6, Y21, AA7b, AA28, GG4, GG9, GG11, GG23b, c, GG31, JJ21, JJ42, KK45)

    2 Transf or fig in var phrr (also as *breeches*):
    a *wear the britches* and varr: To have the real authority (usu said of a woman or a wife). **chiefly Sth, S Midl**
    1666 (1972) Alsop *Character Province MD* 85, I never observed . . that ever the Women wore the Breeches. **1723** *New-Engl. Courant* (Boston MA) 23 Sept 1/2, They . . pretend a greater Authority than ordinary over their Wives, . . tho' they are Hen-peck'd at Home . . and dare as well die as claim the Breeches. **a1814** in 1857 Dow *Hist. Cosmopolite* 412 **CT,** [They] according to the vulgar saying, *put the petticoat on the MAN and wear the breeches themselves.* **1909** *DN* 3.387 **eAL, wGA,** *Wear the britches* . . . To rule a household: usually said of a woman. **1952** Brown *NC Folkl.* 1.375, She wears the breeches in that family. **1965–70** *DARE* (Qu. AA21, . . *Joking expressions . . about a wife who gives the orders and a husband who takes them from her*) 52 Infs, **chiefly Sth, S Midl,** She wears (the) britches; **NV9,** She's got the britches; **VA27,** Wear the britches.
    b *be too big for one's britches:* To assume more than one's proper authority. **widespread**
    1835 Crockett *Account* 152 **TN,** I liked him well once: but when a man gets too big for his breeches, I say Good bye. **1899** (1912) Green *VA Folk-Speech* 43, Too big for his breeches. **1909** *DN* 3.382 **eAL, wGA,** *Too big for one's britches.* **1927** *AmSp* 2.348 **WV,** I always said that man was too big for his britches. **1939** *AmSp* 14.264 **IN,** The recalcitrant youngster is 'gittin' too big for his britches.' **1942** McAtee *Dial. Grant Co. IN* 67 (as of 1890s), *Too big for his breeches,* . . conceited, arrogant. (Ala., Me., Va.) **1946** *PADS* 6.34 **NC, VA,** To get too big for one's britches. **1952** Brown *NC Folkl.* 1.375, Don't get too big for your britches. Too big for his breeches. **1965–70** *DARE* (Qu. GG19a, . . *Feeling important or independent: "He surely is _____ these days."*) 16 Infs, **scattered,** (Feeling, getting) too big for his britches; (Qu. HH8, *A person who likes to brag*) Inf **VT12,** Too big for his britches; (Qu. HH17, *A person who tries to appear important*) Inf **CA93,** Too big for his britches; (Qu. II36b, *Of somebody who . . gives rude answers . . : "She certainly is _____!"*) Infs **CA96, OH61,** (Too) big for her britches; (Qu. KK9, *When someone undertakes something too big for him to handle:*

"*This time you've* _____ .") 14 Infs, **scattered**, (Tackled, took on, tried) something too big for your britches [and var phr; see *DS*]; (Qu. HH41, *Someone who has a very high opinion of himself;* total Infs questioned, 75) Inf **FL25**, Too big for his britches.

c *keep one's britches on* or *hold (onto) one's britches:* Not to become impatient, excited or angry. **chiefly Sth, S Midl**

1965–70 *DARE* (Qu. GG23a, *If you speak sharply to somebody to make him be patient, you say, "Now just keep your* _____ .") 39 Infs, **chiefly Sth, S Midl**, Britches on; **NC40**, Keep on your britches; (Qu. GG23b, . . *"Hold* _____ *!"*) Infs **MS1, MO18**, Your britches; **IN27**, Onto your britches; (Qu. GG23c, . . *Other expressions [to tell someone to be patient]*) Infs **MO3, OH40, VA11**, Keep your britches on.

d *lose one's britches:* To lose a great deal of money.

1965–70 *DARE* (Qu. U39, *Somebody who has lost all his money: "During the depression he* _____ .") Infs **AL6, IL114, MS1, 80, NJ20, NC31, TX94**, Lost his britches.

e *in var other phrr:* See quot.

1965–70 *DARE* (Qu. A21, *When someone is in too much of a hurry . . "Slow down! Don't* _____ .") Inf **NY123**, Bust your britches; **KY5**, Tie your britches up; (Qu. Y6, . . *To put pressure on somebody to do something he ought to have done but hasn't: "He's a whole week late. I'm going to* _____ .") Inf **NC36**, Warm his britches; (Qu. Y21, *To move about slowly and without energy*) Inf **TX51**, Lead in his britches; (Qu. GG31, *To laugh very hard: "I thought I'd* _____ .") Infs **KY94, MA11, TX104**, Bust my britches; **CT15, PA242, TX27**, Split my britches; **CA134**, Wet my britches; (Qu. JJ21, *If you want to be very positive: . . "Are you really going to do that?" . . "You* _____ .") Infs **KY50, OH29**, Bet your britches; (Qu. JJ42, *To make an error in judgement . . "He usually handles things well, but this time he certainly* _____ .") Inf **AR35**, Tore his britches; (Qu. KK45, . . *A narrow escape*) Inf **MD30**, Got off by the slack of his britches.

3 Underwear. **chiefly Sth, Midl**

1908 *DN* 3.294 **eAL, wGA**, *Britches* . . . A child's drawers. **1966–70** *DARE* (Qu. W14, *Names for underwear*) Infs **AR37, GA6, 23, IL113, IN47, MS7, VA42**, Britches; **NC82**, Long britches.

4 =**britchin 3**.

1950 *WELS* (*The folded cloth worn by a baby in place of pants*) 1 Inf, **cWI**, Britches. **1966–67** *DARE* (Qu. W19) Infs **AZ1, FL33**, Britches; **GA88**, Baby britches; **RI12**, Three-cornered britches.

britches quilt n

1953 Randolph *Down in Holler* 230 **Ozarks**, *Britches quilt* . . . A quilt or comforter made of heavy woolen material. A lighter covering is known as a *shirt-tail quilt*.

britchin n, also attrib Also *britchen, britching* [Alter of *breeching*]

1 The part of a harness that passes around the breech of a draft animal to allow it to push backwards.

1899 (1912) Green *VA Folk-Speech*, *Britchin* . . . That part of horse-harness passing around the hind part of the horse and fastened near the ends of the backband on the shafts to keep the cart from running on the horse in going down hill. **1908** *DN* 3.294 **eAL, wGA**, *Britchin*. **1910** *DN* 3.438 **wNY**, *Britchin*. **1922** Gonzales *Black Border* 291 **eSC, GA coasts**, [Gullah glossary], *Britchin'*—breeching (harness). **1923** *DN* 5.202 **swMO**. **1950** Stuart *Hie Hunters* 187 **eKY**, Old Dinah is the near mule when ye have 'em in the britchen. **1954** *Harder Coll.* **cwTN**, *Britchin's*. **c1960** *Wilson Coll.* **csKY**, *Britchin*. **1969** *DARE* Tape **MA58**, ['brɪtʃɪn]. **1970** *DARE* (Qu. K32a, *With a team of horses, what do you call the horse on the driver's right hand?*) Inf **PA226**, Britchin horse.

2 A spanking.

1930 Shoemaker *1300 Words* 5 **cPA Mts** (as of c1900), *Britching*—A spanking administered with a paddle on breech (buttocks).

3 pl: A baby's diaper.

1926 *DN* 5.398 **Ozarks**, *Britchin's* . . . Diapers. **1953** Randolph *Down in Holler* 230 **Ozarks**, *Britchin's* . . . Diapers, also known as *hippin's*. **1954** *Harder Coll.* **cwTN**, *Britchin's* diapers.

britchless See **breechless**

britchmans See **breechman**

britheren See **brethren**

British bulldog n

A children's outdoor game; see quots. (Cf 1969 Opie-Opie *Children's Games* 138)

1966 *DARE* (Qu. EE33, . . *Outdoor games*) Inf **NH1**, British bulldog—draw a line with one player on one side and the other players on the other side. Call "British bulldog" and the single player tries to catch the others. Those caught join his side. **1981** Pederson *LAGS Urban Material* **swTN**, *Line and running games* . . . [2 infs] British bulldogs. "One person is 'it'; others run across and try to tackle them (sic)." Apparently, the person who is 'it' does the tackling.

British lady n

=**redwing blackbird**.

1920 Thomas *KY Superstitions* 28, If you kill the "British lady" (the red-winged blackbird), you will marry the next man you meet . . . Mountains.

British soldier n

1 A red **spider lily** (prob the extensively naturalized *Lycoris radiata*).

1952 Brown *NC Folkl.* 1.523, *British soldier* . . . The spider lily.—Central and west.

2 =**star moss**.

1968 Pochmann *Triple Ridge* 106 **cWI**, Star moss invites close inspection . . the male plants send up tiny brown spires, and the females sport a globular bloom of bright red about the size of a pinhead—known locally as "British soldiers." **1978** Whipple *Vintage Nantucket* 235 **MA**, Still we saw an infinite variety of flora: woolly . . carpets of reindeer and Iceland moss—tundra plants that seemed out of place on the warm September beach, as did the bright red British soldier lichens that paraded through the underbrush.

British tobacco n [Because formerly used as snuff]

=**coltsfoot 1**.

1876 Hobbs *Bot. Hdbk.* 16, British tobacco, Coltsfoot leaves, Tussilago farfara. **1930** Sievers *Amer. Med. Plants* 24, *Tussilago farfara*—Other common names . . . British tobacco, gowan.

britten n [Metath of *bittern*]

Perh the **red-necked grebe**, but cf **shitepoke**.

1969 *DARE* (Qu. Q5, . . *Wild ducks*) Inf **RI4**, A shore bird called britten—slang name [is] shikepoke.

brittle adj

Limber, flexible.

1965–70 *DARE* (Qu. B35, *Ice that will bend when you step on it, but not break*) Infs **NY8, WA18**, Brittle; **NV6, PA13**, Brittle ice; (Qu. KK25, *Something that bends or yields easily*) Infs **IL54, 64, VA26**, Brittle.

brittlebrush n

1 =**brittlebush**.

1924 Austin *Land of Journeys' Ending* 53 **AZ**, Tufts of bunch-grass . . may be found contesting the steep bajadas with globose, downy-white brittle-brush, which in the fore-summer makes a golden glow of bloom. **1931** U.S. Dept. Ag. *Misc. Pub.* 101.164, *E[ncelia] farinosa* . . . Flowering stems become dry and brittle after the seeds mature . . . Vernacular names include brittlebrush . . and whitebush.

2 A **bitterbrush 1** (here: *Purshia tridentata*).

1963 Craighead *Rocky Mt. Wildflowers* 90, *Purshia tridentata* . . . Other names: Antelope Brush, Brittlebrush . . . A much-branched evergreen shrub 2–10 ft. tall.

brittlebush n

A low composite shrub (*Encelia* spp, esp *E. farinosa*) with gray-green leaves and usu yellow flower heads, native chiefly to the deserts of the Southwest. Also called **incienso**. For other names of *E. farinosa* see **golden hills, whitebush**

1908 Hornaday *Camp-Fires* 182 **sAZ**, The White Brittle-Bush, as seen standing alone on bare black lava, is truly a thing of beauty. **1941** Jaeger *Wildflowers* 286, *Brittle-bush* . . . Encelia farinosa. **1965** Teale *Wandering Through Winter* 21 **CA**, The desert brittlebush was as interesting . . . Across the tops of several clumps of this drought-resistant member of the sunflower family extended a thin scattering of yellow blooms. **1974** Munz *Flora S. CA* 158, *E[ncelia] farinosa* . . . Brittle-bush.

brittlewood n

A shrub of the genus *Rhamnus*, esp *R. purshiana* and **Carolina buckthorn**.

1897 Sudworth *Arborescent Flora* 298, *Rhamnus caroliniana*, . . Indian Cherry . . . Common Names [include] . . Brittlewood. **1974** (1977) Coon *Useful Plants* 235, *Rhamnus purshiana*—Cascara sagrada, brittle wood.

brittly adj Cf **brickle** adj **1**
Brittle.
    1967–70 *DARE* (Qu. KK24, *Something that breaks easily*) Infs **SC**32, **VA**75, Brittly.

bro See **brother A1**

broad adj
Of speech: vulgar, coarse.
    1824 Irving *Tales of a Traveller* 1.278 **NY,** Laughing outrageously at a broad story. **1899** (1912) Green *VA Folk-Speech,* Broad-spoken . . . Out-spoken, using coarse language. **1969** *DARE* FW Addit **csVA,** *Broad talking* or *broad statement*—speech that includes obscenity and cussing.

broad n [From **abroad** n, mistaken for an indef art with a noun: *a broad*] esp **S Midl** *old-fash*
A journey or trip.
    1823 Cooper *Pioneers* 1.218 **cNY,** I heer'n say that the Judge was gone a great 'broad, and that he meant to bring his darter hum. **1841** *S. Lit. Messenger* 7.40/1, You must give up your *broad* to-day, Corally, for I want to haul rails right away to fix the fences. **1903** *DN* 2.307 **AR, seMO,** *Broad* . . . A trip; a visit. 'I didn't know you had got back from your broad.' (Very common in Arkansas.) **1912** Green *VA Folk-Speech, Broad* . . . A trip for pleasure. "Don't come back till your broad is out." **1921** (1923) Greer–Petrie *Angeline Seelbach* 25 **KY,** I was sorry the Jedge was in sich a swivvit to git back to Louisville, bekase I didn't half git my broad out. **1943** in 1944 *ADD* **VA** (as of c1900), Broad. **1952** *DE Folkl. Bulletin* Oct 11, "I've had my broad out"—said by someone on a visit and ready to go home ("broad" is apparently a back-formation from "abroad").

broad awake adj phr
Completely or wide awake.
    1887 (1895) Robinson *Uncle Lisha* 18 **wVT,** Of course Uncle Lisha was broad awake.

broad bean n
    1 also *English broadbean:* A vetch *(Vicia faba)* which produces large, flat, edible beans.   Also called **horse bean, Windsor bean**
        1923 Amer. Joint Comm. Horticult. Nomenclature *Std. Plant Names* 523, *Vicia . . . faba . . . Broadbean.* **1950** Gray–Fernald *Manual of Botany* 931. **1968** *DARE* (Qu. I14, *Kinds of beans that you eat in the pod before they're dry*) Inf **VA**26, Broad beans; (Qu. I20) Inf **CT**4, English broad beans. **1981** *Burpee Seeds* 104, *English Broadbean . . .* Inedible, glossy green pods 7 in. long contain 5 to 7 large, oblong, flat, light green beans for use as green shell beans like limas.
    2 See quot.
        1976 *Wanigan Catalog* 5, *Broad . . .* Not the Broad or Windsor bean of Europe, but a flat wide green snap, with white kidney seeds . . . Late.

broadbill n
    1 A scaup, esp the **greater scaup,** the **lesser scaup,** the **redhead,** and the **ring-necked duck.**
        1831 (1927) Hone *Diary* 1.40 **NYC,** A man had . . 600 broadbills. **1844** DeKay *Zool. NY* 2.323, *Fuligula marila . . .* It is only known on this coast under the name of *Broad-bill.* **1858** Baird *Birds* 791, *Broad-bill [Aythya marila].* **1888** Trumbull *Names of Birds* 51, At Seaford (Hempstead) L.I., it *[Aythya americana]* is the *Red-Headed Broad-Bill. Ibid* 55, *Aythya marila . . .* In Connecticut at Stonington, mouth of Connecticut River, Stony Creek, and Stratford, *Broad-Bill . . .* I find latter name in like use in New Jersey at Barnegat, Tuckerton, Pleasant-ville (Atlantic Co.), and Cape May City, and in Virginia at Richmond. **1917** (1923) *Birds Amer.* 1.135, *Scaup Duck . . .* Other Names . . . Broad-bill. **1918** Grinnell *Game Birds CA* 159, *Lesser Scaup Duck . . .* Other names . . . Broad-bill. **1953** Jewett *Birds WA* 131, *Aythya americana . . .* Other names: . . Red-headed Broadbill. **1966–67** *DARE* (Qu. Q10) Inf **FL**29, Broadbill; (Qu. Q5) Inf **NY**10, Lesser broadbill. **1975** Newell *If Nothin' Don't Happen* 32 **nwFL,** "And what in the horrible hell is a scaup?" Uncle Winton asked her. "It's a broadbill," she told him. "You got plenty of 'em down at the mouth of the river." "She means bluebills, Uncle Wint," Tarley said.
    2 =**shoveler.**
        1848 Bartlett *Americanisms, Broadbill. (Anas marila.)* **1888** Trumbull *Names of Birds* 43, *Spatula clypeata . . shoveller . . .* The name *Broad-Bill,* given in Yarrell's British Birds, Coues's Key, etc., though eminently appropriate, seems to have been very thoroughly taken up in our country by other species. **1925** (1928) Forbush *Birds MA* 1.218,

Spátula clypeáta . . . Shoveller. Other names: . . Broadbill. **1936** *Oriole* 1.4, *Shoveler.* Broadbill (general in the United States; also in British provincial use; in allusion to the spatulate bill, as are also the following names).
    3 also *broadbill booby,* ~ *dipper, hard-headed broadbill:* =**ruddy duck.**
        1888 Trumbull *Names of Birds* 110, *Erismatura rubida . . . Ruddy Duck . . .* At Bath, Me., and Newport, R.I., *Broad-bill . . .* at Fairhaven, Mass., *Broad-bill Dipper.* **1917** (1923) *Birds Amer.* 1.152, *Ruddy Duck—Erismatura jamaicensis . . .* Broadbilled Dipper . . . Hard-headed Broad-bill. **1943** Musgrove *Waterfowl IA* 71, *Ruddy Duck . . .* Other names: . . stifftail, broadbill, bumblebee coot. **1954** Sprunt *FL Bird Life* 85, *Ruddy Duck: Oxyura jamaicensis . . .* Local Names: . . Broadbill booby.
    4 also *broadbill swordfish:* =**swordfish.**
        1927 Grey *Tales Swordfish* 107 **CA,** Few novices at the game ever held a broadbill longer than a few moments. *Ibid* 157, The broadbill swordfish was the one fish in the world which could not be caught through luck. **1946** LaMonte *N. Amer. Game Fishes* 34, *Xiphias gladius . . .* Names: Broadbill, Broadbill Swordfish. **1972** Sparano *Outdoors Encycl.* 372, *Swordfish*—Common Names: . . broadbill, broadbill swordfish. Scientific Name: *Xiphias gladius.*

broadbill booby n
    1 See **broadbill 3.**
    2 See **booby** n[1] **2.**

broadbill dipper n
    1 See **broadbill 3.**
    2 See **dipper.**

broad-billed coot n
=**scoter.**
    1888 Trumbull *Names of Birds* 107, *Oidemia americana . . .* At Bell-port and Moriches, L.I., as *Broad-billed Coot.* **1917** (1923) *Birds Amer.* 1.148, *Scoter—Oidemia americana . . .* Broad-billed coot. **1982** Elman *Hunter's Field Guide* 237, *American Scoter . . . Common & Regional Names:* . . broad-billed coot.

broadhorn n
    1 =**ark 1;** see quot 1968.   [In ref to the two long oars, one projecting from each side]
        1832 Paulding *Westward Ho* 1.73 **PA,** The broad-horn in which Colonel Dangerfield and his family embarked on their voyage down the Ohio formed an oblong square, on which was erected a rather rude cabin. **1851** *Knickerbocker* 37.182, The river is dark as night; but we see, every now and then, 'broad-horns' and coal-flats, with a twinkling light. **1941** FWP *Guide MO* 96, Huge, square-cornered, flat-bottomed craft, variously called "flat-boats," "Kentucky flats," or "broadhorns," were built to carry the bulky downstream freight. **1968** Adams *Western Words, Broadhorn . . .* A boat similar to a flatboat, whose movements were usually regulated . . by two great oars, or sweeps, that projected like horns from each side of the boat. The boats were usually 150 feet long and 25 feet wide, were manned by eight or ten men, and were used for carrying various cargoes.
    2 A longhorn.   *?obs*
        1890 *Stock Grower* 11 Jan 4/2 *(AmSp* 17.124), Ten years ago, when there were 2,000,000 of cattle, 1,500,000 of them were of the native or Texas breeds, or were the broadhorn. **1900** Garland *Eagle's Heart* 164, Reynolds and Mose rode out toward the slowly "milling" herd, a hungry, hot, and restless mob of broadhorns, which required careful treatment. **1968** Adams *Western Words.*

broadleaf tree n
A **magnolia:** see quot.
    1950 *PADS* 14.17 **SC,** *Broadleaf tree . . .* The magnolia grandifolia.

broad-mouth n
    1954 *Harder Coll.* **cwTN,** *Broad-mouth . . .* One who talks too much.

broad-open daylight n
Full daylight.
    1933 Miller *Lamb in His Bosom* 17 **GA,** Well, I don't know as I ever done that in broad-open daylight—pukin' like a dog in the grass. **c1960** Wilson Coll. **csKY,** *Broad-open daylight . . .* Actual daylight, not twilight. "He slept till broad-open daylight."

broad shelf n
A shelf, usu in a pantry, on which food is prepared for baking.

1967 *DARE* Tape **MA117**, There was a big broad shelf in front the window, with another board on top and you'd go in there and do your bakin' [in the buttery]. **1970** *DARE* FW Addit **cwPA**, The *broad shelf*—at the end of the pantry, a wide shelf used for kneading dough.

broadside n

1941 *LANE* Map 301 **cwVT**, *Broadside (pork)* . . . Common, a side of fat salt pork.

broad teeth n

1969 *DARE* FW Addit **ceCT**, Broad teeth—adult or 2nd teeth in a horse or cow.

broadus n |'brɔdəs, -təs| Also sp *braughtus, brawdus, brawtus, broatus, brotus* [Etym uncert; perh by coalescence" of *brotta* "a few drops, a small quantity, a little in addition" *(EDD)* with AmSpan *barata* a bargain sale (Santamaría *Dicc. Americanismos*). It certainly = Caribbean creole *braata* (see *DJE*), prob from Port *barata* bargain, a loanword into Afr pidgins or creoles. No Afr lang source has been found.] **SC, GA coast**

Something extra or given in addition, **lagniappe.**

1877 Bartlett *Americanisms* 69, *Brotus.* (Pron. *brought us.*) A word found exclusively in the mouths of negro market women and itinerant street hucksters and schoolboys, in Charleston, S.C.,—who always ask for it in their purchases of peanuts, plums, chinquapins, chestnuts, &c. *Brotus* means the superfluity of a helping,—the running over of a measure which has been "heaped up and shaken down." It is the extra and gratuitous surplusage which the vendor of peanuts gives her customer for his patronage. **1908** *S. Atl. Qrly.* 7.345 [Gullah], Buh Rabbut 'im duh play des' sweet 'pon de quills; an', w'en 'im finish all 'im chune, 'e play 'em one fuh brotus. **1909** *DN* 3.381 **SC**, *Throw in* . . . Add gratis to a purchaser. So far as I know there is not in east Alabama a noun equivalent to the *broadus* of South Carolina (around Charleston). **1922** Gonzales *Black Border* 290 **eSC** [Gullah glossary], *Brawtus*—broadus, lagniappe. **1930** Stoney–Shelby *Black Genesis* 16 **seSC**, Br' Dog gib he knife annudder lick on he shoe, for braughtus. **1944** *PADS* 2.41 **SC**, *Brawtus* ['brɔtəs]. **1948** *Hench Coll.* **GA coast**, Some [regionalisms] around Savannah: . . . This is for broadus (for good measure). *Ibid* **seSC**, A woman who grew up in Charleston, S.C., tells me of a Charleston word *broadus* . . . Examples: A grocery clerk piles a measure high with dried beans and says, "Here are your beans. I put some on top for broadus." . . A mother gives her child an extra spoonful of ice-cream in her saucer and says, "That's for broadus." **1950** *PADS* 14.17 **coastal SC**, *Brotus, broatus, broadus* ['brɔtəs, 'brɔdəs]. **1966–67** *DARE* (Qu. U15, *When you're buying something, if the seller puts in a little extra to make you feel that you're getting a good bargain, you call that _____*) Inf **GA15**, ['brɔdəs]; **SC4**, 10, Broadus [brɔdəs]; **SC43**, Broadus—used mostly by country people. **1982** *Smithsonian Letters* **ceGA**, A Southern mammy punishing her child would put it across her knee and give it a couple of slaps on the "bounky," probably saying at the last stroke, "And here's one for 'brawdus'. " Also a storekeeper would put in an extra candy "for brawdus."

broad-wing n Also *broad-winged buzzard, broad-winged hawk, broad-wing hawk* [See quot 1938]

A hawk *(Buteo platypterus)* with a showy, black-and-white barred tail. Also called **chicken hawk 1, gentle hawk, hen hawk, little hawk**

1812 Wilson *Amer. Ornith.* 6.92, [This] *Broad-Winged Hawk . . Falco Pennsylvanicus* . . . was perched on the dead limb of a high tree. **1844** DeKay *Zool. NY* 2.11, The *Broad-winged Buzzard. Buteo Pennsylvanicus* . . . is a rare species in our State . . . In Virginia and Maryland, it is more common. **1938** Oberholser *Bird Life LA* 169, Its name Broad-winged Hawk has arisen from its relatively ample wings and its excellent powers of flight. **1945** *MA Audubon* March 39, There are some pairs of nesting Red-shoulders, Sharp-shins or Broad-wings. **1950** *WELS (Kinds of hawks in your neighborhood)* 1 Inf, **seWI**, Broad-winged hawk; 1 Inf, **csWI**, Broad-wing hawk. **1965–70** *DARE* (Qu. Q4) 12 Infs, **scattered, but chiefly east of Missip R**, Broad-wing hawk; **CA115, WI12**, Broad-winged hawk.

broatus See broadus

broat-warsht See bratwurst

brockle n [From **brockle-faced**]

1961 Adams *Old-Time Cowhand* 162, An animal covered with splotches or spots of different colors was called a "brindle" or "brockle."

brockle-faced adj Also *brock-face(d), brocky-faced* [Obs Engl dial *brock* a badger, *brock-faced* white-faced, marked in the face with a streak like a badger] **chiefly West**

Used of a cow: having a mottled, pied, or blotchy face; also n *brockle(d) face.*

1665 in 1896 Hempstead NY *Records* 1.166, One cow Coolered Black with a Brockell face. **1749** (1901) Hempstead *Diary* 539 *(DAE)*, [I] set out with my cattle . . . 1 black brockle faced. **1899** *Mth. S. Dakotan* 1.176, [He] walked slowly 'round and lovingly rubbed the brockeled face of the off ox. **1914** *DN* 4.103 **KS**, *Brock* . . . Speckled; flecked with white; as, a brock face cow. **1936** Adams *Cowboy Lingo* 67 **West**, Brockle-faced steer. **1941** O'Donnell *Great Big Doorstep* 80 *(Hench Coll.)*, That Philip. Look how ugly he is today, so ole and church-eyed and brocky-faced and discouraged. [Ed: Meaning uncert] **1951** *Hench Coll.* [In a letter from the editor of *Wranglin' Notes*], With the improvement of cattle herds in the West, brocklefaced is not as common a term as it used to be . . . It means "blotched", usually red and white in a Hereford . . and shows that the animal is not pure Hereford stock. **1963** Burroughs *Head-First* 173 **CO** (as of c1915), That brock-faced heifer'll make a big cow. She's good breeding stock. **1967** *Yankee* Nov 28, Ever hear tell of a 'brockle-faced kaow' (cow).

brodiaea n

Std: a perennial western plant with an underground corm, few grasslike leaves, and hyacinth-like flowers in usually loose umbels. Also called **grass nut, groundnut, hyacinth, wild hyacinth** For other names of var spp see **blue dicks, firecracker flower, golden star, Ithuriel's spear, prettyface, snakelily**

brodie n, also attrib [After Steve *Brodie* who claimed to have jumped off the Brooklyn Bridge in 1886] **West**

A 360-degree turn made by a skidding or uncontrolled vehicle; hence *half brodie* a 180-degree turn.

1962 *AmSp* 37.267 **sCA** [Language of traffic policemen], *Brodie marks* . . . An extensive pattern of spinning skid marks on pavement. **1966** *DARE* FW Addit **MT, NE**, *Brodie*—a turn of 360 degrees made when one skids on ice. Also *half-brodie*—a 180-degree turn. **1982** *DARE* File **cnUT** (as of 1960s), Not only is it dangerous to do a brodie on an icy highway, it is a very frightening experience.

brogan n Usu |'brogən|, sometimes |'bro͵gæn| Also sp *broghan,* pronc-sp *brogum* [Dimin form of Gael *brōg* shoe]

1 also redund comb *brogan shoe*: A heavy work shoe. **widespread, but esp common in Sth, S Midl** See Map

1835 Hoffman *Winter in West* (NY) 1.200 **Chicago IL**, In another [corner of the room], a pair of Cinderella-like slippers would *chassez* cross with a brace of thick-soled broghans. **1891** Garland *Main-Travelled Roads* 212 **WI**, He slipped his heavy government brogan shoes off his poor, tired, blistered feet. **1903** *DN* 2.295 **Cape Cod MA**, [brogæn]. **1907** *DN* 3.206 **nwAR**. **1908** *DN* 3.294 **eAL, wGA**. **1917** *DN* 4.409 **NEng, IL, KY, LA, NY, SC**. **1941** *LANE* Map 366, 1 inf, **seME**, *Brogans,* old-fashioned low shoes of heavy cowhide; 1 inf, **cVT**, Brogans, tied or clasped. **1941** Faulkner *Men Working* 72 **MS**, Paw . . slipped his cracked brogans off his sockless feet. **1950** *WELS (Men's low, rough work shoes)* 14 Infs, **WI**, Brogans. **1965–70** *DARE* (Qu. W11, *Men's low, rough work shoes*) 285 Infs, **widespread, but esp common in Sth, S Midl**, Brogans; **MA40, SC26**, Brogan shoes; (Qu. W42b) 46 Infs, Brogans; **MN37**, Brogums. **1966–68** *DARE* Tape **NC54**, When I's growin' up, the only thing we had was brogan shoes; **SC14**, Brogan shoe.

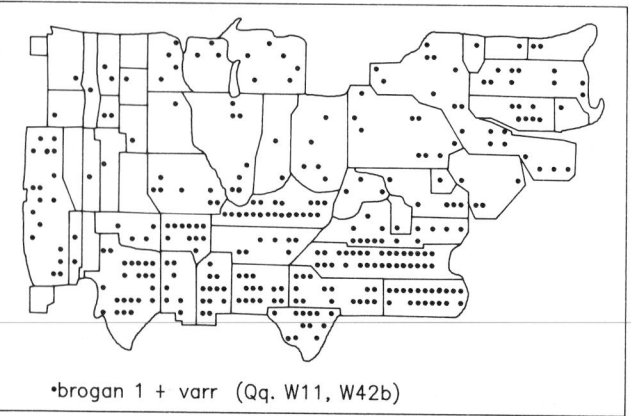

•brogan 1 + varr (Qq. W11, W42b)

2 also *broganite:* By ext, see quots. *joc*
   1950 *WELS (Humorous or uncomplimentary words for big feet)* 1 Inf, **csWI,** Broganites. **1966–69** *DARE* (Qu. X38, . . *Unusually big or clumsy feet)* Infs **ME9, VT16,** Brogans.
3 A large wooden boat usu equipped with sails. **Chesapeake Bay** Cf **bugeye** n²
   1881 Ingersoll *Oyster-Industry* 242, *Brogan.*—A kind of large boat used by the oystermen of the Chesapeake. **1953** *Sun* (Baltimore MD) 18 Oct mag sec 19/2 **Chesapeake Bay,** These log boats continued to grow in size and a new variation, the "brogan," was developed. This craft measured 40 to 45 feet in length. **1968** *DARE* (Qu. O9, . . *Kinds of sailboats)* Inf **MD36,** Brogan ['brogæn]—built like a canoe, 2 sharp or pointed sails, 1 jib—also operated by motor. **1976** Warner *Beautiful Swimmers* 70 **eMD,** The log canoe became a double-masted brogan, which in turn sired the sleek and rakish bugeye.

broganite See **brogan 2**

broghan See **brogan**

brogue v Freq with *about, around, over* [Folk-etym of **bogue** v infl by *brogue* a heavy, coarse shoe] **chiefly sAppalachians**
   To walk, hike, or trudge; to wander or go about aimlessly.
   1883 Zeigler *Heart of Alleghanies* 51 **wNC,** "I've brogued it through every briar patch an' laurel thicket.". . "What do you mean by 'brogued it'?". . "Crawled, thets what hit means." **1917** *DN* 4.409 **wNC,** *Brogue* . . To go afoot. "Where are you a-goin'?"—"Jes' broguin' about." **1926** Kephart *Highlanders* 277 **sAppalachians,** I'm jes' broguin' about. **1928** Chapman *Happy Mt.* 13 **seTN,** Waits brogued over and sat down by his side. **1952** Brown *NC Folkl.* 1.523, *Brogue* . . To walk about.—West. **1954** *Harder Coll.* **cwTN,** *Brogue around* . . To wander about. **1968** *DARE* Tape **DE3,** I usually went fishing or broguing around somewhere. **1969–70** *DARE* (Qu. Y25, *To walk heavily, making a lot of noise: "He came _____ into the house.")* Infs **GA77, VA39,** Broguing.

brogum See **brogan**

broiler house n, also attrib Also *broiler factory* [*broiler* a chicken fit for broiling] **chiefly Sth, S Midl**
   A building in which poultry is raised.
   1944 *Sun* (Baltimore MD) 29 Nov 7/2, Overproduction last Summer caused heavy financial loss to many broiler-house operators in the peninsula. **1950** *WELS Suppl.*, 1 Inf, **csWI,** Broiler factory—facetious for chicken house in which broilers are raised. **1966–69** *DARE* (Qu. M1, . . *Kinds of barns . . according to their use or the way they are built)* Inf **GA84,** Broiler house—baby chicks here; (Qu. M17, *A building where chickens or hens are kept)* Infs **AL33, MS74,** Broiler house; (Qu. M22, . . *Other kinds of buildings . . on farms)* Infs **AR40, MO20,** Broiler house; **AL2,** Broiler house—same height as a layer house. [5 Infs old, 1 Inf mid-aged] **1968** *DARE* Tape **MD39,** Broiler house.

broke See **break** v A

brokebone fever See **breakbone fever**

broked See **break** v A2, 3

broke down adj phr Also *broken down*
   Very tired, exhausted.
   1873 in 1961–62 Albemarle Co. Hist. Soc. *Magazine* 20.42 **VA,** It is a dreadfully long walk; I was quite broken down when I got there. **1966–70** *DARE* (Qu. X47, . . *Other ways . . of saying, "I'm very tired, at the end of my strength.")* Infs **GA1, MS80, VA24, 42,** Broke down.

broken See **break** v A2, 3

broken arms n pl Cf **broken victuals**
   Leftover food.
   1954 Armstrong *Satchmo* 29 **New Orleans LA** (as of c1910), When he came home he brought with him a lot of "broken arms" which were the left overs from the tables he served.

brokenbone fever See **breakbone fever**

broken clabber n [**clabber** n¹ **1**]
   1906 *DN* 3.128 **nwAR,** *Broken clabber* . . Thick curdled milk which has been stirred and mixed.

broken dose n
   A small quantity of medicine administered at intervals.
   1806 (1905) Lewis *Orig. Jrls. Lewis & Clark Exped.* 4.73, We gave him broken dozes of diluted nitre. **1899** (1912) Green *VA Folk-Speech,*

Broken-doses . . Small and often repeated doses. "It is better to take quinine in broken-doses." **1903** *DN* 2.307 **seMO,** *Broken dose* or *doste* . . A little at a time. 'I always give quinine in broken doses.' **1907** *DN* 3.229 **nwAR, seMO,** *Broken dose* or *doste* . . A little (medicine) at a time.

broken-mouthed adj **West**
   Of old sheep: having lost some teeth.
   1913 (1979) Barnes *Western Grazing* 172, Broken-mouthed ewes are those sheep some of whose teeth have been broken off in feeding. **1935** *AmSp* 10.270 **NE,** *Broken-mouthed.* Aged sheep, especially ewes, that have lost some of their teeth. **1971** Green *Village Horse Doctor* 251 **TX,** These ewes all showed some age and were broken-mouthed.

broken sleep n Cf **broke of one's rest**
   Restless or intermittent sleep.
   1965–70 *DARE* (Qu. OO32b, *If a person can't sleep steadily but keeps on waking, he might say, "Every night this week I've _____.")* Infs **KY65, MA6, 37, NY233, PA227,** Had broken sleep.

broken stick n Cf **crooked stick**
   See quots.
   1946 *PADS* 6.7 **swVA, eNC,** *Broken stick* . . An unreliable person or thing. "If you're counting on me, you're counting on a broken stick." **c1960** *Wilson Coll.* **csKY,** *Broken stick* . . Something or somebody undependable or inadequate.

broken vein n **chiefly Sth, S Midl** See Map *esp common among Blacks*
   A varicose vein.
   1965–70 *DARE* (Qu. AA29, . . *The blue, swollen veins that a woman often gets on her legs while expecting a baby)* 40 Infs, Broken veins. [19 of 40 Infs Black]

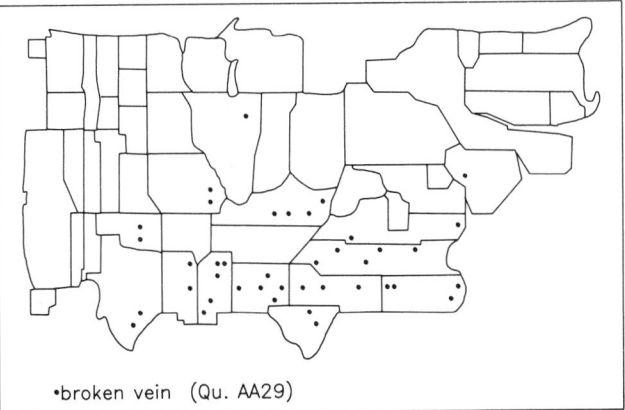

•broken vein (Qu. AA29)

broken victuals n pl Cf **broken arms**
   Leftovers, food remaining from a meal.
   1861 Holmes *Venner* 1.168 **wMA,** Walk up to that table, Mr. Peckham, and help yourself! . . Send a cart, if y'like, 'n' carry off them leavin's . . . Only let me tell ye this . . you'll be known through the taown [sic] . . as the Principal of the Broken-Victuals Institoot! **1911** Clayson *Hist. Narr.* 57 **wWA** (as of c1880), She always took home with her to her tent, or slab shanty, from every family she worked for sufficient broken victuals for herself and Sam.

broke of one's rest adj *arch* Cf **broken sleep**
   Deprived of one's rest.
   1830 (1930) Phelps *Diary* 214 **IL,** I was then sick, being broke of my rest and being exposed to the cold so much. **1884** Baldwin *Yankee School-Teacher* 126 **VA,** I've been broke o' my rest s' much I'm pretty near used up. **1891** (1967) Freeman *New Engl. Nun* 187, I ain't goin' to be broke of my rest this way.

broker n
   A fishing trip that ends with a poor catch.
   1966 *DARE* FW Addit **ME15,** On a fishing trip, fishermen generally divide the profits after expenses for the boat are taken out. If there is no money left over, they've had a "broker." **1968** *DARE* (Qu. P9, *When you're fishing but not catching any)* Inf **AK1,** Made a broker—a halibut fishing trip with poor catch (goes broke).

broke up adj

In poor health; injured.

1955 *DE Folkl. Bulletin* 1.17, If he is really in bad health he will tell you, "I'm all broke up." **1969** *DARE* FW Addit **NC**, All broke up . . Injured. "Old fashioned."

‡brokity adj [Prob *broke* + alter of ppl suff *-ed* + *-y*]

Broken.

1960 Williams *Walk Egypt* 162 **GA**, Carried two sacks trash—ole brokity cups and dishes, rags, sticks.

bromegrass n Also *brome* **Nth, esp Upper MW, Gt Lakes**

A grass of the genus *Bromus.* Also called **cheat 1, chess, wild oats** For other names of var spp see **bronco grass, rattlesnake grass, rescue grass, ripgut**

1793 *Amer. Philos. Soc. Trans.* 3.161/2, *Bromus,* Brome-grass. **1965–70** *DARE* (Qu. L9a) 82 Infs, **chiefly Nth, esp Upper MW, Gt Lakes,** Brome(grass); (Qu. L9b) Infs **CO**38, **UT**15, Brome; (Qu. S9) Infs **MN**12, **NV**5, Bromegrass; (Qu. S26c) Inf **OR**3, English brome. **1968** *Portage Daily Register* (WI) 17 June 3/4, The mixture will be fifteen pounds of tall fescue per acre and ten pounds of Brome grass.

bronc See **bronco** adj, n

bronc-breaker, bronc-buster, bronc-fighter See **bronco-buster**

bronch See **bronco** n

bronchial adj Usu |braŋkiəl|; freq metath, *esp among male and old speakers and speakers with little formal educ,* |branəkəl|; occas |braŋkəl| Pronc-spp *bronchal, bronical, bronikal*

Std sense, var forms.

1931–33 *LANE Worksheets* **cwVT**, Bronical /branəkl/ for bronchial. **1946** *PADS* 6.7 **swVA, eNC,** *Bronical* . . . Bronchial. "I had bronical trouble." . . Common. **1953** Randolph *Down in Holler* 230 **Ozarks,** *Bronikal* . . . Bronchial. **1965–70** *DARE* (Qu. BB12, *The kind of cough that comes with bronchitis*) 157 Infs, **widespread,** Bronical; 10 Infs, **scattered,** Bronchal; (Qu. BB9, . . *A severe cough*) 8 Infs, **scattered,** Bronical (condition, cough, trouble); **CT**21, **NC**2, Bronchal (condition, pneumonia). [Of all Infs responding to Qu. BB12, 66% were old, 27% grade school educ, 43% male; of those giving the response *bronical,* 77% were old, 44% grade school educ, 54% male.] **1969** *DARE* FW Addit **cwIL,** Bronchial trouble—['branəkəl]. Overheard in conversation. **1970** *Thompson Coll.,* Bronical trouble—Asthma. Detroit 1950's, Los Angeles 1960's, Pike Co. Georgia 1971.

bronco adj Also sp *broncho* and abbr *bronc* [Span] **West, esp SW**

Wild, mean, rough.

1866 *Weekly New Mexican* 21 July 1/4 *(DA),* Then the Territory did not keep fast horses and other things, and go to bronco bailes and play whiskey poker. **1887** Francis *Saddle & Mocassin* 146 *(DA),* Sam's too broncho: he gets all-fired mean sometimes when he's full. **1910** *Century Illustr. Mag.* 57.763/2, Away to the north . . were the Bacatete Mountains, the stronghold for ages of the wild or bronco Yaquis. **1910** Mulford *Hopalong Cassidy* 138 *(DA),* That ain't a bad cayuse you got there . . . Is it very bronc? **1947** Westerners Los Angeles Corral *Brand Book* 75, He always felt that a man who made a false step wasn't necessarily all bad or "broncho" as he expressed it. **1967–70** *DARE* (Qu. K16, *A cow with a bad temper*) Inf **OR**10, Riley, mean, bronco.

bronco n |braŋko| Also sp *broncho,* abbr *bronc, bronch* [**bronco** adj]

A wild, unbroken, or vicious horse; also generalized, in wider use, of any horse.

1893 Roosevelt *Wilderness Hunter* 418 **WY**, I saddled up the bronc' and lit out for home. **1910** Raine *O'Connor* 72 *(OEDS),* You're going to . . learn to stick to your saddle when the bronc and you disagree. **1937** [see **coyotey**]. **1944** *Natl. Geog. Mag.* 85.656/1 **ID,** But the greatest fun is the rodeo—a real Wild West spectacle in which hard-working ranch cowboys ride unbroken broncos and steers fresh from the ranges. **1948** *Range Riders Western* May 30/2 *(DA),* Two tired broncs stamped their hoofs restlessly. **c1960** *Wilson Coll.* **csKY,** Broncho . . . A wild horse, a very late word in the region; also *bucking broncho.* **1965–70** *DARE* (Qu. K42, *A horse that is rough, wild, or dangerous*) 178 Infs, **widespread,** Bronco.

bronco-buster n Also *bronc-breaker, ~ buster, ~ fighter, ~ peeler, ~ rider, ~ scratcher, ~ snapper, ~ stomper, ~ twister* **West**

One who breaks wild horses to the saddle.

1888 *Century Illustr. Mag.* 13.507/1 **West,** The flash riders, or horse-breakers, always called "bronco-busters," can perform really marvelous feats. **1911** *DN* 3.550 **WY**, Broncho twister, same meaning as "broncho buster." **1914** Brininstool *Trail Dust* 114 *(DA),* He used to brag he was the boss Bronc-peeler at this ridin' game. **1916** Titus *I Conquered* 92 *(DA),* You'd have made a fine bronc twister. **1938** Balch *Tiger Roan* 56 *(DA),* An expert bronc-rider himself . . . Sleed had been smart enough to see that there was more money to be made. **1943** *Natl. Geog. Mag.* 83.618/1 **AR,** Veteran buckaroos whoop with delight when a bronco-buster gets "piled." **1961** Adams *Old-Time Cowhand* 297, When the hosses on one ranch were broke, they moved to 'nother . . . The roughstring rider's got many slang titles too, such as "bronc breaker," "bronc buster," "bronc stomper," "bronc snapper," "bronc scratcher," "jinete," and "bronc fighter." **1966** *DARE* Tape **NM**14, We generally have one or two men that are exceptionally good riders and know how to handle these [unbroken] horses, and they get most of the worst horses . . . they call them bronc-stompers.

bronco-busting n Also *bronc-stomping*

Breaking wild horses to the saddle.

1891 *Harper's Mag.* 83.208/1 **SW,** Bronco busting is a distinct art. **1947** *Trail Riders Bul.* Feb. 20/2 *(DA),* That's how I come tuh give up bronco bustin' an foun' me a healthier climate. **1950** *PADS* 14.74 **FL,** *Bronc-stomping* . . . Breaking horses. Cowboy speech.

bronco fits n pl

Of a horse: see quot.

1963 Faulkner *My Brother Bill* 163, She [a mare] would have what the Negroes called "bronco fits." All at once she would begin kicking everything in sight.

bronco grass n

A **bromegrass** (here: *Bromus secalinus*).

1967–68 *DARE* (Qu. S9) Inf **CA**87, Bronco grass—like a barley stem, will grow 2½ feet high—more beards on each stem; (Qu. S15) Inf **OR**5, Bronco grass—or devil's darning needle—long needle, inch or so, gets into clothing—had to push them on through.

bronc-peeler, bronc-rider, bronc-scratcher, bronc-snapper, bronc-stomper See **bronco-buster**

bronc-stomping See **bronco-busting**

bronc-twister See **bronco-buster**

bronical, bronikal See **bronchial**

bronnigan See **brannigan 2**

bronzeback n Also *bronzebacker*

=**smallmouth bass.**

1887 Goode *Amer. Fishes* 56, "Bronze-backer" is one of its *[Micropterus dolomiei]* pet names among the anglers. **1946** LaMonte *N. Amer. Game Fishes* 134, *Micropterus dolomiei* . . Names: . . Bronze Back. **1978** *Outdoor Life* Sept 56, The smallmouth bass is changing its habits . . . The bronzeback is adapting to new territory.

bronze bells n

A **fritillary** (here: either *Fritillaria atropurpurea* or *F. lanceolata*).

1897 Parsons *Wild Flowers CA* 264, Bronze Bells . . . *Fritillaria lanceolata.* **1915** (1926) Armstrong *Western Wild Flowers* 38, Bronze Bells . . *Fritillaria atropurpurea.*

bronze curlew n

Either the **glossy ibis 1** or the **white-faced ibis.**

1918 Grinnell *Game Birds CA* 269, White-faced Glossy Ibis *Plegadis guarauna* . . . Other Names—Bronze Curlew. **1928** Bailey *Birds NM* 101, *White-faced Glossy Ibis: Plegadis guarauna* . . . We were not near enough to see the iridescence that gives them the name, Bronze Curlew. **1954** Sprunt *FL Bird Life* 43, *Eastern Glossy Ibis: Plegadis falcinellus* . . . Local Names: . . Bronze Curlew.

bronze gas n

See quots.

1965 *DARE* FW Addit **OK**18, Bronze gas—same as leaded gas. **1967** *DARE* (Qu. N15a, *Gas stations . . usually have two kinds of gasoline: a cheaper kind that's called* _____) Inf **CO**3, Bronze.

bronzehead n

The **goldeneye** duck (here: *Glaucionetta clangula*).

1923 U.S. Dept. Ag. *Misc. Circular 22, Goldeneye . . . Vernacular Names . . . In local use . . .* bronzehead (for female and young) (Oreg.).

bronze John n

1 Yellow fever. [*bronze* skin color produced by yellow fever + *John*, perh folk-etym personification of Fr *jaune* yellow]

1869 *Overland Mth.* 3.130/1, "Bronze John" is pretty well known [in the South] for yellow fever. **1955** Warren *Angels* 95 **LA**, *"La fièvre jaune,"* she said. "Bronze John. Ten thousand died."

2 See quot.

1941 FWP *Guide OK* 121, In general use in the oil-field world are the following expressions: . . Bronze John—The sun.

brood adj

Of a male pig: kept for breeding; hence n *brooder*.

1966–68 *DARE* (Qu. K52, *A male pig kept for breeding is a _____*) Inf **AR47**, Brooder; **MO10**, Brood male; **SC19**, Brood hog.

brood n¹ See **broody**

brood n² See **brother A6**

brooder (hen) See **broody**

brooder house n Also *brooder, brooder coop, ~ pen, ~ shelter* **widespread exc West; esp freq N Cent** See Map Cf **broody**

A chicken coop, hen house.

1931–33 *LANE Worksheets* ceMA, Brooder coop . . . Chicken coop. **1939** *LANE* Map 112 **esp nNEng**, Brooder (house)—a shelter for newly-hatched chickens on chicken farms. **1965–70** *DARE* (Qu. M17, *A building where chickens or hens are kept*) 45 Infs, **scattered, but esp Gt Lakes**, Brooder house; **AL19, MO34**, Brooder; **OK11**, Hen brooder; (Qu. M16, *The small shelter for a hen that can be moved about from place to place*) 31 Infs, **scattered, but esp N Cent, Gt Lakes**, Brooder (house); **OH27, PA201, WI77**, Brooder coop; **MI19**, Brooder pen; **NY102**, Brooder shelter; **MS87**, Chicken brooder; (Qu. M22, . . *Other kinds of buildings . . on farms*) 21 Infs, **scattered, but esp N Cent, KY**, Brooder (house). **1973** Allen *LAUM* 1.255 **throughout Upper MW**, Chicken coop . . . [2 infs:] Brooder . . . [14 infs: Brooder] house.

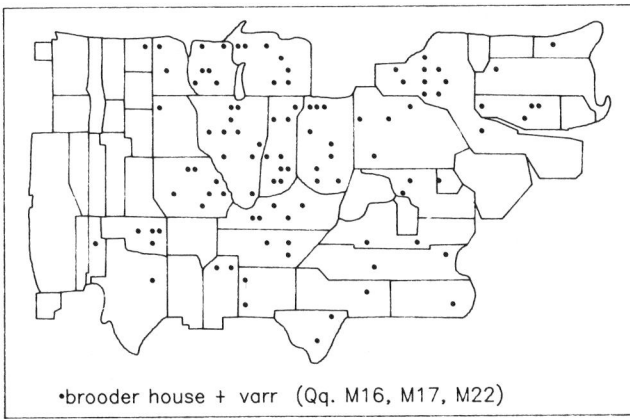

•brooder house + varr (Qq. M16, M17, M22)

brood(ing) hen See **broody**

broodish adj [*brood* v + *-ish*, perh infl by *brutish*]

Brooding, moody, sullen.

1981 *Durham Morning Herald* (NC) 26 Nov 1D, "He was kind of broodish," says James Wingo . . . "In the old days, George [Foreman] liked to throw parties, but he'd have these bodyguards to keep him away from people. He'd listen to you, but he'd be ready to get on you if you said something wrong. I didn't know he had changed until I went to see him. He was clean-headed, talking about the Lord. Instead of being broodish, he was real gentle. It scared me."

broody n Also *brood, brooder (hen), brood(ing) hen, broody ~* [Engl dial; cf *EDD* broody 1, 2] **widespread, but least freq Sth, S Midl** See Map Cf **setting hen**

A hen that is incubating eggs.

1939 *LANE* Map 214 **throughout sNEng**, A hen . . [that] is hatching out eggs . . is called a *setting hen, . . brood ~, broody ~, brooding ~, . . brooder.* **1965–70** *DARE* (Qu. K72, *When the hen stops laying and begins to sit on the eggs to hatch them, she's a _____*) 61 Infs, **chiefly Nth, N Midl, West**, Broody (hen); 35 Infs, **chiefly Nth, N Midl**, Brood

(hen); **IL33, 116, KS20, LA15, MO26, MT3, PA147, VA89**, Brooding (hen); **CO19, IL33, NY32, 65, 117, OK33, VA33**, Brooder. **1973** Allen *LAUM* 1.254, *Setting hen . . . Broody* and *broody hen* are widely scattered, although with no instances in South Dakota . . . [2 infs:] brooder, ~ hen. [2 infs:] brood hen. [2 infs:] brooding hen.

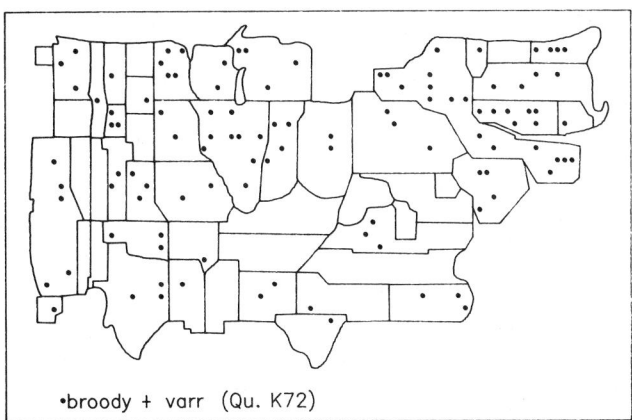

•broody + varr (Qu. K72)

brook n, also attrib Occas *brooklet* **orig chiefly NEng, now widespread but esp common NEast** See Map Cf **branch, creek** n¹ B2, **run**

A small stream.

1612 Smith *Map VA* 2, Here are mountains, hils, plaines, valleyes, rivers and brookes, all running most pleasantly into a faire Bay. **1668** in 1901 Derby CT *Town Rec.* 10, A little Brook or spring that Runs into the beaver River North. **1734** in 1885 Boston Registry Dept. *Records* 12.71, All Fish caught in Rivers, Ponds, and Brooks, shall be . . sold in the Market. **a1817** (1821) Dwight *Travels* 2.149 **NEng**, It is impossible for a brook of this size to be modelled into more diversified, or more delightful, forms. **1843** (1940) Arnold *Diaries* 166 **VT**, Finished the road down the brook-hollow. **1892** Eggleston *Hoosier Schoolmaster* 229, From the ancient Hoosier folk-speech . . . Brook is . . absent. A small stream was . . called a *branch.* **1912** *DN* 3.566 **cNY**, Brook . . . Small stream tributary to a creek . . . Little used on Long Island, near Philadelphia, in Pennsylvania, Illinois, or Missouri, but common in New England. **1939** *LANE* Map 41, *Brook* is the usual term throughout New England for a fresh-water stream of small or moderate size, but *river,* which is applied to many small tributaries as well as to the larger watercourses, competes with it. Few *brooks* flow directly into the sea . . they empty into *rivers* or (salt) creeks. **1965–70** *DARE* (Qu. C1, . . *A small stream of water not big enough to be a river*) 230 Infs, **widespread, but esp common NEast**, Brook; **NY92**, Feeder brook; **MO26, VA8**, Brooklet; **NY213**, Little brooklet; **NJ1**, Spring brook; **NY183**, Windfall brook. **1968** *Amherst Rec.* (MA) 27 Nov 2/1, A temporary foot bridge is being built for residents of the South side of the brook.

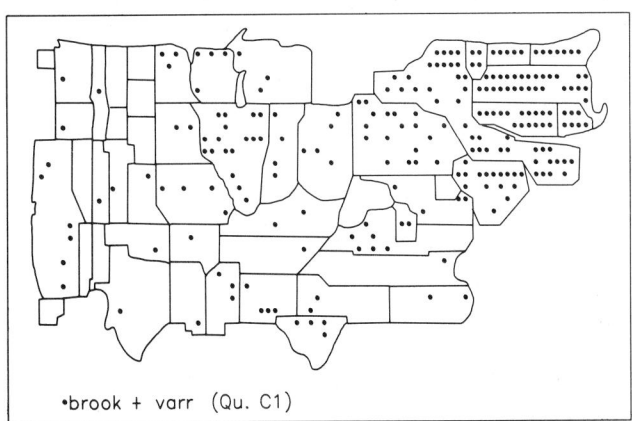

•brook + varr (Qu. C1)

brook-creek n

1916 *DN* 4.344, Brook-creek . . . A brooklike creek. Georgia.

brookflower n

The Virginia **waterleaf** *(Hydrophyllum virginianum).* Also called **burr flower**

1900 Lyons *Plant Names* 196. **1949** Moldenke *Amer. Wild Flowers* 251, Wander through moist woods almost anywhere from Quebec and Ontario. . southward to South Carolina and Kansas and you are likely to find extensive colonies of . . . brookflower or Virginia waterleaf.

brookie See **brook trout**

brooklet See **brook**

Brooklyn Indian n

A Jew.

1967 *Western Folkl.* 26.189, *Brooklyn Indians*—Jews . . heard in service during World War II. **1982** *DARE* File **NYC** (as of c1965), To call a Jew a *Brooklyn Indian* wasn't to insult him; it was taken as a jocular epithet.

brook mint n

=**water mint.**

1967 *DARE* (Qu. I35, *Kitchen herbs . . grown and used in cooking*) Inf **NJ2**, Brook mint—brought into garden from wild.

brook sunflower n [From its commonly growing by streams]

A **beggar ticks 1** (here: *Bidens laevis*).

1900 Lyons *Plant Names* 63, *B[idens] laevis* . . . Brook Sunflower. **1901** Lounsberry *S. Wild Flowers* 525, *Brook sunflower. Bidens laevis.* **1959** Carleton *Index Herb. Plants* 19, Brook Sunflower: Bidens lævis.

brook trout n Also *brookie*

A freckled trout *(Salvelinus fontinalis).* Also called **coaster** n³ **1, mountain trout, native trout, red-spotted trout, salter, sea trout, speckled trout, squaretail, trout 1**

1836 Dunlap *30 Years Ago* 1.57 **VT**, I am not one of your brook trout to be played back and forth with a hair line. **1933** *New York Times (NY)* 9 Apr 3/5, This is the larges[t] annual distribution of "brookies" ever undertaken in New Jersey . . . Because brook trout require cold water, their distribution is being confined chiefly to streams in the northern half of the State. **1949** Caine *N. Amer. Sport Fish* 84, Brook Trout—*Salvelinus fontinalis*. . . Colloquial Names . . . Brookie. **1956** Harlan *IA Fish* 58, *Salvelinus fontinalis* . . brookies. **1965–70** *DARE* (Qu. P1) 57 Infs, **scattered**, Brook trout. **1972** Sparano *Outdoors Encycl.* 355, *Salvelinus fontinalis* . . brookies.

broom n

1 See **broom grass.**

2 See **broom sedge.**

broom ball n [Cf *DCan* 1933 →]

1967 *DARE* (Qu. EE27, *Games played on the ice*) Inf **MN11**, Broom ball—similar to hockey, players don't wear skates and use brooms and a ball.

broom beardgrass See **broom grass**

broom brush n

1 A **Saint-John's-wort** (here: *Hypericum prolificum*).

1888 *N.Y. World (DA)*, The Shakers . . were the first to make brooms of broom brush, and, in fact, originated the entire broom business. **1893** *Jrl. Amer. Folkl.* 6.138, *Hypericum proliferum*, broom brush; West Va. **1933** Small *Manual SE Flora* 873, *H[ypericum] prolificum* . . . Broombrush.

2 See **brush broom** n².

broom crowberry n

An evergreen heathlike shrub (here: *Corema conradii*) of the northeastern US.

1857 Gray *Manual of Botany* 393, *Corèma,* . . *Broom-Crowberry* . . . Much-branched little shrubs. **1976** Bailey–Bailey *Hortus Third* 312, Broom crowberry.

broom dance n

See quots.

1954 Piper *175 Folk Dances* 24, *Broom Dance*—One lady or man with broom in center of floor while others are dancing. When music stops all change ptns [=partners] (one in center drops broom and gets a ptn). The one left with no ptn gets the broom until the next break. **1967–68** *DARE* (Qu. EE2, *Games that have one extra player*) Inf **NY2**, Broom dance—six girls and five fellas—sixth girl has a broom; (Qu. FF5a, *Names for different steps . . in dancing*) Inf **PA**81, Broom dance.

broom dirndl See **broomstick skirt**

broom grass n Also *broom (beardgrass)*

=**beardgrass.**

a1686 (1912) Alvord–Bidgood *First Explor.* 189, "Old fields" is a common expression for land that has been cultivated by the Indians and left fallow, which are generally overrun with what they call broom grass. **1891** Jesup *Plants Hanover NH* 52, *A[ndropogon] scoparius* . . . (Broomgrass.). **1903** Porter *Flora PA* 15, *Andropogon scoparius* . . . Broom Beard-grass. **1910** Graves *Flowering Plants* 48 **CT**, *Andropogon scoparius* . . . Broom Beard Grass. **1946** *PADS* 6.7 **eNC**, *Broom grass* . . . Long grass of savannas, used for making brooms. Common. **1950** Gray–Fernald *Manual of Botany* 231, *A[ndropogon] scoparius* . . . Broom-beardgrass, Broom. **1965–70** *DARE* (Qq. L8, 9a, 9b) 27 Infs, **chiefly Inland Nth**, Broom grass; (Qu. S9) Infs **FL35, IL33, IN3, MI108, NY71, TX33, VA38, WI37**, Broom grass.

broom hickory n

A **pignut** (here: *Carya glabra*).

1813 Muhlenberg *Catalogus Plantarum* 88, Heart h[ickory]—broom h[ickory]. **1837** Darlington *Flora Cestrica* 547, Pig-nut Hickory. Broom Hickory . . . The young saplings, of this species, were formerly much used for making splint brooms. **1897** Sudworth *Arborescent Flora* 115, *Pignut (Hickory)* . . . *Common Names* . . . Broom Hickory (Mo.). **1950** Peattie *Nat. Hist. Trees* 131, The name of Broom Hickory was given it by the early settlers because narrow strips were split from the wood and made into brooms. **1979** Little *Checklist U.S. Trees* 73.

broomie See **broomtail 1a**

broom me out exclam

1953 Randolph *Down in Holler* 230 **Ozarks**, *Broom me out!* . . An exclamation comparable to "Well, I'll be damned!"

broom pine n [See quot1976]

=**longleaf pine 1.**

1791 (1958) Bartram *Travels* 58, The trees were tall, and generally of the species called Broompine. **1847** Wood *Class-Book* 515, *P[inus] palustris* . . Broom Pine. **1876** Hobbs *Bot. Hdbk.* 90, Broom pine . . Pinus palustris. **1900** Lyons *Plant Names* 291, *P[inus] palustris* . . Broom Pine. **1976** Bruce *How to Grow Wildflowers* 26, These are . . enormously long in . . the Longleaf Pine of farther south—so long in the latter species that one common name, "Broom Pine," alludes to the practice of making brooms from bundles of the dried needles.

broomrape n

1 Std: a parasitic plant of the family Orobanchaceae, esp of the genus *Orobanche*. [*OED* 1578 →] Also called **cancerroot 1, ground cone**

2 A **beardgrass** (here: *Andropogon barbinodis*).

1941 *Torreya* 41.45, *Andropogon barbinodis* . . . Broom-rape.

broom sage See **broom sedge**

broom sage broom n chiefly **Sth** Cf **sage grass broom**

A broom with bristles made from the broom sage.

c1960 *Wilson Coll.* **csKY**, *Broomsage broom* . . . Coarse home-made broom to sweep porches. More often sage-grass broom. **1965–70** *DARE* (Qu. F36, *. . Kinds of brooms*) Infs **AL52, MD14, MS37, 45, 72, NC31, SC43, TX99**, Broom sage (broom).

broom sedge n Also *broom* Pronc-sp *broom sage (grass)* chiefly **Sth, S Midl**

=**beardgrass**, esp *Andropogon virginicus*.

1819 'Agricola' *Essays* 26 (DAE), Worn-out fields, which have grown up in broom sedge, may be highly improved by . . ploughing them deep. **1859** Perry *Turpentine Farming* 9, After this, the land needs no cultivation, but every kind of turf should be turned over, such as low bush huckleberry, gallberry, . . savanna grass and broom-sage grass. **1907** *DN* 3.235 **nwAR, seMO**, *(Broom)-sage* . . . Sedge-grass. **1908** *DN* 3.294 **eAL, wGA**, *Broom-sage*. **1933** Small *Manual SE Flora* 44, *A[ndropogon] scoparius* . . . Broom-sedge; . . *A. virginicus* . . . Broom-sedge. **1939** *Hall Coll.* **wNC**, *Broom sage* . . . broom sedge. Any of several species of *Andropogon* . . called also *broom* . . . Old timers used to use it for brooms to sweep off yards with. **c1960** *Wilson Coll.* **csKY**, *Broom sage* . . . Andropogon, Sp . . . Universally used; *broom sedge* is known but is literary. Also called *sage grass*. **1965–70** *DARE* (Qu. L8) Inf **KY86**, Broom sage; **IN35**, Broom sedge; (Qu. L9a, *. . Grass . . grown for hay*) Inf **WV7**, Broom; **WV16**, Broom sage; (Qu. L9b) Inf **TX32**, Broom sage; (Qq. S8, 9, 20, 21, 26d) 17 Infs, **esp Sth, S Midl**, Broom sage (or) broom sedge; **CT40**, Broom.

broom skirt See **broomstick skirt**

‡broomstick n

=**praying mantis.**

    1968 *AmSp* 43.53 **KS,** Praying mantis . . *broomstick* . . 1 [Inf].

broomstick dirndl See **broomstick skirt**

broomstick marriage n Cf **jump the broom**

A common-law marriage.

    1899 (1912) Green *VA Folk-Speech, Broomstick-marriage* . . . Two people living together as man and wife without legal marriage, are said to have been married by jumping over the broomstick.

broomstick skirt n Also *broomstick dirndl, broom dirndl, ~ skirt*

A cotton skirt or dirndl which is given a pleated effect by wrapping it wet around a broom handle.

    1950 *WELS Suppl.,* 12 Infs, **WI,** Broomstick skirt—a dirndl; 1 Inf, **ceWI,** Broomstick skirt—Heard in the early 1940s; a full cotton skirt tied around a broomstick while moist; when removed the skirt has a wrinkly, pleated effect now obtained by a permanently pleated material called "squaw cloth;" 1 Inf, **cnWI,** Broomstick skirt—I first met up with it in West Virginia as a youngster. However, my husband, who is practically a native of Wausau, agrees that it is a full, gaily colored skirt which after being washed is wrapped and bound around a stick so that it dries with many small pleatlike wrinkles; 1 Inf, **neWI,** Broomstick dirndl; 1 Inf, **seWI,** Broom skirt, broom dirndl.

broomstraw n, also attrib **chiefly Sth**

=**beardgrass.**

    1785 (1925) Washington *Diaries* 2.365, Had the Roots, shrubs (which had been grubbed) and tussics of broom Straw . . raked of[f] and burnt. **1954** *PADS* 21.39 **SC,** *Straw field* . . . A field . . overgrown with broom sedge. Also called *broomstraw field.* **1966–69** *DARE* (Qu. F36, *Other kinds of brooms*) Infs **SC**43, **WA**6, Broomstraw broom; (Qu. S21, . . *Other weeds*) Infs **NC**72, **SC**7, 31, Broomstraw. **1969** *DARE* Tape **NC**66, Broomstraw fields.

broom tag n

    1941 FWP *Guide CO* 282, Square dances and waltzes were enlivened at intervals with a 'broom tag,' when a man without a partner thumped a broom upon the floor as the girl he wanted to dance with came past.

broomtail n

1 A horse with a broom-like tail. **chiefly West**

a also *broomie:* A mare.

    1913 (1979) Barnes *Western Grazing* 119, Hair ropes ("mecates") spun from the very choicest mane hair taken from some bunch of "broom tails" (mares) which the boys rounded up on an afternoon and spent hours in throwing in order to obtain the hair. **1929** *AmSp* 5.66 **NE,** A "broom tail" [is] a gentle old mare. **1941** FWP *Guide WY* 461, Broom tail . . . A wild mare. **1945** Thorp *Pardner* 298 **SW,** Broomtail—a range mare, so called because her tail grew long. All range mares were classed as "broomies." Some people called them "willows." **1967** *DARE* (QR p84) Inf **CO**22, Broomtails—brood mares.

b A usu small wild horse of poor quality; a mustang, pony.

    1914 *DN* 4.162 **NW,** *Broom-tail* . . . A pony with a short, bushy tail. **1935** Sandoz *Jules* 409 **wNE,** Fritz tried the next one, slick-headed, a bad broomtail that sagged his smoky belly to the ground. **1939** FWP *ID Lore* 244. **1939** FWP *Guide MT* 413. **1940** FWP *Guide NV* 76. **1941** FWP *Guide UT* 103, The breed degenerated, producing "hammer-heads" and "broomtails," but occasionally, in the wild herds, there is a throwback with the build, spirit, speed, and bearing of the pure-blood Arabian. **1952** Dobie *Mustangs* 193, The inferior ones [=wild horses] came to be called "broomtails," though that term was often extended to all mustangs. **1958** *AmSp* 33.270 **ewA,** Horse . . . *Fuzztail, broomtail.* **1965–70** *DARE* (Qu. K37, . . *A horse of mixed colors*) Inf **IA**1, Broomtail; (Qu. K42, *A horse that is rough, wild, or dangerous*) Inf **OK**18, Broomtail; (Qu. K43, *A horse . . bred by accident*) Inf **CA**105, Broomtail; (Qu. K44, *A bony or poor-looking horse*) Infs **CO**44, **TX**42, Broomtail.

c See quot.

    1965–70 *DARE* (Qu. K41, *A horse with its tail cut short*) Infs **AZ**10, **CA**124, **MI**2, **MT**4, **TX**36, Broomtail.

2 A mule.

    1965–70 *DARE* (Qu. K50, *Joking nicknames for mules*) Infs **AR**52, **CA**124, **GA**72, **IL**19, **TX**89, Broomtail.

broomweed n, also attrib **chiefly KS, OK, TX**

=**snakeweed** (here: *Gutierrezia* spp).

    1908 *Sat. Eve. Post* 21 Nov 9/3 **TX,** Once he [=a coyote] paused, in a patch of broomweed, to send his doleful cry to the stars. **1948** Stevens *KS Wild Flowers* 396, *Gutierrezia*—Broom Snakeweed . . . *Gutierrezia sarothrae* . . . Broomweed . . . *Amphiachyris dracunculoides*—Annual Broomweed. **1964** Wallace *Frontier Life* 53 **OK,** Adding color and beauty to the landscape were Black-eyed Susans, . . and another little tree-like bush called Broom-weed with little spots of yellow at the end of the numerous yellow-green branches. **1965–70** *DARE* (Qu. S21) 13 Infs, **chiefly Sth,** Broomweed; (Qu. S6) Inf **OK**52, Broomweed; (Qu. S20) Inf **TX**66, Broomweed; (Qu. BB50a, . . *Favorite remedies . . for a cough*) Inf **OK**58, Broomweed tea. **1970** Correll *Plants TX* 1573, *Xanthocephalum [Gutierrezia]* . . . Broomweed. **1976** Dodge *Roadside Wildflowers* 45, *Broom snakeweed* . . . Snakeweed is also known as turpentine weed and broomweed.

brooze See **bruise**

bros See **brother** A4

‡broth n

    1968 *DARE* (Qu. DD4, *Moisture in the mouth, colored brown by snuff or chewing tobacco*) Inf **NC**54, Broth [brɔf].

brother n

A Forms.

1 Pronc-sp *bro.* **esp Sth, S Midl** *chiefly among Black speakers*

    1838 (1852) Gilman *S. Matron* 33 **SC,** "Bro' Jim ride more better dan Maus John, for true," said one. [Footnote] Brother. The terms daddy, maumer, uncle, aunty, broder and titter (brother and sister), are not confined to connexions among the blacks, they seem rather to spring from age. **1950** *WELS (Nickname meaning brother)* 2 Infs, **cwWI,** Bro. **1965–70** *DARE* (Qu. Z5, . . *Brother*) 49 Infs, **esp Sth, S Midl,** Bro [bro]; **TN**46, Baby bro. [Of all Infs responding to the question, 9% were Black; of those giving this response, 57% were Black.] **1971** Roberts *Third Ear* [Black], *Bro'* . . a black male. (Abbreviation for "brother.") **1977** Smitherman *Talkin* 255, Many of the terms that blacks use to refer to blacks are also used in addressing one another; for example, . . "Say Bro, what's yo name?"

2 Pronc-spp *b', bre'er, brer, buh, bur.* *orig among Southern Blacks*

    1880 Tourgée *Bricks* 186 **NC,** "Bre'er Nimbus" was still the heart and life of the community. **1909** *S. Atl. Qrly.* 8.43 [Gullah], In *brother,* adjunctively used, elimination is practically complete: *Brer,* as used in Upper Georgia, and *Brudder,* as used in Virginia, fade to one labial and a murmur, *Buh,* often simply an extraneous *b,* as in *Buh Owl an' B' Cootah.* Disjunctively the form is *bubba.* **1922** Gonzales *Black Border* 219 **eSC** [Gullah], One time Buh Hawss en' Buh Mule tu'n out duh pastuh duh Sunday. **1927** Adams *Congaree* 7 **SC** [Black], Tell we, Bur Scrip. **1954** *PADS* 22.30, [Joel Chandler Harris], like many other writers of Negro dialect, used *er* to represent [ə] . . . hence the spelling *Brer* to represent [brə]. **1966–69** *DARE* (Qu. Z5, . . *"Brother"*) Inf **AL**30, Bur [bʌr]; **MS**36, [brʌ]; **NC**18, Brer [brə]; **RI**17, Brer [brer]; **SC**2, Her mother had one named Tom, called him [bə'taʳum].

3 Pronc-spp *breddah, bredduh, brudder, brudduh, budda, budder.*

    1884 Harrison *Negro Engl.* 257 **Sth,** Brudder, brer. **1888** Jones *Negro Myths* 1 **eGA,** One time Buh Rabbit, him meet Buh Alligatur, an eh ax um: "Budder, you tek life berry onconsarne." **1922** Gonzales *Black Border* 290 **eSC** [Gullah glossary], *Bredduh*—(also brudduh) brother, brethren (formal). **1928** Peterkin *Scarlet Sister Mary* 14 **seSC** [Gullah], Although she could remember her mother faintly, Maum Hannah and Budda Ben were the only parents she knew. **1950** *PADS* 14.16 **SC,** *Breddah* ['brɛdə]: n. pl. Brothers, brethren. **1966–68** *DARE* (Qu. Z5) Inf **NY**123, Brudder; **OK**31, ['brʌdɚ].

4 Pronc-spp *bros, broz, brud, bruth.* **esp NEast**

    1950 *WELS (Brother)* 2 Infs, **WI,** Brud. **1965–70** *DARE* (Qu. Z5) 14 Infs, **chiefly NEast,** Brud [brʌd]; **CT**5, 12, **NJ**19, 30, 54, 63, **NC**30, **PA**225, Bruth [brʌθ]; **CT**16, Bros, broz; **DC**11, [brʌz]; **MA**123, [brʌdz]; **OH**28, [brɔz]; **PA**241, [brʌz]—bros was heard several times by FW.

5 Pronc-sp *bruuder.* **Ger settlement areas**

    1951 Danner *PA Dutch Dict.* 14, Brother—bruuder [uu as in English hoot]. **1968** *DARE* (Qu. Z5) Inf **MI**44, ['brudə]—that's just German for "brother"; **MI**68, [brudə] in German families.

6 Other varr: see quots.

    1950 *WELS (Brother)* 2 Infs, **WI,** Brots. **1965–70** *DARE* (Qu. Z5) Inf **HI**6, Bra; **MA**3, **NY**215, Brats; **SC**26, [brat], ['brɛdə]; **VA**13, [brʌb]; **NJ**6, Brood; **NC**55, [brɔɚ]; **NJ**54, **NY**123, [brʌv]; **KY**25, [brʌdi]; **CT**16, ['brudi]; **NY**109, ['brʌʃi]; **NY**96, ['brʌvɚ].

B Senses.

1 usu foll by name: A preacher. **chiefly Sth, S Midl** See Map
  1928 Peterkin *Scarlet Sister Mary* 341 **SC,** When the hymn was sung, Brer Dee read out of the Book. **c1960** *Wilson Coll.* **csKY,** *Brother . . .* Title for an unprofessional or part-time lay preacher. **1965–70** *DARE* (Qu. CC10, . . *An unprofessional, part-time lay preacher*) 40 Infs, **chiefly Sth, S Midl, scattered NEast,** Brother (+ name); **PA223,** Lay brother. **1969** *DARE* Tape **KY17,** Brother Rookers said he was at their house one time; **TX49,** Brother Watts. **1970** *DARE* File **neTX,** Brother Carter is the Reverend Mr. Carter.

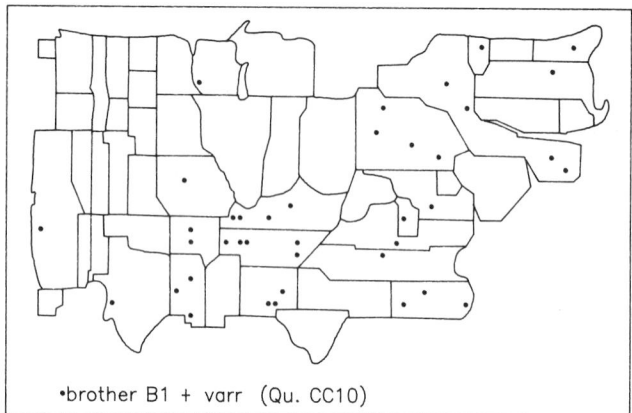

•brother B1 + varr (Qu. CC10)

2 A fellow, chap—used as a term of address. **Cf bo**
  1912 *DN* 3.572 **wIN,** *Brother . . .* A title applied to a stranger in addressing him. "Say, brother, can you tell me how far it is to Veedersburg?" **1965–70** *DARE* (Qu. II10a, *Asking directions of somebody on the street when you don't know his name—what you'd say to a boy: "Say, _____, where's the post office?"*) Infs **CA22, IL50, NY166, 238, 239,** Brother; **HI13,** Eh, brudda; (Qu. II10b, . . *To a man*) Infs **DE3, NJ69, NY206, 239, PA104, RI17,** Brother.

brotheren See **brethren**

brother I'm bobbed n Also *brother (I'm) Bob*
  A parlor game in which a blindfolded person is struck or "bobbed;" see quots.
  1844 Thompson *Major Jones's Courtship* 112 **GA,** "Lets play brother Bob." "Yes, lets play that," ses all of 'em, "won't you be brother Bob, Majer? . . When anyone taps you, you must say, 'Brother, I'm bob'd!' and then they'll ax 'Who bob'd you?' and if you guess the rite one, then they must take your place and be bob'd till they gess who bob'd 'em." **1890** *DN* 1.63 **KY,** *Bobbed . . .* Used in a game played, usually at a country party, called "Brother, I'm bobbed." A boy is blindfolded and seated in a chair; another strikes him on the head with a book, when the hoodwinked boy says, "Brother, I'm bobbed!" "Who bobbed you?" "Jack Smith." If he guesses the right boy, that boy is to be bobbed. **1905** *DN* 3.71 **nwAR,** *Brother, I'm Bob* [or] *Brother, I'm bobbed . . .* Name of a game. **1908** *DN* 3.294 **eAL, wGA,** *Brother, I'm bobbed . . .* The name of a game played by young people.

brother rounds n [Imit] **Cf jugarum**
  A **bullfrog**; the sound it makes.
  1939 *LANE* Map 231 **neCT,** The bullfrog says [ˌbrʌðəˈræondʒ]; **nwRI,** [ˈbrʌðəˈraʊndz], nickname for the bullfrog.

brothren See **brethren**

brots See **brother A6**

brotus See **broadus**

brouge See **bruise**

broughten See **bring B**

brought-on ppl adj Also *brung-on* **chiefly S Midl** *somewhat old-fash* **Cf fotch-on**
1 Commercially made, **boughten**; imported.
  1895 *DN* 1.370 **wNC, eTN,** *Brought on:* not home-made. "The clothes you have on I see are brought on." **1905** *DN* 3.71 **nwAR,** *Brought on . . .* Not domestic, imported. 'These eggs were brought on.' Common. **1917** *DN* 4.409 **wNC, IA, KY.** **1931** *AmSp* 7.92 **eKY.** **1937** Eaton *Handicrafts* 60 **sAppalachians,** The "brung on" cotton warp and woolen yarn were inferior to the old homespun. **1946** TN Folk Lore Soc. *Bulletin*

12.4.5, How does she like that new brought-on paper for her walls? **1969** *DARE* (Qu. U2, . . *A piece of clothing not made at home—one that you buy*) Infs **KY42, 45,** Brought-on. [Both Infs old]
2 Of a person: from outside the community, foreign.
  1911 *DN* 3.537 **eKY,** "Is he brung-on or is he a citizen?" **1939** (1954) FWP *Guide KY* 429, At first the mountain people were very suspicious of the "brought on women" [=nurses or midwives] and continued to have their babies "cotched by the grannies." **1942** (1971) Campbell *Cloud-Walking* 27 **seKY,** She heared tell of brought-on schools set up in the mountain country with teacher folks from the level country.

brought to straw See **called to straw**

brought up in a barn adj phr For varr, see *DS* **scattered, but esp freq NEast, N Cent** See Map **Cf raised in a barn**
  =**born in a barn.**
  1965–70 *DARE* (Qu. II21, *When somebody behaves unpleasantly or without manners: "The way he behaves, you'd think he was _____."*) 134 Infs, Brought up in a barn.

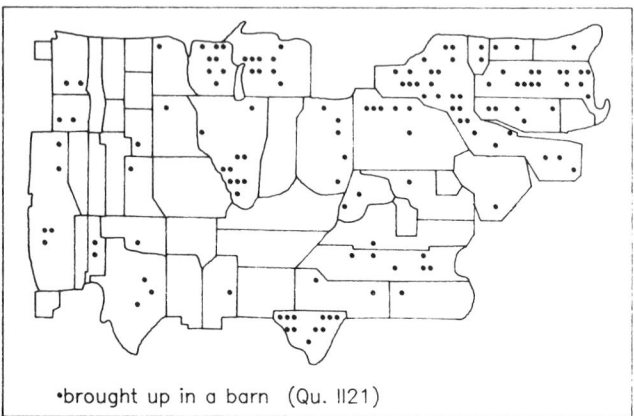

•brought up in a barn (Qu. II21)

‡brouse v
  1944 *PADS* 2.18 **sAppalachians,** *Brouse . . .* To cohabit.

brow n, v **ME Cf brow log**
  In logging: a platform or loading dock on which logs are stacked prior to sawing; to stack (logs) on such a platform.
  1934 *Hanley Disks* **swME,** Now they haul them [=logs] by trucks, skid them out on the . . skidway . . . Some calls it a brow . . . They cut down a couple of trees about thirty or forty feet long and they brow them up so that they come even with the bumpers of the trucks. They haul them out on the brow . . roll the logs off onto that. **1946** Attwood *Length Maine* 13, *Brow*—The bank from which logs are rolled onto a sawmill. **1966** *DARE* Tape **ME6,** What they call browing the logs . . . They have a brow they roll 'em onto, then roll 'em right down to the saw . . . It's built up of pine logs, hardwood logs. They'll have 'em eighteen, twenty feet long so they can pile the logs right onto 'em and the team can come back and get another load while they're sawing those.

browce See **browse v 1**

brow log n **Cf brow Pacific NW**
  In logging: see quot 1958.
  1958 McCulloch *Woods Words* **Pacific NW,** *Brow log*—A big log parallel to the road or track, placed so as to protect trucks and cars during loading and unloading at landings and log dumps. It takes the bump of logs accidentally dropped or swung out of control. **1961** Labbe–Goe *Railroads* 257 **Pacific NW.** **1968** Adams *Western Words.*

brown n
1 See **brown trout.**
2 See **brownie n¹ 1.**
3 See **brownie n¹ 2.**
4 See **brownie n¹ 3.**
5 Perfection, a turn. **Cf do up brown**
  1968–69 *DARE* (Qu. KK3a, . . *The perfect condition—for example, in cooking: "It's done to _____."*) Infs **CT25, NH5, NY136, RI6, WI70,** A brown; **SC66,** A crispy brown; **IL115,** Golden brown; (Qu. KK50, *When something is planned out carefully, down to the last detail: "He had it all worked out _____."*) Inf **PA245,** To the brown.

6 A Mexican. *derog*
1981 Pederson *LAGS Urban Material* **TX,** *Mexicans:* . . [3 infs] browns.

brown v See **brownie** v

brown adder n Cf **adder**
Perh =**water moccasin** (here: *Natrix* spp).
1961 Douglas *My Wilderness* 276 **ME,** I got to know the brown adder with sharp teeth—a non-poisonous snake that is common in Maine.

brown ant n
An ant of the subfamily Myrmicinae.
1965–70 *DARE* (Qu. R18) 29 Infs, **scattered, but esp Nth, N Midl,** Brown ant.

brown ash n
1 =**black ash 1.**
1832 Browne *Sylva* 157, In the extensive country comprising the northern section of the United States . . the White Ash and the Black Ash, which is sometimes called *Water Ash* and *Brown Ash,* are the most abundant in the forests. **1874** *VT State Bd. Ag. Report* 2.549, In Whiting part of this swamp produces brown ash, birch, soft maple and elm. **1891** Jesup *Plants Hanover NH* 27, *F[raxinus] sambucifolia* . . . (Black or Brown Ash.) Swamps; common. **1903** Small *Flora SE U.S.* 918, *Fraxinus nigra* . . . Black Ash. Brown Ash. Water Ash. **1979** Little *Checklist U.S. Trees* 136, *Fraxinus nigra* . . . *Other common names* . . brown ash.
2 =**green ash.**
1897 Sudworth *Arborescent Flora* 328, *Fraxinus pennsylvanica* . . . Brown Ash (Me.). **1910** Graves *Flowering Plants* 317 **CT,** *Fraxinus pennsylvanica* . . . Red, Brown or River Ash. Frequent. Along streams and in swamps, sometimes in drier places.

brownback n
1 also *brownback dowich:* =**dowitcher.**
1844 DeKay *Zool. NY* 2.255, The Dowitchee, Red-breasted Snipe, Quail Snipe or Brown-back, arrives on the coast of New-York towards the latter part of April. **1898** (1900) Davie *Nests N. Amer. Birds* 136, *Dowitcher* . . . Known by several names, such as . . Brown-back, and Gray-back. **1923** U.S. Dept. Ag. *Misc. Circular* 13.51, *Dowitcher* . . . *Vernacular Names* . . . *In local use.*—Brownback (Me., N.H., Mass., R.I., N.J., Va., Mo.). **1956** *MA Audubon Soc. Bulletin* 40.20, *Dowitcher.* Brown-back (Maine, N.H., Mass., R.I. Upper parts of body blackish brown, light cinnamon brown, and yellowish white); Brownback Dowich.
2 also *brownie:* =**pectoral sandpiper.**
1888 Trumbull *Names of Birds* 175, *Pectoral Sandpiper* . . . Known also to some at Rowley and Ipswich [MA] as *Brown-back* . . . "generally called *Brownie*" in the vicinity of Newburyport [MA]. **1925** (1928) Forbush *Birds MA* 1.406, *Pectoral Sandpiper* . . . *Other names:* . . *Brown-back; Brownie.* **1951** Pough *Audubon Water Bird* 321, Brownback *See* Pectoral sandpiper and Dowitcher . . . Brownie *See* Pectoral sandpiper.
3 =**marbled godwit.**
1889 *Century Dict.* 697/3, *Brownback* . . . A name of the great marbled godwit, *Limosa fedoa.*
‡4 Prob a **junebug.**
1969 *DARE* (Qu. R5, *A big brown beetle that comes out in large numbers in spring*) Inf **MO**19, Brownbacks.

brownback dowich See **brownback 1**

brown bass n
=**smallmouth bass.**
1946 LaMonte *N. Amer. Game Fishes* 134, *Micropterus dolomieu* . . . *Names:* . . Brown Bass. **1966–70** *DARE* (Qu. P1, . . *Freshwater fish* . . *that are good to eat*) Infs **AR**4, 56, **PA**168, Brown bass; **NC**72, Bass—largemouth, brown, white.

brown bean n See also **Swedish brown bean**
Any of several common beans of chiefly brown color, as the chili bean, kidney bean, or pinto bean.
1965–70 *DARE* (Qu. I17, *Beans* . . *that are dark red when they are dry*) Infs **CA**87, 111, 132, 210, **CO**27, **MN**11, **UT**3, Brown beans; **OK**1, We don't have [kidney beans], we have brown beans; (Qu. I20) Infs **IA**9, **OR**3, Brown beans; **TN**20, Brown bunch beans. **1968** *Fredericksburg Standard* (TX) 4 Sept 6/6, *Public School Lunchroom Menu* . . . hot dogs,

brown beans, green salad, doughnuts. **1968** *DARE* Tape **CA**87, Brown beans . . . Mexican beans.

brown bells n pl Cf **bronze bells**
A fritillary (here: *Fritillaria micrantha*).
1925 Jepson *Manual Plants CA* 242, *F[ritillaria] parviflora* . . . Brown Bells. **1959** Munz–Keck *CA Flora* 1340.

brown betty n
1 A baked dessert made of apples, bread crumbs, and molasses or brown sugar. **chiefly Nth** Also called **apple (brown) betty**
1864 *Yale Lit. Mag.* 29.187 *(DA),* Tea, coffee, pies and 'brown Betty' must next be sacrificed. **1936** Lutes *Country Kitchen* 41 **sMI,** A light dessert followed—an apple dumpling, perhaps, brown Betty, or a custard. **1941** *LANE* Map 292, *Brown betty,* of apples and bread crumbs, baked. **1950** *WELS (Way of using stale bread)* 1 Inf, **nwWI,** Brown Betty. **1967–69** *DARE* (Qu. H63, *Kinds of desserts*) Infs **CA**97, **IL**5, **NY**230, **PA**13, 49, Brown betty. **1973** Allen *LAUM* 1.297, *Brown Betty,* scattered in southern New England, is used also by one U[pper] M[idwest] inf., a Nebraskan with New York state parents.
2 =**black-eyed Susan 2,** esp *Rudbeckia hirta.*
1894 *Jrl. Amer. Folkl.* 7.92, *Rudbeckia hirta,* . . Brown Betty, Passaic, N.J. **1959** Carleton *Index Herb. Plants* 19, *Brown Betty:* Rudbeckia hirta. **1968** *DARE* (Qu. S7) Inf **PA**104, Brown Betty.

brownbird n
1 Prob a **knot** or similar sandpiper.
1882 Godfrey *Is. Nantucket* 157 **eMA,** Large numbers of the upland grayback, otherwise known as the brown-bird, made their appearance here on the marshes.
2 Either the *rufous-sided towhee* or the **brown towhee.**
1939 *Natl. Geog. Mag.* Mar 353, Most people know it, but not everyone calls it "towhee." Many speak of it as "brown bird" and others call it "bush bird."
3 also *brown merganser:* =**red-breasted merganser.**
1955 *MA Audubon Soc. Bulletin* 39.379, *Red-breasted Merganser* . . Brown Bird, Brown Merganser (Mass. The female and young, which have more brown in the plumage, are more uniform than the parti-colored adult male.).
4 A **fox sparrow** or similar sparrow.
1967–70 *DARE* (Qu. Q21, . . *Kinds of sparrows*) Inf **VA**47, Fox sparrow—brownbird—because of brown back and brown flecked breast; **WA**30, Brownbirds—sparrow.
5 =**brown thrasher.**
1967–69 *DARE* (Qu. Q14, . . *Other names for* . . *brown thrasher*) Inf **CA**120, Brownbird; (Qu. Q14, . . *Other names for* . . *thrush*) Inf **WA**24, Brownbird.

brown blackbird n Also *brown-headed blackbird, brown-headed oriole*
=**cowbird 1.**
1917 (1923) *Birds Amer.* 2.243, Cowbird . . . *Other Names* . . . Brown-headed Blackbird; . . Brown-headed Oriole. **1968** *DARE* (Qu. Q14, . . *Other names* . . *for* . . *cowbird*) Inf **WI**12, Brown blackbird.

brown brant n
=**cackling goose.**
1918 Grinnell *Game Birds CA* 234, Cackling Goose . . . Other names: . . Brown Brant. **1923** U.S. Dept. Ag. *Misc. Circular* 13.37, Cackling Goose . . . Vernacular names . . . *In local use.*—Brown brant (Calif.).

brown bread n, also attrib Also *Boston bread, Boston brown bread* **chiefly NEng**
A dark, usu steamed bread made with molasses and usu a mixture of cornmeal and rye or wheat flour.
1831 *Boston Eve. Transcript* 7 Mar 2/1, "It is not their hilly country nor their fine climate, but their sweet *brown bread,*" to which the rosy cheeks of New England's lads and lasses are to be attributed. *Ibid* 7 Oct 2/1, A *dejeuner* of rye coffee and brown bread toast. **1889** (1971) Farmer *Americanisms, Brown Bread* . . . The component parts of the American comestible of this name are two-thirds maize meal and one-third rye meal; formerly confined to New England and now, in consequence, known in other parts of the Union as *Boston-bread.* **1915** Eaton *Idyl* 26 **MA,** I haven't eaten brown bread Joes since I was a boy. **1941** *LANE* Map 287 **throughout NEng,** *Brown bread* [1 inf: Boston brown bread] is made of corn meal, rye or wheat flour (usually ⅓), and molasses. It is steamed or baked in a loaf or a large roll. Until recently it was regularly

served (with baked beans) on Saturday nights. **1950** *WELS (Special kinds of bread)* 4 Infs, **WI**, Brown bread; 2 Infs, **WI**, Boston brown bread; 1 Inf, **csWI**, Steamed brown bread. **1966–69** *DARE* (Qu. H14, *Bread that's made with cornmeal*) Infs **ME7, MA83, NH6, 11, RI16**, Brown bread; (Qu. H18, . . *Special kinds of breads*) Inf **CT29**, Steam brown bread, made with cornmeal, rye meal, flour; **CT37**, Brown bread—meal and molasses; **MA5**, Brown bread, made with sour milk or buttermilk, sweetened with molasses, made with rye and Indian meal, white flour only in later times. Used to be made in brick ovens, baked long, with one and a half inch crust all over; **MA125**, Brown bread, made of molasses and raisins—looks like gingerbread. It's eaten on Saturday with beans; **NH6**, Brown bread—cup of cornmeal, one of graham flour, one of flour; **NY88**, Brown bread, made with molasses and has cornmeal. It is steamed not baked; **PA234**, Brown bread—with molasses; **VT3**, Brown bread, made with molasses, maple syrup, cornmeal, whole wheat flour, sour milk. [22 other Infs, **chiefly Nth,** gave the resp 'brown bread,' but with no defining explanation.]

brown-breasted nuthatch n
=**red-breasted nuthatch.**
   1966 *DARE* (Qu. Q23) Inf **ME8**, Brown-breasted nuthatch.

brown bullhead n
1 Std: a catfish *(Ictalurus nebulosus)* native to eastern North America. Also called **black catfish, bullhead 1b, bullpout, horned pout, miller's thumb, minister, mud catfish, Sacramento cat, Skuylkill cat, speckled bullhead, speckled cat 2, squaretail catfish, stone catfish, yellow catfish 2**
2 =**yellow bullhead.**
   1956 Harlan *IA Fish* 112, *Yellow bullhead—Ictalurus natalis* . . . Brown bullhead.

brown buzzard n
=**black vulture.**
   1970 *DARE* (Qu. Q13) Inf **MS87**, Buzzards—brown buzzard, black buzzard.

brown-capped chickadee n
A **chickadee** n[1] **1** (here: *Penthestes atricapillus* or *P. hudsonicus littoralis*).
   1916 Seton *Woodcraft Manual Girls* 318, *Chickadee (Penthestes atricapillus)* . . . it is well known in the winter woods of eastern America up to the Canadian region where the brown-capped or Hudson Chickadee takes its place. **1955** Forbush–May *Birds* 350, *Acadian Chickadee* . . . Hudsonian Titmouse; Brown-capped Chickadee. **1966** *DARE* (QR, near Qu. Q23) Inf **ME8**, Brown-capped chickadee.

brown chippy n Also *brown chippie*
=**brown towhee.**
   1904 Wheelock *Birds CA* 248, The Californian Towhee is the brown chippie . . of common parlance throughout most of California west of the Sierra Nevada. **1917** (1923) *Birds Amer.* 3.61, *Cañon Towhee* . . . *Other Names* . . . Brown Chippy . . . It is often called the Brown Chippy from the very persistence of the loud metallic *chip,* whether heard in the streets of towns or out in the dense chaparral and scrub bushes that line the mountain cañons.

brown coot n Also *browny coot*
=**scoter.**
   1888 Trumbull *Names of Birds* 107, *Oidemia americana* . . . The females and young . . are almost invariably regarded by duckers as a species distinct from the old males, and . . they are very generally classed under that of *Gray Coot* . . and less commonly *Brown Coot.* **1917** (1923) *Birds Amer.* 1.148, *Scoter Oidemia americana* . . . Brown Coot. **1955** *MA Audubon* 39.377, Brown Coot (Mass. The female and young.); Browny Coot (Maine).

brown cottontail See **brown rabbit**

brown crane n
=**sandhill crane.**
   1805 (1904) Lewis *Orig. Jrls. Lewis & Clark Exped.* 2.255 **MT,** Saw several of the large brown or sandhill Crain today with their young. **1946** Hausman *Eastern Birds* 230, *Sand-hill Crane Grus canadensis tabida* . . . Other Names . . . Brown Crane. **1955** Forbush–May *Birds* 156, *Sandhill Crane—Grus canadensis tabida* . . . Other names: Brown Crane.

brown creeper n
1 A small long-tailed brown bird *(Certhia familiaris).* Also called **tree creeper**
   1808 Wilson *Amer. Ornith.* 1.122, The Brown Creeper is an extremely active and restless little bird. **1965–70** *DARE* (Qu. Q23, *The insect-eating bird that goes head-first down a tree trunk*) 15 Infs, **scattered, but esp Nth,** Brown creeper.
2 A woodpecker: see quot. Cf **brown woodpecker**
   1967 *DARE* (Qu. Q17, . . *Kinds of woodpeckers*) Inf **MA50**, Brown creeper.

brown daisy n
=**black-eyed Susan 2,** esp *Rudbeckia hirta.*
   1894 *Jrl. Amer. Folkl.* 7.92, *Rudbeckia hirta,* L., brown daisy, Concord, Mass. **1940** Clute *Amer. Plant Names* 86, *Rudbeckia hirta* . . brown daisy. **1967** *DARE* (Qu. S7) Inf **PA4**, Brown daisy.

brown duck n
A **black duck 1** (here: *Anas rubripes*).
   1923 U.S. Dept. Ag. *Misc. Circular* 13.9, *Black Duck . . . Vernacular Names . . . In local use . . .* Brown duck (N.J.). **1966–70** *DARE* (Qu. Q9) Inf **NY40**, Brown duck—it is a mud-hen [FW: but Inf doesn't use that word]; (Qu. Q5) Infs **FL35, NJ30, NY20, OH20, TN65,** Brown duck. **1982** Elman *Hunter's Field Guide* 143, *Black Duck . . . Common & Regional Names: . .* brown duck.

brown eagle n
1 =**bald eagle 1.** [From the color of the immature plumage]
   1815 MA Hist. Soc. *Coll.* 2d ser 4.274, It is probably the brown [eagle] . . we have noticed in the winter season. **1844** DeKay *Zool. NY* 2.5, The *Brown or Bald Eagle. Haliaetos leucocephalus* . . is found in every part of the United States, feeding upon fish, wild fowl and small quadrupeds. **1946** Hausman *Eastern Birds* 196, *Haliæëtas leucocephalus leucocephalus* . . . Brown Eagle (young). **1955** *MA Audubon* 39.442, *Bald Eagle* . . Brown Eagle (N.H., Mass., Conn. . .).
2 =**golden eagle.**
   1917 (1923) *Birds Amer.* 2.82, *Golden eagle—Aquila chrysaëtos* . . . *Other Names* . . . Brown Eagle.

brown-eyed crowder pea See **brown-eyed pea**

brown-eyed daisy n
=**black-eyed Susan 2.**
   1968 *DARE* (Qu. S7) Infs **WI23, 54,** Brown-eyed daisy.

brown-eyed pea n Also *brown-eyed crowder pea*
=**black-eyed pea.**
   1968 *DARE* (Qu. I19, *Small white beans with a black spot where they were joined to the pod*) Infs **AR17, GA28, PA40,** Brown-eyed peas; **LA15,** Brown-eyed crowder pea.

brown-eyed Susan n
1 also *brown-eyed Sue, brown-eye(d) Susie:* =**black-eyed Susan 2.**
   1896 *Jrl. Amer. Folkl.* 9.193, *Rudbeckia hirta,* . . brown-eyed Susan, Brockton, Mass. **1936** IL Nat. Hist. Surv. *Wildflowers* 364, *Rudbeckia hirta* . . . Other names are Brown-eyed Susan . . and Yellow Oxeye Daisy. **1948** *Ardmoreite* (Ardmore OK) 11 July 21/4 *(DA),* Dixie and I enjoyed . . the brown-eyed Susans especially. **1965** *Bee* (Phillips WI) 19 Aug 3/6, Oat fields are golden, the roadsides shine with nodding goldenrods, there are still brown-eyed susans. **1965–70** *DARE* (Qu. S7, *A kind of daisy, bright yellow with a dark center, that grows along roadsides in late summer*) 108 Infs, **widespread,** Brown-eyed Susan; **GA3, PA77, TX13, VA28,** Brown-eyed Susie(s); **GA5,** Brown-eye Susie; **NY10,** Brown-eyed Sue; (Qu. S26a, . . *Other* . . *roadside flowers*) Infs **GA18, 53, MI116, NY120, VA75,** Brown-eyed Susan(s); (Qu. S26d, *Wildflowers that grow in meadows*) Infs **GA18, 38, IL10, PA68,** Brown-eyed Susan(s); **VA2,** Brown-eyed Susan—flower stands up. **1968** *DARE* FW Addit **VA15,** *Brown-eyed Susan* . . . book name [is] black-eyed susan. **1968** *DARE* Wildfl QR Pl.253 Inf **IA25,** Brown-eyed Susan. *Ibid* Pl.254 Inf **MN30,** Brown-eyed Susan.
2 =**gaillardia.**
   1963 Craighead *Rocky Mt. Wildflowers* 212, *Blanketflower* . . . Other names: Brown-eyed Susan . . . only species of genus in n. Rocky Mts. **1967** *DARE* (Qu. S26a, . . *Other* . . *roadside flowers*) Inf **TX19,** Brown-eyed Susan—gaillardia.

3 An **oxeye** (here: *Heliopsis helianthoides*).
1967 *DARE* Wildfl QR Pl.252 Inf **SC**41, Brown-eyed Susan.
4 A **sunflower** (here: *Helianthus angustifolius*).
1967 *DARE* Wildfl. QR Pl.249a Inf **MI**57, Brown-eyed Susan.

brown-eyed Susie See **brown-eyed Susan 1**

brown-eye gravy n Also *brown-eyed gravy* Cf **black-eye gravy, red-eye gravy**
A gravy made with water and meat drippings.
1966 *DARE* Tape **AL**2, Brown-eyed gravy . . . Where the ham was cooked, the fat that it was cooked in, and you poured water in that and it made a very, to me, delicious gravy. **1967** *DARE* (Qu. H37) Inf **AR**52, Brown-eye gravy—you pour water in your hot grease and meat leavings; **AR**55, Brown-eye gravy.

brown-eye Susie See **brown-eyed Susan 1**

brown fly n Also *brown horsefly*
A fly prob of the family Tabanidae.
1966–70 *DARE* (Qu. R11) Inf **NC**10, Brown fly; (Qu. R12) Inf **MD**45, Brown fly—same as dog fly, sheep fly; **NC**85, Brown fly—stings, leaves marks, not sure of correct name; **OK**52, Brown horsefly; (Qu. R13) Inf **DC**2, Brown fly—sting badly; **MI**54, Brown fly—something like a horsefly, a little bigger and brown.

brown frash(er) See **brown thrasher**

brown fritillary See **brown lily**

brown German See **German brown trout**

brown hare See **brown rabbit**

brown hashed potatoes See **hash browns**

brown hawk n
Either the **sharp-shinned hawk** or the Swainson's hawk *(Buteo swainsoni).*
1881 *Amer. Naturalist* 15.209 **sCA**, The brown hawk *(Buteo insignatus)* [sic], is . . not seen . . often . . , owing to its frequenting quiet secluded places. **1955** *MA Audubon Soc. Bulletin* 39.441, Sharp-shinned Hawk. Brown Hawk (Conn. The young.). **1968–69** *DARE* (Qu. Q4) Infs **CA**80, **MO**32, **NY**219, **OH**70, Brown hawk.

brown-headed blackbird, brown-headed oriole See **brown blackbird**

brown horsefly See **brown fly**

brownie n[1]

1 also *brown:* A penny. **chiefly S Atl, esp SC** See Map
1928 Peterkin *Scarlet Sister Mary* 295 **SC** [Gullah], Me an' my chillen don' want not a brownie you got! Not one. **1942** Hall *Smoky Mt. Speech* 73 **wNC, eTN**, Brownie ('penny'). **1950** *PADS* 14.17 **SC**, Brown . . . Brownie. . . A cent piece. **1965–70** *DARE* (Qu. U21, . . *Words for "one cent"*) 23 Infs, **chiefly S Atl, esp SC**, Brownie. **1981** Pederson *LAGS Urban Material* **swAL**, *Money:* . . [1 inf] brownies.

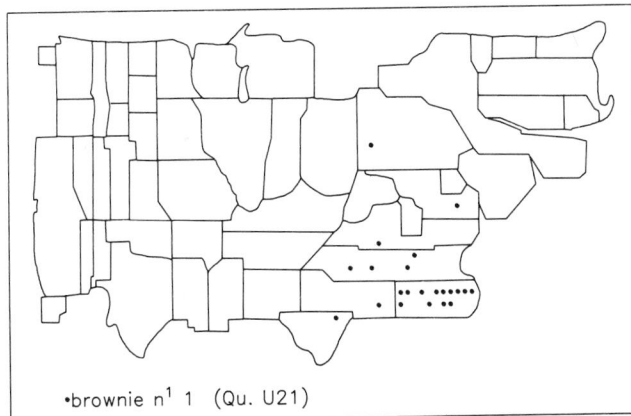

•brownie n[1] 1 (Qu. U21)

2 also *brown;* In marble play: see quots.
1955 *PADS* 23.12 **cwTN**, Brownie . . . A clay marble. Ohio (1900). **1958** *PADS* 29.30 **NY**, Brown . . . A baked clay marble, "ten for a penny." **1967** *DARE* (Qu. EE6b, *Small marbles or marbles in general*) Inf **OH**15, Brownies.

3 also *brown:* =**brownnose** n. **Inland Nth** See Map *esp among young and coll educ speakers* Cf **brownie** v
1965–70 *DARE* (Qu. JJ3b, *When a schoolchild makes a special effort to "get in good" with the teacher in hopes of getting a better grade: "She's an awful _____."*) 12 Infs, **Inland Nth**, Brownie; **IL**98, **MI**69, Brown; [**MI**55, Working on her brownie]; (Qu. II20a, *A person who tries too hard to gain somebody else's favor: "He's an awful _____."*) 11 Infs, **Inland Nth**, Brownie. [Of 20 total Infs, 14 were young, 6 mid-aged; 14 coll educ, 4 hs educ, 2 grade school educ]

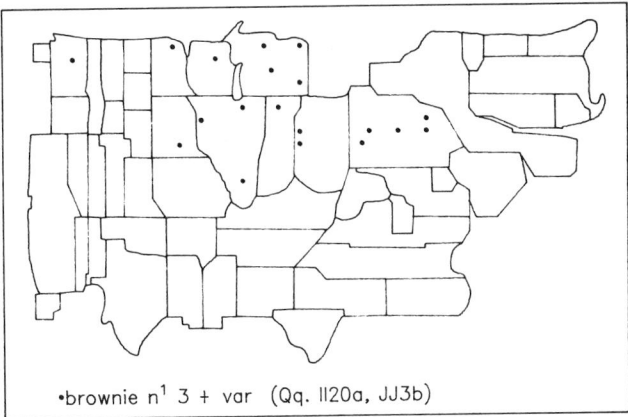

•brownie n[1] 3 + var (Qq. II20a, JJ3b)

4 A dark-skinned mulatto.
1945 Saxon *Gumbo Ya-Ya* 13 **LA**, When them ships come in, that's when I made money. All them sailors wanted a brownie. High yellows fared poorly then.

5 =**black-bellied plover**.
1933 *Hanley Disks* **seMA**, These small birds that he killed were what you see around salt marshes, seashore—well, there's plovers and brownies they call them, yellow legs and such kinds of birds. **1955** *MA Audubon* 39.445, Black-bellied Plover . . . Brownie (Mass. Adults in winter plumage are mostly brownish gray, and the young buffy, on white . . .).

6 See **brownback 2**.

7 See **brown trout 1**.

brownie n[2] [See quot 1945]
Among railroad workers: a demerit.
1929 *Bookman* 69.525, I thought the most I'd get would be thirty days and thirty brownies but darned if he didn't fire me off the road. **1931** *Writer's Digest* 11.41. **1945** Hubbard *Railroad Ave.* 335, Brownies—Demerits. This system is traced back to George R. Brown, general superintendent of the Fall Brook Railway (now part of the New York Central) in 1885. He thought the then current practice of suspending men for breaking rules was unfair to their families and substituted a system of demerit marks. Too many demerits in a given period resulted in dismissal. The Brown system, with many variations, has since been widely adopted by the railroad industry. **1967** *DARE* Tape **ID**9, So many brownies and you are automatically fired. **1969** *AmSp* 44.254.

brownie v Also *brown* Often with *in* or *up (to)* [Abbr for **brownnose** v] **esp Inland Nth** *esp among young and coll educ speakers* Cf **brownie** n[1] **3**
=**brownnose** v.
1961 *AmSp* 36.150 **CO** [Teen-age slang], *To brown* or *to get nose* with a teacher . . . are used to imply currying favor by personal appeals, but apparently without consciousness by today's young people of the more basic, vulgar meaning of *to brown nose*. **1965–70** *DARE* (Qu. II20b, *A person who tries too hard to gain somebody else's favor: "He's always trying to _____ the boss."*) Infs **NJ**69, **TX**72, Brown; **MO**29, Brown in; **IL**97, Brown up to; **IN**7, **MI**75, **PA**93, Brownie; **IL**141, **MI**118, Brownie up (to); (Qu. JJ3a, *When a schoolchild makes a special effort to "get in good" with the teacher in hopes of getting a better grade: "He's trying to _____ again."*) Inf **IL**98, Brown up; **IA**27, **IN**1, **MN**28, **PA**59, 163, 185, **WI**34, Brownie; **PA**167, **WA**22, Brownie up; **PA**93, Brownie her. [Of 20 Infs, 11 were young, 7 mid-aged; 15 were coll educ, 3 hs educ.]

brown kitties n [Folk-etym]
Bronchitis.

1941 in 1944 *ADD* 225/1, Brown-kitties = bronchitis. Used by a few elderly speakers. **1970** *DARE* (Qu. BB9, *A sickness in which you have a severe cough and difficult breathing*) Inf **VA**42, Brown kitties.

brown lark n Also *brown titlark*

=**pipit.**

1812 Wilson *Amer. Ornith.* 5.89, *Brown Lark: Alauda rufa* . . . flies in loose scattered flocks; is strongly attached to flat, newly-ploughed fields. **1831** Audubon *Ornith. Biog.* 1.49, *The Brown Titlark* . . . *Anthus Spinoletta* . . . is met with in every portion of the United States which I have visited. **1917** (1923) *Birds Amer.* 3.169, *Anthus rubescens* . . . *Other Names* . . . Brown lark. **1946** Hausman *Eastern Birds* 470, American pipit *Anthus spinoletta rubescens*—Other Names . . . Brown Lark.

brown lily n Also *brown fritillary*

A **fritillary** (here: *Fritillaria atropurpurea, F. biflora* or *F. lanceolata*).

1897 Parsons *Wild Flowers CA* 264, Brown Lily . . . *Fritillaria lanceolata.* **1915** (1926) Armstrong *Western Wild Flowers* 38, *Brown Fritillary—Fritillaria atropurpurea.* **1923** Davidson–Moxley *Flora S. CA* 89, *F. biflora* . . . Brown Lily. **1968** *DARE* (Qu. S26a, . . *Other* . . *roadside flowers*) Inf **CA**79, Brown lilies.

‡**brown locust** n

=**cicada.**

1966 *DARE* (Qu. R7) Inf **OK**52, Brown locust—larger [than the green locust]—also called a jar fly.

brown mallard n

A **black duck 1** (here: *Anas rubripes*).

1982 Elman *Hunter's Field Guide* 143, *Black Duck* . . . *Common & Regional Names:* . . brown mallard, beach duck.

brown marlin See **marlin**

brown martin n

=**purple martin.**

1969 *DARE* (Qu. Q14) Inf **KY**9, Brown martin.

brown merganser See **brownbird 3**

brown mockingbird n

1 also *brown mocker:* =**brown thrasher.**

1917 (1923) *Birds Amer.* 3.179, *Brown Thrasher—Toxostoma rufum* . . . Brown Mocker; Brown Mockingbird. **1946** Hausman *Eastern Birds* 453, Brown Thrasher *Toxostoma rufum*—Other Names: . . Brown Mockingbird. **1955** *MA Audubon* 39.128, *Brown Thrasher.* Brown mockingbird (Mass. This species is an occasional, though expert, imitator of the notes of other birds.).

2 See quot.

1969 *DARE* (Qu. Q14) Inf **KY**49, Brown mockingbird—size of thrush, yellow breast. [FW sugg: yellow-breasted chat.].

brownnose v *orig among speakers in the military; now widespread but chiefly among young and mid-aged speakers* Cf **brownie** v

To be excessively deferential or ingratiating; to toady.

1939 *AmSp* 14.25 **SC** [Military college slang], *Brown nose* . . . To curry favor, especially for rank. **1948** *AmSp* 23.248 **nTX** [College slang], *Brown nose* . . To curry favor. **1950** *WELS* (*Uncomplimentary word for a person who tries too hard to gain somebody else's favor: "He's always _____"*) 1 Inf, **ceWI**, Brownnosing. **1965–70** *DARE* (Qu. II20b, . . *"He's always trying to _____ the boss."*) 88 Infs, **widespread,** Brownnose; **MI**33, Brownnose with [Of all Infs responding to the question, 12% were young, 25% mid-aged; of those giving this resp, 25% were young, 51% mid-aged]; (Qu. JJ3a, *When a schoolchild makes a special effort to "get in good" with the teacher . . : "He's trying to _____ again."*) 62 Infs, **widespread,** Brownnose; **MA**1, 28, Brownnose the teacher [Of all Infs responding to the question, 13% were young, 24% mid-aged; of those giving this resp, 45% were young, 37% mid-aged]; (Qu. II19, *When you think somebody has been put ahead of you . . , you might say, "I'd rather quit than _____."*) Infs **MN**35, **NY**238, **OH**47, Brownnose; (Qu. KK36, *Talking about a person who is easily fooled: "It's easy to _____."*) Inf **RI**11, Brownnose him.

brownnose n, also attrib Also *brownnoser* [**brownnose** v] *chiefly among young and mid-aged speakers* Cf **ass-licker, bluenose 4**

A toady, apple-polisher.

1939 *AmSp* 14.25 **SC** [Military college slang], *Brown nose* . . . A cadet who curries favor. **1946** *AmSp* 21.247 [Army speech], The Bronze Star Medal . . often known as the *Officers' Good Conduct Medal,* sometimes, more bitterly, as the *Brown Nose Medal* or *Brown Star.* **1948** *AmSp* 23.248 **nTX** [College slang], *Brown nose* . . . One who curries favor. **1950** *WELS* (*A person who tries too hard to gain somebody else's favor: "He's an awful _____."*) 2 Infs, **WI**, Brownnoser; 1 Inf, **ceWI**, Brownnose; (*When a student tries to be extra nice to the teacher in hopes of getting a better grade: "She's an awful _____."*) 4 Infs, **WI**, Brownnose (two Infs noted this was a WWII or army term). **1965–70** *DARE* (Qu. II20a, *A person who tries too hard to gain somebody else's favor*) 79 Infs, Brownnose; 113 Infs, Brownnoser [Of all Infs responding to the question, 12% were young, 26% mid-aged; of those giving the resp *brownnose,* 33% were young, 38% mid-aged; of those giving the resp *brownnoser,* 20% were young, 48% mid-aged]; (Qu. JJ3b, *When a schoolchild makes a special effort to 'get in good' with the teacher in hopes of getting a better grade: "She's an awful _____."*) 17 Infs, Brownnose; 98 Infs, Brownnoser [Of all Infs responding to the question, 14% were young, 25% mid-aged; of those giving the resp *brownnose,* 53% were young, 35% mid-aged; of those giving the resp *brownnoser,* 38% were young, 32% mid-aged]; (Qu. II19, *When you think somebody has been put ahead of you . . , you might say, "I'd rather quit than _____."*) Infs **AL**25, **NY**76, Be a brownnose; (Qu. HH20a, *An idle, worthless person: "He's a _____."*) Inf **VA**107, Brownnoser. **1966** Barnes–Jensen *Dict. UT Slang* 6, *Brown nose* . . . A man who will do anything to please the boss.

brown paper n, v Cf **ass-wiper**

=**brownnose** n and v.

1968 *DARE* (Qu. II20a, *A person who tries too hard to gain somebody else's favor: "He's an awful _____."*) Inf **MD**23, Brown paper; (Qu. JJ3a, *When a schoolchild makes a special effort to "get in good" with the teacher . . : "He's trying to _____ again."*) Inf **MD**22, Brown paper.

brown-paper oven n

1936 Lutes *Country Kitchen* 57 **sMI,** [An oven that would just turn a piece of white writing paper to a nice delicate brown . . . was the way we tested the oven.] *Ibid* 61, This was then . . baked about half an hour in the brown-paper oven, or, according to modern standards, 375 degrees.

brown pine n

=**longleaf pine 1.**

1842 Buckingham *Slave States* 1.177, The Georgia pitch-pine is abundant, and it is . . . called by a great variety of names, such as the southern, the red, the brown, the yellow, and the long-leaved pine. **1897** Sudworth *Arborescent Flora* 30, *Pinus palustris* . . Brown Pine (Tenn.).

brown popcorn See **popcorn flower**

brown rabbit n Also *brown cottontail, brown hare*

Prob a cottontail (*Sylvilagus* spp.).

1965–70 *DARE* (Qu. P30) 19 Infs, **scattered chiefly east of Missip R,** Brown rabbit; **NY**103, Brown cottontail; **MA**6, Brown hare.

brown recluse spider n

A **violin spider** (here: *Loxosceles reclusa*).

1965–70 *DARE* (Qu. R28) 15 Infs, **chiefly Sth, Midl,** Brown recluse spider.

brown-rump nuthatch n

Perh =**red-breasted nuthatch.**

1968 *DARE* (Qu. Q23) Inf **WI**8, Brown-rump nuthatch—rare.

brown snapper n

=**red grouper 1.**

1884 Goode *Fisheries U.S.* 1.410, The "Red Grouper" . . . north of Florida . . is called the "Brown Snapper," or "Red-bellied Snapper." **1935** Caine *Game Fish* 74, *Red grouper—Epinephelus morio* . . . Synonyms: Brown Snapper. **1946** LaMonte *N. Amer. Game Fishes* 53, Red Grouper *Epinephelus morio* . . . Names: . . Brown Snapper.

brown snipe n

1 =**dowitcher.**

1844 Giraud *Birds Long Is.* 263, *Scolopax Noveboracensis* . . . Brown or Red-breasted Snipe. **1888** Trumbull *Names of Birds* 160, *Red-breasted Snipe* . . Gray Snipe: Brown Snipe. **1946** Hausman *Eastern Birds* 283, Eastern Dowitcher . . . Other Names—Brown Snipe, Gray Snipe [etc].

2 =**marbled godwit.**

1923 U.S. Dept. Ag. *Misc. Circular* 13.58, *Marbled Godwit* . . . *Vernacular Names* . . . *In local use* . . . Brown snipe (Utah).

3 Perh **Wilson's snipe.**
1969 *DARE* (Qu. Q7, . . *Other kinds of game birds around here*) Inf **KY**11, Brown snipe.

brown Susan n
=**black-eyed Susan 2.**
1968 *DARE* (Qu. S7) Inf **MO**10, Brown Susans.

brown swallow n
Perh a **bank swallow 1.**
1967–70 *DARE* (Qu. Q20, . . *Kinds of swallows*) Infs **MI**67, **WV**21, Brown swallow(s).

brown Swedish bean See **Swedish brown bean**

brown thrasher n Also *brown frash(er),* ~ *thrash,* ~ *thresh(er),* ~ *thrust*
A long-tailed bird *(Toxostoma rufum)* resembling the thrush and closely related to the mockingbird. Also called **brownbird 5, brown mockingbird,** ~ **thrush 1, corn planter, fox-colored thrush, French mockingbird, ground thrush, mavis, missionary bird, mockbird, planting bird, red mavis, red thrush, rust robin, sandy mockingbird, song thrush, thrasher, thrush**
1810 Wilson *Amer. Ornith.* 2.83, [The] *Ferruginous Thrush . . Turdus Rufus . .* is the Brown Thrush, or Thrasher of the middle and eastern states. **1902** *DN* 2.230 **sIL,** *Brown-thrasher . . .* The brown-thrush. **1917** (1923) *Birds Amer.* 3.179, *Brown Thrasher*—Toxostoma rufum. **1965–70** *DARE* (Qu. Q14) 317 Infs, **widespread,** Brown thrasher; **GA**1, **MS**60, **NC**10, **VA**46, Brown thrash; **MD**15, **MO**37, Brown thrust; **NC**54, Brown frash, brown frasher; **IA**29, Brown thresh; **OK**52, Brown thresher; (Qu. Q17) Inf **IN**7, Brown thresher; (Qu. Q21) Inf **PA**89, Brown thrasher.

brown thrush n
1 =**brown thrasher.** [See quot 1955]
1805 (1905) Lewis *Orig. Jrls. Lewis & Clark Exped.* 6.190, 18th [April] . . . the brown thrush or mocking bird has appeared. **1955** *MA Audubon* 39.128, *Brown Thrasher . . .* Brown Thrush (General. Latter term from its thrushlike coloration—brown above, spotted below). **c1960** *Wilson Coll.* **csKY,** Brown Thrasher—Known to many people as *Brown Thrush.* **1965–70** *DARE* (Qu. Q14) 113 Infs, **scattered, but esp Midl,** Brown thrush. **1968** Pochmann *Triple Ridge* 168 **cWI,** Other thrush are visible in the spring: the veery . . , the wood thrush . . , and the brown thrasher, commonly called the brown thrush around Richford.

2 =**wood thrush 1.**
1955 *MA Audubon* 39.128, *Wood Thrush.* Brown Thrush (Maine). **1962** Imhof *AL Birds* 402, *Wood Thrush—Hylocichla mustelina . . .* Other Names: Brown Thrush.

brown thrust See **brown thrasher**

brown titlark See **brown lark**

brown towhee n
A western **towhee** with chiefly brown plumage. Also called **brown chippy, camp bird, long-tailed chippy, robin**
1881 *Amer. Naturalist* 15.212, A very common bird from the mountains to the coast, in California, is the brown towhee *(Pipilo fuscus).* **1939** *Natl. Geog. Mag.* 75.363, The *California* and *Cañon Towhees . .* are subspecies of the bird popularly known as the "brown towhee." **1967** *DARE* (Qu. Q21) Inf **OR**4, Brown towhee.

brown trout n
1 also *brown, brownie, English brown trout, European (brown) trout:* A common European trout *(Salmo trutta)* introduced into the U.S. towards the end of the 19th century. Also called **German brown trout**
1898 U.S. Natl. Museum *Bulletin* 47.487, *Salmo trutta, . .* the . . Brown Trout . . . has been largely introduced in the streams and lakes of the United States. **1933** *NY Times* 9 Apr 3/5 *(Hench Coll.),* This special planting of 20,000 includes brown, rainbow and native trout. **1949** Caine *N. Amer. Sport Fish* 75, *Brown Trout—Salmo trutta . . . Colloquial Names*—Brownie, English Brown Trout, European Brown Trout. **1965–70** *DARE* (Qu. P1) 52 Infs, **chiefly Nth, also east of Appalachians,** Brown trout; **PA**141, Brownies; **CO**38, Browns—the German brown; **NY**207, Trout—browns. **1966–70** *DARE* Tapes **MI**27, 120, Brown trout; **MI**42, Brown. **1975** Evanoff *Catch More Fish* 80, The brown trout *(Salmo trutta)* is also called the . . English brown trout . . and European trout . . . Now it is found in most of our northern states and mountain states.

2 =**smallmouth bass.**
1935 Caine *Game Fish* 7, *Small-mouthed Black Bass—Micropterus dolomieu . . . Synonyms: . .* Brown Trout.

brown wasp n
A wasp of the genus *Polistes.*
1850 Cooper *Rural Hours* 252 **nNY,** The large, brown wasps, so abundant elsewhere, are unknown about the village. **1939** *LANE* Map 239 *(Wasp),* Small yellowish wasps that build comb-shaped paper nests . . . are commonly known simply as *wasps.* The following specific terms are applied to wasps of this group: *common wasp . . yellow wasp, . . brown wasp* [by 2 infs, both **MA**]. **1967–70** *DARE* (Qu. R21) Infs **MA**5, **NC**85, **NY**71, **VA**70, Brown wasp.

brown widgeon n
=**baldpate 1.**
1949 Sprunt–Chamberlain *SC Bird Life* 122 **SC,** *Baldpate: Mareca americana . . . Local Names:* Widgeon; Brown Widgeon.

brown widow n Pronc-sp *brown widder*
A brown spider *(Latrodectus geometrica)* similar to the black widow *(Latrodectus mactans).*
1965 *DARE* (Qu. R28, . . *Spiders . . around here*) Inf **OK**11, Black widder, fly widder, brown widder.

brown woodcock See **woodcock**

brown woodpecker n
Prob =**flicker.**
1968–70 *DARE* (Qu. Q17) Infs **MO**27, **MA**26, **PA**163, **TN**65, **WV**3, Brown woodpecker.

brownwort n
The Maryland **figwort** *(Scrophularia marilandica).*
1971 Krochmal *Appalachia Med. Plants* 230, *Scrophularia marilandica . . .* Brownwort.

browny coot See **brown coot**

browse v [*browse* young shoots and twigs of trees or shrubs]
1 also pronc-sp *browce:* To beat or whip (someone) as punishment; hence vbl n *browsing.* [**browse** n] **NEng** *somewhat old-fash*
c1869 in 1949 *PADS* 11.30 **ME,** He whacked and whelted Simon Spear. / . . Yes, browsed him like a Saxon / For speaking disrespectfully / Of God and Andrew Jackson. **1914** *DN* 4.153 **NH,** *Browcing.* In *to give a browcing,* to give a good thrashing. **1941** *LANE* Map 397 **eMA, cwVT,** Specific terms denoting a whipping given with a particular kind of instrument . . : *switching, browsing . . .* [brawsɪn, brɑɒsɪn].
2 often with *around:* To wander about idly; to loaf or dawdle. [By ext of *browse* to feed on browse (said of animals)] Cf **bruise** v
1884 Harrison *Negro Engl.* 263 **Sth,** To browse 'roun' er hen-'ouse = to try to steal hens. **1965–70** *DARE* (Qu. A10, . . *Doing little unimportant things: somebody asks, "What are you doing?" and you answer, "Nothing in particular—I'm just _____."*) Infs **MA**41, **NC**83, Browsing around; (Qu. X43b, *If you sleep later than usual one day on purpose, you'd say, "I _____."*) Inf **MO**17, Just browsed around; (Qu. Y21, *To move about slowly and without energy*) Inf **TX**35, Browse; (Qu. Y27, *To go about aimlessly, with nothing to do: "He's always _____ around the drugstore."*) Infs **AL**19, **IL**99, **MI**116, Browsing; (Qu. KK31, *To go about aimlessly looking for distractions: "He doesn't have anything to do, so he's just _____ around."*) Infs **DE**1, **GA**72, **IA**43, **MD**23, **NY**131, **OR**1, **PA**242, **TX**35, Browsing; (Qu. KK60, *Having nothing in particular to do: "I'd just as soon go with you this afternoon—I'm _____ anyway."*) Inf **IN**32, Browsing.

browse n
A thin flexible shoot of a bush or tree (on which an animal might browse) used as a whip.
1941 *LANE* Map 397 **neMA,** *A whipping . . .* Browsing, with [ə braws], i.e. a branch of a tree. *Ibid* Map 398 **nwMA, cwVT,** Terms for an implement used in whipping children: . . a slender, flexible rod . . cut from a tree or bush . . *browse . . .* [brɑɒs].

browsy adj [**browse** v 2]
=**breachy 1.**
1968 *DARE* Tape **PA**71, They're [=Angus cattle] not as easy to handle; they're browsy; they want to get out.

broz See **brother A4**

bruce harp n Cf **juice harp**

A Jew's harp.

1967 *DARE* FW Addit **cOR,** Bruce harp—a jaw harp. **1968** *DARE* (Qu. FF8, . . *Small [musical] instrument that you hold between the teeth and pluck on*) Inf **NC53,** Bruce harp.

bruck See **break** v A2

brud See **brother** A4

brudder See **brother** A3

brudduh See **brethren, brother** A3

bruderen See **brethren**

bruff adj [*EDD bruff* adj.² 2 "Somewhat rough and blunt in manner."] *?obs*

1899 (1912) Green *VA Folk-Speech, Bruff.* . . Rough; short in manners and speech.

brug See **brag** v

bruise v Usu with *around* Also sp *brooze, bruze;* pronc-sp *brouge* **chiefly Sth, S Midl** *old-fash* Cf **browse** v 2

1 also with *along:* To wander about idly.

1855 (1929) DeLong *Jrls.* 8.343 **CA,** Bruised around town, reced [sic] several compliments &c stopped with Carmalieta. **1880** Harris *Uncle Remus Songs* 124 **GA,** 'Twa'n't long 'fo' yer come Mr. Man, broozin' 'roun'. **1893** Shands *MS Speech* 21, *Bruze around* . . . A negro phrase meaning *to wander around, to go about without any set purpose.* **1908** *DN* 3.294 **eAL, wGA,** *Bruise* . . . To go or wander about . . . Fairly common. **1927** *AmSp* 2.349 **WV,** *Brouge* . . to sport around. "What have you been doing to-day?" "Oh! just brouging around." **1952** Brown *NC Folkl.* 1.523, *Bruise (along)* . . . To go around slowly with no particular aim; to stroll.—Central and east.

2 in phr *bruise around among:* To associate with; see quots.

1952 Brown *NC Folkl.* 1.523, *Bruise around (among)* . . . To go (among), to associate with. "He's *bruising around among* the women."—Granville county. Obsolescent. **c1960** *Wilson Coll.* **csKY,** *Bruising around* . . . Going with, associating with. "Ed has been bruising around among the women lately."

bruised blood n [*OED* "Obs. or dial."]

1899 (1912) Green *VA Folk-Speech, Bruised-blood* . . . Clotted blood under the skin. "His lip was cut, and his mouth was full of bruised-blood."

bruiser n

1965–70 *DARE* (Qu. X20, . . *A black eye*) Infs **CA196, CO20, IL35, MD17, MN33, VA74,** Bruiser.

brujo n, also attrib Also *bruja* [Span]

A witch, sorcerer; one who practices black magic.

1940 Fergusson *Our Southwest* 254, Crescenciana used to tell me that any old hag we met with her blouse stuck full of pins was a bruja . . . Brujas may cause illness, crop failure, loss of love, and general bad luck. **1942** Kennedy *Palmetto Country* 177 **FL,** The *brujos* are most noted for their skill in casting spells, usually by means of a potion or charm . . . Professional *brujos* and *brujas* do a thriving business at Key West and Tampa . . . Thousands of Afro-Cubans, as well as many Hispanic-Cubans, live in mortal fear of having a *brujo* spell cast over them. **1967** *DARE* (Qu. CC14, *Words . . used here, where one person supposedly casts a spell over another*) Inf **TX31,** Brujo ['bruhou].

bruk See **break** v A

brukwus(s) See **breakfast**

brulé n |bru'le, 'brulɪ| Also sp *brulée, bruley, brusley* [Fr] **LA**

1 also attrib: A burned-over area of swamp or woodland. Cf *DCan*

1834 (1878) Aime *Plantation Diary* 34 **LA,** Plant cane . . . have not yet suckered, except in the "brulé". **1916** *DN* 4.346 **LA,** *Brulée* [brul'e] . . . An open place in a swamp, generally resulting from the destruction of trees by fire or storm. **1925** Heming *Living Forest* 89 (*DA*), "What's a brule country?" I asked. "A forest of burnt timber." **1967** LeCompte *Word Atlas* 229 **seLA,** Open place in swamp, generally resulting from destruction of trees by fire . . . *brûlé* . . . In English this word is pronounced [brulɪ] and is spelled either "bruley" or "brusley."

2 See quot.

1916 *DN* 4.346 **LA,** *Brulée* [brul'e] . . . A drink made by mixing fruit juices and brandy, and burning out the brandy.

brumbershoot See **bumbershoot**

brung See **bring** B

brung-on See **brought-on**

Brunswick stew n [From *Brunswick* Co VA, where it originated] **chiefly Sth, esp VA, NC, GA** See Map

A stew orig prepared with vegetables and small game such as squirrel or rabbit.

1856 Davis *Farm Bk.* 56 (*DA*) **AL,** Our dinner consisted of the following Bill of Fare . . . Soup Gumbo Brunswick Stew. **1899** (1912) Green *VA Folk-Speech, Brunswick Stew* . . . A stew made of squirrel or chicken meat, lima beans and green corn cooked together and seasoned with pepper and salt. **1924** *Hist. VA* 5.123 (as of c1800), The Baugh family . . settled for a time in Brunswick County, Virginia, and the family were the originators of The Brunswick Stew, the famous Southern dish. **1942** Faulkner *Go Down* 204 **MS,** General Compson . . spent those two weeks sitting in a rocking chair before a tremendous iron pot of Brunswick stew, stirring and tasting. **1942** Rawlings *Cross Creek Cookery* 115 **nFL,** *Brunswick Stew* . . . in the . . Florida backwoods, we make the dish at hog-killing time . . . The basis is fresh pork, and is likely to consist, in humbler circles, of small pieces of lean pork that have escaped the sausage grinder, along with the liver, the lights, and the heart. **1965–70** *DARE* (Qu. H45, *Dishes made with meat*) 16 Infs, **chiefly VA, NC, GA,** Brunswick stew; (Qu. H36, *Kinds of soup*) 9 Infs, **VA, NC, GA,** Brunswick stew; (Qu. H49, *Dishes made by boiling potatoes with other foods*) Infs **GA11, NC16, TN24,** Brunswick stew; (Qu. H55, . . *Kinds of stew;* total Infs questioned, 75) Infs **GA8, MS1, 60,** Brunswick stew; (Qu. H50, *Dishes made with beans, peas, or corn*) Infs **MS60, NC72, 88,** Brunswick stew; (Qu. H43) Inf **GA62,** Brunswick stew—made out of head; **GA70,** Brunswick stew—without cornmeal.

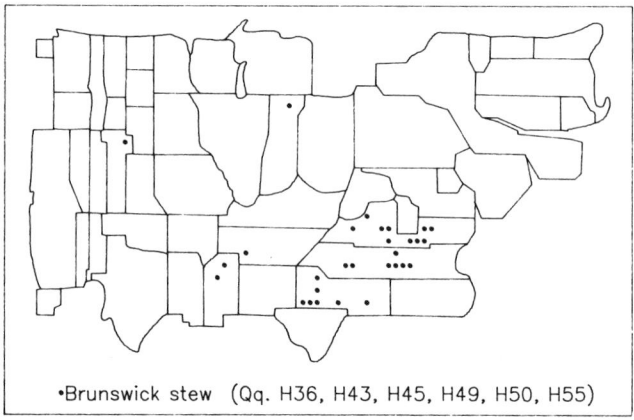

•Brunswick stew (Qq. H36, H43, H45, H49, H50, H55)

brursh See **brush** n, v¹ **4**

brush n, v¹

A Forms (also for v²).

1 pronc |breš|, pronc-sp *bresh.* **chiefly Sth, S Midl**

1837 Sherwood *Gaz.* GA 69, *Bresh,* for brush. **1867** Lowell *Biglow* xxviii **NEng,** *E* sometimes takes the place of *u,* as . . *bresh.* **1907** *DN* 3.229 **nwAR, seMO. 1908** *DN* 3.294 **eAL, wGA. 1909** *DN* 3.419 **Cape Cod MA. 1911** *DN* 3.537 **eKY. 1922** Gonzales *Black Border* 291 **sSC, GA coasts** [Gullah glossary], *Bresh* — brush, brushwood; brush, brushes, brushed, brushing. **1923** *DN* 5.202 **swMO. 1940** Harris *Folk Plays* 88 **NC,** Where's my bresh? **1940** *AmSp* 15.49 **S Midl. 1946** *AmSp* 21.97 **sIL,** Older people pronounce *brush* 'bresh.' **1961** Kurath–McDavid *Pronc. Engl.* 143, *Brush* regularly has the vowel /ʌ/ . . in the North and the North Midland. In the South and the South Midland . . . It is . . used by all cultured speakers and by the great majority of the middle group, while the vowel /ɛ/ . . predominates decisively in folk speech, except for the Low Country of South Carolina and most of Georgia. In the speech of the middle group, /ɛ/ is largely confined to the southern Appalachians and to the points of land along Chesapeake Bay. **1965–70** *DARE* (Qu. F35) Inf **NY24,** Bresh broom; (Qu. F36) Infs **AL30, 34, 52, AR56, FL51, IN12, NC33, VA39, 69,** Bresh broom; **LA31,** Bresh; **FL49,** Yard bresh; (Qu. GG27a) Inf **DC8,** Bresh up. **1976** [see A4 below].

2 pronc-sp *brash.* **chiefly S Midl**

1911 *DN* 3.537 **eKY. 1917** *DN* 4.408 **wNC,** *Brash.* Variant of *brush.* Also Ky. **1923** *DN* 5.202 **swMO,** *Bresh,* or *brash* . . Brush. **1923** *DN*

5.202 swMO. **1976** Garber *Mountain-ese* **Appalachians**, He cut the tree down and then had to burn all the brash.

3 pronc |breɪš, breɪš|, pronc-spp *braish, braysh*.

1902 *DN* 2.230 **sIL**, Bresh (or [breɪš, breɪɑš]). Different pronunciations for brush. **1926** Kephart *Highlanders* 352 **sAppalachians**, Braysh or bresh (brush). **1944** *ADD* 79 **eWV** (as of 1930s), 'Did you braish your hair?' **c1970** [see **A4** below].

4 other forms: See quots.

1916 *DN* 4.272 **NE**, Blursh . . . Variant of *brush*. "Hand me that blursh, I'm all over cat hairs." **1942** Hall *Smoky Mt. Speech* 95, Brush occurs with a very retroflex vowel on one of the speech-records: [breɚʃ], or perhaps [brɝʃ]. **1944** *ADD* 79 **eWV** (as of 1930s), Brursh. **c1970** Pederson *Dial. Survey Rural GA* **seGA**, [Brush is most frequently pronounced [brʌš]; it also occurs as [brʌɪš, breš, breɪš], and rarely as [brɝš].] **1976** Allen *LAUM* 3.282, Nearly all U[pper] M[idwest] infs. have the eastern dominant pronunciation with /ʌ/. The South Midland folk variant with /ɛ/, rhyming with *mesh*, turns up in . . southern Iowa. A West Virginia and Virginia variant with /ɝ/ occurs six times, but some of the instances may be due simply to phonetic assimilation. They are chiefly in the speech of the least educated infs. A pronunciation with /ʊ/, found three times in southern Iowa, is probably to be associated with /ɝ/ . . . All variant pronunciations seem to be on the way out.

B As noun.

1 also attrib: See quots.

1859 (1968) Bartlett *Americanisms*, Brush, for *brushwood*, is an Americanism, and moreover is not confined to undergrowth, but comprises also branches of trees. **1899** (1912) Green *VA Folk-Speech*, Bresh . . . Brush. The small branches and twigs of trees. *"Bresh heaps,"* when piled to be dried and burnt. **1907** *DN* 3.241 **eME**, Brush . . . Branches of evergreen trees. "The one who buys the boughs never knows he's cheated till the brush is thrown off." **1960** *Wilson Coll.* **csKY**, Brush . . . Limbs of trees cut off; also small bushes cut for firewood, fencing, etc.

2 A prairie coneflower **1** (here: *Ratibida columnaris*). Cf **comb**

1896 *Jrl. Amer. Folkl.* 9.192, *Echinacea angustifolia* . . and *Lepachys columnaris*, . . respectively comb and brush, Burnside, So. Dak. **1900** Lyons *Plant Names* 316, *R. columnaris* . . . Long-headed or Prairie Cone-flower, is also called Brush.

3 A switch, whip. **chiefly Sth, S Midl** Cf **brush** v²

1903 *DN* 2.308 **seMO**, Brush (often bresh) . . . Switch. 'He hit the horse with a brush.' **1907** *DN* 3.229 **nwAR, seMO**, Brush . . n. and v.tr. Switch. **1908** *DN* 3.294 **eAL, wGA**, Brush . . . A branch of a tree or shrub, especially such a branch used for a switch. **1940** Stuart *Trees of Heaven* 255 **KY**, I jest got me a bresh and I whopped Boliver.

4 pl: See quots.

1908 *DN* 3.294 **eAL, wGA**, Brush . . . A small tree or shrub. "We had to cut the brushes in the corn field." **1954** *Harder Coll.* **cwTN**, Brushes . . . Wild-growing small trees and shrubs; [we] clean brushes from a field.

5 =**flybrush**.

1949 Nelson *Backwoods Teacher* 27 **sAppalachians** (Hench Coll.), Feelia gave special attention to me and Sally with the "bresh"—a limb with the leaves on it—with which she shooed flies from the table.

6 also *brush cut*: A crew cut. **esp NY, MI** See Map

1965–70 *DARE* (Qu. X5, . . *Kinds of men's haircuts*) 28 Infs, Brush (cut).

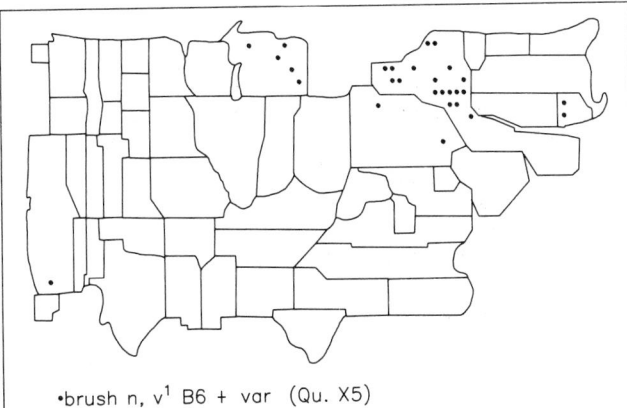

•brush n, v¹ B6 + var (Qu. X5)

C As verb.

1 often with *off, out,* or *up*: To clear land of undergrowth; to cut a trail. **chiefly Nth**

1857 (1949) Thoreau *Jrl.* 10.86 **MA**, Others are ditching and getting out mud and cutting up bushes along fences,—what is called "brushing up." **1939** *LANE* Map 122 **cwVT**, Brushed . . . [Cut] a road or path through the underbrush in the woods. *Ibid* **seMA**, Cleared the land . . . *We breshed it off.* **1939** *FWP Guide AK* 96, Supplies were usually transported from the coast or river landings over the snow in winter, with some preliminary "brushing out" of the trail when necessary. **1947** *Sun* (Baltimore MD) 18 Oct 7/1 (Hench Coll.), But a crew [of forest rangers] may be brushing out telephone lines several miles away. **1950** *WELS* (What do you call it when you dig out roots and underbrush to make a new field) 3 Infs, **WI**, Brushing. **1965–70** *DARE* (Qu. L36) 12 Infs, **esp Nth**, Brushing. **1973** Allen *LAUM* 1.272 **MN**, We cleared the land . . . Brushed, ~ out.

2 See quot. Cf *OEDS* v.² 7

1923 *DN* 5.233 **swWI**, Bresh . . . To do light work at trimming trees while chopping is being done; to do light work of any kind. "He ain't workin' steady—jest breshin' round, I guess."

brush v² [*OEDS* →1783 "*Obs.*"] **chiefly Sth, S Midl** *old-fash*

To beat or thrash; hence vbl n *brushing* a thrashing or whipping.

1842 *Amer. Pioneer* 1.183 **DE**, During the Christmas holydays, Washington thought the Hessians would be drinking, and it would be a good time to give them a brushing. **1865** Kellogg *Life & Death* 194 **KY**, The Surgeon, himself, said that he "brushed his [slaves] up a little when they needed it." **1903** *DN* 2.308 **seMO**, Brush (often bresh) . . . Switch . . . 'I gave the boy a right smart brushing.' **1906** *DN* 3.128 **nwAR**, Brush . . . To whip (though not severely). "If your boy runs away, why don't you brush him?" **1908** *DN* 3.294 **eAL, wGA**, Brush . . . To beat with a switch or brush.

brush ape n

1 A rustic, hillbilly. *derog*

1933 *AmSp* 8.1.53 **Ozarks**, Weed-bender . . . A derisive name for the unprogressive hillman. *Hill-billy . . brush-ape . . and puddle-jumper* are also heard occasionally. **1933** Williamson *Woods Colt* 69 **Ozarks**, "Let's go," says the marshal. "I want to git out of here before a bunch of these brush apes swarm down out of the woods an' take him away from me."

2 See quots.

1939 *FWP ID Lore* 244, Brush ape—one who clears away brush. **1958** McCulloch *Woods Words* **Pacific NW**, Brush ape—Logger. **1968** Adams *Western Words*, Brush ape—A logger.

brush arbor n, also attrib Also *brush house* Pronc-sp *brush harbor* [**arbor** B1] **chiefly Sth, Midl** Cf **bush house**

A large shelter or structure covered with brushwood and usu used as a place for religious meetings.

1851 Woods *16 Months* 62 **PA**, W. is now putting up a brush arbor, to guard us more effectually against the heat of the sun. **1898** Lloyd *Country Life* 217 **AL**, He would like for the members to build a brush arbor and put up plenty of seats. **c1937** in 1977 *Amer. Slave Suppl. 1* 1.11 **AL**, "Marse Lee" had a church called a "brush house", had a floor and seats, and the top was covered with pine boughs. **1941** *FWP Guide IN* 122, In a class by themselves are the religious songs of the 'brush-arbor' and other camp meetings—'white spirituals,' which have been brought across the Ohio River from Virginia, the Carolinas, and other Southern states. **1942** *Hench Coll.* **swVA**, Brush harbor. **c1960** *Wilson Coll.* **csKY**, We're a-going to build a bresh-arbor for Brother Jones to preach in. **1965** *DARE* (Qu. FF16) Inf **OK9**, Creek Indians have brush arbor dances. **1966–67** *DARE* Tape **OK22**, We sat outside under a brush arbor and hung our chart on poles; **SC38A**, Brush arbor. **1967** Green *Horse Tradin'* 248 **TX**, It was in the late summer, which was about the time of year that people in the country used to have "Brush Arbor Meetin's." *Ibid* 249, I rode down to the brush arbor tabernacle . . . I took my spurs off . . instead of wearing them under the brush arbor. **c1974** Jones *Ozark Hill Boy* 5 **AR** (as of c1910), The ten day protracted meeting was a great event for all the community. It was usually conducted in the school house or under a brush harbor in mid-summer.

brush-arbor whiskey n

1953 Randolph *Down in Holler* 230 **Ozarks**, Brush-arbor whiskey . . . Cheap but potent moonshine, *popskull, foxhead*. Sold chiefly to the class of people who attend camp meetings and brush-arbor revivals.

brush broom n¹ Also *bresh broom* [**brush** n, v¹ B1] **Sth, S Midl** Cf **yard broom**

A large broom made of twigs or husks and used for outdoor sweeping.

1864 (1938) Cate *Two Soldiers* 30 **GA,** I had every man to turn out with his brush broom to clean the battery for inspection. **1880** Harris *Uncle Remus Songs* 125 **GA,** Mr. Man, he go off, he did, down in de bushes atter han'ful er switches . . prepa'r'n his bresh-broom. **1908** *DN* 3.294 **eAL, wGA.** **1942** (1971) Campbell *Cloud-Walking* 4 **seKY,** There weren't no end to her fixing and doing — sweeping up her back yard with a brush broom to make it clean like a floor. **1954** *PADS* 21.21 **SC,** *Brush broom, bresh broom, yard broom.* **1960** (1962) Lee *Mockingbird* 46 **AL,** Dill led Jem away and crammed him beneath the steps, poking him with the brushbroom. **c1960** *Wilson Coll.* **csKY.** **1965–70** *DARE* (Qu. F36, . . *Kinds of brooms*) 26 Infs, **Sth, S Midl,** Brush broom; AL30, 34, FL51, NC33, VA69, Bresh broom. [Note: these Infs indicated either that this broom is made of bound twigs or is used to sweep yards. 63 other Infs, scattered throughout Nth, Sth, and S Midl, said "brush (or bresh) broom," but did not specify the kind of broom.] **1966** *DARE* Tape MS75, She was so mad, she grabbed Roberta and a bresh broom. [FW:] What's a brush broom? [Inf:] That's some bushes cut together. You know, . . you go out and cut some old bushes down and make you a bresh broom to sweep your yard with.

brush broom n² Also *bresh broom, broom brush* [*brush* an implement with bristles used for scrubbing, sweeping, painting, etc] **chiefly NEast, esp upstate NY** See Map
A whisk broom.

1910 *DN* 3.438 **cwNY,** *Brush-broom* . . . A whisk-broom made from broom-corn. **1939** *LANE* Map 155 **NEng,** *Brush broom, broom brush* . . a small broom-shaped implement with a short straight handle. **1950** *WELS* (*Kind of broom used around the house*) 7 Infs, **WI,** Brush broom. **1965–70** *DARE* (Qu. F35, *A small broom that you hold in one hand, and use it in places that are hard to get at*) 25 Infs, **chiefly NEast, esp upstate NY,** Brush broom; NY24, Bresh broom. **1965** *DARE* Tape **MA**92, Those hanging up there under the brush brooms.

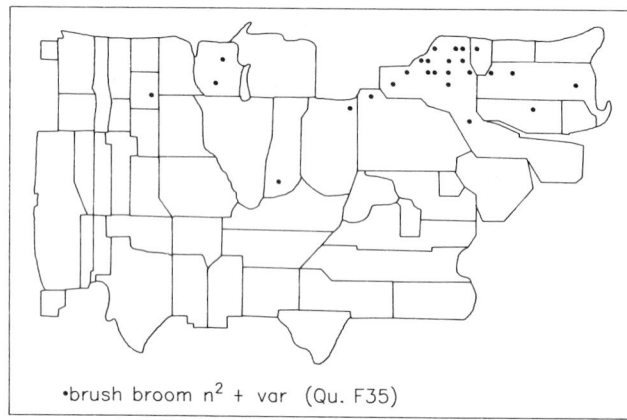

•brush broom n² + var (Qu. F35)

brush buster See **brush popper**

brush colt n Cf **ketch colt, woods colt**
1 See quot.
1965–70 *DARE* (Qu. K43, *A horse that was not intentionally bred, or bred by accident*) 22 Infs, **scattered Sth, Midl,** Brush colt.
2 Transf: an illegitimate child.
1949 Webber *Backwoods Teacher* 18 **Ozarks,** His daddy was an ol' rounder. I wouldn't say this to jist anybody, but he got hisself more'n one bresh-colt. **1966** *DARE* (Qu. Z11b, . . *A child of unwed parents*) Inf SC10, Brush colt. **1973** Allen *LAUM* 1.344 **swIA,** *Illegitimate child* . . . Brush colt.

brush cut See **brush** n, v¹ B6

‡**brush deer** n
=**mule deer** or a subsp thereof.
1928 Anthony *N. Amer. Mammals* 522, *Brush Deer* . . . Resembling typical *hemionus* but with much black on underparts, and antlers comparatively small. **1970** *DARE* (Qu. P32, . . *Other kinds of . . deer*) Inf CA191, Brush deer.

brush drag n
1 A crude fishing device made of tied branches and drawn through the water to fence in fish.
1801 *MA Spy* 21 Oct 3/2, A number of persons . . had met at Franklin, with a view of fishing the Miami, with what is called a brush drag. **1857**

Spirit of Times 7 Mar 6/1 (*DA*), They cut them [grapevines] away, and interweaving them with the thick branches of the buckeye and paw-paw, soon constructed what they called a 'brush drag'; and commenced [sic] on the upper part of some deep pool of water, they stretched it across from shore to shore. **1953** Randolph *Down in Holler* 230 **Ozarks,** *Brush drag* . . . A crude seine made of willow boughs, tied together with bark.
2 See quot.
1953 Randolph *Down in Holler* 230 **Ozarks,** Sometimes *brush drag* is used to mean a primitive harrow, made of brush weighted with stones.

brushes n
=**cornflower 1.**
1900 Lyons *Plant Names* 89, *C. cyanus* . . . Brushes. **1959** Carleton *Index Herb. Plants* 19, Brushes: Centaurea cyanus.

brush hand See **brush popper**

brush harbor See **brush arbor**

brush hen n
Either of two birds: the **yellow-billed cuckoo** or the **black-billed cuckoo.**
1932 Bennitt *Check-list* 36, *Yellow-billed cuckoo* . . . brush hen. *Ibid, Black-billed cuckoo* . . . brush hen.

brush hog n [Var of **bush hog**]
1965–69 *DARE* (Qu. L35, . . *Tools used for cutting underbrush*) Infs IL66, NY182, OH60, Brush hog; OK3, Brush hogs — pulled by tractor; (Qu. L36) Inf OK52, Brush hog — has own engine, cuts down even small trees (up to 2″ [in diameter]). [All Infs old]

brush house See **brush arbor**

brush in v phr *old-fash*
See quots.
1845 (1930) W. Sewall *Diary* 274 **ME,** Sowed my grass seed, timothy and clover seed . . . Brushed in same. **1909** *DN* 3.409 **nME,** *Brush-in* . . . To smooth land just laid down with a drag of birch trees.

brush-in n *old-fash*
1909 *DN* 3.409 **nME,** *Brush-in* . . . A drag made of birch trees fastened to a beam and used to smooth over land newly sown with grass seed.

brush mouth n
1949 Turner *Africanisms* 232 [Gullah], [brʌʃ mɐʊt] 'a drink of whiskey,' i.e., 'brush mouth.'

brush mover n See also *DS* B25
A heavy rainfall.
1932 *Hench Coll.* **VA,** Apropos of the present drought and a brief rain this evening, a friend told of a Negro preacher who prayed, "Oh, Lo'd, send us gentle rains. But please, Lo'd, don't send no gully-washers or bresh-movers." **1968** *DARE* (Qu. B25, . . *A heavy rain*) Inf VA42, Brush mover.

‡**brush pine** n
1969 *DARE* (Qu. T17, . . *Different kinds of pine trees*) Inf GA80, Brush pine.

brush popper n Also *brush buster, ~ hand, ~ rider, ~ thumper, ~ whacker* **West**
A cowboy who works in brush country.
1929 Dobie *Vaquero* 207 **TX,** Sam was a brush popper. Like many another brush whacker, he was wont to emerge from a thicket with enough wood hanging in the fork of his saddle to cook a side of yearling ribs. *Ibid* 241, He was the best brush hand that I have ever known and he was a born horseman. **1945** Thorp *Pardner* 262 **SW,** Some of the riders on these mavericking roundups ("brush-poppers," as we used to call them) took a lot more chances than any other riders going. **1961** Adams *Old-Time Cowhand* 214, The brush rider . . . was an expert at runnin' cattle in the brush . . . [He] went by such names as "brush buster," "brush thumper," "brush hand," "brush whacker," and "brush popper," the latter bein' the most pop'lar title.

brush rabbit n
A kind of cottontail (*Sylvilagus bachmani*).
1907 White *AZ Nights* 10, And me squatting behind that ore dump about as formidable as a brush rabbit! **1935** Pratt *Manual Animals* 350, *S[ylvilagus] bachmani* . . . Brush rabbit. **1966–70** *DARE* (Qu. P30, . . *Wild rabbits*) Infs ND9, OR10, Brush rabbit; CA23, Brush rabbit or bush rabbit; CA25, Cottontail — a little bigger than a brush rabbit; CA87, Brush rabbit — common, tail turns up; CA181, Brush rabbit — same as

cottontail; **CO**41, Brush rabbit—like cottontail, only smaller; **MN**16, Brush rabbit or snowshoe. **1982** Elman *Hunter's Field Guide* 370, The smallest and darkest of all, the brush rabbit *(S. bachmani),* ranges throughout the West.

brush rack n
1953 Randolph *Down in Holler* 230 **Ozarks,** Brush rack . . . A raft or platform of small sticks tied together. The term is sometimes applied to a rude brush shelter for chickens or swine.

brush rattler n
Prob a **timber rattlesnake.**
1969 *DARE* (Qu. P25, . . *Kinds of snakes*) Inf **MI**101, Brush rattler, sand rattler. [FW: Inf thinks these are the same.]

brush rider See **brush popper**

brush roast n
1939 FWP *Guide NC* 105, "Brush roasts," or oysters cooked on a wire netting over an open wood fire, are a popular out-of-doors shore meal.

brush scythe n Also *brush sy* **chiefly Nth** See Map Cf **bush scythe**
A cutting tool used to remove brush and undergrowth.
1634 in 1869 Winthrop *Life & Letters* 2.126 **MA,** Sithes for grass, and two brush sithes. **1811** *Niles' Natl. Reg.* 1.101/1 **PA,** The brush scythe will cut up the brambles. **1858** Warder *Hedges* 63 **OH,** They must be cut off near the ground, either with a brush-scythe, or better, with the mowing-machine. **1950** *WELS (Hand tool used for cutting underbrush)* 15 Infs, **WI,** Brush scythe. **1965–70** *DARE* (Qu. L35, *Hand tools used for cutting underbrush and digging out roots*) 14 Infs, **chiefly Nth,** Brush scythe; **MI**23, 56, Brush sy; (Qu. L37, *A hand tool for cutting weeds and grass*) Infs **MA**66, **MO**19, **MT**4, **VA**10, Brush scythe; **AK**8, **MN**15, Brush sy.

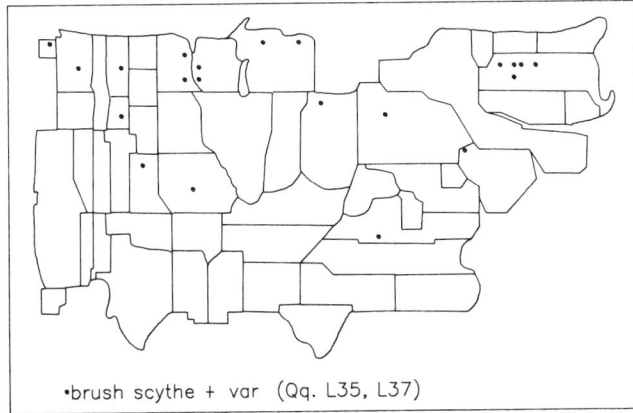

•brush scythe + var (Qq. L35, L37)

brush splitter n
1961 Adams *Old-Time Cowhand* 155, The old "longhorn" [cattle] of the brush country of Texas were called "brush splitters," and "cactus boomers."

brushtail n See **bushtail**

brush thrush n
Perh a **hermit thrush.**
1967 *DARE* (Qu. Q14, . . *Other names . . for . . thrush*) Inf **WA**20, Winter robin, brush thrush.

brush thumper, brush whacker See **brush popper**

brush whip v Cf **brush** v²
1950 FWP *Guide ID* 241, Brush-whip . . . To rebuke mildly.

brush wolf n
=**coyote.**
1923 *Frontier* Mar 11 **Gt Lakes,** Presently a brush wolf yapped. **1946** Stanwell–Fletcher *Driftwood* 24, A little "brush wolf," or coyote, stared at us from a high bank, and vanished. **1967–68** *DARE* (Qu. P32) Inf **MN**5, Brush wolf; **MN**15, Coyote—local name for brush wolf. **1982** Elman *Hunter's Field Guide* 344, Coyote . . . Common & Regional Names: prairie wolf, brush wolf.

brusley See **brulé**

brustle n, v Also sp *brussel* [Alter of *bristle*] **chiefly NEng**
Std senses, var forms.

1815 Humphreys *Yankey in England* 104 **NEng,** Brussels, bristles. **1818** Fessenden *Ladies Monitor* 171 **VT,** Brussels for bristles. **1899** (1912) Green *VA Folk-Speech,* Brussels . . . A variant of *bristles.* **1904** *DN* 2.424 **Cape Cod MA,** Brustle up . . . Used first of a setting hen, then figuratively of a person who acts indignant or offended. **1914** *DN* 4.69 **ME, nNH,** Rural Locutions . . . Brustle, n. and v. Bristle. **1930** *AmSp* 6.97 **cNY,** Brustled up: Excited over. "He's all brustled up over the insult." **1939** *LANE* Map 207 **throughout NEng,** Bristles . . brustles. c1960 Wilson *Coll.* **csKY,** Brustles . . . Older name for *bristles.*

brute n **chiefly S Midl, occas NEng** *euphem* Cf **gentleman cow, male**
A bull.
1891 in 1973 *AmSp* 48.89 **nGA,** Running as fast as they could to get ahead of the brutes. **1913** Kephart *Highlanders* 295 **sAppalachians,** Critter and beast are usually restricted to horse and mule, and brute to a bovine. A bull or boar is not to be mentioned as such in mixed company, but male-brute and male-hog are used as euphemisms. **1939** *AmSp* 14.89 **eTN. 1939** *LANE* Map 190 **scattered in NEng,** Euphemisms used when a direct reference to the bull is avoided on grounds of delicacy . . *the beast, the brute.* **1949** Arnow *Hunter's Horn* 97 **KY,** I allus say 'brute' at school in class, but . . th agriculture book it says 'bull.' **1965–70** *DARE* (Qu. K22, . . *A bull*) Infs **AZ**15, **AR**4, **NC**30, Brute; **GA**72, **KY**29, Stock brute; **MO**37, Big old brute; **NC**30, He-brute; (Qu. K23, *Words used by women or in mixed company for a bull*) Infs **KY**23, **MO**32, **NC**30, **TX**40, Brute; **KY**46, Cow brute; **KY**29, Male brute.

brute beast n *arch*
1952 Brown *NC Folkl.* 1.523, Brute beast . . . An animal.

bruth See **brother** A4

brutherin, bruthren See **brethren**

brutz n [Ger *brüten* to brood over]
A depressed or moody state of mind; also adj *brutzing* depressed, moody.
1970 *DARE* (Qu. GG35a, *To feel depressed or in a gloomy mood: "He has the _____ today."*) Inf **IL**143, Brutz [brʊts]; **PA**243A, [bruts]—Pennsylvania Dutch—sort of to bitch or bellyache; (Qu. GG35b, . . *"She's feeling _____ today."*) Inf **IL**143, Brutzing; **PA**243A, Brutzing.

bruuder See **brother** A5

bruze See **bruise**

bry n |braɪ| Also sp *brie, brij* [Du *brij* porridge] **chiefly in Dutch settlement areas** Cf **balkenbry, bree**
A buttermilk pap usu made with barley and eaten with sugar or syrup.
1970 *DARE* Tape **MI**122, Something she [=Inf's mother] used to fix [was made] with barley and she called it [braɪ], [Inf sp:] b-r-i-e . . . You'd eat it with brown sugar on it . . . It's not as thin as soup. It's more like rice pudding except that it's barley. And that's a typically Dutch dish. **1981** *DARE* File **nwIA,** The word *brij* occurs especially in the names of two Dutch dishes, both of which involve a brewing or mixing process— *balken brij,* and *soepen brij* (which is also simply called *brij*). Soepen brij is white. It's a buttermilk pap—barley boiled in buttermilk. It has to be eaten with syrup on it. Balken brij contains scrap meat from a hog. Traditionally, the mixture was placed in a flour sack and hung from the balken (beams or rafters) where it cured and dried for at least a month or two. It is eaten sliced and fried, with syrup. Balken brij is usually made in early November at hog-butchering time and often eaten around Christmas.

B.T.M. n Also *B.T. emptem* [Abbr for *bottom; OEDS* 1919 →] *joc*
The buttocks.
1966–67 *DARE* (Qu. X35, *Joking words for the part of the body that you sit on*) Infs **WA**6, **WY**5, B.T.M.; **OH**12, B.T.M. bottom [laughter]; **CO**6, B.T. emptem [bi ti ɛmtɛm].

bub n¹ See **bubby** n¹ 1

bub n² |bʌb| [Orig uncert; prob hypocoristic form of *brother*] Cf **bubba** n¹, **bubby** n²
1 also *bubs:* A brother. **widespread, but rare in NEng**
[**1837** *Knickerbocker* 10.521 **NYC,** Have you at present any of the *chastised idiot-brother . . .* What I want is what *you* call *whipped sylla-bub.*] **1859** (1968) Bartlett *Americanisms, Bub and Bubby.* Contractions for brother, often applied to small boys. **1876** *Congressional Record* 28 Jan 725/2 **NEast,** You [addressing Mr. Eugene Hale of ME]

have been known in the last three or four Congresses as "*Blaine's little bub.*" **1950** *WELS (Nicknames and affectionate words meaning "brother")* 2 Infs, **WI**, Bub, bud, buddy, bubber . . . Brother, esp. for small boy. **1965–70** (Qu. Z5, . . *Nicknames and affectionate words meaning "brother")* 35 Infs, **scattered exc NEng**, Bub; NY121, Bud, bubs.

2 A friend, buddy.

1930 Shoemaker *1300 Words* **cPA Mts** (as of c1900), *Bub*—A friend, a pal.

3 Used as a term of address for:

a A boy. **chiefly Nth** *somewhat old-fash*

1839 (1969) Briggs *Advent. Franco* 2.189 **NYC**, "Speak louder, Bub," said one of the vice presidents, encouragingly. **1869** Stowe *Oldtown Folks* 138 **MA**, "Hulloah, bub!" shouted they, "where ye goin'?" **1885** Twain *Huck. Finn* 105 **Missip Valley**, Don't cry, bub. What's the trouble? **1894** *DN* 1.340 **wCT**. **1895** *DN* 1.396 **NEng, NY, nIL, seMI, seMN**, *Bub*: a boy; corresponding masc. of "sis"; not restricted to vocative case as reported . . . [I know it only as a vocative in Me.—E.S.S. In Conn. it is sometimes used as a sort of title for the boy of the family, sometimes clinging to an only son after he is grown up; in this sense it may appear in other cases, but never as a mere common noun.—E.H.B.] **1905** *DN* 3.4 **cCT**. **1907** *DN* 3.182 **seNH**. **1910** *DN* 3.438 **wNY**. **1929** *AmSp* 5.121 **ME**. **1941** *LANE* Map 379 **NEng**, Names used in addressing boys: . . *buddy* . . [2 infs]; *bub* . . [9 infs; 1 considers term old-fash]; *bubby* . . [2 infs; 1 considers term old-fash]. **1966–69** *DARE* (Qu. II10a, . . *A boy: "Say, _____, where's the post office?"*) Infs **ME5, NY123, 206**, Bub; **MA58**, Bub—old-fashioned; **MA68**, Bub—old-fashioned; some didn't like that, but they used it. [4 of 5 Infs old]

b A man, fellow.

1872 Twain *Roughing It* 51 **MO**, Well, I shall have to tear myself away from you, bub. **1889** *Century Illustr. Mag.* 37.411/2 **VA**, 'Lookee here, bub,' said one o' the men, 'that won't do.' **1904** White *Blazed Trail Stories* 4 **ceMI**, Say, bub, you look as interested as a man killing snakes. *Ibid* 11, Don't you lose any hair, bub. **1940** *AmSp* 15.219 **VT**, I had from my western Vermont environment 'No sirree Bub' (not 'Bob'; no comma heard . .). **1970** *DARE* (Qu. II10b, . . *A man: "Say, _____, how far is it to the next town?"*) Inf **NY241**, Bub.

bubaleh See **bubeleh**

bubba n[1] Also sp *bubber, bubbuh* [Prob hypocoristic form of *brother*] Cf **bub** n[2], **bubby** n[2]

Used chiefly as a term of address for:

1 A brother. **chiefly Sth, S Midl** See Map *esp common among Blacks*

1922 Gonzales *Black Border* 291 **sSC, GA coasts** [Gullah glossary], *Bubbuh* . . *Budduh*—(familiar) brother. **1927** Adams *Congaree* 78 **cSC** [Black], Bubber, where you been? **1930** *DN* 6.80 **cSC**, Bubber . . Brother. A frequent nickname, used by friends as well as by relatives. The nieces and nephews of a man so nicknamed will call him "Uncle Bubber". Frequently used in the third person: "Your bubber," "my bubber," etc. **c1960** *Wilson Coll.* **csKY**, Bub, bud, buddy, bubber . . . Brother, esp. for small boy. **1965–70** *DARE* (Qu. Z5, . . *Nicknames and affectionate words meaning "brother")* 65 Infs, **chiefly Sth**, Bubba; 10 Infs, **esp Sth, Midl**, Bubber. **1966** *DARE* Tape **SC16**, And bubba, you will get all you want [directed at local Black preacher assisting FW in interview].

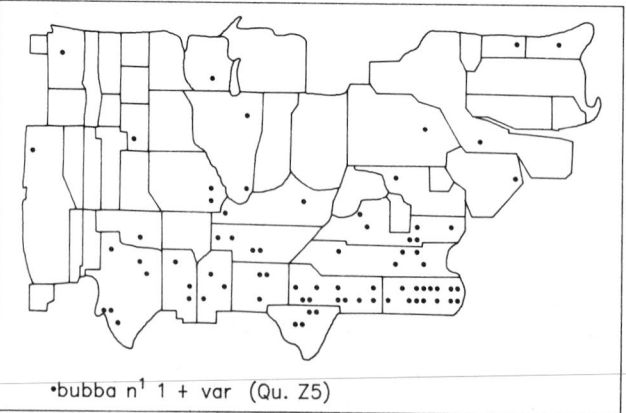

•bubba n[1] 1 + var (Qu. Z5)

2 A boy.

1966 *DARE* (Qu. II10a, . . *A boy: "Say, _____, where's the post office?"*) Inf **SC26**, Son, occasionally bubba.

bubba n[2] [Cf Scots dial *bubba* grandfather]

1968 *DARE* (Qu. Z3, . . *Words . . for "grandfather")* Inf **PA131**, Bubba.

bubba n[3] See **bubbe, bubeleh**

bubbe n |'bʊbə, -bi, 'babi, 'bɔ-| Pronc-spp *bobby, bubba, bubby* [Yiddish] See also **bubeleh**

A grandmother—also used as a term of address.

1967 *DARE* (Qu. Z4, . . *Words . . for "grandmother")* Inf **MA4**, [bɔbi]. **1970** Feinsilver *Yiddish* 358, "Bubby" for *bobbe* or *buhbe*, Grandma—Like "keppy" for *keppele* and "Hypy" for *chupe*, "bubby" is an Anglicized diminutive. **1982** Rosten *Hooray for Yiddish* 71, *Bubbe*; bobe (standard); bube (standard). From Slavic: *baba*: grandmother; midwife. (There is a Hebrew *buba*, but it means "little doll" and is not the Yiddish word for grandmother.) . . Grandmother. **1982** *Wall St. Jrl.* (NY NY) 15 March 1/4, [Headline:] Is the Stock Market Really Efficient? Go Ask a Bubba. *Ibid*, Prof. Schacter explained that "bubba psychology is the study of what Jewish grandmothers know without benefit of graduate training." Any bubba worth her salt, he continued, would intuitively understand that the economists' ideas are silly. **1982** *DARE* File **csWI**, My idea was to have a radio program for the local Jewish community. We could have had the bubbies [bʊbiz] and zeydies giving radio plays in Yiddish, and other programs to deal with holidays and issues. *Ibid* **NYC** (as of 1950s–60s), My cousins used to call my grandmother "Bobby" ['babi].

bubbelly See **bube**

bubbe-mayse n Also *bobbe mayse* [Yiddish]

An old wives' tale.

1970 Feinsilver *Yiddish* 97, *Bobbe mayse*—Lit., Grandma's story. Old wives' tale. The term derives from *Bovo Buch* (Bovo Book), the title of a Yiddish narrative poem of the early sixteenth century . . . intended as satire . . . Three hundred years later it was rewritten in modern Yiddish prose and renamed *Bovo Mayse* (Bovo Story), and this led to the corrupted name of *bobbe mayse*—presumably because it was chiefly old or gullible women who took it seriously. **1982** Rosten *Hooray for Yiddish* 72, *Bubbe-mayse*; bobe-mayse; baba-myseh. Pronounce it *bub-eh my-*seh or *baw-beh my-*seh. 1. (Literally) Grandma's story. 2. An absurd account or explanation. 3. An old wives' tale. **1983** *DARE* File **NYC**, If your mother tells you that going to bed with your hair wet will make you sick, that's a ['bʊbə,maɪntsə].

bubber n[1], also attrib [Prob from **bubby** n[1]] *?obs*

See quots.

1889 (1971) Farmer *Americanisms*, *Bubber*.—A nickname for an old woman with large pendulous breasts. Rarely heard. **1950** *AmSp* 25.171 (as of 1820), *Bubber, n* and *a*. A stout or stoutly mammelated old woman. Used in Salem, Mass. (or was in 1820 *et seq.*): 'Bubber Jones.'

bubber n[2] See **bubba** n[1]

bubbin See **bubby** n[1] 1

bubble n[1]

1 In marble play: see quot.

c1970 Wiersma *Marbles Terms* **swMI**, Bubble—A marble of clear glass with bubbles in it—particularly rare.

2 See quot. [In ref to the bubble in a level]

1982 *Grit* (Williamsport PA) 4 July 17, [In] Portland, Ore., " . . carpenters refer to the strange behavior of the mildly eccentric in the same terms used by their trade." Thus, someone who's "half a bubble off" is as welcome as a planed board that shows up crooked on a level. (That one shows up in Illinois too.)

3 See **bubble-top**.

4 A woman's breast. Cf **bubby** n[1] 1

1968–70 *DARE* (Qu. X31, . . *Words . . for a woman's breasts*) Infs **PA239, SC58, TX53, 106**, Bubbles; **GA13**, Love bubbles. **1971** *AmSp* 46.82 **Chicago IL**, Breasts: breasts, tits, . . bubbles.

bubble n[2]

An automobile.

1939 *LANE* Map 185 **seNH**, *Automobile* . . [bʌ˞bɫ], common term (shortened from the jocular *automobubble?* . .).

bubble and squeak n [From the sounds which the food makes when being cooked] **chiefly NEast**

A dish consisting of some combination of cabbage, potatoes, onions, and meat: see quots.

1930 (1932) *Good Housekeeping Inst. Book of Meals* 79, *Bubble and squeak (English)* . . . Put a layer of sautéed meat in a greased casserole, then a layer of onions and then a layer of potatoes, . . and continuing until the casserole is filled. Over all pour the mock turtle soup and enough cold water to cover . . . A baking powder biscuit crust . . may be put on the casserole after the thickening is added. **1936** Lutes *Country Kitchen* 180 **sMI**, My father liked Bubble-and-Squeak. That may have been the British in him breaking out . . . for I never heard of it anywhere else in Michigan . . . Half a cupful of fat, equal quantities of pork or bacon, and butter, are put into a heavy aluminum kettle . . . A medium-sized cabbage has been finely shredded . . and a number of potatoes peeled and sliced. **1942** Berrey–Van den Bark *Amer. Slang* 91.48, Bubble and squeak, *hash in New England, elsewhere a fried cabbage and beef dish.* **1951** *Good Housek. Home Encycl.* 373/2 *(OEDS)*, In the modern version of bubble and squeak the meat is usually omitted. **1967** *DARE* (Qu. H45, . . *Dishes made with meat*) Inf **NY**12, Bubble and squeak—a camping dish (cottagers do it); a meat pie with biscuit crust. **1975** Gould *ME Lingo*, *Bubble and squeak*—Numerous Maine cookbooks treat this as endemic, and most recipes have no similarity to the English dish of the same name. In Maine it's a left-over contrivance: cold cooked beef, cold smashed potatoes, cold cabbage, shredded onion, etc., browned in pork fat and served with vinegar. It's hearty, and cleans out the refrigerator.

bubble buster n

A non-existent item used as the basis of a practical joke: see quot.

1968 *DARE* (Qu. HH14, . . *Ways of teasing a beginner or inexperienced person* . . *"Go get me _____."*) Inf **IN**32, A bubble buster.

bubblegum machine n chiefly **Sth, S Midl** *joc* Also called **bubble-top, gumball machine**

A police car; the light on top of the car.

1966–68 *DARE* (Qu. N4, . . *A police vehicle with a . . flashing light on top*) Infs **DE**4, **FL**4, **GA**17, 63, **OK**31, Bubblegum machine; **MA**1, Police car, bubblegum machine. **1975** Gould *ME Lingo*, *Bubblegum machine*—From the light globe on the top, a Maine State Police car on the highway. **1982** *DARE* File **NC**, Bubblegum machine—the revolving light on the top of a police car.

‡bubble gun n *joc*

1969 *DARE* (Qu. P37b, . . *Nicknames for a shotgun*) Inf **KY**11, Bubble gun, shot and molasses, old stand-by.

bubbler n

1 also *bubbling fish:* =**freshwater drum. Missip-Ohio Valleys**
1819 Rafinesque in *Western Rev.* 1.372, Grunting Bubbler. *Amblodon grunniens* . . . The vulgar names of this fish are White-perch, White-pearch, Buffaloe-perch, grunting perch, bubbling-fish, bubbler, and muscle-eater . . . A remarkable peculiarity of this fish consists in the strange grunting noise, which it produces, and from which I have derived its specific name . . . Another peculiarity which it has of producing large bubbles in quick succession while digging through the mud or sand of the river, in search of the Muscles or Unios. **1828** Flint *Condensed Geog.* 1.120, Bubbler, *amblodon* . . . Its name is derived from the singular grunting noise, which it makes,—a noise, which is familiar to every one, who has been much on the Ohio. **1872** Schele De Vere *Americanisms* 383, The *Bubbler* . . when drawn from the waters of the Ohio . . makes an extraordinary bubbling noise, as if protesting against such ill-treatment. **1911** *Century Dict.*, Bubbler . . . Also called *bubbling-fish.* **1946** LaMonte *N. Amer. Game Fishes* 148.

2 A drinking fountain, esp one outdoors; orig the valve which caused the water to bubble in such a fountain. **Nth, N Midl; esp freq in WI**

[**1911** *Survey* [E. Stroudsburg] 22 Apr 146/2 **nwIL**, The Board of Public Improvements has ordered that bubbling fountains must take the place of the drinking cup.] **1914** Kohler Co. *Porcelain Ware* 258 **WI**, Drinking Fountains . . . Fitted with . . nickel-plated brass self-closing bubbling valve . . adjustable for a continuous flow of water . . . Can also furnish . . continuous flow bubbler with above fountains. **1926** *Sanitary & Heating Age* 105.582 **nIL**, Century Self Closing and Self Covering Bubblers, Century Combination Bubblers and Faucets, . . Sanitary Lavatory and Sink Fountains, Multiple Bubbler Fountains, Wall Bracket Fountains. **1948** Cain *Moth* 32 **cnMD**, She made me take a drink from the water bubbler. **1950** *WELS Suppl.*, Bubbler—a drinking fountain. Heard in Madison, Milwaukee, Fond du Lac, Appleton, and Deerfield, WI; Rockford, IL; Boston and Worcester, MA; Westchester Co., NY; NJ.

1967 *DARE* FW Addit **cePA**, Bubbler—an outside drinking fountain. **1969** *DARE* File, Bubbler (drinking fountain)—heard used in Cincinnati and Canton, Ohio. **1978** *WI Week-End* 16 Aug 8 **cwWI**, Be sure to take a drink from one of the street bubblers or in a restaurant if you attend Pure Water Days. **1980** *DARE* File **neCO** (as of early 1940s), We called the outdoor fountain in parks *bubblers.* **1981** WI Acad. *Trans.* 85 **WI**, Since the type of porcelain fountain with the bubbler on it became popular for outdoor use, and the water cooler and other types of dispensers were still used indoors, . . a significantly higher percentage of speakers . . use 'bubbler' for the outdoor fountain.

bubble-top n Also *bubble* [From the light on top of the car] **Nth, N Midl**
=**bubblegum machine.**
1967–69 *DARE* (Qu. N4, . . *A police vehicle with a . . flashing light on top*) Infs **IN**65, **MN**16, **NJ**28, **PA**209, **WA**22, Bubble-top; **PA**204, Bubble-top, or just plain bubble.

bubbling fish See **bubbler 1**

bubbly-jock n [Engl and Scots dial; perh imit of its gobble]
1930 Shoemaker *1300 Words* **cPA Mts** (as of c1900), *Bubbly-jock*—A turkey gobbler.

bubbuh See **bubba** n[1]

bubby n[1] Usu |ˈbʌbi|, infreq |ˈbʊbi| [*OED* →1725, "*Obs.* or *dial.*" Cf Ger *bübbi* teat]

1 also *bubbin* and abbr *bub:* A woman's breast. **scattered, but esp S Midl** *somewhat old-fash* Cf **booby** n[2], **bubble** n[1] 4
1806 (1905) Lewis *Orig. Jrls. Lewis & Clark Exped.* 4.186, When this vest is worn the breast of the woman is concealed, but without it . . they are exposed . . and grow to great length, particularly in aged women in many of whom I have seen the bubby reach as low as the waist. **1899** (1912) Green *VA Folk-Speech*, *Bubby* . . A woman's breast. **1907** *DN* 3.221 **nwAR, sIL**, *Bubbies.* **1910** *DN* 3.438 **wNY**, *Bubbies.* **1941** Schulberg *What Makes* 275 **Hollywood CA**, The fact that her name is Harrington must be just as sexually exciting to Sammy as that moist red mouth or those snooty bubs of hers. **1949** *PADS* 11.4 **wTX**, *Bubbies.* **1950** *PADS* 14.17 **SC**, *Bubbies.* **1953** Brewer *Word Brazos* 67 **eTX** [Black], Milly stealed 'im a big piece of cake from de Missus' cupboard an' put it in her bosom . . . Ole Massuh Cooper was eyein' her when she go outen de door, but he don' say nothin' . . . Den he wanna whip her for stealin' de piece of cake, an' he say, "Milly, you' bubbies ain't big ez dey was when you gone outen heah while ago." **c1960** *Wilson Coll.* **csKY**, Bubbies . . . A woman's breasts. "She shore's got big bubbies." **1965–70** *DARE* (Qu. X31, . . *A woman's breasts*) 27 Infs, **scattered, but esp S Midl**, Bubbies (*usu pronc* [ˈbʌbiz]); **MD**9, [ˈbʊbiz]; **LA**26, [ˈbʌbəz]; **TN**42, Bubs; **CA**106, Bubbins. [Of all Infs responding to the question, 60% were old, 27% grade school educ, 31% coll educ, and 50% male; of those giving this response, 74% were old, 42% grade school educ, 16% coll educ, and 65% male.]

2 See **bubbybush.**

bubby n[2] |ˈbʌbi| [Prob hypocoristic form of *brother;* but cf *OED bubby[2]* "the word looks more like Ger. *bube, bub,* boy"] Cf **bub** n[2], **bubba** n[1]
Used as a nickname or term of address for:
1 A brother. **esp Midl**
1859 (1968) Bartlett *Americanisms*, Bub and *Bubby.* Contractions for brother, often applied to small boys. **1965–70** *DARE* (Qu. Z5, . . *Nicknames and affectionate words meaning "brother"*) 12 Infs, **esp Midl**, Bubby.

2 A boy. **chiefly Nth**
1841 *Knickerbocker* 17.39 **seNY**, 'Bubby,' added he, looking at a white-headed little boy with . . affectionate good humor. **1889** Murfree *Despot* 232 **eTN**, Ye ain't a-goin' hongry this winter, air ye, bubby? **1889** (1971) Farmer *Americanisms*, *Bubby.*—A pet name for a baby. Compare with *Babsy.* "When she was ready to go home, she did so without carriage or baby. Shortly after *bubby* kicked up high jinks, and the joker clerk was sent for to take him away."—*San Francisco Weekly Examiner*, 1888. **1897** Barrère–Leland *Slang* 1.177, Bub, bubby (American), a term very commonly applied to a little boy. It came from Pennsylvania, where it was derived from the German *bube*, which is commonly abbreviated to *bub.* **1905** *DN* 3.4 **cCT**, Bub or bubby. **1941** *LANE* Map 379 **RI**, Names used in addressing boys: . . *bubby* . . [2 infs; 1 considers term old-fash]. **1967** *DARE* (Qu. II10a, . . *A boy:* "Say, _____, where's the post office?") Inf **IL**16, Buddy, bubby.

‡**3** A sweetheart.

1950 *WELS (Nicknames or affectionate names for a sweetheart)* 1 Inf, ceWI, Bubby.

bubby n[3] See **bubbe**

bubbybush n [From the resemblance of the flower to a **bubby** n[1] **1**] **sAppalachians**

1 also *bubby, bubby-blossom, ~ flower, ~ root, ~ rose, ~ shrub, sweet bubby:* Either of two **sweet shrubs**: esp **Carolina allspice**, but also *Calycanthus fertilis.* Cf **sweet betsy**

1779 in 1789 Anburey *Travels* 2.396 **VA,** A shrub peculiar to this province . . bears a small flower, which the inhabitants term the bubby flower; . . the name . . arises from a custom that the women have of putting this flower down their bosoms, . . till it has lost all its grateful perfume. **1883** Harris *Nights with Remus* 70 **GA,** Ole Brer Rabbit, he mouter had some bubby-blossoms wrop up in his hankcher. **1893** *Jrl. Amer. Folkl.* 6.141 **nwNC,** *Calycanthus glaucus,* bubby-bush. Banner Elk, N.C. **1913** Morley *Carolina Mts.* 47 **wNC,** Another shrub that belongs to us and eastern Asia and that tempts one to nibble is what the people here call "sweet bubbies." It appears in old-fashioned Northern gardens under the name of sweet-scented or flowering or strawberry shrub. **1943** Peattie *Great Smokies* 172 **eTN, wNC,** Strawberry shrub, with its dark red nipple-form flowers (called "bubby-blossoms" by the mountain folk) and its strange odor, something like fermenting strawberries. **1945** McAtee *Nomina Abitera* 12 **sAppalachians,** Strawberry Shrubs . . . are familiar garden shrubs, the globular flowers of which probably inspire the common names of bubby, bubby-blossoms, bubby bush, bubby-shrub. One is fragrant and, therefore, called sweet bubby. **1960** Williams *Walk Egypt* 107 **GA,** It was sweet shrub—bubby blossoms, the old folks called them, from their sweet reddish-brown puckers like a woman's nipples . . . they came along in April. **1964** Campbell *Great Smoky Wildflowers* 50 **eTN, wNC,** Sweet shrub—*Calycanthus floridus* . . . Shrubs up to 6 or 8 feet tall bear a profusion of deep maroon or brownish flowers . . . 1–1½ inches in diameter. This shrub usually has a spicy fragrance . . . Other names are *bubby-bush* and *Carolina allspice.* **1968** *DARE* FW Addit **VA15,** Bubby-rose—common in woods; book term is "sweet shrub." **1975** Hamel–Chiltoskey *Cherokee Plants* 58, Sweet shrub, . . bubby root, . . *Calycanthus floridus.*

2 =**strawberry bush 1.**

1917 *DN* 4.409 **wNC,** *Bubby bush.* Burning bush (Evonymus Americanus).

bubby duck n Cf **booby** n[1] **2**

=**ruddy duck.**

1945 McAtee *Nomina Abitera* 32, Ruddy Duck . . Bubby duck, Winnieshiek [sic] Bottoms, Iowa.

bubby-flower, bubby-root, bubby-rose, bubby-shrub See **bubbybush**

bube n Also dimins *bubbelly, bubelicks* [Ger *Bube* boy, *Bubli* little boy] **Ger settlement areas in PA, IL**

A boy; a baby.

1928 *AmSp* 23.108 **swIL,** Common words [in the German settlement area] are . . *bube,* boy. **1930** Shoemaker *1300 Words* **cPA Mts** (as of c1900), *Bubelicks*—An endearing term to a baby. **1939** Aurand *Quaint Idioms* 12 **PaGer area,** The dear little *bubbelly* (baby) is so sweet-like; she is so nice-behaved. [**1951** Danner *PA Dutch Dict.,* Baby—buppli.]

bubeleh n |'bubələ| Also sp *bubaleh, bubele,* and abbr *boobee, bubba, bubee, bubie, buby* [Yiddish; dimins and varr of **bubbe**] Used as an affectionate form of address.

1970 Feinsilver *Yiddish* 139, Bubele—Honey-child, sweetie-pie, puddin'. This affectionate term has been heard often on TV . . . The bilingual "Buby" has also been taking on. **1980** Pearl *Jonathan David Slang,* Bubaleh . . . literally, "little grandmother." An affectionate term, the equivalent of dear, honey, etc. . . Bubie . . . *See* bubaleh. **1982** Rosten *Hooray for Yiddish* 73, Bubeleh; babele (Galician/Slovakian Yiddish); bubee (Yinglish, diminutive, affectionate). Be sure to pronounce the *u* as in "put," not as in "but." 1. The affectionate form of *bubbe, baba, bobe, bawbe.* 2. Little grandma. 3. Grandchild. 4. Term of endearment used between a husband and wife, parent and child, relatives, friends. 5. Synonym for "dear," "darling," "honey." . . In theatrical circles, where hugs and kisses and terms of endearment luxuriate in all seasons, *bubeleh* and *bubee* (pronounced to rhyme with "goody") have become familiar Yinglish words. **1982** *Wall St. Jrl.* (NY NY) 29 Mar 17/1–2, A clear distinction should be made between bawbee, which means [in Yiddish] a wise and compassionate grandmother, and boobee

("oo" pronounced as in "look"), which is a term of endearment or comradeship. Bubba can have either meaning depending on how it is pronounced.

bube lice n |'bubə, 'bubi| and varr (see quot 1966–68) [PaGer *bube, buwe,* dimins *bubli, buwli* boy] **PA** Also called **boy lice, boogey lice**

= **beggar ticks 1.**

[**1910** *PA German* 11.546, Bubelause—Com. Beggar-ticks—Bidens frondosa L. **1911** *Ibid* 12.105, Bubeleis—Beggar-ticks—Bidens frondosa L. **1922** in 1926 PA Ger. Soc. *Proc.* 33.3.69, *Beggar's Ticks. Bidens,* genus. *Bu we leis,* (G), Boy Lice. *Meed Leis,* (G), Girl Lice . . . "Buwe" and "Meed" indicate the shape of the seeds and "Leis" their sticking to the clothing. "Buweleis" includes those species of *Bidens* whose seeds are narrow in proportion to their length. **1924** Lambert *PA Ger. Dict.* 35, *Buwe leis* . . . tickseed, Spanish needles, all species of Bidens whose seeds are narrow in proportion to their length.] **1966–68** *DARE* (Qu. S14, . . *Prickly seeds, small and flat, with two prongs at one end, that cling to clothing*) Infs **PA3,** 162, Bube [bubə] lice; **PA18,** 136, Bube [bubi] lice; **PA44,** Bube [bubi] lice, boy lice—lice that sticks to boys; **PA1,** 53, Buva [buvə] lice; **PA11,** Puber [pubɚ] lice.

bubelicks See **bube**

bubie See **bubeleh**

bubs See **bub** n[2] **1**

buby See **bubeleh**

buccaroo See **buckaroo** n

buche n [Fr *bûche* log] *perh not fully naturalized*

=**backlog 1.**

1967 LeCompte *Word Atlas* 151 **seLA,** Large log burned at back of fireplace . . bûche [used by 6 of 21 infs].

buck n[1], freq attrib [ME *bukke* stag, he-goat] *occas considered taboo, esp in 1*

1 An animal, spec:

a A male sheep. **widespread, but infreq in Sth** See Map Also called **sheep buck**

1812 *Niles' Natl. Reg.* 2.240/1 **cnKY,** The product [of wool] was as follows: A Buck, *(Judas)* 12 lbs. 4 oz. **1852** MI State Ag. Soc. *Trans.* 3.25, Best pen of 5 buck lambs. **1915** *DN* 4.181 **swVA,** *Buck* . . . Ram. *Ram* is considered vulgar. **1916** *DN* 4.388 **neOH,** *Buck* . . . Ram. *Buck* is the usual popular word. *Ram* is well known, but is used more for the scientific term. **1927** *AmSp* 2.349 **wcWV. 1941** *LANE* Map 200 **NEng,** Six informants who offer both *ram* and *buck* say that the latter may be used in all situations, while *ram* is never used in the presence of women . . . Three informants exactly reverse this distinction . . , while another restricts both those terms to men and uses only *male sheep* in the presence of women . . . *Buck* is described as the usual term by . . [9 infs]; as rare by . . [4 infs]. Terms for a castrated male sheep were incidentally recorded in a few cases: . . *buck* [2 infs]. **1947** *PADS* 8.31 **swOH,** *Buck:* Usually *buck sheep.* **1949** Kurath *Word Geog.* 62, *Ram* is current everywhere in the Eastern States as the name of the male sheep, but outside the Southern area *buck* and *buck sheep* occur by the side of *ram,* especially in rural sections. **1954** *Harder Coll.* **cwTN,** *Buck:* taboo for *ram,* which is also taboo. **1965–70** *DARE* (Qu. K63a, . . *A male sheep*) 372 Infs, **widespread, but rare in Sth,** Buck; **CT36, KY64, MI87A, NY24,** Buck sheep; **MI101,** Buck ram; (Qu. K63b, . . *A male sheep that*

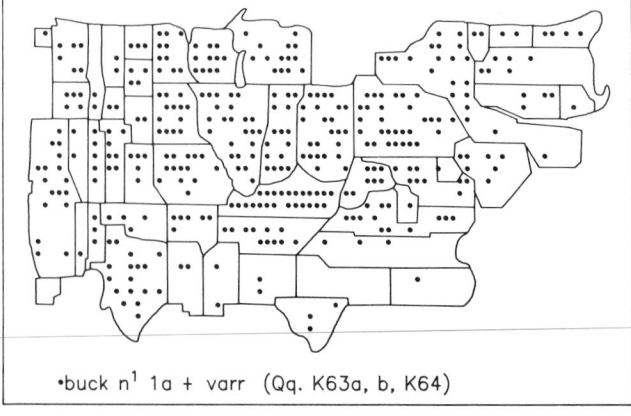

•buck n[1] 1a + varr (Qq. K63a, b, K64)

has been castrated; total Infs questioned, 75) Inf **FL15,** Buck; (Qu. K64, . . *Words used by women or in mixed company for a male sheep;* total Infs questioned, 75) Inf **MS74,** Buck; **NM3,** No special word—just *buck.* [Of all Infs responding to Qu. K63, 44% were comm type 5, 66% male; of the Infs giving the response *buck,* 55% were comm type 5, 74% male; of the 611 Infs giving the std term *ram,* 41% were comm type 5, 63% male.] **1973** Allen *LAUM* 1.248, The dominant term for the male sheep is *ram,* with *buck,* also quite widely distributed, a strong second. The relative frequency is 67% to 45%. In addition 7 scattered instances of *buck sheep* occur. . . Although one eastern Iowa inf. of South Midland background described *buck* as an old-fashioned taboo term, no others expressed any such feeling. It was reported in use by about the same proportion of men as of women. The only contrast in use of *buck* and *ram* seems to be the rural/urban division, as *buck* and *buck sheep* are much more common among rural infs.

b A male goat. **chiefly Nth, Midl** *somewhat old-fash* Cf **buck v¹ B2a**

1869 Brace *New West* 237 **CA,** The Cashmere goat was first imported. . as early as 1846. In the fall of 1861, W. Landrum from a grower in the State of Georgia. **1928** *DN* 6.57 **Ozarks,** The names of male animals must not be mentioned when women are present—such words as . . *buck* . . are absolutely taboo. Some writers think that *buck,* meaning a male goat or deer, is not generally objectionable. . . It is a strange thing, however, that *Buck* is quite admissible when used as a man's given name. **1941** *LANE* Map 200, Some informants use *buck* only of male animals other than sheep: of a male goat . . **[nCT, sRI, eMA],** of a male goat or deer . . **[cCT],** or as a general term including male sheep as well as goats, deer and rabbits . . **[sRI, sME]. c1960** *Wilson Coll.* **csKY,** *Buck* . . . Ram. There seems to be some prejudice against *buck,* much like the avoidance of saying *bull.* Sometimes for male goat. **1965–70** *DARE* (Qu. K67a, . . *A male goat;* total Infs questioned, 75) Infs **FL27, 37,** Buck; **OK43,** Old buck goat; (Qu. K68, . . *A goat that habitually strikes people with its horns*) 13 Infs, **chiefly Nth, N Midl,** Buck; **CT17, KS5, MD26, NY13, 32, 102,** Buck goat; **MD38,** Bad buck. [19 of 23 Infs old]

c *usu* **buck rabbit:** A male rabbit. **chiefly Sth, Midl**

1838 *Knickerbocker* 11.447 **KY,** Your land is so poor, that a single buck-rabbit would make a famine in your whole country. **1841** *S. Lit. Messenger* 7.39/2 **GA,** What the plague then makes her run and *stomp* about the house like a buck-rabbit? **1859** Taliaferro *Fisher's R.* 96 **cVA** (as of 1820s), His eyes looked like a skeered buck rabbit. **1874** Taylor *World on Wheels* 46 **seKS,** Three or four exaggerated creatures lie in a heap in a corner . . . They are ears with bodies to them. It is your first sight of a buck-rabbit. **1878** Pinkerton *Strikers* 318 **sePA,** The train . . [is] called through that locality the "buck-rabbit" train, from the fact that it stops at every little station. **1941** [see **1b** above]. **1965–70** *DARE* (Qu. P30, . . *Wild rabbits*) 9 Infs, **chiefly S Midl,** Buck rabbit; **MS47,** Swamp bucks; **MS89,** Cane buck or buck rabbit. [5 of 11 Infs Black]

d Used as a name for one of a pair of oxen. *old-fash* Cf **bright n 1**

1852 Hawthorne *Blithedale* 120 **eMA,** I discerned Hollingsworth, with a yoke of oxen hitched to a drag of stone . . . "Haw, Buck!" quoth he. "Come along there, ye lazy ones! What are ye about, now? Gee!" **1855** Douglass *My Bondage* 209 **MD,** I was introduced to this huge yoke of unbroken oxen, and was carefully told which was "Buck," and which was "Darby"—which was the "in hand," and which was the "off hand" ox. **1871** Eggleston *Hoosier Schoolmaster* 106 **IN,** They's a right smart sight of defference-ah atwext them air two oxen-ah, jest like they is atwext defferent men-ah . . . Berry-ah jest stands stock still-ah and don't hardly breathe-ah . . . Buck-ah, that ornery ole Buck-ah . . acts jest like some men-ah what is fools-ah. **1907** *DN* 3.241 **eME,** *Buck and Bright* . . . The inevitable names of a yoke of oxen. **1953** Van Wagenen *Golden Age* 42 **ceNY** (as of 1800s), The most common names for oxen were just two, Buck and Bright . . . This usage was surely almost universal over New York and New England . . . The nigh ox was called Buck. **c1960** *Wilson Coll.* **csKY,** Buck and Bawl—names for oxen formerly . . . also *Buck and Berry.*

e A bull or steer—often used in fig phr *since Buck was a calf.* **chiefly Sth** Cf **Hector n**

1952 Brown *NC Folkl.* 1.376, *Proverbial Sayings* . . . Haven't seen you since Buck was a calf. **1966–69** *DARE* (Qu. A16, . . *A very long period of time: "I haven't seen him _____."*) Infs **GA84, NC31,** Since Buck was a calf; (Qu. FF21b, . . *About old jokes*) Inf **LA2A,** I haven't heard that one since Buck was a calf; [(Qu. CC17, . . *Imaginary animals or monsters*) Inf **NC77,** Ole Buck—has a bull's head; said to come out of Trent woods; tell kids that if they weren't good old Buck would get them

at Christmas]. **1966** *DARE* FW Addit **SC,** Buck—bull calf. **1983** *Salt Lake Tribune* (UT) 6 Jan sec C 2/5 **NC,** Old Christmas will be celebrated Saturday at Rodanthe with . . Santa Claus, a dance and the appearance of "Old Buck," a legendary steer that haunts Trent Woods.

f Any of various (usu male) aquatic animals: see quots.

1883 *Century Illustr. Mag.* 4.376/2, Other names have been conferred on account of their pugnacity or voracity, as, tiger, bull, sow, and buck bass. **1931–33** *LANE Worksheets* **RI,** Buck shad—A male shad. Apparently the sex distinction is common. **1955** *Sun* (Baltimore MD) 16 June 16, Distinctive names apply to diamond-back terrapin, too. The male is a "bull" and the female a "cow," of [sic] if young, a "hen." "Buck" and "doe" are also heard. **1967–68** *DARE* (Qu. P1, . . *Fresh-water fish . . that are good to eat*) Inf **SC40,** Buck shad (a male shad); (Qu. P7, . . *Small fish used as bait*) Inf **IN51,** Buck minners; **TX74,** Steel-buck minnow.

g A crab near its molting stage.

1968 *DARE* FW Addit **NYC,** Buck—soft-shell crab, turning hard, forming new shell. **1976** Warner *Beautiful Swimmers* 29 **MD,** The male [crab] grabs the female from above, makes sure that she is face forward, and carries her lightly underneath him with his walking legs for two or three days prior to her moult . . . To the watermen the two crabs are now doublers or a "buck and rider."

2 A male human being, spec:

a also *buck-a-dandy:* A young, dashing, or virile man; a fop. **chiefly Midl, Sth**

1774 (1900) Fithian *Jrl.* 1.89 **VA,** Balantine, either to shew himself a true full-blooded Buck, or out of mere wantonness & pastime turned the Bones . . . into many improper and indecent postures. **1870** Nowland *Early Indianapolis* 148, Mr. Walpole having several daughters in the heyday of life, caused a considerable sensation with the young bucks of the settlement. **1894** *DN* 1.328 **NJ,** *Buck:* a fop. Used contemptuously; "he's a pretty buck, now ain't he?" Also *buck-a-dandy,* with the same meaning. **1903** *DN* 2.308 **seMO,** *Buck* . . . A fashionable young man. Often used as a nickname and considered complimentary. **1908** *DN* 3.295 **eAL, wGA. 1950** *WELS* (*A man with the reputation of running after women*) 1 Inf, **seWI,** Buck. **c1960** *Wilson Coll.* **csKY,** *Buck* (or *young buck*) . . . sometimes any dashing, obvious young man: "Who's that young buck with the rubber-tire buggy?" **1966–70** *DARE* (Qu. HH2, . . *Citified person*) Inf **SC10,** City buck; (Qu. Z12, . . *A small child: "He's a healthy little _____."*) Inf **VA46,** Buck. **1976** Warner *Beautiful Swimmers* 182 **MD,** "Look here," he added, showing me one of his great forearms. "See all those little knots . . . Come from shaft tonging for arsters wintertime. That's real buck work."

b also *bucky:* Used as a man's nickname or familiar form of address. **chiefly Midl**

1840 *S. Lit. Messenger* 6.508/1 **GA,** "Pay for your own slug, buck," said Hopper, snapping down a six-and-a-quarter cent piece on the table. **1843** (1916) Hall *New Purchase* 134 **IN,** Well, Johnny, my buck, I'm willing to talk with Mr. Carlton, or any larn'd man. **1855** Simms *Forayers* 136 **SC,** How are you, old buck, this warm weather? **1899** (1912) Green *VA Folk-Speech* 98, *Buck* . . . The nickname for William. **1902** *DN* 2.230 **sIL,** *Buck* . . . A man's nickname, as 'Buck Sanders.' **1903** *DN* 2.308 **seMO,** *Buck* . . . Often used as a nickname and considered complimentary. **1952** *Sun* (Baltimore MD) 13 Oct 12/7, Perhaps the most purposeless argument ever started in this column is that over the significance of Buck as a nickname for boys . . . a lively lady of nearly 80 years . . doesn't agree that Buck is properly applied only to boys named Charles. Back in the days when she lived on a farm in Prince Georges county, her grandfather called her younger brother "Billy Buck" and the name stuck to him through life. *Ibid* 24 Oct ed. B 18/7, Most of my correspondents and acquaintances seem to have accepted the conclusion that men and boys named Charles (or Charley) have first claim on the nickname "Buck." **1968** *DARE* (Qu. Z5, . . *Nicknames . . meaning "brother"*) Inf **VA2,** Bucky—my boys calls each other bucky when they're playin.

c A Black man, esp a young, strong one—usu considered derog. **chiefly Midl, Sth**

1835 *Vade Mecum* (Phila.) 17 Jan 3/6 *(DA),* A buck nigger is worth the slack of two or three hundred dollars. **1842** *Spirit of Times* (Phila.) 18 April (Th.) *(DAE),* A 'long nine' with a fierce looking buck of a colored fellow hanging to the end of it. **1859** (1968) Bartlett *Americanisms,* A "*buck* nigger" is a term often vulgarly applied to a negro man. Western. **1885** Twain *Huck. Finn* 189 **MO,** There was nigger boys in every tree, and bucks and wenches looking over every fence. **1909** *DN* 3.393 **nwAR,** *Buck* . . . Formerly, a fop; now applied almost exclusively to male

negroes as the opposite of *wench.* **1966–70** *DARE* (Qu. HH28, . .
Nicknames . . for people of foreign background) Infs **OH42, SC69,**
Negro: buck; (Qu. H74a) Inf **GA3,** Strong as a buck nigger. **1971** Landy
Underground Dict., Buck . . . Virile young Black male. Term used by
whites and considered derogatory by Blacks.

d An Indian man—usu considered derog. **chiefly West**

1836 (1934) Ford *Summer* 298 **CO,** The Buck Indians ride along in
company, or seat themselves in the shade, and send the squaws home to
have something prepared to eat by the time they arrive. **1859** (1942)
Patterson *Travel Diary* 161 **West,** Several of the [Cheyenne Indian]
"bucks" have been crossing the stream—swimming their horses—and
trading. **1878** Beadle *Western Wilds* 242, We found another party of
Pueblos on a general spree. One able-bodied "buck" was staggering
along the street, his wife after him. **1903** White *Forest* 204 **MI,** In the
stern sit two or three bucks wearing shirts, jean trousers, and broad black
hats. **1936** Barnard *Rider* 61 **OK,** We cowpunchers had no use for the
boomers. They came into our country, plowed up good grass, and started
to nesting and working like the devil. Even the buck Indians did not
work! **1966–67** *DARE* (Qu. HH28, . . *Nicknames . . for people of
foreign background*) Inf **AZ6,** Navajo Indian: blanket buck; **WA13,**
Indian man: buck.

e freq with *old:* An old man—often considered derog. **Nth, N
Midl** *somewhat old-fash; esp among women*

1940 Stong *Hawkeyes* 184 **IA,** Old Joseph Smith, who seems to have
been a fair sort of old buck, except for his insistence on making his
lechery legal. **1950** *AmSp* 25.87 **OR,** In central Oregon, *buck* is the
regular term for anyone who herds cattle. Experienced hands refer to
themselves as 'old bucks' or occasionally 'waddies' and reserve *cowboy* as
a somewhat contemptuous description of transient workers on cattle
ranches. A student described the help employed during fall roundup on
her father's ranch as 'three old bucks and some cowboys.' **1965–70**
DARE (Qu. HH40, . . *Uncomplimentary words for an old man*) 12 Infs,
scattered Nth, N Midl, Old buck; **MD28, MI28, 108, MT1, NV7,
PA130, RI6,** Buck; (Qu. X48b, . . *If a person is not so young any more . . ,*
"He's . . . .")* Inf **PA136,** An old buck; (Qu. AA23, . . *Joking names
that a woman might use to refer to her husband: ". . My* . . . .")* Inf
MO36, Old buck. [14 of 19 total Infs were women; 15 of 19 were old.]

f A rustic or countrified person. Cf **buckwheat 5**

1959 McAtee *Oddments* 4 **cNC,** Buck . . . hillbilly. **c1960** *Wilson Coll.*
csKY, *Buck* (or *young buck*) . . . Hillbilly or smart-alec. **1966** *DARE*
(Qu. HH1, . . *Rustic or countrified person*) Inf **NC9,** Country buck.

g in phr *son of a buck(er):* See quots. **scattered west of Appalachians** See Map *euphem*

1950 *WELS* (*Humorous substitutes for stronger exclamations: "Why
the son of a* . . . . *!"*) 2 Infs, **WI,** Buck. **1965–70** *DARE* (Qu. NN24,
. . *Humorous substitutes for stronger exclamations: "Why the son of a*
. . . . *!"*) 23 Infs, **scattered west of Appalachians,** Buck; **LA45,** Gun,
bucker, buck. [Of all Infs responding to this question, 13% were young,
50% male; of those giving this response, 29% were young, 75% male.]

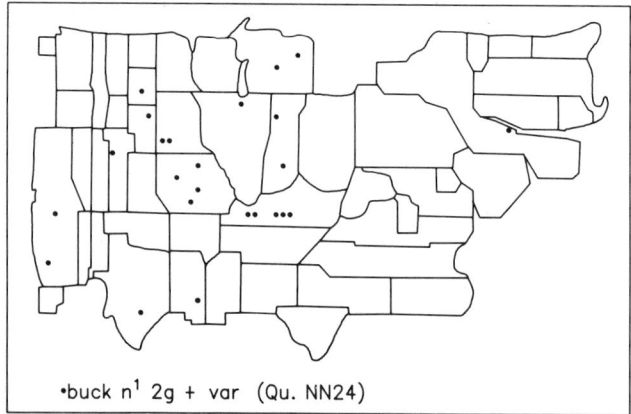

•buck n¹ 2g + var (Qu. NN24)

h A man (in contrast to a woman). Also transf: a men's toilet.
See also **buck v¹ A6** Cf **doe**

1909 Ware *Passing Engl.* 52/1, *Buck* or a *doe* (Anglo-Amer.). A man or
woman, obviously from the habit and mode of thinking by backwoods'
men . . . 'It's kinder rough to rattle 'em along like freight in this way
(coffined, dead), but where you ain't got no plantin' facilities of yer own
it's got to be done. Was the lamented a buck or a doe?'—1883. **1960**

Partridge *Slang* 426, *Buck* or *Doe.* Man or woman . . . [Derived from]
the backwoods—[first recorded in] 1830. **1967** *DARE* (Qu. M21b, . .
Joking names for an outside toilet building) Inf **CO38,** Does and bucks
—two separate buildings. **1981** *DARE* File **West,** In some restaurants,
especially steak houses with Western themes, the men's and women's
restrooms are labeled *Bucks* and *Does* or *Stallions* and *Heifers.*

3 Money. [Abbr for *buckskin* a deerskin formerly used as a unit
of exchange] Note: except as indicated below, *buck* as referring
to money is widespread and occurs freq within all social groups.

[**1826** Biggs *Narrative* 19 **sIL,** McCauslin then sent for the interpreter,
and the indians asked 100 Buckskins for me, in merchandize . . . the
indians then went to the traders houses to receive their pay, they took but
seventy bucks worth of merchandize at that time.]

a usu *the bucks* or *big buck(s):* A large amount of money;
wealth. **?esp N Cent, Upper MW**

1942 Berrey–Van den Bark *Amer. Slang* 377.5, *Make a fortune* . . . get
(up) in the bucks *or* (big) money. *Ibid* 467.1, *Money.*—the bucks.
1948 Fredric Brown *The Dead Ringer* 1 (*DAS*), Everybody was in the
bucks. **1950** *WELS* (*Words for money in general:* "He's certainly got
_____.") 5 Infs, **WI,** (The) bucks; (*Expressions about someone who
has plenty of money*) 4 Infs, **WI,** In the bucks. **1965–70** *DARE* (Qu.
U19a, . . *Money in general:* "He's certainly got the_____.") 9 Infs, **esp
N Cent, Upper MW,** Bucks; **NJ48,** Buck, loot, cash; **MO14,** Dough; few
bucks; (Qu. U37, . . *Words . . about somebody who has plenty of money*)
Inf **IL58,** Loaded; got the bucks; **MI44,** In the bucks; loaded; **NY249,**
He's in the big buck bracket; (Qu. CC11, *When somebody has had a lot of
good luck, you say he_____*) Inf **IA13,** He's been in the bucks; **WI59,**
Is in the bucks. **1972** Butler *The Big Buck and the New Business Breed*
[title]. **1979** *Natl. Rev.* 25 May 659/1, The recent wave of campaign
reform legislation has succeeded in removing the big buck from national
politics. **1981** *Monona Community Herald* (WI) 30 Sept 4/1, Roadside
billboards are ugly—a scar on our beautiful Wisconsin countryside. It's
pollution by anyone's standards. And it's big bucks too!

b A dollar bill. *widely used but esp freq among young and
middle-aged Infs*

1965–70 *DARE* (Qu. U26, . . *Nicknames . . for a paper dollar*) 315 Infs,
widespread, Buck; 25 Infs, **scattered,** One buck; **IL48,** Paper buck. [Of
all Infs responding to the question, 33% were young or mid-aged; of those
giving these responses, 45% were young or mid-aged.]

c A silver dollar. **chiefly west of Appalachians** See Map

1965–70 *DARE* (Qu. U27, . . *Names for a silver dollar*) 58 Infs, **chiefly
west of Appalachians,** Buck; 10 Infs, Silver buck; **PA94,** Hard buck;
TN52, One buck. [Of all Infs responding to the question, 71% were old;
of those giving these responses, 90% were old.]

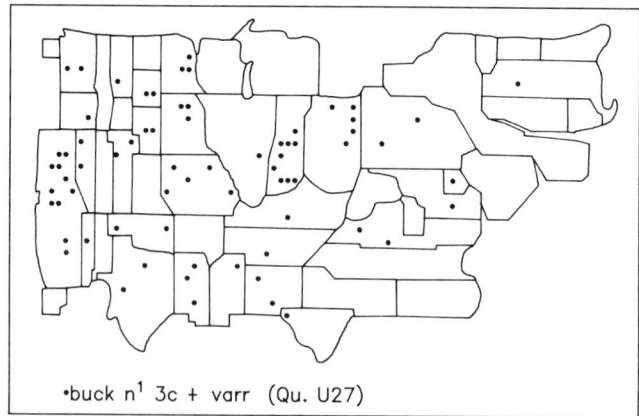

•buck n¹ 3c + varr (Qu. U27)

d as *half (a) buck:* A fifty-cent piece.

1965–70 *DARE* (Qu. U24, . . *A fifty-cent piece*) 143 Infs, **widespread,**
Half a buck; 15 Infs, **scattered,** Half buck. [Of all Infs responding to the
question, 50% were men; of those giving these responses, 68% were men.]

4 also *buckstand, buckhorse:* A device to hold wood for sawing.
chiefly Nth, N Midl exc Rocky Mts, NW See Map Cf **sawbuck**

1816 in 1817 Paulding *Letters from South* 1.189 **NY,** He bought himself
a buck and saw, and became a redoubtable sawyer. **1848** Bartlett
Americanisms 393, *Buck.* A frame or stand of peculiar construction on
which wood is sawn for fuel. In New England it is called a *saw-horse.*
1939 *LANE* Map 162, (*Sawbuck*) 1 inf, **cMA,** Buck; 1 inf, **csCT,** Sawing
buck. **1949** Kurath *Word Geog.* 59, *Saw buck, wood buck,* sometimes

simply *buck,* are characteristic of the entire German settlement area in Eastern Pennsylvania, upper reaches of the Potomac in West Virginia, and on the Yadkin in North Carolina. **1950** *WELS ([Device) to hold wood when you're going to saw it)* 2 Infs, WI, Buck [X-shaped ends connected by a bar]. **1965–70** *DARE* (Qu. L59, . . *An implement with an X-frame to hold firewood for sawing)* 33 Infs, **chiefly Nth, N Midl,** Buck; **GA**16, **IA**43, Wood buck; **CT**6, 17, **MI**101, Buckhorse; **NJ**50, Buckstand; (Qu. L58, . . *An implement with an A-shaped frame that you put boards on to saw them)* Infs **IL**108, **MI**93, **NC**41, Buck. **1967** LeCompte *Word Atlas* 153 **seLA,** *Wooden device to hold logs for sawing . . .* buck horse [1 of 21 infs]. **1973** Allen *LAUM* 1.221 **Upper MW,** *Sawbuck (for firewood) . . .* Buck [2 infs] *. . .* Wood buck [3 infs].

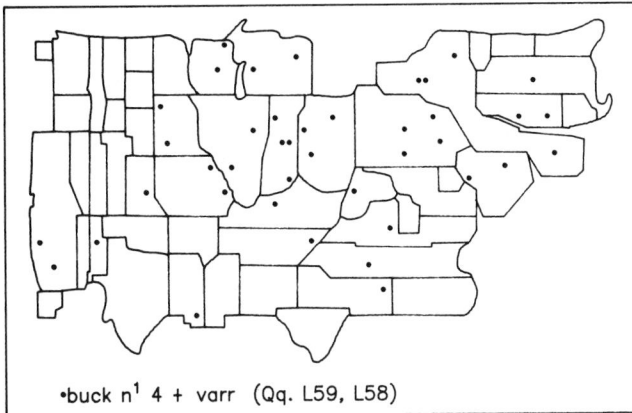

•buck n¹ 4 + varr (Qq. L59, L58)

5 See quot. Cf **buck v² 3, buck adj**
   1958 McCulloch *Woods Words* 208 **Pacific NW,** *Water buck*—Anybody carrying water to a crew.

6 See quot. [Perh abbr for **bucket,** but see **2h** above] Cf **bakkie, buck v¹ A6**
   1967 Cerello *Dakota Co. MN* 47, *Buck . . .* The toilet— "When we were young children we were taught to say buck instead of the word toilet . . . Mother always told us to say buck because it was not so crude." Common.

7 also *buck tie:* See quots. Cf **buck v¹ B6a**
   1951 Grant *Cowboy Encycl.* 34, Buck Tie. A method of tying up a prisoner in the old West. The wrists were lashed together, the hands and arms passed over the knees and a rifle or stick shoved between the joints of the knees and elbows. **1968** Lester *To Be a Slave* 36 (as of c1850s), My master used to throw me in a buck and whip me. He would put my hands together and tie them. Then he would strip me naked. Then would make me squat down. Then he would run a stick through behind my knees and in front of my elbows. My knee was up against my chest. My hands was tied together just in front of my shins. The stick between my arms and my knees held me in a squat. That's what they call a buck.

8 See **buckskin 1.**
9 See **bucks.**
10 See **buck fence.**
11 See **buck euchre.**
12 See **buck-and-wing** n.

buck n², also attrib [**buck v¹ A1a**]
1 Usu of a horse: the act of bucking; the power to buck. **West**
   1877 Bartlett *Americanisms* 71 **TX,** A correspondent of the "Chicago Tribune," writing from Texas, . . writes . . . "The *buck* consists of the mustang's springing forward with quick, short, plunging leaps, and coming down stiff-legged, with his head between his forelegs, and as near the ground as possible." **1883** Sweet–Knox *Mexican Mustang* 69 **TX,** If there had been any buck in them, it would have developed itself at an early stage in the journey. **1890** L.C. D'Oyle *Notches* 34 *(DA),* In two months from now the worst 'buckers' amongst them will not have a 'buck' left in them. **1891** *Harper's Mag.* 83.206/2 **West,** After a series of bucks, more or less severe, during which his spurs go time and again into the pony's flanks, the mastery is established where it properly belongs. **1922** Rollins *Cowboy* 132 **West,** There might be at the base of the saddle's horn a "buck strap," which was a loop that offered a convenient hand-hold during pitching. **1929** [see **buck v¹ A1b**]. **1944** Adams *Western Words* 22, This buck consists of long jumps straight ahead without any twists. **1961** Adams *Old-Time Cowhand* 311, A "buck hook" is a blunt-nosed, up-curved piece added to the frame of the spur

and used to lock in the cinch or in the side of a plungin' hoss, and of course is barred at rodeos.
2 See **buck buck 1.**
3 A pile of hay. [**buck v¹ B7;** cf *EDD buck* sb.¹¹ a fork-load of peas from the field or rick]
   1967 *DARE* FW Addit **ceOR,** Buck load of hay— 500–1000 pounds of hay. After it's bunched, it's picked up with a hay buck. **1973** Allen *LAUM* 1.185 **SD, NE,** *A small pile of hay in the field . . . haybuck* [2 infs] probably reflect[s] the large-scale hayfarming operations of the western prairies, where it is not uncommon for huge rakes or sweeps to bunch hay into large piles, each of which is large enough to be a buck or load on a haywagon. *Ibid* 186, Supplementing the fieldwork lexical items are . . *buckpile,* three times . . . Comment: *. . hay buck:* Larger than a bunch . . . A buck, or load, in each pile *. . pile:* Larger than a 'shock'; piled by a hay buck.
4 See **buck rake** n.

buck n³ [Abbr for *buckhorn knife,* formerly used as a token in poker; see quot 1938 at **2a**]
1 Responsibility.
   1947 *Sat. Eve. Post* 8 Mar 148/3, It puts the buck squarely up to the newspaper publishers, who are, after all, the men who print the leakage. **1962** Steinberg *Man from MO* 246 (as of 1945), One of [President] Truman's assistants said that he developed a mania for making decisions and was unhappy when there were none to render at the moment. On his desk he placed a three-sided gadget with the motto: *The buck stops here.*
2 usu in phr *pass the buck:*
a To shift or avoid responsibility or commitment; hence *buckpassing* (also attrib), *buck passer.*
   1912 W. Irwin *Red Button* 341 *(DA),* The Big Commissioner will get roasted by the papers and hand it to the Deputy Comish, and the Deputy will pass the buck down to me, and I'll have to report how it happened. **1924** *DN* 5.289, *Buck,* in *to pass the buck . . .* To shift responsibility. **1933** *New Republic* 76.37/1, [Heading:] *Some Expert Buck-Passing.* **1933** E. Cunningham *Buckaroo* 110 *(OEDS),* 'Why, you lying buckpasser!' cried Dud, indignantly. [**1938** Asbury *Sucker's Progress* 27, The picturesque custom of using a buck . . originated on the Western frontier during the late 1860's or early 1870's. The buck could be any object, but was usually a knife, and most Western men in those days carried knives with buckhorn handles, hence the name. As first used, the buck simply marked the deal . . . a player who didn't wish to deal was permitted to ante and "pass the buck."] **1948** *Dly. Ardmoreite* (Ardmore Okla.) 29 Apr. 14/6 *(DA),* So far, this has turned into something of a buck-passing game. **1965–70** *DARE* (Qu. II32, . . *To manage . . to shift the responsibility: "He said it wasn't his fault and tried to _____.")* 367 Infs, **widespread,** Pass the buck; **MO**21, Pass the buck on; **MS**1, Pitch the buck; **MS**21, Jump the buck; **CA**87, Buck-passer; [**NY**40, Pass the bucket]; (Qu. A16, . . *When somebody takes too long about coming to a decision, you might say, "I wish he'd quit _____.")* Inf **FL**21, Passing the buck; (Qu. BB27, . . *When somebody pretends to be sick often to get out of doing something . . he's _____)* Inf **CA**137, Passing the buck; **MO**29, Gold-bricking; passing the buck; (Qu. II31) Infs **NH**10, **NY**219, Pass the buck; (Qu. JJ45, . . *When someone avoids giving a definite answer: "We tried to pin him down, but he just kept _____.")* 12 Infs, **chiefly SC coast, Nth,** Passing the buck.
b To converse informally. Cf **chew the rag**
   1967–68 *DARE* (Qu. II12, . . *Meeting somebody on the street and speaking only a few words with him: "We just _____.")* Inf **CO**17, Spoke; passed the buck; **MD**36, Passed the buck; said a couple words; (Qu. KK13, . . *Words for arguing: "They stood there for an hour _____.")* Inf **AR**52, Chewing the fat; passing the buck.
‡c To die. Cf **buck n⁷**
   1966 *DARE* (Qu. BB56, . . *Joking expressions for dying: "He _____.")* Inf **MS**10, Passed the buck.

buck n⁴ [Perh from Engl dial *buck* the liquid in which cloth is boiled in bleaching] **S Atl** Cf **beer 1**
Fermented mash used as an alcoholic drink or cooked in a still to make moonshine.
   1933 Rawlings *South Moon* 91 **FL,** The boy was prowling around the wooden barrels of mash . . . "You git out o' there, Lant!" Piety spoke sharply. "You'll spile your Uncle Zeke's buck." "That un't hardly buck yit, Py-tee. Hit's slow, like. Hit ain't made a cap yit and hit's 'most due to run." . . Zeke dipped a gourd in one of the barrels of seething mash. "You want some o' the beer, Lulu?" **1938** Matschat *Suwannee*

R. 135 **GA,** Freeman was busy skimming the boiling syrup . . cane beer, with a sweet-sour taste, would be made from the fermented skimmings and, later, would form excellent "buck" for a wildcat still. **1940** *Sat. Eve. Post* 6 Apr 55 **seGA, neFL,** Occasionally he'd drink a gourd of cane buck . . . [He] wondered if the buck made him say what he said then. **1966–70** *DARE* (Qu. DD21c, . . *Illegally made whiskey*) Inf **FL**52, Shine, home brew, buck; (Qu. DD25, . . *Nicknames . . for beer*) Inf **FL**7, Swill (covers buck, i.e. homemade beer); **GA**19, Buck (beer moonshine is made from); **GA**26, Corn buck—beer that is made into moonshine; **GA**30, Buck—corn beer before moonshine is distilled; **NC**49, Buck— out of a barrel before it is ready to run; (Qu. DD28a, . . *Liquor other than beer, wine, or whiskey*) Inf **FL**7, They make good cane buck around here; **SC**26, Persimmon buck (beer); (Qu. DD28b, . . *Fermented drinks . . made at home*) Inf **FL**7, Beer, corn buck, mulberry wine; **FL**34, Buck— homemade beer; **FL**52, Buck—grapes and yeast; very local; **GA**7, Corn buck: corn, sugar, meal fermented—not distilled; **GA**26, Corn buck.

buck n⁵ [Engl dial *buck* the body of a cart or wagon] Cf **buckboard**

1881 *Harper's Mag.* 62.786/2 **NY,** The "buck" is a more modern word to describe the long plank attached to runners—a device which was developed from the old custom of holding the small single sleds together in a train.

buck n⁶ Also *buckhead* [*EDD buck* sb.⁷ 3, a hook or ring for attaching the trace to a plowbeam]

A clevis; a ring for attaching a farm implement to a clevis.

1942 Faulkner *Go Down* 293 **MS,** That chronicle . . compounded was the entire South . . that slow trickle of molasses and meal and meat, of shoes and straw hats and overalls, of plowlines and collars and heel-bolts and buckheads and clevises. **1970** *DARE* FW Addit **VA**38, Buck—a clevis; common.

‡**buck** n⁷ [Abbr for **bucket**] Cf **buck** n³ 2c

1966 *DARE* (Qu. BB56, . . *Joking expressions for dying:* "He _____.") Inf **MS**71, Kicked the buck.

buck v¹, hence *bucking* vbl n [From **buck** n¹, infl in some senses by *butt* v]

A Intransitive.

1a Usu of a horse: to leap upwards, arching the back and descending with the forelegs rigid and the head held low. **chiefly West** Cf **bucking** vbl n¹, attrib

1869 *Overland Mth.* 3.127, A mustang is generally any thing in the world but "religious," for he will both "sull," (have the sulks) and "buck." **1869** McClure *3000 Miles* 302 **MT,** The native horses become singularly skilled in "bucking," and there are few riders who can keep the saddle or make them yield to the lines. **1883** Sweet–Knox *Mexican Mustang* 681, The majority of Texas ponies buck, or pitch as it is sometimes termed. **1902** *DN* 2.230 **sIL. 1907** *DN* 3.221 **nwAR. 1962** Atwood *Vocab. TX* 56, When a bronc wants to dislodge the rider, he is usually said to *pitch* . . or to *buck. Ibid* 101, Other distinctions that are given by only a few informants probably also reflect nothing but the feeling that different words should have different meanings; that, for example, . . a horse *bucks* by using his back feet and *pitches* with all four (or vice versa). **1971** Bright *Word Geog. CA & NV* 170, To rear / of a horse trying to throw the rider / . . buck 86% [of infs] . . . Front and back legs.

b in var phrr: See quots.

1929 *AmSp* 5.65 **NE,** If the "pony" jumps forward with each "buck" or "pitch," it "pitches a plungin'," does a "sunning buck," or "bucks straight way." **1937** *DN* 6.619 **swTX,** If the horse eschews *pioneer bucking* and does all his pitching in one spot, he is described as *bucking on a dime.* **1944** Adams *Western Words, Bucking on a dime*—Said when a bucking horse does his bucking in one spot . . . *Buckin' straight away*—This buck consists of long jumps straight ahead without any twists, whirling, or rearing, an easy horse for some to ride, yet poison for others. Straight-away buckers are usually big and strong and rough in their actions.

c Of a person: to move jerkily or erratically.

1869 Brace *New West* 204 **CA,** There was a woman and child inside the coach who commenced *bucking* so, and there ain't none of them passengers as ever have pistols. **1872** in 1952 *AmSp* 27.76 **CA,** The spasmodic and futile capering and "bucking"—to use an expression peculiar to California—of a headless, demoralized and undisciplined rabble. **1966** *DARE* (Qu. BB11, . . *A deep cough that you can't get rid of:* "Listen to him _____.") Inf **AL**4, Cough, buck, snort.

2 To charge (an obstruction), to meet head on, to push; also fig.

1856 in 1901 Allen *Life Phillips Brooks* 1.151 **MA,** I am beginning to buck into Hebrew. **1870** in 1872 Schele de Vere *Americanisms* 327 **TX,** You'll have to buck at it like a whole team, gentlemen, or you won't hear the whistle near your diggings for many a year. **1921** Paine *Comr. Rolling Ocean* 106 *(DA),* A good many of the boys seem to look up to you as a sort of leader since we bucked through that big gale of wind. **1945** *AmSp* 20.147 [Army slang], *Buck.* To study or cram for a test. **1948** *Time* 10 May 23/1, Favorite Son Martin had run a poor third behind Harold Stassen (whose backers had bucked hard for him) and Tom Dewey. **1950** *WELS* (To force your way through: "I had to _____ through a big crowd to get here.") 1 Inf, **cwWI,** Buck. **1967** Fetterman *Stinking Creek* 74 **KY,** I walked all the way down there with the frost bucking up between my toes.

3 To resist.

1857 *San Francisco Call* 21 May 3/1 *(DA),* A great many gamblers left. They think it hardly worth while to 'buck' against the present law prohibiting the pursuit of their 'science.' **1906** Canfield *Diary Forty-Niner* 81 (as of 1851), Anderson has been asked to deliver the oration and although he bucked at first he finally accepted. **1948** *Lawton* (Okla.) *Constitution* 2 July 2/3 *(DA),* As the possessor of superior wisdom, he bucks the bi-partisan foreign policy, embodied in the European Aid Program. **1966–68** *DARE* (Qu. JJ23, . . *To refuse to give in or yield:* ". . I _____.") Inf **NC**45, Bucked; (Qu. JJ24, . . *To refuse firmly:* ". . I _____.") Inf **NC**37, Bucked; (Qu. KK11, . . *To make great objections . . "When we asked him to do that, he _____."*) Inf **IN**5, Bellyached; bucked; balked; **IL**5, Bucked like a bay steer. **1969** *DARE* Tape **CA**137, I just bucked against that, I said nothin' doing.

4 with *for:* To strive diligently for something, esp for recognition or advancement. *esp in military use*

1881 in Hayes *Guiteau* 73 *(DA),* I was bucking very strong for the job. **1944** *Sun* (Baltimore MD) 29 Nov 3/6–7 *(Hench Coll.),* "Well," he said, "I bucked for a job back at the rear echelon today." **1948** *AmSp* 23.77 [Army slang], 'Bucking' referred to activity to attract favorable notice, although 'Bucking for a Section Eight' meant conduct designed to lead to a discharge. **1956** U.S. Air Univ. *Air Force Dict., To buck for,* to exert oneself for something, as for a promotion. *Slang.* **1967–69** *DARE* (Qu. II20a) Inf **NC**76, Bucking for a raise; (Qu. II33) Inf **MO**11, Bucking for promotion. **1978** *DARE* File **csWI,** So, you're bucking for Associate Professor, eh?

‡**5** To yield, bend. [Perh abbr for *buckle*]

1966 *DARE* (Qu. JJ23, . . *To refuse to give in or yield:* ". . I _____.") Inf **SC**11, Didn't buck.

6 See quot. Cf **bakkie, buck** n¹ 6

1967 Cerello *Dakota Co. MN* 47, Buck . . . Go to the toilet—"It was a common thing when we were youngsters to say, 'Please excuse me, but I must go and buck' . . . I don't rightly know why I still use the term buck for going to the toilet, but I guess it just sounds more polite." Common euphemism.

B Transitive.

1 often with *off:* To throw or dislodge by bucking (see **A1a** above); also fig. **scattered, but esp west of Missip-Ohio Valleys**

1871 *Atlantic Mth.* 28.570/1 **CA,** [The colt] had "nearly bucked her to pieces." **1885** Harte *Maruja* 101 **CA,** "I'll bet he don't buck his saddle off with me on it," said the Doctor, grimly. **1948** *Time* 10 May 24/2, His own Republican state legislature bucked off every reform proposal like an unbroken pony with a burr under the saddle. **1956** *Hench Coll.* **VA,** A farmer was showing us some slab wood he had gotten for us for our fire place. Some of it was large and heavy, the kind we wanted. About one extra large piece, "It will buck you, lifting that log," he said. **1965–70** *DARE* (Qu. OO30a, . . *A horse throwing the rider:* "John got a bad horse and was _____.") 63 Infs, **scattered, but esp west of Missip-Ohio Valleys,** Bucked (off); **MA**42, Bucked him off; **IL**114, Throwed; thrown; buck; (Qu. OO30b, . . *"Last week the same horse _____ (his brother)."*) 16 Infs, Bucked; **AR**52, **CA**28, **IN**25, **MI**94, **WA**30, Bucked off; **CA**23, 131, **MI**98, **NY**9, Bucked him off. [Of all Infs responding to these questions, 64% for each question were male; of those giving these responses, 75% for Qu. OO30a were male, 72% for Qu. OO30b were male.] **1971** Bright *Word Geog. CA & NV* 169, [In context *he fell off the horse,*] (got) bucked off [was used by 10% of the infs].

2 To move or act against, spec:

a To butt, move against with the head.

1859 (1968) Bartlett *Americanisms, To Buck.* Used instead of *butt,* applied to animals pushing with their head and horns, and metaphorically of players at football and such games, pugilists, etc. **1861** *Harper's*

Mag. 23.276/1 **MA**, Mr. Fusilbury . . . was in a dream of philosophy, bucking a lamp-post. **1909** Ware *Passing Engl.* 52/2, *Bucking match (Negro).* Fight with heads . . . "Stacey appeared to be the more belligerent of the two, insisted on having the quarrel out, and challenged Kline to fight him without fists or weapons. This is the usual manner among Philadelphia negroes to denominate a 'bucking match', which is not an infrequent method of settling disputes." **1910** *DN* 3.452 **seVT**, *Buck* . . . To butt. Used especially of sheep and goats. **1911** Davies *Football* 122, Emrich takes the ball and bucks the Army's centre for a touchdown. **1939** [see **bucker** n[1] 1]. **1965–70** *DARE* (Qu. K68, . . *A goat that habitually strikes people with its horns)* 18 Infs, **chiefly Nth, N Midl**, Bucking goat; MI23, Buckin' ram. [18 of 19 Infs old]

b To fight the elements.

1883 *Colo. Springs Republic* 31 Dec. 2/2 *(DA)*, Trainmaster Downey has been bucking snow . . . since Saturday night, and has not succeeded in getting through with his four engines yet. **1902** McKee *Land of Nome* 145 **AK**, The *Jeannie,* a steam-whaler, specially fitted to "buck" the ice, was the only vessel known to have discharged its passengers and freight at Nome. **1956** U.S. Air Univ. *Air Force Dict., Buck* . . . Of airplanes or aircrews: To fly into, against, or through rough *weather, gunfire,* or the like. *Slang.* **1966** *DARE* Tape MI21, Bucking wind in a boat.

c Fig: to work in opposition to, fight against, resist.

1902 Lorimer *Letters* 32 **IL**, Jim's father had a lot of money till he started out to buck the universe and corner wheat. **1907** Mulford *Bar-20* 154 **West**, I won't buck the cavalry, but I'll keep it busy huntin' for me. **1929** *Publishers' Weekly* 115.2456/2 **MA**, It is wasted time and energy to try to buck any legitimate movement, and I think it is time and energy wasted for you men to attempt to buck the book clubs. **1948** *Time* 12 Apr 26/1 **cwMO**, If they bucked the machine, they were liable to personal harm. **1966–70** *DARE* (Qu. JJ23, . . *To refuse to give in or yield: " . . I _____."*) Infs NJ16, NC13, TX102, Bucked him; (Qu. II19) Inf NJ8, Buck him.

d in var phrr: See quots.

1900 *DN* 2.24 **NJ, PA, NYC**, *Buck* . . . In phrase 'to buck society,' to call on a lady. **1928** *AmSp* 4.68, Many of these men [=stage-hands] carry *cards* (Union membership certificates), some have *permits,* or short time cards, but most are *bucking the extra board,* and may be *bumped,* if a *card-man* applies for work. **1930** Irwin *Amer. Tramp, Buck.*—To oppose; to contend with. In railroad circles, one "bucking the board" is working as an extra employee, being paid only when taking the place of a regular employee on leave, or when work is heavy. **1960** Criswell *Resp. to PADS* 20 **MO**, Buck the board of trade—to speculate on the Kansas City wheat market. Many local men lost their shirts this way about sixty years ago. Never hear the term now.' **1968** *DARE* (Qu. JJ26, *If somebody has been doing poor work or not enough, the boss might say, "If he wants to keep his job he'd better _____."*) Inf MN15, Buck the line; toe the line.

3 To flush (game).

1969 *DARE* (Qu. P39a, *When a hunter or a dog finds a game animal and makes it start running you'd say he _____ it.*) Inf KY53, Bucked.

4 To push, spur on.

1897 Flandrau *Harvard Episodes* 158 **MA**, He wanted Sears Wolcott on the Signet [club] . . . His best motives for wishing to "buck" Sears in were hardly formulated in his own mind. **1969** *DARE* (Qu. Y5, . . *To urge somebody to do something he shouldn't: "Johnny wouldn't have tried that if the other boys hadn't _____."*) Inf MO19, Bucked him into it.

5a To bet or lose (money) in gambling; to play or gamble against. **chiefly West**

1851 Hooper *Widow Rugby's Husband* 20 **AL**, No matter how I make an honest rise, I'm sure to 'buck it off' at farrer. **1851** in 1922 Clappe *Shirley Letters* 121 **CA**, Little John was then at the Humboldt betting, or, to speak technically, "bucking" away large sums at monte. **1914** *DN* 4.162 **NW**, *Buck* . . . To struggle stubbornly against. "He bucked the roulette wheel all that morning. **1916** *DN* 4.320 **KS**, Buck the tiger . . . To enter upon any hazard with a purpose to win. Also *buck the game.* **1948** *Sat. Eve. Post* 10 July 74/3 **NV**, Professional gamblers will not buck a new game until they have carefully studied the layout and have assured themselves that it is on the level.

b spec, in phr *buck the tiger:* To play against the faro bank. **chiefly West** *hist* Cf **tiger** the game of faro

1859 *Police Gazette* 12 Mar. 4/4 *(DA)*, A third amused the company by informing them as to the luck he had had that day 'bucking the tiger.' **1888** Ferguson *Experiences* 136 **CA** (as of 1850), I ought perhaps to balance the foregoing instance by relating another a little more cheering,

on account of the tender age of one who boldly "bucked the tiger." **1907** Mulford *Bar-20* 91 **SW**, I calculates as how me an' him'll buck th' tiger for a whirl—he's shore lucky. **1938** Asbury *Sucker's Progress* 15, *Bucking the tiger*—Playing Faro. **1943** *AmSp* 18.7. **1944** Adams *Western Words, Bucking the tiger*—Playing faro. During the early days the professional gambler of the frontier carried his faro outfit in a box upon which was painted the picture of a Royal Bengal tiger. Tigers were also pictured upon his chips and oilcloth layout, and the game became known as the *tiger.*

6a usu in phr *buck and gag:* See quot 1909. *hist* Cf **buck** n[1] 7

1848 *Protestant Monitor* (Alton, Ill.) 24 May 3/1 *(DA)*, A man is not considered a soldier until he . . . has been bucked and gagged once or twice. **1851** *Sacramento Transcript* 26 Mar. *(DA)*, Jackson was sentenced to be bucked, receive forty-five lashes, and have his head shaved. **1864** Pittenger *Daring & Suffering* 228, The guards came up, and seizing Pierce, . . and tying his hands before his knees, with a stick inserted across under his knees and over his arms, in the way that soldiers call "bucking," they left him there all night. **1868** Goss *Soldier's Story* 47, To punish him for his attempt at escape, he was "bucked." **1909** *DN* 3.393 **nwAR**, *Buck* . . . To tie the wrists together, draw the knees up between the arms, and put a stick over the arms and under the knees. If the person thus bucked is also gagged he is quite helpless and for that reason thieves and robbers sometimes *buck and gag* anyone interfering with them. **1942** Kennedy *Palmetto Country* 67 **FL** (as of mid 19th cent), Besides flogging, there was the "buck-and-gag" method of punishing slaves, whereby they were doubled about a hoe, shovel, or board, and left to lie in the hot sun.

b also *buck-paddle:* To lay a person across a log or other object in preparation for paddling or flogging; to beat a person thus positioned. Cf **board** v

1879 (1880) Tourgée *Fool's Errand* 80 **NC**, "Is the rest of the incident true,—that about dragging the ministers from the pulpit, bucking them across a log, and beating them?" "Well, I heard afterwards that they did break up the meeting, and give the preachers a little brushing. They might have bucked 'em across a log; more'n likely they did: it's a powerful handy way to larrup a man." **1955** Warren *Angels* 57 **KY**, God-durn you, Jack, you let that gal hang herself and I'll buck-paddle you—I'll sell you down-river.

c To haze; spec, to swing a child against a stationary object or another child. **chiefly S Midl** Also called **bump** v 1, **rambutt**

1890 *DN* 1.63 **KY**, *Buck* a fellow: to take a boy and swing him against a tree. **1900** *DN* 2.24 **TN** [College slang], *Buck* . . . 1. To haze. **1909** *DN* 3.393 **nwAR**. **1939** Harris *Purslane* 202 **NC**, Most of the children scampered away, intent on exploring the woods, hunting sweet gum, wading in the water, and bucking the boys that needed it. **1946** *PADS* 6.7 **eNC**, *Buck* . . . To tame a tough or mommock a small boy by seizing his arms and legs and banging his fundament against the fundament of another boy or against a tree or wall. It takes two "initiators" to do the bucking. Pamlico. Common among boys.

7a To gather hay, esp with a **buck rake.**

1950 *WELS (What do you do to hay in the field after it has been cut?)* 1 Inf, **cwWI**, Rake with side delivery or dump rake into winrows; buck with buck rake; load onto hay rack with loader. **1966–68** *DARE* (Qu. L11, *What do you do to hay in the field after it's cut?)* Inf MN15, Rake it into winrows; buck it together (go down winrows till rake gets full); stack it; SD8, Buck it—with a farm hand, put into cocks. **1969** O'Connor *Horse & Buggy West* 219 **AZ**, The hired man drove a buck rake. This had either three or four horses and they "bucked" or pushed a much larger and heavier rake in front of them to put into stacks the rows of hay I had raked up.

b To lift or push (esp bales of hay or sacks of grain produce). Cf **bucker** n[1] 5

1950 *AmSp* 25.87 **OR**, As a verb, *buck* means . . to carry objects, especially sacks in connection with combining wheat . . . in common use. **1967** *DARE* (Qu. L15, . . *Putting hay into a building for storage)* Inf MO18, Bucking bales. **1981** *DARE* File **eOR** (as of 1920s), A sack "bucker" or sack "buck" . . drove a team around the harvested field picking up the sacks of wheat . . which were dropped from a "chute" on the combine in batches of five. He picked up the sack and "bucked" or pushed it up to the level of the load where he deposited it. If stationary combined, the sack sewer took the sack . . sewed it, tipped it up on his knee, bucked the sack to the sack pile again. *Ibid* **sID** (as of 1960s), A friend of mine spent his summers working on a farm, where one of the most tedious but physically demanding tasks was bucking bales—"tossing" them from the truck to the barn.

8 To conceive a child. Cf **buck up** v phr **4**
1931–33 *LANE* Worksheets **NH**, Bucked a child by so and so.

9 In marble play: see quot. Cf **bunk** v[1] **3b**
1958 *PADS* 29.30 **WI**, Buck . . . To bounce a marble against a wall in the attempt to hit other marbles placed in a line below it.

10 See quot. Cf **A4** above
1968–70 *DARE* (Qu. II20b, . . *A person who tries too hard to gain somebody else's favor: "He's always trying to _____ the boss."*) Infs **FL**48, **PA**162, Buck.

buck v[2], hence *bucked* ppl adj and *bucking* vbl n, also attrib [**buck** n[1] **4**]

1 To saw logs into sections, freq with the aid of a **buck** n[1] **4** or *bucksaw*; to cut wood. **chiefly Nth**
1870 *Phila. Press* 8 Jan. *(DAE)*, [The] Pennsylvanian does not saw wood; he 'bucks' it. **1889** (1971) Farmer *Americanisms*, Buck . . . A frame into which a saw is fixed for sawing wood . . . The operation of cutting-up wood with this instrument is called *bucking*. **1927** *DN* 5.440. **1939** *LANE* Map 162 **MA**, [2 infs]. **1942** *AmSp* 17.220 **Nth**. **1949** Peattie *Cascades* 161 **Pacific NW**, Down the hill the felled trees lay in packed windrows. There single sawyers and axmen bucked the trees into logs and chopped the limbs away. **1956** *AmSp* 31.149 **nwCA**. **1958** McCulloch *Woods Words* **Pacific NW**, Buck . . . To cut trees into logs . . . *Buck for grade*—To cut a tree into *various* log lengths to produce the greatest quantity of high grade material, as opposed to butchering the tree into *equal* lengths regardless of grade . . . *Bucked*—Logs cut up in the woods; mostly called felled and bucked. **1967** *DARE* Tape **WA**20, Timber was bucked into logs in the woods; **WA**24, They buck them [=felled trees] in two. **1967–68** *DARE* FW Addit **NY**98, We'll probably have to buck that [fallen tree] up this afternoon; **WY**5, I bucked them [=trees] down, let them lay in a few years, then burned them; **WA**, Buckin' wedge—wedge to hold wood from clamping up on the saw. **1975** Gould *ME Lingo*, Buck—To cut a felled tree into pulpwood and cordwood of four-foot lengths . . . In the mill yard the former *bucking* is done by power saws and is now called *slashing*. The tool used for *bucking* is the bucksaw.

2 To pile logs. Cf **buck** v[1] **B7**
1918 *DN* 5.54 **WA**, Buck . . . To pile up logs. **1968** Adams *Western Words*, Buck . . . To pile logs. **1969** Sorden *Lumberjack Lingo* **NEng, Gt Lakes**, Buck . . . To yard felled trees in the woods.

3 To bring or carry, esp wood or water. Cf **buck** n[1] **5**
1905 U.S. Forest Serv. *Bulletin* 61.31, Buck . . . To bring or carry, as to buck water or wood. [General] **1968** *DARE* Tape **CA**100, Buck water —carry water via horses or donkeys (in the logging camps). **1968** Adams *Western Words*, Buck . . . To bring or carry, as *to buck water*.

buck v[3] [Engl dial *buck* to wash]
To wash (something): see quot.
1949 Webber *Backwoods Teacher* 104 **Ozarks**, Women . . sheared a few sheep every June and "bucked" the wool clean at the creek, and carded it, as they did their cotton, by hand.

buck v[4] Cf **bunk** v[1] **2**, *DJE* **buck 5**
To meet accidentally, bump into.
1904 (1916) Porter *Freckles* 78 **cnIN**, If you was to buck into Mr. McLean in your prisint state, without me there to explain matters the chance is he'd cut the liver out of you.

buck adj, also absol [**buck** n[1] **2, 5**]
Of the lowest grade in a military rank.
1918 Witwer *Baseball to Boches* 109, Here I am nothin' but a buck private, and I been in the army goin' on four months! **1922** *Ardmore* (Okla.) *D. Press* 14 Jan 1/5 *(DA)*, The former leather-necks, gobs, bucks, shavetails, etc., had finally taken their places. **1930** *AmSp* 5.382 (as of 1914–18), *Buck*. Short for buck private. A soldier without any rank. **1956** *AmSp* 31.227, *Buck general* is a brigadier general, lowest in the group of generals. **1956** U.S. Air Univ. *Air Force Dict.*, Buck private. The lowest military rank, immediately below private first class . . . *Buck sergeant*. The lowest grade of sergeant, immediately above corporal and immediately below staff sergeant.

buck a bull off the bridge v phr Also *buck (or butt) the bull ~*
To meet the most difficult challenge or perform the most difficult task.
1916 *DN* 4.342 **seOH**, *Buck a bull off of the bridge*. To feel well; e.g. "I can buck a bull off of the bridge." **1946** *PADS* 6.35 **eNC**, To butt the *bull* off the bridge. (To do wonders, according to the speaker.) **1949**

Hench Coll., An English teacher at Randolph Macon College, Ashland, Va., (who grew up in Norfolk, Va.) . . talking about the courses he is teaching . . said: I thought I'd bucked the bull off the bridge when I put into our English courses a course in Chaucer; but [another teacher in another college] goes even further and teaches some Middle English.

buckache n [Alter of **buck ague**, infl by *ache*]
=**buck fever 1**.
1965 *DARE* (Qu. P36, *When a hunter sees a deer . . and gets so excited he can't shoot, he has _____*) Inf **MS**1, Buckache; buckitis.

buck-a-dandy See **buck** n[1] **2a**

buck ague n Also *buck ager(s)* [**buck** male deer + **ague**]

1 =**buck fever 1**. **chiefly W Midl, Gulf States** See Map Also called **ague B3** Note: *buck ager(s)* is esp freq among speakers with little formal educ, *buck ague* among speakers with some coll educ.
1844 (1846) Kendall *Santa Fé Exped.* 1.173 **TX**, I underwent a severe attack of the "buck-ague" while on the little hunting excursion . . in plain English . . I was too nervous even to hit a barn door at twenty steps. **1851** *S. Lit. Messenger* 17.46/1 **VA**, It is not every one who can stand and look upon large game, in momentary expectation of shooting;—the heart thumps harder, the throat parches, . . there is an undoubted case of *Buck-ague*. **1898** Lloyd *Country Life* 14 **AL**, That old home feelin would creep up like a buck ager and then wear off about the same way. **1903** *DN* 2.308 **seMO**, *Buck-ague* (often buck-ager). **1906** *DN* 3.129 **nwAR**, Buckager(s). **1908** *DN* 3.295 **eAL, wGA**, *Buck-ager*. **1923** *DN* 5.200 **swMO**, *Buck ager* . . . Nervousness or excitement induced by eagerness to bag game or to excel in marksmanship or in other sport. **1929** Ellis *Ordinary Woman* 97 **CO** (as of early 1900s), She cautions him to be sure and get it in the head, so as not to spoil the meat, calling to us to stay out of range of the gun; then she helped him corner the pig. He drew a bead on it, and let go. Afterward Mama said Henry had 'buck ague'; anyhow, he got the pig in the leg. **1933** Willoughby *Alaskans All* 146, An instant's 'buck ague,' a single quiver of the arm, and there would have been a wounded beast in the boat. **1941** Stuart *Men of Mts.* 144 **neKY**, I took the buck-eggers. The shootin' was so fast . . I got too excited. **1950** *WELS* 1 Inf, **cWI**, Buck ager. **1965–70** *DARE* (Qu. P36, *When a hunter sees a deer . . and gets so excited he can't shoot, he has _____*) 68 Infs, **chiefly W Midl, Gulf States**, Buck ager(s); 20 Infs, **chiefly W Midl, Gulf States, NW**, Buck ague; **WV**7, Buck ['eɪgɪ]; (Qu. BB28, . . *Imaginary diseases*) Inf **IL**17, Buck ager. [Of all Infs responding to Qu. P36, 28% had grade school educ or less, 26% had coll educ; of those giving the responses *buck ager(s)*, 49% had grade school educ or less; of those giving the response *buck ague*, 45% had coll educ.]

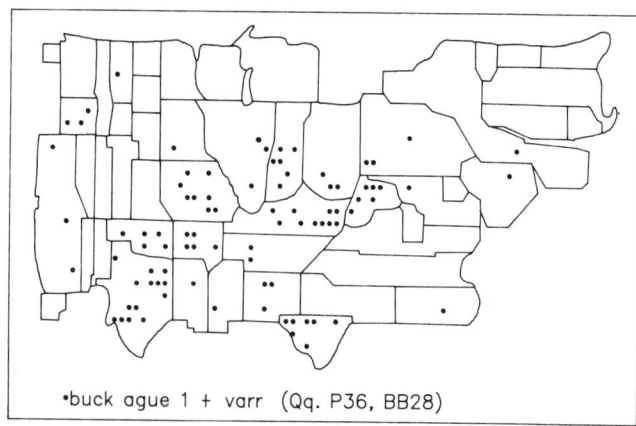

•buck ague 1 + varr (Qq. P36, BB28)

2 =**buck fever 2**.
c1915 in 1966 *AN&Q* 4.121 **IL**, So this assurance of ease begetting riches affected him deeply and it was not long before he had developed an ailment akin to what hunters term 'buck ague.' . . a . . lapse from self control. **1943** Cohn *Love in America* 179 **MS**, Any afternoon on Madison Avenue . . one is likely to see more pretty women in an hour than one would in a week in Paris, while the visiting Englishman, fresh from the land of big feet and teeth to match, suffers buck-ague as he walks. **c1960** *Wilson Coll.* **csKY**, Buck ague (or ager) . . . Fright when trying to shoot a deer; transferred to any other nerve-racking time.

3 =**ague B1**. **Midl**
1906 *DN* 3.129 **nwAR**, Buckager(s), bucks . . . Severe chills with fever. "I've ben havin' the buckagers." **1960** Hall *Smoky Mt. Folks* 60 (as of

1937), *Buck-aggers*: chills and fever. **1965–70** *DARE* (Qu. BB13, . . *Chills and fever*) Infs **IN**33, **OK**42, Buck ager; **AL**4, **IL**14, **MS**59, **TX**39, Buck agers. [All Infs old]

buckalew bird n
=red-throated loon.

1951 *AmSp* 26.90, The cognomen *buckalew bird* has been reported from New Jersey, as from the cries of the loon, but the name *Baccalieu bird,* applied to various species that nest on the Newfoundland isle of that name, may have been transferred southward and restricted to this species *[Gavia stellata].*

buck and billy n [*EDD buck* sb.[3] 3 the 'driver' used by players in the games of 'buckstick,' 'spell and knur' + alter of *billet* piece of wood]
=cricket n[2].

1901 *DN* 2.137, *Buck-and-billy* . . . Name of a game, practically the same as *pussy* [a game with a bat and a block of wood] . . the pussy is called the "billy," the bat the "buck." Rome, N.Y.

buck-and-wing n, also attrib Also *buck (dance)* [From var dance steps: see quot 1968; abbr form perh infl by **buck** n[1] **2c**] widely known, but used esp Sth, S Midl See also **cut the buck 1**
A lively dance usu performed by one person: see quot 1968.

1840 *Spirit of the Times* 2 May 103/2 *(OEDS),* The extra clearing in turn for the finishing buck dance. **1895** *N.Y. Dramatic News* 23 Nov 13/4 *(DA),* Burt Jordan, an exceedingly agile buck and wing dancer, was a hit at Keith's last week. **1902** Lorimer *Letters* 177 **IL,** Get something that won't keep people guessing whether you follow the horses or do buck and wing dancing for a living. **1907** Mulford *Bar-20* 158 **SW,** In the center of the room was a large man dancing a fair buck-and-wing to the time so uproariously set by his companions . . . as though his life depended on speed and noise. **1945** Saxon *Gumbo Ya-Ya* 240 **LA** (as of a1863), The slaves were often summoned to the Big House to sing and dance the buck and wing for guests. **1967–69** *DARE* (Qu. FF5a, . . *Steps . . in dancing—in past years)* Inf **AL**50, Buck; also buck-'n'-wing; **DE**3, Buck-and-wing dancing—a form of tap dancing; **MA**40, Buck-'n'-wing dance—a stage dance; **NJ**57, The buck-and-wing; **NC**49, **SC**31, 32, 34, Buck dance. **1968** Stearns *Jazz Dance* 191, The word *Wing* was used to describe a combination known as Buck and Wing—the general designation for tap dance (and almost anything else) at the turn of the century. Introduced on the New York stage in 1880 by James McIntyre, the Buck and Wing began to swing—unlike the Clog, which preceded it—and launched a new style of Negro-derived dancing. As it surfaced in those days, the Buck was close to a Time Step and the Wing was a simple hop with one foot flung out to the side. **1977** Nevell *Time to Dance* 170 **sAppalachians,** The choreographer of the buckdance is the instinct of the buckdancer, and the length of the dance is dependent upon the individual's energy.

buck-and-wing v
To dance the **buck-and-wing.**

1926 Ferber *Show Boat* 25, She . . roamed the streets of strange towns alone; learned to strut and shuffle and buck-and-wing from the Negroes whose black faces dotted the boards of the Southern wharves as thickly as grace notes sprinkle a bar of lively music.

buck-ankled adj Cf buck-kneed
1969 *DARE* (Qu. X37, . . *People's legs if they're noticeably bent, or uneven, or not right)* Inf **GA**84, Buck-ankled.

buckaroo n, also attrib |ˌbəkəˈru, ˈbʌkəˌru| Also *buckeroo, buccaroo, buckaree, bucker;* formerly *baccaro, ba(c)quero, bakhara, buccahro, bucharo, buckhara, buckayro, bukkarer* Note: esp in the early forms the second syllable is stressed. [Alter of Span *vaquero* cowboy. For an extended discussion of the etym and forms, see *AmSp* 17.10–15, 35.51–55, 53.49–51, 54.151–53] chiefly West, esp Pacific
One who herds cattle or breaks wild horses; a cowboy.

1827 in 1858 Dewees *Letters TX* 66, These [=rancheros] are surrounded by . . peons and bakharas, or herdsmen. **1847** (1850) Colton *3 Yrs.* 206 **cwCA,** Our baccaros. **1847** in 1950 *AmSp* 25.87 **OR,** *Bacquero.* **1861** in 1942 *CA Folkl. Qrly.* 1.270 **Desert SW,** Bucharos—men who herd stock, and perform other duties on a stock ranch. **1862** Winthrop *John Brent* 21 **CA,** Bukkarer. **1873** Perrie *Buckskin* 172 **CA,** A large stock of cattle . . had been in the charge of five good trusty *Buccahros* or herdsmen. **1889** *Century Dict.,* Bucker . . . [Abbr. of *buckayro* . . .] A cowboy . . . Western U.S. **1890** Farmer–Henley

Slang, Buckhara . . . A name given in California to a cattle-driver or cowboy. **1907** White *AZ Nights* 51, If you were going to be a buckeroo, you couldn't go into harder training. **1910** Hart *Vigilante Girl* 60 **nCA,** I can talk what they call 'buckayro' Spanish. It ain't got but thirteen words in it, and twelve of them are cuss words. **1913** *DN* 4.26 **NW,** *Buckaroo* . . . A broncho buster, cowpuncher, cowboy. **1919** *DN* 5.54 **Pacific NW,** *Buckaree* . . . Vacquero. Around Pasco, Walla Walla and Pendleton, Oregon, Thomas was considered some buckaree. Port Angeles Tribune–Times. **1922** Rollins *Cowboy* 39, In Oregon he [=the cowboy] frequently was called "baquero," "buckaroo," "buckhara," or "buckayro," . . each subject to be contracted into "bucker." **1925** *AmSp* 1.152 **West,** Buccaroo. **1934** Weseen *Dict. Amer. Slang* 93, Buckaree—A cowboy, especially in the Southwest . . . Buckeroo—A cowboy of the Spanish-California type; a bronco buster. *Buckaroo* is a variant. **1937** *DN* 6.619 **MT,** Buckaroo. **1962** Atwood *Vocab. TX* 53, *Buckaroo . .* supposedly a widely used western term, has never caught on in Texas. **1967–69** *DARE* (Qu. H47, . . *Kinds of fried potatoes)* Inf **NV**1, Buckaroo potatoes—fry bacon first; slice raw potatoes and onion; add a little butter; add water and simmer; (Qu. H49, . . *Dishes made by boiling potatoes with other food)* Inf **CA**136, Buckaroo stew; mulligan stew; (Qu. I20, . . *Kinds of beans)* Inf **OR**13, Buckaroo beans; (Qu. L1, . . *A man who is employed to help with work on a farm)* Infs **CA**31, **NV**2, Buckaroo. **1971** Bright *Word Geog. CA & NV* 193, Cowboy—cowboy 81% [of informants] . . buckaroo 16% . . vaquero 7%. **1978** *AmSp* 53.50, Buckaroo . . . The first-syllable vowel is *a* through the first half of the nineteenth century . . . Thereafter, *u* comes in and all forms begin with /bək/. **1981** *KS Qrly.* 13.65, *Buckaroo . .* the preferred term for "cowboy" in northern Nevada and adjacent parts of the Great Basin ranching country.

buckaroo v [buckaroo n] chiefly NW
To work as a cowboy.

1967 *DARE* (Qu. L1, . . *A man who is employed to help with work on a farm)* Inf **OR**10, Ranch hand (cattle and buckarooing); farm hand (working the ground); (QR p75) Inf **NV**1, Started to buckaroo—to be a cowboy. **1967** *DARE* FW Addit **OR,** He buckarooed out—he ran cows out of the town. **1969** *DARE* Tape **CA**163, Out there at Eagle Lake . . is an old cow camp that's always been in my family . . [it was] headquarters for camping and we'd go out there buckarooing during the year while the cattle were out there grazing.

buck-ass naked See buck naked

buck bathing pple, vbl n, also attrib [Cf buck naked] C Atl coast
Nude swimming.

1931 *Atlantic City News* 7 Aug. 4/3 *(DA),* Devotees of 'buck bathing' who dance in the nude in and out of the surf are also unwelcome in Brigantine. **1934** Hench Coll. **VA coast,** "Buck bathing" is the name for bathing naked. Sometimes a group of people, usually older persons, married couples that know each other well, go bathing at night, naked. This is called buck-bathing. Others, more frank and bold, go buck-bathing in secluded spots even in the day. **1937** *Ibid,* Nowadays if a party of people go bathing absolute naked, it is called buck-bathing. Examples: We had a buck-bathing party last night. Let's go buck-bathing. **1957** Battaglia *Resp. to PADS 20* **eMD,** *(Without any clothes on at all: "They went in swimming _____.")* In the raw (buck bathing). **1968** *DARE* (Qu. W20, . . *No clothes on . . "There was Johnny, _____.")* Inf **NJ**24, Buck bathing.

buckbean n
1 Std: a bog plant *(Menyanthes trifoliata)* of Europe and North America. Also called **bitterroot 3, bogbean, buckberry 2, marsh trefoil, water shamrock**
2 =false lupine.

1915 (1926) Armstrong *Western Wild Flowers* 246, Golden Pea. Buckbean. *Thermopsis montana* . . . The erect, straight pods, two or three inches long, are silky. **1963** Craighead *Rocky Mt. Wildflowers* 102, Buckbean . . . is sufficiently unpalatable to game and livestock to thrive when more palatable plants on the same range are heavily overgrazed. **1973** Hitchcock–Cronquist *Flora Pacific NW* 273, *Thermopsis* . . . Buck-bean; Golden-pea; Golden-banner.

buck beer n [Alter of bock beer] Cf buck n[4] old-fash or obs
=bock beer.

1859 (1968) Bartlett *Americanisms,* Buck Beer. (German, *bock bier.*) The strongest kind of German beer, said to be so called from causing the drinker to caper like a goat *(bock).* **1869** *New No. West* (Deer Lodge,

Mont.) 13 Aug 3/1 *(DA),* His 'buck' beer is the delight of Teutonic bibulists. **1872** Schele de Vere *Americanisms* 142, Whilst *Lager*beer is so weak that judicial proof has been brought into a Court of Justice of its inability to intoxicate a man even when several gallons have been drunk, the *Buck*beer, on the contrary, is one of the strongest made in Germany, and hence represented by a he-goat, from which it derives its name, and whose effigy may be seen in countless *beer saloons* all over the country. **1881** Nye *Bill Nye & Boomerang* 37 **WY,** He looked like the man who first discovered and introduced Buck beer into the country.

buckberry n

1 Any of var shrubs: **bear huckleberry 1,** a **deerberry** (here: *Vaccinium stamineum*), **maleberry,** or **coralberry 1** (here: *Symphoricarpos orbiculatus*).

1824 (1979) Doddridge *Notes Indian Wars* 86 **WV,** An indifferent kind of fruit, called buckberries, used to grow on small shrubs . . . This fruit has nearly vanished from the settled parts of the country. **1894** *Jrl. Amer. Folkl.* 7.93, *Andromeda ligustrina, . .* seedy buckberry, West. Va. **1920** Stephens *Life at Laurel* 14, Such substitutes as nature . . is able to plant in Kansas—sumach and buckberry [etc]. **1960** Vines *Trees SW* 948, It is also known under the vernacular names of Coralberry, Snapberry, Buckberry [etc]. **1965–70** *DARE* (Qu. I44, . . *Berries . . grow wild around here*) 10 Infs, **chiefly S Midl,** Buckberries. **1966** Wilson *Coll.* **csKY,** Buck berry. **1969** *DARE* FW Addit **KY**65, Buckberry—a small caney shrub that spreads quickly in fields. It has small red berries that are eaten by birds.

2 =**buckbean 1.**

1966 *DARE* Wildfl QR Pl.169 Inf **WA**15, Buckberry.

‡buckberry road n Cf huckleberry train

1970 *DARE* (Qu. N37, *Joking names for a branch railroad that is not very important or gives poor service*) Inf **KY**80, Buckberry road.

buckboard n, also attrib [buck n⁵]

1 also *buck wagon, bucking board:* A wagon having a platform fastened directly to the axles or bolsters with a seat above it; orig the board constituting the platform. **widespread, but less freq in Sth, S Midl** See Map

1839 Hoffman *Wild Scenes* 1.10 **neNY,** Did he ever see a teamster riding upon a buckboard? a stout, springy plank, laid upon the bare bolsters of a waggon! **1864** (1873) Webster *Amer. Dict.,* Buckboard, Buckwagon. **1883** M.F. Sweetser *Summer Days* 126 *(DAE),* The buckboard which . . . some one else calls 'a cross between a see-saw and a hammock,' is the favorite vehicle for driving parties. **1896** *DN* 1.413, *Buckboard:* Place—Monroe Co., Pa. This word means a light, four-wheeled vehicle that has, in place of a body, a number of narrow elastic wooden slats on which a seat is placed with or without springs under it. If it has a top it is called a "covered buckboard." In Frederick Co., Md., this word means the front running part of a vehicle with a broad, stout, elastic board fastened into it in such a way that the rear end of the board is somewhat elevated. On this the driver sits and rests his feet on the axle, enabling him easily to mount or dismount. It is used almost entirely for breaking horses. The description of "buckboard" given above applies to a vehicle in Frederick Co., Md., called a "buck-wagon," and is used largely by butchers in hauling meat, calves, sheep, etc., around the country. **1909** *DN* 3.393 **neOK,** *Buck wagon . . .* Sometimes applied to the vehicle known by the trade name of *buckboard.* **1932** *AmSp* 7.163 **NE** (as of 19th cent), To many of these towns, especially the "inland towns," mail was brought by a "buck board star route," a route over

which the mail carrier drove in a "buck board," a light buggy which took the place of the earlier "stage" or "mail stage." **1950** *WELS* (*Kinds of horse-drawn vehicles still used in your neighborhood—to carry light loads*) 5 Infs, **WI,** Buckboard; (*Kinds of horse-drawn vehicles still used in your neighborhood—to carry people*) 2 Infs, **WI,** Buckboard. **1965–70** *DARE* (Qu. N41c, . . *Horse-drawn vehicles to carry light loads*) 208 Infs, **widespread, but less freq in Sth, S Midl,** Buckboard; **NY**216, Buck wagon; (Qu. N41a, . . *Horse-drawn vehicles . . to carry people*) 70 Infs, **chiefly Nth, Pacific,** Buckboard; **NY**219, Buckboard wagon; **MI**49, Buck wagon—buggy without any top on it; **ND**3, Bucking board—two people; (Qu. L42, *What kind of thing do you call a "rig"?*) Infs **MA**68, **MI**71, **WI**51, Buckboard.

2 A type of sleigh. Cf **buck sled**

1966–67 *DARE* (Qu. N40a, . . *Sleighs . . for hauling loads*) Inf **PA**55, Buckboard; (Qu. N40b, . . *Sleighs for carrying people*) Inf **MI**36, Buckboard—two-seater, high front. [Both Infs old]

3 See quot. Cf **DS** EE31

1949 *AmSp* 24.106 **seSC,** Buckboard . . . Joggling board.

buckboard herring See bucky n 1

‡buckboard prospector n

1940 FWP *Guide NV* 59, A buckboard prospector (he usually has an auto now) is the fellow who does his prospecting almost entirely from the seat of his vehicle.

buck-born naked See buck naked

buckbrush n, also attrib esp West Cf buckbush

1 Any of var shrubby browse plants.

1874 Long *Wild-Fowl* 179 *(DAE),* He may find good shooting, . . . when the buck-brush is so close that the boat cannot be easily pushed through it. **1903** *DN* 2.350 **CO,** Buck-brush . . . Coarse brush. **1932** *DN* 6.226 **West,** *Brush.* This is the almost invariable word in the West for low growth, whether in woodland or open; *the brush* is the common form . . . *Buck-brush, sagebrush,* and *brushwood* are common compounds. **1949** Peattie *Cascades* 179, Throughout the West it is customary to designate many known and all unknown brush species as buckbrush or snowbrush. There is no reason to it, nor is there intended to be; buckbrush in one locality will be snowbrush in another, and vice versa. **1958** McCulloch *Woods Words* **Pacific NW,** Buckbrush—A doggone nuisance when cruising timber or running a line or hunting for corner posts. Any kind of brush for which a better name is lacking. **1967** *DARE* (Qu. S26a) Inf **MO**18, Buckbrush. **1967** *DARE* Tape **OR**13, Buckbrush—a mountain plant; deer feed on it.

2 By ext: an area of such plants.

1981 *KS Qrly.* 13.65, *Buck brush . .* an assorted and usually tangled area of shrubs and brush.

3 Any of var other shrubby plants as:

a A **snowberry,** esp *Symphoricarpos occidentalis* and *S. orbiculatus.*

1894 *Jrl. Amer. Folkl.* 7.90, *Symphoricarpus occidentalis, . .* wolf-berry, buck-brush, W. Neb. **1920** *Torreya* 20.25, *Symphoricarpos occidentalis . . .* Buckbrush . . N. Dak. **1937** *Ibid* 37.100, *Symphoricarpos* sp. . . buck-brush, deerberry, Missouri. **1965** Weaver *Native Vegetation* 29 **NE,** There are three species; the one with purplish fruits . . . has several names, coralberry, Indian currant, and buck brush. **1976** Dodge *Roadside Wildflowers* 70, Sometimes called buckbrush, the shrubs are numerous in foothill canyons above 5,000 feet from west Texas and Colorado to Nevada [and] Arizona . . . *Symphoricarpos oreophilus.*

b A **deerweed 1** (here: *Lotus scoparius*). **CA**

1897 Parsons *Wild Flowers CA* 152, *Deer-Weed. Wild Broom . . .* is known as "deer-weed" and "buck-brush," as both deer and stock are said to feed upon it and flourish, when pasturage is scarce, though they rarely touch it when other food is plenty.

c Any of several western spp of **ceanothus.** For other names of these spp see **California lilac, chamise 2, chaparral B1, deer brier, deer brush, greasebush, hornbrush, mountain lilac, Oregon tea tree, snowbrush, soapbloom**

1911 Jepson *Flora CA* 255, *C. cuneatus . . . Buck Brush.* Rigid divaricately branched shrub of a gray-blue hue, 5 to 8 ft. high. **1940** *Jrl. Mammalogy* 21.388 **CA,** This farm was originally covered with such plants as . . buck brush *(Ceanothus cuneatus).* **1966** *DARE* Wildfl QR Pl.126 Inf **WA**10, Buckbrush if pink; strictly laurel or mountain balm if white. **1973** Hitchcock–Cronquist *Flora Pacific NW* 290, *Ceanothus* L. Buckbrush; Buckthorn; Ceanothus; Wild-lilac.

d A **cliffrose** (here: *Cowania mexicana*).

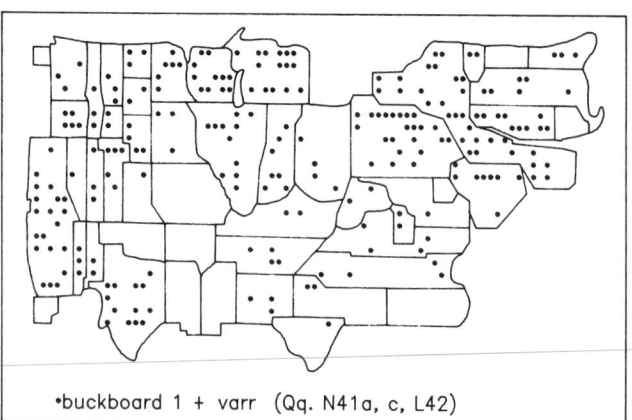

•buckboard 1 + varr (Qq. N41a, c, L42)

1913 (1979) Barnes *Western Grazing* 61 **Rocky Mts,** The buck brush (Cowania mexicana), also called quinine bush, . . and sages, all furnish a large amount of excellent forage for sheep, cattle, goats and horses. 1968 Abbey *Desert Solitaire* 24 **seUT,** The cliffrose is practical as well as pretty. Concealed by the flowers at this time are the leaves, small, tough, wax-coated, bitter on the tongue—thus the name quinine bush—but popular just the same among the deer as browse when nothing better is available—buckbrush.

e =**buttonbush 1.**

1920 *Torreya* 20.25, *Cephalanthus occidentalis* . . . Buckbrush, Reel-foot Lake, Tenn.; Peruque, Mo.

f A **forestiera** (here: *Forestiera pubescens*).

1926 *Torreya* 26.6, *Adelia pubescens* . . . Buck-brush, Graham Mts., Ariz.

g =**mountain mahogany.**

1931 U.S. Dept. Ag. *Misc. Pub.* 101.43, Mountain-mahogany is somewhat cumbersome . . but the great weight of popular usage is overwhelmingly in its favor. Numerous other . . local names for these shrubs include . . buckbrush, deer brush [etc]. 1941 FWP *Guide UT* 21, Also called "buck brush" the latter [=mountain mahogany], related to the true mahogany, is of value as a browsing brush for deer.

h A **bitterbrush 1** (here: *Purshia tridentata*).

1931 U.S. Dept. Ag. *Misc. Pub.* 101.52, *Bitterbrush (Purshia tridentata)* . . . as well as numerous other western shrubs, is frequently called buckbrush. 1967 *DARE* Wildfl QR Inf **OR**12, Bitter brush—also *buckbrush,* because bucks eat it.

i A **cinquefoil** (here: *Potentilla fruticosa*).

1931 U.S. Dept. Ag. *Misc. Pub.* 101.55, *Bush cinquefoil* . . known locally also as buckbrush . . is a much-branched, often sprawling, shreddy-barked shrub.

j =**squaw apple.**

1931 U.S. Dept. Ag. *Misc. Pub.* 101.66, *Squaw-apple (Peraphyllum ramosissimum)* . . . is of an almost innumerable series of western shrubs called buckbrush.

k =**wolfberry** (here: *Lycium* spp).

1931 U.S. Dept. Ag. *Misc. Pub.* 101.142, *Wolfberries (Lycium spp.)* . . . are common and characteristic and a wealth of vernacular names has been bestowed upon them, including . . buckbrush.

l =**chuparosa 2.**

1931 U.S. Dept. Ag. *Misc. Pub.* 101.144, *Thurber anisacanth* . . known locally as buckbrush, honeysuckle, and taparosa, grows 1½ to 5 feet high.

m A **honeysuckle** (here: *Lonicera utahensis*).

1931 U.S. Dept. Ag. *Misc. Pub.* 101.147, *Utah honeysuckle* . . known locally as big buckbrush . . is a low thin-leaved shrub.

n Either of two birches: **dwarf birch** (here: *Betula nana*) or **scrub birch.**

1955 U.S. Arctic Info. Center *Gloss.* **AK,** Buckbrush . . . A Canadian and Alaskan term applied to 'dwarf arctic birch,' 'dwarf' or 'bog birch,' and 'buffalo-berry.'

o A **buffalo berry** (here: *Shepherdia argentea*).

1955 [see **buckbrush 3n**].

p A **spirea.**

1967 *DARE* Wildfl QR Pl.93a, 94a Inf **WA**30, Buckbrush.

q A **saltbush** (here: *Atriplex canescens*).

1967 *DARE* Wildfl QR (St. John) Inf **OR**12, Four-winged saltbush—locally, a *buckbrush. Buckbrush* applies to many local brushes eaten by wild game.

4 attrib: Backwoods, unsophisticated.

1953 *Jrl. Amer. Folkl.* 66.339 **Ozarks,** The respectable townspeople regarded the vagaries of the "buckbrush parsons" as a joke.

buck buck n

1 also *buck; buck, buck, how many . . up; bucket(t)y buck:* A game usu in which one player climbs another's back and requires that person to guess the number of certain objects out of sight; rarely *buck* a player in the game. [See quot 1969]

1899 Champlin *Young Folks' Games* 120, *Buck,* a game played by two person [sic], one of whom places his arms across his breast, or rests them on his knees, and bends forward, resting his head against a fence, tree, or wall. This is called "giving a back." The other player sits astride the back of the first, and holding up one or more fingers, says, "Buck, Buck, how many horns do I hold up?" . . The "buck" is sometimes blindfolded, and a third person often acts as umpire, to see that there is fair play . . . In

another form of the game, a child hides his head in another's lap, and the latter says: "Mingledy, mingledy, clap, clap, clap, / How many fingers do I hold up?" 1949 *AmSp* 24.314 **cVA,** The game . . *mummly, mummly, buck* is known elsewhere. It has been played . . in central Virginia for three generations . . . The name for it there is *bucketty buck* . . . The words of the version that I know are: Bucketty buck, bucketty buck, / How many fingers do I hold up? 1957 *Sat. Eve. Post Letters* **sePA,** Buck buck, how many's up: half of the players bent their backs; half of the players jumped on their backs. If they guessed correctly the number of players on their back, the benders became jumpers. *Ibid* **MA,** Game—Buck, buck, how many passengers have I got up. 1958 *KY Folkl. Rec.* 4.174 **seKY,** "Buckety Buck, Buckety Buck"—Two teams of boys, with one choosing to "face the wall," that is, the leader with hands against the wall, next one with head between his legs and clasping his thigh, and so on. Then the Buckety Buck is formed, the others, one at a time, run and jump on the backs of it. When all are up, the one farthest up holds up some fingers of one hand and says: "Buckety buck, buckety buck, / How many fingers do I have up?" The one under him makes a guess. If he doesn't get it right, they must still "face the wall." If he gets the correct number of fingers, his team gets to ride the buckety buck. 1967–68 *DARE* (Qu. EE33, . . *Outdoor games*) Inf **MD**8, Buck, buck, how many horns are up? Player puts hands against wall, bends over; another person climbs on his back and holds up a number of fingers. "It" must guess how many. If he succeeds, rider becomes "it"; **MA**3, Buck buck: one player near lamppost; other players held the others' waists. The end player would then leap onto the backs of the group and then ask the group how many fingers. [1969 Opie *Children's Games* 298–99, A remarkable feature of this game is that its oral formula, including the meaningless word 'buck,' appears to have survived from classical antiquity . . . In *The Satyricon* of Petronius Arbiter, written about A.D. 65, . . there is an incident at Trimalchio's feast involving his favourite serving boy: 'Trimalchio, not to seem moved by the loss, kissed the boy and bade him get on his back. Without delay the boy climbed on horseback on him, and slapped him on the shoulders with his hand, laughing and calling out "Bucca, bucca, quot sunt hic?"] 1971 *AmSp* 46.84 **Chicago IL,** *Buck-buck-how-many-fingers- up.*

2 A game in which one group of players climbs on the backs of a second group in order to build as large a pile as possible or to cause the supporting players to collapse. **Nth, N Midl** *chiefly urban* Also called **buffalo heap, Johnny-on-the-pony, monkey pile**

1968 *Chicago Daily Tribune* (IL) 15 Sept mag sec 79, Buck buck . . . [is] a guy's game. Big guys. O.K., two lines, two teams. First guy, No. 1 team, stand in front of the wall and brace your arms against it. Head down. All the way. Next guy, in back of him, arms on his shoulders, lean against him. Head on his back. O.K., next guy. One team, six guys. No. 2 team, first guy, start running—from across the street? O.K. Land on No. 1 team. Yeah, we held him. Next guy—run—jump—land. That's two; we're holding two. This next one's a big kid, men. 1968–69 *DARE* (Qu. EE33, . . *Outdoor games*) Infs **PA**76, 94, Buck buck; **PA**133, Buck buck: team lines up against pole or fence; other team jumps on their backs, tries to break them down; **RI**11, Buck buck: boy leans against wall, people try to climb up on him. 1977–78 Foster *Lexical Variation* 43 **NJ,** The only example . . of a boy's game is the anarchic *pile on* (Table 10) . . . Omitted are five responses of *buck buck, horse,* or *Johnny hump a pony,* a game with more sophisticated rules but the same result. 1981 *DARE* File **Chicago IL,** To play buck buck, you see how many men you can pile on top of each other. Two guys on their hands and knees form the base. The trick is to know how to build the pile right so that other people on your team can climb up without tipping it over. The team with the most people on its pile wins.

buckbush n

Either of two **snowberries: coralberry 1** (here: *Symphoricarpos orbiculatus*) or **wolfberry** (here: *S. occidentalis*).

1896 *Jrl. Amer. Folkl.* 9.190, *Symphoricarpos vulgaris* . . buckbush, S.W. Mo. 1900 Lyons *Plant Names* 361, *S[ymphoricarpos] occidentalis* . . . Buck-bush . . . *S. Symphoricarpos* . . . Buck-bush. 1918 Visher *Geog. SD* 93, The buck-bush, is a transition stage between grassland and woodland, and the sage bush between grassland and desert. 1930 *VA Qrly. Rev.* 6.242, Wild ferns grow at its shaded end, grass and buck bushes and tea roses vie for space in the rough-faced lawn. 1937 Stemen *OK Flora* 510.

buck dance n See **buck-and-wing** n

buck dance v, hence *buck dancer* n, *buck dancing* vbl n

To dance the **buck-and-wing.**

1896 *N.Y. Dramatic News* 29 Aug. 8/3 *(DA)*, Conwell and O'Day, buck dancers, made a gigantic hit at Ferris Wheel park. **1897** Ade *Pink Marsh* 73, I use' to know cullud boy in Tuhkish bath place 'at got job on 'e stage doin' buck-dancin'. **1959** Lomax *Rainbow Sign* 36 **AL** [Black], That boy would be buck dancin! Doin everything to make the sound fit in — dancin and twistin and runnin all around. Then he make some kind of special step, slide up to the gal, put his arm around her waist, and start marchin back. **1977** Nevell *Time to Dance* 169 **sAppalachians**, Buck-dancing is the simplest and yet the most enigmatic kind of southern mountain dancing. Essentially, buckdancing is a dance for one but can be for more than one; the dance itself involves nothing more than moving your feet in time to the music. The origins of buckdancing are unclear. The name probably came from the Indians who may have had a ceremonial dance danced by a brave costumed as a buck deer. *Ibid* 170, Make no mistake about it, it is not easy to buckdance. *Ibid* 188, We just did the old buck and wing dances, that's all we ever dance around here, some call it 'flatfoot,' or 'cloggin,' 'buckdancin' ' but it's all the same.

buck darting vbl n

1894 *DN* 1.328 **NJ**, *Buck-darting:* a zigzag method of sailing employed on tide-water creeks.

buck dice n [Prob abbr for **bucket** + *dice*]

1968 *DARE* (Qu. EE40, . . *Table games . . using dice*) Inf **NJ27**, Buck dice — shake dice out of bucket.

buck 'em See **buck up** n

bucker n[1] [**buck** v[1]]

1 One that butts. **chiefly NEast** Cf **bunter** n **1**

1939 (1962) Thompson *Body & Britches* 227 **ceNY** (as of late 19th cent), Bill was a bucker. Have ye met any? He didn't hit with his fists; he banged with his head, very hard. He bucked the railroader all to hell. **1967–69** *DARE* (Qu. K68, . . *A goat that habitually strikes people with its horns*) Infs **IL70, MN15, NJ4, NY45, 62, 65, 126, PA51, 201**, Bucker.

2 A horse that bucks.

1881 Romspert *W. Echo* 205 **West**, To see a big tender-foot back a bucker is about as funny a thing as I ever witnessed. **1907** White *AZ Nights* 95, He was a very hard bucker, and made some really spectacular jumps. **1948** *SW Rev.* 33.27/2, He is not ashamed of being "grassed" by a good bucker. **1967–68** *DARE* (Qu. K42, . . *A horse that is rough, wild, or dangerous*) Infs **CT7, NC48**, Bucker.

3 Transf: a person who balks or rebels.

1887 *Scribner's Mag.* 2.508/1 **CO**, So I heard, last year, a politician speak of a bolter of the Republican ticket as a "bucker." **1889** (1971) Farmer *Americanisms*, Bucker. — In political parlance one who refuses to follow the lead of his party. **1898** *Boston Journal* 10 July 10/1 *(DA)*, Yet the army is never without its buckers.

4 A gambler.

1898 Harte *Stories in Light* 89 **CA**, Selecting a faro bank as his base of operations, he began to bet heavily and with apparent recklessness . . . After winning ten times in succession the luck turned, and the unfortunate 'bucker' was cleared out not only of his gains, but of his original investment. **1900** Smithwick *Evolution of a State* 75 **TX**, One of the "buckers" was in my shop one day and . . was struck with an idea . . . He departed with his prize and after dark repaired to the monte bank.

5 One who lifts or stacks bags of grain or produce.

1931 *AmSp* 7.123 **eID**, The *bucker* piles the full sacks [of potatoes] awaiting shipment or storage. **1981** [see **buck** v[1] **B7b**].

bucker n[2] [**buck** v[2]]

1 One who saws felled trees into logs. **Nthn logging areas, esp Pacific NW**

1900 *Treasurer's Bur. Statistics* Nov. 1116 *(DA)*, A logging crew consists of 1 foreman . . . 2 swampers, 2 buckers, 3 hook tenders. **1918** *DN* 5.23 **wWA**, Bucker . . . One who strips and cuts up a tree that has been felled. **1938** (1939) Holbrook *Holy Mackinaw* 259 **NEast**. **1941** FWP *Guide WA* 73, "Fallers" chopped the trees down, while "buckers" cut or "bucked" them into 24, 32, or even 40-foot lengths. **1949** Peattie *Cascades* 163 **Pacific NW**, Below the buckers, crawler tractors were bulldozing trails and skidding large sawlogs among stumps and rotten windfalls to a landing pile. **1956** *AmSp* 31.149 **nwCA**. **1967** *DARE* Tapes **WA24, 29**, Bucker; **WA30**, A faller is a guy that falls trees and the bucker is the guy that saws 'em in two. **1969** Sorden *Lumberjack Lingo* **NEng, Gt Lakes**.

2 See quot. Cf **buck** n[1] **5**

1905 U.S. Forest Serv. *Bulletin* 61.31, Bucker . . . One who brings or carries [esp wood or water].

bucker n[3], **buckeroo** See **buckaroo** n

bucket n Cf **pail** See also **slop bucket** Note: *bucket* remains widespread in its early, more spec sense of a wooden vessel used to draw or carry water.

1 A usu round, tapered vessel used esp to carry liquids or small objects; a pail. **formerly chiefly Sth and Midl, now more widespread**

1622 Mourt's Relation *Iournall Plimoth* 12 **MA**, We found . . also an English Paile or Bucket. **1851** Woods *16 Months* 53 **CA**, Another takes the dirt to be washed, in pans or buckets, from the hole to the cradle. **1871** Eggleston *Hoosier Schoolmaster* 141 **seIN**, Ralph met Hannah carrying her bucket of milk (they have no pails in Indiana). **1876** Twain *Tom Sawyer* 26 **MO**, Tom appeared on the sidewalk with a bucket of whitewash. **1949** Kurath *Word Geog.* 13, *Pail* . . is the regular name throughout the North for the well-known container with flaring sides and a bail . . . Containers of this type are now made of metal but were formerly of wood. Most New Englanders use *pail* indiscriminately for the metal and the wooden varieties . . but along the coast . . many apply *pail* only to the modern metal container and call the older wooden one a *bucket* . . . It is fairly clear that early New England had both *pail* and *bucket* and that *pail* had largely replaced *bucket* at least in western New England before the westward expansion into New York State, i.e. by the time of the Revolution. The development in the Midland and the South is the precise opposite. *Ibid* 48, The boundaries between *bucket* . . and . . *pail* . . are sharp, and they follow the boundary between the Midland and the North very closely. **1950** WELS (*What is commonly used around the house to carry water or other liquids?*) 2 Infs, **WI**, Bucket; 2 Infs, Bucket — old-fashioned; 1 Inf, Pail; also bucket, but bucket is slightly derogatory — unless made of wood. A paint pail (new) becomes a bucket when it is cleaned out and reused for painting. **1967** *DARE* FW Addit **CO21**, Bucket — not a pail on the place. **1971** *AmSp* 46.170 **Chicago IL**, 'Wooden container for carrying liquid': *bucket* . . [28 infs]; *pail* [20 infs]. *Ibid* 171, 'Metal or plastic container for carrying liquid': *pail* . . [31 infs]; *bucket* . . [8 infs]. **1971** Metcalf *Riverside Engl.* 28 **CA**, It is clear that both *pail* and *bucket* are in general California use, with *bucket* predominating, and that people generally mean different things by *pail* and *bucket*, though different people make different types of distinctions. **1973** Allen *LAUM* 1.195–96, *Bucket* (wooden vessel) . . . *Bucket* is slightly favored in the U[pper] M[idwest] . . . the Iowa pattern strongly indicating a Midland orientation; northern Iowa 46% for *bucket* and 57% for *pail*; southern Iowa 84% for *bucket* and only 20% for *pail*. *Ibid* 197, *Pail* (the metal vessel) . . . The two terms, *pail* and *bucket*, for a metal vessel for water or milk exhibit a rather sharp Northern-Midland contrast. *Ibid* **MN**, Inf says 'pail' is a more "fancy" word than 'bucket'. **1983** *AmSp* 58.7 **neSD**, The . . process . . in which two terms become interchangeable having no apparent difference in meaning . . is illustrated by *pail/bucket* . . . This sharp Northern and Midland contrast has been lost [among the 16 infs].

2 A specific type of such a vessel according to its construction or use, as:

a *cedar bucket:* One made of cedar and used esp to hold water. **chiefly S Midl, Sth**

1956 Ker *Vocab. W. TX* 121, Wooden vessel for water . . . cedar bucket . . (Responses: 8). **1962** Atwood *Vocab. TX* 45, *Cedar bucket* (7[% of infs]). **1964** Faulkner *As I Lay Dying* 10 **MS**, When I was a boy I first learned how much better water tastes when it has set a while in a cedar bucket. **1965–70** *DARE* (Qu. F31) Inf **AL34**, Cedar bucket (general use); **LA2**, Used for water: cedar bucket (old-fashioned), but could be made out of anything; **MS1**, Cedar bucket — for water; **VA45**, Cedar bucket. **1966** *Cynthiana Democrat* (KY) 5 May 3/6, *Absolute Auction* . . . cedar bucket, brass jardenier; spool bed.

b *well bucket:* One typically keg-shaped and used to draw water from an open well. **Nth, esp NEast** *old-fash*

1907 *DN* 3.182 **seNH**, Bucket . . . A large *wooden* pail or pail-like receptacle, e.g., a well-bucket. **1910** *DN* 3.438 **cwNY**. **1916** *DN* 4.388 **neOH**, Bucket . . . Usually it denotes a wooden vessel without a bail; but the *well-bucket* has a bail. **1939** *LANE* Map 129 **NEng**, The wooden *well bucket* [18 infs] (usually made of oak and keg-shaped), [and] the *wooden bucket* for drinking water . . were in use until fairly recently. **1950** WELS (*What used to be let down into an open well to draw water out?*) 1 Inf, **csWI**, Well bucket. **1973** Allen *LAUM* 1.196, 1 inf, **nwSD**, Well bucket.

c freq *sap bucket*, also *sugar* ~: One used in collecting maple sap. **Nth, east of IL**

1845 Judd *Margaret* 12 **ME**, Here were . . frows, sap-buckets, a leach-tub. **1907** *DN* 3.182 **seNH,** *Bucket* . . . A *large wooden* pail or pail-like receptacle, *e.g.,* . . a sugar-bucket. **1910** *DN* 3.438 **cwNY,** Sap bucket. **1912** *DN* 3.568 **cNY, VT,** Sap bucket. **1916** *DN* 4.388 **neOH,** Sap bucket. **1939** *LANE* Map 129, 18 infs, **NEng,** Sap bucket; 3 infs, **MA,** Sugar bucket. **1947** *PADS* 8.7 **VT,** Sap bucket. **1947** *AmSp* 22.152 **NEast, PA,** Sap bucket. **1966–69** *DARE* (Qu. F31) Inf **MA5,** Would use "sap pail" as well as "sap bucket"; **MA29,** Sap buckets; **NH6,** Sap buckets used for maple sap; **NY20,** Sap bucket—metal, once of wood; used for maple syrup; **OH11,** Wooden sap buckets; **VT16,** Wooden: butter bucket, sap bucket. **1968** *DARE* Tape **CT3,** Bucket— used to collect sap and is attached to the tree; **IN36,** Bucket—used for tapping sugar maples.

d usu *coal bucket:* One used to carry coal. **widespread, but esp freq Midl** See Map

1887 *Courier–Jrl.* (Louisville KY) 25 Jan 3/7, At Auction . . 1 Elegant French-Plate Pier Mirror; . . 20 dozen new Coal buckets and Vases. **1904** *DN* 2.417 **nwAR,** *Bucket* . . . Pail, hod . . . 'The coal-bucket is in my room.' **1932** *AmSp* 7.167 **NE,** "Coal bucket" was the Nebraska pioneers' word for the more eastern "coal scuttle." **1961** *AmSp* 36.26 **nOH,** The native terms, *coal scuttle* and *coal hod,* have lost ground to *coal bucket* . . . Coal bucket . . increases in use with the youth of the informant. **1965–70** *DARE* (Qu. F44, . . *A container for coal to use in a stove*) 381 Infs, **widespread, but esp freq Midl,** Coal bucket; 21 Infs, **chiefly Atl, N Cent,** Bucket; **AR19, KS19,** Hod-bucket; **CA139,** Scuttle-bucket, shuttle-bucket; **TX26,** Scuttle-bucket. **1971** *AmSp* 46.171 **Chicago IL,** 'Small container for coal near a stove': . . *(coal) bucket* [18 infs]. *Ibid* 182, Words with Midland designations that identify concepts unfamiliar to younger Chicagoans, though the words may be so widespread that they perhaps have general currency among older informants: . . *coal bucket* . . . [W]ords with Midland and Southern designations that were of general currency in an earlier era and are found in the speech of very old Chicagoans with no overt Midland or Southern associations: . . *coal bucket.* **1973** Allen *LAUM* 1.224, *(Coal) bucket,* a Pennsylvania and Midland word, is more common in the Midland speech territory of Iowa and Nebraska, but its frequency in Minnesota, in contrast with only three occurrences in the related Wisconsin survey, attests further northern extension of Midland features.

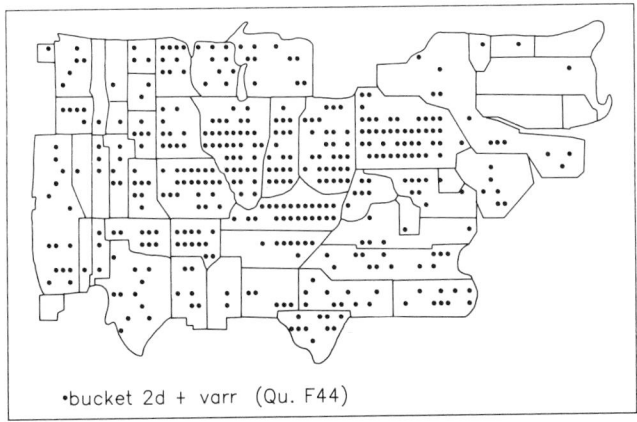

•bucket 2d + varr (Qu. F44)

e usu *dinner* (or *lunch*) *bucket:* A container with a lid for carrying one's lunch; a lunch box; also transf.

1871 (1892) Johnston *Dukesborough Tales* 58 **GA,** Here came Joel at full speed, . . his paddle in one hand and his dinner-bucket, without cover, hanging from the other. Twenty yards behind him ran Seaborn, who had been delayed by having to stop in order to pick up Joel's hat and the bucket-cover. **1904** *DN* 2.417 **nwAR,** Dinner-bucket. **1928** Aldrich *Lantern* 31 **IA,** Sometimes the contents of the dinner buckets were also frozen and one had to thaw them out before eating. **1929** *AmSp* 4.369 **swPA,** Dinner bucket. **1939** *LANE* Map 130 *(Dinner pail),* 17 infs, **NEng,** Dinner bucket; 1 inf, **seCT,** *Dinner pail, ~ bucket,* for school children; 1 inf, **eCT,** 'Some say *dinner bucket.* 'Tain't! It's a pail'; 1 inf, **cMA,** 'Some people say *dinner bucket,* but I don't know why they should'; 1 inf, **cNH,** Dinner bucket, 'slang'; 1 inf, **nME,** Lunch bucket. **1950** Faulkner *Stories* 27 **MS,** We tied the mule to a sapling and hung our dinner bucket on a limb. **1956** Ker *Vocab. W. TX* 124, For a metal container for carrying dinner or lunch, the Northern *pail* and its compounds, *dinner pail* and *lunch pail,* rival the Midland and Southern *lunch bucket* and *dinner bucket.* For *bucket* and its compounds there are recorded only four more responses than for *pail* and its compounds. **1966–69** *DARE* (Qu. F22b, . . *"He had his lunch in a _____."*) Infs

AR14, CA87, IL36, MI52, OH46, Lunch bucket; OK51, Miners had a lunch bucket with a shelf on it; CA105, MI48, Dinner bucket; MA14, OH75, Bucket; AR38, MS72, Tin bucket; (Qu. F31) Inf MI18, A lunch bucket . . is actually a pail. I think buckets usually contain food or drink of some kind; WI62, Lunch bucket; MN42, Dinner buckets—for a thermos and a lunch. **1966–69** *DARE* Tape MI22, Dinner bucket— lunch pail; MI91, The fellow sits down at the factory, and he picks up a lunch bucket, and . . he's eating his lunch. **1970** *Thompson Coll.,* Lunch bucket—lunch catering wagon. Detroit, 1950s; Los Angeles, 1960s.

f *candy bucket:* One used for bulk shipments of mixed candy. **old-fash** See also **bucket candy**

1930 Dobie *Coronado* 49 **TX** (as of 1904), The doctor had made copies of the stone and plates on some wooden lids of old-fashioned candy buckets, but when the Kirkpatrick home burned they burned also. **1945** Wilson *Passing Institutions* 111 **KY,** By the time the last piece was said, the boys returned with a candy bucket.

g *scrub* (or *mop*) *bucket:* One used in household cleaning.

1967–69 *DARE* (Qu. F31) Inf **CO20,** Bucket—same as pail, but used in only a few terms as: wooden bucket, scrub bucket exclusively; **IL5,** Scrub pail, scrub bucket; **PA40, 150,** Scrub bucket; **OH18,** Mop pail or scrub bucket; **MN42,** Bucket . . used for "mop bucket"; **CA149,** Tin ones also called mop buckets.

3 freq in adv constrs: The quantity that a bucket contains, spec a large quantity of rain. [Cf *OEDS* bucket v. *2.b* "Of rain, etc: to pour down heavily"] **chiefly Nth and N Midl, east of Missip R** See Map

1950 *WELS (A heavy rain that keeps on falling)* 1 Inf, **cwWI,** Raining in buckets; *(When it's raining very heavily, you say it's _____.)* 2 Infs, **WI,** Raining buckets; 1 Inf, **csWI,** Coming down in buckets; 1 Inf, **seWI,** Falling by the buckets. **1965–70** *DARE* (Qu. B26, *When it's raining very heavily, you say, "It's raining _____."*) 24 Infs, **chiefly Nth, N Midl,** Buckets; **IL2, 23, MI37, 106, WV20, WI10,** By the buckets; **IL58, MI54, NY92,** Coming down in buckets; **MA72, NY215, VA55,** In buckets; **IL35,** By the bucket; **CO7,** Came down by the buckets; **ND3,** Poured down with buckets; **MA44,** Pouring buckets; (Qu. B25) Inf **NY35,** Came down in buckets. **1968** *DARE* FW Addit **NY70,** "It poured in buckets"—said of very heavy rain.

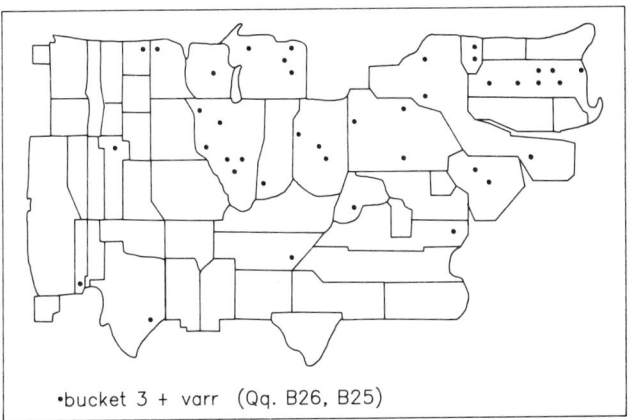

•bucket 3 + varr (Qq. B26, B25)

4 attrib: Of a calf: fed from a bucket instead of from the cow. Cf **bucket-fed**

1928 *AmSp* 4.129 **NE,** Calves . . . must then be hand fed and become . . "bucket" . . calves. **1958** *AmSp* 33.269 **eWA,** Bucket bunter. A calf being fed milk from a bucket rather than from the cow. (The striking motion which a calf makes when sucking or when drinking from a bucket is called *bunting.*) **1961** Adams *Old-Time Cowhand* 155 **West,** Sometimes stockmen purchased calves in the corn belt, or from farmers, and shipped 'em to their ranches to restock their range. These were called "bucket dogies." **1970** Tarpley *Blinky* 159 **neTX,** *Other responses* come chiefly from the city; one of these is *bucket calf,* meaning that the calf must be fed from a bucket.

5 An object used in a children's game; also the game itself: see quot.

1904 *DN* 2.394 **cNY,** *Bucket* . . . 1. A skaters' game. Otsego Co. 2. In the game of the same name, a small willow having several wide-spreading branches cut off like the legs of a stool. It is placed upright and tended by the player who is "it." *Bucket-tender* . . . In the game of *bucket* the person who tends the bucket . . or who is "it." Otsego Co.

6 usu *bucket of bolts:* A motor vehicle, esp an old or dilapidated car.

1938 Runyon *Take it Easy* 331 **NYC,** Clem came out and got in the old bucket with us and I drove him home. **1942** Berrey–Van den Bark *Amer. Slang* 724.4, *Racing car*. . . bucket. **1950** *WELS (Nicknames for an old broken-down car)* 1 Inf, **csWI,** Bucket of bolts. **1954** *AmSp* 29.94 **sCA,** *Bucket*. . . Any car. 'I swapped my bucket for another one a couple of days ago.' *Bucket of bolts* . . . A car that rattles quite a bit, or used derisively of any car. **1963** *AmSp* 38.43 **RI** [Truckers' talk], *Bucket of bolts* . . . An old truck. **1965–70** *DARE* (Qu. N5, . . *An old or broken-down car*) 18 Infs, **esp Inland Nth, N Midl,** Bucket o' bolts. **1971** *Tak Truck Talk, Bucket of bolts:* a dilapidated truck; one that rattles while being driven. May be used derogatorily or affectionately in reference to a truck in sound condition.

7 The buttocks.

1942 Berrey–Van den Bark *Amer. Slang* 462.1, Bucket. . *the posteriors or rectum.* **1960** Wentworth–Flexner *Slang, Bucket*. . . The rump, the buttocks. **1966–69** *DARE* (Qu. X35, . . *Joking words for the part of the body that you sit on*) Infs IL7, KY5, 70, NC1, OH66, PA74, Bucket.

8 A jail.

1955 *PADS* 24.147 [Underworld talk], He is locked up in the *can,* the *bucket,* . . or any other jail. **1965–67** *DARE* (Qu. V11, . . *Joking names . . for a . . jail*) Infs UT3, WA28A, Bucket.

9 =scoter.

1956 *AmSp* 31.182, The scoters . . have names referring to their black color, hardiness, and inedibility, all in one combination, such as *iron pot* and *old iron pot* (N.J.), *bucket* (probably short for *tar bucket,* Md.), *tar-bowl* (Delaware River), and *tarpot* (Del., Md., Wis., Ill.).

‡bucket-a-day stove n

1968 *DARE* FW Addit **DE3,** Bucket-a-day stove—coal stove for heating water.

bucket candy n Also *bucket mixture* **esp SC** *old-fash*
The type of small candies packed in and sold from a bucket.

1950 *PADS* 14.17 **SC,** *Bucket mixture, bucket candy*. . . An assortment of small candy consisting of gumdrops, lozenges, bonbons of various flavors, etc., purveyed in and sold from a large bucket. **1966–67** *DARE* (Qu. H82b, . . *Kinds of cheap candy that used to be sold years ago*) Inf **OR15,** Bucket candies; **SC22,** Bucket candy—a general mixture of all sorts of loose candy—came in twenty-five pound buckets; **SC34,** Bucket candy—assorted hard candy supplied to a grocer in bulk and packed in a bucket; **SC26, 29, 42, 43, TX26,** Bucket candy.

bucket-fed adj For varr see quots Cf **bucket** n **4**
Hand-fed; transf: dependent, pampered.

1927 *AmSp* 2.349 **wcWV,** *Bucket-led*. . refers to a calf that has been taught to feed from a bucket. "He is too much of a bucket-led man for me." **1928** *AmSp* 4.129 **NE,** Generally calves are penned away from the cows. They must then be hand fed and become "skim milk," "bucket," "bucket fed," or "bucket head" calves. **1947** *Denver Post* 2 Mar. c. 3/4 *(DA),* It thrilled me no end to read of those intrepid archers risking their lives against those ferocious bucket-fed buffalo.

bucket man n **West**
A man who carries buckets of sheep disinfectant; also transf and derog: a cowboy.

1897 Hough *Cowboy* 281 **West,** The honest cowboys . . were spoken of with contempt . . . Sometimes they were called . . . "bucket men" by ex-cowboys who would have scorned to carry a "bucket of sheep dip." **1939** Carlisle *Southwestern Dict.,* Bucket men . . . Men assisting at the dipping vats [where sheep are disinfected], one of whose duties being to bring buckets of sheep-dip solutions to pour into the vats. **1942** Berrey–Van den Bark *Amer. Slang* 913.19, *Loyal hand. (Terms used by rustlers for one who is loyal to his employer.)* Bucket man, pliersman, pure, saint, sheep dipper. **1944** Adams *Western Words,* Bucket man—A contemptuous name given the cowboy by the rustler.

bucket mixture See **bucket candy**

bucket of blood n Also *bloody bucket* [Orig uncert, but see quot 1961] *somewhat old-fash*
A saloon or speakeasy; a cheap dive.

1938 Asbury *Sucker's Progress* 329 **CO** (as of late 1800s), The city seldom harbored fewer than a score of tough skimming [=gambling] houses, . . such notorious resorts as the Palace, the Bucket of Blood, the Morgue. **1945** Saxon *Gumbo Ya-Ya* 58 **New Orleans LA** (as of late 1800s), The Bucket of Blood Saloon, on the corner of Rousseau and St.

Mary, was a popular rendezvous for the more virile males of the Channel. **1951** *Western Folkl.* 10.80 **NM,** *Barroom Slang from the Upper Rio Grande.* — The Setting:. . boar's nest (strictly man's place);. . bucket of blood. **1961** Adams *Old-Time Cowhand* 330 **West,** There were some tough saloons on the early frontier, and they soon got the name of "Bucket of Blood." The original "Bucket of Blood" was Shorty Young's dive in Havre, Montana, and since its rep'tation spread the term became used in describin' other dives. **1966–70** *DARE* (Qu. D39, . . *A small eating place where the food is not especially good*) Inf **MD17,** Bucket of blood; **MD37,** Bucket of blood—a local restaurant noted for fights; **MI106,** Bucket of blood—a liquor store; (Qu. DD30, . . *A place where liquor is (or was) sold and consumed illegally*) Inf **CA7,** The bucket of blood (local place); **AL10, IL115,** Bloody bucket; (QR, near Qu. FF24) Inf **CA133,** In old days, a saloon that was a real dive was called "a bucket-o'-blood"; (Qu. C35, *Nicknames for the different parts of your town or city*) Inf **LA27,** Around where an old saloon used to be is still called the "bloody bucket." [All Infs mid-aged or old]

bucket of bolts See **bucket 6**

bucket of lard n Also *lard bucket, bucket of blubber* *chiefly among men*

1965–70 *DARE* (Qu. X50, . . *Nicknames for a person who is very fat*) 26 Infs, **scattered,** Bucket of lard; **LA8,** Old mushy bucket of lard; **AL22, SC19, SD1,** Lard bucket; **PA182,** Bucket of blubber. [Of all Infs responding to this question, 47% were male; of those giving this response, 77% were male.]

bucket of light n

1939 FWP *Guide NJ* 506, Hill people drop by for their provender or for an occasional "bucket of light"—gallon of kerosene.

bucket of steam See **steam**

bucket road n
A badly kept road with bucket-like holes in the surface.

1967 *DARE* (Qu. N27b, *When unpaved roads get very rough, you call them _____*) Inf **CA10,** Bucket roads (in Texas).

bucket-stretcher See **stretcher**

bucketty buck See **buck buck 1**

bucket woman n

1945 Saxon *Gumbo Ya-Ya* 372 **seLA,** The women who sell hot lunches, sandwiches, pies and doughnuts along the wharves are *bucket women* or *pan ladies,* because their wares are usually sold from buckets, huge flat pans or baskets.

buckety buck See **buck buck 1**

buck euchre n Also *buck* . [See **buck pitch**] **chiefly Gt Lakes**
A var of **euchre** n **1:** see quot 1981.

1950 *WELS (Card games played a good deal in your neighborhood)* 2 Infs, **WI,** Buck euchre. **1968–69** *DARE* (Qu. DD35, . . *Favorite card games*) Inf **IL40,** Black spade—what some call buck euchre; **MN42,** Buck euchre; (Qu. EE2) Inf **IN83,** Buck euchre. **1981** *DARE* File **WI,** In regular euchre 4 people play together as 2 partnerships. In buck euchre, 3, 4, or 5 players may play, but all play for themselves. It used to be played more than it is now. *Ibid* **neMN,** I've played more buck than I have four-handed.

buckey See **bucky** n[1]

buckeye n, also attrib

1 Std: a tree of the genus *Aesculus.* Also called **chestnut 2, horsechestnut** For other names of var species see **bottlebrush buckeye, Ohio ~, painted ~, red ~, Texas ~, yellow ~**

2 also *buckeye's weed:* Perh a plant of the genus *Ipomoea;* see quot.

1969–70 *DARE* (Qu. S5, . . *The wild morning glory*) Inf **CA107,** Buckeye; (Qu. K14) Inf **CA199,** [Milk is] tainted, often with buckeye's weed.

3 Orig a backwoodsman near the Ohio River valley; now any resident of Ohio.

1823 James *Acct. of Exped.* 1.20 **OH,** In allusion to this circumstance, the indigenous backwoodsman is sometimes called buck-eye, in distinction from the numerous immigrants who are introducing themselves from the eastern states. **1835** (1906) Bradley *Jrl.* 243 **OH,** He is an old Buckeye farmer and resides on the Scioto, at the village of Piketon. **1857** *S. Lit. Messenger* 24.317, A handsome young Buckeye / Who lived in the West, in the State of Kentucky. **1895** Myers *Bosses & Boodle* 64,

It has been claimed that this device [=a buckeye tree] on this seal [of Gov. St. Clair] gave the appellation of "Buckeyes" to Ohio and her people. **1949** *AmSp* 24.26, Almost every American has heard of *Buckeye* for an Ohioan. **1967** *DARE* (Qu. HH1, . . *A rustic or countrified person*) Inf **CO3**, Buckeyes—Ohio.

4 One whose work is of low quality; the inferior work itself. [See quot 1846] *old-fash*

1843 (1916) Hall *New Purchase* 148, Endowed with our buck-eye-preacher's pathos and unction. **1846** Cist *Cincinnati Misc.* 2.97/1, The buckeye . . . could not be used in building, nor for fences, nor even for fuel. As a tree it consequently stood very low in the estimation of early settlers, and by a figure of speech very forcible to them, it was applied to lawyers and doctors whose capacity and attainment were of a low grade. **1906** *Atlantic Mth.* 98.640/1 **NYC**, The serious painters whose work is found in exhibitions, and the despised "buckeye" painter who paints for the department stores and cheap picture shops. **1912** Thornton *Amer. Gloss.*, *Buckeyes.* Worthless oil paintings, made for auctions: see *New York Evening Post*, June 7, 1881. **1920** Lewis *Main Street* 137 **MN**, The walls of Mrs. Cass's parlor were plastered with "hand-painted" pictures, "buckeye" pictures, of birch-trees, news-boys, puppies, and church-steeples on Christmas Eve.

5 A small cigar factory. *obsolescent*

1915 in 1933 Mack *Factors of Instability* 4 **NYC**, While the corner saloon peddles out cheap cigars which keeps the little "Buckeyes" running, the fine cafes are the most valuable distributing centers for our finer grades of cigars, cigarettes, and tobacco. **1942** Kennedy *Palmetto Country* 271 **FL**, The first cigar factory to be established in Key West was . . in 1831. Other *chinchares,* or "buckeyes" as the Americans called them, were established in rapid succession. **1947** *New Yorker* 15 Feb 59 **NYC**, A buckeye is a small shop in which cigars are made by hand in a back room and sold across the counter out front . . . There are just a few buckeyes left in New York, but as recently as thirty years ago there was one on almost every block downtown.

6 also *buckeye (bark) whiskey:* Whiskey to which buckeye nuts have been added during production.

[**1867** *Harper's Weekly* 11.773/3 **Sth**, It [=smuggled liquor] is nearly all *very bad*, owing to the quantity of buck-eye bean used in its preparation, to give it what is called a *bead*. The buck-eye grows in all parts of the South and West, and is said to be very poisonous. It is held in superstitious veneration by the lower classes and negroes, who believe that to carry one in the pocket is a remedy for some diseases.] **1954** *Harder Coll.* cwTN, Buck-eye whiskey: "Buck-eye poison give you the jake leg." **1966** *DARE* (Qu. DD21b, . . *Bad liquor*) Inf **AL4**, Rot gut; wild cat; buckeye; corn whiskey. **1974** Dabney *Mountain Spirits* 24 **Appalachians**, "Buckeye bark whiskey" got its name from the fact that moonshiners put buckeyes (inedible nuts that grow in the hills) into the newly-run liquor to give it a bourbon red color.

7 See bugeye n[2].

8 =conkers.

1933 Hench *Coll.*, When I was a young boy in Pittsburgh, Penna., say, from 1897 to 1905, the game of "buckeye" or "buckeyes" was played by two in which the aim of the game was to break another person's buckeye with your own buckeye and thus be "king over one." . . A buckeye was pierced with a hole and strung on a shoe-string or leather thong. Then the winner of the "first hit" . . took aim by sweeping his buckeye and string through the air . . several times, and then took a swipe at the other buckeye being held up by the opponent on the end of *his* string.

9 In marble play: a kind of marble, esp a damaged one. **esp Sth, Inland Nth**

1965–70 *DARE* (Qu. EE6d, . . *Special marbles*) 17 Infs, **esp Sth, Inland Nth** Buckeyes; **AL26**, Buckeyes—used to shoot taw; **NC14**, Buckeyes —moonies before they have moons in them; moonies—buckeyes which have been hit so much they get cracks or moons in them; (Qu. EE6a, . . *Kinds of marbles—the big one that's used to knock others out of the ring*) Inf **FL22**, Buckeye—has a small chip or mark; is special because of the mark on it.

10 A type of candy with a peanut butter center and chocolate coating, resembling a buckeye nut.

1970 *DARE* (Qu. H82b, . . *Cheap candy that used to be sold years ago*) Inf **OH102**, Kisses; buckeyes. **1983** *NADS Letters* **sOH**, At a meeting in Cincinnati last spring, a local group was selling a candy called "buckeyes" as a fundraising activity. The candy, I was told, was made to look like the nuts of the buckeye tree. *Ibid* **swOH, IN**, Buckeye candy . . is a homemade variety of Reese's cups. The center is a ball of peanut butter which is covered with chocolate mixed with paraffin to make it stick . . .

The candy is [so] named because it looks like a horsechestnut/buckeye.

11 A sheriff. [See quot 1889]

1889 Howe *Hist. Coll. OH* 202, They [=local Indians at Marietta, Ohio, in 1788] . . were especially impressed with the high sheriff who led the procession with drawn sword; . . his fine physical proportions and dignified bearing excited their highest admiration, which they expressed by the word "Hetuck," or in their language "big buckeye." It was not spoken in derision, but was the expression of their greatest admiration, and was afterwards often jocularly applied to Colonel Sproat, and became a sort of nickname by which he was familiarly known among his associates. **1968** *DARE* (Qu. V10a, . . *Joking names . . for a sheriff*) Inf **OH43**, Buckeyes—the Indians called the first sheriff "Big Buckeye." We used it as kids.

buckeye v, hence *buckeyed* ppl adj

To make or become ill, usu from eating **buckeye** nuts.

1868 IA State Ag. Soc. *Rept. for 1867* 13.129, From half a pound to one pound of lard put down the animal's throat when "buckeyed," is a pretty safe antidote for the poison. **1912** *DN* 3.572 **wIN**, *Buckeye* . . . To disconcert or fuddle. A cow is unsteady and often staggers after she has eaten buckeyes. **1923** *DN* 5.202 **swMO**, *Buck eye* . . . To poison with buck-eye, cockle-burr or other poisonous plants. Also to make sick with tobacco. "That ol' long green shore did buck-eye me!" **1953** Randolph *Down in Holler* 230 **Ozarks**, *Buck-eye* . . . To poison. The hillfolk use the roots of the buckeye tree (*Aesculus glabra*) in poisoning fish. An animal which staggers or acts strangely is said to be *buck-eyed.* **1968** *DARE* (Qu. K28, . . *Diseases that cows have*) Inf **OH58**, Buckeyed—on buck-eyes.

buckeye bark whiskey See buckeye n 6

buckeye bean n

An unidentified bean: see quot.

1968–69 *DARE* (Qu. I19, . . *Small white beans with a black spot where they were joined to the pod*) Inf **MN16**, Buckeye beans; **NJ54**, Buckeyes.

buckeyed adj[1] See buckeye v

buck-eyed adj[2] [*buck* to project (cf *buck teeth*); perh infl by *bug-eyed*] **chiefly Sth, Midl** *esp among Black speakers* See Map Section

Characterized by unusual eyes: see quots.

1950 *WELS* (Words used to describe people according to their eyes) 1 Inf, **WI**, Buck-eyed—same as cock-eyed (with 'a kind of a cross' in the eye, or a whiteness in the eye). **1965–70** *DARE* (Qu. X21a . . *People . . if [the eyes] stick out*) 10 Infs, **esp Sth, Midl**, Buck-eyed; (Qu. X21c, . . *People . . if the eyes are very round*) Infs **KY94, VA39**, Buck-eyed; [**MS73**, Buck-eyed;] (Qu. X26a, . . *If a person's eyes look . . inward*) Infs **MS59, OK54**, Buck-eyed; (Qu. X26b, . . *If a person's eyes look . . outward*) Inf **LA46**, Buck-eyed. [9 of 16 Infs are Black; 7 of 9 Black Infs are women].

‡**buckeye log** n Cf *DS* BB56, 57

In phr *jump the buckeye log:* see quot.

1952 Brown *NC Folkl.* 1.523, *Buck-eye log, to jump* . . To die. "Ol' Daisy [a horse] has jumped *the buck-eye log.* First time I ever knowed her to do that." — Swain county.

buckeye's weed See buckeye n 2

buckeye whiskey See buckeye n 6

buck farmer See buckwheat 5

buck fence n Also *buck, flying buck* [From **buck** n[1] 4] now esp **CO, WY**

A type of rail fence: see quot 1967–68.

1910 in 1914 Stewart *Letters* 85 **WY**, You would see long lines of "buck" fence, a flock of sheep near by, and cattle scattered about feeding. **1940–41** Cassidy *WI Atlas* ceWI, A 'buck fence' was made with a series of overlapping sections composed of a rail laid on the ground at one end and a 'buck' at the other; the buck being simply 2 stakes crossed. **1949** Kurath *Word Geog.* 55, Other types of fences are built of rails: . . the *herring-bone fence* = *stake-and-rider fence* = *buck fence* (Eastern Pennsylvania) = *rip-gut fence,* in which the rails are supported by crossed stakes. **1960** *PADS* 34.42 nwCO, Buck fence 'rail fence, stake and rider fence.' *Ibid* 43, The Eastern localisms *doodle* and *buck fence* point to Midland prominence. **1961** *AmSp* 36.269 **CO**, Eastern dialect items that are rare in Colorado—*snake doctor, buck fence* . . must certainly be considered relics. **1967–68** *DARE* (Qu. L61, . . *Fences made of solid logs*) Inf **CO44**, Buck fence—

[Saw]buck and a rider and slanted poles . . . Weight of the one above holds the others in place [FW illustr: Poles lie between one arm of sawbuck and vertical post at center of sawbuck]; (Qu. L62, . . *Fence made of split logs*) Inf **WY1**, Buck fence—made of poles nailed on [FW illustr: Poles nailed to one arm of sawbuck]; (Qu. L65, . . *Other kinds of fences*) Inf **WV3**, Buck fence; **WY5**, Buck fence—poles nailed on [FW illustr: Poles nailed to one arm of sawbuck]. [All Infs old] **1968** *DARE* FW Addit **VA15**, "Buck" is the same as "flying buck," a rail fence type.

buck fever n [*buck* male deer]

1 The nervous excitement felt by an inexperienced hunter at the sight of game. **widespread, but esp freq in Nth** Also called **buck ague 1, deer fever** See also *DS* P36

1841 *S. Lit. Messenger* 7.224/2 **WV**, If you see a deer . . you'll be sure to git the buck fever. **1890** Custer *Following* 218 **KS**, The elks were so much larger than other game that the officers often lost their first shots from buck-fever. **1902** White *Blazed Trail* 140 **ceMI**, What few running shots offered, he missed, mainly because of buck fever. **1950** *WELS* 47 Infs, **WI**, Buck fever. **1965–70** *DARE* (Qu. P36, *When a hunter sees a deer . . and gets so excited he can't shoot, he has _____*) 612 Infs, **widespread, but esp freq in Nth**, Buck fever. **1978** Gould *Greenleaf* 94 **ME**, Not us, Sheriff. But I hear there's a lot of buck fever over in Lincoln County just now. You been out yet?

2 By ext: nervousness accompanying exposure to a new situation or responsibility.

1941 *Sun* (Baltimore MD) 23 Dec 4/5 (*Hench Coll.*), The fact that enemy submarines have missed three merchant ships off California in the last three days, while hitting one, led to unofficial speculation today that the Japanese underseas skippers have "buck fever." **1943** *Sun* (Baltimore MD) 7 Jan 13/2, Lieutenant Lawson admits to "buck fever" when he saw the first Japanese ship; perspiration ran down his thighs and into his sea boots. **1958** McCulloch *Woods Words* **Pacific NW**, *Buck fever*—Actually means to get stage fright and be afraid to fire at a deer. Also means a man who gets frightened at the thought of work: very lazy. **1966** *AN&Q* 4.122, *Buck fever* . . In its transferred sense—the little school's fear of the big powerful university—the usage came on strong on the sports pages of the 1920s–30s. **1981** Maurer *Lang. Underworld* 183, *Buck fever:* Fear of risking one's money. (Sucker word.)

buck fly n

1 =**deer fly.**

1859 (1968) Bartlett *Americanisms, Buck-fly.* An insect which torments the deer at certain seasons. **1968–69** *DARE* (Qu. R12, . . *Flies . . that fly around animals*) Infs **GA20**, Horse fly; deer fly; buck fly; **PA198**, Buck fly; horse fly; cattle fly; **VA7**, Green fly; buck fly; cow fly (same as face fly and cattle fly); horse fly.

2 also *bucky fly*: Prob a **punkie.**

1968–69 *DARE* (Qu. R11, . . *A very tiny fly that you can hardly see, but that stings*) Inf **VA2**, Buck fly; **RI4**, Bucky fly.

‡buck fright n

=**buck fever 1.**

1967 *DARE* (Qu. P36) Inf **MN2**, Buck fright.

buck grass See **buckhorn 2**

buckhead n[1]

1 A person of mixed race; see quots.

1946 *Social Forces* 24.439 **SC**, *Brass Ankles and allied groups of South Carolina* . . . These peoples are located mainly on the coastal plain area of the State. They are called by a variety of names, depending upon the county but show a general resemblance to each other. They are termed . . Buckheads in Bamberg. **1947** *AmSp* 22.83, The majority of the names . . have obviously been applied by the socially and economically dominant group in the society, namely, the whites. The superiority that the undiluted dominant class feels toward a diluted one is reflected in derisive terms like *Brass Ankles, Buckheads, Clay-Eaters*. [Note:] We have no information about *Buckheads*, which may not turn out to be quite as derisive as it sounds. (Could it possibly be a variant of *bugheads?*) **1963** Berry *Almost White* 27 **cSC**, South Carolina abounds in groups who are "neither fish nor fowl." There are . . the Buckheads of Bamberg, the Goins of Williamsburg, and the Turks of Sumter. *Ibid* 36, There are many names which are truly mysterious—Brass Ankle, Melungeon, . . Buckhead. *Ibid* 111, From a librarian: "Our bookmobile doesn't stop at that Buckhead school . . . If they asked us to stop there, I guess we would stop all right." *Ibid* 185, The Buckheads of Bamberg County are no longer the objects of malicious gossip except among the most uncompromising race purists.

2 See quot.

1969 *DARE* (Qu. U26, . . *Nicknames . . for a paper dollar*) Inf **GA77**, Frog-hides; skins; buckheads.

buckhead n[2] See **buck** n[6]

buckhorn n

1 also *buck's horn*: =**staghorn sumac.** *obs*

1629 Parkinson *Paradisi* 611 **VA**, *Rhus Virginiana.* The Virginia Sumach, or Buckes horne tree of Virginia. **1712** Royal Soc. London *Philos. Trans.* 27.424 **VA**, Virginia *Sumach* . . . The first-branches are very soft and velvety, like the *Horns* of a young *Deer*, for which reason it is called *Buckhorn* by the *Country People*.

2 also *buck grass*: A club moss (here: *Lycopodium clavatum*).

1889 *Century Dict.* 705/2, Buckhorn . . . A name for the club-moss, *Lycopodium clavatum*. *Ibid* 3552/2, *L[ycopodium] clavatum* . . . has also been called *stag's-horn, buck's-horn*. **1900** Lyons *Plant Names* 233.

3 See **buckhorn cholla.**

4 See **buckhorn plantain.**

5 A pine knot. Cf **lightwood**

1969 *DARE* (Qu. T8, . . *Joints of pine wood that burn easily and make good fuel*) Inf **MO39**, Buckhorn; knots.

6 Perh a morel.

1968 *DARE* (QR, near Qu. S21) Inf **MD18**, Buckhorn—this is a white mushroom; edible; grows in damp places.

7 also *buck's horn*: A large hot pepper. Cf **cowhorn 1**

1969 *DARE* (Qu. I22b, . . *Peppers—large, hot*) Inf **MO37**, Buckhorn; the buck's horn.

8 also *buckhorn brake*: =**cinnamon fern.**

1889 *Century Dict.* 658/2, Buckhorn-brake . . [is] a name sometimes applied to the flowering fern, *Osmunda regalis*. **1892** *Jrl. Amer. Folkl.* 5.105, *Osmunda regalis*, buck-horn. Worcester Co., Mass.

9 A freshwater mussel (*Tritogonia verrucosa*). Also called **pistolgrip**

1982 U.S. Fish & Wildlife Serv. *Fresh-Water Mussels* I, Buckhorn . . . *Tritogonia verrucosa* . . . Shell brown or black . . entire shell tuberculate.

buckhorn brake n

1 The royal fern (*Osmunda regalis*).

1874 *Shaker Med. Preparations* **ceNY**, Buckhorn brake—*Osmunda spectabilis*.

2 See **buckhorn 8.**

buckhorn cholla n Also *buckhorn, buckhorn cactus* Cf **staghorn cholla**

A **prickly pear** (here: either *Opuntia acanthocarpa* or *O. versicolor*).

1897 *Land of Sunshine* 6.138, The most familiar cacti of the Southwest in a state of nature are the huge and ghostly zahuaro; the buckhorn cactus, . . whose stems make the familiar "lattice-work canes;" [and] the prickly pear. **1948** *Desert Mag.* July 8/3 (*DA*), On the mountainside nearby were mountain lilac in blossom, . . . agave and buckhorn cactus. **1973** *AZ Highways* 49.3.14, The Staghorn Cholla (*Opuntia acanthocarpa*), also known as the Buckhorn Cholla. *Ibid* 29, The Buckhorn [sic] or Staghorn Cholla (*Opuntia acanthacarpa*) [sic] branches like a deer's antlers. **1982** *NY Times* (NY) 3 Jan sec 10 17/2 **AZ**, Also present are tangles of buckhorn.

buckhorn elm n

Perh a **white elm.**

1968 *DARE* FW Addit **NY96**, Buckhorn elm—used for ax handles. Called so because the limbs bend down and then curl up like a sheep's or goat's horn.

buckhorn plantain n Also *buckhorn, buck plantain*

A plantain (here: *Plantago lanceolata*). Also called **black plantain, English plantain, hock cockle, niggerheads, ribbon grass, ribgrass, ribwort, ripple, soldiers**

1847 Darlington *Weeds & Plants* 220 (*DAE*), *Plantago lanceolata*, . . . Ribgrass, English Plantain, Buckhorn Plantain. **1950** Gray–Fernald *Manual of Botany* 1316; *P[lantago] lanceolata* . . . Buckhorn. **1965–70** *DARE* (Qu. S21, . . *Weeds that are a trouble in gardens and fields*) 38 Infs, **chiefly NEast, N Cent**, Buckhorn; **DC2**, Buckhorns; **OH33**, Plantain—narrow leaf and buck plantain are the two kinds; (Qu. S9, . . *Kinds of grass that are hard to get rid of*) Infs **IL6, 29, 58, 78, MI114, OH80**, Buckhorn.

buckhorse See **buck** n[1] 4

buckie n[1] See **bucky** n[1]

buckie n[2] [Scots *buckie, bucky* a mischievous boy] Cf **buck** n[1] 2b

  1930 Shoemaker *1300 Words* 7 **cPA Mts** (as of c1900), *Buckie*—A lively boy or youth.

bucking vbl n[1], attrib [**buck** v[1] **A1a**] **West**
Associated with a bucking horse.

  1929 *AmSp* 5.60 **NE**, A saddle used for breaking horses or for riding at the rodeo might be a "bucking saddle," one having exceptionally large "swells" which enable the rider to sit more securely. **1933** *AmSp* 8.1.28 **nwTX**, *Buckin' roll*. A roll, sometimes merely a rolled-up coat, placed in front of rider to prevent his striking the saddle—scorned by the best riders, nevertheless useful to lessen fatigue and soreness if there were many horses to break at one time. *Buckin' strap*. A strap something like the handle of a grip or suitcase. It was placed on a saddle for tenderfoot riders to grab for security. **1939** FWP *Guide MT* 413, *Bucking rolls*—Leather pads on the pommel that enable a rider to clamp his knees to the saddle. **1940** *AmSp* 15.376 **NE**, Mr. Dehart himself had 'traded' for a horse who turned out to be a 'bucker.' He fixed up (to use his language) a 'bucking stick,' a crotched stick fastened to the belly band which runs up to the bridle bit rings. This arrangement kept the horse from getting his head down so that he could buck. **1944** Adams *Western Words*, *Bucking rein*—Usually a single rope attached to the hackamore or a bucking horse. By gripping this, the rider has an aid in keeping his balance, but in contests he is not permitted to change hands. *Bucking rim*—A round-headed projection on the cantle of some saddles. **1967** *DARE* Tape **TX25**, Bucking chute . . . bucking rein.

bucking vbl n[2] [Etym unknown]

  1889 (1971) Farmer *Americanisms, Bucking.*—A species of *voudooism* . . consisting of superstitious and barbarous rites. "The queerest thing about the poor white is, that not one was ever known to make any kind of religious profession. There is, so far as I know, but one thing in which they believe, and that is what is termed further South voudooism, or, as they term it here, *bucking.*—*Troy* [NY] *Daily Times*, Feb. 8, 1888.

bucking vbl n[3] See **buck** v[2]

bucking board See **buckboard** 1

bucking paddle See **buck paddle**

bucking pole n
=**buck rake** n.

  1966 *DARE* (Qu. L16, . . *Machines used . . in handling hay*) Inf **ND3**, Buckin' pole—two wheels, fork front, picks up windrows, stacks it in field.

bucking season n [Cf *OED bucking* vbl. sb.[2] "The copulation of certain animals," 1535–1657] **West** Cf **buck up** v phr 4
The season for breeding sheep.

  1931 *AmSp* 6.359 **Rocky Mts**, Late in December or January the "bucking" season begins, and breeding is accomplished. **1949** *PADS* 11.4 **wTX**, *Bucking season* . . . The season for breeding sheep. Common. **1954** Jordan *Hell's Canyon* 171 **ID**, Meanwhile the golden fall had blazed and died, bucking season had passed, and we were approaching the shortest day of the year. **1968** Adams *Western Words, Bucking season*—In sheep raising, the mating season when breeding is done, usually late in December or January so that the lambs will be born in the spring.

buckitis n [*buck* male deer + *-itis*]
=**buck fever** 1.

  1965–69 *DARE* (Qu. P36, *When a hunter sees a deer . . and gets so excited he can't shoot, he has _____*) Inf **GA77**, The nervous jerks, buckitis; **MS1**, Buckache, buckitis; **OH60**, Buckitis [FW sugg].

buckjump v, hence *buckjumping* ppl adj, vbl n

1 =**buck** v[1] **A1a**; hence *buckjumper* a horse that bucks. **chiefly West**

  1851 Kelly *Excursion* 2.123 **CA**, [The horse] commenced rearing, kicking, plunging, and buck-jumping without intermission for fully ten minutes. **1878** in 1885 Bishop *Lady's Life* 147 **CO**, Two stockmen from the Plains, one of whom rode a violent buck-jumper. **1897** *Outing* 30.217/1, Lordly salmon, gamy trout and buckjumping ouananiche are fit for any man to play. **1907** White *AZ Nights* 96, Sometimes we skipped and hopped and buck-jumped through and over little gullies.

  1922 Rollins *Cowboy* 284, Between "bucking" and "pitching," there was no difference except that of geography. The Northwesterner called the horrid motion "bucking" or "buck jumping". **1946** *Sun* (Baltimore MD) 15 Apr 14/2 (Hench Coll.), Assault, the surprise Texas speedster who buckjumped by four lengths in the six-furlong Experimental Handicap last Tuesday.

2 To recoil like a bucking horse.

  1903 *McClure's Mag.* 22.97/2 **Desert SW**, They tried me with a pencil and paper, but I balked, laid my ears back, and buck-jumped. **1930** *AmSp* 6.97 **cNY**, The man moaned as the tree buck-jumped, breaking one of his knees.

buckjump n
=**buck** n[2] **1.**

  1861 *Harper's Mag.* 23.8/1 **CA**, The Captain . . . generally rides downhill at a full gallop, and when that is impracticable, compels his animal to slide or make "buck jumps" over the worst places. **1968** Adams *Western Words, Buck jump*—the plunging and leaping of a horse trying to shed his rider. The expression is particularly used when a horse leaps as he bucks.

buck-kneed adj [Cf *EDD buck* v.[6], *bucksheened* "having the shin-bones bent or crooked"]
Having the knees turned inward; knock-kneed.

  1967 Green *Horse Tradin'* 81 **swTX** (as of 1920s), I traded this mule for two old wore-out, mossy-headed, buck-kneed, big-ankled, bog-hocked, cow horses. **1968–69** *DARE* (Qu. X37, . . *People's legs if they're noticeably bent*) Inf **KY40**, Buck-kneed; **MO39**, Buck-kneed (the knees go in); **OH74**, Buck-kneed—the knees come together.

buck laurel n Cf **deer laurel**
Perh a **rosebay** (here: *Rhododendron maximum*).

  1940 Richter *Trees* 69 **OH**, A foot path . . came to . . the buck laurel and big whortleberry bushes in the swamp.

buckle v

1 usu with *down*, also with *in, under, up*, formerly with *to* : To work hard; to apply oneself ardently; to toe the line. **widespread, but now most common in Nth, least common in Midl**

  1806 (1970) Webster *Compendious Dict., Buckle* . . . *to* . . apply. **1848** Bartlett *Americanisms* 51, *To buckle-to*. To get about any task with energy and a determination to effect the object . . . "I have no objections, said the schoolmaster, to sing you a psalm tune, since you're anxious to hear it; but after that you must *buckle-to*, and stick to the elements.—*Knickerbocker Mag.*" **1865** *Atlantic Mth.* 15.301/1 **CT**, If he would only buckle down to serious study. **1880** Twain *Tramp Abroad* 193 **NY**, I buckled in and read all of those books, because he wanted me to. **1885** Twain *Huck. Finn* 125 **MO**, "Come—buckle to your paddle, and let's get along." I buckled to my paddle and they laid to their oars. **1908** *DN* 3.295 **eAL, wGA**, Buckle down to it. **1941** *AmSp* 16.21 **sIN, MO**, Buckle down. **1950** WELS (If somebody has been doing poor work or none at all: "If he wants to keep his job, he'll have to _____.") 6 Infs, **WI**, Buckle down; ("He was pretty careless at first, but I made him _____.") 3 Infs, **WI**, Buckle down (to work); (To work very hard: "He was slow to begin with, but now he's _____.") 1 Inf, **cnWI**, Buckling down. **1954** Harder Coll. **cwTN**, Buckle down on it. **1959** *VT Hist.* new ser 27.127, Buckle down . . . To apply oneself . . . Common. **1965–70** *DARE* (Qu. JJ26, *If somebody has been doing poor work or not enough, the boss might say, "If he wants to keep his job he'd better _____."*) 46 Infs, **chiefly Nth**, Buckle down; **VA74**, Buckle down to work; **IA17, MI17**, Buckle up; **IL82, IA13**, Buckle under; **OH15**, Buckle in; **MA10**, Buckle; (Qu. KK29, *To start working very hard: "He was slow at first but now he's really _____."*) 46 Infs, **widespread, but most common in Nth**, Buckle down (to it); **CA202**, Buckled in; **IL14**, Buckled in to it; **CA166, IA32**, Buckling down; [Of all Infs responding to Qq. JJ26 and KK29 respectively, 36% and 37% were young or mid-aged; of those giving these responses, 57% and 52% were young or mid-aged.]; (Qu. JJ25, *To show somebody that you're the boss: "He thought he could take the place over, but I made him _____."*) Infs **OH80, PA76**, Buckle down; **IL100, WV1**, Buckle under; **CA206**, Buckle up; (Qu. JJ24) Inf **SC3**, Buckle down; (Qu. A22, . . *"To start working hard"*: "She had only ten minutes to clean the room, but she _____ (and had it done in no time).") Infs **IL19, MN16, NC87, TX51**, Buckled down.

2 also with prep or adv: To hurry.

  1848 in 1935 *AmSp* 10.40 **Nantucket MA**, *Buckle till. Buckle to it.* Work fast. **1903** *DN* 2.295 **Cape Cod MA**, *Buckle* . . . To run fast. **1952** Brown *NC Folkl.* 1.523, *Buckle off* . . . To hurry off.

buckle n

A type of coffee cake, usu made with blueberries.

1959 Masterton *Blueberry Hill Cookbook* 271 **VT**, Blueberry buckle. This one does as well for breakfast as for dessert. Serve warm with cream . . . Toss the fresh blueberries in a little flour; then add them [to the batter]. Spread the batter in a greased and floured 9-inch square pan. *Topping* . . sprinkle over batter. Bake. **1979** Flagg *Cape Cod Cooking* 124, *Blueberry buckle* . . . Blend butter and sugar, add egg and beat well. Stir in the milk. Sift flour, baking powder and salt together and stir into liquid mixture. Add the blueberries. Spread in a well buttered 9″ square pan. Sprinkle with topping . . . Bake. **1983** *Better Homes & Gardens* July 89, *Blackberry Buckle—A buckle is a dessert that features a cakelike topping baked with fruit* . . 2½ cups fresh *or* frozen unsweetened blackberries *or* blueberries. **1983** *DARE* File **swMI**, We grew up eating blueberry buckle; usually we picked the berries ourselves.

buckleback n, adv Also pronc-sp *puckleback* [PaGer *buckel* upper back] **sePA**

Piggyback.

1914 *DN* 4.158 **sePA**, *Buckle-back, adv.* Pickaback. **1967** *DARE* (Qu. Y31, *If a child asked his father to carry him on his back, he might say, "Give me a _____."*) Inf **PA**18, Puckleback ['pukəl bæk]; clutch [FW: Inf has slight PaGer accent.]

buckled up adj [Cf nEngl and Scots dial *buckle* to marry] Married.

1950 *WELS* (*Joking ways for saying people got married: they _____*) 1 Inf, **ceWI**, Buckled up. **1969** *DARE* (Qu. AA15a, *. . Joking ways . . of saying that people got married . . "They _____."*) Inf **CT**27, Got buckled up.

buckler n [*buckle* to bend, warp + *-er*]

A late soft-shell stage of the molted crab, when the shell yields only slightly to pressure.

1879 *St. Nicholas* 7.1.84/2 **ceNJ**, I don't know what a crab is usually called at first, whether a soft or hard crab. We say he is a "Buckler." A buckler is always very poor to begin with; but he eats everything he gets hold of, which, of course, fattens him up some. Then he is called a "Comer." **1884** Goode *Fisheries U.S.* 1.776, The terms "Soft Crab," "Paper-shell," and "Buckler" denote the different stages of consistency of the shell.

buckle to a hen's nest n

1969 *DARE* (Qu. NN12b, *Things that people say to put off a child when he asks, "What are you making?"*) Inf **NY**191, Buckle to a hen's nest.

bucklety-whet adv

Lickety-split.

1859 Taliaferro *Fisher's R.* 67 **nwNC** (as of 1820s), I lammed away at him [=a buck deer], and away he went round the mounting, and the bullet arter him . . . Presently round they come like a streak uv sunshine, both buck and bullit, bullit singin' out, 'Whar is it? whar is it?' 'Go it, my fellers,' says I, and away they went round the Loaf like a Blue Ridge storm. Afore you could crack yer finger they was around agin, bucklety-whet.

buckle up v phr

=**buck up** v phr **3.**

1859 Taliaferro *Fisher's R.* 176 **nwNC** (as of 1820s), He . . buckled up to the 'squire, like a little dog does to a big one when he wants to show out. *Ibid* 177, I tell you the train-ile [=perspiration] streamed out'n both on us, but Sol buckled up ter me like a man.

buck load n

A large shot of liquor.

1846 Porter *Quarter Race* 14 **nAL**, Colonel, let us have some of your *byled* corn — pour me out a buck load — there — never mind about the water, I drank a heap of it yesterday. **1899** (1912) Green *VA Folk-Speech*, Buck-load . . . A large drink of liquor.

buck mouse n *obs*

=**white-footed mouse**.

1857 U.S. Patent Office *Annual Rept.: Ag. for 1856* 90, The white-footed wood-mouse is known under the names of "Deer Mouse," "Buck Mouse," and "White-footed Field Mouse."

buck naked adj Also *buck-ass naked, buck-born ~, stark buck ~* [Origin uncert, but perh alter of *butt* buttocks] **chiefly S Atl, Gulf States** See Map Cf **buck bathing, buff n 2, bum naked, butt naked**

Entirely unclothed.

1928 Peterkin *Scarlet Sister Mary* 33 **SC** [Black], Fo Gawd's sake put on some clothes. You ain' stand up buck naked like dat. You's a grown 'oman now. **1936** (1951) Mitchell *Gone* 885 **GA** [Black], Den he try ter snatch de chile frum me, buck nekked as she wuz. **1937** in 1977 *Amer. Slave Suppl. 1* 1.403 **AL** [Black], One of de slaves, buck naked wid de dogs a runnin' atter him. **1961** Hamner *Spencer's Mt.* 33 **cVA**, All the driver had seen . . were countless little naked behinds disappearing under the porch . . ; later the whole army of little white-headed, buck-naked children had poked their heads out from under the house. **1965–70** *DARE* (Qu. W20, *. . No clothes on at all . . "There was Johnny, _____."*) 44 Infs, **chiefly S Atl, Gulf States**, Buck naked; **AL**50, Buck-ass naked; **SC**26, Buck-born naked; **TX**53, Stark buck naked. [Of all Infs responding to the question, 35% were young or mid-aged; of those giving these responses, 55% were young or mid-aged.] **1975** Newell *If Nothin' Don't Happen* 91 **nwFL**, The horse never had seen Uncle naked before, so it just jerked the bridle over its head and run away . . . It was about two miles home and there wasn't nothing for Uncle Wint to do but walk it — buck naked.

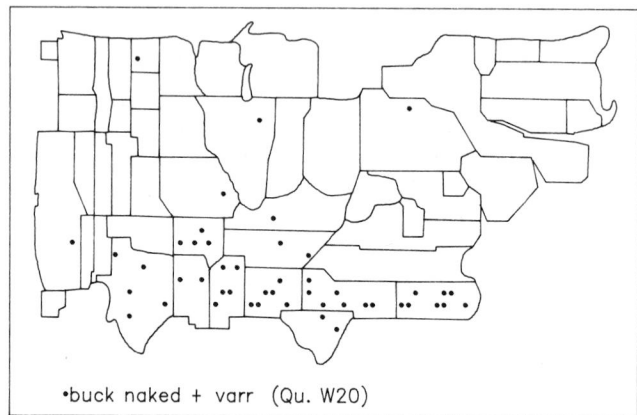

•buck naked + varr (Qu. W20)

buck net n, also attrib [Perh from *buck* to butt, push against] **Chesapeake Bay**

A gill net for catching fish.

1931 *Sun* (Baltimore MD) 26 Feb 5/6–7 (Hench Coll.), Opponents of purse nets and buck net fishing in the Chesapeake Bay squeezed through to a narrow victory in the House today . . . Many of the delegates, it developed, were not certain of the exact nature of buck nets, and some of the delegates from tidal counties insisted that rock and striped bass — the fish for which protection is sought — were never taken in this type of net. *Ibid* 27 Feb 12/1, Only a handful of fishermen now . . [use] purse, or buck nets. **1939** *Sun* (Baltimore MD) 3 Mar 12/1 (Hench Coll.), Seven years ago the Legislature enacted a bill banning the use of purse and buck or gill nets in the Chesapeake Bay . . . Several weeks ago a bill to repeal the ban on the buck nets was introduced in the House of Delegates.

buck nun n [*buck* n[1] 2] **chiefly West**

A celibate man; a man who lives alone.

1907 White *AZ Nights* 286, I might as well go be a buck nun and be done with it. **1944** Adams *Western Words*, Buck-nun — A recluse, a man who lives alone. **1961** Adams *Old-Time Cowhand* 202, Men selected to winter in them camps were usually single men with few or no home ties, and didn't mind the life of a buck nun. *Ibid* 342, You take some old buck-nun who'd never been hogtied with matrimonial ropes, and he didn't savvy she-stuff. **1967** Cerello *Dakota Co. MN* 47, *Buck nun* . . . A priest or other celibate clergyman — "I always felt sorry for the poor sisters that taught us, but those buck nuns really had the life . . . they owned cars, could come and go as they pleased, had money . . . " [Heard in] 6 communities.

bucknut n

=**jojoba**.

1937 U.S. Forest Serv. *Range Plant Hdbk.* B148, Jojoba . . is also locally called bushnut, bucknut, . . and pignut — all such designations alluding to the nutlike fruit.

bucko n [Transf from naval slang for a ship's officer who effects his will through physical violence]

1 A blustering or domineering person; a bully.

1903 Norris *Pit* 87 **Chicago IL**, *This* time I want to . . . get a twist on

those Porteous buckoes, and raise 'em right out of their boots. **1930**
Williams *Logger-Talk* 17 **Pacific NW,** *Bucko:* Any hell-roarer. **1945**
Colcord *Sea Language* **ME, Cape Cod, and Long Island,** *Bucko.* Desig-
nates an officer who used brutal methods of discipline, a bucko mate.
Alongshore, it means a bully, especially in the sardonic appellation "My
bucko!"

2 In logging: a person who steers log rafts.

1925 *AmSp* 1.135 **Pacific NW,** In the spring the logs are driven down
the rivers to the mills by "river drivers," the best among them being
honored with the title of "white-water buckos." The lumberjacks got this
"bucko," perhaps, from the "bucko mates" [=bullying officers of ships]
of the Great Lakes. **1968** Adams *Western Words.*

3 usu with *my:* A fellow—used as a term of address, often
disparagingly. [Cf *W3 bucko* 2, "*chiefly Irish:* young fellow"]

1907 White *AZ Nights* 136, "What?" say I. "Elucidate, my bucko. I
don't take no such blanket order. Spread your cards." **1910** McCutcheon *Rose* 384, "[Jail is] just where you'll land, my handsome bucko,"
said the malevolent Colonel. **1945** [see **1** above].

buck out v phr **West** Cf **buck** n³ **2c,** *DS* BB56
    To die.

1939 Carlisle *Southwestern Dict.,* To buck out . . . Cowboy slang. To
die. **1944** Adams *Western Words,* Buck out—To die. Commonly used
to express a tragic death. *Buck out in smoke*—To die in a gun battle.

buck paddle n Also *bucking paddle* [Cf **buck** v¹ **B6b, buck** v³]
    An implement used for administering physical punishment.

1861 Jacobs *Incidents Slave Girl* 98 **Sth,** Others were tied hand and feet,
and tortured with a bucking paddle, which blisters the skin terribly.
1955 Warren *Angels* 13 **KY** [Black], I says you ain't keerful you gonna git
cowhide and cat-o-nine and buck-paddle laid on till you cain't yell.

buck-paddle v See **buck** v¹ **B6b**

buck party n [**buck** n¹ **2**] *?obs*
    A stag party.

1838 Neal *Charcoal Sketches* 26 **sePA,** "To-morrow . . I leave town for
a week to try a little trout fishing in the mountains." . . "Then I shall go
with you, Mr. Pumpilion," said the lady . . . "Quite *on*possible," returned Pumpilion . . ; "it's a buck party, if I may use the expression—a
buck party entirely." **1872** Schele de Vere *Americanisms* 587, *Buck-
party,* like stag-party, denotes a company without ladies. **1889** (1971)
Farmer *Americanisms,* Buck Party.—An assembly composed entirely
of the male sex.

buck passer, buck-passing See **buck** n³ **2a**

buck pitch n [See quot 1983] Cf **buck euchre**
    A var of the card game **pitch.**

1969–70 *DARE* (Qu. DD35, . . *Favorite card games*) Inf **KY**70, Pitch
—same as buck pitch; **KY**72, Buck pitch. **1982** *Contract Bridge Letters*
scWI, Buck pitch is "Pitch" played by 3 players instead of 4 players,
playing as partners. **1983** *DARE* File **csWI,** Buck pitch—"buck"
means people play cutthroat, every man for himself; no partners; usually
three people.

buck plantain See **buckhorn plantain**

buck plow n [Prob from **buck** v¹ **A2**] Cf **buck rake** n
    1968 *DARE* (Qu. L18, . . *Kinds of plows*) Inf **MO**35, Single plow behind
the horse: the old, buck plow.

buckra n, also attrib Also *buckrah, buckruh, bucra;* formerly
boccarorra, buckera [Efik *mbakára* he who surrounds or governs, White man; cf *DJE backra* 1688 →] **chiefly coastal SC
and GA** *orig Gullah, now more widespread*

1 A boss, master.

1886 Amer. Philol. Assoc. *Trans.* 17.45, *Buck-ra* (for boss or master in
South Carolina). **1892** Harris *On Plantation* 75 **GA,** Miss Chicken
Hawk she coyspon' wid Mr. Eagle, which he was de big buckra er all de
birds. **1949** *AmSp* 24.106 **eSC,** *Buckra* . . . White man. 'My buckra'
(my employer-patron). ('Negro usage.') **1967** Wilson *Folkways Mammoth Cave No. 2* 22 **KY,** *Buckra.* A rare word that must have come from
the few slaves of the region, as it is an African word meaning *bossman* or
leader. Only a few older people can recall having heard it used.

2a Any white person; white people—now usu considered
derog.

1787 Franklin in *Amer. Museum* 2.212/2, They are pleased with the
observation of a negro, and frequently mention it, that Boccarorra

(meaning the white man) make de black man workee, make de horse
workee, make de ox workee, make ebery ting workee. **1800** (1980)
Brown *Arthur Mervyn* 379 **MD,** The blacks looked upon each other . . .
Their habitual deference for every thing *white,* no doubt, held their
hands from what they regarded as a profanation. At last Bob said, in a
whining, beseeching tone—Why, missee, massa buckra wanna go for
doo, dan he wanna go fo' wee [=Why, Miss, (if) the white gentleman
won't do it (i.e., leave at your request), then he won't do it for (on account
of) us]. **1838** Gilman *S. Matron* 104 **seSC** [Black], Ole Maus Osborne
dead . . . and one buckra been come for mak de bounds of de land. **1922**
Gonzales *Black Border* 255 **sSC, GA coasts** [Gullah], Stan' up gal, en'
'low de buckruh fuh look 'punto [=at] yo' foot. *Ibid* 291, *Buckruh*—a
white person or persons; the white people. **1930** *DN* 6.80 **cSC,** *Buckra*
. . . A white person. c**1970** Pederson *Dial. Surv. Rural GA* **seGA,**
(Insulting words for White people) 12 infs, Buckra. [10 infs Black] **1977**
Dillard *Lexicon* 154, Buckra "white person." *Ibid* 177, [Note:] Correctly glossed as an Africanism, this word [=*buckra*] is in widespread use
among whites, especially in the Georgia-South Carolina area.

b in phr *po(or) buckra:* A poor white person; white trash.

1836 Simms *Mellichampe* 2.190 **SC,** 'Tis only poor buckrah dat does
trouble nigger. **1891** Sloan *Fogy Days* 41 (*DA*), Didn't love poor bucra
overseer, Your terror was the patter-roll [=patrol]. **1930** *DN* 6.83 **cSC,**
Po' buckra . . . Used from Columbia, South Carolina, to the coast for the
lower class of white people. The Virginia expression "poor white trash" is
never heard. The adjective *po'* (poor) does not refer to economic status,
but to a lack of breeding or culture. *Po' buckra* is often used as an
attributive adjective. **1949** *State* (Raleigh, N.C.) 24/3 (*DA*), Sometimes
they would have a falling-out, and the white children would say 'nigger,
nigger, nigger,' and the colored ones would say 'po' buckra, 'po'
buckra.' **1966–70** *DARE* (Qu. HH18, *Very insignificant or low-grade
people*) Inf **SC**2, Poor buckra ['poɑˌbʌkrɑ]—low socially; not necessarily
bad; **SC**11, Poor buckra [FW sugg]; **SC**68, Poor buckra (white). c**1970**
Pederson *Dial. Surv. Rural GA* **seGA,** (Insulting words for White people)
1 inf, Po' buckra. [Inf Black]

3 attrib: Of the white race; by ext, white in color.

1840 (1847) Longstreet *GA Scenes* 47 **ceGA** [Black], Fedder fly all ober
de buckera-man meat. **1847** Child *Fact & Fiction* 197 **seSC** [Black],
Myself found the body of my likeliest boy under the tree where buckra
rifles reached him. **1922** Gonzales *Black Border* 291 **sSC, GA coasts**
[Gullah glossary], *Buckruh-bittle*—white man's food. *Buckruh-Nigguh*
—white man's Negro, used contemptuously. *Ibid* 301, "Da' buckruh'
hogmeat flabuh me mout' " . . That white man's pork flavored my
mouth. **1926** Smith *Gullah* 33, *Buckra,* white man, then simply
"white," as *buckra yam,* white potato, *buckra chalk,* white chalk. **1945**
FWP *Lay My Burden Down* 169 **cnSC,** You never see classy buckra man
a-paterolling [=engaged in patrolling, i.e., as an officer on the lookout for
possible runaway slaves].

buck rabbit See **buck** n¹ **1c**

buck rake n Also *buck* [Prob infl by both **buck** v¹ **B7a** and
buck n a male animal, usu with horns] **chiefly West** *somewhat
old-fash* Also called **bucking pole, hay buck 1, hay sweep**
    A large rake, usu pushed by a horse or tractor, used to gather hay.

1893 *Funk's Stand. Dict.* (*OEDS*), *Buck-rake,* a two-horse hay-rake
having hornlike teeth projecting 6 or 8 feet in front for gathering and
transferring hay to a stacker. **1895** *DN* 1.396 **eMA,** *Bull rake:* very
heavy hand rake. N.Y.c [*Buck rake,* Mass. e.] **1943** *Sun* (Baltimore
MD) 15 Mar 6/3, A buck rake picks up hay in the field and carries it to
the barn without having to be touched by hand. **1950** *WELS* (*What . .
you do to hay in the field after it has been cut*) 1 Inf, **WI,** Rake with side
delivery or dump rake into winrows, buck with buck rake; load into hay
rack with loader; (*Tools and machines used . . in handling hay*) 1 Inf,
Buck rake; 1 Inf, Buck rake—tractor drawn (hay rack if no buck rake is
used). **1965–70** *DARE* (Qu. L16, . . *Machines used . . in handling hay*)
Infs **CA**18, **CO**19, **IN**63, **MT**5, Buck rake; **AZ**10, Buck rake—to push
the hay around; **CA**36, Buck rake—picks up six shocks or more at a
time; **CA**63, Buck rake—4 horses; shovels hay to hay press that bales it;
ND9, Old days: buck rake, stacker; **OK**1, Mowing machine—previously
used with a sulky rig and a buck rake; **OK**43, Sulky rake (put into
windrows); buck rake (takes windrows to bales); **WY**4, Buck rake or
push rake—not used here anymore; (Qu. L23) Inf **OR**10, Buck rake.
1967 *DARE* Tape **OR**2, Buck—thing that picks up hay after it's raked. It
is pushed, as is the header. **1981** *DARE* File **WY,** A buck rake for
collecting bales of hay is sort of a front-end loader put on the chassis of an
old truck. It has an hydraulic lift so that the operator can move it up and
down while he's charging toward another bale and can collect about a
dozen bales almost without stopping. He unloads them in a pile out in

the field, where they're stored. You need these out west, where the fields are too big to load all the bales by hand. *Ibid* **csWI,** The buck rake was for gathering hay that was already in winrows. After you had a load, you could dump it by pushing a pedal with your foot. The loader would then come and pick up the piles. *Ibid* **eOR,** In '23 or '24 I worked on a horse-drawn combine in eastern Oregon. There I saw a horse-pushed buck rake. It had the teeth . . inset a couple of feet from each end. Shafts extended back, four shafts for a three horse team if I remember rightly. When used, singletrees would pull against the ends of the shafts—turning would be slow.

buck rake v [buck rake n]

1967 *DARE* (Qu. L11, *What . . you do to hay in the field after it's cut*) Inf **CO**19, Buck rake (bunch into piles), or run into windrows, then bale.

buckram n Cf buckler

A molted crab whose shell is beginning to harden; the stage of hardening subsequent to **papershell.**

c1830 Godman in *Waldie's Select Library* II.87/3 *(DAE),* Twelve hours later the shell is sufficiently stiffened to require some slight force to bend it, and the crab is said to be in *buckram.* **1933** Maryland State Dept. Educ. *Our Underwater Farm* 25 *(Hench Coll.),* Crabs with a thin new hard shell are called "buckrams." Their meat is watery and useless for food. **1934** *Sun* (Baltimore MD) 2 Apr 6/2–3 *(Hench Coll.)* **seMD,** Floats . . have to be fished several times during each twenty-four hours, in order that the soft crab may be taken out at once and placed in grass, otherwise they would become papershell or buckram crabs, which are illegal to market. **1935** *Ibid* 1 June 7/6 *(Hench Coll.),* The bill also would make it "unlawful to take or destroy any hard crab, sponge crab, buckra[m] crab, peeler or soft crab within the protection of this law." **1976** Warner *Beautiful Swimmers* 27 **Chesapeake Bay,** Take a fair number of buckrams or crabs with the semi-stiff shells that are hardening up after moult.

buck root n Cf congo root

A **scurf pea** (here: *Psoralea canescens*).

1765 (1942) Bartram *Diary of a Journey* 33.15/1, Rode to observe A lovely species of onobrichis with large aromatick root & very regular branched stalk 3 foot high₍.₎ people calls it here buck root & say it is very good for inward pains. **c1937** in 1970 Yetman *Voices* 87, De woods was full of dem wild hogs, and lots of fish in de holes where he could sicken 'em with buck root and catch 'em with his hands, all he wanted. **1950** Gray–Fernald *Manual of Botany* 898, *P. canescens . . . Buckroot . . .* Sandy woods, Fla. and Ala., n., locally, to se.Va.

buckruh See buckra

buckrush n

=**hobblebush.**

1911 *Century Dict.* **1932** Randolph *Ozark Mt. Folks* 278, A great owl flapped silently and low over the buckrush in the abandoned garden-patch. **1956** McAtee *Some Dialect NC* 54, Buckrush . . hobble-bush *(Viburnum grandifolium).* Yancey County.

bucks n Also (the) buck [Abbr]

1 =**buck fever 1.**

1906 *DN* 3.129 **nwAR,** Buckager(s), bucks . . . Inaction due to excessive nervous tension. "He would have shot the deer, if he hadn't had the buckagers." **1967–70** *DARE* (Qu. P36, *When a hunter sees a deer . . and gets so excited he can't shoot, he has _____*) Inf **CO**4, The buck; **IL**25, Buck; **IL**115, The buck and gets so worked up he can't pull the trigger; **MO**7, Bucks.

2 =**ague B1.** Cf **buck ague 3**

1906 *DN* 3.129 **nwAR,** Buckager(s), bucks . . . Severe chills with fever.

bucksaw n [Perh from buck n¹ 4, but perh metathesis of sawbuck] Nth, N Midl

A device to hold wood for sawing.

1966–69 *DARE* (Qu. L58, . . *An implement with an A-shaped frame that you put boards on to saw them*) Infs **MA**47, **PA**23, **WI**71, Bucksaw; (Qu. L59, . . *An implement with an X-frame to hold firewood for sawing*) Infs **IN**42, **RI**4, **WA**18, **WI**71, Bucksaw.

buck-scared adj Also buck-shy

Afflicted with **buck fever 1.**

1968 *DARE* (Qu. P36, *When a hunter sees a deer . . and gets so excited he can't shoot, he [is] . . _____*) Inf **WI**62, Buck-scared; **CA**15, Buck-shy.

buck's horn See buckhorn 1, 7

buck's horn brake n obs

=**ostrich fern.**

1821 in 1832 MA Hist. Soc. *Coll.* 2d ser 9.153 **VT,** Onoclea . . struthiopteris, Buck's horn brake.

buckshot n, often attrib

1 Soil that, on drying, forms pellets resembling buckshot. **lower Missip Valley**

1861 (1955) Holmes *Brokenburn* 14 **cwMS,** It has been such a long, muddy winter and spring. No one knows what mud is until he lives on a buckshot place and travels buckshot roads. **1871** Somers *S. States* 144 **MS,** The soil is a dry deep red loam—what is called, in the language of the country, "a buckshot soil." **1884** Murfree *Where the Battle* 13, He began . . by comparing Tennessee soil to the alluvial richness of the buckshot cotton lands of Mississippi. **1903** *DN* 2.308 **seMO,** *Buckshot land . . .* Poor clay soil, called 'buckshot' on account of small lumps which it generally contains. **1916** *DN* 4.268 **seLA,** *Buckshot dirt . . .* Crumbly soil. **1941** FWP *Guide AR* 274, The bottom land of these streams is known as buckshot; if plowed when wet, it forms blocks of sticky earth that become hard and untillable. **1966–70** *DARE* (Qu. C31, . . *Heavy, sticky soil*) Infs **AR**14, **LA**9, **MS**32, 86, Buckshot; **LA**3, Buckshot clay; **LA**7, Buckshot land—in a bottom; makes small clods look like little pebble rocks; (Qu. C30, . . *Loose, dark soil*) Inf **MS**86, Buckshot gumbo—a dark soil that is very sticky.

2 See quot.

1940 FWP *Guide TX* 577 **cwTX,** Along the canyon floor are found thousands of small, perfectly round stones, locally called "buckshot rocks."

buckshot fever n

=**buck fever 1.**

1969 *DARE* (Qu. P36, *When a hunter sees a deer . . and gets so excited he can't shoot, he has _____*) Inf **IN**58, Buckshot fever.

buck-shy See buck-scared

buckskin n, also attrib

1 also *buck:* A horse of a light yellowish dun color and often with a dark stripe down the back and a dark mane. **widespread** (though often considered to be a westernism) *esp among old and male Infs* Also called **coyote B4**

1874 VT State Bd. Ag. *Rept. for 1873–74* 2.402, The buckskin McClellan was a regular hollow or sway back. **1894** *Outing* 24.101/2 **ND,** That Clip of hers . . is a pretty mustang. He's a bright buckskin with a dark stripe. **1935** Sandoz *Jules* **wNE** (as of 1880–1930), Daisy was a compact, dark little buckskin, with shaggy black mane and a tail that dragged the ground. **1950** *WELS* (*Kinds of horses named according to their colors*) 4 Infs, **WI,** Buckskin; (*Horse of a dirty white color*) 1 Inf, Buckskin; (*Horse of mixed colors*) 1 Inf, Buckskin. **c1960** *Wilson Coll.* **csKY,** Buckskin horse . . . Cream-colored or yellow horse. Rarely used. "Grandpa's got a new buckskin horse." **1965–70** *DARE* (Qu. K39, . . *Other . . horses according to their colors*) 180 Infs, **widespread,** Buckskin; **SD**8, Buck [Of all Infs responding to the question, 66% were male, 73% old; of those giving these responses, 81% were male, 82% old.]; (Qu. K38, *A horse of a dirty white color*) 22 Infs, **chiefly Midl, Inland Nth,** Buckskin; (Qu. K37, . . *A horse of mixed colors*) Infs **CT**17, **MA**75, Buckskin. **1967** *DARE* Tape **ID**13, Buckskin—light tan colored horse with lighter mane and tail.

2 A log without bark. **Nthn logging areas**

1938 (1939) Holbrook *Holy Mackinaw* 259 **Nth,** Buckskin. A log from which bark has fallen off. **1942** *AmSp* 17.220 **Nth.** **1950** *Western Folkl.* 9.116 **nwOR.** **1956** Sorden–Ebert *Logger's Words* **Gt Lakes.** **1958** McCulloch *Woods Words* **Pacific NW,** Buckskin—a. A peeled log. b. An old bark-free snag, or a windfall.

3 See quot. [Formerly, a deerskin used as a unit of exchange] Cf **buck n¹ 3, frogskin,** *DS* U26

1966 *Wilson Coll.* **csKY,** Buckskin—money.

4 =**lake trout.**

1904 *Salmon & Trout* 287 **neMI,** "Buckskins" is the name given them [lake trout] around Thunder Bay in Lake Huron.

buckskin pine n Also buckskin tree [Prob from its turning yellow in the fall]

See quots.

1967 Borland *Hill Country* 331, The larch is also called the tamarack, sometimes known as hackmatack, and in the mountain West it is often called the buckskin tree. **1968** *DARE* (Qu. T17, . . *Kinds of pine trees*) Inf **LA**15, Buckskin pine.

buck sled n Cf **buckboard 2, bunk sled**
A type of sleigh.
   1966–70 *DARE* (Qu. N40a, . . *Sleighs . . for hauling loads*) Inf **NJ**46, Buck sled; **NJ**50, Buck sled; straight sled; **NJ**65, Buck sled — short, for heavy duty. [All Infs old] **1981** *DARE* File **seWI**, A buck sled is a bobsled — an ordinary sled with runners. People use it just for enjoyment.

buckstand See **buck** n[1] **4**

buck the bull off the bridge See **buck a bull off the bridge**

buck the Indian n
   1945 Boyd *Hdbk. Games* 58, *Buck the Indian* . . . Two teams face each other and join hands in a line . . . The head player of one team runs and tries to break through the opponents' line . . . If he breaks the line, he takes all the players below the break . . and places them as he thinks best in his own line. The head of the opposing team now has his turn, and so on, the players down the line taking turns according to the line-up.

buck the tiger See **buck** v[1] **B5b**

buck thistle n
=**bull thistle** (here: *Cirsium vulgare*).
   1900 Lyons *Plant Names* 81, *[Cirsium] lanceolatus* [= *C. vulgare*] . . . Buck Thistle.

buckthorn clover n
See quot.
   1959 *VT Hist.* new ser 27.127, Buckthorn clover . . . Hay that contains brush and coarse weeds.

buckthorn weed n
A **fiddleneck 1** (here: *Amsinckia intermedia*).
   1911 Jepson *Flora CA* 350, *Amsinckia intermedia* . . . Buckthorn Weed. **1915** (1926) Armstrong *Western Wild Flowers* 428, Buckthorn Weed — *Amsinckia intermedia.*

buck tick n
Perh =**beggar ticks 1.**
   1970 *DARE* (Qu. S15, . . *Weed seeds that stick to clothing*) Inf **VA**77, Buck tick — fuzzy, cling.

buck tie See **buck** n[1] **7**

buck tongue n [From *buck* a male deer, and the shape of the leaf] Cf **deer's-tongue 1**
=**vanilla plant 1.**
   1970 *Foxfire* Spring–Summer 35 **nGA**, I had a leaf then, buck tongue or deer tongue. When it first grows up it makes a *real* leaf t'call [turkeys] with.

bucktown n
?The rough part of town.
   1968 *DARE* (Qu. C35, *Nicknames for the different parts of your town*) Inf **IA**30, Bucktown — some ornery people lived there; **OH**42, Bucktown.

buck up v phr [**buck** v[1]]
1 usu imper: To take courage, apply oneself. Cf **buckle v 1**
   1844 *Graham's Mag.* Jan 38/1 **sePA**, "Well, now, for my part, I don't see the trouble," said Mrs. Fitzgig; "why can't a man buck up?" **1902** Lorimer *Letters* 153 **Chicago IL**, I want to see you grow . . so strong and big that you will force us to see that you are out of place among the little fellows. Buck up! **1922** Brown *Old Crow* 385 **seMA**, Buck up, old man. Here's another chance for you. **1950** *WELS* (*To get somebody out of an unhappy mood you might say:* "_____.") 2 Infs, **WI**, Buck up. **1965–70** *DARE* (Qu. GG27a, *To get somebody out of an unhappy mood, you might say . . ,* "Everything's going to be all right, so _____.") 16 Infs, **scattered**, Buck up; **KS**6, Buck up now; (Qu. JJ26, *If somebody has been doing poor work or not enough, the boss might say, "If he wants to keep his job he'd better _____."*) Infs **IL**50, **MA**28, **MO**3, Buck up. [17 of 20 Infs are coll educ]
2 with *to*: To court, seek the affections of. *old-fash*
   1832 *Polit. Examiner* (Shelbyville, KY) 8 Dec. 4/1 *(DA)*, I seed her at church one day fixed up kinder pretty snug; so . . . darn my seelskin pumps if I dont buck up to her next Fust day. **1846** in 1956 Eliason *Tarheel Talk* 168 **NC**, Miss _____ was there and the way I bucke up to her made the old folk stare . . . . I did talk soft stuff to her in streakes. I

toled the gal I loved her. **1868** Paulding *Book of Vagaries* 265 **NY**, Single gentlemen . . . should beware how they "buck up" to widows. **1899** (1912) Green *VA Folk-Speech*, Buck-up-to . . . To make advances of courtship. "I saw Bob bucking up to her at the party." c**1960** *Wilson Coll.* **csKY**, *Buck up to* . . . used to mean "pay court to."
3 usu with *to*: To stand up to, defy.
   1846 Porter *Quarter Race* 45 **MS**, I . . never paid no 'tention to him, till he bucked up too me an give me a feller rite under the ear, an I tell ye it made my hed kinder dizzy. **1909** *DN* 3.409 **nME**, *Buck up* . . . To rebel. **1912** *DN* 3.572 **wIN**, *Buck up* . . . To stand up manfully; to meet one squarely. "Don't be afraid; buck right up to him." **1942** Warnick *Garrett Co. MD* 4 (as of 1900–18), *Buck up to.* **1957** *AmSp* 32.285 **NC**, To *buck up* to somebody means to talk and act as good or big as that somebody. c**1960** *Wilson Coll.* **csKY**, *Buck up to* . . . Defy, "tell off": "He just bucked up to that big boy who hit him."
4 To place rams with ewes for breeding. Cf **bucking season**
   [**1867** T[homas] D. Price *MS. Diary* 5 Oct. *(DAE)*, Commenced bucking in afternoon.] **1913** (1979) Barnes *Western Grazing* 380, *Bucking up.* — Placing the bucks with the ewes. A band of sheep is sold "bucked up" to lamb on certain dates.

buck up n Also *buck 'em* [Cf **buck** v[1] **B5**] **MI** Cf **buck euchre, buck pitch**
A card game: see quots.
   1966 *DARE* Tape **MI**24, Buck up [card game] — 4 players, 3 cards to a person; each player contributes to the pot and whoever takes a trick gets one-third of the pot. Contribution to the pot builds. **1982** *Contract Bridge Letters* **seMI** (as of 1936), Buck up . . . can be played by 3 to 17 players, although the largest I ever saw was 9 players . . . If any player fails to win a trick he is "bucked" for the full amount of the pot. *Ibid*, *Buck-up* . . . is played in Michigan State Police circles, emphatically on personal time and emphatically without publicity . . I believe a variant of the card game "Burn." *Ibid*, Buck up (Also called Buck 'Em). *Ibid* (as of 1930s–40s), Buck 'em . . . the dealer dealt three cards to all players (generally six or seven) and then turned up a card, which was trump.

buck wagon See **buckboard** n **1**

buckwheat n
1 Std: a cereal grain *(Fagopyrum esculentum).*
2 A plant of the genus *Eriogonum.* Also called **antelope brush, desert trumpet, dog tongue, Indian tobacco, napkin-ring buckwheat, skeleton weed, sulphur flower, trumpet, umbrella plant, whiskbroom, wild buckwheat, yellow turban**
   1946 Peattie *Pacific Coast* 105 **cwCA**, Dryness intensifies the smell of sage and buckwheat and greasewood. **1948** Sierra Club *Bulletin* March 45, *Oxytropis Parryi* was a depressed dwarf scarcely to be distinguished on the tundra-like flat among the low condensed buckwheats, drabas, phloxes, and daisies with which it grew.
3 See **buckwheat cake.**
4 =**wild buckwheat.**
   1966 *DARE* Wildfl QR Pl.15b Infs **NC**36, **SC**41, Buckwheat. **1968–69** *DARE* (Qu. S21, . . *Weeds . . that are a trouble*) Inf **PA**206, Buckwheat weed; (Qu. S26a, . . *Roadside flowers*) Inf **CA**79, Buckwheat; (Qu. S26d, *Wildflowers . . in meadows*) Inf **WI**72, Buckwheat.
5 also *buckwheater, buck farmer*: A rustic; a greenhorn. **chiefly Nth, N Midl** Cf **buck** n[1] **2f**
   1866 *Beadle's Monthly* 1.248/1 **PA**, The most novel and sometimes very funny experiences are with the aborigines, or, as they are called, the "Buckwheats." They derive their appellation from the fact that, as the oldest inhabitants, who lived out among the barren hills of the country, they raised buckwheat as the only production of the ground, which they would take to the towns to pay their tavern bills, exchange for articles of clothing, etc. **1900** *DN* 2.15 [College slang], A countryman, or a greenhorn of any description, is a *buckwheat*, a *wheat*, a *hay-rube.* **1904** *DN* 2.395 **sNJ**, *Buckwheat* . . . A countryman; a rustic; a "hecker." **1905** U.S. Forest Serv. *Bulletin* 61.31, *Buckwheater* . . . A novice at lumbering. [General]. **1941** *LANE* Map 450, The map shows a great variety of terms, largely derogatory and jocular, applied to a person who lives in the country — specifically to an old farmer who seldom visits the village or city. The following terms were recorded in more than one community: . . *buck farmer* [wMA, nCT, sRI], . . *buckwheat* or *buckwheater* [nwCT]. **1958** McCulloch *Woods Words* **Pacific NW**, *Buckwheat show* — a. Easy logging. b. A poor logging outfit made up of greenhorns. *Buckwheater* — A green hand, newcomer to the woods. **1968** *DARE* (QR, near Qu. C34) Inf **VA**13, "Buckwheat College" is the

Laurel Fork school [FW: Laurel Fork and area has population of 30].
1969 Sorden *Lumberjack Lingo* **NEng, Gt Lakes,** (as of 1850–1920),
Buckwheater.

6 See quot 1969; hence v *buckwheat:* see quot 1905. [Perh
from its being felled by a **buckwheat 5**]

1905 U.S. Forest Serv. *Bulletin* 61.39, *Hang up, to* . . . to fell a tree so
that it catches against another instead of falling to the ground . . . Syn.: . .
buckwheat [Appalachians]. **1969** Sorden *Lumberjack Lingo* **NEng,
Gt Lakes** (as of 1850–1920), *Buckwheat* . . A tree felled so that it lodges
against another tree. Same as hang up, lodge.

7 in phr *show where the bear shit in the buckwheat* and varr: To
tell someone off, put someone in his place.

1917 *DN* 4.342, *Show how the bear came out of the mountains.* To teach
something; e.g. when in a game of cards the bidder—confident of
winning—says he will "show how the bear came out of the mountains."
Also *show how the bear came out of the buckwheat.* **1947** *Progress*
(Charlottesville VA) 24 Jan 1/5 (Hench Coll.), He [an old Arkansan]
recalled that one of his last scholastic acts was to compete in a spelling bee
in which he outspelled "the whole kit and kaboodle of 'em." "Them
fellers was just going into the low fifth and a-leavin' me behind in the
fourth. But I sure showed 'em where the bear sat in the buckwheat."
1966–67 *DARE* (Qu. JJ22, *To express your opinion—for example, at a
public meeting: "I went to the meeting, and _____.")* Inf **MI32,** Told
'em where the bear shit in the buckwheat; (Qu. JJ25, *To show somebody
that you're the boss: "He thought he could take the place over, but I . .
_____.")* Inf **WA30,** Showed him whose boar shit in the buckwheat
patch. **1983** *DARE* File **wOR,** He showed them where the bear crapped
in the buckwheat.

buckwheat bannock n [*buckwheat* + **bannock**] Cf **buckwheat
cake**

1909 *DN* 3.409 **nME,** *Buckwheat bannocks* . . . Thick fritters made of
buckwheat.

buckwheat brush See **buckwheat tree**

buckwheat cake n Also *buckwheat, ~ hotcake, ~ pancake*
chiefly Gt Lakes, Appalachians See Map Cf **pannicake, wheat
cake**

A pancake, esp one made with buckwheat flour.

1772 Kalm *Travels N. Amer.* 1.273 (as of 1748), Buck-wheat cakes . .
are likewise usual at *Philadelphia* and in other *English* colonies, especially in winter. **1814** (1915) Pleasants *Diary* 417 **PA,** Agreed to come
on . . Wednesday night for buckwheat cakes . . . In the evening intended
to go to the buckwheat cake par[t]y. **1830** *Collegian* (Harvard) 41, For
tea, [take] six muffins, a dozen buck-wheats, and 6 cups of shells. **1941**
LANE Map 289 *(Griddle cake)* 12 infs, **CT, RI, MA, sVT,** Buckwheat
cake; 2 infs, **wCT, sVT,** Buckwheat pancake. **1950** *WELS (Names . . for
pancakes)* 9 Infs, **WI,** Buckwheat cakes. **1956** Ker *Vocab. W. TX* 271,
Flat cake (wheat flour) cooked on a griddle: . . buckwheat [1 infor-
mant]. **1965–70** *DARE* (Qu. H20b, . . *Names for pancakes*) 33 Infs,
chiefly Gt Lakes, Appalachians, Buckwheat cakes; **ME2, MI82, NY70,**
Buckwheat pancakes; **MD41,** Buckwheat hotcakes; (Qu. H18), Inf
MD24, Buckwheat cakes—pancake made with buckwheat flour; served
with gravy. **1973** Allen *LAUM* 1.283, *Buckwheat cakes* or [*buckwheat*]
pancakes is the form offered by [5 infs in **IA, NE, ND**].

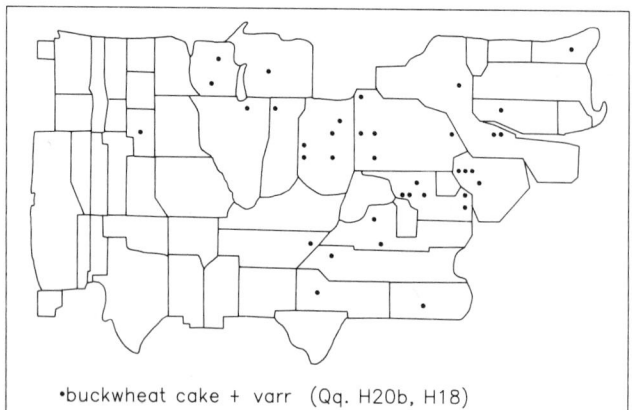

•buckwheat cake + varr (Qq. H20b, H18)

buckwheat cedar n Cf **buckwheat pine**

1966 *DARE* (Qu. T5, . . *Kinds of evergreens, other than pines*) Inf **MI10,**
Buckwheat cedar.

buckwheat crop n

1967–68 *DARE* (Qu. AA20, *A marriage that takes place because a
baby is on the way*) Inf **NY123,** Buckwheat crop; **IL5,** A buckwheat
crop—means that the baby's on the way (because buckwheat gets ripe
much more quickly than other grains).

buckwheater See **buckwheat 5**

buckwheat fly n

A **cluster fly** or similar fly.

1968–69 *DARE* (Qu. R12) Inf **NY105,** Buckwheat fly = cluster fly,
often found in old houses; **NY220,** Buckwheat fly.

buckwheat itch n

See quot 1909.

1909 *DN* 3.409 **nME,** *Buckwheat itch* . . . A skin eruption supposed to
be caused by eating buckwheat. **1953** Van Wagenen *Golden Age* 71
ceNY (as of 1800s), There were certain unfortunates who by sad mis-
chance were allergic to buckwheat so that if they indulged in this royal
food to excess they developed a skin eruption, inelegantly but correctly
designated as the "buckwheat itch." [**1968** *DARE* (QR, near Qu. H14)
Inf **NJ8,** Never ate buckwheat cakes in summer since they would give
you hives.]

buckwheat-nose n Also *buckwheat-nosed adder* obs
=**hognose snake.**

1842 DeKay *Zool. NY* 3.51, The Hog-nosed Snake. *Heterodon platyrhinos* . . . This well known species . . . is also called *Deaf Adder,
Spreading Adder, Hog-nose* and *Buckwheat-nose;* the latter from some
fancied resemblance between that grain and its rostral plate. **1848**
Bartlett *Americanisms* 34, *Blauser.* The name given by the Dutch settlers
to the hog-nosed snake, from its habit of distending or blowing up the
skin of its neck and head. The other popular names in New York are
Deaf-adder and Buckwheat-nosed.—*Nat. Hist. of New York.*

buckwheat note n Also *buckwheat character, ~ grain* [Prob
from the shape, but cf **buckwheat 5**] *usu derog* Cf **fasola**
=**shape note.**

1853 Gould *Hist. Church Music* 55, The characters . . were . . , by way
of reproach, called, by some, buckwheat notes. *Ibid* 140, Still, however,
we have reason to believe that *buckwheat* notes are not all eaten up, but
are to this time preserved and used in many places in the great west.
1883 (1884) Howe *Story Country Town* 17 **KS,** He had a collection of
religious songs preserved in a leather-bound book, the notes being
written in buckwheat characters on blue paper. **1895** Howells *Recollections* 143 **OH** (as of 1825), The books were printed in what they called
patent notes, or, in ridicule, *buckwheat* notes. **1903** *Atlantic Mth.*
92.80/2 **IA,** The younger people . . had attended singing school and
learned to read buckwheat notes. **1933** *Musical Qrly.* 19.400, The
urban fosterers of music *comme il faut* . . in the musical magazines of the
early post-Civil War period reviled the proponents of "measle-toed" and
"square-toed" music, or assured them that their "buckwheat notes"
were about "good enough for niggers." **1933** *AmSp* 8.1.52 **Ozarks,**
Shape notes . . . The peculiar notation which the Ozark singing-teachers
still use rather than the ordinary *round* or *sol* notes. Sometimes called
buckwheat notes. **1933** Jackson *White Spirituals* 419 **S Midl,** The
shape-noters have from the start had to defend their practices. When it
was a matter merely of one notation against another, the controversy
took the form of mutual ridicule. The adherents to the traditional
notation called the rural innovation "buck-wheat grains." **1951** *PADS*
15.53 **neIN,** *Buckwheat notes* . . . In musical notation, from the shape of
some . . notes used before the present style was adopted. **1955** (1960)
Scholes *Oxford Companion Music* 569, The ancient English system of
sol-fa . . . has, however, since 1832 . . been a good deal superseded by a
seven-note 'buck-wheat' system corresponding to the later Tonic Sol-fa.
The 'Bible Belt' or 'Fundamentalist Region' of the Southern States is
nowadays the home of these two systems.

buckwheat pancake See **buckwheat cake**

buckwheat pine n Cf **buckwheat cedar**

Perh a **white pine,** but see quot 1969.

1873 Walling *Atlas MI* 20/1, Upon a somewhat similar soil [=the very
best quality] is found the "Buckwheat," and "grove" pine, which are
usually freely interspersed with hemlock. **1969** Sorden *Lumberjack
Lingo* **NEng, Gt Lakes** (as of 1850–1920), *Buckwheat pine*—Trees that
taper very rapidly and knots show from the ground. Not of much value.
Sometimes occur as double pine or triple pine.

buckwheat tree n Also *buckwheat brush* [See quot 1960]

An evergreen large shrub or small tree (*Cliftonia monophylla*) native to southeastern Georgia and the Gulf States. Also called **black titi 1, ironwood, titi**

1813 Muhlenberg *Catalogus Plantarum* 45, *Mylocarium . . . Buckwheat tree.* **1818** Nuttall *Genera N. Amer. Plants* 276, Mylocarium [ligustrinum] . . . (Buckwheat-tree) . . . a tall evergreen shrub . . . [which grows] on the margins of swamps in Georgia and Florida. **1897** Sudworth *Arborescent Flora* 277, *Cliftonia monophylla . . .* Common names [include] Titi . . . Buckwheat-tree (Fla., La.). **1938** Matschat *Suwannee R.* 262 **FL**, Other flowers were mint, forming a sea of blue flowers . . and the titi, or buckwheat tree. **1951** Teale *North with Spring* 58, Florida is the land of the woolly-bucket tree, the buckwheat tree, the fishfaddle tree and the pondapple tree. **1953** Greene–Blomquist *Flowers South* 68, *Titi, Ironwood, Buckwheat-Brush* . . Another source of excellent honey. **1960** Vines *Trees SW* 644, *Buckwheat-tree . . .* The fruit resembles that of a buckwheat, and hence the common name of the plant.

bucky n[1] Also sp *buckey, buckie* **esp sNEng**

1 also *buckboard herring:* An **alewife** or similar fish.

1877 Bartlett *Americanisms* 71, *Buckey,* an alewife. Western Connecticut. **1896** *DN* 1.413 **RI**, *Buckies* . . buckboard herring. **1931–33** *LANE Worksheets* **RI**, *Bucky*—A slim salt-water fish; cooked fresh or smoked. Same size as scup, very bony. After the civil war it was sent south to colored folks . . . A fish eaten year around by backwoodsmen. *Ibid, Bucky*—A species of saltwater herring. *Ibid* **CT**, *Bucky*—A variety of fish. A bonefish is similar to a bucky.

2 A whelk (*Buccinum* spp).

1939 Natl. Geog. Soc. *Fishes* 209, In recent years, such species of mollusks as the indefatigable periwinkle, dog whelk, and "buckie" . . are now found on the coast of southern New England and Long Island Sound. *Ibid* 318, From behind comes a "buckie," or *Furbelowed Whelk.*

bucky n[2] See **buck** n[1] 2b

bucky adj[1] [*EDD* **bucky** rank, sour]

Having a strong or rank flavor.

1939 *Hench Coll.,* A colleague told me of hearing a person (raised in Henrico County, Va.) speak of the meat of a boar that is at least three years old and hasn't been castrated as "bucky meat."

bucky adj[2] [Perh rel to **bucky** adj[1]]

1 Out of order, not working right.

1950 *WELS (Out of order: "My sewing machine is _____.")* 1 Inf, **cWI**, On the blink; out of commission; bucky; out of whack.

2 Unprofessional.

1968 *DARE* (Qu. X5, . . *Kinds of men's haircuts*) Inf **MD**41, ['bʌkɪ] cut—home job, done on child by his parents.

bucky fly See **buck fly 2**

bucra See **buckra**

bud n[1]

1 A switch or rod.

1891 (1900) French *Otto* 174 **AR**, I jes *will* guv 'er the bud [Footnote: Switch]—leastways, I'll skeer 'er up. *Ibid* 237, But what fur did he kill the feller? Why cudn't he of given him the bud an' taken the money back? [Footnote:] 'To give the bud' or 'give the hickory' is Arkansas for to thrash. **1912** *DN* 3.581 **wIN**, Lay the bud to . . . To whip with a stick. "The teacher laid the bud to him for pinching Lucy." **1946** Greer–Petrie *Angeline Steppin'* 38 **csKY**, If it tuck puttin' the *bud* to him, I was a-gwine to larn that boy of mine manners.

2 See quot.

1944 Adams *Western Words, Buds*—A mark of ownership made by cutting down a strip of skin on the nose of an animal.

bud n[2] [Prob hypocoristic form of *brother*] Cf **buddy** n, **bub** n[2]

1 Used chiefly as a nickname or term of address for:

a A brother or eldest son. **widespread, but esp common in Sth, S Midl** *somewhat old-fash*

1851 (1969) Burke *Polly Peablossom* 19 **GA**, "An't you joking, *bud?*" asked Polly [of her brother]. **1871** Eggleston *Hoosier Schoolmaster* 15 **sIN**, The older son of Mr. Means was called Bud Means. What his real name was Ralph could not find out, for in many of these families the nickname of "Bud" given to the oldest boy, and that of "Sis" which is the birthright of the oldest girl, completely bury the proper Christian name. **1895** *DN* 1.385 **cwIN, wFL. 1896** Harris *Sister Jane* 99 **GA**, Tell Mandy Satterlee that her brother would like mighty well to see her . . . Jest tell Mandy that Bud wants to see her . . . She allers useter call me Bud. **1905**

DN 3.60 **NE.** *Ibid* 71 **nwAR.** **1945** *AmSp* 20.84 **TX**, Should . . [a man] belong to the younger generation he would refer to his brother as 'my bud.' This is an expression widely used by men and women throughout the state. 'My bud's in the Marines on Guadal,' a girl will say. Or, 'Me and my bud bought that steer yonder.' **1950** *WELS (Nicknames and affectionate words meaning brother)* 13 Infs, **WI**, Bud. [11 Infs women] **1965–70** *DARE* (Qu. Z5, *Nicknames and affectionate words meaning "Brother"*) 204 Infs, **widespread but esp freq in Sth, S Midl**, Bud. [Of all Infs responding to the question, 67% were old; of those giving this response, 75% were old.]

b Any boy.

1874 Uncle Bob *Letters to the Children* 196 (Hench Coll.), Now, Bud, don't you scribble any of your nonsense to Uncle Bob. **1902** *DN* 2.230 **sIL. 1903** *DN* 2.308 **seMO**, *Bud* . . . Brother. A small boy. The northern expression 'bub' is never used. Often used as a name, as: 'Bud Watkins.' **1905** *DN* 3.71 **nwAR. 1908** *DN* 3.295 **eAL, wGA. 1944** *ADD* 79/2 **cNY**, *Bud* is used instead of the given name of a boy. One instance. **1950** *WELS (Somebody when you don't know his name . . a boy: "Say, _____, where's the post office?")* 15 Infs, **WI**, Bud. [12 Infs women] **1952** Burnett *Vanity Row* 4 **N Cent**, Gamblers . . would often hand him a quarter . . and say: "Keep it, bud." **1965–70** *DARE* (Qu. II10a, . . *Somebody on the street when you don't know his name . . a boy: "Say, _____, where's the post office?")* 37 Infs, **scattered**, Bud.

c Any man. **esp Atlantic**

1902 Wister *Virginian* 39 **WY**, They called to him; "This way, Budd!" **1905** *DN* 3.71 **nwAR. 1915** *DN* 4.181 **swVA**, *Bud* . . . Often used instead of the Christian name. "Uncle Bud's a comin' to our house." **1965–70** *DARE* (Qu. II10b, . . *Somebody on the street when you don't know his name . . a man: "Say, _____, how far is it to the next town?")* 9 Infs, **chiefly N Atl**, Bud; (Qu. NC52, Hey bud, you've got a hole in your britches; (Qu. GG23c) Inf **OH**95, Cool it, bud; (Qu. NN10a) Inf **MO**13, Hi bud. [9 of 12 total Infs were men] **1968** *DARE* (QR, near Qu. II25) Inf **GA**23, Bud [Inf's name for Inf **GA**22]. **1968–69** [see **buddy** n 1c].

2 A close friend. [Prob abbr for **buddy**]

1967–68 *DARE* (Qu. II1, . . *A close friend . . "He's my _____.")* Inf **AL**8, Best bud, bosom pal; **MI**75, Bud, pal; (Qu. II3, . . *People are very friendly toward each other: "They're _____.")* Inf **AL**8, Best of buds. [Infs young and mid-aged]

bud v[1]

1 To feed upon buds.

1887 *Forest & Stream* 28.131/2 **VT**, Last night I saw a number of grouse budding upon a neighboring apple tree. **1892** Duval *Young Explorers* 123 **TX**, He [=a bear] was up thar buddin', fur at this time of the year they lives mostly on the buds and twigs of some sorts of trees. **1937** (1963) Hyatt *Kiverlid* 9 **KY**, He knew what kind of day fish would bite, and the kind of weather the squirrels would be "budding" the trees.

2 See quot.

1967 Key *Tobacco Vocab.* 95 **CT**, Bud . . . To remove the newly forming blossom so that it won't produce seeds and thereby give all the energy of the plant to the leaves.

bud v[2] [Prob from **buddy** n 2, but cf also **bud** n[2] 2, **butty** n[1]]

1905 *DN* 3.71 **nwAR**, *Bud together* . . . To associate together. Used by Logan Co., Ark., miners.

bud v[3]

1914 *DN* 4.69 **ME, nNH**, *Bud,* or *bud in* . . . To work. "You keep right on a-buddin'!"

bud brush See **bud sagebrush**

budda, budder See **brother A3**

buddhahead n Also sp *buddahead* [*Buddha* + **head** n[1] C1b] **chiefly HI, also CA**

A person of Oriental ancestry.

1967 *DARE* (Qu. HH28, . . *Nicknames . . for people of foreign background*) Inf **HI**13, Buddhahead. **1971** Landy *Underground Dict.* **CA**, *Buddahead* . . . Oriental person. **1972** Carr *Da Kine Talk* 113, *Buddahead* (Sanskrit via Japanese + English). A name given by non-Japanese or by AJAs (Americans of Japanese ancestry) from the Mainland, to Japanese Americans born in Hawaii. **1980** Folb *Runnin' Down* 57 **swCA** [Black], Dey stop me and dey say, "What you doin' here *black boy?*" I say, "Wait a minute buddaheads, you talkin' crazy, Jack."

buddy n Also sp *buddie* [Prob hypocoristic form of *brother,* perh infl in sense **2** by **butty** n[1] (see quot 1929 at **2**)] Cf **bud** n[2], **bubby** n[2]

1 Used as a nickname or term of address for:

a A brother or eldest son. **widespread, but chiefly Midl, Sth** *somewhat old-fash*

1858 *Harper's Mag.* 16.284/2, 'Look, sister, see; the sky's got the measles!' 'No, buddy,' said she, correcting him, 'it's only freckled.' **1862** in 1980 *DARE* File **AR** [Letter], And buddie you have been in a fight. **1895** *DN* 1.385 **cwIN, wFL. 1905** *DN* 3.60 **NE. 1908** *DN* 3.295 **eAL, wGA**, *Bud, buddie* . . . used as a familiar name for the oldest brother. I still call my oldest brother Buddie [speaker is male]. **1950** *WELS (Nicknames and affectionate words meaning brother)* 5 Infs, **WI**, Buddy. [All Infs born before 1900] **1965–70** *DARE* (Qu. Z5, *Nicknames and affectionate words meaning "brother"*) 148 Infs, **chiefly W Midl, Sth**, Buddy; **IA**35, Real buddy. [Of all Infs responding to the question, 67% were old; of those giving these responses, 76% were old.]

b Any boy. *esp among men*

1892 Harris *On Plantation* 44 **GA**, "Bless your soul, buddy," exclaimed Mr. Locke. **1902** *DN* 2.230 **sIL**, *Bud* or *buddie* . . . Form of a stranger's address to a boy. Also a nickname. **1905** *DN* 3.71 **nwAR. 1908** *DN* 3.295 **eAL, wGA. 1941** *LANE* Map 379 **wCT, Cape Cod MA**, Names used in addressing boys . . *buddy*. [2 infs] **1950** *WELS (Somebody when you don't know his name . . a boy: "Say, _____, where's the post office?")* 10 Infs, **WI**, Buddy. **c1960** *Wilson Coll.* **csKY**, *Bud, buddy*—addressing a strange boy, as when asking directions. **1965–70** *DARE* (Qu. II10a . . *Somebody on the street when you don't know his name . . a boy: "Say, _____, where's the post office?")* 117 Infs, **widespread**, Buddy; **NC**76, Hey, buddy. [Of all Infs responding to this question, 47% were male; of those giving these responses, 57% were male.]

c Any man. **chiefly Nth, N Midl, Atlantic** *chiefly among men*

1903 *Everybody's Mag.* 8.174/1 **TX**, "We'll try to make it comfortable for you, buddy," said the cattleman gently. **1950** *WELS (Somebody when you don't know his name . . a man: "Say, _____, how far is it to the next town?")* 2 Infs, **WI**, Buddy. **1965–70** *DARE* (Qu. II10b, . . *Somebody on the street when you don't know his name . . a man: "Say, _____, how far is it to the next town?")* 34 Infs, **chiefly Nth, N Midl, Atlantic**, Buddy; **KY**44, Hey, buddy; (Qu. KK55c) Inf **FL**52, No sir, buddy; (Qu. NN10a) Infs **DE**3, **KY**6, **MD**5, Hi, buddy; (Qu. NN10b) Inf **SC**68, Hello, buddy; (Qu. NN11) Infs **NC**52, **TN**26, So long, buddy. [Of all Infs responding to Qu. II10b, 47% were male; of those giving these responses, 83% were male. All of the 8 Infs giving these responses to the other questions were male.] **1968–69** *DARE* FW Addit **csNC**, Buddy—commonly used as address in conversation; e.g. "Let me tell you, Buddy." Sometimes just Bud is used. *Ibid* **eNC**, Buddy—used often in familiar conversation as form of address.

2 A friend or companion—earlier esp in mining or military use; formerly used of men only.

1896 *DN* 1.413 **nePA**, *Buddy*: intimate companion. "We were always great buddies together." **1901** *DN* 2.137 **ePA, seOH** [College slang]. **1917** Sinclair *King Coal* 30 **CO**, A man might sink to sleep as he lay at work, and if his "buddy," or helper, happened . . to delay a minute too long, it would be all over with the man. **1922** R. Parrish *Case & the Girl* 204 *(DAE)*, Lieutenant, this is Captain West, over across the pond with the Engineers; we were buddies for about two months. **1929** *AmSp* 4.389, It is incontrovertible that *bud* and *buddy* are diminutives of *brother*, but to assert that its derived meaning of *comrade* is a brute fact, leaves all the interesting things still to be said. My surmise is that here is another of those fascinating words of dual origin . . . When I was a boy in the Pennsylvania coalfields, one of the commonest words in the miners' speech was *butty*, or *buttie*, . . meaning work-fellow . . . the man with the pick and the man with the shovel are literally *butties*, working all day long buttock to buttock . . . But the boys of the community thirty years ago adopted the word for the idea which later at school they were to express by *chum*. **1959** Faulkner *Mansion* 75 **MS** (as of 1925), "Captain Strutterbuck was in both wars . . . That Spanish one about twenty-five years ago, and the last one too . . . ""Howdy," Strutterbuck said. "Were you a buddy too?" **1965–70** *DARE* (Qu. II1, . . *A close friend* . . *"He's my_____."*) 599 Infs, **widespread**, Buddy; (Qu. II2a, *When two people begin to be friendly: "He has just recently _____ with John."*) 58 Infs, **widespread**, Become buddies; (Qu. II2b, *When two people have become friendly you might say, "It's been quite a while that Mary and Jane have been _____."*) 20 Infs, **scattered**, Buddies; (Qu. II3, *Expressions to say that people are very friendly toward each other: "They're _____."*) 28 Infs, **Nth, N Midl, West**, Buddies.

buddy v Also freq *buddy up* [**buddy** n] **chiefly W Midl, Sth**

1 To be a friend or companion.

1930 Irwin *Amer. Tramp* 38, "Me and Slim buddy up and take a trip"—Slim and I struck up a friendship and went for a trip together. **1940** *AmSp* 15.334 [College slang], *Buddy up*. Become very friendly. **1944** *Hall Coll.* **TN**, A real pal that any fellow can feel proud to buddy with. **1960** Wentworth–Flexner *Slang* 67, *Buddy up*. To be a close friend to someone; to move about with another; to share living quarters. *Often in the phrase, "They buddy together."* **1960** Partridge *Slang* 426, *Buddy Up, to.* To become friends ([recorded from] 1915). **1965–70** *DARE* (Qu. II2a, *When two people begin to be friendly: "He has just recently _____ with John."*) Infs **AZ**2, **FL**8, **GA**44, **TX**26, Buddied; **GA**30, **IN**45, **KY**59, **NC**51, **OH**45, **SC**40, **WA**22, Buddied up; **SC**19, Buddy together; **AL**5, Buddying around; **SC**3, Started buddying; **MA**61, They're buddying together; (Qu. II2b, . . *"It's been quite a while that Mary and Jane have been _____."*) Infs **GA**9, 44, **MI**80, Buddying. **1966** *DARE* Tape **FL**39, You don't wade too deep [into the swamp] and buddy up with a snake.

2 To seek friendship for personal gain, to curry favor.

1966–67 *DARE* (Qu. JJ3a, *When a schoolchild makes a special effort to "get in good" with the teacher* . . *"He's trying to _____ again."*) Infs **GA**3, **LA**2, Buddy up to her (*or the teacher*).

buddy adj **chiefly NEast** See also **bud run**

Of maple sap or syrup: having a flavor characteristically produced when the tree buds begin to open.

1933 *Sun* (Baltimore MD) 11 Apr 10/6 *(Hench Coll.),* The best [sugar maple] sap is produced early in the season . . . "Buddy sap" is the name applied to the late runs of sap, especially that runnning about the time a tree's buds burst. **1947** *AmSp* 22.152 **Nth, east from OH**, *Buddy sap*. A late run of sap, especially that running about the time when buds on the trees start to open. Usually green or yellowish in color, with a peculiar odor, and not as good for making sirup as the earlier run. *Buddy sirup.* Sirup made from buddy sap. When this is made it usually is kept for the producer's family use. **1947** *VT Life* 1.3.4/2, Some days after the usual season a sort of "Indian summer" season began and sap ran for some days. It was "buddy," but it ran and syrup was made, even if dark in color and potent in flavor. **1959** *VT Hist.* new ser 27.127, In maple sugaring, *buddy* is sometimes used to describe the flavor of the last run of syrup . . . Common. **1980** *NYT Article Letters* **NH**, Here, we are likely to say that the sap has turned 'buddy', meaning that the buds are beginning to show on the branches and the sap has a bitter taste. According to 'Red' Cotton of nearby Hiram, Maine, buddy syrup used to be sold to the manufacturers of chewing tobacco; **ceNY**, Buddy syrup is last run and rather strong.

buddy bee martin n Cf **bee martin 1, billy martin** =**kingbird.**

1970 *DARE* (Qu. Q14) Inf **VA**47, Buddy bee martin (kingbird).

buddy-buddy n [Redup of **buddy** n]

See quot 1960.

1946 *CA Folkl. Qrly.* 5.383 [Navy slang], A sailor is a *gob* or *swab*, and in direct address . . . *Buddy*, or—often sarcastically—*Buddy-Buddy*. **1960** Wentworth–Flexner *Slang, Buddy-buddy* . . . **1** A close friend. *W.W.II Army and USN use.* →**2** One who is not a friend; an enemy; a disliked person. *This sarcastic use is by far the most common since c1945. The reduplication has been used to strengthen the word "buddy" and also to reverse its meaning.* →**3** An overly friendly person; one who tries too hard to make friends, join a group, or be hep. **1966–70** *DARE* (Qu. II3, *Expressions to say that people are very friendly toward each other: "They're _____."*) Infs **CA**24, 107, **GA**23, **KY**21, **NC**14, Buddy-buddies; (Qu. Y17) Inf **NY**96, Buddy-buddies again.

buddy-buddy adj Also *buddy-bud* [**buddy-buddy** n] Cf **palsy-walsy**

Friendly; often, too friendly.

1960 Wentworth–Flexner *Slang, Buddy-buddy* . . . Too friendly; insincere; presuming. **1965–70** *DARE* (Qu. II3, *Expressions to say that people are very friendly toward each other: "They're _____."*) 62 Infs, **widespread**, Buddy-buddy; 43 Infs, **widespread**, All buddy-buddy; **CO**38, **IN**61, **MA**33, **MI**69, Real buddy-buddy; **NY**64, Very buddy-buddy; **LA**14, Buddy-bud; (Qu. II2a, . . *"He has just recently _____ with John."*) Infs **FL**26, **OH**13, 21, 57, **PA**247, Become buddy-buddy; **MA**53, Been buddy-buddy; **PA**165, Getting buddy-buddy; **NM**4, Got buddy-buddy; **IA**15, Gotten buddy-buddy; **NY**3, Buddy-buddy; (Qu. II2b, . . *"It's been quite a while that Mary and Jane have been _____."*) Infs **MA**2, 6, **PA**151, **TN**1, **VA**43, Buddy-buddy. [Of all Infs responding to Qu. II3, 25% were mid-aged; of those giving these responses, 39% were mid-aged.]

buddydoon n [Perh var of **bloodynoun**]

  1970 *DARE* (Qu. CC17, *Imaginary animals or monsters that people around here tell tales about*) Inf **SC68**, ['bʊdɪdʊn]—goes [hwʊm] repeatedly at night. A sound, not a monster. Heard in the swamps.

buddy gee n Also sp *buddy ghee* [**buddy** n + *gee,* man, male friend] *among Black speakers*

A friend, buddy, fellow Black.

  1946 (1972) Mezzrow *Really Blues* 330, Buddy ghee: *pal.* **1960** Wentworth–Flexner *Slang*, Buddy gee—A young man. *Some jive use c1930.*

buddy up See **buddy** v

budge n[1] [*budge* to move]

  1 A fit of nervousness.

  1824 in 1857 Webster *Private Corresp.* 1.373 **VA**, Madame Neckar was a very sincere and excellent woman, but she was not very pleasant in conversation, for she was subject of what in Virginia we call the "Budge," that is, she was very nervous and fidgety. She could rarely remain long in the same place, or converse long on the same subject. **1904** Glasgow *Deliverance* 102 **VA**, Having unfortunately crossed her knees in the parlour after supper, she suffered untold tortures from "budges" for three mortal hours rather than be seen to do anything so indelicate as to uncross them.

  2 A movement of one's body. [*EDD budge* sb.[3] 3 "Ir."]

  1969 *DARE* (Qu. LL18, *To do no work at all, not even make any effort: "She hasn't _____ all day."*) Inf **IN83**, Made a budge; made a move.

budge n[2] [Perh abbr for **budget 1**]

A place inside the breast of a coat, shirt or dress where small articles are kept.

  1903 *Springfield Daily Republican* (MA) 25 Mar 6/5 **MA**, The little chap . . who had been digging about the mysterious interior of his blouse, known better to the boys as his "budge," suddenly withdrew his hand, and in it was a small United States flag. **1947** *WELS Suppl.* **WI**, Budge—place inside the breast of a coat, used by children and parents. "Put it (i.e. a small object) in your budge." **1959** *VT Hist.* new ser 27.127, Budge . . . A place in the front of a dress where women sometimes stuff their handkerchiefs. Occasional. Essex.

budge n[3]

Intoxicating liquor, booze; hence adj *budgy* drunk.

  1874 in 1965 *AmSp* 40.128, *Budge* . . . Intoxicating liquor. *Slang* . . . Like a sober old judge I'd lave [sic] off the budge. **1893** *KS Univ. Qrly.* 1.138, He was full of budge. **1893** in 1932 *AmSp* 7.259 **NE**, *Budge*— whiskey. **1902** White *Blazed Trail* 187 **ceMI**, Every time he got a little "budge" in him, he instituted a raid on the town. **1915** *DN* 4.213, *Budgy,* see *bosky* [=intoxicated].

budge adj [Etym unknown] **chiefly NEng**

Intimate, familiar.

  1890 *DN* 1.18 **seNH**, *Budge:* intimate, familiár. 'To be very budge with a person.' Hilarity seems not to be implied. *Ibid* 77, *Budge* . . . Common in Saco, Me. Noticed from 1864 to 1868 by Professor B.I. Wheeler. **1892** *DN* 1.214, *Budge* . . . "Common in Boston in my youth." **1902** (1968) Clapin *Americanisms*, *Budge* . . . Used in New England, and as far south as New Jersey, for intimate, familiar. "She and your sister are quite *budge.*"

‡budge-eyed adj [Prob var of *bulge-eyed*] Cf **buck-eyed** adj[2]

  1970 *DARE* (Qu. X21a, *. . Words . . used to describe people according to their eyes . . if they stick out*) Inf **NC86**, Budge-eyed.

budget n [ME *bowgette* a leather bag or wallet]

  1 A pouch or wallet; a package, bundle. [*OED* "*Obs.* exc. *dial.*"] **chiefly Appalachians**

  1818 (1920) Clark *Diary* 2322 **CT**, He brought a . . pair of stockings I left there & the budget old Mrs Canfield sent to Augustine. **1845** Judd *Margaret* 286 **ME**, Her father handed her from the saddle, Chilion undid the budget that was strapped to the crupper. **1853** Hammett *Stray Yankee in TX* 214, "I shall make a formal call upon you for . . any information you may possess in the premises." "You will be perfectly safe, Sheriff," added the District Attorney, "in opening your budget [=in telling what you know] . . . So please make a clean breast of it at once." **1899** (1912) Green *VA Folk-Speech* 99, *Budget* . . . A bundle. "He had a *budget* of clothes under his arm." **1907** (1970) Martin *Betrothal* 102 **sePA**, They were all gathered on the kitchen porch to enjoy the budget of mail which, since the sending forth of the invitations, had come to be the

most important feature of their day. **1917** *DN* 4.409 **NC Mts.** **1929** *AmSp* 5.17 **Ozarks.** **1931** *AmSp* 7.90 **eKY.** **1939** *AmSp* 14.156 **WV.** **1955** Warren *Angels* 50 **KY**, I walked this-heah country . . totin a little budget on my back., and sold thimbles and notions and nutmegs out-a my budget to them as would buy. **1969** *DARE* File, *Budget*—bag, sack. Usage of . . old native of western North Carolina, in Appalachians.

  2 Used as the name of a newspaper.

  1936 Ayer & Son *Directory Newsp.* 689, *Valley City* [ND] . . . Teachers' College Budget . . . Collegiate . . . [Established] 1916. **1937** *Amer. Newspapers 1821–1936* 222/3 **KS**, Topeka Budget . . N[ov] 15 1884–Ja 5 1888 . . . Topeka Budget . . . 1890–94. *Ibid* 247/2 **ME**, [Bangor] Weekly Budget . . . 1880. *Ibid* 585/3 **OR**, [Lexington] Budget . . . 1888–90. *Ibid* 733/3 **WI**, [Black Earth] Advertiser . . . 1868? as Monthly budget. **1947** Brigham *Hist. Amer. Newsp.* 1.599 **NY**, [Lansingburgh] Northern Budget, 1797–1798 . . . after which the paper was removed to Troy and continued under the same name [until about 1820]. *Ibid* 738, [Schenectady] Western Budget, 1807–1810. *Ibid* 739, Schoharie Budget, 1817–1819. **1968** Budget (Sugarcreek OH) 25 July, [Masthead:] Serving the Sugarcreek Area and Amish-Mennonite Communities Throughout North America. **1973** U.S. Lib. Congr. Catalog Pub. Div. *Newsp. Microform U.S.* 548/3, Elyria [OH] Budget. Je 13, 1860–? *Ibid* 613/2, Lancaster [PA] . . . Budget . . . 1930–1949. **1975** Ayer Directory Pub. 320, Meredosia [IL] . . . Budget . . . Estab. 1905. *Ibid* 710, Sugarcreek [OH] . . . Budget . . . Estab. 1890. *Ibid* 910, Douglas [WY] . . . Budget . . . Estab. 1886. **1981** U.S. Lib. Congr. Catalog Pub. Div. *Newsp. Microform U.S.* 69/3, Lost City [WV] Budget . . . 1902.

  3 Transf: a person who embodies traits esp of fussiness or fretfulness—used as the second element in var compounds. **chiefly Nth, N Midl, West** See Map Cf **box** n **5a, flutterbudget, fussbudget, pot** n, **sputterbudget, tattlebudget**

  1965–70 *DARE* (Qu. GG14) 264 Infs, **widespread, but least freq in Sth,** Fussbudget; **NY68**, Fussabudget; **NY25, 28,** Fussybudget; **IA3,** Sputterbudget; (Qu. HH11b) 122 Infs, **chiefly Nth, N Midl, West,** (Old) fussbudget; **WA20,** Female fussbudget; **IA3, NY27,** Sputterbudget; (Qu. HH11a) 107 Infs, **chiefly Nth, N Midl, West,** (Old) fussbudget; **NY27,** Sputterbudget; (Qu. A18) Inf **RI14,** A reg'lar old fussbudget; (Qu. GG27b) Inf **NC36,** Be a fussbudget; (Qu. GG38) Infs **AL30, CA169,** Fussbudget; (Qu. GG39) Inf **IL78,** Fussbudget; (Qu. GG41) Infs **CA22, OH5,** Flutterbudget; (Qu. HH9) Infs **CA4, MI51, NY145,** Flutterbudget; **ME13,** Flitterbudget; (Qu. JJ4) Inf **ME22,** Tattlebudget.

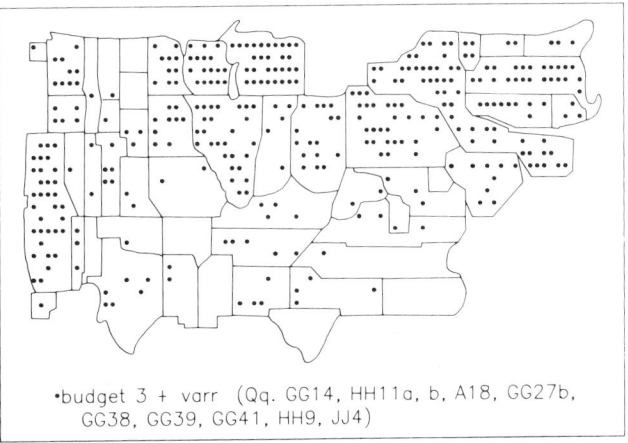

  •budget 3 + varr (Qq. GG14, HH11a, b, A18, GG27b, GG38, GG39, GG41, HH9, JJ4)

budgeway See **booshway**

‡budging adv [Prob alter of *bulging*]

  1968 *DARE* (Qu. LL28, *Expressions meaning entirely full: "The box of apples was _____."*) Inf **LA40**, Budging full; brim full.

budgy See **budge** n[3]

bud run n Cf **bug run, frog run** See also **buddy** adj

See quot 1959.

  1959 *VT Hist.* new ser 27.127, Bug run . . . var: bud run. The last run of the sap during maple sugaring season . . . Bud run is so-called because of the buds on the trees. Common. **1965** Needham–Mussey *Country Things* 39 **VT**, The minute the buds begin to swell on the tree, the syrup starts to take on a leathery taste . . . What little sap runs after that is called the bud run; that sugar is generally just sold for tobacco sweetening.

bud sagebrush n Also *bud sage, bud brush* [See quot 1931]
A low shrubby, spiny **sagebrush** (*Artemisia spinescens*). Also called **button sagebrush, desert sagebrush, horse sagebrush, spring sagebrush**

1925 Jepson *Manual Plants CA* 1142, *A. spinescens . . . Bud Sage . . .* Desert mesas and plains, 2000 to 3000 ft. **1931** U.S. Dept. Ag. *Misc. Pub.* 101.172, *Bud sagebrush . .* is . . variously known as bud brush, bud = sage (the term bud referring to the conspicuous bud or buttonlike, clustered flower heads). **1968** Abbey *Desert Solitaire* 29 **seUT,** Descend to the alkali flats of Salt Valley and you find an entirely different grouping: shadscale, four-winged saltbrush, greasewood, spiny horse-brush, asters, milk vetch, budsage, galletagrass.

budworm n Also *tobacco budworm*
The larva of a noctuid moth (here: *Chloridea virescens*).

1944 *PADS* 2.65, *Bud-worm . .* A worm, smaller than the *tobacco-worm,* that feeds on the bud and the upper leaves. S. Va., n. N.C. **1966** *PADS* 45.8 **KY,** *Budworm . . .* A green worm about one and one-half inches long with light stripes. The insect causes damage to the bud of the tobacco plant . . . "The budworm cuts right through the bud." **1967** *Key Tobacco Vocab.* **GA, KY, MO, NC, PA,** Budworm; **TN,** Before the tobacco blooms [the budworm] is in the bud and he eats out inside. **1968–69** *DARE* Tape **IN45,** Then before long . . the budworm comes in the tobacco and you have to spray for the budworm; **KY35,** When they [=tobacco plants] get up here just a little way, there'll be little—bud-worms we call them—get right down in the bud of this plant, and they don't eat the leaf, they just eat up the bud.

buff n
1 See **buffalo** n A.
2 The bare skin; hence adj phr *in the buff* naked. [*OED buff* sb.[2] 3, 1602 →] **chiefly Nth**
1848 in 1935 *AmSp* 10.40 **Nantucket MA,** Stripped to the buff. State of nudity. **1855** (1940) Chambers *Jrl.* 136 **MT,** Campbell & a half Breed was caught . . their horses stolen & themselves stripped to the Buff. **1899** Peck *Peck's Uncle Ike* 28 **WI,** In some lodges a man is taught a useful lesson by stripping him to the buff and taking a clapboard and letting a common laborer maul him until he finds out that he is not the whole business. **1899** (1912) Green *VA Folk-Speech, Buff . . .* The bare skin. **1968–69** *DARE* (Qu. W20, *If somebody has no clothes on at all—for example, . . "They went swimming _____."*) Inf **IL86,** In the buff; **WI64,** In the buff (read more commonly than heard); **CA161,** In their buff. **1969** *Rolling Stone* 28 June 4/1, The girls call themselves the Groupies and claim they recorded their song in the buff.
‡3 See quot.
1918 *DN* 5.23, *Buff . . .* Girl. Southern Idaho.

buffalo n
A Forms. Usu *buffalo;* pronc-spp *buf(f)ler* (now infreq); abbr *buff.* For arch spp see *DAE*
1848 (1855) Ruxton *Life Far West* 15, A 'clever' man was Bill Bent as *I* ever know'd trade a robe or 'throw' a bufler in his tracks. **1884** *Bismarck Tribune* Aug. (*DAE*), The ball struck the unsuspecting animal in the thigh, inflicting a slight wound. But the old 'buff' took the fling as an insult. **1928** Vestal *Kit Carson* 20 **NM,** Kit heartily agreed with an old trapper who declared, 'Civilized doin's cain't shine with fat buffler, anyways you fix it.' **1949** Guthrie *Way West* 86 (as of 1847), "We ain't seen a Pawnee." "Not likely to, yet. They'll be west with the buffler." **1968** Adams *Western Words, Buffler*—A trader's name for a buffalo. **1968** *DARE* (Qu. K12) Inf **MD15,** Buffler.
B Senses.
1 freq attrib: A cow without horns. **chiefly C Atl, NC** See Map
1804 *Frederick-Town Herald* (MD) 11 Feb 4/2 **MD,** Two Stray Heifers came to the Subscriber's plantation . . one of them a buffaloe, marked with a crop off both ears and slit in the right. **1819** *Amer. Farmer* 1.315/2 **neVA,** The buffaloe breed of cattle, or those without horns, will not answer well for working. **1858** (1867) Flint *Milch Cows* 78 **MA,** Hornless cattle . . have been crossed with the common stock . . to produce hornless grades. These are not unfrequently known under the name of buffalo cattle. **1899** (1912) Green *VA Folk-Speech, Buffalo . . .* Cattle without horns. "Pied buffalo-cow." **1902** (1968) Clapin *Americanisms, Buffalo-cow.* A common expression, among colored people of Virginia, for a cow without horns, because its head somewhat resembles that of the female *buffalo,* whose horns are very short. **1939** *AmSp* 14.89 **TN,** *Buffalo.* A lean calf. 'The buffalo is grazing on the mountain.' **1965–70** *DARE* (Qu. K12, *A cow that has never had horns*) 18 Infs,

chiefly **C Atl, NC,** Buffalo (cow); **MD15,** Buffler; (Qu. K13, *A cow that has had her horns cut off*) Inf **MD13,** Buffalo. [15 of 19 total Infs are old, 16 male.]

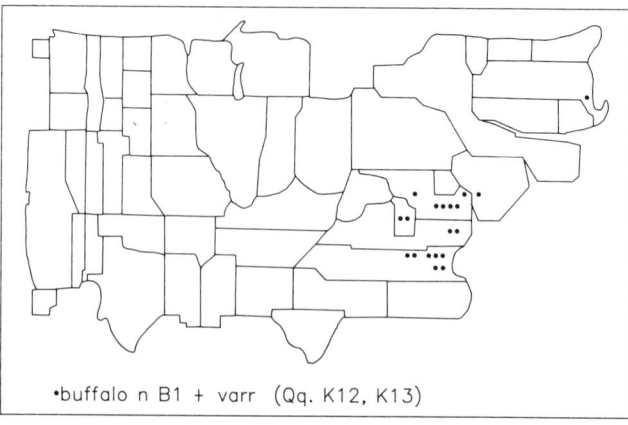

•buffalo n B1 + varr (Qq. K12, K13)

2 also *buffalohead,* rarely *bullhead:* A nickel.
1942 Berrey–Van den Bark *Amer. Slang* 559.11, *Five-cent piece . . .* buffalo, a buffalo nickel. **1945** in 1960 Wentworth–Flexner *Slang* 72, Then slip me a bullhead. I need a java. **1950** *WELS* (*Joking names and nicknames for $.05*) 12 Infs, **WI,** Buffalo; 2 Infs, Buffalohead. **1954** Harder *Coll.* **cwTN,** *Buffalo:* A five cent piece; a nickel. **1965–70** *DARE* (Qu. U22, *. . A five-cent piece*) 59 Infs, **scattered, but most freq in Sth, esp SC,** Buffalo; **CA36, MI76, NY233,** Buffalohead; **MI94, NY133, PA175,** Buffalo nickel; **NY249,** Old buffalo.
3 A Belgian. **seMI**
1967–68 *DARE* (Qu. HH28, *Names and nicknames . . for people of foreign background*) Infs **MI69, 78,** Buffalo—Belgian. **1979** *DARE* File **MI,** A native of Detroit, born 1907, says that when he was a boy the Belgians in the city were called Buffaloes. The Belgians were great bicyclists and often took part in bicycle races. So racing bicycles were known as buffalo bicycles or bikes.
4 See quot.
1976 Warner *Beautiful Swimmers* 80 **eMD,** "During that night a strong wind from the northwest arose and when we went to the floats in the morning we found that every one of the little crabs had shed its 'fingers' and we called them 'buffaloes.' They were of no use whatever." . . A very rough wind will still cause floated crabs to fight more than usual and thus autotomize or purposely drop off a threatened limb at the socket as a defensive measure. Old-timers, in fact, still call the limbless crabs buffa-loes; they know that nine out of ten will "hang up" or fail to moult successfully because of their injuries.
5 See **buffalo fish.**

buffalo v, hence *buffaloed* ppl adj Pronc-sp *buffaloo* [*buffalo bison*] **chiefly Inland Nth, West**
1 To overawe, frighten, confuse, bamboozle.
1896 *DN* 1.413 **cTX,** *Buffaloo:* to confuse, "rattle." **1905** *DN* 3.71 **nwAR,** *Buffalo . . .* To frighten off. 'They have him buffaloed.' Rare. **1914** *DN* 4.162 **NW** Buffalo . . . To cheat; 'bambozzle.' "The traders buffaloed the Indians out of their furs." **1927** *AmSp* 2.175 **Pacific,** *Buffalo*—get under control, hypnotize. **1928** French *Ranchman NM* 27 (as of 1883), On my inquiry whether there was no objection on the part of his fellow-citizens, my informant told me that he had them all 'Buffaloed.' **1929** *AmSp* 5.72 **NE,** When a cow becomes confused it is "buffaloed." **1946** Greer–Petrie *Angeline Gits an Eyeful* 9 **csKY,** He shore did have her *buffaloed!* All he had to do wuz speak and she jump'd. **1950** *WELS* (*To frighten*) 3 Infs, **WI,** Buffalo. **1965–70** *DARE* (Qu. GG24, *. . To frighten: "Now don't let those fellows _____* you."*) 17 Infs, **13 west of Missip R,** Buffalo; (Qu. CC12b, *If a person has a lot of bad luck you might say, "He's been _____."*) Inf **MI78,** Buffaloed; (Qu. CC14, *. . Where one person supposedly casts a spell over another*) Infs **MI87, PA115,** Buffalo; (Qu. GG2, *. . Confused, mixed up*) Inf **KY42,** Buffaloed; (Qu. GG3, *To tease: "See those big boys trying to _____ [that little one]."*) Inf **WA16,** Buffalo; (Qu. GG20, *. . Very much surprised*) Inf **IA22,** Buffaloed; (Qu. JJ23, *To refuse to give in or yield: "He tried to scare me off but I _____."*) Infs **MI4, WA20,** Wouldn't be buffaloed; **MN33,** Buffaloed him; **CA105,** Buffaloed him out; (Qu. JJ42, *. . "He usually handles things well, but this time he certainly _____."*) Inf **RI1,** Had us buffaloed; (Qu. KK36, *. . A person who is easily fooled:*

"It's easy to _____.") Infs **NY**234, **PA**126, Buffalo him; (Qu. **NN**25b, *Weakened substitutes for "damn" or "damned": "Well, I'll be _____."*) Inf **MA**30, Buffaloed. [25 of 30 total Infs old]

2 By ext: to strike on the head with the barrel of a gun.

1961 Adams *Old-Time Cowhand* 178, The West never used the butt for a club because the barrel was more potent, quicker, and a lot safer. This is what he called "buffaloin'." *Ibid* 179, If the average cowhand did use a gun in a fight, and he was at close range, he preferred to use it to buffalo his enemy. Partin' his hair with a six-gun barrel might leave 'im with a knot on his head that'd sweat a rat to run 'round, but he'd eventually wake up.

buffalo apple, buffalo ball See **buffalo bean**

buffalo bass n

=**warmouth.**

1933 LA Dept. of Conserv. *Fishes* 342, The Warmouth Bass has come to bear many confusing popular names. These are . . . Buffalo Bass [etc.].

buffalo bean n Also *buffalo apple, ~ ball, ~ plum* [So called from its growing in buffalo country] **West** Cf **buffalo pea**

=**ground plum,** esp *Astragalus crassicarpus.*

1896 *Jrl. Amer. Folkl.* 9.185, *Astragalus caryocarpus* . . Buffalo-apple, N. Dak[ota]. Buffalo-bean, N. Dak.; Burnside, S. Dak. **1906** Rydberg *Flora CO* 202, *Geoprumnon* . . . Buffalo Beans, Ground Plums. **1918** Visher *Geog. SD* 81, The Legume family . . includes some of the more abundant plants of these plains, notably . . buffalo-bean, loco, lupine, and wild alfalfas. **1939** *Natl. Geog. Mag.* 76.219/1, Buffalo plums like purple shadows lingered past their season. **1966** *DARE* Tape **OK**31, And then we had . . . some little ol' things that grew on little ol' bitty vines, and we called 'em buffalo balls. We'd even eat them. And they were kinda sour, but they were kinda tough . . . They were kinda greenish color, and they were 'bout big as a . . quarter, some of 'em. **1973** Hitchcock–Cronquist *Flora Pacific NW* 246, Ground or buffalo plum, pomme de terre . . *A. crassicarpus.*

buffalo beetle n Also *buffalo bug, ~ moth*

=**carpet beetle.**

1928 Metcalf–Flint *Destructive & Useful Insects* 746, Of the many species of carpet beetles, or, as they are sometimes called, buffalo beetles, which occur in this country, all have a somewhat similar life history. **1939** *LANE* Map 237 **cVT**, (*Moth; Moths*) . . . [Buffalo bug], destroys woolen goods and carpets. **1964** Borror–DeLong *Intro. Insects* 348, Buffalo moth, *Anthrenus scrophulariae.*

buffalo berry n

Either of two shrubs (*Shepherdia argentea* or *S. canadensis*) which produce red or yellow berries. Also called **bullberry 1, oleaster, rabbitberry.** For other names of *S. argentea* see **beefsuet tree, silverberry, stinking willow, tap-nah;** for other names of *S. canadensis* see **nannyberry, sallow-thorn, soapberry, soopolallie, wild olive**

1805 *Thomas' MA Spy or Worcester Gaz.* (MA) 17 July 2/3, Scions of a new discovered berry, called the buffaloe berry. **1932** *AmSp* 7.168 **NE,** The "buffalo berry," the berry of a small bush especially common along the banks of the Missouri, Platte, Elkhorn, and Loup Rivers, was also a favorite berry for jellies and canning. **1938** (1952) FWP *Guide SD* 17, Buffalo-berry bushes grow thickly in the "draws" of the western section. **1967** *DARE* FW Addit **ND,** Buffalo berries — bright red berries about the size of a pea. Grow on bushes from 6–10 feet high along the Missouri River bottoms — near Bismarck . . . Very bitter to taste. "They make good jell."

buffalo bird n

1 =**cowbird 1.** *hist*

1876 Dodge *Black Hills* 125, Found in the Hills proper . . [is the] Buffalo-bird — a large species of jay. **1912** *Animals of Amer.* 43 (*DA*), It is interesting to note that . . the Buffalo had one little companion and friend — the cowbird or Buffalo bird. 'Sometimes the cowbirds walk sedately behind their grazing monster; sometimes they flit over, snapping at flies; often they sit along the ridgepole of his spine.' **1934** *Natl. Geog. Mag.* 66.118/2, In early accounts of prairie life they [cowbirds] were known as "buffalo birds" for the same reason.

2 =**lark bunting.**

1936 Roberts *MN Birds* 2.381, *Lark Bunting: Calamospiza melanocorys . . . Other names: . .* "Buffalo-bird." **1938** Matschat *Suwannee R.*

buffalo bug See **buffalo beetle**

buffalo burr n

A yellow-flowered **nightshade** (here: *Solanum rostratum*) with a prickly seed capsule. Also called **burr tomato, Kansas thistle, sand burr, Spanish nettle**

1894 *Jrl. Amer. Folkl.* 7.95, *Solanum rostratum* . . buffalo-bur, So. Neb. **1931** Clute *Common Plants* 98, The buffalo-bur (*Solanum rostratum*) . . . doubtless perfected its trick of catching hold of all sorts of animals by practicing on the buffalo. **1968** *DARE* FW Addit **CO**7, Buffalo burr — a yellow one — the seeds look like a buffalo and are burrs. Also called nightshade — *Solanum rostratum.*

buffalo cider See **buffalo gall**

buffalo clover n

1 An annual red-flowered clover (*Trifolium reflexum*).

1764 in 1925 Fries *Rec. Moravians* 2.565, *Buffalo Clover* is a particularly large clover, of which these animals, that is the Buffaloes, are very fond. **1767** in 1890 NC *Colonial Rec.* 7.1007, Buffalow Clover was extremely thick here it is a species of grass much like the red clover not much coveted by any cattle but the Buffalow. **1805** (1904) Lewis *Orig. Jrls. Lewis & Clark Exped.* 2.320, I observe a considerable quantity of the buffaloe clover in the bottoms. **1970** Correll *Plants TX* 809, *Trifolium reflexum* . . Buffalo clover.

2 A lupine (here: *Lupinus texensis*).

1930 Dobie *Coronado* 108, Yet the hills could hardly be so lush with buffalo-clover — as we used to call the bluebonnet. **1951** *PADS* 15.15 **TX. 1982** Heat Moon *Blue Highways* 134 **ceTX,** Roadside wildflowers — bluebonnets, purple winecups, evening primroses, and more — were abundant as crops, and where wide reaches of bluebonnets (once called buffalo clover, wolf flower, and, by the Spanish, "the rabbit") covered the slopes, their scent filled the highway.

3 Bush clover.

1942 *Torreya* 42.161, *Lespedeza striata* . . Buffalo clover, southeastern States. **1970** *DARE* (Qu. S21) Inf **PA**234, Buffalo clover — yellow blossom.

buffalo cod n

1907 [see cultus cod].

buffaloed See **buffalo** v

buffalo fever n West *obs* Cf **buck fever 1**

Excitement felt at the sight or prospect of hunting wild buffalo.

1844 (1954) Gregg *Commerce* 235 **Cent,** I have often heard backwoodsmen speak of the 'buck ague,' but commend me to the 'buffalo fever' of the Prairies for novelty and amusement. Very few of our party had ever seen a buffalo before in its wild state; therefore at the first sight of these noble animals the excitement surpassed anything I had ever witnessed before. **1862** *Harper's Mag.* 25.452/1 **SW,** I took the "buffalo fever" at once in its severest form, had my gun ready in the twinkling of an eye, and . . sallied forth.

buffalo fish n Also *buffalo*

Usu =**bigmouth buffalo** but sometimes =**smallmouth buffalo.**

1804 (1904) Clark *Orig. Jrls. Lewis & Clark Exped.* 1.96, Cought [sic] a Buffalow fish. **1820** Rafinesque *Ohio R. Fishes* 55, *Catostomus bubalus* . . . It is called every where Buffalo-fish, and Piconeau, by the French settlers of Louisiana. **1837** Peck *Gaz. IL* 271, *Peoria Lake* . . . abounds with various kinds of fish, such as sturgeon, buffalo, bass of several species, . . etc. **1902** Jordan–Evermann *Amer. Fishes* 39, Common Buffalo Fish — *Ictiobus cyprinella.* **1920** Forbes–Richardson *Fishes of IL* 69, *Ictiobus Cyprinella* . . . This is a very abundant fish — one of the three species most commonly shipped from the Illinois and the Mississippi under the name of "buffalo-fish." **1931** *Amer. Mercury* 23.220 **NM,** They . . caught in the [Rio Grande] river a generous supply of coarse fish, mostly catfish and a kind of sucker known as buffalo fish. **1933** LA Dept. of Conserv. *Fishes* 439, *Megastomatobus cyprinella* . . . The Common Buffalofish. **1950** Bissell *Stretch on River* 169, Even the carp and buffalo are taking it easy tonight. **1966–67** *DARE* Tape **AR**36, Buffalo — kind of fish; **IL**9, Lots of carp and buffalo; **LA**5, Then you have the buffalo.

buffalo fly See **buffalo gnat 2**

buffalo fuel See **buffalo wood**

buffalo gall n Also *buffalo cider* *obs*

The bile or the stomach fluid of the buffalo, used as drinks.

1846 Sage *Scenes Rocky Mts.* 132, I have become . . acquainted with a kind of beverage common among mountaineers . . . termed "bitters." . .

It is prepared by the following simple process, viz: with one pint of water mix one-fourth gill of buffalo-gall. **1872** Schele de Vere *Americanisms* 367, *Buffalo-Cider* is the ludicrous name given to the liquid in the stomach of a buffalo, which the thirsty hunter drinks, when he has killed his game at a great distance from water. **1968** Adams *Western Words, Buffalo cider.*

buffalo gnat n [Prob from the humped shape of the fly, resembling a buffalo, but see also quot 1968]

1 =**black fly.**

1822 J. Woods *English Prairie* 278 *(DA),* As the first part of it [=summer] was so dry, we had no buffalo gnats, and but few prairie flies or musquetoes. **1934** *Sun* (Baltimore MD) 27 Apr 14/1 **AR,** Spring farming operations were stopped today in many sections of Arkansas as the worst scourge of Buffalo gnats in years clouded the skies and killed thousands of dollars worth of live stock. **1968** Adams *Western Words, Buffalo gnat*— A small insect that tortured the buffaloes in the summer. **1968** *DARE* Tape **LA 31,** Sometimes we have buffalo gnats. Not a reg'lar thing here but they do come once in a while. Further north than here they have the buffalo gnats.

2 also *buffalo fly:* =**horn fly.**

1889 U.S. Dept. Ag. *Rept. of Secy.* 346, The . . . "Horn Fly" . . . has also been called the "Texas Fly," the "Buffalo Fly," and the "Buffalo Gnat."

buffalo grass n Cf **false buffalo grass**

Any of several grasses as:

a A widely distributed, creeping, perennial grass *(Buchloë dactyloides).* Also called **curly mesquite 2, mesquite grass, vine mesquite**

1784 (1929) Filson *Kentucke* 24, Where no cane grows there is abundance of wild-rye, clover, and buffalo-grass, . . affording excellent food for cattle. **1834** Peck *Gaz. IL* 9, Horses and cattle find . . pea vines, buffalo grass, wild oats, and other herbage in the timber, for summer range. **1875** Bourke *Diary* 31 May **WY,** In general, this country may be denominated a grassy plain; but great tracts occur where the tuna cactus and sagebrush dispute the supremacy of the buffalo and bunch grass. **1889** Nelson *50 Yrs.* 33 **West,** The food of the animal is a peculiar kind of grass which is called buffalo-grass. This grows from one to three inches high, and is as thick as the hairs on a dog's back. **1894** *Jrl. Amer. Folkl.* 7.104, *Buchloe dactyloides* . . buffalo-grass, W. Neb. **1929** *AmSp* 5.55 **NE,** Nebraska ranches in the "hill country" are covered with "buffalo grass," a short grass which grows very thick on the ground and is very good for cattle. **1940** Gates *Flora KS* 124, *Buchloe dactyloides* . . . Buffalo Grass. **1950** *WELS (Kinds of grass hard to get rid of)* 1 Inf, **seWI,** Buffalo grass. **1970** Correll *Plants TX* 249, *Buchloë dactyloides* . . . Buffalo Grass.

b =**water star-grass.**

1920 *Torreya* 20.19 **TN,** *Heteranthera dubia* . . . Buffalo grass.

c =**Saint Augustine grass. HI**

1929 Neal *Honolulu Gardens* 29, Buffalo grass . . . *[Stenotaphrum secundatum].* **1967** *DARE* (Qu. S9) Infs **HI**2, 4, 11, Buffalo grass.

d =**tobosa grass.**

1941 *Torreya* 41.46, *Hilaria mutica* . . . Buffalo grass, Amarillo, Tex.

e Blue grama *(Bouteloua gracilis).*

1953 Nelson *Plants Rocky Mt. Park* 39, *Grama grass* or *blue grama, Bouteloua gracilis* . . erroneously called buffalo grass. **1954** Faulkner in *Holiday* Apr 36/2 **MS,** That Mexican cotton seed which someone had given the Natchez doctor was clearing the land fast now, plowing under the buffalo grass of the eastern prairies. **1968** Adams *Western Words, Buffalo grass*— A perennial low-growing grass common on the former buffalo ranges of the West. Also, a species of grama grass.

buffalohead See **buffalo** n B2

buffalo-headed duck See **bufflehead 2**

buffalo heap n

=**buck buck 2.**

1984 *DARE* File **csWI** (as of 1930s), Piling people on top of one another was called making a *buffalo heap;* it was just something we did for fun.

buffalo horn n

1887 *Scribner's Mag.* 2.507 **CO,** The latter fixes his attention on the saw-like, serrated crowns, or summits, which are . . typical . . of true mountainous form. There are plenty of such features in the Rocky Mountains, and natives call them "buffalo-horns."

buffalo mange n

=**Texas itch.**

1934 *W2, Buffalo mange.* Texas itch.

buffalo moth See **buffalo beetle**

buffalo nut n

1 =**oilnut 2.**

1848 Gray *Manual of Botany* 398, *Oil-nut. Buffalo-nut* . . . A low straggling shrub. **1901** Lounsberry *S. Wild Flowers* 148, Not until the buffalo-nut had been experimented with at Biltmore was it successfully propagated.

2 The water chestnut *(Trapa natans).*

1931 Clute *Common Plants* 99, The buffalo nut *(Trapa natans),* however, is an inhabitant of watery places and has nothing to do with the buffalo, except that the hard black two-horned fruit has considerable resemblance to the head of the animal. **1959** Carleton *Index Herb. Plants* 20, *Buffalo Nut:* Pyrularia pubera; Trapa natans [sic].

buffaloo See **buffalo** v

buffalo pea n [So called from its growing in buffalo country] **West**

1 A **milkvetch,** but esp **ground plum.**

1900 Lyons *Plant Names* 52, *A. crassicarpus* . . . Ground Plum, Buffalo Apple, Buffalo Bean, Buffalo Pea. *Fleshy legumes* edible. **1911** [see **3** below]. **1919** Cather *My Antonia* 145 **NE,** The buffalo-peas were blooming in pink and purple masses along the roadside. **1931** Clute *Common Plants* 98, It is not at all likely that the buffalo ate the buffalo pea. **1959** Carleton *Index Herb. Plants* 20, *Buffalo Pea:* Astragalus caryocarpus.

2 American vetch *(Vicia americana).*

1896 *Jrl. Amer. Folkl.* 9.186, *Vicia Americana* . . buffalo pea, Burnside, S.Dak[ota]. **1936** Winter *Plants NE* 99, American Vetch. Buffalo Pea. Common in prairies in eastern part of the state.

3 A lupine *(Lupinus* spp). **TX**

1911 *Century Dict. Suppl., Buffalo-pea* . . . In Texas the term is used indiscriminately of species of *Astragalus* and *Lupinus* forming natural pasturage.

4 =**false lupine** (here: *Thermopsis divaricarpa* and *T. montana).*

1959 Carleton *Index Herb. Plants* 20, *Buffalo Pea* . . . Thermopsis divaricarpa. **1963** Craighead *Rocky Mt. Wildflowers* 102, *False Lupine* . . . *Other names:* Golden Pea, . . Buffalo Pea.

buffalo pecker n *obs* Cf **buffalo bird**

Perh =**cowbird 1.**

1806 (1905) Lewis *Orig. Jrls. Lewis & Clark Exped.* 5.201, Killed a buffaloe pecker [Thwaites: picker] a beautifull bird.

buffalo perch n

1 =**freshwater drum.**

1807 (1919) *TN Hist. Mag.* 113, Purchased of the Indians 2 large buffalo perch. **1820** Rafinesque *Ohio R. Fishes* 24, *Aplodinotus grunniens* . . . Buffalo-perch . . . The structure of its teeth is very singular and peculiar . . . [They] are common in many museums, where they are erroneously called teeth of the Buffalo-fish. **1828** Flint *Condensed Geog.* 1.120, Bubbler, *amblodon.* Buffalo perch. Found in all the waters of the Ohio . . . It is a fine fish for the table. **1911** *Century Dict.,* Buffalo-perch . . . the bubbler or fresh-water drumfish.

2 =**smallmouth buffalo.**

1847 *Boston Jrl. of Nat. Hist.* 5.266, Buffalo Sucker. Brown Buffalo . . . The young is nearly elliptical in its outline, and is often sold in the market as a distinct species, under the name of *Buffalo Perch.* **1911** *Century Dict.,* Buffalo-perch . . . *Ictiobus bubalus;* a buffalo-fish.

buffalo pine n

Perh **a bull pine 1b.**

1966 *DARE* (Qu. T17, . . *Kinds of pine trees)* Inf **SD**2, Buffalo pine— long needles.

buffalo plum See **buffalo bean**

buffalo pond See **buffalo wallow**

buffalo sod n **KS**

Sod from ground where **buffalo grass** has grown.

1877 in 1937 Ruede *Sod-House* 28 **KS,** When the prairie is thoroughly soaked by rain or snow is the best time for breaking sod for building. The regulation thickness is 2½ inches, buffalo sod preferred on account of its superior toughness. **1943** Holt *G.W. Carver* 49 **KS** (as of 1886), With a plow they cut the buffalo sod four inches thick and twelve inches wide. **1944** Wellman *Bowl* 82 **KS,** It certainly had been powerful hot and dry, even for the Short Grass. Here it was, June yet, and the buffalo sod already curing and crumbling as in August.

buffalo stamp n *obs*

1873 Beadle *Undeveloped West* 205 **KS,** "Buffalo stamps," are tracts of hard blue soil. **1878** Beadle *Western Wilds* 131 **KS,** The rock lies . . but a few inches below the surface, which is largely dotted with "buffalo stamps." These are said to have been caused by buffaloes crowding together, stamping and licking the ground, led thereto by a saline element in the soil.

buffalo tree n

1 =oilnut 2.

1883 Hale *Woods NC* 154, *Buffalo Tree.* (Pyrularia oleifera . . .) — A bush 3 to 6 feet high, abundant through our mountain range.

2 A magnolia.

1965–70 *DARE* (Qu. T15) Inf **OK**11, Buffalo tree; (Qu. T5) Inf **TX**85, Magnolia—also called buffalo tree. **1970** *DARE* Tape **TX** 87, The buffalo tree is what most people call the magnolia . . . The legend goes that here in Texas . . . this herd of buffalo was headed by this one huge white bull . . . One day a white man came along, and he killed this beautiful white animal . . . There came a tree on the banks of the bayou, and on that tree . . was a beautiful white blossom, and the Indians knew . . . they were forgiven for . . letting the white man come in and kill the buffalo.

buffalo wallow n Also rarely *buffalo waddle,* ~ *wash;* obs *buffalo pond* [See quot 1889] chiefly West *old-fash* Cf hog wallow

A bowl-shaped depression in the earth.

1782 in 1940 McJimsey *Topog. VA* 162, To an Elm Standing on Souths line at the edge of a small Buffaloe pond [="A shallow pond to which buffalo resort to wallow in hot weather"]. **1834** Pike *Prose Sketches* 18 **nTX,** Traveled all day, and encamped again in the prairie, at a hole where buffalo had been rolling, called by hunters a buffalo wallow, and containing water. **1873** Beadle *Undeveloped West* 83 **WY,** They lost all their stock, and took refuge in a "buffalo wallow" a few rods in circumference—a splendid natural earth-work. **1889** (1971) Farmer *Americanisms, Buffalo Wallow* . . . formed in the following manner. A heavy rainfall deluges the hard and level country . . . a portion of the soil, a little more moist than that adjoining, opens in cracks, such as can be seen in any ordinary dried-up mud hole. Another hard rain comes: these cracks are filled up by earth washed from their edges, which, packed more tightly, and retaining moisture longer than before, cracks again wider in drying. This process is repeated again and again, until quite a depression is made in the soil, which is now so tightly packed as to retain water for a considerable time. When the buffalo is shedding his coat in the spring, he is constantly endeavouring to get rid of the superfluous hair, and, in the absence of trees against which to rub, he is frequently rolling and rubbing himself on the ground. These small water-holes are his especial delight. The buffalo is in no way necessary to the formation of the *buffalo wallow,* it being found in parts of the country where there are no buffalo. **1914** *DN* 4.103 **KS,** *Buffalo-waddle* . . . A buffalo wallow. **1966–67** *DARE* (Qu. C6, . . *A piece of land that's often wet, and has grass and weeds growing on it*) Inf **OK**25, Buffalo wallow [wɑlə̈]; (Qu. C21, *A deep place cut in sloping ground by running water*) Inf **NE**7, Buffalo wash. **1973** Allen *LAUM* 1.235, The single occurrence of *buffalo wallow* in South Dakota echoes an earlier day when buffalo roamed the open prairie and, by rolling over in a wet spot or muddy place, so deepened the depression that it persisted until plows cut through the tough buffalo grass.

buffalo weed n

The giant **ragweed** (*Ambrosia trifida*).

1900 Lyons *Plant Names* 27, *A. trifida* . . . Buffalo-weed. **1950** Gray–Fernald *Manual of Botany* 1469, *Great R[agweed], Buffalo-weed* . . . Alluvium, rich openings and waste places. **1970** U.S. Dept. Ag. *Selected Weeds* 368, *Giant ragweed, buffaloweed* . . . Throughout all the United States excepting the Pacific coast area and areas in the Southwest, Florida, northern Maine, and extreme northern Great Lakes States.

buffalo wolf n

A subsp of the **gray wolf** (here: *Canis lupus nubilus*).

1846 in 1956 Sage *Letters & Papers* 1.193, Of these there are five distinct classifications, viz: The big white or buffalo wolf; the shaggy brown, the black; the gray, or prairie wolf; and the cayeute, (wa-chunka-monet,) or medicine-wolf of the Indians. **1928** Anthony *N. Amer.*

Mammals 153, *Gray Wolf; . . Buffalo Wolf* . . . Usual color pattern gray sprinkled with black or dusky on upper parts. **1947** *True* 21.90/1, They [=wolf hunters] could be found . . everywhere that the buffalo wolf roamed . . . The commonest name today is gray wolf, but the wolfer called him the buffalo wolf due to the way in which he haunted the herds. **1968** Adams *Western Words, Buffalo wolf*—A very large gray wolf that preyed upon buffaloes. **1982** Elman *Hunter's Field Guide* 548, Black and white color phases were far more common in the . . subspecies *C.l. nubilus* . . which fed on the immense herds of bison (it was also called buffalo wolf).

buffalo wood n Also *buffalo fuel* [Prob transl of Fr *bois de vache*] Cf chip n[1] 1

Dried buffalo manure.

1848 (1932) Robinson *Jrl. Sante Fe* 13, The men scattered themselves about to pick up . . . buffalo-fuel. **1855** Stone *Put's Calif. Songster* 16 (*DA*), It's fun to cook with buffalo wood. **1968** Adams *Western Words, Buffalo chip*—Dried buffalo manure frequently used for fuel on the plains in the early days. Also called *buffalo wood.*

buff-backed heron n FL

=cattle egret.

1954 Sprunt *FL Bird Life* 31, Cattle Egret: *Bubulcus ibis* . . . Local Names: Buff-backed Heron. **1957** Pough *Audubon W. Bird Guide* 28, Cattle Egret *Bubulcus ibis.* (Buff-backed Heron).

buffelhead, buffel-headed duck, buffel's head See bufflehead 2

‡buffer strip n [Perh from *W3* std sense "a grassed strip between strips of cropland subject to erosion"] See also *DS* N44

1973 Allen *LAUM* 1.381 **ND,** The strip of grass between a sidewalk and the street . . . *buffer strip* [1 respondent].

buffet n, also attrib

A Forms. Usu |bəˈfeɪ|; also |ˈbʌˌfeɪ|; less freq |buˈfeɪ, buˈfeɪ|; now rarely |ˈbʌfɛt|.

1 Hist or old-fash pronc-spp *baufat, beaufatt, beaufet, bofat,* and *bof(f)et,* and std *buffet,* representing proncs such as |ˈbɔfət, 'bofət, 'bɑfət, 'bʌfɛt|. Note: the initial stress and final |-t| remain characteristic of Brit pronc for most senses of *buffet* n.

1828 Webster *Amer. Dict.,* *'Buffet* . . . the name has become, in a great measure, obsolete, except among the common people, by whom it is pronounced *bofat.* **1848** G.E. Ellis *Letter* (Bartlett MS.) (*DAE*), Our old ladies in the country have a sort of corner cupboard, or *dresser* wh[ich] they call a *baufat* [sic], probably derived from the French *buffet.* **1869** Stowe *Oldtown Folks* 34 **MA,** Silver table-spoons and teaspoons graced the beaufet in the corner. **1889** *Century Dict., Beaufet* . . . An erroneous form of *buffet*[2]. *Ibid, Buffet*[2] ('bufet, or, as F[rench], büfä). **1899** (1912) Green *VA Folk-Speech, Bofet* . . . A buffet, generally in a corner, with glass doors, for holding crockery and such like. Boffet. **1912** *Ibid, Beaufatt* . . . A corner-closet, with glass doors for holding "chaney." **1950** *WELS,* 2 Infs, **sWI,** Buf-fet. **1966–70** *DARE* (Qu. E5) Infs **GA**8, **MS**85, [ˈbʌfɛt]; **MD**21, [bʌfɛt]—correct; [ˈbʌfɛt]—modern word; **WA**1, [bʌfɛ]; some people say [bʌfɛt] [laughter]; **NC**25, [ˈboʊfæt].

2 Proncs with initial stress: |ˈbʌfeɪ| widespread, but least freq NEast, N Cent; occas |ˈbʌˌfeɪ, ˈbufeɪ| esp Sth; rarely |ˈbufeɪ, ˈbuˈfeɪ, ˈbofeɪ|. Cf Intro "Language Changes" IV.2

1965–70 *DARE* (Qu. E5) 105 Infs, esp Sth, S Midl, West, [ˈbʌfeɪ]; 10 Infs, esp Sth, [ˈbʌˈfeɪ]; 9 Infs, chiefly Sth, [ˈbufeɪ]; **CT**11, 42, [ˈbufeɪ]; **AK**3, [ˈbuˈfeɪ]; **MN**16, [ˈbofeɪ]; (Qu. H70) Inf **PA**196, [ˈbʌfeɪ]; (Qu. FF1) Inf **WA**22, [ˈbufeɪ] dinner; (Qu. FF2) Inf **VA**58, [ˈbʌfeɪ] supper.

3 Proncs with ultimate stress: |bəˈfeɪ| widespread; also |buˈfeɪ, buˈfeɪ| widespread, but infreq in Midl, West.

1950 *WELS* (*Piece of dining-room furniture:* "buh-fay" or "boo-fay") **WI,** 42 Infs, "Buh-fay"; 7 Infs, "Boo-fay"; 1 Inf, Thirty years ago, it was "boo-fay" in our neighborhood—now it's "buh-fay." **1965–70** *DARE* (Qu. E5) 317 Infs, widespread, [bəˈfeɪ]; 41 Infs, widespread, but infreq in Midl, West, [buˈfeɪ]; 39 Infs, widespread, but infreq in Midl, West, [buˈfeɪ]; **NY**88, [bəˈfeɪ] draw; (Qu. D39) Inf **MO**9, [bəˈfeɪ]; (Qu. E3) Inf **NM**12, [bəˈfeɪ]; (Qu. H70) Infs **AZ**12, **NY**24, **PA**248, [bəˈfeɪ]; **MA**9, [buˈfeɪ]; (Qu. FF2) Inf **ME**11, [buˈfez]; **PA**165, [bəˈfez]; **VA**109, [bəˈfeɪ].

4 Addit proncs: see quot.

1966–69 *DARE* (Qu. E5) Infs **GA**53, 81, 85, **NY**130; **NM**8, **NY**61, **PA**52, [boˈfeɪ]; **MN**16, [ˈbofeɪ]; **LA**33, [ˈbʏfe]; **PA**67, [bɨˈfe]; **TX**35, [bjuˈfeɪ].

B Senses.

1 A corner cupboard for holding tableware. **chiefly NEng old-fash** For addit quots see **A1** above

1789 (1905) Bentley *Diary* 1.118 **MA**, He found all doors open, & the plate in the Buffet. **1859** (1968) Bartlett *Americanisms, Buffet.* This name is still applied, in the rural parts of New England, to a three-cornered cupboard. **1859** Stowe *Minister's Wooing* 18 **NEng**, Right across the corner stands the "buffet," as it is called . . wherein are displayed the solemn appurtenances of company tea-table. **1869** Stowe *Oldtown Folks* 182 **MA**, The apparition . . only appeared in a certain room . . which had across one of its corners a sort of closet called a buffet. **1880** *Harper's Mag.* 61.879/2 **wMA**, Being asked . . how the settlers in that region were prospering, he replied that they were "as poor as the devil's bofat." . . A bofat . . is a little corner closet where the family rum was generally kept.

2 A liquor bar, speakeasy, tavern.

1890 *Voice* (N.Y.) 1 May (*DAE*), A curb-stone reporter avouches that Democratic drinkers no longer 'take a drink' . . . but they patronize the 'buffet.' **1928** McKay *Home to Harlem* 103 **NYC**, Jake had gained admission to Madame Adeline Suarez's buffet flat, which was indeed a great feat. He was the first longshoreman, colored or white, to tread that magnificent carpet . . . And . . to luxuriate with charmingly painted pansies among the colored cushions and under the soft, shaded lights of Madame Suarez's speakeasy. **1942** Berrey – Van den Bark *Amer. Slang* 109.4, *Illicit liquor establishment . . .* beer flat, buffet apartment *or* flat, *a "speakeasy" in a private home.* **1958** *AmSp* 33.299 **NE**, The establishments dealing in on-sale beer are called *taverns, bars, buffets, grills, parlors, or clubs.*

buffle-brained adj [Engl dial *buffle* fool; see **bufflehead 1**] Stupid, foolish.

1900 in 1966 *AmSp* 41.22 **ME**, *Buffle-brained . . .* Foolish. "Eternally cussed . . . was the buffle-brained feller." **1914** *DN* 4.69 **ME, nNH**, *Buffle-brained . . .* Stupid.

buffle duck See **bufflehead 2**

bufflehead n [*buffle* buffalo, fool *(OED "Obs.")* + *head*]

1 A stupid person, blockhead. [Engl dial; cf Ger *Büffelkopf*]

1930 Shoemaker *1300 Words* 7 **cPA Mts** (as of c1900), *Buffle-head—* A stupid, dull person.

2 also *buffalo-headed duck, buffelhead, buffel-headed duck, buffel's head, buffle(-headed) duck:* A small American diving duck *(Bucephala albeola).* Also called **baldpate 3, bobblehead, bumblebee duck, butterback, butterball 1, butterbox, butter duck 2, cock dipper, dapper, devil diver, diedapper, diedipper, dipper duck, dopper, ghost duck, hell-diver, little black and white duck, little brown duck, marionette, pintail whistler, pocket dipper, robin-dipper, saltwater teal, Scotch dipper, skunkhead, spirit duck, splatter-ass, winter duck, woolhead**

1731 (1754) Catesby *Nat. Hist. Carolina* 1.95 *Anas minor purpureo capite.* The Buffel's Head Duck. **1813** (1824) Wilson *Amer. Ornith.* 8.51, The Buffel-headed Duck, or rather as it has originally been, the Buffaloe-headed Duck . . is fourteen inches long, and twenty-three inches in extent. **1858** Baird *Birds* 798, The name buffle head is a corruption of buffalo head. **1888** Trumbull *Names of Birds* 81, *Buffle-head* or *Buffel's Head Duck . . . Buffle Duck: Buffalo-headed Duck.* **1917** (1923) *Birds Amer.* 1.140, Buffle-head—*Charitonetta albeola*—Other Names . . . Buffle-headed Duck; Buffalo-headed Duck . . It was named Buffle-head (or Buffalo-head) because of its large fluffy head. **1917** *DN* 4.423 **NEng**, *Buffle-head (Charitonetta albeola).* Marionette; Butterball. **1982** Elman *Hunter's Field Guide* 211, *Buffle head (Bucephala albeola)—*Common & Regional Names: . . buffalo-head.

buffler, bufler See **buffalo n A**

bug n[1] Note: The std colloq sense of *bug* "insect" is prob due to merging of the sense of *bud* (cf OE *budde* beetle) with *bug* (as in *bugaboo; bugbear, boggart,* etc) toward the end of the 15th cent.

1 also dim *buggy:* A louse. **chiefly east of Missip R** See Map

1965–70 *DARE* (Qu. R25, *Joking names for a head louse, or body louse*) 42 Infs, **chiefly east of Missip R**, Bug; NJ22, Buggies.

2 A stupid person.

1900 *DN* 2.25 **MA** [College slang], *Bug . . .* 1. A stupid person. **1919** *DN* 5.69 **NM** [High school speech], *Bug,* a stupid person.

3 Used in ref to derangement, mental instability, or obsession:

a also attrib: A deranged thought, insane idea; hence *bugs* insanity.

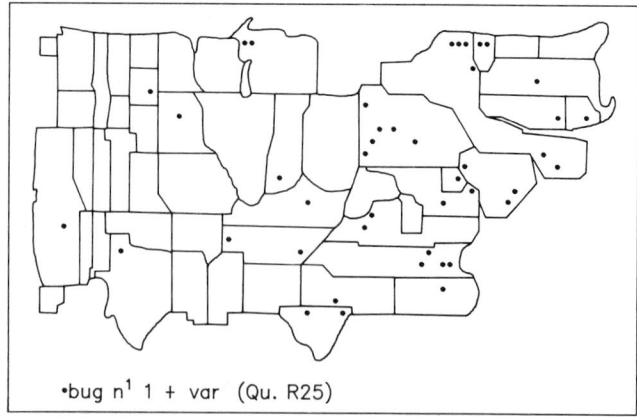

•bug n[1] 1 + var (Qu. R25)

1909 Porter *Roads of Destiny* 208, He's got bugs. Sitting on ice, and calling his best friends pseudonyms. **1912** *DN* 3.572 **wIN**, *Bugs . . .* Insanity. "He acts as if it were a case of bugs." **1915** *DN* 4.232 **OH** [College slang], *Bug . . .* An insane person . . said to have *bugs,* i.e. whimsical notions, in his brain. **1936** Hargan *Glossary of Prison Language* (Hench Coll.), Bug doctor—a psychiatrist or psychologist. Bug tests—psychological tests. **1951** *AmSp* 26.194 **NYC** [Reformatory argot], *Bug doctor:* A psychiatrist or psychologist.

b An insane person.

1915 [see **3a** above]. **1922** O'Neill *Hairy Ape* 68, On'y a bug is strong enough for dat!

c A powerful desire, craze, or obsession.

1915 *DN* 4.243 **MT**, *Bug . . .* Desire or 'craze.' "He's afflicted with the fishing bug." **1919** *DN* 5.69 **NM** [High school slang], *Bug . . .* used when a person talks or thinks on one subject continually . . . "She has the bug when it comes to dress." **1931** Runyon *Guys* 149 **NYC**, He has a bug that he is a wonderful judge of guys' characters. *Ibid* 271, Charlotte . . has a society bug and needs plenty of coconuts at all times to keep her a going concern. **1957** *New Yorker* 13 July 48 **NYC**, Stanley Kramer . . has succumbed to the Cecil B. deMille bug. **1966–68** *DARE* (Qu. AA4a, . . *Expressions . . about a man who is very eager to get married*) Inf **AL4**, Bug's hit him; **AR18**, Love-bug bit him; **DE2**, Got the bug; (Qu. DD10, . . *"He isn't smoking any more—a month ago he _____."*) Inf **HI9**, Killed the bug; (Qu. KK28, *Feeling ambitious and eager to work*) Inf **MI18**, Got the work-bug.

d now usu in comb: A person obsessed by a single idea; an enthusiast. Cf **box n 5, budget n 3**

1904 Porter *Cabbages & Kings* 337, The chief had got together the same old crowd of moneybugs with pink faces and white vests to see us march in. **1915** *DN* 4.232 **OH** [College slang], *Bug . . .* a specialist. **1919** *DN* 5.69 **NM** [High school slang], *Bug . . .* used when a person who is always talks or thinks on one subject continually. "He is such a bug." **1947** *Denver Post* (CO) 2 Feb sec A 11/2, Basketball bugs believe Colorado never had a prep team like the Windsor Wizards. **c1960** Wilson *Coll.* **csKY**, *Bug . . .* An enthusiast. **1965–70** *DARE* (Qu. AA7a, . . *A woman who is very fond of men*) Inf **AZ1**, Lovebug; (Qu. DD3a, . . *A person who uses snuff*) Inf **CA105**, Snoosebug; (Qu. GG36a, *The kind of person who is always poking into other people's affairs*) Inf **FL35**, Newsbug; (Qu. HH10, *A very timid or cowardly person*) Inf **MD40**, Fraidybug; (Qu. HH11a, *Someone who is too particular or fussy . . a man*) Inf **RI4**, Fussybug; (Qu. HH11b, *Someone who is too particular or fussy . . a woman*) Inf **PA75**, Fussbug; (Qu. HH21, *A very awkward, clumsy person*) Inf **PA214**, Bumblebug; (Qu. JJ9, *Somebody who studies too hard or all the time*) Inf **LA46**, Bug.

4 Used in ref to dishonesty or deceit:

a usu in phr *put a* (or *the*) *bug on:* A trick or hoax. Cf **bug v 1**

1848 Thompson *Major Jones's Travel* 126 **GA**, We got to Stunnington, in Connecticut, whar they say the peeple live on fish so much that they smell like whale oil and have scales on their backs. This may be a bug what they put on me, but one thing I do know—and that is that they is great whalers. **1853** Hammett *Stray Yankee in TX* 96, I smell a bug. Dave and that are strannger's ondly playin' possum, . . but they can't pull the wool over this child's eyes. **1967** *DARE* (Qu. II33, *To get an advantage over somebody by tricky means: "I don't trust him, he's always trying to _____."*) Inf **OH33**, Put the bug on you.

‡b An unreliable person, a cheat.

1885 Twain *Huck. Finn* 200 **MO**, Spose people left money laying around where he was—what did he do? He collared it. Spose he contracted to do a thing; and you paid him, and didn't set down there and see that he done it—what did he do? He always done the other thing . . . That's the kind of a bug Henry was; and if we'd a had him along 'stead of our kings, he'd a fooled that town a heap worse than ourn done.

c in var phrr suggesting duplicity: See quots.

1954 *Harder Coll.* **cwTN,** *Bug up his ass* . . . Said of someone who has dishonest intentions. **1968–70** *DARE* (Qu. JJ19, *If somebody has dishonest intentions, or is up to no good, you might say, "I think he's got _____."*) Inf **NY84,** Bug up his sleeve; **NY219,** Bugs in his bonnet; **TN53,** Bug under the rug.

5 Used in ref to disease:

a often *the bug:* A disease-causing organism; hence, a cold or illness, esp the flu. **chiefly NEast** See Map

1914 *DN* 4.162 **NW,** *Bug* . . . Bacillus; germ. "They found the bugs in his system all right." **1947** *AmSp* 22.54 [Pacific war language], The *bug.* Malaria. **1967–70** *DARE* (Qu. BB9, *A sickness in which you have a severe cough and difficult breathing—it often starts with a cold, and lasts a week or two*) Infs **NJ9, 69, NY80,** The bug; **IN60,** A bug; **ME5,** Called a bug today; **CT12,** Bug; **MD9,** Bug—modern term; (Qu. BB13, . . *Chills and fever*) Inf **CT21, MA65, MO20, NY7, PA196,** The bug; **NY130,** A bug (for an infection); **NY27,** Bug; (Qu. BB28, *Joking names that people make up for imaginary diseases: "He must have the _____."*) Infs **NJ54, NY167, 200,** Bug; (Qu. BB49, . . *Diseases [that] are common*) Inf **NY7,** The bug; **CT3,** The bug—word used today for flu; **OH11,** Bugs.

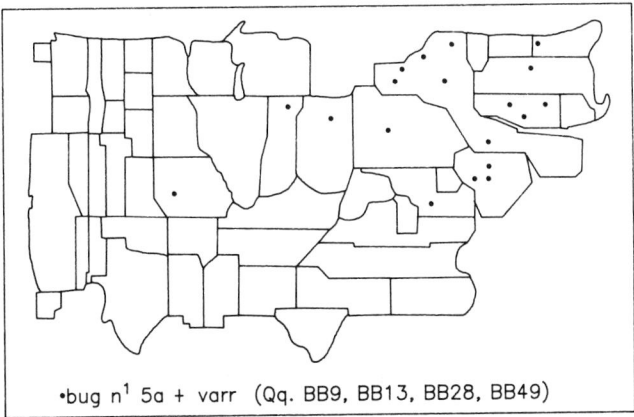

•bug n¹ 5a + varr (Qq. BB9, BB13, BB28, BB49)

b usu with *the,* freq pl: Tuberculosis. **chiefly Mid and S Atl, SW** See Map Cf **con** n¹, **lung fever**

1942 Berrey – Van den Bark *Amer. Slang* 130.21, *Tuberculosis* . . . bug, a tubercle. **1950** *WELS* (*Nicknames for tuberculosis*) 1 Inf, **WI,** The Bug [common]; 1 Inf, The Bugs [occas]; 1 Inf, Bugs [common]. **1965–70** *DARE* (Qu. BB10, . . *Nicknames* . . *for tuberculosis*) Infs **AZ2, FL19, 33, MD24, MN2, NC18, 52, TX18, 70 UT3,** The bug; **AZ16, IL46, SC67, TX9, 36, VA11,** The bugs; **NC88, SC70,** Bugs; **SC58,** So and so's in the sanatorium; he's got a bug.

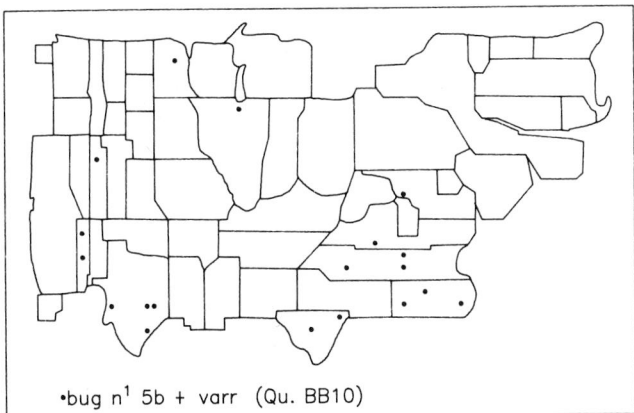

•bug n¹ 5b + varr (Qu. BB10)

6 Nasal mucus. [Engl dial] **scattered, but esp MI, WI** Cf **booger** n¹ 3

1950 *WELS* (*Sticky mucus that forms in the nose*) 1 Inf, **WI,** Bugs; 1 Inf, Bugs (used by children). **1965–70** *DARE* (Qu. X16, *Sticky mucus that forms in the nose—children's words for this*) Infs **CA80, MD35, MI20,**

110, **TX53, WI34,** Bug; **AZ8,** [bʊg]; **WI76,** [bʌg]—common term; **MI2,** Bugs; **DE3,** Nose bugs.

7 pl: =**jimmies.**

1968 *DARE* (Qu. H82b, . . *Candy that used to be sold*) Inf **NY121,** Bugs—ice cream dipped into little chocolate pellets.

8 used in jocular place-names for presumed insect-infested small settlements: See quots. **chiefly Sth, S Midl**

1960 Williams *Walk Egypt* 225 **GA,** "They having a dance to Cardiff and we going." . . She giggled. "Better men in Bugtown. Don't need a banty, I can get me a rooster." **1966–68** *DARE* (Qu. C34, *Nicknames for nearby settlements, villages, or districts*) Inf **NC23,** Bughill; **AR39, TX4,** Bugscuffle; **OK25,** Bugscuffle (Elliott, TX); **CO41, IN49,** Bugtown; **OK51,** Bugtussle—7 or 8 miles out; **TX43** Bugtussle—gone now; **LA2,** Bugtussle—joking name for a local unscreened church where they have to fight the bugs. **1970** Stewart *Amer. Place-Names* 64, Generally the name [with the element *bug*] is humorously derogatory, and stands upon informally named communities without being officially recognized, though it occasionally gets upon standard maps, e.g. *Bug Hollow* KY. Repeated names of this sort are *Bug Tussle* and *Bug Scuffle,* implying places where a person would have to combat bugs, especially bedbugs. **1981** Brooks *Complete Directory TV* 78/1, The $25 million given them [="Beverly Hillbillies"] by John Brewster, of the OK Oil Company, for drilling rights to their land in Bugtussle, Tennessee, was deposited in Milburn Drysdale's Commerce Bank.

9 A small marine creature: see quots. See also **bog** v¹ 2, **bugging**

1945 *AN&Q* 4.187 **NY,** Bug scallop . . . According to the New York State Conservation Department, this is an undersize scallop averaging about three or four months . . . The "bug scallop" has a small or bug-like fleshy portion and is well below the acceptable minimum for commercial use . . . The term is known to have been in use for a long time, but how long could not be easily determined. **1966** *DARE* Tape **SC18,** Shrimp are sometime called bug.

10 A fishing worm.

1950 *WELS Suppl.* **cwWI,** We'll have to dig some more bugs [=worms for fishing].

11 See **bug light 2.**

12 See **bugger** n¹ **B2.**

13 See **mudbug.**

14 In var phrr:

a *go to the bugs:* To go to destruction; to come to nothing. *obs* Cf *go to the dogs*

1828 in 1977 Whiting *Early Amer. Proverbs* 48, But no matter about the affair, let it all go to the bugs. **1833** Neal *Down-Easters* 1.124 **NEng,** If it hadn't a ben for 'Diah I might 'a gone to the bugs arter all. **1856** J.D. Whitney *Life & Lett.* 160 (*DA*), Shall I let the survey go to the bugs and return home immediately?

b *put the bug on:* See quots.

1848 [see **4a** above]. **1967** [see **4a** above]. **1968** *DARE* (Qu. Y6 . . *To put pressure on somebody to do something he ought to have done*) Infs **LA15, MD20,** Put the bug on him.

c *bug under the chip:* An ulterior motive. **chiefly Sth, S Midl**

1885 *Congressional Record* 998/1 **VA,** I know as well what the bug is under this chip as I know that the resolution is pending here. [**1909** Porter *Options* 9 **NY speaker in GA,** How about this write-up of the Atlanta, New Orleans, Nashville, and Savannah breweries? . . . What's the chip over the bug?] **1914** *DN* 4.104 **KS,** *Bug under the chip* . . . Something which does not appear on the surface. "I don't know the reason of the offer, but there must be a bug under the chip." **1916** *DN* 4.298 **Sth,** *Bug under the chip* . . . Common in the South: one sent to pick up chips often found an insect under them. The meaning is, I think that something untoward is concealed. **1946** *Newsweek* 15 July 36/3 **AZ,** To those uneasy over the alliance he gave his word that there are "no such bugs under the chips." **1967–70** *DARE* (Qu. V1, . . *Somebody is trying to deceive you, . . something is going on behind your back*) Infs **TN53, TX5, 65,** Bug under the chip.

d *bug in one's ear* and varr: A hint; a friendly warning. See also **14h** below Cf *flea in one's ear*

1905 *DN* 3.72 **nwAR,** *Bug in one's ear* . . . Hint. 'I want to put a bug in your ear.' **1909** *DN* 3.361 **eAL, wGA,** *Put a bug in one's ear* . . . To tell one a secret, put one on to a secret. **1912** *DN* 3.586 **wIN. 1927** *AmSp* 2.362 **WV. 1929** *AmSp* 4.466 **N Cent, Upper MW. 1949** *Western Folkl.* 8.98 **CA,** To get a bug in his ear — To get a novel suggestion or an inspiration to act. The more usual form appears to be "to put a flea in his ear." **1950** *WELS* (*To give somebody a hint for his own good:* "He *didn't guess that she was up to anything, but I* _____.") 13 Infs, **WI**, Put a bug in his ear. **1965–70** *DARE* (Qu. JJ27, *To give somebody a hint for his own good: "He had no idea that she was up to anything, but I put* _____.") 267 Infs, **widespread**, Bug in his ear; **TX35**, Dropped a bug in his ear; **KS13, MD26, NY96**, Bug in his head; **NJ7**, Bug in him; **CA196, KS18, MS37, TX99**, Bug; (Qu. JJ43) Infs **IA11, MD36, MO6, SC26**, Put a bug in his ear; **CA3, 87, MT3**, Bug in his bonnet; **KY72**, Bug in his hat; bug in his bonnet.

e *ride one bug-hunting:* To punish. **W Midl, Sth**

1906 *DN* 3.153 **nwAR**, *Ride bug-hunting . . .* To chastise, whip. "If you do that, I'll ride you bug-hunting." **1909** *DN* 3.363 **eAL, wGA**, *Ride one (a) bug huntin(g) . . .* To punish one, whip or chastise one. "You better mind or he'll ride you a bug huntin'." **1923** *DN* 5.202 **swMO**, *Bug huntin', to 'ride a man bug huntin',* to subject him to merciless sarcasm or ridicule, or to beat or maul him severely. **1958** *PADS* 29.8 **wTN**, *Bug hunting:* Phrase *ride him bug hunting* means to rub his nose in the dirt. Rep[orted] from Humphreys [County].

f *cute as a bug's ear:* Small and endearingly attractive.

1931 *AmSp* 203 **MO** [College slang], *Cute as a bug's ear:* attractive, dainty. **1965** *DARE* File **csWI** [Speaker an elderly woman], Yes, it was cute's a bug's ear! **1968** *DARE* (Qu. Z12, . . *A small child*) Inf **CA94**, Cute as a bug's ear.

g *bug up one's ass* and varr:

(1) A stimulus, goad, obsessive desire.

1954 *Harder Coll.* **cwTN**, *Bug up (one's) ass, to have a . . .* Of one who works very hard or has only one idea in mind. **1967–70** *DARE* (Qu. A19) Inf **CO47**, Put the bug in my butt and get going; (Qu. GG16) Inf **SC69**, Got a bug up his butt.

(2) See **4c** above.

h *bug(s) in one's bonnet* (or *hat*):

(1) See **14d** below.

(2) See **4c** above. Cf **beans up one's nose 2**

bug n[2] [Cf Engl dial *bug* conceited, Norw *bugge* important man; prob infl by **bug** n[1]] *often derog*

An important person or one who thinks himself so; a big shot. See also **big bug, city bug**

1843 (1916) Hall *New Purchase* 325 **IN**, On one occasion he was in Woodville when a half drunken brute thus hallooed against him — "thare goes that darn'd high larn'd bug what gits nine hundred and ninety-nine dollars and ninety-nine cents of the people's eddekashin money." **1885** (1913) Murfree *Prophet of Smoky Mts.* 201 **eTN**, Them crazy bugs in N-N-Nashvul sent him a book ev'y time they made a batch o' new laws. **1915** *DN* 4.197, *Bug . .* a "swell." "He thinks he is a big bug." **1968** *DARE* (Qu. U37, . . *Somebody who has plenty of money*) Inf **NH14**, Rich bug.

bug v [**bug** n[1]]

1 To cheat or deceive. **chiefly Sth** Cf **bug** n[1] **4**

1843 in 1969 Turner *Cotton Planter's Manual* 62 **AL**, You will first observe the bloom, and the description given, and you will agree with me at once, that Mr. Sears has been *bugged* by an okra flower. **1898** Lloyd *Country Life* 51 **AL**, The pritty little pullet was sent to her to kinder even for the way in which she got bugged when she took old Lige in out of the weather. **1966–67** *DARE* (Qu. II33, *To get an advantage over somebody by tricky means: "I don't trust him, he's always trying to* _____.') Inf **TX10**, Trick; bug; (Qu. LL23, *Cheated, treated dishonestly: "These apples are wormy, I think you got* _____.') Infs **GA7, SC19**, Bugged; **GA1**, Bugged on.

2 usu intr and foll by *out:* Of the eyes: to (cause to) bulge, esp in astonishment. See also **bug eye** n[1]

1877 Wright *Big Bonanza* 57, His eyes bugged out like the horns of a snail. **1896** *DN* 1.413 **cNY, nOH**, *Bug out . . .* "His eyes bugged out, he bugged out his eyes," showing astonishment. **1905** *DN* 3.72 **nwAR**. **1916** *DN* 4.320 **NY, NE**. **1923** *DN* 5.202 **swMO**. **1929** (1951) Faulkner *Sartoris* 225 **MS**, They was a-settin' thar gapin' at the rise when he come over hit, . . buggin' their eyes at him. **1950** Moore *Candlemas Bay* 170 **ME**, That pug knot . . hauled her hair back so tight it bugged her eyes out. **1950** *WELS* (*Eyes that stick out noticeably: his eyes* _____) 4 Infs, **WI**, Bug out; 1 Inf, Bug out like shoe buttons. **1966–69** *DARE* (Qu. X21a, . . *Eyes . . if they stick out*) Infs **NY211, NC24, VT16**, Bug out; **ME22**, Bugged out; **IA27, TN13**, Bugged-out eyes.

3 with *down:* See quot. Cf **bug** n[1] **5**

1933 *Hanley Disks* **seMA**, Bug down [ˈbʌg ˈdaʊn] — get sick on the job.

4 To bother, annoy, vex. *earlier chiefly among young speakers, now widespread*

1949 *Music Lib. Assoc. Notes* 7.40/2, *Bug*, popularized by swing musicians and now much used by be-boppers: to be annoying. **1954** Armstrong *Satchmo* 164 **LA**, I suspected something was bugging her from the way she used to give me hell. **1958** *AmSp* 33.225 [Jazz slang]. **1958** *PADS* 30.44 [Jazz slang], *Bug . . .* To bother, especially to get one in such a state that he cannot play well. Extended to mean getting annoyed at anything. **1965–70** *DARE* (Qu. GG13a) 362 Infs, Bugs; **NY88**, Is bugging; (Qu. Y7) 203 Infs, Bugging; (Qu. II29b) 170 Infs, Bugs me; **NH14**, Bugs me up; **FL52**, Bugs me to death; (Qu.BB40) 54 Infs, Bugged; 21 Infs, Was (or is) bugging; **CT23, LA35**, Bugs; (Qu. GG3) 46 Infs, Bug; (Qu. GG24) 20 Infs, 5 *young*, Bug; (Qu. Y2) 11 Infs, *6 young*, Bug. [Of all Infs responding to Qq. Y7, BB40, GG13a, and II29b, from 10% to 12% were young and 25% mid-aged; of those giving these responses, from 19% to 22% were young and from 28% to 33% mid-aged. Of all Infs responding to Qu. GG3, 11% were young; of those giving this response, 30% were young.] **1975** Morris *Usage* 96, *Usage panel question*—The word *bug* has acquired the sense in recent years of "to irritate, vex, or exasperate." Would you accept this: "His habitual lateness for appointments really *bugs* me"? In writing—Yes: 29% . . . In casual speech—Yes: 83%.

5 See quot. Cf **buck** v[1] **B2c**

1945 Saxon *Gumbo Ya-Ya* 455 **LA** [Black], To 'bug' is to fight . . . 'I'm gonna git Shot Gun Sammy and his whole dern crew, / Gonna git Bucket Leg Pete we gon' bug wit' you.'

6 usu with *out*, occas with *off:* To retreat or leave, esp in haste. [See quot 1956]

1955 *AmSp* 30.116 [Air Force slang], *Bug out; booger off; leap off . . .* Leave suddenly and rapidly. **1956** *U.S. Air Univ. Air Force Dict.* 94, *Bug . . .* To retreat in panic or haste, as in 'they bugged out of Seoul,' or the 'Bug-out Boogie!' *Slang* used in Korean war. **1966–69** *DARE* (Qu. Y18, *To leave in a hurry*) Infs **AL41, ID5, WA33**, Bug out; **NY210**, Bug it; move out; (Qu. Y19, *To begin to go away*) Inf **MO26**, Bug out; **MI32**, Bug; (Qu. X10b) Inf **WA22**, For crying out loud, bug out; (Qu.II22) Infs **NY211, RI6**, Bug off; (Qu. II31) Inf **IL71**, Bug out. **1971** Wood *Vocab. Change* 368/2 **Sth**, Additional volunteered words [for *truancy*]: bug out, ran out of school.

7 See quot. Cf **bugalug**

1967 *DARE* (Qu. Y21, *To move about slowly and without energy*) Inf **NY29**, Bug along.

bugaboo n Also *boogerboo, bugabo* Pronc-spp *boogieboo, buggyboo* [Obs *buggybow*] Cf **booger** n[1]

1 A ghost or imaginary monster; the devil. **esp Sth, S Midl**

1787 *Columbian Mag.* 464/2 **sePA**, The maid . . threatens to leave them [=children] in the dark for the *bug-aboos*, if they are not quiet. **1835** Crockett *Life VanBuren* 188 **S Midl**, All they hear on this subject from Blair and Ritchie is nothing but the *bugaboo* of an old *coat* and *breeches* hung up to scare them. **1899** (1912) Green *VA Folk-Speech*, *Bugabo . . .* A ghost. **1943** [see **booger** n[1] **1a**]. **c1960** [see **2a** below]. **1966–70** *DARE* (Qu. CC17, *Imaginary animals or monsters*) Inf **GA84**, Bugaboo; (Qu. EE41, *A hobgoblin that is used to threaten children and make them behave*) Inf **VA50**, Buggyboo [ˈbʌgiˌbu]; **MT5, NC88**, Boogerboo; **MD31**, Boogieboo. **1971** Bright *Word Geog. CA & NV* 202, *Devil* / also veiled and jocular terms/ . . . *bugaboo* 8% [of responses; "urban and northern California rural"]. **1973** Allen *LAUM* 1.384 **nwND**, *Devil . . .* The second group of expressions is almost exclusively restricted to speech with a child . . . One inf. has heard *bugaboo* in this connection.

2a A source of concern or dread, often an imaginary one.

1791 in 1911 *MD Hist. Mag.* 6.355, That bugaboo of the Indians is quite removed out of the way. **1843** in 1912 Thornton *Amer. Gloss.* 115, Diseased potatoes form the last *bugaboo* story for the newspapers. **1873** Miller *Modocs* 107 **CA**, Grandmothers never hold up before naughty children a bigger or more delusive bug-a-boo than this universal fear of Indians. **1908** Lincoln *Cy Whittaker* 204 **MA**, Tramps are our bugaboos here in Bayport. **1937** (1977) Hurston *Their Eyes* 184 **FL**, So they all went outside to see if Tea Cake could handle the boogerboo. **c1960** *Wilson Coll.* **csKY**, *Bugaboo . . .* Ghost or some nonsensical fear. "She's always scared of some bugaboo." **1967** *DARE* Tape **AL26**, That's been a bugaboo of me all my life . . . in other words, I just didn't know how to meet people.

b See quot. [Perh by confusion with ~~hullabaloo~~]

1905 *DN* 3.72 **nwAR**, *Bug-a-boo . . .* Commotion, ado. 'He raised a big bug-a-boo about nothing.' Common.

3 Nasal mucus: see quots.

1899 (1912) Green *VA Folk-Speech*, *Bugabo* . . . Hardened mucus in a child's nose. **1950** *WELS* (*Sticky mucus that forms in the nose*) 1 Inf, seWI, Bugaboos. **1968–69** *DARE* (Qu. X16, *Sticky mucus that forms in the nose—children's words for this*) Infs CA42, 151, CT9, NJ22, NY41, Bugaboo; CA99, Bugaboos.

4 =**booger** n[1] **2.**

1899 (1912) Green *VA Folk-Speech*, *Bugabo* . . . A louse.

5 A mistake, blunder. [Perh infl by *boo-boo*]

1969–70 *DARE* (Qu. JJ41, *An embarrassing mistake: "Last night she made an awful _____."*) Inf **KY**21, Boogieboo; **KY**85, Boogerboo.

bugaloo See **boogaloo**

bugalug v Cf **bug** v 7

1912 Green *VA Folk-Speech*, *Bugalug* . . . To move about in an aimless way: "What are you doing *bugalugging* about here."

bug-back n, also attrib

A kind of carriage.

a1833 (1911) Bagby *VA Gentleman* 2, But the drivers of the high-swung, bug-back family carriages of the period knew that turning "mighty well." *Ibid* 5, The freckle-face ten-year-old brother, . . standing up behind and hanging back by the carriage straps, yelled with delight every time the bug-back "went down" [when driven over a hole in the road].

bugbane n [*bug* + *bane* poison]

1 also *bugwort*: A plant of the genus *Cimicifuga*. Also called **black cohosh 1, black snakeroot 1, carrion flower 2, fairy candles, rattletop, stink feather.** For other names of var spp see **baneberry 2, battleweed, blueberry 3, blue ginseng 2, cohosh 1b, deerweed, false cohosh, feather wands, papoose root, rattlebox, rattle cohosh, rattlepod, rattleroot, rattlesnake root, rattlesnake weed, rattleweed, rattlewood, richweed, snakeroot, squawroot, squaw-weed, star lance, summer cohosh, summer rockets, Virginia snakeroot, yellow ginseng**

1822 Eaton *Botany* 347, *Macrotys* . . . *serpentaria* (bugbane, black snakeroot, cohosh . .). **1848** Gray *Manual of Botany* 16, *Cimicifuga* . . . Bugbane. **1876** Hobbs *Bot. Hdbk.* 16, Bugbane, Black cohosh, Cimicifuga racemosa. Bugbane, American Hellebore, Veratrum viride. *Ibid* 17, Bugwort, Black cohosh, Cimicifuga racemosa. **1903** Porter *Flora PA* 135. **1959** Carleton *Index Herb. Plants* 20, Bugbane: Actaea (v); Cimicifuga(v); Erigeron (v). **1976** Bruce *How to Grow Wildflowers* 167, Bugbane, *Cimicifuga racemosa* . . . Other names for this plant are Black Cohosh and Black Snakeroot.

2 also *bugwort*: =**Indian poke 1.**

1900 Lyons *Plant Names* 389, *V[eratrum] viride* . . . Bugbane, Bugwort. **1930** U.S. Dept. Ag. *Misc. Pub.* 77.6, *American False-Hellebore . . . Other common names . . .* Bugbane, bugwort. **1971** Krochmal *Appalachia Med. Plants* 262, *Veratrum viride . . . Common Names: . .* big-bane [sic].

3 =**baneberry 1.**

1959 [see **1** above]. **1975** Hamel–Chiltoskey *Cherokee Plants* 55, White bugbane. *Actaea pachypoda*.

4 =**fleabane.**

1959 [see **1** above].

bug day n

See quot 1972.

1939 FWP *Guide NC* 98, "Pa was a-plantin' his potatoes when Alex come along and says, 'Mr. Jones, stop right where you are. Them 'taters won't git a chanct to make. The bugs'll git 'em. This here is bug day.'" Naturally Pa stops and waits till bug day has passed. **1972** Cooper *NC Mt. Folkl.* 90, Bug days—days which should be avoided when planting potatoes to prevent bugs from destroying the green leaves.

bug dust n

1 Dust or small pellets of coal produced by coal mining machinery. **chiefly Midl coal-mining areas**

1920 Du Pont & Co. *High Explosives* 89, Bug dust. —The fine coal or other material resulting from a boring or cutting of a drill, sometimes improperly used as a tamping or stemming material in coal mining. **1929** *AmSp* 4.369 **sePA.** **1940** (1978) Still *River of Earth* 35 **KY,** I wouldn't work in a coal mine if there was gold tracks running in. I'll be buried a-plenty when I'm dead. Don't want bug-dust in my face till then. **1947** Natl. Coal Assoc. *Gloss., Bug dust*—The coal cuttings

produced by undercutting coal with a cutting machine. Locally, any small sized coal. **1965** *DARE* File swPA (as of early 1920s), Bug dust—coal dust. **1973** *PADS* 59.29 **chiefly W Midl,** *Bug dust* [from its powder-like consistency] . . fine particles of coal and other material which result from cutting, drilling, and shooting.

2 Something insignificant or of little value—sometimes used as an expression of disgust.

1936 *AmSp* 11.275 **cTN,** *Bug dust.* Cheap smoking tobacco. 'Watch him puff the bug dust.' **1958** *VT Hist.* new ser 26.262, Doesn't amount to a bug-dust *Ibid* 283, Doesn't amount to a pinch of bug dust. (pinch of snuff.) **1967–70** *DARE* (Qu. HH20b, *Of an idle, worthless person you might say, "He doesn't amount to _____."*) Inf IA5, Bug dust; (Qu. NN13, *When you think that the thing somebody has just said is silly or untrue: "Oh, that's a lot of _____."*) Inf **KY**85, Bug dust. **1982** *DARE* File **cnMA** (as of c1918), "Oh bug dust," an expression of disgust, annoyance, etc.

bug dust v [**bug dust** n 1]

To remove small particles of coal from an area in a coal mine; hence n *bug duster*, vbl n *bug dusting*.

1947 Natl. Coal Assoc. *Gloss., Bug dusting*—Removing bug dust from the kerf . . or undercut. **1973** *PADS* 59.29 **chiefly W Midl,** *Bug dust . . .* to remove the highly explosive bug dust from an area, hole, or cut, especially before shooting. *Ibid, Bug duster . .* clean-up man.

bug-eater n chiefly **West** *derog*

1 An insignificant or worthless person.

1840 in 1965 *AmSp* 40.180, Now I'm no bug-eater 'bout politics, sartin—and you'll see it. **1852** Baldwin *Southern & SW Sketches* 99 **VA** [Black], Congo is a *scrounger;* he's up a gum, and no bug-eater I tell you; he carries a broad row, weeds out every thing—hoes de corn, and digs de taters. **1878** *Field & Forest* 3.132/2 **CO,** Right there the durned bug-eater set / As sly and knowin' as a cat, / Watchin' that ar' hole in the ground. / 'Hello! buggy' sez I. [Footnote:] Our old teamster informed us that in Rocky Mountain parlance, a worthless fellow is called a 'bug eater.' **1891** Sloan *Fogy Days* 134 *(DA)*, I was going to get even with them before I left, to show them I wasn't the kind of a bug-eater they took me for. **1967** *DARE* (Qu. NN24, *Humorous substitutes for stronger expressions: "Why the son of a _____."*) Inf NE11, Bug-eater.

2 A resident of Nebraska.

1872 *Harper's Mag.* 44.318/1, Below will be found a careful compilation of the various nicknames given to the States and people of this republic . . . Nebraska, Bug-Eaters. **1888** *AN&Q* 1.155/2, *Bug-eaters* . . . The term is applied derisively to inhabitants of Nebraska by travellers on account of the poverty-stricken appearance of many parts of the State. **1889** *Ibid* 3.83/2, *Bug-eaters* . . . I imagine this name as applied to the people of Nebraska comes from the fact that at a time when that State was in part overrun by locusts (or "hoppers"), the proposal was made to turn the insects to good account by making them an article of food, after the manner of the Arabs. Several entomologists and journalists actually got up a dinner at which the locusts were served up in various styles.

bug eye n[1], also attrib Also *bugsy eye* [**bug** v 2]

A very round or bulging eye.

1950 *WELS* (*Eyes that stick out noticeably: He has _____ eyes*) 9 Infs, WI, Bug eyes. **1952** Dorson *Bloodstoppers* 70 **nMI,** I did not laugh . . when Bert Damour fixed me with bug eyes in a saloon booth and explained how the bonesetter cured his stiff neck with mumbled words and a pinch of salt thrown into boiling water. **1954** *Harder Coll.* **cwTN,** *Bug-eyes:* Them's ones sticks out on a stem. c**1960** *Wilson Coll.* **csKY,** *Bug eyes . . .* Protruding eyes. **1966–69** *DARE* (Qu. X21a, *. . Eyes . . if they stick out*) Infs CO33, IA27, KY5, 45, MI70, MN28, MO26, Bug eyes; MN34, MS73, Bug eye; MN15, Bugsy eyes; (Qu. X21c, *If the eyes are very round*) Infs CA22, IA36, MA5, NY73, Bug eyes.

bugeye n[2], also attrib Also *(Baltimore) buckeye* [Perh from Engl and Scots dial *buckie* shellfish, or perh from the appearance of hawseholes in the bow (see quot 1882). See etym discussion in 1963 Brewington *Chesapeake Bay Canoes* 89–91] **chiefly C Atl coast, esp Chesapeake Bay** See Map

Formerly a dugout, later a flat-bottomed centerboard boat usu having two masts and triangular sails and used chiefly for oyster fishing.

1881 Ingersoll *Oyster-Industry* 164, The size of the tonging canoe ranges from 15 or 16 feet to 30 feet or more, the larger ones being called 'bugeyes.' **1882** *Century Illustr. Mag.* 24.352/2, The Baltimore clipper was the parent of several types of vessels. The famous oyster pungies . . are allied to it, but the latest . . form is the Baltimore buckeye . . . their most remarkable feature . . is the long, beak-like cut-water, flanked by broad breast-plates at the knight-heads in the bow, in which the hawse-holes look like eyes. **1885** C.P. Kunhardt *Small Yachts* 234 *(OEDS),* The buckeyes . . . are an exaggeration of the dugout canoe. **1946** *PADS* 6.7 **eNC,** Bug-eye . . . A small boat with a triangular sail. Pamlico. Common. **1948** *Sun* (Baltimore MD) 5 Nov 20/2 *(Hench Coll.),* No true bugeyes have been built . . since 1918 . . since the oyster dredging industry has gone into a decline and the non-perishable freight once hauled in sail is carried by power-boat and motor truck. Many so-called "bugeye yachts" have been built in recent years. **1957** *AmSp* 32.289, These [*buckeye* and *bugeye*] should be treated as the same word. Bugeye is the preferred form in Maryland, where the type originated. Buckeye seems to be used more often in print in the 19th cent., probably because of the faintly vulgar connotation of 'bug-'. **1963** Brewington *Chesapeake Bay Canoes* 40, The first bugeyes [c1870] ranged from about fifty feet to sixty feet on deck. The bottoms were built of five or more logs with framed topsides, carvel planked up to the deck . . . The entire body was decked over except for a small cabin forward and the hatches . . . the keel was quickly superseded by the centerboard. Their sail plan in most instances followed that of the brogan: jib, foresail and mainsail, leg-of-mutton style. **1965–70** *DARE* (Qu. O9, . . *Kinds of sailboats*) Infs **DE3, MD15, 42, NJ16, NC27,** Bugeye; **DE4,** Buckeye—that's the proper name but we call them bugeye; two masts and sharp sails; **MD36,** Bugeye—like log canoe (built from three pieces of timber, hewed out with an ax) but sails are square; **MD45,** Bugeye—sharp at both ends; two masts; **NC80,** Schooner (2, 3, or 4 masts), sloop (1 mast), bugeye (1 mast)—difference in the sails; **NC81,** Bugeye—hewn out of logs; 2 mast; (Qu. O10, . . *Other kinds of boats*) Inf **MD15,** Bugeye—like log canoe, but larger. [9 of 10 Infs old; all Infs male] **1982** Heat Moon *Blue Highways* 392 **Chesapeake Bay,** From the attic window, Miz Alice once had watched big schooners out of Baltimore sail seaward and also many of the two thousand Chesapeake oystering boats beat along the bay: skipjacks, bugeyes, pungies, sloops, now all extinct but for the skipjack.

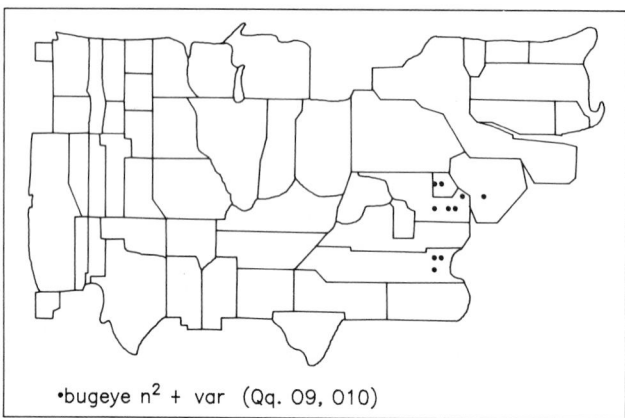

•bugeye n² + var (Qq. O9, O10)

bugfish n Also *bughead, bugshad* [See quots]
=menhaden.

1853 in 1956 Eliason *Tarheel Talk* 262 **neNC,** Bug fish. **1857** *Harper's Mag.* 14.442/1, Other varieties [of refuse fish] are sometimes taken, and among them the bug-fish . . . Its characteristic peculiarity is only discovered on opening the mouth, in which it carries a sort of parasitical bug. **1887** Goode *Amer. Fishes* 386, [For *Brevoortia tyrannus*] Virginia gives us "Bug-fish," "Bug-head" and "Bug-shad," referring to the parasitic crustacean found in the mouths of all Southern Menhaden. **1941** *Nature Mag.* 10.134, In Virginia, bug-fish is the word; it refers to parasitic crustaceans (not bugs, i.e. insects) that are often found in the mouth of the menhaden.

buggabear See boogerbear

buggar See bugger v 2

buggarman See boogerman 2

bugged up adj [Cf bug n²] *obs* Cf *DS* W48
Dressed up.

1893 (1958) Wister *Out West* 159, Texas Vocabulary . . *Bugged up*—dressed up. **1898** Wister *Lin McLean* 3 **WY,** "Bugged up to kill!" exclaimed one, perceiving Lin's careful dress.

bugger n¹ Usu |ˈbʌgə(r)|; also, **chiefly Sth, S Midl,** |ˈbʊgə(r), ˈbu-| (pronc-sp *booger*). See Map Note: the coalescence in form and sense of ME *bougre* heretic and *bugge* hobgoblin means that it is not always possible to distinguish ModE *booger* and *bugger*. See also **booger n¹**

A Forms. See also quots at **B**
1908 *DN* 3.292 **eAL, wGA,** *Booger* . . . Occasionally used in the sense of *bugger.* **1944** *PADS* 2.28 **NC,** *Booger* [ˈbʊgɚ] . . . The act of sodomy. **1965–70** *DARE* (Qu. Z12, . . *Joking words meaning 'a small child':* "He's a healthy little _____.") 59 Infs, **chiefly Sth, S Midl,** Booger [ˈbʊgə, ˈbʊgɚ]; (Qu. K42) Inf **PA166,** Booger [ˈbʊgɚ]; (Qu. Z16) Infs **LA6, TX4,** Bad little booger; **VA42,** Booger; **AR55,** Hard-headed little booger; (Qu. HH21) Inf **DE7,** Stupid booger; (Qu. KK37) Inf **LA17,** Crafty old booger; (Qu. NN24) Inf **LA2,** Booger.

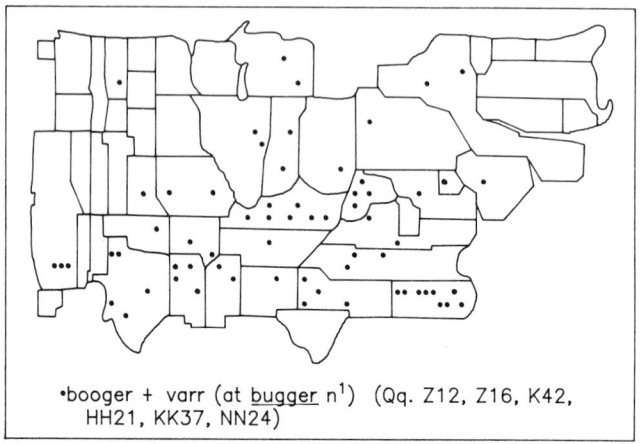

•booger + varr (at bugger n¹) (Qq. Z12, Z16, K42, HH21, KK37, NN24)

B Senses.

1 A fellow, guy; also transf. *sometimes derog*
1854 (1923) Holmes *Tempest & Sunshine* 144 **KY,** Mebby if I'd known all you city buggers was comin', I'd a kivered my bar feet. **1894** *DN* 1.340 **wCT,** Bugger. **1922** (1926) Cady *Rhymes VT* 132, *Planting potaters in Vermont* . . . "Here, take this knife and jest incise / These buggers right between the eyes." **1938** Matschat *Suwannee R.* 30 **sGA,** The Injuns, they was smart boogers. **1939** *AmSp* 14.232, The English meaning of *bugger* as *sodomite* is universal in Canada, and not its innocent usage as equivalent to *fellow* or *chap* as in the American Middle West. **1941** Stuart *Men of Mts.* 97 **neKY,** He's a hard booger to kill. **1950** in 1977 *Pissing in the Snow* 169 **Ozarks,** Here is one place I will beat the old booger easy, no matter what he does! **1965–70** *DARE* (Qu. HH21, *A very awkward, clumsy person*) Inf **DE7,** Stupid booger; (Qu. HH40, *Uncomplimentary words for an old man*) Infs **NJ25, 57,** Bugger; (Qu. HH44, *Joking or uncomplimentary names for lawyers*) Inf **MA1,** Bugger; (Qu. II20a, *A person who tries too hard to gain somebody else's favor:* "He's an awful _____.") Inf **CA81,** Bugger; (Qu. KK37, . . *A very sly person*) Infs **MD47, HI13,** Bugger; **LA17,** Crafty old booger; (Qu. NN9b, *Exclamations showing great annoyance:* "He's run off with my hammer again, _____!") Inf **RI3,** Damn bugger; **NM35,** Darn bugger; **CA145,** The bugger; (Qu. NN24, *Humorous substitutes for stronger exclamations:* "Why the son of a _____.") Infs **MO25, NJ53,** Bugger; **LA2,** Booger [laughter]. **1967** *DARE* Tape **MI42,** Poor bugger [ˈbʌgɚ] if he'd want to get any more pets like that. **1975** Gould *ME Lingo,* Bugger—With hardly any impolite and negative connotation, this word is used in Maine as a synonym for chap, fellow, jeezer, joker, etc.

2 rarely *bug*: A child, esp an impish one—freq used affectionately.

1892 *DN* 1.235 **MI,** *Booger* [ˈbʊgɚ] . . . Used playfully in speaking to or of a baby or small child. **1894** *DN* 1.340 **wCT,** [ˈbʌgɚ] . . is a harmless word meaning much the same as "chap" or as "tacker" [=small tot] . . and used by schoolgirls and all sorts of people who certainly never attach any other meaning to it. **1905** *DN* 3.60 **NE,** *Booger.* **1908** *DN* 3.292 **eAL, wGA,** *Booger.* **1912** *DN* 3.566 **cNY,** *Booger.* **1915** *DN* 4.181 **swVA,** *Bugger* . . . Terms of endearment to a child. **1935** Sandoz *Jules* 395 **wNE** (as of early 1900s), Jules came up with the interested infant held out awkwardly before him . . . "By golly, somebody come and take the bugger," he would beg. **1938** Rawlings *Yearling* 420 **FL,** Well, if I was a scrawny little big-eyed booger like you, I'd stay home. **1941** *LANE* Map 379 **NH,** Terms properly applied to a mischievous or naughty child but frequently used as affectionate names without any connotation of reproach . . . [bʌ˙gə]. **1946** *PADS* 6.7 **eNC**, Booger. **1950** *PADS* 14.16 **SC**, Booger. **1950** *WELS* (Nicknames and affectionate names meaning a young child: "He's a healthy little _____.") 1 Inf, **cWI**, Bug. **c1960** Wilson Coll. **csKY**, Booger . . . Term of affection. "Come here, you little booger, and hug your grandma's neck." **1965–70** *DARE* (Qu. Z12, Nicknames and joking words meaning 'a small child': "He's a healthy little _____.'") 54 Infs, **chiefly Sth, S Midl**, Booger; 38 Infs, **scattered**, Bugger; **AL53, KS10, MO35, OK1, SC3**, Booger; [Of all Infs responding to Qu. Z12, 43% were male; of those giving these responses, 52% were male] (Qu. Z16, A small child who is rough, misbehaves, and doesn't obey) Infs **MD41, MO16**, Bugger; **LA6, TX4**, Bad little booger; **VA42**, Booger; **AR55**, Hard-headed little booger. **1966** *DARE* Tape **AL13**, They're cute lil' ol' buggers ['bʌgəz].

3 An animal.

1937 Sandoz *Slogum* 52 **NE** (as of 1900–1920), He played with the young antelope . . . He found the little bugger in a clump of bull-tongue cactus. **1955** Warren *Angels* 103 **KY**, The dog came into the room . . . "Pat him," Hamish Bond's voice commanded, "pat the pore ole booger." **1967–68** *DARE* (Qu. K42, A horse that is rough, wild, or dangerous) Inf **PA166**, Booger [bʌgə]; **HI2**, Wild bugger ['bʌgə]. **1969** *DARE* Tape **CA145**, They [=rams] got no protection, the poor buggers ['bʌgəz]; **NY159**, A weasel had done that, but I caught the bugger ['bʌgə].

bugger n² See **booger** n¹

bugger v [Cf **bugger** n¹, **booger** n¹]

1 freq passive: To damn—used in exclamations of astonishment. [*OEDS* 1794 →] **NEng**

1914 *DN* 4.151 **csME**, Buggered . . . Used commonly in mild ejaculations by men. "I'll be buggered!" **1943** *LANE* Map 599 (Damn it!) **ME**, Expressions containing the verbal forms . . *bugger* . . . [bʌgəɪ ɪt ɔˑəl, . . bʌgəɪ ɪt]. **1945** Colcord *Sea Language* **NEng coast**, To bugger is to confuse or perplex; "I'll be buggered!" an exclamation of mild astonishment. That seamen—at least, those of fifty years back—had not the remotest idea of the real meaning of the word is amply proved . . by the fact that they used it freely in the presence of respectable women. (Cf. the English word beggar, which is evidently an attempt to soften the term.)

2 usu with *up;* also *booger* (or *boogie, buggar*) *up:* To damage, spoil; to confuse, disorder; hence ppl adj *buggered up* damaged, battered, crippled, confused. [*OEDS* 1923 →]

1931 *AmSp* 6.230 **cnNE**, Boogered up . . . Battered, spoiled, damaged. "After the accident we found that the car was all boogered up." **1934** (1947) O'Hara *Appointment* 74, He's probably forgotten about it, and my going there will bugger things up proper. **1942** Warnick *Garrett Co. MD* (as of 1900–1918), Booger up . . to treat roughly (always used in the past tense) "all buggered up." **1942** *AN&Q* 1.157/2, The term "buggering up" is in fairly common use in the machine trade. It indicates faulty or amateurish work, often a kind of temporary patching that only leaves the way open for worse trouble later on. *Ibid* 2.143/1 **MD**, The expression "buggered up" was in common use in my boyhood days about sixty years ago in Carroll County, Maryland (on the south side of Mason and Dixon's line); and it is still used in the sense of "defaced" or "damaged." It was applied to both persons and things. A man's face, injured in an accident, was said to be "all buggered up"; and the same expression is used for a tool that has been damaged or dulled. **1950** *PADS* 13.16 **cTX**, Booger . . . To disfigure, as the threads of a bolt. "He boogered it up." **1958** *AmSp* 33.268 **eWA**, Boogered up. Crippled. **1959** Lomax *Rainbow Sign* 67 **AL** [Black], He just keep right on jobbin and rippin until the man really boogied up for true. By the time he get to the hospital, that man'll be just solid blood. **1959** *VT Hist.* new ser 27.127, Buggared up . . . Confused. Rare. **1965** *DARE* File **swPA** (as of early 1920s), If you made something and it didn't turn out right, it was said you buggered it up. **1968** *DARE* Tape **OH72**, You've got a good strong clear head line on this hand. That one is buggered up a little, but that may be due to some type of work or athletics. **1982** *Barrick Coll.* **sePA**, Booger—v.t. damage. "It boogered the sink." (1966) "One zipper's boogered a little." (1972).

bugger n³ Cf **bugging**

1946 *Natl. Geog. Mag.* 89.779/1 **ME**, When a down-Easter gets to doing something unusual and different, he is so much an individual that he invents his own expressions to go along with it. So the [sandworm] diggers refer to their bonanza as "bugging" and to themselves as "buggers."

buggerbear See **boogerbear**

bugger-den n [**booger** n¹]

1902 *DN* 2.230 **sIL**, Bugger-den . . . 1. A place supposed to be used by a bugger. 2. Any grewsome place or cavern.

buggerman See **boogerman**

bugger's woods n Cf **booger** n¹, **bugger-den**

1970 *DARE* (Qu. C33, . . Joking names . . for an out-of-the-way place, or a very unimportant place) Inf **VA72**, Bugger's woods ['bʌgəz wʊdz].

buggery See **boogery**

buggery boo n [Blend of **booger** n¹ + **bugaboo**]

1939 (1962) Thompson *Body & Britches* 421 **cnNY**, The Buggery Boo apparently was what we call the Bogie-Man: . . into the bed she quickly fled / For fear of the buggery boo.

bugging vbl n [Cf **bug** n¹ **9**] Cf **bog** v¹ **2**

Gathering small marine creatures.

1946 [see **bugger** n³]. **1966** *DARE* Tape **SC18**, When somebody talks about going fishing, we know he means going shrimping . . or bugging. Shrimp are sometime called bug.

buggins n [Prob var of **booger** n¹; also cf Engl dial *buggin* hobgoblin]

1968 *DARE* (Qu. X16, Sticky mucus that forms in the nose—children's words for this) Inf **AK8**, Buggins ['bʊgɪnz].

buggy n¹

1 A railroad caboose.

1899 *Boston Daily Globe* (MA) 18 Mar 12/2, 31,271 freight cars passed through Concord, N.H. Estimating the total length of these cars, with the engines and buggies, we find that they would completely fill both tracks on the main line between Boston and Concord. **1904** *Ibid* 28 Feb 40/6, After the cars are all coupled the caboose, or as it is better known, the buggy, is hitched on to the rear. It is a peculiar little car, and is the home of the crew while on the rail. **1916** *DN* 4.356. **1943** *AmSp* 18.163. **1945** Hubbard *Railroad Ave.* 335, Buggy—Caboose: rarely applied to other cars. **1951** *PADS* 15.65 **NH**. **1977** Adams *Lang. Railroader* 24, Buggy: A caboose, so called because of its semielliptic springs instead of the coil springs used on freight cars.

2 freq in comb: An automobile, now esp an old or modified one.

1930 Irwin *Amer. Tramp, Buggy.*—An automobile; a contraction of the term "gasoline buggy," by which the earlier automobiles were known. **1960** Wentworth–Flexner *Slang, Buggy* . . . An automobile; esp. an old dilapidated automobile. *Since c1925; has been very common, esp. in jocular use.* **1965–70** *DARE* (Qu. N1, . . An ambulance) Inf **CA130**, Gut-buggy; **LA10**, Go-away buggy; (Qu. N2, The car used to carry a dead body for burial) Inf **VA38**, Black buggy; (Qu. N3, The car . . that takes arrested people to the police station) Inf **MI56**, Bluesuit buggy; (Qu. N5, . . An automobile, especially an old or broken-down car) Infs **CT5, LA10, MO29, NY107, NY236, TX33**, Buggy; **GA40, KY94, VA41**, Struggle-buggy; **MN38, VA41**, Old buggy; **TX5**, Dune buggy; **VA70**, Georgia buggy; **NY142**, Go-buggy; (Qu. N6, An old car that has been fixed up to make it go fast or make a lot of noise) Inf **NY100**, Pop-buggy; **TN53**, Drag-buggy, jitter-buggy, souped-up buggy.

3 See **baby buggy 1**.

4 See **baby buggy 2**.

5 in var phrr, spec:

a *get* (or *stay*) *in the buggy:* To comply with requirements, get on the ball. Cf *stay on the wagon*

1927 *AmSp* 3.132 **NE** [College slang], Freshmen are encouraged to study in such terms as . . "stay in the buggy." **1966–68** *DARE* (Qu. JJ26, If somebody has been doing poor work or not enough, the boss might say, "If he wants to keep his job he'd better _____.'") Infs **OK45, WI22**, Get in the buggy. [Both Infs old]

b *haul buggy:* See **haul ass**.

buggy n² See **bug** n¹ **1**

buggy adj

1 Infested with lice. [**bug** n¹ **1**]

1967 *DARE* (QR, near Qu. R25) Inf **NJ2**, Some children at school might have "buggy tops" or are "thatched" to refer to heads with lice. **1967** *DARE* FW Addit **cnNY**, Buggy—lousy.

2 also *bugs:* Foolish, crazy, demented. Cf **bug** n¹ **3**

1905 *DN* 3.72 **nwAR**, Buggy . . . Mentally deficient. 'Don't mind him; he's buggy.' Slang. **1912** *DN* 3.572 **wIN**, Buggy . . . Insane. **1915** *DN* 4.232 **OH** [College slang], Bugs . . . Eccentric or crazy. **1919** *DN* 5.71

NM [High school slang], *Buggy,* foolish, silly. **1922** O'Neill *Hairy Ape* 11 **NYC,** Yuh're bugs, dats all—nutty as a cuckoo. **1950** *WELS* *(Words about someone who is insane)* 2 Infs, **WI,** Bugs; 1 Inf, Buggy; *(Someone who is queer but harmless)* 1 Inf, Cuckoo; batty; bugs. **1962** Wilson *Folkways Mammoth Cave* 36 **KY,** *Buggy* as *potato vines.* Potato beetles sometimes fairly ruined the *taters* . . . But the bugs of the simile were not on potato vines. **1965–70** *DARE* (Qu. GG2, . . *Confused, mixed up*) Inf **CA**202, Buggy; (Qu. HH3, *A dull and stupid person*) Inf **MO**7, Buggy; (Qu. HH6, *Someone who is out of his mind*) Infs **GA**13, **ME**19, **NY**24, 73, Buggy; **HI**6, Buggy as a bedbug; **LA**46, **MN**33, Bugs. **1969** *DARE* Tape **IL**97, How much can you be expected to retain that feeling and not go buggy?

3 Bug-eyed.
   1965–70 *DARE* (Qu. X21a, . . *Words used to describe people according to their eyes—for example, if they stick out*) Infs **CA**134, **PA**44, Buggy.

buggy v
   To go away, leave.
   1954 *PADS* 21.22 **SC,** *Buggy* . . . To go away, to leave . . . Dutch Fork. *Ibid* 30 **MO,** *Buggy* along . . meaning to go on horseback or in a buggy.

buggyboo See **bugaboo**

‡buggy boss n
   1961 Adams *Old-Time Cowhand* 62 **West,** The absentee owner . . usually made a trip or two each year to the ranch to check with their foreman or manager to whom they had assigned the runnin' of the outfit. The cowhands had various names for them absentee owners . . when on his inspection tours if he didn't ride a hoss well, but preferred ridin' 'round in a buggy, he was called the "Buggy Boss."

‡buggy carriage n Cf **baby buggy 1**
   = **baby carriage 1.**
   1967 *DARE* (Qu. N42, *Vehicles for a baby or small child—the kind it can lie down in*) Inf **TN**6, Buggy carriage.

buggy coach n Cf **baby coach**
   = **baby carriage.**
   1976 *PA Folklife* Spring 30, *Buggy coach,* a baby carriage.

buggyman See **boogerman 2**

buggy road n Also *buggy trail*
   An unpaved road (as in "horse and buggy" days).
   1968 *DARE* (Qu. N27b, *When unpaved roads get very rough*) Inf **WI**39, Buggy trail. [Inf young] **1968** *DARE* Tape **CA**100, Buggy road—single lane dirt or gravel road; old-fashioned.

buggy whip n, also attrib
   1 An imitation cigarette; see quot.
   1944 *Hench Coll.* **cVA,** Several persons happened to speak of buggy-whip as a substitute for cigarettes as used by kids. It is essentially a sort of sawdust bound by cord.
   2 A cartwheel; see quot.
   1968 *DARE* (Qu. EE9c, *The children's trick of turning over rapidly . . if children spread their arms and turn over sideways*) Inf **VA**9, Buggy whip (old-fashioned): "Ah Janie you're turnin' a buggy whip."
   3 attrib: Having new shoots originating from old tree stumps.
   1968 *WI Conserv. Bulletin* Sept–Oct 9, Most of the North had been logged-off and some areas had been burned. The result was extensive areas of brush and "buggy-whip" regeneration of trees.

bughead See **bugfish**

bugheway See **booshway**

Bughill See **bug** n[1] **8**

bughole n
   A small cavity in rock.
   1946 *CA Folkl. Qrly.* 5.167 **MT** [Mining terms], Whenever a drill lurches suddenly from hard rock to soft, or into a small cavity or "bug hole" of some sort, without drilling a hole large enough to release the drill, old miners acquainted with the Cornish terminology say, "There's a Dutchman in the hole." **1950** Reeves *Man from SD* 72 (as of 1916), His eyes scanned the base of the rimrock for the dark opening of the cave. Several times we thought we saw it, but when we had climbed the steep side of the gulch, we found only small bugholes in the limestone cliffs, not Crystal Cave.

Bughollow See **bug** n[1] **8**

bughouse n
   1 A jail. **chiefly Sth, S Midl**
   1956 Ker *Vocab. W. TX* 405, Jail (jocular terms) . . . bughouse [1 inf]. **1965–70** *DARE* (Qu. V11, . . *Joking names . . for a county or city jail*) 12 Infs, **chiefly Sth, S Midl,** Bughouse. [9 Infs comm type 5, 9 Infs grade-school educ] **1970** Tarpley *Blinky* 270 **neTX,** *Other names for the jail* . . . bug house.

‡2 A hospital. [Perh infl by *bughouse* insane asylum]
   1966 *DARE* (Qu. C35, . . *Different parts of your town*) Inf **MI**8, Around the hospital (the bughouse): "He lives near the bughouse."

‡3 See quot.
   1970 *DARE* (Qu. M21b, *Joking names for an outside toilet building*) Inf **KY**93, Bughouse.

bug hunt n
   1981 *Broaddus Coll.* **ceKY** (as of 1958), Bug hunt—a game of marbles in which two players take turns shooting at each other's taw.

bug-hunting See **bug** n[1] **14e**

bug juice n
   1a also obs *bug poison:* Whiskey or other strong liquor, usu of inferior quality.
   1869 *New No. West* (Deer Lodge, Mont.) 22 Oct. 1/5 *(DA),* Citizens glad to see us—freedom of the city—'bug juice,' ad lib. **1889** (1971) Farmer *Americanisms, Bug-juice.*—The Schlechter whiskey of the Pennsylvania Dutch . . a very inferior spirit. Also called *bug-poison.* These terms are now applied to bad whiskey of all kinds. **1903** *DN* 2.308 **seMO.** **1908** *DN* 3.295 **eAL, wGA.** **1908** Porter *Gentle Grafter* 11 **TX,** This little turn in bug juice is, verily, all to the Skibo . . . Andy pours himself out four fingers of our best rye and does with it as was so intended. **1950** *WELS* *(Liquor in general)* 1 Inf, **WI,** Bug juice; *(Bad liquor)* 1 Inf, Bug juice. **1960** Wentworth–Flexner *Slang, Bug-juice* . . . Liquor, esp. inferior whisky . . . *All uses orig. from the tobacco-colored secretion of grasshoppers.* **1966–70** *DARE* (Qu. DD21a, . . *Any kind of liquor*) Inf **NC**33, Bug juice; (Qu. DD21c, . . *Whiskey, especially illegally made whiskey*) Inf **NC**87, Bug juice; (Qu. DD27, . . *Wine*) Inf **IA**22, Bug juice. **1975** *Cosmopolitan* Aug 212/3 **LA,** Hey, Maginty, drinking that bug juice and laying out all night, you look awful, man.

b Transf: a soft drink.
   1942 Berrey–Van den Bark *Amer. Slang* 92.8, Bug juice, *any artificial juice and water.* **1960** Wentworth–Flexner *Slang, Bug-juice* . . . Any beverage, esp. a synthetic or artificially colored beverage; any soft drink. **1975–83** *DARE* File **WI,** Bug juice—Kool-aid; **NEng,** Bug juice is Kool-aid; heard at every summer camp I've ever gone to in New England; **NY,** At Boy Scout camp in Stony Point, N.Y. in the 1950s, I recall, *bug juice* was (?still is) a (the) term for a sort of generic Kool-Aid of different flavors.

2 Gasoline.
   1942 Berrey–Van den Bark *Amer. Slang* 72.11, Gasoline. Bug juice. **1942** *AmSp* 17.103 [Truck driver lingo], *Bug juice.* Gasoline. **1960** Wentworth–Flexner *Slang, Bug-juice* . . . Gasoline. **1983** *DARE* File **cWI** (as of 1920s), Bug juice—gasoline. Used by adolescent boys: "Anybody got any money for some bug juice?"

3 The saliva or squashed remains of insects.
   1967 *DARE* FW Addit **IL,** Bug juice—insect intestines, especially on an automobile windshield. **1983** *DARE* File **PA** (as of c1900), [Children would] catch a grasshopper, hold him by the legs and say "Spit tobacco juice!" Grasshopper tobacco juice was bug juice and it stained white petticoats very badly.

4 See quots.
   1960 Wentworth–Flexner *Slang, Bug-juice* . . . The residue of tobacco in the bowl of a frequently used pipe. **1983** *DARE* File **cnOH** (as of c1928), *Bug juice:* the stuff that gathers in the stem and bowl of a tobacco pipe and has to be cleaned out.

5 Liquid insecticide; insect repellant.
   1944 *PADS* 2.65 **sVA,** *Bug-juice* . . . A poison, such as Paris green, used to kill insects attacking tobacco (and other plants). The term is often used facetiously. **1952** Brooks *Mighty Leaf* 295, A lot of tough lugs [of tobacco] of poor color is given but a few seconds. (Such a lot will be converted into "bug juice," an insecticide.) **1973** *New York Times* (NY) 18 Feb sec 10 1, [We] outfitted ourselves with brilliant red and blue backpacks, Sierra Club cups, waterproof matches, . . Dr. Cutter's bug juice, tube tents, . . the camping rig of all time. **1983** *DARE* File **KY** (as of c1900), Bug-juice: Citronella or any kind of mosquito or insect repellant.

bug lamp, bug lantern See **bug light 2**

bugle n

1 The nose; also the mouth, the head. **chiefly Atlantic, upper Missip Valley**

1865 in 1912 Paine *Mark Twain* 1.275 **CA**, Tore his coat, / Clutched his throat, / And split him in the bugle. **1921** *DN* 5.111 **CA** [College slang], *Bugle* . . . Head. From the noise made with the head. *Bugle-warmer* . . . Head covering; hat. **1930** *Amer. Mercury* 21.420/1 **NYC**, It ain't no skin off of Hymie's bugle. **1951** *Milwaukee Jrl.* (WI) 27 Aug Green Sheet 4/5 [Cartoon "Major Hoople"], My pappy, Jasper Hoople, had the same bugle on him, same size, same color! **1966–70** *DARE* (Qu. X9, *Joking or uncomplimentary words for a person's mouth . . "I wish he'd shut his _____."*) Inf **FL25**, Bugle; (Qu. X14, *Joking words for the nose*) Infs **DE3, IN75, MA72, MI120, MO1, NJ25**, Bugle; (Qu. X15, *. . Names . . for different kinds of noses, according to shape or size*) Infs **CT6, 27, IA45, NC30**, Bugle (nose); (Qu. X45, *. . Joking expressions . . about snoring*) Inf **NY66**, Sounding off the bugle. **1970** Major *Afro–Amer. Slang*, Bugle: (1940's) the human nose.

2 See **bugleweed**.

‡**bugle-eyed** adj

1969 *DARE* (Qu. X21c, *If the eyes are very round*) Inf **NY167**, Bugle ['biugɛl]-eyed.

bugle-mouthed bass n

1975 Evanoff *Catch More Fish* 96, The carp (*Cyprinus carpio*) is also called the German carp, European carp, . . and bugle-mouthed bass.

bugle oil n

An imaginary substance used as the basis of a practical joke.

1921 *DN* 5.94, *Bugle oil*. Young recruit sent for at Officers' Training Camp, Fort Benjamin Harrison, Indiana.

bugleweed n Also *bugle, buglewort*

A **water horehound** (here: *Lycopus virginicus*). Also called **archangel 2, gypsy weed, horehound, sprig of Jerusalem, wolf-foot, wood betony** Note: *bugle(weed)* is also sometimes used, esp in nursery catalogs, for a ground cover of the European genus *Ajuga*.

1824 Bigelow *Florula Bostoniensis* 9, *Lycopus Virginicus* . . . Bugle weed. **1874** *Shaker Med. Preparations* **ceNY**, Bugle—*Lycopus virginicus.* **1900** Lyons *Plant Names* 233, *L[ycopus] Virginicus* . . Bugleweed, Buglewort, Sweet Bugleweed. **1946** Reeves–Bain *Flora TX* 163, *L[ycopus] virginicus* . . . (Bugle Weed.). **1961** *Western Folkl.* 20.16 **KS**, Bungle [sic] weed (lycopus) from the herb garden was a cure for dysentery; its small purple flower was gathered annually in July or August, dried in the shade, and kept in paper sacks. **1971** Krochmal *Appalachia Med. Plants* 166, *Lycopus virginicus* . . . Virginia bugleweed, bugleweed, buglewort, . . sweet bugleweed, water bugle.

bug light n [Prob from the resemblance to the light of the **lightning bug**]

1 A small harbor or channel light.

1882 Godfrey *Is. Nantucket* 217 **MA**, The Cliff lights, sometimes called "Bug lights," . . are situated on the beach northwest of Nantucket Harbor. **1899** in 1919 Hale *Letters* 341 **CA**, My room is called the "Buglight," because it is a little house all by itself set upon four legs over a sort of piazza where we read and sew. **1945** *Chicago Daily News* (IL) 28 Sept 6/5 **MA** (as of 1850s), He became keeper of a bug-light in Boston Harbor and sometime after that buried the money.

2 also *bug, ~ lamp, ~ lantern, ~ torch:* A low-intensity lamp used as a lantern or flashlight.

c1849 Paige *Dow's Sermons* I.75 *(DA)*, You may wander outside in the darkness of ignorance—guided by the bug-lamps of instinct. **1918** *DN* 5.23, *Bug* . . . A home-made lantern used by men fishing for whitefish in the north Idaho lake district. **1924** R. Cummins *Sky-High Corral* 104 *(DA)*, He produced a candle and a can from his pack and made a 'bug' lantern by cutting a hole in the side of the can and poking the candle through it. **1932** *Santa Fe Mag.* Jan 34/2, A trainman's lantern is referred to as a *bug torch*. **1947** Natl. Coal Assoc. *Gloss., Bug light*—Slang term for a miner's electric cap lamp. **1963** *Alaska Sportsman* Mar 15 (Tabbert *Alaskan Engl.*), In place of flashlights, they made what they called bugs out of empty Log Cabin syrup cans. They would cut out one end, shove a miner's candle up a criss-cross cut in the bottom and fix a wire handle on top, which made a nice light for carrying out of doors. **1973** *PADS* 59.30 **chiefly W Midl** [Coal mining terms], *Bug light* [from their resemblance when worn and seen from a distance underground to "lightning bugs"], . . = *cap lamp; safety lamp. Ibid, Bug light belt* . . . = *belt* ["a large belt carrying a holder for a battery which powers the miner's cap lamp"]. **1977** Adams *Lang. Railroader, Bug:* . . A flashlight lantern. *Ibid, Bug torch:* A flashlight lantern.

‡**bugling** vbl n

1967 *DARE* (Qu. X55b, *Words for breaking wind from the bowels*) Inf **MN1**, Bugling.

bug poison See **bug juice 1a**

bug run n Cf **bud run, frog run**

1959 *VT Hist.* new ser 27.127, Bug run . . . The last run of the sap during maple sugaring season, so-called because of the insects which are drowned in the sap . . . Common.

bugs See **buggy** adj 2

‡**bugsarn** v Cf **consarn**

1911 *DN* 3.541 **NE**, *Bugsarn* . . expressing annoyance, or exasperation. "Bugsarn (it), it's going to rain." Not common.

Bugscuffle See **bug** n[1] **8**

bugshad See **bugfish**

bugsy eye See **bug eye** n[1]

bug torch See **bug light 2**

Bugtown, Bugtussle See **bug** n[1] **8**

bugwort See **bugbane 1, 2**

buh See **brother** A2

buhn See **burn** A

build v

A Forms.

Past and past pple: usu *built;* also *builded, builted.*

1887 (1967) Harris *Free Joe* 215 **cGA** [Black], I builted one [=a fire] in dar dis mornin'. **1939** *Sat. Eve. Post* 25 Nov 58 **FL**, It's an awful thing when a woman has done builded her life on a man and she finds his legs is made of sand. **1952** in 1958 Brewer *Dog Ghosts* 30 **TX** [Black], He . . jes' sets on de steps of his li'l' two room house, what he done builted attuh his ole house burnt down. **1953** Brewer *Word Brazos* 30 **eTX** [Black], 'Fo' dey builded de chu'ch houses, de Baptis's an' de Mefdis's used to sometime use de same buildin'. **1967** *DARE* Tape IL5, In 1844 Joseph Smith was killed by a mob and then, in two years time, while they builded covered wagons, the Mormons, sixteen different men tried to be leader.

B Senses.

1 To sew or tailor.

1877 Bartlett *Americanisms* 76, *To build clothes.* Tailors use this expression for making clothes. "Guess we can *build* you a neat pant off these goods, sir." **1951** *PADS* 15.69 **nLA**, *Build* . . . Of clothing: to make. "Mother is building a dress."

2 To prepare something to eat or drink.

1907 *Collier's* 5 Oct 21/3, Mother's at the kitchen stove / Building lemon pie. **1930** Ferber *Cimarron* 208 **OK**, They built angel-food cakes whose basis was the whites of thirteen eggs. **1954** *PADS* 21.22 **SC**, *Build* . . . To make. Reported only concerning the making of coffee in an urn. **1967** *DARE* (Qu. H73, *Words for preparing coffee: the housewife says, "I think I'll go and _____ some coffee."*) Inf **CO47**, Build—also used for any other thing such as "build a stew, build a pie, etc." **1969** *DARE* FW Addit **MA58**, Build me a cake. Old-fashioned. **1970** *Eaton Coll.* **neWI**, Build a pie.

3 in phr *build a smoke:*

a To roll a cigarette.

1937 *DN* 6.621 **swTX**, The cowpuncher does not "roll a cigarette"; instead he *builds a smoke.*

b To produce smoke when firing a gun.

1953 Randolph *Down in Holler* 231 **Ozarks**, *Build a smoke* . . . To fire a gun repeatedly. "Tom sure did build a smoke behind that feller, but he never did hit him." **1968** Adams *Western Words* 42, *Build a smoke under his hoofs*—To shoot at someone's feet.

build pigpens v phr

See quot 1953.

1936 *AmSp* 11.314 **Ozarks**. **1953** Randolph *Down in Holler* 231 **Ozarks**, *Build pigpens* . . . To deceive someone, to cheat a customer. Woodcutters pile firewood pigpen-fashion in their wagons, to make the load appear larger than it really is. I have heard a backwoods politician charge the President of the United States with *buildin' pigpens.*

build the fence v phr Also *build their fence(s), make the fence* **esp S Midl** *old-fash, euphem*

To marry (usu after the conception of a child).

　1935 Sheppard *Cabins* 172 **NC,** He is a demanding and passionate lover . . . Perhaps he overpersuades her and they "plant their corn before they build their fence." **1947** (1964) Randolph *Ozark ·Superstitions* 202, Nothing can convince some of these women that premature babies ever have fingernails. When a baby is born less than nine months after its parents have been married, the old gossips always look for the nails. "Caint fool me," said one old woman. "Them young-uns planted their corn 'bout six weeks 'fore they built their fences. I *seen* fingernails on that baby!" **1967–70** *DARE* (Qu. AA20, *A marriage that takes place because a baby is on the way*) Inf **MO4,** Build the fence before they're caught; filled the crack before the fence was made; **TX103,** They planted the corn before they built the fence; **VA31,** She jumped the broomstick; they made the garden before they built the fence; [All Infs old]; [(Qu. Z11b, *Nicknames and joking words for a child of unwed parents*) Inf **SC46,** "The fence was built before the worm [=bottom rail] was laid." Used by my granny, but not since. [Inf old]]

build-up n Cf **scrub, work-up**

　1966 *DARE* (Qu. EE11, *Bat-and-ball games for just a few players [when there aren't enough for a regular game]*) Inf **SD5,** Build-up.

build up to (someone) v phr

To court, woo (someone).

　1896 *DN* 1.413 **neTX,** Build up to: court.

built from the ground up adj phr

Of a person: stocky, sturdy.

　1886 in 1950 *AmSp* 25.31 **New Orleans LA,** Andy Bohne is a well-knit and spunky little chap, and built from the ground up. **1951** *PADS* 15.53 **cIN. 1954** *Harder Coll.* **cwTN,** Built from the ground up . . . Of a person: well built. **c1960** *Wilson Coll.* **csKY,** Built from the ground up . . . Stocky, heavy-set; or close to the ground. "That Taylor boy is built from the ground up."

bulchyn n [*OED bulchin* "*Obs.* or *dial.*"; *EDD* "*Obs.*"]

　1899 (1912) Green *VA Folk-Speech* 99, Bulchyn . . . A young male calf.

bulge n, v Usu |bʌlj|; also, *esp in Sth, S Midl,* |bʊlj|; *occas* |bulj| Pronc-spp *belge, boolge*

A Forms.

　1892 *DN* 1.233 **KY,** Bulge [bʊlj]. **1906** *DN* 3.129 **nwAR,** Bulge . . . Pronounced [bʊlj]. **1907** *DN* 3.229 **nwAR, seMO,** Bulge (buld) [sic] . . . Advantage. **1917** in 1944 *ADD* 82 **sWV,** Boolges. **1938** *Hench Coll.,* A man who lived in Youngstown, Ohio, and Philadelphia, Pa., used this pronunciation in such contexts as "The wall belges out at this place." **1942** Hall *Smoky Mt. Speech* 40, *Bulge* and *bulk* are always sounded with [ʊ]. **1960** *PADS* 34.54 **CO,** The appearance of [bʊldʒ] *bulge* in those communities with a large number of Southern and South Midland terms — makes it likely that this old-fashioned pronunciation reflects a Southern and South Midland relic. **c1960** *Wilson Coll.* **csKY,** *Bulge out* [buldʒ] . . . To appear overfull.

B As noun.

1 An advantage — usu in phr *get the bulge on (someone).* **esp Midl**

　1841 *Spirit of Times* 18 Dec 498/3 *(DA),* Kate got the bulge on her at the start. **1880** Twain *Tramp Abroad* 40 **CA,** *Now* I guess I've got the bulge on you by this time! **1896** Harris *Sister Jane* 161 **GA,** They hain't nobody under the sun can git the bulge on a mule 'ceptin' it's a nigger. **1903** *DN* 2.308 **seMO,** Bulge . . . Advantage. 'He'll get the bulge on you if you don't watch out.' **1906** *DN* 3.115 **sIN. 1907** *DN* 3.229 **nwAR, seMO. 1908** *DN* 3.295 **eAL, wGA. 1919** Kyne *Capt. Scraggs* 72 **CA,** You'd have the bulge on me forever after. You could blackmail me until I dassen't call my ship my own. **1947** *New York Times* (NY) 12 Oct sec 5 1/8, Yale enjoyed a 10–0 bulge that did not begin to tell the story of its domination of the contest. **1952** Brown *NC Folkl.* 1.524, *Bulge, to get the . . .* To get the advantage of one.

2 See **bulger** n[1] **1.**

C As verb.

Usu foll by prep: To enter or approach abruptly; to barge (in). **esp S Midl**

　1834 Crockett *Narrative* 96 **TN,** They [=dogs] bulged in, and in an instant the bear followed them out. *Ibid* 105, As soon as we struck, I

bulged for my hatchway, as the boat was turning under sure enough. **1849** *Knickerbocker* 34.407/1, The Hosiers' . . war a standin on the shores of the Big Drink, when long bulged the old 'Meteor,' a reglar screamer, I tell ye. **1885** Twain *Huck. Finn* 313 **MO,** Whilst we was a-standing there in the dimmish light, here comes a couple of the hounds bulging in, from under Jim's bed. **1933** Williamson *Woods Colt* 189 **Ozarks,** You cain't go bulgin' up to a strange cabin when there ain't no menfolks there. **1961** Adams *Old-Time Cowhand* 36, In goin' on duty to relieve the guard, a new man approached the herd singin' to let 'em know he was comin' so he wouldn't bulge up on 'em unawares. **1967** *DARE* (Qu. Y25, *To walk heavily, making a lot of noise: "He came _____ into the house."*) Inf **MO18,** Banging, bulging, bursting.

bulger n[1]

1 also *bulge:* A very large or impressive thing. *obs*

　1835 Crockett *Account* 37 **TN,** We . . soon came in sight of the great city of New York, and a bulger of a place it is. **1872** Schele de Vere *Americanisms* 587, *Bulger* . . in the United States generally designates anything very large. "That's a bulger of a story." **1885** Twain *Huck. Finn* 338 **MO,** So the thing was working very well, Tom said . . . So he said, now for the grand bulge! **1960** Wentworth–Flexner *Slang* 71, *Bulge* . . . Any unusually big or important thing. *c1835.* Obs.

2 Spec: a large marble. [*EDD* Suppl, nScotl a1905; *SND bulsher* a playing marble] Cf **bully** n[1]

　1968 *DARE* (Qu. EE6a, *Names for different kinds of marbles — the big one that's used to knock others out of the ring*) Inf **LA37,** ['bul,ju].

3 See quot.

　1956 *Hall Coll.* **wNC,** They logged on sled and what they called bulgers. Bulgers are black gum logs.

bulger adj

Large.

　1889 (1971) Farmer *Americanisms* 101, *Bulger.* — A *bulger* town, tree, fish — anything uncommonly large. A Western phrase, probably from *bulge* to swell. Also known in England. **1890** Farmer–Henley *Slang* 1.362, *Bulger* . . (common). — Large; synonymous with *buster.*

bulger n[2], exclam [Orig unknown]

　1970 *Thompson Coll.* **cnAL** (as of 1920s), Boys in my neighborhood used to "go in bulger [bʊljər]" with another by hooking little fingers of right hands together and yanking their hands apart. They were entitled to lambaste anyone they were "in bulger with" upon hearing him use a "bad word". The beating continued until the one beaten cried "bulger!"

bulkhead n

1 An outside cellar entrance with sloping doors. **chiefly NEng** See Map

　1854 (1969) Thoreau *Walden* 132 **eMA,** Some trader among the Green Mountains . . stands over his bulk-head and thinks of the last arrivals on the coast. **a1862** (1865) Thoreau *Cape Cod* 73, An old woman came out and fastened the door of her bulkhead. **1890** *DN* 1.9, *Bulkhead,* used in New England of the covering of an opening into a cellar. *Ibid* 18, In Eastern Massachusetts 'bulkhead' is invariably used. **1907** *DN* 3.182 **seNH,** *Bulkhead* . . . Outside cellar-entrance with nearly horizontal doors under which is the upright door leading directly into the cellar. "The barrel rolled down into the bulkhead against the cellar-door." **1934** *Hanley Disks* **cMA. 1942** Hale *Prodigal Women* 478 **MA,** He heard the door of the bulkhead fall back, and heard Betsy walking in the cellar; the scrape of the shovel, the tumble and rattle of the coal; he heard

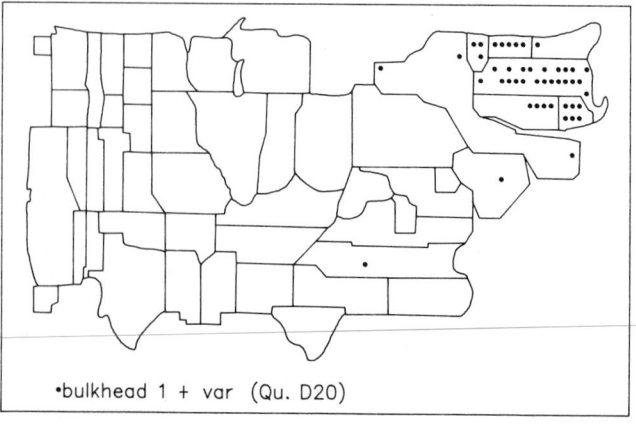

•bulkhead 1 + var (Qu. D20)

the bulkhead close. **1947** *Harper's Mag.* 194.472/2, He went out and sat on the bulkhead in the backyard, safe from interruption. **1965–70** *DARE* (Qu. D20, *Names for a sloping outside cellar door*) 45 Infs, **chiefly NEng**, Bulkhead; NC41, Bulkhead door. **1968** Coatsworth *ME Memories* 22, We walked about the little building, past the clumps of lilacs and climbed on a cellar bulkhead, trying to peer through a shutter into the dark interior.

2 A storm cloud. **Cf bullhead 8**

1967 *DARE* (Qu. B9, *What do you call the big clouds that roll up high before a rainstorm?*) Inf **SC43**, Bulkheads.

bull n, also attrib

1 Std sense—formerly often avoided as a taboo word esp in Sth, S Midl. Cf *DS* K22, 23 and **beast B2, brute, cowbrute, gentleman cow, male-cow**

1913 Kephart *Highlanders* 295 **sAppalachians**, Critter and beast are usually restricted to horse and mule, and brute to a bovine. A bull or boar is not to be mentioned as such in mixed company, but male-brute and male-hog are used as euphemisms. **1943** *New Yorker* 23 Oct 66/2 **cTX** (as of c1905), It was largely cattle country, but the word "bull" was seldom used in the company of ladies; the less offensive word "male" was employed to get the idea over. **1949** Kurath *Word Geog.* 62, The plain term *bull* is current everywhere, and in the North Midland and New York State other expressions are rare. In New England, the South, and the South Midland, however, the plain term is not used by older folk of one sex in the presence of the other. Even many of the younger generation prefer the veiled expressions of the Victorian era. **1953** Randolph *Down in Holler* 96, Schele De Vere says that many Southerners use ox, male-cow, or even gentleman-cow instead of bull, but the Ozarkers usually say *male, cow-critter, brute,* or *cow-brute.* **1954** *Harder Coll.* **cwTN**, *Bull*—Taboo, words used [instead]: yearling, male. **c1960** *Wilson Coll.* **csKY**, *Bull*—Rarely used in mixed company. Brute, animal, beast, male-cow are often substituted. Bullfrog, however, is acceptable; bull fiddle is less common. Among men there is no restraint, with many other compounds used. **1962** Atwood *Vocab.* TX 57, *Male bovine (with original equipment).* The plain term *bull* was given by 77 per cent of the Texas informants, with a steadily increasing frequency in the younger groups. Among the euphemisms that still survive are *male . .* and *surly.* **1970** Tarpley *Blinky* 165 **neTX**, *Male cow . .* In ordinary usage, only 2.5% of the informants have any qualms about saying that a male cow is a *bull.* Among informants under 40, the use of *bull* is unanimous. Four informants, three of them non-city females over 40, substitute *surly, bullie,* or *yearling,* for they were forbidden in childhood ever to say *bull,* and they still avoid that word. **1971** Bright *Word Geog. CA & NV* 168, *Bull* / special words used by farmers? by women? in presence of women? / . . . Very few, perhaps a dozen, expressed any kind of taboo or special attitudes concerning this item.

2 also attrib: The male of var non-bovine animals.

1894 *DN* 1.329 **NJ**, *Bull:* terrapin 3 or 4 inches across the belly. Five are required for a "count," or 60 to a dozen. **1955** *Sun* (Baltimore MD) 16 June ed.B 14/7 *(Hench Coll.),* Distinctive names apply to diamond-back terrapin, too. The male is a "bull" and the female a "cow," or if young, a "hen." "Buck" and "doe" are also heard. **1960** Williams *Walk Egypt* 3 **GA**, They were going on a coon hunt. A big bull coon had been seen up on Atkins' Ridge, eating the new corn and challenging charity. **1969** *DARE* (Qu. K52, *A male pig kept for breeding*) Inf **KY39**, Bull pig. **1982** Elman *Hunter's Field Guide* 637, *Moose (Alces alces) . . .* A mature bull of either type weighs from 1,000 to 1,400 pounds or so.

3 An ox used in logging. *hist* Cf **bull team**

1925 *AmSp* 1.135 **Pacific NW**, The oxen were always "bulls" to the loggers. **1942** *AmSp* 17.218 [Logger talk], Oxen are bulls. **1958** McCulloch *Woods Words* 20 **Pacific NW**, *Bull . . .* The old reliable ox used to skid logs in the bull team days. *Ibid* 23, *Bulls*—Loosely used to mean oxen in many cases.

4 See **bull of the woods.**

5 attrib: Something or someone who is bull-like in size or strength. See also **bull block, bull chain, bull gang, bullwork**

1889 (1971) Farmer *Americanisms* 101, "Bull" is in America a general prefix for "large." **1925** *AmSp* 1.136 [Logger talk], The largest donkey engines were called "bull donkeys," the largest planers in the mills were "bull planers," and "bull steak" and "roast bull" were and are common table terms. **1942** *AmSp* 17.220 [Logger talk], *Bull.* As a noun, either an ox or any kind of boss. As a prefix, . . [it often connotes] the utter superlative in size, power, authority, or virtue. **1958** McCulloch *Woods Words* 20 **Pacific NW**, *Bull . . .* In front of an endless number of other words means big, strong, etc., as bull donkey.

6 See **bullring.**

7 =**Virginia rail.**

1917 *DN* 4.423 **LA**, *Bull.* The Virginia rail (Rallus virginianus).

8 See **bull trout.**

9 See **bull duck.**

10 See **bull rail.**

bull v, hence *bullin(g)* ppl adj [*OED* bull v¹] **chiefly S Midl**
Of a cow: to be in heat; to be put with a bull.

1899 (1912) Green *VA Folk-Speech* 99, *Bulling . . .* A cow in heat is said to be bulling. **1923** *DN* 5.202 **swMO**, *Bull . . .* Said of a cow desirous of mating. "That cow's a-bullin'." Also to breed a cow. "That cow ortuh be bulled." Neither term is used in mixed company. **1930** Shoemaker *1300 Words* 5 **cPA Mts** (as of c1900), *Bullin*—A cow that is in a state ready for service. **1944** Wellman *Bowl* 84 **KS** (as of c1900), Instantly the cow raised her ugly head . . . She had recognized the far-off call of a bull. Suddenly she extended her muzzle and put every fiber of her gaunt being into the long, yearning bellow. Til nodded. "Breachy," he said aloud. "Breachy an' bulling!" **1956** *Hall Coll.* **eTN**, When that cow is a-bullin'. **c1960** *Wilson Coll.* **csKY**, *Bulling*—Term for a cow in heat, among men only. **1983** *MJLF* 9.33 **ceKY**, *Bulling . . .* When a cow is in heat, she puts her fore legs on the back of another cow and pretends she is a bull. This is called bulling.

bullace n

1 also, by back-formation, *bully:* A damson plum.

1671 in 1897 SC Hist. Soc. *Coll.* 5.308, Delightfull forrests . . [are] full of divers sorts of excellent fruits as strawberrys, mulberrys, . . Bullys[,] Nutts[,] with a multitude besides. **1797** Thomas *Newengland Farmer* 266 (*DAE*), The black bullace, is a globular, tart fruit, of the size of grapes. **1850** Emerson *Rept. Trees & Shrubs* 450, *Wild Bullace Tree, P[runus] insititia,* [is] a bush or small tree, found on the banks of Charles River, in Cambridge. **1892** Apgar *Trees Nth. U.S.* 98, Bullace Plum. **1946** Tatnall *Flora DE* 146, *P[runus] insititia . . .* Bullace Plum. **1976** Bailey–Bailey *Hortus Third* 919, *Prunus insititia . . .* Bullace.

2 also *bullace grape, bullance, bullis(on), bullus:* Either **bird grape 1** or **muscadine grape. chiefly Sth, esp S Atl**

1857 in 1954 *AmSp* 29.226 **SC**, With eyes dilating, big as Bullace grapes. **1887** (1967) Harris *Free Joe* 102 **cGA**, Ag'in bullaces is ripe you'll git your heart sot on 'possum. **1893** Shands *MS Speech* 21, *Bullis . . .* A word much used by the negroes of the southern central portion of Mississippi for *muscadine.* Its plural is *bullises.* **1908** *DN* 3.295 **eAL, wGA**, *Bullace . . .* Muscadine. Pronounced *bullus.* **1933** Small *Manual SE Flora* 838, *Muscadinia [Vitis] Munsoniana . . .* Bullace-grape. **1939** Harris *Purslane* 90 **cNC**, A bullance vine, where nature had fashioned a seat exactly to fit a little girl, tempted Nannie Lou. **1950** *PADS* 14.17 **SC**, *Bullace, bullis* ['blɪs], *bullison . . .* The bullace grape. **1953** Greene–Blomquist *Flowers South* 72, Closely related to this *[Vitis rotundifolia]* is the bullace grape *[V. Munsoniana]* of Fla. and Ga. **1960** Vines *Trees SW* 727, *Muscadine Grape*—*Vitis rotundifolia . . .* Vernacular names are . . . Bullace Grape. **1965–70** *DARE* (Qu. I46, *. . . Fruits that grow wild around here*) 17 Infs, **S Atl, esp SC**, Bullace; FL37, GA23, SC62, Bullaces; SC11, Bullison; (Qu. I44, *. . Kinds of berries*) Infs FL8, 36, GA16, Bullaces; (Qu. DD28b) Infs SC26, 40, Bullace wine. **1970** Correll *Plants TX* 1018, *Vitis rotundifolia . . .* Bullace-grape.

bull ant n **chiefly FL, GA**

Prob =**carpenter ant.**

1965–70 *DARE* (Qu. R17, *. . Big black ants that sting*) Infs FL11, 16, 27, 29, GA20, 35, Bull ant; GA3, Black bull ants; (Qu. R18, *Other . . ants*) Infs FL9, 34, 51, GA20, VA43, Bull ant; GA3, Black bull ant.

bull bag n Also *bull's bag, bull bollix*

A **lady's slipper** or similar plant.

1968–70 *DARE* (Qu. S1) Inf **NJ21**, Bull bag; (Qu. S26c) Inf **NJ8**, Bull's bag—like ladyslipper, only bigger and purple; **PA245**, Ladyslipper: bull bollix [=ballocks].

bull band n Also *bull banding* **chiefly wMD, sePA** Cf **belling** vbl n²

=**shivaree.**

1916 *DN* 4.343 **nwMD**, Bull band. = Calithumpian band. **1935** *AmSp* 10.171 **sePA**, Bull-banding is at present the generally accepted name for a serenade for a newly-married couple; a shivaree, or callithumpian. **1949** Kurath *Word Geog.* 78, Bull band, bull banding in the German settlements of the Great Valley of Pennsylvania [for the serenading of newlyweds]. **1949** *AmSp* 24.252, Bull-band(ing) [occurs for serenade or shivaree] in the Pennsylvania German sector. **1968** *DARE* (Qu. AA18, . . *A noisy neighborhood celebration after a wedding, where the married couple is expected to give a treat*) Inf **MD21**, Bull band (used to have this—no longer); **MD27**, Bull band. **1970** *DARE* FW Addit **cePA**, Bull banding.

bullbat n

1 =**nighthawk**. [See quot 1968] **chiefly S Atl, Gulf States, SW, scattered S Midl** See Map

1851 (1874) Glisan *Jrl. Army Life* 89 **OK**, Of the birds and animals not usually eatable, there are the . . bull-bat, wren, yellow-bird, [etc]. **1928** Peterkin *Scarlet Sister Mary* 89 **SC**, Bull-bats darted about catching gnats and mosquitoes. **1930** Shoemaker *1300 Words* 7 **cPA Mts** (as of c1900), *Bull-bat*—The night hawk. **1934** Vines *Green Thicket* 60 **cnAL**, He had enough feathers from wild things to make a feather bed . . . He had a little old trunk nearly full of feathers and down from . . bullbats. **1939** *Hall Coll.* **wNC, eTN**, Bull bat, not the same as whippoorwill; ain't got the whiskers that the whippoorwill has. **1950** *PADS* 14.16 **SC**, *Bullbat* . . The Florida nighthawk. **1955** *AmSp* 30.179, *Bat*, alone, had served to designate the nighthawk in some localities (N.Y., Md., Va., N.C., Fla, Ontario) but probably as a nickname for *bullbat*, a widespread appellation, from a sound made by the bird, not from its size. **1965–70** *DARE* (Qu. Q3, . . *Birds that come out only after dark*) 76 Infs, **chiefly S Atl, Gulf States, SW, scattered S Midl**, Bullbat. **1968** Abbey *Desert Solitaire* 208 **seUT**, Now and then a nighthawk, high in the air, will fold wings and plunge earthward; the noise of the wind rushing through its feathers when the bird extends wings and pulls out of the dive is like a distant roar, a bovine bellow. And so, among its many other names, the nighthawk *Chordeiles minor* is also called a bullbat, at least in the Southwest.

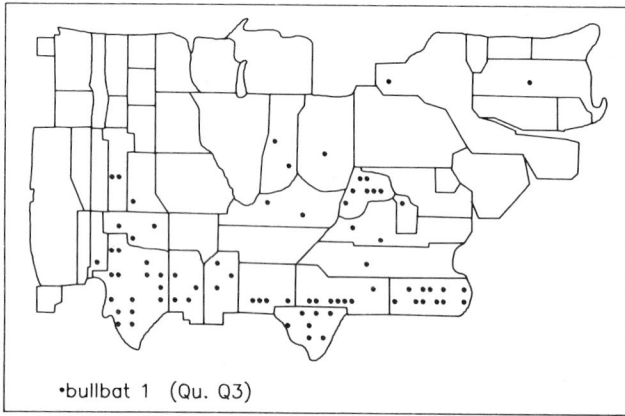

•bullbat 1 (Qu. Q3)

2 also *big bullbat:* =**whippoorwill**.

1933 *Sun* (Baltimore MD) 28 July 8/7 (Hench Coll.), As a boy on the Eastern Shore I had the reputation of being the best bull bat destroyer in the community. We kids used to arm ourselves with long laths and stand at intervals along the streets or lanes till the bats came swooping by in the dusk . . . The bull bat, as is not very commonly known, is the whippoorwill. **1945** McAtee in *AN&Q* 5.11/2 **TX**, Despite the dominance of *whippoorwill,* there are a number of local names for the bird: "big bullbat" (Texas; the nighthawk is the ordinary bullbat).

3 A bat (order Chiroptera).

1950 *PADS* 14.16 **SC**, *Bullbat* . . the common leather-winged bat.

bull bay n chiefly Sth

=**southern magnolia**.

1883 Smith *Report for 1881 & 1882* 292, Magnolia fœtida . . . Bull Bay. **1897** Sudworth *Arborescent Flora* 193, **AL, GA, MS**, Bull Bay. **1960** Vines *Trees SW* 281, *Magnolia grandiflora* . . . Vernacular names are Bull-bay [etc]. **1967** *DARE* (Qu. T5) Inf **TX35**, Bull bay. **1976** Bruce *How to Grow Wildflowers* 145, Another "bay," Bull-bay *(Magnolia grandiflora),* an evergreen tree with a similar range, thrives in central Delmarva. *Ibid* 151, *Magnolia grandiflora,* Bull-bay ("bull" being an allusion to its large size), Southern or Great-flowered Magnolia . . is . . the best known of the native species in this country.

bull-beggar n [Engl dial *bull-beggar* a hobgoblin]

A woodchuck (perh *Marmota monax*).

1969 *DARE* (Qu. P31, . . *Names or nicknames . . for the . . woodchuck*) Inf **MA58**, Bull-beggar.

bullberry n

1 also *bull-brush:* =**buffalo berry**. **chiefly West**

1839 (1973) Farnham *Travels Prairies* 2.52, There is in this valley, and in some other parts of the mountains, a fruit called bullberry. **1855** (1940) Chambers *Jrl.* 105 **MT**, A rich dessert of sugar & Bull berries is given about 12 M. **1926** *Torreya* 26.6, *Lepargyraea argentea* . . . Bull-brush, Graham Mts, Ariz. **1965** Guthrie *Blue Hen's Chick* 16 **MT**, Flushed by frost, bullberries sparkled in their silver thickets, red as Indian beads. **1965–70** *DARE* (Qu. I44) Infs **MT5, NM8, ND1, 5, UT13**, Bullberries. **1967** Schilla *Prairies* 18 **ND** (as of 1880s), The pips from roses, buffalo or bulberries, and from any other edible berry they could find, were dried.

2 Prob a bilberry.

1931–33 *LANE Worksheets* **RI**, Bullberry . . . Kind of berry, black in color.

bullbird n

=**red phalarope**.

1955 *AmSp* 30.177, Why the red phalarope, so gracefully built as to be known as a fairy snipe, is called *bullbird* (N.J.) . . is quite beyond me.

bull block n

In logging: see quots.

1920 *DN* 5.80 **Pacific NW**, Bullblock. A very large pulley block. Logging term. **1950** *Western Folkl.* 9.116 **OR**, *Bull block.* Huge pulleys through which the main line is passed. These pulleys sometimes weigh more than half a ton. **1958** McCulloch *Woods Words* 21 **Pacific NW**, *Bull block*—Originally a large mouthed block wide enough to permit the butt rigging to pull through in ground lead days; now applied to the main line lead block in high lead yarding. **1968** Adams *Western Words* 42, *Bull block.*

bullboat n Also *bullhide boat, ~ canoe* hist

A skin boat: see quots 1859, 1889.

1830 (1940) Ferris *Rocky Mts.* 30, He was consequently placed in a bull-hide boat, in charge of two men. *Ibid* 33, We crossed the Platte in bull-hide canoes. **1835** (1927) Evans *Exped. to Rocky Mts.* 196, By means of this "bull boat" and the body of a small wagon . . we were enabled to get every thing across with safty [sic]. **1859** (1965) Marcy *Prairie Traveler* 83, Another method of ferrying streams is by means of what is called by the mountaineers a *"bull-boat,"* the frame-work of which is made of willows bent into the shape of a short and wide skiff, with a flat bottom . . . Green or soaked hides are cut into the proper shape to fit the frame, and sewed together with buckskin strings . . . Two men can easily build a *bull-boat* of three hides in two days which will carry ten men with perfect safety. **1889** *Century Dict.,* Bull-boat . . . A rude boat made by the North American Indians, usually a shallow crate covered with the raw hide of the bull elk. **1889** (1971) Farmer *Americanisms* 101, *Bull-boat.* In the remote West the name of an ox-hide boat, once commonly enough used for crossing rivers; similar in shape to the ancient British coracle. **1968** Adams *Western Words* 42, *Bullboat*—A lightweight boat used by the fur traders and Indians on the Missouri River and its tributaries.

bull bollix See bull bag

bullbrier n

A greenbrier (here: *Smilax bona-nox* and *S. rotundifolia*).

1853 Hammett *Stray Yankee in TX* 22, [I aided] his rude attempts at road-making whenever a mass of bull-brier or bamboo-vines . . called for action. **1889** (1971) Farmer *Americanisms* 101, *Bull-briar* or *bamboo-briar.*—This plant derives its former name from the size which it attains in the rich alluvial bottoms of the South-west, where alone it is to be found. Its root is of a farinaceous character, and is much esteemed by the Indians for bread-making purposes. "Bull" is in America a general prefix for "large." **1910** Graves *Flowering Plants* 125 **CT**, *Smilax rotundifolia* . . . Bull Brier. **1916** *Torreya* 16.237 **VA**, *Smilax bona-nox* . . . Bull-brier. **1938** Rawlings *Yearling* 40 **nFL**, Bull-briers, tougher than his father's muscles, snared him, and he could only push his way around them or crawl beneath. **1960** Vines *Trees SW* 73, *Smilax bona-nox* . . . Vernacular names used are . . . Bull-brier. **1969** *DARE* (Qu. S15) Inf **MA57**, Bullbriers. **1970** Correll *Plants TX* 412, *Smilax rotundifolia* . . . Bull-brier.

bull-brush See bullberry 1

bull bucker n Also *bull buck* chiefly Pacific NW Cf bucker n^2 1

In logging: the person in charge of the **fallers** and the **buckers**.

1936 in 1949 Powers *Redwood Country* 116 **nCA,** The chopping boss—bull buck—plans the strips. **1956** *AmSp* 31.149 **nwCA,** *Bull buck* . . . The man in charge of fallers and buckers. **1958** McCulloch *Woods Words* 21 **Pacific NW,** *Bull buck*—The boss of the fallers and buckers; also called bull bucker. **1965** *Perrin Coll.* **cwWA,** The bull bucker has charge of men who fall trees and saw them into log lengths. **1967** *DARE* Tape **OR**1 [Conversation about occupations in the woods], [Inf:] There's the timber faller, the bull buck . . . [FW:] What's a bull buck? [Inf:] He's the faller's boss. Sometimes he's a scaler . . . He measures the logs. **1968** Adams *Western Words* 42, *Bull bucker*—In logging, the man in charge of the gang whose job is to *buck* the fallen trees. He records the daily cut of fallers and buckers.

bull-built adj
Husky, burly.
1935 Davis *Honey* 129 **OR,** He was a bull-built old man with a rattly voice that had been developed by talking above the noise of the sawmill.

bull cactus n
Perh a **prickly pear.**
1968 *DARE* (Qu. S26a) Inf **NV8,** Bull cactus—has chewable spines.

bull chain n
In logging: see quot 1956.
1949 Powers *Redwood Country* 103 **nCA,** There was a well-stocked log pond, the logs being sections of redwood limbs. A bull chain continually dragged these up to a mechanical sawyer. **1956** *AmSp* 31.149 **nwCA,** *Bull chain* . . . The big chain that hoists logs up the chute from millpond to sawmill. **1968** Adams *Western Words.*

bull cook n [bull n 2 + cook]
Orig the man who fed the draft animals in logging camps; later a camp handyman or helper.
1917 in 1919 *DN* 5.54 **wWA,** *Bull cook.* Mr. Bill (Jerusalem) Miller has taken the situation of bull cook at the camp. **1925** *AmSp* 1.136, Once the wood-splitter and water-carrier of the logging camp was simply "choreboy"; but this bunkhouse lackey became "bull cook" in the West. **1926** *Ibid* 650 [Hobo lingo], *Bull cook*—a camp flunkey. **1942** *AmSp* 17.218 [Logger talk], Oxen are bulls; the bullcook fed them. The rest of his hours the bullcook spent as camp handyman and choreboy. **1944** Nute *Lake Superior* 209, One night, in a camp that tolerated a broken-down Scotch bull cook, much too fond of his whiskey, the service was getting well under way. **1956** *AmSp* 31.150 **nwCA,** *Bull cook* . . . The person who sweeps out bunkhouses and lights heating stoves. **1958** McCulloch *Woods Words* 21 **Pacific NW,** *Bull cook* . . . A man who puts in firewood, makes beds, does odd jobs around camp. A roustabout, descended from the "lobby hog" of New England logging camps. **1975** Gould *ME Lingo* 26, *Bullcook*—A lumbercamp *choreboy* or handyman. The one thing he never did was cook. While the word *choreboy* is used, the *bullcook* was usually a mature man with, 'twas said, a strong back and a weak head.

bullcook v [bull cook n]
To do odd jobs.
1956 *Seattle Daily Times* (WA) 19 Feb mag sec 10, Today we still have the "bullcooks" and, if one is concerned with a number of small tasks, none of which are of vital importance, one is said to be just "bullcooking." **1958** McCulloch *Woods Words* 21 **Pacific NW,** *Bull cook* . . . To do odd jobs. *Bull cooking machine*—A cat rigged up to do odd jobs around the operation.

bull coot n
=**white-winged scoter.**
1888 Trumbull *Names of Birds* 99, *Oidemia deglandi* . . . On Long Island at Bellport *Bull Coot.* **1917** (1923) *Birds Amer.* 1.150, *Oidemia deglandi* . . . Bull Coot. **1955** *AmSp* 30.177 **CT, NY,** Bull coot—White-winged scoter. **1968** *DARE* (Qu. Q9) Inf **NJ52,** Bull coot.

bullcorn n **TX**
Nonsense.
1967 *DARE* (Qu. NN13, *When you think that the thing somebody has just said is silly or untrue*) Infs **TX**11, 26, Bullcorn. **1970** Tarpley *Blinky* 298 **neTX,** *Mild expression of disgust* . . bull corn. **1981** *Newsweek* 1 June 31 **TX,** There would be some guy sitting in Arizona or Florida saying, 'My social security helped me to retire here.' Well, that's bullcorn.

bullcorn v [bullcorn n]
1970 *DARE* (Qu. GG3, *To tease: "See those big boys trying to _____ [that little one]."*) Inf **TX**104, Bullcorn.

bulldagger n [Alter of *bulldike(r)*] *esp among Black speakers, freq derog*
A masculine-appearing lesbian.
1965 Brown *Manchild* 197 **NYC,** There were a lot of girls who just liked girls. I remember once my little sister asked my mother, "Mama, is that a lady or a man?" It was a stud. Mama just looked at her and said, "That's a bull-dagger, baby." **1967–70** *DARE* (QR, near Qu. HH39) Inf **FL**52, [Hermaphrodite]—Homosexual women—older folk say bulldagger; **MO**8, Bulldagger. **1968** *DARE* FW Addit **New Orleans LA,** Bulldagger—hermaphroditic lesbian; extremely masculine in manner. **1970** Abrahams *Deep Down* 264 **Philadelphia** [Black], *Bulldagger*—A lesbian. Variant pronunciation, bulldiker . . . The actual origin of *bulldagger* is simply a long series of mispronunciations and corruptions of the word hermaphrodite, extraordinary as that may seem at first sight. The series is even more extraordinary in that *all* the corruptions of the original word still co-exist simultaneously, namely: *harumphodite, morphodite, dike, dyker;* and *bull-dyker* or *bull-dagger* with the addition of the male "bull" element. **1971** Roberts *Third Ear* [Black], *Bull dagger* . . a lesbian. **1972** Claerbaut *Black Jargon* 59, Bulldagger . . a female homosexual; lesbian. **1980** Folb *Runnin' Down* 127 **sCA,** Lesbian (*bulldagger*). *Ibid* 231, *Bulldagger, bulldike*—Lesbian (often associated with a particularly masculine-acting female).

bull daisy n Cf **cow daisy**
1 A **black-eyed Susan 2** (here: *Rudbeckia hirta*).
1940 Clute *Amer. Plant Names* 86, *R. hirta* . . . Bull's-eye daisy, bull-daisy. **1959** Carleton *Index Herb. Plants* 20, Bull daisy: . . Rudbeckia hirta.
2 =**oxeye** (here: *Chrysanthemum leucanthemum*).
1940 Clute *Amer. Plant Names* 79, *C. leucanthemum* . . . Bull-daisy. **1959** Carleton *Index Herb. Plants* 20, *Bull daisy:* Chrysanthemum leucanthemum.

bull dice See **boss dice**

bull-dick pine See **bull pine 1c**

bulldocia n [Perh a blend of *bull* boastful talk, *bulldoze,* and *braggadocio*] Cf **braggadoshe**
Boastful and threatening language.
1934 Hurston *Jonah's Gourd Vine* 104 **FL,** Mens on dese camps is full uh bulldocia 'till dey smell uh good size fist.

bulldog n
1 A type of hooded stirrup.
1933 White *Dog Days* 197 **CA,** The stock saddle, then, was the choice. But one did not merely go in and buy a saddle. He had all sorts of important details to decide upon . . . Are we plunging on "ox-bow" stirrups or hooded? If the latter, are we picking the box type, the bulldog, or the long, flapping tapaderos that reach almost to the ground? **1961** Adams *Old-Time Cowhand* 113, [The style of covered stirrups] takes the name of their shape, such as "bulldogs," short ones; "monkey nose," short upturned front; or "eagle-bill," longer hooked front.
2 A kind of men's haircut.
1967–68 *DARE* (Qu. X5) Inf **UT4,** Bulldog; **WY4,** Bulldog—cut so it stands straight up all over about an inch long.
3 A marble.
c1970 Wiersma *Marbles Terms* **swMI,** Bulldog: clear glass marble with specks of something in the glass which looks like "bull's fur."
4 A snapdragon. [From resemblance to a jowly bulldog]
1947 Percival *Old-Fash. Flowers* 140, Bulldogs, *Antirrhinum.* **1963** *AmSp* 38.31, *Bulldog* . . . Snapdragon.
5 =**marsh marigold.** Cf **bull flower, bull's-eye 1**
1963 *AmSp* 38.31, *Bulldog* . . . Marsh marigold.
6 An ant of the subfamily Formicinae. Cf **bull ant**
1966 *DARE* (Qu. R18) Infs **FL**32, 35, Bulldogs.
7 See **bulldog fly.**
8 See **bulldog toe.**

bulldog v[1], hence vbl n *bulldogging,* n *(bull)dogger* **West**
To throw a calf by twisting its neck.
1907 White *AZ Nights* 148, The two "Bulldoggers" immediately pounced upon the victim. It was promptly flopped over on its right side. One knelt on its head and twisted back its foreleg in a sort of hammerlock; the other seized one hind foot, pressed his boot heel against the other hind leg close to the body, and sat down behind the animal. Thus the calf was unable to struggle. *Ibid* 151, One of the men seized the

tightened rope in one hand, reached well over the animal's back to get a slack of the loose hide next the belly, lifted strongly, and tripped. This is called "bull-dogging." **1907** *Outing* 51.329/1 **AZ,** 'No more necked calves,' they announced, 'catch 'em by the hind legs, or bull-dog 'em yourself.' **1920** Hunter *Trail Drivers TX* 297, He [the cowboy] "bull-dogs" them by twisting the neck. **1923** Cook *50 Yrs.* 151 **WY,** This was my first and only experience at bulldogging an elk. **1933** *AmSp* 8.1.28 **nwTX,** Bull dog. **1941** *Natl. Geog. Mag.* 79.300/1 **OK,** He's too old now to bulldog a steer or bust a bronco. **1942** *AmSp* 17.74 **NE,** When a waddie [cowboy] throws a calf by grasping the skin of its opposite flank while it's running, he *flanks* the animal; when he throws it by twisting its neck, he *bulldogs* it; when he throws it by giving its tail a sudden jerk, he *tails* it. **1965** *AmSp* 40.257, *Bulldogger, dogger.* A cowboy who wrestles steers to the ground. **1967–70** *DARE* Tape **TX24,** He'd bulldog one and I'd bulldog one [=calves]; **TX41,** There's a bulldogging contest [in a rodeo]; **TX87,** [At a rodeo] you still have the old flavor; I mean there'd be your bulldogging of the calves; **TX89,** Well they have wild horse riding, bulldogging, calf roping, wild cow milking [at a rodeo].

bulldog v[2] Also *dog* [Cf *OED bull* v.[4] 1824 →] Cf **barrel-dog-ging**

1949 *AmSp* 24.8 **KY** [Moonshiner argot], *Bull dog* . . . To heat used barrels by setting them against a large oil drum in which a fire is built in order to sweat out the whisky which has soaked into the barrel staves. '. . . bull-dog them barrels and get ten gallons of likker.' Also *dog, sweat.*

bulldog fly n Also *bulldog*
=**horsefly.**

1893 Roosevelt *Wilderness Hunter* 115 **MT,** There was a spell of warm weather which brought out a few of the big bull-dog flies, which drive a horse—or indeed a man—nearly frantic. **1967** *DARE* Tape **MN4,** It's a hell-hole for flies . . . We've got our own special breed here we call the bulldog . . . I don't know of any other name for 'em. This bulldog fly that we've got here . . doesn't seem to cover too much of a territory. But it's a terrific hazard and always has been as far as livestock is concerned.

bulldog gravy n **KY** Cf **bull fuck**
See quots.

1939 (1954) FWP *Guide KY* 436, *Bulldog gravy*—The diet of the miner and his family consists chiefly of beans—and more beans—corn bread made without milk, and "bulldog gravy", a mixture of flour, water, and a little grease. **1969** *DARE* (Qu. H37) Inf **KY15,** Bulldog gravy—joking name for thickened gravy made with meat juice and flour; **KY37,** Bulldog gravy. **1970** *DARE* File **seKY,** Bulldog gravy—a cream gravy made of country-cured bacon drippings (not thin-cut store bacon).

bulldog toe n Also *bulldog (shoe) old-fash*
A rounded high toe on a man's shoe; the shoe itself.

1946 (1972) Mezzrow *Really Blues* 7 **Chicago IL** (as of c1915), He [the cop] yanked me out of the car and kicked me so hard with his bulldog toe, I flew right into the precinct house. **1965–70** *DARE* (Qu. W42b, . . *Men's square-toed shoes*) Infs **HI1, NJ1, 16, 30, NY37,** Bulldog toes; **CT12,** Bulldog toes—round, high toes; **DC4,** Bulldog toe—raised a little; **MA6, NY219, PA57,** Bulldog (shoes); **HI9,** Bulldog shoes—men's, round-toed, like a [bull]dog's face. [All Infs old] **1968** *DARE* Tape **NY42,** For play we had heavy . . high shoes, ankle high shoes . . with bulldog toes that you could get scuffed around . . those are stiff toes . . sort of built up in the front . . give your toes plenty of room to stretch and grow in and also to take the knocking around that a small boy would give them. **1969** O'Connor *Horse & Buggy West* 279 **AZ** (as of early 1900s), Peg-top pants had been the rage along with long suit coats with enormously padded shoulders . . . With this costume went high buttoned shoes with "bulldog" toes.

bull driver n

1 =**bullwhacker.**

1970 *DARE* Tape **CA199,** I was the bull driver . . . You know, it seems impossible today to . . think about goin' out with a bunch of oxen, no drove lines on 'em or nothin', just a-talkin' to 'em and go out in the woods and drag out your logs and load 'em—it seems impossible, and you tell people you done it and they'd laugh at you.

2 A rustic.

1930 Shoemaker *1300 Words* 7 **cPA Mts** (as of c1900), *Bull-driver*—A rough farmer from the back country.

bull duck n Also *bull* [See quot 1955] Cf **bullhead 2c**
=**ring-necked duck.**

1955 *AmSp* 30.176, Thus the ring-necked duck is known as *bull* or *bull duck* in Georgia not because it is large of its kind, for it is not, but

probably from its also being named *bullhead* and *bullneck.* **1966–70** *DARE* (Qu. Q5) Infs **FL7, GA20,** Bull duck.

Bull Durham exclam [Trademark for a brand of tobacco] *euphem*
Nonsense!

1928 McKay *Home to Harlem* 48 **NYC,** "Bull Durham!" cried Zeddy. "What was I going to let on about anything for?"

bullet See **bully** n[1]

bullet grape n [By folk-etym from **bullace 2**]
Either the **frost grape** or the **muscadine grape.**

1828 Rafinesque *Med. Flora* 132, V[itis] vulpina . . . It bears a multitude of vulgar names, such as . . . Bullet Grape. **1880** Darlington *Amer. Weeds* 84, *Vulpine or Foxy Vitis.* Fox-Grape, *of the Southern States;* also called "Muscadine," and "Bullet- or Bull-Grape." **1960** Vines *Trees SW* 727, *Muscadine Grape—Vitis rotundifolia* . . . Vernacular names are . . . Bullet Grape. **1966** *DARE* Tape **SC12,** But they must not have been bulletses [sic], bulletses—I reckon they call 'em bullets because they's hard as a marble . . until after frost. **1970** *DARE* (Qu. I46) Inf **FL49,** Bullet grapes.

bullet hawk n [See quot 1844]
Any of several hawks, such as the **Cooper's hawk,** the **duck hawk,** the **marsh hawk,** the **pigeon hawk 1,** or the **sharp-shinned hawk.**

1844 DeKay *Zool. NY* 2.15, *The Pigeon Hawk. Falco columbarius . . .* has been termed the *Bullet Hawk,* in allusion to its swiftness. **1913** *Pacific Coast Avifauna* 9.44, The flight of the Duck Hawk is so marvelously fast that even ducks have not a chance to escape . . . The writer remembers standing, with several companions, on the shore of Summit Lake. "Bullet hawk", called one of the men. **1917** (1923) *Birds Amer.* 2.66, *Sharp-shinned Hawk . . . Other Names . . .* Bullet Hawk; Little Blue Darter. **1923** WV State Ornith. *Birds WV* 141, Cooper's Hawk . . . Common Names—Blue Darter, Bullet Hawk. **1950** *PADS* 14.17 **SC,** *Bullet hawk . . .* The marsh hawk. Probably so called because of the *bullet-like* dart made upon his prey. **1965–70** *DARE* (Qu. Q4) Infs **AZ9, CA62, 120, NJ52, 56, SC9, UT4,** Bullet hawk.

bulletine n

1966 *DARE* (Qu. EE32, *A homemade merry-go-round*) Inf **NM12,** Bulletine [bʊlɛtin].

bull-eye n See **bull's-eye 4a**

bull-eye v Cf *DS* P35b and **bull's-eye 2**
To hunt by shining a light into the eyes of an animal.

1968 *DARE* (Qu. P35b, *Illegal methods of shooting deer*) Inf **LA40,** Bull-eyeing [ˈbʊlˌaɪən]—this word used for hunting rabbits with a headlight. **1979** Hallowell *People Bayou* 134 **sLA,** Randall Stelly goes out with a flashlight to "bull-eye" some alligators in the crevey back of the camp.

bull-eyed daisy See **bull's-eye daisy 1**

bull-eyed lamp See **bull's-eye 2**

bull-face tobacco n
A kind of tobacco.

[**1707** Sloane *Voyage* lxiii **Jamaica,** Tobacco . . is of several sorts . . : that with the broad Leaves is call'd Bulls Face.] **c1770** in 1833 Boucher *Glossary* 50 **MD,** In *twist-bud, thick-joint, bull-face, leather-coat,* I'd toil all day. **1969** *DARE* FW Addit **KY16,** Bull-face tobacco—the tobacco grown by old mountaineers in the area. It was rarely sold but cured for home use.

bullfeathers exclam [By analogy with *horsefeathers*]
Nonsense!

1980 *AR Gaz.* (Little Rock) 11 Mar 1/3, We made up our mind to say hush the way Miss Ina did. But we never thought fast enough. It always came out "You're kidding?" or "No jive?" Or in really incredulous situations, "Bullfeathers!"

bull fever n
=**buck fever 1.**

1839 Townsend *Narr. Rocky Mts.* 53 **Plains States,** Just then I was attacked with the *"bull fever"* so dreadfully, that for several minutes I could not shoot.

bull fiddle n

1 A bass viol; hence *bull fiddler* one who plays a bass viol.
1883 Sala *Amer. Revisited* 2.160 **NE,** A "bull-fiddle"—which is Amer-

icanese for violoncello. **1909** *DN* 3.409 **cnME,** *Bull fiddle* . . . A bass viol. **1942** Handy *Father of Blues* 237 **MT** (as of 1890s), As usual the bull-fiddler sawed away in *G.* **1942** Berrey–Van den Bark *Amer. Slang* 188.7, Bull-fiddle voice, *a deep bass voice.* **c1960** *Wilson Coll.* **csKY,** *Bull*—Rarely used in mixed company . . . Bullfrog, however, is acceptable; bull fiddle is less common.

2 By ext: see quots. Cf **dumb bull**

1942 Berrey–Van den Bark *Amer. Slang* 577.4, *Bull fiddle, the contrabass, also a stringed instrument made from a tin can.* **1968** *DARE* FW Addit NY94, *Bull fiddle*—a "musical" instrument used at a horning. It consisted of a sawhorse and a long smooth plank, both with rosin on them. The board was drawn across the horse to produce a noise.

bullfin n
=**bowfin.**
> **1904** *DN* 2.395 **cNY,** *Bull-fin* . . . The bow-fin or mud-fish *(Amia calva)* . . . Apparently a corruption of *bow-fin.*

bull flower n
A **marsh marigold** (here: *Caltha palustris*).
> **1900** Lyons *Plant Names* 76, *C[altha] palustris* . . . Bull-flower. **1959** Carleton *Index Herb. Plants* 20, *Bull Flower: Caltha palustris.*

bullfly n chiefly **Nth**
Prob a blowfly.
> **1781** Peters *Genl. Hist.* CT 259, The Bull-fly is armed with a coat of mail. **1911** *Century Dict.,* *Bullfly* . . . An insect, the gadfly, so named from its tormenting cattle. **1951** *Eaton Coll.* **neWI,** Bull . . . bloater fly. **1965–70** *DARE* (Qu. R12) Infs **IN**26, **OR**1, **WA**1, Bullfly; **MN**5, Bullfly, a large biting fly like a horsefly; **MN**16, Bullfly—the big ones; blue-green; **WI**23, Bullfly, blue.

bullfoot See in phrr *beans from bull's foot* (at **beans, not to know c**) and **B from (a) bull's foot, not to know**

bull-footed adj
> **1954** *PADS* 21.22 **SC,** *Bull-footed* . . . Awkward, clumsy . . . Also *bumble-footed.*

bullfrog n
1 Std: A large frog of the genus *Rana.* Also called **belly-deep, bizmaroon, bloodick, bloodynoun, brother-rounds, bull paddock, bullyrum, clunker 2, cowfrog, drummer, French frog, goodadoon, grandaddy, green frog, gurrump, honker, Irish nightingale, Johnny bull, jugarum, lunker, more-rummer, squawker, wart frog, yellowthroat**

2 =**belly-flop 2.**
> **1968** *DARE* (Qu. EE29, *When swimmers are diving and one comes down flat onto the water, that's a* _____) Inf **OH**70, Bullfrog.

3 See quot.
> **1981** *DARE* File **OK,** Bullfrog—the game of leapfrog.

bullfrog rock n
Perh fluorite.
> **1941** Corle *Desert Country* 30 **NV,** The quartz was just full of free gold and it was the original genuine green bullfrog rock.

bullfrogs, rain v phr For varr see quots **chiefly Sth, S Midl** See Map
To rain very hard.

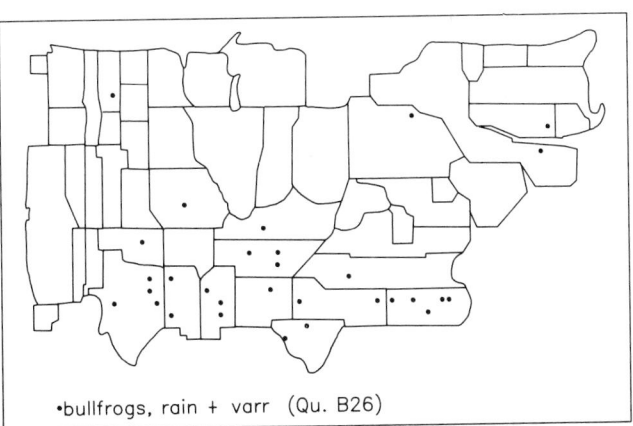

•bullfrogs, rain + varr (Qu. B26)

1954 *Harder Coll.* **cwTN,** It's raining bullfrogs and pitchforks. **1965–70** *DARE* (Qu. B26, *When it's raining very heavily, you say, "It's raining* _____.") 27 Infs, **chiefly Sth, S Midl,** (Down) bullfrogs; **MO**19, **MT**5, **PA**78, **TN**23, Pitchforks and bullfrogs.

bull fuck n **Pacific NW** *joc* Cf **bull gravy**
Gravy.
> **1966–67** *DARE* (Qu. H37, *What words do you have for gravy? Any joking ones?*) Inf **OR**3, Bull fuck; **OR**13, Sop, bull fuck; **WA**11, Dip, bull fuck; **WA**30, Bull fuck.

bull gang n Cf **bullwork**
A crew of manual laborers.
> **1938** Stuart *Dark Hills* 138 **KY,** My first work was with the gin gang. The "bull gang" it was called by many. We cleaned out manholes and laid sewer lines from the new privies the firm was building. We unloaded coke and coal by the trainload. We picked up scraps of rusty steel and sent it in on trucks to be worked over again. We pulled ragweed and crab grass from beside the long bright metal sheds with tops of glass. We worked ten hours each day. **1940** *Sun* (Baltimore MD) 10 May 5/1 (*Hench Coll.*), Structural steel workers, pipefitters, welders, acetylene cutters, hydraulic engineers and what the construction industry chooses to label ["]bull gangs, gave a four-[s]tar performance. **1941** O'Donnell *Great Big Doorstep* 59 **LA** (*Hench Coll.*), "Are you a rough-neck?" "Yes. I'm in the bull-gang so far." **1944** *PADS* 2.65, *Bull-gang* or *the bulls* . . . Men who handle (load or unload) the hogsheads [of tobacco] as they are taken to the warehouses for storage and aging. **1946** Stuart *Tales Plum Grove* 66 **seKY,** Crushing limestone rock at the quarry where my job was helping the other three on the "bull-gang" use the hand drill. **1951** *PADS* 15.75 [Oil field jargon], There are various attributive combinations using animal names: *bull wheel, bull rope, bull gang.* **1958** McCulloch *Woods Words* 21 **Pacific NW,** Bull gang . . . A rig-up crew . . . A road building or repairing crew, or any other crew bulling through a job by main strength rather than by machine.

bullgine n Also sp *bulljine* [Blend of *bull* + *(en)gine*] Cf **engine**
A locomotive or steam engine.
> **1846** Durivage *Stray Subjects* 38 *(DA),* [He made] himself agreeable to his officers by jumping Jim Crow, playing on the bones, and imitating the 'bull-gine.' **1890** Farmer–Henley *Slang* 1.367, *Bull-jine* . . . A sailor's term for a locomotive. **1900** Garland *Eagle's Heart* 150, That's the bull-gine on the Great Western; we got two railroads now. **1914** *DN* 4.104 **KS,** Bullgine [ˈbulˌjaɪn]. **1942** (1965) Parrish *Slave Songs* 202 **GA,** He remembers another fragment which runs like this: "Clear the track an' let the bullgine back." **1945** Hubbard *Railroad Ave.* 335, *Bullgine*—Steam locomotive. **1962** *AmSp* 37.132 **nCA** [Logging railroad language], *Bulgine* [ˈbʌldʒɪn] . . . A locomotive. **1968** Adams *Western Words* 42.

bull-goaded adj
See quot 1976.
> **1964** Faulkner *Hamlet* 143 **MS,** He stood against the desk, huge, bull-goaded, impotent and outraged. **1976** Brown *Gloss. Faulkner* 40 **MS,** *Bull-goaded* . . extremely pestered or irritated, as by a bull (ox) goad.

bull goose n, also attrib [*EDD Suppl.* *bull-goose* a gander]
1 =**double-crested cormorant.**
> **1955** *AmSp* 30.177 **IL,** Bull goose—Double-crested cormorant.

2 A leader, boss.
> **1932** *Sun* (Baltimore MD) 24 Aug 15/3 **nOH,** When Cleveland firemen speak of James E. Granger, the fire chief, they do not say "the chief," "the old man" or "the boss." He is known as the "bull goose," a name he himself attached to the chief before him because a bull goose keeps all the other geese in line and enforces discipline. **1953** Randolph *Down in Holler* 231 **Ozarks,** Bull goose . . . The leader, the boss, the head man. A native of Springfield, Mo., said to me: "Old Foster is the *bull goose* out at the Army Hospital," meaning that Colonel Foster was the commandant. **1962** Kesey *One Flew Over* 18 **OR,** Which one of you claims to be the craziest? Which one is the biggest loony? . . . Who's the bull goose loony here? *Ibid* 19, I been a bull goose catskinner for every gyppo logging operation in the Northwest and bull goose gambler all the way from Korea, was even bull goose pea weeder on that pea farm at Pendleton—so I figure if I'm bound to be a loony, then I'm bound to be a stompdown dadgum good one.

bull grape n [Prob alter of **bullet grape** or **bullace 2**]
Either the **frost grape** or the **muscadine grape.**
> **1880** [see **bullet grape**]. **1893** *Jrl. Amer. Folkl.* 6.139 **AL,** *Vitis vulpina,*

bull grape. **1900** Lyons *Plant Names* 394, *V[itis] vulpina* . . . Bull Grape. **1960** Vines *Trees SW* 727, *Muscadine Grape — Vitis rotundifolia* . . . Vernacular names are . . . Bull Grape. **1960** Williams *Walk Egypt* 224 **GA**, It was only two tree stumps covered with a bull-grape vine. **1966–70** *DARE* (Qu. I46) Infs **SC**4, 9, 70, (Wild) bull grape(s). **1975** *Foxfire 3* 316 **nGA**, *Chicken grape (Vitis vulpina)* (possum grape, river grape, winter grape, frost grape, bull grape).

bullgrass n

1 A grass of the genus *Paspalum*: rarely *P. plicatulum*, usu *P. boscianum* which is also called **redshank grass, water grass. chiefly Sth, S Midl**

   1894 *Jrl. Amer. Folkl.* 7.104, *Paspalum undulatum* . . bull-grass, Ala. **1933** *Torreya* 33.82, *Paspalum boscianum* . . . Bull grass. **1965–70** *DARE* (Qu. L8) Inf **NC**24, Bullgrass hay; (Qu. L9a) Inf **TN**53, Bullgrass; (Qu. S8) Inf **GA**5, Bullgrass; (Qu. S9) Infs **AR**10, **GA**7, **LA**25, **NC**24, **TX**37, Bullgrass.

2 A **cordgrass** (here: *Spartina patens*).

   1910 Graves *Flowering Plants* 68 **CT**, *Spartina Michauxiana* [now *S. patens*] . . . Bull Grass.

3 See quot.

   1940–41 Cassidy *WI Atlas* **cwWI**, Bull grass — a type of grass growing on low wet land; bulrushes.

4 also *bull muhly:* A **muhly grass** (here: *Muhlenbergia emersleyi*).

   1950 Hitchcock *Manual Grasses* 410, *Muhlenbergia emersleyi* . . . *Bullgrass* . . . A good soil binder on steep slopes. **1960** Correll *Plants TX* 232, *Bull muhly* . . . Rocky grassy slopes in the Trans-Pecos. **1970** in 1983 *Carleton Coll.*, Bull grass = *Muhlenbergia emersleyi.* Texas.

bull gravy n Cf **bull fuck**

   1949 *PADS* 11.4 **wTX**, *Bull gravy* . . . Cream gravy. Vulgar.

bull-grinder n

A wooden toy that cranks two blocks back and forth in crossed grooves.

   1980 *Foxfire 6* 162 **nGA**, *Bull Grinder* . . . The Ozark bull grinder was something people say started in the Ozarks. Of course, bull grinders ain't the only name it had. I've heard them called do nothings and smoke grinders . . . It's a little toy that's good for absolutely nothing except for passifying [sic] oneself with something to do other than twiddling his thumbs. **1983** *NADS Letters* **Austin TX**, In engineering schools "bull-grinders" were turned out by students who had to demonstrate lathe-work and milling techniques since the trammel requires a dovetail assembly for base and rod. They can be easily made of wood and become a novelty for sale at crafts fairs.

bullgrip n [See quot 1931] Cf **bullbrier**

A greenbrier.

   1920 *Torreya* 20.19 **SC**, *Smilax* spp. — Bull-grip. **1931** Clute *Common Plants* 97, Horse-brier and bull-grip (*Smilax rotundifolia*) are reserved for a kind of smilax whose power to stop and hold the unwary traveller is well known.

bull grouse n

=**dusky grouse**.

   1955 *AmSp* 30.177 **OR**, Bull grouse — Dusky grouse.

bullhead n

1 Any of var fish with notably large heads, spec:

a A fish of the family Cottidæ, esp the **mottled sculpin** and **cabezon**.

   1814 in 1825 *Lit. & Philos. Soc. NY Trans.* 380, *Eighteen-spined Bullhead. (Cottus octodecim-spinosus.)* **1882** *U.S. Natl. Museum Bulletin* 16.696, U[ranidea] *richardsoni* . . . *Bull-head.* **1887** Goode *Amer. Fishes* 302, In the lakes and streams of the Northern States are numerous species of *Uranidea* and allied genera . . also called "Bull-heads". **1939** Natl. Geog. Soc. *Fishes* 241, *Cabezone (Scorpænichthys marmoratus)* . . . The . . cabezone, also known as the blue cod and bullhead, is one of the commonest of the shallow-water sculpins, family Cottidæ, found along the western coast of the United States. *Ibid* 279, Squawfish . . are gourmands, feeding on such fishes as are convenient, including bullheads, *Cottus*. **1946** LaMonte *N. Amer. Game Fishes* 87, *Cabezone Scorpænichthys marmoratus* . . . Bullhead. **1968–69** *DARE* (Qu. P4) Infs **CA**31, 36, 111, 168, Bullhead(s); (Qu. P2) Inf **CA**105, Ocean bullhead — same as capizonia [sic]; fish off rocks for them.

b also *bullhead cat(fish), bullshead:* A fish of the family Ictaluri-

dae. **chiefly Nth** See Map See also **brown bullhead, flat ~, yellow ~, horned pout**

   1887 Goode *Amer. Fishes* 378, *Ameiurus nebulosus* . . . "Bull-head." **1896** U.S. Natl. Museum *Bulletin* 47.140, *Ameiurus nebulosus* . . . Common Bullhead. **1946** *Richmond Times – Dispatch* 17 Mar Sec II 6-B/2 *(Hench Coll.),* Many different breeds of catfish range the United States, but the three principal varieties here [Toano, Va] are known by the names of "channel" or "willow" cat, . . "bullhead," a variety tasty as the best, but darker and with a tremendous head. **1954** *KS Acad. Sci. Trans.* 57.178, *Bullhead Catfish.* — Although no young-of-the-year bullheads were collected in this sample . . . the growth of this species in Fall River Reservoir is near the average for lakes of Oklahoma . . . Average size . . of 13 Fall River bullhead catfish [etc]. **1963** *Progress* (Charlottesville VA) 6 July 13/2-3 *(Hench Coll.),* "Well, it depends on who is talking. It is most likely to be a bull head or a flat head cat fish." He said that . . there are four kinds of bull heads in Virginia, called by dozens of names . . all bull heads . . . So it is only practical to say that bull heads collectively are one kind of catfish found in our waters. **1965–70** *DARE* (Qu. P1) 125 Infs, **chiefly Nth**, Bullhead(s); **KY**84, Bullhead cat; (Qu. P3) 26 Infs, **Inland Nth**, Bullhead(s); **OH**3, Bullshead; (Qu. P2) Inf **CA**23, Bullhead or ocean catfish; **CA**31, Bullheads; (Qu. P7) Infs **FL**32, **NJ**16, 17, **PA**121, Bullhead; **NJ**39, Bullhead minnows; (Qu. P14) Infs **IL**4, **IA**14, **MN**12, 35, 42, Bullhead(s). **1967–68** *DARE* Tape **LA**5, [Between bullhead and mud cat,] the bullhead gets the biggest . . . Around here on the average twelve pound 'bout the biggest that I've knowed of 'em to be caught around here; **IN**36, Bullheads. **1975** Evanoff *Catch More Fish* 94, Then there are the bullheads or horned pouts . . . There are three kinds: the black bullhead, the brown bullhead, and the yellow bullhead . . . The bullheads are found mostly in the states east of the Rockies.

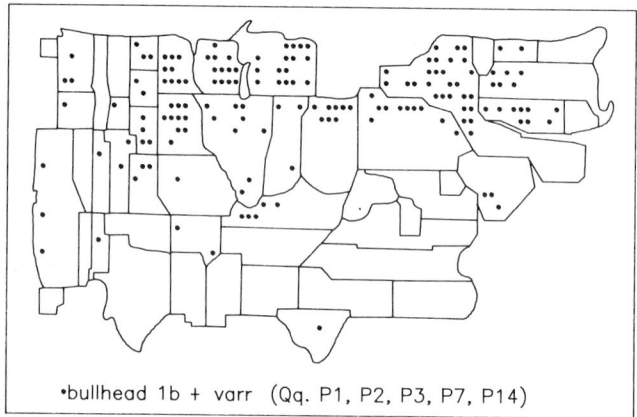

•bullhead 1b + varr (Qq. P1, P2, P3, P7, P14)

c =**mummichog**.

   1907 in 1908 *NJ State Museum Annual Rept.* 155, *Fundulus heteroclitus* . . . Killifish . . . Called "dabbler" and "bull-head."

2 Any of var birds with notably large heads:

a also *bullhead plover;* Either of two plovers: the **black-bellied plover** or the **golden plover**.

   1856 in 1861 *Spirit of Times* 27 Sept 51/3, We didn't get a shot at those bull-heads after all. **1888** Trumbull *Names of Birds* 190, *Charadrius squatarola* . . . *Black-Bellied Plover* . . . On Long Island at Shinnecock Bay, and in New Jersey at Manasquan, Tuckerton, Atlantic City, Somers Point, Cape May C.H., and Cape May City, *Bull-Head. Ibid* 195, *Charadrius dominicus* . . . *American Golden Plover* . . . Bull-Head. **1888** (1890) Warren *Birds PA* 97, Bullhead plover. *Ibid* 98, [Footnote:] The name Bull-head is given to both the Golden and Black-bellied Plovers. *Ibid* 99, My informant states . . that he had always been told, when a boy, that "Bull-heads" were abundant every year. **1892** *Auk* 9.144 **MA**, The young birds [=black-bellied plover], commonly called Beetle-heads, Chuckle-heads, or Bull-heads, have the entire upper parts brownish grey-black covered with irregular spots of white and pale yellow. **1954** Sprunt *FL Bird Life* 164, Black-Bellied Plover: *Squatarola squatarola* — Local Names: . . Bull-head. **1955** *MA Audubon* 39.445, Bull-head (Mass. . .); Bull-head Plover (Conn.).

b =**goldeneye**.

   1888 Trumbull *Names of Birds* 79, *Glaucionetta clangula americana* . . . At Havre de Grace, Md., *Bull-head.* **1923** U.S. Dept. Ag. *Misc. Circular* 13.22, *Goldeneye (Glaucionetta clangula)* . . . bullhead (Md.). **1946** Hausman *Eastern Birds* 157, American Goldeneye . . . Other Names . . . Bullhead. **1970** *DARE* (Qu. Q5) Inf **VA**47, Bullhead.

c Any of three similar ducks: the **greater scaup, lesser scaup,** or the **ring-necked duck.**

 1923 U.S. Dept. Ag. *Misc. Circular* 13.18, *Scaup Ducks . . . Collective Vernacular Names . . . In local use . . .* Bullheads (Fla., Ala.). **1932** Howell *FL Bird Life* 145, *Ring-necked duck: Nyróca colláris . . .* Other Names: . . Bullhead. **1949** Sprunt–Chamberlain *SC Bird Life* 131. **1954** Sprunt *FL Bird Life* 79, Lesser Scaup Duck: *Aythya affinis . . .* Local Names: . . Bullhead. **1955** *AmSp* 30.176 **GA,** The ring-necked duck is . . also . . named *bullhead.* **1962** Imhof *AL Birds* 149, Greater Scaup *Aythya marila . . .* Other names: . . Bullhead.

d =**solitary sandpiper.**

 1931 Read *LA French* 6, Solitary Sandpiper, or Bull Head *(Helodramas solitarius solitarius).*

3 also *bullhead clam:* A freshwater mussel *(Plethobasis cyphus).*

 1931–33 LANE Worksheets **seRI,** Bullheads [old clams] don't bring such a good price. **1961** *W3,* Bullhead . . . also *bullhead clam.*

4 A prickly seed, esp **puncture vine.**

 1967–68 *DARE* (Qu. S14) Infs **AZ**9, **TX**26, 54, Bullheads; **KS**1, Mexican sand burrs—other people call them bullheads; (Qu. S13) Inf **OR**13, Bullheads; (Qu. S15) Inf **TX**36, Bullheads. **1969** *DARE* File **AZ,** *Bullhead;* a sticktight *(Bidens* sp.)—from the two horns. **1982** *NADS Letters* **neOK,** The plant whose seed pod is . . known as *bullhead . . is Tribulus terrestris,* Calthrop family. The common name given for it in the *Audubon Society Field Guide to North American Wildflowers* is puncureweed. This term . . seemed to be in frequent use here while I was growing up, during the 50's, it now seems to be used much less often.

5 A snake, perh a **bull snake.**

 1966 *DARE* (Qu. P25) Inf **WA**6, Bullhead.

6 See **ballhead.**

7 See **buffalo n B2.**

8 A cloud that forms before a storm.

 1968–69 *DARE* (Qu. B9, . . *The big clouds that roll up high before a rainstorm)* Inf **DE**4, Bullheads—these are the little clouds with tails on them; they mean a storm; **KY**49, **NJ**17, Bullheads.

9 also *bullrock:* See quots. Cf **hardhead**

 1920 Thomas *KY Superstitions* 263, A "bullrock," also called a "jackrock" (a small round rock), in the ashes keeps hawks away from chickens. **1968–69** *DARE* (Qu. C25, *Other kinds of stone around here . . [round], smooth and hard)* Infs **IN**58, **OH**81, Bullhead.

bullhead buffalo n Also *bullmouth buffalo, bullnose ~*
=**bigmouth buffalo.**

 1933 LA Dept. of Conserv. *Fishes* 439, The Common Buffalofish . . has come to be known under many popular names . . . Bull Head Buffalo, Bull Nose Buffalo, Bull Mouth Buffalo.

bullhead cat(fish) See **bullhead 1b**

bullhead lily n
A **spatterdock** (here: *Nuphar luteum).*

 1891 *Jrl. Amer. Folkl.* 4.147 **NH,** Nuphar advena was *Bullhead Lily.* **1892** *Ibid* 5.91, *Nuphar advena . .* bull-head lily. **1910** Graves *Flowering Plants* 183 **CT,** Yellow Pond Lily. Spatter-dock. Frog, . . Bull-head or Horse Lily.

bullhead minnow n Cf **bullhead 1**
A minnow of the genus *Pimephales.*

 1960 Amer. Fisheries Soc. *List Fishes* 16, Bullhead minnow . . . *Pimephales vigilax.* **1970** WI Acad. *Trans.* 58.280, *Pimephales vigilax . . .* Bullhead minnow.

bullhead plover See **bullhead 2a**

bull-heaving n

 1966 Peden *Land* 235 **IN,** "Well," said Dick tolerantly, . . "I think maybe all this bull-heaving is unnecessary . . ." "What is bull-heaving?" I asked . . . "It is an expression of frustration," happily explained Dick. "Horses suffer from frustration the same as people. When a horse is kept stall-tied instead of standing loose or running free in the pasture, he gets bored. Sometimes he pulls back and sucks air into his stomach and roars and pumps and pulls his stomach in and out."

bullhide boat, bullhide canoe See **bullboat**

bullhide squall n

 1966 *DARE* (Qu. O19, *Different kinds or degrees of wind that are important when you're in a boat)* Inf **FL**13, Bullhide squall—a real bad one.

bull hives n pl
Large welts appearing on the skin.

 1942 in 1944 *ADD* **nWV,** The serium [serum] caused Bull Hives to break out on me, they covered my body for almost a week.

bull hole n Cf **bunny-in-the-hole, roly-hole**
In marble play: see quot.

 1969 *DARE* Tape **KY**40 [In the game of roly-hole], You'd take 'n dig you three holes in a line and then out to one side there you'd dig another hole. You'd call that the bull hole . . . And when you'd get back up to the top then if you could make it without missin' why then you could go to the bull hole, and if you hit the bull hole, why, you won the game.

bullhorn n
Prob =**unicorn plant,** but cf **beggar ticks 1.**

 1966 *DARE* (Qu. S14, *Other prickly seeds, small and flat, with two prongs at one end, that cling to clothing)* Inf **NM**13, Bullhorns.

bull-in-the-ring n

1 also *bully-in-the-ring, bull(y)-in-the-barnyard:* A children's ring game in which the player who is "it" (the *bull*) tries to break out through a circle of clasped hands. [*SND bull i' the park, ~ ring*] **scattered, but esp PA** See Map

 1883 Newell *Games & Songs* 90, In New York, a violent form of the same sport [=Here I Brew, and Here I Bake] goes by the name of "Bull in the Ring." **1901** *DN* 2.137 **cnNY,** *Bully-in-the-barnyard . . .* Name of a game; same as bull in the barnyard. **1940** Marran *Games Outdoors* 146, *Bull in the Ring,* "It" tries to break through a ring of players . . [but] "it" is allowed only to break through the clasped hands of the ring players and is not allowed to crawl under the arms or the legs of the players. The player who catches and tags "it" after he escapes from the ring becomes the "bull" for the next game. **1950** *WELS* (Names of . . ring games) 1 Inf, **WI,** Bull in the Ring. **1953** Brewster *Amer. Nonsinging Games* 171 **AZ,** Bull in the Ring. **1965–70** *DARE* (Qu. EE33, . . *Outdoor games)* 50 Infs, **scattered, but esp PA,** Bull-in-the-ring; **PA**130, Bull-in-the-ring; one tries to break out of a circle formed by others holding hands; **MN**33, Bull-in-a-ring—one in the middle that tried to break out; (Qu. EE1, *Games . . in which [children] form a ring)* Infs **DE**3, **MA**14, **PA**203, Bull-in-the-ring; **PA**22, Bully-in-the-ring.

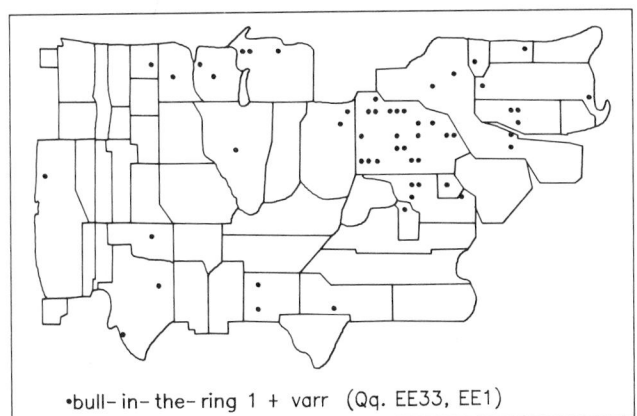

•bull- in- the- ring 1 + varr (Qq. EE33, EE1)

2 See **bullring.**

bullis, bullison See **bullace 2**

bull-jive See **jive v**

bull kelp n
A large brown seaweed of the genus *Nereocystis.*

 1982 *Modern Maturity* June–July 51 **cwCA,** But look carefully; it's easy to mistake the dark-brown floats of bull kelp for the heads of sea otters or harbor seals.

bull minnow n
Perh =**bullhead minnow.**

 1968–70 *DARE* (Qu. P7) Inf **DE**4, Bull minners; **VA**75, Bull minnows.

bull moose n

1 In logging: see quot. Cf **bull goose 2, bull of the woods 1**

 1958 McCulloch *Woods Words* 21 **Pacific NW,** *Bull moose*—a. A large anything. b. The push, or head man on a logging show.

2 A nickel, five cents. Cf **buffalo** n B2

1968 *DARE* (Qu. U22, . . *A five-cent piece*), Infs **IN**19, **MO**10, Bull moose (nickel).

bullmouth buffalo See **bullhead buffalo**

bull muhly See **bull grass 4**

bullneck n

1 Any of var **scaups**, but esp the **canvasback duck**, the **greater scaup**, the **lesser scaup**, and the **ring-necked duck**.

1709 (1967) Lawson *New Voyage* 150, Bull-Necks [=scaup]. These are a whitish fowl, about the bigness of a Brant; they come to us after Christmas, in very great flocks, in all our Rivers. **1888** Trumbull *Names of Birds* 48, *Aythya vallisneria* . . . Known to many gunners about Morehead, N.C., and on New River, Onslow Co., same state, as Bull-Neck . . and in last-named locality, as Red-Headed Bull-Neck. *Ibid* 56, *Aythya marila* . . . By others at Wilmington [N.C.], [known as] Bull-Neck. **1917** (1923) *Birds Amer.* 1.133, Canvas-back — *Marila valisineria* . . . Other Names . . . Bull-neck. **1923** U.S. Dept. Ag. *Misc. Circular* 13.21, *Ring-necked Duck [Marila collaris]* — Vernacular Names . . . In local use . . . bullneck (Fla.). **1955** *AmSp* 30.176, It [bullneck] has been given to the canvasback (N.C., Wis., Calif., . .), is the most common name for the ring-necked duck in parts of the Southeast (N.C., Ga., Fla.), and means either of the scaups in North and South Carolina. [*DARE* Ed: All are scaups.]

2 also *bull-necked teal:* **=ruddy duck.**

1888 Trumbull *Names of Birds* 111, *Erismatura rubida* . . . Commonly known at Chicago, and in the Putnam Co. portion of the Illinois River, and by some at Norfolk, Va., as Bull-Neck. **1917** (1923) *Birds Amer.* 1.152, *Ruddy Duck — Erismatura jamaicensis* . . . Other Names . . . Bull-neck. **1938** Oberholser *Bird Life LA* 141, Ruddy Duck — *Erismatura jamaicensis rubida* . . . Probably no duck has so many different names as this well-known bird. Some of those commonly heard are . . 'bullneck'. **1955** *AmSp* 30.176, [Bullneck] means . . the ruddy duck rather generally. The last-named bird is also called the *bull-necked teal* (Wis., Ill.).

3 also *bullneck goose:* **=cackling goose.**

1909 Field Mus. Nat. Hist. *Zool. Ser.* 353, *Branta canadensis minima* . . Cackling Goose . . . These birds are locally known as 'bull necks' by the sportsmen. **1923** U.S. Dept. Ag. *Misc. Circular* 13.37, *Cackling Goose (Branta canadensis minima)* . . . In local use . . . bullneck, bullneck goose (Wis.).

bull nettle n

1 A **spurge nettle. chiefly N Cent, Cent, TX, LA** See Map

1876 *Congressional Record* 18 May 3166/2 **MO**, He . . beat down the wild-brier and bull-nettle . . . felled the forest, and hewed out his humble home. **1908** *DN* 3.295 **eAL, wGA**, Bull-nettle . . . A large species of nettle. **1939** Tharp *Vegetation TX* 60, Bull-Nettle *(Jatropha)* [here: = *Cnidoscolus*]. **1944** Wellman *Bowl* 125 **KS**, A barren sandy area which lay thick-scattered with spiny bull-nettles to bring grief to bare feet. **1954** Harder *Coll.* **cwTN**, Bull nettle . . . A plant that causes itching and swelling. **1965–70** *DARE* (Qu. S17, . . *Plants . . that will cause itching and swelling*) 44 Infs, **chiefly N Cent, Cent, TX, LA**, Bull nettle(s); (Qu. S14) Inf **CO**20, Bull nettle; (Qu. S15) Infs **AR**41, **IL**25, Bull nettle; (Qu. S21) Infs **IL**19, 80, 126, 143, **IN**49, **LA**17, **MO**32, **TX**104, Bull nettle(s); (Qu. S26a) Inf **TX**84, Bull nettle. [Note: some of these Infs may refer instead to sense **2.**] **1970** Correll *Plants TX* 954, *Cnidoscolus texanus* . . . Bull nettle. **1972** Brown *Wildflowers LA* 100, Bull Nettle — *Cnidoscolus stimulosus*.

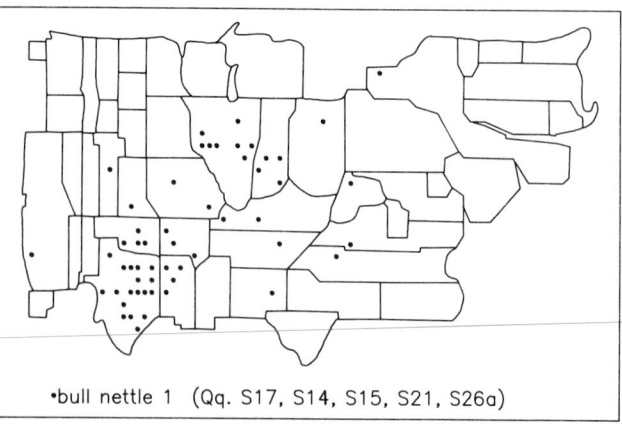

•bull nettle 1 (Qq. S17, S14, S15, S21, S26a)

2 Either of two **nightshades** (*Solanum carolinense* or *S. elæagnifolium*).

1894 *Jrl. Amer. Folkl.* 7.95, *Solanum Carolinense* . . bull-nettle, Perrysville, Ind. **1941** *Torreya* 41.51, *Solanum eleagnifolium* . . . Bull-nettle, Missouri. **1967** *S. Folkl. Qrly.* 31.300 **csKY**, Even youngsters with almost perfect skin seem bent on achieving perfection . . . Instead of ordinary face powder, try powdered dirt-dobber nests, or bull-nettle tea. **1970** Correll *Plants TX* 1396, *Solanum elæagnifolium* . . . Bull-nettle. **1971** Krochmal *Appalachia Med. Plants* 236, *Solanum Carolinense* L. — (Solanaceae) — Common names: . . bull nettle. **1974** (1977) Coon *Useful Plants* 251, *Solanum carolinense* . . bull nettle.

bullnose n **Delmarva**

A quahog too old for use.

1881 Ingersoll *Oyster-Industry* 242, Bull-Nose. An old, overgrown, heavy quahaug, unfit for food. (Cape May.) **1894** *DN* 1.329 **csNJ**, Bull nose: a useless hard clam. **1911** *Century Dict.*, Bullnose . . . An overgrown hard clam or quahaug, *Mercenaria*, too coarse for use. [Chesapeake Bay.]

bullnose (bell) See **bullnose pepper**

bullnose buffalo See **bullhead buffalo**

bullnose pepper n Also *bellnose (pepper), bullnose (bell), bull pepper* [*EDD* bull-nosed flattened] **chiefly NEast, Sth, S Midl** See Map

A large green pepper with a blunt or flattened end.

1859 IL State Ag. Soc. *Trans. for 1857–58* 3.508, The squash, the bull nose, the sweet mountain and sweet Spanish are [good varieties of peppers] for pickling. **1950** *WELS (What do you call large, hot peppers?)* 1 Inf, **csWI**, Bullnose peppers. **1965–70** *DARE* (Qq. I22b, d, *Names for different kinds of peppers*) 30 Infs, **chiefly Atlantic, Sth**, Bullnose peppers; **DE**3, Bullnose pepper — may be either sweet or hot. Name refers to shape; **CT**2, Bullnose pepper — the kind you stuff; **CT**4, Hot bullnose peppers; **MA**74, Bullnose — good to stuff; **TX**54, Bullnose bell; **MO**34, **TX**105, Bellnose (pepper); **NY**36, **PA**245, Bull pepper.

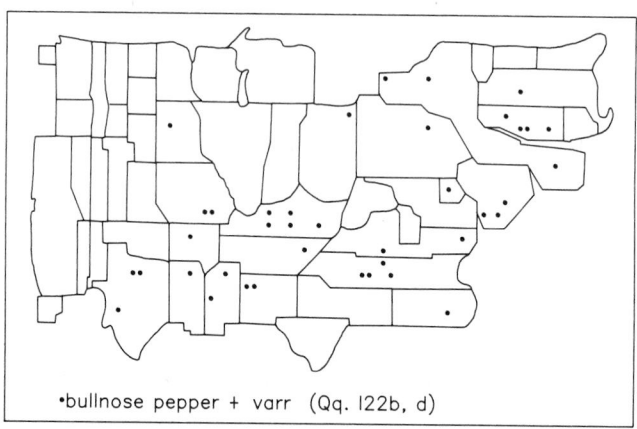

•bullnose pepper + varr (Qq. I22b, d)

bullnut n Also *bullnut hickory, pullnut*
=mockernut hickory.

1859 (1968) Bartlett *Americanisms*, Bull-nut. A large kind of hickory-nut. **1884** Sargent *Forests of N. Amer.* 134, *Carya tomentosa* . . . Mocker Nut. Black Hickory. Bull Nut. **1898** *Bot. Gaz.* 26.254, *Carya tomentosa*, . . pull-nut, mocker-nut, Sulphur Grove, Ohio. **1960** Vines *Trees SW* 132, Mockernut Hickory . . . Vernacular names are . . Bigbud Hickory, Bullnut Hickory, and Fragrant Hickory. **1968–70** *DARE* (Qu. I43) Infs **IL**142, **NJ**50, Bullnuts; (Qu. T16) Inf **IL**104, Bullnuts.

bull of the woods n Also *bull*

1 A foreman or boss esp in a logging camp. **chiefly Nth, Pacific NW**

1872 Schele de Vere *Americanisms* 250, Sumner [was known] as the *Bull of the Woods.* **1925** *AmSp* 1.136 **Pacific NW** [Logger talk], "Little Bull," "Big Bull," "Baldy the Bull," and the like are common nicknames for camp foremen. **1930** *DN* 6.86 **cWV**, Bull, or *bull of the woods,* a bully, a "tough guy"; in some camps possibly a boss of a crew, perhaps because the "boss" has to be tougher than his men, in order to control them. **1946** Peattie *Pacific Coast* 233, The bullwhacker yielded precedence only to the big boss of all the works, the "bull of the woods" as he was called on the Saginaw [in MI]. For a brief period he carried this title in our Northwest. **1959** *AmSp* 34.77 **nCA**, Bull of the woods. **1966**

DARE Tape **MI**10, The camp foreman in the area according to whatever status he happened to have was either the strawboss or the bull of the woods or the push. **1967–70** *DARE* (Qu. HH43a, *The top person in charge of a group of workmen, the* _____) Infs **AZ**6, **CA**106, 197, **NY**92, **WA**20, Bull of the woods; **CA**145, Bull; (Qu. HH43b, *The assistant*) Inf **OH**89, Shop bull. **1968** *AmSp* 43.286 [Railroading], *Bull of the woods*. The roundhouse or car shop foreman.

2 By ext: one who is, or thinks he is, an important person. **chiefly Sth, S Midl, Pacific** See Map

1894 in 1950 *PADS* 13.12 **AL**, In those days Blev Scroggins wore the bell and called himself bull of the woods. **1945** *AmSp* 20.234 **MN** [College slang], *Bull of the woods*. Big shot, important person. **1965–70** *DARE* (Qu. HH17, *A person who tries to appear important, or who tries to lay down the law in his community: "He'd like to be the* _____ *around here."*) 12 Infs, **chiefly Sth, S Midl**, Bull of the woods; **IL**96, Big bull; **CA**81, Bull of the community; **TX**36, Bull of the town; **TX**18, Uncut bull; (Qu. GG19b, *When you can see from the way a person acts that he's feeling important or independent: "He seems to think he's* _____."*) 13 Infs, **chiefly Pacific, Sth**, Bull of the woods; **OH**81, Bull.

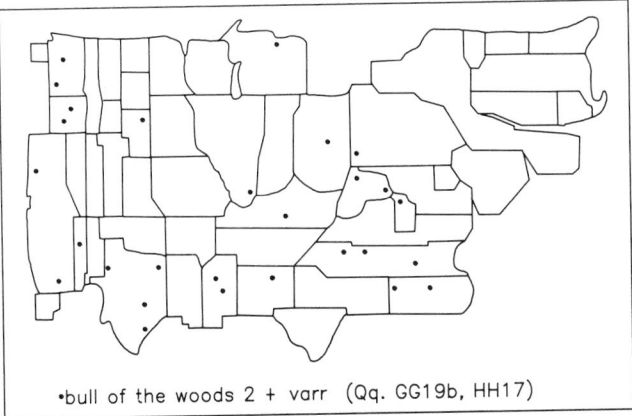

•bull of the woods 2 + varr (Qq. GG19b, HH17)

bull onion n [Cf *EDD Suppl.* *bull-neck* an onion that does not form a bulb but grows somewhat like a leek]
?A thick-necked onion; also used in phr *bull onions and Irish potatoes* a buildup of storm clouds.

1969 *DARE* (Qu. I6, *The kind of onions that come up fresh early in the year, and you eat them raw*) Inf **NC**68, Bull onions, salad onions. **1969** *DARE* FW Addit **Outer Banks NC**, It's coming up bull onions and Irish potatoes [storm clouds].

bullox v [Folk-etym for **bollix**]
1949 *AmSp* 24.152 **nwIA** (as of c1910), *Bullox* . . means to confuse, mess, or disarrange things . . . I always thought it meant literally the clumsiness of a bull or ox and that . . it had been jammed together into one word.

bull paddock n Also *bull pad, bull paddy* [*bull* + **paddock**] **NEng**
=bullfrog 1.
1886 in 1890 *DN* 1.73, In New England "bull-paddock" is a popular synonym for bull-frog. **1890** *DN* 1.72, *Bull-frog, bull-paddy,* and *bull-paddock* are familiar on Cape Cod . . *bull-pad* [has been heard] near Boston. **1892** *DN* 1.213 **ceMA**, *Bull-frog* and *bull-paddy.* **1907** *DN* 3.182 **seNH**, The bull-paddock goes "paddy got dhrunk, paddy got dhrunk." **1939** *LANE* Map 231 **scattered, but esp NH, eMA**, Bull paddock; 3 infs, Bull paddy; 1 inf, *Bull paddock,* older term, formerly very common. **1941** *Nature Mag.* 34.138, Bullfrog . . . In the Northeast, most of the names applied to this species contained in part or in entirety the term paddock, a Scottish and Old English word for frog. Thus bull-paddock and bull-paddy are recorded as used on Cape Cod, and bull-pad at Boston, Massachusetts. These designations seem to have had somewhat wider usage, as they are also rather indefinitely ascribed to New England. **1969** *DARE* (Qu. P22) Inf **MA**68, Bull paddock.

bull peep n [*bull* + *peep* sandpiper]
1 **=white-rumped sandpiper.**
1917 (1923) *Birds Amer.* 1.234, *White-rumped Sandpiper—Pisobia fuscicollis* . . . Bull Peep. **1925** (1928) Forbush *Birds MA* 1.410, *Pisobia bairdi* . . . Baird's Sandpiper . . . Bull-Peep. *Ibid* 408, *Pisobia fuscicollis* . . . *White-rumped Sandpiper* . . . Bull-peep. **1946** Hausman *Eastern*

Birds 279, *White-rumped sandpiper Pisobia fuscicollis* . . . Bull Peep. **1955** *AmSp* 30.177 **MA**, Bull peep—Semipalmated plover, White-rumped sandpiper, Baird's sandpiper, Sanderling.

2 **=sanderling.**
1917 (1923) *Birds Amer.* 1.239, *Sanderling—Calidris leucophæa* . . . Bull Peep. **1917** *Wilson Bulletin* 29.2.79, *Calidris leucophæa* . . . bull-peep, Cape Cod, Mass. **1925** (1928) Forbush *Birds MA* 1.423, *Crocethia alba* . . . *Sanderling* . . . Bull Peep. **1946** Hausman *Eastern Birds* 291, *Sanderling Crocethia alba* . . . Bull peep. **1955** [see **1** above].

bullpen n Also *bull-in-the-pen* **chiefly Midl** *old-fash* Also called **old soak**
A children's ball game: see quot 1980.
1857 *Spirit of Times* 19 Dec 241/1 **GA** (as of 1827), About twenty boys and girls were assembled, . . some . . conning their lessons, and some playing—the boys at bull-pen, the girls at jumping the rope. **1897** (1952) McGill *Narrative* 32, The game "Bull Pen" was very exciting, not only to see the bulls drop flat on the ground to dodge the ball, but to see the last one on the line run the lines and through the pen to get a near shot from any part of the line. **1915** *DN* 4.181 **swVA**, *Bull pen.* **1935** Davis *Honey* 92 **OR**, As long as nobody caught or crowded them, dodging people was a game, like bull-pen or wounded soldier, only a good deal more gratifying to be ahead in. **1940** Kennedy *Schoolmaster* 225 **IN**, In my boyhood we were still playing the games of my father's and grandfather's time—Anty-over, Bull Pen, Old Sow Out. **c1960** *Wilson Coll.* **csKY**, Bull-pen. **1966–69** *DARE* (Qu. EE2, *Games that have one extra player—when a signal is given, the players change places, and the extra one tries to get a place*) Inf **NC**77, Bull-in-the-pen—one inside the ring and a ball you'd throw; (Qu. EE11, *Bat-and-ball games for just a few players [When there aren't enough for a regular game]*) Inf **KY**41, Bull-pen; (Qu. EE33, . . *Outdoor games*) Infs **AR**39, **KY**6, Bullpen; **KY**24, Bullpen—[In a] ring of people "it" threw a ball at one, if he hit one, he was "it"; **SC**19, Bullpen; **TN**12, Bullpen (with a ball)—[Four players stand at corners of a square] throw ball, try to hit [four] children in center. [6 of 7 Infs old] **1966** *DARE* Tape **AL**4, Bullpen ['bʊlpɛn] . . Put everybody in a pen; throw ball at them; player hit had to come out—and was out of the game. **1980** *Foxfire* 6 278 **nGA**, Bullpen . . . The object of the game is to get all the men out on one team by hitting each one of them with the ball. One team of four players mans the bases, and the other players get in the center or in the bullpen.

bull pepper See **bullnose pepper**

bull pine n
1 Any of var pines as:
a Any of four pines native chiefly to California: **bishop pine, Coulter pine, Digger pine, Monterey pine.**
1884 Sargent *Forests of N. Amer.* 195, *Pinus Sabiniana* . . . Bull Pine. **1898** *Jrl. Amer. Folkl.* 11.280, *Pinus Sabiniana* . . bull pine, digger pine, Cal. **1910** Jepson *Silva CA* 99, Bishop Pine . . . is often called . . . "Bull Pine," a slur name of the logging men because they hold it as next to useless for lumber. **1967–70** *DARE* (Qu. T17) Infs **CA**24, 36, 101, 120, 137, 144, Bull pine(s); **CA**31, Bull pine—Monterey pine; **CA**62, Bull pine—in mountains; **CA**87, Bull pine—or Coulter pine; **CA**105, Bull pine—same as bishop or Monterey pine.

b Any of several more widely distributed western pines as **Jeffrey pine, limber pine, lodgepole pine** or **ponderosa pine.**
1884 Sargent *Forests of N. Amer.* 193, *Pinus Jeffreyi* . . . Bull Pine . . . *Pinus ponderosa* . . . Bull Pine. **1897** Sudworth *Arborescent Flora* 16, *Pinus flexilis* . . . Bull Pine (Colo.). *Ibid* 20, *Pinus ponderosa* . . . Bull Pine (Cal., Wash., Utah, Idaho, Oreg.). *Ibid* 22, *Pinus jeffreyi* . . . Bull Pine (Cal.). **1952** Peattie *Black Hills* 23 **SD**, Ponderosas . . have had several aliases—rock pine, bull pine, western yellow pine. **1966–69** *DARE* (Qu. T17) Inf **AK**1, Bull pine = lodgepole pine; **CA**130, Bull pine—same as jack pine; **CA**208, Bull pine—same as Jeffrey; **ID**4, Bull pine—Ponderosa, I think; **ID**5, Bull pine—ponderosa; **KS**6, Bull pine—not native; **MT**4, **NE**3, **OR**1, **SD**3, **WA**3, 8, Bull pine.

c also *bull-dick pine:* Any of three pines native chiefly to the eastern half of the US: **loblolly pine 1** (here: *Pinus taeda*), **shortleaf pine 1** (here: *P. echinata*), or **pond pine** (here: *P. serotina*).
1891 (1894) Coulter *Botany W. TX* 3.554, *Pinus mitis,* . . *'Bull pine.'* **1897** Sudworth *Arborescent Flora* 26, *Pinus taeda* . . . Bull Pine (Texas and Gulf region). *Ibid* 29, *Pinus echinata* . . . Bull Pine (Va.). **1901** Lounsberry *S. Wild Flowers* 2, Bull Pine.—*Pinus echinata.* **1908** Britton *N. Amer. Trees* 31, *Pond Pine—Pinus serotina* . . . is also known as . . . Bull Pine . . and Spruce Pine. **1950** Moore *Trees AR* 17, *Pinus*

taeda . . . Like the shortleaf pine, when it grows in open situations it remains very limby and short and is called "bull pine." **1950** Peattie *Nat. Hist. Trees* 24, *Pinus taeda* . . . Other Names: . . Bull Pine. **1960** Vines *Trees SW* 25, *Pinus echinata* . . . Vernacular names are . . . Bull Pine. **1966–70** *DARE* (Qu. T5) Inf **AR**24, Bull pine; (Qu. T17) Infs **MD**43, **NJ**21, 52, **VA**26, 27, 43, Bull pine; **LA**18, Bull pine—same as hill pine, field pine, or shortleaf; **MD**9, Bull pine—also called scrub; **MD**32, Bull pine—wood no good for furniture; **MD**42, Bull pine—same as cabbage pine; **TX**51, Bull pine—same as shortleaf; **VA**24, Bull pine—pitch pine; **WV**4, Bull pine native; others are set out; **TN**14, Bull-dick pine—Same as scrub pine.

d Other pines not specifically identified.

1967–69 *DARE* (Qu. T17) Inf **CT**17, Bull pine—sappy, used mostly for kindling; **NH**16, Bull pine; **PA**29, Bull pine—not big, scrubby.

2 also *bull sap(ling)*: A scrub pine or similar tree that does not furnish high quality timber.

1902 White *Blazed Trail* 59 **MI**, Thorpe found himself waist-deep in the pitchy aromatic top of an old bull-sap, clipping away at the projecting branches. **1956** Rayford *Whistlin' Woman* 223 **swAL**, In those days, you could find a perfect mast most anywhere in the woods, but, nowadays, you're lucky to find a bull sapling. **1970** *DARE* (Qu. T17) Inf **CA**195, Bull pine—slang for second growth timber. **1975** Gould *ME Lingo* 27, *Bull pine*—A pasture pine; i.e., one that grows in open country and thus doesn't shoot up straight and tall like a forest tree. A *bull pine* has big limbs close to the ground and won't make good boards. It will go for pulp.

bull pipes n

A **horsetail** (here: *Equisetum arvense*).

1974 (1977) Coon *Useful Plants* 131, *Equisetum arvense*—Scouring rush . . bull pipes.

bull plover n [See quot 1955]

=**black-bellied plover.**

1844 DeKay *Zool. NY* 2.215, The large *Whistling Plover,* or *Bull and Beetle-head Plover* as it is called in its autumnal dress, appears with us from the south in May. **1955** *MA Audubon* 39.445, *Black-bellied Plover* . . . Bull Plover (Conn. It is the largest of New England plovers.).

bullpluck n

=**bullhead 1b.**

1967 *DARE* (Qu. P1) Inf **NY**10, Bullpluck.

bullpout n

=**bullhead 1b.**

1823 Cooper *Pioneers* 2.55 **cNY**, Bull-pouts, salmon-trouts, and suckers. **1887** (1895) Robinson *Uncle Lisha* 184 **wVT**, Antoine . . having dug some worms, and borrowed a pole and line of a compatriot, went fishing for bullpouts. **1911** *Century Dict.,* Bullpout . . . A siluroid fish, especially *Amiurus nebulosus,* of the eastern and middle United States: more widely known as *catfish.* Also called *horned pout* and *bullhead.* **1931–33** LANE *Worksheets* seRI, Bullpout . . . catfish; cnRI, Bullpouts. **1975** Gould *ME Lingo* 27, *Bullhead*—Maine word for our only fresh water catfish, the hornpout. Sometimes "bullpout." Their barbels give them an ugly look, but they are good panfish—although not esteemed by trout-loving Mainers.

bull-proof See bull-strong

bullpuncher n Also *bull teamster*

1 =**bullwhacker.**

1874 *Chambers's Jrl.* 51.543/2, Commissariat beeves, guarded by the commissariat 'bull-punchers'. **1887** Roberts *W. Avernus* 19 **TX**, He followed the profession of a 'bull-puncher,' that is, he went in charge of the cattle destined for slaughter and canning in the distant North. **1893** *Scribner's Mag.* 13.711/2, A young "bull-puncher" in a Wisconsin logging camp became in middle life Congressman, then United States Senator. **1949** Peattie *Cascades* 145 **wOR** (as of early 20th cent), John Larrity, the bullpuncher, and his second man were heaving the turn of logs together by the power of screwjacks. *Ibid* 159, The tractor-puncher —heir of the bullpuncher and donkey-puncher—could yard timber down any old mountainside. **1958** McCulloch *Woods Words* 22 **Pacific NW**, *Bull puncher*—A man who drove ox teams in the early days when logging was done with bulls . . . *Bull teamster*—Same as bull puncher. **1966** *PADS* 46.24 **cnAR**. **1967** *DARE* FW Addit **LA**2, Bullpuncher—a man that drives oxen.

2 also *bullpunch:* An ox goad.

1940–41 Cassidy *WI Atlas,* 1 Inf, Bull punch—[an] ox goad; 1 Inf, Bull-puncher—ox goad.

bull quartz n

Massive quartz, lacking the more usual crystalline structure.

1897 *Land of Sunshine* 6.170 **sCA**, Great dykes of porphyry, mica schist and "bull quartz" are here in evidence, running from north to south. **1966** *DARE* (Qu. C26) Inf **NM**11, Bull quartz. **1983** *Rock & Gem* Dec 40, It's amazing how gold can weave itself through cracks and crevices in bull quartz.

bull rail n Also *bull*

Either of two birds: the **king rail 1** or the **Virginia rail.**

1955 *AmSp* 30.177, Why . . the little Virginia rail . . [is called] *bull* and *bull rail* (La., Texas) is quite beyond me. *Ibid* **WI**, Bull rail—King rail.

bull rake n chiefly Nth, Midl *old-fash*

A heavy wide hand rake used for gathering hay; occas a wheeled implement.

1895 *DN* 1.396 **cNY**, Bull rake; very heavy hand rake. **1907** *DN* 3.183 **seNH**, Bull-rake . . . The largest kind of hand hay-rake . . . Rare. **1909** *DN* 3.409 **cnME**, Bull rake . . . A large hand rake similar to a horse rake. **1913** *DN* 4.55 Cape Cod **MA**, Bull-rake . . . A large drag-rake, drawn by hand. **1949** *PADS* 11.18 **CO**, Bull rake . . . A swivel-wheeled implement for hay harvest. **1954** *Harder Coll.* **cwTN**. **1965–70** *DARE* (Qu. L16) Infs **CO**7, **IN**63, **MA**25, **MO**20, 27, 38, **OK**52, Bull rake; **MO**3, We used to use bull rakes when we stacked it [=hay]; **MA**5, Bull rake—used to rake scatterings; **MA**42, [A] big hand rake, six foot wide; [a] bull rake rakes up scatterings from loading it on [a] rack; **UT**3, Bull rake, mowing machines, rakes; **WY**1, Used to use slide stacker, bull rake or sweep. **1969** *DARE* Tape **CT**29, The bull rake doesn't mean that it's propelled by a bull, it means that it's bull work, [that] makes it a bull rake . . . The bull rake is simply a large hand rake that . . was used to get into areas where it wasn't possible to get with the horse rake. **1969** *DARE* FW Addit **neCT**, A bull rake [is] a five foot wide rake pulled by hand in places the horse rake wouldn't fit.

bull rattle n Cf cow rattle

Either of two related plants: **bladder campion** or **white campion 1.**

1900 Lyons *Plant Names* 231, *L[ychnis] alba* . . . Evening-blooming Lychnis, Bull-rattle. *Ibid* 345, *S[ilene] vulgaris* . . . Bladder Campion, Behen, Bull-rattle. **1910** Graves *Flowering Plants* 178 **CT**, *Lychnis alba* . . . Bull-rattle. Roadsides, fields, and waste places. **1923** W.N. Clute *Amer. Plant Names* 63 *(DA),* Bladder Campion.—Cow-paps, cow-bell, bull-rattle. **1959** Carleton *Index Herb. Plants* 20, Bull Rattle: Lynchis [sic] alba; Silene latifolia.

bull redfish n Also *bull red* esp **LA**

=**red drum.**

1898 U.S. Natl. Museum *Bulletin* 16.1453, *Scienops ocellatus* . . . Bull Red-Fish. **1933** LA Dept. of Conserv. *Fishes* 175, The fishermen believe that the schools of these "bull" Redfish inhabit the bays and lagoons during the summer months. **1941** O'Donnell *The Great Big Doorstep* 51 **LA** (Hench Coll.), A bull-red gunna give you plenny fun to land. The bull is the she-male, and that's a funny thing. **1946** LaMonte *N. Amer. Game Fishes* 79, Channel Bass *Sciænops ocellatus* . . . Names . . . Bull Redfish. **1968** *DARE* (Qu. P2) Inf **LA**37, Bull red.

bullring n Also *bull, bull-in-the-ring, bull's ring* Cf **bull hole, bully** n[1]

In marble play: a game in which players try to knock marbles out of a ring; the ring itself.

1891 *DN* 1.76 **NYC, nNJ**, Words used in playing at marbles . . the large circular ring is a "bull", or "bull's ring". **1940** *Recreation* (NY) 34.110 **nOH**, A list of the many games of marbles played throughout the country . . . Bull. **1955** *PADS* 23.12 **cwTN**, Bull . . . A large round ring for playing marbles; hence bull ring. **1958** *PADS* 29.31 **OH**, Bull-ring . . . A marble game for any number of players using any number of marbles desired; the shooters try to clear the ring, keeping the marbles they knock out; if a player hits another player's marble, he collects one from him—in this respect the game differs from *keeps.* **1967–70** *DARE* (Qu. EE7) Infs **IL**130, **IA**29, **LA**43, Bullring; **AL**20, Bull-in-the-ring. **1968–69** *DARE* Tape **IA**35, One was called bullring, where they had a giant circle, maybe two feet round, and they put about five marbles apiece in this big ring . . and the one that drawed the shoot first would shoot his marble in, as many as he got outside this big ring would be his to keep; **IA**40, The marble games that have been played in Council Bluffs are ringers or bullring; **IN**83, Then there's bullring; . . each player put[s] in so many marbles and when the game is over why if you put in five you got ten . . in your pocket; **LA**46, Bullring . . everybody puts so many marbles in the ring . . and then you start to shoot from behind the ring . . and all the marbles you knock out the ring belong to you. **1969** O'Connor *Horse & Buggy West* 83 **AZ** (as of 1910), The principal one [marble game played by grade-school boys] was called Bull Ring. The ring was casually drawn on the ground and could be as large or as small as desired . . . Each player put in an agreed number of marbles in the center of the ring and he kept all he shot out of the ring legally. *Ibid* 84, The skill of the better bull-ring experts was something to contemplate with awe and wonder. **c1970** Wiersma *Marbles Terms* **csIA** (as of 1930s), *Bull-Ring.*

bull-roarer n

1 also *bull-roar:* A noisemaker consisting of a slat of wood attached to a thong and whirled in the air:

a used as a children's toy. **chiefly S Midl** Also called **buzzer n¹, dumb bull**

[**1885** *All the Year Round* 56.249/1, The "bull-roarer" is a toy familiar to most children. It is a long, thin, narrow piece of wood, sharpened at both ends; attached to a piece of string, and whirled rapidly and steadily in the air, it emits a sound which gradually increases to an unearthly kind of roar.] **1889** *Century Dict.* 1.717, Bull-roarer. **1963** *Chr. Sci. Monitor* (Boston MA) 26 Apr 6/6 **nwNC**, The bullroarer features a thin cedar paddle attached to a rhododendron handle with a doubled length of stout cord. **1972** Cooper *NC Mt. Folkl.* 34, For many decades and until stores became plentiful, the children's Christmas toys and gifts were mainly homemade. There were dolls, yarn balls, whistles, geehaw whimmydiddles or ziggerboos, rattle traps, noise-makers or bull roars and flipperdingers. **1975** McDonough *Garden Sass* 222 **AR**, *Bull Roarers* . . . "You take a flat piece of wood — put a hole through the end — tie a string to it and you throw it around your head, and it goes to roaring — it kind of makes a roaring sound . . . This was a very simple thing that was used by primitive people." **1979** *DARE* File, I grew up in the hills of Eastern Kentucky. In my boyhood my friends and I made *bull roars.* We did not call them *noise makers.* **1980** *Foxfire 6* 194 **nGA**, *Dumb Bull or Bull Roarer or Buzzer.*

b used in ceremonial rites.

1885 *All the Year Round* 56.249/1, The *bull-roarer* is to be found in almost every country in the world . . . And as an instrument employed in religious rites or mysteries, it is found in New Mexico, in Australia, in New Zealand, and in Africa to this day. **1951** Fergusson *New Mexico* 37 **swNM** [Among Pueblo Indians], Different dances require different music, often mimetic. Bull-roarers swung by a strong man make the sound of wind. *Ibid* 405, Bull-roarer — a slat of wood tied to the end of a thong: used in religious rites.

2 A noisemaker used at a **shivaree**: see quot. Cf **dumb bull**

1944 Wellman *Bowl* 78 **KS**, Pans were beaten, and there were several of those creations of the devil called "bullroarers" — a device made by boring a hole in the bottom of a large can, and putting through this a whang-leather cord which is secured from slipping all the way through by a large knot. The operator of the bullroarer pulls along his leather cord a piece of resin, and the brutal, nerve-twisting bellow that rises shockingly to the sky is a horrid thing.

bullrock See **bullhead 9**

bull sap(ling) See **bull pine 2**

bull's bag See **bull bag**

bull's breakfast n joc

1927 *AmSp* 2.349 **WV**, *Bull's breakfast* . . a straw hat. "You have a new bull's breakfast this week."

bull's-eye n

1 also *bullseye, bull's-eye watch:* A thick, small-faced watch often contained in a detachable, shell-like case. *hist*

1833 Neal *Down-Easters* 1.78 **ME**, Lugging out a heavy silver watch . . a genuine bull's-eye with a huge copper logging-chain, a bell-metal face. **1858** Holmes *Autocrat* 245 **MA**, With some trouble he dragged up an ancient-looking, thick, silver, bull's-eye watch. He looked at it for a moment, — hesitated, — . . then opened the watch and handed me the loose outside case without a word. **1859** (1968) Bartlett *Americanisms* 55, *Bull's-eye.* A small and thick old-fashioned watch. **1860** Holmes *Professor* 39 **MA**, A friend of mine had a watch given him, . . a "bull's-eye," with a loose silver case that came off like an oyster-shell from its contents. **1881** *Harper's Mag.* 63.88/1, Our fat old bull's eye watch said half past ten. **1889** (1971) Farmer *Americanisms* 102, *Bull's Eye.* — A small, thick turnip-shaped watch . . . Sometimes called *British bull's-eye.* **1892** Duval *Young Explorers* 217, As soon as Uncle Seth had

finished his yarn, he slowly extracted his bullseye silver watch from his fob.

2 also *bull's-eye lantern, bull-eyed lamp:* A lantern having a convex lens in one side.

1883 *Harper's Mag.* 67.204/1, The words were hardly out of his mouth when the hovel gleamed with a lurid fire . . . The thieves yelled with dismay, and one ran away from the light, slap into the danger, and was dazzled again with opening bull's-eyes, and captured like a lamb. **1902** White *Blazed Trail* 61 **MI**, On soft moccasined feet they stole about in the evening with a bull's-eye lantern fastened on the head of one of them for a "jack" [=jacklight]. **1960** Williams *Walk Egypt* 120 **GA**, A rifle hung over the mantel or stood in the corner of every house, as much a piece of living as the bull-eyed lamp dangling by the back door.

3 also *bulls eye:* A penny candy.

1848 Bartlett *Americanisms* 53, *Bull's eyes* . . . A coarse sweetmeat mixed with flour, and streaked various colors, greedily devoured by children. — *Hartshorne's Shropshire Glossary.* The same word is used here. **1965** *Yankee* Oct 105 **neMA**, Now in her seventies, she does a "boomin'" business making and selling fudge and old-fashioned penny candies like root beer barrels, mummies, bulls eyes. **1965–70** *DARE* (Qq. H82a, b) Infs IL97, 98, MA5, OH37, Bull's-eyes; NY41, Bull's-eyes — licorice flavored.

4 In marble play:

a also *bull-eye, bull's-eye aggie:* A marble having eye-like markings. Cf **cat's-eye 1**

1874 Uncle Bob *Letters to the Children* 85 (Hench Coll.), He can discuss admirably about how many agates, st[r]ipes, whites, bull-eyes, etc., he has. **1906** Lovett *Old Boston Boys* 42, A boy's stock of marbles was usually carried in a bag with a running string, and consisted of "Alleys," "Jaspers," "Chinees," "Pewees," "Agates," "Bulls' Eyes," and several other kinds. **1935** *AmSp* 10.158 **seNE**, *Bull's-eye* . . . a ringed agate, which is an especially valuable possession. **1955** *PADS* 23.10 **cwTN**, *Aggie, bull's-eye* . . . An agate marble that gives the appearance of having the likeness of a bull's eye in it. **1958** *PADS* 29.31 **IL**, *Bull's eye.* **1965–70** *DARE* (Qu. EE6a, . . *The big [marble] that's used to knock others out of the ring*) Inf IL9, Bull's-eye; (Qu. EE6d, *Special marbles*) Infs AL20, CT30, NY52, OR1, PA1, 221, Bull's-eyes; SC26, Bull-eyes. **c1970** Wiersma *Marbles Terms* **wMI** (as of 1935), *Bull's eye* . . . Small marbles that were made out of glass and were painted in such a way that they looked like the bull's eye of a target. *Ibid* **swMI**, Bull's-eye aggie.

b A game played by shooting marbles into a ring or a hole in the ground. Cf **bunny-in-the-hole**

1935 *AmSp* 10.158 **seNE**, *Bull's-eye.* Played around a ring of some three feet or more in diameter containing a number of *commies.* **1965–70** *DARE* (Qu. EE7) Infs NC53, OR1, SC40, Bull's-eye; SC54, Bull's-eye; the ring is in the shape of an eye [drawing in text shows almond-shaped ring]. **1973** Ferretti *Marble Book* 41, *Bullseye.* Shooting at a hole in the ground or at the marked-off center of a designated area. Those who play it say it is a skill game; those more honest admit there's a large element of "luck." *Ibid* 71, *Bun-hole* in England is *bunny-in-the-hole* in New England . . . In the American midwest it is called *bullseye.*

5 A children's game: see quot.

1967–70 *DARE* (Qu. EE18, *Games in which the players set up a stone, a tin can, or something similar, and then try to knock it down*) Infs OH103, TX35, VA54, Bull's-eye.

6a =**oxeye daisy** (here: *Chrysanthemum leucanthemum*).

1848 (1932) Robinson *Jrl. Santa Fe* 10, The vegetables growing here . . are the common prairie grass, rosin weed, bull's eye, red root. **1894** *Jrl. Amer. Folkl.* 7.91 **ME, WV**, *Chrysanthemum leucanthemum* . . bulls-eye. **c1960** Hall Coll. **wNC, eTN**, Bull's-eye (ox-eye daisy) — not common.

b See **bull's-eye daisy 1**.

7 =**marsh marigold**.

1933 Small *Manual SE Flora* 511, *C[altha] palustris* . . . Bull's-Eyes. **1959** Carleton *Index Herb. Plants* 20, *Bull's eye:* Caltha palustris.

8 See quot.

1941 *Jrl. Amer. Folkl.* 54.58 **sIL**, Carry a bull's eye (horse chestnut) in your pocket (for rheumatism).

bull's-eye daisy n

1 also *bull-eyed daisy, bull's-eye:* =**black-eyed Susan 2**, esp *Rudbeckia hirta*.

1896 *Jrl. Amer. Folkl.* 9.193, *Rudbeckia hirta* . . bull's eyes . . Paris, Me. **1940** Clute *Amer. Plant Names* 86, *R. hirta* . . . Bull's-eye daisy.

1965–70 *DARE* (Qu. S7) Infs **CT**2, **MA**25, **NY**122, 205, **VT**10, Bull's-eye (daisy); **PA**165, Bull-eyed daisy.

2 =**oxeye** (here: *Chrysanthemum leucanthemum*).

1940 Clute *Amer. Plant Names* 79, *C. leucanthemum . . .* Bull's-eye daisy. **1959** Carleton *Index Herb. Plants* 20, *Bull's eye daisy:* Chrysanthemum leucanthemum (also Rudbeckia hirta).

bull's foot n

1 See in phrr *beans from bull's foot* (at **beans, not to know c**) and **B from (a) bull's foot, not to know.**

2 =**coltsfoot 1.**

1873 in 1976 Miller *Shaker Herbs* 159, *Tussilago farfara* Bullsfoot. **1931** Clute *Common Plants* 105, What particular foot should be associated with *Tussilago farfara* is hard to determine for among its vernacular names are . . bull's foot . . and colt's foot.

bullshead See bullhead 1b

bullshipper n [Euphem for *bullshitter*]

1967 *DARE* (Qu. HH7a, *Someone who talks too much, or too loud: "He's an awful _____."*) Inf **TX**5, Blabbermouth, chatterbox, bullshipper.

bull-shy adj

Bashful, timid.

1937 Sandoz *Slogum* 55 **wNE** (as of 1900–20), It wasn't natural for a heifer to be as bull-shy as that one [= a young girl].

bull sickle root n

Perh **coltsfoot 1** or **sickleheal.**

1977 *Mais Jamais* 17 **LA**, The herbs and roots they had to collect [to make a cough syrup] were mamou roots, Bull Sickle roots, Prickly Ash bark, [etc.].

bull snake n [See quots 1894 and 1974] formerly widespread SE; now esp Missip–Ohio Valleys and westward See Map Cf blue bullsnake, elegant bullsnake

A large, relatively slow-moving colubrid snake (*Pituophis melanoleucus*) with numerous subspp, but most often marked with a center row of brown or black dorsal blotches. Also called **bullhead 5, gopher snake 1, pine snake 1**

1784 (1929) Filson *Kentucke* 27, Serpents are not numerous, and are such as are to be found in other parts of the continent, except the bull, the horned and the mockason snakes. **1817** Brown *Western Gaz.* 357 **AL**, Palmetto flatts, fit only for the present occupants, gouffres, salamanders, and bull snakes. **1852** in 1854 U.S. War Dept. *Explor. Red River* 211 **LA**, *Pituophis,* Holbr . . . The names of Bull, Pine, and Pilot snake, are commonly given to different species of this genus. **1894** U.S. Natl. Museum *Proc.* 17.328 **FL**, From its loud hissing it is called "bull snake," and "pine snake" from its living in the pine woods. **1907** White *AZ Nights* 219, I mind when they catched the great granddaddy of all the bull-snakes. **1929** Sale *Tree Named John* 55 **MS**, Dey don' bite you—de bull snake jes ties hisse'f roun' you en whups you to death wid 'is tail. **1965–70** *DARE* (Qu. P25) 142 Infs, **chiefly Missip–Ohio Valleys and westward**, Bull snake. **1967** *DARE* Tape **AZ**2 [Describing the Hopi snake dance, as performed by a local non-Indian group], As they go past, each dancer is handed a writhing bull snake. The Indians themselves use rattlesnakes, but we here use the bull snakes. **1974** Shaw–Campbell *Snakes West* 106, The gopher snake . . is often called bull-snake, no doubt because the original pioneer namer ran into a large individual.

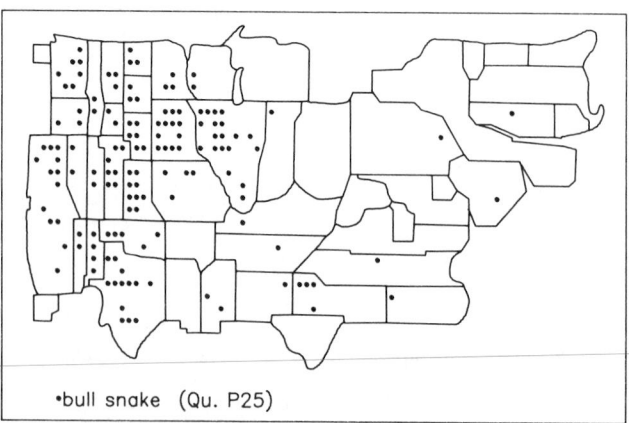

•bull snake (Qu. P25)

bull snipe n

=**marbled godwit.**

1955 *AmSp* 30.177 **ND**, Bull snipe—Marbled godwit.

bull sparrow n

Any of several somewhat similar sparrows: see quot.

1955 *AmSp* 30.177, Bull sparrow [is a name for the] English sparrow [in] N.C., . . Vesper sparrow [in] Ga., Fox sparrow [in] Ky., Texas, Song sparrow [in] Md.

bull sprig n

=**pintail 1.**

1955 *AmSp* 30.177 **CA**, Bull sprig—Pintail (the male).

bull's ring See bullring

bull-strong adj Also *bull-proof, bull-tight* chiefly Midl

Of a fence: strong enough to restrain a bull—often used in phr *horse-high, bull-strong, and pig-tight* and varr; also fig.

1850 *Harper's Mag.* 19.712/1, A Buncombe fence, Sir, is a fence that is bull strong, horse high, and pig tight! **1873** Beadle *Undeveloped West* 40 **IA**, A 'lawful fence' required five [strands of wire], which, the local courts consider, will make it 'horse-high, bull-strong, and pig-tight.' **1895** in 1950 *PADS* 13.12 **AL**, An old man had a mortgage on his land that was 'bull-proof and pig-tight.' **1942** McAtee *Dial. Grant Co. IN* (as of 1890s), *Bull-strong . .* strong as a bull, or of a fence, strong enough to turn a bull; such a fence would be bull-tight. *Ibid* 66, A perfect fence would be horse-high, bull-strong, and pig-tight. **1942** (1960) Robertson *Red Hills* 209 **SC**, "Boys," said Cousin Charlie [=a confederate veteran], his eyes sparkling with excitement, "let me tell you that eternal vigilance must always be the watchword for the Democratic Party. Boys," he shouted, "you got to keep your fences horse-high, bull-strong, and pig-tight." **1948** *Dly. Ardmoreite* (Ardmore OK) 4 July 9/4 *(DA)*, She gave the reins to her father and hopped off the horse and scaled the bull tight fence like a squirrel. **1954** Harder Coll. **cwTN**, Bull-proof and pig-tight. **1967–69** *DARE* (Qq. L63, 65, *Kinds of fences*) Inf **PA**204, Bull-strong fence; **MO**5, Bull-tight fence.

bull swallow n

The purple martin.

1955 *AmSp* 30.177 **IL**, Bull swallow—Purple martin.

bull's-wool See bull-wooly

bull tad n [*bull* + *tad* abbr for *tadpole*]

The larva of a bullfrog.

1968 *DARE* (Qu. P20) Inf **NC**49, Bull tads—makes [sic] a bullfrog.

bull team n [bull n 3] West hist

A team of two or more pairs of oxen used esp in logging.

1855 *Golden Era* (S.F.) 1 Apr 4/2 *(DA)*, The music of your voice . . . shall be used in the humbler occupation of swaying a bull-team. **1879** *Harper's Mag.* 59.878/1 **CO**, I wonder what they'd 'a said if they'd had to ride in a bull team, or drag a hand-cart all the way! **1948** *Popular Western* June 64/1 *(DA)*, He hadn't seen any logging operations for a long time, not since he'd hauled by bull team the logs that formed his squat shack and barn and chicken house. **1949** Peattie *Cascades* 145 **wOR** (as of c1900), The sixteen oxen—the "bullteam"—stood with heads down, the log chain slack under the eight yokes. **1956** *Seattle Daily Times* (WA) 19 Feb mag sec 10 **wWA**, [He] questioned whether the photograph of a bull team logging at Juanita . . could have been taken as late as 1907. **1968** *DARE* Tape **CA**103, In the early days they used bull teams. They built skid roads . . . Generally eight oxen in a bull team.

bull teamster See bullpuncher

bull teeth n pl

Buck teeth.

1966 *DARE* (Qu. X12, . . *Large front teeth that stick out of the mouth*) Inf **GA**13, Bull teeth.

bull thistle n

Any of var large thistles: see quots.

1864 Randall *Practical Shepherd* 271 **NY**, The hay, however, came from a new field, and contained an excessive quantity of bull-thistles. **1900** Bacheller *Eben Holden* 212, It'll be . . nice, smooth land and no stun on it . . . No bull thistles, no hard winters, [etc]. **1909** *DN* 3.409 **cnME**, Bull thistle . . . A large variety of thistle. **1931** Clute *Common Plants* 97, The bull thistle (*Cnicus horridus*) is one of our thorniest thistles. **1961** Wills–Irwin *Flowers TX* 244, Bull Thistle *Cirsium horri-*

dulum. **1963** Craighead *Rocky Mt. Wildflowers* 206, *Bull Thistle—Cirsium vulgare.* **1965–70** *DARE* (Qu. S21, . . *Weeds . . that are a trouble in gardens and fields*) 11 Infs, **chiefly Nth, esp N Cent,** Bull thistle(s); (Qu. S26e, . . *Wildflowers*) Infs **MA**58, **OH**69, **TN**11, **VA**24, 26, Bull thistle; (Qu. S13) Inf **WA**1, Bull thistle; (Qu. S17) Inf **WI**78, Bull thistle; (Qu. S26a) Inf **PA**234, Bull thistle. **1967** *DARE* Wildfl QR Pl.24.3, 24.4 Infs **CA**24, **CO**15, 29, Bull thistle. **1968** *DARE* FW Addit **VA**15, Bull thistle—common, roadside. Cirsium vulgare.

bull thorn n Cf bullhorn

1967 *DARE* (Qu. S15, . . *Weed seeds that cling to clothing*) Inf **CA**1, Bull thorn.

bull-tight See bull-strong

bull toad n Cf bullfrog 1

A frog or toad.

1939 *LANE* Map 231 **seMA,** The difference between *bullfrog* and *bulltoad* is not clear. *Ibid* 232 **seMA,** Bull toad = tree toad. **1949** *McDavid Coll.* **cnNY,** From a male farmer, 85 yrs: Bull toad—not the same as bullfrog; a big garden toad. **1967** *DARE* (Qu. P22) Inf **TN**22, Bull toad.

bulltoad's umbrella n

Prob a toadstool.

1968 *DARE* (Qu. I38) Inf **MD**21, Bulltoad's umbrellas.

bull tongue n, also attrib

1 also *bull tonguer, bull tongue scooter:* A plow with a long narrow plowshare used esp to cultivate hillsides. **chiefly Sth, S Midl** See Map

1833 Holley *Texas* 139, Many farmers use the coulter and bull-tongue ploughs. **1886** *Harper's Mag.* 73.58/2 **seKY,** Ploughing is commonly done with a "bull-tongue," an implement hardly more than a sharpened stick with a metal rim. **1893** Shands *MS Speech* 21, *Bull tongue plow* . . . A kind of plough with a very narrow share shaped somewhat like a bull's tongue, hence the name. **1898** Lloyd *Country Life* 87 **AL,** Many a man can write big about the farmers and the farm, when at the same time he wouldn't know a bull-tongue scooter from a buzzard-wing sweep, or a stack of hay from a hornet's nest. **1903** *DN* 2.308 **seMO,** *Bull-tongue.* **1906** *DN* 3.115 **sIN,** *Bull-tongue* . . . A small shovel on a plow. **1907** *DN* 3.229 **nwAR, seMO,** *Bull-tongue.* **1908** *DN* 3.295 **eAL, wGA,** *Bull-tongue* . . . A kind of 'scooter' plow. **1913** Kephart *Highlanders* 42 **sAppalachians,** For the rough work of cultivating the hillsides a single steer hitched to the "bull-tongue" was better adapted [than a horse or a mule]. **1916** *DN* 4.345 **TN, LA,** *Bull tongue plow.* **1935** *Yale Rev.* 25.176 **KY,** Plough it early when the thaws first come. Break it with a damn good bull-tonguer. **1946** *PADS* 6.7 **eNC** (as of 1900–10), *Bull-tongue.* **1954** *Harder Coll.* **cwTN,** *Bull tongue shovel*—A type of plow used between rows of plants. **1965–70** *DARE* (Qu. L18) 23 Infs, **chiefly Sth, S Midl,** Bull tongue plow; (Qu. L25) Infs **FL**34, **KY**16, 27, 29, **NC**30, Bull tongue (plow).

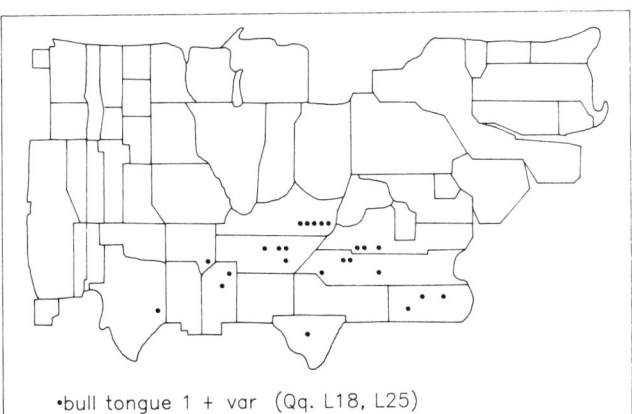

•bull tongue 1 + var (Qq. L18, L25)

2 =arrowhead 1.

1933 *Torreya* 33.82, *Sagittaria* spp.—Bull-tongue, Cameron Parish, La. **1942** *Ibid* 42.157, *Sagittaria lancifolia* . . . Bull-tongue, langue du [sic] boeuf, Louisiana . . . *Sagittaria* spp.—White bull tongue, Louisiana.

3 =golden club.

1933 *Torreya* 33.82, *Orontium aquaticum* . . . Bull-tongue, Okefinokee Swamp, Ga.

4 =pickerelweed 1.

1942 *Torreya* 42.158, *Pontederia cordata* . . . Bull-tongue . . . Louisiana, Lynch; blue bull-tongue, Louisiana, C. Cottam.

bull-tongue cactus n [Prob from tongue-shaped pads] Cf bull cactus

Perh a **cow-tongue prickly pear.**

1935 Sandoz *Jules* 30 **wNE** (as of 1880–1930), In the hollows were tight, tub-sized nests of bull-tongue cactus, the sections broader than a man's hand. *Ibid* 405, A section of bull-tongue cactus the size of a man's hand, with thorns half an inch long. **1937** Sandoz *Slogum* 12 **NE** (as of 1900–20), A patch of bull-tongue cactus beside the road. *Ibid* 102, On the hip of the bluff the bull-tongue cactus were a mat of satin flowers, greenish yellow, large as the cup of her two palms.

bull train n [bull n 3] West hist

A wagon train drawn by oxen, used esp for hauling freight in the West.

1878 Campion *Frontier* 99 **CO,** A Kansas City "bull-train," lately come in, had passed an encampment of over six hundred tents. **1903** (1965) Adams *Log Cowboy* 131 **NM,** Put your freight on a bull train, and it always goes through on time. **1929** Dickson *Covered Wagon Days* 173 **MT** (as of 1860s), The streets were lined with bull-trains and pack-animals. **1939** FWP *Guide KS* 80, The wagons were made up into "bull-trains," which proceeded on the trails at regular intervals, from 10 to 12 miles apart, and were manned by crews of "bull whackers".

bull trout n Also bull

The **Dolly Varden** trout.

1882 U.S. Natl. Museum *Bulletin* 16.319, *S[alvelinus] malma* . . . *Bull Trout.* **1939** FWP *Guide MT* 119, Native blackspot trout ("flats") and Dolly Varden ("bulls") abound in northwestern lakes and larger streams. **1946** LaMonte *N. Amer. Game Fishes* 118, Dolly Varden *Salvelinus malma* . . . Names: Bull Trout. **1966** *Flathead Courier Vacation Guide* (Polson MT) Summer 3, Bull trout or Dolly Vardens range from the 18 inch minimum upwards to 20 pounds and these are more readily taken during early spring or winter. **1966** *DARE* (Qu. P1) Inf **MT**4, Bull trout.

bull-tucker n [bull + tuck, of a trumpet: to sound (EDD v.[1]) + -er]

A frog, esp a **bullfrog 1.**

1890 *DN* 1.72 **Philadelphia PA,** *Bull-tucker:* a frog. **1941** *Nature Mag.* 34.139, Bull-tucker (the second element of which may come from an old Scottish word meaning the sound of a drum) has been noted for Needham, Massachusetts, and Philadelphia, Pennsylvania . . . Bull-frog.

bullus See bullace 2

bullwacker See bullwhacker

bullweed n [ME bulwed; OED c1450 →]

1 A knapweed (here: *Centaurea nigra*).

1889 Murfree *Despot* 35 **eTN,** A tall bull-weed, that swung, purple and burly, among the rocks, was dry. **1911** *Century Dict., Bullweed* . . . Knapweed, *Centaurea nigra*. **1940** in 1968 Haun *Hawk's Done Gone* 15 **eTN,** But old bull weeds covered with ice don't look any more like soldiers to me than sweet williams look like men. **1967** *DARE* (Qu. S21) Inf **TN**6, Bullweed.

2 See quot.

1949 *McDavid Coll.* **swNY,** *Bull weeds* 'bulrushes.'

bullwhack v West hist Cf bull train

To drive an ox team; hence ppl adj *bullwhacking;* transf: full of rough activity.

1869 McClure *3000 Miles* 102 **Rocky Mts** *(DA),* You will often find some graduate of Yale 'bull-whacking' his own team from the river to his mines, looking as if he had seldom seen soap and water. **1906** *DN* 3.129 **nwAR,** *Bull-whackin'* . . . Driving oxen. "What's Jim doin'?" "O, he's a bull-whackin'." **1910** Stanton *When the Wildwood* 106 **Plains States,** We often hear the expression "land poor," but I never realized what it meant until I "bullwhacked" over the sandy desert from Omaha to Denver. **1941** FWP *Guide MO* 244, Kansas City had its beginning in two roaring frontier settlements: the Missouri River town of Kansas, and the bullwhacking, feverish town of Westport, four miles to the south on the Santa Fe Trail.

bullwhack n

A whip.

1885 *Mag. Amer. Hist.* 13.98, In Texas and western Louisiana the "bull-whack" is a terrible whip with a long and very heavy lash and a short handle. It is used by drovers to intimidate refractory animals. **1902** (1968) Clapin *Americanisms* 83, *Bull-whack.* A heavy whip used in the South-West, for driving cattle.

bullwhacker n Also sp *bullwacker* [**bull** n **3** + **whacker**] **chiefly West** *hist*

One who drives oxen, esp in logging and transporting freight.

1858 *Valley Tan* (Salt Lake City) 17 Dec. 2/2 *(DA)*, This valley . . . will set an example that will make the blush of shame mantle upon the cheek of the bull-whacker. **1887** Custer *Tenting* 229 **TX,** There is no sound like the snap of the lash of a 'bull-whacker'. **1929** *AmSp* 5.58 **NE,** The "hand" who formerly drove wagons from the "ranch" to the "cow town" for supplies, etc., was a "bull whacker," "mule skinner," or "freighter." **1941** Fisher *Illusion* 186 **cwNV** (as of 1860–80), Always, day and night, C Street was a hullabaloo of bull-wackers, mule-skinners, and beasts. **1947** Jones *Evergreen Land* 248 **WA,** There wasn't ever no more beautiful a sight . . than to see them bulls bending into the yoke and bringing the log to the landing . . . You could hear the chains clanking and the bullwhacker mumbling all the time and once in a while letting out a yell. **1961** Sackett–Koch *KS Folkl.* 109, *Bull Whacker* . . . The driver of a team of oxen in the freighting business. **1972** *Yesterday* 1.2.23 **WI,** Higher up the ladder in terms of pay and prestige were the teamsters who were called bullwhackers.

bull whitening n

=**white-winged scoter.**

1925 (1928) Forbush *Birds MA* 1.274, *Oidemia deglándi . . . White-winged Scoter . . .* Bull white-wing. **1955** *AmSp* 30.177 **NEng,** Bull whitening—White-winged scoter (the male).

bull woof See **woof**

bull-wooly n Also *bull-wool, bulls-wool* [Cf *OEDS* *bull's wool, bullswool* coarse woollen cloth or yarn]

Coarse cloth made of cotton and wool: see quot 1912.

1912 Green *VA Folk-Speech* 99, *Bull-woolley . . .* Coarse, homespun cloth, of cotton and wool. In old times the people declared their determination to "wear *bull-woolley* and vote agin the tariff." **1942** Berrey–Van den Bark *Amer. Slang* 561.3, Bull-wool, bulls-wool, *cheap clothing.*

bullwork n [**bull** n **5**] Cf **bull gang**

Manual labor.

1944 *AmSp* 19.104, The hard work on her [=a ship] is *muling* or *bull-work.* **1960** Wentworth–Flexner *Slang* 73, *Bull work . . .* Hard work. *Logger, miner, rancher, and maritime use. Not common.* **1969** *DARE* FW Addit **neCT,** Bull work—hard work.

bull worm n

Perh the **hickory horned devil.**

1968 *DARE* (Qu. R27, . . *Kinds of caterpillars or similar worms*) Inf **NC49,** Bull worm—head full of horns, black feet.

bullwort n

A Maryland **figwort** (*Scrophularia marilandica*).

1889 *Century Dict.*, *Bullwort . . .* The plant *Scrophularia aquatica.* **1971** Krochmal *Appalachia Med. Plants* 230, *Scrophularia marilandica . . .* Bullwort.

bully n[1] Also *bullet* [*EDD* *bully,* sw Engl dial]

A large marble.

1899 (1912) Green *VA Folk-Speech* 99, *Bully . . .* A large marble. **1969** *DARE* (Qu. EE6a, *Names for different kinds of marbles—the big one that's used to knock others out of the ring*) Inf **TX58,** Bullet or bully.

bully n[2] See **bullyrum**

bully n[3], v[1] Also *bully net*

A long-handled crawfish net; to use such a net.

1941 Faherty *Big Old Sun* 152 **FL** (Hench Coll.), "Deaver, I put the bully net in your boat," she said. *Ibid* 155, "Yonder's grass," Deaver said. "There'll be crawfish. Where's your bully net?" **1966** *DARE* (Qu. P13, . . *Other ways of fishing*) Inf **FL24,** To bully. Bullies [are] round piece[s] of wire on a stick with net. **1966** *DARE* Tape **FL24,** Years ago we bullied the crawfish with this bully. You had this rim and this net on it and it was on a pole . . of maybe 12 feet or 14 . . and you'd have another pole with a long—we call it a tickler—you run it under the rock that the crawfish lives under . . and that worries him and he comes out. Then you shove your bully down and get him.

bully n[4] See **bullace 1**

bully v[2] [Scots *bully* v to play at "bully", a fighting game played with chestnuts on a string] Cf **egg picking**

To hit boiled eggs together until one breaks.

1941 *Hench Coll.,* A fellow-teacher, who grew up in the Hazelton–Sunbury area of Pennsylvania, tells me this: "To bully eggs" refers to an Easter game. One person has a hardboiled egg and bumps the end of it against the end of another person's egg. The person whose egg breaks, loses.

bull yearlings, rain v phr Cf **pitchforks, rain**

To rain very hard.

1967 *DARE* (Qu. B26, *When it's raining very heavily, you say, 'It's raining _____.'*) Inf **SC43,** Down bull yearlings; **TX1,** Pitchforks and bull yearlings.

bully-fight v [Cf *SND* *bully* v]

1966 *PADS* 46.24 **cnAR,** *Bully-fight . . .* To engage in a form of hand-to-hand combat for the purpose of determining which of two contestants is stronger.—"Them two boys was bully-fighting."

bully-gator n

=**alligator** n[1] **10.**

1970 *DARE* (Qu. EE28, *Games played in the water*) Inf **TX104,** Bully-gator.

bully-in-the-barnyard, bully-in-the-ring See **bull-in-the-ring**

bullymarum See **bullyrum**

bully net See **bully** n[3], v[1]

bullyrum n Also *bully, bullymarum* [Echoic] Cf **-ma-** See also **bizmaroon, jugarum**

A bullfrog 1.

1938 *Sun* (Baltimore MD) 28 Apr 8/8, Catching "bullies" was a favorite sport of mine in boyhood on the old Elk river—and how I could cook 'em . . . The whole frog was good enough to eat, but the hind legs were as choice as the breast of a milk-fed chicken. **1967** *DARE* (Qu. P22) Inf **NY10,** Bullymarum ['bʊləmə,rʌm]; **PA1,** Bully, bullyrum, chugarum.

bully-woolies n pl [**bull-wooly**] *old-fash* Cf **woolies**

Long underwear.

1965–70 *DARE* (Qu. W14, *Names for [long] underwear*) Inf **DC4,** (Men's) Longies, bully-woolies; **MI72,** (Men's) Longies, bully-woolies—years ago they used to say [that]; **MO29,** (Women's) Drawers, bully-woolies; **NY130,** (Women's) Bully-woolies (it used to be this); **NY233,** (Women's) Bully-woolies—ancient!; **VA73,** (Men's) Bully-woolies, long-johns, (Women's) Bully-woolies, union suit. [4 of 6 Infs Black]

bulrusher n [Engl dial] Cf **-er** affix

A bulrush.

1885 Twain *Huck. Finn* 18 **MO,** After supper she got out her book and learned me about Moses and the Bulrushers.

bulvine n [Blend of *bull* + *bovine*]

1968 *DARE* (Qu. K24, *What does the word 'ox' mean around here?*) Inf **PA103,** Castrated bulvine.

bum n[1] Also *bummy*

The buttocks.

1899 (1912) Green *VA Folk-Speech*, *Bum . . .* The buttocks. **1930** Clendening *Human Body* 187, I heard a Virginian speak of a little girl's being spanked on the "bummy." **1953** Randolph *Down in Holler* 87 **Ozarks,** The hillman uses *bum* and *bummy* to mean buttocks. **1965–70** *DARE* (Qu. X35, *Joking words for the part of the body that you sit on*) 14 Infs, **chiefly Nth, N Midl,** Bum. **1967** *DARE* Tape **MA28,** They'd pat a waitress on the bum, think nothing of her.

bum n[2], also attrib Also *bummer* **west of Missip R**

A motherless lamb that is raised by hand.

1931 *AmSp* 6.358 **West,** Skillful nurse maids will catch such a ewe, blindfold her, skin her lamb, and sew its pelt on an "orphan" or a "bum," that is, a lamb whose mother has deserted it. **1938** (1952) FWP *Guide SD* 85, *Bum:* a lamb raised by hand. **1940** FWP *Guide NV* 78, A term that is common to both sheep and cattle is *leppy,* sometimes spelled *leppie,* for a motherless lamb as well as a calf or colt. A *bummer* is another name for these baby lambs. **1942** Henry *High Border* 326 **nRocky Mts,** Sometimes there are lambs for whom it is not possible to provide a foster mother; they are often fed by hand and are known as bum or bummers. **1950** Reeves *Man from SD* 78 (as of 1926–1946), I built a small bum pen and put the orphans on a diet of cow's milk. **1954** Jordan *Hell's Canyon* 67 **ID** (as of 1933–40), Bum. **1959** Martin *Gunbarrel* 75 **WY**, "What's a bum lamb?" I inquired. "A bum is one that has lost his mother or whose mother won't claim him." **1968** Adams *Western Words* 45, *Bum . . . Bummer.*

bum n³ Also *bummer* [Perh alter of **bomber 1**] **SC, FL** *esp among Blacks* Cf **bumblebee n 6**
    1966–67 *DARE* (Qu. EE6a, . . *Kinds of marbles—the big one that's used to knock others out of the ring*) Inf **SC5**, Bum; **SC10, 26**, Bum—big; **FL48, 51, SC65**, Bummer; **SC68**, Bum or bummer—same as a marble, only bigger; used to stead [=replace] railroad ball bearings. [6 of 7 Infs Black] **1973** Allen *LAUM* 1.404 **IA**, *Bummer:* Large marble [1 inf].

bum n⁴ [Imit; cf *EDD* bum v.³ "To strike, knock" and sb.⁶ "A blow"]
A bump.
    1967–69 *DARE* (Qu. X60, . . *A lump that comes up on the head when you get a sharp blow or knock*) Infs **IL37, NC40**, Bum; (Qu. Y1, . . *A person suddenly falling down: "He slipped on the steps and took quite a _____."*) Infs **IL48, NC40**, Bum.

‡**bum** n⁵ Cf **bum v³**
    1966 *DARE* (Qu. Y4, . . *A very uncomplimentary remark*) Inf **NC35**, Bum.

bum v¹ [**bum n²**]
    1938 (1952) FWP *Guide SD* 85, *To bum a lamb:* to take it away from its mother and raise it by hand.

bum v² [*bum* to loaf] **wGt Lakes**
To play hooky.
    1966–69 *DARE* (Qu. JJ6, *To stay away from school without an excuse*) Inf **IL97**, Bum; **MI32**, Bummed; **MI93**, Bum school. **1973** Allen *LAUM* 1.378 **MN**, Several singletons appear in the U[pper] M[idwest]: . . *was bumming from school.*

bum v³ Cf **bum n⁵**
    1970 *DARE* (Qu. Y3, *To say uncomplimentary things about somebody*) Inf **NY249**, Bad-mouth, bum, run down.

bum adj Also *bummy* *somewhat old-fash* Cf **bum, on the**
Ill, though not seriously so.
    1931 *AmSp* 6.231 **cnNE**, *Bummy . . .* Of a person, slightly ill . . . "I feel kind of bummy with this cold." **1943** *LANE* Map 493 **scattered, but esp sNEng**, Bum [19 infs]. **1950** *WELS* (*If someone asked "How are you?", what would you say if you felt: not good*) 1 Inf, **WI**, Bum; 1 Inf, Bummy. **1956** McAtee *Some Dialect NC* 7, *Bum . . .* ill. "I feel bum." **1965–70** *DARE* (Qu. BB39, *On a day when you don't feel just right, though not actually sick, you might say, "I'll be all right tomorrow—I'm just feeling _____ today."*) 27 Infs, **scattered**, Bum; **WY2**, Little bum; **NV8**, Very bum; (Qu. BB5, *A general feeling of discomfort or illness that isn't any one place in particular*) Infs **IA8, MN38, MA6**, Feel bum; **OH53, WY5**, Feeling bum; **MO15**, Bum; **IA8**, Bum all over; **DC11**, I feel bummy; (Qu. BB41, *Not seriously ill, but sick enough to be in bed: "He's been _____ for a week."*) Infs **NV8, SD3**, Feeling bum; **SD3**, Bum; (Qu. X52, . . *A person . . who had been sick was looking _____*) Inf **OH54**, Bum. [34 of a total of 35 Infs old]

bumba n Also sp *bumpa* [Cf *DJE* bumbo the buttocks]
    1968 *DARE* (Qu. X35, . . *The part of the body that you sit on*) Inf **GA43**, Bumba ['bʌmbə]. **1984** *DARE* File, In 1975 my son learned the word *bumpa* ['bʌmpə] from a Black child at a local nursery school. It means the 'bottom,' and has been our family word ever since.

bumbasol See **bumbersol**

‡**bumbasto** n [Prob based on **bum n¹**, perh infl by Engl dial *bumbaste* to beat on the buttocks]
    1969 *DARE* (Qu. X35, . . *The part of the body that you sit on*) Inf **RI1**, Bumbasto [bəm'bæsto].

bumbay n
A children's game: =**Johnny-on-the-pony.**
    1977 *NY Times* (NY) 6 July 29/5, Nobody really knows why . . Johnny-on-a-pony is "bumbay" in St. Louis.

bumbee n [Scots]
A bumblebee.
    1923 Price *Dreams* 4 *(Hench Coll.)*, Them bum-bees mean [for me] to right about, It['s] back to the big open woods fer me. **1950** *PADS* 14.17

SC, Bumbee . . . The bumblebee. A Scottish usage surviving in lower S.C. **1982** *Barrick Coll.* **sePA**, Bum-bee—bumblebee.

bumberella n Also *bumberall, bumberell, bumbrella, bumerell* [Humorous alter of *umbrella*]
An umbrella.
    1896 *DN* 1.413 **c,wNY**, Bumberall . . . umbrella. **1902** (1968) Clapin *Americanisms*, Bumberell. **1913** *DN* 4.52, Bumberell, bumerell. **1965–70** *DARE* (Qu. W1c, *Joking names . . for an umbrella*) 13 Infs, **scattered**, Bumberella; **PA126**, Bumbrella.

bumberry brier n [Prob alter of *brambleberry*]
    1982 Ginns *Snowbird Gravy* 116 **nwNC**, They said the way it got its name, Pick-Breeches, was them there, what they call in the Jack Tales, "bumberry briars." There was an old name, now, "bumberry." I wouldn't know what they call it anymore. They was bumberry briars up there, and they don't grow any blackberries. You can build a fence with 'em. It ain't nothing can get through 'em, that kind of briars. You can lay a lot together, and cattle or nothing won't try 'em.

bumbershoot n Also *blundershoot, brumbershoot, bumbler-shoot, bumbleshoot, bumpershoot, bumptershoot, bumshoot* [Perh blend of **bumberella** + *-shoot*, perh infl by *chute*]
An umbrella.
    1896 *DN* 1.413 **NY, nOH**, Bumbershoot. **1905** *DN* 3.60 **NE**, Bumbershoot. **1906** *DN* 3.129 **Ozarks**, Bumbershoot. **1908** *DN* 3.295 **eAL, wGA**, Bumbershoot. **1913** *DN* 4.52, Bumberell . . . bumbershoot. **1941** *LANE* Map 367 7 infs, **scattered**, Bumbershoot; 1 inf, Bumshoot, "older term"; 1 inf, Bumbleshoot, "jocular, used by children." **c1960** *Wilson Coll.* **csKY**, Bumbershoot . . . Joking name for *umbrella.* **1965–70** *DARE* (Qu. W1c, . . *Joking names . . for an umbrella*) 440 Infs, **widespread**, Bumbershoot; 51 Infs, **chiefly east of Missip R**, Bumbleshoot; 45 Infs, **scattered**, Bumpershoot; **NY68**, Blundershoot; **OH16**, Brumbershoot; **AR18**, Bumblershoot; **RI17**, Bumptershoot; (Qu. W1a, *What do you open up and hold over your head when it rains?*) **MD9, MI2, MA38, NJ55, NY88, RI1**, WI12, 27, Bumbershoot; (Qu. W1b, *If you use an umbrella when the sun is too hot, you call it a _____*) Infs **CA107, DC4, MI2, 97, OK47, SC21, UT4**, Bumbershoot.

bumbersol n Also *bombersoll, bumbasol, bumbersoll, bumpersol* [Blend of **bumbershoot** + *parasol*]
An umbrella.
    1901 *DN* 2.137 **cNY**, Bumbersoll. **1906** *DN* 3.129 **Ozarks**, Bumbershoot, Bumbersol. **1911** *DN* 3.541 **NE**, Bumbersoll. **1913** *DN* 4.52, Bumberell . . . bumbersoll. **1940–41** Cassidy *WI Atlas* **seWI**, Bumbersoll. **1942** Berrey–Van den Bark *Amer. Slang* 75.39, Bombersoll, bumbersoll. **1965–70** *DARE* (Qu. W1c, *Joking names . . for an umbrella*) Infs **AR11, 51, CA22, 157, LA11, TX1**, Bumbersol; **TX4, 40**, Bumbasol; **MO29**, Bumpersol.

bumbersome adj Cf **bunglesome**
    1965 *McDavid Coll.* **sSC**, Bumbersome—clumsy.

bumble n
‡**1** See quot. Cf **bum n⁴**
    1968 *DARE* (Qu. X60, . . *A lump that comes up on your head when you get a sharp blow or knock*) Inf **PA110**, Bumble ['bʌm,bəl].
2 See **bumbler bee.**

bumblebee n
1 Std: a bee of the genus *Bombus.*
2 See **bumblebee coot.**
3 See **bumblebee peep.**
4 =**ruby-throated hummingbird.**
    1956 *AmSp* 31.183 **NC**, Bumblebee . . . Ruby-throated hummingbird.
5 also *bumblebee fuzz:* A **cockleburr 1.**
    1966–69 *DARE* (Qu. S13) Inf **NC44**, Bumblebees—cuckleburrs; **PA204**, Bumblebee fuzz.
6 See quots. Cf **bum n³, yellow jacket**
    c1970 Wiersma *Marbles Terms*, Bumble bee(s): A marble the size of a crockie [larger than regular size, but not as large as a boulder] with a brown and yellow striped design. **1970** *DARE* (Qu. EE6a, *Names for different kinds of marbles—the big one that's used to knock others out of the ring*) Inf **FL48**, Bumblebee; (Qu. EE6b, *Small marbles or marbles in general*) Inf **GA93**, Bumblebee. [Both Infs Black]
7 A bushbean: see quot.
    1970 *Wanigan Catalog* 5, Bumblebee—B[ush] A large, size 7, very fat

oval, white bean having a large red butterfly-like area at the eye . . . A great heirloom in Northern New England.

bumblebee adj **Sth, S Midl**

Of a crop: dried up, stunted.

1918 *DN* 5.20 **NC,** *Bumble-bee cotton,* cotton so low that the bees can lie on their backs and suck the juice from the blooms. **1934** *AmSp* 9.79 **nLA.** **1938** Stuart *Dark Hills* 274 **KY,** "Pa, why do you call the corn bumblebee corn?" "Because a bumblebee can suck on the tassel and its tail touches the ground." **1942** Perry *Texas* 136, "Bumblebee cotton" is cotton so feeble and low to the ground that a bumblebee can lie on its back and kick the locks out of the bolls. **1946** Stuart *Tales Plum Grove* 168 **seKY,** The corn is burnt up. You know it here. The corn aint goin' to git no taller. It's tasselin' and it's bumblebee corn. **1946** *AN&Q* 6.104/1 **OK.** **1965** *DARE* File **Ozarks** (as of c1910), When drought caused a poor cotton crop it was said to be bumblebee cotton. **1970** *DARE* Tape **WV14,** [FW:] What's bumblebee corn? [Inf:] Well, that's real short corn where the bumblebees wear the ground out a-sitting on their hind ends a-suckin' the tassels.

bumblebee coot n Also *bumblebee, bumblebee buzzer* =**ruddy duck.**

1888 Trumbull *Names of Birds* 110, *Ruddy Duck* . . at Portsmouth, N.H., *Bumble-Bee Coot.* **1949** Sprunt–Chamberlain *SC Bird Life* 85, Bumblebee coot. **1950** *PADS* 14.17 **SC,** *Bumblebee coot* . . The ruddy duck. **1955** *AmSp* 30.184, The ruddy duck has been designated *bumblebee* (Ill.), *bumblebee buzzer* (Ark.), and *bumblebee coot* (N.H., Mass., N.Y., Wis., Iowa). **1982** Elman *Hunter's Field Guide* 192, *Ruddy Duck:* (*Oxyura jamaicensis,* also classified as *Erismatura jamaicensis rubida*)—Common & Regional Names: . . bumblebee coot.

bumblebee duck n

1 also *bumblebee coot, ~ dipper:* =**bufflehead 2.** [See quot 1955 *MA Audubon*]

1917 (1923) *Birds Amer.* 1.140, *Buffle-head—Charitonetta albeola*. . . Bumblebee Duck. **1955** *AmSp* 30.184, The bufflehead has been termed *bumblebee coot* and *bumblebee dipper* (Maine), as well as *bumblebee duck* (Mass., Conn.). **1955** *MA Audubon* 39.316, *Buffle-head* . . . Bumble-bee Coot (Maine. From its small size and rapid wing motion; coot is applied generally to sea fowl along the New England coast.); Bumble-bee Dipper (Maine. Part of the preceding note applies; dipper means diver.); Bumble-bee Duck (Mass., Conn.). **1982** Elman *Hunter's Field Guide* 211, *Bufflehead (Bucephala albeola)*—Common & Regional Names: . . bumblebee dipper.

2 =**ruddy duck.**

1951 Pough *Audubon Water Bird* 322, Bumble-bee duck See . . . Ruddy duck.

bumblebee dust See **dust**

bumblebee fuzz See **bumblebee n 5**

bumblebee peep n Also *bumblebee*

Either of two similar sandpipers: the **least sandpiper** or the **semipalmated sandpiper.**

1946 Hausman *Eastern Birds* 286, *Semipalmated Sandpiper Ereuntes pusillus* . . . Other Names . . . Bumblebee Peep. **1955** *AmSp* 30.184, Records of the use of *bumblebee* for definite species occur for the least sandpiper (Mass., N.J., Va.) and semipalmated sandpiper (N.J., Va.). These birds, respectively, are called also *bumblebee peep* (Mass.). **1956** *MA Audubon* 40.19, *Least Sandpiper* . . . Bumblebee, Bumblebee Peep (Mass. From its small size.).

bumblebee root n

A **trillium** (here: *Trillium erectum*).

1892 *Jrl. Amer. Folkl.* 5.104, *Trillium erectum,* . . bumble-bee root. New England. **1930** Sievers *Amer. Med. Plants* 48, *Purple Trillium* . . . *Other common names* . . . Bumblebee root. **1971** Krochmal *Appalachia Med. Plants* 256, *Trillium erectum* . . . Bumblebee root.

bumblebee weed n

A **self-heal** (here: *Prunella vulgaris*).

1899 *Plant World* 2.198 **PA,** *Bumblebee-weed* for *Brunella vulgaris* L., probably because of this bee's fondness for visiting the flowers. **1968** *DARE* (Qu. S21, . . *Other weeds*) Inf **MD30,** Bumblebee weed—roundish leaf, runs over ground, bluish, small flower, bumblebees attracted to it.

bumblebee whiskey n Also *bumblebee stew*

Strong whiskey; moonshine.

1867 Harris *Sut Lovingood Yarns* 33 **TN,** I tuck me a four finger dost [=dose] ove bumble-bee whisky. **1956** *Wall St. Jrl.* (NY NY) 21 Sept 1/1, About one out of every four gallons of hard liquor produced in the United States last year was moonshine—also known by devotees as . . bumblebee stew. **1968** Adams *Western Words, Bumblebee whisky*—What a cowboy calls a strong whisky with a sting.

bumbler bee n Also *bumble, bumbler, bumbly bee*

A bumblebee.

1876 (1882–83) Whitman *Specimen Days* 85 **NJ,** The great wild bee, the bumble-bee, or "bumble," as the children call him. **a1883** (1911) Bagby *VA Gentleman* 90, I hope the bridge will never be mended, but stay just as it is until the bumbler-bees—humble-bees? not any, I thank you—I speak Virginian, not the lingo of Bosting, or even of Ingling . . until the bumbler-bees, and other borers, reduce it to wood-dust and scatter it atom by atom into the stream. **1911** Dreiser *Jennie* 17 **IN,** "There goes a bee," said George, noting a bumbler winging by. **1968–69** *DARE* (Qu. R21, . . *Stinging insects*) Infs **KY40, MD42,** Bumbly bee; **MO39,** Bumble.

bumblershoot, bumbleshoot See **bumbershoot**

‡**bumble spider** n

1950 *WELS* (*Other kinds of spiders*) 1 Inf, **cwWI,** Bumble spider.

‡**bumble wood** n

1968 *DARE* FW Addit **nwPA,** "Bumble wood" used by a carpenter to refer to an unidentified wood or to "just any old wood."

bumblings n Cf **bumblebee whiskey**

See quot 1926.

1917 *DN* 4.409 **wNC,** *Bumblings* . . . Whiskey. **1926** Kephart *Highlanders* 137 **sAppalachians,** All of the moonshine whiskey used to be pure, and much of it still is; but every blockader knows how to adulterate . . . Some add washing lye . . then prime this abominable fluid with pepper, ginger, tobacco, or anything else that will make it sting. Even buckeyes, which are poisonous themselves, are sometimes used to give the drink a soapy bead. Such decoctions are known in the mountains by the expressive terms "pop-skull," "bust head," and "bumblings" ("they make a bumbly noise in a feller's head").

bumbly n Cf **bumblebee n 6**

c1970 Wiersma *Marbles Terms* **NJ,** Bumblies—a striped marble with a white background.

bumbly bee See **bumbler bee**

‡**bumboscis** n [Alter of *proboscis*]

1967 *DARE* (Qu. X14, *Joking words for the nose*) Inf **OH16,** Bumboscis [bəmˈbɑskəs].

bumbosity See **bombosity**

bumbrella See **bumberella**

bum, bum, bum, where are you from n

A children's game: =**lemonade station.**

1966 *DARE* Tape **AL3,** "Bum, bum, bum, where are you from?" I think that's a good game . . . You choose sides . . One side goes 'n' sees the other side. They decide on something they're gonna do . . . Ironing or milking a cow . . . They approach the other side and the leader says "Bum, bum, bum, where you from?" The other side says . . "Boston . . or New York or anything" . . . They say, "What's your trade?" They say "Sweet lemonade." And you go to make a motion whatever it is . . . If they guess it, they see if they can catch 'em before they get back to . . their home.

bumby(e) See **bimeby**

bum cluck n

=**bittern.**

1940 Todd *Birds W. PA* 64/1, He adds that "Bum Cluck" is the local vernacular name of this bird [=bittern].

bumcutter n

=**black-crowned night heron.**

1976 Warner *Beautiful Swimmers* 123 **Chesapeake Bay,** The night herons, locally known as sedge hen or "bumcutters."

bumerell See **bumberella**

bumfidgets n Cf **fidget n 1** and *DS* GG13b

1950 *PADS* 14.18 **SC,** *Bumfidgets* . . . An aggravated state of nervousness; fidgets. "Children, stop the noise; it gives me the bumfidgets."

bum fodder n [**bum** n¹ + *fodder*] Cf **bung fodder**

Toilet paper.

1912 Green *VA Folk-Speech,* Bum-fodder . . . Paper used in water-closet. **1940** *Hench Coll.* **ceNC,** A Univ. of Va. colleague told me that as a boy he . . called toilet paper "bumfodder."

bumfoozle v, hence ppl adj *bumfoozled* [Alter of *bamboozle*]
chiefly wGt Lakes Cf **bamfoozle 1, bumfuzzle**

To confuse.

1905 *DN* 3.60 **NE,** *Bumfoozle, bumfuzzle . . .* Bewilder. "I was bumfoozled." **1912** *DN* 3.572 **wIN,** *Bum-foozled . . .* Perplexed. **1950** *WELS (To deceive somebody)* 2 Infs, **WI,** Bumfoozle. **1965–70** *DARE* (Qu. GG2, . . *Confused, mixed-up*) Infs **IL143, MI17,** Bumfoozled; (Qu. KK36, *Talking about a person who is easily fooled: "It's easy to _____.")* Infs **IN35, NM4,** Bumfoozle him.

bumfuddled ppl adj Rarely *bumfoodled* [Alter of **bumfuzzle,** prob infl by *befuddle*]

Confused.

1956 McAtee *Some Dialect NC* 7, Bumfuddled . . . confused, rattled. **c1960** *Wilson Coll.* **csKY,** Bumfuddled . . . Greatly confused. **1966** Barnes–Jensen *Dict. UT Slang,* Bumfuddled . . . confused. **1966–70** *DARE* (Qu. GG2, . . *Confused, mixed up*) Infs **FL35, KY73, NC22,** Bumfuddled; **WI12,** Bumfoodled [bəm'fudld].

bumfuzzle v, hence ppl adj *bumfuzzled* [**bum** + **fuzzle** to confuse] **chiefly Sth, S Midl** See Map Cf **bamfoozle 1, bumfoozle**

To confuse.

1905 *DN* 3.60 **NE,** *Bumfuzzle.* Ibid 72 **Ozarks,** *Bumfuzzle . . .* To confuse. **1915** *DN* 4.181 **swVA,** *Bumfuzzled . . .* Confused. **1938** Stuart *Dark Hills* 388 **KY,** I didn't know you was that sharp after the way you bumfuzzled the Superintendent's office. **1950** *PADS* 14.18 **SC. 1956** McAtee *Some Dialect NC* 7. **c1960** *Wilson Coll.* **csKY. 1965–70** *DARE* (Qu. GG2, . . *Confused, mixed-up*) 77 Infs, **chiefly Sth, S Midl,** Bumfuzzled; (Qu. KK36, *Talking about a person who is easily fooled: "It's easy to _____.")* Infs **CA101, TX10, 32,** Bumfuzzle him; (Qu. A21) Inf **MS16,** Be so bumfuzzled; (Qu. GG15) Inf **VA31,** Bumfuzzled. **c1970** *Halpert Coll.* **wKY,** Bumfuzzled—puzzled, ludicrously confused.

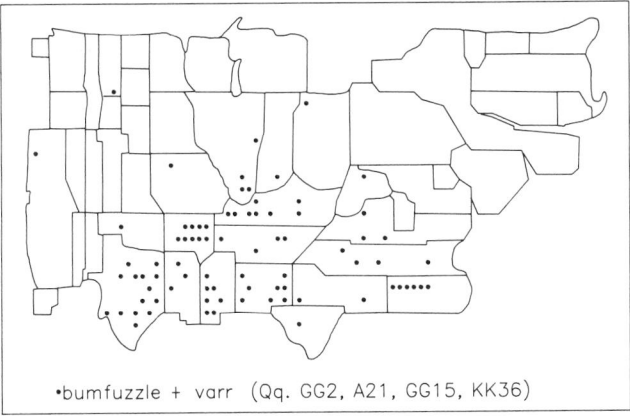

•bumfuzzle + varr (Qq. GG2, A21, GG15, KK36)

‡**bumfuzzler** n

1966 *DARE* (Qu. FF27, *Joking names . . for television*) Inf **MS67,** Bumfuzzler.

bumgillian See **balm of Gilead 2a**

‡**bum-head** n Cf **butt-head**

1966 *DARE* (Qu. K12, *A cow that has never had horns*) Inf **NC3,** Bum-head.

‡**bum ice** n

1973 Allen *LAUM* 1.157 **csND,** *Bum ice:* Ice refrozen after a thaw [1 inf].

bum jacket n [**bum** n¹] **SC**

A short jacket.

1967 *DARE* (Qu. W4, . . *Men's coats or jackets for work and outdoor wear*) Inf **SC29,** Bum jacket, frequently denim, sometimes lined, loose fitting, waist length, very durable; **SC34,** Bum jacket, will be recognized in any store, optionally lined, any cloth, waist length, rugged work jacket; **SC42,** Bum jacket. **1967** *DARE* Tape **SC35,** Say just a everyday coat, call it a bum jacket.

bummer n¹ See **bum** n²

bummer n² See **bum** n³

bummox n [Perh blend of *bum* + *lummox,* but cf *EDD* bummick a cow or ox]

A lummox.

1941 *LANE* Map 464 **swCT,** *Awkward person, Lummox . . .* [1 inf] [bʌməks].

bummy adj

1 See **bum** adj.

2 See quot.

1931 *AmSp* 6.231 **cnNE,** *Bummy.* Spoiled, unfit for use . . . "The potatoes on top were good, but those farther down were all bummy."

bummy n See **bum** n¹

bum naked adj [**bum** n¹] Cf **buck naked**

1965–70 *DARE* (Qu. W20, *If someone has no clothes on at all—for example, "There was Johnny, _____." or "They went in swimming _____.")* Infs **MS60, NY24, 226,** Bum naked; **KY94,** Buck-bum naked. [2 of 4 Infs Black]

bum one's gums See **bump one's gums**

bum, on the adj phr **esp Nth** Cf **bum** adj

Unwell; see quot 1968–70.

1950 *WELS (If someone asked "How are you?", what would you say if you felt: not good)* 1 Inf, **nwWI,** On the bum. **1960** Bailey *Resp. to PADS 20* **KS,** "I'm on the bum today" means "I don't feel well or something went wrong." **1968–70** *DARE* (Qu. BB39, *On a day when you don't feel just right, though not actually sick, you might say, "I'll be all right tomorrow—I'm just feeling _____ today.")* Infs **CA196, NJ22, OH44, PA70,** On the bum; (Qu. BB5, *A general feeling of discomfort or illness*) Infs **NJ25,** Feel on the bum; **MI78,** On the bum.

bump n

1 A pimple; less freq, a boil. **chiefly Sth, S Midl** See Map

1899 (1912) Green *VA Folk-Speech,* Bump . . . swelling or protuberance; a large pimple. **1944** *PADS* 2.7 **Sth,** Bump . . . A euphemism for a pimple. **1956** McAtee *Some Dialect NC* 7, Bump . . . pimple. **c1960** *Wilson Coll.* **csKY,** Bump . . . Pimple, boil, hickey. **1965–70** *DARE* (Qu. X59, . . *Small infected pimples that form, usually on the face*) 35 Infs, **chiefly Sth, S Midl,** Bumps; (Qu. BB33a, . . *A swelling under the skin, bigger than a pimple, that comes to a head*) Infs **DC11, GA8, NC77, TX61,** Bump.

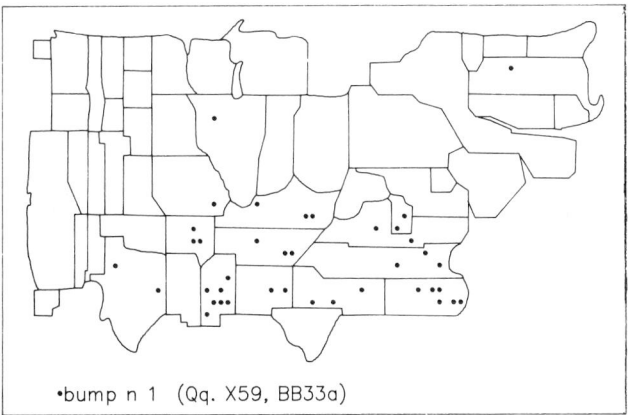

•bump n 1 (Qq. X59, BB33a)

2 pl *bumps:* A rash. *esp among Blacks*

1965–70 *DARE* (Qu. BB24, . . *Names for a rash that comes out suddenly*) 18 Infs, **scattered,** Bumps; (Qu. BB25, . . *Common skin diseases*) Inf **SC10,** Bumps. [Of all Infs responding to these questions, 6% were Black; of those giving this response, 37% were Black]

3 The buttocks. [Perh infl by **bum** n¹ and/or *rump*] Cf **bumper** n¹

1966–69 *DARE* (Qu. X35, *Joking words for the part of the body that you sit on*) Infs **MI2, 107,** Bump.

bump v

1 =**buck** v¹ **B6c.**

1893 Shands *MS Speech,* Bump . . . This word is used principally by school-boys. The process of bumping is as follows: four boys take hold of another, each one seizing a leg or an arm, and swing him so that the rear of his anatomy strikes against a tree with considerable force. *Buck* is the term used for this in Kentucky.

2 Of a cow: to be obviously pregnant; to be about to give birth. [Prob from obs *bump* to bulge]

1965–70 *DARE* (Qu. K10, . . *A cow that is going to have a calf*) Inf **NY**13, She's bumping a calf (when you can feel it); **AR**4, **MS**1, She's bumping; **TX**37, Bumping a hard calf; **GA**12, Bumping up; **GA**9, She's bumping up.

bumpa See **bumba**

bump-coaster n

An amusement park device: ?a roller-coaster.

1935 Davis *Honey* 207 **OR,** Riding merry-go-rounds and Ferris-wheels and bump-coasters.

bumper n[1] [*bump* protuberance + *-er* characterizing suff]

The buttocks.

1950 *WELS* (*Joking words for the part of the body that you sit on*) 1 Inf, **WI,** Bumper, bumpers; 1 Inf, **Bumper. 1966–68** *DARE* (Qu. X35) Infs **MI**67, **NC**9, **VA**13, Bumper.

bumper n[2] [*bump* to push or hit abruptly]

A boost.

1945 Saxon *Gumbo Ya-Ya* 376 **LA** [Black], *Gimme a bumper* means a lift onto a wagon.

bumper n[3] [Etym unknown]

A nickel.

1942 Kennedy *Palmetto Country* 135 **FL,** And the Cap'm didn't fuss so very much when Daddy won a coupla bumpers [nickels] at it hisself.

bumper n[4] See **bumps** n[2]

bumpershoot See **bumbershoot**

bumpersol See **bumbersol**

‡**bumpity** n Cf **bump** n 3

1968 *DARE* (Qu. X35, *Joking words for the part of the body that you sit on*) Inf **WI**70, Bumpity.

bumpity-bumps adv phr Cf **belly-bump 1**

1941 *LANE* Map 576 (*Belly-Bump*), The map shows adverbial expressions recorded in the phrase *To coast (slide, go) belly-bump,* meaning 'to coast down-hill lying prone on the sled' . . . 1 inf, **ceMA,** [bʌ^mpɪtɪbʌmps].

bump-knot n

1966 *DARE* (Qu. X60, . . *A lump that comes up on your head when you get a sharp blow or knock*) Inf **NC**35, Bump-knot.

bump one's gums v phr Also *bum* ~

To argue; to talk (esp loudly or vociferously); hence vbl n *gum-bumping.*

1965–70 *DARE* (Qu. KK13, *Other words for arguing*) Inf **AZ**9, Bumming their gums; **IN**83, Bumped their gums; **NC**7, Bumping gums; **AL**48, Bumping their gums; (Qu. X10b) Inf **WI**64, Quit bumping your gums; (Qu. HH17b) Inf **FL**52, Gum-bumping.

bumps n[1] Also *bumps-up* Cf **bunk** v[1] **3b**

A marble game: see quots.

1935 *AmSp* 10.158 **seNE,** *Bumps-up.* Played with *commies* against a wall or board. A single marble is 'put up' a few inches away, and the players take turns trying to make a marble thrown against the wall hit the one put up or any one previously thrown. The first hit takes all thrown. **1967** *DARE* Tape **WY**1, Bumps. We'd get up agin' a building, usually that was the first game we started in the Spring . . . We'd . . bump the marble agin' the . . building and then it would fall back on the ground. The next man bumped and tried to get . . within a span of the first span . . one hand span. If he did, that was his marble. **1967** *DARE* (Qu. EE7, . . *Marble games*) Infs **WY**1, 4, Bumps.

bumps n[2] Also *bumper* Cf **bampa**

One's grandfather—used as an affectionate form of address.

1968–69 *DARE* (Qu. Z3, . . *Words . . for "grandfather"*) Inf **WI**13, Bumps; **MA**21, Bumper.

bumptershoot See **bumbershoot**

bumptious adj

1893 Shands *MS Speech, Bumptious* . . . The Negroes . . use this word to mean *irascible, easily angered.*

bumpy n Also *boompie* Cf **bum** n[1], **bumper** n[1]

The buttocks.

1966 *DARE* (Qu. X35, *Joking words for the part of the body that you sit on*) Inf **SC**19, Bumpy; **SC**66, Boompie.

bumpy-butt n [Prob from the bird's bobbing gait]

=**purple gallinule.**

1945 McAtee *Nomina Abitera* 33, Purple Gallinule . . . Bumpy-butt, Florence South Carolina.

bum-riding vbl n Also called **bizzing, hooky bobbing**

1967 *DARE* FW Addit **nwMI,** Bum-riding is hanging onto the bumper of a car and sliding along the icy streets, one's shoes the only runners. *Common.*

bum-rub n [**bum** n[1]]

1942 Whipple *Joshua* 211 **UT** (as of c1860), Did you ever hear of a bum-rub? She was giving her clothes a *bum-rub!* She had all her dishtowels and sheets folded up and was sitting there on them, and when I asked her why, she said a bum-rub saved the wear and tear of so much ironing!

bumshoot See **bumbershoot**

bumsky adj [*bum* inferior + **-sky**]

Of poor quality.

1916 *DN* 4.354 **LA,** *Bumsky.* "What a bumsky shot." Exclamation of woman who missed her approach in a golf match.

bum's rush n chiefly **Nth, N Midl, West** See Map

Freq in phr *give one the bum's rush:* a forcible ejection or dismissal; a brush-off, snub.

1926 Finerty *Criminalese* 10, Bums rush—Throwed out. **1927** *DN* 5.441 [Underworld Jargon], *Bum's rush* . . . The act of being thrown out. **1932** *Sun* (Baltimore MD) 17 June 1/5–6 *(Hench Coll.),* [Headline:] Marylander, Seeking To Withdraw In Favor Of Coolidge, Is Given Bum's Rush From Stadium By Convention Police. **1933** *Ibid* 15 Aug 1/3 *(Hench Coll.),* We don't propose to be given the bum's rush on any of these codes. **1941** *Yankee* Dec. 4/3 *(DA),* We'll give him an able demonstration of what we used to call in the old days the 'bum's Rush.' **1948** *Dly. Oklahoman* (Okla. City) 7 June J/6 *(DA),* Ritchie . . . declared Nebraska and Iowa Democrats 'were given the bum's rush' during the president's Omaha visit. **1965–70** *DARE* (Qu. II5b, *When you don't want to have anything to do with a certain person because you don't like him, you might say, "I'd certainly like to give him the _____."*) 36 Infs, chiefly **Nth, N Midl, West,** Bum's rush; (Qu. AA12, *If a man loses interest in a girl and stops seeing her, you'd say he _____*) Infs **NY**10, **OH**23, Give her the bum's rush; (Qu. AA11, *If a man asks a girl to marry him and she refuses, you'd say she _____*) Inf **CT**11, Gave him the bum's rush. **1966** Barnes–Jensen *Dict. UT Slang, Bum's rush* . . . A forceful ejection of one not authorized to be present.

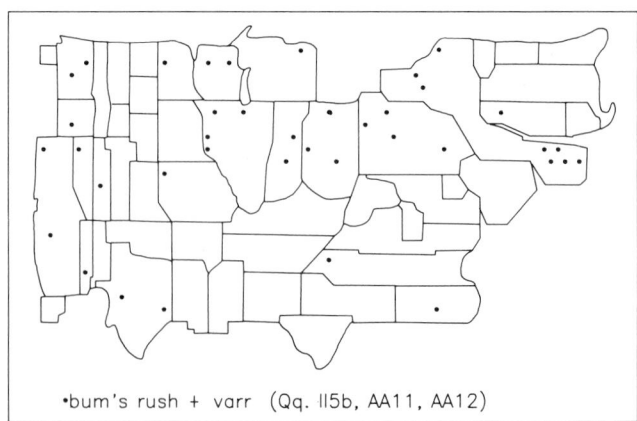

•bum's rush + varr (Qq. II5b, AA11, AA12)

bumstead n [From *Dagwood Bumstead* character in comic strip *Blondie* by Chic Young]

=**dagwood.**

1966 *DARE* (Qu. H42, *The kind [of sandwich] in a much larger, longer bun, that's a meal in itself*) Inf **NM**12, Bumstead.

bumswiggle v Cf **hornswoggle**

1952 Brown *NC Folkl.* 1.524, *Bumswiggle* . . . To surprise.

bumswizzled adj

=**hornswoggled.**

1916 *DN* 4.272 **NE**, *Bumswizzled* . . . Used in "I'll be bumswizzled."
[In Pa., *gumswizzled*].

bum wad n [**bum** n[1]] Cf **bum fodder**

1936 Hench *Coll.* **VA**, I was reminded today of the term "bum wad"
which I had heard when I was a boy. It meant toilet paper or anything else
used for the same purpose.

bumwood n

=**poisonwood** (here: *Metopium toxiferum*).

1884 Sargent *Forests of N. Amer.* 54, *Rhus Metopium* . . . Poison
Wood. Coral Sumach. Mountain Manchineel. Bum Wood. **1897** Sudworth *Arborescent Flora* 274, *Rhus metopium*. *Poisonwood* . . . *Common names* [include] . . . Bumwood, Hog Plum, Doctor Gum.

bun n[1]

1 A sweet roll or pastry. **esp MD, VA, NJ** See Map

1965–70 *DARE* (Qu. H32, . . *Fancy rolls and pastries*) 24 Infs, **esp MD,
NJ, VA,** Bun(s); (Qu. H26, *A round cake of dough, cooked in deep fat,
with a hole in the center*) Inf **VA9,** Bun. **1968** *DARE* FW Addit **MD,**
Bun is a generic name for sweet pastry.

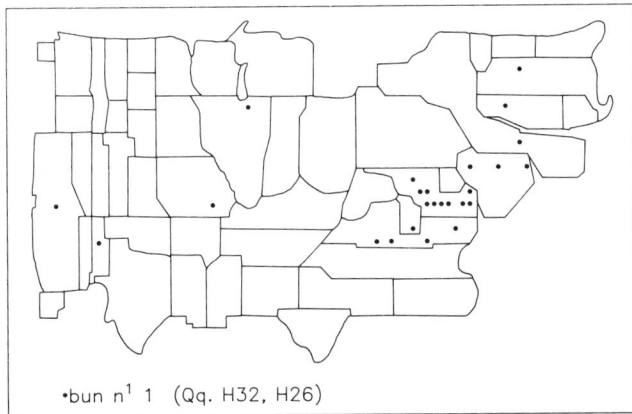

•bun n[1] 1 (Qq. H32, H26)

‡**2** A roll or wad of money.

1966 *DARE* (Qu. U19b, *Talking of paper money: "He always carries a
big _____."*) Inf **DC4,** Bun.

bun n[2] [Alter of *bung*]

1967–69 *DARE* (Qu. F15, *What you turn to let the vinegar or cider run
out of a barrel*) Infs **MA48, OH**11, Bun.

bun n[3] Often *buns* Cf **bum** n[1]

The buttocks.

1960 Wentworth–Flexner *Slang* 76, *Bun* . . . The human posterior.
1967–68 *DARE* (Qu. X35, *Joking words for the part of the body that you
sit on*) Infs **NY**10, **PA**167, Bun; **CA**80, Buns. **1971** Landy *Underground
Dict.* 42, *Buns* . . . buttocks. **1983** *Gentlemen's Qrly.* Mar 48/1 **NY,**
People still come up to me [=Richard Thomas] in airports or shopping
malls and pinch my buns . . . They think I'm one of their best friends.
1983 *WI State Jrl.* (Madison) 8 Jun 1/4 [Remark of an alderman at a city
council meeting], He said city officials should "work our buns off, as my
wife would put it, to get the best welfare director we can get" to solve the
administrative problems.

bun n[4] [Etym uncertain]

A state of inebriation—usu in phr *have* (or *get*) *a bun on.*

1901 Hobart *John Henry* 16 **NYC,** You've got another bun on! How
dare you trail into my flat with your tide high enough to float a
battleship? **1912** *DN* 3.572 **wIN,** *Bun(dle)* . . . A load of liquor. "He has
a bun on to-night." **1915** *Amer. Mag.* 80.93/1 **NYC,** I suppose . . that
we ought to get a slight bun on—but I have to work to-morrow. **1922**
Collier's 7 Oct 26/2 **NYC,** You got a bun on downstairs and I couldn't do
nothin' with you. **1950** WELS *(A drinker who is just beginning to show
the effects of liquor)* 1 Inf, **WI,** Getting a bun on; *(A person who is partly
drunk)* 1 Inf, Got a bun on. **1965–70** *DARE* (Qu. DD13, . . *Beginning
to show the effects of the liquor*) Infs **MI**47, **SD**1, Getting a bun on;
NY202, Has a bun on; (Qu. DD14, . . *Partly drunk*) Inf **MI**10, Got a little
bun on; (Qu. DD15, *A person who is thoroughly drunk*) Inf **WI**30, Had a
bun on.

bun v See **burn** v A

bunch n

1 A swelling or protuberance of the skin; a tumor or cyst.
chiefly Nth, esp NEast

1857 *Lawrence (Kansas) Republican* 11 June 3 *(DAE),* See that he [the
ox] does not have a . . . Missouri stick . . . which will gall his neck, or
produce a bunch. **1874** VT State Bd. Ag. *Report* 2.428, Their bite is
poisonous to a certain extent, as bunches can be felt around their bites.
1965–70 *DARE* (Qu. X60, . . *A lump that comes up on your head when
you get a sharp blow or knock*) 16 Infs, **chiefly Nth,** Bunch; (Qu. BB30, . .
*A hard painful swelling (often on a finger) that seems to come from deep
under the skin*) Infs **ME**10, **VT**3, Bunch. **1967** *DARE* FW Addit **MA**30,
"He's got a bunch on his guts" is said when a person has what looks like a
tumor. **1975** Gould *ME Lingo* 27, *Bunch*—A Maine-ism for what a
surgeon might call a growth, mass, cyst: "This *bunch* came on my arm,
and I went right to the doctor."

2 A herd (of range animals). **West** Cf **bunch quitter**

1881 U.S. Bur. Indian Affairs *Report* 86 **OK,** Have visited them at their
camps a number of times and nearly always find them at home, looking
after their little bunches of stock. **1889** *Harper's Mag.* 78.874/1 **CO,** In
the mountains . . last summer there were two bunches of mountain
bison. **1903** (1965) Adams *Log Cowboy* 49 **NM,** Stalling's bunch was
some three or four miles to the rear and left of this band. **1905** *DN* 3.72
Ozarks, *Bunch* . . . Group, collection, flock, herd, drove . . . 'Bunch of
cattle.' **1929** Dickson *Covered Wagon Days* 95 **NW** (as of 1864), It was
a bunch of hosses over on this side along the ravine. *Ibid* 139, When
yoking up we would drive the bunch into the circle if we corraled or
alongside our wagon otherwise. **1929** *AmSp* 5.67 **NE,** A number of
cattle . . a "bunch." **1968** Adams *Western Words, Bunch*—A group of
cattle.

‡**3** A litter (of pigs).

1970 *DARE* (QR near Qu. K54) Inf **FL**48, They don't say litter [of pigs]
down here, they say bunch.

bunch v[1]

1 To herd (range animals) into a limited space. **West**

1869 *Overland Mth.* 3.126/2 **TX,** Two men often "bunch" on the
march, *i.e.,* unite their herds for convenience in driving. **1869** McClure
3000 Miles 99 **Rocky Mts,** The horses not captured by the Indians have
been "bunched" at either end of the hostile country, and I doubt whether
there will be regular coaches. **1883** Sweet–Knox *Mexican Mustang* 173
TX, We . . were in camp one night, with the cattle bunched out on the
prairie, under guard. **1907** White *AZ Nights* 108, It was somewhere
near noon by the time we had bunched and held the herd of some four or
five thousand head. **1968** Adams *Western Words, Bunch*—To herd a
group of cattle together.

2 Of a horse: to lower the head and arch the back before
bucking.

1955 Warren *Angels* 153 **KY,** She [=a boat] looked like a horse and him
bunching for a jump. [**1961** Adams *Old-Time Cowhand* 295 **West,**
Ever' rider tried his best to keep a hoss from gettin' his head between his
forelegs. This was the first step in buckin', and when a hoss's head was
held high he couldn't do much serious buckin'.]

3 See quot.

c1954 *Harder Coll.* **cwTN,** *Bunch:* To cover celery to keep it white. "I've
heerd *blanching* and *bleaching,* but allus called it *bunching* it; you rake
dirt up to it, leave the top out."

bunch v[2] [Etym unknown]

To quit a job; to leave something unfinished.

1927 *AmSp* 2.391 [Vagabonds], To *bunch,* or to *drag it,* means to quit.
1942 Berrey–Van den Bark *Amer. Slang* 11.6, *Stop; cease* . . . bunch.
Ibid 213.3, *Abandon* . . . bunch. **1950** WELS *(To let something go
undecided . . . "Let's just _____.")* 1 Inf, **nwWI,** Bunch it. **1966**
DARE Tape **MI**10, If you left your job voluntarily, you bunched it.
1968 Adams *Western Words, Bunch her*—In logging, to quit work.
1978 Kalibabky *Hawdaw* 2 **neMN,** "Hey, Joe! You stilla workin' inna
schkool?" "No, I bunched dat job."

bunch bean n esp **Sth, Midl** See Map

Prob a bush bean, but see quots.

1787 (1925) Washington *Diaries* 3.212 **VA,** At Muddy hole . . ordered
. . the 9th square allotted for experiments (to be previously dunged as
others had been) in order to receive the bunch Nomeny [sic for *hominy*]
bean. **1946** *AmSp* 21.189 **seKY,** *Bunch beans* . . . bush string beans.
The explanation given by the mountain people is that these beans grow
in bunches on the plant, or that one picks them in bunches. **1947** *AmSp*
22.156 **sIN.** **1954** *Harder Coll.* **cwTN,** Bunch butter beans . . . White

and specked butter bunch. **c1960** *Wilson Coll.* **csKY,** *Bunch beans . . .* A variety of beans grown to be eaten as green beans; opposed to the climbing varieties, like Kentucky Wonder. **1965–70** *DARE* (Qu. I20) 36 Infs, *esp Sth, Midl,* Bunch beans; LA12, Bunch beans—low, bushy, not vines; NC87, Bunch beans—like a string bean, but not as good; KY37, 44, White bunch beans; TN20, Brown bunch beans; AR20, Case-knife bunch beans; [DE1, Bunch limas]; (Qq. I14–18) Infs AR20, AZ2, GA72, IL117, NC1, 8, SC57, TN1, 4, Bunch beans; AR17, Yellow pod bunch bean; MS87, Bunch snap bean.

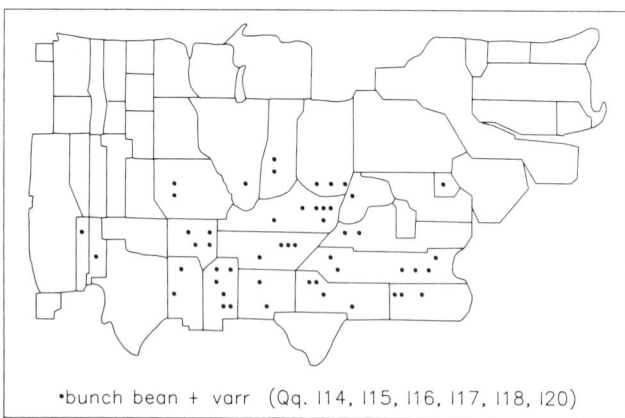

•bunch bean + varr (Qq. I14, I15, I16, I17, I18, I20)

bunchberry n

1 A low-growing perennial plant *(Cornus canadensis)* with whorled leaves and clusters of bright red berries. Also called **bearberry 10, bunch plum, Canadian dogwood, crackerberry 1, cuckoo plum, dwarf cornel, low cornel, puddingberry**

1845 Judd *Margaret* 106 **NEng,** She came to the shadows of the woods . . where she got box-berry flowers and fruit, bunch-berry and star-of-Bethlehem flowers. **1880** *Harper's Mag.* 61.501/1 **MN,** The carpet was . . more suggestive—though starred with scarlet bunch-berries—of death and decay even than the grave-yard on the slope. **1912** Mathews *Amer. Wild Flowers* 318, Bunchberry . . . An exceedingly dainty little plant common on wooded hilltops, and remarkable for its brilliant scarlet berries which grow in small, close clusters. **1941** Chase *Windswept* 420 *(Hench Coll.)* **ME,** Scarlet bunchberries in the damp woods, already faded in the open stretches, still fresh and glowing among the ferns, [were] tucked in the napkins at night to give a festive air to supper. **1955** [Dexter ME] *Moosehead Gazette* Feb 17/3 *(Hench Coll.),* Forest floors are literally carpeted with vines of the [p]artridge berry, bunchberry and emerald mos[s]es in infinite variety. **1961** Douglas *My Wilderness* 214 **NH,** The banks of the creeks in June are thick with bright bunchberries (Canadian dogwood). **1966** *DARE* Wildfl QR Pl.150 Inf NH4, Bunchberry; WA10, Dwarf cornel or bunchberry. **1967–69** *DARE* (Qu. S26c) Inf MI53, Bunchberry; (Qu. S26e) Inf MA67, Dwarf cornel—commonly known as bunchberry.

2 =**Texas lantana.**

1960 Vines *Trees SW* 897, Lantana is an attractive shrub, despite the species name, *horrida* . . . The following vernacular names have been recorded for Lantana in the United States . . : Bunch-berry [etc].

3 =**French mulberry.**

1970 Correll *Plants TX* 1339, *Callicarpa americana* . . . Bunchberry . . . Fruit showy, rose-pink or lilac to violet or red-purple.

buncher n Cf bundle n, v[1] B1

A tool or machine for handling grain or hay.

1968–69 *DARE* (Qu. L16, *Machines used around here in handling hay*) Inf MA47, Buncher—drops bales together; (Qu. L28, *Tools used in the past for cutting grain*) Inf PA127, Reaper or buncher—put it into piles.

bunches exclam

In marble play: see quot.

1963 *KY Folkl. Rec.* 9.62 **eKY,** *Demand for right to place marbles in a position other than the present position:* bunches.

bunchflower n

A liliaceous plant of the genus *Melanthium* with clusters of creamy or greenish-yellow flowers.

1822 Eaton *Botany* 350, *Melanthium . . . racemosum . .* bunch flower. **1845** Phelps *Lectures on Botany (DA),* App 127/1, *Melanthium hybridum,* bunch-flower. **1894** *Jrl. Amer. Folkl.* 7.102, *Melanthium Virgini-*

cum . . bunch-flower, West Va. **1938** Madison *Wild Flowers OH* 18, *Bunchflower . . .* Fls. greenish-yellow . . . Meadows and wet woods. **1976** Bruce *How to Grow Wildflowers* 171, It turned out to be *Melanthium virginicum,* the Common Bunchflower.

bunch grape n chiefly S Atl

A **summer grape** (here: *Vitis æstivalis*).

1916 *DN* 4.344 **FL,** *Bunch grape . . .* Any grape vine that bears grapes in bunches, as distinguished from one, like the scuppernong, in which the fruit occurs in small clusters of two, three, or four. **1966–68** *DARE* (Qu. I46) Inf NC25, Bunch grapes; NC79, Bunch grape—smaller than fox [grape], grow on beach. **1975** *Foxfire 3* 317 **neGA,** *Summer grape (Vitis æstivalis) . .* pigeon grape, bunch grape. **1976** Bailey–Bailey *Hortus Third* 1250, Bunch Grape: *V[itis] æstivalis.*

bunchgrass n

1 Alkali sacaton. *esp* **West**

1837 Irving *Rocky Mts.* 1.129 **ID** (as of 1832), Their horses . . [grazed] upon the upland bunch grass, which grew in great abundance, and, though dry, retained its nutritious properties. **1853** (1928) Knight *Diary* 50 **OR,** The men have driven the stock a mile and a half out, to dry bunch grass. **1877** Wright *Big Bonanza* 208 **NV,** The bunch-grass is considered to be as good for horses as barley, as it bears a heavy crop of seed. **1912** Wooton–Standley *Grasses NM* 83, *Sporobolus airoides . . . Bunch grass.* **1942** Whipple *Joshua* 141 **UT,** Bunch grass would grow on barren hills, and although the clumps were green now in the early Spring, even when strawlike with the heat of August they were still nutritious. **1965–70** *DARE* (Qu. S9, . . *Kinds of grass that are hard to get rid of*) Infs CA207, CO15, ID1, KS15, NM6, Bunch grass; (Qu. S8) Inf UT13, Bunch grass. **1966** *DARE* FW Addit WA 3, Bunch grass—grows in clusters belly-high, grew in Palouse County. Wild horses grazed belly-deep in it.

2 A fescue (here: *Festuca scabrella*).

1894 *Jrl. Amer. Folkl.* 7.104, *Festuca scabrella . .* bunch-grass, Cal. **1965–70** *DARE* (Qu. S9, . . *Kinds of grass that are hard to get rid of*) Infs MA6, 68, MI45, NY232, Bunch grass; (Qu. S21, . . *Weeds . . that are a trouble in gardens and fields*) Infs NY97, VT10, Bunch grass; (Qu. L8) Infs CA193, NY66, Bunch grass. [Note: some of these Infs may refer instead to other senses of **bunch grass.**]

3 =**beardgrass.**

1910 Graves *Flowering Plants* 48 **CT,** *Andropogon scoparius . . .* Bunch Grass. **1933** Small *Manual SE Flora* 43, *Andropogon . . .* Bunchgrasses. **1950** Gray–Fernald *Manual of Botany* 231 *A[ndropogon] scoparius . . . Bunchgrass.*

4 A needlegrass (here: *Stipa viridula*).

1911 Jepson *Flora CA* 43, *S[tipa] viridula . . .* Feather bunch-grass.

5 =**bear grass 1b.**

1951 *PADS* 15.29 **TX,** *Nolina* spp . . . Bunch, . . or basket, grass. **1970** Correll *Plants TX* 404, *Nolina texana . . .* Bunch-grass.

bunchgrasser n [bunchgrass + -er]

See quot 1920.

1920 *DN* 5.80 **eOR,** *Bunchgrassers . . .* People living out in the foothills. **1968** Adams *Western Words.* **1977** Jones *OR Folkl.* 24 (as of 1850s), Some [Oregon settlers] retreated from the rain, back east over the Cascades, preferring a drier climate; the settlers who resituated east were honored with the epithet *bunch-grassers.*

bunch in v phr

To help as a group.

1952 Brown *NC Folkl.* 1.244, The neighbors of men who wished to build a dwelling would "bunch in" and aid him.

bunching onion See bunch onion

bunch moss n Also *chaparral big bunch moss*

=**ball moss.**

1949 Moldenke *Amer. Wild Flowers* 311, Somewhat similar to the Spanishmoss is the *ballmoss* or *bunchmoss.* **1951** *PADS* 15.28 **TX,** *Diaphoranthema recurvata . . .* Bunch . . moss . . . *Tillandsia baileyi . . .* Big or Mexican, bunch or ball, moss; chaparral big bunch moss.

bunch onion n Also *bunching onion, green bunch ~, green bunching ~* chiefly Nth

A scallion *(Allium* spp).

1960 Bailey *Resp. to PADS* 20 **KS,** Bunch onions . . . Common. **1966–69** *DARE* (Qu. I6, . . *Onions that come up fresh early in the year, and you eat them raw*) Infs CT2, ME5, VT16, Bunch onions; WA13,

Green bunch onions; (Qu. I7) Inf **NY66**, Bunch onions; (Qu. I5) Inf **CA63**, Bunch onions—they come in a bunch. **1981** *Burpee Seeds* 126, Green bunching onions (scallions) can be pulled quite early in the season. *Ibid* 127, *White* [onion sets] . . . Excellent for pickling when small as for bunching onions.

bunch pink n

A sweet William *(Dianthus barbatus).*

1857 Gray *Manual of Botany* 54, *Sweet-William* or *Bunch Pink.* **1877** VT State Bd. Ag. *Report* 4.99, The quantity of . . bunch pinks and candytufts coming from self-sown seed is quite startling. **1892** *Jrl. Amer. Folkl.* 5.92, *Dianthus barbatus,* bunch pink. Vt.; So. Ohio.

bunch plum n NEng

=**bunchberry 1.**

1840 *S. Lit. Messenger* 6.518/2 **ME,** There were the fringed polygula [sic], the butter-cup, wild geranium, bunch-plum, ivy-berry. **1892** *Jrl. Amer. Folkl.* 5.97, *Cornus Canadensis,* bunch plums; pudding-berry. N.H. **1898** *Ibid* 11.228, *Cornus Canadensis* . . bunch plum, South Berwick, Me. **1929** *Torreya* 150 **ME,** *Cornus canadensis* "Bunch-plum."

bunch quitter n West

A horse or cow that stays apart from the **bunch** n **2.**

1937 Sandoz *Slogum* 157 **wNE,** A range boss motions a puncher to round up the bunch quitters. **1938** (1952) FWP *Guide SD* 84, *Bunch-quitter:* An animal that voluntarily quits the herd. **1958** *AmSp* 33.269 **eWA,** *Bunch quitter.* An animal which leaves a herd when it is being pressed and travels alone. Some animals do this habitually. **1968** Adams *Western Words, Bunch quitter*—A horse that has the habit of leaving the remuda and pulling for the home ranch or parts unknown.

bunch squash n

Perh a pattypan squash *(Cucurbita pepo* var).

1968 *DARE* (Qu. I23) Inf **SC57**, White bunch squash—flat, white, scalloped edges.

bunch up v phr

To clear the table.

1968 *DARE* (Qu. G10, *When the meal is all over, what do you have to do to the table?*) Inf **MD19**, Bunch it up. **1981** *Broaddus Coll.* **ceKY,** Bunch the dishes up—remove the dishes from the table.

bunch waterlily n

A **floating heart** (here: *Nymphoides aquatica).*

1951 *PADS* 15.37 **TX,** *Nymphoides lacunosum* . . . Water gentian; water apple-blossom; bunch waterlily.

bunchy adj

Chubby.

1942 Warnick *Garrett Co. MD* (as of 1900–1918), *Bunchy* . . . short and stout. "She's a little, short, bunchy girl."

buncle n [Abbr for **carbuncle**]

1969 *DARE* (Qu. BB33b, . . *A swelling under the skin . . . very big or serious*) Inf **GA72**, Buncle.

bunco n, also attrib Also sp bunko scattered, but chiefly N Cent See Map

A table game using dice.

1921 *Outing* 78.132/2 **Chicago IL,** [Advt:] "Joker" Tops . . . Have them at home for Bunko Parties. **1948** *News-Dispatch* (Michigan City,

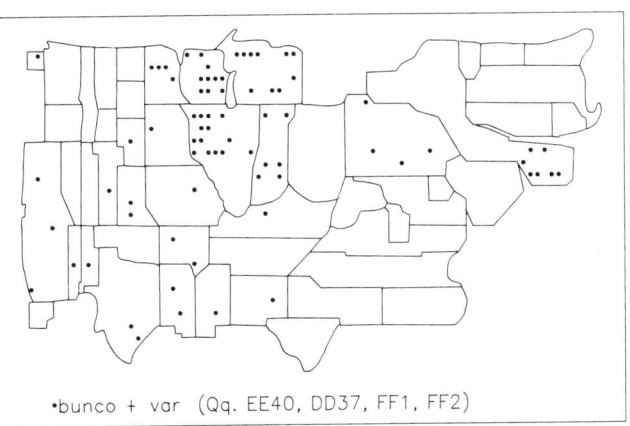

•bunco + var (Qq. EE40, DD37, FF1, FF2)

Ind.) 3 Apr. 6/5 *(DA),* Bunco was played. **1965–70** *DARE* (Qu. EE40, *What table games are played around here, using dice?*) 73 Infs, **esp N Cent,** Bunco; **MI44,** Progressive fifty, played with dice; used to be called bunco years ago; (Qu. DD37, . . *Table games)* Infs **IL4, MI44,** Bunco; (Qu. FF2, . . *Kinds of parties)* Infs **AL25, CA61, KY73, NY51,** Bunco parties; (Qu. FF1, . . *A kind of group meeting)* Inf **MO36,** Bunco. **1969** *Zion-Benton News* (Zion IL) 24 Apr sec 2 2/1, Our Lady of Humility parish will hold a card and bunco party.

buncombe See bunkum adj

bundance n [Aphet abundance]

1908 *DN* 3.295 **eAL, wGA,** *Bundance* . . . An abundance.

bundle n, v[1] |bʌndl| also, in Sth, S Midl, |bʌnl| Pronc-sp bun'le

See also **bindle**

A Forms.

1908 *DN* 3.282 **eAL, wGA,** *d* medial is lost in –ndl combinations, as in [bʌnl]. **1916** *Scribner's Mag.* 59.356/2 **VA** [Black], We come away, fetchin' bun'les an' barskets an' buckets. **1941** *AmSp* 16.12 **eTX** [Black], *Bundle* . . . ['bʌnl]. **1942** Hall *Smoky Mt. Speech* 87, [d] after [n] is in most cases not sounded before [l] . . . bundle. **1966** *DARE* Tape **NC51,** We used to . . fold it an' tie it ahead of it an' make just a ['bʌnl].

B As noun.

1 A **sheaf** of grain. **widespread exc wMD, sPA, WV** See Map

1827 *Albany Gazette* 25 Sep. 2/3 *(DA),* The agent has provided a few bundles of wheat in the sheaf, for the purpose of operation, and solicits the public patronage. **1906** *DN* 3.126 **nwAR,** *Bundle* . . . Sheaf. How many bundles of oats do you reckon there are here? **1910** *DN* 3.438 **cwNY.** **1917** *DN* 4.389 **neOH, IL, KS, KY, NY,** *Bundle* . . . Sheaf of unthresht grain. **1939** *LANE* Map 126, Both *bundle* and *sheaf* are common, being often used side by side. Some regard *sheaf* as bookish (Biblical). **1946** *PADS* 5.13 **VA.** **1949** Kurath *Word Geog.* 67, In the Southern area and in the South Midland *bundle* is the regular word for a sheaf of wheat. Elsewhere in the Eastern States *bundle* and *sheaf* occur side by side, the former predominating in the entire New England settlement area, the latter in Pennsylvania and adjoining parts of West Virginia. In Philadelphia and its immediate vicinity *sheaf* is used to the exclusion of *bundle,* and in the adjoining Pennsylvania German section to the west *sheaf* is much more common than *bundle.* **1950** *PADS* 13.17 **wTX.** **1951** *PADS* 15.53 **TX.** **1954** *Harder Coll.* **cwTN.** **c1960** *Wilson Coll.* **csKY.** **1965–70** *DARE* (Qu. L30a, *When grain is cut it is (or used to be) tied up in* _____) 663 Infs, **widespread except wMD, sPA, WV,** Bundles; (Qu. L12, . . *Small piles of hay standing in the field)* Infs **CT39, IA22, ME19,** Bundles; **AL14, VA46,** Hay bundles. **1973** Allen *LAUM* 1.274, In the UM it *[sheaf]* survives weakly in Minnesota and Iowa . . . In the great wheat-growing regions of the UM *bundle* itself is the usual term.

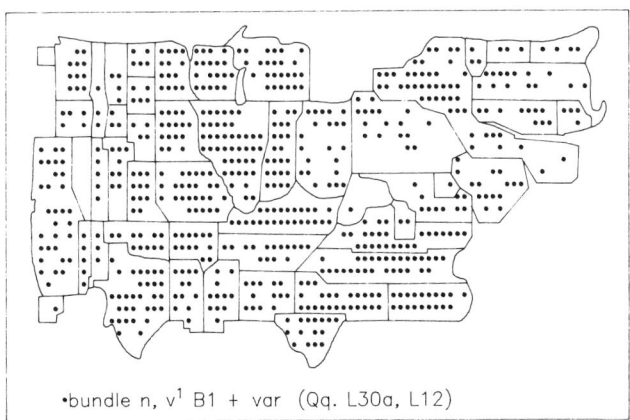

•bundle n, v[1] B1 + var (Qq. L30a, L12)

2 A woman; one's wife.

1904 Number 1500 *Life in Sing Sing* 246, *Bundle* . . a woman. **1935** *AmSp* 10.13 [Underworld argot], *Bundle.* 1. A woman. (Obs.) **1966** *DARE* (Qu. AA22, *Joking names . . [for a man's wife]: "I have to go down and pick up my* _____ .") Inf **SC10,** Bundle.

C As verb.

1 To share a bed with a person of the opposite sex while fully clothed (or with some other impediment to sexual intercourse); also n *bundler,* vbl n *bundling.* **chiefly NEast** *hist*

1775 (1922) Schaw *Jrl. of a Lady* 135, The Lady is a fair American . . . None of your bundlers a' faith for me. **1781** Peters *Genl. Hist. CT* 325,

It would be accounted the greatest rudeness to speak before a lady of a garter, knee, or leg, yet it is thought but a piece of civility to ask her to *bundle;* a custom as old as the first settlement in 1634. **1824** Irving *Hist. NY* 218, Among other hideous customs, they attempted to introduce among them [the Dutch] that of *bundling,* which the Dutch lasses . . seemed very well inclined to follow. **1825** Neal *Brother Jonathan* 1.118 **CT,** I wonder that you have a decent woman left among you. The very "bundling" of the Dutch settlers; that mischievous, wicked habit, which is now spreading through the frontier settlements. **1902** (1968) Clapin *Americanisms, Bundle (to.).* A term designating a custom, formerly practiced in New England, of men and women sleeping on the same bed with all their clothes on, when there was not house-room to provide better accommodation. **1946** *Natl. Geog. Mag.* 89.774, [Caption:] *Some Early New England Couples Did Their Courting in Bed, Called It Bundling* . . . Young folks, fully clothed, tucked under covers, a center-board separating them. **1960** Korson *Black Rock* 248 **PA,** Occasionally a boy was asked to submit to a bundling bag that covered him from armpits to the ends of his toes, and it had pull strings yet! The girl's father tended to the strings himself. **1968** *DARE* FW Addit NY93, *Bundling* —Method of courting in bed with a post between.
2 By ext: to court, woo.
1941 *LANE* Map 404 *(Courting her)* 1 inf, **sME,** Bundling—old-fashioned. **1952** Brown *NC Folkl.* 1.524 **wNC,** *Bundling* . . . Courting. **1968–70** *DARE* (Qu. AA1, . . *When a man goes to see a girl often and seems to want to marry her, he's* _____ *her*) Inf **MA116,** Bundling; **VA11,** Bundling—old-fashioned.

‡bundle v[2] [Alter of *bungle*]
1969 *DARE* (Qu. JJ42, *To make an error in judgement* . . *"He usually handles things well, but this time he certainly* _____*."*) Inf **KY5,** Bundled a job.

bundler See **bundle** v[1] **C1**

bundlesome adj
Bulky.
1940 Stuart *Trees of Heaven* 149 **neKY,** The women from the hills, dressed in tattered dresses, bundlesome coats. **1940** in **1944** *ADD* **WV,** *Bundlesome* . . . The dresses the women wore to the parties in the country were not only warm but also very bundlesome. **1972** *NYT Article Letters* **MT,** *Bundlesome* . . . unwieldy. Heard once.

bundle stick n
1932 Hanley *Disks* **swCT,** We took part of the dough and rolled it out and cut it in strips and twisted it up and fried it and they were called bundle sticks.

bundle stiff n Also *bundle-bum* [Folk-etym for **bindle stiff**]
An itinerant worker.
1927 *DN* 5.441 [Underworld], *Bundle-bum* . . . A bindle-stiff of the lowest order. **1939** FWP *ID Lore* 244, A bundle-stiff (itinerant worker) wheeled in . . and hit the push-up (foreman) for a job. **1941** FWP *Guide WA* 423, The migratory harvesters, once known as "bundle stiffs," now seek other employment.

bundling See **bundle** v[1] **C1**

bundock n See **boondock** n

bung n[1] [From *bung up* to bruise, batter]
1 A bump, knot (on the head). Cf **bunk** n[4]
1966–68 *DARE* (Qu. X60, *A lump that comes up on your head when you get a sharp blow or knock*) Infs **FL31, WI50,** Bung.
‡2 See quot.
1965 *DARE* Tape NY245, We used to [play] what they called bung . . . We used to take a cut piece of . . rubber pipe that you would stand on its small end and hit with a hockey stick like you would a hockey puck today.

‡bung n[2] See **pung**

‡bung n[3] [Alter of *bun*]
1969 *DARE* (Qu. X3, *When a woman puts her hair up on her head in a bunch, you call this a* _____) Inf **RI4,** Bung.

bung v Freq *bung out* [Perh alter of *bug,* but cf **bung** n[1] **1**]
To stick out, protrude.
1896 *DN* 1.414 **NY,** *Bug out* . . . "His eyes bugged out, he bugged out his eyes," showing astonishment . . . *Bung out:* same as *bug out,* above. **1911** Porter *Harvester* 338 **IN,** Won't her eyes bung when I tell her about this? **1942** Whipple *Joshua* 45 **UT** (as of c1860), She had seen him . .

biting his lower lip until it bunged out as if to keep back a whole flock of swear words.

bungalow apron n, also attrib *esp* **NY**
A housedress that ties at the waist.
1966–69 *DARE* (Qu. W22, . . *A loose, full housedress that ties at the waist*) Infs **NY37, 49, 165, 199,** Bungalow apron; (Qu. FF22a, . . *Clubs . . for women*) Inf **FL29,** Bungalow-apron club.

bung-belly n
=**black-eyed pea.**
1899 (1912) Green *VA Folk-Speech* 100, *Bung-bellies* . . . Name given to *black-eye* or *cornfield* peas.

‡bung cheese n [Etym unknown]
Cottage cheese.
1941 *LANE* Map 299, 1 inf, **seME,** Bung cheese, the regular term.

bung cloth n *joc* Cf **belly pad, blanket 3,** and *DS* **H20b**
A pancake.
1938 Tripp *Flukes* 233 [Among NEng whalers], The bill of fare was sometimes varied with pancakes, called, "bung-cloths", by the boat-steerers, and rice and curry.

bungdown adj [*bung* for *bunged* battered + *down*]
1975 Gould *ME Lingo* 28, *Bungdown* . . . This probably comes from "bang." It means battered, used up, belabored: a *bungdown* truck, a *bungdown* hat, the same old *bungdown* reasons for sobriety.

bunged up ppl adj[1]
Beaten, bruised; damaged, run-down; ill.
1899 (1912) Green *VA Folk-Speech,* Bung up . . . To be bruised or swollen from a blow. "His eyes are bunged up." **1908** *DN* 3.295 **eAL, wGA,** *Bunged up* . . . Lacerated, beaten up. "He is all bunged up." **1909** *DN* 3.409 **cnME,** *Bunged up* . . . Ill; out of breath. **1910** *DN* 3.438 **cwNY,** *Bunged up* . . . Bruised or sore; worn out; full of aches. "I ache all over, and feel so bunged up I must go to bed." **1935** Sandoz *Jules* 409 **wNE** (as of 1880–1930), An old-timer with a bunged-up hip. c1960 *Wilson Coll.* **csKY,** *Bunged up* . . . Out of order, injured. **1966–69** *DARE* (Qu. X20, . . *A black eye*) Inf **NC82,** Bunged up; (Qu. DD24, . . *Diseases . . from continual drinking*) Inf **GA9,** Bunged-up liver; (Qu. KK70, *Something that has got out of proper shape: "That house is all* _____*."*) Infs **GA7, IL72,** Bunged up. **1968** *DARE* FW Addit NY96, Bunged up—Injured, shaken up and bruised, usually in an accident. **1975** Gould *ME Lingo* 28, To be all *bunged* up . . used, bruised, beaten, spent.

bunged up ppl adj[2] [*bung* to plug with a stopper, also infl by *bung* anus]
See quots.
c1960 *Wilson Coll.* **csKY,** *Bunged up* . . . Constipated. **1965–70** *DARE* (Qu. BB21, . . *Constipated*) 11 Infs, **scattered,** Bunged up.

bunger See **banjo A**

bungersome See **bunglesome**

bung eye n [**bung** v] *esp* **Nth**
A protruding eye; hence adj *bung-eyed.*
1965–70 *DARE* (Qu. X21a, . . *Eyes . . [that] stick out*) Infs **AZ8, MA5, 58, NY101, 105, 232, VT3,** Bung-eyed; **NY68, 201,** Bung eyes; **OH70,** Bung eye.

bung fodder n [*bung* anus + *fodder;* cf **bum fodder**]
See quots.
1908 *DN* 3.295 **eAL, wGA,** *Bung-fodder* . . . Toilet paper or substitute therefor. **1912** Green *VA Folk-Speech,* *Bum-fodder* . . . *Bung-fodder.* Paper used in the water-closet.

‡bungkajeenis n [Fanciful extension of *bum* buttocks or *bung* anus; cf **bunky**]
The buttocks.
1969 *DARE* (Qu. X35, . . *The part of the body that you sit on*) Inf **GA77,** Bungkajeenis [ˌbəŋkəˈʤinɨs].

bungler n Cf **apple pandowdy, buckle** n
A type of pastry.
1956 McAtee *Some Dialect NC* 54 **nwNC,** *Bungler* . . . Cobbler. "Now we'll have a good old cherry bungler."

bunglesome adj Also *bungersome* somewhat old-fash
Awkward, clumsy.

1889 *Century Dict.* 3.721/2, *Bunglesome . . .* Bungling; clumsy. **1899** (1912) Green *VA Folk-Speech, Bungersome . . .* Clumsy. **1915** Porter *Michael O'Halloran* 377 **IN,** But this sheet is going to be rather bunglesome. Ma, could you do anything about it? **1927** *AmSp* 3.138 **ME,** An awkward one [=person, is called] "bunglesome." **1954** *PADS* 21.22 **SC,** *Bunglesome, bungersome . . .* Of awkward, clumsy shape for handling, applied to packages, bundles, etc. Not applied to persons, so far as reported. **c1960** *Wilson Coll.* **csKY,** *Bunglesome . . .* Awkward.

bungo n, also attrib [AmSpan *bongo,* prob from an Afr language] *Spanish settlement areas; hist* Cf *DJE bungay*
A type of canoe.
1763 Roberts *Acct. FL* [Plate betw pp 10 & 11], A Bungo. **1842** in 1911 TX Dept. State *Diplomatic Corresp.* 3.953 **TX,** I have made a voyage to the Island of Cozumel for which purpose I had occasion to charter a Bungo. **1856** in 1948 *Western Folkl.* 7.6, Whole bungo loads were killed while they were endeavoring to escape by the lake. **1902** (1968) Clapin *Americanisms, Bungo.* A Southern name for a species of small boat. **1948** *Language* 24.253, *Bongo* is undoubtedly African. Neither Raimundo nor Mendonça mentions the word; but Fernando Ortiz has pointed out that it is the name of a ferry-boat in Cuba and Central America; that it is derived from West African *boñgo* 'canoe or large raft'; and that Congo *dongo* is used in the same sense.

bung out v phr Cf **bunch** v[2]
To quit, give up.
1938 FWP *Guide NH* 409, Many people, finding they could not farm successfully near Kinsman Notch, moved to better land; those left behind would remark that the deserters had 'bunged out'.

bungs up adj phr [See quot]
Staggering drunk.
1975 Gould *ME Lingo* 28, *Bungs up—*Rolling badly in a heavy sea, a vessel is *bungs up,* i.e., careening so the *bungs* in her planking are visible. Accordingly, a gentleman *feeling no pain* might be *bungs up* on his way home.

bungums n [*bung* to bruise, batter + *'em* them + *-s*] Cf **knucks** and see *EDD* for descr of the game as played in Yorkshire
A marbles game: see quot 1955.
1955 *PADS* 23.12 **cwTN,** *Bungums . . .* A marbles game in which the players attempt to roll marbles into holes in the ground, and under certain conditions the winner has to allow the others to shoot at his knuckles. **1967** *DARE* (Qu. EE7, *Kinds of marble games*) Inf **NY10,** Bungums.

bung up and bilge free adj phr Also *bungs ~* **coastal NEng**
Properly stowed, in good order; hence used as an expression of approval.
1850 Melville *White-Jacket* 183 **NEng,** "Bung up, and bilge free!" he cried, in an ecstasy. **1916** *DN* 4.333 **Nantucket MA,** *Bung-up and bilge-free . . .* Well, — referring to the way casks are stowed in the hold of a whaler. **1926** Ashley *Yankee Whaler* 126, *Bung up and Bilge Free:* The best position for a cask. **1945** Colcord *Sea Language* **ME, Cape Cod, Long Island,** *Bung up and bilge free.* Properly disposed or packed. From the whaleman's description of the proper stowage of casks of whale oil. **1975** Gould *ME Lingo* 28, *Bungs up and bilge free—*This term derives from the bung in a barrel. Casks in the hold had to be stowed *bungs up,* so bilge water couldn't intrude. It is a term for being shipshape, and anybody who is *bungs up and bilge free* is behaving properly, perhaps a mite sanctimoniously.

‡**bungy** n *euphem* Cf *DS* K22
=**gentleman cow.**
1939 *LANE* Map 190 (*Bull*) 1 inf, **eME,** [bʌ⁻ŋgɪ⁺], used by women.

bun-hole See **bunny-in-the-hole**

bun in the oven, have a See **oven**

bunk adj See **bunkum** adj

bunk n[1] [Etym uncert, but see *OED bunk* sb.[2]]
1 =**poison hemlock 1.**
1900 Lyons *Plant Names* 114, *C[onium] maculatum . . .* Bunk, Poison Parsley [etc]. **1930** Sievers *Amer. Med. Plants* 46, *Poison Hemlock . . .* Other common names . . . Bunk, heck-how, poison root [etc].
2 =**chicory 1.**
1900 Lyons *Plant Names* 101, *C[ichorium] Intybus . . .* Chicory . . . Bunk. **1959** Carleton *Index Herb. Plants* 20, *Bunk . . .* Cichorium intybus.

3 =**cornflower 1.**
1959 Carleton *Index Herb. Plants* 20, *Bunk:* Centaurea cyanus.

bunk n[2]
1 See **bunkhouse.**
2 See **bunk sled.**

bunk n[3] See **bunkum** n

bunk n[4] [**bunk** v[1] 2]
1968 *DARE* (Qu. X60, . . *A lump that comes up on your head when you get a sharp blow or knock*) Inf **NY65,** Bunk.

bunk n[5] [See quot]
=**bohunk 1.**
1931–33 *LANE Worksheets* **cCT,** Bunk. Nickname for Lithuanians. Inf considers word to be a contraction of bohunk.

bunk n[6] Cf **buck** n[1] 2b
A boy—used as a term of address.
1968 *DARE* (Qu. II10a, *Asking directions of somebody on the street when you don't know his name—what you'd say to a boy: "Say, _____, where's the post office?"*) Inf **MD9,** Bunk [bʌŋk].

bunk v[1] [Prob alter of *bump,* infl by **bunt** v[3]]
1 To throw oneself down on a sled. Cf **belly-bunk, bunt** v[3]
1909 *DN* 3.409 **cnME,** *Bunk . . .* In coasting down hill, to start a sled.
2 usu with *into:* To bump into; to meet (someone) accidentally. **NYC, esp Brooklyn**
1942 *New Yorker* 30 May 14/1 **Brooklyn NY,** What do you think of that? Bunking into you on a subway train. **1942** *Time* 1 June 58 **NYC,** I bunked into a friend of mine on Moitle Avenoo. **1967** *DARE* (Qu. II17, *If you happen to meet someone that you haven't seen for a while: "Guess who I _____ this morning."*) Inf **NY34,** Bumped into—In Brooklyn the word bumped is often "bunked". **1967** *DARE* File **NYC,** "I bunked into something" meaning "I bumped . . . " was used by my mother, Jewish, who grew up on the East Side in NYC and also by a friend who is Italian Catholic who was raised in the Bronx. **1968** *DARE* FW Addit **Brooklyn NY,** *Bunk*—To bump (into something). **1980** *Sat. Review* Aug 77 **NYC,** It used to be that we walked into rooms or buildings or walls, or we'd bump into our friends (except in New York, where we'd *bunkinta* them).
3 In marble play:
a also *bunker:* To defeat an opponent; to win (marbles) as a result.
1892 *DN* 1.220 **MO,** The expression *to bunker* means to win a game; as, "I bunkered him," meaning "I won." **1943** *Hench Coll.* **seVA,** A . . student . . said to me that . . in the game of marbles, boys use *bunk* to mean "to win." e.g. Did you bunk any marbles? How many did you bunk?
b To shoot a marble against a wall so that it rebounds and hits another marble.
1968 *DARE* Tape **NY52,** You took your shooter marble which was your prize marble and bounced it against the wall and then I would run out and hit marbles that the other players had put in a space . . the one that . . what they termed bunked their marble first was chosen either by calling out "first bunk" or else they scratched a line in the dirt and shot a marble at it.

bunk v[2] [*bunk* to leave in a hurry, scram]
To play hookey.
1969 *DARE* (Qu. JJ6, *To stay away from school without an excuse*) Infs **RI4, 6,** Bunkin'.

bunk-and-toggle fence n Also *bunk fence, stake-and-bunk fence* **esp ME**
A type of rail fence: see quots.
1907 *DN* 3.242 **eME,** *Bunk and toggle fence . . .* A heavy log fence . . . *Bunk fence . . .* Same as bunk and toggle fence. **1909** *DN* 3.409 **cnME,** *Bunk and toggle fence . . .* A fence similar to a stake and rider fence. **1951** *S. Folkl. Qrly.* 16.117 **ME,** *Bunk, stake-and- . . .* A fence of 4 rails, the ends supported by 2 stakes, which in turn were mounted on bunks or blocks. **1968** *DARE* (Qu. L61, *Fences made of solid logs*) Inf **NJ16,** Bunk and toggle fence—logs on top of each other with holes for stake; not used here.

bunker n[1] [Abbr for **mossbunker**] **N and C Atl**
=**menhaden.**
1842 DeKay *Zool. NY* 3.259, The Mossbonker. . . *Alosa menhaden . . .*

At the east end of the island [=Manhattan], they are called *Skippangs* or *Bunkers.* **1887** Goode *Amer. Fishes* 386, New Jersey uses the New York name with its local variations, such as "Bunker" and "Marshbanker." **1940** *High Sport for the Fisherman in Colonial Virginia Waters* [Folder] *(Hench Coll.),* After the boat is anchored, bunkers, a non-edible fish caught in nets, are ground in a meat chopper and scattered on the water to make a slick. **1945** *Hench Coll.* **ceVA** [Letter], It is uniformly called the alewife, menhaden, or bunker. **1953** MD State Dept. of Educ. *Our Underwater Farm* 15 *(Hench Coll.)* Menhaden are also known as alewives, bunkers, fatbacks, and bug fish. **1959** Wash. *Post* 14 Aug A21/6 *(Hench Coll.),* Using menhaden—bunkers—for bait, they caught 17 cobia. **1966–70** *DARE* (Qu. P2, . . *Saltwater fish . . good to eat*) Inf **NC**12, Bunker; (Qu. P4, *Saltwater fish . . not good to eat*) Inf **VA**79, Bunker; **NJ**16, Greentail bunker; (Qu. P7, *Small fish used as bait*) Inf **NY**47, Bunker; (Qu. P14, *Commercial fishing . . [what kind]*) Inf **VA**46, Bunker; (Qu. O10, . . *Kinds of boats*) Inf **NC**12, Bunker boats. **1976** Warner *Beautiful Swimmers* 127 **Chesapeake Bay,** The menhaden has even more names than the herring . . . Chesapeake watermen simply say menhaden or bunker.

bunker n[2] [**bunk** v[1] **3b**]
In marble play: a shooter, taw.
   1968–70 *DARE* (Qu. EE6a, . . *Marbles—the big one that's used to knock others out of the ring*) Infs **CT**6, **DC**11, 12, Bunker.

bunker n[3]
   1909 *DN* 3.409 **cnME,** *Bunker* . . . A kernel of popcorn that pops perfectly.

bunker n[4] [**bunk** v[1] **1**] Cf **bunt** v[3]
   1909 *DN* 3.409 **cnME,** *Bunker* . . . In coasting, the one who starts a sled.

‡**bunker** n[5] [Perh alter of **bunter 1,** but cf **bunk** v[1] **2**]
A goat that butts.
   1969 *DARE* (Qu. K68, . . *A goat that habitually strikes people with its horns*) Inf **NY**198, Bunker.

bunker v See **bunk** v[1] **3a**

‡**bunker head** n Cf **bulkhead 2, bullhead 8**
   1968 *DARE* (Qu. B11, . . *Other kinds of clouds*) Inf **AL**48, Bunker heads—big clouds forming up before rain.

bunk fence See **bunk-and-toggle fence**

bunkhouse n Rarely *bunk, bunk shack* **chiefly West** See Map
A building (or occas a vehicle) that provides sleeping or living quarters for groups of workers such as ranch hands, loggers, railroad crews.
   1877 U.S. Treas. Dept. *Mines* 8.332 **CO,** Bunk-house [of the Little Annie Mill]. **1915** *DN* 4.243 **MT,** Bunk shack . . . "A sleeping house." **1916** *DN* 4.272 **KS, NE,** Bunk house . . . Rough little log or frame houses used for farm hands or others on ranches, when additional sleeping accommodations are needed. **1927** *AmSp* 2.349 **WV,** Bunk house . . . a sleeping place in a camp. **1933** *AmSp* 8.1.31 **nwTX,** Bunk-house. House where the cowboys sleep, removed from the central ranch-house. **1958** McCulloch *Woods Words* 24 **Pacific NW,** Bunkhouse—The loggers' home, where they bunk down, keep their gear. **1965–70** *DARE* (Qu. L2, *The extra house on a large farm where a hired man and his family live*) 46 Infs, **chiefly West,** Bunkhouse; **PA**235, Bunk; (Qu. M22, . . *Other kinds of buildings . . on farms*) 15 Infs, **chiefly West,** Bunkhouse. [19 Infs

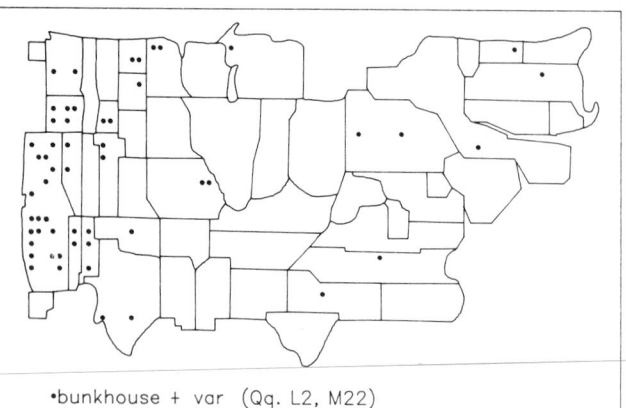

•bunkhouse + var (Qq. L2, M22)

specified that a bunkhouse is for single men only.] **1969** *DARE* Tape **CA**161, [Grain farmers] had a bunkhouse and a cookhouse for the hired help. **1977** Adams *Lang. Railroader* 25, Bunkhouse: A freight car filled with bunks, such as those used by a section gang.

bunkie See **bunkmate**

bunking vbl n, also attrib
Spending the night at the home of a friend.
   1968 *Union City Daily Messenger* (TN) 26 Apr 6/6, Miss Vivian Whitworth recently attended a bunking party. **1983** *DARE* File **nwTN,** Bunking, as used in this area, refers to a group of people, generally junior high or younger girls, getting together to spend the night.

bunkmate n Also *bunkie* **West**
A person with whom one shares sleeping quarters.
   1859 Vielé *Following* 218 **swTX,** I rewarded [his affection for the dog] by giving him Jack for his "bunkie"! **1877** Habberton *Jericho Road* 16 ?**IL,** Folding his blanket double and piling it over his bunkmate, . . the Parson stretched himself in his bunk with no covering whatever. **1902** White *Blazed Trail* 58 **MI,** Thorpe had assigned him as bunk mate the young fellow who assisted . . in the felling. **1903** (1965) Adams *Log Cowboy* 68 **NM,** We had undergone an experience which my bunkie, The Rebel, termed "an interesting experience." **1918** *DN* 5.23 **NW** [College slang], Bunkie . . . A roommate. **1948** *SW Rev.* 33.29.2 **wTX,** The next morning Bud's bunkie sat watching him shave.

bunko See **bunco**

bunk shack See **bunkhouse**

bunk sled n Also *bunk (sleigh)* [*bunk* heavy timber on which logs rest] **Nth**
A sled for carrying loads, esp timber.
   1907 *DN* 3.241 **eME,** *Bunk* . . . A lumberman's sled. *Ibid* 242 **eME,** *Bunk-sled* . . . A lumberman's sled across which is a piece of timber supporting the ends of logs. **1965–70** *DARE* (Qu. N40a, . . *Different kinds of sleighs . . for hauling loads*) Infs **NY**23, **OH**12, Bunk sled; [**MN**15, **MT**4, Double-bunk sleigh]; **MA**19, Bunk; **NY**5, Bunk sleigh; [**MT**4, Single-bunk sleigh]; (Qu. N40c, *Different kinds of sleighs for carrying other things*) Inf **MI**108, Bunk sleigh; **WI**77, Logging bunk. **1967** *DARE* Tape **MN**4, We used to have what we would refer to as bunk sleighs. **1967** *DARE* FW Addit **cnNY,** A bunk sleigh is a logging sleigh with bunks to hold logs.

bunkum adj Also sp *buncombe* Rarely *bunk, bunkumsquint* [Etym uncert; *-um* perh a pseudo-Latin element as in *crinkum-crankum*] **old-fash**
Excellent, first-rate (esp of food); strong; healthy.
   1834 *Military & Naval Mag.* 3.24, My companions caused to be put up in parcels, a quantity of candy and cakes; "for," said Santin, " . . these will be *bunkum* about taps." **1859** *Harper's Mag.* 19.712/1, 'Was the fence alluded to a good, strong fence?' . . 'It was a Buncombe fence, Sir!. . A Buncombe fence, Sir, is a fence that is bull strong, horse high, and pig tight!' **1874** (1937) Nichols *40 Yrs.* 315 **OH,** 'Who is nominated for President?' 'James K. Polk, of Tennessee!' 'Bunkum! First Rate!' **1880** *Harper's Mag.* 61.615/1 **MA,** I had heard the word "bunkum" often used by bumpkins, but always with reference to something of an edible character, as an apple being "bunkum," or a piece of cake or pie. **1904** *DN* 2.395 **MS, NY,** Bunkum . . . Fine, good, first-class, "Those buckwheat cakes are just bunkum." **1905** *DN* 3.72 **nwAR,** Bunkum (buncombe) . . . Excellent. Not uncommon. **1908** *DN* 3.295 **eAL, wGA,** Bunkum . . . Fine, excellent. **1910** *DN* 3.452 **seVT,** Bunkum . . . Sturdy, strong . . In good health. "How are you?" "I'm pretty bunkum." "That wagon isn't very bunkum." **1911** *DN* 3.541 **NE,** Bunkumsquint . . . Fine, excellent. **1941** *AmSp* 16.74 **seNE,** Bunkum or bunk . . a term of encomium, applied especially to food.

‡**bunkum** n Also *bunk* [Cf **bum** n[1]]
   1966 *DARE* (Qu. X35, *Joking words for the part of the body that you sit on*) Inf **SC**4, Bunk, **KY**38, Bunkum—old-fashioned euphemism.

bunkum town n [Perh rel to **bunk** n[5]]
   1966 *DARE* (Qu. II25, . . *Part of a town where the poorer people, special groups, or foreign groups live*) Inf **MS**71, Bunkum town.

bunk up v phr
To vomit.
   1943 *LANE* Map 504 1 inf, **ceVT,** Bunk it up.

‡**bunky** n Also sp *bounky* [Perh rel to **bun** n[3]] Cf **bunkum** n
   1982 *Smithsonian Letters* **ceGA,** A Southern mammy punishing her

child would put it across her knee and give it a couple of slaps on the "bounky."

bun'le See **bundle** n, v[1]

‡bunner n
1967 *DARE* (Qu. Z5, . . *Words meaning "brother"*) Inf **HI**1, Bunner ['bʌnɚ].

bunnet, bunnit See **bonnet** A

bunny n[1] See **bunny tail**

‡bunny n[2] Cf **mouse**
A black eye.
1966 *DARE* (Qu. X20) Inf **WA**11, Bunny.

bunny boot n
A large boot orig made of white felt, later of insulated rubber.
1954 *Jessen's Weekly* (Fairbanks) Sept 23 (Tabbert *Alaskan Engl.*), *Bunny Boots*—All felt, Assorted small, med., large. Excellent cond. 1955 *U.S. Arctic Info. Center Gloss.* 14, *Bunny boot.* A nickname used by U.S. military personnel for the white felt boot issued for arctic use by the Quartermaster Corps. 1965 Bowen *An Alaskan Dictionary* (Tabbert *Alaskan Engl.*), *Bunny boots.* Huge white felt boots, built exactly like Army field boots but much larger . . . Bunny boots are the warmest footgear worn in the Northland excepting the Eskimo Mukluk. 1974 *News-Miner* (Fairbanks AK) (Tabbert *Alaskan Engl.*), New white *Bunny Boots* [pictured are rubber insulated boots].

bunny burner n
A makeshift stove used in camping: see quot.
1967 *DARE* Tape **WA** 28, Bunny burner . . a tuna fish can full of paraffin with a . . wick in the center.

bunny-in-the-hole n Also *bun-hole, bunny hole* Cf **baby-in-the-hole, bungums**
A children's game in which a player tries to roll a marble (or ball) into a hole dug by an opponent (or rarely into the cap of an opponent).
1945 Boyd *Hdbk. Games* 45, *Bunny in the hole* . . . The players place their caps (or dig shallow holes) close to a fence or wall, one beside the other . . . *It* rolls the ball from the line, endeavoring to get it into a cap. 1958 *PADS* 29.31 **MA**, *Bunny hole* . . . Same as *bun-hole* and *bunny in the hole.* A hole is dug in mud with the heel, and players, usually two, roll their marbles or nudge them with bent forefinger toward the hole; the player who holes in the last marble takes all. 1967–68 *DARE* (Qu. EE7, *Kinds of marble games*) Inf **MA**82, Bunny-in-the-hole; **VT**5, Bunny in the hole — make a small hole in the ground with a circle around it, about ten or twelve inches; you hit a marble outside the ring and tried to knock it in the hole. c1970 Wiersma *Marbles Terms, Bunny in the hole* . . . A game in which players attempt to shoot the marble into a hole in the ground. 1973 Ferretti *Marble Book* 71, *Bun-hole.* A hole in the ground is scooped out in the shape of a saucer, not deep but slightly concave, and marbles are shot at it from a shooting line about eight to 15 feet away . . . *Bun-hole* in England is *bunny-in-the-hole* in New England.

bunny-in-the monk n
?=**bunny-in-the-hole.**
1940 *Recreation* (NY) 34.110, A list of the many games of marbles played throughout the country follows . . . Bunny in the Monk.

bunny mullein n
=**mullein.**
1969 *DARE* (Qu. S20, *A common weed that grows on open hillsides: it has velvety green leaves close to the ground, and a tall stalk with small yellow flowers on a spike at the top*) Inf **CT**21, Bunny mulleins ['mʌlɪnz].

bunny tail n Also *bunny* Cf **dust bunny**
1966–69 *DARE* (Qu. E20, *Soft rolls of dust that collect on the floor under beds or other furniture*) Infs **MS**48, **NE**7, Bunny tails; **CA**167, Bunnies.

buns See **bun** n[3]

bunt n [Transf from *bunt* the bulging part of a ship's (square) sail]
The sagging middle part of a fish net.
1970 *DARE* Tape **VA**79, They continue doing that until they get up to what they call the bunt, where the cork lines and lead lines are heavier so it will hold the fish when you get 'em up there.

bunt v[1], hence *bunting* vbl n [**bunt** n]
Of a seine net: to swell, form a bag; to cause a seine to swell.
1847 in 1956 Eliason *Tarheel Talk* 262, [Seine] hung in mud & bunted out Breast . . . Hung in mud . . . & bunted seine & lost ½ the haul. 1956 Eliason *Tarheel Talk* 262, *Bunt*—to allow seine to belly. 1968 *DARE* Tape **NC**59, Each boat would pull [this net] . . . until they'd get it up to where they wanted it — they called it bunting . . . It would just pen the fish up in a small place where they could get to 'em.

bunt v[2] **Nth** Cf **bunter**
To butt.
1910 *DN* 3.452 **seVT**, *Bunt* . . . To butt, to push with the head. Applied to the action of hornless animals, as a small calf, a sheep, or even a person. c1950 *WELS Suppl.* **csME**, An angry ram bunts you. 1965–70 *DARE* (Qu. K68, *A goat that habitually strikes people with its horns*) Infs **IN**69, **MI**98, **MN**23, **OR**4, Bunting goat; **NY**163, Buntin' goat; **MN**34, It's bunting; **MA**6, He bunts you; **NY**23, Bunts; **NY**68, They bunt don't they?

bunt v[3] Cf **belly-bunt 1, bunk** v[1] 1
1892 *Jrl. Amer. Folkl.* 5.146 **ME**, When a boy throws himself upon a sled . . he *bunts*, or *bumps*, or *plumps*, etc., upon it, according to the manner of speech in his locality.

bunt adv [Imit of the sound and action of **bunt** v[2]]
1871 (1882) Stowe *Fireside Stories* 210 **NEng**, Dick would see us, and put down his head, and run at us full chisel, and come bunt agin the fence.

bun, take the v phr
To win the prize, "take the cake."
1887 in 1950 *AmSp* 25.31 **seLA**, *Bun, take the.* 'To take the cake.' . . 'But "the pale and yellow babe of her white sister" takes the bun.' 1896 *DN* 1.414 **cNY**, *Bun:* "That takes the bun," that's very good. 1942 Berrey–Van den Bark *Amer. Slang* 373.4, *Be rewarded* . . . Take the cake, –the bun.

bunter n [**bunt** v[2]]
1 A goat that strikes people with its horns. **chiefly Nth** See Map
c1950 *WELS Suppl.* **csME**, *Bunter:* The ram that bunts (butts) you often. 1965–70 *DARE* (Qu. K68, . . *A goat that habitually strikes people with its horns*) 49 Infs, **chiefly Nth**, Bunter.

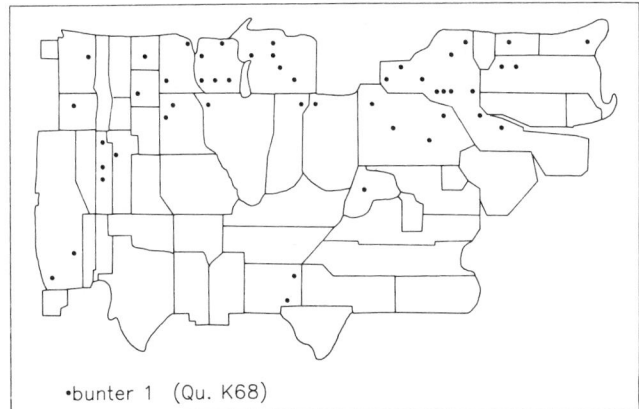

•bunter 1 (Qu. K68)

2 A calf or a hornless cow.
1852 in 1906 Thoreau *Writings* 9.306, These appendages [=horns] are indispensable to the beauty of the animal, as appears from the great calf look of a cow without horns, or a "bunter." 1984 *DARE* File **IN**, By pushing and bunting each other, calves establish their "pecking order" in the herd. In any herd, the best bunter leads the line, goes first through the gate, and takes the first drink of water at the watering trough.
3 See quot.
1919 *Jrl. Amer. Folkl.* 32.378 **seSC**, Bunter means bad child.

buntie, bunting n See **bunty** n

bunting vbl n See **bunt** v[1]

bunty n, also attrib Also *buntie, bunting* [Engl dial *bunty*] **chiefly Appalachians**
A tailless fowl.

1872 Schele de Vere *Americanisms* 380 **PA,** A tailless fowl is . . called a *bunty.* **1891** in 1950 *PADS* 13.5 **cAL,** I think the buntin' hen is setting somewhere, and there's six eggs in my drawer that old Browny laid on my bed. **1930** Shoemaker *1300 Words* 5 **cPA Mts,** *Buntie*—A Rumpless, or tailless fowl, originally from the north of Ireland. **1950** *PADS* 13.5 **cAL,** *Bunting hen* . . . Among the Negroes . . a buntin' hen is a hen without a tail or a rumpless hen. The term is probably derived from *bunty,* which *DAE* defines as a tailless fowl. **1954** *Harder Coll.* **cwTN,** *Buntin' (bunty) hen* . . . A tailless hen. **1956** McAtee *Some Dialect NC* 7, *Bunty* . . . Lacking a tail. "My little bunty hen."

bunty adj
Short and squat.
  1870 *Nation* 11.57/1 **PA,** To be "bunty" was to be squat in stature. **1870** *N&Q* 42.249/2 **sePA,** *Bunty* . . squat. **1968** *DARE* (Qu. EE24a, *When there's snow, children go down the hill on a* _____) Inf **OH**72, Bunty sled—a short sled you sat on, your knees stuck up.

bur n¹ See **burr** n¹

bur n² See **brother** A2

burble n [*OED burble* a pimple, a boil →1622; *EDD burbles* "small tingling pimples, such as are caused by the stinging of nettles or small insects"]
  1930 Shoemaker *1300 Words* 9 **cPA Mts** (as of c1900), *Burbles*—Little red pimples on face after shaving too close.

burbot n
Std: a freshwater fish *(Lota lota)* of the cod family, marked by a single barbel under the chin. Also called **aleby trout, barbot, cusk, dogfish, eelpout 2, freshwater cod, gudgeon, la loche, lawyer, ling 1a, lingcod 2, lush, maria, methy, mother of eels 2, mud blower, mud shark**

burch See **burk**

bur clover See **burr clover**

burden n Pronc-sp *burding* Cf **-ing**
A Forms.
  [**1867** Lowell *Biglow* xxvi **MA,** In that delightful old volume . . . I find *burding, garding,* and *cousing.*] **1917** Torrence *Granny Maumee* 69 [Black], I'm goin' tek de burding . . off'n you.
B Senses.
1 A crop.
  1890 *DN* 1.73 **NH, MA,** *Burden:* crop. "A good burden of grass." Used by a farmer near Portsmouth, N.H. . . Common on Cape Cod.
2 A small stack of tobacco, less than a basket, framed up for marketing. **esp MD**
  1939 *Sun* (Baltimore MD) 12 Apr 13/5 (*Hench Coll.*), The new method . . for handling Maryland's tobacco is designed to save packing in hogsheads before sale, as the "hacks" or "burdens" will, under the new system, be packed in hogsheads in the auction room and shipped to the factories. **1952** *Hench Coll.,* A tobacco-grower from Tidewater Maryland, east of Washington, D.C. . . was talking about taking tobacco to market. "I took several burdens to market," he said, "but the price was so low I brought them back home." My friend asked him what a "burden" was, and the grower answered, "A small stack." My friend judged that a burden was a small stack judged roughly for its size, but not weighed. **1966** *DARE* Tape DC5, [FW:] What do you call those wooden frames? [Inf:] Oh, we call it a tobacco basket. [FW:] Tobacco basket is the whole thing all bound up, with the frame at each end? [Inf:] Yes sir, when you get 'em up like that, we call it a hack of tobacco, or a burden . . . When it's laid up, one on the bottom, one on the top just like that, we call it a burden or a hack. **1967** Key *Tobacco Vocab.* **MD,** [One informant] says a "burden" is two baskets tied together, but the warehousemen say it's tobacco tied between sticks.

burden v [**burden** n B2]
  1967 Key *Tobacco Vocab.* **MD,** *(To place tobacco in a bulk)* To burden it down on them baskets.

burdock n, also attrib
1 A plant of the genus *Arctium.* **chiefly Nth, N Midl** See Map
Also called **beggar's button 1, bird dock, burdog, burr, clotburr 2, cockle 3, cockle button, cuckold dock, cuckoo-button, hardock, hurr burr, rhubarb, stick button.** For other names of var spp see **buzzy** n², **cockleburr 3, kiss-me-quick, love leaves, nigger lice**

1676 Royal Soc. London *Philos. Trans.* 11.629 **VA,** There grow wild in the Woods . . *Yellow-Dock, Bur-Dock.* **1874** *Shaker Med. Preparations,* Burdock—Lappa Major. **c1960** *Wilson Coll.* **csKY,** Burdock . . . Common barnyard weed, often playing a part in folk medicine. **1965–70** *DARE* (Qu. S13, . . *A common wild bush with bunches of round, prickly seeds; when they get dry they stick to your clothing—what are these called around here?*) 246 Infs, **chiefly Nth, N Midl,** Burdock; **VA**43, Burdock burrs; (Qu. S26d, *Wildflowers that grow in meadows*) 132 Infs, **chiefly Nth,** Burdock; (Qu. S15) Infs **CT**12, **IN**19, **MI**31, **NY**30, 75, 113, **OH**88, **PA**89, Burdock; **OH**87, Burdock burrs; **IL**52, **IN**30, **NY**134, 191, **OH**5, Burdocks; (Qu. S21) 13 Infs, **Nth, esp NEast,** Burdock(s). **1971** Krochmal *Appalachia Med. Plants* 58. *Ibid* 60.

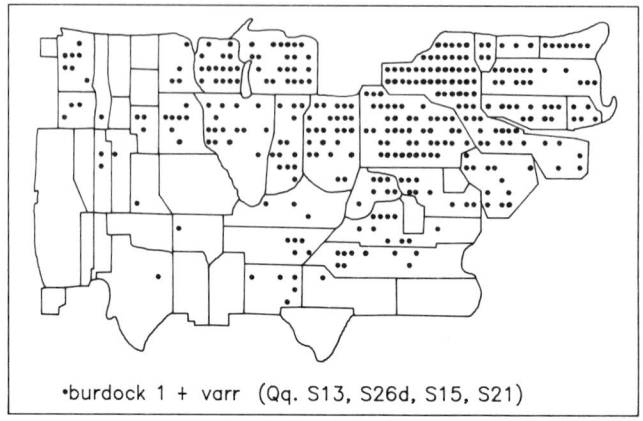

•burdock 1 + varr (Qq. S13, S26d, S15, S21)

2 often *sea burdock:* A **cockleburr 1** (here: *Xanthium strumarium*).
  1824 Bigelow *Florula Bostoniensis* 342, *Xanthium strumarium* . . . *Sea Burdock* . . . A very rough plant, growing at the edges of beaches, &c. near the salt water . . . The fruit is an oval burr. **1900** Lyons *Plant Names* 398, *X. strumarium* . . . Small or Lesser Burdock, Sea Burdock. **1950** Gray–Fernald *Manual of Botany* 1474, *Sea-Burdock.*

‡**burdog** n [Folk-etym]
=**burdock 1.**
  1968 *DARE* (Qu. S15, . . *Other weed seeds that cling to clothing*) Inf **MN**12, Burdogs—a bud that grows in clusters—like a cocklebur in size.

burfine See **burr vine**

burfish n Also sp *burrfish*
A **porcupine fish,** esp of the genus *Chilomycterus.* Also called **balloonfish 1, cucumber fish, pincushion, rabbitfish, swellfish**
  1674 Josselyn *Two Voyages* 113 **NEng,** *Blew-fish[p] Bull-head[p] Burfish.* **1884** Goode *Fisheries U.S.* 1.170, The Porcupine fish — *Diodontidae* . . . These fishes are commonly known by such names as 'Burr Fish,' 'Ball Fish,' 'Swell Fish,' and 'Toad Fish.' **1906** NJ State Museum *Annual Rept. for 1905* 366, Genus *Chilomycterus* . . . The Burr Fishes. **1933** John G. Shedd Aquarium *Guide* 161, This is the common Burrfish of the Atlantic coast. Its spines are short with broad bases forming an almost complete coat of armor. **1955** Zim *Fishes* 138, *Burrfish* or Spiny Boxfish is a very common species with short, stout spines. **1976** Warner *Beautiful Swimmers* 225 **Chesapeake Bay,** Much rarer were the bizarre species variously called burrfishes or spiny boxfishes . . . these little fish have been described in scientific literature as "a solid bony box with holes for the mouth, eyes, fins and vent, more or less inflatable."

burg n Also sp *berg, burgh* **scattered, but esp N Cent, Cent** See Map *sometimes humorous or disparaging*
A town, village, hamlet.
  1843 *Spirit of Times* 25 Mar 43/1 (*OEDS*), Two 'individs' in this 'burg' will give our friend Greer 'the run of his teeth' whenever he visits New York. **1846** Smith *Theatrical Apprent.* 151 (*DA*), It so happened that the stranger who had played poker with us, also disembarked at the same burgh. **1880** *Hist. Dane Co. WI* 1219, He owns 163 acres of land, and water-power in the berg of Elvers, valued at $14,000. **1903** (1965) Adams *Log Cowboy* 71 **NM,** The wagon and a number of the boys went into the burg. **1914** *DN* 4.162 **NW,** *Berg* . . . A town or city. **1920** Lewis *Main Street* 23 **MN,** Why, what's the matter with 'em? Good hustling burgs. It would astonish you to know how much wheat and rye and corn and potatoes they ship in a year. *Ibid* 67, She didn't think Gopher Prairie was "the livest little burg in the state." **1950** *WELS (An*

out-of-the-way place or an unimportant village) 11 Infs, **WI,** (Little) berg. **1965–70** *DARE* (Qu. C33, *Joking names . . for an out-of-the-way place, or a very unimportant place)* 57 Infs, **chiefly N Cent, Cent,** (Small, little) burg; (Qu. C34, *Nicknames for nearby settlements, villages, or districts)* 9 Infs, (Little) burg(s); (Qu. C35, *Nicknames for the different parts of your town or city)* Infs **IN22, MS**11, **PA**94, **VT**2, Burg; (Qu. MM22, . . *"How are things _____?")* Inf **MI**40, In your burg. **1969–70** *DARE* Tape **IN**54, Muncie was just a . . little burg then; **TX**72, There were somewhere close to two thousand people in this burg, if you can imagine.

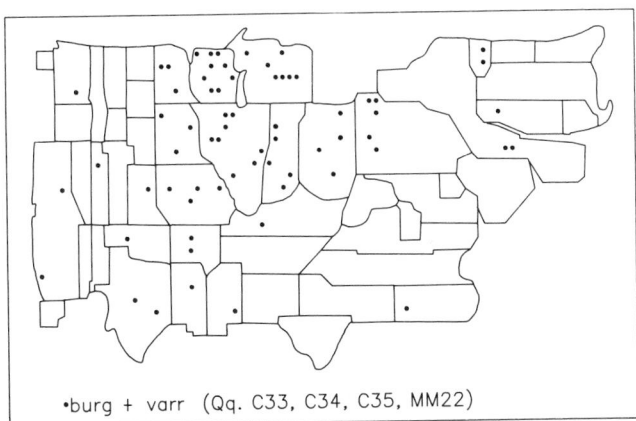

•burg + varr (Qq. C33, C34, C35, MM22)

‡**burgalize** v, hence *burgalizer* n [Prob *burgle* + *ize*]
    1969 *DARE* (Qu. V6) Inf **RI**4, Burgalize ['bɝɡəlaɪz]; **MD**31, Burgalizer ['bɝɡlaɪzɚ].

burgall See **bergall**

burgamot See **bergamot**

burgoo n [Perh Arabic *burghul* cracked wheat]   Note: stress, formerly approx equal, is now strong on the 2d syllable.
1 Orig an oatmeal-like gruel; now also a thick soup or stew. **chiefly NEng**
    1830 Ames *Mariner's Sketches* 184 **MA,** We were 'fed and foddered,' . . with a small allowance of meat, soup, vegetables, *burgoo* milk and buttermilk. [Footnote to *burgoo:*] Thin hasty-pudding made of oatmeal. **1889** *AN&Q* 3.312/1, Burgoo.—This word, a sailor's name for "porridge," is passed over in the *Century* and *New English* dictionaries with no regular etymology. Several months since, a writer in *The Athenæum* published an excellent . . identification of this word with the Arabic *burghul,* or *burghu* (corn, grain, also porridge or gruel). **1918** *DN* 5.15 **MA,** Burgoo . . . Thick soup, porridge. "The fog was as thick as burgoo." **1942** ME Univ. *Studies* 56.60, When it was *thick fog* or *thick o' fog* it was said to be *thick as bur'-goo,* which was a name for sea soup. **1945** Colcord *Sea Language* 45 **ME, Cape Cod, Long Island,** Burgoo. The sailor's name for oatmeal porridge. **1975** Gould *ME Lingo,* Burgoo—Once oatmeal porridge or gruel, the word now means any of several stews, usually thick.
2 also sp *burgou(t),* also attrib: A highly seasoned stew made of any combination of fowl, game, other meats, and vegetables, usu cooked in a large pot outdoors.   **esp KY**
    1853 McConnel *Western Characters* 363, Around a burgou pot, or along the trenches of an impromptu barbecue. **1885** *Mag. Amer. Hist.* Jan 98/2, Burgoo.—A Southern and Southwestern term akin to barbecue . . . The feast, however, was furnished by hunters and fishermen—everything, fish, flesh and fowl, being compounded into a vast stew. **1941** *AN&Q* 1.38/2 **KY,** It was a Frenchman in John Morgan's cavalry who introduced the "burgoo" which has become a culinary tradition in Kentucky. The Bluegrass dish was first made during the Reconstruction days, and blackbirds, because of food scarcity, were the chief ingredient. Was the addition of meat a French variation? And does this account for the occasional spelling "burgout"? **1944** *Chicago Daily News* (IL) 4 May 21/1, Burgoo Stew . . is such an old and ancient dish in Kentucky that no two people tell the same story of its origin and no two people will give you the same recipe. **1964** Amer. Heritage *Cookbook* 474 **KY,** Burgoo . . . came to be associated with Kentucky, and to be even thicker [than the original porridge] by virtue of including hens, squirrels, beef, hogs, lambs, and a wide assortment of vegetables and seasonings. It was . . served at picnics, horse sales, church suppers, and on Derby Day.

1969–70 *DARE* (Qu. H36, . . *Kinds of soup)* Inf **IL**82, Burgoo; (Qu. H45, *Dishes made with meat)* Inf **KY**79, Burgoo. **1969** *DARE* Tape **IL**80, The burgoo [bə'gu], the soup, is made in an outdoor kettle, and they put in chicken and beef and pork probably, and all different kinds of vegetables and cook it over an open fire. **1969** *DARE* FW Addit **KY**59, *Burgoo:* A soup or stew cooked outdoors and eaten for breakfast after a fox hunt.
3 By ext: a picnic at which burgoo is served.
    1889 *Century Dict.* 726 **KY,** *Burgoo* . . . A barbecue, picnic, or woodland feast at which the soup burgoo is served. **1929** Burman *Mississippi* 60, We was taking some chairs and things for a big burgoo and political meeting. **1969** *DARE* Tape **IL**80, The burgoo [bə'gu] itself, the celebration is kind of a homecoming for the people in this area, and people generally try to come back and see all their friends at that time. It's usually about two days.

burgou(t) See **burgoo 2**

burhead n
=**cleavers.**
    1900 Lyons *Plant Names* 167, *G[alium] Aparine* . . . Bur-head. **1940** Clute *Amer. Plant Names* 52, *Galium aparine* . . . bur-head.

burial n
Baptism by total immersion.
    1947 *Sun* (Baltimore MD) 15 Sept 3/4 **GA,** Floyd L. Fowler, farmer-preacher who said he had been conducting primitive services in the area "for six or eight weeks," led his overalled followers in open-air Sunday worship and then baptized several by "burial" beneath the waters of a gloomy, overhung creek.

burial association See **burial society**

burial case n
A coffin, esp one made of metal.
    1851 Cist *Sketches Cincinnati* 191, *Foundery* castings.—This . . is carried on in every possible variety, in which iron can be cast, from a butt hinge to a burial case. **1870** in 1875 Twain *Sketches New & Old* (Hartford) 198, I am talking about your high-toned, silver mounted burial-case. **1943** *LANE* Map 524, Many informants . . use *coffin* indiscriminately of the older and the newer kind of burial case . . . 1 inf, seMA, Coffin, the outer case, also called the burial case . . . 1 inf, ceMA, Burial case = casket. **1945** Mencken *Amer. Lang. Suppl.* 1.570, [Footnote:], Caskets, Coffins, Burial-Cases, and Other Morticians' Goods. **1948** Bean *Yankee Auctioneer* 10 **wMA,** Here we turn out Prophylactic brushes, Proper–McCallum hosiery, International Silverware, Pepsi-Cola and burial cases.

burial ground n   Cf **burying ground**
A cemetery, often a small one for a family's use.
    1934 Hanley *Disks* **nwRI,** This old Jonah Hopkins . . gave a piece of land over here for a burial ground, for all of the Hopkinses. **1965–70** *DARE* (Qu. BB61a, *Other words . . for a cemetery)* 120 Infs, **scattered,** Burial ground. [Of all Infs responding to the question, 31% were coll-educ; of those giving this response, 43% were coll-educ.] **1966** *DARE* Tape **SD**3, There was an Indian burial ground. **1973** Allen *LAUM* 1.366, Although some settlers maintained the already disappearing custom of having a family interment plot on a farm, the infrequency and the archaic character of the Northern expressions *burial ground* and *burying ground* in the U[pper] M[idwest] attest the fact that today it is historical only.

burial society n Also *burial association, burying society   esp among Blacks* Cf **bury-league**
    1911 *Century Dict. Suppl., Society* . . . *Burial society,* a friendly or mutual benefit society which provides a certain sum for the burial of each of its members. **1929** (1951) Faulkner *Sartoris* 373 **MS,** The negro burying-ground lay beyond the cemetery proper, and Isom led her to Simon's grave. Simon's burying society had taken care of him. **1954** Faulkner *Fable* 169 **Sth,** State police . . had been . . charging . . through the pool halls and burial associations and the kitchens and bedrooms of Negro tenements. **1961** Oliver *Blues Fell* 276 [Black], So for years they contribute to burial societies. **1967** *DARE* (Qu. FF1) Inf **LA**8, Burial Society—not a social organization. [Inf Black] **1976** Brown *Gloss. Faulkner* 41, The Negro burial association is a sort of mutual-insurance organization to provide money for the funerals of its members, but it often has religious and social functions as well. **1977** Dillard *Lexicon* 58 [Black], The member who has *passed* . . is taken care of by his church and his burial society, or *buryin' society.*

‡**burinki** n, also attrib [AmSpan *Borinqueño* native of Puerto Rico]

 1973 *AmSp* 48.307 **HI,** In Hawaii, the Puerto Rican community are called *burinki,* and African-style hair is called *burinki hair.*

burk v, n Also *burch* **esp GA**

 To vomit; an instance of vomiting; an expulsion of intestinal gas.

 c1960 *Wilson Coll.* **csKY,** *Burk* . . George Adwell's interpretation of a baby's belch, which is as good as the more common burp. He says a belch is of air, but a burk brings up some food. He ought to know, since he has two small children. **1966–69** *DARE* (Qu. X55, *Words for breaking wind from the bowels*) Inf **GA3,** Burk; **GA7,** Burch; (Qu. BB17, . . *Words . . for vomiting*) Inf **GA77,** Burk up.

burl n See **boil** n[1], v

burlap bag n Also *burlap (sack)* [Perh *burel* coarse woolen cloth + *lap* a fold or flap of cloth] **widespread, but less freq in West** See Map Cf **croker sack, gunny sack**

 A large coarse-cloth container made of jute or hemp and used esp for bagging grains and farm produce.

 1939 *LANE* Maps 149, 150, [Many infs responded both *burlap bag* and *burlap sack* for a "container made of cloth"]. **1946** *PADS* 5.13 **VA,** *Burlap bag* . . . not common except along the Potomac. **1949** Kurath *Word Geog.* 56, *Burlap sack* or *bag* is the most common term in the Eastern States for the rough loose-woven sack in which potatoes and other farm produce are shipped. It is regularly current throughout the North and the North Midland, and not uncommon in Tidewater Virginia and on the Kanawha. **c1960** *Wilson Coll.* **csKY,** *Burlap sack* . . . A coarse cloth bag, usu a large one. *Burlap bag* is less commonly used. *Grass sack* is used by most people. A few sometimes say *gunny sack.* **1962** *AmSp* 37.173 **seNC,** *Burlap bag* was generally preferred. **1962** *PADS* 38.44 **neIL,** Burlap bag. **1965–70** *DARE* (Qu. F23, *A container . . of rough loosely-woven, brown cloth*) 359 Infs, Burlap bag; 90 Infs, Burlap sack; 30 Infs, Burlap; (Qu. F19, *A cloth container for grain*) 18 Infs, Burlap bag; 8 Infs, Burlap sack; **OK42,** Burlap; (Qu. F20, . . *For feed*) 17 Infs, Burlap bag; 10 Infs, Burlap sack; 4 Infs, Burlap. **1971** *AmSp* 46.171 **Chicago IL,** [Of 37 infs, 28 said *burlap* (*bag* or *sack*)].

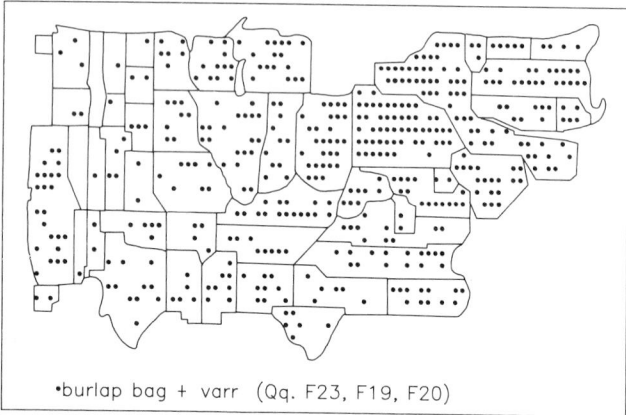

•burlap bag + varr (Qq. F23, F19, F20)

‡**burlap hair** n Also *burlap top*

 1967 *DARE* (Qu. X1a, *Names . . for false hair, worn by men*) Inf **WA20,** Burlap hair, burlap top.

burlap sack See **burlap bag**

burm See **berm**

bur marigold n See **burr marigold**

burn v Usu |bɝn, bən|; occas |bɜɪn|; rarely |bɑrn| See Pronc Intro 3.II.12. Pronc-spp *barn, bu(h)n*

A Forms.

1 Pronc varr.

 1899 (1912) Green *VA Folk-Speech* 101, *Bunt,* v. For *burnt.* **1901** *DN* 2.181 **KY** [Black], *Burn bu'n* (buhn). **1932** in 1944 *ADD* **nVA,** *Burnt* . . . |bɑ(:)rnt|. Repeatedly by speaker aged 17. 'An' then it barnt on down . .' **1942** *AmSp* 17.150 **seNY,** [For the vowel in the word *burn,* 44 infs responded [ɝ], 38 [ɜ] and 15 [ɜɪ]. **1966** *DARE* Tape **GA1,** [The wood scraps] was just throwed out, and burnt [bɜɪnt].

2 Pret and past pple: usu *burned, burnt;* occas assim to *burn;* arch *brent.*

 1923 *DN* 5.202 **swMO,** *Brent* . . . Burned. "The wood's all done brent up." **1930** *AmSp* 5.425 **Ozarks,** When the Ozarker uses *brent* instead of *burnt* he is preserving a very old form, and one employed by many of the great Elizabethans. **1966** *DARE* (Qu. NN20b, *Exclamations caused by sudden pain—a slight burn*) Inf **SC9,** Oh lord, I got burn. **1967** LeCompte *Word Atlas* 345 **seLA,** *(Tired)* 1 inf, Burn out.

B Senses.

1 To brand (livestock); to alter a livestock brand; hence n *burnt brand.* **West**

 1890 in 1942 *AmSp* 17.125, The Nolan and Fisher Live Stock association is doing some good work in ferreting out burnt brands. **1931** (1960) Dobie *Open Range* 181, They offered him $5,000 if he would tell them how he achieved the Star Cross and would quit burning it on their cattle. **1936** Adams *Cowboy Lingo* 121, Trail cattle which changed ownership often . . might . . have their hides thoroughly etched, or, in the language of the cowboy, be 'burnt 'til they look like a brand book.' *Ibid* 158, The practice of 'burning' cattle, of altering brands . . was raised to the dignity of an art by the rustler. **1945** Thorp *Pardner* 17 **SW,** He rode the range on horses not bearing the Bar W brand, to look at other herds and strays and see if he could spot any "burnt" cattle. **1968** Adams *Western Words* 46, Burn cattle—To brand cattle . . . Burning rawhide—Branding; used mostly in reference to rustlers. **1968** *DARE* (Qu. K18, . . *Kind of mark . . to identify a cow*) Inf **NC79,** Burn a place on them.

2 To fire (bricks).

 1966–69 *DARE* Tape **KY14,** That old home there is an old brick home and the bricks was burned right there; **NM8,** They would set that (the wood) afire and burn brick; **NC52,** They call 'em burning brick. It took a week or more to burn a kil' of brick.

3 usu with *off,* rarely *away, up;* Of fog: to lift, dissipate. **scattered, but esp NEng, CA**

 1926 *DN* 5.386 **ME,** *Burn off,* or *up* . . . Clear away, applied to fog, "The fog will burn up before noon." **1939** Hench *Coll.,* A person from . . eastern Virginia was visiting friends at Wood's Hole, Mass. On a foggy morning, the Virginia person said, "Oh, I hope this fog will burn off after a while." At that, one of the Wood's Hole persons said jokingly, "You shouldn't say that. That's a New England expression." **1939** *LANE* Map 89, The terms *burning off* and *lifting,* which usually refer to the disappearance of fog under the influence of the morning sun, were offered . . by a number of informants. **1959** *VT Hist.* new ser 27.128, *Burn off* . . . To clear off so that the sun will shine after a heavy fog or mist. **1965–70** *DARE* (Qu. B19, *When fog begins to go up into the air, you say it's* _____) 22 Infs, **scattered, but esp NEng, CA,** Burning off; **TX84,** Burning away; **MA5,** [It will] clear away, burn off; New Englanders elsewhere are laughed at for saying this; (Qu. B20) Inf **FL3,** Burning off; **MS17,** Sun burns fog off; **OK25,** Sun's burning it off; (QR, near Qu. B2) Inf **CA15,** In the western coastal area of San Francisco when the sun comes out fog is said to "burn off" there.

4 To distill.

 1951 *DE Folkl. Bulletin* 1.2.7, Burn (to distill—as of brandy).

5 sometimes with *down:* To kill, usu with a gun.

 1934 *AmSp* 9.26 [Prison parlance], *Burn down.* To shoot someone. **1942** Faulkner *Go Down* 235 **MS,** The negro he was shooting at outed with a dollar-and-a-half mail order pistol and would have burned Boon down with it only it never went off. **1965** Brown *Manchild* 170 [Black], Do you really want to burn this cat, man? **1966** *AmSp* 41.72 **sePA.** **1972** Claerbaut *Black Jargon* 59, *Burn* . . . to kill, often by shooting.

6 To cook. *among Blacks; joc*

 1970 *DARE* (Qu. H7, . . *A housewife . . might say, "I have to go and _____ supper."*) Inf **OH102,** Burn. [Inf Black] **1970** Major *Afro-Amer. Slang,* Burn: (1940's) to cook food. **1972** Claerbaut *Black Jargon,* Burn . . . to cook food.

7 To set off (firecrackers). [Cantonese calque] **HI**

 1972 Carr *Da Kine Talk* 125 **HI,** *Burn firecrackers* . . . The Cantonese verb *shiu* means 'to burn', 'to roast', and the term *shiu in foh* means 'fireworks'. *Sieu pau-jeung* (in another spelling of the Cantonese) means 'burn firecrackers.'

burn n[1]

1 Of smoking tobacco: the characteristic of burning slowly without bursting into flame.

 1933 *Sun* (Baltimore MD) 17 Nov 9/3–5 *(Hench Coll.),* Maryland tobacco, is noted for its "burn". In this respect Maryland excels most other tobaccos. **1946** *Sun* (Baltimore MD) 11 Jan 12/2, The Maryland tobacco is also a neutral blender, which means it can be blended with other tobaccos to improve the "burn" but without disturbing the aromas of those other tobaccos. **1967** Key *Tobacco Vocab.* **NC,** They don't test the burn for cigarette tobacco as they do for cigar tobacco; **GA,** The thick leaf doesn't have a burn that is satisfactory; **PA,** They carried tallow candles along and they tested the burn when they went in to check a crop; **CT,** Try the burn.

2 See quot. Cf **hickey**

1968 *DARE* FW Addit **cnNY,** A burn is a mark on the skin where someone has sucked it hard and brought the blood to the [surface].

3 Perfection. [**burn** v **B6,** prob infl by *to a turn* to perfection]

1970 *DARE* (Qu. KK3a, b, . . *The perfect condition . . in cooking: "It's done to _____." . . A piece of work: "It's done to _____.")* Inf **AL62,** A burn.

burn n², also attrib [See quot 1981] **AK**

=**berm** n **2c.**

1961 *Alaska Sportsman* June 33 (Tabbert *Alaskan Engl.*), The present homestead practice of bulldozing the timber into big piles or burns is wrong from every angle. **1979** *Fairbanks Daily News-Miner* 21 May 3 (Tabbert *Alaskan Engl.*), He said three crews were fighting another Delta Junction blaze today that has burned about 900 acres, mostly in burn piles on farmland. *Ibid* 6 June 3 (Tabbert *Alaskan Engl.*), The fire started May 10 and by the time it was brought under control May 19 about 5,000 acres had burned. Burn piles were still smoldering, however, and one of these is being blamed as the source of the latest outbreak. **1981** Tabbert *Alaskan Engl.* 383, It would be interesting to discover whether *burn pile* or *berm pile* was used earliest. If it was *burn pile,* the /n/ of *burn* could easily have assimilated to the place of articulation of the following /p/, yielding /bɜ-mpayl/. The first part may then have been associated with *berm* by those who knew the term.

burn-bank See **berm 1**

burn candle v phr

In voodoo practice: to attempt to harm a person by ritual burning of a candle.

[**1945** Saxon *Gumbo Ya-Ya* 538 **sLA** [Witchcraft: Black Art], To cause suffering, light a black candle at the bottom, write the person's name on a piece of paper, and wrap around the burning candle . . . To harm a person . . write his name three times on a piece of paper and burn a black candle on it.] **1952** Harwin *Home is Upriver* 107 **sMissip R,** "They're burning candle on me. You hear? My own girl an' them Casons." " . . They're burning candle on me. And when it goes out, I'll be—dead." . . "This'n is the only cure for their candle. If this'n is going when theirs goes out, I won't—die."

burn daylight v phr *old-fash*

1899 (1912) Green *VA Folk-Speech* 101, *Burn-daylight* . . . To light candles before there is need; waste of time.

burned hazel n [Folk-etym] **sePA**

=**brennessel.**

1967–68 *DARE* (Qu. S17, . . *Other kinds of plants . . that will cause itching and swelling*) Inf **PA6,** Burned hazel; **PA136,** ['bɑrn,esəl]—same as nettles.

burned piece See **burnt piece**

burning vbl n

=**barrel-dogging.**

1954 *Courier–Jrl.* (Louisville KY) 25 Apr mag sec 8/1, Barrel dogging —also called steaming, burning . . really has come into its own in Nelson, Marion, Green . . counties.

burning bush n [Cf *Exodus* 3:2–3]

1 Any of several shrubs or trees of the genus *Euonymus.* Also called **arrowwood c, bursting heart, spindle tree, strawberry bush, wahoo.** For other names of *E. americanus* see **bleeding heart 2, bubbybush 2, cat's-paw, fishwood, hearts-a-bustin'-with-love, puppy toes.** For other names of *E. atropurpureus* see **bitter ash, bleeding heart 2, Indian arrow, Indian bitter, pegwood, purple strawberry, skewerwood, strawberry tree**

1785 Marshall *Arbustrum* 45, *Ever-green Spindle Tree* . . . From their [=its fruits] red appearance [it] obtained the name of the Burning Bush. **1911** (1916) Porter *Harvester* 302 **IN,** This is burning bush, so called because it has pink berries that hang from long, graceful stems all winter, and when fully open they expose a flame-red seed pod. **1938** *Sun* (Baltimore MD) 21 Nov 2/7 (Hench Coll.), Two bushes, whose common names are the "burning bush" and "strawberry bush," . . finished off the

tour. **1939** FWP *Guide TN* 21, Peculiar to the highlands is the "burning bush," called by the mountain folk "hearts-a-bustin'-with-love," because of its brilliant berries in autumn. **1971** Krochmal *Appalachia Med. Plants* 116. **1972** GA Dept. Ag. *Farmers Market Bulletin* 11 Oct 8/1, Hearts-a-Bustin is only one of the many common names for *Euonymus americanus.* Others include "Puppy Toes," "Strawberry Bush," . . and "Burning Bush".

2 =**bittersweet.**

1893 Owen *Voodoo Tales* 71 **MO,** He hid himself in a thicket of plums and burning-bush (bittersweet).

3 =**summer cypress** (here: *Kochia scoparia*).

1936 Winter *Plants NE* 193, *K[ochia] scoparia* . . . Burning-bush. An escape from cultivation in Nebr. **1950** Stevens *ND Plants* 133, *Kochia scoparia* . . . Burning Bush. Summer Cypress . . . Introduced as an ornamental on account of its . . often bright red color in fall. **1976** Bailey–Bailey *Hortus Third* 626, *Burning bush* . . . lvs. narrowly linear, turning purplish-red in autumn.

4 A flowering quince.

1956 McAtee *Some Dialect NC* 7, Burning bush . . . The Japanese quince (*Chaenomeles japonica*).

burning fluid n, also attrib Also *burning oil* *arch*

An alcohol mixture used for fuel in lamps.

1855 MA General Court *Acts & Resolves* 903, Establishments for the manufacture of camphene or burning fluid. **1887** *Courier–Jrl.* (Louisville KY) 16 Jan 14/2, We used "burning fluid" and camphine lamps in those days. **1932** *Old-Time N. Eng.* Oct. 61/2 (*DA*), 'Camphene' (burning fluid) lamps had a bad reputation for explosiveness, particularly if a little ether was part of the mixture. **1963** Adamson *Household Hints* 135 **NEng** (as of late 1800s), But, alas, homemade "burning oil" and low-grade kerosene were dangerous because of explosive gases. *Ibid* 139, *Burning fluid—How to make*—Alcohol, of 98 percent, 9 pts.; good camphene, 1 qt. . . The only safety is in filling lamps in daytime, or far from fire and lights.

burning fly n

1 Perh a **greenhead** (*Tabanus* spp).

1791 (1958) Bartram *Travels* 385 **TN,** Another [fly] . . of a splendid green and the head of a gold colour; the sting of this last is intolerable, no less acute than a prick from a red-hot needle, or a spark of fire on the skin; these are called the burning flies.

2 =**punkie.**

1968 *DARE* (Qu. R11) Inf **MN16,** Burning fly.

burning maple n

=**red maple.**

1968 *DARE* (Qu. T14) Inf **AL41,** Burning maple—same as red maple.

burning nettle n Also called **brennessel**

A **nettle,** usu *Urtica urens* which is also called **dog nettle.**

1900 Lyons *Plant Names* 384, *Urtica urens* . . . Burning Nettle. **1968** *DARE* (Qu. S17, . . *Other kinds of plants . . that will cause itching and swelling*) Infs **MN23, WI58,** Burning nettle. **1970** Correll *Plants TX* 502, *Urtica urens* . . . Burning nettle.

burning oil See **burning fluid**

burnings n, intj

In marble play: see quots.

1883 Newell *Games & Songs* 186, "Burnings" signifies breathing on a marble, and thereby getting certain advantages. **1955** *PADS* 23.13 **cwTN,** *Burnings:* Prob. fr. game of dice. The act of breathing or blowing on a marble in order to obtain certain advantages. *—interj.* Fen burnings, or no burnings. The counter cry to *burnings.*

burning weed n

Perh =**burning nettle.**

1950 *WELS (Other kinds of plants that will cause itching and swelling)* 1 Inf, **swWI,** Burning weed. **1968** *DARE* (Qu. S17, . . *Plants . . that will cause itching and swelling*) Inf **MN34,** Burning weed; **LA31,** Burning weed or stinging weed—has narrow dark-green leaves, grows in edge of marsh, it'll just naturally burn you up.

burn-off n [**burn** v **B3**]

1967 *DARE* (QR, near Qu. B19) Inf **CA15,** When the sun comes out, fog is said to burn off. It's called the burn-off in Sunset and Richmond Districts of San Francisco.

burn one on v phr [Cf *tie one on*]

?To get drunk.

1969 Gordone *No Place* 22 **NY** [Black], Dam'dest thing. Las' night I stayed here [at a bar]. Burnt one on. Fell asleep right here.

‡burn one's foot v phr *joc* Cf **break one's leg**

To become pregnant.

1966 *DARE* (Qu. AA28, . . *Joking . . expressions . . to say that another [woman] is going to have a baby*) Inf **MS16**, She stumped her toe; she burnt her foot.

burnout n

1 A particularly destructive fire, esp one that razes buildings. **S Midl**

1906 *DN* 3.129 **nwAR,** *Burn-out* . . . Fire. "R.A. Childers has got his mill rebuilt after his burn-out." **1939** *Hall Coll.* **eTN,** *Burn-out* . . . A fire. We had a burn-out at Newport. They burnt out the courthouse. Hit's been eight or ten years ago. **1959** Wilson *Bodacious Ozarks* 146, A running fire is still a *burn-out.*

2 Extermination of unwanted animals by the burning of their habitat.

1969 *DARE* Tape **GA51,** That's the year we had the big burnout [of rattlesnakes].

3 A children's game:

a See quot.

1941 FWP *Guide AR* 301, Back in the shade are clumps of rattan, whose long, snake-like withes are used as whips by country boys to play "burn-out". The boys select five- or six-foot lengths of limber rattan, lock their left hands, and lay on until one or the other has had enough.

b See quots.

1967 *DARE* (Qu. EE33, *Other outdoor games*) Inf **TX11,** Burnout— get 100 steps apart, throw the baseball back and forth stepping one step closer on each throw till one can take it no more. **1983** *DARE* File **nCA** (as of 1950s), Burnout was played by two people who threw a ball to one another, each time standing closer together and throwing harder, trying to get the other person to drop the ball.

‡burnout shower n [**burnout** n **1**]

A gift-giving party to benefit a family whose home has burnt down.

1966 *DARE* (Qu. FF3, *Do people give "showers" or "gift parties" around here? What kinds?*) Inf **AR41,** Burnout shower.

burn pear v phr

1980 *DARE* File **TX,** There's a phrase which has appeared in Texas newspapers a good deal in the recent drouth. It is 'burning pear,' meaning burning the spines off prickly-pear cactus with a blow torch in order to have something a little sustaining for cattle.

burns exclam

In marble play: see quots.

1934 *AmSp* 9.75 **ND,** *Burns.* Shouted by a player when his marble hits a stone. It entitles him to shoot again. **1955** *PADS* 23.13 **cwTN,** *Burns: interj.* A call by a player which allows him to roll his marble again after his shooter has hit some object that deflects from the desired direction. **c1970** Wiersma *Marbles Terms* **swMI,** Burns—A call entitling a player to shoot again when his shooter hits a stone.

burnt-eye pepper n

1966 *DARE* (Qu. I22a, . . *Different kinds of peppers—small, hot*) Inf **SC19,** Burnt-eye.

burn the breeze See **burn the wind**

‡burn the city n

1901 *DN* 2.137 **seNY,** *Burn the city* . . . A game.

burn the earth See **burn the wind**

‡burn the leather v phr Cf **burn the wind**

1950 *WELS* (*Ways of telling someone to hurry*) 1 Inf, **ceWI,** Burn the leather.

burn the wind v phr Also *burn the breeze* (or *earth, prairie, track*)

To run or travel very fast.

1881 Romspert *W. Echo* 164, Of course, the first day the mustangs will burn the prairie. **1903** (1965) Adams *Log Cowboy* 37 **NM,** I was a half a mile in the lead, burning the earth like a canned dog. **1910** Raine *B. O'Connor* 57 (*DAE*), When he finds out how the horse he's after is burning the wind, his suspicions grow stronger. **1933** *AmSp* 8.1.28 **nwTX,** *Burning the breeze.* Going at full speed. **1934** Weseen *Dict. Amer. Slang* 94, *Burn the breeze*—To ride at full speed. **1946** Wilson

Fidelity Folks 180 **swKY,** When something went fast in the older days, we said it "burned the wind." **1956** McAtee *Some Dialect NC,* Burn the wind: . . Go fast. **1968** Adams *Western Words,* *Burn the breeze*—To ride at full speed. One cowhand, in telling of a fast ride he had made, said, "When I pushed on the reins, I had that hoss kickin' the jackrabbits out of the trail." **1969** *DARE* (Qu. Y20, *To run fast: "You should have seen him _____!"*) Inf **CA120,** Burn up the track.

burn thunderwood v Cf **thunderwood**

To be angry.

1960 Williams *Walk Egypt* 214 **GA,** Mr. Harl sho burning thunderwood.

burnt land bird n [See quot 1956]

=**nighthawk.**

1927 Forbush *Birds MA* 2.306, *Chordeiles virginianus virginianus* . . . Other names: . . Burnt Land Bird. **1956** *MA Audubon* 40.81, *Common Nighthawk* . . . Burnt-land Bird (Mass. From a habitat.).

burnt piece n Also *burned piece*

A plot of land cleared for planting by burning.

1860 *Harper's Mag.* 20.290/2 **NH,** Here was the fellow who had come . . twenty miles to see the circus. He had left his "burned-piece" just in the nick of time. **1909** *DN* 3.409 **ME,** *Burnt piece* . . . A piece of woodland burnt over after the wood has been cut off.

burnt-tail jinny n Cf **jack-o'-lantern 1**

1950 *PADS* 14.18 **SC,** *Burnt-tail Jinny* . . . The will-o'- the- wisp. The feminine mate or counterpart of Jack-o'-Lantern.

burntweed n Cf **fireweed**

=**willow herb** (here: *Epilobium angustifolium*).

1893 *Jrl. Amer. Folkl.* 4.142, *Epilobium angustifolium,* . . burnt weed. **1959** Carleton *Index Herb. Plants* 20, *Burnt Weed:* Epilobium angusti-folium.

burn up anybody's mill pond v phr

To accomplish a great feat; "set the world on fire."

1898 Lloyd *Country Life* 222 **eAL,** I don't think you will ever burn up anybody's mill pond, nor either go to congress.

burn up one's tail v phr

1954 *Harder Coll.* **cwTN,** *Burn up (one's) tail* . . . work very hard.

burny See **-y**

bur oak See **burr oak**

burr n[1] Also sp *bur*

1 Any of var plants which produce burrs, but here esp **cockle-burr;** also the seed vessels or flowerheads of such a plant. [*OED* c1330 →] **chiefly Nth, N Midl** See Map Cf distributions of **cockleburr, cuckleburr**

1965–70 *DARE* (Qq. S13, 14, 15) 145 Infs, **chiefly Nth, N Midl,** Burr(s).

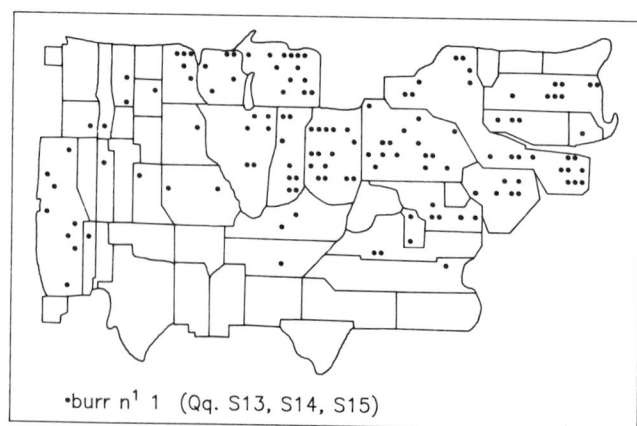

•burr n[1] 1 (Qq. S13, S14, S15)

2 The seed vessels or hulls of other plants which resemble burrs as:

a The husk of a nut, such as that of a chestnut or walnut. [*OED* 1684 →] **esp NEast**

1692 (1878) S. Sewall *Diary* 1.366 **MA,** Bring home some Chesnuts in the Burs to set. **1778** Carver *Travels N. Amer.* 499 **N Cent,** The Button

Wood is a tree of the largest size, . . . covered with small hard burs which spring from the branches, that appear not unlike buttons. **1840** *Knickerbocker* 16.164 **VA,** Bob Tarleton, a strapping fellow, with a head like a chestnut-burr, . . stepped up. **1852** Ellet *Pioneer Women* 207 **WV,** The children here loaded their little pockets with chesnuts, and for a while forgot the pinching cold of the half frozen leaves and frost covered burrs among which they were scattered. **1874** (1902) Roe *Opening Chestnut* 146 **NY,** She . . took the burr from his hand, and daintily plucking out the chestnut tossed the burr rather contemptuously away. **1940** Richter *Trees* 4 **OH,** Months before the chestnut burrs had begun to show, Worth Luckett looked for a woods famine. **1941** *LANE* Map 277 *(The hard case of the walnut or hickory nut which encloses the meat)* 22 infs, **throughout NEng,** Burr. **1965–70** *DARE* (Qu. I39, *What do you call the thick outside covering of a walnut?*) 24 Infs, **chiefly NEast,** Burr.

b A pine cone.

1859 Perry *Turpentine Farming* 24 **NC,** In the first place, we shall find that where pines are situated so that they are not exposed, and are perfectly sound, they will drop their burs clear and regular every year, which is a proof that they are healthy and doing well. In localities where they are much exposed, on the contrary, and are unsound, they will be found to have old burs hanging to them from year to year. **1905** U.S. Forest Serv. *Bulletin* 63.6 **NEng,** The seed of the white pine is borne in a cone, sometimes called a "bur." **1966–69** *DARE* (Qu. T6) Inf **AR48,** Pine burrs (FW: = cones); **NC12,** Burrs or cones; **SC4,** Cone—on the tree—(pine) burrs—on the ground; (QR, near Qu. T3) Inf **CO37,** Pine cones consistently called burrs in Colorado; (QR, near Qu. T6) Inf **CA136,** Cones are called *burrs* around here; **GA28,** Pine cones [are called] *burrs.* **1969** *DARE* FW Addit **GA51,** Burr is the same as a pine cone.

c The hull of a strawberry.

1966–70 *DARE* (Qu. I47, *When you pull the stem out of a strawberry, what do you call the green part that comes off with the stem?)* Infs **AL15, AR47, GA72, 75, IL117, KY84, MT2, SC3, 32,** Burr(s).

3 also *burrhead, chestnut burr:* By ext: a men's very short haircut. **chiefly Cent, Missip-Ohio Valleys, TX** See Map

1950 *WELS (Kinds of men's hair-cuts)* 1 Inf, **csWI,** Burr cut. **c1960** *Wilson Coll.* **csKY,** Burr haircut . . . With the hair cut short all over the head. **1965–70** *DARE* (Qu. X5, *What names do you have around here for different kinds of men's haircuts?)* 60 Infs, **chiefly Cent, Missip-Ohio Valleys, TX,** Burr; **KY77, OK31, TX98,** Burr cut; **MN2,** Burrhead; **NC33,** Chestnut burr.

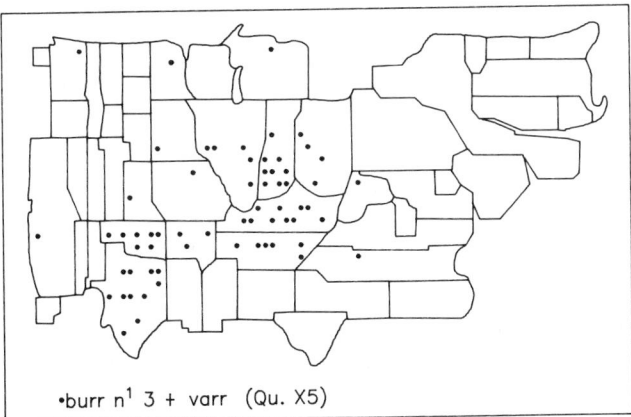

•burr n¹ 3 + varr (Qu. X5)

4 The fitting for a bolt; a nut.

1980 *DARE* File **nwIA, SD,** The word "burr" is regularly used for the nut screwed on a bolt. **1982** *Smithsonian Letters* **IN** (as of 1920s), Nuts and bolts are a common term now but when I was a boy the "nut" was called a "burr." **1982** *DARE* File **csWI** [Service Station Operator], "Burr" is an old-time name for a nut.

‡**burr** n² [?From **berm 3**]

1968 *DARE* (Qu. N25, *The unpaved part of a graded road along the edge of the pavement)* Inf **PA76,** Burr [bɝ].

burr v See **burrow**

burr artichoke n

An artichoke *(Cynara scolymus).*

1900 Lyons *Plant Names* 128, *C[ynara] Scolymus* . . . Artichoke, Bur Artichoke. *Fleshy scales* of flower heads edible when freed from the

bristles or "choke." **1949** Brown *Amer. Cooks* 644 **NC,** For those not familiar with southern food terms, let us explain that Jerusalem artichokes are known as just artichokes, while globe or French artichokes are called "burr artichokes."

burr clover n Also sp *bur clover;* also *burr-leaf clover* **esp CA** See also **button clover**

Any of several, usu prickly-podded, plants of the genus *Medicago.*

1868 *Overland Mth.* 1.180/1 **CA,** Burr clover, whose seed is enclosed in a prickly capsule, alfalfa, bunch grass, and alfilarea represent the general pasture of the mountains. **1966–70** *DARE* (Qu. L9b) Inf **TN24,** Burr clover—has a yellow bloom; (Qq. S8, 9, 13, 15, 21) Infs **CA2, 12, 125, 150, 173,** Burr clover; (Qu. S15) Inf **CA117,** Burr-leaf clover. **1970** Correll *Plants TX* 804, *Medicago* . . . Bur-clover. Medick.

bur reed See **burr reed**

burrer See **burrow**

burrfish See **burfish**

burr flower n [See quot 1822]

A **waterleaf** (here: either *Hydrophyllum canadense* or *H. virginianum*).

1822 Eaton *Botany* 311, *Hydrophyllum* . . . *virginicum* (burr-flower) . . . The flowers have the appearance of a burr several weeks before they expand . . . *[Hydrophyllum] canadense* . . (rough burr-flower). **1876** Hobbs *Bot. Hdbk.* 17, Burr-flower, *Hydrophyllum Virginicum.* **1900** Lyons *Plant Names* 196. **1959** Carleton *Index Herb. Plants* 20, *Burr Flower:* Hydrophyllum virginianum.

burr forget-me-not n

A **stickseed 1** (here: *Lappula texana*).

1951 *PADS* 15.39 **TX,** *Lappula texana* . . . Tick– or stick-seed; bur forget-me-not.

burr grass n Also *grassbur*

A grass of the genus *Cenchrus.* Also called **bear grass 3a, hedgehog grass, sand burr, sand spur.** For other names of var spp see **cadillo, devil burr, feathertop, sand grass**

1829 Eaton *Botany* 165, *Cenchrus* . . . *echinatus* L. (burr-grass). **1843** Torrey *Flora NY* 2.431, *Cenchrus tribuloides* . . . Bur-grass. Hedgehog Grass . . . A troublesome weed in some places, on account of the adhering prickly burs. **1871** *Amer. Naturalist* 4.690, Bur-grass is to be found only beyond the limits of New England. **1894** Coulter *Botany W. TX* 510, *Cenchrus* . . . (Bur-grass) . . . [has] spines minutely barbed backward, causing the burs to stick to anything with which they come in contact. **1970** Correll *Plants TX* 189, *Cenchrus incertus* . . . Grassbur, coast sandbur.

burrhead n¹

1 A Black person. **scattered, but esp Sth** *derog* Cf **head** n¹ **C1**

1927 *DN* 5.441 [Underworld jargon], *Burr-head* . . . A nigger. **1950** *PADS* 14.18 **SC,** *Burrhead* . . . A Negro. **1962** Atwood *Vocab. TX* 73, Terms that are undoubtedly derogatory are *coon* . . and *burrhead.* **1964** *PADS* 42.27 **Chicago IL,** Abusive terms . . . Negro . . *burrhead.* **1964** Will *Hist. Okeechobee* 283 **FL** (as of early 1920s), To cap it all, in Moore Haven John J. had used negroes on his farm, and now, by Neds, he was fixing to bring a batch of the burrheads into Clewiston. **1965–70** *DARE* (Qu. HH28, . . *People of foreign background . . Negroes)* 28 Infs, **scattered, but esp Sth,** Burrhead; [(Qu. C35, . . *Different parts of your town or city)* Inf **OH49,** Burrhead; (Qu. II25, . . *Part of a town where the poorer people, special groups, or foreign groups live)* Inf **OH49,** Burrhead]. **1970** Tarpley *Blinky* 265 **neTX,** *Burrheads* is found only in the age groups over 30 and chiefly among men but entirely outside the city. **1973** Allen *LAUM* 1.347 **swIA,** [One inf called a Negro a *burrhead*].

2 See **burr n¹ 3.**

burrhead n² [Perh infl by **burro 1**]

1967 *DARE* (Qu. K50, *Joking names for mules)* Inf **TX26,** Burrhead.

burrheaded adj Also *burrhead* Cf **burr n¹ 3, burrhead n¹**

Having tight, curly hair—used of Black people.

1930 Stoney–Shelby *Black Genesis* 171 **seSC,** Half o' dem chillen buckra like dey Pa, an' de res', while dey ain' been hairy like dey Ma, been black as soot, an' burrhead! **1948** Faulkner *Intruder* 19 **MS,** You goddamn biggity stiff-necked stinking burrheaded Edmonds sonofabitch. **1950** Faulkner *Stories* 235 **MS,** And she sent the money and he got a burr-headed nigger boy about my size. **1970** *DARE* (Qu. X28,

Joking words used around here for a person's head) Inf **KY**85, Burr-headed, a Negro with long natural hair.

burrito n [MexSpan "little donkey"] **orig SW** *now being spread through commercialization* Cf **burro** n **2**

A combination of meat, cheese, beans, or other foods, wrapped in a tortilla, sometimes deep-fried, and served with a sauce.

1965–70 *DARE* (Qu. H50, *Dishes made with beans, peas, or corn*) Inf **CA**178, Burrito; **CA**4, Bean burrito; (Qu. H45, *Dishes made with meat, fish, or poultry*) Infs **CA**11, 59, **TX**5, Burritos; (Qu. H65, *Foreign foods favored by people around here*) Infs **CA**107, 184, **TX**77, Burritos. **1967** *DARE* Tape **AZ**8, Some of the names . . for these various [Mexican] dishes are *tostada, burrito* . . A burrito is a tostada with a bean and onion and garlic-flavored paste. Sometimes grated cheese is used . . . There are also chicken burritos, beef burritos. **1975** *Sunset* July 55 **sCA** [Caption], In Los Angeles almost anything goes into a burrito. This downtown stand makes theirs with sliced pastrami in oversized 12-inch tortillas. **1978** *New Yorker* 4 Dec 59 **csTX**, Even the drive-in Dairy Queen offers tacos, enchiladas, and burritos along with its standard shakes, burgers, and fries. **1983** *DARE* File **csWI**, Nowadays you don't have to go to the Southwest for Mexican food. Tacos, enchiladas, burritos, and tostadas all seem to be available at fast-food chains throughout the country.

burr-leaf clover See **burr clover**

burr marigold n Also sp *bur marigold*
=**beggar ticks 1.**

1822 Eaton *Botany* 205, *Bidens frondosa* (burr-marygold [sic] . . .). **1901** Lounsberry *S. Wild Flowers* 527, *Bidens lævis* . . . While the bur-marigolds . . are closely related to the Rudbeckias, they suggest to us the coreopsis even more. **1950** Stevens *ND Plants* 286, *Bidens cernua* . . . Bur Marigold. **1971** GA Dept. Ag. *Farmers Market Bulletin* 20 Jan 8/1, Beggar-tick (often called bur-marigold, stick-tight, beggar-lice . .). **1973** Hitchcock–Cronquist *Flora Pacific NW* 496, Bur-marigold. **1976** Bruce *How to Grow Wildflowers* 272, A wet meadow overlay the same sort of soil, producing the same sort of conditions. It was bright all summer long with hardhack and meadowsweet, milkweed, asters, ironweed, boneset, Joe-pye weed, bur-marigolds, vervains, and a dozen others.

burro n, also attrib Usu |ˈbɝo| [Span *burro* donkey] **chiefly SW**

1 A donkey—sometimes applied to a mule.

1844 (1954) Gregg *Commerce* 133 **NM**, In fact the chief riding animal of the peasant is the burro. **1856** (1928) Jaeger *Diary Fort Yuma* 103 **AZ**, The burro train got at the Gila House. **1892** *DN* 1.188 **TX**, Búrro. **1962** Atwood *Vocab. TX* 57, The most common term for this animal is *donkey* . . which occurs throughout the area surveyed. However, the Spanish *burro* . . is almost as popular; it has clearly spread from the western portions [of the state]. **1965–70** *DARE* (Qu. K50, *Joking nicknames for mules*) 11 Infs, **scattered, but esp West**, Burro; (Qu. A18, *. . A very slow person: "What's keeping him? He certainly is_____!"*) Inf **CO**24, Slow as a burro; (QR, near Qu. K50) Inf **CO**22, A burro is a jackass; [(Qu. N37) Inf **AZ**7, Burro train]. **1965–70** *DARE* Tapes **CA**89, **IN**32, **TX**24, Burro; **AZ**1, What made Arizona? Bacon, beans, burros, and balin' wire—The Four B's; **NM**3, There was a one-armed Mexican . . with a little [ˈbuˑˌro] . . . The other men would have them a [ˈbuɝə]. **1967** LeCompte *Word Atlas* 196 **seLA**, (*A farm animal smaller than a mule or horse*) [1 of 21 infs, Burro]. **1967** *DARE* FW Addit **ceTX**, Burro. A small donkey. The word "ass" is not used much around here.

2 =**burrito.**

1971 O'Connor *Complete Stories* 40 **AZ**, Put a few tablespoonfuls of fried beans in a tortilla and roll them up in it and you have a "burro," a delicious lunch. **1983** *DARE* File **swCA**, The Mexican-American women in the cannery where I used to work brought "burros" in their lunches—a tortilla wrapped around meat, eggs, or beans.

burr oak n Also sp *bur oak* **chiefly N Cent, Upper MW, Cent** See Map

An oak tree (here: *Quercus macrocarpa*). Also called **blue oak 1, mossycup oak, overcup oak, scrub oak, white oak**

1815 Drake *Natural View Cincinnati* 82, The most valuable timber trees are the . . white, black, low-land chesnut and bur oaks. **1897** Sudworth *Arborescent Flora* 155, *Quercus macrocarpa* . . . Bur Oak. **1940** Clute *Amer. Plant Names* 162, *Quercus macrocarpa* . . . Bur Oak. **1965–70** *DARE* (Qu. T10) 98 Infs, **chiefly N Cent, Upper MW, Cent**, Burr oak; (Qq. T15, 16) Infs **IL**143, **MO**38, **OK**46, **WV**8, Burr oak.

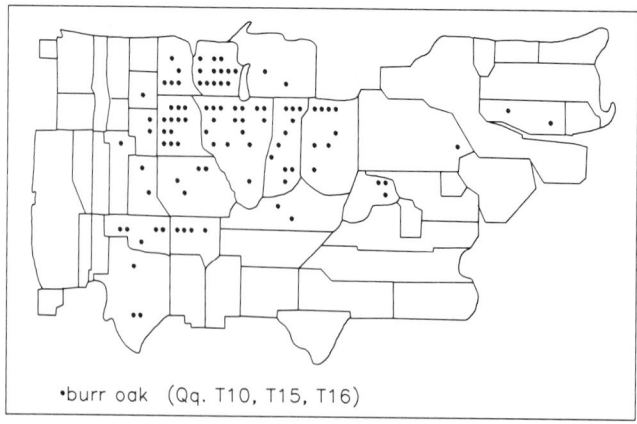

•burr oak (Qq. T10, T15, T16)

burrobrush n **West**

1 A bushy, slender-branched shrub of the genus *Hymenoclea*. For other names of var spp see **cheese bush**

1931 U.S. Dept. Ag. *Misc. Pub.* 101.154, *Hymenoclea monogyra* . . . The common name "burrobrush" alludes to the usual observation that nothing but burros will eat it. **1938** Van Dersal *Native Woody Plants* 142, *Hymenoclea monogyra* . . . Burrobrush . . . *Hymenoclea salsola* . . . White burrobrush. **1944** AZ Univ. *Biol. Sci. Bulletin* 6.354, *Hymenoclea*. Burro Brush . . . Shrubs, more or less bushy. **1981** Benson–Darrow *Trees SW Deserts* 301.

2 =**blackbrush 2.**

1937 U.S. Forest Serv. *Range Plant Hdbk.* B61, Blackbrush, also called . . , especially in southern Utah and northern Arizona, burrobrush, is an intricately branched shrub.

3 A **burr sage** (perh *Franseria deltoidea*).

1966 *DARE* (Qu. T16) Inf **NM**13, Burro brush or rabbit brush—looks like a willow.

burrobush n

The white **burr sage** (*Franseria dumosa*).

1941 Jaeger *Wildflowers* 279 **Desert SW**, Burro bush is our second most widespread and dominant xeric plant, . . erroneously it is generally called burro **weed**. **1946** Sierra Club *Bulletin* Dec 18 **CA**, Even burro bushes look dead and cacti shrivel.

burro deer n
=**mule deer.**

1895 Remington *Pony Tracks* 130, After hunting down the valley for a few days for "burro deer" and wild turkey, we found that the tobacco was promptly giving out. **1928** Anthony *N. Amer. Mammals* 522, Desert Mule Deer; Burro Deer . . . Large, very much paler than typical *hemionus*. **1982** Elman *Hunter's Field Guide* 480, Mule Deer . . . Common & Regional Names: Muley, burro deer.

burro fat n **Desert SW**
=**bladderpod 3.**

1925 Jepson *Manual Plants CA* 407, *I[someris] arborea* . . . Burro Fat. **1927** *Natl. Geog. Mag.* 51.566/2 **sCA**, Some authorities call *Isomeris arborea* bladderpod; others propose the name burro-fat. **1944** AZ Univ. *Biol. Sci. Bulletin* 6.131, The burro fat, which is the most common shrub in our range, is readily recognized by . . its long-stalked inflated pods. **1953** *AmSp* 28.100 **SW**, Burro fat . . . Bladderpod (*Isomeris arborea*). **1981** Benson–Darrow *Trees SW Deserts* 94, Burro Fat . . . The fruit varies from globose-inflated to broadly linear and scarcely inflated.

burro goldenweed See **burroweed 3**

burro grass n

A perennial range grass (*Scleropogon brevifolius*) native to the southwestern US. Also called **needlegrass**

1931 Dayton *Important Browse* 165, Tar-bush . . . is . . frequently in association with creosote bush, mesquite, burrograss, and tobosagrass. **1953** *AmSp* 28.100 **SW**, Burrograss . . . *Scleropogon brevifolius*. **1969** *DARE* (Qu. S9) Inf **TX**68, Burro grass. **1971** Green ~~Village Horse Doctor~~ 175 **TX**, The only grass in the pasture was tough bunch grass, commonly referred to as burro grass, which sheep seldom eat except in the early summer when tender shoots come out close to the ground.

burro load n

See quots.

1944 Adams *Western Words* 25, *Burro load*—This term is often used as a unit of measure, as we use *peck* or *bushel*, especially in the hauling of firewood bought by the *burro load*. **1966** *DARE* FW Addit NM6, A burro load of wood is three ricks, two on [the] sides, one on top [of the burro].

burrow v Usu |'bɝ-o|; sometimes |'bɝ-ə| Pronc-spp *burr, burrer, burruh* See Pronc Intro 3.I.12.d

Std senses, var forms.

1899 (1912) Green *VA Folk-Speech* 101, *Burr* . . . To burrow. **1922** Gonzales *Black Border* 291 **sSC, GA coasts** [Gullah glossary], *Burruh*—burrow, burrows, burrowed, burrowing. **1922** (1926) Cady *Rhymes VT* 182, He lets the chipmunks *burrer*. **1936** *AmSp* 11.159 **eTX**, The vowel in the final syllable of all the words listed below is usually [ə] . . . burrow.

burroweed n Also sp *burrow-weed*

1 A **pickleweed** (here: *Allenrolfea occidentalis*).

1913 Wooton *Trees NM* 64, *Burro Weed (Allenrolfea occidentalis)* is a very peculiar, almost leafless alkali-loving shrub with cylindrical jointed green succulent branches . . . It is sparingly eaten by burros; hence the common name. **1942** Whipple *Joshua* 94 **UT** (as of c1860), There was a cow sampling the saltbrush, there another munching the humble burrow-weed. **1953** *AmSp* 28.100 **SW**, *Burroweed* . . . *Allenrolfea occudentalis* [sic].

2 The white **burr sage** (*Franseria dumosa*). **CA**

1925 Jepson *Manual Plants CA* 1108, *F[ranseria] dumosa* . . . *Burroweed.* Low rounded bush 10 to 20 in. high. **1959** Munz–Keck *CA Flora* 1104. **1981** Benson–Darrow *Trees SW Deserts* 308, In California the plant is known sometimes as burro weed, as it provides forage for donkeys and cattle.

3 also *burro goldenweed*: A **goldenweed** (here: *Haplopappus tenuisectus*).

1931 U.S. Dept. Ag. *Misc. Pub.* 101.157, The related *Aplopappus fruticosus* . . , known as burroweed in southeastern Arizona, . . produces the same harmful effect as *A. heterophyllus*. **1960** Vines *Trees SW* 1004, *Burro Goldenweed* . . . Western woody subshrub with numerous branches from the base. **1981** Benson–Darrow *Trees SW Deserts* 328, Burro weed is significant as an invader of depleted range lands, and often it constitutes the principal vegetational cover.

4 =**yerba de pasmo**.

1931 U.S. Dept. Ag. *Misc. Pub.* 101.158, *Yerba-de-pasmo* . . . is also frequently known as burroweed, chamisa, chill weed, and winged baccharis.

burrowing owl n Also *burrow owl*

A small, long-legged, chiefly terrestrial owl *(Speotyto cunicularia),* native to the western half of the US as well as Florida, which nests in burrows (such as those of prairie dogs). Also called **billy owl, cuckoo owl, elf owl 2, ground owl, howdy owl, Johnny owl, posthole owl, prairie-dog owl, prairie owl 1, snake owl**

1823 James *Acct. of Exped.* 2.97, Mr. Peale killed a burrowing owl. **1852** Stansbury *Expedition* 37 **UT**, A little, white, burrowing owl also . . is frequently found taking up his abode in the same domicile; and this strange association of reptile [=rattlesnake], bird, and beast [=prairie dog] seem to live together in perfect harmony and peace. **1874** Coues *Birds NW* 322, The Burrowing Owl is the only bird of its family inhabiting, in any numbers, the entire treeless regions of the West, and may be considered characteristic of the plains. **1904** Wheelock *Birds CA* 178, Although the Burrowing Owl is more or less shy, it is not at all difficult to study its habits. **1928** Bailey *Birds NM* 328, The droll little Burrowing Owls, stilted up on their long bony legs, bowing as you approach, . . afford much amusement and interest when in the land of "dog-towns." **1953** Jewett *Birds WA* 363, On Smith Island a burrowing owl was living in a rabbit hole. **1965–70** *DARE* (Qu. Q2) Infs **CA**115, 136, **FL**4, **ND**9, **TX**5, **WA**15, Burrowing owl; **CA**117, Burrow owl.

burrowing spider n Also *burrowing wolf spider*

A **wolf spider**.

1931 *Sun* (Baltimore MD) 2 May 10/6 *(Hench Coll.),* The turret or burrowing spider belongs to the family of hunters called *Lycosidae,* known as wolf spiders, and this branch of the family receives its name from the watch tower or turret constructed around the mouth of the burrow. **1980** Milne *Audubon Field Guide Insects* 896, *Burrowing Wolf Spiders (Geolycosa* spp.)

burrow owl See **burrowing owl**

burrow pit See **barrow pit 1**

burrow-weed See **burroweed**

burr pine n Cf **burr** n¹ **2b**

A **shortleaf pine.**

1967–69 *DARE* (Qu. T17) Infs **KY**16, **LA**10, Burr pine—same as shortleaf [pine].

burr ragweed See **ragweed**

burr reed n Also sp *bur reed*

A colony-forming plant of the genus *Sparganium,* which produces burr-like seed capsules. Also called **ox-tongue**

1821 in 1832 MA Hist. Soc. *Coll.* 2nd ser 9.156 **cwVT**, Plants, which are indigenous in the town of Middlebury, [include] . . . *Sparganium ramosum,* Bur-reed. **1840** MA Zool. & Bot. Surv. *Herb. Plants & Quadrupeds* 1.219, Lake Burr Reed . . . grows near New Bedford, in ponds. **1843** Torrey *Flora NY* 2.248, *Branching Bur-reed* . . . [grows in] ditches and borders of swamps: common. *Ibid* 249, *Smaller Bur-reed* . . [grows in] ponds, lakes, and slow-flowing streams, in the interior of the State. **1976** Bailey–Bailey *Hortus Third* 1061, *Sparganium* . . . Bur reed.

burr sack n [?Abbr for *burlap*] Cf *DS* F23

=**coffee sack.**

1981 *Broaddus Coll.* **ceKY** (as of 1958), Burr sack—the same as a "coffee sack," only made out of fodder twine.

burr sage n

A plant of the genus *Franseria.* Also called **ragweed** For other names of var spp see **burrobrush 3, burrobush, burroweed 2, rabbit bush, sand burr, snakeweed**

1931 U.S. Dept. Ag. *Misc. Pub.* 101.153, *Bur-Sages (Franseria* spp. . .) . . . With one exception the shrubby species of bur-sage are not known to have any particular forage significance. **1959** Munz–Keck *CA Flora* 1104, *F. dumosa* . . . *Burro-weed. Bur-Sage.* Low intricately branched rounded shrub. **1981** Benson–Darrow *Trees SW Deserts* 302, *Bur Sage, Western Ragweed* . . . The head . . a bur in fruit, often resembling a cocklebur.

burr thistle n

1 =**cockleburr 1.**

1828 Rafinesque *Med. Flora* 275, *Xanthium* . . . Burthistle. **1876** Hobbs *Bot. Hdbk.* 24, Burr thistle, *Xanthium strumarium.* **1900** Lyons *Plant Names* 398, *Xanthium strumarium* . . . Bur Thistle.

2 =**bull thistle.**

1936 Winter *Plants NE* 165, *C[irsium] lanceolatum* . . . Common Bur Thistle. **1959** Carleton *Index Herb. Plants* 20, *Bur Thistle:* Cirsium lanceolatum. **1968** *DARE* (Qu. S15) Inf **CA**101, Burr thistle.

burr tomato n [Prob because the tomato-like red berry is enclosed in a round prickly seed capsule]

=**buffalo burr.**

1918 Visher *Geog. SD* 90, The bur-tomato *(Solanum rostratum)* is another annual which is sometimes conspicuous in similar situations.

burruh See **burrow**

burr vine n Also sp *burfine* [Folk-etym for *vervine,* alter of *verbena*]

Any of var vervains, esp *Verbena stricta* and *V. urticifolia.*

1897 *Jrl. Amer. Folkl.* 10.52, *Verbena angustifolia, stricta,* and *urticæfolia,* . . bur-vine, Southwestern Mo. **1941** FWP *Guide WV* 140, Burfine root is excellent for coughs and the flu. **1968** *DARE* (Qu. S15) Inf **VA**24, Burr vine—used for stomach cramps.

burrying See **burying**

bursh See **bush** n¹, v¹

burshel See **bushel**

burst v Cf **bust** v

Std senses, var forms.

Past and past pple usu *burst;* also *esp among those with little formal educ, bursted.*

1826 Cooper in 1927 *AmSp* 2.485, Bursted. **1872** Schele de Vere *Americanisms* 587, *Bursted,* a false participle from *burst,* is often used in the South to give emphasis to the word. **1905** *DN* 3.72, *Bu(r)st* . . Break . . . 'Her throat bu(r)sted.' **1908** *DN* 3.295 **eAL, wGA**, Busted . . .

bursted, is commonly heard. **1953** Atwood *Survey of Verb Forms* 7, The preterite . . in the context "The pipe (burst)." . . The form *burst* strongly predominates among all types throughout N. Eng.; more than three-fourths of all informants use this form alone or alongside some variant . . . *Bursted* /bɔstəd/ occurs among a relatively small group of N. Eng. informants (44/413), most of whom (32) fall in Types IA and IIA [old-fashioned, with little or moderate education] with no particular geographical concentration. **1965–70** *DARE* (Qu. F32, . . *A sudden flood in the cellar . . "A water pipe must have _____."*) 422 Infs, **widespread,** Burst; 185 Infs, **widespread,** Bursted; (Qu. W24b) 7 Infs, **scattered,** You're bursted out (like a locust); (Qu. GG30) 15 Infs, **scattered,** Bursted (out laughing, etc); (Qu. KK22) 13 Infs, **scattered,** Bursted (to pieces, smithereens, etc); (Qq. C32, U39, AA29, BB36, KK8, KK53) 7 Infs, **scattered,** Bursted [in var phrr]. [Of all Infs responding to Qu. F32, 28% had less than 2 yrs high school educ, 32% had coll educ; of those giving the response *bursted,* 46% had less than 2 yrs high school educ, 18% had coll educ.] **1968–69** *DARE* Tape GA77, We bursted ['bɔstɪd] ice many a morning to water the stock; MO9, Our home just bursted, you know [in a tornado].

burst a gut See **bust a gut 2**

burst a hame (string) See **bust a hame string**

bursted vessel See **busted vein**

burster n Cf **blue norther** and *DS* B18
   1895 in 1935 Twain *Notebook* 262, Then came a "burster"—kind of hurricane—out of the south—the twin of the Texas "Norther"—and knocked the mercury down 36 degrees in four hours.

bursting heart n [See quot 1860]
=**burning bush 1** (here: *Euonymus atropurpureus* and *E. americanus*).
   1860 Curtis *Cat. Plants NC* 102, *Euonymus Americanus . . . Bursting Heart . . .* The fruit . . . is of a bright crimson color when mature, and . . . finally bursts open exposing its bright scarlet seeds. **1866** *Land We Love* (Charlotte NC) May 80 *(DA),* Bursting Heart . . . The bright crimson berries of this plant, open their embossed covering into four leaves, and display within the smooth scarlet seeds, which give it the name of bursting heart. **1883** Hale *Woods NC* 165, Strawberry Bush . . . [is] a shrub 2 to 5 feet high, found in all the Districts, and known by the names of Burning Bush, Fish-wood, and Bursting Heart. **1930** U.S. Dept. Ag. *Misc. Pub.* 77.59, *Euonymus atropurpureus . . . Other common names.—Burningbush, . . bursting-heart.* **1966** Grimm *Recognizing Native Shrubs* 175, Strawberry-Bush . . . Also known as Bursting-heart.

burst one's buttons See **bust one's buttons**

burweed n
   1 =**cockleburr 1.**
   1828 Rafinesque *Med. Flora* 275, *Xanthium . . .* Burweed. **1903** Small *Flora SE U.S.* 1148, *Xanthium . . .* Burweed. **1912** Blatchley *IN Weed Book* 151, *Xanthium spinosum . . .* Burweed. **1959** Carleton *Index Herb. Plants* 21, *Bur Weed . . . Xanthium canadense.* **1968** *DARE* (Qu. S21) Inf MD29, Burweed.
   2 A tropical tiliaceous plant (*Triumfetta* spp).
   1900 Lyons *Plant Names* 379, *Triumfeta* [sic] *. . .* Burweed. **1933** Small *Manual SE Flora* 841, *Triumfetta . . .* Burweed.
   3 =**bedstraw.**
   1959 Carleton *Index Herb. Plants* 21, *Bur Weed . . . Galium aperine.*

bury v
To be buried; of a family: to have its members buried (in a specific place).
   1934 *Hanley Disks* nwRI, This old Jonah Hopkins . . gave a piece of land over here for a burial ground, for all of the Hopkinses . . to bury on. **1958** Humphrey *Home from the Hill* 6 TX, You heard of anybody dying that buries here? *Ibid* 8, If it's a lady—a white woman—and her folks always buried with us and the poor soul hasn't got no family now.

bury ground See **bury patch**

bury hole n Cf **bury patch**
A grave.
   1940 Richter *Trees* 9 OH (as of early 19th cent), Her own father wouldn't know the place if he rose from his bury hole. **1965** *DARE* File swPA (as of 1920s), *Bury hole*—Grave.

burying n Pronc-spp *berrin, berrying, burrying* Sth, S Midl
A funeral; interment.

1815 Humphreys *Yankey in England* 103, Berrying, burying. **1895** *DN* 1.385 cwIN, wFL, Burying . . . funeral. **1899** (1912) Green *VA Folk-Speech* 101, Burrying . . . A funeral. **1902** *DN* 2.230 sIL, Burying [bɛrɪ-ɪn] . . . Funeral, a word which is not used. **1903** *DN* 2.308 seMO, Burying . . . Interment. **1907** *DN* 3.221 nwAR, Burying . . . Funeral. **1908** *DN* 3.295 eAL, wGA, Burying . . . The common word for interment with funeral ceremonies. **1927** Kennedy *Gritny* 82 sLA [Black], Dey goin' take 'uh all de way to Gritny to wake 'uh, an' have de berrin'. **1933** Rawlings *South Moon* 74 FL, Son, I don't know what Py-tee kin do about a fitten buryin'. They jest ain't enough o' Willy to fix nice in the coffin. **1944** *PADS* 2.28 eKY, wNC, Buryin' . . . ['bʌrɪən, 'bærɪən] . . . Burial. **1946** *PADS* 6.7 eNC, Burying. c**1960** *Wilson Coll.* csKY, Burying . . . The whole funeral and not merely the interment. The actual funeral, in older times, might be later, much later.

burying ground n Also *burying grounds, ~ hill, ~ lot, ~ place, ~ point, ~ yard* old-fash
A cemetery.
   1808 (1910) Ayer *Diary* 58 MA, We went up to the burying hill. I stood a long time without the gate. **1811** (1816) Hyde *Writings* 69 CT, In the afternoon walked with my friend into the burying-ground, and busied myself in perusing inscriptions. **1899** (1912) Green *VA Folk-Speech* 101, Burrying-ground . . . A grave-yard. **1912** *DN* 3.567 cNY, Cemetery . . . Often a new or well-kept grave-yard. "Burying-ground" is used for an old cemetery. **1923** *DN* 5.202 swMO, Buryin' ground. **1929** *AmSp* 5.120 ME, Burying ground. **1931** *AmSp* 7.92 eKY, Buryin'-ground. c**1960** *Wilson Coll.* csKY, Burying ground . . . A term that is only used now. **1965** *Amherst Rec.* (MA) 29 July 7/1–3, Pack your lunch and make for the old burying grounds. **1965–70** *DARE* (Qu. BB61a, *Other words used around here for a cemetery*) 121 Infs, **widespread,** Burying ground; IL35, NC18, Burying lot; ID5, NY121, Burying place; (Qu. BB61b, *Any joking names for a cemetery*) Inf MI89, Burying ground; AR21, Burying place; VA106, Burying yard; MA5, Pauper's burying ground. [Of all Infs responding to Qu. BB61a, 9% were young, 24% mid-aged, 67% old; of those giving these responses, 2% were young, 16% mid-aged, 82% old.] **1975** Gould *ME Lingo* 29, Along the Maine coast a *buryin'* ground is often called a *buryin'* point.

burying society See **burial society**

burying yard See **burying ground**

bury league n *among Black speakers* Cf **burial society**
A mutual organization in which the members pay each other's funeral expenses.
   1928 Peterkin *Scarlet Sister Mary* 218 SC [Black], They could not be happy . . except in crowds or groups. They had societies, bury-leagues, sick benefit circles, lodges. **1942** (1965) Parrish *Slave Songs* 192 GA, If they have not been so provident as to take out an insurance policy, join a "Bury League," or pay to some society or lodge dues which range from ten to twenty-five cents a week.

bury patch n Also *bury ground* joc Cf **burying ground**
A cemetery.
   1965–70 *DARE* (Qu. BB61a, . . *Words . . for a cemetery*) Inf PA29, Bury patch; OR3, Bury ground; (Qu. BB61b, . . *Joking names for a cemetery*) Infs KS15, PA29, Bury patch.

burysies exclam [*bury* v + *-s* pl + *-ies 2*]
In marble play: a call enabling a player to bury his marble.
   1981 *DARE* File sCA (as of c1946), *Burysies*—a term by which one asserts the right to bury one's marble, ostensibly to prevent it from being struck by another player. Also "no burysies." Term in use among third grade marble-playing boys in Ivanhoe School (Silver Lake District) Los Angeles.

bury the tomahawk v phr
   1939 *Hall Coll.* eTN, Buryin' a tommy hawk . . . Copulating.

bus n¹, also attrib Usu |bʌs|, rarely |bɔs| See Pronc Intro 3.I.23
A Form.
   1942 Hall *Smoky Mt. Speech* 41, The occasional employment of [ɔ] for [ʌ] in *bus, fuss, gush* suggests hypercorrection.
B Sense.
A horse-drawn vehicle for carrying people. **chiefly NEast** See Map *old-fash*
   1965–70 *DARE* (Qu. N41a, . . *Kinds of horse-drawn vehicles . . to carry people*) 13 Infs, **chiefly NEast,** Bus; MD29, Bus—in town, drawn by two horses, enclosed; MI24, Bus—two horses; owned by a livery stable;

could rent it; **MD10, MI93, NY105, TN11, VA33,** Horse-drawn bus; **CA107,** Hotel bus; **MA68,** School bus; (Qu. N40b, *Different kinds of sleighs for carrying people*) Inf **NY66,** Bus sleigh; **NY156,** Nigger buses; **RI17,** Buses. [21 of 23 total Infs old]

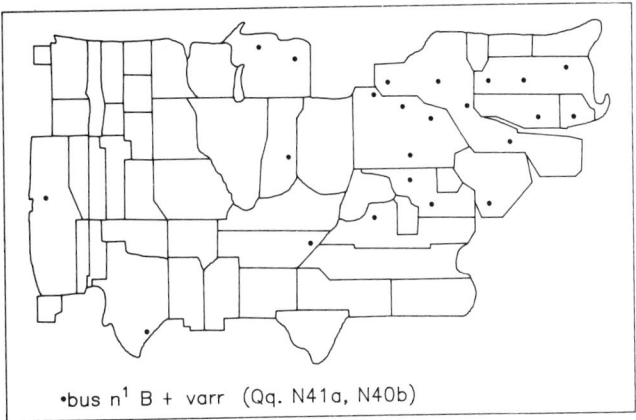

•bus n¹ B + varr (Qq. N41a, N40b)

bus n² See **buss** n

bus v See **buss** v

bush n¹, v¹ Usu |buš|, also |buš|, |bɚš| See Pronc Intro 3.I.5.c, 3.I.23 Pronc-spp *boosh, bursh*

A Forms.
   1939 *AmSp* 14.156 **WV,** Bush = boosh; push = poosh. **1941** *AmSp* 16.112 **VA,** The sounds of [u] in *bush* and *push* . . . may be heard in all parts of the state. **c1960** *Wilson Coll.* **csKY,** Bush is sometimes [bʌrš]. **1967** *Mt. Life* Spring–Summer 15 **ceKY,** The limbs of the ivy burshes. **1968** *DARE* FW Addit **eMD,** *Bush* and *push* have [u]; **nwMD,** Bush [buš].

B As noun.
   1 usu prec by *the:* An area of wild or unsettled land, spec:
   a A piece of land covered by forest or shrubbery. **esp NEng old-fash**
   1779 (1881) Lovell *Orig. Jrl.* 102 **ME,** The Gentlemen took to the Bush and escaped being made prisoners. **1872** Schele de Vere *Americanisms* 89, The word *bush* . . has retained in America the original meaning of the Dutch *bosch* more faithfully than in England, where it generally designates a single shrub, while here . . it means rather a region abounding in trees and shrubs. *Ibid* 178, Should he [the settler] dread the *bush,* he may choose one of those beautiful forest glades. **1902** (1968) Clapin *Americanisms* 86, *Bush.* A land covered with rank shrubbery. The primeval or virgin forest land. A thicket of trees. Uncultivated land covered with trees and undergrowth. **1905** *DN* 3.4 **cCT,** *Bush* . . . Woods. **1929** *AmSp* 5.154 **eNY,** The word *bush* . . was formerly current (in the meaning of forest) . . a borrowing from the Dutch. *Ibid* 157, The word *bush* was in use during the 18th century meaning *woods,* though not apparently in very common use. It remains more or less current down to the middle of the 19th century . . . The word is hardly used now except in *sugar bush* or *maple bush.* **1931–33** *LANE Worksheets* **cwVT,** Natives call any patch of woods a bush. **1959** *VT Hist.* new ser 27.128, Bush possession . . . Squatter's rights. Obsolete. **1966–67** *DARE* (Qu. HH1, . . *A rustic or countrified person*) Inf **FL10,** From the bush; (Qu. BB46, . . *About someone who has been very sick but now is getting better: "He's _____."*) Inf **NY8,** Out of the woods or bush. **1969** Sorden *Lumberjack Lingo* **NEng, Gt Lakes,** *Bush.* The woods or the back country . . . More commonly in Canada than in the lake states.
   b also attrib: A vast and remote region. **Nth, esp AK**
   1891 (1905) Ryan *Told in Hills* 191 **WA,** From their tones one would gather the impression that all the splendors of a metropolis were as nothing when compared with the luxuries of "shack" life in the "bush." **1953** *Jessen's Weekly* 22 Jan (Tabbert *Alaskan Engl.*), The operators commented that . . the average commercial pilot flying the bush has many years of experience. **1972** *River Times* (Fairbanks AK) Aug 4/3, We're still a bush airline . . . and proud of it! **1973** *Tundra Times* (Fairbanks AK) 11 Apr 1/1, State 8th Legislature's Tight Fist Leaves Bush Fighting for Programs. **1976** *News-Miner* (Fairbanks AK) 16 Feb (Tabbert *Alaskan Engl.*), Bush education, particularly, could be hurt if the community college system were separate from the statewide university system. *Ibid* 23 Sept, Justice in the bush villages should be locally controlled rather than imported from the urban areas. **1979** *UpCountry*

July 38 **NH,** The shortest way there is by bush plane, weather permitting, from Sherbrooke, across the border in Quebec.
   2 =**Afro** n. *chiefly among Black speakers*
   1965–70 *DARE* (Qu. V5, . . *Different kinds of men's haircuts*) Infs **AL61, KY59, MS80, OH16, PA239, TN50, TX36, VA39,** Bush. [5 of 8 Infs Black] **1972** Claerbaut *Black Jargon* 59, *Bush* . . . a large, kinky, bushy hairstyle.

C As verb.
   1 To **top out** a building on completion of construction.
   1954 *PADS* 21.22 **SC,** *Bush: v.t.* To *bush* a building is to fasten a green *bush* to the topmost part of the framework when the frame is completed.
   2 To spread (clothing) out on shrubbery to dry.
   1967 Cerello *Dakota Co. MN,* We always used to bush the wash early in the mornings . . . sometimes our clean wash had leaf stains on it from bushing it on certain types of shrubs.
   3 To cut or clear away brush; hence *busher* n.
   1966–69 *DARE* Tape **CT36,** There's your man in the woods that help load the log, he's a busher . . he cuts the paths for the men of the log team; **NC21,** Last year I had a . . fellow over there bushin' . . and he's standing out there . . with a bush hook in his hand.

bush n² [Prob alter of **push**, but cf **booshway**]
   1968 *DARE* (Qu. HH17, *A person who tries to appear important . . "He'd like to be the _____ around here."*) Inf **NY68,** The bush! [laughter].

bush n³ See **bushwa** n²

bush v² Pronc-spp *booch, butch* [Cf *EDD, SND* booshie a call to cows] Cf **boss** n¹ **2**
Come!—used to call pigs.
   1939 *LANE* Map 226 **swCT,** Calls to pigs . . . [buəʃ]. **c1950** *Atlas Checklists* **ceMO,** (*Call to hogs at feeding time*) Bush, co-bush. **1968** *DARE* (Qu. K84, *The call . . to get the pigs in at feeding time*) Inf **IN32,** Bush. **1973** Allen *LAUM* 1.265, (*Call to pigs at feeding time*) Booch, *booch* (S.D.) . . . Butch [Minnesota; said with laughter].

busha n [Alter of **babushka**] *not fully naturalized*
   1 See **babushka**.
   2 also *bushi:* A grandmother.
   1969 *DARE* (Qu. Z4, . . *Grandmother*) Inf **IN75,** Bushi ['buši]; **MI75,** Busha ['bušə] (among Polish people).
   3 A grandfather.
   1969 *DARE* (Qu. Z3, . . *Grandfather*) Inf **IN75,** Busha ['bušə].

bush and bog n, also attrib Also *bush and bob, bush and ball* **chiefly S Atl**
A heavy-duty type of plow or harrow.
   1957 *University of Virginia News Letter* 33.13 1 Apr 1/2 (Hench Coll.), Sometimes heavy bush and bog discs are pulled through the hardwood areas . . . This can be done with a bulldozer or a tractor drawn bush and bog. **1965–70** *DARE* (Qu. L18, *Kinds of plows*) Infs **CT17, FL34, NC13,** Bush and bog plow; **GA3,** Bush and bob plow; (Qu. L20, *The implement used in a field after it's been plowed to break up the lumps*) Infs **GA77, SC1, 63,** Bush and bog harrow; **GA7,** Bush and ball harrow. **1968** *DARE* FW Addit **GA28,** *Bush and bog harrow* is an implement for cutting rough ground. **1969** *SC Market Bulletin* 11 Sept 3, Would consider taking on trade of either Bush and Bog or Scrape Blade or pan with 3 point hitch.

bush arbor n **Sth**
=**brush arbor.**
   1889 Edwards *Runaways* 232 **GA,** As he approached the edifice, which stood in a pine thicket and boasted of a bush-arbor awning in front, he heard the voice of a preacher breaking loudly upon the afternoon calm. **1941** *FWP Guide SC* 101, The services were held in log chapels, in private homes, and out of doors, with 'preaching sheds' and bush arbors serving as shelter from the elements when no other was available. **1966** *DARE* Tape **AL11,** They'd move in the woods and have meetin' . . . everybody'd be there, laid by the cross and things. They had a big bush arbor there where they had the meetin'. **1970** *Thompson Coll.* **cnAL,** *Bush arbor* . . . A place in the woods where the pure-dee, stomp-down real old-time religion is preached. Sometimes a part . . . is walled off with baggin' (apparently burlap such as is used around bales of cotton).

bush around v phr Cf *kick around, beat around the bush*
   To consider, discuss (something).

1970 *DARE* FW Addit **nwMO,** *Bush around*—"We'll bush this around."

bush ax n chiefly **Sth, S Midl, esp Mid Atl** See Map
A tool for cutting underbrush.

1946 *PADS* 6.7 **eNC,** *Bush ax* . . . A thin, curve-bladed ax used for cutting bushes, etc. **1965–70** *DARE* (Qu. L35, *Hand tools used for cutting underbrush and digging out roots*) 39 Infs, **chiefly Sth, S Midl, esp Mid Atl,** Bush ax; (Qu. L37, *A hand tool used for cutting weeds and grass*) Infs **MD38, NC87, VA77,** Bush ax.

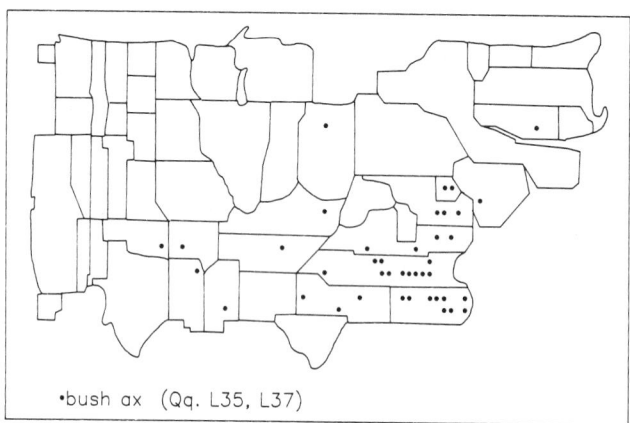

•*bush ax* (Qq. L35, L37)

bush baby n Also *bush child* **Sth** Cf **woods colt**
An illegitimate child.

1940 Fletcher *Raleigh's Eden* 88 **NC,** That girl she no good, she done already have one bush baby, maybe two, nobody knows. **1954** *PADS* 21.22 **SC,** *Bush chillun.* **1962** Atwood *Vocab. TX* 66, *Illegitimate child* . . . Uncommon . . terms, occurring from one to six times each, include . . *bush child.* **1966–67** *DARE* (Qu. Z11b, . . *Joking words for a child of unwed parents*) Inf **SC44,** Bush babies; [**MS36,** Find him behind a bush].

bush bacon n *joc* Cf **Adirondack steak, Arkansas chicken**
1941 *AmSp* 16.16 **eTX** [Black], Go in the woods and get you a bush-bacon. That's a rabbit.

bush baptist n
See quot 1983.

1967 *DARE* (Qu. CC4, . . *Nicknames . . religious groups*) Inf **TX35,** Bush baptists. [**1983** *New York Times* (NY) 17 Mar 4/6 **Australia,** The Macquarie [dictionary] . . has 67 entries derived from the word bush, meaning countryside, from bush baptist (a person of vague but strong religious beliefs) to bushranger (a bandit).]

bush bird n
A rufous-sided towhee.

1917 (1923) *Birds Amer.* 3.58, *Pipilo erythrophthalmus erythrophthalmus* . . . *Other Names* . . . Bush-bird; Turkey Sparrow . . . *Nest:* On the ground, under a clump of grass, weeds, or bushes. **1936** *Sun* (Baltimore MD) 17 Feb 7/2 *(Hench Coll.),* One side [of Eastern shore ornithologists] asserts it has seen "robins" hopping about in the snow; the opponents are scornful—they're not robins, but . . bush-birds. **1939** *Natl. Geog. Mag.* 75.353/2 **West,** Most people know it, but not everyone calls it "towhee." Many speak of it as "brown bird" and others call it "bush bird."

bush blade See **blade** n 3

bush broom n
=**brush broom** n¹.
1966–68 *DARE* (Qu. F36, *Other kinds of brooms*) Infs **AR2, PA119,** Bush broom.

bush-buster n Cf *DS* HH1
A hillbilly.
1933 in **1944** *ADD* **nwAR, swMO,** *Bush-buster* . . . =*hillbilly* . . . Heard occas.

bush child See **bush baby**

‡**bush corn** n
Prob field corn; see quot.
1968 *DARE* (Qu. I34, *If you don't have sweet corn, you can always eat young _____*) Inf **MO10,** Bush corn.

bush cranberry n
A cranberry or similar plant.
1838 Parker *Jrl. Rocky Mts.* 203, The pambina is a bush cranberry. **1926** Harris *W Va Legislative Handbook* 488 *(Hench Coll.),* Ques. What about Cheat Mountain huckleberries? Ans. It is a bush cranberry. When ripe it is from a light red to a deep red.

bush daisy n
Perh an **oxeye daisy.**
1968 *DARE* (Qu. S26a, . . *Roadside flowers*) Inf **CA41,** Bush daisy.

bushed adj [**bush** n¹ **B1**]
Isolated, feeling the effects of **cabin fever.**
1941 *Jrl. Amer. Folkl.* 54.31 **CO,** A few of the older inhabitants, particularly those obviously suffering from isolation ("bushed") will not tell these stories to "outsiders". **1949** Guthrie *Way West* 41 **KY** (as of 1847), I don't hardly feel like we've started [on the Oregon Trail] yet. Way most of 'em act, would think we was bushed in the mountains some place.

bush eel n
A **rattlesnake.**
1835 (1955) *Crockett Almanacks* 3 **wTN,** They shall be treated with . . bush eels (i.e. rattlesnakes) fried in butter.

bushel n, v Usu |'bušəl|; also |'bušəl|, |'bɜ˞šəl| See Pronc Intro 3.I.5c Pronc-spp *booshel, burshel*
A Forms.
1 Pronc varr.
1930s in **1944** *ADD* **eWV,** Usu. booshel [buʃəl]. Occas. burshel [bɜ˞ʃl]. '10 burshels of wheat.' [buʃl] is rare. **1963** Edwards *Gravel* 134 **eTN** (as of 1920s), I bought em from him for a bale of hay an three burshels of corn. **1968** *DARE* FW Addit **nwMD,** Bushel pronounced ['bušl].
2 Sg used as pl.
c1960 Wilson *Coll.* **csKY,** *Bushel* . . . Often used as a plural. **1969** *DARE* FW Addit **MA14,** Must have peeled 10 bushel of potatoes.
B As noun.
A measure of milk.
1823 in **1913** *DN* 4.47 ["Western dialect"], *Bushel* . . . A measure by which milk is gauged. **1903** *DN* 2.308 **Ozarks,** *Bushel (of milk)* . . . A quantity (of milk). 'She is a right good cow and will give a bushel of milk.'
C As verb.
In logging: to fall trees, buck logs, etc, by piece work; hence n *busheler,* vbl n *busheling.* **NW**
[**1938** (1939) Holbrook *Holy Mackinaw* 259 **Nth,** By the bushel . . . Contract work, but usually applied to contract falling and bucking.] **1948** *Sat. Eve. Post* 24 Jan 44/4 **wWA,** Buckers and fallers . . are known in the woods as bushelers. **1956** *AmSp* 31.150 **nwCA,** *Bushelling* . . . Paying on a piecework basis for felling and bucking timber. **1958** McCulloch *Woods Words* **Pacific NW,** *Bushel*—a. To fall, or buck, or do other woods jobs by piece work rather than by day wage. b. To accept a piece rate job or a small contract . . . *Busheler*—A logger working at piece rates or a small contractor, not yet a gypo. **c1965** *DARE* File **nwWA,** *Busheler* . . . Workman who falls timber and bucks it into log lengths . . . "Busheler" dates from early years when pioneers sold their harvest products by the bushel. **1967** *DARE* Tape **WA29,** A busheler ['bušlə˞] is a person that contracts his work. He gets paid by the thousand —every thousand feet [he cuts].

busheler, busheling See **bushel** C

bushel of wheat, bushel of rye exclam For varr, see quots Cf **all not hid can't hide over**
In the game of hide-and-seek: see quot 1953.
1950 *WELS* 1 Inf, **seWI,** "It" called before starting to seek: "A bushel of wheat, a bushel of rye; who's not ready, holler I." **1952** Brown *NC Folkl.* 1.38. **1953** Brewster *Amer. Nonsinging Games* 42 **NE,** One player is counted out to be "It." He is then blindfolded or hides his face between his hands and counts to one hundred. While he is counting, the other players scatter and hide. As soon as he has finished, he calls out, "All not hid, holler 'I!'" If no one yells, he calls next, "A bushel of wheat and a bushel of clover; all not hid can't hide over!" and, finally, "All eyes open; here I come!" **1965–70** *DARE* (Qu. EE15) Infs **IN30, 39,** Bushel of wheat, bushel of rye, all hain't hid holler 'I'; **IN30,** Bushel o' wheat, bushel o' clover, all hain't hid can't hide over; **TN16,** Bushel of wheat, bushel of rye, all ain't ready holler 'I'; **MD20,** Busheree, busherye, who's

not ready holler 'I'. **1968** *DARE* FW Addit **GA**33, *Hide-and-go-seek call:* A bushel of wheat, a bushel of clover. All not hid, can't way cross.

busher See **bush** n¹, v¹ **C3**

bushes n pl

Usu prec by *the:* An insignificant place; the sticks.

1965–70 *DARE* (Qu. C33, . . *An out-of-the-way place, or a very unimportant place*) Infs **MA**62, Bushes; **TX**68, The bushes; **MD**26, **VA**39, Back in the bushes; **PA**205, Road hangs over the bushes there; **NC**53, In the bushes.

bush-hacking n Cf **bush hog** v

1911 *DN* 3.537 eKY, *Bush-hacking* . . . A social gathering upon invitation to assist the host in clearing new land of trees or underbrush, he in turn providing a feast, dance, or other diversion for his helpers.

bush hog n [Trademark *Bush-Hog* a rotary cutter (orig manufactured in Selma AL), 1954 →] **chiefly Sth, S Midl** See Map Cf **brush hog**

A rotary mower for cutting underbrush.

1965–70 *DARE* (Qu. L35, . . *Tools used for cutting underbrush*) 18 Infs, **scattered, but esp Sth**, Bush hog; **FL**29, Bush hog—mower; **IN**19, Bush hog—with a tractor; **LA**2, Bush hog—not a hand tool; pulled behind a tractor with whirling blade like a giant lawn mower; **NY**113, Bush hog is a heavy scythe; **TN**26, Bush hog—machine behind tractor with whirling steel blade; (Qu. L36) Inf **GA**80, Bush hog—a bulldozer type machine; clears surface; pulled by a tractor; **KY**53, Bush hog—machine that cuts brush; **TN**1, Bush hog—like a power mower, only bigger; "modern" way. **1966** *Cynthiana Democrat* (KY) 28 Apr 6/7, *Public Auction* . . 2 John Deere bush-hogs (heavy duty). **1967** *Marshall News Messenger* (TX) 18 Aug 12/4, Let us cut your lot or pasture. New tractor and bush-hog. **1968** *Alexandria Daily Town Talk* (Alexandria–Pineville LA) 16 Feb sec B 11/1, NAA 1953 Ford tractor, excellent condition with bush hog $1480. **1969** *DARE* Tape **GA**84, Such as cuttin' with a rotary mower, which is commonly called a bush hog. **1981** *UPI Dispatch* (Dover TN) 25 June, An Ohio man bled to death late Wednesday after the bush hog tractor he was driving apparently overturned and trapped him underneath its moving blades. *Ibid* (Marion IL) 27 Aug, [He] was operating a bushhog in doing some mowing and clearing work Thursday in a pasture and orchard at his farm home.

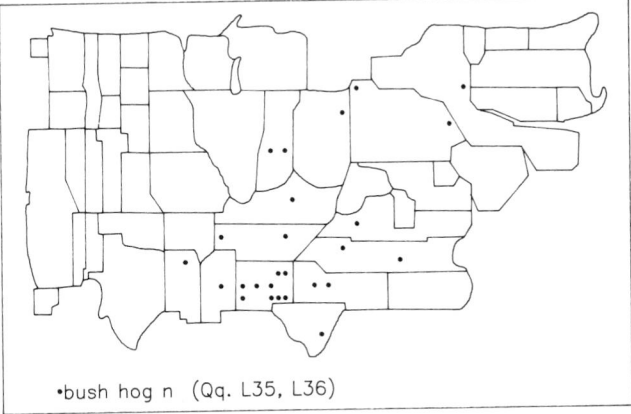

•bush hog n   (Qq. L35, L36)

bush hog v **chiefly Sth, S Midl**

To clear land with a **bush hog** or similar implement; hence vbl n *bushhogging* the clearing of land.

1966 Marckwardt *Linguistics* 49, A casual but fairly regular reading of the Bloomington (Indiana) *Daily Herald Telephone* at the time that this particular chapter was being written added the terms *bush-hogging* and *mammy bench* to my vocabulary. **1967** *DARE* (Qu. L36, . . *When you dig out roots and underbrush to make a new field*) Inf **OH**35, Grubbing, bulldozing, bush hog, clearing. **1968–69** *DARE* FW Addit **AL**, Farmers speak of clearing as bushhogging; **NC**5, *Bushhogging* means clearing land. **1973** *Benton Courier* (AR) 26 Jan 8, [Advt:] MAJOR'S BACKHOE & BUSH HOGGING service. Footings, lines, septic tanks. **1981** *UPI Dispatch* (New Castle KY) 9 July, A farm tractor he was using to "bushhog" brush struck a tree and overturned. *Ibid* (Opelika AL) 23 Aug, He fell off a tractor while he was bushhogging near his home. *Ibid* (Memphis TN) 31 Aug, If you wanted to bushhog down wheat, you can do that.

bush honeysuckle n

A yellow-flowered, deciduous shrub of the genus *Diervilla.* See also **gravelweed**

1822 Eaton *Botany* 266, *Diervilla* . . *humilis* . . bush honeysuckle . . . Variable in size, 1 foot to 6. **1967** *DARE* (Qu. S26c) Inf **AL**27, Honeysuckle—both bush and vine.

bush hook n **chiefly Sth, NEast** See Map

A hand tool for cutting bushes and underbrush.

1834 Smith *Letters Jack Downing* 19 (*DAE*) **ME**, The crittur had just come out of his bush pasture, and had his bush-hook with him. **1847** Howe *Hist. Coll. OH* 493, Their tools are usually coarse, among which is the German scythe, short and unwieldy as a bush-hook. **1884** Roe *Nature's Serial Story* 3 **NY**, The angular fields, . . marked by trees and shrubs that, . . in their earlier life, ran the gauntlet of the bush-hook. **1965–70** *DARE* (Qu. L35, *Hand tools used for cutting underbrush and digging out roots*) 45 Infs, **chiefly Sth, NEast**, Bush hook; (Qu. L37, *A hand tool used for cutting weeds and grass*) Infs **GA**5, 7, **IL**93, **MA**42, **NC**21, 85, **NY**205, 206, Bush hook. **1966** *DARE* Tape **NC**21, I had a colored fellow over there bushin' . . . and he was standin' out there . . with a bush hook in his hand.

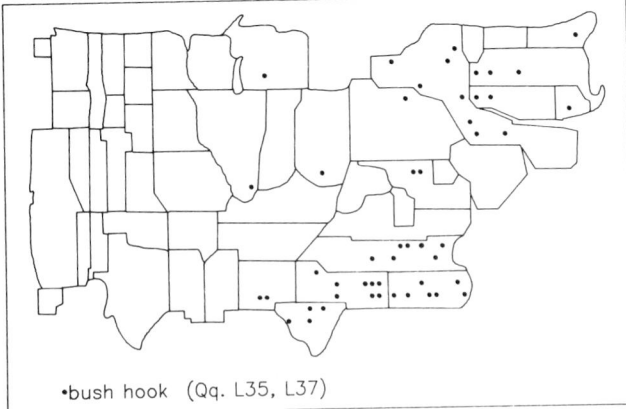

•bush hook (Qq. L35, L37)

bush house n

=**brush arbor.**

1936 *AmSp* 11.275 cTN, *Bush house.* Brush arbor. 'The meetin' is being held in a bush house.'

bushi See **busha** 2

bushka See **babushka**

bush laurel n

1 =**sheep laurel** (here: *Kalmia angustifolia*).

1941 *LANE* Map 249, (*Sheep laurel*) 1 inf, **cwCT**, Bush laurel, poison to cattle.

2 =**sugar sumac.**

1979 Little *Checklist U.S. Trees* 252, *Rhus ovata* . . . *Other common names* . . bush-laurel.

bush-light n

1838 Gilman *S. Matron* 82 seSC [Black], Torches were seen glowing in the range of whitewashed huts, and a bush-light was flaming near Jacque's habitation, which was so brilliant that I perceived the coffin and the groups gathering round it. [Footnote to *bush-light:*] A fire of light wood kindled on a small mound of earth.

bush line n

A weighted fishing line that is fastened to a bush or other stable object on the bank.

1952 Harwin *Home is Upriver* 99 **MS**, Kip and Lenny fished: snaglines and bushlines. **1967–68** *DARE* (Qu. P13, . . *Other ways of fishing*) Inf **LA**26, A bush line is a simple line, sinker, and hook with pole stuck in bank; **SC**40, A bush line is the same as a set line, one hook. **1983** *DARE* File c**AR**, A bush line is a setline for fishing . . . It's a line and a baited hook—used for catfish. It's set out at night and checked in the morning and tied to a bush or a tree.

bush meeting n

=**camp meeting.**

1889 (1971) Farmer *Americanisms* 108, *Bush meeting.* A gathering in the woods for the purpose of open-air preaching, and other religious exercises. **1902** (1968) Clapin *Americanisms, Bush-meeting.* A gathering in the woods, for religious purposes, and differing from the camp-meeting in the fact of lasting only one day. Bush-meetings are at the present mostly done away with, except among the Negroes of the South. **1940** *AmSp* 15.83 **swPA, nWV,** *Bush meeting,* a camp meeting or open air religious gathering. **1942** Warnick *Garrett Co. MD* 4 (as of 1900–1918), *Bush-meeting* . . religious services held in a grove. **1946** Driscoll *Country Jake* 185 **csKS,** *Bush meetings* were so called because they were held in sheds, somewhat like those we built for our cattle, framed with crotch poles and horizontal members, and roofed with brush, cut from the surrounding thickets. **1970** *DARE* FW Addit **seVA,** Bush-meetings—religious revival meetings held outdoors or in tents. Old-fashioned.

bush morning-glory n Also *morning-glory bush*

A **morning glory** (here: *Ipomoea leptophylla*). Also called **bigroot 3, man-in-the-ground, man-of-the-earth 2, manroot, moonflower, wild potato vine, wild rhubarb**

　1897 *Jrl. Amer. Folkl.* 10.51, *Ipomoea leptophylla* . . morning glory bush, Cal. **1900** Lyons *Plant Names* 203, *I. leptophylla* . . . Nebraska to New Mexico and Texas. Bush Morning-glory. **1924** *Torreya* 24.40, The Bush Morning-glory, *Ipomoea leptophylla,* which grows on the plains just east of the Rocky Mountains from Nebraska to Texas, is said to have even a larger root. **1967** *DARE* FW Addit **CO** 7, Bush morning glory . . . twiny or twining morning glory.

bushnipple n [PaGer *buschgnippel* clodhopper] Cf *DS* HH1

A backwoodsman.

　1930 Shoemaker *1300 Words* 6 **cPA Mts** (as of c1900), *Bush-nipple*—Woodsman or hermit. (Originally forest ranger) Pa. Dutch. **1940** Richter *Trees* 269 **OH** (as of early 19th cent), The last time Sayward saw him, he looked like an old bushnipple.

bushnut n **Desert SW**

=jojoba.

　1931 U.S. Dept. Ag. *Misc. Pub.* 101.94, *Jojoba* . . known by a variety of vernacular names, including bushnut. **1937** U.S. Forest Serv. *Range Plant Hdbk.* B148, Jojoba . . is also locally called bushnut.

bushpea n esp **Sth**

=false lupine.

　1911 *Century Dict. Suppl., Bush-pea* . . . A plant of the leguminous genus *Thermopsis;* false lupine. **1933** Small *Manual SE Flora* 674, *T[hermopsis] mollis* . . . *Bush-pea* . . . Blue Ridge to Appalachian Plateau, Ala. to Va. **1941** Walker *Lookout* 47 **TN,** On top of Lookout . . is found a wild bush pea which opens its yellow flowers in April. **1975** Duncan–Foote *Wildflowers SE* 68, *Bush-pea* . . . *Thermopsis fraxinifolia* . . . Perennial . . with several to numerous zig-zagging branches.

bush rabbit n **West**

Prob =brush rabbit.

　1907 White *AZ Nights* 79, The little fellow was ear-marked all right, so we rode on, and never would have discovered nothin' if a bush rabbit hadn't jumped and scared the calf right across in front of our hosses. **1966–69** *DARE* (Qu. P30) Infs **CA**31, 160, 176, **ND**3, **OR**10, Bush rabbit(s); **CA**23, Brush rabbits or bush rabbits; **CA**120, Bush rabbit—little, not as big as cottontail.

bush rat n

A backwoodsman; a woodsman.

　1935 Davis *Honey* 184 **OR,** Some old bush-rat in the neighborhood showed him how to make it still easier. **1968** Adams *Western Words,* *Bush rat*—In logging, a woodsman.

bush scythe n Pronc-sp *bush sy* **chiefly NEng** See Map Cf **brush scythe, bush hook**

A tool for cutting underbrush.

　1856 MI State Ag. Soc. *Trans. for 1855* 54, D.O. and W.S. Penfield, Detroit, [exhibited] three bush scythes. **1874** VT State Bd. Ag. *Report for 1873–74* 194, Other bushes and shrubs will be constantly obtruding themselves, but it is possible to subdue them . . by cutting them off near the ground with a bush-scythe. **1909** *DN* 3.409 **cnME,** *Bushscythe* . . . A short heavy scythe for cutting bushes. **1965–70** *DARE* (Qu. L35, *Hand tools used for cutting underbrush and digging out roots*) 11 Infs, **NEng,** Bush scythe; **NY**24, Bush sy [sɑɪ]; **NY**102, Bush scythe—same as bush hook; **CT**6, **NH**14, Bush scythe—for cutting underbrush; (Qu. L37, *A hand tool used for cutting weeds and grass*) Infs **CT**14, 26, **MA**11, 42, 66, 68, **NH**3, Bush scythe.

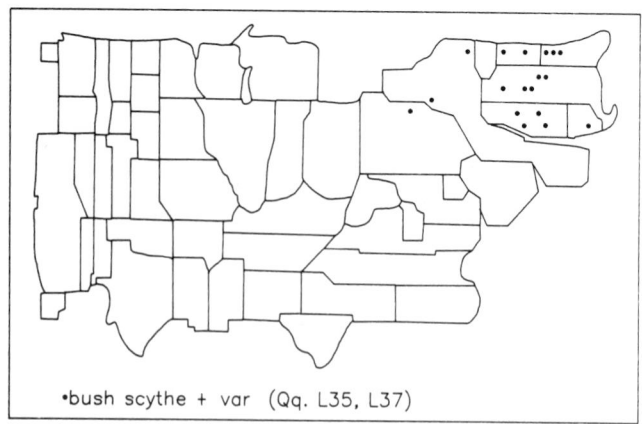

•bush scythe + var (Qq. L35, L37)

bush sparrow n

=song sparrow.

　1858 *Atlantic Mth.* 2.594/2 **MA,** In several localities these two species [the song sparrow and vesper bird] are distinguished by the names of Bush-Sparrow and Ground-Sparrow, from their supposed different habits of placing their nests, one in a bush and the other on the ground. **1967** *DARE* (Qu. Q21, *Different kinds of sparrows*) Inf **CO**22, Dirty urchin sparrow—town sparrow; and a more progressive one—bush sparrow.

bush sy See **bush scythe**

bushtail n Also *brushtail*

Among loggers: a horse.

　1931 *AmSp* 7.52 **Sth, SW** [Lumberjack lingo], Horses are called "bushtails." **1968** Adams *Western Words* 38, *Brush tail*—A logger's name for a horse, as contrasted to *hardtail* or *shavetail,* his names for a mule. Also called *bush tail.* **1969** Sorden *Lumberjack Lingo* **NEng, Gt Lakes,** *Bush tail*—A horse.

bush up v phr **chiefly Ozarks**

To hide, esp in dense shrubbery or woods.

　1926 *DN* 5.398 **Ozarks,** *Bush up* . . . To hide in the shrubbery. "Tom he went an' bushed up down back o' th' church-house." **1931** Randolph *Ozarks* 19, Paw he lit a shuck for th' timber, an' bushed up thar till th' war was plumb done. **1933** Williamson *Woods Colt* 178 **Ozarks,** You tell your paw I'm goin' to bush up for a while . . . I reckon I'll strike for Turkey Gap, an' then kind of work in along Little Yellow River somewhere. **1954** Harder *Coll.* **cwTN.**

bushwa n[1] See **booshway**

bushwa n[2], exclam Also sp *booshwah,* also abbr *bush* [Prob euphem for *bullshit,* perh also infl by CanFr *bois de vache* buffalo dung, or *bois de cheval* horse dung] **chiefly Nth** *somewhat old-fash*

Nonsense.

　1920 in 1944 *ADD* **cNY,** ['buʃwɑ]. Chiefly an exclam. **1924** *DN* 5.264 **CO,** *Bushwah.* **1927** *AmSp* 2.275 [Stanford University expressions], *Booshwah*—talking for talk's sake. **1936** (1947) Mencken *Amer. Lang.* 301, At the same time the college boys and girls launched *bushwah* . . and a number of other such thinly disguised shockers. **1938** *New Republic* 31 Aug 104/2, There has been a lot of bushwa tossed around about how moving pictures aren't worthy of their audiences. **1938** Farrell *No Star* 206 **Chicago IL** (as of 1914), "The Athletics might come back," said Danny. "Bushwah," said Bill. **1965–70** *DARE* (Qu. NN13, *When you think that the thing somebody has just said is silly or untrue: "Oh, that's a lot of _____."*) 19 Infs, **chiefly Nth,** Bushwa; **MO**39, Bush. [17 of 20 Infs old]

bushwhack v, hence *bushwhacking* vbl n, ppl adj, *bushwhacker* n Also sp *bushwack*

1 To live in the backwoods.

　1809 Irving *Hist. NY* 2.107, They were gallant bush-whackers and hunters of raccoons by moon-light. **1868** *Putnam's Mag.* 1.22 **NY,** An old Dutch Continental, / Bushwhacked up there a spell. **1885** *Harper's Mag.* 71.591/2, The General was a natural bushwhacker, in the sense of having an intuitive knowledge of country.

2 To pull (a boat) up a river by grasping bushes. *hist*

　1826 Flint *Recollections* 86 **Missip R,** We began to pull the boat up the stream, by a process, which, in the technics of the boatmen, is called "bush-whacking." **1834** Baird *View Valley Missip.* 48, Instead of spending many months in warping a barge, or "cordelling," and "poling," and "bushwhacking" a keelboat from New Orleans to Pittsburg.. a steam-boat now makes the voyage in fifteen or twenty days. **1861** Winthrop *Open Air* 84 *(DA),* Bushwhacking thus for a league, we circumvented the peril, and came upon the river flowing fair and free. **1936** (1938) Asbury *French Quarter* 76 **Missip Valley,** In high water some were bushwhacked up the river—that is, the boat was kept close to shore, and the crew moved it along by pulling on the bushes which grew on the bank. **1941** FWP *Guide AL* 89, If low hanging branches were within reach the crew could stand on deck, grasp them, and pull the boat along. Known as "bush-whacking," this method was practiced only on the smaller streams. **1941** Dorsey *Master of Missip.* 23 **IL** (as of early 19th cent), By this ancient device of 'bushwhacking,' the craft moved laboriously ahead.

3 To attack (an enemy or game) by surprise.

1866 Smith *Bill Arp* 116 **GA,** The truth is, that the Confederate cavalry can fight 'em, and dog 'em, and dodge 'em, and bushwhack 'em, and bedevil 'em for a thousand years. **1918** Mulford *Bar-20* 193 *(DA),* Here he is over this end of th' trail an' giving you a fine chance to sneak up an' bushwhack him. **1926** *West Virginia Legislative Hand Book* 428 *(Hench Coll.),* A word was coined that makes us wince yet. It is a West Virginia word of local origin. Bushwhacker. The dictionary says that it is a guerrilla that beats through the bushes. But that is not the way we understand it. It refers to the man who strikes from the concealment of the leafy growth. And when the leaden ball sang from the foliage covering the hill, the word was bushwhacking. **1935** Davis *Honey* 4 **OR,** He also killed the three lambs for having got themselves where a coyote could bushwhack them. **1935** *Sun* (Baltimore MD) 20 Jul 15/6 *(Hench Coll.),* They [=bushwhack boats] are a sixteen-foot flat-bottom row boat, with a long sculling oar at the stern, used to "bushwhack ducks." *Ibid,* The Havre de Grace [Maryland] "bushwhackers" . . . "set out the decoys . . . and back off a few hundred yards to let the ducks alight. Then they creep down on them." **1968** Adams *Western Words* 47, *Bushwhack*—To ambush . . . *Bushwhacker* . . . one who ambushes. **1969** DARE (Qu. P35b, *Illegal methods of shooting deer*) Inf **NY**198, Bushwhack. **1970** DARE Tape IL118, People, for real or imagined slights, got into bushwhacking each other and having gun fights with each other.

4 To hike cross-country; to knock aside bushes to go or search through uncleared forest.

1937 FWP *Guide ME* 415, The veteran hunter scorns 'bushwhacking' (leaving tote roads and woods trails to plow through the forest). **1937** *Sun* (Baltimore MD) 19 June 1/5 *(Hench Coll.),* State authorities tonight sought to enlist the entire population of Suffolk county in their search for . . [a] missing Long Island matron. Federal agents, on the other hand, appeared ready to abandon the bush-whacking, foot-by-foot coverage of the countryside. **1945** *Sky Line Trail* June 5/I *(DA),* A small amount of bushwhacking allows the visitor to make his way to camp over Odaray Plateau. **1948** Sierra Club *Bulletin* Mar 122 **WY,** About an hour of talus hopping and bushwhacking is necessary to reach the gulley at the base of the East Arrowhead Chimney where the route begins. **1968** Adams *Western Words* 47, *Bushwhacker*—A woodsman. **1972** *NYT Article Letters,* Bushwhacking—hiking without trails through thickets.

5 See quots. *joc*

1914 DN 4.104 **KS,** Bushwhack . . . To 'borrow' with intent to return. **1961** Sackett–Koch *KS Folkl.* 111, Bushwhack . . . To borrow with intent to return. "Somebody bushwhacked my plow." [To *bushwhack* sometimes means to steal.]

6 To beat someone to something, esp by using secretive means.

1939 Towne *Her Majesty Montana* 106 *(Hench Coll.),* The war [over ownership of certain timber] soon developed into a bushwacking contest. It was a case of get all the logs possible and get them fast. As soon as the tree was felled, it was branded either with the Hammond or the Thompson brand and theoretically became the property of the outfit which had branded it.

‡bushwhack n See **bush whiskey**

bushwhacker n

1 See **bushwhack** v.

2 An illegitimate child. **Cf bush baby**

1949 *AmSp* 24.106 **ceGA,** Bushwhacker . . . Bastard. **1966** DARE (Qu. Z11b, *Nicknames and joking words for a child of unwed parents*) Inf **SC**19, Bushwhacker.

bushwhacking See **bushwhack** v

bush whiskey n Also *bushwhack*

Illegally made whiskey, moonshine.

1955 *Sun* (Baltimore MD) 2 March 38/4 [Ed B] *(Hench Coll.),* A 46-year-old Virginian was sentenced to two years in the House of Correction yesterday for illegal possession and transportation of 162 gallons of "very good bush whisky." **1970** DARE (Qu. DD21c, . . *Illegally made whiskey*) Inf **VA**69, Bushwhack.

‡bushy bird n

=**catbird 1.**

1965 DARE (Qu. Q14, . . *Other names . . for . . catbird*) Inf **MS**1, Bushy bird.

business wagon n **CT** **Cf bus** n[1]

See quots.

1934 *Hanley Disks* **csCT,** He had what we called a business wagon. 'Twas a long body with no seat where you could put trunks in. **1965–70** DARE (Qu. N41a, . . *Horse-drawn vehicles . . to carry people*) Inf **CT**17, Business wagons, half-business wagons; (Qu. N41b, . . *To carry heavy loads*) Inf **CT**13, Business wagon; (Qu. N41c, . . *To carry light loads*) Infs **CT**14, 17, Business wagon.

busk v [Engl dial; see *EDD* busk v.[7]] **Cf busk** n, **buss** n, v[1]

To kiss.

1941 Percy *Lanterns* 194 **Missip Delta,** Although I knew they were crocodile tears, I felt like busking that old man on his bald spot.

busk n [busk v] **Cf buss** v[1]

1968 DARE (Qu. AA9, . . *A loud or vigorous kiss*) Inf **IA**18, Busk—old-fashioned.

‡busky n

1967 DARE (Qu. X35, *Joking words for the part of the body that you sit on*) Inf **CA**13, Busky ['bʊski].

buss n Also sp *bus, buzz* Also *busser, buzzer* **chiefly Midl**

A kiss.

c1770 in 1833 Boucher *Glossary* **MD,** At night reward me with a *smouch,* or *buss.* **1927** *DN* 5.471 **Appalachians.** **1930** Shoemaker *1300 Words* 4 **cPA** (as of c1900), Buss—A kiss. **1930** *AmSp* 5.424 **Ozarks.** **1935** *AmSp* 10.172 **sePA,** Bus for kiss. **1950** WELS (*Other words for a kiss, or kissing*) 12 Infs, **WI,** Buss; 1 Inf, Buzz. **c1960** *Wilson Coll.* **csKY,** Buss . . . A loud kiss. **1965–70** DARE (Qu. AA9, . . *A loud or vigorous kiss*) 32 Infs, **scattered, but esp Midl,** Buss; **NM**5, Loud buss; **FL**5, **MI**62, **PA**184, Buzz; **MO**17, Buzzer, busser. [27 of 37 Infs old]

buss v[1] Also sp *bus* **chiefly S Midl** *somewhat old-fash*

To kiss; hence vbl n *bussing* kissing, a kiss; also fig.

1851 Hooper *Widow Rugby's Husband* **AL** *(ADD),* She bussed me so's you might a heard it a quarter. **1859** Taliaferro *Fisher's R.* 180 **nwNC** (as of 1820s), He poured out a cupful, and gin it to the 'squire fust, who bussed the cup a little, and then I bussed it. **1889** *AN&Q* 3.255/2 **NJ,** In one part of the State to 'bus' a girl means to kiss her. **1908** *DN* 3.295 **eAL, wGA,** Buss . . . To kiss. Not common. **1924** Raine *Land of Saddle-Bags* 103 **sAppalachians,** The venerable word *buss* (to kiss) has fallen into disrepute in the dictionaries. But it is still uncontaminated in the Mountains. **1927** *DN* 5.471 **Appalachians,** Buss. **1930** *AmSp* 5.424 **Ozarks,** Buss. **1931** *AmSp* 7.90 **eKY,** Buss. **1939** *AmSp* 14.89 **cTN,** Buss. **1946** PADS 5.14 **VA,** Buss . . . fairly common. **1956** McAtee *Some Dialect NC* 7, Buss . . . Now chiefly Dial. **1962** Atwood *Vocab. TX* 67, [13% of the infs said *bussing* was a synonym for *kissing*]. **1968** DARE (Qu. AA9, . . *A loud or vigorous kiss*) Inf **NC**49, Bussing.

buss v[2] Also sp *bus* [Perh alter of **bust** v] **Cf bussen**

To strike.

1872 Schele de Vere *Americanisms* 587, To *buss*—also a Western term . . quite as much English as American, in the sense of to punch. **1889** *AN&Q* 3.255/2 **NJ,** In one part of the State to 'bus' a girl means to kiss her, whilst the same word in another part implies the act of striking her.

bussen ppl adj Also *bussened* [Strong past pple of *burst;* cf *EDD* bussen-bellied ruptured (at *burst* II 1)] *obs*

Ruptured.

1845 in 1956 Eliason *Tarheel Talk* 263 **ceNC,** Bussened . . . [He] was struck with a Indianrubber ball in his privates and some of the Boys say he is Bussened. **1899** (1912) Green *VA Folk-Speech,* Bussen, p.a. Affected with rupture or hernia.

busser See **buss** n

‡**buss-eyed** adj Cf *DS* X21a

1940 *Sat. Eve. Post* 3 Feb 15/3 **sMS,** The winner can call the loser a slew-footed, buss-eyed cattywampus.

busshead See **busthead 1**

buss wagon See **buzz wagon**

bussy n [**buss** n]   chiefly sAppalachians

A sweetheart.

1895 *DN* 1.370 **eTN,** *Bussy:* sweetheart. "Ef you'd a ben thar you mout (might) a got a bussy." **1924** Raine *Land of Saddle-Bags* 103 **Appalachians,** *Bussy,* a sweetheart. **1926** *DN* 5.398 **Ozarks. 1927** *DN* 5.468 **Appalachians. 1931** *AmSp* 7.90 **eKY,** Leave him be; he's Matilda's bussy. **1939** *AmSp* 14.90 **cTN. 1940** *AmSp* 15.447 **eTN,** *Cobbed.* Embarrassed. 'Maria's bussy cobbed her.' **1944** *PADS* 2.18 **sAppalachians.**

bust v [Alter of **burst**]

1 To plow (land); freq in phr *bust (out) the middles* to plow between the rows of a crop.   **chiefly Sth, S Midl** Cf **buster 4, middlebuster**

1902 *DN* 2.230 **sIL,** *Bust out* . . . 'To bust out the middles,' to plow the balks. **1903** *DN* 2.308 **seMO,** *Bust out* (the middles) . . . To plow midway between the rows. **1907** *DN* 3.221 **nwAR,** *Bust out* . . . "To bust out the middles." **1908** *DN* 3.295 **eAL, wGA,** *Bust out (middles)* . . . To plow between rows. **1923** *DN* 5.202 **swMO,** *To bust out middles* = to plow out the space between rows of growing crops. **1942** Perry *Texas* 53, You got to plow that land first. Meant to get her busted last fall . . . you'll hitch up those mules and bust that land. **1953** *PADS* 19.9 **cnNC, FL,** *Bust the middles* . . . To plow out the "middles," i.e., between rows. **1954** *Harder Coll.* **cwTN,** *Bust middles* . . . To plow out middles. **1966** *PADS* 45.9 **cnKY,** *Busting the middle* . . . Plowing the middle of the rows. **1967** Key *Tobacco Vocab.* **KY, NC,** *Bust(ing) the middle;* **GA,** When they plow it . . . they'd side it up, and then they'd go back and bust the middle; **MO,** The middles of that crop should be busted, shouldn't it? **TN,** The tobacco grows on each side . . and you just bust the middle out.

2 To tame (a horse); hence n *buster.*   **West**

1888 *Century Illustr. Mag.* 13.507/1, **West,** The flash riders, or horse-breakers, always called "bronco busters," can perform really marvelous feats. **1891** *Harper's Mag.* 83.210/1, Two rides will usually bust a bronco so that the average cow-puncher can use him. **1933** *AmSp* 8.1.28 **TX,** *Bust.* To break, in the sense of to tame for saddle use. **1941** *Natl. Geog. Mag.* 79.300/1 **OK,** He's too old now to bulldog a steer or bust a bronco. **1961** Adams *Old-Time Cowhand* 292, The buster's job was spoken of as "bustin'," "gentlin'," "snappin' broncs," or "twistin' out." No man hired to break hosses ever abused 'em.

3 To rope a cow's forefoot, thereby throwing the animal.   **West**

1941 FWP *Guide WY* 460, *Bust*—To throw an animal by forefeet. **1944** Adams *Western Words, Bust*—To throw an animal violently. **1958** Blasingame *Dakota Cowboy* 262 **SD** (as of 1907), I had no intention of doing anything but "busting" him [a calf], to stop his chasing back and forth. [Picture of cowboy having roped calf's front foot]

4 Of a shellfish: to lose its hard shell; hence vbl n *busting.*   Cf **buster 5**

1933 *Hench Coll.* **seVA,** A friend . . told me that a "buster" is a hard-shelled crab that is on the point of breaking out of its shell into a soft-shelled one. The closer to the actual act of "busting" a crab can be caught, the better he is as a soft-shelled crab.

bust n [By ext from std *bust* a failure, esp a financial failure]

A mistake.

1965–70 *DARE* (Qu. JJ41, *An embarrassing mistake*) 14 Infs, **esp Cent, NEast,** Bust; (Qu. JJ42, *To make an error in judgment and get something quite wrong: "He usually handles things well, but this time he certainly _____."*) Infs **TX**1, 35, Made a bust; **OK**51, Pulled a bust. **1967** *DARE* Tape **TN**29, I got corrected . . . because I made a bad bust in speakin' about a . . . I pronounced a word [wrong].

bust a gut v phr   For numerous similar phrr, see *DS* A21, 22, GG30, 31

1 To exert great effort, to do one's utmost.

1912 *DN* 3.572 **wIN,** *Bust a gut* . . . To make a supreme effort. **1954** *Harder Coll.* **cwTN,** *To bust a gut* . . . To strain very hard. c**1960** *Wilson Coll.* **csKY,** *Bust a gut* . . . Try very hard to do something, explode with anger or effort. **1965–70** *DARE* (Qu. A21, *When someone is in too much of a hurry you might say, "Now just slow down! Don't _____."*) Infs **IL**128, **IN**71, **IA**8, **NY**56, **WA**3, **WV**16, Bust a gut; **MN**36, Bust

your gut; (Qu. A22, . . *'To start working hard': "She had only ten minutes to clean the room, but she _____."*) Infs **MD**40, **NY**34, Bust a gut.

2 also *burst a gut:* To hurt oneself by laughing too hard; to laugh very hard.

1950 *WELS* (To laugh very hard: "I thought I would _____.") 1 Inf, **cwWI,** Bust a gut. **1954** *Harder Coll.* **cwTN,** *Bust a gut* . . . To laugh very hard. **1965–70** *DARE* (Qu. GG31, *To laugh very hard*) 52 Infs, **scattered,** Bust a gut; **SC**40, Bust my gut; (Qu. GG30, *To suddenly break out laughing: "When he told her that, she just _____."*) Infs **CO**39, **MI**63, **SD**8, Busted a gut; **NY**234, Burst a gut; **MN**36, Bust a gut; (Qu. FF21b, *A joke that is so old . . . people say: "The first time I heard that one I _____."*) Infs **IA**22, **OH**47, I busted a gut.

3 To act in an explosive or uncontrolled manner.

1950 *WELS* (When a person becomes over-excited, and loses control: "I thought he was going to _____.") 2 Infs, **se,cwWI,** Bust a gut. **1967** *DARE* (Qu. GG15, . . *A person who became over-excited and lost control: "At that point he really _____."*) Inf **CO**43, Bust a gut.

bust a hame string v phr   Also *burst a hame (string)* Cf **hame n 2**

1 To make a sudden great effort; transf: to become excessively angry.

1903 (1965) Adams *Log Cowboy* 357 **NM,** My father decided that he would go to a funeral or burst a hame string. **1942** McAtee *Dial. Grant Co. IN* 17 (as of 1890s), *Bust a hame string* [make a supreme effort]. **1944** *PADS* 2.19 **sAppalachians,** *Hamestring, to bust a* . . . To make a supreme effort. **1950** *WELS* (When a person becomes over-excited, and loses control: "I thought he was going to _____.") 1 Inf, **seWI,** Burst a hame. **1954** *Harder Coll.* **cwTN,** *Bust a hamestring* . . . To strain too much; to display a sudden burst of energy . . . *Bust (one's) hames* . . . To display a sudden burst of energy. c**1960** *Wilson Coll.* **csKY,** *Bust (or burst) a hamestring* . . . Become very angry or over-energetic. **1967–70** *DARE* (Qu. A21, *When someone is in too much of a hurry you might say, "Now just slow down! Don't _____."*) Inf **AR**53, Bust a hame; **ID**5, Bust a hame string; **IL**113, Burst a hame string.

2 To break out in a fit of laughter.

1967–69 *DARE* (Qu. GG30, *To suddenly break out laughing: "When he told her that, she just _____."*) Inf **IN**54, Burst a hame string; (Qu. GG31, *To laugh very hard*) Infs **CA**36, **ID**5, Bust a hame string.

3 See quot.

1923 *DN* 5.202 **swMO,** *Bust . . . To bust a hame string* = to fail in an undertaking.

bustard n

=Canada goose.

1759 Venegas *Hist. CA* 1.39, About the harbour of Monte-Rey are bustards . . and other birds. **1899** Newton *Dict. Birds* 65, The distribution of the Bustards is confined to the Old World — the bird so-called in the Fur-Countries of North America . . being the Canada Goose, *Bernicla canadensis.*

bust a tug v phr [*tug* a harness trace]   **chiefly Nth**

1 =**bust a hame string 1.**

1899 Garland *Boy Life* 405 **IA,** I'll be with you next year, boys, or bust a tug. **1937** Sandoz *Slogum* 264 **NE** (as of 1900–20), So, this was what they could say — and him busting a tug to help the damned fools. **1968** *DARE* Tape **NY**111, He's going to be all American or bust a tug.

2 also *bust a trace:* =**bust a hame string 2.**

1969–70 *DARE* (Qu. GG31, *To laugh very hard*) Infs **NY**223, **PA**234, Bust a tug; **TN**24, Bust a trace.

busted See **wind-busted**

busted vein n   Also *bursted vessel* Cf **broken vein**

A varicose vein.

1967–68 *DARE* (Qu. AA29, *The blue, swollen veins that a woman often gets on her legs while expecting a baby*) Infs **SC**32, **VA**13, Busted veins; **SC**58, Bursted vessels.

buster n [**bust** v + *-er*]

1 Something extraordinary of its kind.   **esp Midl** Cf **booster**

1842 *Spirit of the Times* 22 Oct 402 (*AmSp* 40.180), If Fashion runs at Camden, she will have to run against Blue Dick and not Boston. She will beat Blue Dick — but he is a 'buster!' **1845** Cist *Cincinnati Misc.* 1.134, Finally I see a country man leading a black colt — wasn't he a buster! **1852** Stowe *Uncle Tom's Cabin* 144, Lor, Pete, . . han't we got a buster of a breakfast! **1904** (1916) Porter *Freckles* 84 **cnIN,** The Portland company cut this for elm butts last year . . . It was a buster! **1905** *DN* 3.4 **cCT,** *Buster* . . . A big one. **1907** *DN* 3.209 **nwAR. 1908** *DN* 3.295

eAL, wGA, *Buster* . . . A large thing, a whopper. **c1960** *Wilson Coll.*
csKY, *Buster* . . . Something large for its expected size. **1965–70** *DARE*
(Qu. LL5, *Something impressively big*) 10 Infs, **esp Midl,** Buster; (Qu.
B24, . . *A sudden, very heavy rain*) Inf **AL**24, Buster; (Qu. B25, . . *Joking
names for a very heavy rain*) Infs **MN**36, **WI**75, Buster. **1967** *DARE*
Tape **TX**49, That's a buster, that's a big bale.

2 A large or well-grown child.
1930 Shoemaker *1300 Words* 7 **cPA Mts** (as of c1900), *Buster*—An
extra size child or boy. **1968** *DARE* (Qu. Z12, . . *'A small child': "He's a
healthy little _____."*) Infs **NC**82, **OH**61, Buster.

3 A fellow, dandy—also used as a term of address, esp to a boy
or young man. Cf **bud** n[2]
1843 *S. Lit. Messenger* 9.732/1 **Sth,** Applause, laughter, cheers and
cries of "go on," "go it, Smith," and "he's a buster, ain't he?" **1905** *DN*
3.4 **cCT,** *Buster* . . . A dashing fellow. **1907** *DN* 3.209 **nwAR,** *Buster.*
1942 McAtee *Dial. Grant Co. IN* (as of 1890s), *Buster* . . . familiar
salutation to a boy; "Hello _____". (Va.). **1961** *Life* 19 May 27/2, I
said to myself, "O.K., Buster, you volunteered for this thing. Now it's up
to you to do it." **1968–69** *DARE* (Qu. II10a, *Asking directions of
somebody on the street when you don't know his name—what you'd say
to a boy: "Say, _____, how far is it to the next town?"*) Infs **IL**47, **NY**48,
WI30, Buster.

4 A breaking plow. [**bust** v 1] See also **clod crusher 1, middlebuster, sod buster**
1966–68 *DARE* (Qu. L18, *Kinds of plows used around here*) Inf **LA**22,
Buster; **MS**21, Busters.

5 A crab or other decapod about to break out of its shell. Cf
bust v 4, **comer** 2
1879 *St. Nicholas* 7.1.84/2 **ceNJ,** He keeps on eating till he is bigger still;
then he is called a "Shedder"; and he still keeps on eating and gets bigger
still, and then cracks a little, and is called a "Crack-buster." He still grows
till he is called a "Buster," and then sheds. Then he is called a "Soft
Crab." **1887** Goode *Fisheries U.S.* 638 **nNJ,** The crabs are separated
into two lots, the "busters" and soft crabs going into one compartment,
and the "comers" into the other. **1904** *DN* 2.395 **MA,** *Buster* . . . A crab
which is preparing to shed its shell and which is in a somewhat more
advanced stage than a shedder. **1941** FWP *Guide LA* 12, *Buster* . . .
Popular name for the blue crab *(Callinectes sapidus)* when it is small and
in the shedding stage, at which time the old shell is pried off and the crab
prepared as a "soft shell." **1943** *Ecology* 24.11/1 **LA,** As the crawfish
grows beyond the limits of its hardened exoskeleton, a white "waist"
appears. . (this stage is termed the "buster"). **1968** *DARE* Tape **MD**15,
You take a hard crab. Every two–three months he'll shed, during the
summer season. But he goes from a hard crab to a peeler. Then a peeler is
when he's first began to make a new crab within his shell. Then he
becomes a buster. That's about the time he's supposed to crack out of his
old shell as a soft crab. **1968** *DARE* FW Addit **seNY.** **1976** Warner
Beautiful Swimmers 27 **Chesapeake Bay,** Invariably the females will be
"red-sign," which means they will moult very soon, if not "busters" that
have already started. *Ibid* 213, A buster . . is a peeler that has just started
to moult.

6 also in combs *belly-buster, shoulder-buster:* A shotgun. Cf
Betsy
1968–69 *DARE* (Qu. P37b, . . *A shotgun*) Infs **IL**4, **MN**38, Shoulder-
buster; **MO**10, Buster; **NY**142, Belly-buster.

7 A firecracker.
1966–69 *DARE* (Qu. FF14, . . *Different kinds of firecrackers*) Infs
MA14, **NC**36, Buster.

8 See **bust** v 2.

busthead n
1 also attrib, also *bustskull* and pronc-sp *busshead:* Whiskey,
esp illegally made or bad whiskey. **chiefly Sth, S Midl** Cf
conk-buster, head n[1] C2
1857 *S.F. Call* 27 Feb 4/1 *(DA)* **CA,** A big strapping six-footer, full of
'bust head' and Dutch courage . . . slapped his fists together, swearing he
was 'spiling for a fight.' **1905** *DN* 3.72 **nwAR,** *Busthead whiskey* . . . Bad
whiskey. **1926** Kephart *Highlanders* 137 **sAppalachians,** Every blockader knows how to adulterate [moonshine] . . . Some add washing lye . . .
then prime this abominable fluid with pepper, ginger, tobacco, or
anything else that will make it sting . . . Such decoctions are known in the
mountains by the expressive terms "pop-skull," "bust head," "bumblings" ("they make a bumbly noise in a feller's head"). **1929** *AmSp*
4.386 **KS,** Bust-head. **1942** Faulkner *Go Down* 156 **MS,** He . . gets
himself a whole gallon of bust-skull white-mule whiskey. **1952** Brown
NC Folkl. 1.524, *Buss-head* . . . Illicit whiskey. **c1960** *Wilson Coll.*

csKY, *Bust-head* or *bust-skull* . . . Illicit, and usually, strong whiskey.
1967–68 *DARE* (Qu. DD21b, . . *Bad liquor*) Infs **AL**31, **TX**35, Busthead; (Qu. DD21c, . . *Illegally made whiskey*) Inf **VA**15, Busthead; [(Qq.
DD34, FF1) Inf **GA**44, Busthead—a drinking party]. **1972** *Foxfire
Book* 317 **nGA,** "Busthead" and "popskull" are names applied to
whiskey which produces violent headaches due to various elements
which have not been removed during the stilling process.

2 A headache from drinking bad whiskey.
1939 *AmSp* 14.90 **cTN,** *Bust head.* Headache. 'I've got a killing bust
head.' **1954** Siberts *Nothing But Prairie* 52 **SD** (as of 1892), The next
morning they had such a bust head that I had to feed the stock and cook
breakfast.

3 =**ballhead.**
1978 *Pioneer Amer.* June 92, The dugout . . . is commonly called a
Tennessee River busthead.

bust-headed adj
?Stubborn.
1932 Stribling *Store* 434 **AL,** Augustus, you're nothing but a blind,
bust-headed Vaiden!

busticate v
To break into pieces; hence adj *busticated* broken.
1916 *DN* 4.272 **KS, MA, NE, NC, OH, PA,** *Busticate* . . . Extension
and intensive of *bust.* "I fell down and busticated the milk pitcher." *Ibid*
320, *Busticated* . . . Unfit for use by reason of bursting, breaking. **1928**
Ruppenthal *Coll.* **KS,** I found my suspender was busticated. **1968**
DARE (Qu. K22, . . *Completely shattered*) Inf **PA**138, Busticated. **1982**
DARE File **cnMA** (as of c1915), We children used *busticated* in a casual,
rather breezy way about toys we had broken. "What's wrong with this
little wagon?" "Oh, just busticated, I guess."

bustification n [*bust* n + -*ification*]
1906 *DN* 3.129 **nwAR,** *Bustification* . . . Used facetiously of an explosion, disaster, or quarrel.

bustified ppl adj [*bust* v + -*ified*]
1939 McGuire *FL Cracker Dial.* 179, *Pusselgutted* . . . Pot-bellied,
"bustified".

bust one's buttons v phr Also *burst* ~ For numerous similar
phrr, see *DS* A21, 22, GG30, 31
1 To strain one's clothing by laughing too hard; to laugh very
hard.
1921 Thorp *Songs Cowboys* 146, They are bustin' their buttins with
laughin', they are laughing fit to kill. **1950** *WELS (To laugh very hard:
"I thought I would _____.")* 2 Infs, **WI,** Burst a button; 1 Inf, Bust my
buttons off. **1966–68** *DARE* (Qu. GG31, *To laugh very hard*) Inf
VA21, Bust my buttons; **AR**3, Bust a button; **WA**9, Bursting buttons;
SC24, Burst a button; [**SC**58, Bust my belly button].

2 To strain oneself physically or emotionally.
1950 *WELS (When a person becomes over-excited, and loses control: "I
thought he was going to _____.")* 1 Inf, **WI,** Burst his buttons; 1 Inf,
Bust a button; *(To be in too much of a hurry, or to do something before the
right time for it "Calm down! Don't _____.")* 1 Inf, Bust your buttons.
1967–69 *DARE* (Qu. A21, *When someone is in too much of a hurry, you
might say, "Now just slow down! Don't _____."*) Infs **ID**5, **IN**7, Bust
your buttons; **PA**215, Bust a button.

3 To swell with pride.
1966–67 *DARE* (Qu. GG19a, . . *When you can see from the way a
person acts that he's feeling important or independent*) Inf **MO**2, About
to bust his buttons; (Qu. GG19b) Inf **NC**36, So proud that his buttons are
bursting.

bust out the middles See **bust** v 1

bustskull See **busthead** n 1

bust the middles See **bust** v 1

bust the wind v phr
=**burn the wind.**
c1960 *Wilson Coll.* **csKY,** *Bust the wind* . . . To go fast . . . "He busted
the wind in his new car."

busty adj [Perh rel to Scots *busteous* rough, fierce *(SND)*]
1936 *AmSp* 11.314 **Ozarks,** *Busty* . . . Self-assertive, loud, smart-
alecky.

but n[1] [Scots] Cf **ben** n[1]
The outer room of a house, esp of a **but-and-ben.**

1950 *WELS Suppl.,* 1 Inf, **cwWI,** *But and ben.* Of a house: front and back parts.   **1959** *VT Hist.* new ser 27.128, *But . . .* Kitchen or general living quarters. Occasional among the Scotch.

but n² See **butt** n²

but-and-ben n, also attrib [**but** n¹ + **ben** n¹]   **Scots settlement areas**

A two-roomed cottage.

1937 Eaton *Handicrafts* 48 **Appalachians,** This type of cabin is known as a "but-and-ben," a term used in Scotland.   **1958** *VA Qrly. Rev.* 34.249 **KY, NC,** It was a but-and-ben, made of two cabins, each a single room with a loft above, and joined by a roof of narrow boards, split thickly with a froe.   **1975** McDonough *Garden Sass* 34 **AR,** More elaborate than these simple homes was the dog-trot style of house, which consisted of two separate log pens with a covered breezeway between them. This was also referred to as a possum trot, turkey run, wind-sweep, or But-and-Ben style.

butch See **bush** v²

butcher n, v Usu |'bʊčɚ|, occas |'bučɚ| Pronc-sp *bootcher* and, for pple, *boochren, bouchren*   See Pronc Intro 3.I.5.c

Std senses; var forms.

1775–76 in 1947 *AmSp* 22.1.2.30 **CT,** *Butchering boochren . . . bouchren.*   **1905** *DN* 3.56 **NE,** Occasionally [u] is heard in *butcher.*   **1910** *DN* 3.438 **cwNY,** *Butcher . .* [bučr].   **1926** *AmSp* 5.386 **ME,** *Butcher* ['bučɚ] *. . .* Ordinary dealer in meat.   **1975** Gould *ME Lingo* 20, *Booot-cher*—Acceptable Maine way to say butcher.

butcher calf n Also *butcher (beef)*   **chiefly TX, OK, LA**   See Map   Cf **bob calf**

1965–70 *DARE* (Qu. K20, *A calf that is sold for meat*) 27 Infs, **chiefly LA, OK, TX,** Butcher calf; **IL125, LA15, 18, MS58, TX3,** Butcher; **MO19,** Butcher beef.

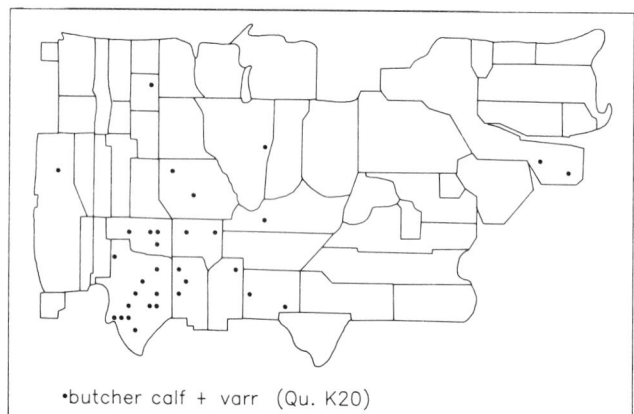

•butcher calf + varr (Qu. K20)

butchering n

1940 *Hench Coll.* **cnVA,** *Butchering* may be a noun meaning any part of the fresh pork newly butchered as in "I sent her some of the butchering."

butchski, butchsky See **bootchkey**

‡**butch team** n

1957 Battaglia *Resp. to PADS 20* **eShore MD,** *(If six oxen are hitched together, you have three _____)* Butch team and lead team.

butnut See **buttnut**

butsel n Also sp *botsel* [From Ger *Bürzel* rump]   *PaGer*

1967 *DARE* (Qu. K73, *. . The rump of a cooked chicken*) Inf **PA21,** Butsel ['bʌtsəl]—the tail; same for boys; **PA27,** Botsel ['bɑtsəl]—Dutch.

butt n¹

1 also attrib, also *butts:* A chunk of salt pork.   **esp SC**

1930 *DN* 6.80 **cSC,** *Butt meat . . .* Fat salt pork.   **1950** *PADS* 14.18 **SC,** *Butts . . .* Chunks of pork, mostly fat, trimmed from other pieces, as hams, and salt cured . . . Also *butt meat.*   **c1960** *Wilson Coll.* **csKY,** *Butts . . .* Trimmings or chunks of pork. Also *butt meat.* "I've saved some butts to cook turnip sallet with."   **1966** *DARE* (Qu. H38, *Other words for bacon (including joking ones)*) Inf **NC20,** Butts; **SC26,** Butts bacon; **SC22,** D.S. butts [=dried, salted butts].

2 See quot.

1956 *AmSp* 31.137 **swPA,** *Butts . . .* Logs suitable for firewood.

3 The hull of a strawberry.   Cf **cap** n¹ 5

1966–70 *DARE* (Qu. I47, *When you pull the stem out of a strawberry, what do you call the green part that comes off with the stem?*) Infs **FL33, 48,** Butt. [Both Infs Black]

4 A person who embodies a specific trait—used as the second element in var compounds.   Cf **box** n 5, **budget** 3

1967–69 *DARE* (Qu. HH11a, *Someone who is too particular or fussy —if it's a man*) Inf **TX31,** Fuss-butt; (Qu. HH21, *A very awkward, clumsy person*) Inf **TX74,** Fumble-butt; (Qu. II35, *A person who is disliked because he seems to think he knows everything*) Inf **WA22,** Smart-butt.

butt n² Also sp *but* [Cf *OED butt* sb.⁸ a promontory, "*Obs.* exc. in local names" and *OED butt* sb.⁵ a hillock, mound, "*Obs.* exc. *dial.*"]   esp **sAppalachians**

A ridge or similar feature that stands out prominently from the surrounding area.

1820 in 1940 *AmSp* 15.162 **VA,** To two white Oaks on a but of the river mountain.   **1821** *Ibid,* To a dogwood on the butt of a spur of said Mountain.   **1835** *Ibid,* The *Big Butt* north of Clinch river, is a high projection of one of the mountains separating the waters of Clinch and Sandy.   **1923** Eby *Geol. & Mineral Resources* 75 **VA,** "Robert's Butt" the end of the spur lying between Toms and Little Toms creeks, just north of Coeburn.   **1926** Kephart *Highlanders* 374 **sAppalachians,** Big Butt is what Westerners call a butte.   **1960** Hall *Smoky Mt. Folks* 57, *Butt:* the abrupt end of a mountain ridge, as in Mollies Butt, at the end of Mollies Ridge.

butt n³ [Cf *OED bottle* sb.³ bundle of hay]

1949 Guthrie *Way West* 66, Rebecca Evans, a sociable and good-humored woman with a front like a butt of hay.

butt v¹ [Aphet]

To abut.

1637 in 1894 Watertown MA *Records* 3, Ordered that there be no Land granted to any person butting upon another mans Land before he have notice of it.   **1719** in 1884 Southold NY *Town Rec.* 2.483, Note the above mentioned lots that butt against ye creeks run into ye same creeks.   **1853** Kennedy *Blackwater Chron.* 6 **WV,** A large spur—apparently the Backbone itself—keeps straight to the south, and butts down on the Cheat.   **1967–69** *DARE* FW Addit **cnNY,** One town butts the next town; i.e. it touches it; **sLA,** St. Charles [Street] butts on the river [speaker from the North].

butt v² [*butt* n, the thick end of a thing]

To beat an opponent in cutting a section off a log; see quot 1949.

1848 Thompson *Green Mt. Boys* 364 **VT,** Her oldest son, having at length been enabled to butt his mother, to use a chopper's phrase, that is to get off his cut first, in a trial of skill on the same log, she concluded to betake herself to household duties.   **1884** Ingersoll *Country Cousins* 14 **CT,** I had an uncle . . . who was a famous chopper . . . When he was past seventy, he had a man working for him . . . and my uncle offered to 'butt' him.   **1949** *AmSp* 24.288, If I undertake to butt you, this means that we are to start at the same moment to chop thru the log, but I will cut at the place nearer the butt . . . Thus I am giving you odds.

butte n **chiefly West** See Map

See quot 1845.

1659 in 1893 Providence RI Rec. Comm. *Early Rec.* 3.76, Also six acres of Land . . neere unto the Two litle hills call*ed* Bailyes Buttes.   **1845**

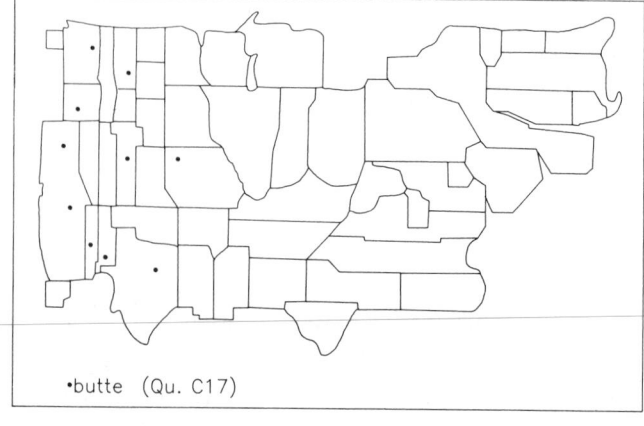

•butte (Qu. C17)

Frémont *Rept. Rocky Mts.* 161, The French word *butte...* is naturalized in the region of the Rocky mountains; and, even if desirable to render it in English, I know of no word which would be its precise equivalent. It is applied to the detached hills and ridges which rise abruptly, and reach too high to be called hills, and not high enough to be called mountains. **1882** *Century Illustr. Mag.* 24.510/2, Everything in the way of hill, rock, mountain, or clay-heap is called a butte in Montana. **1932** *DN* 6.226 **West. 1942** Stegner *Mormon Country* 39 **UT,** The country spreads away in broad, colored plains broken by buttes and mesas and split by canyons and washes. **1965** *Silver City Press Frontier* (NM) July 50/3, That there were varied and numerous cultures is proven by the ruins now found in the dry arroyos and on buttes overlooking the rivers. **1965–70** *DARE* (Qu. C17, *. . A small, rounded hill*) 10 Infs, **West,** Butte.

butte primrose n
An **evening primrose** (here: *Oenothera caespitosa*).
    1938 FWP *Guide ND* 14, In the Badlands grow the .. butte primrose. **1950** Stevens *ND Plants* 215, *Butte Primrose...* Frequent on bare, clay buttes or flats west of Missouri River. **1973** Hitchcock–Cronquist *Flora Pacific NW* 310.

butter and egg day n
    1965 *DARE* (QR, near Qu. U1a) Inf **OK**7, Butter and egg day—[In the] old days when [we] traded produce.

butter and egg money See **egg money**

butter-and-eggs n
    1 also *butter-and-egg plant:* A yellow-flowered **toadflax** (here: *Linaria vulgaris*). Also called **allmouth 2, bread-and-butter 2, buttercup 6, butterflower 4, butterweed 6, cat britches, chopped eggs, dead men's bones, devil's flax, dragon's mouth, eggs-and-bacon, flaxweed, hens-and-chickens, impudent lawyer, Jacob's ladder, rabbitflower, ranstead weed, snapdragon, wild flax, wild snapdragon, wild tobacco, yellow toadflax**
    1847 Darlington *Ag. Botany* 225 (*DAE*), Toad-flax. Ranstead-weed. Butter and Eggs. **1907** *DN* 3.183 **NH,** *Butter and eggs.* **1931** Harned *Wild Flowers Alleghanies* 443, "Butter and Eggs," another familiar name, refers to the deep orange and paler yellow of the flowers. **1961** Douglas *My Wilderness* 252 **nME,** Butter-and-eggs toadflax (*Linaria vulgaris*) is less conspicuous. **1965–70** *DARE* (Qu. S11) 182 Infs, **widespread,** Butter-and-eggs; **RI**17, Butter-and-egg plant. **1966–67** *DARE* Wildfl QR Pl. 196 Infs **AR**45, **NC**36, **OR**12, Butter-and-eggs. **1967** *DARE* Tape **MA** 6, They have .. toadflax here, butter-and-eggs we call it. **1967** *DARE* FW Addit **CO**7, Butter and eggs—toadflax.
    2 A daffodil.
    1876 Hobbs *Bot. Hdbk.* 17, Butter and eggs, Double flowered variety of Narcissus aurantius. **1894** *Jrl. Amer. Folkl.* 7.101, *Narcissus Pseudonarcissus* .. butter and eggs, Martha's Vineyard, Mass. **1899** (1912) Green *VA Folk-Speech* 102, Butter and eggs . . . The Jonquil.
    3 An owl's clover (here: *Orthocarpus erianthus*).
    1897 Parsons *Wild Flowers CA* 151, *Butter-and-Eggs. Orthocarpus erianthus . . . Corolla.*—Deep sulphur-yellow; the .. upper lip deep purple. **1961** Thomas *Flora Santa Cruz* 318 **CA,** Butter-and-Eggs . . . Open fields and grassy slopes. **1973** Hitchcock–Cronquist *Flora Pacific NW* 429.

butter and sugar corn n Also *butter and sugar sweet corn*
NEast
A hybrid sweet corn (*Zea mays* var. *rugosa*) with both yellow and white kernels.
    1966 *Shopping Notes* (Yarmouth ME) 18 Aug 10, Farm Fresh Daily *Butter & Sugar Sweet Corn.* **1967–69** *DARE* (Qu. I33) Inf **MA**1, Butter-and-sugar corn; **RI**3, Butter-and-sugar corn—yellow and white; (QR, near Qu. I33) Inf **PA**166, Butter-and-sugar [corn]. **1969** *DARE* Tape **CT**26, Butter-and-sugar corn [grown by Inf].

butterback n
=**bufflehead 2.**
    1888 Trumbull *Names of Birds* 83, Bartram, in Travels through North and South Carolina, etc, 1791, speaks of the Buffle-head being "called Butterback." **1917** (1923) *Birds Amer.* 1.140, *Buffle-Head—Charitonetta albeola . . . Other Names* . . . Butter-back.

butterball n
    1 =**bufflehead 2.**
    1814 Wilson *Amer. Ornith.* 8.51, *Buffel-headed Duck . . . This* pretty little species, usually known by the name of the *Butter-box,* or *Butter-*

ball, is common to the sea shores, rivers and lakes of the United States. **1888** Trumbull *Names of Birds* 83, *Buffle-Head . . .* At Niagara Falls, Lake St. Clair, Chicago, Snachwine (Putnam Co.), Ill., Washington, D.C., Charleston, S.C., and Savannah, Ga., Butter-ball. **1942** *Sun* (Baltimore MD) 31 Dec 13/3 (*Hench Coll.*), Soldiers in the Aleutians are dining on mallards, teal and butterballs. **1950** *WELS (Kinds of wild ducks)* 5 Infs, **WI,** Butterball(s). **1965–70** *DARE* (Qu. Q5) 23 Infs, **scattered,** Butterball. **1982** Elman *Hunter's Field Guide* 211, *Bufflehead (Bucephala albeola)*—Common & Regional Names: butterball.
    2 =**ruddy duck.**
    1888 Trumbull *Names of Birds* 110, *Ruddy Duck . . .* occasionally at Havre de Grace, Md., Norfolk, Va., Newberne, N.C., Savannah, Ga., and commonly in Golden City, Mo., Palatka and Sandford, Fla., *Butter-Ball.* **1950** *PADS* 14.18 **SC,** *Butterball . . .* The ruddy duck. **1968** *DARE* FW Addit **NV,** Butterball—Joking name for the ruddy duck. **1982** Elman *Hunter's Field Guide* 192, *Ruddy Duck . . .* Butterball.
    3 also *butterball teal:* Either the blue-winged teal or the green-winged teal. [See quot 1955]
    1923 U.S. Dept. Ag. *Misc. Circular* 13.12, *Green-winged Teal (Nettion carolinense) . . . In local use.*—Butterball (Me.). **1938** FWP *Guide IA* 325 **eIA,** The mallard, "butterball teal," brandt, .. and many other varieties visited here in great numbers. **1955** *MA Audubon* 39.314, *Green-winged Teal.* Butterball (Maine. As being sometimes excessively fat.) *Ibid, Blue-winged Teal . . .* Butterball.
    4 A **buckwheat 2** (here: *Eriogonum ovalifolium* var *celsum*). Also called **cushion buckwheat, snowball**
    1915 (1926) Armstrong *Western Wild Flowers* 92, Butter Balls . . . *Eriogonum orthocaulon.* **1968** *DARE* (QR, near Qu. S26e) Inf **CA**60, Desert flowers . . . butterballs or snowballs—a white, round flower, grows on an eighteen-inch stalk if [there is] enough moisture.
    5 See **butterball squash.**

butterball cat n Cf **butter cat**
Perh a **yellow bullhead.**
    1968 *DARE* (Qu. P1, *. . Freshwater fish . . that are good to eat*) Inf **LA**15, Butterball cat—a short one; fat, and runs about three-four pounds.

butterball squash n Also *butterball* [From its color and shape]
A winter squash (*Cucurbita moschata*) similar to a butternut squash.
    1968 *DARE* (Qu. I23) Inf **MN**12, Butterball squash—a yellow squash, like a small pumpkin, smooth hide; **OH**49, Butterballs—round, dark orange.

butter bean n
    1 A lima bean, esp a small one. **chiefly Sth, Midl** See Map
    1821 Cobbett *Amer. Gardener* L3 in Par. 197 **NY,** The *Lima*-bean .. is sometimes called the *butter*-bean. **1841** *S. Lit. Messenger* 7.37/1 **GA,** I clambered up a frail ladder, to assist the young tendrils of the butter-bean to catch the threads loosely suspended from post to post. **1900** Lyons *Plant Names* 285, *P[haseolus] lunatus . . .* Butter Bean. **1946** *PADS* 5.14 **VA,** *Butterbeans . . .* Lima beans; common everywhere. **1949** Kurath *Word Geog.* 73, *Butter beans* is a common expression for lima beans in all of the Southern area. Many people in this section differentiate between the large *lima beans* and the smaller *butter beans.* **1950** *PADS* 14.18 **SC,** *Butterbean . . .* Sieva bean; lima bean. **1954** Armstrong *Satchmo* 106 **LA,** I sure did enjoy the way she cooked those fresh

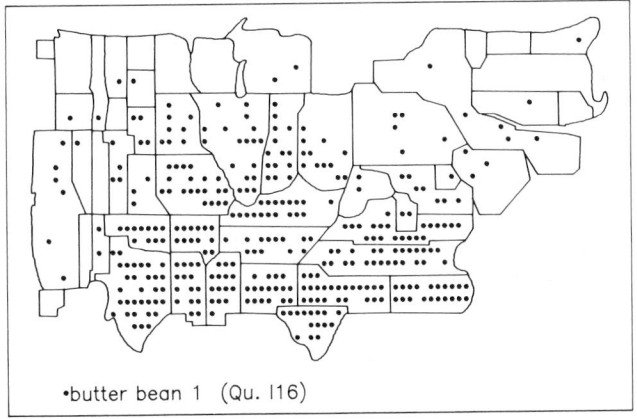

•butter bean 1 (Qu. I16)

butter beans, the beans they call Lima beans up North. *c1960 Wilson Coll.* **csKY**, *Butter-bean* . . . The small Lima bean, often called elsewhere, small Lima or sivvy (sieva) beans. **1963** *TN Folk Lore Soc. Bulletin* 29.79, *Butterbeans*—Everybody called the small *Lima* bean a *butterbean* and never heard of the big kind until fairly recently. *Sieva* or *sivvy beans* as names for this small bean were also unknown, probably showing that South Caroline [sic] settlers did not drift up this way in pioneer times. **1965–70** *DARE* (Qu. I16, *The large flat beans that are not eaten in the pod*) 364 Infs, **chiefly Sth, Midl**, Butter beans. **1969–70** *DARE* Tapes GA77, TX99, Butter beans. **1976** *Bailey–Bailey Hortus Third* 854, *Phaseolus lunatus* . . . Butter Bean.

2 A wax bean. **esp NEng**
   1941 *LANE* Map 259, Butter beans . . are frequently defined as identical with wax beans. **1949** *Natl. Geog. Mag.* 96.159/1, In the South and some other parts of this country lima beans are commonly called "butter beans." In New England this colloquialism is sometimes used to refer to yellow-podded ("wax") varieties of snap beans. **1967** Wilson *Folkways Mammoth Cave No. 2* 27 **KY**, *Butterbean.* The small Lima bean grown everywhere in the region . . . the *yellow-podded bush beans*, known elsewhere as *butterbeans*, are called *wax beans.* **1973** *AmSp* 48.61, *Phaseolus lunatus*, is characteristically grown in the South and formerly was often denominated by the Midland term *butter bean* . . . Some Northern speakers now use *butter beans* to refer to dried lima beans, the green ones still being called *lima beans* . . . And a few . . transfer the term *butter beans* to a still different product, wax beans, and call butter beans *baby limas.*

‡**3** One's navel. *joc*
   1970 *DARE* (Qu. X34, . . *The navel*) Inf VA35, Butter bean, nabel, bird's nest.

butter bean teeth See **butter teeth**

butterbill coot n Also *butterbill, butterbilled coot, butter-boat-bill(ed coot)* Cf **butternose coot**
=**scoter.**
   1838 Audubon *Ornith. Biog.* 4.163, In the States of Maine and Massachusetts, this species is best known by the name of "Butter-boat-billed Coot." **1844** DeKay *Zool. NY* 2.329, *Fuligula albeola.* This little duck is known under the various popular names of . . . Butter-bill [etc]. *Ibid* 335, *Fuligula Perspicillata* . . . Black Sea Duck or Butter-boat-bill, is very common on the coast of New York during the winter. *Ibid* 336, *Fuligula Americana.* This duck, which is known . . farther east by the name of Butter-bill, is described in the books under the name of American Scoter Duck. **1888** Trumbull *Names of Birds* 107, *Oidemia americana* . . In Maine, at Eastport, Millbridge, Frenchman's Bay, Ash Point (near Rockland), Bath, Portland, and Pine Point, at Portsmouth, N.H., in Massachusetts at North Scituate, Barnstable, Fairhaven, New Bedford, and Falmouth, and at Stony Creek, Conn., Butter-bill. **1909** Field Mus. Nat. Hist. *Zool. Ser.* 343, *Oidemia americana* . . . American Scoter Duck . . . *Local name:* Butter-bill Coot. **1917** (1923) *Birds Amer.* 1.148, *Oidemia americana* . . . Butter-bill; . . Butter-billed Coot. **1943** Musgrove *Waterfowl IA* 68, *American Scoter* . . . Other names: butter-bill, . . butter-billed coot. **1966** *DARE* Tape ME10, Butter-bill coot is a very light yellow. Looks just like butter on each side of that bill.

butterbird n
1 =**bobolink.** [See quot 1883]
   1859 (1968) Bartlett *Americanisms* 41, *Bobolink* . . . Other popular names by which it is known in different parts of the country are Rice-bird, Rice-bunting, . . Butter-bird. **1883** *Standard* 26 Dec *(OED)*, They [=bobolinks] . . grow so fat that they receive the name of 'butter birds.' **1946** Hausman *Eastern Birds* 548, *Bobolink* . . . *Other Names* . . . Butterbird, Bob Lincoln, Robert. **1950** *WELS*, 1 Inf, **cWI**, Bobolink—butterbird.

2 =**piping plover.**
   1925 (1928) Forbush *Birds MA* 1.470, *Charadrius melodus* . . . *Other names: Beach-bird; Beach-plover; Butter-bird.* **1946** Hausman *Eastern Birds* 252, *Piping Plover* . . . *Other Names* . . Clam Bird, Butterbird, Mourning Bird.

butter-boat-bill(ed coot) See **butterbill coot**

butterbowl n Cf **butterball 2**
=**ruddy duck.**
   1888 Trumbull *Names of Birds* 110, *Ruddy Duck* . . . We hear also at Norfolk *Butter-Bowl.* **1968** *DARE* (Qu. Q5, . . *Kinds of wild ducks*) Inf MI76, Butterbowl.

butterbox n Cf **butterball 1**
=**bufflehead 2.**
   1814 [see **butterball 1**]. **1844** Giraud *Birds Long Is.* 336, Buffel Headed Duck . . . In New-Jersey it is called "Butter Box," or "Butter Ball." **1888** Trumbull *Names of Birds* 83 (as of 1824), Buffle-Head . . . Wilson writes: "Usually known by the name of the *Butter-Box.*" **1917** (1923) *Birds Amer.* 1.140, *Buffle-Head—Charitonetta albeola* . . . Butterbox. **1982** Elman *Hunter's Field Guide* 211, *Bufflehead (Bucephala albeola)*—Common & Regional Names: . . butterbox.

butterbread n [PaGer *butterbrot*] **chiefly PaGer area**
Bread spread with butter.
   1907 (1970) Martin *Betrothal* 111 **csPA**, I had only butterbread and coffee soup. **1916** *DN* 4.337 **csPA, MI**, *Butter bread.* [Ger. *Butter-brot.*] Bread spread with butter. **1935** *AmSp* 10.171 [PaGer]. **1939** Aurand *Quaint Idioms* 28 [PaGer], Do you want *Butter bread* (bread and butter). **1950** Klees *PA Dutch* 282, *Butterbread* and *jellybread* and *applebutterbread* are descriptive compounds. **1953** *AmSp* 28.245 **csPA**. **1968** *Helen Adolf Festschrift* 37, *Butterbread* (Pennsylvania German *Butterbrot*) for 'bread and butter.'

butterbump n [Prob alter of *bittern* + echoic element; cf **thunder pumper**]
=**bittern.**
   1917 (1923) *Birds Amer.* 1.181, *Bittern—Botaurus lentiginosus* . . . Butterbump. **1946** Hausman *Eastern Birds* 110, American Bittern *Botaurus lentiginosus* . . . Butterbump. **1950** FWP *Guide ID* 89, The racket it [=American bittern] makes has been variously compared with that of bellowing cattle, with the gurgle of an old wooden pump, and with the driving of a peg into a bog; and it has passed in folklore under such names as thunder-pumper, stakedriver, butter-bump, and bog-bull.

‡**butterbung** n
=**flicker.**
   1967 *DARE* (Qu. Q17, . . *Kinds of woodpeckers*) Inf MA5, Flicker = butterbung.

butter cat n [Prob so called from the color and slick skin of the catfish]
=**yellow bullhead.**
   1955 Carr–Goin *Guide Reptiles* 63 **FL**, *Ameiurus natalis* . . . Yellow Cat; Butter Cat . . . Ground color brownish-yellow, darker above, fading to yellow on the belly. **1967** *DARE* (Qu. P1, . . *Freshwater fish . . good to eat*) Inf SC40, Butter cat.

butter cellar n
   1968 *DARE* FW Addit **NY73**, *Butter cellar*—A room in the cellar of a house, especially cool, where butter was kept.

butter clam n **Pacific Coast** See also **money shell**
A Washington clam (*Saxidomus* spp).
   1949 Palmer *Nat. Hist.* 358, *Butter Clam* . . . *Saxodomus* [sic] nuttalli . . . Delicious. **1966–70** *DARE* (Qu. P18) Infs CA191, WA11, Butter clams; AK9, Clams—butter, razor; WA20, Little-neck or butter clam. **1974** Abbott *Seashells* 533, Common Washington Clam . . . A very common species which is edible. Also called the butter clam.

butter cream n
   1952 Tracy *Coast Cookery* 296, *Sour cream.* Smooth, mild, artificially soured cream, called butter cream in the Midwest.

butter cress n
A **buttercup 1** (here: *Ranunculus acris*).
   1900 Lyons *Plant Names* 316, *Ranunculus acris* . . . Butter cress. **1959** Carleton *Index Herb. Plants* 21, Butter cress: *Ranunculus acris.*

buttercup n [From the color]
1 Std: a plant of the genus *Ranunculus.* Also called **beggar's button 2, butter daisy 1, butterflower 2, crowfoot 1a, gold cup, water crowfoot.** For other names of var spp see **alkali buttercup, butter cress, butter rose, celery crowfoot, devil's claw, devil's guts, goldweed, granny threads, green eelgrass, hellweed, horse-gold, king cup, lantern leaves, meadow cup 2, moss, queen's button, ram's claws, water celery, yellow bachelor's button**

2 A cinquefoil, usu *Potentilla anserina* and *P. canadense.*
   1896 *Jrl. Amer. Folkl.* 9.187 **ME**, *Potentilla Canadensis* . . running buttercup. **1898** *Ibid* 11.226, *Potentilla Canadensis* . . little buttercup, South Berwick, Me. **1900** Lyons *Plant Names* 303, *Potentilla Anserina*

... Buttercup. *Ibid* 304, *Potentilla Canadensis* ... Running Butter-cup. **1910** Graves *Flowering Plants* 234 **CT**, *Potentilla canadensis* ... Running Buttercup. **1966** *DARE* Wildfl. QR Pl. 92b Inf **MI7**, "Butter-cup," we call it; it is not a buttercup.

3 =yellow bells.
1915 (1926) Armstrong *Western Wild Flowers* 38, *Yellow Fritillary—Fritillaria pudica* ... The local Utah names, Crocus, Snowdrop, and Buttercup are absurd. **1966** Barnes–Jensen *Dict. UT Slang* 7, Butter-cup ... A name frequently given to the orange Fritillaria *(Fritillaria pudica).* **1967** *DARE* Wildfl QR Pl.3.2 (Craighead) Inf **CO15**, Butter-cups.

4 A daffodil. esp sAppalachians
1956 McAtee *Some Dialect NC* 54, Buttercup ... The daffodil *(Nar-cissus pseudonarcissus).* **1958** *PADS* 29.8 **TN**, In our early days ... we fought over *buttercups* as opposed to *daffodils* or *jonquils.* We still say *buttercup* for the early variety that grow everywhere. **c1960** *Wilson Coll.* **csKY**, *Buttercup* ... Daffodil or other early narcissus, usually a yellow one, however. **1967** Wilson *Folkways Mammoth Cave No. 2* 27 **KY**, *Buttercups.* Probably the most common name for daffodils. They are also called *March flowers, Easter flowers,* and *jonquils.* **1970** *DARE* FW Addit **VA35**, Buttercups—daffodils.

5 An evening primrose (here: *Oenothera macrocarpa*).
1961 Wills–Irwin *Flowers TX* 164, Flutter-mill *Oenothera missouriensis* [=*Megapterium missouriense*] .. known also as ... Buttercup. **1968** *DARE* FW Addit **VA15**, *Buttercup* ... common; evening-primrose is the book name.

‡6 =butter-and-eggs 1.
1966 *DARE* Wildfl. QR Pl.196 Inf **SD6**, Buttercup; some say snap-dragon.

‡7 A globeflower (here: *Trollius laxus*).
1966 *DARE* Wildfl QR Pl.61 Inf **ND4**, Buttercup.

buttercup squash n chiefly Nth
A cultivated variety of fall squash *(Cucurbita maxima).*
1949 *Natl. Geog. Mag.* 96.162/2, Several years ago a North Dakota horticulturist bred a small variety of turban squash as a substitute for the sweet potato ... This little Buttercup squash has flesh surprisingly similar to sweet potato in taste and quality. **1965–70** *DARE* (Qu. I23) 49 Infs, **chiefly Nth**, Buttercup squash. **1966** *Shopping Notes* (Yar-mouth ME) 18 Aug 10, Farm Fresh Daily ... *Green Beans & Wax Beans .. Buttercup Squash.* **1966** *DARE* Tape **MI28**, Buttercup squash .. [is] sort of a flat squash, and it has like a cap on it, on the stem end ... The main part of the squash is a dark green and this little kinda cap part is a light green with little stripes through it ... very sweet, tasty squash.

buttercup waterlily n [From its shape and color]
=spatterdock (here: *Nuphar luteum*).
1968 *DARE* Wildfl QR Pl. 56 Inf **MN37**, Buttercup waterlily.

butter daisy n
1 =buttercup 1.
1900 Lyons *Plant Names* 316, R[*anunculus*] *acris* ... Butter-daisy. **1911** *Century Dict., Daisy* ... *Butter-daisy,* a name of species of *Ranun-culus.* **1940** Clute *Amer. Plant Names* 4, R[*anunculus*] *acris* ... Butter-daisy ... *R. bulbosus* ... Butter-daisy ... *R. repens* ... Butter-daisy. **1959** Carleton *Index Herb. Plants* 21, *Butter daisy:* Ranunculus acris.

2 =marsh marigold.
1969 *DARE* (Qu. S22, .. *The bright yellow flowers that bloom in clusters in marshes in early springtime*) Inf **KY11**, Butter daisies.

butter duck n
1 =surf scoter.
1857 Swan *NW Coast* 347 **swWA**, The Colonel saw a "butter-duck" in a shallow creek ... These ducks are the black surf-duck *(Fuligula perspicillata).* **1966–68** *DARE* (Qu. Q5) Inf **KS12**, Butter duck; **LA10**, Butter duck—a little plump, black duck; **OK18**, Butter duck—small, black, might also be called black-jacks; **WV8**, Butter duck—small, looks like fish duck. [Note: some of these Infs may refer instead to **butter duck 2.**]

2 =bufflehead 2.
1888 Trumbull *Names of Birds* 83, Buffle-Head ... Savannah, Ga. ... *Butter-Duck.* **1917** (1923) *Birds Amer.* 1.140; *Buffle-head ... Other Names.*—Butter Duck. **1946** Hausman *Eastern Birds* 159, *Bufflehead ... Other Names*—Butter Duck. **1982** Elman *Hunter's Field Guide* 211, *Bufflehead (Bucephala albeola)*—Common & Regional Names: .. butter duck.

‡butter duffle n
Prob =bufflehead 2.
1968 *DARE* (Qu. Q5) Inf **MN38**, Butter duffle or fish duck.

butterfish n
1 Any of var salt-water fish, esp of the families Pholidæ, Serran-idæ, and Stromateidæ. **chiefly Atlantic**
1882 U.S. Natl. Museum *Bulletin* 16.541, *Epinephalus punctatus [Ce-phalopholis fulvus]* ... Butter-fish. **1898** U.S. Natl. Museum *Bulletin* 47.2419, *Pholis Gunnellus* ... Butter Fish. **1906** NJ State Museum *Annual Rept. for 1905* 263, *Trachinotus carolinus* ... Butter Fish. **1931–33** *LANE Worksheets,* 1 inf, **csCT**, A scup is same as butterfish; 1 inf, **seMA**, Butterfish—variety of fish; 1 inf, **seRI**, Butterfish ... similar to scup. **1933** John G. Shedd Aquarium *Guide* 97, *Cephalopholis fulvus ruber* ... Butterfish. **1939** FWP *Guide FL* 317, The pompano, also known as butterfish for its fine-textured flesh and delicious flavor, is Florida's rarest and choicest food fish. **1939** Natl. Geog. Soc. *Fishes* 68, *Poronotus triacanthus* has several names, being known as butterfish in Massachusetts and Norfolk (the name used for *Peprilus alepidotus* at Beaufort, N.C.). **1955** Taber *Stillmeadow Daybook* 134 **swCT**, Then when she bought the butterfish, the old man wanted to clean them and she said casually, "Thank you no, it's for the turtles." **1965–70** *DARE* (Qu. P2, .. *Saltwater fish .. that are good to eat*) 12 Infs, **chiefly Atlantic,** Butterfish; (Qu. P4) Inf **NC80**, Butterfish—some call 'em sunfish; (Qu. P14) Infs **DC4, MA55, NC1, 87, RI15**, Butterfish.

2 =golden shiner.
1820 Rafinesque *Ohio R. Fishes* 48, It *[Notropis chrysocephalus]* re-sembles the common Shiner or Butterfish of Pennsylvania. *Cyprinus chrysoleucos* Mitchell. **1873** Thaxter *Among Isle of Shoals* 88 **ME, NH**, Perch are found in inexhaustible quantities about the rocks, and lump or butter-fish are sometimes caught. **1968–69** *DARE* (Qu. P1, .. *Fresh-water fish .. that are good to eat*) Infs **IN58, PA66**, Butterfish; (Qu. P7, *Small fish used as bait*) Inf **NY47**, Butterfish.

3 A moray eel.
1889 (1971) Farmer *Americanisms* 110, *Butter Fish (Muraenoides).*—A common slimy fish; hence its popular name, the idea conveyed in which is akin to that in "butter fingers," i.e., it is difficult to handle.

4 =soft-shell clam. Cf mannose
1842 DeKay *Zool. NY* 4.153, The American Butter-fish, *Gunnellus mucronatus* .. is frequently found among rocks along the seashore, and in the mud. **1881** Ingersoll *Oyster-Industry* 242, *Butter Fish,* the long neck clam, *Mya arenaria* (Virginia). **1970** *DARE* Tape **VA55**, They ain't but two kinds ... a clam and a butterfish we dig out the bottom ... they're soft shellfish ... some calls 'em mannoses.

butterflies n
1 =vanilla leaf 2.
1934 Haskin *Wild Flowers Pacific Coast* 119, Carefully cut away the central leaflet, and you will see that the two remaining ones represent a spreading, green-winged butterfly. This resemblance is very striking, and because of it children call the plant "butterflies."

2 =butter-and-eggs 1.
1966 *DARE* (Qu. S11, .. *Other names .. for .. wild snapdragon*) Inf **SC10**, Butterflies.

butterflower n [From the color] Cf butterweed
1 =marsh marigold.
1900 Lyons *Plant Names* 76, *C. palustris* ... Great Butter-flower.

2 =buttercup 1.
1910 Graves *Flowering Plants* 188 **CT**, *Ranunculus acris* ... Butter or Blister Flowers. **1940** Clute *Amer. Plant Names* 4, R[*anunculus*] *acris* ... Butter-flower ... *R. bulbosus* ... Butter-flower ... *R. repens* ... Butter-flower. **1959** Carleton *Index Herb. Plants* 21, *Butter flowers:* Ranunculus acris.

3 =dandelion.
1968 *DARE* (Qu. S11, .. *Other names .. for .. dandelion*) Inf **WI37**, Butterflower.

4 =butter-and-eggs 1.
1968 *DARE* (Qu. S11, .. *Other names .. for .. wild snapdragon*) Inf **NY37**, Butterflower.

butterfly n
1 =snow angel.
1967–68 *DARE* (Qu. EE26, .. *Games .. children play in the snow*) Inf **CO7**, Butterflies (snow angels); **WI68**, Butterflies—lay down and move

your arms and legs; **IA3,** Making butterflies—same as making angels; **IA27,** Make butterflies.

2 A freshwater mussel (here: *Ellipsaria lineolata*). [From the shape and markings]

1982 U.S. Fish & Wildlife Serv. *Fresh-Water Mussels* Part II, *Butterfly* . . . Shell yellow or brown with interrupted, usually green rays, often of chevron-like markings.

butterfly banner(s) n
=Dutchman's breeches 1.

1933 Small *Manual SE Flora* 550, *B. Cucullaria* . . . Butterfly-banner. **1959** Carleton *Index Herb. Plants* 21, *Butterfly banners:* Dicentra cucullaria.

butterfly bird n
1 =painted bunting 1.

1955 *AmSp* 30.184 **SC, FL, TX,** *Butterfly bird* . . . The nonpareil or painted bunting gets this name . . in allusion to the varied, bright coloration of its plumage.

2 The chestnut-collared **longspur** (*Calcarius ornatus*).

1955 *AmSp* 30.184, *Butterfly bird* . . . the chestnut-colored [sic] longspur has been so called from a resemblance due to both color and motion in its song-flight.

butterfly bush n
1 A shrub of the genus *Buddleia,* with opposite wing-like leaves.

1923 Amer. Joint Comm. Horticult. Nomenclature *Std. Plant Names* 50, *Buddleia* . . . Butterflybush. **1942** Hylander *Plant Life* 437, Butterfly Bush *(Buddleia)* is an ornamental . . native to the tropics of America, Asia and Africa. **1958** Grau *Hard Blue Sky* 317 **sLA,** It was so quiet you could hear the butterfly bushes on the side of the house brush against the boards. **1966** *DARE* (Qu. S10) Inf **NM6,** Beauty bush or butterfly bush—blue flower.

2 =butterfly weed 1.

1966–70 *DARE* (Qq. S26a, e) Infs **KY35, NC36, OH65, VA57,** Butterfly bush; **NJ29,** Butterfly bush—orange clusters; **SC36,** Butterfly bush—orange colored, same as Indian paint-box; **VA26,** Butterfly bush—yellow; (Qu. S26d) Inf **KY24,** Butterfly bush—[same as] Indian paintbrush. Bookword is butterfly weed, *asclepias tuberosa.* **1966** *DARE* Wildfl QR Pl. 171 Inf **NC36,** Butterfly bush.

3 Perh tamarisk.

1967 *DARE* (Qu. T13, . . *Other names . . for tamarack*) Inf **NE6,** Butterfly bush.

butterfly coot n
=old-squaw.

1955 *AmSp* 30.184 **MA,** *Butterfly coot* for the old squaw duck . . probably alludes to the active flight of this species, which dives from the wing, as well as to its pied coloration.

butterfly flower n
1 also *butterfly plant:* **=butterfly weed 1.**

1911 (1916) Porter *Harvester* 418 **IN,** They came to the large beds of orange pleurisy root . . . The Bird Woman calls it butterfly flower. **1940** Clute *Amer. Plant Names* 90, *A. tuberosa* . . . Butterfly-flower. **1941** FWP *Guide SC* 409, The . . butterfly plant snuggles down in the hot summer. **1966–69** *DARE* (Qu. S10) Inf **FL11,** Butterfly plant; (Qu. S26a) Inf **AR28,** Butterfly flowers; (Qu. S26c) Inf **MI108,** Butterfly plant; (Qu. S26d) Inf **TN6,** Butterfly plant.

2 =butterfly weed 2.

1949 Moldenke *Amer. Wild Flowers* 92, Of entirely different aspect are the . . *butterflyflowers (Gaura)* . . . Many species abound in the South and the Middle West.

3 A solanaceous plant of the genus *Schizanthus.*

1959 Carleton *Index Herb. Plants* 21, *Butterfly flower:* Asclepias tuberosa; Clarkia elegans; Schizanthus (v). **1976** Bailey–Bailey *Hortus Third* 1018, *Schizanthus* . . . Butterfly flower.

4 A **farewell-to-spring** (here: *Clarkia elegans*).

1959 [See **butterfly flower 3**].

butterfly milkweed See butterfly weed 1

butterfly pea n

Any of the perennial legumes of the genera *Clitoria* and *Centrosema* which have showy papilionaceous flowers, but esp:

a A somewhat trailing plant (*Clitoria mariana*) found chiefly east of the Mississippi River (exc Nth) with bluish to lavender corolla and nearly erect standard. Also called **clabber-spoon, pigeon-wings, turkey pea**

1848 Gray *Manual of Botany* 97, *Clitoria* . . . Butterfly Pea . . . *Centrosema* . . . Spurred Butterfly Pea. **1901** Lounsberry *S. Wild Flowers* 284, The butterfly pea seems almost too delicate and chaste a blossom to be disputing the soil with hoary mints. **1931** Clute *Common Plants* 94, The butterfly-pea . . refers to the shape of the blossoms which are fancied to resemble butterflies. **1941** Walker *Lookout* 58 **seTN,** Butterfly-pea is one of the many kinds . . growing on the mountain. **1975** Duncan–Foote *Wildflowers SE* 84, Butterfly-pea . . . One to several flowers open at a time, persisting longer than a day.

b A usu vigorously twining plant (*Centrosema virginianum*) chiefly of the Central and Gulf States, with purplish to white corolla, spreading standard, and small spur at the base.

1848 [see **a** above]. **1903** Small *Flora SE U.S.* 651, *Centrosema* . . . Butterfly Pea. **1953** Greene–Blomquist *Flowers South* 60, During the summer months . . the spurred butterfly-peas show up in open grassy places and in ground cover in open woods. **1972** Brown *Wildflowers LA* 77, *Butterfly Pea* . . . A delicate twining herbaceous vine, often climbing to a height of 6 feet.

butterfly plant See butterfly flower 1

butterfly ray n [From the shape]
A short-tailed stingray, esp of the genus *Gymnura.*

1873 in 1878 Smithsonian Inst. *Misc. Coll.* 14.2.34, *Pteroplatea Maclura* . . . Butterfly-ray. **1896** U.S. Natl. Museum *Bulletin* 47.86, *Pteroplatea maclura*—(Butterfly Ray.). **1953** Roedel *Common Fishes CA* 28, *California Butterfly Ray—Gymnura marmorata* . . . Found from Pt. Conception south into Central America. **1960** Amer. Fisheries Soc. *List Fishes* 9. **1979** McPhee *Giving Good Weight* 101, Rays—including a twenty-five-pound spiny butterfly ray, out of its place, which is the deep ocean.

butterfly root See butterfly weed 1

butterfly tongue n [See quot 1934] Cf elephant's head
A **lousewort** (here: *Pedicularis canadensis* and *P. groenlandica*).

1915 (1926) Armstrong *Western Wild Flowers* 504, Elephants' Heads, Butterfly-tongue *Pedicularis Groenlandica* . . . A handsome plant, with quaint flowers. **1934** Haskin *Wild Flowers Pacific Coast* 331, Butterfly-Tongue . . . In this flower the beak is extremely long, slender, and up-curled like a butterfly's tongue. **1959** Carleton *Index Herb. Plants* 21, Butterfly Tongue: *Pedicularis canadensis.*

butterfly violet n
A common blue violet (*Viola sororia*).

1948 Stevens *KS Wild Flowers* 112, *Butterfly Violet* . . . The narrow, spurred beardless lower petal suggesting the body, and the 4 upper petals sufficiently resembling the wings, of a butterfly to let imagination complete the picture. **1968** *DARE* (Qu. S11, . . *Other names . . for blue violet*) Inf **PA99,** Butterfly violet.

butterfly weed n [See 1931 quots at 1]
1 also *butterfly milkweed, ~ root, ~ wort:* A usu orange-flowered milkweed, *Asclepias tuberosa,* native to much of the US (except Pacific and Rocky Mountain states). Also called **archangel 4, butterfly bush 2, butterfly flower 1, Canada root, chiggerweed 2, colicroot 1, flux root, fluxweed, harvest root, Indian bokay, Indian nosy, Indian paint, Indian paintbox, Indian paintbrush, Indian plume, Indian posy, Indian potato, orange root, pleurisy root, rubber root, silkweed, swallowwort, tuber root, white root, wind root, windweed, wine tree, witchweed, yellow milkweed**

1789 in 1793 Amer. Philos. Soc. *Trans.* 3.xviii, The best among pleuretic remedies must be the *pleuresy-root* . . called also *butterfly root.* **1819** Thomas *Travels W. Country* 222, *Asclepias decumbens* butterfly weed. **1830** *Huntingdon (Penna.) Courier* 15 Sep. 4/5 *(DA),* Harvest Root or Butterfly Wort, (Asclepias Tuberosa). **1899** Bergen *Animal Lore* 118, *Asclepias tuberosa,* the butterfly milkweed. **1931** Clute *Common Plants* 95, The butterfly-weed . . is so named from the fact that it is beloved by butterflies. **1931** Harned *Wild Flowers Alleghanies* 396, Many silky parachutes, to which the seeds are attached and by which they are carried on the wind, give rise to the names, Silkweed and Butterfly-Weed. **c1937** (1970) Yetman *Voices* 214 **OK,** When we got sick, we would take butterfly root and life-everlasting and boil it and make a syrup and take it for colds. **1965–70** *DARE* (Qu. S20) Inf **GA70,** Butterfly weed; (Qu. S21) Inf **KY89,** Butterfly weed; (Qu. S26a) Infs **KS41, TN11, VA75,** Butterfly weed; (Qu. S26d) Infs **AR49, KY89,**

NJ45, **PA**99, Butterfly weed; (Qu. S26e) Inf **DC**2, Butterfly weed. **1971** Krochmal *Appalachia Med. Plants* 70, Butterfly milkweed . . . has been used . . to treat rheumatism. **1976** Bruce *How to Grow Wildflowers* 189, Except for the gorgeous Butterflyweed, *A. tuberosa*, garden writers are unanimous in calling milkweeds weedy and undesirable, or at best coarse.

2 Any of var plants of the genus *Gaura* with terminal spikes or racemes of small white, pink or red flowers, but esp *G. coccinea.* Also called **bee plant 3, butterfly flower 2, honeysuckle, morning honeysuckle, wild honeysuckle** For other names of var spp see **bee-blossom 1, kisses, lizard tail, velvetleaf, velvetweed, waving butterfly**
1932 Rydberg *Flora Prairies* 580, *Gaura* . . . Butterfly Weed. **1968** Barkley *Plants KS* 250, Gaura biennis . . . Butterflyweed . . . Gaura coccinea . . . Butterflyweed . . . Gaura parviflora . . . Butterflyweed. **1976** Dodge *Roadside Wildflowers* 53, Butterflyweed . . . First flowers appear at the base of the spike gradually being replaced by several above with unopened buds continuing to the top of the blossom spike, and withered flowers at the bottom.

3 =**mariposa lily.**
1959 Carleton *Index Herb. Plants* 21, *Butterfly weed:* . . Calochortus (v).

butterfly wort See **butterfly weed 1**

butter gold n [From the color of the petals]
=**marsh marigold** (here: *Caltha palustris*).
1967 *DARE* (Qu. S22, . . *The bright yellow flowers that bloom in clusters in marshes in early springtime*) Inf **PA**35, Butter gold.

butterheads n [From the yellow color of the flower heads]
=**brass buttons.**
1915 (1926) Armstrong *Western Wild Flowers* 562, *Brass Buttons, Butter-heads. Cotula coronopifolia* . . . The flower-heads are about half an inch or less across, like the bright yellow center of a Daisy, without rays.

butter-hearted adj
1952 Brown *NC Folkl.* 1.524, *Butter-hearted* . . . Tender-hearted.

butter horn n Also *butter-nut horn*
A rich pastry often made in the shape of a horn or crescent.
1965–70 *DARE* (Qu. H32, . . *Fancy rolls and pastries*) Infs **CA**112, 126, 174, **HI**1, **IL**113, **IA**47, Butter horn(s); **MI**9, Butter horn — pastry rolled into the shape of a horn, butter between, frosting on them; (Qu. H19) Inf **MN**1, Butter horns [are] raised rolls; (Qu. H28, *Different shapes or types of doughnuts*) Inf **WA**13, Butter horn; (Qu. H29, *A round cake, cooked in deep fat, with jelly inside*) Inf **WA**13, Small butter horn. **1982** *Prairie Kitchen Companion* 183, *Butter-nut horns* (Ruggies) . . . Blend flour and butter. Drop in egg yolk and sour cream . . . Mix nuts, sugar cinnamon, and raisins . . . Roll each wedge . . to form a crescent shape. Bake horns at 375 degrees. **1983** *DARE* File **wOR**, Mother used to buy butter horns [a generic term for sweet rolls like Danishes] at the bakery.

butterinsky See **buttinsky 1**

butter letter See **letter**

buttermilk n

1 An orphaned calf. [Because such calves are often fed on the skim milk left after butter is churned] Cf **buttermilker**
1940 FWP *Guide NV* 76, *A buttermilk* . . . A motherless calf. **1961** Adams *Old-Time Cowhand* 155 **West,** An orphan calf was also called a . . . "buttermilk."

2 attrib: Having the characteristics of a marsh; boggy.
1843 (1916) Hall *New Purchase* 49 **IN,** They had been sufficiently fortunate as to get a taste of "buttermilk land," — "spouty land," — and to learn the nature of "mash land." *Ibid* 227, The blasted fool . . wades clean . . through the bio[=bayou]! and the buttermilk slash tother side!

buttermilk cheese n
Cottage cheese.
1949 *AmSp* 24.106 **ncGA, nwSC,** Buttermilk Cheese . . . Cottage cheese. **1967** *DARE* (Qu. H60, *The lumpy white cheese that is made from sour milk*) Inf **TN**5, Buttermilk cheese.

buttermilk clouds See **buttermilk sky**

buttermilker n Cf **buttermilk 1**
1968 *DARE* (Qu. K20, *A calf that is sold for meat*) Inf **NY**72, Veal —

that's where they're fed on new milk; buttermilker — when they're fed on skim milk.

buttermilk-lily n
The large-flowered **trillium** (*Trillium grandiflorum*).
1940 Clute *Amer. Plant Names* 15, *T. grandiflorum* . . . Buttermilk-lily.

buttermilk sky n Also *buttermilk clouds* **scattered, but esp NCent, Inland Sth** See Map Cf **mackerel sky**
The sky when filled with small, curd-like or patchy clouds; the clouds themselves.
1946 in 1974 IN Univ. Lilly Library *Exhibition Carmichael* sig [?]7ᵛ [in a list of sheet music on exhibit], "Ole Buttermilk Sky," with Jack Brooks, 1946. **1956** *Hand Coll.* **swOH,** Buttermilk clouds are followed by rain. *Ibid,* Mares' tails and fishes' scales were terms used to designate high cirrus clouds in the form of streamers and what is sometimes called buttermilk sky. **1961** Douglas *My Wilderness* 266 **ME,** Katahdin has been like a haunting melody since the day in the late twenties when I first saw it against a buttermilk sky. **1965–70** *DARE* (Qu. B11, *Other kinds of clouds*) 19 Infs, **esp NCent, Inland Sth,** Buttermilk clouds; 8 Infs, **scattered,** Buttermilk sky; **CA**21, Buttermilk clouds — fluffy, patchy sky; **CO**7, Buttermilk clouds — dappled all over; **IN**3, Buttermilk clouds — little broken-up clouds that look like buttermilk (clabbered); **MS**26, Buttermilk clouds — small clouds in great abundance; **IL**75, Buttermilk sky — little broken pieces, like cottage cheese; (Qu. B10, . . *Long trailing clouds*) Infs **GA**55, **IL**17, **NY**123, Buttermilk sky; **MS**17, **NE**7, Buttermilk clouds.

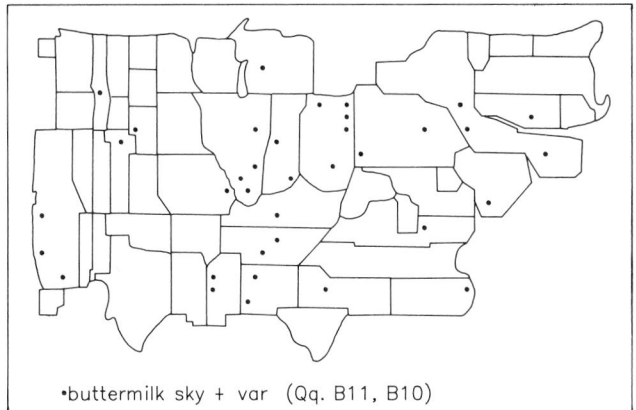

•buttermilk sky + var (Qq. B11, B10)

buttermilk snake n
A subsp (*Coluber constrictor anthicus*) of the **racer 1.**
1953 Schmidt *N. Amer. Amphibians* 188, Northeastern Louisiana, . . and in adjacent Texas and Arkansas. *Common names.* — Buttermilk snake. **1974** Shaw–Campbell *Snakes West* 82, The racer of eastern Texas and Louisiana, which is called the "buttermilk snake," is speckled.

butter money n [*EDD*] Cf **egg money**
1956 McAtee *Some Dialect NC* 7, Butter money . . . receipts from the sale of butter, eggs, etc., a perquisite of the farmer's wife.

buttermunk n

1 =**bittern.** [Perh imit] Cf **butterbump**
1889 *Jrl. Amer. Folkl.* 2.64 **swME,** Buttermunk . . . bittern. **1955** *MA Audubon Soc. Bulletin* 39.313, *American Bittern* . . . Butter-munk (Maine).

2 =**black-crowned night heron.**
1925 (1928) Forbush *Birds MA* 1.336, *Black-crowned Night Heron. Other names:* Quawk; *Buttermunk.* **1955** *MA Audubon Soc. Bulletin* 39.312, *Black-crowned Night Heron* . . . Buttermunk (N.H., Mass. Apparently by corrupt transfer from the American Bittern, which is called Butter-bump.).

‡**butterneck squash** n
Perh a summer crookneck squash.
1969 *DARE* (Qu. I23, . . *Kinds of squash*) Inf **NY**162, Buttercut [sic], butterneck — the two best kinds, very common.

butternose coot n Also *butternose* [See quot 1955]
=**scoter.**
1888 Trumbull *Names of Birds* 107, *Oidemia americana* . . . In Massachusetts at Pigeon Cove (Cape Ann), *Butter-nose.* **1925** (1928) Forbush

Birds MA 1.271, *Oidemia americana . . . Scoter. Other Names: . .*
Butternose. **1955** *MA Audubon* 39.377, *American Scoter [Oidemia americana] . . .* Butter-nose (Mass.); Butter-nose Coot (R.I. [The bill of the male is yellow at base]). **1982** Elman *Hunter's Field Guide* 237, *American Scoter . . . Common & Regional Names: . .* butter-nose.

butternut n

1 also *butternut tree:* Std: a large nut-bearing timber tree *(Juglans cinerea).* Also called **buttnut, filnut, lemon nut, oilnut, white walnut**

2 =**cypress spurge.**

1892 *Jrl. Amer. Folkl.* 5.102 **ME**, *Euphorbia Cyparissias* [sic], butternut.

3 freq attrib: A brown dye color made from an extract of **butternut 1**; homespun fabric colored with such a dye. **esp S Midl** *old-fash*

1810 *Thomas' MA Spy or Worcester Gaz.* (MA) 21 Feb 2/3 neNY, Two pair home-made pantaloons, the one dark colored the other light butternut. **1848** (1870) Drake *Pioneer Life* 74 **KY**, My equipments were a substantial suit of butternut-linsey, a wool hat. **1863** Gilmore *S. Friends* 106 **NC**, He was dressed in a suit of "butternut homespun." **1883** *Harper's Mag.* 67.626/2 **NC, SC**, A big young fellow in butternut flannel appeared. **1893** Frederic *Copperhead* 163 **nNY**, The cooper looked in a puzzled way at the huge butternut-yarn stockings. **1903** *DN* 2.308 **seMO**, *Butternut-color . . .* A home-made dye made from white-walnut or butternut leaves. The color is yellowish brown. In the olden times it was the favorite dye for coloring home-made jeans. **1907** *DN* 3.229 **nwAR**. **1912** Crumpton *Adventures* 110 **AL** (as of 1862), They were all dressed in butternut jeans. **1916** Howells *Leatherwood God* 11 **OH**, His hickory shirt and his butternut trousers held up by a single suspender. **1982** *Greenfield Recorder* (MA) 23 Oct 7 (as of c1900), Those discarded black bark shells were not wasted! They made a dark brown dye of them. It was a "fast" color (didn't fade) and was commonly used to color the men's linen work shirts and pants—hence the name "butternut jeans."

4 pl: Work clothes made from fabric dyed with **butternut 3**. **esp S Midl**

1892 *DN* 1.235 **cwMO**, *Butternuts.* The popular name for overalls of a butternut brown. **1895** *DN* 1.385 **cwMO**, *Butternuts.* **1905** *DN* 3.393 **nwAR**, *Butternuts . . .* Overalls of a butternut brown. **1953** Randolph *Down in Holler* 231 **Ozarks**, *Butternuts . . .* Brown overalls or work clothes. **1954** *Harder Coll.* **cwTN**.

5 See quot.

1935 *AmSp* 10.170 [PaGer], *Butternut.* A Brazil nut or niggertoe.

butter-nut horn See **butter horn**

butter onion n

Perh a bunching onion such as *Allium fistulosum.*

1966 *DARE* FW Addit NH11, Butter onions—small onions used in pickling.

butter pea n **Sth, Midl**

Perh a plant of the genus *Phaseolus,* but see quots.

1965–70 *DARE* (Qq. I14–18, 20) Infs AR52, FL9, GA8, 17, 28, IN57, MS59, 63, SC32, Butter pea(s); AL11, Butter peas—smaller than limas or butter beans; AL30, Butter peas—like an English pea, but when shelled look like butter beans; hard to shell; GA9, Butter peas—rounder than a butter bean, smaller; GA81, Butter pea—smaller, not as flat [as butter bean]. **1970** *DARE* FW Addit VA42, Butter peas—a pea similar to a lima bean, but very fat.

butterprint n [See quot 1889] **esp N Cent**

=**velvetleaf 1.**

1872 IL Dept. Ag. *Trans. for 1871* ix, The Indian Mallow (*Abutilon Avacennæ* [sic]) . . [is] variously known as "stamp weed," "velvet leaf," "butter print." **1889** *Century Dict.,* Butter-print . . . The name alludes to the large round seed-capsule, which is neatly marked above with radiating furrows. **1900** Lyons *Plant Names* 8, *A[butilon] Abutilon . . .* Butter-print. **1967** *DARE* Tape IA10, They's some of them butterprint, too. There're little seeds in 'em, they're round and . . they get dry, they shatter out. **1968–70** *DARE* (Qu. S21, . . *Other weeds . . that are a trouble in gardens and fields*) Infs IL143, IN30, OH69, Butterprint; IL62, Velvet-leaf or butter-print—a great big leaf, the seed part is shaped like an old-fashioned butter mold. **1970** Correll *Plants TX* 1041, Butterprint.

butter rose n

A **buttercup 1** (here: *Ranunculus acris*).

1935 Muenscher *Weeds* 243, *Ranunculus acris . . .* Butter-rose. **1959** Carleton *Index Herb. Plants* 21, *Butter Rose:* Ranunculus acris.

butter sawfish n [*butter* prob refers favorably to quality as a food fish]

Perh a fish of the family Pristidæ.

1969 *DARE* (Qu. P1, . . *Fresh water fish . . that are good to eat*) Inf IN58, Butter sawfish.

butter skin n [*butter* + **skin**] Cf **buckskin 3, butter money,** and *DS* U26, U28a,b,c

c1960 *Wilson Coll.* **csKY**, *Butter skin . . .* Slang name for money, esp. a bill.

butter snipe n

=**Wilson's snipe.**

1956 *AmSp* 31.187 **IL, ID**, *Butter-snipe . . .* the common snipe.

butter teeth n Also *bread-and-butter teeth, butter bean teeth*
Buck teeth.

1965–70 *DARE* (Qu. X12, *Large front teeth that stick out of the mouth*) Infs AL10, IN13, OH40, OK42, SC10, Butter teeth; IL143, Bread-and-butter teeth; GA59, Butter bean teeth.

butter tub, sit in a v phr For varr see quots **NEast**
To have good fortune.

1916 *DN* 4.336 **Nantucket MA**, *Sit in the butter tub . . .* To have a piece of good luck; esp. to marry well. **1968–69** *DARE* (Qu. CC11, *When somebody has had a lot of good luck, you say he _____*) Inf NY123, Fell in the butter tub; CT16, Is sitting in the butter tub; (Qu. AA15c, . . *Joking ways . . of saying that a woman is getting married . . "She _____."*) Inf NY126, Set herself in a butter tub.

butterweed n [*butter* usu in ref to yellow color of flowers]

1 =**horseweed 1.**

1837 Darlington *Flora Cestrica* 471, *Canadian Erigeron. Vulgò*—Horse-weed. Butter-weed. **1876** Hobbs *Bot. Hdbk.* 17, Butter weed, Canada fleabane, Erigeron Canadense. **1937** (1963) Hyatt *Kiverlid* 79 **KY**, We picked wild mustard . . an' dandelion an' butter-weed—an' I don't know what all. **1965** Teale *Wandering Through Winter* 244 **KY**, Here in the rich soil the horseweed . . or butterweed . . . *Leptilon canadense . .* had attained its maximum growth.

2 Any of several **ragworts.**

1845 (1849) Phelps *Lectures on Botany* App 166/1 *(DAE),* Senecio lobata, butter-weed. **1936** McDougall *Plants of Yellowstone* 135, Arrowleaf butterweed (*Senecio triangularis*) . . . Serra butterweed (*Senecio serra*). **1959** Carleton *Index Herb. Plants* 21, *Butter Weed:* Abutilon theoprasti [sic]; Erechtites hieracifolia; Erigeron canadensis; Lactuca canadensis; Senecio (v). **1963** Craighead *Rocky Mt. Wildflowers* 225, *Senecio integerrimus . . . Other names:* Squaw-weed, Butterweed, Ragwort. **1972** Brown *Wildflowers LA* 216, *Butterweed. Senecio glabellus . . .* The color of a few scattered plants is conspicuous, but does not compare to the sheet of gold when one sees acres of them in bloom.

3 =**velvetleaf 1.**

1892 *Jrl. Amer. Folkl.* 5.93 **IL**, *Abutilon Avicennæ,* butter-weed.

4 A **wild lettuce** (here: *Lactuca canadensis*).

1896 *Jrl. Amer. Folkl.* 9.192, *Lactuca Canadensis . .* butter weed, wild lettuce, Sulphur Grove, Ohio. **1959** [see **2** above].

5 A **fireweed** (here: *Erechtites hieracifolia*).

1940 Clute *Amer. Plant Names* 81, *E. hieracifolia . . .* Butter-weed. **1959** [See **2** above].

6 =**butter-and-eggs 1.**

1966 *DARE* (Qu. S11, . . *Other names . . for . . wild snapdragon*) Inf GA2, Butterweed.

7 =**dandelion.**

1969 *DARE* (Qu. S11, . . *Other names . . for . . dandelion*) Inf KY40, Butterweed—old-fashioned.

buttery n Usu |ˈbʌtri|, occas |ˈbʌtəⁱ| Pronc-sp *buttry* **Nth, esp NEng** See Map *old-fash*

A pantry or larder.

1654 in 1916 MA (Colony) Probate Court (Essex Co.) *Records* 1.164, In the shop Kitching & buttery. **1894** Frederic *Marsena* 206 **nNY**, Take the lamp, run to the buttery, and bring the bottle. **1901** *DN* 2.137 **NY**,

Buttery . . . In Washington Co., N.Y., still used distinctively to denote the provision room, while pantry denotes the utensil room. In Otsego Co. and Seneca Co., buttery is used for both, and pantry is rarer. **1903** *DN* 2.296 **seMA,** *Buttery* [bʌtri] . . . Pantry. **1903** *DN* 2.350 **NY, seIA,** *Buttery* [bʌtrɨ]. **1922** (1926) Cady *Rhymes VT* 81, Your wife the whole affair has seen / Behind the buttery winder screen. **1937** Sandoz *Slogum* 223 **NE** (as of 1900–20), The woman . . called back something about an apple cake in the buttery. **1941** *LANE* Map 344, [*Buttery* is widespread throughout NEng, usu pronounced ['bʌtrɨ]]. **1965–70** *DARE* (Qu. D8, *The small room next to the kitchen (in older houses) where dishes and sometimes foods are kept*) 45 Infs, **esp NEng,** Buttery [usu pronc ['bʌtri], occas ['bʌtɚi]]. [Of all Infs responding to the question, 71% were old; of those giving this response 91% were old. 19 Infs labeled the word "old-fashioned."] **1970** *AmSp* 45.65, In large sections of rural New England, upstate New York, and northern Pennsylvania the pantry is commonly called the *buttry* . . . The term . . has been lost in the American Midland and South, but survives in the New England settlement area. **1973** Allen *LAUM* 1.170 **Upper MW,** The 5 active users of *buttry* in Iowa and the one in Minnesota are complemented by a large number in a more extended area who remember the term but consider it old-fashioned and out-of-date. **1979** *UpCountry* 1.38 **ME,** My grandmother brought water and towel from the buttery and washed my hands.

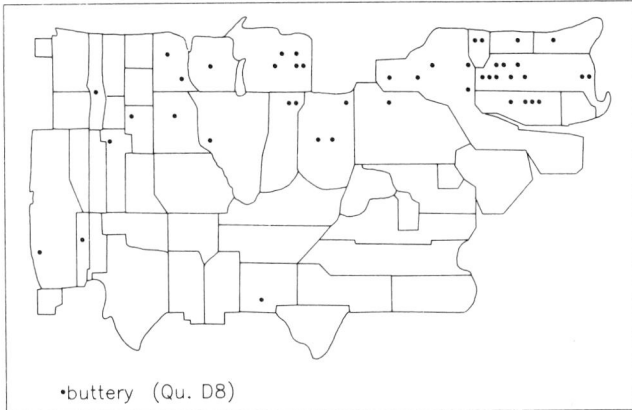

•buttery (Qu. D8)

butt fiend n
A heavy smoker.
1967–69 *DARE* (Qu. DD9a, . . *Expressions . . used about a person who smokes a great deal. "He's a ———."*) Infs **MA**1, 7, 19, **NH**18, Butt fiend.

butt-head n, hence adj *butt-headed*   **chiefly S Atl, AL**   See Map   Cf **muley**
A cow (or less freq a goat or deer) that has no horns.
1908 *DN* 3.295 **eAL, wGA,** *Butt-head* . . . A muley cow, a cow or bull without horns. Often given as a name to such a cow. **1909** *DN* 3.351 **eAL, wGA,** *Butt-headed* . . . Having no horns. **1938** Rawlings *Yearling* 314 **FL,** He'll [=a fawn] be butt-headed 'till summer. *Ibid* 380, The bucks is sheddin' their horns right now. They'll be butt-headed all through the spring. **1946** *PADS* 6.8 **eNC,** *Butt-headed* . . . Hornless; applied to cattle. **1965–70** *DARE* (Qu. K12, *A cow that has never had horns*) 48 Infs, **chiefly S Atl, AL,** Butt-headed; 21 Infs, **chiefly S Atl, AL,**

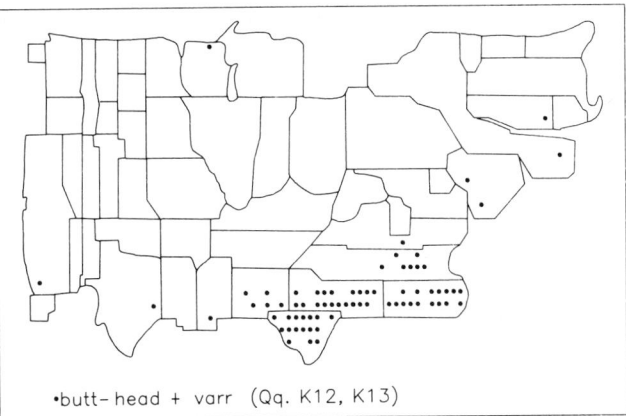

•butt-head + varr (Qq. K12, K13)

Butt-head; **FL**17, **GA**22, 87, Butt-headed cow; (K13, *A cow that has had her horns cut off)* Infs **FL**27, 48, Butt-headed. **1966** *DARE* Tape **FL**36, If they was buttheads, you'd rope around the neck. **1969** *SC Market Bulletin* 9 Jan 2, Want—Nubian buck, butt headed.

butt-headed adj **chiefly S Atl**
1 See **butt-head.**
2 Stubborn.
1909 *DN* 3.51 **eAL, wGA,** *Butt-headed* . . . Headstrong, obstinate, bull-headed. **1966** *DARE* (Qu. GG18, *Other words meaning 'obstinate.'*) Infs **MS**5, **SC**10, 11, Butt-headed.
3 Of a goat: inclined to butt or strike with the head.
1967–68 *DARE* (Qu. K68, . . *A goat that habitually strikes people with its horns*) Infs **GA**68, **TX**35, **SC**63, Butt-headed.
4 See quot.
1965 Will *Okeechobee Boats* 130 **FL,** Bernice was 64 feet 11 inches long, butt headed (square bowed to you).

buttie See **butty** n[1]

butting See **button A**

butting-line n [Aphet form of *abutting* + *line* boundary]
1948 Hurston *Seraph* 38 **wFL** [Turpentine collecting], The limit of a "drift," a territory of one chipper, is known as the "butting-line or block."

buttinsky n [*butt in* to meddle + *-sky*]
1 also sp *buttinski,* also *butterinsky:* One who interferes; a meddler.
1902 Ade *Girl Proposition* 70 *(OEDS),* The friend belonged to the Buttinsky Family and refused to stay on the Far Side of the Room. **1903** *Cincinnati Enquirer* 9 May 13/2 *(DA),* Piker . . a cheap grafter; a noser; a butterinsky. **1912** Raine *Brand Blotters* 156 **AZ,** You're making a heap of formality out of this, Mr. Buttinsky. **1914** *DN* 4.208, *Buttinski,* meddler. **1919** *DN* 5.64 **NM,** *Buttinski,* one who interferes. **1922** Lewis *Babbitt* 252, If you think I'm a buttinsky, then I'll just butt in. **1950** *WELS* (*Someone who joins you or your group without being asked, and won't leave*) 16 Infs, **WI,** Buttinsky; *(Somebody who is always meddling)* 4 Infs, Buttinsky. **1963** Mencken–McDavid *Amer. Lang.* 256, Along with it [=*-heimer*] came *-sky* or *-ski,* as in *allrightsky, buttinski,* and *damfoolski,* but of these only *buttinski* shows any sign of surviving. **1965–70** *DARE* (Qu. II18, *Someone who joins himself on to you and your group without being asked and won't leave*) 111 Infs, **widespread,** Buttinsky; (GG36a, *The kind of person who is always poking into other people's affairs: "She's an awful ———."*) 21 Infs, **scattered,** Buttinsky; (Qu. Y9) Inf **MO**17, Buttinsky; (Qu. GG39) Inf **NY**70, Buttinsky; (Qu. HH26) Inf **NE**1, Buttinsky; (Qu. II22) Inf **NM**6, He's a buttinsky. [Of all Infs responding to these questions, 53% were female; of those giving this response, 64% were female.]
2 A goat that butts. *joc*
1950 *WELS* (*A goat that habitually strikes people with its horns*) 1 Inf, **seWI,** Buttinsky. **1968–69** *DARE* (Qu. K68) Infs **CA**111, **UT**8, Buttinsky.

‡**buttle** n [Engl dial *buttle* to pour out drink]
A tap, spigot.
1970 *DARE* (Qu. F15, *What you turn to let the vinegar or cider run out of a barrel*) Inf **MA**124, Buttle ['bʌtəl].

butt naked adj **Cf bum naked, buck naked**
Completely nude.
1966–70 *DARE* (Qu. W20, *If somebody has no clothes on at all—for example, "There was Johnny,———." or, "They went in swimming ———."*) Infs **AR**15, **NY**237, Butt naked; **MI**72, Butt nekkid. [2 of 3 Infs Black]

buttnut n Also sp *butnut*
=**butternut 1.**
1897 Sudworth *Arborescent Flora* 108, *Juglans cinerea* . . . Common names: . . Buttnut (N.J.). **1922** (1926) Cady *Rhymes VT* 15, And then you sight the butnut tree / And up beyond, the ledges. *Ibid* 90, The butnuts grow tremendous sound, And every sore thumb knows it. **1931–33** *LANE Worksheets* 3 infs, **nw, csCT,** Buttnut . . . Butternut.

buttock down v phr
1972 Cooper *NC Mt. Folkl.* 90, Buttock down—sit down.

button n Usu |'bʌtn, 'bʌʔn|, rarely |'bʌtɪŋ| See Pronc Intro 3.I.20   Pronc-sp *butting*   Cf **-ing**

A Forms.

1922 *DN* 5.135, *Butting* for *button.* **1940** *AmSp* 15.371 **nePA,** Also, [t]> a very clear and emphatic [ʔ] before [l] and [n̩] . . . *Button* ['bʌʔn̩].

B Senses.

1 A young man, boy; an inexperienced or impertinent fellow. **West**

1915 *DN* 4.224 **wTX,** *Button* . . . A fresh fellow. "What a button he is!" **1936** McCarthy *Lang. Mosshorn* (Range Term) **West,** *Button* . . . A young fellow around an outfit. **1945** *AmSp* 20.306 **cwTX,** He was quite a button. (Quite a boy.) **1961** Adams *Old-Time Cowhand* 90 **TX,** The range-bred button (boy) never had a chance to go barefooted and let his feet spread. **1980** *DARE* File [Newspaper clipping], *Button* — a beginner who's trying to learn the skills of cowboying.

2 in var phrr: A game in which players try to guess whose hands hide a button.

a *button, button, who's got the button* and varr. **chiefly Nth, N Midl and West** See Map

1883 Newell *Games & Songs* 150, *Hold Fast My Gold Ring.* The children sit in a circle, with hands closed; one takes the ring, and goes around with it, tapping the closed fists of the players as if inserting the ring . . . Each child, in turn, is then required to guess who has the ring, and, if successful, takes the leader's place; if unsuccessful, he pays forfeit . . . This is known in Massachusetts as, Button, button, who's got the button? **1945** Boyd *Hdbk. Games* 81, *Button, button.* **1965–70** *DARE* (Qu. EE3, *Games in which you hide an object and then look for it*) 79 Infs, **Nth, N Midl, West,** Button, button, who's got the button; 20 Infs, **scattered Nth, N Midl, West,** Button, button; **CA**182, **IL**92, **PA**163, **VT**11, **VA**30, Button, button, where's the button; **PA**16, 165, Button, button, who has the button; (Qu. EE33) Inf **VA**78, Button, button, who has the button; **PA**134, Button, button, who's got the button; **NY**200, Button, button; (Qu. EE1) Inf **MA**6, Button, button; (Qu. EE4) Inf **NY**10, Button, button, who lost the button.

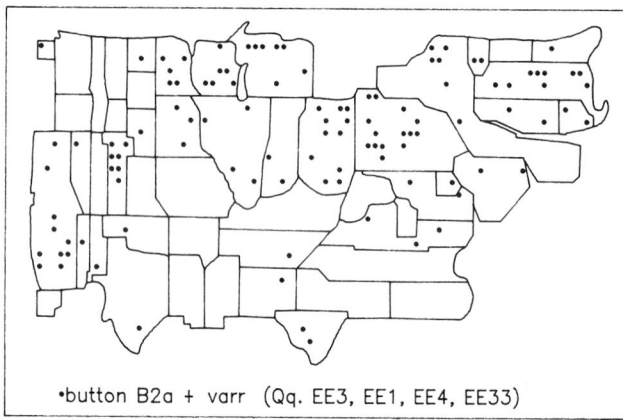

•button B2a + varr (Qq. EE3, EE1, EE4, EE33)

b *who's got the button.*

1965–70 *DARE* (Qu. EE3) 182 Infs, **widespread,** Who's got the button; (Qu. EE2) Inf **CA**82, Who's got the button; (Qu. EE33) Inf **SC**24, Who's got the button.

c *hide the button* and var. **chiefly Nth, N Midl** See Map

1965–70 *DARE* (Qu. EE3) 51 Infs, Hide the button; **NC**22, Hiding the button.

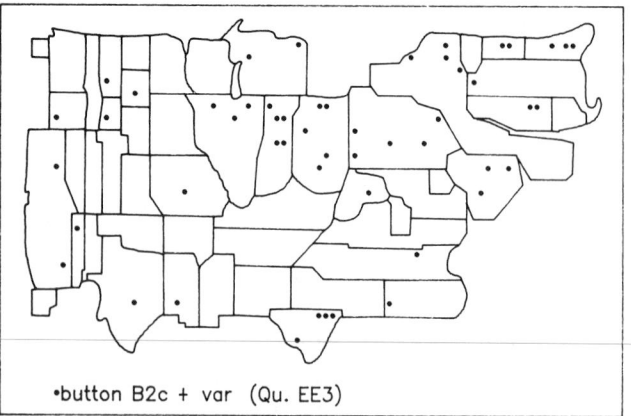

•button B2c + var (Qu. EE3)

d other phrr.

1965–70 *DARE* (Qu. EE3) Infs **NY**220, **OR**1, **RI**3, Find the button; **FL**10, **OK**1, Drop the button; **TX**33, Hunt the button; (Qu. EE1) Inf **WI**18, Pass the button; (Qu. EE33) Inf **MS**73, Pass the button.

3 pl: One's wits, brains. **chiefly Nth, N Midl** See Map

1949 *NYT Book Rev.* 25 Sept 14, Whether you have all your buttons. **1960** Wentworth–Flexner *Slang* 82, *Button(s) missing, have a (few)* to be crazy; to be eccentric. *Colloq. Also common in Eng.* **1965–70** *DARE* (Qu. HH5, *Someone who is queer but harmless*) 21 Infs, **Nth, N Midl,** Doesn't (don't) have all his buttons; **NY**105, Hasn't got all his buttons; **TX**101, Lost his buttons; **NE**3, Not a full row of buttons; (Qu. HH3, *A dull and stupid person*) Inf **NY**137, Hasn't got all his buttons; (Qu. HH4, *Someone who has odd or peculiar notions*) Infs **NJ**18, **NY**219, Doesn't (don't) have all his buttons; (Qu. HH6, *Someone who is out of his mind*) Infs **IA**17, **VA**33, Hasn't (got) all his buttons; **DE**3, **NJ**33, Lost (all) his buttons. **1983** *DARE* File **neNJ,** "She doesn't have all her buttons" . . . Less intelligent than average.

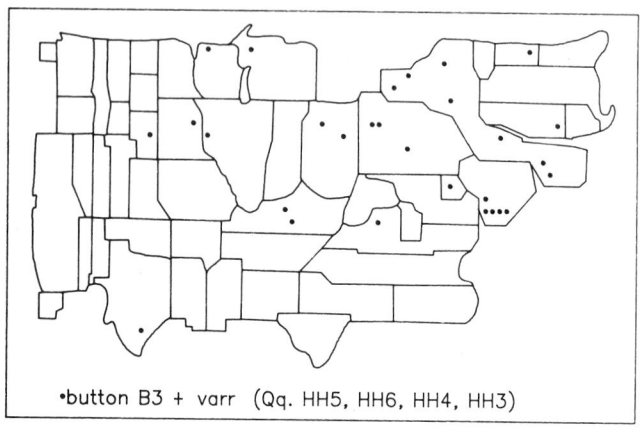

•button B3 + varr (Qq. HH5, HH6, HH4, HH3)

‡**4** The hull of a strawberry. Cf **butt** n¹ 3

1968 *DARE* (Qu. I47) Inf **GA**23, Button.

‡**5** The rump of a chicken.

1968 *DARE* (Qu. K73, *. . Rump of a cooked chicken*) Inf **MD**13, Button.

buttonball n Also *buttonball tree* [From the spherical fruit, which resembles a type of button] **chiefly NEast** See Map =**sycamore;** also its fruit.

1821 *MA Hist. Soc. Coll.* 2 ser. 9.153 **VT,** Button-ball tree. **1897** Sudworth *Arborescent Flora* 206, *Platanus occidentalis* . . . Buttonball Tree (Mass., R.I., Conn., N.Y., N.J., Pa, Del., Miss., La., Mo., Ill., Iowa, Mich., Nebr., Ohio). Buttonball (R.I., N.Y., Pa., Fla.) . . . *Platanus racemosa* . . . Buttonball Tree (Cal.). Buttonball (Cal.). **1931–33** LANE *Worksheets,* 4 infs, **CT,** Buttonball (tree) — sycamore tree. **1949** Kurath *Word Geog.* 77, *Button ball* is current in a well-defined area extending from eastern Connecticut to the Finger Lakes in New York State . . . The term is also used in the environs of Philadelphia by the side of *button wood.* **1950** WELS (Sycamore) 1 Inf, **ceWI,** Buttonball. **1965–70** *DARE* (Qu. T13, *. . Other names . . for . . sycamore*) 61 Infs, **chiefly east of Missip R, esp NEast,** Buttonball; (Qu. T15) Inf **NJ**6, Buttonball; (Qu. T16) Inf **CT**23, Buttonball tree. **1970** Tarpley *Blinky*

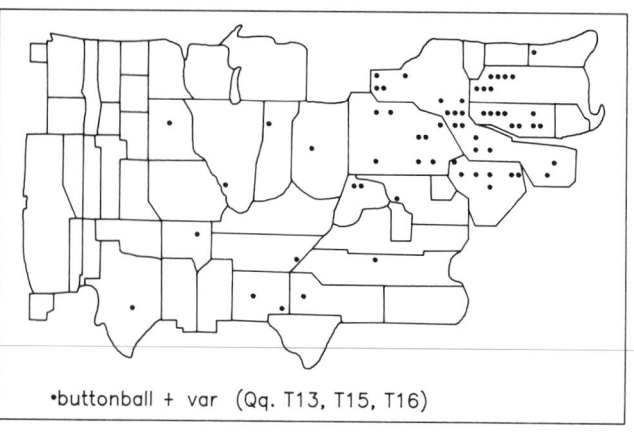

•buttonball + var (Qq. T13, T15, T16)

63, Only one Northeast Texan—a man who reads a great deal—offers *buttonball* as a synonym for *sycamore*. **1971** GA Dept. Ag. *Farmers Market Bulletin* 19 May 8/1, The sycamore tree .. with its massive mottled trunk and "button balls" swinging high in the air.

buttonball bush n
=**buttonbush 1.**
  1951 Teale *North Spring* 84 **FL**, Buttonball and elderberry bushes were crowded together in clumps on some of the islands.

buttonball tree See buttonball

buttonburr n [From the shape]
=**cockleburr 1** (here: *Xanthium strumarium*).
  1900 Lyons *Plant Names* 398, *Xanthium strumarium* . . . Buttonbur.

buttonbush n
1 A much-branched shrub *(Cephalanthus occidentalis),* usu under 10 feet tall, with globose white flower clusters. Also called **bottlebush, buckbrush 3e, buttonball bush, button flower 1, button tree 3, button willow, buttonwood 2, crane willow, crooked wood, crouper bush, elbow brush, globeflower, honeyball, little snowball, pinball, pond dogwood, river bush, Spanish pincushion, swamp dogwood, swamp sycamore, swampwood**
  1754 in 1934 Eliot *Field Husbandry* 124 **CT**, There was not the same Success attending the cutting these Button Bushes as the other Sorts. **1911** (1916) Porter *Harvester* 226 **IN**, "Which bush .. relieved the poor souls scorching with fever?" . . . "Buttonbush, because those balls resemble round buttons. Aren't they peculiar? See how waxy and gracefully cut and set the leaves are." **1968** *DARE* Wildfl QR Pl.210 Inf**NY**91, Button bush. **1976** Bruce *How to Grow Wildflowers* 189, Another common but interesting native is *Cephalanthus occidentalis,* Button Bush, often a neat, globular bush with long, ovalish deep green leaves and perfectly spherical heads of fuzzy white flowers.

‡2 = **sycamore.**
  1967 *DARE* (Qu. T13, *. . Other names . . for . . sycamore*) Inf **OH**16, Buttonbush.

button clover n
A **burr clover** (here: *Medicago orbicularis*).
  1970 Correll *Plants TX* 805, *Medicago orbicularis . . . Button clover . . .* Pod prickleless, flattened and tightly coiled into 5 or 6 spirals.

button daisy n
A **black-eyed Susan 2** or a similar composite plant.
  1967 *DARE* (Qu. S7) Inf **HI**11, Button daisy—white; **OH**33, Button daisy.

button factory, one o'clock at the phr For varr see quot
  1965–70 *DARE* (Qu. W24c, *Sayings to warn a man that his trouser-fly is open*) 15 Infs, **scattered,** One o'clock at the button factory; **TX**28, One o'clock in the button factory; **AR**33, Something o'clock at the button factory.

button flower n
1 =**buttonbush 1.**
  1819 Thomas *Travels* 222 *(DA)*, I noticed the following vegetables growing indigenously, near the Wabash, between Vincennes and Fort Harrison . . . *Cephalanthus occidentalis* button flower.

2 =**Canada anemone.**
  1966 *DARE* Wildfl QR Pl.67 Inf **MI**31, Button flower—colloquial; field anemone.

‡button-head n Cf butt-head
  1968 *DARE* (Qu. K13, *A cow that has had her horns cut off*) Inf **LA**22, Button-head.

buttonhole n joc
1 The navel. **chiefly S Midl**
  1965–70 *DARE* (Qu. X34, *. . The navel*) 10 Infs, **chiefly S Midl,** Buttonhole.
2 The buttocks.
  1965–68 *DARE* (Qu. X35, *. . The part of the body that you sit on*) Infs **OK**11, **WV**7, Buttonhole.

buttonhole cousin n Also buttonhole connection, ~ relation Cf shirt-tail relation
A distant relative; a family friend.
  1913 *DN* 4.4 **ME**, *Buttonhole connection* or *relation . . .* A person but

slightly or remotely related. **1959** *VT Hist.* new ser 27.128, Buttonhole cousin. Distant cousin, not highly esteemed. Occasional [usage]. **1969** *DARE* (Qu. Z7, *Words for any other relatives*) Inf **NY**165, Buttonhole cousin. **1975** Gould *ME Lingo* 30, *Buttonhole relation*—A third or fourth cousin, at least; somebody distantly related but not close enough to bother about. Sometimes a family friend who is no kin at all, but is held dear. Similar to *woodpile cousin.*

‡buttonholes for the ice cream n
=**cat's fur to make kitten britches.**
  1968 *DARE* (Qu. NN12b, *Things that people say to put a child off when he asks, "What are you making?"*) Inf **PA**175, Buttonholes for the ice cream.

button mangrove See buttonwood 3

button pepper n
Perh a cherry pepper *(Capsicum annuum).*
  1965 *DARE* (Qu. I22b) Inf **FL**18, Button peppers—small and round, just like a button.

button rattlesnake-root See button snakeroot 1

buttonrod n [See quot 1975]
=**pipewort.**
  1933 Small *Manual SE Flora* 257, *Eriocaulon . . . Button-rods.* **1969** *Milwaukee Jrl.* (WI) 19 Jan "Picture Journal" 8 **nFL**, He .. described the large cell structure in the onionlike leaves of the buttonrod or pipewort plant. **1975** Duncan–Foote *Wildflowers SE* 240, *Buttonrods . . .* Members of this genus are conspicuous when in flower because of the dense white heads of flowers, "buttons," on the tip of leafless stems.

button sagebrush n Also button sage [From the buttonlike, clustered flower heads]
=**bud sagebrush.**
  1931 U.S. Dept. Ag. *Misc. Pub.* 101.172, Button sage(brush) . . . is a low rounded aromatic prickly or spiny twigged shrub.

button scale n
  1968 *DARE* Tape **GA**48A, Button scale . . . is a scale in the [alligator] hide . . . [it will] turn into .. hard bone.

buttons, give one the v phr Cf DS AA11, 12, 13
=**mitten, give one the.**
  1954 *Harder Coll.* **cwTN**, Give one the buttons . . . 1. to stop seeing someone; 2. to refuse to marry.

button snakeroot n
1 also *button rattlesnake-root:* =**blazing star 3.** [See quot 1949]
  1775 Adair *Amer. Indians* 156 **S Atl**, A thick whip, . . composed of plaited silk grass, and the fibres of the button snake-root stalks. *Ibid* 160, This purifying physic, is warm water highly imbittered with button-rattle-root, which . . they apply only to religious purposes. **c1800** in 1848 GA Hist. Soc. *Coll.* 3.1.79, Every new moon, he drinks for four days the possau, (button snakeroot,) an emetic. **1837** Darlington *Flora Cestrica* 449, *Spiked Liatris. Vulgo*—Blue Blazing Star. Button Snakeroot . . . The *root* of this handsome plant is a popular medicine. **1876** Hobbs *Bot. Hdbk.* 17, Button snake root, Water eryngo, Eryngium aquaticum. Button snake root, Liatris spicata. **1949** Moldenke *Amer. Wild Flowers* 216, Closely related are the *blazingstars . . . Liatris,* also known as *buttonsnakeroots* because of their globular basal tubers and the fact that herb doctors formerly thought them useful in the treatment of snakebites. **1970** Correll *Plants TX* 1539, *Button-snakeroot . . .* Perennial herbs from underground corms.

2 A plant of the genus *Eryngium.* [See quots 1830, 1972] Also called **button thistle 2, coyote thistle, rattlesnake master** For other names of var spp see **corn snakeroot, false thistle, Mexican thistle, purple thistle**
  1830 Rafinesque *Med. Flora* 218, *Eryngium,* L. Button Snakeroot . . . Said to be the best cure for rattle snake bites. **1876** [see **1** above]. **1901** Mohr *Plant Life AL* 643, *Eryngium yuccifolium . . .* Button Snakeroot . . . The root .. is used medicinally. **1936** IL Nat. Hist. Surv. *Wildflowers* 215, The . . . Button Snakeroot is common in open places in all prairie portions of the state. **1972** Brown *Wildflowers LA* 124, *Button Snake-root . . .* Inflorescence .. with dense .. heads, globose to ovoid about ¾ inch in diameter.

button squash n
A **buttercup squash** *(Cucurbita maxima)* or similar squash.
  1967–68 *DARE* (Qu. I23) Inf **WI**47, Button squash; **PA**166, Button

squash—green, size of softball with a button where the blossom comes off; **TX3,** Button squash—white, round, about three inches across. [**1981** *Burpee Seeds* 137, *Fall and Winter Squash . . . Buttercup . . .* Blossom end has prominent "button."]

button thistle n

1 =**bull thistle** (here: *Cirsium vulgare*).

1900 Lyons *Plant Names* 81, [*Cirsium*] *lanceolatum* [=*C. vulgare*] . . . Button Thistle.

2 =**button snakeroot 2.**

1911 Jepson *Flora CA* 289, *Button-thistle . . .* Low places in valley fields and flats in the hills.

button tree n

1 =**sycamore.**

1751 (1972) Douglass *Summary* 2.213 **CT,** The Button Tree, or *Platanus Occidentalis,* is of a fine Parabolick Form fit for Avenues, but its verdure is of short Continuance, and the Tree is not long lived. **1859** (1968) Bartlett *Americanisms* 61, *Buttonwood* or *Button Tree.* (*Platanus occidentalis.*) The popular name, in New England, of the sycamore tree; so called from the balls it bears, the receptacle of the seeds, which remain on the trees during the winter. **1945** Saxon *Gumbo Ya-Ya* 170 **sLA,** Other things used for cure and prevention of illness included hair plant, button tree, . . angel's balm and mouse's eyes. **1968** *DARE* (Qu. T13, . . *Other names . . for . . sycamore*) Inf **VA15,** Button tree—old-fashioned.

2 =**white mangrove.** *obs*

1823 Vignoles *Observations Floridas* 52 **FL,** At Cape Sable . . are fresh water wells: these wells are distinguished by a tuft of button trees or white mangroves, being the only trees on the point.

3 =**buttonbush 1.**

1785 Marshall *Arbustrum* 30, *Cephalanthus occidentalis.* Button-tree This shrub grows pretty common by creek sides and ponds. **1815** Drake *Natural View Cincinnati* 76, The botanical resources of this . . *Forest of the Miami country* [include] . . . *Cephalanthus occidentalis Button tree.* **1900** Lyons *Plant Names* 90, Button tree.

buttonweed n

1 A plant of the genus *Diodia*. For other names of var spp see **Jacob's ladder, poor joe, poorland weed, povertyweed.**

1822 Eaton *Botany* 472, *Spermacoce . . . diodina . .* button weed. **1857** Gray *Manual of Botany* 171, *Spermacóce . . .* Button-weed. **1937** Stemen *OK Flora* 507, *Diodia teres . . .* Rough Button-weed . . . *Diodia virginia . . .* Large Button-weed. **1965–70** *DARE* (Qu. S21, . . *Other weeds*) 17 Infs **scattered, but esp N Cent, N Midl,** Buttonweed(s); (Qu. S26d) Inf **NJ69,** Button weed—color of a daisy, bitter as gall, three feet tall. [Note: some of these Infs may refer instead to **buttonweed 2.**] **1970** Correll *Plants TX* 1495. **1972** Brown *Wildflowers LA* 176, Buttonweed —*Diodia virginiana.*

2 =**velvetleaf 1.**

1892 *Jrl. Amer. Folkl.* 5.93, *Abutilon Avicennae . .* button-weed. Chestertown, Md. **1900** Lyons *Plant Names* 8, *Abutilon [avicennae*] . . . Buttonweed. **1936** IL Nat. Hist. Surv. *Wildflowers* 193, *Abutilon Theophrasti . . .* It is annual and has several names, such as Indian Mallow . . . Buttonweed and Pie Marker. **1967** *DARE* Tape IA1, [In a list of weeds that grow in corn:] Foxtail, mostly smartweeds, buttonweeds.

3 A knapweed (here: *Centaurea nigra*).

1900 Lyons *Plant Names* 89, *Centaurea nigra . . .* Button-weed.

4 A mallow (here: *Malva rotundifolia*).

1941 *Torreya* 41.49, *Malva rotundifolia . . .* Button-weed, Garret County, Md.

5 A bachelor's button.

1968 *DARE* (Qu. S11, . . *Other names . . for . . bachelor's button*) Inf **MD29,** Buttonweed.

button willow n [See quot 1897]

=**buttonbush 1.**

1897 Parsons *Wild Flowers CA* 98, *Button-Bush. Button-Willow . . .* Its leaves are willow-like, and its spherical flowerheads . . resemble small cushions filled with pins. **1901** *Torreya* 1.117, *Cephalanthus occidentalis . . .* Button-willow. **1966–67** *DARE* (Qu. S21 . . *Weeds . . that are a trouble in gardens and fields*) Inf **AR55,** Button willow; (Qu. T15, . . *Swamp trees*) Infs **OK52, PA11,** Button willow. **1967** *DARE* FW Addit **AR55,** Them little old button willows will just springle out [=sprout in various directions], a whole bunch in one wad. **1967** *DARE* Wildfl QR Pl. 210 Inf **TX34,** Button willow. **1970** Hyatt *Hoodoo* 1.422 **MS,** Well,

there's a little willow that grows about that big . . and it spreads all out—it's called button willow . . . [Hyatt:] *Cephalanthus occidentalis . . .* Probably button bush—unrelated to true willows.

buttonwood n

1 also *buttonwood tree:* =**sycamore.** [Prob for the buttonlike fruits, but see also quot 1982] **chiefly NEast** See Map

1674 in 1901 Cambridge MA *Records* 2.223, A button wood tree to make two beames of. **1833** Watson *Historic Tales Philadelphia* 85, Professor Kalm visited . . in 1748 . . . He describes the site as having on the river side in front of it a great number of very large sized water-beech or buttonwood trees; one of them, as a solitary way-mark to the spot, is still remaining there. **1907** *DN* 3.183 **seNH,** Buttonwood. **1940** Richter *Trees* 187 **sOH,** This here pied old buttonwood she had surely seen before. **1949** Kurath *Word Geog.* 76, *Button wood* is found in two separate areas: (1) in Eastern New England . . and (2) in Pennsylvania east of the Alleghenies together with the greater part of New Jersey. **1950** *WELS,* (Sycamore) 1 Inf, **cWI,** Buttonwood. **1965–70** *DARE* (Qu. T13, . . *Other names . . for sycamore*) 80 Infs, **chiefly NEast,** Buttonwood; (Qu. T15) Inf **FL13,** Buttonwood; (Qu. T16) Inf **NY213,** Buttonwood. **1982** *Smithsonian* June 14/3 **OH,** Professor Cassidy's bettywood tree might have been the sycamore (*Platanus occidentalis*), which the pioneers knew as buttonwood. Its fine-grained wood was used for buttons because it resisted splitting.

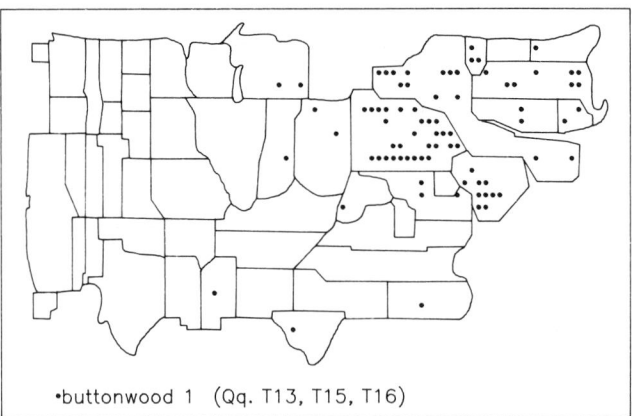

•buttonwood 1 (Qq. T13, T15, T16)

2 also *buttonwood bush,* ~ *shrub:* =**buttonbush 1.**

1802 Drayton *View of SC* 62, Button wood. (*Cephalanthus Occidentalis*). **1828** Rafinesque *Med. Flora* 100, *Cephalanthus occidentalis. English Name*—Button-wood Shrub. **1938** Rawlings *Yearling* 303 **nFL,** Penny dropped to his haunches behind a buttonwood bush. **1966** *DARE* Wildfl QR Pl.210 Inf **NH4,** Buttonwood.

3 also *button mangrove, silver buttonwood:* An evergreen tree (*Conocarpus erectus*) native to southern Florida which produces conelike rounded fruits. [See quot 1967] Also called **mangrove**

1884 Sargent *Forests of N. Amer.* 87, *Conocarpus erecta* [sic] . . . *Button Wood . . .* Wood very heavy and hard, . . burning slowly like charcoal, and highly valued for fuel. **1961** Douglas *My Wilderness* 130 **Everglades FL,** Within the first twelve inches of the sea, there are four zones where four species grow—the red mangrove at salt water's edge, next the black mangrove, then the white mangrove, and, highest of all, the buttonwood, long sought after for charcoal. **1967** Will *Dredgeman* 69 **FL,** In spite of its having been cut for charcoal for the past half century, there were still plenty of buttonwood trees . . . The globular fruit are supposed to resemble old fashioned shoe buttons. **1976** Fleming *Wild Flowers FL* 39, Buttonwood . . . The name refers to its purplish green, buttonlike fruits. **1979** Little *Checklist U.S. Trees* 95, *Conocarpus erectus . . . Button-mangrove . . . Other common names*—buttonwood, silver buttonwood. **1980** *DARE* File, On Longboat Key just off Sarasota, Florida, is a tree which people call *buttonwood.* There's also a Buttonwood Drive on the Key.

4 also *white buttonwood:* =**white mangrove.**

1884 Sargent *Forests of N. Amer.* 87, *Laguncularia racemosa . . . White Button Wood. White Mangrove . . .* Very common; saline shores of lagoons and bays. **1897** Sudworth *Arborescent Flora* 308, *Common Names.* White Buttonwood (Fla.). White Mangrove (Fla.). Buttonwood (Fla.). **1934** *Torreya* 34.138, The White Mangrove or White Buttonwood . . . is not a true mangrove and belongs to quite a different family. **1979** Little *Checklist U.S. Trees* 158, *White-mangrove . . . Other common names*—white buttonwood, buttonwood.

buttonwood bush, buttonwood shrub See **buttonwood 2**

buttonwood tree See **buttonwood 1**

buttony, buttony n [Cf *EDD* buttony sb.]
=**button B2.**
    1968–69 *DARE* (Qu. EE3, *Games in which you hide an object and then look for it*) Infs **PA**59, 224, Buttony buttony; **NJ**3, Buttony, buttony ['bʌtni], who's got the button? **NJ**9, Buttony, buttony ['bʌtni].

buttricks n [Euphem for *buttocks*]
    The buttocks.
    1966–69 *DARE* (Qu. X35, *Joking words for the part of the body that you sit on*) Inf **NH**6, Buttricks [bʌtrɪks]; **RI**4, Buttricks ['bʌtrɪks] "a clean name for it;" **TX**38, Buttricks.

buttry See **buttery**

butt the bull off the bridge See **buck a bull off the bridge**

butty n[1] Also sp *buttie* [*EDD* butty sb.[1] "A fellow-workman . . an intimate friend" 1790 →] **esp PA** See also **buddy n 2**
    Among miners: a partner; a helper.
    1878 Pinkerton *Molly Maguires* 125 **PA**, He must naturally begin at the bottom round of the ladder, and gradually, if at all, rise in the scale to the rating of a miner. It required time and hard work to reach that position. The place of "butty," or helper, even, was not so very easy of acquirement. **1921** *Nation* 113.400/1 **ME**, Beside that barrel there filled up with chips / I reeled, the happiest hours of my life, / I wouldn't say how many thousand blocks, / While Fred, my butty, plug-drilled and broke stone. **1929** *AmSp* 4.389, When I was a boy in the Pennsylvania coalfields, one of the commonest words in miners' speech was *butty*, or *buttie*, as I have always preferred to spell it, meaning work-fellow. In the cramped, underground honey-combs where bituminous coal is dug, the man with the pick and the man with the shovel are literally *butties*, working all day long buttock to buttock, or in the vulgar but comradely abbreviation, butt to butt. The word was used generally in a technical sense, without any endearing connotation of spiritual nearness. But the boys of the community thirty years ago adopted the word for the idea which later at school they were to express by *chum*. **1943** Korson *Coal Dust* 130 **PA**, Alone in his room or with a partner he called a "butty," he [the pick miner] worked without supervision except for inspections of his product on the tipple. **1968** Adams *Western Words* 48, *Butty.*

butty n[2] [*butt* + hypocoristic **-y**]
    1967 *DARE* (Qu. X35, *Joking words for the part of the body that you sit on*) Inf **CO**20, Butty.

buva lice See **bube lice**

buy a piece of the ground v phr *joc*
    To be bucked off a horse.
    1968 *DARE* FW Addit **LA**32, If you're riding a horse and fall off they say, "he bought a piece of the ground."

buy clothes for the baby, not to See **baby n 3**

buy cotton v phr
    To do nothing.
    1960 (1962) Lee *Mockingbird* 14 **AL**, I never knew how old Mr. Radley made his living—Jem said he "bought cotton," a polite term for doing nothing.

buy on one's face See **face, run one's**

buzz n[1] Also *buzzer, buzzy* [Hypocoristic var of *brother*] *somewhat old-fash*
    Used as a nickname for a brother.
    1950 *WELS* (Nicknames . . brother) 6 Infs, **WI**, Buzz; 2 Infs, Buzzy. **1967–69** *DARE* (Qu. Z5, . . *Words meaning "brother"*) Infs **KY**25, **LA**11, **MD**31, 49, **MN**30, 39, **PA**49, 131, Buzz; **CA**6, **WI**27, Buzzer; **MD**17, **MA**15, Buzzy. [11 of 12 Infs old]

buzz n[2] See **buss n**

buzz v Cf **buss v[1], n**
    To court.
    1928 *Ruppenthal Coll.* **KS**, To buzz . . (army) to have a date, to step out. **1941** *LANE* Map 404 **nNEng** (Courting), 5 infs, Buzzing. **1973** Allen *LAUM* 1.371 (He is courting her) 1 inf, **cwMN**, Buzzing her. [Inf notes that the word has been recently introduced in the community.]

buzzard n, also attrib **esp C Atl**
    In unofficial place names: see quot.

1965–70 *DARE* (Qu. C34, . . *Nearby settlements, villages, or districts*) Inf **DC**12, Buzzard Point; **NC**15, Buzzard Town; **MD**31, Buzzard's Glory . . in old days buzzards swarmed there; **NJ**31, Buzzard's Roost; (Qu. C35, *Different parts of your town or city*) Inf **LA**24, Buzzard Lane—old fashioned for Eagle Street; **GA**92, Buzzard Roost; **VA**47, Buzzard Swamp—old cattle-raising and butchering area—buzzards ate guts; **TN**11, Buzzard's Roost—old-fashioned for colored section; (Qu. II25, *The part of a town where the poorer people, special groups, or foreign groups live*) Inf **VA**31, Buzzard's Row.

buzzard bait n **esp S Midl**
    A thin, sickly animal.
    1905 *DN* 3.72 **nwAR**, *Buzzard-bait* . . . An emaciated horse. **1954** *Harder Coll.* **cwTN**, *Buzzard bait* . . . An animal that is ailing. **1965–66** *DARE* (Qu. K15, *A thin, bony, or poor-looking cow*) Inf **MS**60, Buzzard bait; (Qu. K44, *A bony or poor-looking horse*) Inf **AL**2, Buzzard bait.

buzzard-blow-'e-nose n Also *buzzard nose* Cf *DJE* John-Crow (Blow-) Nose
    A stinkhorn (prob *Mutinus caninus*).
    1950 *PADS* 14.18 **SC**, *Buzzard-blow-'e-nose* . . . The stinkhorn. **1966** *DARE* (Qu. S21, . . *Other weeds that are a trouble in gardens and fields*) Inf **FL**1, Coffee weeds, buzzard nose, and just weeds.

buzzard bread n Also *buzzard's bread*
    See quot 1950.
    1950 *PADS* 14.18 **SC**, *Buzzard bread* . . . The seed balls of the plane tree, also called sycamore. **1970** *DARE* (Qu. S15) Inf **SC**67, Buzzard's bread.

buzzard coot n
    =**surf scoter.**
    1956 *AmSp* 31.184 **MD, VA**, Buzzard coot . . . Surf scoter . . . From its black color and large size among ducks.

buzzard curlew n
    =**long-billed curlew.**
    1888 Trumbull *Names of Birds* 198, In New Jersey . . . *Long-billed Curlew;* at . . . Somers Point [NJ], *Buzzard Curlew* (its flight resembling that of a turkey-buzzard). **1955** *AmSp* 30.182 **NJ**, Buzzard curlew (the long-billed curlew . .) alludes to the skill of the species in soaring flight.

buzzard fly n
    =**black fly.**
    1968 *DARE* (Qu. R12) Inf **GA**25, Buzzard fly—same as black fly.

buzzard grass n
    1966 *DARE* (Qu. S9, *Other kinds of grass that are hard to get rid of*) Inf **FL**9, Buzzard grass.

buzzard lope n **chiefly Sth**
    1 also *buzzard dance, ~ flop*: A dance imitating the movements of a buzzard: see quot 1938. *esp among Black speakers*
    1890 *Standard Dict.* 24 Apr.*(DA)*, Buzzard Lope—'the latest social institution of America . . . a dance taught to a Georgian negro by the turkey buzzard.' **1908** *DN* 3.295 **eAL, wGA**, *Buzzard-lope* . . . A kind of breakdown dance. **1938** Burman *Blow for a Landing* 129 **MS** [Black], "Dance the buzzard dance, Iz," mumbled a black-bearded trapper, wearing a coonskin cap. The towering figure began to wheel in long, doleful circles. His arms became gaunt, flapping wings: his head swung jerkily from his cadaverous neck, peering, searching. **1942** (1965) Parrish *Slave Songs* 108 **GA coast**, Since 1915 I have known that such a dance as the Buzzard Lope could be found in the neighborhood of St. Simon's; but the Negroes of that section always told me it was done on some far-off island, such as St. Catherine's or Sapelo. **1954** *PADS* 21.23 **SC**, *Buzzard lope* . . . A dancing step. **1958** Randolph *Sticks* 9 **Ozarks**, The old man got to showing how he could do the Buzzard Flop, which is a kind of buck-and-wing dance. **1967** *DARE* Tape **TX**49, She [=Inf's wife] could do this step you call the buzzard lope . . . It comes from the niggers.
    2 By ext: an ungainly running gait.
    1952 Brown *NC Folkl.* 1.524 **c,eNC**, *Buzzard lope* . . . Running in an awkward, loose-jointed manner; to run in this fashion. **1956** McAtee *Some Dialect NC* 7, *Buzzard lope* . . . An awkward running gait.

buzzard nose See **buzzard-blow-'e-nose**

‡**buzzard religion** n
    1970 *DARE* (Qu. CC7, . . *A person who goes to church very seldom or not at all*) Inf **NC**87, Buzzard religion—comes for funerals.

buzzard roost n

1 See quot 1906.

1889 Twain *CT Yankee* 231, After suffocating body and mind . . in . . that intolerable old buzzard-roost. **1906** *DN* 3.129 **nwAR**, *Buzzard-roost* . . . A dilapidated building.

2 also *buzzard's roost:* The upper balcony of a theater. **chiefly Sth, S Midl, esp SC, TX** See Map Cf **chicken roost 1, crow's nest 4**

1965–70 *DARE* (Qu. D40, . . *Upper balcony in a theater*) 48 Infs, **chiefly SC, TX, OK, LA, MS**, Buzzard('s) roost.

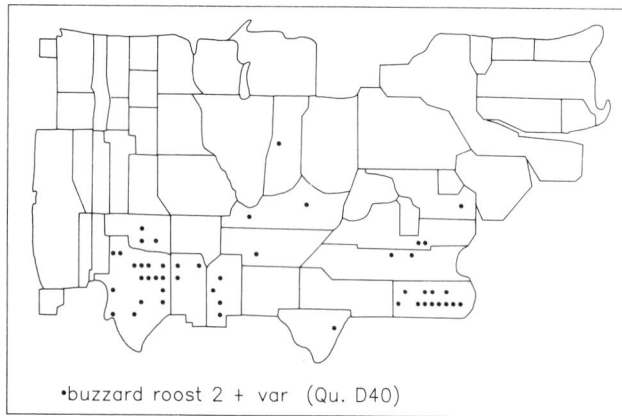

•buzzard roost 2 + var (Qu. D40)

3 See **buzzard** n **1**.

buzzard's bread See **buzzard bread**

buzzard's roost See **buzzard roost 2**

buzzard storm n Cf **blackbird storm**

1954 *Harder Coll.* **cwTN**, *Buzzard storm* . . . A period of very cold weather in spring.

buzzard talk, make v phr

1952 Brown *NC Folkl.* 1.524 **c,eNC**, *Buzzard talk, to make* . . . To quarrel.

buzzard-wing sweep n Also *buzzard sweep, ~ wing* **Sth, S Midl**

A type of plow: see 1970 quots.

1854 in 1927 Jones *FL Plantation Rec.* 575 **NY**, Buzzard Sweeps old patern [sic]. **1898** Lloyd *Country Life* 87 **AL**, Many a man can write big about the farmers and the farm, when at the same time he wouldn't know a bull-tongue scooter from a buzzard-wing sweep, or a stack of hay from a hornet's nest. **1970** *DARE* (Qu. L18, *Kinds of plows*) Inf **TN62**, Buzzard-wing sweep—wings like a bull-tongue, used for potatoes. **1970** *DARE* Tape **VA38**, [FW:] What is a sweep shaped like? [Inf:] Well, It has wings to it . . . old people used to call 'em buzzard wings. Well, it *was* shaped kinda like a buzzard wing. The main part of the plow was in the middle . . and the narrow [part] went on out on the end to go up under your plants. They called it buzzard wing.

buzz buggy, buzz-buzz See **buzz wagon**

buzzer n[1]

1 =**bull-roarer 1a.**

1980 *Foxfire* 6 195 **nGA**, We just called it a buzzer . . . Take a flat piece of this wood and tie a string to it and tie that to a stick and [swing it around and] it'll buzz. I reckon that string a'twistin'll make it roar . . . I've made them and about scared the dogs to death!

2 See quot.

1954 *Harder Coll.* **cwTN**, *Buzzer* . . . A mosquito.

3 also *buzz fly:* Perh a **deer fly.**

1966–69 *DARE* (Qu. R12, . . *Other kinds of flies*) Inf **NM6**, Buzzer; **IL58**, I call 'em buzzers; (Qu. R7) Inf **CA111**, Buzzers; (Qq. R13, 15a) Inf **MN33**, Buzz fly—the large black noisy one; **DE3**, Buzz flies.

buzzer n[2] See **buzz** n[1]

buzzer n[3] See **buzzy** n[2]

buzzer n[4] See **buss** n

buzz fly See **buzzer** n[1] **3**

buzz off v phr **Nth**

1a imper: Go away!

1946 Chandler *High Window* 75 **sCA**, Buzz off. **1960** Wentworth–Flexner *Slang* 83, *Buzz off* . . . To go away; to leave; specif., to beat it. *Usu. a command.* **1967–70** *DARE* (Qu. NN12a, *Things that people say to put a child off when he asks too many questions*) Inf **OH**71, Buzz off; (Qu. NN22b, *Expressions used to drive away children*) Infs **MI**118, **NH**18, **OH**84, Buzz off.

b Fig: to die.

1970 *DARE* (Qu. BB56, *Joking expressions for dying: "He _____."*) Inf **MA**122, Buzzed off.

2 imper: Shut up!

1960 Wentworth–Flexner *Slang* 83, *Buzz off* . . . To stop making noise; to be quiet, *Not common.* **1967–69** *DARE* (Qu. S10b, *To tell a person to stop talking—not very politely*) Infs **MA**2, **RI**15, Buzz off.

buzz tail n

A **rattlesnake.**

1970 *WI Conserv. Bulletin* Mar–April 21, Woody captured his first rattler at the ripe old age of 10. Each year he captures 200 to 300 buzz tails.

buzz wagon n Also *buss wagon, buzz buggy, buzz-buzz* Cf **clunk 1** and *DS* N5

A car, esp an old one.

1909 in 1919 Hale *Letters* 447 **csRI**, I heard of this tea through Weedens, who flew there in their buzz-buzz from Providence. **1914** *DN* 4.104 **KS**, *Buzz-wagon* . . . Automobile. **1915** *DN* 4.224 **wTX**, *Buzz-wagon* . . . Popular term for *automobile.* **1918** *DN* 5.23 **NW**, *Buzz-wagon* . . . A cheap automobile. **1919** *DN* 5.64 **NM**, *Buzz-buggy, -wagon,* an automobile. "The White family bought a new buzz-buggy last week." **1939** *LANE* Map 185 *(Automobile),* 1 inf, **seCT**, Buzz wagon. **1950** *WELS (An automobile)* 1 Inf, **seWI**, Buss wagon. **1960** Wentworth–Flexner *Slang* 83, *Buzz-buggy* . . . An automobile; an early model automobile, whether gas, steam, or electric powered. *Some c1915 use.*

buzzy n[1] See **buzz** n[1]

buzzy n[2] Also *bazzy, buzzer*

=**burdock 1** (here: *Arctium lappa*).

1896 *Jrl. Amer. Folkl.* 9.191, *Arctium Lappa* . . buzzies, Southold, L[ong] I[sland]. **1900** Lyons *Plant Names* 43, *A[rctium] Lappa* . . . Bazzies. **1968** *DARE* File **RI** (as of 1920s), Buzzy—a large round weed seed that clings to your clothing . . . This is the only word I know; *burr* is a book word. **1968** *DARE* (Qu. S13) Inf **NY**90, Buzzers.

by prep

1 To, at, in, into (the home or place of). [Cf *OED by* prep. 3 'at the house of' →1535, and Ger *bei*]

1895 *DN* 1.385 **wFL**, *By* (of a house): *into* or *to.* "Come by my house and stay all night" = not pass by, but stop at the house. **1905** *DN* 3.72 **nwAR**. **1911** *DN* 3.541 **NE**, *By* . . . Used in sense of *to.* **1923** *DN* 5.244 **LA**, Stop by my house. **1930** *DN* 6.84 **cSC**, *By* (in the expression come by my house—meaning stop at my house). **1935** Sandoz *Jules* 193 **wNE** (as of 1880–1930), "Where's Jules?" he asked. "I think he will be home soon. He is by Mintens' over on the hill." **1948** *AmSp* 23.109 **swIL**, I go *by* my house now. (To). **c1950** *WELS Suppl.* **csWI**, He went by the doctor's. *Ibid* **seWI**, Nagels were by your house last evening? **1981** *DARE* File **seWI**, *By* . . . Still used by those one generation removed from [those who use] German as a second language. It expresses the notion of "stop in to see" or "drop by to visit," e.g. "Did you go by grandma's today?"

2 With; in connection with; in the possession of.

1911 *DN* 3.541 **NE**, *By* . . . Used also in sense of *with,* "He was by my Eddie," chiefly by foreign settlers. **1923** *DN* 5.209 **swMO**, I've had this coat by me fer twenty year. **1966** *DARE* Tape **MI**35, They've done a lot by their houses. **1967–69** *DARE* (Qu. BB60, *When friends and relatives gather . . the night before the funeral, you call that*) Inf **NC**77, Sit up by him; (Qu. K10, *Words used about a cow that is going to have a calf*) Inf **TX**54, By calf; (Qu. NN10a, *Expressions . . used when you meet somebody you know quite well*) Inf **PA**50, So how goes it by you?

3 In the opinion of.

1938 *Sun* (Baltimore MD) 1 Sep 8/4 *(Hench Coll.),* [Headline:] Anything Roosevelt Says Or Does Is All Right By Him. **1965–70** *DARE* (Qu. GG21a, *If you don't care what a person does, you might tell him, "You can go ahead and do it _____."*) Infs **AR**52, **PA**57, **WA**1, (It's)

OK by me; (Qu.KK26, *Something that makes no difference at all to you:
"He can think what he likes, it _____ me."*) Infs **AZ**10, **LA**40, **NY**80,
209, **VA**11, **WI**13, (Is) OK by (me); (Qu. NN2, *Exclamations of very
strong agreement*) Inf **CA**21, OK by me.

4 in phr *by sun;* According to the position of the sun; hence,
before sunset; less freq, after sunrise. **chiefly Sth, S Midl**

1828 (1930) W. Sewall *Diary* 122/1 **ME,** Having settled up fairly with
every person, sat [sic] off about two hours by sun with my family and
moveables. **1886** *Amer. Philol. Assoc. Trans.* 17.45 **Sth,** *By sun* (as
hour by sun = before sunset). **1893** Shands *MS Speech* 22, *By sun* . . .
Negro and illiterate white for *before sunset.* Among the lower classes of
society, it is usual to reckon time by the sun; so "an hour or two hours, by
sun" . . means an hour or two hours before sunset. **1899** (1912) Green
VA Folk-Speech 232. **1903** *DN* 2.317 **seMO,** *Hour by sun* . . . An hour
before sunset. **1906** *DN* 3.119 **sIN.** **1908** *DN* 3.322 **eAL, wGA,** *Hour
by sun* . . . An hour before sunset or after sunrise. **1915** *DN* 4.227 **wTX,**
Hour by sun . . . An hour after sunrise or before sunset. **1917** *DN* 4.409
wNC, SC, KY, *By* . . . After. "An hour by sun"; i.e., past sunrise. **1933**
Miller *Lamb in His Bosom* 24 **GA,** It was an hour by sun when Lonzo
said; "Reckon I'd better go." **1954** *PADS* 21.23 **SC,** *By sun* . . . Before
sundown. **1954** *Harder Coll.* **cwTN.** **1956** McAtee *Some Dialect NC* 7,
By sun . . . the time before sundown estimated by the height of the sun
above the horizon; "an hour by sun." **c1960** *Wilson Coll.* **csKY.**

‡5 in phr *sick by one's stomach:* In the area of. Cf **at** prep **2**

1968 *DARE* (Qu. BB16a, *If something a person ate didn't agree with
him, he might be sick _____ his stomach*) Inf **WI**44, By. [Inf not of Ger
heritage]

by adv [*EDD by(e adv.* 4 "Past, gone by, finished, over"; *SND by*
2 *adv.* 'extended also to time to mean "past, finished"']
Past.

1803 (1898) Hunt *Diary* 7 **sePA,** It has been fine pleasant weather for
some time by. **1965–70** *DARE* (Qu. X43a, *If you sleep later than usual
one day by accident, you'd say, "I _____."*) Inf **MS**59, Slept by; (Qu.
X43b, *If you sleep later than usual one day on purpose, you'd say, "I
_____."*) Inf **TX**35, Slept by; [**TX**26, Slept by my regular time]. **1968**
DARE Tape **MD**1, That's all by, now.

by conj [Cf *DJE by* conj 2] *Gullah*
Because.

1928 Peterkin *Scarlet Sister Mary* 36 **SC** [Gullah], I ain' had sin,
Auntie—I'm just a-growin. I'm just fat by I eat so much victuals lately.
Ibid 111, I was a-leanin out de window by it's so awful hot to-day. *Ibid*
283, E's weary by e had a hard task last night.

by a little See **by the littles**

by-am-by See **bimeby**

by bird adv phr Also *by the crow*
By the most direct route; as the crow flies.

1967 *DARE* Tape **AZ**2, Yes, their home is, oh, actually it's about three
miles from my house—by car. By bird it would be a whole lot closer.
1982 Heat Moon *Blue Highways* 158 **AZ,** "How far's the border?"
"About ten miles by the crow, but fifty miles by car."

by-blow n [*OED* 1595 →]
=**catch colt 2.**

1947 *AmSp* 22.183, 'By-blow' for a bastard. **1950** *WELS* (*A child
whose parents were not married*) 1 Inf, **cWI,** By-blow. **1965–70** *DARE*
(Qu. Z11b, *A child of unwed parents*) Infs **CA**97, **HI**1, **IN**39, **LA**14,
MA69, By-blow.

by Christopher See **Christopher**

bye n [By ext from *bye* a goal or starting line in games and
sports] **esp NY**
In children's games: =**base B2.**

1966–70 *DARE* (Qu. EE14, *. . The place where the player who is 'it' has
to wait*) Infs **MI**81, **NY**120, 152, 223, 234, **WI**66, (The) bye.

by guess and by gosh adv phr Also *by guess and by God,
~ golly, ~ gorry* For other varr, see quot 1965–70 **chiefly Nth,
N Midl** See Map
Haphazardly; without planning ahead; at random.

1914 *DN* 4.104 **KS,** *By guess and by golly* . . . Hit or miss. "I didn't have
anything to go by. I just did it by guess and by golly." **1923** *DN* 5.203
swMO, *By guess and by God* . . . Without measure or pattern. "I built
that shack b' guess an' b' God." **1927** *AmSp* 3.140 **ME,** By guess and by

God. **1930** Smiley *Gloss. New Paltz* **seNY,** You better go up there and
see what those men are doing. We cant have them working by guess and
by God. **1963** Burroughs *Head-First* 132 **CO,** Here we left the ditch,
proceeding "by guess or by God" through dense groves of aspen.
1965–70 *DARE* (Qu. KK48, *When you work something out as you go,
without having a plan or pattern to follow: "I didn't have anything to go
by, so I just did it _____."*) 59 Infs, **chiefly Nth, Pacific,** By guess and
by gosh; 26 Infs, **chiefly Nth, esp NEast,** By guess and by God; 23 Infs,
chiefly Nth, N Midl, By guess and by golly; **ME**5, 16, **MA**6, 38, 56,
VT16, By guess and by gorry; **CT**21, **GA**15, By guess and by godfrey;
IN5, 68, By guess and golly; **MA**14, By God and by guess; **MT**5, By guess
and by damned; **IL**5, By guess and by gar; **RI**15, By guess and by
gracious; **NY**113, By guess and by guy; **OH**24, By guess and by jingo;
GA5, By guess and with God; **WI**71, By guess or by gosh. **1976** Warner
Beautiful Swimmers 197 **Chesapeake Bay,** Pound men generally judge
size "by guess and by golly."

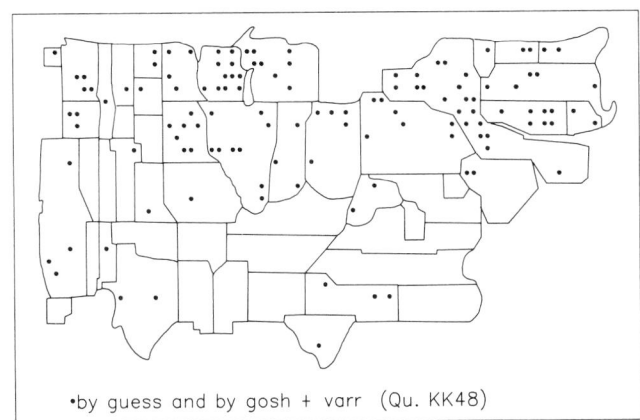

•by guess and by gosh + varr (Qu. KK48)

by head See **head** n **B5**

bylin' See **boiling** n

by littles See **by the littles**

bylow knife n [Prob var of **barlow knife**]

1954 Armstrong *Satchmo* 79 **LA,** She started up at once, pulling her
bylow knife out of her stocking and calling Benny all the black so and so's
she could think of.

bymby See **bimeby**

byo n[1] Also sp *beijo* [Prob Ger dial—see quot 1924; but cf also
such Engl parallels as "rock-a-bye baby," "bye baby bunting"]
PA
A cradle.

1902 (1968) Clapin *Americanisms* **sePA,** *Byo.* A cradle. Used in speak-
ing to a child. Perhaps from by-lo, as in by-lo-land. **1916** *DN* 4.337 **PA,**
Byo ['baɪo] Cradle. "Put the baby in the byo." **1924** Lambert *PA Ger.
Dict., Beijo* . . . cradle . . . d[ialectal] German, buie, boje, puje. **1982**
NADS Letters **sePA,** *Byo* 'cradle' . . . [used] by an educated person,
['bajo].

byo n[2] See **bayou A**

by one's head See **head** n **B5b**

bypasser n [Metath]
A passerby.

1904 *DN* 2.417 **nwAR,** *By-passer* . . . Passer-by. 'A by-passer discovered
the fire and gave the alarm' Fayetteville Daily, Nov. 25, 1904.

bys adv [*by* + *-s* adv-forming suff] Cf **anywheres, somewheres**

1980 *Barrick Coll.* **csPA,** *Bys* . . . Was you bys? Did you go bys?

by sun See **by** prep **4**

by the crow See **by bird**

by the hardest adv phr

1935 Hurston *Mules & Men* 164 **FL** [Black], De ole man got on [the
cow's back] by de hardest. [Footnote: with great difficulty].

by the littles adv phr Also *by a little, by littles*
Gradually, little by little.

1967–69 *DARE* (Qu. LL7, *In small amounts, by small degrees: "She
didn't get the money all at once, they sent it to her _____."*) Inf **KY**34,

By a little; **KY5,** By littles. **1968** Haun *Hawk's Done Gone* 46 **eTN,** Dona kept on telling me things by the littles. *Ibid* 285, So I got up the steps by the littles.

by times adv phr [Alter of *betimes*]

1 Early.

  c1960 *Wilson Coll.* **csKY,** *By times* . . . Early.

2 Occasionally.

  1841 (1940) Arnold *Diaries* 149 **VT,** Mrs. A. distressed by times through the day.

by'ud See **beard A**

byword n chiefly S Midl

One's favorite expression, usu a mild oath.

1914 *DN* 4.104 **KS,** *By-word* . . . A mild oath, as "by Godfrey's cordial," "by jacks." **1923** *DN* 5.203 **swMO,** *By-word* . . . A favorite word or expression. **1939** *Hall Coll.* **eTN, wNC,** *By-word* . . . An innocuous oath; a mildly profane expression; a favorite expression. **1953** Randolph *Down in Holler* 232 **Ozarks,** *By-word* . . . One's favorite expression. A boy in our village shouted in the street that the schoolmaster was a son-of-a-bitch. Later the boy's mother explained that "Tommy didn't mean no harm. Son-of-a-bitch has been his *by-word,* ever since he was a baby." **1954** *Harder Coll.* **cwTN,** *By-word* . . . A curse or oath. **1963** Edwards *Gravel* 180 **eTN** (as of 1920s), My Uncle Ben . . had a by-word which many people remember. It was nearly a cuss-word but Uncle Ben intended it only as a by-word, which was allowable. "Dom" —that was it.

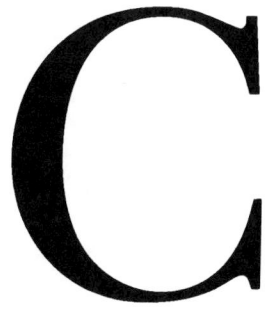

c' See **co'**

ca- See **ker-**

caa See **car** n[1]

caard See **card** n[1] A

cab n See **baby cab**

cab v See **cabbage** v

caba n [Fr *cabas* basket] *old-fash*
A flat basket or small valise.
  1865 Webster *(OEDS), Cabas* . . a lady's flat work-basket or reticule; —often written *caba.* **1877** in 1937 Ruede *Sod-House* 26 **PA,** Jim carried his army coat in a shawl strap and I had our dinner in the caba. **1885** *Boston (Mass.) Jrnl.* 7 Sept 2/4 *(OED),* The origin of the word 'caba' applying to the small hand-bag or satchel . . . The French cabas, a frail basket, hand basket, etc., was used upon ladies' work-boxes imported thirty years ago. **1892** *KS Univ. Qrly.* 1.95, *Caba:* an old valise. (Penn.) **1968** *DARE* FW Addit **PA**169, Valise: caba ['kæbə]. [Remembered by elderly teacher]

cabalero See **caballero**

caballada n Usu |ˌkæbə'jɑdə| or |'kævə'jɑd|, represented by *cavayard* and rel spp For the many varr, see quots; folk-etyms *cavalry yard, calf yard* [AmSpan] **SW** See also **cavvy** Also called **remuda**
A group of saddle horses or mules.
  1821 (1904) Austin *Jrl. TX* 7.288, Found that Erasmo had captured a Caviard of mules & horses which some traders were taking in from the Comanches. **1824** in 1858 Dewees *Letters TX* 53, Corasco . . was driving a large cavyyard of horses and mules to Louisiana. **1836** *Ibid* 208, They . . obtained a fine cavalyard of horses. **1836** Edward *Hist. TX* 107, They will carry back a Mexican cavy-yard. **1841** McCalla *Advent. TX* 37, These daring Indians ['Camanchees'] had . . taken off . . fifty or sixty horses . . , forty of which were from one *caballado,* their word for *herd of horses.* **1844** (1846) Kendall *Santa Fé Exped.* 1.97 **TX,** Nothing can exceed the grandeur of the scene when a large *cavallada,* or drove of horses, takes a "scare." **1844** (1954) Gregg *Commerce* 18 **SW,** [The Indians] drove off the entire *caballada* of near five hundred head of horses, mules and asses. **1846** Sage *Scenes Rocky Mts.* 1.246, Stealing our whole cavallard, consisting of ten head of horses and mules. **1853** Hammett *Stray Yankee in TX* 97, Two or three more [men] were mounted, and sent into the prairie in search of the 'caviarde' of horses. *Ibid* 117, With a Texan, . . a drove of horses [is] a caviarde. **1858** in 1966 Boller *MO Fur Trader* 66 **MO,** The horse-guard drives the cabablada [sic] to pasture. **1862** *Los Angeles Star* 5 Apr 2/2 *(Western Folkl.* 7.7) s**CA,** Three charges of horse stealing . . . a third charge for running off a cavallado of horses from the verdugo rancho. **1874** McCoy *Cattle Trade* 11, For the benefit of our northern readers . . the term "ranch" is used in the Southwest instead of "farm," the ordinary laborer is termed a "cow-boy," and the herd of horses a "cavvie yard." **1892** *DN* 1.188, *Caballáda:* a "bunch" or drove of horses. Generally pronounced *cavyyard* by Americans. The forms *cavallad, caballad, cavallard* (B.) are the more common in Texas. **1901** *Munsey's Mag.* 25.404/2 *(OEDS),* Each man roped a fresh horse from the cavvyyard. **1901** in 1902 KS State Hist. Soc. *Coll.* 7.52, I was driving the *cavayado.* **1908** (1924) Mulford *Orphan* 25, He was soon able to count seven warriors who were driving another 'cavvieyeh' of horses. *Ibid* 40, Caviya. **1910** Hart *Vigilante Girl* 159 n**CA,** "The Spanish ladies of that elder day would have condemned both your riding habit and your habit of riding out alone as being too masculine." "Which means, I sup-

pose," . . "that when I take my ride this afternoon I must go forth with a complete *caballada,* and not alone?" **1931** *AmSp* 6.241 **NE Territory** (as of 1840s), New horses added to the army's "calf-yard," horse herd, were called "recruits." **1932** Bentley *Spanish Terms* 107, *Caballada* English modifications *caballado, cavvieyard, cavayer, cavvayah, cavallada, caballad, cavayard, covoy* (Spanish, ka: bɑ: jɑ́: ða: *and* ka: bɑ: ljɑ́: ða:; *English, the same and* kæ vi: ár) The "string" or drove of horses, that is, supply of mounts, maintained by a ranching outfit, particularly on a special expedition, such as a round-up or an exploring trip . . . The usage of the term includes not only horses, from which the word is derived, i.e., *caballo* but also mules. **1933** White *Dog Days* 158, Wes and I have . . come at last upon our "cavvayard". **1941** *AmSp* 16.181 **SW,** Vulgarized English – Spanish such as . . *caballado, cavalade, cavayard, cavvy.* **1942** *CA Folkl. Qrly.* 1.271 **CA,** Caviyard, cavvyiard . . . Corrupted by Mexicans to "cavayah" and by Americans to "cavvy". A drove of horses. **1942** Dale *Cow Country* 47, The band of horses was . . known as . . the *caballado,* sometimes corrupted into "cavvy yard," "cavalry yard," or "cavvy." **1945** Thorp *Pardner* 299 **SW,** Cavyard (also known as the "cavvy"). **1966** Giles *Great Adventure* 10 **West** (as of 1830s), Fouchette and Bastro brought the notional mule back into the cavvyard and the brigade strung out again. **1981** *KS Qrly.* 13.2.65 **NV,** Cavvy / Caviata . . the group of saddle horses owned by a ranch and used during round-up and other times as the pool of working mounts for buckaroos; a typical cavvy contains several horses for each rider in order to provide a "string" of rotating mounts during lengthy work periods; the familiar Texas term "remuda" is not used in northern Nevada.

caballero n Also sp *cabalero* [Span *caballero* a man on horseback] **SW**
A horseman; a gentleman.
  [**1824** Poinsett *Notes on Mexico* 33, At being compelled to present such a bill of fare to cavalleros.] **1837** Irving *Astoria* iii.85 *(headline) (DAE),* A Californian caballero. **1846** (1848) Bryant *What I Saw in CA* 314, In the rear were two *caballeros,* riding fine spirited horses, with gaudy trappings. **1892** *DN* 1.188, "Spanish and Mexican Words Used in Texas" . . . *Cabálléro:* a horseman, a cavalryman—more generally, a gentleman. **1910** Hart *Vigilante Girl* 159 n**CA,** You are not *muy caballero!* . . If you were a true-for-sure cavalier, you'd ride out with me yourself. **1927** Cather *Death Comes* 60 **NM,** "But you are a caballero, Father Vaillant!" Lujon exclaimed. **1936** McCarthy *Lang. Mosshorn* (Range Term) **SW,** Cabalero . . . A hardened but gay cowboy who can jump on his horse any minute and tell the world to go to hell. **1968** Adams *Western Words,* Caballero.

caballo n |kə'baIo, kə'vælo| Also sp *cavallo, cavoya* [Span] **West, esp SW**
A horse.
  1843 (1845) Green *Jrl. Texian Exped.* 205, How, then, . . do you catch your cavallos and chickens? **1859** in 1957 *Western Folkl.* 7.19 **TX,** The sun has mounted to the zenith, and now makes dusty viejentes and panting caballo . . glad to take a rancho. **1907** White *AZ Nights* 23, "Get your cavallos and follow me," said he. **1907** *Everybody's Mag.* 17.90 **TX,** Throw a pot of coffee together while I attend to the *caballo.* **1932** Bentley *Spanish Terms* 109, *Caballo* . . [kə'baio] *and* [kə'vælo]. A horse . . . It is occasionally heard in light conversation. **1940** FWP *Guide NV* 76, Caballo (kɑvɑyo). **1958** *AmSp* 33.270 e**WA,** Horse . . cavoya [kə'vɔijə]. **1968** Adams *Western Words* 49, Caballo—Horse; from the Spanish . . . but generally the cowboy calls his horse *hoss.*

cabarista, cabaros See **cabestro**

cabase See **cabeza**

cabbage n Usu |'kæbɪǰ|; less freq |'kɛbɪǰ, 'kjæbɪǰ, 'kɑbɪǰ| Pronc-sp *kebbidge*

A Forms.

1 Pronc varr.

1867 Lowell *Biglow* 229 'Upcountry' **MA**, Kebbidge-heads. **1933** *AmSp* 8.4.59 **Delmarva**, [æ] occasionally becomes [ɛ] in . . *cabbage* [kɛbɪʒ]. **1936** *AmSp* 11.239 **eTX**, The tendency toward . . [palatalization] is stronger than in general American . . . [as in] ['kjæbɪʒ]. **1938** *AmSp* 13.4 **VT**, In *cabbages* etc . . . [ɑ] occurs as the only pronunciation in Lemington. **1941** *LANE* Map 255, Pronunciations of the type of [ka·bɪʒ, kɑ·b–] are regarded as older though still in use by . . [6 infs]. [Pronunciations of the type ['kɛbɪʒ] occur occasionally throughout New England.]

2 Gram varr.

a as a plural: See quots. **esp S Midl, NEng**

1905 *DN* 3.72 **nwAR**, *Cabbage* . . . 'Pass them cabbage.' 'Those are fine cabbage.' Not common. **1910** in 1944 *ADD* **FL, GA**. **1926** Kephart *Highlanders* 371 **sAppalachians**, Tomato, cabbage, molasses and baking powder are always used as plural nouns . . . "I'll have a few more of them cabbage." **1941** *LANE* Map 255, [About half the informants make 'cabbage' plural, e.g. "Those are nice large cabbage."] **1953** Randolph *Down in Holler* 48 **Ozarks**, Cabbage is always plural . . . An ordinary hillman says "pass me them cabbage," but an educated mountain girl who wishes to be very elegant may say "those cabbage." A fiddle tune popular at the country dances is called "Bile *Them* Cabbage Down." **1954** *Harder Coll.* **cwTN** [Letter], I had cabbage for supper and they were pretty good. **1956** McAtee *Some Dialect NC* 7, *Cabbage* . . . Cooked cabbage referred to as plural, "They stunk so when I was cooking them that I threw them all out."

b as count noun instead of mass noun: See quot.

1931 *PMLA* 46.1318 **sAppalachians**, The plural of nouns is used excessively and indiscriminately . . . "Pass the cabbages, please."

B Senses.

1 See **cabbage leaf 1**.

2 also *cabbage leaf:* Money. [From the green color of US paper currency, which may be peeled like leaves from a wad] **chiefly NEast, Sth** See Map

1926 (1927) Black *You Can't Win* 213 **UT**, "You carry this head of cabbage, Kid," passing me a pack of greenbacks. **1939** *AmSp* 14.90 **eTN**, *Cabbage leaves.* Paper money. 'He has a wad of cabbage leaves in his hip pocket.' **1942** Berrey–Van den Bark *Amer. Slang* 467.1, *Money . .* cabbages. *Ibid* 467.2, Cabbage . . *a dollar.* **1965–70** *DARE* (Qu. U19a, *Words used around here for money in general: "He's certainly got the _____."*) 34 Infs, **chiefly NEast, Sth**, Cabbage; (Qu. U26, *Names or nicknames around here for a paper dollar*) 11 Infs, **chiefly NEast, Sth**, Cabbage leaf; **IL2, MD43, NY100, NC87, VT16, WI12**, Cabbage; (Qu. U19b, *Talking of paper money: "He always carries a big _____."*) Inf **CT42**, Roll of cabbage; **LA3**, Wad of cabbage; (Qu. U37, *. . Somebody who has plenty of money*) Inf **MA15**, Got the old cabbage.

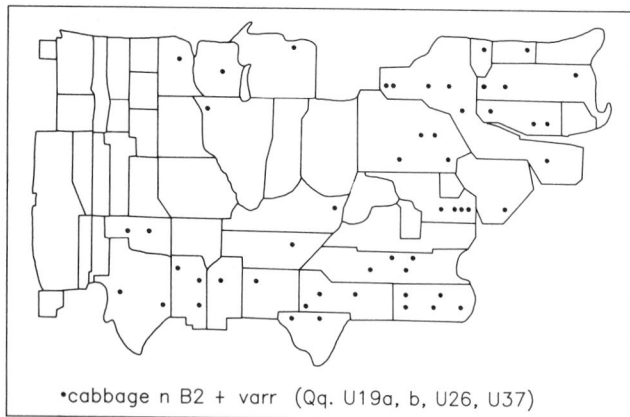

•cabbage n B2 + varr (Qq. U19a, b, U26, U37)

3 See **cabbagehead**.

4 attrib: Used in jocular or derisive nicknames for German settlement areas.

[**1967** *Dict. Canadianisms* 103, *Cabbagetown . .* any run-down urban area; slum.] **1967–69** *DARE* (Qu. C35, *. . Nicknames for the different parts of your town or city*) Inf **PA2**, Cabbage Hill; **IL3**, Cabbage Town, old-fashioned word for the German section; (Qu. II25) Inf **MI51**, Cabbage Town . . . That's where the Germans lived.

5 freq attrib: =**cabbage palm**. **FL**

1766 in 1953 McMullen *Topog. Terms FL* 79, Set out from Cabbage-bluff, so called from the great number of palm or cabbage-trees growing there. **1773** *Ibid* 80, Clear cabbage Land—by the Spaniards called the Palmaro. **1806** (1970) Webster *Compendious Dict.* 40, *Cabbage-tree . .* a tropical tree affording a head like a cabbage, used as food. **c1940** Eliason *Word Lists FL* 2, *Cabbage tree . . .* Cabbage palmetto, sabal palmetto. *Palm* tree is never used. "They cut down that ol' *cabbage tree* in the back lot." **1950** *PADS* 14.74 **FL**, *Cabbage, cabbage-tree . . .* The palmetto palm. *Cabbage bitter . . .* The tender part of the palmetto leaf, just below the bud. *Cabbage boot . . .* The part of the palmetto leaf . . attached to the tree. *Cabbage log . . . Cabbage stalk . . . Cabbage woods.* **1965** Will *Okeechobee Boats* 41 **FL**, The present day Caloosahatchee is pretty enough in its way with oaks and cabbage trees lining its banks. **1966** *DARE* (Qu. T1) Inf **FL4**, Cabbage island . . . Cabbage heads, five or ten cabbage palms in the saw grass. **1975** Newell *If Nothin' Don't Happen* 136 **FL**, That cold wind was blowin' dead fans off of them tall cabbages down at the landin'. *Ibid* 215, Our old homeplace, which Dad had built out of cabbage logs. **1977** *DARE* File **cnFL**, Cabbage bitter is bitter because it is close to the tree; it is good for the stomach.

cabbage v Also *cab, cabbage on(to)* [Etym uncert; see *OED cabbage* sb.[2]] *old-fash*

To steal, pilfer; to latch on to.

1806 (1970) Webster *Compendious Dict.* 40, *Cabbage . .* to steal in cutting clothes. **1825** Paulding *John Bull* 82 **NYC**, I took the first opportunity of . . cabbaging a watch out of a window, which hung so invitingly that I could not resist the temptation. **1846** Corcoran *Pickings* 204 **LA**, I aint agoin' to let my karacter be cabbaged away right before my face. **1899** (1912) Green *VA Folk-Speech* 104, *Cabbage . . .* To steal; to keep possession of a part of a customer's cloth of which a garment was made. **1906** *DN* 3.115 **sIN**, *Cabbage.* **1908** *DN* 3.295 **eAL, wGA**, *Cabbage.* **1914** *DN* 4.141, *Cab*, from *cabbage*. To pilfer, snatch dishonestly or meanly, to "crib." . . . Mod. schoolboy slang. **1943** *LANE* Map 566, [In the context *Who swiped my pencil?* the term *cabbaged* is fairly freq.] **1949** *PADS* 11.4 **wTX**, *Cabbage onto . .* To grab; to filch. **1951** *PADS* 15.53 **neIN, TX**, *Cabbage onto.* **1965–70** *DARE* (Qu. V4, *Other words for stealing something valuable . . "Yesterday somebody _____ my watch."*) Inf **MD17**, Cabbaged; **IL126, TX5**, Cabbaged onto it; (Qu. V5b, *If you take something that nobody seems to own, you might say, "Before anybody else gets its, I'm going to _____ this."*) Infs **CT15, NY68**, Cabbage; **AR18, CA2, IL13, 26, KS19, KY72, TX1, 23, 42, 43, 65, 76, WA30**, Cabbage onto. [Of 18 Infs, 17 were old.] **1982** *Barrick Coll.* **sePA**, Cabbage.

cabbage and cornbread exclam

A call in the children's game of **run sheep run**.

1953 Goodwin *It's Good* 200 **sIL**, From a distance you might hear someone yell "cabbage and cornbread" or "red-hot skillet," and you knew that children were playing run, sheep, run.

cabbage bean See **cabbage pea**

cabbage bug See **harlequin cabbage bug**

cabbage candy n

1966 *DARE* (Qu. H82b) Inf **SC3**, Cabbage candy—sliced coconut made into a candy bar—very hard—it would break your teeth to eat it.

cabbage cigar n

1 See **cabbage leaf 1**.

2 A mixture of ground meat and rice rolled in cabbage leaves and steamed; stuffed cabbage.

1977 *Mais Jamais* 60 **LA** [Black], Cabbage cigars . . 1 cup rice—cooked[,] 1 pound ground meat[,] 1 med. onion, chopped fine . . . Brown ground meat and seasonings; . . let simmer for 30 min. Add rice and roll in softened cabbage leaves.

cabbage-eater n Cf **kraut-eater**

A foreigner of German or Russian origin.

1942 Berrey–Van den Bark *Amer. Slang* 385.29, *Russian.* Bear, cabbage or candle eater. **1967** *DARE* (Qu. HH28, *Names and nicknames . . for people of foreign background . . German*) Inf **CO34**, Kraut, cabbage-eater or kraut-eater.

cabbage grass See **cabbage-leaf grass**

cabbagehead n Also *cabbage* [*OED* 1682 →]
A stupid or silly person; hence adj *cabbage-headed* having a large, round head; stupid.
 1846 Corcoran *Pickings* 10 **LA**, A low, chubby, cabbage-headed Dutchman . . entered. **1854** *Harper's Mag.* 8.269/2, Do our placid Dutch friends ever make us darkly to understand what may be meant by the term "Cabbage-head?" **1887** in 1917 Twain *Letters* 482, This whole . . swindle is a pure creation of one of those cabbages that used to be the head of one of those Retreats. **1891** Farmer–Henley *Slang* 4, *Cabbage-head* . . . A fool; a soft-head; a 'go-along.' **1919** *DN* 5.61 [Speech of high school pupils], *Cabbage-head*, a witless person. "Charlie is a cabbage-head, but he cannot help it." California, New Mexico. **1942** Berrey–Van den Bark *Amer. Slang* 150.5, *Stupid* . . cabbage-headed. **1970** *DARE* (Qu. X28, . . *A person's head*) Inf **SC**70, Cabbage-headed.

cabbagehead pea See **cabbage pea**

cabbage house See **cabbage palmetto house**

cabbage-kraut n [Redund cpd]
Sauerkraut.
 1934 (1970) Wilson *Backwoods Amer.* 8 **AR, MO**, Pork joints, pertaters, . . cabbage kraut. **1954** Harder *Coll.* **cwTN**, Cabbage-kraut, ordinary sauerkraut.

cabbage leaf n, also attrib
1 also *cabbage-leaf cigar, cabbage (cigar)*: A cigar of poor quality.
 1851 Hall *Manhattaner* 158 **LA**, The fog . . was . . as disagreeable to breathe as the smoke of a cabbage-leaf regalia cigar. **1875** Twain *Sketches New & Old* (Hartford) 121, Smoking one of those cabbage cigars the San Francisco people used to think were good enough for us. **1891** Farmer–Henley *Slang* 5, *Cabbage-leaf* . . . A bad cigar; usually contracted into *cabbage*. **1907** Twain in *N. Amer. Rev.* 184.681, No Connecticut cabbage-leaf product, but Havana, $25 the box! **1912** Nicholson *Hoosier Chron.* 62, Try one of those cigars . . . If they're cabbage leaf it is n't my fault. **1950** *WELS* (*Cigar:*) 3 Infs, **WI**, Cabbage; 1 Inf, Cabbage leaves. **1966–70** *DARE* (Qu. DD6a, . . *Names or nicknames for cigars*) 14 Infs, **esp Sth**, Cabbage leaf; **PA**134, Cabbage; **MD**29, Stogie, rope, cabbage; [**CT**16, El cabbagio [kə'bažo]].
2 See **cabbage** n B2.
3 See quot.
 1942 Warnick *Garrett Co. MD* 4 (as of 1900–18), *Cabbage-leaves*, . . large ears.
4 A type of playing marble: see quots.
 1935 *AmSp* 10.159 **WI** (as of c1890), The brown and blue stone agates [marbles] are a "crockie" and a "cabbage leaf." **1958** *PADS* 29.31 **WI**, *Cabbage-leaf* . . . A glass marble with greenish internal markings.

cabbage-leaf grass n Also *cabbage grass*
 1968 *DARE* (Qu. S9, *Kinds of grass that are hard to get rid of*) Inf **NY**83, Cabbage-leaf grass; (S21, . . *Weeds . . that are a trouble in the garden*) Inf **MN**33, Cabbage grass—a wider-leaved grass that grew around pigpens, 6″–8″ tall, smooth on top; fuzzy underneath.

cabbage night n Also *cabbage stump night* **Nth** Also called **beggars' night, corn ~, goosie ~, mischief ~, mystery ~, picket ~, tick-tack ~**
The night before Halloween, when young people throw cabbages and refuse on people's porches, and play other pranks.
 1975 *WI State Jrl.* (Madison) 2 Nov 3/1 **swCT**, Miss Moxley had left the house early Thursday evening . . on what the local children call "cabbage night," a pre-Halloween occasion for pranks. **1976** *DARE* File **neNJ** (as of c1965), On cabbage night we [teenagers] would roam the streets in groups, smashing pumpkins or simply looking for trouble. **1977–78** Foster *Lexical Variation* 75 **NJ**, Cabbage Night, the customary name in most of Bergen County, is said to refer to the custom of leaving skunk cabbages on neighbors' porches, although none of the informants admit having performed this activity. **1978–80** *DARE* File **csWI**, 'Cabbage night' was known and used in Dane County in the 1930s. The kids from Madison used it more than the ones from Cottage Grove; **csOH**, Cabbage night—that's what people in Cincinnati call the night before Halloween; **nwMA** (as of c1915), Here in [the] Berkshire Hills the night before Hallowe'en is called Cabbage Stump Night. I am 73 now and can't really remember ever seeing a full cabbage thrown at a

door. The stumps were used for two reasons; 1. Cheap and easily "lifted" from nearby fields after cabbage had been cut. 2. Made more noise against the door . . . They were more easily carried on the "raids" than a full head of cabbage . . . Today there is very little cabbage stump throwing. **1981** *Seventeen Letters* **neNJ**, In Bergen County, New Jersey . . we call the night before Halloween "Cabbage Night." I know in other areas they call it mischief night or goosie night, but I believe we are the only ones who call it cabbage night.

cabbage oyster See **oyster**

cabbage palm n Also *cabbage palmetto, ~ tree* **chiefly FL** See also **cabbage** n B5
A fan-leaved palm (*Sabal palmetto*) which produces an edible terminal bud. Also called **blue palmetto 3, latanier, palmetto, swamp cabbage, tree palmetto**
 1763 Roberts *Acct. FL* 96 **FL**, Interspersed promiscuously, as mulberry, cedar, cocoa, vanilla, moho, and cabbage-trees. **1836** Latrobe *Rambler in N. Amer.* 2.34 **FL**, A wilderness of saw-palmetto, swamps, and groves of cabbage-palm. **1938** Matschat *Suwannee R.* 211 **FL**, The trunk of the cabbage palm is always studded with the bases of dead leafstalks . . . John Bartram wrote that the cabbage palm was eaten both raw and boiled. *Ibid* 292, Palm, Cabbage: *Sabal palmetto*. **1965** Will *Okeechobee Boats* 12 **FL**, Sendin' a rope ashore to a cabbage tree. **1965–70** *DARE* (Qu. T5, . . *Kinds of evergreens, other than pine*) Infs **FL**9, 29, Cabbage palm; (Qu. T15, . . *Kinds of swamp trees*) Inf **FL**9, Cabbage palm; **WA**22, Cabbage tree; (Qu. T16, . . *Kinds of trees . . "special"*) Infs **FL**27, 35, Cabbage palm; **FL**29, 39, Cabbage palmetto. **1966** *DARE* Tape **FL**38, [With] the cabbage palm, the cabbage is the heart of the palm. It kills the tree when you take that out . . . They have to get so big, but if they get too big they're not as tasty. **1975** Newell *If Nothin' Don't Happen* 9, **nwFL**, Cabbage palms, which we mostly just call cabbages.

‡**cabbage palmetto house** n Also *cabbage house* [**cabbage palm, cabbage** n B5] **FL**
A house roofed with cabbage palmetto leaves.
 1943 Pratt *Barefoot Mailman* 5 **FL**, The sun glistened on several cabbage palmetto houses that looked miniature in the distance. *Ibid* 13, They put him in a cabbage house by himself, and brought him food and talked with him from outside.

cabbage patch n
A place or thing of little importance.
 1862 Newell *Orpheus C. Kerr* 1.227 **NY**, How often does man, after making something his particular forte, discover at last that it is only a cabbage-patch and hardly large enough at that for a big hog like himself! **1902** Rice *Mrs. Wiggs* 4 **KY**, The Wiggses lived in the Cabbage Patch. It was not a real cabbage patch, but a queer neighborhood, where ramshackle cottages played hop-scotch over the railroad tracks. **1969** *DARE* (Qu. C33, . . *An out-of-the-way . . or a very unimportant place*) Inf **KY**68, Cabbage patch.

cabbage pea n Also *cabbage bean, cabbagehead pea* **Sth**
A type of pea: see quots.
 1859 Van Buren *Sojourn in South* 155 *(DA)*, The Cabbage Pea, with its large broad pod, makes a fine soup. **1965–70** *DARE* (Qu. I14, *Kinds of beans that you eat in the pod before they're dry*) Inf **NC**79, Cabbage pea—[eat] pod and all; (Qu. I20, . . *Kinds of beans*) Inf **SC**3, Cabbage beans—a short tender bunch bean; **FL**18, Cabbage peas; **FL**49, Cabbagehead peas—white hull, white pea. **1966** *DARE* Tape **FL**41, Black-eyes, conks, crowders, cabbage pea (looks somewhat like the conks).

cabbage pine n
=**bull pine 1d.**
 1968 *DARE* (Qu. T17, . . *Different kinds of pine trees*) Inf **MD**42, Cabbage pine—same as bull pine.

cabbage rose n
 1968 *DARE* (Qu. S11, . . *Other names for . . peony*) Inf **GA**91, Cabbage rose; (Qu. S26a, *Other wildflowers*) Inf **VA**7, Cabbage rose = wild rose.

cabbage salad n **chiefly Nth** See Map
Coleslaw.
 1953 Piercy *Shaker Cook Book* 210, Cabbage Salad. **1966–70** *DARE* (Qu. H52) 93 Infs, **chiefly Nth**, Cabbage salad; **ME**2, Raw cabbage salad; **NJ**37, Shredded cabbage salad. [Of all Infs responding to the question, 70% were old; of those giving these responses, 80% were old.] **1982** *Grit*

(Williamsport PA) 20 June 5/3, Cole slaw . . is renamed cabbage salad in the Catskills.

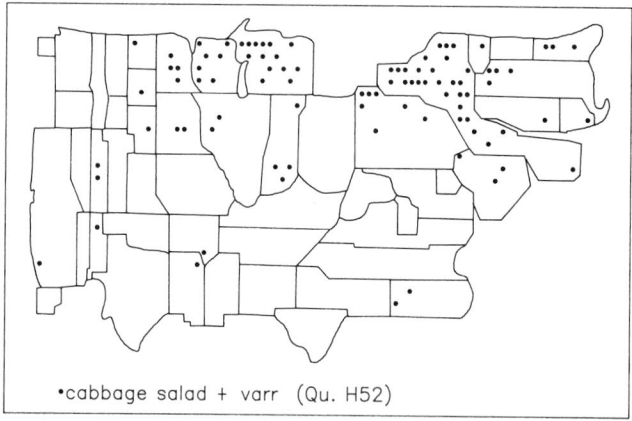

•cabbage salad + varr (Qu. H52)

cabbage slaw n [*cabbage* + **slaw** cabbage salad]
Coleslaw.

c1965 Randle *Cookbooks* (Plain Cookery) 1.2 **neOH,** Cabbage Slaw. **1965–70** *DARE* (Qu. H52) 36 Infs, **scattered,** Cabbage slaw; **CA**1, Hot cabbage slaw; (Qu. I28a) Inf **SC**53, Cabbage slaw. **1967** *DARE* File **csAR,** Cabbage slaw—seen on a menu.

cabbage stack n
See quots.

1958 McCulloch *Woods Words* **Pacific NW,** Cabbage stack—A locie [=locomotive] with a big round spark arrester on the smoke-stack. **1977** Adams *Lang. Railroader* 26, Cabbage stack: An early-day locomotive smokestack that was shaped like a large cabbagehead. The bulbous top served as a repository for the wood ashes. The stacks were used only during the days of the woodburner engines.

cabbage stump night See **cabbage night**

cabbage tree See **cabbage palm**

cabbouze, cabbus See **caboose** n¹ **1**

cabestro n Usu |kə'bestro|, also metath |kə'bresto| For addit varr and pronc-spp see quots [Span *cabestro* halter] **SW**
A hair rope used as a halter or tether.

1805 in 1852 U.S. Congress *Debates & Proc.* 2d sess 16.1082, Their horses they . . always keep . . tied with a long cabras or halter. **1821** (1904) Austin *Jrl. TX* 287, Had a race of about two miles to catch the runaway mule . . . tied head & foot & with a long cabrass & bell on. **1826** in 1858 Dewees *Letters TX* 61, We look us out a spot free from snakes, which we entirely surround with a caboras or hair rope. **1834** (1900) Harris *Reminiscences TX* 100, The hair rope is a Mexican product called a cabris. **1846** *Knickerbocker* 27.251 **SW,** He felt himself violently seized from behind, his arms pinioned, his mouth filled with the end of a hair cabresta. **1846** in 1956 Sage *Letters & Papers* 5.285, Carefully hung in some fitting place, are seen his "riding" and "pack saddles," with his halters, "cavraces," "larrietts," "apishamores," and all the needful *materiel* for camp and travelling service. **1848** Thorpe *Taylor Anecdote* 107 **TX,** He carries a line of braided leather about thiry-five feet in length, called a *"laretto,"* and a line of the same length, made of twisted horsehair, called a *"cabaros".* **1859** (1968) Bartlett *Americanisms, Caberes* . . A rope made of hair. **1892** *DN* 1.188 **TX,** *Cabéstro:* rope made of hair. *Ibid* 245, Often pronounced *cabresto*. **1892** Duval *Young Explorers* 11, I purchased . . a Mexican poncho or blanket, . . [and] a cabressa made of horse hair. **1931** Read *LA French* 132, *Cabresse* . . . A rope made of horsehair; used in the parish of St. Landry. *Cabresse* is adapted, with metathesis of the *r* and change of suffix, from Sp. *cabestro* . . "halter," which signifies a "rope made of hair," in the dialect of the Southwestern United States. The ultimate source is Low Latin *capistrum*, "halter." **1932** Bentley *Spanish Terms* 109, *Cabestro* English modifications *cabresto, cabarista* (Spanish, kɑ: bé: stro:; *English,* kə bé stro: kə bré sto:) A rope halter . . . The word is used to distinguish an improvised rope headgear, or the horsehair rope halter, from the leather manufactured halter.

cabeza n Also sp *cabase, kerbase* [Span] **chiefly West**
The head; freq in phr *off one's cabase*.

1868 *Phoenix* (Sacramento CA) 31 Jan 4/1 *(DA),* The world . . shall yet feel the potency of this *cabeza* and this right arm. **1877** Wright *Big Bonanza* 285, Now, he's got more instink, that dog has, an' more savey, an' pen'tration into human natur, right in that ugly old cabeza of his. **1895** *DN* 1.390 **West,** *Kerbase:* in phrase "off his kerbase" = slightly crazy. **1914** *DN* 4.104 **KS,** *Cabase* . . . Head:—in *off his cabase,* mistaken. *Ibid* 109, *Kerbase* . . . Variant of *cabase.* **1944** Adams *Canal Town* 89 **cwNY,** He'll have me clapt into quod as a ne'erdoweel and a vagabond if I show my cabeza again in town. **1966–70** *DARE* (Qu. X28, *Joking words for one's head*) Inf **AZ**10 [kə'beso]; **CA**189 [kə'besə] —this is common around here; **MI**96 [kə'bizə]; **WA**1 [kə'pesə]—Spanish, but used in the West.

cabezon n Also sp *cabezone* [Span *cabezón* bighead]
Either of two Pacific sculpins: *Leptocottus armatus,* which is also called **staghorn sculpin,** or *Scorpaenichthys marmoratus,* which is also called **biggyhead, blue cod 2, bullhead 1a, drummer, Johnny, salpa.**

1887 Goode *Amer. Fishes* 302, The Cottidæ . . are . . known by such names as "Sculpin" . . and "Cabezon." Only one of these species, *Scorpænichthys marmoratus,* has any sort of economic importance. **1898** U.S. Natl. Museum *Bulletin* 47.1889, *Scorpænichthys marmoratus* . . . Cabezon. *Ibid* 2012, *Leptocottus armatus* . . . Smooth cabezon. **1933** John G. Shedd Aquarium *Guide* 129, *Scorpænichthys marmoratus*—Cabezon. *Ibid* 132, *Leptocottus armatus* . . . Smooth Cabezon. **1939** Natl. Geog. Soc. *Fishes* 241, *Cabezone (Scorpænichthys marmoratus)* . . . The . . cabezone . . is one of the commonest of the shallow-water sculpins . . found along the western coast of the United States. **1946** LaMonte *N. Amer. Game Fishes* 87, The Cabezone [*Scorpænichthys marmoratus*] is . . an example of the scaleless sculpins . . . *Names:* Marbled sculpin . . . Cabezon. **1960** Amer. Fisheries Soc. *List Fishes* 53, Cabezon, cabezone [*Leptocottus armatus*]. **1975** Evanoff *Catch More Fish* 107, The cabezon is another fish often caught by bottom bouncers in California, Oregon, and Washington.

cabin n

1 A cubby or small storage space inside a house. [Cf *W3* ¹*cabin* 8 "a shelved container"]
1969 *DARE* (Qu. D7) Inf **CA**171, Cabin.

2 See **cabin car.**

cabin camp n
Overnight lodgings for automobile travelers consisting of small separate buildings (in contrast to a hotel).

1969 Kantor *MO Bittersweet* 46, First time Irene and I ever stayed at a motel, it was back in the years when they called them cabin camps.

cabin car n Also *cabin*
The caboose on a railroad train.

1879 *Scribner's Mth.* 19.23/2, This road has also cabin cars, with stove, bunks, etc., which it will switch off at any station. **1906** *Car Builders' Dict.* 31, Caboose car . . . Also, but rarely, called conductor's car, cabin car, cabin, or train car. **1945** Beebe *Highball* 207, In the gaudy lexicon of railroad jargon it . . . is caboose, crummy, . . cage, . . parlor, cabin car, and shanty. **1958** McCulloch *Woods Words* 27 **Pacific NW,** *Cabin car*—Another name for a caboose. **1962** *AmSp* 37.132 **Pacific NW,** *Cabin Car* . . . The car for the train crew to ride in. **1977** Adams *Lang. Railroader* 26, Cabin car.

cabine n [Fr *cabine* cabin; cf *cabinet (d'aisances)* toilet] **LA**
An outhouse.

1961 *PADS* 36.12 **sLA,** Other such terms [i.e., those found in Louisiana but not in the Southwest] of less frequency are *cabine* for a privy, [etc]. **1967** LeCompte *Word Atlas* 167 **seLA,** Outdoor toilet. [*Cabine* is the response given by 10 of 21 infs.] *Cabine* is the familiar, *commode* the standard French form for "outhouse."

cabinet n [Etym uncert but see quot 1968] **RI, seMA** Cf **frappe, velvet**
A milkshake.

1957 Rose *Block Is.* 176 **sRI,** Only ten cents for an ice cream soda, fifteen for a college ice, a cabinet or a banana split. **1963** Francis *Engl. Lang.* 121 **RI,** A drink made by beating up milk, flavoring, and ice cream is variously known as a *frappe,* a *cabinet,* a *frost,* or a *milk shake* in different parts of the country. **1968** *DARE* File **MA** (as of 1920s), *Cabinet* is said by Dorothy Cahill of Fall River to have originated in a drugstore there, named by the pharmacist who concocted it. The ice cream was kept in those days in a cabinet that was part of the soda-fountain set-up. **c1970** *DARE* File **Providence RI, Fall River MA,**

Cabinet—an ice-cream milk shake. **1971** *Today Show Letters* **RI,** What they call a *milk shake* in New York and Connecticut and a *frappe* in Massachusetts, they call a *cabinet* in Rhode Island. A *milk shake* in Rhode Island is without ice cream, while a *cabinet* has ice cream. **1982** *Smithsonian Letters* **RI,** Cabinet—In Rhode Island this term more likely refers to a milkshake (using milk, syrup and ice cream) than a piece of furniture. I grew up five miles from the Massachusetts border. As a child I could order a cabinet in R.I., but had to remember to order a frappe just five minutes to the west [*sic*].

cabinet cherry n [See quot 1901]
=black cherry.

   1822 Eaton *Botany* 411, *Prunus virginiana,* wild cherry, rum cherry, cabinet cherry . . . The bark is an excellent tonic. **1901** Lounsberry *S. Wild Flowers* 253, *P[runus] serotina* . . cabinet cherry . . . Its timber of firm texture and splendid colour is much valued for use in cabinet work. **1930** Sievers *Amer. Med. Plants* 11, Black cherry . . . Other common names.—Wild cherry, wild black cherry, cabinet cherry. **1971** Krochmal *Appalachia Med. Plants* 210.

cabinet pudding n NEng
   See quots.

   1896 (c1973) Farmer *Orig. Cook Book* 356 **NEng,** *Cold Cabinet Pudding* [A moulded dessert made of layers of lady fingers, macaroons and custard to which gelatine has been added]. **1947** Bowles–Towle *New Engl. Cooking* 198, *Iced Cabinet Pudding* [Sponge cake, candied fruit soaked in wine. Molded in custard plus gelatin. Served with cubes of currant jelly.] **1979** *DARE* File **cnMA,** Cabinet pudding used to appear on menus in second-rate eating places. I have tried it and recall it as something made out of old cake stuck together somehow. [**1983** *Milwaukee Jrl.* (WI) 21 Dec food sec 10/1, *Can you tell me what cabinet pudding is?* Two puddings bear the name cabinet, one French and one English. The English version, once popular, is rarely made today. The pudding de cabinet of the French kitchen is made with ladyfingers soaked in a liqueur such as kirsch or maraschino . . . The English version is made with bread crumbs, a vanilla-flavored custard and currants. It is baked and can be served with a vanilla-flavored sauce.]

‡cabin-fashion potatoes n Cf **cottage fried potatoes, shanty fried potatoes**

   1968 *DARE* (Qu. H47, *Kinds of fried potatoes favored around here*) Inf **PA176,** Cabin-fashion potatoes—cut up raw, fry in bacon grease.

cabin fever n orig esp NW, now more widespread Cf **shanty fever**
   Nervousness or even slight derangement caused by confinement to close quarters or isolation from other people.

   1924 Shephard *Paul Bunyan* 135 **WA,** But that year they got the spring-fever or the cabin-fever or somethin', and got lazy and laid down on their jobs. **1958** McCulloch *Woods Words* **Pacific NW,** When a man lives too long alone, sticks too much to his own cabin, he gets talking to himself; this is cabin fever . . . Also applied to a small crew working away from other people; men get on each other's nerves after a long period. **1967** *DARE* File **cOR,** Cabin fever—when you want to get out of the house. **1973** *Tabbert Coll.* **AK,** Cabin fever—a psychological aberration supposedly caused by the long, extreme cold and lack of sun in winter. **1978** *UpCountry* May 15 **Cape Cod MA,** There came a winter when Mom was pretty much house-bound . . . To be honest, we both had a touch of cabin fever.

cabio See **cobia**

cablam See **ker-**

cable-stretcher See **stretcher**

cablub See **ker-**

cabm See **captain**

‡caboche n [Fr *caboche* head]
   1969 Cagnon *Franco–Amer. Terms* **RI,** Caboche . . [kabɔš] Head. "You fell on your caboche?"

caboodle n For varr see quots [*ca-* var of **ker-** + **boodle** n **1**]
   See also **kit and caboodle**
   Usu prec by *whole:* A large and miscellaneous collection of things or people.

   1848 Bartlett *Americanisms* 393, *Caboodle. The whole caboodle* is a common expression, meaning the whole . . . It is used in all the Northern States and New England. **1884** Baldwin *Yankee School-Teacher* 27,

I wish the hull keboodle on ye a merry Christmas. **1890** *DN* 1.64, *Compoodle . . .* same as *caboodle.* **1894** *DN* 1.341 **wCT,** *Koboodle . . the hull koboodle* is commonest. **1899** (1912) Green *VA Folk-Speech* 104, *Caboodle . .* crowd; pack; lot; company. The "whole caboodle." **1903** *DN* 2.296 **Cape Cod MA** (as of 1850s), *Caboodle . . .* Crowd. **1905** *DN* 3.5 **cCT,** *Caboodle . . .* The whole lot. *Ibid* 60 **NE,** *Caboodle . . .* Crowd, lot, "outfit." *Ibid* 72 **nwAR,** *Caboodle, capoodle.* **1907** *DN* 3.206 **nwAR,** *Caboodle.* **1908** *DN* 3.296 **eAL, wGA,** *Caboodle.* **1915** *DN* 4.184 **swVA,** *Kapoodle . . .* Group; crowd. **1949** H. Truman in *Time* 18 July 13/2, There was no longer any point to the whole kit & caboodle of anti-inflation controls which he had been demanding. **1950** *WELS* (They made a lot of noise so he sent the whole _____ home) 1 Inf, **cWI,** Gaboodle. **1954** *Harder Coll.* **cwTN,** Caboodle—A whole group of people. **1965–70** *DARE* (Qu. LL10, . . *"They made too much noise, so he sent the whole _____ home."*) 55 Infs, **scattered,** Caboodle; **GA72, IN35, KY74, NM12, VA42, 66,** Capoodle; **FL52, MO21, NY70,** Shoot and caboodle; **NJ51, PA50,** Shoot and capoodle; **ME16,** Parcel and caboodle; **OK9,** Shootin' capoodle; (Qu. LL25, . . *"He sold out the whole place, _____."*) 16 Infs, **scattered,** Caboodle; **TN6, VA42,** Capoodle; **NJ8,** Batch and caboodle; **TX10,** Lock and caboodle; **NY70,** Shit and caboodle, shoot and caboodle; (Qu. LL8b, . . *"She has a whole _____ of cousins."*) Infs **GA12, HI6, MI92, NY94,** Caboodle.

‡cabooma n [*ca-* var of **ker-** + *boom* + *a*] Cf **boomer-peg**
=cricket n².

   1966 *DARE* (Qu. EE10, *A game in which a short stick lying on the ground is flipped into the air and then hit with a longer stick, that's _____*) Inf **FL8,** [kə'bumə].

cabooner n
   A rich strike in mining.

   1945 *CA Folkl. Qrly.* 4.320 **CO** [Cornish words], Cabooner: Bonanza. I never heard this term used in conversation, but I was told the story three or four times of John Prouse, coming into the office of the Hidden Treasure when Alfred Richard had just struck a good body of ore and asking: "How's the cabooner?"

caboos n [Port *cabóz* big-head, a fish similar to the frog-fish or sculpin]
   A goby or gobylike fish.

   1967 *DARE* (Qu. P1, . . *Freshwater fish . . good to eat*) Inf **HI4,** Caboos [kɐ'bus]; in Hawaiian, *'o'opu.*

caboose n¹ [Du *kabuis, kombuis* cook's galley]
   1 for arch spp, see quots: A cook's galley on a vessel. esp N Atl coast arch or obs

   1747 in 1910 Essex Inst. *Coll.* 46.91 **MA,** They shipp'd a Sea which carried overboard . . their Boat and Carpouse. *Ibid,* Another [heavy sea] carried away their Boat, Cabbouze & one Carriage Gun. **1766** *Boston Evening-Post* (MA) 10 Nov 2/2, 'Twas imagined she took fire at sea, as her cabouse was burnt. **1789** in 1886 Boston Registry Dept. *Records* 10.211, Chimnies and cabbusses for vessels. **1805** (1904) Lewis *Orig. Jrls. Lewis & Clark Exped.* 1.255, I permitted the blacksmith to dispose of a part of a sheet iron Callaboos which had been nearly birnt out on our passage up the river. **1848** Bartlett *Americanisms* 60, *Caboose.* The common pronunciation for *camboose* (Dutch *kombuis*), a ship's cooking-range or kitchen. **1899** (1912) Green *VA Folk-Speech* 104, *Caboose . . .* Cambouse. The small house on board a vessel where cooking is done. **1926** Ashley *Yankee Whaler* 126, *Camboose:* Whaler's name for caboose or galley. A ship's kitchen.

   2 A railroad car attached usu behind a freight train, where members of the crew may cook, eat, and sleep.

   1861 H. Dawson *Remin. Life Locomotive Engineer* 90 *(OEDS),* Another midnight ride in the 'Caboose' of a freight train. **1945** in 1953 Botkin *Treas. Railroad Folkl.* 344, In the gaudy lexicon of railroad jargon it [=the caboose] has more names than any other property in the economy of the high iron . . . It is a caboose, . . drone house, . . diner, . . and shanty. **1977** Adams *Lang. Railroader,* Caboose—See anchor, angel's seat, animal car, ape wagon, bazoo wagon, bed house, bouncer, brain cage, brain wagon, buggy, . . cabin car, . . cage, chariot, chuck wagon, clown wagon, cook loft, conductor's car, cook shack, coop, cracker box, crib, cripple's home, . . crumb box, crummy, . . den, doghouse, doodlebug, doss, drawing room, flophouse, flop wagon, galloping goose, glory wagon, go-cart, hack, hay wagon, hearse, hut, kipps, kitchen, library, louse cage, . . monkey cage, monkey house, monkey hut, monkey wagon, palace, parlor, . . pavilion, . . perambulator, . . rest room, saloon, shack, shack house, shanty, shelter house, . . skunk speeder, . . treasure house, van, way car, zoo.

3 *Transf:* any small cramped building or place within a building.

1839 U.S. Congress *Congressional Globe* App 15 Feb 343/1, In his little caboose of a post office I have found electioneering interferences. **1891** Farmer–Henley *Slang, Caboose* . . . (American).—Generally applied to convivial quarters; also to a bachelor's snuggery—a *den.* **1942** Berrey–Van den Bark *Amer. Slang* 44.2, *Cubbyhole; narrow, contracted place.* Caboose. *Ibid* 83.3, *Any dwelling, esp. a mean one* . . caboose. **1958** McCulloch *Woods Words* 27 **Pacific NW,** *Caboose* . . . At times used to mean bunkhouse.

4 =**cuna** n 2.

1920 Hunter *Trail Drivers TX* 1.237, Under a camp wagon is usually suspended an old cowhide called the "caboose," and in that we throw stray pieces of wood . . for use in . . emergencies. **1968** Adams *Western Words* 85.

5 *Transf from* **2:** anything that follows behind or comes last in a sequence, as:

a The buttocks.

1932 in 1947 Stix *Say It Ain't* 300 **NYC,** It used to look very funny from the sidelines with all those wrestlers' cabooses sticking out. **1942** Berrey–Van den Bark *Amer. Slang* 121.71, *Posteriors* . . caboose. **1944** Mencken *Christmas Story* 23 **MD,** Larry and the other comedians began paddling the girls' cabooses with slapsticks. **1969** DARE (Qu. X35, *Joking words for the part of the body that you sit on*) Inf **CA**166, Caboose.

b The lastborn child in a family.

1950 WELS (*The youngest child*) 2 Infs, **ce,seWI,** The caboose.

c One who follows or imitates others; one who allows himself to be duped.

1969 DARE (Qu. Y9, *Somebody who always follows along behind others*) Inf **MI**103, Caboose; (Qu. II34, *If you think somebody is trying to use you to his advantage: "I'm not going to be his _____."*) Inf **SC**65, Tool, caboose, fool.

caboose n² [Prob alter of **calaboose,** but cf **caboose** n¹ 3]

A jail.

1865 *Republican Banner* (Nashville, Tenn.) 12 Oct. 3/2 *(DA),* The 'caboose' is neatly packed with 'pickled' offenders of municipal law. **1939** FWP *These are Our Lives* 346 **NC,** It's going to be kept clean as long as I'm there if they put me in the caboose for cruelty to roaches and water bugs. **1965–70** DARE (Qu. V11, *What joking names do you have around here for a county or city jail?*) 16 Infs, **scattered,** Caboose.

caboose bounce n Also *caboose hop*

A short train consisting of only an engine and a caboose.

1929 *Bookman* 69.526, Caboose bounce: A train made up of just the engine and caboose. Also spoken of as running light. **1940** Cottrell *Railroader* 122, Caboose bounce—An early term for a train composed of only engine and caboose. *Caboose hop*—More widespread term [than *caboose bounce*]. **1943** AmSp 18.163, Caboose bounce, caboose hop. **1951** Porter *Ragged Roads* 19 **OK,** The hobo likes to think he is "beatin'" a ride, and not that he is the recipient of alms extended by a caboose hop. **1958** McCulloch *Woods Words* 27 **Pacific NW,** *Caboose hop.* **1962** AmSp 37.132 **nCA,** Caboose hop. **1977** Adams *Lang. Railroader* 27, Caboose bounce . . caboose hop.

‡**caboose mice** n Cf *DS* BB28

1950 WELS (*Joking or fantastic names for imaginary diseases: "I guess he's got the _____."*) 1 Inf, **cnWI,** Heebie-jeebies, caboose mice.

‡**caboot** n |kə'but| [Var of **boot** n¹ **1,** perh infl by **caboodle**] =**boot** n¹ **1.**

1969 DARE (Qu. U15, *When you're buying something, if the seller puts in a little extra to make you feel that you're getting a good bargain, you call that _____*) Inf **NY**207, A caboot [kə'but]—only around here.

caboras See **cabestro**

caboulder n [*ca-* var of **ker-** + **boulder**]

In marble play: see quots.

1968 DARE File **Long Island NY,** Caboulder, a large marble; [the] purey [and] caboulder—the most valuable marbles. **1973** Ferretti *Marble Book* 41 **NY,** Bumboozer. A very large marble, used as a bowling shooter. Also called a Boulder, or Caboulder or Scaboulder.

cabouse See **caboose** n¹ **1**

cabrace See **cape-race**

cabras, cabrass, cabressa, cabresse, cabresta, cabresto, cabris See **cabestro**

cabrito n [Span "young goat"] **TX**

Suckling goat usu barbecued.

1940 FWP *Guide TX* 87, Goat raisers a few years ago attempted to popularize the meat and adopted the name "chevon" [sic] to distinguish it from mutton. But the campaign [to change the name] failed, and cabrito is still a sectional dish, as well known to the remainder of Texas as the tamale, yet as seldom eaten by the average citizen. *Ibid* 340, Venders offer unusual wares, from a live cabrito (kid) to a penny's worth of dulces (candies or cakes). **1957** Stoker *Concha's Cook Book* 118, *Cabrito Asado con Salsa* Roasted baby goat with Sauce: One-half baby goat or lamb (one that is still sucking milk). **1967** DARE (Qu. H45) Inf **TX**5, Cabrito [kæ'brito]—barbecued little goat; **TX**11, Cabrito [,ka'brito]—small goat roasted over [an] open fire; (Qu. H65, *Foreign foods favored by people around here*) Inf **TX**26, Tacos, macaroni, enchiladas, cabrito (goat meat). **1967–70** DARE Tape **TX**81, A cabrito [kæ'bri·to] is a small Spanish goat and we think it makes the finest barbecue of any kind of meat. Fairly recent in this area; **TX**43, Cabrito . . . They fix it all kind of ways. My favorite way is to barbecue it.

cacely See **scarcely**

cachanilla See **cachimilla**

cache n [Fr "hiding place"] **AK**

By ext from std sense: a small house used for storage of food and equipment; see quots.

1867 *The Esquimaux* (Libbysville, Port Clarence) 5 May 35 (Tabbert *Alaskan Engl.*), He returned . . with ten large fish . . which . . he had stolen from an Indian cache. **1870** Dall *Alaska* 27, Behind these houses are the caches, called *kradowói* by the Russians. They are simply small houses, about six feet square and high, elevated from six to ten feet above the ground on four upright posts. They are well roofed and are used only as storehouses for provisions. **1956** Marshall *Arctic Wilderness* 64, We left about half our food and dog feed for the Wild River part of our journey, storing it in Ernie's cache, a little log cabin built on poles about eight feet high. **1968** DARE Tape **AK**13, He was stationed here . . [at the] Forest Service tent. This was just a cache. [FW:] That looks like a little house, but it really was a cache. [Inf:] Oh yes, it is a little cabin . . on this hill . . . People would stop [there] overnight. **1981** Tabbert *Alaskan Engl.* 173, For more than 100 years now *cache* has been used here to name the small (usually) log cabin which is built up on poles above the reach of animals and which is used to store food, furs, and gear.

cachimilla n Also *cachanilla, cachinilla* [AmSpan] **SW** =**arrowweed 1.**

1911 *Century Dict. Suppl.,* *Cachimilla* . . . A west American composite shrub, *Pluchea sericea,* called *arrow-wood* by travelers because it is used by the Indians in making arrows. It ranges from western Texas to California and northern Mexico. Also called *arrow-weed.* **1913** Wooton *Trees NM* 146, *Arrow Wood* or *Cachinilla (Berthellotia borrealis* [sic]*)* is a common shrub, forming large patches in the valleys of the southern part of the State. **1931** Dayton *Western Browse Plants* 164 *(DA),* Arrowweed [is] . . also known by the vernacular names arrowbush, arrowwood, cachanilla, cachimilla, and osikakamuk.

cachunk See **ker-**

cack n¹ Also sp *kack* [Perh from *cack* excrement; cf other derog terms applied affectionately to children, as **bugger** n¹ **B2**]

A small child.

1895 DN 1.385 **CT,** *Cack:* like *shaver* . . used playfully of a child. **1910** DN 3.445 **wNY,** Little *kack* . . . Child.

cack n² Also sp *kack, kak* [Etym uncert, but perh abbr for **cactus** n²; see quot 1937] **West**

A saddle, esp an old or ill-fitting one.

1936 McCarthy *Lang. Mosshorn* **West** [Range terms], *Kack* . . . A saddle. **1937** DN 6.618 **cwTX,** Other words for saddle besides *ellum* include *hull* and *cack.* The horse objects to a saddle just as he does to thorny cactus on his back; hence the use of the colorful *cack* for saddle. **1939** FWP *ID Lore* 244, Then he throws on the kak (saddle) and screws hisself on tight (assumes a firm position) and tops him off (lets the horse go). **1939** FWP *Guide MT* 414, *Kack*—Saddle. **1940** FWP *Guide NV* 75, Cactus, hull, chair, centerfire, kak, rigging—all names for saddle in Nevada. **1949** PADS 11.4 **wTX,** *Cack* [kæk] . . . An old saddle. Occasional. **1958** AmSp 33.271 **eWA,** *Kack.* Any saddle, but usually an inferior or beat-up one.   **1961** Adams *Old-Time Cowhand* 113 **West,** Some saddles don't fit the hoss they're on, and cause sores, "set fasts," or "kack biscuits," as they're sometimes called. *Ibid,* No matter how good a blanket you use, if the saddle's an old worn-out kack that's been warped out of shape, it doesn't protect the hoss from a sore back.

cack n[3]   See **cackling goose**

cack v[1]   See **cacky** v, n

cack v[2]
To cackle.
   1970 *DARE* Tape **VA**112, They [=marsh hens] cack like a chicken you know, when a chicken lays eggs.

cack v[3] [Abbr for *cactus*]
   1933 *AmSp* 8.1.31 **nwTX,** One of the most interesting and illuminating divisions of the cowboy's vocabulary is his slang . . . *Cack.* To throw cactus on an animal to make it fight.

cack v[4]   See **caulk B**

cackany n Also abbr *cany,* pronc-spp *cock-a-nee-nee, cookania* [Origin unknown] **esp NY** *old-fash* Cf **jack wax**
Molasses candy; **maple wax.**
   1807 Irving *Salmagundi* 10.203, Boil your molasses to a proper consistency . . then pour it off, and let it cool, or draw it out into little pieces about nine inches long, and put it out for use. This manufacture is called by the bostonians *lasses candy*—by the new-yorkers *cock-a-nee-nee.* **1855** Barnum *Life* 21, My stock in trade consisted of a gallon of molasses, boiled down and worked into molasses candy, called in those times "cookania." **1901** *DN* 2.137 **cwNY,** Cackany [kak'eni] . . . Wax of maple, sugar; also home-made molasses candy in small lump, to be held in fingers; something like all-day suckers, but without stick. **1904** *DN* 2.395, *Cany* [kenɪ] . . . When I was a boy in Montgomery County, N.Y., maple wax made by throwing thickened maple syrup on the snow to cool was always called *cany.*

cackey, cackie   See **cacky** v, n

cack'late   See **calculate**

cackle v Also *cackle out,* and redund *cackle-laugh* **chiefly Sth, S Midl** See Map
To burst out laughing.
   1931 *AmSp* 6.270 **KY,** A large class of compounds is formed by combining two words . . to express similar or related ideas . . . cackle-laughin'. **1965–70** *DARE* (Qu. GG30, *To suddenly break out laughing: "When he told her that, she just _____."*) 37 Infs, **chiefly Sth, S Midl,** Cackled; 8 Infs, **chiefly Sth, S Midl,** Cackled out.

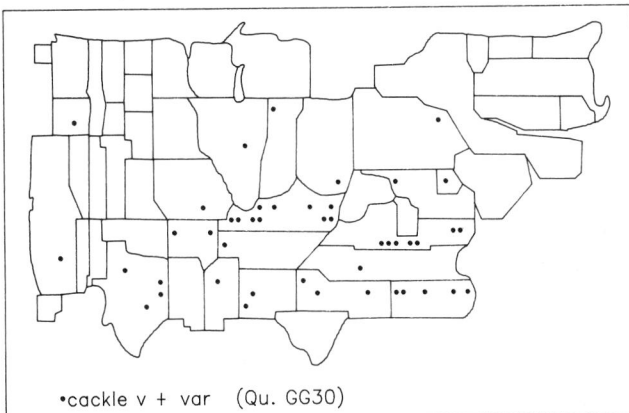

•cackle v + var   (Qu. GG30)

cackle n[1] Cf **cackleberry**
An egg.
   1930 *DN* 6.89 **cWV,** *Two cackles with their eyes open,* two fried eggs. **1946** *AmSp* 21.31 **ceTX,** *Cackle(s)* . . . Egg.

cackle n[2] [Malapropism for *grackle,* infl by *cackle,* sound made by hens and other birds]
A **grackle.**
   1969 *DARE* (Qu. Q11, *Kinds of blackbirds*) Inf **NY**211, Purple cackle.

cackleberry n Also *cackle fruit, cackle jelly* *humorous* Cf **hen fruit**
An egg.

   1916 *DN* 4.272 **NE,** *Cackleberries* . . . Eggs. "Pass the cackleberries." Doane College, Crete, Nebraska. [Also Pa., Kan.] **1922** *DN* 5.151, Cackle-berry. **1925** *AmSp* 1.139 **Pacific NW,** And he [=a logger] goes forth to eat of "cackleberries and grunts (eggs and bacon)." **1925** Krapp *Engl. Lang.* 1.321, Sometimes slang is complicated in its suggestiveness, like *cackleberry,* meaning egg. **1930** *DN* 6.86 **cWV,** *Cackleberries.* **1947** Berrey–Van den Bark *Amer. Slang Suppl.* 27.2, Bombs, cackle jelly, *eggs.* **c1960** *Wilson Coll.* **csKY,** *Cackleberries* . . . Facetious for eggs. "We had bacon and cackleberries for breakfast." **1966** *DARE* (Qu. H33, *Joking names for eggs*) Inf **GA**8, Cackle fruit. **1966** *DARE* Tape **NC**30, At these logging camps they used different words for different items of food, such as: eggs were either cackleberries or hen fruit. **1968** Adams *Western Words, Cackleberries*—A logger's name for eggs.

cacklebird n *humorous* Cf **cackle** n[1], **cackleberry**
A chicken.
   1966 *St. John Valley Times* (Madawaska ME) 23 June 10/1, [Advt:] Cacklebirds 4 to 6 lb average Grown on the Shores of Penobscot [sic] Bay.

cackleburr n [Var of **cockleburr 1**]
   1968 *DARE* (Qu. S13) Inf **IA**22, [ˈkækl̩ˌbɚz].

cackle out   See **cackle** v

cackler n
See quots.
   1926 *AmSp* 1.650 [Hobo lingo], *Cacklers*—white collared office workers. **1927** *DN* 5.441 **NC,** *Cacklers* . . . Office workers;—so called because of their supposed hen-coop effeminacy. **1968** Adams *Western Words, Cackler*—A logger's and miner's term for a clerk. **1969** Sorden *Lumberjack Lingo* 20 **NEng, Gt Lakes,** *Cackler*—A white-collar worker.

cackling goose n Also *cack, cackler* [See quot 1918]
A smaller and darker, chiefly western subsp of the **Canada goose** (here: *Branta canadensis minima*).   Also called **brown brant, bullneck 3, gray brant, greaser, little squeaking goose, squealer, yelper**
   1909 Field Mus. Nat. Hist. *Zool. Ser.* 9.352, Cackling goose . . . winters from southern British Columbia to California; stragglers occur in the Mississippi Valley and Wisconsin. **1918** Grinnell *Game Birds CA* 234, Cackler . . . The high-pitched call-note (whence the name Cackling Goose) is easily distinguished from the notes of the Canada and Hutchins geese. **1923** U.S. Dept. Ag. *Misc. Circular* 13.37, Cackling Goose . . . Vernacular names . . . *In local use* . . . Cackler (Nebr., Calif.). **1940** Gabrielson *Birds OR* 127, In addition to its small size and dark color, this species has a distinctive high-pitched call . . that is recognized by many hunters who, in various localities, call it "China Goose," "Cackler," "Cack," or "Squealer." *Ibid* 128, Neither of us has hunted in this area, but we have examined numerous geese killed there without finding a single "Cackler." **1953** Jewett *Birds WA* 105, Alaskan Cackling Goose . . . Other names: Cackling Goose; Cackler; Cack. *Ibid* 106, According to Kitchin . . he saw a flock of "cacklers" at Westport September 15 to 19, 1930. **1967–69** *DARE* (Qu. Q6) Infs **CA**140, 155, 160, **MN**34, **OR**5, Cacklers; **IA**22, Cackling geese.

cacky v, n Also sp *cackey, cackie, cockey, kacky;* less freq *cack* [Scots, Engl dial *cack, cacky* to void (as) excrement] Cf **hockey** n[2], v
To void excrement; human excrement.
   1886 Amer. Philol. Assoc. *Trans.* 17.37 **eTN,** To cacky, 'alvum exonerare.' Webster gives to *cack* in this sense from Pope. It may still be heard in East Tennessee. **1899** (1912) Green *VA Folk-Speech* 104, Cacky, n. Human excrement. **1916** *DN* 4.320 **KS,** *Cackey, cockey, n.* and *v.i.* Variants of cackie, excrement: a child's word. **1930** Shoemaker *1300 Words* 36 **cPA Mts** (as of c1900), *Kacky*—Excrement. **1978** *DARE* File **cnMA** (as of c1918), One of the terms for human excrement used by some small children was [ˈkækɪ].

cacky adj [**cacky** v, n]
Sticky, mucky.
   1968 *DARE* (Qu. Y40a, *Other words referring to sticky stuff: "I've got to wash my hands, they're all _____."*) Inf **MN**15, Cacky.

ca'c'late   See **calculate**

cacomite n [MexSpan]
1 Either of two plants of the family Iridaceae: a **blue-eyed grass 1** (here: *Sisyrinchium bermudiana*) or a tiger flower (here: *Tigridia pavonia*).

1892 *DN* 1.188 **TX,** *Cacomíte* (from Mexican *cacomitl,* S.): an edible bulbous root. The name is applied to a number of different bulbs, but chiefly to *Sisyrinchium Bermudiana* and *Tigridia pavonia,* both belonging to the family of *Iridiæ.* **1938** *AmSp* 13.116, Edible roots include *cacomite* and *camote* . . . *Tigridia* . . bore the Mexican name of *caco-mite* . . . *Tigridia pavonia,* and . . *Sisyrinchium bermudiana* are known to Texan Americans by this name. **1953** *AmSp* 28.101 **TX,** *Caco-mite* . . . In Texas, Tigridia pavonia, the tiger flower, or *Sisyrinchium bermudiana.*

2 A nodding onion (here: *Allium cernuum*).

1953 *AmSp* 28.101 **NM,** *Cacomite* . . . In New Mexico, *Allium recurvatum.*

cactified adj Cf **-ified**

1950 *PADS* 14.18, *Cactified* . . . Assuming a false appearance of superiority, "stuck up." Upcountry S.C.

cactus n[1]

A Forms.

Pl: usu *cacti, cactuses;* occas *cactus.* See Intro "Language Changes" II.7

1905 *DN* 3.73 **nwAR,** *Cactus* . . . 'Mr. James has some twenty or more cactus.' Common.

B Senses.

1 Std: a plant of the family Cactaceae.

2 A **glasswort** (here: *Salicornia perennis*).

1913 *Torreya* 13.230, *Salicornia ambigua* . . . Cactus, Cameron, La.

3 also *cactus plant:* **=mullein.**

1967 *DARE* (Qu. S20) Inf **MO**12, [From the description it] sounds like a cactus. **1968** *DARE* Tape **GA**30, Most the people now'd call it cactus plants, but they called it mullein and they'd beat that up and make a poultice for the chest.

cactus n[2] [Perh from the discomfort it causes the horse; cf **cack** n[2]] Cf **kyack** n[2]

A packsaddle.

1940 FWP *Guide NV* 75, The saddle, which the cow-country calls *cactus, hull, chair, centerfire, kak, pack,* or *rigging.*

cactus apple n

Perh the fruit of a **yucca,** but cf **banana B2, banana yucca.**

1967–68 *DARE* (Qu. I46, . . *Fruits that grow wild around here*) Infs **CA**4, 90, Cactus apple(s).

cactus berry n

Perh the fruit of a **yucca.**

1967 *DARE* (Qu. I44, . . *Berries [that] grow wild around here*) Inf **CO**20, Cactus berries.

cactus boomer n [*cactus (country)* + *boomer* a drifter] **West** *old-fash*

See quots.

1929 Dobie *Vaquero* 210, A popular nickname for the wild brush cattle was "cactus boomers." **1961** Adams *Old-Time Cowhand* 155 **TX,** The old "longhorn" of the brush country of Texas were called "brush splitters," and "cactus boomers."

cactus plant See **cactus** n[1] **B3**

cactus quail n [From its habitat] **SW**

=scaled quail.

1961 Ligon *NM Birds* 96, The Scaled Quail [is] also widely known as Blue Quail, Cottontop, Blue Racer, and Cactus Quail.

cactus rose n Cf **prickly pear**

Prob the flower of a cactus of the genus *Opuntia.*

1967 *DARE* (Qu. S26a, . . *Roadside flowers*) Inf **CO**22, Cactus rose; (Qu. S15) Inf **CO**22, Cactus rose.

cactus thrush n

Prob a **thrasher** (here: *Toxostoma* spp).

1967 *DARE* (Qu. Q14) Inf **CA**9, Cactus thrush.

cactus woodpecker n

=gila woodpecker.

1914 U.S. Natl. Museum *Bulletin* 50.6.254, *Dryobates Scalaris Cacto-philus* Oberholser. Cactus Woodpecker. **1941** Jaeger *Wildflowers* 19 **SW,** The red-shafted flicker and the little speckle-check or cactus wood-pecker dig holes in the fibrous trunks and branches.

cad n [*OED cad*[2] 2, →1839] *arch* or *old-fash*

1915 *DN* 4.224 **wTX,** Cad . . . Familiar term of address, similar in meaning to *sport* and *pal.* "Hello, cad, where are you goin'?"

cadamize See **macadamize**

cadamy See **macadamy**

‡**cadarup** v [Perh **ker-** + unknown element]

To leap about.

1911 *DN* 3.542 **NE,** *Cada'rup* . . . About the same meaning as *cavort.* "My little girl climbed on the table and cadaruped over it, knocking off a china plate." "Quit cadaruping around here and settle down."

cadder See **caddow**

caddie n[1] [*OED caddie* 2 →1883]

1981 *Milwaukee Jrl.* (WI) 20 Dec sec 2 12/4 **Madison WI,** The people who don the sandwich boards are called caddies. Last summer, Walking Ads hired about 18 caddies at $3.50 an hour.

caddie n[2] See **catty** n[1]

caddow n Also pronc-sp *cadder* [*OED caddow*[2], "Obs. or dial.";* *DOST* 1576 → but no longer current in Scots] *?obs*

A quilt or coverlet.

1789 Robert Carter *Letter* 8 Dec. *(DAE),* The bearer . . . calles on you for . . . a pr. of Cadders or Blankets. **1843** *Amer. Pioneer* 2.446 **OH** (as of 1802), To make rag carpeting, such as sometimes covers kitchen floors now, and to sew two breadths of proper length together, was a good substitute for blankets . . . These cadders (for so we called them,) were a great help in bed . . from their great ability to press a sheet or blanket close. **1899** (1912) Green *VA Folk-Speech,* Caddow.

caddy n[1] See **catty** n[1]

caddy n[2] See **cady**

caddy n[3] [*caddy* small container; convenient household device; see *W3* [2]*caddy* 2]

An antimacassar, a chair **tidy.**

1968 *DARE* (Qu. E10) Inf **VA**28, Caddies.

caddy n[4] See **catty** n[3]

caddy adj Often sp *catty* [Engl dial *caddy* hale, hearty, in good health and spirits; perh infl by *catty* like a cat]

1 Spry, agile, active.

1938 *Hall Coll.* **wNC, eTN,** *Catty,* active, lively, not still a minute. **1939** *Ibid, Catty* . . . "pretty spry". Fairly common. **1956** *Ibid,* I was catty for a little feller. **1958** McCulloch *Woods Words* **Pacific NW,** *Catty* . . . Fast on the feet. **1969** Sorden *Lumberjack Lingo* 23 **NEng, Gt Lakes,** Catty man—Any man who was quick on his feet, generally in reference to a river pig. **1969** *DARE* (Qu. KK27, *A very lively, active old person: "For his age, he's _____."*) Inf **GA**72, Spry, caddy, glib.

2 Stylish, well dressed. [Cf *EDD caddle* "Dainty, fastidious"]

1918 *DN* 5.22 **nwID** [Students], *Catty* . . . Well-dressed (of a girl); becoming (of her clothes). **1966** *DARE* (Qu. W38, *When a man dresses himself up in his best clothes, you say he's _____*) Inf **WA**18, Looking caddy—like sophisticated. [Inf born 1881]

caddy bat See **catty** n[1] **2**

caddy-corner(ed) See **catercorner** adj, adv, v

caddywampus See **catawampus** adj

cade n, often attrib or in comb, as *cade lamb* [EModE *cad,* lamb rejected by its mother and brought up as a pet (*OED cade* sb.[2] 2a)] **seMA, sRI** Cf maps in 1949 Kurath *Word Geog.* Figs 12, 105

1 A domestic animal, usu a lamb, brought up as a pet: see quots.

1889 (1971) Farmer *Americanisms,* Cade.—A calf, a pet. **1931–33** *LANE Worksheets* **sRI,** 2 infs, Cade sheep—sheep raised by hand, a tame sheep; 1 inf, **sRI,** Cade bull—a bull brought up by hand; 1 inf, **sRI,** Cade hen, cade rooster—raised as pet; 1 inf, **nwRI,** Cade sheep—sheep brought up on a bottle . . . cade is also used of pigs. **1959** *AmSp* 34.249, An orphan lamb raised on the bottle . . *cade*—*cade lamb* is the dominant form throughout the Midlands [of England]. In this country [the U.S.] . . *cade* is a localism restricted to the Narragansett Bay area and Cape Cod.

2 Transf: a spoiled or pampered child.

1931–33 *LANE Worksheets,* 1 inf **seMA,** Of a child: he's a cade. **1941** *LANE* Map 379 *(kid, tot),* 1 inf, **sRI,** A regular cade = a spoiled child.

3 Used as an exclam: a call to sheep. Cf *DS* K85
1949 Kurath *Word Geog.* 65 **sRI, seMA,** Calls to sheep . . . Narragansett Bay alone has *cade!,* which is here also the name for a pet sheep.

cade adv [**cade** n 1]
Treated as a pet.
1931–33 *LANE Worksheets,* 1 inf, **sRI,** The sheep was brought up cade.

cademy n [**catty** n¹ **1** perh blended with *academy,* by school association]
=**catty** n¹ **1.**
1943 *Baltimore Sun* 17 Aug 12/7 *(Hench Coll.)* **MD,** My reference to the game of caddy, or catty, has produced an astonishing flood of information . . . Some Marylanders call it cademy.

caderidge See **cartridge**

cadey See **cady**

cadged adj [Perh *caged,* but cf **cadgy**]
1941 *Sat. Eve. Post* 10 May 111/2 **TN,** He got as restless in his chair as a cadged kid.

cadgy adj Pronc-spp *cagey, cagy, caigy, cajy, kagy* [Scots *caigie* wanton; cheerful, sportive; *DSL* 1592 →; see also *EDD, SND*] **chiefly S Midl** Cf **cadged**
Lively, excited, spry; esp of a stallion, sexually aroused, hence apt to be dangerous.
1897 *KS Univ. Qrly.* 6.51, *Cagy* . . keen, or full of animal spirits. **1902** *DN* 2.237 **sIL,** *Kagy* [keji] . . Epithumetic. **1903** *DN* 2.308 **sMO,** *Cagy* . . . Rampant, as applied to stallions. **1906** *DN* 3.115 **sIN,** *Cagy.* **1909** *DN* 3.393 **nwAR,** *Cagy* . . . Vicious, rampant (of stallions). **1916** *DN* 4.321 **KS,** *Cagey, cajy* ['keji] . . . Having strong sexual desire; esp. of a male. "The stallion is quite cajy after seeing a mare go by." **1917** *DN* 4.409 **wNC,** *Caigy* . . . Full of sexual desire . . . In N. Eng. applied to a high-spirited horse. **1923** *DN* 5.203 **swMO,** *Cagey* . . . Passionate, sensual. Cf. *Horny.* **1926** Kephart *Highlanders* 354, A few words, caigy (cadgy), coggled, [etc] . . almost exhaust the list of distinct Scotticisms. **1927** *AmSp* 2.350 **WV,** *Cagey* . . full of sexual desire and usually used in referring to males. **1944** *PADS* 2.25 **OH,** *Caigy* ['kedʒɪ] . . inflamed with sexual desire. **1953** Randolph *Down in Holler* 107 **Ozarks,** *Cagey, pruney, rollicky,* and *horny* are the conventional words for sensual, and are not used in polite conversation. **1961** Sackett–Koch *KS Folkl.* 112, *Cagey, cajy* . . . Having sexual desire. **1976** Garber *Mountain-ese, Cagey* . . sexually adventurous . . . Pa, that Ellie May is so cagey she's agoin' to git into trouble.

cadi See **cady**

cadillo n [Span, burdock or similar plant]
A **burr grass** (here: *Cenchrus echinatus*).
1970 Correll *Plants TX* 189, *Cadillo* . . . Burs about 4–6 mm. thick basally . . . Coastal States, N.C. to Tex.

cadridge See **cartridge**

cadulix n [Origin unknown] *?obs*
1930 Shoemaker *1300 Words* **cPA,** Cadulix—Male genital organ.

cady n Also sp *caddy, cadey, cadi, kady, katy* [Scots *cadie* ['kedi] a man's or boy's cap—see *SND Suppl.*]
A hat or cap.
1846 *Spirit of the Times* 6 June 170/2 *(DAE),* I may be able to discover my lost 'Cady'. **1891** Farmer–Henley *Slang* 14, *Cady* . . . A hat . . . Sometimes written *cadey* and *caddy.* **1912** *DN* 3.572 **wIN,** *Cady* . . . A hat. The term is applied to any kind of hat worn by a man. "Get your cady and we'll go." **1947** Ballowe *The Lawd* 3 **LA,** Cuffee's eyes were fixed upon the straw hat with the blue band that the stranger wore. "Efn Ah had ma ruthers," he said, "Ah'd take his katy." "Not me," Sambo, his partner, said. "Ah'd grab his yaller shoes." **1960** Wentworth–Flexner *Slang* 84, Cady, caddy, cadi, kady, katy . . . A man's hat or cap. *Underworld use since c1850; now somewhat archaic.*

Caesar pine n
The cluster pine (*Pinus pinaster*).
1969 *DARE* (Qu. T17, . . *Different kinds of pine trees*) Inf **NC76,** Caesar—started in the fifties, special for salt weather—same [as] Maritime [pine].

cafe n, also attrib Pronc-spp *caffey, caffy, caif, calf* **chiefly West, Sth** See Map

A small coffeehouse or restaurant, now esp one considered inexpensive or inferior.
1835 Ingraham *South-West* 1.112 **LA,** We repaired to an adjoining café, à la mode New-Orleans. **1891** *Harper's Mag.* 84.49/2 **NYC,** I was inspired with the idea of taking our guest off to a café concert over in the Bowery. **1921** Thorp *Songs Cowboys* 74 **CO,** You kin brag of city caffeys . . / Of their meals served a la carty. **1921** *DN* 5.78 [The jocularizing of French words], *Caif, calf, caffy,* café. **1965–70** *DARE* (Qu. D39, *Nicknames . . for a small eating place where the food is not especially good*) 28 Infs, **chiefly Sth and West,** Cafe.

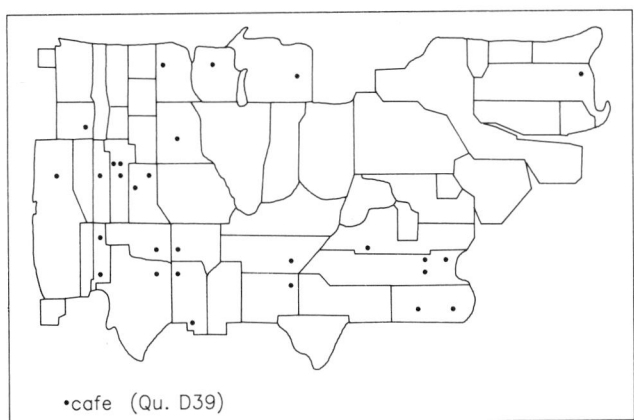

•cafe (Qu. D39)

caflooey, cafluey See **ker-**

caflugalty See **cafugelty, ker-**

caflummox See **flummox, ker-**

cafugelty n Also *caflugalty* [Prob alter of Scots *carfuffle, carfuchle* disagreement, quarrel (*SND carfuffle* n 2), perh blended with Scots *curfuggle* mess, disorder. Cf also **diffucalty, ker-**] *old-fash* or *obs*
See quots.
1914 *DN* 4.154 **NH** (as of a1900), *Cafugelty* . . . Trouble; a row. **1932** *AmSp* 7.330 **Baltimore MD,** [Johns Hopkins students' jargon], Caflugalty—difficulty.

cag See **keg**

cage n
c1970 Wiersma *Marbles Terms,* Cage—[a] clear marble with colorful center stripes. 'He has five blue cages.' [Heard in Monrovia CA]

cage-the-bird n
See quot 1969.
[**1949** Shaw *Cowboy Dances* 278 **West,** Bird in a Cage and Allemande Six.] **1969** *DARE* (Qu. FF5a, *Different steps and figures in dancing—in past years*) Inf **KY40,** Cage-the-bird (a square-dance step).

cage vine n [Perh for **cowitch** + *vine*]
1970 *DARE* (Qu. S17, . . *Other kinds of plants . . that will cause itching and swelling*) Inf **VA38,** Cage vine—a vine that runs up trees—like wild grape vine—has long bean-like pods.

cagey See **cadgy**

cagg See **keg**

Cagian See **Cajun** n¹

cag out v phr [Cf Engl dial *cag* crawl, move slowly (*EDD cag* v²)]
To break down, cease functioning.
1975 Gould *ME Lingo* 39, *Cagged*—To conk out . . to quit; "Hardly left my moorin' when the engine cagged out."

cagy See **cadgy**

cah See **carry** A1

cahoo See **cahot**

cahoot n¹, usu pl |kə'hut| Also *cahoots, cohoot(s)* [Etym obscure: Fr *cahute* cabin, *cohorte* company, group, and even Amer **cahot** pothole in a road, have been proposed though none is fully acceptable; *co-* "with" seems to be understood and is perh reinforced by intensive **ker-**; *hoot* remains unexplained]

1 usu in phr *in cahoots with:* Partnership, freq implying or involving collusion, secrecy, hence further, dishonesty. **widespread**

1829 Kirkham *Engl. Grammar* 193, Provincialisms . . . Md. Va. Ky. or Miss. . . Hese in cohoot with me. *He is* in *partnership* with me. **1839** U.S. Congress *Congressional Globe* 25 Cong. 3 Sess. 211/3 **OH,** I will splice the member from North Carolina to you, and for a short time will consider you one person, or in *"cahoot".* **1862** G.K. Wilder *MS. Diary* 14 May *(DAE),* Mc wished me to go in cahoots in a store. **1888** Jones *Negro Myths* 5 **GA coast,** Deese yer Cooter [turtles] . . . all come inter cohoot an conclude to fool Buh Deer. **1905** *DN* 3.73 **nwAR,** *Cahoot, cahoots* . . . Collusion; (less often) partnership. 'He's in cahoot with the worst crowd of boys in school.' **1966–70** *DARE* (Qu. V1, *When . . somebody is trying to deceive you . . you say "_____."*) Inf **IL**143, They're in cahoots; (Qu. JJ3a, . . *"He's trying to _____ again."*) Inf **MI**17, Get in cahoots with the teacher; (Qu. JJ36, *To work out a . . secret plan*) Infs **CA**115, **PA**118, Be in cahoots; (Qu. KK67, *When people think alike on something: "On that particular thing we _____."*) Infs **CA**120, **CT**25, **IL**96, Are in cahoots.

2 in phr *the whole cahoot:* the entire bunch (of people). Cf **caboodle**

1892 *DN* 1.235 **MO,** Cahoot. A favorite word in the phrase, "The whole cahoot" = "the the whole lot of them." Kansas City.

3 A children's game involving secrecy among the players who are not "it": see quots.

1925 *Book of Rural Life* 2264, *In Cahoots* . . can be successfully played only where people are well known, for it is necessary to be able to recognize the voices of everybody present . . . One is blindfolded, and is asked by the other, "Are you in cahoots?" This means, "Do you know the name of the person who was the last to say anything?" **1969** *DARE* (Qu. JJ36) Inf **CA**115, There's a game called [kə'huts] — one goes out of the room and the others plan something, and then he comes in and tries to find out what it is.

4 in phrr *go* (or *be*) *in cahoot(s):* To share (as a financial burden or claim).

1966–69 *DARE* (Qu. II9, *If several people have to contribute in order to pay for something, you say, "Let's all _____."*) Inf **NC**1, Go in cahoot; **AR**31, **SC**59, Go in cahoots; **CA**137, Be in cahoots; (Qu. II8, *When one person wants to share . . something with another person, he might say: "Let's _____ on that."*) Infs **IL**96, **LA**2, **MO**39, Go in cahoots; **GA**1, Go [kə'huč].

cahoot v [**cahoot** n¹]

To consort; to connive.

1886 Mitchell *Roland Blake* 261, The women ken cohoot together down at the old house, and me and you, we'll go a-fishin'. **1948** *Chicago Daily Tribune* (IL) 1 Aug 6, Why don'tcha feud fa'r an' squar' — with shootin' arns instead o' gossip thet he's cahooting with speerits?

cahoot adv [**cahoot** n¹]

Into partnership or connivance.

1857 *NY Herald* (NY) 20 May 11/1, They agree to go cahoot with their claims against Nicaragua. **1903** *DN* 2.308 **seMO,** *Cahoots* . . . Partnership. 'Going cahoots' is equivalent to 'dividing spoils.' **1966–69** *DARE* (Qu. II9, *If several people have to contribute in order to pay for something, you say, "Let's all _____."*) Inf **SC**7, Go cahoot; **GA**1, Go [kə'huč]; **GA**72, Go cahoots.

cahoot n² [Prob *ca*- var of *ker*- + *hoot* something trifling]

1970 *DARE* (Qu. GG21) Inf **TN**53, I don't give a cahoot.

cahootin' See **callyhooting**

‡cahoozin n [Var of **cahot**]

1968 *DARE* (Qu. N30, *What do you call a sudden short dip in a road?*) Inf **NY**27, Cahoozin [ˌkə'huʒn̩] — hole, dip shaped, in snow, worn down from sleighs.

cahot n |kə'ho; kə'hu| Also sp *cahoo* [CanFr *cahot*] **esp nNEng**

A depression in a road (often snow-covered) which causes vehicles to lurch; a **thank-you-ma'am.**

[**1807** Heriot *Travels* 269 **Canada,** After a heavy fall of snow, the loaded slays which pass along in the vicinity of the towns, alternately take up in their front, and deposit a quantity of snow, and thus form in the roads furrows and ridges in a transverse position, which are called *cahots;* until these are filled up, travelling becomes fatiguing and unpleasant.] **1874** *VT State Bd. Ag. Report* 2.659, The highways leading to our larger

villages . . are frequently so full of pitchholes or 'cahoos' as to render them totally unfit for travel. *Ibid* 661, Pitch holes or 'cahoos', in winter roads, are a dangerous nuisance. **1959** *VT Hist.* new ser 27.128 **nVT,** *Cahoo* . . cahot, kiss-me-quick; thank-you-ma'am. A drift of snow, usually on a flat, open space where the wind blows. It might cover a large rut and cause the front part of a cutter, wagon, or automobile to drop into the hole. **1967–68** *DARE* (Qu. N30, . . *A sudden short dip in a road*) Inf **NY**20, Dip, [kə'ho]; old-fashioned.

cahr See **carry A1**

cahush See **cohosh**

caian See **carrion**

caif See **café**

caigy See **cadgy**

caile See **coil** v

caint, cain't See **can** v¹ **1b**

cain't see See **can't see**

caious See **cous**

caird See **carry A2**

caire(y) See **carry A1**

cairn See **carry A3**

caitch See **catch** v **A1**

Cajan See **Cajun** n¹

cajon n |kɑ'hon| [Span "box"] **SW**

A box canyon.

1862 (1929) Hayes *Pioneer Notes* 276 **sCA,** For midsummer, the wind was bleak that blew down through the Cajon. *Ibid* 278, The woods of Lytle Creek are a verdant thread coming from the Cajon and broken as it bends toward Jurupa. **1900** *Amer. Geog. Soc. NY Jrl.* 32.34, *Cajon:* A box canyon. Local in Southwest.

Cajun n¹ Also *Cagian, Cajan* [Alter of *'Cadian,* aphet form of *Acadian* (see *DA 'Cadian*)]

1 A member or descendant of the community of French Canadians who colonized the Bayou Teche area of Louisiana after 1755; also the language of this community. **LA** Cf **boogerlee 1**

[**1842** in 1943 *AmSp* 18.119, *Acajan*]. **1868** *Putnam's Mag.* 12.54, Among them were Creoles, *Cagians,* the descendants of the old Acadians, and a few mulattoes. **1885** *Outing* 5.337/1, The Cajan fisherman will gladly teach you his art of catching trout. **1927** Kennedy *Gritny* 63 **sLA** [Black], Good time an' plenny fun laughin' at de Cajuns. **1962** Atwood *Vocab. TX* 73, For a person of Acadian French origin the Louisiana word *Cajun* . . is fairly frequent in East and South Texas, but becomes rare in other areas. **1979** Hallowell *People Bayou* 2 **sLA,** This was Cajun French, some of whose clipped staccato phrasing dates back to seventeenth century usage. *Ibid* 88, A few years ago, . . two young anthropologists . . broke new ground to the extent of designating as Cajun anyone with certain crucial characteristics — close family ties, Catholicism, rural living, and the French language. The definition is at least easy and practical, and loosely reflects the present consensus of what a Cajun is.

2 Transf and applied generally as a derisive epithet: see quots. Cf **coonass**

1932 *AmSp* 7.265 **LA, TX,** *Cajun* . . . Properly designating a Louisianan of supposed Acadian French descent, the term is slurringly used to designate an oil-field man from Louisiana or Texas. **1968** *DARE* (Qu. HH1, *A rustic or countrified person*) Inf **LA**35, Cajun.

3 See quot 1946. **AL**

1934 Carmer *Stars Fell on AL* 260 **swAL,** I want to take you to a Cajan school. [*Ibid* 262, I gazed back . . to see among the curly-headed boys and girls of olive complexion a number of yellow-haired, blue-eyed blonds — as Nordic in appearance as Dakota Swedes. The teacher [said] . . . "Yellow and black hair often run in the same family."] *Ibid* 263, "These girls get married when they're sixteen and the boys go to work farmin' or in the turpentine woods — long before they're ready for high school. There's just one Cajan high school I've heard of. The Roman Catholics gave 'em that over at Chestang." **1941** FWP *Guide AL* 367, In the heavily wooded region around Citronelle are several *Cajan Settlements,* occupied by a people of undetermined racial origin. The name, Cajan, is not applied correctly, for these people are not related to the Cajuns of the Gulf Coast, who are descended from the Acadians of

Canada. The Alabama Cajans know little of their ancestry, but they are believed to be descended from early French, Spanish, and English settlers who married Indian women. **1946** *Social Forces* 24.4.439/2 **AL, MS,** Cajans in the hilly areas of Washington, Mobile, and Clarke counties [Alabama] as well as adjoining parts of Mississippi . . . Name "Cajan" derived from fanciful resemblance to the Louisiana Cajuns or Acadians . . . Cajuns are a poor hill people of the wooded country who subsist by lumbering, turpentine extraction, and various odd jobs. **1963** Berry *Almost White* 90, The Cajuns of Alabama support themselves by lumbering and the extraction of turpentine. *Ibid* 27, Alabama [has] its Creoles and Cajuns. **1967** *DARE* (Qu. HH29a, *Names around here for people of mixed blood—part Indian*) Inf **AL30,** ['kejənz] — [We] have them in this county.

'cajun n[2] Pronc-sp for *occasion*

1922 Gonzales *Black Border* 219 **sSC, GA coasts** [Gullah], 'E fuhgit fuh tell 'um suh 'e yent hab cajun fuh switch fly 'long 'e tail. [He forgets to tell him that he won't have occasion to switch flies with his tail.]

cajunck, cajung, cajunk See ker-

Cajun pony n

Perh =**creole pony.**

1941 FWP *Guide LA* 432, *Cajun pony* — These small and hardy ponies, with their flashing eyes, long manes and tails, and fuzzy varicolored coats are known by a variety of names: . . Cajun pony.

cajy See cadgy

cake doughnut n widespread, but esp Inland Nth, West

A doughnut leavened with baking powder or soda rather than yeast. Cf **friedcake 1**

1960 *PADS* 34.64 **CO,** Raised doughnut, cake doughnut [are used esp by younger speakers]. **1965–70** *DARE* (Qu. H28) 31 Infs, **scattered, but esp Inland Nth, West,** Cake doughnut. **1967** *Independence Enterprise* (OR) 12 Jan 3, [Bakery items in a supermarket] Apple sauce cake donuts Doz. 39¢. **1980** *DARE* File **Chicago IL** (as of 1940s), *Cake doughnut* — doughnut made with baking powder dough.

cake jesmus See Cape jasmine

cake money n

1967 *DARE* FW Addit **eGA, AL,** Cake money — money to be used for no particular purpose, for just a good time. Equivalent to *pin money.*

cake social n For varr see quots Cf ice-cream social

A social gathering at which cake is served or sold.

1967–69 *DARE* (Qu. FF1) Inf **MO37,** Cake social; **MN6,** Cake and pie social; **MD38,** Box socials — [named] according to what's sold — cake social, candy social; **PA81,** A cake social, at the Grange. A cake sale, pie sale — pick out the pie or cake you want, measure the woman's waist and pay so much an inch.

cake turner n [*cake* abbr for *griddlecake, hotcake, pancake* + *turner*] chiefly C Atl, eN Midl See Map *somewhat old-fash* Cf egg turner, flipper n[1] 2

A spatula.

1902 (1969) Sears *Catalogue* 590, *Cake Turners* . . Enameled wood handles . . . Price, each . . . 3c. **1965–70** *DARE* (Qu. F3, *When you're frying things — for example, eggs — you turn them over with a _____*) 34 Infs, **chiefly C Atl, eN Midl,** Cake turner. [29 Infs old]

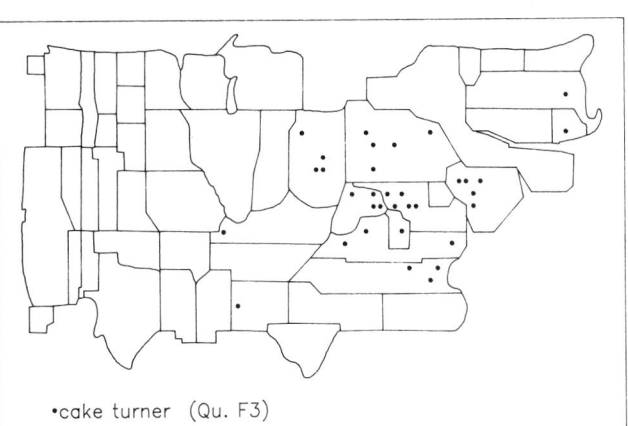

•cake turner (Qu. F3)

cakewalk n

1 A social entertainment, once especially favored by Blacks, in which a cake was the prize awarded for the fanciest steps or figures executed by those who walked or paraded around it; for recent variation, see quot 1978.

1879 *Harper's Mag.* 59.799/1, Reader, didst ever attend a cake walk given by the colored folks? . . They are usually given to aid some poor person or some deserving charity, and after the walk there is always a dance. **1890** *DN* 1.60 **swOH,** *Cake.* Take the *cake:* to be the best or very excellent. From the darky festival known as a *cake-walk,* in which a cake is in the centre of a room, and the contestants promenade around it, the couple "putting on most style" winning the cake. **1894** Twain *Harriet Shelley* 109, The negroes have a name for this grave deportment-tournament: a name taken from the prize contended for. They call it a Cake-Walk. **1950** Blesh – Janis *Ragtime* 96, Born in Tennessee, the son of freed slaves, he [Edmonds] recalls that "the cakewalk was originally a plantation dance, just a happy movement they did to the banjo music because they couldn't stand still. It was generally on Sundays, when there was little work . . that the slaves both young and old would dress up in hand-me-down finery to do a high-kicking, prancing walk-around. They did a take-off on the high manners of the white folks in the 'big house,' but their masters, who gathered around to watch the fun, missed the point. It's supposed to be that the custom of a prize started with the master giving a cake to the couple that did the proudest movement." **1968** Stearns *Jazz Dance* 71, Cakewalking in a white circus was a step up for Negro dancers, but it did not last, and as the Cakewalk lost popularity in the teens, the circuses dropped it. *Ibid* 123, During its origin the Cakewalk, as performed by plantation Negroes, was a satire on the fine manners of the Southern gentleman. **1971** Southern *Music Black Amer.* 273, In 1876 the celebration of the Centennial of American Independence at Philadelphia [had an exhibit of] a plantation scene featuring the singing of Negro folksongs by ex-slaves and free-born blacks. A special attraction was the performance of an old folk dance dating back to ante-bellum times, called "chalk-line walk" or "cakewalk." Originally, the dance had been performed on the plantation by slave couples who competed for a prize, generally a cake, awarded to the pair that pranced around with the proudest, high-kicking steps. On some plantations the dancers moved with pails of water on their heads. Those who spilled the least water and yet maintained erect posture were declared the winners. **1978** *DARE* File **IL,** It is rather ironic that the only cakewalk I have ever seen in my life I saw in Chicago in 1978. It was a black affair, a "debutante" ball at a posh hotel in the Loop. There was a meal served at the beginning. When it was time for dessert, the lights were dimmed until the ballroom was almost completely dark; then uniformed waiters entered marching rhythmically to the sound of the band with cakes held high. One couldn't see the actual cakes of course for they were on servers covered by translucent covers that glowed in the dark with many colors: pink, green, etc. The waiters marched around the entire ballroom several times; then the lights were turned up and cake was served. Whether it was the same cake on the servers I don't know.

2a A marching or dancing game (often a fundraising event) generally played on a marked floor, with the prizes (often cakes) for those on the lucky numbers when the music stops; see quots.

1930 *Randolph Enterprise* (Elkins WV) 18 Dec 1/1, After the supper a cake walk program was carried out and about a dozen cakes walked off. The band from the Odd Fellows Home . . furnished music. **1940** *Play Party Games* 41 (as of 1915), *West Virginia Cake Walk* — A cake, jar of pickles or other desirable object was exhibited, and all the couples who were interested paid 10¢ to join the cake walk. A circle was formed around a leader who held a long fishing pole. A time-keeper held a watch set on a certain length of time, and the cake-walk began. Each couple in turn was permitted to pass under the fishing pole, which was lowered at the instant the time-keeper signalled that the time was up. The couple immediately in front of the pole took the cake. In some cases a generous couple would put the cake up again, to raise more income for the cause. *Ibid* 49, *Arkansas Cake Walk* — The cake walk that we know here is as follows: A large double circle is blocked off into numbered sections which are sold for 10 cents each. Couples stand in the sections until a sufficient number have been sold. Then the music (preferably string ensemble) starts, and the couples walk until the music stops. A number is drawn and the ocuple [sic] standing on the section of corresponding number receive a cake. **1954** *Harder Coll.* **cwTN,** Cake-walk — Party at which members are assigned cards placed in a circle. Then they march until the signal is given for them to halt. The one standing on the lucky card gets the cake. **1965–70** *DARE* (Qu. FF5a, *Names for different steps and figures in dancing — in past years*) 123 Infs, **widespread,** Cakewalk. **1966** *DARE* Tape NM12, Each lady would bake a cake. All the cakes would be put on a table. When the music started, the men would walk around the table and when the music stopped, wherever they stopped, that one would get the cake. That was a cakewalk. **1966** *DARE* FW Addit **VA**12, Cakewalk—a large circle was chalked on the floor and the couple would walk around the room in time to music. When the music would suddenly stop, if a couple was in the circle they received a cake. **1969** *Zion-Benton News* (Zion IL) 24 April, Win a cake at the Cake Walk.

b A game similar to **musical chairs.**

1966–70 *DARE* (Qu. EE2, *Games that have one extra player—when a signal is given, the players change places, and the extra one tries to get a place*) Infs **MI**34, Musical chairs (what the ladies call it when the ladies play it); the kids call it 'cakewalk' or 'chairwalk;' **MS**8, The cakewalk (musical chairs); **TX**88, Cakewalk (same as musical chairs); (Qu. FF1) Inf **KY**75, [For a] cakewalk, cakes [were] numbered, a circle of chairs numbered; [players would] walk around the chairs to music; when the music stopped, the participants sat . . . [A player] won the cake whose number corresponded to the number on his chair. Players paid a set amount to join the cakewalk. Another event used to make money. **1970** *DARE* Tape **PA**249, Cakewalk—A form of musical chairs with a cake for a prize.

3 Fig: a task requiring no effort; cf the more common *piece of cake.*

1942 Berrey–Van den Bark *Amer. Slang* 642.6, [An] *Easy game.* Breather, cakewalk, cinch, . . duck soup. **1967** *DARE* (Qu. KK42a, *Expressions about a person who does something very easily; "For him that would be _____."*) Inf **TX**26, A cakewalk. **1981** *Capital Times* (Madison WI) 6 Aug 4/1, Lewis acknowledged that rebuilding the controller corps would not be "a cakewalk" but said it could be done within a year or two.

‡**cake-waltz** n [?Var of **cakewalk**]

c**1937** in 1977 *Amer. Slave Suppl. 1* 1.170 **AL**, But dey danced till day sometimes, . . would waltz, cake-waltz, and one-step and sech.

cala n[1], also attrib [From one or more West African languages, as Nupe *kàrà* a fried cake; Yoruba, Igbo, Efik *àkàrà* an oily cake made from beans ground and fried. Cf also Common Bantu **kádà* to fry, roast] **New Orleans LA** Cf *DJE ackra*

A fritter, usu made of rice, sometimes of ground black-eyed peas: see quot 1945.

1880 Cable *Grandissimes* 133 **LA**, Frowenfeld entered after him, *calas* in hand. **1883** Buel *Mysteries of Cities* 521 **New Orleans LA**, We were received by an aged negress, whose face was familiar to me as that of the 'cala-woman,' from whom I had often bought that dainty. **1931** Read *LA French* 118, *Cala* . . . A sweetened rice cake, served with the morning *café au lait,* and formerly sold by the Creole negro women in the French Quarter of New Orleans. **1945** Saxon *Gumbo Ya-Ya* 32 **New Orleans LA**, A cala is a pastry which originated among Creole Negroes —a thin fritter made with rice and yeast sponge . . . yeast was concocted the night before, of boiled potatoes, corn meal, flour and cooking soda, left in the night air to ferment, then mixed with the boiled rice and made into a sponge. The next morning flour, eggs, butter and milk were added, a stiff batter mixed, and the calas formed by dropping spoonfuls into a skillet. *Ibid* 33, Some vendors sold not only calas of rice, but also calas of cow-peas, crying, *Calas tout chauds, Madame, Calas au riz calas aux fèves!* **1958** Hughes–Bontemps *Negro Folkl.* 417, Cala Vendor's Cry —One cup of coffee, fifteen cents calas, Make you smile the livelong day. Calas, tout chauds, Madame, Tout chauds! Git 'em while they're hot! Hot calas! **1983** Reinecke Coll. **New Orleans LA**, Cala ['kala]—a hot cake for breakfast, made of grated cooked rice. No longer sold, but still talked of.

cala n[2] Also *cally* [Abbr for *California ham*]

A type of picnic ham.

1910 IL Ag. Exper. Station (Urbana) *Bulletins* 281, Picnics or Calas (formerly termed California hams) are cut 2½ ribs wide . . . They . . are sold almost entirely as sweet-pickled, smoked and boiled meats. The lighter averages (4 to 8 pounds) are sometimes termed Boston Shoulders, and were formerly butted shorter than Calas and only slightly rounded; but Chicago and other western packers now trim them like Calas and designate both as Picnics. **1945** *Chicago Daily News* (IL) 6 Sept 18/1, [Advt:] Juicy "miracle" cooked callies[,] Sweet delicious callies for wonderful dinners or sandwiches. Cooked to the peak of perfection. **1967** *Watertown Daily Times* (NY) 14 June 23, Smoked Calas U.S. Gov't. Inspected Short Shank 39¢ lb. **1968** Hahn *Cooking of China: Recipes* 69, Red-cooked Pork Shoulder . . . A 4- to 5-pound fresh pork picnic

shoulder or cala with the rind left on. **1971** *AmSp* 46.79 **Chicago IL**, Cally ham.

calabacilla n Also sp *calabazilla, calabacita, calavacita* [Mex-Span dimins of *calabaza*] **SW**

Any of several squash or gourds: see quots.

1886 Havard *Flora W. & S. TX for 1885* 522, *Cucurbita perennis,* Gray. (Calabacilla.) . . . The pulp of the green fruit is used with soap to remove stains from clothing. **1892** *DN* 1.188 **TX**, *Calabacílla:* a gourd with round fruit the color of an orange (*Cucurbita foetidissima*). **1925** Jepson *Manual Plants CA* 660, Calabazilla [is] . . also called Chili Cayote and used by Spanish-Californians, the root as a cleanser, the leaves medicinally. **1966–67** *DARE* (Qu. I23, *What kinds of squash do people grow around here?*) Inf **NM**5, Calabacita—small, green, usually stuffed; **TX**4, Calavacitas—white and green [about three inches long]; (Qu. H50) Inf **TX**28, Calabacita con carne—squash and beef and pork chunks, sometimes has corn in it.

calabasate n [Span *calabazate*]

Candied pumpkin.

1967 *DARE* (Qu. H80, *Kinds of candy often made at home*) Inf **TX**31, Calabasate (pumpkin); grapefruit peel; leche quemada (sweet boiled milk); riznaga.

calabash See **calabash gourd**

calabash cousin n [See quots] **HI**

See quots.

1967 *DARE* (Qu. Z7, . . *[Nicknames] for any other relatives*) Inf **HI**1, Tutu—aunt or grandmother; calabash cousin—not a real relative but a person closely accepted by the family; from dipping into the same calabash of poi. **1972** Carr *Da Kine Talk* 113, Calabash cousins . . . Very close friends, but not blood relatives, who in most cases have grown up together and who 'eat from the same calabash'. The compound term was apparently coined in Hawaii.

calabash gourd n Also *calabash, gourd calabash*
=**bottle gourd.**

1820 in 1931 Bernice P. Bishop Museum *Special Pub.* 17.19 **HI**, They call for their food wherever they happen to be sitting or lying, which is brought to them in Calabashes. **1835** Simms *Partisan* 364, Needn't mind the calabashes, he says, We can get them every where along the road. **1861** Wood *Class-Book* 364, Calabash . . . The hard, woody rind of the fruit is used as ladles, bottles, &c. **1900** Lyons *Plant Names* 213, Gourd, Calabash Gourd, Bottle Gourd. **1901** Mohr *Plant Life AL* 747, *Common Gourd Calabash* . . . A rank coarse climber. **1976** Bailey-Bailey *Hortus Third* 633, Calabash G[ourd] . . . In many sizes and shapes, from 3 in. to 3 ft. long.

calabazilla See **calabacilla**

calabogus See **calibogus**

calaboose n, also attrib |ˈkæləˌbus| For varr see quots [Span *calabozo* dungeon] **scattered, but chiefly Sth, West** See Map *informal, often humorous*

A jail, esp one in a village or small town.

1792 Pope *Tour U.S.* 43 **AL**, Their Fate will be confinement . . . in the *Callibouse at Mobille.* **1866** *Eastern Slope* (Washoe NV) 13 Oct 1/6 (*DA*), Now he is a poor drunkard, and earns barely a . . . living as a calaboose shyster. **1892** *DN* 1.188 **TX**, *Calabózo:* jail, guard-house,

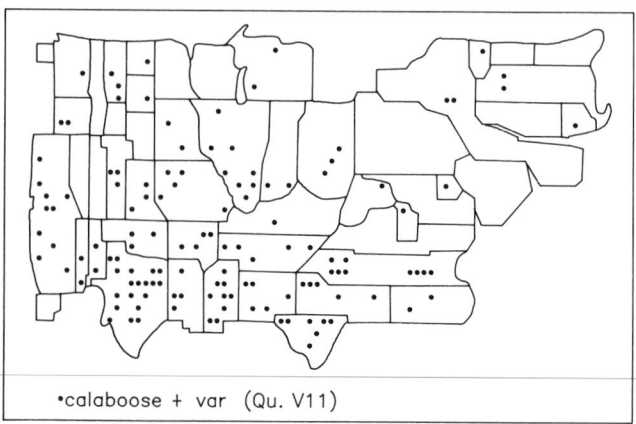

*calaboose + var (Qu. V11)

prison. The common form is *calaboose*. **1894** Twain *Pudd'nhead Wilson* 169 **MO**, If I got the twins into the common calaboose . . well, once in the calaboose they would be disgraced, and uncle would n't want any duels with that sort of characters, and would n't allow any. **1908** *DN* 3.296 **eAL, wGA**, *Calaboose* . . A town lock-up: never applied to a larger county or state prison. **1908** Fox *Lonesome Pine* 198 **KY**, Did you git board in the calaboose? **1929** Sale *Tree Named John* 44 **MS**, Dey 'uz gwi be fo'ced to have de law on 'im en maybe put 'im in de callyboose, too. **1937** in 1977 *Amer. Slave Suppl. 1* 1.262 **AL**, Some of the plantations had a "calaboose" in which to put unruly slaves, which was built of logs strongly fastened together, and imbedded in the ground, making it almost impossible to get out. **1940** FWP *Guide TX* 396, *Calaboose* . . . jail. **1963** Burroughs *Head-First* 44 **CO** (as of 1915), Having shoved him inside the *calaboso* [here = a chicken house], I pushed the hasp over the staple and replaced the padlock. **1965–70** *DARE* (Qu. V11, *What joking names do you have around here for a county or city jail?*) 131 Infs, **scattered, but chiefly Sth, West**, Calaboose; AR18, Cattle boose.

calabosh n
=**caboodle**.
    1952 Brown *NC Folkl.* 1.524 **wNC**, *Calabosh* . . . The entire crowd.

calaboso, calabózo See **calaboose**

Calaforny See **-y**

calamanco n, also attrib Also sp *callamink, callemink, callimanco, cal(l)imanker, collimancoe* and abbr *manker* [Origin unknown; *OED* 1592 →] *old-fash*
1 A glossy woolen fabric striped or checked on one side.
    1744 (1907) Hamilton *Itinerarium* 17 Aug 181 **NY**, He had a weather-beaten black wig, an old striped collimancoe banyan and an antique brass spur upon his right ankle, and a pair of thick-soaled [sic] shoes tied with points. **1795** Dearborn *Columbian Grammar* 134, *Improprieties*, commonly called *vulgarisms*, . . . Callemink for Calamanco. **1839** Longfellow *Hyperion* 1.7 (1889 *Century Dict.*), A morning gown, though, I am sorry to say, not a calamanco one, with great flowers. **1845** Judd *Margaret* 36 **MA** (as of c1800), On the right [of the store] were rolls of Kerseymeres, callimancoes, thicksets, durants, fustians, shaloons, antiloons, ratteens, duffils and serges of all colors. **1901** Jewett *Tory Lover* 106 **NH**, I dove into my pockets an' come upon this old piece o' callamink I'd wrapped some 'baccy in.
2 Transf: a calico or tortoiseshell cat.
    1947 *WELS Suppl. 1* Inf, **WI**, Cal(l)imankers, Calamanco — Tortoise-shell cats. **1950** *WELS* 1 Inf, **cwWI**, Tortoise shell, calico, brindle, callimanker. **1966–70** *DARE* (Qu. J5, . . *Cat of mixed colors*) Inf **AL6**, Callimanker; **MA122**, Manker, Calico.

calamity n, usu pl **Nth** *old-fash* Cf **clatterment, collateral**
Odds and ends; a miscellaneous assortment of personal belongings.
    1871 *Winnebago Co. (Wis.) Press* 3/2 (*DA*), We learn that our people have given Mr. Riggs a wide berth and that he has packed his 'calamities' and left town. **1884** Hill *Tales Pioneers* 282 **CO**, A crop-eared, one-eyed mule, a few battered cooking utensils, a few rations of 'grub,' and a corresponding amount of 'traps and calamities,' comprised the outfit. **1914** *DN* 4.153 **NH** (as of c1900), *Calamity* . . . Old stuff, such as is bought at an auction. **1941** *LANE* Map 346, Field workers asked for names applied to old, broken, useless things . . such as accumulate in the house or yard and are eventually thrown away or otherwise disposed of . . . 1 inf, **ceVT**, A pile of old calamity.

Calamity Jane n [Nickname for Martha Jane Canary Burke (1852–1903) famous markswoman who brought "calamity" to those who opposed her]
1a A woman who foresees or predicts calamity; a worrier or fussbudget.
    1942 Berrey–Van den Bark *Amer. Slang* 184.2, Calamity Jane, *a pessimistic female*. **1968–70** *DARE* (Qu. GG14, *Names and nicknames for someone who fusses or worries a lot, especially about little things*) Infs **CA66, 197, MA100**, Calamity Jane.
b One who suffers calamity.
    1966 *DARE* (Qu. KK33, *Other ways of saying 'in succession': "He had a cold, then the measles, then chicken pox _____."*) Inf **FL38**, First one thing and then another, a Calamity Jane.
2 See quot.
    1968 Adams *Western Words* 50, *Calamity Jane* — What the gamblers called the queen of spades.

calamus n Also *calamus grass*, ~ *root, calmus*
=**sweet flag**.
    1822 Eaton *Botany* 155, *Acorus . . . calamus* (sweet flag, calamus . .). [Habitat] Water or wet. **1849** Smith *Acct. Journey NEast TX* 26, The *Calamus grass* alone, or mixed with the wire, and other natural grasses, covers the prairies of the black soil. **1883** (1971) Harris *Nights with Remus* 174 **GA**, In one een' dey wuz a piece er calamus-root en some collard-seeds. **1894** *Jrl. Amer. Folkl.* 7.103, *Acorus Calamus*, . . calmus, N.J. **1938** FWP *Guide IA* 470, Calamus . . received its name from a wild marsh plant that formerly grew in abundance around the town pump. The plant has a three-petaled flower resembling a miniature iris, and long thin blades of olive green. **1967–70** *DARE* (Qu. S26b, *Wildflowers that grow in water or wet places*) Infs **OH82, TN6**, Calamus; (Qu. S26d, *Wildflowers that grow in meadows*) Inf **NJ1**, Calamus; (Qu. S26e, *Other wildflowers*) Inf **MD18**, Calamus; **NJ67**, Calamus root; (Qu. BB22, . . *Home remedies . . for constipation*) Inf **SC31**, Calamus root. **1976** Bruce *How to Grow Wildflowers* 279, The rhizome is the "calamus" of old-time medicine.

calate See **calculate**

calathump(ian) See **callithumpian** n

calavacita See **calabacilla**

Cal beer See **California beer**

calchon See **colchon**

calculate v Usu |'kælk(j)ə,leɪt|; also, **in NEng**, |'kæl,leɪt| Pronc-spp *cack'late, ca'c'late, calate, calc'late, calcilate, calkilate, cal'late, callate, callerate, cowc'late, kalkerlate, kalkilate, kal'late* **formerly chiefly NEng, now more widespread** *somewhat old-fash* Cf **allow, figure, reckon**

A Forms. See further in **B** below
    1823 Cooper *Pioneers* 2.293 **cNY**, You over calkilate your aim, Natty. **1843** (1916) Hall *New Purchase* 176 **IN**, John . . could "kalkilate in his head faster nor Jerry Simpson with chalk or coal." **1848** Lowell *Biglow* 8 **MA**, You'll begin to kal'late. **a1883** (1911) Bagby *VA Gentleman* 79 **NEng**, When people begin to build houses "on the square," they begin to calculate — or, to give the word its idiomatic meanness, "cack'late" — and when they begin to "cack'late," they begin to keep an account of expenses — which is the infallible premonitory symptom of the virus of Yankeeism striking into the bone. **1904** Day *Kin o' Ktaadn* 198 **ME**, I jest calkilate. **1916** *DN* 4.340 **seOH**, Calculate. Pronounced *kalkerlate*. **1959** *VT Hist.* new ser 27.128, *Calculate* . . . You cal'latin' to stay tunight? **1966** *DARE* Tape **ME26**, Callate.

B Senses.
1 To suppose, reckon, guess.
    1810 Pike *Expeditions* 152, We had reason to calculate, that they had good guides. **1815** Humphreys *Yankey in England* 104, *Calculate*, used frequently in an improper sense, as reckon, guess. **a1828** (1887) Bernard *Retrospections* 307 **ME**, Capital, gentlemen! capital! You are right humorsome, I calculate. What's to pay? **1853** Hammett *Stray Yankee in TX* 116, The Yankee *guesses*, the Southron *reckons*, . . however, the Yankee *calculates*, and pretty shrewdly also, while the Southron *allows*. **1859** (1968) Bartlett *Americanisms* 64, *To Calculate*. This word, which properly means to compute, to estimate, has been erroneously transferred from the language of the counting-house to that of common life, where it is used for the words to esteem; to suppose; to believe; to think; to expect; intend, etc. It is employed in a similar way to the word *guess*, though not to so great an extent. Its use is confined to the illiterate of New England. **1904** *DN* 2.424 **Cape Cod MA**, Callate. **1914** *DN* 4.69 **ME, nNH**, *Cal'late* . . . Calculate; think. "I cal'late she's a right smart cook." **1916** Lincoln *Mary-'Gusta* 28 **eMA**, "Why — why, no," he stammered; "it didn't seem to soak in, somehow. Cal'late my head must have stopped goin'." **1939** (1969) Thompson *Body & Britches* 288 **neNY**, Well, I callerate, if they rig up the calleration they callerate on, we'll go to the Boreas. **c1960** Wilson *Coll.* **csKY**, "I jest calculated that you'd be here." Never shortened to New England cal'late. **1965–70** *DARE* (Qu. JJ34, *When you decide it would be to your advantage to do something, you might say, "Yes, I _____ I'll be better off that way."*) Infs **AR51, CT25, GA86, MS21, NY92, PA242, VT16**, Calculate; **MA5, 98, NY93**, Calculate, callate; **NC72**, Calculate, reckon; **MD17**, Feel, guess, (some people say) calculate, reckon. **1977** *Yankee* Jan 113 **ME coast**, But island men when they curse can set your mouth to watering. I calate if I was to explain you'd be titrified.
2 To plan, intend.
    1907 *DN* 3.242 **eME**, He cal'lated to go up, but his health was too

poor. **1912** *DN* 3.572 **wIN,** *Calc'late* . . . To plan; to purpose. "I calc'late to build a new barn next year." **1915** *DN* 4.181 **swVA,** *Calcilate* . . . To calculate; plan; intend. **1917** *DN* 4.389 **neOH,** *Ca'c'late* [kæklet], . . Calculate, consider, intend. "I ca'c'late he'll be here to-morrow." "I ca'c'late to go to town today." *Ibid* 390, *Cowc'late* . . . Calculate, with the 'l' completely vocalized . . . Used by people who would recognize *ca'clate* as illiterate . . . "I cowc'late to be there." **1931–33** *LANE Worksheets* **swCT,** My father always calculated to have a stonewall man come for a month or two out of the year. **1966–68** *DARE* Tape **CT**14, Most farmers around here, that are still farming, still calculate to raise the best heifer calves; **ME**26, Now maybe he didn't callate to hit her.

3 in phr *calculated for:* Considered to be, accepted as, admitted to be.

1865 (1922) Jackson *Col.'s Diary* 189 **cwPA,** He [Gen. Sherman] is calculated for a soldier.

calculation n Pronc-sp *cowc'lation* [**calculate** v]

1917 *DN* 4.390 **neOH,** *Cowc'lation(s)* [kaʊkəl'ešənz] . . . Calculation(s), intention(s), arrangement(s). "They made *cowc'lations* for thirty people."

‡calendar fear n *euphem*

Menstruation.

1968 *DARE* (Qu. AA27, . . *A woman's menstruation*) Inf **NY**76, Calendar fear.

calf n[1] Usu |kæf|, also |kæɪf, kɛef, keəf, ke(ɪ)f, kjæf| Pronc-spp *carf, cyaaf*

A Forms.

1902 *DN* 2.230 **sIL,** *Calf* [kef] and [keəf]. **1904** Day *Kin o' Ktaadn* 153 **ME,** And only t'other afternoon he found a Jersey carf / A-hangin' up acrost a beam and dead's a bag o' charf. **1922** Gonzales *Black Border* 295 [Gullah glossary], Cyaaf. **1936** *AmSp* 11.239 **eTX,** *Calf* [kjæˆf]. **1942** Hall *Smoky Mt. Speech* 23, *Calf* [keef]. **c1960** *Wilson Coll.* **csKY,** *Calf* [kæɪf].

B Senses.

1 See quot.

c1960 *Wilson Coll.* **csKY,** *Calf*—An awkward person, usually an adolescent boy.

2 A timid or cowardly person. Cf *fraidy-calf* at **fraidy-cat**

1967 *DARE* (Qu. HH10) Inf **NY**32, Calf, scaredy-cat.

3 in phr *have a calf:* See quot. Cf *have kittens*

c1960 *Wilson Coll.* **csKY,** *Have a calf:* . . . Show great anger, have a fit.

calf n[2] See **kerf**

calf n[3] See **café**

calf v

To vomit.

1968 *DARE* (Qu. BB17, . . *Vomiting*) Inf **NY**80, Throw up, puke, calfed [kæft]; [(Qu. BB18, *To vomit a great deal at once*) Inf **NY**82, Had an awful calf throwed up.].

calf corn n Cf **bear corn 1, corn lily 3c**

A **bead lily** (here: *Clintonia borealis*).

1897 *Jrl. Amer. Folkl.* 10.145, *Clintonia borealis* . . hound's tongue, calf corn, Hartford, Me. wild corn, corn flower, Oxford County, Me.

calf-eyes n Also *calf's eyes* **prob Sth, S Midl**

A look expressive of tender or sentimental longing.

1949 *PADS* 11.4 **wTX,** *Calf-eyes, to make* . . . To show adoration with the eyes . . . "Mary made calf-eyes at Jim during church." **1954** *Harder Coll.* **cwTN,** To make calf-eyes, to show adoration with the eyes. **c1960** *Wilson Coll.* **csKY,** *Calf-eyes*—A languishing look, as of one lover to another. **1966** *DARE* (Qu. AA8, *When people make too much of a show of affection in a public place*) Inf **FL**28, Making calf's eyes.

calf fry See **fry** n 5

calf-rope, holler v phr Also *call calf-rope, cry ~, say ~, yell ~;* also *calf-rope* exclam [Origin uncert] **chiefly S Midl, Gulf States** See Map Cf **uncle**

Esp in children's games: to give in, surrender; to capitulate.

1878 Eggleston *Roxy* 44 **sIN,** [They] pummeled each other in a friendly way until the challenger, finding that his antagonist had entirely stopped respiration, was forced to "hollow calf-rope," that is, to signify by gestures that he was beaten. **1906** *DN* 3.129 **nwAR,** *Calf-rope* [kæf-

rop] . . . I give up, I surrender. "I'll give it to him till he yells calf-rope." **1908** *DN* 3.296 **eAL, wGA,** I'll make him say calf-rope. **1933** *AmSp* 8.1.31 **nwTX,** In an argument, rassel, or any sort of contest, a fellow could acknowledge his opponent's superiority, and usually stop hostilities immediately, by saying calf-rope. In extreme cases, however, the conquered was made to spell it. *Ibid* 49 **Ozarks,** *Holler calf-rope* . . . To acknowledge oneself beaten. When one boy throws another down in a wrestling match, the defeated wrestler *hollers calf-rope,* usually by crying "enough" or "I give up." **1942** Faulkner *Go Down* 109 **nMS,** *That I reneged, cried calf-rope, sold my birthright, betrayed my blood, for what he calls not peace but obliteration, and a little food.* **1950** *WELS Suppl.,* Calf-rope [a response to the question] "Do you surrender?" [in] children's tussles. At branding time new calves were chased, roped, trussed and rendered helpless for branding. Hence: "Calf-rope." Used in Texas. **1954** *Harder Coll.* **cwTN,** Calf rope—[The truce term in] a children's game in which the winner forces the loser to scream "calf rope," usually after the loser has had his arm twisted until it is almost sprained or broken. *Ibid,* To holler calf rope—to give up, surrender. "I made 'im yell calf rope. I beat 'at old head in for 'im." **c1960** *Wilson Coll.* **csKY,** *Calf rope*—Nuff! **1964** Wallace *Frontier Life* 97 **cwOK** (as of c1900), She [mother] said that someone "yelled calf rope" if he had given up or called for help. **1965–70** *DARE* (Qu. EE20, *When two boys are fighting, and the one who is losing wants to stop, he calls out, "———."*) 52 Infs, **chiefly S Midl and Gulf States,** Calf-rope; **AL**20, Calf-rope (old); uncle; **GA**86, I made him holler calf-rope; **KY**89, You win, calf-rope—when somebody twists your arm; **LA**2, Calf-rope [FW: Inf's high school aged grandson had not heard of this]; **OK**31, Uncle (now), calf-rope (when I was young); **TN**8, Calf-rope (old-fashioned), help (modern); **TN**16, Let's quit, I give up, calf-rope (more in rassling than in fighting); **TX**39, Calf-rope—This is what you make the other fellow say if you want to stop and you're winning; very humiliating to have to say this; I give; **TX**42, Calf-rope—winner makes loser say this, or offers to stop pummeling; king's ex; **TX**45, Calf-rope (old-fashioned) = I give up. **1976** Brown *Gloss. Faulkner* 44, *Calf rope* . . . One child seizes a handful of another's hair (probably originally a girl's pigtail) and keeps pulling until the victim says "calf rope." From this usage, to *say calf rope* gets the general meaning of to "give in, surrender, admit defeat."

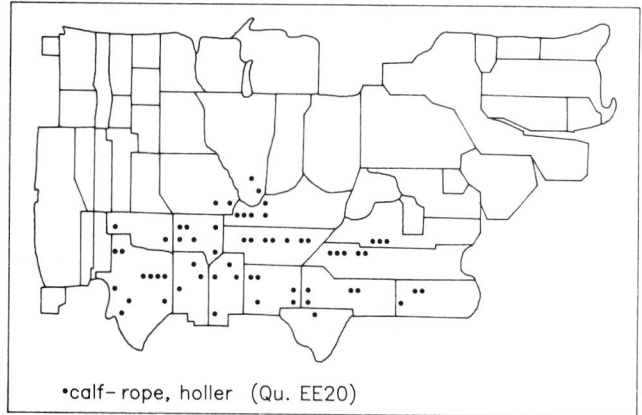

•calf-rope, holler (Qu. EE20)

calf-scramble n

A rodeo contest: see quot 1966–69.

1966 *Walsh Co. Rec.* (Grafton ND) 1 C, Eight 4-H and FFA members won calves in the calf scramble held Tuesday and Wednesday evenings in connection with the Little International livestock shows. **1966–69** *DARE* (Qu. FF16, . . *Local contests*) Infs **AL**16, 30, **AZ**15, **TX**1, 36, Calf-scramble; **MS**67, Calf-scramble—boys capture calves that cattle-growers turn loose; **TX**68, Calf-scramble at rodeo.

calf's eyes See **calf-eyes**

calf's head n [See quots] **chiefly nCA**

=**California pitcher plant.**

1889 *Century Dict.,* Calf's-head . . . [is so called] in allusion to the ventricose hood at the summit of the leaf. **1897** Parsons *Wild Flowers CA* 391, The mountaineers call the plant [*Darlingtonia californica*] "calf's-head," because of the large yellowish domes of the pitchers. **1925** Jepson *Manual Plants CA* 448, *Calf's Head* . . . Leaves enlarged upward into a rounded hood . . with . . a 2-forked appendage. **1949** Moldenke *Amer. Wild Flowers* 60, Similar to this is the famous *Californiapitcherplant* or *calfshead.*

calf's head and pluck n   Cf **pluck**

See quots.

[**1772** (1894) Winslow *Diary* 45 **MA**, One [dish] contain'd three calves heads (skin off) with their appurtinencies anciently call'd pluck.] **1969** *DARE* (Qu. HH3, *Foods made from parts of the head and inner organs of an animal*) Inf **MA**38, Calf's head 'n' pluck [kavzhɛdṇ'plʌk].

calfskin n   [From the leather binding]   *?obs*

The Bible.

1845 Thompson *Pineville* 119 **cGA**, Mrs. Perkins had been in a pet all afternoon, and saluted [=kissed] the "calfskin" as a toad catches flies — so quick that few saw the operation.

calf-slobber(s) n   [See quot 1949 Webber at 2]   **chiefly S Midl, SW** *joc*

1 Saliva.

1954 *Harder Coll.* **cwTN**, Calf-slobbers . . . saliva.

2 Meringue.

1927 *AmSp* 2.390 [Vagabond argot], Meringue, on pastry, is called *calf-slobber.* **1933** *AmSp* 8.1.27 **nwTX**, Calf slobbers. **1949** Webber *Backwoods Teacher* 204 **Ozarks**, She had "brung an aig pie with bananers in it." . . with browned meringue top — "calf slobbers," children called the meringue pies they brought to school, in allusion to the white, stiff foam that forms around a calf's mouth when he sucks. **1949** *PADS* 11.4 **wTX**, Calf-slobbers . . . Meringue. Vulgar. **c1960** *Wilson Coll.* **csKY**, Calf-slobber — Meringue on pies or egg custards. **1966–69** *DARE* (Qu. H64, *The sweet covering spread on top of a cake*) Inf **AL**52, Calf-slobber — heard kids say this; **OK**21, Calf-slobbers; (Qu. H66a, *The sweet liquid that you pour over a pudding*) Inf **TX**35, Calf-slobber — made out of egg whites. **1966** *DARE* FW Addit **swOK**, Calf-slobbers.

calf tail n   Cf **dog-ear tear**

1968 *DARE* (Qu. W27, *What do you call a three-cornered tear in a piece of clothing from catching it on something sharp?*) Inf **OH**48, Calf tail.

calf-time n

In cattle ranching: springtime, when new calves are born.

1848 (1855) Ruxton *Life Far West* 14, 'Twas about 'calf-time,' maybe a little later, and not a hundred year ago, by a long chalk, that the biggest kind of rendezvous was held 'to' Independence, a mighty handsome little location away up on old Missoura. **1968** Adams *Western Words, Calf time* — Springtime on the ranch.

calf tongue n, also attrib   [From the shape and small size of the share. Cf **bull tongue 1**]

A type of plowshare; see quots.

1923 *DN* 5.203 **swMO**, Calf tongue . . . A narrow, steel plow-shovel or point, much narrower, thinner and lighter but similar in shape to a bull tongue. **1954** *Harder Coll.* **cwTN**, Calf tongue plow — A small plow with a narrow blade that has a point shaped somewhat like a calf's tongue.

calf wagon n

=**blatting cart**.

1961 Adams *Old-Time Cowhand* 276, Sometimes a more humane drover would carry a "calf wagon," or "blattin' cart," to save the calves born en route. **1966** *DARE* Tape **NM**14, Calf wagon — during a cattle drive a wagon to carry newborn calves.

calf yard n[1]   Also *calfy yard, cavvy yard*   [Perh Scots *calf-ward* an enclosure for raising calves, perh infl by *cavayard*]

A pen where calves are kept for weaning.

1929 *AmSp* 5.68 **NE**, Many ranchers . . keep the "weaning calves" in the "calf" or "calfy yard" (sometimes "cavvy yard"), a separate pen, so that they can be weaned.

calf yard n[2]   See **caballada**

calibogus n, also attrib   Also sp *calabogus, callebogus, callibogus*   [Origin unknown]   **NEng**

A drink usu made of rum, (spruce-)beer, and molasses, but see quot 1975.

1758 in 1890 *Dedham Hist. Reg.* 1.16, Calabogus Club begun. [**1771** in 1792 Cartwright *Jrl. Labrador* 1.139, They supped with me, and afterwards smoked a few whiffs of tobacco and drank a little callibogus; but they seemed to prefer sugar and water.] **1816** *Old Farmer's Almanac* Apr **MA**, Now I would not have you think that by avoiding the tiger you are to become a sheep — or, to invert what a great *General Court* man once said, that, by avoiding *Callibogus* you are to run upon

Silly! **1859** (1968) Bartlett *Americanisms, Calibogus.* Rum and spruce-beer. **1947** Bowles–Towle *New Engl. Cooking* 274, Other colonial drinks of note were stonewall, a mixture of cider and rum; bogus or calibogus, bogus and rum served cold; and blackstrap, rum and molasses. **1955** Adams *Grandfather* 74 **wNY** (as of 1830s), They hailed Grandfather and offered him a draught of callebogus, which he declined, having no taste for rum-and-molasses and being cautious of strangers. **1975** Gould *ME Lingo* 39, *Calibogus* — A rum or brandy flip made with the usual spices, but unsweetened. Mainers use the word today for almost any kind of a non-temperance treat; even a can of beer.

calic   See **calico** n **B1a**

caliche n, also attrib |kəˈliči| [Span]   **SW, esp TX**

1 A calcareous deposit found near the surface of the soil in arid regions; soil containing such deposits.

1885 *Santa Fe W. New Mexican* 22 Oct. 4/6 *(DA)*, By digging down on the vein through this caliche, you strike the mineral. **1932** Bentley *Spanish Terms* 112, *Caliche* . . . Applied to the calcareous deposits found near the surface of the soil in some parts of Texas, Arizona and the Southwest in general . . any calcareous soil of approximately the composition [77 per cent calcium carbonate] . . is termed caliche in the Southwest. The word is in common use and is not considered technical. **1940** (1966) FWP *Guide AZ* 404, Caliche is the local Arizona name for a lime-earth of cement-like hardness which occurs throughout the southwestern United States. **1965–70** *DARE* (Qu. C26, *What special kinds of stone or rock are there in this part of the state?*) Inf **TX**13, Caliche; **TX**56, Limestone caliche; (Qu. C31, *What do you call heavy, sticky soil?*) Infs **OK**31, **TX**4, Caliche; (Qu. N23, . . *Paved roads*) Infs **TX**27, 68, Caliche; (Qu. N27a, . . *Unpaved roads*) Infs **TX**10, 11, 13, 26, 72, 79, 81, 102, Caliche road. **1969** O'Connor *Horse & Buggy West* 277 **AZ**, It [=the University of Arizona] was located out on the caliche and greasewood desert a mile from the center of Tucson [in 1885]. **1969** *DARE* Tape **TX**71, [FW:] What does agate look like when you find it? [Inf:] It looks just like a rock. It's covered with caliche [kəˈliči] . . a formation they have here in west Texas . . a soft stuff.

2 A playing marble made of or resembling caliche.

1967 *DARE* (Qu. EE6c, . . *Cheap marbles*) Inf **TX**28, Caliches.

calico n, also attrib   Pronc-spp *caliker, callicro*

A Forms.

1891 (1967) Freeman *New Engl. Nun* 92, "I had a pink caliker gownd once," she quavered out. **1912** Green *VA Folk-Speech, Caliker* . . . For calico, printed cotton cloth. **1922** Gonzales *Black Border* 292 **sSC** [Gullah glossary], *Callicro* — calico. **1941** *AmSp* 16.10 **eTX** [Black], Spellings with *o* . . . *Banjo, mosquito, mulatto, Negro, piano, potato, tobacco, tomato* all end in [ə], ['bǽndʒə], etc.; but *calico* usually has a clear [o], ['kjælə,ko].

B Senses.

1a also *calic:* A woman.   [From *calico* cotton fabric; but cf Scots *cailliach* an old woman *(DSL)*, *calik* a gossip *(SND)*, *callack* a young girl *(EDD)*].

1848 *Glance at N.Y.* 28 *(DA)*, Only come up to-night, and I'll show you as gallus a piece of calico as any on de floor . . . . He said something about a piece of gallus calico . . . . Ha! ha! ha! you unsophisticated mortal, he means his sweetheart! **1857** (1923) Beadle *To Nebraska* 176, I told him I was going to the boat to see a lady. Cook laughed and said something about how good calico looked in Nebraska. **1887** in 1950 *AmSp* 25.31 **New Orleans LA**, Tom is a dandy and he likes a piece of new calico . . . If he likes old faded calico let him buy it, but can't he change the color? **1896** *DN* 1.414 **cTX**, Calico: woman, lady. "Look at the calico comin'!" . . . (At Washington and Lee University, Lexington, Va., the students use *calic.* "Are you going to take calic?" = "Are you going with a young lady?") **1905** *DN* 3.73 **nwAR**, Calico. **1909** *DN* 3.409 **cnME**, She's a good piece of calico. **1913** *DN* 4.28 **NW**, Tommy . . . A girl. Also called *calico, flūzy, chippy, molly, bunch of rags, bat,* all of which are not uncomplimentary in certain circles.

b in var attrib uses: See quots.

1898 Lloyd *Country Life* 24 **AL**, I never have took my stand and made my final restin place around in the calico corner, but when them two town girls come and picked me out for a native born idiot. **1900** *DN* 2.26, *Calico* . . . 'Calico course,' a course popular with women students, or one in which the social element is more prominent than the educational. **1961** Adams *Old-Time Cowhand* 338, The fewness of women didn't lessen a cowhand's wish to go a-courtin'. He called this courtin' "gallin' " . . or was said to have the "calico fever."

2 Mosaic disease of tobacco plants.

1967 Key *Tobacco Vocab.* **CT, PA,** Mosaic or calico—A virus disease of tobacco.

3 A fish with mottlings or spots, here:

a =hogchoker. *prob obs*

[**1815** *Lit. & Philos. Soc. NY Trans.* 1.388, *New-York Sole* . . . Belly pale brown, or rather a dirty white, overspread with roundish or circular spots of dusky brown, exhibiting a calico appearance.] **1872** Schele de Vere *Americanisms* 384, *Coverclip* is the curious name by which the sole is known in the waters of New York; but even more mysterious is that of *Calico,* which may be heard quite as frequently. **1873** in 1878 Smithsonian Inst. *Misc. Coll.* 14.2.16, American sole; calico; hog-choker *(New Jersey).*

b =crappie.

1972 Sparano *Outdoors Encycl.* 361, *White Crappie* . . . Calico. *Ibid* 362, *Black Crappie* . . . Calico.

calico v, hence vbl n *calicoing* [calico n B1a] *old-fash*

To court or spend time with a woman.

1887 *Lippincott's* 40.102, For it very frequently happens that the best students do a good deal of "calicoing." **1905** *DN* 3.73 nwAR, *Calico* . . . To call on a young lady. 'I'm going calicoing.' Rare. **1915** *DN* 4.181 swVA, *Calico* . . . To pass one's time with ladies; 'fuss.' "He's out a calicoin' every Sunday."

calico-back n

1 also *calico bird:* The ruddy turnstone. [See quot 1955]

1872 Coues *Key to N. Amer. Birds* 246, *Strepsilas* . . . Turnstone. Brant Bird. Calico-back. **1877** C. Hallock *Sportsman's Gaz.* 164 (DAE), [The name] Calico-back [has reference] to the curiously variegated plumage of the upper parts. **1950** *PADS* 14.18 SC, *Calico-back* . . . The ruddy turnstone. **1955** *MA Audubon Soc. Bulletin* 39.446, *Ruddy Turnstone* . . . Calico-back (Maine, Mass.); Calico Bird (Mass., R.I. The plumage of adults is strikingly varicolored.). **1970** *DARE* (Qu. Q10, . . *Water . . and marsh birds)* Inf **VA**47, Calico-back.

2 See quot 1890.

1890 Webster 204/3 (DAE), *Calicoback* . . an hemipterous insect *(Murgantia histrionica)* which injures the cabbage and other garden plants. **1895** Comstock *Manual Insects* 145, The Harlequin Cabbage-bug or Calico-back . . is very destructive to cabbages, radishes, and turnips in the Southern States.

calico bass n

=crappie, usu *Pomoxis nigromaculatus.*

1882 U.S. Natl. Museum *Bulletin* 16.465, *P[omoxis] sparoides* . . . Calico Bass; Grass Bass . . . A handsome fish, valued as food. **1887** Goode *Amer. Fishes* 69, In Lake Michigan the name "Bar-fish" is in general use, giving place in Illinois to the name "Calico Bass." **1940** *High Sport for the Fisherman in Colonial Virginia Waters* 16 (Hench Coll.) eVA, Among the gamest of the fresh water flock are pike, crappie (calico bass). **1965–70** *DARE* (Qu. P1, . . *[Edible] freshwater fish)* 10 Infs, NEast, Calico bass.

calico bird See calico-back 1

calico bush n

1 also *calico bloom, ~ blossom, ~ flower, ~ tree:* A **mountain laurel 1** (here: *Kalmia latifolia*). Also called **clamoun, ivy, lambkill, laurel, mountain ivy, poison ivy, poison laurel, rose laurel, sheep laurel, spoonwood, wicky, wood laurel**

1802 Drayton *View of SC* 69 **SC,** Calico flower, wild ivy, or laurel . . . whose flowers of red and white, grow in such large clusters together; as to give the whole plant at a small distance, the appearance of having a bit of calico thrown over it. **1814** Pursh *Flora Americae* 1.297, *Kalmia . . . latifolia* . . . A shrub from three to eight feet high, very elegant when in flower; called *Laurel* or in the mountains *Callico-bush. Ibid* 2.688, Kalmia . . . latifolia; *Calico-flower. Ibid* 2.698, Calico-tree. *Kalmia latifolia.* **1910** Graves *Flowering Plants* 309 **CT,** Calico Bush . . . All parts of the plant are poisonous except the wood. **1932** *Country Life* 62.65, From a very thin distribution in certain sections, to impenetrable jungles in others, is found the Mountain-laurel . . , often more familiarly called by the Carolinians Calico-bush. **1941** *LANE* Map 249 (*Mountain Laurel)* 3 infs, **CT, RI,** Calico bush. **1945** *Richmond Times-Dispatch* 14 May 6/2 (Hench Coll.), As . . the pioneers grew accustomed to its beautiful blossoms someone with imagination thought the blossoming plant looked as if it were covered with . . colorful scraps of calico, and today in certain areas it is called the "calico bush." **1961** Douglas *My Wilderness* 175 **wNC,** Mountain people call laurel (whose regional name is ivy) the calico bush or mountain ivy. Its

bloom is pinkish-white. **1968** Haun *Hawk's Done Gone* 7 eTN, And the calico bushes all over the Lead Hill with their white, closed-up blossoms that open when they feel a bee light on them. **1969** *DARE* FW Addit GA51, Calico bloom—[Inf] records calico blossom and calico bush for this. So called because of different colors.

2 =fever tree.

1901 Lounsberry *S. Wild Flowers* 476, Georgia Bark. Calico Bush . . . The most interesting feature perhaps of its attractive blossoms is the way one . . of the calyx lobes of certain of the cyme's flowers becomes a large, pink floral leaf.

3 Texas lantana *(Lantana horrida).*

1960 Vines *Trees SW* 896, Texas Lantana . . . bearing varicolored flowers of red, orange or yellow . . . grows mostly in sandy soil in Texas, Louisiana, Mississippi, and Mexico . . . vernacular names . . Calico-bush. **1970** Correll *Plants TX* 1327, *Lantana horrida* . . Texas lantana, hierba de cristo, calico bush.

calico flower See calico bush 1

calico hind n [From its varying colors and spots]

=red hind 1.

1946 LaMonte *N. Amer. Game Fishes* 56, *Red Hind* . . . *Names: . .* Calico Hind, Grouper.

calico salmon n

=chum salmon.

1914 Greely *Hdbk. AK* 129, The plump, silvery dog salmon, known also as calico salmon, averages ten pounds. **1946** Dufresne *AK's Animals* 278 **AK,** One of these is the huge Dog Salmon *(Oncorhynchus keta),* sometimes called the chum, or calico, salmon. **1975** *AK Mag.* Feb 20/3 **AK,** The *chum* salmon *(Oncorhyncus keta),* also called the dog or calico salmon, has light-colored flesh.

calico tree See calico bush 1

calico wood n

=silverbell (here: *Halesia carolina).*

1884 Sargent *Forests of N. Amer.* 106, *Halesia tetraptera* . . . Rattlebox . . . Calico Wood. **1897** Sudworth *Arborescent Flora* 323, *M[ohrodendron] carolinum* . . . Syn.—*Halesia Carolina* . . . Common Names . . . Calicowood (Tex., Ill.). **1950** Peattie *Nat. Hist. Trees* 545, *Halesia carolina* . . . Other Names: . . Calicowood. **1960** Vines *Trees SW* 842, *Halesia carolina* . . . Vernacular names for the tree are . . Calico-wood.

calico woodpecker n

=red-bellied woodpecker.

1930 OK Univ. Biol. Surv. *Pub.* 2.146, *Red-bellied Woodpecker* . . . *Local Names: . .* zebra woodpecker, calico woodpecker . . . The upper parts of the body and wings are black closely barred with white; top of head and nape red.

california v

See quots.

1933 *AmSp* 8.1.28 nwTX, *California.* To throw an animal; to catch it by its neck (or by its ear) and its flank, and trip it by throwing your foot in front of its legs. The animal jumps, and tripping, goes clear over the thrower's head. This method was used for large and unruly calves. **1968** Adams *Western Words, California*—To throw an animal by tripping it.

California acorn woodpecker See California woodpecker

California bank note n *hist*

A hide used as a medium of currency in pre-Gold Rush California.

1840 (1841) Dana *Two Years* 98, They [the people of Monterey] have no circulating medium but silver and hides—which the sailors call "California bank notes." **1941** Dobie *Longhorns* 239 (as of 1850s), In California, before the Gold Rush, the hides themselves were coins of the realm, commonly known as "California bank notes."

California bay n Also *California bay tree*

=California laurel.

1887 *Overland Mth.* 10.153/1 **CA,** The California bay, or laurel, which may be called a tree from its size, though usually growing in bushy form, is beautiful in color, and is a favorite because of its fragance. **1969** *DARE* (Qu. T16, *What kinds of trees are "special" around here?)* Inf **CA**107, Laurel—also called California bay. **1983** *DARE* File nCA, The leaves of the California bay tree have a fragrance similar to that of bay leaves used in cooking.

California bee plant n Also *Californian* ~

A figwort (here: *Scrophularia californica*). Also called **bee plant 2, jack-in-the-pulpit**

1897 Parsons *Wild Flowers CA* 342, *Californian Bee-Plant. Scrophularia Californica . . .* We are apt to class them in the category of weeds; but the fact that their little corollas are almost always stored abundantly with honey for the bees saves them from this reproachful title. **1898** *Jrl. Amer. Folkl.* 11.276, *Scrophularia Californica . .* California bee-plant, Cal. **1915** (1926) Armstrong *Western Wild Flowers* 490, *California Bee-plant . . .* These plants yield a great deal of honey and are common and widely distributed. **1961** Thomas *Flora Santa Cruz* 310 **CA,** California Bee-Plant. Woods, borders of thickets, occasionally in chaparral, and in coastal scrub.

California beer n, also attrib Also *Cal beer* Cf **beer seed**

A homemade, usu non-alcoholic drink.

1965–70 *DARE* (Qq. DD28a,b) Inf **GA7,** California beer—[made] from a 'seed' put in water with sugar, etc.; **KY75,** California or Cal beer; **LA2,** California beer—made with sugar and beer seed, which start[s] in the bottom of a barrel where they make syrup; **TX89,** California beer; **FL7,** California beer seed. **1970** *DARE* FW Addit **KY75,** California beer or Cal beer—a non-alcoholic beverage made of California beer seed (sent for from magazine ads), sorghum molasses, and water; old-fashioned, but still made by some people. **1981** *DARE* File **cTX** (as of c1920), California beer—a fermented brew made of corn secretly by teenagers.

California black sea bass See **black sea bass 2**

California blanket n *joc*

See quots.

1926 *AmSp* 1.650 [Hobo lingo], *California blankets*—newspapers when used for sleeping purposes. **1927** *DN* 5.441, *California blankets . . .* Newspapers used by homeless men as a substitute for bedding.

California bluebell n

1 also *California(n) bluebell(s):* =**baby blue-eyes.**

1897 Parsons *Wild Flowers CA* 290, *Baby-Blue-Eyes . . .* From the campanulate, half-opened buds, it has been called "Californian bluebell." **1911** *Century Dict. Suppl., Bluebell . . .* California bluebell, the baby-blue-eyes, *Nemophila insignis* [=*menziesii*]. **1959** Carleton *Index Herb. Plants* 22, California Bluebells: Nemophila (v).

2 =**wild canterbury bell.**

1923 Davidson–Moxley *Flora S. CA* 298, California Blue Bell. On low hills and burned areas . . . The proper name of this species is *P[hacelia] minor.* **1948** Stevens *KS Wild Flowers* 160, *Phacelia* is exclusively a New World genus of more than 100 species . . one of the finest of these . . is the annual California bluebell. **1961** Wills–Irwin *Flowers TX* 177, The California Blue-bell, *P[hacelia] whitlavia . .* is commonly grown as a bedding plant.

California bluejay See **California jay**

California blue oak See **blue oak 2**

California brook trout See **California trout**

California buckskin n

1968 Adams *Western Words, California buckskin*—A cowboy's name for baling wire.

California buckthorn n

=**coffeeberry 2a(1).**

1937 U.S. Forest Serv. *Range Plant Hdbk.* B127, It shares its southern range with California buckthorn [*Rhamnus californica*]. **1938** Van Dersal *Native Woody Plants* 223, *Rhamnus californica* California buckthorn. **1960** Vines *Trees SW* 704, California Buckthorn.

California coffeeberry See **coffeeberry 2a(1)**

California coffee-tree See **coffee tree 2**

California collar n *hist*

A noose for hanging a person.

1942 Henry *High Border* 97 **WY** (as of 1870s), Inexorably the vigilantes put the California collar around his neck. **1949** *AmSp* 24.262 **West** (as of c1850s), The [hanging] rope was referred to as a California collar. **1968** Adams *Western Words, California collar*—A hangman's noose, so called because of its frequent use in California in vigilante days.

California dew See **California mist**

California false nutmeg See **California nutmeg**

California goose n

=**blue goose 1.**

1932 Bennitt *Check-list* 18 **MO,** *Blue goose. Chen cærulescens . . .* California goose.

California grass n

=**Saint Augustine grass.**

1967 *DARE* (Qu. S9, . . *Kinds of grass that are hard to get rid of*) Inf **HI11,** California grass—buffalo grass.

California holly n Also *Californian* ~

=**toyon.**

1884 Sargent *Forests of N. Amer.* 84, *Heteromeles arbutifolia . . .* California Holly. **1893** *Jrl. Amer. Folkl.* 6.141, California holly . . . Santa Barbara, Calif. **1897** Parsons *Wild Flowers CA* 90, The common name, "Californian holly," refers more to the berries than to the leaves, as the latter have not the form of holly-leaves. **1898** *Jrl. Amer. Folkl.* 11.226, California holly. **1900** Lyons *Plant Names* 189, California holly. **1967–70** *DARE* (Qu. S26A, . . *Other wildflowers*) Infs **CA4, 65,** California holly; (Qu. T5, . . *Evergreens*) Infs **CA80, 85, 87,** California holly; (Qu. T16, *What kinds of trees are "special" around here?*) Infs **CA79, 204,** California holly.

‡**California house** n

1970 *DARE* (Qu. M21B, *Joking names for an outside toilet building*) Inf **CA204,** California house.

California jay n Also *California bluejay* **Pacific**

Either of two jays: *Aphelocoma californica* or *A. cærulescens.*

1853 U.S. Army Corps Topog. Engineers *Rept. Sitgreaves* 34 **NM,** There were quite a number of birds among the cedars, among them the California jay, (*Cyanocorax Californicus*). **1872** Coues *Key to N. Amer. Birds* 166, *Aphelocoma californica* California Jay. **1910** Wheelock *Birds CA* 490, California Jay.—*Aphelocoma californica.* **1953** Jewett *Birds WA* 462, *Aphelocoma cærulescens immanis . . .* Other names: California Jay. **1965–70** *DARE* (Qu. Q16, . . *Kinds of jays*) Infs **CA78, 115, 136, 150, 160, OR5,** California jay; **CA40, 54,** California bluejay.

California laurel n

A tree *(Umbellularia californica)* with aromatic laurel-like leaves. Also called **balm of heaven, California bay, California olive, laurel, mountain laurel, myrtle, Oregon myrtle, peppernut tree, pepperwood, sassafras laurel, spicebush, spice tree**

1871 *Colo. Gazeteer* 117 *(DA),* It will be recalled, on this occasion, that the last tie laid was manufactured from California laurel, with silver plates bearing suitable inscriptions. **1949** Peattie *Cascades* 188, One other hardwood must be mentioned . . . This is the California laurel.

California lilac n Cf **lilac**

Any of the chiefly Pacific spp of the genus *Ceanothus,* but esp *C. thyrsiflorus,* a large, sometimes arborescent, evergreen shrub with showy usu blue flower-clusters, which is also called **blue blossom, bluebrush, blue myrtle 1, lilac, mountain lilac, tick brush, wild lilac.**

1853 in 1913 Winthrop *Canoe & Saddle* 14 Apr **cwCA,** Of these the only interesting one is the California lilac so called, (*Ceanothus?*), bearing a pretty bluish flower. **1882** *Century Illustr. Mag.* 24. 227/2, Up through the forest region, to a height of about nine thousand feet above sea-level, there are . . five or six species of ceanothus, called deer-brush or California lilac. **1902** (1974) Chestnut *Plants Indians* 367 **CA,** *Ceanothus cuneatus . . .* A low evergreen species of California lilac. *Ibid* 368, *Ceanothus integerrimus . . .* A blue or white flowered species of the California lilac. **1916** Parsons *Wild Flowers CA* lxxvi, Many of the species are commonly known as "California lilac." **1946** Peattie *Pacific Coast* 55, But the most characteristic chapparral plants are the gnarled tree-shrubs, numberless in species and variously called wild or California lilac or blue blossom when their flowers are blue or lavender. **1979** Little *Checklist U.S. Trees* 79, *Ceanothus spinosus . . .* California-lilac . . . *Ceanothus thyrsiflorus . . .* California-lilac.

California lion n

=**mountain lion.**

1850 *Deseret News* (Salt Lake City) 29 June 17/2 *(DA),* It is reported that the *California lion* has been seen, yes killed, in this valley, but who can show us one, or even a stuffed skin? **1895** *Out West Mag.* 2.81/1 **CA,** The American lion is *felis concolor* [sic]—the puma, cougar, mountain-lion or California lion. **1914** Applegate *Recollections* 86 **OR** (as of 1843), The deep basso growl of the gray mountain wolf was heard of nights, as also the scream of the . . . California lion.

California live oak n Also *Californian* ~
=**canyon oak 1.**

1894 *Jrl. Amer. Folkl.* 7.99, *Quercus chrysolepis* . . . Californian live oak, Cal. **1967–70** *DARE* (Qu. T5, *Evergreens*) Inf **CA**181, California live oak; (Qu. T10, . . *Different kinds of oak trees*) Inf **CA**7, California live oak; (Qu. T16) Inf **CA**107, California live oak. **1967** *DARE* Tape **CA**10, You went through Dark Canyon Pass . . there were a lot of oak trees there. [FW:] What kind of oak trees? [Inf:] Live oaks—California live oak. I think there are still a few ragged ones there that you can see.

California maple n
1 =**big-leaf maple.**

1892 Apgar *Trees Nth. U.S.* 86 **West,** *Acer macrophyllum* . . . Large-leaved or California Maple. **1968** *DARE* (Qu. T14, . . *Different kinds of maples*) Inf **CA**97, California maple—large maple leaf, two or three species.

2 =**box elder.** Cf **Canadian maple**

1968 *DARE* (Qu. T13) Inf **CA**105, California maple.

California mist n Also ~ *dew* Cf **Oregon mist, Scotch mist**
A light rain.

1968–70 *DARE* (Qu. B21, *When fine drops of moisture are falling*) Inf **CA**90, California dew; (Qu. B23, . . *A light rain*) Inf **CA**211, California mist.

Californian adj See **California** entries

California nutmeg n Also *California false nutmeg, coast nutmeg, nutmeg tree*

A tree *(Torreya californica)* which produces nutmeg-like fruits. Also called **stinking cedar, yew**

1894 *Jrl. Amer. Folkl.* 7.100, *Torreya Californica* . . nutmeg-tree, Cal. **1897** Sudworth *Arborescent Flora* 102, *Torreya californica* . . California Nutmeg (Cal., Idaho) . . California False Nutmeg . . Coast Nutmeg. **1908** Sudworth *Forest Trees Pacific* 191, California nutmeg is a rare tree of small size. It is called nutmeg from the fancied resemblance of its seed-kernel to the nutmeg of commerce. **1910** Jepson *Silva CA* 167, *Torreya californica* . . California Nutmeg . . . The California Nutmeg is, however, not at all related, either biologically or economically, to the nutmeg of commerce *(Myristica fragrans* Houtt.). **1968** *DARE* (Qu. T5, . . *Kinds of evergreens, other than pine*) Inf **CA**97, California nutmeg *(Torreya californica)*.

California olive n Also *California wild olive* [Perh from the resemblance of the leaves to those of the olive]
=**California laurel.**

1897 Sudworth *Arborescent Flora* 203, *Umbellularia californica* . . *California Laurel* . . . California Olive (Oreg.) **1897** Parsons *Wild Flowers CA* 373, This tree *[Umbellularia californica]* is known in different localities by a variety of names, such as . . . "California olive." **1900** Lyons *Plant Names* 383, *Umbellularia Californica* . . . California Wild Olive.

California overshoe See **California sock**

California pants n
See quots.

1927 (1944) Russell *Trails Plowed Under* 2 (as of 1870s), Maybe he'd wear California pants, light buckskin in color, with large brown plaid, sometimes foxed, or what you'd call reinforced with buck or antelope skin. **1933** *AmSp* 8.1.31, *California pants,* heavy wool trousers, usually striped or checked, of an excellent double weave. **1939** Abbott *We Pointed Them* 8 **West** (as of c1870s), Striped or checked California pants made in Oregon City, the best pants ever made to ride in. **1968** Adams *Western Words.*

California pea (bean) See **pea bean**

California peacock n *joc*
=**roadrunner.**

1956 *AmSp* 31.182, California peacock [a name for a] Roadrunner [in] Utah.

California pine See **California white pine**

California pitcher plant n Also *Californian* ~

A bog plant *(Darlingtonia californica)* of northern California and southwestern Oregon which has hollow pitcher-like leaves topped by a curved hood with a prominent 2-lobed appendage. Also called **calf's head, California side-saddle flower, cobra plant, pitcher plant 2**

1866 Lindley *Treas. Botany* 384/1 *(OED),* The only species, . . known as the Californian Side-saddle flower or Pitcher-plant, is a perennial herb growing in marshy places. **1897** Parsons *Wild Flowers CA* 390, *Californian Pitcher-plant* . . . is one of the most wonderful and interesting of all the forms that grow. **1925** Jepson *Manual Plants CA* 448, *California Pitcher Plant* . . . Plants greenish-yellow . . leaves enlarged upward into a rounded hood. **1949** Moldenke *Amer. Wild Flowers* 60, Similar . . is the famous *Californiapitcherplant* . . found in marshy meadows and along streams . . in northern California and southwestern Oregon. **1973** Hitchcock–Cronquist *Flora Pacific NW* 182.

California poplar n
A black **cottonwood 1** (here: *Populus trichocarpa*).

1967 *DARE* (Qu. T12, . . *Kind of poplar tree that has sticky, sweet-smelling buds*) Inf **IA**1, California poplar. **1979** Little *Checklist U.S. Trees* 208, *Populus trichocarpa* . . *black cottonwood* . . Other Common Names . . California poplar.

California poppy n Also *California state poppy*
A yellow poppy *(Eschscholtzia californica)* native to California. Also called **cup of gold, dormidera, gold poppy**

1907 White *AZ Nights* 277, The animal waded fetlock deep in the gorgeous orange California poppies. **1965–70** *DARE* (Qu. S26a, . . *Roadside flowers*) 9 Infs, **chiefly SW,** California poppy; **CA**65, **NM**13, California poppies; (Qu. S26c, *Wildflowers that grow in woods*) **CA**22, 99, **WA**15, California poppy; (Qu. S26d, *Wildflowers that grow in meadows*) **CA**20, 22, 155, **WA**15, California poppy; (Qu. S26e, . . *Other wildflowers*) Infs **CA**115, 155, 162, 204, **TN**22, **WA**15, California poppy; **CA**9, California state poppy.

California prayer book n Also *Californian* ~ *joc*
A deck of cards (esp as used during "gold rush" days in California).

1851 Kelly *Excursion* 2.64, But by far the greater number were engaged in the study of the "California prayer-book." **1932** *AmSp* 7.430 [Gold-rush English as of c1850], A deck of cards was called a "California prayer-book." **1962** *Western Folkl.* 21.29 **Los Angeles,** California prayer book—a deck of cards. **1968** Adams *Western Words,* California prayer book—A gambler's name for a deck of cards.

California quail n
1 also *California mountain quail,* ~ *valley quail*: A quail *(Lophortyx californica)* with a black topknot, native to California and Oregon. Also called **helmet quail, topknot quail, tufted quail, valley quail**

1826 in 1831 Beechey *Narrative* 2.81 **nCA,** The California quail *(tetrao viginianus)* . . afforded amusement to our sportsmen. **1957** Pough *Audubon W. Bird Guide* 68, California Quail *Lophortyx californica.* **1967–69** *DARE* (Qu. Q7, . . *Game birds*) Inf **CA**130, California mountain quail—called "mountain quail"; California valley quail—also called "valley quail"; **CA**105, California valley quail; **CO**31, California quail.

2 =**Gambel's quail.**

1928 Bailey *Birds NM* 221, The handsome Gambel Quail, locally but incorrectly called California Quail . . may be met in the Lower Sonoran Zone in quail brush . . and creosote. **1964** Phillips *Birds AZ* 29, It [Gambel's quail, *Callipepla gambelii*] is similar to, and sometimes erroneously called the California Quail, a species which does not occur in Arizona.

California rack See **rack**

California redworm n
Prob a beetle larva.

1968 *DARE* (Qu. P6, . . *Kinds of worms*) Inf **NH**14, California redworm—a small redworm, similar to an angleworm—lives under [the] bark of pulp trees.

California reins n pl
See quot.

1961 Adams *Old-Time Cowhand* 120, "Tied," "closed," or "California reins," . . are tied together at the ends or the entire rein's made in one piece.

California room n Cf **Florida room**
1975 *DARE* File **neOH,** California room—a sun room or lounge with big windows.

California rose n
=**bindweed 1** (here: *Convolvulus japonicus*).

1910 Graves *Flowering Plants* 324 **CT,** *Convolvulus japonicus* . . California Rose. **1973** Hitchcock–Cronquist *Flora Pacific NW* 364, California rose. *C[onvolvulus] japonicus.*

California salmon n

=**chinook salmon.**

1879 *U.S. Natl. Museum Proc. for 1878* 1.69 **OR,** *Oncorhynchus Quinnat* . . . California *Salmon.* **1882** *Amer. Naturalist* 16.766 **CA,** The familiar quinnat or California salmon is exchanged for the "tshawytcha" or "chouicha." **1911** *Century Dict.* 5314/3, Quinnat, or California Salmon *(Oncorhynchus tschawytcha).*

California sidesaddle flower n Also *Californian sidesaddle*
flower, saddle flower [From the shape] Cf **sidesaddle flower**

=**California pitcher plant.**

1866 *Treas. Bot.* 384/1 *(OED),* The only species, . . known as the Californian Side-saddle flower or Pitcher-plant, is a perennial herb growing in marshy places. **1876** Hobbs *Bot. Hdbk.* 100, Saddle flower, Darlingtonia Californica. *Ibid* 106, Side-saddle flower, Calif'nia, Pitcher plant, Darlingtonia Californica. **1900** Lyons *Plant Names* 98, California Side-saddle flower. **1911** *Century Dict.,* Sidesaddle-flower . . . *Chrysamphora Californica* has been called *Californian side-saddle flower.*

California skirt n

1968 Adams *Western Words,* California skirt—A stock saddle with round skirts, so called because it is a favorite style in that state.

California slingshot n

Among loggers: see quot 1959.

1959 *AmSp* 34.77 **nCA,** *California sling shot* . . . The name given to crotch line loading. In this logging system two poles are used with the rigging which resembles a slingshot, in the middle. **1968** Adams *Western Words,* California slingshot.

California slippery elm See **slippery elm**

California sock n Also ~ *moccasin,* ~ *overshoe hist*

A makeshift foot covering made of a cloth sack worn instead of a sock or shoe.

1941 (1948) Dane *Ghost Town* 4 **CA,** A man didn't ever have to go without socks if he had a couple of flour sacks. He'd put his foot on the sack near one end and he'd fold the corners and the front end over the top of his foot, and then he'd bring the other end up in back over the heel and wrap it around his ankle and leg and pull his boot on over it; and that was called the "California sock." **1952** Walker *Injun Summer* 78 **CO** (as of c1870s), Plodding over clods in their "California overshoes." (California overshoes are made by folding a tow sack cornerwise, setting the foot so the corner will fit neatly behind the calf of the leg; and the two extra corners are left to tie a firm knot after wrapping rightly [sic] around the foot.) **1967** *Western Folkl.* 26.189, *California overshoes*—footcoverings made of gunny sacks. **1968** Adams *Western Words,* California *moccasins*—A cowhand's name for sacks bound about the feet to prevent them from freezing.

California sorrel n

1968 Adams *Western Words,* California sorrel—A red-gold horse of the palomino type.

California state poppy See **California poppy**

California stingray n

=**bat ray.**

1882 *U.S. Natl. Museum Bulletin* 16.51, *Myliobatis californicus* . . . California Sting Ray. **1896** *Ibid* 47.89. **1933** John G. Shedd Aquarium *Guide* 25, *Aëtobatus californicus*—California Sting-ray. **1983** *DARE* File, I have known the popular term California stingray for *Myliobatis californicus* since my earliest growing-up years in Long Beach, California.

California strawberry See **strawberry**

California sunflower n

A **sunflower** (here: *Helianthus californicus*).

1967 *DARE* (Qu. S7) Inf **CA7,** Black-eye(d) Susan, California sunflower; 100 species of helianthus.

California trout n Also *California brook trout*

=**rainbow trout.**

1882 *U.S. Natl. Museum Bulletin* 16.312, *Salmo irideus* . . California Brook Trout. **1975** Evanoff *Catch More Fish* 81, The rainbow trout *(Salmo gairdneri)* is also called the California trout, Pacific trout, . . etc.

California twist n

1961 Adams *Old-Time Cowhand* 232, A rope cast with a single overhead twist, and no whirlin', was called the "California twist."

California valley quail See **California quail 1**

California white pine n Also *California pine*

Any of several western pines, esp **ponderosa pine.**

1910 Jepson *Silva CA* 79, In the general market the sawmill product is always sold under the name of California White Pine *[Pinus ponderosa].* **1958** McCulloch *Woods Words* 27 **Pacific NW,** *California white pine*—At different times, and at different places, this name was given to western white pine, sugar pine, and western yellow pine. **1960** Vines *Trees SW* 19, Ponderosa Pine—*Pinus ponderosa* . . Other vernacular names are . . California White Pine. **1966** *DARE* (Qu. T17, . . *Different kinds of pine trees)* Inf **ME14,** California pine—long spill.

California wild olive See **California olive**

California woodpecker n Also *California acorn woodpecker,*
Californian woodpecker

A black-and-white woodpecker *(Melanerpes formicivorus)* native to the Pacific coast and the Southwest, noted for its habit of wedging acorns into holes in trees. Also called **carpintero**

1858 Baird *Birds* 114, California Woodpecker . . . In most specimens one or two red feathers may be detected in the black of the breast just behind the sulphur yellow crescent. **1898** Grinnell *Birds Pacific Slope* 26, *Californian Woodpecker.* Abundant resident in the oak regions, and . . in the pines and firs up to 6000 feet in the mountains. **1913** *Pacific Coast Avifauna* 9.54, California Woodpecker . . . is often seen near Centerville, and sometimes follows down the river bottom much farther. **1940** Gabrielson *Birds OR* 374, The handsome, sleek-looking California Woodpecker . . . is the species that so delights in wedging acorns into telephone poles and trees. **1964** Phillips *Birds AZ* 70, *Acorn Woodpecker; Ant-eating Woodpecker; . . California Woodpecker* . . . This white-eyed clown of woodpeckers has a harlequin face. **1967–69** *DARE* (Qu. Q17, . . *Kinds of woodpeckers)* Infs **CA24, 115, 160,** California woodpecker; **GA140,** California acorn woodpeckers.

California yellowtail n Also *yellowtail*

A food and game fish *(Seriola dorsalis).* Also called **amberfish, amberjack 2, jack** n[1], **white salmon**

1896 *U.S. Natl. Museum Bulletin* 47.902, *Seriola Dorsalis*—(Yellowtail). **1947** Caine *Salt Water* 34, The *California Yellowtail [Seriola dorsalis]* is one of the finest game fish of the Pacific, but should not be confused with the yellowtail, *Ocyurus chrysurus,* of the Florida Keys, which is a much smaller fish. **1953** Roedel *Common Fishes CA* 82, California Yellowtail—*Seriola dorsalis.* **1975** Evanoff *Catch More Fish* 160, The fish usually sought by these boats is the California yellowtail . . . Fishing for the yellowtail usually runs from April to October.

Californy See -y

caliker See calico

calimanker See calamanco

Ca'lina See Carolina

calinche See colonche

Ca'liner See Carolina

caliope See calliope

calithumpian See callithumpian n

caliwampus See catawampus adj

calk See caulk

calk down v phr [Scots and Engl dial *calk, cau(l)k* alter of *chalk*
(up, down) to run up an account at a shop]

To charge a purchase.

1950 *WELS (If you buy something but don't pay cash for it, you might say, "I _____.")* 1 Inf, **ceWI,** Put it on the cuff—calked it down.

calkilate See calculate

call v

1 in phr *call one out:* To wake someone. Cf **holler one up**

1954 *Harder Coll.* **cwTN,** *Call him out*—To awaken; same as roust him out.

2 occas with *up:* To lure a bird or an animal by imitating its call.

1831 Audubon *Ornith. Biog.* 1.12, During spring, Turkeys are *called*, as it is termed, by drawing the air in a particular way through one of the second joint bones of a wing of that bird, which produces a sound resembling the voice of the female, on hearing which the male comes up, and is shot. **1860** *Harper's Mag.* 20. 442/1 **ME,** "Tom, can you call moose?" **1939** *Hall Coll.* **wNC,** *Call* . . . To call an animal imitatively; to attract so as to shoot. "They couldn't call 'em up. That is 'calling,' the way of calling up a turkey gobbler, calling with my mouth."

3 usu with *on:* To ask for assistance; hence vbl n *calling on.*

1914 *DN* 4.69 **ME, nNH,** *Call on* . . . To ask for charity. "He called on the town." **1927** *DN* 5.441 **cNC** [Underworld jargon], *Call* . . . To beg. **1975** Gould *ME Lingo* 40, *Call on*—For casual help. On a one-man farm there were many two-man tasks. A farmer needing an extra hand would *call on* his neighbor. *Calling on* is not the same as *changing work.* If payment is offered after *calling on,* a man would rightly reply, "Oh, no, that's all right; I may want to *call on* myself, some day." *Calling on* is also the term for asking welfare relief from the town; when a man couldn't swing his affairs and needed assistance, he would *call on.*

4 also *call off:* To announce or prompt (the steps in a square dance). Cf **call figures**

1873 Beadle *Undeveloped West* 455 **NM,** They [=Mexicans] never have the set "called," as in the States. **1880** *Harper's Mag.* 60. 544/2 **CO** [Black], I can call de dances bully—you bet! **1902** *DN* 2.230 **sIL,** *Call off* . . . To prompt figures in a square dance. **1903** Wiggin *Rebecca* 23 **ME,** He played the violin and "called off" at dances. **1907** *DN* 3.221 **nwAR,** *Call off.* **1910** *DN* 3.438 **cwNY,** *Call off* . . . To announce the figures of a square dance.

5 with *out:* To invite a woman to dance. Cf **call-out 1**

1916 *DN* 4.268 **New Orleans LA,** *Call out* . . . At a carnival ball, when one is masked, to invite (a lady) to dance.

6 also *call in:* To begin. Cf **take in**

1899 (1912) Green *VA Folk-Speech, Call in* . . . School calls in at 9 o'clock. **1950** *WELS* (*If you want to know the time that something begins, for example a church service, you say, "What time does church _____?"*) 1 Inf, **seWI,** Commence, begin, call.

7 with *off:* To list by name.

1840 Cooper *Pathfinder* 1.186 **NY,** Name them? it is no easy matter to call off the stars, for the simple reason that they are so numerous.

8 with *for:* To name after.

1831 (1910) Ayer *Diary* 327, I have this day heard of the death of a dear young friend . . . She was call'd for me, and I was much attach'd to her.

9 in phr *call one out of one's name* and varr: To address a person (or thing) by a name other than the true one; to abuse. [*EDD call* v.[1] III.4.(3) "to call by a nickname, not by one's proper name . . to abuse, vilify."]

1899 (1912) Green *VA Folk-Speech, Call* . . . To call out of name; to call by improper and abusive names. **c1925** in 1944 *ADD* **swWV,** He called me out o' my name. **1934** *W2, Call* (one) *out of* (his) *name.* To call by a wrong name. **1942** Berrey–Van den Bark *Amer. Slang* 298.7, *Swear at.* Call a person out of his name, call names. **1946** Greer–Petrie *Angeline Gits an Eyeful* 7 **csKY,** But la me, that old werman is li'ble to call anything out of hits name. **1953** Goodwin *It's Good* 142 **sIL** [Black], Now Ruby, if anybody calls you out of your name this morning, don't pay any attention to them. Just say to yourself, 'Sticks and stones may break my bones but words can never harm me.'

10 To say, pronounce (a word or name).

1931–33 *LANE Worksheets* **nwVT,** That's the high-tone way of calling it. **1934** Hanley Disks **nRI,** You called it once. **1953** Randolph *Down in Holler* 232 **Ozarks,** *Call* . . . Sometimes it is used instead of pronounce, as when a man says, "I cain't rightly call that word," in reference to some strange term he has seen in print.

11 also *call over:* To mention (one's name). **S Midl** Cf **call one's name**

1917 *DN* 4.409 **wNC,** *Call* . . . Mention. "Ain't you never heard Tommy call my name?" [Also] N. Eng. **1926** Roberts *Time of Man* 69 **KY,** By the time the tobacco was ripe the name no longer caught at her nerves when Artie Pinkston called it in her gossip. **1927** *AmSp* 2.350 **cwWV,** *Call* . . to mention. "Did any one call my name?" **1927** Adams *Congaree* 18 **cSC** [Black], If I stays here he mought think I been talkin' 'bout him an' Jesus know I ain't never called he name to nobody. **1952** Brown *NC Folkl.* 1.525, *Call over* . . . to mention, speak of. "You called over that fellow's name just a minute ago." **1953** Randolph *Down in Holler* 232 **Ozarks,** *Call* . . . If a hillman says "I dassn't call his name," the word means mention rather than recall. **1954** *Harder Coll.* **cwTN,** *Call.* **c1960** *Wilson Coll.* **csKY,** *Call.*

12 usu of names: To recall, remember. [From *call to mind, call to remembrance;* cf *OED call* v.20.b. 1472 →; also infl by *recall*] chiefly **Sth, S Midl**

1887 (1967) Harris *Free Joe* 117 **GA,** I'll bet a hoss I kin call the name 'thout movin' out'n my cheer . . . The name er the man what sont the word is Tuck Peevy. **1926** *DN* 5.398 **Ozarks,** *Call* . . . To remember, recall. "I caint *call* his name." **1939** *Hall Coll.* **eTN,** *Call* . . . For recall. "I caint call his other name." **1944** *PADS* 2.54 **MO, NC, SC, VA,** *Call* . . . To remember. "I can't call his name right now." **1953** Randolph *Down in Holler* 232 **Ozarks,** *Call* . . . To recall, to remember. "I orter know that feller, but I cain't call his name." **1954** *Harder Coll.* **cwTN,** *Call.* **c1960** *Wilson Coll.* **csKY,** *Call* . . . "I can't call your name, but I know your face and where you're from." **1962** Faulkner *Reivers* 128 **MS,** A man, another rich white man, I dont call his name but I can find him. **1965–70** *DARE* Tape **AR43,** I can't call their names now; **MS1,** I can't call either one of 'em's name just now; **OK1,** I can't call it right now; **SC16,** I couldn't call; **TX38,** I just could not call their names and I'd just get panicky; **VA73,** I know his name but I just can't exactly call it right off. **1968** *DARE* (Qu. JJ30a, . . *Expressions for forgetting something*) Infs **MD36, NY60,** Can't call it; (QR, near Qu. E10) Inf **MD50,** I once knew [the name], but can't call it now. **1968** *DARE* FW Addit **GA45,** 47, I can't call it; **eMD,** Can't call it.

call n[1]

1 In a song or rhyme: a solo line or stanza which is followed by a response or refrain—often used in the phr *call and sponse.* chiefly among Black speakers

1922 *DN* 5.189 [Black], *Call and sponse.* Song and refrain impromptu. **1922** Talley *Negro Folk Rhymes* 265, They [Negroes] named the parts of their verse "Call," and (Re)"Sponse." **1942** (1965) Parrish *Slave Songs* 15 **GA coast,** Where there are wide fields, musical half-yodeled calls often bring " 'sponses" from laborers a mile away. **1977** Smitherman *Talkin* 104, The African-derived communication process of call-response . . spontaneous verbal and non-verbal interaction between speaker and listener in which all of the speaker's statements ("calls") are punctuated by expressions ("responses") from the listener . . . You can find call-responses both in the church and on the street.

‡**2** A name. [*call* v **8**]

1966 *PADS* 46.25 **cnAR,** *Call* . . . Name. "There might be several calls for it."

3 in phr *have a call:* An intention.

1944 *PADS* 2.18 **sAppalachians,** *Call, to hev (have) a* . . . To intend, to have a mind to. "I hev a call to go to town today."

call n[2] Also sp *coll* [Abbr for **colcannon**]

See quots.

1926 *AmSp* 1.651, *Coll*—a hobo *de luxe* dish, consisting of baked potatoes mashed, with salt, milk, butter, onion tops and liver sausage reheated. **1927** *DN* 5.441 [Underworld jargon], *Call* . . . A pottage made by boiling bacon, potatoes, and onions together. **1927** *AmSp* 2.389 [Vagabond argot], *Call* is a stew of potatoes and onions, with or without meat; only old-timers use the word. **1960** Wentworth–Flexner *Slang* 85, *Call* . . . Stew, esp. one consisting mainly of onions or potatoes.

callaboos See **caboose** n[1] **1**

callahootin(g) See **callyhooting**

callamink See **calamanco**

call a sale v phr Cf **sale-crying**

To preside at an auction.

1944 Wellman *Bowl* 167 **KS,** Never halting, never pausing, the auctioneer's jargon rose and fell . . . Many never before had heard LeForce "call a sale".

callate See **calculate**

callathump(ian), callathumping See **callithumpian** n

call-ball n Also *call-ballie* Also called **ballie-callie**

1883 Newell *Games* 181, *Call-Ball.* This game (commonly called Callie-ball, or Ballie-callie), was formerly a common sport of schoolboys in New England. The ball was thrown against a house, and at the same time a name called. The lad named must strike back the ball on its rebound.

call book n

Among railroad workers: see quot 1977.

1953 Botkin *Treas. Railroad Folkl.* 170 (as of 1906), All I had to do was to ask to see his service letter . . and get his name on the callbook. **1969** *AmSp* 44.252 **IL,** Freight crews stay in hotels, rooming houses, or company dormitories, where they are awakened by a *call boy* who requires them to sign a *call book,* furnishing proof that they actually have been called. **1977** Adams *Lang. Railroader,* Call book: A book carried by the call boy to be signed by the men called to duty. The book resolved many disagreements and relieved the call boy of blame because it held a record of whether or not the one called had signed.

callboy n Also *caller, call-kid*
Among railroad workers: one who summons the train crews and keeps the **call book.**

    1898 (1970) Hamblen *Genl. Manager* 72 **Chicago IL,** When it became known that Joe's fireman was sick, all the others made it a point to be away from home when the caller made his rounds with orders to call the first man he found off duty. **1940** Cottrell *Railroader* 5, Even language must be transformed, and the young call-kid who says "ten minutes to nine" instead of "eight-fifty" or the machinist apprentice who uses "burr" instead of "nut" immediately feels the cutting edge of ridicule. *Ibid* 46, All others must make themselves available to a call boy, whose responsibility it is to notify the crew at least two hours before their train is to depart. The caller may require those called to "sign the book." **1953** Botkin *Treas. Railroad Folkl.* 170 **CO** (as of 1906), As callboy, I called many a man without his having been formally hired. All I had to do was to ask to see his service letter (phony or good), tell him to see the doctor when he got back from his first trip, and get his name on the callbook. **1966–68** *DARE* Tape NJ25, Callboy . . . A boy who had to be on call to notify a wrecking crew in case of a train wreck. The first job I took was [as] a callboy on the Erie railroad; **SD5,** Callboy. **1969** *AmSp* 44.254 **IL,** *Call boy*—Employee who informs freight crews of the time they must report for duty.

call by v phr **prob S Midl** Cf **come by 2**
To pay a short visit.

    1905 *DN* 3.73 **nwAR,** *Call by* . . . Make a call. 'Can't you call by on your way to town?' **1906** *Everybody's Mag.* 15.465/1 **NC,** He would call by for Mary Adrian. **1946** *PADS* 6.8 **swVA** (as of 1930–43), *Call by.* **c1960** *Wilson Coll.* **csKY,** *Call by*—Come to visit, even for a brief time.

callcannon See **colcannon**

call cows, call dogs See **call hogs**

call-down n Also vbl n *calling-down* **chiefly Nth, Midl**
A reprimand.

    1901 Hobart *John Henry* 11 **NYC,** The four-flush call-down makes you back-pedal. **1909** *DN* 3.409 **nME,** *Calldown* . . . A reprimand. **1933** Hanley *Disks* **ceMA,** My husband . . he's a regular book-fiend—he's always reading . . I give him such call-downs about reading that . . I never let him catch me reading. **c1960** *Wilson Coll.* **csKY,** *Calling-down*—A reprimand. "Our teacher give us a big calling-down." **1965–70** *DARE* (Qu. II27, *If somebody gives you a very sharp scolding, you might say, "I certainly got a _____ for that."*) 39 Infs, **chiefly Nth, Midl,** Calling-down; 10 Infs, **chiefly Nth,** Call-down; (Qu. Y6) Inf **IN60,** Give him a calling-down; (Qu. Y12A, *A fight between two people, mostly with words*) Inf **NY96,** Call-down.

call down v phr **chiefly Nth, Midl**
To reprimand.

    1896 (1898) Ade *Artie* 27 **Chicago IL,** I did n't want to call her down. **1897** *KS Univ. Qrly.* 6.86, *Call down:* to humble one. **1907** in 1953 Botkin *Treas. Railroad Folkl.* 304, You'd better fix the matter before the roadmaster hears of your blunder and calls you down. **1947** *AmSp* 22.182, To call someone down (i.e. to reprimand him). **c1960** *Wilson Coll.* **csKY,** *Call down*—Scold severely. **1966** Barnes–Jensen *Dict. UT Slang* 7, *Call down* . . scold. **1966–69** *DARE* (Qu. Y6, *Words meaning to put pressure on somebody to do something he ought to have done but hasn't: "He's a whole week late. I'm going to _____."*) Inf **MO6,** Call him down; **MI50,** Lay him out, call him down, get after him; (Qu. II27, *If somebody gives you a very sharp scolding, you might say, "I certainly got _____."*) Infs **NH1, NJ30, NY73, WI62,** Called down. **1967** *DARE* FW Addit **NY,** Called down—taken to task for it. **1968** *DARE* Tape **IA33,** I'd had to call her down two or three times. She was a little spoiled; **IN23,** [At the time of a death in the neighborhood] if we got noisy or anything our parents called us down.

callebogus See **calibogus**

called home, be v phr Also *be called aft, call home*
To die; hence ppl adj *called home* dead.

    1942 Berrey–Van den Bark *Amer. Slang* 117.18, *Dead* . . called home. **1968** *DARE* (Qu. BB56, *Joking expressions for dying: "He _____."*) Inf **CT6,** Called home; kicked the bucket. **1975** Gould *ME Lingo* 40, *Called aft*—To die. A sailor not measuring up would be *called aft* to the captain's domain to be censured or punished; so a man would be *called aft* for final judgment.

called out in meeting, be v phr Cf **cry 2**
To have one's intentions of marriage announced in church.

    1939 (1954) FWP *Guide KY* 438 **seKY,** A couple contemplating marriage is "called out in meetin'" at least once prior to the marriage ceremony.

called to straw adj Also *brought to straw* [*OED straw sb.¹* 2.b. *in the straw* in childbed, lying-in (a1661 →); *EDD bring to the straw* to bear, bring forth] **S Midl**
Pregnant; in childbed.

    1931 *PMLA* 46.1307 **sAppalachians,** Maggie's been called to straw. (She is pregnant.) **1933** *AmSp* 8.1.48 **Ozarks,** Called to straw. **1940** (1968) Haun *Hawk's Done Gone* 23 **eTN,** Then it got out that Tiny was called to straw. Old Man Brock didn't take note of Tiny's shape till nigh four months before the time. *Ibid* 117, She was two months called to straw and easy to upset. **1946** TN Folk Lore Soc. *Bulletin* 12.4.4, Pore thing. Eight children. Ever since she wuz brought to straw with that last youngun, she ain't riz. Jes' lies there pint-blank like a ghost woman. **1953** Randolph *Down in Holler* 114, In some parts of the Ozark region *straw* means childbirth. A woman who is *called to straw* is about to have a baby.

callemink See **calamanco**

caller See **callboy**

callerate See **calculate**

call figures v phr Cf **figure v B**
In dancing: to announce the figures or movements which the dancers execute.

    1898 Canfield *Maid of Frontier* 165 **TX,** The dancing was only the old-fashioned quadrille . . . The band, in additon to furnishing music, called the figures. **1927** *AmSp* 2.350 **cwWV,** *Call figures* . . to call the changes for a square dance. "Can any one here call figures?" **1943** Chase *Jack Tales* 86 **wNC** (as of 1880s), They made music and got to playin' Weevily Wheat and Skip to My Lou and runnin' eight-handed reels and all. Jack never did have such a good time and his uncle was an awful good hand to call figures. **1954** *Harder Coll.* **cwTN,** *Call figures* —To call the changes at a dance.

call for quarter See **quarter, call (for)**

call hogs v phr Also *call pigs* (or *cows, dogs*), *drive pigs* and varr [Scots *call* to drive + Scots *hog* yearling sheep or Engl *hog* pig] **scattered, but chiefly Sth, S Midl** See Map *esp freq among Black speakers* Note: this idiom is attested in both Scotland and England.
To snore.

    1912 Green *VA Folk-Speech,* Call hogs . . . To snore. **1942** Berrey–Van den Bark *Amer. Slang* 251.7, Snore. Cut it, drive pigs (to market), hit the knots. **1946** (1972) Mezzrow *Really Blues* 331, Call some hogs: snore. **1965–70** *DARE* (Qu. X45, . . *Joking expressions . . about snoring*) 56 Infs, **scattered, but chiefly Sth, S Midl,** Calling (the) hogs; **MO8,** Call the hogs; **SC26,** Callin' the hog; **TN52,** Calling hogs from the

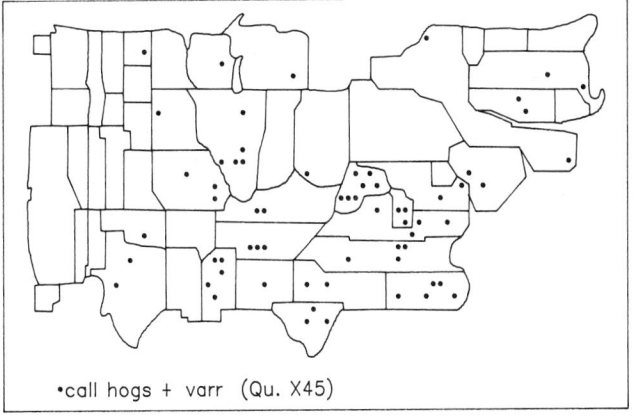

•call hogs + varr (Qu. X45)

bottom; **IL**78, **NY**10A, Calling pigs; **NJ**16, **TX**92, Calling (the) cows; **VA**39, Calling the dogs; **CT**36, Driving pigs. [Of all Infs responding to the question, 6% were Black; of those giving this response, 60% were Black.] **1980** *DARE* File **Buffalo NY** [Black], Calling hogs [=snoring].

call home See **called home, be**

calliathump See **callithumpian** n

callibogus See **calibogus**

callibouse See **calaboose**

callicro See **calico** n

callie-over See **colly-over**

callimanco, callimanker See **calamanco**

calling vbl n Also *calling up*
=telephoning.

1966–70 *DARE* (Qu. P13, . . *Ways of fishing*) Inf **SC**40, Calling them up, telephoning — [there are] two boats, the ringing boat drifts along the edge, turns the telephone and drags the line; the netting or pickup boat gets the stunned fish. This won't work on scaly fish; (Qu. P16) Inf **TN**53, Herding, gathering, calling, tolling fish.

calling down See **call-down**

calling hours n pl Rarely *calling* **chiefly NEast, also OH, IN**
See Map Cf **visiting hours**

1965–70 *DARE* (Qu. BB60, *When friends and relatives gather together at the place where the body is, usually the night before the funeral, you call that*) 34 Infs, **chiefly NEast, also OH, IN,** Calling hours; **IN**76, **OH**57, Calling.

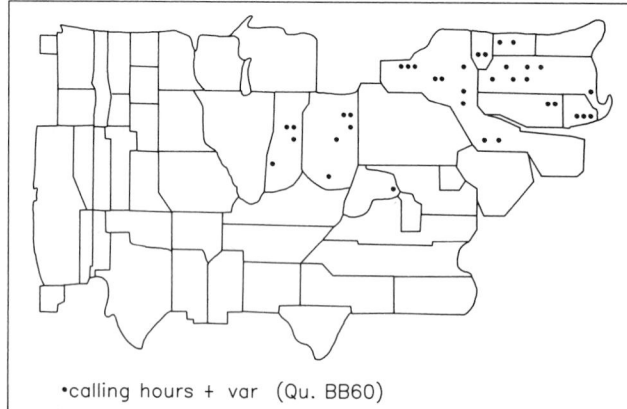

•calling hours + var (Qu. BB60)

calling on See **call** v 3

calling the brands vbl n

1961 Adams *Old-Time Cowhand* 255, The characters of a brand read from top to bottom, from outside to inside and from left to right. The ability to read them brands was referred to as "callin' the brands."

calliope n Std |kə'laɪə͵pi|, often |'kæli͵op| Also sp *caliope;* pronc-spp *callio, kallyope* See also quot 1969 at **A**
A Forms.

1858 *Harper's Mag.* 18.138/1, Some time in the spring of '57 the steamer *St. Nicholas* 'opened' in this [Southern] city with a caliope — the first one ever heard in these parts. **1860** Worcester *Dict.* 193, [kə'laɪopɨ] . . A musical instrument of recent invention, consisting of a series of pipes, having keys, and operated on by steam instead of air. **1912** *DN* 3.572 **wIN,** Calliope . . "It must be a big circus; they have two cal-li-opes." **1914** Lindsay *Adventures* 76 **IL,** I am the Gutter Dream, / Tune-maker, born of steam, / Tooting joy, tooting hope. / I am the Kallyope. **1927** Sandburg *Songbag* 349, [The] mammoth, invincible, crowning feature of the three-ring circus, the last wagon in the parade, [was] the steam "kallyope." **1946** Driscoll *Country Jake* 16 **csKS** (as of c1900), I think I hear the shrill notes of the approaching kally-ope. **1946** McAtee *Dial. Grant Co. IN Suppl. 3* 3, Calliope . . Some modified the word still more into "callio." **1963** Haywood *Yankee Dict.* 23, The children reluctantly returned to school and, when they had settled down, the teacher would explain that the "steam piano" is named calliope for one of the Greek muses, the mother of Orpheus. **1968** *DARE* Tape **OH**44, On a showboat an' in a circus it's called a ['kali͵op] . . in all other locations [kə'laɪo͵pi]. **1969** *DARE* FW Addit **cwIL,** [kə'lælə͵pi].

B Sense.
A steam locomotive.

1940 Cottrell *Railroader* 122, Calliope — A locomotive. Modern four-tone whistles brought on this appellation. **1945** Hubbard *Railroad Ave.* 336, Calliope — Steam locomotive.

callithumpian n, often attrib Usu |͵kælə'θʌmpɪən|, less freq |͵kaʊ'θʌmpɪən| Also sp *cala-, cali-, calla-, calli(a)-, cal-, cow-, -thump(ian), -thumpin(g)* [Engl *gallithumpian* prob from *gally* to frighten, to confuse with noise + *thump* to beat, to walk or dance with energy. See *EDD*] **chiefly NEast** *somewhat old-fash*

A boisterous, rowdy group (or a member of such a group) that assembles with noisemakers, spec:

a For merrymaking in a parade, esp on New Year's Eve or the Fourth of July.

c1830 in 1939 *NY Hist. Soc. Quarterly* 23.16 **NY,** On New Year's Eve different parties of young men and boys parade the streets, shouting, singing, blowing penny-trumpets and long tin horns, . . etc. A celebrated detachment of these Rioters has long assumed the name of the "Callithumpian Band," and has been distinguished for being more noisy and uproarious than the others. **1848** Bartlett *Americanisms* 61, It is a common practice in New York, as well as other parts of the country, on New-Year's eve, for persons to assemble with tin horns, bells, rattles, and similar euphonious instruments, and parade the streets making all the noise and discord possible. This party is called the *Callithumpians,* or the *Callithumpian Band.* **1856** Hall *College Words* 342 **CT,** The band [=Pandowdy, noise-making band of Bowdoin College] corresponds to the Calliathump of Yale. **1909** *DN* 3.409 **cnME,** *Calathumpian* . . One dressed up to represent a ragamuffin in a procession. **1916** *DN* 4.305, *Callithumpian* . . [*DN*: From *Calliope* + *thump?*] Applied to rowdy bands with horns, tin pans, etc., on New Year's Eve, esp. in Baltimore . . . Also Kan., Va. **1941** *LANE* Map 409 **neMA,** [kæʊ'θʌmpɪn], on the fourth of July: 'You dress up as bad as possible, go out and wake everybody up.' **1942** *AmSp* 17.213 **CA,** Callithumpians, or groups of 'horribles' . . used to come at the end of Fourth of July and other processions, wearing all sorts of garbs and disguises [in childhood days of inquirer].

b For a wedding night escapade, sometimes to protest the marriage. Cf **serenade, shivaree, skimmelton**

1848 Bartlett *Americanisms* 61, Callithumpians . . . On wedding nights the happy couple are sometimes saluted with this discord by those who choose to consider the marriage an improper one, instead of a serenade. **1889** *Century Dict.* 931/3, *Charivari* . . Serenades of this sort . . are still occasionally heard in the United States, where they are also known as *callithumpian concerts.* **1913** *DN* 4.4 **ME,** *Callithumpian band* . . . A noisy crowd playing on tin horns and pans which serenaded a newly married couple. *Ibid,* *Callithumpian serenade,* . . A serenade by a callithumpian band. It was often a token of disapproval. **1916** *DN* 4.305, [Footnote:] In Va., a *callithumpian parade* is a farce serenade used especially on the occasion of the wedding of unpopular men. **1930** Shoemaker *1300 Words* 12 **cPA Mts** (as of c1900), *Calli-thumpian*—a noisy gathering at the home of a newly married couple. **1931–33** *LANE Worksheets* **cCT,** Callathumpian reception—a noisy celebration; **csCT,** Callathump . . . A noisy celebration; **nwCT,** Calla-thump—a noisy celebration after a wedding. **1932–34** Hanley Disks **cCT,** Noisy celebration after a wedding, shivaree. They'd have a cal'thump; **neMA,** Calathump is the same as shivaree. **1941** *LANE* Map 409, The map shows the terms *serenade (serenading), horning, shivaree* and *callithump (cal-, cow-, -thumping, -thumpian).* [18 infs offer *callithump,* with comments such as the following:] **wCT,** Our minister married his third wife; we had a pretty good cowthump out of that; **wCT,** Nowadays we call it serenade; we always used to call it callithump; **sCT,** Serenade for a popular couple; callithump, for an unpopular couple; **sCT** Callithump, older term; serenade, modern; **neMA,** A rowdy musical band at a wedding; **eNH,** The [callithumpian band] plays music at a serenade. **1946** *PADS* 6.8 **swVA,** *Calathump* ['kælə'θʌmp] . . . Salem. Reported, 1940. **1960** Korson *Black Rock* 251 **PA** (as of c1900), All newlyweds, rich and poor alike, received a mock serenade on their wedding night from a group of noisemakers and pranksters commonly called a bull band, but also known under a more fancy name, calithumpians. **1965–70** *DARE* (Qu. AA18, . . *A noisy neighborhood celebration after a wedding, where the married couple is expected to give a treat*) Infs **CT**1, **NJ**2, 9, 35, 41, 46, Callathump; **PA**17, 55, Callathumpian band; **PA**35, Callathumpian party; **PA**202, Callathumping band; (Qu. FF4) Inf **CT**3, At a callathump, the bride and groom treat the guests. The men go down with noisemakers and the couple has to invite all inside. [10 of 11 Infs old]

callithumpian adj
Noisy, boisterous, discordant.

1851 in 1951 *AmSp* 26.182 **NC,** Ten of the boys were summonsed before the Faculty to stand their trial for going on a "Calithumpian spree" the night before — they were all dismissed. **1886** *Harper's Mag.* 73.213/2, The call [on the exchange] lasts ten or fifteen minutes, and occasionally has the accompaniment of callithumpian discord. **1946** Blesh *Shining Trumpets* 155, Then the swift notes poured out, a black, calithumpian music.

‡callithumpian duck n
=old-squaw.

1956 *AmSp* 31.186, The sobriquet *Callithumpian duck* (old squaw, Wis.), needs rather more explanation. The term *Callithumpian band* is applied to extemporized groups with unconventional instruments . . and uncertain musical ability . . . The old squaw duck has a variety of calls unusual among its tribe, thus encouraging . . the adjective *Callithumpian* for it.

call-kid See callboy

call off
1 See **call** v **4.**
2 See **call** v **7.**

cal-log See carry-log

call oneself v phr
To consider oneself (to be doing something).

1944 Wentworth *ADD* 91 **WV,** 'What do you call yourself a-doin'?' = What do you think you're doing? What are you doing?, What would you say you're doing there? . . . 'I call myself making better gravy' = (I think that) my gravy making is improving. **1950** Faulkner *Stories* 27 **MS,** A seventy-year-old man, with both feet and one knee, too, already in the grave, squatting all night on a hill and calling himself listening to a fox race that he couldn't even hear unless they had come right up onto the same log he was setting on and bayed into his ear trumpet. **1977** Smitherman *Talkin* 258 [Black], *Call yo'self,* to assume to be doing something, to intend to do a thing, as in "I call myself having this dinner ready on time," or "Girl, what you call yo'self doing?" *Ibid,* "Chile, you call yo'self done iron this, with all these cat faces in it?" **1983** *NYT Mag.* 25 Sept 14/4, Write about Black English sometime . . . *You can't never guess a man* and *mosying along* and *runnin' her big mouth as usual* and *calls herself makin' a soup.* **1983** *DARE* File **cAR,** I called myself looking there [on the bookshelf].

‡call one's food v phr
To eat noisily.

1967 *DARE* (Qu. H11B, *If he makes a noise with his food, he* _____) Inf **NE2,** Calls his food.

call one's hand v phr [Prob transf from card playing]
To question, to call one to account.

c1960 *Wilson Coll.* **csKY,** *Call one's hand*—[to] question one's word or conduct. **1966–68** *DARE* (Qu. JJ24, *To refuse firmly: "He wanted to get some more money, but this time I* _____.') Inf **AL40,** Called his hand; (Qu. JJ35b, *. . Expressions you might use when you have lost patience and are just about ready to tell somebody what you think of him*) Inf **VA25,** Call his hand; (Qu. JJ40, *When you admit that you did something wrong and are willing to take the consequences, you might say: "It was my fault and I'm willing to* _____.') Inf **WA3,** Call my hand. **1967** *DARE* FW Addit **LA11,** Called his hand—to call down people.

call one's name v phr [Prob Biblical; cf Gen 3:20] Cf call v 11
To be called or named.

1899 (1912) Green *VA Folk-Speech, Call* . . . A negro woman who calls her name Sally. **1905** *DN* 3.73 **nwAR,** *Call one's name* . . . Used in the expression, 'What do you call your name?' i.e., 'What is your name?' **1919** *DN* 5.32 **seKY,** *Call* . . . Used in inquiring after one's name, as, "How did ye say ye called yer name?"

call-out n
1 See quot 1916. [**call** v **5**]

1916 *DN* 4.268 **New Orleans LA,** *Call-out* . . 1. An invitation to dance with a masker. 2. A lady who has received an intimation that she will be called out, and is assigned to a special section of seats. "Those seats there are for the call-outs." **1934** Carmer *Stars Fell on AL* 238, [In Mobile, in

anticipation of the Strikers' Ball held on New Year's Eve:] The hearts of post-débutantes and wives grow lighter when an envelope bearing the cherished "call-out" card, a masker's request for the honor of a dance, appears. *Ibid* 239, At the end of the hall, while the captain and his lady wait, they find their partners for the grand march — the first call-out. The Strikers' Ball has begun. **1951** *AmSp* 26.111 **New Orleans LA** [Mardi Gras terminology], *Call out:* One of several dances reserved for the masked members of the carnival organization and their partners; an invitation to participate in such a dance. *Call out boxes:* A previously designated section of the ballroom in which guests of the club who are to participate in call outs are seated. *Call out favor:* A souvenir gift presented by a member of the carnival organization to his partner following each call out.

2 A children's game: see quot.

1966 *DARE* (Qu. EE33) Inf **WA13,** Call-out—facing columns, one of boys paired with one of girls; a starter [positioned at head of columns, midway between the two] calls "start"; boys and girls run around outside of the lines and try to touch hands before the starter can grab the boy and take over his place in line.

call pigs See call hogs

call quarter See quarter, call (for)

call the turn See turn, call the

call the wind v phr
1942 (1965) Parrish *Slave Songs* 15 **GA coast,** When a field needs to be burned over, a sail is flapping idly, or rice is to be fanned, you may hear a Negro "calling the wind": "Co' win'! Co' win'! Co'!" A prolonged whistle follows . . in the African manner of calling the rain.

call-up-a-storm n
The common **loon** (here: *Gavia immer*).

1951 *AmSp* 26.270, *Call-up-a-storm* is a rather lengthy New England appellation for the common loon, whose excessive crying is supposed to presage bad weather. **1955** *MA Audubon* 39.309.

calluses on one's feet, have v phr Cf born with burnt feet
1965 *DARE* File **Ozarks** (as of c1910), A child born in less than nine months after marriage was said to have calluses on its feet from making a nine month trip in less.

cally See cala n²

callyboose See calaboose

cally-cornered See catercorner adj, adv

callyhooting pres pple, adv |ˈkælɪˌhutn, -hutɪŋ, ˈkælə-| Also cahootin', callahooting, callihootin Cf gallihoot, scallyhoot
Usu in phrr *come* (or *go*) *a-callyhootin':* Moving very rapidly and noisily.

1880 Harris *Uncle Remus Songs* 190 **GA,** Dey tells me dish yer train goes a callyhootin. **1883** (1971) Harris *Nights Remus* 132 **GA,** Bimeby Brer Rabbit come a-cally-hootin' back des a-hollerin': "Run, Brer Fox, run!" **1930** Shoemaker *1300 Words* 14 **cPA Mts** (as of c1900), *Calla hooting*—careening along at a breakneck pace. **1950** *PADS* 14.18 **SC,** *Callihootin* [ˌkælɪˈhutn], *cahootin', gallihootin:* adv. At high speed, same as "lickety-split." **c1960** Bailey *Resp to PADS 20* **KS,** "Comes a-cally-hootin'." I have heard this expression used to mean swaggering, gallivanting, blowing-in, and so on . . . Usually when I've heard the expression used it seemed to mean a noise, a disturbance of a disordered type; my guess . . is that it was derived from the confusion and noise that accompany a calliope.

calm n, adj, v Usu |kam|; also, esp in Sth, Midl, infreq in NEng, |kæm|; in NEast rarely |karm, kam|; sp-pronc |kalm| Pronc-spp cam, ca'm, carm, cyaam Cf balm, palm
Std senses, var forms.

1892 *DN* 1.238 **MO, KS,** *Calm.* Generally [kæm]. **1893** Shands *MS Speech* 6, Among the educated classes *palm, calm, psalm, qualm,* and similar words are correctly pronounced, but the illiterate of both colors pronounce the *a* as [æ]. **1904** Day *Kin o' Ktaadn* 100 **ME,** Set *herself* up as straight as Cuffy an' as carm. **1908** *DN* 3.296 **eAL, wGA,** *Calm,* n. and adj. Pronounced [kæm]. **1922** Gonzales *Black Border* 296 **SC, GA coasts** [Gullah glossary], *Cyaam*—calm, calms; "uh cyaam sea." **1923** *DN* 5.203 **swMO,** *Ca'm,* v. or adj. Calm. **1937** *AmSp* 12.168, When a candidate for Congress in the tenth district of New York said [karm] for *calm* . . he was certainly not trying to be elegant, but rather to train himself to use *r* where he had not originally pronounced it, in words like *harm, farm . . . Carm* I heard again . . from a night-nurse [from Connecticut], who .. had a habit of saying: 'Well, is everybody *carm* and collected?' **1941** *LANE* Map 478 *(Calm),* [Usu [kɑm, kam]; esp in Maine, New Hampshire occas [kæm], often described as old-fashioned; rarely [karm].] **1946** *PADS* 6.8 **eNC** (as of 1900–10), Cam [kæm]; *adj.* Calm. **1959** *VT Hist.* new ser 27.128, *Calm* [karm]. **1961** Kurath–McDavid *Pronc. Engl.* 141, *Calm* with the vowel /æ/ of *bag* has extensive currency in the Midland and the South, except in cultivated speech. It is the predominant folk pronunciation throughout this far-flung area, being nearly universal outside of eastern Pennsylvania and parts of South Carolina . . . in the New England settlement area this pronunciation survives only in the speech of a minority of the folk and has been completely eliminated in metropolitan New York and its extensive hinterland. **1984** *DARE* File, *Calm* is sometimes |kɑlm|.

calm of day n Also *calm daylight*
See quots.
    1939 FWP *Guide NC* 98, Daylight is "calm daylight" or "calm of day". **1972** Cooper *NC Mt. Folkl.* 90, Calm of day—early broad daylight.

calmus See **calamus**

calomel root n [?Erron for **calamus**]
=**sweet flag.**
    1936 *Torreya* 36.146, A cook who came from a negro settlement a few miles from Stevenson [Alabama] .. said the people there cultivated the calamus ("calomel root," as they called it), and used it medicinally.

caloop v Also sp *calloope* [Perh *ca-* var of **ker-** + *loop* to encircle, embrace] Cf **cat** v 2
See quots.
    1942 Berrey–Van den Bark *Amer. Slang* 847.10, *"Pet"; "Neck."* .. boodle, bundle, calloope, canoodle. **1968** *DARE* File **Middletown RI** (as of 1900–10), To go (out) calooping. Go out to have a good time, ride, enjoy oneself in trivial pleasures.

cal'thump, calthumpian, calthumping See **callithumpian**

calvary n [Metath for *cavalry*]
    1905 *DN* 3.58 **eNE**, Metathesis .. is very frequent .. *calvary.* **1906** *DN* 3.129 **nwAR**, *Calvary . . .* Cavalry. **1934** *AmSp* 9.313 **KS** [Black], The colored troopers at Fort Riley all say they are in the *Calvary.* **1946** *AmSp* 21.147 [Mispronounced army terms], The officer recounting army organization joined the generality of men in speaking of the mounted 'calvary'. **1983** *Capital Times* (Madison WI) 27 Jan 9/1, His maternal grandparents .. the mismatched "retired" calvary officer and patrician's daughter who spend their days in non-communication.

calve v, also vbl n *calving*
1 See quots.
    1913 Beach *Iron Trail* 373 **AK**, The huge mass [of ice] began to rumble; it "calved," it split, it detonated, and, having finally loosened itself from its bed, it acquired increased momentum. **1939** FWP *Guide AK* 151, At certain stages of each tide masses of ice break away from the glacier and crash into the water. This process is called calving. **1955** U.S. Arctic Info. Center *Gloss.* 15, *Calve . . .* To break off or discharge pieces of ice from a larger ice mass, as from a tidewater glacier.
‡**2** To fall or cave in, to break. [Etym uncert; perh confused with or infl by *cave (in)* collapse and fall (in); see *OED* calve v.²]
    1968 *DARE* (Qu. KK19) Inf **NH14**, Broke down, busted down, [kæːvd] .. used of a barn or piece of machinery breaking and falling in; (Qu. KK20a) Inf **NH14**, Ready to [kæːv].

calzone n [Ital *calzoni,* Span *calzónes* trousers]
A pastry shaped to resemble trousers:
a A filled turnover made from pizza dough.
    1969 *DARE* (Qu. H65) Inf **CA118**, Calzone [kæl'zouni]. **1977** Katzen *Moosewood Cookbook* 159 **cNY**, Calzone .. an Italian pastry, a cheese-filled turnover with a pizza dough. Crisp on the outside, creamy on the inside. **1983** *Isthmus* (Madison WI) 20 May sec 2 3, [Restaurant ad:] Calzones—Italian Turnovers 4.75. **1984** *NYT Mag.* 8 July 40, *Getting To Know Calzone . .* an Italian specialty that had its beginnings perhaps a century or more ago, a filled bun or turnover .. known as calzone.
b A sweet biscuit.
    1977 *Mexican Cook Book* 89 **CA**, *"Pants" Biscuits* Calzones (kahl-*sohnehs*)—This rolled dough makes a bland sweet biscuit, much like the popular American sugar cooky, which is cut into the shape of a pair of pants.

cama n [Span "bed"]
A bedroll used by cowboys.
    1940 FWP *Guide NV* 76, Cama—cowboy's bedroll. **1968** Adams *Western Words* 52, Cama—A name the cowboy sometimes gives his bedroll; from the Spanish, meaning *bed.*

camas n Also sp *camass, quamash;* for addit varr see quots
1 A plant of the genus *Camassia.* **chiefly NW** Also called **biscuit root 2, swamp sego, wild hyacinth** For other names of var spp see **bear grass 2b, false hyacinth, Indian hyacinth, Indian potato, Indian squill, indigo squill, meadow hyacinth, railroad hyacinth, soaproot**
    1805 (1965) Ordway *Jrls.* 290 **wMT**, These natives have a large quantity of this root bread which they call Commass. the roots grow in these plains. **1806** (1808) Gass *Jrl.* 308 **NW**, We also got bread made of roots, which the natives call co-was and sweet roots which they call Com-mas. **1826** (1918) Rogers *Jrl.* 261, A number of Inds. visited our camp today, bringing fish, clams, strawberrys, and a root that is well known by the traders west of the Rocky Mountains by the name of commeser. **1831** (1940) Ferris *Rocky Mts.* 101, I witnessed the process of cooking "Kamas," a small root about the size of a crab apple, which abounds in many parts of this country. **1843** in 1938 Hulbert *Marcus Whitman* 7.297 **OR**, The Grand Round .. is a large Kamsh plain. [**1863** Gibbs *Chinook Jargon* 7 **NW**, *Kám-ass,* or *Lá-kam-ass . . .* Nootka. *The Scilla esculenta,*—a bulbous root used for food by the Indians. Jewitt gives CHAMASS as the Nootka for *fruit,* also for *sweet,* or *pleasant to the taste.*] **1865** (1973) Stuart *Montana as it Is* 58, It [=camas root] is very abundant in Oregon, and was an important article of food to the first settlers. Hence, they derived their "sobriquet" of "camus eaters," "camus" being the name that the root is known by among the whites. **1868** Whymper *Travel AK* 24, He has subsisted for twelve days on fern and "gamass," or lily roots, and a few berries. **1897** *Jrl. Amer. Folkl.* 10.145, *Camassia esculenta . .* "kmass," Cal. **1932** Rydberg *Flora Prairies* 218, *Camassia . . .* Camash, Blue Camas. **1938** *AmSp* 13.177, *Camas*—['kæːməs]. A reproduction in familiar phonemes of the Chinook word for 'sweet,' applied to the camas bulb. **1941** *Torreya* 41.46, *Quamasia esculenta . . .* Camas plant, kamas root, quamish. **1966–70** *DARE* (Qu. S23, *Pale blue flowers with downy leaves and cups*) Inf **WA6**, Camas; (Qu. S24, *A wild flower that grows in swamps and marshes and looks like a small blue iris*) Inf **WY1**, Camas lily; (Qu. S26d, *Wildflowers that grow in meadows*) Inf **WA19**, Camas; (Qu. S26e, *Other wildflowers*) Inf **WA6**, Camas. **1974** (1977) Coon *Useful Plants* 173, *Camassia (various species)*—Quamash, camass . . . The flowers range from blues through white, thus distinguishing this plant from the "death camass" which has smallish yellow flowers. **1976** Bailey–Bailey *Hortus Third* 208, *Camassia . . .* Camass, camas . . . *[Camassia]* Quamash . . . Quamash, common c[amass], camosh.
2 =**death camas.**
    1936 Winter *Plants NE* 13, *T. nuttallii . . .* Nuttall's Camas. **1937** Stemen *OK Flora* 47, *Nuttall's Camass . . .* Bulb large, coated. **1972** Brown *Wildflowers LA* 22, Camass. *Zigadenus glaberrimus . . .* It is related to the *poison camass* and is suspected of being toxic . . . Camass. *Zigadenus leimanthoides . . .* Found in boggy sites in wet pine flatwoods [sic].
3 in phr *knock the camas out:* See quot.
    1946 *CA Folkl. Qrly.* 5.233 **wOR**, He got the camass knocked out of him. To "knock the camass" out of some person or thing is to destroy a vital part or a productive capacity . . . (The saying is not common nowadays, but I recently heard it applied by an old settler to a wrecked automobile.)

camas rat n Also *camass rat, camas pouched rat, camas pocket gopher*
A **pocket gopher** (here: *Thomomys bulbivorus*) native to Oregon.
    1849 *Sk. Nat. Hist. Mammalia* IV.96 *(DA),* The Camas pouched rat is common in N. America, on the banks of the Columbia River. **1868** Wood *Homes without Hands* 35 *(DA),* The Camas Rat *(Pseudostoma borealis) . . .* The name is derived from its food, which consists chiefly of quamash root. **1928** Anthony *N. Amer. Mammals* 288, Camas Pocket Gopher or Camas Rat. **1936** Bailey *Mammals & Life Zones Ore.* 225 *(DA),* If the big camas pocket gopher *(Thomomys bulbivorus)* were twice its present size its longer tail would be the only convenient means of distinguishing the two. *Ibid* 250, The original name of camas rat was undoubtedly based on their fondness for the bulbs of the camas. **1957** Blair et al *Vertebrates U.S.* 683, Camas pocket gopher. Largest of genus . . . Color dark brown or sooty . . . Willamette Valley, Oregon, in rich valley soils.

camass See **camas**

camass rat See **camas rat**

camboose, cambouse See **caboose** n[1] **1**

cambric coffee n [By analogy with **cambric tea**]
Very weak coffee.
  1968 *DARE* (Qu. H74b, . . *Coffee . . very weak*) Inf **PA**128, Cambric
—named after the material.

cambric tea n Also folk-etym *Cambridge tea* old-fash Cf **kettle tea**
A drink made of hot water, milk, sugar, and sometimes a small
amount of tea, usu served to children.
  1888 *Union Signal* (Chicago) 21 Jan. 3 *(DAE)*, [She] offered me tea,
cambric tea to be sure, but in a beautiful cup. **1908** *DN* 3.296 **eAL,
wGA,** *Cambric tea* . . Same as kettle-tea . . but not so commonly
used. **1960** Bailey *Resp. to PADS 20* **KS** *(Names for tea according to the
way it is made: Very weak),* Cambric (water only, sweetened and with
milk). **1966–68** *DARE* (Qu. H72b, . . *Very weak tea; total* Infs questioned, 75) Inf **AR**38, Cambric tea [Inf old]; **ME**20, Cambridge tea—
like rainwater. **1967** *DARE* Tape **OR**1, There was a tea called cambric
tea that was hot water, milk and sugar . . . no tea, it was for children's tea
parties. **1979** *DARE* File **cnMA** (as of c1915), I was disillusioned when I
discovered that the delicious Cambric tea (we could drink as much as we
liked) served by the minister's wife to her children and any others who
were at the rectory was nothing but cream, sugar, and hot water.

came See **come A4**

camel n See **camel walk**

camelback n
1 also attrib, also *camel:* A locomotive with the cab over the
middle of the boiler.
  1872 in **1942** Footner *MD Main* 143, Of the quaint "camel-back"
locomotives hauling long strings of "red hoppers". **1945** Hubbard
Railroad Ave. 336, *Camel* or *Camelback*—Engine with control cab built
over middle of boiler, suggesting camel's hump. Also called *Mother
Hubbard* type.
2 also attrib: A house which is higher in back than in front.
chiefly New Orleans LA Cf camelopard house
  1941 FWP *Guide LA* 158, The "camel-back" house, one-story in front
and two stories in the rear, . . [is] of frequent occurrence in New Orleans. **1968** *DARE* (Qu. D23) Inf **LA**23, Camelback double. **1968**
DARE File **New Orleans LA,** Camelback house—[a] house that is one
story high in front. At the back, above the last room, it is two stories
high. **1971** *Today Show Letters* **New Orleans LA,** Camelback—This
type house usually has five rooms on one level and two rooms above the
two rooms in the rear of the house. **1981** Pederson *LAGS Urban
Material* **New Orleans LA,** Camel back [means that] only the back part
[of a house] is two-story.
3 See quot. [*OED* 1631] Also called **razorback, saddleback**
  1969 *DARE* (Qu. K44, *A bony or poor-looking horse*) Inf **CT**32,
Camelback.
4 See quot.
  1969 *DARE* (Qu. N30, . . *A sudden short dip in the road*) Inf **NC**76,
Camelback.

camel cricket n Also *cave cricket*
A wingless long-horned grasshopper of the subfamily Rhaphidophorinae.
  1859 (1968) Bartlett *Americanisms* 356, *Rear Horse.*—The vulgar
name, at the South, for the orthopterous insect called the Mantis, Camel
Cricket, or Johnny Cock-horse. **1964** Borror–DeLong *Intro. Insects*
135, The cave or camel crickets, subfamily *Rhaphidophorinae,* are
brownish and rather hump-backed in appearance . . and are found in
caves or hollow trees.

camel jockey n Also *camel jock, camel rider* derog
  1967–68 *DARE* (Qu. HH28, *Names and nicknames around here for
people of foreign background*) Inf **MO**26, Camel jocks (India Indians)—
term picked up at the University of Missouri in Columbia; **PA**76,
Syrians: Camel jockeys, sand scratchers; **TX**37, Syrians—camel riders.

camelopard house n [*camelopard* giraffe] Cf **camelback 2**
  1981 *DARE* File **ceRI** (as of c1920), Camelopard [giraffe] house—A
house which had two stories in front and one behind, the back of the roof
sloping more sharply than the front.

camel rider See **camel jockey**

camel walk n Also *camel* chiefly Sth *freq among Black
speakers*
A dance step.
  1921 *Frontier* May 16 *(DA),* The morbid minded may read them as
openly as they danced the shimmy and the camel-walk a year ago. **1946**
Perelman *Keep It Crisp* 31, The lady, her wrists trailing the piano keys, is
bent backward in an arc recalling the Camel Walk of 1922. **1958** *Dance*
March 91 (Stearns *Jazz Dance*) **seGA,** We do git together an hab dance
an pahties an big suppuhs . . . we does duh *Snake Hip* and duh *Buzzard
Lope* . . . an addalas [at the last] dance we did duh *Fish Tail* and duh
Fish Bone and duh Camel Walk. **1965–70** *DARE* (Qu. FF5a) Infs
DC11, **FL**29, **GA**13, **LA**23, **MS**73, **OH**103, **SC**69, **VA**71, Camel walk;
MI72, Boogie-woogie camel walk; **LA**37, Camel; (Qu. FF5b) Infs
PA164, **SC**65, **VA**41, Camel walk. [7 of 13 Infs Black]

camel worm n
Prob an ant lion.
  1958 *PADS* 29.8 **TN,** Camel worm . . ? The larva of an ant lion. It is
described as "what children used to pull out of a hole in the ground with
broom straws in the spring."

camesa See **camisa**

camfire See **camphor**

camiller n Pronc-sp for *camellia* See Pronc Intro 3.I.12.b
  1967 *DARE* (QR, near Qq. S26b, c) Inf **AL**15, Camillers, roses, pansies,
marigolds.

camisa n Also sp *camesa* [Span] **chiefly SW**
A shirt or blouse.
  1831 (1973) Pattie *Personal Narr.* 286 **NM,** The Indian women were all
clad in blue petticoats, cotton *camisas,* with bosom and sleeves ruffled.
1843 (1845) Green *Jrl. Texian Exped.* 320, Any sergeant's wife . . would
trust him for the washing of his camisa. **1930** Shoemaker *1300 Words*
14 **cPA Mts** (as of c1900), Camesa—A shirt worn by women. **1939**
Vestal *Old Santa Fe* 264, The women wore a skimpy *camisa,* loose,
abbreviated sleeves, short red skirts, gay shawls. **1968** Adams *Western
Words* 52, Camisa—A shirt.

camley See **kamleika**

camosh See **camas**

camote n esp **TX**
Any of several plants with edible roots or stems: see quots.
  1772 Ulloa *Noticias* 99, Allí prevalecen el *Maiz,* las *Batatas,* que llaman
Camotes, . . y muchas especies de simientes. [Maize, Sweet Potatoes,
which are called Camotes, and many kinds of seeds prevail there.] **1892**
DN 1.188 **TX,** Camóte (from Mexican *camotli,* S.): sweet potato, yam,
(Batata edulis). Occasionally heard on the Rio Grande. *Camote del
monte* (mountain potato): a shrubby plant with yellow flowers and small
edible tuberous roots (*Peteria scoparia,* Gray). (C.) *Camote del raton*
(mouse potato): *Hoffmanseggia stricta.* (C.) **1892** in **1941** *Torreya*
41.48, *Hoffmannseggia stricta* . . . Camote del raton, Texas. **1925**
Bryan *Papago Country* 27, Their principal vegetable food was the
camote (*Amnobroma* [sic] *sonorae*), an edible root found in the sand
dunes. **1931** U.S. Dept. Ag. *Misc. Pub.* 101.154, *White bur-sage* . . . is
one of the two chief host plants of the curious, parasitic . . sandroot
(*Ammobroma sonorae*), known also as . . camote, whose succulent
stems with a flavor reminiscent of sweetpotatoes, are a valuable source of
food supply to the Cocopa Indians and to desert travelers. **1967** *DARE*
(Qu. I9, *Other names . . for potatoes*) Inf **TX**6, Camote. **1970** Correll
Plants TX 797, *Caesalpinia atropunctata* . . . Camote del raton. *Ibid*
835, *Peteria scoparia* . . . Camote del monte . . . The Spanish name
attributed to this plant implies that the roots are tuberous, rather like
sweet potatoes, and edible.

camp n
1 A summer dwelling, whether modest or elaborate. **chiefly
NEast, Gulf States**
  1880 Sweetser *Picturesque Maine* 62 *(DA),* Here and there . . are commodious buildings for the entertainment of sportsmen, still preserving,
in their generic name of 'camps,' the memory of earlier, less elaborate
shelters. **1906** *N.Y. Ev. Post* 16 June (Resort Sec.) 4 *(DA),* The word
'camp' is ambiguous as applied to abodes in the Adirondack forest, for it
may be used to designate a snug little cabin . . or it may apply to an
extensive establishment. **1945** Saxon *Gumbo Ya-Ya* 422 **LA,** Along a
wharf edging the lake were rough camps of one or two rooms which

could be rented by the day. **1965–70** *DARE* (Qu. D21, *A small, poorly-built house, or one in rundown condition*) Infs **LA**37, **ME**23, **NH**14, **NY**23, **VT**16, Camp. **1967–70** *DARE* Tape **MA**98, Camp [is] a house where you go for vacations, and it would not have any central heating or anything; it would be very casual living. 'Course it used to never have any running water, any toilet, but now we've changed all that; **MI**28, Camp [a cabin in the woods]; **NY**4, What we want now is more people to come here for summer and build real nice summer camps; **NY**7, Camp [summer home]; **NY**199, The camp . . was just a small building . . it was a two-story with a living room downstairs, a kitchen and . . the men's bedroom then upstairs we had the places for the women and children to sleep; **TX**78, Camp [a hunting cabin in the mountains]. **1968–69** *DARE* FW Addit **GA**44, Camp—a lakeside cottage. There are some beautiful camps on Lake Seminole, some of those camps cost $40,000; **neCT**, Camp—a little plot of land with a house on it. **1975** Gould *ME Lingo* 40, Camp—The general word in Maine for a wilderness dwelling, no matter how elegant. It can be a one-room log cabin or the sumptuous retreat of land-owning executives . . . *Camp* can also mean a sizeable complex of buildings, such as a lumber or sporting *camp*.

2 =sugar camp.

1823 Cooper *Pioneer* xx *(DA)*, The sugar-boiler . . was busy in his 'camp.' **1848** (1870) Drake *Pioneer Life* 85 **KY**, There were but few sugar trees on father's land, and he rented a "camp," as the grove was called. **1898** Jones *Squirrel Hunters* 18 **OH**, There are a few of the older crop of sugar trees still remaining; but the great *"camps"* that furnished sweets in abundance have . . fallen victims to the woodman's ax. **1937** *Hall Coll.* **wNC**, Neil Sutton had a camp . . on Little Cataloochee where he made maple sugar. Also made "piggins" (wooden buckets) and other containers. **1965–70** *DARE* (Qu. T4, *The place where . . trees grow together and sap is gathered*) Infs **MD**22, **OH**33, **PA**176, Maple camp; **IA**29, **PA**70, Camp; **IN**73, Maple syrup camp.

3 =fish camp 1.

1965–70 *DARE* (Qu. O7, . . *A place where boats can be rented*) Infs **OK**25, **SC**19, Camp; **TX**76, Boat camp; **AL**32, Boat rental camp. **1979** Hallowell *People Bayou* 190 **sLA**, On summer and fall weekends, fishermen and hunters crowd into the camps and roar around the lake and the bayous in their outboards . . . All the camps follow the same design—a cabin, usually painted green, with a slightly pitched roof and a cypress wood cistern off to one side; a dock jutting into the bayou; and a boardwalk joining the dock to the cabin.

4 See campboat.

campanyero See compañero

campbellite n [Transf from *Campbellite* a member of a Christian denomination which practices baptism by immersion; see quots 1872, 1889]

The white **crappie** (here: *Pomoxis annularis*).

1872 *Harper's Mag.* 45.315/2 **MO**, "What do you call those fish?" "Campbellites," promptly responded the boy. "Why do you call them Campbellites?" "Because they spoil so quick after I get them out of the water." **1889** *Century Dict.*, Campbellite . . . A local name of a sunfish, *Pomoxis annularis*, abundant in the Mississippi. Also called *new-light*. "The names new-light and *Campbellite* are due to the fact that it became abundant and the subject of observation when the religious denomination bearing those names originated." **1906** *DN* 3.129 **nwAR**, Campbellite. **1933** LA Dept. of Conserv. *Fishes* 332, The Sac-a-lait . . . This species' popularity is very well attested by the variety of names . . . They are as follows: Crappie, Bachelor, Newlight, Campbellite [etc]. **1975** Evanoff *Catch More Fish* 90, The white crappie has been called some of the same names as the black crappie and also . . campbellite.

campbell-roof n, also attrib [Folk-etym for **gambrel roof**]

1968 *DARE* (Qu. M1) Infs **NY**99, 117, Campbell-roof(ed) barn.

camp bird n Also *camp jay* Cf **camp robber**

=Canada jay.

1917 *Wilson Bulletin* 29.2.82, *Perisoreus [canadensis].*—I heard camp-bird . . in western Washington. **1928** Bailey *Birds NM* 470, Rocky Mountain Canada Jay: *Perisoreus canadensis capitalis* . . the big, fluffy, gray . . Camp Bird, belongs among the hemlocks and spruces of the Hudsonian Zone. **1946** Hausman *Eastern Birds* 419, Canada Jay—*Perisoreus canadensis canadensis* . . . Camp Jay.

campboat n Also *camp* Cf **camp 3**

A houseboat.

1964 Will *Hist. Okeechobee* 120 **sFL**, Sometimes a [catfish] camp was a houseboat, with a covered porch on which the cats were skinned. These

"floating rigs" became more common later on. **1978** *Pioneer Amer.* June 86 **Missip R**, Fishermen usually occupied houseboats only when fishing away from home (hence the name *campboat,* a term considered synonymous with *houseboat*).

camp coffee n Cf **cowboy coffee**

1975 Gould *ME Lingo* 41, Camp *coffee*—Boiled coffee. The kind boiled in a pot or a No. 10 can over an open fire in the woods; but it is still camp coffee if made the same way on a range.

camp dog n

In construction and logging camps: an employee who looks after beds and belongings.

1927 *DN* 5.441, Camp-dog . . . The hobo at construction camps who takes care of the bunks and belongings of hoboes at work. **1965** *AmSp* 40.259, Camp dog (in construction camps). **1968** Adams *Western Words* 52, Camp dog—In logging, a helper who looks after the camp sleeping quarters and bunks; a flunky.

camp down v phr

To sit or lie down.

1848 (1850) Colton *3 Yrs.* 310, I have seen this *savan* camp down and snore soundly through the night. **1870** Alcott *Little Women* 2.100 **MA**, I'll be hanged if I don't make them . . camp down before her table afterward. **1931–33** *LANE Worksheets* **VT**, I guess I'll camp down for a few minutes.

campfire See **camphor**

camp-fish n

1908 *DN* 3.296 **eAL, wGA**, Camp-fish . . . A camping excursion for purposes of fishing.

camphor n Also, *esp in S Midl*, pronc-spp *camphaw, camphir(e), cam(p)fire, kamfire* (Cf forms in *OED*)

A Forms.

1729 in 1923 *MD Hist. Mag.* 18.333, Camphir. **1834** Davis *Letters Downing* 261, When it gits hold, kamfire and lodnum stand no chance with it! **1908** *DN* 3.296 **eAL, wGA**, Camphire . . . Camphor. **1917** *DN* 4.412 **wNC**, That ain't got no bad taste; it has a leetle farewell to it as though it had campfire in it. **1929** Ellis *Ordinary Woman* 205 **CO** (as of early 1900s), I just melt on the floor, the quilt covering me. One of the men says, 'Look, boys, and see if there is any whiskey or camfire,' and tries to raise me. **1950** (1965) Richter *The Town* 151 **OH** (as of late 19th c), And it's not camphire. It's c-a-m-p-h-o-r, camphaw! **1959** *VT Hist.* new ser 27.128, Camphor ['kæm,fair] . . . Rare. **c1960** *Wilson Coll.* **csKY**, Camphor was sometimes ['kæm,fair] or [kæim-].

B Sense.

See **camphor weed 2.**

camphor daisy n See **camphor weed 2**

camphor plant n See **camphor weed 2, 3**

camphor weed n [From the odor]

1 A western **blue curls 1,** esp *Trichostema lanceolatum* of California.

1898 *Jrl. Amer. Folkl.* 11.277, *Trichostema lanceolatum* . . camphor weed, Cal. **1915** (1926) Armstrong *Western Wild Flowers* 454, *T. lanceolatum* is called Camphor Weed, because of its strong odor, like camphor but exceedingly unpleasant. **1962** Sweet *Plants of West* 29, Blue Curls, Vinegar-Weed or Camphor Weed, *Trichostema* sp., Mint Fam.

2 also *camphor, camphor daisy, camphor plant:* a **golden aster** (here: *Heterotheca subaxillaris*). *esp Gulf States*

1933 Small *Manual SE Flora* 1342, H[eterotheca] subaxillaris . . . Camphor-plant. **1936** Whitehouse *TX Flowers* 158, *Camphor Daisy* . . so called because of the camphor-like odor of the rough foliage, is a common summer pest to the farmer. **1966** *DARE* (Qu. S21, . . *Weeds . . that are a trouble in gardens and fields*) Inf **FL**27, Camphor. **1972** Brown *Wildflowers LA* 208, Camphor-weed . . . A polymorphic, much-branched perennial herb up to 4 feet tall. **1982** *Naples Now* May 36 **sFL**, Along the higher stretches of beaches, one might see *camphorweed*—a golden yellow, daisy-like flower about one inch across—in open clusters above rough-hairy plants one to four feet tall.

3 also *camphor plant:* A **marsh fleabane** (here: *Pluchea camphorata*). *S Atl and Gulf States*

1900 Lyons *Plant Names* 295, *P. camphorata* . . . Salt-marsh Fleabane, . . Camphor plant. **1964** Batson *Wild Flowers SC* 118, *Camphor-Weed* . . . Leaves alternate, finely toothed, up to 4 in. long and strong scented. **1967** *DARE* Wildfl. QR Pl.249b Inf **TX44**, Camphor weed. **1975** Duncan–Foote *Wildflowers SE* 206, *Camphorweed; Stinkweed* . . . Foul-smelling annual or perennial to 1.6 m tall.

camphor worm n Cf **tumblebug**
Prob a beetle larva.
    1970 *DARE* (Qu. P6, . . *Kinds of worms also used as bait*) Inf **FL48**, Camphor worm—little green worm, found on oaks, stinks like a June bug—1 inch long—tumble-turd [is] another name for camphor worms.

camp hunter n
One who provides fresh meat for the workers in a lumber camp.
    1975 Gould *ME Lingo* 41, *Camp hunter—A meatman . . . Meatmen* in lumber camps considered *camp hunter* the preferred term.

camp inspector n *joc* Cf **inspector**
An itinerant logger.
    1950 *Western Folkl.* 9.380 **neCA**, *Camp inspector*. A man who prides himself in working for several outfits each season. **1956** *Ibid* 15.202 **West**, Loggers will tell you that a *camp inspector* is just the opposite of a home guard. A home guard is a steady employee. **1958** McCulloch *Woods Words* 28 **Pacific NW**, *Camp inspector*—A tramp logger who moved from job to job so rapidly that he was never in one place long enough to do more than look at it. On a bet, an Oregon logger once worked in 30 different camps in 31 days, and lost, because the other man worked in 31. **1968** Adams *Western Words*. **1975** Gould *ME Lingo* 41, *Camp inspector—A chopper* who comes into *camp* to hire out, but for some reason doesn't stay too long, as if he were making an inspection visit.

camp jack See **camp tender 1**

camp jay See **camp bird**

camp jerker See **camp tender 1**

camp meat n **chiefly Inland Nth, West** See Map
Deer shot illegally.
    1950 *WELS* 2 Infs, **WI**, Camp meat. **1965–70** *DARE* (Qu. P35a, *Names or nicknames for any deer shot illegally*) 77 Infs, **chiefly Inland Nth, West**, Camp meat.

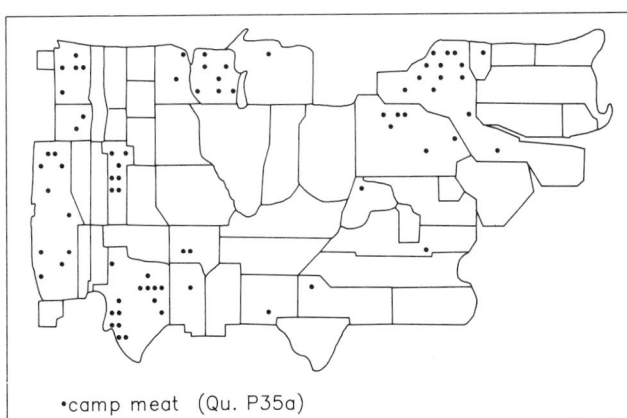

•camp meat (Qu. P35a)

camp meeting n, also attrib Also *grove meeting, wood meeting* **chiefly Sth, Midl** *old-fash*
An open-air encampment lasting several days usu for religious revival sessions.
    1804 Dow *Life & Travels* 285 **GA**, A camp meeting was held on shoulder-bone creek. **1805** (1916) Putnam *Diary* 59, Some days past there was a camp meeting of the Methodists in Lynn. **1810** Lee *Short Hist. Methodists* 279, About this time [1801] *Camp Meetings* were first introduced. But I never could learn whether they began in the upper parts of South-Carolina, in Tennessee, or in Kentucky. **1859** (1968) Bartlett *Americanisms* 66, *Camp-meeting*. A meeting held in the wood or field for religious purposes, where the assemblage encamp and remain several days. These meetings are generally held by the Methodists. The Mormons call it a *Wood-meeting*. **1864** (1922) Jackson *Col.'s Diary* 161, Camp . . is on the Smyrna Camp Ground, an old camp meeting place. **1881** Thayer *From Log-Cabin* 319 **OH**, During the month of June the entire school went in carriages to their annual grove-meeting, at

Randolph. **1942** (1960) Robertson *Red Hills* 160 **SC**, Cotton is an easy crop to grow. We can plant it in April, plow it and hoe it, work hard in the fields until August, and then lay the crop by and go off to camp meetings and all-day singings and fish fries. **1950** (1965) Richter *The Town* 224 **OH** (as of late 19th c), When summer and camp meeting came around, she had to go along and stand in the shadows with him and listen to the praying and preaching. **1966–68** *DARE* Tape **AL11**, Camp meeting . . they'd move in the woods and have meetin' a week; **IL23**, They would have camp meeting out here north of town where some preacher would come, and everybody would rally round, and pray, and sing and all. Everybody would go . . very exciting; **IN7**, [He] was a preacher without a church house to preach in. He preached in barns and in residences, and in those days they had great camp meetings, and so on; **MD44**, Smith Island camp meeting; **SC46**, It'd go on a week or longer . . . You'd have services in the mornin', services afternoon, and services at night. That was just a regular camp meeting, and they'd have preachers from far and near. **1971** Southern *Music Black Amer.* 93, The historic first camp meeting was held in Logan County, Kentucky, in July, 1800, and drew thousands of participants . . . From Kentucky the idea of camp meetings traveled in all directions—northeast into West Virginia, Maryland, Delaware, and up to the northern states; east into Virginia and on into the Carolinas; south into Tennessee and down into the Deep South. The camp meeting was an interracial institution. *Ibid* 94, To both participants and observers, the singing was one of the most impressive aspects of camp meetings. **1976** Boles *Religion Antebellum KY* 24, The services began on Friday of the last weekend of July 1800 . . . This was to be the first "camp meeting," later a southern institution. **1982** *Foxfire* 7 14, The camp meeting, anchored firmly in the American past, continues as a reality in West Virginia, Georgia, the Carolinas, and throughout the Bible Belt of the American heartland. *Ibid* 265, Born in frontier Kentucky around 1800, the camp meeting became a vehicle of civilization, conversion, and social interaction in what was often the coarse, lonely and, the preachers said, godless life of the American wilderness . . . The camp meeting was more than a religious gathering. It was a social event for which folks traveled great distances. Most meetings lasted five to seven days and travelers had to bring supplies for a lengthy stay . . . As the camp meeting became institutionalized, it became an important part of the religious life of the South and Southeast.

camp meeting baby n Cf *DS* Z11b
    1931 Randolph *Ozarks* 51, Some revivals are so notoriously immoral that "camp-meetin' baby" has come to mean an illegitimate child.

camp mover See **camp tender 1**

campoda See **campoody**

camp on one's trail v phr
To follow or remind (someone) persistently.
    1882 Baillie–Grohman *Camps* v *Rocky Mts*, I shall have to ask him to camp, to use another Western expression, on the trails of all sorts of beasts and uncouth characters. **c1960** Wilson *Coll.* **csKY**, *Camp on one's trail* . . . To remind, persistently, someone of something he is to do. **1961** Adams *Old-Time Cowhand* 200, When he [the cowhand] was followin' someone he was said to be "campin' on his trail."

campoody n Also sp *campoda, campoodie* **esp CA** *arch*
A hut or cabin; a village of such dwellings.
    1856 *Butte Record* (Oroville CA) 6 Sep 2/2 *(DA)*, We took a little walk . . . and brought up with a round turn and an invitation at John Davis' Campoda. **1869** Twain *Innocents* 541, Endor . . . is worse than any Indian *campoodie*. **1887** *Rep. Indian Affairs* II *(DA)*, Many live in comfortable board or log houses, and others in 'campoodies' (huts) made of puncheons, pieces of boards &c. **1903** (1950) Austin *Land of Little Rain* 23 **neCA**, Walking in the evening glow, . . I sniffed the unmistakable odor of burning sage. It is a smell that carries far and indicates usually the nearness of a campoodie. *Ibid* 56, A campoodie at noontime, when there is no smoke rising and no stir of life, resembles nothing so much as a collection of prodigious wasps' nests. The huts are squat and brown and chimneyless, facing east, and the inhabitants have the faculty of quail for making themselves scarce in the underbrush at the approach of strangers. **1906** Canfield *Diary Forty-Niner* 9 **CA**, There is an Indian campoody up on the ridge above Brush Creek, where about two hundred Digger Indians are camped.

campo santo n Also sp *campo sancto* [Span] **SW**
A cemetery.
    1856 in 1948 *Western Folkl.* 7.6 **sCA**, It would be better . . that steps be taken for the cession of the Campo Santo to the church proper. **1877**

Field & Forest 3.10 **NM,** The Pueblos have their regular "campos sanctos," or else bury in the floors of their churches. **1943** Hewitt *Mission Monuments* 217 **NM,** A stone terrace was reconstructed, as were the walls of the *campo santo.* **1967–70** *DARE* (Qq. BB61a,b) Infs CA206, TX4, 20, Campo santo. **1968** Adams *Western Words* 52, *Campo santo.* **1975** *Sunset* July 67 **NM,** Camposanto, cemetery with elaborately decorated grave markers, is an unaltered heritage of Spanish occupation.

camp robber n Also *camp robin,* ~ *thief, Canadian camp robber* **chiefly NW, CO** See Map
Any of var birds, esp the **Canada jay,** that frequent camp sites and steal food.

1893 *Outing* 22.424/1 **CO,** Our scavengers, the "camp robbers," were on hand too, waiting their turn. They are pretty little gray-and-black-plumaged birds, the size of a pigeon, but with a dismal squawk which they keep up incessantly. They will carry off anything from a biscuit to an iron spoon, and are useful if they confine their depredations to refuse and garbage. **1903** (1950) Austin *Land of Little Rain* 21 **neCA,** Very clean and handsome . . is Clark's crow . . . It is permissible to call him by his common name, "Camp Robber": he has earned it. Not content with refuse, he pecks open meal sacks, filches whole potatoes, is a gormand for bacon. **1940** FWP *Guide NM* 17 **NM,** On the high timbered mesas and in mountain canyons, the Rocky Mountain magpie *(Pica pica hudsonia)* . . . does not hesitate to filch bright objects and for that reason is called the camp robber, a title bestowed elsewhere on the Canada jay. **1941** FWP *Guide CO* 19, *Camp-robber . . .* Rocky Mountain jay. **1949** Emrich *Wild West Custom* 208, Prospectors . . befriended the friendly and curious jay—the "camp robber" or "camp robin"—and the porcupine. **1955** *MA Audubon* 39.84, *Canada Jay . . .* Camp Thief (Maine. From its pilfering food about woodland camps.). **1965–70** *DARE* (Qu. Q16) 27 Infs, **chiefly NW, CO,** Camp robber; WA20, Canadian camp robber. **1976** Hobbs *Tisha* 80 **AK,** The woods were silent except for here and there a few camp robbers hopping around in the trees, having some last minute arguments.

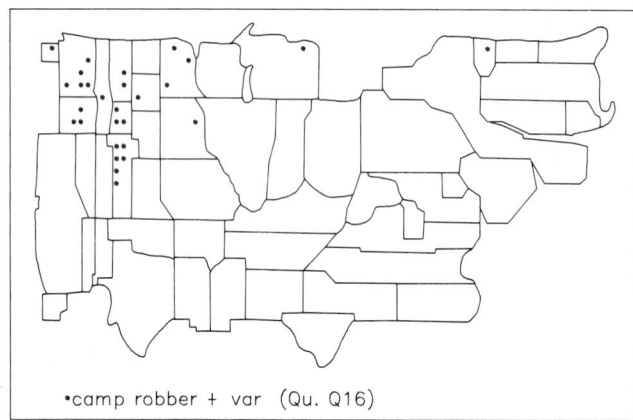

•camp robber + var (Qu. Q16)

camp rustler See **camp tender 1**

camp swamper n Cf **camp tender 1**
1966 Giles *Great Adventure* 2 **NM** (as of 1830s), Half a dozen of them were camp swampers, meat hunters, horse wranglers, what have you. Their job was to take the drudgery out of the season for the beaver men—to pack and unpack morning and night; to stretch and cure pelts; to cook and keep camp; to do any kind of odd job needing to be done.

camp tender n **chiefly Plains States, West**
1 also *camp jack,* ~ *jerker,* ~ *mover,* ~ *rustler:* In sheep herding: see quot 1931.
1913 (1979) Barnes *Western Grazing* 157, With each outfit is a camp rustler, or tender, who goes ahead of the sheep, picks out a camping place, keeps the camp stocked with food and supplies, leaving the herder free to look after his sheep. *Ibid* 380, Among stockmen . . 'Camp Tender, Camp Rustler' [is] a man who accompanies the sheep herd, looks after the packs, locates camp and relieves the herder from such matters. **1931** *AmSp* 6.355 **Plains States,** If an outfit "runs" several bands of sheep, there will be a herder for each band, and a camp tender for every three or four bands. The herder is charged with the care of the flock, while the camp tender brings him supplies and moves his camp (usually a "sheep wagon") about on the range as grazing conditions dictate. The camp tender is frequently known as the "camp mover,"

"camp jerker," or "wagon boss." **1940** FWP *Guide NV* 78, *Camp jack . .* man who cooks and cares for the camp, assisting the herder when necessary. **1952** FWP *Guide SD* 85, *Camp tender . .* the man who keeps the herder in supplies and moves the wagon. **1959** Robertson *Ram* 205 **ID** (as of c1875), The life of the camp movers was entirely different. They could spend considerable time in town where they went for supplies.

2 See quot.
1952 FWP *Guide SD* 85, *Camp tender . .* an old ewe who picks up scraps around the wagon.

camp thief See **camp robber**

campyard n
See quot 1945.
1945 Thorp *Pardner* 36 **SW,** I went to a campyard and put up my horses. Campyards for horsemen were common in the Western towns then, as tourist camps for motorists are now . . . Campyards were very crude—a yard, generally with box stalls on two sides, and shed and a high fence around. In the shed you could make your bedroll down. Generally there was a stove in it, where you could cook if you wanted to. **1951** Porter *Ragged Roads* 135 **OK,** We soon approached a camp yard with several cabins.

camus See **camas**

can v[1]
Std senses, var forms.
1 pres:
a usu |kæn|; also |kɛn, kɪn|. Pronc-spp *ken, kin*
1903 *DN* 2.291 **Cape Cod MA,** Short vowels frequently differed in quality from those of normal English: . . *i* for *a, kin* = *can* (verb). **1905** *DN* 3.399 **nwAR,** I ken do it. **1907** *DN* 3.192 **seNH,** I ken tell. **1908** *DN* 3.296 **eAL, wGA,** *Can . .* commonly pronounced *kin.* **1933** Rawlings *South Moon* 14 **FL,** A man kin step over a split-rail fence. **1935** Sandoz *Jules* 13 **NE,** Lots of things kin happen. **1959** *VT Hist.* new ser 27.128, *Can* [kɪn] . . . Common. Rural areas.

b neg: usu |kænt|; also esp in **Sth, S Midl,** |kɛɪnt|. Pronc-spp *caint, cain't, cayn't, kain't, keint*
1887 *Scribner's Mag.* 2.475 **AR,** I cayn't make her hear me. **1905** Culbertson *Banjo Talks* 11 **SE,** You kain't kotch up. **1909** *DN* 3.393 **nwAR,** *Cain't . . .* Can't. **1915** *DN* 4.225 **wTX,** *Can't.* Always, even by educated people, pronounced *keint.* **1923** *DN* 5.203 **swMO,** Jane caint hol' a can'le t' Mary fer looks. **1968** *DARE* FW Addit **LA, TN, WV,** [kɛɪnt]—common.

2 past:
a usu |kʊd|; occas |kʌd|. Pronc-spp *cood, cud*
1815 Humphreys *Yankey in England* 43, I cood form a more righter judgment of you. **1887** *Scribner's Mag.* 2.482 **AR,** I cudn't leave 'er thataway, cud I? **1889** in 1944 *ADD* **SC,** [kʌd].

b neg: usu |'kʊdn̩t|; also |'kʊdn̩, kʊnt|. Pronc-spp *couldn, cudn't*
1887 *Scribner's Mag.* 2.481 **AR,** I cudn't make out. **1902** *DN* 2.231 **sIL,** *Couldn* [kʊdn] . . . 'He couldn lift it.' **1903** *DN* 2.310 **seMO,** *Couldn.* **1907** *DN* 3.221 **nwAR, sIL,** *Couldn* [kʊdn]. *Ibid* 230 **nwAR, seMO,** *Couldn.* **1942** Hall *Smoky Mt. Speech* 88, There is frequent omission of [d] before [n] in *couldn't* and *didn't:* [kʊnt], [dɪnt].

3 in double auxiliary constructions: See **may can, might could.**

can n
1 A glass jar for preserving food. *old-fash*
1868 MI State Bd. Ag. *Annual Rept.* 7.348, S.B. Rowley, Philadelphia, Pa., [exhibited] 1 lot fruit cans (glass). **1882** Owens *Mrs. Owens' Cook Book* 319 *(DAE),* Fill your cans, as many as will stand in your wash boiler . . . Put cold water in the boiler, nearly to the top of the jars. **1968** *DARE* Tape NY108, Fruit cans. [Inf born 1894]
2 A toilet or outhouse. **scattered, but chiefly West** See Map
1900 *DN* 2.26 **IN, MI, MN, NY, WI** [College words], *Can . . .* Water-closet. **1915** *DN* 4.232 **neOH.** **1942** Hale *Prodigal Women* 480 **MA** (as of 1905–40), I'd like to build a little cabin sort of job back there at the edge of the woods, to work in . . . I'd like to have my own can and shower so if I got started on anything I could sleep out there. **1965–70** *DARE* (Qu. F37, . . *An indoor toilet*) 25 Infs, **scattered, but chiefly West,** Can; AR55, Crapping can; MI91, Pee can; (Qu. M21b, . . *Outside toilet building*) 14 Infs, **chiefly Upper MW,** Can; AR48, 55, ID4, IA1, MN37, SD1, Crapping can; MO5, Cabin can; CT7, Crap can; KS12, Trapping can. **1975** Newell *If Nothin' Don't Happen* 63 **nwFL,** The next time a lady come in seemin' to be in a hurry he said, "Lookin' for the rest room,

ma'am?" . . . She just looked at him like he had lost his mind and said,
"Man, I ain't tired. Where's the can?" **1978** Gould *Greenleaf* 63 **ME,**
This man isn't feeling well, sir. I'm taking him to the can.

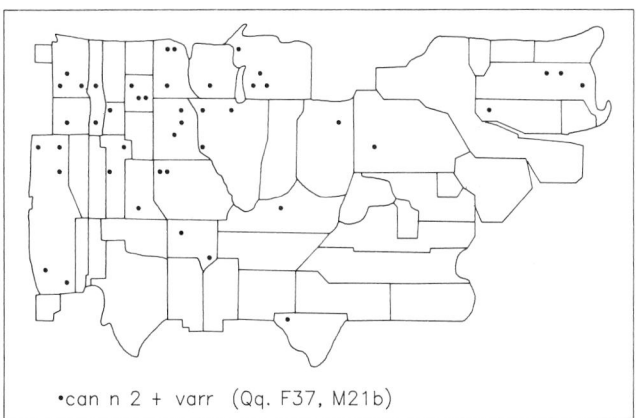

•can n 2 + varr (Qq. F37, M21b)

3 A part of the body, spec:
a The head.
  1915 *DN* 4.198, *Can,* head. "I'll bust your can, if you don't look out."
Ibid 243 **cMT.** **1967** *DARE* (Qu. X28, *Joking words for one's head*) Inf
IL12, Can.
b A woman's breast. [Abbr for **milk can**]
  1965–70 *DARE* (Qu. X31, *Other words used around here for a
woman's breasts*) Infs **CA**15, **FL**39, **HI**8, 9, **PA**1, **WI**12, 57, Cans.
c The buttocks. **chiefly NEast, N Cent, C Atl** See Map
  1935 Hurston *Mules & Men* 116 **FL,** "Y'all been wearin' Ole Massa's
southern can out dis mornin'." [Footnote to *can:* His hips] **1965–70**
DARE (Qu. X35, *Joking words for the part of the body that you sit on*) 62
Infs, **chiefly NEast, N Cent, C Atl,** Can; **CA**15, Cans; **MA**6, Fat can; (Qu.
A20, *Joking ways of telling somebody to hurry*) Inf **MI**63, Come on, get
off your can; (Qu. LL18) Inf **NJ**2, She set on her can.

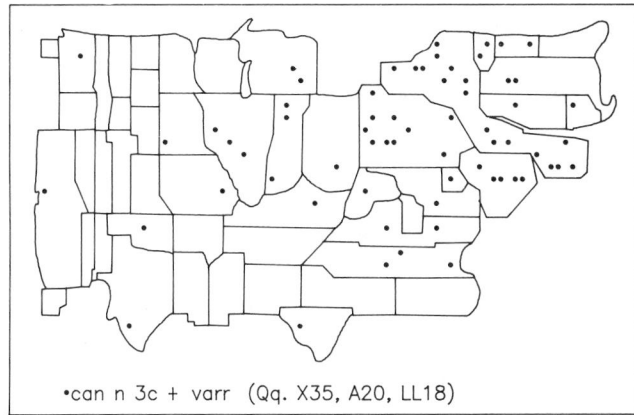

•can n 3c + varr (Qq. X35, A20, LL18)

can v² [Cf *OED canister* v b. "to fasten a canister to the tail of (a
dog)"; 1815 →]
1 To tie a tin can to a dog's tail; hence ppl adj *canned.*
  1903 (1965) Adams *Log Cowboy* 37 **NM,** I was a half a mile in the lead,
burning the earth like a canned dog. **1905** *DN* 3.73 **nwAR,** *Can* . . . To
tie a tin can to a dog's tail and then to set him loose. 'The students canned
his dog for him.' **1956** McAtee *Some Dialect NC* 7, *Can* . . tie an empty
can to the tail of a cat or dog in thoughtless abuse. **c1960** *Wilson Coll.*
csKY, *Can*—To tie a tin can to a dog's tail; formerly regarded as very
funny, esp. at the country store.
2 By ext: see quot 1933.
  1933 *AmSp* 8.1.29 **TX,** Can. To tie a tin can on the dewlap of a cow by
means of a wire run through a slit in the dewlap, to prevent fence-break-
ing. **1961** Adams *Old-Time Cowhand* 159.

can v³ [Cf Engl dial *cand*]
  1896 *DN* 1.414 **wCT, swNY,** *Can* . . to become candied, as of honey.

Canack See **Canuck**

Canada attrib See also **Canadian** entries

Canada anemone n Also *Canadian ~*
An anemone (here: *Anemone canadensis*). Also called **button
flower 2, crowfoot 1b, spring beauty**
  1900 Lyons *Plant Names* 34, *A. canadensis* . . . Canada anemone.
1961 Smith *MI Wildflowers* 135, *Canada or Broad-leaf Anemone* . . . is
more attractive than our other white-flowered anemones because of its
more conspicuous, yellow-centered, brilliantly white flowers and its
habit of growing in clumps. **1966** *DARE* (Qu. S26e, *Other wildflowers*)
Inf **MI**31, Canadian anemone.

Canada balsam n Also *Canadian ~*
=**balsam fir.**
  1806 (1905) Lewis *Orig. Jrls. Lewis & Clark Exped.* 4.46, This tree
affords considerable quantities of a fine clear arromatic [sic] balsam in
appearance and taste like the Canadian balsam. **1848** Gray *Manual of
Botany* 440, *A[bies] balsàmera* . . . Also called *Canada Balsam,* or
Balm-of-Gilead Fir. **1897** Sudworth *Arborescent Flora* 50, *Abies balsamea* . . . *Common Names* . . . Canada Balsam (N.C.). **1968** *DARE*
(Qu. T17, . . *Different kinds of pine trees*) Inf **MD**9, Canadian balsam.
1979 Little *Checklist U.S. Trees* 33, *Balsam fir* . . . *Other common
names*—balsam, Canada balsam.

Canada bird n [*DCan* 1866 →] Cf **Canada sparrow**
=**white-throated sparrow.**
  1917 (1923) *Birds Amer.* 3.37, *White-throated Sparrow* . . . *Other
Names.*—Peabody Bird; . . Canada Bird. **1951** *AmSp* 26.91, *Canada
bird,* for the white-throated sparrow.

Canada black goose n
=**Canada goose.**
  1966 *DARE* (Qu. Q6, . . *Kinds of wild geese*) Inf **GA**1, Canada black
geese.

Canada brant n
=**Canada goose.**
  1917 (1923) *Birds Amer.* 1.158, *Canada Goose* . . Other
Names . . . Canada Brant. **1946** Hausman *Eastern Birds* 125, *Canada
Goose* . . Canada Brant.

Canada corn n [*DCan* 1819 →]
A variety of corn *(Zea mays).*
  1838 MA Ag. Surv. *Report for 1837* 82, This is what we call Canada
corn; a kind I never planted here before. **1848** Fleischman *Nordamer.
Landwirth* 113, Canada Corn, oder Eight Rowed Yellow Small Corn.
1917 Will *Corn among Indians* 72, By Canada corn he probably means
flint corn, as that name was usually applied to the most popular varieties
of that type in the eastern states. **1969** *DARE* (Qu. I34, *If you don't have
sweet corn, you can always eat young* _____) Inf **MA**42, Canada corn.

Canada field pea See **Canada pea 1**

Canada goose n
Std: a large gray and white, black-headed goose (*Branta canadensis* and subspp). Also called **bustard, Canada black goose,
Canada brant, ~ honker, ~ trumpeter, Canadian blue goose,
Canadian snow goose, gray goose, honker, long-necked goose,
reef goose** See also **cackling goose, Hutchins' goose, white-
cheeked goose**

Canada honker n Also *Canadian honker, ~ honky, kennedy*
=**Canada goose.**
  1929 *AmSp* 5.73 **NE** [Cowboy speech], "Kennedies" and "Canadian
Honkies" are geese from Canada. **1965–70** *DARE* (Qu. Q6, . . *Kinds of
wild geese*) 56 Infs, **chiefly Inland Nth, West,** Canadian honkers; 22 Infs,
scattered, but chiefly Inland Nth, Canada honkers.

Canada jay n Also *Canadian jay* [*DCan* 1772 →] **chiefly Nth**
A gray, dark-capped jay (*Perisoreus canadensis*). Also called
**camp bird, carrion bird 1, deer hunter, elk-bird, gorby, grease
bird, lumberjack, meatbird, moosebird, old logger, pork bird,
tallow bird, venison bird, whiskey jack, white-headed jay, woodman's ghost**
  1813 (1824) Wilson *Amer. Ornith.* 3.33, The Canada Jay, *Corvus
Canadensis.* **1917** (1923) *Birds Amer.* 2.225, Canada Jay—*Perisoreus
canadensis canadensis.* **1940** FWP *Guide NM* 17, The Rocky Mountain magpie . . . is called the camp robber, a title bestowed elsewhere on
the Canada jay. **1965–70** *DARE* (Qu. Q16, . . *Kinds of jays*) 26 Infs,
Nth, Canada jay; **MI**2, 36, **NH**14, **NY**6, 106, 233, Canadian jay; (Qu.

Q14) Inf **MI2**, Canadian jay. **1966** *DARE* Tape **MI36**, The Canadian jay or whiskey jack. Oh, they're nice birds.

Canada lynx n Also *Canadian ~* [*DCan* 1820 →] **chiefly Nth**
A **lynx** (here: *Lynx canadensis*).
  1840 MA *Zool. & Bot. Surv. Herb. Plants & Quadrupeds* 33, The Northern or Canada Lynx presents a very striking resemblance to the cat. **1891** Jesup *Plants Hanover NH* 80, *Lynx . . . Canadensis . . . Canada Lynx.* **1966** *DARE* Tape **ME26**, Canadian lynx. **1968** *DARE* (Qu. P31, *. . Names . . for . . wildcat*) Inf **CA105**, Canadian lynx; (Qu. P32, *. . Wild animals*) Inf **NY88**, Canadian lynx.

Canada mayflower n Also *Canadian ~*
A **false lily of the valley** (here: *Maianthemum canadense*).
  1931 Fassett *Spring Flora* 31 **WI**, Canada Mayflower . . . *M. canadense.* **1938** Madison *Wild Flowers OH* 18, *Canada Mayflower. Maianthemum canadense.* Fl[ower]s white. **1966** *DARE* Wildfl. QR Pl.19 Inf **NH4**, Canadian mayflower. **1969** *DARE* (Qu. S26c, *. . Wildflowers that grow in woods*) Infs **MA49**, 67, Canada mayflower. **1975** Duncan–Foote *Wildflowers SE* 254, *Canada-mayflower . . .* The fruits are a favorite fruit of the ruffed grouse.

Canada nuthatch n Also *Canadian ~*
=**red-breasted nuthatch.**
  1903 Dawson *Birds OH* 241, During migrations the Canadian Nuthatch . . moves freely about the smaller limbs of orchard and shade trees, especially conifers. **1953** Jewett *Birds WA* 486, *Sitta canadensis . . .* Other names: Canada Nuthatch; Red-bellied Nuthatch. **1968** *DARE* (Qu. Q23, *The insect-eating bird that goes headfirst down a tree trunk*) Inf **CT10**, Canadian nuthatch.

Canada pea n
1 also *Canada field pea:* A small-flowered **vetch** (*Vicia crassa*). Also called **cow vetch**
  1896 *Jrl. Amer. Folkl.* 9.186, *Vicia cracca, . .* Canada pea, Paris, Me. **1953** Van Wagenen *Golden Age* 231 **NY** (as of 1840s), New York has had a number of different crops that were once important but now are almost forgotten. One of them was the Canada field pea. **1965** Needham–Mussey *Country Things* 140 **sVT**, For a laxative he would dig out a little of this gummy stuff, and roll it up in a round pellet not quite the size of a Canada pea or a field pea; that was one dose. **1976** Bailey–Bailey *Hortus Third* 1155, *Canada pea . . .* Fl[ower]s small, purplish, varying to white.
2 =**marsh pea.**
  1966 *DARE* Wildfl. QR Pl.116 Inf **NC28**, Canada peas.

Canada pest n
A **catchfly gentian** (here: *Eustoma grandiflorum*).
  1894 *Jrl. Amer. Folkl.* 7.95, *Eustoma Russelianum . .* Canada pest . . Mont. **1900** Lyons *Plant Names* 158, *Eustoma . .* Canada-pest.

Canada plum n Also *Canadian ~* **NEast**
A wild **plum** (*Prunus nigra*). Also called **horse plum, pomegranate, red plum**
  1848 *Knickerbocker* 31.31 **NY**, We add the Hawthorn, Poplar, . . Larch and Canada-Plum. **1897** Sudworth *Arborescent Flora* 236, *Prunus nigra . . . Common Names.* Canada Plum (Mass., N.Y., Mich., Ont.). **1968–69** *DARE* (Qu. I46, *. . Kinds of fruit*) Inf **VT13**, Canada plums; (Qu. I53, *Other fruits*) Inf **NH14**, Canadian plums.

Canada robin n Also *Canada waxwing, Canadian robin*
A **waxwing**, usu the **cedar waxwing.**
  1844 DeKay *Zool. NY* 2.44, *Bombycilla carolinensis . . .* This well known bird has various popular names . . . In Massachusetts, it is called *Canada Robin.* **1895** Minot *Land-Birds New Engl.* 152, *Cedarbird . . .* "Canada Robin." **1917** (1923) *Birds Amer.* 3.94, *Bombycilla cedrorum . . .* Canada Robin; Récollet. **1953** Jewett *Birds WA* 540, *Cedar Waxwing . . .* Other names: Cedarbird, . . Canada Waxwing. **1968** *Caribou Co. Sun* (Soda Springs ID) 25 Jan 3/1, We saw a huge flock of stray birds and Grace says they are Bohemian Wax Wings or more familiarly known as the Canadian Robin.

Canada root n
=**butterfly weed 1.**
  1828 Rafinesque *Med. Flora* 74, *Asclepias tuberosa . . . Vulgar Names . .* Silk weed, Canada root, &c. **1876** Hobbs *Bot. Hdbk.* 18, Canada root, Pleurisy root, Asclepias tuberosa. **1930** U.S. Dept. Ag. *Misc. Pub.* 77.18, *Canada-root . . . Part used.*—The roots. **1974** (1977) Coon *Useful Plants* 72, Canada root . . . Other references show that it was cultivated by the Indians for the roots to be cooked.

Canada sparrow n Cf **Canada bird**
Either of two birds: the **tree sparrow** or the **white-throated sparrow.**
  1869 *Galaxy* 8.173, The fox-sparrow . . comes to us in the fall, from the North, where it breeds. Likewise the tree or Canada-sparrow. **1884** *Century Illustr. Mag.* 29.220/1, In winter, especially, they sweep by me and around me in flocks,—the Canada sparrow, . . the shorelark, . . the red-poll, the cedar-bird. **1917** (1923) *Birds Amer.* 3.37, *White-throated Sparrow . . . Other Names*—Peabody Bird; . . Canada Sparrow. *Ibid* 3.40, *Tree Sparrow . . . Other Names.*—Snow Chippy; . . Canada Sparrow. **1963** Gromme *Birds WI* 217, Tree Sparrow . . . Canada sparrow.

Canada thistle n **chiefly Nth**
A widespread, naturalized **thistle** (*Cirsium arvense*). Also called **Canadian thistle, corn ~, creeping ~, cursed ~, dog ~, horse ~**
  1799 Thomas' MA *Spy or Worcester Gaz.* (MA) 31 July 1/1 **VT**, A torvous, stubborn and vexatious plant, known by the name of the Canada Thistle. **1840** MA *Zool. & Bot. Surv. Herb. Plants & Quadrupeds* 122, *C[arduus] arvensis . .* Canada Thistle. **1874** *Shaker Med. Preparations.* **1909** *DN* 3.409 **ME**, Canada thistle. **1965–70** *DARE* (Qu. S21, *. . Other weeds . . that are a trouble in gardens and fields*) Infs **CT9, IL33, 55, MA42, MI80, NY75, WI17, 70, 72, WY5**, Canada thistle(s); (Qu. S26e) Inf **VA26**, Canada thistle. **1967** *DARE* Tape **IA1**, [FW:] What weeds give you the most trouble with corn around here? [Inf:] Foxtail . . . and 'course Canada thistles ['kændə ˌθɪsəlz] and morning glory.

Canada trumpeter n
=**Canada goose.**
  1967 *DARE* (Qu. Q6, *. . Kinds of wild geese*) Inf **NY100**, Canada trumpeters.

Canada violet See **Canadian wood violet**

Canada waxwing See **Canada robin**

Canadian adj See also **Canada** entries

Canadian blue goose n
=**Canada goose.**
  1967–68 *DARE* (Qu. Q6) Infs **MI101, NE11**, Canadian blue geese.

Canadian camp robber See **camp robber**

Canadian dogwood n Also *Canada dogwood* [*DCan* 1947 →]
=**bunchberry 1.**
  1956 St. John *Flora SE WA* 303, *Cornus canadensis* L. *Canada Dogwood; Bunchberry.* **1966** *DARE* Wildfl. QR Pl.150 Inf **WA10**, Canadian dogwood. **1984** *DARE* File **MA**, Canadian dogwood.

Canadian duck n Also *Canada duck*
=**white-winged scoter.**
  1957 *AmSp* 32.184 **WY**, Canadian duck—White-winged scoter. **1968** *DARE* (Qu. Q5, *. . Kinds of wild ducks*) Inf **PA132**, Canada duck.

Canadian gray See **gray goose**

Canadian hemlock n Also *Canada hemlock*
A **hemlock** (here: *Tsuga canadensis*).
  1967–69 *DARE* (Qu. T5, *. . Kinds of evergreens, other than pines*) Infs **MA58, PA3**, Canadian hemlock; (Qu. T15, *. . Kinds of swamp trees*) Inf **MA58**, Canadian hemlock. **1971** Krochmal *Appalachia Med. Plants* 258, *Tsuga canadensis . . . Common Names:* Eastern hemlock, Canada hemlock.

Canadian maple n Cf **California maple 2**
=**box elder.**
  1967–69 *DARE* (Qu. T13, *. . Names . . for . . box elder*) Inf **NY142**, Canadian maple; (Qu. T14, *. . Different kinds of maples*) Inf **IL7**, Canadian maple.

Canadian snow goose n
=**Canada goose.**
  1968 *DARE* (Qu. Q6) Infs **IA29, PA163**, Canadian snow geese.

Canadian soldier n
1 also *Canada soldier, Canadian sailor:* usu a **mayfly**, but see quot 1965–70. **esp OH** See Map
  1926 *Nature Mag.* 8.7, Near shores of lakes or large rivers, may-flies may be seen in great whirling swarms as they perform their mating flight or dance. They also are known as lake-flies, shad-flies or Canadian soldiers. **1965–70** *DARE* (Qu. R4, *A large winged insect that hatches in*

summer . . around lakes . . , crowds around lights, lives only a day or so, and is good fish bait) Infs **MI2, OH2,** 16, 17, 20, 22, 28, 41, 67, 79, **WI**77, Canadian soldier; **NY**103, Canada soldier; **PA**128, Canadian sailor; (Qu. R5) Inf **DC8,** Canadian soldier; (Qu. R15b, *Names for an extra big mosquito)* Inf **OH6,** Canadian soldiers; (Qu. R30) Inf **PA75,** Canadian soldier (grasshopper). **1969** *DARE* File **nOH,** Canadian soldier—the mayfly or Green Bay fly, now in the Cleveland area along Lake Erie.

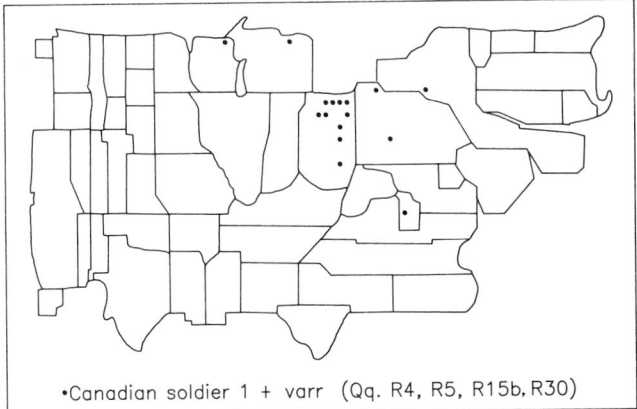

•Canadian soldier 1 + varr (Qq. R4, R5, R15b, R30)

2 =box-elder bug.

1966 *DARE* (QR, near Qu. R29) Inf **GA**12, Box-elder bug—Canadian soldier. **1983** *DARE* File (as of c1930), In Ohio I knew the *box-elder bug* as *Canadian soldier.*

Canadian sparrow n

=tree sparrow.

1957 *AmSp* 32.184 **PA,** Canadian sparrow—tree sparrow.

Canadian tea n

=wintergreen 2.

1900 Lyons *Plant Names* 169, *Gaultheria procumbens* . . Canadian tea. **1930** Sievers *Amer. Med. Plants* 63, Canadian tea. **1971** Krochmal *Appalachia Med. Plants* 128, Canadian tea.

Canadian thistle n

1 =Canada thistle. [*DCan* 1822 →] **chiefly Inland Nth, N Midl**

1836 Weston *Visit U.S.* 102, What are called Canadian thistles . . emigrate to the Southern States in great numbers. **1965–70** *DARE* (Qu. S21, . . *Weeds . . that are a trouble in gardens and fields)* 30 Infs, **chiefly inland Nth, N Midl,** Canadian thistle(s); (Qq. S9,11,13,15,17,20,26a,d,e) 14 Infs, **chiefly Inland Nth, N Midl,** Canadian thistle(s). **1966** *DARE* Wildfl. QR Pl.264 Inf **WI**35, Canadian thistle. **1968** *ID Enterprise* (Malad City) 1 Feb 5/4, Weed control, mainly of morning glory and Canadian thistle—is of prime importance to many farmers.

2 A bull thistle (here: *Cirsium vulgare).*

1968 *DARE* FW Addit **VA**15, *Cirsium vulgare* [is] also known as bull thistle and Canadian thistle. Common on roadsides.

Canadian wood violet n Also *Canada violet*

A white-flowered violet (here: *Viola canadensis).* Also called **hens, June flower**

1821 *Jrnl. Science* III.274 *(DA),* Floral . . calendar for Plainfield, Mass. . . May 3. Lombardy poplar and Canada violet in blossom. **1891** *Century Dict.* 676/3, *Canada violet, Viola Canadensis,* a species common northward and in the mountains of eastern North America, having an upright stem a foot or two high, and white petals purplish beneath. **1969** *DARE* (Qu. S3, *A flower like a large violet)* Inf **VT**13, Canadian wood violet. **1972** Courtenay – Zimmerman *Wild Flowers* 57, *Canada Violet, Viola canadensis* / Medium woods and forests / Flowers pink-backed.

canaigre n, also attrib [See quot 1894 *DN*]

A tall perennial dock *(Rumex hymenosepalus)* with clusters of tannin-rich tuberous roots, native chiefly to the Southwest. Also called **pie dock, sour dock, wild pie-plant, wild rhubarb**

1879 U.S. Dept. Ag. *Rept. of Secy. for 1878* 119 **TX,** In many respects cañaigre root resembled rhubarb. **1894** *DN* 1.324, *Canaigre:* a tall weed of Texas and Northern Mexico, belonging to the dock family *(Rumex hymenosepalus).* The root of this plant is very rich in tannic acid. From Sp. *caña* and *agre,* an old form of *agrio.* **1894** Trimble *Tannins* 2.106,

The use of canaigre in tanning has passed the experimental stage. *Ibid* 107, The Canaigre plant is from one to three feet in height. **1938** Goodding *Native & Exotic Plants* 56 *(DA),* Outside of possible commercial use, the Canaigre is valueless. **1940** FWP *Guide NM* 350, Many crops, ranging from canaigre (a native plant from which a type of tannic acid is extracted) . . have been experimented with. **1970** Correll *Plants TX* 518, Canaigre . . . Baja Calif., Calif., Nev., Wyo., Ariz., Colo., N.M., Chih. and Tex.

canal n Pronc-spp *canall, canawl, canol, cunnal* [Du *kanaal* channel; in LA, Fr *canal*]

A Forms.

1835 Todd *Notes* 64 *(DA),* The Erie canal—here called *canol.* **1853** in 1962 Thompson *Body & Britches* 238 **NY,** I'll tell you of the hardships to me that did befall / While going on a voyage up the Erie can-all. **1927** Kennedy *Gritny* 80 **sLA** [Black], Me an' my brether Booguloo took a skiff soon dis mawnin', an' went down Harvey Cunnal to see my cousin. **1939** (1962) Thompson *Body & Britches* 224 **NY,** [Footnote:] It is generally assumed that we got the pronunciation *canawl* from the Irish. Mr. Joel Munsell, the antiquary-printer, maintained that it was of Dutch origin. **1955** Adams *Grandfather* 43 **Erie Canal NY** (as of 1830s), "Let 'er [the canal] breach," the man said. "It ain't my canawl." **1964** Lomax *Penguin Amer. Folk Songs* 47, We were forty miles from Albany, forget it I never shall, / What a terrible storm we had one night on the E-R-I-E Canal; / . . . The wind began to whistle and the waves began to roll, / And we had to reef our royals on the rag-i-ing 'Canol'.

B Sense.

An irrigation ditch. **West**

1810 (1895) Pike *Expeditions* 621, Both above and below Albuquerque, the citizens were beginning to open canals, to let in the water of the river. **1890** *Stock Grower* 31 May 6/3 *(DA),* In our great southwest are many relics of ancient basins and canals, showing that the pre-historic people had a flourishing agriculture. **1967** *DARE* FW Addit **TX,** Canal—a main irrigation ditch. **1968** Adams *Western Words* 53, *Canal*—The main artificial stream from which irrigation water is obtained. **1970** *DARE* Tape **CA**174, They call them [irrigation] canals out here but it was a ditch to us [in Colorado].

canal boat n [From the size and shape] **chiefly NY** See Map *joc*

A large foot or shoe.

1935 *AmSp* 10.9, The resemblance of feet to various forms of water craft seems to prompt the currency of *tugboats, steamboats, gunboats, battleships, canal boats, sailboats, steamers, canoes,* and *submarines.* **1951** Johnson *Resp. to PADS 20* **DE,** Clodhoppers, canal-boats (shoes). **1965–70** *DARE* (Qu. X38, *Joking names for unusually big or clumsy feet)* 14 Infs, **esp NY,** Canal boats; **NY**1, Shoes like canal boats; (Qq. W42a, b) Infs **NY**52, 92, Canal boats.

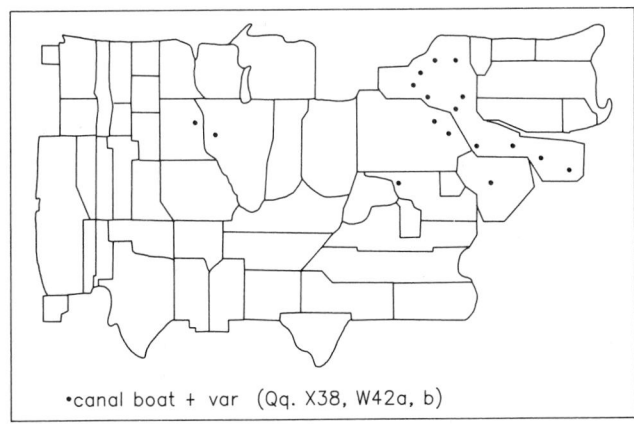

•canal boat + var (Qq. X38, W42a, b)

canal boater n

A large **channel catfish** (here: *Ictalurus punctatus).*

1957 Trautman *Fishes* 415 **OH,** Largest adults (colloquially called channel and blue cats [usually males], canal boaters, black warriors . .) are dark steel-blue with whitish bellies.

‡canal flour n [Perh alter of *canaille* coarse flour]

1872 (1973) Thompson *Major Jones's Courtship* 63 **GA,** "Will you have a hot biskit," ses he, "made out of the best Canal flower from imported wheat?"

canaller n Also sp *canaler, canawler*

1 A worker on a canal or canal boat. **NY** *hist*

1830 *Germanstown* (Pa.) *Telegraph* 14 July 4/1 *(DA)*, A Canawler asked his captain 'what A.M. stood for after a man's name?' **1851** (1976) Melville *Moby-Dick* 248, "Canallers!" cried Don Pedro. "We have seen many whaleships in our harbors, but never heard of your Canallers. Pardon: who and what are they?" "Canallers, Don, are the boatmen belonging to our grand Erie Canal." **1898** Westcott *Harum* 230 **nNY**, The canalers was a rough set in gen'ral . . an' I got my share of cusses an' cuffs. **1930** *AmSp* 6.97 **Erie Canal NY**, *Canawlers:* canalers. "The canawlers would say that the food is unhealthy." **1940** FWP *Guide NY* 478, The 'canawler' half sailor and half landlubber, swore, drank, and fought hard. **1955** Adams *Grandfather* 18 **Erie Canal NY** (as of 1830s), The first canaller to reach the spot, a burly old steam captain, swept the official's feet out from under him. **1962** Wyld *Low Bridge* 83 **Erie Canal,** Shouts like "Canawler, Canawler" were common "up and down the old canawl."

2 A canalboat; see quot 1944. **Gt Lakes**

1941 FWP *Guide MI* 114, Many of them, especially the 'canallers' built to navigate the old Welland canal, had boxlike hulls of maximum dimensions permitted by the locks. **1944** Landon *Lake Huron* 349 **IN, MI, OH, NY,** "Canaler", (a canal ship) with blunt, straight stem, flat stern with almost no cutaway and a short bowsprit.

canary grass n Also *Reed('s) canary grass* **chiefly Nth, N Midl**

A grass of the genus *Phalaris*. For names of var spp see **ribbon grass**

1822 Eaton *Botany* 386, *Phalaris . . . canariensis* (canary grass . . .). **1950** *WELS* (*Kinds of grass . . grown for hay*) 4 Infs, **WI,** Canary (grass); 1 Inf, Reed's canary grass. **1965–70** *DARE* (Qu. L8, *Hay that grows naturally in damp places*) Infs **IN**67, **NY**182, 216, Canary grass; **MO**18, Reed's canary grass; (Qu. L9a, *. . Grass . . for hay*) Infs **CT**24, **IL**46, **IA**14, **PA**103, **WI**17, Canary grass; **MN**16, 31, Reed canary grass; **PA**33, Reed's canary grass; (Qu. S9, *Other kinds of grass*) Infs **IN**67, **WA**24, Canary grass; **MN**16, Reed canary grass. **1972** *WI Conserv. Bulletin* July–Aug 323, Wetlands containing sedge and canary grass were second in preference . . as nesting sites.

canary root n

An unidentified root used in magical practices.

1952 Dorson *Bloodstoppers* 36 **nMI,** Long time ago, if you like a woman and she doesn't love you, and sasses you, you get some canary root and shave it fine.

canary vine n

=**mountain fringe 1.**

1896 *Jrl. Amer. Folkl.* 9.181, *Adlumia cirrhosa . .* canary vine, Madison, Wis. **1911** *Century Dict. Suppl.,* Canary-vine . . . [*Century:* Supposed to have been brought from the Canary Islands.] The climbing fumitory. **1959** Carleton *Index Herb. Plants* 23.

canatillo n Also *cañatillo, cañatilla* **SW**

=**Mormon tea.**

1913 Wooton *Trees NM* 24, Canatillo (*Ephedra* spp.). **1931** U.S. Dept. Ag. *Misc. Pub.* 101.12, *Jointfirs . . .* All the species are known also as Mormon-tea, canatillo [etc]. **1937** U.S. Forest Serv. *Range Plant Hdbk.* B73, Jointfir . . . In the range country, . . the names Mormon-tea and cañatillo are generally used in reference to these plants. **1941** Jaeger *Wildflowers* 5 **Desert SW,** Canatilla. *Ephedra trifurca . . .* A small bush . . distinguished by its long leaves, large, papery fruits, and spinose branches. **1950** *Western Folkl.* 9.340, *Medicinal Herbs of Early Days in Use and Collected in the San Antonio Mission District . . .* Bladder: tea of Grama, Canutillo [sic], Tabardillo, Root of parsley. **1966** Barnes–Jensen *Dict. UT Slang* 31, Mormon Tea . . . Canatillo. **1970** Correll *Plants TX* 81, *Ephedra trifurca . . .* Cañatilla. *Ibid* 83, *Ephedra antisyphilitica . . .* Cañatilla.

canawl See **canal A**

canawler See **canaller**

cancer drops n [From its use as a remedy for cancer]

=**beechdrops 1.**

1876 Hobbs *Bot. Hdbk.* 19, Cancer drops, Beech drops, Orobanche Virginiana. **1940** Clute *Amer. Plant Names* 109, *E[pifagus] Virginiana . . .* Cancer-root, cancer-drops. **1959** Carleton *Index Herb. Plants* 23.

cancerroot n

1 A **broomrape 1,** esp *Orobanche fasciculata* and *O. uniflora.* [See quots 1822, 1840] See also **beechdrops 1**

1712 in 1714 Royal Soc. London *Philos. Trans.* 29.64, To this [=boar thistle] they add a Root, call'd the Cancer Root. **1822** Eaton *Botany* 272, *Epiphegus . . virginianus . .* beech drops, cancer-root . . . Barton says this plant is an astringent; and that it is useful in cases of indolent ulcers and perhaps cancers, applied externally. *Ibid* 369, *Orobanche . . uniflora* (squaw-root, cancer-root) . . . About 3 inches high, of a yellowish white colour. **1840** MA Zool. & Bot. Surv. *Herb. Plants & Quadrupeds* 156, *O[robanche] Americana* L. Cancer Root. Because it has been used as a remedy for this dreadful disease . . . *O. uniflora* L. Small Cancer Root. *Ibid* 157, *E[piphagus] Americana . .* Cancer Root . . . has a drab appearance, and the bark appears to perform the functions of leaves. **1859** Bartlett *Americanisms,* Squaw-Root *(Conopholis americana.)* A medicinal plant put up by the Shakers, also called Cancer-Root. **1897** Parsons *Wild Flowers CA* 172, There are about half a dozen species of cancer-root known upon our Coast, all strange-looking, leafless plants, of very doubtful moral character—for I fear it must be confessed they are thieves. **1910** Graves *Flowering Plants* 359 **CT,** Cancer-root . . . *Epifagus virginiana . . . Conopholis americana . . . Orobanche uniflora.* **1951** Voss *IL Wild Flowers* 81, One-flowered cancer root . . . is found on the roots of asters and goldenrods and does not seem to harm the host plants. **1975** Duncan–Foote *Wildflowers SE* 180, Cancer-root . . . Rich woods; c Fla into Cal, BC, Yukon, and Nfld. Apr–May.

2 A cancerwort (here: *Kickxia elatine*).

1940 Steyermark *Flora MO* 477, Cancer-root (*Kickxia Elatine . .*) . . . Sand and gravel bars of streams, and waste ground. Scattered, southern and central Mo.

3 =**pokeweed 1.**

1971 Krochmal *Appalachia Med. Plants* 190, *Phytolacca americana . .* cancerroot . . . In some areas dried fruits are used as a poultice on sores.

cancer stick n *esp among young speakers*

A cigarette.

1963 *AmSp* 38.276 [American Indian student slang], Cigarettes are called *cancer sticks*. **1964** *AmSp* 39.235 **KS** [Student slang], *Cancer stick . . .* A cigarette . . . *Stick . . .* A cigarette. **1965–70** *DARE* (Qu. DD6b, *Nicknames for cigarettes*) 118 Infs, **widespread,** Cancer stick. [Of all Infs responding to the question, 9% were young and 24% were mid-aged; of those giving this response, 31% were young and 33% were mid-aged.]

cancerweed n

1 Any of several plants thought to be a remedy for cancer.

1802 Drayton *View of SC* 60, Cancer weed. (*Salvia* Lyrata, et Mexicana.) **1806** (1905) Lewis *Orig. Jrls. Lewis & Clark Exped.* 5.108 **OR,** I observe here . . cansar weed [Thwaites: cancerwort]. **1889** *Century Dict.* 786/3, Cancer-weed . . . The rattlesnake-root, *Prenanthes alba,* of the United States, . . which is used as a domestic tonic. **1931** Clute *Common Plants* 123, A number of the ancient plant names recall afflictions which have happily gone quite out of style . . . In the list are . . itch-weed, . . and cancer weed (*Salvia lyrata*). **1941** FWP *Guide MO* 23, Cancer weed (salvia).

2 =**cancer stick.**

1965–70 *DARE* (Qu. DD6b) Infs **GA**19, 30, 72, 77, **MS**6, **PA**8, 230, **TX**89, Cancerweed.

canchalagua n Also sp *conchalagua* [AmSpan] **CA**

A California centaury, esp *Centaurium venustum.*

[**1772** Ulloa *Noticias* 109, La *Calaguala,* y la *Canchalagua . .* son producciones de aquellos inhabitables pinaculos de la condillera. [The *Calaguala* and the *Canchalagua . .* are products of those uninhabitable pinnacles of the mountains.]] **1848** Bryant *What I Saw in CA* 452, There is another plant in high estimation with the Californians, called *canchalagua,* which is held by them as an antidote for all the diseases to which they are subject; but in particular for cases of fever and ague. **1894** *Jrl. Amer. Folkl.* 7.94, *Erythraea Muhlenbergii, . .* conchalagua, Cal. **1922** Smiley *Weeds CA* 153, This is but one of several "canchalaguas" growing within the state, though it is the handsomest. **1959** Munz–Keck *CA Flora* 440, *C. venustum . . .* Canchalagua.

C. and E. Christian See **Christmas and Easter Christian**

candelilla n [AmSpan "little candle"; see quot 1961]

A spurge *(Euphorbia antisyphilitica)* native to Texas. Also called **wax plant**

1940 FWP *Guide TX* 24, The candelilla, or wax plant. **1961** Wills–Irwin *Flowers TX* 148, Closely related is the . . Candelilla . . . The pencil-like stems bear small whitish flowers near their tips in spring. **1970** Correll *Plants TX* 965.

candle n

A Forms. Usu |ˈkændl|; also, **esp in Sth, S Midl**, |ˈkænl| Proncspp *can'le, keandle* [Cf Scots, nEngl dial *can'le, cannle*, etc]

1900 *Bookman* 11.447/2 **eVA**, On the mantelpiece those handsome *keandle*-sticks remind us that, although the candle is archaic for illuminating purposes, *keandle* is a survival in Virginia dialect. **1908** *DN* 3.282 **eAL, wGA**, *Consonant changes* . . . Dentals . . . *d* medial is lost in -ndl combinations, as in bunl, cænl, dwinl, etc. **1923** *DN* 5.203 **swMO**, *Can'le.* **1942** Hall *Smoky Mt. Speech* 81 **wNC, eTN**, [ˈkænl]. **1967** *DARE* File **seLA**, [kænl].

B Senses.

1 Mucus that protrudes from the nose. [*OED candle* sb. 4c 'mucus pendulous at the nose']

1967–69 *DARE* (Qu. X16) Infs **PA34, 227**, Candles.

2 See quots.

[**1898** Gomme *Traditional Games* 2.186, The child who stands on the plank in the centre [of a see-saw] and balances it, is frequently called the "canstick" or "candlestick."] **1931–33** *LANE Worksheets* **cCT**, Candle—The bar that a teeter totter was balanced on.

3 A shoot of new growth on a pine tree.

1950 Moore *Trees AR* 17, The spring "candle" or shoot [of loblolly pine] is grayish green, slender, and often curved or drooping rather than erect. **1968** Pochmann *Triple Ridge* 74 **cWI**, "Those as don't get put in," said Howard, "can be heeled in . . . They'll keep . . till the candles get right long." . . The light-green candles on the white pines were only one-half inch long.

candleberry myrtle n Also *candleberry (tree)* [From the use of the wax covering the "berries" in candle-making]

=**wax myrtle.**

1731 (1754) Catesby *Nat. Hist. Carolina* 1.13, The broad-leaved Candle-berry Myrtle. *Ibid* 1.69, The narrow-leaved Candle-berry Myrtle. **1753** Chambers *Cyclopedia Suppl.* [1.6Gᵛ], Candle *berry tree, . .* an aromatic evergreen . . . also called the *Virginia myrtle.* **1775** (1922) Schaw *Jrl. of a Lady* 203 **NC**, The Myrtle thro' all this swamp is the candle-berry-myrtle, which makes the green candle you have seen at home. **1883** Hale *Woods NC* 171, *Wax Myrtle. Candle-berry Myrtle* . . A well-known shrub with fragrant leaves. **1892** *Jrl. Amer. Folkl.* 5.103, *Myrica cerifera*, candle-berry. Worcester Co., Mass. **1960** Vines *Trees SW* 117, *Myrica pusilla* . . . Vernacular names are Dwarf Candleberry, Bayberry, Waxberry, and Wax-myrtle. **1971** Krochmal *Appalachia Med. Plants* 180, *Myrica cerifera* . . . Common Names: . . candleberry, candleberry myrtle . . . The fruit is the main source of wax used in making candles.

candle bug See **candle fly**

candle cactus n [See **candlewood 3**]

=**ocotillo.**

1901 *Scientific Amer.* 84.140/1 **sCA**, Here is the huge candle cactus so common on the Mexican and Arizonian deserts.

candlefish n, also attrib **Pacific**

1 also *candlestick fish:* =**eulachon.** [See quots]

1879 U.S. Natl. Museum *Bulletin* 14.56, *Osmerus pacificus . . . Oulachan; Candle-fish.* North Pacific. **1881** *Nature* (London) 24.39/2, Oolachan oil . . is obtained from a fish called by the North American Indians Oolachan, or candle-fish, from the fact that when dried the fish itself can be used as a torch or candle. **1947** Jones *Evergreen Lands* 152 **WA**, There he would feed them candlefish oil and he would also burn the oil lavishly. **1962** Salisbury *Quoth the Raven* 242 **AK**, The Eulikon was put to another use which gave it the name candle fish. Because of their remarkable richness in oil the natives were accustomed to dry them and run the pith of the cattail or rush, or strips of cedar bark through them like a candle wick. **1968–69** *DARE* (Qu. P3) Inf **AK9**, Candlefish; (Qu. P4) Inf **AK1**, Candlefish; (Qu. near Qu. P13) Inf **CA111**, Candlefish—name given by Indians to fish that had so much oil they made candles out of it. **1968** *DARE* Tape **CA104**, [Inf:] Now there's a candlestick fish,

is that the same thing [as a grunion]? [FW:] Never heard of it. [Inf:] Well, they have it there [=Trinidad, CA], candlestick fish . . . They're just like a light in the water, they show up. [FW:] Are they fluorescent? [Inf:] Yes, yes . . . [FW:] How do they catch them, they're about eight inches long, do they catch them with a net? [Inf:] . . . That's the way they catch the candlefish is to put the hooks on the line an' just keep, keep bobbin' it up an' down.

2 =**sablefish.**

1884 Goode *Fisheries U.S.* 1.268 *(DA)*, Black Candle-fish *(Anoplopoma fimbria)* . . . At San Francisco it is usually called 'Candle-fish.' **1953** Roedel *Common Fishes CA* 91.138, Sablefish . . . *Unauthorized Names:* Coalfish, candlefish.

candle flare See **candle fly**

candleflower n

1 A **stickleaf** (here: *Mentzelia decapetala*).

1948 Stevens *KS Wild Flowers* 321, One of the vernacular names is 'candleflower,' in allusion to the appearance of the closed flowers as they are usually seen in the daytime.

2 See **candlewood 3.**

candle fly n Also *candle bug, ~ flare, ~ miller* **chiefly Sth, Midl**

=**lightning bug.**

1959 Sanders *Echoes* 16 **swAR**, It seems that the crickets and candle bugs were better Methodists than a lot of the folks around our township; they would attend in great numbers every night. **1965–70** *DARE* (Qu. R4) 9 Infs, **Sth, Midl**, Candle fly; **AR41, FL35**, Candle bug; **AR41**, Candle miller; (Qu. R1) Inf **VA26**, Candle fly; (Qu. R5) Infs **LA14, 15**, Candle bug; (Qu. R10) Inf **MO9**, Candle flare; (Qu. R12) Inf **NC10**, Candle fly; (Qu. R30) Inf **NC27**, Candle bug. **1969** *DARE* FW Addit **swNC**, Candle fly.

candlelight n Also *candlelighting* Cf **early candlelight**

Dusk.

1696 (1878) S. Sewall *Diary* 1.439 **MA**, Just about Candle-lighting the news of it is brought to Town. **1803** in 1956 Eliason *Tarheel Talk* 263 **NC**, They did not depart for home . . . till some time after Candle Light. **1895** *DN* 1.385 **cwIN, cNY**, *Candlelightin':* nightfall. "Evenin' meetin' took up at early candlelightin'." **1899** (1912) Green *VA Folk-Speech* 105, *Candle-light . . .* The time at which candles or lamps are lighted. "The evening service will begin at candle-light." Marriages took place at "early candle-light." **1922** Talley *Negro Folk Rhymes* 74, Can we git dar 'fore candle-light? **1923** *DN* 5.203 **swMO**, *Can'le light . . .* Dusk, twilight. Modified by 'early can'le light' or 'late can'le light.' **1953** Randolph *Down in Holler* 212 **Ozarks**, Dusk is called *lamp-lighting time*, or *candle-light*—often divided into *early candle-light* and *late candle-light;* the expression *early candle-light* is still seen in the country newspapers, announcing church meetings and the like.

candle miller See **candle fly**

candle of the Lord See **Our Lord's candle**

candle-sperm n

Drops of wax from a spermaceti candle.

1927 Kennedy *Gritny* 119 **sLA** [Black], She knew somebody was burning a candle over her to keep bad luck in her way . . . She was sure of it; because she found red pepper and buzzard feathers and candle-sperm tracks on her front door steps.

candlestick fish See **candlefish 1**

candlestick plover n

The western **willet** *(Catotrophorus semipalmatus inornatus).*

1918 Grinnell *Game Birds CA* 416, *Western Willet . . . Other names*—Willet; Candlestick Plover. **1951** *AmSp* 26.277 **CA**, Candlestick plover (for the willet). **1953** Jewett *Birds WA* 264.

candlestick tree n Cf **candle tree 3**

Perh the candlestick senna *(Cassia alata).*

1967 *DARE* FW Addit **LA1**, Candlestick tree—an ornamental annual plant with yellow flowers and large compound leaves.

candle tree n

1 =**catalpa 1.** [From the resemblance of the beans to candles]

1889 *Century Dict.* 789/1, *Candle-tree . . .* In the United States, the *Catalpa bignonioides*, from its long round pods. **1907** Hodge *Hdbk. Amer. Indians* 1.213, The two species native in the United States are the common catalpa . . or candle-tree . . and the western catalpa. **1960**

Vines *Trees SW* 926, *Southern Catalpa* . . . Vernacular names for the tree are Candle-tree [etc].

2 =wax myrtle. [From the use of the wax to make candles]
1960 Vines *Trees SW* 120, *Myrica . . pennsylvanica* . . . Vernacular names in use are Waxberry, . . Candle-tree, and Tallow-tree.

3 A **senna 1** (here: *Cassia alata*). [So called because the erect flower stalks resemble candles]
1961 Wills–Irwin *Flowers TX* 129, Mention should be made of the Candle-tree, *C. alata* . . , a large-leaved tender shrub . . usually cultivated in Texas as a perennial herb.

candlewick n [*OED* 1597 →]
1 =mullein.
1891 *AN&Q* 7.210/1, Candle-wick, or common mullen [sic], is also called *hag's taper.* **1951** Teale *North Spring* 222, Mullein, that plant of many names—candlewick, blanket leg, Adam's-flannel, old man's-flannel, hares' beard, velvet plant, clown's lungwort—was beginning the production of the thick felty leaves of a new year.

2 A **cattail 1** (here: *Typha latifolia*).
1959 Carleton *Index Herb. Plants* 23, Candle Wick: Typha latifolia; Verbascum thapsus.

candlewood n
1 A resinous wood.
1634 Wood *New Engl. Prospect* 17, Out of these Pines is gotten the candlewood that is so much spoken of, . . but I cannot commend it for singular good, because it is something sluttish, dropping a pitchie kinde of substance where it stands. **1700** in 1899 Springfield MA *First Century* 2.357, No Stranger or any that are not proper Inhabitants of the Towne shal . . draw any Candell wood for Tarr from tyme to tyme. **1935** U.S. Congress *Serial Set* 9903 Doc 33.14 (as of early 18th cent), Candlewood used for tar making was prohibited if gathered within 6 miles of the Connecticut River. **1940** Richter *Trees* 232 OH, (as of early 19th cent), When it got late without him, she and Achsa lighted candlewood and went over to the Covenhovens.

2 A **torchwood.**
1908 Britton *N. Amer. Trees* 576, Balsam Torchwood . . . is sometimes called Candle-wood. **1979** Little *Checklist U.S. Trees* 54, *Amyris elemifera* . . . *Other common names*—candlewood.

3 also *candleflower:* **=ocotillo.** [See quots 1915, 1965] **SW**
1889 *Century Dict.* 789/1, Candlewood . . . The genus *Fouquiera* of northern Mexico and the adjacent United States, including several species with erect, slender, very resinous, and often leafless stems, and large bright-scarlet flowers. **1915** (1926) Armstrong *Western Wild Flowers* 294, Ocotillo, Candle Flower . . . From the tip of each wand springs a . . cluster . . of scarlet flowers . . suggesting a flame. **1939** Pickwell *Deserts* 65/2, One of the commonest is "candlewood," the name of the family; another is "coachwhip." **1965** Teale *Wandering Through Winter* 35 CA, One of its [ocotillo's] common names, candlewood, is derived from the fact that it burns with a steady deep yellow flame. **1970** Correll *Plants TX* 1070.

4 A **wax myrtle** (here: *Myrica pennsylvanica*). [See quot 1910]
1910 Graves *Flowering Plants* 143 CT, Bayberry. Candlewood . . . The berries yield a wax or tallow, somewhat used for making candles. **1960** Vines *Trees SW* 120, Vernacular names in use are Waxberry, . . Candleberry, Candlewood, Candle-tree, and Tallow-tree.

candock n [*OED* 1661 →]
A **water lily**, often **spatterdock.**
1807 in 1942 *Torreya* 42.160, *Nymphaea advena* . . . Can-dock, splatter-dock [sic], Philadelphia, Pa. **1959** Carleton *Index Herb. Plants* 23, Can Dock: Numphozanthus advena; Nymphaea alba. **1967** DARE (Qu. S26b, *Wildflowers that grow in water or wet places*) Inf **NJ1**, Candocks.

candy n See **candy kid**

candy v
1969 DARE (Qu. U15, . . *If the seller puts in a little extra to make you feel that you're getting a good bargain, you call that* _____) Inf **CA147**, Candying the customer.

‡**candy** adj [Folk-etym for *candid*]
1946 McCullers *Member* 17 GA, 'If you want my candy opinion,' said Berenice, 'that whole crowd of folks down yonder at the fair just give me the creeps.' *Ibid* 75, Give me your candy opinion.

candy ankle n
A weak or effeminate man.
1938 Stuart *Dark Hills* 148 KY, When we catch a candy-ankle going between the sheds a couple or three of us fellars grab him and away we take him to a barrel of oil. We souse him under too.

candy bee See **candy pulling**

candy boiling See **candy stew**

candy breaking n Also *candy cracking* **S Midl** *old-fash*
See quots.
1923 *DN* 5.203 swMO, Candy breakin' . . . A social gathering where couples are made up by having them match the broken ends of candy sticks. Each lady, usually, is given a broken stick, the opposite end of which is deposited with others in a suitable receptacle from which it may be drawn by a man. **1931** Randolph *Ozarks* 66, In addition to the social opportunities provided by . . holidays, the young folk get together now and then at clearings, log-rollings, house-raisings, cornhuskings and other "workin's", and mingle at an occasional candy-breaking or box-supper or church "sociable", . . [or the] "play-party." **1936** *Jrl. Amer. Folk.* 49.204 Ozarks, Sometimes the making and eating of candy is the principal activity of the evening, such a party being referred to as a "candy-breakin'." **1952** Brown *NC Folkl.* 1.525 wNC, Candy-cracking . . . A party at which candy is broken and served. Obsolescent. **1953** Randolph *Down in Holler* 232 Ozarks, Candy-breakin' . . . A social game where men and women are "paired off" by biting opposite ends of the same piece of candy. **1954** Harder *Coll.* cwTN, Candy breakin'. **1973** *Foxfire 2* 374 nGA, They'd have a dishpan fulla stick candy broke up into little pieces, . . . And th'pan was covered. And a girl and boy would pair off and go and reach under there and get a piece a'candy. If they each got a piece alike [the same color], why they could keep it, but if they didn't, they had t'put it back . . . I remember . . he carried me home that night after th'candy breakin'. **1975** McDonough *Garden Sass* 168 AR, When the candy-making was finished it was usually followed by a game called candy-breakin'. As Polly described it, "We broke this candy up in little pieces and we would have to put that little piece of candy in our mouth, and then our partner would bite the other end off." **1983** Montell *Don't Go Up* 28 csKY, cnTN, People looked forward to candy breakings.

candy bucket See **bucket 2f**

candy can See **cannikin 2**

candycane snake n [So called from the red-and-white markings]
=milk snake 1 (here: *Lampropeltis triangulum syspila*).
1958 Conant *Reptiles & Amphibians* 171, *Red Milk Snake* . . . Also called "red snake" and "candy-cane snake."

candy cone See **ice-cream cone**

candy cracking See **candy breaking**

candy, drop one's See **drop one's candy**

candyflower n **Pacific NW**
A **miner's lettuce** (here: *Montia sibirica*).
1973 Hitchcock–Cronquist *Flora Pacific NW* 108, Alas[ka] to Cal[ifornia], . . e[ast] to Mont[ana] and Utah; w[estern] springbeauty, Siberian m[ontia], candyfl[ower] . . . *M[ontia] sibirica.*

candy grass n
=stinkgrass.
1894 *Jrl. Amer. Folk.* 7.104, *Eragrostis major* . . candy-grass. Central Neb. **1898** *Ibid* 11.283, *Eragrostis major*, . . candy grass, . . Kans. **1901** Mohr *Plant Life* AL 380, Candy Grass . . . A frequent garden weed. **1936** Winter *Plants NE* 27, Candy-grass . . . A common weed over all the state . . . *E. cilianensis.*

candy kid n Also *candy (man)*
A dandy; a favorite.
1913 *DN* 4.16, Candykid. A fine fellow; a showy, stylish person . . . "He's a candykid all right." "She is some candykid." *Candyman.* A dandy fellow; a stylish, showy person. **1924** Henderson *Keys to Crookdom* 400, Candy kid. A lady's man. A pretty boy. **1935** *AmSp* 10.13 [Lingo of the good-people], Candy or candy-kid. One who has a way with women. A *dink*, a *boiler-maker.* **1958** McCulloch *Woods Words* 28 Pacific NW, Candy kid—a. The boss' favorite. b. A mama's boy.

candy knocking n
  1963 Watkins *Yesterday Hills* 105 **cnGA** (as of c1900), At a candy knocking a piece of candy was tied to a string hanging from the ceiling. One person was blindfolded and handed a stick of wood. If he swung at the candy and hit it, he was given a stick of candy.

candy man See **candy kid**

candy party See **candy pulling**

candy pine n [Perh alter of *Canada* + *pine*]
  Perh =**Norway pine.**
  1966 *DARE* (Qq. T8, 17) Inf **ME24,** Candy pine—harder [than soft pine], is all full of pitch or sap.

candy pulling n Also *candy bee, ~ party, ~ pull* **scattered, but chiefly Sth, S Midl, NEast, CA** See Map *old-fash* Cf *SND taffie-join* Cf **taffy pulling**
  A social gathering for young persons at which candy (usu molasses taffy) is made.
  1845 *Lowell Offering* 5.268 **MA,** We used to have sewing parties, tea parties, candy parties. **1846** in 1939 *AmSp* 14.106 **wNY,** The distinguished festival of Podunk is the candy bee . . . The "New Orleans" had been boiling for an hour, and all await in anxious expectation the moment when it shall be hard enough to 'pull.' **1862** (1931) DeLong *Jrls.* 10.377 **CA,** In the evening went to Col Hoge's with Warfield had a candy pull a good dance &c. **1908** *DN* 3.296 **eAL, wGA,** *Candy-pulling* . . . A kind of gathering or party in which the young people make and pull (molasses) candy. *Candy-pull* is not heard. **1923** *DN* 5.203 **swMO,** *Candy pullin'.* **1939** Coffin *Capt. Abby* 66 **ME** (as of c1860s), He went to molasses candy pulls at his uncles' houses. He went to spelling schools and singing schools at the schoolhouse. **c1960** *Wilson Coll.* **csKY,** *Candy-pulling.* **1965–70** *DARE* (Qu. FF2, *What kinds of parties do people favor around here?*) 33 Infs, **scattered, but chiefly Sth, S Midl, NEast, CA,** Candy pulling; **FL31,** Candy pulls; **VA1,** Candy parties; (Qu. FF1) Inf **TX42,** Candy pulling; (QR, near Qu. H80) Inf **CA70,** Used to have candy pulls. [18 Infs indicated that candy pulling parties were old-fashioned or a thing of the past.] **1975** *Foxfire 3* 236 **nGA,** Everybody'd go out for Decoration Day an' have a dinner on th'grounds'r'something like that. An' th'rest of the time th'only thing we ever went to would be a corn-shuckin', or a pea-thrashin', or a singin', or a candy-pullin', 'r'somethin' like that. **1982** Ginns *Snowbird Gravy* 151 **nwNC** (as of c1910), When the syrup was made in the fall, they always had a candy pulling around the syrup mill. They'd boil the syrup and pull it.

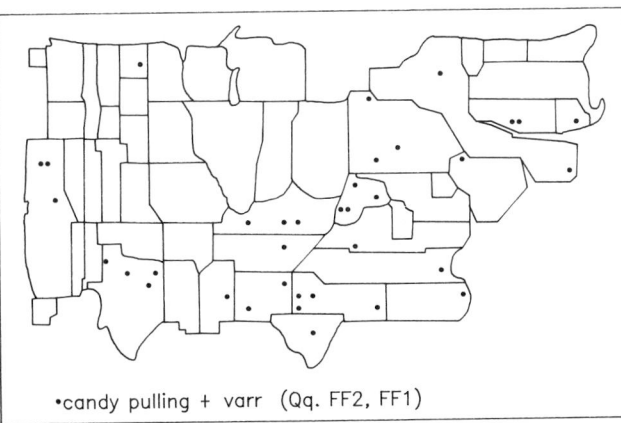

•candy pulling + varr (Qq. FF2, FF1)

‡candy rice n
  1928 Peterkin *Scarlet Sister Mary* 28 **SC,** Budda Ben . . bought pink and white candies that looked like rice grains and sprinkled these all over the whole cake . . . Maum Hannah said that the candy rice would bring good luck to the bride.

candy roaster n
  A variety of squash often roasted or baked with sugar.
  1966–69 *DARE* (Qu. I23, . . *Kinds of squash*) Inf **KY17,** Candy roasters—cook, put in butter, brown sugar, and cinnamon, and bake; (Qu. I26, . . *Kinds of melons*) Inf **NC44,** Droppin' melons, punkins, candy roasters.

candyroot n [See quots 1948, 1968]
  =**milkwort** (here: *Polygala* spp).

1926 *Torreya* 26.92, A New Candy-root from Florida . . . *Polygala aboriginum* Small, sp. nov. **1938** (1955) FWP *Guide DE* 12, Other plants noted on this brief visit were three kinds of meadow-beauties, six of milkwort or candyroot. **1948** Wherry *Wild Flower Guide* 71, Other *Candyroots,* differing in details, occur here. The members of this genus *[Polygala]* are often called . . *Milkwort,* but the name referring to the wintergreen flavor of the roots is preferred here. **1968** McPhee *Pine Barrens* 129, "This is candy root," he said . . . The root of the plant had the taste of a sweet peppermint candy cane. **1972** Brown *Wildflowers LA* 98, Candy Root. *Polygala cruciata. Ibid* 99, Candy Root. *Polygala incarnata* . . . Orange Candy Root . . . *Polygala lutea. Ibid* 100, Candy Root. *Polygala nana* . . . Roots smell like wintergreen candy.

candy side n
  In logging: see quots.
  1942 *AmSp* 17.220, *Candy side.* The 'side' of a high-lead camp which has the best equipment; the opposite of *haywire side.* **1958** McCulloch *Woods Words* 28 **Pacific NW,** *Candy side*—The side, or operating unit, which has the best timber or best logging conditions. **1959** *AmSp* 34.77 **nCA,** *Candy side* . . . That crew of a high-lead camp which has the best equipment. The other side is naturally the 'haywire' one.

candy snake n
  =**glass snake** (here: *Ophisaurus ventralis*).
  1953 Randolph *Down in Holler* 232 **Ozarks,** *Candy snake* . . . The so-called glass snake or joint snake (*Ophisarurus ventralis*), which is really a legless lizard.

candy stew n Also *candy boiling* **KY, NC, VA** *old-fash* Cf **sugar stew**
  A party at which candy is made.
  1837 in 1956 Eliason *Tarheel Talk* 263 **NC,** Waiting to go to a candy stew. **1842** *Ibid,* We had a great deal of company to the candy boiling . . we pulled the candy, and played magical music and redeemed pawns, and then the company went home. **1863** in 1951 *AmSp* 26.182 **NC,** Eat supper . . and had a candy boiling. **a1883** (1911) Bagby *VA Gentleman* 11, Parties of all kinds, from candy-stews and "infairs" up to the regular country balls at the county seat. **1887** *Courier–Jrl.* (Louisville KY) 30 Jan 13/3, A supper in addition to a "candy-stew" was an unheard-of luxury. **1969** *DARE* Tape **NC60,** We used to have . . old time candy boilin's, we'd take this sugar an' put it in the pot an' put vinegar in thar an' water an' cook it . . . then we'd go to pullin' this candy . . . an' then we'd break it up in sticks. **1982** Ginns *Snowbird Gravy* 147 **nwNC** (as of 1930s), We'd have a candy stew—we called it a candy stew—or we'd have a corn shucking or some event, such as grinding molasses, to get together. At the candy stew, we'd make up a bunch of chocolate candy, [sic] Milk, chocolate, sugar. [sic] what have you. Everybody would get around and tell tales, play games.

candystick n [So called because its bright stripes resemble those of stick candy]
  1 =**coral snake 1a.**
  1894 U.S. Natl. Museum *Proc.* 17.334, The only species of Elaps I have found in south Florida . . . is known . . as . . "candy-stick."
  2 also *stick candy:* =**sugarstick. Pacific NW**
  1934 Haskin *Wild Flowers Pacific Coast* 245, One of the most showy of the saprophytes found growing in our deep forests is . . stick candy . . . [which] resembles nothing so much as a brightly striped stick of candy. **1973** Hitchcock–Cronquist *Flora Pacific NW* 341, *Allotropa* . . Candystick; Sugarstick.

candy sticker n [Prob folk-etym for *Canada* + *sticker* prickly plant]
  Prob =**Canada thistle.**
  1968 *DARE* (Qu. S21, . . *Weeds . . that are a trouble in gardens and fields*) Inf **MD20,** Candy sticker—smaller stalk, narrower leaf than bull thistle, has only one bloom on top.

candy wagon n **Pacific NW** Cf **crummy** n **2**
  See quots.
  1942 Berrey–Van den Bark *Amer. Slang* 766.6, Candy wagon, puddle jumper, *a light truck.* **1958** McCulloch *Woods Words* 28 **Pacific NW,** *Candy wagon*—a. A camp commissary. b. A crew truck. **1959** *AmSp* 34.77 **nCA,** *Candy wagon* . . . A station wagon or bus that transports men to and from work in the woods. *Crummie* . . is the more popular word. **1970** *DARE* Tape **CA201,** The men that were working . . on the railroad bed . . [would] have . . the candywagon. They'd take food out to them . . and serve it to them on the job instead of . . bringing them in.

candyweed n

1 =**milkwort** (here: *Polygala* spp, esp *Polygala lutea*). [From the mint-like flavor of the root]
1933 Small *Manual SE Flora* 768, *Polygala* . . . Candyweeds. Polygalas. Ibid 774, *P. lutea* . . . Bog Bachelor's-button. Candyweed. Wild Bachelor's-button. **1949** Moldenke *Amer. Wild Flowers* 51, In pinebarren swamps, pinelands, and sandy bogs on the coastal plain from Long Island to Florida and Louisiana one may commonly find the spectacularly beautiful . . *candyweed*. **1975** Duncan–Foote *Wildflowers SE* 90, *Candyweed* . . . Common. Wet pinelands and savannahs, bogs.

2 =**horehound.**
1951 *PADS* 15.40 **TX,** *Marrubium vulgare* . . . Candy, cough, or croup, weed. Still made into candy or syrups, with sorghum or sugar, for dosing youngsters with throat ailments.

cane ash n [See quot 1897]

=**white ash** (here: *Fraxinus americana*).
1897 Sudworth *Arborescent Flora* 327, *Fraxinus americana* . . . Cane Ash (Ala., Miss., La.) . . . So called from its growing in cane-brakes of the forest. **1926** U.S. Dept. Ag. *Misc. Circular* 66.35, The most common alternative name for white ash is cane ash. **1971** Krochmal *Appalachia Med. Plants* 124, Cane ash . . . grows to 120 feet in height.

cane beer n Also *cane skimmings* Cf **beer**

A fermented beverage made from the skimmings of boiling sugarcane syrup.
1938 Matschat *Suwannee R.* 135 **nFL, sGA,** Freeman was busy skimming the boiling syrup and putting it carefully to one side: cane beer, with a sweet-sour taste, would be made from the fermented skimmings and, later, would form excellent "buck" for a wildcat still. **1965–68** *DARE* (Qu. DD28b) Infs **AL39, GA5, LA6,** Cane beer; **FL17,** Cane skimmings; (Qu. DD25) Inf **GA26,** Cane skimmings; (Qu. DD31) Inf **FL35,** Cane skimmings. **1965** *DARE* Tape FL43, Whoever was operating the mill . . would take the foam off the top of the vats and dip it into a barrel . . . This foam would settle into a liquid and let it set for, oh say, nine, maybe ten days . . and it'd make a wine. It's quite tasty for a wine. It's a little bit sweet, but it's about 90 proof . . . A barrel of . . cane skimmins would usually last a year on the farm.

cane bird n

Prob the **yellow-breasted chat.**
1908 *DN* 3.296 **eAL, wGA,** *Cane-bird* . . . A yellow-breasted swamp bird.

canebrake See **brake** n² b

canebrake rattler n Also *canebrake (rattlesnake)* **Sth**

A subsp of the **timber rattlesnake** (here: *Crotalus horridus atricaudatus*). Also called **velvet-tail, seminole.**
1933 Ditmars *Reptiles World* 260 **Sth,** This variety lives along the coastal region and is called the Cane-Brake Rattlesnake. **1968–69** *DARE* (Qu. P25, . . *Kinds of snakes*) Infs **GA25, 84,** Canebrake rattler. **1968** *DARE* Tape GA35, This one here is a timber rattler, or seminole, or often called canebrake. **1972** GA Dept. Ag. *Farmers Market Bulletin* 24 May 1/3, Species of rattlesnakes found in Georgia are the Eastern diamond back, the timber rattler, the pigmy rattler, and the canebrake rattler . . . The *canebrake rattlesnake,* a very similar species, replaces the timber rattler along the coastal plains.

cane breaker, cane buck See **cane cutter**

cane cactus See **cane cholla**

cane chews n Cf **pummies**
1967 *DARE* File **neLA,** Cane chews—Dry pulp after juice is squeezed from [sugar] cane.

cane cholla n Also *cane cactus* [*cane* walking stick: see quot 1940] chiefly **Desert SW**

Any of var spp of **prickly pear.**
1909 Longyear *Rocky Mt. Wild Flower Studies* 51 *(DA),* The name 'Cane cactus' often applied to this plant is derived from the fact that canes are sometimes made from the old stems that have made a straight growth. **1912** U.S. Natl. Museum *Annual Rept. for 1911* 449, The cane cactus *(Opuntia arborescens)* bears hundreds of large red blossoms. **1937** U.S. Forest Serv. *Range Plant Hdbk.* B106, The round-stemmed species of *Opuntia* are known as chollas or cane cacti. **1940** AZ Univ. *Biol. Sci. Bulletin* 5.34, *Opuntia spinosior* . . . Cane cholla. Ibid 36, This species is the one most favored for making canes, since its main stems are long and straight. **1960** Vines *Trees SW* 774, *Walking-stick*

Cholla. *Opuntia imbricata* . . . It is also known as Cholla, Tree Cactus, Cane Cactus [etc]. **1967** *DARE* (Qu. S26e, . . *Other wildflowers*) Inf **CA4,** Cane cholla. **1973** *AZ Highways* 29, Other Chollas are not so spiny and less conspicuous, such as the Pencil Chollas and Cane Chollas.

cane, come out of the v phr
1906 *DN* 3.129 **nwAR,** *Cane* . . . Retirement, privacy, inactivity. "Come out of the cane and go to work."

canecutter n Also *cane breaker, ~ buck, ~ rabbit* **Sth**

=**swamp rabbit 1.**
1935 Pratt *Manual Animals* 351, *S[ylvilagus] aquaticus* . . . Swamp rabbit; cane-cutter. **1941** *Jrl. Mammalogy* 22.377 **MS,** Log sets took cottontail and swamp rabbits, the latter called "cane-cutters". **1965–70** *DARE* (Qu. P30, . . *Wild rabbits around here*) 14 Infs, **Sth,** Canecutter; MS89, Cane buck; MS16, Cane rabbit; GA89, Cane breaker. **1969** *DARE* Tape GA86, In the swamps you would have buck rabbits, which was a little larger rabbit—some people call 'em canecutters. **1982** Elman *Hunter's Field Guide* 370, The small, dark marsh rabbit . . and closely related but lighter and very large swamp rabbit, or cane-cutter . . , both range from Virginia to Florida and across the Gulf states into Texas.

caneel See **carnelian**

cane gall See **gall 1**

cane grass n

Any of var grasses or grass-like plants: see quots.
1827 (1934) Smith *Travels* 24 **West,** I determined to make a raft, and for this purpose cut a quantity of cain grass. Ibid 33, Cane grass candy. **1834** (1940) Ferris *Rocky Mts.* 222 **UT,** Our camp presented eight leathern lodges and two constructed of poles covered with cane grass. **1916** *Torreya* 16.237, *Spartina cynosuroides* . . . Cane grass, Cat I[slan]d, S.C. **1920** Ibid 20.18, *Potamogeton americanus* . . . Cane grass, Reelfoot Lake, Tenn. **1940** Gates *Flora KS* 135, *Phragmites communis berlandieri* . . . Reed, Canegrass. **1969–70** *DARE* (Qu. S8, . . *Wild grass*) Inf **KY28,** Cane grass; (Qu. S9) Inf **SC67,** Cane grass—like wire and joint grass.

canelian See **carnelian**

cane rabbit See **cane cutter**

Cane River mulatto n

A member of a mixed-blood group living near the Cane River in Natchitoches Parish, Louisiana.
1946 *Social Forces* 24.445 **LA,** The term "Red Bone" is derived from the French Os Rouge, for persons partly of Indian blood. Also called "Houmas" along the Coast and "Sabines" farther west. In Natchitoches are the "Cane River Mulattoes." **1947** *AmSp* 22.82, Cane River mulattoes. **1963** Berry *Almost White* 33, In Louisiana there are a people called "Cane River Mulattoes," the very sound of which throws them into a rage.

cane-seed-eater n [In ref to raising sorghum]

A Mormon.
1942 Whipple *Joshua* 164 **UT** (as of c1860), Though they call us soggum-lappers or cane-seed-eaters, we will yet show them!

cane skimmings See **cane beer**

cane snake n

Perh a **milk snake 1** (here: *Lampropeltis triangulum*), but cf **canebrake rattler.**
1967 *DARE* (Qu. P25) Inf **AL32,** Cane snake.

cane turtle n
1968 *DARE* FW Addit **seLA,** Cane turtle—does not have a hard-hard shell, but harder than that of the soft shell turtle. It has striped neck and legs.

can-i-can See **cannikin 2**

canick See **kinick**

caniddling pie n
1968 *DARE* (Qu. NN12b, *Things that people say to put off a child when he asks, "What are you making?"*) Inf **PA113,** Caniddling pie.

cank v [Cf *EDD* cank sb.² "A fit of ill-humour," *canky* adj "cross, peevish"]

See quots.
1944 *PADS* 2.41 **wNC,** *Cank* . . . To annoy, to fret, to overcome. **1952**

Brown *NC Folkl.* 1.525, *Cank* . . . To annoy. "That's been canking Bill's heart for years."

canker n

1899 (1912) Green *VA Folk-Speech* 105, *Canker* . . . Verdigris, formed on the surface of dirty brass candlesticks.

canker v

1 See quot.

1899 (1912) Green *VA Folk-Speech* 105, *Canker* . . . To corrode; to rust.

2 To begin to decay, to spoil; hence adj *cankered.*

1953 Randolph *Down in Holler* 232 **Ozarks,** *Canker* . . . To become tainted, to decay. A fowl which has hung too long is said to be *high* or *cankered.*

canker bird n [See quots]

=**cedar waxwing.**

1878 *Forest & Stream* 10.319, A correspondent, . . of Taunton, Mass., . . sends us a list of fifty-seven species . . all of them being mentioned by their local names, . . . as moaning dove, chuweet, . . and canker bird (cedar bird). The last named, so called from its supposed habit of destroying great numbers of canker worms. **1917** *Wilson Bulletin* 29.2.84, *Bombycilla cedrorum* . . . Canker-bird, from its habit of feeding on canker worms, Taunton, Mass. **1956** *MA Audubon Soc. Bulletin* 40.129, *Cedar Waxwing* . . . Canker Bird (Mass. As feeding on cankerworms.).

canker lettuce n [See quots 1895, 1916]

A **wintergreen 1** (here: *Pyrola rotundifolia*).

1889 *Century Dict.* 4875/3, *P. rotundifolia*, the larger wintergreen, . . has been called *Indian lettuce* and *canker-lettuce.* **1895** *DN* 1.385 **wMA,** *Canker lettuce:* the plant *Pyrola rotundifolia;* said to be a cure for "canker." **1916** Parsons *Wild Flowers CA* 104, This is called . . "canker lettuce," and a tincture of the fresh plant is used in medicine for the same purposes as chimaphila. **1959** Carleton *Index Herb. Plants* 23, *Canker lettuce:* Pyrola americana.

cankerous adj [Cf Scots, Engl dial *cankered* cross, querulous, ill-natured]

1969 *DARE* (Qu. GG14, . . *Someone who fusses or worries a lot, especially about little things*) Inf **KY21,** Cankerous.

canker rash n Also by metanalysis *canker ash* **chiefly NEast old-fash**

Usu scarlet fever.

1803 *Med. Repository* 341 *(DA),* A bilious malignant fever made its appearance, and continued till August, when the cholera and canker-rash commenced, and continued throughout the year. **1828** Webster *Amer. Dict., Scarlatina* . . . The scarlet fever; called in popular language, the *canker rash.* **1862** *Harper's Mag.* 25.138/1 **ME,** Here lies . . William . . who, after nine days' violent seizure of a canker rash, calmly resigned his infant life to the King of Terrors, June 17, 1787. **1889** *Century Dict.* 791, *Canker-rash* . . a variety of scarlet fever complicated with ulcerations in the throat. **1932** Hanley *Disks* **seMA,** Oh, they [children] have the canker rash and mumps. **1962** Carrell *Autobiog.* 18 **MA** (as of 1880s), I had scarlet fever and canker rash, measles, mumps, chicken pox. **1968** *DARE* File **NY88,** Canker ash—old-fashioned for diphtheria.

cankerroot n

1 =**goldthread.**

1876 Hobbs *Bot. Hdbk.* 19, Canker root, Marsh rosemary, Statice Caroliniana. Canker root, Goldthread, Coptis trifolia. Canker root, Canker weed, Prenanthes alba. **1929** *Torreya* 29.150, Coptis trifolia, "*Canker-root*" was used for children and adults with canker-sores or facial eruptions. **1961** Smith *MI Wildflowers* 139, Goldthread, Canker-root. Coptis groenlandica . . . A decoction of the rootstocks [was used] for treating sore gums and for lessening the pain of teething. **1974** (1977) Coon *Useful Plants* 220, Gold-thread . . cancer-root . . . Medicinal qualities are well known . . . Used as a tincture it is valuable for ulcerations of the mouth. A New York State mother has written me that it is very valuable for "baby's sore mouth."

2 =**sea lavender** (here: usu *Limonium carolinianum*).

1876 [see **1** above]. **1910** Graves *Flowering Plants* 314 **CT,** *Limonium carolinianum* . . . Sea Lavender . . Canker-root . . . The root has long been used in medicine. **1933** Small *Manual SE Flora* 1021, *Limonium* . . . Sea-lavenders. Marsh-rosemarys. Canker-roots. **1959** Carleton *Index Herb. Plants* 23, *Canker root:* Limonium carolinianum.

3 A **rattlesnake root** (here: *Prenanthes alba*). Cf **cankerweed**

1876 [see **1** above].

4 A **cancerwort** (here: *Kickxia elatine*). Cf **cancerroot 2**

1900 Lyons *Plant Names* 144, Sharp-pointed Fluellin . . Canker-root. **1933** Small *Manual SE Flora* 1209, *K[ickxia] Elatine* . . . Canker-root. **1950** Gray-Fernald *Manual of Botany* 1265, *K. Elatine* . . . Canker-root.

cankerweed n

A **rattlesnake root** (here: *Prenanthes* spp, esp *P. alba*).

1874 *Shaker Med. Preparations,* Canker weed . . . Nabalus Albus. **1876** Hobbs *Bot. Hdbk.* 19, Canker root, Canker weed, Prenanthes alba. **1900** Lyons *Plant Names* 256, *N[abalus] albus* . . . Rattlesnake-root, . . Cancer-weed, White Canker-weed, Lion's-foot . . . *N. serpentarius* . . . Canker-weed. **1974** (1977) Coon *Useful Plants* 115, *Prenanthes alba* . . cankerweed . . . It is found in the woods from East to the Midwest.

cankery adj [**canker** n]

Rusty.

1828 Webster *Amer. Dict., Cankery* . . . Rusty. **1899** (1912) Green *VA Folk-Speech* 105, *Cankery* . . . Corroded; rusty.

cankywampus See **catawampus** adj

can'le See **candle**

Cannacker See **Canuck**

canna pail See **cannikin 1**

canned adj Also *canned up* Cf **crocked, fried**

1967–68 *DARE* (Qu. DD14, *When a person is partly drunk, "He's _____.")* Inf **WI17,** Canned; **NY68,** Half-canned; **WI77,** Canned up; (Qu. DD15, *A person who is thoroughly drunk*) Infs **NJ3, NY68, PA161,** Canned; (Qu. N13) Inf **WI77,** Canned-up driver.

cannibal bug n

=**assassin bug.**

1901 Howard *Insect Book* 293, *Assassin Bugs* . . . All are predatory in their habits and . . . some . . are known as "cannibal bugs".

cannibal trout n

Perh a **cutthroat trout.**

1969 *DARE* (Qu. P1) Inf **CA147,** Cannibal trout.

cannikin n [*OED* 1570 →; cf *mannikin, pannikin*]

1 also *cannikin tub, canna pail, canny pail, can pail:* A wooden storage container for sugar, flour, etc. **seNEng**

1904 *DN* 2.426 **Cape Cod MA,** *Harness head tub* . . . A wooden firkin-shaped pail with wooden handle and close fitting cover, used for sugar, crackers, etc. In some parts of the country it is called a *canny pail* or *can pail.* **1916** Macy-Hussey *Nantucket Scrap Basket* 126, *Cannikin Tub*—A wooden pail, with straight sides, hooped and with a close-fitting wooden cover. The term is an old one, but though in constant use today by Nantucketers, most off-islanders are puzzled by it. **1918** *DN* 5.15 **Martha's Vineyard MA,** *Cannikin* . . . A wooden pail or bucket, with wooden bail, used for flour, sugar, etc. Also cannapail. **1931–33** *LANE Worksheets* **RI,** Canna pail—container for flour and sugar; Can pail—wooden bucket for sugar ("Mother's term"); Can pail—wooden container with bail and cover used for sugar: holds twenty pounds.

2 pronc-spp *can-i-can, candy can:* A children's game: see quots. Cf *kick the can*

1968 *DARE* (Qu. EE18, *Games in which the players set up a stone, a tin can or something similar, and then try to knock it down*) Inf **NJ39,** Can-i-can ['kænikæn], **NJ21,** Candy can; (Qu. EE27, *Games played on the ice*) Inf **NJ39,** ['kænikæn]. [**1969** Opie *Children's Games* 166, 'Tin Can Tommy', which is the basic name in London, is widely distributed . . . 'Kick the Can', the usual name in Scotland and the Isles, is also not uncommon in Dublin, Liverpool, Manchester, and much of Wales. Other names: . . 'Can Can' (Tetchill).]

cannon n Also *cannon cracker*

A large firecracker.

1871 Bagg *4 Years at Yale* 297, A party of carousers insist upon . . firing off cannon-crackers in the entries. **1937** Sandoz *Slogum* 231 **NE** (as of 1900–20), The young American flipped a lighted cannon cracker towards her, and she picked it up and threw it back. **1950** *WELS (Firecrackers)* 3 Infs, **WI,** Cannon; 11 Infs, Cannon crackers. **1954** Harder *Coll.* **cwTN,** Cannon—firecracker. **c1960** Wilson *Coll.* **csKY,** Cannons: Child name for large firecrackers. Also *cannon crackers.*

1965–70 *DARE* (Qu. FF14, . . *Different kinds of firecrackers*) 129 Infs, **scattered,** Cannon crackers; 14 Infs, **scattered,** Cannons. [Of all Infs responding to the question, 64% were old; of those giving these responses, 85% were old.] **1967** Borland *Hill Country* 212 **NE,** After the anvil was shot, the big firecrackers, giant crackers or cannon crackers, were set off.

cannonball n, also attrib **chiefly Missip Valley** See Map Cf **fast train, flier 1**

A fast or express train; facetiously, a slow train or branch railroad.

1888 *Chicago Weekly Inter-ocean* 3 Jan 1/5 *(DAE),* The north and south bound cannon-ball trains on the Cincinnati Southern Railroad collided to-day. **1906** *DN* 3.129 **nwAR,** *Cannonball* . . . A fast through train . . . "The happy couple left on the cannonball for St. Louis." . . "They call the cannonball on this road the Arkansas Traveller." **1913** *Jrl. Amer. Folkl.* 26.172, *Cannon-ball* . . . A humorous name for the slow trains of the South. **1927** *DN* 5.441, *Cannon ball* . . . A fast freight, running on a limited schedule. **1953** Botkin *Treas. Railroad Folkl.* 463, *Cannonball Blues* . . . Catch a train they call the Cannonball / From Buffalo to Washington. **c1960** *Wilson Coll.* **csKY,** *Cannonball:* A name for a former fast, through train. **1962** Faulkner *Reivers* 198, The train, the engine passing us in hissing thunder, sparks flying from the brake shoes; it was the long one, the big one, the cannonball, the Special. *Ibid* 199, The train—it was the Special for Washington and New York, the cannonball wafting the rich women in diamonds and the men with dollar cigars in suave and insulate transmigration across the earth. **1965–70** *DARE* (Qu. N35, *A fast train that goes from one big city to another without stopping at all the stations*) 30 Infs, **chiefly Missip Valley,** Cannonball; **IN**1, Wabash cannonball; (Qu. N37, *Joking names for a branch railroad that is not very important or gives poor service*) Inf **CA**17, Cannonball; **WA**18, Cannonball Limited.

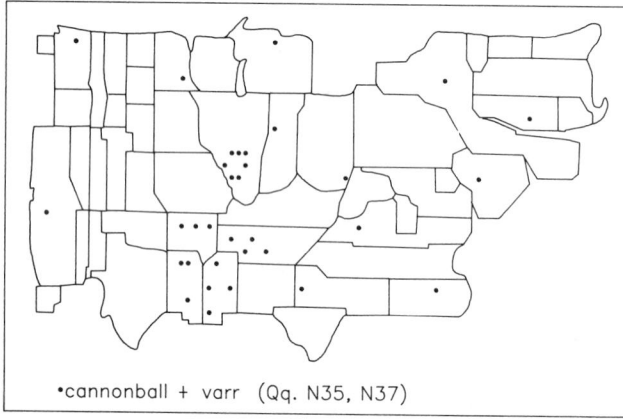

•cannonball + varr (Qq. N35, N37)

cannon cracker See **cannon**

canny pail See **cannikin 1**

canoe n Cf **canal boat**

1968–69 *DARE* (Qu. X38, *Joking names for unusually big or clumsy feet*) Infs **MI**103, **WI**57, Canoes.

canoe v [Cf **canoodle v**]

See quot 1960.

1954 Armstrong *Satchmo* 154 **New Orleans LA,** Her old man had been hearing about me and Daisy canoeing from the first night we'd got together. **1960** Wentworth–Flexner *Slang* 87, *Canoe* . . . To have sexual intercourse; to kiss and caress, esp. intimately; to neck.

canoe birch n [From the use of the bark in making canoes] =**paper birch.**

1810 Michaux *Arbres* 1.25 *(DAE),* Canoe birch *(Bouleau à canot.)* **1814** Pursh *Flora Americae* 2.621, A large tree, highly useful to the natives for constructing their large portable canoes, from which circumstance it is known by the name of *Canoe Birch.* **1897** Sudworth *Arborescent Flora* 140, *Betula papyrifera . . . Common Names* . . . Canoe Birch (Me., Vt., N.H., R.I., Mass., N.Y., Pa., Wis., Mich., Minn., Ont.). **1961** Douglas *My Wilderness* 110 **nMN,** Behind it were a few paper (canoe) birch and a thick stand of black spruce towering eighty or a hundred feet.

canoe-chief n

An Indian.

1935 Davis *Honey* 175 **OR,** I've seen a big old canoe-chief named Spillets or something like that swaller five full-size bottles of Dr. Turnbull's Prescriptions for Expectant Mothers as fast as he could git the corks pulled.

canoewood n Also *canoe tree, canoewood tree* =**tulip tree.**

1762 Gronovius *Flora Virginica* 83 **VA,** *Polyandria . . . Polygynia. Liriodendrun* [sic] . . . White-wood & Canoe-wood-tree nostratibus. **1860** Curtis *Cat. Plants NC* 77, Tulip Tree . . . (Liriodendron Tulipifera . .) . . In some of the Northern States it is called . . *Canoe Wood.* **1900** Lyons *Plant Names* 227, Canoe-wood. **1952** Taylor *Plants Colonial Days* 89, Tulip tree . . Delaware Swedes called it "Canoe tree." **1960** Vines *Trees SW* 280, Canoe Wood.

canol See **canal A**

cañon See **canyon**

can on the rock n Cf **duck on a rock**

c1960 *Wilson Coll.* **csKY,** *Can on the Rock:* A children's game, same as Duck on the Rock.

cañon wren See **canyon wren**

canoodle v, hence n *canoodler,* vbl n *canoodling* Also sp *conoodle, kidoodle* [Perh *ca-* var of **ker-** + *noodle* to act the fool] To fondle, caress; to "spoon."

1859 Sala *Twice Round* 112, [In front of a camera] Jenny arranges Jemmy's hair, and gives the moustache a twist, and there is a sly kiss, and a squeeze, and a pressure of the foot or so, and a variety of harmless endearing blandishments, known to our American cousins (who are great adepts at sweet-hearting) under the generic name of "conoodling." **1891** Farmer–Henley *Slang* 27, *Canoodle* . . . To fondle; bill and coo; indulge in endearments . . . [There are two suggested derivations: (1) from *cannie* . . 'gentle,' and (2) that the primary signification may have been "to act as a noodle," *i.e.,* to play the fool.] For synonyms . . *firkytoodle.* **1942** Berrey–Van den Bark *Amer. Slang* 355.5, *Fondle; caress; pet* . . canoodle. *Ibid* 443, *Lovers; pairs of lovers.* 1 . . . canoodlers. **1946** in 1947 *AmSp* 22.76 **IN,** I knew there was somethin' goin' on between Klara an' Stephen Mandrake. I don't mean that they canoodled or anything, but you just kinda got to feel they had a big liking f'r one another. **1947** *AmSp* 22.76, He [a 75-year-old southern evangelist speaking in Boston] summed up "petting, or kidoodling, or whatever you want to call it," as, "a contact that inflames society." **1975** Gould *ME Lingo* 41, *Canoodlin'*—A Maine nicety for pleasurable dalliance atween the sexes, meaning mostly the casual kind—the kind in the *bushes* or behind the *chip pile.*

canoodle n[1] [**canoodle v**]

A dalliance, flirtation.

1976 De Vries *I Hear Amer.* 47 **IA,** Modesty was going, going, gone, and could chastity be far behind? Many's the canoodle she had seen get started in that climate, as the brittle dialogue snapped and crackled like a brush fire.

canoodle n[2] [*ca-* var of **ker-** + alter of *needle,* infl by **canoodle n[1]**]

1944 Coatsworth *Country Neighborhood* 178 **coastal ME,** Once a week the neighboring women met in one kitchen or another to knit together. They would establish a working rhythm by repeating, "Little canoodle, / Big canoodle, / Take out your canoodle, / Let me see your canoodle, / Compare your canoodle with mine." "Canoodle" apparently meant the knitting needle.

can pail See **cannikin 1**

can't See **can't see**

cant dog n **chiefly NEng**

A wooden lever, metal-spiked at the lower end, and with a hook hinged to the lower side, used in handling logs; a peavey.

1850 Judd *Richard Edney* 51, Silver seized the cant-dog, and aimed at the head-stock man. **1907** *DN* 3.242 **eME,** *Cant-dog* . . . A short, stout pole shod with an iron point and hook, used by river drivers. "You can get Orono cantdogs in Bangor." **1914** *DN* 4.69 **ME, nNH,** *Cant-dog, cant-hook* . . . Lumberman's log-rolling tool. **1966–68** *DARE* Tape **ME**19, Cant dog, . . four feet, four and a half feet . . had a dog on it, so they could roll 'em; **ME**26, Some people call 'em peavies, some call 'em cant dog; **NH**14, In the Sears and Roebuck book they call 'em a cant hook, but up around here they call 'em cant dog . . . a handle in it, a pick and a dog on it . . . a floating hook where you catch into the log. **1975** Gould *ME Lingo* 42, *Cant dog*— The *dog* is the hook that bites into a log on both the *canthook* and the *peavey*.

‡**cantering** adv [Blend of **catering** + **canting** set at an angle]
In a diagonal manner.
  1935 Smiley *Gloss. New Paltz* **seNY**, "We cut off down that way cantering." [It comes] from 'cant'—diagonally. He was speaking of wood-cutting on a side hill, meaning neither directly down the slope nor along it as a contour.

can't-hardlies n [Abbr for *can't hardly wait*]
A state of anxiety or impatience.
  1969 *DARE* (Qu. GG11, *To be quite anxious about something*) Inf **PA**199, Got the can't-hardlies.

can't-help-it n chiefly **S Atl** *joc*
1 pl: An imaginary disease or condition; also, delirium tremens. [Cf *EDD can* v II.2, *can't-help-it* "a violent disinclination for work, &c."]
  1966–70 *DARE* (Qu. BB28, *Joking names that people make up for imaginary diseases: "He must have the _____."*) Infs **GA**33, **KY**70, **NC**83, **SC**7, 19, 27, 70, **VA**30, Can't-help-its; (Qu. DD22, *. . Delirium tremens*) Inf **SC**19, Can't-help-its; (Qu. GG34a, *To feel depressed or in a gloomy mood . . "He has the _____ today."*) Inf **KY**70, Can't-help-its.
2 Menstruation.
  1954 *AmSp* 29.298 [Words for menstruation], *Can't help it.*

cantle boarding vbl n
See quots.
  1941 FWP *Guide WY* 460, *Cantle boarding*—riding loosely and hitting the cantle or back of saddle. **1961** Adams *Old-Time Cowhand* 108 **West**, Some cowhands had a way of ridin' loose and hittin' the cantle as the hoss traveled. This was called "Cantle-boardin'," but it wasn't the sign of a good rider.

cantrip n Also sp *cantrap* [Scots *cantrip, cantraip, cantrap* a charm; a spell; a trick]
A mischievous trick; a magic spell.
  1830 (1940) Ferris *Rocky Mts.* 24, Few [mules] exist but will strive to do you an injury by some infernal cantrap or other. **1939** (1962) Thompson *Body & Britches* 234 **NY**, His patrons preferred a tightrope artist who every night walked from Nelse's place, across the canal and to the top of a tree, pushing a wheelbarrow and at times (by some cantrip which I have not clearly in mind) frying an egg in transit. *Ibid* 417, Another cantrip of love is told in a ballad entitled *The Half-Hitch.*

can't see n Also *can't* Usu in phrr *from can't see to can't see, from can to can't,* and varr—see quots chiefly **Sth**
The darkness before sunrise and after sunset.
  1931 *Scribner's Mag.* 89.127/2 **FL**, "I got boys in the woods from can't to can't," Fatty said. **1937** in 1977 *Amer. Slave Suppl. 1* 1.90 **AL**, De mos' us did wuz wurk from 'can 'til can't. *Ibid* 1.413 **AL**, Most slaves worked on Satu'day jes like dey did on Monday; that was from kin' ter caught, or frum sun ter sun. **1941** Daniels *Tar Heels* 157 **NC**, In the South it was such labor from kin to can't which pushed some of the people to the towns. **1941** FWP *Guide CO* 226, Work begins at sunup and continues until after sundown, or, as the phrase is "from can see to can't see." **1942** Rawlings *Cross Creek* 240 **FL**, "I got boys in the woods from can't-see to can't-see," he said, "getting me squirrels for that pilau." **1943** Writers' Program NC *Bundle of Troubles* 5, Long 'bout cain't-see time. **1946** in 1958 Brewer *Dog Ghosts* 104 **TX** [Black], De nighttime done brung de cain't see to de lan'. **1947** Ballowe *The Lawd* 50 **LA**, After days and days of work from sun to sun, kin to cain't, the wheel was finished. **1950** *PADS* 14.18 **SC**, *Can't see.* **1968** *DARE* FW Addit **LA**39, Kin to can—sunup to sundown, said of a work day. **1969** *DARE* Tape **MA**58, From can see to can't see. **1975** Gould *ME Lingo* 154, *Kin to kaint*—From see to can't see; dawn to dusk.

can't-see-um n chiefly **Nth**
=**no-see-um.**
  1895 *DN* 1.385 **ME**, *Can't see 'em*: Indian name for midges. **1965–70** *DARE* (Qu. R10, *Very small flies that don't sting*) Infs **MN**7, **NH**4, Can't-see-um; (Qu. R11, *A very tiny fly . . that stings*) Infs **AZ**2, **MN**7, **NH**4, **NJ**43, **WA**1, Can't-see-um.

canty-wise adv [*canty* tipped, sloping + *-wise* in manner or state] Cf **catty-ways**
  1968 *DARE* (Qu. MM1, *Words meaning 'opposite to' . . "The shed is _____ the barn."*) Inf **GA**31, Canty-wise from.

Canuck n |kə'nʌk| Also sp *Canack, Cannacker, Canucker, Cunnuck, Kanu(c)k, Knuck, K'nuck* [Perh from CanFr *canaque*, from Haw *kanaka* man, through Northwest fur trade; see *AmSp* 53.176ff] chiefly **Nth**, esp **NEast** See Map *often considered derog* See also *DCan*
A Canadian; also, esp in the northeast, a French-Canadian.
  1835 Todd *Notes upon Canada* 92 *(DA)*, Jonathan distinguishes a Dutch or French Canadian, by the term Kanuk. **1846** Stewart *Altowan* 191 *(DAE)*, The Cannackers, as they were commonly called, set themselves quietly about reviving their fire. **1891** Farmer–Henley *Slang* 23, *Canack, Canuck, Kanuck, K'nuck, . .* A Canadian, usually a *K'nuck*. **1905** *DN* 3.7 **cCT**, *Cunnuck, Canuck* or *Knuck . . .* A Canadian. **1907** *DN* 3.183 **seNH**, *Canuck . . .* A French Canadian. *Ibid* 242 **eME**, *Canuck . . .* A French Canadian. **1926** *DN* 5.386 **ME**, *Canuck* (accent on second syl.). French-Canadian. obsol. **1930** Irwin *Amer. Tramp* 47, *Canuck.*— In the United States, any Canadian; properly, in Canada, a French-Canadian. **1939** Wolcott *Yankee Cook Book* 339 **NEng**, The ritual [of maple sugaring] begins . . . Father and the hired man and Uncle John and Allie from back of the mountain, the Coffin boys and Pops Talley and Jean, the Canuck, bore and hang, estimate the run, hazard weather predictions—there is no lack of willing hands during the sapping season. **1942** ME Univ. *Studies* 56.12, Canadian French were Canucks; South Sea islanders, especially Hawaiians, were kanakas, a name quite unrelated to Canuck. **1958** McCulloch *Woods Words* 29 **Pacific NW**, *Canucker*—A logger from north of the border. **1958** (1971) Kerouac *Subterraneans* 5, I am a Canuck, I could not speak English till I was 5 or 6, at 16 I spoke with a halting accent. **1959** *VT Hist.* new ser 27.129 **nVT**, Canuck . . . French Canadian. **1965–70** *DARE* (Qu. HH28) 165 Infs, chiefly **Nth**, esp **NEast**, Canuck; **MA**45, French Canuck; **CT**23, French-Canadian Canuck. **1968–70** *DARE* Tape CA 103, This lady . . is a Canuck. You know who a Canuck is? [FW:] No. [Inf:] A Canadian; **MI**121, Quite a few of the new settlers came from Ontario—Canadians—Canucks [kə'nʌks] we called 'em. **1969** *DARE* FW Addit **VT**, I can call myself a Canuck, but you'd better not call me one. **1975** Gould *ME Lingo* 42, *Canuck*—The word originated in Maine lumber camps for a French-Canadian working in the Maine woods. It did not mean a French-Canadian anywhere else, and when a British Columbia hockey team called itself the *Canucks* the word was far afield. Over the years, as *Canuck* took on an objectionable tone, the word has been superseded somewhat by *Kaybecker* . . . French-speaking Canadians from Québec were *Canucks*.

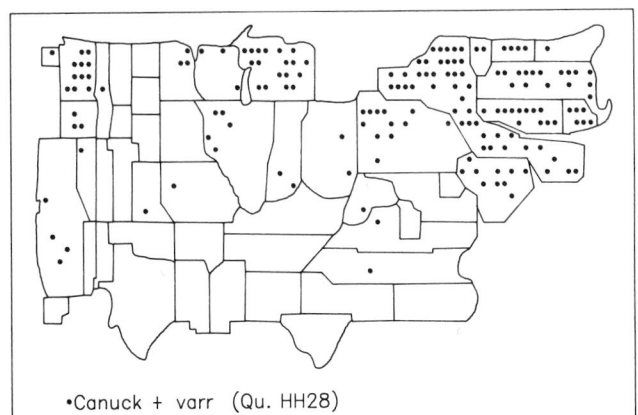

•Canuck + varr (Qu. HH28)

canvasback bluebill n
=**greater scaup.**
  1923 U.S. Dept. Ag. *Misc. Circular* 13.19, *Greater Scaup Duck . . . Vernacular Names . . . In local use . . .* canvasback bluebill (Wis.).

canvasback duck n
Std: a **scaup** (*Aythya valisineria*), largely white with black stippling. Also called **bullneck 1, gray duck, hickory-quaker, horse duck, redhead, redneck, sheldrake, whiteback**

canvasback grass n [?By assoc with the **canvasback duck**]
=**tape grass.**

1920 *Torreya* 20.18, *Vallisneria spiralis* . . Canvas-back grass, Chesapeake Bay, Md. **1941** *Ibid* 41.45, *Vallisneria spiralis* . . Canvasback grass.

cany See **cackany**

canyon n |'kænjən| Also sp *cañon, kanyon, kenyon* [Span *cañon;* see quot 1932] **chiefly West, scattered Nth** See Map
A deep valley with steep sides, with or without water flowing through it.

1839 (1973) Farnham *Travels Prairies* 1.267, About midway from the Great Gap and the Kenyon of the south Fork of the Platte. *Ibid* 1.268, This Kenyon terminates thirty miles above the Gulf. **1872** Twain *Roughing It* 100 **UT,** One could look below him upon a world of diminishing crags and canyons leading down . . to a . . plain. *Ibid* 105 **UT,** Echo Canyon is twenty miles long. It was like a long, smooth, narrow street, with a gradual descending grade, and shut in by enormous perpendicular walls of coarse conglomerate, four hundred feet high in many places, and turreted like mediaeval castles. **1892** *DN* 1.189 [Spanish and Mexican words used in Texas], *Cañon:* a deep gorge or mountain pass. This word may be said to be naturalized in English, which has shifted the accent to the first syllable. **1917** *DN* 4.347 **TX,** *Cañon.* **1932** Bentley *Spanish Terms* 144, *Cañon* is the augmentative of *caño* in Spanish and means therefore a large tube, funnel, or cane . . . The accent has been shifted from the last to the first syllable and the spelling alternates between *cañon* and *canyon.* **1958** *PADS* 30.9, [In the western parts of Nebraska and South Dakota] occur *gulch* and *canyon* for the short and deep valleys peculiar to the eroded hills along many streams. **1965–70** *DARE* (Qu. C15, *A place in mountains or high hills where you can get through without climbing over the top*) 19 Infs, **chiefly West,** Canyon; **NV7,** Canyon — very narrow, high rocks on both sides; (Qu. C19, *What do you call low land running between hills? [with and without water]*) 25 Infs, **chiefly West,** Canyon; **CA4,** Canyon — valley with steep sides, fairly narrow; **CA19,** Canyon — sometimes they have water; **CA177,** Canyon — gorged out, steep; **CA184,** 189, **TX10,** 68, 73, 80, 90, Canyon — steeper (than valley); **CA210,** Canyon — narrower, deeper than a valley; **ID1,** Canyon — steep sides along main river; **ID4,** Canyon — very narrow, impassable; **NM11,** Canyon — if narrow and steep-sided with and without water; **TX5,** Canyon — narrow with steep side[s]; **WA2,** Canyon — deeper than a valley; **WA12,** Canyon — if it's narrow; **WY2,** Canyon — narrow, along river; **WY4,** Canyon — narrower than valley; **WY5,** Canyon — deeper and narrower; (Qu. C21, *A deep place cut in sloping ground by running water*) 26 Infs, **chiefly West,** Canyon; **CA21** Canyon — very wide; **CA82,** Canyon — if large; **CA90,** Canyon — through a mountain; **CA105,** Canyon — if cut real deep; **IA11,** Small canyon; **MT3,** Canyon — larger than a gully, cut by a river; **NV1,** Canyon — very deep. **1983** *Milwaukee Jrl.* (WI) 7 July Accent sec 2/2, The flood [of the Colorado River], in which twice the amount of water rushed through the canyon, will have scoured salt and silt from the canyon's terraces, . . that will allow new growth to take root.

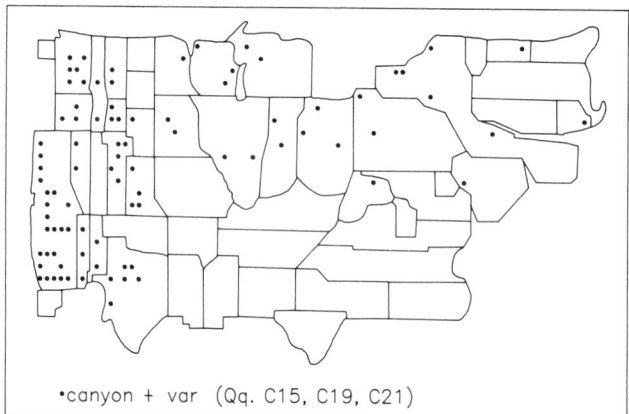

•canyon + var (Qq. C15, C19, C21)

canyon live oak See **canyon oak 1**

canyon maple n **CA**
=**big-leaf maple.**
1970 *DARE* (Qu. T14) Infs **CA**181, 190, Canyon maple; (Qu. T3) Inf **CA**181, Canyon maple — doesn't produce syrup or sugar. **1974** Munz *Flora S. CA* 54, *Acer macrophyllum* . . Canyon Maple.

canyon oak n

1 also *canyon live oak:* An oak tree (here: *Quercus chrysolepis*). **Pacific** Also called **maul oak**
1908 Sudworth *Forest Trees Pacific* 295, Canyon live oak is an evergreen oak, with the soft, scaly trunk bark of a white oak. **1961** Peck *Manual OR* 255, *Quercus chrysolepis* . . Canyon Oak. **1970** *DARE* (Qu. T10) Inf **CA**208, Golden cup — canyon live oak. **1974** Munz *Flora S. CA* 480, *Q[uercus] chrysolepis* . . Canyon Oak.

2 =**Lacey oak.**
1960 Vines *Trees SW* 160, *Lacey Oak — Quercus laceyi* . . Vernacular names are Rock Oak, Canyon Oak, [etc.]. **1979** Little *Checklist U.S. Trees* 232, *Quercus glaucoides . . Lacey oak* . . Other common names . . canyon oak.

canyon wren n Also *cañon* ~
A brown, white-throated wren *(Catherpes mexicanus).*
1878 U.S. Natl. Museum *Proc.* 1.402, *Catherpes Mexicanus,* [var.] *conspersus. — Cañon* Wren. **1928** Bailey *Birds NM* 545, *Canyon Wren: Cathérpes mexicánus.* **1961** Douglas *My Wilderness* 24 **cCO,** Canon wrens serenaded from spruce thickets.

caouane n |'kɑ,wen, -'wæn, -'wɑn, 'ko-| Also sp *caoaine, cawan, kawan* [AmFr *caouane* snapping turtle. Cf AmSpan *caguama* < Carib, and *DJE kaiwaama*] **chiefly LA**
=**alligator turtle 1.**
1884 Goode *Fisheries U.S.* 1.153, The southern species, *Macrochelys lacertina* . . . also occurs in Missouri, where it is said to receive the name 'Caouane.' **1917** *DN* 4.421 **LA,** *Kawan* [kɑweð] . . . A snapping turtle: used among negroes. Usually *tortue kawan.* **1931** Read *LA French* 136, *Caouane* . . . The name caouane is applied to the freshwater alligator snapping turtle . ., which ranges from western Texas to western Florida and as far north as Missouri . . . commonly known as a "loggerhead". **1968** *DARE* (Qu. P24, . . *Kinds of turtles . . around here*) Inf **LA**22, Caouane ['kɑ,weɪn] — a flat-backed, hard shell turtle, its color varies with environment; **LA**44 ['ko,wæn] — a good eating turtle. [FW: standard French *caouane* . . refers to the sea turtle called *loggerhead* in English. The turtle described here is a swamp creature — swamp or river.] **1968** *DARE* FW Addit **seLA,** Caouane [,ka'wæn], a snapping turtle. **1983** *Reinecke Coll.* **New Orleans LA,** *Caouaine* [ka'wɑn or ka'wæn] — turtle used in soup; sold under this name (cawan) in seafood stores in New Orleans. Esp. loggerhead or alligator snapping turtle.

caounty See **county**

caow See **cow**

cap n[1]

1 also *capper:* The top sheaf or bundle of a stack of grain or hay. See also **cap bundle, capsheaf** Cf **hudder, weather bundle**
1954 *Harder Coll.* **cwTN,** *Cap* — A pitchfork-full of hay placed on top of a stack of hay. **c1960** *Wilson Coll.* **csKY,** *Cap* or *cap sheaf* — The bundle or bundles of grain turned bottom upwards on a shock to protect the shocked bundles from getting wet. **1965–70** *DARE* (Qu. L31) 386 Infs, **widespread,** Cap; **IL**104, **KY**53, **NJ**20, **OH**47, **PA**1, **WA**18, Capper.

2a also attrib: The removable circular metal lid of a wood-burning stove. **chiefly S Midl, Sth** See Map and Map Section Cf **damper, eye** n[1] **1, griddle** n

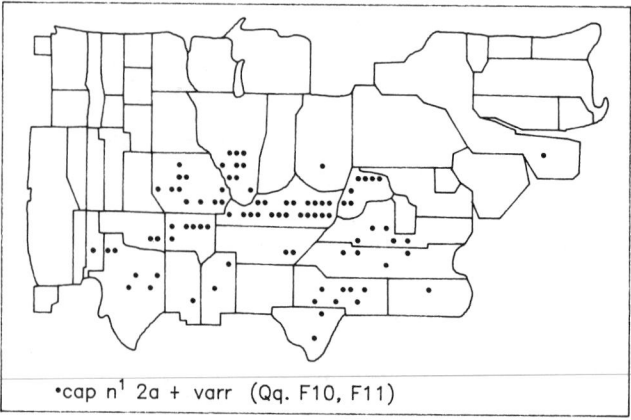

•cap n[1] 2a + varr (Qq. F10, F11)

1905 *DN* 3.73 **nwAR**, When you broil steak like the Yankees do, you take the caps off the stove and hold the meat right over the coals. **1921** *DN* 5.118 **KY**, *Crook* . . . A short, crooked instrument for lifting caps from a kitchen stove. **1950** Stuart *Hie Hunters* 51 **eKY**, Arn walked to the flat-topped cookstove, lifted the cap from the firebox with the cap-lifter. **1954** *Harder Coll.* **cwTN**, *Cap lifter*. **1965–70** *DARE* (Qu. F10) 56 Infs, **chiefly S Midl, Sth**, Cap; 21 Infs, **chiefly S Midl**, Stove cap; (Qu. F11, *The thing you use to remove the lids . . from a wood-burning stove*) 49 Infs, **chiefly S Midl**, Cap lifter; **IL**85, 86, Stove-cap lifter; **KY**8, Cap holder; **GA**8, Cap key, cap wrench. **1977** *Foxfire 4* 128 **nGA**, It's an iron stove up on four legs—a little flat feller. They's two caps . . down here, and then it raises up a little and they's two caps up here.

‡b By ext: see quot.

1969 *DARE* FW Addit **KY**5, The Informant calls the burners of her electric stove *caps*.

3 also *capping,* also attrib: The strip of wood or metal that covers the ridge of a roof. **chiefly Midl**

1965–70 *DARE* (Qu. D30) 11 Infs, **chiefly Midl**, Cap; **MD**39, **MA**37, **NC**67, **VA**47, Capping; **NC**8, Cap of the roof; **AL**41, Cap strip; **KY**83, Crown cap; **NY**172, Drip cap; **MN**2, Roof cap; **KY**52, Roof capping.

4 A movable box set on top of a beehive for the storage of honey; a **super**.

1970 *DARE* Tape **KY**85, The cap [is] a box of honeycombs set on top of a bee-gum. The honey made in the cap is taken from the bees.

5 also *capping:* The green leaves at the top of a berry, usu a strawberry. **chiefly Sth, S Midl** See Map Cf **burr, hull**

1905 *DN* 3.73 **nwAR**, These strawberries have large caps. **1931–33** *LANE Worksheets* **sRI**, *Cap*—Hull of a strawberry. **1950** *WELS* (*The green top that pulls off with the stem of a ripe strawberry*) 1 Inf, **cwWI**, Cap. **1954** *Harder Coll.* **cwTN**. **c1960** *Wilson Coll.* **csKY**, *Cap*—The green part that pulls off the vine with the berry (strawberry, usually). **1965–70** *DARE* (Qu. I47) 210 Infs, **chiefly Sth, S Midl**, Cap; **AR**51, Capping.

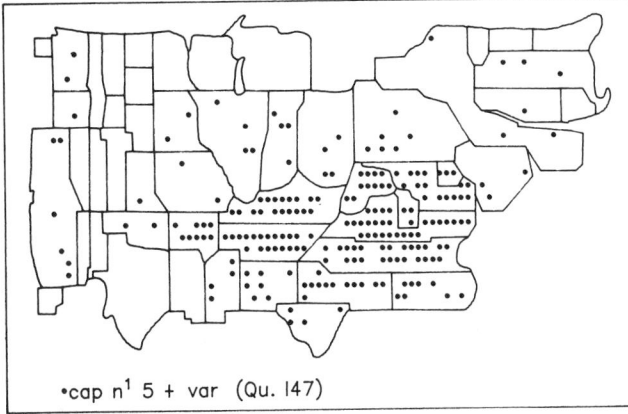

•cap n¹ 5 + var (Qu. I47)

6 freq in phrr *in cap, into cap:* In mining: the narrowing or termination of an ore vein; the state in which veins have contracted or terminated; the contracted vein. **chiefly West, esp CO**

1872 U.S. Treas. Dept. *Mines* 313, The "cap," a term usually employed to express the impoverished condition of the vein, may be due either to the pinching together of the walls of the fissure, or . . to the filling of the vein with barren rock. **1876** Fossett *Colorado* 177, To use common phrases they "widen out" at one point or "pinch up" at another—disclose a "pocket, ore chimney or bonanza," or "go into cap." **1931** Willison *Here They Dug* 122 **CO**, Most of the hard-rock mines are in cap. **1945** *CA Folkl. Qrly.* 4.322 **CO**, In cap: Vein has pinched out. **1968** Adams *Western Words*, *Cap*—In mining, a narrow or pinched place in a vein of ore. A change from paying to barren ground. A barren section in the *gangue*.

7 also attrib: In moonshining:

a See quots.

1949 *AmSp* 24.8 **KY**, *Cap* . . . The metal *still cap* placed over the opening on top of the still to start vapor through the *connections* to the *condenser*. 'You put the cap on and I'll put the paste to her.' **1972** *Foxfire Book* 315 **nGA**, *Cap*—the top third of the still. It is removable so that the still can be filled with a run. *Cap Arm*—the copper pipe connecting the cap with the next section of the still.

b See quot 1949.

1933 Rawlings *South Moon* 91 **FL**, Hit ain't made a cap yit and hit's 'most due to run. **1949** *AmSp* 24.8 **KY**, *Cap* . . . The meal formation of the top of the vat of fermenting beer [=mash]; this finally clears away, settling through the beer. 'It ain't ready to run. The cap ain't broke.'

8 The husk of an ear of corn. Cf **shuck, husk**

1949 Kurath *Word Geog.* 40 **MD**, On the Eastern Shore we find the local term *caps* between the Chester River and the Nanticoke, separating the Midland *husks* from the Southern *shucks*.

9 A kernel of popcorn. [**cap v 5**] Cf **capper 3**

1946 *AmSp* 21.270 **neKY**, *Caps* . . . Popcorn. 'A poke o' caps.'

10 A protective piece fastened on the toe of a shoe. Cf **brad n² 1**

1899 (1912) Green *VA Folk-Speech*, *Cap* . . . A piece of leather put on the toe of a shoe. **1965–70** *DARE* (Qu. W12b, *Metal pieces under the tips of shoes to prevent wear*) 84 Infs, **widespread exc in Nth**, Caps; 10 Infs, **scattered**, Toe caps; **MO**18, Half-caps.

11 A whitecap. [**Abbr**] Cf **cap v 6**

1970 *DARE* (Qu. O15, . . *Kinds of waves*) Infs **SC**66, 69, Cap. [Both Infs Black]

12 also *fence-cap:* See quot. Cf **cap-and-stake fence**

1917 *DN* 4.389 **Wrn Reserve OH, MA, VT**, *Cap, fence-cap* . . . A rectangular piece of wood c. two ft. x six in. x two in. with a large hole near each end. It is placed over the upper ends of two stakes in making a stake-and-rider fence, or sometimes a worm fence.

13 in phr *put a cap on (someone):* See quot.

1966 *DARE* (Qu. BB27, *When somebody pretends to be sick . . you'd say he's* ____) Inf **SC**10, "Putting a cap on somebody"—is fooling somebody (a dunce cap); (Qu. KK36, *Talking about a person who is easily fooled: "It's easy to* ____.') Inf **SC**10, Put the cap on him.

14 in phr *put the cap on the bottle:* To be the "last straw," to "take the cake."

1969 *DARE* (Qu. GG22b, *When you have come to the end of your patience, you might say, "Well, that certainly* ____.') Inf **NY**220, Puts the cap on the bottle.

cap v

1a To surpass, outdo, beat.

1848 Bartlett *Americanisms*, *To cap.* To excel; to surpass. Ex. *To cap all* . . . *To cap the climax*, is to surpass. **1899** (1912) Green *VA Folk-Speech*, *Cap* . . . To surpass. "He capped all." **1954** *Harder Coll.* **cwTN**, Don't that cap anything you ever did see? **1965–70** *DARE* (Qu. GG22b, *When you have come to the end of your patience, you might say, "Well, that certainly* ____.') Infs **KY**21, **MD**41, Caps it; **GA**1, **KY**46, Caps it off; **MA**6, Caps it all. **1970** Major *Afro–Amer. Slang*, *Capped:* (1940's–50's) to have outdone someone.

b in phrr *cap the climax* (or *vortex*): To exceed all expectations, usu in an unfavorable way; to be the "last straw."

1804 *Lancaster* (Pa.) *Intelligencer* 21 Feb (1912 Thornton), Your correspondent caps the climax of Misrepresentation. **1841** U.S. Congress *Congressional Globe* app 10.68/2 **PA**, Our government cowered before him, and this last act of submission has capped the climax. **1907** Porter *Heart of West* 55 **MT**, To-day he caps the vortex. **1965–70** *DARE* (Qu. GG22b, *When you have come to the end of your patience, you might say, "Well, that certainly* ____.') 10 Infs, **scattered**, Caps the climax.

c in phr *cap the stack:* =prec. [**cap n¹ 1**]

1859 Taliaferro *Fisher's R.* 23 **nwNC** (as of 1820s), Thith Famus business caps the stack and saves the grain. **1930** *DN* 6.80 **cSC**, *To cap the stack* . . . To cap the climax. **1967** *DARE* (Qu. GG22b) Inf **SC**34, Caps the stack.

d To outdo someone in a verbal exchange; hence vbl n *capping* the exchanging of ritualized insults. *esp among Black speakers* Cf **backcap** v

1946 (1972) Mezzrow *Really Blues* 331, *Cap:* have the last word, go one better, outdo. **1972** Labov *Lang. Inner City* 307, Exchanging ritualized insults . . . [is called] on the West Coast, such general terms as *cutting, capping,* or *chopping*. **1972** Claerbaut *Black Jargon* 60, *Capped* . . outdid; did better, often referring to a verbal exchange: *He capped you.* **1977** Smitherman *Talkin* 119, Some Black Semantic terms that are somewhat synonymous with signification are: dropping lugs; joanin; capping; sounding. *Ibid* 96, Noting that all black people were, in a sense, imprisoned, he capped: "That's what America means: prison." **1980** Folb *Runnin' Down* viii **Los Angeles CA** [Black], Some social activity—a jam session, a church meeting and social, a "capping" contest, a day's adventure of "low-riding" around the local high school.

2 See quot. [*Engl dial*]

1899 Green *VA Folk-Speech, Cap* . . . To puzzle. "That caps me."

3 Of a vein of ore: to narrow or terminate. [**cap** n[1] **6**]

1869 McClure *3000 Miles* 267 **Rocky Mts,** They know that [the lead] may cap or pinch, or play out entirely.

4 To take the hull off a strawberry. [**cap** n[1] **5**] **Sth, S Midl**

1895 *DN* 1.370 **eTN,** Hit's mighty slow, pickin' an' cappin' berries. **1905** *DN* 3.73 **nwAR,** *Cap* . . . To hull. 'I must cap these strawberries.' **1906** Pittman *Bells of Blue Grass C.* ix.129 *(DA),* Close beside her sat a great basket of fresh strawberries which must be capped before she could set out for church. **1908** *DN* 3.296 **eAL, wGA,** *Cap* . . . To hull (strawberries).

5 To pop corn. Cf **cap** n[1] **9, capper** n **3**

1936 Morehouse *Rain on Just* 197 **NC,** "Get the corn capping," soothed . . Drake. "Don't want a pooty fire for capping." He scattered a crowd at the fireplace still capping corn for the young uns. **1946** *AmSp* 21.270 **neKY,** *Cap* . . . To pop (corn).

6 Of waves: to form a crest, to break. [**cap** n[1] **11**]

1968 *DARE* (Qu. O15, . . *Different kinds of waves*) Inf **MD36,** It's capping—breakers, waves with white foam on top; **MD45,** Sea's a-capping—makes white-topped waves.

cap n[2] See **captain**

cap-and-ball layout n [*cap-and-ball* in ref to archaic firearms with percussion caps + *layout* establishment]

1944 Adams *Western Words, Cap-and-ball layout*—A cowboy's term for a shiftless and unprogressive ranch or outfit.

cap-and-stake fence n [**cap** n[1] **12** + *stake*] Cf *DS* L61, 62

A kind of **stake-and-rider fence.**

1832 (1930) W. Sewall *Diary* 144 **IL,** Commenced making cap and stake fence on my ditch, the other fence being insufficient to keep out hogs.

capberry n

A **thimbleberry** (here: prob *Rubus parviflorus*).

1917 Eaton *Green Trails* 79 *(DA),* The cap-berry was perhaps the most conspicuous, a large shrub with numerous blossoms, not unlike small white roses in appearance.

cap bundle n Also *capping* ~ esp **Midl** See Map

=**cap** n[1] **1.**

1965–70 *DARE* (Qu. L31, . . *Top bundle of a shock*) 25 Infs, Cap bundle; **KY43, WI42,** Capping bundle.

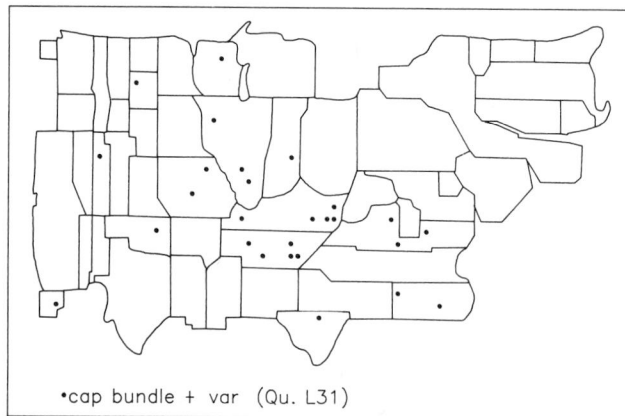

•cap bundle + var (Qu. L31)

‡**cap-buster** n [**cap** n[1] **11** + *buster* breaker]

1966 *DARE* (Qu. O12, *A disturbance caused by wind which seems to run and spread quickly along the surface of water*) Inf **AR5,** Cap-busters —big waves.

cap-cap n Pronc-sp *cop-cop* **LA**

1 =**green heron.** [See quot 1931]

1917 *DN* 4.424 **seLA,** *Cap-Cap.* The green heron (Butorides virescens). **1931** Read *LA French* 19, *Cap-Cap* . . . The Little Green Heron (*Butorides virescens virescens* L.); called thus because of the bird's hollow croak. **1968** *DARE* (Qu. Q8) Inf **LA31,** Cop-cop ['kap,kap].

1983 *Reinecke Coll.* New Orleans **LA,** *Copcop* ['kɑpkɑp]—little green heron, shitepoke. Used in Fr. of La. in imitation of bird's sound. Common in country.

2 Transf: see quots.

1967 LeCompte *Word Atlas* 258 **seLA,** *Cap-cap* "an illiterate Acadian of low social standing." **1968** *DARE* (Qu. HH28, . . *People of foreign background . . Creole*) Inf **LA46,** Cop-cops—cajuns. **1983** *Reinecke Coll.* New Orleans **LA,** *Copcop* . . . Also, metaphorically a backwoods cajun.

cape n [From the shape, resembling the article of clothing] In moonshining: see quot.

1972 *Foxfire Book* 315 **nGA,** *Cape*—the bulge in the main body of the still. It is the point of greatest circumference. *Ibid* 319, The sides of the furnace touched the still at only one point, and that was above the cape at the point where the sides of the furnace tapered in.

Cape Ann turkey n [*Cape Ann* a cape in northeastern Massachusetts] *joc*

=**Cape Cod turkey.**

1844 *Knickerbocker* 24.470, I had left a *real* gobbler at home, to come here and dine on a 'Cape-Ann turkey!' Of all articles tolerated . . I most abominate boiled salt fish. **1939** Berolzheimer *U.S. Cookbook* 72, *Salt Codfish* (Cape Ann Turkey).

cape bonnet n

A bonnet having a cape-like border on the bottom.

[**1799** Weld *Travels* 89 **VA,** There is a kind of bonnet very commonly worn, [in Va.] which, in particular, disfigures them amazingly; it is made with a caul, fitting close on the back part of the head, and a front stiffened with small pieces of cane, which projects nearly two feet from the head in a horizontal direction.] **1838** (1852) Gilman *S. Matron* 131 **SC,** I perceived . . a young girl . . dressed in homespun, with a *cracker,* or cape bonnet of the same material. **1896** Pool *In Buncombe County* 21 *(DA)* **NC,** A woman in a very deep cape bonnet, a bonnet which makes a face look as if it were at the far end of a cavern,—pushed her way up.

cape-brace See **cape-race**

Cape Cod clergyman n *joc ?obs*

A sculpin.

1848 Lowell *Biglow* 30 '**Upcountry**' **MA,** They might have been permitted, by way of mortification, to take some few sculpins (those banes of the salt water angler), . . known in the rude dialect of our mariners as *Cape Cod Clergymen.*

Cape Cod fence n

A picket fence; also *Cape Cod fencing,* materials to make such a fence.

1951 Johnson *Resp. to PADS 20* **DE,** *Cape Cod fence*—The kind of wood fence built around a garden or near a house. **1966** *DARE* (Qu. L64) Inf **ME24,** Cape Cod fence. **1968** *State* (Columbia SC) 2 May sec A 11, [*Advt, with picture of picket fence sections:*] Cape Cod Wood Fencing, 3 Ft. Sections, Painted White, Ideal For Lawn & Garden Borders.

Cape Cod measure n

1881 Greene *Cape Cod Folks* 24, We call it four miles, more or less. That's Cape Cod measure—means most anythin' lineal measure.

Cape Cod protection n *joc obs*

1844 *Lexington Observer* 27 Nov. 1/3 *(DA),* A raw boned yankee made his appearance with a knife and a pine stick in one hand, and a Cape Cod protection, alias a cake of gingerbread in the other.

Cape Cod stifle See **stifle**

Cape Cod turkey n **NEng** *joc* Cf **Albany beef, Arkansas chicken**

A codfish (dinner).

1865 in 1891 Farmer–Henley *Slang,* A salted cod fish is known in American ships as a Cape Cod turkey. **1901** (1961) Greenough–Kittredge *Words* 331, 'Welsh rabbit' is merely a joke, like 'Cape Cod *turkey*' for *codfish.* **1907** *DN* 3.183 **seNH,** *Cape Cod turkey* . . . A joke of the same order as Welsh rabbit and Arkansas Chicken (salt pork). **1909** *DN* 3.409 **neME.** **1939** Wolcott *Yankee Cook Book* 41, The origin of the name "Cape Cod turkey" is obscure. It has come to mean cooked fish; what kind doesn't matter unless you are literal. If you are, it means baked stuffed codfish well-larded with salt pork . . . Then, too, the Irish in and around Boston used the term "Cape Cod turkey" to refer to their Friday meal of fish. **1975** Gould *ME Lingo,* Cape Cod turkey—A salt fish dinner, usually cod-fish.

Cape Cord n Pronc-sp for *Cape Cod* See Pronc Intro 3.I.5.e

1939 Coffin *Capt. Abby* 98 **ME,** You will look fairly long for misspellings, save the natural Yankee ones. Capt. John spelled it Cape "Cord," as a Yankee should, to his dying day.

cape drake See **cape-race**

Cape Flyaway n

See quots.

1942 Berrey–Van den Bark *Amer. Slang* 790.5, Cape Flyaway, Dutchman's Cape, *a cloud on the horizon mistaken for land.* **1945** Colcord *Sea Language* **ME, Cape Cod, Long Island,** *Cape Flyaway.* A cloud-bank on the horizon having the appearance of land.

Cape Horn nut n

1941 *LANE* Map 277, 1 inf, **Martha's Vineyard MA,** Cape Horn nuts, larger than walnuts, with a thinner shell; 1 inf, **Nantucket Island MA,** Cape Horn nuts, old term, still natural.

Cape jasmine n Also *Cape jesmond, ~ jessamine;* pronc-sp *cake jesmus* **Sth**

A gardenia (here: *Gardenia jasminoides*).

1826 Flint *Recollections* 300 **New Orleans LA,** The houses are . . in the midst of orange groves and pretty gardens, in which are . . the delicious cape jessamine, a flowering shrub, . . and a great variety of vines. **1835** Ingraham *South-West* 1.243 **New Orleans LA,** The delicately leaved Cape-jasmine. **1929** (1951) Faulkner *Sartoris* 42 **MS,** She could look down upon Cape jasmine and syringa. **1934** Vines *Green Thicket* 83 **cnAL,** Old-time flowers decorated the yard and were mostly started by the girl's mother, and comprised crape myrtle bushes, old-fashioned lily bushes, cape jasmine. **1966–69** *DARE* (Qu. S17, . . *Plants . . that will cause itching and swelling*) Inf **SC24,** Some people break out from Cape jessamine; (Qu. S26c, *Wildflowers that grow in woods*) Inf **SC57,** Cape jessamine; (Qu. S26e, . . *Other wildflowers*) Inf **MS82,** Cake Jesmus ['kek jɛsməs]; (Qu. T5) Inf **NC18,** Cape jasmine; **GA80,** Cape jessamine. **1969** *DARE* FW Addit **ceNC,** Cape Jesmond—said to be old name for gardenias.

capelin n, also attrib Also sp *caplin(g)* Cf *DNE*

1 A small fish *(Mallotus villosus)* of the smelt family. [See quot 1939] Also called **lodde**

1824 *Salem Observer* 29 May *(DAE)* **MA,** In the capling season, the codfish are such epicures that they will not taste anything but capling. **1871** *Amer. Naturalist* 5.119 **nAtl,** The Capelin . . . is well known as a bait for cod-fish. **1879** *Scribner's Mth.* 19.18/2 **MI,** Grayling, wherever found, are spring spawners, as also are the smelt and the capelin. **1939** Natl. Geog. Soc. *Fishes* 29, The American capelin was so called because early French fishermen saw a resemblance to the European *capelan,* a small cod, but the American fish is classed as a smelt. **1946** Pease *Sequestered Vales* 93 *(DA),* Herring-like fishes called caplin [were] spread out in the dooryard to dry before being placed raw on the table as an appetizer. **1960** Amer. Fisheries Soc. *List Fishes* 12, Capelin . . . A[tlantic]-P[acific] . . . *Mallotus villosus.*

2 A silverside (here: *Menidia menidia*).

1884 Goode *Fisheries U.S.* 456, The Green Smelt of the Connecticut coast *Menidia notata* [is] also called . . . by the boys about Boston the 'Capelin.'

Cape May diamond n [*Cape May* a cape in southern New Jersey]

A piece of quartz worn smooth by water action, freq used in jewelry.

1846 *Dollar Newspaper* (Phila.) 12 Aug. 3/5 *(DA),* Occasionally a pure crystal of quartz, disfigured and despoiled of its natural beauty and proportions by the action of the waves, is found, and this is the famed Cape May diamond, so eagerly sought for, and so highly prized when found. **1866** Reid *After the War* 81, Others . . were dressed in broadcloth, with flashy scarfs and gaudy pins, containing paste, or Cape May diamonds. **1939** FWP *Guide NJ* 566, Many vacationists carry away geological souvenirs, the "Cape May diamonds" found on the beach. **1968** *DARE* Tape **NJ15A,** We have false teeth made out of Cape May diamonds [at the local museum]. **1969** *DARE* (Qu. C26) Inf **NJ59,** Cape May diamond—some rock that polishes up to look like [a] diamond.

Cape May goody n Also sp *Cape May goodie*

1 The fish commonly called **spot** (here: *Leiostomus xanthurus*).

1855 U.S. Natl. Museum *Annual Rept. for 1854* 329, The "Cape May Goody" of the Jersey coast, so called from its great abundance at Cape Island, is very rarely taken in winter. **1889** (1971) Farmer *Americanisms,* Cape May Goody.—The Lafayettefish. A popular name on the Jersey coast where Cape May is situated. **1911** *Century Dict.* 2575, *Goody*[2] . . . The spot or lafayette, a sciaenoid fish, *Liostomus* [sic] *xanthurus:* more fully, *Cape May goody.* **1935** *Old Salt* (Atlantic City) 9 Aug. 3/2 *(DA),* Years ago I used to catch a small pan fish known as the "Cape May goodie." Are they still around? . . Yes. It is the spotfish.

2 Transf: see quots.

1968 *DARE* (Qu. HH16, *Uncomplimentary words with no definite meaning—just used when you want to show that you don't think much of a person*) Inf **PA66,** Cape May goody. **1969** *DARE* FW Addit **Cape May Courthouse NJ,** Cape May goody—A fellow from the country wearing white ducks, sneakers, with fifty cents in his pocket—who goes on the Atlantic or Ocean City boardwalk.

cape merchant n *arch*

The head merchant in a store or warehouse.

1899 (1912) Green *VA Folk-Speech,* Cape-merchant . . . The man who had charge of the general store or magazine.

capen See **captain**

caper n, also attrib

=**marsh marigold** (here: *Caltha palustris*).

1896 *Jrl. Amer. Folkl.* 9.179 **ME,** *Caltha palustris* . . capers. **1900** Lyons *Plant Names* 77, C[altha] *palustris* . . Capers. **1966** *DARE* (Qu. S22, . . *The bright yellow flowers that bloom in clusters in marshes in early springtime*) Inf **ME7,** Capers—same as cowslips; caper greens are eaten as greens; (Qu. I28a) Inf **ME5,** Caper greens.

cape-race n Also *cabrace, cape-brace, cape drake, cape-racer, caybrace, scapegrace* [From its prevalence near *Cape Race* Newfoundland] **NEast**

=**red-throated loon.**

1835 Audubon *Ornith. Biog.* 3.24 *(DA),* In the neighborhood of Boston, and along the Bay of Fundy, They are best known by the names of 'Scape-grace' and 'Cape-racer.' **1875** *Fur Fin & Feather* 119, The smaller species of loon I have heard variously called the spike-bill, the cape-race, the touch-monk, the gun-greaser, the pegging-all [sic], etc. **1917** (1923) *Birds Amer.* 1.15, Red-throated Loon . . . Other Names . . Cape Race; Cape Racer; Scape-grace. **1927** Forbush *Birds MA* 1.28, Red-throated loon. *Other names:* . . cape drake; cape race; cape racer; scapegrace [etc]. **1951** *AmSp* 26.90 **NEast,** Early sailors called the red-throated loon *cape-race* (a name recorded from Newfoundland and Massachusetts), . . and the name has spread to all parts of the northeastern coast, at the same time undergoing considerable rationalization. *Cape-racer* (New Brunswick; Nova Scotia; Maine, Mass.) seems an inevitable derivative . . and *scapegrace* (. . Mass; N.Y.) . . . *cabrace* (Mass.) . . *cape-brace* (Mass.) . . *caybrace* (Mass.).

caper-cornered See **catercorner** adj, adv

caper juice n Cf *DS* DD21a, b

1889 (1971) Farmer *Americanisms,* Caper-Juice.—A slang term for whiskey. Say, fellers, let's take a leetle mo' uv the *Caper Juice* . . . *Portland Transcript,* February 29, 1888.

capful of wind n **NEng**

A light breeze.

1851 Longfellow *Golden Legend* 255, I was whistling to Saint Antonio / For a capful of wind to fill our sail. **1942** ME Univ. *Studies* 56.57, A *capful of wind* for a gust or flaw in light weather. **1945** Colcord *Sea Language* 206 **ME, Cape Cod, Long Island,** A capful o' wind is a nice little sailing breeze. **1975** Gould *ME Lingo,* Capful o' wind—A gentle sailing breeze, and thus one aspect of a pleasant day.

capish v |kə'piš| [It *capisci < capire* to understand] **Nth**

To understand, comprehend.

1965–70 *DARE* (Qu. NN5, *Other ways of saying "Do you understand?"*) Infs **CA166, CT29, IL98, MN2, NY146, PA134,** Capish; **IN35, IA31,** Capish—Italian; **MA75,** Capish—Italian, I guess. **1981** *DARE* File **Madison WI,** Capish [kə'piš]? [Heard in conversation]

capital n

1901 *DN* 2.137 **nNJ,** Capital . . . A game.

capizonia n [Prob alter of **cabezon**]

1968 *DARE* (Qu. P2) Inf **CA105,** Ocean bullhead = capizonia; fish off rocks for them.

caplin, capling See **capelin**

cap-log n

See quot 1962.

1903 Wasson *Cap'n Simeon's Store* 55 **ME** (as of c1850), From the cap-log of the sagging wharf dangled the frayed ends of the parted lines. **1962** *AmSp* 37.251, *Cap-log* . . . The uppermost horizontal log of a wharf.

cap'm, cap'n See **captain**

‡**capnip** n Pronc-sp for *catnip*

1968 *DARE* FW Addit neNY, ['kæp,nɪp] [is] often used by children to smoke in place of tobacco.

capnit fit See **catnip fit**

capon egg n *joc*

An imaginary item used to tease a greenhorn.

1967 *DARE* (Qu. HH14, *Ways of teasing a beginner . . for example, by sending him for a 'left-handed monkey wrench': "Go get me _____."*) Inf **WA22**, Capon eggs.

capoodle See **caboodle**

‡**capoot** n[1] [Prob var of **capush** or **capoodle**, perh infl by *kaput*] =**caboodle 1.**

1968 *DARE* (Qu. LL10, *A whole group of people: "They made too much noise, so he sent the whole _____ home."*) Inf **AK8**, The whole darn capoot [kə'pʊt].

capoot n[2] See **ker-**

caporal n Usu |,kæpə'ræl, ,kɑpə'rɑl| Also (by assoc with military rank) *corporal* [Span "chief"] **SW, esp TX**

A foreman on a ranch.

1892 *DN* 1.245 **TX**, *Caporál:* overseer, man who directs the work, but does not pay the laborers. **1913** (1979) Barnes *Western Grazing* 380, Expressions in common use among stockmen . . . [include] Caporal, . . . the foreman in charge of a sheep outfit. **1920** Hunter *Trail Drivers TX* 229, Billy Henson was our corporal, or boss. **1929** Dobie *Vaquero* 125, His *caporal* (straw boss), jealous and drunk, pointed a gun through the window . . and shot him dead. **1932** Bentley *Spanish Terms, Caporal* (*Spanish,* kɑːpoːˈrɑːl; *English,* kæpərǽl) The manager or assistant manager of a cattle ranch; a ranch boss; an overseer or person in charge. **1944** Adams *Western Words, Caporal* (cah-po-'rhal) — The boss, the manager or assistant manager of a ranch. **1967** *DARE* (Qu. HH43a, *The top person in charge of a group of workmen, the _____*) Inf **TX11**, [,kɔrpə'ræl]; **TX1**, El corporal.

capote See **chapote**

capper n

1 A person employed as a lure or decoy, as in gambling houses or at auctions; a shill. [**cap** v **1a**] **chiefly West**

1853 *Alta California* (S.F.) 25 Apr. 1/7 *(DA)*, Each shop has a glib-mouthed auctioneer and at least two cappers, puffers, or decoy-ducks. **1856** (1975) Taylor *Gold Digger's* 26 **CA**, There's the gambler has his cappers who are looking all about, / And when they can find a sucker they are sure to pan him out. **1941** FWP *Guide WY* 240, The streets were filled with Indians, gamblers, "cappers," saloon-keepers, merchants, miners, and mulewhackers. **1945** Thorp *Pardner* 37 **SW**, Professor Scott . . . sold patent medicines . . . He employed cappers, picked locally, who pretended to be members of the audience and walked up when volunteers were invited to take sample doses of his medicine. **1948** Bean *Yankee Auctioneer* 208 **CT**, It may be that some auctioneers do use cappers or shills to boost the price. **1951** Morgan *Skid Road* 174 **cwWA**, There were "cappers" located at convenient points who made a specialty of teaching high-school boys how to beat the game—instruction which, as these young men subsequently learned, was entirely misleading.

2 See **cap** n[1] **1.**

3 A utensil for popping corn over an open fire. [**cap** v **5**] Cf **cap** n[1] **9**

1939 *Atlantic Mth.* 164.533 **neKY**, Sister Nell finished poppin' the capper of corn . . . He watched Sister Nell shuffle another capper of popcorn over the fire.

capping n See **cap** n[1] **3, 5**

capping vbl n See **cap** v **1d**

capping bundle See **cap bundle**

caps and bells, play v phr [From the traditional foolscap]

To act like a prankster.

1969 *DARE* (Qu. GG32a, *To habitually play tricks or jokes on people: "He's always _____."*) Inf **OH89**, Playing caps and bells.

capsheaf n Also *capsheath, cap sheef, cap shief* [**cap** n[1] **1** + *sheaf*]

1 also attrib: =**cap** n[1] **1**; also fig. **chiefly N Cent** See Map Cf **cap bundle**

1782 in 1919 Baldwin *Life & Letters* 106 nNY, The whole was crown'd with a capshief of Albany politeness. **1899** (1912) Green *VA Folk-Speech, Cap-sheaf* . . . A sheaf of wheat or straw forming the top of the stack. **1957** Battaglia *Resp. to PADS 20* eShore MD, Capsheath. **1965–70** *DARE* (Qu. L31, . . *Top bundle of a shock*) 19 Infs, **chiefly N Cent,** Capsheaf; **IL114,** Capsheaf bundle.

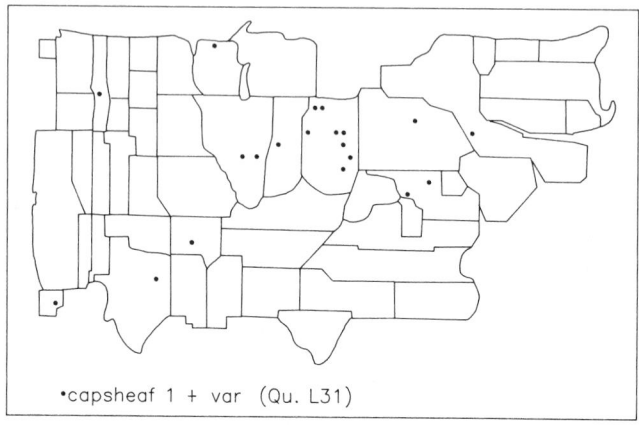

•capsheaf 1 + var (Qu. L31)

2 By ext: the crowning point, the extreme. **chiefly NEast** *arch*

1815 *Thomas' MA Spy or Worcester Gaz.* (MA) 31 May [3]/3, This is the crowner, the capsheaf. **1836** (1838) Haliburton *Clockmaker* (1st ser) 260 **NEng**, Look at our declaration of independence. It was writ by Jefferson, and he was the first man of the age . . . I calculate you couldn't falt it in no particular, it's generally allowed to be his cap shief. **1840** Kennedy *Quodlibet* 26 **MD**, The commissioners came this way and put the cap-sheaf on Michael's worldly fortune. **1851** (1976) Melville *Moby-Dick* 264, The placing of the cap-sheaf to all this blundering business was reserved for . . Cuvier. **1856** *Knickerbocker* 48.508 **NY**, Amelia . . has n't come out much . . and she the cap-sheaf of every body. **1856** Whitcher *Bedott Papers* 88 **cNY**, Of all the strains ever I heerd on I should think that was the cap sheef. **1865** (1868) Trowbridge *3 Scouts* 26 **TN**, If you ain't the capsheaf of all the complainin' women!

3 in phr *put on the capsheaf:* To be the "last straw," to "take the cake." Cf **cap** n[1] **14**

1871 (1882) Stowe *Fireside Stories* 185 **MA**, Ike's bull took the prize. That put the cap-sheaf on for Bill. He was jest about as much riled as a feller could be. **1968** *DARE* (Qu. GG22b, *When you have come to the end of your patience, you might say, "Well, that certainly _____."*) Inf **IN30**, Puts on the capsheaf.

capsicum n [*Capsicum* genus of perennial shrubby plants, incl peppers] Cf **dander**

Fig: anger.

1845 Kirkland *Western Clearings* 83 **MI**, Her husband, whose capsicum was completely roused, began pummelling Ashburn.

captain n Usu |'kæp,t(ə)n|, also |'kæpn̩, 'kæpm̩| and abbr |kæp|; occas |kæbm̩|, |'kæptɪŋ| (cf **-ing B**) Pronc-spp *cabm, cap, capen, cap-m, cap'm, cap'n, captin(g), kepp'n*

A Forms.

1837 Sherwood *Gaz. GA* 69/2, [List of provincialisms to be avoided] *Capting,* for captain. **1840** Hoffman *Greyslaer* 1.84, The bizness is a bad one, anyhow you can fix it, capting. **1867** Lowell *Biglow* xxv 'Upcountry' **MA**, *Capting,* for instance, I never heard save in jest, the habitual form being *kepp'n.* **1891** *DN* 1.121 **cNY**, [kæpn, (kæptn, kæp)]. **1893** Shands *MS Speech, Capen* [kæpn̩]. Negro for *captain.* **1899** (1900) Ade *Fables in Slang* 50, Cap Gibbs . . confronted them with a Red, White, and Blue Sash around him. **1908** *DN* 3.296 **eAL, wGA**, *Cap-m.* **1915** *DN* 4.178 **swVA**, *b* is sometimes developed out of a voiceless p, when in accented syllable: cabm (captain), Babtis (Baptist). **1945** *CA Folkl. Qrly.* 4.319 **CO**, Captain (pronounced Cap'n). **1950**

Faulkner *Stories* 243 **MS,** Captin, will you please tell me. **1958** Humphrey *Home from the Hill* 53 **TX,** *How Cap'm Wade Hunnicutt Kill the Las' Wile Boar in Eas' Texas.*

B Senses.

1 By ext from *captain* of a ship:

a A stagecoach driver.

1835 Shirreff *Tour N. Amer.* 49 **VT,** Captain is a general title for stage drivers.

b A railroad conductor.

1867 Latham *Black and White* 97 *(DA),* Presently the guard, here called 'the Captain of the train,' came to a coloured gentleman, and asked for his ticket. **1889** (1971) Farmer *Americanisms* 123, *Captain.* — The conductor or guard of a train. This official, on whom devolves the chief responsibility for the safety of a train, is, in America, often addressed as *captain* — an analogy being drawn from the phraseology of rail and water traffic. In America the terminology of the latter has been almost universally adopted to describe many phases of the former. **1945** Hubbard *Railroad Ave.* 336, *Captain* — Conductor; often called skipper. This title dates from Civil War days when some railroads were run by the Army and the conductor was in many cases a captain.

2 An unofficial title of respect, sometimes used humorously or ironically. **Sth, S Midl** Cf **colonel**

1746 *London Mag.* 15.324/1, Wherever you travel in *Maryland* (as also in *Virginia* and *Carolina*) your Ears are constantly astonished at the number of *Colonels, Majors,* and *Captains,* that you hear mentioned. **1873** Twain–Warner *Gilded Age* 515 **DC,** When we first came here, I was *Mr.* Sellers, and *Major* Sellers, and *Captain* Sellers, . . but the minute our bill went through the House, I was *Colonel* Sellers every time. **1908** *DN* 3.296 **eAL, wGA,** *Cap-m* . . . Captain. The word is supplanting *boss* as a polite form of address by negroes to white men. **1932** Faulkner *Light in August* 307 **MS,** "And wasn't nobody bothering him, captain," the negro said. "We never even knowed him to call his name." *Ibid* 109, "Who you looking for, cap'm?" the negro said. **1939** *Hall Coll.* **wNC,** Some of the local people address a stranger as captain. **c1960** *Wilson Coll.* **csKY,** Captain is often ['kæpn] or ['kæpm]. Often a courtesy title for a V.I.P. **1966–70** *DARE* (Qu. II10b, *What you'd say to a man: "Say, _____, how far is it to the next town?"*) Infs **GA**30, **SC**32, Cap'n; **GA**1, **MS**56, Captain; **LA**23, Cap; **SC**40, Cap'm; (Qu. NN4, . . *"Would you lend him ten dollars?"* "_____") Inf **DC**13, It'll never happen, cap. **1966** *DARE* Tape **SC**16, In [kæpm] John Richardson's time.

3 One who excels. **chiefly S Midl**

1917 *DN* 4.409 **wNC, KS, KY,** "He's a captain on the floor to dance." "He's a captain to tell a tale." **1927** *AmSp* 2.350 **WV,** He is a captain at playing checkers. **1930** Shoemaker *1300 Words* 12 **cPA** (as of c1900), *Cap* — A leader, a head man, a dignitary. **1939** *Hall Coll.* **wNC,** *Captain* . . . "He's a captain" is a common expression . . . it means "better than the average fellow, a leader." **1960** Hall *Smoky Mt. Folks* 64 **eTN, wNC,** *Captain:* One who excels.

4 In hiding games: the player who is "it."

1966–70 *DARE* (Qu. EE13b, *In games in which all others hide, the one who must try to find the others*) Inf **ID**1, **MO**9, **VA**39, Captain.

Captain Bill vine n [Origin unknown]

1935 Sheppard *Cabins* 309 **NC,** A row of spruce pines screens the front face of the building, and Captain Bill vine overruns the fence.

captain may I n **WI** Cf **mother may I**

A children's outdoor game: see quots.

1950 *WELS* (Hiding-games that start with some special, elaborate way of sending the players out to hide) 2 Infs, **WI,** Captain may I. **1968** *DARE* (Qu. EE33, *Other outdoor games children play*) Inf **WI**47, Captain may I.

captain's walk n **NEng**

=**widow's walk.**

1933 *Hanley Disks* **neMA,** Of course I have a captain's walk! . . Every house should have a captain's walk. **1935** Lincoln *Cape Cod Yesterdays* 43, When he sighted it, he would come down from his "Cap'n's walk", go out to the barn, hitch his horse to the truck-wagon, and cart an empty keg over to the packet landing. **1942** *ME Univ. Studies* 56.73, They built fine houses often with a gallery called the captain's walk. **1963** Haywood *Yankee Dict.,* Captain's Walk — A small platform, fenced in, set upon the highest point on the roof of a house in a New England seaport town. **1967** *DARE* Tape **MA**71, A captain's walk . . . it's sometimes called a widow's walk.

captin(g) See **captain**

capture the flag n

A children's game: see quot 1953.

1953 Brewster *Amer. Nonsinging Games* 69 **AR,** *Capture the Flag* . . . The playing space for this game should measure one hundred by five hundred yards and should be wooded or hilly or both. There are two teams of from fifteen to twenty players each and a referee. The object of the game is to get the opponents' flag and bring it back to the home base without being tagged by those on the other side. **1966–70** *DARE* (Qu. EE3, *Games in which you hide an object and then look for it*) Inf **PA**216, Capture the flag — a flag is hidden by each team and the players on each team had to find the other's flag without being caught; (Qu. EE12) Infs **IL**97, 98, **ME**15A, **MI**89, **PA**26, Capture the flag; **PA**133, Capture the flag, you must get one another's flags — two large teams; (Qu. EE26) Inf **IL**97, Capture the flag; (Qu. EE27) Inf **WI**50, Capture the flag; (Qu. EE33, *Other outdoor games*) Infs **LA**32, **SC**40, **TX**54, 81, **WV**10, Capture the flag.

capuluptic fit n Also *capuluptic spell* [Alter of *cataleptic,* perh infl by *apoplectic* and similar words]

A fit or seizure.

1900 Day *Up in ME* 41, He had a fit the other day. / A sort of capuluptic spell. **1914** *DN* 4.70 **ME, nNH,** *Capuluptic fit* . . apoplectic fit.

‡**capush** n [Perh blend of **caboodle** + **push** n]

=**caboodle.**

1966 *DARE* (Qu. LL10, *A whole group of people*) Inf **MS**30, Capush [kəˈpuš].

car n[1] Usu |kɑr, kɑ, ka| also |kɒ(r)| and, **esp in S Midl,** |kjɑ(r)| See Pronc Intro 3.I.16, 3.II.26 Pronc-spp *caa, cyaa(r), cyar, kear, kyar*

Std senses, var forms.

1887 (1967) Harris *Free Joe* 115 **nGA,** The railroad kyars. **1900** *Bookman* 11.447 **VA,** I was directed to take a certain *kear,* and at a designated street to transfer to another *kear.* **1903** *DN* 2.308 **seMO,** *Cars* . . pronounced with an inserted palatal *y* as . . kyars. **1919** *DN* 5.39 **VA,** *Caa* . . . Car. **1922** Gonzales *Black Border* 295 **seSC, nGA coast** [Gullah glossary], *Cyaa', cyaar.* **1925** *DN* 5.347, Later observation has shown me that the pronunciations of . . *car* . . as [ka] . . are not general — at least in the cultivated speech of Boston . . but, on the other hand, not uncommon. **1930** *DN* 6.85 **cSC,** The pronunciations cyar, . . cyarpet, etc., are common with older people of all classes. **1941** *AmSp* 16.118 **VA,** The off-glide or vanishing y sound in words like *car* and *garden,* . . is . . seldom heard now except in the . . older generation. Among the students tested not a single one said [kɪɑ(r)]. **1942** Hall *Smoky Mt. Speech* 29 **wNC, eTN,** In the following words . . the vowel is usually [ɑ], but in some of them it is very often rounded to [ɒ], [ɒ̣] . . . car. **1961** Kurath–McDavid *Pronc. Engl.* 121, With the exception of Western Pennsylvania and Delmarva, areas that preserve postvocalic /r/ as such have the checked vowel /ɑ/ of *crop, pot, rod,* etc. in *barn, car, garden* etc. In Upstate New York and adjoining parts of New England and Pennsylvania, the /ɑ/ is usually a low-central [ɑ], occasionally a low-front [a]; elsewhere it ranges from a low-back [ɒ] to a low-central [ɑ]. The low-back variant is especially common in the Philadelphia area, where it may even have slight rounding. **1969** *DARE* FW Addit **MA**30, [kjɑ] = car.

car n[2] [Folk-etym for *corf*] See also **eel car, fish car**

A large box suspended in water for keeping marine animals alive.

a1870 Chipman *Notes on Bartlett* 69 *(DA),* Car . . . a square box in which, floating, are preserved live fish. — New England and Middle States. **1947** Coffin *Yankee Coast* 137, I could see cars full of lobsters and baskets of clams down there at the shallow end of our sea-cellar. **1966** *DARE* Tape **FL**24, We put them [=sponges] in, we call them cars. We build a car and we put them in that and have a top on it. We tie them overboard.

car n[3] [Etym unknown]

The hinged metal piece on a canthook.

1968 *DARE* Tape **NJ**39, A canthook has a car or a piece of metal at the end of it that fetches up.

car v See **carry** A1

caracara n, also attrib Also *carcara, carra carra, carrancha* [Brazilian Port *caracará*]

A vulture-like falcon *Caracara cheriway.* Also called **king buzzard, Mexican buzzard, Mexican eagle, Mexican hawk**

1839 Audubon *Ornith. Biog.* 5.351, Caracara Eagle. *Polyborus Braziliensis* . . . Nests of the Caracara found in the Floridas . . were placed on the highest branches of the tall trees in the pine barrens. **1849** *Western Journal* (1906) 139 *(DAE)*, There were the Carra Carra Eagles in great number. **1892** *DN* 1.245 **TX**, *Cáracara:* a sort of vulture, probably the typical Mexican eagle, rather than *zopilóte.* **1894** *DN* 1.324 **TX**, Cáracara . . . *(Polyboros cheriway).* **1895** U.S. Dept. Ag. *Yearbook for 1894* 211 **FL, TX, SW,** Among the birds may be mentioned the white-crowned pigeon, Zenaida dove . . . and caracara eagle. **1911** *Century Dict.*, Caracara . . . [Tupi *caracará* from its hoarse cry.] The popular name of the hawks of the subfamily *Polyborinæ* . . . Also called *carcara* and *carrancha.* **1942** U.S. Natl. Park Serv. *Fading Trails* 261 **FL, TX, SW,** Caracaras . . . are not as timid as most of the hawk tribe and consequently are easy prey for man. **1964** Phillips *Birds AZ* 26, Caracaras are usually very tame, and their habit of sitting on telephone poles, in areas devoid of large cacti, probably led to their extermination south of Tucson by thoughtless gunners.

carajo pole n Also sp *caracho ~* **chiefly SW**
The tall upright stem of the maguey or any similar plant, freq used as a goad.

[**1880** Oswald *Summerland Sketches* 293, He had . . finally strayed to Sisal and exchanged the spit for a muleteer's goad, — vulg., "caracho-pole."] **1902** *Out West* Oct 452, He showed her the *mescal,* and . . told her their many aliases of *maguey,* "carajo poles," *palmilla,* . . bear grass, Spanish dagger or bayonet. **1902** KS State Hist. Soc. *Coll.* 7.52, I hurried him [an ox] along by repeated punches with my *carajo* pole. **1910** Bronson *Reminiscences Ranchman* 287 **cwTX** (as of 1882), An' th' boss music-maker on a perch in th' middle of th' bunch, shaking a little *carajo* pole to beat hell at any of th' outfit that wa'n't working to suit him.

caramel n Usu |ˈkɑrməl| **in Nth, West; in Midl, esp west of Appalachians,** usu |ˈkærəməl|, also |ˈkɛr-, 'ker-, -mɪl, -mɛl| Also sp *carmel, car'mel, carmle*
Std senses, var forms.

1944 *ADD* **cNY** (as of c1920), Carmle, car'mel. *Ibid* **IN, WV,** [karml]. **1965–70** *DARE* (Qq. H80, 81, 82a, b) 44 Infs, **chiefly Nth, West,** Carmel; 34 Infs, **chiefly Midl, esp west of Appalachians,** Caramel.

caran See **carrion**

carancro See **carrion crow 1**

carau n [Prob echoic]
=**limpkin.**

1858 Baird *Birds* 657, Carau; Crying Bird; Courlan . . . The species inhabiting North America is readily distinguishable by its smaller size. **1917** (1923) *Birds Amer.* 1.201, Carau . . . In the Everglades of Florida it is a common bird. **1946** Hausman *Eastern Birds* 233, Limpkin . . . Other Names . . Indian Pullet, Carau.

caravina See **corvina b**

carbon oil n, also attrib [Orig a trademark] **chiefly swPA** Cf **coal oil, cougar juice, lamp oil 1**
Kerosene.

1904 *DN* 2.377, Carbon oil . . . The name under which refined petroleum was sold for an illuminator in Pittsburgh, 1850–55. **c1965** *DARE* File **swPA** (as of 1920s), This was when we had carbon oil lamps. **1968** *DARE* (Qu. F45, *What do you call fuel that's used in an ordinary lamp?*) Infs **PA**77, 92, Carbon oil. **1971** Wood *Vocab. Change* 52 **Sth,** *Carbon Oil* is reported everywhere [in the eight southern states studied] but in Georgia and Louisiana. [16 responses from approx 1,000 infs]

carbox n [Metath *boxcar*] **Sth** See Intro "Language Changes" I.1
A boxcar of a train.

1930 *DN* 6.80 **cSC,** Carbox . . . Boxcar. Fairly frequent. **1949** *AmSp* 24.107 **neGA,** Car-boxes . . . Box cars. **1968** *DARE* FW Addit **csLA,** A carbox is a box car; the word is said to be used only by Negroes, but regularly by them. **1975** Shaw *All God's Dangers* 75 **AL** [Black], That carbox had to be unloaded on the spot or else it stood there overtime and he had to pay rent on it.

carbuncle n Also, **esp in S Midl,** *arbuckle,* and folk-etym forms *carbuckle, carbustle, cowbuncle*
Std senses, var forms.

1890 *DN* 1.64 **KY,** Cowbuncle . . carbuncle. "Who is doctoring Bill Smith's cowbuncle?" **1927** *DN* 5.472 **Ozarks,** Arbuckle . . . A sore or risin', doubtless a corruption of carbuncle. "This hyar arbuckle started from a santy-fay bite, Doc." A santy-fay is a centipede. **1951** *PADS* 15.69 **nLA,** Cowbuncle . . . A carbuncle; a boil. **1967–69** *DARE* (Qu. BB33a, . . *A swelling under the skin, bigger than a pimple*) Inf **CO3,** Carbuckle [ˈkɑrbəkl]; (Qu. BB33b, . . *A swelling under the skin, if it is very big or serious*) Inf **TN27,** Carbuckle [ˈkɑrˌbəkl]; **KY21,** Carbustle [ˈkɑrˌbəsl]

carcajou n Also sp *carcague, corcajou* [CanFr]
1 =**wolverine.** [*DCan* 1703 →]

[**1744** Dobbs *Account* 40 **Canada,** The Beavers have three Enemies, Man, Otters, and the Carajon [*sic*], or Queequehatch.] **1832** Williamson *Hist. ME* 1.133, The *Wolverine,* [Carcajou] is as large as a wolf and of like colour. **1846** Sage *Scenes Rocky Mts.* 126 **swWY,** The "carcague" is a native of the Rocky Mountains, . . partaking the mixed nature of the wolf and bear. **1859** G.A. Jackson *Diary* 521 *(DAE)*, Corcajou came into camp while I was at fire. **1917** Kephart *Camping* 1.262 *(DA)*, The wolverine, also called glutton, carcajou, skunk bear, and Indian devil, is the champion thief of the wilderness. **1946** Dufresne *AK's Animals* 95, The "Indian devil" or carcajou as it is sometimes called gives way to no other animal in the north. **1947** De Voto *Wide Missouri* 165 (as of 1830s), To them the 'carcajou' was literally demoniac: he had an infernal ancestor. **1949** Palmer *Nat. Hist.* 597, Wolverine . . . Known as carcajou, skunk bear, Indian devil.

2 The badger *(Taxidea taxus)* or **lynx.**

1823 Franklin *Narrative Polar Sea* 650, Meles Labradora. American Badger . . . Buffon agreed, describing the American animal under the name of Carcajou. **1864** (1873) Webster *Amer. Dict.* 197/1, Carcajou . . . the American badger *(Meles Labradorica),* found in the sandy plains or prairies of North America. **1895** Gerard in *N.Y. Sun* 30 July *(DA)*, Carcajou, a name properly belonging to the wolverine, but erroneously transferred by certain writers to the American badger, and by old hunters of northern New York to the lynx.

carcara See **caracara**

carcase n [Alter of *carcass; W3* "Brit"]
1899 (1912) Green *VA Folk-Speech*, Carcase . . . The trunk; the body. "He takes good care of his carcase."

carcass n perh esp **Sth, S Midl** *joc*
One's body; one's buttocks.

1957 Battaglia *Resp. to PADS 20* **eShore MD,** (Joking words for the part of the body that you sit on) Carcass. **1960** (1962) Lee *Mockingbird* 252 **AL,** Get your stinkin' carcass off my property. **c1960** Wilson *Coll.* **csKY,** Carcass . . . A humorous reference to the human body. "Get your carcass out of my chair or I'll beat the stuffing out of you." **1969** *DARE* (Qu. NN9b, . . *"He's run off again with my hammer, _____."*) Inf **TX70,** Confound his carcass. **1980** De Vries *Consenting Adults* 197 **IL,** "I'll buzz off if you'd like," I said, ardently. "Park your carcass."

carcel n [Span] **SW**
A jail or prison.

1840 (1973) Turnbull *Travels* 57, The survivor, for safe keeping merely, was sent to the Carcel. **1910** *Sat. Eve. Post* 8 Oct 5/1, The general and the chief of police . . had carted off four *carreta* loads of my machinery to the *cárcel.* **1930** Duffus *Santa Fe Trail* 66 (as of 1819), The old *carcel* in which he had been confined was still standing. **1932** Bentley *Spanish Terms,* Carcel . . . A prison . . . This word is heard occasionally along the border by English-speaking people and is encountered no more frequently in writings of this region. **1968** Adams *Western Words,* Cárcel—Jail; from the Spanish.

card n[1] Usu |kɑ(r)d|; also, **esp in S Midl,** |kjɑ(r)d| See Pronc Intro 3.I.16 Pronc-spp *caard, cyard, keard, keerd, kyard*
A Forms.

1823 [see **B1** below]. **1899** (1912) Green *VA Folk-Speech,* Card . . . Keard. **1900** *Bookman* 11.447 **eVA,** In social calls, at the door the servant receives your kyard. **1901** *DN* 2.181 **neKY** [Black], Cards— keards. **1910** Porter *Strictly Business* 76, I've got the keerds. **1916** *DN* 4.296 **sAppalachians,** "Palatal influence." When these words are "broken" we have: "cy-ard". **1926** Kephart *Highlanders* 351 **sAppalachians,** "I gotta me a deck o' cyards." **1942** Hall *Smoky Mt. Speech* 94, In . . older people, this glide [j] is very common . . *card* . . . Some CCC enrollees . . say [kjɑɚd] for *card.*

B Senses.

1 A "sheet" of baked goods; a pan of other cooked food. *obs*

1823 Cooper *Pioneers* 102 **NY,** A third was filled, to use the language of the housekeeper, with "caards of gingerbread." **1853** (1854) Baldwin *Flush Times* 160 **AL,** He had ravished himself from the supper table, scarcely eating any thing—three or four cups of coffee, . . a card of spare-ribs and one or two feet of stuffed sausages. **1871** *Atlantic Mth.* 28.574/2 **NY,** Through clouds of smoke and steam . . sprang the cooks, . . dropping a card of biscuits and picking them up again in their fists. **1897** Robinson *Uncle Lisha's Outing* 297 **VT,** There were numerous booths where refreshments of mead, spruce beer, and great cards of good old-fashioned yellow gingerbread were temptingly displayed.

2 also attrib, freq in phr *card of matches:* See quot 1940. *old-fash*

1847 *Farmers' Almanack* 9/1 **NY,** A man got up the other night and took, as he supposed, a card of matches and began to break off one by one, trying to light a lamp, until the whole card was used up, without accomplishing his object, when he discovered that he had used up his wife's comb! **1870** O. Optic *Field and Forest* 65 *(DA),* Mr. Mellowtone gave me a card of matches. **1940** *AmSp* 15.449, A *card of matches* in the nineteenth century was a piece of wood, I should say about a tenth of an inch thick and two and a half inches square, divided into matches by slits which ran from the edge to within about half an inch of the opposite edge. **1967** *DARE* Tape **MA5,** That was when they made card matches, wasn't it? Or was that after they made the single matches?

3 See **card man.**

card n²

A curry-comb or similar implement.

1820 *Columbian Centinel. Amer. Federalist* (Boston MA) 8 Jan 4/3, Wool, Cotton, and Cattle Cards. **1859** U.S. Patent Office *Annual Rept. for 1858: Arts & Mfgr.* 1.346, *Improvement in Cards for currying Cattle.* **1860** (1863) Olmsted *Journey* 246 **TN,** He picked up a piece of corn cob and began scraping him. "Hadn't he got a curry comb or card?" **1930** Shoemaker *1300 Words* 14 **cPA Mts** (as of c1900), *Card* —A curry-comb.

‡card v [?Alter of *cart*]

1952 Brown *NC Folkl.* 1.525, *Card* . . . To go home, to move on. "Well, I'd better be carding."

‡card cheese n [Alter of *curd cheese*]

1966 *DARE* (Qu. H60, *The lumpy white cheese that is made from sour milk*) Inf **ME16,** Card cheese is the old name, cottage cheese is the new name.

cardidge See **cartridge**

cardinal n

1 Std: a red grosbeak (*Richmondena cardinalis*). Also called **English cockatoo, firefly 2, redbird, red blue jay, Virginia nightingale, winter redbird**

2 See **cardinal flower.**

3 See quot. [Cf *OED cardinal* sb.3 "A short cloak worn by ladies, originally of scarlet cloth"]

1930 Shoemaker *1300 Words* 9 **cPA Mts** (as of c1900), *Cardinal*—A long cloak, principally used by horse-back riders.

cardinal flower n Also *cardinal (lobelia)* Cf **red cardinal flower**

Either of two lobelias: usu the red-flowered *Lobelia cardinalis,* but also the blue-flowered *Lobelia syphilitica.* The former is also called **highbelia, hog physic, Indian feather, Indian pink, queen of meadow, red betty, red cardinal flower, slinkweed;** the latter is also called **blue lobelia, highbelia, Louisiana lobelia**

1705 Beverley *Hist. VA* 2.24 **VA,** The Cardinal-Flower, so much extoll'd for its Scarlet Colour, is almost in every Branch. **1839** *Boston Weekly Mag.* 1.377/1 **MA,** The cardinal lobelia gleams like the flower of a brighter clime around the borders of the rivulets. **1881** *Harper's Mag.* 63.585/1 **NEng,** The fragrant clethra, whose prim fingers of creamy bloom made a good foil to the cardinals. **1906** Rydberg *Flora CO* 326, *Lobelia* . . . Cardinal-flower. **1913** Porter *Laddie* 11 **IN,** On either side of the entrance he had planted a cluster of cardinal flower that was in full bloom. **1965–70** *DARE* (Qq. S26a,b,c,d,e) 13 Infs, **esp NEast,** Cardinal flower.

cardinal redbird See **redbird 1**

cardinal-spear n [See quot 1975]

A **coral tree** (here: *Erythrina herbacea*).

1933 Small *Manual SE Flora* 716, *E. herbacea* . . . *Cardinal-spear* . . . Coastal Plain, Fla. to Tex. and N.C. **1953** Greene–Blomquist *Flowers South* 59, A closely related perennial herb called cardinal-spear . . is very similar in its leaf, floral, and fruit characteristics. **1975** Duncan–Foote *Wildflowers SE* 84, *Cardinal-spear; Coral Bean* . . . Corolla scarlet, the standard to 53mm long, folded so that the entire flower appears long and narrow.

card man n Also *card*

A union member.

1968 Adams *Western Words, Card man*—What the loggers call a union man; often shortened to *card.*

cardy bird n

A nuthatch (here: prob either *Sitta canadensis* or *S. pusilla*).

1887 (1895) Robinson *Uncle Lisha* 59 **wVT,** Nary one on 'em bigger 'n a cardy bird. [Footnote:] Nuthatch.

care v, n Usu |kɛr, keə, ker, keə, kær, kæə|, also |kjɛr, k(j)ɪr, k(j)ir, kiə(r), kjɜ, kɛː, kɪə| See Pronc Intro 3.I.1.b and 3.I.16 Pronc-spp *kear, keer, kere, kyare*

A Forms.

1823 Cooper in 1927 *AmSp* 2.483, Kear. **1848** Lowell *Biglow* 145 'Upcountry' **MA,** Keer, care. **1871** Eggleston *Hoosier Schoolmaster* 63 **sIN,** You don't keer how much trouble I have. *Ibid* 178, So tak kere. **1903** *DN* 2.308 **seMO,** *Care* . . . Pronounced keer [kir]. 'I'm not *keerin'* is used for I don't care. **1905** Culbertson *Banjo Talks* 45 **SE,** He tuck . . fus' class kyare er me. **1906** *DN* 3.129 **nwAR,** *Care* . . illiterate [kir]. **1908** *DN* 3.296 **eAL, wGA,** *Care* . . . Pronounced [ker], and sometimes with intrusive ɪ [kɪer]. **1931** *AmSp* 6.167 **seVA,** *Care* . . [kɛː] . . . Negroes, *care* . . [kɪə]. **1954** *Harder Coll.* **cwTN,** *Care* . . [kyɪr], sometimes [kyir]. **c1960** *Wilson Coll.* **csKY,** *Care* . . [kjɛr] or [kjir]. **1961** Kurath–McDavid *Pronc. Engl.* 118, *Stairs, care,* etc., have one of three vowels, the /e/ of *eight,* the /ɛ/ of *head,* or the /æ/ of *bag,* in rather clearly defined regional dissemination. In addition, high-front /i∼ɪ/ and mid-central /ɜ/ occur after the /k, č/ of *care, chair* in the folk speech of certain areas. **1967** *DARE* FW Addit **neLA,** Care [kæɪjə].

B As verb.

1 in neg constrs: To be willing, to be pleased—usu used in response to an invitation. **chiefly Midl**

1903 *DN* 2.308 **seMO,** *Care* . . . In negative 'not to care'; a common expression denoting consent. 'Will you go to dinner with me?' 'I *don't care.*' (Not meant to be indifferent.) **1907** *DN* 3.229 **nwAR, seMO.** **1907** *DN* 3.456 **seKY,** *Care* (with negative) . . . To be willing. "If I had a horse and carriage I wouldn't care to take you to Boring." **1931** Hannum *Thursday April* 52 **WV Mts,** "Come and set?" "I wouldn't keer to." The rising inflection of the guest's voice indicated her willingness, so together they dropped down in the cool grass. **1937** *Hall Coll.* **wNC, eTN,** "She don't care to talk" [means] she doesn't mind talking, i.e. she is a great talker. **1969** *WV Hist.* 30.2.467, One of the most baffling expressions our people use . . is "I don't care to . . . " To outlanders this seems to mean a definite "no," whereas in truth it actually means, "thank you so much, I'd love to." **1971** *Down East* Nov 26, Maine Circumlocutions . . such as, "I don't care for him" when the meaning is, "I have no objection to him." **1980** *DARE* File **sIN** (as of c1900), People might think you were brash if you answered straight out "Yes" to an offer of food or drink, so to be polite you said "I don't care." **1981** *High Coll.* **ceKY** (as of c1930), I hope to live my life out so people won't care to look at me, and I won't care to meet nobody . . . You don't have to be hateful. You can be kind. And people don't care to look at you.

2 with *for:* To raise (a child). **chiefly FL, MS, AR, OK, NM** See Map on p. 544

1965–70 *DARE* (Qu. Z17, *To take care of or bring up a child: "All her children were _____ (on the farm)."*) 17 Infs, Cared for.

C As noun.

See quots. Cf **continental** n

1950 *WELS* (*If you don't care what a person does, you might tell him, "I don't give a _____."*) 3 Infs, **WI,** Care; (*If you don't care the least bit about something: "I don't give a _____."*) 3 Infs, Care. **1965–70** *DARE* (Qu. GG21b, . . *"Go ahead—I don't give a _____."*) 22 Infs, **scattered,** Care.

cared See **carry A2**

careen v Pronc-sp *creen* **chiefly S Midl**

1 Of a ship or a building: to lean away from the vertical position; hence ppl adj *careened* leaning to one side.

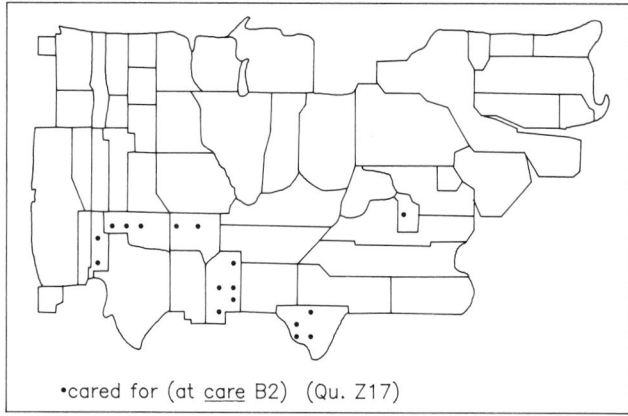

•cared for (at <u>care</u> B2) (Qu. Z17)

1899 (1912) Green *VA Folk-Speech*, *C'reen*, . . To lean to one side as a ship under press of sail. Careen. "The boat *creened* so I thought she'd turn over." **1950** *PADS* 13.17 **cwTX**, *Creen* . . . To bend from a natural position. "The barn is *creening* a little." *Ibid* 14.23 **SC**, *Creen* . . . To lean away from the vertical position, said of houses, barns, etc., whose walls were not properly braced in building. **c1960** *Wilson Coll.* **csKY**, *Creen* . . . To lean awry; to careen. **1965–70** *DARE* (Qu. KK70, *Something that has got out of proper shape: "That house is all _____."*) Infs **MS30, NC72, SC19, 34**, Careened over; **KY84**, Careened.

2 Of a person: to lean or bend sideways.

1917 *DN* 4.410 **wNC**, *C'reen* . . . To bend the body to one side. "I noticed a ketch in my back ever' time I c'reened." **1927** *DN* 5.473 **Ozarks**, *Creen* . . . To lean or fall sidewise. "Th' ol' man went a-creenin' 'roun' all evenin', an' fin'ly he fell right spang inter th' hog-waller." **1928** *AmSp* 4.57 **Ozarks**, The verb *creen* signifies to lean or to twist slowly sidewise, and is evidently an abbreviated form of *careen*.

careful pin n
A safety pin.
1950 *PADS* 14.18 **SC**, *Cayless-pin* . . . *Careless* pin. A straight pin as distinguished from a safety or *careful* pin. *Negro,* coastal area.

careing See **carry** A3

careless See **careless weed** 1

careless pin n
1950 [see **careful pin**].

careless weed n

1 also *careless, keerless weed:* =**amaranth.** **chiefly W Midl, SW** See Map
1807 Scott *Geog. MD & DE* 26, **MD**, Common and white plantain, . . Jameson, careless, poke root. **1849** in 1926 *SW Hist. Qrly.* 29.206 **sCA**, Traveled to the second watering place . . . grass short, but plenty of *Careless Weed* of which our Animals seemed very fond. **1900** *Land of Sunshine* 13.320 **CA**, A species of chenopodium, called "careless weed" by freighters and cattle men, exceeds ten feet in height. **1941** Stuart *Men of Mts.* 152 **KY**, The pig . . . likes ragweeds, pulsey [sic], careless and horse weeds. **1949** *PADS* 11.8 **wTX**, Keerless weed . . A common weed. **1954** *Harder Coll.* **cwTN**. **1965** Teale *Wandering Through Winter* 150 **TX**, All across Texas, a host of . . names have been

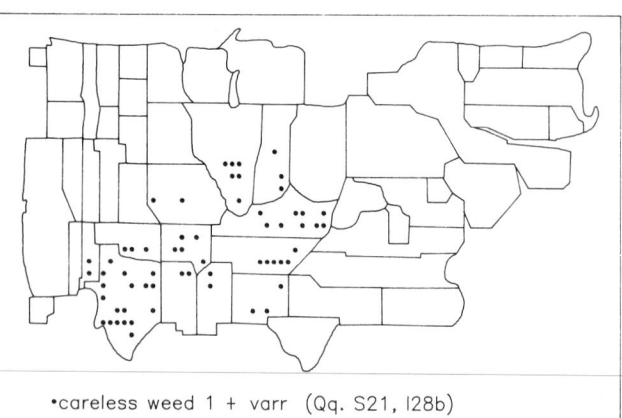

•careless weed 1 + varr (Qq. S21, I28b)

bestowed on the wild plants . . . They run from angel's trumpet . . and careless weed to shame vine . . and kiss-me-and-I'll-tell-you. **1965–70** *DARE* (Qu. S21 . . *Other kinds of weeds*) 55 Infs, **chiefly W Midl, SW,** Careless weed(s); **AL11, 15, OK52**, Thorny careless; **AR24, KY5**, Sticky careless; **AR2**, Red careless; **AR24**, Wild careless; (Qu. I28b, *Kinds of greens that are cooked*) Inf **TX89**, Careless weeds.

2 A **marsh elder** (here: *Iva xanthifolia*).
1940 Gates *Flora KS* 237, Careless Weed . . . Waste places and along streams. **1953** Nelson *Plants Rocky Mt. Park* 179, Carelessweed . . *Iva xanthifolia.* **1968** Barkley *Plants KS* 359, Careless Weed. Rag Sumpweed.

caren See **carrion**

caretaker n **chiefly PA** See Map
A road supervisor.
1965–70 *DARE* (Qu. N33, *A man whose job is to take care of roads in a certain locality*) 20 Infs, **chiefly PA**, Caretaker; **PA104**, Highway caretaker.

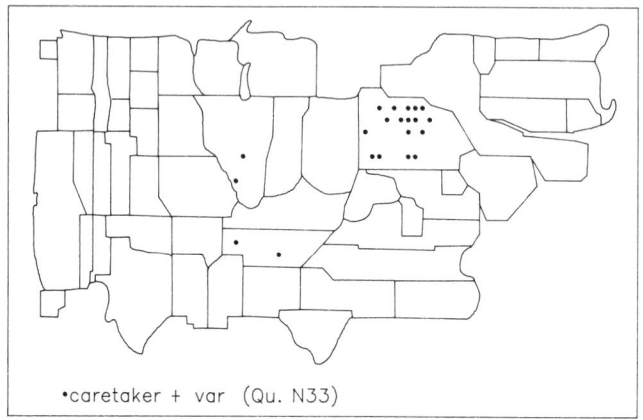

•caretaker + var (Qu. N33)

carey (chicken) See **Mother Carey's chicken**

carf See **calf** n[1]

carf(e) See **kerf**

carga n [Span] **SW** *?obs*
A load to be transported; a unit of weight, usu of approx 300 lbs.
1844 (1954) Gregg *Commerce* 128, Two men are always engaged at a time in the dispatch of each animal, and rarely occupy five minutes in the complet [sic] adjustment of *aparejo* and *carga.* **1892** *DN* 1.189 **TX**, *Cárga:* a load, a charge. *Ibid* 245 [Addendum to prec], *Cárga* . . 336 pounds. **1897** Inman *Santa Fé Trail* 57 (as of early 1800s), The *carga* is then hoisted on top of the saddle if it is a single package. **1968** Adams *Western Words, Carga*—In mining, a load of clean ore ready for the furnace, weighing, in the Mexican measure, 300 pounds.

cargador n [Span] **SW** *?obs*
A freighter, porter; one who loads **carga**.
1811 Humboldt *Political Essay* 1.51, The existence of these vallies prevents the inhabitants from travelling except on horseback, a-foot, or carried on the shoulders of Indians (called *cargadores*). **1844** (1954) Gregg *Commerce* 292, The *cargadores* who were carrying my packages were no doubt as much frightened as myself. **1855** *Los Angeles Star* 1 Dec 2/3 (*Western Folkl.* 7.6), [A traveler, reporting a voyage by way of the Chagres River, complains of] the vexatious banterings of *cargadores.* **1892** *DN* 1.245 **TX**, *Cargadór:* the man in charge of the packs, in a pack train. **1923** Wheeler *Frontier Trail* 198 (as of 1877), A cargador, who keeps the aparejos (saddles) in repair and sees that they are properly fitted to each mule. **1968** Adams *Western Words, Cargador*—In a pack train, the man second in importance to the pack master; he makes up and forms the cargo, equalizes the packs, cares for the mules, repairs the aparejos etc.

car house n **Sth, S Midl** Cf **car shed**
A garage.
1954 *Harder Coll.* **cwTN**, Car house—Building for a car. "Garage" is becoming more common. **1960** (1962) Lee *Mockingbird* 151 **AL**, As far back as I could remember, there was always a Chevrolet in excellent condition in the carhouse. **1962** Atwood *Vocab. TX* 77, Car house. A garage. **1966** *DARE* Tape **NC21**, [I] put it [the sail] overhead in my car

house and it hasn't been out since. **1969** Emmons *Deep Rivers* 58 **eTX** [Black], She kept hearing some kind of noise in my "car house," as she called it.

caribou moss n
Reindeer moss.
[**1904** White *Silent Places* 137 **Canada,** The foundation he made of caribou-moss, gathered dry from the heights.] **1961** Douglas *My Wilderness* 111 **neMN,** As I cleared the edge of the cliff and came to the top, I was on a thick carpet of gray-green caribou moss.

carita See **carreta**

cark v [*OED* →1848; *"obs."*] *relic*
To fret, complain.
1968 *DARE* (Qu. GG16, *Words for finding fault or complaining: "You just can't please him—he's always _____."*) Inf **IN39,** Carking.

car knocker n Also *car knock, ~ tink, ~ toad, ~ tonk, ~ whack(er)* [See quot 1943]
In railroading: a car repairman; a car inspector.
1925 in 1953 Botkin *Treas. Railroad Folkl.* 228, I hammered like hell with my fists and a car-knocker let me out. **1931** *Writer's Digest* 11.41, *Car Toad*—Car repairer; there are many variations of this word viz: car knock, car tonk, car whack, etc. **1943** *AmSp* 18.163, *Car knocker.* Inspector. *Ibid, Car whacker.* From the early custom, when wheel-casting was not as exact as it now is, of tapping the wheels to detect defects such as cracks or seamy flanges—still resorted to if appearance of the wheel raises doubt. **1945** Hubbard *Railroad Ave.* 336, *Car Knocker*... Also called *car whacker;* and *car toad* (because he squats while inspecting), *car tink,* and *car tonk.* **1962** *AmSp* 37.132 **nwCA,** *Car knocker.* **1975** McDonough *Garden Sass* 261 **AR,** These were names that the railroad men had for each other: . . a car repairman was a "car knocker."

carmel, car'mel See **caramel**

Carmelite n Also *Carmel Indian* **swOH**
A person of mixed Black, White, and Indian ancestry associated with Carmel, Ohio.
1940 FWP *Guide OH* 509, *Carmel* . . a trading center for a curious group of people living in the impoverished hills. Called Carmelites, these people are of mixed white, Negro, and Indian blood. With their smooth brown skin and straight black hair they are not unlike Indians in appearance. **1963** Berry *Almost White* 19, From Kentucky they [Melungeons] have moved into Ohio, forming a settlement in Highland County, where they are known as the "Carmel Indians." *Ibid* 35, Sometimes it is the nearby town which gives the people their name. Hence, we have . . the Carmel Indians in Ohio. *Ibid* 136, Lately . . these Carmelites have been moving to Dayton. *Ibid* 185, The Carmelites of Ohio are generally regarded as white people, but of inferior grade. **1981** *DARE* File, These people are no longer called Carmel Indians, but Carmelites, after the village of Carmel ['karml̩].

carmle See **caramel**

carnelian n Also *caneel, canelian, carne, carnel, cornelia(n)*
A red or flesh-red marble made of carnelian or similar material.
1950 *WELS (Names of marbles)* 3 Infs, **WI,** Carnelians; 3 Infs, Cornelians. **1958** *PADS* 29.31, *Carne* . . *carnel* . . Abbr. of *carnelian* (Wis.) . . . *carnelian* . . A marble made of carnelian or similar material. "The best marbles" (S.D.). "Ten or 15 cents apiece" (Neb.). *Ibid* 32, *Cornelia* . . *cornelian* . . Var of *carnelian* (Wis.). **1965–70** *DARE* (Qu. EE6d, *Special marbles*) Infs **FL30, IA9, MN37, 38, SC68,** Cornelians; **IL35,** Caneel; **MO13, NJ43,** Canelians; **IL20,** Cornelia; (Qu. EE6a, *Names for different kinds of marbles—the big one*) Inf **IL26,** Cornelian; **SD1,** Carnelian; **GA58,** Caneel; (Qu. EE6c, *Cheap marbles*) Inf **MT3,** Cornelians. **1968** *DARE* Tape **IA35,** Cornelias . . had a basketweave inside the glass part of the marble. **1973** Ferretti *Marble Book,* [Cover photo:] Cornelian "Blood" Alley.

carnish See **cornice**

carnival v [Cf *caracole*]
Of a horse: see quot 1968.
1945 Thorp *Pardner* 65 **SW,** Many an otherwise gentle horse, if flank-cinched, would carnival and go places with his rider. **1968** Adams *Western Words, Carnival*—To buck in a showy manner.

Carolina n Usu |ˌkɛrəˈlaɪnə, ˌkærə-|; also |kerəˈlaɪnə, karˈlaɪnə, ˌkə-, ˌkɛ-, kə-; -ˈlaɪnə, -ˈlaɪni| Pronc-spp *Ca'lina, Ca'liner, Caroline, Caroliny, Kerliny* Cf **-y**

1891 *DN* 1.158 **cNY,** [karˈlaɪni] 'Carolina'. **1895** *DN* 1.375 **seKY, wNC, eTN,** *Kerliny.* **1926** Kephart *Highlanders* 354 **sAppalachians,** I have never heard a Carolina mountaineer say . . No'th Ca'lina, though . . the syllable *ro* is often elided. **1926** in 1944 *ADD* **SC,** Ca'lina [kəlaɪnə]. **1933** Rawlings *South Moon* 38 **FL,** Caroliny. **1940** in 1944 *ADD* **swPA, nVA,** North Ca'liner. Old illit. speaker. **1940** *Sat. Eve. Post* 20 Apr 13/3, The North Caroliny mountings. **1942** *Sat. Eve. Post* 5 Sept 10/2, We've named dogs from Canady to the Carolines. **1942** Hall *Smoky Mt. Speech* 24, [æ] occurs in: . . Carolina. *Ibid* 25, [ɛ] frequently occurs: . . *Carolina* . . . *Carolina* is sometimes [kɛˈlaɪnə] . . . *Carolina* [kəˈlaɪnə]. **1966** *DARE* (Qu. T13) Inf **NM2,** [karˈlaɪnə] poplars. **1968** *Wilson Coll., Carolina,* in southern Kentucky among older people, is [ˌkəˈlaɪnə]. **1969** *DARE* Tape **GA72,** [ˌkeərəˈlanər].
B Sense.
See **Carolina potato.**

Carolina allspice n Also *allspice*
A **sweet shrub** (here: *Calycanthus floridus*). Also called **apple shrub, bubbybush 1, pimento, pineapple plant, shrub, spicebush, strawberry bush, strawberry shrub, sweet betsy, sweet bush**
1793 Amer. Philos. Soc. *Trans.* 3.xxi, The barks of young Sassafras, and of *Calycanthus Floridus* [Footnote: Called Carolina allspice] much resemble cinnamon. **1830** Rafinesque *Med. Flora* 203, *Sweet Shrub, Allspice* . . . Much esteemed for the blossoms, smelling like Pineapple . . . The seeds taste like Pimento. **1868** (1870) Gray *Field Botany* 131, *Carolina Allspice* . . . Fragrant strawberry-scented blossoms. **1901** Mohr *Plant Life AL* 518, Carolina allspice. **1938** Van Dersal *Native Woody Plants* 79, *Carolina allspice* . . . A large shrub; flowers April–August. **1975** Hamel–Chiltoskey *Cherokee Plants* 58, Sweet shrub, all spice . . . Roots are strong emetics.

Carolina ash n Also *Carolinian ash*
An ash tree (here: *Fraxinus caroliniana*). Also called **Florida ash, pop ash, red ash, swamp ash, water ash**
1785 Marshall *Arbustrum* 50, *Fraxinus americana. Carolinian or Red Ash.* **1897** Sudworth *Arborescent Flora* 331, Carolina ash. **1979** Little *Checklist U.S. Trees* 135, *Carolina ash* . . . *Other common names*—water ash [etc].

Carolina bark n *prob obs*
=**fever tree.**
1876 Hobbs *Bot. Hdbk.* 20, Carolina bark, Florida bark, Pinckneya pubens. **1900** Lyons *Plant Names* 290, Fever-tree *Bark* . . [is called] Carolina bark. **1911** *Century Dict., Bark* . . Georgia, bitter, Carolina, or Florida bark.

Carolina bat See **Virginia bat**

Carolina beechdrops n pl, sometimes construed as sg
=**sweet pinesap.**
1861 Wood *Class-Book* 495, *Carolina Beech-drops* . . . *S[chweinitzia] odorata* . . . Rich shady soils, Md. to N. Car. **1901** Lounsberry *S. Wild Flowers* 376, Carolina beech-drops . . is more rarely found through shady woods than the Indian pipe and is a rather shorter plant. **1959** Carleton *Index Herb. Plants* 24, Carolina beech drops: Monotropsis odorata.

Carolina buckthorn n
1 A buckthorn (*Rhamnus caroliniana*). Also called **arrowwood f, bog birch 1, brittlewood, Indian cherry, polecat tree, stink berry, stinkwood, tree buckthorn, yellow buckthorn, yellowwood**
1813 Muhlenberg *Catalogus Plantarum* 24, *Rhamnus* . . Carolinianus[,] *Buckthorn* . . Carolina. **1883** Hale *Woods NC* 150, *Carolina Buckthorn* (Frangula Caroliniana . .). A thornless shrub . . . The berry is blackish, of the size of a small pea. **1979** Little *Checklist U.S. Trees* 247, *Rhamnus caroliniana.* Carolina buckthorn.
2 A **southern buckthorn** (here: *Bumelia lycioides*).
1897 Sudworth *Arborescent Flora* 319, *Bumelia lycioides* . . . *Common Names* . . . Carolina Buckthorn (N.C.). **1908** Britton *N. Amer. Trees* 779, *Southern Buckthorn* . . . is also called Carolina buckthorn, Southern Bumelia, and Chittimwood.

Carolina cherry n Also *Carolina cherry-laurel, Carolina laurel-cherry, Carolinian cherry*
An evergreen, black-fruited cherry tree (*Prunus caroliniana*). Also called **cherry laurel, evergreen cherry, laurel cherry, laury mundy, mock orange, wild olive, wild orange, wild peach**

1846 Browne *Trees* 272 *(DAE), Cerasus caroliniana,* The Carolinian Cherry-Tree . . . The wood of the Carolinian cherry is fine-grained. **1897** Sudworth *Arborescent Flora* 247, Carolinian cherry. **1953** Greene–Blomquist *Flowers South* 52, *Carolina Cherry-Laurel* . . . [is] an evergreen, small tree with finely serrate, narrowly elliptic shining leaves. **1967** *DARE* (Qu. I46, *Other kinds of fruit that grow wild around here*) Inf **SC**38, Carolina cherry—a black cherry, poison to cows; (Qu. T5, *Kinds of evergreens*) Inf **SC**40, Carolina cherry. **1979** Little *Checklist U.S. Trees* 212, *Carolina laurelcherry* . . . Coastal Plain from se. N.C. to c. Fla. and w. to e. Tex.

Carolina dove n
=**mourning dove 1.**

1874 Coues *Birds NW* 389, *Zenædura Carolinensis* . . . Carolina Dove; Common Dove. **1894** B. Torrey *Fla. Sketch-Book* 147 *(DA),* Herons in the usual variety were present, with ospreys, an eagle, kingfishers, ground doves, Carolina doves, [etc.]. **1917** (1923) *Birds Amer.* 2.46, *Mourning Dove—Zenaidura macroura* . . Carolina Dove. **1940** Todd *Birds W. PA* 706/2.

Carolina eagle n

1970 *DARE* (Qu. Q13, *Names around here for the vulture*) Inf **VA**61, Carolina eagle.

Carolina groundnut See groundnut

Carolina jasmine n Also *Carolina (yellow) jessamine* [From the fragrance]

A yellow-flowered, evergreen vine *(Gelsemium sempervirens).* Also called **evening trumpet flower, false jasmine, jasmine, poison vine, poor man's rope, woodbine, yellow jasmine**

1831 Audubon *Ornith. Biog.* 1.114 **S Atl,** *The Florida Jessamine* . . . is also named *Carolina Jessamine* and *Yellow Jessamine.* **1889** *Century Dict.* 2478/3, The plant . . known in the United States as the wild, yellow, or Carolina jasmine. **1941** Walker *Lookout* 56 **TN,** Of the . . wild vines . . Carolina jasmine is one of the earliest flowering kind. **1976** Bailey–Bailey *Hortus Third* 499, *Gelsemium* . . . Carolina y[ellow] j[essamine], Carolina jasmine.

Carolina junco n

A subsp of the **slate-colored junco** (here: *Junco hyemalis).*

1898 *Atlantic Mth.* 82.492/2 **NC,** But if this is true of the Carolina junco, I failed to satisfy myself of the fact. **1943** Peattie *Great Smokies* 275, The Carolina juncos ("Snowbirds") may be incubating eggs under a snow-covered canopy of rootlets and dried plant remains.

Carolina laurelcherry See Carolina cherry

Carolina locust n

The Carolina grasshopper *(Dissosteira carolina).*

1911 *Century Dict. Suppl., Locust*[1] . . . *Carolina locust,* an American acridiid, *Dissosteira carolina.* **1941** FWP *Guide CO* 19, The greatest scourge of the prairie land is the grasshopper . . . they range from the bulky "lubber," occasionally two inches long, to the small "Carolina locust."

Carolina nuthatch n
=**white-breasted nuthatch.**

1917 (1923) *Birds Amer.* 3.200, White-Breasted Nuthatch *Sitta carolinensis carolinensis* . . Carolina Nuthatch. **1932** Bennitt *Check-list* 46. **1946** Hausman *Eastern Birds* 433, White-Breasted Nuthatch *Sitta carolinensis* . . Carolina Nuthatch.

Carolina pinesap n
=**sweet pinesap.**

1951 *PADS* 15.18, *Monotropsis odorata* . . . Carolina pine-sap.

Carolina pink n

1 also *Carolina pinkroot:* An **Indian pink** (here: *Spigelia marilandica).*

1779 in 1914 *Documents Revol. Hist. NJ* 4.21, To be Sold . . Carolina pink root. **1789** in 1793 Amer. Philos. Soc. *Trans.* 3.xviii, Carolina pink; a southern plant: it will destroy the worms; but caution in the dose is requisite. **1872** Schele de Vere *Americanisms* 399, The *pink*-root (Spigelia marilandica) is by no means limited to Maryland, . . and is quite generally known as *Carolina Pink.* **1938** Madison *Wild Flowers OH* 86, Indian or Carolina Pink . . . Corolla scarlet outside, yellow inside. **1964** Batson *Wild Flowers SC* 91, *Carolina Pink: Spigelia marilandica.*

2 A **wild pink** (here: *Silene caroliniana).*

1964 Batson *Wild Flowers SC* 43, *Carolina Pink: Silene caroliniana* . . . Flowers about 1 in. across, white or pink.

Carolina poplar n Also *Carolina popple, Caroline poplar, North Carolina* ~, *North Caroline* ~, *South Carolina* ~

1 A **cottonwood 1** (here: *Populus deltoides).* Also called **alamo 1, cotton tree, necklace poplar, river cottonwood, water poplar, whitewood, yellow cottonwood**

1860 Curtis *Cat. Plants NC* 72 **NC,** Carolina Poplar *(Populus angulata* . . .) . . . The wood does not appear to be used. **1931** Mattoon *Forest Trees Okla.* 25 *(DA),* The cottonwood, or Carolina poplar, is found along streams throughout the state. **1965–70** *DARE* (Qu. T13, *Other names . . for . . poplars*) Infs **NM**2, 6, 9, **OH**61, **PA**70, Carolina poplar; **NY**165, North Caroline poplar; (Qu. T16, *What kinds of trees are "special" around here?*) Inf **UT**13, North Carolina poplar.

2 =**balsam poplar.**

1965–70 *DARE* (Qu. T12, *The kind of poplar tree that has sticky, sweet-smelling buds*) Infs **CA**163, **NM**9, Caroline poplar; **OR**3, **VA**8, North Carolina poplar; **CO**3, **CT**4, South Carolina poplar; **NY**97, Carolina popple; **CA**163, Caroline poplar—used for shade. **1971** Krochmal *Appalachia Med. Plants* 206, *Populus balsamifera* . . . *Common Names:* Balsam poplar, . . Carolina poplar, cottonwood.

Carolina potato n Also *Carolina arch*

The sweet potato *(Ipomoea batatas).*

1775 (1962) Romans *Nat. Hist. FL* 123, The varieties, in an ascending scale for goodness, [are] 1st Spanish, . . . 2d. Carolina, little superior to the first. 3d. Brimstone. **1819** Schoolcraft *Lead Mines MO* 34, The sweet, or Carolina potatoe was raised last year in considerable perfection. **1884** *Century Illustr. Mag.* 27.442/1, The sweet potato was adopted from the aborigines in all the Southern colonies, and it is yet known in the market as the 'Carolina.'

Carolina racehorse n *joc*

A razor-back hog.

1862 Gilmore *Among the Pines* 212 **SC,** We passed great numbers of swine . . long, lean, slab-sided race, with legs and shoulders like deer . . . "We call them Carolina race horses."

Carolina silver-bell tree See silverbell tree

Carolina tea n
=**yaupon.**

1876 Hobbs *Bot. Hdbk.* 118, Tea, Carolina, Ilex vomitoria. **1901** Lounsberry *S. Wild Flowers* 315, Yaupon . . . The Carolina, or South Sea tea, as also this holly is called, occurs most generally near salt water . . . In the Atlantic States its leaves are annually dried and used by the natives for tea. **1907** Hodge *Hdbk. Amer. Indians* 1.150/1, *Black drink* ("Carolina tea" . .) . . *Ilex cassine.* **1960** Vines *Trees SW* 647, Local names in use are . . Carolina-tea, . . Christmas-berry.

Carolina vanilla n [See quot 1900] **SE**
=**vanilla plant 1.**

1900 Lyons *Plant Names* 378, *T[rilisa] odoratissimus* [sic] . . . Carolina Vanilla . . . *Leaves* have an agreeable vanilla-like odor. **1930** Sievers *Amer. Med. Plants* 20, Carolina-Vanilla . . . Large quantities of the leaves are used in the flavoring of tobacco.

Carolina whiting n

A **kingfish 1** (here: *Menticirrhus americanus).*

1898 U.S. Natl. Museum *Bulletin* 47.1474, *Menticirrhus americanus* . . . Carolina Whiting; Sand Whiting . . . Very common on the sandy coasts of our Southern States, where it is a food-fish of some importance. **1946** LaMonte *N. Amer. Game Fishes* 86, Southern Kingfish . . . Names: Kingfish, . . Carolina Whiting.

Carolina wren n Also *great Carolina wren*

A large reddish-brown wren *(Thryothorus ludovicianus)* with a white stripe over the eye. Also called **graveyard bird, mocking wren**

1810 Wilson *Amer. Ornith.* 2.61 **S Atl,** [The] *Great Carolina Wren* . . . *Certhia Caroliniana,* . . . is frequently seen, early in May, along the shores of the Delaware. **1948** *Bird-banding* 19.101 **TN,** When choosing a nest site, the Carolina Wren shows a decided preference for some type of receptacle or ledge to support and protect the roofed, side-entrance nest. **1968** *DARE* (Qu. 21) Inf **VA**26, Carolina wren—looks like a wren.

Carolina yellow jessamine See Carolina jasmine

Caroline See **Carolina**

Caroline poplar See **Carolina poplar**

Carolinian ash See **Carolina ash**

Carolinian cherry See **Carolina cherry**

Caroliny See **Carolina**

caronie n [Alter of Span *carona* the padding of a saddle next to the animal's back]
   1929 (1978) Watt *Mule Train* 39 eWA (as of 1860s), With each aparejo there was a "caronie," a fancy Spanish embroidered pack blanket, which was laid over the "sweat" blanket.

carot(te) See **carrot 1**

carp n[1] *derog*
   1968 *DARE* (Qu. HH28, *Nicknames . . for people of foreign background: Bohemians*) Inf **IA32**, Carp.

carp n[2] See **kerf**

carpenter n Also *carpenter bird* [See quot 1956] Cf **carpintero**
   Any of several woodpeckers.
   1858 *Atlantic Mth.* 2.870/1 **NEng**, The little Hair-Bird . . is called the "Chipping-Sparrow," as if he were in the habit of making chips, like the Carpenter-Bird. **1956** *MA Audubon* 40.83, Pileated Woodpecker . . . Carpenter Bird (. . Name from its working in wood.). **1967** *DARE* (Qu. Q18, . . *Names . . for woodpeckers*) Inf **ID5**, Carpenter.

carpenter ant n Rarely *carpenter's ant* [*OED* 1883 →]
   A wood-excavating ant of the genus *Camponotus*. Also called **black timber ant, bull ant**
   1901 Howard *Insect Book* 48, It is the earnest hope of the writer that some student will take up . . the large carpenter ant . . [and] study it most carefully. **1951** Johnson *Resp. to PADS 20* **DE** (*The big black ants that sting*) Carpenter ant. **1964** Borror–DeLong *Intro. Insects* 729, Carpenter ant. **1965–70** *DARE* (Qu. R17, . . *Big black ants that sting*) 23 Infs, **chiefly Nth**, Carpenter ant; **NY88**, Carpenter's ant; (Qu. R18, . . *Other kinds of ants*) 24 Infs, **chiefly Nth**, Carpenter ant.

carpenter bee n [See quot 1859; *OED* 1844 →]
   A bee of the subfamily Xylocopinae.
   1859 Gosse *Letters from AL* 143, Those species which thus drill round holes in wood, for the purpose of obtaining a secure and commodious nidus for their young, are appropriately called Carpenter-Bees. **1867** *Amer. Naturalist* 1.157, I send specimens in alcohol of the pupa of *Xylocopa virginica*, the Carpenter Bee. **1910** NJ State Museum *Annual Rept. for 1909* 698, The large carpenter bee [is] common throughout the State. **1941** O'Donnell *Great Big Doorstep* 260 (Hench Coll.) **LA**, The carpenter bees hummed loudly around the bridge. They bored their deep round holes far into the cypress wood. **1967–70** *DARE* (Qu. R27) Infs **NJ22, PA49, 223**, Carpenter bee; **CA191**, Carpenter bee—same as bumblebee; **DC2**, Carpenter bee—size of bumblebee, chews a hole in wood and crawls in, make[s] hole in ceiling of porch.

carpenter bird See **carpenter**

carpenter frog n [See quots]
   A striped brown frog (*Rana virgatipes*).
   1907 *Amer. Naturalist* 41.50 **NJ**, *Rana virgatipes* may be called the Carpenter Frog, for its note sounds much like the blow of a hammer on a board. **1958** Conant *Reptiles & Amphibians* 298, Carpenter Frog . . . Voice: Pu-tunk', pu-tunk', pu-tunk'. Like two carpenters hitting nails a fraction of a second apart. **1961** Collier's 24 Nov 64/3 seGA (Hench Coll.), "Thing that makes the swamp . . is the sounds" . . . After supper we settled down in the cabin in the dark and listened. The hooting of the owls . . increased in volume, joined after a while by the many-toned babble of the frogs: the grunts of the Southern bullfrog, the regular thumps of the carpenter frog, the thin peeping of the oak toad, the rasping trill of the chorus frog. **1969** *DARE* Tape **GA51**, This yer little carpenter frog, he'd [čə'læk, čə'læk, čə'læk], sound like somebody hammerin'.

carpenter leaf See **carpenter's leaf**

carpenter's ant See **carpenter ant**

carpenter's herb See **carpenter weed**

carpenter's leaf n Also *carpenter leaf*
   An evergreen herb (*Galax* spp) formerly used in healing superficial wounds.

1814 Pursh *Flora Americae* 2.446, *Galax rotundifolia* . . . In the . . Virginia mountains this plant is known by the name of *Carpenter's-leaf*, being used in healing all kinds of wounds and cuts. **1830** Rafinesque *Med. Flora* 222, *Galax rotundifolia* . . . Carpenters' leaf. Vulnerary, used for all kinds of wounds, bruises and sores. **1876** Hobbs *Bot. Hdbk.* 20, Carpenters' leaf, Galax rotundifolia. **1959** Carleton *Index Herb. Plants* 24, Carpenter leaf: Galax aphylla.

carpenter's square n
   1 also *carpenter square:* A **figwort** (here: *Scrophularia marylandica*).
   1837 Darlington *Flora Cestrica* 370, Maryland Scrophularia . . . Figwort. Carpenter's Square. **1897** *Jrl. Amer. Folkl.* 10.52, *Scrophularia . . Marilandica*, . . carpenter's square, Southwestern M[issouri]. **1930** Sievers *Amer. Med. Plants* 29, Carpenter square . . . is 3 to 10 feet high with 4-angled stems. **1969** *DARE* (Qu. I28b, *Kinds of greens that are cooked*) Inf **MO6**, Carpenter square. **1970** Correll *Plants TX* 1425, *Carpenter's square* . . . Stem with rounded 4 angles and grooved sides.

   2 A square-cut **earmark** n.
   1968 *DARE* (Qu. K18, . . *Mark . . to identify a cow*) Inf **WV8**, Cut a carpenter's square in top of both ears.

carpenter weed n Also *carpenter's herb*
   =**self-heal** (here: *Prunella vulgaris*).
   1891 *Jrl. Amer. Folkl.* 4.148 **NH**, Carpenter Weed was our only name for Brunella vulgaris. **1892** *Ibid* 5.102. **1897** Parsons *Wild Flowers CA* 322, The *Brunella* was considered particularly efficacious in the disorders of carpenters and common laborers, because its corolla resembled a bill-hook. Hence it was commonly called "carpenter's herb." **1936** IL Nat. Hist. Surv. *Wildflowers* 280, Carpenterweed. Prunella vulgaris . . This genus name was often written Brunella, especially before Linnaeus' time, as it was said to be derived from the German *Bräune*, a throat disease for which this plant was used as a remedy. **1970** Correll *Plants TX* 1357, Carpenter-weed. **1971** Krochmal *Appalachia Med. Plants* 208, Common Names: . . carpenter's herb, carpenterweed.

carpetbag v
   To act like a carpetbagger; to attempt to deceive.
   1934 *AmSp* 9.289 [Black student slang], Carpetbag. To attempt to make a favorable impression on a professor (or anyone in authority) by feigning deep interest in the subject.

carpet beetle n Also *carpet bug, carpet moth* [See quot 1889]
   Any of several insects, esp of the family Dermestidae: see quots.
   1889 *Century Dict.* 831/1, *Carpet-beetle* . . . A popular name of Anthrenus scrophulariæ . . so called from its destructiveness to carpets and other woolen fabrics. **1928** Metcalf–Flint *Destructive & Useful Insects* 746, Carpet Beetles or Buffalo Beetles. **1964** Borror–DeLong *Intro. Insects* 349, Some of the smaller dermestids . . may do serious damage to carpets . . . Two common species of this type are the black carpet beetle, Attagenus piceus . . and the buffalo moth, Anthrenus scrophulariae. *Ibid* 544, The clothes moth of the least importance in the United States is the . . carpet moth, Trichophaga tapetzella. **1967–68** *DARE* (Qu. R30) Infs **NY123, PA53**, Carpet beetle; **IL14**, Carpet beetle—they're moths; **MI67**, Lady bug—also called "carpet bug" and sometimes called a "carpet beetle."

carpet grass n
   1 A grass of the genus *Axonopus*.   **chiefly Gulf States**
   1901 Mohr *Plant Life AL* 120, Carpet grass (*Paspalum compressum*) . . a West Indian species most probably introduced. **1939** FWP *Guide FL* 479, Some fields are being cleared of palmetto growth; once cleared, an occasional clipping is all that is required to grow carpet grass, ideal forage for stock. **1948** Holland's March 50/3 (*DA*), All three are good grasses—and of course there are those old favorites, Bermuda and carpet. **1965–70** *DARE* (Qu. L8, *Hay that grows naturally in damp places*) Inf **TX105**, Carpet grass; (Qu. L9a, *Kinds of grass . . grown for hay*) Infs **LA2, 3, TX35**, Carpet grass; (Qu. S8, *A common kind of wild grass . . spreads by sending out . . roots*) Infs **PA239, TX26, 37**, Carpet grass; (Qu. S9, *Kinds of grass that are hard to get rid of*) Infs **GA84, MS6, NJ58**, Carpet grass; (Qu. S21, *Weeds . . a trouble in gardens and fields*) Inf **NJ58**, Carpet grass. [Note: some Infs may refer instead to sense **2** below.] **1976** Bailey–Bailey *Hortus Third* 131, Axonopus affinis . . Carpet grass.

   2 Any of several other grasses: see quots.
   1882 Godfrey *Is. Nantucket* 36, The carpet-grass and the orange-grass . . were eagerly sought for at that period. **1970** Correll *Plants TX*

153, This lawn grass *[Stenotaphrum secundatum]* is commonly but mistakenly called "carpet grass," a name best reserved for Axonopus.

3 A **frogfruit** (here: *Phyla nodiflora* var. *canescens*).

1976 Bailey–Bailey *Hortus Third* 865, *Phyla nodiflora* . . Carpet grass.

carpet moth See **carpet beetle**

carpet, on the adj phr Also *out on the carpet* **Sth, S Midl, esp NC, TX, AR** See Map
Eager to marry.

1909 *DN* 3.355 **eAL, wGA,** (Out) on the carpet . . . Said of one who is a candidate for matrimony. "They say Widow Jones is out on the carpet again." **1922** *DN* 5.172 **AR,** Out on the carpet . . . In society to find a wife. "You don't mean to say that old widower's out on the carpet." **1952** Brown *NC Folkl.* 1.525, *Carpet, to be on the* . . . To be courting. "Well, I hear he's on the carpet again, and his wife ain't been dead more'n a year." **1956** McAtee *Some Dialect NC* 7, *Carpet, on the* . . . Courting. **1965–70** *DARE* (Qq. AA4a, b, . . *Eager to get married* . . "He's_____." . . "She's_____.") 28 Infs, **esp NC, TX, AR,** (Out) on the carpet (again); [(Qu. AA15c, . . *A woman is getting married,* "She_____.") Inf NJ67, Got on the carpet, jumped off the carpet; PA167, Kicked the carpet.].

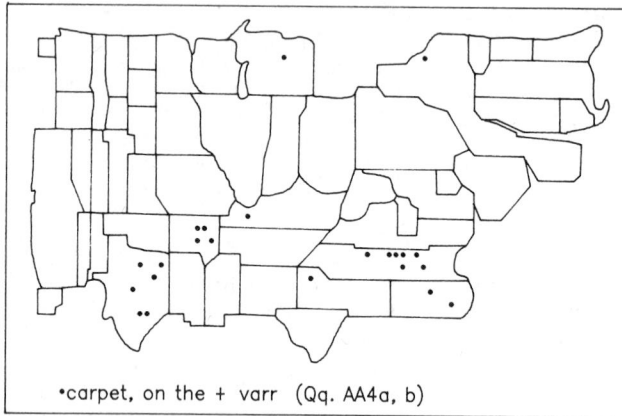

•carpet, on the + varr (Qq. AA4a, b)

carpet pink n [See quot 1934]
=**moss campion.**

1934 Haskin *Wild Flowers Pacific Coast* 93, Carpet Pink. *Silene acaulis* . . . forms densely-tufted, flower-covered mats at high elevations in the mountains. **1936** Thompson *High Trails* 85 **nwMT,** The carpet pink flourishes early.

carpet pussley n [*carpet,* from its spreading habit, + **pussley**]
A type of **pussley.**

1949 *PADS* 11.4 **wTX,** Carpet pussly . . . Purslane. Common rural.

carpet shell n
A venus clam (*Protothaca staminea*) common on the Pacific coast, esp California.

1884 U.S. Natl. Museum *Bulletin* 27.240 **CA,** *Tapes staminea* . . . known as the "Carpet-Shell", "Little-Neck Clam," and "Hard-Shelled Clam", is abundant on the whole Calfornian coast. **1895** *Std. Dict. Engl. Lang.* (Funk) 289/1, *Carpet* . . . *-shell* . . . A small clam (*Tapes staminea*) extensively used as food in California.

carpetweed n [From their habit of growing thickly along the ground]

1 A plant of the genus *Mollugo.* See also **devil's grip, Indian chickweed**

1784 in 1785 Amer. Acad. Arts & Sci. *Memoirs* 1.407, Carpet-weed . . . Blossoms greenish white. **1822** Eaton *Botany* 355, *Mollugo* . . *verticillata* (carpet weed . .) . . . Generally grows in gardens among purslain. **1859** (1968) Bartlett *Americanisms,* Carpet Weed. A small spreading plant, common in cultivated ground (*Mollugo*). **1947** *Amer. Midland Naturalist* 38.42 **MD,** *Mollugo verticillata* (Carpetweed). Common (locally abundant) in cultivated fields.

2 A **bedstraw.**

1959 Carleton *Index Herb. Plants* 24, Carpet Weed: *Galium aristatum.*

3 =**knotweed.**

1963 Zimmerman–Olson *Forest* 195, Carpet weed . . Polygonum aviculare.

4 A kind of caltrop (here: *Kallstræmia hirsutissima*).

1970 Correll *Plants TX* 905, *Kallstræmia hirsutissima* . . Carpetweed. Prostrate annual, forming a dense carpetlike mat.

carpintero n [Span "carpenter"] **SW** Cf **carpenter**
Any of several woodpeckers.

1882 *Amer. Naturalist* 16.357 **CA,** Mr. Bice is of the opinion that the acorns are stored simply for the larvae, which the *carpintero* eats after the maggot has attained a good size. **1911** *Century Dict.,* Carpintero . . . A name of several species of woodpeckers in the southwestern United States, from their tapping and boring wood. One of the commonest species to which the name is given is the California woodpecker . . ; another is the Gila woodpecker.

carpouse See **caboose** n[1] **1**

carps n [Metath of *craps*]
The game of craps.

1901 *DN* 2.137 **Brooklyn NY,** Carps . . metathesis for craps.

carra carra See **caracara**

carrageen n [*Carragheen,* Ireland; *OED* 1834 →]
=**Irish moss.**

1876 Hobbs *Bot. Hdbk.* 20, Carrageen moss, Irish moss, Chondrus crispus. Carragheen moss. **1901** Arnold *Sea-Beach* 80, Carrageen . . *Chondrus crispus.* **1965** Teale *Wandering Through Winter* 333 **ME,** She pointed out a dense, many-branched seaweed, reddish-purple in hue. This was Irish moss or carrageen, *Chondrus crispus.* **1969** *New Engl. Galaxy* Winter 65 **MA,** While busy hands on Scituate sands the "carrageen" may dress.

carrancha See **caracara**

carren See **carrion**

carret See **carrot 1**

carreta n Also sp *carita* [Span] **SW**
A primitive cart with two solid wooden wheels.

1844 (1954) Gregg *Commerce* 67, New Mexicans . . with *carretas* or truckle-carts and oxen, drive out into these prairies. **1883** Sweet–Knox *Mexican Mustang* 367 **TX,** All the goods that were sold in San Antonio were hauled up from the coast on uncouth vehicles called *carretas.* **1888** Lindley *Calif. of South* 83 (*DA*), There was a Mexican *carita,* drawn by two oxen. **1892** *DN* 1.245 **TX,** *Carréta:* a primitive, two-wheeled cart; the wheels are generally solid and held together by wooden pins. The creaking noise made by these wheels is altogether unearthly, and may be heard at long distances. **1940** Fergusson *Our Southwest* 79, He carried with him, enshrined on her own *carreta,* an image of the Virgin, *La Conquistadora,* to whom he prayed for success. **1968** Adams *Western Words,* Carreta—A simple cart with rimless wheels made in one piece, usually cut from an oak log, with a hole cut in the center for the axle.

carriage See **baby carriage**

carriage-wheel wiper n *old-fash* Cf *DS* JJ3b
A toady, bootlicker.

1968 *DARE* FW Addit **cnVA,** A carriage-wheel wiper is someone so eager to please that he would lean up against the carriage wheel, dirtying the front of his coat as he shook the gentleman's hand or kissed the lady's hand.

carri⁽ⁱ⁾n See **carrion**

carring See **carry A3**

carrion n Usu |'kæriən, 'kɛriən|; also |'kærin, -ən| and, **esp in S Midl,** |kjɑ(r)(ə)n| See Pronc Intro 3.I.1.b, 3.I.16 Pronc-spp *caian, caran, car(r)en, carrin, carr(i)'n, cyarn, kyarn(y)*
A Forms.

1806 Berquin–Duvallon *Travels* 123 **LA,** A bird . . called carancro [=carrion crow]. **1843** (1916) Hall *New Purchase* 220 **IN,** "A most powerful rottin darn'd ole carrin [=horse]". **1890** *DN* 1.73 **Cape Cod MA,** Carri'n [kærɪn]: carrion. **1893** Shands *MS Speech,* Cyarn [kjan]. Negro for carrion. **1899** (1912) Green *VA Folk-Speech,* Caren . . . Carrion. Carren. **1908** *DN* 3.328 **eAL, wGA,** Kyarn . . Carion [sic]. A negrism. *Kyarn-crow, kyarny-crow.* **1916** *DN* 4.296 **sAppalachians,** "Palatal influence." . . carrion . . . cy-arn. **1917** *DN* 4.410 **wNC,** Cyarn . . . Carrion. **1933** Miller *Lamb in His Bosom* 43 **GA,** Stunk like carr'n. **1942** Hall *Smoky Mt. Speech* 94, *Carrion* as [kjɑə-n] now seems to be obsolescent . . . The prevailing pronunciation is said to be ['kærən]. **1947** (1964) Randolph *Ozark Superstitions* 246, Carr'n crow. **1965** *DARE* (Qu. Q13) Inf MS60, Caian crow. **1969** *DARE* FW Addit seGA, Carrion [kjɑrən] crow.

B Sense.

See **carrion crow 1.**

carrion beetle n Also *carrion bug*

A beetle of the family Silphidae.

    1854 Emmons *Agriculture NY* 5.261, Carrion beetle. **1911** *Century Dict.*, Carrion-beetle . . . A necrophagous coleopter, a beetle that feeds upon or deposits its eggs in carrion. **1926** Essig *Insects N. Amer.* 380, Carrion Beetles . . . Members of the genus *Necrophorus* . . members of the genus *Silpha.* **1966–70** *DARE* (Qu. R30, *Other kinds of beetles*) Infs IL135, IN69, Carrion beetle; KY47, Carrion beetle—green and stink; ME12, Carrion beetle—large, black, lives on carrion; KY40, Carrion bug—some say stink bug; VA38, Carrion bug. **1980** Milne *Audubon Field Guide Insects* 548, Carrion Beetles (Family Silphidæ).

carrion berry See **carrion flower 1**

carrion bird n

1 =**Canada jay.** [See quot 1955]

    1784 in 1877 Belknap *Papers* 1.390 **NH,** The Dr. saw a blue bird, with a white head, which is said to be a *saw-whetter,* alias *carrion-bird.* **1844** DeKay *Zool. NY* 2.130 **NY,** The Canada Jay. *Garrullus canadensis* . . . Its food consists of berries . . and even carrion, from whence it derives one of its popular names of *Carrion-bird.* **1917** (1923) *Birds Amer.* 2.225, Canada Jay—*Perisoreus canadensis canadensis* . . Carrion Bird. **1936** Roberts *MN Birds* 2.58, Canada Jay: *Perisoreus canadensis* . . Carrion Bird. **1955** *MA Audubon* 39.84, Canada Jay . . . Carrion Bird (Maine. From its feeding upon camp refuse.).

2 See **carrion crow 1.**

carrion bug See **carrion beetle**

carrion crow n

1 also *carancro, carrion, ~ bird, ~ eater:* Either of two scavengers: the **turkey vulture** or the **black vulture. chiefly S Atl, Inland Sth** See Map

    1791 (1958) Bartram *Travels* 96 **S Atl,** The other species may very properly be called the coped vulture, and is by the inhabitants called the carrion crow. **1806** Berquin–Duvallon *Travels* 123 **LA,** There is a bird very common here, which is found in silent flocks near the houses, the size of a small turkey, of an ordinary plumage, ignoble aspect, and heavy flight, living on insects and reptiles, that is called carancro. **1908** [see **carrion**]. **1909** *S. Atl. Qrly.* 8.45 [Gullah], Fly t'ru de yelement lak carrion crow! **1947** [see **carrion**]. **1950** *PADS* 14.43 **SC,** Kyarn crow [kjɑnkro] . . . Carrion crow. **c1960** Wilson *Coll.* **csKY,** The local name for the Black Vulture is *Carrion* [kjɑrn] *Crow.* **1965–70** *DARE* (Qu. Q13, *Names . . for the vulture*) 31 Infs, **chiefly Inland Sth, S Atl,** Carrion crow; AZ2, KY49, NE4, NJ43, OK11, PA89, WV7, Carrion bird; CA10, KY11, 72, NC49, TX37, WI32, Carrion; NY123, SC24, Carrion eater; MS60, Caian crow; LA7, Red-head carrion crow. **1969** *DARE* FW Addit seGA, Carrion crow ['kjɑrən,kroʊ] Black vulture, *Coragyps atratus.*

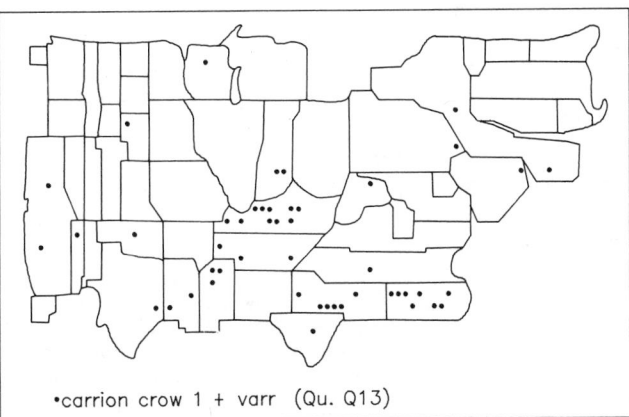

•carrion crow 1 + varr (Qu. Q13)

2 The raven *(Corvus corax)* or a crow.

    1903 (1950) Austin *Land of Little Rain* 19 **neCA,** The least objectionable of the inland scavengers is the raven, frequenter of the desert ranges, the same called locally "carrion crow." **1917** (1923) *Birds Amer.* 2.229, Crow . . . Other Names . . . Carrion Crow.

carrion flower n [From the smell of the flower]

1 also *carrion berry:* A **greenbrier,** usu *Smilax herbacea* which is also called **catbrier, field yamroot, Jacob's ladder, sarsaparilla.**

    1837 Darlington *Flora Cestrica* 567, *Herbaceous Smilax. Vulgo*—Carrion-flower . . . There is no difficulty in recognizing this plant by the abominable fœtor of its flowers,—which is so strong as frequently to deceive the carrion flies. **1942** Derleth *Wisconsin* 36, Great and small, islands dot the Wisconsin . . . hung with grapevines, bittersweet, carrion berry, greenbrier. **1947** *Midland Naturalist* 38.37 **MD,** Carrion-flower . . . [is] rare in seepage swamps, terrace forest, hedgerows, and wood margins. **1967** *DARE* (Qu. S26a, *Roadside flowers*) Inf IA3, Carrion berry—same as carrion flower.

2 also *carrion plume:* Any of several other plants, such as **bugbane 1** or **pitcher plant 1:** see quots.

    1876 Hobbs *Bot. Hdbk.* 20, Carrion flower, Ground Ivy, Nepeta glechoma. **1959** Carleton *Index Herb. Plants* 24, *Carrion flower:* Amorphophallus rivieri; Cimicifuga (v); Sarracenia purpurea; Smilax (v); Stapelia (v). *Carrion plume:* Cimicifuga (v).

carrion fly n

A fly which feeds on carrion, such as a **blowing fly** or a **flesh fly.**

    1926 Essig *Insects N. Amer.* 383, The hairy rove beetle . . . It is now believed that the larvae and adults of this beetle feed upon the maggots of carrion flies. **1968–69** *DARE* (Qu. R13) Inf NJ31, House fly—carrion fly; MA42, ['kæærən] flies—lay the eggs to make the maggots.

carrion plume See **carrion flower 2**

carr'n See **carrion**

carrot n

1 also sp *carret, carot(te):* A tightly rolled bundle of tobacco leaves: see quot 1812. [From its shape] **esp Gulf States**

    1772 in 1916 Mereness *Travels* 537 **FL,** Others took the Cock off his riffle and Sixteen Carrots of Tobacco. **1812** Stoddard *Sketches La.* 227 *(DA),* Carottes of tobacco are still made by the French of Missouri and Louisiana. The leaves, after the large stem has been removed, are laid together lengthwise and compressed; then the bundle is covered with a cloth and tightly wrapped from end to end with a cord, making the tobacco into an almost solid mass from twelve to eighteen inches long and tapering almost to a point at each end. **1857** *IL Dept. Ag. Trans. for 1856–57* 2.360, The Creoles manufactured the tobacco into carrots, as they were called. A carrot is a roll of tobacco twelve or fifteen inches long. **1890** *Congressional Record* 27 Aug 9213/2 **FL,** I have here some carots of Cuban tobacco. **1938** FWP *Guide MS* 94, The leaves [of tobacco] were packed in hogsheads by the larger planters and in "carrets" by the smaller growers.

2 See **carrot weed 1.**

carrot bed n Also *carrot hill, ~ hole*

    1967–70 *DARE* (Qu. M19, *A place for keeping carrots, potatoes . . over the winter*) Inf NJ67, Carrot bed; AL34, Carrot hill; TN1, Carrot hole; AL31, Potato or carrot bed.

carrot blossom See **carrot weed 1**

carrot eater n Also *carrot snapper* [In ref to use of carrots for subsistence by early Mormon pioneers] **ID** *derog*

A person from Utah, usu a Mormon.

    1968 *DARE* FW Addit **ID,** Carrot eater. Someone from Utah. "There's another carrot eater coming to catch all our fish." **c1971** Hall *Snake River Valley* s**ID,** (*Terms for Mormons*) 4 infs, Carrot eaters; 1 inf, Carrot snapper.

carrot flower See **carrot weed 1**

carrotleaf n [See quot 1948]

=**biscuit root 1.**

    1948 Stevens *KS Wild Flowers* 347, *Lomatium daucifolium.* Carrotleaf Lomatium . . . The leaf resembling that of the carrot. **1963** Craighead *Rocky Mt. Wildflowers* 128, *Lomatium dissectum* . . . Other names: Carrotleaf . . . Leaves . . . are dissected 3 or 4 times into linear divisions; this gives them appearance of a large carrot or parsley leaf. **1968** Barkley *Plants KS* 261, *Lomatium foeniculaceum* . . . Carrotleaf Lomatium. Rocky prairies.

carrot-leaved parsley n

A **biscuit root 1** (here: *Lomatium daucifolium*). Also called **carrotleaf, parsley, whiskbroom parsley**

    1930 OK Univ. Biol. Surv. *Pub.* 2.75, *Lomatium daucifolium* . . . Carrot-leaved Parsley.　**1936** Winter *Plants NE* 85, *C. daucifolia* . . . Carrot-leaved Parsley.

carrot plant n [Prob from the shape of the root]
=**dandelion.**

　1968 *DARE* (Qu. S11, *Names . . for dandelions*) Inf **GA38**, Carrot plant.

‡carrot snake n

　1969 *DARE* (Qu. P25, . . *Kinds of snakes*) Inf **GA72**, Carrot snake—mostly in South.　**1984** *NADS Letters* **ceGA**, A student from Sparta, GA, says that his older brothers, who are farmers, use this term, but the student himself has no idea what a *carrot snake* is.

carrot weed n

1 also *carrot, ~ blossom, ~ flower, ~ top:* =**wild carrot.**

　1830 Rafinesque *Med. Flora* 215, *Daucus carotta* [sic] . . . Carrots . . . The wild roots have a stronger smell and taste, very diuretic and useful in strangury arising from blisters.　**1895** Gray–Bailey *Field Botany* 202, *Daucus, Carrot* . . . Umbel concave and dense in fruit, like a bird's nest.　**1949** Moldenke *Amer. Wild Flowers* 147, A related native American species, the *American carrot, D. pusillus* . . . is common in the hill country of California and north to British Columbia.　**1965–70** *DARE* (Qu. S6, *Names . . for Queen Anne's Lace*) Inf **VA43**, Carrot weed; **NJ48**, Carrot; **NC18**, Carrot blossom; **PA245**, Carrot flower; **PA26**, Carrot top; (Qu. S21, *Weeds . . that are a trouble*) Inf **VA43**, Carrot weed.　**1973** Hitchcock–Cronquist *Flora Pacific NW* 324, *Daucus* L. Carrot.

2 A ragweed (here: *Ambrosia artemisaefolia*).

　1900 Lyons *Plant Names* 27, *A[mbrosia] artemisæfolia* . . . Tassel-weed, Stick-weed, Carrot-weed, Bastard Wormwood.

carry v Usu |'kæri, 'kɛri| less freq |'keri, 'kɑri|; esp in **Sth, S Midl,** also |'kjæri, 'kjæ-i|　See Pronc Intro 3.I.2.a, 3.I.16
A Forms.

1 pres: usu *carry;* pronc-spp *cah(r), caire(y), car, cearr, cya', cyar, kearry, kerry, kirry, kyar.*

　1861 Holmes *Venner* 373 **wMA,** Kerry.　**1887** *Scribner's Mag.* 2.475 **AR,** Won' ye lemme cyar the baby a spell?　**1888** Jones *Negro Myths* 7 **GA Coast,** Buh Rabbit . . full him calabash long water an cah um to eh house. *Ibid* 20, Den dey all run up an cahr de meat to dem house.　**1892** Smith *Day at Laguerre's* 190 **VA,** Reckon he kearries mos' of it on his shoes.　**1899** (1912) Green *VA Folk-Speech, Car* . . . Ceaar; caire. To carry.　**1905** *DN* 3.56 **NE,** *Carry* is sometimes *kirry.*　**1905** Culbertson *Banjo Talks* 11 **TX** [Black], Widout no pusson ter kyar' dem roun'.　**1922** Gonzales *Black Border* 295 [Gullah glossary], *Cya'*—carry, carries, carried, carrying. *Ibid* 296, *Cya'um*—carry, carried, etc., him, her, it, them.　**1928** *AmSp* 3.406 **Ozarks,** *Carry* . . is often reduced to something very like the last syllable of *decay.*　**1930** *AmSp* 5.343 **ceVA,** [ɛ] or a very slack [æ] is the vowel in . . *carry. Ibid* 355 **NYC,** [ɛ] appears without vowel glide in . . *carry. Ibid* 397, Carry [has] æ.　**1931** *AmSp* 6.168, The medial [r] in *very, carry, dreary,* and *Mary* is usually well formed in the speech of white people in Tidewater Virginia.　**1936** *AmSp* 11.243 **eTX,** Carry . . *Plantation-Type* . . ['kjæri] . . *Hill-Type* . . ['kjæri], ['kjæi] . . *Negro* . . ['kjæi].　**1939** in 1944 *ADD* **eIL,** [keri].　**1942** *Nation* 155.194/1, Educated foreigners who have learned to say "carry" and not "cairey."　**1968** *DARE* FW Addit **MD13,** [The informant] always pronounces *carry* with an /ɑ/ rather than an /æ/, which is standard for the area.

2 past and past pple: usu *carried;* pronc-spp *caird, cared, cyared, ker'd.*

　1848 Lowell *Biglow* 143 'Upcountry' **MA,** Caird, carried.　**1861** Holmes *Venner* 177 **wMA,** Th' ol' Doctor, he'd h' ker'd 'em through.　**1887** *Scribner's Mag.* 2.475 **AR,** I done cyared 'er a heap.　**1912** Green *VA Folk-Speech, Cared* . . . For *carried.*

3 pres pple: usu *carrying;* pronc-spp *cairn, careing, carring, kyar'yin'.*

　1848 Lowell *Biglow* 143 'Upcountry' **MA,** Cairn, carrying.　**1899** (1912) Green *VA Folk-Speech, Car* . . . carring . . . Careing . . . Carrying. "For careing you to town."　**1905** Culbertson *Banjo Talks* 113 **Sth** [Black], Dey's kyar'yin' on dat-a-way.
B Senses.

1 To escort, accompany.　**formerly freq in NEng; now chiefly Sth, S Midl**　See Map

　1861 Holmes *Venner* 373 **wMA,** I'm go'n' to kerry y' home.　**1875** (1969) Coffin *Caleb Krinkle* 161 **MA,** "Who is there that I can invite?" . . "Bell, . . I am afraid that she will be left at home unless you

carry her."　**1899** (1912) Green *VA Folk-Speech.*　**1927** *AmSp* 2.350 **wcWV.**　**1931** *Scribner's Mag.* 89.353/1 **FL.**　**1931** *AmSp* 7.90 **eKY.**　**1938** *AmSp* 13.5 **seAR.**　**1941** *LANE* Map 402 **throughout NEng,** May I . . carry you home?　**1955** *PADS* 23.41 **Charleston SC.**　c**1960** *Wilson Coll.* **csKY.**　**1965–70** *DARE* (Qu. AA2, . . *"John is going to ＿＿＿ Mary to the dance."*) 99 Infs, **chiefly Sth, S Midl,** Carry.

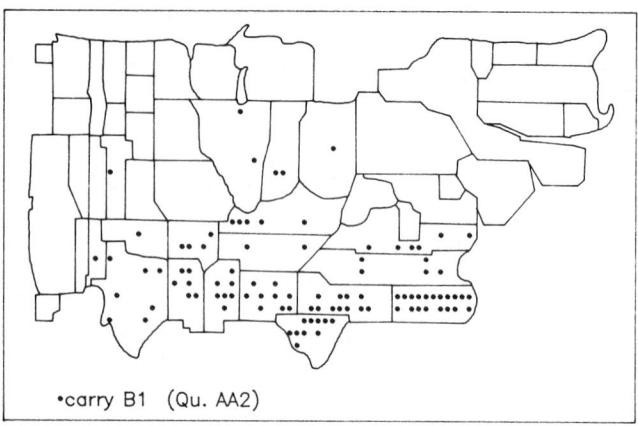

•carry B1　(Qu. AA2)

2 To take, bring.　**chiefly Sth, S Midl**

　1899 (1912) Green *VA Folk-Speech* 106, Caire this letter to the post office.　**1933** Rawlings *South Moon* 24 **FL,** We carried somethin' we figgered 'd make us welcome.　c**1960** *Wilson Coll.* **csKY,** Carry . . . To lug, to tote, to pack.　**1968** *DARE* FW Addit **MD39,** We carried the children gifts.　**1970** *DARE* (Qu. V8b, *Of a person who has been given a paper ordering him into court you might say: "He was ＿＿＿ into court."*) Infs **FL48, NC85,** Carried.

3 To transport in a vehicle; to haul.　**formerly Mid Atl, now widespread**

　1949 Kurath *Word Geog.* 57, Along the Southern coast, less often in the piedmont, *carrying* is used by the side of *hauling.* [Fig 76 "Hauling (wood)" shows *carrying* to be common in South Carolina, North Carolina, Virginia, Maryland.]　**1965–70** *DARE* (Qu. L54, . . *Transporting firewood in a wagon*) 34 Infs, **scattered,** Carrying; **SC7,** Carry off.

4 Esp of horses: to lead.　**chiefly Sth** *old-fash*

　1829 Kirkham *Engl. Grammar* 193, Provincialisms . . . Md. Va. Ky. or Miss. Carry the horse to water.　**1836** Edward *Hist. TX* 107, When this powerful tribe [Comanche] wishes to raise the wind . . they will carry back a Mexican cavy-yard.　**1837** Sherwood *Gaz. GA, Provincialisms* . . . Carry a horse to water, instead of lead or ride him to water.　**1899** (1912) Green *VA Folk-Speech, Carry* . . . "Carry the horses to water."　**1905** *DN* 3.73 **nwAR,** Did you carry the horse to water?　**1913** *DN* 4.4 **ME.** *Ibid* 47 **West,** Carry . . to lead a quadruped.　**1914** *DN* 4.159 **cVA,** *Carry* . . . To lead; ride; drive. "Carry the hawse ovah tuh neah thu cawn-hause."　**1927** Kennedy *Gritny* 57 **sLA** [Black], You mean to say ole Maggie Hutson done got her a husban', aft' de sinful life she bin carryin' all dese years . . ?

5 To profess, maintain.

　1981 Harper–Presley *Okefinokee* 69 (as of 1930), He says to me: 'Mr. Thrift, what kind of religion do you carry?' That's the words he spoke exactly.

carry a corner　See **corner, carry a**

carry a swath　See **swath, carry a**

carry guts to a bear v phr Also *pack ~, tote ~, carry guts to a barrel*

To do the most rudimentary or distasteful task.

　1833 Neal *Down-Easters* 81 **ME,** That air chap's no gentleman . . [he] aint fit to carry guts to a bear.　**1903** *DN* 2.323 **seMO,** *Pack guts to a bear* . . . 'He isn't fitten to pack guts to a bear.' An expression of extreme contempt.　**1914** *DN* 4.70 **ME, nNH,** *Carry guts to a bear, he ain't got sense enough to* . . . Equivalent of "He doesn't know enough to come in when it rains."　**1960** Williams *Walk Egypt* 179 **GA,** Can't tote guts to a bear.　**1967–68** *DARE* (Qu. JJ15a, *Sayings about a person who seems to you very stupid: "He hasn't sense enough to ＿＿＿."*) Infs **MD22, VA29,** Carry guts to a bear; **LA11, 16,** Carry guts to a barrel.

carry-in n, also attrib　**chiefly IL, IN, OH**　See Map and Map Section

A potluck meal.

1965–70 *DARE* (Qu. H70, *When people bring baked dishes .. and share them*) 17 Infs, **chiefly Missip – Ohio Valley**, Carry-in; **IN**1, 60, 65, Carry-in dinner; **CT**16, **IL**70, Carry-in meal; **WI**49, Carry-in dish; (Qu. FF1, *Kinds of socials*) Inf **MO**1, Carry-in. **1967** *Roseville Independent* (IL) 3 Aug 1/4, A carry-in supper will be served at 6:30 p.m. Each member is to bring a dish of food to pass. **1968** *Daily Sentinel – Tribune* (Bowling Green OH) 20 May 8/7, Kenny and Johnny, surprised their mother .. with a carry-in dinner. *Ibid* 13/8, [Headline:] Liberty Women Have Carry-In Dinner. **1968** *Budget* (Sugarcreek OH) 18 July, The above mentioned all except Olans spent Sun. with relatives and friends where a carry-in dinner was held in a park. **1968** *DARE* Tape IN21, We have a carry-in dinner; we have a committee and kind of get together, so many bring meat, and so many bring this and that.

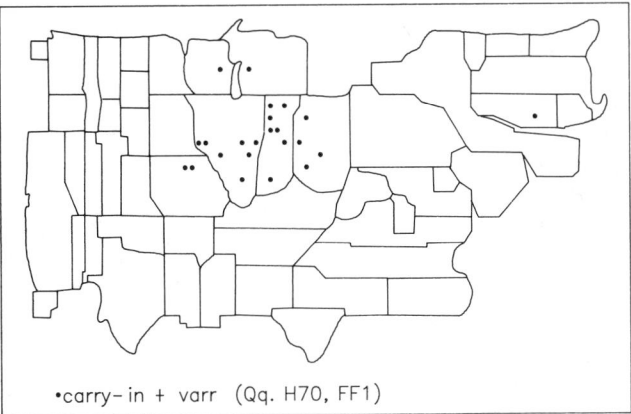

•carry-in + varr (Qq. H70, FF1)

carrying vbl n
The amount that can be carried at one time.
   1940 *AmSp* 15.52 **Appalachians, Ozarks**, I fotched a carryin' (armful) o' wood.'

carry-log n, also attrib Pronc-sp *cal-log* [carry v **B3** + *log*]
1 A vehicle with large wheels, used for hauling logs. Also called **timber wheels**
   1781 in 1875 Virginia *Calendar .. State Papers* 1.569 *(DA)*, [He] is in want of waggons and a carry-log. **1862** *NY Tribune* (NY) 27 Feb 8/5, The only carry-log we could obtain broke in attempting to transport the first gun. **1891** Smith *Farm and Fireside* 52 (*AmSp* 48.89) **nwGA**, A ride on the carrylog tongue would suit me pretty well. **1899** (1912) Green *VA Folk-Speech*, *Carry-log* .. A set of very tall wheels for carrying timber. **1946** *PADS* 6.8 **eNC**, *Cal-log* ['kæˌlɑg] .. Carry-log, a log carrier. A cart with wheels eight or more feet high used for hauling timber logs.
2 By ext: see quot.
   1969 *DARE* (Qu. L13) Inf **GA**84, A carry-log is real old-fashioned, used around 1900 – 1920. It was a frame made of logs with stakes sticking up vertically, on which loose hay was piled. The frame was put on a wagon. Often pronounced ['kɛˌlɔg].

carry me out with the tongs exclam
   1927 *AmSp* 3.135 **ME**, "You could knock me down with a feather" or "carry me out with the tongs!" were expressions of surprise.

carry one on a chip v phr
   1933 *AmSp* 8.1.48 **Ozarks**, *Carry on a chip* .. To treat overly well, to pamper, to spoil. *They jest carried that 'ar boy on a chip till he aint no good for nothin'.*

carry power v phr
To have the innate capacity to influence the minds of others or exert "spiritual" force over them.
   1935 Hurston *Mules & Men* 230 **LA** [Black], Jethro was a great hoodoo man. Jethro could tell Moses could carry power as soon as he saw him. In fact he felt him coming.

carry straws v phr
   1954 *PADS* 21.23 **cSC**, *Carry straws* .. To go courting, "He is carrying straws for Mary." This is taken from the habits of the male bird in the mating season.

car shed n chiefly **Sth, S Midl** Cf **drive shed**
   =**car house.**
   1881 Harris *Uncle Remus Songs* 177 **GA**, In de kyar-shed. **1930** in

1944 *ADD* **eWV**, *Garage* .. *Car shed* is often used instead. **1954** *Harder Coll.* **cwTN**, *Car shed* .. A building for a car, attached to another building. **1965–70** *DARE* (Qu. M22, *Buildings .. on farms*) Infs **IL**4, **KY**86, **MS**81, **NC**21, **OK**18, **TX**51, **VA**38, 70, Car shed.

cart v
1 To haul in a wagon or other utility vehicle. **chiefly Nth, esp NEast** See Map
   1911 Porter *Harvester* 20 **IN**, All the old stock in the storehouse goes out as soon we can cart it. **1939** *LANE* Map 180, The map shows the verbs *hauling, drawing, carting* and *teaming*, recorded in the context *He was hauling (a load of) wood in his wagon.* [Heaviest concentrations of *carting* are in eastern New England and Long Island Sound.] **1949** Kurath *Word Geog.* 57, The area of *carting* extends in an unbroken belt along the shore from Cape Cod to southern New Jersey. **1965–70** *DARE* (Qu. L54, *If someone was transporting firewood in a wagon, .. he was _____ firewood.*) 37 Infs, **chiefly NEast**, Carting.

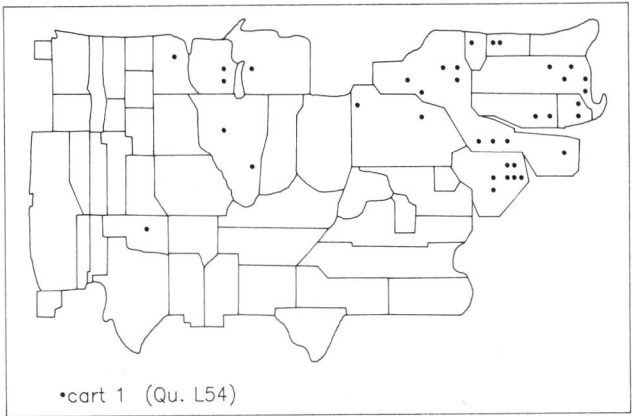

•cart 1 (Qu. L54)

2 To carry. **scattered, but chiefly Nth, N Midl**
   1903 *DN* 2.296 **Cape Cod MA**, *Cart* .. To carry. 'What are you carting them clothes from one room to the other for?' **1965–70** *DARE* (Qu. Y30a, *To take something up and move it .. for example, a paper sack of groceries*) Infs **IL**82, **MA**6, 25, **MI**50, **NY**80, **ND**3, **OR**4, **RI**4, Cart; (Qu. Y30b, .. *For example, a bushel of apples*) 18 Infs, **scattered, but chiefly Nth, N Midl**, Cart. **1981** *DARE* File **cnMA** (as of 1915), We were always *carting* things around when I was a child. You could cart books home from the library, cart old clothes up to the attic. You could even cart along a baby brother or sister when you went on an errand. No cart was involved. You *carried* the books, the clothes, the child.
3 To beat, whisk (an egg).
   1953 Piercy *Shaker Cook Book* 97, "Cart an egg" meant beating it.

cartain See **certain A**

carthrage See **cartridge**

cartin See **certain A**

car tink, car toad See **car knocker**

carton-box n
A cardboard box.
   1946 *AmSp* 21.270 **neKY**, *Carton-box*. A characteristic reduplication.

car tonk See **car knocker**

cartoon n [Alter of *carton*] old-fash
   1907 *DN* 3.183 **seNH**, *Cartoon* .. Pasteboard box or carton, such as slippers or shoes are packed in. Cf *saloon* from *salon*. **1930s** in 1944 *ADD* **nWV**, *Cartoon* .. Freq. **1941–43** *Ibid* **WV**, ['kɑr'tʊn], -['tʌn], –['tɑn]. **1942** *Ibid*, A cartoon of cigarets. Radio. **1959** *VT Hist.* new ser 27.129, Carton [ˌkɑr'tun] .. Occasional in northern Vermont and northern New England.

cartridge n, also attrib; sometimes constr as pl Usu |'kɑ(r)ˌtrɪj, 'ka-, 'kɑ-, 'kɔ-|; also, **esp east of Missip R**, |'kætrɪj, 'kæd(ə)rɪj| less freq |'kɔr-; -tərɪj, -tɪj, -d(ə)rɪj, -dɪj, -tɚj, -trɪč, -dwɪč| Pronc-spp *cad(e)ridge, cardidge, carthrage, cartrich, cᴧtterge, ca(')t(t)ridge, catwich, cottige*
Std sense, var forms.
   1813 (1932) Schillinger *Jrl.* 68 **OH**, Our men employed making cat-tridges. **1834** *Life Andrew Jackson* 94, Not even a single blank catridge

in their pouches. **1890** *DN* 1.6 **cNY,** The sound æ in . . *cartridge* [kæt-]. **1892** *DN* 1.238 **wMO,** [kætrɪdʒ]. **1893** *DN* 1.242 **csME,** *Catridge* . . . Cartridge. *Ibid* 279, The modern [kætrɪdʒ] is probably due to the influence of [pætrɪdʒ]. **1893** Frederic *Copperhead* 152 **nNY,** He can't bite ca'tridges. **1903** *DN* 2.290 **Cape Cod MA,** Other peculiarities of *r* are seen in *pattridge, cattridge.* **1905** *DN* 3.58 **eNE,** Loss of *r* is fairly frequent . . *cattridge. Ibid,* Unvoicing is frequent in . . *cartrich.* **1907** *DN* 3.242 **eME,** *Catridge* . . . Cartridge. **1908** *DN* 3.301 **eAL, wGA,** *Cottige* . . . Cartridge. **1911** *DN* 3.537 **eKY,** How many catridge have you? **1912** Green *VA Folk-Speech, Carthrage* . . . For *cartridge.* **1928** French *Ranchman NM* 225 (as of 1895), 'Why, hell! I didn't have no catridge.' **1940** in 1944 *ADD* **swPA, nWV,** [ˈkɑtɪdʒ]. Old illit. speaker. **1942** Hall *Smoky Mt. Speech* 30, [ˈkætrɪj] (beside [ˈkɑtə‑j]) . . . [ˈkɑtrɪj]. **1960** Hall *Smoky Mt. Folks* 9, He did not trust his marksmanship with his single remaining "cattridge." **1963** Watkins *Yesterday Hills* 25 **cnGA,** Aw, Pa, I just drapped a few little old catterges in the heater to hear them pop. **1965–70** *DARE* (Qu. P38) 364 Infs, **scattered,** Cartridge; 28 Infs, **chiefly east of Missip R,** *chiefly rural and among speakers with little formal education,* Cad(e)ridge; **MI**101, [ˈkɑdwɪč]; **OR**13, Catwich; **GA**65, Cardidge [ˈkɑrdɪj]; **MO**16, Cartridge plant [ˈkorrə‑ɪj].

carving vbl n, also attrib **West** See also **chop v 4, cut v 5**
Separating cattle from a herd; hence n *carver* horse used for this purpose.

1913 (1979) Barnes *Western Grazing* 381, *Cutting Horse.—*A horse used especially for the work of cutting out; a 'carver,' a 'chopper,' Chopping horse. *Cutting Out . . Carving . . .* cowboy expressions to cover the operation of removing from the herd such animals as are needed, like cows, calves and steers. **1942** *AmSp* 17.74 **NE,** Separating cattle from a herd. Old hands still say *carving.* **1968** Adams *Western Words, Carvin' horse—*A cutting horse.

car whack(er) See **car knocker**

cascade v **esp SC**
To vomit.

1848 Bartlett *Americanisms, To Cascade.* To vomit—from the resemblance to a waterfall. It is a common word in England. **1895** *DN* 1.385 **cVA,** *Cascade . .* to vomit. **1943** *LANE* Map 504 *(Vomit)* 1 inf, **cCT,** Cascading. **1950** *PADS* 14.18 **SC,** *Cascade . . .* Euphemism for vomit. Charleston Negro uṣage. **1966** *DARE* (Qu. BB18, *To vomit a great deal at once*) Infs **SC**19, 27, Cascade; (Qu. BB17, *Words . . for vomiting*) Inf **FL**5, Cascaded.

cascara n, also attrib
1 also *cascara buckthorn, cascara tree:* A deciduous large shrub or small tree *(Rhamnus purshiana)* with small greenish flowers, and black berries. Also called **bearberry 4, bearwood, bitterbark 2, brittlewood, chittam wood 4, coffeeberry 2a(2), coffee tree 2, mountain cranberry, pigeonberry, polecat tree, sacred bark, western coffee, wild coffee, wild coffeebush**

[**1897** Sudworth *Arborescent Flora* 299, *Rhamnus purshiana . . . Common Names* . . . Cascara Sagrada (Cal., Oreg.).] **1931** U.S. Dept. Ag. *Misc. Pub.* 101.113, *Cascara buckthorn . .* also called cascara . . . and locally known as cascara sagrada [etc] . . is by far the most important species economically. **1946** Peattie *Pacific Coast* 68, Cascara trees (really a kind of buckthorn) are still stripped, in summer, by seasonal labor . . and you see signs in the woods advertising for cascara barkers, at the peak of the employment period. **1967** *DARE* FW Addit **WA**29, Cascara is the same as chittam; it's used as a physic. **1979** Little *Checklist U.S. Trees* 248, *Cascara buckthorn . . . Other common names* —cascara, cascara sagrada.

2 Esp the dried bark, but also the leaves or berries; any cathartic remedy made from these.

1937 U.S. Forest Serv. *Range Plant Hdbk.* B127, Cascara buckthorn . . . is important chiefly as the source of cascara sagrada (literally, sacred bark) of commerce, which is used medicinally as a laxative . . . However, the name cascara sagrada is also used in the trade for the bark of California buckthorn. **1966–69** *DARE* (Qu. BB22) Infs **CA**53, 97, **LA**14, **MI**96, 100, Cascara; **OR**6, **WA**1, 20, Cascara bark; **RI**17, Cascara sagrada; **CA**36, Cascara tea; **WA**1, Cascara leaves.

cascaron n, also attrib [MexSpan < Span *cascaron* eggshell] **chiefly CA** *old-fash*
~~An eggshell filled with confetti or scented water, used as a~~ decoration or party favor.

1855 *Los Angeles Star* 1 Jan. 2/1 *(AmSp* 30.229), In the city cascarones commanded a premium, and many were complimented with them as a finishing touch to their head dress. **1879** *Scribner's Mth.* 18.615/1, The cascarones looked very pretty . . . They were egg-shells, emptied of their contents by means of a small hole in one end. **1881** Bell *Reminiscences* 200 **sCA,** A *cascaron* is an egg shell filled with gilt paper of all the colors of the rainbow, cut as fine as scissors can cut. **1910** Hart *Vigilante Girl* **nCA** 226, They call them *cascarones;* the eggshells are emptied, and filled—sometimes with those colored papers or confetti, and sometimes with scented waters. It is a carnival custom you find among all the Latin races. **1946** Peattie *Pacific Coast* 161 **CA,** That social, likely enough, was the Shrovetide jollity, winding up with a *cascaron* dance.

cascrom n [Scots *cascrom* a crook-handled spade, used by Highlanders; a kind of foot plow]

1930 Shoemaker *1300 Words* 15 **cPA Mts** (as of c1900), *Casorom* [sic]—A small wooden plough to work by hand around rocks and stumps.

case n¹
1 usu in phr *in good case:* Esp of animals: a condition of body or general health.

1634 in 1884 Maine Hist. Soc. *Documentary Hist.* 3.31, They [the pigs] . . kept themselves in very good Case. **1745** in 1912 Essex Inst. *Coll.* 48.299 **MA,** I was still out of Case but Keept about. **1852** Stowe *Uncle Tom's Cabin* 172, If he [Tom] was kept fat and in good case till he got him into market. **1918** *DN* 5.15 **Martha's Vineyard MA,** *Case . .* Condition. "The sheep were in good case, and I sold them for twenty-two cents a pound." **1955** McAtee *Dial. Grant Co. IN Suppl.* 6, *Case . .* condition. Archaic. "Lige's pigs are in good case."

2 In tobacco curing: a condition in which the leaves contain enough moisture to be handled without breaking. Also called **order**

1640 in 1883 *Archives of MD* 98, Bad Tobacco shall be judged ground leafes Second Crops leafs notably brused . . fro[s]t bitten . . in the house sooty wett or in too high Case. **1724** (1865) Jones *Present State VA* 70, When it [=tobacco] is in proper Case, (as they call it) . . they *strike* it, or take it down. **1864** ME Bd. Ag. *Abstract for 1863* 162 [Letter from **KY**], The fires should be suffered to go out, and the tobacco be suffered to come in case, or get soft again. **1903** *DN* 2.308 **seMO,** *Case . . .* In condition for packing, as applied to tobacco. When hung in a barn the leaves become dry and brittle. Toward spring the leaves soften and when quite pliable are said to be 'in *case.*' They must be 'bulked' promptly as they again dry out and may become worthless. **1944** *PADS* 2.65 **Midl. 1950** Stuart *Hie Hunters* 95 **eKY,** They knew this vapor was carried by the wind among the drying tobacco plants in the wall-less tobacco barns and it moistened them and put them in case. **1966** *PADS* 45.10 **KY. 1967** Key *Tobacco Vocab.* **NC, TN. 1968–69** *DARE* Tape **KY**35, After a rain or the weather's damp enough . . it'll get in case till it's flexible and you won't damage or break it up when you're tryin' to strip it; **OH**58, They'll pile 'em up in a pile, to keep 'em in case . . . So they can handle it without it . . fallin' to pieces . . . "In case" is in damp . . , leathery-like; **IN**45, It's hard to bring in case or hold in case, . . Case is the moisture in the leaf.

3 Transf: a moist or mature condition; see quots.

1941 *AmSp* 16.23 **IN,** *In case.* Moist, damp because of wet weather. 'The crackers are in case.' **1954** *Harder Coll.* **cwTN,** *In case . . .* ready for cutting or harvesting. "Them sodie-beans in case now."

4 An infatuation, crush.

1852 *Harper's Mag.* 5.338/2, Young America sipping cobblers, and roving about in very loose and immoral coats, voted it "a case." The elderly ladies thought it a "shocking flirtation." **1912** *DN* 3.577 **wIN,** *Have a case . . .* To be in love. "I think Joe and Edith have a case." **1927** Hart *Bellamy Trial* 75, Everyone knew they had a terrible case on each other. **1965–70** *DARE* (Qu. AA10, *A very special liking that a boy may have for a girl [or the other way round]— You'd say "He_____ her" [or "She_____ him."]*) 13 Infs, **chiefly Inland Nth, CA,** Has (got) a (bad) case on; **IL**80, Has a case; **IA**38, Had a case on each other; **MD**19, That's a bad case; (QR, near Qu. HH22) Inf **CA**149, He had a case on her, = a crush. [15 of 17 Infs women]

5 An unusual or peculiar person; a character; a disreputable person.

1848–60 Bartlett *Dict. Amer. (OED), Case,* a character, a queer one; as 'That Sol Haddock is a case'. 'What a hard case he is', meaning a reckless scapegrace; *mauvais sujet.* **1884** *Harper's Mag.* 68.922/2, There was a little wheat in all that chaff of a man . . . But the wife is a case. **1899**

(1912) Green *VA Folk-Speech, Case* . . . A person who is peculiar or remarkable in any respect; as a queer *case;* a hard *case;* sometimes without qualification: as, he is a case. **1905** *DN* 3.5 **cCT. 1907** *DN* 3.210 **nwAR, cCT. 1921** *DN* 5.116 **KY. 1930** Shoemaker *1300 Words* 10 **cPA Mts** (as of c1900), *Case*—"A hard case", an unregenerate loafer. **c1960** *Wilson Coll.* **csKY,** *Case* . . . Person or specimen. Ain't Sam a queer case.

6 See quots.
1833 *Sketches D. Crockett* 24 **wTN,** In the slang of the backwoods, one swore . . he would never be "a case"—that is flat, without a dollar. **1930** Shoemaker *1300 Words* 10 **cPA Mts** (as of c1900), *Case*—Anything that is finished; broken beyond repair.

7 usu in phr *get off* (or *on*) *one's case:* A point of vulnerability; an area subject to criticism. *chiefly among Blacks* Cf **case** v
1971 Roberts *Third Ear* [Black], *Case* . . . an imaginary region of the mind in which is centered one's vulnerable points, eccentricities, and sensitivities: e.g. Don't get on my case! **1971** Landy *Underground Dict.,* *Get off my case* (B[lack]) Expression meaning leave me alone. **1972** Claerbaut *Black Jargon* 65, *Get on (your) case* . . to verbally harass or attack someone . . . to verbally chastise or punish someone: *If you don't do it, he'll really get on your case.* **1980** Folb *Runnin' Down* 232 [Black], *Case, stay on (one's)*—Steadily disparage, ridicule, or harass. **1981** *DARE* File **csWI,** I overheard a conversation in which a [White] man interpreted his wife's comments as criticism, and snapped at her "Get off my case, will you?"

8 in phrr *come* (or *get*) *down to cases:* To come to the point, to get to the bare facts of a matter.
1918 Mulford *Bar-20* 21 (DA), Coming down to cases, you ain't really a cow-puncher. **1948** *Time* 19 July 87/3, Then he got down to cases. **1970** *DARE* FW Addit **cwPA,** *Come down to cases:* get down to brass tacks.

case n² also attrib [Etym uncert; perh expressing the idea of unity, all the parts being in a single container; perh Fr *caisse* cash, as in phr *en caisse* cash in hand]
1a A dollar.
1885 *Sante Fe W. New Mexican* 30 July 4/6 (DA), Captain Hoover furnished him street car fare to the extent of two five case notes. **1890** *DN* 1.60 **swOH,** *Case* . . . a dollar. **1893** *KS Univ. Qrly., Case:* dollar, as 'It cost me two cases.' **1908** McGaffey *Sorrows* 196 (DA), He gives me a twenty case note and the card. **1921** *Collier's* 15 Jan 20/4, He takes out his wallet and removes a hundred-case note. **1929** *AmSp* 4.358, "Dollar" . . . is . . *case* (most frequently used in such a phrase as "a two-case note," or "a five-case note").
1b also *caser:* A silver dollar.
1927 *DN* 5.441, *Case* . . . A silver dollar. **1932** *Santa Fe Mag.* Jan 35/1 [Railway slang], A silver dollar is a caser; a dollar bill is a *Jew flag.*
2 attrib: A coin of a particular denomination as against the same amount of money comprised of several coins. **chiefly SC**
1954 *PADS* 21.23 **SC,** *Case dollar* . . . A whole dollar, not a dollar in change. Some take this to mean a silver dollar. **1967** *DARE* (Qu. U27, *Names for a silver dollar*) Infs **SC**40, 43, Case dollar. **1972** *Atlanta Letters* **c,cnGA,** Case quarter, dime, nickel: One single coin . . instead of the change equal to that amount. **1973** *Patrick Coll.* **AL** (as of 1946), A case dollar, case quarter, case dime is one coin of the total amount; two dimes and one nickel make a quarter, but a 25-cent piece is a case quarter. **1980–81** *DARE* File **Columbia SC,** Here . . people refer to a quarter in one piece as a "case quarter." I never heard this expression in NC; **SC** [Black], Case nickel, case dime, case quarter.

case v Cf **case** n¹ **7**
1971 Roberts *Third Ear* [Black], *Case* . . to joke about another's characteristics or foibles; e.g. He cased her at lunch. 2. to reprove or reprimand sternly; e.g. His mother cased him for being late.

case conj See **because** conj

case-expander n Cf **stretcher**
A non-existent tool used as the basis of practical jokes.
1967 *DARE* (Qu. HH14, *Ways of teasing a beginner or inexperienced person—for example, by sending him for a 'left-handed monkey wrench':* "Go get me _____.") Inf **MN2,** Case-expander.

case fly n [For the *case* which the larva builds and lives in]
A caddis fly (*Trichoptera* spp).
1926 Essig *Insects N. Amer.* 172 **West,** The adults are known as caddis flies, caddice flies, or case flies.

case knife n¹ [From its orig being carried in a case] **esp freq in Midl**
1 A table knife.
[**1790** [see **caseknife bean**].] **1885** Twain *Huck. Finn* 308, So I'll mosey along now, and smouch a couple of case-knives. **1903** *DN* 2.296 **Cape Cod MA** (as of 1850s), *Case knife* . . . An ordinary table knife. **1906** Low *Some Recoll.* 29 (as of 1840s), It is most interesting to see them stow the tea away with boxes of firecrackers and mats of cassia. They make such close stowing that you can hardly get a case knife between the chests. **1907** *DN* 3.206 **nwAR. 1908** *DN* 3.285 **eAL, wGA. 1944** *PADS* 2.41 **sVA. 1951** West *Witch Diggers* 36 **sIN,** He finished eating, rose, took the case-knife off the mantel, and put it in the bowl with his spoon. **1954** *Harder Coll.* **cwTN,** *Case-knife* . . . table knife. **c1960** *Wilson Coll.* **csKY,** *Case-knife*—A table knife. "Mammy broke one of her best case-knives yesterday." **1968** *DARE* FW Addit **IN, VA.**
2 A folding knife. [Perh infl by *Case* trademark of W.R. Case & Sons Cutlery Co.]
1930 Shoemaker *1300 Words* 11 **cPA Mts** (as of c1900), *Case knife*—A folding knife, to differentiate from a dagger in early days. **1968** *DARE* (Qu. F39, *A large pocket knife with blades that fold in and out*) Inf **OH**61, Case knife. [**1981** *DARE* File **PA** [Letter from W.R. Case & Sons Cutlery Co.], The origins of Case knives can be traced back to the mid-1800's and the family of Job Russell Case.]

caseknife bean n Also *Dutch caseknife (bean), caseknife bunch bean, caseknife runner* [See quot 1790]
A tall, climbing variety of the common garden bean (*Phaseolus vulgaris*).
1790 Deane *New Engl. Farmer* 20/1, The case-knife bean is so called, because the pod is shaped like that instrument. **1859** *IL Dept. Ag. Trans. for 1857–58* 3.503, There are many varieties of pole beans. The early Dutch caseknife is excellent, both as a snap and shell bean. **1941** *LANE* Map 259 **swMA,** Dutch caseknife beans, smaller than lima beans. **1966–69** *DARE* (Qu. I20, *Other kinds of beans*) Inf **KY**22, Caseknife beans; **AR**20, Caseknife bunch beans. **1978** *Wanigan Catalog* 6, *Case knife* = Brown Seeded P[ole]—A very old name in garden beans, having been listed in 1820 catalogs. This one, from Maine is a tall climber with flat green pods and beans brown, flattened, size 5 seed. Early. *Case knife* Syns: Dutch caseknife, Caseknife Runner—P[ole] Origin in 1820 and a leader by 1860. Still great. Seed size 6, flat, white, with faint gray veining. Late here.

caser See **case** n² **1b**

case weather n [**case** n¹ **2**]
A warm spell in the winter, during which tobacco leaves soften enough to be handled without breaking.
1948 *AmSp* 23.309 **WI,** Here [on racks in the tobacco shed] the crop hangs until *Case Weather* arrives. It may come practically any time after there has been one good frost and the tobacco is thoroughly cured, usually in December or January. **1950** *WELS* (*A fog that comes in cold weather*) 1 Inf, **swWI,** Case weather—old-fashioned; (*The warm weather around the end of the year, or the beginning of the New Year*) 1 Inf, **csWI,** Case weather refers to taking down and stripping tobacco.

case worm n [See **case fly;** *OED* 1606 →]
The larva of a caddis fly (*Trichoptera* spp).
1926 Essig *Insects N. Amer.* 172 **West,** The larvae are . . known as case worms, caddis worms, or to many country boys as fish bait.

cashaw See **cushaw**

cash banana See **cassabanana**

cashes n
=**poison hemlock 1.**
1900 Lyons *Plant Names* 113, *C[onium] maculatum* . . . Cashes, Bunk, Poison Parsley. **1930** Sievers *Amer. Med. Plants* 46, *Poison Hemlock . . . Other common names . . .* Cashes, bunk, heck-how.

cash in v phr [Abbr for **checks, cash in one's**]
To die.
1907 Love *Deadwood Dick* 118, During the war many of them cashed in and the others for the most part left for pastures new. **1907** Mulford *Bar-20* 197 **West,** "Is he comin' up too?" "No, I reckons not. Jimmy, th' bartender, said that he cashed in up at Laramie." *Ibid* 362, "How did Trendley cash in?" asked Porous. "Nobody knows except that bum from th' Tin-Cup. I'll get him later."

cash money n chiefly Sth, S Midl

Money that is in immediately negotiable form: coin or the equivalent, rather than money-orders or checks.

1894 Riley *Armazindy* 4 **IN,** She could raise the means to pay / . . . In cash-money. **1926** Roberts *Time of Man* 18 **cKY,** I'll give you twenty dollars a month in cash money and the house rent free. **1934** (1970) Wilson *Backwoods Amer.* 207 **Ozarks.** c**1937** in 1972 *Amer. Slave* 2.113 **SC,** Any cash money? Where you gwine get 'em? Only cash the gospel! Have to get the gospel. **1942** Rawlings *Cross Creek* 59 **FL,** The first cash money from the first orange crop, a good one, disappeared. **1944** *PADS* 2.32 **wNC.** **1954** *Harder Coll.* **cwTN.** c**1960** *Wilson Coll.* **csKY.** **1968** *DARE* Tape **SC56,** If I had to go to the hospital, I'd be well taken care of without puttin' out any cash money. **1970** *DARE* (Qu. U19b, *Talking of paper money, "He always carries a big _____."*) Inf **TX106,** Roll of cash money.

cashunk See **ker-**

cash up v phr [Cf **cast up**]

1943 *LANE* Map 504 **cwCT,** Vomit . . . [1 inf] Cashed up [inf displayed amusement.]

casino See **cassena**

'casion See **occasion** n

casket n

1958 *Hand Coll.* **neOH,** When you slice a loaf of bread and cut into a hole in the bread, it means death. The hole is a casket.

casket nail n Also *casket tack* Cf **coffin nail, coffin tack**

A cigarette.

1966–69 *DARE* (Qu. DD6b) Infs **DE1, KY65, MN38,** Casket nail; **KY65,** Casket tack; [**MS16, NJ1, NY209, TN6,** Nail in (a, the, your) casket].

casmash, casouse See **ker-**

Caspar Milquetoast See **milquetoast**

caspergou See **gaspergou**

casplash See **ker-**

cassabanana n Also sp *cassebanane,* folk-etym *cash banana* [Perh blend of *casaba* (melon) + *banana*]

1 A vine *(Sicana odorifera)* which produces a long orange-crimson edible fruit; also the fruit.

1911 *Century Dict. Suppl.,* Cassabanana . . . A plant of the family Cucurbitaceae (Sicana odorifera) . . . The fruit is sometimes two feet long, and squash-like, orange or crimson in color, and with a very aromatic odor. **1967** LeCompte *Word Atlas* 317 **seLA,** [17 of 21 infs responded *cassebanane* for "large, cucumber shaped vegetable, usually pickled."] **1968** *DARE* (Qu. I23, *Kinds of squash*) Inf **LA33,** Cassebanane ['kɑsˌbaˌnɑn]—long sausage-shaped squash. **1968** *DARE* FW Addit **seLA,** Cassebanane ['kasˌbanɑn] is squash cooked in somewhat the same way as sweet potatoes; ruddy brown in color. **1976** Bailey–Bailey *Hortus Third* 1041, Cassabanana . . . Grown to some extent in the Gulf region . . . for its ornamental, fragrant fr[uit], which is also edible.

2 =**vegetable sponge.**

1968 *DARE* FW Addit **csLA,** Cash banana The netlike interior of a squash or gourd used for washing dishes. *Ibid,* Cash banana ['kæs bəˌnænə] The inside of a particular kind of squash often used for washing dishes—sometimes for the face.

cassena n Also ~ *berry* Also sp *casino, casseena, cassia, cassina, cassine, cassio, cussenca* chiefly S Atl

=**yaupon;** also a drink made from the plant.

1587 (1964) Laudonnière *Notable History* (transl Hakluyt) [3]ᵛ **FL,** He commaundeth Cassine to bee brewed, which is a drinke made of the leaves of a certaine tree. **1697** (1945) Dickinson *Jrl.* 48 **FL,** They . . went to drinking casseena, smoking and talking. **1854** Simms *Scout* 245 **SC,** Sometimes we regale ouselves on Indian tea, which is made of the Cussenca leaf. **1862** (1955) Holmes *Brokenburn* 164 **neLA,** They . . would like to come to see us Christmas Eve . . . Johnny and I gathered a lot of mistletoe and crimson casino berries. **1897** Sudworth *Arborescent Flora* 280, *Ilex vomitoria* . . . Cassio-berry-bush. **1930** Stoney–Shelby *Black Genesis* 102 **seSC,** De ditch bank been growed up t'ick wid sassyfrass-bush, an' cassina-berry an' t'ing. **1936** Smith–Sass *Carolina Rice* 18, The boundary of the garden would frequently be marked . . with hedges of China briar, jessamine, cassena, or Spanish

bayonet. **1960** Vines *Trees SW* 647, Local names in use are Cassena, Cassine, Cassio-berry-bush [etc]. **1968** *DARE* (Qu. T5, . . *Kinds of evergreens*) Inf **SC63,** Cassena. **1974** (1977) Coon *Useful Plants* 64, Cassiaberry bush . . . is a smallish evergreen tree, occurring from Virginia to Florida.

casson n [*casson* chest; cf Fr *caisson; OED* "Obs."]

A chest for storing clothes.

1930 Shoemaker *1300 Words* 15 **cPA Mts** (as of c1900), Casson—A family chest. **1940** Richter *Trees* 269 **OH** (as of early 19th c), When first he came, he was a dandy with a whole casson, they said, of shirts and fixings.

cassy See **causey**

cast v

1 To throw. *old-fash*

1917 Garland *Son Middle Border* 182 **WI,** Mother put up a basket of food, father cast a quarter of beef into the back-part of the sleigh. **1966–69** *DARE* (Qu. Y10, *To throw something—for example, "The dog came at him, so he picked up a stone and _____ it at him."*) Infs **AR31, GA84, NC41, TX10,** Cast. [All Infs old]

2 To cast a spell.

1934 (1970) Wilson *Backwoods Amer.* 174 **AR, MO,** The prospective profiteer would furnish Wid with a twenty dollar gold piece and so he would plant the coin in the chosen earth and "cast." Provided the spell were right . . . the twenty dollars was due to have foaled four tens.

cast n [Alter of *cask;* see Pronc Intro 3.I.14]

1969 *DARE* FW Addit **CT,** Cast [kæst] is said for cask [kæsk].

caster n, also attrib Also sp *castor* *old-fash*

1 A stand for small containers or cruets used at the dining table; the containers themselves.

1819 *NY Daily Advt.* (NY) 6 Apr 4/5, [Advt:] Castors & Liquor Stands. **1853** (1970) Felt *Customs of New Engl.* 21, *Castor*—As a frame of wood or metal, it holds small bottles with various condiments . . . Now it is seen in most families with comfortable means of support. **1904** *World* (NY NY) 27 Mar World Mag 10/4, On each table is a caster-stand, containing cruets of condiments and seasons. **1928** Aldrich *Lantern* 163 **NE,** There were two red plush chairs, a stylish castor, a green glass pitcher with frosted glasses. **1965–70** *DARE* (Qu. G6, *Other dishes that you might have on the table for a big dinner or special occasion—for example, Thanksgiving*) 30 Infs, **chiefly east of Missip R,** Caster; **PA9, 128,** Caster set; **AL30,** Pickle casters; **MD14,** Salt-and-pepper casters. [Of all Infs responding to the question, 70% were old; of those giving these responses 100% were old.]

2 See quot.

1896 *DN* 1.414 **cNY,** Caster: a sled which has cast-iron shoes.

casterate, casterize See **castrate**

castermine v

1949 *AmSp* 24.107 **neGA** [Black], Castermine . . . Castrate.

casting n *obs*

A coin.

1834 Crockett *Narrative* 78, The boat was loaded with whiskey, flour, sugar, coffee, salt, castings, and other articles suitable for the country. **1844** *Spirit of the Times* 21 Sept 354 (AmSp 40.181), He accordingly forked over the castings, $600 in number. **1846** Corcoran *Pickings* 18, He slipped a Mexican casting into the hand of Fournier. **1851** (1969) Burke *Polly Peablossom* 41 **MO,** A substantial farmer . . by years of toil, had accumulated a tolerable pretty pile of castings.

casting pple

1977 *Yankee* Jan 73 **csME,** Setting *yeast bread* is called *casting.*

cast-iron dog n [From the metal-like appearance of the hairless skin] **SW** *obs* Cf **asthma dog**

The Mexican hairless dog.

1853 in 1930 Brewerton *Overland* 208 **SW,** One of those hairless, rat-tailed New Mexican curs, which the Americans are in the habit of designating as "cast-iron dogs." **1882** Sweet–Knox *Sketches TX Siftings* 60 **TX,** The Mexicans call him *pelon.* The Americans refer to him as the no-hair dog; while the stranger from the north, who sees him for the first time, calls him a cast-iron dog, for that is what he looks like at first glance.

cast-iron sweat n

1912 *DN* 3.567, Conniption . . . Highly nervous state . . . In New York *cast iron swet* [sic] is also common, and I have heard it in Connecticut.

castle bean n
=**bagpod.**

1948 *Miami* (Okla.) *D. News – Record* 30 July 8/2 *(DA)*, Farmers call it [*Sesbania vesicaria*] bladderpod, coffeebean and castle-bean. 1948 *Sun* (Baltimore MD) 10 Nov 16/3 *(Hench Coll.)*, There's a new cattle-killing weed on the loose, from Florida to Texas and Oklahoma. Its botanical name is *glottidium vesicarium*. Farmers call it bladderpod, coffee bean weed, castle bean, says *Farm Journal*.

castor See **caster**

castorate See **castrate**

castor cat n [*castor* beaver + *cat*]
A beaver.

1930 Shoemaker *1300 Words* 13 **cPA Mts** (as of c1900), *Castor cat* — The beaver.

castorwood n Also *castor tree* [*castor* beaver] *obs* Cf **beaver tree**
=**sweet bay 2.**

1859 (1968) Bartlett *Americanisms* 27, *Beaver-tree. (Magnolia glauca)* Called also . . Castor-wood. 1872 Schele de Vere *Americanisms* 208, The *Beaver-tree (Magnolia glauca)*, is so called in the West, while elsewhere it is more generally known as *Castor-tree*.

castrate v Usu |ˈkæstˌreɪt|; occas epenthetic |ˈkæstəˌreɪt, ˈkæstəˌeɪt|; also (perh infl by *circumcise*) |ˈkæstəˌaɪz|, rarely |ˈkæθəˌaɪz| Pronc-spp *casterate, casterize, castorate* See also **castermine**
Std sense, var forms.

1939 *LANE* Map 210 (*Castrate*) **nwRI**, 1 inf, [kæstəˌet]; **seMA,** 1 inf, [kæstəret]; **seMA,** 1 inf, [kæsdəret]; **swCT,** 1 inf, [kæθəˌeɪz]; **cMA,** 1 inf, [kæstəˌaez]. 1965–70 *DARE* (Qu. K70) 17 Infs, **chiefly Sth, S Midl,** Casterate [ˈkæstəˌeɪt]; **MS**58, 81, [ˈkæsəret]; (Qu. K25) Infs **MI**23, 71, OK1, TN26, TX32, WI6, [ˈkæstəˌeɪt]. 1973 DeVries *Forever Panting* 221 **CT,** "It *is* a plain case of delusions of grandeur now — if you can call thinking you've been castrated grand." He pronounced it "castorate," as though from long years of prescribing castor oil. 1973 Allen *LAUM* 1.251 (*Castrate*), **cMN, swNE,** 3 infs, Casterize.

cast up v phr [**cast** v 1]
To vomit.

1966 *DARE* (Qu. BB17, . . *Expressions . . for vomiting*) Inf **SC**24, Cast up.

casuey v
Of a horse: to buck.

1921 Thorp *Songs Cowboys* 106 [Black], He ca-su-ied wid me, most ruinous, / Till ma haid jest popped de ceilin'. [Footnote:] Ca-su-ied, southern Texas word for bucking. 1944 Adams *Western Words, Casueying* — (kɑ-ˈsooyíng) A South Texas term for pitching, but rarely heard in other sections.

caswash See **ker-**

cat n

1 A person; spec:

a A malicious or spiteful woman.

1915 *DN* 4.196, *Cat,* a mean, cunning woman. "If I had an old cat like that for my mother, I'd do something desperate." 1932 *AmSp* 7.330 **MD** [Student jargon], *Cat* — a spiteful woman. 1942 Berrey – Van den Bark *Amer. Slang* 406.4, *Shrewish woman.* Cat.

b A prostitute or woman of questionable morals. *chiefly among Blacks*

1916 *DN* 4.321 **KS,** Cat wagon . . . get meat for (one's) cat . . . To solicit. 1932 *AmSp* 7.330 **MD** [Student jargon], Cat . . . a prostitute. 1934 *AmSp* 9.288 [Black], *Cat.* A low woman; a prostitute. 1937 *AmSp* 12.217 [Black], A dictionary of 1670 defined *cat* as 'a common whore' (a meaning which still survives in the slang 'cathouse' — a brothel). Negroes use it in this obsolete sense. 1958 McCulloch *Woods Words* **Pacific NW,** *Cat* . . An easy dame. 1967–70 *DARE* (Qu. AA7a, . . *A woman who is very fond of men . . she's nice about it*) Inf **NJ**67, Cat; (Qu. AA7b, . . *She's not respectable about it*) Infs **CT**43, **NY**55, **TX**42, Cat; **KY**94, Gay cat. [4 of 5 Infs Black]

c A performer or aficionado of jazz music. *orig among Black jazz musicians*

[1922 J.A. Carpenter *(title of ballet)* Krazy Kat *(OEDS)*.] 1935 *Down Beat* 1 Nov. 8 *(OEDS)*, The slanguage of swing-terms that 'cats' use.

1937 L. Armstrong *Swing that Music* xiii.III *(OEDS)* I wanted to give 'em a load of how we swing that music at home. My 'cats' understood it the same way and began lickin' their chops, as we say it. 1937 *AmSp* 12.183, *Cats.* Those members of the audience who are receptive to jazz music or who understand it. 1955 Shapiro & Hentoff *Hear Me Talkin'* 335, Minton's was just a place for cats to jam. 1958 *AmSp* 33.224 [Jazz], Hundreds of thousands of *cats,* white and colored, . . continue to use the word [ofay] in blissful ignorance.

d A good fellow; a guy. *esp among Blacks*

1938 *AmSp* 13.314 [Black], *Cat.* City slicker without conceit. 1946 (1972) Mezzrow *Really Blues* 331, Cat: *regular fellow, guy.* 1958 *PADS* 30.44, *Cat* . . . Orig., one who was "hep." Obs. in this sense; now, any person. (Thus, a musician can now speak of a "square cat" — a contradiction in terms in the '30's.) 1965 Brown *Manchild* 77 [Black], I knew K.B. about a year before we became ace boon coons. K.B. was the first cat I locked with up at Wiltwyck. 1965–70 *DARE* (Qu. HH2, . . *A citified person*) Infs **LA**8, **VA**69, City cat; (Qu. HH5) Inf **LA**46, Mod cat; (Qu. HH17, . . *"He'd like to be the _____ around here."*) Inf **KY**73, Head cat; **NC**87, Top cat; (Qu. HH19, . . *A tramp*) Inf **PA**247, Sorry cat; (Qq. II10a,b, *Asking directions . . when you don't know his name . . "Say, _____"*) Infs **CA**187, **TN**50, Cat; (Qu. II23) Inf **GA**72, Top cat; (Qu. U32) Inf **NY**249, A nice cat; (Qu. EE11) Inf **SC**69, [The game has] three or four cats (boys) — catcher, pitcher, hitter. [7 of 11 Infs Black] 1980 Folb *Runnin' Down* 36 **Los Angeles CA** [Black], *Dude, cat* . . carry the same potential meaning as *guy.*

e An expert.

1912 *Jrl. Amer. Folkl.* 25.139 **Appalachians,** When one is proficient in anything, he is said to be a *cat* on that thing: "She is a cat on bread."

f Transf and used as a combining form: one who has qualities of timidity, nervousness, or furtiveness. See also as separate entries **fraidy-cat, fuss-cat, scaredy-cat**

1965–70 *DARE* (Qu. GG14, *Names . . for someone who fusses . . a lot*) Infs **MA**100, **NJ**1, **NY**52, **VA**46, Fuss-cat; **NH**10, Worry-cat; (Qu. HH11, *A very timid or cowardly person: "He's _____."*) 102 Infs, Fraidy-cat; 54 Infs, Scaredy-cat; **CA**2, **CT**16, **MA**15, **NY**24, Fraid-cat; **IL**4, **ME**6, **MN**2, **NJ**39, **OH**38, Scared-cat; **MI**67, **NY**66, **TX**36, **WI**70, Scary-cat; **CA**158, **LA**40, **MI**55, Scare-cat; **MO**15, Cowardy-cat; **AZ**6, Scairty-cat; (Qu. HH11b, *Someone who is too particular or fussy — if it's a woman*) Infs **MA**15, **NJ**1, Old fuss-cat; (Qu. HH12, *A person who is always finding fault about unimportant things*) Inf **MA**15, Old fuss-cat; (Qu. JJ4, *A child who is always telling on other children*) Inf **OH**77, Snitch-cat; **MI**32, Squeal-cat; (Qu. JJ7, *Words or expressions for cheating in school examinations*) 16 Infs, **scattered, but rare in SE,** Copy-cat.

2 A kind or sort of person or thing. Cf **breed of cat**

1977 *UpCountry* Nov 14/3 **cwNH,** One might think that . . the equivalent price would be $100 a cord — all things being equal. However, a woodstove and an oil furnace are very different cats.

3 In children's play:

a A game in which a player uses a bat to tap a wooden peg into the air and then bat it as far as possible, toward fielders who try to catch it. **chiefly NEast, esp NY**

a1883 (1911) Bagby *VA Gentleman* 49, He must now learn to cut jackets, play hard-ball, choose partners for cat and chermany. 1896 *DN* 1.414 **seNY,** *Cat:* same as *pussy.* Ibid 422 **cNY,** *Pussy:* a game played with a small bat (usually part of a broomstick) and a small block 1″ by 4″. 1901 *DN* 2.137 **neOH,** *Cat* . . . A game like pickie . . but more elaborate. 1933 Hanley Disks **Boston MA,** *Cat* — Children's Game. With a sharp stick like a cigar, and you tap one end and then hit it. Peewee type. 1965–70 *DARE* (Qu. EE10, *A game in which a short stick lying on the ground is flipped into the air and then hit with a longer stick*) Infs **MA**52, **NY**34, 35, 44, 57, Cat.

b The tapered wooden peg used in **cat** n **3a.**

1883 Newell *Games & Songs* 186, The "cat" is a little billet of wood, about four inches long, and pointed at the ends, which is to be struck with a light stick. 1891 *Jrl. Amer. Folkl.* 4.233 **Brooklyn NY,** *Cat* . . . The "cat" is whittled from a piece of wood, and is usually about six inches in length by an inch in diameter, with sharp pointed ends. *Ibid, Cat* . . . The pitcher throws the cat towards the circle . . . If the cat falls without the circle, the batter hits it on one end . . and as it rises into the air strikes it again. The other boys try to catch the cat . . and if they succeed, the batter is out. 1943 *Sun* (Baltimore MD) 17 Aug 12/7, In Pennsylvania the game was called tip-cat, and the short stick was the cat. 1947 Smith *Baseball* 28 **NY,** Two-hole cat had a parent called "cat" (short for "catapult") in which a small stick named a "cat" was catapulted out of a circle while the boy who was "it" hastened after it and other boys scrambled varying distances, depending on how long it took "it" to recover the stick. **1980** *DARE* File **NYC** (as of c1920), In the game of *one-a-cat*, the stick that was hit [was] called the *cat*.

c also *cat-a-hole, cat ball, cat bat, cat-in, cat-o'-nine-tails, cat-out*: A bat and ball game similar to **cat n 3a**, and a forerunner of baseball, with numerous variations in method of play. **chiefly Sth, S Midl** See also **one old cat**

1890 *DN* 1.63, *Cat*: a game at ball. In two-cornered cat, a boy with bat stands at each corner; there is a catcher behind each boy. If a batter is 'caught out,' or 'crossed out,' he gives up his bat. He is 'crossed out' when the ball is thrown between him and the corner to which he is running. **1931–33** *LANE Worksheets* **seMA**, *Cat ball* . . . An old game; the ancestor of baseball. **1948** *Ardmoreite* (Ardmore OK) 6 July 8/4 *(DA),* 'Cat' could be played with as few as three players; pitcher, catcher and batter. There were but two bases. The player hit the ball at home plate and attempted to get to the other base and back. If he made it he kept on batting until he made an out. **1954** *Harder Coll.* **cwTN**, *Catball* . . . A bat and ball game that requires a minimum of four players. Perhaps receding and even old-fashioned. **c1960** *Wilson Coll.* **csKY**, *Cat-ball* . . . A simple ball game, usually played with two batters and a certain number of strikes before the batters change places. **1965–70** *DARE* (Qu. EE11, *Bat-and-ball games for just a few players*) 17 Infs, **chiefly Sth, S Midl**, Cat ball; NC7, 9, 23, 26, 82, TN16, Cat; TN35, Cat bat; SC54, Cat-a-hole; NC7, Cat-in; OH5, Cat-o'-nine-tails; AL39, Cat-out; (Qu. EE33, *Other outdoor games*) Infs **AR**18, 47, Cat ball. **1966–69** *DARE* Tape NC22, Cat ball is baseball played with 4 players, 2 to a team; NC60, Gittin' out an' playin' cat, we'd call it cat ball; FL8, Cat.

d See **cat and mouse 1.**

e See **cat's game.**

f See **cat's-eye 1.**

4 also attrib: A cylindrical plug of moss or straw mixed with clay and used esp in building chimneys. [Scots; *SND* →1923] Cf **cat-and-clay, cat-and-jam**

1907 Cockrum *Pioneer IN* 187, After this mud mixed with grass was made and large cats or lumps were pounded in between the boards placed to shape the fire place and the logs, until it was as high as needed and then the chimney was started. **1967** *DARE* FW Addit LA1, *Cat*, a wad of mud mixed with grass or (preferably) grey moss (the common local name for Spanish moss) used in making stick-and-mud chimneys. A cat was about 1½–2 feet long and three inches in diameter. It was stuck wet onto the stick frame. **1975** McDonough *Garden Sass* 50 **AR**, Mr. Claude Lawrence, who has the remains of a cat chimney on an old cabin at his homeplace, described a cat as a ball of mud with a grass thread running through it to hold it together.

5 A simple raft. [Perh abbr for *catamaran*]

1966 *DARE* Tape ME26, Made him a cat; it's a raft, four logs wide, spiked together . . . I had a cat, but it was only two logs.

6 Whiskey. Cf **soo cat, wildcat n**

1965–66 *DARE* (Qu. DD21c, . . *Whiskey, esp illegally made*) Infs **OK**11, 52, Cat.

7 in phr *let the old cat die* and var: See quot 1890.

1890 *DN* 1.25, Strange, uncommon, or antiquated words . . [include] *let the old cat die*, used of letting a swing come to rest gradually instead of stopping it. **1892** *DN* 1.212 **cwMA**, I was familiar in my boyhood with . . . *let the old cat die*. Ibid 214 **eMA**, Let the old cat die . . . Common in Boston in my youth. **1929** Ellis *Ordinary Woman* 61 **CO** (as of early 1900s), We always invented our own playthings; made a swing in the barn, fighting to see who would swing the longest, it taking such a time for the cat to die. **1944** *ADD* **cNY** (as of c1910), *Let the old cat die* . . . Usual among children. **1981** *DARE* File **cMA** (as of c1915), "Let the old cat die" was learned from my father.

8 also attrib: A catfish. **chiefly Sth, S Midl**

1705 Beverley *Hist. VA* 2.32, Conger-Eels, Perch, and Cats, &c. **1765** (1942) Bartram *Diary of a Journey* 38/1 **FL**, 'Tis full of large fish, as cats, garr, mullets, and several other kinds. **1892** Lummis *Tramp* 11 **KS**, One of the most expert of these diver-fishermen hooked a "cat" too big for him, and was dragged down and drowned. **1897** (1952) McGill *Narrative* 272 **SC**, Tho' fond of all kinds of fish, he claimed the cat fish stew as his favorite dish, and on a certain occasion he fixed up his cat lines and soon he was at the fishing ground. **1906** *DN* 3.129 **nwAR**. **1908** *DN* 3.285 **eAL, wGA**. **1915** *DN* 4.181 **swVA**. **1918** *DN* 5.18 **NC**. **1968** *DARE* Tape IN45, I think he said it was a big blue cat.

9 =**catamount 1.**

1906 *DN* 3.129 **nwAR**, *Cat* 1. Catamount. "There use to be heaps of cats in the timber around yere." **1947** *Democrat* 16 Oct 1/7 *(DA),* The cat, which was on display . . . measured 36 inches from tip of nose to the tip of her stump tail. **1958** McCulloch *Woods Words* **Pacific NW**, *Cat* . . . A cougar or bobcat. **1966–69** *DARE* Tape AR15, A cat—I'm talkin' about a bobcat now; CA87, An' the cat's forehead is almost impenetrable.

cat v, hence vbl n *catting*

1 often *cat around*, rarely *gay-cat*: To gad about, fool around. *chiefly among Blacks*

1938 *AmSp* 13.317 **NE** [Black], *Cat around* . . . used with a rather indefinite meaning, perhaps 'to fool around.' **1965** Brown *Manchild* 18 **NYC** [Black], This was going to be my first try at catting out. I went looking for somebody to cat with me. **1965–70** *DARE* (Qu. Y29b, . . *About a man who doesn't stay home much:* "He's always _____.") 15 Infs, **scattered**, Catting around; CT43, NY240, Catting; (Qu. Y29a, . . *About a woman*) Inf **KY**94, Gay-catting; (Qu. W39, . . *A person's best clothes*) Inf **NY**210, Cattin' clothes. [8 of 19 Infs Black]

2 To court or pursue a woman. [**cat n 1b**] Cf **alley-cat v, fuss v 2, tomcat v**

1900 *DN* 2.26 **csLA** [College slang], *Cat* . . . To go with bad women. **1916** *DN* 4.272 **NE**, *Cat* . . . "fuss." Not derogatory. **1967** *DARE* (QR, near Qu. AA15) Inf **MI**68, "He's out catting around" is when men are out chasing women. **1968** *DARE* FW Addit **seRI**, *Catting*: To go out (same meaning as calooping). Women 40–70 now use this. **1970** Major *Afro–Amer. Slang* 35, *Catting*: (1920's–30's) when a man is out searching for available women.

3 To fish for catfish; also fig.

1834 Caruthers *Kentuckian* 2.217 **VA**, I'm jist now like I've been at times when I've been out catting [Footnote: Throwing for cat-fish]. **1859** (1968) Bartlett *Americanisms, Catting.* Fishing for "cat." Thus, a story of an old negro, who while fishing was seen to keep only the catfish and throw all others, even of the better kinds, back into the water. On being asked the reason, he replied, "Lilly massa, when I goes a *cattin*, I goes a cattin." **1865** *Spirit of Times & Sportsman* 19 Aug 387/3, When we goes a catting, we goes a catting, and throws trout back into the water to pay 'em for their imperdence of biting. **1897** (1952) McGill *Narrative* 272, He thus philosophized at the unexpected turn in the affair, as he said: "Go, go; I'll call for you at another time. To-day I am fishing for cats, and when I go a catin', I go a catin".

4 To build (a chimney) with plugs of clay and straw. [**cat n 4**]

a**1890** (1944) Robinson *Hist. Morrill* 31 **ME**, The chimneys were made of stones up to the wooden mantel-tree, then cated out, that was, made of splits and plastered with clay.

cataba See **catawba A**

catabias adj, adv Also *catty-bicey, kitty-macbias* For further varr, see quots [Alter of **cater-** + pleonastic **bias**] **chiefly Midl, esp S Midl** Cf **catercorner, catty-whistling**

1 Out of line, askew.

1895 *DN* 1.385 **wKY**, *Catabiassed*: out of line, irregularly arranged. **1950** *PADS* 14.18 **SC**, *Cattibias, catabias* . . [ˌkætɪˈbaɪəs, ˈkɑtəˈbaɪəs]: adj . . . Askew, awry, diagonal. **c1960** *Wilson Coll.* **csKY**, *Catawampus* . . . Askew, out of line . . . There are many other spellings and similar words, including kitty-macbias. **1968** *DARE* (Qu. MM13, *The table was nice and straight until he came along and knocked it _____*) Inf **MD**30, Catty-bias; **NJ**16, Caterbias; (Qu. KK70, *Something that has got out of proper shape*) Inf **PA**126, Catabias; (Qu. MM3, *When someone does something the wrong way round you might tell him "This is the front, you've got the whole thing turned _____.")* Inf **NJ**20, Caterbias.

2 Diagonally; positioned diagonally from.

1950 *PADS* 14.18 **SC**, *Cattibias, catabias* . . adv . . . diagonally. **1965–70** *DARE* (Qu. MM14, *If a drugstore is on one corner of a square and a gas station is on the far corner you might say, "The drugstore is _____ the gas station."*) Inf **NJ**16, Caterbias; **VA**39, Catabias; **MS**15, Catty-bias; **KY**91, Catty-bicey. **c1970** Pederson *Dial. Survey Rural GA*, *(Two roads cross, and two houses are diagonally across the intersection . . . the houses are _____ from each other)* 1 inf, **seGA**, Catabiasin.

catabla, cataca See **catalpa A**

catacorner(ed), cata-corners See **catercorner** adj, adv, v

cat-act n
   1908 *DN* 3.297 **eAL, wGA,** *Cat-act* . . . Agile performance; in the phrase 'to do the cat-act,' i.e., to fall on one's feet.

cataded, catadid See **katydid** A

cataga See **catalpa** A

catagoggle v [Prob from **cattygodlin**]
   1939 *AmSp* 14.90 **TN,** *Cat-a-gogling.* Walking side ways or angling. 'He's cat-a-gogling.'

‡**catagorricky** adv [Alter of **cater-** + (perh) Scots dial *gorroch* to spoil, bungle]
   1969 *DARE* (Qu. MM3, *When someone does something the wrong way round you might tell him: "This is the front, you've got the whole thing turned _____."*) Inf **NC61,** Catagorricky.

cat-a-hole See **cat** n 3c

Catahoula hog dog n Also *Catahoula (cur)* [*Catahoula* parish in Louisiana] **chiefly AR, LA, TX**
   A type of large, speckled hound used to hunt wild pigs.
   1952 *Argosy* (NY) June 25 **LA,** I've never run into anything like the Catahoula Hog Dog. **1958** Humphrey *Home from the Hill* 48 **TX,** He had . . one of the fabulous, blue-spotted, glassy-eyed Catahoula hog dogs, sometimes called leopard dogs. **1967** *DARE* (Qu. J1) Inf **LA2,** Some say a pure-bred Catahoula cur. **1967** *DARE* Tape **LA**10, They use a Catahoula hog dog [to herd and catch wild hogs]. **1967** *DARE* FW Addit **AR**51, Catahoula [ˌkætəˈhulə], a hound that looks like a cross between bluetick and black-and-tan. Said to be a Louisiana dog. **1981** *NADS Letters* **LA,** The Catahoula hog dog (hawg dawg) is now registered by the National Association of Louisiana Catahoulas, Inc. They evidently were bred by the Natchez Indians and allied tribes in Louisiana, and have been known from early days to have been native in east central Louisiana.

catalba, catalca, catalfa, catalfy, catalga See **catalpa** A

catalog woman n West *now hist* Cf **mail-order 1**
   See quots.
   1928 *AmSp* 4.128 **cnNE,** Many a "kincaider's" wife to whom these venders come was a "catalog woman," one obtained through a matrimonial bureau. **1939** *FWP Guide NE* 111, *Catalog woman* . . a wife obtained through a matrimonial bureau. **1968** Adams *Western Words,* *Catalog woman*—What the cowboy called a wife secured through a matrimonial bureau. Usually, as Alkali Allison said, "one of them widders that wants her weeds plowed under."

catalpa n Usu |kəˈtælpə, -ˈtɑlpə, -ˈtɔlpə| For pronc and sp varr see quots at **A** [Creek *kutȟhlpa* winged head, in ref to the shape and marking of the flower] **widespread, but least freq in Sth** Cf **catawba** and see also *Amsterdam Studies in . . Linguistic Science* IV.15.1–10
   A Forms.
   Pronc-spp *catabla* (**esp LA**), *cataca, cataga, catalba, catalca, catalfa* and *catalfy* (**esp IL, IN, KY**), *catalga, catalpy* (**esp IL, IN, KY**), *catapa.* See also as separate entries: **batawfel, macaltha, patalca, talpa, topple**
      c**1960** *Wilson Coll.* **csKY,** [kəˈtælfə] tree. **1965–70** *DARE* (Qu. T9) 420 Infs, **widespread, but least freq in Sth,** Catalpa; **LA**31, Catabla; **TN**67, Catalba [kəˈtɑlbə]; **MO**5, Catalca [kəˈtælkə]; **IL**96, Catalfy [kəˈtælfɪ]; **KS**12, Catapa [kəˈtɑpə]; (Qu. P6) 33 Infs, **chiefly Midl,** [kəˈtælpə, kəˈtɑlpə, kəˈtɔlpə, *or* kəˈtɛlpə] worm; 9 Infs, **chiefly Sth, S Midl,** [kəˈtɑpə, kəˈtɔpə, kəˈtɔupə]; **AL**7, **FL**18, **IA**32, **KY**16, **TX**74, [kəˈtælbə, kəˈtɑlbə, kəˈtɔlbə]; **LA**10, 15, 29, 34, [kəˈtɑblə] worm; **IL**6, **IN**45, 51, **KY**53, 75, Catalpy [kəˈtælpɪ, kəˈtɑlpɪ, kəˈtɔlpɪ]; **IL**14, **IN**83, **KY**11, 72, 86, 88, Catalfy *or* catalfa [kəˈtælfɪ, kəˈtælfə, kətalfə]; **MI**91, [kəˈtæləpə]; **IN**58, [kəˈtɑpɪ]; **KY**93, [kəˈtælkə]; **TN**53, Catalga [kəˈtɑlgə]; **NC**48, Catalpa grub; (Qu. R27) 20 Infs, **chiefly Midl,** Catalpa worm. c**1970** Pederson *Dial. Survey Rural GA,* 1 inf, **seGA,** Cataca [kəˈtɑkɑ]; 1 inf, **seGA,** Cataga [kəˈtɑgə].
   B Senses.
   1 also *catalpa tree:* A shade tree of the genus *Catalpa,* with large heart-shaped leaves, clusters of white blossoms, and long slender pods, native to the southeastern US but naturalized in other areas. Also called **banana tree, bean tree, candle tree, catawba, cigar tree, fish-bait tree, Indian bean, Indian cigar, Indian pipe, lady cigar tree, ladyfinger, monkey cigar tree, pea tree, smoking**

bean, stogie tree, stringbean tree, toby tree, umbrella tree, worm tree
   1731 (1754) Catesby *Nat. Hist. Carolina* 1.49, *The Catalpa Tree* . . . was unknown to the inhabited parts of *Carolina,* till I brought the seeds from the remoter parts of the country . . . 'Tis become an Ornament to many of their Gardens. **1859** (1968) Bartlett *Americanisms, Catalpa.* **1897** Sudworth *Arborescent Flora* 334, *Catalpa catalpa* . . . Common Catalpa. **1965–70** [see Qu. T9 at **A** above].
   2 also *catalpa caterpillar,* ~ *grub,* ~ *worm:* The caterpillar *Ceratomia catalpae,* which feeds on the leaves of the catalpa tree and is valued as fish bait.
   1889 Edwards *Runaways* 32 **GA,** Whenever the catalpa worm crept upon the leaf two runaways fled from Woodhaven and dwelt in the swamps. **1958** Babcock *I Don't Want to Shoot an Elephant* 157 (Hench Coll.), I heard of a resourceful country boy who sold enough catalpas last season to buy himself a jalopy. *Ibid* 158, But if you are in the lower South and it is bream you are after, the orthodox bait is the catalpa caterpillar. **1965–70** [see Qq. P6, R27 at **A** above]. **1975** Evanoff *Catch More Fish* 3, Another highly effective bait for bluegills is a catalpa worm. This big caterpillar is found in catalpa trees and is cut in half and turned inside out, and one of the halves is placed on a hook.

catalpa rain n
   1956 *Hand Coll.* **swOH,** It always rains when the catalpa blooms. They call this a "catalpa rain."

catalpy See **catalpa** A

catamount n Pronc-spp *catamouth, cateymount, cattamount, cattermount, cattymount* **chiefly Sth, S Midl, NEast**
   1 =**lynx.**
   1698 in 1899 Springfield MA *First Century* 2.348 **MA,** Voted to allow Wm Mackcranny Twenty schillings out of the Rates for his killing four Cattamounts. **1832** Williamson *Hist. ME* 1.134, The *Catamount* (the *Indian* Lunkson, or evil devil,) is a most ferocious and violent creature. **1910** *DN* 3.452 **seVT,** *Catamount* . . . Name given to a species of wildcat or lynx. This word is comparatively rare, the name commonly used being "wild-cat." **1930** Shoemaker *1300 Words* 15 **cPA Mts** (as of c1900), *Catamount*—The "big gray wild cat," or Canada lynx. **1954** *Harder Coll.* **cwTN,** *Bobcat* is the usual term. I have heard catamount very seldom. **1965–70** *DARE* (Qu. P31) 14 Infs, **Sth, S Midl, NEast,** Catamount; **KY**16, [ˈkætiˌmæunt]; **MS**21, Cattymounts; **MS**53, Cattermounts.
   2 =**mountain lion.**
   1713 (1870) CT (Colony) *Pub. Rec.* 5.406, If any person shall kill and destroy any grown wolf or wolves, cattamount or panther, within bounds of any town or plantation in this Colony, he shall have forty shillings. **1840** MA Zool. & Bot. Surv. *Herb. Plants & Quadrupeds* 2.37, It is still a question whether the southern animal known as the Panther or Catamount, is the same as the northern. **1930** *AmSp* 5.425 **Ozarks,** The panther or *catamount* is now practically extinct. **1944** *Baltimore Sun* 21 Nov 1/3 (Hench Coll.) **neKY,** They [=dogs] starts to whine when they hears the cateymounts and tucks their tails 'tween their legs. **1965–70** *DARE* (Qu. P31) Infs **GA**84, **LA**14, **MA**58, **NC**36, **SC**19, **TX**11, Catamount; **NC**53, Catamouth [ˈkætəˌmauθ]. **1968–69** *DARE* Tapes **KY**16, Sound like wild cats, catamounts, and everything else; **NC**55, Some people call 'em [a wild cat] a catamount.

cat-and-clay n, freq attrib [**cat** n 4] **S Midl** Cf **cat-and-jam**
   A mixture of clay and sticks or straw used as a building or chinking material for chimneys; occas, the chimney itself.
   1917 in 1944 *ADD* **sWV,** *Cat-and-clay* . . . of a chimney. **1927** *AmSp* 2.350 **WV,** *Cat and clay chimney* . . a chimney built of sticks and daubed with mud. "We must build a new cat and clay chimney this fall." **1936** *AmSp* 11.314 **Ozarks,** *Cat-an'-clay* . . . A rude chimney made of sticks and mud. **1941** FWP *Guide WV* 345, *Cat and clay chimney* . . . Rusty wood-burning stoves have replaced the 'cat and clay' chimney in most homes. c**1960** *Wilson Coll.* **csKY,** *Cat-and-clay* . . . Said of a chimney made of a wooden pen covered with wisps of straw covered with mud. Very rare.

cat-and-dog fight n Also *cat-and-dog* **NEng**
   See quots.
   1907 *DN* 3.183 **NH,** *Cat and dog fight* . . . Two fire-crackers *(snap-crackers)* are broken on one side in the middle, bent back into a V-shape, and placed apex to apex. The powder overflowing between the two apexes is then ignited. The result is a cat and dog fight. Called by New York City children, *scissors* (sizzers). **1965–70** *DARE* (Qu. FF15,

When a firecracker doesn't go off, and you break it in the middle and light the powder, you call it _____) Infs **ME**15, **MA**82, **NH**1, 5, 11, **RI**6, **VT**16, Cat-and-dog fight; **MA**1, Cat-and-dog. **1966** *DARE* FW Addit **cnMA**, *Cat-and-dog fight*—When a small firecracker doesn't go off, you break it in the middle and light the powder. We used to step on them once they were lit (on a hard surface) to make a loud bang. **1981** *DARE* File **cnMA** (as of c1915), With typical New England thrift we used to save the firecrackers that didn't go off. Later we bent them into V-shapes, set them down on the sidewalk in pairs, the points of the *V*'s almost touching. Then we applied our punk to the gunpowder that spilled out, and for two or three seconds we watched the firecrackers dart around in what was known as a cat-and-dog fight.

cat-and-jam n [cat n 4 + ?*jamb*]

A **cat-and-clay** chimney.

  1970 *DARE* (QR, near Qu. D33) Inf **AR**56, Cat-and-jam [is a] chimney made of mud and grass, blue clay and cheap grass.

cat and mouse n

1 also *cat, cat and rat, rat and cat*: The game of tick-tack-toe. [Ger *Katz und Maus* tick-tack-toe] **chiefly Upper MW, WI, Cent** See Map Cf **old cat**

  1950 *WELS (Tick-tack-toe)* 25 Infs, Cat and rat; 3 Infs, Cat and mouse; 5 Infs, Cat. **1965–70** *DARE* (Qu. EE38a, *A game played with pencil and paper where the players try to get three x's or three o's in a row*) 24 Infs, **chiefly Upper MW, Cent,** Cat and mouse; 17 Infs, **chiefly Upper MW, WI, TX,** Cat and rat; **AZ**8, **KS**18, **MN**33, **MT**4, **SD**3, **WI**77, Cat; **MI**34, Rat and cat.

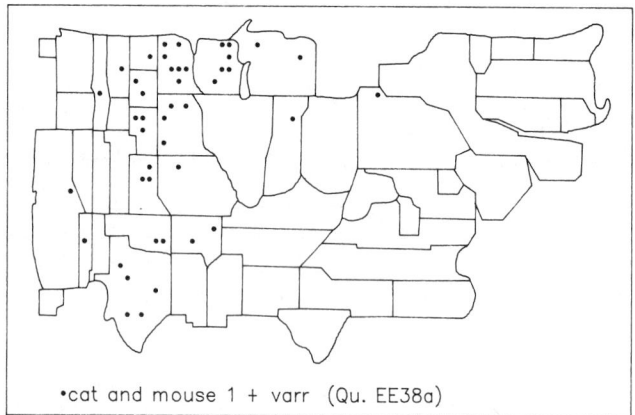

•cat and mouse 1 + varr (Qu. EE38a)

2 freq *cat and rat*: A children's game; see quot 1953.

  1905 *DN* 3.73 **nwAR**, *Cat and mouse* . . . The name of a children's game, also called 'kitten and mouse,' and 'crow and chicken.' **1946** TN Folk Lore Soc. *Bulletin* 12, Some of the mixed games required a good deal of running, as . . . Cat and Rat. **1953** Brewster *Amer. Nonsinging Games* 61 **IN**, *Cat and Mouse* . . . One child is chosen "Kitty" and another is . . "Mousie." The other players form a circle around them. The first player tries to catch the second as the latter runs in and out of the circle. **c1960** *Wilson Coll.* **csKY**, Cat and Rat . . . A chasing game, formerly enjoyed by children.

3 =**fox and geese 2**.

  1950 *WELS (Games played in the snow)* 1 Inf, **ceWI**, Cat and mouse. [Inf drew a picture of a spoked wheel with "home" marked in the center.] One tries to catch another to free himself. No one can catch you when you're home.

cat and rat See **cat and mouse 1, 2**

cat-and-rat rifle n

A small-caliber rifle.

  1940 Mencken *Happy Days* 140 **Baltimore MD**, We had an air-rifle, but wanted a cat-and-rat rifle, which used real cartridges, and our father's harsh and profane prohibition of it only made us want it the more. **1944** Baltimore *Sun* 5 Jan 8/4 *(Hench Coll.)* **MD** (as of c1900), Later on, armed with a 22 rifle of the sort then called "cat-and-rat," we used to wander the countryside looking for spoils.

catapa See **catalpa A**

catapwa See **catawba A**

catarrh n Usu |kə'tɑr|; also |kə'tɑrə, 'kætər, 'kɛtər| Pronc-sp *cattair* **central Missip Valley** Cf **cat-boil**

By ext from std senses: an inflamed or running sore.

  1902 *DN* 2.230 **sIL**, *Catarrh* (['kætɑr] or ['kɛtɑr] . .). An inflamed and purulent sore, generally on the hand, and caused by a bruise. **1903** *DN* 2.309 **seMO**, *Cattair* . . . (Cattarh?) A carbuncle or abscess on the hand. **1907** *DN* 3.221 **nwAR**, *Catarrh* ['kætɑr] . . . An inflamed and purulent sore. **1970** *DARE* (Qu. BB37, *When yellowish stuff comes out of a person's ear*) Inf **IL**118, [kə'tɑr] old-fashioned, ear infection. **1982** *DARE* File **csMO**, A [kə'tɑrə] is a boil-like infection that develops in the mastoid bone and later breaks through with pus.

catasterfy n Pronc-sp for *catastrophe* [Metath]

  1844 Thompson *Major Jones's Courtship* 41 **GA**, I knows you never hearn of jest sich a catasterfy before.

catawampous(ly) See **catawampus** adv

catawampus adj Also *caliwampus, cankywampus, cattywampus* and many other varr—see quots and DS Y38, KK20a, MM2, 3 [Alter of *cater-* + *wampus, wampous,* perh rel to Scots *wampish* to wriggle, twist, or swerve about] See also **kittywampus** adj

1 Askew, awry, wrong. **widely scattered exc NEast** See Map

  1884 Murfree *Where the Battle* 405 **TN**, I kin prove ter ye that ye air all cat-a-wampus on that p'int. **1891** *PMLA* 6.173 **TN**, We might call a rhombus a *catawampus* square. **1903** *DN* 2.309 **seMO**, *Catawampus* . . . Out of shape; skewing. **1905** *DN* 3.73 **nwAR**, *Catawampus*. **1908** *DN* 3.297 **eAL, wGA**, *Catawampus* . . . Also pronounced *cattywampus*. **1911** *DN* 3.542 **NE**, *Catawampus, cattywampus*. **1917** *DN* 4.409 **IL, KS, NE, KY, wNC**, *Catawampus*. **1941** *AmSp* 16.21 **sIN**, *Catawampus*. **1947** Ballowe *The Lawd* 170 **LA**, It looked like all of the white brains were catawampus that day, all except Mrs. Effingham's. **1950** *PADS* 13.17 **cTX**, *Cattawampus*. **1950** *PADS* 14.18 **SC**, *Catawampus, caliwampus, kittywampus* . . . *cattiwampus*. **1965–70** *DARE* (Qu. MM13, *The table was nice and straight until he came along and knocked it* _____) 62 Infs, **widespread exc NEast and Gt Lakes,** Catawampus; **CA**28, **GA**12, **IN**38, **KY**24, **OH**78, **OK**31, Cattywampus; **AL**12, **MO**26, Caddywampus; **NC**13, Cankywampus; **CA**136, Cattawampused; **IN**38, Catterwampus; **OK**15, Cattywamp; **LA**12, Cattywampired; **MS**73, Cattywamping; **LA**40, Cattywhampus; (Qu. KK70, *Something that has got out of proper shape: "That house is all* _____.") 28 Infs, **scattered, but esp West and Gulf States,** Catawampus; **KY**25 **LA**40, **PA**203, **VA**31, Catawhampus; **SC**31, **VA**5, Catawhompered; **LA**12, Catawampered; **TX**33, Catawampist; **OR**13, Catawamus; **OR**10, Catawapus; **MS**73, Catawhampit; **VA**5, Catawhobbled; **IN**60, Catawumpus; (Qu. MM15, *If a carpenter nails a board crossing another board at an angle, you might say, "He nailed the board on* _____.") Infs **IL**130, 143, **WA**33, Catawampus; **SC**67, Caddywampus; **CA**136, Catawampused; **OK**15, Cattywamp; **NC**33, Cattywampus.

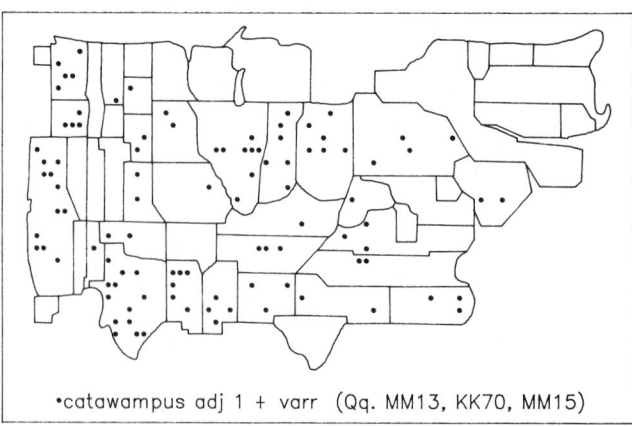

•catawampus adj 1 + varr (Qq. MM13, KK70, MM15)

2 In a diagonal position (with respect to); **catercorner** adj 2. Cf **catabias, catty-whistling**

  1911 *DN* 3.542 **NE**, *Catawampus, cattywampus* . . . Crosswise, diagonal. **1946** *PADS* 5.14 **VA**, *Catty-wampered (cattawampus)* . . . In a diagonal position, or awry.

3 See quot.

  1972 Cooper *NC Mt. Folkl.* 90, Catawampus . . big and fine.

catawampus adv Also *catawampiously, catawampous(ly), catawamptiously, caterwampust, cattiwampus, cattywhompy, cattywobble* and other varr—see quots

1 Utterly, completely. *obs*

1834 *Life Andrew Jackson* 74, That the gineral was catawampously inclin'd tu the United States' service there is little doubt. **1836** (1955) *Crockett Almanacks* 54 **wTN**, Mister, I think you are most catawampiously chawed up. **1840** *Spirit of Times* 25 Jan. 561/2 *(OEDS)*, Him is done up—used up catawampous—kicked up into eberlasting hoki! **1859** (1968) Bartlett *Americanisms*, Catawampously, or *catawamptiously*. Fiercely, eagerly. To be *catawamptiously chawed up* is to be completely demolished, utterly defeated. One of the ludicrous monstrosities in which the vulgar language of the South-western States abounds.

2 Diagonally, obliquely; **catercorner** adv. **chiefly Midl, Sth**

1906 *DN* 3.116 **sIN**, *Caterwampust* . . . Diagonally. **1908** *DN* 3.297 **eAL, wGA**, *Catawampus* . . . cross-ways, obliquely. **1912** *DN* 3.573 **wIN**, *Cata-wampus* . . . Diagonally. **1950** *PADS* 14.18 **SC**, *Cattiwampus, catawampus* . . diagonally. **1962** Bailey *Jayhawker* 25 **KS** (as of 1890s), I thoroughly detested the dirt where he cut catawampus across the boy's playground. **1965–70** *DARE* (Qu. KK52, *To do something in an indirect and complicated way: "I don't know why he had to go _____ to do that."*) Inf **TX**11, Catawampus; (Qu. MM14, *If a drugstore is on one corner of a square and a gas station is on the far corner, "The drugstore is _____ the gas station."*) Infs **CA**177, **IL**45, **IA**45, **OH**52, **WA**16, Cattywampus; **GA**3, **IL**143, Catawampus; **LA**32, **WA**12, Cattywampus across from; **OK**20, 31, Cattywampus from; **MS**57, **MO**25, Cattywhampus; **SC**40, Cattywampus to; **SC**9, Cattywhamper; **SC**31, Cattywhampered to; (Qu. MM16, *If you're walking with somebody to the other corner of a square, and you want to save steps, you might say, "It'll be shorter if we _____."*) Inf **SC**40, Go cattywampus; **OH**87, Go cattywhampus. **c1970** Pederson *Dial. Survey Rural GA*, (*When a person cuts diagonally across a field . . . "He went _____ across the field."*) 1 inf, **seGA**, Cattywobble; cattywhompy.

catawampus v Also sp *catterwampus* [**catawampus** adj]

1 To put out of proper shape.

1906 *DN* 3.130 **nwAR**, *Catawampus* . . . To warp. "The fire just catawampused this boiler."

2 To move diagonally.

1902 *DN* 2.230 **sIL**, *Catterwampusin* . . . The same as preceding [i.e., *cattering . . . Moving diagonally.*]

catawampus n Also *(cata)wampus cat, caterwampus* For var spp, see quots [Perh alter of *catamount*] **chiefly Sth, S Midl**

1 An imaginary monster, a hobgoblin; also fig.

1843 (1916) Hall *New Purchase*, 225 **IN**, [He] is a sort of catawampus, (spiteful) and maybe underhand wouldn't stick to do you a mischief if he thought you made a laff on him. **1866** Smith *Bill Arp* 54, It is a thing that plots, and plans, and schemes for a few weeks, and then suddenly pokes its head out like a catawampus and says *Booh!* **1941** *Sat. Eve. Post* 6 Dec 12/3 **MS**, "Well, I'll be a catty wampus," Skeeter said. "Never saw a dog do that before." **1942** Henry *High Border Country* 318 **MT**, For weeks display boards had bragged that Helena's Diamond Jubilee would be a Ring-Tailed Caterwampus, and the town was dressed for the occasion. **c1960** *Wilson Coll.* **csKY**, *Catawampus cat* . . . One of the folk animals, or *wampus cat*. **1965–70** *DARE* (Qu. CC17, *Imaginary animals or monsters*) Infs **GA**1, 3, **IN**13, **NC**31, **WV**13, Catawampus; **NY**205, **TX**65, **VA**1, Catawampus cat.

2 Transf: see quot. Cf **cat n 1a**

1915 *DN* 4.225 **TX**, *Catawampus* (or *wampus*) *cat* . . . A virago. "She's a regular catawampus cat."

catawampus exclam For varr, see quot [**catawampus** n 1]

1938 Matschat *Suwannee R.* 19 **GA**, He . . dipped out a tin cup full . . [and] drank deeply. "Catawumpus! Kin lick my weight in wildcats, after that." *Ibid* 124, "Great caterwumpus!"

catawampus cat See **catawampus n**

catawampus-corner v phr [**catawampus** n 1 + *corner* force into a difficult position]

1906 *DN* 3.130 **nwAR**, *Catawampus-corner* . . . To worry. "The democracy of Arkansas has been catawampus-cornered and has got nervous prostration." Rare.

catawba n Usu |kəˈtɔbə, kəˈtabə| For pronc and sp varr see quots at **A** [Choctaw *katapa* separated (i.e., from the main body of Siouan peoples)] Note: through similarity of form, *Catawba* (an Indian people of North and South Carolina) and its varr have become popularly identified with **catalpa** and have taken on its senses. **chiefly Sth, S Midl, OH, IN** See Map See also **catalpa**

A Forms.

Pronc-spp *cataba, catapwa*, catawber, catawby, catawfa*, catawpa*, catoby, catowba, kitarber, kitarby, kitawber*. See also as separate entries **batawga, bitawby, fataga, pataga, patawber, shatawba, taba, tataba, tawga, toby tree, typa** Note: starred forms may belong instead with **catalpa**.

1896 *Garden and Forest* 262, Catalpa . . . From a supposition that the name was derived from that of a tribe of South Carolina Indians, the word was corrupted at an early period to Cataba and Catawba. **1952** Brown *NC Folkl.* 1.525, *Catawba* [kəˈtɔbə] . . . Catalpa. **1965–70** *DARE* (Qu. T9) 132 Infs, **chiefly Sth, S Midl, OH, IN**, Catawba; **FL**20, **IL**50, **WI**71, Catawpa [kəˈtɔpə]; **DE**3, Catapwa [kətapwə]; **MD**13, Catawfa [kəˈtɔfə]; **MD**42, Kitarby [kɪˈtɑrbɪ]; (Qu. P6) 45 Infs, **chiefly Sth**, Catawba [kəˈtɑbə, kəˈtɔbə] worm; **AR**51, **TN**22, 30, Catawby [kəˈtɔbɪ]; **TN**7, Catoby [kəˈtobɪ]; **AL**17, Catowba [kəˈtaubə]; **TX**32, Catawber [kəˈtɔbɚ]; **AR**42, Cataba [kəˈtæbə]. **c1970** Pederson *Dial. Surv. Rural GA* **seGA**, 1 inf, Catowba [kəˈtaubə]; 1 inf, I say catalpa [kɪˈtɔlpə] but most people say catowba [kəˈtaubə]; 1 inf, Kitarber [kɪˈtɑə-bɚ] worms; 1 inf, Kitawber [kɪˈtɔbɚ].

B Senses.

1 =**catalpa B1**.

1899 (1912) Green *VA Folk-Speech*, Catalpa . . . Catawba. An ornamental tree. **1908** *DN* 3.297 **eAL, wGA**, *Catawba* . . . Catalpa. **1939** *FWP Guide TN* 19, This region is the natural habitat of the catalpa or "catawba," a fast-growing tree with purple, yellow, and white flowers and large heart-shaped leaves. **1965–70** [see Qu. T9 at **A** above].

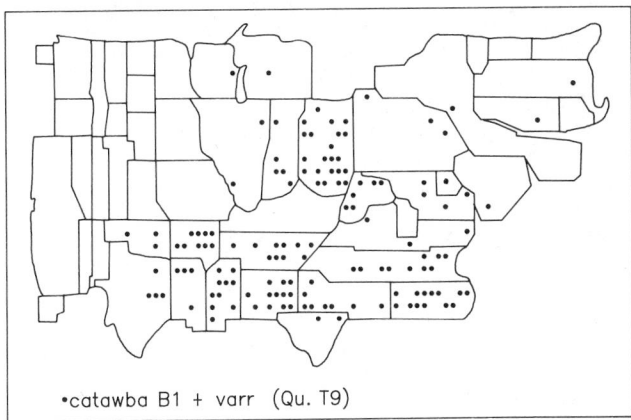

•catawba B1 + varr (Qu. T9)

2 =**catalpa B2**.

1908 *DN* 3.297 **eAL, wGA**, *Catawba* . . . The catalpa worm. "We fished with catawbas." **1947** Dalrymple *Panfish* 153 *(DA)*, 'Catawbies' is a local name in Ohio for the larvae of a butterfly . . . The fisherman who taught me to use them would shake them from the trees on which they naturally feed—the catalpa tree (from which the name 'catawbies' grew). **1960** Lee *Mockingbird* 21 **AL**, The class was wriggling like a bucketful of catawba worms. **1960** Williams *Walk Egypt* 109 **GA**, They got catawba worms. **1965–70** [see Qu. P6 at **A** above].

catawber see **catawba A**

catawby See **catawba A, B2**

catawfa, catawpa See **catawba A**

cat back v

1961 Adams *Old-Time Cowhand* 300, A hoss which jumped 'bout with arched back and stiffened knees at a pretense of buckin' was said to . . "cat back."

catback house n Cf **catslide roof**

1967 *DARE* FW Addit **MA**5, A catback house is a saltbox.

cat ball, cat bat See **cat n 3c**

cat bath n Also *cat cleaning*

A hurried or partial cleaning; a "lick and a promise."

1953 *AmSp* 28.144, Baths involving only a portion of the body are variously called cat bath, spot bath, French dry clean. **1968** *DARE* (Qu. KK49, *When you don't have the time or ambition to do something thoroughly: "I'm not going to give this place a real cleaning, I'll just _____."*) Inf **MN**16A, Give it a cat cleaning.

cat beer n *humorous*

Milk.

1960 Wentworth-Flexner *Slang* 91, *Cat beer* Milk. *Some W.W.II Army use reported; prob. synthetic.* **1966** *DARE* FW Addit **ceMN**, *Cat beer* [is the same as] milk.

cat-bells n

A **spiderwort** (here: *Tradescantia virginiana*).

1966 *DARE* Wildfl QR Pl.7 Inf **TX34**, Cat-bells.

catbird n

1 A slate-gray, black-capped bird *(Dumatella carolinensis)* known for its catlike call. Also called **bushy bird, cat flycatcher, cat mocker, cherry picker 6, chicken bird 2, gray mockingbird, mockingbird, pussy, slate-colored mockingbird**

1709 (1967) Lawson *New Voyage* 148, The Cat-Bird . . makes a Noise exactly like young Cats. They have a blackish Head, and an Ash-coloured Body, and have no other Note that I know of. **1850** Cooper *Rural Hours* 81 **NY**, The cat-birds are mewing about the grounds. **1859** Taliaferro *Fisher's R.* 126 **NC** (as of 1820s), They . . charmed me to the spot, like a black snake charms a catbird. **1885** *Century Illustr. Mag.* 29.682 **AL**, The brown thrushes, the cardinal grosbeaks, and the catbirds were singing in the hedges. **1899** (1912) Green *VA Folk-Speech.* **1965–70** *DARE* (Qu. Q14) 448 Infs, **widespread**, Catbird; (Qu. Q7, . . *Other kinds of game birds*) Inf **DC13**, Catbirds.

2 =**loggerhead shrike.**

1955 Lowery *LA Birds* 411, The terms "butcher bird," "French mockingbird," or "catbird" instead of Loggerhead Shrike would probably be more often recognized in Louisiana as the name for this species. **1962** Imhof *AL Birds* 419, *Loggerhead Shrike . . . Other Names:* French Mockingbird, Catbird, Butcher Bird.

3 The Arkansas **kingbird** (here: *Tyrannus verticalis*).

1955 *AmSp* 30.178 **KS**, The Arkansas kingbird has called *catbird* in Kansas from its harassing cats.

4 Transf: a mischievous or cunning person.

1931 *Scribner's Mag.* 90.624 **FL**, The other of them catbirds, the one thet took after you. **1968** *DARE* FW Addit **VA15**, *Catbird*—uncomplimentary term for a woman who is sly, cunning, nosey, versatile and mocks you behind your back like a catbird.

catbird grape n Also *cat grape*

A wild grape *(Vitis palmata).* Also called **Missouri grape, possum grape**

1920 *Torreya* 20.23, *Vitis palmata* . . Cat grape. **1939** (1954) FWP *Guide KY* 22, Festoons of catbird grape hang from the lower branches and climb over the smaller shrubs, extending to the water's edge. **1976** Bailey–Bailey *Hortus Third* 1163/1, *Vitis palmata* . . Cat grape, Catbird grape.

catbird seat n [Prob from the catbird's habit of delivering its song from a high, exposed position]

A prominent or especially favorable position.

1943 *AmSp* 18.278. **1944** *AmSp* 19.152. **1945** Thurber *Carnival* 8/2, It was Joey Hart . . who had explained what the gibberish meant. "She must be a Dodger fan," he had said. "Red Barber announces the Dodger games over the radio and he uses those expressions—picked 'em up down South." Joey had gone on to explain . . "sitting in the catbird seat" meant sitting pretty, like a batter with three balls and no strikes on him. **1954** *AmSp* 29.282. **1968** *DARE* (Qu. GG19b, *When you can see from the way a person acts that he's feeling important or independent: "He seems to think he's _____."*) Inf **OH49**, In the catbird seat. **1976** *Sat. Review* 26 June 58, Here's the history of "the catbird seat," in the words of Red Barber himself: "When I was in Cincinnati, doing the Reds games, a small group of us used to play penny-ante poker . . . I determined to raise and reraise everybody, hoping to force a pot . . . As he raked in the pot he said 'Thanks for all those raises—from the start I was sitting in the catbird seat.' Inasmuch as I had paid for the expression, I began to use it. I paid for it, I popularized it, and Mr. Thurber took it." **1977** *Ibid* 20 Aug 65/3, Meanwhile, ABC is sitting smugly in the catbird seat, confident of maintaining its prime-time dominance for a third consecutive season. **1981** *NADS Letters* **swIN** (as of 1920), *Sitting in the catbird seat:* I grew up in Posey County, Indiana . . . I have heard this phrase all of my life . . It . . was a favorite phrase of one of the baseball announcers in the late 30's and into the 40's. *Ibid* **cIL**, Catbirds will swing on a wire with their tails stuck up . . . Red Barber, a famous sports broadcaster on radio, used this expression [sitting in the catbird seat]

very frequently. It must be Southern. **1981** Garreau *Nine Nations* 9, The Empty Quarter . . is in the catbird's seat in terms of energy reserves.

cat boil n

An infected swelling on the skin.

1950 *WELS (A swelling on the skin)* 2 Infs, **WI**, Cat boil. **1960** Bailey *Resp. to PADS* 20 **KS** *(A swelling on the skin that comes to a head),* Cat boil. **1966–68** *DARE* (Qu. X59, . . *Small infected pimples . . usually on the face)* Inf **LA25**, Cat boils; (Qu. BB33a, . . *A swelling under the skin, bigger than a pimple)* Infs **MS71, SC4, 24**, Cat boil. **1982** *DARE* File **SC**, *Cat boil*—a hickey, a small boil.

catbrier n Also *catbriar, cat greenbrier* [See quot 1943]

Any of several **greenbriers.**

1839 *S. Lit. Messenger* 5.375/2 **GA**, On the left was a large bay-gall, . . thickly beset with cat-briers and undergrowth. **1888** *Outing* 12.483/2 **NEng**, The first rattle of the ox-cart may start them [=quail] from the stubble-field to the shelter . . of the cat-brier coppice. **1899** (1912) Green *VA Folk-Speech,* Cat-briar . . . A kind of bramble, the briars of which are like the claws of a cat. **1930** Stoney–Shelby *Black Genesis* 187 **seSC**, Tis all tangle up wid jasmine an' cat briar, an' smilax, an' supplejack. **1943** Shimer *Plant Names* 19, The same plant is called Cat briar for its sharp stout prickles, and Green briar because of its bright green bark. **1960** Vines *Trees SW* 77, Cat Greenbrier. *Smilax glauca.* **1967** Borland *Hill Country Harvest* 160 **nwCT**, There is no question where the name "cat-brier" came from, especially if you ever got caught in a tangle of it. **1970** GA Dept. Ag. *Farmers Market Bulletin* 21 Oct 8/1, *Smilax rotundifolia* also called catbrier, greenbrier, bullbrier and other names, grows all over the country—often being a nuisance giving it the more common name of blaspheme-vine. **1970** *DARE* (Qu. S21, . . *Weeds . . that are a trouble in gardens and fields)* Inf **VA38**, Catbriers.

cat britches n

=**butter-and-eggs 1.**

1966 *DARE* (Qu. S11, . . *Other names for . . wild snapdragon)* Inf **AR41**, Cat britches.

catch v

A Forms.

1 pres (exc 3rd pers sg): usu *catch;* often *ketch;* occas *cotch, kotch,* rarely *caitch.*

1815 Humphreys *Yankey in England* 106, Ketch, catch. **1892** Eggleston *Hoosier Schoolmaster* 42, *Ketch* was used by writers of the sixteenth and seventeenth centuries for *catch.* A New Hampshire magistrate in the seventeenth century spells it caitch, and probably pronounced it in that way. **1892** *DN* 1.238 **cwMO, NEng**, *Catch* . . . [kɛč]. **1905** Culbertson *Banjo Talks* 11 **SE**, You kain't kotch up an' you go an' go. **1906** *DN* 3.132 **nwAR**, *Cotch on . . .* To catch on. **1906** *DN* 3.113 **sIN**, *Ketch . . .* The usual form of *catch.* **1926** Kephart *Highlanders* 358 **sAppalachians**, There are many corrupt forms of the verb, such as . . cotch (in all tenses) or cotched. **1947** *AmSp* 22.50 [Gullah], There are . . words . . still used by coastal Carolina Negroes today . . *cotch* (catch or caught). **c1960** *Wilson Coll.* **csKY**, Catch is [kɛč] on all levels.

2 pres 3rd pers sg: usu *catches, ketches;* rarely *catch, ketch.*

1922 Gonzales *Black Border* 309 **sSC, GA coasts** [Gullah glossary], *Ketch*—catch, catches, caught, catching. **1967** *DARE* Tape **LA7**, The cane grow so late here, it be so green and the frost catch it.

3 past and past pple: usu *caught;* freq *catched, cotch(ed), cotcht, ketched, ketcht, kitcht, kotch(ed);* rarely *catch, caughten, ketch, kutch.*

1795 Dearborn *Columbian Grammar* 135, [Improprieties:] Cotch for catch'd or caught. **1837** Sherwood *Gaz.* **GA** 69, [In a list of Provincialisms to be avoided] *Cotch'd,* for caught. **1844** Thompson *Major Jones's Courtship* 47 **GA**, I cotched more cold than coons. **1851** (1969) Burke *Polly Peablossom* 50 **MO**, He was cotch one day stealin' acorns from a blind hog. **1866** Smith *Bill Arp* 127, I rolled some twenty feet into the edge of the woods, and cotch up agin an old pine stump. **1902** Day *Pine Tree Ballads* 246 **ME**, The teacher cotched him that time, though. **1903** *DN* 2.310 **seMO**, *Cotch,* pret. and *pp.* Caught. **1907** *DN* 3.192 **seNH**, *Ketch . . .* To catch. "He ketched it when he got home." **1907** *DN* 3.230 **Ozarks**, *Cotch,* v. pret. and *pp.* Caught. **1908** *DN* 3.301 **eAL, wGA**, *Cotch(t),* pret. and *pp.* of catch. *Ibid* 326, *Ketched,* and sometimes *kotch(ed).* **1910** *DN* 3.454 **seVT**, *Ketcht . . .* Rare. **1914** *DN* 4.78 **ME, nNH**, *Catched . .* caught. **1914** Furman *Sight* 37 **KY**, That whole funeral meeting kotch its breath at them awful words. **1916** *DN* 4.273 **NE, MA, KS**, *Catched.* Occasional preterite of caught. **1922** Gonzales

Black Border 309 **sSC, GA coasts** [Gullah glossary], *Ketch* . . caught.
1939 *Hall Coll.* **ceTN,** *Catched* . . . I didn't want to be catched in the rain
an' no shelter. **1939** *AmSp* 14.91 **eTN,** *Kutch.* Caught. 'We kutch the
chickens this morning.' **1944** *PADS* 2.41 **VA, NC, nSC,** *Catched* [kĕčt,
kæčt] . . Preterit and past participle of *catch.* **1953** Atwood *Survey of
Verb Forms* 8, The pronunciation /kɪtšt/, it will be noted, is very widely
scattered except for parts of n.e. N. Eng. **1965–70** *DARE* (Qu.
OO11a, . . *"Some mice got into the cellar but our cat _____ (them)."*)
959 Infs, **widespread,** Caught; 16 Infs, **scattered,** Ketched; 10 Infs,
scattered, Catched; SC9, 26, Catch; [8 Infs also reported having heard
catched or *ketched* in their communities.] (Qu. OO11b, . . *"That makes
five she's _____ this week."*) 968 Infs, **widespread,** Caught; 15 Infs,
scattered, Ketched; TX29, Catched; MS69, SC26, Catch; MI112,
MI112, Caughten ['kɔtən]; VA13, Cotched [kɔčt]. [8 Infs also reported
reported having heard *catched* or *ketched* in their communities.] **1970**
AmSp 45.67, In parts of the Atlantic States /kĕčt/ is current beside *caught*
as the past tense of *catch,* especially in such conservative areas as New
England, coastal North Carolina, and the Appalachians. **1976** Garber
Mountain-ese, Cotch . . . While I wuz out in the night air I am afeard I
cotch a bad cold.

B Senses.

1 freq with *on:* To understand, comprehend.

c**1960** *Wilson Coll.* **csKY,** *Catch on?* . . Do you understand? **1965–70**
DARE (Qu. NN5, *Other ways of saying, "Do you understand?":* "You
take hold of it this way, _____.") 106 Infs, **widespread,** Catch on;
CA80, IL96, 98, OR1, SC32, WI21, Catch; GA1, Catch that.

2 To ignite; to become ignited.

1939 McGuire *FL Cracker Dial.* 170, *Catch* . . . "To catch a match."
"To strike a match." **1967** Fetterman *Stinking Creek* 45 **KY,** It's hard
coal . . . It just naturally don't want to catch. **1968** *DARE* (Qu. Y43a,
Expressions meaning to light a fire: "_____ the fire.") Inf SC64,
Catch.

3 usu with *on;* Of food: to burn slightly, to scorch. **NEng**

1890 *DN* 1.18 **seNH,** *Caught:* milk is 'caught' when it is slightly
burned. **1939** Wolcott *Yankee Cook Book* 178, Make a dozen dumplings as for soup and drop in . . being careful that the mixture does not
'catch on.' **1981** *DARE* File **cnMA** (as of c1915), *Catch on*—to burn
slightly. Many think a pot roast is better (at least has browner gravy) if it is
allowed to catch on.

4 also with *up:* To become pregnant, to make pregnant; hence
ppl adj *caught* (sometimes with the implication that the pregnancy was inadvertent).

1912 *DN* 3.573 **wIN,** *Catch* . . . To become with young. **1940**
Faulkner *Hamlet* 351 **MS,** So there was a old woman told my mammy
once that if a woman showed her belly to the full moon after she had
done caught, it would be a gal. **1949** Guthrie *Way West* 183 (as of 1847),
So left all their hopes on Brownie, for Rebecca couldn't catch again.
1949 *PADS* 11.5 **wTX,** *Caught* . . . Pregnant. Occasional. **1959** *VT
Hist.* new ser 27.129, Catch awful quick . . To get pregnant easily.
1965–70 *DARE* (Qu. K43, *A horse that was not intentionally bred, or
bred by accident*) Inf NY2, Caught; LA3, Caught-up; IN69, Mare was
caught; FL12, She got caught; IA22, She got caught when we didn't
know it; (Qu. AA28, *What joking or sly expressions do women use to say
that another is going to have a baby? "She('s) _____."*) 15 Infs, Got
caught; CA114, CT40, IL97, IA3, She got caught; CA59, NY2, 37,
Caught; SC3, VA18, Been caught; AL26, OH11, Caught again; NJ39,
SC21, Got caught again; [WV12, Caught the preggies;] IL96, Caught up;
TN46, Got caught up; IL37, She's caught. **1967** *DARE* Tape LA7, She
[=a sow] could be caught up with pigs . . . She'd be showing if she caught
with pig . . . If she caught, she'd have to be 'bout two months
now . . . She ain't never caught up.

5 Of plant seeds, oyster spawn, etc: to take hold (and begin to
grow). Cf **catch n 2**

1843 (1924) Oliver *8 Months* 95, The seed catches quick and grows
well. **1868** Brackett *Farm Talk* 128, Sow oats thin, and fix the ground as
well as for barley, and grass will catch well enough. **1901** *DN* 2.137
ncNY, *Catch* . . . To take root; "the seed caught." **1953** Baltimore *Sun*
20 Aug. B6/4 *(Hench Coll.)* Catch, the act of an oyster seed attaching self
to an empty shell and growing.

6 To freeze. [*OED* 1879 →]

1975 Gould *ME Lingo* 46, *Caught*—Frozen, as a water pipe. "If we
don't get a fire started the pipes'll *catch!*" "The pump was *caught* this
morning."

7 To undergo or suffer (an unpleasant experience); to encounter
an adverse condition (of weather).

1946 *AmSp* 12.189 **seKY,** *Catch* . . to have. 'If you don't watch out
careful, you'll catch a fall.' **1968** *DARE* FW Addit **cwLA,** *To catch*
(*snow, rain, hail, sleet* etc.) is the same as to get rained on. "I didn't catch
no snow; I caught some sleet while ago though." Said by truck driver with
slight French accent.

8 Of a muscle or joint: to experience sudden sharp pain. [**catch
n 3**]

1968 *DARE* FW Addit **CA101,** [Her] shoulder would catch [when she
lifted her arm to comb her hair].

9 To assist in the delivery of a baby. **Sth, S Midl**

1928 Peterkin *Scarlet Sister Mary* 208 **SC** [Gullah], Ma is done too old
to be all de time gwine round a-catchin chillen for people. E ought to let
somebody else do em now. **1931** Hannum *Thursday April* 19 **WV Mts,**
I'm expectin' you to catch me a boy! **1948** Hurston *Seraph* 84 **sFL,**
Arvay was brought up to date on everything that had happened since she
left. Whose babies Dessie had caught, and who were supposed to be the
fathers. **1960** Williams *Walk Egypt* 56 **GA,** Now you can catch a
young'un 'thout the rest of this stuff, but you got to have clean hands to
do it with. [Said by a midwife] **1960** Hall *Smoky Mt. Folks* 45, I've
catched them (babies) here. **1967** Fetterman *Stinking Creek* 88 **KY,** My
dad cotched four hundred children . . . He was a midwife doctor. He
went out on nights wasn't fit for stock to go catch a baby. **1968**
DARE (QR, near Qu. AA30) Inf **GA**57, She caught babies.

10 usu with *up* or *out:* To saddle or harness (an animal). **chiefly
Sth, S Midl**

1830 (1940) Ferris *Rocky Mts.* 20, Immediately after sundown, the
words "catch up," resounded through camp, all hands flew to the horses,
and all was noise and bustle for some minutes. **1902** *DN* 2.237 **sIL,**
Ketch, or *ketch up* . . . To saddle a horse, or harness a team to a wagon or
plow. **1906** *DN* 3.120 **sIN,** *Ketch up.* **1929** Dobie *Vaquero* 15, "Eli," he
called to the horse wrangler, "catch out Ribbon in the morning for
John." **1932** Stribling *Store* 459 **AL,** You catch out your mules, and
we'll go over to Cady's. **1942** Faulkner *Go Down* 76 **MS,** When I seed
him catch up pappy's mare and wagon, I knowed that was it. **1942**
(1971) Campbell *Cloud-Walking* 16 **seKY,** He pulled on his britches to
go catch up the nag for Sary. **1966–68** *DARE* (Qu. L43a, *When
someone is going to get horses ready to work, he might say, "I'll _____
the horses."*) Infs **AL**2, **SC**57, Catch out; **GA**17, Ketch out; **SC**7, Catch.

11 To kill or bag (a game animal). [See quot 1981] **AK**

1950 *Alaska Sportsman* Feb 7 (Tabbert *Alaskan Engl.*), My cousin had
caught this particular bear in the fall. **1974** *Fairbanks Daily News–
Miner* 12 July (Tabbert *Alaskan Engl.*), Victor Kanrilak caught a
walrus. *Ibid* 23 July, Some people had caught caribou. *Ibid* 30 Oct 2,
Ken Jackson caught a bull moose. **1981** Tabbert *Alaskan Engl.* 195,
Often pointed out as a feature of the English of Alaska Natives is use of
the transitive verb *catch* to mean "successfully hunt (such and such an
animal)" . . . Perhaps it reflects some Native language pattern. Or perhaps it was simply an expansion of the range of English's "catchable"
creatures from fish to mammals . . . Still another possibility is that it is
from, or was influenced by, a usage of *catch* which existed in Pacific
island and maritime pidgins . . . [meaning] "get" or "take."

12 To get, obtain. **HI** [Pacific maritime pidgins] Cf **catch v
B11**

[**1911** William Churchill *Beach-La-Mar: The Jargon . . of the Western
Pacific* 38 (Tabbert *Alaskan Engl.*), *Catch* 1. to take, to get, to obtain, to
have.] **1934** *AmSp* 9.58 **HI,** *Catch.* In the sense of 'to take,' 'to get,' 'to
obtain,' 'to have.' This has almost gone out of use in the [American
English] dialect, but was once common in the pidgin. **1972** Carr *Da
Kine Talk* 126 **HI,** *Catch* vs. *get*—"Us go beach—catch da tan."
Swimmers and surfers use *catch* in the sense of *get.* [*DARE* Ed: Cf *catch a
wave*]

13 To arrive at, reach. *Gullah* Cf *DJE* **catch 7**

1888 Jones *Negro Myths* 8 [Gullah], So eh tek eh calabash an hop off
fuh de spring. Wen eh ketch de spring, eh see de Tar Baby. *Ibid* 67, De
Mossa, him tek one long white gown wuh ketch down ter eh foot, an pit
um on.

14 See **catch 'im.**

catch n Pronc-sp *ketch*

1 Any device intended to hold something temporarily while a
task is being performed: see quots.

1919 *DN* 5.32 **seKY,** *Catch* . . . A lifter for stove caps. **1968** *DARE*
(Qu. M11, *What do you put the cow's head through when she stands in
the barn?*) Inf **AL**43, Catch. **1977** *Mais Jamais* 13 **LA,** When the piece
of iron was hot, the horse's foot was put on a catch and the iron was bent

to fit the exact size of the hoof. **1981** *DARE* File, They used to put the horse's hoof in a wooden contraption that was shaped like a bootjack, they called it a catch. They don't use these anymore. The last time I saw one used was at Michigan State University twenty years ago.

2 also *catch crop, self-catch:* A successful germination; a **volunteer** crop. [**catch** v B5]

1868 Brackett *Farm Talk* 128 **MN,** "Send this down this year?" "Yes; that's one reason why I sowed the field to barley,—so as to get a good catch." **1888** VT State Bd. Ag. *Rept. for 1887–88* 10.48, Wheat gives a good catch, barley next, and oats poorest of all. **1940–41** Cassidy *WI Atlas* **cwWI,** Unless lime is put on sour soil, you can get a ketch of alfalfa, but it will only last one year. **1950** *WELS (A crop . . that springs up and grows by itself from old seed)* 2 Infs, **se,csWI,** Catch crop; 1 Inf, **cwWI,** Self-catch. **1966–69** *DARE* (Qu. L10, *After hay has been cut, then it grows back and you cut it again, you'd call that_____.*) Inf **FL**1, Catch crop; (Qu. L24, *A crop . . that springs up . . by itself)* Infs **IL**11, **IN**69, Catch crop; **IL**33, Ketch crop; **MI**12, Self-catch. **1966–67** *DARE* Tape **AR**51, This year I made a little what we call a catch-crop; **ME**18, I asked him how we happened to get so good a catch [of alfalfa].

3 A sudden, sharp pain in the back, side, or neck; a stitch. Cf **catch-pain** [*SND* 1895 →]

1954 *Harder Coll.* **cwTN,** *Catch . . .* A sudden muscular pain in the back. **c1960** *Wilson Coll.* **csKY,** *Catch . . .* A sudden muscular contraction in the back. **1965–70** *DARE* (Qu. BB3b, . . *In the back)* 307 Infs, **widespread but least common in NEast,** Catch; (Qu. BB3c, . . *In the side)* 153 Infs, **widespread,** Catch; (Qu. BB3a, . . *Pain that strikes . . in the neck)* 106 Infs, **widespread,** Catch. **1981** *Broaddus Coll.* **ceKY,** Catch—a sudden, sharp, pain in the side.

4 See **catch colt.**

catch a crab v phr

1 See quot and cf note at *OED crab* sb.[1] 10.

1975 Gould *ME Lingo* 46, *Catch a crab*—To mishandle oars while rowing, so that there is a splash of water. Mainers transfer the term to any mistake, error, bungling, or *gormy* miscue.

2 To do a **belly flop 2.**

1968 *DARE* (Qu. EE29, *When swimmers are diving and one comes down flat onto the water)* Inf **OH**61, Catch a crab.

catch a duck asleep See **catch a weasel asleep**

catch-a-fox n Cf **fox and geese 5**

1969 *DARE* (Qu. EE33, *Outdoor games)* Inf **IL**76, Catch-a-fox—a little bit like London bridge.

catch air v phr

To run very fast.

1975 Newell *If Nothin' Don't Happen* 108 **nwFL,** Tarley said it were such a surprise that he just throwed him right out in the yard, and when he did, old man Yancy went to hollerin', "Help! Murder! Robbers!" And Tarl really caught air.

catch as can adv phr [Alter of *catch-as-catch-can*]

In a haphazard fashion.

1960 Williams *Walk Egypt* 153 **GA,** Cars and horses and wagons were parked catch as can everywhere under elms and oaks and chinaberry.

catch a weasel asleep v phr Also *catch a duck asleep* old-fash

See quot 1905.

1825 Neal *Brother Jonathan* 3.269 **CT,** Caught!-me!-I!-*you!*-catch a weasel asleep! **1833** Neal *Down-Easters* 1.3, If he don't shave putty nigh the grinstun, somebody . . 'll show him what's what, afore he's done with him—ketch a weazle asleep, hey? (cocking his eye at me,) [he'll] wish his cake [were] dough. **1843** (1916) Hall *New Purchase* 215 **IN,** "This . . 'tis worth ten cents in silver. We give twelve in trade." "Ketch a duck asleep!—if that 'ere tow linen thare aint worth fifteen cents in store-tea or coffee ither, I'll bet old Nan—(his rifle) again two-shot gun!" **1859** (1968) Bartlett *Americanisms, To Catch a Weasel asleep.* It is supposed that the little animal is never caught napping, for the obvious reason that he sleeps in his hole beyond the reach of man . . . "You cannot deceive me, any sooner than you can *catch a weasel asleep.*" **1891** Maitland *Amer. Slang Dict., Catch a weasel asleep . .* a task requiring much acuteness. **1905** *DN* 3.5 **cCT,** *Catch a weasel asleep . . .* To take a shrewd person off his guard.

catch bugs See **catch flies**

catch center See **catch on the center**

catch cold, be too slow to See **catch the itch, be too slow to**

catch colt n Also *catch* **chiefly West, Inland Nth** See Maps

1 The offspring of a mare bred accidentally.

1940–41 Cassidy *WI Atlas* **csWI,** *Catch*—Colt that was unintentionally bred. **1958** *AmSp* 33.271, *Ketch-colt.* An offspring obviously not from the herd sire. **1965–70** *DARE* (Qu. K43, *A horse that was not intentionally bred, or bred by accident)* 80 Infs, **chiefly West, Inland Nth,** Catch colt. **1973** Allen *LAUM* 1.345, Catch colt [4 infs used this expression with reference to horses].

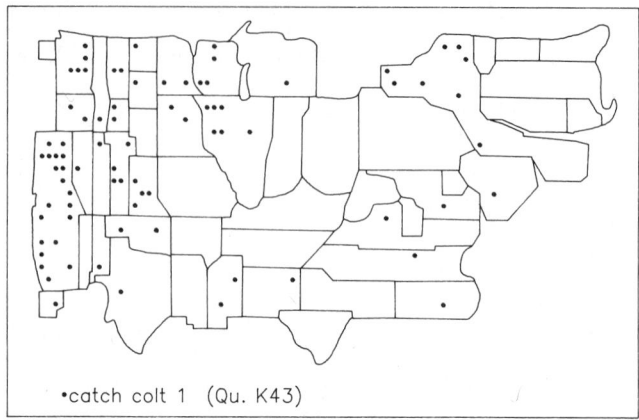

•catch colt 1 (Qu. K43)

2 By ext: a child born out of wedlock.

1901 *DN* 2.13 **cNY,** *Catch-colt . . .* An illegitimate child. **1949** Kurath *Word Geog.* Fig 150, Bastard [6 infs in NY said *ketch-colt*]. **1965–70** *DARE* (Qu. Z11b, . . *A child of unwed parents)* 27 Infs, **chiefly West, esp Rocky Mts,** Catch colt; **OR**3, Catch. **1971** Bright *Word Geog. CA & NV* 192, [3% of infs called an illegitimate child a catch-colt]. **1973** Allen *LAUM* 1.344, Illegitimate child . . catch colt [23 infs].

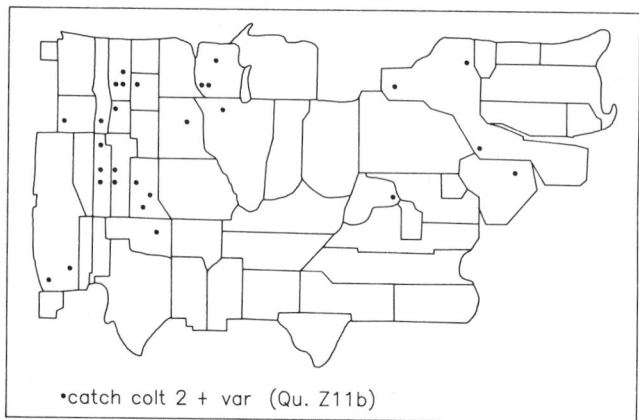

•catch colt 2 + var (Qu. Z11b)

catch crop See **catch** n 2

catch dog n Also *ketch dog* **esp FL, GA** Cf **find dog**

A dog trained to attack animals and detain them.

1860 U.S. Congress *Congressional Globe* App 16 Jun 436/3 **NY,** God forbid that the heart of a single freeman . . should prostitute his body in the service of those [=slave-hunters] who, at home, perform the same labor with well-trained blood-hounds and catch-dogs. **1938** Rawlings *Yearling* 46 **FL,** He's a good ketch-dog. **1942** *Sat. Eve. Post* 5 Sept. 56/2 **FL** [Black], So I had to put the catch dogs on the bull. **1966** *DARE* Tape **GA**3, If you got two catch dogs, turn one loose on each side of the hog. **1967** *Atlanta Constitution* (GA) 6 Mar 5, A farm home possession without equal, one to be cherished and bragged about was "a snaggletoothed ketch dog". "What did he catch?" . . . "Cows, hogs, anything." **1968** Adams *Western Words, Ketch dog*—A dog trained to catch cattle by the nose and hold or throw them until they could be tied, or to worry a steer until a puncher could get to the steer with his rope. **1970** *Foxfire* Spring–Summer 13 **GA,** Since cows and hogs were grazed on open range, mountain families often trained "ketch dogs" also. Their job was to help round up the stock. **1975** Newell *If Nothin' Don't Happen* 10 **nwFL,** Both the hogs and cows ran wild in the Hammock . . We kept track of 'em with catch dogs . . one would catch and hold a cow or a steer till it were marked.

catch 'em See **catch 'im**

catcher n

The children's game of tag.

1917 *DN* 4.420 **seLA,** *Catcher* . . . Same as *tag.*

catch flies v phr Also *catch gnats,* ~ *bugs* Cf **flycatch, fly- catcher**

1 To gawk; stare with one's mouth open.

1941 *AmSp* 16.21 **sIN,** *Catchin' flies.* Said of one who habitually holds his mouth open. **c1960** *Wilson Coll.* **csKY,** *Catch flies* . . . To stare, with mouth open. **1965–70** *DARE* (Qu. X22, *To stare at something with your mouth open*) 30 Infs, **scattered,** Catch flies; **AR**23, 56, **CA**101, **OK**42, **TX**13, **VA**69, 73, Catch gnats; **MO**38, Ain't gonna catch a fly; **CO**7, Catch bugs; **GA**44, Mind you'll catch a fly.

2 To yawn.

1965–70 *DARE* (Qu. X46, *When a person's getting sleepy and opens his mouth wide and takes a deep breath, that's . .* _____) Inf **OR**3, Catch flies; **GA**3, **NJ**63, **OK**42, **TN**1, Catching flies.

catchfly n Cf **flycatcher**

1 A plant of the genus *Silene.* [See quot 1971] Also called **cockle 1, Indian pink, wild pink** For other names of var spp see **bladder campion, Carolina pink 2, fire pink, garden catchfly, moss campion, night-flowering catchfly, sleepy catchfly, starry campion, windmill pink**

1791 in 1793 *Amer. Philos. Soc. Trans.* 3.169, *Catchfly.* **1832** Hale *Flora's Interp.* 34, *Catchfly. Silene* . . . One of the most splendid species, flowers bright scarlet, is found in Ohio and Lower Louisiana. **1967** *DARE* Wildfl QR Pl.53 Inf **WA**30, Catchfly or French Pink. **1971** GA Dept. Ag. *Farmers Market Bulletin* 22 Sept 8/1, The name Catchfly refers to the sticky coating on leaves, stems and flower buds of this wildflower.

2 A white-flowered plant *(Aldenella tenuifolia)* native to the southeastern coastal plain.

1953 Greene–Blomquist *Flowers South* 41, Catch-Fly *(Aldenella tenuifolia)* . . catchfly has a sticky substance on its stems which catches ants and other small insects.

3 A campion (here: *Lychnis viscaria*) of the northeastern US.

1950 Gray–Fernald *Manual of Botany* 629, *Lychnis viscaria* . . German Catchfly. **1976** Bailey–Bailey *Hortus Third* 687, *Lychnis . . Catchfly.*

catchfly gentian n

A plant of the genus *Eustoma.* Also called **bluebell 1h, Canada pest, prairie gentian**

1970 Correll *Plants TX* 1208, *Eustoma* . . Catchfly-gentian. **1972** Brown *Wildflowers LA* 137, Catchfly-gentian—*Eustoma exaltatum.*

catchfly grass n Also *flycatch grass*

A perennial grass *(Leersia lenticularis)* often found in marshy environments.

1829 Eaton *Botany* 273, *Leersia lenticularis* . . catch-fly grass. **1857** Gray *Manual of Botany* 540, *L[eersia] lenticulàris* . . . Fly-catch Grass . . . [grows in] Low grounds, Virginia, Illinois, and southward. **1946** Tatnall *Flora DE* 35, Catchfly grass. **1970** Correll *Plants TX* 113, Catchfly grass.

catch gnats See **catch flies**

catch him intj Also *I catch you* [Imit] Cf **gesundheit, scat** intj

1950 *WELS* (What people say to somebody when he sneezes) 1 Inf, **csWI,** Ketch um!; 1 Inf, **cnWI,** Catch him!; 1 Inf, **csWI,** I catch you!

catch 'im v phr Also *catch ('em)* **chiefly Sth, S Midl** See Map

Sic 'im!—used as a command to a dog.

c1960 *Wilson Coll.* **csKY,** Catch 'im! . . Call to dogs; same as "Sic 'im!" **1965–70** *DARE* (Qu. J8, *To tell a dog to attack an animal or a person, you'd say, "*_____.*"*) 59 Infs, **chiefly Sth, S Midl,** Catch 'im! **LA**15, Catch! **1973** Allen *LAUM* 1.242 **csMN,** Call to a dog to attack another dog [1 inf, Catch 'im]. **1981** *Broaddus Coll.* **ceKY,** Catch 'em—synonymous with "sic 'em."

catching See **catchy**

catching pen See **catch pen**

‡catch-keep exclam

1978 *Smithsonian* May 80 **Brooklyn NY,** Catch-keep means if I catch

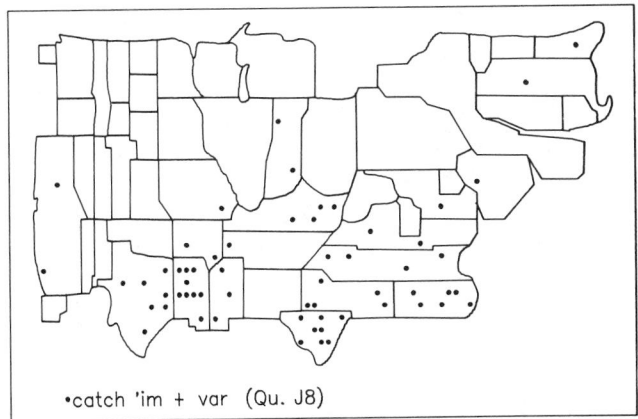

•catch 'im + var (Qu. J8)

one of your pigeons, no way you're gonna get it back. No way. I'm gonna sell it to somebody at a distance, where you'll never see it again.

catch-my-goose n

A children's game: =**fox and geese 5.**

1967 *DARE* (Qu. EE26, *Games . . in the snow*) Inf **AZ**1, Catch-my-goose.

catch on the center v phr Also *catch center*

1 Of a steamboat engine: to be on dead center. *hist*

[**1926** Quick *MS Steamboatin'* 196, Many a cub went to the throttle, trembling in fear that he would center his engine and so make a lot of work for men who would have to turn the wheel past this center point with levers.] **1968** Adams *Western Words* 59, In steamboating, to center an engine or get it caught center, a calamity that might disable the engine at a critical moment, throwing the steamer out of the channel and hanging her up for hours, or even days, on a sandbar . . . the boat might be on rocks or snags and sunk.

2 Fig: see quot.

1869 Twain *Innocents* 45, He had no one to blame but himself when his voice caught on the centre occasionally, and gave him the lockjaw.

catch-pain n [**catch** n 3] **chiefly Sth, S Midl** See Map *esp freq among Black speakers*

A sharp, sudden pain, usu up in the side.

1965–70 *DARE* (Qu. BB3c, *A sudden pain that comes in the side*) 21 Infs, Catch-pain; (Qu. BB3b, *. . In the back*) Inf **FL**49, Catch-pain. [8 of 21 Infs Black]

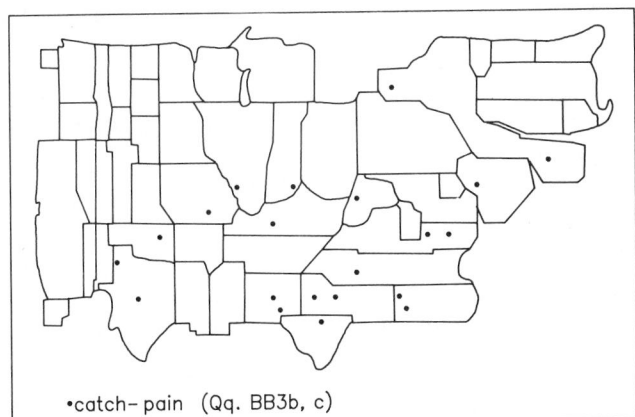

•catch-pain (Qq. BB3b, c)

catch pen n Also *catching pen, catch pasture*

A place where cattle may be penned up.

1958 *AmSp* 33.269 **eWA,** *Catching pen.* An inner corral. **1967–70** *DARE* (Qu. M13, *The space near the barn with a fence around it where you keep the livestock*) Infs **MS**81, **TX**16, Catch pen; (Qu. M14, *The open area around or next to the barn*) Infs **WI**43, Catch pen; **TX**8, Catch pasture. **1967** *DARE* FW Addit **LA**8, Get that lead cow in the ['kɛč͵pɪn], you got 'em all.

catchpenny n

Something cheap or showy made to be sold for a quick profit.

1912 Green *VA Folk-Speech,* Catch-penny . . . Bad work done for gain. **1930** Shoemaker *1300 Words* 10 **cPA Mts** (as of c1900), *Catch-penny*—A quick device to secure money.

catch the cock n Also *catch the sack*
A children's game: see quots.

1933 *Hanley Disks* **cnRI**, Catch the cock. People would run across the schoolyard and tear each other's clothes apart . . . one man stood in the middle and everyone ran past him. All the people he could ketch had to stand in the middle and help him catch the others. *Ibid*, One [game] we called "catch the sack". I believe these people had to run across the school yard and tear each others' clothes apart, and always someone lost a button.

catch the itch, be too slow to v phr Also *be too slow to catch cold*
To be extremely slow.

1952 Brown *NC Folkl.* 1.430, So slow you can't ketch the itch. **1966–67** *DARE* (Qu. A18, . . *A very slow person: "What's keeping him? He certainly is _____."*) Infs **AR34, FL9, 19, MO38, SC26**, Too slow to catch (a) cold; **NC41, OK42**, Too slow to catch the (seven-year) itch.

catch the sack See **catch the cock**

catchweed n [From the prickles, by which it catches on to clothing, etc. *OED* 1776 →]
=**cleavers** (here: *Galium aparine*).

1833 Eaton *Botany* 152, *[Galium] aparine* (catch-weed, goose grass). **1971** Krochmal *Appalachia Med. Plants* 126, *Galium Aparine L* . . . Catchweed.

catchy adj Also *catching*
1 Of weather: changeable, unpredictable.

1894 *DN* 1.331 **NJ**, *Ketchy*: changeable (weather). **1903** *DN* 2.293 **seMA**, *Catchy* . . . Uncertain, liable to sudden changes, said of weather. **1931–33** *LANE Worksheets* **swCT**, Catching weather for haying. **1936** *AmSp* 11.315 **Ozarks**, 'Th' weather's kind o' ketchy' means that it is unsettled, with an uncertain prospect of rain. **1940–41** Cassidy *WI Atlas* **cWI**, Showers and sun alternating is ketchy weather. **1959** *VT Hist.* new ser 27.129, Catchy . . . Changeable.
2 See quot. [Perh infl by *tetchy*]
1895 *DN* 1.396 **cNY**, *Catchy* [kɛči]: impatient, irritable.

catclaw See **cat's claw**

‡**catclaw and underbrush** n
1967 *DARE* (Qu. N37, . . *A branch railroad that is not very important*) Inf **TX1**, Catclaw and underbrush.

cat-clawed ppl adj Also *cat-stitched*
Poorly sewn.

1967 *DARE* (Qu. W29, . . *Things that are sewn carelessly: "They're _____."*) Inf **TX26**, Cat-clawed; **NJ1**, Cat-stitched.

cat cleaning See **cat bath**

cat corn n
1969 *DARE* (Qu. L34, . . *Important crops grown around here*) Inf **MO6**, Cat corn.

cat-cornered See **catercorner** adj, adv, v

cat dirt, cat dung See **cat shit**

cat-ear See **cat's-ear**

catedidist See **katydid** A

cater v Also sp *catter* [Engl dial] Cf **catercorner** v
To move diagonally.

1902 *DN* 2.230 **sIL**, *Cattering* [kætərɪn or ketərɪn] . . . Moving diagonally or obliquely. **1905** *DN* 3.60 **eNE**, *Catter* . . . Move diagonally. "I cattered across the campus." **1959** *VT Hist.* new ser 27.129, Cattering off . . . To deviate from a straight line.

cater- prefix [Engl dial *cater* diagonally]
Used to form var adjs and advs: see **catabias, catagorricky, catawampus, cater-by, caterway, cateslunkit, catifawgus, catty-byward, catty-cross, catty-cue, catty-godlin, catty-strangling, catty-ways, catty-west, catty-whistling**

cater-bias See **catabias**

cater-by adj [cater- + *by,* perh from **bias,** perh *bye* aside; cf **catabias, catty-byward**]
1970 *DARE* (Qu. MM15, *If a carpenter nails a board crossing another*

board at an angle, you might say, "He nailed the board on _____.") Inf **NC88**, Cater-by.

catercorn See **catercorner** adj, adv

catercorner adj, adv Also *catercornered;* also sp *catacorner(ed), catta-, catter-, catti-, catty-;* rarely *caddy-, cally-, caper-, catacorners, cat-cornered, catercawnered, catercorn, catty-corned, catty-cornereds, catty-corners, caty-corner, katter-kornered* [Engl dial *cater* diagonally + *corner*] See also *DS* MM 13–15, *LANE* Map 547, and **kitty-corner** Note: it is not always possible to distinguish adj from adv uses in the quots
A As adj.

1a Askew, out of line. **chiefly Sth, S Midl**

a1883 (1911) Bagby *VA Gentleman* 79, I want to go whar I kin build my house catty-cornered, lop-sided, slanting-dicular, bottom-upward, any way I please. **1899** (1912) Green *VA Folk-Speech*, *Catercornered* . . . A table cloth not put on square is *catercornered.* **1950** *PADS* 14.18 **SC**, *Catticornered; catacornered* . . . Askew, awry. *diagonally.* **1954** Harder *Coll.* **cwTN**, *Cally-cornered* . . . Out of shape. You've knocked it all cally-cornered. *Ibid*, *Catty-cornered* . . . Uneven, not square or at straight angles. **1965–70** *DARE* (Qu. KK70, *Something that has got out of proper shape: "That house is all _____."*) Infs **FL18, KS2, KY40, NC51, VA5**, Catty-cornered; **KY41**, Catty-corner; (Qu. MM13, *The table was nice and straight until he came along and knocked it _____*) 20 Infs, **chiefly Sth, S Midl**, Catty-cornered; **CA176, ME9, NJ55, OH70, VA50, 75**, Catty-corner; **OK1, 48**, Catta-corner; **TX97**, Caddy-cornered; **IN68**, Catercorner; **NJ4**, Catty-corned; **MD13**, Catty-corners.

b By ext: out of sorts, ill-tempered.
1884 Baldwin *Yankee School-Teacher* 177 **VA**, She [=a mule] am de catty-corneres' sort ob beast dat eber I wur 'flicted ter own, dat she am. **1954** Harder *Coll.* **cwTN**, *Catty-cornered* . . . Nervously annoyed, upset. "E's jis' catty-cornered with hisself lately."

2 Diagonal.
1838 Neal *Charcoal Sketches* 196, One of that class . . who, when compelled to share their bed with another, lie in that engrossing posture called "catty-cornered." **1843** (1916) *New Purchase* 221, In spite of our use of "diagonal," and its being rendered into popular language "katter-korner'd-like," the strings were inclined to perpendiculars to the sides. **1896** *DN* 1.414 **cNY**, Cat-a-cornered. **1901** *DN* 2.137 **cNY**, Catter-cornered. **1945** Steinbeck *Cannery Row* 4 **CA**, Lee Chong's grocery was on its catty-corner right and Dora's Bear Flag Restaurant was on its catty-corner left. **1946** *PADS* 5.14 **VA**, Catty-cornered. **1949** *PADS* 11.19 **CO**, Catticorner, catty-corner, catty-cornered . . . In the opposite corner.

3 Triangular.
1954 Harder *Coll.* **cwTN**, Catty-cornered . . . Of a piece of cloth: three-cornered. **1969–70** *DARE* (Qu. W27, . . *A three-cornered tear in a piece of clothing*) Inf **IL96**, Catty-corner hole; **VA102**, Catty-corner tear; **MO19**, Catty-cornered.

B As adv.
Diagonally; positioned diagonally with respect to.
1905 *DN* 3.60 **NE**, Cattercorner, -ed, cattacorner, -ed, cattycorner, -ed . . . Diagonally across from. **1908** *DN* 3.297 **eAL, wGA**, Catacorner(ed), catacorners, cattycornered . . . Diagonally across, out of plumb. **1912** *DN* 3.573 **wIN**, Cata-cornered . . . Diagonally. **1941** *LANE* Map 547, [The map shows many informants giving the responses cater-cornered, catty-cornered; there are rare occurrences of caper-cornered, cat-cornered, catty-corner]. **1950** *PADS* 14.18 **SC**, Catticornered, catacornered . . . diagonally. **1953** Brewer *Word Brazos* 75 **eTX** [Black], Brothuh Ben Turner's house, what was catercawnered crost de road from de chu'ch house. **1965–70** *DARE* (Qu. MM14, *If a drugstore is on one corner of a square and a gas station is on the far corner, you might say, "The drugstore is _____ the gas station."*) 267 Infs, **widespread**, Catty-cornered (to, from, etc); 221 Infs, **widespread**, Catty-corner (to, from, etc); 11 Infs, **chiefly Midl**, Catercornered (from, to); **CT15, IL21, NJ3, NY105, OH43, OH1**, Catercorner (from); **IA5, OK1, TN12**, Catta-corner; **IL5, OK48**, Catta-cornered (to); **MS69**, Cat-cornered across from; **DC11**, Cater-corn; **TX36**, Catty-cornereds from; (Qu. MM16, . . *"It'll be shorter if we _____."*) 37 Infs, **chiefly Sth, Midl**, (Go, walk) catty-corner (across); **CA79, FL36, MO17, 36, OR3, SC3**, (Go, walk) catty-cornered (across). **1968** *DARE* Tape **IN36**, And let 'er [=the fishing line] warsh kinda' catty-corner down along the creek there.

catercorner v Also sp *caddy-corner, cat-a-corner, catercorn, catty-corner*

To move diagonally.

1888 J. Kirkland *McVeys* 59 *(OEDS),* Now suppose the railroad runs diagonally across a field, 'cater-cornering', as he says. **1902** White *Blazed Trail* 53, When the log had been cat-a-cornered from its bed [of ice], the chain was fastened around one end. **1965–70** *DARE* (Qu. MM16, *If you're walking with somebody to the other corner of a square, and you want to save steps, you might say, "It'll be shorter if we _____."*) Infs **TX**10, **WA**1, **WI**70, Catty-corner; **MO**16, Caddy-cornered; **DC**11, Catercorn; **PA**126, Catty-cornered; **NJ**28, Catty-cornered acrost.

catercornered See **catercorner** adj, adv

catering adj, adv |'ke(ɪ)t(ə)rɪn, -ɪŋ, 'kæt-| Also sp *cattering* [cater v]   **chiefly NEng**   Cf **kittering**

Diagonal(ly); askew.

1894 *DN* 1.340 **wCT,** *Caterin':* diagonally. **1941** *LANE* Map 547 *(Cater-cornered)* 2 infs, **nVT,** [kæɾərɪn, keˑtrɪn] [keɪtrɪn] of furniture, 'set diagonally across a corner . . '; of buildings, 'not parallel with the street . . or one another'; 1 inf, **sNH,** [keɪtərɪn]; 1 inf, **eCT,** [ketrɪn] 'askew, out of plumb', [kætrɪn] 'cut on the bias'. **1966** *DARE* (Qu. MM15, *If a carpenter nails a board crossing another board at an angle, you might say, "He nailed the board on _____."*) Inf **MA**6, Catering ['ketəɪn].

caterpillar n

‡**A** Form.

1966 *Wilson Coll.* **csKY,** Caterpillars ['kjælə,pɪləz].

B Senses.

1 A scorpionweed (here: *Phacelia congesta*).

1936 Whitehouse *TX Flowers* 112, Fiddle-Neck (*Phacelia congesta*) is also known as . . caterpillars . . . It has curled flower clusters and lavender-blue flowers.

2 An **amaranth** (here: *Amaranthus cruentus*). [From the appearance of the flowering heads; cf *DJE*]

1970 Correll *Plants TX* 558, *Amaranthus cruentus* . . . Caterpillar, purple amaranth, amaranto rojo.

caterpillar v¹

To have **gooseflesh.**

1891 Cooke *Huckleberries* 336 **CT,** What should I do if I was took sick to your house [in the country]? No doctor, no folks around! It makes me caterpiller to think on 't.

‡**caterpillar** v² [Malapropism, perh for *capitulate*]

1851 (1969) Burke *Polly Peablossom* 53 **MO,** Here all the Yazoo boys expressed great anxiety to know the reason why Ike's gun didn't fire. "Let's licker fust," said Mike, "an' if you don't caterpillar, you can shoot me."

caterpillar hunter n

A ground beetle of the genus *Calosoma*.

1905 Kellogg *Amer. Insects* 254, One of the largest, most conspicuous and well-known Carabids is the searcher, or caterpillar-hunter, *Calosoma scrutator*. **1928** Metcalf–Flint *Destructive & Useful Insects* 56, But certain species [of ground beetles] are known to be very valuable; and, in general, these . . "caterpillar hunters" are probably helpful to man. **1964** Borror–DeLong *Intro. Insects* 334, The . . beetles . . *Calosoma* . . are often called caterpillar-hunters, since they feed chiefly on caterpillars, particularly those which attack trees and shrubs. **1972** *Living Museum* 34.4.115 **IL,** The caterpillar hunter (*Calosoma scrutator* Fabricius) has a bright green back margined with red. It feeds on caterpillars in trees.

caterwampus See **catawampus** n

caterwampust See **catawampus** adv

caterway adv [cater- + way]

1941 *LANE* Map 547 *(Cater-cornered),* 1 inf, **swCT,** Caterway 'diagonally across an intersection of two streets'.

cateslunkit adj [Prob alter of **cater-** + *slunkit* perh a var of *slanted*]

1952 Brown *NC Folkl.* 1.525, *Cateslunkit* . . . Crosswise; a carpenter's term.

cat-eye See **cat's-eye**

cat-eyed adj

1 Having piercing or sharp eyes. *esp freq among Black speakers*

1965–70 *DARE* (Qu. X21b, . . *Eyes [which] are very sharp or piercing*) 52 Infs, **chiefly east of Missip R,** Cat-eyed. [Of all Infs responding to the question, 7% were Black; of those giving this response 38% were Black.]

2 Having watchful eyes.

1944 Adams *Western Words* 29, Cat-eyed—Said of a bad man who has to be constantly watchful to keep from being "downed" by a rival jealous of his reputation.

cateymount See **catamount**

catface n, also attrib   Also *cat's face*

1a A scar or knot on a tree, esp a pine tree cut for turpentine production. Cf **box** n 1, v¹

1879 *Lumberman's Gazette* 3 Dec. *(DA),* Logs that have cat faces or burnt places. **1946** *Democrat* 26 Dec. 1/1 *(DA)* **AL,** The southern fusiform rust which causes swelling and cat-faces on pine trees should be controlled. **1952** Brown *NC Folkl.* 1.525, Catface . . . A knot or bruise in lumber. —Chapel Hill. **1966** *DARE* FW Addit **AL,** Catface. A slash on a pine tree to collect sap for turpentine. The slash is made with a straight edged tool—something like a window scraper. **1967** *DARE* FW Addit **ceOR,** Cat's face. A scarring knot that goes deep and wide in a tree and makes it undesirable for commercial timber. A cat's face tree is left standing. **1982** *Fort Myers News-Press* (FL) 24 Jan 5F, About midnight we started home and set fire to a couple of turpentine "cat faces" on pine trees to warm up.

b By ext: see quots.

1966–68 *DARE* (Qu. T8, *Joints of pine wood that burn easily and make good fuel*) Infs **GA**7, 35, Catface. **1969** *DARE* FW Addit **nwCA,** Catface. Fire-scarred tree. **1981** *DARE* File **sGA,** Catface refers to a hole in tree.

2 A wrinkle or pucker left on a garment when ironed improperly. *chiefly among Black speakers*

1952 Brown *NC Folkl.* 1.525, Catface . . . A wrinkle or pucker in clothing ironed when too dry. —Granville county. **1969** Angelou *Caged Bird* 48 [Black], I had to iron seven starched shirts and not leave a cat's face anywhere. **1976** *DARE* File **seLA** [Black], You left too many catfaces in it. **1977** Smitherman *Talkin* 258 [Black], *Cat faces,* wrinkles in clothes when ironing them, as in "Chile, you call yo'self done iron this, with all these cat faces in it?"

3 See quot.

1973 *DARE* File **neMI,** Catface—The pattern of cracks that develop naturally on a tomato around the stem.

4 A bracket fungus: see quot.

1966 *DARE* (Qu. S19, *Mushrooms that grow out like brackets from the sides of trees*) Inf **FL**4, Catfaces.

‡**cat-face spider** n

1966 *DARE* (Qu. R28, . . *Different kinds of spiders*) Inf **ID**1, Cat-face spider.

cat feathers n pl   Also *cat paws, cat('s) tails*

Balls of dust.

1966–70 *DARE* (Qu. E20) Inf **OH**29, Cat feathers; **MI**108, Cat paws; **NC**36, Cat tails; **NY**230, Cat's tails.

cat fever n [Short for *catarrhal fever*]

A respiratory infection accompanied by chills and fever.

1943 *AN&Q* 3.149/2 **VA,** Cat Fever: the nickname given by Navy personnel in Norfolk, Virginia, to a "new infection" that swamped the city early in December; three days of high fever followed by subsiding temperature, a clammy feeling, and nausea; a revival of a term given by Navy men, in the tropics during the last war, to a grippal fever. **1960** Williams *Walk Egypt* 176 **GA,** The last few months seemed like the siege of the cat fever she had had when she was eight.

catfight n   Cf **dogfight**

The most informal of occasions; one requiring the least dressing-up.

1981 *DARE* File **cnMA** (as of c1915), We didn't wear dreadful-looking things to a *catfight.* "That hat! I wouldn't wear it to a catfight."

catfish n

1 See quot. [Prob euphem for **cat shit**]

1969 *DARE* (Qu. HH22b, . . *A very mean person* . . *"He's meaner than _____."*) Inf **PA**197, Catfish.

‡**2** See quot.

1967 *DARE* (Qu. HH7a, *Someone who talks too much, or too loud,* *"He's an awful _____."*) Inf **TX**27, Catfish.

catfish cloud n

1967 *DARE* (Qu. B10, . . *The long trailing clouds high in the sky*) Inf **LA**11, Catfish clouds.

catfish row n Cf *DS* II25

A section of a town where Black residents live.

1937 *Natl. Geog. Mag.* 72.271 **cnMS,** "Sadaday" night is traditional "darkey night" up-State. Then whites stay off the streets and the black families in pre-Sunday best emerge from "catfish rows" and hold orderly carnival. **1938** FWP *Guide MS* 323 **cwMS,** Between the junction and Vicksburg, U.S. 61 passes a number of large hardwood mills and through a "catfish row" of Negro shacks.

catfish stew n **chiefly SC** See Map

A stew or soup made with catfish.

1897 [see **cat n** 8]. **1965–70** *DARE* (Qu. H45, *Dishes made with meat, fish, or poultry . . around here*) Infs **SC**19, 21, 29, 32, 38, 42, 43, 46, 51, 62, **NC**20, **GA**12, Catfish stew; **SC**7, Catfish stew—tomato soup, onion, fat back, ketchup, hot sauce; boil and add catfish; **SC**26, Catfish stew—hot sauce, catsup, onions, black pepper, salt, potatoes, carrots; **GA**17, Catfish-head stew; [(Qu. FF1, . . *A kind of group meeting called a "social" . . What kinds are there?*) Inf **SC**19, Catfish stew].

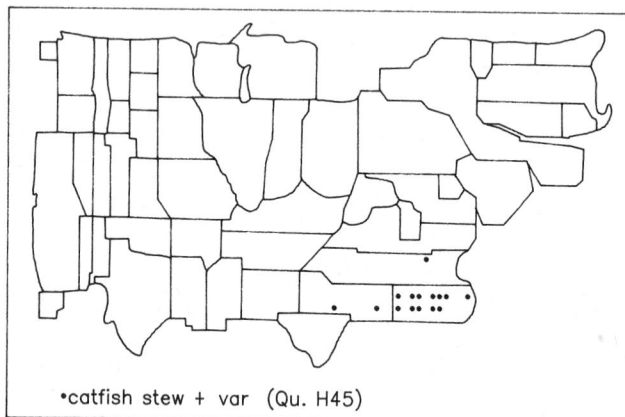

•catfish stew + var (Qu. H45)

cat fit n

A burst of joy or (more often) anger.

1895 *DN* 1.385 **cNY,** *Cat fit:* = conniption fit. **1905** *DN* 3.60 **NE,** *Catfit, catnip-fit* . . Same as *conniption fit.* **1931** Faulkner *Sanctuary* 52 **MS,** I be dawg ef hit dont look like he'll have a catfit. **1949** *PADS* 11.5 **wTX,** *Catfit* . . A fit of anger or joy. "She'll have a cat fit when she hears about it." **1951** *PADS* 15.53 **TX,** *Catfit* . . A conniption. **c1960** *Wilson Coll.* **csKY,** *Cat-fit* . . A fit of anger or joy. "When she got his letter, she had a cat-fit." **1965–70** *DARE* (Qu. KK11, *To make great objections or a big fuss about something: "When we asked him to do that, he _____."*) Infs **CT**37, **ID**5, **IL**5, **MI**18, **ND**2, **OH**89, **PA**130, **VT**16, Had cat fits. **1983** *MJLF* 9.34 **ceKY** (as of 1957), *Cat fit* . . a severe fit.

cat fly n

A small unidentified fly: perh a midge of the family Chironomidae.

1970 *DARE* (Qu. R10, . . *Very small flies that don't sting*) Inf **TN**52, Cat flies.

cat flycatcher n

=catbird 1.

1917 (1923) *Birds Amer.* 3.177, *Dumetella carolinensis* . . . Other Names . . . Cat Flycatcher. **1946** Hausman *Eastern Birds* 452.

catfoot n Cf **cat's-foot**

1 also *cats foot:* A **wild ginger 1** (here: *Asarum canadense*). [Perh from the shape of the leaves]

1876 Hobbs *Bot. Hdbk.* 21, Cats foot, Canada snake root, Asarum Canadense. **1900** Lyons *Plant Names* 49, *A. canadense* . . . Catfoot. **1971** Krochmal *Appalachia Med. Plants* 66, *Asarum canadense* . . . Common Names: . . catfoot, . . wild ginger.

2 A **cudweed 1** (here: *Gnaphalium obtusifolium*). [Prob from the woolly clustered heads]

1950 Gray–Fernald *Manual of Botany* 1464, *G. obtusifolium* . . . Catfoot. **1961** Smith *MI Wildflowers* 399, *Catfoot* . . In open, often in sandy, places. **1970** Correll *Plants TX* 1616, *Cat-foot, fragrant cudweed* . . . Heads in glomerules.

cat game See **cat's game**

cat grape See **catbird grape**

cat greenbrier See **catbrier**

catgut n

1 A **goat's rue** (here: *Tephrosia virginiana*); also its root. [See quot 1840]

1840 MA Zool. & Bot. Surv. *Herb. Plants & Quadrupeds* 65, Goat's Rue . . . The root is slender, tough, and long, and popularly called *catgut.* **1900** U.S. Bur. Amer. Ethnology *Annual Rept. for 1897–98* 1.425 **S Atl,** The catgut or devil's shoestring *(Tephrosia).* **1971** Krochmal *Appalachia Med. Plants* 248, *Tephrosia virginiana* . . . Catgut. **1976** Bruce *How to Grow Wildflowers* 284, *Tephrosia virginiana,* because of its enormously long root, is known as Cat-gut and Devil's Shoestring as well as Goat's-rue.

2 A rawhide rope. **SW**

1933 *AmSp* 8.1.30 **TX,** *Swing a catgut.* To use a rope. **1961** Adams *Old-Time Cowhand* 127 **SW,** A rawhide rope's called a . . "catgut."

3 Bad whiskey; rotgut.

1924 Marks *Plastic Age* 18 **RI,** You told me . . that that stuff [in a flask] was catgut and that you wouldn't drink it on a bet. **1966–69** *DARE* (Qu. DD21b) Infs **MI**19, **RI**13, Catgut.

cat-gut scraper n *joc*

A fiddler.

1891 Maitland *Amer. Slang Dict.,* Catgut scraper, a fiddler. **1930** Shoemaker *1300 Words* 10 **cPA Mts** (as of c1900), Cat-gut-scraper.

cat hair n Cf **cat hide**

1966–67 *DARE* (Qu. U19a, *Words used around here for money in general: "He's certainly got the _____."*) Inf **OH**2, Cat hair—that's my husband's [term]; **OK**51, Cat hair—very common.

cat-hammered adj [Folk-etym for *cat-hammed*]

Of a cow: having thin thighs.

1949 *PADS* 11.18 **CO,** *Cat-hammered* . . . Said of a cow that isn't quick enough into the beef; i.e., with a considerable amount of practically bare bone above the hock.

cat-harn n [Minced form, ult from *God-damn*]

1911 *DN* 3.550 **WY,** *Cat-harn,* about the same as "continental darn." Used vaguely in expressions like "I don't care a cat-harn."

cathead n, also attrib Also *cat's head* **Sth, S Midl**

1 A biscuit, esp a large one.

1930 *DN* 6.86 **cWV,** *Cathead,* a biscuit. **1941** FWP *Guide WV* 403, The West Virginia logger has retained his jargon. Cooks are still 'stomick robbers' . . biscuits, 'cat-heads.' **1958** *PADS* 29.8 **TN.** **1960** Hall *Smoky Mt. Folks* 7, It was a novel experience to eat "cat heads" (biscuits) or corn pone three times a day. **1966** *DARE* Tape **NC**30, Biscuits were called cat's heads [in logging camps]. **1966–68** *DARE* FW Addit **cs,cwNC.** **1967** *DARE* (Qu. H19, . . *A biscuit*) Inf **NC**44, Catheads; **TN**11, Cathead variety is bigger, flakier than a biscuit. **1969** Angelou *Caged Bird* 36 [Black], Her cathead biscuits were at least three inches in diameter and two inches thick. **1972** *Atlanta Letters* **cnGA,** Catheads are biscuits; **nwGA,** Farm workers called a large biscuit a cat-head.

2 See quot.

1966 *DARE* (Qu. H71, . . *The last piece of food left on a plate*) Inf **MS**46, Cathead.

3 Perh =catfish row.

1966 *DARE* (Qu. C35, . . *Different parts of your town or city*) Inf **GA**12, Cathead.

cat hide n Cf **cat hair, frogskin**

1970 *DARE* (Qu. U26, . . *A paper dollar*) Inf **AR**56, Cat hide.

cathole n [Prob in ref to presence of catfish] **chiefly MI**

A small pond or deep place in a river.

1842 Kirkland *Forest Life* 2.177 **MI,** Fears . . led her at once to a deep hollow . . where there was a small circular pond without any apparent outlet—one of those deposits of water called in this country, cat-holes. **1859** MI State Ag. Soc. *Trans. for 1857* 9.578, The very important work of draining our swamps, marshes and "cat holes" has been fairly commenced. **1899** (1912) Green *VA Folk-Speech,* Cat-hole . . . A very deep place in any body of water, either pond, creek or river. **1923** Adams *Pioneer Hist. Ingham Co.* 180 **MI,** One mile east we pass the corner—Young's Corners—it is called, and then for a mile or two we have hills galore, clay knolls and cat-holes, until we come to the log house.

cat-hop n Cf **cat back**
　　1949 *PADS* 11.19 **CO**, *Cat-hop* . . . Mild bucking [of a horse].

cat ice n [See quot 1950] **Nth**
　　A thin layer of ice.
　　1950 *WELS (The first thin ice that forms on a pond)* 1 Inf, **cwWI**, Cat ice [forms] in depressions in fields, edges of pools—just like glass; looks like the eye of a cat, with bubbles in the ice; or a cat would break it stepping on it. **1955** *U.S. Arctic Info. Center Gloss., Cat-ice* . . . Thin ice formed before underlying water receded. **1967–69** *DARE* (Qu. B33a, *The first thin ice*) Infs **PA200, WY4**, Cat ice. **1979** *UpCountry* Feb 26 **ME**, The bay was crested with whitecaps and cat-ice covered the puddles.

catifawgus adj [Alter of **cater-** + uncert element]
　　=**catawampus** adj **1**.
　　c1960 *Wilson Coll.* **csKY**, *Catifawgus* . . . Awry, out of kilter, catawampus.

cat-in See **cat** n **3c**

cat in a bag n Also *cat in a sack*, ~ *the bag* [Ger *die Katze im Sack kaufen* 'to buy the cat in the sack'] **chiefly Inland Nth, N Midl** See Map Cf **pig in a poke**
　　Something one buys or trades without being able to see it; hence something to be wary of.
　　1950 *WELS (Buying or exchanging something that you have not seen: You say you're getting . . . _____)* 1 Inf, **WI**, Cat in the bag; *(Exchanging with somebody when neither one has seen what the other has; you call that _____)* 5 Infs, **WI**, (Getting, buying a) cat in a (the) bag. **1965–70** *DARE* (Qu. U13) 17 Infs, **chiefly Inland Nth, N Midl**, Cat in a (or the) bag; **GA89, IL86, IN3, IA43, KS18, OH81, TN36**, Cat in a sack; **WI12**, Bought a cat in a bag.

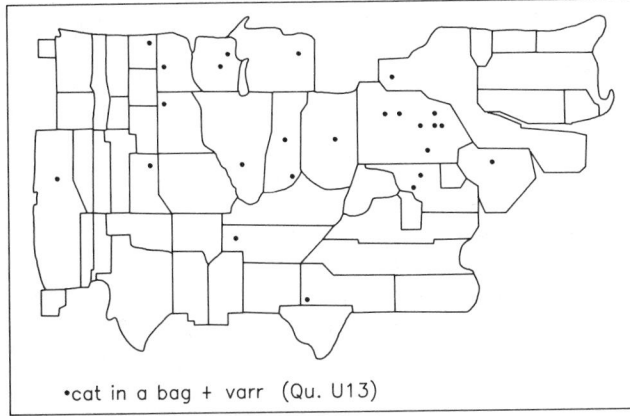

　　　　　•cat in a bag + varr (Qu. U13)

cat in the corner n Also *cat in a corner*
　　A children's game: see quots.
　　1954 *Harder Coll.* **cwTN**, *Cat in the corner* . . . Children's game. Same as puss in the corner. **1969** *DARE* (Qu. EE2, *Games that have one extra player—when a signal is given, the players change places, and the extra one tries to get a place*) Inf **CT23**, Cat in a corner.

cat-I one holt n
　　=**cat** n **3c**.
　　1892 *DN* 1.214, *Cat* . . . "I am very familiar with [the game] . . also with 'Cat-I one holt.' "

catish adj Usu |kəˈtɪš|, also |kɪ'taš, kə-| Also sp *katish, kitash* **chiefly N Cent**
　　Fine, elegant, stylish.
　　1890 *DN* 1.60 **swOH**, *Catish* . . . stylish, elegant; generally preceded by *very*. (Accent on the ultimate.) **1942** *Berrey–Van den Bark Amer. Slang* 37.10, Beautiful . . *catish*. **1967** *DARE* (Qu. W38, *When a man dresses himself up in his best clothes, you say he's _____*) Inf **OH2**, Kitash [kəˈtaš]. **1978** *DARE* File **csWI** (as of 1920s), Catish [kəˈtɪš] stylish. "Oh, your new dress is catish!" **1979** *Verbatim Letters* **neIL** (as of c1900), A word that has been knocking around in our family for several generations . . is . . *kitash* (with a short i sound and ah sound for the a, emphasis on the last syllable). We use it in our family to denote something rather elegant, e.g., "We went to a very kitash party last night, everyone came formal, butlers all over the place." **1981** *DARE* File **csWI** (as of 1930), *Katish* [kəˈtɪš] Pleasantly elegant, very nice, stylish.

"Your dress is really katish!" "May I hold your coat?" "That would be katish!" *Ibid* **sIN**, You certainly have some [kəˈtɪš] stores here.

cat-licker n Also *cat lick* [Alter of *Catholic* + *er*] **chiefly N Cent** See Map *often derog*
　　A Catholic.
　　1960 *Wentworth–Flexner Slang* 91, *Cat lick*—A Catholic. *A jocular and derog. corruption.* **1965–70** *DARE* (Qu. CC4, . . *Nicknames . . for various religions or religious groups*) 16 Infs, **chiefly N Cent**, Cat-lickers. **1981** Pederson *LAGS Urban Material* **AL**, (Roman Catholic) Cat licker. Common in Chicago.

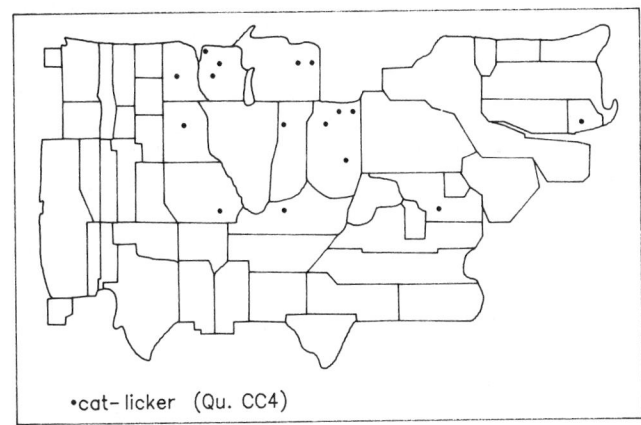

　　　　•cat- licker (Qu. CC4)

cat manure See **cat shit**

cat mewing n *obs*
　　A catcall.
　　1851 (1969) Burke *Polly Peablossom* 105 **LA**, He . . could hear distinctly the terrific cry, "Put 'em out!" "Get out!" and similar demonstrations of public dissatisfaction, mingled with hisses, outcries, cat-mewings, and similar demonstrations.

catmint n, also attrib [*OED* 1265 →]
　　Catnip.
　　1737 (1911) Brickell *Nat. Hist. NC* 20, The Pot-Herbs which are useful in Physick are . . *Derg*, red and white, *Nep* or *Cat-mint*. **1936** IL *Nat. Hist. Surv. Wildflowers* 278, Catnip. Cat Mint. *Nepeta Cataria*. **1969** *DARE* Tape **KY44**, Catmint . . grows up about two feet high and has a big white flower on it and you know you can't grow it around in your back yard.

‡cat-mirer n
　　1970 *DARE* (Qu. B25, . . *A very heavy rain*) Inf **VA82**, Gully-washer, cat-mirer ['kæt 'maɪrə].

cat mocker n
　　=**catbird 1**.
　　1966 *DARE* (Qu. Q14, . . *Other names for . . catbird*) Inf **GA7**, Cat mocker—mockingbird is slightly different, bigger.

cat nettle n
　　An unidentified nettle-like plant; see quot.
　　1967 *DARE* (Qu. S17, . . *Kinds of plants . . that will cause itching and swelling*) Inf **LA2**, Cat nettle—grows around houses; there's another nettle, but I don't know the name of it. It grows in the woods.

cat-nine-tails See **cat-o'-nine-tails 1**

catnip fit n Also metath *capnit fit* Cf **cat fit**
　　A conniption.
　　1905 *DN* 3.60 **NE**, Catfit, Catnip-fit . . . Same as conniption fit. **1914** *DN* 4.70 **ME, nNH**, Catnip, capnit, conniption or *capuluptic fit* . . . A fit. The latter apoplectic. **1922** (1926) Cady *Rhymes VT* 217, Beneath its box he kept the rits / That give the county catnip fits.

catnip, not to know v phr Cf **beans, not to know**
　　1954 *Harder Coll.* **cwTN**, *Catnip* . . . in expression, "He don't know catnip," [means] to lack common sense.

cat-nipper n [**cat** n **3b** + *nipper* perh from Engl dial *nip* to strike a ball with the edge of a cricket bat]
　　1903 *DN* 2.350 **NY**, *Cat-nipper* . . . The stick in playing the game of cat.

catoby See **catawba** A

cat-o'-nine-tails n

1 also *cat-nine-tails:* A **cattail 1** (*Typha* spp) or similar plant.
1858 Holmes *Autocrat* 330 **MA,** It swayed back and forward like a . . cat-o'-nine-tails (bulrush) with a bobolink on it. **1883** *Harper's Mag.* 68.100/1 **N Atl,** A mossy bank with overhanging ferns and cat-o'-nine-tails. **1943** *Sun* (Baltimore MD) 14 Sept 16/7 *(Hench Coll.),* It is true the cat-o'-nine-tails is a whip but it is also the swamp grass you are talking about. **1965–70** *DARE* (Qu. S26b, . . *Wildflowers that grow in water or wet places*) 9 Infs, **scattered,** Cat-o'-nine-tails; **PA167,** Cat-nine-tails; (Qu. S26a, . . *Other wildflowers*) Inf **ME7,** Cat-o'-nine-tails; (Qu. S26d, *Wildflowers that grow in water or wet places*) Inf **NY45,** Cat-o'-nine-tails; (Qu. S26e, . . *Other wildflowers*) Inf **MA67,** Cat-o'-nine-tails; (Qu. S21, . . *Weeds . . that are a trouble in gardens and fields*) Inf **LA43,** Cat-o'-nine-tails.

2 See **cat n 3c.**

catooch n [Fr *cartouche* cartridge] *obs*
1899 (1912) Green *VA Folk-Speech, Catooch* . . . A cartridge box.

catoosa bass n [Prob for *Catoosa* Co., Georgia, from the Cherokee language, perh "high place"]
=smallmouth bass.
1969 *DARE* (Qu. P1) Inf **GA76,** Catoosa bass—same as smallmouth bass.

catouse n |kə'taus| Also sp *katowse* [*ca-* var of **ker-** + **touse**] **NEng**
An uproar, commotion.
1859 (1968) Bartlett *Americanisms, Katowse.* (Germ. Getôse.) A din, tumult, rumpus; as "What a katowse you are making!" New England. **1890** *DN* 1.20 **NH,** My father . . always used 'catouse' [kə'taus] for *touse.* **1903** *DN* 2.296 **seMA,** *Catouse* . . . Uproar. **1914** *DN* 4.70 **ME, nNH,** *Catouse* . . . A rumpus, row, disturbance, fight. **1967–70** *DARE* (Qu. KK11, *To make great objections or a big fuss about something:* "*When we asked him to do that, he _____.*") Inf **MA38,** Made a great [kə'taus] about it; **MA73,** Made a big [kə'taus]; (Qu. KK16, *A great noise or disturbance*) Inf **MA79,** [kə'taus].

cat-out See **cat n 3c**

cat-over-the-roof n
=Antony-over n.
1967 *DARE* (Qu. EE22, *What do you call the game in which they throw a ball over a building . . to a player on the other side?*) Inf **OH20,** Cat-over-the-roof.

catowba See **catawba A**

cat owl n
Any of several owls, such as the barred owl, the **horned owl,** the **long-eared owl** or **short-eared owl.**
1792 Imlay *Western Terr.* 225, [Birds in south central US include] Night hawk, Cat owl, Screech owl, [etc]. **1856** U.S. Dept. Ag. *Rept. of Secy.* 122, The bird [the large-horned owl], also known as the cat-owl, is most common along the shores of the Ohio and the Mississippi but is found from Hudson's Bay to Florida. **1916** Seton *Woodcraft Manual Girls* 306, *Great Horned Owl or Cat Owl (Bubo virginianus)* . . . It is known at once by its great ear tufts, its yellow eyes . . . This is the winged tiger of the woods. **1925** Bailey *Birds FL* 76, *Strix varia* . . Cat owl. **1931–33** *LANE* Worksheets **swCT,** Cat owl . . . A variety of owl; **swCT,** Yorkers call screech owls cat owls; **csRI,** Cat owl . . . A variety of owl. **1946** Hausman *Eastern Birds* 352, *Otus asio* . . Cat Owl. *Ibid* 362, *Asio wilsonianus* . . Cat Owl. **1950** *PADS* 14.18 **SC,** *Cat owl* . . . The great horned owl. **1955** *AmSp* 30.178, The known distribution of the name *cat owl* is for the barn owl (N.C., Ontario), horned owl (general), screech owl (Mass., R.I., N.Y., N.C., Fla., W. Va., Calif.), barred owl (Wis.), long-eared owl (R.I., Pa., N.J., Wis., Ark., La., Texas, Saskatchewan), and short-eared owl (Wis., Mo., Newfoundland, Labrador). **1966–69** *DARE* (Qu. Q2, . . *Owls*) Inf **RI15,** Cat owl; **ME3,** Cat owl—head like a cat; **ME12,** Cat owl—eyes like a cat's eyes; **NJ52,** Cat owl—same as barn owl; (Qu. Q1) Inf **MN16,** Screech owl—also called a cat owl.

cat paw See **cat's-paw 8**

cat paw plant See **cat's-paw 1**

cat paws See **cat feathers**

cat pine n Cf **cat spruce**
=white spruce.
1894 *Jrl. Amer. Folkl.* 7.99, *Picea alba,* . . cat-pine, Buckfield, Me. **1900** Lyons *Plant Names* 288.

cat piss See **cat shit**

cat poison n Cf **cat shit**
1930 *AmSp* 6.97 **cNY,** *Cat poison:* Meanness. "He'd work some of the cat poison out of her liver!"

‡cat-ran-through-the-garret relation n
1914 *DN* 4.151 **ME,** *Cat-ran-through-the-garret relation.* A distant relative.

catridge, ca'tridge See **cartridge**

cat rock n [Prob abbr for *catapult* + *rock*] Cf **cat n 3b**
1949 *PADS* 11.19 **CO,** *Cat rock* . . . A small rock, often used with a sling.

catrup n
Catnip (*Nepeta cataria*).
1900 Lyons *Plant Names* 259, *N. Cataria* . . . Catrup, Cat's-wort, Field Mint. **1971** Krochmal *Appalachia Med. Plants* 184, *Nepeta Cataria* . . . Catrup.

cat's ass n

1 A snarl or knot in a cable or **choker 1:** see quot 1958. Cf **cat's-paw 9**
1942 Berrey–Van den Bark *Amer. Slang* 516.4, *Cat's ass, a kink in a wire cable* [in an oil field]. **1958** McCulloch *Woods Words* **Pacific NW,** *Cat's ass*—a. The snarl which results when a choker slips off a log and cinches up tight. b. A closed choker hook which has slid down the choker until it cannot be unhooked . . d. A knot which has been pulled into a line, particularly a full 360 degree kink.

2 used in emphatic denials: See quot.
1966 *DARE* (Qu. KK55a, *To deny something very firmly:* "*No, not by a _____.*") Inf **OK27,** Cat's ass.

3 A self-important person. [Alter of older *cat's meow, cat's pajamas*] *derog*
1967 *DARE* (Qu. GG19b, . . "*He seems to think he's _____.*") Inf **IL4,** The cat's ass.

4 =**hickey n².**
1967 *DARE* (Qu. X39, *A mark on the skin where somebody has sucked it hard and brought the blood to the surface*) Inf **CO7,** Blood blister, cat's ass.

cat's-breeches n [See quot 1915] **West, esp Rocky Mts, NW**
The ballhead **waterleaf** (*Hydrophyllum capitatum*). Also called **bear cabbage, pussyfoot, ragged breeches, woolen breeches**
1915 (1926) Armstrong *Western Wild Flowers* 418, Cat's Breeches . . . The flowers . . are crowded together in roundish clusters . . . The whole cluster . . becomes in fruit a conspicuous, very fuzzy, round head, covered with bristly white hairs, making the children's quaint common name for this plant quite appropriate. **1937** U.S. Forest Serv. *Range Plant Hdbk.* W98, Ballhead waterleaf is also known as cats-breeches. **1956** St. John *Flora SE WA* 334, Cat's Breeches . . . is often cooked and eaten as "greens". **1963** Craighead *Rocky Mt. Wildflowers* 153, Cats-breeches . . blooms about [the] time first Canada goose goslings hatch and take to the water. **1966** *DARE* Wildfl QR Inf **WA10,** *Hydrophyllum capitatum,* cat's-breeches.

cat's-claw n, also attrib Also *catclaw* **SW**
A prickly or spiny plant of the genera *Acacia, Mimosa, Pithecellobium,* or *Schrankia.*
1849 (1906) Audubon *Western Jrl.* 73 **TX,** Every tree, shrub and plant is thorny to a degree no one can imagine until they have tried a thicket of "tear-blanket" or "cat's claw." **1882** *Bot. Gaz.* 7.9 **AZ,** "Almost as cruel are the bushes of an acacia, appropriately called cats's claws," that crowd in the trail, and reach their slender limbs across the way, armed every half inch with pairs of strong, recurved thorns, that tap your veins unawares. **1893** (1958) Wister *Out West* 151 **TX,** The ground . . generally was of earth, brown and dry; the smaller growths being cactus, cats-claw and broom-weed. **1940** FWP *Guide TX* 80, The major honey bee plants are horsemint, cotton, mesquite, huajilla, and catclaw. **1941** Jaeger *Wildflowers* 97 **Desert SW,** Cat's-claw is a spreading deciduous shrub or small tree, of rocky desert hillsides and washes. **1965** Teale *Wandering Through Winter* 22 **CA,** We stopped beside the cat's-claw, whose curved spines give it the nicknames of "tear-blanket" and "wait-a-minute-bush." **1967–69** *DARE* (Qu. S21, . . *Weeds . . that are a trouble in gardens and fields*) Inf **TX68,** Cat's-claw; (Qu. T16, . . *Trees [that] are special*) Inf **CA9,** Cat's-claw; **NM13, TX1, 11, 22,** Catclaw; **TX13,** Catclaw bush. **1969** *DARE* Tape **TX72,** To me, there's nothing more beautiful than the desert . . in the spring, when the catclaw's blooming.

cat's-ear n Also *cat-ear*

1 =**mariposa lily.** [See quot 1949]
1897 Parsons *Wild Flowers CA* 278, Cat's-Ears. Pussy's-Ears. **1941** FWP *Guide WA* 22, The creamy cat's-ear or mariposa lily. **1949** Peattie *Cascades* 259, The calochortus . . . Its creamy blossom has on the inside a dark purplish spot and long soft hairs like those in a cat's ear. **1966** *DARE* Wildfl QR Inf **WA**10, *Calochortus elegans*—Cat's-ear. **1968–70** *DARE* (Qu. S23) Inf **CA**101, Cat-ears; (Qu. S26c) Inf **CA**204, Cat-ears.

2 A plant of the genus *Hypochoeris.* [*OED* 1848 →] Also called **gosmore, yellowweed**
1900 Lyons *Plant Names* 198, *Hypochoeris* . . . Cat's-ear. **1935** Davis *Honey* 1 s**OR**, The creek-meadow in season was full of flowers—wild daisies, lamb tongues, cat-ears, big patches of camas. **1959** Anderson *Flora AK* 448, *H. radiata* . . . Cat's Ears. **1973** Hitchcock–Cronquist *Flora Pacific NW* 532, *Hypochaeris* [sic] L. Cats-ear.

3 =**pussytoes.**
1900 Lyons *Plant Names* 37, A[ntennaria] dioica . . . Cat's-ear. **1938** (1958) Sharples *AK Wild Flowers* 12, *Antennaria* . . . "Cat's Ear," "Ladies' Tobacco," "Pussy Toes."

cat sense n
Common sense.
1963 Wright *Lawd Today* 109 **Chicago IL** [Black], That woman ain't got cat sense!

cat's-eye n, also attrib Also *cat-eye*

1 also *cat:* A clear marble with an internal design suggestive of the eye of a cat.
1955 *PADS* 23.10 **OH** (as of 1900), Aggie, cat's eye . . . An agate marble that gives the appearance of having the likeness of a cat's eye in it. **1962** *PADS* 37.1 c**KS**, Cat's eye, cat eye. A clear glass marble into which has been inserted by the manufacturer a four-bladed colored design. This is a manufacturer's designation. **1965–70** *DARE* (Qu. EE6d, *Special marbles*) 84 Infs, **chiefly Nth**, Cat's-eyes; 57 Infs, **scattered**, Cat-eyes; **IN**73, Cat-eye marbles; **OH**42, Cats; (Qq. EE6a,b,c) 12 Infs, **scattered**, Cat-eye(s); 8 Infs, **chiefly Nth**, Cat's-eye(s); **AL**8, Cat-eye marbles. **1966–68** *DARE* Tape **IN**1, Cat-eyes are clear marbles that . . actually look like they have stars inside them; **IL**2, Some of those agates . . . the cat's-eyes—that's the collectors; **LA**36, We also have another marble called the cat-eye . . . They're real, real pretty; they have things inside. **c1970** Wiersma *Marbles Terms* sw**MI**, Cat's eye . . . a clear glass playing marble with oval colored portion at center. General. *Cat-eye* . . . A clear glass marble with a colored portion at the center resembling the pupil of a cat's eye. **1973** Ferretti *Marble Book* 41, Cats eyes. Glass marble with football-shaped wedges of color in otherwise clear glass.

2 A glass reflector.
1940 Charlottesville *Daily Progress* 17 Dec 1/2 (Hench Coll.) **VA**, These alterations will be made on the north and west sides and "cat eyes" for night driving will be installed around the curbing.

cat's face n

1 A Johnny-jump-up (here: *Viola tricolor*).
1900 Lyons *Plant Names* 394, V[iola] tricolor . . . Cat's faces. **1931** Harned *Wild Flowers Alleghanies* 326, Pansy (V. tricolor L.) . . . This species has a multitude of common names, among which are Johnny Jump-up, . . Cat's Faces, . . [etc].

2 See **catface.**

cat's-foot n

1 =**ground ivy.** [*OED* 1597 →]
1876 Hobbs *Bot. Hdbk.* 21, Cats foot, Ground ivy, Nepeta glechoma. **1959** Carleton *Index Herb. Plants* 25, Cat's foot: Antennaria (v); Nepeta hederacea. **1974** (1977) Coon *Useful Plants* 157.

2 See **catfoot 1.**

3 =**pussytoes.** [*OED* 1775 →]
1900 Lyons *Plant Names* 37, A[ntennaria] dioica . . . Cat's-foot. **1950** Stevens *ND Plants* 280, *Antennaria.* Catsfoot . . . Early spring flowers, the clusters first showing as little furry balls unfolding, whence the name "catsfoot" or "pussytoes".

cat's foot intj Also *cat's hind foot* [Prob orig euphem for *Christ's foot*] **scattered but esp NEng** Cf **foot** intj
Used as an expression of contempt or disbelief.
1877 Bartlett *Americanisms* 778, Cat's Foot! An exclamation of disbelief. New England. **1894** *Jrl. Amer. Folkl.* 7.253 ce**MA**, Cat's foot—A

singular expression . . . applied to any nonsensical or improbable remark. **1899** (1912) Green *VA Folk-Speech*, Cat's foot . . . An expression of dissent or disapproval. **1909** *DN* 3.419 se**MA**, Oh, cat's foot! . . . Used as an exclamation of contempt or disgust. "Oh, cat's foot!" **1927** *AmSp* 3.138 **ME**. **1939** *AmSp* 14.266 **IN**. **1939** Coffin *Capt. Abby* 56 **ME** (as of c1860s), "Cat's hind foot!" she would say. "There's Hannah traipsing off to the village again, and she was there just last week." **c1970** Halpert Coll. w**KY**, Well, a cat's hind foot! = a mild oath.

cat's fur to make kitten britches n For varr, see quots Cf **layovers to catch meddlers**
A nonsensical reply to a child's question "What's that for?"— used esp when *for* is pronounced [fɝ].
1942 Whipple *Joshua* 293 **UT** (as of c1860), What fur? . . . 'Cat-fur-to-make-kitten-britches!' **1949** *PADS* 11.13 w**TX**, What fur? Cat fur to make kitten britches. (Response to an inquisitive "What for?") Common. Also heard in San Diego. **1950** *WELS* (Things that people say to put a child off when he asks too many questions: "What's that for?" "_____") 6 Infs, **WI**, Cat fur to make kitten britches; 1 Inf, Cat fur; 1 Inf, Cat fur and dog fur to make kitty britches. **1965–70** *DARE* (Qu. NN12a) 149 Infs, **widespread**, Cat's fur to make (*or* for making) kitten britches; 13 Infs, **scattered**, Cat fur to make kitten britches; 14 Infs, **scattered**, Cat's fur; 11 Infs, **scattered**, Cat fur; **TX**1, Cat fur and kitten britches; **TN**42, Cat's fur to make cat britches; **NC**45, Cat's fur to make whistle britches; **NY**92, Cat's fur on a pumphandle; (Qu. NN12b, *Things that people say . . when [a child] asks, "What are you making?"*) 14 Infs, **scattered**, Cat('s) fur (to make kitten britches); **IN**83, Cat's fur fer kitchen britches. **1966** Wilson Coll. cs**KY**, Cat fur . . . Answer to question "What's that fer?" Cat fur to make kitten britches, d'you want a pair? **1970** Thompson Coll. **AL** (as of 1920s), Cat fur to make kitten britches. Reply to "What for?" (Pronounced fur).

cat's game n Also *cat, cat game, cat's tail*
A tie game of tick-tack-toe.
1950 *WELS* (Neither "x" nor "o" wins [at tick-tack-toe], you say it's _____) 6 Infs, **WI**, The cat's; 6 Infs, Cat's game; 6 Infs, (One) for the cat; 2 Infs, Cat got (*or* gets) it; 1 Inf, Cat. **1965–70** *DARE* (Qu. EE38b) 120 Infs, **widespread**, Cat's game; 18 Infs, **scattered**, Cat; **OR**15, Cat game; **CA**37, Cat's tail; [24 Infs, Cat (wins, won, gets it, got it, has it, gets [*or* got], wins) the game)].

cat-shaking n
1948 *AN&Q* 8.107 **KY**, In Lee County, Kentucky, it is customary to hold a cat-shaking whenever a new quilt has been finished in the neighborhood. To it are invited all the eligible bachelors and spinsters. The new quilt is unfolded, and all gather 'round. Each person grasps the edges of the quilt, and at a given signal a cat is tossed right into the middle of it. Everyone shakes nervously. The cat gets wild and the shakers the same. If the cat gets off—and the supposition is that he does, usually!— the person standing nearest to the point at which the beast escapes will be the first to be married.

cat's-head n Cf *DS* X31

1 See quot 1930.
[**1891** Farmer–Henley *Slang* 247, Dairy . . . The paps . . . *English synonyms* . . cat-heads.] **1930** Shoemaker *1300 Words* 9 c**PA Mts** (as of c1900), Cats-heads—A woman's breasts.

2 See **cathead.**

cat's hind foot See **cat's foot**

cat shit n Also *cat (dirt, dung, manure, piss, water), cat's tail* **chiefly PA, NJ, NY** See Map on p. 570 *chiefly among men*
Std sense, in phr *meaner than cat shit:* extremely mean, unkind.
1965–70 *DARE* (Qu. HH22b, *Talking about a very mean person, you might say, "He's meaner than _____."*) 23 Infs, **chiefly NJ, PA**, Cat shit; **KS**8, **NJ**15, 33, 39, Cat dirt; **CO**7, **NY**66, Cat manure; **MD**31, Cat dung; **NY**73, Cat piss; **NJ**53, Cat shit and a damn sight nastier; **IN**39, Cat water; **MD**9, Cat's tail. [Of all Infs responding to the question, 48% were male; of those giving *cat shit*, 96% were male.]

‡cat's jump n
1959 *VT Hist.* new ser 27.129, Cat's jump . . . A short distance.

catslide roof n
1978 Whipple *Vintage Nantucket* 82 **MA**, Among the aesthetic attractions of the "Oldest House" are its clean lines, with the austere, flat facade and the roof rising to a peak and swooping down in a long pitch to one-story height in the rear. On the mainland this design is generally

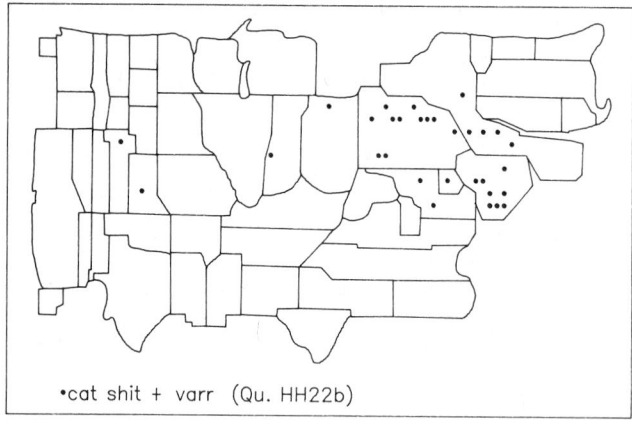

•cat shit + varr (Qu. HH22b)

called a saltbox house; it is rarely called that on Nantucket, where the more picturesque British term "catslide roof" is preferred.

cat's light n
1959 *VT Hist.* new ser 27.147, Cat's light . . . Twilight. Occasional.

cats' nest n
1912 *DN* 3.573 **wIN**, Cats'-nest . . . A house of ill repute.

cat's-paw n, also attrib

1 also *cat paw plant:* =**ground ivy.**
1876 Hobbs *Bot. Hdbk.* 21, Cats paw, Ground ivy, Nepeta glechoma. **1970** *DARE* (Qu. S21, . . *Weeds . . that are a trouble in gardens and fields*) Inf **NY233,** Cat's-paw: paw-like leaf with long leafed runners and purple flowers. **1977** *Mais Jamais* 18 **LA,** Homemade Cough Syrup . . . 1 handful of pine needles 1 cat paw plant 1 Mamon plant.

2 =**pussytoes.**
1900 Lyons *Plant Names* 37, *A. dioica* . . . Cat's-paws. **1936** Winter *Plants NE* 152, *Antennaria* . . . Cat's-Paws. **1963** Craighead *Rocky Mt. Wildflowers* 190, *Pussytoes* . . . *Other names:* Catspaws.

3 A ragwort.
1931 Harned *Wild Flowers Alleghanies* 598, Cat's Paw Ragwort (*S. antennariifolius . .*). Considering the specific name of this plant one must play a bit on his imagination to discover the origin of the common name Cat's-paw.

4 A **strawberry bush 1** (here: *Euonymus americanus*). Cf **puppy toes**
1951 *PADS* 15.16 **sAppalachians,** *Euonymus americanus* L.—Cats-paw. **1967** *DARE* FW Addit **AR49,** Cat's-paw or wahoo. **1975** Hamel–Chiltoskey *Cherokee Plants* 38, Cats paw.

5 =**pearly everlasting.**
1966 *DARE* Wildfl QR Pl.211a Inf **WI34,** Cat's-paw. **1968** *DARE* FW Addit **VA15,** Cat's-paw . . . common in meadows; book term for life-everlasting.

6 A greenbrier. Cf **catbrier**
1968 *DARE* (Qu. S17, . . *Kinds of plants . . that will cause itching and swelling*) Inf **GA38,** Cat's-paw, spylax [sic for smilax] are the same.

7 A ripple caused by a light wind on the surface of a body of water; the wind itself. **chiefly Atl, esp N Atl**
1899 (1912) Green *VA Folk-Speech,* Cat's paw . . . Small patch of ripple on the water from a slight breeze. **1942** ME Univ. *Studies* 56.57, A *catspaw,* for a light puff [of wind] in calm weather. **1965–70** *DARE* (Qu. O12, *A disturbance caused by wind which seems to run and spread quickly along the surface of water*) Infs **CT4,** 13, 14, **GA12, NJ55, NY34,** 103, 151, Cat's-paw; (Qu. O15, . . *Kinds of waves*) Inf **CA191,** Cat's-paw. **1982** *TWA Ambassador* July 47, Cat's paw. A light puff of wind in America, just barely noticeable—enough to cause a patch of ripples on water.

8 also *cat paw:* A dupe, stooge. [From the fable of the monkey and the cat; cf quot 1969] *somewhat old-fash*
1922 *DN* 5.158, Cat's paw . . . The one who does the disagreeable work for another. **1927** *AmSp* 2.350 **wcWV,** Cat's paw . . the tool of another. "The boy was only a cat's paw for his employer." **c1960** *Wilson Coll.* **csKY,** Cat's paw . . . A person who does dirty work for someone else. **1965–70** *DARE* (Qu. II34, *If you think somebody is trying to use you to his advantage: "I'm not going to be his _____."*) 58 Infs, **scattered,** Cat's-paw; **MS56, OR3, SC19, TX43,** Cat paw. [Of all Infs responding to this question, 63% were old, 33% were coll educ; of those giving this

response, 84% were old, 52% were coll educ.] **1969** *DARE* FW Addit **csNC,** A cat and a fox were cooking potatoes in hot ashes and when it was time to get them out, the fox grabbed the cat's paw and used it. Thus it [=*cat's-paw*] is used to mean to be maneuvered into doing someone else's work.

9 Among loggers: a knot or splice. Cf **cat's ass 1**
1958 McCulloch *Woods Words* **Pacific NW,** Cat's paw—a. A non-slipping knot used on a steel cable. b. A line run through an eye and tied back on itself . . . c. A greenhorn's attempt at splicing a wire rope.

cat spruce n [From the odor] Nth, esp NEng
Usu the **white spruce,** but also the **black spruce 1.**
1894 *Jrl. Amer. Folkl.* 7.100, *Picea nigra,* . . cat-spruce, Penobscot Co., Me. yew-pine, spruce-pine, West Va. **1897** Sudworth *Arborescent Flora* 37, *Picea canadensis . . . Common Names . . .* Cat Spruce (Me.). **1941** Williams *Strange Woman* 161 **MN** (as of mid 19th cent), But the lot that spends their days drinking rum down at the Coffee House, . . half of them don't know a cat spruce from a hackmatack. **1950** *WELS* (*Different . . evergreens*) 1 Inf, **cwWI,** Cat spruce. [Inf's mother was from Connecticut] **1966–68** *DARE* (Qu. T5, . . *Kinds of evergreens, other than pine*) Infs **ME8, NH14,** Cat spruce. **1966** *DARE* Tape **ME8,** They call that the cat spruce, the white one, because it does have a rather strong odor.

cat squirrel n

1 An eastern gray squirrel (*Sciurus carolinensis*). **chiefly S Atl, Gulf States** See Map
1826 Godman *Amer. Nat. Hist.* 2.129, The Cat-Squirrel, *Sciurus Cinereus,* . . . is found in great abundance throughout the oak and chestnut forests of this country. **1884** Harris *Mingo* 171 **GA,** The cat-squirrels . . occasionally scamper across the crumbling shingles. **1908** *DN* 3.297 **eAL, wGA,** Cat-squirrel . . . The gray squirrel in distinction from the red or fox squirrel. **1933** *AmSp* 8.1.48 **Ozarks,** Cat-squirrel . . . The grey squirrel as distinguished from the larger reddish fox squirrel. which is also common in the Ozarks. **1933** Rawlings *South Moon* 7 **FL,** Seems to me they's cat-squirrels this side o' the river, 'stead o' fox-squirrels. **1950** *PADS* 14.18 **SC,** Cat squirrel . . . The gray squirrel. **1965–70** *DARE* (Qu. P27, . . *Kinds of squirrels*) 59 Infs, **chiefly S Atl, Gulf States,** Cat squirrel; **AL22,** 62, **AR56, GA93, MI65, TX96,** Gray cat squirrel. **1967** *DARE* FW Addit **LA5,** The cat squirrel is small and lives in the hills. Its belly is always white. **1975** Newell *If Nothin' Don't Happen* 177 **nwFL,** They're just ordinary gray squirrels—what we call cat squirrels down here. I guess they get that name from the funny meowin'-like noise they make when they get real aggravated.

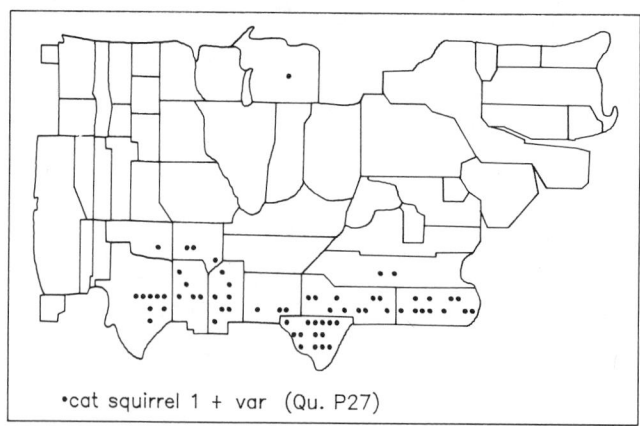

•cat squirrel 1 + var (Qu. P27)

2 A cacomistle (*Bassaris astuta*).
1889 *Century Dict.* 865/3, Cat-squirrel . . . A name of the ring-tailed bassaris, *Bassaris astuta.* [Southwestern U.S.] **1917** *Animals of Amer.* 109/I *(DA),* Dr. Coues speaks of it as the Bassarisk; and the reader may find other references to it as the 'Bassaris,' 'Cat Squirrel' (so called in Texas).

3 A fox squirrel.
1916 *DN* 4.431 **LA,** Cat squirrel . . . The western fox squirrel (*Sciurus rufiventer*).

cat's-tail n
1 See **cattail.**

2 See **cat's game.**

3 See **cat shit.**

cat's tails See **cat feathers**

catstep n

A small terrace on a hill.

1939 Bennett *Soil Conservation* 295, *Terracettes*. Slumping of masses only a few feet wide is the cause of many of the hillside steps, variously known as "cattle terraces," "sheep paths," or "cat steps," found on sloping lands in many parts of the country.

catstep v, hence *catstepping* ppl adj

To walk quietly.

1955 Warren *Angels* 107 **KY,** And I walked up the street, never looking back but bearing in my mind the hard gratification of that image of the white-clad figure cat-stepping behind me, at the humble distance. **1956** Gipson *Old Yeller* 155 **TX,** The horse was a cat-stepping blue roan with a black mane and tail.

catstick n *old-fash*

1 See quots. [cat n **3a, b**]

1859 (1968) Bartlett *Americanisms, Catstick.* A bat or cudgel, used by New England boys in a game at ball. **1872** Schele de Vere *Americanisms* 450, *Catstick,* in England the bat for playing certain games at ball, is an Americanism as far as it is used for any unsplit stick of wood with the bark on, which is small enough to be grasped by the hand.

2 A piece of kindling.

1832 *Daily Eve. Transcript* (Boston MA) 7 Jan 2/1, He "dropt into" the cellar to survey his wood-pile; .. he found that the faithful fellow had thrown down the large logs *whole,* sprinkled them with sawed cat-sticks. **1859** (1968) Bartlett *Americanisms, Catstick* ... In Pennsylvania, Maryland, and further south, the term is applied to small wood for burning. **1867** Lowell *Biglow* lviii, *Cat-stick:* a small stick.

3 Perh =**cat** n **4.**

1899 *Daily Eve. Transcript* (Boston MA) 14 Jan 12/2, The "Caton chimney" of Kentucky is doubtless an emigrant from the Atlantic coast, with tobacco stalks substituted for cat-sticks.

cat-stitched See **cat-clawed**

cat stool n Cf **cat face**

A bracket fungus: see quot.

1968 *DARE* (Qu. S19, *Mushrooms that grow out like brackets from the sides of trees*) Inf **VA24,** Cat stools—that's what we allus called 'em.

cat's tooth n

1 =**bleeding tooth.**

1916 *DN* 4.302 **FL,** *Cat's tooth* ... *bleeding-teeth* [A little shell with two red spots inside, suggesting two bleeding teeth].

2 A gromwell (here: *Lithospermum ruderale*).

1956 St. John *Flora SE WA* 347, *Lithospermum ruderale* ... *Cat's Tooth* ... Nutlets ovoid, .. the shell white, hard, ivory-like. **1966** *DARE* Wildfl QR Inf **WA10,** *Lythospermum*—cat's tooth—the seed is shiny white, like porcelain and pointed.

cat's track n Also *cat tracker, cat-tracking snow*

A light fall of snow.

1967–69 *DARE* (Qu. B39, *A very light fall of snow*) Inf **ME1,** Cat's track; **MA30,** Cat-tracking snow; [**IL2, WI5,** 13, 19, (Not) enough (snow) to track a cat]. **1967** *DARE* FW Addit **csWI,** *Cat tracker*—criterion for determining whether there is enough snow on the ground to use the term a snowfall (i.e., if there is enough snow to track a cat, there has been a snowfall.)

cat-stretcher See **stretcher**

cat's uncle n

See quots.

1936 *AmSp* 11.275 **TN,** *Cat's uncle.* Criminal. 'He is an escaped cat's uncle.' **c1970** *Halpert Coll.* **wKY,** A cat's uncle = a criminal.

cats'-water n

Gin.

1891 Maitland *Amer. Slang Dict., Cat's water,* gin. **1930** Shoemaker *1300 Words* 10 **cPA Mts** (as of c1900), *Cats-water.*

cat's whisker n

1 also *cat's whiskers:* See quots.

1968–69 *DARE* (Qu. GG19a, *When you can see from the way a person acts that he's feeling important or independent: "He surely is _____ these days."*) Inf **NV7,** Cat's whiskers; (Qu. GG19b, .. *"He seems to*

think he's _____.") Infs **GA84, MD33,** Cat's whiskers. **c1970** *Halpert Coll.* **wKY,** He's a cat's whisker [means] a person who feels important.

2 in phr *to a cat's whisker:* To a T, very well, exactly.

1967–68 *DARE* (Qu. KK50, *When something is planned out carefully .. : "He had it all worked out _____."*) Infs **IA5, PA138,** To a cat's whisker.

cat switch n

See quots.

1954 *Harder Coll.* **cwTN,** *Cat switch* ... An instrument used to punish a child. **1982** *DARE* File **csTN,** *Cat switch.* The switch itself was usually a small peach limb, thin, about two feet long, maybe two and one-half ... My belief was that the switch was also used to "switch" cats and children. Cats usually had the free run of houses, and everyone had a lot of cats ... The switch contrasted with the hickory limb, not a switching instrument but one for beating.

catta-corner(ed) See **catercorner** adj, adv

cattail n, also attrib Also *cat's-tail*

1 Std: a plant of the genus *Typha.* Also called **cooper's reed, flag, flat rush, nail rod, reed mace, soft flag, tule** For other names of var spp see **blackhead 5, candlewick 2, cat-o'-nine-tails 1, deer marsh grass, flag grass, Indian leek, Indian onion**

2 Any of var other plants resembling a cat's tail in some way, as:

a A bulrush (here: *Scirpus lacustris*).

1897 *Jrl. Amer. Folkl.* 10.146, *Scirpus lacustris,* .. cat-tail flag, Cal.

b =**horsetail.**

1900 Lyons *Plant Names* 147, *E[quisetum] arvense* ... Cat's-tail. **1959** Carleton *Index Herb. Plants* 25, *Cattail:* Equisetum (v); Hippurus vulgaris; Typha latifolia.

c A mare's tail **2** (here: *Hippuris vulgaris*).

1900 Lyons *Plant Names* 192, *H[ippuris] vulgaris* ... Cat's-tail. **1959** [see **2b** above].

d =**viper's bugloss.**

1900 Lyons *Plant Names* 143, *E[chium] vulgare* ... Blue Cat's-tail. **1959** Carleton *Index Herb. Plants* 25, *Cat's tail:* Echium vulgare; Nepeta hederacea (N. glechoma: Glechoma hederacea).

e =**barnyard grass.**

1920 *Torreya* 20.18, *Echinochloa crus-galli* ... Cat-tail, Charleston, S.C., Savannah, Ga.

f Pearl millet (*Pennisetum glaucum*).

1926 *Torreya* 26.4, *Chaetochloa glauca* ... Cat-tail, Morton, Miss[issippi].

g =**ground ivy.**

1959 [see **2d** above].

‡3 See quot.

1966 *DARE* FW Addit **NC,** *Cattail:* A small, running stream, smaller than a creek.

cattail hen n

=**least bittern.**

1970 *DARE* (Qu. Q10, .. *Water birds and marsh birds*) Inf **VA47,** Cattail hen (least bittern).

cat tails See **cat feathers**

cattair See **catarrh**

cattamount See **catamount**

cattaw(h)ampus See **catawampus** adj

catter n [cat v **2**]

A woman-chaser.

1916 *DN* 4.272 **IL,** *Cat* ... *catter* ... "John is getting to be quite a catter."

catter v See **cater** v

catter-cornered See **catercorner** adj, adv

catterge See **cartridge**

cattering See **catering**

cattermount See **catamount**

catterwampus See **catawampus** adj, v

cattibias See **catabias**

catti-corner(ed) See **catercorner** adj, adv

cat tier n

In tobacco farming: =**comb rail.**

1967 Key *Tobacco Vocab.* 173 **MD,** [The topmost bents in the barn are called] the cat tier [taɪə].

cattiwampus See **catawampus** adj, adv

cattle n pl, also attrib *derog*

Human beings.

1899 (1912) Geen *VA Folk-Speech,* Cattle . . . Human beings, in contempt or ridicule. **1915** *DN* 4.196, *Cattle,* a term of contempt. "The *cattle* had a regular stampede on the carnival grounds last night." **1927** *DN* 5.442 [Underworld], *Cattle* . . . Downtrodden working men who are having their life's blood sucked out by capitalists. **1932** *AmSp* 6.400 **WA,** *Cattle* . . . Girls. "Gee, those cattle make a lot of noise." **1944** *PADS* 2.41 **VA, NC,** *Cattle* . . . Low, contemptible people. **1970** *DARE* (QR, near Qu. P17) Inf **CA191,** Party boats are called cattle boats by local fishermen.

‡**cattle bay** n [Prob euphem for **bull bay**]

1968 *DARE* (Qu. T5, . . *Evergreens, other than pine*) Inf **GA35,** Cattle bay.

cattle bean See **Jacob's cattle bean**

cattle beast n Cf **beast B2**

1946 *PADS* 6.8 **eNC,** *Cattle beast* . . . General term for a bovine animal . . 1900–05. **1962** *AmSp* 37.174 **seNC,** A single cow is frequently referred to as a *cattlebeast.*

cattle beet See **cattle turnip**

cattle boose See **calaboose**

cattle chip See **chip** n[1] 1

cattle corn See **cow corn**

cattle egret n

Std: a small white heron *(Bubulcus ibis)* with buff-colored back found in the U.S. chiefly in Florida but also as far west as Texas. Also called **buff-backed heron, cattle heron, cowbird 4**

cattle gap n chiefly Sth

A grate-like device across a road or a fence line, used to prevent livestock from crossing.

1942 Rawlings *Cross Creek* 183 **FL,** No one came to meet me as my car crossed the cattle-gap. **1966–70** *DARE* (Qu. N31) Infs **FL1, GA40, KY56, MS8, 63,** Cattle gap; **FL27,** Cattle gap—like railroad irons set apart so hooves will go through and cattle can't get out. **1970** Tarpley *Blinky* 68, Place to let cars or trains pass through a fence [1.5% of infs responded with *cattle gap*].

cattle heron n [See quot 1911]

=**cattle egret.**

1911 *Century Dict. Suppl.,* Heron, . . cattle-heron, Bubulcus ibis, so named from following and even alighting on cattle and buffaloes to feed on ticks. **1966** *DARE* (Qu. Q14, . . *Other names . . for . . cowbird*) Inf **FL4,** Cattle herons.

cattle mill v phr Cf **mill** v

To move around circularly, as cattle in a herd do, or are made to do as a means of controlling them.

1916 *DN* 4.347 **cwTX,** *Cattle-mill* . . . To go round in a circle.

cattle moss n

=**Spanish moss 1.**

1951 *PADS* 15.28 **TX,** *Dendropogon usneoides* . . . cattle moss . . . trees are still cut down so that cattle may get at the moss.

cattle paper n

See quot 1961.

1930 Dale–Rader *Readings OK Hist.* 590, Thus there grew up in the West that large class of securities known as "cattle paper." **1961** Adams *Old-Time Cowhand* 163, Them notes and mortgages [against the herd] were spoken of as "cattle paper."

cattle pass n Also *cattle passing*

=**cow pass.**

1965–70 *DARE* (Qu. N31, *A place in the road where animals regularly go across*) 34 Infs, **scattered,** Cattle pass; **MN12,** Cattle passing. **1970**

DARE File, *Cattle pass:* Vermont has numerous road signs with this wording, and few with *cattle crossing;* Massachusetts has only one *cattle pass* sign that I have seen and a thousand *cattle crossing.*

cattle-penning vbl n

1946 *PADS* 6.8 **eNC,** *Cattle penning* . . . Semi-annual event when cattle were driven from grazing grounds in woods and salt marsh hammocks to be marked by owners, sold, etc . . . [Used] before 1905. Common.

cattle-salting grounds n

Prob a salt lick.

1935 Davis *Honey* 122 **OR,** It turned off south at a cattle-salting grounds in the old timber.

cattle show n **MA**

A country fair.

1815 *N. Amer. Rev.* 2.136 **MA,** The Cattle show . . at Pittsfield. **1823** (1922) Anthony *New Bedford* 67 **MA,** Cornelius and Susan, Nat. and Anna, started this afternoon for Worcester to attend the cattle show at that place, and return by way of Boston to be at the cattle show at Brighton. **1884** Barber *Diary* **cnMA,** Started for [Athol] Cattle Show at 9 AM. Went up to the grounds & staid until 5 p.m. **1934** Hanley *Disks* **cwMA,** The first cattle show—in Massachusetts, I guess it was—was held at the park here. **1981** *DARE* File **cnMA** (as of c1915), *Cattle show*—This was the old term for what later came to be the Athol Fair. I suppose it was originally a cattle show . . . It was the county fair type of thing.

cattle spinach n [See quot 1941]

A **saltbush** (here: *Atriplex polycarpa*).

1923 in 1925 Jepson *Manual Plants CA* 328, *Atriplex polycarpa* . . Cattle Spinach. **1938** Van Dersal *Native Woody Plants* 66, *Atriplex polycarpa* . . Cattle spinach. **1941** Jaeger *Wildflowers* 51 **Desert SW,** Cattle Spinach, . . *Atriplex polycarpa* . . . The common name, "cattle spinach," was given because of its high value as a browse plant.

cattle town See **cow town**

cattle turnip n Also *cattle beet*

A rutabaga.

1967–69 *DARE* (Qu. I3, . . *Large yellowish root vegetable*) Infs **MA5, 68,** Cattle turnip; **MA68,** Cattle beet.

cat-tongue n

1912 Green *VA Folk-Speech,* Cat-tongues . . . Very long, slender, small oysters.

cat track n Also sp *catt'rack* [Folk-etym for *cataract*]

Any eye disease.

1919 *DN* 5.33 **seKY,** *Cat-tracks* . . . Trachoma, "sore-eyes," . . . This figure is perhaps derived from the red spots and streaks seen in the eyes. **1922** Gonzales *Black Border* 292 [Gullah], *Catt'rack*—cataract, cataracts (eye). **1923** *DN* 5.242 **KY,** *Cat tracks.* Any disease of the eyes.

cat tracker, cat-tracking snow See **cat's track**

cattridge See **cartridge**

catty n[1] Also sp *caddie, caddy*

1 A children's game: see quot 1965–70; also the wooden peg used in the game. [**cat** n 3a, b; see also quot 1964] **chiefly MD, NJ, NY, PA** See Map

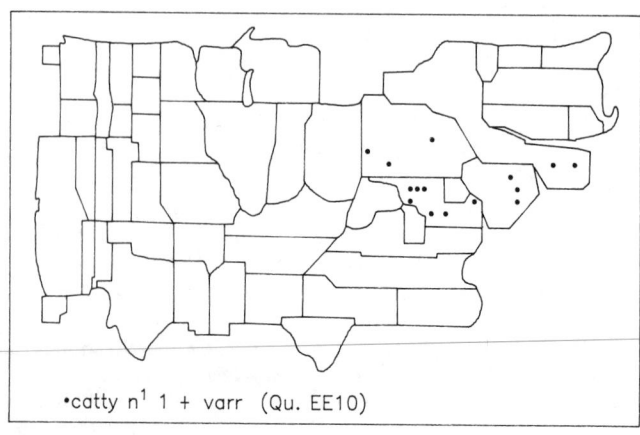

•catty n[1] 1 + varr (Qu. EE10)

1903 *DN* 2.350, *Catty*... The cat in the game of tip-cat. **1940** Mencken *Happy Days* 29, Every boy knew it as familiarly as he knew the rules of run-a-mile or catty. **1943** *Sun* (Baltimore MD) 17 Aug 12/7 **DE, MD, NC,** The game of caddy, or catty, .. "was played mostly on open lots. The piece of broomstick sharpened at both ends was called the pussy. You made a ring on the ground with the caddy stick about five feet in diameter; the pussy was placed in the center and batted from there." . . [Others] say there was a pitcher who threw the caddie, not the pussy, or cat, toward the ring. **1957** Battaglia *Resp. to PADS 20* eShore **MD,** *(Game in which you flip a short stick into the air and try to hit it with a longer stick)* Catty. [**1964** Gomme *Traditional Games* 17, *Bandy Cad or Gad* . . "Cad" is the same as "cat" in the game of "Tip-cat;" it simply means a cut piece of wood. [Nodal and Milner's Lancashire Glossary.]] **1965–70** *DARE* (Qu. EE10, *A game in which a short stick lying on the ground is flipped into the air and then hit with a longer stick*) 9 Infs, chiefly **NJ, PA,** Catty; **MD**15, 23, 25, 27, 31, Caddy; **NY**40, [kædi]— short for kitty-cat; [used as name for the game] thirty years ago.
2 attrib in *caddy bat:* Transf: a game played with a bat and ball. [cat n 3c]
1965–69 *DARE* (Qu. EE11, *Bat-and-ball games for just a few players*) Infs **AL**52, **MS**1, **NY**40, Caddy bat.

catty n² [caddy adj 1]
1958 McCulloch *Woods Words* **Pacific NW,** *Catty*... An expert in logging jobs.

catty n³ Also sp *caddy*
A catfish of the family Ictaluridae.
1838 Neal *Charcoal Sketches* 98 sePA, If you don't trot, .. boss will be down upon you and fetch you up like a catty on a cork-line—jerk! **1850** *Knickerbocker* 36.105 **NY,** There he will squat under a big, projecting rock .. now soberly hauling up an eel, now a "catty." **1968** *DARE* (Qu. P7) Inf **PA**121, A bullhead or catfish, called a caddy or catty.

catty adj See **caddy** adj

catty-bias, catty-bicey See **catabias**

catty-byward adj [Alter of **cater-** + *by-* from **bias** + *-ward* in a stated direction; cf **catabias**]
1952 Brown *NC Folkl.* 1.608, *Wiehard and catty byward* . . . Diagonal; "antigodlin."

catty-corned, catty-corner(ed), catty-cornereds, catty-corners See **catercorner** adj, adv, v

catty-cross adv [Alter of **cater-** + aphet form of *across*] See also *DS* MM14
=**catercorner** adv.
1970 *DARE* (Qu. MM14, *If a drugstore is on one corner of a square and a gas station is on the far corner you might say, "The drugstore is _____ the gas station."*) Inf **VA**39, Catty-cross.

catty-cue adj [Alter of **cater-** + *cue* perh from *askew*]
=**catercorner** adj 1a.
1967 *DARE* (Qu. MM13, *The table was nice and straight until he came along and knocked it _____*) Inf **IA**4, Catty-cue ['kæti,kju].

catty-godlin adj, adv [Alter of **cater-** + *godlin* as in **antigodlin**]
=**catercorner** adj 1a, adv.
1967 *DARE* (Qu. MM13, *The table was nice and straight until he came along and knocked it _____*) Inf **LA**2, Cattygodlin; (Qu. MM14, *If a drugstore is on one corner of a square and a gas station is on the far corner you might say, "The drugstore is _____ the gas station."*) Inf **AZ**1, Catty-godlin.

catty-ker-wampus adj [Alter of *catawampus;* cf **ker-**]
=**catawampus** adj **1.**
1959 McAtee *Oddments* 4 **NC,** *Catty-ker-wampus* . . leaning.

cattymount See **catamount**

catty-strangling adv [Alter of **cater-** + (perh) *straggling* with intrusive *n*]
=**catercorner** adv.
1936 *AmSp* 11.314 **Ozarks,** *Catty-strangling* . . . Diagonally across. 'Bob's east forty lays jest catty-stranglin' across th' creek from my place.'

‡catty tail n [Perh from *cat-o'-nine-tails*]
1967 *DARE* (Qu. EE41, *A hobgoblin that is used to threaten children and make them behave*) Inf **MO**21, Catty tail—refers to a whip; probably imaginary.

cattywamp(ered), cattywamping See **catawampus** adj

cattywampus See **catawampus** adj, adv, n

catty-ways adv [Alter of **cater-** + *ways*]
=**catercorner** adv.
1966 *DARE* (Qu. MM14) Inf **SC**11, Catty-ways.

catty-west adv [Alter of **cater-** + *-west* as in **galley-west**] Cf **catawampus** adv **2, cat-west**
Crookedly.
1941 *LANE* Map 547 *(Cater-cornered)* 1 inf, sME, Catty-west, of plowing, not of walking.

cattywhamper(ed), cattywhampus See **catawampus** adj, adv

‡catty-whistling adv [Alter of **cater-** + alter of *-wise* as in *crosswise,* *slaunchwise,* etc] Cf **antigodlin 2**
=**catercorner** adv.
1967 *DARE* (Qu. MM14) Inf **LA**2, Catty-whistlin'.

cattywhompy, cattywobble See **catawampus** adv

cat wagon n [cat n 1b + *wagon*]
A travelling brothel.
1916 *DN* 4.321 **KS,** *Cat wagon* . . . Until the enactment of the 'white slave' law of 1913, prostitution was carried on in some degree in rural communities by means of traveling wagons, usually covered[,] and drawn by horses. **1968** Adams *Western Words, Cat wagon*—A name given to a wagon that carried women of easy virtue who plied their trade along the cattle trails or on the range.

catwater n
1 See quot.
1958 *VT Hist.* new ser 26.264, Poorer than catwater.
2 See **cat shit.**

cat-west adv [Var of **galley-west** infl by such words as **catawampus, catercorner**]
Into disarray, confusion, destruction.
1946 *PADS* 6.9 eNC, *Cat-west, to knock* . . . To knock out of the way; to settle "the hash of"; . . . "The car hit him and knocked him cat-west." "I'll knock you cat-west if you don't stop pestering me." . . Occasional among teen-age boys. **1969** Calhoun *Ball of String* 10, Old Man Wicker was in the woods gathering mushrooms, and the ball of string plumb knocked him cat-west.

catwich See **cartridge**

catwort n [*OED* a1450] Cf **catmint**
Catnip.
1971 Krochmal *Appalachia Med. Plants* 184, *Nepeta Cataria* . . . Catwort.

caty-corner See **catercorner** adj, adv

catydid See **katydid** A

caucus n Usu |'kɔkəs, 'kakəs| occas |'kɔɚkəs| Pronc-spp *corcus, corkus* See Pronc Intro 3.I.23
A Forms.
1915 *DN* 4.182 swVA, Corcus. Variant of *caucus.* **1917** *DN* 4.410 **KS, NEng, wNC, neOH,** Corkus . . . Variant of *caucus.* **1925** Dargan *Highland Annals* 240 *(ADD)* **sAppalachians,** Corcus. **1926** Kephart *Highlanders* 350 wNC, eTN, Corkus (caucus). **1942** Hall *Smoky Mt. Speech* 32 wNC, eTN, It is reported that everyone pronounces *caucus* /'kɔɚkəs/.
B Sense. [?Infl by *ruckus*]
1936 *AmSp* 11.376 seUT, He has often heard *caucus* used colloquially as meaning a brawl or disorderly meeting, as in 'The party turned into a caucus,' or 'The revelers started (or raised) a caucus.'

caught, caughten See **catch** v **B4, A3**

caught short adj phr
Expecting a child out of wedlock.
1960 Williams *Walk Egypt* 296 **GA,** Aunt Baptist did little granny-wifing these days, just girls caught short, and Negroes.

cauliflower n Pronc-spp *colleyflower, cullyflower* See also **curly flower**
Std sense, var forms.
1968 *DARE* (Qu. I4, . . *Vegetables . . less commonly grown around here*) Inf **NY**70, Cullyflower. **1976** Garber *Mountain-ese, Colleyflower* . . cauliflower. "We raise our own colleyflower."

cauliflower (nose) n [Prob by analogy with *cauliflower ear* an ear misshapen or deformed by injury (as from boxing)]
1968 *DARE* (Qu. X15, . . *Kinds of noses*) Inf **PA76,** Cauliflower.

caulk v |kɑk| (represented in *DARE* quots by sp *calk*) or |kɔk| (repr by *cawk*) See Pronc Intro 3.III.4
A Forms. Cf **cork** v² 2
1965–70 *DARE* (Qu. O6, *If a wooden boat is leaking, what do you have to do to stop the leak?*) 334 Infs, **scattered,** Cawk (it), cawk it up, cawk the seams; 156 Infs, **scattered,** Calk (it, them).
B Sense.
Often *caulk off,* also *caulk a nod,* rarely sp *cack:* To take a nap, go to bed. [Orig naut] **now chiefly NEng**
[**1891** Farmer–Henley *Slang, Caulk subs.* and *verb* (nautical).—1. Sleep; to sleep. In substantive form it sometimes appears as *caulking.* To *caulk* formerly meant 'to pick out a soft plank,' *i.e.,* to lie down on deck; to sleep with one's clothes on.] **1939** *AmSp* 14.77 [Naval Academy terms], *Caulk off.* Sleep, especially during the day. **1942** ME Univ. *Studies* 56.79, "To caulk off." To take a nap. There is no probable explanation of the expression. **1946** *CA Folkl. Qrly.* 5.387 [Naval Slang], Whoever *knocks off* work in order to rest or sleep *conks out, conks off, caulks off.* **1967–70** *DARE* (Qu. X40, . . *Other ways . . to say, "I'm going to bed."*) Inf **MA72,** Caulk off; **CT43,** Caulk a nod. **1975** Gould *ME Lingo, Caulk off*—To take a nap. The term comes from the shipyard; a man's snoring is likened to the noise of *caulking* mallets. *Cork off, conk off,* and *conk out* are, of course, misuses of the correct imagery.

caulked ppl adj Pronc-sp *cawked* [**caulk** B]
1936 *AmSp* 11.275 **TN,** Cawked. Exhausted. 'I'm all cawked.'

caulker n [*OED* →a1854, "?something 'to keep out the wet' "; but cf *corker*] arch
A drink of liquor.
1851 Burke *Polly Peablossom* 74 **MS,** "That's the best red eye I've swallered in er coon's age," said the speaker, after bolting a caulker. **1891** Maitland *Amer. Slang Dict., Caulker . .* more often *Corker,* a drink.

causen See **because** conj

cause why conj [Engl dial; cf *EDD* cause conj 2]
For the reason that.
1854 (1932) Bell *Log TX–CA Trail* 230 **TX,** I certainly shall not be so [disappointed] again, cause why, I will expect nothing.

causey n, v Pronc-spp *cassy, cussey old-fash* Note: while *causey* is the source of *causeway,* it has largely been replaced by the latter.
A raised road surface, causeway; to pave or surface (as a causeway).
a1817 (1821) Dwight *Travels* 1.497 **MA,** The sides of the Causeys are stoned, capstained, and railed. *Ibid* 2.478 **NY,** About three miles of the road was causeyed with logs. **1890** *DN* 1.73 **NH,** Cassy [kæsi]: *causeway.* More than one town in New Hampshire. **1929** *AmSp* 5.131 **ME,** "Cussey" or "causey" was [what is now known as a] causeway. **1941** FWP *Guide SC* 326 **eGA,** In the swamplands nearer the coast, ditches of clear dark water flow between the railroad and highway, to drain the 'causeys' (causeways) on which the roads are stabilized.

cautch n [Perh rel to **culch** 2]
1891 *Jrl. Amer. Folkl.* 4.159 **neMA,** Cautch . . food improperly cooked or otherwise ruined. **1895** *DN* 1.385 **neMA,** Cautch: underdone (food).

caution n Pronc-sp *corshin* Cf **case** n¹ 5, **corker** n 1
An unusual or remarkable person, action, or occurrence.
1835 Hoffman *Winter in West* (NY) I.197 **IL,** The way in which the icy blast would come down the bleak shore of the lake "was a caution." **1835** (1906) Bradley *Jrl.* 253 **MI,** Such myriads of emigrants and strangers as now crowd this city [Detroit] are, as they say here, a caution. **1899** (1912) Green *VA Folk-Speech, Caution . . .* Something to excite alarm or astonishment; something extraordinary. **1907** *DN* 3.210 **nwAR, cCT,** Caution. **1941** *AmSp* 16.21 **sIN,** Caution. Used as a noun, with the meaning of *dandy, corker,* etc. 'That Henry sure is a caution.' The word may mean the subject is an incorrigible, a wit, a spendthrift. **c1960** *Wilson Coll.* **csKY,** Caution n. Often /kɔršən/. A sort of half-complimentary name for a person who is unlike most of his acquaintances. **1968** *DARE* (Qu. NN7, *Exclamations of surprise . . "Well, _____ .'*) Inf **NJ44,** Ain't that a corshin.

‡**caution strip** n
1966 *DARE* (Qu. N17, . . *The separating area in the middle of a four lane road*) Inf **MS72,** Caution strip.

cauvaut See **cavort** 1

cavalade See **caballada**

cavalla n [Span] **S Atl and Gulf coasts**
1 A cero (here: *Scomberomorus cavalla*).
1896 U.S. Natl. Museum *Bulletin* 47.875, *Scomberomorus cavalla . . .* Kingfish; Cavalla; Cero; Sierra. **1902** Jordan–Evermann *Amer. Fishes* 287, *Kingfish; Cero; Cavalla . . .* Of all the host of Florida game-fishes that are used as food this is the greatest. **1972** Sparano *Outdoors Encycl.* 376, *King Mackerel . . . Common Names: . .* cavalla, cero.
2 See **cavally.**

cavallad(a), cavallado See **caballada**

cavalla jack See **cavally**

cavallard See **caballada**

cavalli, cavallo n¹ See **cavally**

cavallo n² See **caballo**

cavally n Also *cavalla (jack), cavalli, cavallo* **S Atl and Gulf coasts** Cf **cavalla**
=**crevalle a,** esp *Caranx hippos.*
1624 Smith *Genl. Hist. VA* 5.172, Some of them yet knowne to the *Americans,* as the Purgoose, the Cauallo, the Gar-fish, Flying-fish and Morerayes. **1709** (1967) Lawson *New Voyage* 159, Cavallies are taken in the same Places. They are of a brownish Colour, have exceeding small Scales, and a very thick Skin. **1775** (1962) Romans *Nat. Hist. FL* lii, The fish caught here are . . . such as seamen know by the following names, viz. *King-fish, barracoota, . . cavallos, . .* and an immense variety of others. **1799** (1803) Elliott *Jrl.* 255, Along the Florida Reef, and among the Keys, a great abundance and variety of fish may be taken: such as . . cavallos. **1892** *DN* 1.189 **TX,** Cavalli: a species of fish found in the Gulf of Mexico. **1902** Jordan–Evermann *Amer. Fishes* 306, *Carangus hippos,* the cavalla or jack, is the most abundant . . of the genus. **1946** LaMonte *N. Amer. Game Fishes* 36, Common Jack Crevalle . . . Names . . . Cavalla Jack. **1972** Sparano *Outdoors Encycl.* 377, *Jack Crevalle . . . Common Names: . .* cavally, cavalla.

cavalry yard, cavalyard See **caballada**

‡**cavascacious** adj
1919 *DN* 4.18 **swME,** Cavascacious . . . pleasant, agreeable. Used in Maine—cf. an article in the Lewiston (Me.) *Journal* of July 29, 1912. "A cavascacious day." "A cavascacious time."

cavault See **cavort** 1

cavayado, cavayard, cavayer See **caballada**

cave n

1 An underground chamber suitable for keeping foodstuffs. [Cf Fr *cave* cellar] **chiefly N Midl** See Map Cf **bank** n¹ 1
1933 *AmSp* 8.1.48 **Ozarks,** Cave . . . A cellar. Many hillmen use natural caves to store their food in, but the same word is used to designate a *dug* cellar. **1950** *WELS* (*A place for keeping carrots, turnips, potatoes, etc over winter*) 1 Inf, **WI,** Cave. **1954** *Harder Coll.* **cwTN,**

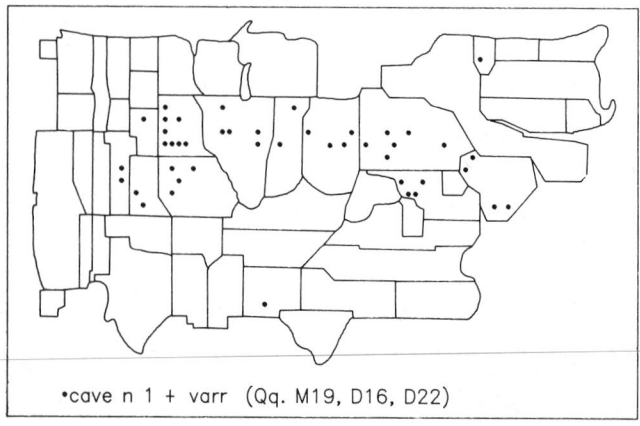

•cave n 1 + varr (Qq. M19, D16, D22)

Cave . . . Fruit cellar. **1965–70** *DARE* (Qu. M19) 38 Infs, **chiefly N Midl,** Cave; **IL26, OH95,** Vegetable cave; **IN30,** Fruit cave; **OH80,** Root cave; (Qu. D16, . . *Parts added on to the main part of a house*) Inf **MD30,** Cave—partly or totally underground, for storing food, attached to house; (Qu. D22, *Underground place to go to in case of a violent windstorm*) Inf **OH90,** Cave—where they stored food; (QR, near Qu. D40) Inf **IL55,** Instead of having a cellar, some houses had a little cave built beside the house, near the kitchen door. It had a double door on it—outside door and then steps and a door at the bottom, with a mound of dirt over it, used to keep foods in.

2 An underground shelter. **scattered, but esp N Midl** See Map
1965–70 *DARE* (Qu. D22, *Underground place to go to in case of a violent windstorm*) 45 Infs, **esp N Midl,** Cave; **CO19, GA13, IA11, 31, IN54, KS8, 14, 16, NE2,** Storm cave; **IA4, PA60,** Caves; **KS5,** Cyclone cave; **NC67,** Fallout shelter or cave.

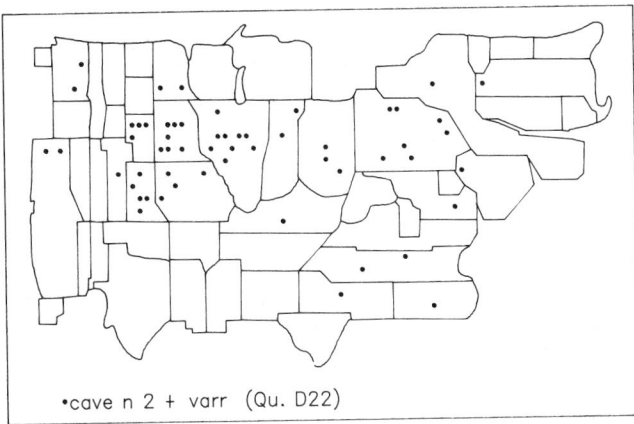

•cave n 2 + varr (Qu. D22)

3 See **cave-in.**

cave v Also *cave around* **chiefly Midl**
To rave, rage.
1902 *DN* 2.230 **sIL,** *Cave* . . . To get in a passion . . . 'When I told him about it he jes caved.' **1903** *DN* 2.309 **seMO,** *Cave* . . . To rave or ramp. (Perhaps a contraction of cavort.) **1906** *DN* 3.116 **sIN,** *Cave.* **1907** *DN* 3.221 **nwAR, sIL,** *Cave. Ibid* 229 **nwAR, seMO,** *Cave.* **1916** *DN* 4.273 **NE, KS,** *Cave round* . . . To be angry, make a rumpus. "He lost his temper and caved round for a while." *Ibid* 321 **KS,** *Cave* . . . To be noisily or demonstratively angry. "When he learned what we were doing he just caved and roared." **1935** Davis *Honey* 173 **OR,** If they cave around about price, it's li'ble to start questions bein' asked. **1949** Arnow *Hunter's Horn* 352 **KY,** He might quarrel and rave and cave all through supper. **1953** *AmSp* 28.248 **csPA,** *Cave.*

cave cricket See **camel cricket**

cave-in n Also *cave, cave-off* **chiefly Sth, S Midl**
A landslide.
1957 Battaglia *Resp. to PADS 20* **eShore MD** (*When a mass of earth and rock breaks loose from a high place and comes rushing down*), Cave-in. **1965–70** *DARE* (Qu. C16, *When a mass of earth and rock comes loose from a high place and rushes down, you call it a _____*) Infs **CT32, GA36, KY21, LA33, MS11, TX45,** Cave-in; **LA9, 20,** Cave; **IA14, LA12,** Cave-off.

caviard(e), caviata See **caballada**

caving adv [cave v]
Raving; extremely.
1907 *DN* 3.229 **nwAR, seMO,** *Cave* . . . He was cavin' mad.

caviyard See **caballada**

cavort v [Perh ca- var of ker- + alter of *vault* (*OED* v.²)] **orig chiefly Sth, S Midl, now widespread**
1 formerly sp *cauvaut, cavault, covault;* To prance; to behave in a frisky manner; hence n *covault.*
1794 in 1924 Steele *Papers* 1.106 **NC,** The Hon. J—e "Cauvauted", don't laugh at the expression, it suits the idea I meant to convey. **1821** in 1830 Royall *Letters AL* 121, I tell ye what, they were prime; and they made such a fuss, and *covaulted,* and was going to fight. *Ibid* 122, *Covault* is of Tennessee birth . . . It signifies an unruly or ungovernable man; also an untame horse, or any thing that cannot be controuled.

1829 *Virginia Lit. Museum* 16 Dec. 419 *(OEDS), Cavault* or *Cavort,* ranting, highflying.—West. **1899** (1912) Green *VA Folk-Speech, Cavort* . . . To prance about; said of a horse. To bustle about nimbly; said of a person. **1903** *DN* 2.309 **seMO,** *Cavort* . . . Curvette; prance. Often applied to the actions of drunken men . . 'He was cavorting around town all day.' **1905** *DN* 3.60 **NE,** *Cavort.* **1907** *DN* 3.229 **Ozarks,** *Cavort.* **1908** *DN* 3.297 **eAL, wGA,** *Cavort.* c**1960** *Wilson Coll.* **csKY,** *Cavort* . . . Act oddly, show off, strut, prance. **1966–67** *DARE* (Qu. Y22, *To move around in a way to make people take notice of you: "Look at him _____."*) Infs **ID4, TX9,** Cavort.

2 =**cave** v.
1893 Shands *MS Speech* 22, *Cavort* . . . commonly used in Mississippi by all classes to mean *to rage, to create a disturbance.* **1905** *DN* 3.393 **nwAR,** *Cavort* . . . "He caved and cavorted around, but he had to give in." **1906** *DN* 3.116 **sIN,** *Cavort* . . . To rage. "He just cavorted."

‡cavortion n [cavort v 1]
1908 *DN* 3.297 **eAL, wGA,** *Cavortion* . . . Rough behavior, rude manners.

cavoy See **caballada**

cavoya See **caballo**

cavrace See **cabestro**

cavvayah, cavvayard, cavvie yard, cavvieyeh, cavviyard See **caballada**

cavvy n [Var of *cavayard,* for which see **caballada**] **West, esp Rocky Mts** Cf **remuda**
1 =**caballada.**
1937 *DN* 6.618 **swTX,** The word *cavvy* seems to be a variant of *remuda.* **1939** FWP *ID Lore* 244, Jist about when the hand is chasun after a cavvy (horse herd), the coolie yells beans. **1939** FWP *Guide MT* 413, *Cavvy*—Herd of horses (from Spanish *caballada*). **1940** FWP *Guide NV* 76. **1940** *Sat. Review* 22.9/2, When I joined a northwestern Colorado roundup I was assigned a "string" from the "cavvy" or loose herd—which on another range might have been known as the "remuda." **1968** Adams *Western Words, Cavvy*—A remuda, or band of saddle horses; used more commonly on the northern ranges. *Ibid, Cavvy man*—The horse wrangler, who keeps the saddle horses together.
2 See quot.
1911 *DN* 3.550 **WY,** *Cavvy, cavvies,* stray cattle of which the owners are known, which are taken along and returned to their proper range.

cavvyard, cavvyiard See **caballada**

cavvy yard See **calf yard** n¹, **caballada**

cavy(y)ard See **caballada**

‡caw v [?Var of **co** or **coy**]
Come!—used to call cows.
1966 *DARE* (Qu. K80, *The call that's used around here to get the cows in from the pasture*) Inf **GA16,** Caw, caw, caw etc.

cawan See **kawan**

cawhalux, cawhop See **ker-**

cawk v¹ See **caulk**

cawk v² [Imit; cf *EDD cawk* v² "To cry out, make a noise like a hen when disturbed on her nest"]
=**call** v 2.
1907 Cockrum *Pioneer IN* 437, Turkeys . . were easily fooled. The hunter . . would locate where an old gobbler was gobbling and go as near without being seen as he thought safe, and then would commence to "cawk," using a bone taken from the turkey's wing for that purpose, with which he could very closely imitate the calling noise made by the hen turkey. c**1940** *Hall Coll.* **wNC, eTN,** In wild turkey hunting, the hunter would "cawk," using a bone taken from the turkey's wing.

cawked See **caulked**

cawky See **corky**

cawn See **corn** n

cawnder, cawnuh See **corner** n¹ A

cawt-house See **courthouse**

caybrace See **cape-race**

cayeute See **coyote** n A

cayn't See **can** v[1] **1b**

cayoodle See **kyoodle**

cayota, cayote See **coyote** n **A**

cayote cactus See **coyote cactus**

cayuse n, also attrib |'kaɪjus, ˌkaɪ'jus| Also sp *skyuse* [*Cayuse* an Indian people of Washington and Oregon] **chiefly West, esp NW**

A range horse; an Indian pony.

1843 (1973) Farnham *Travels Prairies* 2.157 **seWA,** Skyuse horses never make such disagreeable mistakes. **1903** *DN* 2.350 **seWA,** *Cayuse . . .* An Indian pony; any 'scrub' of a horse. **1928** (1978) Watt *Mule Train* 19 **eWA** (as of 1860s), On the Boise pack trail in early days some boys had a cayuse pack train . . . Mules were much easier to work with, and they would carry much heavier loads than the Indian cayuses. **1939** FWP *Guide MT* 413, *Cayuse*—Horse of doubtful lineage, usually an Indian pony. **1940** FWP *Guide NV* 76, *Cayuse.* **1941** *AmSp* 16.181 **SW,** *Cayuse.* **1958** *AmSp* 33.269 **eWA,** *Cayuse.* **1965–70** *DARE* (Qu. K37, *A horse of mixed colors*) Inf NY163, Cayuse—western; WA5, [ˌkaɪ'jus]; (Qu. K42, *A horse that is rough, wild, or dangerous*) Infs OR2, WA5, [ˌkaɪ'jus]; CA87, WA3, ['kaɪju]; AZ2, Cayuse—wild and tamed; (Qu. K43) Inf ID3, [ˌkaɪ'us].

cayuse v [**cayuse** n]

Of a horse: to buck.

1961 Adams *Old-Time Cowhand* 301 **TX,** What cowboys in other sections called "buckin'," the Texan called "pitchin'," and a term used in South Texas, though seldom heard in other sections, was "cayusein'."

cayuse wind n Cf *DS* B18

1968 Adams *Western Words* 413, *Cayuse wind*—A cold east wind, opposite of *chinook.*

caze See **because** conj

cazen n, v Also sp *kazen* [Alter of *causing* pple of *cause* v; cf *causen* at **because** conj]

See quot 1911.

1911 *DN* 3.537 **eKY,** *Cāzen, v. tr.* To cause; e.g., "You cazened me to do it." *Ibid, Cāzen, n.* Cause, e.g., "You are the cazen of all the trouble." **1931** *PMLA* 46.1307 **sAppalachians,** "Kazen," v. and n. is also heard.

C.E. See **Christmas and Easter Christian**

ceanothus n

Std: any of var plants of the genus *Ceanothus,* whether deciduous or evergreen, spiny shrubs or small trees, with white to blue to purplish flower-clusters and a three-lobed fruit capsule. For names of var spp see **barranca bush, bennie bush, bluebrush, buckbrush 3c, California lilac, cuyamaca bush, deer brush, indigo brush, ione bush, island myrtle, jim brush, lady bloom, lilac, mahala mats, mountain lilac, musk bush, myrtle, New Jersey tea, Oregon tea tree, redheart, sand scrub, snowbrush, whitethorn, wild lilac**

cearr See **carry** A1

cease v[1] Usu |sis|, rarely |siz|; occas, **Sth,** *esp among Black speakers* |sist| Pronc-sp *ceast* See Pronc Intro 3.I.23

A Forms.

1928 Peterkin *Scarlet Sister Mary* 336 **SC** [Gullah], Pray widout ceastin until . . you soul gets white as snow. **1942** *AmSp* 17.155 **seNY,** [*Cease* was pronounced [sis] by 41 infs, [siz] by 2.] **1962** Atwood *Vocab. TX* 39, Two Negro informants put a *t* in . . *ceasting.*

B Sense.

Of wind: to decrease. **chiefly Sth, Ozarks** See Map *freq among Black speakers*

1939 *LANE* Map 92 **sVT,** The wind is going down . . . [sᴚisɨn], [sɪsɪn tə blo sə had]. **1949** McDavid *Coll.* **cnNY,** From a male farmer and forest ranger, 77 yrs: Of wind, to cease down = to die down. **1953** Randolph *Down in Holler* 150 **Ozarks,** That there wind *denotes* rain . . . I hope it ceases afore mornin'. **1962** Atwood *Vocab. TX* 39, When a strong wind begins to abate, it is said to be . . *ceasing.* **1965–70** *DARE* (Qu. B13, *When the wind begins to decrease . . it's* _____) 17 Infs, **chiefly Sth, Ozarks,** Ceasing; **MO**8, Beginning to cease; **GA**71, Going to cease. [8 of 19 Infs Black]

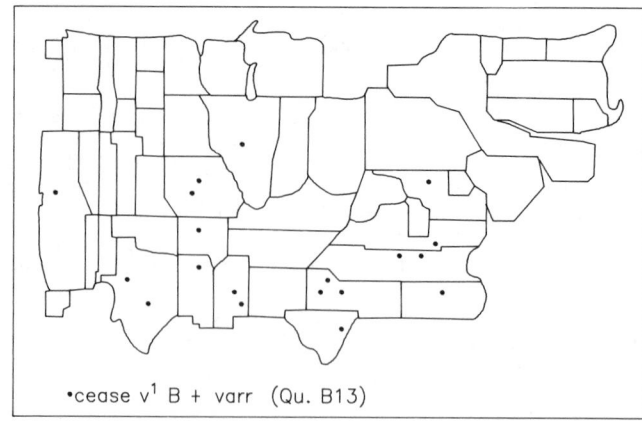

•cease v[1] B + varr (Qu. B13)

cease v[2], hence ppl adj *ceased* (Pret and ppl forms *ceasded, ceasted* result from pronc of *cease* as |sist|, whether by phonetic intrusion of *t* [see **cease** v[1] **A**] or by a present tense form **ceast* inferred from the pple *ceased;* cf **-ed** pret suff **1**) [Aphet form of *decease*] **chiefly Sth** *chiefly among Black speakers*

To die; as ppl adj, dead.

1927 Kennedy *Gritny* 80 **sLA** [Black], She talkin' 'bout de ole lady call Aun' Milly,—layin' yonder 'ceasted. (Deceased.). *Ibid* 217, Now that Gussie was 'ceased, there wasn't no use for any elder to stand up and preach about his sinful ways. **1954** *PADS* 21.23 **SC,** *Ceasted:* past tense and past part. Deceased. Negro usage. **1965** *DARE* (Qu. BB55, *To say that a person died—serious expressions*) Inf MS29, Ceased. **1967** *DARE* FW Addit AR55, Ceasted—died. [Inf says usage is old-fash, by Black speakers.]

cebolleta n [Dimin of Span *cebolla* onion, bulb]

A **rain lily 1** (here: *Cooperia drummondii*).

1970 Correll *Plants TX* 417, *Cooperia Drummondii . . . Cebolleta . . .* Bulb large, subglobose.

cedar n

1 A shrub or tree of the genus *Juniperus.*

1897 Sudworth *Arborescent Flora* 92, *Juniperus virginiana . .* Cedar (Conn., Pa., N.J., S.C., Ky., Ill., Iowa, Ohio, Mont.); . . *J. occidentalis . .* Cedar (Idaho, Mont.). **1900** Lyons *Plant Names* 208, *Juniperus, . . J. Oxycedrus . .* Berry-bearing Cedar . . . *J. Virginiana . .* Virginian Cedar. **1939** Tharp *Vegetation TX* 42, Cedar (*Juniperus* spp). **1961** Douglas *My Wilderness* 61 **swUT,** Neighbors of the piñon pine were junipers, which Utahans call cedars. **1979** Little *Checklist U.S. Trees* 153, *Juniperus . .* (Family Cupressaceæ) *. .* Other common names . . "cedar."

2 An arborvitæ (*Thuja* spp).

1894 *Jrl. Amer. Folkl.* 7.100, *Thuya occidentalis . .* cedar, Penobscot, Co., Me.

3 See **cedar pencil.**

cedar apple n

A brown, rounded growth on cedar trees (*Juniperus* spp) caused by var rusts (*Gymnosporangium* spp). Also called **cedar ball.**

1849 Lyell *Second Visit* 2.244 **VA,** The cedar (*Juniperus virginiana*) is often covered at this season with what is termed here the cedar apple (*Podisoma macropus*), supposed by many of the inhabitants to be the flower or fruit of the tree itself. **1876** (1882–83) Whitman *Specimen Days* 87 **NJ,** These cedar-apples last only a little while however, and soon crumble and fade. **1948** Boyce *Forest Pathology* 176, "Cedar apples" on eastern red cedar [are] caused by *Gymnosporangium juniperivirginianae.* On the left [in photo] the telia are dry, on the right moist and jellylike.

cedar ball n

=**cedar apple.**

1889 *Century Dict., Cedar-apple . . .* Also called *cedar-ball.* **1908** *DN* 3.297 **eAL, wGA,** *Cedar-ball . . .* The cedar-apple. **1954** *Harder Coll.* **cwTN,** Cedar balls: Large reddish-yellow balls that appear on cedar trees. **1956** *KY Folkl. Rec.* 2.54 **KY,** Wear a cedar ball in pocket to cure kidney disease.

cedar bird n Also *cedar lark* [See quot 1899]

=**cedar waxwing.**

1791 (1958) Bartram *Travels* 298, Ampelis garrulus, crown bird or cedar bird. These birds . . are to be seen in all the regions from Canada to New Orleans. **1844** Giraud *Birds Long Is.* 163, *Ampelinæ . . . bombycilla . . . Cedar bird.* **1850** Cooper *Rural Hours* 99 **cNY**, As for the cedar-birds, everybody knows them. **1899** (1912) Green *VA Folk-Speech*, Cedar-bird . . . A small bird that feeds on cedar berries. **1902** (1904) Rowe *Maid of Bar Harbor* 31 **ME**, Blithe and merry as the red-capped cedar birds. **1911** *Century Dict.*, Cedar-bird . . . Also called *cedar-lark.* **1934** Vines *Green Thicket* 60 **cnAL**, Cedarbirds. **1967–68** *DARE* (Qu. Q23) Inf **LA15**, Cedar bird.

cedar bird v

To deceive or trick; to make a patsy or fall guy (of someone).

1984 *DARE* File **wNC** (as of 1915–20), The locutions "He was cedar birded" and "He got cedar birded" were current in the community. I'm not sure about the origin; perhaps from a view that the cedar bird was a negligible or fictitious or discreditable creature.

cedar brake n

1 See **brake** n² c.

2 The **mountain cedar.**

1960 Vines *Trees SW* 33, *Juniperus . . ashei . .* Cedar Brake.

cedar braker n Also *cedar breaker* (erron or by folk-etym) [**brake** n² c] **West**

A range animal grazing wild in cedar brakes.

1936 Adams *Cowboy Lingo* 73, Wild stock which ranged high in the cedar thickets were called 'cedar-breakers.' **1944** Adams *Western Words* 30, Cedar braker—One of the wild stock which range high in the cedar brakes.

cedar bucket See **bucket 2a**

cedar chopper n **TX** Cf **cedar savage 2**

A rustic, a hayseed.

1962 Atwood *Vocab. TX* 74 **cTX**, The rustic type of person . . *cedar chopper* and *charcoal burner,* both of which are recorded only in Travis County. **1967–68** *DARE* (Qu. HH1, . . *Rustic or countrified person*) Infs **TX4, 54**, Cedar chopper; (Qu. HH18, *Very insignificant or low-grade people*) Inf **TX54**, Cedar choppers.

cedar elm n [Etym unknown]

An elm tree *(Ulmus crassifolia)* found chiefly in the southern and southeastern US. Also called **basket elm, cork elm 3, lime elm, red elm, rock elm, scrub elm, Texas elm**

1884 Sargent *Forests of N. Amer.* 122, *Ulmus crassifolia . . . Cedar Elm.* **1897** Sudworth *Arborescent Flora* 180 **TX**, *Ulmus crassifolia . . . Cedar Elm.* **1931** Mattoon *Forest Trees Okla.* 60 *(DA),* Cedar Elm . . in the southeastern part of the State. **1960** Vines *Trees SW* 210, *Cedar Elm—Ulmus crassifolia . . .* Texas, Oklahoma, Arkansas, and Louisiana; east to South Carolina, north to New York, and west to Kansas. **1970** *DARE* (Qu. T11, . . *Elm*) Inf **TX106**, Cedar elm.

cedar fever n Also *cedar itch, cedar poisoning*

A skin irritation caused by cedar oil and characterized by itching.

1950 *WELS (Common itching diseases)* 1 Inf, **ceWI**, Cedar itch. **1958** McCulloch *Woods Words* **Pacific NW**, *Cedar fever*—An itch sometimes affecting men working with western red cedar logs or poles. There was also a cedar asthma, attributed to the dust around cedar lumber and shingle mills. **1966** *DARE* (Qu. S17, . . *Plants . . that will cause itching and swelling*) Inf **MI9**, Some people get cedar poisoning.

cedar grass n [Prob because it somewhat resembles cedar fronds]

A submerged water plant *(Naias flexilis)* with slender, much-branched stems and grasslike leaves, common throughout much of the US.

1920 *Torreya* 20.18, *Naias flexilis . . .* Cedar grass, Horn Point, Va.

cedar itch See **cedar fever**

cedar lark See **cedar bird**

cedar moss n Also *water cedar* **SE**

A **hornwort,** esp *Ceratophyllum demersum.*

1920 *Torreya* 20.20, *Ceratophyllum demersum . . .* Cedar moss, Reelfoot Lake, Tenn. **1933** Small *Manual SE Flora* 509, *Ceratophyllum . . .* Cedar-mosses. **1937** *Torreya* 37.97, *Ceratophyllum demersum . . .* Water-cedar, Wakulla, Fla.

cedar pencil n Rarely *cedar* [From the wood of which the pencil is made] **chiefly Sth, S Midl** See also **pencil cedar**

A pencil, usu unpainted and cheap.

1869 Twain *Innocents* 398 **MO**, It seems to come as natural . . as it is to put a friend's cedar pencil in your pocket. **1891** Farmer–Henley *Slang,* Cedar . . . (prison).—A pencil. **1899** (1912) Green *VA Folk-Speech,* Cedar-pencil . . . Lead-pencil used for writing. **1908** *DN* 3.297 **eAL, wGA,** Cedar-pencil . . . Pencil, lead-pencil. **1949** *PADS* 11.5 **wTX,** Cedar pencil . . . An unpainted pencil. **1965–70** *DARE* (Qu. JJ10a, . . *Kinds of pens and pencils*) Infs **AR52, LA2, MS1, 6, TX36, 37,** Cedar pencils; **GA86, KY85,** Cedar pencils—same as penny pencils; **MA68,** Cedar pencil—no enamel on it.

cedar pine n

1 =**spruce pine 1. chiefly Sth**

1884 Sargent *Forests of N. Amer.* 201 **S Atl, Gulf States,** *Pinus glabra.* Cedar pine. Spruce pine. White pine. **1897** Sudworth *Arborescent Flora* 29 **MS,** *Pinus glabra . .* Cedar Pine. **1908** Rogers *Tree Book* 50, [The *Spruce Pine (P. glabra)*] is known as "cedar pine" in Mississippi. **1960** Vines *Trees SW* 27, *Pinus . . glabra . .* Cedar Pine. **1969** *DARE* (Qu. T17, . . *Pine*) Inf **GA77,** Cedar pine.

2 =**Jersey pine.**

1860 Curtis *Cat. Plants NC* 20, *Jersey Pine. (P. inops . .* [=*P. virginiana]*) . . . In some parts of the country it is known also under the names of *Cedar, River,* and *Scrub Pine.* **1897** Sudworth *Arborescent Flora* 27 **NC,** *Pinus virginiana . .* Cedar Pine.

cedar poisoning See **cedar fever**

cedar racer n **TX** See *racer* in Map Section

The striped **whipsnake** (here: *Masticophis taeniatus*).

1958 Conant *Reptiles & Amphibians* 150, *Central Texas Whipsnake . . .* Also called "cedar racer" . . . An alert, fast-moving snake of brakes and valleys.

cedar robe n [*cedar* + *-robe* abbr for **wardrobe**] **esp LA, MS**

A **wardrobe** made of cedar.

1967 LeCompte *Word Atlas* 120 **seLA,** Smaller, modern piece of furniture to hang clothes in . . . cedar robe [used by 8 of 21 infs]. **1970** *DARE* (Qu. E1, *A piece of furniture . . you hang clothes in*) Inf **MS85,** Cedar robe. **1971** Wood *Vocab. Change* 370 **Sth,** [Piece of furniture in which clothes can be hung] Additional volunteered words: . . *cedar robe.*

cedar savage n

1 Among loggers: one who works with cedar logs or poles.

1956 Sorden–Ebert *Logger's Words* 8 **Gt Lakes,** Cedar-savage, A man who cuts or peels cedar logs, poles or posts. **1958** McCulloch *Woods Words* 31 **Pacific NW,** *Cedar savage*—A logger working in a cedar pole camp, or for a shingle bolt outfit. **1966** *DARE* Tape **MI10,** His cousin who worked in the deep swamps generally, hewing ties or cutting shingle timber, was generally called a cedar savage.

2 A rustic; a farmer. *derog* Cf **cedar chopper**

1958 *AmSp* 33.263 **MN,** The subsistence farmer with his small cleared plot of unproductive soil. To him some townspeople have given the opprobrious name *jack pine savage* or *cedar savage.*

cedar-swamp v

To cut cedar in a swamp.

1968 *DARE* Tape **NJ51,** I've always cedar-swamped after I got older.

cedar water n

See quots.

1968 McPhee *Pine Barrens* 16 **NJ,** The characteristic color of the water in the streams is the color of tea—a phenomenon, often called "cedar water", that is familiar in the Adirondacks, as in many other places where tannins and other organic waste from riparian cedar trees combine with iron from the ground water to give the rivers a deep color. In summer the cedar water is ordinarily so dark that the riverbeds are obscured. **1982** Heat Moon *Blue Highways* 372 **cNJ,** Bog iron (cannonballs fired at Valley Forge were made here) and tannins had turned the transparent water the color of cherry cola. This "cedar water," as it is called, sea captains once carried on long voyages because it remained sweet longer than other waters. Even today, it is remarkably free of pollutants since all streams that flow through the Pines have their source here.

cedar waxwing n

A brownish passerine bird *(Bombycilla cedrorum)* with prominent crest and secondaries with red waxlike tips, fond of berries (esp cedar berries and cherries); it ranges throughout much of the US except the Southwest and Rocky Mountain states. Also called **apple bird 2, Canada robin, canker bird, cedar bird, cherry bird, hammerlock, paraquet, polite bird, Quaker bird, ricebird 2, seal, spider bird, wax bird**

1844 Giraud *Birds Long Is.* 163 **NY,** *Ampelinæ . . . bombycilla . . . Cedar Waxwing . . . Cedar Bird.* **1917** (1923) *Birds Amer.* 3.94, *Cedar waxwing—Bombycilla cedrorum.* **1967–68** *DARE* (Qu. Q23) Inf **TX40,** Cedar waxwing; (Qu. Q10, . . *Water . . and marsh birds*) Inf **MI67,** Cedar waxwing; (QR, near Qu. Q23) Inf **GA18,** Cedar waxwing (don't nest here).

ceiling n
By ext from std sense: an attic, loft.

c1960 *Wilson Coll.* **csKY,** *Up in the ceiling*—reference to attic or loft.

'ceitful adj [Aphet form of *deceitful*]
Deceitful.

1922 Gonzales *Black Border* 292 **sSC, GA coasts** [Gullah glossary], *'Ceitful*—deceitful. **1927** Adams *Congaree* 8 **cSC** [Black], Dat nigger act just like a 'ceitful Congaree nigger. **1970** *DARE* (Qu. II20b) Inf **SC69,** 'Ceitful.

celandine n Infreq sp *cellandine*
A yellow-flowered plant *(Chelidonium majus)* naturalized in the eastern US. Also called **celandine poppy 2, swallowwort**

1822 Eaton *Botany* 234, *Chelidonium . . . majus . . .* (celandine). **1938** Matschat *Suwannee R.* 89 **nFL, sGA,** Seeds of cellandine. **1968** *DARE* (Qu. S26a, . . *Wildflowers . . roadside flowers*) Inf **PA99,** Celandine; (Qu. S26d, *Wildflowers . . in meadows*) Inf **RI15,** Common celandine.

celandine poppy n
1 A perennial plant *(Chelidonium diphyllum)* common in woods. Also called **wood poppy**

1857 Gray *Manual of Botany* 25, *Stylóphorum . . . Celandine Poppy.* **1891** *Century Dict.* 6013/2, *Stylophorum . . diphyllum* is the celandine poppy or yellow poppy of the central United States . . . Its light-green leaves resemble those of the celandine, and, like it, contain a yellow juice.

2 =celandine.

1959 Carleton *Index Herb. Plants* 25, Celandine poppy: *Chelidonium majus.*

celery n Usu |'sɛl(ə)ri,-ɪ|, occas |'sæl-| Pronc-sp *salary*
Std sense, var forms.

a Pronc varr.

1899 (1912) Green *VA Folk-Speech, Salary . . .* Celery. c1960 *Wilson Coll.* **csKY,** *Celery* is hardly distinguishable from /'sælər/. **1968** *DARE* (Qu. H56) Inf **WI60,** Celery ['sælri] pickles.

b Used as a count noun rather than a mass noun.

1941 Faulkner *Men Working* 198 **MS,** I wisht they wouldn't give us so many of them celeries.

celery cabbage n
Chinese cabbage.

1950 *WELS* (Greens) 2 Infs, **eWI,** Celery cabbage. **1967** *DARE* (Qu. I28a, . . *"Greens" . . those that are eaten raw*) Inf **OH22,** Celery cabbage.

celery crowfoot n Also *celery-leafed crowfoot, celery-leaved crowfoot*
A **buttercup 1** (here: *Ranunculus sceleratus*).

1822 Eaton *Botany* 424, *Ranunculus . . . sceleratus* (celery crowfoot.). **1840** MA Zool. & Bot. Surv. *Herb. Plants & Quadrupeds* 1.26, Celery-leafed Crowfoot. **1901** Mohr *Plant Life AL* 514, Celery-leaved or Cursed Crowfoot . . . Canadian Zone to Louisianian area. Throughout Atlantic North America west to British Columbia and Arizona. **1940** Clute *Amer. Plant Names* 5, *Ranunculus sceleratus . . .* Celery-leaved crowfoot.

celery grass n
=tape grass.

1920 *Torreya* 20.18, *Vallisneria spiralis . .* Celery grass, Horn Point, Va.

celery-leafed crowfoot, celery-leaved crowfoot See celery crowfoot

cellandine See celandine

---

cellar n[1] Usu |sɛlə(r)|; in ·Nth, esp NEng, also |sʌlə(r), sʊlɚ| Pronc-spp *sulla(r), suller*

A Forms.

1895 Brown *Meadow-Grass* 132 **NEng,** Well, you go down sullar an' bring me up a little piece o' pork. **1904** Day *Kin o' Ktaadn* 21 **ME,** Yet, standin' down there in the suller, A-sniffin' an' snuffin' away. **1908** (1911) Gale *Friendship Village* 31 **WI,** The most I've got in my sullar, I guess, is a gallon jar o' watermelon pickles. **1917** *DN* 4.389 **neOH, KY,** *Cellar . . .* My pronunciation has always been [sɛlr], but [sʌlr] is heard. **1922** (1926) Cady *Rhymes VT* 266, Then sign it with a careless scrawl / And stick it in the suller wall. **1959** *VT Hist.* new ser 27.129, Cellar ['sʊlər] . . . Common. Rural areas. **1975** Gould *ME Lingo* 79, *Down sulla* is the opposite of "up attic."

B Senses. [Note: it is not always possible to differentiate the following senses. See *DAE* for hist documentation]

1 A storeroom or storage place, usu for produce or foodstuff, above or below ground. [*OED* a1225 →] Cf *DS* M19 and **cold cellar, fruit cellar, root cellar**

1950 *AmSp* 25.165 **CO,** In Colorado the primary meaning of cellar is a storeroom. In the northeastern potato-growing area of the Platte, potato cellars are dugouts in the side of a hill, or pits covered with sod or dirt. In this section . . the word *cellar* alone means primarily a storeroom for food, usually underground. Seldom does it designate a room below the first floor of a house. But in the southwestern potato-growing area of the San Luis Valley, potato cellars are sturdy adobe brick structures built entirely aboveground because of the high water table . . . In this section all cellars are storerooms and are never below ground. **1965–70** *DARE* (Qu. M19, *A place for keeping carrots, turnips, potatoes . . over the winter*) 263 Infs, **widespread,** Cellar; (Qu. M18, *The separate building where milk is kept cool*) 14 Infs, **scattered,** Cellar; **IL128, MO25, NV8,** Milk cellar; **WV13,** Spring cellar. **1970** *DARE* Tape **MI121,** There were . . several potato storage cellars. **1971** Bright *Word Geog. CA & NV* 147, 26 [informants] thought of it [=cellar] as an old-fashioned word and 21 as a place used only for storing food. Of the last group, all but 2 were from rural areas.

2 A basement; the underground part of a house or building. [*OED* 1331 →] **widespread, but least freq Plains States, Rocky Mts** See Map Cf **basement 1**

1894 Frederic *Marsena* 111 **nNY,** She did all the housework there was to do, from cellar to garret. **1923** *DN* 5.243 **LA,** *Cellar . . .* Basement. Owing to the watery soil the floor is above ground. **1965–70** *DARE* (Qu. D18, *The part of the house below the ground floor*) 614 Infs, **scattered throughout US, but esp freq in NEast,** Cellar; (Qu. D19, *Referring to the part of the house below the ground floor, you might say, "I'm going . . ."*) 302 Infs, **widespread,** (Down) cellar; 200 Infs, **chiefly Nth, N Midl, esp NEast,** Down cellar; **AL43, AR1, KY55, NY107, SD3,** Down to cellar; **PA239,** Down in cellar; **DC7, FL3,** (To) the cellar; **MO9, OH4,** Cellar. **1968** *DARE* Tape **IN51,** We had cellars then, they call 'em basements now.

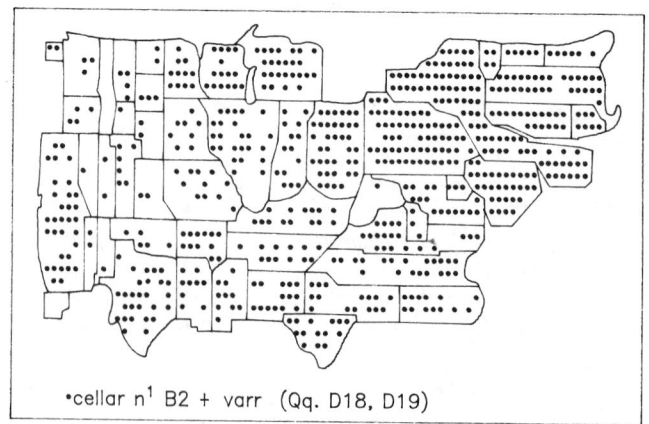

•cellar n[1] B2 + varr (Qq. D18, D19)

3 An underground room, usu separate from other buildings, used for protection or refuge. See also *DS* D22 and **cyclone cellar**

1915 *DN* 4.225 **wTX,** *Cellar . . .* Universal for *storm-house.* c1960 *Wilson Coll.* **csKY,** *Cellar . . .* Usually not under the house but separate, sometimes in the side of a bank. Many cellars were built for storm houses after the destructive tornado of March, 1923. **1965–70** *DARE* (Qu.

D22, *Underground place to go to in case of a violent windstorm*) Infs **OH**15, 74, Outside cellar; **NJ**28, Outside cellar—built like a little cave, used to be used by farmers; **NY**72, Dirt cellar—old-fashioned; they run right in the bank.

cellar n² See **saltcellar**

cellar bang n [In ref to the noise made when it is closed] Cf *DS* D20 and **cellarway**
=**bulkhead 1.**
   1971 *DARE* File **MA** (as of c1900), *Cellar bang*—a sloping outside cellar door.

cellar barn n Cf **basement barn**
=**bank barn.**
   c1951 Johnson *Resp. to PADS 20* **DE**, *(Barn built on a hillside with entrances on two levels)* Cellar barn. **1967–68** *DARE* (Qu. M1, . . *Kinds of barns*) Inf **NJ**45, Cellar barn—bottom of stone, top ordinary, built into a hill, for example; **IL**24, Cellar barn—built on two levels, on a slope.

cellar case n [**cellar** n¹ **B2** + **case** abbr for *casement*] **NEng** *old-fash* Cf *DS* D20 and **cellarway**
See quot 1890.
   1890 *DN* 1.18 **seNH**, *Cellar-case:* outside entrance to a cellar, with a sloping door. **1891** *DN* 1.215 **neMA**, *Cellar-case . . . Cellar-door* was used . . up to 1864. **1895** Brown *Meadow-Grass* 161 **NEng**, She had prepared for her return by leaving the doors of the cellar-case open.

cellar house n [**cellar** n¹ **B2, 3**]
An underground storage room or shelter; a building which has a cellar.
   1966–69 *DARE* (Qu. D22, *Underground place to go to in case of a violent windstorm*) Infs **OH**90, **VA**22, Cellar house; (Qu. M19, *A place for keeping carrots, turnips, potatoes, and so on over the winter*) Infs **IN**2, **KY**6, **NY**107, Cellar house; (Qu. M22, . . *Buildings . . on farms*) Inf **OH**39, Cellar house. **1970** *DARE* Tape **WV**14, Tell you what a cellar house is. That's just a building above a cellar.

cellar kitchen n **chiefly NEast** *old-fash*
A kitchen in a basement or cellar.
   1830 Watson *Annals Philadelphia* 202 **PA**, *Cellar Kitchens*, Now so general, are but of modern use. **1847** Child *Fact & Fiction* 247 **N Atl**, She was mostly confined to the cellar kitchen, from which she looked out upon stone steps and a brick wall. **1934** *Hanley Disks* **MA**, If they had an underground part, they used to have what they used to call a cellar kitchen. **1941** *LANE* Map 343, 3 infs, **eMA**, Cellar kitchen. **1967** *DARE* (Qu. D18, *The part of the house below the ground floor*) Inf **NJ**3, Cellar kitchen. **1980** *Greenfield Recorder* (MA) 8 Nov, The hearth stone in the old "cellar kitchen" of the Hemenway house in North Leverett, is smooth-surfaced, but not quite all flat.

cellar neck n *old-fash*
=**cellarway.**
   1886 *Amer. Philol. Assoc. Proc.* 17.xii **sePA**, "Cellar-neck" *(Keller-hals)* is frequently heard for cellar-way. **1914** *DN* 4.104 **KS**, *Cellar-neck . . . Cellar way.*

cellarway n **chiefly NEast, N Cent** See Map Cf **cellar bang, cellar case, cellar neck**
An indoor or outdoor entrance to a cellar.

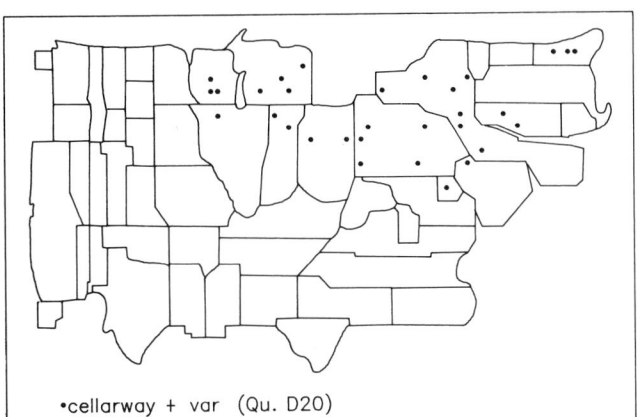
•cellarway + var (Qu. D20)

1761 in 1861 *MA Hist. Soc. Coll.* 4th ser 5.512 **MA**, Two or three were found lying on that part of the floor which was left, and in the cellar-way. **1892** *DN* 1.235 **nwMO, MI**, *Cellar-way . . .* also applies to an entrance from within the house. **1897** (1969) French *Missionary Sheriff* 172, She had the ill-hap to fall down her cellar-way, injuring her spine. **1907** *DN* 3.242 **eME**, *Cellar-way . . .* Outside cellar entrance with nearly horizontal double doors beneath which is the upright door opening directly into the cellar . . . 2. Stairway leading from the kitchen or any other room down into the cellar. **1962** Carrell *Autobiog.* 16 **MA** (as of 1880s), Our well water was hard so father had a barrel in the cellar way, which had a drain go into it to catch rain water. **1965–70** *DARE* (Qu. D20, . . *A sloping outside cellar door*) 28 Infs, **chiefly NEast, N Cent**, Cellarway; **IL**29, **MI**66, **PA**213, Outside cellarway. **1965–68** *DARE* FW Addit **ME**, *Cellarway*—Entrance to the cellar from the outside; **PA**, Cellarway—part of house. **1968** *DARE* Tape **WI**26, I throwed my dirty clothes in the cellarway.

cement n, v, adj Usu |ˌsɪˈment, sɛ-, sə-|; also, **chiefly Sth, S Midl**, |ˈsiˌment, -mɪnt|; occas |sment, siˈment|
Std senses, var forms.
   1892 *DN* 1.238 **MO, MI, NEng**, [sɪˈment]. **1928** *AmSp* 3.407 **Ozarks**, The hillman usually places a strong emphasis upon the first syllable of . . *police, cement* and *hurrah*. **1934** *W2*, *Cement* ([siˈment] . . . *the older* [ˈsɛmənt] *is now little used*). **1939** *LANE* Map 43 throughout **NEng**, *Cement road . . .* [səment], [smɛnt], [sɪment] . . . *Cement* always has end stress, except in [community] 315, where the exceptional form [ˈsɛmənt], probably an imitation of British usage, is the only one offered. **1941** in 1944 *ADD* **nWV**, [ˈsiˌment]. **1942** Hall *Smoky Mt. Speech* 52, Cement [ˈsiˌment]. **1950** *WELS* (*Used in building roads:* see-ment [or] se-*ment*) [All but 4 of the 50 Infs gave se-*ment* as their choice. Three Infs listed *see-ment* and one spelled out *sment*. Several added that *see-ment* is used occas, by older people, or humorously.] **1965–70** *DARE* (Qu. N23) 318 Infs, Cement. [Usu pronc [siˈment, səˈment]; **in Sth, S Midl, and occas West**, also [ˈsiˌment, ˈsiˌmɪnt].]

cement-stretcher See **stretcher**

cemetery n Usu |ˈsɛmətɛri, -ɪ|, occas by syncope |ˈsɛmətrɪ|; also |ˈsɪ-| Pronc-spp *cemetary, simmetery*, joc forms *cement-tary, cement tree*
Std senses, var forms.
   1873 *Newton Kansan* 3 July 3/2 (*DAE*), For a city cemetry. **1891** *DN* 1.159 **cNY**, [sɛmətrɪ], 'cemetery'. **1927** Kennedy *Gritny People* (*ADD*) **LA** [Black], Simmetery. **1940** in 1944 *ADD* **swPA, nWV**, [ˈsɪmətɛri]. **1941** [see **cent a**]. **1943** *LANE* Map 525 **NEng**, The word *cemetery* is regularly stressed on the first syllable. The presence or absence of a secondary stress on the third syllable is usually reflected in the quality of the vowel: thus [ˈsɛmɪˌtɛrɪ] but [ˈsɛmɪtərɪ, ˈsɛmɪtrɪ]. **1968** *DARE* (Qu. BB61b, . . *Joking names for a cemetery*) Inf **MN**15, Cement-tary; **WI**47, Cement tree.

cemetery pink n
A pink (*Dianthus* spp).
   1967 *DARE* (Qu. S26e, . . *Wildflowers*) Inf **MA**5, Cemetery pinks. **1980** *Greenfield Recorder* (MA) 21 June B3, In the flower bed close by the back door was oftentimes a bunch of spice pinks, or clove pinks often so-called because of their fragrance. As they were so often planted on the graves where the slate stone markers were, they also were known as "cemetery pinks."

cenizo n Also *ceniza* [Span] **chiefly SW**

1 A **saltbush** (here: *Atriplex canescens*).
   1892 *DN* 1.246 **TX**, *Cenizo:* a shrub of southern Texas, not identified. Probably from Spanish *ceniza*, ashes, the leaves being ash-colored. **1900** Lyons *Plant Names* 54, *A[triplex] canéscens . . .* S. Dakota to Mexico and California. Bushy Atriplex, Cenizo. **1937** *U.S. Forest Serv. Range Plant Hdbk.* B27, Other names sometimes applied to this well-known bush [fourwing saltbush (*Atriplex canescens*)] include buckwheat shrub, cenizo. **1940** *FWP Guide TX* 97, There are remedies for everything, even for *susto*—fright. (The cure for this is cenizo leaves, boiled.). **1960** Vines *Trees SW* 236 **TX**, *Atriplex canescens . .* It is known also by the vernacular names of . . Cenizo. **1980** *DARE* File **wTX**, *Ceniza*—a gray-leaved plant which after rain has lavender flowers.

2 A **silverleaf** (here: *Leucophyllum frutescens*). **esp TX**
   1936 Whitehouse *TX Flowers* 131, *Cenizo* (*Leucophyllum texanum*) covers hillsides in the southern and southwestern parts of the state. **1951** *PADS* 15.19, *Leucophyllum frutescens . . .* Cenizo, Texas. **1960** Vines *Trees SW* 920, The . . vernacular name, Cenizo, is much used in

the Southwest and means "ash-like" with reference to the pale leaves. **1961** Wills–Irwin *Flowers TX* 200, *Cenizo . . .* produces an abundance of flowers from June to September.

cent n Usu |sɛnt|, freq, **chiefly Sth**, |sɪnt| See Pronc Intro 3.I.4
Std senses, var forms.

a Pronc var.

1934 *AmSp* 9.210 **Sth,** *Ten cents* [tɪn sɪn(t)s]. **1941** *AmSp* 16.5 **eTX** [Black], Before *m, n,* in . . *cemetery, cent, general,* . . [ɛ] becomes [ĩ], sometimes [ẽĩ]. *Ibid* 119 **VA,** *Ten cents* . . [tɪn sɪnts].

b sg for pl: Cents. **chiefly Sth**

1918 *DN* 5.39 **ce,seVA,** *Cent . . .* Cents. This use of the singular for the plural is quite common . . . "Those eggs cost forty *cent* a dozen." **1966–68** *DARE* (Qu. U22, *Other words . . for a five-cent piece*) Inf NC50, Five cent, five pennies; (Qu. KK17, . . *"It isn't worth _____.")* Inf GA7, Two cent. **1966–68** *DARE* Tape AL11, Oh, twenty-five, thirty cent [sɛnt]; GA25, If he could make twenty-five cent [sɛnt] a day he was a-doin' fine; GA51, I'd get a dollar forty cent [sɛnt] for his hide. **1972** *Atlanta Letters* **GA,** One dollar and thirteen cent.

c double pl *centses:* See **-es 2.**

center n[1], also attrib **Nth**
In logging: see quots.

1942 *ME Univ. Studies* 56.132, *Center.* Sticks of *pulpwood* caught upon rocks in a stream or river, with other sticks piled upon them. **1956** *Seattle Times Pictorial* 22 Apr 34–5 (*Perrin Coll.*), Ben Larson, log driver from Lewiston, moved fast and headed for shore with his peavey as a "center" of snarled logs began to tremble—a warning it would shift. **1956** Sorden–Ebert *Logger's Words* 8 **Gt Lakes,** *Center,* A few logs held on a single rock or obstruction in a river during a log drive. Center-jam, A log jam on an island in the center of the stream. **1958** McCulloch *Woods Words* 31 **Pacific NW.**

center n[2] [*cent* penny + *-er*]
In marble play: see quot.

1968 *DARE* (Qu. EE6c, *Cheap marbles*) Inf NY123, Centers—a penny a piece.

center catch ball n Also *center-ball*
A children's game: see quot 1909.

1901 *DN* 2.137, *Center-ball . . .* A game. **1909** (1923) Bancroft *Games* 355, *Center catch ball . . .* All of the players but one stand in a circle . . . The odd player stands in the center of the circle and tries to catch the ball, which is tossed rapidly from one circle player to another. Should he be successful, the one who last touched the ball changes places with him.

center fire adj, also used absol [Transf from *center-fire bullet,* one which must be struck in the center by the hammer of the gun] **West, chiefly WA to AZ**
Of a saddle: having one cinch attached in the center rather than two at the ends of the saddle.

1907 White *AZ Nights* 288, A sidesaddle had arrived from El Paso. It was "centre fire," which is to say it had but the single horsehair cinch, broad tasselled, very genteel in its suggestion of pleasure use only. **1933** White *Dog Days* 197 **CA,** One did not merely go in and buy a saddle. He had all sorts of important details to decide upon . . . One broad cinch or two narrower ones?—"center fire" or "double barrel"? **1940** FWP *Guide NV* 75, A buckaroo's paraphernalia includes the following: the saddle, which the cow-country calls *cactus, hull, chair, centerfire, kak, pack,* or *rigging.* **1964** Jackman–Long *OR Desert* 110, Oregon cowboys rode a center-fire saddle. **1966** *DARE* FW Addit **WA,** Center fire rigs—single cinch on a saddle.

center man n Also *center marble*
In marble play: a large marble or taw.

1966–69 *DARE* (Qu. EE6a, . . *Marbles—the big one that's used to knock others out of the ring*) Inf GA74A, Center man; MS21, Center marble; (Qu. EE6d, *Special marbles*) Inf KY40, Center man—big one.

center shot n

1 A marksman who can hit the center of a target. *arch*

1842 *Amer. Pioneer* 1.225 **VA,** And as to the use of the rifle, he was said to be one of the quickest and surest centre shots to be found. **1850** Garrard *Wah-to-yah* 326 **SW,** 'Our hearts are big,' and we are all center shots. **1883** Zeigler *Heart of Alleghanies* 218 **SC, wNC, VA** (as of 1770s–80s), Their fame as "center shots," with the rifle, was well known to the British regulars, who feared to meet them.

2 A shot which hits the center of a target; anything which succeeds or "hits the mark." *old-fash*

1853 Hammett *Stray Yankee in TX* 120, They give me some stuff [=medicine] that tasted like iron hoops stewd down, but t'wouldn't make a center shot nither. **1903** (1965) Adams *Log Cowboy* 78 **NM,** It was a centre shot.

centipede n Pronc-spp *santerfee, santiped, santy fay;* folk-etym *sandy Pete* [Of multiple sources: forms without final *d* or *t* are from AmSpan *cientopié* (or Port *centope(i)a*); forms with final *d* or *t* are from Engl or directly from Fr *centipède*]
Std sense, var forms.

1889 in 1944 *ADD,* Sandy Pete. **1918** *DN* 5.37 **OK,** Santerfee . . . Centiped [sic]. Also *santiped.* **1923** *DN* 5.219 **swMO,** *Santy fay . . .* Centiped [sic]. **1927** *DN* 5.472 **Ozarks,** A santy-fay is a centipede.

centipede grass n **S Atl, HI**
An introduced turf-forming grass *(Eremochloa ophiuroides).* Also called **lazy-man's grass**

1950 Hitchcock *Manual Grasses* 787, *Eremochloa ophiuroides* . . Centipede grass. **1965–70** *DARE* (Qu. S9, . . *Grass . . hard to get rid of*) Infs FL22, HI2, NC52, SC67, Centipede grass. **1966** *Lake Co. Citizen* (Tavares FL) 1 Apr 5/3, For Centipede grass this recommendation should be cut in half. The fertilizer should be applied with a spreader. **1966** *DARE* Tape FL5, We've tried zoysia, St. Augustine, and centipede. **1969** *SC Market Bulletin* 44.37.4/3, Centipede grass $1.25 per bushel. **1971** GA Dept. Ag. *Farmers Market Bulletin* 26 May 1/4, South Georgians find the hybrid Bermudas, zoysia and centipede to be better choices.

centses See **cent c**

century n, also attrib Usu |'sɛnč(ə)rɪ, -i|, rarely |'sɛntərɪ|
A Form.

1917 *DN* 4.389 **neOH, KY,** *Century* [sɛntərɪ].
B Sense.
A hundred dollar bill; one hundred (dollars).

1859 Matsell *Vocabulum* 18, *Century.* One hundred dollars; one hundred. **1907** Mulford *Bar-20* 192 **West,** Aristotle said he'd give a century fer five minutes' palaver with him, but he shied th' town an' didn't come back. **1927** *DN* 5.442 [Underworld jargon], *Century . . .* A hundred dollar bill. **1967–69** *DARE* (Qu. U20, . . *It cost a hundred _____*) Inf TN1, Century notes; (QR, near Qu. U28c) Infs CA113, 147, Century—a hundred dollar bill.

century plant n [From the legend that it blooms once in 100 years]
=agave.

1843 (1860) Stephens *Incidents Yucatan* 2.44, Growing on the roof are two maguey plants, Agave Americana, in our latitude called the century plant, but under the hot sun of the tropics blooming every four or five years. **1847** Wood *Class-Book* 539, *A[gāve] Americāna.* American Aloe. Century Plant. **1925** Fries *Rec. Moravians* 2.572 **NC,** *Century Plant* grows abundantly here on the Uplands. **1948** Peattie *Inverted Mts.* 276 **SW,** The century plant or mescal . . forms veritable "forests" in places. **1965** Teale *Wandering Through Winter* 118 **TX,** The dead stalks of the century plant, *Agave scabra,* rose above the lower vegetation. **1966–69** *DARE* (Qu. S26, . . *Wildflowers*) Infs NM13, TX66, Century plant(s). **1973** *AZ Highways* Mar 29/2, Century Plant is misnomer for the Agave . . . the Century Plant is ready to bloom after ten years. **1983** *DARE* File **CA,** I grew up in an area of California where the agave was a common plant, but I remember it referred to as century plant, not agave.

ceonosa n
Perh=**ceanothus.**

1861 *Harper's Mag.* 23.13/1 **cwCA,** The air is fragrant with the scent of wild roses, honey-suckle and ceonosa.

ceounty See **county**

'cep(t) v [Aphet form of *accept, except*]

1922 Gonzales *Black Border* 292 **sSC, GA coasts** [Gullah glossary], *'Cep', 'cep'm, 'cep'n'* . . except, excepts, excepted, excepting; accept, accepts, accepted, accepting. **1972** *Atlanta Letters* **GA,** He was cepted in de lodge when he jined.

cerillo n Also *cerilla* |sɛ'rijo, sə'rijə| [MexSpan *cerillo* wax match] **TX**

A match.

1892 *DN* 1.246 **TX**, *Cerilla* or *cerillo:* slender wax taper. Wax match of Mexican manufacture, far superior in the way of matches to anything manufactured in the United States. **1967** *DARE* (Qu. F46, . . *Matches you can strike anywhere*) Inf **TX3**, Cerillos [sæˈijəz]. **1980** *DARE* File **wTX**, Cerillo [sɛˈrijo], match.

cer'nly See **certainly**

cerril(l)o See **cerro**

cerro n Also dimins *cerrillo, cerrilo* [Span] **SW**

A hill or peak—freq used in place names.

1831 (1973) Pattie *Personal Narr.* 297, The principal mountains coast Rio del Norte, following its western banks. Some peaks, or *cerros,* are to be distinguished. **1861** U.S. Congress *Serial Set* 1058 Doc. 90.3.99 **NM**, From this mesa rise the volcanic cones of the "Cerrillos." **1933** *AmSp* 8.3.8 **SW**, *Cerro* is a hill and *cerrillos,* little hills. **1946** *So. Sierran* Oct. 3/3 *(DA)*, Cerro Gordo, Inyo Mountains, elevation 9217 feet, was climbed Monday by twelve persons.

certain adj, adv Usu |ˈsɚˌt(ə)n, -ɪn| and in r-less areas |ˈsɜtn, ˈsʌtn|; also, **esp NEast, Sth, S Midl** |ˈsɑ(r)t(ɪ)n| (This last form is the preservation of a regular pre-colonial pronunciation which changed in 17th cent to |ɚ|.) Pronc-spp *sart(a)in, sartan, sarten, saa't'n, saht'n, sutt(i)n;* infreq *sarting* (cf **-ing**), *cart(a)in, corten, soitain*

A Forms.

1773 in 1956 Eliason *Tarheel Talk* 308 **NC**, Cartain. **1785** *Ibid,* Sartain. **1789** *Ibid,* Sartin. **1801** *Ibid,* Cartin. **1834** Smith *Letters Jack Downing* v **ME**, This is a sartan sine that I am popular. **1835** in 1956 Eliason *Tarheel Talk* 308 **NC**, Corten. **1841** (1952) Cooper *Deerslayer* 336 **NY**, What is proved is sartain. **1843** (1916) Hall *New Purchase* 460 **IN**, Well, you ain't proud . ., that's sarten. **1848** Lowell *Biglow* 145 'Upcountry' **MA**, Sartin, *certain. Ibid* 146, Suttin, *certain.* **1891** *DN* 1.119 c**NY**, |sɑrtn|. **1893** Shands *MS Speech* 54, *Sartin* . . . Negro for *certain.* This pronunciation is also used to some extent by the illiterate whites of Mississippi, as by those of almost every other part of the United States. **1901** *DN* 2.181 ne**KY** [Black], *Certain* saht'n. **1911** *DN* 3.537 e**KY**, *Certain* . . . [sɑrtɪn]. **1914** *DN* 4.79 **ME**, n**NH**, Sartin. **1916** Lincoln *Mary-'Gusta* 29 **MA**, All I seem to be real sartin of just now is that the Campbells are comin'. **1922** Gonzales *Black Border* 324 s**SC**, **GA** coasts [Gullah glossary], Saa't'n Sutt'n—certain. **1930s** in 1944 *ADD* **NYC**, Soitain. Radio. **1941** *AmSp* 16.10 e**TX** [Black], *Certain* . . ['sʌtn, 'sɜtn]. **1943** *LANE* Map 590 **NEng**, *Certainly!* . . . Expressions described as older or old-fashioned though still in use: *sartin* by [27 infs; see map for other proncs]. **1953** Randolph *Down in Holler* 26 **Ozarks**, The word certain is generally *sartin* in the backwoods, but I have heard an Arkansas legislator, in a public address, pronounce it *sarting.*

B As adv.

1 Certainly. **esp NEng, also C and S Atl**

1837 Smith *Col. Crockett's Exploits* 33 **S Midl**, If the fife had had an extra tune to its name, sartin it wouldn't have been quite so hide-bound on such an occasion. **1884** Jewett *Mate of Daylight* 197 **ME**, I walked off into the bedroom, for I thought I should laugh, certain. **1891** Cooke *Huckleberries* 17 **NEng**, Yes, I be, yes, I be—sartain. **1899** (1912) Green *VA Folk-Speech, Certain* . . . Certainly; assuredly. " 'Tis *certain* so." **1905** *DN* 3.5 c**CT**, *Certain* . . . Certainly. **1908** Lincoln *Cy Whittaker* 53 **MA**, You've sartin made the place rise up out of its tomb; you have so. **1910** *DN* 3.458 **FL**, **GA**, I hav sartain got a misery in my *innards.* **1943** *LANE* Map 590 **NEng** *Certainly!* The map shows expressions used for emphatic or emotional affirmation, enthusiastic agreement and the like: *certainly, oh ~, why ~, certain (sartin).* **1966** *DARE* File **MD**, It's a fine day 'certain'—an Eastern Shore expression for "It's certainly a fine day." Used in any expression where "certainly" would be used.

2 in phr *for certain:* Assuredly, as a certainty. [*OED* c1320] **chiefly Sth**

1872 Schele de Vere *Americanisms* 450, *Certain* belongs to a class of adjectives which Americans constantly use as adverbs. "He's done it sure and *certain.*" It is frequently strengthened by the addition of *for.* "We shall be burnt out *for certain.*" **1905** Culbertson *Banjo Talks* 146 **SE**, "An' dey's better, heap, fer sartin', w'en b'iled down." **1938** Matschat *Suwannee R.* 124 n**FL**, s**GA**, Ye're a noticin' womern, for sartin. **1966-68** *DARE* (Qu. B6) Inf **VA18**, Rain for certain; (Qu. NN1) Inf **TX33**, For certain.

3 in phr *certain sure* (and varr): Most certainly. [Engl dial] **chiefly Mid and S Atl, NEng, Ohio Valley**

1856 *Knickerbocker* 48.432, The old man would certain sure get riled. **1859** (1968) Bartlett *Americanisms* 75, I'll go to-morrow sure and *certain.* **1887** (1967) Harris *Free Joe* 104 **GA**, She oughter know him certain an' shore. **1894** Riley *Armazindy* 8 **IN**, I know *I* did—certain-shore! **1899** (1912) Green *VA Folk-Speech, Certain sure* . . . Without doubt or question; without fail; in truth and fact. **1916** Lincoln *Mary-'Gusta* 92 **MA**, Sartin sure I will. **1938** Matschat *Suwannee R.* 85 n**FL**, s**GA**, Oh, sure for sartin. **1943** *LANE* Map 590 **NEng**, *Certainly!* . . . Expressions described as older or old-fashioned though still in use: . . *sartin sure* by [6 infs, about one-fourth of those responding with the term].

4 in phr *certain and declare:* Most certainly; decidedly.

1970 *Foxfire* 4 Spring-Summer 78, Certain'n'declare no. I don't believe I ever did.

C In adj phrr.

1 in phr *for certain:* See **for** prep **B4.**

2 in phr *certain sure* (and varr): Very sure.

1852 Watson *Nights Block-house* 81 **Ohio R Valley**, If he succeeded, his escape was sartin' sure. **1908** Lincoln *Cy Whittaker* 242 **MA**, Sure and sartin. *Ibid* 319, He was sartin sure of the thirty thousand for a spell. **1935** *Atlantic Mth.* 156.49/1 n**AL**, The old folks axed us if we was certain sure we knowed our minds. **1938** Matschat *Suwannee R.* 148 n**FL**, s**GA**, So durn sartin sure hit weren't so. **1960** Williams *Walk Egypt* 125 **GA**, She was certain-sure that he had heard all the tales . . . Certain-sure they did not call her Hug-Me-Tight. **1961** *Mt. Life* Fall 9 s**Appalachians**, They'll be larrupin' good fer sartain shore.

certain and declare See **certain B4**

certain and sure See **certain B3**

certainly adv Pronc-spp *cer'nly, cert(ɔ)ny, certingly, sart(a)inly, sartnly, soitainly, sutenly, su'tinly, sutney, sut'n'y* Cf **certain A** Std senses, var forms.

1815 Humphreys *Yankey in England* 108, Sartinly. **1841** (1952) Cooper *Deerslayer* 157, Sartainly something *did* move the water. **1873** Harte *Mrs. Skaggs* 58 **CA**, Certingly a sort of a skunk and suthin of a fool. **1887** Page *In Ole VA* 36 [Black], She sut'n'y did cry over it. *Ibid* 41, He sutney set a heap o' sto' by me. **1893** Shands *MS Speech* 76, *Sutenly* . . . Negro for *certainly.* **1899** (1912) Green *VA Folk-Speech, Certny.* **1903** *DN* 2.290 **Cape Cod MA** (as of 1840s), It's sartnly so. *Ibid* 321 se**MO**, Certingly. **1917** Torrence *Granny Maumee* 67 [Black], De man what buys guitars at dat price su'tinly plays on de golden strings. **1926** Ferber *Show Boat* 359, I cer'nly was. **1927** Kennedy *Gritny* 18 s**LA** [Black], She cert'ny a p'ovokin' ole sole 'bout dat hog she got yonder. **1930s** in 1944 *ADD* **NYC**, Soitainly.

certain sure See **certain B3, C2**

certingly, cert(ɔ)ny See **certainly**

cess n [Alter of *cease; OED* "obs"] *arch* Cease, cessation.

1912 Green *VA Folk-Speech, Cess* . . . For *cease:* He talked for two hours without *cess.*

C.H. See **courthouse**

chaa'ge See **charge** v **A**

chac See **chock** n¹

cha-cha n [Echoic]

1 =**katydid B1.**

1944 *PADS* 2.41 nw**NC**, Cha-cha [ˈtʃæˈtʃæ] . . . The katydid . . . Rare.

2 The brown-headed **nuthatch** (*Sitta pusilla*). Cf **chay-chay 2**

1962 Imhof *AL Birds* 383, Brown-headed Nuthatch . . . Cha-cha.

cha-cha-cha intj **LA, TX**

A call to animals to urge them forward or urge them to come.

1967 LeCompte *Word Atlas* 188 se**LA**, *Call to cows in pasture / to get them home /* . . [5 of 21 infs] cha-cha-cha . . . The response "cha-cha," to my knowledge, is not used in other speech communities, though it is widespread in this area, not only as a call to cows, but also as a call to dogs. [P. 193 shows 1 inf using it for the latter.] **1967** *DARE* Tape **TX49**, You'd naturally say cha, cha, cha [to horses], you know, and they'd lay down and pull.

chachalaca n [AmSpan, imit of the bird's cry]

1 also *chachalac, chiacalacca, chiac-chia-lacca:* A turkeylike bird (*Ortalis vetula macalli*) native to Texas.

1851 *Acad. Nat. Sci. Philadelphia Proc.* 5.222 **wTX,** Long legged Sand piper[s] . . were exceedingly numerous about Matamoras, during the following winter, and were served at the tables of the Hotels and Restaurants very prodigally, as well as the *Chiac-chia-lacca.* **1858** Baird *Birds* 611, *Ortalida McCalli . . . Chiacalacca.* **1878** *U.S. Natl. Museum Proc.* 1.159 **sTX,** The Chachalac, as the present species is called on the Lower Rio Grande, is one of the most characteristic birds of that region. **1894** *Scribner's Mag.* 15.598/1 **sTX,** Through the dense foliage of mesquite and granjeno sounds the harsh cackle of the toothsome "chachalaca." **1955** *AmSp* 30.229, *Chachalaca.* A Texan guan or a related species of bird. **1965** Teale *Wandering Through Winter* 130 **TX,** A flock of more than twenty chachalacas fed along the path.

2 =roadrunner.

1917 *Wilson Bulletin* 29.2.81, *Geoccoccyx* [sic] *californianus . . .* chachalaca.

chad n[1]

=red-bellied woodpecker.

1917 (1923) *Birds Amer.* 2.160, *Red-bellied Woodpecker . . . Other Names . . .* Chad.

chad n[2] [Cf **chat** n[3]]

The small bit of paper released when a ballot is punched or a paper punch is used.

1980 *DARE* File **IL,** [Letter of procedure to election officials:] Check your ballot cards carefully for any "chads" which might be hanging loose. [Used by the staff since computer ballot cards were introduced.] **1981** *Los Angeles Times* (CA) 19 May sec 2 1/3, What the city is trying to avoid is a repeat of April's Great Chad Chore, when more than 40,000 ballots had to be recounted because their chads—the punched-out portions—failed to break loose. **1981** *DARE* File **CA,** The word "chad" has been in use since punch-out ballots first came into use in this state, at least ten years ago in most of the bigger cities . . . It is used only by people in the ballot-counting business, not by other users of computer cards, who seem to call the same bits of cardboard "confetti." **1982** *Capital Times* (Madison WI) 11 Nov 51/1 **NY,** Learning what to call the . . paper remnant that flutters down after you use a hole punch ("chad") pacifies his soul.

chad n[3] [Prob alter of **shad**]

1970 *DARE* (Qu. P7, *Small fish used as bait*) Inf **MS81,** Chad.

chad-cherries n [Echoic]

=red-bellied woodpecker.

1913 *Auk* 30.497 **Okefenokee GA,** *Centurus carolinus . . .* 'Shamshack'; 'Ram-shack'; 'Chad-cherries' . . . The 'Sham-shack' has a variety of call-notes, which . . . has doubtless given rise to the local names. **1955** *Oriole* 20.10 **GA,** *Red-bellied Woodpecker.—Chad-cherries . .* in reference to common utterances of this polyphonic bird.

chaff n

1 See **chaff bed.**

2 See quot.

1968 *DARE* (Qu. T6, *The pointed leaves that fall from pine trees*) Inf **MD13,** Pine chaff, fallen needles that gather under [the] tree.

3 Nonsense, ridicule; small, unimportant things or acts.

1859 Matsell *Vocabulum, Chaff.* Humbug. **1959** *VT Hist.* new ser 27.129, Chaff . . . Nonsense; foolishness; small things of not much consequence. **1968** Adams *Western Words* 59, *Chaff*—A fur trapper's word for ridicule.

chaff v [*OED chaff* v[2]]

To talk nonsense, to joke; to banter, tease, make fun of; to trick; hence vbl n *chaffing.*

1859 Matsell *Vocabulum, Chaffing.* Talking; bantering. **1872** Burnham *Memoirs U.S. Secret Service* iv, *Chaff,* to talk nonsense; to deceive, or gammon. **1912** Green *VA Folk-Speech, Chaff . . .* To assail with sarcastic raillery; banter; make game of; tease; worry; joke. **1953** Van Wagenen *Golden Age* 235 **ceNY,** Always they laughed and gossiped and chaffed a little. **1959** *VT Hist.* new ser 27.129, Chaff . . . To make fun of. Common.

chaff bed n Also *chaff, chaff tick* [*OED* 1683 →] **chiefly East** *old-fash*

A mattress or sack filled with chaff instead of feathers.

~~**1684** in 1896 Hempstead *NY Records* 1.431 **NY,** Two chaff beds and two boulsters.~~ **1784** Smyth *Tour U.S.A.* 1.76 **VA,** A miserable thin chaff bed, somewhat raised from the floor, in a corner of the room, which

alternately served him for his chair, his table, and his couch. **1841** Bache *Fire-Screen* 170, Here, a chaff bed, stained and torn; there, a pair of elegant glass shades. **1940** Yoder *Rosanna* 62 **PA,** The bed was high and the chaff tick was filled with finely cut straw. **1941** FWP *Guide WV* 440, The rate was cheaper for sharing a bed with 'one or more bedfellows'; or taking a 'chaff' instead of a feather bed.

chaffey See **chaffy 3**

chaffseed n [From the chaffy appearance of the seeds]

A perennial plant (*Schwalbea americana*) with dull purplish-yellow flowers, native to the eastern US.

1822 Eaton *Botany* 450, *Schwalbea . . . americana . . .* (chaff-seed). **1857** Gray *Manual of Botany* 294, *Schwálbea . . . Chaff-seed . . . S. Americàna . . .* Wet sandy soil, from Sandwich, Massachusetts, and New Jersey, southward, near the coast: rare. **1976** Bailey–Bailey *Hortus Third* 1019, *Chaffseed . . .* Late spring to summer. Wet sandy soil, e. Mass. to Fla., e. to La.

chaffy adj

1 Dried up, chaff-like.

1966 *DARE* (Qu. I8, *When root vegetables get old and tough*) Inf **FL19,** Chaffy [tʃæfi].

2 Of tobacco: light, thin, straw-colored.

1967 Key *Tobacco Vocab.* **MD,** Chaffy—thin, light; **NC,** Chaffy . . it doesn't carry much weight and has filling qualities; **TN,** Chaffy—Like the chaff of straw. Refers to the golden color. An excellent condition; **MO,** Chaffy (a dry conditon).

3 also *chaffey:* Bantering; boisterous; happy.

1859 Matsell *Vocabulum, Chaffey.* Boisterous; happy; jolly. **1874** in 1917 Twain *Letters* 233, He was as chaffy as he was sixty years ago. **1915** *DN* 4.213, *Chaffy,* full of banter. "I don't enjoy reading chaffy stories."

chafing gear n

Any kind of material fastened on a fish net or boat to prevent wear by rubbing; see quot 1978.

1966–67 *DARE* Tape **SC18,** The body of the net and behind it a long, slender bag which is covered by chafin' [tʃefɪn] gear to keep from wearing your net out;**TX14,** Chafing gear around the tail of these nets, which we used to make out of heavy webbing to keep the tail of the net from dragging on the rocks and shell on the bottom. **1978** Merriam *Illustr. Lobstering* 20 **ME,** *Chafing Gear*—Rags, rubber, or canvas tied around painter or hawser to prevent chafing or rubbing. Also refers to the slats on the side of the boat that prevent wear when hauling up traps.

‡chagalag n

1967 *DARE* (Qu. N5, . . *An automobile, especially an old broken-down car*) Inf **HI13,** Chagalag [tʃægəlæg].

chahdge See **charge** n

chain cactus n Also *chain cholla, chain-link cactus* Cf **chain-fruit cholla**

A **prickly pear** in which the fruits are sometimes linked together: for var spp see quots.

1957 Jaeger *N. Amer. Deserts* 282, *Chain Cactus. Opuntia fulgida.* So named because the persistent fruits hang in chainlike clusters. **1960** Vines *Trees SW* 772, *Opuntia spinosior . . .* is also known under the vernacular name of Chain Cholla. **1976** Bailey–Bailey *Hortus Third* 792, [*Opuntia*] *imbricata . . . Chain-link cactus.*

chaince See **chance** A

chain cholla See **chain cactus**

chain dishcloth n Also *chain dishrag, ~scratcher, ~scrubber*

A metal pad made of small interconnected links used to scour pots and pans.

1966–69 *DARE* (Qu. G14, *The rough metal pad that's used to scour pots and pans*) Infs **MA6, 38,** Chain dishcloth; **MD30, MO8,** Chain dishrag; **MA69,** Chain scratcher, chain scrubber. [**1980** *DARE* File **VT,** [In a catalog] *Pot Cleaning Chain* The kind grandma used, heavy steel, never wears out.]

chained lightning See **chain lightning**

chainey briar See **China brier**

chain fern n

A large fern of the genus *Woodwardia* having spore capsules closely linked along the leaf rib.

1868 (1870) Gray *Field Botany* 366, *Woodwardia*, chain-fern . . . A small genus of rather large Ferns . . . Fruit-dots oblong, close to the midribs. **1913** *Torreya* 13.251 **seNY,** Along a small stream flowing through the barrens, the narrow-leaved chain-fern, *Lorinseria areolata* (L.) Presl., grew in company with the common cinnamon fern. **1941** FWP *Guide WV* 19, The southern chain fern, a native of the Carolinas, has established itself on Droop Mountain. **1976** Bailey–Bailey *Hortus Third* 1174, *Chain fern* . . . Sori in rows parallel to the midrib.

chain-fruit cholla n Also *chainfruit, chain-fruited cholla* Cf **chain cactus**
=**jumping cholla.**
   1957 Jaeger *N. Amer. Deserts* 64, The chain-fruited cholla *(Opuntia fulgida . .) . .* has a candelabra-like form and often long, curiously joined, and drooping chains of fruit. **1973** *AZ Highways* Mar 29, Tall, with a top-heavy candelabra-like form, are the Chain-Fruit Chollas *(Opuntia fulgida),* distinctive by its droopy, curiously jointed chains of fruit. **1982** *NY Times* (NY) 3 Jan sec 10 17/2 **AZ,** Also present are tangles of . . chainfruit.

chain gang n
1 In railroading: one of several crews operating (extra) trains by turns.
   1939 FWP *ID Lore* 245 [Railroading], *Chain gang*—freight men. **1943** *AmSp* 18.163, *Chain gang.* When a number of extra trains in excess of regular trains are being run, regular crews may be assigned to take trains in turn rather than to specific scheduled runs; they are operating a chain gang. **1967** *DARE* Tape **ID6,** I was in regular freight, what they call chain gang; **ID9,** Chain gang. **1969** *AmSp* 44.255, *Chain gang*—Employees on the board who operate nonscheduled freight runs in rotation (The term may be due to the fact that long hours and a lack of schedule, especially in the early days of railroading, made employees complain that they felt like convicts.)
2 In lumbering: see quot.
   1967 *DARE* Tape **MI47,** Them days, everything was loaded with cant hooks and chain gangs. It was three men to a gang—a top loader, and a man to send up logs with a cant hook to keep the logs straight on the skids, and a teamster.
3 In cattle raising: see quot.
   1968 Adams *Western Words* 60, *Chain gang*—A cowboy's name for the wagon crew on roundup.

chain-gang pea n
=**black-eyed pea.**
   1960 Williams *Walk Egypt* 210 **GA,** Onion, okra, cabbage, and chain-gang peas ripened. **1984** *NADS Letters* **ceGA,** No one here (despite all of our prisons and actual prison road gangs) has ever heard a "real" person use this term. One student did report, however, that he had seen a movie in which poor people who couldn't pay fines were sent to work on public pea farms where *chain-gang peas* were grown. He couldn't name the movie, however. It is the unanimous opinion of my students, nevertheless, that *chain-gang peas* must be black-eyed peas.

chaining vbl n
In logging: see quot.
   1969 Sorden *Lumberjack Lingo* **NEng, Gt Lakes,** *Chaining*—Skidding logs with horses and chains, as opposed to the use of a go-devil or dray.

chain lightning n, also attrib Also *chained lightning* chiefly **NEast, West** *old-fash*
1 Lightning which moves rapidly in a forked or zigzag course; often fig: something which moves at great speed.
   1834 Davis *Letters Downing* 37 **NY,** I'm goin there like a streek of chain-lightning. **1872** Schele de Vere *Americanisms* 451, *Chain-lightning,* the Western term for "forked lightning," is generally rendered more redundant by being changed into *chained lightning.* **1879** Taylor *Summer-Savory* 109 **wNY,** One of those darting spiders that outlines chain-lightning has you by the nape of the neck. **1905** *DN* 3.5 **cCT,** *Chained lightning* . . . Forked lightning. **1910** *DN* 3.439 **wNY,** *Chain lightning* . . . In such sentences as: "He's quicker than chain lightning,"*i.e.,* remarkably quick. **1918** Mulford *Man from Bar-20* 141 *(DA),* He's dangerous, chain-lightnin' with his guns. **1930** Stoney-Shelby *Black Genesis* 154 **seSC,** Dere came a crackle o' chainlightnin' close by dem, an' a great roll o' t'under.
2 Strong, usu inferior liquor. [In ref to its powerful and rapid effect] Cf **white lightning**

1843 (1846) Haliburton *Attaché* (1st ser) 1.262, The drinks ain't good here; they hante no variety in them nother; no white-nose, apple-jack, stone-wall, chain-lightning, rail-road. **1867** Lowell *Biglow* 15 '**Up-country' MA,** I know ye ez I know the smell of ole chain-lightnin' whiskey. **1878** *Appletons' Jrl.* 5.416 **West,** Western people . . prefer to call whiskey *corn-juice* . . . And when they go farther and call it *chain-lightning,* they vividly set forth the style of its working. **1942** Berrey–Van den Bark *Amer. Slang* 99.8, *Strong liquor* . . . chain(ed) lightning *(esp. strong whiskey).*

chain-link cactus See **chain cactus**

chain of lightning n
=**yellow jacket.**
   1969 *DARE* (Qu. R21, . . *Stinging insects*) Inf **VT**13, Chain of lightning—yellow jacket: they come at you so fast.

chain pickerel n Also *chain pike, chainsides*
A **pickerel 1** *(Esox niger)* distinguished by the reticulated pattern on the sides and a duckbill-like snout. Also called **duck-billed pike, eastern pickerel, federation pike, grass pickerel, green jack, green pike, jack, jackfish, lake pickerel, pike, pond pickerel, red-finned pike, snake**
   1887 Goode *Amer. Fishes* 277, Its peculiar markings have given it the name of "Chain Pickerel." **1946** LaMonte *N. Amer. Game Fishes* 128, *Eastern Pickerel . . . Names:* Chain Pickerel, . . Chain Pike. **1968** *Julesburg Grit–Advocate* (CO) 7 Feb n.p. **NE,** The four species for which no entries were submitted were blue catfish, chain pickerel, buffalo, and sucker. **1972** Sparano *Outdoors Encycl.* 367, *Common names:* Chain pickerel, jack, chainsides. **1975** Evanoff *Catch More Fish* 86, The one usually caught and sought is the chain pickerel *(Esox niger).*

chain, rattle one's v phr Also *pull* or *yank one's chain*
To cause someone to act in an unusual or unwelcome manner.
   1968–69 *DARE* (Qu. BB40, . . *Somebody acting strangely: "All of a sudden he got up and left. What do you suppose_____him?"*) Inf **PA**185, Rattled his chain; **PA**209, Yanked his chain; (Qu. II22, *Expressions to tell somebody to keep to himself and mind his own business*) Inf **VA**2, Who pulled your chain?

chains and rings n
A children's game.
   1967 *DARE* (Qu. EE33, . . *Outdoor games*) Inf **MA**1, Chains and rings.

chain scratcher, chain scrubber See **chain dishcloth**

chainsides See **chain pickerel**

chain snake n [From the pattern of its black and white markings]
A **king snake 1** (here: *Lampropeltis getulus getulus*).
   1743 (1754) Catesby *Nat. Hist. Carolina* 2.52, As it wanted a Name, the best I could think of was, that of *Chain-Snake,* from some Resemblance of a Chain that seems in many Places to environ the Body. **1789** Morse *Amer. Geog.* 61, The Snakes which infest the United States, are the following, viz. The Rattle Snake . . Chain [Snake]. **1842** DeKay *Zool. NY* 3.37, The Chain Snake. *Coluber getulus* . . . Their northern and eastern range does not extend beyond New York, and they are found as far south as Louisiana. **1875** *Field & Forest* 1.30 **MD,** I observed . . a reptile which proved to be the Chain, or Thunder snake (Ophibolus getulus). **1935** Pratt *Manual Animals* 210, Chain-snake . . . Color black, with . . yellow or white dorsal bands which . . join one another, giving the effect of a chain. **1958** Conant *Reptiles & Amphibians* 167, Eastern kingsnake *Lampropeltis getulus getulus* . . . The "chain snake" —a shiny black serpent clad with large, bold links of white or cream.

chain-stretcher See **stretcher**

chainwork n Cf **change work**
A series of exchanges of work; see quot.
   1967 *DARE* (Qu. L5, *When a farmer gets help on a job from his neighbors in return for his help on their farms later on*) Inf **OH**31, Chainwork: one farmer helps another, then that one helps another and so on.

chainy See **china A**

chain, yank one's See **chain, rattle one's**

chair n Usu |čer, čεə|; in **SC, sNEng, Upstate NY** also |-e-|; in **NEast and Mid Atl** also |-æ-|; in folk speech, in **Sth and S Midl,** scattered in **PA, NEng** |-i-, -ɪ-|; rarely |-ɜ-| See **Pronc Intro**

3.I.1.b and quots 1961, 1976 Pronc-spp *chear, cheer, cher, chir, chur*

A Forms.

1774 in 1956 Eliason *Tarheel Talk* 308 **NC,** Cheer. **1822** *Ibid,* Chir. **1857** *Putnam's Mag.* 10.352/2 **CT,** Hev' a cheer? **1887** (1967) Harris *Free Joe* 101 **GA,** Fling a cheer at 'er! **1890** *DN* 1.67 **KY,** *Chair* [čæɚ]: sometimes [čǎ]. *Ibid* 71 **LA,** *Cheer, chur:* chair. **1899** (1912) Green *VA Folk-Speech, Cheer* . . . Chair. Chear. Chers. **1916** *DN* 4.340 **seOH,** Chair [čiɚ]. **1917** *DN* 4.409 **wNC, SC, KY, IL, NEng,** Cheer. **1938** Matschat *Suwannee R.* 156 **nFL, sGA,** If ye go a-courtin', they'll set ye in a chur. **1940** Richter *Trees* 155 **sOH** (as of early 1800s), And the young gal sot in the old woman's cheer. **1946** Stuart *Tales Plum Grove* 106 **seKY,** "Get you some chears," says Jake. "Let's sit under the shade and take it easy." **c1960** *Wilson Coll.* **csKY,** *Chair* is often [čer] or [čir]. **1961** Kurath–McDavid *Pronc. Engl.* 118–19 and map 40, [*Chair* is pronounced with /ɛ/ esp in PA, nWV, NJ, also NY, sNEng, wVT, and SC. /e/ is found as well in SC, esp the Low Country, and sNEng, Upstate NY. /æ/ occurs in all of NEng, esp neNEng, NEng settlements in NY, Upper South incl VA, adjoining parts of MD, sWV, NC. In folk speech /i ~ ɪ/ is used widely in the Sth and S Midl with scattered survivals in PA, NEng; /ɜ/ occurs in the same general area, but less frequently.] **1976** Allen *LAUM* 3.30, [In *theirs, care, chair:*] The common /ɛ/ of New England, Upstate New York, and North Midland speech is even more dominant in the U[pper] M[idwest], where there appear only a few surviving instances of the receding /æ/ and the occasional /e/ of New England.

B Senses.

1 In logging: =**barber chair.**

1958 McCulloch *Woods Words* **Pacific NW,** *Chair*—Part of the tree trunk left on the stump as a result of the tree falling before the back cut was through far enough to make a clean break between stump and butt log.

2 A cowboy's saddle.

1940 FWP *Guide NV* 75, A buckaroo's paraphernalia includes the following: the saddle, which the cow-country calls *cactus, hull, chair, centerfire, kak, pack,* or *rigging.*

chairback n, also attrib Also *armchair back* [*OEDS* 1858 →] Cf **chair set**

An antimacassar.

1880 *Harper's Mag.* 61.656/1, She . . carries home an embroidered 'Chairback'—the more dignified name that she gives nowadays to her 'tidy.' **1950** *WELS* (*Knitted or crocheted pieces placed on the back or arms of a chair for decoration and cleanliness*) 7 Infs, **WI,** Chairbacks; 2 Infs, Chairback sets. **1965–70** *DARE* (Qu. E10) 58 Infs, **widespread,** Chairbacks; TN31, 35, Armchair backs; MA63, PA136, Chairback sets.

chairbacker n Also *chairback (preacher), chair pusher* [See quot 1980] **Sth, S Midl** Cf **stump knocker, table tapper**

An unprofessional, part-time lay preacher.

1955 *PADS* 23.35, The average white Southerner may use the term *jackleg preacher* freely as a gloss for such more local terms as *chair-backer, stump-knocker, table-tapper,* and *yard-ax*—designations for a part-time voluntary preacher, normally without formal seminary training and generally with a low degree of competence. **1970** *DARE* (Qu. CC10) Inf NC87, Chairback, chair pusher; VA46, Chairback preacher. **1971** Wood *Vocab. Change* 262 **OK, TN,** An unprofessional, part-time lay preacher [3 infs, Chair backer]. **1980** *NADS Letters* ceVA [Black speaker], A chair back preacher was a man who was uneducated and he did not have his own church. He preached on the street corner and carried a chair with him which he used for his pulpit. *Ibid* SC, I [Raven McDavid] also got it *[chairbacker]* from some of my SC informants, I am not sure whether they were all black or not. The metaphor is simple: the preacher straddles a chair, hanging onto the back (which is turned toward the audience) and bangs on it or twists it or whatever as the spirit enters into him.

chair bark oak n [Perh folk-etym for **cherry bark oak**]

1965–70 *DARE* (Qu. T10, . . *Kinds of oak trees*) Infs AL11, MS31, WV7, 21, Chair bark oak.

chair board n Infreq *chair boarding*

=**chair rail.**

1854 *S. Lit. Messenger* 20.559/2 **nVA,** The wainscoting of walnut, and extending unbroken around the whole apartment to the height of what is called the chair-board. **1881** Vanderbilt *Social Flatbush* 67 **NY,** A wooden molding, called a "chair board," often . . extended around the

room, about three feet from the surbase. **1950** *WELS* (*Strip of wood . . along the bottom of a wall inside a room, joining to the floor . . . more than 8 inches*) 1 Inf, **swWI,** Chair boarding. **1966–70** *DARE* (Qu. D37, *The strip of wood about eight inches high along the bottom of the wall*) Infs DC12, MD21, 27, NC3, PA142, Chair board; (Qu. D38, . . *Higher than eight inches;* total Infs questioned, 75) Inf NC16, Chair board; (QR, near Qu. D37) Inf AR38, Chair board— around the wall; if people leaned back in chairs they would not mess up the walls. The chair top hits this board. Sometimes this is called a ['deˌdo].

chair buy v

To buy by mail order rather than at a store.

1967 Cerello *Dakota Co. MN* 48, It was my one wish to become rich enough some day and chair buy everything in the monkies' [=Montgomery Ward] catalog . . . The only disadvantage of chair buying as I can see it is that you don't get a chance to inspect what you're buying.

‡chair-fast adj [Prob by analogy with *bedfast*]

Confined to a chair, unable to move around on one's own.

1937 Sandoz *Slogum* 354 **NE** (as of 1900–20), Sundays he read Ruedy's books, . . talking to the old woman by the hour, pretty well chair-fast now by her arthritis.

chair pusher See **chairbacker**

chair rail n Also *chair railing board* Cf **chair board**

A protective strip of wood on a wall to prevent damage from the backs or rockers of chairs; wainscot; baseboard.

1968–70 *DARE* (Qu. D37, *The strip of wood about eight inches high along the bottom of the wall*) Infs NY239, VT7, Chair rail. **1968** *DARE* FW Addit NY88, Chair railing board—a board around a wall in a room about as high as the back of a chair to keep chairs from damaging the plaster when people leaned back in them. **1969** *AmSp* 44.12 **NW** [Painters' jargon], Chair rail . . . A protective rail run about the walls [*AmSp:* of a room] to protect them from damage [by] contact with tables or chairs. **1972** *Atlanta Letters* **GA,** He had sent her to the store earlier for "cheer" rail. My builder husband says it this way, too, when he's talking about chair rail.

chair set n Also *arm(chair) set* Cf **chairback**

An antimacassar.

1950 *WELS* (*Pieces placed on the back or arms of a chair for decoration and cleanliness*) 12 Infs, **WI,** Chair sets. **1954** *Harder Coll.* **cwTN,** Chair set. **1965–70** *DARE* (Qu. E10) 77 Infs, **widespread, but least freq in Sth, NEng,** Chair sets; 10 Infs, **scattered,** Armchair sets; MA124, Arm sets.

chair tidy See **tidy** n

chair walk n [Perh infl by **cakewalk 2b**]

The game of **musical chairs.**

1966 *DARE* (Qu. EE2, *Games that have one extra player—when a signal is given, the players change places, and the extra one tries to get a place*) Inf MI34, Chair walk.

chaland n Also sp *chalon* [LaFr < Fr *chaland, chalan;* see quot 1956] **seLA**

A small, flat-bottomed boat.

[**1931** Read *LA French* 135, Other La.-Fr. names for small, flat-bottomed boats, constructed of planks, are French *chaland* and *péniche.*] **1944** Kane *Deep Delta Country* 86 **seLA** (as of late 1800s), Soon, too, came the "chalons," floating department stores in miniature. **1956** Knipmeyer *Settlement Succession* 163 **LA,** Small rectangular flat-bottomed boats . . . The *chaland* is one type which is restricted to the lower bayou country . . . usually well built of inexpensive planking and is never painted . . . ten to fourteen feet long, two and a half to three feet wide, and from eight to twelve inches deep . . . *Chaland* has a broad meaning which includes rectangular, flat-bottomed boats of almost any size. [Footnote:] This usage is Louisiana French . . . Standard French has *chaland,* a barge or scow, and *chalan,* a rectangular, flat-bottomed river boat. **1967** LeCompte *Word Atlas* 220 **seLA,** Small, flatbottomed, rectangular boat . . [5 of 21 infs] chaland . . . *Chaland* is standard French for "flatboat."

chalina See **czarnina**

chalk n[1], also attrib **chiefly Gulf States, scattered W Midl** See Map Cf **chalk-eye** n, **chalkie**

A cheap or low-grade marble, usu made of chalk or similar material.

1908 *DN* 3.297 **eAL,wGA,** *Chalk* . . . A playing marble made of a chalk-like compound. "You can't stick no chalk on me." **1965–70** *DARE* (Qu. EE6c, *Cheap marbles*) 26 Infs, **chiefly Gulf States, scattered W Midl,** Chalks; **AR**28, **MS**1, Chalk marbles; (Qu. EE6b, *Small marbles*) Infs **LA**15, **MS**71, Chalks. [Of 28 Infs, 24 were old, 18 had grade school educ or less.]

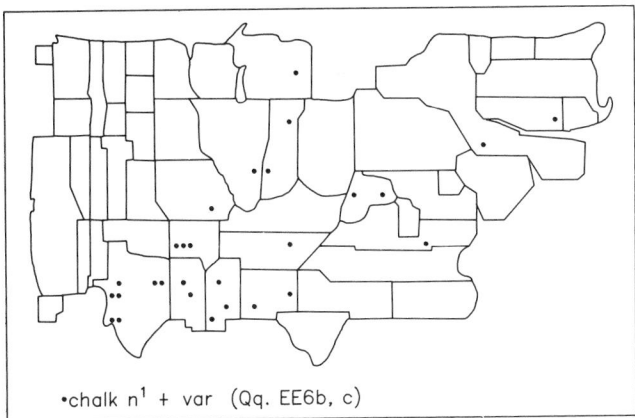

•chalk n¹ + var (Qq. EE6b, c)

chalk n² See **choc** n²

chalk-eye n Cf **chalkie**
=**chalk** n¹.
1969 *DARE* (Qu. EE6c, *Cheap marbles*) Inf **KY**24, Chalk-eyes.

chalk-eye v Pronc-sp *chawk eye*
1946 Greer–Petrie *Angeline Gits an Eyeful* 3 **csKY,** Hit wouldn't do fur me to ketch my little Jeems Henry *a-chawk eye'n* [=acting as golf caddy] fur great big, stroppin' men like that.

chalk-eyed adj
1904 *DN* 2.424 **Cape Cod MA,** *Chalk-eyed* . . . White eyed.

chalkie n, also attrib Also sp *chalky* [**chalk** n¹ + *-ie* familiarizing suff] **chiefly west of Missip R** *somewhat old-fash*
=**chalk** n¹.
1955 *PADS* 23.13 **OH** (as of 1900), *Chalky* . . . A marble made of chalk. **1958** *PADS* 29.31 **GA, OK, WA,** *Chalky.* **1965–70** *DARE* (Qu. EE6c, *Cheap marbles*) 15 Infs, **chiefly West of Missip R,** Chalkies. [14 of 15 Infs old] **1966** *DARE* Tape **OK**42, A chalkie, that's the lower-grade marble . . . chalkie marbles. **1971** Bright *Word Geog. CA & NV* 116, Chalkies 12 [responses].

chalk-line n [See quot 1945] **NEast** Cf **cream-shitter**
=**green heron.**
1843 DeKay *Zool. NY* 2.224, The *Poke, Chalk-line, Fly-up-the-creek,* or *Schyte Poke* as he was called by our Dutch progenitors, . . . is common throughout the State, and, from some curious notions respecting its habits, is held in general contempt. **1888** (1890) Warren *Birds PA* 63, Green Heron; Shite-poke; Chalk-line; Fly-up-the-creek. **1910** Eaton *Birds NY* 1.263, The Green Heron, . . or Chalk-line, is perhaps the most familiar member of this family in most parts of New York. **1945** McAtee *Nomina Abitera* 27, Green Heron . . . Chalk-line (from the whitish "line" of feces it lets fly), Massachusetts . . , New York . . , Chester County, Pennsylvania. **1951** Pough *Audubon Water Bird* 323.

chalk line, walk the See **walk the chalk line**

chalk maple n
A maple *(Acer leucoderme)* distinguished by its light-colored bark. Also called **sugar maple, whitebark maple**
1933 Small *Manual SE Flora* 825, [*A[cer] leucoderme* . .]—(*Chalk-maple.*) . . inner edge of Coastal Plain and Piedmont, Ga. to La., Ark. and N.C. **1960** Vines *Trees SW* 672, *Acer* . . *leucoderme* . . . It is sometimes planted as a shade tree in the South and has been cultivated since 1900 . . . Chalk maple may be distinguished by the green leaves (not glaucous) which are velvety-pubescent beneath, and by the very white bark. **1979** Little *Checklist U.S. Trees* 40.

chalk plant See **chalk weed**

chalk rabbit See **chalk the rabbit**

chalk rose n
A **stickleaf** (here: *Mentzelia decapetala*).

1948 Stevens *KS Wild Flowers* 321, The names 'sand-lily' and 'chalk-rose' are often used locally, but the plant *[Mentzelia decapetala]* . . is far removed . . from the lily family, and in respect to the flower is more like the cactus than the rose.

chalk the rabbit n Also *chalk rabbit, chalk the arrow* or *walk*
A children's game: =**arrow chase.**
1905 *DN* 3.73 **nwAR,** *Chalk the rabbit* . . . Name of a boys' out-door game. **1923** Acker *400 Games* 109, *Chalk the Arrow* (Arrow Chase). **1950** *WELS* (*Outdoor games*) 1 Inf, **ceWI,** Chalk the rabbit. **1953** Brewster *Amer. Nonsinging Games* 40 **MO,** *Chalk the Walk* . . . two groups, one to do the hiding and the other to be the hunters. Those who are to hide must make marks with chalk on sidewalks, fences, buildings, etc. to show the direction in which they are going. **1966** *DARE* File **neIN,** Chalk the rabbit (Follow the arrow)—a kind of chase game; **nMI,** Chalk the rabbit—arrows on the sidewalk, follow the trail. **1970** *DARE* (Qu. EE33, . . *Outdoor games*) Inf **IL**116, Chalk rabbit—old-fashioned. Kids steal chalk and make arrows on the sidewalk with it directing [others] to hidden players.

chalk weed n Also *chalk plant*
A **baby's breath 1** (here: *Gypsophila paniculata*).
1940 Clute *Amer. Plant Names* 166, Chalk-plant. *Gypsophila paniculata. Ibid* 260, *Gypsophila paniculata.* Chalk-weed, baby's breath.

chalky n See **chalkie**

chalky adj
Brittle; see quot.
1965–70 *DARE* (Qu. KK24, *Something that breaks easily: "She broke her arm again; her bones must be _____.")* Infs **AL**40, **AR**51, **CA**105, **IN**31, 41, **LA**2, **MS**45, **NC**79, **OK**9, 45, **TX**10, 32, Chalky.

chalon See **chaland**

chalupa n |čǝˈlupǝ| [MexSpan "small canoe; small oval corn cake"] **chiefly SW**
A dish usu of flat tortillas with meat, beans, and condiments.
[**1895** *Jrl. Amer. Folkl.* 8.61 **Mex,** There were enchiladas, chaloupas, fried chicken, cold turkey, and I dare not say what else.] **1939** Berolzheimer *U.S. Cookbook* 583, Taos salmon chalupas with Spanish onion rings. **1967** *DARE* (Qu. H45, *Dishes made with meat, fish, or poultry that everybody around here would know*) Inf **TX**29, Chalupa. **1967** *DARE* Tape **TX**41, Chalupa [čǝˈlupǝ] . . . Tortilla of corn . . . We have beans on it . . mayonnaise and cheese and tomatoes on it . . . [it's] flat. **1980** *Milwaukee Sentinel* (WI) 19 June sec 4 3/3, [Recipe:] *Chalupa* . . *pinto beans* . . *pork roast* . . *onion* . . *chili powder* . . *cumin* . . *oregano* . . *green chilies—Corn chips.* **1980** *DARE* File **TX,** In Laredo a chalupa is a flat tortilla with meat and beans on it.

chamber n, also attrib Usu |ˈčembǝ(r)|, infreq |ˈčæmbǝ(r)| Pronc-spp *charmber, chaumber, chawmber*
A Forms.
1899 (1912) Green *VA Folk-Speech, Chaumber* . . . Chamber . . . Charmber. **1902** Eggleston *Dorothy South* 293 **VA,** The word chamber was pronounced "chawmber." **1917** *DN* 4.389 **neOH, VT,** *Chamber* [čæmbr]. **1941** *LANE* Map 337 **NEng,** [*Chamber* is occasionally pronounced [čæmbǝ] throughout New England].
B Senses.
1 An upper room or floor of a house, freq used as a bedroom.
chiefly NEng
1639 (1908) Winthrop *Jrl.* 1.311 **Boston MA,** Briscoe . . came in and went up to his chamber to lodge there. **1694** in 1852 MA Hist. Soc. *Coll.* 4th ser 1.105, Ye houses are built generally low; but very few of ym have an upright chamber; ye lower rooms are built very high. **1746** in 1915 NH *Prov. & State Papers* 33.98, The use of the Stairs in the Said Entry to pass up & Down to the Chamber & Garret. **1800** (1907) Thornton *Diary* 178 **PA,** Took her up in my Chamber while I dressed. **1902** (1904) Rowe *Maid of Bar Harbor* 265 **ME,** Roses everywhere, in chambers, parlor, and hall. **1917** *DN* 4.389 **neOH, VT,** *Chamber* [čæmbr] . . . Chamber, room, usually on the upper floor of a house; also the whole of the upper floor. **1926** *AmSp* 2.79 **ME. 1926** *DN* 5.386 **ME. 1937** FWP *Guide ME* 87, On the second floor there were usually two large rooms at the front of the house called 'chambers.' **1941** *LANE* Map 337 **NEng,** *Bedroom* . . . *Chamber* is restricted by many informants to a bedroom on the second (or third) floor . . . Many other informants use this term to denote any room on an upper floor, not necessarily a bedroom. In houses where the second floor is not partitioned into separate rooms, the *chamber* may be the entire upper floor.

Ibid Map 345. **1946** *PADS* 6.44 **ME,** *Chamber:* Always upstairs, and as *the chamber* a large, often unfinished or "open" room, but also *front chamber* for a finished bedroom on the front of the house. **1950** *WELS (A sleeping room in a house)* 3 Infs, **WI,** Chamber—old-fashioned; *(Room for visitors to sleep in)* 3 Infs, **WI,** Guest chamber [1 Inf terms it old-fashioned]; 1 Inf, Bed chamber—occasional; 1 Inf, Chamber—old-fashioned; 1 Inf, Chamber [is] used by an aunt of mine. **1959** *VT Hist.* new ser 27.129, Chamber . . . Bedroom or other room. Sometimes used with another word, as It's up in the north *chamber* bedroom; or, in the woodhouse *chamber.* Usually, in phrases, such as in the front *chamber* or in the shed *chamber.* Common. Older people.

2 An upper floor or room of a barn, house or other building, used for storage, esp of corn. **chiefly NEng** Cf **barn chamber**
   1644 (1914) Essex Inst. *Coll.* 50.320 **MA,** Corne upon the ground, 3li.; corne upon the chamb., 18s. **1667** (1887) East Hampton NY *Records* 1.120, Mary & I had brought the corne into the chamber. **1864** ME Bd. Ag. *Abstract for 1863* 25, He harvested and carried into his chamber a good crop of sound corn. **1939** *LANE* Map 106 **NEng,** Whatever corn is raised is usually kept in the same building as the grain (in the *corn house* or the *granary* . .), or else in the barn, the attic or the loft of the ell or wood house (in the *corn chamber*). [*Chamber* was given by six infs; comments: "corn was often stored in the chamber in the ell"; "*corn chamber,* over the wood shed"; "*corn chamber,* in the barn loft"; "over the wood shed"; "in the ell chamber . . on the upper floor of the ell."] **1967** *DARE* Tape **MA**117, Kept that corn up in the attic—up overhead in the kitchen—up in the chamber. **1968–69** *DARE* (Qu. D4, *The space up under the roof, usually for storing things*) Inf **VT**3, Shed chamber; **MA**42, Woodshed chamber. **1979** *UpCountry* Jan 38 **csME,** The beans were stored in kegs in the unfinished chamber over the ell.

3 A room on the main floor of a house, usu used as a sitting room and a bedroom. **VA**
   1863 Hopley *Life South* 1.204 **VA,** The lady led me into the "chamber," as the family sitting-room of a Virginia house is called, comprising bed-room and nursery as well. **a1883** (1911) Bagby *VA Gentleman* 12, There was . . a large hall or passage, a parlor and dining-room, "the chamber" proper for the old lady and for everybody, and a fine old-time staircase leading to the guest-chambers. **1902** Eggleston *Dorothy South* 292 **VA,** The chamber, in an old plantation house, was that room on the ground floor in which the master of the plantation, whether married or unmarried, slept. It was the family room always. Into it came those guests whose intimacy was sufficient to warrant intrusion upon the penetralia. **1946** *PADS* 5.14 **VA,** *Chamber* . . A sitting room on the first floor, usually with a bed; in the Tidewater area, among older people. **1949** Kurath *Word Geog.* 46 **eVA,** The Virginia Tidewater has . . *chamber* . . for a downstairs bedroom-living room. **1950** *Hench Coll.,* George Zeliner, Native of Dinwiddie County [VA] was talking about a house he had seen . . in the mountains north of Syria, VA . . . "Next to the kitchen," said George, "is the chamber." Some one asked him what he meant. He answered, "Their bed-room and sitting room. The parlor is for seeing guests—in case you have a parlor. The chamber is their own room."

4 occas in combs: A vessel for urine or waste; a chamber pot. *euphem, somewhat old-fash* Cf **pot chamber**
   1829 in 1956 Eliason *Tarheel Talk* 264 **NC,** Chamber [for chamber pot]. **1899** (1912) Green *VA Folk-Speech, Charmber* . . . A chamber pot. **1907** *DN* 3.221 **nwAR, sIL,** Chamber. **1950** *PADS* 13.17 **cTX,** *Chamber* in the sense of a room is known from reading, but it is not used in conversation because *chamber* is the common word for a chamber pot. **1950** *WELS (Utensil kept under a bed for use at night)* 36 Infs, **WI,** Chamber [2 term it old-fashioned, 1 uses it occasionally]; 1 Inf, Bed chamber—old-fashioned. **c1960** *Wilson Coll.* **csKY,** *Chamber* . . . much more modest as a word than *pot.* Short for chamber pot. **1965** Guthrie *Blue Hen's Chick* 7 **MT,** For a toilet, a privy, with the complements of chambers and slop jars on frozen nights. **1965–70** *DARE* (Qu. F38) 404 Infs, **widespread,** Chamber; 8 Infs, **scattered,** Bed chamber; **KS**4, **VA**22, Night chamber; **VA**22, Glass chamber. [Of all Infs responding to the question, 70% were old; of those giving these responses, 83% were old.]

‡5 A cow's udder.
   1969 *DARE* (Qu. K4) Inf **GA**77, Bag [is] old-fashioned; [called] chamber today.

‡6 See quot.
   1969 *DARE* (Qu. X29, *Joking or uncomplimentary words for a person's face*) Inf **GA**77, Chamber.

chamber bucket n Also *chamber pail*
   A chamber pot.
   1967–70 *DARE* (Qu. F38, *Utensil kept under the bed for use at night*) Infs **PA**136, 242, Chamber bucket; **SC**70, Chamber pail.

chamber lye n [**chamber 4;** *OED chamber-lye* 1577 →] **chiefly Sth, S Midl, West**
   Urine; occas, a mixture containing urine used for medicinal purposes.
   1899 (1912) Green *VA Folk-Speech, Charmber-lye* . . . Urine. **1928** *DN* 6.63 **Ozarks,** Modest Ozark women never say *urine,* but use the word *chamber-lye,* even when talking to a physician. **1933** *AmSp* 8.1.48 **Ozarks,** *Chamber-lye* . . . Urine. Also a mixture of urine and sweet oil, often administered to infants as a medicine for various digestive ailments. **1935** Davis *Honey* 322 **OR,** They didn't know enough to pour chamber lye out of a boot. **1942** Whipple *Joshua* 37 **UT,** Chamber lye, she decided; there was nothing better for chapped skin. **1945** Saxon *Gumbo Ya-Ya* 561 **LA,** Chamber lye: urine. **c1960** *Wilson Coll.* **csKY,** *Chamber lye* . . . Now very rarely heard.

chambermaid n
1 A person who does the daily cleaning chores in a stable. *joc*
   1928 *Ruppenthal Coll.* **KS,** Chambermaid in a livery stable—(humorous or disparagement) one whose duties were largely to clean livery stables . . [or] any task regarded as menial. **1968** Adams *Western Words* 60, Chambermaid to the mules—The logger's title for a stable caretaker.

2 In railroading: see quot.
   1943 *AmSp* 18.163, Chambermaid. Machinist in roundhouse.

chamber mug n **chiefly NEng**
   A chamber pot.
   1948 Bean *Yankee Auctioneer* 142 **wMA,** Miniature music boxes are another collector's item that always commands a ready sale . . . I heard of one which was hidden in the cover of a chamber mug. **1950** *WELS* 1 Inf, **csWI,** Chamber mug. **1956** Eliason *Tarheel Talk* 187 **NC** (as of c1750–1860), The common indoor receptacle was regularly called a *chamber* or *chamber mug,* never anything coarser. **1965–70** *DARE* (Qu. F38, *Utensil kept under the bed for use at night*) 10 Infs, **chiefly NEng,** Chamber mug. [9 Infs old]

chamber pail See **chamber bucket**

chamberwork n *old-fash*
   Housework; housecleaning.
   1870 Parton *Ginger Snaps* 20 **NEast,** Having done chamber-work, or cooking, for such a number of years in New York, they don't need *any* lady to instruct them how! **1885** U.S. Bur. Indian Affairs *Report* 161 **NC,** The girls also take great interest in the household duties, such as sewing, cooking, chamber-work, &c. **1931–33** *LANE Worksheets* **seMA,** *Chamberwork* . . Sweeping, dusting, making beds. **1940–41** Cassidy *WI Atlas,* Doing the chamber work! Clearing the table, straightening up. [Inf 70 yrs old] **1950** *WELS* 1 Inf, **csWI,** *Chamber* used by an aunt of mine: "I have to do my chamber work" = make beds, dust, empty pots.

cham-chack n Also *cham-chat, chamchucker* [Imit] **chiefly S Atl**
   =**red-bellied woodpecker.**
   1932 Howell *FL Bird Life* 307, *Centúrus carolínus* . . *Cham-chack.* **1938** Matschat *Suwannee R.* 26, **nFL, sGA,** Cham-chack and white-shirt peck cypress. **1949** *AmSp* 24.107 **FL,** *Cham-chat* . . . A variety of small woodpecker. **1949** Sprunt–Chamberlain *SC Bird Life* 332 **SC,** *Centurus carolinus carolinus* . . . Cham-chack. **1950** *PADS* 14.19 **SC,** *Cham-chack* . . . The red-bellied woodpecker. **1955** *Oriole* 20.1.10, *Red-bellied Woodpecker* . . . Cham-chack, Cham-chat, Cham-chucker (all in reference to common utterances of this polyphonic bird).

chameleon n [Prob for **carnelian**]
   A type of marble.
   1966 *DARE* (Qu. EE6d, *Special marbles*) Inf **SD**3, Chameleons [kə'miljənz].

chamis(a) See **chamise**

chamisal n, also attrib Also sp *chemese, chemisal, chemise, chemizal, chimisal* [AmSpan *chamiso* + *-al,* "a grove of"] **CA**
   A dense growth or thicket of **chamise 1;** occas transf to the

individual shrub: see quots 1897 and 1898.   Also called **chamise brush**

1853 House of Representatives. Ex. Doc. 91 (Bentley *Spanish Terms*), *Traveling* . . is rendered very trying by . . patches of dense masses of shrubbery known as the chemizal. **1867** Harte *Condensed Novels* 244, Except the occasional pattering of a squirrel, or a rustling in the *chimisal* bushes, there were no signs of life. **1897** Parsons *Wild Flowers CA* 60, Chamisal. The chamisal forms a large part of the chapparal of our mountain slopes . . . It is an evergreen shrub, with small clustered, needle-like leaves. **1898** *Jrl. Amer. Folkl.* 11.226, *Adenostoma fasciculatum* . . *chemisal*, chemise brush, greasewood, Cal. **1902** U.S. Bur. Plant Industry *Bulletin* 12.31, These chaparral areas . . have become landmarks, the word chamisal, sometimes corrupted into chemisal, chemise, or chemese being adopted as a local name. **1931** Dayton *Western Browse Plants* 53 *(DA)*, Chamiso is especially characteristic on long steep slopes where it forms a chamisal, or dense impenetrable thicket. **1967** *DARE* (Qu. C28, *A place where underbrush, weeds, vines and small trees grow together so that it's nearly impossible to get through)* Inf **CA4**, Chamisal [ˌčɑmiˈsɑl].

chamise n, also attrib   Also sp *chamis, chamisa, chamiso, chamiza, chamizo, chemise* [AmSpan *chamiso* < Span *chamizo* half-burnt stick of kindling wood; *chamiza* brush used as kindling wood]

1 A resinous evergreen shrub *(Adenostoma fasciculatum)* most abundant in the coast ranges of California where it forms dense thickets: see **chamisal**.   **chiefly CA**   Also called **greasewood**

1848 Emory *Notes Reconnoissance* 77, In one view could be seen clustered, the . . green wood acacia, chamiza, . . and a new variety of sedge. **1869** Brace *New West* 94, The chaparral, with which we made such a disagreeable acquaintance, is generally a thorny, impervious shrubbery, made up of the Chinquapin . . and the Chamiso. **1893** *Jrl. Amer. Folkl.* 6.141, *Adenostoma fasciculatum*, chamise; chamise brush. S. Barbara Co., Cal. **1915** (1926) Armstrong *Western Wild Flowers* 228, Chamise . . . sometimes covers miles of mountain slopes, looking a good deal like heather when it is not in bloom. **1937** U.S. Forest Serv. *Range Plant Hdbk.* B8, In southern California, chemise provides protection for very valuable watersheds from erosion. **1940** FWP *Guide NM* 111, *Chamizo*—Brush used as kindling wood. **1962** Sweet *Plants of West* 18, Chamise . . . burns very quickly with a bright flame and supplies quick heat for cooking.

2 Any of var other shrubs which often form similar thickets, esp **wingscale** in the West generally, but also **buckbrush 3c** and **squawbush** in the Southwest and **toyon** in California.

1937 U.S. Forest Serv. *Range Plant Hdbk.* B27, Fourwing saltbush . . . in New Mexico . . is almost wholly known as chamiza, and that name (or its variants, chamise and chamiso) is in common use elsewhere. *Ibid* B41, Wedgeleaf ceanothus, known locally as . . chamise, chaparral, and greasebush, . . . frequently forms extensive, impenetrable thickets. **1960** Vines *Trees SW* 236, *Atriplex canescens* . . . is known also by the vernacular names of . . Chamiso, Chamiza, and Costillas de Vaca. *Ibid* 696, Knife-leaf Condalia . . . is known under the vernacular names of . . Squaw-bush, Chamis, [etc]. **1968** Abbey *Desert Solitaire* 29 **seUT**, Along the washes and the rare perennial streams you'll find a third community: . . rabbitbrush or *chamisa*.

chamise brush n   Also sp *chamiso brush, chemise ~* [AmSpan *chamiso* + *brush*]   **CA**   **=chamisal.**

1893 *Jrl. Amer. Folkl.* 6.141, *Adenostoma fasciculatum*, chamise; chamise brush. S. Barbara Co., Cal. **1897** *Outing* 30.552/1 **CA**, The deer's favorite browse is chemisal—"chemise brush" it is commonly called. **1904** *New York Tribune* (NY) 17 July sec 4 3/1 **CA**, One afternoon they located a grizzly, and ran him into a field of chamiso brush.

chamise lily n   Also sp *chemise lily* [*chamise* < AmSpan *chamiso* + *lily*, so called from its growing in association with **chamise**]   **CA**

1 **=dogtooth violet** (esp *Erythronium giganteum*).

1897 Parsons *Wild Flowers CA* 136, Fawn-lily. Dog's-tooth violet. Chamise-lily. *Erythronium giganteum* . . . Indeed, in Mendocino County they are commonly known as "chamise-lilies." **1915** (1926) Armstrong *Western Wild Flowers* 28, In California [*Erythronium* spp] are often called Chamise Lily. **1934** Haskin *Wild Flowers Pacific Coast* 25, Giant dog-tooth violet . . . Other local names are . . adder's-tongue, curly lily, and chemise lily.

2 **=chaparral lily.**

1911 Jepson *Flora CA* 95, Chaparral Lily . . . Near the coast called Redwood Lily; towards the interior Chaparral or Chamise Lily. **1959** Munz–Keck *CA Flora* 1342, *L[ilium] rubescens* . . . Chaparral Lily. Redwood Lily. Chamise Lily.

chamiso See **chamise**

chamiso brush See **chamise brush**

chamiza, chamizo See **chamise**

champ See **chomp** v

champean, champeen See **champion**

champer off v phr [Alter of *chamfer* + *off*; *OED* 1788]

1914 *DN* 4.155 **Cape Cod MA**, *Champer off* . . . Chop, rasp or hack away bit by bit. "If the board's too wide, champer off a bit with the hatchet."

champion n, adj   Usu |ˈčæmpɪən|; occas |čæmˈpin| Pronc-spp *champean, champeen*

Std senses, var forms.

1905 *DN* 3.60 **NE**, *Champeen*. Frequent pronunciation of *champion*. **1922** *DN* 5.134 **cWest**, *Champeen*. **1923** (1946) Greer–Petrie *Angeline Doin' Society* 24 **csKY**, He was the champeen player of Merry Oaks. **1934** Carmer *Stars Fell on AL* 44, Next'll be Monkey Brown, champeen of Tuscaloosa County. **1941** Faulkner *Men Working* 121 **MS**, Hub was telling me 'bout . . picking right 'longside the Arkansaw champeen. **1941** *Time* 6 Oct 53/1 **NYC**, Brooklynites . . . swarmed into Manhattan . . to welcome home their "champeens." **1943** Stuart *Taps* 204 **eKY**, Say, you are that champean lassie maker in Kentucky, ain't ye? **c1960** *Wilson Coll.* **csKY**, Champion is often [ˌtʃæmˈpin].

cha-muck-a-muck n [Cf Chinook jargon *muck-a-muck* food]

A relish; see quot.

1953 Randolph *Down in Holler* 233 **Ozarks**, Cha-muck-a-muck . . . A relish of mixed pickles, highly seasoned. May Kennedy McCord, of Springfield, Mo., says that it is identical with what used to be called *chow-chow*. Some Indians at Pack, Mo., told me that it is a Cherokee word.

chance n   Usu |čæn(t)s|; also, **esp NEng and VA**, |-ɑ-|; occas, **esp sAppalachians**, |-e(ɪ)-|; occas |čænst|; infreq |čænč|; rarely |čɪnč(t)|.   Pronc-spp *chaince, chanch, chanc(e)t, chanst, charnce, chaunce*

A Forms.

1815 Humphreys *Yankey in England* 104, Chaunce, chance. **1853** Simms *Sword & Distaff* 335 **SC**, You won't let the chaince slip of getting yourself into good quarters. **a1883** (1911) Bagby *VA Gentleman* 56, If he is a tidewater man, he does not say "chance," but "charnce." **1890** *DN* 1.8 **Baltimore MD**, [čens]. **1900** *Bookman* 11.449 **VA**, The English or Cavalier "a" was retained by Virginians in the entire class of words now represented by medial "a" in American educated speech . . . For example: . . the sound of the Virginia "a" in words as . . advance, chance, dance . . . This broad sound of "a" . . is unquestionably the most distinguishing feature of the Virginia dialect. **1903** *DN* 3.309 **seMO**, *Chanst* . . . Chance. **1904** Day *Kin o' Ktaadn* 181 **ME**, It was certainly a glorious chanst for them hungry an' lazy Injuns. **1907** *DN* 3.229 **nwAR, seMO**, *Chanst*. **1914** *DN* 4.70 **ME, nNH**, *Chanst*. **1931** Goodrich *Mt. Homespun* 40 **sAppalachians**, Aunt Liza said I did "mighty well for the chaince" I'd had in my "raising." **1933** Rawlings *South Moon* 53 **FL**, Give the young folks a chancet to git acquainted. **1942** Whipple *Joshua* 9 **UT**, Give me a chanct! **1943** *LANE* Map 570 **chiefly nNEng**, *Another chance* . . . [tʃɑn(t)s], [tʃɛnts], [tʃɔnts]. **1950** *PADS* 13.22 **sKY**, *Chanct* . . . Chance. Fairly common among uneducated. **1954** *Harder Coll.* **cwTN**, Chance [čɪnč], also [čɪnčt]. **1956** *Hall Coll.* **wNC**, That's about all the chance [čeɪns] I have of makin' a livin'. **1970** *DARE* File **nwTN**, Chanch [čænč].

B Senses.

1 usu with an adj: A quantity, amount, or number.   **chiefly Sth, S Midl**

1805 (1965) Ordway *Jrls.* 316 **KY**, The men returned with a fine chance of Elk meat. **1822** Woods *2 Yrs. Residence* 294 **IL**, I have got a few beefs, and a tolerable chance of corn. **1842** *Knickerbocker* 20.491 **GA**, There's a mighty chance of lawyers' lies in the papers. **1843** (1916) Hall *New Purchase* 92 **IN**, She . . pulled off what she called "a right smart chance of rattles." *Ibid* 294, A small chance of Pukes. **1881** Pierson *In the Brush* 6 **KY**, He has broken a right smart chance of brush. **1902** *DN*

2.231 **sIL. 1903** *DN* 2.309 **seMO. 1908** *DN* 3.297 **eAL, wGA. 1915** *DN* 4.181 **swVA. 1957** *AmSp* 32.284 **NC**, *Chance* ('amount'). **1968** *Filson Club Hist. Qrly.* 158 **KY**, To gather a fine chance of berries, that is, an indefinite amount.

2 By ext: a distance; a length of time. *old-fash, rare*

1840 Simms *Border Beagles* 2.98 **MS**, It's on the other road, and a smart round about chance to get to it. **1845** (1968) Simms *Wigwam & Cabin* (1st ser) 55 **sNC**, There I stood, a pretty considerable chance. **1927** *AmSp* 2.350 **WV**, *Chance, a right smart* . . a long distance.

3 A specimen, an example. *old-fash*

1830 Royall *Letters AL* 190 **wPA**, Honorable *Mr. Mitchell*, is a poor *chance*, as we say in the West. He had a letter for me, and after keeping it a long time, refused to see me, and carefully kept his back towards me . . . I hope Pennsylvania will not send him again. **1849** *Knickerbocker* 34.113 **GA**, He strode a 'right smart chance of a critter,' that could n't be beat in 'them diggins'. **1858** in 1956 Eliason *Tarheel Talk* 264 **NC**, Myself an Mr White went down to the Mockerron landing an it was a bad chance. thare was A grateal of work to do on the road being so wet. **1888** *KS State Hist. Soc. Coll.* 4.245, We found Chicago then, as I first heard the expression—"a right smart chance of a place"—with some 30,000 or 40,000 inhabitants. Nothing beautiful about it. **1917** *DN* 4.409 **NC Mts**, A poor chance of a place to spend the night.

4 See quot.

1923 *DN* 5.203 **swMO**, *Chance* . . . Doubt. 'Ithout a chance hit'll be a-rainin' ag'in mornin'.

5 An area of land suitable for logging; a timber claim. [Cf *DAE chance* a person's lot of land; used in Maryland 1667–1700]

1946 Peattie *Pacific Coast* 230 **WA**, A homestead claim of 160 acres was yours, almost for the asking. Clear an acre, build a cabin that looked more or less (generally less) like a home, putter about it for a bit, and lo! a timber "chance" was yours, on which stood, perhaps, ten million feet of the finest timber on earth. **1956** Sorden–Ebert *Logger's Words* **Gt Lakes**, A good chance is one where conditions are favorable for easy logging. **1958** McCulloch *Woods Words* 31 **Pacific NW**, *Chance*—A logging operation, or show. **1975** Gould *ME Lingo*, *Chance*—In the sense of opportunity, referring to the area where a chopper is cutting trees. Paid by board feet or cords, a man would have a good *chance* or a poor *chance* depending on the growth.

chance along n

1975 Gould *ME Lingo*, *Chance along*—To coastal sailors, a *chance along* is a fair wind with favorable weather.

chance blow n

=**chance child**.

1852 (1971) Melville *Pierre* 131 **NEng**, Some chance-blow of a splendid, worthless rake, doomed to inherit both parts of her infecting portion—vileness and beauty.

chance child n [Engl dial] Cf **come-by-chance**

An illegitimate child.

1950 *WELS* (A child whose parents were not married) 1 Inf, **csWI**, Chance child. **1967** *DARE* (Qu. Z11b) Inf **ID5**, Chance child. **1973** Allen *LAUM* 1.344 **ND**, A child born out of wedlock . . . [1 inf] chance child.

chance off v phr

To raffle (something) off.

1930s in 1944 *ADD* **eWV**, *Chance off.* To raffle off (a turkey, or the like). **1948** *AmSp* 33.69 **cwNJ**, The local American Legion post was recently selling chances on a refrigerator that was to be raffled . . . The sign propped up against it read: To be chanced off. **1968** *Co. Rec.* (Denton MD) 8 May sec 1 4/6, Plans were perfected for chancing off a lovely silk coverlet.

chancet See **chance**

‡**chancey's mare** n [Perh for *chance's mare* or *chauncey's mare*]

=**shank's mare**.

1967 *DARE* (Qu. Y24, . . *To go on foot: "I can't get a ride, so I'll just have to _____."*) Inf **TX18**, Ride chancey's mare.

chanch, chanct See **chance A**

chancy adj

1 Lucky, fortunate; good-natured. [Scots]

1928 Chapman *Happy Mt.* 29 **seTN**, They fought for the chanciest

places. **1930** Shoemaker *1300 Words* 12 **cPA Mts** (as of c1900), *Chancy*—A person willing to take chances, fortunate, good-natured.

2 Doubtful; uncertain. [*OED* 1860 →]

1903 *DN* 2.296 **Cape Cod MA** (as of 1850s), *Chancy if.* Doubtful if. 'If we wait for him, chancy if he comes.' **1914** *DN* 4.151 **eME**, *Chancy if* . . . Doubtful if.

chanery, chaney See **china A**

chaney brier See **China brier**

changa n [AmSpan]

An introduced **mole cricket** (*Scapteriscus vicinus*).

1901 U.S. Dept. Ag. *Yearbook* 510, The *"changa,"* . . a kind of a mole-cricket, which has become very troublesome. It is believed this insect was introduced from South America in guano. **1928** Earle *Sugar Cane* 174, The Mole Cricket, or Changa . . is a soil insect. **1965** Blickenstaff *Insects* 290, Changa . . . *Scapteriscus vicinus* Scudder.

change v[1] *Infreq change over; ppl adj changed* **chiefly Sth, sAppalachians** See Map *euphem* Cf **alter** v

To castrate; infreq, to spay (a domestic animal).

1915 *DN* 4.181 **swVA**, *Change* . . =*alter*, to castrate. **1931–33** *LANE Worksheets* **seMA**, Changed, spayed—of a female dog. **1933** Rawlings *South Moon* 149 **FL**, We better be changin' them two boars, Aunt Py-tee, if you aim to make fitten barrows outen 'em. **1939** *LANE* Map 210 **NEng**, Castrate . . [approx 15 infs responded with] *change (over)*. **1946** *PADS* 5.15 **VA**, *Change* . . Castrate; fairly common. **1950** *PADS* 14.19 **Charleston SC**, *Change* . . . Same as *alter*. "Git a bull an' change um for a ox." **1965–70** *DARE* (Qu. K70, . . *Castrating an animal*) 25 Infs, **scattered Sth, sAppalachians**, Change; (Qu. K25, . . *Steer*) Inf **WY4**, Changed bull; (Qu. K58, . . *A castrated pig*) Inf **OH41**, Changed pig. [22 of 27 Infs old, 17 rural] **1973** Allen *LAUM* 1.251 **IA**, Castrate . . . [2 infs] change.

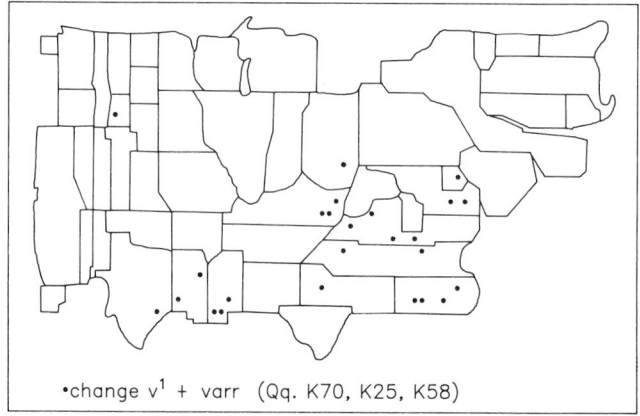

•change v[1] + varr (Qq. K70, K25, K58)

change n, v[2] See **change work**

changeance intj

In marble play: see quot.

1980 *NADS Letters* **cnAL**, The cries "changeance" and "no changeance" permit and prohibit change of toy [=taw].

change baby n [From *change of life* menopause + *baby*]

1952 Giles *40 Acres* 39 **eTN**, Kenneth is what is called around here a "change baby." Long after Miss Bessie thought her childbearing days were over he made an unexpected, and it may be even an unwelcome, appearance.

change bird n

=**winter wren**.

1951 *AmSp* 26.270 **SC**, *Change bird* for the wood wren in South Carolina, where this bird's spirited whistling is supposed to presage a turn in the weather.

changed ppl adj

1 Of milk: slightly sour. **chiefly Nth** Cf **blinky**

1950 *WELS* (Milk . . *beginning to turn sour*) 1 Inf, **WI**, Changed—old-fashioned; 1 Inf, Changed milk. **1966–70** *DARE* (Qu. H58) Infs **ME16, NY218, PA234**, Changed; **NY21**, Changed milk.

2 See **change** v[1].

change help, change labor See **change work**

change off v phr *chiefly W Midl, Missip Valley*

Of the wind: to alter in direction; to decrease in velocity.

1954 *Harder Coll.* **cwTN,** Change off—Of the wind: suddenly to begin to blow in another direction. **1965–70** *DARE* (Qu. B15, *When the wind suddenly begins to blow in a different direction*) Infs **AL**61, **AR**6, **IL**2, 7, **IN**71, **LA**40, **MS**72, **TN**33, 34, **WV**7, Changed off; **MO**2, Changed off directions; **AR**17, Changing off; (Qu. B13, *When the wind begins to decrease*) Inf **OH**36, Changing off.

change over See change v[1]

changes n pl *euphem*

Menstruation.

1930 Shoemaker *1300 Words* **cPA Mts** (as of c1900), *Changes*—Female sickness. **1968** *DARE* (Qu. AA27, . . *Menstruation*) Inf **VA**31, Changes.

change time See **change work**

change up v phr

1 To exchange or shift positions; to change one's clothes.

1905 *DN* 3.73 **nwAR,** *Change up* . . . 1. To exchange. 'They changed up places.' 2. To shift positions . . . [e.g. at] card games . . . parties. **1908** *DN* 3.297 **eAL, wGA,** *Change up* . . . To exchange positions. **1940** *Qrly. Jrl. Speech* 26.265 **VA,** One who *changes clothes* is "changing up."

2 See quot.

1905 *DN* 3.73 **nwAR,** *Change up* . . . To reform, do better.

change-up n

See quots.

1905 *DN* 3.74 **nwAR,** *Change-up* . . . A change. 'There'll have to be a change-up soon.' Universal. **1908** *DN* 3.297 **eAL, wGA,** *Change-up* . . . A change. **1959** McAtee *Oddments* 4 **NC,** *Change-up* . . change . . . "He has had a change-up."

change words v phr

To exchange words, speak.

1942 Hurston *Dust Tracks* 35 **FL,** Let me change a few words with him—and I am of the word-changing kind—and he was ready to change ends. *Ibid* 51, Don't change too many words if you aim to fight.

change work v phr, n For varr, see quots *chiefly Nth, N Midl*
See Map Cf **exchange work**

To give and receive help reciprocally; an exchange of labor.

1899 Garland *Boy Life* 194 **IA,** A good part of the fall's labor consisted in "changing works" with the neighbors, thus laying up a stock of unpaid labor ready for the home job. **1914** *DN* 4.70 **ME, nNH,** *Changing wuks.* **1917** *DN* 4.389 **neOH, ME, NH, VT, MA, NY, KS,** *Change works.* **1927** *AmSp* 2.350 **WV,** Will we change works in harvest this year? **1947** Botkin *Treas. New Eng. Folkl.* 675, It was custom both among men and women to join forces on a smaller scale and have a little neighborly visiting by what was called "change-work." **1950** *WELS* 9 Infs, **WI,** Changing work; 1 Inf, Changing works; 2 Infs, Change help; 2 Infs, Changing help; 1 Inf, Change; 1 Inf, Changing; 1 Inf, Changing time. **1954** *Harder Coll* **cwTN,** Change work . . . To exchange work. **1965–70** *DARE* (Qu. L5, *When a farmer gets help on a job from his neighbors in return for his help on their farms later on*) 37 Infs, **chiefly Nth,** Changing work; 19 Infs, **chiefly Nth,** Change work (*or* help, labor); 13 Infs, **chiefly N Cent, Plains States,** Changing help; 8 Infs, **Nth,** Changing (labor, time, *or* works); **NJ**50, **PA**80, Changed work; **MN**7,

Change of work; **IA**36, Change. **1969** *DARE* Tape **KY**56, The neighbors change work with one another, or maybe a family, if there're three or four members of a family who have different crops, why they'll change work with each other. **1975** Gould *ME Lingo, Changing work* . . . A farmer would help his neighbor make hay, and in return the neighbor would help him cut firewood.

changies exclam

In marble play: a call allowing a player to change marbles.

1955 *PADS* 23.13 **cwTN, cwAL,** *Changies: n. interj.* A call that allows the player to change shooters. **1962** *PADS* 37.1 **cKS,** *Changies.* **c1970** Wiersma *Marbles Terms* **swMI,** Changies . . . In marble play: a call entitling a player to change a lost marble and so give up one he values less.

changing chairs n *somewhat old-fash*

The game of **musical chairs.**

1965–70 *DARE* (Qu. EE2, *Games . . the players change places, and the extra one tries to get a place*) 20 Infs, **scattered,** Changing chairs. [17 Infs old]

changing-clothes n

A second set of clothes, a change of clothing.

1970 *DARE* File **TN,** *Changing-clothes*—a second set of clothes, such as a child or poor person would not have. "I knew him when he didn't have changing-clothes," meaning you have known the person for a long time. **1970** *DARE* Tape **VA**71, They wouldn't let their mothers even take them changin'-clothes, from Saturday to Sunday.

‡**changing life** n [Prob alter of *change of life*]

1968 *DARE* FW Addit **NY**61, Changing life = menopause.

chanille n Cf *caneel,* var of **carnelian**

1968 *DARE* (Qu. EE6d, *Special marbles*) Inf **GA**18, Chanilles [šəˈnilz].

chank v |čæŋk|, also |čɔŋk| Also sp *chaunk, chawnk, chonk* [Prob alter of *champ* or **chomp** v] *chiefly W Midl, NEast*

To eat noisily, chew loudly.

1844 Stephens *High Life in NY* 1.50 **CT,** But there sot the old man a chonking an apple. **1895** *DN* 1.385 **CT,** Chank. **1901** *DN* 2.137 **NY,** Chank. **1905** *DN* 361 **NE,** Chonk [čɔnk] [sic]. **1906** *DN* 3.310 **nwAR,** Chomp, chonk. **1908** *DN* 3.298 **eAL, wGA,** Chonk . . . To eat noisily. **1909** *DN* 3.393 **nwAR,** Chank. **1909** Porter *Girl Limberlost* 393 **IN,** They just chanked into it. **1914** *DN* 4.70 **ME, nNH,** Chank, chawnk. **1917** *DN* 4.389 **neOH,** Chawnk [čɔnk] . . . Chank. General . . . In Vt. & Mass. used with comic intent and not associated with *chank.* **1927** *DN* 5.473 **Ozarks,** Chaunk. **1941** *LANE* Map 315 **NEng,** Jocular and derogatory terms meaning 'to chew noisily' [9 infs, Chank(ing); 4 infs, Chonk(ing)]. **1953** Brewer *Word Brazos* 109 **eTX** [Black], He stop chawnkin' on a good ole juicy drumstick. **1954** *Harder Coll.* **cwTN,** Chaunk . . . To crush between the teeth. Old-fash.

chank n [chank v]

A noisy or forceful act of chewing or biting.

1950 Reeves *Man from SD* 226, After every meal he retired to his bunk house for twenty minutes to chank raw carrots a measured number of chanks, for their vitamin content.

chankings vbl n pl Pronc-spp *chawnkin's, chonkings* [**chank** v] *chiefly NEng*

The rejected parts or chewed remains of fruit, esp apples, and occas other foods.

1882 *Century Illustr. Mag.* 25.299/1 **NY,** The ground . . covered with the "chonkings" of the frozen apples, the work of the squirrels in getting at the seeds. **1895** *DN* 1.385 **CT, ME, MA, VT,** Chankings: parings of apples and other fruits, or the core and other rejected parts of an apple. **1910** *DN* 3.452 **seVT,** Chankings. **1914** *DN* 4.70 **ME, nNH,** Chankin's, chawnkin's. **1917** *DN* 4.389 **neOH,** [čæŋk] is common. **1927** *AmSp* 3.139 **ME coast,** Apple "chankings," (champing). **1941** *LANE* Map 315, **swCT,** Where did all these [čæŋkɪnz] come from?; **cwMA,** [čæŋkɪnz], gristle, shells and the like, which must be spit out because they cannot be chewed; **cwMA,** [čæŋkɪnz], half-eaten grains of corn, etc., left by squirrels and rats. **1946** *AmSp* 21.307 **NEng,** When eating an apple or other fruit with rough or thick skin, my mother would say, 'Put your chankings in the stove.'

chanky-chank n [Perh echoic]

1982 Heat Moon *Blue Highways* 112 **sLA,** I drank a Dixie and ate bar peanuts and asked the bartender where I could hear "chanky-chank," as

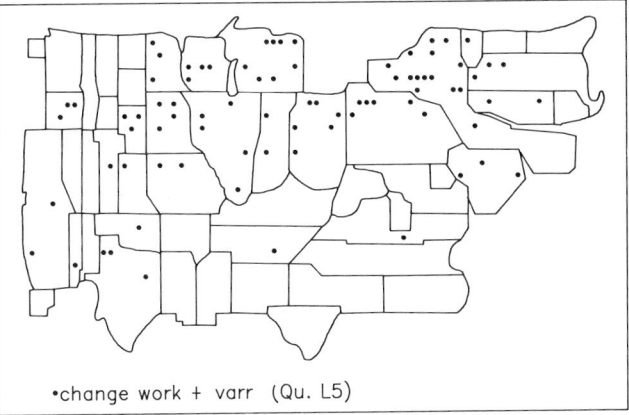

•change work + varr (Qu. L5)

Cajuns call their music. *Ibid,* An accordion (the heart of a Cajun band), a fiddle, guitar, and ting-a-ling (triangle) cranked out chanky-chank.

channel bass n chiefly Sth
=**red drum.**

   1887 Goode *Amer. Fishes* 102, In the Carolinas, Florida and the Gulf we meet with the names "Bass," and its variations, . . "Channel Bass." **1897** *Outing* 29.331/2 **FL,** The channel-bass, or "redfish," which sometimes attains a weight of fifty pounds. **1933** LA Dept. of Conserv. *Fishes* 174, The Redfish . . is also called the Red Drum and the Channel Bass. **1946** LaMonte *N. Amer. Game Fishes* 79, Channel Bass—*Sciaenops ocellatus* . . . *Distribution:* New York to Texas. **1966–70** *DARE* (Qu. P2, . . *Saltwater fish . . good to eat*) Infs **AL**22, **NC**12, 27, **SC**7, **VA**41, 47, Channel bass; **MD**36, Red channel bass. **1967** *DARE* Tape **TX**18, Up on the east coast, Virginia, up in there, they call 'em channel bass, but we call 'em redfish. **1969** *DARE* FW Addit **eNC,** Channel bass—also called red drum and old drum.

channel catfish n Also *channel cat* chiefly Missip Valley and adjacent areas See Map

   A catfish, such as the **blue catfish 1** or the **white catfish 1,** but most commonly *Ictalurus punctatus* which is also called **black warrior 2, blue catfish 2, blue fulton, canal boater, Edisto cat, fiddler catfish, lady cat, loggerhead, marble cat, old whiskers, silver catfish 1, speckled catfish 1, spotted cat, squealer.**
   1820 Rafinesque *Ohio R. Fishes* 62, *Pimelodus maculatus* . . . Vulgar names Spotted, White, and Channel Catfish. *Ibid* 63, *Pimelodus pallidus* . . . Vulgar names white and channel Catfish. **1887** Goode *Amer. Fishes* 377, The Channel Cat or Blue Cat, Ictalurus punctatus, abounds in all the larger Western and Southern streams, living in river channels. **1908** *DN* 3.297 **eAL, wGA,** Channel-cat . . . A kind of catfish. **1940** Stong *Hawkeyes* 246 **IA,** I have never seen a yellow or channel cat that weighed more than three or four pounds. These are Aryan mudcats and they are delicious. **1944** *PADS* 2.54 **nwAR, SC, LA,** Channel cat . . . A catfish. **1950** *PADS* 13.17 **cTX,** Channel cat . . . A fresh-water catfish which may be a *yellow channel cat* or a *blue channel cat.* The meat of the channel cat is considered tastier than that of the *mud cat.* **c1960** *Wilson Coll.* **csKY,** Channel cat . . . A long, slender, stream-lined catfish, very much unlike the shorter, more bulgy bullhead, the usual catfish. **1965** Teale *Wandering Through Winter* 173 **OK,** In Oklahoma channel cats have reached a weight of sixty pounds and a length of three and a half feet. **1965–70** *DARE* (Qu. P1, . . *Freshwater fish . . good to eat*) 79 Infs, **chiefly Missip Valley and adjacent areas,** Channel cat(s); 13 Infs, **chiefly Missip Valley,** Channel catfish; **IA**29, Small channel cat; (Qu. P3, *Freshwater fish . . not good to eat*) Infs **NC**53, **WI**58, Channel cat; (Qu. P14, . . *Commercial fishing*) Infs **GA**65, **LA**15, **MS**25, **TX**104, Channel cat. **1967** *DARE* Tape **IL**9, I personally prefer catfish about four pounds and that would have to be a mudcat. I don't want a channel cat . . a mudcat is sweet. **1969** *Rockford Labor News* (IL) 7 Feb 15/4, Channel catfish, 14–oz., Fries, Slaw, Roll . . $1.95.

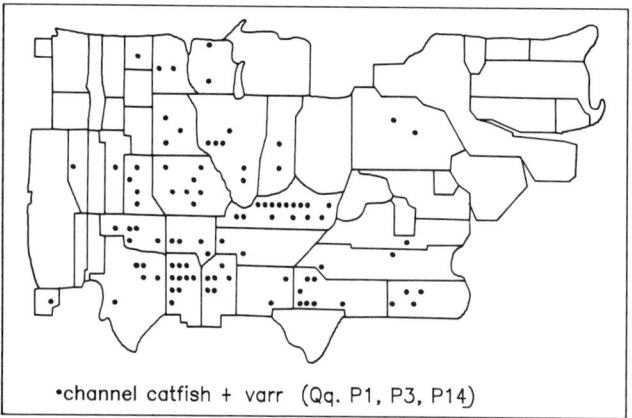

•channel catfish + varr (Qq. P1, P3, P14)

channel digger n [From its seeking food in channel bottoms]
=**paddlefish.**

   1949 Brown *Amer. Cooks* 239 **KS,** Around Kansas City, Kansas, they do catch spoonbill catfish called "channel diggers," which weigh up to 60 pounds.

channel mullet n **LA**

   A **kingfish 1** (here: *Menticirrhus americanus*).

1933 LA Dept. of Conserv. *Fishes* 181, The Kingfish, Channel Mullet or Whiting—*Menticirrhus americanus.* **1968** *DARE* (Qu. P2, . . *Saltwater fish . . good to eat*) Infs **LA**37, 44, Channel mullet; (Qu. P14, . . *Commercial fishing*) Inf **LA**44, Channel mullet. **1968** *DARE* FW Addit **coastal seLA,** Channel mullet—common local name for whiting.

channel trout n
=**rainbow trout.**

   1976 *DARE* File **nwMI,** At Rock Harbor [on Isle Royale] salmon trout are called channel trout.

channel weed n
=**tape grass.**

   1837 Darlington *Flora Cestrica* 557, Spiral Vallisneria . . . Channel-weed. **1941** *Torreya* 41.45, *Vallisneria americana* . . channel weed.

chanst See **chance** A

chany See **china** A

chaoui n |šaˈwi| [See quot 1931] **LA**
=**raccoon.**

   [**1803** Berquin–Duvallon *Vue Colonie* 101 **LA,** Les quadrupèdes sauvages sont: . . le pichou, espèce de grand renard, le chaoui, autre espèce plus petite, . . et quelques autres animaux moins répandus. [The wild quadrupeds are: . . the 'pichou,' a type of large fox, the 'chaoui,' another smaller kind, . . and some other, less widespread animals.]] **1931** Read *LA French* 87, Chaoui is derived from Choctaw or Mobilian *shaui,* "raccoon". The first syllable sounds like French *chat* . . the second syllable is exactly like French *oui* . . and the stress lies on the second syllable. **1968** *DARE* (Qu. P30, . . *Other names . . for . . racoon*) Inf **LA**34, Chaoui [ˌšaˈwi].

chap n

1 also attrib: A young child; a baby.   **chiefly Sth, S Midl** Cf **chappie**

   1883 (1971) Harris *Nights with Remus* 133 **GA,** "Go en shake han's, honey, en tell Daddy Jack howdy. He laks good chilluns." Then to Daddy Jack: "Brer Jack, dish yer de chap w'at I bin tellin' you 'bout." **1902** *DN* 2.231 **sIL,** Chap . . . A babe or child. **1907** *DN* 3.221 **nwAR, sIL.** **1908** *DN* 3.297 **eAL, wGA. 1926** *DN* 5.398 **Ozarks,** Chap . . . Child. "My least chap's ben right puny all summer." **1935** Hurston *Mules & Men* 79 **FL,** "Why don't you run dem chaps 'way from here?" . . He started to chase them off home but I made him see that it was a happy accident that they had chosen the lane as a playground. That I was enjoying it more than the chaps. **1940** (1978) Still *River of Earth* 118 **KY,** The kiver was opened and thar the chap was, hits little face red and wrinkled. *Ibid* 128 **KY,** I recollect your ma when she was a chap. **1953** Randolph *Down in Holler* 233 **Ozarks,** Chap . . . A child, usually a little boy. The plural is used for children of both sexes. Chap never means an adult in the Ozarks. **1965–70** *DARE* (Qu. Z14b, *If a child expects to have its own way or have too much attention*) Inf **AR**52, A spoiled chap; (Qu. Z16, *A small child who is rough, misbehaves, and doesn't obey*) Inf **AR**22, Mischievous chap; (Qu. JJ2a, *A child going to school, one in the lower grades*) Inf **VA**39, Chap; (Qu. E22, *If a house is untidy . . "It looks like _____."*) Inf **GA**10, A chap's playhouse; (Qu. Z12, . . *'A small child': "He's a healthy little _____."*) 33 Infs, **widespread,** Chap. [Note: this response prob includes the standard sense, *chap* 'fellow, man.'] **1982** Ginns *Snowbird Gravy* 102 **nwNC,** Now, it ain't wrong to steal if you get to where you have to for food. If you got a little bunch of chaps, and you go and ask for it first.

2 A young woman; a girl.

   1860 Holmes *Professor* 150 **MD,** Pootiest and nicest little chap I've seen since the schoolma'am left. **1954** *PADS* 21.23 **SC,** Teen-age girls are called chaps in the Dutch Fork.

chap v[1] [chaps] West Cf **chapping**

   To strike one with **chaps.**

   1937 Sandoz *Slogum* 290 **NE** (as of 1900–20), He wanted a crack at the fancy woman, too, by God. He'd chap Wampy Joe for her right now.

chap v[2] [chap n 1]

   To produce children.

   1964 Faulkner *As I Lay Dying* 165 **MS,** You and me aint nigh done chapping yet, with just two.

chaparajos n pl |ˌšæpəˈre(h)os, ˌčæp-| Also sp *chap(p)arejos, chaperajos* [Prob blend of **chaparreras** + **aparejo**] chiefly West, esp SW
=**chaps.**

1887 *Outing* 10.115/1, We had all discarded our *chaparajos,* and the horses were lightly blanketed. **1888** *Century Illustr. Mag.* 35.505/2 **MT,** The broad hat, huge blunt spurs, and leather *chaperajos* of the riders. **1891** Lummis *NM David* 82, Clumsy leathern *chapparejos* over their blue overalls. **1892** *DN* 1.189 **TX,** *Chaparájo, -s:* leather overalls worn by cowboys to protect their legs from thorny bushes. Probably from Spanish *chapa,* a protecting strip of leather on seams. The form *chaperajo* is found sometimes. **1940** *FWP Guide NM* 111, *Chaparejos*—Chaps. **1967** *DARE* FW Addit **CO,** *Chaparajos*—leather leg protectors.

chapararros, chapareras, chapareros See **chaparreras**

chaparral n |ˌšæpəˈræl| For var spp see quots at **A** [MexSpan] chiefly **SW**
A Forms.

1842 (1845) Green *Jrl. Texian Exped.* 59 **TX,** Suddenly the head of the line was turned . . into a dense and most difficult chaparral. **1843** in 1965 *AmSp* 40.128, Dey hid demselves in de chapparel. **1850** (1968) Taylor *Eldorado* 94 **CA,** The road passed between low hills, covered with patches of chapparal. **1851** *Alta California* 16 Nov (*DAE*), It was then deemed futile to enter the chapparral with so few men. **1851** (1854) Bartlett *Personal Narr.* 1.256, The road first entered a thick chapporal of mezquit. **1854** (1932) Bell *Log TX–CA Trail* 30 **NM,** Fine wood by digging up the roots of chaparall. **1857** *Recoll. West. Texas* 51 (*DAE*), A cluster of chaperelle that grew in the centre of the level and interminable solitude. **1873** Beadle *Undeveloped West* 819 **TX,** He . . reached the *chappural.* **1878** Tuttle *Border Tales* 33 (*DAE*), The most timid . . ran into the chapperell to hide away. **1913** [see **B1** below]. **1967** *DARE* Tape **TX**29, Chaparral [šæpəˈræl].

B Senses.
1 Any of numerous thicket-forming shrubs or shrubby trees, esp of the genera *Acacia, Ceanothus, Condalia,* or *Forestiera;* also the thicket itself.

1879 *Harper's Mag.* 59.92/2 **FL,** In the close chaparral the heat was intense. **1892** *DN* 1.189 **TX,** *Chaparrál:* primarily a thicket of *chaparros,* stone oaks or scrub oaks, then any kind of extensive bushy thicket . . . In very common use. **1897** *Jrl. Amer. Folkl.* 10.52, *Lippia cuneifolia* . . chapparal, Mexican heliotrope, Tex. **1907** Mulford *Bar-20* 64 **West,** The assassins had waited in the chaparral for Johnny to pass. **1913** *Torreya* 13.233 c**LA,** Styracaceae . . . *Styrax americana* . . . Chaparrelle. **1946** Peattie *Pacific Coast* 55 s**CA,** Chaparral . . . the whole plant complex, largely evergreen and permanently of dwarf stature, which covers the intermediate altitudes of the Coast Ranges of southern California with a compact growth of what some claim are really trees, or as much of trees as conditions allow . . . The woodcutter calls all Ceanothus simply "chaparral." **1947** Bedichek *Advent. TX Naturalist* 116, Chaparral means an extense of bushes, or, perhaps, place of bushes. The ranch people in the Brush Country of Texas use chaparral in two ways: (1) to designate what the Mexicans call *chaparro prieto,* or black brush, *Acacia amentacea;* and (2) to designate thorny brush in general . . . In California chaparral means the manzanita. **1965–70** *DARE* (Qu. C28, *A place where underbrush, weeds, vines and small trees grow together so that it's nearly impossible to get through*) Infs **AZ**15, **CA**82, 105, 113, **OR**10, **TX**17, 22, Chaparral.
2 Fig: a tangle, thicket.

1875 Twain *Sketches New & Old* (Hartford) 153, Her hair was frizzled into a tangled chapparel. **1878** *Congressional Record* 15 June App 453/2, They see in every democratic Representative upon this floor a Mexican bandit skulking in the political chaparral.
3 See **chaparral cock.**

chaparral berry n
1 =**buffalo berry.**
1881 in 1942 *Annals of WY* 14.119, Gazelle and Ma made some Chapparel berry pies and cookies.
2 An **agarita** (here: *Berberis trifoliata*). **SW, esp TX**
1892 *DN* 1.189 **TX,** The berries called in Texas *chaparral* berries are the fruit of a species of *Berberis* (*B. trifoliata*). **1920** Hunter *Trail Drivers TX* 134 **TX,** I walked all day with nothing to eat but chapparal berries. **1936** Whitehouse *TX Flowers* 30, Agarita. Texas Barberry (*Berberis trifoliolata*), known also as agrito . . , chaparral berry, and wild currant. **1951** *PADS* 15.32 **TX,** Chaparral berry . . . Good for jellies, preserves, . . and delicious raw. **1967** *DARE* (Qu. I44, . . *Berries . . [which] grow wild*) Inf **TX**26, Chaparrals.

chaparral big bunch moss See **bunch moss**

chaparral bird See **chaparral cock**

chaparral broom n chiefly Pacific
A groundsel tree (here: *Baccharis pilularis*). Also called **cotton bush, coyote brush, fuzzy-wuzzy, kidneyroot, kidneywort**
1911 Jepson *Flora CA* 473 **CA, OR,** Bacharis . . . pilularis . . . Chaparal Broom. **1931** U.S. Dept. Ag. *Misc. Pub.* 101.160, Kidneywort . . also known as . . chaparral broom, . . . is typically a coastal or seashore plant, growing (usually in colonies) on dunes and low sand hills. **1954** CA Div. Beaches & Parks *Pt. Lobos Wild Flowers* 32, *Baccharis pilularis.* Chaparral Broom. **1961** Peck *Manual OR* 793, Baccharis . . . pilularis . . . Chaparral Broom. **1973** Hitchcock–Cronquist *Flora Pacific NW* 494, Chaparral broom . . . Bluffs and thickets along the coast.

chaparral cock n Also *chaparral,* ~ *bird,* ~ *hen,* ~ *fowl* chiefly **SW**
=**roadrunner.**
1853 *San Diego Herald* 22 Oct 2/4 (*AmSp* 26.224), A party of gentlemen . . returned Thursday evening, laden with spoil. To say nothing of quail, grouse, chapparal cock, and rabbits. **1892** *DN* 1.246 **TX,** *Chaparral* . . . Also the name of the chaparral cock, or roadrunner, *Geococcyx Californianus.* **1926** TX Folkl. Soc. *Pub.* 5.88, As crazy as a *paisano* (road-runner or chaparral bird). **1953** *AmSp* 28.278 **TX,** Chaparral fowl (road runner . .). *Ibid* 281 **TX,** Chaparral hen. **1967** *DARE* (Qu. Q7, . . *Game birds*) Infs **TX**1, 42, Chaparral bird; (QR, near Qu. Q23) Inf **NM**13, Roadrunner = chaparral = paisano. **1969** *DARE* FW Addit **NM,** *Chaparral hen*—a bird of New Mexico. Also called roadrunner, chaparral cock, ground cuckoo, and snake killer. **1970** Anderson *TX Folk Med.* xviii, The roadrunner (*paisano* or chaparral cock), so thoroughly Texan and so appropriately part of the Southwestern landscape, was boiled, baked, and fried and used as a cure for boils and as a preventive for snakebites. *Ibid* 9, Boil a chaparral [roadrunner] and make it into a soup.

chaparral deer n
Perh a subsp of the mule deer.
1886 Van Dyke *Southern CA* 80, One of them, the little chaparral deer, is almost extinct, and never was abundant.

chaparral fowl See **chaparral cock**

chaparral fox n
1932 Bentley *Spanish Terms* 119, *Chaparral fox*—Occasionally applied to a sneak or a sly tricky person.

chaparral hen See **chaparral cock**

chaparral lily n
A tall lily (*Lilium rubescens*) which produces fragrant white, purple-spotted flowers aging to wine color. Also called **chamise lily 2, lilac lily, redwood lily, ruby lily**
1897 Parsons *Wild Flowers CA* 72, Chaparral Lily . . . Lilium rubescens . . . The favorite haunts of this lily are high and inaccessible ridges, among the chaparral, or under the live-oak or redwood. **1911** Jepson *Flora CA* 95, Lilium . . . rubescens . . . Chaparral Lily. **1915** (1926) Armstrong *Western Wild Flowers* 36 **CA, OR,** Ruby Lily—Chaparral Lily—Lilium rubéscens. **1959** Munz–Keck *CA Flora* 1342, Chaparral Lily. **1976** Bailey–Bailey *Hortus Third* 663, Chaparral l[ily] . . . Coast Ranges, s. Ore. to cent. Calif.

chaparral pea n Also *pea chaparral*
A spiny evergreen shrub (*Pickeringia montana*) native to California. Also called **stingaree bush**
1897 Parsons *Wild Flowers CA* 230, Upon wild mountain-slopes . . the chaparral pea often makes dense, impenetrable thickets. **1925** Jepson *Manual Plants CA* 515, Pickeringia . . . montana . . . Pea Chaparral. **1969** *DARE* (Qu. S26e, . . *Wildflowers*) Inf **CA**140, Chaparral pea.

chaparral tea n
A leatherweed (here: *Croton corymbulosus*).
1886 Havard *Flora W. & S. TX for 1885* 514, Encenilla; Chaparral Tea . . . Very common weed of valleys and prairies. An infusion of the flowering tops, either green or dried, makes excellent tea. **1920** Saunders *Useful Wild Plants* 159, Similarly used is the . . Chaparral Tea (*Croton corymbulosus . .*). The flowering tops are the part employed, and an infusion of them is palatable to many.

chaparras See **chaparreras**

chaparrelle See **chaparral**

chaparreras n pl |ˌšæpəˈrɛrəs, ˌčæp-| Also sp *chapararros, chapareras, chapar(r)eros,* shortened forms *chaparras, chaparro(s)* [MexSpan] **chiefly SW** *old-fash*
=chaps.

[**1861** Tylor *Anahuac* 335 **Mexico,** Chaparreros, over-trousers of goatskin with the hair on, used in riding.] **1865** *Atlantic Mth.* 15.61/1 **Mexico,** The Don insisted on my assuming . . . Mexican riding-costume: cool linen drawers, cut Turkish fashion; over these . . the leathern *chapareros* or overalls. **1889** (1971) Farmer *Americanisms, Chaparajos* or *Chaparro.* — Trousers made of stout leather, and stitched with leather cording. **1892** *DN* 1.246 **TX,** *Chapareras.* **1895** Remington *Pony Tracks* 79 **TX,** Mr. Johnnie Bell . . was walking about in his heavy *chaparras,* a slouch hat, and a white "biled" shirt. **1899** *Philistine* 9.126 **NY,** To promote him further would be to invite him to swing his chapararros astride the neck of Freedom. **1909** Porter *Roads of Destiny* 95 **TX,** Lonny is one of them, a knight of stirrup and chaparreras. **1926** Burns *Billy the Kid* 170 **NM,** He put on cowboy habits with his first pair of chapareras.

chaparro n[1] [AmSpan]
Any of var undergrown oaks.

1892 *DN* 1.189 **TX,** *Chaparrál:* primarily a thicket of *chaparros,* stone oaks or scrub oaks. **1925** Lummis *Mesa* 133 **cAZ,** Clambering down the steep and sinuous trail among the chaparro. **1944** Adams *Western Words, Chaparro* . . An evergreen oak.

chaparro n[2], **chaparros** See **chaparreras**

chaperajos See **chaparajos**

chaperelle See **chaparral**

chapo adj, n Infreq *chopo, chupo* [MexSpan] **chiefly SW**
Short, chubby, chunky; a person or horse with such characteristics.

[**1857** *Los Angeles Star* 7 Feb 2/3 (*Western Folkl.* 7.7), Un chapo pelon.[A short bald person].] **1893** Lummis *Land of Poco Tiempo* 122 **NM,** That *chopo* [Footnote: A short, heavy-set man] Hercules, Francisco, the strongest man of the Tiguas. **1908** (1966) Thorp *Songs Cowboys* 30 **West,** You're a safe conveyance my little Chopo. **1931** Lomax *Cowboy Songs* 300 **AZ,** Little brown Chapo bore the cowboy o'er the far away frontier. **1932** Bentley *Spanish Terms* 119, *Chapo* . . ['čɑpo . . 'čæpo] Short or chubby; often used as a proper name or nickname. Incidentally, it is a favorite name among Americans for small saddle horses. As an adjective it is used in such an expression as "He is a little *chapo* fellow." . . the word is not uncommon in spoken English in the Southwest. **1968** Adams *Western Words, Chapo* — A short-coupled horse with a chunky build; also called *chupo.*

chapolin See **chapulin**

chapote n Also ~ *prieto;* infreq *capote, sapote, zapote* [MexSpan]
=black persimmon.

[**1846** (1941) Gregg *Diary* 1.239 **TX,** Among other wild fruits of this vicinity, that called by Mexicans *chapote* and generally by Americans, black persimmon (or Mexican or Mustang persimmon) a black fruit about half the size of the common persimmon.] **1892** *DN* 1.246 **TX,** *Chapóte or zapóte:* in Texas, a shrub or tree of the ebony family, Mexican persimmon . . . *Diospyros Texana.* **1902** (1968) Clapin *Americanisms, Chapote* . . . In Texas, a shrub or tree of the ebony family (Diospyros Texana), otherwise called black persimmon. Also, *sapote, zapote.* **1936** Whitehouse *TX Flowers* 94, *Mexican Persimmon (Diospyros texana)* is also called 'possum plum, "chapote," and black persimmon. **1937** Parks *Plants TX* 95, The plant received the name of Capote as the Mexican women use the ripe persimmon in making a hair dye. [**1956** Gipson *Old Yeller* 88 **TX,** They especially liked the wild black persimmons that the Mexicans called chapotes.] **1960** Vines *Trees SW* 839, *Diospyros* . . *texana* . . . Chapote, and Chapote Prieto. **1967** *DARE* (Qu. T5, . . *Evergreens*) Inf **TX29,** Chapote.

chapparal(l) See **chaparral**

chapparejos See **chaparajos**

chapparel, chapparral, chapperell See **chaparral**

chappie n Also sp *chappy* [**chap** n 1]
A child; a young person.

1932 *Scribner's Mag.* 91.284 **FL,** Thank you, ma'am. They'll fit one o' the chappies, shore. **1942** Rawlings *Cross Creek* 71 **Carolinas,** Yet all of the Widow Slater's brood, the "chappies" as she called them, Carolina fashion, had a luminous quality. **1945** O'Hara *Pipe Night* 49 **PA,** I have a little spot of annecdotes [sic] . . to tell you which may amuse the chappies around Lebuses.

chapping vbl n, also attrib [**chap** v[1]] **West**
A contest in which two players alternately strike one another with **chaps;** punishment in which one is struck with **chaps.**

1910 Raine *Bucky O'Conner* 60 (*DA*), A chapping would sure do him a heap of good. **1926** Branch *Cowboy* 31 **West,** The rest of the outfit might avenge the dignity of their calling by a "chapping"—a laying on of leather after the manner of ancient disciplinarians, the offender's own pair of chaps sometimes the instrument. **1937** Sandoz *Slogum* 288 **NE** (as of 1900–20), A chapping match was announced between a couple of young horse breakers . . . They . . sat down on the floor, facing, their lean legs dovetailed, each with half a chap held by the upper end. Joe drew the long straw for the first lick; Norm swung his body back to the floor, and snapped his long legs up over to take the snapping leather across his britches with all the steam Joe could put behind it. Then Joe's legs went up and Norm got his lick in. So it went on, up and down, like clockwork—the whack, whack, of good leather loud along the ridgepole of the house. **1939** FWP *Guide NE* 109, A chapping match, in which two swains drew lots and took turns whacking each other with half of a horsebacker's leather chaps (unlaced to allow the two legs to fall apart), the victor being rewarded with the pick of a girl, if he had none. **1944** Adams *Western Words, Chapping*—The act of whipping one with a pair of chaps. This is often done in rough horseplay when a group of cowboys get together for a kangaroo court. When used against someone of vile and unpopular disposition, it can be severe punishment.

chapporal, chappural See **chaparral**

chaps n pl Usu |šæps|, also |čæps| Pronc-spp *shaps, schap(p)s* [Abbr for **chaparreras;** see also **chaparajos**] **West**
Leather leggings resembling trousers without a seat, worn chiefly by cowboys or ranch hands over regular trousers to protect the legs when riding through chaparral or brush.

1884 Shepherd *Prairie Exper.* 41 **WY,** The cow-boys, with their *schaps,* i.e. leather-leggings and flopping wide-brimmed hats, are trooping off. **1894** *DN* 1.324 **TX,** *Chaps.* **1896** *Christian Educ.* Jan 7/1 (*DAE*), A cowboy with spurs, schapps, sombrero and lariat, was a new sight to Miss Selby. **1904** (1969) Robins *Magnetic North* 181, Anybody must needs be a devil of a fellow who went about in 'shaps,' as his California cousins called chaparejos. **1926** Branch *Cowboy* 23, Chaps, worn when there was riding to be done, were also a part of the cowboy's courtin'-clothes. **1930** James *Lone Cowboy* 264 **MT,** Some folks wonder why cowboys wear shaps. **1949** *PADS* 11.5 **wTX,** Chaps [šæps] . . . Chaparejos, but the full word would sound affected. Common. **1960** *PADS* 34.66 **CO,** The wide spread of . . *chaps* (frequently *shaps*) in the popular speech . . makes [it] fully naturalized. **1967** *DARE* FW Addit **ID,** [šæps]; **IL** [čæps]; **ceTX,** [čæps], leather leggings to protect horsemen from brush; **CO,** [šæps].

chapulin n Also *chapolin* [MexSpan] **SW**
1 A grasshopper.

1932 Bentley *Spanish Terms* 119, *Chapolin* . . [čæpo'lin] Literally "a grasshopper". [**1942** Santamaria *Dicc. Americanismos, Chapulín.* (Voz azt. *Acridium peregrinum.*) m. Saltamontes; langosta que en mangas enormes ataca las sementeras; acridio que forma una de las plagas de este Continente. [*Chapulín.* (Aztec term. *Acridium peregrinum.*) Grasshopper; locust which attacks cultivated lands in enormous hordes; locust which forms one of the plagues of this continent.]] **1967** *DARE* (Qu. R6, . . *Grasshoppers*) Inf **TX28,** Chapulin.
2 By ext: see quot.

1932 Bentley *Spanish Terms* 119, *Chapolin* . . used derisively by extension to apply to a person of a mean or petty disposition.

chaqueta n [Span] **SW**
A jacket of leather or heavy cloth.

1892 *DN* 1.246 **TX,** *Chaquéta:* a jacket; more specifically in Texas, a jacket made of leather or very heavy cloth, worn by cowboys as a protection against thorns of the *chaparral.* **1930** Duffus *Santa Fe Trail* 171, The New Mexican men, in their braided *chaquetas,* their laced *calzoneras* or trousers, their brilliant sashes, their boots of embossed leather . . were as shamelessly lurid as their wives and sweethearts. **1968** Adams *Western Words, Chaqueta*—A jacket sold by the early traders; from the Spanish *jaqueta.*

char See **chore** n

charbon n Also sp *chorbon* **chiefly LA**

1 A disease of cattle, perh anthrax: see quots.

1836 *Niles' Natl. Reg.* 51.96/3 **LA,** A disease termed *chorbon* is causing great mortality among the stock of Louisiana—some planters have had all their horses carried off by it, and in many instances it has proved fatal to man. **1945** Saxon *Gumbo Ya-Ya* 114 **LA,** Kenner's Saint Rosalia procession began in 1899, after a promise made to the saint for her proficiency in stopping a plague of charbon, which was destroying the cattle and mules so essential to the livelihood of the Italian farmers of the vicinity. **1965–70** *DARE* (Qu. K28, . . *Diseases . . cows*) Infs **LA**7, 10, 15, 24, 29, 31, 39, 40, **MS**72, **TX**12, Charbon; (Qu. K47, . . *Diseases . . horses or mules*) Infs **LA**10, 12, 22, 31, 39, 40, **TX**4, 12, Charbon. **1967** *Merck Vet. Manual* 361, Anthrax (Splenic fever, Charbon, Milzbrand) An acute, infectious, febrile disease, of virtually all animals and man, caused by *Bacillus anthracis.*

2 attrib in *charbon fly:* An insect (perh a tabanid) believed to cause the charbon disease of cattle.

1968 *DARE* (Qu. R12, . . *Flies . . that fly around animals*) Inf **LA**15, Charbon fly.

charco n [Span] **SW**

A pool, puddle or water hole; occas a spring.

1890 *Stock Grower & Farmer* 9 Aug 4/3 *(DA),* In a day or so the rain came and the water holes and the 'charcos' were again filled. **1892** *DN* 1.189 **TX,** *Chárco:* a puddle, shallow water hole. *Ibid* 246, Also, sometimes, a bold spring, generally gushing forth from a ledge of rocks. **1907** Porter *Heart of West* 168 **TX,** But when he staggered to his feet his first move was to find his soap and towel and start for the *charco.* **1922** Bryan *Routes to Desert* 321 **AZ,** Charcos are pools of water that occur along the channels where flood waters spread out over adobe flats. **1942** Castetter *Pima & Papago Ag.* 43 **sAZ,** Often there were natural water holes or pools of standing water of variable size along channels where flood waters spread out over adobe flats and washes, in which case they were known as *charcos,* usually three to five feet deep.

charcoal n, also attrib *old-fash, derog* Cf **coal** n

A Black person; one with dark skin.

[**1870** Macrae *Americans* 2.35 **Sth,** To call him "a charcoal nigger" was the blackest insult of all, making him the furthest remove from the nobility of whiteness.] **1900** *DN* 2.26, Charcoal blossom . . A young negress. *Ibid* **AL,** Charcoal-lily . . A boy very dark in color. **1926** Van Vechten *Nigger Heaven* 285, Charcoal: Negro.

charcoal burner n

A rustic, hillbilly.

1962 Atwood *Vocab. TX* 74 **cTX,** The rustic type of person . . *charcoal burner* . . recorded only in Travis County.

charcoal iron n Also *charcoal-burning iron old-fash* See also **box iron, coal iron, cold iron**

A flatiron heated by coals burning in a raised box-like compartment.

1965–70 *DARE* (Qu. F29, . . *Irons—not electric*) 17 Infs, **scattered,** Charcoal iron; **OK**51, **SC**29, Charcoal-burning iron. [15 of 19 Infs old]

charcoal out v phr Cf **fry out**

To barbecue.

1980 *DARE* File **VA,** *Charcoal out,* used several times in reference to barbecuing dinner over a grill in the back yard.

charcoal pit See **coal pit**

chare See **chore** n

charge v Usu |cha(r)j|, rarely |cherj| Pronc-sp *chaa'ge*

A Forms.

1902 *DN* 2.231 **sIL,** Charge [charj] or [cherj]. **1922** Gonzales *Black Border* 292 **sSC, GA coasts** [Gullah glossary], *Chaa'ge*—charge, charges, charged, charging.

B Senses.

1 In moonshining: to fill a still. [**charge** n **2**]

1946 *AmSp* 21.193, Still operators regularly 'charge a still,' by filling the still with high wine for redistillation. **1974** Maurer *KY Moonshine* 115, *Charge* . . To fill the still with beer.

2 To stand or lie down and remain still—used as a command to a dog. **chiefly Nth** See Map

1950 *WELS* (Command to a dog to be still on the ground) 7 Infs, **WI,** Charge. **1965–70** *DARE* (Qu. J9a, *To tell a dog to lie down on the*

ground *and keep still)* 19 Infs, **chiefly NEast,** Charge; **NJ**53, **NY**213, Charged; (Qu. J9b, *To tell a dog to stand without moving*) 18 Infs, **chiefly Nth,** Charge; **GA**12, Down; charge.

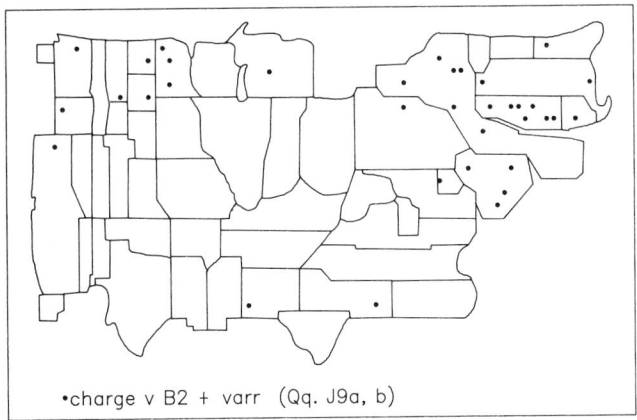

•charge v B2 + varr (Qq. J9a, b)

3 To attack—used as a command to a dog. **chiefly Nth, esp NEast**

1965–70 *DARE* (Qu. J8, *To tell a dog to attack an animal or person*) Infs **CT**7, **IL**10, **KS**18, **NJ**2, 25, **NY**188, **PA**79, 128, 135, **WI**62, Charge. [All Infs old, rural]

charge n Pronc-sp *chahdge*

1 An amount or quantity (of anything consumed); one filling.

1887 (1895) Robinson *Uncle Lisha* 30 **wVT,** He got out from another a twist of greenish-black tobacco, and whittling off a charge and grinding it between his palms, filled and lighted his pipe. **1968** *DARE* (Qu. DD18, *A drink of liquor, or the amount of liquor taken in one swallow*) Infs **IA**22, 47, Charge. **1979** Lewis *How to Talk Yankee* **NEng,** Chahdge . . A quantity . . . "I et an awful *chahdge* for breakfast."

2 Spec: in moonshining, the quantity of **beer 1** needed to fill the still; one filling of the still.

1933 Rawlings *South Moon* 220 **FL,** I'm about in time to he'p you run a charge, dogged if I ain't. **1949** *AmSp* 24.8 [Moonshine argot], *Charge* . . . One filling of the still from the fermenter vats. This *beer* is boiled until the alcohol has evaporated, when another *charge* is put into the still. **1974** Maurer *KY Moonshine* 65, In addition to grain and possibly fruit, the moonshiner needs malt, a considerable quantity of flour to seal the cap on the still between *charges,* and commercial yeast.

charged ppl adj Also *charged up* [*charge* to load]

Feeling the effects of drink or drugs; filled.

1880 Twain *Tramp Abroad* 48, The pleasant talk and the beer flow for an hour or two, and by and by the professor, properly charged and comfortable, gives a cordial good night. **1938** *AmSp* 13.182 [Underworld jargon], *Charged.* Var. of *overcharged.* Stupefied or drowsy as a result of having taken more narcotics than necessary to produce euphoria. **1966** *DARE* (Qu. DD14, . . *Partly drunk*) Inf **DC**8, Getting charged up. **1971** Landy *Underground Dict., Charged up* . . . Under the effect of narcotics. **1979** *DARE* File **NC** [Black], Charged—full of. He's charged up with cold.

charge it to the dust and let the rain settle it v phr Also *charge it to the sand* ~

See quots.

1946 *PADS* 6.35 **swVA,** *Charge* it to the sand ((dust)) and let the rain settle it. (Charge it on the books but it may not be paid. Generally said jokingly.) **1968** *DARE* FW Addit **nwLA,** *Charge it to the dust and let the rain settle it* = that's somebody else's responsibility. I'm not going to worry about it. A "flip" expression, "snippy." **1984** *DARE* File **wNC** (as of c1915), *Charge it to the dust and let the rain settle it.* In my experience, this phrase asserts the futility of charging (i.e., recording a debt) in a particular case. No actual debt-recording occurs because such action is considered a waste of effort.

charge (someone) off v phr

To end or deny a relationship.

1969 *DARE* (Qu. Y51, . . *"To avoid" . . "He's not your kind—you'd better _____ him."*) Inf **IL**78, Charge him off; (Qu. II6, *If you meet somebody who used to be a friend, and he pretends not to know you*) Inf **IL**78, Charged me off.

charging-school n
See quot 1983.

1975 Thomas *Hear the Lambs* 86 **nwAL** [Black], I still mean to learn all I can . . . I learned a lot teaching my own little charging-school. **1983** *DARE* File **neAL**, A charging-school . . . is a school where tuition was paid. *Ibid*, During the great depression . . the public schools . . could operate only from five to seven months a year. When the schools had to close, those parents who could afford it, would commission a teacher or teachers to carry on their children's education . . . They were allowed to use the public school facilities without charge and were paid directly by the parents.

chariot n
In railroading: a caboose.

1945 in 1953 Botkin *Treas. Railroad Folkl.* 344, It is a caboose, crummy, way car, . . chariot. **1945** Hubbard *Railroad Ave.* 337, *Chariot*—Caboose, or general manager's car. **1977** Adams *Lang. Railroader* 31.

charivari See shivaree

Charles See Charlie 2

Charleston brim n [*Charleston* South Carolina + *brim* alter of bream]
A **sheepshead** (here: *Archosargus probatocephalus*).

1973 *DARE* File **Savannah GA**, *Charleston brim*—the sheephead (fish). Common.

Charleston buzzard n Also *Charleston eagle* **SC**
=black vulture.

1949 Sprunt–Chamberlain *SC Bird Life* 150, *Coragyps atratus* . . . Charleston Buzzard. **1950** *PADS* 14.19 **SC**, *Charleston buzzard, Charleston eagle* . . . The black vulture. **1966** *DARE* (Qu. Q13, . . *Vulture*) Inf **SC21**, Charleston Eagle, nickname for buzzard.

Charley See Charlie

Charley horse n [Orig uncertain: see 1949 *AmSp* 24.100–104] widespread, but least freq NEast and Sth
A pain or soreness, usu in a muscle and often the result of a bruise.

1888 in 1949 *AmSp* 24.103, I could dance in those days, because, you see, I never was bothered with "Charley Horse." **1913** *Amer. Mag.* July 68/1 **West**, Everybody got jov'al, and the barkeep at Sierra Joe's got a charley-horse tryin' to keep up with his orders. **1965–70** *DARE* (Qu. BB4, . . *A pain* . . *"He's had a _____ in his arm for a week."*) 42 Infs, **chiefly N Midl, West, scattered Inland Nth**, Charley horse; (Qu. BB3a, . . *A pain that strikes you suddenly in the neck*) Infs **CT31, NC61, WI76**, Charley horse; (Qu. BB3b, *A sudden pain* . . *in the back*) Infs **OR4, SD2, UT3, WA9, WI34**, Charley horse; (Qu. BB3c, *A sudden pain* . . *in the side*) Infs **IN35, OK18, 42**, Charley horse; (Qu. BB28, *Joking names that people make up for imaginary diseases*) Inf **OK1**, Charley horse (not invented); (Qu. Y11, . . *A very hard blow*) Inf **VA2**, Gave him a charley horse.

Charlie n Also sp *Charley*
1 Used as a casual term of address when a person's name is not known; a representative name for a male. *sometimes derog*

1965–70 *DARE* (Qu. II10a, *Asking directions of somebody on the street when you don't know his name* . . *to a boy: "Say, _____, where's the post office?"*) Infs **IL47, SC45**, Charlie; (Qu. II10b, . . *To a man*) Infs **NM4, PA236**, Charlie; (Qu. CC12b) Inf **NC18**, Hard luck Charlie; (Qu. U32) Inf **IL43**, Good-time Charlie; (Qu. V9) Inf **CA87**, White-line Charlie. **1971** Jennings *Cowboys* 226, Charlie—Such a frequent name in the Old West that qualifying nicknames to go with it appear to be required.

2 also attrib, occas *Charles, Chuck*: A white man; by ext, white people, white society in general. [Abbr for **Mister Charlie**] *among Black speakers; derog*

1963 *Freedomways* 3.55 **NYC** [Black], They all was beamin' like they had Charley's number; and Charley was settin' there fussin'. **1968–69** *DARE* (Qu. HH28, *Names and nicknames*) Inf **GA83**, Charlie—nickname for White people by Blacks; **PA66**, Caucasian: Patty, Chuck, Cracker. **1969** Gordone *No Place* 40 **NY** [Black], Couldn't copy Charlie's good points an' live like men. So we copied his bad points . . . All it did was make us hate him all the more an' ourselves too . . . Seems to me, the worse sickness a man kin have is the Charlie fever. **1970** Major *Afro-Amer. Slang*, Charles: white man; see *Charlie. Charlie*: a corrup-

tion of "Mister Charlie," any white man; originally, the overseer or boss. *Chuck*: a white man; see *Charlie*. **1970** *DARE* Tape **NY242**, The man is usually Charlie, the employer is rarely a Black person. **1977** Smitherman *Talkin* 252 [Black], *Charley, Charles, Chuck*, derogatory references to white male.

3 also *Charlie Whitehouse*: A chamber pot.

1968 *DARE* (Qu. F38, *Utensil kept under the bed for use at night*) Infs **IA30, PA110**, Charlie; **PA163**, Charlie Whitehouse.

‡4 Menstruation.

1968 *DARE* (Qu. AA27, . . *Woman's menstruation*) Inf **IA32**, Charlie.

5 A dollar.

1968–70 *DARE* (Qu. U19a, . . *Money*) Inf **NC87**, Charlie; (Qu. U20, . . *Dollars*) Inf **WI48**, Charlie; (Qu. U23) Inf **WI48**, Quarter Charlie; (Qu. U24) Inf **WI48**, Half a Charlie. **1971** Landy *Underground Dict.*, *Charlie* . . . One dollar; five Charlies = five dollars.

Charlie died See Charlie's dead

Charlie Noble n [See quot 1975]
A galley stovepipe; by ext, any stovepipe or smokestack.

1940 *AmSp* 15.450, *Charley Noble*. The funnel or smokestack on a ship. **1945** Colcord *Sea Language* 51 **ME, Cape Cod, Long Island**, *Charley Noble*. The galley stovepipe. Sometimes used for a stovepipe (not chimney) alongshore. **1946** *CA Folkl. Qrly.* 5.383 [Naval slang], *Charley Noble* is no gallant and heroic seaman, but the galley smokestack. **1967** *DARE* File **East coast**, *Charlie Noble*—the smokestack on the galley of a boat. **1975** Gould *ME Lingo*, *Charley Noble*—A galley stovepipe aboard ship: hence, any flue or chimney. The allusion is thus explained: "The First Lord of the Admiralty acknowledges your recent inquiry, and begs to state in reply that according to the records in the archives of His Majesty's Navy, an American Master Merchant Mariner, in the early 1800's, a Mr. Charles Noble of Nobleboro, of Maine, discovered one day at sea that his galley stovepipe was made of brass, and he gave an order that it should be kept bright." So, wherever a gleaming brass flue was seen at sea—there would be Charley Noble! This Maineism has gone around the world.

Charlie-on-the-spot n Cf Johnny-on-the-spot
A reliable or punctual person.

[**1805** *Thomas' MA Spy or Worcester Gaz.* (MA) 20 Feb 4/1, I mean to have my Sunday shirt / Wash'd and mended, early, / And I will be upon the spot, / As punctual as "Charley."] **1835** Crockett *Account* 112, Did I not tell you . . that I would not vote on the appropriation bill, but when you came to any thing else, I was 'Charlie on the spot?' **1942** Berrey–Van den Bark *Amer. Slang* 2.14, *Prompt; punctual* . . . Charlie or Johnny on the spot; 434.4. *Reliable person* . . . Charlie-on-the-spot.

Charlie's dead phr For varr see quots esp CA
Used as a warning that one's slip is showing.

1942 Berrey–Van den Bark *Amer. Slang* 89.9, *Your slip is showing*. Charlie's dead. **1950** *WELS* (*Expressions* . . *a woman's slip is showing*) 1 Inf, **seWI**, Charlie died. **1967–70** *DARE* (Qu. W24a, . . *To warn a woman slyly that her slip is showing*) Infs **CA15A, 151, 188, NV9**, Charlie's dead; **CA106**, Charlie is dead; **CA87**, Uncle Charlie's dead; **CA170**, Charlie's showing.

Charlie Taylor n West
A butter substitute made of sorghum and bacon grease.

1933 *AmSp* 8.1.27 **nTX**, *Charley Taylor*. Syrup or sorghum into which bacon or ham grease from the platter has been poured and stirred. **1939** Wellman *Trampling Herd* 237 **West**, A really accomplished cook would give his outfit something to brag about with such a gustatory array as . . Charlie Taylor (a substitute for butter made from a mixture of sorghum molasses and bacon grease). **1950** *Western Folkl.* 9.139, Characteristic frontier names for common foods include . . *Charlie Taylor* for a butter made of sorghum and bacon grease.

Charlie Whitehouse See Charlie 3

charm n
1930 Shoemaker *1300 Words* 11 **cPA Mts** (as of c1900), *Charm*—A premonition of death, a "Banshee".

charmber See chamber A

charm root n
1942 (1965) Parrish *Slave Songs* 31, The author gives a picture of a distorted "charm root" which explains the use of eccentric wood growths in the decoration of the Negro graveyard.

charm stick n

A divining rod.

1967 *DARE* (Qu. CC13a, . . *A forked stick that's used to show where there's water underground*) Inf **TN**13, Charm stick.

charm string n

A string of buttons: see quots.

1947 (1964) Randolph *Ozark Superstitions* 61, Years ago, many an Ozark girl collected buttons from her friends and strung them together into a sort of necklace called a charm string . . . "each donor of a choice button came under the charm, and nothing could break the friendship between that person and the owner of the charm string." **1967** *DARE* (Qu. W33, . . *Jewelry . . woman's forearm*) Inf **AZ**1, Charm string. **1976** *Miami Herald* (FL) 15 Jan sec B, One of the prize displays at the local button show is an authentic "charm string" collection, popular at the turn of the century. "Young girls . . sometimes collected buttons or received them as gifts. They would be strung and counted. Supposedly, when the girl reached 999 buttons, her final prize would be Prince Charming, who would come and take her away and they would live happily ever after."

charn See **churn** A

charnce See **chance** A

charnier See **chenier** 1

charnina See **czarnina**

char-pit v

1919 *DN* 5.54 **WA**, *Char pit*. To burn out (stumps). August Schmitz is quite busy char pitting stumps. He has about fifty to smoke out.

charro n, also attrib [MexSpan] **SW**

1 A Mexican cowboy or horseman, usu in a spec costume (see quot 1932); by ext, the costume he wears.

[**1898** Lummis *Awakening* 20 **Mexico**, Yet Leon is a prosperous and contented city, full of little and big manufactures of yarn . . and the beautiful *charro* suits of velvety kid-skin.] **1932** Bentley *Spanish Terms* 120, *Charro* . . . A horseman or one skilled in horsemanship. *Charro* is commonly used in English contexts when referring to the suit which has become the more or less official national costume, the *charro* suit. It consists of a large grey, black, or brown felt sombrero decorated with silver or gold embroidery, a short jacket, also embroidered, over a soft shirt with a colored necktie; trousers that fit snugly and flare at the bottom and are trimmed with braid and ornamented with buttons. The suit may be made of soft-tanned leather, buckskin, or of cloth . . . The riding appurtenances, saddle, bridle, spurs, etc., of the *charro* are elaborately decorated to harmonize with the *charro* costume . . . its use in Mexico is decreasing except for parade or other similar functions. **1940** *FWP Guide NM* 111, *Charro*—Gaudy clothes of embroidered fabrics. **1967** *DARE* (Qu. FF16, . . *Local contests or celebrations*) Infs **TX**27, 31, Charro days. **1967** *DARE* Tape **TX**31, The charro days is a celebration inaugurated here in which everybody dresses up in Mexican costumes, and then they have this annual parade . . . held right before Lent.

2 An ill-bred, coarse person.

1939 Carlisle *Southwestern Dict.*, Charro . . . Coarse one; churl; ill-bred person. **1940** *FWP Guide NM* 111, Charro . . . Also an ill-bred person.

chart class n [From the chart used as an aid in learning] *old-fash*

Kindergarten; the first year of school.

1949 (1958) Stuart *Thread* 4 **KY**, I had pupils from the chart class to and including the eighth grade. **1969** *DARE* Tape **KY**5, We'd begin at the chart class . . . they call 'em kindergartens nowadays . . . learn our ABC's an' how to count a hundred on this chart.

charted See **chartered** 1

charter v [Prob back-form from **chartered**] Cf **chartered** 1

Of whiskey: to age in charred kegs.

1939 *FWP Guide TN* 426 [Moonshining], Under the leaves in the hollows they stashed (cached) away the fresh corn in ten-gallon kegs and let it charter (char) for months.

chartered adj [Prob alter, by folk-etym, of *charred*] **Sth, S Midl**

1 also *charted;* Of whiskey: refined by straining through charcoal or aging in charred kegs.

1959 Faulkner *Mansion* 13 **MS**, The rich man himself in the house, the warm kitchen, with in his hand a toddy not of the stinking gagging homemade corn . . but of good red chartered whiskey ordered out of Memphis. **1967** *DARE* FW Addit **GA**21A, *Charted moonshine*— moonshine treated with charcoal in some way. It is yellow, while ordinary moonshine is white. **1970** *DARE* (Qu. DD21c, *Nicknames for whiskey*) Inf **TN**53, Chartered whiskey.

2 Of kegs used in whiskey production: charred.

[**1963** Carson *Social Hist. Bourbon* 36 **KY**, There occurred a fortuitous discovery by the bourbon distillers that aging in charred white oak barrels enormously improved the whiskey which slumbered for several summers in the casks. There are many legends about the origin of charring. But it appears to have been completely a matter of chance.] **1965–66** *DARE* (Qu. DD29, . . *Containers for liquor;* total Infs questioned, 75) Inf **MS**60, Chartered kegs. **1971** Thompson Coll. **GA** (as of 1920s), Chartered-oak keg [kæg] . . said to be used to age whiskey in.

chase n

1 also *chase 'em, chase the shooters, chase-ups, chasies, (poon) chasing:* A marble game in which opponents shoot in turn at the other's marble as they move along, one thus always pursuing the other.

1922 *DN* 5.186 **MN**, *Chase* . . . A game in which one boy throws a marble and the other throws his so as to hit it and thus win it. **1935** *AmSp* 10.159 **seNE**, *Chase-ups*. Played with two *shooters* only, each hit meaning the forfeit of a *commie*. **1940** *Recreation* (NY) 34.110, Chase. **1949** *PADS* 11.9 **CO**, Chase. **1955** *PADS* 23.13 **cwTN, cwAL**, Chase. **1958** *PADS* 29.31 **WI**, *Chase . . . chase 'em*. **1965–70** *DARE* (Qu. EE7, . . *Marble games*) 35 Infs, **scattered**, Chase; **PA**185, Chase the shooters; **AK**9, **WA**6, Chasing; **RI**12, Poon chasing—throw at a marble; if you hit it, you win it; **OR**10, Chasies. **1968** *DARE* Tape **IA**37, If you hit the other player's marble he was out of the game. You kept that up with four or five, maybe six players, until you boil it down to the last two, an' then when the other marble got hit, why then the game was over . . . That was a game called chase. **c1970** Wiersma *Marbles Terms* **MI**, Chase. **1973** Ferretti *Marble Book* 66, Boss-out . . . In the United States it is called *chasies*.

2 A game of tag.

1967–69 *DARE* (Qu. EE33, . . *Outdoor games*) Infs **CA**93, **SC**32, Chase—name for tag; **AL**41, 54, Chase.

3 A game in which one team hides from the other.

1969 *DARE* (Qu. EE12, *Games in which one captain hides his team and the other team tries to find it*) Infs **PA**216, **VT**16, Chase.

chase v

1 Among loggers: to pass or hand (something) from one person to another.

1925 *AmSp* 1.137 **Pacific NW** [Logger talk], "Chase" is the password. "Chase that Java and canned cow over here" . . . "Chase us a slab of that bull." **1968** Adams *Western Words*, *Chase the cow*—A logger's request for someone to pass the milk at the dining table.

2 In logging: see quot.

1958 McCulloch *Woods Words* **Pacific NW**, *Chase*—To hook or unhook logs at the landing.

3 To run, hurry; depart rapidly.

1966 *DARE* (Qu.Y18, *To leave in a hurry: "Before they find this out we'd better _____!"*) Inf **MS**10, Chase.

chase a cloud v phr

1944 Adams *Western Words*, *Chase a cloud*—To be thrown high from a horse.

chase a rabbit v phr *euphem*

To go to the toilet.

1941 *LANE* Map 354 **cMA**, *Privy* . . . To chase a rabbit.

chase 'em See **chase** n 1

chase oneself v phr

1 usu in imper phr *(go) chase yourself:* To leave, depart; to mind one's own business. **esp Nth**

1883 Peck *Mirth for Million* 79 **WI**, O, you go and chase yourself. That is not small pox Pa has got. **1896** Crane *Maggie* 126 **NYC**, Go chase yerself. **1896** (1898) Ade *Artie* 119 **Chicago IL**, Aw, go chase yourself. **1923** Paine *Comrades* 206 **ND**, Let him rest, Kid. You chase yourself below and look things over. **1965–70** *DARE* (Qu. II22, . . *Tell somebody to keep to himself and mind his own business*) Infs **CA**87, **IL**25, 111, **MA**73, **NJ**16, **WI**62, Go chase yourself; (Qu. NN12a, . . *To put a child off when he asks too many questions*) Infs **NJ**50, **WI**62, (Oh,) go chase yourself; (Qu. NN22b, . . *To drive away children*) Infs **PA**108, **WA**12, Go chase yourself; (Qu. NN26b, *Weakened substitutes for "hell"*) Infs **ME**22, **TN**23, Go chase yourself. [Prob understood as "go to hell"]

2 To hurry, move rapidly.

1967 *DARE* (Qu. A22, . . *To start working hard:* "She had only ten minutes to clean the room, but she _____ (and had it done in no time).") Inf **MI**68, Chased herself.

chase one's face v phr
=**chase oneself 1.**

1966 Barnes–Jensen *Dict. UT Slang* 8, Chase your face . . . get away, get out of here.

chaser n

1 In logging: see quots. [**chase** v 2] **chiefly Pacific NW**

1919 *DN* 5.55 **WA**, *Chaser* . . . The man who follows the logs as they are dragged through the forest and frees them from impediments. **1925** *AmSp* 1.136 **Pacific NW**. **1938** (1939) Holbrook *Holy Mackinaw* 259 **Nth**, *Chaser.* Man who unhooks logs from choker, high-lead logging. **1956** *AmSp* 31.150 **nwCA**, *Chaser* . . . A logger who unhooks logs as they are brought in from the woods. **1958** McCulloch *Woods Words* **Pacific NW**, *Chaser* a. In the early days of ground lead yarding the chaser followed or chased the logs from the woods to the landing to see that they did not hang up en route, to replace chokers which were always falling out of the open choker hooks used in those days, and to open and close yarding blocks, allowing the butt rigging and log to pass by. b. Now the chaser mostly unhooks the chokers from logs at the landing. Sometimes the name is given to a loader. **1977** Churchill *Don't Call* 44 **nwOR** (as of c1918), A chaser, in logging terminology, she explained, was a worker who followed the logs in from felling areas. The big machines with their heavy drums of steel cables reeled the logs in, like a fisherman reeling in a fish. In the old ground logging days the logs came plowing in flat on the ground. They often hung up on roots or stumps. The job of a chaser was to free them. Chasing was a miserable job and about as dangerous as chewing on a dynamite cap, since the chaser was often within reach of moving lines, the deadly whip of a vine maple limb, and the crushing weight of a toppled tree or snag.

2 =**nigger chaser.**

1967–70 *DARE* (Qu. FF28, . . *Kinds of fireworks*) Infs **KY**81, **MI**100, **MO**30, **OH**5, Chasers. **1976** Flexner *America Talking* 152, Fireworks . . *serpents* . . which burned with a serpentine motion; also called *snakes,* a similar type was called *chasers.*

3 A wind; see quot.

1967 *DARE* Tape **TX**41, Texas twister, but around here it's mostly called chaser.

chase the fox n Also *chasing the fox* Cf **fox and dog(s), fox and geese**

Any of various children's games in which one player (or one couple) is pursued by the others; see quot.

1967–70 *DARE* (Qu. EE1, . . *Games . . in which they form a ring*) Inf **CO**3, Chase that fox — house game, two lines, "Up and down that center we go — the last couple is out"; (Qu. EE26, . . *Games . . in the snow*) Inf **MO**21, Chase the fox; **NJ**3, Chase the fox (ring in the snow); (Qu. EE27, *Games played on the ice*) Inf **AR**47, Chase the fox — one guy takes out and he hides and the others try to catch up with him (when the creek used to freeze); (Qu. EE33, . . *Outdoor games*) Inf **TX**13, Chase the fox — one would be the fox with a head start and the others would be dogs and try to catch the fox; **NC**84, Chasing the fox; (Qu. EE16, *Hiding games that start with a special, elaborate method of sending the players out to hide*) Inf **TN**37, Chasing the fox.

chase the gator n Cf **alligator** n[1] **B 10**

A tag game played in the water.

1966 *DARE* (Qu. EE28, *Games played in the water*) Inf **GA**3, Chase the gator — same as tag but the one who has to catch others is called the gator.

chase the shooters See **chase** n 1

chase the squirrel n

In various games or dance figures: see quots.

1952 Brown *NC Folkl.* 1.80 **NC** (as of c1927), *Chase the Squirrel* . . a sort of steeplechase. One boy is given a start; then the rest chase him, singing . . . and following exactly in his tracks. The object is to see if they can catch him by taking the same risks he does. **1966–67** *DARE* (Qu. FF5a, . . *Steps and figures in dancing*) Inf **NC**4, Chase the squirrel; (Qu. EE1, . . *Games . . in which they form a ring*) Inf **CO**3, Chase the squirrel.

chase-ups, chasies, chasing See **chase** n 1

chasing sheep n
=**run sheep run.**

1967 *DARE* (Qu. EE12, *Games in which one captain hides his team and the other team tries to find it*) Inf **AL**32, Chasin' sheep.

chasing the duck See **duck** n[1]

chasing the fox See **chase the fox**

chasing the ring n

1968 *DARE* (Qu. EE1, . . *Games . . in which [children] form a ring*) Inf **GA**28, Chasing the ring.

chassay v Also sp *chassé, chassez* [Fr *chasser* to chase; past pple *chassé*] Cf **sashay**

To move in a rapid slide or glide; to dance the chassé; to move along.

1835 [see **brogan 1**]. **1850** Garrard *Wah-to-yah* 95 **CO**, By this time, I had made acquaintance of many young men and girls, and often I chassaed up to the scalps, and joined in the chorus. **1884** Harrison *Negro Engl.* 263 **SE**, To chassay 'roun' = to dance around, to be polite. *Ibid* 278, Chassay forrard! = move forward. **1929** *AmSp* 5.76 **NE**, I think I'll chasse over to Jones' place to pass a word. **1944** Adams *Western Words*, *Chasséd.*

chaste tree n [By ref to *agnus castus* pure lamb]

An aromatic shrub or small tree *(Vitex agnus-castus)* widely planted and somewhat naturalized in the southern US. Also called **hemp tree, Indian spice, monk's peppertree, sage tree, wild lavender, wild peppertree**

1900 Lyons *Plant Names* 395, *Vitex Agnus-castus* . . Chaste-tree. **1933** Small *Manual SE Flora* 1144, *Vitex Agnus-Castus* . . Chaste-tree. **1969** *SC Market Bulletin* 9 Jan 4, Chaste tree. **1979** *Little Checklist U.S. Trees* 294, *Vitex agnus-castus* . . Common chaste-tree . . is a shrub or sometimes small tree.

chat n[1] See **yellow-breasted chat**

chat n[2] Also sp *chatt* [Cf *OED chat* "A small poor potato", 1840 →] Cf **shat**

See quots.

1959 *VT Hist.* new ser 27.129, Chatts . . . Potato peelings. Occasional. Windsor. **1970** *DARE* File **eVT** (as of c1950), Chats — potato peelings.

chat n[3], also attrib [Cf *EDD chat* sb.[1] "A piece of stone blended with lead ore" and *W3 chat*] **Cent** Cf **chad** n[2], **shat**

Gravelly tailings from mines, often used to surface roads; also a small bit of this material.

1915 *School Sci. & Math.* 566, In Missouri a considerable amount of road material is obtained from the tailings of the concentrating mills at the zinc mines. This material, which is put on the market as "chats," consists of small angular fragments of chert and limestone. **1939** *FWP Guide KS* 440, The chert [=residue from the zinc mines], or "chat", as it is more commonly known, is used in this region as railroad ballast, for road surfacing, and in concrete aggregate. **1953** Randolph *Down in Holler* 13, The fine gravel which is heaped up about lead-mines in the Joplin, Missouri, district is correctly known as chert, but the local people always call it *chat,* to ryme with *hat.* **1965** *DARE* FW Addit **OK**19, Chat [čæt] — coarse gravel. **1968** *DARE* (Qu. C26, . . *Kinds of stone or rock*) Infs **MO**4, 10, 25, Chat; (Qu. N27a, . . *Kinds of unpaved roads*) Infs **MO**4, 10, Chat road. **1968** *DARE* Tape **MO**25, They have mounds of this chat [as a by-product of lead mining] . . . it's in little bitty things like small gravel only it's white and it looks more like a lime rock and they call it a chat. **1984** *Joplin Globe* (MO) 13 Sept, Allen said chat has been carried from Galena by the truckloads, and is on many graveled roads throughout the county.

chater n [Etym unknown]

A small frog that makes shrill noises in spring; a "peeper."

1979 *DARE* File **nwOH**, About March 15 to 20 the sun warmed the pond enough to bring out the little frogs or as we called them the "Peepers" or "Chaters." They are about the size of a man's thumb nail.

chatt See **chat** n[2]

chatterbox n [See quot 1915] **chiefly Pacific NW**

The giant **helleborine** (here: *Epipactis gigantea*).

1915 (1926) Armstrong *Western Wild Flowers* 74, *Chatter-box* . . . Although the flowers are very handsome this curious tremulous motion . . gives them a quaint likeness to an old woman in a sunbonnet, with a hooked nose and chattering jaw. **1934** Haskin *Wild Flowers Pacific Coast* 73, "Chatter-Box" . . . The flowers which strongly suggest those of the lady's slipper are green and purple. **1950** FWP *Guide ID* 69, A member of the lily family, it [hellebore] has very showy green flowers that strongly resemble the lady's slipper. The lower portion hangs as though on a hinge and moves easily, so giving the plant its folk name of chatterbox. **1976** Bailey–Bailey *Hortus Third* 430.

chatter-bump n
A bump or hole in a road that makes a vehicle rattle.
1966 DARE (Qu. N27b, *When unpaved roads get very rough*) Inf **MI2,** Full of chatter-bumps.

chattering flycatcher n
=**yellow-breasted chat.**
1785 Pennant *Arctic Zool.* 2.385 **NC, SC,** Chattering (Fly-catcher) . . . Lives by the banks of great rivers; and makes so loud a chattering, as to reverberate from rock to rock. **1858** Baird *Birds* 248, *Icteria viridis* . . . Chattering flycatcher.

chattering plover n
=**killdeer.**
1731 (1754) Catesby *Nat. Hist. Carolina* 1.71 *Pluvialis vociferus.* The chattering Plover. **1789** Morse *Amer. Geog.* 59, Chattering Plover or Kildee. **1917** (1923) *Birds Amer.* 1.259 *Oxyechus vociferus* . . . Chat-tering Plover. **1946** Hausman *Eastern Birds* 256, *Oxyechus vociferus* . . Chattering Plover.

chatwood n, also attrib [Engl dial *chat* a twig or small branch suitable for kindling]
Kindling wood.
1911 *Century Dict.,* Chat-wood . . . Little sticks; fuel. **1947** Adams *Banner* 95 **NY** (as of 1817–47), Near Syracuse they spent the night in an abandoned barge and breakfasted over a chatwood fire.

chaugset See **chogset**

chaumber See **chamber** A

chaunce See **chance** A

chaunchy adj, adv |ˈčɔnčɪ| [Perh blend of **chinchy** and *raunchy*] s**LA**
1 Worthless; in a cheap, tawdry manner.
1968 DARE (Qu. LL2, . . *Too small to be worth much: "I don't want that little _____ potato."*) Inf **LA35,** Chaunchy. **1968** DARE FW Addit **csLA,** If a woman dresses too loud without taste with too much makeup and earrings down to here you say she's dressing chaunchy.
2 =**chinchy.**
1968 DARE FW Addit **csLA** [Waitress], Chaunchy [čɔ̌čɪ] =stingy.

chaunchy n
1967 DARE FW Addit **LA34,** Chaunchy [čɔnčɪ]—nickname for Mexi-cans along the Sabine River around Zwolle; also called pepper-bellies.

chauncy n
1969 DARE (Qu. H57, *Tasty or spicy side dishes served with meats*) Inf **KY41,** Apple chauncy [ˈčɔnsi]—apples, raisins, spices, vinegar, sugar.

chaunk See **chank** v

chaw n See **chew** n

chaw v See **chew** v

chawbacon n Cf DS HH1
A rustic, hick, country person.
1834 *Life Andrew Jackson* 76, If a few dozen chaw-bacons be us'd up for the public benefit as solemn warnins tu the obstropulous tu be quiet, isn't the glory of the nation increas'd by it. **1899** (1912) Green *VA Folk-Speech,* Chaw-bacon . . . A countryman. **1941** LANE Map 450 **nwCT,** Chaw-bacon, heard from lumbermen. **1946** in 1953 Botkin *Treas. Railroad Folkl.* 183, No countrified allusions to "the 9.30" or the "down train" or the "express," as the chaw-bacons in some hick town would call them.

chaw beef See **chaw raw beef**

chaw-chaw n [Echoic]
=**red-bellied woodpecker.**
1959 AmSp 34.73, Chaw-chaw (red-bellied woodpecker).

chawed See **chewed**

chawed rosum n Pronc-sp for *chewed rosin;* cf **rosin**
1953 Randolph *Down in Holler* 233 **Ozarks,** Chawed rosum . . . Some-thing conspicuously excellent. "This here gun," said a hunter brandish-ing a new rifle, "is the *chawed rosum* an' no mistake!"

chawed up See **chewed** 1

chawers See **chewers**

chawing See **chewing** 1

chawing-up vbl n Cf **chew out**
A bawling-out.
1883 Twain *Life on Missip.* (Boston) 44 **AR,** Leave him to me; he's my meat . . . You lay thar tell the chawin-up's done.

chawk eye See **chalk-eye** v

chawmber See **chamber** A

chaw-mouth n
A very talkative person.
1964 *PADS* 42.39 **Chicago IL,** [Names for Irish:] *Chaw-mouth* . . which refers to the Irishman's talkativeness. **1967** Cerello *Dakota Co. MN* 48, He's an absolute chaw-mouth and tells everything he knows—and at times even more.

chawnk See **chank** v

chawnkin's See **chankings**

chaw raw beef v phr Also *chaw (roast) beef*
To use one's teeth to untie knots in (wet) clothing.
1895 *Searcher* 1.50/2, There is a peculiar practice that obtains among boys "in swimming time;" I refer to the practice of "chawing roast beef." When a boy is out in the water his mischievous companions seize the opportunity of taking his shirt and tying it into hard knots . . . If the sleeves are wet, the knots are all the more difficult to untie . . . The idea seems to have originated in the habit of the victim chewing on the knots, as it is almost impossible to untie them with the fingers alone. **1899** *Philistine* 9.125 **NY,** He'll suck eggs, catch mice for the fun of clipping their ears and tails, and make you "chaw beef" if he gets a chance. **1942** McAtee *Dial. Grant Co. IN* 73 (as of 1890s), *Chaw raw beef* . . untie with the teeth knots tied in clothing at swimming "holes" by practical jokers. **c1970** DARE File **IL,** Chaw raw beef—used as a child, to use the teeth to untie a swimmer's clothes that have been wetted and knotted.

chawswizzled adj [Fanciful formation; cf *bamboozled, horn-swoggled*]
1905 DN 3.60 **NE,** Chawswizzled . . . Confounded. "I'll be chawswiz-zled."

chaw wax See **chewing wax**

chay v [Ir; cf EDD *chay,* intj "[tʃē.] Used to quiet cows."]
Come!—used as a call to cows.
1949 AmSp 24.107 ceSC, Chay! A call to summon cows. **1980** McDavid Coll. **SC,** Chay! to my surprise I first encountered (and in fact only encountered) in a field trip up the north side of the Santee in the fall of 1946. It came up from more than one of my informants in Kingstree (Williamsburg Co.), and from at least one of those in Manning (Claren-don County) . . . As I recall it was a prolonged tense /e/, with perhaps a smidgin of inglide at the end, tone level, beginning and continuing mid or mid-high, with a fall at the end.

chay-chay n [Echoic]
1 The blue-gray **gnatcatcher** *(Polioptila caerulea).*
1949 Sprunt–Chamberlain *SC Bird Life* 413, *Polioptila caerulea caer-ulea . . . Local Names:* Chay-chay. **1959** AmSp 34.73, *Chay-chay* (brown-head nuthatch; blue-gray gnatcatcher).
2 The brown-headed **nuthatch** *(Sitta pusilla).* Cf **cha-cha** 2
1959 [see **1** above].

chayote n Also sp *cheyote* [MexSpan]
A squash-like plant *(Sechium edule)* grown for the edible fruits and root tubers. Also called **mirliton, vegetable pear**
1911 *Century Dict.,* Chayote . . . The fruit of *Chayota edulis,* a cucur-bitaceous plant . . . Also *cheyote.* **1942** Rawlings *Cross Creek Cookery* 55 **FL,** The chayotes grow pendulous, pear-shaped, their color the palest jade-green. **1967–68** DARE (Qu. I23, . . *Squash*) Inf **HI1,** Chayotes; (Qu. I53, . . *Fruits*) Inf **CA80,** Chayote. **1976** Bailey–Bailey *Hortus Third* 258, The chayote . . . is adaptable also to the coastal parts of the United States from South Carolina southward and to southern Califor-nia.

che- See **ker-**

cheap cutter n Also *cheap critter*

A person inferior in character or intellect.

1926 *AmSp* 2.82 **ME,** In the community at large an unvirtuous person is a "cheap critter (or cutter)." **1929** *AmSp* 5.118 **ME,** One who was shallow-pated, pretentious and probably dishonest was a "cheap cutter."

cheapie n

In marble play: a marble of low value.

1958 *PADS* 29.31 **WI,** *Cheapie* . . . A cheap marble. **1968** *DARE* (Qu. EE6c, *Cheap marbles*) Infs **NY**120, **TX**54, Cheapies.

cheap John n, also attrib [*OED* 1826–27 →]

1 A person dealing in inferior goods; by ext, one who does things in a gaudy, niggardly, or inferior style; a stingy or niggardly person.

1880 *Harper's Mag.* 61.348/1 **ME,** Outside stood Isaacson—a travelling cheap-John who had opened a stock of secondhand garments for ladies and gentlemen in a disused fish-house on the wharf. **1908** *DN* 3.298 **eAL, wGA,** *Cheap John* . . . A niggardly or stingy person, one who does things in a cheap style: often used attributively. **1912** *DN* 3.573 **wIN,** *Cheap John* . . . One who does things in cheap style; especially one who sells goods of any kind on the street corners. **1955** Harris *Look of Old West* 93, A neatly pressed pair of trousers with the crease down each leg would have marked you instanter as a cheap John. **1968** *DARE* (Qu. U33, . . *A stingy person*) Inf **NC**79, Cheap John.

2 Cheap goods; something inexpensive, inferior, or in poor taste.

1855 Helper *Land of Gold* 164 **CA,** Notwithstanding all its Peter Funk and Cheap John establishments, it sustains a better character than any other city in the state. **1872** Twain *Roughing It* 325 **NV,** None of your cheap-John turn-outs for me. I'm here to have a good time, and money ain't any object. **1905** *DN* 3.74 **nwAR,** *Cheap John* . . . In poor taste, low-bred, vulgar. "We don't want any cheap John shows in this lecture course." **1944** Clark *Pills* 302 **Sth,** Every store was in the jewelry trade, stocks ranged from small handfuls of essential items to wide cases filled with elaborate displays of baubles and "cheap john."

cheap screw See **screw**

‡cheap tail n

=**lamb's leg.**

1968 *DARE* (Qu. X16, *Sticky mucus that forms in the nose*) Inf **IN**3, Cheap tails. [*DARE* Ed: perh for *sheep tail*]

cheapwad n [Perh blend of *cheapskate* + *tightwad*]

A cheapskate.

1970 *DARE* (Qu. U35, *Words meaning thrifty but not in a complimentary way*) Inf **VA**73, Cheapwad.

chear See **chair**

cheat n [Prob from its deceptive resemblance to good grain]

1 also *cheatgrass, cheet:* =**bromegrass.**

1784 Smyth *Tour U.S.A.* 2.121 **MD,** To prevent my seed being mixed with darnel, cheat, or false grain, which had begun to infest my plantation and fields of wheat, I steeped all my seed in a brine of salt. **1806** (1905) Lewis *Orig. Jrls. Lewis & Clark Exped.* 5.107 **West,** A third species [of native grass] resembles the cheet. **1834** *Life Andrew Jackson* 165, He wou'd jist see if he cou'dn't spifflicate the ivybush of Uncle Sam in sich way that he cou'dn't tell cheat from timothy. **1887** Eggleston *Graysons* 331 **cIL,** Tom stopped the noisy fanning-mill to shovel back the wheat and to rake away the cheat. **1900** Lyons *Plant Names* 69, *Bromus secalinus* . . Cheat Grass. **1944** *PADS* 2.32 **NC, sVA,** *Cheat* . . . "Grows in a wheat field—looks like wheat, but ain't; it's said to be poison." **c1960** Wilson *Coll.* **csKY,** *Cheat* . . . A grass that grows in wheat and around the edges of plowed fields. **1965–70** *DARE* (Qu. S9, . . *Kinds of grass that are hard to get rid of*) 9 Infs, **chiefly NW,** Cheatgrass; (Qu. S15, . . *Weed seeds that cling to clothing*) Infs **AR**10, **WA**1, 12, Cheatgrass (seeds); (Qu. S21, . . *Weeds . . in gardens and fields*) Infs **MD**23, **WA**6, Cheatgrass; (Qu. S13, . . *Round, prickly seeds*) Inf **OR**1, Cheatgrass; (Qu. L9a, . . *Grass . . grown for hay*) Inf **OR**10, Cheatgrass; (Qu. L24) Inf **MD**13, Cheat.

2 Darnel.

1899 (1912) Green *VA Folk-Speech, Cheat* . . . Darnel, a deleterious grass growing among wheat. **1900** Lyons *Plant Names* 228, *L[olium] temuléntum* . . . Darnel . . cheat. **1915** *DN* 4.181 **swVA,** *Cheat* . . . Darnel. **1923** in 1925 Jepson *Manual Plants CA* 107, *Lolium temulentum* . . Cheat. **1930** OK Univ. Biol. Surv. *Pub.* 1.51, *Lolium temulentum* . . Cheat.

cheater n

1a Something which makes a job or activity easier.

1941 *AmSp* 16.240 **Detroit MI** [Auto workers], *Cheater.* Rear view mirror. **1963** *AmSp* 38.205 [Skiing slang], *Cheaters* . . . Slang for metal skis. When metal skis were first introduced by racers, they were called *cheaters* because of their easier maneuverability. **1968** Adams *Western Words, Cheaters*—In gambling, marked cards. **1969** *AmSp* 44.12 **WA** [Painter jargon], *Cheater* . . . A paint roller used to apply paint—it cheats men out of hours of work.

b pl: Eyeglasses; infreq sunglasses. **esp Nth, N Midl, West** See Map

1931 *AmSp* 6.330 [Carnival terms], *Cheaters* . . . Eye-glasses. **1950** *WELS* (*Eye-glasses*) 11 Infs, **WI,** Cheaters. **1965–70** *DARE* (Qu. X23, . . *Eyeglasses*) 165 Infs, **esp Nth, N Midl, West,** Cheaters. **1970** Major *Afro–Amer. Slang, Cheaters:* (1930's) dark eyeglasses; later, supplanted by *Shades.*

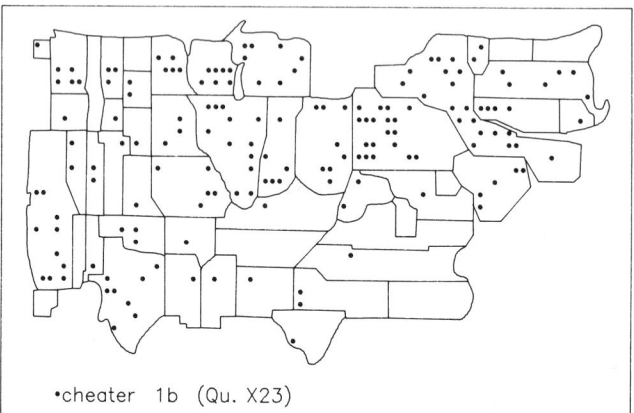

•cheater 1b (Qu. X23)

c pl: False teeth.

1950 *WELS* (*False teeth*) 1 Inf, **cWI,** Cheaters. **1966–69** *DARE* (Qu. X13b, . . *False teeth*) Infs **GA**72, **MI**10, **WA**9, Cheaters.

d also *cheater bar:* A length of pipe put over the handle of a wrench to increase leverage.

1959 *AmSp* 34.77 **nCA** [Logging], *Cheater bar* . . . A length of pipe used to tighten the binders on a truck load. **1960** Climax Molybdenum Co. *Manual* 46, *Cheater*—A pipe placed on the end of a wrench to give more leverage. **1961** *PADS* 36.27 **West** [Construction terms], *Cheater* . . . A short length of pipe which slips over the handle of a wrench to give additional length and leverage. **1966** *Daily Oklahoman* (Oklahoma City OK) 11 Dec mag sec 11/3 [Oil terms], "Cheaters" are pieces of pipe used to extend the length of manually operated tools.

e See quot.

1983 *DARE* File **seME,** One local name . . used by Mainiacs on the off-islands of Maine [is]—a cheater. Most of the smaller islands have short roads (a total of less than three miles on Matinicus) and the natives resent paying licenses. So the cars they buy are usually cheaters, so-called because they cheat in more ways than one. First, they usually buy cars which are cheap because they cannot pass inspection to qualify for a license. Second, they buy them from individuals who do not charge a sales tax . . . Third, they sneak these cars on a ferry by borrowing a license plate from another car.

2 Among loggers: one who measures the board feet in a log; a camp clerk. Cf **cheat stick** See also *DCan*

1958 McCulloch *Woods Words* **Pacific NW,** *Cheater*—a. Timekeeper. b. Scaler. **1969** Sorden *Lumberjack Lingo* **NEng, Gt Lakes,** *Cheater*—Nickname for the camp clerk or the scaler.

cheater bar See **cheater 1d**

cheatgrass See **cheat 1**

cheat stick n, also attrib Cf **cheater 2**

In logging: a rule used by a scaler to determine the number of board feet in a log.

1942 *AmSp* 17.220 [Logging], *Cheat stick.* A scaler's rule. A sawyer's pay is gauged by the scaler. **1958** McCulloch *Woods Words* **Pacific NW. 1959** *AmSp* 34.77 **nCA** [Logging], *Cheat stick rigger* . . . A scaler. **1968** Adams *Western Words* 42, He [the bull bucker] records the daily cut of fallers and buckers, going from log to log, measuring the small end of each with wooden calipers or a "cheat stick," which gives a reading in board feet for a log of known length. **1972** *Yesterday* 1.2.23, The scalers . . estimated the board feet in the harvested logs. According to one old logger, this specialist could use his "cheat stick" ruler and Scribner's or Doyle's formula so as "not to give or take more wood than would make a perch for a Chickadee."

chebang See **ker-**

chebec n Also sp *chebeck, chebeque* [Echoic]
The least **flycatcher** (*Empidonax minimus*).
    1903 Dawson *Birds OH* 332, *Least Flycatcher . . . Synonym.—Chebec . . . Sewick—sewick,* or as some prefer to hear it, *che-bec,* sounds frequently in a very business-like tone of voice from the tip of the dead branch which serves the bird as a base of operations. **1914** Eaton *Birds NY* 2.199, The Least flycatcher or Chebeck, as it is usually called, is a common summer resident of all portions of the State. **1946** Hausman *Eastern Birds* 405, *Least Flycatcher . . . Other Names*—Chebec, Chebeque. **1972** *WI Conserv. Bulletin* 37.4, The dominant expression of the least flycatcher is its *che-bec* call. It is so prominent, in fact, that people in some parts of our country simply call this flycatcher the *che-bec.* The accent is on the second syllable.

checacho, chechaco, chechak(h)o, chechaquo See **cheechako**

chechinquamin, chechinquarnin See **chinquapin**

che-choker See **cheechako**

check n¹
  1 A cross point of furrows which have been plowed at right angles to one another to mark the planting point and facilitate plowing between and across the rows; also the square so marked; hence *checkrow* a row of squares so set off. [**check** v 1]
    1787 (1925) Washington *Diaries* 3.194 **neVA**, In each of these checks or crosses, one root, when it was large and looked well, was put. **1864** *Rep. Agric. Soc. Maine* 160 (DA), It is then to be laid off with a plow . . & a small hill made in or on the check . . for the reception of the plant. **1888** VT State Bd. Ag. *Report* 10.26, He . . puts the crop in check rows, to be able to cultivate thoroughly both ways. **1945** FWP *Lay My Burden Down* 168 **Sth**, Checking corn is running a straight row clean 'cross the field both ways, and it make a check 'bout two feet square.
  2 in pl: A game in which the players toss, catch and arrange a set of small objects in a variety of figures; see quot 1899. [Cf *EDD check* sb.² 3] *old-fash* See also **jack** n² 1
    1774 (1957) Fithian *Jrl. & Letters* 189 **eVA**, A small game with Peach-stones which they call *checks.* **1899** (1912) Green *VA Folk-Speech, Checks . . .* A game among children, in which five marbles are thrown and caught on the back of the hand; or one is thrown up, and before it is caught as it falls the others are picked up, or placed in ones, twos, threes, or fours. **1908** *DN* 3.298 **eAL, wGA**, *Checks . . .* An indoor game with marbles, being a series of movements of catching and placing the marbles (usually five) in various combinations, forms, etc.
  3 often pl: A playing piece in the game of checkers; the game itself. [Abbr for *checker(s)*] **Sth, S Midl**
    1844 Thompson *Major Jones's Courtship* 146 **GA**, Mary and me was playin a game of drafts, and I was jest about to pen her with three kings, when one of the checks happened to drap off the board. **1908** *DN* 3.298 **eAL, wGA**, *Check . . .* A piece used in the game of checkers. Rare. **1954** Harder *Coll.* **cwTN**, *Checks . . .* checkers (table game). **c1960** Wilson *Coll.* **csKY**, *Checkers . . .* Common game. Often checks. **1968–69** *DARE* (Qu. DD37, . . *Table games*) Inf **SC58**, Check; **AL51**, Checks.
  4 A checkrein; occas a driving rein. [Abbr] Cf **checkrein**
    1868 Woodruff *Trotting Horse* 202 (DAE), In order to prevent him from throwing down his head . . the well-known Kemble-Jackson check . . was invented. **1887** Tourgée *Button's Inn* 122 **nOH**, Throw me that off rein, if you please . . . Just shift those inside checks, won't you? **1902** *DN* 2.231 **sIL**, Check or check-rein . . . Driving rein on a horse. **1967** *DARE* FW Addit **nwSC**, Check—leather from the top of the bridle to the hames to require a horse to hold his head up.
  5 Money; a dollar. *old-fash*
    1889 (1971) Farmer *Americanisms, Checks.*—Money; cash. A term derived from poker where counters or *checks* bought, as one enters, at certain fixed rates, are equivalent to current coin. **1932** *AmSp* 7.330 **MD** [Johns Hopkins Univ slang], *Check*—a dollar.
  6 See **checkerboard** 1.

check v
  1 also *checkrow*: To plant (or mark) a field in squares so that it can be plowed or cultivated both crosswise and lengthwise.
    1768 (1925) Washington *Diaries* 1.265 **VA**, At the first and last of wch. just began to check Corn G'd. **1871** IL State Ag. Soc. *Trans. for 1869–1870* 8.239 **IL**, After the field has been thoroughly prepared . . proceed to check it off from east to west with a three-rowed marker. **1944** *PADS* 2.32 **NC, VA**, *Check . . .* To sow corn in squares so that one may plow the cornfield lengthwise or crosswise. **1945** FWP *Lay My Burden Down* 168 **Sth**, That man would make them niggers on the plantation plow up a great big field . . and then check it for corn. And checking corn is running a straight row clean 'cross the field both ways. **c1960** Wilson *Coll.* **csKY**, *Check . . .* To plant corn where rows or furrows intersect. Formerly common. **1965–70** *DARE* (Qu. L22, . . *A crop he intends to plant* . . *"This year I'm going to _____."*) Infs **AR56, IN3, 63, KY80, NJ20, PA21, TN62, WI24**, Check corn; **MI83, ND3**, Checkrow corn. **1970** *DARE* FW Addit **KY84**, Check tobacco, old-fashioned—they make lines across a field to mark where the tobacco hills should be planted.
  2 To tease, taunt. [Engl dial]
    1941 Percy *Lanterns* 301 **MS**, A bunch of boys starts off jest talkin', then they starts kiddin', jest for fun, you know, and then they start checkin'. That's kiddin' what's rough.
  3 in phr *check you (later)*: Good-bye—used as a formula of leave-taking.
    1970 *DARE* (Qu. NN11, *Informal ways of saying "good-bye"*) Infs **FL48, TN46**, Check you later; **TN54**, I'll check you. [All Infs Black]
  4 See **check out** 2.

check n² [Scots *chack, check* a snack] **Appalachians**
A snack or light meal.
    1775 (1934) Fithian *Jrl.* 2.6 **sePA**, This is an Irish settlement—They speak in a shrill, acute, Accent, & have many odd Phrases . . . "Will you just take a Check?"—She meant a late Dinner. **1817** (1916) *MD Hist. Mag.* 11.368, Thence 15 Miles to the half way house fed & took a Check. **1839** Marryat *Diary* 1.197 **Ohio R Valley**, "Will you have a *feed* or a *check?*"—A dinner, or a luncheon? **1872** Schele de Vere *Americanisms* 452, *Check* is in Pennsylvania the name of an impromptu meal of cold provisions. **1949** Kurath *Word Geog.* 36 **WV**, On the Kanawha we find *check* and *jack-bite* . . beside the Southern *snack* for a bite between meals. **1952** Brown *NC Folkl.* 1.526, *Check . . .* A light meal.

checked adder See **checkered adder**

checkedy adj
Checkered.
    ?1917 *Star* (Kansas City MO) 3 Feb (*Ruppenthal Coll.*), Get out your old checkedy dress. **1968** *Foxfire* Fall-Winter 42 **nGA**, I seed that checkedy sole print in the soft ground.

checker n
  1 with *the*: The very thing; the appropriate thing. *old-fash*
    1854 (1923) Holmes *Tempest & Sunshine* 84 **KY**, By Jupiter! . . that's just the checker. **1911** Quick *Yellowstone Nights* 97 **SD**, When I hadn't but four sections . . I thought 'twas about the checker f'r a man with three boys. **1965** Gould *You Should Start* 19 **ME**, He said . . he had a beauty . . . He said it [=a chainsaw] was just the checker, and he was glad to see me have it because he was partial to it and wanted it to have a good home.
  2 The game of checkers.
    1968–69 *DARE* (Qu. DD37, . . *Table games*) Infs **MO39, VA27**, Checker.
  3 See quot.
    1930 *AmSp* 5.389 **N Atl** [Among fishermen], *Checkers . . .* Temporary adjacent enclosures or pens on deck to keep the fish from sliding about when the vessel rolls; there are usually four in the form of a divided square. The heavy planks of which they are made are called *checkerboards.*
  4 See **checker mallow.**

checkerbacker n
=**downy woodpecker.**
    1917 *DN* 4.409 **wNC**, *Checkerbacker . . .* Downy woodpecker.

checker-bark juniper See **checkered-bark juniper**

checkerbelly n Also *checkerbreast*
=**white-fronted goose.**

1918 Grinnell *Game Birds CA* 218, *Anser albifrons gambeli* . . . Checker-breast; Checker-belly. **1930** Phillips–Lincoln *Amer. Waterfowl* 287, White-fronted Goose *(Anser albifrons albifrons)* . . Checker-belly. **1953** Jewett *Birds WA* 110, *Anser albifrons frontalis* . . . Other names: White-fronted Goose; . . Checker Breast.

checkerberry n Also sp *chequerberry* [Etym uncert]

1 rarely *chidkerberry:* A **wintergreen 2** (here: *Gaultheria procumbens*).

1776 in 1877 *PA Mag. Hist. & Biog.* 1.173 **PA,** Some families [had] no other bread but patatoes for sometime, which with Checkerberry tea was seen the only food for a woman with a Sucking Child. **1843** *Amer. Pioneer* 2.125 **PA, NY,** The vivid green leaves and bright scarlet berries of the "Partridge bush," or "Checkerberry." **1891** Jesup *Plants Hanover NH* 26, *Gaultheria* . . Wintergreen or Checkerberry. **1900** Lyons *Plant Names* 169, *G[aultheria] procúmbens* . . . Canada and northeastern U.S. . . Checkerberry. **1948** Peattie *Berkshires* 57 **MA,** Most country children are familiar with the pleasant aromatic flavor of the young tender leaves of the checkerberry or wintergreen. **1951** Hough *Singing in Morning* 241 **seMA,** One of the most curious of the wild berries that may be found hereabouts . . is the checkerberry or wintergreen, more often called boxberry by our own people. **1965–70** *DARE* (Qu. I44, . . *Berries* . . *wild*) Infs **ME1, MA29, 66, 72, RI5, 9,** Checkerberries; (Qu. S26a, . . *Wildflowers*) Inf **ME7,** Checkerberry; (Qu. S26b) Inf **MA6,** Checkerberries. [*DARE* Note: some of these Infs may be referring instead to sense 2 or sense 3.] **1971** Krochmal *Appalachia Med. Plants* 128, *Gaultheria procumbens* . . . Checkerberry wintergreen, . . checkerberry, chequerberry, chidkerberry.

2 A **bearberry 2** (here: *Arctostaphylos uva-ursi*).

1784 in 1785 Amer. Acad. Arts & Sci. *Memoirs* 1.444, *Arbutus* . . . Foxberry. Checkerberry . . . The berries are rather of an agreeable taste, and are sometimes eaten by children in milk. **1941** *LANE* Map 274 **sVT,** [čɛkəberɨz], grow on a small vine 'called *mountain laurel* in the White Mountains.'

3 also *chickaberry, chickerberry:* =**partridgeberry 1.** Cf **chickberry**

1823 Cooper *Pioneers* 1.128 **cNY,** Is the poor devil to . . put them [=logs] in his pocket, . . as you would a handful of chesnuts, or a bunch of chicker-berries? [*DARE* Ed: sense uncert] **1872** Schele de Vere *Americanisms* 402, Partridge-berries. It is also known as *chequer*-berry, and in New England occasionally as *chick*-berry. **1900** Lyons *Plant Names* 249, *Mitchélla* . . . *répens* . . . Checker-berry. **1911** *Century Dict.*, Chickaberry . . . A corruption of *checkerberry*. **1971** Krochmal *Appalachia Med. Plants* 176, *Mitchella repens* . . . checkerberry.

4 A kind of candy.

1896 *DN* 1.414 **cNY,** *Checker-berries:* little red pepper candies.

checkerbloom n [See quot 1954] **chiefly CA**

A **wild hollyhock** (here: *Sidalcea malvaeflora*).

1911 Jepson *Flora CA* 260, *S[idalcea] malvaeflora* . . . Checkerbloom. **1949** Moldenke *Amer. Wild Flowers* 113 **CA,** The genus Sidalcea contains many, very showy flowers. Outstanding is the *checkerbloom, S. malveaflora,* which lives on open hillsides along the California coast. **1954** CA Div. Beaches & Parks *Pt. Lobos Wild Flowers* 16, From late February until May, Checker Bloom forms pink masses in the meadows near the sea . . . Veined petals . . give this flower its common name. **1976** Bailey–Bailey *Hortus Third* 1042.

checkerboard n

1 also *check,* freq attrib: A crew or group containing both black and white people.

1926 *AmSp* 1.650 [Hobo lingo], *Checker-board crew*—a mixed crew of white and negro workers. **1960** Wentworth–Flexner *Slang, Check crew (gang, mob, team,* etc.) Working groups composed of both Negro and white members . . . *Checkerboard* . . . A town, neighborhood, public gathering place, factory, etc., which contains both Negro and white elements. **1968** Adams *Western Words, Checkerboard crew*—In logging, a mixed crew of white and Negro workers.

2 A plank used to make a **checker 3.**

1930 [see **checker 3**].

checkerbreast See **checkerbelly**

checkered adder n Also *checked* ~ **chiefly NEng** Cf **chequered snake**

A **milk snake 1** (here: *Lampropeltis triangulum*).

1839 MA Zool. & Bot. Surv. *Fishes Reptiles* 227, *Coluber eximius* . . is

known by the names of . . chicken snake; milk snake; and chequered adder. **1842** DeKay *Zool. NY* 3.39, In this State, its most usual popular name is *Milk Snake,* although it has various other appellations. It is called *Chicken Snake, Thunder and Lightning Snake, House Snake,* and *Chequered Adder.* **1844** Stephens *High Life in NY* 2.172 **CT,** I say, par, did you ever see a checkered adder a charmin a bird . . ? **1952** Ditmars *N. Amer. Snakes* 43, "Milk" Snake, House Snake, Checkered "Adder", *Lampropeltis triangulum triangulum* . . . White beneath, with oblong spots of black, sometimes imparting a "checkerboard" effect. **1965–70** *DARE* (Qu. P25, . . *Snakes*) 11 Infs, **NEng,** Checkered adder; **CT36, MA68,** Checked adder. **1979** *Greenfield Recorder* (MA) 22 Sept A4/4, I remember once finding a good-sized checkered adder in the dooryard near a retaining wall and rushing into the house to get my mother.

checkered-bark juniper n Also *checker-bark* ~ [From the squarish plates of the bark] **AZ, NM, TX**

=**alligator juniper.**

1911 *Century Dict. Suppl.,* Juniper . . . Alligator-juniper or *checkered-bark juniper* . . . The names allude to the checkered bark, which is sometimes nearly four inches thick. **1960** Vines *Trees SW* 31, The vernacular name, Alligator Juniper, has been given the tree. Other names are Checker-bark Juniper and Tascate. **1979** Little *Checklist U.S. Trees* 155, Checker-bark juniper.

checkered paint n Cf **striped paint**

A non-existent item used as the basis of a practical joke.

1967–69 *DARE* (Qu. HH14, *Ways of teasing a beginner or inexperienced person . . by sending him for a "left-handed monkey-wrench")* Infs **KY10, MA33, NY141,** (Can of) checkered paint.

checkered woodpecker n

=**red-bellied woodpecker.**

1955 *Oriole* 20.1.10, Red-bellied Woodpecker . . . Checkered Woodpecker (the back is black-and-white banded, not checkered).

checker lily n [From the often mottled or "checkered" flowers]

A **fritillary,** usu *Fritillaria lanceolata* or *F. meleagris.*

1911 Jepson *Flora CA* 93, *F. lanceolata* . . Checker Lily . . . Perianth deeply bowl-shaped, dark purple mottled with greenish yellow. **1961** Thomas *Flora Santa Cruz* 118 **CA,** Checker Lily . . . Usually growing on wooded slopes, occasionally in exposed places. **1973** Hitchcock–Cronquist *Flora Pacific NW* 691, Checker lily . . . *F. atropurpurea* . . . *F. lanceolata.*

checker mallow n Also *checker* Cf **checkerbloom**

=**wild hollyhock** (here: *Sidalcea* spp).

1953 Nelson *Plants Rocky Mt. Park* 105, Wild hollyhock or New Mexican checkermallow, *Sidalcea neo-mexicana* . . . A plant with . . rose-purple flowers resembling miniature hollyhocks. **1959** Munz–Keck *CA Flora* 130, *Sidalcea* . . . Checker. **1973** Hitchcock–Cronquist *Flora Pacific NW* 292, Checker-mallow; Sidalcea. Fl[owers] white to deep pink or pinkish-lavender.

check in v phr

1 To die. Cf **check out 1** and **checks, cash in one's**

1912 Raine *Brand Blotters* 338 **AZ,** They couldn't take me alive at all, and I reckon before I checked in a few of them would. **1943** *LANE* Map 521 **neNH, MA,** Jocular and disrespectful synonyms of *died:* . . [3 infs] *checked in.*

2 To go to bed.

1965–70 *DARE* (Qu. X40, . . *Going to bed*) 12 Infs, **chiefly Atlantic,** Check in.

checkline n

1 A checkrein; see quots.

1939 *LANE* Map 177 **csMA,** The short straps running from cheek piece to hames or saddle, serving to hold up the horse's head . . . checkline. **1967** *DARE* FW Addit **nwSC,** Checklines—lines attached from left/right lines to the inside of the right/left horse's bit so that *both* horses could be directed to turn without depending on one horse to lead another.

2 A driving rein, **checkrein. chiefly S Midl** See Map

c1960 Wilson *Coll.* **csKY,** Check lines . . . Lines to guide a horse. **1965–70** *DARE* (Qu. L51, *The leathers or ropes that a driver holds to guide a horse*) 28 Infs, **chiefly S Midl,** Checklines.

check out v phr

1 To die. *euphem*

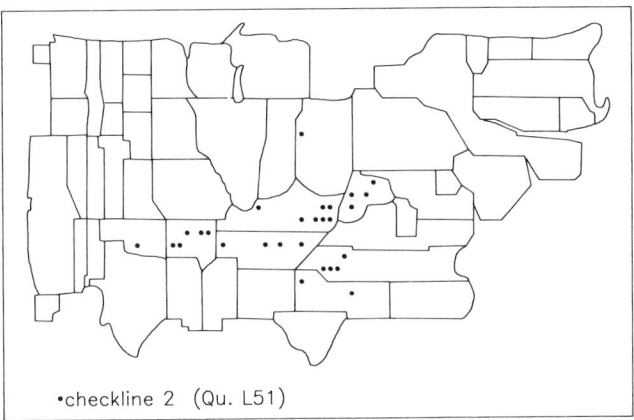

•checkline 2 (Qu. L51)

1936 *AmSp* 11.200, American Euphemisms for Dying . . . Checked out. **1943** *LANE* Map 521 **NH, neMA,** Jocular and disrespectful synonyms of *died:* . . [3 infs] *checked out.* **1957** *AmSp* 32.279 [Jazz argot], *Check out.* To die. **1965–70** *DARE* (Qu. BB56, *Joking expressions for dying*) Infs **IL29, MI27, 47, 81, SC2, VA30,** Checked out; **MA48,** Checking out; (Qu. BB57, . . *Suicide*) Inf **MS10,** Got tired of living and checked out; (Qu. BB54, *When a sick person is past hope of recovery*) Inf **IL29,** About to check out.

2 rarely *check:* To leave, esp hurriedly. **chiefly Sth**
    1965–70 *DARE* (Qu. Y18, *To leave in a hurry*) Infs **AL30, 43, GA9, NC41, SC2, 11, TX5, WV2,** Check out; **TX86,** Check; (Qu. Y19, *To begin to go away from a place*) Infs **GA44, MO27, NC55,** Check out; (Qu. Y20, *To run fast*) Inf **SC11,** Check out; (Qu. II31, . . *"He saw that he was wrong, so he started to _____."*) Inf **FL22,** Check out; (Qu. JJ31a, *What you'd say to a bus driver: "Please stop at the next corner—I want to _____."*) Inf **TX70,** Check out.

checkquered snake See **chequered snake**

checkrein n Cf **checkline 2**
    One of a pair of lines used to guide a horse or a team of horses.
    1902 *DN* 2.231 **sIL,** *Check* or *check-rein* . . . Driving rein on a horse. **1903** *DN* 2.309 **seMO,** *Check-reins* . . . Driving lines. 'I held the horses till one of the check-reins broke and then they ran away.' **1966–68** *DARE* (Qu. L51, *The leathers or ropes that a driver holds to guide a horse*) Infs **MO9, NC30, TN1,** Checkreins.

checkrow See **check** n[1] **1, check** v **1**

checks exclam
    1969 *DARE* (Qu. EE17, *In a game of tag, if a player wants to rest, what does he call out so that he can't be tagged?*) Inf **IL97,** Checks.

checks, cash in one's v phr Also (*hand, pass, throw,* or *turn*) *in one's checks* (or *chips*) and varr: see quots [See quot 1955; also sometimes understood as a *check* bank draft: see quot 1965–70] **scattered, but esp Nth, Midl** *euphem* Cf **cash in**
    To die.
    1871 Hay *Jim Bludso* 7 **Missip Valley,** How Jimmy Bludso passed in his checks / The night of the Prairie Belle. **1898** Lloyd *Country Life* 66 **AL,** But if I had to be nagged and bedeviled, and kicked around and crowded out like some old men I have seen I would rather pass in my checks and quit as soon as my time could come. **1912** *DN* 3.577 **wIN,** Hand in one's checks. **1918** *DN* 5.73 **NM,** Cash in checks, to die . . . Hand in checks, to die. **1922** *DN* 5.165 **IN,** Hand in one's checks. **1927** *AmSp* 2.356 **WV,** *Hand in your checks.* **1943** *LANE* Map 521 **NEng,** Jocular and disrespectful synonyms of *died:* [Freq *passed in his checks*; occas *cashed (in) his checks*; infreq *handed (or turned) in his checks, passed in his chips*]. **1955** Funk *Heavens to Betsy* 29, *To cash in* (*hand in,* or *pass in*) *one's checks* (or *chips*) Whichever the phraseology, it adds up to the one result—to die. The allusion is to the American game of poker, in which a player may at any time drop from the game and turn in (hand in, or pass in) his chips or checks to the banker in exchange for cash. **1965–70** *DARE* (Qu. BB56, *Joking expressions for dying*) 26 Infs, **chiefly Nth, Midl,** Cashed in his chips (*or checks*); 12 Infs, **chiefly Nth, N Midl,** Passed in his chips (*or checks*); **HI1, MI68, NY209, VA13,** Turned in his checks (*or chips*); **MI114, SD5,** Threw in the (*or his*) chips; **MA69,** Cash in your chips; **NY23,** Cashed his chips; **VA11,** Checking in his checks; **MD15,** Cashed his check; **CA59,** Signed his last check, took the last paycheck; (Qu. BB54, *When a sick person is past hope of recovery*) Inf **NY66,** Cashed in his chips; **CA7,** Ready to cash in his chips; **IL5,** Ready

to pass in his checks; (Qu. BB57, . . *Committed suicide*) Inf **CA53,** Threw in his chips; (Qu. BB18, *To vomit a great deal*) Inf **CA7,** Darn near cashed in my chips.

check-stretcher See **stretcher**

check you (later) See **check** v **3**

chedge water See **chinch water**

chee n See **cheese** n **A**

chee intj [Cf *EDD chee* an exclamation of incredility]
    1972 Carr *Da Kine Talk* 129 **HI,** *Chee!* or *Shee!* vs. *Gee!* . . . *Chee* and *shee* are local pronunciations of the American *gee.* Unvoicing of the initial affricate, producing *chee* (and its change to a fricative in *shee*) could have been an influence of the Chinese language.

cheechako n Usu |čĭ'čako, čĭ'čɔko| For var spp, see quots [Chinook jargon] **AK, Pacific NW**
    A newcomer, tenderfoot.
    1897 *Chicago Record* (IL) 2 Mar 4/4 **AK,** Many a "Chechaco" (tenderfoot) on his way to the mines, with a pack on his back, has thrown down everything and struck back for town . . cursing the country and its mosquitoes. **1900** Spurr *Through Yukon Gold Diggings* 51 (Tabbert *Alaskan Engl.*), The veteran miner in Alaska is a splendid, open-hearted, generous fellow; the newcomer, or "chicharko," is a thing to be avoided. **1901** *Pall Mall Mag.* 23.56 **cwAK,** 'Nome is a good camp, but too many cheechakers', that is 'tender feet', new comers. **1902** M. Clark *Roadhouse Tales, or Nome in 1900* 112 (Tabbert *Alaskan Engl.*), He thoroughly prospected the claim and found there was no gold in this one place, so he cleaned up nearly all the corner, and then laid for a "che-choker" to buy the claim. He soon found his man. **1904** (1969) Robins *Magnetic North* 271 **AK,** It is curious to see how soon travellers get past that first cheechalko feeling that it is a little 'nervy' . . to walk into another man's house uninvited. **1905** (1966) London *White Fang* 202 **AK,** The men who came . . were newcomers. They were known as *chechaquos* . . . They made their bread with baking powder. This was the invidious distinction between them and the Sour-doughs. **1933** Marshall *Arctic Village* 355, You help him poor man, help him cheechawker. **1939** Franck *Lure of AK* 118, Sourdoughs and Cheechakoes ("cheechalker" is the way Alaska really pronounces its word for tenderfoot) mingle freely in the streets of Fairbanks. **1939** FWP *Guide AK* xl, Chechakho "just arrived," hence, tenderfoot (Chinook). **1943** Brandt *AK Bird Trails* 24 (as of 1924), This was another hard run for the cheechockar (tenderfoot). **1944** Williamson *Far North* 46 **AK,** At Cook Inlet you might be on Monday morning a mere cheechakho, as a tenderfoot was called. **1955** U.S. Arctic Info. Center *Gloss.,* Cheechako, chechako, cheechaco . . . A term for a newcomer, derived from Northwest Coast Indian words meaning 'to come lately.' **1958** McCulloch *Woods Words* **Pacific NW,** Cheechako—A greenhorn. **1962** Salisbury *Quoth the Raven* 48 **seAK** (as of 1920s), Bill Gardner was out after deer, or to show the checacho how to hunt for deer. **1966–68** *DARE* (Qu. HH2, . . *A citified person*) Inf **AK5,** [čĭ'čako]; **AK8,** In Alaska a newcomer is a [čĭ'čɔko] (not necessarily derisory); (Qu. HH15, *A very inexperienced person*) Inf **AK5,** Cheechako; (Qu. HH31, *Somebody who is not from your community, and doesn't belong*) Inf **WA16,** Cheechako [čĭ'čako].

chee-chee n [Echoic]
    =**myrtle warbler.**
    1959 *AmSp* 34.73, Chee-chee (myrtle warbler).

chee-dee n [Echoic]
    =**pinewoods sparrow.**
    1968–70 *DARE* (Qu. Q22, . . *Common sparrow*) Infs **LA15, TX85,** Chee-dee.

cheeger See **chigger**

cheek v

1 also vbl n *cheeking:* See quots. **West**
    1911 *DN* 3.550 **WY,** *Cheek a horse,* to move the horse's head to the side, toward the saddle, when mounting. **1944** Adams *Western Words,* *Cheeking*—Grasping the cheek strap of the bridle just above the bits and pulling the horse's head as far toward the saddle as possible while mounting to prevent the horse from running or bucking. If a man does not know a horse, he is sure to cheek him the first few times. Cheeking pulls the horse toward you if he starts in motion, and this has the advantage of almost swinging you into the saddle without effort. Swinging in the opposite direction would make mounting more difficult.

2 To stand or dance cheek-to-cheek.

1951 *AmSp* 26.237, *Cheek.* The couple necked and cheeked through the dance.

3 To display or act with impudence or "cheek;" to bluff.

1900 *DN* 2.26 *Cheek* . . . In phrase 'cheek it,' to go into recitation unprepared as if prepared. **1951** *AmSp* 26.237, He had the nerve to cheek his way into the party. **1960** Wentworth–Flexner *Slang, Cheek it*—To bluff; to deceive, esp. a teacher or employer, by pretending to have knowledge or ability not actually possessed.

cheek cheek widow n [Echoic]
=chuck-will's-widow.

1897 (1952) McGill *Narrative* 183 **SC,** It was a bright and serene summer night, and Sam and Sarah sat together in the wide passage of their house listening to the music of the "cheek, cheek widows" in the surrounding groves of pine forest.

cheench See **chinch** n¹ **1**

cheep v [Imit of the sound of a bird] **chiefly S Midl**
To tell or reveal; to betray a confidence.

1903 *DN* 2.309 seMO, *Cheep* . . . To mention; to hint at; 'Don't cheep it to any one.' **1906** *DN* 3.130 nwAR, *Cheep* . . . To betray a secret. **1940** in 1968 Haun *Hawk's Done Gone* 22 **eTN,** I never did cheep it to Joe. **1946** Greer–Petrie *Angeline Gits an Eyeful* 11 csKY, I cawshun'd him to keep his mouth shet and never cheep it to nobody. **1952** Brown *NC Folkl.* 1.526 **c, eNC,** *Cheep* . . . To reveal confidential matter. **c1960** *Wilson Coll.* csKY, *Cheep* . . . Betray a secret. "He didn't cheep until I told him he could talk." **1966** *DARE* (Qu. JJ44, . . *Someone who can be trusted to keep a secret: ". . he'll _____."*) Inf **AR3,** Never cheep it.

cheeper n
A small frog or toad such as the **spring peeper.**

1950 *WELS* (*Small frogs that sing or chirp loudly in spring*) 1 Inf, **nMI,** Cheepers. **1965–70** *DARE* (Qu. P21) 10 Infs, **chiefly Nth, Midl east of Missip R,** Cheepers; **IL115, PA214,** Spring cheepers; (Qu. R8, . . *Creatures that make a clicking or shrilling or chirping kind of sound*) Inf **MA16,** Cheepers—small toads.

cheepie bird See **chipping sparrow**

cheer See **chair**

cheer rail See **chair rail**

‡cheerwater n [A liquid that cheers one up]
Liquor, alcohol.

1949 Guthrie *Way West* 230 **West** (as of 1847), Savin' that cheerwater for kingdom come?

cheese n
A Forms.
Sometimes used as pl, hence back-formed sg *chee.* **chiefly S Midl**

1894 *DN* 1.340 wCT, *Cheese* is sometimes used as plural = cheeses. **1895** *DN* 1.376 **KY, wNC, TN,** *Chee,* singular; *cheese,* plural. **1905** *DN* 3.74 nwAR, *Cheese, pl.n.* 'Those cheese haven't come yet.' **1908** *DN* 3.298 eAL, wGA, *Cheese* . . . Used as a plural. "Pass me them cheese." **1923** *DN* 5.203 swMO, *Cheese* . . . The term is used, however, as if plural in form. "These cheese air right good." **1941** *LANE* Map 300, [Freq, **esp in nNEng,** *most cheese are;* also, **esp sNEng,** *most cheeses are;* less freq, *most cheese is.*] **1954** *Harder Coll.* cwTN, Them cheese.

B Senses.

1 also *cheesecake (plant), cheeseflower, cheese mallow, cheese plant, cheesetts, cheese weed:* The fruit of a **mallow** or the **mallow** (*Malva* spp) itself. [*OED* 1527 →]

1878 Taylor *Between the Gates* 137, The mallows . . whence you used to gather the little green "cheeses." **1890** Howells *Boy's Town* 54 **OH,** There was a garden outside of the schoolroom; hollyocks grew in it, and the boys gathered the little cheeses, as they called the seed-buttons which form when the flowers drop off, and ate them. **1896** *Jrl. Amer. Folkl.* 9.183, *Malva rotundifolia* . . cheeses, Cumberland County, Me. cheesetts, Oxford County, Me. **1900** Lyons *Plant Names* 238, *Málva* . . . Mallow . . . the shape of the fruit suggesting the popular name "Cheeses." . . *M. sylvéstris* . . . Cheese-flower, Cheese-cake plant. **1936** IL Nat. Hist. Surv. *Wildflowers* 195 **IL,** The Common Mallow or Cheeses was introduced from Europe, has become naturalized . . . The flattened fruits, divided into as many 1-seeded parts as

there are styles, are while green the edible "cheeses." **1959** Carleton *Index Herb. Plants* 26, *Cheese cake:* Malva sylvestris . . *Cheese flower:* Malva (v) . . *Cheeses:* Malva moschata. **1965–70** *DARE* (Qu. S21, . . *Weeds*) Infs **MI31, WI66,** Cheese mallow(s); **CA208, UT4,** Cheese weed; (Qu. S26a, . . *Roadside flowers*) Inf **MI67,** Cheeses; **NV8,** Cheese weed; (Qu. S11, . . *Other names . . bachelor's button*) Inf **IL25,** Cheesecake, because it looks like wrapped-up cheese. [*DARE* Ed: misidentification] **1969** *DARE* File **MI** (as of c1920), *Cheese plant*—wild geranium, because the seed pods "look like little cheeses," and were eaten by children. [*DARE* Ed: misidentification]

2 also *cheese souse, souse cheese:* =**headcheese.**

1968–70 *DARE* (Qu. H43, *Foods made from parts of the head and inner organs of an animal*) Infs **MD44, VA56,** Souse cheese; **FL49,** Cheese; **VA45,** Cheese souse.

3 in phr *piece of cheese:* A stooge, patsy.

1966 *DARE* (Qu. II34, *If you think somebody is trying to use you to his advantage: "I'm not going to be his _____."*) Inf **MI13,** Piece of cheese.

4 A light-skinned Black person. Cf **charcoal**

1970 *DARE* (Qu. HH29b, . . *People of mixed blood—part Negro*) Inf **NC87,** Oh, you're not going with coal now, you're going with cheese—when a man quits dating a dark girl and starts going with a light one.

cheese v

1 Of small children: to vomit or spit up milk curdling in the stomach. [Engl dial]

1974 *DARE* File **nOH,** Put a diaper over your shoulder until they stop cheesing.

2 To apple-polish, play up to. Cf **cheese-eater**

1970 *DARE* (Qu. JJ3a, *When a school child makes a special effort to "get in good" with the teacher . . "He's trying to _____ again."*) Inf **FL48,** Cheese.

cheese and crackers intj [Alter of *Jesus Christ*] euphem

1 also *cheese and crust:* Used as a mild oath.

1924 *DN* 5.260, Cheese and crust. **1966–68** *DARE* (Qu. NN30, *Exclamations beginning with the sound of "j"*) Infs **OR1, WA1,** Cheese and crackers; Inf **NY92,** Cheese and crust all maggots [almighty God].

2 See quot.

1967 *DARE* (Qu. NN18, *When somebody sneezes, what do people say to him?*) Inf **WA28,** Cheese and crackers.

cheese block n [In ref to a wedge cut from a round cheese]
In logging: see quot 1958.

1905 U.S. Forest Serv. *Bulletin* 61.33, Cheese block. **1950** *Western Folkl.* 9.116 nwOR, Cheese block. Wedge-shaped block of steel used to prevent logs from rolling off bunks. **1958** McCulloch *Woods Words* **Pacific NW,** *Cheese block*—A triangular wood or metal block placed on top of a bunk to bear against the under side of a loaded log, to prevent it from rocking. **1968** Adams *Western Words.*

‡cheese-bound adj [In ref to the supposed constipating effect of cheese]

1950 *WELS* (*Other words for being constipated*) 1 Inf, **seWI,** Cheesebound.

cheeseburg n [Abbr for *cheeseburger*] Cf **hamburg**
A hamburger with a slice of cheese.

1968 *DARE* (Qu. HH41, . . *Roll or bun sandwiches . . in a round bun or roll*) Infs **CT6, 8, 11,** Cheeseburg. **1968** *DARE* File **cNY,** Cheeseburg [sandwich listing on wall menu, Main Street Lunch].

cheese bush n
A **burrobrush 1** (here: *Hymenoclea salsola*).

1941 Jaeger *Wildflowers* 282, Cheese-bush. Hymenoclea Salsola . . . Called cheese-bush because of the cheesy odor of the crushed herbage.

cheese butter n

c1950 *WELS Suppl.* ceWI, Cheese butter (from German *Käsebutter*): [Made by] adding some thick cream to cottage cheese to make it smooth.

cheesecake (plant) See **cheese** n **B1**

cheesecakes n pl [Alter of *Jesus*] euphem Cf **cheese and crackers 1**

1924 *DN* 5.264 **NYC,** *Cheesecakes:* oh sweet _____.

cheese-eater n [See quot 1960] **chiefly Sth** *chiefly among Black speakers* Cf also **cheese** v 2, **eat cheese**
A cheater; informer; apple-polisher.
1960 Wentworth–Flexner *Slang, Cheese eater*—One who cheats, doublecrosses, or informs. *Euphem. for rat,* which orig. meant an informer or stool pigeon. **1970** *DARE* (Qu. II20a, *A person who tries too hard to gain somebody else's favor*) Infs **FL48, 52,** Cheese-eater; (Qu. JJ3b, *When a school child makes a special effort to "get in good" with the teacher*) Inf **FL48,** Cheese-eater. [Both Infs Black] **1981** Pederson *LAGS Urban Material* **FL, GA, MS,** [*(A seeker of praise and attention)* 3 infs, all Blacks, Cheese eater. Pederson: common in high school in Atlanta, Georgia 1974–8].

cheeseflower See **cheese** n B1

cheese-head n
A stupid, awkward person.
1919 *DN* 5.61 **NM** [High school slang], *Cheese-head,* a green, awkward person. "Anything that cheese-head says doesn't hurt me." **1939** Chandler *Big Sleep* 75 *(DAS),* You let this cheesehead . . insult me? **1942** Berrey–Van den Bark *Amer. Slang* 433.3, *Stupid person* . . . Cheesehead.

cheese mallow See **cheese** n B1

cheese pepper n
A small hot pepper (here: *Capsicum annuum* var).
1968 *DARE* (Qu. I22a, *. . Peppers—small hot*) Inf **NJ21,** Cheese peppers.

cheese plant See **cheese** n B1

cheese pumpkin n **NEast**
A cultivated variety of pumpkin (here: *Cucurbita moschata*).
1931–33 *LANE Worksheets* **CT,** *Cheese pumpkin*—a variety of pumpkin. Field pumpkin made poor pie; cheese pumpkin made good pie. **1968–69** *DARE* (Qu. I23, *. . Squash*) Inf **NJ50,** Cheese pumpkins; **NY209,** Cheese pumpkins (cream-colored). **1976** Bailey–Bailey *Hortus Third* 343, *Cucurbita moschata . .* 'Cheese' [pumpkin], fr. dark cream-colored, depressed-globose, ribbed, to 6 in. long and 14 in. in diam., flesh deep orange, juicy, suitable for canning or stock feed.

cheese rennet n Also *cheese rennet herb* [*OED* 1601 →]
A **bedstraw.**
1900 Lyons *Plant Names* 168, *Galium verum . .* Cheese-rennet, Runnet, Curdwort . . coagulates milk. **1959** Carleton *Index Herb. Plants* 26, *Cheese rennet:* Galium arvensis. **1971** Krochmal *Appalachia Med. Plants* 126, *Galium aparine . . .* cheese rennet herb.

cheeserind n [From its appearance: a thin light-colored wooden strip encircling the cockpit]
Of a boat: see quot 1978.
1950 Moore *Candlemas Bay* 38 **ME,** Guy came to his feet in a horrified scramble, all anyhow, pulling himself up by the boat's cheeserind. **1978** Merriam *Illustr. Lobstering* **ME,** *Cheeserind*—Board inside the washboard around the hull. It is usually topped by an iron strip. Also called coaming.

cheese souse See **cheese** n B2

cheesetts, cheese weed See **cheese** n B1

cheesy adj
1 Low-grade, worthless, trashy; cheap, stingy. [*OEDS* 1896 →]
1932 *AmSp* 7.330 **MD** [Johns Hopkins slang], *Cheesy*—bad; disgusting; of no value. **1935** *AmSp* 10.13 [Underworld], *Cheesy.* Of an inferior quality. **1950** *WELS (Low-grade, or of poor quality: a piece of merchandise)* 3 Infs, **WI,** Cheesy. **1965–70** *DARE* (Qu. KK6, *Something low-grade or of poor quality*) 30 Infs, **chiefly Nth, C Atl,** Cheesy; (Qu. D24) Inf **MA1,** Cheesy; (Qu. LL2, *. . Too small to be worth much*) Inf **MO30,** Cheesy; (Qu. U36b, *. . A person who saves in a mean way or is greedy in money matters*) Inf **NC87,** Cheesy.
2 See quot.
1931 *AmSp* 6.231 **cnNE,** *Cheesy.* Pale, peaked. "You look sort of cheesy this morning, aren't you well?"

cheet See **cheat** 1

cheeweeh, cheewink See **chewink**

chego See **chigger**

chemese See **chamisal**

‡**chemical head** n
= **conk** n[3] 1.
1974 Matthews *My Race* 24 **NYC** [Black], He still had his Chemical Head, with a black scarf tied around his head knotted in the front.

chemisal See **chamisal**

chemise See **chamisal, chamise**

chemise brush See **chamise brush**

chemise lily See **chamise lily**

chemizal See **chamisal**

chemmy lizard n [Perh alter of *shimmy* chemise]
1958 *VT Hist.* new ser 26.278, To act like they had lots of body lice and chemmy lizzards.

chenaie See **chenier** 2

chench water See **chinch water**

chenier n [LaFr < Fr *chêne* oak] **chiefly LA**
1 also sp *charnier, chenière:* A clump of scrub oak on open ground: a **shinnery.**
1804 (1930) Dunbar *Jrl.* 309 **MS,** At this place we began to see the wood called 'charnier' which is to be found all the way down the Washita below this place. **1967** LeCompte *Word Atlas* 241 **seLA,** *Clump of oak trees growing in open country . .* [9 of 21 infs] chenière.
2 also sp *chenaie, cheniere, chinnery:* A sandy, wooded ridge or hummock; see also quot 1971.
1847 *DeBow's Rev.* 3.257 **LA,** They have acquired the name of the chenaies. **1885** *Outing* 5.337/2 **LA,** In the intervening hours, however, you can fish from the bank, seated on some *chénière* in the shade of umbrageous oaks. **1908** *Sat. Eve. Post* 24 Oct 11/1 **West,** A tiny figure . . racing along the trail, . . across a stretch of "chinnery" where the sand was deep and the gallant old mare labored direfully. **1941** FWP *Guide LA* 687, *Chênière*—an oak-covered ridge elevated slightly above the coastal marshes. **1971** Detro *Generic Terms* 161 **LA,** The term *"chênière" . .* occurred during the period 1901–1968 as a toponymic generic in three areas of Louisiana: in coastal southwest Louisiana; in the Barataria Basin and along its coastal area; and in an area immediately west of the city of Monroe. The term *"chênière"* was applied principally to coastal relief features although it signified full rapid streams, wetlands —swamp, and woodlands as well. *Ibid* 165, The term was present in the vernacular but was pronounced as if spelled in English "Shinny." **1972** Brown *Wildflowers LA* 79, *Indigo . . .* Locally common on . . sandy cheniers. *Ibid* 136, Catchfly-gentian . . . Sandy cheniers and damp depressions. **1979** Hallowell *People Bayou* 20 **sLA,** At an elevation of about ten feet, the dry, sandy soil of the ridges provides the trees a roothold that permits them to survive. For this reason, the Cajun French word, *chenière* (oak tree) has been applied to the elevations . . . The chenières were created as waves driven by southerly winds . . eroded the silt and clay, carrying them out to sea and piling the sand that remained into long ridges. Here young live oaks soon took root.
3 See quot.
1968 *DARE* (Qu. EE7, *. . Marble games*) Inf **LA37,** Chenier [šɪnjer].

cheniere See **chenier** 1, 2

chenook See **chinook salmon**

Chenuk n [Prob alter of **Canuck,** perh infl by **chinook**]
1892 *KS Univ. Qrly.* 1.96 **KS,** *Chenuk:* a Canadian.

cheny See **china** A

chequerberry See **checkerberry**

chequered snake n Also sp *checkquered ~* Cf **checkered adder, coral snake**
An unidentified snake.
1674 Josselyn *Two Voyages* 115 **NEng,** The Checkquered snake, having as many colours within the checkquers shaddowing one another, as there are in a Rainbow. **1827** Williams *View W. FL* 29, The garter, riband, green, chequered, and glass snakes, make up the account of this species, in West Florida.

cher See **chair**

cherce See **choice** n, v

cherink See **chewink**

cherk See **chirk**

chermany n [Etym uncert] **esp VA** *old-fash*

A variety of baseball.

a1883 (1911) Bagby *VA Gentleman* 49, He must now learn to . . choose partners for cat and chermany. **1899** (1912) Green *VA Folk-Speech*, *Chermany* . . . A boys' game with a ball and bats. **1904** Conway *Autobiog.* 1.35 **nVA** (as of 1840s), Our recess games were chiefly chermany and bandy. **1911** *Century Dict.*, *Chermany* . . . In the southern United States, a variety of the game of base-ball.

Cherokee See **Cherokee rose**

Cherokee bean n Also *Cherokee* **SE**

=**coral tree**, esp *Erythrina herbacea.*

1926 *Torreya* 26.5, *Erythrina herbacea* . . . Cherokee, Sapelo I[slan]d, G[eorgi]a. **1933** Small *Manual SE Flora* 715, *Erythrina . . . Coral-beans. Cherokee-beans.* **1955** *S. Folkl. Qrly.* 19.234, The *Cherokee Bean* (Erythrina herbacea) . . was used both as a food and as an ornament by the Cherokee Indians; it is still used in some parts of Florida as a Christmas tree decoration. **1961** Douglas *My Wilderness* 148 **sFL**, The satinleaf, paradise tree, fiddlewood, Cherokee bean, tetrazygia, myrsine, smilax, and wax myrtle were strange. **1979** Little *Checklist U.S. Trees* 127, *Southeastern coralbean* . . . Other common names . . Cherokee-bean.

Cherokee plum n Cf **Chickasaw plum**

An unidentified plum (*Prunus* spp), perh a cultivated variety.

a1782 (1788) Jefferson *Notes VA* 36, Cherokee plumb. *Prunus sylvestris fructu majori.* **1786** (1925) Washington *Diaries* 3.32 **neVA**, Hoed the ground behind the Garden again and planted therein, in three rows, 177 of the wild, or Cherokee plumb. **1842** Buckingham *Slave States* 1.180 **SE**, The Cherokee plum, now putting forth its blossoms, was like the black[t]horn of England in May, and produces a small, round, harsh, and sour fruit, like the sloe.

Cherokee robin n

The rufous-sided **towhee** (here: *Pipilo erythrophthalmus*).

1917 *DN* 4.424 **LA**, Cherokee robin. The towhee (Pipile [sic] erythrophthalmus). **1957** *AmSp* 32.183 **LA**, Cherokee robin—Eastern towhee.

Cherokee rose n Also *Cherokee* **Sth**

Either of two evergreen, white-flowered roses: usu *Rosa laevigata,* but also *Rosa bracteata* which is also called **Chickasaw rose, prairie rose**

1823 (1959) Douglas *Jrl.* 26 **PA**, Roses Champneya, Cherokee, and two others. **1829** Eaton *Botany* 368 **Sth**, *Rosa . . . laevigata . . .* (cherokee rose.) **1838** (1852) Gilman *S. Matron* 53 **Sth**, He . . asked me some questions about the Cherokee rose-hedge. *Ibid* 89, It was his delight to . . enter the avenue where the Cherokee hedge shut out the view. **1888** *Harper's Mag.* 76.867/1 **Sth**, Their only exit lay at the end of the Cherokee hedge. **1896** Harris *Sister Jane* 19 **GA**, The Cherokee rose was rapidly covering the broken-down fences with its glistening green shield and its fragrant white flowers. **1951** Capote *Grass Harp* 58 **Sth**, The Judge, a fine-looking man dressed in narrow-cut suits with a black silk band sewn around his sleeve and a Cherokee rose in his buttonhole. **1960** Vines *Trees SW* 435, *Rosa . . bracteata . . .* Vernacular names . . Cherokee Rose . . Macartney Rose is often called Cherokee Rose in some localities but true Cherokee Rose, *R. laevigata . .* has three leaflets. **1965–70** *DARE* (Qu. S26a, *. . Roadside flowers*) Infs **GA3, 84, 89, MS38, SC46**, Cherokee rose(s); **MS73**, Wild Cherokee rose; (Qu. S26b, *Wildflowers . . in water or wet places*) Inf **MS23**, Cherokee rose; (Qu. S26e, *. . Wildflowers*) Inf **TN22**, Cherokee rose; **LA4**, Wild Cherokee.

cherook n Also sp *chorook, churook* [Echoic] **chiefly LA**

A sandpiper, usu *Pisobia melanotos* or *Tryngites subruficollis.*

1917 *DN* 4.424 **LA**, Chorook. 1. The pectoral sandpiper (Pisobia maculata) . . . 2. The buff-breasted sandpiper (Tryngites subruficollis). **1923** U.S. Dept. Ag. *Misc. Circular* 54 **LA**, *Pectoral Sandpiper* . . . cherook (also spelled chorook, churook; there is a tendency to apply this name to all sandpipers). **1946** Hausman *Eastern Birds* 288, *Buff-breasted Sandpiper . . . Other Names*—Hill Grassbird, Cherook, Little Brownbreast. **1962** Imhof *AL Birds* 246, *Pectoral Sandpiper* . . . Cherook, Krieker, Grass Snipe.

cherrup See **chirrup**

cherry n Usu |'čɛrɪ, -ɪ|, also |'čɝ·ɪ, -ɪ|; see also quot 1961 and Pronc Intro 3.I.2.a **Pronc-sp** *churry*

A Forms.

1930s in 1944 *ADD* **eWV**, *Cherry* . . . |tʃɝɪ| churry. Not common. **1934** *Ibid* **NYC**, |tʃɝɪ|. **1961** Kurath–McDavid *Pronc. Engl.* 124, The word *cherry* . . predominantly has the checked vowel /ɛ/ of *ten* in all parts of the Eastern States, regularly so in cultivated speech. In folk speech, and to some extent in the speech of the middle group, four other vowels occur besides /ɛ/: the checked /ɪ/ of *crib* in parts of New England and Upstate New York, the /ɝ/ of *first* chiefly in parts of Pennsylvania and West Virginia, the /ʌ/ of *sun* in parts of the Lower South, and the free /e/ of *eight* in parts of South Carolina and Georgia. **1976** Allen *LAUM* 3.34, With even greater uniformity than in the eastern states U[pper] M[idwest] speakers have the mid-front /ɛ/ before /r/ in *cherry* and *merry.* The principal modification is simply that of appreciable retroflexion of the vowel as indicated by [ɚ] and occuring sporadically without patterned distribution in the area.

B Senses.

1 =**hickey** n[2].

1967–70 *DARE* (Qu. X39, *A mark on the skin where somebody has sucked it hard and brought the blood to the surface*) Infs **IL17, MO29,** Cherry.

2 See **cherry top.**

cherrybark oak n Also *cherry oak*

A red **oak** (here: *Quercus falcata*). Also called **pagoda oak, Spanish oak, turkey oak**

1960 Vines *Trees SW* 188, *Q[uercus] falcata* var. *pagodaefolia . . .* the bark has a tendency to be tighter and resemble the bark of Wild Cherry, hence giving it the name of Cherry-bark Oak in some areas . . . [T]he true Cherry-bark Red Oak, *Quercus falcata* var. *leucophylla.* **1968–70** *DARE* (Qu. T10, *. . Oak trees*) Inf **IL119**, Cherrybark oak; **IN35**, Cherry oak. **1979** Little *Checklist U.S. Trees* 231, *Quercus falcata . .* cherry-bark oak.

cherry bell n

=**mullein.**

1968 *DARE* (Qu. S26a, *. . Roadside flowers*) Inf **PA89**, Cherry bells, same as *Verbascum.*

cherry birch n

=**sweet birch.**

1810 Michaux *Arbres* 1.26 *(DA)*, *(Betula lenta).* Black birch, cherry birch. **1850** Cooper *Rural Hours* 385 **cNY**, The *cherry birch,* or black birch, is also a northern variety, and very common here. **1897** Sudworth *Arborescent Flora* 142, *Betula lenta . .* Cherry Birch (N.H., R.I., N.Y., Pa., Va., Del., N.C., S.C., Fla., Wis., Mich., Ont.). **1961** Douglas *My Wilderness* 203 **MD**, In March I also like to hunt down the cherry birch. Its bark is aromatic and was once used to obtain the oil of wintergreen. **1971** Krochmal *Appalachia Med. Plants* 76, *Betula lenta . .* cherry birch.

cherry bird n Also *cherry robin*

=**cedar waxwing.**

1805 (1905) Lewis *Orig. Jrls. Lewis & Clark Exped.* 6.187, This day a flock of *cherry* or *cedar* birds were seen . . . [They] are frequently destructive to the cherry orchards, and in winter in the lower parts of the states of Virginia and Maryland feed on the buries of the Cedar. **1884** *Harper's Mag.* 68.616/1 **NY**, The Carolina wax-wing, *alias* cedar or cherry bird. **1913** Morley *Carolina Mts.* 67, No sooner does the fruit turn red on the few trees lovingly watched by their owners than there appear upon the scene a large and happy flock of cedar waxwings, for no slight reason named "cherry-birds." **1939** Lincoln *Migration* 102, The well-known 'cherry bird' . . sometimes takes a heavy toll of small fruit. **1949** Sprunt–Chamberlain *SC Bird Life* 422 **SC**, Although its fondness for cherries in many areas has given it a local name of "Cherry Bird," [the Cedar Waxwing] seems equally fond of cedar berries. **1969** Longstreet *Birds FL* 124, *Cedar Waxwing*—Other names: Cedar Bird; Seal; Cherry Robin; Canadian Robin.

cherry bomb n Also *cherry boom, ~ pop, ~ salute* [From its shape and color] Cf **apple 5**

A large, red, round, powerful firecracker.

1965–70 *DARE* (Qu. FF14, *. . Kinds of firecrackers*) 382 Infs, **scattered,** Cherry bombs; **VA37**, Cherry booms; **CA133**, Cherry pops; **NY73**, Cherry salutes; (Qu. FF28, *. . Fireworks*) Infs **GA54, NY228**, Cherry bombs. [Of all Infs responding to Qu. FF14, 64% were old; of those giving *cherry bombs,* 46% were old.] **1975** Doctorow *Ragtime* 94 **NY** (as of 1900s), He . . had . . designed . . an unusual firecracker packed not cylindrically but in a spherical container. With its fuse looking like a stem it was named a Cherry Bomb.

cherry-dill pickle See **cherry pickle**

cherry hot pepper See **cherry pepper**

cherry laurel n Also *laurel cherry* **chiefly S Atl**
=**Carolina cherry.**
   1897 Sudworth *Arborescent Flora* 246, *Prunus caroliniana . . . Laurel Cherry . . . Common Names . . .* Cherry Laurel (Fla.). **1960** Vines *Trees SW* 388, *Prunus . . . caroliniana . . .* Cherrylaurel. **1966–68** *DARE* (Qu. T5, . . *Kinds of evergreens*) Infs **FL9, LA18, MS38, NC16,** Cherry laurel; (Qu. T15, . . *Swamp trees*) Inf **NC16,** Cherry laurel. **1978** *MS Qrly.* 31.501 **SC,** Or it is equally possible that he is describing the very common cherry laurel of the coastal dunes and swamps. **1979** Little *Checklist U.S. Trees* 212, *Carolina laurelcherry . . . Other common names* — laurel cherry, cherry-laurel.

cherry oak See **cherrybark oak**

cherry pepper n Also *cherry hot pepper, ~ red ~*
A cherry-like, cultivated pepper (here: *Capsicum annuum* var *annuum*).
   1960 Vines *Trees SW* 908, Cherry Pepper, *C[apsicum] frutescens* var. *cerasiforme* Irish, has erect or leaning spherical fruit up to one inch across, yellow or purple, very pungent. **1965–70** *DARE* (Qu. I22a, . . *Peppers — small hot*) 14 Infs, **chiefly NEast,** *chiefly rural,* Cherry peppers; **MS87,** Cherry hot peppers; **PA166,** Cherry red peppers; **PA178,** Hot cherry peppers; (Qu. I22b, . . *Large hot*) Infs **CO47, MA8,** (Hot) cherry peppers; (Qu. I22c, . . *Small sweet*) Infs **AZ8, NY20,** Cherry peppers. **1976** Bailey–Bailey *Hortus Third* 219, Cherry pepper.

cherry picker n

1 A large hooked nose. [See quot 1939] *joc*
   [**1939** *AmSp* 14.261 **sIN,** A particularly prominent and hooked nasal organ is 'a cherry-picker's nose,' the possessor of which could hook it over a limb and thus support himself while he picked cherries with both hands.] **1968** *DARE* (Qu. X15, . . *Kinds of noses*) Inf **NC79,** Cherry picker; **NJ18,** Cherry picker — hang on a limb and pick cherries with both hands. **1984** *DARE* File **scWI,** My best friend has been 'Cherry Picker' since our boyhood around 1920 because of his large hooked nose, supposedly big enough to hook over a branch while picking cherries with both hands.

2 In railroading:
a A switchman: see quot 1945.
   1942 Berrey–Van den Bark *Amer. Slang* 771.22, *Switchman.* Cherry picker. **1945** Hubbard *Railroad Ave.* 337, *Cherry picker* — Switchman, so called because of red lights on switch stands.
b See quot.
   1945 Hubbard *Railroad Ave.* 337, *Cherry picker . . .* Also any railroad man who is always figuring on the best jobs and sidestepping undesirable ones (based on the old allusion, "Life is a bowl of cherries").

3 also attrib: A basket on a boom, mounted on a truck, for raising or lowering a person.
   1968 *Amherst Rec.* (MA) 27 Nov 2, Workers from New England Tree Experts, Inc. work from a "cherry picker" bucket high above the town common. **1981** Pederson *LAGS Urban Material* **TX, AL, FL, TN,** [(*Snorkel truck* [of a fire department]), 5 infs, cherry picker]. **1982** *DARE* File **NH,** I overheard an exchange the other day between a lineman and his friend on the street who was shouting up to the guy in the cherry picker.

4 In logging: see quots.
   1950 *Western Folkl.* 9.116 **nwOR,** *Cherry picker.* A crane for reloading logs spilled along a railroad right-of-way. **1958** McCulloch *Woods Words* **Pacific NW,** *Cherry picker* — A light loading machine for picking up logs lost along a railroad or truck road; also used in prelogging and relogging to some extent.

5 See quot. Also called **walnut picker**
   1968 *DARE* (Qu. W42a, . . *Men's sharp-pointed shoes*) Inf **NC79,** Cherry pickers.

6 =**catbird 1.** Cf **cherry bird**
   1967 *DARE* (Qu. Q14, . . *Catbird*) Inf **MO5,** Cherry picker.

cherry pickle n Also *cherry-dill pickle*
See quot 1984.

1965–70 *DARE* (Qu. H56, . . *Kinds of pickles*) Infs **IL3, WI47, 58, 71,** Cherry-dill pickles; **IA2,** Cherry pickles. **1984** *DARE* File **csWI** (as of 1930–40), The cherry-dill pickles in Cottage Grove . . were cucumbers, accompanied in their brine by dill and by cherry leaves, not fruit.

cherry pop See **cherry bomb**

cherry red pepper See **cherry pepper**

cherry robin See **cherry bird**

cherry salute See **cherry bomb**

cherry soup n esp **WI**
A cold soup whose main ingredient is sour cherries.
   1968–69 *DARE* (Qu. H36, *Kinds of soups favored around here*) Infs **WI11, 76,** Cherry soup. **1981** *DARE* File **Madison WI** [On a restaurant menu], Cold Hungarian cherry soup [includes cream, Hungarian wine, cherries]. **1982** *Milwaukee Jrl.* (WI) 21 July food sec 1, Cold cherry soup, creamy and sweet, is a refreshingly different way to enjoy sour cherries. The soup, a Hungarian recipe, can be garnished with sweet cherries. *Ibid* 8, Cherry soup . . is a traditional dish in Hungarian homes on Christmas Eve. **1982** *DARE* File **csWI,** My mother devised a recipe for cherry soup in 1960 based on a German recipe. She said it was usually eaten with pancakes in Germany. It consists of sour cherries and juice thickened slightly with cornstarch and flavored with sugar and lemon juice. We usually ate it as the main meal.

cherrystone n Also *cherrystone clam*
A small **quahog.**
   1880 Twain *Tramp Abroad* 574, I have selected a few dishes, and made out a little bill of fare . . Cherry-stone clams. **1931–33** *LANE Work-sheets* **RI,** *Cherry stone* — a clam slightly larger than a littleneck. **1939** *LANE* Map 235 **ceMA,** *Round clam . . .* [čɣrɪstoʊnz]. **1947** Coffin *Yankee Coast* 294 **ME,** Quahaugs, or round clams. Cherrystones, littlenecks to the outside world. **1968–70** *DARE* (Qu. P18, . . *Shellfish*) Infs **DE4, RI4, VA55,** Cherrystone(s); (Qu. H45) Inf **VA48,** Fried cherrystone clams. **1968** *DARE* Tape **DE2,** We always go out and catch clams . . . I like to pick up the little cherrystones because David likes clam on the half-shell; **DE4,** I sort 'em in the wintertime . . . There's the little necks, the cherrystones, and the chowder clams. **1982** Heat Moon *Blue Highways* 345 **ME,** I bought two pounds of steamed quahogs (also called "littlenecks" and "cherrystones" when small.)

cherrystone juniper n
A one-seeded **juniper** *(Juniperus monosperma).* Also called **red-berry juniper, sabina, white juniper**
   1938 Van Dersal *Native Woody Plants* 148, *Juniperus monosperma . .* Cherrystone Juniper. **1960** Vines *Trees SW* 35, *Juniperus . . . monosperma . . .* Cherry-stone Juniper. **1970** Correll *Plants TX* 78. **1979** Little *Checklist U.S. Trees* 155, *Juniperus monospermum . .* Other Common Names — cherry-stone juniper.

cherry tomato n
=**ground cherry.**
   1897 *Jrl. Amer. Folkl.* 10.51, *Physalis,* . . cherry tomatoes, Eastern end of Long Island. **1976** Bailey–Bailey *Hortus Third* 868, *Physalis . . . peruviana . . .* Cherry tomato, strawberry tomato, gooseberry tomato.

cherry top n Also *cherry*
A police car with a red light on its roof; by ext, a policeman.
   1966–70 *DARE* (Qu. N4, *A police vehicle with a red, blue, or yellow flashing light on top*) Infs **IN1, KS8, OH99, TX28, WA22,** Cherry top; **NY198,** Cherry; (Qu. V9, . . *Nicknames . . a policeman*) Inf **MO20,** Cherry top.

cherup See **chirrup**

chesky n Also sp *cheskey, czezski* [See quot 1945]
A Czech or Bohemian.
   1945 Mencken *Amer. Lang. Suppl. 1* 602, In regions where Czech immigrants are numerous *cheskey* is frequently heard. Monsignor [J.B.] Dudek says that it is "an attempted transliteration of the Bohemian adjective *český* (Czech)." **1950** *WELS* (People of foreign background: *Bohemian*) 1 Inf, **ceWI,** Chesky. **1964** *PADS* 42.40 **IL,** Both of the very old forms *czezski* (or *chesky*) and *butchsky* were offered by an old German who remembered using those terms in her youth on the West Side of Chicago, where many poor European nationality groups begrudgingly shared territory.

chess n [*OED* 1736 →]
=bromegrass.

1751 in 1934 Eliot *Field Husbandry* 65 **CT**, Otherwise Tares, Cockle, Chess, and the like . . will increase from Year to Year. **1835** Shirreff *Tour N. Amer.* 83 **NY**, I had observed the wheat crops of America abounding with a species of grass passing by the name of chess, which I imagine to be the *Bromus secalinus* of botanists. **1847** U.S. Patent Office *Annual Rept.: Ag.* 102, In July the wheat fields of Ohio are said to abound in cheat or chess. *Ibid* 455, Chess-seed will grow, and . . wheat will not turn to chess. **1863** U.S. Dept. Ag. *Rept. of Secy. for 1862* 103 **NH**, If he sows chess seed with his wheat, he will be quite likely to harvest a mixture of wheat and chess. **1889** Vasey *Ag. Grasses* 73 **Sth**, (Chess; cheat.) It is an old tradition which some farmers still cling to that chess is a degenerate wheat. **1970** U.S. Ag. Research Serv. *Selected Weeds* 44, *Bromus secalinus*—Chess.

chess pie n Also *chess-cake pie, chess tart* [Prob alter of *chest;* cf **coffin 3**] **chiefly Sth, S Midl**
A pie or tart with a filling mainly of eggs, butter and sugar.

1932 (1946) Hibben *Amer. Regional Cookery* 290 **MD**, Chess-Cake Pie. **1949** Trahey *Taste TX* 236, The Texan . . . [will] take pie, preferably pecan, chess pie and almost any deep-dish cobbler. **1952** Tracy *Coast Cookery* 230 **TN**, Chess pie. **c1960** *Wilson Coll.* **csKY**, *Chess pie* . . . A very rich pie, made largely of egg yolks. Very modern in area. **1965–70** *DARE* (Qu. H63, . . *Desserts*) 16 Infs, **Sth, S Midl, esp wKY**, Chess pie; TN66, VA74, Lemon chess pie; TN66, Coconut chess pie, Germans' chocolate chess pie. **1970** *DARE* File **AR, KY**, *Chess pie*—A rich, creamy pie, so called because it could be kept in the chest. **1972** Hewitt *NYT Heritage Cookbook* xvii, And no section on Southern cooking would be complete without recipes for such delectable desserts as Lane cake, Lady Baltimore cake, chess tarts and Moravian Sugar cake.

chessy adj
Full of **chess.**

1842 Kirkland *Forest Life* 1.153 **MI**, My wheat was unaccountable chessy, though I turned water upon it and kept it moist all summer.

chest bib n
=**granny rag 1.**

1970 Anderson *TX Folk Med.* xvii, And so does a "granny rag"—a flannel cloth smeared with suet or with lard, camphor, dry mustard, turpentine, or coal oil and some other "medicines" for good measure; sometimes called a "chest bib," such a concoction might be sewed on the victim for the winter.

chest clothes n [Because they are stored in a chest]
1970 *DARE* (Qu. W39, . . *A person's best clothes*) Inf **VA48**, Chest clothes.

chester drawers n Also *chester (drawer)* [Pronc-sp (and perh folk-etym) for *chest of drawers*]
1965–70 *DARE* (Qu. E3, *A piece of furniture in which you lay clothes flat*) Infs **AR56, PA134, UT3**, Chester drawers; **FL49**, Chester. **1967** LeCompte *Word Atlas* 232 **seLA**, Chester drawer [response of 4 of 21 infs]. **1970** Tarpley *Blinky* 85 **neTX**, The familiar piece of bedroom furniture containing a series of wide drawers is identified most often as *chest of drawers* [38%] . . or *chester drawers* [29.5%]. The latter is slightly more prevalent in the 14–30 age group.

chesterfield n
1 also attrib: A sofa. [*OEDS* 1900 →] **esp CA**
1950 *WELS* (*A piece of upholstered furniture that seats two people*) 1 Inf, **cwWI**, Chesterfield. **1951** *AmSp* 26.256 **Upstate NY**, The only common terms which seem peculiar to Canada are *chesterfield* (large overstuffed sofa) and *coil* (pile of hay raked up in the field). **1954** *PADS* 21.5 **CA**, The word *chesterfield*, meaning "davenport, couch, or sofa," and found elsewhere on this continent principally in Canadian English, occurs in three-quarters of the questionnaires filled out in the area north of the ten southernmost counties of California and west of the Sierra Nevada. East of the Sierra in Northern California it appears in only one-quarter of the individual responses, and in Southern California it is known to only one person in twenty. **1965–70** *DARE* (Qu. E9, *A piece of upholstered furniture that seats three people*) 11 Infs, 6 in **CA**, Chesterfield; **CA149**, Chesterfield love seat; (Qu. E7, *The piece of upholstered furniture that you can stretch out on to rest*) 9 Infs, 4 in **CA**, Chesterfield. **1971** Bright *Word Geog. CA & NV* 144, *Chesterfield* 45% [of the infs]. The majority described it as a large, heavy piece with upholstered arms and back. **1971** *Today Show Letters* **AL** (as of 1930s), No one had a sofa, divan, or davenport but instead nearly everyone had a chesterfield.

1973 Allen *LAUM* 1.164, *Chesterfield* . . . is familiar to residents of the U[pper] M[idwest] communities along the Canadian border, but they have not adopted it.

2 also *Lord Chesterfield:* A dandy, charmer.
1950 *WELS* (*A person who enjoys dressing up, or who spends too much on clothes*) 1 Inf, **seWI**, Chesterfield. **1965–66** *DARE* (Qu. AA6a, . . *A man who is fond of being with women and tries to attract their attention*) Inf **AR12**, Chesterfield; (Qu. HH2, . . *A citified person*) Inf **MT2**, Lord Chesterfield; (Qu. II37, *Somebody who is very courteous or polite*) Inf **MS63**, Chesterfield.

‡**chester tree** n [Alter of *chestnut*]
1968 *DARE* (Qu. T16, . . *Trees* . . "*special*") Inf **MD**13, Chester tree [Inf's word for *chestnut*].

chestnut n
1 Std: a tree of the genus *Castanea*, in the US usu *C. dentata*. Also called **chinquapin B1**
2 =**buckeye 1.**
1759 (1775) Burnaby *Travels* 7 **VA**, They are likewise adorned and beautified with . . scarlet-flowering chesnuts, fringe trees, flowering poplars.

3 Anything trite, as an old joke or story; something which has been too often told or performed. **chiefly Nth, N Midl** See Map *somewhat old-fash*
1880 (1910) Ranous *Diary* 199 **NYC**, Think of doing that awful old *Nancy Lee*—such a chestnut! **1886** in 1950 *AmSp* 25.31 **New Orleans LA**, Change of bill weekly and no chestnuts. **1923** *DN* 5.233 **swWI**, *Chestnut bell* . . . A small bell worn on the shirt or waistcoat of a dandy and covered by the coat; the bell, actuated by a spring, was rung whenever an outworn funny story was told. (Obs.) **1948** *Time* 5 Apr 106/2, He has omitted such chestnuts as *The Raven* and *O! Captain! My Captain!* **c1960** *Wilson Coll.* **csKY**, *Chestnut* . . . A worn-out joke or saying. Very rare in area. **1965–70** *DARE* (Qu. FF21a, *A joke that is so old it doesn't seem funny any more*) 58 Infs, **chiefly Nth, N Midl**, Chestnuts; **NJ20, NY69, 232, OH44**, Old chestnuts. [Of all Infs responding to the question, 64% were old, 31% coll educ; of those giving this response, 90% were old, 50% coll educ.]

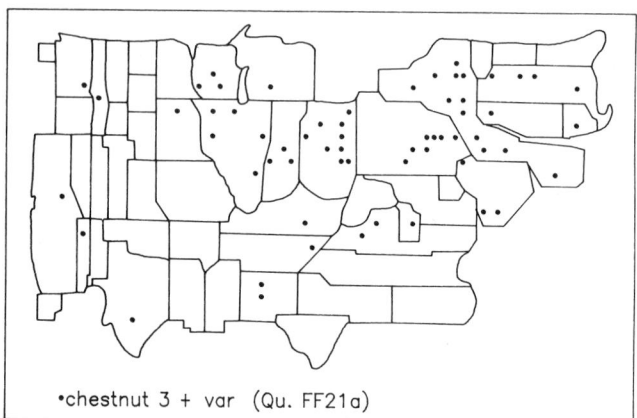
•chestnut 3 + var (Qu. FF21a)

chestnut burr See **burr** n¹ **3**

chestnut oak n Also *chestnut-leaved oak* [From the shape of the leaf]
Any of var oaks such as **chinquapin oak 1, 2, basket oak 1,** and *Quercus prinus.*

1703 in 1894 Providence RI Rec. Comm. *Early Rec.* 5.176, The Northwest Cornner is a Chessnut Oake Tree. **1785** Marshall *Arbustrum* 125, *Quercus Prinus.* Chestnut-leaved Oak. **1835** *Survey of Property* Nov., Pettigrew P. (N.C. Univ.) *(DA)*, Beginning at a big chuznut oak corner Tree. **1884** Murfree *TN Mts.* 60, Now and again the forest quiet was broken by the patter of acorns from the chestnut-oaks. **1906** *DN* 3.130 **nwAR**, *Chestnut oak* . . . A kind of oak the leaf of which resembles the chestnut leaf. **1941** Walker *Lookout* 64 **TN**, Among the trees that have furnished crossties, the chestnut oak, perhaps leads. Its bark was long sought for use in tanning leather. **1960** Vines *Trees SW* 152, *Quercus* . . *muhlenbergii* . . . Chestnut Oak. *Ibid* 153, *Dwarf Chinquapin Oak—Quercus prinoides* . . . It also has the vernacular names of Scrub Chestnut Oak, Dwarf Chestnut Oak. **1965–70** *DARE* (Qu. T10, . . *Kinds of oak trees*) 75 Infs, **esp S Midl, also NEast, C Atl,**

Chestnut oak; (Qu. T16) Inf **NY**213, Chestnut oak. **1967** Borland *Hill Country* 161 **nwCT,** Among the oaks there is one sometimes called basket oak. It is also known as a chestnut oak, because of the shape of its leaves.

chestnut scrub oak n
=**chinquapin oak.**

1970 *DARE* (Qu. T10, . . *Kinds of oak trees*) Inf **MA**100, Chestnut scrub oak.

chestnut-sided nuthatch n
=**red-breasted nuthatch.**

1966 *DARE* (Qu. Q23, *The insect-eating bird that goes headfirst down a tree trunk*) Inf **ME**8, Chestnut-sided nuthatch.

chestnut soil n
Any of a group of brown-colored soils typical of drier grasslands.

1927 *AmSp* 2.350 **WV,** Chestnut soil . . the thin soil on northern exposures. **1954** Thornbury *Geomorphology* 78, Chestnut soils are brown or grayish brown soils that developed under short-grass vegetation in areas slightly drier than those that produced chernozems. **1968** *DARE* (Qu. C30, . . *Loose, dark soil*) Inf **MD**20, Chestnut soil.

chestnut sore n
Ringworm.

1969 *DARE* (Qu. BB25, . . *Common skin diseases*) Inf **MA**58, Chestnut sores—ringworm.

chestnut stabber n [Ref to immigrant street vendors selling roasted chestnuts]
A person of Italian heritage.

1968 *DARE* (Qu. HH28, . . *People of foreign background: Italian*) Inf **NY**76, Chestnut stabber.

chestnutty adj [chestnut 3] arch
Old, stale.

1884 *Free Press* (Detroit MI) 14 May 2/1 (*DAE*), Excitement about it soon dies away, and references to it are regarded as chestnutty in the press and in the pulpit. **1887** *Chicago Daily Tribune* (IL) 27 Nov 27/6, "Ha! ha!" laughed a Dearborn-street clerk as his employer finished a story with a very ancient and chestnutty smell.

chestnut white oak n
An unidentified oak: cf **chestnut oak, white oak.**

1708 (1879) S. Sewall *Diary* 2.222 **eMA,** Southward of the Swamp is a small Chestnut White-Oak. **1814** Pursh *Flora Americae* 2.633, This large and useful tree is known by the name of Chesnut White Oak, Swamp Chesnut Oak, and, to the south, White Oak. **1968** *DARE* (Qu. T10, . . *Kinds of oak trees*) Inf **DE**3, Chestnut white oak.

chest of draw See draw n

chest-pounder n [From the gesture of tapping the chest in confession]
A Roman Catholic.

1930 *AmSp* 5.238 **NY** [Colgate Univ. slang], *Chest-pounder:* a Roman Catholic. **1968** *DARE* (Qu. CC4, . . *Nicknames . . religions or religious groups*) Inf **NY**66, Chest-pounders, Catholics.

chest robe n [Blend of chest of drawers + wardrobe] Cf cedar robe
1968 *DARE* (Qu. E1, *A piece of furniture that stands against the wall, and you hang clothes in it*) Inf **MD**37, Chest robe.

chesty adj, adv
Arrogant, conceited; in an arrogant or self-important manner.

1899 (1900) Ade *Fables in Slang* 90, All during the Seventeen Years Zoroaster and Zendavesta continued to walk Chesty and tell People how Good they were. **1915** *DN* 4.214, *Chesty,* egotistical. "The man has gotten wonderfully chesty since he became governor." Colloquial. **1946** (1972) Mezzrow *Really Blues* 331, Chesty: conceited. **1950** *WELS* (*Feeling important or independent*) 3 Infs, **WI,** Chesty. **c1960** *Wilson Coll.* **csKY,** *Chesty* . . . Conceited, arrogant. **1967–70** *DARE* (Qu. GG19a, . . *Feeling important or independent*: "He surely is _____ these days.") Infs **CO**34, **MN**10, **TX**43, Chesty; (Qu. GG5, *When someone does something unexpectedly bold or forward*) Inf **IL**113, Chesty.

chetlins See chitterlings

chev See chive

---

chevalier de batture n [Fr "knight of [the] embankment"]
=**spotted sandpiper.**

1917 *DN* 4.424 **LA,** *Chevalier de batture.* The spotted sandpiper (Actitus macularia). [**1923** U.S. Dept. Ag. *Misc. Circular* 13.54 **Quebec,** *Pectoral Sandpiper* . . . chevalier (cavalier, a French term applied to most of the sandpipers).]

chew v Usu |čŭ|; also, esp in NEng, |čiu|; often |čɔ|. Pronc-sp chaw
A Forms.

1738 in 1944 *ADD* **VA,** *Chaw* . . . Chew. **1857** Twain in 1929 *IA Jrl. Hist. & Politics* 27.424, Suffice it to say that the little press "chawed up" half a bushel of the devotees. **1894** *DN* 1.329 **NJ,** *Chaw:* common pron. for *chew.* **1899** Garland *Boy Life* 334 **nwIA,** No hired man shall chaw my hair off again, and don't you forget it. **1903** *DN* 2.296 **Cape Cod MA,** *Chaw* . . . Chew. **1905** *DN* 3.5 **cCT,** *Chaw.* **1906** *DN* 3.116 **sIN,** *Chaw.* **1908** *DN* 3.298 **eAL, wGA,** *Chaw,* v. and n. Chew. **1935** Sandoz *Jules* 37 **wNE** (as of 1880–1930), He would n't chaw slow elk, starving. **1954** *PADS* 21.23 **SC,** *Chaw* is not usually felt to be slang; it is a widespread nonstandard variant of *chew.* **c1960** *Wilson Coll.* **csKY,** *Chew* is usually |čŭ|; sometimes |čɔ|. **1961** Kurath–McDavid *Pronc. Engl.* 168, After /l, č, s/ as in *blew, chew, suit* (of clothes), all dialects on the Atlantic seaboard have /u/, without a preceding /j/. However, in the New England settlement area a fair number of the less educated speakers say /bliu, čiu, siut/. **1966–67** *DARE* File **NC, MI,** [čɔ].

B Senses.

1 To eat; to eat noisily.

1894 *Century Illustr. Mag.* 47.518, "Now there's Schenectady. You can chew all right there . . ." "I had heard of Buffalo as a good 'chewing town.'" **1905** *DN* 3.74 **nwAR,** *Chew* . . . Eat. Students often say, 'Let's go chew.' **1926** [see **2** below]. **1968** *DARE* (Qu. H11b, *If he makes a noise with his food, he _____.*) Inf **WI**52, Chaws. **1977** Watts *Dict. Old West* 83, To *feel like chawin':* to be hungry.

2 To talk.

1926 *AmSp* 1.251 [Hobo argot], *Chew*—to eat or talk. **1930** Irwin *Amer. Tramp* 50, Chew . . . to talk. **1948** (1951) Lait–Mortimer *NY Confidential* 42 **NYC,** The stoop-sitters in far Flatbush are chewing about it.

3 also with *at, on, up:* To annoy, nag, scold, bawl someone out.

1884 Hill *Tales Pioneers* 198 **CO,** I went *in quest* of him, and I just chawed him up. **1942** Warnick *Garrett Co. MD* (as of 1900–18), *Chew* . . scold. **1965–70** *DARE* (Qu. Y6, . . *Put pressure on somebody*) Inf **CO**47, Chew his ass; (Qu. Y7, *When one person never misses a chance to be mean to . . or to annoy another:* "I don't know why she keeps _____ me all the time.") Inf **NY**201, Chewing; **VT**16, Chewing at; **TX**18, Chewing on; (Qu. Y8, *To keep after a person so as to get him to do things*) Inf **OK**42, Chewing on him; (Qu. BB40, . . *Somebody acting strangely:* ". . . What do you suppose _____ him?") Inf **CA**140, Was chewing on; (Qu. II27, . . *A very sharp scolding*) Inf **OK**27, Chewed up one side and down the other. **1975** Gould *ME Lingo,* Chew . . . "to *chew* anybody up and down." This means to bawl him out in good shape.

4 To embarrass, to put (someone) down.

1908 *DN* 3.298 **eAL, wGA,** *Chaw* . . . To get the better of one in a contest of obscene repartee, to hack or guy one in this way. **1952** Brown *NC Folkl.* 1.526, *Chaw* . . . To embarrass. "What that fellow said to you last night certainly did *chaw* you." **1953** *PADS* 19.9 **NC,** *Chawed* . . . Embarrassed. "That compliment sort of chawed me."

5 To argue, protest.

1965–70 *DARE* (Qu. KK13, *Other words for arguing*) Infs **IL**29, **MA**18, **NY**22, 84, **PA**206, Chewing; **IL**36, Chewing back and forth; **NY**46, Chewing things over; **OH**91, Chawing; **TX**10, Chewed it up. **1975** Gould *ME Lingo,* Chew . . . It can mean "protest": "He *chewed* a bit when he got the bill, but he paid it."

6 To undertake and carry through. [Prob infl by phr *bite off more than one can chew*]

1967–68 *DARE* (Qu. Y50, *To undertake or carry out a job:* "That's a big job for just one person to _____.") Infs **AL**20, **NY**65, **PA**148, Chew.

‡7 To brownnose, applepolish.

1970 *DARE* (Qu. JJ3a, *When a schoolchild makes a special effort to "get in good" with the teacher in hopes of getting a better grade:* "He's trying to _____ again.") Inf **TX**97, Chew—teenage expression mainly.

chew n Also chaw
1 in phr *get a chaw on (someone):* An attachment, grasp.

1895 *DN* 1.370 **eTN,** *Chaw:* hold, attachment. Of a flirt: "She's tryin' to git a chaw on a feller." **c1970** *Halpert Coll.* **wKY,** To get a chaw on someone = to get a hold or attachment.

2 An argument or disagreement. **[chew v 5]**

1966 *DARE* (Qu. KK15, *A disagreement or quarrel*) Inf **ME9,** A chew. **1966** *DARE* Tape **ME26,** They get in a chew over the cows getting over the line.

3 An Irish person.

1929 Ellis *Ordinary Woman* 202 **CO** (as of early 1900s), But soon George starts to complain that it was run by a bunch of 'red necks,' 'chaws,' 'flannel mouths,' 'Micks'—all names for Irishmen.

chewallop See **ker-**

chew-bubble n

c1970 *DARE* File **TN,** *Chew-bubble*—bubble-gum.

chew down v phr [Alter, perh by folk-etym, of *jew down*]
To haggle or bargain to receive a lower price.

1965–70 *DARE* (Qu. U12, *. . You argued with the person selling . . till you made him lower the price*) 13 Infs, **chiefly Nth,** Chewed him down.

chewed ppl adj Pronc-sp *chawed* [Cf **chew v B3, 4**]

1 usu with *up:* Embarrassed, discomfited, surprised.

1843 (1916) Hall *New Purchase* 412 **IN,** The Majur was most teetotally discumfiisticutted, and near about as good as chaw'd up. **1901** White *Westerners* 305 **SD,** They agreed that they'd be tee-totally chawed up! **1936** *AmSp* 11.368 **nLA,** *Chawed up . . .* Embarrassed; confused; surprised; as, 'I surely was chawed up when I found that out.' **1951** *PADS* 15.69 **nLA,** *Chawed up . . .* Embarrassed; confused. "Mary was all chawed up because she didn't have no new dress." **1959** *VT Hist.* new ser 27.129, Well, I'll be sweetly chawed up! . . . Rare. Essex. **c1960** *Wilson Coll.* **csKY,** *Chawed up . . .* Defeated or embarrassed or severely scolded . . . *Chawed up . . .* Scolded severely and, usually, unjustly.

2 Angry, beaten, defeated.

1942 *Amer. Mercury* 55.92 **AL** [Black], I know you feel chewed. **1950** *PADS* 14.19 **SC,** *Chawed . . .* Defeated, beaten. In a literal or figurative sense. **1956** *Vogue* 15 Oct 73, 'Chewed Up' . . by Paul Klee . . . is, oddly, reminiscent of the American Southernism, 'chawed,' meaning *mad.* **c1960** [see **1** above].

chewee See **chewink**

cheweeka n

1 =**killdeer.** [Echoic]

1936 *Oriole* 1.7 **GA,** Killdeer.—Cheweeka (in imitation of its notes). **1949** Sprunt–Chamberlain *SC Bird Life* 215 **SC,** *Charadrius vociferus vociferus . . .* Cheweeka. **1950** *PADS* 14.19 **SC,** Cheweeka [čĭ'wikə] . . . The killdeer.

2 See quot.

1950 *PADS* 14.19 **SC,** *Cheweeka . . .* An insignificant, puny person. "You little cheweeka!" Coastal area.

cheweet See **chewink**

chewers n pl Pronc-sp *chawers* somewhat old-fash
Teeth; false teeth.

1942 Berrey–Van den Bark *Amer. Slang* 121.74. *Teeth . . .* Chewers. **1950** *WELS* (*Joking names for teeth*) 2 Infs, **WI,** Chewers; 1 Inf, Chawers; (*False teeth*) 1 Inf, Chewers. **1965–70** *DARE* (Qu. X13a) 31 Infs, **scattered,** Chewers; (Qu. X13b, *. . False teeth*) Infs **CA31, FL15, MN37, RI4,** False chewers. [32 of 36 Infs old] **1970** Major *Afro–Amer. Slang, Chewers:* (1940's) teeth.

chewfest n [**chew v B3, 5** + *fest*]
An argument, quarrel.

1967–69 *DARE* (Qu. Y12a, *A fight between two people, mostly with words*) Infs **CO33, IL97, MN15,** Chewfest.

‡chew fire v phr [Blend of *chew nails* + *breathe fire*]
To be upset, angry, annoyed.

1949 Arrow *Hunter's Horn* 298 **KY,** Back a year ago you was a chewen fire cause Andrew wasn't gitten th youngens through th eighth grade.

chewhack, chewhallop See **ker-**

chewing n

1 also *chawing:* Chewing tobacco; a chew of tobacco.

1906 *DN* 3.130 **nwAR,** "Gimme a chew of chawin'." . . . "Got any chewin'?" **1915** *DN* 4.225 **wTX,** *Chawin' and spittin' . . .* Tobacco:—

facetious. **1933** Williamson *Woods Colt* 253 **Ozarks,** He's plumb out of chawin', an' gittin jerky about it. **1933** *AmSp* 8.3.25 [Prison slang], *Chewin'.* Chewing-tobacco. **1940** *Esquire* Sept 134 **KY,** Have you got any homemade chawin on you? **1967** *DARE* (Qu. DD2, *The portion or quantity of tobacco chewed at one time*) Inf **HI6,** Chewing.

2 usu *chewins:* Food.

1907 *Cosmopolitan* 43.645/2, We went down the river "on our own," hustling our 'chewin's.' **1927** *DN* 5.442 [Underworld], *Chewins . . .* Food. **1930** Irwin *Amer. Tramp* 50, *Chewins.*—Food, that which is chewed. **1970** *DARE* (Qu. H6, *Words for food*) Inf **PA245,** Chewing.

3 A scolding. [Abbr for *chewing-out*—see **chew out**]

1965–70 *DARE* (Qu. II27, *. . Somebody gives you a very sharp scolding . . "I certainly got a _____ for that."*) Infs **CA147, CT42, MI10, MO25, PA245, RI15, TX72,** Chewing.

chewing match n **chiefly Nth**

1 An argument, quarrel. **[chew v B5]**

1950 *WELS* (*A fight between two people: mostly with words*) 6 Infs, **WI,** Chewing match. **1960** *VT Hist.* new ser 28.204, Match. A chewing match. (A heated argument.) **1965–70** *DARE* (Qu. Y12a, *A fight between two people, mostly with words*) 13 Infs, **chiefly Nth,** Chewin(g) match; (Qu. KK15, *A disagreement or quarrel*) Inf **MA14,** Chewing match.

2 occas *rag chewing match* (or *contest*): A meeting where there is a great deal of talking. **[chew v B2]**

1950 *WELS* (*Joking words for a meeting where there is a lot of talking*) 4 Infs, **WI,** Chewing match; 1 Inf, Rag chewing match; 1 Inf, Rag chewing contest. **1967–69** *DARE* (Qu. KK12), Infs **CT25, MA14, 18, NY131, OR4,** Chewing match.

chewing-out See **chew out**

chewing wax n Also *chaw wax* [**wax n**]
Chewing gum.

1940 Wilson *Wabash* 250 **IN,** Had they stayed longer, they might also have acquired the universal feminine habit of chewing burgundy pitch —one of the precursors of modern American chewing gum, or "chawwax," as it is still called in some parts of Indiana. **1966** *Wilson Coll.* **csKY,** *Chewing wax.* Chewing gum.

chewink n Also *cheeweeh, cheewink, cherink, chewee(t)* [Echoic]
The rufous-sided **towhee** (here: *Pipilo erythrophthalmus*).

1793 Morse *Amer. Universal Geog.* 1.191, Towhe Bird, Pewee, Cheeweeh. **1832** Williamson *Hist. ME* 1.143, The *Pewit,* or *Cheeweeh,* lives in the summer months about barns and out buildings, where the swallows have nests, in which she lays her eggs with theirs. **1884** Burroughs *Birds & Flowers* 134 (*OED*), The cheewink is a shy bird also. **1911** Porter *Harvester* 169 **IN,** Almost at the same time a chewink had something to say. **1949** Sprunt–Chamberlain *SC Bird Life* 522 **SC,** *Pipilo erythrophthalmus erythrophthalmus . . . Local Names:* Joree; Chewink. **1955** *MA Audubon* 39.254 **NEng,** Cherink (Maine); Chewee (Maine, N.H.); Cheweet (R.I.); Chewink (General). **1959** *AmSp* 34.73, Chewee, cheweet (Eastern towhee). **1967** Borland *Hill Country* 128 **nwCT,** The towhees are also called chewinks and ground robins. "Towhee" and "chewink" come from the calls.

chewins See **chewing 2**

chew it fine v phr **West**
To explain fully or simply; to consider thoroughly.

1936 Adams *Cowboy Lingo* 217, If the cowboy did not understand you and failed to grasp your meaning of a statement, he would ask you to 'chew it finer,' or 'cut the deck a little deeper.' **1941** FWP *Guide WY* 122, The tales 'traded' give life and currency to such expressions as 'cow sense', 'chew it finer'. **1971** Jennings *Cowboys* 226, Chew It Fine— From "chew it over" or "think it over," and, in this case, think it over thoroughly; also means to explain at greater length or put in simpler terms.

chew of tobacco n

In phrr *not worth a chew of tobacco, not to care a ~:* The smallest amount, the most trivial thing.

1804 (1969) Irving *Jrls. & Notebooks* 1.151, You can only take my life & that I dont care a chew of tobacco for. **1922** *DN* 5.158 **NE,** *Chaw of tobacco . . .* "He wasn't worth a chaw of tobacco when he came back." **1927** *AmSp* 2.350 **WV,** *Chaw of tobacco, not worth a . .* entirely worth-

less. "Don't buy that cow. She's not worth a chaw of tobacco."
1966–68 *DARE* (Qu. HH20c, *Of an idle, worthless person . . "He isn't worth _____."*) Infs **GA**1, **NJ**39, Chew of tobacco.

chew on all one's teeth v phr
To eat hurriedly.
    1950 *WELS* (*When you eat in a hurry because you have to go somewhere, you say, "I'll _____."*) 1 Inf, **ceWI**, Chew on all my teeth.

chew one's bit(s) v phr [Cf *champ (at) the bit,* in ref to a horse] **chiefly Sth, S Midl**
1 To be anxious or impatient; to be upset or angry.
    1939 *AmSp* 14.90 **eTN**, *Chewing his bits.* A fit of anger. 'John's chewing his bits.' **1967–70** *DARE* (Qu. AA4a . . *A man who is very eager to get married*) Inf **LA**31, Chewing the bit; (Qu. GG11, *To be quite anxious about something*) Inf **SC**32, Chewing his bits; (Qu. GG7, . . *Annoyed or upset*) Inf **IL**143, Chewing the bit.
2 To argue or talk too much or too loud.
    1968–69 *DARE* (Qu. HH7b, *Someone who talks too much or too loud*) Inf **VA**15, Chewing the bits; (Qu. KK13, *Other words for arguing*) Inf **GA**77, Chewing the bits.

chew one's cabbage twice v phr Also *boil one's cabbage twice* Cf **chew one's tobacco 2**
To repeat oneself.
    1888 *AN&Q* 1.6/2, "I Don't Boil my Cabbage Twice." In the country, especially in the country towns of Pennsylvania, this is a very common expression, generally pronounced, "I don't bile my cabbage twict." It signifies that the person uttering it does not intend to repeat an observation. **1978** *DARE* FW Addit **cnMA** (as of c1915), "I don't chew my cabbage twice" means "I am not going to repeat myself." **1981** De Vries *Sauce* 203 **IN**, Even Daisy had sometimes had to chew her cabbage twice, when her Hoosier twang had had met with a "Beg Pardon?" **1983** *DARE* File **csWI** (as of 1930s), The expression "I don't chew my cabbage twice" was familiar to me, but it was considered crude and rude to say it that way.

chew one's gums v phr [Alter of *beat one's gums*]
    1969 *DARE* (Qu. HH7b, *Someone who talks too much or too loud*) Inf **IL**30, Chewing his gums.

chew one's own meat v phr
=**chew one's tobacco 1.**
    1902 (1968) Clapin *Americanisms, Chew (to) one's own meat.* To attend to one's own business; to do a thing oneself.

chew one's tobacco v phr In var phrr **chiefly Sth, S Midl**
1 *to chew one's own tobacco:* To rely on oneself. *arch*
    1858 Hammett *Piney Woods Tavern* 59 **TX**, It's allers best for every man to chaw his own tobackker. **1898** Lloyd *Country Life* 202 **AL**, Chew your own tobacco. Hold your head up. Look the sun in the face.
2 *to chew (one's) tobacco more than once* and varr:
a To repeat what one has said. Cf **chew one's cabbage twice**
    1893 Shands *MS Speech* 23, *Chaw tobacco more than once* . . . A very common phrase among negroes and illiterate whites. It means *to repeat.* **1906** *DN* 3.130 **nwAR**, *Chaw one's tobacco* [tǝbǽkǝ] *twice* . . . To repeat a remark. "I don't chaw my tobacker twice." **1938** *AmSp* 13.4 **seAR**, I don't chew my tobacco but once. **1954** Harder *Coll.* **cwTN**, I don't chaw my tobacco but oncet. **1954** *PADS* 21.23 **SC**, I don't *chaw* my tobacco ('backer) but once. Sometimes is added "and I spit where I please." This is an intentionally offensive and challenging refusal to repeat one's words.
b To mull something over before acting.
    1927 *AmSp* 2.350 **WV**, *Chaw one's tobacco twice* . . to consider for a long time before acting. "He will chaw tobacco twice on that proposition."
c To be stingy.
    1927 *AmSp* 2.350 **WV**, *Chaw one's tobacco twice* . . . To be stingy. "Mr. Thompson does not buy much tobacco, because he always chaws it twice."
3 *to chaw one's tobacco mighty fast:* See quot.
    1902 *DN* 2.231 **sIL**, *Chaw one's tobacco mighty fast.* An expression denoting perturbation or subdued anger.

chew out v phr, hence *chewing-out* vbl n   *esp among younger speakers*
To bawl out, scold, reprimand.

1948 *NY Folkl. Qrly.* 4.18, A verbal admonishing from a superior would be recorded by the victim with "I just got eaten out" or "I got chewed out." **1960** Wentworth–Flexner *Slang* 97, *Chew out* . . . to bawl out . . . *Very common during W.W.II; still in frequent use among civilians as well as servicemen.* **1965–70** *DARE* (Qu. II27, . . *A very sharp scolding*) 135 Infs, **scattered**, Chewing-out; **CA**37, **LA**46, **MO**4, **NM**4, **NV**4, Chewed out; **MN**33, **VT**16, My ass chewed out; **MI**123, Chew out; [Of all Infs responding to the question, 12% were young, 25% middle-aged; of those giving these responses, 23% were young, 39% middle-aged.] (Qu. Y12a, *A fight between two people, mostly with words*) Infs **CA**59, 140, **MN**28, Chewing-out; **LA**3, **WA**3, Chewing each other out; (Qu. Y6, . . *To put pressure on somebody*) Infs **CA**59, **NY**1, **SC**70, **VA**24, 109, Chew him out; (Qu. Y7) Inf **MA**58, Chewing me out; (Qu. JJ35b) Infs **GA**67, **MN**21, (Like to) chew him out. **1968** Adams *Western Words, Chew out*—To administer a tongue-lashing.

Chewsday See **Tuesday**

chew the cud v phr
    1944 Adams *Western Words, Chew the cud*—To argue, to carry on a long-winded conversation.

chew-tobacco n
1 also attrib: Chewing tobacco.
    1834 Caruthers *Kentuckian* 1.103, "Not your chaw-tobacco parson, I hope?" "And why not? What if he *would* roll his chaw-tobacco into one cheek at you, while he coupled you up [=married you] with the other?" **1965–70** *DARE* (Qu. DD1, . . *Forms . . chewing tobacco*) 17 Infs, **scattered**, Chew-tobacco; **CA**191, **NC**40, **NY**111, **OH**92, **TN**33, Chaw-tobacco. **1966** *Wilson Coll.* **csKY**, *Chew-tobacco* . . . chewing tobacco.
2 A grasshopper of the family Acrididae. [From the insect's emitting a brown fluid when squeezed] Cf **bug juice 3**
    1968 *DARE* (Qu. R6, . . *Grasshoppers*) Infs **DE**4, **NJ**39, Chew-to-bacco; **NJ**21, Chew-terbaccers.
3 See quot.
    1968 *DARE* (Qu. H82a, *Cheap candies*) Inf **SC**51, Chew-tobacco—joking name for licorice.

chew wax n
    1967 *DARE* (Qu. H82b, *Kinds of cheap candies . . years ago*) Inf **PA**40, Chew wax—had flavoring in it.

chew wet v phr
    1916 *DN* 4.321 **KS**, *Chew wet* . . . To chew succulent vegetables, or other food, with the mouth open so that a clacking sound escapes.

Cheyenne leg n Also *Cheyenne cut* **West**
A type of **chaps**: see quot 1944.
    1944 Adams *Western Words, Cheyenne cut*—A type of wing chap developed in Wyoming, the wing being narrower and straight. The under part of the leg is cut back to the knee, with no snaps below that point. **1946** Mora *Trail Dust* 89, The "Cheyenne leg," which is the lower inside leg piece cut away at a curve, is very popular, and deserves to be. **1955** Harris *Look of Old West* 214, *Cheyenne leg.*

Cheyenne pepper n [Alter of *cayenne*]
    1966–68 *DARE* (Qu. I22a, . . *Peppers—small hot*) Infs **GA**9, **LA**15, Cheyenne peppers.

Cheyenne saddle n Also *Cheyenne (roll)* [*Cheyenne,* town in Wyoming] **West**
A type of saddle: see quot 1944.
    1891 *Harper's Mag.* 83.204/1 **Plains States**, The Texas saddle has a much flatter seat than the Brazos tree; the Cheyenne saddle a still flatter one, with a high cantle and a different cut of pommel arch. **1907** Mulford *Bar-20* 134 **West**, He sat in his Cheyenne saddle like a centaur. *Ibid* 358, The saddle, a famous Cheyenne and forty pounds in weight, was black, richly embossed, and decorated with bits of beaten silver which flashed back the sunlight. **1944** Adams *Western Words, Cheyenne roll* . . a saddle with a leather flange extending over, to the rear, of the cantleboard . . . This saddle was brought out about 1870 and became very popular throughout the seventies and eighties, especially east of the Rockies. **1977** Watts *Dict. Old West, Cheyenne roll* . . . The saddle with such a roll was referred to as a *Cheyenne* or *Cheyenne saddle* and was originated by Frank Meanea, a saddlemaker from that town.

cheyn(e)y See **china A**

cheyote See **chayote**

Chi n[1] See **Chicago A**

chi n[2] See **chy**

chia n Also *chia seed*, ~ *sage* [MexSpan *chía*] **SW**
A **sage**, esp *Salvia columbariae.*
  1876 Hobbs *Bot. Hdbk.* 22, Chia seed, Salvia Hispanica. **1897** Parsons *Wild Flowers CA* 298, Chia. Sage. Salvia Columbariæ. **1938** *AmSp* 13.115 [Nahuatl words], In Arizona various species of spring-blooming salvia bear the name *chia,* especially among the Indians. **1967–68** *DARE* (Qu. S26e, . . *Wildflowers*) Inf **CA4**, Chia; **CA60**, Chia sage. **1976** Bailey–Bailey *Hortus Third* 999, Chia . . . Calif. to cent. Baja Calif., e. to Utah and Ariz.

chiacalacca, chiac-chia-lacca See **chachalaca 1**

chib See **chive**

chibbole n Also sp *chibbal* [Engl dial, alter of *cibol*]
A scallion.
  1896 (1968) Earle *Colonial NY* 136 (as of 1740s), There were also plenty of vegetables: *cibollen* (chibbals), *peasen* (pease), *chicoreye* (chiccory), . . and many others. **1941** *LANE* Map 258 **seNH**, *Scallion* . . . Chibbole [čɪbowz].

chib-chab n [Echoic]
Either the **downy woodpecker** or the **hairy woodpecker.**
  1930 OK Univ. Biol. Surv. *Pub.* 2.118, *Hairy Woodpecker . . . Local names:* . . chib-chab. *Ibid* 123, *Southern Downy Woodpecker . . . Local Names:* . . chib-chab.

chic adj Std |šik|, sp-pronc |čɪk| Pronc-sp *chick*
Std sense, var forms.
  1920 *DN* 5.78, *Chick, chic.* "Your new garments are very chick." **1925** Parrish *Perennial Bachelor* 250 **MD** (as of 1850–1900s), See, isn't that *chick?* **1948** *This Week Mag.* 16 Oct 29/2 (*DA*), One of them Hollywood flowered shirts is right chick on the right rooster. **1970** *DARE* File **KS**, That dress is really [čɪk]. **1975** Morris *Usage* 122 , *Chic* should be pronounced *sheek,* not *chik.*

chica See **chico** n[2], adj

chicadee See **chickadee** n[1]

Chicago n Usu |šɪˈkɑgo, šə-, -kɔ-|, occas |č-|, less freq with intrusive *r;* see also quots 1939, 1976. Shortened form *Chi* |šai| Pronc-sp *Chicagyo*
A Forms.
  1914 *Nebraska State Journal* 12 June (*DN* 4.127), If women's votes aridify The town that's briefly know as '*Chi*', I can't begin to tell you The funny things that we shall view. **1922** Gonzales *Black Border* 292 **sSC, GA coasts** [Gullah glossary], *Chicagyo*—Chicago. **1927** *DN* 5.442 [Underworld jargon], *Chi* . . . The abbreviation for Chicago, the hobo capital of America. Pronounced 'shy.' **1939** *LANE* Map 22 **NEng,** *Chicago.* [Usu [šɪˈkɑgo, -kɔ-]; also [-gou, -goʊ], esp ME, and usu regarded as older; infreq [-gə, -gu, -gʊ]; occas [šə-], infreq [ˈškɑgo], [čɪˈkɑgo, čə-]. Infreq [šae], 'for short.'] **1945** O'Hara *Pipe Night* 49 **PA,** The poor man's Bing Crosby is still making with the throat here in Chi. **c1960** *Wilson Coll.* **csKY,** *Chicago* is often [šɪˈkɑr̩go]. **1965** *PADS* 44.67 **Chicago IL,** The distinctive features in the speech of the native Negro in Metropolitan Chicago include: . . Phonemic differences . . /ɑ/ for /ɔ/ in *Chicago.* **1967** *DARE* FW Addit **ceNC,** Chicago [čəkɑrgo]. **1976** Allen *LAUM* 3.351, There are two widespread pronunciations of *Chicago,* one with a medial stressed unrounded vowel occurring as [ɑ] or [ɑ] and one with rounded [ɔ] or, more commonly, [ɒ]. They exist in a 1:2 ratio in the UM, with an apparent slight Northern weighting for the unrounded vowel. . . . The final syllable . . general pattern with some allophones of /o/ is broken in the speech of 14 infs. by the appearance of /ə/, all but one of whom are in Midland speech territory, principally Iowa and Nebraska . . . Another minor variable is evident in the uncommon use of the affricate /č/ instead of /š/ as the initial consonant [by 5 infs].
B Senses.
1 See quot.
  1905 *DN* 3.74 **nwAR,** *Chicago* . . . A bowling game.
2 also attrib: A type of pastry, freq jelly-filled; a **long-john. WI, MN, ND** Cf **bismarck**
  1950 *WELS* (*Doughnuts*) 1 Inf, **WI,** Chicagos; (*Different shapes or sizes*) 2 Infs, Chicagos; 1 Inf, Chicago fried cakes; (*A round cake cooked the same way, but with jelly inside*) 1 Inf, Chicagoes; (*A long cake cooked the same way*) 2 Infs, Chicago(s); 3 Infs, Chicago doughnuts; 1 Inf, Chicago fried cake. **1966–68** *DARE* (Qu. H29, *A round cake, cooked in deep fat, with jelly inside*) Inf **WI58**, Chicago; **ND1**, Chicago Bismarck; (Qu. H30, *An oblong cake, cooked in deep fat*) Inf **MN16**, Chicago.

3 In marble play: see quot.
  1968 *DARE* (Qu EE7, . . *Marble games*) Inf **WI60**, Chicago—draw a big circle, put marbles inside and try to shoot them out. Whoever shoots the marble out gets to keep it.

Chicago fire n [From its bright red foliage: in allusion to the Chicago fire of 1871] **WI**
=**summer cypress.**
  1950 *WELS Suppl.* **csWI,** Chicago fire—Kochia; **csWI,** Chicago fire—fire bush, Mexican fire bush; **seWI,** Chicago fire—commonly, fire bush; **csWI,** When I was a little girl about 1910, the Chicago fire (Kochia bush) was most popular around Baraboo and Prairie du Sac.

Chicago mallard n
Any of three ducks: the common merganser, **hooded merganser,** or **red-breasted merganser.**
  1956 *AmSp* 31.182, *Name* . . . Chicago mallard . . . *Bird* . . . Mergansers . . . *Known Distribution of the Name* . . . Wis.

Chicagyo See **Chicago A**

chicalote n [MexSpan] **SW**
A **prickly poppy** (here: either *Argemone platyceras* or *A. mexicana*).
  1889 *Century Dict.* 4.954, Chicalote . . . A Mexican name given in southern California to a species of thorn-poppy. **1897** Parsons *Wild Flowers CA* 74, Thistle-poppy. Chicalote. Argemone platyceras. **1970** Correll *Plants TX* 664, *Argemone mexicana . . . Devil's fig,* . . *chicalote, Mexican poppy.* **1976** Dodge *Roadside Wildflowers* 14, One of the common and distinctive drouth resistant perennials of the Southwest is the thistle poppy, prickly poppy, or chicalote.

chicaric n [Echoic]
=**ruddy turnstone.**
  1877 Hallock *Sportsman's Gazetteer* 164 (*DA*), The names Chicaric and Chickling have reference to their rasping notes. **1917** *Wilson Bulletin* 29.2.80 **eMA,** *Arenaria interpres.*—Chicaric. **1955** *MA Audubon Soc. Bulletin* 39.446, *Ruddy Turnstone* . . . Chicaric (Mass. Sonic.).

chicayote See **chilacayote**

chiccory See **chicory**

ch'ice See **choice** n, v

chichado n [?Alter of **chicharra**]
Prob a cicada.
  1843 (1969) Lewis *Odd Leaves* 98 **LA,** An unusual stillness rested over the swamp . . not even a frog or chichado was to be heard.

chicharko See **cheechako**

chicharra n |čɪˈčɑra| Also *chicharro* [Span] **TX**
A cicada.
  1892 *DN* 1.246 **TX,** *Chichárra:* harvest fly, Cicada spumaria. **1967** *DARE* (Qu. R5, *A big brown beetle . . flies with a buzzing sound*) Inf **TX28**, Chicharro [čɪˈčɑro]; (Qu. R7, *Insects that sit in trees or bushes in hot weather and make a sharp, buzzing sound*) Inf **TX28**, Chicharro.

chicharron n Also sp *chicheron, chickeron* [Span] **SW**
A **crackling** n 1.
  1856 C.W. Webber *Tale of the South Border* 48 (Bentley *Spanish Terms*), Chicharrones are cracklings, and are one of the greatest delicacies the Mexicans know! *Ibid* 109, Everyone . . holding in one hand a tin cup . . and in the other a tortilla and chickerones. **1892** *DN* 1.246 **TX,** *Chicharrón:* crackles; bacon left in the pan after it is fried. **1932** Bentley *Spanish Terms* 120, *Chicharron* English modifications *chicherones, chikerones . . .* The designation *chicharrones* is more commonly used by some Americans along the border than is the English "cracklings."

chi-chi n |či či| [Japanese *chichi* milk; the breast] **HI**
A woman's breast.
  1967 *DARE* (Qu. X31, . . *A woman's breasts*) Inf **HI8**, Chi-chi; **HI9**, Chi-chi [či či], everybody uses it (Japanese).

chi-chi-chi intj [Abbr for *chick*]
Used as a call to chickens.
  1967 LeCompte *Word Atlas* 191 **seLA,** *Call to chickens* . . . [2 of 21 infs] chi-chi-chi. **1968** *DARE* (Qu. K79, *How . . you call the chickens*) Inf **LA33**, Chi-chi-chi-chi.

chichiquamin See **chinquapin**

chick n *esp among young speakers and among Black speakers; sometimes derog*

A young, usu attractive woman.

1927 Lewis *Elmer Gantry* 114 **KS**, He didn't want to marry this brainless little fluffy chick. **1938** *AmSp* 13.316 **NE** [Black], *Chick . . girl.* **1950** *WELS (Nicknames or affectionate names for a sweetheart)* 1 Inf, **cWI**, Chick. **1955** *AmSp* 30.302 **MI**, *Chick . . . Girl, usually pretty.* **1958** *PADS* 30.44 [Jazz musicians], *Chick . . . A girl.* **1963** *AmSp* 38.172 **KS, MI** [College slang], A very pretty female date: . . *chick.* **1965–70** *DARE* (Qu. HH34, *General words . . for a woman*) 140 Infs, **scattered**, Chick; **GA53, NC36**, Slick chick [Of all Infs responding to the question, 12% were young, 26% mid-aged, 7% Black; of those giving this response 25% were young, 33% mid-aged, 19% Black.]; (Qu. W36, . . *A woman who uses a lot of cosmetics)* Inf **FL51**, Decked-out chick; (Qu. Z6, . . *Words meaning "sister")* Inf **NY241**, Fly chick; (Qu. AA3, . . *A sweetheart)* Infs **MO26, PA221**, Chick; (Qu. AA7a) Inf **NY241**, Real sweet chick; (Qu. AA12) Inf **FL51**, Let that chick go. **1970** Major *Afro–Amer. Slang, Chick:* a young woman, especially an attractive one. **1970** *DARE* Tape **NY242**, Chick . . sometimes is a put-down [for] a girl who's somewhat of a bitch, depending upon the intonation.

chick adj See **chic**

chickaberry See **checkerberry 3, chickenberry 1**

chickabiddy n [*chick* + *-a-* + *biddy* n[1]]

1 An immature chicken—sometimes used as a call.

1848 Bartlett *Americanisms, Chickabiddy.* A young chicken. **1872** Schele de Vere *Americanisms* 380, *Chickabiddy* for the little ones [chicks]. **1942** Berrey–Van den Bark *Amer. Slang* 120.27, Chickabiddy, chicky, *esp. a small chicken.* **1967** *DARE* File **csMA** (as of 1940s), *Chickabiddy*—a call to chickens.

2 A hen.

1930 Shoemaker *1300 Words* **cPA Mts** (as of c1900), *Chickabiddy*— An old hen; a mother hen.

3 A loved one, esp a child.

1848 Bartlett *Americanisms, Chickabiddy . . .* Used also as a term of endearment to children, and not peculiar to America. **1942** Berrey–Van den Bark *Amer. Slang* 185.2 *Pet names; terms of endearment. (Frequently prefaced "my" or "little.") . . .* Chickabiddy.

chickaboo See **jigaboo**

chickadee n[1] Also sp *chicadee, chick-a-dee-dee* [Echoic]

1 A bird of the genus *Penthestes.* Also called **titmouse** For other names of var spp see **brown-capped chickadee**

1838 (1949) Thoreau *Jrl.* 1.60 **NEng**, The chickadee is more than usually familiar. **1845** *Knickerbocker* 25.200 **NY**, There was no sound but the note of the little 'chick-a-dee-dee,' so familiar to the pine woods in winter. **1872** Schele de Vere *Americanisms* 377, The *Chickadee* (Parus atricapillus), elsewhere known by the quaint title of Hoary Titmouse, bears its name also from its utterance: it is the tiny, black-cap titmouse. **1904** Waller *Wood-Carver* 73 (DAE), The chicadees are fairly singing somersaults around one another. **1905** *DN* 3.5 **cCT**, *Chicka-dee . . .* The black-cap titmouse. **1965–70** *DARE* (Qu. Q23) 23 Infs, **chiefly Nth**, Chickadee; (Qu. Q14) Infs **MI2, MA46, NY6, TN56, VT10, WI78**, Chickadee; (Qu. Q21) Infs **CA210, MD22, 48, MN2, NH5, PA104, RI15**, Chickadee; (Qu. Q22) Infs **MA40, PA245**, Chickadee.

2 A loved one; a sweetheart; a child; also used ironically. [From the bird's friendly, endearing nature]

1860 Holland *Miss Gilbert* 62 **NY**, When a feller gets tied to a wife, and has a lot of little chickadees around him. **1889** Munroe *Golden Days* 272 **CA** (as of 1849), Ain't he just a chick-a-dee-dee with the cheek of a government mule! **1942** Berrey–Van den Bark *Amer. Slang* 185.2, *Pet names; terms of endearment. (Frequently prefaced "my" or "little.") . . .* Chickadee, chickapin. **1950** *WELS (Nicknames or affectionate names for a sweetheart)* 1 Inf, **ceWI**, Chick-a-dee. **1967** *DARE* (Qu. AA3, . . *A sweetheart)* Inf **OH34**, Chickadee.

3 See quot.

1956 Sorden–Ebert *Logger's Words* **Gt Lakes**, *Chickadee,* A road monkey whose job it was to clean the horse manure from the ice road.

4 In marble play: see quot. [From the colors and design]

1958 *PADS* 29.31 **IL**, *Chickadee . . .* A glazed or baked marble of very good quality and with a glossy, porcelain-like finish, mottled or "blotchy" in several colors but with no regular design; slightly smaller than regular mibs.

chickadee n[2] See **chickaree**

chick-a-dee-dee See **chickadee** n[1]

chickamy chickamy craney crow n For varr see quots **chiefly Sth, S Midl** Cf **craney crow, fox and hen, hawk and chickens, old witch**

A children's game in which one player (the hawk or witch) tries to catch the others (the chickens) who are usu protected by another player (the hen).

1877 *Lumberman's Gaz.* 24 May 356 [Political cartoon], Chickie! My Chickie! My Craney Crow. You've had your "day" and down you go. **1935** Hurston *Mules & Men* 78 **FL**, That most raucous, popular and most African of games, "Chirck, mah Chick, mah Craney crow." **1946** TN Folk Lore Soc. *Bulletin* 12.21, Chick-a-my-Craney-Crow [a children's singing game]. **1952** Brown *NC Folkl.* 1.48–51, 'Old Witch' and 'Chickamy, chickamy, Craney Crow' have the same theme and the differences between them are only superficial . . . [Also called] 'Chicky My Chick My Craney Crow.' . . 'Chick-O-My, Chick-O-My, Craney-Crow.' **1953** Goodwin *It's Good* 201 **sIL** [Black], We didn't need five murders in ten minutes on the radio to give us a thrill. Eluding the witch in chickany, chickany, crany crow . . was thrill enough. **1953** Brewster *Amer. Nonsinging Games* 71 **TN**, *Chickamy Chickamy Craney Crow* . . . One player is the hawk, another is the hen, and the rest are chickens. [*DARE* Ed: the hawk is freq a witch, who tries to catch the chickens while the hen tries to protect them]. *Ibid* 76, Chickamy. **1957** *Sat. Eve. Post Letters* **WI**, Chickory (*or* chickeney) cranery crow. **1966** *DARE* Tape **MS76**, ['čɪkəmə'krenɪ'kro]. **1968** *DARE* FW Addit **VA**, Chickany, chickany, craney crow / Went to the well to wash my toe / When I came back, my chicken was gone. / What time is it, old witch?

chickapea See **chick-pea**

chickapen See **chinquapin A**

chickaree n Also sp *chiparee, chickeree, chickery;* rarely *chickadee* [Echoic]

=**red squirrel.**

1804 in 1909 *MD Hist. Mag.* 4.9 **PA**, These squirrels are exceedingly active and the mountaineers call them the Chiparee squirrel. **1825** in 1974 *Fauna Americana* 185, *Sciurus hudsonius, . .* vulgarly *the Chick-a-ree.* **1849** (1911) Thoreau *Week on Concord* 242 **NEng**, The larger red squirrel or chickaree, sometimes called the Hudson Bay squirrel. **1857** Paige *Dow's Patent Sermons* 3.171, The birds have ceased their summer carrolings—the chickeree shells his nut in quietness—no sound is heard. **1893** *Jrl. Amer. Folkl.* 6.143 **VA**, *Chickaree . . .* red squirrel (*Sciurus hudsonius*). **1940** *Jrl. Mammalogy* 21.175 **NV**, *Tamiasciurus fremonti fremonti . . .* Fremont chickaree.—The only tree squirrel encountered was the chickaree. **1948** Peattie *Inverted Mts.* 337 **SW**, At elevations ranging above eighty-five hundred feet . . are . . red spruce squirrels commonly called chickarees. **1949** Kurath *Word Geog.* 74, *Chipmunk . . . Ground squirrel . . .* Scattered relics of two old local terms occur: *grinnie* around Pittsburgh, *chickery* south and east of Philadelphia. **1968–69** *DARE* (Qu. P27, . . *Squirrels)* Infs **MD20, NJ31, 39, 53**, Chickaree; **NJ55**, Chickadee.

Chickasaw n

1 also attrib: A multi-colored horse orig favored by the Chickasaw Indians.

1745 *South-Carolina Gaz.* (Charleston SC) 16 Dec [2/2], *Several* valuable Saddle Horses, of the *Chickasaw* and *Choctaw* Breed to be sold. **1761** *Ibid* 8 Aug [3/2], Strayed or Stolen . . a grey gelding . . with a *Chicasaw* head. **1816** in 1824 Knight *Letters* 76 **VA**, The toughest, and longest-lived field horses are said to be the Chickasaws, or small calico-coloured ponies; often serving for thirty years. **1968** *DARE* (Qu. K37, . . *A horse of mixed colors)* Inf **MD29**, ['čɪkə.sɔ], mouse-colored with gray or white stripes; **VA27**, ['čɪkɪsɔ] horse, a western horse from Ohio; **WV7**, [čɪkɪsɔʊ], gray mixture.

2 See **Chickasaw plum.**

3 =**spreading dogbane.**

1897 *Jrl. Amer. Folkl.* 10.50, *Apocynum androsaemifolium . .* Chickasaw, wildweed, Paris and Hartford, Me.

Chickasaw plum n Also *Chickasaw* **chiefly S Midl**

A small thorny plum (here: *Prunus angustifolia*) which produces white flowers followed by red or yellow fruits. Also called **hog plum, mountain cherry, sand plum, yellow plum**

1760 in 1922 Fries *Rec. Moravians* 1.229 **NC**, The wagon came back from Springhill . . loaded with . . rosemary, Chickasaw plums and a kind of pine with very long leaves. **1775** Adair *Amer. Indians* 360 **sTN, nAL, nMS,** They have a large sort of plums, which their ancestors brought with them from South-America, and which are now become plenty among our colonies, called Chikkasah plums. **1819** (1821) Nuttall *Jrl.* 100 **AR,** The land on the Indian side, contiguous to the river, abounded with thickets of Chicasaw plum-trees. **1872** Schele de Vere *Americanisms* 57, The *Chickasaw* Plum derives its name from an Indian tribe residing in the portion of Arkansas where the bush (Prunus chicasa) is found in great abundance along the banks of Red River. **c1960** *Wilson Coll.* **csKY,** *Chickasaw plum* . . The common wild plum, growing in thickets around old house sites and said to have been here when the white men came. **1960** Williams *Walk Egypt* 63 **GA,** A mother quail towing a skein of babies into the thickets of Chickasaw plum. **1969–70** *DARE* (Qu. I46, . . *Fruits that grow wild*) Infs **KY**5, 84, Chickasaw plum(s). **1972** Brown *Wildflowers* LA 67, Chickasaw Plum —*Prunus angustifolia.*

Chickasaw rose n Infreq *wild chickasaw*

A **Cherokee rose** (here: *Rosa bracteata*).

1835 Ingraham *South-West* 2.108 **MS,** The "chickasaw rose," which is a beautiful hedge thorn, grows luxuriantly. **1865** *Atlantic Mth.* 15.424/1 **eGA,** The deserted house was embowered in great blossoming shrubs, . . among which predominated that of the little Chickasaw roses. **1967** *DARE* (Qu. S26e, . . *Wildflowers*) Inf **LA**4, Wild cherokee —a running white rose, white petals, yellow stamen, runs along in trees and on the ground. There's a brier brought in here for fencerows called the wild chickasaw, but a lot of people call it the wild cherokee. It makes a round clump with a tough root system, and comes up mostly in pastures. **1972** Brown *Wildflowers* LA 70, Chickasaw Rose . . *Rosa bracteata.*

chick-bean See **chick-pea**

chickberry n

1 =**partridgeberry 1.** Cf **checkerberry 3**

1859 (1968) Bartlett *Americanisms,* Chequer Berry. (Mitchella.) A handsome little creeping plant, the only species of its genus, more commonly known as the Partridge Berry. Also called Chickberry. **1872** Schele de Vere *Americanisms* 402, Partridge-berries. It is also known as *chequer*-berry, and in New England occasionally as *chick*-berry.

2 See **chickenberry 1.**

chickee n[1] Also sp *chikee* [Prob from Creek; perh akin to Choctaw *chuka* house] **FL**

A hut first made by the Seminole Indians usu having open sides and a roof of palmetto fronds.

1948 Hanna *Lake Okeechobee* 327 **FL,** Their substitute for a house, the chikee, became more loosely constructed. It consisted of a wood platform some three or four feet above the ground, covered by a palm-leaf roof supported by poles. **1961** Douglas *My Wilderness* 145 **Everglades FL,** His huts (there were three of them) were in the center of the hammock. They are called chickees. Their sides were open; they stood high off the ground; their roofs were peaked, like those in Ireland. **1964** Will *Hist. Okeechobee* 68 **FL,** Each hut or chickee was nothing but a steep thatched roof of palmetto fans with eaves head high from the ground. **1975** Newell *If Nothin' Don't Happen* 123 **nwFL,** He had him a shack built up, roofed over and sided up with palmetto fans, somethin' like a Indian chickee.

chickee n[2] See **chickie**

chicken n Usu |ˈčɪkən|; also |ˈčɪkɪŋ| Pronc-spp *chickin(g)* Cf **-ing**

A Forms.

1 Pronc varr.

1837 in 1956 Eliason *Tarheel Talk* 308 **NC,** Chickings. **1843** (1916) Hall *New Purchase* 54 **IN,** Nan, sort a turn them thare chickins. **1844** Thompson *Major Jones's Courtship* 35 **GA,** The chawk rattled on the board like a flock of chickins pickin corn off a clap-board. **1922** Gonzales *Black Border* 292 **sSC, GA coasts** [Gullah glossary], Chickin —chicken, chickens. **1969** *DARE* Tape **GA**79, Chicken [ˈčɪkɪŋ].

2 pl: usu *chickens*, rarely *chicken*.

1922 [see **1** above]. **c1950** *WELS Suppl.,* **csWI** [Woman of German descent], We're going to buy 50 chicken and put them in our freezer.

B Senses.

1 Any of var gallinaceous birds: see quots.

1812 (1920) Luttig *Jrl.* 14 Oct 86 **WY,** 4 Men went out to hunt . . got this Day 21 Chickens. **1895** *Outing* 27.42/1 **MT,** Quickly the heavy

sound of chickens' wings notified us that game had been found. **1907** Anderson *Birds IA* 233, Though the species has been dignified by . . Pinnated Grouse . . , in the vernacular of sportsmen, hunters, and all who have known the bird in its native haunts, the name has always been . . "Prairie Chicken" or simply "Chicken." *Ibid* 234, On a few occasions I have seen Chickens roosting in trees in the winter time, but this is unusual. **1918** *DN* 5.55 **WA,** *Chicken* . . . Chinese pheasant. Game Warden J.W. Pike planted thirty-eight of the chickens in three different districts of the county. **1953** *AmSp* 28.278, [These are called *chicken:*] The spruce grouse (Alaska); ruffed grouse (Manitoba); pinnated grouse (Wis., Minn., Iowa, N. Dak., Manitoba); sharp-tailed grouse (Wis., N. Dak., Mont., Oreg., Alberta, Manitoba, Saskatchewan), and the ring-necked pheasant (Wash.). **1958** McCulloch *Woods Words* **Pacific NW,** *Chicken* —Any bird found in the woods between the size of robins and eagles. **1968** *DARE* (Qu. Q7, . . *Game birds*) Inf **NH**14, Chicken, = partridge; **NY**41, 44, Chicken. **1976** *Fairbanks Daily News–Miner* (AK) 26 Aug, "Chicken" is the common name for the ptarmigan, which is abundant in the area.

2 =**ruddy turnstone.**

1888 Trumbull *Names of Birds* 186, [Ruddy Turnstone] at Chatham [MA] *Chicken* simply. **1917** (1923) *Birds Amer.* 1.268. **1953** *AmSp* 28.278 **MA,** The turnstone, a familiar and, when encouraged, a confiding, shore bird, also has been termed *chicken.* **1955** *MA Audubon Soc. Bulletin* 39.446, *Ruddy Turnstone* . . . Chicken . . (Mass. The term "chicken" seems to refer to clucking notes.).

3 A person; spec:

a A fellow, guy. Cf **child B1, coon** n[1] **1**

1853 in 1956 Eliason *Tarheel Talk* 265 **NC,** Tha cant sker this chicken.

b A child. [*OED* ?a1400 →]

1899 (1912) Green *VA Folk-Speech,* Chicken . . . A person of tender years; a child; used with a negative in satirical implication of mature age. "She's no *chicken.*" **1941** *LANE* Map 379 **cMA,** Terms . . used as affectionate synonyms of *child* [include *chicken,* offered by 1 inf]. **1967** *DARE* (Qu. Z16, *A small child who is rough, misbehaves, and doesn't obey*) Inf **TX**35, Spoilt chicken.

c also attrib: A young woman; a **chick;** also a woman of questionable morals.

1915 *DN* 4.225 **wTX,** *Chicken* . . . Uncomplimentary term for *woman.* **1924** *DN* 5.289, *Chicken* . . . Female of somewhat doubtful virtue. **1942** Berrey–Van den Bark *Amer. Slang* 828.2, Chicken house . . *a sorority house. Ibid* 829.10, *Girls' dormitory* . . . chicken house. **1950** *WELS (Nicknames or affectionate names for a sweetheart)* 1 Inf, **ceWI,** Chicken. **1966–69** *DARE* (Qu. AA3, *General words . . for a woman*) Infs **CA**107, **ID**2, **MI**67, **NE**11, **OH**37, Chicken; (Qu. AA3, *Nicknames or affectionate names for a sweetheart*) Inf **WA**1, Chicken; (Qu. AA22, *Joking names . . wife*) Inf **SC**44, Little chicken. **1981** Pederson *LAGS Urban Material* **Houston TX,** [*Whore house,* 1 inf, chicken shack.]

d A young sailor or soldier, often the close "buddy" of another older one.

1888 Billings *Hardtack* 52 **NEast,** A Marblehead man called his chum his "chicken," more especially if the latter was a *young soldier.* **1890** *Congressional Record* 21 Apr 3637/1 **MA,** In the hospital I saw an admirable illustration of the affection which a sailor will lavish on a ship's boy to whom he takes a fancy, and makes his "chicken," as the phrase is. **1928** Ruppenthal *Coll.* **KS,** Chicken . . . (army) a youthful soldier. **1956** *AmSp* 31.191 [Marine Corps slang], A novice is usually a chicken.

4 Any of several games:

a One in which the main point is to show lack of cowardice; see quots.

1953 Bradbury *Fahrenheit 451* 27, Go out in the cars . . trying to see how close you can get to lamp-posts, playing 'chicken' and 'knock hubcaps.' **1961** *AmSp* 36.150 **Denver CO** [Teen-age slang], *Chicken,* often heard in reference to the deplorable games of daredevil young drivers . . . [T]he games of *chicken,* one of which is to let a car run without hands on the wheel until one passenger panics and grabs the wheel, are supposedly games or tests of cowardice and bravery. **1965–70** *DARE* (Qu. EE5, *Games where you try to make a jackknife stick in the ground*) Infs **IL**97, 98, **NY**81, **TX**41, 68, 88, Chicken; (Qu. EE28, *Games played in water*) Inf **IL**116, Chicken; **PA**247, Chicken— Child dares another to do what he does; (Qu. EE33, . . *Outdoor games*) Inf **NJ**57, Chicken—you dare a chicken [=cowardly] kid to stand on the railroad tracks while the train is coming; **SC**54, Chicken—bicycle riders charge each other, and the one who swerves is chicken; new.

b See **chicken fight 2.**

5 See quot.

1943 *AmSp* 9.288 **PA** [Black College slang], *Chicken.* A more or less foolish, or sheepish, grin.

6 A soft roll of fuzz that collects on the floor under beds or other furniture.

1950 *WELS* 1 Inf, **WI**, Chickens. **1951** Johnson *Resp. to PADS 20* **DE**, Chickens. **1968** *DARE* (Qu. E20) Inf **NY**123, Chickens.

7 also *chicken dance,* ~ *scratch,* ~ *trot, hot chicken:* A dance consisting of steps which imitate the motions of a chicken. *esp among Black speakers* Cf **funky chicken**

1965–70 *DARE* (Qu. FF5b, *More recent dance steps*) 11 Infs, **esp Sth, S Midl**, Chicken; **VA**39A, Hot chicken; (Qu. FF5a, *. . Steps and figures in dancing—in past years*) Infs **KY**87, **PA**239, Chicken; **WA**1, 9, Chicken scratch; **MD**31, Chicken dance; **WA**9, Chicken trot (?). [10 of 17 Infs Black] **1977** Smitherman *Talkin* 256 [Black], Most popular dances, from roughly 1950 to the present: *applejack, chicken.*

C Phrases.

1 in phr *when chickens have teeth:* Never.

1950 *WELS* (*Something that will never happen: He'll pay his debts _____.*) 1 Inf, **seWI**, When chickens have teeth.

2 in phr *have a chicken to pick:*

a =**crow to pick, have a.** **Midl**

1965–70 *DARE* (Qu. KK14, *Something that people disagree about: "I have a _____ to pick with you."*) Infs **KY**53, **MO**5, 20, **OK**9, Chicken.

b See quot.

1968 *DARE* (Qu. KK35, *When someone wants to pass on a compliment about you, in exchange for one about himself, he says, "I have a _____ for you."*) Inf **VA**25, Chicken to pick.

3 in phr *get* or *catch it where the chicken got it* (or *got the ax*): See quots.

1942 Berrey–Van den Bark *Amer. Slang* 322.6, Be punished . . catch it where the chicken got it. **c1960** *Wilson Coll.* **csKY**, Get it where the chicken got the ax . . . Get punished properly and adequately.

chicken v See **chicken out** v phr **1**

chicken adder See **chicken snake 2**

chicken and egg n

A zinnia.

1966 *DARE* (Qu. S11, *. . Zinnia*) Inf **NC**44, Chicken 'n' egg.

chicken and slicks See **chicken slick**

chicken asshole See **chicken butt**

chickenberry n [Folk-etym var of **checkerberry**]

1 also *chickberry, chickaberry:* A **wintergreen 2** (here: *Gaultheria procumbens*).

1872 Schele de Vere *Americanisms* 402, It [*Gaultheria procumbens*] is also known . . in New England occasionally as *chick*-berry. **1894** *Jrl. Amer. Folkl.* 7.93 **CT**, Chickaberry. **1900** Lyons *Plant Names* 169, Chicken-berry. **1911** *Century Dict.*, Chicken-berry . . Same as *checkerberry*, in both senses [*Mitchella repens; Gaultheria procumbens*]. **1930** Sievers *Amer. Med. Plants* 63, Chickenberry.

2 =**partridgeberry.**

1832 Williamson *Hist. ME* 1.130, *An additional Catalogue of Native Plants . . . Chicken-berry, (Mitchella Repens.)* **1896** *Jrl. Amer. Folkl.* 9.190, Chicken berry. **1900** Lyons *Plant Names* 249, *M[itchella] repens . .* Chicken-berry. **1911** [see **1** above].

chickenbill n

1 also *chicken-billed rail:* =**sora.**

1925 (1928) Forbush *Birds MA* 1.357, *Porzana carolina . .* Chickenbill. **1936** Roberts *MN Birds* 1.445, *Porzana carolina . .* Chicken-billed Rail. **1946** Hausman *Eastern Birds* 240, *Porzana carolina . .* Chicken-billed Rail. **1963** Gromme *Birds WI* 217, Chicken-billed rail.

2 See **chicken duck.**

chicken-billed grebe n

=**pied-billed grebe.**

1936 Roberts *MN Birds* 1.158, *Pied-billed Grebe . . . Other names: . . Chicken-billed Grebe . . . Field Marks.*—The bill is short, stout, and much arched, like the bill of a chicken—"Chicken-billed Grebe". **1963** Gromme *Birds WI* 215.

chicken-billed rail See **chickenbill 1**

chicken bird n

1 also *chicken plover, chicken turnstone:* =**ruddy turnstone.** [See quot 1955] **chiefly MA**

1875 *Fur Fin & Feather* 65 **MA**, Wilson's snipe, or red-breasted, black-breasted, or chicken plover. **1888** Trumbull *Names of Birds* 186, [Ruddy Turnstone] In Massachusetts at . . Martha's Vineyard . . chicken-bird. **1925** (1928) Forbush *Birds MA* 1.478, *Arenaria interpres morinella . . .* Other names: chicken-bird; chicken-plover. **1955** *MA Audubon Soc. Bulletin* 39.446, *Ruddy Turnstone . . .* Chicken Bird, Chicken Plover (Maine, Mass.) Chicken Turnstone (Mass. The term "chicken" seems to refer to clucking notes.).

2 =**catbird 1.**

1917 (1923) *Birds Amer.* 3.177, *Catbird—Dumetella carolinensis . . .* Chicken Bird. **1946** Hausman *Eastern Birds* 452, *Catbird . . . Other Names . .* Chicken Bird.

chicken bone n

1 A wishbone.

1844 Thompson *Major Jones's Courtship* 88 **GA**, You come under little sister's chicken bone, and I do believe she know'd you was coming when she put it over the dore. **1908** *DN* 3.298 **eAL, wGA**, Chicken-bone . . . Specifically the wish-bone.

2 A brittle candy resembling a chicken bone in shape.

1969 *DARE* (Qu. H82b, *Kinds of cheap candy that used to be sold years ago*) Inf **PA**181, Chicken bones. **1981** *DARE* File **sID** (as of c1930), Chicken bones were peanut butter flavor inside and rolled in finely ground toasted coconut. They were deliciously crunchy, and pillow-like in shape; **swID** (as of 1930s and 1940s), Chicken bones were about an inch and a half long, 3/8″ wide, golden brown, with toasted coconut outside and a brittle peanut butter filling inside.

chickenbone special n

See quots.

1970 *DARE* (Qu. N37, *. . A branch railroad . . not very important or gives poor service*) Inf **NC**87, Chickenbone special, because the Negroes have greasy bags of fried chicken so they won't have to pay for the diner. **1971** Walls *Chickenbone Special* 82 **NC**, "That's this old 'Chickenbone Special' for you." . . The name is thought to have originated back in the late fifties among a group of black graduate students at Temple University in Philadelphia . . . [R]eminiscing about life in the Carolinas, they discovered that most if [sic] them had come north at one time or another on the same train. Further, they remembered the lunches packed by anxious mothers for sons and daughters who could not afford the prices charged on railroad dining cars. Invariably, those lunches contained at least one piece of fried chicken, as they still do.

chicken-broke-its-neck exclam

In the game of Antony-over: =**pigtail** exclam.

1969 *DARE* (Qu. EE23b, *In the game . . if you fail to get the ball over the building and it rolls back, what do you call out*) Inf **KY**40, Chicken-broke-its-neck.

chicken butt n Also *chicken asshole* Cf **bird-peck, chickie 4**

1966–69 *DARE* (Qu. X34, *. . Other names and nicknames for the navel*) Inf **MS**1, Chicken butt; [**MA**15, Butt of the chicken;] **VT**16, Chicken asshole.

chicken buzzard n

1970 *DARE* (Qu. Q13, *. . Vulture*) Inf **MI**112, Chicken buzzard.

chicken-cock n *old-fash*

A rooster.

1859 (1968) Bartlett *Americanisms* 524, Head and tail up, like chicken-cocks in laying-time. **1875** Twain *Sketches New & Old* (Hartford) 32 **CA**, Well, thish-yer Smiley had rat-tarriers and chicken cocks. **1903** *DN* 2.309 **seMO**, Chicken-cock . . . Rooster.

chicken coffee n

1981 *DARE* File **NEng** (as of 1920s), *Chicken coffee*—coffee adulterated with chicory root.

chicken coop n For pronc, see **coop** n[1] **A**

1 A building for housing poultry. **chiefly Nth** See Map Note: *chicken coop,* meaning a small, often portable, cage or enclosure for poultry, is widespread throughout the US.

1891 Ryan *Pagan* 234 **Alleghany Mts**, Jake was listening . . from behind the chicken-coop. **1939** *LANE* Map 112, **NEng**, Coop, chicken *coop* and *hen coop* usually denote a small shelter for one hen and her brood . . . *Hen coop* (rarely *chicken coop*) is used by some of our informants also for a small *hen house* provided with roosts. **1965–70** *DARE* (Qu. M17, *A building where chickens or hens are kept*) 68 Infs, **chiefly Nth,** Chicken coop. **1979** *Blair & Ketchum Country Jrl.* 77 **VT,** When the price of heating oil doubled, our woodshed resumed its former ways after long service as a chicken coop.

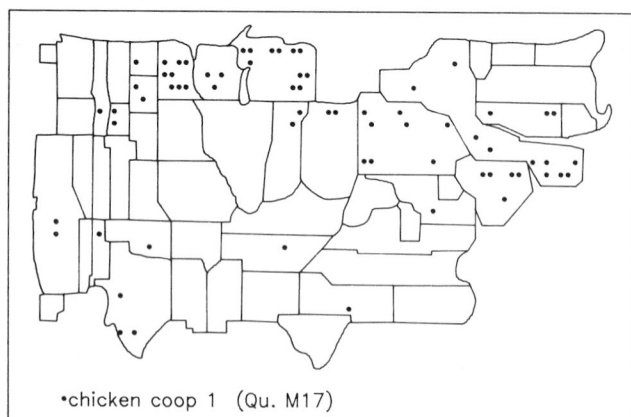

•chicken coop 1 (Qu. M17)

2 A police car or patrol wagon.

1967 *DARE* (Qu. N3, *The car or wagon that takes arrested people to the police station or jail*) Inf **MN2,** Chicken coop.

3 An outdoor toilet.

1970 *DARE* (Qu. M21b, *Joking names for an outside toilet building*) Inf **KY72,** Chicken coop.

chicken corn n

1 A variety of sorghum. **Sth**

1856 U.S. Congress *Congressional Globe* 17 Apr 960/2, Chinese sugar cane is nothing more than what we call chicken corn down in Georgia, and is of no sort of value. **1901** Mohr *Plant Life AL* 339, *Sorghum vulgare . . . Chicken Corn, Durrha, Sugar-Corn.* **1950** Hitchcock *Manual Grasses* 775, Chicken corn (*S. vulgare* var. *drummondii* . .), described from New Orleans, La., was early introduced from Africa and became naturalized in Mississippi and Louisiana, but it is apparently dying out.

2 Field corn *(Zea mays).*

1967–68 *DARE* (Qu. I34, *If you don't have sweet corn, you can always eat young* _____) Inf **MI44,** Chicken corn, regular corn that is not sweet corn; **NY5,** Chicken corn, not recommended; **NY45,** Chicken corn.

3 Money. **Cf chicken feed 2**

1954 *Harder Coll.* **cwTN,** Chicken corn. [Money, general word.]

4 A gold- and orange-colored candy shaped like a kernel of corn. **Cf chicken feed 3**

1968 *DARE* (Qu. H82b, *Kinds of cheap candy that used to be sold years ago*) Infs **NJ26, NY49, 53,** Chicken corn. **1980** *DARE* File **ePA,** We called them chicken corn when I was growing up.

chicken corn soup n, also attrib **chiefly PA** See Map Cf **rivel soup**

A soup made with chicken, corn and rivels (small pieces of egg and flour dumpling).

1964 *Amer. Heritage Cookbook* 425, Chicken Corn Soup was a favorite in Lancaster County, Pennsylvania, where it was often served on picnics during the summer. A 4-pound stewing chicken . . 10 ears fresh corn . . *Rivels:* 1 cup flour Pinch of salt 1 egg Milk. **1965–70** *DARE* (Qu. H36, *Kinds of soup favored around here*) 13 Infs, **PA,** Chicken corn soup; **PA242,** Chicken corn soup—corn, chicken and rivels (egg and flour drops like noodles); (Qu. H45, *Dishes made with meat, fish, or poultry*) Infs **MD27, PA13, 22, 29, 150,** Chicken corn soup; (Qu. H50, *Dishes made with beans, peas, or corn*) Infs **MD27, PA18, 136, 150, 242,** Chicken corn soup; (Qu. FF1, . . *A "social"*) Inf **PA242,** Chicken-corn-soup supper; (Qu. FF16, . . *Local contests or celebrations*) Inf **PA7,** Chicken-corn-soup supper.

chicken crow n Also *chicken crowing* (or *hollering*) *time* [Euphem for *cockcrow* dawn] **S Midl**

Dawn, early morning.

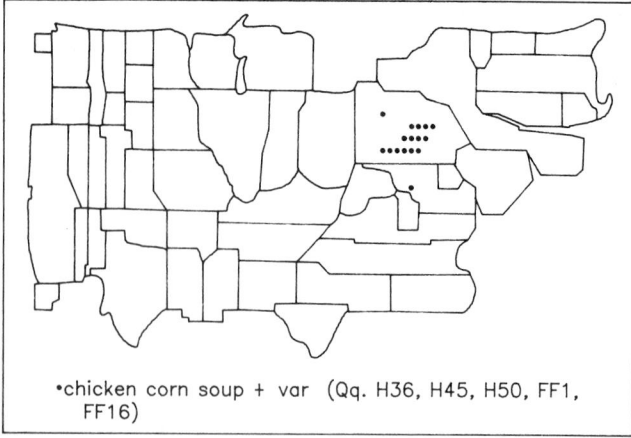

•chicken corn soup + var (Qq. H36, H45, H50, FF1, FF16)

1902 *DN* 2.233 **sIL,** For early morning, we have heard 'chicken hollerin time' used. **1906** *DN* 3.130 **nwAR,** Chicken-crowin' time . . . Cockcrow. "It was chicken-crowin' time when the rag was over." **1930** *Herald–Advt.* (Huntington WV) 30 Nov **KY, WV Mts,** In the days of yore, the young folks were wont to "set up" and "spark" till "chicken crow." **1940** (1968) Haun *Hawk's Done Gone* 66 **eTN,** I knowed they wouldn't be back till chicken crow. **1953** Randolph *Down in Holler* 182 **nwAR,** I've *sot up* till *chicken-crow* with that gal . . but it was just *time throwed away.*

chicken dance See chicken n B7

chicken drownder See goose drownder

chicken duck n Also *chickenbill*

A **coot** n[1] **1** (here: *Fulica americana*).

1917 *Wilson Bulletin* 29.2.79 **VA,** *Fulica americana.*—Chicken duck, chicken-bill. **1967–70** *DARE* (Qu. Q5, . . *Wild ducks*) Infs **MO38, VA47,** Chicken duck; (Qu. Q9, *The bird that looks like a small, dull-colored duck and is commonly found on ponds and lakes*) Inf **VA47,** Chicken duck.

chicken-eater n chiefly Sth, S Midl

1 Any of several animals which eat chickens, spec:

a also *chicken-eating sow:* See quot 1954.

1919 *DN* 5.33 **seKY,** Chicken-eatin' sow . . . Vulgar name applied to sows, the sharp pointed "appendix" just under the tail representing the bill of a chicken which the sow has eaten! **1954** *Harder Coll.* **cwTN,** Chicken eater . . . A hog, dog, mule, or other animal that eats chickens. **1959** Sanders *Echoes* 40 **swAR** (as of c1910), Our chicken-eating sow caught and made quick work of him.

b =**chicken hawk 1.**

1873 Figuier *Reptiles & Birds* (transl Gillmore) 578, The Peregrine Falcon . . inhabits North America, where it is frequently called the Chicken-eater. **1970** *DARE* (Qu. Q4, . . *Hawks*) Inf **VA70,** Chicken-eater.

c =**chicken snake.**

1968 *DARE* (Qu. 25, . . *Snakes*) Infs **LA26, NC80,** Chicken-eater.

2 A preacher. *esp among Black speakers; humorous* See also **chicken preacher**

1954 *Harder Coll.* **cwTN,** Chicken-eater . . . A preacher. (Humorous.) **1966–70** *DARE* (Qu. CC10, . . *An unprofessional, part-time lay preacher*) Infs **FL48, 51, NC83, SC26, 69,** Chicken-eaters [All Black Infs]; (QR, near Qu. CC10) Inf **IL4,** Chicken-eater, nickname for a preacher, because women used to bring a preacher roast chicken on Sunday.

3 also adj *chicken-eating:* A Methodist.

1966–70 *DARE* (Qu. CC4, . . *Religions or religious groups*) Infs **NC36, TX18,** Chicken-eating Methodists; **TX43,** Chicken-eaters = Methodists; **VA5,** Chicken-eating people = Methodists.

chicken-eating adj

1 Ineffectual, despicable, trifling.

1889 Edwards *Runaways* 142 **GA,** What have you got to do with hit, you little chick'n-eatin' thing you?

2 See **chicken eater 3.**

chicken-eating sow See chicken-eater 1a

chickeney cranery crow See **chickamy chickamy craney crow**

‡**chicken-eyed** adj

1970 DARE (Qu. X21c, *If the eyes are very round*) Inf NC88, Chicken-eyed.

chicken feed n

1 also attrib: Cornmeal.

1865 Kellogg *Life & Death* 109 **GA,** Two buckets of mush for ninety men. 'Chicken feed,' the boys called it, and it seemed a very appropriate name, for it was nothing but coarse corn meal and water, with a little salt, half cooked. **1966** DARE (Qu. H14, *Bread that's made with cornmeal*) Inf NC33, Chicken feed bread.

2 Something trifling, of little importance; esp, a small sum of money, small change.

1837 Smith *Col. Crockett's Exploits* 49 **lower Missipp Valley,** I stood looking on, seeing him pick up the chicken feed from the greenhorns . . men are such darned fools as to be cheated out of their hard earnings. **1908** DN 3.298 **eAL, wGA,** Chicken feed . . . Small change, nickels and dimes. **1950** WELS (*An amount of money that seems impressive*) 4 Infs, **WI,** [That's] not chicken feed. **1968–70** DARE (Qu. U19a, . . *Money in general*) Infs **GA**77, **KY**28, Chicken feed; (Qu. U21, . . *"One cent"*) Inf **MN**34, Chicken feed; (Qu. KK42a, *Expressions about a person who does something very easily: "For him that would be _____."*) Infs **IL**131, **KY**72, Chicken feed.

3 A type of candy. Cf **chicken corn 4**

1945 *Reader's Digest* Dec 103/1, The candy, of course, sold for a penny. There was butter-corn, or 'chicken feed,' a favorite confection, gold and orange kernels in a glass bin. **1950** WELS (*Candies sold especially for children*) 1 Inf, **ceWI,** Mixed hard candies. Sometimes called chicken feed. **1983** NADS Letters **Brooklyn NY** (as of 1920s & 1930s), The description of "candy rice" [in *NADS*] sounds like what we used to call "chicken feed". Could they be the same?

chicken feeder n Cf **chicken horse**

=**crowbait.**

1970 DARE (Qu. K44, *A bony or poor-looking horse*) Infs **CA**205, **OR**10, Chicken feeder; (Qu. K15, *A thin, bony, or poor-looking cow*) Inf **CA**205, Chicken feeder.

chicken fight n

1 also *chicken fighter:* A violet (*Viola* spp). [See quot 1891] **chiefly S Midl, esp KY, MD** See also **rooster fight**

1891 *NY Herald* (NY) 29 Mar 14/4 **cKY,** We found . . wild lettuce and 'chicken fights' or wild violets, which are so misnamed because children catch two blossoms together at the curve in the stem and with a quick pull break off the poor little blue heads. **1898** *Jrl. Amer. Folkl.* 11.223, *Viola palmata* . . var. *cucullata,* . . chicken-fights, Cecil Co[unty], Md. **1941** *Torreya* 41.49, *Viola* spp.—Chicken-fights, Garrett County, Md. **1942** Warnick *Garrett Co. MD* (as of 1900–1918), *Chicken-fights* . . violets. **c1960** *Wilson Coll.* **csKY,** Chicken-fights . . . Violets or a contest with them to see which head can be pulled off first. Called also *rooster-fighters.* **1967** DARE FW Addit **cnSC,** Chicken fights—a wild violet; put the blooms together, cross them and see which one's head will come off first. **1967–70** DARE (Qu. S11, . . *Blue violet*) Infs **KY**11, 49, 53, Chicken fights; **KY**83, Chicken fighters; (Qu. S3, *A flower like a large violet with a yellow center and small ragged leaves*) Inf **MO**38, Johnny-jump-up is what most people call these little chicken farters [sic] I spoke of.

2 also *chicken, chicken fighting:* A children's game similar to cockfight: see quots.

1968–70 DARE (Qu. EE28, *Games played in water*) Inf **MI**118, Chicken—you try [to] knock other off shoulders; **MI**123, Chicken fighting—(also on land) you try to knock person off someone's shoulders; **NY**119, Chicken fights—two people on two other people's shoulders; try to knock each other off; **OH**97, Chicken—try to knock the other person off the shoulders of another.

chicken fighter See **chicken fight 1**

chicken fighting See **chicken fight 2**

chicken fit n

=**cat fit.**

1845 Hooper *Advent. Simon Suggs* 31 **AL,** Hoop-ee! *won't* they roll over the floor, and have chicken-fits, a dozen at a time! **c1960** *Wilson Coll.* **csKY,** Dog fit . . . A nervous outburst . . . Also *chicken fit.*

chicken fixings n pl [**fixing**]

1 Chicken prepared as food; elaborate or "fancy" food. **formerly W Midl** *old-fash* Cf **common doings, doing**

1838 Flagg *Far West* 2.72 **IL,** The first inquiry made of the guest by the village landlord is the following: "Well, stran-ger, what'll ye take: wheat-bread and *chicken fixens,* or *corn-bread* and common doins?" **1843** (1916) Hall *New Purchase* 303 **IN,** A snug breakfast of chicken fixins, eggs, ham-doins, and corn slap-jacks. **1854** (1923) Holmes *Tempest & Sunshine* 46 **KY,** We don't have any of your chicken fixin's nor little three-cornered hankerchers laid out at each plate. **1872** Schele de Vere *Americanisms* 472, *Chicken Fixings,* the universal dish of the West and the South. **1874** (1895) Eggleston *Circuit Rider* 20 **IN,** Mrs. Lumsden's "chicken fixin's," and butter-cakes, and "punkin-pies." **c1960** *Wilson Coll.* **csKY,** Chicken fixin's . . . Baked chicken with its dressing and gravy.

2 By ext: anything elaborate or fancy.

1870 (1935) Duval *Advent. Big Foot* 302 **TX,** The Mexican war had ended, and that chap with the gold epaulets on his shoulders and the 'chicken fixings' on his coat-sleeves had mustered us out of the service and paid us off. **1886** Proctor in *Knowledge* 1 April 179/1 (DAE), Chicken-fixings, . . now applied sometimes to any particularly fine arrangements as distinguished from 'common doings.' **1914** DN 4.70 **ME, nNH,** *Chicken-fixin's* . . . Anything fancy, in food, dress, or otherwise. "With all the little chicken-fixin's on."

chicken flesh See **chicken skin**

chicken flutter n

1 also attrib; also *chicken flip:* A dance movement imitating the fluttering of a chicken. *old-fash*

1835 Crockett *Account* 34, It would do you good to see our boys and girls dancing. None of your stradling, mincing, sadyin; but a regular sifter, cut-the-buckle, chicken-flutter set-to. **1835** *S. Lit. Messenger* 1.550/2 **Sth,** Horse-galloping dances . . . chicken flutter for the gentlemen. **1912** *Boston Journal* 25 Nov. 1/4 (DA), Boston's elect danced the grizzly bear and the chicken flip in the Grand Salon. **1962** Nathan *Dan Emmett* 86 (as of 1848), The "chicken flutter," to judge by its name, was either a jump with wing motions of the arms or simply the popular name of the "pigeon wing." It appears in this context: ["Uncle Gabriel," a minstrel dance] De niggers dey come all around and kick up a debil of a splutter, / Dey eat de coon and clar de ground to dance de chicken flutter.

2 Fig: a state of excitement. Cf **chicken fit**

1903 DN 2.296 **Cape Cod MA,** *Chicken-flutter* . . . Undue excitement, as 'He's in a chicken-flutter.'

chickenfoot n

=**Florida gallinule.**

1923 U.S. Dept. Ag. *Misc. Circular* 13.44, Florida Gallinule . . . Vernacular Names . . . In local use . . . Chicken-foot (Mich.); chicken-foot coot (Ont.).

chicken-foot ice n [See quot 1981]

See quots.

1965 DARE (Qu. B33a, *The first thin ice that forms over the surface of a pond or pool*) Inf **OK**1, Chicken-foot ice. **1981** NADS Letters **NY,** I . . heard the term . . . many years ago. The ice cracks and heals so that it has a scar pattern which looks like chicken tracks or chicken feet. You can see it for yourself anytime a thin layer of ice has formed and the air is not too windy or too still. *Ibid* **seMI,** My father (age 62, a lifetime resident of the Detroit area) immediately recognized the term 'chicken-foot ice' . . . The name refers to the pattern of lines in the ice (rather like 'crow's feet' in reference to wrinkles at the corner of the eye).

chicken-fried steak n Also *chicken-fry steak* **chiefly West**

A steak, usu an inexpensive cut, breaded and fried.

1966–68 DARE (Qu. H45, *Dishes made with meat, fish, or poultry*) Infs **IA**24, **OK**26, Chicken-fried steak; (Qu. H22, . . *Food dipped in batter and fried in deep fat*) Inf **OK**26, Chicken-fried steak. **1967** DARE FW Addit **CO,** Chicken-fry steak—fixed like breaded pork cutlet only deep-fat fried. All over Colorado. **1968** *Territorial Enterprise & VA City News* (VA City NV) 15 Mar 3, [Restaurant dinner menu:] Chicken Fry Steak. **1978** DARE File **wKS,** Chicken-fried steak—a cube steak or minute steak breaded and fried; **ID,** Chicken-fried steak.

chicken-gizzard plant n Also *chicken gizzard*

A bloodleaf (here: *Iresine herbsti*).

1955 *S. Folkl. Qrly.* 19.235 **FL,** The showy leaves of the *Chicken Gizzard Plant* (Iresine herbsti) with heavy purple veining and crimped tips looks [sic] like chicken gizzards. **1969** *Capital Times* (Madison WI) 31 May green sec 1/6, Iresine herbstii [sic], a showy plant with wine-red, rounded leaves and light red veins . . . Popularly, this is known as Chicken-gizzard or Bloodleaf.

chicken granny n Cf **granny** n

1936 *AmSp* 11.314 **Ozarks,** *Chicken-granny* . . . One who raises chickens for the market. Usually applied to 'furriners,' derisively. The word *granny* means midwife.

chicken grape n

=**frost grape.**

1807 Scott *Geog. MD & DE* 112, A middle sized grape, of a purple colour, growing in clusters, like the chicken grape. **1872** Schele de Vere *Americanisms* 412, The *Bermuda* Vine (Vitis riparia) is the *Chicken Grape* of Southern States, famous for its fragrant blossoms. **1886** Mitchell *Roland Blake* 260 **Sth,** Mrs. Ludlam says she is 'waitin' for them chicken-grapes to git a little more sun.' **1900** Lyons *Plant Names* 395, *Vítis . . . cordifólia* . . . Chicken Grape. **1967–68** *DARE* (Qu. I46, . . *Kinds of fruits that grow wild*) Infs **NJ**21, 24, 39, **PA**13, 29, 136, Chicken grapes.

chicken guts n pl const as sg [From the twisted shape]

1 See quot. Cf **chicken fixings 2**

1951 Longstreet *Pedlocks* 12 **NY** (as of 1860s), It showed a proud young man in Rebel gray, with the gold trimming the soldiers called "chicken guts" on the cuffs.

2 An ampersand.

1950 *PADS* 14.19 **SC,** *Chicken guts* . . . A child's name for the symbol &.

chicken halibut n chiefly Pacific

1 A California halibut.

1930 *AmSp* 5.389 **N Atl** [Among fishermen], *Chicken halibut* . . . A young halibut weighing up to 25 pounds, and much esteemed as a delicacy. **1940** White *Wild Geese* 206 **OR** (as of 1890s), By gum! . . a chicken halibut! Thar's *eatin'!* **1946** LaMonte *N. Amer. Game Fishes* 98, *Paralichthys californicus* . . Chicken Halibut. **1953** Roedel *Common Fishes CA* 55, *California Halibut—Paralichthys californicus . . . Unauthorized Names:* Chicken halibut. **1975** Evanoff *Catch More Fish* 221, The California halibut . . is also called the . . chicken halibut.

2 See quot.

1919 *DN* 5.64 **CA** [Among high school students], *Chicken-halibut,* a term of disparagement used to signify disgust. "He's the only chicken-halibut in the family."

chicken hawk n

1 Any of var hawks which prey or are thought to prey upon chickens. Cf **broad-wing, hen hawk**

1827 Williams *View W. FL* 30, *Of Eagles. Falco,* we have . . Hen Hawk. *F. gallinareus.* Chicken Hawk. *F. pullenarius.* **1844** DeKay *Zool. NY* 2.14, [Duck Hawk] is . . known under the various popular names of *Hen Hawk, Chicken Hawk* and *Pigeon Hawk.* **1934** Vines *Green Thicket* 60 **cnAL,** He had enough feathers from wild things to make a feather bed . . . He had a little old trunk nearly full of feathers and down from . . chicken hawks. **1950** *PADS* 14.19 **SC,** *Chicken hawk* . . . Florida red-shouldered hawk; northern red-shouldered hawk. **c1960** *Wilson Coll.* **csKY,** *Chicken-hawk* . . . Any large hawk, esp. the Red-tailed or Red-shouldered, but not the Marsh, which is a Rabbit Hawk.

2 A children's tag game; see quot.

1968 *DARE* (Qu. EE33, . . *Outdoor games*) Inf **VA**13, Chicken hawk —all players raced to a place designated the pen. The last one was the hawk, all the rest were chickens. As the hawk tagged chickens they joined him as hawks. The game continued until all were caught.

3 See **hawk** n.

chicken head n

1 also *chicken's head:* A **lousewort** (here: *Pedicularis canadensis*).

1897 *Jrl. Amer. Folkl.* 10.52, *Pedicularis Canadensis* . . . chickens' heads, Southold, L[ong] I[sland]. **1954** *Harder Coll.* **cwTN,** Chicken head . . . weed, also known as rooster head.

2 See quot.

1919 *DN* 5.61 **NM** [High school slang], *Chicken-head,* a dull person. "How did that chicken-head get this far is more than I understand."

chicken hen n

1939 *LANE* Map 214 **seMA,** [čɪkɪn hɛn], a hen with chicks.

chicken hollering time See **chicken crow**

chicken horse n Cf **chicken feeder**

See quot 1940.

1940 (1966) FWP *Guide AZ* 68, The unsatisfactory, the smallest, and the old horses are killed for dog and chicken feed—hence the term "chicken horses" used in many localities. **1944** Adams *Western Words,* Chicken horse.

‡**chicken in a jar** n Cf *DS* P35a

1950 *WELS (Any deer shot illegally)* 1 Inf, **cwWI,** Chicken in a jar.

chicken in the yard adj phr

All right.

1969 *DARE* (Qu. KK4, *When things turn out just right, you might say, "Everything is _____ now."*) Inf **GA**72, Chicken in the yard.

chicken ladder n Cf **chicken roost 2**

1940 (1966) FWP *Guide AZ* 401, One of their old mines, called the Old Bat Hole, still contains the "chicken ladders" that they used to bring the ore to the surface. The shaft was on a sixty degree angle and about every ten feet a layer of mesquite logs 4 feet long and 3 feet wide were placed . . to serve as rest stations for the men who carried the ore in rawhide buckets strapped to their backs.

chicken lettuce n

1949 Webber *Backwoods Teacher* 264 **Ozarks,** A thistle called "chicken lettuce."

chicken lobster n [*chicken,* implying tenderness and good flavor] **NEng**

A lobster weighing from 1–1¼ pounds.

1969 *DARE* FW Addit **MA**56, *Chicken lobster*—a lobster about a pound and a quarter. **1978** Merriam *Illustr. Lobstering* **ME,** *Chicken Lobster*—A lobster size classification of between one and one-and-a-quarter pounds. Said by many to be the tenderest eating, though others say the large lobsters are no different.

chicken marks See **chicken scratch 1**

chicken meat n

The white meat of a turtle.

1948 Hurston *Seraph* 2 **FL,** There were soft-shell turtles that made a mighty nice dish when stewed down to a low gravy, or the "chicken meat" of those same turtles fried crisp and brown.

chicken money n *obs* Cf **egg money**

1 Spending money; small change.

1853 Simms *Sword & Distaff* 299 **Sth,** Did you suppose that the widow, who is so rich, would go to the country and take no money with her—even if it were only a stocking-full of shillings for chicken money.

2 Proceeds from selling chickens.

1856 Stowe *Dred* 2.156 **NC,** Drinking up all my chicken-money down to 'Bijah Skinflint's.

chicken mustard n

An unidentified plant; see quot.

1967 *DARE* (Qu. S21, . . *Weeds*) Inf **TN**13, Chicken mustard, first spring weed.

chicken necker n *derog*

An amateur who interlopes on professional crabbers.

1976 Warner *Beautiful Swimmers* 149 **MD,** "Them no good chicken neckers come in here and lay their lines right over us." Chicken neckers was a term I was to hear often in the next twenty-four hours. Lester was talking about outsiders and rank amateurs, since there is a widespread belief among dilettante crabbers that chicken necks are the best crab bait.

chicken nest n [Cf Fr *nid de poule* pothole, lit 'chicken nest']

A pothole.

1969 *DARE* (Qu. N27b, *When unpaved roads get very rough*) Inf **PA**204, Chicken nests, not used very often.

chicken of the sea n

1 An albacore or similar fish.

1949 Brown *Amer. Cooks* 42 **CA,** Tuna fish is aptly called "chicken of the sea" along the West Coast. **1975** Evanoff *Catch More Fish* 220, The Pacific albacore (Thunnus germo) is also called . . chicken-of-the sea.

2 =puffer.

1970 *DARE* (Qu. P2, . . *Saltwater fish . . good to eat*) Inf **VA**46, Chicken of the sea = swell toad.   1970 *DARE* FW Addit **VA**112, *Chicken of the sea*—same as blow toad and sugar toad. Bookword is northern puffer.

chicken on the wing n [From the shape of the flower] =fringed polygala.

1944 Nute *Lake Superior* 322 **nwMI**, Late June and early July find . . the forest floor . . dotted with . . the lovely little "chicken on the wing" or fringed polygala.

chicken out v phr

1 infreq *chicken:* To back out, change one's mind, lose one's nerve.

1943 Wolfert *Torpedo 8* 13, I just wanted to . . make sure you weren't chickening out on me.   1950 *WELS* (*A coward*) 1 Inf, **cwWI**, [He's] chickened out; (*When somebody says he will do something and then changes his mind and won't*) 1 Inf, **ceWI**, Chickened out.   1954 *Harder Coll.* **cwTN**, *Chicken out* . . . To renege, or *back out.* Occasional. Derogatory.   1961 McCullers *Clock* 69 **Sth**, You would of been the first to chicken.   1965–70 *DARE* (Qu. II31, . . *"He saw that he was wrong, so he started to_____."*) 43 Infs, **scattered**, Chicken out; (Qu. II32, . . *To shift the responsibility*) Infs **CA**15, **NJ**10, **SC**45, Chicken out; (Qu. II33, . . *I don't trust him, he's always trying to_____*) Inf **MI**24, Chicken out; (Qu. JJ38, *When somebody agreed to do something, then changed his mind*) Infs **OK**20, 31, Chickened out; (Qu. P36, *When a hunter sees a . . game animal and gets so excited he can't shoot*) Inf **OH**74, Chickened out; **NC**49, Chickening out; (Qu. AA12, *If a man loses interest in a girl and stops seeing her*) Inf **WI**72, Chickened out; (Qu. AA13, *When two people . . stop going together*) Inf **MI**118, Chickened out; (Qu. BB57, *If someone committed suicide*) Inf **CA**59, Chickened out.

2 in phr *chicken one out:* To dare someone to prove he is not a coward.

1965 *DARE* (Qu. Y5, . . *To urge somebody to do something he shouldn't:* "*Johnny wouldn't have tried that if the other boys hadn't_____.*") Inf **OK**7, Chickened him out.

chicken owl n

=great horned owl.

1925 Bailey *Birds FL* 77, Great Horned Owl . . *Bubo virginianus virginianus (Chicken owl)* . . . does take many chickens.   1966–68 *DARE* (Qu. Q2, . . *Owls*) Infs **GA**7, **NJ**52, Chicken owl.

chicken-peck See **bird-peck**

chicken pecking See **chicken scratch 1**

chicken pepper n

A **buttercup 1** (here: *Ranunculus abortivus*).

1900 Lyons *Plant Names* 315, *Ranúnculus . . . abortívus* . . . Canada and eastern U.S. to Colorado. Chicken Pepper.

chicken plover See **chicken bird 1**

chicken preacher n Cf **chicken eater 2, gospel bird**

1970 Tarpley *Blinky* 237 **neTX**, Local preachers who are unordained and serve only part-time . . . *Chicken preacher* [not common] denotes the myth about preachers' fondness shown for chicken when they dine with members of the congregation.

chicken pulling n Also *chicken pull, pulling the chicken* **SW** Cf **gander pulling**

See quot 1936.

1928 Breakenridge *Helldorado* 84 **Phoenix AZ**, On Sunday afternoons it was customary to have horse-races and chicken-pulling . . . Chicken-pulling is a Mexican game.   1936 Adams *Cowboy Lingo* 204, The Mexican *vaquero* had a sport called 'pulling the chicken,' in which the rooster was buried in the earth, his head only being left above the ground, and the contestants were mounted on horses. They dashed by, one after the other, and as they passed the rooster each man swung himself from the saddle and reached for its head. The chicken naturally dodged more or less, rendering it no easy matter to catch him. Finally secured, however, by a lucky grab, the body was brought out by a jerk which generally broke the neck, and the horseman, chicken in hand, dashed away at his best speed, all the rest giving chase for the possession of the rooster.   1940 Fergusson *Our Southwest* 344 **NM**, Horse- and foot-races and 'chicken pulls' are nearly inevitable. To pull a live chicken out of soft dirt, where it has been buried and its head dodges helplessly, may look savage, but it's fun for the boys.

chicken rain n Cf **cow storm**

A light rain.

1969 *DARE* (Qu. B23, . . *A light rain, that doesn't last*) Inf **IN**58, Chicken rain.   1983 *NADS Letters* **cwNY**, Farmers around Rochester, New York call rain that is so slight they need not put the chickens in the coop a *chicken rain.*

chicken roost n

1 =buzzard roost 2.

1905 *DN* 3.74 **nwAR**, Chicken roost . . . Theatre balcony . . . Common.   1967–70 *DARE* (Qu. D40, . . *The upper balcony in a theater*) Infs **AR**55, **IL**64, **IN**49, **SC**69, **TX**29, 31, Chicken roost.

2 =chicken ladder.

1945 *CA Folkl. Qrly.* 4.322 **CO** [Mining], *Chicken roosts:* Ladder made of sprags, or spreaders, four feet apart and two feet higher going up an incline through gunneys to get into a stope.

chicken saddle n

1944 Adams *Western Words, Chicken saddle*—A slang name for an unusually small saddle.

chicken scratch n, freq pl

1 also *chicken scratching, ~ marks, ~ pecking:* Handwriting which is difficult to read.   Also called **chicken tracks, hen scratching**

1956 McAtee *Some Dialect NC* 8, Chicken scratching: hen scratching . . . Poor handwriting.   c1960 *Wilson Coll.* **csKY**, *Chicken-scratching* . . . Poor penmanship, used facetiously.   1965–70 *DARE* (Qu. JJ11, *Joking names for handwriting that's hard to read*) 104 Infs, **scattered**, Chicken scratches; 48 Infs, **scattered**, Chicken scratching; 25 Infs, **scattered**, Chicken scratch; **HI**13, Chicken scratch writing; **RI**11, Chicken marks; **NC**38, Chicken pecking. [Of all Infs responding to the question, 13% were young, 6% were Black; of those giving these responses, 28% were young, 18% were Black.]

2 See **chicken** n B7.

chicken sense n

1939 *Hall Coll.* **Smoky Mts.**, *Chicken sense* . . . Little sense.

chicken shad n

A young shad.

1874 U.S. Dept. Ag. *Rept. of Secy. for 1873* 452 **CA**, The "chicken-shad," as they are called among the pound-fishermen, instead of being a distinct species are the yearlings of the *præstabilis.*   1884 Roe *Nature's Serial Story* 216 **NEng**, The males will come back next spring, and these young males are called 'chicken shad' on the Connecticut.

chicken's head See **chicken head 1**

chicken skin n Also *chicken flesh* =gooseflesh.

1950 *PADS* 14.19 **SC**, *Chicken-flesh* . . . Goose-flesh.   1967–69 *DARE* (Qu. X58, *When you are cold, and little points of skin begin to come on your arms and legs*) Infs **HI**8, 9, **IL**51, **MN**2, Chicken skin.   1973 Allen *LAUM* 1.406 **ND**, [1 inf, Chicken flesh; 1 inf, Chicken skin.]

chicken slick n Also *chicken and slicks, chicken slickum*

A kind of chicken and dumpling stew.

1940 Harris *Folk Plays* 292 **NC**, *Chicken slick*, chicken stew.   1966 *DARE* (Qu. H45, *Dishes made with meat, fish, or poultry*) Inf **NC**5, Chicken slicks or chicken slickum—cook an old hen with water and season, then drop small dumplings into water; **OK**21, Chicken and slicks (same as dumplings).

chicken snake n [Because it eats chickens and eggs] See also **chicken-eater**

1 =rat snake. chiefly **Sth, Missip Valley, TX, OK** See Map

1791 (1958) Bartram *Travels* 173 **SE**, The chicken snake is a large, strong and swift serpent . . . They are a domestic snake, . . being great devourers of rats, but they are apt to disturb hen roosts and prey upon chickens.   1835 Parker *Trip to TX* 152, The large black snake . . is here called the "chicken snake," because it sometimes robs hen's nests.   1894 U.S. Natl. Museum *Proc.* 17.326 **FL**, *Callopeltis guttatus* . . . is known by . . "chicken snake".   *Ibid* 327, *Callopeltis quadrivittatus* . . . Why the larger specimens are called "chicken snakes" is easy to understand.   1926 TX Folkl. Soc. *Pub.* 5.66, If you don't believe that . . a witch snake exists, examine the head of a young chicken snake.   1945 FWP *Lay My Burden Down* 164 **SE**, Old Mistress went to the wellhouse and she found a chicken snake and killed it.   1965–70 *DARE* (Qu. P25) 130 Infs, **chiefly Sth, Missip Valley, TX, OK**, Chicken snake [Note: some of these

Infs are prob referring to sense **2** and perh to sense **3**]; **AR**51, Black snake
or chicken snake; **AR**52, Racer or chicken snake; **FL**32, Chicken snake
or tree snake; **GA**25, Chicken snake same as white-oak snake; **GA**65,
Chicken snake (same as rat snake); **GA**72, Chicken snake changes color
when he's mad.from black to gray; **GA**84, Chicken snake: non-poisonous, eats eggs, is gray, 5 feet long; **LA**3, Chicken snake—same as
black snake; **OK**42, Black snake—also called chicken snake. **1974**
Shaw–Campbell *Snakes West* 99, The corn snake, for example, is
sometimes called the chicken snake.

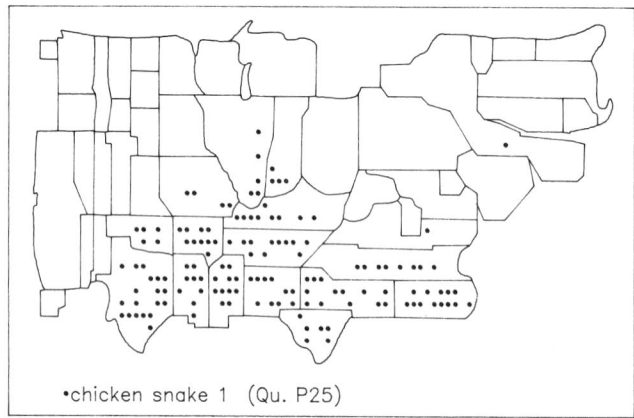

•chicken snake 1 (Qu. P25)

2 also *chicken adder:* =**king snake 1.**

1709 (1967) Lawson *New Voyage* 139 **NC,** The Egg or Chicken-Snake is
so call'd, because it is frequent about the Hen-Yard, and eats Eggs and
Chickens. **1839** MA Zool. & Bot. Surv. *Fishes Reptiles* 227, *Coluber
eximius* . . is known by the names of . . chicken snake; milk snake; and
chequered adder. **1842** DeKay *Zool. NY* 3.39, In this State, its most
usual popular name is *Milk Snake,* although it has various other appellations. It is called *Chicken Snake, Thunder and Lightning Snake, House
Snake,* and *Chequered Adder.* **1911** *Century Dict.,* Chicken snake.
c1960 *Wilson Coll.* **csKY,** *Chicken snake* . . . A smallish, non-poisonous
snake that is quite common in agricultural areas. **1965–70** *DARE* (Qu.
P25) Inf **AR**55, Chicken snake or king snake; **AZ**15, Chicken snake;
LA8, Chicken snake—got little dots on him; **NM**13, Chicken snake—
king snake; **SC**34, Chicken snake: has white on his back; **SC**66, King
snake or chicken snake; **TX**52, Chicken snake; **NH**4, Chicken adder.

3 =**coachwhip snake.**

1894 U.S. Natl. Museum *Proc.* 17.326 **FL,** *Bascanion flagellum* . . . is
known as the "coach whip" and sometimes the larger ones are called
"chicken snakes," like several other of the larger colubrine snakes.

4 =**indigo snake** (here: *Drymarchon corais couperi*).

1938 Matschat *Suwannee R.* 209 **GA,** A long indigo snake that was
sleeping among the vines . . . At the noise . . reared upward . . . she
laughed aloud; the big snake dropped to the ground . . . "Chicken
snake," Pompano said.

chicken sparrow n

Perh an **English sparrow.**

1969 *DARE* (Qu. Q21, . . *Kinds of sparrows*) Inf **VT**13, Chicken sparrow.

chicken squab n

A **puffer.**

1968 *DARE* (Qu. P2, . . *Saltwater fish . . good to eat*) Inf **NJ**27,
Chicken squab = blowfish tail.

chicken stew n

1953 *PADS* 19.9 **NC,** *Chicken stew* . . . A get-together at tobacco
barns . . when tobacco is being cured, at which time many people gather
and stew chickens over the flue where the tobacco is being cured. It is
quite a social event in those areas where tobacco is raised.

chicken thief n [Perh because the leaf clings to things it touches]

A **stickleaf** (here: *Mentzelia oligosperma*).

1970 Correll *Plants TX* 1085, *Chicken-thief* . . . Rounded to matted
semiwoody perennial with enlarged roots.

chicken tracks n pl, also attrib chiefly Nth, N Midl See Map
Cf hen tracks

=**chicken scratch 1.**

1953 in 1960 Wentworth–Flexner *Slang,* The teacher had us all try to

write the first letters of the alphabet . . . when she saw mine she
said . . . 'I'd better put you in the chicken tracks row.' **1965–70** *DARE*
(Qu. JJ11, *Handwriting that's hard to read*) 38 Infs, **chiefly Nth, N Midl,**
Chicken tracks. [Of all Infs responding to the question, 13% were young,
35% coll educ; of those giving this response, none were young, 53% coll
educ.]

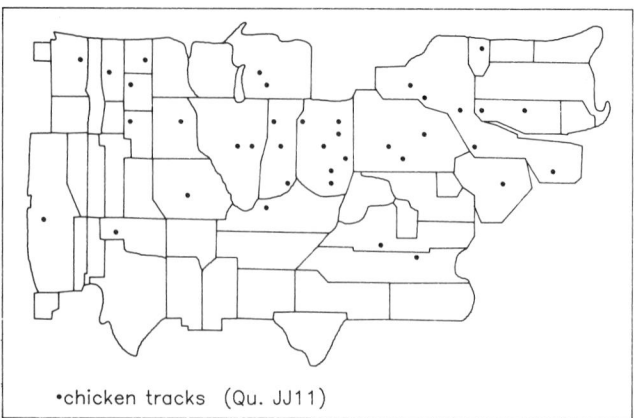

•chicken tracks (Qu. JJ11)

chicken trot See chicken n B7

‡chicken trouble n

Hiccups.

1969 *DARE* (Qu. X54) Inf **MA**30, Chicken trouble.

chicken turnstone See chicken bird 1

chicken turtle n

A long-necked, freshwater turtle *(Deirochelys reticularia)* native
chiefly to the South Atlantic and Gulf States.

1952 Carr *Turtles* 319, The chicken turtle is recognized by rural
people . . in many places in the south and is generally rated by them as
even more succulent than the rest, although with this judgment I cannot
agree. **1966** *DARE* (Qu. P24, . . *Turtles*) Inf **NC**12, Chicken turtle.
1972 Ernst–Barbour *Turtles* 178, The chicken turtle apparently was
named for its palatable flesh. It was once common in the markets of
southern cities but is not often sold today. It is still eaten locally in the
South.

chickenweed n

1 The common **ragwort** (here: *Senecio vulgaris*).

1899 (1912) Green *VA Folk-Speech,* Chicken-weed . . . A weed the
seeds of which are mixed with chickens' food as a remedy. **1900** Lyons
Plant Names 342, *Senécio . . . vulgáris* . . . Chicken-weed. **1959** Carleton *Index Herb. Plants* 26, *Chicken weed:* Senecio vulgaris; Stellaria
media. **1968–70** *DARE* (Qu. S21, . . *Weeds*) Infs **GA**70, **PA**92, 198,
VA57, Chickenweed(s). [Note: any of these Infs may refer instead to
sense **2** or **3.**]

2 =**chickweed 1a** (here: *Stellaria media*).

1900 Lyons *Plant Names* 25, Stellaria media . . . Chickenweed. **1959**
[see **1** above].

3 A **bedstraw.**

1926 *Torreya* 26.6 **MD,** *Galium* . . . Chicken-weed, because small
chickens get caught in it.

chicker v [Prob alter of *checker;* cf check v 1]

1916 *DN* 4.337 **scPA,** *Chicker* . . . To cultivate. "I saw him chickering
his corn yesterday."

chickerberry See checkerberry 3

chickeree See chickaree

chickeron See chicharron

chickeroo See chickoo

chickery See chickaree

chickewit See chickwit

chickgrass See chickweed 1a

chickie n Also sp *chickee, chickey, chicky*

1 occas in var combs with *chick;* usu repeated: Used as a call to
chickens. **widespread, but esp freq in Midl and Sth** See Map
Note: *chick,* with repetition, is used throughout US.

1949 Kurath *Word Geog.* 65, Calls to Chickens . . . The calls *chick!* and *chickie!* are current throughout the Eastern States, but in certain sections other expressions are used as well. **1962** Atwood *Vocab. TX* 54, All of the chicken calls recorded in Texas involve *chick* and *chickee,* repeated in various patterns. **1965–70** *DARE* (Qu. K79) 203 Infs, **esp Midl, Sth,** Chickie chickie (etc.); 29 Infs, **esp Midl, Sth,** Chickie chick (in var combs and repetitions); [461 Infs, **widespread,** Chick chick (etc)]. **1968** Haun *Hawk's Done Gone* 63 **eTN,** I was shucking away and calling the chickens at the same time, "Chickey, chickey—pee, turks, pee, pee, pee, pee." **1970** Tarpley *Blinky* 155 **neTX,** By far the most common announcement of feeding time is *chick-chick-chick.* Outside the city and among the lowest educational levels, *chickie-chickie* gains in frequency of use. **1973** Allen *LAUM* 1.267, Although no sharp areal division can be drawn, the simple *chick* . . has a significant Northern orientation, and the hypocoristic *chickie* is distinctly Midland in its weighting.

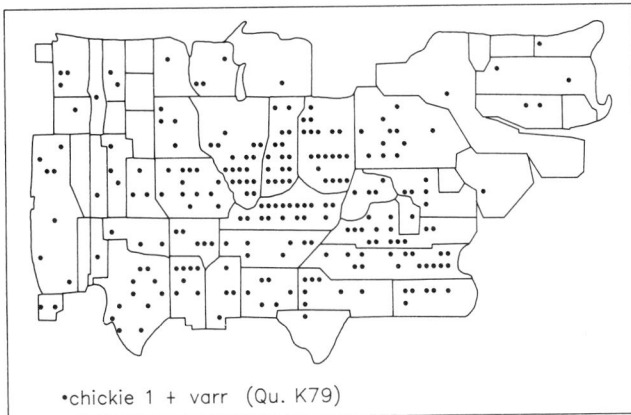

•chickie 1 + varr (Qu. K79)

2 See quots.
1960 Wentworth–Flexner *Slang,* Chickie . . . A warning or command to cease an improper activity in order to avoid detection . . . *Very pop[ular] among N.Y.C. adolescents and juvenile delinquents since c1945.* **1983** Lutz Coll. **neNJ,** Chicky! A word of warning. It was the usual word among school children (about 1915–1925) in Ramsey, when warning others of the approach of a teacher or the principal; it was "Chicky!" It meant that one should stop whatever behavior the authorities would condemn, even it it was merely drawing cartoons in study hall.

3 One's wife or sweetheart—used as an affectionate term of address.
1966–68 *DARE* (Qu. AA3, *Nicknames or affectionate names for a sweetheart*) Inf **NY105,** Chickie; (Qu. AA22, *Joking names . . wife*) Inf **AL10,** Chickie.

‡**4** The navel. Cf **chicken butt,** and *chicken-peck* at **bird-peck**
1968 *DARE* (Qu. X34) Inf **IN35,** Chickie.

chickie my chickie my craney crow See **chickamy chickamy craney crow**

chickin(g) See **chicken** n

chicklets See **chitlets**

chickling n [Imit] *prob obs*
=**ruddy turnstone.**
1877 Hallock *Sportman's Gazetteer* 164 *(DA),* The names Chicaric and Chickling have reference to their rasping notes. **1888** Trumbull *Names of Birds* 186.

chicklins See **chitterlings**

chick-o-my, chick-o-my craney crow See **chickamy chickamy craney crow**

chickoo intj (Often repeated) Also *chickeroo* **Sth, S Midl**
Used as a call to chickens.
1940 (1978) Still *River of Earth* 170 **KY,** We raised thirty-six dommers. They scarcely pecked at the bran we threw out, for there was such a plenty of food in the fields and patches. You could holler "chickeroo" the day long and they wouldn't come. **1966–68** *DARE* (Qu. K79, *How . . you call the chickens*) Infs **GA46, MO21, SC23,** 40 Chickoo; **FL7,** Chickoo chickoo. **1970** Tarpley *Blinky* 154 **neTX,** *Call to chickens to come get the feed* . . [2 informants] chickoo-chickoo.

chickory See **chicory**

chickory cranery crow See **chickamy chickamy craney crow**

chick-pea n Infreq also *chickapea, chick-bean, chicky-pea*
1 A cultivated bean-like or pea-like plant *(Cicer arietinum).* Also called **garbanzo**
1900 Lyons *Plant Names* 100, Cicer arietinum . . Chick Pea. **1950** Gray–Fernald *Manual of Botany* 932, The *Chick-Pea, Cicer* . . *arietinum.* **1966–70** *DARE* (Qu. I20, . . *Beans*) Inf **FL30,** Chick-peas; (Qu. I18, *The smaller beans . . white when they are dry*) Inf **NY35,** Chickbeans; (Qu. I43, . . *Nuts . . wild*) Inf **VA69,** Chicky-pea. **1976** Bailey–Bailey *Hortus Third* 271, Cicer . . arietinum . . Chick Pea.
2 =**cowpea.**
1968–69 *DARE* (Qu. I19, *Small white beans with a black spot*) Infs **MO36, NJ58,** Chick-peas; **IL113,** Chickapeas—friends from Oklahoma say this.

chickrod n Cf **chickwit**
A weakfish **1.**
1931–33 *LANE* Worksheets **CT,** [ˈčɪkrəd] Chickrod is known commercially as sea trout.

chick sale(s) See **chic sale(s)**

chick-the-willow n Also *chick-(the)-will* [Echoic]
=**chuck-will's-widow.**
1888 (1890) Warren *Birds PA* 180, The Chuck-will's-widow . . . Residents of Florida assured me that the "Chick-will," as the bird is there known, was found in that state only as a summer resident. **1966** *DARE* (Qu. Q3, . . *Birds that come out only after dark*) Inf **SC19,** Chick-the-will; **SC26,** [ˈčɪkdə,wɪlə].

chickweed n See also **Indian chickweed, red chickweed, water chickweed**
1 often with a qualifier: Any of numerous plants of the family Caryophyllaceae, as:
a rarely *chickgrass:* A plant of the genus *Stellaria.* Also called **starwort, stitchwort** For other names of var spp see **adder's mouth 3, chickenweed 2, Easter bell, rabbit grass, satin flower, snappers, tongue grass, white bird, winterweed**
1784 in 1785 *Amer. Acad. Arts & Sci. Memoirs* 1.431 **MA,** Alsine . . . Chickweed . . . If it be boiled when young, it can hardly be distinguished from spring spinach. **1840** MA Zool. & Bot. Surv. *Herb. Plants & Quadrupeds* 88, Stellaria . . . media . . . Formerly Alsine media . . Chickweed. **1899** (1977) Norris *McTeague* 43 **nCA,** There were huge loaves of rye bread full of grains of chickweed. **1955** U.S. Arctic Info. Center *Gloss., Common chickweed.* An herb, Stellaria media. **1965–70** *DARE* (Qu. S21, . . *Weeds*) 73 Infs, **scattered,** Chickweed; **IL47,** Plain chickweed; (Qu. S9, . . *Grass . . hard to get rid of*) 21 Infs, **chiefly Nth,** Chickweed; **MD4,** Chickweed or chickgrass; (Qu. S26a, . . *Roadside flowers*) Inf **NY227,** Chickweed; (Qu. S26d, *Wildflowers . . in meadows*) Inf **RI15,** Chickweed. [Note: some of these Infs may refer instead to other subsenses of **chickweed 1.**] **1971** Krochmal *Appalachia Med. Plants* 242, Stellaria media . . . Chickweed, . . common chickweed.
b also *mouse-ear chickweed:* A plant of the genus *Cerastium.* Also called **Chinese clover** For other names of var spp see **powder horn, snow-in-summer**
1829 Phelps *Familiar Lect.* 357, Cerastium . . . vulgatum, (mouse-ear, chick weed . .). **1843** Torrey *Flora NY* 1.100 Cerastium nutans . . . Nodding Chickweed . . . Low moist and rather shady places. **1845** (1849) Phelps *Lectures on Botany* App. 88/1, Sticky chickweed. **1874** *Shaker Med. Preparations,* Chickweed—Cerastium Vulgatum. **1950** Gray–Fernald *Manual of Botany* 624, Cerastium . . . Mouse-ear Chickweed. **1955** U.S. Arctic Info. Center *Gloss., Chickweed* . . . Any plant of the genera Cerastium or Stellaria, annual or perennial, low matted herbs with small, opposing leaves and white, terminal flowers. **1973** Hitchcock–Cronquist *Flora Pacific NW* 113, Cerastium . . . Chickweed; Cerastium.
c usu *forked chickweed:* =**whitlow-wort.**
1840 MA Zool. & Bot. Surv. *Herb. Plants & Quadrupeds* 95, Queria . . . Canadensis . . . Forked Chickweed. **1843** Torrey *Flora NY* 1.100, Anychia dichotoma . . Common Forked Chickweed . . . Dry woods and hill-sides. **1950** Gray–Fernald *Manual of Botany* 613, P[aronychia] canadensis . . . P. fastigata . . . Forked Chickweed.
d usu *jagged chickweed:* A naturalized, white-flowered weed *(Holosteum umbellatum).*

1900 Lyons *Plant Names* 193, Jagged Chickweed . . . Nat. in U.S. **1952** Strausbaugh–Core *Flora WV* 368, *Jagged Chickweed* . . . Petals eroded. **1973** Hitchcock–Cronquist *Flora Pacific NW* 115, Jagged chickweed . . . Eurasian weed, common.

e usu *sea chickweed:* A **sandwort** (here: *Arenaria peploides*).

1900 Lyons *Plant Names* 28, *A. peploides* . . . Sea Chickweed. **1910** Graves *Flowering Plants* 175 **CT**, Sea Chickweed . . . Sandy and stony shores of the Sound. **1950** Gray–Fernald *Manual of Botany* 619, *A. peploides* . . . Sea-Chickweed.

f usu *gravel chickweed:* =**knawel.**

1900 Lyons *Plant Names* 338, *S[cleranthus] annuus* . . . Gravel Chickweed. **1910** Graves *Flowering Plants* 172 **CT**, Gravel Chickweed. Frequent. Dry, sandy or sterile fields and roadsides.

g A white-flowered weed *(Myosoton aquaticum).*

1950 Gray–Fernald *Manual of Botany* 616, *Giant Chickweed* . . . *M[yosoton] aquaticum.* **1952** Strausbaugh–Core *Flora WV* 360.

2 A **smartweed.**

1951 *PADS* 15.30 **TX**, *Persicaria longistyla* . . . chickweed.

3 =**chickweed wintergreen.**

1966 *DARE* Wildfl. QR Pl.165b Inf **OH37**, Chickweed.

4 =**bluet 2.**

1968 *DARE* (Qu. S11, . . *Other names . . bluets*) Infs **DE3**, 4, Chickweed.

chickweed wintergreen n Also *chick wintergreen, wintergreen chickweed*

A plant of the genus *Trientalis.* Also called **chickweed 3, starflower** For other names of var spp see **May star, star anemone, star-of-Bethlehem, wild potato**

1814 Bigelow *Florula Bostoniensis* 88, *Trientalis Europaea.* Chickweed Wintergreen. **1821** MA Hist. Soc. *Coll.* 2d ser 9.157, Plants . . indigenous in the township of Middlebury [VT] . . Chick wintergreen. **1829** Phelps *Familiar Lect.* 310, *Trientalis . . . americána,* (chick wintergreen). **1840** MA Zool. & Bot. Surv. *Herb. Plants & Quadrupeds* 155, *Trientalis . . . Americana* . . . Chick Wintergreen. A small, beautiful plant, not green through winter. **1843** Torrey *Flora NY* 2.11, *Trientalis Americana* . . . Chickweed Wintergreen. **1850** Cooper *Rural Hours* 85 **cNY**, Some persons call this chick wintergreen, a name which is an insult to the plant. **1950** Gray–Fernald *Manual of Botany* 1142, *Trientalis . . . Chickweed-wintergreen.* **1959** Carleton *Index Herb. Plants* 126, *Wintergreen-chickweed:* Trientalis (v).

chickwhit See **chickwit**

chick-will See **chick-the-willow**

chick wintergreen See **chickweed wintergreen**

chickwit n Also *chickewit, chickwhit, chigwit* **chiefly CT** Cf **chickrod**

A **weakfish 1,** esp *Cynoscion regalis.*

a1870 Chipman *Notes on Bartlett* 37 *(DAE),* Chickwhit. **1889** (1971) Farmer *Americanisms,* Chickwit. — The *blue-fish* of Connecticut. **1892** *Outing* 20.54/1 **eVA**, He did say where it be called the 'gray trout,' 'sun trout' and 'shad trout,' the 'chickwit,' 'squit,' 'succoteague' and 'squitee.' **1902** (1968) Clapin *Americanisms,* Chickwit (Ind.) An obsolete name of the squeteague or weakfish (Cynoscion regalis), which is still, however, sometimes heard in Connecticut. Also, *chickewit, chigwit.* **1931–33** *LANE Worksheets* **seCT**, Chickwit . . a variety of fish, same as weakfish.

chicky See **chickie**

chicky my chick my craney crow See **chickamy chickamy craney crow**

chicky-pea See **chick-pea**

chico n[1] Also *chico brush, ~ bush* [AmSpan]

A **greasewood** (here: *Sarcobatus vermiculatus*).

1913 Wooton *Trees NM* 64, The Greasewood (Sarcobatus vermiculatus) . . . is often called *chico* bush in the northwestern part of the State. **1929** Ellis *Ordinary Woman* 26 **CO** (as of early 1900s), The Indians . . would come in from the agency — no roads — galloping their horses over the chico till they looked like waves. **1941** FWP *Guide CO* 15, Gray saltbush, or chico-brush — better known as greasewood — grows in alkaline soil and in the shale beds of the lower foothills. **1945** Wodehouse *Hayfever Plants* 102, The greasewood or chico (*Sarcobatus*

vermiculatus . . .) is an erect shrub one to three feet high with spinescent tangled and matted branches. **1960** Vines *Trees SW* 243, Chico.

chico n[2], adj Also *chica* [Span] **SW**
=**chiquito;** see quot 1932.

1897 Hough *Cowboy* 26 **SW**, The Spanish diminutives are in common use in the English speech of this region, as *chico, chiquito.* **1907** Porter *Heart of West* 212 **csTX**, But if you'll run in, *chica,* and throw a pot of coffee together . . I'll be a good deal obliged. **1908** (1966) Thorp *Songs Cowboys* 30 **West**, You're always in fix and willing to go / Whenever you're called on, my chico Chopo. **1932** Bentley *Spanish Terms* 121, *Chico* . . . "Small" or "small one." *Chico* is frequently used by Americans as a nickname or pet name. Often it is given to a boy and is carried with him to manhood. **1940** FWP *Guide NM* 111, *Chico* — Small.

chicopin See **chinquapin A**

chicory n Also sp *chiccory, chickory*

1 A widespread, usu blue-flowered, edible weed *(Cichorium intybus).* **chiefly Nth, C Atl** Also called **blue daisy, blue dandelion, blue devil n 6, blue sailors 1, blueweed 2, bunk** n[1] **2, coffeeweed 2a, endive, horseweed, ragged sailor, succory**

1847 Darlington *Ag. Botany* 98, *Cichorium Intybus* . . . Wild Succory. Chiccory. **1880** Twain *Tramp Abroad* 576, Continue the boiling and evaporation until the flavor and aroma of the coffee and chiccory has been diminished to the proper degree. **1965–70** *DARE* (Qu. S26a, . . *Roadside flowers*) 17 Infs, **chiefly N Cent, NEast,** Chicory; **CT8,** Wild chicory; (Qu. I28a, . . *"Greens")* 12 Infs, **chiefly N Atl, C Atl,** Chicory; **MD41,** Chicory greens; (Qu. S21, . . *Weeds*) 12 Infs, **chiefly Nth,** Chicory; (Qu. I4) Inf **CT29,** Chicory; (Qu. I28b) Infs **CA24, RI1,** Chicory; (Qu. I35, . . *Kitchen herbs*) Inf **MA98,** Chicory; (Qu. S9, . . *Grass . . hard to get rid of*) Inf **NY222,** Chicory; (Qu. S23, *Pale blue flowers*) Inf **IL50,** Chicory; (Qu. S26d, *Wildflowers . . in meadows*) Infs **PA60, WI20,** Chicory; (Qu. S26e, . . *Wildflowers*) Infs **NJ45, RI15,** Chicory.

2 See quot. [Because chicory is often added to or substituted for coffee]

1897 *KS Univ. Qrly.* 6.86 **West**, *Chickory:* all kinds of coffee.

chic sale(s) n, also attrib Usu cap Also *chick sale(s)* [See quot 1929] **scattered, but chiefly NEast, N Midl, West** See Map *somewhat old-fash, joc*

An outhouse, outside toilet.

[**1929** Sale *Specialist* [6], There's Chic Sale, Doc Sale's boy / From Urbana, Illinoy. *Ibid* 11, You are face to face with the champion privy builder of Sangamon County.] **1950** *WELS (An outside toilet building)* 5 Infs, **WI,** Chick Sales; 2 Infs, Chick Sale; 1 Inf, Chic Sales; 1 Inf, Chick Sales Classic Palace; 1 Inf, Chick Sale Special. **1962** Atwood *Vocab. TX* 53, *Chic Sale.* **1965–70** *DARE* (Qu. M21b, *Joking names for an outside toilet building*) 119 Infs, **scattered, but chiefly NEast, N Midl, West,** Chic sale(s); **DC2, MD48,** Chic sale house; **NY127,** Chic sale special; (Qu. M21a, *An outside toilet building*) Inf **MO4,** Chic sale. [Of all Infs responding to Qu. M21b, 6% were young, 26% coll educ; of those giving these responses, none were young, 50% coll educ.] **1970** Tarpley *Blinky* 149 **neTX**, Chick Sales. [1 inf] **1971** Bright *Word Geog. CA & NV* 150, *Chic Sale(s).* [75 infs, Central and Southern Nevada, scattered in California] **1973** Allen *LAUM* 1.181, Chic Sale. [6 infs, 2 in Iowa, 4 in Nebraska]

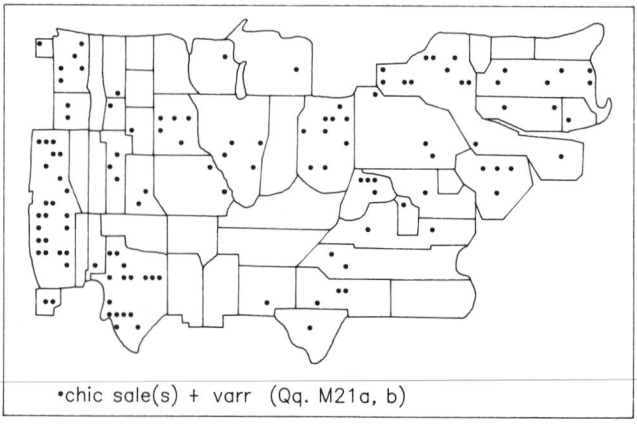

•chic sale(s) + varr (Qq. M21a, b)

chicus n
=cleavers.
1971 Krochmal *Appalachia Med. Plants* 126, *Galium aparine* . . . chicus.

chidkerberry See **checkerberry 1**

chidling See **chitterlings**

chief n[1], also attrib
An American Indian; a person with some Indian ancestry.
1940 FWP *Guide NM* 157, In the 1850's a Navajo sarape was one of the most desired garments on the frontier; it brought $60 on the open market, and was so tightly woven it could hold a bucket of water . . . the so called "chief blanket" of broad bold red, white, and blue stripes were traded and treasured by Indians as far north as Canada. **1966–69** *DARE* (Qu. HH28, *Names and nicknames . . Indians*) Infs **MI**103, **NC**45, **PA**230, Chief; (Qu. HH29a, *. . People of mixed blood—part Indian*) Inf **MO**11, Chief. **c1971** Hall *Snake River Valley,* (Terms for Indians) 1 inf, **swID**, Chiefs.

‡**chief** n[2] [Aphet form of *kerchief*]
1967 *DARE* (Qu. W3, *A piece of cloth that a woman folds over her head and ties under her chin*) Inf **MO**38, A chief.

chief cook and bottle wash(er) n
A factotum or handyman—also used as an ironic title for one in a menial position.
1840 *Magician* (Harrisburg PA) 29 Aug 2/3 *(DA),* Taking it for granted that the Kitchen Orator will be appointed 'Chief Cook and Bottle Wash' at the White House, he hopes, no doubt, to receive a sub-appointment as a reward. **1878** Campion *Frontier* 3, He offered himself for the post of what he inelegantly called, 'chief cook and bottle-washer to the outfit.' **1927** Ruppenthal *Coll.* **KS,** Chief cook and bottle washer—one upon whom most work falls, esp. in a household, camp, etc. **1966** *DARE* (Qu. HH17, *A person who tries to appear important*) Inf **NM**6, Chief cook and bottle washer. **1976** Garber *Mountain-ese* **Appalachians,** Chief-cook-and-bottle-washer . . handy-man, jack-of-all trades. We only have one office worker, she is chief cook and bottle washer.

chifforobe n, also attrib Usu |ˈʃɪfərob|; also |ˈʃɪfro(b)| For pronc varr, see quot 1965–70 Also sp *chiffarobe, chifferobe, chiffing robe, chifrobe, shifferobe* [Blend of *chiffonier* + *wardrobe*]
scattered, but esp freq Sth, S Midl See Map
A piece of furniture with drawers and space for hanging clothes.
1908 Sears *Catalogue* (Spring) 419, The Chifforobes as illustrated on this page are a modern invention, having been in use only a short time . . . Each article possesses the essential features of both wardrobe and chiffonier. **1937** (1958) Brewer *Dog Ghosts* 94 **TX** [Black], She looks on top of de chifferobe an' tecks down a spank-brand new breeches quilt what Mirandy, Jim's fuss wife, done quilted jes' 'fo' she died for de chilluns to sleep unnuh. **1948** *Sewanee Rev.* 270 **TN,** This shifferobe belongs to Hazel Wickers. **1954** *Harder Coll.* **cwTN,** Chifforobe. **c1960** Wilson *Coll.* **csKY,** Chifforobe. **1965–70** *DARE* (Qu. E1, *A piece of furniture that stands against the wall, and you hang clothes in it*) 116 Infs, **esp Sth, S Midl,** Chifforobe; **GA**17, **KY**15, **LA**6, **NJ**23, **SC**19, 22, 26, [ˈʃɪf(ə)ro(b)]; **GA**13, **PA**88, [ˈʃɪfɚˌrob]; **KY**28, [ˈʃɪˌfɪnrob]; **MI**61, [ˈʃɛfəˌrob]; **TN**30, [ˈʃɪəfərob]; **SC**9, [ʃɪfɪreɪd, ʃɪfɪrod]; **MS**72, Chiffing robe; (Qu. E3, *A piece of furniture in which you lay clothes flat*) 23 Infs, **esp Sth, S Midl,** Chifforobe; (Qu. W39, *. . A person's best clothes*) Inf **GA**77, Chifforobe clothes. **1968** *State* (Columbia SC) 3 May sec C 5,

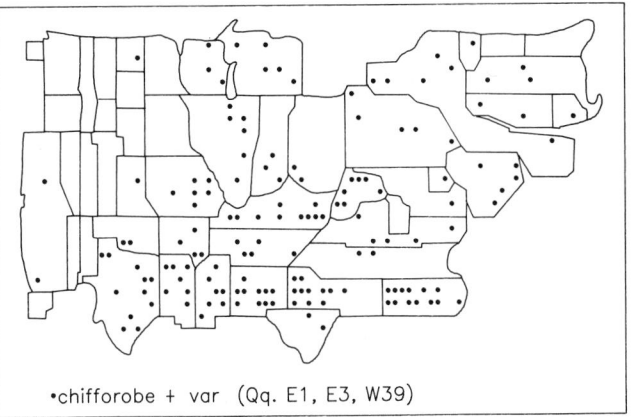

•chifforobe + var (Qq. E1, E3, W39)

Used furniture—chiffarobe. **1970** Tarpley *Blinky* 85 **neTX,** Two informants in the 60–70 age group use *chifrobe,* a term which usually designates a tall piece of furniture with a closet on one side and drawers on the other.

chigaderos n pl Also *chinkaderos,* abbr form *chinks* [Am-Span] **West**
=**armitas.**
1936 Adams *Cowboy Lingo* 34 **West,** The 'armitas' were simply well-cut blacksmith's aprons, usually made of home-tanned or Indian buckskin and tied around the waist and knees with thongs. They protected the legs and clothes and were cooler to wear in summer than 'chaps.' They were often called 'chinkaderos,' 'chigaderos,' or shortened to 'chinks,' and were more or less 'dress-up' garments. They were seldom seen on the later-day range. **1946** Mora *Trail Dust* 90, Chinks, or Armitas, are a kind of skeleton chap, and were worn quite a bit on some coast ranges and in Nevada. They are generally made of buckskin, the sides and bottoms often fringed. They are made up like a carpenter's long apron without a bib. The fronts were fastened with thongs or light straps around the leg, tied or snapped. **c1971** Hall *Snake River Valley,* (Outer covering worn to protect one's legs), 1 inf, **eOR,** Chinks, chinkaderos. **1977** Jones *OR Folkl.* 43, *Chaps:* leg coverings worn over a buccaroo's pants to protect him from the brush and weather. Also called *chinks* when made of leather.

chigger n |ˈčɪgɚ, ˈčɪgə| Pronc-spp *cheeger, chego, chigo(e), chigre, chigroe* [Alter of Cariban *chigoe*] Cf **jigger** Note: since both *chigger* and *jigger* are used of two similar tiny parasites, a mite (sense **1** below) which is widely distributed in the US, and a flea (sense **2** below) found chiefly in the South, there is overlapping both of the creatures' occurrence and of the names, with some popular confusion.

1 A harvest mite (*Trombicula* spp). Also called **jigger, redbug**
1851 (1969) Burke *Polly Peablossom* 68 **Sth,** The etarnalest out-of-the way for bar, . . an' cheegers, an' lizzards. **1852** (1949) Thoreau *Jrl.* 3.173 **MA,** The worst kind of chigo, or tick, to get under your skin is yourself in an irritable mood. **1872** Schele de Vere *Americanisms* 394, The Seed-tick is, in all probability, the same insect as the hated *Jigger* or *Chigre,* of Kentucky. **1899** (1912) Green *VA Folk-Speech,* Chigger . . . A small, red acarus or tick that buries itself in the skin. **1905** *DN* 3.60 **NE,** Chigger . . . Chigoe, or chîgre. An insect, a minute spider . . . Cf. also the slightly commoner *jigger.* Ibid 74 **nwAR,** Chigger . . . Chigoe, 'red-bug.' . . The form 'jigger' is rare. **1908** *DN* 3.298 **eAL, wGA,** Chigger . . . A tiny insect, the red-bug. **1915** *DN* 4.225 **wTX,** Chigger . . . The spelling and pronunciation chigoe are never used. **1928** Metcalf–Flint *Destructive & Useful Insects* 845, Chiggers, Jiggers, or Red Bugs . . *Trombicula* spp. **c1960** Wilson *Coll.* **csKY,** Chigger . . . A small red mite, *Trombicula irritans,* which becomes a pest in summer. Farther south it is a *red bug;* farther north it is a *jigger.* Originally *chigoe,* maybe. **1964** Borror–DeLong *Intro. Insects* 789, The majority of the harvest mites (also called chiggers or redbugs) which attack man belong to the family Trombiculidæ. **1965–70** *DARE* (Qu. R22, *Very small red insects . . get under your skin . . cause itching*) 451 Infs, **widespread,** Chigger; **TX**26, Chigroes [ˈčɪgrouz]; **GA**77, Redbug chiggers; (Qu. R23a, *Insects . . that fasten themselves to the skin and suck blood*) Infs **AR**56, **CA**20, **GA**3, 35, **PA**168, 180, Chiggers. [Note: some of these Infs may refer to sense **2.**]

2 also *chigoe flea:* A flea (*Tunga penetrans*) that burrows into the skin. Also called **jigger**
1859 (1968) Bartlett *Americanisms,* Chigoe, spelt also *chigre, chigger, jigger,* etc. (*Pulex penetrans.*) Sand-fleas, which penetrate under the skin of the feet, particularly the toes. **1889** (1971) Farmer *Americanisms,* Chigoe (*Pulex penetrans*) . . . It is found in the West Indies and along the Mexican coast. The name *chigoe* has many variants—*Jigger, nigua, chego, chigo, chigre, chigger, tungua, pique.* **1903** *DN* 2.318 **seMO,** Jigger or chigger . . . Chigoe; a minute flea. **1928** Metcalf–Flint *Destructive & Useful Insects* 841, Chigoe Flea . . . This insect must not be confused with chigger mites, since both are called chiggers. **1949** *PADS* 11.19 **CO,** Chigger, jigger . . . A flea that burrows under the skin. **1951** *AmSp* 26.14, Jigger (or chigger) is the common Southern name for a minute insect with a proclivity for burrowing in human flesh. **1964** Borror–DeLong *Intro. Insects* 652, The chigoe flea or jigger, *Tunga penetrans.*

3 Prob by transf because of the sting: see quots.
1950 *WELS* (A very tiny fly that you can hardly see but that stings sharply) 1 Inf, **WI,** Chigger; 1 Inf, Chigger, jigger. **1968–69** *DARE* (Qu. R11, *A very tiny fly . . that stings*) Infs **CT**11, **MO**20, **WI**37, Chigger.

4 =**beggar ticks 1.**

1949 *PADS* 11.19 **CO,** *Chigger, jigger . . .* Along banks, a weed that has a tiny sharp seed that gets under the skin. **1968** *DARE* (Qu. S14, . . *Prickly seeds, small and flat, with two prongs at one end, that cling to clothing*) Inf **PA**73, Chiggers.

chigger flower See **chiggerweed 2, 3, 4**

chiggerweed n chiefly **S Midl**

1 A dog fennel (here: *Anthemis cotula*).

1896 *Jrl. Amer. Folkl.* 9.191, *Anthemis Cotula,* . . chigger weed, Ind . . . So called because supposed to harbor the "chigger," a troublesome mite which burrows under the skin. **1931** Clute *Common Plants* 59, The dog-fennel *(Anthemis cotula),* which bears several other names of a derogatory nature, may as well have chigger-weed added to the list. **1969** *DARE* (Qu. S26a, . . *Roadside flowers*) Inf **KY**40, Chiggerweed = dog fennel.

2 also *chigger flower:* =**butterfly weed 1.**

1899 Bergen *Animal Lore* 118 **swMO,** *Asclepias tuberosa,* the butterfly milkweed, is called 'chigger flower,' from the belief that insects known as chiggers harbor in it. **1941** FWP *Guide SC* 409 **neSC,** Sandy pine groves where . . the scrubby little chigger weed or butterfly plant snuggles down in the hot summer, its deep orange flower resembling in color the 'red bug' or chigger. This innocent milkweed is avoided by many who believe the minute mites have pre-empted the plant as a citadel from which to attack. **c1960** *Wilson Coll.* **csKY,** *Chigger weed . . .* The butterfly milkweed, *Asclepias tuberosa.* **1964** Campbell *Great Smoky Wildflowers* 54 **eTN, wNC,** *Butterfly-weed—Asclepias tuberosa . . .* also known as *chigger weed.* **1965–70** *DARE* (Qu. S26a, . . *Roadside flowers*) Infs **TN**13, **VA**21, Chiggerweed [=butterfly weed]; (Qu. S26d, . . *Wildflowers . . in meadows*) Infs **KY**5, 89, **TN**6, Chiggerweed [=butterfly weed]; **MO**37, Chigger flower [=butterfly milkweed]; (Qu. S20) Inf **GA**70, Chiggerweed [=butterfly weed]. **1966–67** *DARE* Wildfl QR Pl.171 Infs **AR**44, 45, **SC**41, Chiggerweed. **1967** *Ozark Visitor* (Point Lookout MO) Feb 6/2, Further down the trail the orange of chiggerweed stood out against the lespedeza which was finding its way into the Ozark country. **1971** Krochmal *Appalachia Med. Plants* 70, *Asclepias tuberosa . . .* chigger flower.

3 also *chigger flower:* =**black-eyed Susan 2.**

c1960 *Wilson Coll.* **csKY,** *Chigger flower . . . Rudbeckia hirta,* the Black-eyed Susan; always was full of chiggers. **1966–70** *DARE* (Qu. S7, *A kind of daisy, bright yellow with a dark center that grows along roadsides in late summer*) Infs **AL**59, **NC**64, **OH**68, **SC**19, **TX**71, Chiggerweed.

4 also *chigger flower:* =**Queen Anne's lace 1.**

1968–70 *DARE* (Qu. S6, . . *Queen Anne's lace*) Infs **KY**18, **VA**38, 43, 101, Chiggerweed; **VA**7, Chigger flower.

5 An oxeye (here: *Chrysanthemum leucanthemum*).

1969 *DARE* FW Addit **KY**21, Chiggerweed—oxeye daisy *(Chrysanthemum leucanthemum).* **1969–70** *DARE* (Qu. S26d, *Wildflowers that grow in meadows*) Inf **KY**11, Chiggerweed, white with orange center; **VA**43, Chiggerweed, white with yellow center (oxeye daisy).

6 =**beggar ticks 1.** Cf **chigger 4**

1976 Garber *Mountain-ese* **Appalachians,** *Chigger-weed . .* stickweed.

chigo(e) See **chigger**

chigoe flea See **chigger 2**

chigre, chigroe See **chigger**

chigwit See **chickwit**

Chihuahua n Also *Chihuahua spur* [*Chihuahua* state and city in Mexico] **West**

A spur with a large rowel; also the rowel itself.

1936 Adams *Cowboy Lingo* 36 **West,** The large Mexican spurs, 'Chihuahuas.' **1939** Rollins *Gone Haywire* 110 *(DA),* Th' hombres that skedaddled jus' now musta bin sheepherders, for two o' 'em was wearin' only one spur, an' the rowels was Chihuahuas . . . What do I mean by Chihuahuas? Why, big rowels like th' Mexicans mostly uses. **1940** FWP *Guide NV* 76, The buckaroo's spurs are referred to as *steel, gads, hooks, gut lancers,* or *chihuahuas.* **1944** Adams *Western Words,* Chihuahuas . . . Large Mexican spurs. Made in one piece with wide heel bands, the genuine Chihuahua spur is often a beautiful piece of workmanship, inlaid with silver in the most intricate designs, even to the spokes of the rowels. **1967** *DARE* FW Addit **CO,** [In a museum:] Chihuahua spur— huge rowel and large leather foot "over-piece."

chihuahua intj Also *ay chihuahua* [Mex Span] **SW** *euphem*
Used as a mild expletive.

1930 Dobie *Coronado* 362 **SW,** Chihuahua, name of a state and city in Mexico—used as a harmless expletive. **1962** Atwood *Vocab. TX* 70, *Exclamations of disgust . . .* Mild terms . . . *chihuahua.* **1967** *DARE* (Qu. NN21a, *Exclamations caused by sudden pain—a pinched finger*) Inf **TX**28, Ay chihuahua.

Chihuahua cart n
See quots.

1930 Dobie *Coronado* 362 **SW,** Chihuahua cart, a heavy wooden cart. **1944** Adams *Western Words,* Chihuahua cart—A heavy wooden cart with solid wooden wheels. **1955** Harris *Look of Old West* 159 (as of 1860s–80s), A somewhat smaller version, the Chihuahua cart, carrying about half the load [of the Mexican oxcart] and requiring only three yoke of oxen, was also popular for freighting, especially on the more rugged routes.

Chihuahua town n Also *Chihuahua hill, little Chihuahua* **SW**
A section of a town or city populated primarily by persons of Mexican ancestry.

1966–67 *DARE* (Qu. C35, *Nicknames for the different parts of your town or city*) Inf **NM**6, Chihuahua town—area of about 2 blocks, a Spanish area; **NM**11, Chihuahua hill; **TX**5, Little Chihuahua—south El Paso.

chikee See **chickee** n[1]

chilacayote n For var spp see quots, esp 1947 [MexSpan] **SW**
Any of several gourds (*Cucurbita* spp), esp *C. foetidissima.*

1893 *Jrl. Amer. Folkl.* 6.142, *Cucurbita perennis,* Chili cojote; calabazilla. So. Cal. [**1895** *Jrl. Amer. Folkl.* 8.44 **Mex,** *Chilcoyote* looks much like the Chirimoya; if eaten by a person who is heated, will bring on chills and fever.] **1938** *AmSp* 13.116, In various southwestern States several species of gourds having fruits with an edible pulp (especially eaten as a dessert) are termed *chilacayote,* a name descended from Nahuatl *tzilacayotli.* Of this the first element is *tzilac* 'flat, smooth,' and the second *ayotli* 'gourd'—a word also seen in *chicayote,* a name of the calabaza and other gourds, as was recorded in dictionaries of about three decades ago. **1947** (1976) Curtin *Healing Herbs* 45 **SW,** Calabazilla—Cucurbita foetidissima . . *Chilicoto, chilicoyote, chilicayote, cucurbitác, chilicojote, chilicothe.* **1951** *PADS* 15.41 **TX,** *Curcurbita* [sic] *foetidissima . . .* chilicoyote. **1968** *DARE* (Qu. S26e, . . *Wildflowers*) Infs **CA**60, 87, Chilacayote.

chilaquiles n [See quot 1938]
See quot 1892.

1892 *DN* 1.189 **TX,** *Chilaquíles:* a Mexican dish of vegetables seasoned with red peppers, or of pieces of fried *tortilla* in red pepper sauce. **1938** *AmSp* 13.116 **TX,** A vegetable dish seasoned with these [chilchote] is known as *chilaquiles,* a name which we owe to Nahuatl *chilaquilitl,* whose second element *(quilitl)* denotes 'an edible herb.'

chilblain n, usu pl Also *chilbain, childblain, chillbaum, chublain* somewhat old-fash

A Forms.

1873 Harte *Mrs. Skaggs* 63 **nCA,** I've got a fevier. And childblains. **1965–70** *DARE* (Qu. BB13, . . *Chills and fever*) Infs **IL**66, 97, **IA**11, **OH**66, 80, **PA**202, **TN**48, **TX**33, Chilblains; **OH**95, Chilbains, old-fashioned; **OH**56, Chillbaum [Inf's spelling]; **PA**29, Chublain ['čublen]. [9 of 11 Infs old]

B Sense.
=**gooseflesh.**

1968–70 *DARE* (Qu. X58, *When you are cold, and little points of skin begin to come on your arms and legs, you have _____*) Infs **GA**72, **VA**101, Chilblains; **MO**10, Chilbains.

chilchipin See **chilipitin**

chilchote n [MexSpan] **TX**
A green pepper (*Capsicum* spp).

1892 *DN* 1.189 **TX,** *Chilchóte:* green peppers, sweet peppers. **1938** *AmSp* 13.116, The Texan word *chilchote,* signifying 'green or sweet peppers,' is derived from Nahuatl *chilchotl.*

chilcoyote See **chilacayote**

child n
A Forms.

1 sg: usu |čaɪld|; also, **chiefly Sth, S Midl**, *esp freq among Black speakers*, |čaɪl|. Pronc-sp *chile* See Pronc Intro 3.I.22

1887 *Scribner's Mag.* 2.474 **AR** [Black], De onlies' chile she got dyin' of. **1901** *DN* 2.181 **KY** [Black], Child chile. **1922** Gonzales *Black Border* 293 **sSC, GA coasts** [Gullah glossary], *Chile*—child, children. **1969–70** *DARE* (Qu. Z16) Inf **MO**15, Disobedient chile; (Qu. NN10a) Inf **TN**46, Hey chile. **1969** *DARE* FW Addit **NC** [Black], |čaɪl|, child, term of endearment, especially with children.

2 pl: usu |ˈčɪldrən|; also, **chiefly Sth, S Midl**, by metath (and assim) |ˈčɪl(d)ɚn|; also, **chiefly Sth, S Midl** *esp among Black speakers*, by assim |ˈčɪlən|, |ˈčʊlən|; occas, **chiefly nNEng, Sth, S Midl**, |ˈčɪldən|; occas, **esp Sth**, |ˈčɪ(ə)rən, ˈčɪlrən|; infreq |ˈčɪldrɪŋ, ˈčold(r)ən|; rarely |ˈčɪlwɪn|; *relic* (Scots) |ˈčɪldə(r)|. Pronc-spp *childer, chil(d)ern, child'n, childring, childun, childurn, chil'en, chillen, chillern, chillun, chillurn, chil'ren, chirren, chuldren*

1824 in 1956 Eliason *Tarheel Talk* 308 **NC**, Childring. **1843** (1916) Hall *New Purchase* 310 **IN**, I've no more nor two beds and them's all tuk up by me and the childurn. **1844** Thompson *Major Jones's Courtship* 81 **GA**, "Bomination take the retch," ses the old woman, "to run away from his wife and childern." **1845** Thompson *Pineville* 162 **GA**, His ready reply was, that he was " 'bleeged" to do the best he could to get meat for her and the "childer." **1859** Taliaferro *Fisher's R.* 97 **nwNC** (as of 1820s), Nur shall my chiliun talk it. **1871** (1882) Stowe *Fireside Stories* 170 **MA**, The child'n they brought in lots o' wild grapes. **1873** Harte *Mrs. Skaggs* 67 **nCA**, Sandy Claws . . gives things to chillern,—boys like me. **1883** (1971) Harris *Nights with Remus* 314 **Sth** [Black], Bless you, I know childun w'at'd keep dish yer whole place tarryfied. **1891** (1900) French *Otto* 163 **AR** [Black], She do dem chil'en good as a mudder. **1895** (1969) Crane *Red Badge* 102, Ye'd oughta see th' swad a' chil'ren I've got. **1901** *DN* 2.181 **KY** [Black], Children chillun. **1903** *DN* 2.290 **Cape Cod MA**, Childern . . for *children*. **1905** *DN* 3.56 **eNE**, Once in a while, [ɪ] passes into [ʊ] or [ʌ]:—*chuldren*. **1905** Culbertson *Banjo Talks* 11 **Sth** [Black], W'en biggitty chillen, long to'des night. **1908** *DN* 3.298 **eAL, wGA**, *Chil(d)ern* . . . Children. **1930** *AmSp* 6.171 **seVA** [Black], [tʃɪlən] for *children*. **1931** *AmSp* 6.230 **neOR**, 'Chillun' roam the hills. **1933** Miller *Lamb in His Bosom* 96 **GA**, He wanted to go on first before Seen and the chillurn. **1936** *AmSp* 11.245 **eTX**, Children [Plantation-Type speech] [ˈčɪldrən]; [Hill-Type] [ˈčɪldɚn], [ˈčɪlɚn]; [Black] [ˈčɪlən], [ˈčʊlən]. **1938** Faulkner *Unvanquished* 84 **MS** [Black], Take care of Miss Rosa and the chillen. **1941** *LANE* Map 378 **chiefly nNEng**, Our children . . . [tʃɪldɚn]; **scattered nNEng**, [tʃɪlən]; **sNH**, [tʃɪlən]; **seNH**, [tʃɪlrən]; **Cape Cod MA**, [tʃoldən, tʃoldrɪn]; **csME**, [tʃɪldrɪŋ]. **1942** Hall *Smoky Mt. Speech* 87, After [l], syncope of [d] is . . occasional in *children* [ˈtʃɪlɚn]. *Ibid* 98, Metathesis . . . Children [ˈtʃɪldɚn]. **1947** Guthrie *Big Sky* 16 **West** (as of 1830s), God Almighty! He's got chirren beyond countin'. **1950** *PADS* 13.22 **sKY**, Childern. **1950** *PADS* 14.19 **SC**, Childer [čɪldə] . . . Children. Obsolescent. **c1960** *Wilson Coll.* **csKY**, Children [čɪldən] common . . . [čɪlən] humorous. **1963** Carson *Social Hist. Bourbon* 103 **csKY**, Now, chillun, tomorrer we is goin' to take up mixin' in the mash. **1965–68** *DARE* FW Addit **LA**18A, Children [ˈčɪlɚn]—common among women here, though when thinking about it they carefully enunciate the [ld]; **LA**18, [ˈčɪlɚn], mostly Negro; **LA**35, [ˈčɪlən], **neLA**, [ˈčɪlrən]; **MS**, *Chillun*—used by Negroes to mean children. **1966–67** *DARE* (QR, near Qu. Q4) Inf **CA**74, [ˈčɪlwɪn]; (QR, near Qu. U3) Inf **FL**8, [čɪrən]. **1966–69** *DARE* Tape **AL**33, [čɪlərn]; **AL**43, [čɪlən]; **CA**143, [čɪrən].

3 double pl: *childrens*. Also pronc-spp *childerns, chilluns* **Sth, S Midl**

1895 Riley *Rhymes of Childhood* 18 **cIN**, 'Cause all the little childerns there's so straight an' strong an' fine. **1928** Chapman *Happy Mt.* 14 **seTN**, And girl childrens grown and married and having childrens themselves. **1929** (1951) Faulkner *Sartoris* 11 **MS** [Black], "Chris'mus!" Joby exclaimed, with the grave and simple pleasure of his race, . . "Y'ear dat, chilluns?" *Ibid*, Aunt Jenny, for all her widowhood, was one of the chilluns too, to Joby. **1966–67** *DARE* Tape **AL**14, We used to play with white childrens . . all the time; **AL**24, I have twelve here childrens [ˈčɪlrənz].

B Senses.

1 in phr *this child*: I, me—used in ref to oneself. *arch*

1839 *Daily Picayune* (New Orleans LA) 24 Mar 2/2, Neba min; you'll hab a chance to catch dis child some oder time. **1845** Thompson *Pineville* 181 **GA**, You jest fool with this child . . and if I don't blow you to kingdom come—you see if I don't! **1848** (1855) Ruxton *Life Far West* 90, Thar arn't a devil as hisses thar, as can 'shine' with this child, I tell you. **1850** Garrard *Wah-to-yah* 220 **NM**, This child's no niggur, an'

he says it's onhuman—agin natur—an' they ought to choke. **1851** Burke *Polly Peablossom* 99 **GA**, This child haint had that much money in a coon's age. **1871** *Harper's Mag.* 44.157/2 **TN**, I have pascience to write eny more, but dont you never go back on this child. **1947** Guthrie *Big Sky* 70 **West** (as of 1830s), This child don't feel easy in his mind about them sick ones in the boat.

2 in pl: Listeners.

1981 *DARE* File **ceKY** (as of c1930), *Children* stands for the audience, whether that audience is one person or several, young or old . . . "My goodness sakes, children! I was just talking to my husband about the grapes business."

childblain See **chilblain**

childer(n) See **child** A2

childerns See **child** A3

child-fetching vbl n [fetch v] **sAppalachians**

Aiding in birth; delivering a child.

1931 Hannum *Thursday April* 7 **WV Mts**, Godamighty, Thursday April! I hain't no hand with child-fetchin'! **1942** (1971) Campbell *Cloud-Walking* 15 **seKY**, Sary was a right good hand at child-fetching.

childing vbl n, ppl adj [OED "Obs. or arch."]

Child-bearing; pregnant.

1943 Peattie *Great Smokies* 115 **TN, NC**, But whatever the hazards of "childing"—as Shakespeare and the mountain people put it—the new baby itself is the most welcomed thing on earth. **1972** Cooper *NC Mt. Folkl.* 89, A-childing—gestating; pregnant.

child in the bushes See **baby in the bushes**

child'n See **child** A2

child nurse n

A midwife.

1968 *DARE* (Qu. AA30, *An older woman who comes in . . to help when a baby is going to be born*) Inf **PA**79, Child nurse.

child of the earth n

1 A wind scorpion (*Eremobates* spp).

1966–67 *DARE* (Qu. R21, . . *Stinging insects*) Inf **NM**13, Child of the earth (a scorpion); **TX**5, Child of the earth, looks like a large termite; (Qu. R28, . . *Kinds of spiders*) Inf **AZ**2, Child of the earth spider.

2 See quot.

1970 *DARE* (Qu. R30, . . *Beetles*) Inf **CA**173, Potato bug or child of the earth, yellow-colored, hard-shelled, common in yards or new buildings.

childrens See **child** A3

children's bane n Also *children's death* [See quot 1911]
=spotted cowbane.

1828 Rafinesque *Med. Flora* 107, *Cicuta maculata* . . Children's bane. **1900** Lyons *Plant Names* 101, *C. maculata* . . Children's bane. **1911** *Century Dict. Suppl.*, Children's-bane . . *Cicuta maculata*: so called because its root causes death to children who mistake it for an edible root. Also called *children's death*.

childring, childu(r)n See **child** A2

chile See **child** A1

chile colorado See **chili colorado**

chile joint See **chili joint**

chil'en See **child** A2

chileno n [Perh AmSpan *Chileno* from Chile] **West**

A type of bridle bit: see quot 1946.

1946 Mora *Trail Dust* 85, The ring bit, often called a Chileno, is just a severe curb. In place of the curb strap the lower jaw goes into a steel ring that is hung from the top of the mouth port. With one who rides the reins or is very heavy-handed, this bit can be quite severe: but on a well-reined horse with a loose-rein rider, there is positively nothing wrong with it. **1961** Adams *Old-Time Cowhand* 119 **West**, A "ring bit" is one with a metal circle slipped over the lower jaw of the hoss and a whole set of hardware in his mouth. This cruel Spanish bit's sometimes called a "Chileno," and ain't looked on with favor by American cowmen.

chile rel(l)ano, chile relleno See **chili relleno**

chilern See **child** A2

chili n [*chili* a hot pepper] **West** *derog* Cf **chili eater**
A Mexican.

1936 Adams *Cowboy Lingo* 198, To the cowboy a Mexican was a 'greaser,' 'oiler,' 'shuck,' 'chili,' 'chili-eater,' or 'bean-eater.' **1956** Ker *Vocab. W. TX* 374, Mexican (nicknames) . . . *Chili,* reported from Hartley and Borden counties. **1967** *DARE* (Qu. HH28, . . *People of foreign background . . Mexican*) Inf **TX27,** Chili.

chili bean n

1 The type of bean (usu reddish brown) used to make chili con carne. **chiefly Midl, West**

1906 *DN* 3.130 **nwAR,** *Chili bean* . . . A large reddish-brown bean used to make chili. **1950** *WELS (Beans [not pods] that are dark red when they are dry)* 6 Infs, **WI,** Chili beans. **1965–70** *DARE* (Qu. I17) 52 Infs, **chiefly Midl, West,** Chili beans; **CO3,** Mexican chili beans; (Qu. H50, *Dishes made with beans, peas, or corn*) 8 Infs, **CA,** Chili beans; (Qu. H45) Inf **CA64,** Chili beans; (Qu. H65) Inf **CO5,** Chili beans. **1976** *Wanigan Catalog* 6, *Chili*—Smooth, red, nearly round size 4 seed produced on vining, 3′ plants. Not as close as Pink bean to the Southwestern type of chili bean.

2 See quot.

1968 *DARE* (Qu. EE6b, *Small marbles or marbles in general*) Inf **LA20,** Chili beans.

chilicayote See **chilacayote**

chili chaser n [**chili**]
See quots.

1956 *AmSp* 31.100 **SW** [Smugglers' argot], The *chili chasers,* border patrolmen. **1968** Adams *Western Words, Chili chasers*—The cowman's name for border patrolmen on the Mexican border.

chili choker, chili chomper See **chili eater**

chilicojote See **chilacayote**

chili colorado n Also sp *chile ~* [MexSpan]
A red pepper *(Capsicum axi).*

[1844 Kendall *Santa Fé Exped.* 2.160 **Mex,** Seated upon the ground, a female might be seen with a few chiles colorados, or red peppers, for sale.] **1884** Hill *Tales Pioneers* 283 **CO,** The scarlet ribbons in her dark hair rivaled in brilliancy the wreathes of 'chili-colorado' that festoon the walls of a Mexican plaza in the Indian summer time. **1910** Porter *Strictly Business* 22 **NY,** Chili colorado bestows upon it zest, originality and fervour. **1938** *AmSp* 13.117, The condiment *chili colorado.* **1947** Curtin *Healing Herbs* 62 **NM,** Capsicum axi Vell., often referred to as the *chile colorado* by the Spanish-Americans of New Mexico.

chilicothe n [MexSpan: see quot 1938] **CA**

1 =**bigroot 1.**

1897 Parsons *Wild Flowers CA* 26, Wild Cucumber. Big-Root. Chilicothe . . . *Megarrhiza Californica [=Marah fabaceus].* **1911** Jepson *Flora CA* 270, E[chinocystis] macrocarpa (the Chilicothe) has a very spiny oblong pod 4 in. long. **1923** Davidson–Moxley *Flora S. CA* 345, *Micrampelis. Chilicothe. Big-root* . . . Common and widely distributed in the chaparral belt. **1938** *AmSp* 13.116, In various southwestern States several species of gourds having fruits with an edible pulp . . are termed *chilacayote* . . . A modified form *chilicothe* as applied to certain wild cucumbers has Californian currency.

2 See **chilacayote.**

chilicoto, chilicoyote See **chilacayote**

chili eater n Also *chili choker, ~ chomper, ~ picker* **chiefly West** *derog* Cf **chili**
A Mexican, esp one considered to be of low class.

1919 *DN* 5.63 **NM** [High school slang], *Chili-eater, -picker,* low class Mexicans. "I went over to Barellas to a dance and all the chili-eaters were there." **1938** *AmSp* 13.117, *Chili,* a sauce . . so preferred by the Mexican that he is sometimes called a *chili-*eater. **1944** Adams *Western Words, Chili eater*—Another nickname for the Mexican. Commonly used to mean *low-caste* or *low-brow.* **1970** Tarpley *Blinky* 258 **neTX,** *Nicknames for Mexican people* . . [infreq] chili chokers, chili pickers. **c1971** Hall *Snake River Valley,* 1 Inf, **csID,** Chili chompers.

chili jalapino See **jalapeño**

chili joint n Also *chili stand* Also sp *chile* **chiefly SW**
A small, cheap restaurant, particularly one that serves poor quality food.

1906 *DN* 3.130 **nwAR,** *Chili-joint, chili-stand* . . . A booth, shed, or room in which cheap luncheons, consisting mainly of chili or Hamburg steak, are served. **1927** Eubank *Horse & Buggy Days* 31 *(DA),* We made the round trip in less than three hours, scouted a couple of oil wells and ate dinner in a Wichita chili joint. **1940** Fergusson *Our Southwest* 339, Le's figure on a junta for nooning at the chile joint. **1967** Green *Horse Tradin'* 105 **TX,** There was a chile joint on one corner close to the trade square where I ate dinner. **1967–70** *DARE* (Qu. D39, . . *A small eating place where the food is not especially good*) Infs **TX26, 84,** Chili joint.

chilipepino See **chilipitin**

chilipepper n [From its reddish color] **CA**
A **rockfish** (here: *Sebastodes goodei*).

1953 Roedel *Common Fishes CA* 122, Chilipepper—*Sebastodes goodei.* **1960** Amer. Fisheries Soc. *List Fishes* 37, Chilipepper . . *Sebastodes goodei.* **1968** *DARE* (Qu. P2, . . *Saltwater fish . . good to eat*) Inf **CA65,** Chilipepper, channel fish.

chilipequin See **chilipitin**

chili picker See **chili eater**

chilipitin n Also *chilipepino, chilipequin, chil(l)ipiquin, chilitepin(o),* and earlier spp *chilchipin, chiltapin;* also abbr *pepino, piquin* [MexSpan *chiltipiquin*] **chiefly SW, esp TX**
=**bird pepper.**

[1825 Bullock *Residence in Mexico* 2.139, Two hundred and forty of chiltecpin, or small red pepper.] **1892** *DN* 1.246 **TX,** *Chiltapín:* bird-pepper; a shrubby plant of the nightshade family, with yellowish or red berries, used by Mexicans as a condiment. *Capsicum baccatum* . . . From the Mexican *chiltecpin.* **1894** Amer. *Anthropologist* 7.299 **sTX,** The mescal . . has added to it several kinds of roots and berries, the most important being the chilchipin, said to be the basis of the fiery Tabasco sauce. **1938** *AmSp* 13.112 **TX,** Bird-pepper, the *Capsicum baccatum* of the botanist, is termed *chiltapin* in Texas, especially by the Mexicans . . . A Texan form *chilchipines,* denoting the very fiery pepper growing wild in Texas and Mexico, which forms the basis of the relish called tabasco sauce. **1949** Trahey *Taste TX* 11, For me, chili simply ruins good beans, although I do like a few chilipiquines (the little wild Mexican red peppers) cooked with them. **1951** *PADS* 15.39 **TX,** *Capsicum baccatum* . . . Bird or Mexican pepper . . chilipitin. **1960** Vines *Trees SW* 908, *Capsicum . . frutescens* . . . Vernacular names are Chilipitin, Chillipiquin, Chili Pepper. **1965–70** *DARE* (Qu. I22a, . . *Peppers—small hot*) Infs **TX3, 6, 69,** Chilipitin [-pə'tin] peppers); **TX11,** Chilipitin peppers, also called bird peppers; **TX41,** Chilipitin [-pɪ'tin] peppers; **TX43,** Chilipitin peppers; **TX67,** Chilipitin peppers, also chilipequin; **TX28,** Chilipitins; **TX29,** Chilipitins [-pɪ'tinz]; **TX10,** Chilipequin [-pə'kin]; **TX31,** Chilipiquin ['či:lɪpɪ,kin]; **TX5,** Piquin; **CA24,** Chilipepinos [-pəpinos]; **WA11,** Pepinos; **TX21,** ['čɪltə,pen]; **OR1,** Chiletepins [-'tepenz]; **CA87,** Chilipepino.

chili relleno n |re'jeno, -jano| Also sp *chile relleno, chili* (or *chile) rel(l)ano* [MexSpan *chile* + *relleno* stuffed] **chiefly SW but widely recognized elsewhere**
A stuffed pepper; by ext, the type of pepper used for the dish.

1895 *Jrl. Amer. Folkl.* 8.60 **San Antonio TX,** But "chile con carne," "tamales," "tortillas," "chile rellenos," . . were always on sale. **1932** (1946) Hibben *Amer. Regional Cookery* 184 **NM,** *Stuffed Peppers (Chilis Rellenos).* **1949** Trahey *Taste TX* 173, Chili Rellanos (Stuffed Peppers). **1967–70** *DARE* (Qu. H45, *Dishes made with meat, fish, or poultry*) Infs **CA174, TX29,** Chili(s) rellenos; **CA54,** Chile relano, a stuffed pepper; (Qu. I22b, . . *Peppers—large hot*) Inf **TX4,** Chiles rellenos, a variety for stuffing, not really too hot; (Qu. I22d, . . *Peppers—large sweet*) Inf **TX81,** Chili rellenos [rə'jenoz], eaten raw or stuffed with cheese and rolled in egg and fried. **1981** *DARE* File, I was first introduced to chilis rellenos in southern California, where some of my relatives called them [re'jenoz] and others called them [re'janoz].

chili stand See **chili joint**

chilitepin(o) See **chilipitin**

chill v, hence *chilled* ppl adj **chiefly NEast**
To freeze.

1847 Walker in 1940 Drury *Pioneers Spokanes* 196 **ME,** Mr. E. lost an old cow, which being exposed to the wind chilled to death. **1943** *LANE* Map 648 **ME, NH,** *Froze* . . . Verbs denoting a milder degree of freezing . . *skiffed, chilled.* **1968–69** *DARE* (Qu. B33b, . . *The first thin ice that forms over the surface of a pond or pool: "The pond is just _____ over."*) Infs **NY72, 92,** Chilled; (Qu. OO15b, *About freezing your ears:*

"If he had been out last night he would have _____ *(his ears)."*) Inf **MA**30, Chilled his souse. **1969** *DARE* Tape **GA**72, It makes very bad liquor if you let it chill down, we call it — if it freezes down an' quits workin' an' forms a ice-cap over the top.

chill n

1967 *DARE* FW Addit **swWA**, Chills — new roots of the salmonberry; the Indian word was *chits* from which white kids developed *chills*. Old-fashioned. (Same as Thimbleberry.)

chill and fever doctor n Also *chills ~*

See quot 1923.

1923 *DN* 5.203 **swMO**, *Chill an' fever doctor* . . . Depreciatory reference to a doctor, meaning that his professional ability is limited only to the treatment of the simplest diseases. **1949** Webber *Backwoods Teacher* 137 **Ozarks**, Ol' Uncle Johnny used to set hisself up as a power doctor but all he was was jist a chills-an'-fever doctor an' I can cyore chills an' fever myself.

chillbaum See **chilblain**

chill bumps n pl Also *chill bugs, chilly bumps, cold-chill bumps* chiefly **Sth, S Midl** See Map
=**gooseflesh**.

c**1960** *Wilson Coll.* **csKY**, *Chill bumps* . . . Goose pimples. **1965–70** *DARE* (Qu. X58, *When you are cold, and little points of skin begin to come on your arms and legs, you have* _____) 83 Infs, **Sth, S Midl**, Chill bumps; **AR**47, Cold-chill bumps; **GA**59, **MO**9, Chilly bumps; **CA**106, Chill bugs. [Of all Infs responding to the question, 64% were old, 6% were Black; of those giving these responses, 41% were old, 24% were Black.] **1972–82** *DARE* File **S Midl, GA, SC**, Chill bumps . . . gooseflesh; **eVA**, Goose bumps? Chilly bumps is what we always say — chilly bumps.

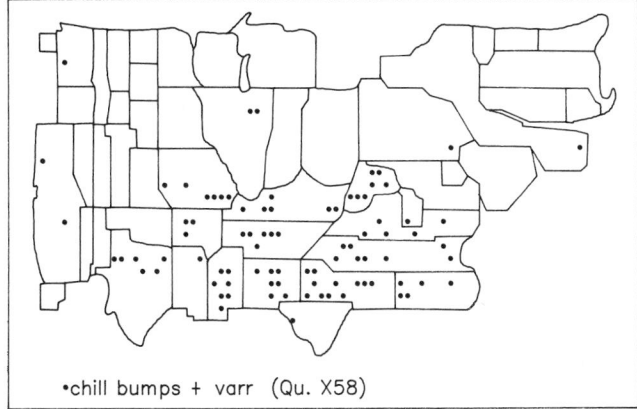

•chill bumps + varr (Qu. X58)

chilldee See **killdeer**

chilled plow n Also *chill plow,* pronc-sp *chilt ~*

A plow with share and moldboard made of steel surface-hardened by a chilling process.

[**1876** Knight *Amer. Mech. Dict.* 1747/1, The chilled cast-iron plowshare was patented by Ransome of Ipswich, England, 1803. The under side and points are hardened, and the top wears away, leaving a comparatively thin edge of hard, chilled iron.] **1884** Knight *New Mech. Dict.* 193, *Chilled Plow.* A plow the mold-board of which is cast on a chill to harden it and increase its wearing and polishing qualities. **1902** (1969) Sears *Catalogue* 678, *Full Chilled Plows* . . . Made on the same lines as the original Oliver Plows. These are general purpose plows and can be used anywhere that a chilled plow will work. As a sand soil plow they have no equal. **1968** *DARE* (Qu. L18, *Kinds of plows*) Infs **KY**75, **PA**135, **VA**26, 27, 46, 77, Oliver chill plow; **CA**97, Oliver chilled plows — named for the process in making them; **OH**43, Chilled plow — old-fashioned; **MO**32, Chilt plow.

chillen, chillern See **child A2**

chill-grass n [Evid used medicinally against chills; cf *DJE fever grass*]

An unidentified grass.

1970 Anderson *TX Folk Med.* 14 **ceTX**, Take a handful of chill-grass roots about the size of a match stick and five or six inches long and put them in a pot with three cups of water.

chill, have (something) down v phr

To know something extremely well; have something "down cold."

1900 *DN* 2.26, **CT, IA, MA, MI, NY, OH, RI**, *Chill* . . . In phrase 'have anything down chill.' To have perfect mastery of anything. **1915** *DN* 4.232 **neOH** [College slang], *Chill, adj.* Substitute for *cold*, in phrase to *have down chill*, to know thoroughly.

chillipiquin See **chilipitin**

chill plow See **chilled plow**

chills and fever doctor See **chill and fever doctor**

chill tonic n chiefly **Sth, S Midl**

A tonic or medicine thought to cure chills.

1935 Carson *90 Degrees* 33 **Sth**, A practice is made of "advancing" such things as fat meat, sugar, snuff, . . chill tonics, kidney pills. **1944** Clark *Pills* 235 **Sth**, Chill tonics returned almost as much money as the cotton crops. **1965–67** *DARE* (Qu. BB50d, *Favorite spring tonics*) Infs **OK**7, **TX**9, Chill tonic; **MS**68, Grove's chill tonic; **TX**40, Grove's tasteless chill tonic — but it wasn't tasteless.

chillun(s), chillurn See **child A2, 3**

chilly bumps See **chill bumps**

chilly hawk n Cf **killy hawk**
=**sparrow hawk 1**.

1970 *DARE* (Qu. Q4, . . *Hawks*) Inf **FL**48, Chilly hawk.

chilly-lou n [Echoic]

A whippoorwill.

1966 *DARE* (Qu. Q14) Inf **NC**35, [čílɪlu].

chil'ren See **child A2**

chiltapin See **chilipitin**

chilt plow See **chilled plow**

chim n Also *chimmy* [Abbr for **mummichim**]

A **mummichog** or similar fish.

1939 *LANE* Map 234 **Martha's Vineyard MA**, [A minnow or any small salt-water bait fish, 3 infs, Chimmies]. **1949** Kurath *Word Geog.* 23 **MA**.

chimbl(e)y, chimbli See **chimney**

chime n [*OED* →1793] arch

A rhyme; hence *chimer,* one who composes rhymes.

1897 (1952) McGill *Narrative* 49, One of the girls . . made a chime, which became the slang phrase of the school. *Ibid* 51, Now comes the Barnwell youth who was another of our chimers. We were classified in the Mount Zion school in 1837, and he too, not unlike many boys of the tender age, imagined he possessed a poetic vein.

chiming bells n **West**
=**bluebell 1g.**

1950 Stevens *ND Plants* 238, *Mertensia lanceolata* . . . *Chiming Bells* . . . A very attractive, early spring flower on hills in western North Dakota. **1953** Nelson *Plants Rocky Mt. Park* 133, *Mertensia, chiming bells,* or *American bluebells.* — These plants are easily recognized by their numerous pendent, bell-shaped blue blossoms. **1975** Zwinger *Run River* 13 **UT**, At the foot of the slope there are lush clumps of magenta monkeyflowers and thin-leafed chiming bells, blooming in splendid profusion.

chimisal See **chamisal**

chiml(e)y See **chimney**

chimmy See **chim**

chimney n, also attrib Usu |ˈčɪmnɪ|; also, chiefly **Sth, Midl**, occas **NEng**, |ˈčɪm(b)lɪ|; occas |ˈčɪmənɪ|; infreq |ˈčɪm(b)əlɪ| Pronc-spp *chimbl(e)y, chimbli, chiml(e)y* [Cf Scots and nEngl dial *chymlay, chimblay* 16th cent →]

A Forms.

1706 in 1907 NH *Prov. & State Papers* 31.574, My will ffurther is that . . my two sons . . build two Chimlys of Brick in the middle of sayd House. **1818** Fessenden *Ladies Monitor* 171, A list of some provincial words and phrases, which ought to be avoided by all who aspire to speak or write the English language correctly . . . *chimbly* for chimney. **1837** Sherwood *Gaz.* GA 69, *Chimbly,* for chimney. **1845–58** in 1956

Eliason *Tarheel Talk* 309 **NC**, *Chimney* [spelled] *chimbly* 1845 . . , *chimley* 1857 . . , *chimbley, chimley* 1858 . . , *chimblis* 1858. **1885** Twain *Huck. Finn* 47 **MO**, I couldn't get up the chimbly, it was too narrow. **1890** *DN* 1.67 **KY**, *Chimbly* or *chimly* [čimlɪ]: for *chimney*, by children. Not so often heard now. [*DN*: Also in New and Old England, and *chimbly* is reported from Louisiana.] **1905** *DN* 3.74 **nwAR**, *Chim(b)ly* . . . as a rule, the kind of chimney with a fireplace at the bottom. **1917** *DN* 4.409 **wNC, neOH, IL, KS, KY, NEng**, *Chimney*. **1922** Gonzales *Black Border* 293 **sSC, GA coasts** [Gullah glossary], *Chimbly*. **1929** Sale *Tree Named John* 118 **MS**, Den dey got in de chimbley en kick de mortar f'um twix' de bricks. **1930** *AmSp* 5.206 **Ozarks**, *Chimley*. **1936** *AmSp* 11.237 **eTX**, *Chimney*: ['tʃɪmlɪ], ['tʃɪmblɪ] (both illiterate). **1939** *Hall Coll.* **wNC**, *Chimley*. **1940** Richter *Trees* 21 **OH**, I'm up higher'n a chimley! **1941** *LANE* Map 332, The map shows the word *chimney* (or *chimley, chimbley*) . . . Pronunciations of the type of [čɪm(b)lɪ] are described as common or most natural by . . [9 infs]; and as older though still in use by . . [26 infs]; [infreq exx of [čɪm(b)əlɪ, čɪmɪnɪ].] **1942** *AmSp* 17.170 **sIL**, *Chimly* (for 'chimney') . . 6 [informants]. **1942** Hall *Smoky Mt. Speech* 99, *Chimney* ['tʃɪmlɪ]. **1957** Faulkner *Town* 257 **MS**, Even when it was staring him in the face out yonder at Miz Hait's chimley . . he still missed it. **1961** Sackett–Koch *KS Folkl.* 112, *Chimly* . . . *Chimney*. **1965–70** *DARE* (Qu. Q2) Inf **OH**42, Chimley owl; (Qu. Q20) Infs **AR**20, 28 39, **LA**2, **NC**35, Chimley sweep(er); **NJ**28, Chimley swallow; (Qu. DD9a) Inf **OH**87, Chimley. **1966–68** *DARE* Tape **AL**3, [čɪmlɪ]; **CA**73, [čɪmənɪz]; **IN**5 [*Chimley*, used by Inf's schoolchildren, is corrected by her to *chimney*]. **1975** *Foxfire* 3.244 **nGA**, I wished I just had one little rock from that old chimbley. **1976** Allen *LAUM* 3.303, Seven infs, all but one living in Midland speech territory, have an anaptyptic vowel in *chimney*, which they pronounce as /čɪməni/. *Ibid* 330, [Only 14 instances of the forms /čɪmli/ and /čɪmbli/ occur, in the eastern half of the Upper Midwest except for a few in northern North Dakota. Almost all of these infs have no more than grade school educ.]

B Senses.

1 A fireplace, hearth. **chiefly Sth, S Midl** [*OED* "Obs. exc. dial."]

1837 in 1926 *AmSp* 2.31 **?IL**, Make a little fire in the *chimney*. **1903** *DN* 2.309 **seMO**, *Chimney* (often chimbley) . . . Fireplace. **1906** *DN* 3.116 **sIN**, *Chimney* . . . Fireplace. "They sat at the chimney." **1939** *Hall Coll.* **wNC**, Beans and fruit are sometimes dried in the 'chimley,' i.e., fireplace. **1942** Faulkner *Go Down* 69 **MS**, My chimbley cooks good. **1966** *DARE* FW Addit **SC**, Ash bread—Make dough . . wrap in paper, rake back the coals, cover with ashes—it's made in the [čɪmblɪ].

2 A heavy smoker. **Nth, N Midl** *esp among coll educ speakers*

1900 *DN* 2.26 **NY** [College slang], *Chimney* . . . A person much addicted to smoking. **1965–70** *DARE* (Qu. DD9a, . . *A person who smokes a great deal: "He's a _____."*) 14 Infs, **Nth, N Midl**, Chimney; **CA**7, **IN**68, **NY**30, **VA**33, Regular chimney; **OH**87, Chimney. [14 of 19 Infs coll educ]

3 See quot.

1979 Hallowell *People Bayou* 124 **sLA**, Crawfish are builders as well as excavators . . . They wall each burrow to a height of three or four inches with mud brought up from the hole into what south Louisianans call a chimney.

4 A saltcellar.

1970 *DARE* (Qu. G3, *A container for salt that's put on the table . . open*) Inf **SC**70, Salt chimney.

chimney bat n

1 See **chimney swift**.

2 =**nighthawk**.

1955 Forbush–May *Birds* 282, *Eastern Nighthawk* . . . Other names: . . Chimney Bat. **1968** *DARE* (Qu. Q20, . . *Kinds of swallows*) Inf **MD**32, Chimney bat.

chimney bird See **chimney swift**

chimney corner adj

Unofficial, not genuine, popularly made up.

1915 *DN* 4.181 **swVA**, *Chimbley corner law* . . . Self-made law. **1916** *DN* 4.321 **KS**, *Chimney corner law* . . . The opinions, views, beliefs, etc., of the unskilled as to what is law. "Chimney corner law is expounded on the street corners and in the village store." **1923** *DN* 5.203 **swMO**, *Chimbly corner laws* = Customs that have been transmitted from generation to generation until they finally assume the nature of unwritten laws. The same term applies also to unprofessional and usually erroneous interpretations of the statutes. **1927** Ruppenthal *Coll.* **KS**,

Chimney corner lawyer—one who is unlearned in law but professes to advise. **1939** *Hall Coll.* **ceTN**, *Chimley-corner scripture* . . . A popular saying or adage supposed by some to be a Biblical text. A local CCC foreman who used the expression gave the following example . . . : "Better to put your seed in the belly of a whore than to spill it on the ground."

chimney corner pink n Also *chimney corner* Cf **chimney pink** A **cornflower 1** or similar flower.

1968 *DARE* (Qu. S11, . . *Bachelor's button*) Inf **IN**14, Chimney corners. **1968** *DARE* Tape **IN**14, Then I have a bed of ragged robins . . or some of the older people call them chimney corner pinks, of all colors.

chimney dick See **chimney swift**

‡**chimney leg** n

1950 *WELS* (*People's legs: very thick*) 1 Inf, **seWI**, Chimney legs.

chimney martin See **chimney swift**

chimney pink n Cf **chimney corner pink**
=**bouncing Bet 1.**

1893 *Jrl. Amer. Folkl.* 6.138, *Saponaria officinalis* . . . Chimney pinks. N.H.

chimney rock n

A type of rock or stone suitable for building chimneys.

1870 U.S. Congress *Congressional Globe* App 26 Mar 225/2 **MO**, The marbles of our western border have heretofore served as "chimney rock" for the cabin of the luxurious border farmer. **1968–69** *DARE* (Qu. C26, . . *Special kinds of stone or rock*) Inf **WV**3, Sandstone—[they] quarry it for chimneys, [it] splits in large pieces, called chimney rock; (Qu. D31, *In front of a fireplace . . stonework on the floor*) Inf **CA**134, Chimney rock.

chimney shelf n esp **NEng** Cf **clock shelf**

A shelf over a fireplace.

1881 Greene *Cape Cod Folks* 293, The bare, shining floor, the unpainted table, the chimney-shelf. **1941** *LANE* Map 328, 1 inf, **swCT**, *Chimney shelf*, used for more common purposes, 'They don't put so much rubbish on the mantel shelf;' 1 inf, **cnCT**, *Chimney shelf*, over the fireplace; *mantel shelf*, elsewhere: 'You can take down a mantel shelf but not a chimney shelf.' **1949** *AmSp* 24.107 **FL**, *Chimney shelf* . . . Mantel. **1968** *DARE* (Qu. E6, *A small shelf hanging on the wall with small decorative articles on it*) Inf **NH**14, Chimney shelf.

chimney sparrow, chimney swallow See **chimney swift**

chimney sweep n Also *chimney sweeper* chiefly **Sth, S Midl** See Map

=**chimney swift.**

1903 Dawson *Birds OH* 1.337, In nesting the Chimney "Sweeps" seek out the smaller chimneys of dwelling houses, and usually only one pair occupies a single shaft. **1905** *DN* 3.74 **nwAR**, *Chimley-sweep* . . . Chimney-swallow. **1908** *DN* 3.298 **eAL, wGA**, *Chim(b)ly-sweep(er)* . . . Chimney-swallow. Universal. *Chimney-sweeper* . . . The chimney-swift. The latter is rarely or never heard. **1917** *DN* 4.424 **LA**, *Chimney swift* . . . Chimney Sweep. **1934** Vines *Green Thicket* 60 **cnAL**, He had enough feathers from wild things to make a feather bed . . . He had a little old trunk nearly full of feathers and down from . . chimney sweeps (swifts). **1950** *PADS* 14.19 **SC**, *Chimney*

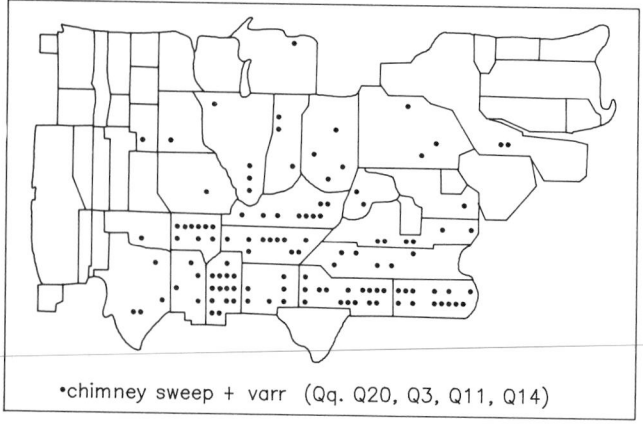

*chimney sweep + varr (Qq. Q20, Q3, Q11, Q14)

sweep . . . The chimney swift. **1965–70** *DARE* (Qu. Q20, . . *Kinds of swallows*) 86 Infs, **chiefly Sth, S Midl,** Chimney sweep; 26 Infs, **chiefly SE,** Chimney sweeper; **AR**28, 39, **LA**2, Chimley sweep; **AR**20, **NC**35, Chimley sweeper; (Qu. Q3 . . *Birds that come out only after dark*) Infs **AR**48, **IL**76, **LA**44, **MS**21, **MO**10, **NC**24, Chimney sweep; **SC**19, Chimney sweeper; (Qu. Q11) Inf **AL**6, Chimney sweep; (Qu. Q14) Infs **GA**89, **TN**56, Chimney sweep; **GA**91, Chimney sweeper. **1966** *Wilson Coll.* **csKY,** Chimney sweeper . . . Chimney swift.

chimney sweepers n

A corn smut.

1850 U.S. Patent Office *Annual Rept. for 1849: Ag.* 393, The sooty powder on the flowering parts of corn-plants, called smut, chimney-sweepers, and dust-brand, is formed of the spores of another *uredo.*

chimney swift n Also *chimney bat, ~ bird, ~ dick, ~ martin, ~ sparrow, ~ swallow* **widespread exc West, Sth** See Map Cf **chimney sweep** Also called **bat** n[1] **2, house swallow, swallow, swift**

A somewhat swallow-like, sooty black bird *(Chaetura pelagica)* which often nests in chimneys.

1789 Morse *Amer. Geog.* 60, Upwards of one hundred and thirty American Birds have been enumerated . . . The following catalogue is inserted to gratify the curious . . . Chimney [swallow]. **1813** (1927) Gerry *Diary* 68 **PA,** We saw 5000 chimney martins go round in a circle and then descend one chimney of the [Reading] court house, where they roost. **1849** (1906) Audubon *Western Jrl.* 129, I saw fifteen or twenty swifts, about double the size of our common chimney swift at home. **1888** (1890) Warren *Birds PA* 182, The Chimney-bird, unless resting on its nest or clinging to the sooty chimney sides, is always seen flying. **1955** *Oriole* 20.1.9 **GA,** Chimney Swift . . . Chimney Martin ("martin" here meaning merely "bird"). **1955** Forbush–May *Birds* 284, *Chimney swift . . .* Other names: . . Chimney-bird; Chimney Bat. **1965–70** *DARE* (Qu. Q20, . . *Kinds of swallows*) 188 Infs, **widespread exc West, Sth,** Chimney swift; 111 Infs, **widespread exc West, Sth,** Chimney swallow; **NJ**31, Chimney swaller; **NJ**28, Chimley swallow; **MD**32, Chimney bat; **NJ**52, Chimney dick; (Qu. Q3, . . *Birds that come out only after dark*) 14 Infs, **chiefly Nth,** Chimney swift; **DC**4, **IA**22, **MD**13, 48, **NJ**3, **OH**78, Chimney swallow; (Qu. Q14) Inf **GA**89, Chimney swift; (Qu. Q21) Inf **LA**33, Chimney sparrow, local name for chimney swift (any small dull-colored bird is called sparrow). **1969** Longstreet *Birds FL* 83, Chimney Swift. Other names: Chimney Swallow; Chimney Bat; Chimney Sweep.

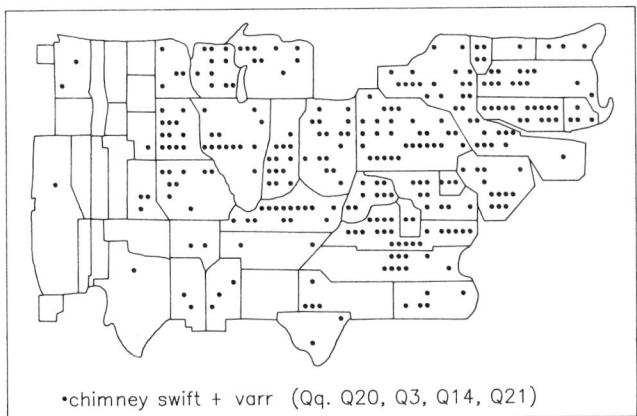

•chimney swift + *varr* (Qq. Q20, Q3, Q14, Q21)

chim wood See **chittamwood 4**

chin n, also attrib

Talk; chatter.

1894 (1899) Ford *Peter Stirling* 14 **NEast,** I'll wait till I've graduated, and had a chin with my governor about it. **1919** *Detective Story Mag.* XXVIII. Nov. 60 *(DA),* All we got to do is to frame up a good spiel to make him bite. And that's your little job. You always were there with the chin stuff. **1959** *VT Hist.* new ser 27.129, Chin: *n.* and *v.* Talk conversation. Chittenden. Common. **c1960** *Wilson Coll.* **csKY,** Chin . . . Idle talking or talk.

chin v, hence *chinning* vbl n, ppl adj

1 To talk (to), address; to chatter, gossip, argue.

c1871 Twain *Screamers* 77 **MO,** When I stood before the "Republican" office and looked up at its tall unsympathetic front, it seemed

hardly *me* that could have "chinned" its tower ten minutes before. **1890** Custer *Following* 308 **KS,** Men called out to each other very pointed remarks about snoring, or too much 'chinning,' as they said, when they wanted to sleep. **1899** *DN* 2.26 [College words], *Chin* . . . To "buzz," interrogate, gossip, talk to. **1951** *AmSp* 26.237 ?**NE,** *Chin* . . . 'The two spent their whole time chinning about this and that.' **1967–70** *DARE* (Qu. II15, . . *Stop and talk a while*) Infs **IL**46, **MN**2, Stop and (*or* to) chin awhile; **CT**10, Chin a little; (Qu. KK13, . . *Arguing*) Inf **MI**92, Chinning; **KS**7, And chinned; (Qu. II12, . . *Speaking only a few words*) Inf **NY**234, Chinned. **1967** *DARE* File **IL, WI,** We started chinning [čɪnɪn] around [=talking]. **c1970** *Halpert Coll.* **wKY, eTN,** Chinning = gossiping; talking endlessly.

2 To hold under one's chin.

1946 Greer–Petrie *Angeline Steppin'* 32 **csKY,** She was a chunk of a little gal I could a chinned.

china n, often cap, also attrib Usu |'čaɪnə|; also, **esp in Sth, S Midl, occas NEng** *chiefly among old speakers and speakers with little formal educ* |'čaɪni, 'čeni, -ɪ|; also |čaɪnɚ| See Pronc Intro 3.I.12.b Pronc-spp *chainy, chanery, chan(e)y, cheny, cheyn(e)y, chinar, chine(e), chin(e)y, chinie, chinny*

A Forms.

1647–48 in 1891 *Scribner's Mag.* 10.345/2, Cheyny £4 . . . One parcel cheyney plates and saucers. **1707** in 1907 **NH** *Prov. & State Papers* 31.553, My silver scollup dish and my white codell pote and cheny basan. **1843** (1916) Hall *New Purchase* 133 **IN,** What do you allow sang's (ginseng) done with out thare in Chi-ne? *Ibid* 445, Well! bust my rifle, if I allowed thare was sich a powerful heap of silver and chanery [=china] in these here diggins! **1861** Holmes *Venner* 153 **wMA,** All the borrowed chaney slippin' round on the waiters 'n' chippin' 'n' crackin'. **1891** (1967) Freeman *New Engl. Nun* 91, I had a tea-set, real chiny, with a green sprig on't. **1893** Shands *MS Speech* 23, *Chany* [čeni] . . . Negro for *china,* used in speaking of *chinaware.* **1899** Eggleston *Hoosier Schoolmaster* 173 **IN,** You can't make nothin' else out of him, no more nor you can make a Chiny hog into a Berkshire. **1904** *DN* 2.423 **Cape Cod MA,** China (Chiny). **1905** *DN* 3.74 **nwAR,** *Chinny* . . . A boy's name for a) marble. **1908** *DN* 3.297 **eAL, wGA,** *Chaney, chaney-tree, chaney-berry-tree . . .* The common soap-berry tree of Southern U.S. **1912** Wason *Friar Tuck* 238 **WY,** They were the souls o' furniture-movers who had died without repentin' of all the piano-lamps an' chiny-ware they had broke. **1931** in 1944 *ADD* **NEng coast,** [čaɪnə(r)] Chinar. **1936** *AmSp* 11.160 **eTX,** Among older or less well educated people in rural districts, . . *China, extra,* . . are pronounced with [ɪ] in the final syllable: . . ['tʃaɪnɪ] (especially in the phrase 'Poland-China hogs'). **1941** Stuart *Men of Mts.* 292 **neKY,** Just to think of him fooling with women in Chinee, Ja-pan, and all them low-down strollops in Africa and South America. **1950** *PADS* 14.19 **SC,** Chaneyberry ['tʃenɪˌbɛrɪ] . . . A widespread pronunciation of *chinaberry . . . Chaney* is a dialect pronunciation of *China.* **1955** *PADS* 23.13 **cwTN,** *Chiney, chinie, chinee.* **1961** Kurath–McDavid *Pronc. Engl.* 168, *Sofa, china . . .* These words usually end in /ə/. But in folk speech [ɨ ~ ɪ] occur with some frequency in northern New England, in West Virginia, and in the Upper South, and relics of it appear elsewhere. **1965** *Dict. Queen's English* **NC,** *Chainy* (for china) (as in rainy): She set out her finest chainy for the dinner. I wouldn't do that for all the tea in Chainy. **1966** *Wilson Coll.* **csKY,** [čaini]. **1976** Allen *LAUM* 3.290, *China,* occurs as /čaini/ in the speech of [15 infs, almost all in the oldest and least educated group].

B Senses.

1 A playing marble, often made of china.

1892 *DN* 1.220 **MO,** Marbles themselves are almost universally called *chineys.* **1895** *DN* 1.385 **Boston MA,** *Chinees:* white clay marbles, covered with geometrical figures in colors. **1905** [see A above]. **1906** Lovett *Old Boston Boys* 42, A boy's stock of marbles was usually carried in a bag with a running string, and consisted of "Alleys," "Jaspers," "Chinees," "Pewees," "Agates," "Bulls' Eyes," and several other kinds. **1916** *DN* 4.268 **New Orleans LA,** China [čaɪni]. **1922** *DN* 5.186 **MA, MN,** *Chiney . . .* A marble made of china. **1942** Whipple *Joshua* 376 **UT,** He was big for seven years, . . always shooting 'chinies' with the Peabody boys in the dooryard. **1955** *PADS* 23.13 **cwTN,** *China alley* (also *chiney, chinie, chinee[s]*) . . . A marble made of china ware, often with rings painted in different colors. **1965–70** *DARE* (Qu. EE6d, *Special marbles*) 11 Infs, **Inland Nth, N Midl, West,** Chinies; **KY**36, **NV**3, 7, China marbles; **OH**68, Chinas; **RI**12, China king; (Qu. EE6c, *Cheap marbles*) Infs **LA**8, 25, **TX**12, China marbles; **CA**107, **LA**40, Chinas; (Qu. EE6b, *Small marbles*) Infs **LA**23, 40, Chinas; **RI**17, Chinies—clay agates. **1971** Bright *Word Geog. CA & NV* 205, Marbles . . . chinas / chinies.

2 freq in combs *china chippers, ~ choppers, ~ clippers;* also *chinaware;* rarely *Chinese choppers:* A set of false teeth; infreq, teeth. **esp Nth, N Midl** *joc*

1942 Berrey–Van den Bark *Amer. Slang* 121.74, *Teeth . . .* China. **1950** *WELS (False teeth)* 14 Infs, **WI,** China (choppers, clippers); 1 Inf, Chiny teeth; 1 Inf, Chinaware; *(Joking names for teeth)* 1 Inf, China. **1953** Hall *Coll.* **swNC,** China clippers . . . A set of false, store teeth. **1965–70** *DARE* (Qu. X13b, *Joking names for false teeth)* 40 Infs, **esp Nth, N Midl,** China clippers; 13 Infs, **chiefly NEast,** China(s); **CA59, GA75, MI123, NJ8, NY167, OK31, PA69, 93,** China choppers; **NJ2, 56, NY92, 229 NC52, PA234, SD3,** Chinaware; **MA122,** China chippers; **WY4,** Chinese choppers; **GA75,** China teeth; (Qu. X13a, *. . Teeth)* Inf **CA36,** China clippers; **NC52, NY92,** Chinaware.

3 See **Chinaberry 1, 2.**

4 See **Chinaroot.**

Chinaball n Also *~ tree* **chiefly LA**

=Chinaberry 1.

1939 *AmSp* 14.259, *Chinaberry . .* the common name in Louisiana of an imported tree, *Melia azedarach* L., which now grows wild in the State . . . By some natives of Louisiana it is also called *China-ball* (tree); by natives of other states it is, I believe, generally called the *China tree* or the *Chinaberry* (tree). **1954** Armstrong *Satchmo* 10 **New Orleans LA** (as of c1910), Whenever I did something she thought I ought to get a whipping for, she sent me out to get a switch from the big old chinaball tree in her yard. **1967** LeCompte *Word Atlas* 240 **seLA,** Chinaball [13 of 21 infs] . . chinaberry tree [2 infs]. **1968** *DARE* (Qu. T5, *. . Evergreens)* Inf **LA37,** Chinaball. **1969** *DARE* FW Addit **OK,** *Chinaball* = chinaberry (because of the shape of it). **1977** *Mais Jamais* 18 **LA,** [As a remedy for fever] strip the leaves off a chinaball tree branch and mash the leaves.

China bean n

=black-eyed pea.

1868 (1870) Gray *Field Botany* 109, China Bean. [*Vigna sinensis*]. **1903** Small *Flora SE U.S.* 654, *Vigna . .* China Bean.

China bedbug See **China bug 2**

Chinaberry n

1 also *China, Chinaberry tree:* An introduced shade tree *(Melia azedarach).* **chiefly S Atl, Gulf States** See Map Also called **bead tree, Chinaball, China tree 1, Chinese umbrella, false sycamore, Indian lilac, paternoster tree, pride-of-China, pride-of-India, umbrella tree**

1847 *Knickerbocker* 29.197, The China is the favorite shade-tree of this and many of the southern towns. **1890** *Harper's Mag.* 82.106/2 **FL,** The high gray towers . . were crowned with ornaments like the berries of the chinaberry-trees. **1896** Harris *Sister Jane* 84 **GA,** I hear a flutter in the chaney-berry tree, and look up and see a jaybird. **1898** Lloyd *Country Life* 63 **AL,** I was so glad to git home that I hugged the old chaneyberry tree that stood out in the back yard. **1922** Gonzales *Black Border* 292 **sSC, GA coasts** [Gullah glossary], *Chanyberry* —Chinaberry, or Pride of India tree. **1932** (1974) Caldwell *Tobacco Road* 8 **GA,** He saw Ellie May peering at him from behind the chinaberry tree. **1950** *PADS* 14.19 **SC,** *Chaneyberry* ['tʃɛnɪˌbɛrɪ] . . . A widespread pronunciation of *chinaberry.* **1965–70** *DARE* (Qu. T16, *. . Trees)* 62 Infs, **chiefly S Atl, Gulf States, esp SC, AL, TX,** Chinaberry; (Qu. I44, *. . Berries)* Infs **AL6, FL51, GA11, NM5, NC60, SC26,** Chinaberries; (Qu.

I43, *. . Nuts)* Inf **OK17,** Chinaberries; (Qu. S26e) Inf **OK28,** Chinaberry tree. [Note: some of these Infs may refer instead to **chinaberry 2.**]

2 also *China, Chinaberry tree:* **=soapberry 1.**

1897 Sudworth *Arborescent Flora* 295, *Sapindus marginatus . . . Wild China . . .* Soapberry . . Chinaberry (N. Mex.). **1908** *DN* 3.297, *Chaney, chaney-tree, chaney-berry-tree . . .* The common soap-berry tree of Southern U.S. **1940** Gates *Flora KS* 221, Soapberry, Chinaberry. Rocky hillsides. **1967** *DARE* (Qu. T16, *. . Trees . . "special")* Inf **AL30,** Texas china. **1973** Stephens *Woody Plants* 358, *Sapindus drummondii . . .* Soapberry, chinaberry . . . It is an attractive tree and is often used for yard planting.

3 **=red baneberry.**

1963 Craighead *Rocky Mt. Wildflowers* 52, *Baneberry. Actaea arguta . . . Other names:* Snakeberry, Chinaberry.

China brier n Also sp *China briar* and, **esp in SC,** pronc-spp *cha(i)ney ~*

Usu **stretchberry** *(Smilax bona-nox),* but also *S. laurifolia.*

1745 *London Mag.* 14.551/2 **GA coast,** The good *Indians* regaled us, and for Greens, boiled us the Tops of China-Briars, which eat almost as well as Asparagus. **a1816** (1848) Hawkins *Sketch* 21 **GA,** The China briar is in the flat, rich, sandy margins of streams. The Indians dig the roots, pound them in a mortar, and suspend them in coarse cloth, pour water on them and wash them. The sediment which passes through with the water is left to subside; the water is then poured off, and the sediment is baked into cakes or made into gruel sweetened with honey. **1899** (1962) Cushman *Hist. Choctaw* 312 **MS,** They made a very palatable jelly from the pounded roots of the China brier, strained through baskets. **1930** Stoney-Shelby *Black Genesis* 133 **seSC,** Dat chaney briar might do, if somebody else was a-huntin' him, but Br' Rabbit would cut t'rough it wid one look. **1939** FWP *Guide FL* 44 **Everglades,** From the jungles come coontie and chinabriar from which a flour is made. **1950** *PADS* 14.19 **SC,** *Chaney briar . . .* The China briar, the *bramboo briar,* smilax. **1954** *PADS* 21.41 **Charleston SC,** *Wild asparagus . . .* The tender shoots of the bull briar, purveyed in season in bunches and used as a vegetable. It is also called *chaney briar.* **1960** Vines *Trees SW* 76, *S[milax] laurifolia . . .* Vernacular names are Bamboo-vine, China-brier [etc]. **1967** *DARE* FW Addit [From a Charleston SC cookbook], *Chainey Briar* = wild asparagus.

China bug n

1 An unidentified insect; see quot.

1850 U.S. Patent Office *Annual Rept. for 1849: Ag.* 137 **VA,** Wheat is at best a delicate and uncertain crop, subject to two great disasters, *rust* and *mildew;* and also the Hessian fly and china bug.

2 also *China bedbug:* An **assassin bug** (here either *Triatoma sanguisuga* or *T. protracta*).

1928 Metcalf–Flint *Destructive & Useful Insects* 837, The bites inflicted by the . . China bedbugs . . are scarcely exceeded in severity by any other insect. **c1970** *DARE* FW Addit **CA,** *Chiny bugs* —flies with red wings. Daughter and grandchildren call chiny bugs "kissing bugs."

China cane n

Perh sorghum *(Sorghum vulgare).*

1949 *AmSp* 24.107 **GA,** *China cane . . .* The small-stemmed, disease-resistant East Indian sugar cane.

china chippers, china choppers, china clippers See **china B2**

china closet See **closet 1**

China clover n

A bush clover (here: *Lespedeza striata*).

1942 *Torreya* 42.161, *Lespedeza striata . . .* Buffalo, Carolina, China, Georgia, and oldfield, clover, southeastern States.

China croaker See **Chinese croaker**

china doll('s) eye See **doll's eyes**

china-eye n [From the resemblance to porcelain]

1930 Shoemaker *1300 Words* 10 **cPA Mts** (as of c1900), *China-eye* —A wall-eyed horse; sometimes applied to a blue-eyed girl.

Chinafish n Also *China rockfish*

A **rockfish:** see quots.

1953 Roedel *Common Fishes CA* 130, *Sebastodes chlorostictus . . Unauthorized Names:* Chinafish. *Ibid* 131, *Sebastodes constellatus . . Unauthorized Names:* Chinafish. *Ibid* 134, *China Rockfish—Sebastodes nebulosus.* **1963** *Fisherman's Encycl.* 543, There are about 60 species of

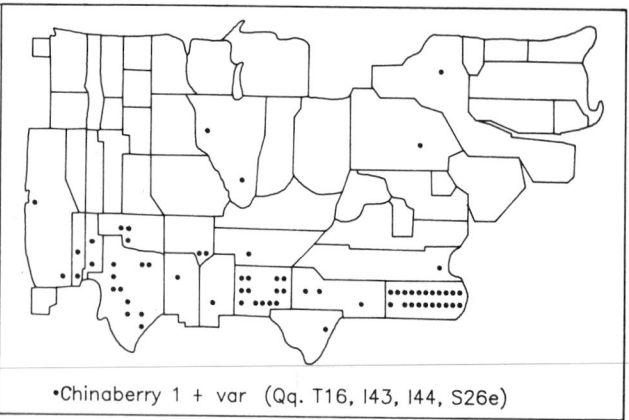

•Chinaberry 1 + var (Qq. T16, I43, I44, S26e)

these rockfish . . on the Pacific Coast . . . Chilipepper . . Chucklehead, Chinafish . . are a few of the more frequently encountered varieties. Most of them are found from central through southern Calfornia, possible [sic] much farther north.

China grass n

1954 *PADS* 21.36 **SC,** *Sapphire grass . . .* The *Liriope spicata* . . . Brought presumably from China, it is also called China grass.

China lettuce n **Pacific NW**

1 also *Chinese lettuce:* Prob a **wild lettuce** such as *Lactuca pulchella.*

1966–67 *DARE* (Qu. S21, . . *Weeds*) Inf **WA**12, China lettuce; **ID**5, Chinese lettuce. **1966** *DARE* FW Addit **OR**12, Blue-flowered lettuce is locally called China [ˈčaɪnɪ] lettuce.

2 =**dandelion.**

1967 *DARE* (Qu. S11, . . *Dandelion*) Inf **WA**30, China lettuce.

China lily n Also *Chinese lily*

A narcissus.

1880 *Harper's Mag.* 62.72/2 **San Francisco CA,** At nearly every window was . . a dish of the favorite Chinese lily, the narcissus, in full bloom. **1968** *DARE* (Qu. S26e, . . *Wildflowers*) Inf **CA**87, China lilies —narcissus.

Chinaman n

1 See quot.

1895 *DN* 1.385 **cwMO,** Chinaman: cup of tea.

2 =**ring-necked pheasant. NW**

1957 *AmSp* 32.184 **MT, WA, OR, CA,** Chinaman—Common pheasant. **1966** *DARE* (Qu. Q7, . . *Game birds*) Inf **WA**15, China pheasant —Chinaman.

3 One who has and dispenses political influence.

1971 *AmSp* 46.83 **Chicago IL,** Political influence: *clout, drag, pull, to have a Chinaman, to have an "in," to have connections.*

4 in phr *Chinaman gets it:* =**cat's game.**

1968–69 *DARE* (Qu. EE38b, *If the game of tick-tack-toe comes out so that neither x nor o wins*) Inf **CA**59, Chinaman gets it; **CA**136, Chinaman got it. **1981** *DARE* File **CA,** When a game of tick-tack-toe is won by neither player, one says "the Chinaman got it."

China match n

1967–69 *DARE* (Qu. F46, . . *Matches you can strike anywhere*) Infs **CA**144, **OR**3, China matches.

China owl n

Perh the **burrowing owl.**

1968 *DARE* (Qu. Q2, . . *Owls*) Inf **CA**91, China owl—a small owl in the desert—along the drain ditch banks they have holes.

China pheasant See **Chinese pheasant**

China plant n

=**red baneberry.**

1966 *DARE* Wildflower QR Pl.62 Inf **CO**7, China plant.

chinar See **china A**

China rockfish See **Chinafish**

Chinaroot n

1 also *China:* Usu **stretchberry** *(Smilax bona-nox),* but also *S. hispida.*

[**1673** in 1876 Bourne *Life John Locke* 326 **NC, SC,** By the last fleet I sent you a parcel of Carolina china-root.] **1682** (1836) Ash *Carolina* 11, The China grows plentifully there, whose Root infus'd, yields us that pleasant Drink, which we know by the Name of China Ale in England. **1731** (1754) Catesby *Nat. Hist. Carolina* 1.52, Of these Roots the Inhabitants of *Carolina* make a Diet-Drink, attributing great Virtues to it in cleansing the Blood, &c . . . 'Tis called there *China* Root. **1817** Brown *Western Gaz.* 146 **LA, FL,** The China root and passion flower are abundant on the rich grounds. **1899** Cushman *Hist. Choctaw* 229 **SW,** To produce a copious perspiration, a hot decoction of the China root swallowed had the desired effect. **1930** Sievers *Amer. Med. Plants* 9, *Bamboo Greenbrier. Smilax pseudo-china . . . Other common names . . .* American chinaroot, . . bullbrier. **1973** Stephens *Woody Plants* 22, *Smilax hispida . . .* Bristly greenbrier, smilax, Chinaroot.

2 A **wild yam** (here: *Dioscorea villosa*).

1971 Krochmal *Appalachia Med. Plants* 110, *Dioscorea villosa . . .* China root. **1974** (1977) Coon *Useful Plants* 128, China

root . . . is rather a twining perennial vine . . . The part used is the smallish root, dried, powdered, and made into a decoction.

China rose Also *Chinese rose* [*OED* 1731 →]

An hibiscus (here: *Hibiscus rosa-sinensis*). Also called **shoe plant, shoe-black plant**

1933 Small *Manual SE Flora* 857, *Hibiscus Rosa-Sinensis* . . Chinese-Rose. **1938** Matschat *Suwannee R.* 36, **nFL, sGA,** Thar hain't no chiny rose growin' here in Okefenokee. **1982** Perry–Hay *Field Guide Plants* 60, *Hibiscus rosa-sinensis*—China rose.

China tree n **chiefly S Atl, Gulf States**

1 =**Chinaberry 1.**

1819 Evans *Pedestrious Tour* 209 **MS,** Here grew the China tree, of a beautiful appearance, and bearing fruit of an inviting aspect, but of an unpleasant taste. **1867** *Old Guard* 5.93 **SC** (as of 1770s), Thinly sprinkled with a secondary growth of scrubby and water oaks, field pines, persimmon, and the frequent China tree. **1897** (1952) McGill *Narrative* 43 **SC,** Indiantown Swamp, the west bank of which was said to have been a settlement of Indians, as was marked even then by a growth of China trees and other indications of a settlement. **1920** *Torreya* 91 **GA,** Here . . it grows on . . China tree *(Melia Azedarach)* and red cedar. **1941** FWP *Guide LA* 403, China tree . . planted by early settlers because they grew rapidly . . and made good firewood. In addition the flowers were used as a moth deterrent, the China "balls" provided pop-gun ammunition for small boys, and the dried seeds were dyed and strung as beads by the girls. **1949** *AmSp* 24.107 **SC,** *Chaney trees . . .* Chinaberry trees. **1979** Little *Checklist U.S. Trees* 172, *Melia azedarach . . . Other common names . . .* chinaberry, chinatree. *Ibid* 270, *Sapindus drummondii . . . Sapindus saponaria . . . Other common names . .* wild chinatree.

2 usu *wild China (tree):* =**soapberry 1.**

1852 in 1854 U.S. War Dept. *Explor. Red River* 6 **LA,** The timber, consisting of overcup, white-oak, elm, hackberry, and wild china, is large and abundant. **1884** Sargent *Forests of N. Amer.* 44, *Sapindus marginatus . . . Wild China. Soapberry.* **1897** Sudworth *Arborescent Flora* 295, *Sapindus marginatus . . .* Wild China (Fla., Miss., La., Tex., Iowa, Kans.). **1908** *DN* 3.297 **eAL, wGA,** *Chaney, chaney-tree, chaney-berry-tree . . .* The common soap-berry tree of Southern U.S. **1933** Small *Manual SE Flora* 828, *Wild-china. Soapberry.* **1960** Vines *Trees SW* 683, *Sapindus drummondii . . .* Vernacular names are . . Wild China-tree, and Indian Soap-plant. **1979** [see **1** above].

chinaware See **china B2**

Chinawood n

Prob a **soapberry 1** (here: *Sapindus drummondii*).

1907 Cook *Border & Buffalo* 62 **SW,** There was a thicket of stunted hackberry and palodura, hard poles of china-wood, close to where the old camp-fire had been. *Ibid* 143, I cut a china-wood pole.

chincapin See **chinquapin A**

chince n[1] See **chinch** n[1] **1**

chince n[2] See **chinch** n[2]

chince v See **chinse** v

chinch n[1] Also freq *chinch bug* [Span *chinche*]

1 also sp *cheench, chince, chinche, chinchy, chintz, cinch:* A bedbug *(Cimex lectularius).* [*OED:* "A name now confined to the U.S."] **chiefly Sth, S Midl** See Map

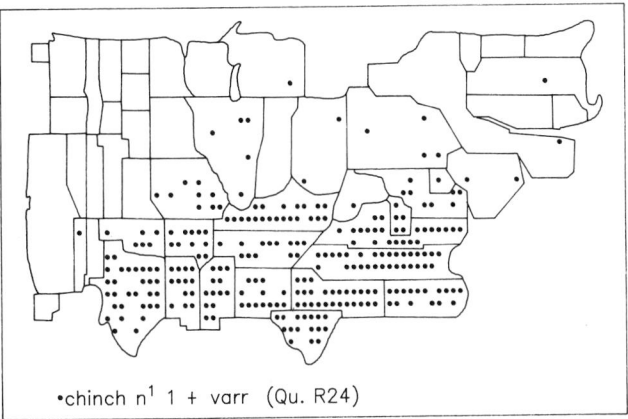

•chinch n[1] 1 + varr (Qu. R24)

1708 (1865) Cook *Sot-weed Factor* 19 **MD**, But Heat and Chinces rais'd the Sinner, / Most opportunely to his Dinner. **1807** (1935) Janson *Stranger in Amer.* 60 **NEng**, The inhabitants called bed-bugs, *chintzes.* **1844** Kendall *Santa Fé Exped.* 1.327 **KS**, The room we were then occupying, .. being so completely overrun with *chinches* and other vermin, that it was impossible to sleep at night. **1892** *DN* 1.189 **TX**, *Chinche:* chinch-bug, bed-bug *(Cimex lectularius).* Ibid 229 **KY**, *Chinches:* bedbugs . . . "The chinches like to eat .. me up in that hotel." **1902** *DN* 2.231 s**IL**, *Chince* or *chinche* . . . A bed bug. **1903** *DN* 2.309 se**MO**, *Chinch* or *chinch-bug* .. chintz-bug. **1908** *DN* 3.298 e**AL, w**GA**, *Chinch.* **1917** *DN* 4.409 w**NC, IL, KY, LA**, *Chinch.* **1923** *DN* 5.203 sw**MO**, *Cheench.* **1947** (1964) Randolph *Ozark Superstitions* 45, Bedbugs—which .. the Ozarker calls "cheenches." **1965–70** *DARE* (Qu. R24, .. *Bedbug*) 248 Infs, **chiefly Sth, S Midl**, Chinch; 23 Infs, **chiefly Sth, S Midl**, Chinch bug; **AR**41, Chinchies; **SC**67, Chinchy bug; **FL**22, **GA**7, Cinch. **1968** Abbey *Desert Solitaire* 31 se**UT**, Watch out for .. chinch bugs.

2 also *chintz bug, cinch ~*: A bug *(Blissus leucopterus)* that is harmful to corn and grain and that smells bad when squashed. Also called **chink bug**

1786 (1925) Washington *Diaries* 3.97 **VA**, Examined the low and sickly looking corn in several parts of this field, and discovered more or less of the Chinch bug on every stalk between the lower blades and it. **1873** Beadle *Undeveloped West* 225 **KS**, The fly is a little troublesome to wheat, but its principal enemy is the chintz bug, so-called here. **1905** *DN* 3.74 nw**AR**, *Chinch-bug* usually means *Blissus leucopterus,* which is harmful to grain. **1965–70** *DARE* (Qu. R30) 22 Infs, **scattered, but esp S Midl**, Chinch (bug); **IN**35, 75, **LA**18, **VA**105, Chinch bug is the same as stink bug; **MN**23, Chinch—smelled if you smashed them; a little yellow on their back; **IL**56, Chinch bug—little, black, 1/8 inch in size, eats corn and wheat; **NY**60, Cinch bug—smells; **NE**3, Chintz bug; **OR**1, Chintz bug—same as pine beetle or stink bug; (QR p125) Inf **GA**54, Chinch bug—gets in roots of grass and kills it. [15 of the 32 Infs mentioned that the bug has an offensive smell.]

3 A body louse *(Pediculus humanus).*

1927 Boston Soc. Nat. Hist. *Proc.* 38.281 **Okefenokee Swamp GA**, One member of the household wanted them [=bats] killed, on the ground that they 'raised chinches.' **1966–69** *DARE* (Qu. R25, .. *A head louse, or body louse*) Infs **FL**4, **MS**53, Chinch; **KY**35, **MS**53, Chinch bug.

4 =sowbug.

1674 Josselyn *Two Voyages* 117 **NEng**, If you chance to break one of the *Bugs* it will stink odiously: they call them *Chinches* or *Woodlice.*

chinch n[2] Also *chince* [OED *chinch* a. and sb.[2], a1300 →1570]
A stingy person, a miser.

1949 *PADS* 11.19 **CO**, *Chinch, chince* [čɪnts] . . . A stingy person. **1966–69** *DARE* (Qu. U33, .. *A stingy person*) Inf **SC**55, Chinch; (Qu. U36a, .. *A person who .. is greedy*) Inf **IN**45, Chinch; (Qu. U36b) Infs **AL**6, **SC**40, Chinch.

chinch n[3] [Alter of *cinch*] **chiefly ePA**
Something easily done; a snap.

1967–68 *DARE* (Qu. KK42a, .. *A person who does something very easily: "For him that would be _____."*) Infs **NY**89, **PA**39, 108, 118, 138, 161, [A] chinch.

chinch v [Alter of **chink** v; cf **chinse** v]
=chink v.

1965–70 *DARE* (Qu. O6, *If a wooden boat is leaking, what do you .. do to stop the leaks?*) 10 Infs, **chiefly lower Missip Valley**, Chinch (it).

chinche See **chinch** n[1] 1

chinchgrass See **chinchweed**

chinching See **chinchy**

chin chopper n

1 See quot 1930. [From a children's tickling rhyme: see quot 1952]

1930 Shoemaker *1300 Words* 11 c**PA Mts** (as of c1900), *Chin-chopper* —A cunning, lovable little brother. [**1952** Brown *NC Folkl.* 1.189 (as of c1928), Eye Winker (touching eye) / Tom tinker (touching other eye) / Nose Dropper (touching nose) / Mouth Eater (touching mouth) / Chin chopper (tickling under chin).]

2 See quot.

1969 Sorden *Lumberjack Lingo* **NEng, Gt Lakes**, *Chin chopper*—Tree that splits in falling.

chinch water n Pronc-spp *chedge water, chench ~*

1966–68 *DARE* (Qu. H74b, .. *Coffee .. very weak*) Inf **GA**1, Chinch [čenč] water; chench = louse, bedbug; **GA**29A, Chedge [čɛj] water.

chinchweed n Also *chinchgrass, cinchgrass* [Prob from its odor]

A low, yellow-flowered plant *(Pectis papposa).* Also called **manzanilla coyote**

1932 Bentley *Spanish Terms* 122, *Chinch weed*—"A low, small, rounded plant, *(Pectis papposa)* vividly green, with bright yellow flowers. It has a strong, rather unpleasant smell. Blooms throughout summer." **1941** Jaeger *Wildflowers* 303 **SW**, *Chinch-weed. Pectis papposa* . . . eastward to Utah and south to Mex. **1941** *Torreya* 41.53, *Pectis papposa* . . . Chinchweed. **1949** Curtin *By the Prophet* 104 **AZ**, *Pectis papposa harv. and gray* . . . Chinchweed. **1967–70** *DARE* (Qu. S21, .. *Weeds*) Infs **KS**8, **KY**34, Chinchweed; (Qu. S9, .. *Grass .. hard to get rid of*) Inf **IN**58, Chinchgrass; (Qu. S8, .. *Wild grass .. in fields*) Inf **SC**67, Cinchgrass.

chinchy n See **chinch** n[1] 1

chinchy adj Infreq *chinching* [**chinch** n[2]] **chiefly Sth, S Midl**
See Map
Stingy, niggardly.

1899 (1912) Green *VA Folk-Speech, Chinching* . . . Miserly; niggardly. **1906** *DN* 3.130 nw**AR**, *Chinchy* . . . Stingy, penurious. **1933** Rawlings *South Moon* 221 **FL**, Put a chinchy couple o' buckets o' fresh meal in each barrel, please sir. **1949** [see *chintzy* adj[1]]. **1950** *PADS* 14.19 **SC**, *Chinchy.* **1960** Williams *Walk Egypt* 69 **GA**, She's chinchy and a cheat. **1962** Atwood *Vocab. TX* 72, *Stingy* . . . *Chinchy* is also still in use, principally among older informants. **1965–70** *DARE* (Qu. U36b, .. *Words .. to describe a person who saves in a mean way or is greedy in money matters*) 33 Infs, **chiefly Sth, S Midl, esp SC**, Chinchy [čɪnči, -ɪ]; (Qu. U33, .. *A stingy person*) Infs **DC**11, **NC**16, **TX**42, Chinchy; **NM**8, Chinchy cuss; (Qu. U34, .. *"Stingy"*) Infs **AR**40, **NM**8, Chinchy; (Qu. U35, .. *Thrifty but not in a complimentary way*) Inf **NC**16, Chinchy; (Qu. U17, .. *A person who doesn't pay his bills*) Inf **TX**31, Chinchy. **1970** Tarpley *Blinky* 240 ne**TX**, A person who is too careful with his money is _____ . . . [6 of 200 infs] chinchy.

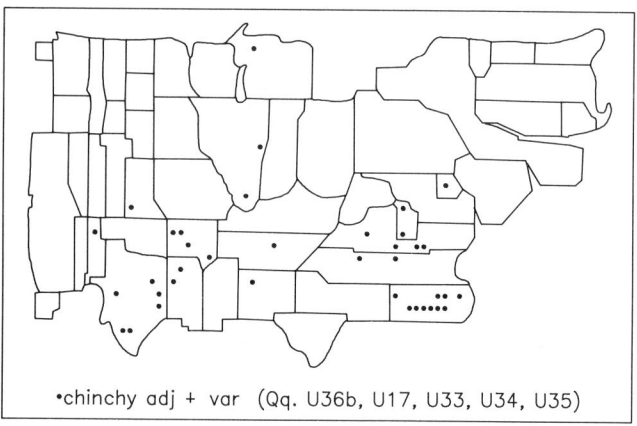

•chinchy adj + var (Qq. U36b, U17, U33, U34, U35)

chinckapin, chincomen, chincopin See **chinquapin** A
chincy See **chintzy** adj[1]
chinded See **-ed** adj-forming suff
chin dropper n Cf **eye-drop** 1

c**1970** Wiersma *Marbles Terms* **MI**, *Chin-dropper* . . . In marble play: a shot in which the marble falls onto the playing area from chin height.

chine, chinee n[1] See **china** A

Chinee n[2], adj Also sp *Chiney* [Back-formation from *Chinese,* understood as a pl] **esp West and Nth** See also **heathen Chinee**
Chinese.

1890 *Congressional Record* 7 June 5791/2 **PA**, It may be claimed that this bill .. has something of a Heathen Chinee Flavor about it and that it is framed with "intent to deceive." **1907** Mulford *Bar-20* 216 **West**, Who owns a mosaic bronch, Chinee flag on th' near side, Skillet brand? **1910** Hart *Vigilante Girl* 375 n**CA**, Think of feeding two train-loads all to once—with one force of girls and one Chiney cook. **1911** *DN* 3.549 **NE**, Folk-etymological singulars .. common . . . Chinee, Portugee.

1961 Adams *Old-Time Cowhand* 22 **West,** Bein' beat at his own game made 'im feel like he might as well been talkin' Chinee to a pack mule. **1965–70** *DARE* (Qu. H65, *Foreign foods*) Inf **NY**61, Chinee food; (Qu. Q7, . . *Game birds*) Infs **OR**13, **WA**30, Chinee pheasant; (Qu. T9) Inf **CA**120, Chinee locust; (Qu. T11) Inf **OK**52, Chinee elm; (Qu. X21c) Inf **NY**60, Round eyes like a Chinee; (Qu. HH28, . . *Chinese*) Infs **NV**7, **NY**60, Chinee; **CT**10, Heathen Chinee. **1968** *DARE* FW Addit **PA**88, 90, 91, *Chinee*—a Chinese.

Chinee pheasant See **Chinese pheasant**

Chinese apple n

A pomegranate *(Punica granatum).*

1980 *DARE* File **NYC** (as of 1948), Chinese apple = pomegranate.

Chinese artichoke n

An introduced **hedgenettle** (here: *Stachys sieboldi*).

1902 Bailey *Cyclop. Horticulture* 4.1714/1 Chorogi. Chinese or Japanese Artichoke. Knotroot. **1942** Amer. Joint Comm. Horticult. Nomenclature *Std. Plant Names* 24, Chinese A[rtichoke]; Japanese A[rtichoke] . . . Betony, . . *Stachys sieboldi.* **1950** Gray–Fernald *Manual of Botany* 1233, *Stachys sieboldii . . Japanese* or *Chinese Artichoke.* **1966** *DARE* (Qu. S21, . . *Weeds*) Inf **MS**8, Chinese artichoke. **1971** GA Dept. Ag. *Farmers Market Bulletin* 6 Jan 8/2, I have chinese artichoke in my orchard that I would like to get rid of.

Chinese bean n

1969 *DARE* (Qu. I16, *The large, flat beans that are not eaten in the pod*) Inf **CA**170, Chinese bean—flat, yellowish; (Qu. I20, . . *Beans*) Inf **CA**113, Chinese beans—all our first vegetable growers were Chinese—these beans are *long* green beans.

Chinese berry n

The fruit of the **Chinaberry.**

1864 (1938) Cate *Two Soldiers* 27, To a half bushel of Chinese berries, picked from the stems, add three gallons of water.

Chinese checks n [check n[1] **3**]

The game of Chinese checkers.

1966 *DARE* (Qu. EE40, . . *Table games*) Inf **FL**37, Chinese checks.

Chinese choppers See **china B2**

Chinese clover n

=**chickweed 1b.**

1959 Carleton *Index Herb. Plants* 26, Chinese clover: Cerastium (v).

Chinese croaker n Also *China croaker* **Pacific coast**

1 =**red roncador 1.**

1946 LaMonte *N. Amer. Game Fishes* 82, *Black Croaker* . . . Names: Red Roncador, Chinese Croaker. **1960** Amer. Fisheries Soc. *List Fishes* 55, Croaker, china—see croaker, black; sargo.

2 =**sargo 2.**

1960 [see **1** above].

Chinese date n

=**jujube.**

1939 FWP *Guide FL* 327, Rarer fruits include . . red berrylike Chinese dates; sticky Chinese limes. **1960** Vines *Trees SW* 700, *Ziziphus jujuba . . .* The tree is also known as the Chinese Date. It is popular with the Chinese and as many as 400 varieties have been cultivated by them.

Chinese fire drill n

1 A scene of great confusion; a chaotic situation.

1961 in 1962 *Western Folkl.* 21.29 **CA,** He . . likened it [=the administration of President Kennedy] to a 'Chinese fire drill' and said orders are being issued and countermanded with such frequency that only 'chaos and confusion' remain. **1962** *AmSp* 37.267 **sCA** [Among traffic policemen], *Chinese fire drill* . . . An accident scene of great confusion, such as a school bus or cattle truck upset. **1969** *DARE* Tape **TX**68, With me and my cousin it's kind of like a Chinese fire drill. **1981** *DARE* File **nwKS** (as of 1950s–60s), It looked like a Chinese fire drill.

2 See quots.

1976 *DARE* File **sID** (as of early 1960s), During every homecoming parade we'd have Chinese fire drills. At a stoplight, everyone in the car would jump out, run around the car, and hop in again before the light turned green. **1981** *NYT Mag.* 20 Sept 18 **NYC** (as of late 1960s), "Chinese fire drill" . . . a collegiate prank in which a group of students would jump out of a car as it stopped for a red light, run around the car several times and jump back in just as the light turned to green. **1983**

NADS Letters **Brooklyn NY,** What I learned forty or more years ago to be known as a "Chinese fire-drill" (when a car stops at a red light and the driver and the passengers get out and run around the car to exchange places).

Chinese goose n

=**white-fronted goose.**

1957 *AmSp* 32.183 **CA,** Chinese goose—White-fronted goose.

‡**Chinese grits** n *joc*

Rice.

1967 Will *Dredgeman* 107 **FL,** There was an ample sufficiency of rice. That is, if you [the cook] weren't too sensitive to such remarks as, "What the hell do you think we are, Chinks? Nobody didn't order no Chinese grits!"

Chinese handball n

A version of handball played outdoors.

1970 *DARE* (Qu. EE33, . . *Outdoor games*) Inf **NY**241, King-queen or Chinese handball—each player gets a cement block section of the sidewalk. First is king, then queen, jack, etc. **1981** *Verbatim Letters* **NYC** (as of 1930s), Chinese Handball was played against any convenient wall and was, in all respects the same game as conventional handball, except that the ball was required to bounce on the ground before it hit the wall.

Chinese houses n Also *Chinese temples* **West**

=**blue-eyed Mary 1,** esp *Collinsia heterophylla.*

1915 (1926) Armstrong *Western Wild Flowers* 488, *Chinese Houses—Collinsia bicolor . . .* The arrangement of the flowers is somewhat suggestive of the many stories of a Chinese pagoda and the plant is common. **1920** Rice *Calif. Wild Flowers* 113 *(DA),* Very popular are the little Chinese Houses, *Collinsia bicolor . .* quite common throughout California. **1923** Davidson–Moxley *Flora S. CA* 327, *C. bicolor . . .* Chinese Temples. Common in foothills and shady canyons. April. **1969** *DARE* (Qu. S26e, . . *Wildflowers*) Inf **CA**140, Chinese house [sic] —comes up on spikelet, light purple with white throat, sort of like wild snapdragon.

Chinese itch See **Chinese rot**

Chinese jump rope n

See quot 1980.

1966 *S. Folkl. Qrly.* 30.256 **KS, IA,** [Title:] *Chinese Jumprope* [Detailed description follows]. **1968** *DARE* (Qu. EE33, . . *Outdoor games*) Inf **UT**10, Chinese jump rope. **1980** *DARE* File **swMI,** Chinese jump rope: two players stand apart facing each other with an elastic jump rope looped around their legs. A third player must jump in and out of the rope in various fashions.

Chinese lantern n

1 A ground cherry, esp *Physalis alkekengi.* [From the appearance of the inflated capsule enclosing the berry]

1901 Bailey *Cyclop. Horticulture* 3.1320/2, *P[hysalis] Alkekéngi,* var. *Franchéti,* Hort.). Chinese Lantern Plant. **1948** Stevens *KS Wild Flowers* 167, *Plains Chinese-lantern . . .* Berry enclosed in the bladdery-inflated calyx. **1966** *DARE* Wildfl QR Pl.37a (Wills–Irwin) Inf **TX**34, Chinese lantern.

2 =**desert fivespot.**

1941 Jaeger *Wildflowers* 142 **Desert SW,** Desert five-spot, Lantern flower, Chinese lantern. *Malvastrum rotundifolium.* **1980** Hogan *Quartzsite* 205 **AZ,** He picked some five-spot Chinese lanterns, rose-pink flowers with a dark red spot hidden at the inner base of each of their five petals.

Chinese lettuce See **China lettuce 1**

Chinese lily See **China lily**

Chinese mallard n **Pacific**

=**coot n[1] 1.**

1918 Grinnell *Game Birds CA* 313, *Fulica americana . . .* Coot; Chinese Mallard. **1953** Jewett *Birds WA* 238, *Northern American Coot . . .* Other names: . . Chinese Mallard. **1956** *AmSp* 31.181 **CA,** Chinese mallard—American coot.

Chinese marbles n

The game of Chinese checkers.

1967–69 *DARE* (Qu. DD37, . . *Table games*) Infs **CO**15, **IA**41, **IL**73, **MO**25, Chinese marbles.

Chinese mustard n

An Asiatic mustard (*Brassica* spp).

    1967 *DARE* (Qu. I28b, . . *Greens . . cooked*) Inf **LA6**, Chinese mustard—light-colored instead of dark.

Chinese onion n

An **arrowhead 1** (here: *Sagittaria latifolia*).

    1913 *Torreya* 13.227, *Sagittaria latifolia* . . . is known as Chinese onion, and muskrat potato at Oshkosh, Wis.

Chinese orange n

=**Osage orange**.

    1969 *DARE* (Qu. T13, . . *Osage orange*) Inf **RI**17, Chinese orange.

Chinese pheasant n Also *China pheasant, Chinee ~, Chinese ringneck, Chinese rooster* **chiefly Nth, esp OR, WA** Also called **Chinaman 2, Chink n³ 2**

=**ring-necked pheasant**.

    1898 (1900) Davie *Nests N. Amer. Birds* 180, It is known by two other names: Chinese and Mongolian Pheasant. **1927** Forbush *Birds MA* 2.15, Ring-necked Pheasant. Other names: . . Chinese Ring-neck. **1946** Hausman *Eastern Birds* 224, Chinese Pheasant, Chinese Ringneck, Oregon Pheasant. **1957** *AmSp* 32.184 **NJ**, Chinese rooster—Common pheasant. **1965–70** *DARE* (Qu. Q7, . . *Game birds*) Infs **MN**12, 29, **OR**15, **WA**2, 11, 15, 24, 28, Chinese pheasant; **OR**4, 5, China pheasant; **OR**13, **WA**30, Chinee pheasant; (Qu. K76, . . *Poultry raised around here*) Inf **OR**2, China pheasants. **1967** *DARE* FW Addit **WA**, *Chinese pheasant, Chink,* or *China pheasant*—brought in from China, 16–18 inches high, about 2½ lbs. Red cone [sic—?for *comb*] and red breast and neck feathers. Honks like a goose. Good eating.

Chinese rose See **China rose**

Chinese rot n Also *Chinese itch*

See quots.

    1938 Hertzler *Horse & Buggy Dr.* 52, We learned . . about diseases one never has seen, such as yaws, beriberi and Chinese itch. **1968–69** *DARE* (Qu. BB24, . . *A rash that comes out suddenly*) Inf **NJ**21, Chinese rot; (Qu. BB28, . . *Imaginary diseases*) Inf **NJ**54, Chinese rot.

Chinese school n

A children's game: see quot 1981.

    1966–70 *DARE* (Qu. EE33, . . *Outdoor games*) Infs **MS**52, **WV**21, Chinese school; **MA**128, Chinese school has just begun. No more laughing no more fun. If you show your teeth or tongue you will get a penalty. The penalty of beating is optional. **1981** *Verbatim Letters* se**KS**, Chinese school—I played this game from 1925–27 when living in Independence, Kansas. A set of steps (usually to the front or back porch) was the scene. Any number could play but was best with from four to six players. One was "it." Each of the steps represented a grade. "It" held a small object, usually a small stone, in a closed fist and the "student" chose one or the other of the fists extended by "it". If the choice was correct, a grade advance was the reward. An empty fist was a "didn't pass". A player could move up a grade, out of turn, if in so doing "it" didn't catch him / her. If caught, the player returned to the first grade to start over. The player completing all grades first was the winner and became the next "it". *Ibid,* I played Chinese School a lot when growing up in Southern Kansas and my sister played it in Nebraska but we may just have taken the knowledge of the game to Nebraska with us. I know it was a great hit at my children's birthday parties in Texas, mainly because a two-story house was a novelty. In Kansas, however, it was always played outdoors. All the children sit on the bottom step. One person is "It" and has a pebble in a hand. The child is simply to guess which hand the pebble is in (touching the hand seems part of it.) If they guess correctly, they go up a step. If wrong, they are out of the game. The winner, of course, is the person who makes it all the way to the top first. Thinking back, it must be dreadfully dull for the people who drop out early. But the game was essential at almost any outdoor activity . . I kind of think that when you got down to two people, it was like a spelling bee. If both guessed wrong, the game went on until one guessed right.

Chinese spinner n

A type of marble; see quot.

    1962 *PADS* 37.1 c**KS**, *Chinese spinner*. A cat eye in which the design did not open out into four blades in the manufacturing process but remains a single wisp of color in the center of the marble. So called because of a fancied resemblance to a Chinaman's eye.

Chinese sumac n Also sp *~ sumach*

=**tree of heaven**.

    1868 (1870) Gray *Field Botany* 83, *Chinese Sumach* . . . is a common shade tree, tall, of rapid growth. **1960** Vines *Trees SW* 600, Vernacular names for the tree are . . Chinese Sumac . . and Devil's Walkingstick.

Chinese tag n

A children's game; see quot 1916.

    1916 Seton *Woodcraft Manual Girls* 45, *Chinese Tag*—Is like the regular game of tag with this difference; the one who is tagged must keep her hand on that part which was hit when she was tagged thus making only one free arm. **1923** Acker *400 Games* 93, Chinese Tag. **1953** Brewster *Amer. Nonsinging Games* 63 **IN**, *Chinese Tag.* **1967–69** *DARE* (QR p 229) Inf **CO**14, Chinese tag—the individual tagged had to hold the place tagged while he tried to tag the next person; (Qu. EE33, . . *Outdoor games*) Inf **RI**3, Chinese tag.

Chinese tallow tree n

A **tallow tree** (here: *Sapium sebiferum*).

    1900 Lyons *Plant Names* 33, *S[apium] sebiferum* . . . Chinese Tallow-tree. **1940** FWP *Guide TX* 315, Along the streets are . . Chinese tallow, camphor and eucalyptus trees. **1979** Little *Checklist U.S. Trees* 271, Chinese tallowtree. Planted as an ornamental and naturalized in Coastal Plain [of the southeastern US] . . . Native of China.

Chinese temples See **Chinese houses**

Chinese thistle n

A **cockleburr 1** (here: *Xanthium spinosum*).

    1898 *Jrl. Amer. Folkl.* 11.230, *Xanthium spinosum* . . Chinese thistle. **1956** St. John *Flora SE WA* 476, *Xanthium spinosum* . . Chinese Thistle.

Chinese tree of heaven n

=**tree of heaven**.

    1861 Wood *Class-Book* 283, *Ailanthus* . . . Chinese "Tree-of-Heaven." . . The rapid growth of this tree is its only recommendation as a tenant of our parks. **1968** *DARE* (Qu. T16, . . *Trees*) Inf **CA**87, Chinese tree of heaven, imported 100 years ago. **1979** Little *Checklist U.S. Trees* 47.

Chinese umbrella n Also *umbrella Chinatree*

Either the Chinese parasol tree *(Firmiana simplex)* or the **Chinaberry 1**.

    1897 Sudworth *Arborescent Flora* 270, *Melia azedarach umbraculifera* . . Umbrella China-tree. **1967–68** *DARE* (Qu. T16, . . *Trees*) Inf **CA**12, Chinese umbrella; **CA**79, Umbrella trees—Texas umbrella, Chinese umbrella.

Chinese yam n

A yam (here: *Dioscorea batatas*) often cultivated as an ornamental. Also called **cinnamon vine 1**

    1868 (1870) Gray *Field Botany* 336, *Chinese Yam*: cult. from China and Japan, for ornament, or for its very deep and long farinaceous roots. **1876** Hobbs *Bot. Hdbk.* 134, Yam, Chinese, Dioscorea Batatas. **1952** Strausbaugh–Core *Flora WV* 250, *Chinese Yam* . . . often cultivated in West Virginia and locally established. **1967** Braun *Monocotyledoneae* 392, *Chinese Yam* . . . An occasional escape, . . formerly sometimes planted, perhaps because of the odd potato-like tubers borne in leaf-axils.

chiney n¹ See **china A**

Chiney n² See **Chinee n²**

chinfest n [chin n + fest]

A gathering at which there is much talk, a gabfest.

    1940 *AmSp* 15.204 [Theater jargon], *Chin-fest.* A conference. **1969** *DARE* (Qu. KK12, *A meeting where there's a lot of talking*) Infs **CT**37, **GA**72, **NY**205, Chinfest.

chin fly n

A botfly (*Gastrophilus nasalis*). Also called **throat bot**

    1866 Carpenter *Six Months* 129 **KY**, You were brought up on a farm, were you not? Then you know what a *chin fly* is. **1928** Metcalf–Flint *Destructive & Useful Insects* 776, There are three kinds of botflies that molest horses in this country. They are known as the common horse botfly, the chin fly or throat bot, and the nose or lip bot.

ching-chang Chinese, ching-ching Chinaman See **Chink n³ 1**

chin-happy See **happy** adj

chinie See **china** A

chin jaw n
Among loggers: =**chin** n.
1942 *AmSp* 17.221 **Nth** [Lumbering], Chinjaw. Small talk; social conversation; its nearest literary equivalent may be 'palaver.' **1968** Adams *Western Words, Chin jaw*—The logger's term for small talk; social conversation.

chink v chiefly **Sth, S Midl** See Map Cf **chinch** v, **chinse**
To fill up the chinks or cracks of; to caulk; hence vbl n *chinking* the act of filling up cracks or interstices.
1748 in 1912 Augusta Co. VA *Chronicles* 1.35, Presentment vs. Court House, . . built of logs, chinked with mud, but cracks 4 to 5 inches wide. **1791** in 1930 Jillson *Dark & Bloody* 111 **KY**, The walls . . are chinked with white clay. **1824** Blane *Excursion* 181 **IL**, This operation is called *chinking;* and before it has been performed, the cabin, in winter, would be uninhabited from the cold, were it not for the great fire that is always kept up. **1829** Flint *George Mason* 10 **MS** (as of 1816), They knew infinitely better than he did how to "daub and chink" a log cabin. **1844** Kendall *Santa Fé Exped.* 1.25 **TX**, Our log-house quarters, however, were closely "chinked and daubed." **1904** *DN* 2.417 **nwAR**, *Chink up . . .* To fill (chinks). **1923** *DN* 5.234 **swWI**, *Chink-and-daub . . .* Of log construction, chinked with wood and daubed with mud or plaster. **1961** Adams *Old-Time Cowhand* 28 **West**, There wasn't 'nough grass left to chink 'tween the ribs of a sandfly. **1965–70** *DARE* (Qu. O6, *If a wooden boat is leaking . . to stop the leaks*) 20 Infs, **chiefly Sth**, Chink (it); **KY56, MS16, SC43**, Chink it up; **GA1**, Chink 'em; **MI65**, Chink it with calking; **GA22**, Chink the crack. [17 of 25 Infs grade school educ or less]

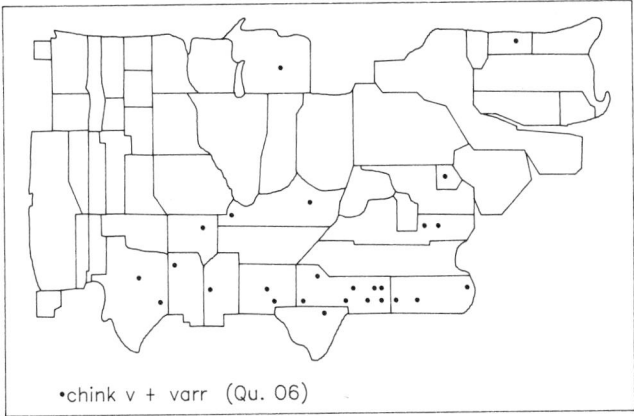

•chink v + varr (Qu. O6)

chink n[1], also attrib Freq in phrr with *daub(ing)* Cf **chinking**
Material used to fill cracks or spaces, esp in log houses.
1804 (1965) Ordway *Jrls.* 166 **ND**, We raised the roof of the meat & Smoak house bringing it up with Timber cross drawing in, So as to answer with chinks & dobbing. **1881** Pierson *In the Brush* 51 **Missip Valley**, The large openings between the logs had been filled with "chink and daubing." **1923** *DN* 5.234 **swWI**, *Chink-and-daub . . .* Of log construction, chinked with wood and daubed with mud or plaster. "He's got a chink-an'-daub cabin up thar in the woods." **1944** Blair *Tall Tale America* 66 **TN**, In the spring, when the dogwood came out, they'd knock away the chinks so that light and air could come into the cabin. **1967** *DARE* (Qu. D12, *The part that's put on in winter around an outside door to give extra protection from the cold*) Inf **IA8**, Chink.

chink n[2] [Echoic of the sound of coins; *OED* 1573 →]
Money.
1834 Crockett *Narrative* 20, If all the hills about there were pure chink, and all belonged to me, I would give them if I could just talk to her. **1844** Stephens *High Life in NY* 1.231 **CT**, I raly think they ought to shell out more chink than they du for my letters. **1909** *DN* 3.394 **nwAR**, *Chink, the . . .* Money. **1912** *DN* 3.573 **wIN**, *Chink . . .* Money. "Possibly he has bought it; he has the chink." **1918** Lomax *Cowboy Songs* 191, Such a slam against my talent made me hotter than a mink, / And I swore that I would ride him for amusement or for chink. **1966** *DARE* (Qu. U37, . . *Somebody who has plenty of money*) Inf **AR40**, Lousy with the chink.

chink n[3], often cap [Alter and abbr of Chinese *ching-ching,* a courteous exclam]
1 also *Chinkie* (*OEDS* 1879 →), *ching-chang* Chinese, *ching-ching* Chinaman, *chink(y)-chink(y)* Chinaman: A Chinese person. *usu considered derog*
1901 *Munsey's Mag.* 24.536 (*DAE*), The leader suggested the 'chink,' and to the one Chinese laundry . . . the little band departed. **1907** Mulford *Bar-20* 180 **West**, Yu cross-eyed lump of hypocrisy! . . . Yu whitewashed Chink, yu. **1912** Wason *Friar Tuck* 401, Just when I made sure it was the Chink, he moved and sat up. **1930** Williams *Logger-Talk* 15 **Pacific NW**, *Chink:* A Chinaman. **1949** *AmSp* 24.156, *Chink* for Chinese. **1959** Mailer *Advt. for Myself* 412, A certain Chinkie. **1961** Adams *Old-Time Cowhand* 185 **West**, He follered his old friend to the Chink's. **1964** *PADS* 42.30–31 [Racial slurs], Oriental . . . Chink [12 responses]. **1965–70** *DARE* (Qu. HH28, . . *People of foreign background*) 269 Infs, **scattered**, Chink; **DC3**, Chink-chink Chinaman; **KY50**, Chinkie; **MA28**, Chinky-chinky Chinaman; **AL8**, Ching-chang Chinese. **1966** *DARE* Tape **AL6**, [Counting-out rhyme:] Chink chink Chinaman, how you sell your geese, Chink chink Chinaman, fifty cents a piece. Chink chink Chinaman that's too dear, Chink chink Chinaman get out of here. **1981** Pederson *LAGS Urban Material*, 1 inf, **Tampa FL**, Ching, ching, Chinaman / Eats dead rats / Doesn't save none for the poor Tom cats; 1 inf, **St. Louis MO** (as of 1935–40), Ching, ching, Chinaman / Eats dead rats / Chews them for gingersnaps.
2 also *chinker:* =**ring-necked pheasant. Nth, esp NW**
1940 Gabrielson *Birds OR* 226, The *Ring-necked Pheasant,* China Pheasant, Denny Pheasant, or Chink, was first shipped from China to Oregon in 1880. **1957** *AmSp* 32.184 **IA, OH, OR, MN, MT, WI**, Chink—Common pheasant. **1966** *Okanogan Independent* (WA) 1 Dec 4/3, *Chinks Aplenty in Basin Now . . .* Pheasants may be hunted from now until December 31. **1966–67** *DARE* (Qu. Q7, . . *Game birds*) Infs **ID5, MT4**, Chink(s); **MT3**, Chinks—Chinese [pheasants]; **WA12**, Chink—ring-necked pheasant; **WA22**, Chinker. **1967** *DARE* FW Addit **WA**, Chinese pheasant, Chink, or China pheasant.
3 =**china** B1.
1950 *WELS* (Marbles: small ones) 1 Inf, **ceWI**, Chinks. **1958** *PADS* 29.31 **WI**, *Chink . . .* A small marble. **1966** *DARE* (Qu. EE6c, *Cheap marbles*) Inf **MT1**, Chinks. **1971** Bright *Word Geog. CA & NV* 116, Chinks 2 [responses].

chinkaderos See **chigaderos**

chinkapen, chinkapin See **chinquapin** A

chink bug n [*OED: "Chink* [sb.4], obs. form of *chinch"*]
=**chinch** n[1] 2.
1969 *DARE* (Qu. R30, . . *Beetles*) Inf **TX59**, Chink bug.

chink-chink Chinaman See **chink** n[3] 1

chinker n[1] See **chink** n[3] 2

chinker n[2] [Prob from *Chincoteague Island* in Chesapeake Bay]
A wild horse; see quots.
1968 *DARE* (Qu. K42, *A horse that is rough, wild, or dangerous*) Inf **CT17**, Chinker ['čɪŋkər]—wild horses around here; you try to sell them quickly. [**1981** *NADS Letters* **eVA** [Answering query about *chinker*], Once again about the ponies on Chincoteague. Although I don't know when the round-ups began, the ponies have supposedly been on the Island for centuries. The annual roundup is in July and is put on by the Assateague fire department—the herd is forced to swim the channel between the 2 islands. The young weaned colts and fillies are sold at auction as pets; the proceeds of the sales ($200–$300 each) go to the Fire Dept. The remaining ponies are returned to Chincoteague. The sold ponies go all over the country.]

chinkerings n Cf *DS* AA27
Menstruation.
1930 Shoemaker *1300 Words* 9 **cPA Mts** (as of c1900), Chinkerings—Feminine sickness.

chinkeyben See **chinquapin** A

Chinkie See **chink** n[3] 1

chinking n [**chink** v]
1 Material used to fill up cracks or spaces, esp of log houses; filling, padding.
1791 in 1930 Jillson *Dark & Bloody* 107 **OH**, It has a dirt floor pounded hard and no chinking in the walls. **1843** (1916) Hall *New Purchase* 52

IN, The interstices of the log-wall were "chinked"—the "chinking" being large chips and small slabs dipping like strata of rocks in geology; and then on the chinking was the "daubing"—viz. a quant. suff. of yellow clay ferociously splashed in soft by the hand of the architect, and then left to harden at its leisure. **1856** (1862) Colt *Went to KS* 69, The rain had dissolved our mud chinking. **1894** *DN* 1.329 **NJ.** **1904** *DN* 2.417 **nwAR.** **1912** Wason *Friar Tuck* 238, We had hard work thawin' out the clay for chinkin', an' we did n't get the cabin as tight as we'd 'a' liked. **1931** Randolph *Ozarks* 24, The spaces between the logs were filled with "chinkin'," which consisted of sticks or stones set in clay, or in a mixture of clay and moss. **1960** Hall *Smoky Mt. Folks* 59, *Chinkin':* sticks and mud used to stop up cracks between logs. **1967** *DARE* (Qu. D12, *The part that's put on in winter around an outside door to give extra protection from the cold*) Inf **CO**7, Chinking.
2 See **chink** v.

chinking moss n
=**Spanish moss 1.**
    1951 *PADS* 15.28 **TX,** *Dendropogon usneoides* . . . Chinkin' moss . . . With mud it was used in chinking cracks in log-cabin walls.

chinkmunk See **chipmunk**

chinkopen, chinkopin See **chinquapin A**

chinks n
1 =**wintergreen 2.** Cf **chickenberry 1**
    1892 *Jrl. Amer. Folkl.* 5.100, *Gaultheria procumbens,* . . jinks or chinks. N.H.; Mass. . . young chinks. Mason, N.H. **1900** Lyons *Plant Names* 169, *Gaultheria procumbens* . . Chinks. **1930** Sievers *Amer. Med. Plants* 63, *Wintergreen* . . Other common names . . . chinks. **1959** Carleton *Index Herb. Plants* 27, *Chinks:* Gaultheria procumbens.
2 See **chigaderos.**

chink sparrow n
Perh an **English sparrow.**
    1966–69 *DARE* (Qu. Q22, . . *The common sparrow*) Infs **MS**47, **NC**64, **NY**183, Chink sparrow.

chink vine n Cf **chinks 1**
Perh a **wintergreen 2** (here: *Gaultheria procumbens*).
    1929 Sale *Specialist* 7, Down through memry; puncheon floors / Outside latch an' friendly doors; / Chink vines, too, an' garden sass / All mixed up with hollyhocks.

chinky adj [Prob alter of **chintzy** adj¹ **1** or **chinchy** adj¹]
    1969 *DARE* (Qu. U36b, . . *A person who saves in a mean way or is greedy in money matters*) Inf **KY**37, Chinky.

chinkyberry n [Var of **Chinaberry 1**]
    1968 *DARE* (Qu. I44, . . *Berries . . wild*) Inf **GA**23, Chinkyberries.

chinky-chinky Chinaman See **chink** n³ **1**

chinkypen, chinkypin See **chinquapin A**

chinky-tin eye See **chinquapin eye**

chin music n [**chin** n]
Incessant, idle talk; foolish, boastful talk; angry words.
    1836 Hildreth *Dragoon Campaigns* 1.26, He was . . a thorough-bred Kentuckian, full of *chin music,* as the species of loquacity which he possessed is termed. **1872** Twain *Roughing It* 332 **NV,** The thing I'm on now is to roust out somebody to jerk a little chin-music for us and waltz him through handsome. **1897** *KS Univ. Qrly.* 6.86 **neKS.** **1915** *DN* 4.211. **1919** *DN* 5.64 **NM.** **1927** *AmSp* 2.350 **WV,** *Chin music* . . foolish or senseless talk. **1929** *AmSp* 5.121 **ME.** **1939** FWP *ID Lore* 241, *Chin music*—incessant (and usually empty) talk. **1951** *PADS* 15.53 **IN.** **1966–69** *DARE* (Qu. Y12a, *A fight between two people, mostly with words*) Infs **ME**5, **MA**74, Chin music; (Qu. II15, . . *Stop and talk a while*) Inf **GA**72, Let's trade chin music; [(Qu. X9, . . *A person's mouth*) Inf **GA**72, Chin music.] **1967** *DARE* FW Addit **TN**22, They like to hear their own chin music (said of people who like to hear themselves talk).

chinnery See **chenier 2**

chinning vbl n, ppl adj See **chin** v

chinning the moon phr
    1944 Adams *Western Words, Chinning the moon*—Said of a horse which bucks high, or stands on his hind feet and paws the air.

chinny adj [**chin** v] *?obs*
Talkative.

1884 Hay *Bread-Winners* 100 **NY,** I forgot all about the old lady, though she was more chinny than the young one.

chinny v Also *chinny up* [Var of **shinny**]
    1966–70 *DARE* (Qu. EE36, *To climb the trunk of a tree by holding on with your legs while you pull yourself up with your hands*) Infs **IL**130, **KS**13, Chinny up; (Qu. OO10a, . . *Climbing trees*) Inf **NJ**21, Chinny.

chinny n See **china A**

chinny-chin-chin n [From the children's story "Three Little Pigs"]
In phr *not by the hair of my chinny-chin-chin* and varr: No, not at all, by no means.
    1965–69 *DARE* (Qu. KK55a, *To deny something very firmly:* "No, not by a _____.") Infs **AZ**1, **CA**72, (Hair of my) chinny-chin-chin; (Qu. KK55b, . . "*Not on your* _____.") Infs **IL**11, **MS**64, Chinny-chin-chin; (Qu. KK55c) Infs **ID**5, **IN**45, Not by the hair on my (*or* of your) chinny-chin-chin.

chinograss n Also *chino grama*
A **grama grass** (*Bouteloua ramosa*).
    1930 Dobie *Coronado* 158 **TX,** It is a land of mountain, canyon, and mesa grown over with greasewood, coarse chino grass, dagger, and thorned brush. **1970** Correll *Plants TX* 246, *Bouteloua ramosa* . . Chino grama, chinograss.

chinook n, also attrib, often cap Usu |ʃɪˈnʊk|, also |ʃə-, čɪ-, čə-, -ˈnʊk| **chiefly NW**
A Forms.
    1938 *AmSp* 13.177 **ID,** *Chinook* . . . [ʃɪˈnʊk] is the most frequent pronunciation, although [čɪˈnʊk] is occasionally heard; the older inhabitants of the Northwest generally pronounce it [čɪˈnuːk], which is a close reproduction . . of the Indian pronunciation. **1962** *AmSp* 37.74, *Chinook* /šəˈnuk/. The pronunciation with initial /č/ appears to be gaining headway, especially among younger speakers.
B Senses.
1 usu cap: A trade jargon, compounded from the Chinook and other Indian languages with English and French elements. [*DCan* 1833 →]
    1855 Schoolcraft *Indian Tribes U.S.* 5.548, A jargon of Indian words in Oregon and Washington, mixed with English, French, and Spanish . . . called the *Chinook Jargon.* **1886** Poore *Reminiscences* 2.110, Finally an officer who had served on the Pacific coast recognized it as "Chinook," a compound of the English, Chinese, and Indian languages used by the whites in trading with Chinook Indians. **1955** U.S. Arctic Info. Center *Gloss., Chinook* . . . A trade jargon used among Indians of the Northwest Pacific Coast. **1968** Adams *Western Words, Chinook jargon*—A trade language used in the Pacific Northwest, composed of elements from *Chinook* . . Nootka, English, French, and other languages.
2 A warm wind most noticeable in winter which blows from the southwest across the Northwestern US and British Columbia. See Map
    1860 in 1940 *Pacific NW Qrly.* 31.347 **WA,** Pleasant warm weather, high winds from S.W., they call it the Chinook wind. **1878** in 1909 Roe *Army Letters* 190 **MT,** The weather had been bitter cold, but during the night a chinook had blown up, and the air was warm and balmy. **1916** Wilson *Somewhere* 181 **WA,** Society belles flung modesty to the chinook

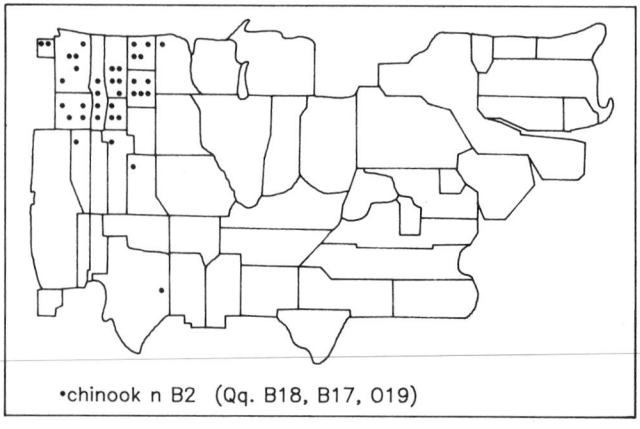

•chinook n B2 (Qq. B18, B17, O19)

wind and took to divided skirts for horseback riding. **1931** *AmSp* 6.230 **neOR,** The 'chinook' is a mild winter wind. **1939** FWP *Guide MT* 413, *Chinook*—A warm southwest wind that removes snow in winter. **1940** OR *Hist. Soc. Hist. Qrly.* 41.103, The highest testimony regarding the Chinook Wind is a hallelujah in the speech of the people, with a coined verb and a folkish, affectionate . . "She chinooks." **1965–70** *DARE* (Qu. B18, . . *Kinds of wind*) 36 Infs, **chiefly NW, Dakotas, AK,** Chinook; (Qu. B17, *A destructive wind that blows straight*) Infs **MT3, WA**12, Chinook; (Qu. O19, . . *Wind* . . *important when you're in a boat*) Inf **TX**35, Chinook [ši'nʊk].

3 See **chinook salmon.**

chinook v [**chinook** n B2]   **NW**
Of the wind: to blow warm in winter.
   1890 in **1940** OR *Hist. Soc. Hist. Qrly.* 41.105, We worked three days getting the sheep to ground part clear of snow; they done well for two days, but it chinooked for a few hours and then froze a heavy crust. **1922** *DN* 5.181 **OR, WA, ID,** *Chinook* . . . To blow warm (an impersonal verb like it rains, from the noun chinook). "We were going for a sleighride, but it chinooked and the snow went off." **1940** [see **chinook** n B2].

chinook bird n [Perh through association with **chinook** winds] **=Bohemian waxwing.**
   1953 Jewett *Birds WA* 536, *Bombycilla garrulus pallidiceps* . . . Other names: . . Chinook Bird; Black-throated Waxwing; Silk-tail.

chinook licorice n Also sp *chinook liquorice* [Perh from the licorice-like smell of the plant]
A lupine (here: *Lupinus littoralis*).
   1893 *Jrl. Amer. Folkl.* 6.140, *Lupinus littoralis,* Chinook liquorice. Washington, D.C. [*DARE* Ed.: prob Washington state rather than Washington, D.C., as the plant does not grow in the east.] **1934** Haskin *Wild Flowers Pacific Coast* 187, *Chinook licorice—Lupinus littoralis* . . . It is found close along the seashore from British Columbia to Northern California.

chinook salmon n Also *chenook, chinook* **chiefly Pacific NW**
An anadromous fish (*Oncorhynchus tshawytscha*) with a comparatively robust body, a dark-blue back usu with numerous small dark spots, silvery below, that is native to the Pacific coast but introduced elsewhere. Also called **blackmouth salmon, California ~, Columbia River ~, fall ~, king ~, quinnat ~, Sacramento ~, saw-kwey, spring salmon, tschawytscha, tyee salmon, winter ~**
   1851 *S.F. Picayune* 15 Oct 2/5 *(DA),* We notice that P.B. Macy & Co. have received a supply of Chenook salmon. **1955** U.S. Arctic Info. Center *Gloss., Chinook* . . . The king salmon. **1962** Salisbury *Quoth the Raven* 240 **AK,** Species of salmon in the North Pacific waters: the *chinook,* or king salmon—sometimes called the tyee. **1967–69** *DARE* (Qu. P1, . . *Freshwater fish*) Infs **AK**1, **MI**108, Chinook (salmon); (Qu. P2, . . *Saltwater fish*) Infs **CA**105, **WA**22, 30, Chinook (salmon); (Qu. P14, . . *Commercial fishing*) Inf **WA**20, Chinook salmon. **1970** WI Acad. *Trans.* 58.292 **WI,** *Oncorhynchus tshawytscha* . . Chinook salmon. **1983** *New York Times* (NY) 17 Apr travel sec 12/2 **British Columbia,** Although there is only one species of Atlantic salmon, there are five Pacific salmon species . . : sockeye (which Americans usually call red), coho (which Americans sometimes call silver), pink (both agree on this one), chum (sometimes called Keta on both sides of the border) and spring (which Americans call chinook or king).

chin pipe n
   1966 *DARE* File **cwWI,** Chin pipe—a [tobacco] pipe with a downcurved stem. "Oh, we always called them chin pipes."

chinquapin n Usu |'čɪŋkəˌpɪn, čɪn-, -kɪ-|; less freq |'čɪŋ-, šɪŋ-, -kɪ-, -pɛn|; rarely |'čɪkpɪn| For var spp see quots [Of Algonquian origin; see quot 1907 and *W3*]
A Forms.
   c1612 (1849) Strachey *VA Britannia* 72 **VA,** They plant their fields and sett their corne, and live after those monthes most of acrons, walnutts, chestnutts, chechinquarnins [sic], and fish. *Ibid* 185, [From 'A Dictionaire of the Indian Language, for the better enabling of such who shalbe thither ymployed':] Chichiquámins, *a kind of graine to eat.* **1615** Hamor *True Discourse* 23 **VA,** So manie fruites, . . many goodly groues of *Chincomen* trees with a huske like unto a Chesnut. **1682** (1836) Ash *Carolina* 64, The Chincopin Tree bears a Nut not unlike the Hazle, the shell is softer. **1710** in **1886** NC *Colonial Rec.* 1.740, The Nottoway

Indian old men being gone to gather Chinkopens. **1724** (1865) Jones *Present State VA* 130, Upon the Leaves of the *Chinckapin* . . I have frequently found a very large Worm not much unlike the Silk-Worm. **1799** *Farmer's Register* (Greensburg, Pa.) 30 Nov (1912 Thornton), She remembered chinquoimines, chesnuts, walnuts, &c. **1819** Dana *Geog. Sketches* 171 **MS,** The soil is . . thickly covered with timber; such as various species of . . hornbeam, chincapin, wildberry. **1849** Bracht *Texas* 64, Chinquepin. **1863** *Times* (London) 16 June 11/5 **VA,** A thick undergrowth of chicopin. **1864** (1922) Jackson *Col.'s Diary* 129 **PA,** I find here . . the chinckapin bush. **1886** *Leslie's Mth. Mag.* 21.150/1, A mess of chinkapins and hickory-nuts. **1899** (1912) Green *VA Folk-Speech,* Chinkapen. **1907** Hodge *Hdbk. Amer. Indians* 1.275, Spelled also chinkapin, chincapin, chinquepin, chinkopin . . . Such forms as chincomen and chechinquamin, found in early writings, make plausible the supposition that a *p* was later substituted for an *m* in the last syllable of the word, which would then represent the widespread Algonquian radical *min,* 'fruit,' 'seed.' The first component of the word, according to Hewitt, is probably cognate with the Delaware *chinqua,* 'large,' 'great.' **1922** Gonzales *Black Border* 293 **sSC, GA coasts** [Gullah glossary], *Chinkypen.* **1942** Hall *Smoky Mt. Speech* 60, *Chinquapin,* which seems always to have the raised vowel: ['tʃɪŋkɪpɪn]. **1947** Dalrymple *Panfish* 84, Chinquapen. **1965–70** *DARE* (Qu. I43) Inf **MS**73, Chickapens; **MS**72, Chinkypens; (Qu. T10) Inf **IN**3, Chinkypin; **CA**150, ['čɪkəˌpɛn]; **MD**37, ['šɪŋkɪˌpɪn]. **1967** *Van Buren Press Argus* (AR) 13 July 4/3, I picked up chinkeybens by the gallon and hickery nuts by the toe [sic] sack full.

B Senses.

1 =**chestnut 1.** **chiefly Sth, S Midl** See Map
   1804 (1930) Dunbar *Jrl.* 244 **MS,** He [the bear] has been feeding luxuriously for some time upon the autumnal fruits of the forest, such as . . chinquapins. **1907** Hodge *Hdbk. Amer. Indians* 1.275, *Chinquapin.* A species of chestnut (*Castanea pumila*) common in the Middle and Southern states. **1931–33** *LANE Worksheets* **CT,** Chinquapin ['čɪŋkəpɪn]. **1940** FWP *Guide TX* 399, Chinquapin, bois d'arc, cedar, and pine trees are abundant. **1965–70** *DARE* (Qu. I43, . . *Nuts* . . *wild*) 101 Infs, **chiefly Sth, S Midl,** Chinquapin(s); **MS**73, Chickapens; **MS**72, Chinkypens; (Qu. T16) Infs **MA**68, **NC**55, **TN**31, **TX**33, **VA**15, Chinquapin; (Qu. T15, . . *Swamp trees*) Inf **OK**1, Chinquapin bush; (Qu. I44, . . *Berries* . . *wild*) Inf **MS**35, Chinquapins.

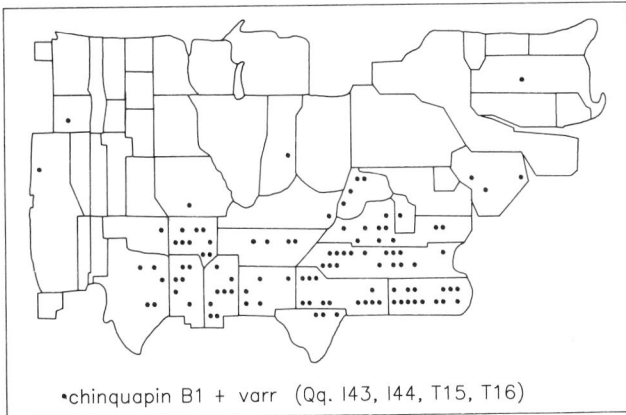

•chinquapin B1 + varr (Qq. I43, I44, T15, T16)

2 See **chinquapin oak 1.**

3 also *golden(leaf) chinquapin, western ~:* A tree or shrub of the genus *Castanopsis.* **chiefly CA, OR**
   1869 [see **chamise 1**]. **1897** Sudworth *Arborescent Flora* 149, *Castanopsis chrysophylla* . . . *Goldenleaf Chinquapin* . . . *Common names.* Chinquapin (Cal., Oreg.) . . . Western Chinquapin. **1907** Hodge *Hdbk. Amer. Indians* 1.275, *Castanopsis chrysophylla* is called western chinquapin and in California and Oregon chinquapin. **1950** Ross *Trees OR* 56, Chinquapin may even have some leaves that suggest the outline of a football, but most Chinquapin leaves have a torpedo shape. *Ibid* 57, Chinquapin has a spiny burr that you won't confuse with the fruit of any other tree . . . Chinquapin leaves . . . are a deep yellow green on top and are coated with minute golden yellow scales underneath. From this yellow under-leaf coating comes the common name Golden Chinquapin. **1984** *DARE* File **cOR,** The chinquapin in the mountains of central Oregon was a low, shrubby bush, but on the coast it could grow to be a large tree.

4 =**water chinquapin.**

1892 *Jrl. Amer. Folkl.* 5.91 **MO,** *Nymphæaceæ. Nelumbium luteum,* chinquapins. **1951** Voss *IL Wild Flowers* 203, American Lotus (Chinquapin . . .) *Nelumbo lutea.* **1966** *DARE* (Qu. S26b, *Wildflowers . . in water or wet places*) Inf AR42, Chinquapins. **1974** (1977) Coon *Useful Plants* 193, *Nelumbium pentapetalum . .* This relative of the famed lotus of the Nile . . is called chinquapin, because of some taste similarity to a "chinquapin chestnut."

5 also *chinquapin perch:* =**crappie.**

1887 Goode *Amer. Fishes* 71, It [*Pomoxys annularis*] is also called "Sac-a-lait" and "Chinquapin Perch" in the Lower Mississippi. **1907** Hodge *Hdbk. Amer. Indians* 1.275, A species of perch (*Pomoxys annularis*), known also as crappie, is called chinquapin or chinkapin perch. **1933** LA Dept. of Conserv. *Fishes* 333, This species, popularity [sic] is very well attested by the variety of names it has been given . . : Crappie, . . Chinquapin Perch. **1946** LaMonte *N. Amer. Game Fishes* 143, *Pomoxis annularis . .* Chinquapin Perch . . and many other localized names. **1947** Dalrymple *Panfish* 84 *(DA),* Here, my friend, are the various names by which you would address that little gamester, the Crappie, depending on where you happened to be at the moment: Bachelor, . . Chinquapen, Chinquapen Perch, Crapet, . . Sand Perch. **1967** *DARE* Tape LA5, They have these . . [čɪkpɪn]. They just little ol' red perch. They don't get as big as the goggle-eyed do.

6 also *chinquapin bream:* An unidentified fish; see quot.

1968 *DARE* (Qu. P1, . . *Freshwater fish . . good to eat*) Infs **LA**15, 26, Chinquapin; **LA**15, Chinquapin breams.

chinquapin eye n Also *chinky-tin eye*

1967–68 *DARE* (Qu. X21c, . . *Eyes . . very round*) Infs **LA**12, **NC**55, Chinquapin eyes; **TX**37, Chinky-tin eyes.

chinquapin oak n Also *dwarf chinquapin oak*

1 also *chinquapin, chinquapin scrub oak:* A timber oak *(Quercus muehlenbergii)* or its acorn. Also called **chestnut oak, chestnut scrub oak, pin oak, rock oak, scrub oak, yellow oak**

1785 Marshall *Arbustrum* 125, *Quercus* Prinus humilis. *Dwarf Chesnut or Chinquepin Oak.* This generally rises with several shrubby, spreading stalks, to the height of two or three feet. **1819** (1821) Nuttall *Jrl.* 205 **AR,** We found the small chinquapin oak by acres, running along the ground as in New Jersey. **1829** Eaton *Botany* 355, *Quercus . . . chinquapin . .* (dwarf chestnut oak, chinquapin). **1890** Howells *Boy's Town* 3 **OH,** There was no end to the small, sweetish acorns, which the boys called chinquepins. **1906** *DN* 3.130 **nwAR,** Chinkapin oak . . . A kind of oak with long acorns. **1907** Hodge *Hdbk. Amer. Indians* 1.275, Two species of oak (*Quercus acuminata* and *Q. prinoides*) are named chinquapin oak and dwarf chinquapin oak, respectively. **1916** Seton *Woodcraft Manual Girls* 281, *Yellow Oak, Chestnut Oak, or Chinquapin Scrub Oak (Quercus Muhlenbergii) . . .* up to 160 feet high. **1965–70** *DARE* (Qu. T10, . . *Oak trees*) 18 Infs, **chiefly IN, KY,** Chinquapin (oak); **MO**37, Chinquapin; **IN**3, Chinkypin; **CA**150, [čɪkəˌpɛn].

2 A sometimes shrubby, often thicket-forming oak *(Quercus prinoides).* Also called **chestnut oak, running white oak, scrub oak, shin oak, yellow oak**

1907 [see **1** above]. **1940** Gates *Flora KS* 225, *Quercus prinoides . .* Chinquapin Oak. **1960** Vines *Trees SW* 153, *Dwarf Chinquapin Oak—Quercus prinoides . . .* It also has the vernacular names of . . Chinquapin Oak.

chinquapin perch See **chinquapin B5**

chinquapin scrub oak See **chinquapin oak 1**

chinquapin weather n

=**blackberry winter.**

1969 *DARE* (QR, near Qu. B32) Inf **GA**89, Chinquapin weather, blackberry weather—cool spell in spring when these plants bloom.

chinquepin, chinquoimine See **chinquapin A**

chinse v, hence vbl n *chinsing* Also sp *chince* [Alter of **chinch** v; *OED* 1513 →]

=**chink** v.

[**1770** in 1792 Cartwright *Jrl. Labrador* 1.65, I ordered some of the workmen to gather moss, and chinse the store.] **1889** (1971) Farmer *Americanisms, Chink, Chince, Chinse, To.*—To fill up the long narrow openings or interstices between the roughly hewn timber of log cabins. **1945** Colcord *Sea Language* 52 **ME, Cape Cod, and Long Island,** *Chinse.* To caulk or fill in a very narrow seam; probably related to chink. **1955** U.S. Arctic Info. Center *Gloss., Chinse . . .* To calk a boat seam or house

crack in a temporary or rude fashion. Chinsing materials are rags, moss or grass, whereas oakum, tar or cement are usual materials used in calking. **1975** Gould *ME Lingo, Chinsing*—The whole hull of a wooden boat is *caulked,* but a minor repair job of driving oakum or cotton into a small seam or crack is called *chinsing.* Thus, any small effort or temporary fix-it. To give a girl-friend a *chinsing* is exploratory.

chinsy See **chintzy** adj[1]

chintz See **chinch** n[1] 1, 2

chintz bug See **chinch** n[1] 2

chintzer n [**chintzy** adj[1] 1]

1968 *DARE* (Qu. U33, . . *A stingy person*) Inf **MD**25, Chintzer.

chintzy adj[1] Usu |ˈčɪn(t)si|; also |ˈčɪn(t)zi| Also sp *chincy, chinsy* [Alter of **chinchy**] **widespread, but esp Nth, N Midl, West**

1 Stingy, miserly, tight.

1940 in 1944 *ADD* nwVA, Chinchy [ˈčɪnči], chinsy, -cy, -[sɪ]. **1949** *PADS* 11.5 wTX, *Chinchy . . .* Stingy. Also heard in San Diego, California, as *chintzy* [ˈtʃɪntzɪ]. *Ibid* 19 **CO,** *Chinchy, chincy . . .* Stingy. **1965–70** *DARE* (Qu. U36b, *Words . . to describe a person who saves in a mean way or is greedy in money matters*) 10 Infs, **esp Nth, N Midl,** [ˈčɪnsi]; **AL**41, **AR**56, **MI**16, **SC**45, **WV**10, [ˈčɪntsɪ]; **CA**107, **CO**22, [ˈčɪntsɪ]; **CA**32, **NY**146, **VA**63, [ˈčɪntzi]; **IN**1, [ˈčɪənsi]; **AK**1, **MA**9, **NY**227, Chintzy; (Qu. U33, . . *A stingy person*) Infs **AK**1, **CO**22, **OK**31, Chintzy; **IN**15, [ˈčɪnsi]; (Qu. U34, . . *"Stingy;"* total Infs questioned, 75) Infs **MS**31, **OK**31, Chintzy; (Qu. U35, . . *Thrifty but not in a complimentary way*) Infs **AL**6, **CA**32, **CO**22, **OR**4, 10, **PA**209, Chintzy; (Qu. H12, *If somebody . . takes little bits of food and leaves most of it on his plate*) Inf **MO**20, Chintzy eater; (Qu. HH10, *A very timid or cowardly person*) Inf **NY**76, Chintzy. [Infs chiefly young or middle-aged, and coll educ.] **1973** Allen *LAUM* 1.355, *Stingy . . . Near, cheap, chintzy, greedy, penurious . .* are additional replies, some offered by only one person. **1977** *UpCountry* Nov 14/3 **NEng,** Being chintzy, I naturally thought about buying cheaper wood.

2 Meager, scanty.

1967–70 (Qu. LL12, *Not full or sufficient: "She gave us a _____ meal."*) Inf **CA**188, [ˈčɪnsi]; **WA**30, [ˈčɪnzi].

chintzy adj[2] [*chintz* an inexpensive cotton fabric; *OEDS* 1851 →]

1 Unfashionable, unsophisticated.

1953 *Syracuse (N.Y.) Post-Standard* 28 May 19/4 *(DAS),* In New York City, the all-white costume is considered '*chintzy*' (that's the newest word for unfashionable) . . . White shoes with a dark dress is [sic] considered very definitely . . . 'chintzy.'

2 Worthless, of poor quality.

1965–70 *DARE* (Qu. KK6, *Something low-grade or of poor quality*) Infs **CA**189, **MI**123, **OR**1, **WA**33, Chintzy; **CA**140, **PA**165, **WI**47, [ˈčɪnsi]; **CA**66, Chintzy deal; (Qu. LL2, . . *Too small to be worth much*) Infs **CA**66, **WA**33, Chintzy; **VA**99, [ˈčɪntzi].

chin-wag v, n

1 To chatter, talk excessively; hence n *chin-wagger* an excessive talker, and vbl n *chin-wagging* excessive talk, a meeting at which there is much talking.

1919 *DN* 5.63 NM [High school slang], *Chin-wagger,* an idle talker. "She is a regular chin-wagger and never says anything worth while." **1942** Berrey–Van den Bark *Amer. Slang* 422.1, *Loquacious person; idle chatter . . .* chatterbox, chin, chinner, chin wagger, clack-box. **1945** Thorp *Pardner* 298 SW, Auger—cowboy word for gossip, talk, parley, conversation, or chin wagging of almost any kind. **1950** *WELS (Joking words for a meeting where there is a lot of talking)* 1 Inf, **WI,** Chin-wagging.

2 A scolding.

1942 Berrey–Van den Bark *Amer. Slang* 295.1, Bawling-out . . calling-down, chin music, chin-wag, cussing-out.

chin-whisker adj Also *chin-whiskered* **Nth** *usu derog*

Among loggers: small-scale, unprofessional.

1930 Williams *Logger-Talk* 21 **Pacific NW,** *Chinwhisker:* Pertaining to a farmer; used as an adjective, as in *chinwhisker outfit.* **1958** McCulloch *Woods Words* **Pacific NW,** *Chin-whiskered*—A kind of a farmer's set-up; not a highball logging outfit. **1969** Sorden *Lumberjack Lingo* **NEng, Gt Lakes,** *Chin-whiskered jobber*—A logger operating on a small scale.

chiny See **china A**

Chiny-loo n [Prob *China-loo,* var of the card game *loo*]
   1969 *DARE* (Qu. DD35, . . *Favorite card games*) Inf **CA**137, Chiny-loo—Trinity County game.

chip n¹

1 A piece of dried animal dung, formerly often used for fuel. **chiefly West**
   1804 Roberts *PA Farmer* 137, I ploughed it five times more, then put on twenty loads of chip, and ten loads of yard dung. **1811** (1935) Hunt *Travel Diary* 281 **Oregon Trail,** The Indians used buffalo chips as fuel. **1857** Chandless *Visit to Salt Lake* 1.122 **swWY, nUT,** Some one pitched on an old camping-place studded with 'ox-chips.' **1897** Hough *Cowboy* 179 **SW,** Some of the boys kicked together enough of the abundant prairie chips—the only fuel within sixty miles of that point. **1903** (1965) Adams *Log Cowboy* 210 **wKS,** We were frequently forced to resort to the old bed grounds of a year or two previous for cattle chips. These chips were a poor substitute. **1932** *AmSp* 7.167 **NEast,** "Chips," when not piled on the floor making a "chip pile" or in a corner of the room, were in a "chip box." **1961** *AmSp* 36.269 **CO,** Chips 'buffalo dung' [also in the sense of 'kindling.'] **1966–67** *DARE* Tape **IA**8, He'd send us boys out on the plains, the prairie there, to pick up cow chips and buffalo chips; **NM**2, Cow chips [cow droppings used as fuel]; **OK**30, We burned chips in those days, cow chips. **1967–70** *DARE* (Qu. L17, . . *Manure*) Infs **KS**4, **NJ**67, Cow chips.

2 In turpentine production:
a The cut made on the surface of a pine tree trunk from which resin exudes.
   1859 Perry *Turpentine Farming* 54, It makes no difference how large or how small the chip is cut, or how far it reaches up, the same grain is cut in either case. **1896** Mohr *Timber Pines* 69 **S Atl, AL, MS,** The height of the chip is increased about 1½ to 2 inches every month.
b The resin from these cuts.
   1859 Perry *Turpentine Farming* 54, If the weather should happen to be warm and damp, the chip will sour before it seasons, and the fly, by coming to this sour chip, will cause the black worm in the pine; it will also be the means of drawing the bug, and putting the cutting, or circle worm into the tree. **1904** *DN* 2.395, *Chip* . . . A term used in the turpentine industry. "At intervals of three or four weeks the resin from the boxes . . , known as the *chip,* is taken out with a flat metal spoon and placed in a bucket, which in turn is emptied . . into a barrel." *Evening Post,* June 1, 1903.

3 also *chip basket:* A basket made of thin wooden strips, usu for carrying fruit. **PA**
   1968 *DARE* (Qu. F17, *What peaches come in*) Infs **PA**128, 131, 167, Chip; **PA**74, 77, 92, Chip basket; **PA**131, Half-bushel chip.

4 A small piece of wood or similar material used to kindle a fire. **chiefly Nth** See Map Section
   1965–70 *DARE* (Qu. D34) 34 Infs, **chiefly Nth,** Chips; **NJ**54, Wood chips; (Qu. T8) Inf **IL**7, Pine chips.

5 in phr *look for chips:* See quot. [From *have a chip on one's shoulder*]
   1968 *DARE* (Qu. GG39, . . *Looking for reasons to be angry*) Inf **NC**79, Looking for chips.

chip v

1 In turpentine production: to cut a **chip** n¹ **2a** in a tree. **S Atl** Cf **box** v¹
   1788 Schöpf *Reise Staaten* 2.221 **SC,** Und eben so oft werden die Boxes wieder nachgehackt oder angefrischt (re-chip'd). [And equally as often the boxes are rechipped or freshened up.] **1859** Perry *Turpentine Farming* 114, At other times he will chip too shallow. **1896** *Pop. Sci. Mth.* 48.469 **Sth,** Once a week from March till October the trees are either chipped or hacked. **1904** *DN* 2.395, *Chip* v. **1933** Rawlings *South Moon* 140 **FL,** "Zeke's figgerin' on turpentinin' if he can't git nothin' else." "Chippin' boxes—I know." **1968–69** *DARE* Tape **GA**22, [The turpentine collector] would cut it [=the tree] on each side there, just above the box, and fix it right for chipping; **GA**23, Then you come along and you chip it for so many years, usually it's three.

2 =**chip together.**
   1887 *Courier–Jrl.* (Louisville KY) 8 May 8/3, The shake-purse didn't count up over $40. The hat was passed to me, but I declined to chip.

chip n²

1 See **chippy** n² **3.**

2 See **chipping squirrel.**

chip adj See **chippy** adj²

chiparee See **chickaree**

chip basket See **chip** n¹ **3**

chip-bearer n [**chip** n¹ **5**]
   1968 *DARE* (Qu. GG39, *Somebody . . looking for reasons to be angry*) Inf **UT**5, Chip-bearer.

chip bird See **chipping sparrow**

chip, carry (one) on a See **carry (one) on a chip**

chip-cheeny n [*chip* v (from the attempt to knock a piece off the opponent's marble with one's top) + *cheeny,* var of **china B1**]
   1969 O'Connor *Horse & Buggy West* 84 **AZ** (as of 1910–12), A game requiring great skill was Chip-Cheeny (spelling my own). The players drew two lines about fifty yards apart, placed a large marble directly between the two lines. The idea was to spin a top, pick it up on the hand, bring the hand down so the spinning top would strike the marble and send it sailing off in the direction of the spin. The first player who got the marble across his goal line was the winner.

chip-de-willow n [Imit]
=**chuck-will's-widow.**
   1967 *DARE* (Qu. Q3, . . *Birds . . out only after dark*) Inf **SC**43, Chip-de-willow.

chip dirt n Also *chip dung,* ~ *manure* [**chip** n¹ **1**] **chiefly NEast** *old-fash*
Material from a **chipyard** used as fertilizer.
   1821 MA Hist. Soc. *Coll.* 2nd ser 9.139 **VT,** I . . filled up the cavity, around the roots, with chip manure. **1850** U.S. Patent Office *Annual Rept. for 1849: Ag.* 103 **NY,** Shallow ploughings given annually, liquid manure, chip-dirt, road scrapings, . . have been turned in with marked advantage. **1874** VT State Bd. Ag. *Report for 1873–74* 2.271, If the ground has settled so that the trees stand too shallow, more soil, (chip dirt is best) should be . . placed around them. **1884** Barber *Diary* 36 **MA,** I put some chipdung into the horse barn cellar. **1945** Wilson *Passing Institutions* 6 **KY,** Chip dirt was also attractive to fishing worms.

chip-fell-out-of-a-white-oak n Also *chip-off-the-white-oak, chip-o'-white-oak*
=**chuck-will's-widow.**
   1932 Bennitt *Check-list* 38, Chuck-will's-widow . . . Chip-o'-white-oak . . . Southern Missouri. [**1946** Hausman *Eastern Birds* 370, Notes . . . like the words . . *chip-fell-white-oak.*] **1955** *Oriole* 8.9, Chuck-wills-widow.—All names are sonic unless otherwise explained. *Chip-fell-out-of-a-white-oak; Chip-off-the-white-oak.*

chip gon See **chipper** n **5**

chip lot See **chipyard**

chip manure See **chip dirt**

chipmunk n Usu |ˈčɪpˌməŋk|, occas |ˈčɪpmək|, infreq |ˈčɪkməŋk|, čɪt-| Also occas sp *chipmonk, chipmuck,* rarely *chinkmunk, chipminck* **chiefly Nth, esp NEast, though becoming more widespread**
Any of var small rodents, usu with stripes along the back: see quots.
   1841 *Knickerbocker* 17.365 **NH,** He ventures the stone, twice aimed, at the unoffending chip-muck. **1841** (1952) Cooper *Deerslayer* 334 **NY,** Have you discovered a chip-munk in a tree? **1854** P.B. St. John *Amy Moss* 13 (*OED*), I would not give a chip-minck's tail for both our scalps, if we were circumvented by that noted rascal. **1880** Howells *Undiscovered Country* 204, From the first of the strawberries to the last of the blackberries, the birds and chipmucks feasted. **1882** Hawthorne *Fortune's Fool* I.xxxiii (*OED*), Hares and striped chipmonks cantered and scudded amidst the huckleberry bushes. **1890** *DN* 1.73 **neIN,** *Chipmuck* [čɪpmək] seems to be the only pronunciation known in northeastern Indiana among the farmers' boys. **1907** *DN* 3.210 **nwAR, cCT,** *Chipmunk* . . . The striped squirrel. **1939** *LANE* Map 229, The word *chipmunk* was offered by nearly half the informants as denoting the well-known ground squirrel. Ten informants . . pronounce the word without [ŋ], as [ˈtʃɪpmʌk]; one . . says [ˈtʃhɪ²kmʌ·ŋk], another . . [ˈtʃɪtmʌŋk]. All other pronunciations are of the type of [ˈtʃɪpmʌŋk]. Two informants call the animal *chipmunk squirrel.* **1949** Kurath *Word Geog.* 74, The chipmunk is regularly so called in the North; the South

and the South Midland just as regularly use *ground squirrel*. In the North Midland the present situation is rather confused. *Chipmunk* predominates in Eastern Pennsylvania, *ground squirrel* in the Pittsburgh area and the Ohio Valley. In the Philadelphia area . . *ground hackie*, is being replaced by chipmunk. Chipmunk is also crowding out *ground squirrel* in central Pennsylvania and in southern New Jersey; it has made its way down the Eastern Shore, and through Maryland to the Shenandoah Valley, supported by literary usage. **1950** *WELS (Chipmunk)* 1 Inf, **ceWI**, [čĭkmʌŋk]. **1961** *AmSp* 36.267 **CO**, Coloradans refer to two entirely different rodents with the terms *chipmunk* and *ground squirrel*. In Colorado *chipmunk* means what both terms mean in the East, genus *Eutamis* or *Tamias*. **1965–70** *DARE* (Qu. P27, . . *Kinds of squirrels*) 129 Infs, **scattered, but esp NEast**, Chipmunk; **MO**38, Chipmunk-squirrel; **CA**95, Desert chipmunk—a little smaller than a ground squirrel, two stripes; **NV**8, Large chipmunk—belongs to squirrel family, has stripes; (Qu. P29, . . *Gophers*) 40 Infs, **chiefly N Cent**, Chipmunk; **KS**5, Chinkmunk; (Qu. P31, . . *Groundhog*) Infs **IL**4, **MO**18, **OH**50, Chipmunk. **1968** *DARE* Tape **IN**30, We call 'em groundhogs and we also call 'em chipmunks. They are the funny little rodent animal that comes out on February the second and prophesies whether we're going to have some more winter or are we going to have a early spring. **1971** Wood *Vocab. Change* 233 **Sth**, [Percentage of use of the term *chipmunk* by state: Tennessee, 35%; Georgia, 26%; Alabama, 32%, Mississippi, 41%; Florida, 28%; Louisiana, 44%; Arkansas, 37%; Oklahoma, 42%].

chipmunk's apple n
A **bearberry 2** (here: *Arctostaphylos uva-ursi*).
1938 (1958) Sharples *AK Wild Flowers* 16, *A. Uva-ursi* . . . Its red berries are sometimes called "Chipmunk's apples" by children. **1953** Nelson *Plants Rocky Mt. Park* 116, Kinnikinnic is covered with . . berries, which turn scarlet in autumn. These are much relished by the small animals and are called "chipmunks apples" by the children.

chip-off-the-white-oak See **chip-fell-out-of-a-white oak**

chip one's teeth v phr
1 To talk, usu too much or too loud; to argue.
1958 McCulloch *Woods Words* **Pacific NW**, *Chipping their teeth*— Said of a group of men sitting around the bunkhouse doing a great deal of talking. **1968–69** *DARE* (Qu. HH7b, *Someone who talks too much, or too loud: "He's always _____."*) Inf **RI**15, Chipping his teeth; (Qu. KK13, *Other words for arguing*) Inf **CA**66, Chipping their teeth.
2 See quot.
1962 *AmSp* 37.268 **sCA** [Among traffic police], *Chip one's teeth* . . . To demonstrate extreme anger. 'He was so mad he was chipping his teeth!'

chip out v phr [Engl dial]
1936 *AmSp* 11.275 **cTN**, To *chip out*. To have a misunderstanding. 'He and his friends have chipped out.'

chip-o'-white-oak See **chip-fell-out-of-a-white-oak**

chippen bird See **chipping sparrow**

chipper n
1 In turpentine production: the worker who cuts the tree trunk so that the resin can run out. [**chip** v **1**]
1896 *Pop. Sci. Mth.* 48.469 **Sth**, The chipper first removes strips about two inches wide. **1904** *DN* 2.395, The chipper stands in front of the box . . and with his hack . . removes a strip of bark and sapwood three-quarters of an inch wide just above the exposed surface caused by cornering. **1939** FWP *Guide FL* 378. **1941** *AmSp* 16.237 **GA**.
2 See quot. [**chip** n¹ **1**]
1942 *AmSp* 17.74 **NE**, *Chipper* . . a rancher who is poor or who is in only moderate circumstances . . . [U]sed . . in a slighting sense . . . Most of the poorer ranchers in the sandhills still gather cow chips (hence the word *chipper*) for their winter fuel.
3 See **chipping sparrow**.
4 A machine which reduces wood to chips.
1956 *AmSp* 31.150 **nwCA** [Logging talk], *Chipper* . . . A machine in which wood waste is cut into chips for by-products. **1968** *DARE* Tape **GA**23, They . . go right into the chipper and it chips up into . . quarter by seven, eight inch chips. **1970** *Torrington Reg.* (CT) 30 Dec, Have you ever seen the "chippers" operating along a roadside? Men cut the brush by hand. Then they feed it into a Brobdingnagian [sic] cousin of an old-fashioned meat grinder.
5 also *chip gon*: see quot.
1970 *Current Slang* 5.1.5 **West** [Railroad jargon], *Chip gon* . . . A high sided gondola car used in hauling wood chips. *Chipper* [same definition].

6 See quot.
1950 *WELS (A kiss, or kissing)* 1 Inf, **ceWI**, Chipper.
7 See quot.
1967 *DARE* (Qu. H28, . . *Doughnuts*) Inf **MI**43, Chippers—chocolate-chip chippers and orange chippers; fried in a ball.
8 See quot. [Perh from *a chip off the old block*]
1968 *DARE* (Qu. Z12, . . "A small child") Inf **OH**76, Chipper.
9 See **clipper 2**.

chipperdale n [Prob alter of **chippy** n² **3**, perh infl by *chippendale*]
See quot 1952.
1938 Rawlings *Yearling* 290 **FL**, Now if the gal's honest, why don't Oliver marry her and be done with it? If she's nothin' but one o' them leetle ol' chipperdales, why do he mess up with her? **1952** Brown *NC Folkl.* 1.527, *Chipperdale* . . . A worthless woman, a strumpet.

chippery adj [*chipper* adj + *-y*]
=**chippy** adj².
1967 *DARE* (Qu. GG29, *To be in a good or pleasant mood*) Inf **MA**28, Chippery.

chippie n¹ See **chippy** n¹ **1**

chippie n² See **chipping sparrow**, **chippy** n² **3**

chippified adj [**chippy** n² **3** + *-ified*]
1968 *DARE* (Qu. W36, . . *A woman who uses a lot of cosmetics*) Inf **AK**8, Chippified looking, made herself look chippified.

chip pile n
1 An area where wood is cut and where a mound of wood fragments accumulates. Cf **chipyard**
1859 IL *Dept. Ag. Trans.* 3.472, Because a man is a farmer, or a countryman, is no reason why . . the back yard or grounds around the back door [should be] filled with rags, bones, chip piles, broken hoe handles, old plows. **1899** Garland *Boy Life* 48 **nwIA**, The first island to appear in the midst of the ocean of slush and mud around the Stewart house, was the chip-pile.
2 See quot.
1906 *DN* 3.130 **nwAR**, *Chip-pile* . . . A game.

chipping vbl n, also attrib
In turpentine production:
a The cutting of the tree surface so that resin exudes. [**chip** v **1**]
1859 Perry *Turpentine Farming* 84, We will suppose the seven weeks' chipping to be now passed over . . ; by continuing to chip, it would require the whole chipping season for two years. **1896** Mohr *Timber Pines* 69 **S Atl**, **AL**, **MS**, The removal of the bark and of the outermost layers of the wood—the "chipping" or "hacking"—is done with a peculiar tool, the "hacker" . . . The chipping is repeated every week from March to October or November. **1941** *AmSp* 16.237 **GA** [Turpentine production], In chipping, *hack-balls* or *hack-weights* are placed on the hack stocks or handles.
b =**chip** n¹ **2a**.
1832 Browne *Sylva* 232 **S Atl**, The chippings extend the first year a foot above the box.

chipping adj See **chippy** adj²

chipping sparrow n Also *chippie*, *chippy*; for other varr see quots **chiefly Nth, N Midl, esp NEast** See Map
Any of var sparrows of the genus *Spizella*, but esp *S. passerina*, which is also called **hair bird, nixie, house sparrow, twit sparrow**.
1791 (1958) Bartram *Travels* 184, *Passer domesticus*, the little house sparrow or chipping bird. **1843** (1973) Porter *Big Bear AR* 16, Game, indeed, that's what city folks call it; and with them it means chippen-birds [=tree sparrows] and shite-pokes. **1852** Stowe *Uncle Tom's Cabin* 1.256 **Nth**, She sat down on his knee, like a chip-sparrow, still laughing. **1886** Burroughs *Signs & Seasons* 75 **NY**, He also found a "chippie" (called also "hair bird") suspended from a branch by a horse-hair, beneath a partly-constructed nest. **1913** Porter *Laddie* 60, In the hollow of a rotten rail a little chippy bird always built a hair nest. **1917** *Wilson Bulletin* 29.2.83, *Spizella passerina* . . chipsney . . Hickman, Ky. **1955** *MA Audubon* 39.255 **NEng**, *Chipping Sparrow*. Chip Bird, Chipper (Mass.); Chipping Bird (N.H); Chippy (General. Its call is a *chip* and its song a succession of similar notes.); Chipping sparrow (Maine, Conn.). **1955** Forbush–May *Birds* 523, *Eastern Chipping*

Sparrow . . . Chippy; Chip-bird. **1965–70** *DARE* (Qu. Q21, . . *Sparrows*) 91 Infs, **chiefly Nth,** Chipping sparrow; 19 Infs, **chiefly NEast,** Chippie (sparrow); **MA26, NE7, RI12, WI62,** Chirping sparrow; **NH5,** Winter chippie; **MA68,** Chip bird; **VA8,** Chip sparrow; (Qu. Q22, . . *Common sparrow*) 25 Infs, **chiefly Nth,** Chippie; **NY126,** Chipping sparrow; **DC4,** Chirper; **MO6,** Cheepie bird.

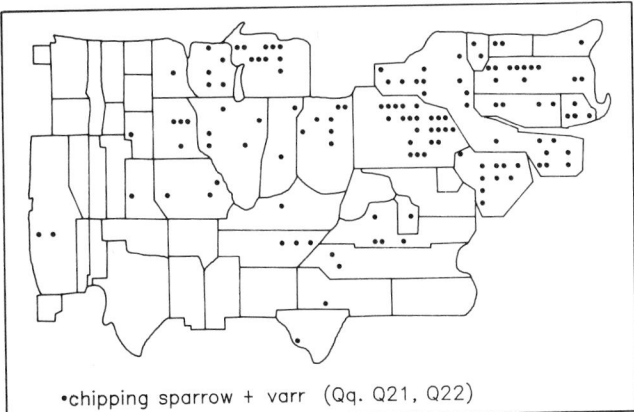

•chipping sparrow + varr (Qq. Q21, Q22)

chipping squirrel n Also *chippy, chip (squirrel)* **chiefly Nth**

A **chipmunk** (*Tamias* spp).

1800 *Raleigh* (N.C.) *Register* 1 July *(DA),* An Advertisement was lately published in several papers, offering a generous price for 10,000 chipping squirrel skins, for exportation. **1844** Stephens *High Life in NY* 2.220 **CT,** I could feel the leetle hand a movin . . like a chip squirrel in its nest. **1928** Anthony *N. Amer. Mammals* 241, *Eastern Chipmunk.—Tamias striatus* and related forms . . Chipping Squirrel. **1949** Kurath *Word Geog.* 74, Chipmunk . . . Sporadic terms are *chippie* and *chip squirrel.* **1950** *WELS* (Chipmunk) 9 Infs, **WI,** Chippy; 2 Infs, Chip; 1 Inf, Chipping squirrel. **1966–69** *DARE* (Qu. P27, . . *Kinds of squirrels*) Infs **MA62, OH87,** Chippy; (Qu. P32) Inf **PA1,** Chipmunk = chippy.

chippy n[1]

1 also sp *chippie;* In marble play: see quots.

1955 *PADS* 23.13 **cwTN,** *Chippie* . . . A marble, usually glass, in a chipped condition. **1969** *DARE* (Qu. EE6c, *Cheap marbles*) Inf **AZ11,** Chippies. **c1970** Wiersma *Marbles Terms* **MI,** Chippie . . a chipped playing marble.

2 also attrib: A miner's drill.

1918 *DN* 5.23 **nID,** *Chippy* . . . A one-man engine for drilling in the face of a tunnel. **1922** *DN* 5.181 **nID,** *Chippy-doctor* . . . One who sharpens steel in the blacksmith shop of a mine. **1968** Adams *Western Words* 63, *Chippy*—A miner's name for his excavating drill.

3 also attrib: In mining: an "elevator," a cage for transporting workers and equipment to or from the level being worked.

1939 FWP *Guide MT* 146, A miner going to work in the Leonard mine changes into digging clothes . . and waits for his turn in the "chippy"—the cage used to raise and lower men. **1949** Emrich *Wild West Custom* 165, Before the passage of safety laws governing the mines, the *chippy cage* in the shaft picked up anything—men, tools, ore. But the *chippy,* with its violent accidents passed.

chippy n[2] [Echoic or phonosymbolic]

1 See **chipping sparrow.**

2 See **chipping squirrel.**

3 also sp *chippie,* infreq *chip:* A disreputable girl or woman; a prostitute. [Perh rel to Fr *chipie* a shrewish woman] **formerly East, Sth; now chiefly Inland Nth and West** See Map

1886 in 1950 *AmSp* 25.31 **New Orleans LA,** This class of females are known by the gang as "Chippies," and most of them come from the slums, and work in the cigar and cigarette factories. **1896** *DN* 1.414 **eMA, NH, NY,** *Chippy:* a young woman who is somewhat free or of questionable character. **1908** *DN* 3.298 **eAL, wGA.** **1916** *DN* 4.321 **KS,** *Chippy* . . . Prostitute. Current in the east in the nineties. Medina Co., O[hio], in the eighties . . . Generally applied to innocent girls who 'pick up.' **1927** *AmSp* 2.350 **WV,** Chippie. **1930** Shoemaker *1300 Words* 10 **cPA Mts** (as of c1900), *Chip*—A cheap, easily led girl. **1931–33** *LANE Worksheets* **ceMA,** Chip . . girl. **1938** Farrell *No Star* 138 **Chicago IL** (as of 1914–15), 'Tis well, you poor man, that you left when you did, that you didn't live to see your daughter runnin' around

like a high-lifer and a chippy with a black devil of a Protestant. **1949** *PADS* 11.5 **wTX,** Chippie. **1950** *WELS Suppl.* **csWI,** Anyone who uses too much makeup is "painted like a chippy." **1965–70** *DARE* (Qu. HH37, *An immoral woman*) 72 Infs, **chiefly Inland Nth and West,** Chippy; (Qu. AA7b, . . *A woman who is very fond of men . . not respectable about it*) Infs **CA114, 134, IL32, 37, IA22, KY94, NE4, VA5,** Chippy; **CA148,** She's a little chippy; (Qu. W36, . . *A woman who uses a lot of cosmetics*) Infs **AZ16, MO38,** (Like a ten-cent) chippy; (Qu. AA6, . . *A man who is fond of being with women*) Infs **KY94, MI68, OR10,** Chippy chaser; (Qu. HH34, *General words . . for a woman*) Infs **CA165, NY241, OR10, UT3, WA30,** Chippy; (Qu. HH28, . . *Of foreign background*) Inf **RI17,** Chippy—English girls; (Qu. X53a, . . *An oversized stomach*) Inf **NY55,** Chippie's playground; (Qu. DD30, . . *Where liquor is (or was) sold and consumed illegally*) Inf **AK8,** Chippy joint.

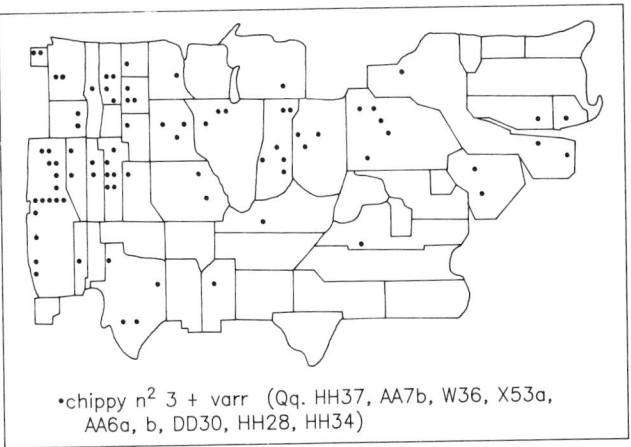

•chippy n[2] 3 + varr (Qq. HH37, AA7b, W36, X53a, AA6a, b, DD30, HH28, HH34)

4 A narrow-gauge railroad track, train, or car.

1918 *DN* 5.23 **nID,** *Chippy* . . . A narrow gauge railroad track or the train that runs on it. **1945** Hubbard *Railroad Ave.* 337, Chippies—Narrow-gauge cars.

chippy v, hence vbl n *chippying* [**chippy** n[2] 3]

See quots.

1930 Williams *Logger-Talk* 21 **Pacific NW,** *Chippy:* An easy woman of semi-professional standing; used more often as a verb as in *You can't chippy on me.* **1977** Dillard *Lexicon* 89, A pimp must never 'chippy' (make love to a woman for the pleasure of it). **1980** *Chicago* Dec 237, [They] had agreed to lead separate love lives, based on what they termed contingency (and which American hookers name, more simply, chippying).

chippy adj[1] [**chippy** n[2] 3]

1915 *DN* 4.214, *Chippy,* of questionable character.

chippy adj[2] Also *chip, chipping* [Alter of *chipper* adj]

Cheerful, lively; spry, fit.

1965–70 *DARE* (Qu. GG29, *To be in a good or pleasant mood*) Infs **DC8, NY57, TN1,** Chippy; **NY213,** Pretty chippy; **IN32,** Chip; (Qu. KK27, *A very lively, active old person; "For his age, he's _____."*) Inf **SC66,** Chippy old man; **IN80,** Pretty chipping; **MO21,** Pretty chip.

chippy bird See **chipping sparrow**

chippy hawk n

Perh a **sparrow hawk 1.**

1968 *DARE* (Qu. Q4, . . *Hawks*) Inf **NY40,** Chippy hawk.

chippying See **chippy** v

chips and whetstones n pl Also *chips (or whets) and grindstones* **chiefly Midl**

Small amounts; various small articles, odds and ends.

1927 *Ruppenthal Coll.* **KS,** Chips and whetstones—Sundry articles; miscellaneous. You may sell produce at the stores, but you must take it out in chips and whetstones, you can't get cash. **1950** *PADS* 14.19 **SC,** *Chips and whetstones* . . . Small amounts; small partial payments. "He pays his account in chips and whetstones." **1952** *AmSp* 27.290 **cIL,** When a father told his children not to exchange their money or other belongings *for chips and whetstones,* he meant not to waste them on worthless trifles. **1953** Randolph *Down in Holler* 234 **Ozarks,** Chips and grindstones . . . Odds and ends, general merchandise. A workman who is paid in *chips and grindstones* gets no cash, but is forced to accept feed, groceries, dry goods, and the like. The phrase *whets and grindstones* is also used. **1954** *Harder Coll.* **cwTN,** Chips and grindstones: Small amounts of leftovers; junk. **1956** McAtee *Some Dialect NC* 8, Chips and whetstones, made of: . . Made of odds and ends, or any available materials; of a rude building or a picked-up meal. **1966-68** *DARE* (Qu. LL7, *In small amounts, by small degrees*) Infs **NM6, 9, NC33, VA11,** (In) chips and whetstones.

chips, cash in one's See **checks, cash in one's**

chipsney See **chipping sparrow**

chip sparrow See **chipping sparrow**

chip squirrel See **chipping squirrel**

chip together *v phr* **chiefly Nth**
To share the responsibility or cost of an enterprise; chip in.
1950 *WELS* (*If several people share the cost of something*) 4 Infs, **WI,** Chip together. **1965-70** *DARE* (Qu. II9, *If several people have to contribute in order to pay for something*) Infs **IN35, ME1, ND1, PA97, 130, SD2, WI12,** Chip together. **1967** *DARE* Tape **MA6,** If anyone was in trouble they all chipped together to help.

chipyard *n, also attrib* Also *chip lot*
An area where wood is cut and where sawdust and wood fragments accumulate.
1850 *Knickerbocker* 36.73 **West,** I first let down her bars, crossed her chipyard, and stood before her habitation. **1879** Taylor *Summer-Savory* 110, Thus a number of residents of La Porte, Indiana, went and camped out for a week in plain sight of the city! It was a sort of chipyard picnic. **1939** *Senior Scholastic Teachers' Ed.* 18 Mar 27/1, I threw down my books in the chipyard. **1968** *DARE* (Qu. M14, *The open area around or next to the barn*) Inf **IN19,** Chip lot—wood was cut there.

chiquito *n, also attrib* Also *chiquita, chiquite* [Span] **chiefly SW** See also **chico** n[2]
A small or dear one—freq used as a nickname or term of address.
1847 Reid *TX Rangers* 108 **CA,** Beneath you, sporting in the limpid element, you behold men and boys, and women with their *chiquitos*. **1857** in 1948 *Western Folkl.* 7.8 **sCA,** Los Angeles Chiquito. **1861** U.S. Army *Rept. Colorado R.* 39 **sCA,** We found a large party of Cocopas . . waiting on the bank, with grinning faces, for the arrival of the "chiquito steamboat," as they call our diminutive vessel. **1886** Harte *Complete Poetical Wks.* 117 **West,** "Chiquita" [Poem title] . . . Chiquita, my darling, my beauty [=a horse]. **1897** Hough *Cowboy* 26 **SW,** The Spanish diminutives are in common use in the English speech of this region, as *chico, chiquito*. **1928** Lummis *Bronco Pegasus* 64 **NM,** Do you remember those days, chiquite?

chir See **chair**

chiravari See **shivaree**

chirck, mah chick, mah craney crow See **chickamy, chickamy, craney crow**

chirivaris See **shivaree**

chirk *adj* Also sp *cherk, churk* **chiefly NEng** *arch*
In good spirits; cheerful, lively.
1789 Webster *Dissertations Engl. Lang.* 387, This word is wholly lost, except in New England. It is there used for *comfortably, bravely, cheerful;* as when one enquires about a sick person, it is said, he is *chirk*. **1815** Humphreys *Yankey in England* 104, Chirk, churk, brisk, lively, in good spirits. **1816** Pickering *Vocab.* 59, It should be remarked, that the adjective *chirk* is used only in the *interior* of New England; and even there, I think, only by the illiterate. It is never heard in the sea-port towns. **1864** (1868) Trowbridge *Cudjo's Cave* 36 **TN,** After that Penn slept a little. "Tank de good Lord," said the old negro the next morning, "You're lookin' as chirk as can be!" **1891** Cooke *Huckleberries* 163 **NEng,** I s'pose 't is more cherk up there than 't is to a solitary widder's like me. **1955** Adams *Grandfather* 282 **NY** (as of c1880s), And there he sat on the live boat foredeck . . as chirk as a chitterdiddle on a pokeweed.

chirk up *v phr*
To become or make (someone) cheerful, lively.
1843 [see **chirky**]. **1844** Stephens *High Life in NY* 1.231 **CT,** All I could do she wouldn't chirk up. **1892** *DN* 1.236 **MO.** **1905** *DN* 3.74 **nwAR.** **1936** Morehouse *Rain on Just* 181 **NC,** But in spite of her righteous intentions, Least Dolly chirked up when . . Hansie followed. **1939** (1962) Thompson *Body & Britches* 158 **NY,** Even the trustee of a

church wasn't to blame if his horse chirked up a bit when some old plug tried to pass him. **1960** Williams *Walk Egypt* 4 **GA,** She had brown curly hair, a round body, and red lips that chirked up into a smile. **1968** Kellner *Aunt Serena* 109 **sIN,** A little syrup of pepsin will chirk you up and make you better off. **1968-69** *DARE* (Qu. GG27a, *To get somebody out of an unhappy mood*) Infs **MI101, NY66, TN30,** Chirk up.

chirky *adj*
=**chirk.**
1843 in 1912 Thornton *Amer. Gloss.* 1.170, All our folks appear more *chirkier* than they really feel, in order to *chirk* her up. [Given as an antiquated rustic expression.]—*Yale Lit. Mag.* i.26 (Feb.). **1967** *DARE* (Qu. GG29, *To be in a good or pleasant mood: "This morning he seems to be feeling _____."*) Inf **IA9,** Chirky [čɜ˞ki].

chirme See **churn A**

chirp *v* Also sp *churp*
1 with *up:* =**chirk up;** hence ppl adj *chirped up.*
1897 *KS Univ. Qrly.* 6.86 **neKS,** Churp up: to encourage. **1897** Stuart *Simpkinsville* 35 **AR,** Mis' Meredith is chirpin' up a'ready. **1966** *DARE* (Qu. GG29, *To be in a good or pleasant mood*) Inf **AR22,** Pretty chirped up.
2 See **chirrup.**

chirp *n* See **chirper** n 1

chirp *adj*
=**chirk.**
1824 *New Bedford Mercury* 28 May (1912 Thornton 1.170), As chirp as a flock of blackbirds. **1863** Dodge *Gala-Days* 233 **NEng,** We walk away as 'chirp as a cricket.' **1966-67** *DARE* (Qu. BB47, *Feeling in the best of health and spirits*) Inf **AL4,** Chirp; (Qu. GG29, *To be in a good or pleasant mood*) Inf **TX37,** Chirp.

chirper *n*
1 also *chirp, chirping frog, spring chirper:* A **spring peeper** or similar frog.
1950 *WELS* (*Small frogs that sing or chirp loudly in spring*) 1 Inf, **csWI,** Chirper. **1966-69** *DARE* (Qu. P21) Infs **IL25, NY23, 212, VA26,** Chirpers; **MO19,** Spring chirpers; **NY58,** Chirp; **SD5,** Chirping frogs.
2 See **chipping sparrow.**
3 A tattletale.
1969 *DARE* (Qu. JJ4, *A child who is always telling on other children*) Inf **GA72,** Chirper.

chirper *adj* [?Blend of **chirp** adj + *chipper*]
In good spirits, chipper.
1967-70 *DARE* (Qu. GG29, *To be in a good or pleasant mood*) Infs **IL143, MI63,** Chirper; (Qu. BB47, *Feeling in the best of health and spirits*) Inf **OH50,** Chirper.

chirping frog See **chirper** n 1

chirping sparrow See **chipping sparrow**

chirpy *adj* See also **chippy** adj[2]
=**chirk.**
1838 Gilman *S. Matron* 53 **SC,** It makes me chirpy to think of Roseland. **1898** (1909) Page *Red Rock* 573 **Sth,** Andy Stamper was chirpy and facetious. **1967** *DARE* (Qu. GG29, *To be in a good or pleasant mood*) Infs **AR55, NC40,** Chirpy.

chirren See **child A2**

chirrup *n, v* Also sp *cher(r)up, chirp* [Echoic]
The clicking or chirping sound used to urge a horse forward; to make this sound; transf: to urge someone on.
1843 (1916) Hall *New Purchase* 138 **IN,** All cherrups and get-ups and even old-rascals-you—all snapping of bridle reins to bring to his recollection Conestogo [sic] whip-crackings—all, all were in vain! **1860** Holland *Miss Gilbert* 93 **CT,** Dr. Gilbert chirruped to the little black pony. **1865** (1889) Whitney *Gayworthys* 247 **NEng,** She's to chirp us all up Boar-back [=a mountain] next Saturday. **1899** (1912) Green *VA Folk-Speech, Cherup . . .* To urge on by cherupping. A noise made with the lips to urge on a horse. **1905** *DN* 3.5 **cCT,** Chirrup . . . To quicken a horse by a clicking sound. **1950** *WELS* (*Humorous expressions meaning to urge somebody to do something*) 1 Inf, **seWI,** Chirped him on. **1966-69** *DARE* (Qu. K36a, *. . To make a horse go faster*) Inf **NY66,** A chirp; **NY219,** Chirp to him; **DC8,** Chirp or whistle—he'll put out more.

chisel-chin n, hence adj *chisel-chinned*

See quots.

1957 Battaglia *Resp. to PADS 20* **MD**, *(If a person's lower jaw sticks out, you say he is _____)* Chisel-chinned. **1968–69** *DARE* (Qu. X6, *If a person's lower jaw sticks out prominently*) Infs **GA**77, **MD**6, **NY**70, **PA**108, Chisel-chinned; **KS**12, **OH**47, Chisel-chin; (Qu. X9, *. . A person's mouth*) Inf **KS**12, Chisel-chin.

chiseler n

1967 *DARE* (Qu. P27, *. . Squirrels*) Inf **WY**1, Chiseler ['čɪzlɚ], a ground squirrel.

chiselhead cat n

A catfish.

1878 U.S. Natl. Museum *Bulletin* 12.72 **cnTN**, Chisel-head Cat. **1969** *DARE* (Qu. P1) Inf **KY**65, Chiselhead cat.

chiseling vbl n

A scolding.

1968 *DARE* (Qu. II27, *If somebody gives you a very sharp scolding . . a _____*) Inf **NH**14, Chiseling.

chiselly See **chizzly**

chiselmouth n Also *chiselmouth jack* [See quot 1896]

A freshwater fish *(Acrocheilus alutaceus)* of the Columbia River. Also called **hard-mouth, square-mouth**

1889 *Oregonian* (Portland OR) 4 Nov 5/1, He . . landed after a most exciting fight, a chinook or a chisel-mouth of large size. **1896** U.S. Natl. Museum *Bulletin* 47.208, Chisel-mouth . . . Upper jaw protractile, covered with a fleshy lip, inside of which is a small, straight, cartilaginous plate, similar to that on the lower jaw, but much smaller and not evident externally; lower lip covered with a firm cartilaginous plate, sharp externally, the upper surface being formed by its beveled edge. **1911** *Century Dict. Suppl.*, Chiselmouth . . . A cyprinoid fish, *Acrocheilus alutaceus*, found in the lower Columbia river and its tributaries, as far up as Shoshone and Spokane Falls. Also called *chiselmouth jack*. **1960** Amer. Fisheries Soc. *List Fishes* 13, Chiselmouth.

chisly See **chizzly**

chism See **jism**

chispa n |'čɪspə| Infreq sp *chisper* [Span *chispa* sparkle; small diamond; little bit or particle] **CA**

A gold nugget.

1853 *S.F. Alta California* 29 April 1/7 *(DA)*, During the week two more 'chispas' were taken out . . . one weighing twelve and the other ten ounces. **1853** (1956) Davis *CA Gold Rush Merchant* 91, Mr. Cruikshank and his partner found a "chisper," or lump of gold & quartz, weighing 15½ lbs. **1874** Evans *A la CA* 239, A moment later he came out with a bound like a deer . . holding high above his head a nugget, or "chispa," of pure gold, weighing over $900. **1923** Saunders *S. Sierras* 94 **CA**, A glitter of something yellow caught his eye, and his fingers closed on some of the little gold nuggets that the Spanish people call *chispas*. **1969** *DARE* FW Addit **CA**114, Chispa ['čɪspə]—Spanish word for melon seed, hence a piece of gold about that size. Smaller than what you'd call a nugget. [Ed note: *chispa* 'melon seed' has not been found recorded elsewhere].

chissum See **jism**

chist n Pronc-sp for *chest* **scattered, but esp NEng, Midl** Addit quots in *ADD*

1844 Stephens *High Life in NY* 2.160 **CT**, I whistled the colt up tu us, and pinted out his harnsome head and chist, and the clean notion that he has got of flingin out his legs. **1853** Simms *Sword & Distaff* 539 **SC**, He's got other we'pons in that chist, prehaps. **1893** Shands *MS Speech* 23, Chist . . . Negro and illiterate white pronunciation of *chest*. **1903** *DN* 2.291 **Cape Cod MA** (as of 1840s), [ɪ] for [ɛ] in *chist*. **1907** *DN* 3.183 **seNH**. *Ibid* 221 **nwAR, sIL**. **1908** *DN* 3.298 **eAL, wGA**. **1909** *DN* 3.409 **nME**. **1911** *DN* 3.537 **eKY**. **1917** *DN* 4.409 **NC Mts, IL, KY, NEng**. **1950** (1965) Richter *Town* 151 **OH** (as of c1900), It's chest . . . Don't let me hear you say chist again. **1954** *Harder Coll.* **cwTN**, Chest [čɪst] . . woman's breast. **1957** *AmSp* 32.285 **NC**, Chist for *chest*.

chisum See **jism**

chit n[1] [*OED* sb.[1] 2, c1624 →]

A child, or by ext, a girl or young woman.

1814 *Intellectual Regale* 1.50, The sentence from the captain of "that lad's soused in Cupid's pickling tubs over head and ears;" and an "ay, ay, the chit has caught him in a net," from the others threw him into a train of reflections on the nature of his feelings for the interesting Isabella. **1828** Webster *Amer. Dict., Chit* . . . A child or babe, in *familiar language*. **1899** (1912) Green *VA Folk-Speech, Chit* . . . A pert young girl. **1930** *AmSp* 5.418 **sNH**, *Chit*: a small child. "The little chit was timid." **1930** Shoemaker *1300 Words* 10 **cPA Mts** (as of c1900), *Chit*—A young, unfledged girl. **1956** Longstreet *Real Jazz* 96, In the late twenties . . every dance left at least a half-dozen of the chits—high school girls, debutantes and convent-bred misses—dead drunk in the corners.

chit n[2] [*OED* sb.[3], 1601 →, "*Obs. exc. dial.*"] **esp NEng**

The germinal part of a grain; a sprout.

1828 Webster *Amer. Dict., Chit* . . . A shoot or sprout; the first shooting or germination of a seed or plant. **1849** Emmons *Agriculture NY* 2.192, The . . yellow corn . . was strongly glazed at this time, and filled all the spaces upon the cob; but the chit shrank some on drying. **1856** U.S. Patent Office *Annual Rept. for 1855: Ag.* 238 **S Atl**, The phosphates . . in wheat, concentrate wholly about the germs, in their mucilage, or "chits." **1886** *Century Illustr. Mag.* 32.41/2, At one end of the [wheat] berry is a tuft of fine vegetable hairs, called the brush, and at the other is the chit, or germ, which contains the germinal principle. **1903** *DN* 2.296 **Cape Cod MA**, *Chit* . . . Sprout on old potatoes. **1931–33** *LANE* Worksheets **cwMA**, Chits are the hard things that encase the seeds [in an apple]. **1977** *Yankee* Nov 256/2 **NEng**, The corn was then washed in several changes of water to remove the lye. It could then be rubbed by hand or in a churn with water to remove the hulls and chits (black tips). **1983** *Greenfield Recorder* (MA) 30 Apr 11, In the old days when corn was taken to the mill to be ground, the whole natural kernel, germ or chit and all was ground, nothing taken out like now.

chit bird n [?Echoic]

1969 *DARE* (Qu. Q21, *. . Sparrows*) Inf **KY**11, Chit bird.

chitlets n pl Also *chicklets, chittlets* [See quot 1962]

The intestines of hogs or fowl prepared as food; **chitterlings 1.**

1939 *LANE* Map 216 **Martha's Vineyard MA**, Giblets . . . chitlets . . . some part or all of the edible internal organs of a fowl . . or else a dish prepared from these. **1962** Atwood *Vocab. TX* 100, Chitlets ([Blend of] *chittlins + giblets*). **1970** Tarpley *Blinky* 200 **neTX**, Food made from hogs' intestines—cut up and fried . . 1.0% [=2 infs] chicklets; 1.0% chittlets.

chitlin bread See **chitterling bread**

chitling n [Prob *chit* n[1] + -*ling*, dimin]

1966 *DARE* (Qu. K54, *. . The smallest pig in a litter*) Inf **MI**8, Chitling.

chitling(s), chitlin(s) See **chitterlings**

chitlin strut See **chitterling strut**

chitney See **jitney**

chits See **chitterlings**

chittam (bark) See **chittamwood 4**

chittam tree See **chittamwood 1**

chittamwood n |'čɪtəm,wʊd, šɪtəm-| Also sp *chittimwood, shittimwood* [*W3* suggests that *chittam* is perh of Muskogean origin while *shittim* is from Heb; because both forms are used for most senses, the two have not been separated here.]

1 also *chittam tree*: A smoke tree (here: *Cotinus obovatus*).

1843 in 1917 Pelzer *Marches* 221 **OK**, Marched 4 miles E.S.E. and encamped on a pretty grove of Elm, hackberry, Tallow tree, and chittim[wood] with good grass and water. **1897** Sudworth *Arborescent Flora* 274, *Cotinus cotinoides* . . . Chittamwood (Ala.). Yellowwood (Ala.). Smoke-tree (Ark.; R.I., cult.). **1900** Lyons *Plant Names* 119 **SE**, *C[ótinus] cotinoídes* . . . Chittam-wood. **1901** Mohr *Plant Life AL* 34, The American smoketree or chittamwood *(Cotinus cotinoides)* in its isolated localities in north Alabama and southwestern Missouri. **1966–67** *DARE* (Qu. T16) Inf **OK**52, Chittam tree—has little blooms like yellow sawdust and berries; **TN**22, Chittam tree ['šɪtəm]—same as yellowwood. **1970** Correll *Plants TX* 988, *Cotinus obovatus* . . American smoke-tree, chittam-wood.

2 A bumelia (here: either *Bumelia lanuginosa* or *B. lycioides*). **chiefly Sth, SW**

1884 Sargent *Forests of N. Amer.* 102, *Bumelia lanuginosa* . . . Gum Elastic. Shittim Wood . . . A clear, very viscid gum exuded from the freshly-cut wood is sometimes used domestically. **1897** Sudworth *Arborescent Flora* 319, *Bumelia lanuginosa*... Shittimwood (Tex.)... *Bumelia lycioides*... Chittimwood (Tex.). **1900** Lyons *Plant Names* 71 **SE**, *B. lycioides*... Chittim-wood. **1933** Small *Manual SE Flora* 1034, *B[umelia] lanuginosa*... Evergreen (or deciduous-leaved northward) shrub, or tree... (*Gum-elastic. Black-haw. Shittim-wood.*)... Coastal Plain and occasionally other provinces, Fla., to Tex., Kans, Ill., and Ga. **1952** Blackburn *Trees* 101, *Bumelia lanuginosa* (s United States) *Wooly bumelia, chittimwood.* **1960** Vines *Trees SW* 833, *Bumelia..lanuginosa*... Chittamwood. **1966–67** *DARE* (Qu. T15, .. *Swamp trees*) Inf **AL2**, Chittamwood; (Qu. T16) Inf **TX22**, [ˈʃɪtəmˌwʊd], evergreen.

3 A silverbell (here: *Halesia carolina*). **chiefly Sth, SW**

1894 *Jrl. Amer. Folkl.* 7.25.94 **WV**, *Halesia tetraptera*.. shittim-wood. **1900** Lyons *Plant Names* 250, *M[ohrodéndron] Carolínum*... Virginia to Florida, west to Illinois... Shittim-wood. **1960** Vines *Trees SW* 842, *Halesia... carolina*... Silver-bell.. Chittimwood.

4 also *chim wood, chittam, ~ bark, chittem, ~ bark, ~ wood, chittern, chittim, ~ bark, ~ tree, chittum, shittim-wood, shittim bark:* A buckthorn.

1897 Parsons *Wild Flowers* CA 68, In Oregon it is known as "chittem-wood". **1897** Sudworth *Arborescent Flora* 299, *Rhamnus purshiana*... Shittimwood (Oreg., Idaho, Wash.). **1900** Lyons *Plant Names* 318 **Pacific NW**, *R[hámnus] Purshiána*... Shittim-wood... Bark, Chittam or Chittim bark. **1930** Sievers *Amer. Med. Plants* 21, *Cascara Buckthorn... Other common names*... Chittem-bark, chittam wood. **1931** U.S. Dept. Ag. *Misc. Pub.* 101.113, *Cascara buckthorn*.. locally known as.. chittim, .. and shittimwood, ranges from British Columbia to western Montana and northern California. **1935** Davis *Honey* 102 **OR**, Closest to the door, within easy reach in case of unexpected illness, was a chittim-tree. **1940** (1951) FWP *Guide OR* 23, Chittam bark, digitalis or foxglove, and other medicinal plants are collected for the market. **1958** McCulloch *Woods Words* **Pacific NW**, *Chittam*—The cascara tree or its bark. At one time it was collected by a few old time loggers on Sundays off. Now the professional bark gatherers have it pretty well cleaned up. The name is also used as chittem, chittam, chittern, and other variations. **1966–69** *DARE* (Qu. BB22, .. *Home remedies.. for constipation*) Infs **CA137, WA1**, Shittim bark; **OR6**, Cascara bark—called chittam; (Qu. T16, .. *Trees*) Inf **CA101**, Chim wood, towards coast. **1967** *DARE* FW Addit **WA29**, *Chittam*—used as physic (a tea). **1973** Hitchcock–Cronquist *Flora Pacific NW* 290, Cascara, chittam bark.. R[hamnus] purshiana.

chittediddle See **chitterdiddle**

chittem, chittem bark, chittemwood See **chittamwood 4**

chitterdiddle n Also *chittediddle, chittidee* [Cf **katydid A**] =**katydid B1.**

1804 (1905) Lewis *Orig. Jrls. Lewis & Clark Exped.* 6.127 **West**, The green insect known in the U'States by the name of the *sawyer* or *chittediddle*, .. was first heard to cry on the 27th of July. **1955** Adams *Grandfather* 282 **NY** (as of 1830s), And there he sat on the live boat foredeck.. as chirk as a chitterdiddle on a pokeweed. **1970** *DARE* (Qu. R7, *Insects that sit in trees or bushes in hot weather and make a sharp, buzzing sound*) Inf **AL59**, Chittidee [ˈtʃɪdidi].

chitterings See **chitterlings**

chitterling bread n Also *chitlin bread, chittlin(g) ~* **Sth** Cf **crackling bread**

Corn bread made with **chitterlings 1.**

1908 *DN* 3.298 **eAL, wGA**, *Chittlin(g)-bread*... Cornbread cooked with bits of chitterling in it, — a heavy, greasy diet greatly enjoyed by the negroes. **1967** *DARE* (Qu. H14) Inf **TX33**, Chitlin bread. **1972** *Atlanta Letters* **GA**, Chitterling bread—common in plantation days, made with corn meal and chitterlings.

chitterlings n pl (rarely sg) Usu |ˈtʃɪtlɪnz|, infreq |ˈtʃɪtlɪŋz|; sppronc |ˈtʃɪtə(r)lɪŋz| Freq sp *chitlins;* for other varr see quots [*OED* c1280 →] **chiefly Sth, S Midl**

1 Intestines, usu of hogs, prepared as food. See Map Cf **chitlets**

1841 *S. Lit. Messenger* 7.39/2 **Sth**, I have never yet learned to relish chitterlings. **1890** *AN&Q* 5.6/2 **eKY**, Chetlins (that is, chitterlings) are a favorite article of food in that district of the country. **1906** *DN* 3.130 **nwAR**, Chitlins. **1908** *DN* 3.298 **eAL, wGA**, Chitlin(g). **1930** *AmSp* 6.159 **NYC**, Chitterlings. **1931** *Scribner's Mag.* 89.127 **FL**, Cracker Chidlings By Marjorie Kinnan Rawlings Real Tales from the Florida

Interior. **1946** *PADS* 5.15 **VA**, Chittlins. Hog's intestines; in general use east of the Blue Ridge. **1949** Kurath *Word Geog.* 64, Chittlins is the name of the small intestines of a pig in the Southern area, where they are eaten by the simple folk. The trisyllabic *chitterlings* is rare. **1950** Faulkner *Stories* 372 **MS**, First, each had that quantity of stewed bird chitterlings which the other could scoop with two hands from the pot. **1950** *PADS* 14.19 **SC**, Chitlings, chittlings. c**1960** Wilson Coll. **csKY**, Chitlings (chitlins or chitterlings). **1961** *PADS* 36.7 **sLA**, Chittlins .. 27 [% of 70 infs]. **1962** Atwood *Vocab. TX* 64, Chittlin(g)s. This word-and-thing combination is well known throughout Texas.., except in the Trans-Pecos areas. **1965–70** *DARE* (Qu. H43, *Foods made from parts of the head and inner organs of an animal*) 102 Infs, **chiefly Sth, S Midl**, Chitlin(g)s; **LA**14, Chitlings [tʃɪtlɪnz] "I never heard anyone pronounce it chitterlings [tʃɪtəlɪŋz] in my life."; 36 Infs, **chiefly Sth, S Midl**, Chitterlings, [no transcription given]; 10 Infs, Jitlins, [no transcription given]; **NY**99, [jɪtlɪŋz], **KY**94, Chitterlings, jitlins—Kentucky oysters. People use this term for chitterlings; **CT**2, Chitterings [tʃɪtərɪŋz]—(like potato chips); **MT**3, Chittles; (Qu. H45, *Dishes made with meat, fish or poultry that everybody around here would know, but that people in other places might not*) Inf **NC**36, Chitlin struts (Negro party where chitlins are served); **TN**5, Chitlins; (Qu. FF1, *Do you have around here a kind of group meeting called a "social" or sociable*?) Inf **AL**5, Chitterling [ˈtʃɪtlɪn] supper; **SC**69, Chitterling supper; (Qu. FF2, *What kinds of parties do people favor around here*?) Inf **DC**11, Chitterling parties. **1970** Tarpley *Blinky* 200 **neTX**, *Food made from hogs' intestines*—cut up and fried 80% [160 infs] chitlins (chitterlings); 2.0% [4 infs] chicklins. *Ibid* 201, Almost all of the answers represent some variation of *chitterlings*, but the tri-syllable pronunciation is never heard... in Northeast Texas all classes of people eat them. *Chittlins* in fancy frozen packages may even be purchased in Dallas super markets. **1972** Claerbaut *Black Jargon* 60, Chitlins.. chits.. chitterlings. **1972** Hilliard *Hog Meat* 43 **Sth** (as of early 1800s), Chitterlings (the large intestine), reputedly treasured only by Negroes, were relished by whites as well, and the traditional "chitlin supper" came to be an annual epicurean delight. **1973** Allen *LAUM* 257, The southern *chittlins*, with the fuller variant *chitterlings*, for the intestines of a pig, is used by two Negro infs. in Minnesota and Iowa. **1977** Smitherman *Talkin* 257 [Black], Chitlins, chitterlings, the insides of the pig, originally thrown away by the slave-master and considered fit only for the slaves; Big Mommas took this "waste" and, by careful cleaning and cooking, turned it into a delicacy. **1981** *Great Amer. Writers' Cookbook* 75 **MS**, Chitterlings (pronounced chittlins) I like to eat them in cafes because they stink up the house, cooking.

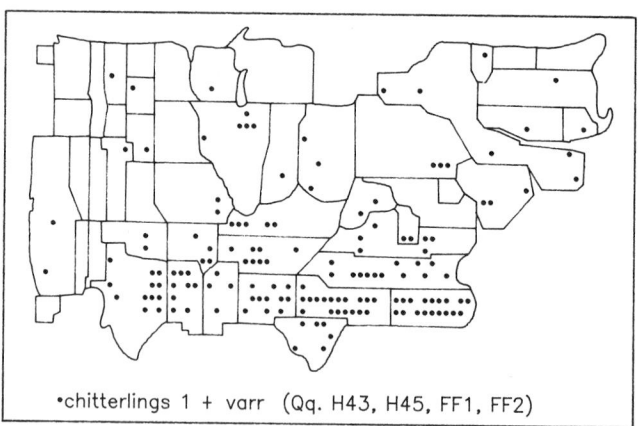

•chitterlings 1 + varr (Qq. H43, H45, FF1, FF2)

2 Intestines; fig: guts, nerve. [*EDD chitterlings* 3 "The intestines of a human being."]

1840 (1847) Longstreet *GA Scenes* 10, My soul if I don't jump down his throat, and gallop every chitterling out of him. **1848** Burton *Waggeries* 50, If my *sow*-licitude is hurtin' yer chitterlings, why be smashed into a hog's pudding. **1933** Rawlings *South Moon* 313 **FL**, I never figgered he'd have the chitlin's when the time come. **1938** Rawlings *Yearling* 168 **FL**, Not him. His chitlin's is made o' iron.

‡3 Transf: see quot.

1944 *PADS* 2.18 **sAppalachians**, Chitlins... The hands.

chitterling strut n Also *chitlin strut* [**chitterlings** + **strut** n] **S Atl**

See quots.

1949 *AmSp* 24.107 **SC,** *Chittlin' strut* . . . An eating orgy featuring beer and chittlings (prepared hog intestines). **1953** *PADS* 19.9 **w, cNC,** *Chitterling strut* . . . A social event, taking place during hog-killing time, at which folk dances are played. **1966** *DARE* (Qu. H45) Inf **NC36,** Chitlin struts (Negro party where chitlins are served). **1972** *DARE* File **cwGA,** *Chitlin-strut*—a blowout at which chitlins are one of the comestibles. "They ain't hardly none of us, nor them neither, fitten to waller in a hog-pen with or go to a chitlin-strut with even." Humourous (but realistic) use of "low colloquial" speech.

chittern See **chittamwood 4**

chittidee See **chitterdiddle**

chittim, chittim bark, chittim tree See **chittamwood 4**

chittimwood See **chittamwood**

chittles See **chitterlings**

chittlets See **chitlets**

chittlin(g) bread See **chitterling bread**

chittling(s), chittlins See **chitterlings**

chittum See **chittamwood 4**

chiv See **chive**

chivaree, chivari See **shivaree**

chivarras n pl Also *chivarros* [MexSpan] **SW**
Chaps made of goatskin.

1892 *DN* 1.189 **TX,** *Chiváro, -s:* leggin; used almost altogether in the plural. Origin unknown; probably from Spanish *chavarí,* a kind of cloth, or from *chiva,* a goat. *Ibid* 1.246, [Addenda to prec:] *Chivárro, -s* (. . not *chivaro, -s*). Add: also *chivarra, -s.* **1930** Dobie *Coronado* 362 **SW,** *Chivarras,* leggins, chaps. **1932** Bentley *Spanish Terms* 119, In the case of *chaps* made of goatskin the hair is abundant, wavy, and may be black or white. These latter are properly known as *chivarras.* **1944** Adams *Western Words, Chivarras.*

chive n Usu |šɪv| Also sp *chev, chib, chiv, shiv(e), sheive* [*OED* 1673 →]
A knife or razor, esp one considered to be a weapon.

1918 *DN* 5.42 [Hobo cant], *Shiv* . . . A razor. **1927** *DN* 5.462 [Underworld jargon], *Shiv*—A razor. **1927** *AmSp* 2.282 [Prison lingo], *Shiv*—A knife. **1930** Shoemaker *1300 Words* 10 **cPA Mts** (as of c1900), *Chive*—A bone or wood handled knife carried by Gipsies. **1930** *AmSp* 6.132 [Underworld slang], *Chev* . . . Knife or razor . . . *chev man* . . . One who fights with a chev. **1931** *AmSp* 7.105 [Underworld argot], *Chive* . . (pronounced shiv.) knife. "A file makes a A-1 chive, if you grind it right." **1935** *AmSp* 10.179 **PA Ger area,** *Chive* for a knife carried by backwoodsmen. **1947** Dadswell *Hey There Sucker* 97, *Shiv* . . knife, usually of the pocket variety. **1954** Armstrong *Satchmo* 224 **LA,** She always kept her chib handy, and with that wide long blade she would soon carve up anybody who tried to get out of line. **1960** Wentworth–Flexner *Slang, Shiv chiv chive shive chev sheive* . . . A knife, esp considered as weapon . . . *Since 1925 the spelling has tended toward "shiv." The variant spellings are given above in decreasing order of prominence.* **1967–68** *DARE* (Qu. F39) Infs **LA43,** Niggers call it a [šɪv]; **OR14,** [šɪv]. **1970** Major *Afro–Amer. Slang, Chib (chiv):* (1940's) an especially long and sharp switchblade knife. *Ibid, Shiv:* a switch blade knife; in prison, a homemade knife.

chiven n Also sp *chivin*
=**fallfish.**

1857 (1864) Thoreau *ME Woods* 187, Many fishes, apparently chivin, came close up to us. **1887** Goode *Amer. Fishes* 428, In Massachusetts it [*Semotilus corporalis*] is often called . . the "Chiven" from its resemblance to the English Chub or Cheven. **1946** LaMonte *N. Amer. Game Fishes* 158, *Fallfish* . . . Names: . . Chivin, White Chub, Windfish, Corporal.

chiveree See **shivaree**

chivin See **chiven**

chivirari See **shivaree**

chivy cat See **civvy cat**

chizzle wink See **chizzywink**

chizzly adj Also sp *chiselly, chisly, chizly* [Perh blend of *chilly* + *drizzly*] **esp Nth**

Of weather: chilly; sometimes also damp.

1896 *DN* 1.414 **c,wNY, nOH, seMI,** *Chiselly:* unpleasant, disagreeable. **1928** Ruppenthal *Coll.* **KS,** Chisly, chizly . . chilly—used often with affected chatter of teeth, as onomatopoetic. **1939** *LANE* Map 99, 1 inf, **RI,** *Chizzly* [tʃɪzlɨ]. [*DARE* Ed: unclear if ref is to severely cold, or brisk, invigorating weather]. **1946** McAtee *Dial. Grant Co. IN Suppl. 3* 3, *Chiselly* . . facetious variant of chilly. **1967** *DARE* FW Addit **swWA,** A chilly, drizzly day is chisley ['čɪzəli]. **1981** *NADS Letters* **MI, IL, MN,** *Chizzly* . . . I've know this since I was a child in Michigan . . my mother used it there . . my wife knew it in southern Illinois. I have a hunch that the inserted /z/ is the /z/ from *freezing* . . . I have heard it here in Minnesota, too. *Ibid* **MI,** *Chizzly*—This is a word my family (we are from Dearborn, Michigan) has always used, but I can't say I've heard it much from anyone else. I understand it to mean bone-chilling weather—cold and usually damp. *Ibid* **NY, OH,** Wife of Chicago informant tells me that . . *chizzly* . . is heard in both Ohio and NY. "Means chilly—not quite ice-cold, but penetrating. It sometimes refers to chills when one seems to be getting a cold or flu, but usually it is a response to weather."

chizzywink n Also *chizzle wink, jizzywig* [Etym uncert: prob in part echoic, but cf *-wig* (as in *earwig*), *DJE merrywing* mosquito, and *EDD winkie* tiny] **chiefly FL Cf blind mosquito**
A midge (family Chironomidae).

1947 Douglas *Everglades* 41 **FL,** Winds carried to them from the reedy lake clouds of feeble white insects lake people call "chizzle winks," which breed and die in myriads in a short few days. **1964** Will *Hist. Okeechobee* 96 **FL,** There was another insect called the chizzy-wink . . . He looked like a mosquito only a little larger, but with a light gray body and fuzzy legs. **1965** Will *Okeechobee Boats* 129 **FL,** As settlers on the lake increased, so did freight boats too, till they were thicker than chizzywinks around a lantern. **1966** *DARE* (Qu. R4, *A large winged insect that hatches in summer in great numbers around lakes or rivers, crowds around lights, lives only a day or so*) Inf **GA3,** Jizzywig [jɪzəwɪg]. **1967** Will *Dredgeman* 51 **FL.**

chlorine fly n
Perh a **mayfly.**

1966 *DARE* (Qu. R4, *A large winged insect that hatches in summer in great numbers around lakes or rivers*) Inf **GA11,** Chlorine fly.

cho See **choo**

choack cherry See **chokecherry**

choak dog See **chokedog**

choaty adj obs Cf *EDD*

1899 (1912) Green *VA Folk-Speech, Choaty* . . . Fat; chubby, used of children.

choby See **chopa spina**

choc n[1] See **chock** n[1]

choc n[2], also attrib Also *chalk, chock* [Abbr for **Choctaw 2**] **chiefly OK, TX, KS**
An inferior type of beer: see quots.

1929 *AmSp* 4.387 **KS,** Another common malt beverage is called *choc* or *chalk*—a thin whitish ale made of barley and hops. I am told that the name was originally *Choctaw* or *Choc-a-taw,* and that the drink came to Kansas by way of Oklahoma. **1931** *AmSp* 7.53 **Sth, SW** [Lumberjack lingo], "Choc" is a low-grade beer originally made by the Choctaws. **1941** *FWP Guide OK* 302, Krebs became known for its production of a drink called Choctaw or "choc" beer, made of hops, tobacco, fishberries, barley, and alcohol. **1965–66** *DARE* (Qu. DD28b, . . *Fermented drinks . . made at home*) Infs **OK25, 42,** Choc; (Qu. DD25, . . *Nicknames . . beer*) Inf **OK11,** Choc. **1970** Green *Ely* 445 **TX** (as of c1915), The colored people I am told has a formula the Teacher never heard of. It can be made from a wash pot to a coffee pot. One is called rip gizzard. The other is chock beer.

cho cho n |čo čo| Also *choch* |čoč| [Basque "child, young man"] **OR**
A small child, a boy.

1967 *DARE* (Qu. Z12, . . *A small child*) Inf **OR10,** Cho cho [čo'čo] (Basque); choch ['čoč]; [both] not used in a sentence, more as a replacement for a name, instead of calling by name. **1967** *DARE* Tape **OR18,** [FW:] Are there any words in the Basco [=Basque] language that are used today kind of commonly as part of your English speech? . . . [Inf:] Cho cho [čočo] means boy or sonny.

chock n[1] Usu |čɔk| Also sp *chac, choc* [LaFr] **chiefly LA**
A **boat-tailed grackle** or similar bird.
    1917 *DN* 4.423, *Boat-tailed grackle . . .* Chock; Crow-jack; Crow Blackbird. [**1931** Read *LA French* 26, *Choc . . .* Blackbird. This word probably arose in imitation of the cries of the various species of Grackles or Crow Blackbirds. *Choc* is pronounced like *chock* in English *chock-ful.*] **1967–68** *DARE* (Qu. Q11) Inf **LA**31, Chock [čɔk] (=grackle); [(Qu. Q14, . . *Thrush*) Inf **TX**37, [šɔː]]. **1983** *Reinecke Coll.* **New Orleans LA**, *Chock, chac* [tʃɑk]—a grackle, medium-sized black bird with long tail. Used in La. French, either from onomat. or from unrecognized Indian use.

chock n[2] See **choc** n[2]

chock n[3] See **shock** n

chock v See **shock** v

chockablock adj, adv   Pronc-spp *chockerblock, chuckablock*
[See quot 1945] **esp NEng**
Very full; completely (full).
    1850 Melville *White-Jacket* 388 **NEast**, I'm blessed if we ar'n't about chock a' block here! **1903** *DN* 2.293 **Cape Cod MA**, *Chock a block . . .* Full; satisfied. 'I can't eat any more; I'm chock a block.' **1914** *DN* 4.70 **ME, nNH**, *Chuck-a-block, chock-a-block . . .* Very full. **1916** Macy–Hussey *Nantucket Scrap Basket* 126 **MA**, "Chock," "chock-full," "chock-a-block" and "chock-a-block full"—are all nauticalisms in general use, but more commonly used among a seafaring people than elsewhere, and Nantucketers employ these various terms on all occasions. Each has its particular shade of meaning when correctly used. **1931** in 1953 Botkin *Treas. Railroad Folkl.* 308, When they arrived at the transfer track, it was chockablock—not a damned car could this foreman shove in. **1942** McAtee *Dial. Grant Co. IN* 18 (as of 1890s), *Chuckablock . . .* full. **1945** Colcord *Sea Language* **ME, Cape Cod, Long Island**, *Chockablock.* Said of a *purchase* or *tackle* when both blocks have been brought together and no more slack can be taken on the rope. "I'm chockablock and belayed," said an innkeeper on the Maine coast, in turning away a would-be guest. Ashore (colloquial), it means completely; often abbreviated to chock, as in chock-full. **1953** *PADS* 19.9 **w,cNC**. **1959** *VT Hist.* new ser 27.130, *Chuck full . . .* var. chuck-a-block full. Crammed; full to the utmost. **1965–70** *DARE* (Qu. LL28, . . *Entirely full*) Infs **CA**97, **CT**29, **DC**1, **GA**11, **LA**32, **MD**43, **NY**66, **RI**17, **VA**69, Chockablock; **MA**5, Chockablock full; **CT**19, Chockerblock; **VT**16, **WI**61, Chuckablock; (QR, near Qu. GG3) Inf **CA**113, The campgrounds were just chuckablock full.

chock-a-la-taw n [See quot 1951] **LA**
=**marsh hawk.**
    1917 *DN* 4.424 **LA**, *Chock-a-la-taw.* The marsh hawk (Circus hudsonius). **1951** *AmSp* 26.94, The marsh hawk, primarily, but sometimes related species, is called *chock-a-la-taw* in Louisiana, a corruption of either *chocolatier* (chocolate dealer) or *chocolatière* (chocolate pot), both referring to the brown color of the more commonly seen immature birds.

chockcherry See **chokecherry**

chockerblock See **chockablock**

chocolate See **chocolate drop 1, chocolate root**

chocolate baby n   Cf **nigger baby**
A chocolate candy in the shape of a baby.
    1968–69 *DARE* (Qu. H82b, . . *Cheap candies . . years ago*) Infs **NJ**30, **NY**119, **RI**5, Chocolate babies.

chocolate drop n
1 also *chocolate* (*bar* or *bunny*): A Black person. **esp Sth, S Midl** *derog*
    1900 *DN* 2.27 **neOH** [College words], *Chocolate-drop,* a young negress. **1941** *LANE* Map 452b, 1 inf, **ceCT**, [hʌklbeɹɪ, čɔklɪt drɔp], jocular names. **1950** *WELS* (*Nicknames . . Negro*) 1 Inf, **seWI**, Chocolate drop. **1962** Atwood *Vocab. TX* 73, Other words that occur more than once include . . *chocolate drop.* **1964** *PADS* 42.30 **Chicago IL** [Racial slurs], Negro . . . Chocolate drop. **1965–70** *DARE* (Qu. HH28, . . *Negro*) 12 Infs, **chiefly Sth, S Midl**, Chocolate drop; **RI**6, Chocolate bunny; [(Qu. HH29b, . . *People of mixed blood—part Negro*) Inf **NC**87, Chocolate; **IL**11, Has chocolate in his blood]. **1970** Tarpley *Blinky* 264 **neTX**, *Teasing and derogatory names for Negroes . . .* [Infreq] chocolate bars, chocolate drops.

2 See quot. [Perh from the shape of a chocolate kiss]
    1968 *DARE* (Qu. C17, . . *A small, rounded hill*) Inf **PA**128, Chocolate drop.

chocolate flower n
A **cranesbill 1** (here: *Geranium maculatum*).
    1892 *Jrl. Amer. Folkl.* 5.93 **NH**, *Geranium maculatum,* chocolate-flower. **1930** Sievers *Amer. Med. Plants* 62, Wild Geranium. *Geranium maculatum . . . Other common names . . .* Chocolate-flower, crowfoot, . . shameface. **1971** Krochmal *Appalachia Med. Plants* 134, *Geranium maculatum . . .* chocolate flower.

chocolate lily n [From the color]
A **fritillary** (esp *Fritillaria biflora,* but also *F. atropurpurea* and *F. camschatcensis*).
    1897 Parsons *Wild Flowers CA* 266, *F. biflora,* the black, or chocolate, lily, is the species common in the south, and blooms early. **1966** Heller *Wild Flowers AK* 93, Chocolate, Black or Kamchatka Lily . . . Flowers chocolate colored, the 3 sepals and 3 petals joined, forming a nodding bell. **1967** *DARE* (Qu. S26c, *Wildflowers . . in woods*) Inf **CA**20, Chocolate lily. **1973** Hitchcock–Cronquist *Flora Pacific NW* 691, Checker lily, chocolate l[ily] . . . *F. atropurpurea.*

chocolate man See **chocolate soldier**

chocolate mouse n [From the shape] **esp WI**
A type of children's candy.
    1968 *DARE* (Qu. H82a, *Cheap candies*) Infs **WI**5, 49, Chocolate mice; **WI**13, Chocolate mice—we bought them in Chicago, probably unique to Jefferson; (Qu. H82b, . . *Years ago*) Infs **CT**16, **WI**5, 46, Chocolate mice. **1980** *DARE* File **Akron OH** (as of c1920), "Chocolate mice" were candies about an inch long, shaped like mice, and with a dark coating (perhaps chocolate), sold to children as "penny candies."

chocolate root n Also *chocolate, ~ plant* [See quots 1832, 1890] **chiefly NEng**
=**water avens.**
    1832 Williamson *Hist. ME* 1.121, The Chocolate plant . . Its root, when boiled, makes a drink in taste and goodness like chocolate. **1890** *Century Dict.* 2504/3, The roots of . . the water avens, *Geum rivale,* . . from their reddish-brown color are sometimes known by the names of chocolate-root and Indian chocolate. **1893** *Jrl. Amer. Folkl.* 6.141, *Geum rivale,* chocolate. Buckfield, Me.; Franconia, N.H. **1910** Graves *Flowering Plants* 235 **CT**, *Geum rivale . .* Chocolate-root. **1959** Carleton *Index Herb. Plants* 27, Chocolate Root: Geum (v). **1976** Miller *Shaker Herbs* 130, *Water Avens—Geum rivale—*Chocolate Root.

chocolate soldier n Also *chocolate man* [From the shape]
A type of children's candy.
    1967–69 *DARE* (Qu. H82a, *Cheap candies*) Inf **MA**43, Chocolate men; **NH**15, Chocolate soldiers or chocolate men—may or may not be sold now; (Qu. H82b, . . *Years ago*) Inf **MI**72, Chocolate soldiers; **NH**15, Chocolate soldiers or chocolate men.

Choctaw n, also attrib Also older sp *Choktah*
1 A type of horse.
    1775 Adair *Amer. Indians* 411 **swTN, nMS, nAL**, He rode a young Choktah horse, which had been used only to a rope round his neck. **1830** *Boston Transcript* 26 Nov 3/1 *(DA)*, Two gentlemen and a lady, mounted each on a Choctaw poney, and evidently from far-famed Chickasha. **1945** Saxon *Gumbo Ya-Ya* 561, Des cheveaux Choctaw: in southern Louisiana, a small horse. (The Choctaws were short.)

2 A kind of homemade beer or whiskey, more often called **choc** n[2].
    1965 *DARE* (Qu. DD21c, . . *Whiskey, especially illegally made*) Inf **MS**64, Choctaw; (Qu. DD28b, . . *Fermented drinks . . made at home*) Inf **OK**11, Choctaw beer.

Choctaw root n
An **Indian hemp** (here: *Apocynum cannabinum*).
    1931 Clute *Common Plants* 29, A familiar plant, still used for basket-making and similar purposes, and commonly called Indian hemp (*Apocynum cannabinum*), was once known as Choctaw root. **1971** Krochmal *Appalachia Med. Plants* 52, *Apocynum cannabinum . . .* choctaw root. **1974** (1977) Coon *Useful Plants* 62, *Apocynum cannabinum . .* coctaw-root [sic] . . . Poisonous to stock as well as man and yet medicinal when used by the knowing.

choggie n [Abbr for **chogset** + -*ie* famil suff] **NEng**
=**cunner** n[1] **1.**
    1965 *PADS* 43.25 **seMA**, *Minnow . . .* [1 inf] choggies. **1969** *DARE* (Qu. P4, *Saltwater fish . . not good to eat*) Inf **RI**17, [čɔgiz].

chogset n Usu |'čɔgsɪt, -sɛt, -sət, -zɪt| Infreq sp *chaugset* [Of Algonquian origin] **NEng**
=**cunner** n[1] **1.**

 1842 DeKay *Zool. NY* 4.173 **NEng,** The Bergall has various popular names; Chogset, a name derived from the Mohegan dialect, but its purport unknown. **1872** Schele de Vere *Americanisms* 66, More generally known is the *Chogset* (Ctenolabrus ceruleus), frequently called *Burgall* or *Blue Fish,* and found on the whole Eastern coast. **1899** Bergen *Animal Lore* 62 **seMA,** Chaugset (Indian) . . cunner, *Tautogolabrus adspersus.* **1939** *LANE* Map 234 *(Minnow),* 1 inf, **seRI,** [čɒgsət]; 1 inf, **seRI,** [čɒgzɪt]; 1 inf, **ceRI,** [čɒgsɪt]; 1 inf, **seMA,** [čɒgsɛt]; 2 infs, **seMA,** [čɒgsɪt].

choice n, v Usu |čɔɪs|; also |-ɔɪ-, -ɜɪ-, -əɪ-, -ɚ-| Pronc-spp *cherce, ch'ice.*

A Forms.

 1894 in 1941 Warfel–Orians *Local-Color Stories* 738 **sAR** [Black], I'd even gin 'im he's ch'ice o' sets. **1930** *AmSp* 5.340 neMA, [ɔɪ] [oɪ]. The first element tends to be tense in *choice.* **1931** *AmSp* 6.164 swVA, [ɔɪ] in *choice, joist, noise, join,* is often modified. Among the white people in Williamsburg, the sound commonly appears as a diphthong of uncertain character, [əɪ], [ʌɪ] or [oɪ]. **1940** in 1944 *ADD* **NYC,** Choice . . |əɪ|, |ʌɪ|. Less educated. **1941** *Ibid* **NYC,** Cherce |tʃɚs|. **1942** Hall *Smoky Mt. Speech* 46, In the Smokies, the diphthong [ɔɪ] varies [ɔɪ], [ɔ·ɪ], [oɪ]. The general preference seems to be for [oɪ] in *choice, join.* **1942** *AmSp* 17.149 seNY, *Choice* has [ɔɪ] 14 [informants], [ɜɪ] 2 [informants].

B As verb.

See quot. Cf *DJE*
 1914 *DN* 4.153 **NH,** Choice . . . To choose.

choice adj chiefly **NEng**
Appreciative, careful.

 1775 in 1875 J. & A. Adams *Familiar Letters* 128 **MA,** I shall be very choice of them. **1840** (1841) Dana *2 Yrs.* 335 **MA,** They had many of the latest sailor songs . . which they were very choice of. **1859** Tomlinson *KS in 1858* 99 **NEast,** While living here in Kansas he was very choice of her, scarcely allowing her to stir out. **1902** (1904) Rowe *Maid of Bar Harbor* 333 **ME,** They have been in my husband's family for generations . . and he's very choice of them. **1939** Wolcott *Yankee Cook Book* 336, Because he was very choice of it, they were to have only one drink apiece. **1949** *McDavid Coll.* swNY, He was so choice of it [=his watch]. **1950** *Eaton Coll.* neWI, The old map is falling apart and we're rather choice of it.

choicy adj Also sp *choicey*

1 Choosy, particular, fussy.

 1909 Wason *Happy Hawkins* 208 **TX,** "I ain't nowise choicy," sez I, "call me anything you want." **1923** *DN* 5.203 swMO, Choicey . . . Particular . . . "Don't get too choicey." **1935** Sandoz *Jules* 299 wNE (as of 1880–1930), Girls were scarce and could be choicy. **1954** *Harder Coll.* cwTN, Choicy: choosey. **1957** *DE Folkl. Bulletin* 1.28, Choicy (choosy). **1966** *DARE* FW Addit cwAL, You shouldn't be so choicy! **1967–69** *DARE* (Qu. H12, *If somebody eating a meal takes little bits of food and leaves most of it on his plate*) Infs MD19, OH80, 88, TN11, Choicy; IN52, Choicy with his food. **1968** *DARE* Tape MD19, These days I hate to cook because everybody's so choicy.

2 Of high quality.

 1923 *DN* 5.203 swMO, Choicey . . . choice . . . "That meat's right choicey."

chok See **chook** intj

choke v[1] **Nth**
In logging: to put a cable or similar line tightly around a log in order to move it.

 1958 McCulloch *Woods Words* **Pacific NW,** Choke—To pass a line around a log or other object and pull it tight. **1967** *DARE* Tape WA24, Then you choke the logs. **1969** Sorden *Lumberjack Lingo* **NEng, Gt Lakes,** Choking—Binding logs together with a cable when hoisting them to load a sleigh or railroad car.

choke v[2] [Var of *chock* to block, make fast] Cf **chunk** v **1b**

 1949 (1958) Stuart *Thread* 198 **KY,** They helped us choke wheels and use handspikes.

choke intj See **chook** intj

choke a horse v phr For varr see quots **chiefly Nth** *joc*
In var phrr indicating excess: See quots.

 1844 Thompson *Major Jones's Courtship* 185 **GA,** Drunk more yarb tea than enough to kill a horse. **1965–70** *DARE* (Qu. U19b, . . *Of paper money*) Infs IL144, NJ1, Enough (dough) to choke a horse; ME21, Wad big enough to choke a horse; IL114, It would choke a cow; MI55, Wad that would choke an ox; (Qu. U37) Inf MN33, Money enough to choke a horse; (Qu. U38a) Inf MA58, Roll'd choke a horse; (Qu. U38b) Inf CT23, Enough to choke a horse; (Qu. B3) Inf MN33, Hot enough to choke a horse; (Qu. HH22c) Inf MN33, Choke his own horse to death; (Qu. H74a) Inf MD8, Strong enough to choke a horse; (Qu. LL9b) Inf CA155, To choke a horse.

chokeberry n

1 A plant of the genus *Aronia.* Also called **choke-huckleberry, chokepear, shadbush, shore berry**

 1778 Carver *Travels N. Amer.* 1.511 **Gt Lakes,** The Choak Berry. The shrub thus termed by the natives grows about five or six feet high, and bears a berry about the size of a sloe, of a jet black. **1899** Garland *Boy Life* 123 nwIA, The roots of ferns, black haws, chokeberries, sheep-sorrel, . . anything at all that happened to be in season or handy. **1901** Mohr *Plant Life AL* 71, The chokeberry, which is here of arborescent habit, presents a beautiful sight when loaded with its bright scarlet fruit. **1938** Matschat *Suwannee R.* 207 nFL, sGA, Chokeberry bushes and blackberry vines were in full bloom. **1941** Walker *Lookout* 61 **TN,** Chokeberry has . . many favorable spots . . where its loads of garnet red berries add beauty to the late summer woodlands. **1966–68** *DARE* (Qu. I44, . . *Berries* . . *wild*) Infs MA6, OH3, Chokeberries; (Qu. DD28b, . . *Fermented drinks* . . *made at home*) Inf MN15, Chokeberry wine. **1967** *DARE* Wildfl. QR Pl.103 Infs LA21, OH37, Black chokeberry. **1976** Bruce *How to Grow Wildflowers* 117, Closely related to *Amelanchier* is a genus of three species found only in eastern North America: *Aronia,* the Chokeberries.

2 =**chokecherry 1.**

 1832 Williamson *Hist. ME* 1.117, The *Prune* genus embraces . . . the *Choke-cherry,* or as some may call it the choke-berry of two varieties. **1967** *Merck Vet. Manual* 1062, *Prunus* sp. Chokeberries or wild cherries.

chokebore britches n Also *choke-bore(d) pants,* pronc-sp *chokeboard* [*chokebore* a shotgun barrel that narrows toward the muzzle] **West**
Trousers that narrow towards the bottom, esp riding breeches.

 1944 Adams *Western Words, Choke-bored pants*—A name given the flare-hipped, tight-kneed riding breeches of the Easterner. **1958** McCulloch *Woods Words* **Pacific NW,** *Choke-bore pants*—Breeches worn by dudes in the woods and much sneered at by loggers. **1959** Martin *Gunbarrel* 231 **WY,** She wore "chokeboard" trousers with wrap-around leggings, but her high-heeled kid pumps left a two-inch margin of silk stocking exposed. **1967** *DARE* (Qu. W9) Inf WA30, Chokebore britches.

choke-bored adj
Tall and thin.

 1958 McCulloch *Woods Words* **Pacific NW,** *Choke-bored*—A thin man, or a long-legged skinny man.

chokecherry n, also attrib Arch spp *chock-, choack-*

1 A cherry, usu *Prunus virginiana,* but also **black cherry.** chiefly **Nth** See Map

 1784 in 1785 Amer. Acad. Arts & Sci. *Memoirs* 1.449 **MA,** The Black Choke Cherry. A low shrub. **1822** (1898) Fowler *Jrl.* 143 **NM,** In the

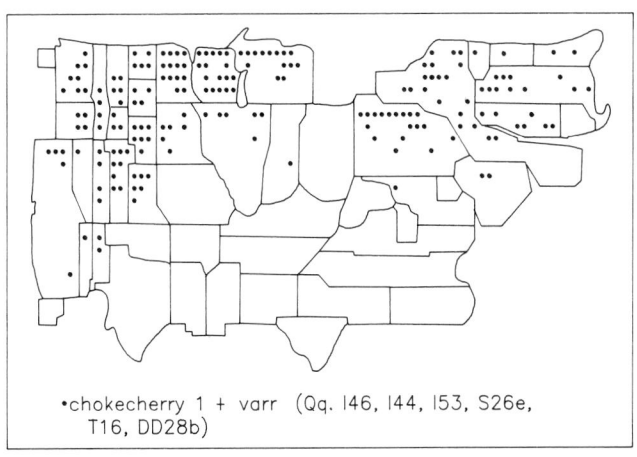

•chokecherry 1 + varr (Qq. I46, I44, I53, S26e, T16, DD28b)

bottoms along the Cricks Cotten Wood Black elder and Willows With the Chock Cherry Black Curren . . . the Choack Cherry is on[e] of the Handsomest Bushes I Have Seen. **1834** Pike *Prose Sketches* 28 **cnNM,** I found I was freezing, and stopped in a cliff of rocks, and made a little fire of choke-cherry bushes. **1859** (1942) Patterson *Travel Diary* 146 **NE,** We find a thicket of brushwood — rose bushes, choke cherries, currants and young cottonwood. **a1862** (1864) Thoreau *ME Woods* 310, The prevailing shrubs and small trees along the shore were: *osier rouge* and alders . . choke-cherry. **1958** Blasingame *Dakota Cowboy* 27 **SD** (as of 1904), There was a heavy stand of timber — cottonwood, ash, elm, and many plum, chokecherry, and Juneberry thickets lined the river. **1965–70** *DARE* (Qu. I46, . . *Fruits . . wild*) 172 Infs **chiefly NW, Rocky Mts, Upper MW, and Nth,** Chokecherries; (Qu. I44, . . *Berries . . wild*) 14 Infs, **chiefly Nth,** Chokecherries; (Qu. I53) Inf **SD2,** Chokecherries; (Qu. T16, . . *Trees*) 8 Infs, **chiefly Nth,** Chokecherry; (Qu. S26e, . . *Wildflowers*) Infs **CT26, NJ45,** Chokecherry; (Qu. DD28b, . . *Fermented drinks . . made at home*) 12 Infs, **chiefly Inland Nth,** Chokecherry wine; **NY23,** Chokecherry with dandelion wine; **NE10,** Wild chokecherry wine. **1971** Krochmal *Appalachia Med. Plants* 210, *Prunus serotina* — Common Names: . . choke cherry.

2 =**chokeberry 1.**

1967 *DARE* Wildfl. QR Pl.103 Inf **OR8,** Black chokecherry.

chokedamp n [*OED* 1741 →]

Blackdamp.

1943 Korson *Coal Dust* 221, From the manner in which it killed its victims, blackdamp was nicknamed chokedamp. **1968** Adams *Western Words, Chokedamp* — Mine gas that causes choking or suffocation when there is insufficient oxygen. **1973** *PADS* 59.31 **PA, MD,** *Chokedamp . . = blackdamp.*

chokedog n Arch sp *choakdog*

An anglepod (*Gonolobus* spp).

1845 (1849) Phelps *Lectures on Botany* App. 107/2, *Gonolobus . . obliquus*, (false choak-dog . .). **1876** Hobbs *Bot. Hdbk.* 23, Choke dog, Angle pod, Gonolobus obliquus. **1959** Carleton *Index Herb. Plants* 27, *Choke dog: Gonolobus* (v).

choke 'em n [Because of its parasitic effect on host plants]
=**dodder.**

1966 *DARE* Wildfl. QR (Wills–Irwin) Pl.34A Inf **TX34,** Choke 'em.

choke-huckleberry n
=**chokeberry 1.**

1931 Clute *Common Plants* 69, One taste of each is enough . . to indicate why the aronias are often called choke-huckleberries.

chokem See **choker 2**

chokepear n [*OED* 1530 →]
=**chokeberry 1.**

1838 Kettell *Yankee Notions* 95 **NEng,** Fruit he would not eat, except choke pear. **1839** Buel *Farmer's Companion* 269 **CT,** It is as easy to cultivate the vergaleu as it is the choke pear. **1892** *Jrl. Amer. Folkl.* 5.95 **seME,** *Pyrus arbutifolia . .* choke-pear. **1947** Bowles–Towle *New Engl. Cooking* 266, Pickled Choke Pears.

choker n

1 also *choker line:* In logging: a wire rope or cable hooked around a log for pulling it; hence *choker hook, chokerman, choker setter* or *chokesetter:* see quots. [**choke** v¹] **Nth, esp Pacific NW**

1905 U.S. Forest Serv. *Bulletin* 61.33 **Pacific NW,** *Choker . . .* A noose of wire rope by which a log is dragged. **1918** *DN* 5.55 **WA,** Axel Sandros . . lost his life Thursday afternoon, when a choker hook, pulled from under a log, struck him on the head. **1942** *AmSp* 17.220 **Nth** [Logger talk], Each fastens on three *choker lines* that have been noosed around logs by *chokesetters*. *Ibid* 221, *Choker.* A loop of wire rope, used to noose a log in high-lead logging. *Chokerman* or *choker-setter.* The man who places the choker around a log that is to be yarded. **1945** (1946) Macdonald *Egg & I* 49 **WA,** He told me to put the chokers on the fir trees and to shout directions for the pulling. **1956** *AmSp* 31.150 **nwCA,** *Choker.* **1958** McCulloch *Woods Words* **Pacific NW,** *Choker setter —* On a logging crew, the next step above the beginning job of whistle punk. The choker setter puts the wire choker around logs to be yarded. Sometimes he is called a rigging man, sometimes a rigging slinger. *Chokerman —* A man who sets chokers. **1966–67** *DARE* Tape **MT4,** The chokerman . . would clear out and get ready to hook the cables onto the logs that they'd pull in with a cable by a steam donkey; **OR1,** [FW:]

What occupations fit in under someone working "in the woods"? [Inf:] Well, there's the timber faller and the bull buck . . and then they have chokesetters, rigging slingers; **WA24,** You had your hold-back line, you'd drop that down with chokers on it . . . A choker is a piece of line with a choker hook on it. They made 'em different lengths, 14 to 20 feet long. **1982** *Smithsonian Letters,* I was raised in the lower Columbia river logging country . . (Early 1900) . . . The crew in the woods the Hooktender (who was the head of the crew) and the choker setters (who put the cable around the logs) and the whistle punk who signaled the donkey puncher (operator) when to go and when to stop by means of a wire which reached from the logging area to the whistle on the donkey.

2 also *chokem:* Something that chokes one when eaten, or that promotes constipation; see quots.

1925 *AmSp* 1.137 **Pacific NW** [Logger talk], Cheese is "choker." **1928** Ruppenthal Coll. **KS,** Chokem, choke'm . . . (army) cheese. **1930** Irwin *Amer. Tramp, Choker.* — Cheese. Largely used in the harvest fields and in the lumber camps, and so called from its effect on the bowels. **1958** McCulloch *Woods Words* **Pacific NW,** *Chokem —* Cheese. **1970** Thompson Coll. **AL** (as of 1920s), Cold sweet potatoes (chokers) don't go down too pretty good.

choke rag n Also *choke strap* [Cf older *choker* in similar use (*DAS*)]

A necktie.

1944 Adams *Western Words, Choke strap* — The derisive reference to a necktie, something for which the cowboy has little need. **1953** Randolph *Down in Holler* 234 **Ozarks,** Choke rag . . . An old-fashioned necktie. **1954** Harder Coll. **cwTN,** *Choke rag:* A necktie. Humorous. **1969** Sorden *Lumberjack Lingo* **NEng, Gt Lakes,** *Choke strap —* A necktie.

choker hole n [**choker 1**]

In logging:

1 See quot.

1958 McCulloch *Woods Words* **Pacific NW,** *Choker hole —* A small hole blasted or dug under a log so the choker can be passed under the log, getting it ready to yard.

2 Transf: a doughnut. *joc*

1925 *AmSp* 1.137 **Pacific NW** [Logger talk], For dessert . . some "choker holes (doughnuts)." **1968** Adams *Western Words, Choker holes —* A logger's name for doughnuts.

choker hook, choker line, chokerman See **choker 1**

chokerman's brute n

1958 McCulloch *Woods Words* **Pacific NW,** *Chokerman's brute —* A kind of sickness; used to describe any illness not otherwise known or named.

choker setter, chokesetter See **choker 1**

choke strap See **choke rag**

choke-tater n [*choke* abbr for *artichoke* + *tater* potato]

A tuber of the Jerusalem artichoke (*Helianthus tuberosus*).

1893 Owen *Voodoo Tales* 145 **MO,** The choke-taters or artichokes, (not the green vegetable rosettes served to "white folks," but the tubers of the great "Jerusalem sunflowers" . .) were buried in the ashes.

choke up v phr

To make an unwilling payment; "cough up."

1967–68 *DARE* (Qu. U8b, . . *I paid ten dollars for it*) Inf **WI57,** Choked up; (Qu. U18, . . *"I finally made him _____."*) Inf **TX27,** Choke it up.

choke vine n

A bindweed **1.**

1967 *DARE* (Qu. S5, . . *Wild morning glory*) Inf **NY6,** Choke vine.

choky adj

Having the throat constricted from nervousness or stage fright.

1872 (1973) Thompson *Major Jones's Courtship* 136, I felt kind o' choky, but after they was all done hollerin . . I . . begun my Oration.

cholera n Usu |ˈkɑlə·ə, ˈkɔ-| rarely |ˈko-|; occas, **esp in Sth,** second vowel is syncopated; **freq in SE, less common in other areas** final vowel is |-i| or less often |-ɪ|; Pronc-spp *chol(l)ery* Cf **-y**

Std senses, var forms.

1848 Lowell *Biglow* 2 **NEng,** Zekle, ses she, our Hosee's gut the chollery or suthin anuther. **1891** *DN* 1.117 **cNY,** [kɑlə·i, kɑlri] . . *cholera.* **1900** Stockton *Afield* 321 **CT,** I've got the cholery. **1942** Warnick *Garrett Co.*

MD 1 (as of 1900–18), Feminine names ending with an "a" were pronounced as if ending in "ie" or "y", as were also some common words as extry, cholery, and sody. **1946** Greer–Petrie *Angeline Steppin'* 31 **csKY,** Pervided they didn't ketch the cholery. **c1960** *Wilson Coll.* **csKY,** Cholera is commonly ['kɑlɚɪ]. **1965–70** *DARE* (Qu. K7) Inf **AR47,** Eatin' too much would be called cholera ['kɑlrɪ]; (Qu. K28) Inf **GA17,** ['kɑlərɪ]; **GA77** ['kɒlɚæ]; **LA22,** ['kaʊrɪ]; (Qu. K47) Inf **LA18,** [kɑlrɪ]; (Qu. K78) Inf **OK49,** Used to get ['kɔlɛri] but not any more; **MO1,** ['kɑlɚi]; **FL26,** Cholery.

‡cholera drop n

1968 *DARE* (Qu. I25, . . *Cucumbers*) Inf **NY45,** Cholera drops—old-fashioned. [FW: Inf's grandparents thought these vegetables [=cucumbers and tomatoes] were poison.]

cholera morbus n Usu |'kɑlɚə 'mɑ(r)bəs, -'morbəs|, also |'kɑlɚi-, 'kɑlə-, 'kɑlɪ-|; see further quot 1965–70; also sp *cholera morabus; coleramorbus; colly marbles, ~ mobbles, ~ morbus; collarmoggis;* and by folk-etym *colored marbles* [*OED* 1704 →] See also **gollywobbles**

Std sense, var forms.

1844 Thompson *Major Jones's Courtship* 127 **GA,** It would jest be my luck if sum bominable thing like a war or a coleramorbus, or a starvation was to come along. **1942** Hall *Smoky Mt. Speech* 33 eTN, wNC, The most striking thing here is the complete unrounding which the vowel often undergoes, as in *cholera morbus* ['kɑlɚɪ 'mɑɚbəs]. **1946** Stuart *Tales Plum Grove* 98 **seKY,** She took somethin' like the collarmoggis and it took her outten this world like a flash of lightnin'. **1965–70** *DARE* (Qu. BB19, *Joking names for looseness of the bowels*) Inf **AR55,** [ˌkɑlɪ'mɔbəs]; **NH11,** Cholera morbus; **NJ53** ['kɔlərə 'morbɪs]; **SC27,** Colly mobbles; **VA52,** [kɔlɪməbəs] (from green apples); (Qu. BB28, *Joking names . . imaginary diseases*) Inf **AZ6,** [kɑlʊri mɑrbəlz]; **AR56,** ['kɑlə ˌmɑbəs]; **NC41,** Colly morbus; **RI15,** ['kɑlɚəmorbəs]; (Qu. BB49, . . *Diseases . . common*) Infs **KY19,** 24, [ˌkɑlə-i 'mɑrbəs]; **IL143,** ['kɑlɚimɑrvɪs] (stomach ache); **MS33,** Cholera morabus; (QR, near Qu. GG36) Inf **CA36,** [kɑlɚimorbɪs], the stomach cramps that come from eating green apples. **1966–68** *DARE* FW Addit **SC,** *Colly-mobbles*—a virus: vomiting and your bowels are running off at the same time. Now [kɑlərə maurbəs]; **MN23,** Colored marbles, i.e. colly marbles or cholera morbus, a belly-ache and diarrhea from too many green apples. **1969** *DARE* Tape CT41, We'd get ['kɔlərə ˌmɑbəs] . . . that comes from eating green apples.

cholery See cholera

cholic root See colicroot 3

cholla n, also attrib |'čɔɪjə| Pronc-sp *choya* [MexSpan] SW =prickly pear.

1846 Robinson *Life in CA* 102, A large tract covered with *choyas,* or prickly pears. **1901** Van Dyke *Desert* 3 **AZ,** In the draws and flat places the fine sand lies thicker, is tossed in wave forms by the wind, and banked high against clumps of cholla, or prickly pear. **1907** White *AZ Nights* 186, The hill I had to climb was steep and covered with chollas, so I didn't get along very fast. **1961** Douglas *My Wilderness* 82 **AZ,** Here too is . . the cholla cactus (or staghorn). This is the cactus that has joints like sausages and thrives on destruction. For when animals trample on it, the broken pieces have a chance to hitchhike to new growing places. **1967** *DARE* (Qu. S26, . . *Wildflowers*) Inf **CA4,** Cholla = staghorn cholla or cane cholla. **1973** *AZ Highways* Mar 29, Pronounced *"choy-ah,"* Cholla is the common alias for *Cylindropuntia* . . . In Mexican it means "head." **1981** *DARE* File, The jumping cholla ['čɔɪjə] of the Arizona desert has segments so loosely attached to the main plant that they actually seem to jump out at anyone who passes close to them.

chollery See cholera

cholo n Usu |čo(ʊ)lo(ʊ)|, also |ča-, šo-| [AmSpan] chiefly SW usu derog

A Mexican, esp a low-class one; a half-breed.

1851 (1976) Melville *Moby-Dick* 196, Archy . . whispered to his neighbor, a Cholo. **1881** Bell *Reminiscences* 60 **sCA,** That is to say, he called the Governor hard names; called his chivalrous followers vagabonds and *cholos.* **1949** *PADS* 11.19 **CO,** Cholo ['šolo] . . . A Mexican. **1967–69** *DARE* (Qu. HH28, . . *Mexicans*) Infs **CA4,** 66, Cholo; **CA113,** [čoʊloʊ], a low-class Mexican; **WA22,** [čalo]; (Qu. HH18, *Very insignificant or low-grade people*) Inf **CA66,** Cholo—a low-grade Mexican. **1969** O'Connor *Horse & Buggy West* 63 **AZ** (as of early 1900s), Since the Anglo-Saxon American was top dog he looked down on the ordinary Mexican. He called him a "greaser" and a "cholo." **1971** Bright *Word*

Geog. CA & NV 195 **s,cCA,** *Mexican* / neutral and derogatory terms / . . *cholo* 11% [of infs]. **1971** Landy *Underground Dict., Cholo* . . pachuco [=Mexican-American young person, usually rowdy, tough] . . . 2. Term used by whites meaning a Mexican. 3. Person of mixed blood, commonly used in Mexican-American community. **1976** Maeno *Melville Dict.* 49/2, *Cholo*—A person of mixed Spanish and American Indian blood.

chomp v Usu |čɑmp|, occas |čɔmp| Pronc-sp *chump* [Engl dial and US var of std Engl *champ*] Note: *champ* is now generally less common than *chomp* in US: responses to *DARE* Qq. H11a, b, AA4a, GG11, and KK28 include 3 instances of *champ* as against 45 of *chomp*

A Forms.

1848 Bartlett *Americanisms, To chomp.* To champ; to chew loudly and greedily. *Champ* is an old word, but not often used now, except in connection with a horse.—Forby's *Vocab. Chomp* is quite common in New England, and is applied to persons who eat fast or greedily. **1893** Shands *MS Speech* 23, *Chomp* . . . This pronunciation of *champ* is the one always used by negroes in Mississippi . . . Educated people of Mississippi, however, generally give this word the correct pronunciation. **1904** *DN* 2.424 **Cape Cod MA** (as of 1850s), *Chomp* . . . To champ. **1906** *DN* 3.130 **nwAR,** *Chomp.* **1908** *DN* 3.298 **eAL, wGA,** *Chomp.* **1941** *LANE* Map 315, **eMA, NH, RI,** *Chew* [9 infs gave a form of *chomp* or *champ,* 3 with the vowel [ɔ], 3 with [æ], 2 with [ɒ], 1 with [ɑ]. Of these, 5 said, "of horses", with one adding "also of human beings". The Rhode Island inf said "of a glutton".] **1954** *Harder Coll.* **cwTN,** *Chomp* . . . 1. To chew, as tobacco; or bits, as "a mule chomps his bits." 2. To chew loudly. **1959** *VT Hist.* new ser 27.129, *Chomp* . . . To chew. Common. Rural areas. **1965–70** *DARE* (Qu. H11b, *If he makes a noise with his food*) 15 Infs, **scattered,** Chomps; **AR53,** Chomps like a hog; **KY34,** Chomps too hard; **NC55,** A-chomping his food; **IL82,** Still chomping; (Qu. H11a, *If somebody eats rapidly and noisily*) Infs **IL82, MD41, NE2, NJ46, OR13,** Chomps his food; **AZ8, OH63, PA150,** Chomps; **KY15,** Chomps like a pig; **IL134,** Chomping; **TX99,** Sounds like a pig chomping corn; **KY28,** Is chompin' his food; (Qu. AA4a) Inf **KY94,** Chumping at the bit. **1969** *DARE* File **cTX,** The squirrels chomped a hole in my chair.

B Senses.

1 usu in phr *chomp at the bit(s):* To be impatient, eager, or anxious.

1965–70 *DARE* (Qu. AA4a, . . *A man who is very eager to get married*) 11 Infs, **scattered,** Chomping at the bit (to get married); **KY94,** Chumping at the bit; (Qu. AA4b) Inf **CA36,** Chomping at the bit; (Qu. KK28, *Feeling ambitious and eager to work*) Infs **GA31, LA17,** 32, **NE11,** Chomping(g) at the bit; **AR52, GA84, TX70,** Chompin' at the bits; (Qu. GG11, *To be quite anxious*) Inf **LA28,** Just a-chompin'; (Qu. GG17, . . *Longing*) Inf **LA32,** Chompin' at the bit; (Qu. GG23c, . . *Tell someone to be patient*) Inf **TX52,** Don't chomp at the bit so. **1966** Barnes–Jensen *Dict.* UT *Slang, Chomp* . . champ. "The horse is chomping at the bit." **1976** Garber *Mountain-ese* **sAppalachians,** *Chomp-at-the-bits* . . be eager. Mike is chompin' at the bits to get in the game and play.

‡2 Fig, of a boat: to move vigorously forward.

1890 (1919) Hale *Letters* 254 **RI,** Then we descended to the tug, a very respectable conveyance, but open-deck, and waving farewell to the Saale, sate on a settee in rugs, chomping up to Southampton.

chomp n

The amount of tobacco bitten off a cake or wad at one time for chewing; a chunk.

1954 *Harder Coll.* **cwTN,** *Chomp* . . . Same as *plug.*

chomper n

1 A noisy eater.

1969 *DARE* (Qu. H11a, *If somebody eats rapidly and noisily*) Inf **PA221,** Is a chomper.

2 also *chonker;* in pl: Teeth; false teeth. *humorous*

1950 *WELS* (*Joking names for teeth*) 2 Infs, **WI,** Chompers; (*For false teeth*) 1 Inf, Chompers. **1954** *Harder Coll.* **cwTN,** *Chompers* . . . Teeth. Humorous. **1965–70** *DARE* (Qu. X13a, . . *Teeth*) 70 Infs, **scattered,** Chompers; **UT7,** Chonkers; (Qu. X13b, . . *False teeth*) 25 Infs, **scattered,** Chompers. **1976** Garber *Mountain-ese* **sAppalachians,** *Chompers* . . teeth, dentures.

chongo n [MexSpan "bun of hair"]

1 A woman's top-knot, a bun.

1967 *DARE* (Qu. X3, *When a woman puts her hair up on her head in a* bunch) Inf **TX28**, Chongo [ˈčoŋgou]. **1981** *NADS Letters,* In the sense of "a woman's top-knot," chongo is used in Anthony, New Mexico, directly on the Texas border; in Belén, New Mexico, just south of Albuquerque; and in Las Vegas, New Mexico, near the Colorado border.

2 Transf: a steer with a drooped horn; such a horn.

1893 Lummis *Land of Poco Tiempo* 127 **NM**, In an instant more, in stone's-throw of safety and the farther goal, a mighty hand clutches him by the flying chongo—and all is up. **1941** Dobie *Longhorns* 330, This steer was what the Mexicans call a *chongo*—a steer with a drooped horn. A horn drooped down over the steer's eye may not make him any wilder, but it makes him look wilder. **1956** Gipson *Old Yeller* 31 **TX**, He was what the Mexicans called a *chongo* or "droop horn." . . He wasn't as tall and long-legged as the chongo bull.

‡chonk n

A large marble.

1971 Bright *Word Geog. CA & NV* 116, Marbles . . . Chonks . . . "Very large." 1 [response].

chonk v See **chank** v

chonker See **chomper** 2

chonkings vbl n

1 See **chankings**.

2 See quot.

1968 *DARE* (Qu. DD2, *The portion or quantity of tobacco chewed at one time*) Inf **CT3**, Chonkins.

choo intj |ču|, also |čo|, usu repeated. Also sp *chou, cho* [Fr *chou,* pronc |ču|, may overlap here with Engl *choo* |ču| (Ir & E Midl of Engl) and with **chook** |čuk| (SW Engl & Is. of Wight): see *EDD;* all these used chiefly with pigs. Cf also **shoo,** used chiefly with chickens] Cf *DCan* **choo** a call to sled dogs

Used as a call to pigs and sometimes other animals.

1848 Bartlett *Americanisms,* Choo! . . . (Old Fr. *chou.*) Used to drive away pigs and set dogs upon them. **1931** Read *LA French* 26 **sLA**, Chou . . . One cries *chou! chou!* to call or drive away pigs. **1939** *LANE* Map 226 *(Calls to pigs)* [1 inf, **cwNH**, [čɔə], repeated; 1 inf, **swME**, [ču], repeated]. **1968** *DARE* (Qu. K84, *The call . . to get the pigs in at feeding time*) Inf **LA39**, Choo choo choo [ˈču ˈču ˈču]; (Qu. K80, *The call . . to . . cows*) Inf **LA20**, Cho cho cho [ˈčo ˈčo ˈčo].

choog v See **chug** v 1, 2

chook intj Usu |čuk|, less freq |čʌk, čɔk, čok|, infreq |čuk| or prec by |kə-| or foll by |-ɪ|; usu repeated. Also sp *choog, chok(e), chu(c)k* [SW Engl dial *chook,* of which **choo** may be a var; see also *EDD* **choogey** pig] chiefly **eNEng, Sth** Cf **choo**

Used as a call to pigs.

1848 Bartlett *Americanisms,* Chuk. A noise made in calling swine. Always repeated at least three times. **1893** *DN* 1.266, In Virginia a long call for hogs is [čok]. **1899** (1912) Green *VA Folk-Speech,* Chuck. Word for calling hogs. *Chok. Chook.* **1903** *DN* 2.296 **Cape Cod MA**, Chook! *chook!* . . . A call to pigs to be fed. **1939** *LANE* Map 226 (Calls to pigs), [Freq use, usu repeated 3–5 times, **chiefly in ME, coastal NEng**, of [čuk, čug]; less freq [čʌk, čɔk, čok]; infreq [čuk]; occas [kəčuk, -g]; 2 infs gave a form with a final [-ɪ].] **1949** Kurath *Word Geog.* 65, In northeastern New England and on Nantucket, Martha's Vineyard, and Block Island *chook!, choke!* has survived. *Chook!, choke!* is in general use in the Virginia Piedmont and occurs also on both sides of Chesapeake Bay and to some extent on the North Carolina coast as far south as the Neuse. Other variants of this call in the South are *choog!, chuck!, kə-chook!, kə-choo!.* c1950 *Atlas Checklists* **swWI**, Call to hogs at feeding time: chook, chook. **1967–70** *DARE* (Qu. K84, *The call . . to get the pigs in at feeding time*) Infs **CT39, NY148**, Chook, chook; **VA89**, Chook; **LA23, PA37**, [čuk] (repeated); **NC81**, [čoːk] (rising tone on each repetition); **VA43**, [čɔɔk] repeated. **1971** Wood *Vocab. Change* 179, 299 **AR, LA, MS, TN**, Chook, chook [used by 6 infs as a call to hogs].

chook n See **chuke** n¹

‡chookabama n

A dragonfly.

1949 *AmSp* 24.107 **SC**, Chookabamas [ˈčukəˌbæməz] . . . Dragonflies.

chookee n Also sp *chuckee*

1 See quots. [Echoic]

1917 *DN* 4.428 **LA**, Orchard oriole (Icterus spurius). Chuckee. [**1938** Oberholser *Bird Life LA* 592, It [=the Orchard Oriole] uttered in a

subdued voice the 'chuckee' note.] **1968** *DARE* FW Addit **seLA**, Chookee—a small field-sparrow-like bird that flits through low grass. **1983** *Reinecke Coll.* **LA**, Chookee . . [tʃuˈki] orchard oriole. Used in La. French.

2 Transf: see quot.

1968 *DARE* FW Addit **seLA**, Chookee [čuˈki]—a country hick.

chookee adj

1983 *Reinecke Coll.* **LA**, Chookee [tʃuˈki]—foolish, cowardly.

chookie See **chuck** intj 2

chooning vbl n [**tune,** pronc [čun]]

1939 FWP *Guide TN* 144, The ballads usually come without music and a tune has to be improvised, the lines often being modified to fit the melody. This improvisation, called "chooning it" is done with surprising quickness and ease.

choose v

A Forms.

1 past: usu *chose;* occas *choosed;* infreq *chosen, chosed, chosened.*

1837 Sherwood *Gaz. GA* 69, Choosed, for chose. **1884** Harrison *Negro Engl.* 252 **SE**, Pres. choose (also = wish; I don't choose any)—*Past.* choosed, chosen, chosed, chosened. **1905** *DN* 3.102 **nwAR**, Strong verbs often become weak in the speech of the ignorant and the partly educated. Cf . . choose (they *choosed up*). **1906** *DN* 3.116 **sIN**, *Choose-chosed.* Verb made weak. "You choosed to go." **1908** *DN* 3.283 **eAL, wGA**, Choosed.

2 past pple: usu *chosen;* obs *choosen;* occas *chose, choosed;* infreq *chosened.*

1695 in 1929 *AmSp* 4.310 **seNY**, Choosen [as past pple]. **1774** *Ibid,* Chose [as past pple]. **1884** Harrison *Negro Engl.* 252 **SE**, Choose . . . *Pass. Part.* choosed, chosened. **1893** *DN* 1.276 **nwCT**, Choose . . [pret and past pple] chose. **1928** Green *In the Valley* 167 **NC**, He said he'd choosed one.

B Sense.

Usu in neg constrs, esp in declining food at the table: To want or wish to have. chiefly **NEng, Sth**

1872 Schele de Vere *Americanisms* 453, Choose, to, is used by low-bred people, with the peculiar meaning of to choose not to take what is offered. A dish offered at table is declined with the words, "I don't choose any." **1884** [see A1 above]. **1885** Howells *Rise Lapham* 80 **MA**, But I spoke up the way I did because I didn't choose Irene should think I would stand any kind of a loafer 'round. **1895** *DN* 1.385 **IN**, Choose . . . to decline a dish at table. **1902** *DN* 2.231 **sIL**, Choose . . . Used negatively in declining a dish at table. **1903** *DN* 2.309 **seMO**. **1905** *DN* 3.74 **nwAR**. **1906** *DN* 3.116 **sIN**. *Ibid.* 130 **nwAR**, Choose . . . To like, care for . . . "I don't choose to come." **1908** *DN* 3.298 **eAL, wGA**. **1914** *DN* 4.159 **cVA**. **1915** *DN* 4.181 **swVA**. **1927** *NY Times* (NY) 3 Aug 1/8, President Coolidge today dramatically and unexpectedly . . issued the following statement to the correspondents here: "I do not choose to run for President in nineteen twenty-eight." **1941** *LANE* Map 320 *(I don't care for any)* [3 infs, **ME**, I don't choose any.] **1971** *DARE* File **Cape Cod MA**, You know, Nonnie, I'd choose another cup of coffee.

choosed See **choose** A1, 2

choosen See **choose** A2

‡chooser adv [By analogy with *rather, sooner,* or the like]

1967 *DARE* (Qu. JJ32, *If you have to make up your mind between two things—for example, a dog and a cat, you might say, "I'd _____ (have a dog)."*) Inf **CA15**, Chooser.

choose-up n

An informal baseball game for which the captains take turns choosing the players.

[**1910** *DN* 3.439 **wNY**, Choose up, v. phr. (Sometimes *choose up sides.*) To select two nines for a game of baseball, the two captains choosing in turn a man each till the number is complete.] **1950** *WELS (Bat-and-ball games for a few players)* 2 Infs, **WI**, Choose-up; [1 Inf, Choose up sides]. **1965–70** *DARE* (Qu. EE11, *Bat-and-ball game for just a few players*) Infs **KY24, NJ55, WA13**, Choose-up; **NY119**, Choose-up game; [**DC8, NJ33, NY2**, Choose up sides.]

choosing match n **West**

Among cowboys: the selection of work horses; see quot 1944.

1944 Adams *Western Words,* Choosin' match—The selection of mounts on a ranch. The choice rotates according to seniority with the firm, and each puncher chooses his string from the remuda of the ranch. His choice is final, and even the foreman respects it. **1971** Jennings *Cowboys* 64, But getting the strings [of horses] together in the first place was usually done by a choosing match.

chop v Usu |čɑp|, also occas |čæp| Note: *chap* and *chop*, to cut or to become cut, were both present in Middle English and have continued into English and American folk use. *Chap* appears to have been the earlier, *chop* developing as a variant. The present split in senses—*chop* to cut with a heavy blow, and *chap*, of the skin, to develop small cuts or fissures—began in Early Modern English and is now established in std use.

A Forms.

1884 Harrison *Negro Engl.* 279 **SE,** To chap de cotton-rows = to hoe the rows of cotton. **1906** *DN* 3.116 **sIN,** *Chop,* pronounced chap [čæp]. To cut, as wood.

B Senses.

1 also with *out:* To cut weeds or to thin crops (esp cotton) with a hoe or similar implement; hence vbl n, also attrib, *chopping.* **chiefly Sth, Midl**

1820 in *Henderson's N.C. Almanack* (1823) 25 *(DAE),* The hands may begin to thin by chopping out the cotton with their hoes. **1908** *DN* 3.298 **eAL, wGA,** *Chop cotton* . . . To thin out the young cotton plants with hoes. **1933** Miller *Lamb in His Bosom* 15 **GA,** She would always rather sew than chop cotton. **1939** FWP *Guide NC* 94, The southerner "chops" his cotton instead of hoeing it. **1950** *AmSp* 25.230 **ceMS,** *Chop out.* To thin the number of young cotton plants, in order to allow room for growth for those remaining. **1954** *Harder Coll.* **cwTN,** *Chop out:* To thin out the stand of corn, or other plants, with a hoe. **1954** *PADS* 21.23 **SC,** *Chop out.* **1956** *Hall Coll.* **wNC,** *Chop the balks out.* To clear out weeds in the balks, i.e. between the rows of corn. **c1960** *Wilson Coll.* **csKY,** *Chop* . . . To hoe, not necessarily to chop out or thin the plants, as of corn. **1964** Wallace *Frontier Life* 74 **OK** (as of 1893–1906), We found other attractions to interfere with cotton chopping. **1966–70** *DARE* (QR, near Qu. L32) Inf **GA52A,** Chopping cotton—with a hoe—thin it out; (Qu. L35, *Hand tools used for cutting underbrush and digging out roots*) Inf **LA40,** Chopping ax; **KY84,** Chopping hoe; **KS15,** Chopping knife; (Qu. L36, . . *Dig out roots and underbrush to make a new field*) Inf **NC30,** Chop it. **1966–67** *DARE* Tape **GA1,** Give it a chopping. That's thin your cotton or hoe your corn; **SC24,** Chopping cotton, if it was too thick you thinned it out . . . and also you chopped the grass out as you thinned, **AL24,** [I] went to field and chopped cotton; **TX10,** Just chopping the cotton. They chopped it—and that was all.

2 To chap; split; hence ppl adj *chopped* chapped. **chiefly Midl**

1828 Webster *Amer. Dict., Chop* . . . To break or open into chinks or fissures; to crack; to *chap* . . . *Chop,* n . . . A crack or cleft. See *Chap,* which, with the broad sound of *a,* is often pronounced *chop.* **1899** (1912) Green *VA Folk-Speech, Chop* . . . To crack: open in slits. The hands chop. **1903** *DN* 2.309 **seMO,** *Chopped* . . . Chapped. 'My face is badly chopped since the weather turned cold.' **1906** *DN* 3.116 **sIN,** *Chopped* . . . Chapped, as of hands. **1909** *DN* 3.394 **nwAR,** *Chopped* . . . Chapped. "My lips are awful chopped." **1942** Warnick *Garrett Co. MD* (as of 1900–1918).

3 See quot.

1899 (1912) Green *VA Folk-Speech, Chop* . . . To mark a tree by making three chops with an axe on each side, showing the boundary between tracks of land. Line-trees are chopped every three years by law.

4 To separate cattle from a herd. **West** Also called **cut** v **5** See also **carving, chopping horse**

1913 (1979) Barnes *Western Grazing* 381, *Cutting Out,* . . *Chopping* . . . removing from the herd such animals as are needed. **1942** *AmSp* 17.74 **NE,** Separating cattle from a herd. Old hands still say *carving* or *chopping* instead of cutting. **1977** Watts *Dict. Old West.*

chop n[1] [*chop* act of cutting, sharp blow with a heavy instrument]

1 also attrib, often pl: Cracked or coarsely ground grain. [Engl dial: cf *EDD chop* sb.[2] 4] **now chiefly Sth, Midl** See also **Indian chop**

1733 in 1925 Fries *Rec. Moravians* 2.768, The toll will therefore be one-eighth for corn-meal, one-tenth for flour, corn chops and rye chops, and one-twelfth for malt chops. **1830** Collins *Emigrant's Guide* 132 **MD,** When it [=rye] is ground only (as it is used for bread in England) they here call it "chop," and give it to cattle. **1852** MI State Ag. Soc. *Trans. for 1851* 3.151, Chop feed is good for them in small quantities, say

half a pint to a sheep. **1905** *DN* 3.74 **nwAR,** *Chops* . . . Cracked (Indian) corn. 'Chops are good for chickens.' **1908** *DN* 3.298 **eAL, wGA,** *Chops* . . . Cracked Indian corn. Universal. **1922** *Outing* July 184/3 **PA,** When the cow had licked up the last bit of chop, she looked around at the milker. **1927** *Ruppenthal Coll.* **KS,** When milling was largely done by water power, we pioneer settlers called the broken grain chop or chop feed, when the grains had been but slightly broken, as if they were "chopped" into fragments. **1960** Korson *Black Rock* 30 **PA,** He was a fella that used to build mills—grist mills—to grind. He made flour and chop and stuff like that. **1966** *DARE* (Qu. M4a, . . *Spaces or sections between the [studding] in a barn*) Inf **OK18,** Chop boxes—for feed for horses. **1967** *DARE* FW Addit **LA1,** *Chops*—corn ground coarser than meal—fed to chicken and oxen.

2 A crack or cleft in the skin. [*OED* →1767] *arch*

1899 (1912) Green *VA Folk-Speech, Chop* . . . Cleft or crack in the hands or face.

3 also *chopping:* The sharp bark of a hunting dog. Cf **chop-mouth, chop-tongue**

1897 *Outing* 30.127/1 **MA,** Of a sudden the character of the baying changed from the noisy yapping of a lot of playful puppies to the persistent chopping of the driving hound—the fox was up. **1968** McPhee *Pine Barrens* 138 **NJ,** What began as a long, drawling bay becomes shorter and shorter as the scent grows stronger, until the sound of the hounds becomes what the hunters call a chop. The chop intensifies, and when it reaches a certain pitch and tempo the hunters know that the hounds are about to "jump a fox"—the moment when the chase begins.

4 See **chophill.**

chop n[2]

Usu pl: A part of the face: originally the jaw, or cheek, later the mouth, lips, or teeth.

1899 (1912) Green *VA Folk-Speech, Chops* . . . The upper or lower part of the mouth; the jaws. **1927** *AmSp* 2.276 **Pacific Coast, Sth,** *Chops*—cheeks. **1930** Shoemaker *1300 Words* **cPA Mts** (as of c1900), *Chops*—Fat cheeks, or jowls. **1946** (1972) Mezzrow *Really Blues* 331, Chops: lips. **1965–70** *DARE* (Qu. X9, . . *A person's mouth*) 11 Infs, **scattered,** Chops; **MO8,** Chop; (Qu. X10b, *To tell a person to stop talking—not very politely*) Inf **AR28,** Shup [sic] your chops; **NY240,** Shut your chops; **SC10,** Stop blow your chop; (Qu. X13a, . . *Joking names . . teeth*) Infs **MI103, NJ54, TX86,** Chops; **MO8,** Pork chops; (Qu. X13b, . . *False teeth*) Inf **NY240,** Chops; **MO8,** Pork chops, pug chops; (Qu. X29, . . *A person's face*) Inf **NY52,** Chops—That sounds as if I would mean just the mouth, but I mean the whole face; (Qu. HH7b, *Someone who talks too much, or too loud*) Inf **FL52,** Beating his chops; (Qu. KK13, . . *Arguing*) Inf **FL2,** Beating up their chops. [9 of 21 Infs Black] **1970** Major *Afro–Amer. Slang* 37, *Chop(s):* (1925 and later) . . . lips or the mouth; a musician's lips. **1972** Claerbaut *Black Jargon* 60, *Chops* . . . 1. teeth. 2. lips.

chop n[3] [Hindi *chāp* stamp, brand; transf from trade usage]

1 Quality; esp in phr *first chop* highest quality.

1810 (1912) Bell *Journey to OH* 49, He thinks himself a gentleman of the *first chop,* & takes the liberty of coining words for himself. **1844** Stephens *High Life in NY* 1.48 (1958 Taylor–Whiting *Dict. Amer. Proverbs*), My boys aint men of the common chop. **1945** Colcord *Sea Language* **ME, Cape Cod, Long Island,** *First-chop.* Of first-class quality; from the Chinese merchant's chop-mark. Pidgin English, brought home by sailors. **1950** Starnes *Another Mug* 110 *(DAS),* Imported champagne of the very first chop.

2 Rank, position.

1882 Howells *Modern Instance* 236 **Boston MA,** But I hate to live in a town where I'm not first chop in everything.

chopa blanca n Also *chopa, choper* [AmSpan]

A Bermuda chub *(Kyphosus spectatrix).*

1882 U.S. Natl. Museum *Proc.* 5.281 **Gulf Coast,** *Liostomus xanthurus* . . . *Chopa Blanca; Spot; Flat Croaker; Post Croaker* . . . A good pan-fish, but not very important from its small size. **1887** Goode *Amer. Fishes* 129, The Spot, or Lafayette, *Liostomus xanthurus* . . is known . . at Pensacola as the "Spot" and "Chopa blanca." **1939** *AmSp* 14.255, *Chopa* . . . *Kyphosus sectatrix* [sic] . . . In Pensacola, Florida, I have heard the name pronounced [čɑpə] . . . This fish is also known as a *Bermuda chub, chub, chopa blanca,* and *rudder fish.* **c1940** Eliason *Word Lists* **FL** 6, *Choper* [čopɚ]: A shiny little salt-water fish that is a scavenger.

chopa spina n Also *choby* [AmSpan]
=**pinfish.**
> **1882** U.S. Natl. Museum *Proc.* 5.278 **Gulf Coast,** *Lagodon rhomboides . . . Chopa spina . . .* A fish . . little valued as food, and seldom brought to the market. **1935** Caine *Game Fish* 55, *Lagodon rhomboides . . Synonyms:* Choby, Chopa Spina. **1946** LaMonte *N. Amer. Game Fishes* 71, *Lagodon rhomboides . .* Chopa Spina.

chop-ax n [For *chopping-ax*] Cf **club ax**
> **1898** Lloyd *Country Life* 242 **AL,** As ugly as a chop-ax.

chop block See **chopping block**

chop cotton See **chop wood 2**

choper See **chopa blanca**

chophill n, usu pl Also *chop, choppie* [Cf *OED chop sb.*[1] 6] **NE** Cf **sand hill**
A small, low, usu barren hill that appears as if roughly chopped up.
> **1928** *AmSp* 4.126 **nw, cnNE,** Around the lakes are "choppies" or "chophills," billows of low hills that are for the most part bare of grass. **1935** Sandoz *Jules* 80 **wNE** (as of 1880–1930), The broken chops reared into high ridges. *Ibid* 269, Many turned back at the first soft yellow chophills. **1937** Sandoz *Slogum* 49 **NE** (as of 1900–20), Now there was a complete cattle rustlers' layout on Hab's claim in Lost Valley, deep in the chophills. **1956** Lincoln (Nebr.) *Sunday Journal and Star* 21 Oct 4–B (*AmSp* 33.79), A hunter poises high on a Sandhills "choppie" to fire at a grouse. **1958** *AmSp* 33.80 **NE** (as of c1943), *Choppies . . .* 'Small rough hills, usually about lakes. Freezing pushes them up.'

chophouse n [*OED* 1690 →]
A restaurant, esp one of poor quality.
> **1806** (1970) Webster *Compendious Dict., Chophouse . .* a house to eat provisions at. **1840** Bird *Robin Day* 31 (*DAE*), I summoned courage enough to enter a little tavern or chophouse. **1873** Miller *Modocs* 340 **CA,** The food was cold refuse of some low chop-house. **1907** Field *Six-Cylinder* 74 **NYC,** A moment later we drew up in front of a well-known chop-house. **1950** *WELS* (*Nicknames . . a small eating place*) 1 Inf, **ceWI,** Chophouse. **1967–70** *DARE* (Qu. D39, *. . A small eating place where the food is not especially good*) Inf **CA**19, Chophouse —very bad; **CA**194, Chophouse.

chop log n Also *chopping log*
A log on which small wood was cut up and poultry killed.
> **1867** Hill *Homespun* 124 **NEng** (as of 1842), There is an indiscriminate spirting of fresh blood all around the chop-log. **1912** Green *VA Folk-Speech, Chop-log . .* A log at a wood-pile on which smaller logs and limbs are cut. **1940** Richter *Trees* 166 **OH** (as of c1800), The women . . laughed . . for behind the chopping log was where they told their youngest that babies came from.

chop-mouth n, also attrib [chop n[1] 3] Cf **chop-tongue**
A hound with a strong, repeated bark.
> **1967** *DARE* Tape **LA** 3, A chop-mouth dog [is one] with just a steady, steady chop. **1970** *Natl. Geog. Mag.* 138.672 **Ozarks,** Mr. Riley identified another [fox-hunting dog] as a "chop-mouth"; I judged that one to be a baritone.

chopo See **chapo**

chopped ppl adj
1 See **chop v B2.**
2 Annoyed. Cf *DS* GG4
> **1970** *DARE* FW Addit **TX**81, *Chopped,* meaning annoyed, peeved, also known as *hacked off.*

chopped eggs n [From the yellow-and-orange colors of the flower]
=**butter-and-eggs 1.**
> **1900** Lyons *Plant Names* 226, *L. vulgaris . . .* Chopped eggs.

choppel n Cf *DS* H43
=**headcheese.**
> **1973** Allen *LAUM* 1.288 **seNE,** *Head cheese* commonly names a food preparation composed of parts of the head, and sometimes of the feet, of swine, cut up fine, seasoned, boiled, and pressed . . . Several terms, apparently more or less equivalent in meaning, appear on the checklist returns as voluntary write-ins of the respondents . . . Nebraska . . has *head souse, . . choppel, . . knip.*

chopper n
1 One skilled in using an ax; spec, in logging: one who fells trees and cuts logs. **chiefly Nth** Cf **faller**
> **1785** in 1908 Mathews *A. Ellicott* 44 **MD,** My Brother Joseph at Present runs the guide Line for the Choppers. **1828** Cooper *Prairie* 103, What will the Yankee Choppers say? **1851** (1856) Springer *Forest Life* 92 **ME,** First, then, come the "boss," or the principal in charge. Then the choppers, meaning those who select, fell, and cut the logs, one of whom is master chopper. **1909** *DN* 3.410 **nME,** *Chopper . . .* One skilled in the use of the axe. **1925** *AmSp* 1.135 **Pacific NW** [Logger talk], "Choppers" go out in the winter to fell and trim the trees. **1956** *AmSp* 31.150 **nwCA** [Logging], *Chopper . . .* Formerly, one who cuts down trees. *Faller* is now used more often. **1968** *DARE* Tape **CA**103, Choppers were instructed to leave [a leaning] tree alone.

2 also attrib: A machine used in cutting up hay. **chiefly Nth** See Map
> **1904** MacKaye *Panchronicon* 17 **NH,** Ef a feller'll jest take a grip on the North Pole an' go whirlin' round it, he'll be cuttin' meridians as fast as a hay-chopper. **1950** *WELS* (*Tools and machines used for different steps in handling hay*) 7 Infs, **WI,** Hay chopper; 6 Infs, Chopper; 2 Infs, Chopper, occasionally; (*Wagon used for carrying hay*) 2 Infs, Chopper wagon. **1965–70** *DARE* (Qu. L16, *Machines used . . in handling hay*) 18 Infs, **chiefly Nth,** Chopper; **CT**9, **IA**1, 39, **IN**59, **MD**29, **NY**189, **OH**27, **WV**12, Field chopper; **IA**26, **IL**38, **IN**69, **MS**19, **PA**56, **VA**111, **WI**51, Hay chopper; **CT**9, Chopper and blower; (Qu. L13) Inf **MI**12, Chopper wagon.

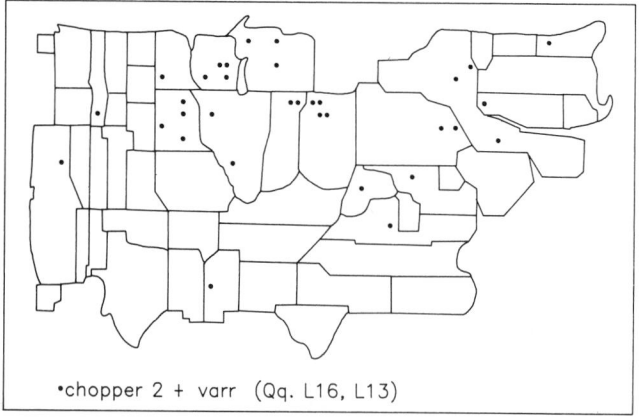

•chopper 2 + varr (Qq. L16, L13)

3 See **chopping horse.**

4 A cowboy who cuts cattle from a herd. [chop v B4]
> **1944** Adams *Western Words, Chopper*—A man employed in cutting out cattle.

5 See quot 1935. Cf **cutter n[1] 2**
> **1935** *AmSp* 10.270 [Language of livestock mart], *Choppers.* Aged ewes in medium flesh—not good enough to grade as fat. **1968** Adams *Western Words, Chopper.*

6 =**bluefish 1.**
> **1972** Sparano *Outdoors Encycl.* 378, *Bluefish—Common Names: . . chopper . . . Scientific Name: Pomatomus saltatrix.*

choppie See **chophill**

chopping vbl n
1 also pl: A piece of land upon which the trees have been or are being felled; infreq, the trees felled on such land. **chiefly Nth, esp NEast** Cf **fallow n B**
> **1817** *Thomas' MA Spy or Worcester Gaz.* (MA) 11 June 3/1 **NY,** Artemas Shatluck, on that day, in a piece of chopping that he was clearing, fell a tree across a stump. **1838** Holmes *Rept. Aroostook R.* 54 **ME,** Some prefer to let the "*chopping,*" or trees that are fell, lie until the next spring, before they burn them. **1907** *DN* 3.242 **eME,** *Chopping . . .* A piece of timber-land where the trees have been felled. **1909** *DN* 3.410 **nME,** *Chopping.* **1967** *DARE* Tape **PA**17, A chopping . . was maybe three or four acres of nice wood. **1967** *DARE* FW Addit **csPA,** *Choppings* [ˈčɑpɪnz]—cut off timber land that had scrub oaks on it. **1968** Adams *Western Words* 64, *Chopping.* **1969** Sorden *Lumberjack Lingo* **NEng, Gt Lakes,** *Choppings*—The area where lumberjacks are cutting down trees.

2 See **chop n[1] 3.**

chopping bee n Also *chopping, chopping frolic; wood-chopping (bee), ~ party*

A **bee** n[2] or social gathering for cutting down timber.

1809 *Thomas' MA Spy or Worcester Gaz.* (MA) 12 July 3/4, At Bristol (Ver.), June 7, at a chopping-Bee, a limb of one of the falling trees struck one of the men. **1853** Ramsey *Annals TN* 720 (as of late 1700s), Weddings, military trainings, house-raisings, chopping frolics, were often followed with fiddle, and dancing, and rural sports. **1860** *Harper's Mag.* 20.712/2 **OH,** One of his neighbors had a "chopping-bee" on Christmas-day . . . The axes flew rapidly . . , making the woods ring with the joyous music. **1893** T.D. Price *MS Diary* 20 April *(DA),* A. Jones made a chopping for Wolcott. **1967–70** *DARE* (Qu. FF2, . . *Parties*) Inf IL4, Wood-chopping bees; IL9, Wood-chopping parties; VA42, Wood-choppings. **1968** *Filson Club Hist. Qrly.* 157 **KY** (as of early 1800s), The Shakers themselves engaged not only in the popular cornhusking but also in other competitive races such as "spinning frolics" and "chopping bees."

chopping block n Also *block, chop block*

Std sense, in var betting phrr suggesting self-certainty, assuredness: see quots.

1914 *DN* 4.70 **ME, nNH,** "Bate ye two fingers on the choppin' block, an' resk it." A common form of laying a wager. **1967–68** *DARE* (Qu. JJ20, *If you felt very sure about something*) Inf LA14, Put my neck (or nuts) on the chop block; LA3, Put my neck on the chopping block; LA20, Bet my arm on a chopping block; LA35, Bet my head on a block; KS19, Put my head on a block.

chopping frolic See **chopping bee**

chopping horse n Also *chopper* [**chop** v B4] **West** Cf **carving** =**cutting horse.**

1913 (1979) Barnes *Western Grazing* 381, *Cutting Horse.*—A horse used especially for the work of cutting out; a "carver," a "chopper," chopping horse. **1920** Hunter *Trail Drivers TX* 297 **wTX,** The specially trained horses used for this work, so intelligent that you can remove the bridle after the animal to be cut out is indicated, and the horse will separate the cow from the bunch with unerring instinct, are called "cutting horses," "carving horses" or "chopping horses." **1933** *AmSp* 8.1.29 **nwTX,** *Choppin' horse.* **1944** Adams *Western Words* 34, *Chopping horse.*

chopping log See **chop log**

chop sack n

A sack for carrying **chop** n[1] 1; a **burlap bag.**

1968 *DARE* (Qu. F20, *A cloth container for feed*) Inf PA176, Chop sack. **c1970** *DARE* File **PA** (as of 1920s), *Chop sack*—burlap sack.

chop suey n **HI** *humorous*

A person of mixed ancestry.

1967 *DARE* (Qu. HH28, . . *People of foreign background*) Inf HI1, Chop suey—of very mixed ancestry. **1981** *Pidgin To Da Max* **HI,** *Chop suey* . . . all mixed up. [Cartoon caption, first speaker:] "I get Japanese, Chinese, Filipino, Irish, German, Hawaiian, French —" [second speaker:] "Real chop suey, yeah?"

chop-tongue n, hence adj *choptongue(d)* =**chop-mouth.**

1909 *S. At. Qrly.* 8.47 **seSC** [Gullah], A hound having a short yelp instead of a full, lingering . . voice, is known as a *chop-tongue dog*—a *dog with a short or chopped bay.* **1922** Gonzales *Black Border* 293 **sSC, GA coasts** [Gullah glossary], *Chop'tongue*—hounds with short yelp; the cry of the modern English fox-hound, as distinguished from the long bell-like notes of the Carolina deer-hounds. **1950** *PADS* 14.19 **SC,** *Choptongued* . . . Descriptive of a dog with a short yelp instead of a full round, bell-like voice, when warm on the trail.

chop wood v phr

1 To snore. [Var of *saw wood*] *joc*

1967–70 *DARE* (Qu. X45, *Joking expressions . . snoring*) Infs KY94, MN37, MO26, Chopping wood.

2 also *chop cotton:* To get busy, work hard.

1966–67 *DARE* (Qu. JJ26, *If somebody has been doing poor work or not enough . . "If he wants to keep his job he'd better _____."*) Inf AR28, Chop wood; (Qu. KK29, *To start working very hard; "He was slow at first but now he's really _____."*) Inf TX33, Choppin' cotton.

chorbon See **charbon**

chore n Usu |čor|, rarely |kour, kouə| Pronc-spp *char, chare* Std senses, var forms.

1815 Humphreys *Yankey in England* 104 **NEng,** *Chares, chores,* trifling employments at or near home. **1867** Lowell *Biglow* xliii **NEng,** *Chore* is also Jonson's word, and I am inclined to prefer it to *chare* and *char,* because I think that I see a more natural origin for it in the French *jour,* whence it might come to mean a day's work, and thence a job, than anywhere else. **1933** *AmSp* 8.3.81 **seLA,** *Chore.* I find that a fair sprinkling of students from . . that part of Louisiana east of the Mississippi River, pronounce the word *core* [kour] or [kouə]. When asked why they pronounce it so, they usually reply that they do so on the analogy of the word *chorus.*

chore v, hence vbl n *choring* **chiefly Nth, N Midl** See also **choresing**

Also *chore around:* To perform regular daily tasks; to do necessary work.

1788 (1873) May *Jrl.* 88 **OH,** Five hands at work on the house. Two playing the whipsaw, and the rest choring in the woods, such as felling trees from three to five feet through. **1839** Kirkland *New Home* 87 **csMI,** I was obliged to employ Mrs. Jennings to "chore around," to borrow her own expression. **1885** Thayer *Tannery to White House* 68 **MA,** Teaming, farming, choring, . . was preferable to tanning leather. **1914** *DN* 4.70 **ME, nNH,** *Chore* . . . To work. "Sam, he chores down to Billin's's." **1923** *DN* 5.203 **swMO,** *To chore aroun'* = to putter about at unimportant work. **1930** *AmSp* 6.97 **cNY,** *Choring:* Doing odd jobs. "He is choring on the Canal." **1940** Richter *Trees* 301 **sOH** (as of c1800), Sayward chored on by herself. Her grubbing hoe kept cutting off the woody sprouts. **1942** Whipple *Joshua* 33 **UT,** Brother Lee's out chorin', now. **1965** Gould *You Should Start* 4 **ME,** I pulled on my storm clothes and made ready for my morning trek to chore the cow. **1967** *DARE* Tape IA12, Everybody has to get out an' chore when they chore. **1968** *Filson Club Hist. Qrly.* 157, I did not feel well; still I . . chored around at various things. **1969** *DARE* (Qu. L4b, . . *The time early in the morning and at night when you have to feed livestock, clean stalls and so on*) Inf IN67, Have to go chore.

chore pron See **your**

chore boy n **chiefly Nth, West**

In logging or on a ranch: one who does odd jobs.

1893 *Scribner's Mag.* 13.711/2 **nGt Lakes,** For a crew of sixty men, the cook has a helper, called in camp parlance the "cookee," and a "choreboy" to fetch wood and water and help wait on table. **1904** White *Blazed Trail Stories* 12 **MI,** A fat cook . . and a chore "boy" of seventy-odd summers were the only human beings in sight. **1905** U.S. Forest Serv. *Bulletin* 61.33, *Chore Boy.* One who cleans up the sleeping quarters and stable in a logging camp, cuts firewood, builds fires, and carries water. **1925** *AmSp* 1.136 **Pacific NW** [Logger talk], Once the wood-splitter and water-carrier of the logging camp was simply "choreboy". **1958** McCulloch *Woods Words* **Pacific NW,** *Chore boy*—A young bull cook.

‡chored ppl adj

Burdened with chores.

1898 Westcott *Harum* 173 **nNY,** Polly wa'n't but little older 'n me, an' bein' the youngest girl, was chored most to death herself.

choresing pple [*chores* n pl]

Doing one's regular daily tasks.

1954 *WELS Suppl.,* In Sioux County, Iowa, the singular [=*chore*] is never heard. I would say normally, "At chores time, farmers are out choresing." A former pastor always said *choring* and as a kid I was sure he didn't know English.

chore time n Also *chores time,* occas *choring time* **widespread, but chiefly Nth, N Midl, West** See Map Cf **feeding time**

The time for doing daily or routine tasks.

1939 *LANE* Map 217, [The map shows *chore time* to be current throughout NEng. Commentary:] *Chore time* is very commonly defined as a general or inclusive term, denoting the time when the farmer must not only feed the stock but perform all the rest of his routine work, such as milking, 'bedding down' the cattle, filling the wood box and 'cleaning up.' **1950** *WELS* (*The time of day when this work is done*) 12 Infs, **WI,** Chore time; 2 Infs, Chores time. **1955** Potter *Dial. NW OH* 82, The time when animals are attended to is generally called *chore time,* the term in regular use throughout the Great Lakes area. **1965–70** *DARE* (Qu. L4b, . . *The time early in the morning and at night when you have to* *feed the livestock, clean stalls, and so on* . . *"I've got to go now, it's ———— . . ."*) 432 Infs, **widespread, but chiefly Nth, N Midl, West,** Chore time; [**MO**4, Do-the-chore time;] **AR**40 Evening chore time, morning chore time; 29 Infs, **chiefly Nth,** Chores time; **IN**67, **OH**82, Choring time. **1971** Bright *Word Geog. CA & NV* 172, *Feeding time* 45% [of infs] . . *chore time* 29% . . . These two terms more or less complemented each other. *Chore time* was used particularly in the area between Mariposa and Selma, and was also more widely used in the southeastern part of the state. **1973** Allen *LAUM* 1.258 **Upper MW,** *Chore time* is the most common . . expression. [Also reported were *chores time* by 5 infs, and *choring time* by 2 infs.]

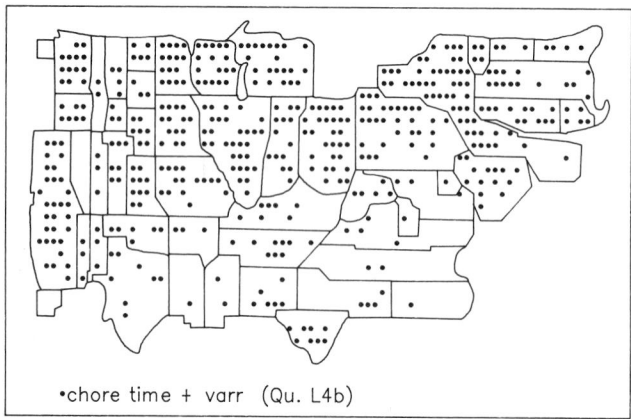

•chore time + varr (Qu. L4b)

chorizo n Also sp *choriso* [Port *chouriço;* Span *chorizo; OEDS* 1846 →]   **NW, HI**   Cf **chourisse**

A type of sausage: see quots.

1967 *DARE* (Qu. H45, *Dishes with meat, fish, or poultry*) Inf **OR**10, Chorizo [čơ'rišo] — like pork and pepper and garlic. **1968** *Mountain Home News* (ID) 8 Feb 5/5, A supper of Basque made chorizos and coffee was served. **1972** Carr *Da Kine Talk* 96 **HI,** *Choriso* (or *chorizo*) is another Portuguese sausage, usually sold in tins. (*Chouriço* is the dictionary form of this word.) **1984** *DARE* File **swID,** One of the most popular kinds of pizza was made with chorizo.

chorook See **cherook**

‡**chorus girl** n [Var of *chore girl,* trademark]

1967 *DARE* (Qu. G14, *The rough metal pad that's used to scour pots and pans*) Inf **TN**23, Chorus girl.

chorus jig n **NEng**

An intricate figure in a **contra dance:** see quot 1977.

1938 FWP *Guide NH* 118, The morning star, Virginia reel, quadrille, Hull's victory, patronella, chorus jig, and moneymusk are still danced. **1966** *DARE* (Qu. FF5a, . . *Steps and figures in dancing — in past years*) Inf **MA**6, Chorus jig. **1977** Nevell *Time to Dance* 95 **NEng** (as of c1934), He liked the intricate dances, like 'Chorus Jig,' where you've got 'contra corners' to turn.

chose, chosed, chosen(ed) See **choose** A

chou See **choo**

chouder See **chowder** n

chouette n [Fr] **LA**

The Florida **screech owl** (here: *Otus asio floridanus*).

1917 *DN* 4.424 **LA,** Chouette. = *chat houant.* **1931** Read *LA French* 26, *Chouette* . . . The most common name for the Florida Screech Owl. **1938** Oberholser *Bird Life LA* 332, *Florida Screech Owl* . . . the French in Louisiana call it 'chouette'. **1945** Saxon *Gumbo Ya-Ya* 549 **LA,** When 'Chouette' (screech owl) or 'Gimme Bird' sings around a house, it means there will be a death in the house.

chounse v [Alter of *jounce* shake up]

1 To shake up, as a pillow. **Sth, Midl** *?old-fash*

1942 McAtee *Dial. Grant Co. IN* 18 (as of 1890s), *Chounse* . . to shake up, as a pillow or tick to disperse the lumps. **1943** *AmSp* 18.306 **swAL** (as of c1900). **c1960** Wilson *Coll.* **csKY,** *Chounse* . . . To shake up as one shakes a pillow.

2 To punish, "shake up;" hence n *chounsing* punishment.

1941 *LANE* Map 397 **nwCT,** The map shows terms for a whipping given as punishment to a naughty child, recorded in the context (*If you*

don't behave,) you'll get a whipping . . [čauntsın, i.e. trouncing [reported by 1 inf]. [*DARE* Ed questions interpretation of [tʃauntsın] as "trouncing."]

choupique n, also attrib |'šu,pık| Also sp *choupic,* pronc- and folk-etym spp *shoe-peg, shoe-pick* [See quot 1939] **LA** =**bowfin.**

1763 LePage du Pratz *Hist. LA* 2.104, The *Choupic* is a very beautiful fish; many people mistake it for the trout. **1885** *Outing* 5.336/2 **LA,** For the rest, there are gais [sic, error for gars?], own cousins to the alligator, buffalo, *gaspergoos,* . . and *choupics.* **1927** Kennedy *Gritny* 160 **sLA** [Black], "Wid a sack full o' dirty ole shoe-pick feesh." . . A fish so fat and greasy, and so plentiful in all the muddy bayous and ditches, that everybody called it "Gawd's feesh." **1931** Read *LA French* 88, *Choupique* is almost the only name given in Louisiana to this fish even by those who cannot speak French. **1939** *AmSp* 14.255, *Choupique* . . . *Amia calva* . . . a French derivation of Choctaw *shupik,* 'mudfish,' is the popular name for the bowfin, both in English and in French, throughout Southern Louisiana. Du Pratz gives a lengthy description of the 'Tchoupic.' **1945** *AmSp* 20.48 **LA,** *Choupic* . . . As a pre-school boy in New Orleans this word was as familiar to me as 'green-trout' (black bass), 'gaspergou,' or perch. It is pronounced by the English-speaking natives 'shoe-pick.' **1967** *DARE* Tape **LA**5, They call it green cypress trout, choupique ['šupık], and grindles. **1968** *DARE* (Qu. P1, . . *Freshwater fish* . . *good to eat*) Inf **LA**20, Cypress trout or choupique ['šu,pık]; **LA**22, Choupique ['šu,pık] = bowfin or grindle; (Qu. P3, . . *Not good to eat*) Inf **LA**26, Choupique ['šu,pɛk]; **LA**40, Choupique ['šu,pık]. **1970** Stewart *Amer. Place-Names,* Applied to swamps and bayous in LA, it is American-French 'mudfish,' but is probably from an Indian (Muskogean?) word 'muddy,' and in some instances to be taken in this meaning; sometimes, by folk-etymology, rendered by Americans as Shoe-Peg. **1983** Reinecke *Coll.* **New Orleans LA,** Choupique ['šupık] — bowfin, mudfish, Amia Calva, eaten only by poor Blacks. From La. French, ult. from Choctaw "shupik" with same meaning.

chourisse n [?Fr rendering of Span *chorizo*] =**chorizo.**

1968 *DARE* (Qu. H43, *Foods made from parts of the head and inner organs of an animal*) Inf **LA** 33, Chourisse [ču'ris] — like sausage except meat is cut, not ground; heavily seasoned and put into casing; smoked.

chouse v[1] [Perh var of *touse* handle roughly]

1 See quot.

1895 *DN* 1.385 **OH,** Chouse: to put forcibly into.

2 also sp *chowse:* To persecute, annoy; esp, to handle cattle roughly; hence vbl n *chousing,* ppl adj *choused.* **West**

1903 *DN* 2.309 **seMO,** Chouse [čauz] . . . To persecute, to intimidate. 'I don't want to be choused around by lawyers.' **1904** (1944) Biggers *From Cattle Range* 67 **wTX,** Cattle . . would be thrown into the herd, "choused" around for several days. **1929** Dobie *Vaquero* 14, But to get back to the mossy horns. "Chousing" them was extremely hazardous. They were all outlaws, *ladinos,* as wild as bucks, cunning, and ready to fight anything that got in front of them. **1944** Adams *Western Words,* *Chouse* — This word, as used by the cowboy, means to handle cattle roughly, to make them nervous, to annoy them and stir them up unnecessarily. **1958** Blasingame *Dakota Cowboy* 47 **SD,** Every Indian camp had dogs running around and a lot of them learned to chouse stock. If a man could catch them at it and shoot the leaders, the others generally quit. **1966** *DARE* Tape **NM**14, We had to be very careful not to chouse nor abuse the drag cattle. **1967** Green *Horse Tradin'* 33 **swTX** (as of 1920s–30s), I wouldn't be ready to show them for a day or two . . until they filled up and got over looking chowsed and drawn from shipping. **1969** Green *Wild Cow Tales* 295 **TX** (as of 1930s), Nobody got any chousin' about gettin' water on the floor from thawin' out the clothes. **1971** Jennings *Cowboys* 57 **West,** And I don't care how you settle your differences, just don't chouse the outfit, hear?

3 with *along:* To saunter.

1930 Knibbs *Songs Lost Frontier* 73 **West,** Jake and Roany was a-chousin' along, / And Jake was a-singin' what he called a song.

chouse v[2] [*OED* a1659 →]

To cheat, defraud.

1828 Webster *Amer. Dict.,* Chouse . . . To cheat, trick, defraud; followed by *of,* in Hudibras; but in America, by *out of;* as, to *chouse* one *out of* his money. [*It is now vulgar.*] **1879** in 1917 Twain *Letters* 354, Some villains were trying to chouse some negro orphans out of $700. **1889** (1971) Farmer *Americanisms,* Chouse . . . to defraud . . . In America . . the word is still looked upon as orthodox, and is applied to all kinds of fraudulent dealing and deceit. **1899** (1912) Green *VA Folk-Speech*, *Chouse* . . . To cheat; swindle. He *choused* him out of his money. **1952** Brown *NC Folkl.* 1.527, *Chouse* . . . To cheat.

chowchow n [Prob from the call; cf **cow-cow**]
1 Usu the **yellow-billed cuckoo,** but also the **black-billed cuckoo.**
    1898 (1900) Davie *Nests N. Amer. Birds* 255, *Yellow-billed Cuckoo* . . . This bird is known by several names, such as Rain Crow, Rain Dove and Chow-chow, which are likewise applied to the Black-billed species. **1917** *Wilson Bulletin* 29.2.81 **KY,** *Coccyzus americanus.* —Chow-chow, phantom or spirit bird. **1927** Forbush *Birds MA* 2.240, *Coccy̆zus americánus* . . . Chow-chow. **1932** Bennitt *Check-list* 36 **MO,** *Yellow-billed cuckoo* . . . chow-chow. **1937** FWP *Guide ID* 95, The yellow-billed cuckoo (rain crow, rain dove, storm crow, chowchow) has a black bill . . . His song is a succession of spasmodic gurgles. **1956** *MA Audubon* 40.80, *Yellow-billed cuckoo.* Chow-chow. *Ibid,* Black-billed cuckoo . . . Chow-chow.

2 =**red-bellied woodpecker.** Cf **chaw-chaw**
    1959 *AmSp* 34.73, *Chow-chow* (red-bellied woodpecker; yellow-billed cuckoo).

chowder n, also attrib Older sp *chouder* [Prob Fr *chaudière* pot: see discussion in *OED; DNE* 1745 →]
1 freq in comb: A thick soup or stew usu of seafood, salt pork, onions, potatoes, freq also other vegetables. **orig and chiefly NEng,** now also **Nth, CA, C Atl** See Map
    1751 *Boston Evening–Post* (MA) 23 Sept. 2/1, First lay some Onions to keep the Pork from burning, / Because in Chouder there can be no turning. **1826** Flint *Recollections* 354 **LA,** We had public chowder-parties, where sixty people sat down under grape-vine arbours, to other good things beside fish. **1905** *DN* 3.5 **cCT,** *Chowder* . . . A dish of fish, pork, etc. **1947** Bowles–Towle *New Engl. Cooking* 46, Every New England girl who lived within sound of the sea, four or five generations ago, counted a chowder kettle as an essential part of her "setting out." **1955** Taber *Stillmeadow Daybook* 157 **swCT,** Plenty of true chowder crackers split and buttered and warmed. **1964** Amer. Heritage *Cookbook* 425, *Corn Chowder*—This chowder originated in Massachusetts, but it is also made in the South with tomatoes added. **1965–70** *DARE* (Qu. H36, . . *Soups*) 80 Infs, **chiefly Atlantic, Pacific,** (Clam) chowder; 18 Infs, **chiefly NEng,** Fish chowder; 9 Infs, **NEast,** Corn chowder; 11 Infs, **chiefly Atlantic,** (Abalone, catfish, conch, fish and clam, meat, New England clam, oyster and clam, parsnip, quahog *or* red clam) chowder; (Qu. H45) 25 Infs, **chiefly Nth,** (Fish, catfish, conch, *or* seafood) chowder; 9 Infs, **Nth,** (Manhattan) clam chowder; (Qu. H49) 20 Infs, **Nth,** (Corn, fish, *or* potato) chowder; (Qu. H50) 16 Infs, **NEast,** Corn(-tomato) chowder; (Qu. H57) 4 Infs, (Green tomato) chowder; (Qu. H65) Inf **OH15,** Chowder.

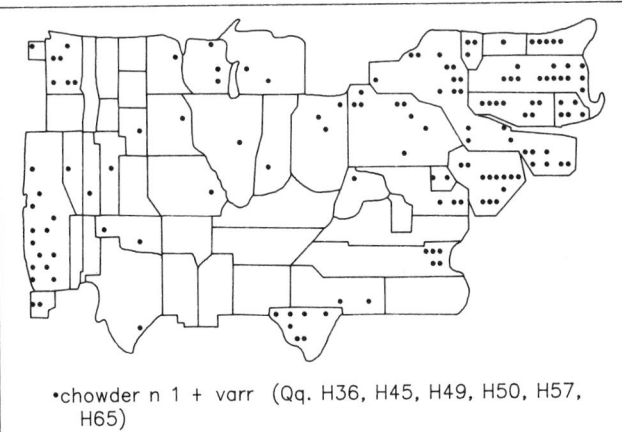

•chowder n 1 + varr (Qq. H36, H45, H49, H50, H57, H65)

2 in full *chowder party:* A gathering at which chowder is served.
    1848 Bartlett *Americanisms* 82, Nearly 10,000 persons assembled in Rhode Island, for whom a *clambake* and *chowder* were prepared. **1853** (1854) Baldwin *Flush Times* 80 **AL,** In the science of getting up . . a picnic or chowder party, or fish fry, the Virginian . . was first. **1884** *Century Illustr. Mag.* 28.555/2 **ceNY,** A chowder was given a few weeks ago at the head of our little bay. **1906** *Eve. Post* (NY NY) 6 Nov 8/4, The Bowery . . went about the business . . with as much good nature as if it were "Big Tim's" annual "chowder."

3 See quot. Cf **chop** n[1] **1**
    1954 *PADS* 21.24 **neSC,** *Chowder* . . . The entire cornstalk, ears, and shucks ground for cattle feed.

chowder intj Also *chowderation* **NEng** Cf *DS* NN8a, b
Darn! —used as an exclam or mild oath.
    1827 *Natl. Gaz. & Lit. Reg.* (Philadelphia PA) 11 Oct 1/4 **Boston MA,** Once in our Bay, I vum by chowder, / The *Tea* was made of good *Gunpowder.* **1914** *DN* 4.70 **ME, nNH,** *Chowder* . . . Expletive. **1959** *VT Hist.* new ser 27.130 **cw, nwVT,** Chowder! . . . chowderation! . . . Rare. Essex.

chowder v
    1975 Gould *ME Lingo, Chowder*—In additon to edible chowder, this word has the Maine meaning of wobbling, chattering, wavering, vibrating, and fretting. A drill that wobbles as it bores a hole is said to *chowder,* not only as to its wobbling but as to the noise it makes. Wind can rattle shutters until somebody will say, "The whole house chowdered all night."

chowderation See **chowder** intj

chowderhead n, hence adj *chowder-headed*   **chiefly NEng** *somewhat old-fash*
A stupid person, a dolt.
    1833 Neal *Down-Easters* 1.119 **NEng,** Thats our Amos! if taint I'm a chowderhead. **1851** (1976) Melville *Moby-Dick* 66 **NEast,** I wonder now if this here has any effect on the head? What's that stultifying saying about chowder-headed people? **1867** Lowell *Biglow* lviii **MA,** *Chowder-head:* a muddle-brain. **1871** in 1875 Twain *Sketches New & Old* (Hartford) 299, That lets you out, you know, you chowder-headed old clam. **1904** *DN* 2.424 **Cape Cod MA,** *Chowder-head* . . . A stupid person. **1922** *DN* 5.159. **1932** in 1963 Fitzgerald *Letters* 498, I do not destinate to signify that you were a wiseacre, witling, dizzard, chowderhead. **1941** *LANE* Map 465 *(Fool)* 1 inf, **swME,** Chowderhead. **1967** Serling *President's Plane* 62 **DC,** The stupid chowderheads would cut Shakespeare.

chowder party See **chowder** n 2

chowse See **chouse** v[1] 2

chowy adj
Of weather: unsettled.
    1905 Wasson *Green Shay* 79 (*AmSp* 37.251) **ME,** Don't you know how ungodly chowy and hubbly it gits down there with the flood tide settin' in ag'in an easterly breeze o' wind? **1974** *AmSp* 49.62 **swME,** *Chowy* . . Unsettled (of the weather).

choya See **cholla**

Chriskingle See **Kriss Kringle** 1

Chris on you See **Christmas at you**

Chris root See **Christmas flower** 1

Christ-apple See **apple** n 3

Christ bird n
=**robin** (here: *Turdus migratorius*).
    1942 Thomas *Blue Ridge Country* 218, Through the southern mountains the Robin is often called the "Christ Bird" because of this legend. [A robin comforts Christ on the cross, getting his breast feathers stained with blood.]

Christ-dust n *obs*
Flour.
    1884 Baldwin *Yankee School-Teacher* 49 **VA** [Black],"I see you making up some Christ-dust f' supper!" (This is the common name for flour, signifying its rarity in the daily fare . . .).

Christer n
1 An overly pious or zealous person, esp a teetotaler. *derog ?old-fash* Cf **Christian**
    1924 'W. Fabian' *Sailor's Wives* 90 (*OEDS*), You never were a Christer in college. **1927** *AmSp* 3.20, The word "Christer" has American currency, or at least good collegiate currency . . . It is applied to one who is active in the college Christian Association or to one who is of "high" ideals generally. It is always a term of opprobrium. **1930** Williams *Logger-Talk* 17 **Pacific NW,** *Christer:* A professional Christian; also a general term of opprobrium. **1932** Dos Passos *1919* 143, In spite of not drinking and being somewhat of a christer, having odd ideas about reform and remedying abuses. **1951** *Cornell (Univ.) Daily Sun* 23 Oct

4/2 (DAS), Non-drinkers are called all sorts of names—one in popular usage is 'Christer.' **1967** *DARE* (Qu. DD33b, *A person who is actively against drinking*) Inf **OR**1, Christer.

2 Transf: see quot.

1979 Lewis *How to Talk Yankee* **NEng**, *Christer* . . . various meanings. Can be a hell raiser, or one who goes *ramming* [=on the town]. In general, anything excessive. "*Wan't that thunderstorm a christer!*"

christial See **crystal**

Christian n Sth Cf Christer 1

A non-drinker; one who oppposes drinking.

1966–70 *DARE* (Qu. DD11, *When somebody gives up drinking*) Infs **GA**19, 30, (He's) made a Christian; (Qu. DD33a, *A person who drinks no liquor at all*) Infs **GA**19, **VA**73, Christian; (Qu. DD33b, *A person who is actively against drinking*) Infs **KY**34, **NC**54, Christian (man).

Christian door n chiefly NEng

A wooden door with stiles and rails supporting the panels and forming a cross.

1937 FWP *Guide MA* 597, The Cole House . . has a 'Christian' door with eight panels forming a double cross—supposed to protect the house from witchcraft. **1941** FWP *Guide IN* 245, The 'Christian door,' closing a stairway from the third floor to the attic, has cross pieces connecting the panels to form a tree cross. **1965** Teale *Wandering Through Winter* 333 **ME**, The woman who answered our knock at the double-Christian doors of the old house was five feet, two inches tall. **1965** (1975) Sloane *Wood* 29 **NEng**, In the pioneer days, doors were often symbols . . . A godly man might prefer a Christian door with stiles (vertical pieces) and rails (horizontal pieces) that formed a Christian cross.

Christian flycatcher n [See quots]

=crested flycatcher.

1908 *DN* 3.298 **eAL, wGA**, *Christian-flycatcher* . . . A bird that builds under the eaves of houses or in hollows, always using a cast snake-skin in the nest. Perhaps a corruption of *crested-flycatcher*. **1951** *AmSp* 26.91 **AL**, *Christian flycatcher* . . for the crested flycatcher.

Christ killer n derog

A Jew.

1941 *LANE* Map 455, *Nicknames for a Jew* [8 infs, Christ-killer]. **1945** Mencken *Amer. Lang. Suppl. 1* 617 **MD**, Names for Jew . . . *Christ-killer,* which is not recorded in any of the dictionaries (though Berrey and Van den Bark list *Christ-killer* as "a Socialist soap-box speech"), was familiar in my boyhood, but has passed out with the decay of Bible searching. **1950** *WELS* (*Nicknames . . Jewish*) 2 Infs, **WI**, Christ killer. **1964** *PADS* 42.32 **Chicago IL**, Terms used abusively for *Jew* . . . Christ-killer. **1967–69** *DARE* (Qu. HH28) Infs **NJ**1, **NY**84, **PA**227, **SC**54, **TX**37, Christ killer. **1970** Tarpley *Blinky* 254 **neTX**, *Nicknames for Jewish people* . . . 1.5% [of infs said] Christ killers.

Christkindle v, hence vbl n Christkindling Also sp Kris Kringle [Ger Christkindl Christ child] Ger settlement areas See also belsnickeling, mummer

A Christmas caroling celebration.

1950 Klees *PA Dutch* 353, *Christkindling* . . . Though it has died out in Pennsylvania, it persists . . in North Carolina, and therefore I give it its North Carolina name. Almost every night during the Christmas holidays a group of young people gathered at a country crossroads to make the rounds of near-by houses and farms. Often they wore disguises—blackened faces or masks and old clothes . . . At each house or farm visited, the leader of the band, who back in Pennsylvania was known as the *wünscher,* stepped forward and . . wished the master of the house and all his family . . a merry Christmas, a happy New Year . . . After . . his part, the whole company burst into song . . . Thereupon several youths shot off guns, while others beat on drums or pans or blew a horn . . . The masqueraders were treated at every farm to cider, apples, and Christmas cookies. **1964** Smith *PA Germans* 122 **VA**, In eastern Rockingham County residents had heard of belsnickeling, but claimed that when they "dressed-up clown-like during Christmas time and wore masks and visited, it was called going Kris Kringling!" As early as the eighteenth century the Pennsylvania Germans also had a *Christ-Kindel* or Christ-child who brought gifts to good children. Christ-Kindel became Kriss Kringle sometime during the first half of the nineteenth century, and a century ago merged into the popular Santa Claus of today.

Christ-kinkle See **Kriss Kringle 1**

Christly adv, adj Also Christless NEng

Damned—used as a generalized oath.

1968–69 *DARE* (Qu. LL37, *To make a statement as strong as you can:* "I could have wrung her neck, I was so _____ mad.") Inf **VT**12, Christly; (Qu. NN31, *Exclamations beginning with the sound of "cr_____".*) Inf **NH**14, Christly [FW: Conv, roughly similar to "damn," etc—as in "That's a christly thing."]. **1979** Lewis *How to Talk Yankee* **NEng**, *Christless* . . . Along with "christer" and "christly" this is a mildly blasphemous, all-purpose word. "I never did think we'd get that *christless* truck out of the ditch."

Christmas n

1 Something used in celebrating Christmas. **chiefly Sth, S Midl**

a A gift.

1857 in 1945 Easterby *SC Rice Plantation* 136, Joe and Will went to Waverly to see Christmas given out to the negroes there. **1895** *DN* 1.386 **wFL**, *Christmas:* . . a Christmas gift. **1905** *DN* 3.74 **nwAR**, *Christmas* . . . Christmas present. 'Ask the express agent if my Christmas has come in yet.' Not common.

b Whiskey.

1895 *DN* 1.386 **wFL**, *Christmas* . . anything used in celebrating Christmas; *e.g.* fireworks or potables. **1908** *DN* 3.298 **eAL, wGA**, *Christmas* . . . Whisky especially in the Christmas egg-nog. "Has it got enough Christmas in it?" **1915** *DN* 4.225 **wTX**, *Christmas* . . . Whiskey. "Has this pie got any Christmas in it?" **1952** Brown *NC Folkl.* 1.527, *Christmas* . . . Liquor—usually a supply supposedly for the Christmas holidays.

c Fireworks.

1895 [see **1b** above]. **1905** *DN* 3.74 **nwAR**, *Christmas* . . . Fireworks. 'My brother buys his Christmas every year.' Common.

2 Payday; the day on which one receives something.

1927 *AmSp* 3.24 **eTX** [Sawmill talk], On payday "the ghost walks" or it is "Christmas." **1968** Adams *Western Words*, Christmas—What the logger calls payday.

3 in var phrr indicating slowness or expressing impatience at having to wait: See quots. **chiefly Sth, S Midl** See Map

1884 Harrison *Negro Engl.* 270 **SE**, Tell [=till] Cris'mus = indefinite time. **1903** *DN* 2.309 **seMO**, *Christmas is coming* . . . An expression of impatience at delay. **1907** *DN* 3.229 **nwAR, seMO**, . . "Git a wiggle on you, Christmas is coming." **1942** McAtee *Dial. Grant Co. IN* 18 **IN, MO** (as of 1890s), "Christmas is coming", expression of impatience at delay; "_____ and so are you". **1951** *PADS* 15.65 **cwNH** (as of 1920–30), *Christmas, so's: phr.* Slowness is implied in this retort to the expression, "I'm comin'." **1952** Brown *NC Folkl.* 1.384, *Christmas* . . . As slow as Christmas. **1965–70** *DARE* (Qu. A18, . . *A very slow person*) 28 Infs, **chiefly Sth, S Midl**, Slow as Christmas; **GA**73, 80, As slow as Christmas; **TX**42, Just like Christmas; **NC**62, Slow as Christmas coming; **FL**51, **NC**11, Slower than Christmas.

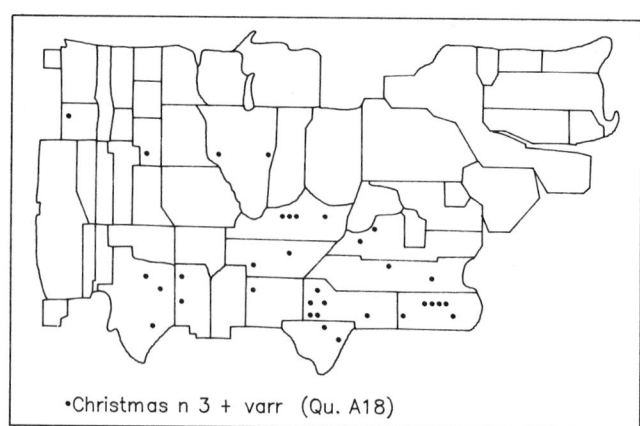

•Christmas n 3 + varr (Qu. A18)

Christmas intj [Euphem; *OEDS* 1897 →] chiefly Nth, esp NEast See Map Cf jiminy Christmas

Christ!—in var phrr, used as a mild oath.

1924 *DN* 5.260, *Substitutes for "Christ"*—Christmas: oh _____, giminy _____. **1950** *WELS* (*Exclamations beginning with the sound of "cr-"*) 1 Inf, **seWI**, Christmas. **1965–70** *DARE* (Qu. NN31, *Exclamations beginning with . . "cr-"*) 24 Infs, **chiefly Nth, esp NEast**, Christmas; **CT**29, 36, **MA**33, Oh Christmas; **SC**67, **SD**5, Criminy Christmas; **WA**16, **WV**3, Holy Christmas; **AK**5, Christmas tree; **CT**39,

For Christmas sakes; (Qu. NN30, *Exclamations beginning with . . "j"*) Infs **CO4, NY123, WA1, 20,** Gee Christmas; **OH71, OK1,** Jesus Christmas; **PA66,** Jeebie Christmas; **VT16,** Jumped-up Christmas; (Qu. NN29c, . . *"Holy _____!"*) Infs **CA155, KY70, NY66, 73, PA11,** Christmas; (Qu. NN27b, . . *"For _____ sakes!"*) Inf **NY45,** Christmas; (Qu. NN32, *Exclamations like 'I swear'*) Inf **WA6,** Holy Christmas.

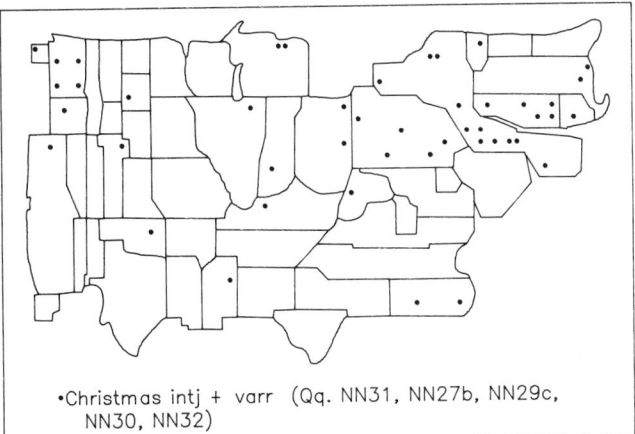

•Christmas intj + varr   (Qq. NN31, NN27b, NN29c, NN30, NN32)

Christmas and Easter Christian n Also abbr *C. and E. ~, C.E.* For varr see quots   See also **Easter Christian** and *DS* CC7
A person who seldom attends church.
    1967–70 *DARE* (Qu. CC7, . . *A person who goes to church very seldom or not at all*) Infs **CT12, NY136, TX80,** Christmas and Easter (Christian *or* goer); **NE4,** Christmas Catholic; **NY36,** C. and E. Christian; **IA45,** C. and E. man; **CA106,** C.E. people; **NJ46,** C.E.'s.

Christmas at you exclam Also *Chris on you*   Cf **Christmas gift**
See quots.
    1949 *AmSp* 24.107 **FL,** *Christmas at you!* A christmas greeting. **1968** *DARE* (Qu. FF10, . . *To greet each other on Christmas morning*) Inf **UT10,** Chris on you.

Christmasberry n
    1 =toyon.
    1897 Sudworth *Arborescent Flora* 235 **CA,** *Heteromeles arbutifolia . . . Tollon . . .* Christmas Berry. **1923** in 1925 Jepson *Manual Plants CA* 508, *Photinia arbutifolia . .* Christmas Berry. **1948** *Pacific Discovery* Mar–Apr 30/2 **CA,** The common toyon or Christmas berry is probably a relict since it has relatives . . in the Orient. **1974** Munz *Flora S. CA* 747, *Heteromeles . .* Christmas-Berry.
    2 A holly, usu **yaupon** but also *Ilex opaca.*
    1926 *Torreya* 26.5, *Ilex vomitoria . . .* Christmas berry, Jekyl Id., Ga. **1930** (1972) Cate *Our Todays* 10, A tea [was] made from the leaves of the ilex cassine, . . or "Christmas berry," sometimes called yaupon, which grows in abundance on the islands and mainland of the coast of Georgia. This beautiful shrub . . with its small glossy leaves and bright red berries presents a lovely picture in the winter. **1932** Lovell *Golden Isles* 58 **GA,** The grounds were inclosed by hedges of *Ilex cassine* or Christmas berry. **1937** *Torreya* 37.98, *Ilex opaca . . .* Christmas-berry, Jekyl Id., Ga. **1960** Vines *Trees SW* 650, Although the leaves of *I. cassine* were sometimes mixed with those of *I. vomitoria,* the former contains [sic] no caffeine. Vernacular names in use are Christmas-berry [etc.]. **1967** *DARE* (Qu. T5, . . *Evergreens*) Inf **SC63,** Christmas berry, cassina, red berries at Christmas.
    3 A red-berried shrub (*Crossopetalum ilicifolium*) native to southern Florida.
    1933 Small *Manual SE Flora* 819, *R. ilicifolia . . .* Depressed shrub with pubescent twigs . . drupe subglobose, . . red. —(*Christmas-berry.*) **1953** Greene–Blomquist *Flowers South* 70, Examples [of the family Celastraceae] are bittersweet, euonymus, and the less known Christmas-berry . . of s. Fla.
    4 A **wolfberry,** usu *Lycium carolinianum,* but also *L. californicum.*
    1938 Van Dersal *Native Woody Plants* 331, Christmasberry (*Lycium californicum, Lycium carolinianum . .*). **1953** Greene–Blomquist *Flowers South* 106, *Christmas-Berry (Lycium carolinianum) . . .* is a spiny shrub . . with red berries . . . Fla. to Tex., n. to S.C. **1976** Fleming

Wild Flowers FL 72, Christmas berry blooms all year in hammocks, shell mounds, and coastal areas that flood with salt water.
    5 A **greenbrier,** prob *Smilax lanceolata.*
    1969 *DARE* FW Addit **GA51,** *Christmas berry* = the red-berried Smilax.

Christmas box n *arch* or *obs*
A Christmas present.
    1810 in 1929 Weems *Mason Locke Weems* 3.29, Liberal allowance made to those . . who take several copies of Washington and Marion for Christmas Boxes to their young relations. **1823** Cooper *Pioneers* 1.227 **NY,** He gave me this packet to offer you as a Christmas-box. **1896** *DN* 1.413 **wNY,** "Christmas box," any Christmas gift . . . occasionally.

Christmas box exclam See **Christmas gift**

Christmas bush n
    1 A **yaupon** (here: *Ilex vomitoria*).
    1926 *Torreya* 26.5, *Ilex vomitoria . . .* Christmas bush, . . Jekyl Id., Ga.
    2 A **boneset 1** (here: *Eupatorium odoratum*).
    1960 Vines *Trees SW* 991, Christmas-bush *Eupatorium . . .* Vigorous shrubby plant attaining a height of 3–10 ft.

Christmas cactus n [From its blooming around Christmastime]   Cf **desert Christmas cactus**
A red-, pink-, or white-flowered cactus (*Schlumbergera bridgei*) often cultivated as a pot plant.
    1921 *Frontier* Nov 23, She stooped to inhale the fragrance of a hyacinth, and caress the smooth green Christmas cactus leaves. **1943** Damon *Sense of Humus* 65 **NH,** The Christmas cactus on a little bracket at the side punctually justifies its name. **1966** *DARE* FW Addit **WA,** *Christmas cactus*—leafy cactus plant that blooms in December.

Christmas Catholic See **Christmas and Easter Christian**

Christmas-crack n *obs*
A toy pistol: see quot.
    1890 Howells *Boy's Town* 111 **OH,** There were all sorts of pistols; but the commonest was one that the boys called a Christmas-crack; it was of brass, and when it burst the barrel curled up like a dandelion stem when you split it and put it in water.

Christmas Eve n ?chiefly **Sth, S Midl**
The day before Christmas; hence also *Christmas Eve day, ~ morning, ~ night.*
    1905 *DN* 3.74 **nwAR,** *Christmas eve night . . .* Christmas eve . . . Common. **1906** *DN* 3.130 **nwAR,** *Christmas eve day . . .* December 24 . . . Christmas eve morning . . . The forenoon of the day before Christmas. **1928** *AmSp* 4.80 **Sth,** Christmas Eve Night. **1938** Stuart *Dark Hills* 193 **KY,** I left him fixing a flat tire on Cumberland Mountain on Christmas Eve day. **1944** *PADS* 2.7 **Sth,** *Christmas Eve . . .* The twenty-four hours preceding Christmas, usually supplemented with *day* or *night* to specify. **1945** *PADS* 3.9 **NY,** *Christmas Eve . . .* we make distinctions: "the morning of Christmas Eve," "Christmas Eve about four o'clock."

Christmas-Eve gift See **Christmas gift**

Christmas evergreen See **Christmas green**

Christmas-Eve tree See **Christmas tree 3**

Christmas fern n Also *Christmas shield fern*
A **sword fern:** usu *Polysticum acrostichoides,* which is also called **bear's bed 2.**
    1878 Williamson *Ferns KY* 99, *Aspidium acrostichoides . . .* Winter Fern—Christmas Fern. **1884** Miller *Dict. Engl. Names of Plants* 164, *Aspidium acrostichoides.* Christmas Shield-Fern, of N. America. **1947** *Amer. Midland Naturalist* 38.26 **MD,** Polystichum acrostichoides (Christmas Fern). Occasional (locally common) in seepage swamps. **1961** Douglas *My Wilderness* 194 **MD,** The fronds of the ferns now [=in March] begin to stir. There are several dozen species in the Potomac area. Christmas, cinnamon, maiden-hair, bracken, hay-scented, leathery grape—these are present. **1967** *DARE* (Qu. S26a, . . *Roadside flowers*) Inf **MA5,** Christmas fern. **1973** Hitchcock–Cronquist *Flora Pacific NW* 53, *Polystichum . . .* Holly-fern; Christmas-fern; Sword-fern. **1976** *Greenfield Recorder* (MA) 23 Oct [Hemenway column], "Ferning." That was the gathering and bunching of sword (Christmas) ferns and . . lady fern for use by florists and decorators. **1976** Bruce *How to Grow Wildflowers* 22, In sheltered pockets I would easily find evergreen woodferns and Christmas fern.

Christmas flower n [From its blooming at Christmastime]

1 also *Chris root, Christmas plant, Christmas rose:* Either of two hellebores (*Helleborus niger* or *H. viridis*).

1876 Hobbs *Bot. Hdbk.* 23, Christmas rose, Black hellebore, Helleborus niger. **1896** *Jrl. Amer. Folkl.* 9.180, *Helleborus viridis* . . Christmas rose, Chris root, Sulphur Grove, Ohio. **1900** Lyons *Plant Names* 186, *H. niger* . . . Christmas-flower, Christmas Rose . . . *H. viridis* . . . Chris-root, Christmas Rose. **1952** Strausbaugh–Core *Flora WV* 394, *H. viridis* . . . Green Hellebore. Christmas Flower . . . Cultivated as an ornamental, locally escaped; has been found wild in [six] . . counties. **1959** Carleton *Index Herb. Plants* 27, Christmas plant . . . Christmas rose: Helleborus niger.

2 also *Christmas star:* A **poinsettia** (here: *Euphorbia pulcherrima*).

[**1946** *Chicago Daily Tribune* (IL) 23 Dec 14/3, Other specimens in the holiday arboretum are . . the Christmas flower, which is the Mexican name for the poinsettia.] **1953** Greene–Blomquist *Flowers South* 66, This remarkable plant family . . . includes such ornamentals as the Christmas-flower *(Poinsettia)*. **1982** Perry–Hay *Field Guide Plants* 58, *Euphorbia pulcherrima* . . . Poinsettia, Christmas flower; Christmas star.

Christmas fool n Similarly ~ *fooling* **WI, MN, ND, areas of Norw settlement** Cf **Belsnickel 2, Christkindle**

See quots.

1938 FWP *Guide ND* 79, In many Norwegian towns, Jule Bokke or Christmas Fools still make the rounds of the homes between Christmas and New Year. They are young people dressed in costume and masked, who call on neighbors and are given food and drink at each home visited. **1968** *DARE* (Qu. FF9, *A Christmas gathering, at church or at someone's home, where there are songs and presents*) Inf **MN12**, During Christmas fortnight went ['juləbukɪŋ] or Christmas fools—dressed in disguise and went visiting (Norwegian). **1976** *Capital Times* (Madison WI) 28 Dec 39 **cwWI,** "Do you want to see the Christmas Fools?" . . . This was your introduction to "Julebukking" ("Christmas Fooling"), one of the customs dating back to pagan times in Norway.

Christmas gift exclam Pronc-spp or eye-dial *C(h)ris'mus gif; Christmas giff* Also ~ *give;* ~ *box,* ~ *present,* ~ *treat,* less freq, *Christmas-Eve gift* **chiefly Sth, S Midl** See Map

Used as a greeting on Christmas day; orig the first person saying it received a present from the person(s) spoken to.

[**1844** *Knickerbocker* 23.16, Threatening to catch him for a Christmas gift next morning, [she] disappeared up the stairs.] **1881** Harris *Uncle Remus Songs* 44 **GA** [Black], I'm gwineter bounce in on Marse John en Miss Sally, en holler Chris'mus gif' des like I useter. **1884** Harrison *Negro Engl.* 270 **SE,** To holler 'Cris'mus gif' = to cry 'Christmas gift'. **1890** Howells *Boy's Town* 112 **OH,** The first thing when you woke you tried to catch everybody, and you caught a person if you said "Christmas Gift!" before he or she did; and then the person you caught had to give you a present. Nobody ever said "Merry Christmas!" as people do now; and I do not know where the custom of saying "Christmas Gift" came from. It seems more sordid and greedy than it really was; the pleasure was to see who could say it first; and the boys did not care for what they got if they beat. **1903** *DN* 2.309 **seMO,** Christmas gift! . . . Merry Christmas! **1906** *DN* 3.130 **nwAR,** *Christmas gift* . . . Merry Christmas. Negroes and the lower class of whites use the expression literally as a begging formula. It is felt to be appropriate only on Christmas morning. In other cases it means nothing more than "Merry Christmas." **1908** *DN* 3.298 **eAL, wGA,** *Christmas gift* . . . A greeting on Christmas morning. The person who is caught, i.e., who is greeted first, is expected to give a present to the one who catches him. The custom is passing away. **1915** *DN* 4.181 **swVA,** *Christmas gift.* **1946** *PADS* 6.9 **VA, NC, cGA,** *Christmas gift.* **1949** Kurath *Word Geog.* 80, In the North and in most of the North Midland *Merry Christmas!* is the universal Christmas salutation, and this expression is now freely used by the younger generation in the South and the South Midland, especially in urban areas. The simple folk of the South and the South Midland still say *Christmas gift!* This salutation is also still heard from older people in southern Pennsylvania (from the Susquehanna westward) and is in rather common use in the Ohio Valley, in West Virginia as well as in Ohio. It seems fairly clear that both the South and the Midland had this expression from early times, and that *Merry Christmas!* has largely displaced *Christmas gift!* in Pennsylvania and on Delaware Bay in fairly recent times. **1950** *PADS* 14.19 **SC,** *Christmas-give, -gift, -giff.* **1954** *Harder Coll.* **cwTN,** Christmas-Eve gift. **c1960** *Wilson Coll.* **csKY,** *Christmas-Eve Gift!* Formerly common as a greeting on Christmas Eve; usually a gift, like candy or nuts, was expected. **1965–70** *DARE* (Qu.

FF10, . . *To greet each other on Christmas morning*) 183 Infs, **chiefly Sth, S Midl,** Christmas gift; **GA70, MO20, TX98,** Christmas-Eve gift; **PA13,** My Christmas gift; **MD20,** Christmas present; **SC40,** Christmas treat. **1970** Tarpley *Blinky* 233 **neTX,** Among the older informants, *Christmas gift* is the usual greeting heard early on Christmas morning. *Christmas gift* has increasing popularity as the level of education and size of community decline . . . Geographically, *Christmas gift* is most popular in the northeastern counties. [Reported by 49.5% of infs. *Christmas present* was given by less than 1%.] **1971** Wood *Vocab. Change* 40 **Sth,** The usual Christmas greeting is *Merry Christmas.* Less general but still reported is *Christmas gift.* A few of the choices in Tennessee and Georgia are *Christmas box. Christmas gift,* as natives of the region will point out, is a part of a Christmas morning game and thus has a different function from that of exchanging the greeting *Merry Christmas.*

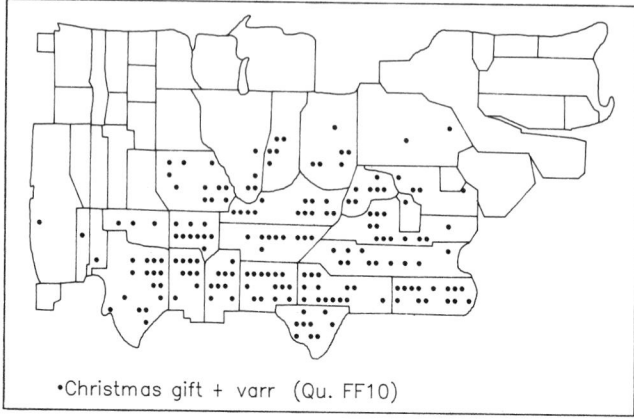

•Christmas gift + varr (Qu. FF10)

Christmas green n Also *Christmas evergreen*

A **ground pine** (here: *Lycopodium complanatum*).

1876 Hobbs *Bot. Hdbk.* 24, Christmas evergreen, Festoon pine, Lycopodium rupestre. **1897** *Jrl. Amer. Folkl.* 10.147, *Lycopodium complanatum* . . trailing Christmas Green, West Va. **1910** Graves *Flowering Plants* 31 **CT,** Christmas Green . . . Well known and much used for Christmas decorations.

Christmas holly n

1 A **holly** (here: *Ilex opaca*).

1940 Steyermark *Flora MO* 334, *Christmas Holly (Ilex opaca* . . *).* The red berries and dark green evergreen leaves of the holly are popular as Christmas decorations. **1960** Vines *Trees SW* 649, *Ilex* . . *opaca* . . . Vernacular names are Yule Holly, Christmas Holly, and White Holly. The foliage and fruit are often used for holiday decorations.

2 =**toyon.** Cf **Christmasberry 1**

1968 *DARE* (Qu. T16, . . *Trees* . . *"special"*) Inf **CA79,** Christmas holly.

Christmas melon n

Perh a **winter melon.**

1950 *WELS* 1 Inf, **cwWI,** Christmas melon . . occasional. **1971** *Thompson Coll.* **GA,** Santa Claus melons. We used to call them Christmas melons.

Christmas plant See **Christmas flower 1**

Christmas plover n

Either the **black-bellied plover** or the **willet.**

1951 *AmSp* 26.277 **Key West FL,** The black-bellied plover and willet are known as *Christmas plovers* from their being most commonly noted at that season.

Christmas present See **Christmas gift**

Christmas rose See **Christmas flower 1**

Christmas shield fern See **Christmas fern**

Christmas star See **Christmas flower 2**

Christmas treat See **Christmas gift**

Christmas tree n

1 usu in descriptive phr: A woman who uses excessive make-up, or who overdresses. *joc*

[**1960** Wentworth–Flexner *Slang, Christmas* . . . Any ostentatious display, as of clothing, jewelry . . . *orig. "all lighted up like a Christmas tree."*] **1965–70** *DARE* (Qu. W36, . . *A woman who uses a lot of* *cosmetics*) Infs **AR3, FL28, OH41, TX54 VA48,** (Looks like a) Christmas tree; **CA132,** Painted up like a Christmas tree; (Qu. W37, *When a woman puts on her good clothes and tries to look her best*) Inf **KY60,** Dressed up like a Christmas tree; (Qu. W40, . . *A woman who overdresses*) Infs **KS15, OH66, TX43,** (Looks like a) Christmas tree; **NY92, PA26,** Dressed (*or* lit up) like a Christmas tree.

2 in phr *lit up like a Christmas tree:* Drunk.

1969 *DARE* (Qu. DD15) Inf **CA158,** Lit up like a Christmas tree.

3 also attrib, infreq *Christmas-Eve tree:* A Christmas gathering or party, usu with presents and songs. **chiefly Sth, nNEng, also S Midl** See Map

1929 Dobie *Vaquero* 162 **swTX,** On Christmas Eve a group of us young people drove down in buggies to attend a Christmas tree on the Picketwire. **1950** *WELS (A Christmas gathering (at a home or at church) where there are songs and presents)* 6 Infs, **WI,** Christmas tree; 1 Inf, **WI,** Christmas tree party; 1 Inf, Christmas tree program. **1954** *Harder Coll.* **cwTN,** Christmas tree: A Christmas gathering . . "Christmas tree's today, ain't it?" **1965–70** *DARE* (Qu. FF9, *A Christmas gathering, at church or at someone's home, where there are songs and presents*) 107 Infs, **chiefly Sth, OK, AR, nNEng,** Christmas tree; 8 Infs, **chiefly Sth, S Midl,** Christmas-tree party; **MS29, NC40, NY18, 32,** Christmas-Eve tree; **SC40,** Community Christmas tree, family Christmas tree. **1967** *San Juan Mission News* (San Juan Bautista CA) 24 Nov 7/3, The annual Haydon Christmas Tree has been set for December 22nd.

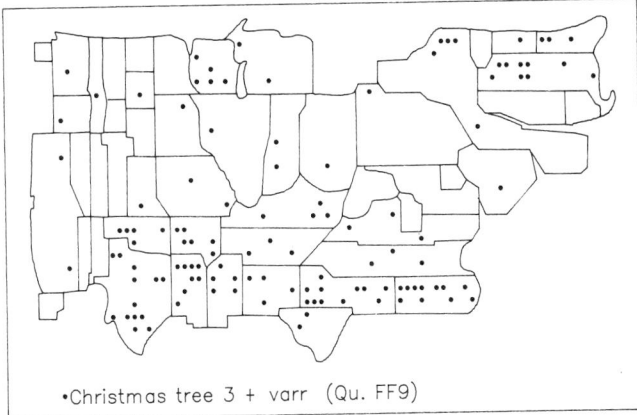

•Christmas tree 3 + varr (Qu. FF9)

4 in phr *knock one off the Christmas tree:* To astonish; to berate. *somewhat old-fash*

1913 *DN* 4.2 **ME,** *Knock off the Christmas tree* . . . To call one down; to bring one to time. "So I just knocked him off the Christmas tree." **1929** *Ruppenthal Coll.* **KS,** That certainly knocked me off the Christmas tree when I heard it.

5 A yaupon (here: *Ilex vomitoria*).

1941 *Torreya* 41.49, *Ilex cassine* . . . Christmas tree, Okefinokee Swamp, Ga.

6 A **poinsettia** (here: *Euphorbia pulcherrima*). Cf **Christmas flower 2**

1972 Carr *Da Kine Talk* 127 **HI,** The red poinsettia, potted and offered for sale in luxuriant bloom in December, is sometimes called the Christmas tree by old-timers in the immigrant groups. In Japan and Korea, the poinsettia appears so regularly on American Christmas cards that it is thought of as a kind of Christmas tree and this idea has been transferred to Hawaii.

Christmas trick n

An act performed rarely—orig on an annual holiday, such as Christmas.

1855 in 1956 Eliason *Tarheel Talk* 265 **NC,** Papa waded the river for his Christmas trick. **1957** *AmSp* 32.285 **Sth,** In older times Christmas seemed to come hardly once a year; hence a *Christmas trick* would be an event that is very unusual. For example, one might say to someone who has never visited him, 'Why don't you play a Christmas trick and come see me sometime?'

Christopher intj Freq ~ *Columbus,* also *holy* ~, infreq ~ *Jerusalem, Jesus* ~, *Jiminy* ~, *by* ~ **chiefly Nth, also N Midl**

Used as a mild oath: see quots.

1854 (1923) Holmes *Tempest & Sunshine* 82 **KY,** Christopher Columbus! One of my servants! **1924** *DN* 5.260, *Substitutes for "Christ"* . .

Christopher . . [Christopher] Columbus. **1950** *WELS (Exclamations beginning with the sound of "cr-")* 11 Infs, **WI,** Christopher (Columbus); 1 Inf, **WI,** Well for Keristofher Columbo. **1959** *VT Hist.* new ser 27.130, By Christopher! . . . Occasional . . . By the jumped-up Christopher! . . . Rare. **1965–70** *DARE* (Qu. NN31, *Exclamations beginning with the sound of "cr-")* Infs **CA9, ID5, IL36, NY126, 146, OH18, 28, SD8,** Christopher Columbus; **HI1, MA68, MT3, 4, NY2, OH47, PA227,** Christopher; **MA6,** Christopher Jerusalem; (Qu. NN29c, *Exclamations beginning with "holy")* Infs **IA23, MI3, 93,** Christopher; (Qu. NN30, *Exclamations beginning with sound of "j")* Inf **WI12,** Jesus Christopher; **IL100,** Jiminy Christopher.

Christyde n [For *Christmastide*] *arch or obs*

1899 (1912) Green *VA Folk-Speech, Christyde* . . . Christmas.

chrome dome See **dome**

chronic v

To malinger; hence n *chronics* an imaginary disease.

1967 *DARE* (Qu. BB27, *When somebody pretends to be sick . . you'd say he's _____*) Inf **LA3,** Chronicking; (Qu. BB28, *Joking names . . imaginary diseases*) Inf **LA3,** [The] chronics.

chronical adj

1914 *DN* 4.70 **ME, nNH,** *Chronical* . . . Chronic. "The chronical Bright disease."

chub n

1 also *chubs:* A fat or stocky person—orig applied to a Texan, now used more generally as a nickname.

1869 *Overland Mth.* 3.129 **SW,** For the Texan sobriquet "Chub" I know of no explanation, unless it be found in the size of the Eastern Texans. It is related of the Fifteenth Texas Infantry, for instance, that . . no member was of a lighter weight than a hundred and eighty pounds. **1942** Berrey–Van den Bark *Amer. Slang* 429.2, *Fat person* . . . chub. **1967–70** *DARE* (Qu. X50, *Names or nicknames for a person who is very fat*) Infs **CA189, GA77, NC47, 88, PA108,** Chub; **IL19,** Chubs; (Qu. Z12, *Nicknames . . "a small child"*) Inf **NE8,** Chub.

2 See quot.

1953 Randolph *Down in Holler* 234 **Ozarks,** *Chub* . . . A sweetheart, a lover. Rose O'Neill, of Taney County, Mo., says that this was a common word along Bear Creek in the early nineteen hundreds and applied to either sex.

3 See **chubsucker.**

chub v

1 To fish by using chubs or cut-up pieces of other fish as bait. [Perh infl by **chum** v]

1967–69 *DARE* (Qu. P16, *When fishermen throw bits of bait in the water to attract fish*) Infs **NY2, 164, PA29, SC69, TX11,** Chubbing.

2 To bottom-fish.

1969 *DARE* (Qu. P17, . . *[To] fish by lowering a line and sinker close to the bottom of the water*) Inf **CA137,** Chubbing.

chubasco n [Span] **CA, TX**

A strong wind or squall coming from Mexico.

1947 *AN&Q* 7.62, Pacific coast fishermen refer to the "Chubasco" as a cyclone at sea. This storm is likely to strike at any time across the Gulf of Tehuantepec. **1967–70** *DARE* (Qu. B18, . . *Kinds of wind*) Inf **CA82,** [čəbæsko]; **TX22,** [ču'asko] [sic]—squall; (Qu. B12, *When the wind begins to increase*) Inf **CA82,** Chubasco—if it comes from the south; (Qu. B17, *A destructive wind that blows straight*) Inf **CA189,** [čəbɔsko]. Spanish—a wind from Mexico, common on the coast here.

‡chubby adj

1954 *Harder Coll.* **cwTN,** *Chubby:* chummy, excessively friendly.

chubhole n

1954 *Harder Coll.* **cwTN,** *Chubholes* . . . Holes, usually filled with water, that are in a roadway . . . Also known as *chuckholes.*

chublain See **chilblain**

chub mackerel n

Std: a foodfish (*Scomber colias*) of the North Atlantic. Also called **thimble-eye, tinker mackerel**

chubnose buffalo n

=**bigmouth buffalo.**

1933 LA Dept. of Conserv. *Fishes* 440, The Common Buffalofish [*Ictiobus cyprinellus*] . . has come to be known under many popular names. For the sake of making these names available, they are all enumerated here: Redmouth Buffalo, . . Chub Nose Buffalo.

chubs See **chub** n 1

chubsucker n Also *chub*

1 A common **sucker** of the genus *Erimyzon*.
1817 *Acad. Nat. Sci. Philadelphia Jrl.* 1st ser 1.93, *C. gibbosus* . . . This species I discovered in the river Connecticut, near Northampton, where it is named Chub Sucker. **1842** DeKay *Zool. NY* 4.193, The *Brilliant Chubsucker, Labeo oblongus,* . . is familiarly known under the name of *Chub,* and *Chubsucker.* **1887** Goode *Amer. Fishes* 436, The "Chub Sucker," *Erimyzon succetta,* the "Sweet Sucker" or "Creek-fish," is one of the most abundant and widely diffused of the Suckers, being found from Maine to Texas. **1960** *Amer. Fisheries Soc. List Fishes* 17, Creek chubsucker . . *Erimyzon oblongus;* Lake chubsucker . . *Erimyzon sucetta;* Sharpfin . . *Erimyzon tenuis.*

2 A **fallfish** or similar fish.
1931–33 *LANE Worksheets* cwCT, Chub sucker — a mudfish, same as dace.

chu'ch See **church** n

chuchupate n [AmSpan]

1 =**lovage**, esp *Ligusticum porteri*.
1937 U.S. Forest Serv. *Range Plant Hdbk.* W106, Loveroots. *Ligusticum spp* . . . are known as chuchupate in the Southwest. *Ibid* W107, Porter loveroot . . , also called osha and chuchupate, may be regarded as a more southern and coarser-leaved sister species of fernleaf loveroot. **1947** (1976) Curtin *Healing Herbs* 139, *Chuchupate* (southern New Mexico) *Ligusticum porteri* . . . The popular names *chuchupate* and *oshá* are of Indian origin.

2 A **biscuit root** 1 (here: *Lomatium californicum*).
1961 Thomas *Flora Santa Cruz* 261 CA, *L. californicum* . . . Chu-Chu-Pate. Occasional, usually on shaded slopes.

chuck v

1 To throw, toss; also fig. [*OED* 1593 →] **scattered, but esp freq NEast** See Map
1890 *DN* 1.60 wPA, wOH, Chuck: e.g. "to chuck one a blow on the ear." **1899** Edwards *Defense* 2 GA, Did she ever chuck anything at you? **1914** in 1937 Moses *Repr. Amer. Dramas* 339/1 NYC, You're afraid to put her to the test: you're afraid she will chuck you. **1915** *DN* 4.232 neOH [College slang], Chuck . . . To throw out as bait; try on. "To chuck a bluff." **1922** Rollins *Cowboy* 125 West, Many a tenderfoot, unmindful of this order of procedure, has "hit the ground," "sunned his moccasins" or "landed," . . has been "spilled," "chucked," or "dumped." **1930** Shoemaker *1300 Words* 11 cPA Mts (as of c1900), Chuck — To get rid of. **1943** *LANE* Map 667 *(Threw),* 7 infs, MA, CT, Chucked. **1959** *VT Hist.* new ser 27.130, Chuck . . . To throw out. **1965–70** *DARE* (Qu. Y10, *To throw something*) 31 Infs, **chiefly NEast**, Chucked; (Qu. C24b, *"The dog wouldn't go away, so he took a stone/rock and _____ it at him."*) 13 Infs, **scattered**, Chuck; AL14, CT7, VA47, WI5, Chucked; (Qu. Y51, . . *"He's not your kind — you'd better _____ him."*) Inf WI64, Chuck; (Qu. EE18) Inf GA23, Chucking; (Qu. EE26) Inf MD15, Chuck snowballs; (Qu. II9, *If several people have to contribute in order to pay for something*) Inf PA245, Chuck in; PA114, Chuck together; (Qu. II8, *When one person wants to share or divide something with another*) Inf PA114, Chuck together.

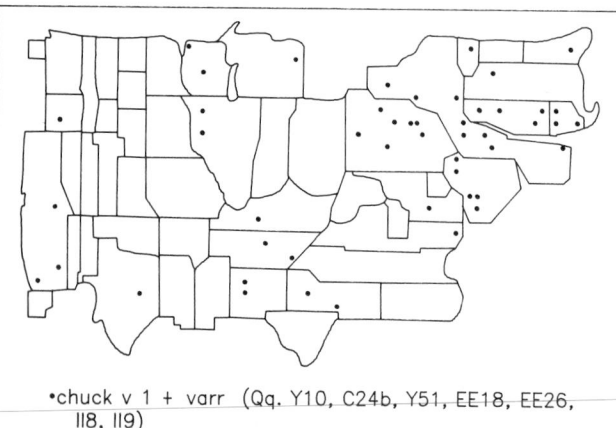

•chuck v 1 + varr (Qq. Y10, C24b, Y51, EE18, EE26, II8, II9)

2 To hide, conceal. [Perh infl by *tuck*]
1915 *DN* 4.162 NW, Chuck . . . To put away; conceal . . . "Before the arrival of officers, both sides chucked their guns." **1968** *DARE* (Qu. Y47, *To hide something away for future use*) Inf MN30, Chucked away.

3 See **upchuck**.

chuck n[1]

1 A chunk; a thick, large, or rough piece. [*OED* 1674 →]
1955 Warren *Angels* 153 KY, He was red-faced, and the face square-hacked like you had done the job out of a big chuck of red cedar with a hand-ax and hadn't been too careful about the smooth-off. **1969** *DARE* (Qu. C25, . . *Kinds of stone*) Inf CA113, Chuck of granite.

2 Food; a meal. [*OEDS* 1850 →]
1865 *Harper's Mag.* 30.325/1 NEast coast, [I] finished chuck on twelve o'clock. **1892** *KS Univ. Qrly.* 1.95 KS, Chuck: lunch. **1905** *DN* 3.74 nwAR, Chuck . . . Dinner. **1907** White *AZ Nights* 112, When the last man had returned from chuck, Homer made the dispositions for the cut. **1915** *DN* 4.225 wTX, Chuck . . . Food, or "grub." **1916** *DN* 4.344 seSC, KS, Chuck . . . The leavings of food . . . In N.W. Colorado the call to meals at the cook-wagon is "chuck, come and get it." **1965–70** *DARE* (Qu. H6, *Words for food in general*) 11 Infs, **scattered**, Chuck.

3 Money.
1895 *DN* 1.386 Boston MA, Chuck . . . money.

chuck n[2] Infreq *chuck of the wood* [Abbr for **woodchuck**] **chiefly Nth**

=**woodchuck** n[1].
1781 Peters *Genl. Hist. CT* 250, The Woodchuck . . , when eating, makes a noise like a hog, whence he is named Woodchuck, or Chuck of the Wood. **1809** *Thomas' MA Spy or Worcester Gaz.* (MA) 8 Nov [4]/1 MA, Then if to go farther I was put in doubt, / By a Chuck at the mouth of a hole. **1880** *Harper's Mag.* 61.586/1 NH, "Hullo! there's a 'chuck," shouted 'Mandy, and off he went . . to wage war with a sober old woodchuck. **1950** *WELS (Other names . . woodchuck)* 1 Inf, nwWI, Chuck. **1965–70** *DARE* (Qu. P31, . . *Other names . . groundhog*) Infs KY53, MA47, 68, NY68, OH16, PA73, 141, 205, Chuck. **1982** Elman *Hunter's Field Guide* 408, *Marmot (Marmota)* — Common & Regional Names: chuck, whistler.

chuck n[3] Also *chucky* [Scots and Engl dial: see *EDD, SND*]
A playing marble; a game using such marbles.
1956 *AmSp* 31.37 MA, A chuck . . is a pebble or marble used in a game of marbles called chuck or chucky.

chuck n[4] [Chinook jargon; *DCan* 1860 →] **NW** See also **salt-chuck**
Water; a body of water.
1899 U.S. Fish & Wildlife Serv. *Fishery Bulletin* 18.70 AK, At the end of this arm is a narrow passage, or "skookum chuck," as it is called in this country, leading into a bay. *Ibid* 72, Into this salt chuck another stream empties. **1930** Williams *Logger-Talk* 21 Pacific NW, Chuck: A body of water, as in *salt chuck* for Puget Sound, *Pilchuck* for red river. **1939** *FWP Guide AK* xl, Chuck . . . water, stream (Chinook). **1958** McCulloch *Woods Words* Pacific NW, Chuck . . . Short for saltchuck, the ocean. **1967** *DARE* Tape WA20, Chuck is water. The Indian name for water is [čʌk].

chuck n[5] [Alter of *shuck*]
1968 *DARE* (QR, near Qu. L9) Inf VA14, Chucks or husks from the ear [of corn].

chuck n[6] [Abbr for **chuckhole**]
1973 Allen *LAUM* 1.401 nwIA, The road is full of 'chucks'.

chuck n[7]
=**chuck-will's-widow**.
1954 Sprunt *FL Bird Life* 257, In common with the others of its peculiar family, the Chuck builds no nest. **1955** *Oriole* 8.9, Chuck-wills-widow. All names are sonic unless otherwise explained . . . Chuck. **1962** Imhof *AL Birds* 314, Chuck-will's-widow . . . Other names: . . Chuck.

Chuck n[8] See **Charlie** 2

chuck intj Usu repeated

1 See **chook** intj.

2 also *chucky, chookie:* Used as a call to chickens. **chiefly Inland Nth**

1948 Davis *Word Atlas* App, 2 infs, **MI,** Chuck-chuck [as a call to chickens]. **1955** Potter *Dial. NW OH* 239, [The map shows three instances of *chuck-chuck!* as against fifty-four instances of *chick(ie)-chick(ie)!*]. **1965–70** DARE (Qu. K79, *How . . you call the chickens*) 12 Infs, **chiefly Inland Nth, esp PA,** Chuck chuck; **PA191, WY4,** Chuck chuck chuck; **HI2,** Chuck; **NY13, OH81, PA92,** Chucky chucky; **PA163,** Chucky. **1971** Wood *Vocab. Change* 183, 300 Sth, [As a call to chickens, *chuck, chuck* was given by 8 infs, in **TN, AL,** and **GA**]. **1973** Allen *LAUM* 1.267, *Calls to chickens at feeding . . .* [1 inf, **MN**] chookie, chookie. *Ibid* [From the check list:] *Chuck* (?[čʊk]) occurs 7 [sic] times in the Northern speech zone [6 **MN** infs, 1 **IA,** 1 **ND**].

chuckablock See **chockablock**

chuck-a-luck n Also *chuck-luck, chuckle-luck, chucker-luck, chutter-luck* esp **West, Sth**

A dice game: see quot 1968.

   1843 Green *Exposure of Gambling* 90 *(DAE),* Chutter-luck . . . This game is played with three dice . . and a box to throw them from. **1856** *Liberator* (Boston MA) 26.12/4 **IL,** Leper and Doolin got into a quarrel over a game called 'chuckle luck.' **1888** Grigsby *Smoked Yank* 104 **AL** (as of 1864), Chuck-luck, faro, poker, . . tricks and games of every variety were played and carried on openly. **1907** White *AZ Nights* 165, And a man's so sick of himself by the time he gets this far that he'd play chuck-a-luck, let alone faro or monte. **1929** Dobie *Vaquero* 140, The gambling dens ran day and night but were in full blast from midnight on. Keno, poker, monte, chuck-luck, rouge et noir, roulette, faro, casino—every kind of game that the professional gambler might ask for or the tenderfoot be fleeced for was there. **1938** Asbury *Sucker's Progress* 52, Chuck-a-Luck is one of the oldest of dice games. . . . About 1820 it began to be known in some sections of the country as Chucker-Luck, and by the Civil War this had begun to give way to Chuck-Luck and Chuck-a-Luck. In recent years it has often been called Bird Cage. **1965–70** DARE (Qu. EE40, . . *Table games . . using dice*) Infs **CA114, MO1, NC36, PA163, TX3, WA28,** Chuck-a-luck; (Qu. DD37, . . *Table games played . . by adults*) Infs **MI113, WA28,** Chuck-a-luck. **1968** Adams *Western Words, Chuck-a-luck*—A gambling game of English origin brought to this country about 1800 and now the most popular dice game in the West. It is played with three dice tumbled in a bottle-shaped wire cage called a *chuck cage* and a board with squares numbered from one to six. In placing stakes on any square, the player bets the bank even money that one of the dice will show the number chosen.

chuck-a-luck adj

   1892 *KS Univ. Qrly.* 1.96 **KS,** Chuck-a-luck: loaded (of dice).

chuckatuck n [Imit] Cf **chicaric**

=**ruddy turnstone.**

   1917 (1923) *Birds Amer.* 1.268, *Ruddy Turnstone . . . Other Names . . .* Chuckatuck. **1959** *AmSp* 34.74, *Chuckatuck* (ruddy turnstone).

chuckawalla See **chuckwalla**

chuckaway n, also intj **West**

=**chuck** n[1] **2.**

   1873 *Newton Kansan* 20 Feb. 3/4 *(DAE),* An Indian scout . . . asked first for chuckaway. **1933** *AmSp* 8.1.27 **nTX,** *Chuck-away (John).* Call used in lieu of *dinner is served,* and to which often the threat was added, *If you don't come and git it, I'll throw it out.* **1936** Barnard *Rider* 67 **OK,** Lockridge refused to give any, and told him he would give them some chuck-away, but if so many of them ever came again he would give them nothing. **1956** Ker *Vocab. W. TX* 142, Chuck-a-way—come to meat.

chuck block n

=**chuck box.**

   1967 DARE FW Addit **CO,** Chuck block—fits back end of wagon—the grub box.

chuck boat n **Nth** Also called **wanigan**

Among loggers: a boat for carrying food and other provisions.

   1958 McCulloch *Woods Words* **Pacific NW,** *Chuck boat*—Same thing to a log drive that the chuck wagon is to the round-up; following down the river to feed the river drivers. **1969** Sorden *Lumberjack Lingo* **NEng, Gt Lakes,** *Chuck boat*—A wanigan. A boat with supplies that followed the log drive downstream.

chuck box n, also attrib **chiefly West**

A box for carrying provisions, usu attached to a **chuck wagon 1.**

   1904 *DN* 2.396 [Lumbering terms], *Chuck-box . . .* A complete pantry attached to the rear of a cowboy's camp wagon. **1933** *AmSp* 8.1.27 **nTX,**

Chuck box. A sort of travelling kitchen cabinet affixed to the back of the *chuck wagon,* having many pigeon-holes and compartments for stowing away food and utensils needed . . at any time the *outfit* had to stay away from headquarters at meal time. **1944** Adams *Western Words, Chuck-box*—Bolted to the rear of the chuck wagon is the chuck-box. It has a hinged lid that, when let down and supported by a stout leg, forms a wide shelf or table. This is the cook's private property, and woe unto the nervy puncher who tries to use it for a dining table. Occasionally this privilege is granted to the wrangler, who generally eats after all the others have finished and are changing horses, but never to a rider. **1956** Ker *Vocab. W. TX* 193. **1966** DARE Tape NM13, Hinged and let down; that was the chuck box lid, and the cook was the private owner of that chuck box lid; that was his; NM14, Chuck box lid—almost a symbol for the cook's privacy.

chuckee See **chookee** n

chucker-luck See **chuck-a-luck** n

chuckers n [Cf **chuck** n[3]]

=**dibs.**

   1956 *AmSp* 31.37 **MA,** A chuck (whence perhaps the *chuckers* of our *Chuckers on that!*) is a pebble or marble.

chuckhole n [The sense of *chuck* here is uncert]

1 A depression or hole in a road; hence adj *chuckholed, chuckholey.*

   1836 (1929) Willson *Journey* [20], The abundance of traveling . . wears the road into deep holes; these we call chuck-holes. **1860** (1937) Lewis *Diary Pike's Peak* 14.209, Broke right hind wheel . . . in sand chuck hole. **1887** Kirkland *Zury* 537 **IL,** Chuck-hole . . . A sudden depression in a road-rut. **1907** White *AZ Nights* 30, Their tongues was out, and every once in a while they'd stick in a chuck-hole. Then a man would get down and put his shoulder to the wheel, and everybody'd take a heave, and up they'd come, all a-trembling and weak. **1949** *PADS* 11.19 **CO,** *Chuck hole . . .* A hole in a road that chucks wagons and riders up and down. **1950** *WELS (Something with a rough surface . . a street)* 3 Infs, **WI,** (Full of) chuck holes; 1 Inf, Chuckholed; 1 Inf, Chuckholey. **1965–70** DARE (Qu. N27b, *When unpaved roads get very rough*) 69 Infs, **scattered, but least freq in Sth,** (Full of) chuckholes; **OK42,** Has chuckholes; **PA235,** Lot of chuckholes; **HI1, IN1,** Chuckholey; (Qu. N30, . . *Dip in the road*) Infs **IN69, IA11, MN33, NY27, SD2,** Chuckhole.

2 A small place in which to hide something, a cubbyhole.

   1967 DARE (Qu. D7, *A small space . . where you can hide things or get them out of the way*) Inf **IL15,** Chuckhole.

chuck house n

1 A cookhouse, an eating place. **chiefly West** Cf **chuck boat**

   1910 *Sat. Eve. Post* 1 Oct 74/2 **ND,** About fifty tons of flour, twenty-five barrels of coffee and fifty half-barrels of salt fish are used in the chuck houses on the farm each year. **1930** Irwin *Amer. Tramp, Chuck house.*—A mine or mill eating-house. A restaurant. **1956** Ker *Vocab. W. TX* 116. **1958** McCulloch *Woods Words* **Pacific NW,** *Chuck house*—A cookshack; most important part of a logging camp. **1969** Sorden *Lumberjack Lingo* **NEng, Gt Lakes,** *Chuckhouse*—The cook shacks in a logging camp.

2 By ext: see quot.

   1918 *DN* 5.23 **nID,** *Chuck-house . . .* A boarding house, in connection with a mine or mill.

chuckled adj Cf **chucklehead 1**

   1969 DARE (QR, near Qu. Q5) Inf **IL32,** Widgeon—male has a chuckled head [FW: speckled].

chucklehead n

1 =**black-bellied plover. chiefly NEng**

   1888 Trumbull *Names of Birds* 190, *Black-bellied plover . . .* Again, at Bath and Portland [Maine], Chuckle-head. **1892** *Auk* 9.144 **MA,** The young birds [=black-bellied plover], commonly called Beetle-heads, Chuckle-heads, or Bull-heads, have the entire upper parts brownish grey-black covered with irregular spots of white and pale yellow. **1917** (1923) *Birds Amer.* 1.256, *Black-bellied Plover . . .* Chuckle-head. **1923** U.S. Dept. Ag. *Misc. Circular* 68 **ME, MA,** *Black-bellied Plover . . .* chuckle-head. **1946** Hausman *Eastern Birds* 258, *Black-bellied plover . . .* Some twenty-five or more local names, among which are . . . Beetlehead, Chucklehead.

2 =**green heron.**

   1895 (1907) Wright *Birdcraft* 253, *Green Heron . . .* That this Heron is the commonest and best known of its family, is attested by the numerous local names it bears. "Fly-up-the-creek," "Chalk-line," and "Chucklehead" being a few of the list to which every small boy feels it his duty to add one.

3 See **chuckleheaded catfish**.

4 A rockfish.

   1953 Roedel *Common Fishes CA* 130, *Greenspotted Rockfish . . . Unauthorized Names:* Chinafish, red rock cod, chucklehead.

5 =**channel catfish**.

   1967 Cross *Hdbk. Fishes KS* 205, Channel catfish . . . Head with low rounded pads above and behind eyes ("chucklehead").

chuckleheaded catfish n   Also *chucklehead, chucklehead cat(fish), chuckleheaded cat* **esp Missip Valley**
=**blue catfish 1.**

   1911 *Century Dict. Suppl., Cat[1] . . .* Chuckle-headed cat, the fork-tailed channel catfish, *Ictalurus furcatus.* **1920** Forbes–Richardson *Fishes of IL* 178, Blue Cat; Chuckle-headed Cat; Fulton Cat . . . This species is found throughout the Mississippi Valley and the Gulf States, being most abundant southward. **1946** LaMonte *N. Amer. Game Fishes* 161, Blue Catfish . . . Names: . . Chuckleheaded Cat. **1953** Randolph *Down in Holler* 234 **Ozarks**, Chucklehead . . . A blue catfish *(Ictalurus furcatus),* thinner and reputedly tougher than the ordinary channel cat. **1968** *DARE* (Qu. P1, . . *Freshwater fish . . good to eat*) Inf **TX**52, Chucklehead catfish. **1975** Evanoff *Catch More Fish* 94, The blue catfish *(Ictalurus furcatus)* is . . also called the . . chucklehead cat, and *poisson bleu.*

chuckle-luck See **chuck-a-luck** n

chuck line n   Often in phrr *ride (the) chuck line* **West**

A succession of places where a cowboy can get a free meal; hence *chuck liner* or *chuck line rider* one who frequents such places; a moocher.

   1903 (1965) Adams *Log Cowboy* 280 **West,** He was riding the chuck-line all right, but Miller gave him a welcome, as he was the real thing. **1928** French *Ranchman NM* 153, We received a visit from one of those gentlemen known throughout the West as 'Chuck-liners'. **1933** *AmSp* 8.1.32 **nTX,** *Ride a chuck line.* To secure free board by visiting from one ranch to another. The average ranchman received chuckline riders cordially, glad to have company. The word was often used figuratively to designate any moocher. **1958** Blasingame *Dakota Cowboy* 159 **SD** (as of 1905), If a "doings," . . was whispered from camp to camp by chuckline riders — those unemployed newsmen who rode from place to place, dropping a good story for a meal — every one of us perked up his ears. **1961** Adams *Old-Time Cowhand* 9 **West,** Any worthy cowboy might be forced to ride chuckline durin this season [winter], but the professional chuck liner was jes' a plain range bum, despised by all cowboys. He was the kind that took advantage of the country's hospitality and stayed as long as he dared wherever there wasn't any work for 'im to do and the meals were free and reg'lar.

chuck-luck See **chuck-a-luck** n

chuck of the wood See **chuck** n[2]

chuck up v phr

1 See **upchuck**.

2 See quot.

   1970 *DARE* (Qu. Y37, *To make a place untidy or disorderly*) Inf **VA**46, Chuck up.

chuck wagon n, also attrib

1 A wagon carrying provisions and equipment for cooking, usu on a ranch or in a lumber camp. **chiefly West**

   1890 D'Oyle *Notches* 26 *(DAE),* The sun blistered the paint upon the 'mess-box' behind the 'chuck-waggon.' **1907** White *AZ Nights* 17, We'd bog down the chuck-wagon if we tried to get back to the J.H. But now after the rain the weather ought to be beautiful. **1913** *DN* 4.26 **NW,** *Chuck-wagon . . .* The provision wagon used on round-ups. Also called *grub-wagon.* **1966** *DARE* Tape **OK**30, Wagon they used on any trail, we'd always call it a chuckwagon or some of 'em called it a mess wagon. **1967** *San Augustine Rambler* (TX) 27 July 2/1, All sorts of jobs are available for trail bosses, wranglers, chuck wagon honchos, cowpokes, and so forth.

2 Transf: a small eating place.

   1950 *WELS (Nicknames . . a small eating place)* 1 Inf, **seWI,** Chuck wagon. **1960** Wentworth–Flexner *Slang, Chuck-wagon . . .* Any small roadside or neighborhood lunch counter. *c1940.*

3 An informal buffet-style meal; hence *chuck wagon* adj, adv, informal, in the manner of a buffet. **esp West**

   1954 in 1960 Wentworth–Flexner *Slang NV,* "In [Las] Vegas you scoff either downtown at the Golden Nugget . . or else you eat chuck wagon on the strip." *Oral,* Las Vegas shill. **1966** *Flathead Courier* (Polson MT) *Vacation Guide* Summer sec B 1/5, [Advt:] Chuck Wagon Buffet Dinners served every Sunday afternoon. Seafood Chuck Wagon every Friday evening. **1967** *Snowflake Herald* (AZ) 13 July 1/3, From 5:30 p.m. to 8:30 p.m. a Chuck Wagon supper is planned with entertainment and games to be followed by a dance. **1967** *Henderson Co. Graphic-Reporter* (Stronghurst IL) 17 Aug [15]/1, [Advt:] Try the Friday Night Chuckwagon At The National in Roseville . . . All you can eat for $1.50.

4 A large sandwich made with various kinds of meat and cheese.

   1967–70 *DARE* (Qu. HH41, . . *Sandwiches . . in a round bun or roll*) Inf **AR**47, Chuck wagon — different kinds of meat, and a lot of it; **TN**66, **VA**69, Chuck wagon. **1981** *NADS Letters,* Several students tell me that chuck wagon sandwiches are made of roast beef (one student thinks that ham may be substituted) and cheese on a sesame seed bun. These informants have themselves used the term in San Bernadino, California; Anthony, New Mexico; Albuquerque, New Mexico; Belén, New Mexico; and Las Vegas, New Mexico. They tell me these sandwiches are available here in Las Cruces.

5 A caboose.

   1942 Berrey–Van den Bark *Amer. Slang* 485.5, Chuck wagon . . *a caboose.* **1977** Adams *Lang. Railroader* 32, Chuck wagon: A caboose.

chuck-wagon chicken n *joc*

   1944 Adams *Western Words,* Chuck-wagon chicken — Cowboy's slang name for fried bacon.

chuckwalla n, also attrib   Also sp *chuckawalla,* infreq *chukawalla,* pronc-sp *chuckwaller* [MexSpan *chacahuala*]

A lizard *(Sauromalus obesus)* native to the Southwest.

   1893 *N. Amer. Fauna* 7.174 **West,** The 'chuck-walla,' by which name this remarkable lizard is universally known to both Indians and whites (except the Mormons), inhabits many of the Lower Sonoran Desert ranges in the southern part of the Great Basin. **1914** Brininstool *Trail Dust* 103 *(DA),* Let me see the chuckawalla and the Gila monster too. **1942** Lillard *Desert Challenge* 248 **sNV,** I reckon my critics never drank alkali water and lived on whang leather and Chukawalla lizards. **1968** Adams *Western Words,* Chuckwaller — A chuckwalla, a large plant-eating lizard found in the desert regions of the Southwest.

chuckwalla's delight n

A bushy, yellow-flowered desert plant *(Bebbia juncea).* Also called **sweet bush**

   1941 Jaeger *Wildflowers* 286 **Desert SW,** Sweetbush, Chuckawalla's Delight. Bebbia juncea aspera . . . Chuckawallas feed greedily on the flowers. **1947** *Desert Mag.* May 28/3 *(DA),* Chuckawalla's Delight.

chuckweed n

Prob =**chickweed 1a.**

   1968 *DARE* (Qu. S21, . . *Weeds*) Inf **AK**7, Chuckweed — comes up esp after rain, has a little white flower.

chuck-will's-widow n   Infreq *chuck-will-widow, chuck-will-willow,* pronc-sp *chuck-willuh* [Echoic] **chiefly Sth**

A brownish-gray, night-flying bird *(Antrostomus carolinensis).* Also called **chick-the-willow, chip-de-willow, chip-fell-out-of-a-white-oak, chuck** n[7]**, Dick married-a-widow, Dutch whippoorwill, fontis cat, funny sacks, great bat, mangeur maringouin, Spanish whippoorwill, stick-for-the-red-oak, whippoorwill**

   1791 (1958) Bartram *Travels* 98, Caprimulgus rufus called chuckwill's-widow, from a fancied resemblance of his notes to these words: they inhabit the maritime parts of Carolina and Florida, and are more than twice the size of the night hawk or whip-poor-will. **1872** Coues *Key to N. Amer. Birds* 180, Chuck-will's-widow . . . South Atlantic and Gulf States, strictly; resident in Florida. **1917** *DN* 4.424 **LA,** *Chuck-will's widow (Antrostomus carolinensis) . . .* A heavy thick-headed nocturnal bird. **1922** Gonzales *Black Border* 293 **eSC, GA coasts** [Gullah glossary], *Chuckwilluh* — Chuck-Will's Widow, used to indicate the wide-open mouth of a hungry child. **1938** Matschat *Suwannee R.* 26 **nFL, sGA,** An occasional chuck-will's-widow. **1949** Sprunt–Chamberlain *SC Bird Life* 315 **SC,** *Chuck-will's-widow . . . Caprimulgus carolinensis . . .* Much confusion attends the identity of the Chuck-will's-widow and the Whip-poor-will. **c1960** *Wilson Coll.* **csKY,** Chuck-will's-widow . . . The largest of the goatsuckers, known to few people, though it is fairly common in the farming areas outside the park. Most people think it merely a strange-voiced whippoorwill. **1961** Douglas *My Wilderness* 144 Everglades FL, That morning I discovered a new friend—chuck-will's-widow . . . Its call sounds the words "chuck-will's-widow" perfectly, the accent being on the *wid* in widow. **1965–70** DARE (Qu. Q3, . . *Birds . . out only after dark*) Infs **GA**18, **RI**15, **SC**46, **TX**33, **VA**46, Chuck-will's-widow; **SC**2, Chuck-will-widow; **SC**4, Chuck-will-willow; (Qu. Q19, . . *Birds similar to the whippoorwill;* total Infs questioned, 75) Infs **MS**47, 53, 66, 73, Chuck-will's-widow. **1975** Newell *If Nothin' Don't Happen* 65 nwFL, In all my life I never heered but one real northern whippoorwill. It didn't sound like our birds, but put the accent on the "will." Like this: "Whip-poor-*will*," . . The ones we have down here holler, "*Chuck*-will's-*wid*ow."

chucky adj Cf **chuggy**
Of a road: having **chuckholes;** rough.
   1950 WELS (*Something with a rough surface . . a street*) 1 Inf, **cwWI**, Chucky. **1966–68** DARE (Qu. N27b, . . *Unpaved roads . . very rough*) Infs **CO**3, **IL**25, **MN**36, **NM**8, **OH**70, Chucky.

chucky n See **chuck** n[3]

chucky intj See **chuck** intj 2

chucky bean n [Appar var of **shucky bean**]
   c**1970** DARE FW Addit KY, Chucky beans . . beans left to mature then shelled, cooked, and eaten. Same as shelly beans.

chuco n, also attrib Also *chuke* [Abbr for **pachuco**]
See quot 1970.
   1967 DARE (Qu. W42a, . . *Nicknames . . men's sharp-pointed shoes*) Inf **TX**27, Chuco shoes. Mexican teen-age boys, juvenile delinquents, are called pachucos or chucos ['čuko]. **1970** Current Slang 4.3–4.15 NM, *Chuke . . .* A Mexican or a Mexican-American (derogatory).

Chuesday See **Tuesday**

chufa n, also attrib |čufə(r)| Also sp *chuffa* [Span] **chiefly Sth**
=**nut grass 1.**
   1855 Amer. Inst. NYC *Annual Rept. for 1854* 605 **DC**, Earth Almond, or Chufa, . . from the south of Spain . . . The tubers resemble in taste a delicious chestnut or cocoa-nut, and like them, may be eaten raw or cooked. **1898** Jrl. Amer. Folkl. 11.282, Cyperus esculentus . . chufa, Kans. **1912** Baker *Book of Grasses* 269, This latter species *[Cyperus esculentus] . .* [is] also called "Chufa." **1932** Scribner's Mag. 91.288 FL, They had planned . . to buy hogs and raise peanuts and chufas **1966–67** DARE (Qu. I42, . . *Peanuts*) Inf **AR**52, Chufas ['čufəz] are a little like peanuts; **FL**30, ['čufəz]—like a peanut, grown to feed to pigs; **FL**31, ['čufəz]. **1970** GA Dept. Ag. *Farmers Market Bulletin* 28 Oct 7/3, Chuffa grassnuts, 25¢ pkg. c**1970** Pederson Dial. Surv. Rural GA, *(Nuts that ripen underground)* 8 infs, seGA, [tʃuufəʳz]; 6 infs, [tʃuufəz]. **1974** (1977) Coon *Useful Plants* 124, Cyperus esculentus—Chufa.

‡**chuffer** n [Perh alter of *chaff*]
Rubbish; trash.
   1941 LANE Map 346 *(Rubbish),* 1 inf, swME, *Chuffer,* heard from an old man who lived for some time in Ohio.

chuffle-jawed adj [*chuffle* is prob a form of *chavel,* an early form of *jowl:* see OED *jowl, jole* sb.[1]] Cf DS X6
Having large or full jaws.
   1950 PADS 14.20 SC, *Chuffle-jawed . . .* Same as *whampsy-jawed.*

chuffy adj[1] [Engl dial *chuff, chuffy:* see EDD *chuff* adj.[1], adv.[1], and sb.[2]]
Surly, ill-tempered.
   1899 (1912) Green *VA Folk-Speech, Chuffy . . .* Blunt; rude; surly. **1954** PADS 21.24 SC, *Chuffy . . .* Surly.

chuffy adj[2] [Scots and nEngl dial *chuff, chuffy:* see EDD *chuff* adj.[2]] **chiefly SMidl**
Fat, plump; healthy-looking.
   1899 (1912) Green *VA Folk-Speech, Chuffy . . .* Fat, plump, or round, especially the cheeks. **1930** Shoemaker *1300 Words* 13 cPA Mts (as of c1900), *Chuffy*—Fat faced, healthy looking. **1939** Hall Coll. wNC, *Chuffy . . .* Fat . . . "She's alright, but she's a little chuffy." **1942** Warnick *Garrett Co. MD* (as of 1900–18). **1953** Randolph *Down in Holler* 234 Ozarks, Chuffy . . . Plump. "Lucy's man is a kinder low, chuffy feller." c**1960** Wilson Coll. csKY. **1968** DARE (Qu. X50, . . *A person who is very fat*) Inf **LA**29, Chuffy. **1976** Garber *Mountain-ese* 15 **sAppalachians.**

chug v Usu |čʌg|, also |čʊg, čug| [Prob imit, but cf **joog**]
1 also *choog:* To hit, punch, strike. **chiefly Sth, S Midl**
   1891 PMLA 6.174 TN, We also *chug* a man in the short ribs with the fist. I think I have heard both *chug* and *chüg.* **1892** KS Univ. Qrly. 1.96 KS, *Chug:* to strike a blow, as in, Chug him one. **1893** [see **2** below]. **1908** DN 3.299 eAL, wGA, *Chug* [čʊg] . . . To punch, strike a punching blow. **1941** Sat. Eve. Post 13 Sept 15/3 SC, 'Move over and let me choog around with this knife blade' . . . He chooged and the blade slid through the sand. **1968** DARE (Qu. Y14a, *To hit somebody hard with the fist*) Inf **MD**17, Chug [čʌg] him a good one.
2 also *choog:* To throw something into water. Cf **chuck** v 1
   1891 PMLA 6.174 TN, *Chug (choog)* is the verb used to denote the act of casting anything into the water when especial attention is directed toward the noise which it makes in coming in contact with the surface of the water. **1893** Shands MS Speech, *Choog* or *Chug* [čʊg or čəg]. Both used in Tennessee in the same sense as in Mississippi, i.e. *to cast into the water* or, sometimes, *to punch;* as, "He chugged me in the ribs."
3 also *chugalug:* To drink a great deal (usu of beer) rapidly, esp without pausing. *esp among younger speakers*
   1956 in 1960 Wentworth–Flexner *Slang,* "If you chug-a-lug that [bottle of beer] I'll pay for the next one." *Oral,* St. Louis bar. *Onomatopoetic from sounds of swallowing and imbibing.* **1965–70** DARE (Qu. DD17, *To drink a great deal, or too fast: "He doesn't just drink, he _____.")* Infs **LA**34, 45, **MA**44, **NY**89, **PA**165, **TX**33, 74, **WI**63, Chugalugs; **IN**61, **SC**54, Chugalug; **NY**142, Chugs a lug; **CA**191, **IL**97, **IN**75, **NY**156, **OH**84, 99, **OK**25, **WI**57, Chugs; **IL**84, 99, Chugs it down; **MA**1, Chug. [Of all Infs responding to the question, 64% were old; of those giving these responses, none were old.] **1972** Dict. Contemp. & Colloq. Usage, Chug, chug-a-lug . . . To drink without pausing for breath, said esp. of drinking beer.
4 See quot. [Perh alter of **jig** v]
   1967 DARE (Qu. P13, . . *Other ways of fishing . . besides the ordinary hook and line*) Inf **MI**63, Down on the river you "chug" [čʌg]—long copper wire, sinker, close to bottom, move it up and down; (Qu. P15, . . *Fishing . . from a slowly moving boat*) Inf **MI**63, Trolling or chugging—that's the river where they do that, gotta have a good bottom.

chug n[1] [Abbr for **chughole**] Cf **chuck** n[6]
See quots.
   1927 DN 5.473 Ozarks, *Chug . . .* A slight depression in the road. "Hit rained jes' 'nough t' fill all them leetle chugs full o' water." **1948** Courier–Jrl. (Louisville KY) 7 Feb, My husband . . stopped for road directions one night . . . An old man told him: "Go to the next chug in the road and turn right . . ." Chugs are holes that used to scar old-time roads like poxmarks. They were called chug-holes, or chugs, from the noise made when a wagon hit one. The driver went "Ug!" and the seasoned hickory of his front axle let out a low groan of twisted agony. The two sounds always blended into something like "Chug!" A small sinkhole was the beginning of many a chug. But most of them were caused by somebody digging out a stump, then neglecting to fill up the hole. There was a difference between chugholes and mudholes. Mudholes were bothersome only in rainy weather, or after a hard freeze. But chug-holes broke as many axles in dry weather as in wet. They were a nuisance the year around.

chug n[2] [**chug** v 3]
A large swallow of liquid.
   1968–69 DARE (Qu. DD18, *A drink of liquor, or the amount of liquor taken in one swallow*) Infs **IN**75, **PA**161, Chug.

chug n[3] [Perh blend of *chew* or *chaw* + *plug,* perh infl by *chunk*]
   1968–70 DARE (Qu. DD2, *The portion or quantity of tobacco chewed at one time*) Infs **CA**72, **GA**91, Chug.

chugalug See **chug** v 3

chugarum See **jugarum**

chug-full adj [Alter of *chock-full*] **S Midl**
Completely full, full to overflowing.
   1905 DN 3.74 nwAR, *Chug . . .* In the expression '*chug full,*' entirely. 'That pitcher's *chug full.*' **1908** DN 3.298 eAL, wGA, The tub was chug full of honey. **1915** DN 4.182 swVA, *Chug full . . . = chock full.* c**1960** Wilson Coll. csKY, *Chuckfull* (or *chockfull*) . . . Very full, even crammed or stuffed. Also *chugfull.*

chugged up adj [Cf **chug-full**]
Clogged.

1970 *Thompson Coll.* **cnAL** (as of 1930s), Chugged up . . . Choked up, stuffed up. Chimleys and stovepipes used to get "all chugged up" with sutt [sic], and colds affected some people in such a manner that they became "all chugged up".

chuggy adj [**chug** n¹]
=**chucky** adj.
  1961 *McDavid Coll.* **cOK,** Chuggy — rutty. **1967** *DARE* (Qu. N27b, . . Unpaved roads . . very rough) Infs **AL28, TX23,** Chuggy.

chughole n [Alter of **chuckhole 1**] *chiefly S Midl, esp KY* See Map
=**chuckhole 1.**
  1905 *DN* 3.74 **nwAR,** *Chug-hole* . . . Mud-hole. 'This road's full of chug-holes.' Common. **1923** *DN* 5.203 **swMO,** *Chug hole* . . . An abrupt depression in a road or highway. Also Chuck hole. **1946** Stuart *Tales Plum Grove* 95 **seKY,** Flem sat upon the coffin and rode over the chugholes. **1949** *PADS* 11.5 **wTX.** *Ibid* 19 **CO. 1954** *Harder Coll.* **cwTN. 1959** Sanders *Echoes* 50 **swAR,** I shall never forget the early thirties. I was working my routes from early to late, over roads that were full of chug holes you could bury a dog in. **c1960** *Wilson Coll.* **csKY,** *Chughole* . . . A hole in the road with steep sides, giving a vehicle a jerk when it plunges into it. **1965–70** *DARE* (Qu. N27b, . . Unpaved roads . . very rough) 16 Infs, **chiefly KY,** Full of chugholes; **IN3, TX11,** (Has) chugholes; (Qu. N30, . . A sudden short dip in the road) Infs **KY33, 35, OK28,** Chughole; (QR, near Qu. N29) Inf **IN3,** Washboardy road has chugholes. **1976** Garber *Mountain-ese* 15 **Appalachians.**

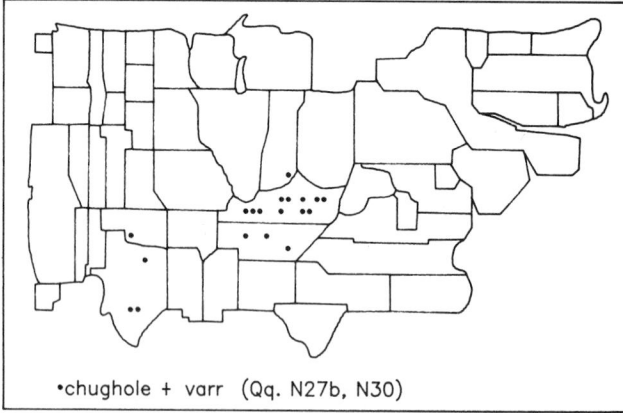

•chughole + varr (Qq. N27b, N30)

chuk intj See **chook** intj

chukawalla See **chuckwalla**

chuke n¹ Also *chook* [Alter of CanFr *tuque*] **Nth, esp states bordering Canada**
A knitted stocking cap.
  1966 *Rhinelander Daily News & New North* (WI) 1 Mar, Standard, I reported was the "chuke and mittens" outfit of the North Country. I was surprised to find so few hereabouts who recognized the word "chuke." . . "Chuke" may have been a northern Michigan colloquialism. [Also mentioned as known in New York & Vermont] **c1970** *DARE* File **WI** (as of 1920s), *Chook* — a knitted headpiece similar to a stocking cap without the tassel . . knitted . . for boys when I was growing up. **1980** *NYT Article Letters* **ceNY,** Chook . . was a term used for a woolen head piece, known as a skating cap. A rolled edge could be pulled over the ears. My father was of French-Canadian descent (Eastern Townships) and he always referred to this when I went out to skate or play. It is not the long woolen cap worn by Les Racquetteurs (Snowshoe Clubs) in Quebec.

chuke n² See **chuco**

chuldren See **child** A2

chum n¹, also attrib [Etym uncert but cf obs Engl & Scots dial *chum* food *(DSL, EDD)* and Newfoundland *chum* food cooked to a formless mass *(DNE)*]
1 Chopped up fish scattered on the water by fishermen to attract fish.
  1857 *Porter's Spirit of Times* 7 Nov 3.150, **NYC,** After chumming our fishing-place, and watching the bits of chum that floated upon the surface of the surf, we would see a break made by a large bass. **1876** *Fur, Fin & Feather* Sept. 131 *(DAE),* The chummer cuts up the bait . . and

thus manufactures the chum. The chummer's principal duty is to 'chum.' This performance consists in throwing out quantities of chum from the stand to the particular spot in the water where the fisherman will cast his line. **1931–33** *LANE Worksheets* **RI,** Chum [čʌm] — A lot of fish, ground up fine, thrown into water, mackerel eat it; you put lines in later and catch mackerel. **1966–70** *DARE* (Qu. P7, *Small fish used as bait*) Infs **CA191, GA11, NY76,** Chum; **NY89,** Chums; (Qu. P13) Inf **VA79,** Chum; (Qu. P16) Inf **MD45,** Chum fishing; (QR, near Qu. P8) Inf **DC2,** Chum-line: series of handfuls of chum put out and carried by the tide. **1975** Evanoff *Catch More Fish* 157, The chum usually used for giant tuna is the menhaden or bunker. **1975** Gould *ME Lingo,* Chum — Chopped bait, scattered in the water to attract fish to the hook or net. Anglers for tuna have a meat grinder on the coaming and crank chum overboard as they troll. **1978** Merriam *Illustr.* **ME,** Chum — Cut-up fish used for the bait to toll (attract) mackerel.
2 The remains of fish after pressing out the oil. *?obs*
  1859 *ME Bd. Ag. Ag. ME* 4.182, Pogies will be caught for the chum and not for the oil. **1875** *Chicago Daily Tribune* (IL) 27 Sept 3/5 **ME,** The chum, as that which remains after the oil is extracted is called, is sold for a fertilizer.

chum v Cf **chub** v **1**
1 To attract fish with **chum** n¹ **1;** hence vbl n *chumming* the act of fishing by such means.
  1857 [see **chum** n¹ **1**]. **1876** [see **chum** n¹ **1**]. **1882** *Forest & Stream* 18.363/3 **NY,** "Chumming" is much more sport, the fish then being captured with rod and reel. **1965–70** *DARE* (Qu. P16, *When fishermen throw bits of bait in the water to attract fish*) 204 Infs, **scattered, but esp N and C Atl, CA,** Chumming; **DC2, GA12, IN13,** Chumming up (an area); **SC21,** Chumming the waters; **ME16, MA80,** Chum; (Qu. P15) Inf **VA41,** Chumming. **1975** Evanoff *Catch More Fish* 115, One such trick is to chum under a pier or bridge to draw fish to your spot. **1977** *Yankee* Jan 112 **ME,** Chopped clams mixed with oil and spread across the water is excellent for tolling fish, and this is called chumming.
2 Transf: see quot.
  1975 Gould *ME Lingo, To chum* is to entice, coax, wheedle.

chum n² See **chum salmon**

chummer n, also attrib
One who prepares and scatters **chum** n¹ **1** in fishing.
  1876 [see **chum** n¹ **1**]. **1932** Miller *I Cover Waterfront* 33 *(DA),* He was the chummer. This meant he had to stand on the edge of the bait tank and throw out live sardines to start the tuna biting. **1969** *DARE* Tape **MA40,** They had stands built out over the water for fishin', and they would go out and sit in a chair on the end of those stands, and the boys from the mainland used to go down there to wait on them, to bait their hooks and throw the chum to the trout fish, and they were called chummer boys.

chumming See **chum** v **1**

chummy n [**chum** n¹ **1**]
  1979 *Capital Times* (Madison WI) 20 July 39/4, After having moved south to Portland, I found that they referred to the northern fisherman as a "chummy." That's derived from a term describing oily, cut fish that fishermen spread on the water to draw schools of mackerel (these small pieces are known as "chum bait").

chump See **chomp** v **2**

chump change n [Prob *chump* blockhead, fool] *among Black speakers*
A small amount of money.
  1968 *Current Slang* 3.2 **sCA** [Black], *Chump change* . . . Spending coins. **1970** Major *Afro–Amer. Slang.* **1971** Roberts *Third Ear* [Black]. **1980** Folb *Runnin' Down* 232 **sCA** [Black], *Chump change* . . . Small amount of money . . . Only enough money for the most basic needs.

chump off v phr [*chump* blockhead, fool]
To dupe or get the better of (someone).
  1967–70 *DARE* (Qu. U8b, *Similar expressions meaning "I paid ten dollars for it."*) Inf **LA14,** Chumped off; (Qu. KK36, . . A person who is easily fooled: "It's easy to _____.") Inf **NY241,** Chump him off [Inf Black]. **1972** Claerbaut *Black Jargon,* Chump (you) off . . to verbally defeat someone; to get the better of one in a battle of words: *Aw, that cat will chump you off.*

chumpy adj [*chump* blockhead, fool]
  1915 *DN* 4.214, *Chumpy,* lacking judgment. "I was chumpy last night."

chum salmon n Also *chum* [?Chinook jargon *tsum, tzum* spots, writing] **NW**

A Pacific salmon (here: *Oncorhynchus keta*). Also called **calico salmon, dog salmon, fall salmon**

1908 *Pop. Sci. Mo.* Dec. 169 *(DA),* The dog Salmon *(Oncorhyncus Keta)* is known also as calico salmon and *chum.* **1962** Salisbury *Quoth the Raven* 241 **seAK,** Species of salmon in the North Pacific waters: . . the *chum,* or ketah — often called the dog salmon. **1967** *DARE* (Qu. P1, . . *Freshwater fish . . good to eat)* Inf **AK1,** Chum; (Qu. P14, . . *Commercial fishing . . what . . the fishermen go out after)* Inf **WA20,** Chum. **1977** *New Yorker* 2 May 65/1 **AK,** With few exceptions, the Pacific salmon that run in these Arctic rivers are of the variety known as chum. *Ibid,* Athapaskan Indians, harvesting from the Yukon, put king salmon on their own tables and feed chum salmon to their dogs.

chumsy adj [*chum* pal, close friend]

1966 *DARE* (Qu. II3, *Expressions to say that people are very friendly toward each other)* Inf **NC45,** Chumsy.

chun n [Korean]

1972 Carr *Da Kine Talk* 109 **HI,** The taste for Korean food has grown in Honolulu since the time of the Korean conflict . . . *Chun* is meat or fish cut into small pieces and rolled in flour before being fried.

chu'n See **churn A**

chune See **tune**

chunk n [Prob alter of **chuck** n[1] infl by **junk** n 1]

1a A thick, short, heavy piece of wood; a block of wood; also fig. [*OED* 1691 →]

c1770 in 1833 Boucher *Glossary* l **MD,** Instant I caught a *chunk,* and, at a blow, / To pieces *smash'd* my notice-giving foe . . . *Chunk;* a short piece of wood; a thick stick; a bludgeon. **1816** Pickering *Vocab.* 60, *Chunk . .* is also used in the *Northern* States, to signify a thick, short block or bit of wood. **1843** (1916) Hall *New Purchase* 171 **IN,** The seats were long benches with very ricketty limbs, expanded two a piece at each end, and double planks resting on rude chunks. **1887** (1967) Harris *Free Joe* 184 **ceGA,** " 'Twuz a gal." "A gal!" exclaimed Mrs. Stucky. "Yes'n, a gal, an' *ef* she wa'n't a zooner you may jess take an' knock my chunk out.' " **1904** *DN* 2.417 **nwAR,** *Chunk . . .* Support used in raising an object. 'We can use that beam for a chunk when we raise the shed.' **1905** *DN* 1.5 **cCT. 1908** *DN* 3.299 **eAL, wGA. 1927** *DN* 5.473 **Ozarks,** Jeff he caint shoot nohow less'n he restes his rifle-gun on a chunk. **1941** *LANE* Map 330 *(Log)* 15 infs, **scattered throughout NEng,** Chunk. **1958** McCulloch *Woods Words* **Pacific NW,** *Chunk* — A piece of a log sawed or broken off.

b A piece of firewood, esp a **backlog 1** or a partially burned piece of wood. Cf **chunk of fire**

1781 *PA Jrl. & Weekly Advt.* (Philadelphia PA) 23 May 1, *Chunks,* that is brands, half burnt wood. This is customary in the middle colonies. **1822** Hawley *Jrl.* 44 **OH,** In the room of andirons, many families make use of what are here called *chunks,* which are the two brands of a large forestick, or billets of wood, cut on purpose for this use. **1892** Eggleston *Hoosier Schoolmaster* 61 **IN,** [Footnote:] The commonest use of the word *chunk* in the old days was for the ends of the sticks of cord-wood burned in the great fireplaces. As the sticks burned in two, the chunks fell down or rolled back on the wall side of the andirons. By putting the chunks together, a new fire was set a-going without fresh wood. **1908** *DN* 3.299 **eAL, wGA,** *Chunk . . .* A partly consumed piece of firewood. **1917** *DN* 4.389 **IL, IA, KS, LA, MA, NH, NY, neOH, VT,** *Chunk* [tʃʌŋk] . . . A piece of firewood too large for a cook-stove, and used in a heating stove. Also *chunk-wood.* "He is drawing a load of chunks." . . "Chunk-wood for sale." **c1950** *Atlas Checklists* **MN,** Back chunk; **WI,** *Chunk* — Large piece of wood at back of fire. **1965–70** *DARE* (Qu. D33, . . *In the fireplace . . the big log that goes behind the others)* Infs **AL61, CT7, 37, MD19, NY2, 68, OH74,** Chunk; **IA47, NY83, 116, TN31,** Back chunk; **FL37, LA20, NH10,** Chunk of wood; **LA20,** Big chunk; (Qu. T8, *Joints of pine wood that burn easily and make good fuel)* Infs **MD20, TN24,** Pine chunks; **IN44,** Chunks. **1967** *DARE* FW Addit **LA6,** Chunk — piece of partly-burned stick of wood in a fire. **1982** *Barrick Coll.* **csPA,** *Chunk* — a stick of wood, esp. firewood.

2 usu in phr *chunk of a _____:*

a Something fair-sized or large; a stocky, sturdy or robust person or animal; something considerable.

1822 Woods *2 Yrs. Residence* 185 **IL,** A hog of two hundred lbs. weight is here called a *fine chunk of a fellow.* **1823** Doddridge *Logan* [39] **WV,** I was then a thumpin chunk of a boy, may be ten or a dozen years old.

1832 Hall *Legends West* 50 **KY,** If a man got into a chunk of a fight with his neighbour, a lawyer would clear him for half a dozen muskrat skins. **1853** Simms *Sword & Distaff* 52 **SC,** A stout chunk of a horse, of frame not unsuited to his own, bore his weight. **1903** *DN* 2.309 **seMO,** *Chunk-of-a-pony . . .* A pony-built horse. **1944** *PADS* 2.25 **cwNC,** *Chunk of a boy.* **1953** Hall *Coll.* **wNC,** The cubs as big as a good chunk of a dog. **c1960** *Wilson Coll.* **csKY,** *Chunk of a boy . . .* A good-sized or promising specimen of boyhood. **1966** *DARE* (Qu. X50, . . *A person who is very fat)* Inf **MI13,** Chunk.

b Something nice, fairly good.

1893 Shands *MS Speech* 23, *Chunk . . .* Illiterate white for something *moderately good* or *nice;* as, "They had a chunk of a wedding"; i.e. a moderately nice wedding.

c A small person or animal.

1906 *DN* 3.116 **sIN,** *Chunk-of-a . . .* Small, undersize. "He's a chunk-of-a horse, boy, dog." **1927** *AmSp* 2.350 **WV,** *Chunk of a boy,* no more nor a (adj. phrase), only a boy. **1937** Sandoz *Slogum* 71 **NE** (as of 1900–20), He would n't ask for anything nicer than a cute little chunk like Cellie here. **1939** Hall *Coll.* **eTN,** I was just a chunk of a boy when my father killed his last panther. **1969** *DARE* (Qu. Z12, . . *A small child)* Inf **KY70,** Chunk.

3 also attrib: A strong, stout horse, smaller than a draft horse.

1818 Palmer *Jrl.* 131 **KY,** The other words and sayings that are peculiar to the United States . . are as follows . . . *Chunk,* a small horse. **1829** Flint *George Mason* 111, Away scamper chunks, donkeys, mules, and negroes. **1892** *DN* 1.209 **NEng,** *Chunk:* a closely-built horse. **1907** *DN* 3.243 **eME,** *Farm chunk, . .* "35 head of horses will be offered at this sale, including several *farm chunks.*" Rare — Bangor newspaper. **1972** Green *More Horse Tradin'* 216 **TX** (as of 1920–30), A fellow that was ridin' south rode by our camp leadin' a pretty good farm chunk kind of work mare that was about eight years old.

4 usu in phr *too big a chunk:* More than one can handle.

1965–70 *DARE* (Qu. KK9, *When someone undertakes something too big for him to handle)* Infs **IA22, IL9, 14, MA6, MN12, ND2, SD3,** Bit off too big a chunk; **ND1,** Bit off a big chunk; **TX5,** Bitten off a chunk too big to swallow; **MN42,** Really bit off a chunk; **SC40,** Took too big a chunk.

‡5 in pl: Mastitis.

1968 *DARE* (Qu. K7, *What sickness can a cow get in her udder . . if she's left unmilked too long)* Inf **CA101,** Chunks.

‡6 =**Antony-over** n.

1966 *DARE* (Qu. EE22, . . *The game in which they throw a ball over a building . . to a player on the other side)* Inf **SC7,** Chunk.

chunk v [**chunk** n]

1a To insert pieces of wood or other material to make a building weathertight. [Perh infl by **chink** v]

1782 in 1929 Summers *Annals* 1.761 **swVA,** Ordered that the Clerk of this Court hire some persons to chunk and daub the Courthouse. **1813** (1932) Schillinger *Jrl.* 72 **OH,** Our men employ'd to Day . . cutting A Door into the Lower part of the Picket block house & chunking the same. **1843** (1924) Oliver *8 Months* 237 **IL,** The logs are not laid quite close, an interval of two or three inches being left between each, which is afterwards *chunked* and *daubed,* i.e., filled up with bits of wood, and plastered with clay or mortar. **1960** Williams *Walk Egypt* 8 **GA,** The walls of the house were fieldstone chunked with *dobbin,* a rarity here where most houses were built from green pine.

b To block (a wheel) with a **chunk** n **1a** or other object. Cf **choke** v[2]

1937 Sandoz *Slogum* 12 **NE** (as of 1900–20), Then came the long pull out of the Niobrara Canyon, the six- or eight-horse teams straining in the collar, . . the men . . chunking the wheels at the nearest thing to a level place to give the horses time to blow.

2 To throw or toss; to throw (something) at, pelt; to strike forcefully. **chiefly S Atl, Gulf States** See Map

1834 *Life Andrew Jackson* 61 **SE,** There also they were hunted up and chunkt or bagnetted. **1884** Harrison *Negro Engl.* 269 **SE,** To chunk de chickens = to throw at the chickens. **1887** (1967) Harris *Free Joe* 102 **GA,** Ef you want to chunk anybody, chunk me. **1899** Edwards *Defense* 112 **GA,** She paused just long enough to bestow a whack upon the little darky for "chunkin' " chips at the dog. **1903** *DN* 2.309 **seMO. 1906** *DN* 3.130 **nwAR. 1908** *DN* 3.299 **eAL, wGA. 1911** *DN* 3.537 **eKY. 1916** *DN* 4.344 **seSC. 1918** *DN* 5.18 **NC. 1927** *DN* 5.473 **Ozarks,** *Chunk . . .* To discard, to waste, to throw away. "He jes' kep' a-chunkin' his money away." **1950** *PADS* 14.20 **SC. 1950** *WELS Suppl.,* He chunked some wood into the stove. **1962** Atwood *Vocab. TX* 75, Threw *(a rock)* . . . a considerable number of informants substitute the word *chunked* (39 [%]). **1965–70** *DARE* (Qu. Y10, *To throw something*) 98 Infs, **chiefly Sth, esp S Atl, Gulf States,** Chunked; **LA**14, Chunked him; **AL**6, **SC**10, 26, Chunk; (Qu. C24b) 48 Infs, **esp S Atl, Gulf States,** Chunked; **FL**27, **GA**73, **NC**8, 11, 17, Chunked a rock; **GA**89, Chunked the dog; 11 Infs, **chiefly S Atl, Gulf States,** Chunk; (Qu. L15) Inf **AL**31, Chunking it; (Qu. V2b) Inf **NC**79, Fur as I could chunk him; (Qu. EE26) Inf **DE**2, Build a fort and chunk snowballs back and forth.

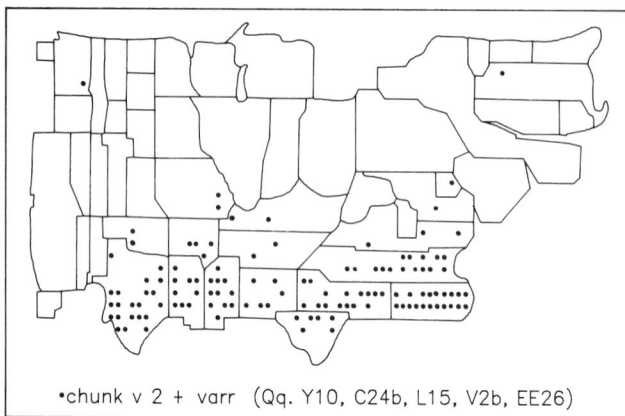

•chunk v 2 + varr (Qq. Y10, C24b, L15, V2b, EE26)

3 freq with *up*: To stoke a fire. **chiefly SE** Cf **chunk n 1b**

1840 *S. Lit. Messenger* 6.398/2 **eVA,** Chunk the fire Charles, and see if you cannot make it burn better. **1884** Harrison *Negro Engl.* 271 **SE,** To chunk up de fier [sic] = to make the fire burn. **1899** (1912) Green *VA Folk-Speech,* Chunk . . . To punch or poke the fire with a stick or poker. **1908** *DN* 3.299 **eAL, wGA. 1909** Denny *Blazing the Way* 439 **WA,** The women and children often helped to pile brush and set fires and many a merry party turned out at night to "chunk up" the blazing heaps. **1923** *DN* 5.204 **swMO,** Chunk up. **1939** *Hall Coll.* **wNC,** He was chunkin' fire in that thing. **1948** Faulkner *Intruder* 233 **MS,** Made him comfortable sitting against a tree, even chunking the fire up to dry his wet feet. **1950** *PADS* 14.20 **SC,** Chunk. **1954** *Harder Coll.* **cwTN,** Chunk up. **c1960** *Wilson Coll.* **csKY,** Chunk up the fire . . . Build it up again by pushing the brands together or adding new wood. **1967** Green *Horse Tradin'* 190 **TX,** Cookie got the night's dishes done up and the fire chunked up. **1972** *Foxfire Book* 339 **nGA,** Chunk the fire easy, starting slowly, and gradually building it up in intensity.

4 freq with *out* or *up*: In logging: to clean an area of chunks, stumps, trash; also fig. **Nth**

1905 U.S. Forest Serv. *Bulletin* 61.33 **Pacific NW,** Chunk . . . To clear the ground, with engine or horses, of obstructions which can not be removed by hand. *Ibid* 33 **Gt Lakes, nNEng,** Chunk up, to. To collect and pile for burning the slash left after logging. **1919** *DN* 5.81 **NW,** Chunk out, to. To clean out the chunks from skid roads. Logging terms. **1958** McCulloch *Woods Words* **Pacific NW,** Chunk out—a. To remove logs, stumps, and trash from a right-of-way before road building. b. In the old days of logging, to yard out windfalls or chunks which would interfere with the yarding of logs. c. A logger who got in a fight and cleaned out a saloon said he chunked it out. **1969** Sorden *Lumberjack Lingo* **NEng, Gt Lakes,** Chunk out—To clean skid roads, especially to remove chunks.

5 To thrust, to push with a stick or piece of wood.

1981 Mebane *Mary* 12 **cnNC** (as of 1930s), My job was to stand over the pot and "chunk" the clothes down to keep the water from boiling over.

chunk bottle See **junk bottle**

chunked adj Often |'čʌŋkɪd| Also compar *chunkeder*

1 Short and thick. **chiefly NEast**

1844 Stephens *High Life in NY* 1.115, She had on a great loose awk'ard-looking gown, that made her seem twice as chunked as she used to. **1886** Harte *Complete Poetical Wks.* 294, For you know I am "chunkèd" and clumsy, as she says are all boys of my size. **1910** *DN* 3.452 **seVT,** Chunkèd . . . Solid, fleshy, stoutly built. "He's a chunkèd baby." **1914** *DN* 4.154 **NH,** Chunked . . . Thick and short. **1968** *DARE* (QR, near Qu. I15) Inf **NY**75, Butter beans are a little chunkeder or thicker than limas.

2 Impudent, bold. *obs.*

1853 Hammett *Stray Yankee in TX* 227, If it aint that owdacious critter of Miss Mash's, a helpin' hisself in broad daylight, septin' the fog; that's putty chunked. **1859** (1968) Bartlett *Americanisms,* Chunked. Any person who is impudent or bold, at the South-west, is said to be *chunked.*

chunk-floater n Also *chunk-mover, ~ washer* **chiefly Sth, S Midl**

A sudden heavy rain.

1961 *AmSp* 36.153 **sIL,** It's goin' to be a gully washer and a chunk floater. **1962** Atwood *Vocab. TX* 38, An unusually heavy rain that does not last very long . . . A good many humorous phrases have a limited currency . . . Among these are *chunk floater, chunk mover.* **1965–70** *DARE* (Qu. B25, . . *Joking names . . a very heavy rain*) Infs **AL**1, **LA**2, **MS**63, **TX**35, 51, Chunk-mover; **AR**52, **MS**2, **OK**51, **TN**30, Chunk-floater. **1972** Cooper *NC Mt. Folkl.* 90, *Chunk-washer*—a heavy rain.

chunkhead n

=**copperhead snake 1.**

1818 *Amer. Jrl. Science* 1.84, *Scytalus Cupreus* or Copper-head Snake . . is known by a variety of names in different parts of the State of New York: . . *copper-head, copper-snake, chunk-head,* [etc]. **1863** in 1920 *Colonial Soc. MA Pub.* 20.232, If we add that our political Copperheads, like their reptile type, are so "slow and clumsy in their motions" that they deserve the additional cognomina of "Chunk-heads" and "Deaf-adders," we shall have made the analogy complete.

‡**chunking** vbl n [Cf **chunk v 5**]

1966 *DARE* (Qu. Y16, *A thorough beating*) Inf **GA**9, Chunking.

chunk-mover See **chunk-floater**

chunk of fire n **chiefly S Midl** Cf **fire, come to borrow**

A burning coal, a firebrand.

1831 in 1918 Ruffin *Papers* 2.31 **NC,** I shall be glad to see you in March: *do not come for a chunk of fire.* **1834** Pike *Prose Sketches* 30 **AR,** I threw away my chunk of fire. **1856** Cartwright *Autobiog.* 215 **KY,** He threw down his chunk of fire. **1899** (1912) Green *VA Folk-Speech,* Chunk-of-fire . . . The burning end of a *chunk* of wood. Fire was carried in *chunks* from one place to another before matches came into use. **1929** Dobie *Vaquero* 7, Carrying a chunk of fire so that it would not go out was something of an art and required expedition. If anybody wanted to "borrow" fire, he generally made his call brief. Hence arose the old saying, once common but now dying out, "You must have come after a chunk (or coal) of fire," in protest to a brief call. **1939** *Hall Coll.* **wNC,** Chunk of fire . . . A burning coal; a 'fire coal.' . . He reached down and got a chunk of fire in his mouth. **c1960** *Wilson Coll.* **csKY,** Chunk of fire . . . A burning brand or some coals borrowed to start a new fire.

chunk pickle n Also *junk pickle* (cf **junk n 1**) **esp Nth**

A usu sweet pickle made from cucumbers cut in thick pieces rather than slices.

1960 Bailey *Resp. to PADS 20* **KS** (*Types of pickles*), Chunk. **1965–70** *DARE* (Qu. H56, . . *Kinds of pickles*) Infs **IL**15, 124, **MI**82, **VA**26, **WI**11, Chunk pickle(s); **CO**30, Virginia chunk pickle; **IL**13, Chunk pickle—pickled with cauliflower and onion; **IL**29, Chunk—sweet; **MI**28, Chunk pickles—a sweet pickle, a sweet cucumber pickle; **MN**34, Sweet chunk; **NY**162, Chunk pickles—cucumbers; **NY**233, Chunk pickles—because of cut; **OH**59, Chunk pickles—small cukes; **WA**6, Chunk pickles—sweet; **IL**134, Junk.

chunk stove n [**chunk n 1b**]

A wood-burning stove.

1938 (1955) FWP *Guide DE* 501, A "Winter King" iron chunk stove stood the year around in a box of sand in the middle of the room. **1968** *DARE* (QR p24) Inf **NY**72, Wood stove, also called chunk stove. **1968** *DARE* FW Addit **PA**169, Chunk stove. **1976** *PA Folklife* Spring 29/2 **PA,** A stove . . might be named according to its function *(laundry stove, cook stove),* form *(pot belly stove, ten-plate stove),* or the size of wood or coal burned in it *(chunk stove, egg stove).*

chunk up v phr [Prob alter of *chuck up;* see **upchuck**]

To vomit.

1966 *DARE* (Qu. BB17) Inf **SC**2, Chunk up.

chunk-washer See **chunk-floater**

chunky n

An unidentified sucker perh of the genus ~~Moxostoma;~~ see quot.

1915 *DN* 4.182 **swVA,** Chunky . . . A fish like but smaller than the "red-horse."

chunky pipe n [Cf **junky** and *DAE junk* 1] Cf *DJE junka(-pipe)*
A tobacco pipe prob having a shortened or "junked" stem.
   1943 Chase *Jack Tales* 113 **wNC** (as of 1880s), I wish I was back home settin' in my mother's chimley corner smokin' my old chunky pipe.

chuparosa n [MexSpan *chuparrosa*]
   1 A low-growing, red-flowered shrub *(Justicia californica).*
   1912 Lumholtz *New Trails* 207 **AZ,** As we followed the fairly distinct Indian trail . . I observed the chuparosa *(beloperone californica),* the flowers of which are eaten by the Papago. **1941** Jaeger *Wildflowers* 245 **SW,** *Chuparosa. Beloperone californica* . . . Low, rounded shrub, the single California representative of a tropical American genus. **1959** Munz–Keck *CA Flora* 685, *B[eloperone] californica* . . . Chuparosa. **1981** Benson–Darrow *Trees SW Deserts* 217.
   2 An often low-growing, usu red-flowered shrub *(Anisacanthus thurberi).* Also called **buckbrush 3l, desert honeysuckle, honeysuckle, taparosa**
   1944 AZ Ag. Exp. Sta. *Bulletin* 6.298, *Anisacanthus thurberi* . . . Chuparosa . . . is one of the better browse plants of the desert. **1960** Vines *Trees SW* 932, It is also known under . . Chuparosa. Palatable to cattle and sheep, and sometimes grazed closely. **1976** Bailey–Bailey *Hortus Third* 79.

chupid adj Also *chupit* Pronc-spp for *stupid* Cf *DJE*
   1922 Gonzales *Black Border* 293 **eSC, GA coasts** [Gullah glossary], *Chupid Chupit*—stupid.

chupo See **chapo**

chur n See **chair**

chur exclam
   1968 *DARE* (Qu. K79, *How . . you call the chickens to you at feeding time*) Inf **NJ**50, Chur [čɚ čɚ čɚ čɚ] very high pitched.

church n Pronc-spp *chu'ch, chutch*
   Std senses, var forms.
   1890 *DN* 1.68 **KY,** Illiterates say, "I'm goin' to *jine* the chu'ch." **1899** (1912) Green *VA Folk-Speech, Chutch.* **1922** Gonzales *Black Border* 293 **sSC, GA coasts** [Gullah glossary], *Chu'ch*—church, churches. **1967** *DARE* FW Addit **AR**55A, [čɔɪč]—Negroes and upper-class whites; poor whites say [čɚč].

church v
   1 also *church-maul:* To try before the church; to discipline by church action.
   1829 *Western Mth. Rev.* 3.114 **NEng,** It is notorious, that a woman was churched there, for cutting off the ends of the fingers of her gloves, and exposing the tips of her dainty and delicate fingers. **1844** Stephens *High Life in NY* 1.55 **CT,** Jest tell him, the next time he threatens to church you for what I'm a doing down here in York, that . . . you'll "stop his supplies." **a1870** Chipman *Notes on Bartlett* 83 *(DAE), Church-maul,* To.—To call to account, to discipline, by ecclesiastical methods.—N.E. [=NEng], vulgar. **1895** *DN* 1.386 **cwIN,** *Church* . . . to try or investigate before the church on the charge of some offence unbefitting a church member. **1902** Wilson *Spenders* 132 **MT,** Only I hope the First M.E. Church of Montana City never hears of her outrageous cuttin's-up . . . They'd have her up and church her, sure. **1909** *DN* 3.394 **nwAR,** *Church* . . . To put on trial before the church. "Tom Jones was churched for drinking." **1945** *PADS* 3.9 **NC,** *To church,* as I have known the term, means to call before local church authorities for some offense. The penalty is not necessarily expulsion but may be censure or some form of penance—or even acquittal.
   2 To expel from a congregation, to remove from church membership. **chiefly S Midl**
   1917 *DN* 4.409 **NC Mts,** *Church* . . . To expel from a congregation. **1927** *AmSp* 2.350 **WV. 1944** *PADS* 2.26 **cwOH, cwNC. 1963** Edwards *Gravel* 81 **eTN** (as of 1920s), The church trial, not an infrequent happening, smacks . . of the county criminal court, except . . that the sentence is not to be jailed but to be "churched"—that is, turned out of the church, deprived of membership. It is a sort of condemnation to purgatory. **1972** *Atlanta Letters* **GA,** *Church* . . . To turn (someone) out of the church. **1977** Miles *Ozark Dict.,* Kicked out of the congregation. "Them gals was churched for card-playin'."
   3 To attend church.
   1967 *DARE* Tape **WA**28, We churched together.

church clothes n For varr see quot
   =Sunday-go-to-meetin' clothes.

   1965–70 *DARE* (Qu. W39, *Joking . . a person's best clothes*) Infs **CO**20, **IL**30, **PA**26, 130, **VA**63, Church clothes; **ND**1, **SC**10, Sunday-go-to-church clothes; **ID**5, Church suit; **OR**1, Going-to-church clothes; (Qu. W38, *. . In his best clothes*) Inf **TX**68, In his church clothes.

church house n
   A church (building), a meeting house. **chiefly S Midl, Sth**
   1895 *DN* 1.386 **wFL,** *Church house:* church, "meetin'-house," building used for religious services. **1902** *DN* 2.231 **sIL,** *Church-house* . . . A church. **1903** *DN* 2.309 **seMO,** *Church-house* . . . Church; meeting house. **1904** *DN* 2.417 **nwAR. 1910** *DN* 3.456 **seKY. 1916** *DN* 4.321 **KS, LA. 1917** *DN* 4.409 **wNC, KS. 1938** Matschat *Suwannee R.* 128 **nFL, sGA,** They built up big heaps of dirt to put their church-house and their cabins on. **1967–69** *DARE* FW Addit **KY**44, 47, **TN,** Church house—a church building. **1970** *DARE* Tape **AR**56, They had a church house down there and a graveyard.

church is out phr
   Something is over, finished; no chance remains.
   1966 *Current Slang* 1.1.2, *Church is out.* Something is over, or a chance is gone . . . *Church is out* for me in that course. **1975** Newell *If Nothin' Don't Happen* 173 **nwFL,** He'd go right in and get that cat by the back of the neck and go to backin' up, shakin' it just as hard as he could . . . Whenever he got that neck holt, church were out!

church-maul See **church** v 1

church mother n Also *mother of the church   among Black speakers* Cf *DJE mother*
   See quots.
   1970 *Thompson Coll.* **Detroit MI** (as of 1940s) [Black], Church mother . . . A woman, usually of some years, who works for, sometimes sings in the choir of, "the church . . . " [They] usually wear white, sometimes have more or less distinctive (for their churches) uniforms . . . some wear capes; hats often have streamers . . . sometimes ribbons. **1970** *DARE* Tape **OK**58, Church mother, she's over the young ones under her, and the older girls, they're her children. She advises them, and she's next to the pastor. **1977** Smitherman *Talkin* 110, The hierarchy of the traditional black church . . . God (The Father, Spirit, and the Holy Ghost) . . Minister, Reverend, Elder (God-sent men) . . Mother of the Church . . Old folks (Elders).

church mouse n
   1966 *DARE* FW Addit **ME**15, Church mouse—one who goes to church a great deal.

‡church mouse preacher n [Alluding to the common simile "poor as a church mouse"]
   1968 *DARE* FW Addit **seOH,** Church mouse preacher—used of a newly ordained minister who couldn't get a prestigious appointment. Used by 10-year resident who came from Georgia originally.

church owl n
   =barn owl 1.
   1911 *Century Dict.* 455, *Barn-owl* . . . Also called *church-owl.* **1923** WV State Ornith. *Birds WV* 20, Barn Owl . . . Common Names: . . Church Owl . . . The eggs are laid in . . hollows in trees, . . sides of wells, mining shafts, dovecots or barns, and church steeples.

‡church rider n Cf **circuit rider** 1
   1967 *DARE* (Qu. CC10, *. . Unprofessional, part-time lay preacher*) Inf **IL**11, Church-rider.

‡church slider n
   A backslider.
   1967 *DARE* (Qu. CC7, *. . A person who goes to church very seldom or not at all*) Inf **TX**37A, Church slider.

churk See **chirk**

churn v, n Pronc-spp *charn, chirme, churm, chu'n*
   A Forms.
   1899 (1912) Green *VA Folk-Speech, Charn* . . . Churn. **1905** Culbertson *Banjo Talks* 66 **Sth,** Yeard de chu'n a hour ergo, Dashin', splishin', splash'. **1912** Green *VA Folk-Speech, Churm* . . . Form of *churn. Chirme.*
   B As verb.
   To beat.
   1953 Randolph *Down in Holler* 234 **Ozarks,** Churn . . . To beat, to drub, to paddle. "If that young-un don't behave, I'll churn his behind

every step of the way home." **1954** *Harder Coll.* **cwTN,** *Churn* . . . To hit or beat someone.

churn-butted adj Also n *churn butt* **Nth**

In logging: of a tree: having an enlarged base.

1905 *U.S. Forest Serv. Bulletin* 61.33, *Churn butted.* **1958** McCulloch *Woods Words* **Pacific NW,** *Churn butt*—The swollen butt of a tree or log. **1969** Sorden *Lumberjack Lingo* **NEng, Gt Lakes,** *Churn butted*—A tree greatly enlarged at the base. Same as bottle butted, swell butted.

churn dash calf n

See quots.

1944 Adams *Western Words, Churn-dash calf*—One, although belonging to a milk cow, which has not the full benefit of the mother's milk. **1961** Adams *Old-Time Cowhand* 154, A calf raised on skimmed milk was referred to as a "pail fed," "skimmy," or a "churn dash calf."

churn-dasher n

In marble play: see quot.

1944 *PADS* 23.34 **seKY,** *Churn-dasher* . . . A taw streaked with white and blue and, like the "aggie," a harder, better marble than those shot at in the ring.

churn gig n

A fishing device (fish gig) that stirs up the water clumsily.

1931 Randolph *Ozarks* 263, The short gigs are thrown or pitched, and are even more difficult to handle than those of the ordinary type, which are contemptuously called "churn-gigs" by the devotees of the shorter weapon.

churn-head n, hence adj *churn-headed* **West**

See quot 1936.

1936 Adams *Cowboy Lingo* 82, 'Churn-heads,' 'jug-heads,' or 'crock-heads.' By these terms the cowboy meant that the horse spoken of was hard-headed, had a lack of intelligence, and had to be pulled around considerably before he was made to understand what was wanted of him. **1944** Adams *Western Words.* **1945** Thorp *Pardner* 196 **SW,** Letty was ridin' that churn-headed horse, Two Bits, you know.

‡churning vbl n

Perh for *chumming* (see **chum** v 1).

1969 *DARE* (Qu. P16, *When fishermen throw bits of bait in the water to attract fish*) Inf **MI108,** Churning, chumming.

churn-twister n *derog*

Among cowboys: a farmer.

1936 Adams *Cowboy Lingo* 197 **NW, SW,** The farmer . . . was apt to be referred to by such contemptuous titles as 'churn-twister,' 'plow-chaser,' or 'fool hoeman.' **1942** North *Saga Cowboy* 90, The contemptuous reference to "churn twisters" and "plough chasers," . . are obvious in their relation to farmers. **1944** Adams *Western Words.*

churny adj

Agitated, stirred up.

1969 *DARE* (Qu. KK39, *Stirred up, upset*) Infs **CT39, IL98, TX70,** Churny; **MO20,** Muddy and churny.

churook See **cherook**

churp (up) See **chirp** v 1

churry See **cherry**

Chusday, Chuseday See **Tuesday**

chutch See **church** n

chute n **lower Missip Valley**

A small sluggish channel, usu between an island and the main landmass; see also quot 1971.

1859 Twain in **1963** Ramsay–Emberson *Twain Lexicon* 44, He actually ran the chute of Glasscock's Island, downstream, in the night. **1862** *NY Daily Tribune* (NY) 11 June 8/2 **Memphis TN,** When we came to a bayou or chute, the Fleet would divide, part going the irregular way, and part keeping the direct course. **1873** Twain–Warner *Gilded Age* 42 **Missip R,** Sometimes she [=the steamboat] approached a solid wall of tall trees as if she meant to break through it, but all of a sudden a little crack would open just enough to admit her, and away she would go plowing through the "chute" with just barely room enough between the island on one side and the mainland on the other; in this sluggish water she seemed to go like a race horse. **1968** *DARE* (Qu. C14, *A stretch of still water going off to the side from a river or lake*) Inf **LA24,** Chute.

1971 Detro *Generic Terms* 239 **LA,** The principal connotation of the term *"chute"* was to signify a narrow river channel between an island and the nearest riverbank. Other connotations recorded during the period 1901–1968 were (in rank order): standing water—point bar; full sluggish streams; wetlands—seasonally flooded inland basins or flats; artificial or severely modified watercourses; partially intermittent sluggish streams; and full relatively rapid streams.

chutter-luck See **chuck-a-luck** n

chy n Also sp *chi* [Russ] **AK**

Tea; a meal or snack at which tea is served.

1866 in **1942** James *First Scientific Explor.* 218 **AK,** Went out after chi and got several small birds. *Ibid* 266, First we were called to *chi.*, that is, the first morning meal consisting of tea and crackers or bread. [**1885** Schwatka *Along Alaska's River* 291, He returned to the shore, having uttered but one word that we could comprehend, *chy* (tea).] **1945** *Alaska Sportsman* Feb 33 (Tabbert *Alaskan Engl.*), We loved the Russian custom of afternoon chi, or tea. The slightest pretense for a call at the door brought forth an invitation to come in for a cup of chi.

chyike v [From the shout "chy-ike" used in driving animals]

1889 Nelson *50 Yrs.* 62 **West,** I was one of the horse-stealing party, and helped to drive off the herd. We chyiked them into the ravine and clean through it like a streak of lightning.

cicada n

Std: a wedge-shaped dark-colored buzzing insect of the family Cicadidae. Also called **August fly, brown locust, chicharra, dog-day cicada, harvest fly, heat bug, hot bug, jarfly, July fly, lyre-man**

cicada killer n

A digger wasp (here: *Sphecius speciosus*).

1895 Comstock *Manual Insects* 653, The Cicada-killer, *Sphecius speciosus.* It is a formidable insect, measuring one and one fourth inches in length. **1980** Milne *Audubon Field Guide Insects* 845, Cicada Killer (Sphecius speciosus).

cicel n

=sweet cicely.

1969–70 *DARE* (Qu. I28b, . . *Greens . . cooked*) Infs **KY48, 81,** Cicel.

cider n esp **NEng** *old-fash*

In phr *all talk and no cider:* Action, substance, results.

1807 Irving *Salmagundi* 7.132 **NY,** The people, in fact, seem to be somewhat conscious of this propensity to talk, by which they are characterized, and have a favorite proverb on the subject, viz. 'all talk and no cider.' **1849** (1914) Kingsley *Diary* 50 **CT,** Fine stories are cold comfort, when it is as they say "All talk and no cider." **1872** Schele de Vere *Americanisms* 591, *All talk and no cider* . . is stated to have originated at a party in Bucks County, Pennsylvania, which had assembled to drink a barrel of superior cider; but politics being introduced, speeches were made, and discussion ensued, till some malcontents withdrew on the plea that it was a trap . ., politics and not pleasure being the purpose of the meeting, or, as they called it, *All talk and no cider!* **1905** *DN* 3.5 **cCT,** *Cider* . . . Substance. In the expression 'all talk and no cider.' **1912** Green *VA Folk-Speech* 19, All talk and no cider.

cider v

Of apples: to make into cider.

1962 *Mt. Life* Spring 18 **sAppalachians,** He . . "ciders" his apples (when he doesn't "brandy" them).

cider applesauce n Freq *boiled-cider applesauce* **NEng**

Applesauce made with **boiled cider;** apple butter.

1907 *DN* 3.183 **seNH,** *Cider apple-sauce* . . . Boiled cider apple-sauce; "apple butter." **1939** Wolcott *Yankee Cook Book* 282 **NEng,** *Vermont boiled-cider apple sauce [An original old recipe]* "Boil yr. cider on the stove till it's down to a thick mush. This will require lots of replenishing. It takes a terrible lot of cider. Either use this in mincemeat, so, or mix it with straight apple sauce to eat." **1941** *LANE* Map 293 **cVT,** Boiled cider apple sauce. **1966–67** *DARE* (Qu. H57, *Tasty or spicy side-dishes served with meat*) Inf **MA5,** Sweet cider applesauce; (Qu. H63, *Kinds of desserts*) Inf **NH6,** Boiled-cider-dried-apple sauce—made of boiled cider and dried apples.

cider brandy n Also *cider champagne* **NEng** [*OEDS* 1703 →]

An alcoholic beverage made from fermented cider.

1800 *Columbian Centinel. MA Federalist* (Boston MA) 22 Jan 4/4, For Sale. A quantity of Cider-Brandy and Gin. **1894** *DN* 1.331, "Cider brandy" is the natural word to New Englanders. **1905** *DN* 3.5 **cCT**, *Cider brandy* . . . Same as apple brandy. **1933** *Hanley Disks* **neMA**, Cider brandy . . . apple jack. **1968–69** *DARE* (Qu. DD28b, . . *Fermented drinks . . made at home*) Infs **CT**3, **MA**30, Cider brandy; **MA**62, Cider champagne.

cienaga n Usu |si'ɛnəkə, -gə|, also |'sɪnɪgi, -ə| Also sp *cienega*, infreq *cienoga;* pronc-spp *ciniky, senaca;* dimin forms *cienagita, cienaguilla, -o, cieneguita* [Span] **chiefly SW**

A marsh or swamp, a wet meadow.

[**1848** (1962) U.S. Army *Abert's NM Rept.* 65, After a short march, we reached "Cienega," a very well watered place, as its name denotes.] **1859** (1968) Bartlett *Americanisms, Cienega* . . . A marsh. New Mexico and Texas. A small marsh is called a *cieneguita.* **1882** (1964) Garrett *Billy the Kid* 18 **swTX**, Two horsemen were rushing across the cienega which lies between the plaza and the mountains. **1887** F. Francis *Saddle & Moccasin* 132 (*DAE*), We passed the Clanton Cienega. *Ibid* 152, 'Where did you kill the antelope?' . . . 'In the big draw, back of Clanton's ciniky.' **1892** *DN* 1.189 **TX**, *Ciénega.* **1920** Grey *Man of Forest* 104 **sAZ**, "What's a *senaca*?" . . . "Thet's Mexican for park, I guess." **1924** Austin *Land of Journeys' Ending* 175 **CO**, Every tiny *rincon* and cienaguilla has its mud-walled ranch house. **1932** *DN* 6.227 **West**, Cienaga. This term for a wet meadow, or one which has been wet and is now dried up, is said to be "common in the Southwest," which means, of course, wherever there are wet meadows. I judge it to be rather confined to the Rio Grande valley, which was the country first settled by the Spaniards, and where, in the river bottoms, there are more wet meadows than in the desert country to the east or west. One meets the word sometimes in English, generally spelled *senaca.* **1932** Bentley *Spanish Terms* 123, *Cienega* or *cienaga* (. . *English*, sínigi: or sínigə) . . . A marsh, swamp, or morass; a marshy valley. **1933** *AmSp* 8.3.9 **SW**, A marshy place is called a *cienaga*, but if small is a *cienagita*, while a collection of small marshy spots is known as *cienaguillos.* **1965** *Silver City Press Frontier* (NM) [16/3], Springs and cienogas (small marshes in the high country) give the streams inception, and they are added to by other springs and seeps. **1966** *DARE* (Qu. C6, . . *A piece of land that's often wet, and has grass and weeds growing on it*) Inf **NM**11, Cienega [sɪnɪgi]. **1966** *DARE* Tape **NM**12, Because . . all down in there was all cienaga [si'ɛnəkə] . . a marsh. **1981** *DARE* File **sCA**, The street named [la si'ɛnɪkə] has lots of restaurants along it; **swCA** [la si'ɛnɪgə, si'ɛnəgə].

ciffy cat See **civvy cat**

cig n Also *ciggy* [Abbr for *cigar(ette)*] **esp Nth and West** See Map

A cigarette; less freq, a cigar.

a1889 in 1897 Barrère–Leland *Slang*, Dancing the jig, / Every fellow with a *cig*, / And a *cig* of confounded bad tobacco. **1907** Mulford *Bar-20* 59 **West**, "Mebby he rustled some grub out with him—I saw him tiptoein' out of th' gallery this mornin' when I come back for my cigs." **1914** *DN* 4.127 **NE**, *Cig*, from cigarette. **1915** *DN* 4.236 **neOH** [College slang], *Cig*. Cigar: meaning also 'cigarette.' Also *ciggy.* **1965–70** *DARE* (Qu. DD6b, *Nicknames for cigarettes*) 40 Infs, **scattered, but esp Nth, West**, Cig. [Of all Infs responding to the question, 26% were mid-aged; 30% were coll educ; of those giving this response, 38% were mid-aged, 50% were coll educ.]

cigamagar, cigamarute See **-ma-** infix

cigar n [From the shape] Cf **cigar tree**

The bean of the **catalpa B1**.

1877 *Field & Forest* 2.51 **sePA**, I verily believe that some . . boys . . took their first lessons in smoking, by using the "beans" or "cigars" of the Catalpa.

cigar box n, also attrib

1 A cheaply constructed building.

[**1878** Taylor *Between the Gates* 252, We have been circling about that cigar-box of a town.] **1970** *DARE* (Qu. II25, . . *The part of town where the poorer people, special groups, or foreign groups live*) Inf **PA**242, Cigar box row.

2 See quot.

c1970 Wiersma *Marbles Terms* **MI**, *Cigar box* . . . In marble play: a game in which marbles are dropped from chest height toward a hole in the cover of a cigar box.

cigarette cactus n
=**pencil cholla.**

1967 *DARE* (Qu. S26e) Inf **CA**4, Pencil cholla = cigarette cactus.

cigarette flower n

A **wax mallow** (here: *Malvaviscus drummondii*).

1967 *DARE* Wildfl QR (Wills–Irwin) Pl.25d Inf **TX**34, Cigarette flower.

cigarette moss n
=**ball moss** (here: *Tillandsia baileyi*).

1951 *PADS* 15.28 **TX**, *Tillandsia baileyi* . . cigarette moss. The beautiful and conspicuous deep rich purple flowers in their closely rolled shapes, suggest cigarettes.

cigarfish n [From its shape] **chiefly Gulf States**

A **scad** (here: *Decapterus punctatus*).

1882 U.S. Natl. Museum *Proc.* 5.268, *Decapterus punctatus* . . . *Cigarfish* . . . Rather common at Pensacola. **1887** Goode *Amer. Fishes* 230, The Round Robin, *Decapterus punctatus*, [is] called at Pensacola, the "Cigar-fish." **1967** *DARE* (Qu. P4, *Saltwater fish . . not good to eat*) Inf **TX**14, Cigarfish.

cigar orchid n [See quot 1975]
=**cowhorn orchid.**

1950 Correll *Native Orchids* 347, *Cyrtopodium punctatum* . . . Common names: Bee-swarm Orchid, . . Cigar Orchid. **1961** Douglas *My Wilderness* 147 **Everglades FL**, These were all new to me. So were the orchids that grow in them—grass pink orchid, cigar orchid, mule-ear orchid, . . . Tiny shoots of the cigar orchid were already coming up out of the stalks of an old one, even though it still had blooms. **1975** Natl. Audubon Soc. *Corkscrew* 27, *Cigar Orchid* . . . Its long conical pseudobulbs are responsible for its common names.

cigar tree n Also *cigar plant* [From the shape of the pod or bean] **chiefly Midl** See Map Cf **Indian cigar**
=**catalpa B1.**

1872 *Amer. Naturalist* 6.727 **IN**, The beautiful catalpa, or "cigar-tree" *(Catalpa bignonioides)*, grew as a common species among the underwoods. **1933** Small *Manual SE Flora* 1241, Catalpa . . . *Cigar-trees.* **1965–70** *DARE* (Qu. T9, *The common shade tree with large heart-*

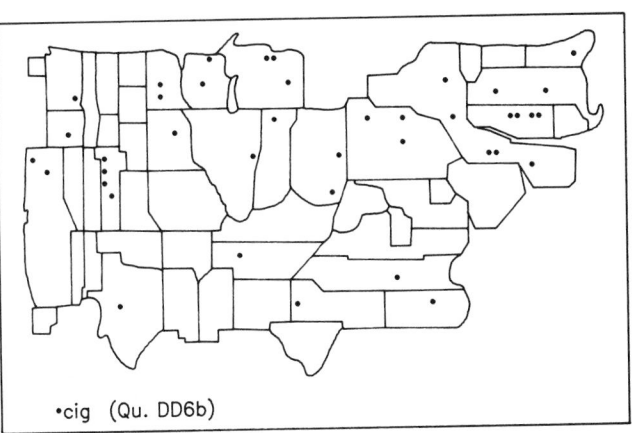

•cig (Qu. DD6b)

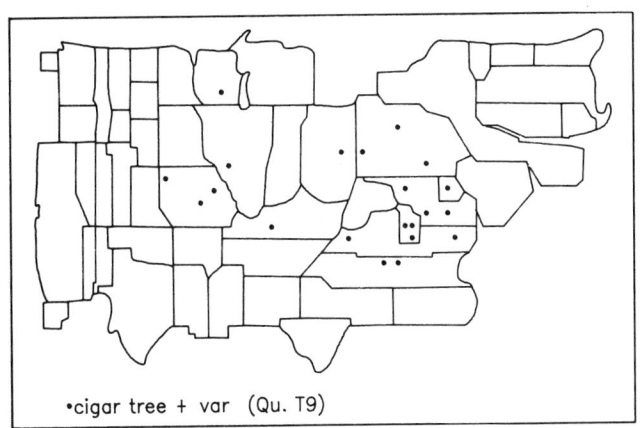

•cigar tree + var (Qu. T9)

shaped leaves, clusters of white blossoms, and long thin seed pods or "beans") 20 Infs, **chiefly Midl,** Cigar tree; NC16, Cigar plant.

ciggy See **cig**

cilantro n Also *culantro* [Span]
Coriander.
1967 *DARE* (Qu. I35, . . *Kitchen herbs grown and used in cooking*) Inf TX28, Cilantro ['silɑntro]. [*DARE* FW: *culantro* is the name I know this by.] **1976** *NY Times* (NY) 5 June 13/3 **Chicago IL,** The vegetable section burst with feathery bunches of parsley and pungent fresh cilantro, . . prickly cactus leaves, and at least eight kinds of chili peppers. **1977** Sunset *Mex. Cook Book* 6 **CA,** Coriander (cilantro). Fresh coriander looks like large, lacy parsley. But it has its own spicy, pungent aroma and flavor. You may find it under the name of Chinese parsley when sold in Oriental markets. **1982** *DARE* File **CA, CO,** *Cilantro*—sign seen regularly in supermarket produce sections above the fresh coriander. **1984** *Capital Times* (Madison WI) 9 May 48, A blend of south-of-the-border garlic, tomatoes and chiles subtly seasoned . . . [Seasonings include] bay leaf . . cinnamon . . cloves . . cilantro leaves . . capers.

cimarron n Also sp *cimmaron, simarron* [AmSpan *cimarrón* wild] **West, esp SW**
1 A wild or solitary creature.
1892 *DN* 1.246 **TX,** *Cimarrón* or *simarrón;* wild, speaking of plants. Also used as a noun for shy, bashful children. **1944** Adams *Western Words, Cimarron* . . . Spanish, meaning *wild, unruly.* The Mexican uses it for an animal, horse, bovine, or even human, which, deserted by all its friends, runs alone and has little to do with the rest of its kind. Literally, it signifies one who flees from civilization and becomes a fugitive or wild person.
2 A mountain sheep (*Ovis canadensis*).
[**1844** (1954) Gregg *Commerce* 138 **SW,** The *canero cimarron* or bighorn of the Rocky Mountains.] **1849** in 1850 U.S. Congress *Serial Set* 562 Doc 64.201 **NM,** The big-horn, or cimarron, is also seen skipping playfully from rock to rock upon the narrow overhanging crags. **1897** Lewis *Wolfville* 81 **AZ,** First we-alls knows, these yere Britons would be runnin' cimmaron in the hills. **1982** Elman *Hunter's Field Guide* 503, The desert tribe [*Ovis canadensis*] furnishes half a dozen examples of subtle differences among localized races, from the small, pale, slim-horned sheep of southern Nevada to the darker, heavier-horned Arizona bighorn and the pale little Mexican *cimarrón* with its thin flaring curl.

cimbal See **cymbal**

cimlin See **cymling**

cimmaron See **cimarron**

cinch n[1], also attrib [Span *cincha*]
1 also sp *cincha, cinche, cincho, sinch(e):* A saddle girth or bellyband. **scattered, but esp West, Nth** See Map
1859 in 1890 Hall *Hist. CO* 2.521, [I] nailed shoes on Old Chief to-day, and Black Hawk and I made Hackamore and sinche. **1878** E. Tuttle *Border Tales* 35 (*DAE*), The whole is fastened by a broad 'belly-band' termed a *sinch,* which by a method of drawing up loops of rope . . . known as sinching, is tightened until a load of three hundred pounds may be piled high on top. **1892** *DN* 1.189 **TX,** *Cíncha:* saddle girth, generally made of plaited hair ropes. The usual form in Texas is *cinch.*

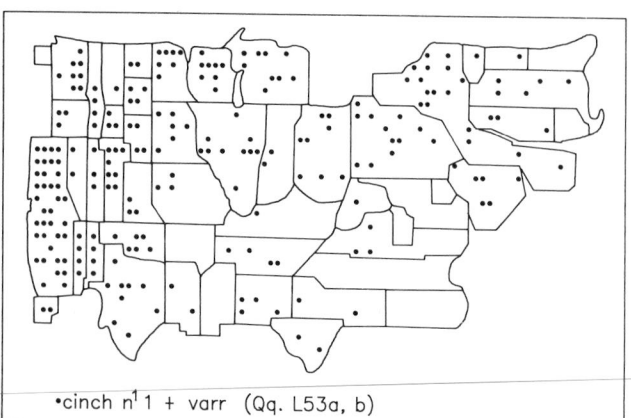

•cinch n[1] 1 + varr (Qq. L53a, b)

Ibid 246 **TX,** *Cincha* . . . Add: More specifically, the girth nearer the shoulders of the horse . . . The form *cinche* is also common, and the masculine form *cincho* is also used. **1906** *DN* 3.131 **nwAR,** Cinch. **1927** Siringo *Riata* 67 **SW** (as of 1879), The cinchas on these saddles being broad, and in the center of the saddle, it is difficult to keep the saddle tight on the pony's back. **1929** *AmSp* 5.61 **NE.** **1944** Adams *Western Words, Cinch*—From the Spanish *cincha* . . meaning *girth.* This is a "broad, short band made of coarsely woven horsehair or sometimes of canvas or cordage, and terminating at each end with a metal ring" . . . Together with the latigo, it is used to fasten the saddle upon the horse's back. **1961** *PADS* 36.9 **sLA,** Cinch. **1965–70** *DARE* (Qu. L53a, *The band that goes under a horse's middle to hold a saddle on*) 216 Infs, **scattered, but esp West,** Cinch; CA111, MI116, MN4, NJ44, Cinch strap; OK52, Saddle cinch; (Qu. L53b, . . *If it's part of a work harness*) 10 Infs, **chiefly West,** Cinch; NY9, Cinch strap.
2 A sure or easy thing. **scattered, but esp NEast, Atlantic**
1888 *World* (NY NY) 22 July 9/4, The bettor of whom the pool-room book-maker stands in dread, however, is the racehorse owner, who has a cinch bottled up for a particular race. **1890** *DN* 1.60 **swOH,** Cinch . . . a sure thing. (Really the belly-band or surcingle of a saddle. Hence the phrase "to have a cinch" on a thing; *i.e.* to have it tied up securely. Hence, "cinch" in general means a sure thing.) **1908** *DN* 3.299 **eAL, wGA.** **1965–70** *DARE* (Qu. KK42a, . . *About a person who does something very easily:* "For him that would be _____.") 109 Infs, **scattered, but esp Atlantic, NEast,** Cinch; RI17, Lead-pipe cinch; NY199, Pipe cinch; (Qu. KK42b) Inf SC34, Cinch; (Qu. JJ20, . . *Very sure*) Inf MN10, It's a cinch; (Qu. NN2, . . *Strong agreement*) Inf MN10, It's a cinch. **1969** *DARE* Tape CT41, I didn't marry him to get a cinch and sit on my behind and let him support me.
3 also sp *sinch:* A card game; see quot 1974. **chiefly Midl** Also called **double pedro, high five**
1889 in 1938 *DAE,* [Newspaper:] I found that sinch is the great Northwestern game of cards, a recent invention, and played everywhere and by everybody . . . It is a variation of High, Low, Jack. **1906** *DN* 3.131 **nwAR,** Cinch . . . High five, also the five-spot of trumps and of the other suit of cards of the same color as trumps. **1927** *AmSp* 2.350 **WV.** **1950** *WELS* (Table games) 1 Inf, **cwWI,** Cinch. **1965–70** *DARE* (Qu. DD35, . . *Favorite card games*) Infs IL135, IN35, KY24, 85, PA71, 164, 165, Cinch; IA18, Cinch—a 5 card in each hand game—played 60 years ago. **1974** Gibson *Hoyle* 65, Cinch: Known also as "double pedro" and "high five" . . this game is actually an elaboration of *Auction Pitch* . . including features of *Pedro,* with additional features that characterize it as a game in its own right. It is a four-player game . . . the trump suit includes the five of the other suit of the same color.
4 also *cinch notice:* A warning or deficiency notice sent by a college to a student.
1921 *DN* 5.111 **CA** [Students' terms], Cinch, cinch-notice . . . A warning sent by the college authorities with the object of tightening the student's hold on his work. **1968** *AmSp* 43.76, Some colleges in California and Nevada, also borrowing from cowboy lore (or, less poetically, from the stable), use terms like *cinch notice* and *cinch* to refer to their deficiency reports . . . The idea of squeezing or being squeezed is, obviously, inherent in the meaning of the terms.

cinch n[2] See **chinch** n[1] **1**

cinch v
1 To tighten the girth on a horse. **West**
1871 Miller *Songs of Sierras* 1.272, We drew in the lassoes, seized saddle and rein, / Threw them on, cinched them on, cinched them over again. **1892** *DN* 1.189 **TX,** Cinch . . to put the cinch on a horse, to tighten the girth. Sometimes two *cinchas* are used; they are then called *cinchas de gineta. Ibid* 236, Cinch [sɪnč]: to pull a saddle-girth tight. Kansas City [MO]. I have heard of this word in New Mexico and Colorado, as well as in Kansas. It may well have been brought from New Mexico by the "prairie schooners," which had Kansas City and vicinity for their eastern terminus. *To get a cinch* on a person = *to get a "bind," a hold,* on him. **1929** *AmSp* 5.61 **NE,** A cowboy "cinches up" a "bronc" rather than "saddles" one. **1933** *AmSp* 8.1.27 **nTX,** Cinch up. To tighten a girth. **1944** Adams *Western Words, Cinch up*—(As verb, and never merely *cinched.*) The act of fastening the saddle upon the horse's back by drawing the cinch up tight with the latigo straps.
2 To secure, fasten.
1968 *DARE* Tape CA103, Cinch 'em [logs] down from one side to the other. **1969** *DARE* (Qu. K81, *To make a cow stand still*) Inf CA124, Cinch cow up with rope.
3 To make sure of.

1905 *DN* 3.61 **NE,** *Cinch* . . . Clinch, make sure of. **1906** *DN* 3.131 **nwAR,** *Cinch a bargain* . . . To close an agreement. **1908** *DN* 3.299 **eAL, wGA,** *Cinch* . . . To make sure of.

4 To squeeze into a small place; also fig.

1875 *Scribner's Mth.* 10.277/1 **San Francisco CA,** A man who is hurt in a mining transaction is "cinched." **1881** *New York Times* (NY) 18 Dec 4/3, It is unfairly said that the Northern Pacific Company intends to "cinch" the settlers by exacting large prices for its lands. **1910** *Outlook* 96.2/1, If the rich man strives to use his wealth to destroy others, I will cinch him if I can. **1967** *DARE* (Qu. Y32, *To squeeze yourself into a small space*) Infs **CO20, NV5,** Cinch up; [**CA113,** Cinch up your girdle]. **1967** *DARE* Tape **CA8,** She [=a woman being laced in a corset] is probably just cinched in.

5 also sp *sinch:* See quot 1889. Cf **cinch** n[1] **3**

1889 in 1938 *DAE,* [Newspaper:] Prevent him from making as many points as he agreed to make. If he fails to make good his offer, he is 'sinched'. **1927** *AmSp* 2.350 **WV,** *Cinch* . . . We cinched them for six straight hands.

6 See quot. Cf **cinch** n[1] **4**

1921 *DN* 5.111 **CA** [Students' terms], *To cinch* . . . To cause the authorities to send out a notice to a student.

cincha See **cinch** n[1] **1**

cinch bat n

Perh a **nighthawk.**

1968 *DARE* (Qu. Q3, . . *Birds* . . *out only after dark*) Inf **SC57,** Cinch bat.

cinch binder n **West**

A horse which balks, rears, or falls over backward when cinched too tightly; also fig.

1916 Wilson *Somewhere* 180 **WA,** I had another aunt named Obedience, only she proved to be a regular cinch-binder. **1940** FWP *Guide NV* 75, *Cinch binder* . . a horse that when cinched too tightly refuses to move or falls over backwards. **1944** Adams *Western Words, Cinch binder*—A horse which rears on its hind legs, loses its balance, and falls backward. **1946** Mora *Trail Dust* 65, [Caption:] The Cinchbinder. A poison bronc.

cinch bug See **chinch** n[1] **2**

cinche See **cinch** n[1] **1**

cincher n

=**cinch** n[1] **1.**

1914 *DN* 4.104 **KS,** *Cincher* . . . = *Cinch,* a saddle girth. **1967** *DARE* (Qu. L53a) Inf **MO14,** Cincher.

cinchgrass See **chinchweed**

cinch notice See **cinch** n[1] **4**

cincho See **cinch** n[1] **1**

cinci n [Abbr for *Cincinnati*]

1 A small glass of beer; the glass itself.

1981 *DARE* File **Chicago IL** (as of c1912–16), Cinci—a glass approximately 4½″ tall, 2½ in diameter . . . No doubt anything could be served in it. But I remember seeing only beer in the saloon connected to the barbershop my Father and I patronized . . . "Draw two cincis" is an expression I have heard on occasion, indicating to me those who ordered them wanted to dampen rather than wet their whistles. *Ibid* **cwNY** (as of c1920s), *Cinci* . . small beer—i.e. a short beer. *Ibid* **cwNY,** *Cinci* . . . a short glass of beer.

2 See **Cincinnati B2.**

Cincinnati n

A Form.

See **-a.**

B Senses.

1 attrib: Used in ref to pork. [*Cincinnati* Ohio, a center of the pork-packing industry since the mid 19th cent] *joc* Cf **Albany beef, Cape Cod turkey**

1864 *Harper's New Mth. Mag.* 29.433/1 **CT,** Here is the list: . . 200 pounds Borden's meat biscuit; 20 pounds "Cincinnati cracklings"— *pork scraps.* **1877** Bartlett *Americanisms* 121, *Cincinnati Oysters,* Pigs' feet. **1884** *New York Weekly* 23 June [Waiters' Lingo] (*AmSp* 20.71), 'Cincinnati quail—have it fat,' was the next order. The cook cut off a large slice of fat pork and put it on a plate. **1889** Barrère–Leland *Slang*

252/2 (*DAE*), *Cincinnati Olives* (American), pigs because a large quantity of olive oil is manufactured out of Cincinnati lard. **1938** Asbury *Sucker's Progress* 271, For some forty years hogs and Cincinnati were so nearly synonymous in the public mind that pigs-feet were called 'Cincinnati oysters,' and in many places were so listed on restaurant menus. **1946** *McDavid Coll.* **ceSC,** Cincinnati turkey—salt pork; **seGA,** Cincinnati chicken—salt pork. **1950** Brown *Amer. Cooks* 668 **OH,** The dish called "Cincinnati chicken" is really made of a big pork tenderloin. **1970** *DARE* (Qu. H38, . . *Bacon*) Infs **VA35, 42,** Cincinnati chicken.

2 also *cinci:* A marble game; see quots.

1908 *DN* 3.299 **eAL, wGA,** *Cincinatti* [sic] . . . The name of a game of marbles. **1958** *PADS* 29.31 **OK, WA,** *Cinci, Cincinnati* . . . A marble game played with a small ring; all marbles must be shot with two knuckles flat to the ground to prevent fudging. **1963** *KY Folkl. Rec.* 9.60 **eKY,** [Marble] *Games played on a football-shaped pattern:* Cincinnati. **1967–70** *DARE* (Qu. EE7) Inf **CA197,** Cincinnata; **WY1,** Cincinnati; **TX1,** Hogando Cincinnati. **1967** *DARE* Tape **WY1,** Cincinnati was a game two or three boys could play. The ring was . . oval in shape . . . If [a player's] marble hit some of the marbles in the Cincinnati ring . . he went right on playing. **1970** *Thompson Coll.* **cAL** (as of 1920s), Cincinnati . . type of marble game. The players . . bellowed "everything goes in Cincinnati!" "Hard down study knucks!" **1980** *NADS Letters* **cnAL,** Cincinnati . . . A space the size of a bed-room floor was required . . . the ring is about four feet long [oval]; a line from which the first shots are made is several feet away.

cinder n attrib

In var phrr referring to the railroad: see quots.

1926 *AmSp* 1.265, The cinder bull double-crossed me. **1927** *DN* 5.442 [Underworld jargon], *Cinder trail* . . . (1) The railroad. (2) Tramp life in general. **1930** Irwin *Amer. Tramp, Cinder Sifter.*—A tramp, especially one travelling along the railroads. **1945** Hubbard *Railroad Ave.* 337, *Cinder cruncher*—Switchman or flagman. *Cinder skipper* is yard clerk. *Cinder dick*—Railroad policeman or detective. *Cinder snapper*—Passenger who rides open platforms on observation car. **1950** *WELS* (*Detective*) 1 Inf, **csWI,** R.R. dick, cinder cop. **1966** Barnes–Jensen *Dict. UT Slang, Cinder bull* . . a railroad detective.

cinder beetle n

An imaginary beetle. Cf **ice worm**

1944 Wellman *Bowl* 107 **KS,** It was an innocent story—about a purported incursion of "cinder beetles" which were alleged to be working their way into Kansas, causing extensive damage by eating the kingbolts out of wagons, and sometimes even devouring iron footscrapers off front doorsteps.

cindy-in-the-meadow n

=**spiderwort.**

1968 *DARE* (Qu. S24, *A wild flower that grows in swamps and marshes and looks like a small blue iris*) Inf **VA24,** Cindy-in-the-meadow.

ciniky See **cienaga**

cinnamon bear n Also *cinnamon*

A color phase of the black bear (*Ursus americanus*).

1829 Richardson *Fauna Boreali–Amer.* 1.15, The *Cinnamon Bear* of the Fur Traders is considered by the Indians to be an accidental variety of this species [*Ursus americanus*]. **1855** Marryat *Mountains & Molehills* 228 **CA,** The cinnamon's weight was quoted at 400 lbs. **1910** Hart *Vigilante Girl* 119 **nCA,** A heated controversy broke out aboard as to whether it was a grizzly or a cinnamon bear, the verdict finally being that it was a grizzly. **1928** Anthony *N. Amer. Mammals* 74, *Black Bear.*— *Euarctos americanus* . . Names . . . Cinnamon Bear. **1946** Peattie *Pacific Coast* 82, Some of the bears formerly called cinnamons were undoubtedly grizzlies. **1949** Palmer *Nat. Hist.* 592, Black Bear, Cinnamon Bear—*Euarctos americanus.* **1966** *DARE* (Qu. P32, . . *Wild animals*) Inf **NM13,** Cinnamon bear. **1982** Elman *Hunter's Field Guide* 585, Cinnamon black-bear sow with cub.

cinnamon fern n Also *cinnamon-colored fern*

A large fern (*Osmunda cinnamomea*) which produces both cinnamon-colored and green fronds. Also called **breadroot 2, buckhorn 8, fern snakeroot, fiddlehead, flowering fern**

1847 Wood *Class-Book* 634, *O[smunda] Cinnamomea.* Cinnamon-colored Fern. **1878** Williamson *Ferns KY* 137, *Osmunda cinnamomea* . . . Cinnamon Fern. **1938** Matschat *Suwannee R.* 253 **nFL, sGA,** Cinnamon ferns were abundant. **1961** Douglas *My Wilderness* 194 **MD,** The fronds of the ferns now [=in March] begin to stir. There are several dozen species in the Potomac area. Christmas, cinnamon, maiden-hair, bracken, hay-scented, leathery grape—these are present.

‡cinnamon head n Cf **cymling-head**

1939 AmSp 14.90 eTN, Cinnamon head. Feebleminded. 'Joe's a cinnamon head.'

cinnamon honeysuckle n [Prob from the odor]

The clammy azalea (*Rhododendron viscosum*).

1894 Jrl. Amer. Folkl. 7.93 WV, Rhododendron viscosum . . cinnamon honeysuckle. **1901** Mohr Plant Life AL 653, Azalea viscosa glauca . . . Cinnamon Honeysuckle.

cinnamon oak n

=**bluejack 1.**

1897 Sudworth Arborescent Flora 176, Quercus brevifolia . . Cinnamon Oak (Fla.). **1960** Vines Trees SW 178, Bluejack Oak . . . Vernacular names are . . Cinnamon Oak. **1979** Little Checklist U.S. Trees 233, Quercus incana . . cinnamon oak.

cinnamon owl n

Perh a **screech owl** (here: *Otus asio*).

1968 DARE (Qu. Q2, . . Owls) Inf IA22, Cinnamon owl.

cinnamon sedge n

=**sweet flag.**

1900 Lyons Plant Names 13, Acorus . . . Calamus . . . Cinnamon Sedge . . . Aromatic. **1930** U.S. Dept. Ag. Misc. Pub. 77.56, Sweetflag . . . Other common names . . . Cinnamon sedge . . . The . . rootstocks . . . have an agreeable aromatic odor. **1959** Carleton Index Herb. Plants 28, Cinnamon sedge: Acorus calamus.

cinnamon squash n

Perh =**cymling 1.**

1966–68 DARE (Qu. I23, . . Kinds of squash) Infs MD12, NC15, Cinnamon squash.

cinnamon stone n

An essonite garnet.

1953 Pough Rocks & Minerals 295, The Garnets . . Essonite or "cinnamon [sic] stone," light brown in color.

cinnamon teal n [From the color]

A teal (here: *Anas cyanoptera*). Also called **red-breasted teal**

1874 Coues Birds NW 568, The Cinnamon Teal was found breeding in Idaho. **1917** DN 4.424 LA, Cinnamon teal (Querquedula cyanoptera). **1938** Oberholser Bird Life LA 119, Cinnamon Teal—Querquedula cyanoptera. **1955** Lowery LA Birds 168, Cinnamon Teal. Anas Cyanoptera. **1967–69** DARE (Qu. Q5, . . Wild ducks) Infs CA78, 140, CO7, IA22, MN42, RI4, Cinnamon teal.

cinnamon vine n

1 =**Chinese yam.** [See quot 1948]

1895 Gray–Bailey Field Botany 430, Cinnamon Vine. Cult. from China and Japan . . , for ornament, or for its very deep and long farinaceous roots. **1948** (1965) Neal Gardens HI 229, Cinnamon Vine. Dioscorea batatas . . . Minute cinnamon-scented male flowers are borne on one or two narrow spikes at leaf axils. **1968** Barkley Plants KS 101, Cinnamon vine. Cultivated, escaped in Kansas river floodplain near Manhattan. **1976** Bailey–Bailey Hortus Third 1239, Cinnamon vine: Dioscorea Batatas.

2 A clematis.

1966 DARE Wildfl QR Pl.73 Inf NC28, Cinnamon vine.

cinnamon wood n [See quot 1971]

=**sassafras.**

1900 Lyons Plant Names 335, S. albidum . . . Cinnamon-Wood. **1960** Vines Trees SW 298, Sassafras . . . Cinnamon-wood. **1971** Krochmal Appalachia Med. Plants 228, Cinnamon wood . . . All parts of the tree have a spicy aroma.

cinquefoil n Usu |'sɪŋkfɔɪl, -ˌfoɪl|, infreq |'sɪŋkˌfiəld, 'sɪŋkwɨˌfɔɪl| Pronc-spp *sinkfiel(d), sankfield*

A plant of the genus *Potentilla*. Also called **buttercup 2, five-finger, meadow stars, starflower, strawberry** For other names of var spp see **barren strawberry, bog strawberry, buckbrush 3i, cowberry 3, false strawberry, five-fingered Jack, gold cup, hardhack, high strawberry, old-field cinquefoil, prairieweed, purple marshlocks, purplewort, silverweed 1, sinkfield, tundra rose, yellow rose, yellow strawberry**

1778 Carver Travels N. Amer. 515, Balm, Nettles, Cinque Foil, Eye-bright, Sanicle. **1893** Jrl. Amer. Folkl. 6.141 WV, Potentilla Canadensis, sinkfield. **1915** DN 4.190 swVA, Sinkfiel(d) . . Variant [DN: by folk etymology] of cinquefoil. **1937** in 1944 ADD 529 neKY, The cattle guards are gone now & the sankfield & dewberry briars have covered up the crossties. **1949** Peattie Cascades 255 Pacific NW, Potentillas are also called cinquefoils, a name that originated in Europe. **1968–69** DARE (Qu. S21, . . Weeds) Inf OH5, ['sɪŋkˌfoɪl]; PA89, ['sɪŋkwɨˌfɔɪl]; (Qu. S26a, . . Roadside flowers) Inf PA99, ['sɪŋkfɔɪl]; PA191, Cinquefoil; (Qu. S26c, Wildflowers . . woods) Inf RI15, Cinquefoils; (Qu. S26d, Wildflowers . . meadows) Inf MD18, Sinkfield; (Qu. S26e) Inf MA42, [sɪŋkfɔɪl], creeping like a vine with little yellow blossoms. **1968** DARE FW Addit VA15, Cinquefoil ['sɪŋkˌfiəld]—common, roadsides and meadows.

cions See **scions**

cioppino n Usu |čə'pi,no|, also |šə'pɪŋ| [Ital] **chiefly CA**

A fish and shellfish stew cooked with tomatoes, wine, spices and herbs.

1954 (1962) Hunt Cape Cod Cookbook 91 MA, Cioppino Sauce . . . Cioppino Fish and Shellfish. **1964** Amer. Heritage Cookbook 463, Cioppino . . sea bass . . shrimp . . lobster . . clams or mussels . . olive oil . . . onion . . garlic . . green pepper . . tomatoes . . red wine . . parsley. **1967–69** DARE (Qu. H45, Dishes made with meat, fish, or poultry that everybody around here would know) Inf CA15, Cioppino [šə'pɪŋ]—Italian; Ca107, [Inf's sp:] Chappino [šə'pɪŋ], made with crabs in shell, fish, etc., all boiled up together; CA112, Crab coppino [sic]—hot stew, tomato sauce, onions, garlic, pieces of live crab cooked in it. **1968** Brown Amer. Cooking 103 [Caption], One of California's famous dishes, a casserole of cioppino, is served in an elegant apartment in San Francisco. The main ingredients for the dish—mussels, shrimp, crab, fish and clams—came from the sea close by. **1978** Time–Life Amer. Regional Cookbook 145, Cioppino (Far West) . . a highly seasoned seafood stew, is at its best when made with a mixture of both finned- and shellfish. **1981** DARE File cwCA, Cioppino, [čə'pino]—A stew made with mussels, crab, fish, any seafood, in a tomato base. **1984** Gourmet 44.108, On a recent trip to the San Francisco area we were lucky enough to visit Sam's Anchor Cafe in Tiberon. The cioppino was marvelous . . . A spicy blend of seafood, this dish is a San Francisco favorite.

cipher n Also obs sp *cypher*; rarely *ciphen*

1 Zero, naught. [OED 1399 →] **chiefly Nth, Midl** See Map *old-fash*

1788 in 1912 Ford Notes N. Webster 1.226 CT, Mercury at 6 below cypher. **1815** Drake Natural View Cincinnati 94, From nine years observations, at Cincinnati, it appears that the thermometer falls below cypher twice every winter. **1899** (1912) Green VA Folk-Speech 115, Cipher . . . The character of the form 0. **1950** WELS (The figure that follows the figure "1" when you write ten (10) is called _____) 11 Infs, WI, Cipher. **1965–70** DARE (Qu. LL15, To write ten (10), what figure do you put after "1"?) 61 Infs, **chiefly Nth, Midl**, Cipher. [Of all Infs responding to the question, 63% were old; of those giving this response, 90% were old.] **1983** MJLF 9.35 ceKY, Ciphen . . a cipher, zero.

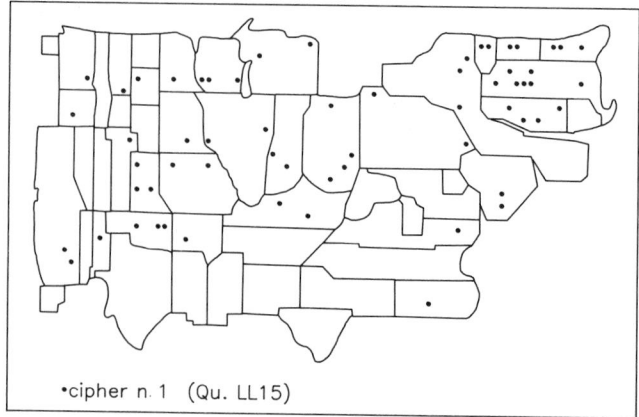

•cipher n. 1 (Qu. LL15)

2 By ext: any number, figure, or letter.

1940 Stuart Trees of Heaven 170 neKY, They [=bankers] have everything down in ciphers and in the word [=in writing] in big books. **1968** DARE (Qu. JJ11, Joking names for handwriting that's hard to read: "I can't make anything out of his _____.") Inf VA29, Ciphers.

3 Fig: an insignificant person, a nonentity.

1967 *DARE* (Qu. HH16, *Uncomplimentary words with no definite meaning—just used when you want to show that you don't think much of a person: "Don't invite him. He's a _____."*) Inf **MI67,** Cipher.

cipher v Also obs sp *cypher*

1 also with *out:* To figure (arithmetic problems), to calculate; by ext, to think out. *old-fash*

1806 (1970) Webster *Compendious Dict.* 51, Cipher, . . to cast accounts. **1836** (1838) Haliburton *Clockmaker* (1st ser) 112 **NEng,** I read till I came to his calculations, but I never could read figures, 'I can't cypher.' **1885** Twain *Huck. Finn* 168 **MO,** Leave me alone to cipher out a way so we can run in the day-time. **1887** *Scribner's Mag.* 2.479 **AR,** That ar's cyphered right, ain't it? **1889** (1971) Farmer *Americanisms* 147, Cipher, To.—To ponder; to think out; the transition from the primary meaning to calculate, to the idiomatic usage is obviously an easy one. **1898** Westcott *Harum* 154 **NY,** S'posen you come 'round to my place tomorro' 'bout 'leven o'clock, an' mebbe we c'n cipher this thing out. **1923** *DN* 5.204 **swMO,** Cipher . . . To scheme, to manipulate, as in negotiating a trade. **1937** Eaton *Handicrafts* 222 **wNC,** [The] family . . . often work together around the rug frame, deciding among themselves just how to fill in certain parts of the pattern which had been left for them to "cipher out."

2 also with *about* or *around:* To snoop, nose around (into other people's business).

1889 *Century Dict.* 1005/3, Cipher . . . In *fox-hunting,* to hunt carefully about in search of a lost trail; said of a dog. [New Eng.]. **1930** *Herald-Advt.* (Huntington WV) 30 Nov, If a "furriner" comes "cipherin' about" up the hills, he is not making mathematical calculations, but is snooping about, perhaps too closely into other people's business. **1953** Randolph *Down in Holler* 234 **Ozarks,** Major E.H. Criswell, of Lexington, Mo., says that a man who *ciphers around* "goes nosing into other people's business, trying to detect something that will enable him to make trouble. He is a busybody rather than an idler."

3 usu with *around:* To loaf, idle. [Cf *OED cipher [sb.]* 2 "A person who fills a place, but is of no importance or worth"]

1929 *AmSp* 5.17 **Ozarks,** Cipher around . . . To do nothing, to idle about. **1942** Berrey–Van den Bark *Amer. Slang* 248.3, *Idle; loaf; loiter* . . . cipher around. **1983** *MJLF* 9.35 **ceKY,** Cipher . . to loaf . . . *Cipher around* . . loaf around.

cipher down v phr

To defeat an opponent in a **ciphering** match by solving arithmetic problems more quickly.

1927 *AmSp* 2.350 **WV,** Cipher down . . to turn an opponent down at a ciphering match. **1946** McAtee *Dial. Grant Co. IN Suppl. 3* 3, Cipher down, . . surpass in a ciphering match; parallel to "spell down." **c1960** *Wilson Coll.* **csKY,** Cipher down . . . To defeat in an arithmetic match . . . Old usage; now rarely heard or known.

ciphering vbl n [*OED* 1611 →] **chiefly S Midl**

Arithmetic; hence *ciphering match* a contest usu between two sides in solving arithmetic problems quickly but accurately.

1905 *DN* 3.75 **nwAR,** Ciphering-match . . . A contest between sides or teams in solving arithmetical problems. **1927** *AmSp* 2.350 **WV,** Ciphering match . . a contest in which sides are chosen for the purpose of testing accuracy and speed in arithmetic. **1941** FWP *Guide AR* 87, Here [in one-room schoolhouses] church services were sometimes held, and such favorite social gatherings as ciphering matches and spelling bees. **1942** McAtee *Dial. Grant Co. IN* (as of 1890s), Ciphering-match . . school exercise paralleling the familiar spelling-match. **c1960** *Wilson Coll.* **csKY,** Ciphering . . . Older name for arithmetic. "Reading, writing, and ciphering to the Rule of Three." *Ciphering match* . . . A quick drill in arithmetic, usually done on a slate; the first one getting the correct answer won. **1963** Edwards *Gravel* 77 **eTN** (as of 1920s), What'll ye do if the old man finds out that you're slightin the readin, writin, and cipherin an sich as that?

circe, circi See **sirsee**

circis See **circus**

circle n, also attrib

1 The area a rider covers during a day in a roundup, from which cattle are herded in to a given spot; such an operation or act. **West**

1888 *Century Illustr. Mag.* 13.857/2 **West,** This morning work is called circle riding . . . As the band goes out, the leader from time to time detaches one or two men to ride down through certain sections of the country, making the shorter, or what are called inside, circles, while he . . makes the longest or outside circle himself. **1889** (1971) Farmer *Americanisms* 147, Circle riding.—A cowboy's term. At *round-ups,* or when cattle are on the march, the plains are scoured for stray beasts, sometimes for fifteen or twenty miles back. This is effectually done by *circle riding.* The herdsmen scatter in different directions, returning on lines that tend to the common centre like, says Roosevelt "as if the lines of a fan were curved." Two or three of the band take shorter and larger circles than the rest; each man engaged in the *circle riding* driving in any strays he may have come across. **1927** James *Cow Country* 82 **West,** We was just catching horses for the second circle of the day when the two rode up. **1930** Raine *Cattle* 300 **West,** Half an hour after the circle starts down the prong one can see for miles small bunches of cattle in motion. **1939** FWP *Guide MT* 414, Circle—Area a roundup rider must inspect in a day. Several men riding separate circles cover the range thoroughly. **1977** Watts *Dict. Old West,* Circle . . . Used on round-up as *go on circle;* when the riders would scatter to all points of the compass to work the cattle generally toward the center.

2 See **traffic circle.**

circle buck n Also *circle bucking* [*circle* + **buck** n[2] **1**] Cf **spinner**

Of a horse: see quots.

1944 Adams *Western Words,* Circle buck—The bucking of a horse in long, rapid, and evenly timed leaps in a circle of thirty or forty feet, the horse leaning inward toward the center of the circle. **1950** *PADS* 14.74 **FL,** Circle-buckin' . . . The manner in which a horse sometimes bucks, staying in a circle of about fifteen feet in diameter.

circle horse n [**circle 1**] **West**

See quot 1941.

1941 FWP *Guide WY* 461, Circle horse—One selected for his stamina to cover territory in a roundup. **1944** Adams *Western Words,* Circle horse—A horse used on circle during the roundup. The wilder horses are used for this task. They do not have to be specially trained, but they do have to be tough and have bottom. **1958** Blasingame *Dakota Cowboy* 82 **SD** (as of 1900–10), The long-legged, strong, seemingly tireless circle horse was ridden when a big region was to be encircled for a roundup. **1966** Thorp *Songs Cowboys* 309 **West,** A circle horse is one chosen with sufficient stamina ("bottom," in cowboy lingo) to endure the greater mileage. **1966** *DARE* Tape **OK30,** They'd have one or two, generally the biggest and strongest horse, they'd called them circle horses. They'd use them in building a roundup . . . They'd push the cattle in close to where the wagon was camped.

circle rider n [**circle 1**] **West**

See quot 1944.

1888 *Century Illustr. Mag.* 13.860/1 **West,** As soon as . . the last circle-riders have come in . . we begin to work the herd. **1922** Rollins *Cowboy* 220 **West,** Horsemen, widely separated in skirmish line, started miles from a designated corral, and, as "circle riders," converging on it, drove slowly before themselves everything that moved on legs. **1926** Branch *Cowboy* 56, Up this gorge the circle-riders make their way, and dividing into couples, start at a lope for the lurking-places of the cattle. **1944** Adams *Western Words,* Circle rider—One of the horsemen, who, on roundup, widely separate into small parties, starting miles from a chosen holding spot, then ride toward it, driving slowly before them all cattle encountered. **1966** Thorp *Songs Cowboys* 309 **West,** The circle riders are those who take the outer perimeter.

circle-swing n

1953 Randolph *Down in Holler* 244 **Ozarks,** A *circle-swing* is a bit more elaborate [than **flying Dutchman 3**], with many seats. I saw a circle-swing, powered by a mule, in operation at Reeds Spring Junction, Mo., as recently as 1938.

circuit rider n Also *circuit (preacher),* infreq *circuit-riding preacher* somewhat old-fash

1 A minister, esp a Methodist, serving several churches within a circuit, usu in a frontier or sparsely populated area.

1830 *NY Annual Reg.* 291, Other towns have no settled ministers—supplied by circuit and other preachers. **1837** Wetmore *Gaz. MO* 333, When Patsy gets her eye on the greyhound, she'll feel a heap gladder than when the circuit rider comes round. **1838** Flagg *Far West* 2.61 **IL,** A little, portly, red-faced man . . announced himself a "Baptist circuit-rider!" **1872** Eggleston *End of the World* 245 **IN,** Then he stepped to the door and called in the circuit preacher. **1932** Faulkner *Light in August*

229 **MS,** Dissertations composed half of . . bleak and bloodless logic . . , and half of immediate hellfire and tangible brimstone of which any country Methodist circuit rider would have been proud. **1953** Brewer *Word Brazos* 74 **eTX** [Black], De membuhship cain't in no wise pay a full-time preachuh, an' dat's de why de bishop allus sen' 'em a circuit-ridin' preachuh to preach de Word to 'em evuh fo'th Sunday. **1965–70** *DARE* (Qu. CC10, . . *Unprofessional part-time lay preacher*) 51 Infs, **scattered,** Circuit rider; **NC22, OH11, TN24,** Circuit rider—a Methodist; **NC61,** Circuit; **PA104,** Circuit preacher. [Of all Infs responding to the question, 68% were old; of those giving these responses, 80% were old. 18 Infs called the term old-fashioned.] **1966** *DARE* Tape **OK19,** There was a circuit rider who came through and he just came about once every two weeks. **1982** *Foxfire* 7 20 **nGA,** Add to that the Methodists, with their ubiquitous circuit riders. *Ibid* 28, *Baptists* . . . The old horseback-riding circuit preachers of yesteryear have their own special place.

2 By ext: see quot.

1967 Key *Tobacco Vocab.* **GA, KY, MD, NC, TN,** Circuit rider—supervisor of tobacco buyers . . used by buyers among themselves.

circumbendibus n [Fanciful formation borrowed from English lit use: Farmer–Henley *Slang* 1681 →] *old-fash*
Circumlocution, a roundabout way.

1834 *Life Andrew Jackson* 224, Now, gineral, I tell you without any circumbendibus, what the people say. **1848** Bartlett *Americanisms, Circumbendibus.* A circuitous, roundabout way, either of getting to a spot, or of telling a story. **1899** (1912) Green *VA Folk-Speech, Circumbendibus* . . . A roundabout way. **1942** Berrey–Van den Bark *Amer. Slang* 43.2, *Something curved* . . . circumbendibus, *a roundabout way. Ibid* 188.1, *Speech; talk* . . . circumbendibus, detour, *a circumlocution.*

circumstance n Pronc-spp *circumstahnce, sarcumstance, suckemstance*

A Forms.

1841 (1952) Cooper *Deerslayer* 455 **NY,** Now, gifts come of sarcumstances. Thus, if you put a man in a town, he gets town gifts. **1843** (1916) Hall *New Purchase* 151 **IN,** The sarcumstance of the chopp'd log satisfied me. **1861** Holmes *Venner* 2.302 **wMA,** I shell, . . make sech noo arrangements as circumstahnces compel. **1867** Lowell *Biglow* 2d ser 16 '*Upcountry*' **MA,** A moultin' fallen cherubim, ef he should see ye, 'd snicker, / Thinkin' he warn't a suckemstance. **1926** Kephart *Highlanders* 371 **sAppalachians,** Reckon Pete was knowin' to the sarcumstance?

B Senses.

1 An addition or extension: see quots. [*OED circumstance* 9c →1792, "*Obs.*"] *arch* or *old-fash*

1885 in 1937 *AmSp* 12.76 **NE,** The Florida "Cracker's" highest ambition was to get well enough off to buy himself a framed house with a "circumstance" (meaning a tower or observatory), rising above the surrounding woods, so that he could see over the whole country. **1937** *AmSp* 12.76 **nwNE,** A generation ago the mothers called the full ruffle on the bottom of a kitchen apron a 'circumstance.' [Footnote: Told me by Mari Sandoz, whose childhood home was in the sandhills.] " 'I didn't have enough goods for a circumstance,' the housewife might say regretfully. Her regret was for practical rather than aesthetic reasons. The full ruffle caught any grease that might fall in hurried cooking, saving the hose and shoes of the wearer." In the sandhill region of Nebraska an extension to the bed of a lumber wagon was sometimes called a 'circumstance.' If long poles were being carried, for example, the protruding ends needed support.

2 in phr *not a circumstance to* and varr: Nothing in comparison with. **now chiefly Sth, S Midl** Cf *DS* LL32

1836 *Crockett's Yaller Flower Almanac* 19 (*DAE*), Orson the wild man of the woods, is nothing to him—not a circumstance. **1845** Judd *Margaret* 284 **NEng,** It an't a circumstance to what it used to be. **1905** *DN* 3.5 **cCT,** *Circumstance* . . . In the expression 'not a circumstance to,' not to be compared with. **1907** *DN* 3.210 **nwAR. 1908** *DN* 3.299 **eAL, wGA. 1910** *DN* 3.439 **cwNY. 1946** *PADS* 6.9 **eNC** (as of 1900–10). **c1960** Wilson *Coll.* **csKY,** She's not a circumstance (that is, not to be compared with) to Mary.

3 usu in comb *mere circumstance* and varr: A person or thing of little consequence, importance, or value.

1838 Flagg *Far West* 1.145 **MO,** The race of John Gilpin or of Alderman Purdy were, either or both of them, mere circumstances to ours. **1840** *Knickerbocker* 16.154, My uncle was a little wiffet of a man; one that in Kentucky we would not call even an 'individual'; nothing

more than a 'remote circumstance.' **1856** Simms *Eutaw* 394 **SC,** To be beaten by [*"*]such a mere circumstance of a gal-child," as he himself phrased it, was a circumstance of mortification. **a1910** in 1917 Twain *What is Man* 155, Next comes King John, and he was a poor circumstance.

4 Transf: a unique or unusual person; an exemplar.

1853 Simms *Sword & Distaff* 350 **SC,** And a pretty sizeable sarcumstance of a child he is! **1952** Brown *NC Folkl.* 1.527 **cnNC,** *Circumstance, a* . . . An unusual or distinctive person.

‡**circumvengemous** adv [From **circumbendibus**]

1927 *AmSp* 2.350 **WV,** Circumvengemous . . in a roundabout manner. "Mother told the story very circumvengemous."

circus n Pronc-sp *circis*

1 freq attrib: Something gaudy, garish, or overdone. **chiefly Nth**

1940 Harris *Folk Plays* 88 **NC,** I'll jes' keep on my circis jacket till I git warm. *Ibid* 103, He . . grabbed me up, and pushed me in his circis cart, and shut the door, and cranked up. *Ibid* 292, *Circis cart,* automobile. **1960** Wentworth–Flexner *Slang* 106, *Circus* . . . Any large, colorful spectacle. *Ibid* 639, *Circus* . . . This prefix word serves as an adjective = spectacular, exciting, elaborate, garish, specifically created or done in a spectacular manner to impress others. **1965–70** *DARE* (Qu. W36, . . *A woman who uses a lot of cosmetics*) Infs **MA79, PA224,** Looks like a circus; **MA5, NY209,** Painted up like a circus horse; **WI50,** Circus clown; **PA175,** Circus queen; **OR1,** Going to the circus; **SC6,** Painted up like a circus; **CA59,** Painted up like a whore on circus day; (Qu. W40, . . *A woman who overdresses*) Infs **IL43, PA224,** Circus horse.

2 =**traffic circle.**

1967–69 *DARE* (Qu. N20, . . *A circular arrangement on one level at a big intersection, where cars can go around till they come to the road they want*) Infs **NY219, OH20,** Circus.

circus beetle n Also *circus bug* [See quots] **SW**
=**pinacate bug.**

1957 Jaeger *N. Amer. Deserts* 170, Circus Beetle. Eleodes armata. Called circus bugs . . because of their queer way, when disturbed, of standing with the body raised vertically. **1965** Teale *Wandering Through Winter* 21 **CA,** Advancing laboriously over the bare ground moved a swollen, jet-black beetle . . . Disturbed, it stopped, lifted its body almost vertically in the air, balanced itself on long, katydid-like hind legs and stood on its head in the sand. We were seeing the famed circus or pinacate beetle of the dry Southwest.

cironcified See **suffancified**

cisco n Occas sp *sisco;* infreq *ciscoette, cisco herring* [Abbr for CanFr *ciscoette*] **chiefly Gt Lakes**
Any of several fish of the genus *Coregonus.* For other names of var spp see **blackfin cisco, bloater 1, bluefin 1, grayback, kiyi, lake herring, longjaw, mooneye, shortjaw, tullibee, whitefish**

1848 Bartlett *Americanisms, Cisco.* The popular name of a fish of the herring kind which abounds in Lake Ontario, particularly in Chaumont Bay at the east end, where thousands of barrels are annually caught and salted. **1875** *Amer. Naturalist* 9.135, I received . . a collection of deep-water "Siscoes" taken in Lake Tippecanoe, Kosciusko Co., Indiana. **1902** Jordan–Evermann *Amer. Fishes* 138, The bloater is known also as . . cisco or ciscoette. **1965–70** *DARE* (Qu. P1, . . *Freshwater fish . . good to eat*) Infs **ID1, MI103,** Cisco; **MI20,** Cisco herring; **MI84,** Ciscoes; (Qu. P14, . . *Commercial fishing*) Infs **MI108, MN10, 15,** Cisco; (Qu. P4, *Saltwater fish . . not good to eat*) Inf **MN10,** Cisco. **1976** *DARE* File **nMI,** Ciscos are a deep-water trout, 300 to 450 feet, deeper water version of herring.

ciscoette See **cisco, siscowet**

cisco fly n [cisco n + *fly*] **WI**
=**mayfly.**

1872 *Fur, Fin, & Feather* 200 (*DA*), Cisco fishing at Geneva Lake, Wis. . . . Their coming is heralded by the cisco-fly. **1950** *WELS* (*Large winged insect*) 1 Inf, **csWI,** Cisco flies. **1950** *WELS Suppl.,* [3 Infs called Mayflies "Cisco flies"]. **1968** *DARE* (Qu. R4, *A large winged insect that hatches in summer in great numbers around lakes or rivers, crowds around lights, lives only a day or so, and is good fish bait*) Inf **WI62,** Cisco fly.

cisco herring See **cisco**

ciscoquette, ciscovet See **siscowet**

cisor n [Abbr for *incisor;* perh also folk-etym *sizer* in ref to its large size]

1968 *DARE* (Qu. X12, . . *Large front teeth that stick out of the mouth*) Inf **NY66,** Cisors; (Qu. X13a, . . *Joking names* . . *for teeth*) Inf **PA70,** Cisors ['saɪzɚz].

cistern n [Prob alter of *citron*]

Perh =**citron melon.**

1969 *DARE* (Qu. I26, . . *Kinds of melons*) Inf **NC76,** Cisterns ['sɪstɚnz] —have to cook them. They look like watermelons.

cistern trough n Also *cistern troft*

=**eaves trough.**

1956 Ker *Vocab. W. TX* 98 (*Troughs to take water off roof*) 1 inf, Cistern troughs. 1965 *DARE* (Qu. D28, *What hangs below the edge of the roof to carry off rain-water?*) Inf **OK1,** Cistern trofts. 1970 Tarpley *Blinky* 76 **neTX,** *Troughs to take the water off the roof* . . . 1.5% [=3 infs] cistern troughs.

cite v

To show, prove to (one).

1906 *DN* 3.131 **nwAR,** *Cite me* . . . In the common slang expression, "You'll have to cite me; I'm from Missouri." . . [*DN:* Spelled in the newspapers, "sight."] *Cite to* . . . To quote, cite. "Can you cite me to a single case of the kind?" **c**1970 Halpert *Coll.* **wKY,** You'll have to cite me (show me), 'cause I'm from Missouri.

citireen n [?Alter of *citizen*]

1929 *AmSp* 5.17 **Ozarks,** Citireen . . . An old resident, an old-timer, an old fogy of either sex, particularly one familiar with all the old signs and superstitions. 1953 Randolph *Down in Holler* 235 **Ozarks,** Citireen [sɪtɚ'in].

citizen n

1 A fellow, guy, esp one considered rough or uncouth.

1897 Clover *Paul Travers' Adv.* 67 (*DAE*), Paul was left in inky darkness with two presumably tough citizens. 1910 Raine *B. O'Connor* 41 (*DAE*), Chinks, greasers, and several other kinds of citizens driftin' that way. **c**1960 *Wilson Coll.* **csKY,** Citizen . . . Usually a tough one, a tough guy.

2 A local resident, in contrast with a newcomer.

1911 *DN* 3.537 **eKY,** Citizen . . . A native of a locality, as distinguished from a new-comer. 1917 *DN* 4.409 **KY, wNC,** Citizen . . . A native: as distinguished from *furriner.*

citron n

1 also *wild citron:* =**mayapple.** [From the shape and color of the fruit]

1937 *Torreya* 37.97, *Podophyllum peltatum* . . . The fruit, citron, Missouri. 1940–41 Cassidy *WI Atlas,* Citron—may-apple. 1966–69 *DARE* (Qu. S4, . . *May apple*) Infs **GA7, IL110, PA78,** Wild citron. 1973 *DARE* File **WI,** Citron—the May-apple, *Podophyllum peltatum.*

2 See **citron melon.**

3 =**least bittern.**

1917 *Wilson Bulletin* 29.2.78, *Ixobrychus exilis.*—Citron (undoubtedly a corruption of bittern), near Alexandria, Va.

citronalis n [Prob alter of *citronellas*]

A **horse-balm 1** (*Collinsonia canadensis*).

1884 Baldwin *Yankee School-Teacher* 105 **VA,** Aunt Molly . . bent tenderly over the citronalis, which flung her the sweetest of greetings.

citron grass n

=**sweet flag.**

1953 Piercy *Shaker Cook Book* 235 **OH,** Sweet flag is the root of citron grass and is related to the spice Calamus mentioned in the Scriptures.

citron melon n Also *citron*

A white-fleshed cultivated variety of the watermelon (*Citrullus vulgaris*).

1806 (1905) Clark *Orig. Jrls. Lewis & Clark Exped.* 4.175, The substance is about the consistancy of the rind of a citron Mellon and ¾ of an inch thick, yellow celindrick, and regularly tapering. 1876 Hobbs *Bot. Hdbk.* 24, Citron melon, variety of watermelon, Citrullus vulgaris. 1950 *WELS (Kinds of melons)* 2 Infs, **WI,** Citron; 1 Inf, Citron—resembling lemons; 1 Inf, Citron—green rind, white center; 1 Inf, Citron, not edible as fresh, used for pickles and jellies. 1965–70 *DARE* (Qu. I26, . . *Kinds of melons*) Infs **CA36, CT6, 16, IN34, NJ8,** Citron melons; **LA40,**

MA6, 55, SC57, Citrons; (Qu. I4, . . *Vegetables* . . *less commonly grown*) Inf **MO8,** Citron; (Qu. I53, . . *Fruits*) Infs **MN29, MA5,** Citron.

city bird See **city sparrow**

city bug n [**bug** n[2]]

A person from the city.

1936 *AmSp* 11.275 **eTN,** City bug. A person who lives in the city. 1940–41 Cassidy *WI Atlas,* City bug—one from the city, as seen by farmers. 1967–69 *DARE* (Qu. HH2, . . *A citified person*) Infs **CT28, MO38,** City bug.

city cracker See **cracker 2**

city jake n [Joc alter of *country jake* (at **country** n B2a)]

1966–70 *DARE* (Qu. HH2, *Names and nicknames for a citified person*) Infs **DC8A, IA3, MD20, TX95,** City jake.

city light n

The low beam of a headlight.

1950 *WELS Suppl.* 4 Infs, **Milwaukee WI,** Low beams on a car are called city lights. 1965–70 *DARE* (Qu. N10, . . *The bright and dim lights on a car*) Infs **IL66, 69 , 85, 87, TN33, 34, 36, WI71,** City lights; **IL78, 83, NJ36, TN31, TX53,** Country lights and city lights.

city sparrow n Also *city bird, town sparrow* **chiefly S Midl, esp KY, SC**

=**English sparrow.**

1962 Imhof *AL Birds* 495, *Passer domesticus* . . *Other Names:* . . Town Sparrow. 1965–70 *DARE* (Qu. Q21, . . *Kinds of sparrows*) Infs **AR5, KY76, SC32, 34, 57, TX99,** City sparrow; (Qu. Q22, *Joking names or nicknames for the common sparrow*) Infs **KY31, 43,** City sparrow; **KY9,** City bird; **VA52,** City spars [sic].

‡city squash n *joc*

1949 McDavid *Coll.* **cnNY,** From a retired male farmer, 85 yrs: Depreciatory term—a *city squash* as contrasted with a *country pumpkin* (bumpkin).

civer See **cover**

civerlize See **civilize v 1**

civet cat n

1 A cacomistle.

1852 in 1854 U.S. War Dept. *Explor. Red River* 200 **LA,** *Bassaris Astuta.* Licht. Civet cat. [Found at] Cross Timbers. 1917 *Animals of Amer.* 108 (*DA*), The name Civet Cat applied to this animal is really a misnomer, as the Civet Cats are found only in the Old World, but this name has been used locally in the West in place of the more proper one of Ring-tailed Cat. 1961 Douglas *My Wilderness* 96 **AZ,** The Mexican wolf, the civet cat, the badger, and the gray fox are there too.

2 also *civet (kitty), civit cat;* infreq pronc-sp *civits cat:* =**skunk. chiefly west of Missip R** See Map Cf discussion in 1973 Allen *LAUM* 1.321, and see also **civvy cat, civic cat**

1950 *WELS (The skunk)* 1 Inf, **WI,** Civet cat; 1 Inf, Civits cat. 1956 Ker *Vocab. W. TX* 196, Black and white striped animal that makes a bad odor—civet cat [4 infs] . . civit cat [1 inf]. **c**1960 *Wilson Coll.* **csKY,** Civet-cat (or civvy-cat) . . . A name for skunk; very rarely heard. 1962 Atwood *Vocab. TX* 54, Animal with the bad odor . . . A few informants use *civet cat* (6[%]) and *civvy cat* (2.2[%]), although some state that this means a different kind of varmint. 1965–70 *DARE* (Qu. P26, . . *A*

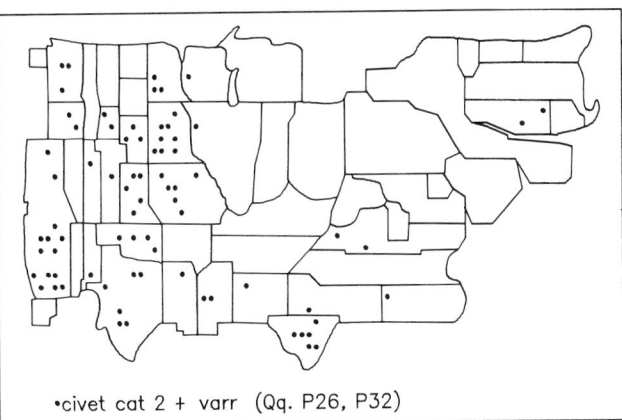

•civet cat 2 + varr (Qq. P26, P32)

skunk) 65 Infs, **chiefly west of Missip R**, Civet cat; **FL**27, **IA**36, **KS**18, **MO**39, **WA**22, Civet; **CA**91, Civet kitty; (Qu. P32, . . *Other kinds of wild animals*) Infs **CA**52, **FL**7, 35, **IA**8, 14, **VA**8, Civet cat. **1970** Tarpley *Blinky* 151 **neTX**, *Civet cat* is generally defined as a small cat-like animal with spotted yellowish fur and dreaded because of the musklike scent it excretes; nevertheless, three informants in adjoining counties in the western half of the region give this name in answer to the question which specifies that the animal is black and white. **1971** Bright *Word Geog. CA & NV* 185, *Civet (civic / civvy) cat* 13% [of infs, rural areas] . . . This was described as smaller than *skunk* or *polecat*, which were generally considered synonymous, although a few thought *skunk* the larger of the two.

3 See quot. [?Erron]

1968 *DARE* FW Addit **CA**105, Civet ['sɪvət] cat — raccoon.

civet kitty See **civet cat 2**

civey cat See **civvy cat**

civic cat n [Alter of **civet cat**] **West**
=**civet cat 2.**

1956 Ker *Vocab. W. TX* 196, Civic cat [2 infs]. **1966** *DARE* (Qu. P26, . . *Skunk*) Inf **WA**18, Civic ['sɪˌvɪk] cat. **1970** Tarpley *Blinky* 150 **neTX**, Civic cat [less than 1.5% of infs]. **1971** [see **civet cat 2**].

civil adj

1 Of people: polite, courteous, quiet. [Cf *OED civil a.* 11, 12] **chiefly Sth, S Midl**

1806 (1970) Webster *Compendious Dict.* 52, *Civil* . . civilized, kind, obliging, polite. **1902** *DN* 2.231 **sIL**, *Civil* . . . Polite; obligingly polite; gentle mannered. **1907** *DN* 3.221 **nwAR, sIL**, *Civil* . . . Polite. **1916** in **1944** *ADD* 115 **sMts**, *Civil* . . . Quiet, peaceful. **1940** *AmSp* 15.447 **eTN**, *Civil*. Quiet and reserved. 'Lizzie's very civil.' **1944** *PADS* 2.41 **wNC, sVA**, *Civil* . . . Respectable; considerate of others. **1952** Brown *NC Folkl.* 1.527, *Civil* . . . Polite, courteous, kind.

2 Of weather: fine, temperate. **N Atl** [*DNE* 1887 →]

1930 *AmSp* 5.389 **N Atl** [Among fishermen], *Civil morning* . . . A fine morning. **1942** Berrey–Van den Bark *Amer. Slang* 3.1, Beaut of a day, clever-, civil or daisy day, dazzler, *a fine day*. **1957** Beck *Folkl. ME* 169, A good day is referred to as either a "proper," a "civil," or a "pretty" day.

civilize v [civil 1 + -ize]

1 also pronc-sp *civerlize*: To exchange civilities or greetings with. **Sth** *?obs*

1843 (1973) Porter *Big Bear AR* 98 **NC**, Arter howd'ying and civerlizin' each other I sot down. **1864** Nichols *40 Yrs.* 1.387 **Sth**, When people salute each other at meeting, he [=the Southerner] says they are howdyin' and civilizin' each other.

2 To spruce up in dress. Cf *DS* W38

1920 Hunter *Trail Drivers TX* 442, We would civilize up a bit when we went to a dance, that is, we would take off our spurs and tie a clean red handkerchief around our neck.

civilly adv Cf **purely**

See quots.

1919 *DN* 5.33 **seKY**, *Civilly* . . . Certainly, positively, indeed. "I jist civilly had to git up an' light a rag fer home." **1923** *DN* 5.242 **KY**, *Civilly* . . . Intensive for *certainly, surely.* "I civilly just had to hand him my hardware" (gun).

civit cat, civits cat See **civet cat 2**

civvy cat n Also sp *civey cat*, pronc-spp *ciffy cat, chivy cat* [Alter of **civet cat**] **chiefly SW, Cent**
=**civet cat 2.**

1927 *DN* 5.473 **Ozarks**, *Civvy-cat* . . . A civet, a little striped skunk, very similar to the phoby-cat of the Southwest. **1944** *PADS* 2.55 **cMO**, *Civvy-cat* . . . A species of skunk. **1950** *PADS* 14.20 **SC**, *Civey cat* . . . The polecat. From *civet cat.* **1956** Ker *Vocab. W. TX* 196, Chivy cat [1 inf]. **c1960** Wilson *Coll.* **csKY**, *Civvy-cat.* **1962** [see **civet cat 2**]. **1965**–**70** *DARE* (Qu. P26, *Names and nicknames . . a skunk*) 18 Infs, **chiefly SW, Cent**, Civvy cat; **OK**52, Ciffy ['sɪfɪ] cat — throws the same scent, smaller than a skunk and spotted; (Qu. P32, . . *Wild animals*) Infs **OK**42, **TX**67, Civvy cat. **1971** [see **civet cat 2**].

cla See **declare**

clabber n[1], also attrib [Abbr for **bonnyclabber**]

1 also *clabber milk*: Sour milk that has thickened or curdled. **chiefly Sth, Midl and West** See Map and Map Section Cf

clabber n[1] (Note: the form *clabbered milk* is used throughout the US) Also called **bonnyclabber, clotted milk, loppered milk, thick milk**

1828 Webster *Amer. Dict.*, Clabber or bonny-clabber . . . Milk turned, become thick or inspissated. **1838** Gilman *S. Matron* 52 **SC**, When I told Aunt Patty that Southern folks ate clabber, she rolled up her eyes. **1905** *DN* 3.75 **nwAR**, *Clabber* . . . Sour milk composed of curd and whey which are not yet separated. **1906** *DN* 3.131 **nwAR**, *Clabber (milk).* **1908** *DN* 3.299 **eAL, wGA**, *Clabber.* **c1937** in **1972** *Amer. Slave* 2.246 **SC**, Didn' get nothin from de dairy but old clabber an dey been mighty thankful to get dat. **1946** *PADS* 5.15 **VA**, *Clabber.* **1949** Kurath *Word Geog.* 70, *Clabber* is the Southern expression, *clabber milk* that of the South Midland. *Clabber* is in general use south of the Pennsylvania state line; it is used to some extent even in the southern counties of Pennsylvania. The Ohio Valley from Wheeling downstream has *clabber*, less commonly *clabbered milk*, and the latter expression seems to have replaced *lobbered milk* in the Western Reserve of Ohio. **1950** *WELS* (*Milk that becomes thick as it turns sour*) 6 Infs, **WI**, Clabber. **1954** *Harder Coll.* **cwTN**, Clabber milk. **c1960** *Wilson Coll.* **csKY**, Clabber. **1965**–**70** *DARE* (Qu. H59, *Milk that becomes thick as it turns sour*) 348 Infs, **chiefly Sth, Midl and West**, Clabber; 52 Infs, **chiefly Sth, Midl**, Clabber milk; (Qu. H58, *Milk that's just beginning to become sour*) 13 Infs, **chiefly S Midl**, Clabber; **AK**8, **MO**21, Clabber milk; **MD**30, Turning to clabber; (Qu. BB50a) Inf **CA**7, Hot clabber milk. **1970** *DARE* Tape **VA**112, She was a-makin' biscuits out of clabber. **1973** Allen *LAUM* 1.291, Southern *clabber* . . occurs with strength in the dominantly Midland areas of southern Iowa and Nebraska. *Clabber milk* and *clabbered milk* . . retain strength in basically Northern speech territory in the U[pper] M[idwest].

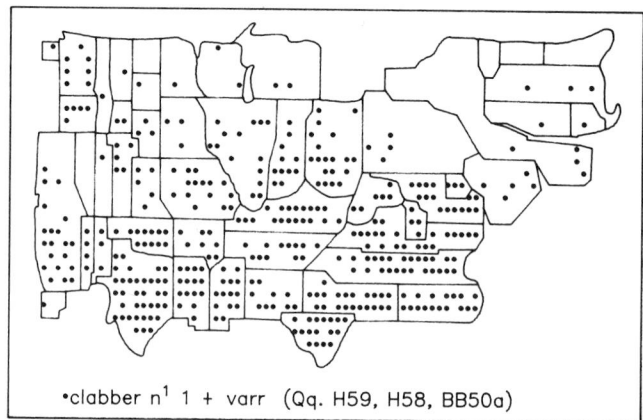

•clabber n[1] 1 + varr (Qq. H59, H58, BB50a)

2 See **clabber cheese.**

3 in var fig phrr: See quots.

1918 *DN* 5.33 **seKY**, *Clabber* . . . Used in the figure, "Steve ups with a cant-hook an' knocks him as cold as clabber." **1966**–**68** *DARE* (Qu. B3, *If a day is very hot, you say it's* _____) Infs **SC**9, Hot enough to melt clabber; **SC**51, Hot as hell / hades!, hot enough to fry eggs, hot enough to melt clabber [heard].

clabber v [**clabber** n[1]]

1 Of milk, to sour and become thick; to form curds; to cause to sour or thicken; also fig.

1880 Webster *Amer. Dict.*, *Clăb'ber* . . . To turn thick in the process of souring, — said of milk. **1905** *DN* 3.75 **nwAR**, *Clabber* . . . To become thick after souring. 'Goat's milk clabbers almost as soon as you set it down.' **1908** *DN* 3.299 **eAL, wGA**. **1938** Rawlings *Yearling* 222 **FL**, She needed rain-water, too, to clabber the milk. The milk turned rankly sour in the heat but would not clabber. **1949** Gipson *Hound-Dog Man* 115 **csTX**, It were enough to clabber a kid's blood. **1967**–**68** *DARE* (Qu. H58, *Milk that's just beginning to become sour is* _____) Infs **PA**74, **WI**20, Clabbering; **CA**39, Starting to clabber; **MO**38, First curdles then clabbers.

2 also *clobber*, and usu with *up*: To become cloudy, cloud over.

1933 Williamson *Woods Colt* 47 **Ozarks**, Looks like it might be clabberin' up to rain. **1950** *WELS Suppl.* **nwWI**, When clouds begin to form, you say it's "clabbering up." [Inf first heard this in California.] **1953** [see **clabber** adj]. **1954** *Harder Coll.* **cwTN**, Clabber: v. To cloud over. **1959** *VT Hist.* new ser 27.130, Clabber up . . . To look like clabber. It's *clabbering up* to rain. **1967**–**69** *DARE* (Qu. B6, *When* *clouds begin to increase)* Infs **OR**1, **TX**22, Clabbering up; (Qu. B5, *When the weather looks as if it will become bad)* Inf **PA**216, Clobbering up for a rain. **1967** *DARE* FW Addit **CO**21, It's going to clabber up and rain. **1972** *Atlanta Letters* **GA,** It looks like it will clabber up and rain.

clabber adj Also *clabbered, clabbery* [**clabber** n¹ **1**] Cf **mackerel sky**
Cloudy, threatening to storm; also fig.

> **1940** FWP *Guide OH* 78, A clabbered sky (mackerel sky, says the New Englander), smoke settling instead of rising, gnats bunching and dancing in mid-air . . mean wet weather. **1953** Randolph *Down in Holler* 235 **Ozarks,** Clabber . . . Cloudy, as when the sky *clabbers* up before a storm. But sometimes it is used figuratively. Asked what he thought about the prospects of war, a backwoods congressman said, "It looks mighty *clabber* to me." **1954** *Harder Coll.* **cwTN,** *Clabber* . . . Cloudy. **1969** *DARE* (Qu. B8, *When clouds come and go all day)* Inf **AL**54, Clabbery cloudy; (Qu. B10, . . *The long trailing clouds high in the sky)* Inf **AL**54, Clabbery [ˈklæbɚɪ].

clabber n² For varr see quots [Abbr and alter of *klaberjass*]
The card game klaberjass or one similar to it.

> **1932** *Collier's* 11 June 7/1 **NYC,** I go around to Good Time Charley's little speak in West Forty-seventh Street . . . and play a little klob with Charley. **1952** Culbertson *Card Games* 278, Well-known in central Europe, Klaberjass reached the United States early in this century via the immigrant colonies along the Eastern seaboard. In the writings of Damon Runyon and others, the game is frequently mentioned, as Klob, Clob, Klab, Kalaber, and, often, Kalabriàs. *Ibid* 282, *Clabber*—This is a game similar to Klaberjass. **1968** *DARE* (Qu. DD35, . . *Favorite card games)* Inf **IN**42, Clabber—like euchre but with more cards; **IN**49, Clabber. **1974** Gibson *Hoyle* 64, *Clabber,* or *clob, clobber, clobberyash, clubby:* Names for the game now called *Klaberjass.*

clabber biscuit n
A biscuit made with **clabber** n¹ **1.**

> **1939** Harris *Purslane* 2 **cNC,** Dele hastily made a fire, fried some shoulder, baked clabber biscuits, and left Nannie Lou to tend the oven. **c1960** Bailey *Resp. to PADS 20* **KS,** Clabber biscuit. **1966** *DARE* Tape **FL**36, [FW:] She mentions the fat clabber biscuits; what are these? [Inf:] They're biscuits made with clabber. **1966–68** *DARE* (Qu. H19, . . *Biscuit)* Inf **FL**19, Clabber biscuits; **FL**36, Fat clabber biscuit.

clabber cheese n Also *clabber, clabbered cheese, clobber cheese* **chiefly Sth, S Midl** Cf **bonnyclabber cheese**
Cottage cheese.

> **1904** *DN* 2.417 **nwAR,** *Clabber-cheese* . . . Sour milk cheese. **1946** *PADS* 5.15 **VA,** *Clabber cheese* . . Cheese made of the drained curd of sour milk; not common. **1948** Davis *Word Atlas* App. **ceIL,** 1 inf, *Clobber cheese.* **1949** Kurath *Word Geog.* 71, In the Southern area *curds (curd cheese)* and *clabber cheese* are widely used, . . the latter in the greater part of the Carolinas and in parts of West Virginia. **c1960** *Wilson Coll.* **csKY,** *Clabber cheese,* formerly the commonest name; few people made this cheese and regarded it in general as cheap stuff, anyway. A few older people still use the word. **1961** Folk *Word Atlas N.LA* 191, *Cottage cheese* . . in the South *curds, curd cheese,* and *clabber cheese* are common. **1961** Sackett–Koch *KS Folkl.* 112, *Clabber cheese* . . . Sometimes used. **1961** *PADS* 36.7 **sLA,** *Clabber cheese.* **1962** Atwood *Vocab. TX* 61, The most widespread of these [regional usages] is *clabber cheese . .* , which occurs in all parts of the state, but which is strikingly characteristic of older informants. **1965–70** *DARE* (Qu. H60, *The lumpy white cheese that is made from sour milk)* 11 Infs, **chiefly S Midl, Mid Atl,** Clabber cheese; **GA**17, **MD**44, Clabber; **KY**63, **MO**17, **NE**8, Clabbered cheese. [9 Infs old, 7 mid-aged] **1967** Faries *Word Geog. MO* 105, *Cottage cheese* . . Of the regional terms . . two seem to have significance in Missouri: the South and South Midland *clabber cheese* (130 occurrences) and the Midland *smear case.* **1971** Wood *Vocab. Change* 44 **Sth,** A kind of cheese once made at home is sometimes known as *clabber cheese* . . . *Cottage cheese,* however, is the first choice of almost half of the informants. **1973** Allen *LAUM* 1.293, *Clabber cheese,* a South Midland and southern Atlantic coastal term, is reflected in the U[pper] M[idwest] with a few instances along the Des Moines River in southern Iowa and near the Missouri River in southwestern Iowa and southeastern Nebraska.

clabber-cod n [**clabber** n¹ + **cod** n¹ **1**]

> **1953** Randolph *Down in Holler* 104 **Ozarks,** Country boys sometimes speak of having the *clabber-cod,* some condition of the testicles associated with venereal disease.

clabberd See **clapboard**

clabbered See **clabber** adj

clabbered cheese See **clabber cheese**

clabbergrass n
=**cleavers.**

> **1940** Clute *Amer. Plant Names* 259, *Galium aparine.* Clabber-grass.

clabberhead n [Engl dial *clabber* mud]

> **1940** *AmSp* 15.215 **wFL,** *Clabberhead* . . a foolish or dirty talking person.

clabber milk See **clabber** n¹ **1**

clabbermouth n

> **1944** Wellman *Bowl* 15 **KS,** This old clabber-mouth robbed me on them sand hills he sold.

clabbermouthed adj

> **1940** *AmSp* 15.221 **cwTX,** And if you think you are not getting a 'square deal,' why then 'don't be clabber-mouthed (silent) about it.'

clabber pine n
An unidentified tree; see quot.

> **1965** *DARE* (Qu. T16, *What kinds of trees are "special" around here?)* Inf **FL**18, Clabber pine.

clabber-spoon n [Prob from the spoon-shaped petal]
=**butterfly pea a.**

> **1944** AL Geol. Surv. *Bulletin* 53.135, (*Clitoria Mariana* L.) ("Clabber-spoon.") . . . Flowers . . are . . upside down.

clabber up See **clabber** v **2**

clabbery See **clabber** adj

clabbid, clabboard, clabbord See **clapboard**

clabby adj [Alter of *clabbery*]

> **1966** *DARE* (Qu. H58, *Milk that's just beginning to become sour)* Inf **NC**44, Clabby.

clabo(a)rd See **clapboard**

clack, at a adv phr [*clack* sharp sound of two objects striking each other]
At one time, in one group.

> **1958** *PADS* 29.30 **MO,** *At a clack* . . . Together; referring to the marbles (usually "two at a clack", sometimes three, rarely four) placed at one time in a *pink.*

clacker n [Imit]
1 A cheap metal token used as "scrip" instead of regular money.

> **1943** Korson *Coal Dust* 72 **sAppalachians,** The same colloquial terms were used for scrip and store orders, such as "stickers," "clackers," "flickers," and "drag." **1970** *Thompson Coll.* **cAL** (as of 1920s), Clacker . . a metal token good in trade at a company store.

2 pl: Teeth, esp false teeth. **chiefly Nth**

> **1950** *WELS* (*False teeth)* 1 Inf, **cwWI,** Clackers. **1965–70** *DARE* (Qu. X13b, *Joking names for false teeth)* 10 Infs, **Nth, esp NEast,** Clackers; **PA**115, Telly-clackers; (Qu. X13a, *Joking names . . teeth)* Inf **IN**75, Clackers.

3 See quot.

> **1967** *DARE* (Qu. W12b, *Metal pieces under the tips of shoes to prevent wear)* Inf **NY**10, Clackers.

clacky n
1 See quot.

> **1970** *DARE* (Qu. BB53b, . . *A doctor who is not very capable or doesn't have a very good reputation)* Inf **PA**237, Clackies.

2 See quot.

> **1970** *DARE* (Qu. H37, . . *Gravy)* Inf **VA**39, Clacky [ˈklæki]—hard, no-good gravy.

claggy adj [Engl dial and Scots *claggy* sticky, glutinous, muddy: see *SND* and esp *EDD* claggy adj 3] *arch*

> **1895** *DN* 1.386 **Sth,** *Claggy:* heavy (of bread, etc).

claik n [Scots: see *SND* claik n¹ **4**]

> **1959** *VT Hist.* new ser 27.130 **nVT,** Claik [klek] . . . A visit. Occasional along [sic] the Scotch.

clair See **clear**

clam n

1 The mouth.   Cf **clamshell**

1825 Neal *Brother Jonathan* 1.143 **CT**, Shet your clam, our David.
1833 Neal *Down-Easters* 1.93 **NEng**, Shet your clam! **1968–69** *DARE*
(Qu. X9, *Joking or uncomplimentary words for a person's mouth*) Infs
NY209, **PA148**, Clam.

2 in phr *happy as a clam* and varr: Exceedingly happy, very
content. [See quot 1945] **chiefly NEng**

1834 *Harvardiana* 1.121 *(DAE)*, He could not even enjoy that peculiar
degree of satisfaction, usually denoted by the phrase 'as happy as a
clam.' **1868** Saxe *Poems* 447 **VT**, Thy life is one of very little ease; /
Albeit men mock thee with their similes / And prate of being "happy as a
clam"! **1905** *DN* 3.11 **cCT**, Happy as a clam. . Also commoner, 'happy
as a clam at high water.' **1922** *DN* 5.165 **NH, CT**, Happy as a clam at
high tide, happy as a clam in the mud. . . Very happy. **1945** Colcord *Sea
Language* **ME, Cape Cod, Long Island**, *Clam, happy as a.* Alongshore,
this phrase is happy as a clam at high water; that is, when no enemy can
reach him. The landsman has abbreviated it to the meaningless happy as
a clam. **1968** *DARE* (Qu. GG29, *To be in a good or pleasant mood*) Inf
NC82, Happy as a clam in high water. **1975** Gould *ME Lingo, Clam,
happy as a*—The ultimate in jubilation and contentment. The full
expression is *happy as a clam* at high tide. When the tide is full, nobody is
digging clams.

3 See quot.

1970 *DARE* (Qu. DD4, *Moisture in the mouth*) Inf **NY241**, Clam (or
spit).

4 See **clam digger 2**.

5 A marble.

1973 Ferretti *Marble Book* 42, *Clams.* Marbles. *Ibid* 80 **NH**, Marbles
as a winter sport . . . Dig a hole at the base of a snow bank . . . The
marbles are here considered "clams" . . . The first person tosses his clam
toward the hole, drops it in the snow. . or . . rolls his marble [in a trench]
toward it . . . Cold hands a small price to pay for being a winning clam.

clam, clamb v See climb 1, 2d

clambake n, also attrib chiefly N Atl Cf bake n

A party or social gathering at which clams and other food are
prepared and eaten outdoors; the food prepared at such a gathering.

1835 *Vade Mecum* (Phila.) 5 Sep. 2/1 *(DA)* A Clam Bake—Our
curiosity [sic] has been gratified, as to the nature of the festival understood by this term. **1848** Bartlett *Americanisms* 82, Nearly 10,000
persons assembled in Rhode Island, for whom a *clambake* and *chowder*
were prepared. **1883** *Pall Mall Gaz.* 24 Sept 12/1, At a recent . . festival
in Connecticut a gigantic clambake was cooked which was 25 ft. long and
10 ft. wide, and consisted of 2,000 ears of corn, 600 pounds of lobster,
600 pounds of fish, 1,000 chickens, innumerable oysters and clams, two
barrels of sweet potatoes and two of the ordinary kind, and the whole
topped off with two immense plum puddings and 150 water melons.
1890 McAllister *Society* 186 **RI**, All pronounced this kind of clambake
picnic a species of *fête* not to be indulged in knowingly a second time.
1905 *DN* 3.5 **cCT**, *Clam-bake* . . . A kind of picnic where the principal
part of the meal consists of clams baked on the ground. **1939** Wolcott
Yankee Cook Book 23 **RI**, It has been said that the chief contribution of
the Indians to the New England pioneers was the clambake. **1965–70**
DARE (Qu. H45, *Dishes made with meat, fish, or poultry*) Infs **CT29**,
NY65, **RI9**, Clambake; (Qu. FF2, . . *Kinds of parties*) Infs **GA11**, **PA113**,
RI11, 13, Clambakes; (Qu. FF16, . . *Local contests or celebrations*) Infs
NJ6, **RI15**, Clambakes; (Qu. FF1, . . *A "social"*) Inf **NY109**, Clambake;
(Qu. H70, *When people bring baked dishes, salads, and so forth to a
meeting-place and share them together*) Inf **NY210**, Clambake.

clambed See climb 2d

clam broth n

1973 Ferretti *Marble Book* 36, Other kinds of glass marbles sought by
collectors are the . . *clam broth.*

clam catcher n

A New Jerseyite.

1845 *St. Louis Reveille* (MO) 14 May 2/4, The inhabitants of . . New
Jersey . . [are called] Clam-catchers. **1888** Whitman *November Boughs*
70, Those from Maine were call'd Foxes; New Hampshire, Granite Boys;
. . New Jersey, Clam Catchers. **1949** *AmSp* 24.27, *Clam-catcher* for a
Jerseyman.

clam chaser n

=**sanderling**.

1956 *AmSp* 31.186 **NC**, Clam chaser [=] Sanderling . . . A clam would
not seem to require much chasing, but the birds do seek small ones
moved about by receding waves.

clam cracker n

=**cownose ray**.

1881 Ingersoll *Oyster-Industry* 242, *Clam cracker*, a fish, a species of
ray, *Rhinoptera quadriloba*, which molests the oyster beds. (Savannah.). **1966** *DARE* (Qu. P4, *Saltwater fish . . not good to eat*) Inf **GA11**,
Clam crackers.

clamded See climb 2d

clam digger n

1 A nickname for a person from var northeastern towns.

1949 *AmSp* 24.26 **ME**, A citizen of . . Wells is a *Clam-digger.* **1968**
DARE Tape **NY44**, People who come from Canarsie are called clam
diggers.

2 pl; also *clams*: The hands.   *joc*

1969 *DARE* (Qu. X32, *Joking or uncomplimentary words for the hands*)
Inf **VT16**, Clam diggers; **WA11**, Clams.

clam duck n

=**black duck 1**.

1946 Hausman *Eastern Birds* 138, *Anas rubripes* . . Clam Duck. **1955**
Forbush–May *Birds* 59, *Anas rubripes rubripes* . . . *Other names:* . .
Clam Duck. **1955** *MA Audubon* 39.314, *Black Duck* . . . Clam Duck
(Mass.).

clam gun n chiefly Pacific NW joc

A shovel or other tool used to dig clams; any digging tool.

1927 *AmSp* 2.392 [Vagabond argot], A short-handled one [=shovel] is a
clam-gun. **1937** C.R. Snow "The Elements of Clam Gunnery" *Alaskan
Sportsman* Feb 13 (Tabbert *Alaskan Engl.*), A clam gunner . . . is a
person adept in the pursuit of clams with a clam gun. The latter
instrument usually is a shovel of the common or garden variety. **1938**
(1939) Holbrook *Holy Mackinaw* 259 **Nth**, *Clam gun.* A shovel. **1940**
White *Wild Geese* 204 **NW** (as of 1890s), "I'll fetch the clam gun," said
Len. He slipped down through the cabin and galley and into the cargo
hatch, to return with an implement that elsewhere would be called a
potato fork. **1940** (1951) FWP *Guide OR* 372, The small sharpened
shovels used to dig blue clams, along the river are called "clam guns."
1942 *AmSp* 17.221 **Nth** [Logger talk], *Clam gun.* A shovel, used by a
gopher, gandy dancer, or road monkey. **1958** McCulloch *Woods Words*
Pacific NW. **1959** *AmSp* 34.77 **nCA** [Logging], *Clam gun* . . . A
shovel. **1966–67** *DARE* Tape **WA20**, Clam gun—it's really a shovel,
about 5 inches of blade, about 5 inches wide and a handle about 30
inches long; **WA17**, You have a fork made like a hoe with long prongs on
it . . . clam gun.

clam it v phr Cf clam n 1

1969 *DARE* (Qu. X10b, *To tell a person to stop talking—not very
politely*) Inf **NC61**, Clam it; (Qu. GG23c, . . *To tell someone to be
patient*) Inf **NY190**, Clam it.

clammed See climb 2d

clammish adj

=**clammy**.

1969 *DARE* (Qu. HH24, *Somebody who doesn't talk very much, who
keeps his thoughts to himself*) Inf **CA113**, Clammish.

clam mouth n

1967 *DARE* (Qu. HH24, *Somebody who doesn't talk very much, who
keeps his thoughts to himself*) Inf **NY12**, Clam mouth.

clammy adj

Close-mouthed, silent.

1967 *DARE* (Qu. JJ44, *Expressions about someone who can be trusted
to keep a secret: ". . he'll _____."*) Inf **PA32**, Stay clammy.

clamoun n

=**calico bush 1**.

1900 Lyons *Plant Names* 209, *K[almia] latifolia* . . . Mountain Laurel,
. . Clamoun, . . Wicky. **1960** Vines *Trees SW* 828, *Kalmia . . latifolia*
. . . Vernacular names are . . Calico-bush, Clamoun, and Southern
Mountain-laurel.

clamp v[1] **chiefly W Midl** See Map Cf **band** v[1] **2**

To castrate a young animal by means of a clamp or rubber band; hence vbl n *clamping.*

 1965–70 *DARE* (Qu. K70, *Words . . for castrating an animal*) Infs **AR**40, **IN**27, 59, **KY**58, 64, 72, **MO**11, Clamp; **OH**35, **SC**57, Clamp [FW: Conv]; **AL**2, Clamp—new term, use rubber band when they are small; **DC**5, Clamp—use rubbers [=rubber bands] now; **IL**125, Clamp —calves only; **IN**30, Clamp—calves and sheep; **KY**6, Clamp—present usage; **KY**86, Clamp—nowadays; **MO**38, They clamp 'em now so much; **TN**30, Clamp—used if castration is done by applying clamps; **MA**25, Nowadays they talk about clamping; **PA**132, Clamping—a different process, used in warm weather.

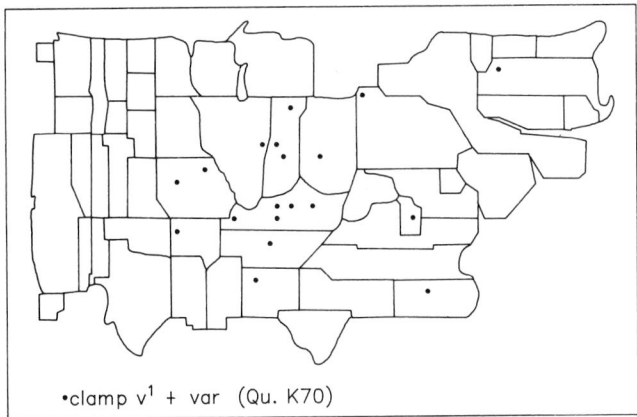

•clamp v[1] + var (Qu. K70)

clamp v[2] [Engl dial: cf *EDD clamp* v.[4], *OED clamp* v.[3]]
=**clomp 1.**

 1968 *DARE* (Qu. Y25, *To walk heavily, making a lot of noise*) Inf **NY**122, Clamping ['klæmpən].

Clamper n, also attrib **chiefly nCA** *hist*

A nickname for a member of **E Clampus Vitus;** as *Clampers,* the organization.

 1928 Ritchie *Forty-Niners* 248 **nCA** (as of 1850s), Membership in the 'Clampers'—convenient foreshortening of the hog-Latin name—became a patent of nobility in the chivalry of the mines. *Ibid* 249, On the steps of the abandoned Methodist chapel the most bellows-lunged Clamper appears with an eight foot tin horn—the "hewgag." **1941** (1948) Dane *Ghost Town* 237 **nCA,** The Clampers! Say, I can see them yet . . . Their mascot was a billy-goat, tastefully gilded, and their banner a hoop skirt with the words on it: *This is the flag we fight under.*

clampers n pl

1 The teeth.

 1968–70 *DARE* (Qu. X13a, *. . Joking names . . teeth*) Infs **CA**42, **NC**88, Clampers.

2 also *clamps, climpers:* See quot.

 1906 *DN* 3.131 **nwAR,** *Clamp(er)s* . . . In the expression, "put the clampers on," meaning to check, to restrain. "Don't you worry; I'll put the clampers on him." . . [Also] *climpers.*

clam pie n **N Atl**

A pie made with clams.

 1844 in 1965 *AmSp* 40.128, Oh! they had a clam pie Over There! **1939** Wolcott *Yankee Cook Book* 64, Cape Cod Clam Pie . . . 2 quarts soft-shelled clams . . cornstarch . . pastry . . salt and pepper. **1968–69** *DARE* (Qu. H45, *Dishes made with meat, fish, or poultry*) Infs **NJ**23, **NY**43, 45, 220, Clam pie. **1979** Flagg *Cape Cod Cooking* 41, *Clam pie*—Here again, there are many, many different recipes—one crust, two crust, pie crust or biscuit crust, potatoes or no potatoes, etc.

clamps See **clampers 2**

clam roller n

 1983 *DARE* File **csME,** A "clam roller" is synonymous with a "clam creel," locally. It is the lath container rounded in design for gathering clams . . and probably got its name because clams are literally *rolled* in it when they are washed at the tide's edge. The laths are spaced about an inch apart, so the water flows thru', & the mud, etc., is washed out.

clamshell n, also pl **NEng** Cf **clam 1**

The mouth; the jaws.

 1834 Smith *Letters Jack Downing* 104 **ME,** Says I squire Dudley shut up your clack, or I'll knock your clam-shells together pretty quick'. **1848** Bartlett *Americanisms, Clam-shell.* The lips, or mouth. There is a common though vulgar expression in New England, of "Shut your *clam-shell,*" that is, Shut your mouth, hold your tongue. **1867** Lowell *Biglow* 2d ser 19 **'Upcountry' MA,** You don't feel much like speakin', / When, ef you let your clamshells gape, a quart o' tar will leak in. **1904** *DN* 2.424 **Cape Cod MA,** *Clam-shell . . .* Mouth.

clamshell orchid n

A tree orchid *(Encyclia cochleata)* native to Florida.

 1933 Small *Manual SE Flora* 392, Lip much shorter than the sepals and petals; blade very broad, concave and clamshell-like . . . *Clamshell-or-chid.* **1953** Greene–Blomquist *Flowers South* 22, *Clam-Shell Orchid* . . . A distinctive species by its shell-like, purple lip. **1976** Bailey–Bailey *Hortus Third* 1268.

clang See **cling** v

clap n

1 also *claptrap:* The mouth. [Cf *clapper* the tongue of a talkative person, *OED* 1638 →]

 1966–68 *DARE* (Qu. X9, *Joking or uncomplimentary words for a person's mouth*) Infs **NJ**9, 39, **OH**16, Clap; **NY**166, Claptrap; (Qu. II22, *. . To tell somebody to keep to himself*) Inf **ME**19, Keep your clap still.

2 See quot.

 1968 *DARE* (Qu. W12b, *Metal pieces under the tips of shoes to prevent wear*) Inf **IA**27, Claps, toe claps.

clapboard n, v Usu |'klæbə(r)d, -bord|; also |'klæp,bord| Pronc-spp *clabberd, clabbid, clab(b)oard, clab(b)ord* **scattered, but chiefly NEast** See Map

A Forms.

 1656 in 1892 Dedham MA *Early Rec.* 3.140, Granted to Daniell Morse two Seders to make Clabbord. **1756** (1901) Hempstead *Diary* 678 *(DAE),* I was at Daughter Starr's puting in some Clabords in ye Leantoo Chamber. **1887** Kirkland *Zury* 537 **IL,** Clap-board . . . Roofing made by splitting logs. **1902** *DN* 2.229 **sIL,** When *boards* are used to side a house they are called clabberds. **1906** *DN* 3.116 **sIN,** *Clab-board.* **1907** *DN* 3.221, **nwAR, sIL,** *Clapboard . . .* Pronounced [klæbərd]. **1941** *LANE* Map 350 *(Clapboards),* [Throughout eNEng, [klæb(o)ədz, -b(o)ədz]; in wNEng, [klæb(o)ərdz, -b(o)ərdz]; **MA, CT, RI,** [klæp-]]. **1949** *AmSp* 24.107 **GA, SC,** *Claboard fence . . .* Paling fence (generally of wood split with a froe). **c1960** Wilson *Coll.* **csKY,** *Clapboard* ['klæbəd] or ['klæp,bord]. **1975** Gould *ME Lingo* 50, *Clabbids*—Clapboards.

B As noun.

Also attrib: A board used for covering the roof or sides of a house, each board overlapping the one below it; collectively, *clapboarding.*

 1632 (1790) Winthrop *Jrl.* 1.31 **MA,** It was for the warmth of his house, and the charge was little, being but clapboards nailed to the walls. **1843** (1916) Hall *New Purchase* 52 **IN,** The roof was thick ricketty shingles, called clapboards. **1904** *DN* 2.417 **nwAR,** *Clapboard . . .* Hewn board used, as a rule, to shingle roofs and sides of buildings. **1965–70** *DARE* (Qu. D27, *Strips of wood used to cover the outside of a frame house*) 180 Infs, **chiefly NEast, scattered east of Missip R,** Clapboards; **MS**18, **MO**7, **NJ**30, **NY**200, **OH**51, Clapboard; **NJ**1, Clapboard siding; **NJ**38, Clapboarding; **NY**152, **OK**9, ['klæbə-dz]. **1967** LeCompte *Word Atlas*

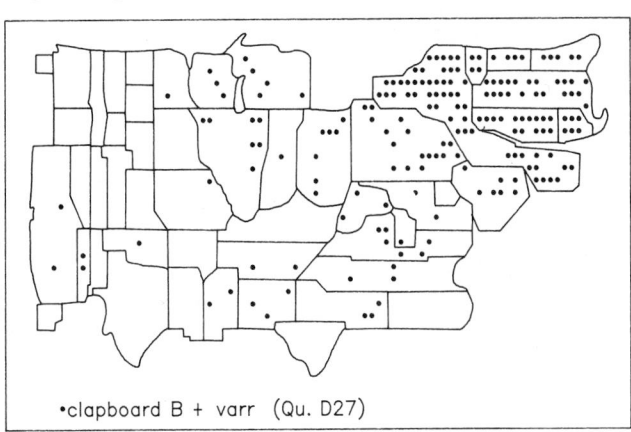

•clapboard B + varr (Qu. D27)

114 **seLA,** Overlapping boards on outside of house . . [1 inf responded] clapboards. **1968** *DARE* Tape **CA**97, The clapboarding on the front porch was planed, which I understand is unusual . . but the original planed clapboards are still there; **IN**30, These stones [of the chimneys] were held together with that [chinking] and . . were made quite tall on the house so the sparks wouldn't fall down on the clapboard [klæbord] roof . . when they were made from sawmill slabs. **1973** Allen *LAUM* 1.176 **Upper MW,** Both *weatherboards* and the common eastern *clapboards* seem to be declining in favor of the generic *siding.*

C As verb.

To apply or furnish with clapboards; hence ppl adj *clapboarded.*

1637 in 1861 New Plymouth Colony *Records* 12.26 **MA,** The house to be . . clap boarded w[i]thin. **1705** in 1878 Boston Registry Dept. *Records* 3.172 **MA,** [To] board or clabboard the outside of said house. **1840** (1841) Dana *2 Yrs.* 223 **MA,** The sides of the between-decks were clapboarded. **1905** *DN* 3.6 **cCT,** *Clapboard* [klæbord] . . . To cover with clapboards. **1931–33** *LANE Worksheets* **cCT,** Clapboarded . . . The barn is all clapboarded; **eMA,** Clapboarded fence—fence with overlapping boards.

clapbrush See **clapweed**

clape n [Echoic] **esp NY**
=flicker.

1844 DeKay *Zool. NY* 2.192, The Clape, or Golden-Winged Woodpecker, *Picus Auratus* . . . is called *High-hole, Yucker, Flicker.* **1850** Cooper *Rural Hours* 99 **cNY,** A handsome Clape, or golden-winged woodpecker, a pretty wood-pewce [sic: for *pewee*] and a very delicate little black-poll warbler. **1917** (1923) *Birds Amer.* 2.164, [*Colaptes auratus*] The Flicker is the most interesting bird of all the Woodpeckers . . . Another person hearing the loud one-syllable call across the fields or the swamp lot has named the bird the Clape. **1949** Sprunt–Chamberlain *SC Bird Life* 330, *Colaptes auratus auratus* . . . it has another call resembling the word "clape," which is a local name for the bird in some places. **1968** *DARE* (Qu. Q17, . . *Woodpeckers*) Inf **NY**58, [klep].

claphat adj [See quot 1950] *derog*
Hasty, hurried.

1909 *S. Atl. Qrly.* 8.47 **seSC** [Gullah], A woman, hasty and sudden in speech and deed, is resentfully styled *"dat clap-hat bitch!"* **1950** *PADS* 14.20 **SC,** *Claphat* . . . Hasty, reckless. A woman hasty in speech and deed is frequently referred to as "that claphat wench," as one who claps on her hat and goes in haste. Derogatory. **1965** *Dict. Queen's English* 1 **NC,** *Claphat* (for hasty): He always acted in a claphat manner.

clap in, clap out n Also occas *slap in, slap out,* infreq *snap out* and *clap out* **esp Sth, S Midl, NEng**
A young people's match-making game played in various ways; see quots.

1894 Frederic *Marsena* 9 **nNY,** He never shrank from bearing his part in . . "clap in and clap out," . . or whatever other game was to be played, and he went through the kissing penalties and rewards involved without apparent aversion. **1899** Champlin *Young Folks' Games* 195, *Clap in and clap out* . . . The boys stand each behind a chair, and the girls go into another room. One of the players, who acts as keeper of the door between the two rooms, asks one of the boys to choose a girl. The doorkeeper then opens the door and calls the girl thus chosen, who must sit down in one of the chairs. If she sit in front of the boy who chose her, he kisses her and she keeps her seat, but if not, all the boys clap their hands as a sign that she is wrong, and she must leave the room again. **1905** *DN* 3.94 **nwAR,** *Slap in, slap out* . . . The name of a game called in New England 'clap in, clap out.' **1907** *DN* 3.183 **seNH,** Clap in, clap out. **1908** *DN* 3.299 **eAL, wGA,** Clap-in, clap-out. **1908** Lincoln *Cy Whittaker* 175 **MA,** The children played "Post Office" and "Copenhagen" and "Clap in, Clap out," while the grown folks looked on. **1915** Masters *Spoon River* 202 **IL,** I went to the dances at Chandlerville, / And played snap-out at Winchester. **1953** Brewster *Amer. Nonsinging Games* 154 **IN,** *Clap In, Clap Out* . . . All the girls in the group leave the room together. After having selected his girl, each boy stations himself behind an empty chair. Each girl, in turn, is called back into the room. As she enters, every boy in the room tries to get her to sit in his chair. If she seats herself in the right one, the boy gets another chair and sits down beside her. If she sits in the wrong one, all the boys clap their hands and she must guess again. This continues until all the players are paired off for the evening. **1964** Wallace *Frontier Life* 88 **swOK** (as of early 1900s), On rainy days which confined us indoors, the teacher let the older ones play "Clap In and Clap Out," which produced gales of laughter if the boy guessed wrongly which girl had chosen him to sit by her, and the girls could clap their hands

when he had to go out again. **1965–70** *DARE* (Qu. EE33, . . *Outdoor games*) Infs **TX**79, **VT**5, Clap in, clap out; **MN**37, Clap out; (Qu. EE2, *Games that have one extra player . . the extra one tries to get a place*) Inf **FL**18, Clap in, clap out. **1966–70** *DARE* Tape **AL**3, Slap in, slap out . . . The boys go out and the girls stay in, or vice versa . . . All the girls stand behind the chairs . . . There is a keeper at the door who lets 'em in, one at a time . . . [Each girl's] chair is named and it's got to match. [The boy's name, fruit, candy, etc, may be used. When the boy sits in the wrong chair everyone claps.]; **TX**78, Clap in, clap out. **1968** *DARE* FW Addit **VA**12, *Clap In and Clap Out*—Players sat in a circle. One player left the room. Meanwhile the remaining players choose one of their group. After choosing, they clapped. He returned and when he sat by the chosen person, they clapped again.

‡**clapjack** n [Var of **flapjack** 1]
1940–41 Cassidy *WI Atlas,* Clapjack. Pancake.

clap out See **clap in, clap out**

clapper n

1 A member of a religious group which uses handclapping as a regular feature of its services.

1967 *DARE* (Qu. CC4, . . *Nicknames . . for various religions or religious groups*) Inf **MI**67, Some of the Negro churches (religions) have been called 'clappers' and 'shouters' and 'stompers'.

2 A member of a community of mixed race living in Schoharie County, New York. [Prob from the family name *Clapper,* but see quot 1937]

1914 *Jrl. Amer. Folkl.* 27.305 **ceNY,** In certain communities whose members are designated as "sloughters," "clappers," and "honies," according to the locality in which they live, the folk-tales have degenerated to a degree which renders them unfit for repetition. **1937** Gardner *Folkl. Schoharie* 43 **ceNY,** "Clapper" is the term which many Schoharians apply to a person suffering from the "clap," an Elizabethan word which, according to the New English Dictionary, is obsolete. But in the Schoharie Hills it is still in current use and, furthermore, forms part of the name of a settlement known as "Clapper Hollow." **1963** Berry *Almost White* 23 **ceNY,** In Schoharie County there are several groups of supposedly Indian ancestry—the Honies, . . the Clappers of Clapper Hollow, and the "Arabs" of Summit. *Ibid* 34, It is quite common for whole communities to be known by the family name which is most prevalent among them. For instance, there are the Van Guilders and the Clappers in New York.

3 See **clapper rail.**

clapperclawing vbl n [Scots and Engl dial; *EDD* clapperclaw "to scratch, maul, fight in an unskillful manner; *gen.* used of women"]
A fight, beating; a tirade.

1834 *Life Andrew Jackson* 118 **TN,** That numbers must kick the bucket in this clapperclawin was a ded sartinty. **1939** FWP *Guide TN* 134, A tirade is a "clapper-clawing."

clappered milk n [Alter of *clabbered milk;* cf *bonnyclapper* at **bonnyclabber**]
=**clabber** n[1] **1.**

1973 Allen *LAUM* 1.292 **MN,** Clappered milk [1 inf].

clapper rail n Also *clapper* [From its call]
A rail (here: *Rallus longirostris*). Also called **marsh hen, meadow hen, mud hen, pull-doo, sage hen, saltwater hen, sedge hen, tomtit**

1813 (1824) Wilson *Amer. Ornith.* 7.117 **Atlantic,** The Clapper Rail, or, as it is generally called, the Mud-hen, soon announces its arrival in the salt marshes, by its loud, harsh and incessant cackling. **1858** Baird *Birds* 747, *Clapper Rail; Mud Hen* . . . The bird is . . an inhabitant of the seacoast . . abundant from New Jersey to Florida. **1946** Hausman *Eastern Birds* 237, Northern Clapper Rail *Rallus longirostris crepitans* —Other Names—Common Clapper, Marsh Clapper. **1966–70** *DARE* (Qu. Q7, . . *Game birds*) Infs **SC**21, **VA**79, Clapper rail; (Qu. Q10, . . *Water . . and marsh birds*) Infs **VA**79, 84, Clapper rail. **1967** *Weston Chron.* (MO) 8 Sept 5/6, There will be no open season on king or clapper rails, but . . Virginia and yellow rails may be hunted in Missouri from September 1 to November 9.

‡**claprack** n
=**stoneboat.**

1970 *DARE* (Qu. L57, *A low wooden platform used for bringing stones or heavy things out of the field*) Inf **CA**204, Claprack.

claptrap See **clap 1**

clapweed n Also *clapbrush* [*clap* gonorrhea]
=Mormon tea.
   1937 *Torreya* 37.95, *Ephedra* spp . . . Clapweed, southern Utah and Nevada . . . Most of the vernacular names . . refer to a supposed value for the treatment of venereal diseases. **1945** McAtee *Nomina Abitera* 7, Clapbrush (Death Valley region . .), clapweed (southern Utah, Nevada . .). **1970** Correll *Plants TX* 83, *Ephedra antisyphilitica* . . . Clapweed.

clapwort n [*clap* gonorrhea]
=squawroot 1.
   1828 Rafinesque *Med. Flora* 248, *Clapwort*. Astringent, antiseptic and syphilitic, deemed in the West a specific for gonorrhea and syphilis. **1876** Hobbs *Bot. Hdbk.* 24, *Clapwort* . . Orobanche Americana.

clar adj, adv See **clear**

clar v See **clear, declare**

clarances See **clearance(s)**

clare adv See **clear**

clare v See **declare**

clarin' See **clearing**

clark n, v Usu |klɑrk| Also infreq *clarke* Pronc-spp for *clerk* See Pronc Intro 3.I.1.f *old-fash*
   1634 in 1894 Watertown MA *Records* 1.1.1 [The] Towne Clark . . shall keep the Records and Acts of the Towne. **1843** (1916) Hall *New Purchase* 141 **IN**, By authority of this here license from the clark of our court. **1899** (1912) Green *VA Folk-Speech, Clark* . . . Writer of a court. Clerk. Clarke. **1911** *DN* 3.537 **eKY**, *Clerk* . . . Pronounced clärk. **1940** *AmSp* 15.46, *Clerk* [klɑ(r)k] is peculiar in American dialect to Kentucky. **1944** *PADS* 2.18 **sAppalachians**, Clark [klɑrk]: *n.* and *vb.* A clerk; to clerk.

clarry n[1] See **clary** n[1]

clarry n[2] See **clary** n[2]

clart v [Scots and nEngl dial *clart* smear with dirt, befoul]
   1 See quot.
   1944 *PADS* 2.28 **eKY**, *Clart* [klɑrt] . . to defecate . . . Rare.
   2 To adhere.
   1903 *DN* 2.350, *Clart* . . . To stick.

clart n [**clart** v **1**]
   1944 *PADS* 2.28 **eKY**, *Clart* . . . Feces . . . Rare.

clarty adj Also *clearty* [**clart** v **2**]
   See quots.
   1896 *DN* 1.414 **cNY**, *Clarty* . . sticky: said of soil that sticks to the plough. **1902** (1968) Clapin *Americanisms, Clearty*. A Scotch word sometimes heard in sense of sticky, as of soil that sticks to the plough.

clary n[1] Also sp *clarry* [Scots; see *SND clary 1*]
   1936 *AmSp* 11.191 **swWY**, *Clarry* or *clary*. Dressings for bread, as butter, jam, honey, jelly, etc.

clary n[2] Also sp *clarry* [*OED* c1485 →]
   A *sage,* usu *Salvia sclarea,* but also *S. pratensis.*
   1873 in 1976 Miller *Shaker Herbs* 154, *Clary—Salvia sclarea* . . . Clarry. **1973** Hitchcock–Cronquist *Flora Pacific NW* 407, Meadow clary, meadow see-bright . . *S[alvia] pratensis* . . . Clary, clear-eye, see-bright . . *S[alvia] sclarea.*

clash n [Scots and nEngl dial; see *EDD, SND*] *arch*
   1899 (1912) Green *VA Folk-Speech, Clash* . . . Idle talk.

clatch See **klatch** n

clatchy adj [Scots and Engl dial *clatch* mess; cf *SND, EDD*]
   1911 *DN* 3.542 **NE**, *Clatchy* . . . Cluttered. "This room is as clatchy as a second-hand store."

clatter n
   1 A blow. [Yorkshire dial; *EDD clatter* sb.[1] 2 "A blow accompanied by a rattling sound from a fall or otherwise"] *obs*
   1859 Taliaferro *Fisher's R.* 119 **nwNC** (as of 1820s), I seen it in his foxy looks that he 'tended to gin me a clatter.
   2 See quot. [Scots and nEngl dial]
   1899 (1912) Green *VA Folk-Speech, Clatter* . . . Idle gossip. Fast and

idle talk; rattle with the tongue; confusion; talk or gabble. Confused noise.
   3 in phr *at one clatter:* All at once, at one time. [Cf Scots *in a clatter* at once, immediately]
   1906 *DN* 3.131 **nwAR**, *Clatter* . . . In the expression, "at one clatter," i.e., at one stroke. **1914** *DN* 4.104 **KS**, *Clatter* . . . In the phrase *at one clatter,* at one time. **1923** *DN* 5.204 **swMO**, *Clatter* . . . All at once. "I bust down two wheels at one clatter."
   ‡**4** Transf: a crowd, a group of people.
   1967 *DARE* (Qu. LL10, *"They made too much noise, so he sent the whole _____ home"*) Inf **WA**30, Clatter.
   ‡**5** pl, also *clatterers:* False teeth.
   1968–70 *DARE* (Qu. X13b, *Joking names for false teeth*) Inf **CA**196, Clatterers; **OH**70, Clatters.

clatterbones n pl [Scots]
   Bones rattled together as for a percussion instrument.
   1960 Williams *Walk Egypt* 94 **GA**, The girls switched by, tongues going like clatterbones, never seeing the boys, of course.

clatterbox n [**clatter 2** + **box** n **5a**; *EDD* 1892]
   1969 *DARE* (Qu. HH7a, *Someone who talks too much or too loud*) Inf **GA**72, Clatterbox.

clatter brain n attrib [**clatter 2**; cf *EDD* clatter-brains "a noisy do-nothing person"]
   1939 *AmSp* 14.90 **eTN**, *Clatter brain.* Gossiper. 'The old clatter brain woman is busy.'

clatterer n
   1 See quot.
   1967 *DARE* (Qu. HH11b, *Someone who is too particular or fussy . . a woman*) Inf **IA**3, Clatterer.
   2 pl: See **clatter 5.**

clatter goose n [Engl dial]
   =brant 1.
   1917 (1923) *Birds Amer.* 1.161, *Branta bernicla glaucogastra* . . Clatter Goose.

clatterment n Pronc-sp *klediment* [Cf Scots *clatter-traps, clutterment;* see also *OED cladment*] Cf **accoutrements**
   See quots.
   1895 *DN* 1.371 **TN Mts**, *Clatterments:* belongings, accoutrements. "Sam, what did you do with all the clatterments that belong to the mowin' scythes and the harness?" **1979** Cash *Among Klediments* 12 **eTN, swVA**, A klediment can be almost anything that has earned a right to be a part of things close to you. It can be precious antique furniture gathered from grandmother, pieces of china, little handmade doilies, the straw mats on your floor, or the priscilla curtains you made yourself. A klediment can be a thing you love . . . A klediment can be a thing you just won't throw away . . . A klediment can be a person dear to you.

clatter up v phr Cf **clatty 1**
   1970 *DARE* (Qu. Y37, *To make a place untidy or disorderly*) Inf **TX**76, Clutter up or clatter up.

clatterwhacking n Also sp *clatterwacking* [**clatter 2**]
   A clatter, racket; noisy talking.
   1851 Burke *Polly Peablossom* 148 **MS**, I hearn the darndest clatterwacking and noise in the road behind us. **1859** (1968) Bartlett *Americanisms, Clatterwhacking.* A clatter, racket. **1946** *PADS* 6.9 **swVA**, *Clatterwhacking* . . . Clatter, palaver.

clatty adj [Scots, Ir, and nEngl dial; cf *EDD, SND*]
   1 Cluttered, messed up; slovenly; confused. Cf **clatter up**
   1899 (1971) Farmer *Americanisms, Clatty.*—Dishevelled; untidy. A similar meaning attaches to the word in Lowland Scotch. **1905** *DN* 3.61 **NE**, *Clatty* . . . Cluttered, confused. **1911** *DN* 3.542 **NE**. **1916** *DN* 4.273 **NE**, *Clatty* . . . Mussy, slovenly. Reported by one contributor as brought from eastern Pennsylvania. "You are such a clatty dishwasher." [*DN*: . . Reported from Mass. among immigrants from N. Irl . .] **1946** *PADS* 6.9 **swVA**, *Clatty* . . . Cluttered.
   2 See quot. [Cf *EDD* clatty 3, "Of weather: wet, rainy."]
   1911 *DN* 3.542 **NE**, *Clatty* . . . Meaning damp, or moist.

clavergrass See **cleavers**

clavers n pl Cf *DS* EE41, NN12b
   1952 Brown *NC Folkl.* 1.527, *Clavers will get you, the* . . . This would appear to be a threat, perhaps like *lay-overs to catch meddlers.*

claw v

1 with *off* or *out:* To get out of an embarrassing or threatening situation; to make excuses. [See quot 1945]

1838 Kettell *Yankee Notions* 28 **NEng,** Thinks I to myself . . "there's no clawing off, this hitch. I *must* begin." **1890** *DN* 1.18 **seNH,** *Claw out:* make excuses, get out of an embarrassment, and the like. Elsewhere 'claw off' is said. **1892** *DN* 1.215 **NC, TN,** *Claw out.* **1945** Colcord *Sea Language* **ME, Cape Cod, Long Island,** *Claw off.* To beat off a lee shore; hence, to get out of a threatening situation.

2 See quot.

1914 *DN* 4.70 **ME, nNH,** *Claw* . . . Start, hurry. "Claw fer hum!"

3 See quot.

1970 *DARE* (Qu. Y3, *To say uncomplimentary things about somebody*) Inf **CT43,** Claw.

claw cactus See **crab cactus**

clawfish n [Folk-etym for *crawfish*]
=**crawfish** n **B1.**

1966–69 *DARE* (Qu. P19, . . *Small, freshwater crayfish*) Infs **ME20, MA32,** Clawfish. **1966** *DARE* Tape **NC1,** Down in South Florida in the Gulf they have a fish . . that's something similar to a lobster only he don't have the big claw—which the proper name of it is a crawfish but they really call him a lobster . . . This Clawfish doesn't have it.

claw-off n [**claw** v **1**]

1929 *AmSp* 5.129 **ME,** It was only a "claw-off" meant it was only an excuse.

claw off v, **claw out** See **claw** v **1**

clawt See **cloth**

claw thumper See **crawthumper**

claybank adj, often used absol [From the color] **formerly more widespread, now chiefly Sth, S Midl** See Map
Of a horse: yellowish-brown or cream-colored.

1853 *Oregonian* (Portland) 5 Nov. 1/6 *(DA),* Well, ses he, getting off an hitching his ole clay-bank to a swinging limb, 'count me in.' [**185!** *Putnam's Mag.* 5.188/2 **NH,** I mounted a clay-bank colored nag, and rode to the hunt.] **1885** Murfree *Prophet of Smoky Mts.* 108 **wNC, eTN,** The mountain colt, a clay-bank, with a long black tail full of cockleburrs, . . reared violently under the surprise of the lash. **1907** *DN* 3.229 **nwAR, seMO. 1908** *DN* 3.299 **eAL, wGA. 1910** Mulford *Hopalong* 117, I'll whale th' stuffin' outen you, you wall-eyed claybank! **1940** FWP *Guide TX* 451, Old-timers still remember him as a boy who . . rode a clay-bank pony into town to get his mail. **1944** Wellman *Bowl* 101 **KS,** Trotting his handsome claybank horse along the road. **1950** *WELS* (*Kinds of horses . . according to their colors*) 1 Inf, **WI,** Claybanks; (*Horse of a dirty white color*) 1 Inf, Some call them a "claybank." **1965–70** *DARE* (Qu. K38, *A horse of a dirty white color*) 30 Infs, **chiefly Inland Sth, TX, wNC, sIN,** Claybank; (Qu. K39, . . *Names . . for horses according to their colors*) Infs **AR15, FL12, GA1, IL87, IN32, MS53, NC33, 36,** Claybank; [**PA163,** Claybank colored].

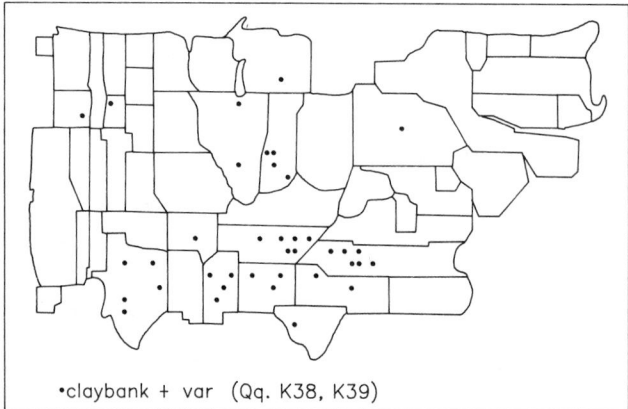

•claybank + var (Qq. K38, K39)

clay dauber n Also *clay wasp*
=**mud dauber 1.**

1851 *DeBow's Rev.* 11.56 **LA,** *Mason Wasp* or clay dauber. **1965–68** *DARE* (Qu. R20, *Wasps that build their nests of mud*) Infs **MS63, NY107, SC11,** Clay dauber; **MD18,** Clay wasp.

clay-eater n **chiefly S Atl** *usu derog* Cf **dirt-eater**

1 One who eats clay; by ext, a poor or low-class person; hence adj *clay-eating.*

1841 Simms *Kinsmen* xiv *(DAE),* He was a little, dried up, withered atomy,—a jaundiced 'sand-lapper' or 'clay-eater' from the Wassamasaw country. **1854** Pike *Ida May* 440 **NC, SC,** The poor whites . . are called "clay-eaters" in Carolina . . . [S]ubsisting principally upon "turpentine whiskey," and appeasing their craving for more substantial food by filling their stomachs with a kind of aluminous earth which abounds everywhere, they are squalid and emaciated to a frightful degree; with yellowish, drab-colored complexions, eyes that are dull and cold as the eyes of a dead fish, and faces whose idiotic expression is only varied by a dull despair, or a devilish malignity . . . They . . are looked down upon by the negroes with a contempt which they return by a hearty hatred. **1863** Gilmore *S. Friends* 43, A woman whose dress and appearance designated her as one of the species of "white trash" known in North Carolina as "clay-eaters." *Ibid* 47, It was fortunate for the clay-eating feminine that her conversation had disgusted us. **1896** Harris *Sister Jane* 31 **GA,** They were as lanky and as lousy-looking a set as I had ever seen—pale, cadaverous, and careworn—veritable "clay eaters," as I have heard sister Jane call them. **1950** Faulkner *Stories* 587 **MS,** He say it was already two of um waiting there then. Clay-eaters. *Ibid* 593, Coming down here every year and staying two months, without nothing to see and nowheres to go except these clay-eaters and Nigras. **1950** *PADS* 14.20 **SC,** *Clay-eater, chalk-eater* . . . One who eats clay, especially a kind of clay found in Aiken, Calhoun, Greenwood, and probably other counties. Said to cause a bluish complexion. Addicts moving away from the source of supply have it shipped to them. In default of clay they eat starch or chalk. **1963** Berry *Almost White* 35, In a remote quarter of South Carolina the mixed-bloods are known as "Clay-eaters."

2 A person from or resident of North Carolina, South Carolina, or Georgia.

1891 Maitland *Amer. Slang Dict., Clay-eater . . ,* a native South Carolinian. The "poor-whites" in some of the back counties of that State eat considerable quantities of soft, white clay. **1939** *AmSp* 14.26 **SC** ["A Citadel Glossary"], *Clay-eater* . . . A native of the low-country of South Carolina or Georgia. **1949** *AmSp* 24.26, Nicknames for the people of the different states . . . *Clay-eater* for any kind of Carolinian. **1970** Major *Afro–Amer. Slang, Clay-eater:* a native of the lowlands of Georgia and South Carolina.

clayer n [Cf *EDD clay* sb.[1] 4]
A clay marble.

1955 *PADS* 23.13 **OH, cwAL,** *Clays* . . . Marbles made of red clay or brick; also *clayers.*

clayey See **clayie**

clay gall See **gall 2**

clayie n Also sp *clayey* [*clay* + -ie 3]
A small, cheap marble made of clay.

1958 *PADS* 29.31 **AR,** *Clayey.* **1967–68** *DARE* (Qu. EE6c, *Cheap marbles*) Infs **AK9, CA87, CO14, 21, 42,** Clayies. **1973** Ferretti *Marble Book* 42, *Clayeys.* Small marbles of clay. Never used as shooters but rather as target or object marbles. Held in low esteem.

clay, meaner than adj phr [Var of **dirt, meaner than**]

1968 *DARE* (Qu. HH22b, . . *A very mean person . . "He's meaner than _____.'*) Infs **OH71, 72,** Clay.

clay pea n **Sth**
An unidentified legume: see quots.

1908 *DN* 3.299 **eAL, wGA,** *Clay-pea* . . . A reddish variety of the cowpea. **1966–70** *DARE* (Qu. I20, . . *Beans*) Infs **NC15, SC19, 29, VA46,** Clay peas. **1971** *Foxfire* 5.1&2.101 **GA,** Ever'body planted these old clay peas. I ain't seen 'em in over twenty years. Th'seeds of 'em's about t'run out. People used t'always plant 'em in their corn field.

clay road n **scattered east of Missip R, esp S Atl** See Map Cf **sand-and-clay road**
An unimproved road on clayey ground.

1856 Olmsted *Journey Slave States* 63 **VA,** We picked our way . . through a deeply corrugated clay-road. **1891** *Century Illustr. Mag.* 41.483/1 **GA,** Flung as if by chance beside a red clay road . . a settlement appears. **1965–70** *DARE* (Qu. N27a, . . *Kinds of unpaved roads*) 29 Infs, **chiefly Sth, esp SC, GA, FL,** Clay road; **AZ11, SC57,** Red-clay road; (Qu. N23 . . *Kinds of paved roads*) Infs **AL47, FL31, NC79,** Clay (road).

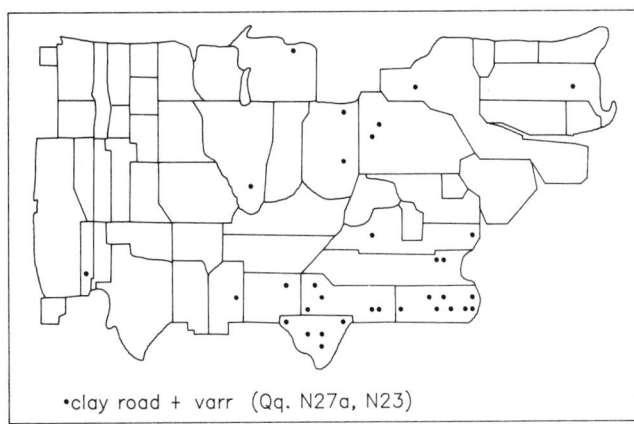

•clay road + varr (Qq. N27a, N23)

clay root n
See quots.
1945 Saxon *Gumbo Ya-Ya* 562 **LA,** Clay root: the exposed roots of a tree which has been blown out in such a way that a large hole is left where the tree was standing. **1952** Brown *NC Folkl.* 1.527 **c,eNC,** Clay-root . . . An uprooted tree. **1966** *PADS* 46.25 **cnAR,** *Clay root* . . . An uprooted tree that has fallen or blown over, leaving a large hole in the ground where it grew.

clay swallow n
Prob =**cliff swallow.**
1968 *DARE* (Qu. Q20, . . *Kinds of swallows*) Inf **IA22,** Clay swallow.

clay wasp See **clay dauber**

clayweed n
=**coltsfoot 1.**
1900 Lyons *Plant Names* 381, *T[ussilago] Farfara* . . Clay-weed. **1930** Sievers *Amer. Med. Plants* 24, Clayweed.

‡cleak n |klik| [Alter of *cleat*]
1970 *DARE* (Qu. W12a, *Heavy pieces of metal fastened under the soles of boots to keep them from slipping*) Inf **TN50,** Cleaks.

clean v
A Forms.
Usu *clean;* also, as pres and pple, *clen;* pronc-sp *clem.*
1936 *AmSp* 11.191 **swWY,** To *clen.* To clean. 'Clen the room.' **1940–41** Cassidy *WI Atlas* **swWI,** Git them clen up. **1968** Coatsworth *ME Memories* 155, Instead of cleaning up, you "clem" up.
B Sense.
With *out* or *up:* To leave or go — used imper.
1915 *DN* 4.182 **swVA,** *Clean out,* In the imperative, — go at once. **1946** *PADS* 6.9 **eNC** (as of 1900–10), *Clean up* . . . Begone! Used in driving away an unwanted dog.

clean adj
1 Wakeful. ?obs
1838 (1852) Gilman *S. Matron* 94 [Gullah], When sister Nelly put Maus Ben to bed de night o' de fire, Maus Ben ax 'em for sing one hymn for 'em, cause *he eye clean.* [Footnote: Watchful]
2 also *cleaned:* Dressed up, well-dressed. *among Black speakers*
1967–70 *DARE* (Qu. W38, *When a man dresses himself up in his best clothes*) Infs **FL51, MO29, MA8, NY240,** Clean; **MA8,** Cleaned; **DC11,** Clean as doctors' hands; (Qu. W37, *When a woman puts on her good clothes and tries to look her best*) Infs **AL60, FL51, MO29,** Clean. [All Infs Black] **1972** Claerbaut *Black Jargon* 60, *Clean* . . . well dressed, attractively attired: *The dude is clean, man.* **1977** Smitherman *Talkin* 257 [Black], *Clean,* dressed up. **1980** Folb *Runnin' Down* 109 **sCA** [Black], "I'm always high signin'. Got to be clean and ready!" *Ibid* 111, The cover term that is most often used to characterize the well-dressed person is *clean.* It carries with it the connotation of being not only sharply dressed . . but physically clean . . , neat . . , and dressed in your good clothes . . . And, in a real sense, clean is "untouchable." "You clean, nobody cain't touch you den. He's decked out clean, Clean, *Clean!* . . He's decked to kill." **1983** *DARE* File **LA,** Clean, among Black jazz musicians, means wearing a suit.

clean dozens See **dozens**

cleaned See **clean** adj 2

cleaner n
1962 [see **clearie**].

cleaners exclam Also *cleans, cleansies*
=**clearance(s).**
1963 *KY Folkl. Rec.* 9.65 **eKY,** To ask for permission to clean path of shooter to marbles being shot at: cleaners . . cleans . . cleansies.

cleanly adj
Clean, free from dirt.
1807 (1919) Bedford *Tour to New Orleans* 60 **VA,** Scrubbed off some of the dirt that abounded on our skin and exchanged our dirty, wet clothes for more cleanly. **1933** Rawlings *South Moon* 8 **FL,** The day's work had been cleanly. Feet were not soiled.

clean off v phr Also *cleanse up*
1968–69 *DARE* (Qu. B7, *When clouds begin to decrease*) Inf **MD32,** Cleaning off; **MA55,** [glɛnzəp].

clean one's clock v phr [Cf **clean the clock**]
To beat someone thoroughly.
1966–69 *DARE* (Qu. Y15) Infs **ND3, PA223,** Cleaned his clock; (Qu. Y16) Inf **WA1,** Cleaned his clock. **1980** De Vries *Consenting Adults* 109 **IL,** If you don't keep the hell away from Colly I'll clean your clock. I'll fix your wagon, but good.

clean one's plow v phr esp S Midl
To beat, whip, or punish someone.
1931 *AmSp* 7.121 **eID,** When some young man threatens *to clean your plow* he intends to defeat you in a fistic encounter. **1933** *AmSp* 8.1.48 **Ozarks,** *Clean his plow* . . . To beat, to injure severely. *Th' sheriff was goin' t' put Bill in jail, but Bill's pappy jest cleaned his plow with a rock.* **1949** *PADS* 11.5 **wTX,** *Clean (one's) plow:* . . . To whip. "I'll clean his plow for that." **1949** Webber *Backwoods Teacher* 88 **Ozarks,** I'm awful fed up with her. But I really cleaned her plow las' time she come buttin' in, actin' so stuck-uppity. **1954** Harder *Coll.* **cwTN.** **1960** Hall *Smoky Mt. Folks* 64 **eTN, wNC,** *Clean someone's plow:* to lick or punish: "I'll clean your plow (for that)" is a common warning to unruly children or other malefactors. **1962** Atwood *Vocab. TX* 77, *Clean your plow.* "Give a good whipping."

clean-peel n attrib
=**clearseed.**
1949 *AmSp* 24.107 **SC,** *Clean-peel peach* . . . Clearstone peach.

cleans See **cleaners**

cleanser n eNEng, esp Boston area
A dry cleaner.
1958 *AmSp* 33.158, The area in which *cleaning* and *cleaners* become *cleansing* and *cleansers* shows a striking coincidence with the major portion of the classic Atlas 'tonic' area of eastern New England . . . in Boston and its environs, extending westerly as far as Worcester, they [cleansers and cleansing establishments] began to appear in profusion. **1961** *AmSp* 36.225, In the area pivoting on Boston, *cleanser* seems to be a survival of a genuine regionalism, probably now found chiefly in the names of firms. *The Boston Directory* for 1907, pp. 2051–52, has the headings *Cleansers* and *Cleansing Works,* with not a cleaner in sight . . . The 1958 Yellow Pages for Portland, Maine, . . lists 10 cleansers to 18 cleaners. Other New England cities outside the *[tonic]* area have a much lower proportion: Burlington, Vt., one to 12; Concord, N.H., one to 11; Manchester, N.H., 4 to 21. **1966** *PMLA* 81.2.11, A Middle Western academician transplanted to MIT quickly learns to order *tonic* for his children, not *soda pop,* and to send his clothes to a *cleanser.*

cleanse up See **clean off**

cleansies See **cleaners**

clean the clock v phr Also *wipe the clock* (or *gauge*) [See quot 1958]
In railroading: to apply the air brakes, bringing the train to a sudden stop.
1929 *Bookman* 69.526, Should the engineer "wipe the gauge" or "clean the clock", it means that he has brought the train to a sudden stop by setting the air brakes. **1958** McCulloch *Woods Words* **Pacific NW,** *Clean the clock* — To apply emergency air brakes. This causes the indicator needle on the gauge (or clock) to drop back to zero and the

"clock" is then empty. **1962** *AmSp* 37.132 **nCA** [Logging railroads], *Clean the clock; wipe the clock; wipe the gauge.*

clean the plow off v phr Cf **clean one's plow**

1968 *DARE* (Qu. GG22b, *When you have come to the end of your patience, you might say, "Well, that certainly _____."*) Inf **VA**15, Cleans the plow off.

clean the ring v phr

In marble play: to remove all marbles from the playing circle by skillful shooting.

1966–67 *DARE* Tape **LA**8, You want get five games the quickest, that mean clean the ring, get all marbles outa the ring first; **NM**9, He can clean the ring, that is if he's smart enough to hit each time, but the first time he misses, then the boy who was standing in line next is the one who'd come next, and right on down the line.

clean thing n

A proper, honest, or honorable action.

1835 Crockett *Account* 193, I don't like it. It isn't the clean thing. **1849** (1914) Kingsley *Diary* 69 **CT**, The Directors are doing the clean thing, and for the first time have taken thier [sic] proper position in this company. **1905** *DN* 3.6 **cCT**, *Clean thing . . .* An honorable thing. **c1960** *Wilson Coll.* **csKY**, *The clean thing . . .* A straightforward, honest, correct action.

cleanup n, also attrib **West**

1 In mining: the process of separating grains of valuable minerals from an accumulation in a sluice or stamping mill.

1866 U.S. Congress *Congressional Globe* 18 June 3231/1 **NV**, When what they technically call in mining the clean-up comes, very often the clean-up exhibits the lofty sum of nothing, while thousands have been expended in the effort. **1953** Roy G. Southworth *Jessen's Weekly* July 16 *(Tabbert Coll.)* **AK**, Mine operators . . . were inclined to be a bit careless or too hurried at cleanup time to make certain that every bit of foreign matter had been removed from the gold. **1968** Adams *Western Words, Cleanup*—In mining, the process of periodically separating the valuable mineral from the gravel and rock which have collected in the sluices or at the stamping mill.

2 The minerals accumulated in such a process; the "take."

1871 Harte *East West Poems* 39 **West**, Which the truth not to wickedly stifle / Was his last week's "clean up,"—and *his all.* **1939** FWP *ID Lore* 243 [Mining jargon], *Clean-up*—mineral taken from a sluice-box. **1939** FWP *Guide AK* xl, *Clean-up . .* reckoning up the "take" at the end of a season, hence the "take." **1959** Hart *McKay's AK* 30, *Cleanup:* The amount of gold accumulated at the end of a season regardless of the method used to extract the ore. **1976** Hobbs *Tisha* 83 **AK**, He brought over another jar that was filled with nuggets ranging in size from pinheads to little pebbles. The two jars had their whole season's cleanup in them—maybe two thousand dollars worth of gold.

clear n, v, adv, adj Usu |klɪr|; also **chiefly Sth, S Midl** |klær, klɑr|, occas |klɛ(r), klær, klɜˑ|; occas |klɪən| Pronc-spp *clair, clar, cl'ar, cla'r, clare, clearn, cle'r*

A Forms.

1843 (1916) Hall *New Purchase* 227 **IN**, The nevy he runs clare up two miles. **1853** Simms *Sword and Distaff* 336 **SC**, I'm cl'ar to say that the charitablest thing you kin do, when you see how the cat wants to jump, is jest to open the window, and give her a cl'ar track. **1884** Harrison *Negro Engl.* 257 **SE**, Cla'r de track! *Ibid* 272, To cle'r up the th'oat = to clear the throat. **1892** *DN* 1.209 **MA**, *Clearn through* [klɪən] . . . Perhaps it is *clean* influenced by *clear* . . . [DN: Also at Southwest Harbor, Me., [klɪən] has been heard.] **1903** *DN* 2.309 **seMO**, *Clear* [klar] . . . I clar forgot my deeds. **1905** *DN* 3.58 **NE**, Rarely *n* is added in the phrase *clear(n) through.* **1907** *DN* 3.229 **Ozarks**, *Clear* [klar] . . . Quite, entirely. **1909** *DN* 3.352 **eAL, wGA**, *Clearn up* or *clean up* new ground is often heard. **1910** *DN* 3.456 **seKY**, Clear [klɑr]. **1923** *DN* 5.204 **swMO**, *Clair*, v. To clear, as land for cultivation. adj. Clear. **1926** Kephart *Highlanders* 79 **sAppalachians**, The weather clars. **1929** (1951) Faulkner *Sartoris* 235 **MS**, They was cl'ar of the niggers, and cussed him. **1933** Rawlings *South Moon* 105 **FL**, You'd of seed him clare. **1936** *AmSp* 11.12 **eTX**, The usual pronunciation . . is [bjɪɚ], [klɪɚ], etc., and [bjɪˑɚ], [klɪˑɚ], etc., with a raised and pinched [ɪ] which is not high enough to be transcribed [i]. In addition to this usual form, however, the words *beer, clear, . .* are occasionally heard with [ɛ]: [bjɛə], [bjɛɚ]; [klɛə], [klɛɚ]. **1942** Hall *Smoky Mt. Speech* 16, *Clear . .* [klɪɚ], [klɛɚ], [klɜˑ]. **c1960** *Wilson Coll.* **csKY**, *Clear . . .* Sometimes /klɑr/ or /klær/. **1967–68** *DARE* FW Addit **seAR**, [klɛr, klɛ:]; **GA**, [klɛr]; **seGA**, Cleared [klɛrd].

B As adj.

1 Of food or drink, esp of tea or coffee: plain; without anything added. **chiefly Nth** See Map *somewhat old-fash* Cf **bare-footed 1**

1856 (1862) Colt *Went to KS* 83 **NY**, Willie . . . said, "Willie *rather have white bread*," and the little fellow will eat it clear, and relish it much better than children with pampered appetites do their rounds of goodies. **1899** (1912) Green *VA Folk-Speech, Clear . . .* Free from dilution; as "*clear* brandy." **1950** WELS (Food taken alone: "Would you like milk or lemon for your tea?" "No, thanks, I'll take mine _____.") 17 Infs, **WI**, Clear. **1965–70** *DARE* (Qu. KK61) 26 Infs, **Nth**, Clear.

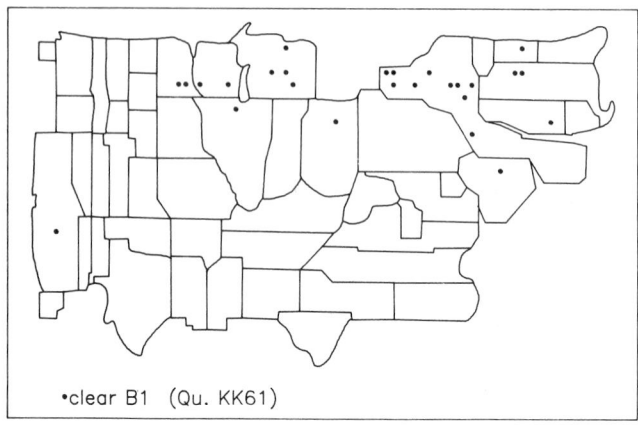

•clear B1 (Qu. KK61)

2 Pure, genuine. **NEng**

1835 Thompson *Advent. Peacock* 91 **VT**, "These Dutch minxes," coolly observed the latter, "are clear pepper-pots for grit." **1843** (1846) Haliburton *Attaché* (1st ser) 2.126 **ME**, All these forks and spoons, and plates and covers, and urns, and what nots, rael, genu*wine* solid silver, the clear thing, and no mistake. **1941** *LANE* Map 308 *(Genuine Maple Syrup)* 1 inf, **nwCT**, Clear.

3 See quot.

1951 *Eaton Coll.* **neWI**, Clear . . . Simplest, obviously best means (of doing something). That'd be the clear thing; if we had a [piece of equipment], that'd be the clear rig.

C As adv.

Prec an adj or v: Entirely, all the way.

1903 [see **A** above]. **1916** *DN* 4.342 **eOH, LA**, *Clear done.* Completely finished. **1965–70** *DARE* (Qu. LL28, *. . Entirely full: "The box of apples was _____."*) 19 Infs, **scattered N Midl, West**, Clear full; (Qu. JJ30a, *. . Expressions for forgetting something: "I _____."*) Infs **FL**14, **LA**2, **VA**38, 42, Clear forgot; (Qu. KK20b, *Something that looks as if it might collapse any minute: "Our old washing machine is _____."*) Inf **MD**24, Clear gone.

D As noun.

See **clearie**.

clearance(s) exclam, also in comb Also *clearings* Pronc-sp *clarances* [Also in Scots; see *SND*] Also called **clears, clearsies**

In marble play: used as a call claiming the privilege of removing obstacles between marbles; also the privilege itself.

1843 (1916) Hall *New Purchase* 42 **IN**, Man-lay!—Clearings!— 'fen!—knuckle-down! **1876** *N&Q* 54.348/2, *Fen (or Fend?).*—Boys in all parts of the United States employ this word, especially when playing marbles, to prevent any change in the existing conditions of the game, as, for instance, *fen-placings*, to prevent an alteration in the position of the marbles; *fen-clearances*, to prevent the removal of an obstacle; or *fen-everything.* Is this word an "Americanism," or did the children of the original colonists bring it with them across the Atlantic? **1892** *DN* 1.219 **DC**, When you said "fen clarances" your opponent had no right to *clear* away the rubbish lying between his marble and yours. The phrase "fen everything" deprived your opponent of all privileges, such as *clarances.* **1932–34** *Hanley Disks* **csCT**, *Clearance . . .* Marble-game call to gain right to remove matter [small stone, etc.] impeding clear shot. **1950** WELS (In playing marbles . . . *To get the right to do something*) 1 Inf, **WI**, Clearance; 1 Inf, No clearance. **1958** *PADS* 29.31 **WI**, *Clearance(s).* **1973** Ferretti *Marble Book* 42, *Clearance!* A defensive shout which permits one to clear away roughness or debris before shooting.

clearey See **clearie**

clear-eye n [Folk-etym of 15th cent form *clary*]
A **sage** (here: *Salvia sclarea*).
    1876 Hobbs *Bot. Hdbk.* 24, Clear eye, Wild clary, Salvia Verbenaca.
1973 Hitchcock–Cronquist *Flora Pacific NW* 407, Clear-eye . . S[alvia] sclarea.

clearie n Also sp *clearey*; also *clear, clearsie* [*clear* + *-ie*]
A transparent glass marble.
    1950 *WELS* (Marbles . . large ones) 1 Inf, ceWI, Clearies. **1958** *PADS* 29.32 WI, *Clearie* . . A clear glass marble, larger than the small clay marbles. **1962** *PADS* 37.1 cKS, *Clearies.* Transparent marbles of various colors. The manufacturer's designation for them is *marine puries. Clears.* Also *cleaners* or *clearies.* **1967–68** *DARE* (Qu. EE6d, *Special marbles*) Infs IN39, MI89, MA1, OR10, 14, SC65, Clearies; IL116, Clears. **c1970** Wiersma *Marbles Terms* NJ, cwNY (as of 1938–40), *Clearie* . . a clear glass playing marble. *Ibid* swMI (as of c1960), *Clearsie* . . a translucent playing marble of any color. **1971** Bright *Word Geog. CA & NV* 116 swCA, Clearies 1 [response]. **1973** Ferretti *Marble Book* 42, Cleareys. Clear glass marbles, often tinted and bubbly inside.

clearing n Pronc-sp *clarin'* S Midl
See quot 1929.
    1859 Taliaferro *Fisher's R.* 218 nwNC (as of 1820s), Nor could a man clear a piece of ground without inviting his neighbors, and having a "clearin'." They "swopped work." **1929** *AmSp* 5.17 Ozarks, *Clarin'* . . . A social gathering, the real purpose of which is to clear the host's land of timber and underbrush. People bring axes and saws and work hard all day, while the owner's part is to provide good food, and perhaps some whiskey for the frolic in the evening. **1954** *Harder Coll.* cwTN, Clearin' . . . A land cleaning bee; a group of men will gather to clean trees and shrubs, and sometimes stones from land.

clearings See **clearance(s)**

clear-mouth n Cf **chop-mouth**
A hunting dog that bays with a pure-toned voice.
    1970 *Natl. Geog. Mag.* 138.673/1 AR, A dog he described as a "clear-mouth" seemed to be the tenor of the pack.

clearn See **clear**

clearnut n attrib Cf **clearstone**
=**clearseed**.
    1949 *AmSp* 24.107 SC, Clearnut peach . . . Clearstone peach.

‡**clear quill** n [*clear* B2]
Something genuine.
    1940–41 Cassidy *WI Atlas*, The clear quill—pure, genuine.

clears exclam
=**clearance(s)**.
    1963 *KY Folkl. Rec.* 9.65 eKY, To ask for permission to clean path of shooter to marbles being shot at: . . clears.

clearseed n Also *clearseed peach* [*clear* free from contact + seed] chiefly Gulf States, S Atl See Map Also called **clearnut, clearstone**
A peach in which the flesh does not adhere to the seed; a **freestone**.

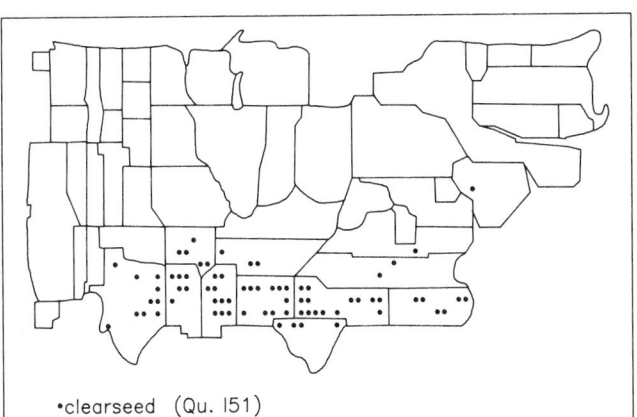

•clearseed (Qu. I51)

1908 *DN* 3.299 eAL, wGA, *Clear-seed* . . . A free-stone peach. **1939** Harris *Purslane* 74 cNC, Up the hill to the right was the peach orchard with its luscious yellow clear-seeds and big red presses flavoring the air. **1949** [see **clearstone**]. **1954** *PADS* 21.24 SC, *Clear seed* . . . Freestone as applied to peaches. **1962** Atwood *Vocab.* TX 60, *Freestone peach.* A considerable majority of Texas informants in all areas speak of a *free-stone peach* (72 [%]). *Clearseed* (15 [%]), which is rather concentrated in southern Arkansas, has invaded certain of the northern portions of Texas (Map 107). It is clearly archaic. **1965–70** *DARE* (Qu. I51, *The kind of a peach where the hard center is loose*) 73 Infs, **chiefly Sth**, Clearseed. **1971** Wood *Vocab. Change* 43, *Clear seed* is most frequently reported in Georgia, Alabama, and Mississippi.

clearsie See **clearie**

clearsies exclam
=**clearance(s)**.
    c1970 Wiersma *Marbles Terms* swMI, *Clearsies* . . in marble play: a call entitling a player to clear away some obstruction and thus make his shot easier.

clearstone n Also *clearstone peach* [*clear* free from contact + stone] **chiefly Sth** See Map *esp common among Black speakers*
=**clearseed**.
    1820 *Patterson's Almanac* 19 swPA, A small clearstone peach, the skin a greenish yellow, the flesh of the same colour; dry without much flavour. **1941** *LANE* Map 267 (*Freestone peach*) 1 inf, cNH, [kɬɪə] stone. **1949** Kurath *Word Geog.* 72, *Clear-seed peach* and *clear-stone peach* [are characteristic] of South Carolina and of a curious belt running northward through the eastern piedmont of North Carolina to the James in Virginia. **1965–70** *DARE* (Qu. I51, *The kind of a peach where the hard center is loose*) 16 Infs, **Sth**, Clearstone [8 of 16 Infs Black].

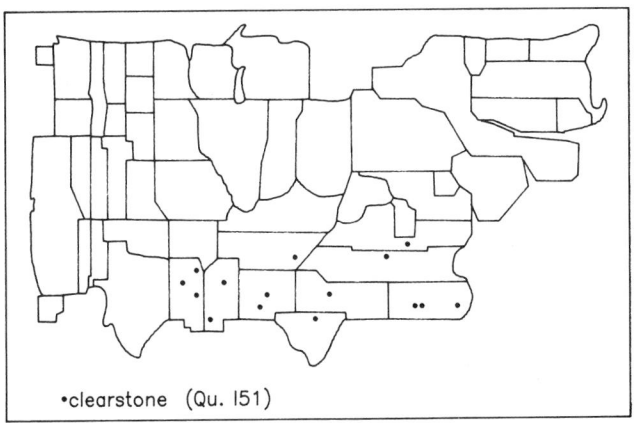

•clearstone (Qu. I51)

clearty See **clarty**

clearweed n [See quot 1843]
=**richweed 1**, esp *Pilea pumila*.
    1843 Torrey *Flora NY* 2.223, *Adike pumila* . . . In some places it is known by the name of *Clearweed*, from the semitransparency of its stems. **1876** Hobbs *Bot. Hdbk.* 24, Clearweed . . Urtica pumila [=*Pilea pumila*]. **1900** Lyons *Plant Names* 16, *Pilea pumila* . . Clearweed. **1937** Stemen *OK Flora* 102. **1940** Gates *Flora KS* 148. **1950** Stevens *ND Plants* 118. **1963** Evers *IL* 25, In the vicinity of the spring at the base of the bluff, clearweed [*Pilea pumila*], wild hydrangea, false nettle, and touch-me-not are common. **1963** Zimmerman–Olson *Forest* 168, Clearweed [*Pilea pumila*] . . varies according to the favorability of the habitat. **1965** Weaver *Native Vegetation* 24, Clear-weed.

cleats n [ME *clete* < OE *clite* coltsfoot]
=**coltsfoot 1**.
    1900 Lyons *Plant Names* 381, *T[ussilago] Farfara* . . Cleats. **1930** Sievers *Amer. Med. Plants* 24, Cleats.

cleavenut See **cleavestone**

cleavers n Also *clavergrass, cleaver's herb, cleaverwort, cleverwort, clivers* [From its adhering to clothing, etc]
A **bedstraw**, usu *Galium aparine*, which is also called **beggar's lice 5, burhead, burweed 3, catchweed, cheese rennet, chicus, clabbergrass, cling-rascal, goose grass, goosehill, goose-share,**

gosling grass, gravel-grass, grip, harvest lice, lady's bedstraw, loveman, milksweet, poor robin, robin-run-the-hedge, scratchweed, snatchweed, stick-a-back, sweetheart, turkey grass.

a1782 (1788) Jefferson *Notes VA* 35, Clivers, or goose-grass, *Galium spurium*. **1840** MA Zool. & Bot. Surv. *Herb. Plants & Quadrupeds* 144, *Galium aparine . . . cleavers*. **1900** Lyons *Plant Names* 167, *Galium Aparine* . . Cleavers (Clivers), Cleaverwort, . . Claver-grass. **1940** Clute *Amer. Plant Names* 52, *Galium aparine*. Cleavers . . . Cleaverwort. **1970** GA Dept. Ag. *Farmers Market Bulletin* 2 Sept 8/1, Cleavers— goosegrass or bedstraw, common names for Galium Aparine, is a weak almost perennial herb that can't stand upright unless it is climbing on and supported by surrounding vegetation . . . Despite the terminal "s" cleavers is singular. **1971** Krochmal *Appalachia Med. Plants* 126, *Galium Aparine*—Common Names: . . cleavers, cleaver's herb, cleverwort.

cleavestone n, also attrib Also *cleavenut*
=clearseed.

1941 *LANE* Map 267 **Cape Cod, Block Is., neLong Island,** 6 infs, Cleavestone (peach). **1949** *AmSp* 24.107 **SC,** *Clearnut peach; cleavenut peach* . . . Clearstone peach. **1949** Kurath *Word Geog.* 72, On lower Cape Cod (Chatham to Provincetown) *cleave-stone peach* occurs as a relic. A single instance of this term was noted on the southwestern prong of Long Island. [Fig. 129 also shows 3 instances of *cleave-stone peach* in c,ceNY]. **1969** *DARE* (Qu. I51, *The kind of peach where the hard center is loose*) Inf **MA**55, Cleavestone. **1971** Wood *Vocab. Change* 298 **TN, GA,** 3 [instances of] Cleavestone.

cleek cleek n Also *clee-clee* [Echoic]
=sparrow hawk 1.

1917 *DN* 4.424 **LA,** *Cleek cleek.* The sparrow hawk (Falco sparverius). **1959** *AmSp* 34.74, *Clee-clee, cleek-cleek* (sparrow hawk).

cleft See **cliff**

clem, clen See **clean** v **A**

cler See **clear**

clevel n Also sp *clevil* [sEngl dial; see *EDD*] arch or obs
1892 *DN* 1.210 **MA,** *Clevel* or *clevil:* a grain of corn.

clever adj

1 Healthy, chipper; spry. [*OED* "dial.": cf *EDD, SND*] See also **cleverly** adv **3,** adj

1775 in 1875 Essex Inst. *Coll.* 13.196 **neMA,** Father was very clever last Saturday P.M. **1815** *Thomas' MA Spy or Worcester Gaz.* (MA) 14 June 4/4, I somehow did not feel quite clever, but hoped for the best. **1968** *DARE* (Qu. KK27, *A very lively, active old person: "For his age, he's _____."*) Inf **DE**7, Pretty clever.

2 See quot. [*OED clever* a. 5 "Now *dial.*, also in *U.S.*"] arch
1899 (1912) Green *VA Folk-Speech,* Clever . . . Pretty. Handsome . . tall.

3 Pleasant, good-natured, affable. **formerly NEng, now chiefly Sth, S Midl** See also **cleverness**

1758 in 1872 Essex Inst. *Coll.* 12.148 **MA,** This afternoon secured a place to have ye Small Pox in, with a very clever family. **1768** *Boston Post Boy* 20 June 211, That Young and Old, the Cross and Clever / Join hands, and live so well together. **1844** in 1935 *Filson Club Hist. Qrly.* 9.233 **KY,** The Yocums were clever neighbors; great for log rolling; but quarrelsome among themselves. **1883** Eggleston *Hoosier Schoolboy* 119 **sIN,** You've always been 'clever' to me, and I don't want to see no harm done you. **1904** *DN* 2.417 **nwAR,** Clever . . . Good-natured, accommodating. **1905** *DN* 3.6 **cCT.** **1906** *DN* 3.116 **sIN.** **1908** *DN* 3.299 **eAL, wGA.** **1911** *DN* 3.537 **eKY.** **1915** *DN* 4.182 **swVA.** **1917** *DN* 4.409 **wNC, IL, KY, NE.** **1950** *PADS* 14.21 **SC.** **1965** Will *Okeechobee Boats* 38 **FL** (as of c1920), Cap'n Clay Johnson was a right clever hearted man, and generous as well—too generous. **1966–69** *DARE* (Qu. U32, . . *A very generous person*) Infs **KY**40, 42, **NC**30, 55, Clever; **KY**44A, He's the cleverest thing you ever seed. **1968** *DARE* FW Addit **csNC,** Clever—friendly or nice. When I was a kid, that was the only meaning I knew.

4 Agreeable but somewhat simpleminded. **chiefly NEng** Cf *DS* HH2, 3, 5

1781 *PA Jrl. & Weekly Advt.* (Philadelphia PA) 9 May 1/3, Americans generally mean by *clever,* only goodness of disposition, worthiness, integrity, without the least regard to capacity; nay, if I am not mistaken, it is frequently applied where there is an acknowledged simplicity or mediocrity of capacity. **1823** *Natl. Intelligencer* 1 May (*DN* 4.48)

[Yankee dialect], Clever . . . Goodnatured, silly, inoffensive. **1907** *DN* 3.183 **seNH,** Clever . . . 2. Used of persons who are goodnatured and perhaps a little deficient mentally. **1931–33** *LANE Worksheets* **MA,** Clever . . below normal intelligence. **1943** *LANE* Map 468 *(Good-natured),* Clever may mean (a) good-natured; (b) good-natured but stupid, weak willed or clumsy; (c) good-natured but shiftless and irresponsible; (d) foolishly obliging, so good-natured as to be at the mercy of others; (e) gullible or spineless; (f) ignorant; (g) stupid, brainless; (h) foolish but harmless; (i) indolent, shiftless or worthless. **1972** *NYT Article Letters* **cNY,** People who were not very intelligent but harmless and always agreeable were [called] "clever" [in my grandparents' generation].

5 Of animals: docile, gentle; well-trained. **NEng**

1816 Pickering *Vocab.* 62, In speaking of any thing but *man* we use the word much as the English do. *We say a clever horse, &c.* **1839** *S. Lit. Messenger* 5.432/1 **ME,** He . . looked as big as a clever young ox. **1904** *DN* 2.417 neMA, seNH, I have heard *clever* (=*gentle*) used of horses. **1907** *DN* 3.183 **seNH,** Clever . . . Used of animals in the sense of *gentle, kind.* **1913** *DN* 4.55 **ME,** Clever . . . Easily managed: docile: noted from Lebanon. "Oxen must be pretty clever to be bossed around the way they are." **1931–33** *LANE Worksheets* **CT,** Clever [klɛvə] . . free from vicious traits—said of horses. **1943** *LANE* Map 468 **scattered throughout NEng,** Another common meaning of *clever* is 'gentle' as applied to animals.

6 Of a woman: aggressively flirtatious; promiscuous.

1931–33 *LANE Worksheets* **csCT,** Clever girl—prostitute. **1969** *DARE* (Qu. AA7a, . . *A woman who is very fond of men and is always trying to know more—if she's nice about it*) Inf **CA**114, Eager, clever. **1981** Broaddus *Coll.* **ceKY** (as of 1958), Clever woman—a sexually loose woman.

‡7 See quot.

1931–33 *LANE Worksheets* **VT,** Clever ['klɛvə] . . homely.

clever adv

In phr *treat one ~:* Well; in a friendly way.

1865 Crockett *Life* 57 **TN,** The old man appeared quite willing, and treated me very clever. **1940** Cather *Sapphira* 289 **VA,** (as of 1860s), The new miller treated him real clever, and let him sleep in old Master's mill room. **1941** in 1944 *ADD* **KY,** Clever . . . [If you'll come visit us,] we'll treat you clever. **1946** Greer–Petrie *Angeline Gits an Eyeful* 20 **csKY,** . . They wuz all jest as *common* and shore treated us *clever.*

cleverly adv

1 Conveniently. [*OED* →1791, "*Obs.*"] arch or obs
1892 *DN* 1.210 **seMA,** Cleverly. "As soon as I cleverly can; i.e. possibly or reasonably can."

2 Entirely. [*OED* →1884, "Now *dial.* and *U.S.*"]
1841 in 1898 Poe *Tales* 68, We had let our sails go on the run, before it [=a hurricane] cleverly took us. **1843** (1846) Haliburton *Attaché* (1st ser) 125 **CT,** Mister landlord . . . comes to me, as soon as I was cleverly up this mornin'. **1884** Murfree *Where the Battle* 78 **TN,** It'll be cleverly dark by the time Mirandy gits ter her house. **1917** *DN* 4.409 **wNC,** Cleverly . . . Fully. "He wasn't cleverly grown—just a slick-faced boy."

3 Very well. **NEng** obs Cf **clever** adj **1, cleverly** adj
1776 in 1854 Adams *Works* 9.417 **MA,** We are now cleverly situated. I have got a set of servants as good as I can expect to find. **1815** Humphreys *Yankey in England* 104, Cleverly, very well. **1847** Hurd *Grammatical Corrector* 23, Cleverly, for *quite well,* or *in good health;* as "How is your friend to-day? He is *cleverly;* or he is getting along *cleverly.*" This use of the term is not allowable, even in conversation.

4 Barely.
1788 in 1853 Jefferson *Writings* 2.457, While our second revolution is just brought to a happy end with you, yours here is but cleverly under way. **1918** *DN* 5.33 **seKY,** Cleverly . . . Barely. " 'Lish's Rob's jist cleverly begun to crap (farm)." **1923** *DN* 5.242 **KY,** Cleverly . . . Only; just. "Spark's jist cleverly begun to farm."

cleverly adj **NEng**

In good health.

1784 in 1875 J. & A. Adams *Familiar Letters* 212 **MA,** She is cleverly now, although she had a severe turn for a week. **1816** Pickering *Vocab.* 63 **NEng,** In answer to the common salutation, *How do you do,* we often hear, I am *cleverly.* **1834** Smith *Letters Jack Downing* 82 **ME,** I've been amost sick for a week . . . But I'm getting cleverly now. **1847** [see **cleverly** adv **3**].

cleverness n [**clever** adj **3**]
Amiability.

1890 Howells *Boy's Town* 82 **OH** (as of 1850s), A citizen's character for cleverness or meaness was fixed by his walking round or over the rings. Cleverness was used in the Virginia sense for amiability; a person who was clever in the English sense was smart.

cleverwort See **cleavers**

clevil See **clevel**

clevis n, also attrib *Usu* |'klɛvɪs|, also |'klɪvɪs| Pronc-spp *clev(v)y, clevys, clivis, clivvy*
Std sense, var forms.
   1828 Webster *Amer. Dict., Clevy, Clevis* . . . An iron bent in the form of an oxbow, with the two ends perforated to receive a pin, used on the end of a cart-neap . . . *New England.* **1899** (1912) Green *VA Folk-Speech, Clevis* . . . Clevy. Clevvy. Clevyses. **1908** *DN* 3.299 **eAL, wGA,** *Clivis* . . . Clevis, an attachment on a plow. **1910** *DN* 3.452 **seVT,** *Clevy* . . . A bent iron with the shape of an ox-bow having holes in the ends for the insertion of a bolt. It is used to couple the *whippletrees* to the evener. *Clevy-pin* . . . The bolt of the clevy. **1931–33** *LANE Worksheets* **RI,** Clevis pin [klɛvɪs pɪn] . . used to attach yoke to wagon tongue. **1946** *PADS* 6.9 **eNC,** *Clivvy* . . . Clevis. **c1960** *Wilson Coll.* **csKY,** *Clevis* /'klɪvɪs/ . . . A device to connect a plow to the doubletree or singletree.

clew n[1] [Scots, Ir, and nEngl dial; cf *EDD*] *old-fash*
1 A ball (of yarn).
   1950 *PADS* 13.22 **sKY,** *Clew* . . . A ball of yarn used for darning or knitting; . . "Grandma takes her clew o' yarn and knits when she goes visitin'." **c1960** *Wilson Coll.* **csKY,** *Clew* . . . A ball of yarn. Now rare.
2 Transf: a hair bun. Cf *DS* X3
   1950 *PADS* 13.22 **sKY,** *Clew* . . . A ball of hair rolled up at the nape of a woman.

clew v [Prob *clew* obs past tense of *claw,* still found occas in Scots and Engl dial; cf *SND claw* v. 3 "To beat, strike"]   See also **clew** n[2]
To strike.
   1927 *DN* 5.473 **Ozarks,** *Clew* . . . To strike. "An' then I jes' clewd him side o' th' head." **1954** *PADS* 21.24 **neSC,** *Clew* . . . *past tense* and *past part., clewed, clewted.* To strike a person, usually on the head with the fist. **1954** *Harder Coll.* **cwTN,** *Clew* . . . To hit.

clew n[2] Also sp *clue* [**clew** v; see also *EDD* **clew** sb.[2]] *arch* or *old-fash*
A blow.
   1870 (1935) Duval *Advent. Big Foot* 165 **TX,** I took him a "clue" over the head that would have stunned a beef, but he never winked. *Ibid* 239, I gave him a "clew" on the side of the head . . that knocked him senseless to the floor. **1901** *DN* 2.138 **cNY,** *Clew* . . . A blow, slap . . . Uncommon.

clew bird n Cf **clippo, filliloo bird, milermore bird, noon-bird, twill-do bird**
See quots.
   1951 Randolph *We Always Lie* 68 **Ozarks,** The fishermen in Taney County, Missouri, still tell tourists about the clew-bird . . . "It looks like a crane, only bigger . . . Mostly it sets its bill solid in them gravels, an' then spins round like a top, so fast you cain't tell what color it is." **1953** Randolph *Down in Holler* 235 **Ozarks,** *Clew-bird* . . . A fabulous heron that sticks its bill in a gravel bar and whistles loudly through its rectum.

click n Also *clicker* **Nth**
A heel plate; a metal piece put on the sole of a shoe to prevent wear or slipping.
   1950 *WELS Suppl.,* For the metal plates school-children had put on shoes during wartime the words used were *taps* or *clickers.* **1966–70** *DARE* (Qu. W12b, *Metal pieces under the tips of shoes to prevent wear*) Infs **IA32, NH1, NJ69,** Clicks; **ND3,** Clickers; (Qu. W12a, *Heavy pieces of metal fastened under the soles of boots to keep them from slipping*) Inf **MN23,** Clickers.

click beetle n Also *click bug* [See quot 1905]
A beetle of the family Elateridae.
   1905 Kellogg *Amer. Insects* 267, The click-beetles, Elateridæ, are readily distinguished . . by . . their curious capacity, whence their name, of springing into the air with a sharp click when laid back downward. **1950** *WELS* (*Creatures that make a clicking, shrilling, or chirring sound*) 1 Inf, **ceWI,** Click beetle. **1964** Borror–DeLong *Intro. Insects* 353, Elateridæ . . The click beetles constitute a large group, and many species

are quite common. These beetles are peculiar in being able to "click" and jump. **1965–70** *DARE* (Qu. R8, . . *Creatures that make a clicking or shrilling or chirping kind of sound*) 8 Infs, **scattered,** Click beetle; **IL119,** Click beetle—if you turn it over on its back it pops up; it makes a clicking sound; (Qu. R30, . . *Other kinds of beetles*) 9 Infs, **scattered,** Click beetle; **SC43, 63,** Click bug; (Qu. R5) Inf **CO20,** Click beetle—brown, makes clicking sound. **1968** *Thief River Falls Times* (MN) 12 Jan 4, The mature wire worm is known as the "click beetle."

‡clickel tree n
A hackberry: see quot.
   1969 *DARE* (Qu. T13, . . *Hackberry*) Inf **IN58,** Cackleberry, clickel trees.

clicker n [Imit]
1 =**yellow rail.**
   1946 Hausman *Eastern Birds* 241, Yellow Rail . . . *Other Names*— . . Yellow Crake, Clicker. **1955** Forbush–May *Birds* 164.
2 See **click.**

clickers n pl *joc* Cf **clacker 2**
False teeth.
   1950 *WELS* (False teeth) 1 Inf, **cwWI,** Clickers. **1967–69** *DARE* (Qu. X13b, . . *False teeth*) Infs **CA128, MI75, NY34, OH34,** Clickers.

clide, clied See **cloy**

cliff n *Usu* |klɪf|; also, **scattered,** |klɪft| Pronc-sp *clift,* hist sp *cleft;* also pl *clivs* Cf **acrost, crost** and Pronc Intro 3.I.23   Addit quots in *ADD*   Note: *clift,* the older form of *cleft,* was confused with *cliff* in the 15th cent and treated as a variant of it esp in the 16th–18th cents; see *OED* **cliff.**
Std sense, var forms.
   1650 (1923) Bland *New Brittaine* **VA,** Berkeley Island . . being fortified with high Clefts of Rocky Stone. **1702** in 1968 CT (Colony) *Pub. Rec.* 4.380, A young chestnut tree . . stands within a seat of said pond under a clift of rocks. **1805** (1965) Ordway *Jrls.* 1.235, High bluffs & clifts along the Shores. **1859** (1968) Bartlett *Americanisms* 87 **West,** *Cliff* . . . Usually pronounced *clifts.* **c1885** Eggleston in *AmSp* 30.113 **IN,** *Clift* for *cliff,* another form set down to the Negro, is common among country people. **1908** *DN* 3.299 **eAL, wGA,** *Clift.* **1917** *DN* 4.409 **IL, KY, wNC, NEng,** *Clift.* **1939** *Hall Coll.* **eTN, wNC,** *Clift* . . [klɪft] A cliff. **1946** *AmSp* 21.270 **neKY,** *Clivs* . . . Pl of *cliff.* **1966–70** *DARE* Tapes **AR41, 56,** [klɪft]. **1976** Allen *LAUM* 3.301 **cwSD,** /klɪft/. *Ibid* 16, The excrescent *t* infrequently found with *orphan, skiff,* . . and *cliff* is a minor social marker.

cliff brake n
A fern of the genus *Pellaea.*   See also **rock brake**
   1867 Gray *Manual of Botany* 659, *Pellæa.* Cliff-Brake . . . *P. atropurpùrea* . . . Dry calcareous rocks: not common, but of wide range. **1941** Walker *Lookout* 56, Purple cliffbreak [sic] finds congenial homes in the limestone ledges. **1961** Douglas *My Wilderness* 88 **AZ,** Then I find the tiny Arizona spurge and several small ferns—bristle-tip cliff brake, dwarf cliff brake, and Lindheimer lip fern.

cliff harlequin n
=**mountain fringe 1.**
   1933 Small *Manual SE Flora* 549, *A[dlumia] fungosa* . . . Mountain-fringe. Cliff-harlequin.

cliff lettuce n
An unidentified green: see quot.
   1973 Kluger *Wild Flavor* 72 **sIN,** There were other greens . . that have fascinating colloquial names: "woolly britches," . . "cliff lettuce," and "wild cabbage."

cliff pink n
A **catchfly 1** (here: *Silene rotundifolia*).
   1941 Walker *Lookout* 53 **TN,** A dainty cliff pink . . ventures . . on both sides of the mountain.

cliffrose n
A plant of the genus *Cowania.*   Also called **buckbrush 3d**   For other names of *C. mexicana* see **bitterbrush 2, quinine bush**
   1931 U.S. Dept. Ag. *Misc. Pub.* 101.49, Cliffrose (*Cowania stansburiana*) . . is known also by a variety of local names, including quinine-bush, bitterbrush, bitter aloes. It sometimes appears in literature under the name *Cowania mexicana.* **1960** Vines *Trees SW* 426, Heath

Cliffrose—Cowania ericæfolia. **1968** Abbey *Desert Solitaire* 24 **seUT**, There's a cliffrose standing near the shed behind the trailer, shaking in the wind, a dazzling mass of blossoms, and another coming up out of solid sandstone beside the ramada, ten feet tall and clothed in a fire of flowers.

cliff swallow n

A swallow *(Petrochelidon pyrrhonota)* which builds gourd-shaped mud nests on cliffs, bridges, and similar sites.   Also called **barn swallow 2, blue swallow 1, eave swallow, jug swallow, mud dauber 2, mud swallow, Rocky Mountain swallow**

1825 Bonaparte *Amer. Ornith.* 1.65 **West**, The Cliff Swallow advances from the extreme western regions, annually invading a new territory farther to the eastward. **1844** DeKay *Zool. NY* 2.41, *The Cliff Swallow* . . . breeds with us, and its nest, composed of mud or clay with a narrow tubular neck, resembles a coarse retort. **1965–70** *DARE* (Qu. Q20) 79 Infs, **scattered**, Cliff swallow.

cliffweed n

=**alumroot 1.**

1828 Rafinesque *Med. Flora* 241, *Heuchera acerifolia* . . Vulgar Names—Alumroot . . Cliffweed. **1876** Hobbs *Bot. Hdbk.* 24, *Cliffweed*, Maple leaf alum root, *Heucheria* [sic] *acerifolia.*

clift See cliff

clifted adj [*clift* alter of std *cleft* + *-ed* pret suff **1**]

Split.

1929 *AmSp* 4.356 **ME**, Dote . . . "White birch always gets doted if it ain't clifted."

clim See climb 1, 2b

climate v

To satisfy as to weather conditions.

1929 *AmSp* 5.17 **Ozarks**, Climate, v. To afford proper climatic conditions. "My kin-folks they went to Newbrasky oncet, but 'peared like th' North couldn't climate 'em, noways."

climated adj [Aphet for *acclimated*]

Acclimated.

1849 (1914) Kingsley *Diary* 92 **nCA**, Relinquishing the idea of going to the diggings this winter [to] get ourselves climated ready for spring. **1863** Gilmore *S. Friends* 61 **NC**, It gits a feller's stumac used to Tophet 'fore the rest on him is 'climated. **1906** *DN* 3.131 **nwAR**, *Climated* ['klaɪmətəd] . . . Acclimated. "These horses are climated." **1929** Ellis *Ordinary Woman* 43 **CO** [as of early 1900s], She was always brewing sage tea for some tenderfoot, who was getting 'climated.'

‡climate fever n

1969 *DARE* Tape TX62, My mother said . . they called it, they said that was climate fever, that was the name for it. But I imagine it was typhoid fever.

climax, cap the See cap v 1b

climb v

Std senses, var forms.

1 pres: usu *climb;* also pronc-sp *clam(b),* (**esp Sth, S Midl,** *esp in representation of Black Speech*); rarely *clim;* eye-dial *clime.*

1884 Harrison *Negro Engl.* 252 **SE**, *Pres.* clime (climb). *Ibid* 261, To clam up arter sump'n' = to seek for something by climbing. **1901** *DN* 2.181 **KY** [Black], *Climb*—clime. **1908** *DN* 3.299 **eAL, wGA**, *Clam* . . . To climb. **1912** Green *VA Folk-Speech* 116, *Clamb* . . . For *climb.* **1937** in 1958 Brewer *Dog Ghosts* 98 **TX** [Black], So he tecks his li'l' brothuh by one han', his fiddle in t'othuh'n, clams thoo de barb-wire fence wid 'em, an' goes on ovuh to de cotton-seed house. **1954** *Harder Coll.* **cwTN**, *Climb* . . . pres.—climb, clim.

2 past, past pple: usu *climbed;* also:

a *clum, clumb* |klʌm|, rarely *clumbed.*   **widespread** *esp among speakers with little formal educ*

1835 (1961) Strang *Diary* 60 **NY**, I . . clumb above water. **1835** (1927) Evans *Exped. to Rocky Mts.* 208 **IN**, With great difficulty we clum over a steep ledge. **1851** Burke *Polly Peablossom* 147 **MS**, He was the durndest, rantankerous hoss-fly that ever clum er tree! **1903** *DN* 2.309 **seMO**, *Clum.* **1906** *DN* 3.116 **sIN**, *Clum.* **1907** *DN* 3.229 **Ozarks**, *Clum.* **1908** *DN* 3.299 **eAL, wGA**, *Clum(b)* . . . Sometimes *clumbed.* ~~**1913** *DN* 4.10 **MN**, *Clum.*~~ ~~**1914** *DN* 4.105 **KS**, *Clum.*~~ **1916** *DN* 4.273 **NE, KS, IL, PA**, *Clumb.* **1927** *AmSp* 3.139 **eME**, *Clumb.* **1950** *PADS* 14.21 **SC**, *Clum, clumb.* **1953** Atwood *Survey of Verb Forms* 8, In the

rest [=all but the northernmost edge] of Pa., as in N.J., w. Md., W. Va., and the Shenandoah Valley of Va., the form *clum* /klʌm/ is heavily favored . . . in inland N.C. *clum* and *clim* are about equally distributed. **1965–70** *DARE* (Qu. OO10a, . . *"When we were children we often _____ trees."*) 92 Infs, **scattered**, Clum (up). [Of all Infs responding to the question, 67% had less than coll educ; of those giving these responses 80% had less than coll educ]; (Qu. OO10b, . . *"Some trees were dangerous—we shouldn't have _____ (those)."*) 100 Infs, **scattered**, Clum. [Of all Infs responding to these questions, 26% had less than hs educ; of those giving these responses, 45% had less than hs educ.]

b *clim, klim* |klɪm|, occas *climmed.*   **chiefly Atl States, esp nNY, wNEng** See Map

1775 (1906) Litchfield *Diary* 321 **MA**, He . . clim up the mast. **1843** (1916) Hall *New Purchase* 145 **IN**, And she know'd the varmint wasn't going to rest till he klim down the inside of the chimbly. **1890** *DN* 1.71 **LA, NEng, IN**, *Clum, clom, clim.* **1907** *DN* 3.183 **seNH**, *Clim.* **1939** Hall *Coll.* **eTN, wNC**, *Clim* or *clum.* **1953** Atwood *Survey of Verb Forms* 8, In N.Eng. (except Cape Cod), N.Y. (except the lower Hudson Valley), and the northernmost edge of Pa., the form *clim* /klɪm/ strongly predominates . . over the other strong forms. **1960** *PADS* 34.58 **CO**, *Climmed* . . . Older folk speech. **c1960** *Wilson Coll.* **csKY**, *Clim* or *clumb* . . . Past and past participle of *climb; clumb* is still very common. **1965–70** *DARE* (Qu. OO10a) 29 Infs, **chiefly east, esp nNY, wNEng**, Clim (up); (Qu. OO10b) 24 Infs, **chiefly east, esp nNY, wNEng**, Clim (up); NC53, VA1, Climmed. [Of all Infs responding to these questions, 26% had less than hs educ; of those giving these responses, 56% had less than hs educ.] **1972** Cooper *NC Mt. Folkl.* 90, Clim.

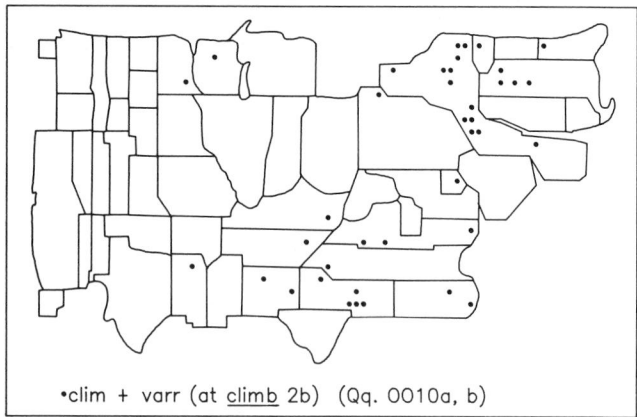

•clim + varr (at <u>climb</u> 2b)   (Qq. OO10a, b)

c *clomb(e), clome* |klom|, occas *clomed,* rarely pple *clomben (arch).*   **chiefly Midl, esp VA, NC**

1835 (1955) Crockett *Almanacks* 18 **wTN**, The bear did not come, he only clomb up higher. **1886** in 1919 Hale *Letters* 158 **MA**, I . . clomb from a chair into a sorry saddle. **1889** (1971) Farmer *Americanisms, Clomb.*— The preterite of climb . . . The old past participle, *clomben,* is also still heard in New England. **1912** Green *VA Folk-Speech, Clomb* . . . For climbed. **1927** *AmSp* 3.2 **Ozarks**, [Pres] climb—[Pret] clim, clum, clome—[Past pple] clum, clome. **1930** *AmSp* 5.264 **Ozarks**, *Clumb* or *clim* . . . *clombe.* **1951** VA Univ. *Univ. Studies* 5, The use of [klom] (rather than the usual Southern [klɪm] or [klʌm]) as the preterite of climb (Figure 7). The center of currency of this form is clearly the Piedmont, although [klom] is common along the Fall Line. **1952** Brown *NC Folkl.* 1.527, *Clumb, clomb* . . . Past tense and past participle of *climb.* **1953** Atwood *Survey of Verb Forms* 8, The Piedmont area of Va. (as well as some areas to the westward) is distinguished by the presence of *clome* /klom/ along with *clim* and *clum;* in inland N.C. . . . there are a few occurrences of *clome.* **1965–70** *DARE* (Qu. OO10a) Infs MN23, TX1, Clome; VA35, Clomed; (Qu. OO10b) Infs IL135, MN23, TX1, VA35, 75, Clome. **1972** Cooper *NC Mt. Folkl.* 90, Clome.

d *clam, clamb, clambed, clamded, clammed* |klæm, klæmd, klamdɪd|.   **chiefly Sth** *esp among Black speakers*

1825 Neal *Brother Jonathan* 1.164 **CT**, Ye . . never clamb a tree, for nothin—arter owls. **1884** Harrison *Negro Engl.* 252 **SE**, *Past.* clambed, clum, . . clam. **1908** *DN* 3.299 **eAL, wGA**, *Clam* . . . Pret. *clammed* or *clum.* **1953** Atwood *Survey of Verb Forms* 9, *Clam* /klæm/ is used by two N. Eng. and four Southern informants, two of whom are ~~Negroes. *Clammed* /klæmd/ (presumably with a present form /klæm/) is~~ used by one N. Eng. and seven Southern informants, including four Negroes. **1965–70** *DARE* (Qu. OO10a) 11 Infs, **chiefly Sth**, Clam; (Qu.

OO10b) Infs **FL**48, **MS**24, 44, **MO**1, 8, **TX**97, **VA**39, Clam. [9 of 14 total Infs Black] **1968** *DARE* FW Addit **GA**46, Clamded [klamdɪd] used as past tense of *climb* by Negro cleaning woman. **1969** Emmons *Deep Rivers* 59 **eTX** [Black], And she "clam right up Raymond's leg like it was a tree."

e less freq *cloom, cloomb* |klum|. **esp VA, NC**

1940–41 Cassidy *WI Atlas* **ceWI**, Cloom . . Climbed. **1943** Chase *Jack Tales* 18 **wNC** (as of 1880s), He cloomb on up on the scaffle, rockled and reeled this-a-way and that-a-way. **1953** Atwood *Survey of Verb Forms* 8, There are seven occurrences of *cloom* /klum/, nearly all of which are in the Piedmont area of Va. and adjoining areas of N.C. **1960** *PADS* 34.58 **CO**. **1968** *DARE* FW Addit **GA**46, [klum] used as past tense of *climb* by Negro cleaning woman. **1972** Cooper *NC Mt. Folkl.* 90, Cloom.

f occas *climb.*

1922 Gonzales *Black Border* 293 **sSC, GA coasts** [Gullah glossary], *Climb . . .* climbed. **1953** Atwood *Survey of Verb Forms* 9, The uninflected *climb* /klaim/ is used by two Negro informants. **1965–70** *DARE* (Qu. OO10a) Infs **GA**1, **KY**34, **ME**6, 16, **SC**10, 26, Climb. [2 of 6 Infs Black; 5 have less than hs educ.]

climber n

=**racer 1.**

1968 *DARE* (Qu. P25) Inf **DE**3, Climbers—shiny black snake with white under the throats; climbs trees.

climb fool's hill See **fool's hill**

climbing bittersweet n

A **bittersweet** (here: *Celastrus scandens*).

1848 Gray *Manual of Botany* 83, *C. scandens . . . Climbing Bitter-sweet . . .* Woody, sarmentose and twining. **1901** Lounsberry *S. Wild Flowers* 319, *Climbing Bitter-sweet . . .* Country people collect the roots to use in various medicinal ways. **1950** Stevens *ND Plants* 201, *Climbing Bittersweet.* Woody vine, . . twining around trees or bushes. **1960** Vines *Trees SW* 660, Known by the vernacular names of Climbing Bitter-sweet, Staff-vine [etc.].

climbing boneset n Also *boneset*

=**climbing hempweed.**

1847 Wood *Class-Book* 316, *M[ikania] scandens . . . Climbing Boneset . . .* Branches short, nearly naked, each bearing a small corymb of whitish, or pink-colored flowers. **1901** Lounsberry *S. Wild Flowers* 500, Another common name by which it [=*Mikania scandens*] is designated is "boneset." **1910** Graves *Flowering Plants* 377 **CT**, Climbing Boneset . . . Swamps and along streams. **1946** Reeves–Bain *Flora TX* 248, Climbing Boneset . . . Late summer, fall. **1976** Bruce *How to Grow Wildflowers* 262, What is for all intents a climbing eupatorium is *Mikania scandens . . .* 'Climbing Hempweed'. . or 'Climbing Boneset' is a rather delicate vine.

climbing buckwheat n

=**bindweed 3.**

1822 Eaton *Botany* 402, *Polygonum scandens* (climbing buckwheat . .). **1931** Clute *Common Plants* 83, The devil's tether (*Polygonum convolvulus*), however, is devoid of thorns and is otherwise known as climbing buckwheat. **1950** Gray–Fernald *Manual of Botany* 588, *Climbing Buckwheat . . P[olygonum] cilinode.* **1961** Smith *MI Wildflowers* 101, Climbing Buckwheat—*Polygonum cilinode.*

climbing colicweed See **colicweed 3**

climbing false buckwheat n

A polygonaceous twining perennial plant (*Bilderdykia scandens,* formerly *Polygonum scandens*) native chiefly to the eastern half of the US. Also called **bindweed 3, hedge bindweed 2, hedge cornbind**

1891 Jesup *Plants Hanover NH* 35, *P[olygonum] dumetorum . . scandens . . .* (Climbing False Buckwheat). **1931** Harned *Wild Flowers Alleghanies* 151, Climbing false buckwheat (P[olygonum] scandens . .). **1950** Stevens *ND Plants* 123, *Polygonum scandens . .* Climbing False Buckwheat.

climbing glory n

A **morning glory.**

1969 *DARE* (Qu. S5) Inf **NY**183, Climbing glory.

climbing hempweed n Also *climbing hempvine, hempvine*

A plant of the genus *Mikania.* Also called **climbing boneset**

1848 Gray *Manual of Botany* 194, *Climbing Hemp-weed . . .* Climbing perennials, with . . heart-shaped and petioled leaves, and . . flesh-colored flowers. **1892** Coulter *Botany W. TX* 177, *Mikania . . . (Climbing hemp-weed) . . .* The flowers, achenes, etc., as in Eupatorium. **1933** Small *Manual SE Flora* 1328, *M. scandens . . . Climbing hemp-vine . . . M. cordifolia . . .* The most vigorous of the climbing-hempweeds. **1948** Wherry *Wild Flower Guide* 131, *Hemp-vine . . .* Highly desirable for the swampy wild garden. **1961** Douglas *My Wilderness* 132 **Everglades FL**, A vine called the climbing hempweed was taking hold in the sand.

climbing lane n

On a highway: the outer lane, for slow traffic.

1977 *DARE* File **TX**, The truck lane is called the climbing lane, even when there's not much of a hill.

climbing orangeroot n

A **bittersweet** (here: *Celastrus scandens*).

1900 Lyons *Plant Names* 89, *C. scandens . . .* Climbing Orange-root. **1930** U.S. Dept. Ag. *Misc. Pub.* 77.4, Climbing orange-root . . . is found in woods and thickets. **1960** Vines *Trees SW* 660, Known also by the vernacular names of . . Jacob's Ladder, and Climbing-orangeroot.

climb over fool's hill See **fool's hill**

‡**climb the mountain** v phr

1954 *Harder Coll.* **cwTN**, *Climb the mountain . . .* To say foolish things. " 'E's done went 'n climbed the mountain. Ain't no backin' off now."

climb the wood, climb the wooden hill, climb the wooden stairs See **wooden hill**

clime See **climb 1**

climmed See **climb 2b**

climpers See **clampers 2**

clinch bar n *old-fash*

A **crowbar.**

1941 *LANE* Map 154 (*Crowbar*) 1 inf, **cVT**, [klɪntʃbɑ·], 'for removing roofs'. **1966–69** *DARE* (Qu. L39, *An iron bar with a bent end, used for pulling nails, opening boxes*) Infs **AR**21, **CA**152, **ME**14, **MA**47, **NM**3, **TX**40, Clinch bar. [All Infs old] **1966** *DARE* Tape **MA**86, She'd taken one of my clinch bars and stuck [it] in behind the brick there . . . She tipped that damn thing right out onto the floor.

clinch peach n Also *clinchstone*

=**clingstone.**

1970 *DARE* (Qu. I52, . . *A peach where the hard center is tight to the flesh*) Inf **VA**48, Clinch peach. **1973** Allen *LAUM* 1.306, *Clingstone (peach) . . .* Clinchstone, from a northern Minnesota French-Canadian farmer.

cling v

Std senses, var forms.

Past, past pple: usu *clung;* also *arch* or *obs clang, clinged.*

1815 in **1930** *AmSp* 5.264, Daniel Sandiford gave *crope* as the past tense of *creep,* and *clang* as a correct preterite of *cling.* **1884** Harrison *Negro Engl.* 252 **SE**, *Pres.* cling—*Past.* clinged.—*Pass. Part.* clinged. **1903** *DN* 2.293 **Cape Cod MA** (as of 1850s), There is a tendency to make strong verbs weak . . . *Clinged.*

cling n See **clingstone**

clinged See **cling** v

clinger, cling-fast (peach), clinging-pit peach, clingingstone See **clingstone**

cling-john n *?obs*

See quots.

1867 Lowell *Biglow* lviii, *Cling-john:* a soft cake of rye. **1889** (**1971**) Farmer *Americanisms*, *Clingjohn.*—A rye cake lightly baked.

cling peach See **clingstone**

cling-rascal n

=**cleavers.**

1900 Lyons *Plant Names* 167, *G. Aparine . . .* Cling-rascal. **1940** Clute *Amer. Plant Names* 52. **1959** Carleton *Index Herb. Plants* 28, *Cling rascal:* Galium aparine.

clingstone n Also *clingstone peach, cling (peach), clinger, clingfast (peach), clinging-pit peach, clingingstone, clingseed (peach)* Cf **freestone**

A peach in which the flesh adheres to the seed.

1705 Beverley *Hist. VA* 4.78, The best sort of these [=peaches and nectarines] cling to the Stone, and will not come off clear, which they call Plum-Nectarines, and Plum-Peaches, or Cling-Stones. **1831** *Daily Eve. Transcript* (Boston MA) 23 July 1/1, *Cling-stone* peaches were exhibited, of high flavor and sound healthy flesh. **1905** *DN* 3.6 **cCT**, *Clingstone*. . . A kind of peach. **1906** *DN* 3.131 **nwAR**, *Cling*. . . A clingstone peach. **1940** Brown *Amer. Cooks* 849 **VA**, *Peach Cobbler* . . . If you are using freestone peaches, pare and halve them; if clingstones, only pare and gash them, leaving them whole. **1941** *LANE* Map 267, [Clingstone (peach) and cling (peach) are widespread **throughout NEng**; 8 infs, VT, NH, MA, RI, Cling-fast peach]. **1949** Kurath *Word Geog.* 47, The North and Midland . . . *cling(-stone) peach* . . against *plum peach* and *press peach. Ibid* 72, *Cling-stone peach* is the regular term throughout the New England settlement area. The Midland has *cling-stone peach* and *cling peach.* **1950** *WELS* (Peach with the hard center tight to the flesh) 34 Infs, **WI**, Clingstone (peach); 9 Infs, Cling (peach); 1 Inf, Clingingstone. **1962** Atwood *Vocab. TX* 60, The only words that have any currency are *clingstone (peach)* (51[%]) and *cling (peach)* (30). Neither the Virginia *plum peach* (4) nor the Carolina *press peach* (1.8) can be said to have established itself; both usages are confined to informants over sixty. **1965–70** *DARE* (Qu. I52) 451 Infs, **widespread**, Cling (peach); 388 Infs, **widespread**, Clingstone (peach); NY79, 97, OH89, Clinger; AR17, GA28, LA18, Clingseed (peach); NY58, RI3, Yellow cling; MI44, Yellow clingstone; IN79, Lemon cling; NY70, Clinging-pit peach. **1973** Allen *LAUM* 1.305, Clingstone (peach) . . . Clingstone . . dominates the U[pper] M[idwest], but *cling* is widespread as a minority variant, with slightly greater frequency in the Midland areas of Iowa and Nebraska . . . *clinger* and *clingingstone* appear once each in Minnesota and Nebraska.

cling weed n
Perh a **bedstraw.**
1966 *DARE* (Qu. S15) Inf **NM13**, Cling weed—sticks to you, but seeds don't; has small yellow blossom.

clink n Cf **chinks 1**
=**wintergreen 2** (here: *Gaultheria procumbens*).
1971 Krochmal *Appalachia Med. Plants* 128, *Gaultheria procumbens* . . clink. **1974** (1977) Coon *Useful Plants* 135, Clink.

clinker n[1]
1 See quot.
1895 *DN* 1.371 **eTN**, *Clinkers:* insects. "The clinkers are mighty thick in this yere cabin."
2 See quot.
1905 *DN* 3.75 **nwAR**, *Clinker* . . . A cheat . . . Rare.
3 See quot.
1905 *DN* 3.75 **nwAR**, *Clinker* . . . An industrious or diligent person.

clinker n[2] [Alter of *clinger*]
=**clingstone.**
1903 *DN* 2.309 **seMO**, *Clinker* . . . A clingstone peach.

clip v *euphem*
To castrate.
1949 *AmSp* 24.107 **SC**, *Clip*. . . To castrate. **1968** *DARE* (Qu. K70, . . *Castrating an animal*) Infs **IL27, MN42**, Clip.

clip n See **clipper 1**

clip and clean adv phr
Completely, entirely.
1929 *AmSp* 5.128 **ME**. **1930s** in 1944 *ADD* **eWV**, He missed me clip & clean. **1975** Gould *ME Lingo*, Clip and Clean—Completely. "The jolt took out his front tooth clip and clean."

clipe n [*SND* clype, kleip, n.[4] "A blow;" cf *clip* to hit, strike]
1930 Shoemaker *1300 Words* 10 **cPA Mts** (as of c1900), *Clipe*—A blow, a stroke from a staff or club.

clip in v phr
1916 Macy–Hussey *Nantucket Scrap Basket* 127 **MA**, "Clip In"—To run in for a short visit, as "I think I'll clip in to Mary's on the way home." It implies a hurried call, and if the visitor announces that he just clipped in, he is not expected to tarry more than a few minutes.

clipper n
1 also *clip:* A likable, attractive, shrewd, or lively young woman; see also quot 1975. **Nth** *old-fash*

1836 (1838) Haliburton *Clockmaker* (1st ser) 177, She was a real handsum looking gall . . a real clipper, and as full of fun and frolic as a kitten. **1901** *DN* 2.138 **neNY**, *Clip* . . . A lively girl; "she's a clip." **1922** (1926) Cady *Rhymes VT* 184, I like a girl that's quite "a clip," / A boy, by George! that's quite "a case." **1929** Suckow *Cora* 298 **IA**, Her employer, was boasting about his good secretary. "She's a clipper." **1930** Shoemaker *1300 Words* 11 **cPA Mts** (as of c1900), *Clip*—A knowing, shrewd girl. *Ibid* 12, *Clipper*—A fast or forward girl. **1932** in 1933 *AmSp* 8.3.72 [In list of "old back country words"], *A clip* "a shrewd girl." **1975** Gould *ME Lingo* 53, Most lingering Maine references to *clippers* allude to women and similar things of beauty—fast, trim, tall, showy, dressy, clean, etc.

2 also *chipper:* =**hellgrammite.**
1901 Howard *Insect Book* 212, In 1889 Professor W.W. Bailey . . collected the names in use in Rhode Island alone for this insect, and they are . . . conniption bugs, clipper [etc]. **1911** *Century Dict.*, *Clipper*[2] . . . The larva of *Corydalus cornutus*, . . used for bait by anglers. **1948** *Field & Stream* July 42/2 (*DA*), Various stages of the dobson are known as conniption bugs, chippers, water grampus, . . and hell-divers.

3 A child's sled: see quots. [Perh abbr for trademark *Yankee Clipper,* but perh simply *clipper* something that moves swiftly]
1931–33 *LANE* Worksheets **RI**, Clipper ['klɪpə] . . Boy's sled. Low to the ground. Round runners extended beyond sled. **1943** *LANE* Map 573–574 **RI, cMA**, A low sled with solid sides coming to a point in front, often home made . . *clipper* [reported by 4 infs].

4 in pl: Teeth; false teeth. *joc* Cf **China B2**
1967–69 *DARE* (Qu. X13b, . . *False teeth*) Infs **CO36, CT23, 34, OH43**, Clippers; (Qu. 13a, . . *Teeth*) Inf **TX28**, Clippers.

‡clippo n Cf **clew bird, filliloo bird, twill-do bird**
An imaginary bird: see quot.
1968 *DARE* Tape **GA25**, Clippo ['klɪpo] . . . He's different, he flies with his back down and his breast up all the time. It's impossible to kill one of them birds and get him because he falls up.

clitbur See **clotburr 2**

clitch v [*OED* clitch v.5., *EDD* clitch v.2]
To stick together; hence adj *clitchy* sticky.
1816 Pickering *Vocab.* **NEng**, *Clitchy.* Clammy, sticky, glutinous . . . Used in a few instances by old people . . but it is very rarely heard. **1891** *Jrl. Amer. Folkl.* 4.159 **neMA**, *Clitch.*—A most expressive word, meaning to stick, to catch. It is not the same as "clutch."

clivers See **cleavers**

clivis See **clevis**

clivs See **cliff**

clivvy See **clevis**

cloak See **cluck n**

clob n See **clabber n**[2]

clob v [Imit]
=**clomp 1.**
1967–69 *DARE* (Qu. Y25, *To walk heavily* . . "He came _____ into the house.") Infs **NC72, PA48**, Clobbing.

clobber n[1] [Var of **clabber n**[1]]
1 also *clobbered milk,* rarely *clobber milk:* =**clabber n**[1] **1.** chiefly **Nth, esp NEast**
1899 (1912) Green *VA Folk-Speech, Clabber* . . . Curdled milk. Bonny-clabber. Clobber. **1902** *DN* 2.231 **sIL**, *Clabber.* Pronounced [klɑbər], or as if spelled clobber. **1949** Kurath *Word Geog.* 71, In New England relics of *clobbered, clabbered,* and *labbered* have survived by the side of the usual *lobbered* and *loppered.* **1950** *WELS* (Milk that becomes thick as it turns sour) 1 Inf, **cWI**, Clobbered. **1954** *Harder Coll.* **cwTN**, *Clabber milk.* "Clobber" is a pronunciation heard also. **1965–70** *DARE* (Qu. H59, *Milk that becomes thick as it turns sour*) 15 Infs, chiefly **Nth, esp NEast**, Clobbered (milk); KY82, MN23, MA10, Clobber; (Qu. H58, *Milk that's just beginning to become sour is _____*) NY12, VT8, Clobbered. **1970** Tarpley *Blinky* 190 **neTX**, (Milk that has turned sour and thickened) Clobbered milk [rare]. **1973** Allen *LAUM* 1.291, U[pper] M[idwest] variants probably due to confusion with *clabber milk* are *clobber milk* (once in Minnesota), *clobbered milk* (once each in Minnesota and South Dakota).

2 Mastitis. [By ext from **1**; the milk in the udder becomes lumpy]

1969 *DARE* (Qu. K7, *What sickness can a cow get in her udder—for example, if she's left unmilked too long?*) Inf **NY205**, Clobber.

clobber n² [Metath]
=**cobber** n¹ **2.**
   1969 *DARE* (Qu. H63, . . *Favorite desserts*) Inf **KY5**, Clobber, fried pies; **KY8**, Cakes, pies, clobber or deep-dish pies, fried pies (old-fashioned).

clobber n³ [**clob** v + -*er*]
1 See quot.
   1970 *DARE* (Qu. W11, *Men's low, rough work shoes*) Inf **NY249**, Clobbers.
2 also *clobber-foot:* See quot.
   1967–68 *DARE* (Qu. X38, . . *Unusually big or clumsy feet*) Inf **IL2**, Clobbers; **DE5**, Clobber-foot.

clobber n⁴ See **clabber** n²

clobber v See **clabber** v **2**

clobber cheese See **clabber cheese**

clobbered milk See **clobber** n¹ **1**

clobber-foot See **clobber** n³ **2**

clobber milk See **clobber** n¹ **1**

clobber up See **clabber** v **2**

clobberyash See **clabber** n²

clobhobble See **clodhop**

‡**clock bird** n
   A cuckoo.
   1970 *DARE* (Qu. Q14) Inf **MS81**, Clock bird (=cuckoo).

clock dials n [Prob so-called from the disk-shaped style] Cf **dumb watches**
   A pitcher plant **1** (here: *Sarracenia purpurea*).
   1951 Teale *North With Spring* 274 **cNJ**, Radiating pitcher plants are 'clock dials.'

clockface n
   A prickly pear.
   1982 *NY Times* (NY) 3 Jan sec 10 17/2 **AZ**, Clusters of hedgehog cactus, and prickly pear with names like clockface and cows-tongue, have wedged roots into the rock.

‡**clockify** v [**clock** + -*ify*]
   To repair clocks.
   1953 Randolph *Down in Holler* 45 **Ozarks**, One of Rose O'Neill's neighbors near Walnut Shade, Missouri, boasted that he could *clockify,* meaning that he knew how to repair clocks.

clock mantel See **clock shelf**

clocks n
   Alfilaria; also its seed capsule.
   1897 Parsons *Wild Flowers CA* 194, Children call them [seed capsules] "clocks," and love to stand the seed up in their clothing and watch the beaks wind slowly about, like the hands of a timepiece. **1915** (1926) Armstrong *Western Wild Flowers* 276, Other names are Pinkets, Pinclover, Storksbill, and Clocks. **1967–69** *DARE* (Qu. S15) Infs **CA20**, Clocks—alfilaria—has a corkscrew-shaped burr when dry—also called clocks—wound themselves up; **CA189**, Clocks.

clock shelf n Also *clock mantel* chiefly **Nth** Cf **chimney shelf**
   A small shelf on a wall; a mantel.
   1941 *LANE* Map 328 *(Mantel shelf)* 2 infs, **MA, VT**, Clock shelf. **1948** Davis *Word Atlas* App, **MI, IL, IN, OH**, *Clock shelf* [reported from 11 of 59 communities]. **1956** Ker *Vocab. W. TX* 97, Shelf over fireplace . . . Clock shelf [reported by 1 inf]. **c1960** *Wilson Coll.* **csKY**, *Clock-shelf* . . . Sometimes used for mantel or for a shelf in a corner where a small clock is placed. **1965–70** *DARE* (Qu. E6, *A small shelf hanging on the wall with small decorative articles on it*) 18 Infs, **esp N Cent**, Clock shelf; **IN19**, Clock mantel; **NC76**, Clock shelves; (Qu. D36, . . *The shelf over the fireplace*) Inf **VT16**, Clock shelf. **1973** Allen *LAUM* 1.162, *Clock shelf* has greater frequency [in mailed replies] than in the fieldwork, with 10 instances in Minnesota, 34 in Iowa, 17 in the Dakotas, and 16 in Nebraska, for a total of 9%.

clod n

1 also *country clod:* =**clodhopper 1.** [*OED* 1605 →]
   1942 Berrey–Van den Bark *Amer. Slang* 391.3, *Rustic; Bumpkin . . .* Country clod. **1950** *WELS* (*A city person's names . . for a country person*) 2 Infs, **WI**, Clod. **1964** *AmSp* 39.307, In Arizona and California it is the *clods* who live, not in the *sticks,* but in the *tules. Clod* has become part of general American slang, but *tule* remains localized in the Southwest. **1965–70** *DARE* (Qu. HH1, . . *A rustic or countrified person*) 14 Infs, **scattered**, Clod. **1967** *IN Engl. Jrl.* 2.2, People from the country who look awkward and out of place in town . . . *Clod.*

2 By ext: used as a disparaging epithet for:
a also *clod-head:* A dull or stupid person. *esp among younger speakers*
   1963 *AmSp* 38.170 [Kansas Univ slang], A rather stupid student . . . *clod* [reported by 7 of 123 students]. **1965–70** *DARE* (Qu. HH3, *A dull or stupid person*) 84 Infs, **scattered**, Clod; **IA45**, Clod-head. [Of all Infs responding to the question, 36% were young and mid-aged; of those giving these responses, 61% were young and mid-aged.] **1968** *Current Slang* 3.2.16 **sCA**, Harry has flunked every test, he's such a *clod.* **1974** *AmSp* 49.203, (*Terms for low intelligence*) Names of Groups . . . clod.
b An awkward or clumsy person. *esp among younger speakers*
   1950 *WELS* (*A very awkward or clumsy person*) 1 Inf, **seWI**, Clod; 1 Inf, **csWI**, Clumsy clod. **1957** Battaglia *Resp. to PADS 20* **eMD**, Clumsy clod. **1965–70** *DARE* (Qu. HH21) 132 Infs, **widespread**, Clod; **MI67, SC54**, Clumsy clod. [Of all Infs responding to the question, 37% were young and mid-aged; of those giving these responses, 55% were young and mid-aged.]
c A gauche or unmannerly person.
   1965–70 *DARE* (Qu. II36a, *Somebody who talks back or gives rude answers*) Infs **CA53, IN5, MI75, VA54**, Clod; (Qu. AA6b, . . *A man who is fond of being with women . . if he's rude*) Infs **MI75, OH61, VA31, 54**, Clod; (Qu. HH18, . . *Low-grade people*) Infs **MI103, MO7**, Clods; (Qu. II7, *Somebody who doesn't seem to "fit in"*) Inf **HI13**, Clod; (Qu. II21, . . *When somebody behaves unpleasantly*) Infs **LA46, MI75**, Clod.

3 =**clodhopper 3.** [Perh infl by *clog;* cf *EDD* clods miner's shoes]
   1967–69 *DARE* (Qu. W11, *Men's low, rough work shoes*) Infs **MN2, 37, NY186, 209, 219**, Clods; (Qu. W42b, . . *Nicknames for men's square-toed shoes*) Inf **NY209**, Clods.

4 also *clod-foot:* =**clodhopper 4.** [Cf **clog**]
   1967–69 *DARE* (Qu. X38, . . *Unusually big or clumsy feet*) Infs **IL97, MI96, MO26, NY20, PA182**, Clod(s); **PA40**, Clumsy clods; **IL57**, Clod-foot.

clod v

1 See quot 1899. [Also in Scots, Ir and Engl dial: see *EDD, OEDS*]
   1893 Twain in *Niagara Book* 95, Trying to clod apples out of that forbidden tree. *Ibid* 98, She has been climbing that tree again. Clodded her out of it. **1899** (1912) Green *VA Folk-Speech,* Clod . . . To pelt with clods; to throw lumps of dirt.
2 =**clomp** v **1.** See also **clob** v
   1966–70 *DARE* (Qu. Y25, *To walk heavily, making a lot of noise: "He came _____ into the house."*) Infs **MI120, NC36, OH70, PA148**, Clodding.

clod breaker See **clod crusher 1**

clod buster n

1 also *clod melter, clod roller:* A heavy rain. **scattered, but esp Sth, S Midl**
   1950 *PADS* 14.21 **SC**, *Clod buster . . .* A fairly heavy rain. Hill country. **1954** *Harder Coll.* **cwTN**, Clod buster: A heavy rain. **1962** Atwood *Vocab. TX* 38, *Torrential rain . . . clod roller* [1 inf]. **1967–69** *DARE* (Qu. B25, . . *A very heavy rain*) Infs **AL52, MI47, OH47, UT8**, Clod buster; (Qu. B24, . . *A sudden, very heavy rain*) Inf **OH47**, Clod buster. **1970** Tarpley *Blinky* 54 **neTX**, (*Very heavy rain that doesn't last long*) Clod-buster [rare] . . . Clod-melter [rare]. **c1970** *DARE File* **Ozarks** (as of c1910), A heavy fall of rain was a clod buster or a gully washer.

2 =**clodhopper 1;** by ext, a clumsy or awkward person.
   1950 *WELS* (*A city person's names . . for a country person*) 1 Inf, **csWI**, Clod buster. [**1954** in 1967 *Dict. Canadianisms* 155, You'll . . . end up marrying a clod-buster's daughter and spend the rest of your life raising chickens.] **1968** *DARE* (Qu. HH21, *A very awkward, clumsy person*) Inf

PA71, Clod buster. **1973** Allen *LAUM* 1.349 **neND, nwIA,** A rustic . . . clod buster [reported by two infs].

3 See quot.

1969 *DARE* (Qu. W42b, *Men's square-toed shoes*) Inf **IL96,** Clod busters.

4 See **clod crusher 1.**

clod crusher n

1 also *clod breaker, clod buster, clod masher:* A spiked roller used for pulverizing lumps of earth. [*OED* 1842 →] See also **float** n

1850 U.S. Patent Office *Annual Rept. for 1849: Arts & Mfgr.* 523, There is no difficulty in combining the effect of the plough, harrow and pulverizer, or clod-breaker, in the same machine. **1872** (1876) Knight *Amer. Mech. Dict.* 1.572/2, One form of clod-crusher consists of a series of cast-metal rings, or roller-parts, placed loosely upon a round axle. **1891** Farmer–Henley *Slang, Clod-Crushers . . .* In agriculture an implement for pulverising clods. **1950** *WELS (What is generally used to break up lumps in a field?)* 7 Infs, **WI,** Clod crusher. **1966–70** *DARE* (Qu. L20, *The implement used in a field after it's been plowed to break up the lumps*) Infs **AL62, IL93, MS28, NY32, VA49, WI17,** Clod crusher; **NC13, TN24,** Clod breaker(s); **CA63, 79, 105, DC5, OR7, TN30, WA8,** Clod masher; **GA14,** Clod buster.

2 =**clodhopper 1.**

1914 *DN* 4.207, *Clod . . -crusher,* country bumpkin.

3 also *clod masher:* =**clodhopper 4.**

1897 Barrère–Leland *Slang* 1.243, *Clod-crushers* (American), an epithet used by Americans to describe the large feet which they believe to be the characteristics of Englishwomen. **1970** *DARE* (Qu. X38, *Joking names for unusually big or clumsy feet*) Inf **VA46,** Clod mashers.

cloddered milk n [*EDD* *clodder* a stiff curdle or mass] =**clabber** n[1] **1.**

1967 *DARE* (Qu. H59, *Milk that becomes thick as it turns sour*) Inf **IL3,** Cloddered milk—a Cornish word.

cloddy-hop See **clodhopper 1**

clod fitter n [Prob Scots *fit* to tread, kick + *-er;* ult from Scots, nEngl dial *fit* foot]

1967 *DARE* (Qu. X38, . . *Unusually big or clumsy feet*) Inf **AZ8,** Clod fitters [fɪtɚz].

clod-foot See **clod** n **4**

clod-head See **clod** n **2a**

clod-heel n

=**clod** n **1.**

1968 *DARE* (Qu. HH1, . . *A rustic or countrified person*) Inf **CA36,** Clod-heel.

clodhop v Also *clodhobble, clobhobble* [Back-formation from **clodhopper**]

To walk clumsily.

1966–69 *DARE* (Qu. Y25, *To walk heavily, making a lot of noise: "He came _____ into the house."*) Infs **CA107, CO47, WA33,** Clodhopping (it); **PA66,** Clobhobbling [klɑb-], clodhobbling [klɑd-].

clodhopper n

1 also *cloddy-hop, clod jumper:* A rustic. [*OED* c1690 →]

1856 Simms *Eutaw* 302 **SC,** Five hundred British bayonets, opposed to a thousand clodhoppers, never retreat. **1899** (1912) Green *VA Folk-Speech, Clod-hopper . . .* A farmer's labourer. **1912** *DN* 3.573 **wIN,** *Clod-hopper . . .* A rustic; a hayseed. **1917** Garland *Son Middle Border* 196 **WI,** A hundred citified young men and women, fairly entitled to laugh at a clod-jumper like myself. **1930** Shoemaker *1300 Words* 11 **cPA Mts** (as of c1900), *Clod-hopper—*A country clown. **1950** *WELS (A city person's names . . for a country person)* 10 Infs, **WI,** Clodhopper. **c1960** Wilson *Coll.* **csKY,** *Clodhopper . . .* A rustic, a yokel. Less common is *clod-jumper.* **1965–70** *DARE* (Qu. HH1, . . *A rustic or countrified person*) 79 Infs, **widespread,** Clodhopper; **WI27,** Cloddyhop.

2 By ext: an awkward, stupid, or unmannerly person. ?esp Nth

1919 *DN* 5.63 **NM,** *Clod-hopper,* an awkward, gawky person. **1924** *DN* 5.289, *Clod-hopper . . .* Boor; lout. **1941** *LANE* Map 464 *(Awkward Person, Lummox)* 1 inf, **nwVT,** He's a regular bull in a china shop, clodhopper. **1950** *WELS (A very clumsy or awkward person)* 2 Infs, **WI,** Clodhopper. **1965–70** *DARE* (Qu. HH21, *A very awkward, clumsy person*) 13 Infs, **esp Nth,** Clodhopper; (Qu. HH3, *A dull and stupid*

person) Infs **NJ8, OH87, OR4,** Clodhopper; (Qu. AA6b, . . *A man who is fond of being with women . . if he's rude*) Inf **OH57,** Clodhopper. **1966** *DARE* FW Addit **MS7,** Clodhopper—applied contemptuously to people.

3 A large shoe, esp a coarse or heavy work shoe. [*OED* 1836]

1912 *DN* 3.573 **wIN,** *Clod-hopper . . .* A coarse kind of shoe. **1950** *WELS Suppl.* 3 Infs, **ce,cwWI,** Clodhoppers—big largish shoes. **1954** Harder *Coll.* **cwTN,** *Clodhoppers . . .* Shoes. **c1960** Wilson *Coll.* **scKY,** *Clodhoppers . . .* Heavy work shoes, brogans. **1965–70** *DARE* (Qu. W11, *Men's low, rough work shoes*) 175 Infs, **widespread,** Clodhopper; (Qu. W42b) 19 Infs, **scattered,** Clodhoppers.

4 By ext: a large or clumsy foot.

1950 *WELS (Big feet)* 20 Infs, **WI,** Clodhoppers. **1965–70** *DARE* (Qu. X38, . . *Unusually big or clumsy feet*) 469 Infs, **widespread,** Clodhoppers.

‡5 A mud dauber (here: of the subfamily *Sphecinae*).

1966 *DARE* (Qu. R20, *Wasps that build their nests of mud*) Inf **AR5,** Dirt dauber [has a] long nest; clodhopper build[s] nest like a ball; [both] look like wasps.

clodknocker n **chiefly Sth, esp S Atl** Cf **clodhopper**

1 A rustic.

1946 *PADS* 6.9, *Clod-knocker . . .* In some parts of the South also applied to a countryman in a derogatory sense. **1970** *DARE* (Qu. HH1, . . *A rustic or countrified person*) Infs **NC87, VA71,** Clodknocker. [Both Infs Black]

2 A large or clumsy shoe or foot.

1918 *DN* 5.20 **NC,** *Clod-knocker,* foot. **1942** Berrey–Van den Bark *Amer. Slang* 935 [Western slang], Clodhoppers, clod-knockers, *esp. large feet.* **1946** *PADS* 6.9 **swVA, eNC,** *Clod-knocker . . .* A heavy shoe. **1968–70** *DARE* (Qu. W11, *Men's low, rough work shoes*) Infs **GA81, MD13, NC87,** Clodknockers.

3 A marble: see quots.

1966 *DARE* (Qu. EE6a, . . *Kinds of marbles—the big one*) Inf **NC9,** Clodknocker. **1973** Ferretti *Marble Book* 42, *Clodknockers.* Ordinary marbles to be shot at.

clod masher See **clod crusher 1, 3**

clod melter, clod roller See **clod buster 1**

cloes, clo'es See **clothes**

clof(f) See **cloth**

clog n Also *clog foot* [Prob by ext of *clog* heavy, clumsy shoe (*DAE* 1733 →)] See also **clod** n **4**

A large or clumsy foot.

1968–70 *DARE* (Qu. X38) Infs **CT43, NJ25,** Clogs; **VA102,** Clog feet.

clog and chunk fence n

1939 *FWP Guide KS* 318, The "clog and chunk" fence consisted of a single strand of wire suspended between two posts. A cord about ten feet long, attached to the wire with a slip knot, would, when fastened to the right forefeet of horses or cattle, allow the animals to graze the length of the wire.

clog foot See **clog**

cloghopper n

1 =**clodhopper 2.**

1969 *DARE* (Qu. HH21, *A very awkward, clumsy person*) Inf **WI76,** Cloghopper.

2 =**clodhopper 4.**

1950 *WELS (Big feet)* 1 Inf, **seWI,** Cloghopper. **1969** *DARE* (Qu. X38, *Unusually big or clumsy feet*) Inf **WI76,** Cloghoppers.

clomb, clombe, clomben See **climb 2c**

clomber See **clomper**

clome, clomed See **climb 2c**

clomp v[1] [Alter of *clump*]

1 To walk heavily.

1903 *DN* 2.296 **seMA,** *Clomp . . .* To tread heavily or with much noise. **1914** *DN* 4.155 **seMA,** *Clomp . . .* To step heavily. **1950** *WELS (Walk heavily)* 7 Infs, **WI,** Clomping. **c1960** Wilson *Coll.* **csKY,** *Clomp . . .* To walk heavily and noisily. **1965–70** *DARE* (Qu. Y25, *To walk heavily, making a lot of noise: "He came _____ into the house."*) 116 Infs, **scattered,** Clomping (along); **NJ46, VA31,** Clomp, clomp; **MO32,** Clomp; **KY10,** A-clomping.

‡**2** To limp.

1968 *DARE* (Qu. BB1, *When a person has been injured so that when he walks he steps more heavily on one foot than the other, "He _____."*) Inf **CA**53, Clomps—he puts one leg down heavier than the other.

clomp v² [Alter of *clamp*]

To clamp, fasten.

1941 *Sat. Eve. Post* 13 Sept 52 **SE,** Clomp it [=an outboard motor] on the back [of the boat]. *Ibid,* I'll clomp it with my elbow.

clomper v Also *clomber* [c,nEng dial; cf *EDD*]

1967–70 *DARE* (Qu. Y25, *To walk heavily, making a lot of noise: "He came _____ into the house."*) Inf **KY**33, Clombering; **KY**72, Clompering.

clomper n

1 A heavy boot. [**clomper** v; cf *EDD* clomper sb.¹ 2 "A heavy hob-nailed boot"]

1903 *DN* 2.296 **seMA** (as of 1850s), *Clomper . . .* Heavy boot. **1916** *DN* 4.265 **seMA,** To take his great "clompers" off before he walks on the new "settin'-room mattin'."

2 in pl: False teeth. [Perh var of **chomper 2**]

1966–70 *DARE* (Qu. X13b) Infs **MS**68, **NC**88, **OK**54, Clompers. [2 Infs Black]

clonk v [Var of **clomp**]

1968–70 *DARE* (Qu. Y25, *To walk heavily making a lot of noise*) Infs **MD**21, **NJ**63, **WI**72, Clonking.

‡**clonker** n [**clonk**]

1967 *DARE* (Qu. X38, *Joking names for unusually big or clumsy feet*) Inf **IL**7, Clonkers.

clonk out v phr [Alter of *conk out,* perh infl by *clonk* to strike *(DAS)*]

To become or be made unconscious.

1967–68 *DARE* (Qu. BB14, *To suddenly become unconscious and fall*) Infs **KS**3, **PA**167, Clonked out; (Qu. BB15, *Somebody who is unconscious from a hard blow: "He's been _____ for ten minutes."*) Inf **PA**167, Clonked out.

clook See **cluck** n

clook-clook n Also *clou-clou* [Prob echoic]

=**yellowlegs 1.**

1959 *AmSp* 34.74, *Clook-clook, clou-clou* (greater and lesser yellowlegs).

clooky See **cluck** adj

cloom, cloomb See **climb 2e**

‡**clopper** n

A slipper.

1968 *DARE* (Qu. W21, *Soft shoes that people wear only inside the house*) Inf **CA**87, Cloppers.

clorte See **cloth**

close v

To turn off (a light).

1942 in 1944 *ADD* **nWV, Philadelphia PA,** 'Close the lights' = turn out the lights. **1967–69** *DARE* (Qu. Y42, *Expressions for putting out a lamp or light*) Infs **GA**54, **IL**45, **MN**2, **NY**119, Close the (or a, those) light(s); **MA**3, Close. **1972** Carr *Da Kine Talk* 127 **HI,** *Close the light* and *open the light* vs. *turn out the light* and *turn on the light* These loan translations have apparently entered Hawaii's English from a language that uses the verbs *close* and *open* for electric switches, just as English uses these verbs for water faucets. **1972** *DARE* File **Boston MA,** A Cambridge, Massachusetts landlady—Italian out of Boston's North End—put notes in the bathrooms at her house saying "Please close the lights when you leave." **1978** Kalibabky *Hawdaw* 2 **neMN.** **1982** *NADS Letters,* I grew up in New York City (born in 1948) . . . there are two expressions which always seem curious to my Oregon-born husband and also, to friends in various parts of the country . . . the other is one I remember my grandmother and other Eastern European immigrants of her generation using. It is "close the lights" for "turn off the lights".

close adj, adv Usu |klos|, also |klost| (see Pronc Intro 3.I.23); occas, **esp in NEng,** |klɛs, klʌs(t)| Pronc-spp *clost(e), clus(s), clust* Hence compar *clos(e)ter,* superl *closetest* [Cf *EDD* clost]

Std senses, var forms.

1815 Humphreys *Yankey in England* 104, *Clus, close.* **1892** *DN* 1.238 **cwMO,** *Closter.* **1893** Shands *MS Speech, Closte.* **1904** Day *Kin o' Ktaadn* 84 **ME,** An I heered 't was clus' on midnight. *Ibid* 87, A reg'lar chaps like I have been, a-stayin' clust to home. **1905** *DN* 3.394 **nwAR,** *Clost . . . Closter.* **1906** *DN* 3.116 **sIN,** *Clost.* **1908** *DN* 3.299 **eAL, wGA,** *Clost.* **1926** *AmSp* 1.415 **seGA,** An' ev'ry circle he'd come in closeter. **1926** Kephart *Highlanders* 103 **sAppalachians,** A man cain't lay cluss enough to you to keep warm. **1929** (1951) Faulkner *Sartoris* 235 **MS,** He pushes hit too clost. **1939** *LANE* Map 484 **cwCT,** [klʌs]. **1943** *Ibid* Map 714 **neME,** [kləs]. **1959** *VT Hist.* new ser 27.130, Close [klʌs] . . . Obsolescent. **1967–69** *DARE* Tape **AZ**4, That was the closetest mine; **NC**54, The closetest doctor was fourteen miles; **TX**24, They [=sheepherders] worked these ewes and lambs out every morning, and they'd have to keep the bred ewes there pretty clost.

close n¹

A marble game: see quot.

1958 *PADS* 29.32 **WI,** *Close: n.* A marble game played against a wall; the winner is the player who gets his marble closest to the objective.

close n² See **clothes**

close aboard adj phr [Cf *DNE* close aboard near, alongside; with *of* near to] **N Atl**

Very near.

1916 Macy–Hussey *Nantucket Scrap Basket* 127, "Close Aboard"— Very near. **1945** Colcord *Sea Language* 20 **ME, Cape Cod, and Long Island,** *Aboard.* Inside the bulwarks, on deck, or (figuratively) in collision: "She was almost aboard of us before we saw her." In this use, the preferred intensifier is close, often pronounced "clost." **1957** Beck *Folkl. ME* 167, A person at a distance is seen "in the offing" but soon comes "close aboard." [**1982** *DNE* 100, *Close . . close aboard . . .* Near to. 'close aboard of the church.']

close-clapped adj [*close* adv + pple of *clap* to press down: see *SND* clap v. 2; *OED* lists *close-clapped* (under *close* adv. C Combinations 2) but without supporting quot]

Chunky.

1960 Williams *Walk Egypt* 18 **GA,** With the close-clapped set of his body, he looked like an owl possessed by mistake of pants.

closed gentian n

A **gentian,** usu *Gentiana andrewsii* or *G. clausa,* which produces a scarcely-opened flower. Also called **blind gentian, bottle ~**

1848 Gray *Manual of Botany* 361, *G[entiana] Andrewsii . .* (Closed Gentian). **1900** Lyons *Plant Names* 171, *G[entiana] Andrewsii . .* Closed Gentian. **1950** Gray–Fernald *Manual of Botany* 1162, *G[entiana] Andrewsii . .* Closed Gentian . . . *G. clausa . .* Closed Gentian. **1959** Carleton *Index Herb. Plants* 28, *Closed Gentian:* Gentiana andrewsi [sic]. **1966–68** *DARE* (Qu. S26a, *Roadside flowers*) Inf **WI**58, Closed gentian; (Qu. S26b, *Wildflowers . . wet places*) Inf **NH**4, Soapwort—some call it (not correctly) closed gentian; (Qu. S26c, *Wildflowers . . in woods*) Inf **NC**36, Gentian—both open and closed; (Qu. S26d, *Wildflowers . . in meadows*) Inf **MA**6, Gentians—fringed and closed.

closed log fence n

1968 *DARE* (Qu. L61, *Fences made of solid logs*) Inf **MN**33, Closed log fence—laid lengthways; solid.

closed winter n

1933 *AmSp* 8.4.50 **NE,** A *closed winter* was a *hard winter,* one characterized by heavy snowfalls and blizzards.

close fence n [Perh *OED* close sb.¹ 2 an enclosed field, but perh *close* adj]

1852 Bickley *Hist. Tazewell Co. VA* 204 (as of 1779), The garden was about sixty yards from the house, and as no sawmills were in existence at that day in this county, slab-boards were put up in the manner called "wattling" for palings. These were some six feet long, and made what is called a close fence.

close-herd v, hence vbl n *close-herding* **West** Cf **loose-herd**

1 To keep cattle in a compact group; also transf.

1874 McCoy *Cattle Trade* 348 *(DA),* Like other extensive Colorado ranchmen, he outrides the country instead of close herding his stock. **1885** in 1967 *Chadron Rec.* (NE) 4 Sept 3/7, The cattlemen intend to round up everything on that range and close-herd what they do not ship. **1887** *Scribner's Mag.* 2.508/2 **CO,** A friend tells me he has heard a sheriff talk of "close-herding" several prisoners in his charge. On the plains it means the difficult art of keeping cattle in a compact body, close together. **1936** Adams *Cowboy Lingo* 73 **West,** To hold a herd of cattle on a new range until they felt at home was to 'locate' them . . . To hold them in a compact mass was 'close-herding' them. **1949** *PADS* 11.19 **CO.**

2 Fig: see quot.

1939 FWP *Guide MT* 414, *Close herdin'*—Cheek-to-cheek dancing.

close one n [Var of older, widespread *close call* or *close shave*] **chiefly Nth, N Midl** See Map

A narrow escape.

1965–70 *DARE* (Qu. KK45) 88 Infs, **chiefly Nth, N Midl,** Close one; **VT**12, Clost one.

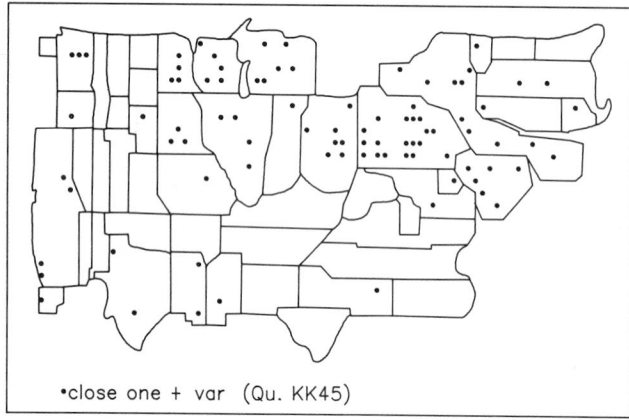

•close one + var (Qu. KK45)

close range n [*close* enclosed]

See quots.

1882 Chase *Editor's Run* 93 **NM,** Those who are able are buying land along water courses, enclosing their purchase, and as much government land back of it as they desire, with wire fence. This is "close range." **1968** Adams *Western Words, Close range*—a range enclosed with a wire fence.

‡**closestone** n

=**clingstone.**

1973 Allen *LAUM* 1.306, *Clingstone (peach)* . . . *Closestone,* from a southern Minnesota farmer of Ohio parentage.

closet n

1 also *china closet, cold closet, dish closet, kitchen closet, pot closet:* A small room adjoining a kitchen used for storage of food and/or dishes; a pantry. **chiefly Nth, esp RI** See also **bake closet**

1867 *Harper's Mag.* 36.64/2 **MA,** It [=the medicinal oil] is on the third shelf, right-hand side of the pot-closet. **1941** *LANE* Map 344, The map shows terms denoting, in general, a small room adjoining the kitchen, where food or dishes or both are stored. [The map shows 27 infs, **esp RI,** *Closet;* 9 infs, **RI, eCT, eMA,** Kitchen closet; 1 inf, **RI,** Dish closet; 1 inf, **RI,** Cold closet. Commentary:] *kitchen closet,* a small pantry . . *closet,* right off'n the kitchen . . *closet,* dark; *pantry,* light . . *closet,* for food and dishes . . *closet,* for victuals and dishes . . 'There are many different kinds of closets.' A neighbor keeps her victuals in the closet . . *closet,* 'where you cook (i.e., prepare food for heating) and mix. I don't use *pantry,* but many do.' . . *pantry,* not for cooking; *kitchen closet,* for dishes. **1949** Kurath *Word Geog.* 52, On the Narragansett Bay . . *closet* is the usual designation for the pantry. **1965–70** *DARE* (Qu. D8, *The small room next to the kitchen (in older houses) where dishes and sometimes foods are kept)* Infs **CO3, DC1, GA19, NH10, NC16, RI1,** Closet; **LA37A,** Closet, or kitchen closet; **FL11, TX51,** Kitchen closet; **MA72,** Dish closet; **NJ55,** Dish closet—wouldn't have food; **NJ69,** China closet. **1973** Allen *LAUM* 1.170, *Pantry* . . 1 inf, **neMN,** Closet; 1 inf, **swMN,** China closet.

2 also attrib: A toilet or outhouse. [*OED closet of ease* 1662]

1902 Sears *Catalogue* 652, *Plumbing Goods and Supplies* . . We quote only such articles as are most commonly used in the country, but . . can furnish anything you may wish in this line—Closets, Bath Tubs, [etc. *Closets* are illustrated by pictures of toilets.] *Ibid* 655, *Closet Seat with Cover.* [Illustr shows a toilet seat.] **1941** *LANE* Map 354 *(Privy)* 15 infs, **scattered throughout NEng,** Closet. **1948** *AmSp* 23.264 **Ozarks,** *Closet*

meant *privy.* **1949** *PADS* 11.5 **wTX.** **1949** Kurath *Word Geog.* 36, Expressions that occur in Western Pennsylvania, in northern West Virginia, and in adjoining parts of Ohio are: *closet* . . for the outdoor toilet. *Ibid* 53, *Closet,* in the Ohio Valley. **c1960** *Wilson Coll.* **csKY,** *Closet*—Privy. Very proper. "Pappy built mammy a new closet." **1962** Atwood *Vocab. TX* 53, *Outdoor toilet* . . . *Closet* (13 oc[currences]). **1965–70** *DARE* (Qu. M21a, *An outside toilet building*) 20 Infs, **scattered, but esp Sth,** Closet; **PA71,** Outside closet; (Qu. M21b, *Joking names for an outside toilet building*) Infs **IN30, NH14,** Closet; **AL11,** Old closet; (Qu. F37, . . *An indoor toilet*) 17 Infs, **scattered,** Closet; **ME16,** Flush closet. **1973** Allen *LAUM* 1.180, *Privy* . . . *Closet* and *watercloset* have a 13% and 12% frequency in Minnesota and North Dakota respectively, but only 4.2% in Iowa, with 7% in South Dakota and 8% in Nebraska. **1979** *DARE* File **cnMA,** The *closet* as in *go to the closet* meaning 'go to the toilet' was common enough when I was in grammar school (1923) so that the reprimand of our teacher, annoyed by whispering when she went to the supply closet for some paper, was greeted with guffaws. What she said was: "It's a pity you can't be quiet for the time it takes a teacher to step to the closet."

closeter, closetest See **close** adj, adv

closet fly n

=**cluster fly.**

1968 *DARE* (Qu. R12) Inf **OH**61, Closet fly.

close-up n Also called **fudging, inchings** n 2

In marble play: a move to gain a more favorable position; see quot.

1963 *KY Folkl. Rec.* 9.64 **ceKY,** *Trying to get closer shot by placing the hand in a position nearer to the marble being shot at:* close-up.

closies n pl

In marble play: see quot.

c1970 Wiersma *Marbles Terms* **swMI** (as of c1960), *Closies* . . marbles that hit together.

clost, closte, closter See **close** adj, adv

clot See **cloth**

clotburr n

1 also sp *clott-burr:* =**cockleburr 1** (here: *Xanthium spinosum*).

1822 Eaton *Botany* 517 *Xanthium* . . *strumarium* (clott-burr . . .). **1900** Lyons *Plant Names* 398, *Xanthium* . . Clotbur. **1911** Jepson *Flora CA* 456, *X[anthium] spinosum* . . Spiny Clotbur. **1974** Munz *Flora S. CA* 241, *X[anthium] spinosum* . . Spiny Clotbur.

2 also *clotebur, clitbur:* =**burdock 1.**

1876 Hobbs *Bot. Hdbk.* 24, *Clotbur* . . Arctium lappa. **1900** Lyons *Plant Names* 43, *A[rctium] Lappa* . . Clotbur (Clote-bur, Clit-bur). **1933** Small *Manual SE Flora* 1480, *A[rctium] minus* . . Clotbur. **1971** Krochmal *Appalachia Med. Plants* 58, *Arctium Lappa* . . Common Names . . clotbur. *Ibid* 60, *Arctium Minus* . . Common Names . . clotbur.

clotch See **klatch** n

clotcher See **klatcher**

clotebur See **clotburr 2**

cloth n Usu |klɔθ, klɑθ|, infreq |tl-|; pronc-spp *clawt, clof(f), clorte, clot,* used esp in representations of Black speech See Pronc Intro 3.I.17

Std senses, var forms.

1853 Simms *Sword & Distaff* 199 **SC** [Black], I no see no clot'. **1880** Harris *Uncle Remus Songs* 39 **GA** [Black], Dat ain't all, honey, but 'twon't do fer ter give out too much cloff fer ter cut one pa'r pants. **1888** Jones *Negro Myths* 114 **GA** [Gullah], Dem all gone up fuh tek dem las look at Buh Wolf . . . Dem raise up de clorte wuh bin ober eh face, an eh look dist as natrul. **1905** Culbertson *Banjo Talks* 25 **SE** [Black], Cotton-clof. **1922** Gonzales *Black Border* 152 **sSC, GA coasts** [Gullah], "Wuh kinduh clawt" you got?" "Homespun, gingham, calico . . . " **1936** *AmSp* 11.236 **eTX,** [k] > [t] by assimilation to the following [l]. Examples . . . With *cl-: climate,* . . *close,* . . *cloth* . . . ['tlaɪmɪt] . . [tlous], etc. In East Texas these pronunciations are widespread. They are not limited to the illiterate, but belong to the common speech.

clothes n pl Usu |klouz|, sometimes |klouðz|; infreq |tlouz| Pronc-sp *croase;* eye-dial *cloes, clo'es, close*

Std senses, var forms.

1815 Humphreys *Yankey in England* 104, *Close,* clothes. **1829** Tenney *Female Quixotism* 1.120 **sePA** [Black], But what debil put him in your head, Betty, to dress in masser [=master's] croase, and go in de grobe [=grove]? **1848** Lowell *Biglow* 143 "Upcountry" **MA** [Glossary], *Close, clothes.* **1887** (1967) Harris *Free Joe* 105 **GA**, The chap a-straddle of him is got store clo'es. **1905** Culbertson *Banjo Talks* 25 **SE** [Black], De gals jes' come an' go, A-spo'tin' sto'-cloes [=a-sporting store-clothes]. **1936** *AmSp* 11.234 **eTX**, *Clothes* is regularly [klouz], ([tlouz]). **1937** *AmSp* 12.269 **cVA**, An' 'tain't no wonder; ole, ragged, flappin' close (clothes). **1969** *DARE* (Qu. E1) Inf **NY**180, [kloŏz] tree.

clothesline night n Cf **mischief night**
=**cabbage night.**

     1980 *Verbatim Letters* **cwVT**, In the 1950's the night before Halloween was called 'clothesline night'. I suspect that clotheslines were festooned with yards of toilet paper.

clothes locker See **locker**

clothes-peg n [*W3 "Brit"*]

     1949 *PADS* 11.19 **CO**, *Clothes peg* . . . A clothes pin; not so common as *clothes pin.*

clothespress n [*clothes* + **press;** *OED* 1713 →]

1 A piece of furniture for storing clothing: a **wardrobe,** shelved cabinet, or chest of drawers.

     1773 in 1902 Singleton *Social NY* 83, [Joseph Cox . . London] . . makes . . clothes presses and chests, china shelves. **1870** U.S. Patent Office *Annual Rept. for 1868* 2.462/1 **IA**, *Clothes Press* . . . A series of winged or swinging bars is inclosed in a frame provided with a door, and having a cloth covering in front and rear. **1908** *DN* 3.299 **eAL, wGA**, *Clothespress* . . . Wardrobe. **1910** *DN* 3.439 **cwNY**, *Clothes-press* . . . Wardrobe. **1941** *LANE* Map 338 *(Clothes closet)* 3 infs, **CT, csMA**, *Clothes press,* 'a piece of furniture'; 1 inf, **sRI**, *Clothes press,* 'a closet or a piece of furniture with drawers'; 1 inf, **cMA**, *Clothes press,* 'a piece of furniture with four drawers, with or without a mirror'; 1 inf, **cMA**, *Clothes press,* 'a piece of furniture with shelves for clothing'; 1 inf, **csMA**, *Clothes press,* 'a piece of furniture with several drawers'; 1 inf, **csMA**, *Clothes press,* 'a piece of furniture 4 feet wide, 7 feet high, with drawers and a space to hang clothes in'; 1 inf, **cVT**, *Clothes press,* 'a chest of drawers', 1 inf, **cnVT**, *Clothes press,* 'a piece of furniture, higher than a bureau, with or without drawers'. **1950** *WELS (Place where you hang clothes: separate)* 4 Infs, **WI**, Clothespress; *(Piece of furniture where clothes are laid flat)* 2 Infs, **WI**, Clothespress. **1959** *VT Hist.* new ser 27.130, Clothespress . . . A wardrobe, receptacle for clothes. **1965–70** *DARE* (Qu. E1, *A piece of furniture that stands against the wall, and you hang clothes in it)* 43 Infs, **scattered,** Clothespress; **CA**115, Clothespress—New England word; **DE**2, Clothespress—this is built into the wall; **OH**18, Clothespress—that's permanent, old-fashioned; **SC**46, Clothespress—not common; [Note: *clothespress* was the first or only response of nearly half of these Infs, but 10 Infs indicated that the word was old-fashioned or known only from the speech of older relatives.] (Qu. E3, *A piece of furniture in which you lay clothes flat)* Infs **AR**14, **GA**75, **NH**6, **NY**41, **NC**48, **OR**4, Clothespress; **LA**2, Clothespress—for everyday clothes—had a curtain over the front, shelves to lay folded clothes on. **1971** Wood *Vocab. Change* 49 **SE**, The piece of furniture in which clothes can be hung is ordinarily called a *wardrobe.* Its synonyms *clothes press* and *press,* occur in Tennessee, Georgia, Alabama, Florida, and Oklahoma.

2 Transf: a clothes closet. **chiefly NEast, eN Midl** See Map

     1903 *DN* 2.350, *Clothes press* . . . Used instead of 'closet' in the Berkshire region of Massachusetts. **1912** *DN* 3.567 **cNY**, *Clothes-press* . . . Small, dark room where clothing is hung. **1934** Hanley Disks **cwRI**, I call it a clothespress . . . It's just built-in. [Inf says she doesn't think the very old houses before her time have built-in clothespresses.] **1949** Kurath *Word Geog.* 52, Throughout the New England settlement area and the North Midland, including the Shenandoah Valley and northern West Virginia, *clothes press* is still a common term for the clothes closet in rural areas. On Narragansett Bay, where *closet* is the usual designation for the pantry, and in Western Pennsylvania and the adjoining counties of Ohio and West Virginia, *clothes press* is current among all social classes in the country as well as in the cities. **1962** Atwood *Vocab. TX* 43, *Place to keep clothing* . . . *Clothes press* . . is almost non-existent in Texas. **1965–70** *DARE* (Qu. E2, *A built-in space in a room for hanging clothes)* 31 Infs, **chiefly NEast,** Clothespress; (Qu. D7, *A small space anywhere in a house where you can hide things or get them out of the way)* Infs **CT**39, **NY**75, 105, **PA**70, Clothespress. **1971** Wood *Vocab. Change* 49 **Sth,** When a storage room is a part of the floor plan, it is ordinarily called a *closet* or a *clothes closet* . . . *Press* and *clothes press* have scattered occurrences. **1973** Allen *LAUM* 1.168 *(Clothes closet [built in])* 2 infs,

sMN, Clothes press. **1980** *NYT Article Letters,* My 87 year old mother, who is from upstate New York and originally from the Hudson River area, still calls a closet a 'clothes press'.

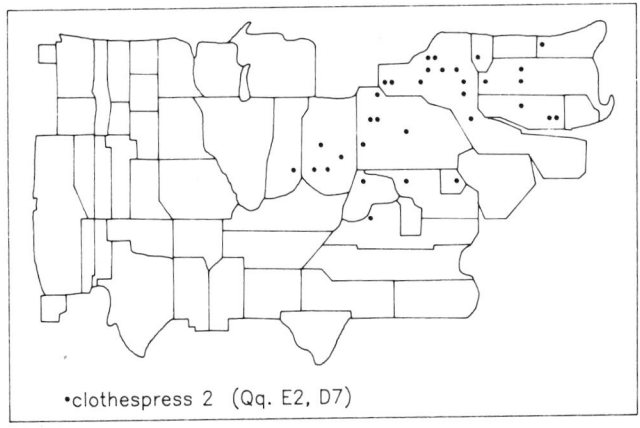

•clothespress 2 (Qq. E2, D7)

clothes rack n **chiefly Nth, N Midl** See Map

A framework for hanging clothes.

     1857 Strother *VA Illustr.* 46, He . . strode out, upsetting the waterbucket and knocking over the clothes-rack in his progress. **1950** *WELS (Place where you hang clothes: separate)* 3 Infs, **WI**, Clothes rack. **1965–70** *DARE* (Qu. E1) 110 Infs, **chiefly Nth, N Midl**, Clothes rack. **1973** Allen *LAUM* 1.168 **seSD**, *Clothes closet* (movable) [*Clothes rack* was said by 1 inf].

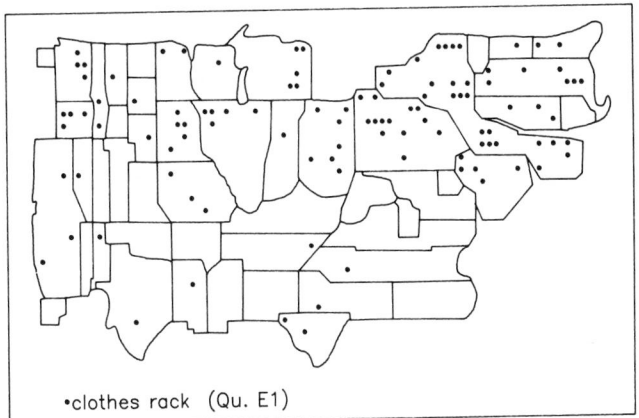

•clothes rack (Qu. E1)

clothes room n [Perh from Du *kleedkamer*] **Nth, esp N Atl**

A clothes closet.

     1857 Vaux *Villas & Cottages* 137 **NY**, In the attic . . a space for lumber is marked on the plan; but this might be used as a clothes-room. **1865** (1889) Whitney *Gayworthys* 176 **NEng**, She vanished up the end staircase, and hid herself away in the old clothes-room. **1941** *LANE* Map 338 *(Clothes closet)* 13 infs, **esp coastal NEng,** Clothes room. **1948** Davis *Word Atlas* 179, *Small room for hanging clothes* . . . 2 infs, **cnIN, cOH**, Clothes room. **1967–70** *DARE* (Qu. E2, *A built-in space in a room for hanging clothes)* Infs **MN**10, **NY**68, Clothes room; **NY**75, Clothes room, clothes closet; **NY**128, Closet, clothes room, clothespress; **NY**233, Clothes room. **1973** Allen *LAUM* 1.168, *(Clothes closet* [built-in]) 1 inf, **ceIA**, Clothes room: Older term than 'closet.'

clothes slice See **slice**

clothes tree n **chiefly Nth, esp NEast** See Map on p. 694

A piece of furniture, often a freestanding post with extended arms, for hanging clothes.

     1892 *Boston Journal* 19 Dec 1/7 (*DAE*), Our English Oak Clothes-Tree . . keeps your clothing from all wrinkles, dries and ventilates it, and preserves it from being 'mussed.' **1965–70** *DARE* (Qu. E1, *A piece of furniture that stands against the wall, and you hang clothes on it)* 43 Infs, **chiefly Nth, esp NEast,** Clothes tree; **VT**8, Clothes tree—no sides or doors.

cloth-of-gold n

1 A beach heather (here: *Hudsonia ericoides*).

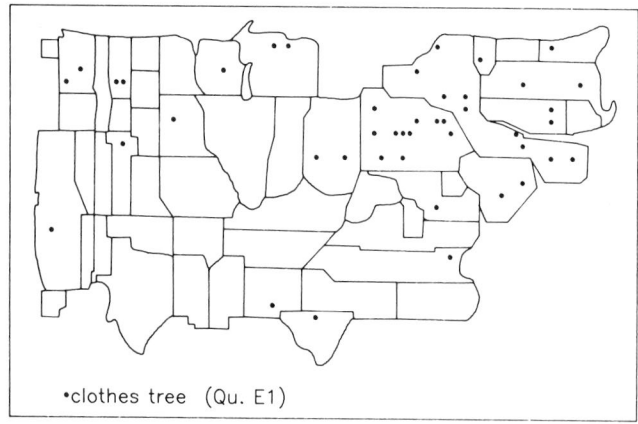

•clothes tree (Qu. E1)

1948 Wherry *Wild Flower Guide* 67, *H[udsonia] ericoides* . . known as Gold-heather or Cloth-of-gold, grows in Atlantic pinelands.

2 Perh a **yellow-puff.**

1965 Teale *Wandering Through Winter* 150, All across Texas, a host of . . names have been bestowed on the wild plants . . . They run from angel's trumpet . . to shame vine, . . cloth-of-gold, . . and kiss-me-and-I'll-tell-you.

cloth's low phr Cf *cotton is low* at **cotton** n 4

1966 *DARE* (Qu. W24a, . . *Expressions . . to warn a woman slyly that her slip is showing*) Inf **NC3**, You're slipping, cloth's low.

clott-bur See **clotburr**

clotted milk n

=**clabber** n[1] **1.**

1941 *LANE* Map 298 *(Sour milk)* 1 inf, **cMA**, [klʌtəd mɪɫk]. 1967–68 *DARE* (Qu. H59, *Milk that becomes thick as it turns sour*) Infs **CA97, IA17, NY65**, Clotted milk.

clou-clou See **clook-clook**

cloud n[1] Freq *black cloud, dark cloud* Cf **smoke**

A Black person or crowd of Black persons; hence v phr *cloud up*: see quot 1941.

1913 *DN* 4.163 **NW**, *Dark cloud,* . . A negro. 1939 *AmSp* 14.89 **eTN**, *Black cloud.* A crowd of negroes. 'The black cloud lives in bush town.' 1941 *LANE* Map 452B 1 inf, **ceMA**, [dak klɑad]; 1 Inf, **cnMA**, If you see two or three negroes coming along together, you say [ðɛə kʌmz ə klɑod] or [ɪt̬ s klɑodɪn ʌˑp].' 1944 *PADS* 2.55 **cnMO**, *Cloud* . . . A Negro . . . Used mainly by uneducated whites. 1952 Brown *NC Folkl.* 1.521 **c,eNC**, *Black cloud* . . . A crowd of Negroes. 1967–69 *DARE* (Qu. HH28, *Names and nicknames . . for . . Negro*) Infs **MD26, NY93, RI6, SC39**, Black cloud(s). 1970 Tarpley *Blinky* 264 **neTX**, *Teasing and derogatory names for negroes:* . . other responses: . . black clouds. *Ibid* 265, Clouds.

cloud n[2] Also *cloudy*

A type of marble.

1908 *DN* 3.299 **eAL, wGA**, *Cloud* . . . A clouded playing-marble. 1982 *DARE* File **ceKS**, *Cloudy* . . . A type of marble.

cloudberry n

A raspberry (here: *Rubus chamaemorus*). Also called **baked-apple berry, maroshka, outberry, salmonberry**

a1782 (1788) Jefferson *Notes VA* 37, Cloudberries. Rubus chamaemorus. 1876 Hobbs *Bot. Hdbk.* 24, Cloud berry, High blackberry, Rubus villosus. 1938 (1958) Sharples *AK Wild Flowers* 125, "Cloudberry" . . . An inhabitant of peat bogs . . . Edible fruit composed of a few soft drupelets. 1961 Douglas *My Wilderness* 215 **NH**, In open places the white petals of wild raspberries are on display and, less conspicuous, those of the cloudberry (*Rubus Chamaemorus*). 1981 Tabbert *Alaskan Engl.* 277.

cloudbust n Also *cloudburster, cloudbuster*

A cloudburst.

1939 *Hall Coll.* **wNC, eTN**, Cloud-bust. 1941 *Esquire* 15.4.161 **neKY**, There's coming in a cloud-bust. 1942 Berrey–Van den Bark *Amer. Slang* 71.8, *Rain* . . cloud burst. 1966–70 *DARE* (Qu. B25, . . *Joking names . . for a very heavy rain*) Infs **AL21, 43, CA1, 137, MA58, MI80, OK53**, Cloudbuster; **CA136, PA182, SC43**, Cloudburster; **CO47**,

Cloudbust; (Qu. B24, *A sudden, very heavy rain*) Infs **FL48, GA22, VA69**, Cloudbuster; **CO47, GA22**, Cloudbust; (QR, near Qu. B27, *A sudden rush of water coming from a heavy rain*) Inf **VA1**, Cloudbust. 1983 *MJLF* 9.35 **ceKY**, *Cloud bust* . . . a rain heavier than a *pour down,* lighter than a *gulley washer.*

cloud grass n

Perh a **grass-of-Parnassus.**

1954 *Harder Coll.* **cwTN**, Cloud grass.

‡**cloudspout** n

A cloudburst or waterspout.

1967 *DARE* (Qu. B27, *A sudden rush of water coming from heavy rain*) Inf **LA11**, Downpour, cloudspout—as it comes from [the] sky.

cloud up See **cloud** n[1]

cloudy See **cloud** n[2]

clout n[1]

1 rarely *clouk:* A piece of cloth; now esp a piece used for babies' diapers. **scattered, but esp Midl** See also **baby-clout, breech-clout** [Note: *clouting diaper* (quots 1733, 1754) = a type of cloth *(diaper)* suitable for babies' breeches]

[1733 *S.C. Gazette* 282/1 *(DAE),* Just Imported, and to be Sold . . . , platilas and clouting diaper. 1754 *Ibid* 20 June 2/2, Archibald & Richard Park Stobo Have just imported . . napkinning and clouting diapers, fringed diaper and damask table cloths.] 1859 Elwyn *Glossary, Clout* . . . Its other meanings we have kept as we had them from our ancestors, *i.e.,* a kitchen-cloth, etc. 1899 (1912) Green *VA Folk-Speech, Clout* . . . Any piece of cloth: as, a baby's clout. 1926 *DN* 5.398 **Ozarks,** *Clout* . . . Sometimes used to mean *diaper,* and the combination *britch-clout* is heard occasionally. 1950 *PADS* 14.21 **SC**, *Clout* . . . A quilted pad used to protect the outer clothes of infants, a pilch. 1966–70 *DARE* (Qu. W19, . . *The folded cloth worn by a baby in place of pants*) Infs **KY40, 42, MA5, NJ55, TN13, UT7**, Clout. 1967 *DARE* FW Addit **MA5**, *Clout*—diaper, noun and verb. Grandmother of Inf used the word c1860. 1968 *DARE* Tape **MD31**, In my younger days they called it a clouk or a hippen. Today they call 'em didies ['daɪdiz] . . . Yeh, they called 'em a [klɑʊk].

2 A blow; a beating. See also **clout** v **2**

1859 Elwyn *Glossary, Clout,* for *a blow on the head.* Though an old word, I have heard it but once in this country. 1899 (1912) Green *VA Folk-Speech, Clout* . . . A blow with the hand; a cuff. 1930 Shoemaker *1300 Words* 11 **cPA Mts** (as of c1900), *Clout*—A blow on the head or neck. 1966–70 *DARE* (Qu. Y11, . . *A very hard blow*) Infs **IA5, 15, MI100, NY67, 111, TX5, WV2**, Clout; **ME5**, Give him a good clout; (Qu. Y16, *A thorough beating*) Inf **MA13**, Clout.

3 Political influence or power. **orig Chicago IL, now widespread**

1937 Gosnell *Machine Politics* 82 **Chicago IL**, [Quoting a Chicago precinct captain:] No one . . gets anywhere in politics or business on his merits. He has to have the 'clout' from behind. 1958 *AmSp* 34.230 **Chicago IL**, He got the job because he had clout. 1967 *PADS* 47.5 **Chicago IL**, *Clout* 'influence.' 1978 Safire *Political Dict.* 123, Clout, in its power sense, applies to the ability of an individual or group to put across a program, decide a nomination, sway votes. In its influence sense, clout means the ability to reach and persuade those in power; it is one step removed from the power source.

4 A person who exercises political power in another's favor.

1980 *Capital Times* (Madison WI) 11 Feb 17/3 **Chicago IL**, They were so pleased with her that they gave her a glowing recommendation. Isn't that nice? Some cynical Chicagoans might ask: "Who's her clout? City Hall contracts for $25,000 don't just come down the chimney with Santa."

clout n[2] [Perh blend of **clod** n + *lout,* but cf *EDD clout* sb.[3] a clod of earth; a foolish or base person]

An awkward, stupid, or unmannerly person; a person considered to be rough or countrified.

1950 *WELS* (A man with the reputation of running after women) 1 Inf, **cWI**, Clout. 1965–70 *DARE* (Qu. HH21, *A very awkward, clumsy person*) Infs **IL92, MI28, 51, MO12, OR4, WA25**, Clout; (Qu. HH1, . . *A rustic or countrified person*) Infs **NE9, WI62**, Clout; (Qu. HH3, *A dull and stupid person*) Infs **MD26, NY59**, Clout.

clout v

1 To diaper. [**clout** n[1] **1**] *?obs*

1967 [see **clout** n[1] **1**].

2 To hit, slug. [clout n¹ **2**]

1895 *DN* 1.396 **cNY,** *Clout . . .* to strike. **1930** Irwin *Amer. Tramp,* *Clout.* — To steal, generally by force . . . To strike. **1955** Willingham *To Eat a Peach* 201 **TN,** If I'd acted that way when I was his age, my old man would have clouted the hell out of me. **1966–70** *DARE* (Qu. Y14a, *To hit somebody hard with the fist*) 15 Infs, **chiefly east of Missip R,** Clout; (Qu. Y14b, *To hit somebody with the open hand*) Infs **CA**15, **MI**108, Clout.

3 To exercise political power (for). **esp Chicago IL**

1958 *AmSp* 34.230 **Chicago IL,** He clouted himself a job. **1980** *Capital Times* (Madison WI) 11 Feb 17/3 **Chicago IL,** When Brady was asked about the fat contract for his former partner and close friend, he also denied that his power had anything to do with it. "I did not clout for her," he declared.

clove n, also attrib [Du *kloof, klove*] **NY, esp Hudson R Valley**
A ravine or valley; a mountain pass.

1777 in 1901 *Documents Revol. Hist. NJ* 1.433 **NY,** The other Part [of Washington's army is] to be commanded by Mr. Green, at the Clove, and Parts adjacent. **1827** in 1928 Roosevelt *Amer. Backlogs* 16 **NY,** Passing through a steep and precipitous canyon, a 'clove-road' as it was called in the vernacular. **1896** *DN* 1.414 **NY,** *Clove:* a narrow gap or valley, = *notch* in N.E. This word is used in the Catskills. De Vere is mistaken in giving the form *cove* for the Catskills. *Cove* is used in some varieties of English . . , but is not the same as the Catskill word, which is clearly the Dutch *kloof.* **1929** *AmSp* 5.154 **eNY,** *Clove . .* for a ravine. **1939** (1962) Thompson *Body & Britches* 73 **NY,** For them was named Smith's Clove, a cleft in the mountains, sometimes called the Kitchen of the County. **1983** *Lutz Coll.* **seNY,** *Clove* — As a term for a gap or pass or notch in the hills, the word appears in some place names in Rockland and Orange Counties, N.Y., and farther north in the Catskills. It seems to have been applied especially to a gap through which travelers could most easily cross a ridge.

clove apple n
See quot 1949.

1939 Wolcott *Yankee Cook Book* 284, Do you remember the clove-apple on grandmother's parlor whatnot long ago? Call it a "pomander" today, but it still remains an apple solidly embedded with cloves and guaranteed to last half a century. **1949** Brown *Amer. Cooks* 818 **VT,** *Clove apple . . .* A hard winter apple stuck with as many cloves as it will hold and allowed to dry in the air while the spice prevents its decay.

‡cloven bread n
1970 *DARE* (Qu. H32, *. . Fancy rolls and pastries*) Inf **SC**67, Cloven bread ['klovn breɪd] made with citron, pecans, and fruits that are used in fruitcake.

clove pink n [From the odor]
A cultivated pink (*Dianthus* spp).

1983 *Greenfield Recorder* (MA) 21 May (Hemenway column, as of 1920), At each side of the stone walk, near the fence, there were flower beds that had yellow day lilies, . . sometimes spice pinks (also called clove pinks).

clover-eater n *obs* Cf **clay-eater 2**
1869 *Overland Mth.* 3.129 **SW,** For no particular reason that I am aware of, a Virginian is styled a "Clover-eater."

clover kicker n Cf **kicker**
1968–69 *DARE* (Qu. HH1, *. . A rustic or countrified person*) Infs **MI**78, **PA**199, Clover kicker.

clown n
=**white-breasted nuthatch.**

1956 *AmSp* 31.186 **CA,** Clown [=] White-breasted nuthatch . . . From its topsy-turvy clambering over trees.

cloy v Usu |klɔɪ|; also, **esp NEng,** |klaɪ| Pronc-sp *cly;* hence past, past ppl, and rarely pres spp *clide, clied, clyed* Cf *DJE* **cly**
Std sense, var forms.

1890 *DN* 1.77 **NJ,** *Clied:* to surfeit. 'To clied horses on grass.' **1895** *DN* 1.386 **ME,** *Clied* (*i.e.* cloyed): surfeited, unwilling to eat more. Appears to have become an adjective in some localities, the verb having become obsolete, and then to have been taken up in this form and used as a verb . . . [*DN*: In W. Conn. the use of the verb and of the participle as adjective presents nothing remarkable; even the current pron. [klaɪ] is quite in line with other words in the dialect.] **1904** *DN* 2.424 **Cape Cod MA,** *Cloyed . . .* Pronounced [klaɪd]. **1907** *DN* 3.183 **seNH,** *Cly . . .* To cloy. "I've eaten so much I am clied." **1909** *DN* 3.410 **nME,** *Clied.* **1956** *VT Hist.*

new ser 24.79 (as of 1800s), "She was clyed." Possibly the spelling is "clide." It meant "full of."

club n

1 Formerly of a man's hair, now only of a woman's: a bunch or gathering, a knot or bun. [From the knobbed shape; *OED* 1785–95 →] once general, now **chiefly S Midl**

1791 *MA Mag.* 3.221/2, What would become of the ladies' *bishops* and *cushions,* and of the *clubs* and *tight breeches* of our bucks? **1855** Griswold *Republican Court* 53 (as of 1788), His [=Alexander Hamilton's] hair is turned back from his forehead, powdered, and collected in a club behind. **1886** Longfellow *Life of H.W. Longfellow* 1.19 **ME,** A . . gentleman . . wearing . . the old-style dress . . his hair tied behind in a club, with black ribbon. **1940** (1942) Clark *Ox-Bow* 190 **NV** (as of 1885), He looked like a Mex, though his hair was done up in a club at his neck, like an Indian's, and his face was wide, with high, flat cheeks. **1954** *Harder Coll.* **cwTN,** *Club . . .* The knot of hair on a woman's head formed by putting the hair up. **1968–70** *DARE* (Qu. X3, *When a woman puts her hair up on her head in a bunch*) Infs **KY**38, 85, **TN**24, 27, 52, **VA**35, 42, Club.

2 See **clubfoot** n **1.**

club v¹ [club n **1**] *obs*
To put hair into a knot at the back of the head.

1813 (1939) Hartsell *Memora* 11.110 **PA,** One of the Cheroke Indians . . caut his hare that was clubed up.

club v² [Imit]
=**clomp** v **1.**

1969 *DARE* (Qu. Y25, *To walk heavily, making a lot of noise: "He came _____ into the house."*) Inf **KY**11, Clubbing.

club ax n
An ax, esp one with a heavy head.

1937 in 1977 *Amer. Slave Suppl. 1* 1.264 **AL,** In talking of splitting wood Isaam spoke of the ax he used which he called a "club ax"; and when asked what kind of ax it was he picked up the ax in his yard (an ordinary chopping ax) and showed it to the writer. **1966–68** *DARE* (Qu. L35, *Hand tools used for cutting underbrush and digging out roots*) Infs **GA**22, Club ax; **NC**49, Grubbing hoe; club ax for bigger stuff; **SC**9, Club ax — an ordinary cutting ax.

clubby n See **clabber** n²

clubby adj [Cf *EDD* **clubby** adj.¹ "Thick-set, sturdy"] Cf **club** v²
1 See quot.

1966 *DARE* (Qu. W42b, *. . Men's square-toed shoes*) Inf **WA**1, Clubby.

2 See quot.

1968 *DARE* (Qu. HH21, *A very awkward, clumsy person*) Inf **NC**82, Clubby, ill at ease.

club fist n **esp Appalachians** Also called **fist stalk**
A children's game played by interlocking the fists: see esp quot 1883.

1883 Newell *Games & Songs* 134 **GA, PA,** *Club Fist.* A child lays on a table his clenched fist, with the thumb elevated; another grasps the raised thumb with his own fist, and so on until a pile of fists is built up. A player, who remains apart from the group, then addresses the child whose hand is at the top: "What's that?" "A pear." "Take it off or I'll knock it off." . . The fist [is] withdrawn as speedily as possible, to escape a rap from the questioner. When only one is left, the following dialogue ensues: "What have you got there?" "Bread and cheese." [A chain of questions & answers follows, ending:] "Where's the cat?" "Behind the church-door. The first who laughs, or grins, or shows the teeth has three pinches and three knocks." Then follows a general scattering; for some child is sure to laugh. **1952** Brown *NC Folkl.* 1.66, *Club fist.* [7 versions of the game are listed.] **1953** Brewster *Amer. Nonsinging Games* 29 **NM,** *Clubfist . . .* When only one player has one hand free from the tower of fists, he calls to the player whose fist is on top, "What have you got there?" The other answers, "Clubfist." Then at the command "Take it off or I'll knock it off," he either removes his fist or has it removed forcibly by a blow from the questioner. **1956** *KY Folkl. Rec.* 2.125 **wKY. 1959** McAtee *Odd-ments* 7 **NC,** *Club Fist* — a bedtime rigmarole — What you got there? Bread and butter. Where is my share? Cat's got it . . . First one speaks a word will get a box with five red nails in it. **1966** *DARE* Tape **AL**3, Club fist . . . "What you got there?" . . "Club fist." **1968** Haun *Hawk's Done Gone* 276 **eTN,** He was all the time learning her something. How to . . play . . club fist as his ma had showed him when he was little. **1980** *Foxfire 6* 281 **nGA,** *Club Fist.*

clubfoot n

1 also *club*: A large or clumsy foot.

1954 *Harder Coll.* **cwTN,** *Club feet:* Large feet. **1965–70** *DARE* (Qu. X38, *Joking names for unusually big or clumsy feet*) 108 Infs, **scattered,** Clubfeet; NC55, Clubfoot; **KY40, OR14,** Clubs.

2 See **clubfoot** adj.

3 See quot.

1931–33 *LANE Worksheets* **cnCT,** A scallion is a club foot; it runs to tops.

clubfoot adj Also *clubfooted* [**clubfoot** n]

Having large, clumsy feet; hence n *clubfoot* one who stumbles; a clumsy person.

1954 *Harder Coll.* **cwTN,** *Clubfoot:* adj. Of a mule: that stumbles, *clubfooted. Clubfoot:* n. A mule that is a stumbler. **1965–70** *DARE* (Qu. X38, *Joking names for unusually big or clumsy feet*) 23 Infs, **scattered, but esp MO, OK, KY,** Clubfooted; (Qu. Y25, *To walk heavily, making a lot of noise: "He came _____ into the house."*) Inf CO47, Clubfooted Bill, [came] in like a clubfooted elephant; (Qu. HH21, *A very awkward, clumsy person*) Infs CA8, 158, IL4, Clubfoot; **CA120, TX43, UT4, VA80,** Clubfooted.

club in v phr [*club* an association of people]

To contribute to a common purpose.

1904 Day *Kin o' Ktaadn* 72 ME, The boys, I ricollick, they all clubbed in / An' bought a brindle bull ca'f's untanned skin.

club moss n

Std: a plant of the genus *Lycopodium.* Also called **creeping Jennie 2, crowfoot 4, evergreen, foxtail, ground pine** For other names of var spp see **buckhorn 2, Christmas green, coral evergreen, elkhorn 2, elk moss, ground cedar, ground festoon, liberty, moonfruit pine, prince's pine, running pine, running vine, staghorn moss, trailing vine**

cluck v [From the characteristic noise made by a hen wanting to set. Attested in Engl from 1611 *(OED),* but US distrib suggests also independent borrowing in some regions from Ger *glucken, klucken* and perh Norw *klukke.* See also **cluck** n] **Nth, esp PA, WI, Upper MW**

Of a hen: to be broody or setting; hence *clucking hen, clucker,* a broody or setting hen.

1937 *AmSp* 12.104 [**Upper MW**], A setting hen may be . . a *clucker,* a *clucking hen.* **1939** *LANE* Map 214 *(Setting hen),* Only five informants offer different terms . . , calling a hen that is actually hatching a *setting hen,* but one that only wants to sit either a *broody hen* . . or a *clucker* [1 inf, **swCT**]; 1 inf, **cCT,** [klʌkə]; 1 inf, **swCT,** *Clucking hen,* 'because she goes round clucking'; 1 inf, **nwRI,** *Clucking hen,* not heard from natives; 1 inf, **csMA,** [klʌkɪn hen]; 1 inf, **ceCT,** [ʃi z klʌkɪn]; 1 inf, **cCT,** [ðə hen z klʌkən]. **1949** Kurath *Word Geog.* 32 PA, Clucker. **1950** *WELS (When a hen stops laying and begins to sit on her eggs, you say she _____)* 15 Infs, clucking; 2 Infs, **wWI,** Clucks; 1 Inf, **cWI,** Is a clucker. **1962** Atwood *Vocab. TX* 57 **cTX,** *Setting hen* . . occasionally *clucker.* **1965–70** *DARE* (Qu. K72, *When the hen stops laying and begins to sit on the eggs . . , she's a _____*) Infs **AK8, MD22, MA66, MI38, MN15, PA92, VA25, WI54,** Clucking hen; **LA39,** She's clucking; **MI56, 107, NY77, PA174, 187, 198, SD3,** Clucker; **NC76,** Clucker—comes from New Jersey; heard some people from there use it. **1973** Allen *LAUM* 1.255, Setting hen . . . Clucking hen [4 infs, **MN**] . . . Clucker [2 infs, **nwMN, ceND**]. **1981** *Broaddus Coll.* **ceKY** (as of 1958), *Clucking hen*—a setting hen.

cluck n, also attrib Usu |klʌk|, also |kluk, klok| Also sp *cloak, clook, glook, kluck* [Borrowed independently in several regions from Ger *glucke, klucke* (PaGer *gluuk*) broody hen, and perh also Norw *klukk* broody (adj), *klukkhøne* broody hen; cf **cluck** v, adj]

1 A broody or setting hen, a hen with chicks. **chiefly PA, N Cent, Upper MW** See Map

1914 *DN* 4.104 KS, Cluck . . . Hen. "The old cluck takes good care of her chicks." **1935** *AmSp* 10.170 **sePA** [English of PA Germans], Kluck, a setting hen or a mother hen. **1937** *AmSp* 12.104 [**Upper MW**], A setting hen may be a *cluck.* **1939** *LANE* Map 214 *(Setting hen)* 1 inf, **csCT,** Cluck, heard from natives of German ancestry; 1 inf, **cwMA,** [klʌk, ~ hen]. **1949** Kurath *Word Geog.* 32, For a setting hen one commonly hears in Pennsylvania the term *clook* . . riming with *cook,*

sometimes *cluck* or *clucker.* **1950** *WELS (When a hen stops laying and begins to sit on her eggs, you say she _____)* 5 Infs, **seWI,** (Is a) cluck; 1 Inf, **cWI,** Old cluck; *(A hen that is on the eggs to hatch them)* 16 Infs, **esp ce,seWI,** Cluck; 1 Inf, **swWI,** Old cluck; *(The small shelter for a hen)* 2 Infs, **eWI,** Cluck coop; 1 Inf, **ceWI,** Cluck box. **1951** *AmSp* 26.253 NY, Cluck (klʌk, kluk) (setting hen). **1962** Atwood *Vocab. TX* 57, *Setting hen* . . . 64 instances of a form spelled *clook, cluck, glook,* and occasionally *clucker.* The usage is concentrated in Central Texas . . and is characteristic of, but not confined to, informants of German language background. **1965–70** *DARE* (Qu. K72, *When the hen stops laying and begins to sit on the eggs . . , she's a _____*) 48 Infs, **chiefly PA, N Cent, Upper MW,** Cluck; OH77, [kluk]; PA75, Cloak [klok]; PA21, Old cluck; [PA158, ['briˌgluk] or breeding hen]; (Qu. M16, *The small shelter for a hen that can be moved*) Infs PA204, 235, WI51, 68, Cluck box; PA204, Cluck pen. **1967** *DARE* Tape MN8, We used to call 'em [=portable shelters for hens] . . little cluck coops. We made 'em out of old boxes. **1968** *Helen Adolph Festschrift* 36 **cePA,** *Kluck*—Most people in the area use this Pennsylvania German term when referring to a setting hen. **1973** Allen *LAUM* 1.255, Setting hen . . . Cluck [29 infs, **chiefly MN**] . . . Cluck—used by local Scandinavian people [1 inf, **nwND**] . . . Clook [2 infs, **csMN, neNE**]. **1982** *Barrick Coll.* **csPA,** Clook [kluk] . . . Setting hen, or hen with chicks.

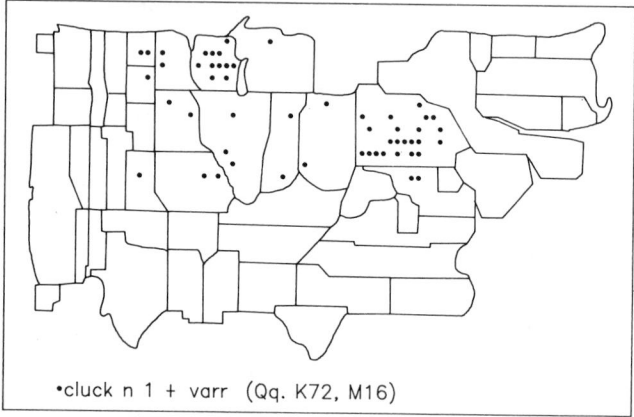

•cluck n 1 + varr (Qq. K72, M16)

2 See quot. [?Confusion between **cluck** n **1** and *clutch*]

1902 *DN* 2.231 **sIL,** Cluck . . . A sitting [sic for *setting*] of eggs.

cluck adj Usu |klʌk|, also |klɑk| Also *clucky* Pronc-sp *clooky* [sEngl dial *cluck, cluck-hen (EDD* at *cluck*), nEngl and Scots *clock-hen (EDD* at *clock* v.[2] sb.[2]); but US distrib suggests also independent borrowing in some regions from Ger *gluckhenne* broody hen; Norw *klukk* broody (adj), *klukkhøne* broody hen, setting hen] **chiefly PA, N Cent, Upper MW**

Of a hen: setting or wanting to set, broody.

1923 *DN* 5.204 **swMO,** Cluck . . . Said of a brooding hen. "That ol' hen's cluck." *i.e.,* setting, or with chickens. **1939** *LANE* Map 214 *(Setting hen)* 1 inf, **cwMA,** [klʌk hen]. **1940–41** Cassidy *WI Atlas* **csWI,** Clucky hen—a hen that wants to sit on eggs. **1950** *WELS (When a hen stops laying and begins to sit on her eggs, you say she _____)* 1 Inf, **WI,** Is cluck; 1 Inf, Cluck hen; 1 Inf, Goes cluck, goes broody. **1965–70** *DARE* (Qu. K72, *When the hen stops laying and begins to sit on the eggs . . , she's a _____*) Infs **IA1, MI38, 91, MN23, ND1, OH70, PA163, 166, TX4, WI14, 24,** Cluck hen; **MI23, 38,** Clucky hen; **OH89,** Clooky hen. **1973** Allen *LAUM* 1.255, Setting hen . . . Cluck hen [6 infs, **MN, IA, ND**] . . . Cluck hen . . /klɑk ~/ [1 inf, **seMN**] . . . Clucky hen [1 inf, **cIA**]. **1975** *DARE* File neMN, Terms . . naturalized in the English usage of the Norwegian-American community . . [include] cluck hen, clucky.

clucker n

1 A damaged bivalve mollusk: see quots. Cf **rattler**

1894 *DN* 1.329 **sNJ,** Clucker: frozen oysters. **1899** (1912) Green *VA Folk-Speech* 119, Clucker . . . An oyster that has been kept so long out of the water as to lose its liquor, and sounds hollow when the shell is struck, is called a *"clucker."* [**1967** *Dict. Canadianisms* 155, Clucker . . . the two shells of a scallop still joined at the hinge after the scallop has died naturally.]

2 See **cluck** v.

clucking hen n

1 See **cluck** v.

2 =**limpkin**. [*DJE* 1679 →]

1917 (1923) *Birds Amer.* 1.201, *Limpkin—Aramus vociferus . . . Clucking-hen.* **1946** Hausman *Eastern Birds* 233, *Limpkin. Aramus pictus . . . Clucking Hen.*

clucky See **cluck** adj

clue See **clew** n²

cluff v [Prob alter of *clove*, past tense of *cleave*] *arch*

1884 Harrison *Negro Engl.* 252 **SE**, *Pres.* cleave (to split)—*Past.* cluff (I cluff him in two)—*Pass. Part.* cluff.

clum, clumb, clumbed See **climb 2a**

‡clumber v [Prob alter of Engl dial *clumper* to tread heavily and clumsily; prob also infl by *lumber*] Cf **clumper**

1970 *DARE* (Qu. Y25, *To walk heavily*) Inf **TX**98, Clumbering along.

‡clumbly adj [Prob alter of *crumbly*]

1965 *DARE* (Qu. C32, *When soil breaks up easily in your fingers, it's* ———) Inf **OK**1, Clumbly [ˈklʌmblɪ].

clump n [*EDD* clump sb.¹ 2 "A heavy, inactive person"] =**clod** n **2b**.

1950 *WELS* (*A very awkward or clumsy person*) 1 Inf, **seWI**, Clump. **1969** *DARE* (Qu. HH21, *A very awkward, clumsy person*), Inf **CT**35, Clump.

clumper n [*EDD* clumper sb. 4 *pl.* "Thick, heavy shoes"]

A work shoe.

1845 *Knickerbocker* 26.417 **NJ**, Stilton made me ten pairs of 'clumpers.' **1859** Elwyn *Glossary*, Clumpers. *Very thick and heavy shoes.* Forby, who says wooden shoes are so called in Holland, gives a Belgic word, *klompen*, for its origin. We used the word, as boys, in the above sense. Shoes with thick soles we called a "real pair of *clumpers.*" **1966** *DARE* (Qu. W11, *Men's low, rough work shoes*) Inf **MT**4, Clumpers [ˈklʌmpɚz].

clumpety-clump adv [Echoic]

1968 *DARE* (Qu. Y25, *To walk heavily*) Inf **VT**8, Clumpety-clump.

clump mustard n

A wallflower.

1967 *DARE* FW Addit **CO**, Clump mustard—wallflower *(Erysimum capitatum)*.

clumse n [Prob back-form < *clumsy*, but perh also rel to Engl dial *clumse* speechless, loutish (< Norw *klumsa*)] *?obs*

1899 (1912) Green *VA Folk-Speech* 119, Clumse . . . A stupid, awkward person. "What a great *clumse* you are."

clumsy-jack n [jack n¹]

1908 *DN* 3.299 **eAL, wGA**, Clumsy-jack . . . A clumsy, awkward fellow.

clunk n

1 also *clunker:* An old, dilapidated vehicle or other mechanical device. [Prob echoic] **chiefly Nth, West** See Map

1938 *AmSp* 13.307 [Bus driver lingo], Clunk. A bus, usually old and worn-out. **1942** Berrey–Van den Bark *Amer. Slang* 766.3, *Decrepit car.* Clunk, crate of worms, . . junk heap. **1947** Jones *Evergreen Land* 181

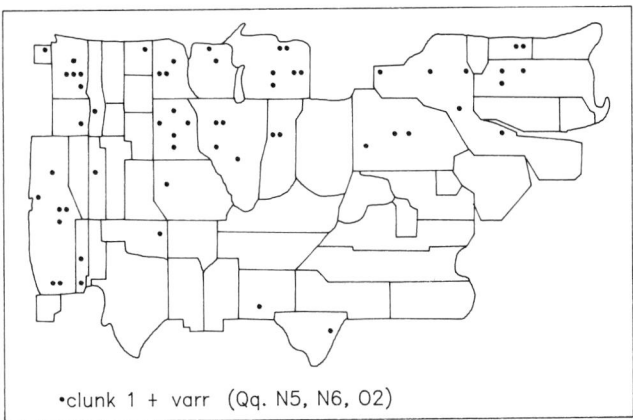

•clunk 1 + varr (Qq. N5, N6, O2)

WA, They had those old DC-4's—those old four-motor Douglas clunks. **1950** *WELS* (*Old broken-down car*) 2 Infs, **WI**, Clunk; 2 Infs, Clunker; (*Joking names for a pocket watch*) 1 Inf, Clunker. **1956** *AmSp* 31.227 [Air Force slang], Clunker . . . An aircraft that performs poorly. **1957** *AmSp* 32.193 **MA, NH** [Among target club members], *Clunker* . . . An old, dilapidated, or poorly rebuilt handgun . . . Sometimes modified into *old clunk.* **1960** Wentworth–Flexner *Slang*, Clunk . . . An old or worn-out piece of machinery; an old bus or car. *c1935.* **1963** *AmSp* 38.43 **RI** [Truckers' speech], Clunker [An old truck]. **1965–70** *DARE* (Qu. N5, . . *Automobile, especially an old or broken-down car*) 44 Infs, **chiefly Nth**, (Old) clunker; **ID**3, **WA**3, 6, 12, 30, **WI**34, (Old) clunk; (Qu. N6) **UT**5, Clunker; (Qu. O2, . . *An old, clumsy boat*) Infs **CA**80, 86, **MI**10, 80, 90, **MA**1, **NH**18, **PA**76, (Old) clunker; **MN**33, **WI**34, (Old) clunk.

2 also *clunker:* A hard blow.

1943 in 1960 Wentworth–Flexner *Slang*, Clunk . . . "One clunk on the knuckle." **1968–70** *DARE* (Qu. Y11, . . *"Joe really hit him a* ———.'*) Infs **CT**43, **NY**96, Clunker.

3 also *clunkhead:* A dull, stupid person; a clumsy or careless person.

1934 Runyon *Blue Plate Special (DAS)*, Because you'll be listed among the clunks. **1950** *WELS* (*A very awkward or clumsy person*) 2 Infs, **WI**, Clunk. **1952** in 1960 Wentworth–Flexner *Slang* 112, "Some clunkhead sent me three live quail!" Arthur Godfrey, radio, Jan. 1. **1966–68** *DARE* (Qu. N12, . . *Somebody who drives carelessly or not well*) Inf **WA**8, Clunk; (Qu. HH16, *Uncomplimentary words . . used . . of a person: "Don't invite him. He's a* ———.'*) Inf **IA**46, Clunk. **1974** *AmSp* 49.205, (*Terms for low intelligence*) Clunkhead.

clunker n

1 See **clunk 1, 2**.

2 =**bullfrog 1**. [Echoic; cf **lunker**]

1966 *DARE* (Qu. P22, . . *A very large frog that makes a deep sound*) Inf **MI**10, Clunker.

clunkhead See **clunk 3**

‡clupper n Cf **clumper**

1969 *DARE* (Qu. X38, . . *Unusually big or clumsy feet*) Inf **MA**56, Cluppers [ˈklʌpəz].

clus, cluss, clust See **close** adj, adv

clusterberry n

=**mountain cranberry**.

1900 Lyons *Plant Names* 386, *V[accinium] vitis-idæa* . . Cluster-berry.

cluster fly n

1 A large, dark-brown fly *(Pollenia rudis)*. Also called **attic fly, buckwheat fly**

1882 U.S. Natl. Museum *Proc.* 5.636 **NY**, The flies . . . hang from the cornice of a room in large clusters, like swarming bees . . . "*Cluster flies.*" **1965** Teale *Wandering Through Winter* 284 **VT**, She had been busy sweeping up cluster flies . . . These elongated insects are part of every north-country winter . . . When autumn comes and the temperature falls below a certain point, the flies seek out darkened crannies . . . When the temperature rises inside the buildings, the insects are attracted to light and cluster on the inside of windowpanes; hence their common name. **1968–70** *DARE* (Qu. R12) Inf **NY**105, Cluster fly, same as buckwheat fly; (Qu. R13) Inf **IL**126, Cluster flies—get in attic—black in color. **1975** *DARE* File **csWI**, Attic flies—some call them cluster flies.

2 See quot.

1968–69 *DARE* (Qu. R10, *Very small flies that don't sting, often seen hovering in large groups or bunches outdoors in summer*) Inf **NY**155, Cluster fly; **NY**113, Cluster flies.

cluster lily n **West**

=**brodiaea**, esp **blue dicks**.

1897 Parsons *Wild Flowers CA* 262, Cluster-lily . . *Brodiæa capitata.* **1915** (1926) Armstrong *Western Wild Flowers* 16, *Brodiæa capitata*—There are several other names, such as Cluster Lily and Hog-onion. **1963** Craighead *Rocky Mt. Wildflowers* 17, Wild Hyacinth *Brodiaea douglasii* . . Other names: Cluster-lily.

clutch n¹

1 A clump (of trees). [Cf *EDD* clutch sb.² 2 "A quantity, number"]

1929 *AmSp* 5.22 **sMD,** While motoring through Southern Maryland recently he was directed by a native to go up past that "clutch of woods," meaning ten or a dozen trees in a clump. He was . . not [familiar] with a "clutch of trees."

‡**2** A piggyback ride.

1967 *DARE* (Qu. Y31, *If a child asked his father to carry him on his back, he might say, "Give me a _____.")* Inf **PA**18, ['pukəl bæk], clutch.

3 See **klatch** n.

clutch n² See culch 1

clutter hole n

1966 *DARE* (Qu. D7, *A small space anywhere in a house where you can hide things or get them out of the way)* Inf **ME**5, Clutter hole.

clutter work n

1966 *DARE* (Qu. KK32, *Do you use the word "busywork" around here?)* Inf **WA**12, We call it clutter work.

cly, clyed See cloy

co v Often repeated, usu |ko| or |ku|, rarely |'koə| or |'kuə|; also, in combs, |ˌkə-| Pronc-spp *coo, ko, ku, cur* [Abbr for *come*] **chiefly east of Missip R** See also **coaf, co-boss(ie), co-boy, co-bush, co-calf(ie), co-chick, co-cow, co-dack, co-day, co-dub(bie), co-ee, co-ets, co-jack, co-nan(nie)** v phr, **co-sheep(ie)** v phr, **cossie, co-wench, coy, cubbie**

Come!—used to call farm animals.

1914 *DN* 4.155 **NH,** [ko ko ko] . . . Call of cattle. *Ibid, Kujack* or *kōjock.* Horse call. **1949** Kurath *Word Geog.* 14, The Northern cow call is *boss!, co-boss!, kə-boss!,* or *come boss!* . . This call has survived also in the New England settlements on the Ohio around Marietta . . . East of the Susquehanna, Pennsylvania German and Dutch calls and the simple *co!* still compete with the Northern *boss!* On the coast of New England and on Long Island Sound the simple *co!* and an old-fashioned *coaf!* are heard. The *co!* of southern New Jersey probably comes from the New England shore. *Ibid* 21, The cow calls *co!* and *coaf!* . . are heard only in the coastal section of Eastern New England and to some extent on Long Island Sound. Elsewhere in New England only calls containing *boss!* are heard. **1965–70** *DARE* (Qu. K80, . . *Call . . to get the cows in from the pasture)* 10 Infs **east of Missip R,** [ko (ko ko)]; **CT**17, ['ko'ko] and ['ku 'ku]; **AL**33, **NJ**21, **TX**105, [ku]; **GA**7, ['koə]; **FL**27, 36, **GA**17, **NC**12, Co-(baby, babe, Annie, Sally); (Qu. K82, . . *Horses)* Inf **AL**20, [ko]; **LA**33, [koʊ]; **TN**53, Cur-cur-cur; (Qu. K83, . . *Calf)* Inf **NJ**56, [ko]; **VA**70, [ko'bæ]; (Qu. K84, . . *Pigs)* Infs **MA**74, **PA**218, Co-pig(s); (Qu. K85, . . *Sheep)* Inf **ME**12, [kə'jɛk, kə'jæk]. **1967** LeCompte *Word Atlas* 187 **seLA,** Call to horses / to get them home / . . co-co-co. [1 inf] **1973** Allen *LAUM* 1.260 **MN,** Calls to calves . . . Coo [1 inf]. *Ibid* 262 **IA,** Calls to horses . . . Coo [1 inf].

co- See ker-

co' n Also *c', co'n, coz, cun* [Abbr for *cousin*] **eSC** *Gullah*

A friend, relative, or associate—used as a polite term of address.

1867 Allen *Slave Songs* 29 **Port Royal Island SC,** Abbreviating this, after their fashion, they get *co'n* or *co'* (the vowel sound *u* as in *cousin*) as the common title when they speak of one another; as C'Abram, Co'Robin, Co'n Emma, C'Isaac. **1909** *S. Atl. Qrly.* 8.40 **eSC,** The *Gullah* negroes, at the *Fisherman's Landing,* cry to each other, "Oh, no; Coz!", as Shakespeare used *coz* in "Macbeth." **1928** Peterkin *Scarlet Sister Mary* 227 **SC,** Cun Andrew [in direct address]. *Ibid* 329, 338.

coach n

1 See **baby coach.**

2 See **coach horse.**

coach v [Prob ext of *coach* to prompt]

To coax.

1967–70 *DARE* (Qu. Y5, *Words meaning to urge somebody to do something he shouldn't)* Inf **FL**51, Coached him into it; **NE**1, **WY**4, Coached him. [All Infs have grade school educ.]

coach-abower n [Ir; see *EDD*] *old-fash*

1930 Shoemaker *1300 Words* 10 **cPA Mts** (as of c1900), *Coach-abower* —The sound of an invisible coach and horses on a gravel road, usually considered an omen of death.

coach-dog bean n Also *coach dog* [From its spotted pattern and color, like that of a "coach dog," a Dalmatian] **NEng**

An early-maturing dry bean (horticultural variety of *Dolichos*) which is spotted black-and-white.

1959 Carleton *Index Herb. Plants* 8, Bean: . . Old varieties from New England include . . Coach Dog, . . and Harlequin. **1963** *AmSp* 38.31, *Coach-dog bean.* A variety of American bean, *Dolichos.* **1978** *Wanigan Catalog* 6 **ME,** Coach Dog . . . Syn[onym]: Polka Dot.

coach-dray n

See quot 1978.

1955 Warren *Angels* 51 **KY** (as of c1850), Then I got me a little ole spavin mule and a little ole coach-dray fer my totin. **1978** *DARE* File [Private correspondence, Robert Penn Warren], As for coach-dray, I can be sure that I encountered it in use (probably in Louisiana) . . I expect a coach-dray would be a sort of buckboard with a cover or cab-like thing over the seat . . It doesn't sound like Kentucky to me, somehow.

coach horse n Also *coach old-fash* Cf **hackney**

A bob-tailed draft horse.

1950 *WELS* (*A horse with his tail cut short)* 1 Inf, **WI,** Coach horse (common usage); 1 Inf, Coach horse (occasional usage). **1965–70** *DARE* (Qu. K41) Infs **IN**3, **OK**10, **VA**43, Coach horse; **IL**66, Coach—a horse that has been docked; **MO**4, Coach. [All Infs old]

coachwhip n Also *coachwhip cactus* [Perh from the long slender branches] **SW**

=**ocotillo.**

1903 Small *Flora SE U.S.* 784, *Fouquiera* [sic] *spléndens* . . Jacob's Staff. Ocotillo. Coach-whip. **1913** Wooton *Trees NM* 125, The plant is sometimes called *Coach Whip Cactus,* but it is a very decided misnomer, because the plant is in no way related to the cacti. **1960** Vines *Trees SW* 762, *Ocotillo—Fouquieria splendens* . . . Vernacular names for the plant are Coachwhip-cactus, [etc].

coachwhip snake n Also *coachwhip;* rarely *whipcoach* (See Intro "Language Changes" I.1) [So called because the scalation of the long tail suggests a braided whip] **chiefly S Atl, Gulf States** See Map

A whipsnake (*Masticophis flagellum*) of the South and Southwest which has various color phases within the seven subspecies. See also **black racer 2, chicken snake 3, horse whipper, prairie racer, red racer**

1714 in 1974 Shaw–Campbell *Snakes West* 87, There be likewise . . Snakes made like a Coachwhip as long and as small, that will twist their head round a horse's leg, and with their tayl lash a horse with great violence until ye blood comes. **1743** (1754) Catesby *Nat. Hist. Carolina* 2.54, *Anguis flagelliformis.* The Coach-whip Snake. This is a very long slender Snake, particularly the hind Part, . . and from the Resemblance of a Coach-Whip has received its name. **1827** Williams *View W. FL* 29, The coach-whip is most frequently seen in the pine barrens; he perfectly resembles a coach-whip, with a black handle; but is very innocent. **1908** *DN* 3.299 **eAL, wGA,** Coach-whip . . . A black snake, so called from its resemblance to the old fashioned plaited leather coach-whip. Compare *black-runner.* **1925** *TX Folkl. Soc. Pub.* 4.51, I once heard an old-time Texas native call to his son to " . . be sure that a coach-whip doesn't catch and whip you." **1965–70** *DARE* (Qu. P25, . . *Snakes . . found around here)* 80 Infs, **chiefly S Atl and Gulf States,** Coachwhip (snake); **GA**72, **MS**63, Whipcoach. **1968** *Clarke Co. Democrat* (Grove Hill AL) 30 May np, Also, there is the myth about the ability of the coachwhip to beat a person to death, then stick his tail up his victim's nostrils to see if he is

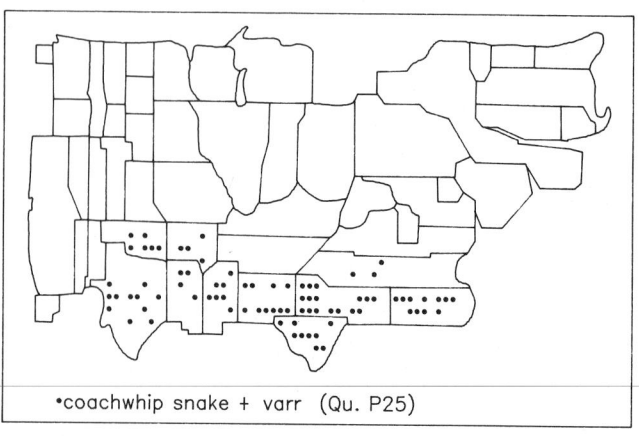

•coachwhip snake + varr (Qu. P25)

still breathing. **1977** Watts *Dict. Old West, Coachwhip snakes*—(S and Texas). A name given to a number of harmless snakes that resembled coach whips.

coaf v Usu |ko(ʊ)f, kɔ(ə)f|, also |kʊf, kuf, kov| [Prob abbr for *come off;* cf **co** v] *esp* **sNEng**

Come!—used to summon cows.

1939 *LANE* Map 218–219, [Especially on the southern coast of NEng and on Long Island Sound, *coaf* occurs freq, pronounced [ko(ʊ)f, kov, kɔɔf, kʊf, kuf].] **1968** *DARE* (Qu. K80, . . *Call . . to get the cows in*) Inf CT14, [kʊːʊf].

coag See **coge it**

coakum n Also sp *cocum, cokan, cunicum* [Perh from an Algonquian word for "red": cf **skoke** n[1], **atamasco (lily)**] See also **cokaberry**

=**pokeweed 1.**

1814 Bigelow *Florula Bostoniensis* 112 **MA**, *Poke, Cocum* . . . One of the most common and conspicuous plants in waste grounds, by road sides, &c. **1832** Williamson *Hist. ME* 1.127, *Poke*, . . an abbreviation of *Pocum*, is frequently called *Cocum*, and erroneously, *Garget*. **1876** Hobbs *Bot. Hdbk.* 24, Coakum, Garget, Phytolacca decandra. **1896** *Garden and Forest* 9.262/2, *Coakum* . ., with its variants Cocum and Cunicum, is a word of Indian (Tarascan) origin, but not of Indian application . . . The colonists of Massachusetts . . formed the word through a corruption of Mechoacan. **1930** Sievers *Amer. Med. Plants* 46, Coakum . . . has a very thick, long, fleshy, conical, branching root which is poisonous. **1959** Carleton *Index Herb. Plants* 29, Cokan: Phytolacca americana. **1971** Krochmal *Appalachia Med. Plants* 190, *Phytolacca americana . . . Common Names:* . . coakum, cocum, cokan, . . scoke, skoke, Virginia poke.

coal n *among Black speakers* Cf **charcoal**

A dark-skinned Black person.

1942 *Amer. Mercury* 55.89 **Harlem NYC**, Who, me? Man, I don't deal in no coal. Know what I tell 'em? If they're white, they're right! If they're yellow, they're mellow! If they're brown, they can stick around. But if they come black, they better git way back! Tell 'em bout me! **1970** *DARE* (QR, near Qu. HH29b) Inf NC87, "Oh, you're not going with coal now, you're going with cheese"—when a man quits dating a dark girl and starts going with a light one. [Inf Black]

coal v *chiefly* **NEast** Cf **coaling**

Also *coal off*: To make charcoal; to cut timber for making charcoal.

1945 Beck *Jersey Genesis* 129 (as of c1860), To "coal" in New Jersey is to make charcoal. **1965** (1973) Sloane *Wood* 47, Looking north from Cornwall over Connecticut's Berkshires, one sees an unending series of rolling hills. From the Revolution to the Civil War this land had given most of its tree growth to feed iron furnaces. Every thirty-five years . . the hills were harvested. In the Berkshires, people called it being "coaled." **1967** *DARE* Tape PA17, They coaled these mountains all off, burnt the wood and made the charcoal. **1969** Sorden *Lumberjack Lingo* 25, Coal off—To cut a forest clean for charcoal wood.

coal bank See **bank** n[1] 2

coal bucket See **bucket** 2d

coal buggy n

A small wagon used to haul coal in a mine.

1938 Stuart *Dark Hills* 31 **KY**, It was great fun to ride in a coal buggy back into the darkness under a hill.

coal-burner n

1 See quot.

1930 Shoemaker *1300 Words* 15 **cPA Mts** (as of c1900), *Coal-burner* —One who made charcoal for old-time iron furnaces.

2 Fig: see quot. Cf **stem-winder**

1950 *PADS* 14.21 **SC**, *Coal-burner.* Applied by Negroes to a preacher who is up to the minute and pleasing in every way. A complimentary title. Obsolescent. This word arose at the time when the *coal-burning* locomotives, superior to the older wood-burners, were introduced.

coaley See **coaly** n

coalfish n [Prob from the dark color]

1 =**pollack.** [*OED* 1603 →]

1838 MA Zool. & Bot. Surv. *Repts. Zool.* 129, *Merlangus carbonarius.* The Coal Fish. It is often met with in our market in considerable

quantities, and . . is called, by our fishermen, the 'pollack.' **1972** Sparano *Outdoors Encycl.* 383, *Pollock . . . Common names:* . . coalfish.

2 =**cobia.**

1887 Goode *Amer. Fishes* 144, The Cobia or crab-eater, *Elacate canada*, known in the Chesapeake Bay as the "Bonito" or the "Coalfish." **1972** Sparano *Outdoors Encycl.* 376, *Cobia . . . Common Names:* . . coalfish.

3 =**sablefish.**

1902 Jordan–Evermann *Amer. Fishes* 498, It *[Anoplopoma fimbria]* is the beshow, coal-fish.

coal-flour n [Alter of **cold flour**]

Parched corn ground into flour.

1860 Claiborne *Life Dale* 2.36 (as of 1793), Our accoutrements were a 'coonskin cap, bearskin vest, short hunting-shirt, . . a wallet for parched corn, coal flour, or other chance provision. **1942** *Amer. Legion Mag.* May 53/3, And he'd look for other powerful, simple foods—such as rockahominy, or pinole or coal-flour. Under whatever name, it's corn, parched in clean ashes until it bursts, then sifted and blown clean and pounded to a coarse flour.

coal hearth n Cf **coaling**

=**coal pit 1.**

1967 *DARE* Tape PA17, There was a coal hearth there . . where they burnt this stuff. They dig it out and then they pile this wood, cut the wood and pile it on there to burn this charcoal.

coal hod See **hod** n[1] 1

coalie-over See **colly-over**

coaling n [**coal** v] *old-fash*

A place where charcoal is made.

1905 Valentine *Hecla Sandwith* 268 **cPA**, Dave . . drove off with him as far as Custard's, a lonely inn not far from the coalings. **1941** Nixon *Possum Trot* 54 **AL**, No longer was there a "coaling" for producing charcoal. **c1960** Wilson Coll. **csKY**, Coaling: . . A place where charcoal was burned or timber grown for that purpose.

coaling-ground n

1976 Garber *Mountain-ese* **Appalachians**, *Coalin'-ground* . . coal storage.

coal iron n Cf **fire iron** 2

=**charcoal iron.**

1965–70 *DARE* (Qu. F29, *Different kinds of irons—not electric— used . . for smoothing clothes*) 17 Infs, **scattered,** Coal iron; LA12, Cold iron ['koʊl ˌdaːn] or coal iron ['koʊl ˌaːn]—used charcoal inside. [16 of 18 Infs old]

coal juice n [From the liquor's being filtered through charcoal]

Moonshine.

1969 *DARE* Tape GA72, We have a variety of names for this homemade whiskey in this county . . . We call it coal juice.

coal kiln n Pronc-sp *coal kill* [**coal** charcoal] *old-fash*

=**coal pit 1.**

1776 (1934) Fithian *Jrl.* 2.162, A Fog of Smoke rises from off it as from a Coal Kiln. **1847** in 1927 Jones *FL Plantation Rec.* 318, 2 work on the mill, 3 make Coal kill. **1859** Taliaferro *Fisher's R.* 176 **nwNC** (as of 1820s), He was sweatin' like a coal-kill. **1967** *DARE* Tape MA5A, They'd have these two-wheel wagons pile this . . wood in, onto them and push it into the coal kiln [kɪl].

coal off See **coal** v

coal of fire, come after a See **fire, come to borrow**

coal oil n [See quot 1949] **widespread, but least freq in Nth, S Atl** See Map Cf **lamp oil** Note: for use of the term in folk remedies, see *DS* BB50a–d, BB51a, which show its occurrence scattered **chiefly Lower Missip Valley and SW**

Petroleum or a refined derivative, esp kerosene.

1859 U.S. Patent Office *Annual Rept. for 1858: Arts & Mfgrs.* 1.276, This lamp . . is more especially designed for burning coal oil and similar substances that are rich in carbon. **1883** Twain *Life on Missip.* (London) 267 **Missip Valley**, "Out with that coal-oil, now, lively, *Lively!*" **1947** (1964) Randolph *Ozark Superstitions* 43 **nwAR, swMO**, "There's coal oil on them rags," an old woman remarked, "an' it cures the roup." **1949** Kurath *Word Geog.* 34, The regular word for kerosene is *coal oil* . . in all of Pennsylvania, except for the Pittsburgh area and the New

England counties in the northern fringe of the state. This term has spread far to the south as a trade word, beginning with the 1860's. We find it not only in West Jersey and in Delamarvia, but in all of Maryland west of the Bay, on the upper reaches of the Potomac in West Virginia, in the Shenandoah Valley, and on the Rappahannock in Virginia; furthermore, in southern Ohio and adjoining parts of West Virginia, beside the more common *lamp oil* of the Pittsburgh area. **1951** *AmSp* 26.255 **wNY. 1958** McCulloch *Woods Words* 36 **Pacific NW. 1958** *PADS* 29.8 **TN,** *Coal oil:* Kerosene oil. "We said *coal oil* but we knew it was *kerosene.*" **c1960** *Wilson Coll.* **csKY. 1965–70** *DARE* (Qu. F45, . . *Fuel that's used in an ordinary lamp*) 441 Infs, **widespread, but least freq in Nth, S Atl,** Coal oil. **1971** Wood *Vocab. Change* 12 **Gulf Sth,** The words *coal oil* and *kerosene* are of particular interest since they show how brief a period is required for the spread of regional words and for one of them to decline in our esteem. These two industrial names appeared in the 1850's. *Ibid* 52, After the middle of the nineteenth century, the introduction of a manufactured oil for lamps led to the dissemination of the names *carbon oil, coal oil, kerosene,* and *lamp oil.* **1973** Allen *LAUM* 1.225, Although Northern *kerosene* consistently dominates the U[pper] M[idwest] . . Pennsylvania's *coal oil* long was a strong competitor throughout the area. In the three northern states, however, its present incidence is almost entirely in terms of overheard or distantly recalled occurrence . . it is actually alive only in southern Iowa and Nebraska.

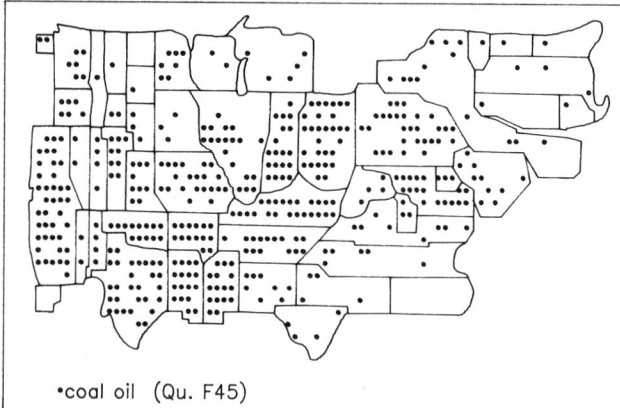

•coal oil (Qu. F45)

coal-oil aggie n

In marble play: an **agate 2.**

1967 *DARE* (Qu. EE6d, *Special marbles*) Inf **LA8,** Coal-oil aggie.

coal pit n [*coal* charcoal] *now hist*

1 also *charcoal pit:* Orig a pit in which charcoal was made; later a mound of hardwood covered with turf and burned to make charcoal.

1805 (1904) Clark *Orig. Jrls. Lewis & Clark Exped.* 1.252 **ND,** We are now burning a large Coal pit, to mend the indians hatchets, & make them war axes. **1930** *AmSp* 5.418 **NH,** *Coal-pit:* a hole in the ground where charcoal was made in former days. "Alder wood was burned in the coal-pits a hundred years ago." **1947** *AmSp* 22.277, In a letter of December 2, 1814, [Dudley A.] Tyng enclosed the following notes by the anonymous Harvard teacher: 'The following are the only American words, or English words used in an American sense, which I now recollect . . . *Coal-pit.* Wood piled for charring, and covered with earth: also the charcoal before it is removed.' **1967** *DARE* Tape **MA5A,** If you're plowing where they ever burnt an old coal pit, you'll see little pieces of charcoal—a primitive method of making charcoal in the woods where the wood was buried or covered with turf when burnt. **1968** McPhee *Pine Barrens* 45 **NJ,** Charcoal pits were actually aboveground. They had the shape of beehives and were twenty feet high. To make them, colliers stacked cordwood in vertical tiers and covered the wood with chunks of sandy turf, known as floats. The colliers dropped burning kindling into a hole in the top and then sealed it over. They poked holes in the sides with a stick called a fagan, and kept watch over the pit day and night.

2 also attrib; Fig: a pie made with apples piled high like wood in a coal pit.

1828 *Yankee* July 227/1 **Portland ME** *(DAE),* Then they all repair to the house, or the refreshment is brought out to them, where a motherly quantity of lusty pumpkin and coalpit or two-story apple platter pies are provided.

coal-scuttle blond n Also sp *coal-skuttle* ~ *among Black speakers; joc* Cf **coal** n

A Black woman.

1938 *AmSp* 13.151 **IN,** *Coal-skuttle blonde.* A dark negro girl. [Author: Common usage among Blacks.] **1942** *Amer. Mercury* 55.88 **Harlem NYC,** Dat broad I seen you with wasn't no peola. She was one of them coal-scuttle blondes with hair just as close to her head as ninety-nine is to a hundred. *Ibid* 94, *Coal scuttle blonde*—black woman.

coals, rake (one) over the v phr, hence vbl n *raking over the coals* For var phrr see quots

1 To reprimand severely; to speak of abusively.

1834 Smith *Letters Jack Downing* 87, But if Dr. Burnham dont give me satisfaction, I'll call a caucus of the party and have him over the coals and du him over. **1844** Stephens *High Life in NY* 1.190, The way the gals du haul him over the coals is a sin to Crocket. *Ibid* 215, Haul our Sam over the coals and sarmonize him. **1880** Harris *Uncle Remus Songs* 20 **GA,** He sorter rake me over de coals. **1896** *DN* 1.414 **c,seNY,** Call over the coals: for *haul over the coals.* **1965–70** *DARE* (Qu. II27, . . *A very sharp scolding*) 33 Infs, **scattered,** Raking over the coals; 7 Infs, **chiefly Nth,** Taken (took, taking) over the coals; **OH8,** Calling over the coals; **SC68,** Carrying over the coals; **IA34,** Chewing over the coals; **VT16,** Going over the coals; (Qu. Y3, *To say uncomplimentary things about somebody*) Inf **MN33,** Rake them over the coals; (Qu. Y6, *Words . . to put pressure on somebody to do something he ought to have done*) Infs **GA82, VA60,** Rake him over the coals.

2 To cause to suffer much misfortune.

1967 *DARE* (Qu. CC12b, *If a person has a lot of bad luck . . "He's been ———."*) Inf **WA22,** Raked over the coals.

coals, rake up the v phr *joc*

To snore.

1969 *DARE* (Qu. X45, *Joking expressions . . about snoring*) Inf **MA30,** Rakin' up the coals.

coaly n Also sp *coaley old-fash*

1 usu cap: The devil.

1953 Randolph *Down in Holler* 177 **Ozarks,** Any black object may be described as . . *black as Coaley's butt.* Coaley is an old-time name for the Devil. In Yell County, Arkansas, children say *black as Coaley's tail,* and a boy from that neighborhood told me that black dogs are usually named Coaley. **1975** Preston *Proverbial Comparisons* 26 **sIN,** Black as Old Coaly . . black as Old Coaly's ass.

2 See quot.

1977 Adams *Lang. Railroader* 34, *Coaly:* A fireman.

coaly v

To soil, blacken.

1967 Cerello *Dakota Co. MN,* He's all coalied up from cleaning the basement . . . The old pot-belly [stove] was forever coalying our house . . I just guess coalied is a nicer word to use than dirty or grimy.

coarse coin n Also *coarse money* [*coarse* in large bits or portions]

1930 Williams *Logger-Talk* 21 **Pacific NW,** *Coarse money* or *coarse coin:* A well-to-do man is *Way up in the coarse money.*

coarse gold n Also *coarse-quartz gold* **chiefly CA**

Gold in sizable grains as distinct from gold dust.

1848 (1849) Bryant *What I Saw in CA* App. 472, The coarse gold is dug out of the crevices among the rocks, in the dry beds of the mountain torrents. **1882** King *Rep. Precious Metals* 79 *(DA),* The gold is a coarse-quartz gold, very little washed, and often connected with its original quartz matrix. **1910** Hart *Vigilante Girl* 142 **CA,** What quantities of golddust, of "coarse-gold," of amalgam, . . were brought down from mines and mills to assay-offices and mints. *Ibid* 51, Sometimes riffles would be clogged with coarse gold; . . often there was nothing in them but "the color"—ghostly flakes of gold set in black sand. **1970** Stewart *Amer. Place-Names* 103 **cCA,** *Coarsegold* CA . . [The name for the community of Coarsegold was] given during the gold rush of 1849, apparently because of the finding of gold in granules or nuggets and not in dust.

coarse-grained adj

Abrasive, unpleasant.

1958 McCulloch *Woods Words* 36 **Pacific NW,** *Coarse-grained*—A man hard to get along with.

coarse money See **coarse coin**

coarse-quartz gold See **coarse gold**

coarse-talking adj
    Having a deep voice.
        1969 *WV Hist.* 30.470, You ought not to be shocked if you hear a saintly looking grandmother admit she likes to hear a coarse-talking man; she means a man with a deep voice (this can also refer to a singing voice . .).

coase See **course**

coast n
    1a The shore of a river or small body of water. [*OED* 1607, *"Obs.;"* cf Fr *côte* coast, shore] **esp LA**
        1814 Brackenridge *Views of LA* 175, The dwellings on the Coast are generally frame, of one story in height. *Ibid* 175, The Coast may be said to begin at Pointe Coupée. From this to La Fourche, two-thirds of the banks are perfectly cleared. **1835** Ingraham *South-West* 2.24, [Footnote:] The banks of the Mississippi are termed *'the coast,'* as far up the river as Baton Rouge. It is usual to say one lives on the *coast,* if he lives on the river shore. **1887** *Century Illustr. Mag.* 35.108 **LA,** We are bound for the Lower Coast. The country on both sides of the Mississippi from New Orleans up to the mouth of the Red River is known as the Upper Coast; that below the city down to the Jetties, as the Lower Coast. Was it a tribute to the might of the great river, this use by the early French settlers of a name for its banks usually applied to the shores of the sea? **1927** Kennedy *Gritny* 18 **sLA,** My cousin, down de coas', had a hog w'at got his th'oat cut clean thoo. **1937** *AmSp* 12.217 **NJ,** Negroes use *coast* for the bank of a river or pond, an obsolete meaning of the word (1607). **1983** *Reinecke Coll.* **New Orleans LA,** Coast [kos]—a stretch of the Mississippi above or below New Orleans, used almost entirely in combination: the lower coast, German coast (i.e., St. Charles and St. John parishes) etc. from La. French "cote" with same meaning.
    b in phr *coast(s) of (the) Nebraska:* Apparently the hilly banks of the Platte River. *hist*
        1852 Stansbury *Expedition* 29 **NE,** The country became more elevated, and presented a range of small hills of a sandy reddish clay, with a sharp outline toward the river, forming the "coast of the Nebraska," and also constituting the bluff bounding the river valley on the south. **1949** Guthrie *Way West* 81 (as of 1847), Evans squinted ahead, searching for the hills [above the Platte River] that people spoke of as the coasts of Nebraska.
    2 An area or region, as on a hillside or mountain slope. [*OED* →1667, *"Obs."*] *relic*
        1895 *DN* 1.371 **TN,** Coast: region. By a mountaineer: "I live on yon coast." **1924** Raine *Land of Saddle-Bags* 100 **Appalachians,** A lad who has never heard of the ocean says, "I live on yan coast."
    3 A hill or slope used for sledding. [Cf Fr *côte* hillside, slope] **MA**
        1775 in 1865 *MA Hist. Soc. Proc.* 8.398, Some of our school lads . . improv'd the Coast from Sherburn's hill down to School street. *Ibid* 399, Their fathers before 'em had improv'd it as a coast for time immemorial. **1889** *Boston Journal* 5 Feb 2/3 *(DA),* During a racing contest at a coast in Albany . . a loaded bob-sled came in contact with some hummocks, breaking the steering apparatus. **1906** Lovett *Old Boston Boys* 30 **MA** (as of 1850s), A squad of coasters would be bunched together at the top of this coast holding their sleds. *Ibid* 33, The most popular coasts were the "Long Coast" . . , the Joy Street coast, . . and the "Big" or "Flagstaff" Hill. **1911** Wharton *Ethan Frome* 179 **wMA,** "Ethan! Ethan! I want you to take me down again!" "Down where?" "The coast. Right off," she panted.
    4a The act of sliding down a hill or slope on a sled.
        1870 Alcott *Old-Fashioned Girl* 44 **MA,** "Let's run," said Polly as they came into the path after the last coast. **1911** Wharton *Ethan Frome* 173 **wMA,** "I guess this'll be their last coast for a day or two," Ethan said, looking up at the mild sky.
    b Transf; in bicycling: the act of moving freely downhill without pedaling.
        1888 G. B. Thayer *Bicycle Tour (New York World) (OED),* The only pleasant anticipation I had in the 3 hours' climb was the coast that was sure to come. **1897** *Outing* 29.461/1, The road outside the town afforded a most delightful coast, and down we flew [on bicycles] without any exertion.

coast v
    1 To slide down a snow-covered hill or slope, to sled; hence vbl n *coasting.* [**coast** n 3] **prob orig Boston area, now chiefly Nth, N Midl** See Map
        1836 *Boston Pearl* 9 Jan (1912 Thornton), Skate, if you like; 'coast,' if you are boy enough. **1848** (1927) Rodman *Diary* 283 **MA,** The boys and Ellen went the latter part of the ev'g to share in the still popular and very fashionable amusement of sled coasting . . . Went from the c[oun-tin]g house earlier than usual to accompany Sue to the coasting course on School Street. **1888** *Jrl. Amer. Folkl.* 1.78, Coast . . . Even now not familiar in parts of New England, where the usual expression is *to slide;* and this seems the more proper and ancient phrase. When a boy from Maine, fifty years ago, came to Boston, and heard other boys talk of "coasting down hill," he did not know what they meant. **1890** *DN* 1.21, *Coast:* to slide down hill . . . It is not the natural word among boys on Cape Cod or in Maine, but it was current in Boston fifty years ago . . as now, and is common in Cincinnati to-day. *Ibid* 58, *Coast,* as a verb, is very common in Western New York. **1926** *AmSp* 2.80 **ME,** In winter the children "slide," rather than "coast," or "sled-ride," as they say in Pennsylvania. **1929** *AmSp* 5.134 **MA,** But "coasting" . . came to have a special meaning, that of sliding down hill. This particular sense, in full harmony with the etymology of the word, used to be confined to New England, where sliding down hill was a winter amusement. Now the word has gone all over the world, and is used in connection with bicycling, automobiling, and the like. **1943** *LANE* Map 575, *Coast* is not general in New England and is often regarded as a rather recent innovation. **1965–70** *DARE* (Qu. EE24b, *When children go down a hill on a sled . . they say they're_____*) 184 Infs, **chiefly Nth, N Midl,** Coasting; (Qu. EE25, *When a child picks up his sled . . , runs with it, and then throws himself down on it, that's a _____*) 8 Infs, **chiefly Nth,** Coasting. [Of all Infs responding to Qu. EE24b, 63% were old; of those giving this response, 84% were old.]

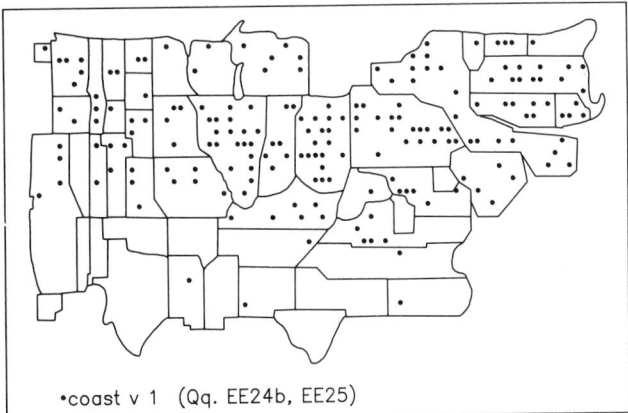

•*coast* v 1 (Qq. EE24b, EE25)

    2 To peddle cargo along the lower Mississippi. [**coast** n 1a]
        1894 *Century Illustr. Mag.* 25.486/1, 'To coast' in flat-boatman's phrase is to peddle a cargo to the French planters on the lower Mississippi, a region always called 'the coast'—no doubt a corruption of the French *côte.*
    3 See **coast on the spurs.**

coast cloud n
    A moisture-laden cloud which passes over a body of water (as the Gulf of Mexico) and produces thundershowers when it meets the air over a land mass.
        1966 *DARE* (Qu. B11, . . *Kinds of clouds that come often around here*) Inf **AR**17, Coast cloud (clouds drifting inland from the [Gulf] coast, just big thunderheads). **1978** *DARE* File **csLA,** Oh, sure, I've used the term "coast cloud" all my life. It means dark clouds which cause afternoon thunderstorms. [Speaker old] *Ibid* **swLA,** The term "coast clouds" is currently used in marine weather forecasting . . . The clouds are formed when moisture-laden air from the Gulf moves in over the land mass and collides with air of a different temperature and moisture content. The resulting cloud formation and turbulence often give way to sudden thundershowers.

coaster n[1] [**coast** v **1**]
    1 One who slides downhill on a sled. **MA** *old-fash*
        1849 (1927) Rodman *Diary* 289 **MA,** On my way I passed some of the

streets thronged with coasters and spectators. **1870** Alcott *Old-Fashioned Girl* 3.42 **MA**, The coasters were at it with all their might . . . Some little girls were playing with their sleds. **1906** Lovett *Old Boston Boys* 38 **MA** (as of 1850s), A big, heavy negro was one day coasting down Mt. Vernon Street on glare ice, and . . a sledge . . moving at a walk came into sight. The coaster had no time to think or swerve from his course.

2 also attrib: A sled or similar device esp suitable for sliding downhill. **NEng**

1931–33 *LANE* Worksheets **swCT**, *Coaster sled*; **sRI**, *Coaster*, a small toboggan; **nRI**, *Coaster*, two sleds tied together. **1943** *LANE* Maps 573–574, [*Coaster* is applied to two kinds of sleds: the] double-sled, consisting of two sets of short runners joined by a reach or a plank . . [also] usually applied to a 'single sled' . . [e.g.] a low sled with solid sides coming to a point in front, often homemade.

3 also attrib: A kind of toy wagon for children. *old-fash*

1911 *Sears Catalogue* 866, A celebrated make of Coaster Wagon improved and fitted with brake. **1968** *DARE* (QR p233) Inf **CA**73, Coasters—name used for wagon when used to go down hills. [Inf old]

4 See **baby coaster.**

coaster n², also attrib

A Texas longhorn steer from the coastal region.

1890 *Stock Grower* 19 Apr 7/2 *(OEDS)*, There are lots of big old-fashioned "coaster" horns among them. **1903** *KS State Bd. Ag. Rept. for 1901 and 1902* 18.154, Fine specimens [of herefords] have been . . landed in the hands of the Philistines, with dire results to the offspring — bodies that could not make a shadow, and horns of the old Texas coaster — all the lack of decent care. **1929** Dobie *Vaquero* 20 **TX**, The 'coasters,' or 'sea lions,' as people sometimes called the longhorned cattle of the coast country, could swim like ducks and were as wild. **1930** Ferber *Cimarron* 80 **TX**, The steers was wild long-legged coasters — and run! Say, they come through between us like scairt wolves, and I lost the count. **1935** *AmSp* 10.270 **NE**, *Coasters*. Texas cattle raised in areas near the Gulf of Mexico. **1961** Adams *Old-Time Cowhand* 155, The old "longhorn" . . of the coast country of Texas were "coasters," or "sea-lions" that "come right out of the Gulf" of Mexico.

coaster n³ chiefly **wGt Lakes**

1 =**brook trout.** [From its presence along coasts or shores]

1949 Hubbs–Lagler *Fishes Gt. Lakes* 34, Brook trout which work along the shores of some of the lakes are called "coasters." **1976** *DARE* File **Isle Royale MI**, A coaster is a speckled brook trout. It gets too big for streams, then goes into the lake; weighs about 9 lbs.

2 also *coast rainbow trout*: =**rainbow trout.**

1956 Harlan *IA Fish* 57, Rainbow Trout *Salmo gairdneri* . . Other Names—Coast rainbow trout, coaster.

coast haole n, also attrib [**haole**] **HI**

A white person ignorant of local customs and hence looked down on as lacking sympathy for things Hawaiian; see quot 1978.

1967 *DARE* (Qu. X57, *A person with light-colored skin and hair*) Inf **HI**1, He's a coast haole [hauli], too blond to be typical of the islands; (Qu. HH31, *Somebody who is not from your community, and doesn't belong*) Inf **HI**1, Coast haole. [The word] has assumed a derogatory tone. **1967** *DARE* Tape **HI**2, We talk about coast haole [hauli] pineapples, which we call flat. They're a little on the less acid side. **1978** *DARE* File [Letter from Elizabeth Carr Holmes], *Coast haole*: new, ignorant of local customs; someone who is despised and looked down on because of his lack of interest and lack of that elusive thing called "aloha" for things Hawaiian. *Coast* is not mainly the West Coast or East Coast. It is anywhere on the Mainland and hence remote from Hawaii.

coasting See **coast** v 1

coasting coat n

1899 (1912) Green *VA Folk-Speech* 119, *Coasting coat,* . . Coursing-coat; a hunting or coursing-coat.

coast nutmeg See **California nutmeg**

coast, on the adv phr **Nantucket MA** *arch*

Nearby.

1859 (1968) Bartlett *Americanisms* 303, *On the coast*. Near, close at hand. A nautical expression, in common use in Nantucket. **1872** Schele de Vere *Americanisms* 341, Nantucket fishermen, besides, have a way of using the words *on the coast,* even when on shore, in the often very ludicrous meaning of "near at hand," and a gallant lover will assure his lady-love that if she will only fix the day, "he'll be sure to be *on the coast* with the parson." **1935** *AmSp* 10.40 **Nantucket MA** (as of 1848), *On the coast.* Neat [Error for *near*].

coast on the spurs v phr, hence vbl n *coasting on the spurs* Also *coast* [*coast* to move freely with little or no effort] **West**

In rodeo parlance:

a To refrain from using spurs or to use them lightly.

1936 McCarthy *Lang. Mosshorn* **West** [Rodeo terms], *Coastin'*. Said when a cowboy attempts to quiet a bronc by holding its head and not spurring. The practice is often exhibited by an inexperienced cowboy who happens to draw the meanest critter in the chutes. **1937** *DN* 6.619 **swTX**, As long as the rider does not deign to scratch the bronco with his spurs, he is *coasting on the spurs.*

b To keep the spurs applied to one spot: see quot.

1961 Adams *Old-Time Cowhand* 310, "Coastin' on the spurs" is ridin' with the spurs locked in the cinch, or under the hoss's shoulder blades, and is not tolerated in contests.

coast rainbow trout See **coaster** n³ **2**

coast redwood n

The California redwood.

1897 Sudworth *Arborescent Flora* 63, *Sequoia sempervirens* . . Common Names . . Coast Redwood (Cal.). **1908** Britton *N. Amer. Trees* 88, This gigantic tree (*Sequoia sempervirens*) is also called . . Coast redwood. **1979** Little *Checklist U.S. Trees* 273, *Sequoia sempervirens* . . *Other common names*—coast redwood.

coat n *old-fash*

1 A petticoat or slip. **Sth**

1859 (1968) Bartlett *Americanisms* 89, *Coat.* Used in the South for *petticoat.* Formerly common, and still provincial, in England. **1882** (1910) Watterson *Oddities* 487, Cousin Sally Dilliard and Mose, like genteel folks, they walked the log; but my wife, like a darned fool, hoisted her coats and waded through. **1883** *Amer. Philol. Assoc. Trans.* 14.46, *Coat,* 'a petticoat.' Still used in the South . . A friend writes me that the word was "so used a generation or two ago in seaboard Massachusetts." **1899** (1912) Green *VA Folk-Speech* 119, *Coats* . . Petticoats. **1922** Gonzales *Black Border* 293 **sSC, GA coasts** [Gullah glossary], *'Coat*— petticoat, petticoats (man's "coat" is always "jacket"). **1950** *PADS* 14.21 **SC**, Coat. Petticoat. "Missy, yo' *coat* duh heng." Your slip is showing. Negro usage of Charleston.

2 A dress. **Sth, S Midl** Cf **coattail 2**

1899 (1912) Green *VA Folk-Speech* 119, *Coats* . . Women's outer garments. **1902** *DN* 2.231 **sIL**, *Coat*. . . A woman's dress. (Obs.) **1903** *DN* 2.309 **seMO**, *Coat* (for a girl or woman) . . . Dress; frock. (Used only by quite old-fashioned people.) **1908** *DN* 3.299 **eAL, wGA**, *Coat* . . . A dress or frock for a woman or child: used chiefly by negroes.

coat bet n, also attrib Pronc-sp *cope bet* [Echoic]

A **tree frog** (here: *Hyla gratiosa*).

1932 Wright *Life–Hist. Frogs* 294, *Hyla gratiosa* . . "Coat Bet." **1969** *DARE* Tape **GA**51, He's got one of the ponds named after the cope bet frog . . . Frog is ahollerin', makes a loud noise . . . Name for that certain kinda frog in this holler is a cope bet . . . My daddy'd tell me that was the name of it . . . The natives'd call it that. That ain't the book name.

coat, have something under one's v phr

To be keeping something secret; to have something up one's sleeve.

1965–70 *DARE* (Qu. JJ19, *If somebody . . is up to no good, you might say, "I think he's got _____."*) Infs **AZ**15, **CA**101, **FL**22, **NC**40, **WV**16, Something under his coat. [All Infs old]

coat o' Joseph n [In ref to Joseph's coat of many colors, Gen 37:3]

A cat with fur of mixed colors.

1969 *DARE* (Qu. J5) Inf **AZ**10, Coat o' Joseph.

coat patches n Cf **poor man's patches**

1970 *DARE* (Qu. S15, . . *Other weed seeds that cling to clothing*) Inf **VA**52, Coat patches—flat, fuzzy.

coat, pull one's v phr *among Black speakers*

To give someone a hint.

1968–70 *DARE* (Qu. JJ27, *"He had no idea that she was up to anything, but I _____."*) Infs **FL**52, **PA**66, **TX**97, Pulled his coat; (Qu.

JJ43, *"He wasn't supposed to know. Somebody must have _____."*) Inf **PA**66, Pulled his coat. [All Infs Black]

coatsfoot See **coltsfoot 1**

coattail n

1 Std sense, in var phrr indicating speedy activity:

a in phrr *get one by the coattail* or *be at one's ~:* To be in close pursuit of someone.

  1966–69 *DARE* (Qu. AA5, *If a woman seems to be . . after one certain man . . : "She's _____."*) Inf **AR**18, Got him by the coattail; **GA**77, At his coattails.

b in phrr *have one's coattails popping* or *on end:* To be in a hurry.

  1950 *PADS* 14.75 **cwFL**, *Coat-tails poppin'.* Description of a person in an angry hurry. **c1960** *Wilson Coll.* **csKY**, *Coat-tails popping (or on end)*—said of someone in a great hurry, actual or seeming.

‡c in phr *have one's coattails out straight:* To be working hard.

  1936 *AmSp* 11.375, Is is true that *coat tails out straight* means in parts of New England "working hard"?

2 See quot. [**coat 2**]

  1899 (1912) Green *VA Folk-Speech* 119, *Coat-tail,* . . The whole skirt of a woman's dress from the waist. "They went about in the rain with their coat-tails over their heads."

coattail it v phr [In ref to one's coattails flying out behind] Cf **coattail 1b**

To run fast.

  1969 *DARE* (Qu. Y20, . . *"You should have seen him _____."*) Inf **NY**209, Coattail it outa here.

cob n[1] Also sp *cobb* [*cob* to strike] *obs*

A blow, usu one applied to the buttocks.

  1828 *Cherokee Phoenix* 10 Apr (1859 Bartlett *Americanisms*), Such negro so offending shall receive fifteen *cobbs* or paddles for every such offence. **1859** (1968) Bartlett *Americanisms* 89, *Cobb.* A blow on the buttock. **1940** FWP *Guide OH* 535 (as of 1812), *Cob* . . When a private was found sitting down at his post, stealing a few winks, the general sentenced him to 'ten cobs on his bare posterior, well laid on, with a paddle four inches wide and one-half inch thick, bored full of holes'.

cob n[2] [Etym uncert: see *OED;* the basic sense appears to be that of a lump or mass, often rounded]

1 A marble game: see quot 1922. [Cf *EDD cob(b* sb.[1] 15 "a game played with nuts" and 17 "a game at marbles"] Cf **cob roller, coobie**

  1922 *DN* 5.186 **KY**, *Cob.* A game similar to "cob" as played in Northhamptonshire. Four small holes are made in the ground, in the shape of an L, with the third hole at the apex. After reaching the first hole, a player is allowed to "span" for each succeeding hole. **1955** *PADS* 23.14 **cwTN**, *Cob* . . A marble game . . . The term as applied to a game of marbles probably came in very early. **1973** Ferretti *Marble Book* 69 **NY**, Holilakes [a marble game] also spawned *cob,* a game in which several players bowl their marbles into a series of four holes in the ground.

2 An apple core. [Engl dial *cob* the seed of a fruit]

  c1970 *DARE* File **swPA** (as of 1920), Cob—apple core.

3 also *cobtail:* A bob-tailed horse. [Perh abbr for *cob-horse* a short-legged, sturdy horse, with its tail cut short; cf **cob** v[1] **2**] **Nth** *old-fash*

  [**1872** Burnham *Memoirs U.S. Secret Service* 92, And, with a few dollars of his hard-earned good money . . he bought and paid for a good stout cob of a horse.] **1950** *WELS* 1 Inf, **ceWI**, *Cob,* a horse with his tail cut short. **1965–70** *DARE* (Qu. K41, *A horse with its tail cut short is called a _____*) Infs **CT**29, **IA**19, **NY**105, Cob; **CT**2, Cobs [kabz] used to be common; **CT**7, [kɑb], not many left today—you don't have the coach horses; **MA**42, [kɑb]—tail cut to about eighteen inches; **NY**233, Cob; **MI**78, **NY**189, **PA**163, Cobtail. [All Infs old]

4 Anything thought to resemble a corncob in quality, shape, or use, as:

a Something rough; a rough person; see quot 1972.

  1942 *AmSp* 17.170 **sIL**, *Cob* (a backwoodsman). [**1972** Hall *Sayings Old Smoky* 52 **eTN**, "What was Cal Smallwood like?" . . "He was a big old rough _____, he was rough as a cob . . . I mean, when he told ye he'd whup ye, ye'd just as well walk up right then."]

b A servile person; a dupe.

  1969 *DARE* (Qu. II34, *If you think somebody is trying to use you to his advantage: I'm not going to be his _____*) Inf **KY**40, Cob.

c attrib: A round or unsquared log.

  1814 in 1947 *AmSp* 22.273, Cob wharf—cob pier [,] one made of round logs.

d A cigar. *joc*

  1970 *DARE* (Qu. DD6a, . . *Nicknames for cigars*) Inf **IL**118, Cob.

e See quot.

  1970 *Thompson Coll.* **cAL** (as of c1920), *Cob*—The paper board cylinder on which toilet paper is usually wound.

5 in pl: Coal. [*EDD cob(b* sb.[1] II.5]

  1977 Adams *Lang. Railroader,* Cobs: Coal.

cob n[3] [Abbr for *cobweb*]

  1973 Allen *LAUM* 1.332 **MN**, Unusual variants [of spiderweb, cobweb] include . . cob.

cob v[1] [Prob assoc with *cob* to strike]

1 In mining: to crush and separate ore; hence vbl n *cobbing.*

  1872 (1876) Knight *Amer. Mech. Dict.* 1.582/1, *Cob* . . . To break ore with a hammer, to reduce its size, to enable its separation from portions of the gangue, and its assortment into grades of quality. **1968** Adams *Western Words, Cobbing*—In mining, ore sorting.

2 To bob the tail of a horse; hence, ppl adj *cobbed.* Cf **cob** n[2] **3**

  1950 *WELS* 1 Inf, **cnWI**, *Cobbed,* a horse with his tail cut short. **1970** *DARE* (Qu. K41, *A horse with its tail cut short*) Inf **NY**233, They cob the tail. [Inf old]

3 To embarrass. Cf **cut** ppl adj **2**

  1940 *AmSp* 15.447 **eTN**, *Cobbed.* Embarrassed. 'Maria's bussy cobbed her.'

cob v[2], hence vbl n *cobbing*

To rub or pelt with corncobs.

  1933 *AmSp* 8.1.48 **Ozarks**, *Cobbing.* A vigorous massage with a corncob soaked in grease or ointment. A *plumb good cobbin'* is indicated in certain skin diseases. **1954** *Harder Coll.* **cwTN**, *Cob,* throw corncobs at someone; rub an animal, or even a person, with a corncob. Common usage.

cob v[3]

To limp, hobble.

  1969 *DARE* File **neKY**, *Cobbing it around* ['kabɪn]. Limping because of an injured foot or leg.

cob v[4] Also *cob onto* [Alter of *cop* to take]

To take, filch, glom v **1**.

  1968–69 *DARE* (Qu. V4, *Other words for stealing something valuable . . "Yesterday somebody _____ my watch."*) Inf **MO**20, Cobbed; (Qu. V5a, *To take something of small value that doesn't belong to you . . "Who's been _____ the cookies?"*) Inf **IA**45, Cobbing; (Qu. V5b, *If you take something that nobody seems to own . . : "Before anybody else gets it, I'm going to _____ this."*) Inf **IN**27, Cob onto. **1980** *DARE* File **csWI**, *Cobbed it off a dead nigger:* Took something of small value. Reported as used among schoolboys in Portage, Wisconsin; also as used facetiously, or evasively, when an item in question was acquired in a conventional way.

cob apple pie See **cob pie**

cobay See **co-boy**

cobb n[1] See **cob** n[1]

cobb n[2] [Prob from one or more West Gmc forms: cf Du *kobbe, kob,* E Fris *kobb(e)*] **NEast**

=**great black-backed gull.**

  1844 Giraud *Birds Long Is.* 361, *Larus marinus* . . . Black-backed Gull, or Cobb. **1872** Coues *Key to N. Amer. Birds* 312, Great Black-backed Gull. Saddle-back. Coffin-carrier. Cobb. **1917** (1923) *Birds Amer.* 1.41, *Great Black-backed Gull . . . Other Names . . .* Cobb; Wagell. **1946** Hausman *Eastern Birds* 311.

cobbing vbl n[1] See **cob** v[1] **1**

cobbing vbl n[2] See **cob** v[2]

cobble n[1], also attrib [Abbr for **cobblestone**]

1 A naturally rounded stone of medium size. **chiefly NEast and West**

1910 *DN* 3.453 **seVT,** *Cobble . . .* A stone of any shape (tho seldom flat) from the size of a peach to the size of one's head. **1939** *LANE* Map 35 **wCT, csMA,** [Among the infs who used *cobble,* four variously described it as "a small stone in a field," "a perfectly round stone," a stone "as big as your fist," and "a large stone."] **1965–70** *DARE* (Qu. C25, *. . Stone . . about . . [the] size of a person's head . . , smooth and hard*) Infs **MA15, 17, 37, NJ8, NY1, 72, 110, 220, 233,** Cobble; **AZ7, ID1, WY4,** Cobble rock; (Qq. C22, 23, 24a, 26) Infs **CA125, 141, NM8, NY110, 220, 233, UT3,** Cobble (rock); (Qu. L60) Inf **OH10,** Cobble fence; (Qu. N27a) Inf **MA4,** Cobble road. **1968** *DARE* Tape **IN9,** Cobble street—just big old rough rock. **1971** *AmSp* 46.170 **Chicago IL,** Cobble (stone) fence. [4 infs]

2 Transf: a peach or cherry seed. Cf *DS* I48, 50

1941 *LANE* Map 268 **ceMA,** Cobble, peach ~ . . the hard-shelled seed of a peach. *Ibid* Map 269 **ceMA,** Cobble . . the hard-shelled kernel of a cherry.

cobble n[2] [Perh from **cobble** n[1]; the suggested etyms in quots are prob erron] **NEast**

A rounded hill—used chiefly in place names.

1887 (1895) Robinson *Uncle Lisha* 81 **wVT,** He moved on to a bald peak of the hill from which a portion of the valley could be seen, with its cleared fields and wooded cobbles. **1890** Townsend *U.S. Index* 135, *Cobble.* From the German, *koble,* meaning "rock". Name applied to a hill or other moderate elevation whose sides have a covering of loose or cobble-stones. *Cobble Hill* (Adirondacks), N.Y., *Cobbleskill,* N.Y. (In the Catskills.) The word is local with Massachusetts and New York. **1929** *AmSp* 5.158 **eNY,** *Cobble,* a hill, not much used, though widely dispersed in the northern part of the district as Rattle Snake Cobble (Glen Falls), Scott's Cobble, and Cheney Cobble (Marcy), Kitty Cobble (Canada Lake). These all seem as though the word has a definite meaning as a kind of hill. In other cases this is not so clear; in Cobble Hill . . and Cobble Mt. . . the particular meaning seems to be lost. **1948** Peattie *Berkshires* 51, The word "cobble" is an old English name for an outcropping of rock. Bartholomew's Cobble [Sheffield] is an island of limestone jutting into the alluvial meadows of the Housatonic Valley, with one side cut into abrupt cliffs by geological caprices, or perhaps by the steady wear of the Housatonic. *Ibid* 52, [One can] find time to travel most of the twenty-five acres that compose the unique Cobble. **1957** Schönfelder *Deutsches Lehngut* 219, [Author questions the German derivation of *cobble*]. **1965** *DARE* File **swMA,** Cobble. A rounded hill, usually of moderate elevation . . . Cobble Mountain reservoir, source of Springfield's water supply, is in a hilly area. Evidence at hand shows *cobble* is not used west of NY State nor south of New England. **1970** Stewart *Amer. Place-Names* 103, *Cobble*—As a now obsolete generic, it is probably of Dutch origin and is preserved in NY with the apparent meaning 'hill'; it stands occasionally as a specific, tautologically, e.g. *Cobble Hill* NY.

cobble n[3]

=**red-throated loon.**

1955 *MA Audubon* 39.309 **NEng,** Cobble (New England. A British provincial name for the young of this species. May it not compare the sharp bill to a cobbler's awl?).

cobble v

1918 *DN* 5.15 **Martha's Vineyard MA,** Cobble. To roll up and break, as surf on a reef. "See how those waves are cobbling up on the ledge."

cobbler n[1] [Perh from **cobble** to patch together roughly]

1 A drink made of wine, sugar, fruit juice, and cracked ice. *somewhat old-fash*

1809 W. Irving *Knickerb.* (1861) 241 *(OED),* The first inventors of those recondite beverages, cock-tail, stone-fence, and sherry-cobbler. **1852** Curtis *Lotus-Eating* 115, Various other select parties are . . watching the sails and sipping cobblers. **1888** Whitman *November Boughs* 101, My recollection of the 'cobblers' (with strawberries and snow on top of the large tumblers,) . . help[s] the regretful reminiscence of my New Orleans experiences. **1939** Wolcott *Yankee Cook Book* 330, Cobblers are of American origin and are great favorites in all warm climates.

2 also *cobbler pie:* A deep-dish fruit pie with crust, often of biscuit dough, on the top and sometimes lining the pan. **chiefly Sth, S Midl** See Map Cf **clobber** n[2]

1859 (1968) Bartlett *Americanisms* 90, *Cobbler . . .* 2. A sort of pie, baked in a pot lined with dough of great thickness, upon which the fruit is placed; according to the fruit, it is an apple or a peach *cobbler.* Western. **1902** *DN* 2.231 **sIL,** *Cobbler.* A thick fruit pie to be eaten with a sauce.

1903 *DN* 2.309 **seMO. 1906** *DN* 3.131 **nwAR. 1908** *DN* 3.299 **eAL, wGA,** *Cobbler.* A pie made in a deep pan with a crust on top only. **1941** *LANE* Map 292 **seCT, seVT,** Apple cobbler; **swMA,** Dutch cobbler. **1965–70** *DARE* (Qu. H63, *Kinds of desserts especially favored by people around here*) 40 Infs, **chiefly Sth, S Midl,** (Fruit) cobbler(s); 31 Infs, **chiefly Sth, S Midl,** [Specific fruit +] cobbler; **AR35, KY28, NC55,** Cobbler pies; **SC56,** Cobblers—called "gobblers" when kids. **1969** *DARE* FW Addit **KY28,** Cobbler pie: a biscuit-like dough is put into the bottom of a large square pan and baked. Fruit is put on this and another layer of dough on top. This is baked; the results are superb, especially with wild blackberries or fresh peaches. **1973** Allen *LAUM* 1.297, For an apple pie with a thick upper crust and no bottom crust, steamed or baked in a pot or crock, the U[pper] M[idwest] term with Midland orientation is *(apple) cobbler* and that with Northern orientation is *deep apple pie.*

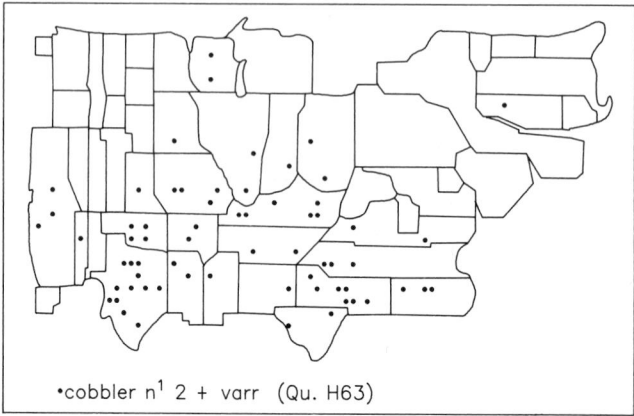

•cobbler n[1] 2 + varr (Qu. H63)

3 Any of var pastries containing fruit.

1965–70 *DARE* (Qu. H30, *An oblong cake, cooked in deep fat*) Inf **GA3,** [kɑblər]; **WA8,** Cobbler—has fruit in it; (Qu. H32, *. . Fancy rolls and pastries*) Infs **FL9, OK51,** Cobblers. **1967** *DARE* File **swWA,** *Cobbler.* Hot berries (preserves) poured over baking powder biscuit. Common.

4 Either of two fish:

a A **mummichog** (here: *Fundulus heteroclitus*).

1896 U.S. Natl. Museum *Bulletin* 47.640, *Fundulus heteroclitus . . . Cobbler.* **1933** John G. Shedd Aquarium *Guide* 61, *Fundulus heteroclitus*—Common killifish; mummichog; cobbler. This fish, known to all boys along the Atlantic shores, is exceedingly tough and tenacious of life. **1960** Amer. Fisheries Soc. *List Fishes* 54.

b The common **pompano** (here: *Trachinotus carolinus*).

1946 LaMonte *N. Amer. Game Fishes* 38, *Common Pompano . . .* Names: . . Cobbler.

cobbler n[2] Also *Irish cobbler*

A white potato, esp **Irish potato 1.**

1950 Bissell *Stretch on River* 143 **Missip Valley,** He [=the messboy] loaded up with cobblers and climbed the ladder. **1950** *WELS* (Nicknames or other names for potatoes) 1 Inf, **cWI,** Irish cobbler. **1965–70** *DARE* (Qu. H47) Inf **VA78,** Irish cobbler; (Qu. I9) Inf **CT2,** Irish cobblers are cobblers (earliest of all potatoes); **CT39,** Irish cobblers; **GA72,** Cobblers are a certain kind, but often used for any kind; **IN48, MI66, NY88,** Cobblers; (Qu. HH30) Inf **KY42,** Irish cobbler—potatoes; **NC33, VA15,** Irish cobbler. **1966** *DARE* Tape **ME 9,** Well, they grow katahdins, kennebecs, russets, a few cobblers. **1976** Olds Seed Co. *Seeds* 23 **Madison WI,** *Irish Cobbler . . .* is an old variety that seems to hold its popularity.

‡cobbler cheese n

1970 *DARE* File **cnMI,** Cobbler cheese—cottage cheese.

cobblerfish n Cf **cobbler** n[1] **4**

A **threadfish** (here: *Alectis ciliaris*).

1882 U.S. Natl. Museum *Bulletin* 16.438, *Cobbler-fishes . . . B[lepharis] crinitus.* **1902** Jordan–Evermann *Amer. Fishes* 308, The genus *Alectis* is not essentially different from *Carangus . . .* The only one in our waters is *A. ciliaris,* the thread fish, cobbler-fish or sun-fish. **1933** John G. Shedd Aquarium *Guide* 83, *Alectis crinitus*—Threadfish; Cobbler-fish.

cobbler pie See **cobbler** n¹ 2

cobblestone n, also attrib *chiefly NEast* See Map
=**cobble** n¹ 1.
   1859 (1968) Bartlett *Americanisms* 90, *Cobble-Stone.* A roundish stone; a small boulder, such as is used for paving. Mr. Halliwell informs us that the word *cobble* is used in this sense in the North of England; and cites from old authors the terms *cobbled stones* and *cobbling stones,* which last suggests that the origin of the word is the use of such boulders by cobblers for a lapstone. **1905** *DN* 3.6 **cCT**, *Cobble stone* . . . A round stone about half the size of one's head. **1907** *DN* 3.210 **nwAR**. **1950** *WELS* 2 Infs, Cobblestone; 1 Inf, Cobblestone—large, flat; make good building stone; 1 Inf, Cobblestones were once used for roads and walks. **1965–70** *DARE* (Qu. C25, *Other kinds of stone*) 30 Infs, **chiefly NEast**, (Large) cobblestone; (Qu. C26) 11 Infs, **chiefly Nth**, Cobblestone(s); (Qu. C24a, *A small piece of stone that you could easily throw*) Infs **CO**41, **CT**10, 14, **NY**75, 112, Cobblestone; (Qq. L60, N23, N27a,b) 42 Infs, **chiefly NEast**, Cobblestones *or* cobblestone (fence, road). **1969** *DARE* Tape **MI**105, No, they're just cobblestone houses, a lot of 'em . . . A lot of 'em are cobblestone, a lot of 'em are face stone. **1971** *AmSp* 46.170 **Chicago IL**, *Cobble(stone) fence.* [4 infs]

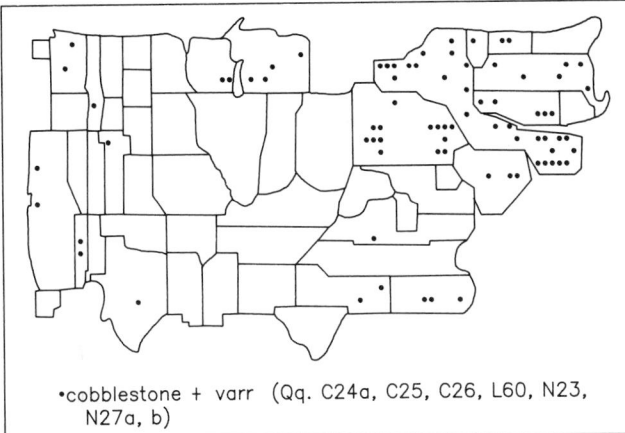

•cobblestone + varr (Qq. C24a, C25, C26, L60, N23, N27a, b)

cob box n
   A stove that burns corncobs.
   1950 *Western Folkl.* 9.137, When *cobs* were used as fuel, the box [=stove] was called a *cob box.*

cob corn n
   Corn that is still on the cob.
   1864 in 1945 Easterby *SC Rice Plantation* 304, Boath Parsels only measured 365 bushels of Cob Corn, which Gives only 182½ bushels of Sheld Corn. **1968** *DARE* (Qu. I33, *. . Ears of corn that are just right for eating*) Inf **NJ**8, [kɑb kɔrn].

cobey See **cobia**

cob-fashion adv *hist* Cf **cobhouse** n 1, v, **cob-pile** v
   In the manner of a **cobhouse** n 1.
   1857 (1864) Thoreau *Maine Woods* 193, They had got a young moose, . . confined in a sort of cage of logs piled up cob-fashion. **1888** Billings *Hardtack* 49, By far the most common way of logging up a tent was to build the walls 'cob-fashion,' notching them together at the corners.

cob-fence n attrib [*cob* perh from **cobble** n¹; perh rel to **cob-fashion**]
   Fig: a rural area.
   1915 Patten *Courtney* 207, The regulars followed the cob-fence route, playing exhibition games each afternoon with minor-league clubs.

cob-floater n *joc* Cf **chunk-floater, lightwood-knot floater**
   A heavy rain.
   1962 Atwood *Vocab. TX* 38, *Torrential rain.* For an unusually heavy rain that does not last long . . . [other terms] occur only once each, but may not necessarily be original: . . *cob floater.* **1970** *DARE* (Qu. B25, *Joking names . . for a very heavy rain*) Inf **IL**19, Cob-floater.

cobhead n [**cobb** n² + *head*] Cf **cubhead**
   A **goldeneye** (here: *Glaucionetta clangula*).
   1888 Trumbull *Names of Birds* 79, *Golden-eye* . . . At Cape May

C[ourt] H[ouse], *Cob-head,* the last name being monopolized, however, by the young birds, which are regarded as a species distinct from the "Whistle-ducks" . . . The name Cob-head is again heard at Cape May City [NJ]. **1923** U.S. Dept. Ag. *Misc. Circular* 13.22, *Goldeneye . . . Vernacular Names . . . In local use . . .* Cobhead (N.J.).

cobhouse n [Cf *EDD* **cob-castle** a flimsy building]
1 A structure built by children out of corncobs; hence any loosely stacked, flimsy structure; also fig. *old-fash*
   1774 (1847) Marcou *Jeremy Belknap* 68 **MA**, They have a neat poultry house, built of sawed strips of wood, in the form of a cob-house, with four apartments. **1818** Birkbeck *Letters IL* 116, In this country they build "cob houses;" a "cob" is the interior part of a head of Indian corn, after the grains are stripped off; with these cobs, . . structures are raised by the little half Indian brats, very much like our "houses of cards." **1830** *MA Spy & Worcester Co. Advt.* (Worcester MA) 21 July 1/3 **SC** (citing *Providence American*), The [Black] victim is chained to a stake, and a pile of light combustible wood built up around him, in the form of a cob-house. **1852** *Knickerbocker* 39.203 **NY**, The 'log' has been placed; the *'back-log'* has surmounted it; the 'top-stick' crowns the apex; the 'fore-stick' rests against the 'and irons;' and the intermediate 'cob-house' of timber, fired by the faithful 'kindling-wood,' is all ablaze. **1913** *Eve. Post* (NY NY) 5 June 2/1, Mayor [Gaynor] made [a] . . statement, comparing the "Curran scandal committee" to a "cobhouse of sensationalism, lying, and scandal . . . All cobhouses fall down at the first jar." **1923** *DN* 5.206 **swMO**, *Down goes his cob-house,* . . "If I don't have a good crop this year, w'y down goes my cob-house."
2 also **cob shed:** A shed for storing corncobs for use as fuel.
   1967–69 *DARE* (Qu. M22, *. . Buildings . . on farms*) Inf **IL**108, Cobhouse, in old days; **NE**8, An older place might have a cobhouse to store fuel. **1972** *Yesterday* 1.4.2 **seWI**, Whatever became of the old home that had a "cob-house" attached which was filled every fall? It was the kids' chore to bring a good supply of cobs into the kitchen every so often. **1973** Allen *LAUM* 178, *Shed . . . Cob house* and *cob shed* occur as minor variants where corn cobs were burned as fuel.

cobhouse v Cf **cob-fashion** adv, **cob-pile** v
   To build in the manner of a **cobhouse** n 1.
   1969 *DARE* FW Addit **MA**42, *Cobhouse,* to alternate. Inf speaking of logs—of a log construction made by alternating logs and piling them higher; construction would then be filled with stone; construction used in building roads near a shore. [Inf old]

cobia n Also sp *cabio, cobio;* pronc-spp *covia, cobey* [Etym unknown]
   A saltwater food fish (*Rachycentron canadum*) with a spindle-shaped body dark brown to buff in color and marked by a dark longitudinal stripe, separate pre-dorsal spines, and a flattened head; common on the South Atlantic and Gulf coasts. Also called **black salmon 2, bonito 2, coalfish 2, crabeater, lemon fish, ling 3, sergeantfish, snook**
   1879 U.S. Natl. Museum *Bulletin* 14.52, *Elacate canadus . . . Cobia; Crab-eater.* **1902** Jordan–Evermann *Amer. Fishes* 323, *Rachycentron canadus.* This fish is an inhabitant of warm seas, ranging in summer as far north on our Atlantic Coast as Cape Cod . . . It is known as sergeant-fish, crab-eater, coal-fish and cobia, and . . it is edible. **1939** *Richmond Times–Dispatch* 16 Aug 15/6 *(Hench Coll.)* **VA**, Captain T.S. Clopton writes from Gloucester Point: I have recently caught several . . cabio, fishing near Cape Charles. **1945** *Ibid* 18 Apr 14/1, Cobia is the name by which the fish will be called in this column . . on authority of the International Game Fish Association. Hitherto it has been called the black bonita or cabio. **1966** *Carteret Co. News–Times* (Morehead City & Beaufort NC) 16 Aug 2/4, Mrs. B.J. White reports that 2 cobia were taken, one weighing 8-pounds and the other 14-pounds. **1966–68** *DARE* (Qu. P2, *What kinds of saltwater fish caught around here are good to eat?*) Inf **GA**28, Cobia; **MD**36, Cobey ['kobi], found near wrecks; black, slippery, shaped like a shark; (Qu. P14, *If commercial fishing is done . . what do the fishermen go out after?*) Inf **NC**27, Covia ['kouvijа]. **1972** Sparano *Outdoors Encycl.* 376, *Cobia . . . Common Names: . .* Cabio, cobio.

cobim See **ker-**

cobio See **cobia**

‡**cob it up** v phr [Prob from *cobble* to repair clumsily]
   1967 *DARE* (Qu. KK63, *To do a clumsy . . job of repairing something*) Inf **MA**1, Cob it up.

‡**cob job** n [Prob from *cobble* to repair clumsily]
A rough or imperfect repair.
   1967 *DARE* (Qu. KK63) Inf **MA1**, What a cob job that is. [FW: Used of a "crappy" welding job on a car.]

cob onto See **cob** v[4]

co-boss(ie) v phr |ˌkə-, ˈko-, -ˈbɔs(i), -ˈbɑs(i)| Also sp *co-bossy, rarely *cow boss* [**co** v + *boss(ie)* a cow] **chiefly Nth** See Map
Come! — used to call cows from pasture.
   1893 *DN* 1.264, When the animal is quite near at hand, this call is shortened into a coaxing *kò-b·âs,* or *k·ò-bâs,* and this again, accented on the ultimate, is often used for a long-distance call, the ò of the first syllable being almost eliminated, as *k'-bâs* or *k'-bâsi.* **1901** *Nation* 18 Apr 314/2, The call 'Co' boss is familiar to most of the inhabitants of our Northern States and Canada. **1907** *DN* 3.242 **eME**, *Co, bos.* **1949** Kurath *Word Geog.* 12, Characteristic Northern expressions that are current in all of New England and the New England settlement area in New York State and northern Pennsylvania, as well as in the Hudson Valley, on Long Island, and in East Jersey, are: . . *co-boss!* **1950** *WELS* (*Call to cows to come in from the pasture*) 21 Infs, **WI**, Co-boss; (*Call to a calf at feeding time*) 1 Inf, C'boss. **1965–70** *DARE* (Qu. K80, *The call . . to get the cows in from the pasture*) 114 Infs, **chiefly Nth**, Co-boss; **FL15, 20, ME5, MI27, NC1,** Co-bossie; **PA198,** [kəbɔsi]; **WI21,** [kəbɔs kəmbɔs]; **MI64,** [kəˈbɔs]; **NC85,** [koˈbɒ]; **RI15,** [kwə] shortened from [ˈkɔˌbɔs]; **ME23,** Cow boss; **NY189,** [gəˈbɔs]; **MO5,** Sook-boss co-boss wo; (Qu. K81, *To make a cow stand still . . you say*) Infs **CA6, NY70,** [ˈkoʊˌbɑs]. **1971** Wood *Vocab. Change* 46, The usual term is *sook cow* or *sook calf(ie)* except in Florida where *co-bossie* is preferred. **1973** Allen *LAUM* 1.259, [*Co-boss* is used by 34 infs, scattered throughout the Upper Midwest; but it is least common in Nebraska. There are two instances of *co-bossy* in Minnesota.]

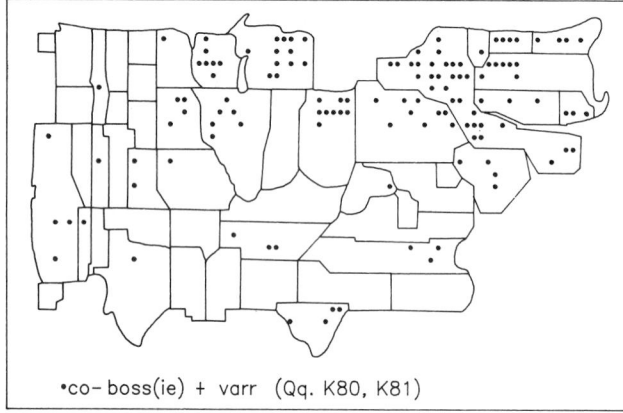

•co- boss(ie) + varr (Qq. K80, K81)

cob owl n
A short-eared owl.
   1970 *DARE* (Qu. Q2, . . *Kinds of fowl found around here*) Inf **VA47,** Cob owl; [same as] marsh owl.

co-boy v phr |ˈko-, kə-, + -ˌbɔɪ| Rarely *cobay, coby* [**co** v]
Come! — used to call cows or horses from the fields.
   1899 (1912) Green *VA Folk-Speech* 119, Cobay . . Call for calves. **1951** Johnson *Resp. to PADS 20* **DE**, Co-boy. **1965–70** *DARE* (Qu. K80, *The call . . used . . to get the cows in*) Inf **FL12,** Co-boy; **NC81,** [ˈko ˌbɔɪ]; (Qu. K82, . . *To get horses*) Inf **DE1,** [ˈko ˌbɔɪ]; **MI2,** [koˈbɔɪ, kəbɔɪ]; **MO5, NC1, 21, 81,** Co-boy; (Qu. K83, *To call a calf*) Inf **FL12,** Co-boy. **1973** Allen *LAUM* 1.262/2 **IA, SD,** [3 infs], Co-boy; [1 inf], Coby.

cob pie n Also *cob apple pie* [Cf *OED cob* sb.[1] II.7, a small lump (of anything); see also **cobbler** n[1] **2,** which coincides in sense and etymological assoc] **RI**
A deep-dish apple pie; **pandowdy.**
   1939 Berolzheimer *U.S. Cookbook* 142 **RI**, Cob Pie (Rhode Island) is Pandowdy sweetened with molasses instead of sugar. **1941** *LANE* Map 292 **seRI**, *Cob (Apple) Pie.* **1949** Kurath *Word Geog.* 23, *Cob pie . .* for a deep-dish apple pie (only on Aquidneck, including Newport) [Rhode Island]. **1952** Tracy *Coast Cookery* 104 **RI**, *Cob-apple pie*—A deep-dish apple pie served upside down. An old Newport recipe.

cob-pile v, hence ppl adj *cob-piled* Cf **cobhouse** v, **cob-fashion**
To stack in a one-over-another, criss-cross, and more or less haphazard fashion.
   1902 Day *Pine Tree Ballads* 9 **ME**, Queer, Gothic old structure of cob-piled bones. *Ibid* 103, They [=logs being driven downstream] loiter in the shallows and . . cob-pile at the falls. **1904** Day *Kin o' Ktaadn* 113 **ME**, Settin' loose a cob-piled million that had jack-strawed at the dam.

cob-popping vbl n
   c1974 Jones *Ozark Hill Boy* 10 **AR** (as of c1920), Cob-popping as a sport was carried on by collecting a bushel or so of corn cobs from the crib and placing them, a few at a time, in a bonfire . . . After the cobs were burned they were removed one by one . . as glowing embers and quickly placed on the chop block. The "popper" would deposit a small lake of "spit" near the ember, roll the glowing cob into the spit and then immediately strike it with a sledge hammer or post maul. The explosive burst resembled the report of a shot gun and the glowing fragments from the cob created beautiful miniature fireworks, spraying ten to twenty-five feet in all directions.

cobra plant n Also *cobra flower, cobra-leaved pitcher plant, cobra lily* [From the upright, snakelike aspect of the leaves] **nCA, swOR**
=**California pitcher plant.**
   1940 (1951) FWP *Guide OR* 20, Watery sphagnum bogs [are] lush with the cobra-leaved pitcher plant and the delicate sundew. **1959** Carleton *Index Herb. Plants* 29, *Cobra-flower:* Darlingtonia californica. **1973** Hitchcock–Cronquist *Flora Pacific NW* 182, *Darlingtonia . . .* California Pitcher-plant; Cobra-plant. **1980** *Nature Conserv. News* Mar/Apr 24, Others include the California pitcher plant or cobra lily (*Darlingtonia californica*).

cob roller n [**cob** n[2] 1]
In marble play: a taw or shooter.
   1966 *DARE* (Qu. EE6a) Inf **GA7,** [ˈkɑb ˈrolə].

cob shed See **cobhouse** n 2

‡**cob spider** n [Cf **cob** n[3] and *OED cob* sb.[4] "*Obs*. . . . A spider"]
   1967 *DARE* (Qu. R28, . . *Different kinds of spiders . . around here*) Inf **OH28,** Cob spiders.

cobtail See **cob** n[2] 3

co-bush v phr [**co** v + **bush** v[2]]
Come! — used to call pigs.
   c1950 *Atlas Checklists* **ceMO**, (*Call to hogs at feeding time*) Bush, co-bush.

cobweb social n
   1950 *WELS* (*Kinds of socials in your community*) 1 Inf, **seWI**, Cobweb social. Put tacks in ceiling and weave them together—a gift at end of each string—then get together and unweave them to get the gift. Takes all day to prepare and undo.

cob wharf See **cob** n[2] 4c

coby See **co-boy**

coca-cola n Also abbr *coke* [Trademarks *Coca-Cola* 1893 → and *Coke* 1945 → a soft drink]
A Forms. Usu |ˈkokə ˈkolə| or |ˈkok|; in **Sth**, also |ˌkoˈkolə|. Pronc-sp *co'cola*
   1919 *DN* 5.33 **seKY**, *Co'-cola . . .* Coca-cola. **1967** *DARE* FW Addit **AL**, [ˌkoˈkolə]. **1978** *News & Observer* (Raleigh NC) 29 Aug [Column by Dennis Rogers], Don't laugh at them [=visiting Yankees]. Love them. Buy them a "Co'Cola," patiently show them how to pour in the peanuts and help them find the true way of life. **1983** *NADS Letters* **nwAL**, Other Furman faculty identified the experience of sticking a hand through the cold ice [in a drink box] to pull out a co-cola or an RC.
B Sense.
By ext from the trademarked name: any of var carbonated soft drinks. **chiefly Sth, S Midl, SW**
   c1960 *Wilson Coll.* **csKY**, Coca-cola (or coke). The name for any carbonated drink. **1965–70** *DARE* (Qu. H78, *Ordinary soft drinks, usually carbonated*) Inf **AR56,** Coke [FW: no distinction among brands generally]; **CA10,** Coke [FW: Inf thinks Coke includes more than Coca-Cola]; **CA59, 85,** Coke—by type; **CA107,** Coke—mostly for Coca-Cola; **CA138,** Coke—if Coke or not; **GA36,** Coke—they claim that's a trademark; **GA75,** Cokes—for anything; **KS14,** Coke—no

matter what kind it is; **LA12**, Cokes—sometimes applied regardless of brand; **LA14**, Coke—without capital C; **MA5**, Coke—for all [soft drinks]; young people now; **MI1**, Pepsi and all of them would be cokes; **MI51**, Coke—many call everything coke; **MN17**, Coke—by type or trade name; **MO11**, Coke—refers to soft drinks in general; **NM2**, Pop, coca-cola; **OH65**, Coke is any soft drink; **SC32, 34**, Coke—any kind; **SC51, TN5**, Coke—generic term; **TN30**, Cokes [FW: generic term used regardless of whether Coca-Cola is meant or not]; **TX99**, Coke—used generally. **1967–68** *DARE* FW Addit **AL**, Coke, coca-cola, co'cola. . In most cases people use the term *co'cola* to refer not only to *Coke* but to any soft drink [or] soda; **OK**, Coke. . has become a generic name for any non-alcoholic beverage drunk in a social situation; **PA**, *A coke bar*—a soda fountain; common; **TN**, Coke—generic term for any bottled, carbonated drink, even to the extent of prompting the question, "What kind of coke do you want?" **1970** Tarpley *Blinky* 195 **neTX**, Younger informants frequently apply the trade name *Coke* or *Coca Cola* to all carbonated beverages. **1980** *Houston Chronicle* (TX) 27 Jan 8, What Texans call non-alcoholic carbonated beverages seems to differ by region. Respondents under 25 tended to use the trade name Coke for any of the beverages. That use is most common in Dallas and West Texas.

cocaho n Also *cocaho minnow*

1968 *LA Conservationist* Jan–Feb 17/2 **LA**, Live minnows, particularly "cocahos", . . are also excellent bait. **1968** *DARE* FW Addit **seLA**, Cocaho, ['kɑkə,hoʊ], also cocaho minnow; small fish used as bait; some have small iridescent spots, others are uniformly shaded from brown on top to white below. Also called storm minnows. They are caught in marshes and ditches.

co-calf(ie) v phr [co v + *calf(ie)*] **esp S Atl**
Come!—used to call calves and sometimes cows.

1949 Kurath *Word Geog.* 64, Co-calfie! competes with *cossie!* in parts of eastern Virginia and North Carolina. **1965–70** *DARE* (Qu. K80, *The call that's used . . to get the cows in from the pasture*) Inf **NC24**, Co-calfie; (Qu. K83, *To call a calf . . at feeding time*) Inf **NC24**, Co-calf. **1971** Wood *Vocab. Change* 303 **Gulf Sth**, [43 respondents, esp freq in Florida, *co-calf(ie)*]

cocash n [See quots]

1 A fleabane, esp horseweed **1**.
1828 Rafinesque *Med. Flora* 1.167, They [i.e. plants of the genus *Erigeron*] were known to the Northern Indians by the name of Cocash or Squaw-weed. **1845** in 1937 U.S. Forest Serv. *Range Plant Hdbk.* W67, E[rigeron] canadensis . . . E. annuus . . and E. philadelphicus . . . These plants were well known to the northern Indians by the name of Cocash or Squaw-weed, as emmenagogues and diuretics. **1902** (1968) Clapin *Americanisms* 125, Cocash . . . A plant (Erigeron canadense) much used by the Northern Indians for medical purposes.

2 also *cocash root, cocash weed:* The red-stalked aster (*Aster puniceus*). Also called **cold-water root, liferoot, meadow scabish, September weed, squaw-weed, swan weed**
1873 in 1976 Miller *Shaker Herbs* 156, Cocash *Aster puniceus* . . . Cocash Weed. **1876** Hobbs *Bot. Hdbk.* 25, Cocash root, Red stalked aster. **1896** *Garden and Forest* 9.262, Cocash (Aster puniceus).—From Natick (Algonk.) *kokoshki,* "it is very rough," a name referring to the hispid character of the stems, which has given the plant one of its popular names—that of the "rough-stemmed Aster." **1907** Hodge *Hdbk. Amer. Indians* 1.316, Cocash. A name of the red-stalk or purple-stem aster (*Aster puniceus*), known also as swan-weed, early purple aster, etc.; from one of the eastern dialects of the Algonquian language, signifying 'it is rough to the touch,' in reference to the stem of the plant.

3 also *cocash weed:* =**golden ragwort.**
1873 in 1976 Miller *Shaker Herbs* 196, Senecio aureus . . . Cocash Weed. False Valerian. **1902** (1968) Clapin *Americanisms* 125, Cocash . . . Also called *squaw-weed.* Both names are also given to another medicinal plant (Senecio aureus) used for diseases of the skin. **1971** Krochmal *Appalachia Med. Plants* 234, Cocashweed . . . is listed as an emmenagogue and vulnerary.

cocenero See **cocinero**

co-chick v phr |'ko-, 'kʌ-, 'kʊ-, ˌkə-, + -čɪk, -či| Also sp *coo-chick, coo-chee* [co v] **chiefly VA**
Come!—used to call chickens.

1868 (1870) Baker *New Timothy* 92 (*DAE*), The voice of Mrs. General Likens coocheeing the poultry to their morning meal, ordering the servants in their duties. **1899** (1912) Green *VA Folk-Speech*, Coochee, . . Word used for calling chickens. Contraction from *come chick.* (?)

1949 Kurath *Word Geog.* 41, The chicken call *coo-chee!, coo-chick!* is also heard only in a part of the Piedmont, from the Rappahannock to the Roanoke in North Carolina, but it has been carried down the points of land to Chesapeake Bay. *Ibid* 65, The Virginia Piedmont and Tidewater south of the Rappahannock have *coo-chee!, coo-chick!*. . Neither the *biddie* of New England nor the *coo-chee!* of Virginia has been carried westward. **1966–70** *DARE* (Qu. K79, *How do you call the chickens . . at feeding time?*) Inf **NC15**, Co-chick; **VA38**, ['kučɪk]; **VA43**, ['kʌči]; **VA105**, [kʊ'či]; **VA70**, [ˌkə'či]. **1971** Metcalf *Riverside Engl.* 15 **CA, NV**, [Call to chickens when feeding them], (Come here) chick. [Also] chickee . . , coo-chee.

cochino n [Span *cochino* hog] Cf **pig's ears**
1967 *DARE* Tape **TX31**, You have different things like what we call cochinos [ko'činos]—it's in the shape of a pig . . . It's more or less brown in color . . . On the style of gingerbread, but it has no actual ginger in it . . . It's just too bad I can't think of these various Mexican cakes, cause they make several kinds.

cochon n [Fr *cochon* swine, pig]
1969 Cagnon *Franco–Amer. Terms* 223 **RI**, Cochon . . [kɔʃɔ̃] Piggy. "You ate all that, you're a big *cochon.*"

cochon de lait n [Fr "sucking pig"]
A pig roast; a suckling pig.
1968 *DARE* (Qu. FF2, . . *Kinds of parties . . people favor . . here*) Inf **LA32**, Cochon de lait [ˌkoʊˌšɑndə'leɪ], in English a pig-roast, but everybody says the French. **1983** *Reinecke Coll.* **New Orleans LA**, Cochon de lait [kə'ʃɔ də lei]—(1) suckling pig . . . (3) a pig roast, given by churches, politicians, etc. in rural Fr. Louisiana. Meaning still common.

cochuck, cochunk See **ker-**

cocinero n Also sp *cocenero, cocinera, cosinero,* and pronc-sp *coshinera* [Span "cook"] **SW**
A cook, esp on a ranch or trail drive.
1845 Green *Jrl. Texian Exped.* 258 **TX**, When not presiding as chief *cocinero* (cook), much of my time was employed at the desk. **1898** in 1921 Thorp *Songs Cowboys* 97 **NM, TX**, And help the "cosinero" rustle wood. **1933** *AmSp* 8.1.27 **wTX**, Cocinera. Pronounced variously, as were all Spanish adoptions, but most often *coshinera.* Cook. **1936** McCarthy *Lang. Mosshorn* **West**, Cocinera . . . A flattering term for the cook. **1937** *DN* 6.621 **cwTX**, The cook is frequently called the *cocenero.*

cock n[1] [Prob from assoc with *cock* penis] *usu considered obscene*

1 The female genitalia. **chiefly Sth, S Midl**
1942 McAtee *Dial. Grant Co. IN* 3 (as of 1890s), Cock . . applied to both the female pudendum and the male penis. **1944** *PADS* 2.18 **sAppalachians**, Cock. (Pudenda muliebra.) Always a vulgar term among the highlanders, no matter what it is used for. In the vulgar sense, it is always applied to females, never to males, as in England. **1950** *PADS* 13.16 **c, cwTX**, Cock . . . Pudenda muliebra. **1954** Harder Coll. **cwTN**, Cock, . . Occas. pudendum. The latter is probably more common than one would suspect. I remember (1930s) that boys in school talked about girls' cocks. The confusion occurs in the phrase, "She's a good piece of cock." **1969** *DARE* FW Addit **se, cwNC**, Cock, female genitals. **1970** Abrahams *Deep Down* 259 **PA**, Cock—Most commonly the female genitalia. **1970** *AmSp* 45.48, It seems that *cock* also has mixed reference, depending on the region. At a point roughly the same as the Mason-Dixon Line, there is a division in meaning. In the North, *cock* refers to the male genitalia, but in the South its use is restricted to the female genitalia. Missouri is a border state in which both meanings are used.

2 Sexual intercourse. *esp among Black speakers* See also **cocksman**
1942 McAtee *Dial. Grant Co. IN* 3 (as of 1890s), Cock . . . Also meant the "deed of kind", as in "plenty of good _____." **1970** Bullins *Electronic* 39 **sCA** [Black], I start in drinkin' and talkin' to girls but none of them are listen'n 'cept for seven bucks. ., and I ain't buyin no cock . . . not in the States. **1970** Abrahams *Deep Down* 36 **Philadelphia PA** [Black], She said, "Kid, now if you can get some cock 'fore my mother get back home, . . you can have it." So I said, "Lay down." **1980** Folb *Runnin' Down* 150 **Los Angeles CA** [Black], Many of the same expressions are used for females in general and for the female genitalia (*pussy, cock, tail*), and for the act of sexual intercourse (to *get some pussy / cock / tail*).

cock n[2] Also *haycock* **chiefly Nth, N Midl** See Map
A conical pile of hay left in the field.

1684 (1977) Mather *Essay Providences* 5.163 **MA,** Several Cocks of English-hay mowed near the house, were taken and hung upon Trees. **1735** (1901) Hempstead *Diary* 306 **CT,** I dried about a Ld of hay yt was in Cock not Cured. **1794** Williams *Nat. & Civil Hist. VT* 98, Of an oval form, resembling the construction of an haycock. **1861** Holmes *Venner* 1.119 **NEng,** I should like to know whether that's a hay-cock or a mountain! **1940** Richter *Trees* 111 **OH** (as of c1880), Hay cocks in the meader. **1946** *PADS* 5.25 **VA,** Hay cock . . A pile of hay in the field at haying time; west of the Blue Ridge, on the Middle Neck and on the Eastern Shore. **1949** Kurath *Word Geog.* 54, Hay cock. For the temporary small heaps of hay in the meadow two regional terms are widely current, *cock* in the New England area and the North Midland, *shock* in the Southern area and in the South Midland. **1965–70** DARE (Qu. L12, . . *The small piles of hay standing in the field*) 165 Infs, **chiefly Nth, scattered N Midl,** Haycocks; 98 Infs, **chiefly Nth,** Cocks (of hay); (Qu. L30b . . *Piles*) 9 Infs, **chiefly N and C Atl,** Cocks; (Qu. L14, *A large pile of hay stored outdoors*) Infs **CA**111, **IN**83, **MA**11, 72, **PA**234, Haycock; (Qu. L11) Inf **MI**78, Pile it in haycocks; **MI**83, Cocks, put in small piles. **1973** Allen *LAUM* 1.185, For a small pile of hay in the field the two principal U[pper] M[idwest] terms, *(hay)cock* and *(hay)shock,* are regionally distributed in correlation with the eastern pattern of *haycock* in the North and North Midland and *hayshock* in the South Midland and South Atlantic Coast.

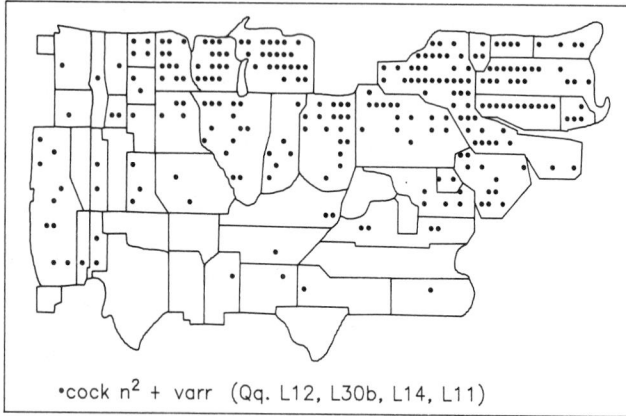

•cock n² + varr   (Qq. L12, L30b, L14, L11)

cock v¹ [**cock** n²] **Nth**

Also *cock up:* To put hay into conical piles; also transf.

1931–33 *LANE Worksheets* **cwCT,** Stacking hay in the field, some say cocking it. *Ibid,* Cocked [kakt], Stacked up; if hay is cocked it's shaped more to shed rain. **1933** *AmSp* 8.2.79 **NEng** (as of 1830s), As busy as cocking hay afore a shower. **1950** *WELS* (What . . you do to hay in the field after it has been cut) 1 Inf, **cwWI,** Cocked into small piles (haycocks), old-fashioned. **1965–70** DARE (Qu. L11, *What do you do to hay in the field after it's cut*) 19 Infs, **Nth,** Cock it (up); (Qu. L12, . . *Small piles of hay standing in the field*) Inf **MI**40, Hay cocks, and piling it was called 'cocking the hay.' **1969** DARE FW Addit **neNY,** The logs was cocked up, [that is] jammed up. Old-fashioned [term].

cock v² [Etym uncert] Cf **coldcock**

To hit someone hard, to knock someone out.

1960 Criswell *Resp. to PADS 20* **Ozarks,** [*Cold-cock,* . .] To knock out, knock unconscious . . . One also hears *cock,* alone, used in this sense. **1968** DARE (Qu. Y11, . . *A very hard blow*) Inf **PA**96, Cocked him.

cock-a-doodle-do(o) n [Cf *cock of the walk* one who dominates] **SW**

A ranch foreman or boss.

1922 Rollins *Cowboy* 165, There was the foreman, who sometimes was referred to as the "cock-a-doodle-do." **1961** Adams *Old-Time Cowhand* 64, The foreman of a good ranch didn't have no easy job, and it was one of great responsibility. He was knowed by such titles as . . "cock-a-doodle-doo."

cock-a-nee-nee See **cackany**

cockbill v [*acockbill* adv, in a tipped-up position]

1945 Colcord *Sea Language* 55 **ME, Cape Cod, and Long Island,** *Cockbill.* To brace yards unevenly or in opposite directions. Alongshore, to hang askew. "I don't like to see pictures all cockbilled on a wall."

cock-brain n [In ref to the small size of a cock's brain]

1915 *DN* 4.206, *Cock-brain,* a light-hearted, foolish person. "To my notion about twenty-five per cent of the youths are cock-brains."

cock-burr n [Var of **cockleburr**]

1884 Lanier *Poems* 172 **GA** (as of 1869), And to quit raisin' cock-burrs, thistles and sich.

cock dipper n [See quot 1955] Cf **dipper**

Either of two ducks: **bufflehead 2** or **goldeneye** (here: *Glaucionetta clangula*).

1923 U.S. Dept. Ag. *Misc. Circular* 13.23, *Bufflehead . . . Vernacular Names . . . In local use . . .* cock-dipper (N.C.). **1955** *AmSp* 30.181, Names of similar suggestion [i.e., the spruce appearance of the black and white colored and conspicuously crested *cock-robin duck*] include *cock dipper* (bufflehead, Va., N.C.; common goldeneye, Md., N.C.).

cocked ppl adj [Perh from *cock* to set (a gun) for firing] **chiefly Nth**

Drunk; hence *half-cocked* partly drunk.

1965–70 DARE (Qu. DD14, . . *A person . . partly drunk*) 9 Infs, **chiefly Nth,** Half-cocked; (Qu. DD15, *A person . . thoroughly drunk*) Infs **NH**2, **NY**193, Cocked; **MA**62, Cocked as a log; **NH**18, Cocked to the gills.

cockershell n [Alter of *cockleshell*]

1970 DARE Tape **CA**68 [Jump rope rhyme], Bluebells, cockershells, eevy-ivy-over.

‡cocker up v phr [Cf *cocker* to pamper, indulge]

1935 Davis *Honey* 324 **eOR,** [She had] a fixed notion that nobody around her was getting enough to eat . . . She disliked harvest hands, and worked from four in the morning till ten at night cockering up grub for them that they wouldn't get tired of.

cockery n [Prob alter of **crockery**]

1968 DARE (Qu. EE6d, *Special marbles*) Inf **OH**56, Cockeries.

cockey See **cacky** v, n

cockeye n Cf **cockeye piddle**

A car with only one working headlight—often used as an exclam in a kind of courting game; see quot.

1980 *Hand Coll.* **KS,** If a boy and girl drove past a car with only one headlight burning (a cockeye), the one who saw the cockeye first, licked his right forefinger, clenched his right hand into a fist, hit his left palm with his right fist, and exclaimed "cockeye" before the other one; got to either kiss or hit his or her companion.

cockeyed adj

1 Lopsided, out of plumb. **scattered, but chiefly NEast** See Map

1965–70 DARE (Qu. KK70, *Something that has got out of proper shape: "That house is all _____."*) 21 Infs, Cockeyed.

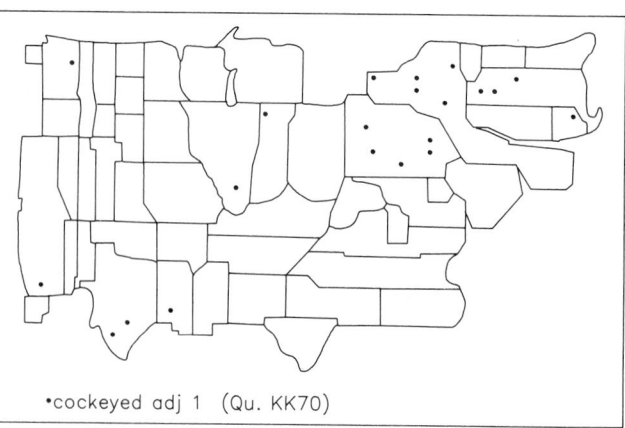

•cockeyed adj 1   (Qu. KK70)

2 Crazy, blasted, damned—used as an intensifier.

1950 *PADS* 14.21 **SC,** Cockeyed . . . A favorite expletive: "I'll tell the *cock-eyed* world." **1967–68** DARE (Qu. R21) Inf **MN**5, Cockeyed sandflies, they're the ones that get my goat; (Qu. NN17, . . *"That _____ fly won't go away!"*) Inf **UT**4, Cockeyed.

cockeyed adv [From **cockeyed** adj 2]

Extremely.

1951 Porter *Ragged Roads* 37 (as of 1900), All of us were so cockeyed poor there was no way to draw a comparison. **1965–70** *DARE* (Qu. LL37, *To make a statement as strong as you can: "I could have wrung her neck, I was so*_____ *mad."*) Infs **CA**107, **GA**68, **MN**16, **MT**3, **NE**11, **UT**4, **WA**1, 20, **WI**30, Cockeyed.

cockeye piddle exclam [Prob blend of **cockeye** and **padiddle**]
    1980 *Hand Coll.* **AR**, It's said to be able to see your girl friend if you see three cars with just one headlight, if you put your thumb into your fist and say, "cockeye piddle." I heard it somewhere in grade school.

cockhold herb See **cuckold** n **1**

cockle n
    1 Any of several plants of the pink family, but esp **corn cockle, cowherb,** or a **catchfly 1.** Cf **white cockle**
    1801 Society Useful Arts *Trans.* 1.25 **NY**, Cockle, drips and sorrel often mingle their seeds with the crop. **1886** *Century Illustr. Mag.* 32.44/1, There still remains an objectionable element in the grain [=wheat] which must be gotten rid of—the seeds of cockle and other weeds. **1896** *Jrl. Amer. Folkl.* 9.182, *Saponaria vaccaria*, . . cockle, Blue Earth County, Minn[esota]. **1898** *Ibid* 11.223 **WY**. **1899** (1912) Green *VA Folk-Speech* 120, Cockle . . . A weed that grows in wheat; corn-rose, or corn-cockle; the small, black seeds that grow in a capsule. **1912** Blatchley *IN Weed Book* 78, *Silene antirrhina* . . . *Tarry Cockle* . . . is very common in wheat and rye. *Ibid* 79, The sticky cockle or night-flowering catchfly (*S. noctiflora* . .) . . may develop into troublesome weeds. **1966** *DARE* Wildfl QR Pl.52 Inf **WI**34, Cockle. **1967–69** *DARE* (Qu. S21, . . *Weeds . . that are a trouble in gardens and fields*) Inf **ID**5, Cockle; (Qu. S26d, *Wildflowers that grow in meadows*) Infs **MI**96, **NY**160, Cockle; (Qu. S26e, *Other wildflowers*) Inf **OH**22, Cockle.
    2 also sp *cuckle:* =**beggar ticks** (esp *Bidens frondosa*).
    1898 *Jrl. Amer. Folkl.* 11.229, *Bidens frondosa* . . cuckles, Alcove, N.Y. **1900** Lyons *Plant Names* 63, *B[idens] frondósa* . . . Cuckles. **1959** Carleton *Index Herb. Plants* 29, *Cuckles:* Bidens frondosa. *Ibid* 34, *Cuckles:* Bidens frondosa. **1965–70** *DARE* (Qu. S14, *Other prickly seeds, small and flat, with two prongs at one end, that cling to clothing*) 6 Infs, **CT, NJ, NY**, Cuckle(s); **CT**2, **NJ**1, 3, **NY**75, 209, Cockles.
    3 also sp *cuckle:* =**cockleburr 1.**
    1965–70 *DARE* (Qu. S13, . . *A common wild bush with bunches of round, prickly seeds; when they get dry they stick to your clothing*) Infs **CT**26, **NY**209, **PA**104, Cockles; **CT**26, **NJ**12, **NY**233, Cuckles.

cockleberry n Also sp *cuckleberry*
    =**cockleburr 1.**
    1928 Ruppenthal *Coll.* **KS**, Cockleberry . . . variant of cockleburr. **1965–70** *DARE* (Qu. S13, . . *Common wild bush with bunches of round, prickly seeds; when they get dry they stick to your clothing*) Infs **MO**21, **MA**40, Cockleberry; **MA**14, Cockleberries; **MD**34, Cuckleberry.

cockleburr n Also sp *cocklebur*
    1 Any coarse weedy annual plant of the genus *Xanthium;* also the burr produced by such a plant. **widespread, but chiefly N Cent, Upper MW, West** See Map Also called **beach burr, burr thistle 1, burweed, clotburr 1, cuckleburr 1** For other names of var spp see **burdock 2, buttonburr, Chinese thistle, dagger cockleburr, ditch burr, louse burr, pigs, sheep burr, Spanish thistle** See also **bristle burr, bumblebee** n **5, burr** n[1] **1, cackleburr,**

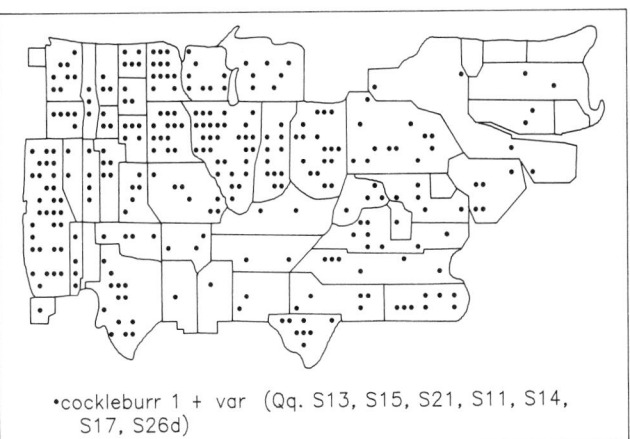

•cockleburr 1 + var (Qq. S13, S15, S21, S11, S14, S17, S26d)

cock-burr, cockle 3, cockleberry, cockle bush, crinkleburr, huckleburr, pickery burr, poky weed, pricker, pricker burr, pricker bush, prickly burr, she-burr, sticker, sticker burr, sticker bush
    1815 Drake *Natural View Cincinnati* 119, The wide alluvial vallies of these rivers . . abound in . . cockle burr *(xanthium strumarium* . .). **1891** Jesup *Plants Hanover NH* 22, *Xanthium* . . . Cocklebur. **1965–70** *DARE* (Qu. S13) 272 Infs, **chiefly N Midl, West,** Cockleburr(s); (Qu. S15) 12 Infs, **chiefly N Cent,** Cockleburr(s); **NM**13, Sonora cockleburr; (Qu. S11) Infs **LA**33, **PA**40, Cockleburrs; (Qu. S14) **OH**65, **PA**165, **VA**71, Cockleburr(s); (Qu. S17) Inf **MD**24, Cockleburr; (Qu. S21) Infs **GA**3, **IA**36, **IL**126, **IN**3, 8, **TN**56, Cockleburrs; (Qu. S26d) Inf **MI**95, Cockleburrs. [Note: Some of these Infs may be referring instead to **cockleburr 2.**] **1966** *DARE* Wildfl QR Pl. 213b Inf **CO**11, Cockleburr.
    2 An agrimony (*Agrimonia* spp).
    1828 Rafinesque *Med. Flora* 34, *Agrimonia eupatoria* . . . Vulgar Names—Cockle-bur, Stickwort, etc. . . . Fruit, a small green bur . . . This bur often sticks to clothes, like other bristly burs. **1900** Lyons *Plant Names* 19, *A. hirsuta* . . . Stick-weed, Cockle-bur. These names . . are applied also to other indigenous species. **1950** Gray–Fernald *Manual of Botany* 865, *Agrimonia* . . . Agrimony. Cocklebur. Harvest-lice . . . Perennial widely distributed genus of herbs. **1974** (1977) Coon *Useful Plants* 223, *Agrimonia gryposepala* . . cocklebur . . . Valuable for sore and husky throats.
    3 =**burdock 1.**
    1900 Lyons *Plant Names* 43, A[rctium] lappa . . . Cockle-bur. **1931** Harned *Wild Flowers Alleghanies* 601, Other names locally applied to Burdock are Cockle-bur, Stick-button, and Beggar's-button. **1959** Carleton *Index Herb. Plants* 29, *Cockle bur:* Arctium lappa.
    4 attrib; also sp *cuckleburr:* Used of something considered inferior.
    1944 Adams *Western Words* 70, *Cocklebur outfit*—A small ranch, a "one-hoss" outfit, a "seedy" outfit. **1967–68** *DARE* (Qu. N37, *Joking names for a branch railroad that is not very important or gives poor service*) Infs **CA**62, **KS**12, Cuckleburr special; (Qu. HH1, . . *A rustic or countrified person*) Inf **LA**11, Cuckleburr bullies [laughter].

cockle bush n
    =**cockleburr 1.**
    1967 *DARE* (Qu. S13) Inf **NJ**1, Cockle bush.

cockle button n Also sp *cuckle button* **chiefly NEng**
    =**burdock 1.**
    1895 *DN* 1.386 **neMA,** *Cuckle-button* ['kʌkl 'bʌtn]: burr of the burdock, from which children make baskets. **1898** *Jrl. Amer. Folkl.* 11.229, *Arctium Lappa* . . cuckle buttons, South Berwick, Me. **1930** Sievers *Amer. Med. Plants* 17, *Arctium minus* . . Cockle button. **1966** *DARE* (Qu. S13) Inf **ME**7, Cuckle buttons.

cockloft n [Prob from the use of attics as roosting places] *old-fash*
    1 A small garret.
    1803 Davis *Travels* 347, He ascended a few steps and opened a trap-door in the rafters, which I had not perceived led to a cock-loft. **1899** (1912) Green *VA Folk-Speech* 120, Cock-loft . . . A garret. **1936** Smith–Sass *Carolina Rice* 33 (as of 1850), The negroes, Robinson noted further, occupied "eighty-four double frame houses, each containing two tenements of three rooms to a family besides the cockloft." **1968** *DARE* (Qu. D4, *The space up under the roof, usually used for storing things*) Inf **NY**56, Cockloft. **1973** Allen *LAUM* 1.169, The old name [for *attic*] *cock-loft* was recalled by a southern Minnesotan both of whose parents came from Canada.
    2 In railroading: the cupola of a caboose. Also called **crow's nest 3b**
    1943 *AmSp* 18.164 [Railroad language], *Cockloft* . . . Cupola of a caboose. **1945** Hubbard *Railroad Ave.* 337.

cockmantail n
    =**ruddy duck.**
    1945 McAtee *Nomina Abitera* 32, Cockmantail, North Carolina coast . . . The ruddy duck has a number of epithets based on peculiarities of its tail, one of which [;] frequent erection, may have to do with this name.

cockney n
    1965–70 *DARE* (Qu. HH28, *Names and nicknames . . for people of foreign background . . English*) Infs **CT**35, **NJ**61, **NY**9, 219, **OR**4, **PA**104, Cockney.

cock of the desert n
=**roadrunner.**
1917 (1923) *Birds Amer.* 2.126 Road-Runner ... *Other Names* ... Cock of the Desert.

cock of the plains n West
=**sage grouse.**
1805 (1904) Lewis *Orig. Jrls. Lewis & Clark Exped.* 2.384, Capt. C. killed a cock of the plains or mountain cock. it was of a dark brown colour with a long and pointed tail. **1872** Coues *Key to N. Amer. Birds* 233, Genus *Centrocercus* . . Sage Cock. Cock of the Plains. **1917** (1923) *Birds Amer.* 2.29, *Sage Hen*—Centrocercus urophasianus . . Other names.—Cock of the Plains; Sage Cock; Sage Grouse. **1918** Grinnell *Game Birds CA* 564, *Sage-hen* . . Other names—Sage Grouse; Sagecock; Cock-of-the-plains.

cock of the roost n [Var of *cock of the walk*] Cf **cock-a-doodle-do(o)**
One who dominates a group or situation; the top man, boss.
1913 Porter *4 Million* 165, The cock-of-the-roost sits aloft like Jupiter on an unsharable seat, holding your fate between two thongs of inconstant leather. **1965–70** *DARE* (Qu. GG19b, . . *"He sure is _____ these days."*) Infs **AL34, CA174, MD12, MI115, MN38, MO2, SC32,** Cock of the roost; (Qu. HH17, . . *"He'd like to be the _____ around here."*) Infs **FL29, HI1,** Cock of the roost; (Qu. EE33, *Outdoor games*) Inf **GA18,** Bull-in-the-ring (last one out is the cock o' the roost).

cock of the woods n [From its large size] **chiefly Nth**
=**pileated woodpecker.**
1817 Paulding *Letters from South* 1.154 **VA,** Of living objects, we sometimes saw a covey of partridges, a cock of the woods, or a ground squirrel. **1923** *DN* 5.234 **swWI,** Cock o' the woods. The great pileated woodpecker. **1965–70** *DARE* (Qu. Q17, . . *Kinds of woodpeckers*) Infs **ME8, MI53, NY97, 191, 219,** Cock of the woods; (Qu. Q18, . . *Joking names . . for woodpeckers*) Inf **NY191,** Cock of the woods. **1967** Borland *Hill Country* 326 **nwCT,** I heard the hammerblows of a pileated woodpecker, the rolling, echoing *Brrrrr* that means the big, colorful Cock of the Woods is at work.

cock one's pistol v phr
To startle, surprise greatly, annoy one.
1960 Criswell *Resp. to PADS 20* **Ozarks,** Cock (one's) pistol . . . Startle, dumbfound. "Now wouldn't that cock your pistol; I never expected him to talk back." Once common. **1965–70** *DARE* (Qu. GG22b, *When you have come to the end of your patience, you might say, "Well, that certainly_____."*) Infs **AR3, IL96, TX51,** Cocks my pistol; (Qu. NN7, *Exclamations of surprise, "They're getting married next week? Well, _____."*) Inf **IL96,** Don't that cock your pistol.

cock oyster n
1949 Brown *Amer. Cooks* 268 **New Orleans LA,** "Cock oysters" are selected by their off-color. They're found in all shades of the rainbow, from delicate pink to violent purple, each of a subtly different flavoring, depending on the iodine and other nutritive and tasty sea salts that painted this pearly lily.

cockroach n
Std sense, used attrib to connote filth, unhealthful living conditions, degradation.
1939 FWP *Guide NJ* 352, The proprietors of these shops [Paterson's own brand of sweatshop . . the family shop] are known as cockroach bosses. **1966–67** *DARE* (Qu. D39, . . *Small eating place where the food is not especially good*) Inf **NE5,** Cockroach joint; **ID5,** Cockroach trap. **1978** *DARE* File **Madison WI,** I couldn't help but pity those graduate students, pacing the hotel corridors in their cockroach suits while awaiting interviews for teaching positions they would never receive.

cockroach killer n *joc* Cf **snake kicker, toad stabber**
A sharp-pointed shoe.
1970 *DARE* (Qu. W42a) Inf **NJ63,** Cockroach killers.

cock-robin duck n
1955 *AmSp* 30.181, Cock-robin duck (hooded merganser, N.J.) probably refers to the spruce appearance of this black-and-white colored, and conspicuously crested, bird.

cockscomb n Also *coxcomb*
1 A cultivated woolflower *(Celosia cristata)* which produces feathery flower spikes.
1791 in 1793 *Amer. Philos. Soc. Trans.* 3.164/2 **sePA,** *Celosia . . castrensis[?]* Cocks-comb. **1945** Saxon *Gumbo Ya-Ya* 364 **LA,** *Cox-combs*—a coarse red flower resembling a rooster's headdress—once enjoyed a great vogue among poorer Creoles. **1961** Wills–Irwin *Flowers TX* 104, Cock's-comb, *Celosia argentea.* **1970** Correll *Plants TX* 553, *Celosia argentea* . . Cockscomb . . . Forma *cristata* . . Cockscomb. **1976** Bailey–Bailey *Hortus Third* 241, *Celosia cristata* . . Cockscomb.

2 =**amaranth.**
1829 Phelps *Familiar Lect.* 272, *Amaranthus albus,* white coxcomb . . . Common garden weed. **1899** Going *Field, Forest, and Wayside Flowers* 354 *(DAE),* Some species of amaranth are cultivated in old fashioned gardens, and called "cockscomb," "love-lies-bleeding," and "prince's feather." **1901** *Harper's Mag.* 104.211/2, They had their own . . little court, brave with hollyhocks and cocks-comb around the fountain. **1936** Winter *Plants NE* 195, *A[maranthus] caudatus* . . , the cultivated Cocks-comb, has drooping inflorescences. **1947** (1976) Curtin *Healing Herbs* 25, Red Cockscomb—Amaranthus paniculatus . . . Cockscomb was brought into this region [the Upper Rio Grande] by the Spaniards. **1967–68** *DARE* (QR, near Qu. S11) Inf **MO4,** The bachelor's button, the corn flower, and cockscomb belong to the same family; (Qu. S26e, *Other wildflowers not yet mentioned*) Inf **TN22,** Cockscomb. **1974** (1977) Coon *Useful Plants* 53, *Amaranthus hybridus* . . red cockscomb.

3 =**death camas.**
1966 Barnes–Jensen *Dict. UT Slang,* Coxcomb . . . A name sometimes given to the Death Camas or "Poison Sego" *(Zigadenus paniculatus).*

4 also *cockscomb weed:* Perh **cockspur 2.**
1969 *DARE* (Qu. S9, *Kinds of grass . . hard to get rid of*) Inf **CT26,** Cockscomb weed; (Qu. S21, *Other weeds . . that are a trouble in gardens and fields*) Inf **CT26,** Cockscomb.

5 An unidentified mushroom: see quot.
1970 *DARE* (Qu. I37, *Small plants shaped like an umbrella that grow in woods and fields . . safe to eat*) Inf **OH95,** Cockscomb.

cockscomb weed See **cockscomb 4**

cocksfoot grass n, also attrib Also *cocksfoot* **NEast** *old-fash*
1 =**orchard grass.** [*OED* 1697 →]
1791 in 1793 *Amer. Philos. Soc. Trans.* 3.161/1 **sePA,** *Dactylis . . glomerata[?]* Cock's foot-grass. **1795** Winterbotham *Amer. U.S.* 3.401, Besides the cultivated grasses, the States of New-England abound with a great variety which are found growing in their native soils and situations . . . Most common are the following . . . Cock's foot grass, Dactylis glomerata. **1839** Buel *Farmer's Companion* 226, *American Cock's-foot* and *Orchard-grass* are different names given to the *Dactylis glomerata* of botanists. **1889** Vasey *Ag. Grasses* 14, Pastures consisting largely of early, strong-growing grasses, particularly cock's foot (orchard grass).

2 =**barnyard grass.** Cf **cockspur 2**
1824 Bigelow *Florula Bostoniensis* 40, *Cocksfoot Panic grass* . . . A common weed in cultivated ground. **1837** Darlington *Flora Cestrica* 49 **PA,** Racemes dense, spikeform . . . *Cock's foot Panicum.* **1840** MA Zool. & Bot. Surv. *Herb. Plants & Quadrupeds* 244, The Cock's-foot Grass, introduced from Europe, and common in gardens, and about yards, seems to follow man in his dispersions over this country. **1849** Emmons *Agriculture NY* 2.81, *Panicum Crus-galli (Cocksfoot grass).* Grown in the yard of the Old State House. **1910** Graves *Flowering Plants* 56 **CT,** *Echinochloa crusgalli* . . . Cockspur or Cocksfoot Grass.

cock's hair, to a See **hair n¹ B**

cock shop n, also attrib [Perh *cock* chief, boss; cf **cock-a-doodle-do(o)**; but cf also **cookshop 2**]
The office of a logging camp.
1938 (1939) Holbrook *Holy Mackinaw* 260, Cock shop. Camp office. **1942** *AmSp* 17.221, Cock shop. The camp office. **1968** Adams *Western Words* 70. **1975** Gould *ME Lingo* 54.

cocksman n [**cock** n¹]
1 A man who is highly successful in sex.
1958 Humphrey *Home from the Hill* 36 **TX,** Why, hello there, Theron. How's the old cocksman? Getting much lately? **1967** *DARE* FW Addit **LA,** Cocksman. A man who is consistently sexually successful. Also known as a real operator. Common usage. **1969** *DARE* (Qu. AA6a . . *A man who is fond of being with women and tries to attract their attention—if he's nice about it*) Inf **MO27,** He's a cocksman.

2 See quot.
1970 Major *Afro-Amer. Slang* 38, Cocksman: a male whore.

‡**cock-sniper** n
    1970 *DARE* (Qu. HH16, *Uncomplimentary words with no definite
meaning . . used . . to show . . you don't think much of a person*) Inf
PA236, Cock-sniper.

cockspur n
1 =cockspur thorn.
    1792 Imlay *Western Terr.* 213, Nut Trees, &c . . . Cockspur *Cratægus
coccinea.* **1858** Warder *Hedges* 25, The Cockspur . . is a native of our
Middle States, and is truly beautiful, with its deep green and highly-pol-
ished leaves.
2 also *cockspur grass:* A grass of the genus *Echinochloa,* esp
barnyard grass. Cf cocksfoot grass 2
    1861 Wood *Class-Book* 787, Cock-spur Grass . . . Coarse grasses with
the fl[ower]s in dense paniculate racemes. **1912** Blatchley *IN Weed
Book* 52, Cockspur Grass . . . Often cut for forage when other grass is
scarce. **1966–67** *DARE* (Qu. S13) Inf SC63, Cockspur; (Qu. S14, *Other
prickly seeds . . that cling to clothing*) Inf AL15, Cockspur; (Qu. S15, . .
Other weed seeds that cling to clothing) Infs SC4, 43, Cockspur(s). **1973**
Hitchcock–Cronquist *Flora Pacific NW* 636, *Echinochloa* . . . Cockspur; Barnyard-grass.

cockspur thorn n Also *cockspur haw,* ~ *hawthorn* [See quot
1979]
    A **hawthorn** (here: *Cratægus crus-galli*). Also called **cockspur 1,
hog apple, Newcastle thorn, pine thorn, pin thorn, red haw, thorn
apple**
    1762 Gronovius *Flora Virginica* 76, *Cratægus foliis ovatis repando-an-
gulatis serratis* . . . Cockspur-Hawthorn. **1795** Winterbotham *Amer.
U.S.* 3.392, *Flowering Trees, Shrubs,* [include] . . Cockspur hawthorn,
Cratægus coccinea. **1838** MA Ag. Surv. *Report for 1837* 1.123, There is
a native shrub abundant in this vicinity most admirably adapted for
fences; the common Cockspur Thorn. (*Cratægus Crus Galli.*) [**1850**
Cooper *Rural Hours* 121 **nNY,** During the war of the Revolution the
long spines of the thorn were occasionally used by the American women
for pins, none of which were manufactured in the country; probably it
was the cockspur variety, which bears the longest and most slender
spines.] **1851** Browne *Trees* 278, The Cock-spur Thorn . . is . . found in
woods and hedges, from Florida to Canada, and as far west as Missouri.
1892 Apgar *Trees N. U. S.* 104, Cockspur Thorn . . . A small tree with a
flat, bushy head . . . Wild and common throughout, and often planted.
1897 Sudworth *Arborescent Flora* 216, *Cratægus crus-galli* . . . Cockspur Hawthorn (Pa.). **1930** OK Univ. Biol. Surv. *Pub.* 2.2.64, *Cratægus
crus-galli* . . . Cock-Spur Haw. Red Haw. **1979** Little *Checklist U.S.
Trees* 111, Cockspur hawthorn . . . *Derivation*—cock's spur, from the
long spines. Other common names . . cockspur-thorn.

cocktail n, also attrib [*cocktail* end, last (the rear or last part of a
bird); but cf *OED cock-crow* early dawn; see also *DJE cock-crow*]
    Among cowboys: the last watch of the working day or night.
    1891 *Outing* 17.411/1 **csCO,** Half-past 2 and the boys are counting the
minutes before calling the 'cocktail guard' that relieves them. **1927**
James *Cow Country* 37, No songs was heard during 'cocktail' that
evening. **1936** McCarthy *Lang. Mosshorn* (Range Term) **West,** *Cocktail* . . . Hours between last meal of the day and first night guard. Not to
be confused with a spirited beverage. **1948** Rollinson *WY Cattle* 205,
We . . returned to camp about 5:00 A.M., called the cook, and aroused
the boys who were to come out on herd. We dubbed this the 'cocktail
relief.' **1961** Adams *Old-Time Cowhand* 278, There were several periods of guard durin' the night, and "cocktail." This was the last watch
before daylight, and the one despised by all herders because it was at a
time when men most loved to sleep.

cocktail finger n [**finger** n 1]
    A finger-shaped piece of crabmeat suitable for a cocktail party
hors d'oeuvre.
    1976 Warner *Beautiful Swimmers* 190 **Chesapeake Bay MD,** Whack
them [=crab claws] with the knife handle at just the right point, break
them apart gently by hand, and pull out a pleasingly whole claw muscle,
suitable for "cocktail fingers," as they say in the trade.

cocktop n
    A haycock.
    1931–33 *LANE Worksheets* **swCT,** Some call them haycocks, some
use cocktop.

cock up See **cock** v[1]

‡**cocky** n
    1967 *DARE* (Qu. K73, . . *The rump of a cooked chicken*) Inf **NY**13, The
cocky ['kɑki].

cocky-sure adj [Alter of *cocksure*]
    1968 *DARE* (Qu. II36a, *Somebody who talks back or gives rude
answers: "Did you ever see such a _____?"*) Inf **VA**29, Cocky-sure
person.

coco n See **coco grass**

‡**coco** v [*coco* head]
    To strike (on the head).
    1927 *AmSp* 2.351 **WV,** *Coco you on the bean* . . to hit one on the head.
"A falling limb cocoed him on the bean."

cocoa n Cf **high yellow**
    One who has brown skin.
    1968 *DARE* (Qu. HH28, *Names . . for people of foreign background: . .
Negro*) Inf **NY**64, Cocoa.

cocoa grass See **coco grass**

cocoa plum See **coco plum**

coco grass n, also attrib Also *coco, cocoa grass, coconut* ~
chiefly **Sth,** esp **LA, MS** Cf **bitter coco, sweet coco grass** See
also **coffee grass, coke grass**
1 also *coco sedge:* =**nut grass 1,** esp *Cyperus rotundus.*
    1823 (1878) Aime *Plantation Diary* 19 **LA,** Dug up coco grass around
sugar house. *Ibid* 81, Some cane, in coco land, having been hoed deeply
during the drought, are withering away; in such circumstances it is better
to cover coco. **1855** Amer. Inst. NYC *Annual Rept. for 1854* 168, In
Louisiana and Mississippi a species known as coco grass is a great trouble
to cotton planters. **1894** *Congressional Record* 17 July 7587/1, In my
State [Mississippi] . . there is a grass that is as damaging to the land as the
thistle can be to the people of the other part of the country, and that is the
cocoa grass. **1897** Stuart *Simpkinsville* 43 **AR,** A heavy dew . . hung in
glistening gems upon the blades of bright green cocoa spears that had
shot up between the drier clods. **1898** *Jrl. Amer. Folkl.* 11.282, *Cyperus
rotundus* . . . coco, coco sedge, Wyo. **1944** AL Geol. Surv. *Bulletin*
53.76, *C. rotundus* . . . Nut-grass. (Called "coco" farther west.) One of
our worst weeds. **1965–70** *DARE* (Qu. S9, *Other . . grass . . hard to get
rid of*) 15 Infs, **Sth,** Coco grass; MS72, Coconut grass; (Qu. S8, . .
*Common kind of wild grass . . grows in fields . . spreads by sending out
long underground roots*) Infs LA31, 33, MS82, Coco grass; (Qu. S21, . .
Other weeds) Inf AR10, Coco; LA20, Coco grass; (Qu. S15, . . *Other
weed seeds that cling to clothing*) Inf LA15, Coco burr. [Note: some of
these Infs may be referring to **coco grass 2.**]
2 A bulrush, esp *Scirpus robustus.*
    1913 *Torreya* 13.228, *Scirpus* spp.—Coco, coco grass, sometimes
sweet coco grass, various localities in Louisiana. **1942** *Torreya* 42.158,
Scirpus robustus . . . Coco, coco grass, Louisiana. **1947** *Jrl. Wildlife
Management* Jan 54/1, Muddy peats subject to admixture of clay from
storm tides are taken over by "coco" marsh, an association of "coco" or
salt-marsh bulrush, saltgrass, and "wiregrass." **1951** *PADS* 15.8,
Scirpus robustus . . . Coco, Louisiana.

co'cola See **coca-cola A**

cocono n [Prob alter of *coquina* a small marine clam used for
soups]
    1949 Brown *Amer. Cooks* 120 **FL,** Tiny local oysters called coconos are
another unusual delicacy.

coconut dipper n Also *cocoanut*
    A long-handled dipper, orig made out of a coconut.
    1899 (1912) Green *VA Folk-Speech* 120, *Cocoa-nut* . . . Made by
sawing off one fourth of the stem-end of a cocoa-nut shell, a handle a foot
long is made by putting a stick through holes bored near the edge . . It is
used for dipping water out of a water-can. **1931–33** *LANE Worksheets*
nRI, Coconut dipper—a dipper with a straight handle.

coconut grass See **coco grass**

coconut head n derog Cf **head** n[1] **C1**
    1967–68 *DARE* (QR, near Qu. X60) Inf **HI**9, Coconut head—a hard
head—a stupid person; (Qu. HH28, . . *People of foreign background: . .
Negro*) Inf **PA**94, Coconut head.

coconut strip n Also *coconut ribbon* chiefly **PA**
    A kind of confection: see quot.

1965–70 *DARE* (Qu. H82b, *Kinds of cheap candy that used to be sold years ago*) 14 Infs, **12 in PA,** Coconut strips; PA138, Coconut ribbon; PA9, Molasses coconut strips.

coconut wagon n

1968 *DARE* File **neDE,** *Coconut wagon.* A truck delivering illicit liquor.

coco plum n Also *cocoa plum* [*coco,* from Span *icaco,* ult from Island Carib *hikáku; OED* 1676–99 →] **chiefly sFL**

A rosaceous tree *(Chrysobalanus icaco)* with simple leaves, small white flowers, and a plum-like fruit. Also called **corker plum, gopher plum**

1699 (1945) Dickinson *Jrl.* 52 FL, In some time after we had been in the house, came in Indian women laden with baskets of berries, mostly of the palm, some seaside coco-plums and seaside grapes. **1911** *Century Dict.* 990, *Chrysobalanus* . . The cocoa-plum, *C. Icaco,* is found throughout tropical America and in southern Florida. Its fruit is edible, resembling a plum, and is used as a preserve. **1971** Craighead *Trees S. FL* 23, The "scorching" from the frost . . was sharply defined on buttonwood and coco plum along a line between the wet and dry glades.

coco sedge See **coco grass 1**

co-cow v phr Also *co-heifer* [**co** v] **NC**

Come! — used to call cattle.

1965–70 *DARE* (Qu. K80, *The call that's used . . to get the cows in from the pasture*) Infs NC3, 8, 21, 87, Co-cow; NC10, Co-heifer; (Qu. K83, *To call a calf . . at feeding time*) Infs NC3, 8, Co-cow; NC10, Co-heifer.

cocum See **coakum**

cod n[1]

1 usu pl: The testicles, scrotum; sometimes the penis. **chiefly S Midl**

1899 (1912) Green *VA Folk-Speech* 120, *Cods* . . . Testicles. **1908** *DN* 3.299 **eAL, wGA,** *Cod* . . . A testicle. **1939** Hall Coll. **nwNC,** *Cod* . . penis. "Somethin' you got in your britches." **1958** Randolph *Sticks* 33 Ozarks, Tommy was cod-deep in guts by this time. **c1960** *Wilson Coll.* **csKY,** He won't play fair: he's always trying to kick somebody in the cods. **1969** *DARE* File **NC,** *Cods.* Testicles.

2 also attrib: The inmost recess of a bay, marsh, or meadow. [Prob so called from its bag-like shape] **S Atl coast** *arch*

1643 in 1940 *AmSp* 15.165 **VA,** Crossing a Codd of a Baye unto a marked white oake. **1649** *Ibid* 166 **VA,** Bounded on the Northwest from Said Poynt at Preslyes Creeke soe over to ye Codd point with a Creeke Called Mattrams Creeke. **1770** in 1953 McMullen *Topog. Terms FL* 89, Apalache . . . river enters the Gulph of Mexico about one hundred miles from the cod of the Bay of Apalache. **1899** (1912) Green *VA Folk-Speech* 120, *Cod,* . . The inmost recess of a bay or sea; also of a marsh; "the cod or farthermost part of it [=a bay]."

cod n[2] See **codfish** n[1]

cod n[3] [Cf **cod** v]

A deception or hoax.

1892 *KS Univ. Qrly.* 1.96, *Cod:* a bit of deceit, as in, He gave the teacher a cod.

cod v Also sp *codd* [Perh akin to *cod* a fool; see *OED* **cod** sb.[5]] **chiefly Nth** *somewhat old-fash*

To deceive in a playful way; to joke, to tease.

1890 *Jrl. Amer. Folkl.* 3.311 **NEng, cIL,** *Cod* . . . To make fun of a person, by giving him false information. "Oh, you're just codding me!" **1903** (1965) Adams *Log Cowboy* 245, They had codded one another until Joe had shown some spirit. **1905** *DN* 3.6 **cCT,** *Codd* . . to fool, or bluff anyone. **1907** Wasson *Home from the Sea* 178 (*AmSp* 37.251) ME, Some of 'em would take and cod Abner about his new git-up of a model, too, till they'd have him real het up over it. **1907** *DN* 3.210 **nwAR,** *Codd.* **1910** *DN* 3.439 **wNY,** *Codd.* **1912** *DN* 3.573 **wIN,** *Cod.* **1932** Smiley *Gloss. New Paltz* NY, They used to cod him about his horses being so slow that they could not keep away from the rats. **1941** FWP *Guide OK* 114, The tall tale is usually not merely a highly improbable piece of fiction, but a method of "codding" a naïve youngster or newcomer. **1950** *WELS* (*To play jokes on people:* "He's always ———.") 1 Inf, **ceWI,** Codding, = teasing — used to hear a lot.

co-dack v phr Usu |kə'dæk|; sometimes |-'deɪk, -'dɛk, -'dɪk(i)| Also sp *co-dak, co-dake, co-dick(ie), kudack* [**co** v + *Dick* a typical name for male animals (cf *EDD* **Dick** sb.[1])] **chiefly NEng**

Come! — used to call sheep.

1896 *DN* 1.414 **n,cNY,** *Coda(k)* [kʌd-eɪk]: for "Come, Dick"? A call for cattle or sheep . . . For sheep only, Otsego Co. **1914** *DN* 4.155 **NH,** *Kudack* . . . Sheep call. **1939** *LANE* Map 225, [*Co-dack* and varr occur sporadically throughout NEng, e.g.: 1 inf, swCT, [kə'dæk], old-fashioned; 1 inf, cnCT, ['kʌm,dɪk kə'dɪk kə'dɪk]; 1 inf, ceCT, [kədɪk]; 1 inf, ncVT, [kə'deɪk]; 1 inf, cwME, [kə'dɛk]]. **1949** Kurath *Word Geog.* 16, The two most common calls to sheep in New England are, or were, *kə-nan!, nannie!* and *kə-day!, kə-dack!, kə-dick!* . . Both these calls were carried westward in the New England migration to the Susquehanna and the Great Lakes. *Ibid* 65, The New England area has *kə-day! (kə-daik!, kə-dack! kə-dick!).* **1965–70** *DARE* (Qu. K85, *The call to sheep to come in from . . pasture*) Inf NY142, Co-dake [kə'dek]; MA58, [kə'dɪk, kə'deɪ]; MA25 [kə'dɪki]; MA42 [kə'dɪk, kə'dɪk]. **1971** Wood *Vocab. Change* 298 TN, [3 infs reported *co-dack,* 1 inf, *co-dick*]. **1973** Allen *LAUM* 1.266 **NE,** Kudack. [1 inf]

co-day v phr Usu |kə'deɪ|, less freq |kɪ-, kæ-, kʊ-, ko-, kɔ-|, |-'daɪ| Also sp *co-die, ka dai, kiday, kuday* [**co** v + *day* from *dake* of **co-dack**] **chiefly NEast, MI** See Map Cf **co-nan(nie), co-sheep(ie)**

Come! — used to call sheep and (rarely) cows.

1893 *DN* 1.267, From Vermont, South Carolina, and Kansas is reported the call [kæ-'deɪ]. **1914** *DN* 4.155 **NH,** *Kuday.* Sheep call. **1917** *DN* 4.395 **NEng, NY, neOH,** *Kiday, kiday, kiday* [kɪd'ei . .]. Call to sheep. Sometimes so divided as to suggest *daiky, daiky, daiky* ['deɪkɪ]. **1939** *LANE* Map 225, [*Co-day* is scattered throughout NEng, usu pronc [kə'deɪ]; 1 inf, sRI, [ko'deɪ]]. **1949** Kurath *Word Geog.* 16, The two most common calls to sheep in New England are, or were *kə-nan!, nannie!* and *kə-day!, kə-dack!, kə-dick!* . . Both these calls were carried westward in the New England migration to the Susquehanna and the Great Lakes. *Ibid* 65, The New England area has *kə-day! (kə-daik!, kə-dack!, kə-dick!).* **1951** *PADS* 15.67 **NH,** *Ka dai* . . . Call to sheep. **1965–70** *DARE* (Qu. K85, *The call to sheep to come in*) 28 Infs, **chiefly NEast, MI,** Co-day [kə'deɪ]; NY117, RI12, [kɪ'de]; NY107, 122, [kʊ'deɪ]; WI21, [ko'de]; CO47, ['kudaɪ]; CT36, Co-die; MA58, Co-dick co-day; NY72, Co-day co-nip co-nam; (Qu. K80, *The call . . used to get the cows in*) Inf NJ10, [kə'daɪ]; NJ29, [kə'taɪ]. **1971** Wood *Vocab. Change* 298 TN, [2 infs, Co-day]. **1973** Allen *LAUM* 1.266, New England and New York state *co-day* or *kuday* /ˌkə'de/ and *co-dack* or *kudack* /ˌkə'dæk/ turn up 4 times [2 Minnesota, 1 Iowa (heard), 1 North Dakota] . . . Only 14 [of 712 mail] respondents . . checked *kuday / kudack,* which are sparsely distributed throughout the U[pper] M[id]west].

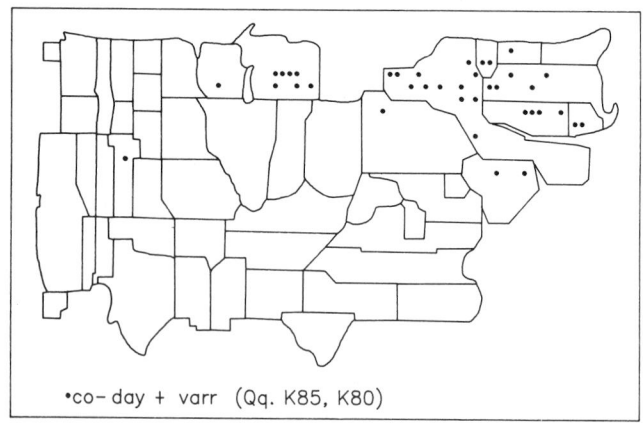

•co-day + varr (Qq. K85, K80)

codd See **cod** v

coddle n [Alter of *caddle* a confused mess]

1942 (1971) Campbell *Cloud-Walking* 25 seKY (as of 1936–41), Trying to figure how to talk to folks with such a pile of learning got Nelt's mind all in a coddle and he went scatter-wit.

coddle v[1] [Alter of *caddle* to potter about]

1906 *DN* 3.117 **sIN,** Coddle . . . To waste time with. "He's coddlin around in the garden."

‡**coddle** v[2] [Perh from **cod** v]

1965 *DARE* (Qu. GG3, *To tease:* "See those big boys trying to ———— *(that little one).*") Inf **OK**13, Coddle [kɑt̬ḷ].

‡**coddled** ppl adj [Perh akin to Engl dial *coddle* to shrink, wither; see *EDD coddle* v.[2] 4]

  1968 *DARE* (Qu. I8, *When root vegetables get old and tough and are not good to eat, you say they are* _____) Inf **MD**37, Coddled.

coddle up v phr [Alter of *cobble up*]

To mend hastily or clumsily.

  1939 *LANE* Map 152 **seNH, neVT,** 2 infs, Coddle up.

coddy adj [Prob from Engl dial *cod* a fool; cf **cod** v]

Eccentric.

  1892 *KS Univ. Qrly.* 1.96, *Coddy:* odd, out of fashion. **1961** Sackett–Koch *KS Folkl.* 112, *Coddy* . . . Unconventional or out of fashion. [Of a woman who wore a long evening dress to go shopping in the afternoon, another woman says, "They always were a little coddy."]

cod end n, also attrib [*cod* bag]

See quots.

  1930 *AmSp* 5.389 **MA,** *Cod-end* . . . The bag at the apex of an otter trawl which collects the fish. *Ibid, Cod-end knot* . . . An ingenious knot for keeping the cod-end closed until it is filled with fish and then releasing it after the bag has been hoisted aboard. **1975** Gould *ME Lingo* 55, *Cod end*—The bag end of a trawl net. If somebody gets bagged in the *cod end,* he's caught up for fair.

codfish n[1] Also *cod* [From its resemblance to the cod, *Gadus morrhua*] **Pacific NW**

=**lingcod 1.**

  1884 Goode *Fisheries U.S.* 1.267, Cultus Cod . . is universally called 'Cod-fish' where the true cod is unknown. **1911** *Century Dict.* 1082, *Cod* . . . A hexagrammoid fish, *Ophiodon elongatus,* of the Pacific coasts of North America, universally called *cod* and *codfish* where the true cod is unknown.

codfish n[2] [From **codfish aristocracy**]

  1967–68 *DARE* (Qu. II23, *Joking names for the people who are, or think they are, the best society of a community*) Inf **OR**1, Codfish.

codfish aristocracy n Also *codfish gentility,* ~ *aristocrat* **chiefly NEast**

Originally the social upper class made up of families enriched by the Massachusetts codfish industry; more generally, a parvenu upper class based on commercial success; a member of that class.

  1849 *Rainbow* (Belleville, Ohio) 30 Nov 2/4 *(DA),* That evil is the instigation or giving rise to what is called Codfish Aristocracy a class of persons who wish to appear before the public as though they were worth thousands. **1856** Whitcher *Bedott Papers* 305 **cNY,** I've noticed that yer *codfish gentility* always dew [feel uneasy]. **1909** *DN* 3.419 **Cape Cod MA,** *Codfish aristocracy* . . . Cheap aristocracy. **1943** Menefee *Assignment* 12, They hate the 'codfish aristocracy,' who looked down their noses at the upstart Irish as long as they could. **1950** *WELS (Joking names for . . the best society in a community)* 2 Infs, **cw,seWI,** Codfish aristocracy. **1966–69** *DARE* (Qu. II23, . . *People who are, or think they are, the best society*) Infs **ME**16, **MA**30, Codfish aristocracy; **MA**68, Codfish aristocrats.

codfish ball n Also *codfish cake* **chiefly NEast** Also called **fish ball 1**

Flaked codfish mashed with potato, molded into a sphere or patty, and fried.

  1845 *Knickerbocker* 26.462, Wonder if they had any 'codfish-balls' or 'bread-puddings?' **1887** in 1965 *AmSp* 40.128, There's cod-fish cakes for Finnegan. **1932** (1946) Hibben *Amer. Regional Cookery* 168 **MA,** Codfish balls. **1944** *Vogue* July 70 *(DA),* I come home and renew acquaintance with . . . baked beans and codfish cakes. **1948** *Richmond* (Va.) *News Letter* 6 May 31/3 *(DA),* Bacon and eggs, sausage, fish roe, codfish balls, . . . are ingredients which you will have to reconsider. **1969** *DARE* (Qu. HH5, *Dishes made with meat, fish, or poultry*) Inf **RI**1, Codfish balls; **NH**6, **NY**43, Codfish cakes; **CT**6, Codfish cakes: like hash but made with fish.

codfisher n

  1958 McCulloch *Woods Words* 36 **Pacific NW,** *Codfisher*—A logger from a camp fronting the ocean, or from a float camp.

codfish flats n

The poor section of town.

  1969 *DARE* (Qu. C35, *Nicknames for different parts of your town or city*) Inf **CT**29, Codfish flats: specific expression for "on the other side of

the tracks." **1969** *DARE* FW Addit **ceCT,** Codfish flats—poor side of town.

codfish gentility See **codfish aristocracy**

codge n[1] See **codger 4**

codge n[2] [Cf *EDD cadging-pouch* a large tobacco pouch]

  1968 *DARE* (Qu. DD2, *The portion or quantity of tobacco chewed at one time: "He's always got a big* _____ *in his cheek."*) Inf **MD**43, Codge [kɑj].

codger n [Perh akin to Engl dial *cadger* an itinerant, an ill-tempered person; see *EDD*]

1 freq with *old:* An elderly person. *often derog, sometimes affectionate*

  1910 *DN* 3.453 **swVT,** *Codger* . . . A disreputable old fellow. **1927** *AmSp* 3.137 **eME,** "A codger" was a singular old person. **1930** Shoemaker *1300 Words* **cPA Mts** (as of c1900), *Codger*—A pleasant, elderly individual. **1950** *WELS (Uncomplimentary words for an old man)* 4 Infs, **WI,** Old codger; 1 Inf, Old codger (may be used affectionately); 4 Infs, Codger. **1965–70** *DARE* (Qu. HH40, *Uncomplimentary words for an old man*) 263 Infs, **widespread,** (Old) codger; (Qu. KK27, *A very lively, active old person*) Infs **CA**140, **LA**14, Lively old codger; **LA**40, **WI**47, Spry codger; **IL**29, Chipper codger; (Qu. X48b, . . *A person . . not so young any more*) Inf **MI**10, Old codger; (Qu. AA23, *Joking names . . a woman may use to refer to her husband*) Inf **MO**17A, Old codger; (Qu. LL3b, *Shrunk, dried up: "He's a little* _____.") Inf **CA**8, Codger. **1967** *DARE* Tape **TX**11, They had a bunch of us youngsters in there that were foremen over those old codgers, veterans of World War I.

2 A strange or unusual person.

  1899 (1912) Green *VA Folk-Speech* 120, *Codger* . . . An old fellow; an odd person. **1906** *DN* 3.117 **sIN,** *Codger* . . . An odd person. "He's an old codger." **1969** *DARE* (Qu. HH5, *Someone who is queer but harmless*) Inf **KY**6, Codger: a peculiar character.

3 A hick.

  1908 *DN* 3.299 **eAL, wGA,** *Codger* . . . A countryman, a rustic. **1967** *DARE* (Qu. HH1, . . *A rustic or countrified person*) Inf **AR**51, Codger.

4 also *codge:* A vagrant. [Cf *EDD cadger* sb.[1] 7]

  1901 *DN* 2.138 **cNY,** *Codge* . . . Like codger . . , but less definite; of any shiftless, worthless person. **1969** *DARE* File **cwNJ,** *Codger's room*—hobo's room—a room sealed off from the rest of the house with an entrance from stairs off the kitchen, where hobos were put up for the night.

5 A small child. *joc*

  1941 *LANE* Map 379 *(Kid, tot)* 1 inf, **sME,** A little [kɔədʒə] = a child. **1965–70** *DARE* (Qu. Z12, *Nicknames and joking words meaning "a small child": "He's a healthy little* _____.") Infs **GA**89, **LA**40, **MI**92, **OH**60, **PA**55, 148, Codger.

codgerdick n [*codger 1* + *Dick* a typical name]

A testy old man.

  1967 *DARE* Tape **SC**34, We're doin', I guess, pretty good accordin' to old codgerdicks . . that's just an old sayin', that old codgerdick . . . Just the oldest, don't nothin' suit him, he's hard to please . . cranky, just like an old maid.

codge up v phr [Prob from Engl dial *codge* botch, mend clumsily, patch; see *EDD*] Cf **coddle up**

  1927 *AmSp* 3.137 **eME,** "A codger" was a singular old person, but "codge it up" was used much as fudge or patch or botch.

codhead n

  1924 *DN* 5.286 **Cape Cod MA,** Just why knee-length leather boots should be called 'codheads' has always puzzled me, yet that is the sole name by which these articles of dress are called by the natives of the Cape, though in these days the gum boot is taking the place of the old leather 'codhead'.

co-dick(ie) See **co-dack**

co-die See **co-day**

codster n [*cod* n[1] 1]

A stallion.

  1930 Shoemaker *1300 Words* 11 **cPA Mts** (as of c1900), Cooser or codster—An entire horse.

co-dub(bie) v phr [*co* v + *dub(bie)* from *dub* v[1] 2 to blunt, hence also *dubbed* and *dubby* blunt: here prob in ref to the hornless calf]

Come! — used to call calves.

1949 Kurath *Word Geog.* 47, The calf call *kədub!* or *kədubbie!* occurs only on Albemarle Sound. *Ibid* 64, *Co-dubbie!* [predominates] on Albemarle Sound.

co-ee v phr Usu |'ko₁(w)i, 'kɔ-|, also |'ku-, 'kʊ-, -₁(w)e, -ə| Also sp *coo-ee, coo-way, cowie, co-way* [**co** v + vowel prolonged for audibility] **chiefly C Atl, S Atl**

Come! — used to call cows and other barnyard animals.

1949 Kurath *Word Geog.* 63, *Co-wench!, co-inch!, co-ee!* in the South, from Delaware Bay to Georgia. **1965–70** *DARE* (Qu. K80, *The call . . to get the cows in*) 11 Infs, **chiefly C Atl, S Atl**, ['ko₁(w)i *or* 'kɔ₁I]; 5 Infs, ['ku₁i *or* 'ku₁wI *or* 'kuₘ,wI]; 4 Infs, Co-way ['ko(ʊ)₁we(I) *or* 'koₑ]; VA38, ['kɔₑi]; VA105, Coo-way ['kʊₑe]; DE5, Co-ee; IL26, Cowie; (Qu. K82, . . *To get horses in*) Inf MS53, ['kuə]; (Qu. K83, *To call a calf*) Inf MD13, ['ko:₁i]; DE1, Coo-ee; (Qu. K84, . . *To get the pigs in*) Inf OH20, ['ku₁i].

co-ets v phr |'ko₁ɛts, -ət| Also *co-ut* [**co** v + ? alter of *up*] Cf **co-ee, cope** v²

Come! — used to call cows.

1965–70 *DARE* (Qu. K80, *The call that's used . . to get the cows in from the pasture*) Inf GA33, ['ko₁ɛts]; AL15, ['ko₁ət].

co-fair n [? Alter of *confrere*]

1949 *AmSp* 24.107 seGA, *Co-fairs*, . . Close friends.

coffee and n [*coffee* + *and* conj B5; cf *cider and* (at *OED cider* 2) 1754 →]

Coffee and a doughnut or roll; sometimes coffee with cream and sugar.

1901 in 1954 Weingarten *Amer. Dict. Slang* 74, Coffee and. **1927** *DN* 5.442 ncNC [Underworld argot], *Coffee an'* . . Coffee and a roll, a meal costing five cents. **1931** "Dean Stiff" *Milk and Honey Route* 15.172 (*OEDS*), The hash house where they sup plentiously [sic] on coffee-ands. **1946** *AmSp* 21.87 **West Coast,** But 'coffee and' or 'coffee with' means 'with cream and sugar.' In skidroad restaurants, 'coffee and' is still sometimes used for coffee and doughnuts, although this term is falling into disuse in that sense. **1980** De Vries *Consenting Adults* 78 **IL,** Stop in with me for a midmorning coffee-and-sometime.

coffee bean n

1 also *American coffee bean, coffee bean tree, Kentucky coffee bean:* =**Kentucky coffee tree;** also its seed.

1819 (1821) Nuttall *Jrl.* 41, Among the trees, we still continue to observe the coffee-bean (*Gymnocladus canadensis*). *Ibid* 178, In this elevated alluvion I still observed the Coffee-bean tree. **1848** *Cultivator* new ser 5.213, I will remark . . that . . two young coffee bean trees (*gymnocladus canadensis*) . . are in a thrifty condition. **1876** Hobbs *Bot. Hdbk.* 25, Kentucky coffee bean, Gymnocladus Canadensis. *Ibid* 61, American coffee bean. **1897** Sudworth *Arborescent Flora* 255, *Gymnocladus dioicus* . . . Common Names . . . Coffee Bean (Ill., Kans., Nebr.). Coffee Bean Tree (Ky., Ark.). **1950** Moore *Trees AR* 86, Kentucky Coffeetree . . . Local Names: Coffee Tree, Coffee Nut, Coffee Bean. **1966–69** *DARE* (Qu. T9) Inf OK18, Coffee bean tree; (Qu. T15) Inf PA89, Kentucky coffee bean; (Qu. T16) Inf KY65, Coffee bean.

2 also *coffee-bean weed:* =either **bagpod** or **coffeeweed 1.**

1942 *Torreya* 42.161, *Daubentonia drummondii* . . . Coffee bean, Louisiana . . . This term and coffee bean weed are applied in various parts of the South to almost any conspicuous wild legume. **1948** *Miami* (Okla.) *D. News–Record* 30 June 8/2 (*DA*), Farmers call it bladderpod, coffee-bean, and castle-bean. **1951** *PADS* 15.34, *Cassiaceae* . . . Mostly called coffee beans and rattle-pod beans. **1960** Vines *Trees SW* 545, Other common names for the Drummond Rattlebox are . . Coffee Bean, and Senna. *Ibid* 547, Other vernacular names are . . Coffee Bean, and Florida Coffee Bean. It is listed . . under the scientific name of *S[esbania] macrocarpa*. **1966–70** *DARE* (Qu. S20) Inf TX52, Coffee bean; (Qu. S21) Inf AR10, Coffee bean; TX37, Coffee-bean weeds; (Qu. S26e) Inf TX85, Coffee bean. **1970** Correll *Plants TX* 836, *Sesbania Drummondii* . . . Rattlebush, poison bean, coffee bean.

3 A garden bean, perh so called from the color and shape; see quots.

1969 *DARE* (Qu. I20) Inf KY40, Coffee beans — brown bean with red hull. **1979** *Wanigan Catalog* 11, Hillbilly or Coffee Bean . . . Ran up to 7' here. Yellow snap bean has a pink blush which turns yellow in cooking. White bloom. 4″ flat pods bear cinnamon colored flat size 3 seed. Late.

4 =**whirligig beetle.** [Perh from the dark color and oval shape]

1951 Teale *North Spring* 274 **NJ,** Whirligig beetles are "coffee beans."

coffee bean tree See **coffee bean 1**

coffee-bean weed See **coffee bean 2**

coffeeberry n

1 =**Kentucky coffee tree.**

1822 Woods *2 Yrs. Residence* 224 **IL,** On the creek bottoms, [there grow] coffee-berry, poplar, pecon, white walnut. **1949** Brown *Amer. Cooks* 37 **AR,** All sorts of substitutes [for coffee] are used, including roast acorns, but chiefly beans from domestic bushes such as the coffeeberry. **1969** *DARE* (Qu. T16, *What kinds of trees are "special" around here*) Infs **KY**24, 25A, Coffeeberry.

2 Any of several plants native to the Southwest and / or West Coast of the US as:

a Either of two West Coast buckthorns:

(1) also *California coffeeberry, coast* ~, *Sierra* ~: A usu evergreen shrub (*Rhamnus californica*), 1–4 m high, with leaves scattered along the branchlets, umbels of small greenish flowers, and green, red, or black berries. Also called **bayberry, bearberry, bearwood, California buckthorn, chittamwood 4, coffee plant 1, coffee tree 2, pigeonbark, pigeonberry, trinitas, wild coffee, yellow-boy, yellowroot, yellowwood, yerba del oso**

1898 *Jrl. Amer. Folkl.* 11.225, *Rhamnus California* . . coffee berry, Cal. **1937** U.S. Forest Serv. *Range Plant Hdbk.* B127, *California Buckthorn—Rhamnus californica*—This evergreen, olivelike shrub is . . variously known as coffeeberry, pigeonberry, yerba-del-oso, and cascara sagrada. **1969** *DARE* (Qu. S26c, *Wildflowers that grow in woods*) Inf CA137, Coffeeberry. [Note: this Inf may be referring instead to **coffeeberry 2a (2).**] **1979** Little *Native Trees U.S.* 246, *Rhamnus californica* . . . Other common names — coffeeberry, California coffeeberry, coast coffeeberry, Sierra coffeeberry.

(2) Cascara sagrada.

1886 Van Dyke *Southern CA* 33, The *madroña*, the coffee-berry, the manzanita, . . form what is called the chaparral. [Note: this quot may refer instead to **coffeeberry 2a (1).**] **1897** Sudworth *Arborescent Flora* 299, *Rhamnus purshiana* . . . Common Names . . . Coffee-berry (Cal.). **1931** U.S. Dept. Ag. *Misc. Pub.* 101.113, Cascara buckthorn (*R. purshiana*), also . . locally known as . . coffee berry, . . is . . the source of the medicinal cascara sagrada. **1946** Linsdale *CA Ground Squirrel* 253, A squirrel watched on an afternoon early in September had its cheek pouches full of coffeeberry fruits. [Note: this quot may refer instead to another sub-sense of **coffeeberry 2.**] **1974** (1977) Coon *Useful Plants* 235.

b =**jojoba.**

1931 U.S. Dept. Ag. *Misc. Pub.* 101.94, Jojoba . . , known by a variety of vernacular names, including . . coffee berry, . . . is a bushy-branched and spreading shrub. **1937** U.S. Forest Serv. *Range Plant Hdbk.* B148, Jojoba, a bushy, bluish-green shrub . . is widely known in the Southwest as coffeeberry . . alluding to the nutlike fruit. **1942** Castetter *Pima & Papago Ag.* 26, On the lowest, drier level adjoining the desert are thickets of *jojoba* or coffeeberry (*Simmondsia californica*).

c A silk tassel (here: *Garrya elliptica*).

1937 U.S. Forest Serv. *Range Plant Hdbk.* B81, Wright silktassel, known by a variety of local names — bearberry, chaparral, coffeeberry, feverbush, grayleaf dogwood, and quinine-bush — is a shrub.

coffeebush n Cf **wild coffeebush**

=**jojoba.**

1931 U.S. Dept. Ag. *Misc. Pub.* 101.94, Jojoba . . , known by a variety of vernacular names, including . . coffee bush, . . . is a bushy-branched and spreading shrub. **1937** U.S. Forest Serv. *Range Plant Hdbk.* B148, Jojoba, a bushy, bluish-green shrub . . is widely known in the Southwest as coffeeberry and is also locally called . . coffeebush.

coffee clutch See **klatch** n

coffee coat n

An informal garment worn by women around the house; a housecoat.

1950 *WELS (Long coat-like garment, often worn over pajamas, worn around the house)* 1 Inf, **swWI,** Coffee-coat. **1976** *DARE* File **Madison WI,** *Coffee coat* — A woman's housecoat that usually snaps, rather than buttons or zips up in front, and is generally made of cotton or polyester. Though housecoats are informal and far from elegant, a coffee coat is usually even lower on the social scale. Coffee coat is both a merchandising term and in common use.

coffee cooler n

1 In military use: an idler, a shirker (but see quot 1939).

1886 Mitchell *Roland Blake* 294 **NEng,** "He is nothing but an old coffee-cooler, Mr. Pennell." "And what is a coffee-cooler?" . . "A man who blows his coffee while the brigade is going by into action." **1896** (1961) Bradley *March MT Column* 47 **csMT** (as of 1876), The 'coffee-coolers,' as the shiftless, superannuated loungers about camp are very aptly termed. **1918** Empey *First Call* 352, *"Coffee cooler."* Slang used in the army for a soldier who is always looking for a soft job. **1928** Ruppenthal *Coll.* **KS,** *Coffee cooler,* . . a soldier who evades duty. **1939** Abbott *We Pointed Them* 177 **West,** They [the government] drawed up the treaty fixing the new boundaries for the [Sioux] reservation . . and they got some of these coffee-coolers to consent to it. [Footnote re *coffee-coolers:*] Yes-men among the Indians who would do anything for a cup of coffee. **1945** Hamann *Air Words, Coffee cooler.* One who seeks easy jobs.

2 See quots.

1914 *DN* 4.162 **NW,** *Coffee-cooler* . . . A prospector. **1968** Adams *Western Words* 70, *Coffee cooler*—A prospector. A loafer.

3 also *cooling saucer:* A saucer for cooling coffee as one drinks it.

1969 *DARE* (Qu. G6, *Other dishes . . for a big dinner or special occasion*) Inf **MA43,** Coffee coolers are the same as coolin' saucers—for coffee—coffee poured into this saucer to cool it.

4 pl: The lips. Cf **crumb crusher 2**

1972 Claerbaut *Black Jargon* 60, *Coffee coolers* . . the lips of a black person.

coffee cow n

1972 Hilliard *Hog Meat* 140 **Sth** (as of 1840–60), The port cities imported much of their cheese and butter and a portion of their beef, while the interior towns depended upon a few "coffee cows" kept in small pastures or lots for dairy products and nearby farmers for occasional supplies of beef.

‡coffee cup n

1967 *DARE* (Qu. S11 . . *Other names . . for: dandelion*) Inf **NY28,** Coffee cups.

coffee-drink n

A wake, funeral watch.

1945 Saxon *Gumbo Ya-Ya* 559 **LA,** There will be a big coffee-drink soon. (A wake.).

‡coffee grains n

The buttocks.

1970 *DARE* (Qu. X35, *Joking words for the part of the body that you sit on—for example, "He slipped and came down hard on his _____."*) Inf **PA244,** Coffee grains.

coffee grass n

Perh a **nut grass 1.**

1968 *DARE* (Qu. S9, *Other . . grass . . hard to get rid of*) Infs **NJ16, 17,** Coffee grass; (Qu. S21, . . *Other weeds*) Inf **NJ17,** Coffee grass.

coffee grinder n [From the sound] Cf **coffee mill 2**

A noisy machine.

1950 *WELS* (*Nicknames . . for an old, broken-down car*) 1 Inf, **seWI,** Coffee grinder. **1969–70** *DARE* (Qu. O11, . . *Other names . . for an outboard motor*) Infs **IL81, MA123,** Coffee grinder.

coffee grinding n [From the arm motion used in grinding coffee]

1940 FWP *Guide NV* 77, In pursuit of his work a cowboy *dallies,* or holds an animal on the rope by wrapping it around the horn of the saddle counter clockwise. *Coffee grinding* is the incorrect way of taking dallies; it means the rope is wound clockwise.

coffee grounds n pl

1976 Warner *Beautiful Swimmers* 142 **Chesapeake Bay MD,** They [=crabbers] avoid beds with "coffee grounds" or too much dark winter-killed stubble.

coffee milk n [Prob transl Fr *café-au-lait* coffee with milk] **LA**

Coffee with hot milk.

1967 LeCompte *Word Atlas* 288 **seLA,** Coffee milk. **1968** *DARE* FW Addit **csLA,** Coffee milk—Inf's name for café-au-lait.

coffee mill n [Transf from the rotary action of a coffee mill]

1 A revolver. Cf **pepperbox**

1887 H.L. Williams *Buffalo Bill* 10 *(DA),* One of the old-pattern Colts, with the barrels revolving, the ancient 'coffee-mill' or 'pepperbox,' laughed at all over the West in the present day.

2 See quot. Cf **coffee grinder**

1969 Sorden *Lumberjack Lingo* 25 **NEng & Gt Lakes,** *Coffee mills*—small, side-wheel steamboats that towed lumber or log rafts.

coffee nut n

=**Kentucky coffee tree; also its seed.** Cf **coffeeberry 1**

1797 in 1928 Filson Club *Hist. Qrly.* 2.166 **KY,** The natural fruit is . . beachnut, Coffee nut & Buck eye. **1884** Sargent *Forests of N. Amer.* 58, *Gymnocladus canadensis* . . Kentucky Coffee Tree . . Coffee Nut. **1901** Lounsberry *S. Wild Flowers* 263, It is related that during the Revolution, the natives in remote places west of the Alleghanies used its seeds as a substitute for coffee, and in fact, they still call the fruit, coffee nuts. **1950** [see **coffee bean 1**]. **1968** *DARE* (Qu. T9) Inf **IN40,** Coffee nut.

coffee plant n

1 Either cascara sagrada or **coffeeberry 2a (1).**

1890 *Congressional Record* 12 June 5992 **CA,** An indigenous plant found on that coast, the common name of which is "coffee plant."

2 An **evening primrose** (here: *Oenothera biennis*).

1893 *Jrl. Amer. Folkl.* 6.142, *Oenothera biennis,* scurvish. Franconia, N.H. fever-plant; coffee-plant. Eastern States . . . Infusion used as a drink in the harvest field. **1959** Carleton *Index Herb. Plants* 29, *Coffee-plant:* Oenothera biennis.

3 =**mullein.**

1970 *DARE* (Qu. S21) Inf **FL48,** Coffee plant or coffeeweed or mullein.

coffeepot n *derog*

1 A small or leaky steam engine.

1945 Hubbard *Railroad Ave.* 2, A leaky old steam engine is, disgustedly, a "teakettle" or "coffeepot". **1958** McCulloch *Woods Words* 36 **Pacific NW,** *Coffee pot* . . a donkey [engine] unusually small or low-powered.

2 also attrib: A small-scale operation, esp a small lumber mill.

1958 McCulloch *Woods Words* 36 **Pacific NW,** *Coffee pot*—A mill . . unusually small or low-powered. **1960** Williams *Walk Egypt* 130 **GA,** A scream cut the song; a coffee-pot sawmill beyond the hill bucked a hardwood knot. *Ibid* 167, The trees were coming down at a sickening rate, for a coffeepot mill nibbled away inexorably. **1965** *DARE* Tape **FL42,** Some of these little, I call 'em coffeepot mills, work fifty to a hundred men—I'd consider that a coffeepot mill, just run on a small scale, little one-horse affair, and they've just about got everything cut out now.

coffee sack n [From its use in shipping green coffee] **chiefly KY** Also called **burr sack, grass sack**

A large **burlap bag.**

1850 Garrard *Wah-to-yah* 307, We carried charcoal from the pit to the intended "shop." With coffeesacks on our shoulders, we lifted until our appearance would have well vied with that of a city charbonnier. **1882** Peck *Peck's Sunshine* 103 **seWI,** The drummer wiped the perspiration from his face with a coffee sack. **1941** *Sat. Eve. Post* 114/2 **KY,** I climbed, lifting rocks in a coffee sack, reaching the poke's neck to her on gaining the tiptop . . . Mother jerked, and the bucket slipped, and the coffee sack emptied in a clatter across the shingles. **1949** Hornsby *Lonesome Valley* 96 **eKY,** "He couldn't carry a tune in a coffee sack," she said. **1950** Stuart *Hie Hunters* 31 **eKY,** Now . . he was free as the wind . . a coffee sack across his back and a mattock in his hand. **c1960** Wilson *Coll.* **csKY,** Coffee sack . . . Large, coarse cloth bag. **1965–70** *DARE* (Qu. F23, *A container made of rough, loosely woven, brown cloth*) Infs **KY28, 40, 41, 52, 57, 63, 71,** Coffee sack; (Qu. F19, *A cloth container for grain*) Infs **KY28, 52,** Coffee sack; (Qu. F20, . . *For feed*) Inf **KY57,** Coffee sack.

coffee shell n [Perh from the shape and color]

A small brown, high-spired snail shell (*Melampus coffeus*) found in areas of mangroves in southern Florida.

1869 in 1870 *Amer. Naturalist* 3.403 **FL,** Many snails . . can be collected, and the Coffee-shell . . is close at hand. [**1974** Abbot *Seashells* 332, *Melampus coffeus* . . —Coffee Melampus—South half of Florida.]

coffee sister n [Ger *Kaffee Schwester* a lover of coffee]

1928 Ruppenthal *Coll.* **KS,** *Coffee sister* . . a person who likes coffee very much; a coffee toper.

coffee-strainer n *joc*

A bushy mustache.

1977 *Jrl. – Courier* (Jacksonville IL) 6 Nov 3/2, George . . was bereft of all hirsute adornment except a bushy mustache, which was a genuine "coffee strainer" indeed.

coffee sugar n

1936 Lutes *Country Kitchen* 74 **MI** (as of c1890), Kegs of salt mackerel sat . . along the wall [of a country store] and the barrels of brown sugar and white sugar (called, I believe, "coffee sugar," being a creamy white and not granulated) kept company with the crackers.

coffee tree n

1 =Kentucky coffee tree. **chiefly Midl**

1784 (1929) Filson *Kentucke* 23, The coffee-tree greatly resembles the black oak, grows large, and also bears a pod, in which is enclosed good coffee. **1931** Clute *Common Plants* 41, The coffee-tree (*Gymnocladus dioica*) was much too harmful to be used as a substitute for coffee, but its hard brown seeds, about the size of coffee beans, make the name appropriate. **1967–70** DARE (Qu. T16, *What kinds of trees are "special" around here?*) Infs **CT**11, **IN**58, **KY**88, **MI**51, Coffee tree.

2 also *California coffee-tree:* Either of two similar buckthorns: cascara sagrada or **coffeeberry 2a (1). chiefly Pacific**

1900 Lyons *Plant Names* 318, R[hamnus] *Californica* . . the California Coffee-tree . . . *Berries* of this have been used as a substitute for Coffee. **1911** *Century Dict.,* Coffee-tree . . California coffee-tree (*Rhamnus Purshiana*). **1979** Little *Checklist U.S. Trees* 248, *Rhamnus purshiana* . . . Other common names . . coffeetree.

coffee-water n

Very weak coffee.

1966–69 DARE (Qu. H74b, *Different words for coffee according to how it's made — very weak*) Infs **GA**62, **KY**28, **MS**17, Coffee-water.

coffeeweed n chiefly S Atl, Gulf States

1 Any of several fabaceous plants, as:

a Any of three spp of *Sesbania:* **rattlebox 5a, b** or **Colorado River hemp.**

1913 *Torreya* 13.231, *Daubentonia longifolia [Sesbania drummondii]* . . . Coffee-weed, Cameron, La. **1941** *Ibid* 41.48, *Sesban macrocarpa* . . . Coffee-weed, Morton, Miss. **1942** *Ibid* 42.16, *Daubentonia [Sesbania] drummondii* . . . Coffee bean, Louisiana . . . This term and coffee weed are applied in various parts of the South to almost any conspicuous wild legume. **1965–68** DARE (Qu. S15) Inf **FL**18, Coffeeweed — seeds like coffee; (Qu. S21) Inf **LA**8, Coffeeweed; **LA**15, Coffeeweed — as high as 10 foot, narrow leaves, has little dark beans; **LA**31, Coffeeweed — Agriculture Department calls 'em rattlebox. **1970** U.S. Ag. Research Serv. *Selected Weeds* 228, Coffeeweed . . . *S[esbania] punicea.*

b A species of *Cassia,* esp **sicklepod 2.**

1933 Small *Manual SE Flora* 660, *Ditremexa [Cassia]* . . . Coffeeweeds. — The seeds of some species are used as a coffee-substitute. **1944** AL Geol. Surv. *Bulletin* 53.125, *C. obtusifolia* . . . Coffee-weed . . . *C. occidentalis* . . . Coffee-weed. **1959** Carleton *Index Herb. Plants* 29, Coffee-weed; Cassia (v). **1966–70** DARE (Qq. S20, S21) 11 Infs, **chiefly S Atl, Gulf States,** Coffeeweed(s). [Note: Some of these Infs may be referring instead to **coffeeweed 1a** above.] **1975** Duncan–Foote *Wildflowers SE* 66, Coffee-weed; Sickle-pod . . . *Cassia obtusifolia.*

c =wild indigo.

1966 DARE (Qu. S20) Inf **GA**7, Coffee weed = indigo.

2 Any of several other plants, as:

a =chicory 1.

1949 Moldenke *Amer. Wild Flowers* 177, The *common chicory* . . . grows from a deep taproot, which is extensively ground up and used as an adulterant for or substitute for coffee (hence the name *coffeeweed* often applied to it). **1971** GA Dept. Ag. *Farmers Market Bulletin* 10 Feb 8, Chicory . . *coffeeweed* — the latter from the use of its ground up root as a coffee adulterant, is from a remarkably versatile group of herbs of the Compositae Family.

b =curled dock.

1961 W3, Coffeeweed . . . Curled dock. **1970** *Smithfield Times* (VA) 20 May 12, It [a herbicide] stops the toughest grasses and weeds, including . . coffeeweed.

c =mullein.

1970 DARE (Qu. S21) Inf **FL**50, Coffee plant or coffeeweed or mullein.

coffee worm n

See quot 1982.

1967 DARE (Qu. P5, . . *The common worm used as bait*) Inf **AL**17, Coffee worm. **1982** *NADS Letters* **cNC,** Coffee worm — People who

grow worms for fishing will toss used coffee grounds into the worms' earth and mix them up. Or you can attract . . the common earthworm . . in your backyard by digging a shallow pit in the ground in the evening, dumping in used coffee grounds, and letting it stand undisturbed overnight. In the morning you should find some good fishing worms in the pit.

coffin n

1 A trunk. [*OED* → 1677]

1968 Adams *Western Words* 70, *Coffin* — A cowboy's term for a trunk.

2 A vehicle that is, or is thought to be, a deathtrap.

1945 Hamann *Air Words, Coffin* . . . A dangerous plane to fly, particularly one that is in a dilapidated, run-down condition. **1967** DARE (Qu. O2, . . *An old, clumsy boat*) Inf **PA**27, Coffin.

3 A pastry crust; a deep-dish pie or its pan. [*OED* "Obs."]

1916 DN 4.239 **ceMA,** *Coffin* . . . Pie crust: called *long coffin, round coffin,* etc., according to the shape. **1949** Brown *Amer. Cooks* 842 **VA,** *Coffin* . . . A pastry-lined dish or pan. **1953** Piercy *Shaker Cook Book* 97 (as of c1800), "Pie Coffin" was a term used to define the case of the pie-shell. *Ibid* 168, From New England the Shaker Sisters brought with them the terms trap, coffin, grated and tart pie. The trap was a deep-dish pie often of meat, fowl or fruit. When this trap was covered with a top crust it was called a coffin, for it was baked in a loaf pan and resembled a coffer or coffin.

coffin-bearer See **coffin-carrier**

coffin board n Also *coffin plank*

1954 *Harder Coll.* **cwTN,** *Coffin boards* . . . Pieces of sawed lumber placed across a casket to protect it. *Coffin planks* . . coffin boards.

coffin-boat n [From its shape and the hunter's supine position] =battery 1.

1859 (1968) Bartlett *Americanisms.* **1889** (1971) Farmer *Americanisms* 157, *Coffin-boat* . . . is a box sufficiently large to contain a man, with a deck about two feet wide surrounding it. To this deck are attached . . floating wings, which . . prevents the water from rushing in . . . When the gunner is in his craft, it is . . nearly on a level with the water.

coffin-carrier n Also *coffin-bearer* [See quot 1956] **NEast coast**
=great black-backed gull.

1872 Coues *Key to N. Amer. Birds* 312, Great Black-backed Gull. Saddle back. Coffin-carrier. **1917** (1923) *Birds Amer.* 1.41, Great Black-Backed Gull *Larus marinus* . . Black-backed Gull; Saddleback; Coffin-carrier; Cobb; Wagell. **1925** (1928) Forbush *Birds MA* 1.69, Great Black-backed Gull. Other names: black-back; . . coffin-bearer. **1956** *MA Audubon* 40.22, Great Black-backed Gull . . . Coffin-bearer (Mass. From the black mantle which appears oblong in silhouette.).

coffin fodder n

One who looks ready to die.

1961 Adams *Old-Time Cowhand* 185, This coffin fodder came in at a side door.

coffin money n

Burial insurance.

1950 Faulkner *Stories* 308 **MS,** "Anyway, I got my coffin money saved up with Mr. Lovelady." Mr. Lovelady was a short, dirty man who collected the Negro insurance.

coffin nail n

1 also *nail in one's coffin:* A cigarette; infreq a cigar. **widespread but esp Nth, Midl, West** See Map and Map Section Cf **coffin tack**

1888 *Texas Siftings* 18 Feb 8/1 *(OEDS),* A youth . . puffed at an ill-smelling coffin nail. **1900** DN 2.28 [College words], *Coffin-nail* or *coffin tack* . . . A cigarette. **1914** DN 4.162 **NW. 1940** AmSp 15.335 **seNE,** To smoke is . . *to put a nail in one's coffin* . . . A cigarette is a . . *coffin-nail.* **1948** *Chicago Daily News* 4 Dec. 4/7 *(DA),* I am a little hurt at the irritable stand taken by the *Journal* . . concerning the vitamin-enriched copy of the coffin-nail advertisements. **1950** WELS (Nicknames for cigarettes) 35 Infs, **WI,** Coffin nail(s). **1965–70** DARE (Qu. DD6b, . . *Cigarettes*) 451 Infs, **widespread but esp Nth, Midl, West,** Coffin nail; 11 Infs, **chiefly Nth,** (Another) nail (for, in, *or* on) (the *or* your) coffin (Qu. DD6a, . . *Cigars*) Inf **IN**22, Coffin nail.

2 Transf: see quot.

1915 DN 4.232, *Coffin nail* . . . A cigarette 'fiend'; one who smokes too much.

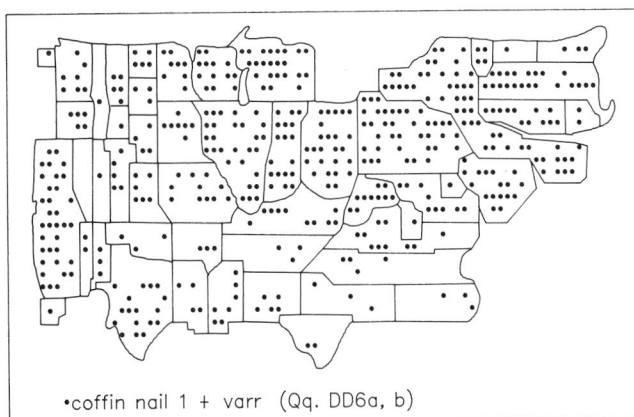

•coffin nail 1 + varr (Qq. DD6a, b)

coffin plank See **coffin board**

coffin screw See **coffin tack**

coffin stick n [Prob a blend of **coffin nail 1** + **cancer stick**]
A cigarette.
    1968–70 *DARE* (Qu. DD6b, *Nicknames for cigarettes*) Infs IL27, KY92, MA123, Coffin stick.

coffin tack n Also infreq *coffin screw, tack in one's coffin* **chiefly Sth, S Midl** See Map and Map Section Cf **coffin nail 1**
A cigarette; infreq a cigar.
    1897 *Chicago Daily Tribune* (IL) 15 July 3/2, [Headline:] *Unconscious from cigaret smoke.* George Decker of Jersey City succumbs to an Excessive Use of 'Coffin Tacks.' **1914** *DN* 4.162 **NW**, *Coffin tack* . . . A cigarette. *Slang.* **1922** *DN* 5.159 [College words], *Coffin-nail or coffin tack* . . . A cigarette. **1965–70** *DARE* (Qu. DD6b, . . *Cigarettes*) 61 Infs, **chiefly Sth, S Midl**, Coffin tack; CA158, KY6, TX26, Coffin screw; ME22, Another tack in your coffin; LA2, Tack in my coffin; (Qu. DD6a, . . *Cigars*) Inf GA16, Coffin tack.

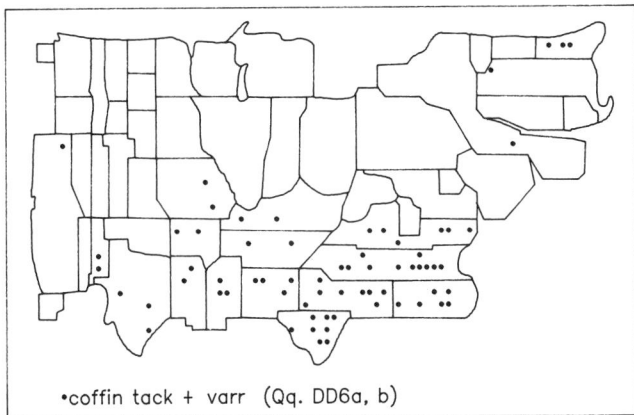

•coffin tack + varr (Qq. DD6a, b)

coffin varnish n **chiefly West** *joc*
Liquor, whiskey, esp that of low quality.
    1935 *AmSp* 10.14 [Underworld jargon], *Coffin varnish. Rotgut* whiskey. **1941** FWP *Guide WY* 461, *Coffin varnish* . . liquor. **1961** Adams *Old-Time Cowhand* 330, The cowman has a lot of slang names for the booze he drinks, and calls it such things as . . "coffin varnish." **1971** Jennings *Cowboys* 93, He said himself ther'd be no coffin varnish in this outfit. *Ibid* 227, *Coffin varnish*—Whiskey, of course.

cog n [Scots and Engl dial *cog* a hollow wooden vessel; a pail]
    1930 Shoemaker *1300 Words* 10 **cPA Mts** (as of c1900), *Cog*—A small wooden pail or dish.

coge it v phr Also sp *coag* [*cogue* to drink drams *(OED "Obs.")*, from *cogue* a small drinking vessel]
    1889 (1971) Farmer *Americanisms*, *Coge it, to.*—To drink heavily and habitually. Sometimes to *coag.*

coggle v[1], hence ppl adj *coggled (up)* [Scots and Engl dial; origin uncert; akin to *cobble* to shake from side to side, *cockle, cocker* to oscillate unsteadily; cf *OED coggle* v.[2]]
To wobble or be unsteady.

1843 (1916) Hall *New Purchase* 142 **IN,** Some carried and fixed tables, pushing and kicking and jamming at them till they consented to stay fixed and not to coggle! **1917** *DN* 4.409 **wNC,** *Coggled up* . . . Rickety; wobbly. "That's the most *coggled up* far [fire] I ever seed." **1926** Kephart *Highlanders* 354, Since the Appalachian people have a marked Scotch-Irish strain, we would expect their speech to show a strong Scotch influence. So far as vocabulary is concerned, there is really little of it. A few words, caigy (cadgy), coggled, . . almost exhaust the list of distinct Scotticisms.

coggle v[2] [Perh a var of *cobble* to repair hastily]
    1902 *DN* 2.231 **sIL,** *Coggle* . . . 1. To cobble. 2. To repair anything hastily for immediate use. 3. To join the ends of a broken chain with a key.

coggly adj [Cf *OED coggly* shaky, unsteady]
    1916 *DN* 4.321 **KS,** *Coggly* . . . Of irregular shape. "They used coggly stones in the wall."

‡**cogilate** v [Prob blend of *cogitate* + *calculate*]
    1914 *DN* 4.104 **KS,** *Cogilate* . . . Variant of *calculate,* suppose, 'reckon.'

cohab n, also attrib [Abbr for *cohabitant*] **UT**
One who lives in illegal cohabitation, spec a polygamous Mormon.
    1888 *Ogden (Utah) Union* 11 June 2/5 *(DA),* The general verdict of returning cohab convicts is, "Had a good time, good usage, good fare, etc." **1890** *Ogden (Utah) Commercial* 25 Oct 1/4 *(DA),* (Headline) *Cohabs in Trouble.* **1942** Stegner *Mormon Country* 125, The third [thing] was the polygamy prosecutions under the Edmunds–Tucker Act, and the coming of deputy marshals snooping for "polygs" and "cohabs." **1942** Whipple *Joshua* 568 **UT,** Zadoc Hunt betrays his Church and deserts his plural wives in order to escape the penitentiary. Zadoc Hunt becomes a 'cohab,' that word to be spat out among God-fearing men as if it were a piece of filth. **1948** *Jrl. Amer. Folkl.* 61.29 **UT,** A 'cohab' . . left in such haste that he didn't even get into his trousers.

cohabitate v [Back-formation from *cohabitation*]
    1968 *DARE* (Qu. AA19, *Words or expressions about a man and woman who are not married but live together as if they were*) Infs NC18, VA11, Cohabitating.

cohash See **cohosh**

cohee n, also attrib Also sp *coohee, kohee* [Perh alter of *quoth he*] *old-fash*
An inhabitant of the mountains of western Virginia or Pennsylvania.
    1789 (1873) May *Jrl.* 144 **WV,** My little log hut was filled with two boats' crews of Yankees, from Marietta, and a number of Kohees, belonging to the [Wheeling, West Virginia] settlement. **1815** in 1956 Eliason *Tarheel Talk* 126 **NC,** The back country people [of Virginia] are called 'Cohees' from some of the back country people using frequently the term 'quote he' and 'quote she' or as they usually speak it 'coo he' and 'coo she.' **1853** *S. Lit. Messenger* 19.40/1, In Western Virginia, . . even about Lexington, the Cohee Athens—your Petitioner is well nigh discarded. **1867** Lowell *Biglow* (2nd ser.) lviii, *Cohees':* applied to the people of certain settlements in Western Pennsylvania, from their use of the archaic form *Quo' he.* **1899** (1912) Green *VA Folk-Speech* 125, *Coohees* . . . Of Scotch origin "Quo' he." *Coohees* was the nickname applied to people in western Virginia, while those in the east were called "Tuckahoes." **1949** *AmSp* 24.28, Mr. F. O. Richey . . tells me [=H. L. Mencken] that the local legend has it that *Cohee* was derived from *quoth he,* which is ascribed to the Quakers. A more likely etymology ascribes its origin to an Indian word signifying a bend in a river. [No further info given]

co-heifer See **co-cow**

coho See **coho salmon**

coho clam n
=**horse clam.**
    1967 *DARE* (Qu. P18, . . *Kinds of shellfish common around here*) Inf WA20, Coho—an Indian name [for horse clams]; in common use.

cohoe See **coho salmon**

cohog See **quahog**

cohogle v [Cf *EDD connyfogle* v.[1] "To hoodwink; dupe, cheat" and *SND carfuffle* v.1 "To throw into confusion"; see also **ker-**]
    1 To hoodwink. Cf **connyswaggle**

1829 *Va. Lit. Museum* 16 Dec 419 *(DAE)*, To *cohogle.* "To bamboozle." Kentucky. **1931** *AmSp* 7.96 **KY**, [Author speculates that *cohogle* may perhaps be related to *cog* to lie or cheat.]

2 To associate. Cf **cahoot** v

1855 *Olympia* (W[ashington] T[erritory]) *Pioneer* 6 July (1912 Thornton), Now the question is, will it pay to cohogle with these owls any longer?

cohoosh See **cohosh**

cohoot See **cahoot** n[1]

cohooter n [*co* var of **ker-** + *hooter* noisemaker] **cME** *obs*

1 A sentinel for a flock of passenger pigeons.

1930 *AmSp* 6.150, They [=passenger pigeons] disappeared here about the middle seventies, and this word died out with them . . . The pigeons fed in large flocks . . . When feeding, . . a flock would have from one to several old cock-pigeons posted on tall dead pines near by, watching. These birds kept up a constant calling, known from the sound as "cohootering," and the sentinels were called "cohooters."

2 A busy, voluble leader in community affairs.

1930 *AmSp* 6.149, Fifty years ago, though perhaps no one would remember it now, in the central part of Maine, a person who made himself prominent in local matters was commonly spoken of as a "cohooter." "Down to the Methodis' old Deacon Blank is the head-cohooter;" or "They're a-gettin up a levee (church fair) an' Mis' Smith is head-cohooter." But the term was oftenest used of men, and of men who talked more than they worked, in my recollection. The word had nothing to do with the phrase "to be in cahoots with." There was nothing derogatory about it save the whimsical implication that the person mentioned was both seen and heard . . . It was about equivalent to the "bell-wether of the flock" . . The people, on Penobscot . . applied the name to their neighbors who made more noise than they did work, and particularly to those who in the prayer-meetings were constant exhorters.

cohooter v [**cohooter** n]

1930 *AmSp* 6.150 **cME**, The people, on Penobscot at least, applied the name [cohooter] to their neighbors . . . It was also used as a verb— "to go cohootering around," that is, talking constantly and to little purpose.

cohoots See **cahoot** n[1]

coho salmon n Also *coho(e)* [See quot 1884; *DCan* 1808 →]

An anadromous fish *(Oncorhynchus kisutch)* with an elongate, somewhat compressed body generally silvery in color, but with small dark spots on the metallic blue back; native to the Pacific coast, but introduced elsewhere, as in Great Lakes. Also called **Arctic trout, hookbill, hooknose, hoopid salmon, quisutch, silver salmon, skowitz**

1884 Goode *Fisheries U.S.* 1.477 (Tabbert *Alaskan Engl.*), This species is almost everywhere known by the name of "Silver Salmon." It has also a series of local names . . . On Frazer River it is known by the Musquam name of "Coho". **1898** U.S. *Fish & Wildlife Serv. Fishery Bulletin* 18.6, In the opinions of the canners . . the coho should rank next after the king salmon in food value. **1955** U.S. *Arctic Info. Center Gloss., Coho, coho salmon.* The silver salmon. **1965–70** *DARE* (Qu. P1, *Freshwater fish that are good to eat*) 10 Infs, **chiefly Gt Lakes**, Coho salmon; **AK1**, **MI108**, **WI171**, Coho; (Qu. P14, *If commercial fishing is done around here, what do the fishermen go out after?*) Infs **IL46**, **MI91**, Coho salmon; **WA20**, Coho. **1968–69** *DARE* Tape **MI101**, They brought the coho salmon in to clean up the alewives; **MI103**, There's coho fishing that's coming back now . . Smoked, they're great, but I've tried broiling them and . . I don't like them; **WI75**, This coho is a tremedously fast-growing fish . . . The coho salmon on the west coast . . live in the saltwater for about . . eight years . . . These cohos that they plant here now . . , they'll be mature fish in just about three years.

cohosh n Also sp *cahush, cohash, cohoosh, cohush* Cf **black cohosh, blue ~, false ~, rattle ~, red ~, summer ~, white ~**

1 Any of several plants used medicinally as:

a =**baneberry 1.**

1789 Morse *Amer. Geog.* 1.189, Among the native . . plants of New England, the following have been employed for medicinal purposes . . . Cohush *(Actæa spicata).* This is a valuable plant. **1855** MI *State Ag. Soc. Trans.* 6.149, In the low grounds are skunk cabbage, birth root, . . cahush, . . and spikenard. **1891** *Jrl. Amer. Folkl.* 4.147, [In New Hampshire] Actaea alba was *Cohush.* **1950** Gray–Fernald *Manual of Botany* 671, Actaea . . . Cohosh.

b also *cohosh bugbane:* A **black snakeroot 1** (here: *Cimicifuga racemosa*).

1822 Eaton *Botany* 347, *Macrotys . . . serpentaria* (bugbane, black snakeroot, cohosh). **1859** (1968) Bartlett *Americanisms* 91, *Cohosh,* sometimes called Black Cohosh or Black Snakeroot *(Cimicifuga racemosa)* a well-known medicinal plant. **1933** Small *Manual SE Flora* 513, *C[imicifuga] racemosa . . . Cohosh-bugbane.* **1960** Williams *Walk Egypt* 215 **GA**, Now I'm gonna send you some cohash. Brew you a tea; it'll make you loose as Saturday night, and twice as green.

c =**blue cohosh 1.**

1828 Rafinesque *Med. Flora* 97, *Caulophyllum thalictroides . . . Vulgar Names*—Cohosh, Cohush. *Ibid* 98, Cohosh was the indigenous name of this plant, and a better one than Blueberry, the usual one in many parts. **1911** *Century Dict., Cohosh . . .* The blue cohosh. **1959** Carleton *Index Herb. Plants* 29, *Cohosh . . . Caulophyllum thalictroides.*

2 An infusion prepared from cohosh.

1948 *Chicago Daily News* (IL) 26 Feb 16/3 **CO** (as of 1880s), [Column title:] *Ever Take A Nip of Cohoosh? . . .* The real tonic that the adults enjoyed administering . . was made of a root called 'black cohosh.'

cohosh bugbane See **cohosh 1b**

cohush See **cohosh**

coil v Usu |kɔɪl|; also, **chiefly Sth, S Midl**, |k(w)ɑɪl|, |kwɔɪl| Pronc-spp *caile, cwoil, quarl, querl, quile, quoil, quorl* Std senses, var forms.

1888 Jones *Negro Myths* 100 **GA coast** [Gullah], Eh hunt tel eh fine one whalin ob er rattlesnake duh quile up on one log [=He hunts till he finds a whale of a rattlesnake that's coiled up on a log]. **1899** (1912) Green *VA Folk-Speech, Querl . . .* To twirl; turn or wind around; coil: as to *querl* a cord, thread, rope. **1902** *DN* 2.242 **sIL**, *Quarl* or *quoil . . .* Different pronunciations of coil, as a snake. **1903** *DN* 2.291 **Cape Cod MA**, *Oi* was regularly pronounced *ai: . . caile* for *coil.* **1906** *DN* 3.122 **sIN**, *Quarl, querl, quoil . . .* To coil. "The snake was quoiled up." *Ibid* 133 **nwAR**, *Cwoil . . .* To coil. "The snake cwoiled around his legs." **1909** *DN* 3.361 **eAL, wGA**, *Quoil.* **1912** *DN* 3.587 **wIN**, *Quoil up.* **1917** *DN* 4.416 **wNC, KY**, *Quile.* **1926** Kephart *Highlanders* 352 **sAppalachians**, The word coil is variously pronounced quile, querl, or quorl. **1927** *DN* 5.470 **Appalachians**, Quiled. **1927** *AmSp* 2.362 **WV**, *Quile.* **1936** *AmSp* 11.35 **eTX**, *Coil . .* [kɔɪl], [kwɑɪl]. **1941** *AmSp* 16.7 **eTX** [Black], *Coil . .* [kwa:ɪl]. **1942** Hall *Smoky Mt. Speech* 93, The still very common pronunciation of *coil* as [kwɑɪl] . . . *Coil* was heard also as [kwɔɪl], which seems to be a compromise between the dialectal and the standard forms. **1960** Criswell *Resp. to PADS 20* **Ozarks**, *Coil . .* [kwɑɪl]. Very common pronunciation fifty years ago and earlier; not now.

coil n[1] **West**

A rope.

1936 McCarthy *Lang. Mosshorn* **West**, *Coil . . .* A rope. **1961** Adams *Old-Time Cowhand* 127, Like ever'thing else in the cowboy's life, he's got a lot of slang names for his ropes . . . His grass rope's called such names as . . "coil."

coil n[2] [Orig unknown]

A haycock.

1959 *AmSp* 34.145, The Canadianism *coil,* recorded regularly in border communities of Ontario, Saskatchewan, and Manitoba, has invaded northwestern Minnesota (in the speech of a farmer near Crookston who said that a coil is made with a fork and a cock with a rake) and perhaps North Dakota (as indicated by a questionnaire response). **1966** *DARE* (Qu. L12, *What do you call the small piles of hay standing in the field*) Inf **MI2**, Coil.

coil one's ropes v phr

1975 Gould *ME Lingo, Coiled His Ropes*—Died. A good seaman coiled his lines neatly after work.

coil snake n

Perh a rattlesnake.

1966 *DARE* (Qu. P25, *Kinds of snakes . . around here*) Inf **MS6**, Coil snake.

co-inch See **co-wench**

coin hill n

1967 *DARE* (Qu. II24, . . *The part of a town where the well-off people live*) Inf **PA11**, Coin hill.

coin wash n

A coin-operated self-service laundry.

1966 *Champaign–Urbana Courier* (IL) 27 Dec 11/2, He and his wife will continue to operate the C & B Coin Wash in Arcola. **1978** *DARE* File **Madison WI**, Coin wash, a self-service laundry.

co-jack v phr [co v] **chiefly NEast**

Come!—used to call horses.

1893 *DN* 1.266, From New York is reported a call, ['koǰak], of which the latter syllable seems to be plainly the name of a horse. **1914** *DN* 4.155 **NH**, *Kujack* or *kōjock* . . Horse call. **1939** *LANE* Map 222, The usual calls are [kə'dʒæk], kə'dʒɒ(k)] and [kə'dʒʌ(k)], in which the second element is not thought of as the name of a horse. **1965–70** *DARE* (Qu. K82, *The call used . . to get horses in from the pasture*) Inf **MA42**, ['kʌǰak]; **NH5**, [kəǰɔk]. **1971** Wood *Vocab. Change* 46 **Gulf Sth**, If he wishes to use a customary word, he calls *kope,* or *co-jack* . . [in calling horses]. *Ibid* 302, Co-jack [offered by 31 of approx 1000 infs].

cokaberry n [Prob alter of **coakum**]

1970 *DARE* (Qu. I44, . . *Kinds of berries . . wild around here*) Inf **IL113**, ['kokə,beriz].

cokan See **coakum**

coke v [*coke* carbonized coal fuel]

In tobacco curing: to dry tobacco with artificial heat.

1966 *PADS* 45.10 **ncKY**, Coke . . . = *fire* . . "I don't coke my tobacco until I have to."

coke n See **coca-cola**

coke grass n

Perh =**coco grass.**

1966–67 *DARE* (Qu. S9, *Other kinds of grass that are hard to get rid of*) Infs **MS16, TX32,** Coke grass.

coke hod See **hod** n[1] **1**

coker sack See **croker sack**

coke stove n

See quot 1966.

1966 *PADS* 45.10 **ncKY**, Coke stove . . A coke-burning stove used to control humidity in the barn while tobacco is curing. (Also *fishback, salamander, curing stove*) . . . "If it starts getting too wet, I light coke stoves in the barn." **1969** *DARE* Tape **KY35**, Take coke stoves an' build several fires down through the barn an' cure it out that way.

coke tobacco n [*coke* carbonized coal fuel]

Low quality tobacco produced by the improper use of a **coke stove** in the firing process.

1966 *PADS* 45.10 **ncKY**, Coke tobacco . . . Tobacco that has a yellowish, streaked appearance caused by improper firing practices. Coke tobacco has a bitter taste and is thought highly undesirable by buyers . . . "I'd rather have house burn tobacco than coke tobacco." **1967** Key *Tobacco Vocab.* **TN,** Coke tobacco. Tobacco improperly fired which becomes yellowish, streaked, and bitter.

cola n [*cola* a tonic extract from the kola nut, used in making soft drinks] **scattered, but esp freq Midl**

A carbonated soft drink.

1938 Matschat *Suwannee R.* 238 **nFL, sGA,** All the trails converged upon the crossroads store with the big jar of barred pink and white candy in its flyspecked window, and the bottles of Cola and cherry phosphate on a counter inside. **1948** *Family Circle* June 85/1 *(DA),* She ordered a cola and sipped it idly, watching her reflection in the mirror. **1968–69** *DARE* (Qu. H78, *Ordinary soft drinks, usually carbonated—what are they called*) Infs **IN1, 65, KY12, 81, MD37, MI88, OH55, 61, PA120, UT6, VA18,** Cola(s).

colation See **collation**

col'-bucking vbl n Also *kol'-breaking* [Perh folk-etym alter of Fr *culbute* somersault]

1950 *PADS* 14.75 **FL,** Col'-buckin', kol'-breaking': . . The manner in which a horse sometimes bucks when he puts his head between his knees.

colcannon n Also sp *callcannon* [IrGael *cāl ceannan* white-headed cabbage] Also called **call** n[2]

A dish made of potatoes and vegetables boiled together.

1834 *Life Andrew Jackson* 125, I almost even now weep, when I think of the brave fellers takin their last leave of Judy and Kate, and their colcannon, and their murphies. **1939** FWP *Guide NJ* 132, The Irish of the same section [Bergen Co.] have a much more cheery custom. Each family prepares for the holiday supper [Hallowe'en] a dish known as "callcannon," a conglomerate of onions, potatoes, and parsnips.

colcha n [Span] **NM** Cf **colchon**

A bedspread.

1935 *New Mexico* 13.15 (1939 Carlisle *Southwestern Dict.*), Miss Leonora Cartin, . . who made a most valuable collection of Spanish *colchas* . . , decided she would like to sponsor such a venture. **1940** FWP *Guide NM* 195, Colchas, or counterpanes, [are] distinctly a New Mexican achievement. On a sheet of hand-woven cloth was worked an all-over pattern in wool with tapestry stitch, in free designs usually taken from native pottery. **1951** Fergusson *New Mexico* 405, Colcha—a coverlet.

colchon n Also sp *calchon* [Span *colchón*] **NM**

A mattress.

1857 Davis *El Gringo* 179 **NM,** The females in particular, prefer the easy *colchon*—folded mattress—to the straight and stiff-backed chairs and settees. **1926** *Century Illustr. Mag.* 113.25/2 **NM,** No doubt before the arrival of the American rocking chair the *colchón* contributed to comfort in the best houses as it still does in humble homes. **1936** Poe *Buckboard Days* 142 **swNM,** I'd like for you to mention among the girls that I've bought two new sheepskins for my *calchon*. **1940** FWP *Guide NM* 112, Colchón—A mattress. In early days it was placed on floor and used as bed.

colcock See **coldcock**

cold adj[1]

1 Lacking enthusiasm, unwilling to participate fully.

1859 (1968) Bartlett *Americanisms* 91, Cold . . . Applied in a peculiar way to those who do not engage in some particular undertaking, e.g. a revival in a church (this seems to be the original use), a railroad company, a bank, or even a conspiracy to cheat some one. He who does not earnestly engage in it is said to be *cold*. "How many shares in the _____ Bank . . ? . . And how many did Jackson take? Oh, he's *cold*, he'd only take one, provided I'd swap horses with him." **1968–69** *DARE* (Qu. CC7, *Words for a person who goes to church very seldom or not at all*) Inf **IN16,** Cold; **KY19,** Got cold.

2 See quot.

1915 *DN* 4.232 **neOH,** Plain; clear; certain. "That's cold enough."

3 Of a check: worthless, fraudulent.

1927 *Cleveland Press* 2 Feb *(DA),* John Horan, wanted in connection with a 'cold' check passed three weeks ago. **1928** *Ruppenthal Coll.* **KS,** Cold check, . . a check given on a bank by one who has no funds deposited in such bank . . . Statutes that penalize giving such checks are called "cold check laws." **1939** FWP *These are Our Lives* 304, Lots of cold checks is passed and we have to run them down. **1970** *DARE* FW Addit **KY80,** Cold check—a check that is worthless.

cold adj[2] *among Blacks*

Very good, excellent.

1942 *Amer. Mercury* 55.94 **Harlem NYC,** Cold . . "He was cold on that trumpet!" **1977** *Capital Times* (Madison WI) 2 May 12 [Black], Thass *cold*, Baby, thass *cold*. [Cartoon caption] **1980** Folb *Runnin' Down* 233 **Los Angeles CA** [Black], Cold . . . Fine, exceptional.

cold adv Cf **plumb**

Simply, plain.

1940 *Sat. Eve. Post* 23 Nov 99/1 **GA,** If he ain't back by sunup tomorrow I'm cold going at him. *Ibid* 7 Dec 25/1, One night a bunch of wild boys took after me, and I had to just cold outrun 'em.

cold and hot See **hot and cold**

cold bird n

A bird thought to predict cold weather; perh =**cold-weather bird.**

1938 in *1972 Amer. Slave* 2.24 **SC,** De people used to have a bird for cold weather, too. Folks say, 'Don' you hear dat cold bird? Look out, it gwine be cold tomorrow.' De cold bird, he a brown bird. If you can see him, he a fine lookin bird, too.

cold-blooded adj

Of horses and cattle: having mixed or inferior breeding; hence n *cold-blood* an animal with such breeding.

1937 *DN* 6.618 **swTX,** A *cold-blooded* horse is not a thoroughbred animal. **1955** *AmSp* 30.18, Any nonthoroughbred, regardless of the purity of its pedigree, is a *cold-blooded* horse. **1961** Adams *Old-Time Cowhand* 159, Cattle not thoroughbreds were called "cold blooded stock," while thoroughbreds were "hot bloods," or "pures." **1977** Watts *Dict. Old West, Cold-blooded stock*—Also *cold-bloods.* Originally in Europe this term was applied to horses of northern descent, as opposed to Arabs and Barbs. In the West it meant cows or horses lacking good blood or breeding.

‡coldbox n
An icebox.
   1968 *DARE* (Qu. D10a, *The place to keep food cool, usually with ice*) Inf CA36, Coldbox—an older one.

cold brand n
=*hair brand*; see quot 1977.
   1944 Adams *Western Words, Cold brand*—A hair brand. **1970** *DARE* (Qu. K18, . . *Kind of mark . . to identify a cow*) Inf VA111, Cold brand. [**1977** Watts *Dict. Old West* 156, Cold branding; the light branding of an animal (sometimes done through a wet blanket) in which only the hair was marked by the hot iron. Used for trail-branding or by cow-thieves.]

cold bumps n pl Also *cold-weather bumps* **chiefly Sth** Cf **chill bumps**
=*gooseflesh.*
   1965–70 *DARE* (Qu. X58, *When you are cold, and little points of skin begin to come on your arms and legs, you have _____*) 12 Infs, **chiefly Sth**, Cold bumps; TN27, Cold-weather bumps.

cold cellar n **NEast** See Map
A root cellar.
   1965 *DARE* File **MA** (as of 1953), *Cold cellar:* room or section of a cellar where root crops, flower bulbs, etc., may be stored for the winter at cool, but above freezing temperatures. **1965–70** *DARE* (Qu. M19, *A place for keeping carrots, turnips, potatoes, and so on over the winter*) 22 Infs, **NEast**, Cold cellar.

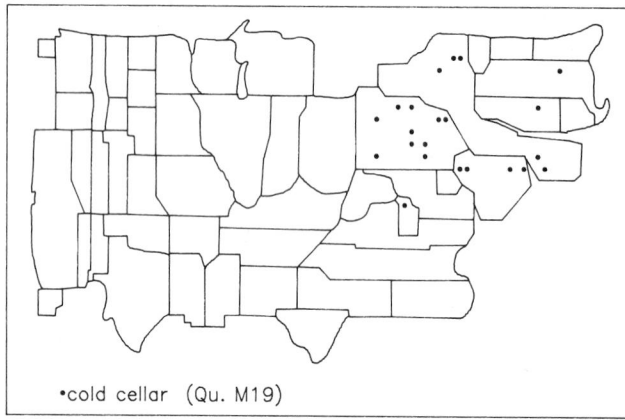

•cold cellar (Qu. M19)

cold-chill bumps See **chill bumps**

cold closet See **closet 1**

coldcock v Also *colcock, coolcock* [*cold* unconscious, senseless + *cock* v²]
1 To knock unconscious.
   1927 *AmSp* 2.351 **WV**, *Cold cocked . .* to be knocked senseless. "Tom was cold cocked when that rock hit him." **1930** *AmSp* 5.389 **MA**, *Cold-cock . . .* To kill when used of vermin; when applied to a man it usually means to stop, to knock unconscious, to disable. **1950** *PADS* 14.21 **SC**, *Colcock* ['kɔlkɑk], *coolcock:* . . To knock out, knock cold, with a connotation of knocking with a blunt instrument on the side or back of the head. Origin undetermined. **1952** Brown *NC Folkl.* 1.527 **wNC**, *Cold-cock . . .* To knock unconscious. **1954** *Harder Coll.* **cwTN**, *Cold-cock* ['kɔl,kɑk], knock out, render unconscious. **1966–70** *DARE* (Qu. Y14a, *To hit someone hard with the fist*) Infs CA107, CO33, IL135, PA223, SC19, 21, 26A, 32, *Cold-cock;* (Qu. Y15, *To beat somebody thoroughly*) Infs IN26, MN42, Coldcocked; (Qu. BB15, *Somebody . . unconscious from a hard blow*) Inf NE11, Coldcocked. **1968** *DARE* FW Addit **nwAR**, Coldcock ['koʊl,kɑk], to deliver a disabling blow, usually to the jaw or head, either with the fist or some object. *Ibid* **swMO**.
2 See quot 1963.
   1937 (1977) Hurston *Their Eyes* 145 **cFL**, He leaned on the counter with one elbow and cold-cocked her a look. **1963** *PADS* 40.4 **FL**,

Cold-cock . . . To hurl, dart, fling in a decisive manner. [*DARE* Ed: *PADS* author's definition of Hurston's use in quot 1937]

cold-crock v [*coldcock,* infl by *crock* to disable]
=*coldcock 1.*
   1960 Criswell *Resp. to PADS 20* **Ozarks**, *Cold-cock, . .* To knock out . . . Also *cold-crock* is very often used.

cold deck n [*cold* not in use, reserved]
1 A stacked pack of playing cards; fig, anything calculated to deceive; hence *cold decker,* one who uses a stacked deck, a cheat.
   1859 *S.F. Call* 3 Apr 4/2 (*AmSp* 22.90), He's got the thing all set to ring in a 'cold deck,' in which case he will deal himself four aces and his opponent four queens. **1876** Harte *Gabriel Conroy* 323 **CA**, You've been . . playin' it very low down on my moral and religious nature, generally ringin' in a cold deck on my spriritual condition for the last five years. **1920** Mulford *J. Nelson* xv.163 (*DA*), I've had all th' visitin' I want with a bunch of cold-deckers. **1946** *Chi. D. News* 17 July 14/7 (*DA*), The boys in the back room can't deal us a cold deck when the voters bring their own cards to the game. **1961** Holt *Phrase and Word Origins* 59, Cold deck. In draw poker, the deck of cards that is in use is thought of as warm, while one that has been stacked in a certain order beforehand, waiting to be secretly substituted, is of course cold. Thus, to be "cold decked" is to be cheated. It dates back almost to the riotous days of the forty-niners. **1968** Adams *Western Words* 70, Cold deck—In gambling, a stacked deck of cards.
2 In card play: a good hand at one deal.
   1889 (1971) Farmer *Americanisms* 158, Cold deck.—A good hand; *cold* or a *cold deck* in poker phraseology is to get a good hand at first, without the necessity of drawing fresh cards. In thieves' slang it means a prepared pack of cards.
3 In logging: a pile of logs held in reserve for later shipping; hence *cold decker,* a machine used to stack such a pile.
   1938 (1939) Holbrook *Holy Mackinaw* 260, Cold deck. A pile of logs left for later loading and hauling. **1941** *AmSp* 16.232 **MT**, Cold deck. **1950** *Western Folkl.* 9.116 **Pacific NW**, Cold deck. **1958** McCulloch *Woods Words* 36 **Pacific NW**, *Cold deck . . .* A big pile of logs yarded up to a swing tree in the woods; or stacked up any place away from the immediate logging; or stored at mill or other location . . . *Cold decker*—A gas driven donkey . . used mostly to build cold decks. **1969** Sorden *Lumberjack Lingo* 25 **NEng, Gt Lakes**, Cold deck.

cold-deck v [*cold deck* n]
1 To introduce a stacked pack of playing cards into a game; hence to deceive, to cheat.
   1884 *Gringo and Greaser* 15 Feb 2/2 (*AmSp* 17.125) **NM**, The miller . . kicked, because said Serna was trying to cold deck said Sanches. **1902** Wilson *Spenders* 123 **MT**, A man wakes up to find that his natural promptin's has cold-decked him. **1943** *AmSp* 18.7, *To Cold Deck.* To introduce a stacked deck into the play. Not restricted to faro; in fact, much more commonly heard nowadays in connection with other types of card game. **1951** *AmSp* 26.98, *Cold deck . . .* They cold-decked me. **1961** [see **cold deck** n 1]. **1968** Adams *Western Words* 70, Cold deck—To introduce a stacked deck into play . . . Also, a general term meaning *to take unfair advantage.*
2 See quot.
   1958 McCulloch *Woods Words* 36 **Pacific NW**, *Cold deck . . .* To stack up logs in a pile.

cold drink n [*cold* + *drink* n] **chiefly Sth, Lower Missip Valley** See Map Cf **coca-cola**

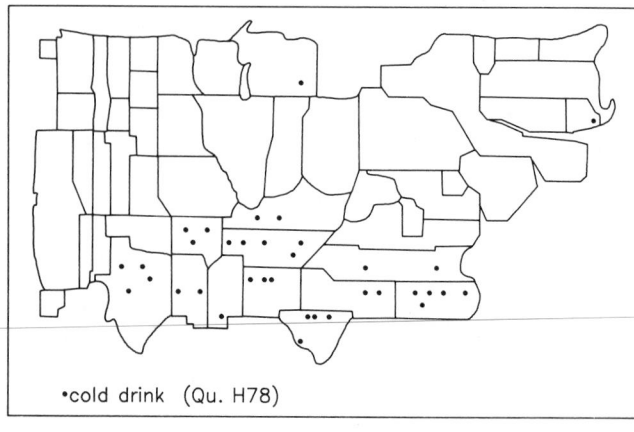

•cold drink (Qu. H78)

Any non-alcoholic, carbonated, and bottled beverage; a soft drink.

1954 *Harder Coll.* **cwTN,** *Cold drink:* Any bottled non-alcoholic drink, not necessarily cold.   **1962** Atwood *Vocab.* **TX** 63, *Cold drink* . . is also in use [in Texas, southern Arkansas, and southeastern Louisiana].   **1966–70** *DARE* (Qu. H78, *Ordinary soft drinks, usually carbonated*) 35 Infs, **chiefly Sth,** Cold drink(s).   **1967** *DARE* FW Addit **swAR,** *Cold drink,* carbonated beverage.   **1970** Tarpley *Blinky* 195 **neTX,** Carbonated beverages in a bottle are more likely to be called *cold drinks* or *soda pop* than any other name. *Cold drink* decreases as informants grow older.

cold duck n
   1970 *DARE* (Qu. FF5b, *More recent dance steps*) Inf **VA**39C, Cold duck; **WV**21, Cold duck [kol dʌk]. [Both Infs Black]

cold flour n Also *cold meal*   Also called **coal-flour, nocake, pinole**
Parched and ground maize mixed with sugar.
   1821 (1904) Austin *Jrl.* **TX** 287, Engaged 2 bushels of cold flour, & 50 lbs bacon.   **1859** Marcy *Prairie Traveler* 33 **West,** The most portable and simple preparation of subsistence that I know of, and which is used extensively by the Mexicans and Indians, is called *"cold flour."* It is made by parching corn, and pounding it in a mortar to the consistency of coarse meal; a little sugar and cinnamon added makes it quite palatable.   **1889** (1971) Farmer *Americanisms* 158, *Cold flour.*—Backwoodsman's fare—simple, modest, and rough, but withal a delicacy and nourishing. It consists of maize meal (the corn itself having been parched before grinding) mixed with sugar, and stirred into a paste with water, spice being sometimes added according to taste, to render it even more palatable. This latter is known in the Spanish districts as *pinole.*   **1902** (1968) Clapin *Americanisms* 126, *Cold flour* . . . Also known as *nocake* (New England), and *pinole* (Spanish districts).   **1938** FWP *Guide MS* 51, *Cold meal.* "Cold meal," was a favorite because of its sustaining qualities in times of war and famine. This parched corn flour would keep without spoiling as long as it was dry, and a man could travel for a week on a quart of it.

cold-footed adj [From *cold feet* apprehension, misgivings] **West**
1 Cowardly, unventuresome; hence n *cold footer* a timid or cowardly person.
   1918 *DN* 5.72 **NM,** *Cold-footed,* . . cowardly, "You are cold-footed on this proposition of marriage."   **1920** Hunter *Trail Drivers* **TX** 429, We were not allowed to cross the cattle on the bridge, so we had to swim for it. Two of my men stayed with me, and the third, a "cold-footer," crossed on the bridge.   **1968** Adams *Western Words* 70, *Cold-footed*—Cowardly.
2 Of a horse: lame.
   1964 Jackman–Long *OR Desert* 394 [Horse buyers' jargon], Cold footed—stringhalted [i.e. lame in the hind legs].

cold-footed adv
=**flat-footed 1.**
   1966 *PADS* 46.30 **cnAR,** A girl very definitely said *no* to a boy if she "turned him down cold footed."

cold footer See **cold-footed** adj **1**

cold-harbor n *obs*
   1899 (1912) Green *VA Folk-Speech* 121, *Cold-harbour* . . . A protection at a wayside for travellers who are benighted, where they found shelter and a lodging place; no food was supplied, but means to cook what the traveller had; he used his own bedding, and feed might be had for his animals . . . The name came thence [from England] into eastern Virginia.

‡cold heat n Cf **cold bumps**
=**gooseflesh.**
   1966 *DARE* (Qu. X58) Inf **SC**10, A cold heat.

cold house n Cf **cold cellar**
   1967 *DARE* (Qu. M19, *A place for keeping carrots, turnips, potatoes, and so on over the winter*) Inf **AZ**2, Cold house.

cold hurt adj
   1946 *PADS* 6.9 **ceNC** (as of 1900), *Cold hurt* . . . Nipped or frozen by the cold. Said of potatoes [=sweet potatoes] that have been slightly affected before being dug or after they have been banked during the winter. Never applied to Irish potatoes.

cold in hand adj phr
Without cash, broke.
   1942 *Amer. Mercury* 55.86 **Harlem NYC** [Black], "What's cookin'?" "Oh, just like de bear—I ain't nowhere . . . Like de bear's daughter—ain't got a quarter." . . "Cold in hand, huh? . . Last night when I left you, you was beating up your gums and broadcasting about how hot you was . . . What you doing cold in hand?" "Aw, man, can't you take a joke? I was just beating up my gums when I said I was broke."

‡cold, in the adj phr [Prob from *out cold* totally unconscious]
   1968 *DARE* (Qu. BB15, . . *Unconscious from a hard blow:* "He's been ——— *for ten minutes."*) Inf **AL**8, In the cold.

‡cold iron n [Alter of **coal iron** + intrusive *d*]
   1967 *DARE* (Qu. F29, *Different kinds of irons—not electric—used . . for smoothing clothes after they're washed*) Inf **LA**12, Cold iron ['koʊl‚daən] or coal iron ['koʊl‚aən]—used charcoal inside.

cold-jaw n [*cold* insensitive]   Cf **cold-jawed**
   1933 *AmSp* 8.1.28 **TX,** *Cold-jaw.* A horse that does not respond to bridle signals, however harsh they may be.

cold-jaw v Cf **cold-jawed**
Of a horse: to act unmanageably, to bolt, despite pressure from the bits.
   1941 Cleaveland *No Life* 341, Streak was beginning to 'cold-jaw' when he started after a cow brute, a trick which if not checked would of course ruin him for range work.   **1971** Green *Last Trail Drive* 57 **TX** (as of 1920), I got a pretty firm hold on her but for some reason she grabbed the bits between her teeth and cold jawed and run away with me.

cold-jawed adj **SW**
Of a horse: having an insensitive mouth, hence difficult to control with the reins.
   1929 Dobie *Vaquero* 206 **SW,** In the heat of the chase they are apt to become "cold-jawed" (hard mouthed) and uncontrollable.   **1937** *DN* 6.618 **swTX,** A *cold-jawed* horse is one difficult to rein in or stop, because he ruins the rider's leverage by getting the *bits* between his teeth and holding on to them tenaciously.   **1945** Thorp *Pardner* 99 **SW,** Randolph . . was riding a horse named Simon, which was cold-jawed. A cold-jawed horse is one that has been abused around the mouth; maybe at some time he had been pulled up hard and the nerves killed by a Mexican ring-bit.   **1961** Adams *Old-Time Cowhand* 119.

cold meal See **cold flour**

cold natured adj
1 Of persons: prone to feel cold.
   1908 *DN* 3.300 **eAL, wGA,** *Cold-natured* . . . Cool-blooded, easily made cold.
2 See quot.
   1937 *Hall Coll.* **eTN,** *Cold-natured* . . . Cold; having a cold climate. "Like Smoky Mountain, 'Waynesville' is cold-natured."

cold nose n, also attrib **sAppalachians** Cf **cold trailer**
Of a hunting dog: a nose especially sensitive to a stale or cold track; a dog with such a nose; hence adj *cold-nose(d)* keen-scented.
   1838 (1852) Gilman *S. Matron* 210 **SC,** After driving about for some time, Bounce, a cold-nose dog, struck a trail.   **1892** Harris *On Plantation* 35 **GA,** He what was called a 'cold nose,' which is a short way of saying that he could follow a scent thirty-six hours old, and yet he was a very shabby-looking dog.   **1939** *Hall Coll.* **eTN, wNC,** *Cold-nosed*—Used of a dog that can pick up and follow a cold trail.   **1970** Green *Ely* 116 **sTN,** They consist of this type of strategy: Two cold-nose pot-lickor hounds to build up the trail. These English hounds were faster than the cold-nose.

cold one n Also *cool one*
A bottle or can of beer.
   1928 *Ruppenthal Coll.* **KS,** *Cold one* . . euphemism for a bottle of beer kept on ice or otherwise cooled. Law violators and those who bought of them avoided the use of terms that denoted intoxicating liquors, so "cold one" was used and did not of itself suggest an alcoholic drink as did beer.   **1965–70** *DARE* (Qu. DD25, . . *Nicknames for beer*) Infs **KY**34, **MD**15, **NJ**23, **NC**67, **OH**46, **VA**39, Cold one; **SC**40, Cool one.   **1981** *DARE* File **Madison WI,** A friend of mine from Michigan offers his guests beer by asking "Can I get you a cold one?"

cold-out adv Cf **cold** adv
Really, completely, plain.

1933 Rawlings *South Moon* 45 **FL,** "Does folkses around here know?" "Don't nobody cold-out know, honey, but me and you." *Ibid* 98, "Ma," he asked, "what happens if them gov'mint buzzards cold-out ketches a feller?" **1938** Rawlings *Yearling* 84 **FL,** I figger, for some reason, that fox were cold-out crazy.

cold-out adj

Whole, entire, full.

1940 *Sat. Eve. Post* 23 Nov 10/1 **sGA,** They's one buck deer in these here woods that's got a cold-out night of hauling tail ahead of him.

coldover n Cf holdover

A leftover.

1970 *DARE* FW Addit **MS** [Black], Food saved for another meal—coldovers.

cold owl n Cf shivering owl

=screech owl.

1949 *AmSp* 24.107 **neSC,** Cold owl . . screech owl.

cold pantry n

1968 *DARE* (Qu. D8, *The small room next to the kitchen . . where dishes and sometimes foods are kept*) Inf **CT9,** Cold pantry, as opposed to butler's pantry between kitchen and dining room, where silver etc. is kept. A cold pantry is used mainly for food storage . . . It is usually behind the kitchen.

cold pile n

1966 *DARE* Tape **SC18,** A cold pile is trash that comes in when the net is brought in and is put on the deck, has shrimp, fish, crabs, sharks, stingamarees and things like that in it, pretty well anything you'll find in the ocean.

cold pimples n pl Cf cold bumps

=gooseflesh.

1965–70 *DARE* (Qu. X58) Infs **AK8, GA28, KY52, LA12, TN24, VA9,** Cold pimples.

cold potato n, also attrib

Someone or something dull, boring, or worthless.

1967–69 *DARE* (Qu. FF23, *. . Joking names . . for . . clubs or lodges*) Inf **KY60,** Cold potato club; (Qu. HH16, *Uncomplimentary words with no definite meaning*) Inf **NY35,** Cold potato; (Qu. HH20b, *Of an idle, worthless person*) Inf **GA77,** A cold potato.

cold scald n [Perh from hog butchering: with a good scald the bristles can be scraped off easily; hence a *cold scald* is one not hot enough, not good] obs Cf good scald at scald

A misfortune.

1839 *Spirit of the Times* 4 May 108/1 *(DA),* It was indeed 'a cold scald.' **1845** *St. Louis Reveille* (MO) 18 June 1/6, That really was a "cold scald" for us, when these *persecuted Saints,* driven from the free State of Missouri, took shelter in the bosom of Illinois.

cold shake n

A dismissal; the cold shoulder.

1883 Twain *Life on Missip.* (Boston) 54, But none of them herded with Dick Allbright. They all give him the cold shake. **1885** Twain *Huck. Finn* 315, If we ever got the least show we would give them the cold shake and clear out and leave them behind. **1968** Adams *Western Words* 70, *Cold shake*—A logger's term for a dismissal. **1969** Sorden *Lumberjack Lingo* 25 **NEng, Gt Lakes,** *Cold shake*—A discharge; a dismissal.

cold shape n

1959 *VT Hist.* new ser 27.156, *Cold shape:* . . Any cold dish, such as a gelatine dish, which stands alone. Common.

cold sheet n [Perh alter of cold shut 2]

1969 Sorden *Lumberjack Lingo* 25 **NEng, Gt Lakes,** *Cold sheets*—Fried cakes, doughnuts. Generally, tough doughnuts.

coldshin n

Any of three ducks: the **ring-necked duck,** the **greater scaup** or the **lesser scaup.**

1951 *AmSp* 26.91, In coastal North Carolina, the ring-necked duck and the two species of scaup are called *coldshins* . . . The word possibly is an echo of *cochin,* a poultry term facetiously applied to these waterfowl. **1953** *AmSp* 28.276, Then too, if I am not mistaken, the name *coachen* (varied to *coachin,* and folk-etymologized as *cold-shin*) in coastal North Carolina really means 'Cochin,' and indicates that . . greater and lesser scaups and the ring-necked duck . . are thought of as breeds of Nature's poultry.

cold shut n [Prob cold + shut, ppl adj used absol] esp NW

1 A link or split ring that is closed by hammering without heat; see quots.

1872 (1876) Knight *Amer. Mech. Dict.* 1.593/2 *Cold shut.* A term meaning that a link is closed while cold, without welding. **1887** *Scribner's Mag.* 2.304/2 **Rocky Mts,** A long chain is . . made fast around a log, with a "cold-shut" or split-ring, such as you put your pocket-keys on, and which can be fastened by hammering. **1956** *AmSp* 31.150 **nwCA,** *Cold shut* . . . A link for joining pieces of chain. **1958** McCulloch *Woods Words* 36 **Pacific NW,** *Cold shut*—A link which can be closed by pounding a pin through a hole on the other side of the link, where it can be burred over to fasten it in place. **1967** *DARE* Tape **WA24,** They'd make . . cold shuts . . . You take a piece of iron . . . You'd flatten it out and put a hole in one end, then you'd bend it around . . . then you welded it on the other side . . . You'd put that in the place of a link . . . You wouldn't have to throw the whole thing [=rigging] away.

2 Transf: a hard doughnut. *joc*

1958 McCulloch *Woods Words* 36 **Pacific NW,** *Cold shut*—A tough doughnut.

cold slaw n [Folk-etym] Cf hot slaw

Coleslaw.

1794 *Thomas' MA Spy or Worcester Gaz.* (MA) 12 Nov 4/2, A piece of sliced cabbage, by Dutchmen ycleped cold slaw. **1896** E. Higginson *Tales* 50 *(DAE),* The cabbage was chopped finely for the cold-slaw . . . Then Mrs. Bridges "set" the table. **1925** Parrish *Perennial Bachelor* 5 **MD** (as of 1850–1900), Mock turtel soup, boiled turkey with oyster sauce, . . beats, cold slaw. **1950** *WELS* (*Dishes made with fresh cabbage*) 13 Infs, **WI,** Cold slaw. **1954** *Harder Coll.* **cwTN.** **c1960** *Wilson Coll.* **csKY,** *Cold slaw:* . . Often used in the area; people are not used to associating cale or cole or kohl with cabbage. **1965–70** *DARE* (Qu. H52, *Dishes made with fresh cabbage*) 111 Infs, **widespread, but least freq in Sth,** Cold slaw.

‡cold snow n

Snow with a hard surface-crust.

1968 *DARE* Tape **IL29,** There's no cold snow anymore. When I was going to school, the snow got so hard on top . . that you could go over the top of fences.

cold soap n Also cold-water soap

Homemade soap made with cold water.

1967–68 *DARE* Tape **IN3,** Nowadays when we make the cold-water soap, it has to be made out of grease; **TX40,** There's cold soap—you just use some cold water, you don't boil that.

cold storage n

1966–70 *DARE* (Qu. V11, *. . A county or city jail*) Infs **IN3, MS1, NJ67,** Cold storage.

‡cold tea n

1907 *DN* 3.242 **csME,** Cold tea . . . Beer.

cold timberline n

See quot 1925.

1903 *Am. Geol. Soc. Bul.* 14.556 *(DA),* On the mountains of central Idaho, the cold timberline is sharply drawn at an elevation of about 10,000 feet, while the dry timberline, equally well defined, has an elevation of about 7,000 feet. **1925** Bryan *Papago Country* 375, The cold timber line, at which the growth of trees is prohibited by low temperature, is not found in this part of Arizona even on the highest summits.

cold-trail v

1 Of a hunting dog: to follow an old and faint scent. **?chiefly S Midl**

1939 *Hall Coll.* **eTN, wNC,** *Cold-trail* . . . To follow a cold trail . . . "We had some dogs, some bear dogs, and we went on and trailed—cold-trailed—'em right onto side . . of Shanty Mountain." **1950** Stuart *Hie Hunters* 16 **eKY,** "I hold him out until Brier-patch Tom Eversole's War Horse cold-trails the fox and gets a hot track," Sparkie said. **1966** *DARE* Tape **AR15,** Sometimes you have to cold-trail 'em [=foxes]. **1968** McPhee *Pine Barrens* 138 **NJ,** Experienced hounds know how to "cold-trail," and they are turned loose first . . . Three or four cold-trailing dogs move around for a while, and soon, as the trail becomes hot, their voices change. **1975** Newell *If Nothin' Don't Happen* 96 **nwFL,** It's sure a funny thing to me how a dog can get plastered by a skunk and in just a few minutes be able to cold-trail some other varmint. I can't figure out how he can smell anything.

2 To control a smoldering forest fire by trenching around apparently cool areas which could possibly rekindle.
   1958 McCulloch *Woods Words* 36 **Pacific NW**, *Cold trail*— To build a fire trail along the dead edge of a fire just to be sure.

cold trailer n [**cold-trail** v 1] Cf **cold nose**
A tracking dog that can follow an old, faint scent; also one that does so silently.
   1937 *Hall Coll.* **eTN, wNC**, *Cold-trailer*. . . A dog trained . . to follow in silence the scent of animals which are being hunted . . . "A cold-trailer won't have any noise." *Ibid* **eTN**, *Cold trailer* . . [a dog that follows a trail] after several hours. **1966** *DARE* Tape **AR15**, All the dogs are not cold-trailers; they'll just stay out there with the one that's doin' the trailin' till it gets warm.

cold-water n attrib **chiefly NEast** *old-fash*
Belonging or pertaining to the temperance movement.
   [**1830** U.S. Congress *Reg. of Debates* 25 Feb 584/1, It may be expedient . . to make our sailors cold water drinkers [=temperance men].] **1840** in 1934 Frear *Lowell & Abigail* 147 **MA**, This eve. a cold water party at Brother Coan's. **1843** (1916) Hall *New Purchase* 109 **PA**, You must all know we are cold water men, and don't believe in whiskey. **1844** (1940) Arnold *Diaries* 168 **VT**, He had a meeting of children, & formed a cold water army 92 present. **1906** *Springfield Republican* 16 Aug 1 *(DA)*, Another [case in point] comes in the action of the prohibition state executive committee in Pennsylvania . . . The cold water convention there nominated William H. Berry.

cold-water (apartment) See **cold-water flat**

cold-water bread n
   1906 *DN* 3.131 **nwAR**, *Cold water bread*, . . Corn bread made of meal, salt, and cold water. "I like cold water bread for breakfast."

cold-water carp n
Prob a carpsucker (*Carpiodes* spp). Cf **white carp**
   1967 *DARE* Tape **LA5**, We do have what they call a cold-water carp down here at times . . they look a little something like a buffalo only they're more whitish color; four to six pounds. **1968** *DARE* (Qu. P1) Inf **IN42**, Cold-water carp.

cold-water flat n Also *cold-water,* ~ *apartment,* ~ *tenement* **scattered, but chiefly NEast** See Map
An apartment with cold water only, or one not equipped with up-to-date plumbing.
   1942 McCarthy *Company She Keeps* 241, He had only to mention the name of the magazine and he would be whisked into . . a cold-water flat in an old-law tenement. **1954** Faulkner *Fable* 372 **Brooklyn NY**, A walk-up, cold-water Brooklyn tenement. **1958** Golden *For 2¢ Plain* 77 **NY**, 171 Eldridge Street, a cold-water tenement . . . Originally the toilets were in the yard in back. Later on came the inside toilets, one to a floor, serving four families. **1964** Markfield *To Early Grave* 31 **NY**, He had found himself a cold-water flat near the Village. **1965–70** *DARE* (Qu. D26, . . *Kinds of apartments*) 13 Infs, **chiefly NEast**, Cold-water flat; 12 Infs, **scattered, but chiefly NEast**, Cold-water; **MI122**, Cold-water apartment.

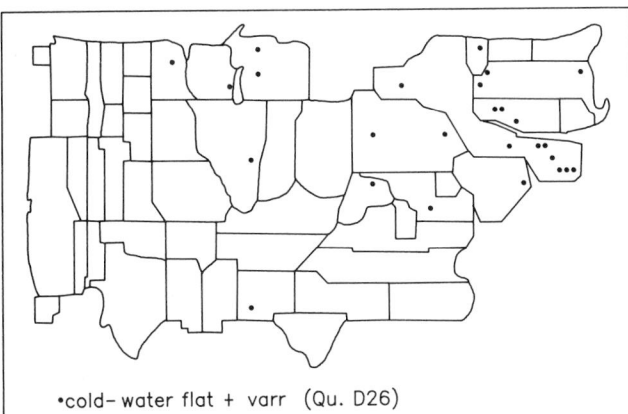
•cold- water flat + varr (Qu. D26)

cold-water pickle See **ice-water pickle**
cold-water root n *obs*
=**cocash 2**.

1873 in 1976 Miller *Shaker Herbs* 156, *Aster puniceus* . . . Cold Water Root. **1876** Hobbs *Bot. Hdbk.* 25, Cold water root, Cocash root, Aster puniceus.

cold-water soap See **cold soap**

cold-water tenement See **cold-water flat**

cold-weather bird n Cf **cold bird**
=**killdeer**.
   1951 *AmSp* 26.275, *Cold-weather bird* denotes the killdeer locally in North Carolina.

cold-weather bumps See **cold bumps**

colear v, n Also sp *coleo, colliar* [Span *colear*] **SW**
To throw an animal by the tail; the act of so doing.
   [**1844** (1954) Gregg *Commerce* 170 **NM**, Among the vaqueros, and even among persons of distinction, *el coleo* (tailing) is a much nobler exercise than the preceding [*correr el gallo,* racing (for) the cock] and is also generally reserved for days of festivity.] **1848** Ruxton *Advent. Rocky Mts.* 94, Not a ranchero . . could more dexterously *colear* a bull. [*Ibid* 82, We arrived at the ranch of LaPunta . . in time to witness the truly national sport of the *coléa de toros*—in English, bull-tailing—for which some two or three hundred rancheros were assembled from the neighbouring plantations.] **1932** *Sat. Eve. Post* 27 Feb 63/3 **CA**, I teach you the *colliar*. **1932** Bentley *Spanish Terms* 126, *Colear* or *coleo* English modification *colliar* . . "To tail" an animal; the act of "tailing." This may consist of merely grasping a creature's tail and holding it or twisting it to obtain action, or throwing the animal by force applied to the tail.

coleramorbus See **cholera morbus**

cole root n
A **colicroot 2** (here: *Aletris farinosa*).
   1892 (1974) Millspaugh *Amer. Med. Plants* 172/1, *Aletris farinosa* . . . Com[mon] Names . . . Cole Root, Crow Corn [etc.]. **1959** Carleton *Index Herb. Plants* 29, Cole-root: Aletris farinosa.

colic ball n
=**oilnut 2**.
   1975 Hamel–Chiltoskey *Cherokee Plants* 27 **NC**, Buffalo nut, colic ball, oilnut . . . Chew nut to make vomit for colic.

colicker n
An animal esp subject to colic.
   1967 Green *Horse Tradin'* 56 **swTX**, He also told me that this mule had been in the barn before and was a chronic "colicker" and could not eat grain.

colicroot n [Because formerly used in the treatment of colic]
1 =**butterfly weed 1**.
   1833 Eaton *Botany* 33, *Asclepias tuberosa*, butterfly-weed, colic-root, pleurisy-root, white root . . . Cathartic, diaphoretic, expectorant. **1892** (1974) Millspaugh *Amer. Med. Plants* 135/1, *Asclepias tuberosa* . . . Com[mon] Names . . . Colic Root. *Ibid* 135/4, The provings, however, point to it as a valuable remedy in . . colic, diarrhoea, dry coughs [etc].
2 A perennial liliaceous plant of the genus *Aletris* with a basal rosette of wide grass-like leaves and small white or yellow flowers in a spikelike raceme, native to the eastern half of the US. Also called **star grass** For other names of the most widely distributed species, *Aletris farinosa,* see **ague grass, agueweed 3, aloeroot, backache root 2, bear grass 2c, betty grass, bitter grass, blackroot 3, blasting root, blazing star 1, cole root, crow corn, devil's bit, false aloe, false stargrass, false unicorn root, huskwood, huskwort, miller's maid, rheumatism root, starwort, true unicornroot, unicorn, unicorn plant, unicorn root, unicorn's horn**
   1837 Darlington *Flora Cestrica* 218, *A[letris] farinosa* . . . Star Grass. Colic root . . . The *root* of this is bitter; and has been used as a remedy for Intermittents. **1861** Wood *Class-Book* 697, *Aletris* . . . Star-grass. Colic-root. **1901** Lounsberry *S. Wild Flowers* 54, Yellow Colic-Root . . . *Aletris aurea* . . . A. *farinosa,* colic-root, star-grass, is a more widely distributed and better known plant than the already mentioned one. In the south also a form with golden yellow flowers . . has been recently described . . as *Aletris lutea*. **1936** IL Nat. Hist. Surv. *Wildflowers* 62, *Aletris farinosa* . . . The Colicroot is a shy inhabitant of out of the way places, and . . . occurs locally from Maine to Minnesota and south to Florida and Arkansas. **1976** Bruce *How to Grow Wildflowers* 167, So I went back and found my first Star-grass or Colic-root, *Aletris farinosa*.

3 also sp *cholic root*: A **wild yam** (here: *Dioscorea villosa*).

1873 in 1976 Miller *Shaker Herbs* 153, Cholic Root. *Dioscorea villosa*. Colic Root. Rheumatism Root. Used in biliary colic. **1894** *Jrl. Amer. Folkl.* 7.101, *Dioscorea villosa* . . colic-root, West Va. **1936** Winter *Plants NE* 14, Wild Yam-root. Colic-root. Common in moist thickets throughout the region. **1974** (1977) Coon *Useful Plants* 128, Colic root . . . is variably recommended to be used for the nausea of pregnant women, for flatulence, for various intestinal disorders and even for hiccough.

4 =**blazing star 3,** esp *Liatris spicata* and *L. squarrosa*.

1873 in 1976 Miller *Shaker Herbs* 233, *Liatris spicata* . . . Colic Root. **1900** Lyons *Plant Names* 212, *L. spicata* . . . Colic-root . . . *L. squarrosa* . . . Colic-root. **1931** Clute *Common Plants* 124, In addition to other plants mentioned . . may be included the various colic-roots, especially *Dioscorea villosa* . . and species of Liatris.

5 A **wild ginger 1** (here: *Asarum canadense*).

1894 *Jrl. Amer. Folkl.* 7.97, *Asarum canadense* . . coltsfoot, N.Y. colic-root, West Va. **1901** Mohr *Plant Life AL* 481, Colic Root. Alleghenian and Carolinian areas. Virginia along the mountains to North Carolina, Georgia, and eastern Tennessee. **1931** Clute *Common Plants* 124, In addition to other plants mentioned, of undoubted medicinal value, may be included the various colic-roots, especially . . *Asarum Canadense*. **1971** Krochmal *Appalachia Med. Plants* 66.

6 A **blazing star 2** (here: *Chamaelirium luteum*).

1892 (1974) Millspaugh *Amer. Med. Plants* 177, *Chamaelirium luteum* . . . Com[mon] Names . . . Starwort, Colic Root.

7 =**spreading dogbane.**

1900 Lyons *Plant Names* 40, *A[pocynum] androsaemifolium* . . . Colic-root, Honey-bloom. **1974** (1977) Coon *Useful Plants* 61, Colicroot . . . As with so many plants used medicinally, it should be remembered that overuse makes it dangerous.

8 also *colicwort*: **Parsley piert** *(Alchemilla arvensis)*.

1900 Lyons *Plant Names* 21, *A. arvensis* . . . Colicwort. **1940** Clute *Amer. Plant Names* 250, Colic-root.

‡colic seed n

1968 *DARE* (Qu. I25, *Names or nicknames for cucumbers*) Inf **NY**113, Colic seeds.

colicweed n [Because formerly used in the treatment of colic]

1 =**yellow corydalis.**

1821 in 1832 MA Hist. Soc. *Coll.* 2d ser 9.149, Plants, which are indigenous in the township of Middlebury, [Vt., include] . . *Corydalis . . glauca*, Colic-weed. **1900** Lyons *Plant Names* 79, *C. flavulum* . . . Pale Corydalis. Colic-weed. **1948** Stevens *KS Wild Flowers* 119, *Corydalis flavula* . . . In some localities the plant is called colicweed, indicating that a decoction of it has been used to relieve abdominal pain. **1959** Carleton *Index Herb. Plants* 29.

2 Either of two similar plants:

a =**Dutchman's breeches 1.**

1822 Eaton *Botany* 253, *Corydalis . . . cucullaria* . . colic weed. **1876** Hobbs *Bot. Hdbk.* 25. **1900** Lyons *Plant Names* 63, Dicentra cucullaria . . . Colic-weed. **1931** Clute *Common Plants* 124, In addition to other plants mentioned, of undoubted medicinal value, may be included . . the colic-weed *(Dicentra cucullaria)*.

b =**squirrel corn 1.**

1900 Lyons *Plant Names* 62, Dicentra Canadensis . . . Colic-weed. **1911** *Century Dict. Suppl.*, Colic-weed . . . The squirrel-corn, *Bikukulla Canadensis;* also, less frequently, the dutchman's-breeches, *B. Cucullaria,* and species of *Capnoides* [=*Corydalis*].

3 also *climbing colicweed*: =**mountain fringe 1.**

1822 Eaton *Botany* 253, [*Adlumia] fungosa* . . climbing colic weed. **1840** MA Zool. & Bot. Surv. *Herb. Plants & Quadrupeds* 40, Climbing Colic Weed; has already been introduced from our woods into the gardens and yards. **1959** Carleton *Index Herb. Plants* 29, Colic-weed: Adlumia fungosa.

colicwort See **colicroot 8**

colima n esp **TX**

A **prickly ash 1** (here: *Zanthoxylum fagara*).

1892 *DN* 1.189 **TX**, *Colíma:* a small tree or shrub, prickly ash *(Xanthoxylum pterola)* . . . Origin unknown. **1902** (1968) Clapin *Americanisms* 127, *Colima,* co-leé-mah (Sp.). In Texas, a species of dwarf prickly ash (Xanthoxylum pterola). **1941** *Torreya* 41.49 **TX**, *Xanthoxylum fagara* . . Colima, Texas. **1967** *DARE* (Qu. T16, *What kinds of trees are*

"special" around here?) Inf **TX**22, Colima. **1970** Correll *Plants TX* 911, *Zanthoxylum Fagara* . . Colima.

colishé n Also sp *colishay*

The gray fox *(Urocyon cinereoargenteus).*

1928 Anthony *N. Amer. Mammals* 143, *Names.*—Gray Fox; Colishé; Tree Fox. **1930** Shoemaker *1300 Words* 13 c**PA Mts** (as of c1900), Colishay—The grey fox.

coll See **call** n[2]

collar n

A brow or ring of land among higher peaks.

1888 (1958) Wister *Out West* 74, We did not get to any peak but up to a collar . . over which we could look into a wild country below.

collar v

1 To get, obtain. [*collar* to seize] *among Blacks*

1942 *Amer. Mercury* 55.85 **Harlem NYC,** The longer you slept, the less you had to eat. But you can't collar nods all day. No matter how long you stay in bed, and how quiet you keep, sooner or later that big gut is going to reach over and grab that little one and start to gnaw . . . You got to get out on the beat and collar yourself a hot. *Ibid* 94, Collar a nod—sleep. *Collar a hot*—eat a meal. **1946** (1972) Mezzrow *Really Blues* 331, *Collar a nod:* get some sleep.

2 To understand, comprehend something. *among Blacks*

1946 (1972) Mezzrow *Really Blues* 331, Collar: understand, get hold of. *Ibid,* Collar all jive: understand all the subtleties. **1958** Hughes–Bontemps *Negro Folkl.* 482, Collar all jive: To understand everything. "Hipsters collar all jive." **1970** Major *Afro–Amer. Slang* 39, *Collar the jive:* (1930's–40's) to grasp what is happening in a situation.

3 To girdle, to ring a tree.

1954 Harder *Coll.* cw**TN**, Collar—To cut a circle of bark from a tree in order to kill it. c**1960** Wilson *Coll.* cs**KY**, Collar . . . To remove a strip of bark from around a tree to deaden the tree.

collar and elbow See **collar and shoulder**

collar and hames n [*collar, hames* parts of a draft harness] **West** *joc*

A stiff collar and necktie.

1961 Adams *Old-Time Cowhand* 78, There's nothin' a cowhand could wear that'd be as useless as a city man's stiff collar and necktie, which he called a "collar and hames." **1966** *DARE* (Qu. W38, *When a man dresses himself up in his best clothes, you say he's* _____) Inf **SD**8, Got his collar and hames on.

collar and shoulder adj phr Also *collar and elbow*

Of an eating establishment or manner of serving food: family style, informal; crowded.

1926 *AmSp* 1.651 [Hobo argot], *Collar and shoulder style*—where everything is placed on the table and one helps himself. **1930** Irwin *Amer. Tramp* 53, *Collar and shoulder style.*—The system adopted at many boarding-houses and construction camps, where the food is placed on the table in front of the boarders, not served to them individually, and where each man serves himself by a fast dive at the platter. **1945** Hubbard *Railroad Ave.* 338, Collar and elbow joint—Boardinghouse. (There isn't too much room at dinner table). **1968** Adams *Western Words* 71, Collar-and-shoulder style—The help-yourself system of food serving used in some lumber camps and loggers' boardinghouses; similar to cafeteria style.

collar and tie adj phr

White-collar.

1927 *AmSp* 3.24 e**TX**, The office men, store clerks etc., are said to hold "collar and tie" jobs. **1968** Adams *Western Words* 71, Collar-and-tie men—A logger's term for the company office men, store clerks, etc.

collard n, freq attrib; usu used in pl when not attrib Pronc-sp *colly* **chiefly Sth, S Midl** See Map

Kale.

1797 Imlay *Western Terr.* 477 **KY**, He likewise makes a small garden for peas, beans, collards, and other vegetables. **1854** Simms *Southward Ho* 320 **AL**, His cabbage invariably turns out a collard. **1869** *Overland Mth.* 3.130, 'Collard' (probably corrupted from *colewort*) is the kind of cabbage found everywhere in the South, whose leaves, not heads, furnish the greens for the inevitable dish of bacon and greens. **1908** *DN* 3.300 e**AL**, w**GA**, Collard greens . . Collards. "I'm a living monument to collard greens, corn liquor, and good nature." *Country newspaper.*

1934 Carmer *Stars Fell on AL* 4, At dinner, I learned soon enough that I did not like corn bread . . nor could I eat okra, or collards. **1960** (1962) Lee *Mockingbird* 56 **AL**, "Don't make a sound," he whispered. "Don't get in a row of collards whatever you do, they'll wake the dead." **1965–70** *DARE* (Qu. I28b, . . *Greens . . cooked*) 156 Infs, **Sth**, Collard(s); 66 Infs, **chiefly Sth, S Midl**, Collard greens; **MD**44, Georgia collards; **WV**3, Colly greens; (Qu. I28a, . . *"Greens" . . eaten raw*) 20 Infs, **Sth**, Collards; 10 Infs, **Sth**, Collard greens; (Qu. H54, *Dishes . . with greens;* total Infs questioned, 75) 18 Infs, **Sth**, Collards; 10 Infs, **Sth**, Collard greens; **AR**38, Collards greens; (Qu. I4, . . *Vegetables . . less commonly grown around here*) 9 Infs, **chiefly Sth**, Collard(s); **IL**76, Collard greens; (Qu. L34, . . *Most important crops*) Infs **SC**63, **NC**60, 80, Collard(s); (Qu. H53) Inf **FL**8, Stewed tomatoes and collards; (Qu. BB34b) Inf **FL**19, Collards; (Qu. R26, . . *Small greenish lice that come on plants*) Inf **GA**9, Collard bugs; **NC**49, Collard worm; (Qu. B3) Inf **TX**33, Hot as a pot of collards.

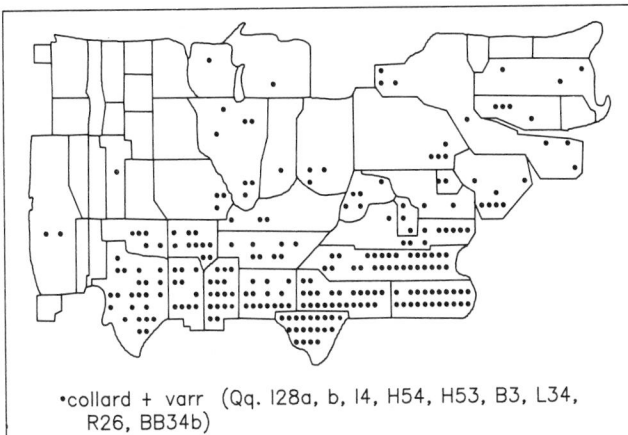

•collard + varr (Qq. I28a, b, I4, H54, H53, B3, L34, R26, BB34b)

collar, fill one's v phr [*collar* part of a draft harness]
To perform adequately.
  1898 Westcott *Harum* 195 **cNY**, I seen right off that you was goin' to fill your collar, fur's the work was concerned.

collar, get in the v phr Also *be in the collar* [*collar* part of a draft harness]
To start working; to work hard.
  1967–68 *DARE* (Qu. A22, . . *"She had only ten minutes to clean the room, but she _____."*) Inf **CA**90, Got in the collar, buddy; (Qu. Y6, . . *"He's a whole week late. I'm going to _____."*) Inf **CO**4, Tell him to get in the collar; (Qu. KK29, *To start working very hard: . . "now he's really _____."*) Inf **OR**3, In the collar.

collar, go up against the v phr [*collar* part of a draft harness]
To work hard, to submit to hardship or inconvenience.
  1978 *DARE* File **KS**, *To go up against the collar* was one of my grandmother's customary expressions. She was born in 1886 and grew up on a farm in southwestern Kansas among Irish immigrants. Some typical examples of the usage: "Well, it means I'll just have to go up against the collar if I'm going to have that garden." "He wasn't willing to go up against the collar to get the job, so he lost his chance."

collarmoggis See **cholera morbus**

collar, under one's adv
In secrecy, "up one's sleeve."
  1967–69 *DARE* (Qu. JJ19, *If somebody has dishonest intentions, or is up to no good . ., "I think he's got _____."*) Inf **IL**9, Something under his collar; (Qu. JJ44, *Expressions about someone who can be trusted to keep a secret*) Inf **GA**77, [He'll] keep that under his collar.

‡collash v [Blend of *collide* + *clash*]
  1908 *DN* 3.300 **eAL, wGA**, *Collash* . . . To clash, collide: a combination word.

collasp v [Metath of *collapse*]
To collapse.
  1916 *DN* 4.273 **NE**, *Collasp.* Occasional for collapse. **1970** *DARE* (Qu. BB14, . . *"Just as she came to the door she _____."*) Inf **MS**88, Collasped.

collateral n **NEng** Cf **calamity**
A clutter of personal belongings; odds and ends of trash.

1914 *DN* 4.70 **ME, NH**, *Collat'ral* . . Money, property, things in one's way. "Clear this darn collat'ral out o' here!" **1941** *LANE* Map 346, The field workers asked for names applied to old, broken, useless things . . such as accumulate in the house or yard and are eventually thrown away. [In northern and central New England, *collateral* was a common response.] **1981–82** *DARE* File **MA** (as of 1953), *Collateral.* A miscellaneous clutter of personal belongings—sometimes used jocularly to refer to valuable things; usually equals the sort of things one would find in the attic; **Cape Cod MA**, The word "collateral" is very familiar to me, meaning possessions that have been allowed to accumulate in some place not their usual place for keeping. "Come on, let's get all this collateral out of here, and put away." This is your word *clutter.*

collation n Also sp *colation* *old-fash*
Refreshments served to one's guests or at a meeting or ceremony.
  1861 Holmes *Venner* 1.167 **wMA**, There's meat and cakes and pies and pickles enough on that table to spread a hahnsome côlation. **1916** Lincoln *Mary-'Gusta* 408 **MA**, Her uncles had tried to remonstrate with her, telling her there were plenty of others to arrange the flowers and attend to what the local newspaper would, in its account of the affair, be sure to call the "collation." **1941** FWP *Guide LA* 274, Afternoon coffee, served with ceremony about 3 o'clock, is still called a *collation.* **1981** *NY Times* (NY) 9 Aug 8 **RI**, My father, a product of Fall River, Mass., would say as I came in from an evening visiting friends, "Did they serve a collation?" As it happens I am punctilious about offering a collation to guests. But very few of them, unless they are at least 80, know it.

collector highway n Cf **feeder**
  1969 *DARE* (Qu. N29, . . *A less important road running back from a main road*) Inf **CA**119, Collector highway—very common word here. A road that collects traffic and feeds it on to a main road.

college n Usu |'kɑlɪj|, rarely |'kɑlɪč| Eye-dial spp *colli(d)ge*
A Forms.
  1843 (1916) Hall *New Purchase* 324 **IN**, It was a right smart chance better to have no collidge no how. *Ibid* 172, This apostul of ourn what spoke the text, never rubbed his back agin a collige, nor toted about no sheepskins. **c1960** *Wilson Coll.* **csKY**, *College,* sometimes ['kɑlɪtʃ].
B Senses.
1 pl: See quot.
  1926 *DN* 5.385 **ME**, *Colleges* . . . College buildings in a collective sense. "Take John to see the colleges." Common.
2 A prison or jail. *joc*
  1859 Matsell *Vocabulum* 20, *College.* A state prison. **1931** *AmSp* 7.105 [Underworld argot], A penitentiary. "He was just released from college." **1970** *DARE* (Qu. V11, . . *Joking names . . for a county or city jail*) Infs **NY**237, 249, College. [Both Infs Black]
3 A privy. **NEng** *euphem*
  1892 *DN* 1.210 **seMA**, *College:* an outhouse. **1931–33** *LANE Worksheets* **csCT**, College ['kɑlɪj] . . outhouse; at camp we called it the college. **1943** *LANE* Map 537, 12 infs, **scattered in NEng**, College, the college [*joc euphem for privy*].

college-called adj
Qualified by virtue of one's education.
  1977 Dillard *Lexicon* 57 [Black], Even an erring preacher can still be a *God-sent man* . . . It is considered worse if he is not really a *God-called preacher* but is only *church-called* or *college-called.*

college football See **football 1**

college hill n
A section of a town, esp where well-off people live.
  1965–70 *DARE* (Qu. C35, *Nicknames for the different parts of your town or city*) Infs **AR**47, **PA**131, 164, **WA**3, College hill; (Qu. II24 . . *The part of a town where the well-off people live*) Inf **OH**13, College hill; (Qu. II25, . . *The part of a town where . . special groups . . live*) Inf **MO**10, College hill; **PA**133, College hill—up by the college, a rich section.

college ice n **NEng** *somewhat old-fash*
An ice-cream sundae.
  1913 *DN* 4.39, *Sundae,* a name now in established usage for college ices. **1942** Hale *Prodigal Women* 34 **MA** (as of 1905–40), They spent every cent of money they could beg, on college ices. **1957** Rose *Block Is.* 176 **sRI** (as of early 1900s), Only ten cents for an ice cream soda, fifteen for a college ice, a cabinet or a banana split. **1967** *DARE* (QR p46) Inf **MA**50, College ice. **c1970** *DARE* File **csMA**, *College ice,* a sundae. **1980** *DARE* File **cnMA** (as of c1915), By the time I was in high school we

had sundaes, but the first ice cream with "sauce" on it that I ever had in a drug store was a college ice.

‡college yoke n

1970 DARE (Qu. FF5b, *More recent dance steps*) Inf **MO**30, College yoke. [Black Inf]

colleyflower See **cauliflower**

colliar See **colear**

collidge See **college A**

collier n[1] Also *collier-aphis*
=**bean aphid.**

1849 U.S. Patent Office *Annual Rept.: Ag.* 339, Another species, which, from their sooty color, are called the black-flies, black dolphins, or colliers. **1911** *Century Dict., Dolphin-fly* . . . Also called, from its black color, the *collier-aphis.*

collier n[2] [Prob Fr *collier* collar, in allusion to its ringed neck]
=**Wilson's plover.**

1917 DN 4.424 **LA**, *Collier.* The Wilson plover (Ochthodromus wilsonius).

collige See **college A**

collimancoe See **calamanco**

collision n

1 A children's game: see quot. Cf **fruit basket upset**

1968 DARE (Qu. EE2, *Games that have one extra player—when a signal is given the players change places, and the extra one tries to get a place*) Inf **IL**27, Collision—just like fruit basket except you use car names instead of fruits.

‡2 A kind of haircut.

1970 DARE (Qu. X5, . . *Names* . . *for* . . *men's haircuts*) Inf **MO**23, Collision—hair is lined all around.

collision, be in v phr

1945 Colcord *Sea Language* 56 **ME, Cape Cod, Long Island,** *Collision, to be in*—Ships do not collide; they are "in collision with" each other . . . This usage is followed alongshore, in regard to vehicles, persons, etc.

collogue v Also *collugue* [Origin uncert, but perh from Fr *colloque* conference, consultation] *old-fash*

1 To intrigue, to conspire. **chiefly S Midl**

1650 in 1936 DN 6.519 **Providence RI,** Then I tould him yt áll hee said did not moue mee seing wt trim hee was in. / hee then replied saying warner how thou Cologest with mee, ye wch I confesse stired mee more then all yt hee said before. **1899** (1912) Green *VA Folk-Speech* 121, *Collogue* . . . To join together, in a bad sense, in league or conversation. "They were *colloguing* together for sometime." **1903** DN 2.309 **seMO,** *Collogue* . . . To conspire. "I'm satisfied they're colloguing to beat me out of my place." **1907** DN 3.229 **nwAR, seMO. 1908** DN 3.300 **eAL, wGA,** *Collogue* . . . To collude. **1936** DN 6.519, *Collogue* . . . The word is now obsolete, or . . dialectal.

2 To be on friendly terms (with someone).

1908 DN 3.300 **eAL, wGA,** *Collogue* . . . to be on intimate terms with. **1932** Stribling *Store* 524 **AL,** "He was crazy to begin with," said Love. "Look at the way he collugues with the niggers, calling 'em Mister and Misses."

3 To confer, consult, chat with.

1935 Davis *Honey* 2 **OR,** [They] had collogued with the same set of neighbors over the same line-up of news and business all their lives long.

collote See **coyote** n **A**

collugue See **collogue**

colly n See **collard**

colly v [Perh from **collar** v **2,** but cf quot 1960] *esp among Blacks*

To understand; see quot 1960.

1941 AmSp 16.245 [Underworld argot], To *Colly.* To understand. 'There's fuzz in the back. Don't you colly?' **1960** Wentworth–Flexner *Slang* 115, *Colly* . . To understand, to comprehend. *Primarily Negro use, used in the rural areas of the South as much as in Harlem and in jive circles; it seems to predate "collar."* **1970** Major *Afro–Amer. Slang* 39, *Colly:* to comprehend, to understand.

colly-fox v [Scots *collie-fox* to idle about]

1943 LANE Map 568, 1 inf, **seNH,** *If a laborer or hired man is idle when he should be at work, he is said to be* . . . ['kɒˑlɪ̆ˌfɒˑksɪn], *of a man who is 'off doing things he has no business to do, making mischief.'*

colly marbles, colly mobbles, colly morbus See **cholera morbus**

colly-over n, exclam Also sp *callie-over, coalie-over*
=**Antony-over.**

1895 DN 1.386 **ceMA,** *Colly over* = *haily over.* **1967–70** DARE (Qu. EE22, *What do you call the game in which they throw a ball over a building* . . *to a player on the other side?*) Inf **PA**7, Callie-over; **PA**242, Coalie [koli]-over; (Qu. EE23a, *In the game of Andy-over* . . *what do you call out when you throw the ball?*) Inf **PA**7, Callie-over; **PA**242, Coalie-over.

collyrobin n [Folk-etym]

Kohlrabi.

1968 DARE (Qu. I4, . . *Vegetables* . . *less commonly grown around here*) Inf **OH**45, Collyrobins—calaraba, like a turnip.

colly up n

1895 DN 1.386 **ceMA,** "*Colly up,*" same or similar game [as **colly-over**] in which the ball is thrown against the side of the building, or on the sloping roof, and caught on return.

collywobbles n Also sp *collywabbles* [Prob folk-etym for **cholera morbus,** perh infl by *colic* and *wobble*] Cf **galleywobbles, gonnywobbles**

1 Depression or nervousness; some imaginary or undefined illness; malaise.

1834 *Life Andrew Jackson* 91, There was a general depression of spirits; the people seem'd to have taken the collywabbles, and every one was afear'd to speak his mind to his neighbor. **1942** *Sat. Eve. Post* 10 Oct 103/2 **Sth,** It's a wonder Larry don't get the collywobbles, playin' around Mud Lake after varmints. **1950** WELS (*Imaginary diseases*) 4 Infs, **WI,** Collywobbles. **1965–70** DARE (Qu. BB28, . . *Imaginary diseases*) 33 Infs, **esp Nth and West,** Collywobbles; (Qu. BB34a, *To feel depressed or in a gloomy mood: "He has the _____ today."*) Infs **CA**36, 115, **CT**13, Collywobbles; (Qu. GG13b, *When something keeps bothering a person and makes him nervous* . . *"It gives me the _____."*) Infs **HI**1, **NJ**16, Collywobbles; (Qu. BB5, *A general feeling of discomfort or illness*) Inf **CT**27, Collywobbles; (Qu. BB39, *When you don't feel just right, though not actually sick*) Inf **CA**59, Have the collywobbles.

2 An upset stomach, stomachache, or diarrhea.

1942 in 1944 ADD **MA,** [The effects of smoking] may be a dizzy feeling, a sensation of nausea, or just a plain case of the 'colly-wobbles.' **1950** WELS Suppl. **ceWI,** Colly-wobbles—a term for "tummy aches" peculiar to the eating of green apples; **seWI,** Collywobbles is a feeling, upset stomach, etc. **1967–70** DARE (Qu. BB19, *Joking name for looseness of the bowels*) Inf **CA**15, Collywobbles; **OH**93, When a person has the runs he has collywobbles. **1967** DARE FW Addit **nIL,** Collywobbles: upset stomach (e.g., from eating green apples); **neTN,** Collywobbles ['kɑlɪˌwɑblz]—a stomachache (joking).

3 By ext: menstruation.

1969 DARE (Qu. AA27, . . *Other names* . . *for* . . *menstruation*) Inf **CT**27, Collywobbles.

4 See quot. Cf **DS** E20

1950 WELS Suppl. **ceWI,** Collywobbles—small rolls of dust on the floor.

colonche n Also sp *calinche* [MexSpan] **SW**

A fermented drink made from the fruit of the tuna plant.

1846 (1848) Bryant *What I Saw in CA* 376, A juicy fruit is produced by the prickly-pear, named *tuna,* from which a beverage is sometimes made called *calinche.* It has a pleasant flavor, as has also the fruit, which, when ripe, is blood red. **1895** *Jrl. Amer. Folkl.* 8.58 **TX,** The pink *colonche* or cider of the tuna; . . is an exceptionally good drink. **1911** Wooton *Cacti in N.M.* 25 (DA), Colonche (Co-lone-chay) is a fermented drink made from these fruits [i.e., tunas].

colonel n Pronc-spp *cuhn'l, cunnle, kunnel;* eye-dial *kurnal, kurnel*

A Forms.

1840 Haliburton *Clockmaker* (3d ser) 88 **NEng,** He rose to be a gineral arterwards, but then he was only a kurnel. **1848** Lowell *Biglow* 143 **'Upcountry' MA** [Glossary], *Cunnle,* a colonel. **1892** Smith *Day at*

Laguerre's 173, A lank, chin-bearded Virginian . . straightened himself out and came forward . . . "I'm Kurnal Jarvis, zur." **1940** *Sat. Eve. Post* 24 Feb 24/2 **csTX** [Black], "Mawnin', Cuhn'l Bliss." **1941** Warfel–Orians *Local-Color Stories* 669 **NC** (as of 1899), 'Well,' sez de kunnel 'you kin hab de 'oman.'

B Senses.

1 Used as an unofficial title of respect, sometimes applied joc or ironically. **chiefly Sth, S Midl**

1744 (1907) Hamilton *Itinerarium* 94 **Albany NY**, Had it been a rattlesnake I should have been entitled to a colonel's commision, for it is a common saying here that a man has no title to that dignity until he has killed a rattlesnake. **1896** Harris *Sister Jane* 11 **GA**, His title of colonel . . was purely a title of respect, a mark of the esteem in which he was held by his friends and neighbors, a tribute to his moral and business qualities. **1899** (1912) Green *VA Folk-Speech* 121, *Colonel* . . . It does not seem that the title of *Colonel* before the Revolutionary war was used as an honorary or derisive title . . . So, Virginians seem to have had a right to titles that have since fallen into contempt, as being used or claimed by men who have no right to them whatever. **1903** *DN* 2.309 **seMO**, *Colonel* . . . A title very commonly bestowed on men of any prominence without reference to military service, especially on country lawyers. **1907** *DN* 3.229 **nwAR, swMO**. **1914** *DN* 4.104 **KS**, *Colonel* . . . Applied to auctioneers. **1926** *DN* 5.398 **swMO, nwAR**, *Colonel* . . . This title is conferred upon prominent mountain men without any reference to military service. Nearly every auctioneer is an honorary colonel, as are many country lawyers and bankers. **1950** *WELS (Familiar or friendly names given to elderly people not related to you)* 3 Infs, **WI**, Colonel. **1969** *DARE* (Qu. V10b, . . *Joking names for a marshall*) Inf **GA**77, Colonel of the town; (Qu. HH17, . . *"He'd like to be the _____."*) Inf **GA**77, Colonel of the town; (Qu. II23, *Joking names for . . the best society*) Inf **VT**12, Colonel so-and-so.

2 A native or resident of Kentucky.

1936 (1947) Mencken *Amer. Lang.* (4th ed) 552, In other cases separate nicknames have arisen, e.g., *Jayhawks* (Kansas), *Colonels* (Kentucky). **1949** *AmSp* 24.28, Today the most popular nickname for Kentuckians seems to be Colonels.

colony house n Also *colony* **chiefly Nth, esp NEast**

A kind of chicken coop.

1950 *WELS (Building for chickens)* 1 Inf, **cwWI**, Colony (for smaller groups); 1 Inf, **csWI**, Colony house. **1967–69** *DARE* (Qu. M16, *The small shelter for a hen that can be moved about from place to place*) Infs **CT**14, **NH**3, **NY**75, 187, **PA**29, Colony house. **1982** *DARE* File **Madison WI**, According to a University of Wisconsin poultry scientist, a colony house is an old-fashioned chicken coop, usually small (12′ x 12′), sometimes with a run in front so the chickens can scratch in the dirt. The term originated in the Northeast, but came to be used throughout the U.S.

color n Formerly sp *colour*

1 Gold; a particle of gold. **West**

1851 (1922) Clappe *Shirley Letters* 92 **CA**, There is a deep pit in front of our cabin, and another at the side of it, though they are not worked as, when "prospected," they did not "yield the color." **1858** in 1942 *CA Folkl. Qrly.* 1.272, [Song:] If I fail in my attempt to bring / A 'decent color' as I onward sing, / Bid me 'dry up,' I'll bear deserved blame / And any miner then may 'jump my claim.' **1873** Miller *Modocs* 43 **nCA**, "Are you really dead-broke?" "Skinned clean down to the bed-rock. Haven't got the colour." **1905** (1909) Beach *Pardners* 19 **AK**, We cross-cut in three places, and never raised a colour, but we kept gophering around till March, in hopes. **1939** *FWP Guide MT* 360, "You know well enough if you pike me down and run me through a sluice, you couldn't get a color," I said. **1941** *FWP Guide WY* 8, Every season hundreds of old and young prospectors strike out for the hills, with shovels and grub stakes, to pan the streams for "colors." *Ibid* 222, The valley here was settled shortly after 1859 by men who had become discouraged in their search for "color." **1968** *DARE* (Qu. CC11, *When somebody has had a lot of good luck, you say he _____*) Inf **AK**1, Struck good colors.

2 In tobacco farming: the hue and brilliance of the leaf.

1940 *AmSp* 15.134, *Color.* A desirable quality in tobacco. Has a technical meaning. **1966** *PADS* 45.10 **cnKY**, *Color* . . . A term referring to the hue and brilliance of tobacco leaf . . . "The lugs should have a light color." **1967** Key *Tobacco Vocab.* 50 **NC**, The amount of body in the tobacco will govern the color; **CT**, Light blond colors are in great demand.

3 A crayon.

1965 *DARE* File **swPA** (as of c1920), Our teacher would say, "Everyone get out your colors and color the picture." **1969** *DARE* FW Addit **csPA**, *Colors* ['kɛlərz] meaning crayons. **1981** *DARE* File **swCA**, As far back as memory serves, I have always called crayons *colors*. This usage is perhaps an abbreviation of *color crayon*.

color v

1967 Key *Tobacco Vocab.* **GA**, *Color:* of tobacco leaf: to turn yellow as it begins to cure. "Hang it up in the barn and let it color."

Colorado beetle See **Colorado potato beetle**

Colorado blue (spruce) See **Colorado spruce**

Colorado bluestem See **bluestem 2**

Colorado bottom grass See **Colorado grass**

Colorado fir n Also *Colorado white fir*
=**white fir.**

1897 Sudworth *Arborescent Flora* 55, *Abies concolor* . . . Common names [include] . . Colorado White Fir. **1908** Britton *N. Amer. Trees* 78, This fir [*Abies concolor*], also called . . Colorado white fir, occurs from the mountains of Oregon . . to . . northern Mexico. **1960** Vines *Trees SW* 5, It [*Abies concolor*] also has the vernacular names of . . Colorado Fir. **1967** *DARE* (Qu. T5, . . *Kinds of evergreens*) Inf **KS**3, Colorado fir. **1979** Little *Checklist U.S. Trees* 34, *Abies concolor* . . Colorado fir.

Colorado grass n Also *Colorado bottom grass* [See quots 1889, 1939]
=**Texas millet.**

1884 Vasey *Ag. Grasses* 36, It has been called . . in some parts . . Colorado bottom grass. **1889** Vasey *Ag. Grasses* 25, *Panicum Texanum* (Texas millet) . . . It is frequently called Colorado grass, from its abundance along the Colorado River in the States. **1939** Tharp *Vegetation TX* 44, *Colorado grass (Panicum texanum);* a coarse weedy grass abundant in the sandy fields of the valley of the Colorado River, is of some considerable value both for fall grazing and for hay. **1967** *DARE* (Qu. L9a, . . *Grass . . grown for hay*) Inf **TX**40, Colorado grass.

Colorado hemp See **Colorado River hemp**

Colorado mockingbird n joc Also called **Arizona nightingale, Rocky Mountain canary**

1968 Adams *Western Words* 71, *Colorado mockingbird*—A burro.

Colorado potato beetle n Also *Colorado beetle*

A yellow, black-striped, chrysomelid beetle (*Leptinotarsa decemlineata*).

1868 MI State Bd. Ag. *Annual Rept.* 7.181, A plant . . of the night-shade family . . was well covered with the Colorado beetle and its slugs. **1948** *Chicago Tribune* (IL) 15 Feb sec 1 30/6, An import license was refused because of the danger of Colorado beetle infestation. **1964** Borror–DeLong *Intro. Insects* 407, Before the introduction of the potato into the United States this species was confined to Colorado and neighboring states, . . and . . . is frequently called the "Colorado" potato beetle. **1966–69** *DARE* (Qu. R30, . . *Beetles . . known . . because of . . odor or color*) Infs **ME**12, **MA**68, **OH**4, Colorado beetle; **MA**30, 58, Colorado potato beetle.

Colorado River hemp n Also *Colorado hemp*

A tall annual legume (*Sesbania exaltata*) of the Southwestern and Gulf States which produces long tough fibers formerly used like hemp by the Indians. Also called **bequilla, coffee bean 2, coffeeweed 1a, indigo, siene bean, zacate**

1900 Lyons *Plant Names* 343, Colorado Hemp. One of several species which yield a strong fibre for cordage. **1925** Jepson *Manual Plants CA* 580, Colorado River Hemp . . . is a fiber plant producing white lustrous smooth and very strong filaments which are used by the Yuma Indians for nets and fish-lines. **1941** Jaeger *Wildflowers* 115 **Desert SW**, Colorado River hemp is gaining favor among orchardists as a cover crop. **1974** Munz *Flora S. CA* 470, *S[esbania] exaltata* . . . Colorado-River-Hemp . . . Frequent in overflow lands, along ditches, etc.

Colorado rook n

1949 Brown *Amer. Cooks* 229 **IA**, Restaurant menus camouflage crow as "Colorado Rook," or put it down playfully under the alias of "Jim Crow" or "Old Crow." But crow has come to stay and the U.S. Department of Agriculture publishes a booklet of recipes for cooking it.

Colorado spruce n Also *Colorado blue (spruce)*
=blue spruce.

1897 Sudworth *Arborescent Flora* 40, *Picea pungens* . . Common names [include] Colorado Blue Spruce (Colo.). **1933** *Colo. Agric. Coll. Bul.* 326-A II *(DA),* Since the chief purposes of tree distribution by the State Forester are for windbreaks, shelterbelts and groves, rather than for ornamentation, the Colorado Blue Spruce is no longer offered by him. **1965–70** *DARE* (Qu. T5, . . *Kinds of evergreens, other than pine*) Infs **IA**41, **MN**29, **MA**25, **OH**28, Colorado blue spruce; **KS**3, **MO**26, **OH**4, 82, Colorado spruce; **CO**9, Colorado blue; (Qu. T16, . . *Kinds of trees . . "special" around here*) Inf **CO**9, Colorado blue spruce.

Colorado turkey n **SW**

1 =wood ibis.

1858 Baird *Birds* 9.682, *Tantalus loculator,* Linn. *Wood Ibis* . . is said to be abundant on the Colorado river, especially about Fort Yuma, and to be there called Colorado turkey. **1917** (1923) *Birds Amer.* 1.179, *Mycteria americana*—Other names.—American Wood Stork; Colorado Turkey; Goard, Gourd, Head; Iron Head; Gannet. **1956** *AmSp* 31.182, With localities substituted for races, there are a good many bird titles of derisive import . . . Colorado turkey [is used for the] Great blue heron [in] Ariz. [and for the] Wood ibis [in] Ariz., Calif.

2 =great blue heron.

1956 [see **1** above].

Colorado white fir See **Colorado fir**

color-blind adj
Given to stealing.

1943 *AmSp* 18.164, *Color-blind.* One who is color-blind is an employee who cannot distinguish between his own money and that of the company. **1966** *DARE* (Qu. V3, . . *A thoroughly dishonest person*) Inf **FL**15, Color-blind—can't tell his money from somebody else's.

colored n Pronc-sp *cullud* [From absol use of *colored* adj]
chiefly Sth
A Black person; Black people.

1916 *Scribner's Mag.* March *(ADD),* Dese here culluds ain't like dem in Tidewater. **1922** Gonzales *Black Border* 295 **sSC, GA coasts** [Gullah glossary], *Cullud*—colored, colored people, the dark race. **1968** *DARE* FW Addit **sLA,** *Colored* means negroes (apparently abbr of "colored people"). "Colored don't come in here much." Young owner of a drive-in, Franklin, LA. "You'll hear the colored call it that." Cameron, LA. I do not recall this in New Orleans. **1969** *DARE* Tape **TN**34, The ratio of colored to white is about 60/40.

colored baby n *euphem*
=nigger baby.

1967 *DARE* (Qu. H82a, *Cheap candies sold especially for school children around here*) Inf **PA**2, Colored babies.

colored eggs n
A children's game: =colors.

1966 *DARE* File **nwWI,** *Colored eggs*—A children's game, not played with colored eggs at all. Each child received the name of a color. When the color is called (red egg, or yellow egg, etc.), the child had to run and avoid being tagged. **1968** *DARE* (Qu. EE33, *Other outdoor games*) Inf **PA**163, Colored eggs: each kid has a color; devil comes and asks for an egg, guesses the color and chases the egg; if the egg gets back to the mother it's safe.

colored eye n

1967 *DARE* (Qu. X20 . . *Other words . . for a black eye*) Inf **MN**10, Colored eye.

colored folks' time See **colored people's time**

colored fox n
=red fox.

1982 Elman *Hunter's Field Guide* 360, *Red Fox . . . Common & regional names: . .* colored fox.

colored marbles See **cholera morbus**

colored people's time n Also *colored folks' time,* abbr *C.P.T.*
Cf **Alaska time, Indian time, Jewish time**
See quot 1966.

1926 Van Vechten *Nigger Heaven* 285, *C.P.T.:* coloured people's time, i.e., late. **1966** *Western Folkl.* 25.38 (as of c1945), *Colored folks' time.* An hour or two later than the prescribed time. **1980** *DARE* File **nFL,** In

Tallahassee if a meeting started at 9 or 9:30 when it was scheduled to have started at 8, people talked about working on colored people's time. **1982** *Sat. Review* May–June 61, *Colored People's Time,* by Leslie Lee. The title is a phrase often abbreviated to "C.P.T." among black people; it means that they live by private clocks, not necessarily matched to white chronometry.

colors n Also called **colored eggs**
A children's guessing game that takes various forms: see quots.

1883 Newell *Games & Songs* 213, *Colors.* A row of children, on the door-steps of a house, or against a chamber wall. Opposite . . two girls . . one the good, the other the bad, angel. Every child selects a color . . . The "Good Angel" knocks . . names a color . . If this color is represented . . the angel takes the child . . When all the children are divided, a "tug of war" ensues . . . This form of the game is probably a recent translation from the German, by New York children. **1953** Brewster *Amer. Non-singing Games* 180 **MO,** *Colors*—Speaking characters in this game are the Angel, the Devil, and the Mother. The rest of the players are the latter's children . . the Mother assigns to each of the other players . . a color. The Angel then returns [and by formula guesses the various colors; the Devil does likewise] . . . As soon as all the other players have been taken, either by the Angel or by the Devil, there is a tug of war between the two groups. **1962** Carrell *Autobiog.* 22, We played [at a children's party] post office, spin the cover, spin the thimble, colors, etc. [Colors was] probably a game my grandmother from eastern Massachusetts taught us. "It" thought [sic] of a color and arms himself with a thimble filled with water. He passes down the line and each child guesses a color. After many false threats, he tosses the water in the face of the child who guesses the right color. **1969** *DARE* (Qu. EE33, *Other outdoor games*) Inf **NY**126, Colors: played on steps; you had to guess what color "it" was thinking of.

color-struck adj *among Blacks*
Conceited because of the light shade of one's skin; preferring light-skinned to dark-skinned people.

1934 Hurston *Jonah's Gourd Vine* 92, You so pretty and you ain't color-struck lak uh whole heap uh bright-skin people. **1963** *PADS* 40.4 **FL,** *Color-struck . .* vain, conceited, or egotistical because of the color of one's skin. **1976** *DARE* File **cLA,** She is color-struck. **1977** Smitherman *Talkin* 251, *Color struck,* adjective denoting one who prefers light-skinned blacks; also high-yellows "stuck" on themselves because of their color.

colory adj

1 Of tobacco: having a yellow or golden hue characteristic of good quality. [**color** n 2] Cf **bright** adj 1

1887 *Courier–Jrl.* (Louisville KY) 7 Feb 7/1, The differences, which are not more than one or two bids, include colory smokers. **1899** (1912) Green *VA Folk-Speech* 121, *Coloury . . .* Having a colour characteristic of good quality. "Fine *coloury* tobacco 21 cts. a pound." **1900** U.S. Dept. Ag. *Yearbook for 1899* 435 **MD, eOH,** These tobaccos are used exclusively for pipe smoking and cigarettes, the following grades being made by the packers: fine yellow, medium bright, good ordinary "colory," fine red. **1960** Heimann *Tobacco* 109, Sudden application of heat lightens the tobacco, a result first prompted by the market demand for yellow, "colory" plug wrappers. *Ibid* 149, There had always been a demand, more or less sporadic, for "colory" tobacco, that is a light, mild leaf of a yellow or golden hue and sweet aroma.

2 Of coffee: see quot.

1899 (1912) Green *VA Folk-Speech* 121, *Coloury . . .* Having a colour characteristic of good quality . . . "Coloury coffee," of a bright bluish tint.

colour See **color** n

colt n Also *colt over the fence* Cf **fence-corner, woods colt**

1968 *DARE* (Qu. Z11b . . *A child of unwed parents*) Inf **LA**46, Colt; **CA**65, Colt over the fence.

colt v [Perh by analogy with *calve*]
To foal.

1965–70 *DARE* (Qu. K45, *When a mare has had a young horse, you say she has just* _____) Infs **GA**17, **PA**187, 191, **TN**10, **TX**13, **WY**4, Colted; **MA**74, Colt.

colt over the fence See **colt** n

‡colt's eye n Cf **buck-eyed** adj[2], **horsey eyes**

1968 *DARE* (Qu. X26b, *If a person's eyes look different directions, looking outward, he's* _____) Inf **NH**14, If one eye looks at an object and the other looks away, it's colt's ['kols] eye.

coltsfoot n [From the shape of the leaf]

1 pronc-sp *coatsfoot*: A low perennial plant *(Tussilago farfara),* formerly used medicinally, which produces a single head of yellow flowers, later followed by rounded leaves. [*OED* 1522 →] Also called **British tobacco, bull's foot, clayweed, cleats, coughwort, cow's foot, foal foot, ginger root 1, horse hoof**

1784 in 1785 *Amer. Acad. Arts & Sci. Memoirs* 1.481, *Tussilago . . . Coltsfoot.* The leaves . . have been much used in coughs and consumptive complaints. **1795** Winterbotham *Amer. U.S.* 3.397, Among the native and uncultivated plants of New-England, the following have been employed for medicinal purposes: . . [399] Colt's foot, *Tussilago farfara.* **1840** MA Zool. & Bot. Surv. *Herb. Plants & Quadrupeds* 1.128, *T[ussilago] farfara.* Garden Colt's Foot . . . Expectorant; its leaves were smoked in ancient times as a cure for diseases of the lungs. **1874** *Shaker Med. Preparations* ceNY, *Coltsfoot herb,* Tussilago farfara. **1960** Hall *Smoky Mt. Folks* 34 **TN,** "When cattle eat colt's foot, they th'ow it up, and ivy (laurel) pizens them." **1969** *DARE* (Qu. S25) Inf **NY195,** Coatsfoot.

2 A **wild ginger 1** (here: *Asarum canadense*).

1762 Gronovius *Flora Virginica* 72, *Asarum aquaticum . . .* Nostratibus errore Coltsfoot. **1843** Torrey *Flora NY* 2.131, *Asarum Canadense . . .* Wild Ginger. Coltsfoot . . . Shady woods, in rich soil . . . The root is a popular medicine. It is aromatic, and has somewhat the taste of ginger. **1897** *Jrl. Amer. Folkl.* 10.54, *Asarum Canadense . .* colt's foot; West. **1971** Krochmal *Appalachia Med. Plants* 66.

3 =**sweet coltsfoot 1. chiefly Nth**

1822 Eaton *Botany* 496, *[Petasites] frigida* (mountain colt's foot. New Hampshire, V[ermon]t). **1840** MA Zool. & Bot. Surv. *Herb. Plants & Quadrupeds* 1.129, Wild Colt's Foot . . . Has been found in the mountain wood in Massachusetts. **1911** *Century Dict.,* Coltsfoot . . . Sweet coltsfoot, the European butter-dock, *Petasites Petasites;* also *P. palmata* of North America. **1955** U.S. Arctic Info. Center *Gloss.,* Coltsfoot . . . Any perennial herb of the genus *Petasites,* with large, edible, basal leaves and numerous, medium-sized, white, purple, rarely yellowish flowers, which grows on wet or boggy soils. **1973** Hitchcock–Cronquist *Flora Pacific NW* 541, *Petasites . . .* Coltsfoot.

4 A **marsh marigold** (here: *Caltha palustris*).

1837 Darlington *Flora Cestrica* 336, *C[altha] palustris . . .* Colt's-foot. **1892** *Jrl. Amer. Folkl.* 5.91, *Caltha palustris . .* coltsfoot. Stratham, N.H. **1907** *DN* 3.184 seNH, Coltsfoot . . . Marsh marigold (Caltha). The leaves are of such a shape as to suggest a colt's foot. **1966–69** *DARE* (Qu. I28a, *What . . do you call "greens" . . eaten raw?*) Inf **ME5,** Coltsfoot greens; (Qu. I28b, *. . Greens that are cooked?*) Inf **MA40,** Coltsfoot; (Qu. S25) Inf **NY195,** Coltsfoot. **1974** (1977) Coon *Useful Plants* 219, *Caltha palustris . .* colt's foot.

5 =**galax.**

1894 *Jrl. Amer. Folkl.* 7.94, *Galax aphylla . .* coltsfoot, Banner Elk, N.C. **1933** Small *Manual SE Flora* 1020. **1964** Campbell *Great Smoky Wildflowers* 38, Galax is often called *Coltsfoot* because of the shape of the leaves.

6 =**oconee bells.**

1901 Lounsberry *S. Wild Flowers* 402, *Little Colt's-Foot . . . Shortia galacifolia.* **1933** Small *Manual SE Flora* 1019, *Shortia.* Oconee-bells, One-flower Coltsfoot.

7 =**water shield 1.**

1927 Boston Soc. Nat. Hist. *Proc.* 38.247 **Okefenokee Swamp GA,** *Brasenia purpurea*—Colt's-foot.

coltsfoot candy n Also *coltsfoot (rock)*

A hard candy flavored with **coltsfoot 1.**

1967–68 *DARE* (Qu. H82b, *. . Cheap candy . . sold years ago*) Inf **NY34,** Coltsfoot rock: fluted, anise-flavored hard sticks; **NY41,** Coltsfoot: semi-hard long sticks; dissolved in mouth. **1976** *Yankee* May 64/2 **PA,** As a child, one great treat was coltsfoot candy. This confection was sandy in color, semi-hard, and a bit porous . . . The name and flavor comes from a plant of the same name *Tussilago farfara,* anciently one of the most popular medicinal herbs.

coltsfoot snakeroot n

A **wild ginger 1** (here: *Asarum canadense*).

1876 Hobbs *Bot. Hdbk.* 25, Coltsfoot snake root, Canada snake root, Asarum Canadense. **1891** *Jrl. Amer. Folkl.* 4.148 **NH,** Asarum Canadense was *Snakeroot;* father said, 'Colt's-foot Snakeroot'. **1971** Krochmal *Appalachia Med. Plants* 66.

colt's tail n

=**horseweed 1.**

1833 Eaton *Botany* 135, *Erigeron canadense,* . . colts tail, flea-bane, pride-weed. **1911** *Century Dict.,* Colt's-tail . . . A name of the fleabane, *Leptilon Canadense.* **1965** Teale *Wandering Through Winter* 244 **KY,** Here in the rich soil the horseweed or Canada fleabane or prideweed or butterweed or colt's tail—*Leptilon canadense . .* had attained its maximum growth.

columba root See **columbo**

Columbia See **Columbia red berry**

Columbian pine n

=**Douglas fir.**

1958 McCulloch *Woods Words* **Pacific NW,** *Columbian pine*—Douglas fir.

Columbia poplar n

Prob **balsam poplar.**

1966–70 *DARE* (Qu. T12, *The kind of poplar tree that has sticky, sweet-smelling buds*) Inf **AR28,** Columbia poplar; (Qu. T13, *. . Other names . . for . . poplar*) Infs **DE3, VA43,** Columbia poplar.

Columbia red berry n Also *Columbia*

Prob a species of *Ribes.*

1968 *DARE* (Qu. I44, *What kinds of berries grow wild around here?*) Inf **CT6,** Columbias. **1968** *DARE* Tape **NY121,** Columbia red berries—they're like a black raspberry, only they're a little bit bigger.

Columbia River salmon n Also *Columbia salmon* **Pacific NW**

=**Chinook salmon.**

1881 *Amer. Naturalist* 15.177 **Pacific NW,** Quinnat . . Chinnook salmon, Columbia River salmon, Sacramento salmon. **1882** U.S. Natl. Museum *Bulletin* 16.306, *Columbia Salmon. . . .* Especially abundant in the Columbia and Sacramento Rivers, where it is the principal salmon. **1902** Jordan–Evermann *Amer. Fishes* 151, *Chinook Salmon*—Oncorhynchus tschawytscha . . Other names by which this fish is known are quinnat salmon, king salmon, Columbia River salmon, Sacramento salmon, tyee, tchaviche, and tschawytscha. **1946** LaMonte *N. Amer. Game Fishes* 106, *Chinook Salmon . . . Names:* . . Columbia River Salmon.

Columbia River smelt n **Pacific NW**

=**eulachon.**

1923 Ward *Encycl. Food* 190, Eulachon, or Candle-fish, or 'Columbia River Smelt,' a rich, delicious, slender little fish of the North-Pacific coast, which reaches a maximum length of about twelve inches. It is placed on the market fresh, smoked, brined, kippered, and canned. **1939** Natl. Geog. Soc. *Fishes* 281, *Thaleichthys pacificus . . .* Fish of this species, called locally Columbia River smelt, occur in February and in early March in the lower Columbia River system.

Columbia River spruce n

=**Sitka spruce.**

1958 McCulloch *Woods Words* **Pacific NW,** *Columbia River spruce*—Sitka spruce.

Columbia River turkey n *joc* Cf **Cape Cod turkey**

A salmon.

1945 *AN&Q* 5.88/2, Columbia River turkey—salmon.

Columbia River tyee See **tyee salmon**

columbia root See **columbo**

Columbia salmon See **Columbia River salmon**

columbo n Also *columba root, columbia root* [Prob by confusion with calumba *(Jatrorrhiza palmata),* roots of which were also used medicinally] **chiefly East**

A species of *Frasera* (see **green gentian**), esp *F. caroliniensis,* a southeastern species having long panicles of yellowish-white purple-spotted flowers. Also called **deer's ears, Indian lettuce 1, meadow pride, monument plant, pyramid flower, yellow gentian**

1803 (1905) Lewis *Orig. Jrls. Lewis & Clark Exped.* 7.244, ½lb. Columbo Rad. [$]1. **1821** Royall *Let. from AL* 138, This is the region of . . the Columbia root. The Columba root has several broad leaves near the ground, in the shape like a hound's tongue, of a yellowish green—the leaf thick and fuzzy—and a stem runs up from these one to two feet. **1822** Woods *2 Yrs. Residence* 219, The following trees and herbs are used in medicine . . . Columbia-root, and sumach, and sassafras trees. **1840** Phelps *Lectures on Botany* (2) 98, *Frasera . . . verticillata,* (American columbo). **1915** (1926) Armstrong *Western Wild Flowers* 368, Columbo, Deer's Tongue—*Frasera speciosa . . .* West, etc. *Ibid* 369, Small Columbo—*Frasera nitida . . .* Cal., Oreg. **1975** Duncan–Foote *Wildflowers SE* 124, *Columbo . . .* Flowers in a pyramidal panicle . . . *Frasera caroliniensis.*

columbus n

A type of sled: see quot 1905.

1905 *DN* 3.70 neMA, *Columbus.* 'A coasting sled composed of two small bobs or pairs of runners connected lengthwise by a long seat or board.' **1943** *LANE* Map 573–4 neMA, The following terms for 'double sled' are given on the map: . . columbus.

column n Usu |ˈkaləm|, sometimes |ˈkaljəm| Pronc-spp *colume, colyum*

Std senses, var forms.

1867 Lowell *Biglow* xxxii, However, *per contra,* Yankees habitually say *colume* for *column.* **1896** *DN* 1.437, *Colume.* **1908** *DN* 3.300 eAL, wGA, *Colume.* **1914** *DN* 4.104 KS, *Colyum.* **1926** Davis *Column* 3, The most important development on America's editorial pages during the past quarter of a century has been the evolution of the "colyum". **1936** *AmSp* 11.311 nNY, *Column* occurs 121 times as [ˈkaləm] and ten times as [ˈkaljəm]. **1943** *AmSp* 17.41 sNY, In *column, coupon,* and *percolator,* there is, of course, no historical justification for [j]. [Two infs had [j] in *column;* 40 omitted it.] **c1960** *Wilson Coll.* csKY, *Column* [ˈkaljəm] often. **1968** *DARE* FW Addit LA17, *Column* [ˈkaljəm]; common, but not used by the educated.

column center n

A non-existent item used as the basis for practical jokes.

1969 *DARE* (Qu. HH14, *Ways of teasing a beginner . . for example, by sending him for a "left-handed monkey wrench"*) Inf IL47A, A bushel of column centers—what you send someone for in an architect's office: a column center is just a dot, the intersection of two lines on the paper.

colyum See **column**

com- See **ker-**

coma n [MexSpan] Cf comal n²

A bumelia (*Bumelia* spp); also its fruit.

1886 Havard *Flora W. & S. TX* for 1885 7.476, *Coma* (*Bumelia lycioides*), becoming a tree 1 foot in diameter and 30 feet high. *Ibid* 524, *Bumelia lycioides* Gaertn. Called Coma by the Mexicans on the Lower Rio Grande where it becomes a tree with a stem a foot thick. Wood tough and compact, making excellent ax-handles. The black berries are edible but not very palatable. **1892** *DN* 1.246 TX, *Comal . . .* A round black berry . . oftener spelled *comá.* **1895** *Jrl. Amer. Folkl.* 8.47 TX, The *Coma* is a small, black, or deep blue berry, much like our own whortleberry, but dead sweet in taste; it grows on a stunted bush, and is ready for use from June to August. **1929** Dobie *Vaquero* 209 swTX, A big mesquite or *coma* thorn in the joint of a horse's leg is as bad as a *viznaga* thorn in his foot. **1932** Bentley *Spanish Terms,* Coma . . . "An evergreen, stubborn, beautiful . . . with dirk-like thorns, and, in season, with blue berries . . . " **1938** *AmSp* 13.112, The beautiful southern buckthorn, *Bumelia lycioides* bears in Texas the Mexican-Spanish name of *coma.* Such, moreover, is the name of its edible round shiny black berry. **1953** *AmSp* 28.101 SW, *Coma* (Mex.Sp.). Southern buckthorn (*Bumelia lycioides*). **1960** Vines *Trees SW* 835, Saffron-Plum Bumelia —*Bumelia angustifolia . . .* Some of the vernacular names are Schott Bumelia, . . Coma, . . and Coma Resinera. **1967** *DARE* Tape TX28, There's another evergreen around here and I don't know what the English name for it is, it's called a coma, coma tree. It's got a little, black, chicle-type—I mean it's a sticky—we used to chew 'em when we're a kid. It looked like chicle . . . [tastes] kinda sweetish. **1970** Correll *Plants TX* 1188, *Bumelia lanuginosa . . Coma . . .* Mostly in uplands or sometimes in bottomlands from Fla. to Mo. and Kan., s. to Tex., s.Ariz. and n.Mex.

comadre n [Span] SW

A godmother; a close woman-friend of a family.

1834 Pike *Prose Sketches* 105, We have been brought up together; our mothers are comadres, (sponsors) and you can never know me better than you do now. **1846** (1962) Magoffin *Down Santa Fé* 154, It pleased her so much she called me *'comadre'* [godmother] all the time. **1863** *Rio Abajo Press* 28 April 1 (*DAE*) **Albuquerque NM,** But he did not find her, and his search for her among comadres, relatives, and friends had no satisfactory result. **1899** *Out West Mag.* 11.324 sCA, The *compadres*

and *comadres* who stand for them do not look unworthy of their charge. **1948** *SW Jrl. Anthro.* 4.43, Each compadre or comadre must be greeted individually even when several are together in one group.

comal n¹ [MexSpan] SW

A griddle of stone, earthenware, or metal.

1844 (1954) Gregg *Commerce* 109 NM, This is afterwards spread on a small sheet of iron or copper, called *comal* (*comalli,* by the Indians), and placed over the fire, where, in less than three minutes, it is baked and ready for use. **1892** *DN* 1.189 TX, *Comál,* a slightly hollow utensil of stone or earthenware on which *tortillas* are cooked or baked . . . From Mexican *comalli.* **1912** Lumholtz *New Trails* 191 swAZ, The ordinary *comal,* made of earthen-ware, is of course useless for travel. **1938** *AmSp* 13.120, Texans of Mexican origin have long been wont to bake tortillas in a slightly concave utensil of stone or of earthenware; often an iron dish is now used instead. This vessel they term a *comal,* a word derived from Nahuatl *comalli,* denoting a crude form of earthenware griddle.

comal n²

The fruit of the **coma.**

1892 *DN* 1.246 TX, *Comal . . .* Also the name of a round, black berry, with a taste somewhat resembling our whortleberry; oftener spelled *comá.* **1938** *AmSp* 13.112, *[Coma]* is the name of its *[Bumelia lycioides]* edible round shiny black berry, which is also termed the *comal.*

comal cactus n

Perh a **prickly pear.**

1970 Anderson *TX Folk Med.* 17, Colds—Make a tea out of the leaves of the comal cactus.

Comanche moon n

1952 Dobie *Mustangs* 67 TX, Long before this [1847] the Comanches had become hostile towards the encroaching *Tejanos,* whom they differentiated from other Americans—a differentiation still pleasing to Texans. A few old ones can remember when the full moon of each month was called the "Comanche moon." *Ibid* 68, In the calendar of the Comanches, September was the "Mexican moon"; in the calendar of the Mexicans, it was the "Comanche moon."

Comanche pill n Cf Montezuma's revenge

A laxative.

1969 *DARE* (Qu. BB22, . . *Home remedies . . for constipation*) Inf TX70, Ex-lax; Comanche pills.

comandante n Also sp commandante [Span] SW

A commanding officer.

1844 (1846) Kendall *Santa Fé Exped.* 2.119, Colonel Velasco . . took his leave, at the same time introducing the commandante of our new guard. **1897** *Outing* 30.74/2, In the old adobe . . Resánoff dined with the comandante. **1904** (1913) Porter *Cabbages & Kings* 12, The comandante . . wrote in his secret memorandum book the accusive fact that Señor Goodwin had on that momentous date received a telegram. **1931** Brown *Progressive Arizona* 9 (Carlisle *Southwestern Dict.*), So I gives the commandante the dinero and we all goes down the calle.

comb n Usu |kom|, rarely |kʊm|

A Form.

1927 Shewmake *Engl. Pronc. VA* 31, *Going,* when unstressed, and followed by *to,* is in rapid or careless speech pronounced *goon* (*oo* as in *wool*). *Comb* and *home* suffer a similar change at times, becoming *coom* and *hoom* (*oo* as in *wool*).

B Senses.

1 The crest or ridge of a mountain. [Scots and nEngl dial]

1930 Shoemaker *1300 Words* 13 cPA Mts (as of c1900), *Comb*—The crest or summit of a mountain ridge.

2 also *combing:* The ridge or peak of a roof; the strip of material covering the ridge. **chiefly Midl, occas Sth** See Map Cf **cone 1**

1824 Doddridge *Notes Indian Wars* 136, The roof was formed by making the end logs shorter, until a single log formed the comb of the roof. **1869** Twain *Innocents* 174 NYC, From the eaves to the comb of the roof stretched . . great curved marble beams. **1884** Harrison *Negro Engl.* 277, De koam er de house = the gable of the house. **1886** Amer. Philol. Assoc. *Trans.* 17.37 Sth, Comb of a house, i.e. 'apex of the roof,' the ridge. It is very common in the South, and known in the West. **1899** (1912) Green *VA Folk-Speech,* Comb . . . Combing . . . "The boy was astraddle of the combing when they saw him." **1905** *DN* 3.75 nwAR, *Comb.* **1908** *DN* 3.300 eAL, wGA, *Comb.* **1959** *Hall Coll.* TN (as of c1900), *Comb.* **1965–70** *DARE* (Qu. D30, *The strip of wood or metal* *that covers the ridge of a roof)* 64 Infs, **chiefly Midl,** Comb; **MD**35, **NJ**56, **WA**12, 14, Combing; **IN**71, **KY**5, **TN**30, 60, Ridge comb; **AR**7, 26, Comb of the house; **WA**11, Roof comb; **KY**77, Straddle comb; (Qu. M1, . . *Different . . kinds of barns)* Inf **PA**166, Comb roof barn, with a ['pikt] roof.   **1968** *DARE* FW Addit **MD**18, *Comb:* Point of roof in barn—corresponds to attic in house.

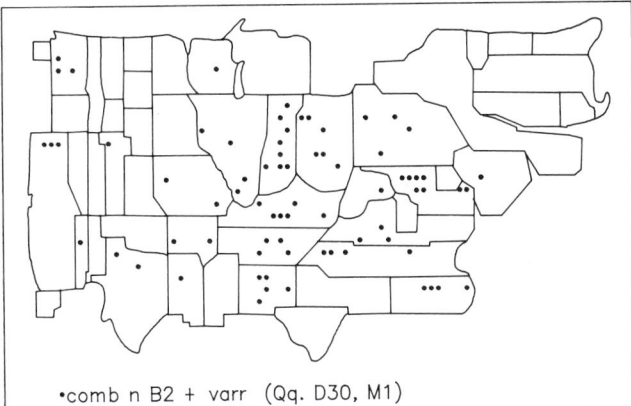

•comb n B2 + varr   (Qq. D30, M1)

3 See **comb tier.**

4 The crest of a wave. *obs* Cf **comber**

1848 Cooper *Oak-Openings* 2.203, Nothing that goes through, or *on,* the water . . can ever be made to keep company with that feathery foam, which under the several names of "white-caps"—an in-shore and lubber's term—"combs," "breaking of the seas,". . glances by a vessel in a blow.

5 A **purple coneflower** (here: *Echinacea angustifolia).* Cf **combflower 1**

1896 *Jrl. Amer. Folkl.* 9.192, *Echinacea angustifolia . .* and *Lepachys columnaris . .* respectively comb and brush, Burnside, So. Dak.   **1940** Clute *Amer. Plant Names* 219, *Brauneria angustifolia.* Comb. Sampson-root.

6 The pistillate head of a stalk of **buffalo grass** n.

1937 Sandoz *Slogum* 230 **NE** (as of 1900–20), He did fewer of the little-boy things, like bringing in the first combs of the buffalo grass.

7 A pine cone. [Folk-etym]

1969 *DARE* FW Addit seGA, Comb [koum], the cone of a pine tree. [Said by young Inf and by others in the area.]

‡**8** A kind of mushroom.

1967 *DARE* (Qu. S18) Inf **MO**8, [koUm]—They're pointed at the end. Have a stalk at the top of 'em.

comb v **West**

To spur a horse: see quots.

1933 *AmSp* 8.1.28 **TX,** *Comb.* To run spurs down the side of a horse's neck to make him pitch.   **1961** Adams *Old-Time Cowhand* 311 **West,** The cowboy's said to "curry 'im out" when he rakes with his spurs; "reefin'," "combin'," and "shove in the steel" are terms also used.

comb, cut one's See **cut one's comb**

comber n [comb n **B4** + *er*]

A long curling wave.

1840 (1841) Dana *2 Years* 71, The heavy swell of the Pacific was setting in, and breaking in loud and high "combers" upon the beach.   **1921** Paine *Comrades of the Rolling Ocean* 84 *(DA),* A thundering comber fell on deck forward with a crash of splintered woodwork.   **1947** *Time* 17 Mar 41/2 **sCA,** Miles of broad beaches . . great combers to jump in.   **1965–70** *DARE* (Qu. O15, . . *Different kinds of waves)* 17 Infs, **coastal US, esp NYC, also Gt Lakes,** Comber; (Qu. O18, *Different currents or actions of the water . . important . . in a boat)* Inf **MI**47, Big comber.

combflower n

1 =**purple coneflower.**

1847 Wood *Class-Book* 338, *E. purpurea . . . Purple Cone-flower or Comb-flower . . .* Disk thickly beset with the stiff, pointed, brown chaff.   **1911** *Century Dict., Comb-flower . . .* The purple cone-flower or blacksampson, *Brauneria purpurea.*   **1940** Clute *Amer. Plant Names* 219, *Brauneria purpurea.* Comb-flower.

2 Teasel.

1966 *DARE* Wildfl QR Pl.215a Inf **OH**82, Combflower, teasel.

3 A sunflower (here: *Helianthus annuus).*

1959 Carleton *Index Herb. Plants* 30, *Comb-flower:* Helianthus annuus.

combinate v, also vbl n *combinating* [Back-formation from *combination]*

To play a numbers game by distributing one's money over every possible combination of digits.

1965 Little *Autobiog. Malcolm X* 85 **Harlem NYC,** Many players practiced what was called "combinating." For example, six cents would put one penny on each of the six possible combinations of three digits. The number 840, combinated would include 840, 804, 048, 084, 408, and 480. *Ibid* 86, Most people tried to play a dollar a day, but split it up among different numbers and combinated.

combination barn n

1967 *DARE* (Qu. M1 . . *Special kinds of barns)* Inf **OR**13, Combination or ranch barn; **WA**20, Combination [barn] with hay mow and lean-to for stock.

combinder n [Perh blend of *combine* n + *binder]*

A combine harvester.

1965–70 *DARE* (Qu. L28, *Tools . . for cutting grain)* Inf **TX**29, Combinder; (Qu. L29, *Machines . . for cutting grain)* Infs **GA**77, **NC**49, Combinder; (Qu. L32b, *In early days, how was the grain separated from the chaff?)* Inf **UT**3, Blown through a combinder; (Qu. L33, *How is the grain separated . . nowadays?)* Inf **GA**77, Combinder.

combinet n Pronc-sp *commonette* [*combin* from *combination* + *-et] old-fash*

A pail with lid and handle, that functions both as chamber pot and slop jar.

1950 *WELS (Utensil kept under a bed for use at night)* 2 Infs, **swWI,** Combinet.   **1965–70** *DARE* (Qu. F38) 12 Infs, **scattered,** Combinet; **MS**45, Commonette is the proper term. [10 of 13 Infs old]

combing See **comb n B2**

combing out vbl n Also *combing down,* ~ *over* Cf **comb one's head 2**

A scolding.

1959 *VT Hist.* new ser 27.130, *Combing out:*. . Also combing down. A scolding. Common.   **1968** *DARE* (Qu. II27, . . *A very sharp scolding)* Inf **MD**30, Combing over.

combings n pl

1961 Adams *Old-Time Cowhand* 250 **West,** The final cattle drove in from circle on roundup were called the "combin's."

combo n Cf **commie**

1968 *DARE* (Qu. EE6c, *Cheap marbles)* Inf **IA**29, Combos—a clay marble—the cheapest. Ten combos to make one tick.

comb one's head v phr

1 See **head n B1.**

2 also *comb one's hair* (or *wool):* To whip, beat; to scold severely.

1795 Murdock *Triumphs* 30, If I don't comb his head with a three-legged stool, there is no snakes in Ireland.   **1891** Dixon *Dict. Idiom. Phrases* 68, *Comb . . .* To comb a man's head—to give him a thrashing.   **1927** *AmSp* 2.351 **WV,** *Comb his wool . .* to find fault with; to scold. "Your mother will comb your wool well when she hears of this."   **1928** Ruppenthal Coll. **KS,** Comb, comb (one's) hair . . . to scold.   **1938** Stuart *Dark Hills* 281 **neKY,** I promised her I'd be back . . by nine o'clock. It's nearly ten now. She'll comb my hair, Jesse.   **1954** *Harder Coll.* **cwTN,** *Comb one's wool . . .* Treat someone severely; scold; whip.   **1967** *DARE* (Qu. II27, *If somebody gives you a very sharp scolding . .* "I certainly got _____.") Inf **NJ**1, Hair combed.   **1968** Adams *Western Words,* Comb his hair—To hit someone over the head with the barrel of a pistol. After a person had his "hair parted" in this manner, he was, in the language of one cowman, apt to "sleep as gentle as a dead calf."

comb rail n [comb n **B2** + **rail**] Cf **comb tier**

In a tobacco barn: one of the **rails** closest to the ridgepole.

1966 *PADS* 45.10 **cnKY,** *Comb rails . . .* The topmost bents [the intersection of the rails and vertical supporting pieces in the framework of a tobacco barn] in the barn. They run just under the ridge pole . . . "The comb rails are on the highest tier."   **1967** Key *Tobacco Vocab.* **MO,** Comb rails.

comb the kinks out of one v phr

To correct faulty notions, to "set someone straight."

1911 Porter *Harvester* 473 **IN,** If you think I hain't got no sense at all I jest dare you to ask Doctor Carey. 'Twouldn't take him long to comb the kinks out of you.

comb tier n Also *comb*

In a tobacco barn: the set of **comb rails.**

1967 Key *Tobacco Vocab.* **PA,** Comb tier; **KY,** Comb.

combustible n [Prob assoc with *combustion* violent agitation]

1975 Gould *ME Lingo, Combustible*—A gale of wind approaching hurricane velocity.

come v Eye-dial sp *cum*

A Forms.

1 pres (exc 3rd pers sg): usu *come;* occas *comes.*

1966–70 *DARE* Tape **SD8,** Most of our storms here comes from the northwest; **VA2,** The railroad cars comes in; **VA112,** They get weaker as the times comes on. **1969** *DARE* FW Addit **seNY,** There are a lot of birds that go south and comes north that flies nights.

2 pres 3rd pers sg: usu *comes;* occas *come.*

1922 Gonzales *Black Border* 293 **sSC, GA coasts** [Gullah glossary], *Come* . . comes.

3 past: usu *came;* often *come;* occas *com(e)d;* pronc-spp *kem, kim.*

1815 Humphreys *Yankey in England* 104, *Cum,* came. **1837** Sherwood *Gaz. GA* 69/1, *Com'd,* for came. **1843** (1916) Hall *New Purchase* 365 **IN,** When I kim to, I couldn't see my bonnit. **1884** Murfree *TN Mts.* 151 **TN,** They kem back a-fotchin' the gal with 'em. **1884** Baldwin *Yankee School-Teacher* 134 **VA** [Black], Dat was long an' long 'nough [=long ago] 'fore you kim t' plague ole Rose. **1892** *DN* 1.276 **wCT,** Come. **1895** *DN* 1.376 **TN, KY, NC,** *Come.* **1903** *DN* 2.293 **Cape Cod MA,** *Come.* **Ibid** 102 **nwAR,** Come. **1907** *DN* 3.184 **seNH,** *Come.* **1910** *DN* 3.439 **wNY,** *Come.* **1917** *DN* 4.413 **wNC, KY,** [kɛm]. Variant *came.* **1927** Kennedy *Gritny* 46 **sLA** [Black], I comed out de wilderness. **1953** Atwood *Survey of Verb Forms* 9, The preterite is recorded in the context "He (came) over to see me." *Came* /kem/ predominates in all classes only in a small area around New York City, though it is heavily favored by cultured informants in all areas. *Come* /kʌm/ occurs in nearly all the communities of N. Eng. being almost as common among younger informants as among the more old-fashioned. Elsewhere, outside of Greater New York City, *come* is used by from two thirds (N.Y.) to all (N.C.) of the Type I informants [=old, with little educ], whereas from one third (N.Y.) to seven eighths (N.C.) of the Type II informants [=with fair educ] use it. All Negro informants use *come.* **1965–70** *DARE* (Qu. OO17a, . . *Yesterday her son _____ home*) 846 Infs, **widespread,** Came; 198 Infs, **widespread exc Gt Lakes and wNMidl,** Come; **KY5,** Comed. [Of all Infs responding to the question, 29% were comm type 5, 63% old, 27% grade school educ or less, 48% male; of those who responded *come,* 47% were comm type 5, 77% old, 50% grade school educ or less, and 63% male.] **1975** Allen *LAUM* 2.12, Despite school insistence upon the distinction between *come* and *came,* a high proportion of all infs use *come* as a preterite instead of the prescribed *came,* some exclusively and others as the conversational and informal alternate.

4 past pple: usu *come;* often *came;* sometimes *comed.*

1916 *DN* 4.301 **wMA,** *Came* . . . Come, chiefly as a past participle, as "I should have *came* this way any way." **1965–70** *DARE* (Qu. OO17b, . . *He was late; he should have _____*) 879 Infs, **widespread,** Come; 105 Infs, **widespread,** Came; **AL33, CA134, PA161, SC11,** Comed. [Of all Infs responding to the question, 25% were mid-aged, 27% grade school educ or less, 48% male; of those who responded *come,* 35% were mid-aged, 44% grade school educ or less, 60% male.] **1969–70** *DARE* Tape **CA120,** The big dredgers have came in; **TX78,** Came.

5 imper, in calls to animals:

a *come.* **chiefly Nth, West** See Map Cf **co** v

1846 Sage *Scenes Rocky Mts.* iii, Come, boss! Poor boss!—bossy, bossy! **c1950** *Atlas Checklists* **WI,** Come boy—Call to get horse in from pasture. **1950** *WELS* (Call to cows to come in from the pasture) 35 Infs, **WI,** Come boss(ie); (Call to the chickens at feeding time) 22 Infs, **WI,** Come chick(ie) chick(ie); (Call to a calf at feeding time) 9 Infs, **WI,** Come boss; 2 Infs, Come boss. **1961** *AmSp* 36.27 **nOH,** The rapid decline of farm knowledge in an urban area is evidenced by the small number of returns on the checklists . . . Come boss(ie) is strong among the old and the uneducated. **1965–70** *DARE* (Qu. K80, . . *Cows*) 209 Infs, Come

(boss, bossie, etc); (Qu. K83, . . *Calf*) 123 Infs, Come (boss, calfy, etc); (Qu. J10, *To call a cat to make it come*) 63 Infs, Come (kitty, pussy, etc); (Qu. K79, . . *Chickens*) 29 Infs, Come (chick, chicky, etc); (Qu. K82, . . *Horses*) 16 Infs, Come (boy, horsie, etc); (Qu. K84, . . *Pigs*) 22 Infs, Come (pig, piggy, etc); (Qu. K85, . . *Sheep*) 15 Infs, Come (sheep, nanny, etc). **1973** Allen *LAUM* 1.243, In the U[pper] M[idwest] a dog is summoned usually by either *Here!* or an expression with *Come! Ibid* 259, *Co boss* and *come boss* . . [occur as calls to cows] everywhere but in southern Iowa. *Ibid* 260, The Northern generics *co bossy(y)* and *come boss(y)* are, with two exceptions, limited to the UM Northern speech area. *Ibid* 262, *Come,* followed by *boy, jack, pony,* or a name . . [occurs as a call to a horse] in Northern speech oriented regions.

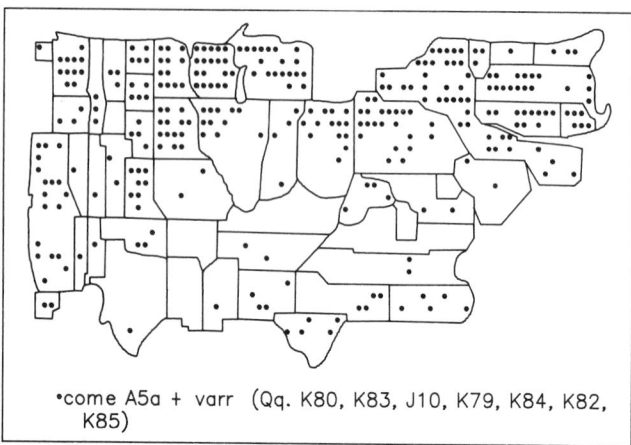

•come A5a + varr (Qq. K80, K83, J10, K79, K84, K82, K85)

b *come on.* **chiefly Sth, S Midl** See Map Cf **sook**

1965–70 *DARE* (Qu. J10, *To call a cat to make it come*) Infs **CA131, KY16, LA20, MD35, MN6, TN1, TX71,** Come on (kitty, minou, etc); (Qu. K79, . . *Chickens*) Infs **KY75, OK8,** Come on (chick); (Qu. K80, . . *Cows*) 19 Infs, Come on (come on, girls, here, now, etc); (Qu. K82, . . *Horses*) 18 Infs, Come on (come on, here, George, in, etc); (Qu. K83, . . *Calf*) 19 Infs, Come on (calf, calfy, etc); (Qu. K84, . . *Pigs*) Infs **NJ31, OK43,** Come on pig; (Qu. K85, . . *Sheep*) Infs **KY29, LA8, 29, MD30, MS21, NH3, NY211,** Come on (sheep, nanny, etc).

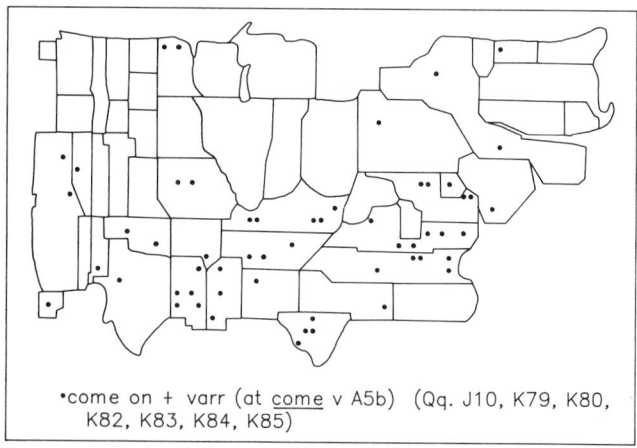

•come on + varr (at come v A5b) (Qq. J10, K79, K80, K82, K83, K84, K85)

B Intr senses.

1 To take an expected shape or reach an expected condition.

1899 (1912) Green *VA Folk-Speech* 122, Come . . . The forming of butter in a churn after the proper churning. "Has the butter come yet, you've been churning at it long enough." **1942** Whipple *Joshua* 167 **UT,** Among the women the talk ran on . . the best way to make soap come. **1964** Wallace *Frontier Life* 73 (as of 1893–1906), Until the butter "came," meaning that the globules of butter fat clung together in a floating mass on top of the milk which at this stage was called buttermilk. **1968** *DARE* Tape **WV11,** Then if it [yeast] didn't ferment, *come* as we called it, Grandmaw would have to go to her neighbors to get a cup of yeast to start her yeast.

2 To happen, take place.

1943 *LANE* Map 595 **seNH, sVT,** The map shows the question *How does it happen (that you are here?)* and a number of equivalent expressions . . *how comes it, how come it.* **1950** *WELS* (*"What time does church _____ ."*) 1 Inf, **csWI**, Come. **1967** *DARE* Tape MI47, How's it come that you never said anything about it? **1969** *DARE* FW Addit **cwNJ**, That's how they come to get married.

3 To become.

1941 *Sat. Eve. Post* 5 Apr 28/3, Hearing this, Whitney came awake and went to Washington. **1965** *DARE* Tape MS1, He didn' know what come of his people. **1967–70** *DARE* (Qu. II2a, . . *"He has just recently _____ with John."*) Inf **VA25**, Come buddies; **VA38**, Came close. **1969** *DARE* FW Addit **seNY**, When I come [=got] big enough.

4 Of the weather: to develop into (a specified condition). **chiefly Gulf States** See also **come on** v phr **1a, come up 2**

1941 Street *Father's House* 190 **MS** *(ADD)*, A wet spell would ruin us and she was coming rain before long. **1950** *WELS Suppl.* **swWI**, It came such a terrible storm. **1965–70** *DARE* (Qu. B5, . . *The weather looks as if it will become bad, . . it's _____*) Inf **TX35**, Going to come a storm; **TX36**, Gonna come a norther; **TX100**, Fixing to come a storm; (Qu. B6, *When clouds begin to increase*) Inf **TX90**, Going to come storm; (Qu. B12, *When the wind begins to increase*) Infs **AR56, LA15**, Coming a norther (in the winter), coming a blowup (in the summer); **KY41**, Coming a storm; (Qu. B27, *A sudden rush of water . . from a heavy rain*) Inf **NC36**, Coming a flood; (QR, p34) Inf **IA12**, That could come a nice heavy rain. **1970** Tarpley *Blinky* 50 **neTX**, *(The weather has been bad, but now it is _____)*—Other responses: coming fair. *Ibid* 54, *(Very heavy rain that doesn't last long)*—Come a flood.

5 Of a specified time or seasonal event: to arrive, come to pass—used in inverted constrs. [Survival of arch subjunc constr; *MED cŏmen* v 10c, c1300 →] **esp S Midl**

1908 *DN* 3.300 **eAL, wGA**, Come Friday a week ago, I went to see him about it. **1914** *DN* 4.70, **ME, nNH**, *Come fall, spring etc* . . . When it comes fall, etc. *Ibid* 159 **cVA**, *Come* . . . When (it) shall come. "We'll go huntin' come cooleh weatheh." **1923** *DN* 5.204 **swMO**, I'm aimin' on a-gorn come Christmas week. **1931** *PMLA* 46.1305 **sAppalachians**, I aim to foal that mare, come grass (in the spring). **1938** Matschat *Suwannee R.* 122 **GA**, Belike come cane-grindin', ye-all will have invites to Cella's pledge-troth to Pompano. **1950** *WELS (She came to see me _____)* 1 Inf, **swWI**, Come Friday, a week ago. **1954** *Harder Coll.* **cwTN**, I'll do that come spring. I'll see you come a Tuesday.

6 Of an infirmity: to develop.

1934 *Hanley Disks* **csNH**, I had an old aunt living then. She had a bad foot come on her and she had to have it amputated.

C Quasi-transitive uses in fixed phrr.

1 *come it:* To achieve something, to succeed in some undertaking.

1840 *Hard Cider Press* 10 Oct 2/1 *(OEDS)*, Kent has come it . . . Kent has Kracked the Krown of King Martin in Maine. **1868** Gregg *Life in Army* 141, Nothing can exceed the luxury of lying down . . and feeling secure from their [=mosquitos'] voracious bills, as they hum around your room, and try to "come it," but find an abatis in their way. **1908** *DN* 3.300 **eAL, wGA**, *Come it* . . . To succeed. "He tried hard, but he couldn't quite come it." **1949** Guthrie *Way West* 213, I'm thinkin' we can come it, but it's hard and chancey. **1972** Cooper *NC Mt. Folkl.* 93, I can't come it—I can't eat more.

2 *come (something) over* (or *on*) *one:* To gain the upper hand or outdo by trickery or guile. *old-fash* Cf **come a dodge**

1829 *Daily Natl. Intelligencer* (DC) 17 June 2/4 **nNY**, A farmer in Fairfield has adopted a new way to "come Paddy over" them [pigeons]: he soaks his corn in *whiskey*, and scatters it about the fields—the pigeons soon become intoxicated, and are thus caught easily by the hand. **1842** *Spirit of the Times* 11 Oct *(DAE)*, Says I, "Mr. Coon," and then he smiled, "You can't quite come it over this child." **1847** (1962) Robb *Squatter Life* 74, "No!" shouted Tom, with mock surprise, "You ain't comin' a hoax over a fellar?—you raaly are the sure enough Jedge?" **1874** (1895) Eggleston *Circuit Rider* 216, He's got a smart way thet comes the sympathies over the women folks and weak-eyed men, and sets 'em cryin' at a desp'ate rate. **1901** *DN* 2.138 **cNY**, Come it on. **1904** *DN* 2.424 **seMA** (as of 1850s), Come it on. **1905** *DN* 3.6 **cCT**, Come it over. **1906** *DN* 3.131 **nwAR**, Come that (game) on . . . To deceive in that way. "You come that game on me." **1907** *DN* 3.206 **nwAR**, Come it over. **1908** *DN* 3.300 **eAL, wGA**, Come it on (or over). **1916** Lardner *You Know Me Al* 156 **IN**, I sent $25.00 to Florie so she can't come no none support business on me.

3 *come agreement onto:* See quot.

1966 *DARE* (Qu. KK67, *When people think alike about something: "On that . . , we _____."*) Inf **SC10**, Come agreement onto it.

4 *come +* (a number of years): To approach, be close to.

1931–33 *LANE Worksheets* **nwCT**, He's coming three. *Ibid* **nwRI**, He's coming three in December. **1942** Perry *Texas* 91, He was a big bay, coming four years old. *Ibid* 136, We frequently refer to our children not as being, say, six years old, but as "coming seven." **1949** Guthrie *Way West* 8 (as of 1847), I was just thinkin'. Got a girl comin' seventeen myself. **1949** *PADS* 11.5 **wTX**, *Coming twenty* (*eighteen*, etc.) . . . Approaching an age of twenty (eighteen, etc.). Common in talking of the age of animals. "That horse is six, coming seven in the Spring." **1954** *Harder Coll.* **cwTN**, That old mule's coming twenty if he's a day old. **c1960** *Wilson Coll.* **csKY**, *Coming twenty (or some other age)* . . . About to be, especially of animals.

come aboard v phr

1945 Colcord *Sea Language* 20 **ME, Cape Cod, and Long Island**, "Come aboard!" is the conventional invitation, without which no seaman would enter another's vessel. On the coast, it is a cordial invitation to a person already at the door.

come-a-Christian n

The castor bean plant *(Ricinus communis).*

1970 Anderson *TX Folk Med.* 32, Fever—Lay a come-a-Christian [palma Christi, the castor-oil plant] on the forehead.

come across v phr

1 To occur to (one).

1887 (1967) Harris *Free Joe* 151 **ceGA** [Black], Hit make me feel right foolish in de head w'en it come 'cross me dat I use ter tote Miss Hallie 'roun' w'en she wuz a little bit er baby.

2 To interrupt.

1951 *DE Folkl. Bulletin* Oct 7/2, *Come across* (interrupt as in, "Excuse me for coming across you.")

3 To make oneself clear.

1970 *DARE* (Qu. NN5, . . *Ways of saying 'Do you understand?'*) Inf **TN58**, Am I coming across?

4 See **come through 1, 3.**

come a dodge v phr Cf **come C2**

1968 Adams *Western Words* 71, *Come a dodge*—A trader's expression meaning *to play a trick.*

come again v phr **chiefly Nth, esp NEast** Cf **come back (again)**

To pay a return visit—used as a farewell expression.

1941 *LANE* Map 428 **throughout NEng**, *Come again*—The map shows the expression *come again . .*, as spoken to a departing visitor. **1944** *ADD* **cNY** (as of 1920s), 'Come again!' Common. Longer expressions are also used, but none shorter. **1958** Francis *Structure of Amer. Engl.* 486, Farmers in upstate New York identify Pennsylvanians by the farewell "Come back" or "Come back again!" where New York Staters would normally say "Come again!" **c1960** *Wilson Coll.* **csKY**, *Come again*—said at parting. **1968–70** *DARE* (Qu. NN11, *Informal ways of saying "good-bye" to people you know quite well*) Infs **IL130, NY73, 126, 169, VT16, WI6**, Come again. **1973** Allen *LAUM* 1.389, As in New England, the most frequent parting expression to a visitor is *Come again,* spread quite evenly but with a possible slight Northern bias.

come-all-you n

A commotion, to-do; free-for-all.

1950 *WELS Suppl.* **cWI**, Come-all-you [kʌm 'al jə]—meaning a great how-de-do, a big hooraw. "What's all this come-all-you about?" Rare, old-fashioned. **1969** *DARE* (Qu. Y13, *A fist fight with several people in it*) Inf **NY199**, Come-all-you.

come-along n

1 A rope halter.

1968 Adams *Western Words* 71, *Come-along*—A rope halter made so that it will tighten when a horse refuses to follow and loosen when the animal obeys.

2 A device used to take up the slack in a cable or chain.

1944 *AmSp* 19.231 **Pacific NW** [Shipyard terms], *Come-along.* A wire-tightening machine. **1950** *Western Folkl.* 9.116 **nwOR**, *Come-along.* Rig to tighten guy wires on the tree jacks. *Ibid* 380 **neCA**, *Come-along.* An instrument used to take up slack in a chain or cable.

3 A timber hook.

1950 *WELS Suppl.* **cnWI**, Come along—timber hook, tool used in lumbering.

4 See quot 1975.

1975 Gould *ME Lingo* 56, *Come-along*—A block-and-tackle or winch used horizontally to move heavy objects over the ground, such as a building or a boat in its cradle. **1984** *DARE* File, My husband bought a come-along when we lived in Maine, and we have used it to winch a car up a steep driveway.

5 In railroading: a hand signal.

1977 Adams *Lang. Railroader,* Come along: A hand signal meaning to come ahead.

come-and-go adj
Easy-going.

1968 *DARE* (Qu. KK46, . . *Taking things as they come and not worrying: "The whole family was sort of_____.")* Inf **MO34,** Come-and-go.

come-and-go party n Also *come-and-go affair*
1965–66 *DARE* (Qu. FF3, . . *"Showers" or "gift parties")* Inf **FL18,** Come-and-go affair: tea and gifts for someone; **OK31,** Come-and-go parties: Bring your gift and leave at any time. Refreshments.

come apart v phr Also *come undone*
Of a horse: to buck.

1961 Adams *Old-Time Cowhand* 295, When a hoss started to buck there were a lot of slang expressions the cowhand used for a description of this act. The hoss "arches his back," . . "comes apart," "comes undone."

come around v phr
1 Of the wind: to shift and come from a more favorable direction.

1951 Hough *Singing in Morning* 229 seMA, "Coming around the right way" means a clockwise turning of the weathervane—and a return of sunshine and calm. **1966–69** *DARE* FW Addit csME, When the wind comes around good [from south to west to north], fair weather will follow; ceNC, I'm sure glad the wind come around. **1967** *DARE* (Qu. B15) Inf **ME10,** The wind changing from northwest to northeast is *comin' around* (good weather); wind from the northwest to the west or southwest is *backenin' in* or *backenin' up* (storm to come).

2 also *come round:* To menstruate.

1914 *DN* 4.104 KS, Come round (or *around*) . . . To begin to menstruate. **1923** *DN* 5.204 swMO, Come aroun' . . . To menstruate. **1954** *AmSp* 29.298 TX, OK, FL, *Illness, inconvenience, or disability* [of menstruation]: . . come around. **1960** Williams *Walk Egypt* 55 GA, Sodom berries dried on the screen frames on the porch. There was nothing better for making a woman "come 'round." **1969** *DARE* (Qu. AA27, *Other names and expressions . . for . . menstruation)* Infs **CA127, MI78, MN2, OH28, WA6,** (She's) coming around.

3 See quot.

1905 *DN* 3.6 cCT, Come around . . . To coax or entice.

4 See quot.

c**1960** *Wilson Coll.* csKY, Come around . . . Invitation to come for a visit or call.

come-around(s) n [come around 2]
1966–69 *DARE* (Qu. AA27, . . *Menstruation)* Infs **MA6, 55,** Come-around; **MO39,** Come-arounds.

come at v phr Cf *drive at*
To suggest, imply, mean.

1872 Twain *Roughing It* 28.207, Here—what do you mean? What are you coming at? Is there some mystery behind all this? *Ibid* 31.224, Is that your idea? Is that what you're coming at? **1894** Freeman *Pembroke* 52, What I was comin' at was—I'd been kind of wrong in my reasonin'. c**1960** *Wilson Coll.* csKY, Come at. To imply or mean: "I can't figure out what he is coming at."

come-at-able adj
Accessible, procurable.

1859 Constitutional Convention of Kansas *Proceedings* 311 (*DN* 5.245), The homestead is not *comeatable* for debts. **1899** (1912) Green *VA Folk-Speech* 122, Comeatable . . . Capable of being approached or come at: that may be reached, attained, or procured. **1923** *DN* 5.245 KS, Comeatable . . . That can be reached or got at.

come-at-able n
Something that is readily accessible.

1840 Simms *Border Beagles* 1.125, I donned my first come atables, and rammed the rest in dad's old saddlebags.

come at oneself v phr
To regain consciousness, come to.

1966 *PADS* 46.25 cnAR, When I did come at myself, I got up.

come-away n
A game played on ice: see quot.

1933 *Hanley Disks* csCT, We use to have what they called come-away, on the ice—a man would stand in the center and try to ketch you as you went by—we had lines on each side to come up to.

come back exclam See *coming back*

come back (again) v phr chiefly Midl, scattered Sth Cf *come again*
To pay a return visit—used as a hospitable parting expression.

1896 *DN* 1.415 NE, Come back again, right soon: for *call again.* **1905** *DN* 3.75 nwAR, Come back, come back again . . . Call again. Usual invitation to a parting caller. **1908** *DN* 3.300 eAL, wGA, Come back, . . . Call again. **1942** Hall *Smoky Mt. Speech* 39 wNC, eTN, Steadily encroaching upon it *[you-ones],* is ['juˌɔl] or [jɔl] (more familiar), as in ['jɔˑl 'kʌm 'bæk] (hospitable invitation to return). **1958** [see *come again*]. **1965–70** *DARE* (Qu. NN11, *Informal ways of saying 'good-bye' to people you know quite well)* Infs **AR27, KY49, OK42 PA242, SC44,** Come back; **IL75, IA27, PA163,** Come back again; **CT6, MO20, NY234,** Come back soon; **OK11, TX81,** Come back and see us; **TX59,** Come back to see us; **MS57, NC76, OK27, VA85,** (You, you-all, y'all) come back (ˌyou hear); (Qu. II39, *What other ways do you have of saying 'thank you')* Inf **NC72,** Come back again; **TX89,** Y'all come back again; **TX98,** Y'all come back now. **1973** Allen *LAUM* 1.389, One-third of the U[pper] M[idwest] infs. [208] use Come back, either alone or in any of various expressions, the most common of which is Come back again. The strong Midland orientation of Come back, a form favored by younger speakers, reflects the absence of these forms from the New England records.

come by v phr
1 To acquire. chiefly S Midl

1899 (1912) Green *VA Folk-Speech* 123, Come-by . . . To obtain. "How did you come-by that horse." **1906** *DN* 3.116 sIN, Come by . . . To acquire, as property; to inherit. **1908** *DN* 3.300 eAL, wGA. **1909** *DN* 3.394 nwAR. **1915** *DN* 4.182 VA. **1923** *DN* 5.204 swMO. c**1960** *Wilson Coll.* csKY. **1966** *DARE* FW Addit MS, Come by it naturally: [said of] an untutored, innate ability of a person to do something.

2 To pay a short visit—freq used as an invitation. chiefly Sth, S Midl Cf *call by, go by, stop by*

1863 Hopley *Life South* 1.58, The Southerners . . deem it a thing impossible that a friend should pass the house and not come in; so that "come by" implies "take *our* road home, and of course come in." **1895** *DN* 1.371 seKY, eTN, wNC, Come by: visit. "Come by and stay to supper." *Ibid* 385 wFL. **1903** *DN* 2.310 seMO, Come by! . . . A common form of invitation equivalent to 'Come and see us.' **1905** *DN* 3.75 nwAR. **1912** Green *VA Folk-Speech* 123, Come-by . . . An invitation: "Come-by and get dinner." **1914** *DN* 4.159 VA. **1923** *DN* 5.204 swMO. **1965–70** *DARE* (Qu. II14, *To pay a short visit)* 15 Infs, **chiefly Inland Sth, SW,** Came (come) by (awhile); 5 Infs, **Sth,** Come by; **AL16,** Come by and chat or sit awhile; **MS56,** Come by and set awhile; **FL26,** Come by for a few minutes; **TX61,** Come by later. **1972** *NYT Article Letters* KY, Come by. Come to visit. "Won't you come by."

come-by-chance n chiefly NEng, Sth, S Midl Cf *come-too-soon*
An illegitimate child; also fig.

1835 Crockett *Account* 89 TN, Squire Williams, my neighbor, said he didn't think so: it [=nullification] was a kind of come-by-chance, that was too wicked to know its own kin. **1895** *DN* 1.386 Cape Cod MA, Come-by-chance: illegitimate child. **1907** *DN* 3.184 seNH. **1914** *DN* 4.154 NH. **1927** *AmSp* 3.135 ME coast, A "forceput" marriage or "come by chance" child, were commonly spoken of. **1953** *AmSp* 28.248 csPA, Come-by-chance . . . An illegitimate child, a bastard. Popular speech. Apparently not an Americanism; *OED* considers it standard. **1965–70** *DARE* (Qu. Z11b) 15 Infs, **esp Sth, S Midl,** Come-by-chance.

come ci v phr [Engl *come* + Fr *ci* here]
See quot 1968.

1968 *DARE* FW Addit LA33, Come ci [ˌkəm 'si]: come here; common in English sentences. *Ibid* seLA, Come ci: come here—common. **1984** *DARE* File seLA, Mothers call "come ci" to their children. The *ci* is French, the *come* English.

come clean v phr

1 To confess or admit to wrongdoing.

1919 C.H. Darling *Jargon Book* 8 (*OEDS*), *Come clean*, to confess everything. **1926** (1927) Black *You Can't Win* 33, Come on, out with it. If you want any help here you've got to come clean. **1943** Laura V. Hamner *Short Grass & Longhorns* 155 (*DA*), The next morning he went up to the White House to "come clean." **c1960** *Wilson Coll.* **csKY,** *Come clean.* To confess, esp. after trying to "lie out of it." **1968** *DARE* (Qu. JJ45, *When somebody avoids giving a definite answer*) Inf **NJ53,** Wouldn't come clean.

2 To clear up a debt.

1967–70 *DARE* (Qu. U18, *If you force somebody to pay money . . he owes you . . "I finally made him _____."*) Infs **IL10, KS6, MI122, MN10,** Come clean.

3 See quot.

1942 (1965) Parrish *Slave Songs* 34, If the chicken "come clean" (loses its feathers), it is sure proof that it has scratched up something intended for its owner's bad luck. So much for black magic.

come clear v phr

1927 *Ruppenthal Coll.* **KS,** *Come clear . .* to be exonerated, to be acquitted on trial. "A man was charged with theft but he came clear."

comed See **come** A3, 4

come day, go day (,God send Sunday) adj phr For var phrr, see quots

Easy-going, indolent, lackadaisical.

[**1899** (1912) Green *VA Folk-Speech* 26, Come day, go day, God send Sunday.] **1918** *DN* 5.29 **NW,** Come-day, go-day, God send Sunday . . . Indolent, unambitious. General. **1960** Bailey *Resp. to PADS 20* **KS** *(Somebody who doesn't worry much about anything: "He's kind of a _____ fellow.")*, Come day, go day, God send Sunday. **1965–70** *DARE* (Qu. KK46, *Other expressions for taking things as they come and not worrying: "The whole family was sort of _____."*) Infs **DC3, GA1, 5, 7, IL97, MD2, 8, 49, MI72, NC79, WA6,** Come day, go day (,God send Sunday); **NJ57,** Come day, go day, God bless Sunday; **VA31,** Come day, go day, Good Lord'll send Sunday. **1967** *DARE* Tape **TX21,** Since I'm living here alone, I just stay come day, go day [laughter]. **1968** *DARE* FW Addit **DE3,** Come day, go day, God send Sunday—easygoing, living only for the present. **1975** Gould *ME Lingo* 56, *Come day, go day, God send Sunday*—Used in the beginning to describe an indifferent seaman who looked forward to the lighter labors of the Lord's Day, this phrase is now used for clock-watchers and whistle-listeners.

come down v phr

1 See **come down on** 1.

2 To become, get.

1937 *Hall Coll.* **eTN, wNC,** "Hit began to come down dusky; the sun was a-settin'." [Hall: Common among old people]. **1965** Will *Okeechobee Boats* 100 **c,ceFL,** The captain was the first one to come down sick. **1970** *DARE* (Qu. BB44, *. . A person just starting some sickness . . "He _____ pneumonia."*) Inf **OK58,** Come down sick with.

come down in a pile v phr

To die.

1950 Reeves *Man from SD* 242, "I'm not a kid any longer," I said, "and what will happen to a woman I marry and bring to this goddam ranch when the time comes for *me* to come down in a pile?"

come down on v phr

1 also *come down:* See quot. *obs*

1895 *DN* 1.415 **cNY,** *Come down, come down on:* to applaud with the feet. "They came down on him."

2 To harass, rebuke. Cf *get on one's case* (**case** n[1] 7), **square out**

1942 ME Univ. *Studies* 52, *To come down on,* that is, to attack from the windward, means to censure, to rebuke, to give one a "blowing up." A fuller expression is to "come down upon one hot and heavy." **1972** Claerbaut *Black Jargon* 60, *Come down on . .* to harass or oppose, often verbally: "He'll come down on you for that."

3 See quots.

1972 Claerbaut *Black Jargon* 60, *Come down on . .* to fight; physically combat. **1980** Folb *Runnin' Down* 233 **Los Angeles CA** [Black], *Come down hard (on one)*—Confront or assault.

come easy, go easy adj phr Also *come easy, come go* [Alter of *easy come, easy go*] **chiefly Sth**

Easygoing.

[**1899** (1912) Green *VA Folk-Speech* 26, *Come easy, go easy.*] **1965–70** *DARE* (Qu. KK46, *. . Taking things as they come and not worrying*) 17 Infs, **chiefly Sth,** Come easy, go easy; **CT25,** Come easy, come go.

‡come-easy, go-easy, come-Sunday-God'll-send-Monday adj phr [Blend of **come day, go day (,God send Sunday)** and **come easy, go easy**]

1919 Kyne *Capt. Scraggs* 101 **CA,** Me, all my life I been a come-easy, go-easy, come-Sunday,-God'll-send-Monday sort o' feller.

come follow me to London n

1970 *DARE* (Qu. EE1, *What games do children play around here, in which they form a ring, and either sing or recite a rhyme?*) Inf **PA242,** Come follow me to London.

come for fire See **fire, come to borrow**

come forward v phr Cf **come out** 2, **come through** 1

To stand up and profess one's faith at a religious meeting.

1967 Fetterman *Stinking Creek* 95 **seKY,** Reckon how many the preacher will get to come forward?

come fresh v phr Also *come in fresh* **scattered exc NEast** See Map Cf **come in** 1, **freshen** 2

Of a domestic animal, esp a cow: to give birth; to begin to give milk thereafter.

1917 *DN* 4.390 **IL,** Come in fresh. **1939** *LANE* Map 193, 3 infs, **scattered,** Come fresh. **1950** *PADS* 14.21 **SC,** *Come fresh . . .* Of cows: to freshen. **c1960** *Wilson Coll.* **csKY,** *Come fresh.* To have a calf and, therefore, be giving milk again. **1965–70** *DARE* (Qu. K10, *. . Of a cow that is going to have a calf*) 33 Infs, **scattered,** (She's) comin(g) (in) fresh (soon); 17 Infs, **scattered,** (She's) (going to, due to, ready to, will) come (in) fresh; **AR18,** Came fresh; (Qu. K11, *When a cow has a calf, you say she _____*) 29 Infs, **scattered,** Come(s) (in) fresh; **FL7, 32, MO38, NC87, OR4, WV13,** Came fresh; **DE1, IL29, NC30, SC7,** (Has) come fresh; **FL26, MN40, NJ56,** (Is) coming fresh; **CA63,** Comes in fresh with a calf; (Qu. K45, *. . A mare . . has just _____*) Inf **CA193,** Come fresh. **1966** *PADS* 46.25 **cnAR,** "The cow will come fresh in September." **1973** Allen *LAUM* 1.246 **Upper MW,** *Come fresh, . .* with an overall average of only 10%, is perhaps favored by more Northern than Midland speakers.

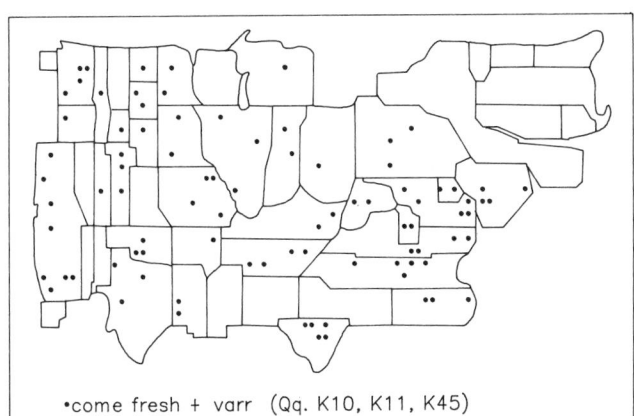

•come fresh + varr (Qq. K10, K11, K45)

come go home with me v phr

1934 Carmer *Stars Fell on AL* 263, That's the way a Cajan says good-by. 'Come go home with me.'

come-here n **seVA**

A person not originally of the community.

1974 *Lancaster Heritage* (Weems VA) July 1 [Black], In Lancaster County everybody has heard and used the term "come-here," as applied to recent, and in some cases not-so-recent, arrivals among its residents . . . The users of "come-here" frankly concede that a whiff of opprobrium often goes with it. **1983** *VA Wildlife* 44.421 **eVA,** "To make it worse, a Come-Here caught the first flounder [of the fishing season]." (A Come-Here is an Eastern Shore resident whose family has lived on the peninsula for fewer than four generations, more or less.) **1984** *Reader's Digest* Aug 41, For more than 30 years, our family has vacationed at a cottage we own on the Chesapeake Bay in Virginia. We had reconciled ourselves to always being "Come Heres" to the local community, but one year when I paid the property taxes, there was a sign of real acceptance for the first time.

come-hither shovel n

1950 *PADS* 14.21 **SC**, *Come-hither shovel*. . . A shovel reshaped so that the blade is at a right angle with the handle, used like a hoe for digging in pluff mud and marshes, for clams, etc.

come in v phr

1 rarely *come in(to) milk;* Of a cow (or rarely of another domestic animal): to give birth; to begin to give milk thereafter. [Engl dial; cf *EDD* come II.1.(16)(d). See also *OED* come 59j.] **widespread, but least freq in Midl** See Map Cf **come fresh, come in profit**

1839 MA Ag. Surv. *Report* 2.60, He gives an opinion, . . that the heifers which "come in" with their first calf at two years old, do better than when their coming in is delayed until three years old. **1863** *Country Gentleman* 21.63/3 **Boston MA**, Hence the object is to have all the cows "come in" near the commencement of the butter or cheese making season. **1895** *DN* 1.386 **CT**, *Come in* (of cows): to calve. **1903** *DN* 2.296 **Cape Cod MA** (as of a1857). **1908** *DN* 3.300 **eAL, wGA**. **1910** *DN* 3.439 **cwNY**. **1914** *DN* 4.70 **ME, nNH**. **1915** *DN* 4.182 **swVA**. **1917** *DN* 4.390 **neOH**, *Come in*. . . To calve. Associated [*DN* ed: not in N. Eng.] with the fact that a cow *comes in* from the woods, where she is likely to stay a few days before calving. **1919** *DN* 5.76, *Come in*. Used in rural Massachusetts of nearly all domestic animals (horses, dogs, cows, sheep), not restricted to cows; therefore Mr. Kenyon's suggestion [in *DN* 4.390] as to the origin of the term probably will not hold. **1923** *DN* 5.245 **KS**, *Come in*. . . Of domestic animals: to bring forth young. **1939** *LANE* Map 193, Two sets of terms are shown on the map . . . One set refers specifically to the birth of the calf: *calve* . . ; the other refers to the enlargement of the cow's udder previous to calving: *freshen, fresh . . , come fresh, be fresh . . , come in, be in, come into milk, come in milk.* [*Come in* was recorded from about 3/4 of the communities surveyed; the varr *come in milk* and *come into milk* were each recorded once.] **1965–70** *DARE* (Qu. K10, . . *About a cow that is going to have a calf*) 52 Infs, **scattered,** (She's) coming in; 16 Infs, **scattered,** (Due, going, fixing, about, *or* pretty near ready) to come in (soon); **AL11, GA74, NH14,** Come in; **NC48, OH3,** Comes in; **CA63, NY163,** Comin' in (shortly *or* with calf); **LA12,** Gone come in; **NC53,** She's gonna come in; (Qu. K11, *When a cow has a calf, you say she* _____) 40 Infs, **scattered,** Comes in; **AR33, CT2, 9, MN40, 42, MS39, NV8, WI52,** Came in; **ME1, MS46, NC53, VA38,** Come in; **KY39,** Is come in; **WI71,** Is coming in; (Qu. K1, *A cow that is giving milk*) Inf **ME1,** She just come in; (Qu. K45, *When a mare has had a young horse, you say she has just* _____) Inf **MS21,** Come in; (QR, near Qu. K54) Inf **CA31,** [A] sow that had come in with eight or ten little piglets. **1973** Allen *LAUM* 1.246, *Come in* [for *calve*] has the clearest regional pattern: Mn. 20%, Ia. 8%, N.D. 24%, S.D. 4%, Nb. 6%. It is not reported in southern Iowa, and in Minnesota it is limited, with one exception, to the oldest settled portions . . . Mail returns from 1,025 infs. support the Northern orientation of *come in* with 31 in Minnesota and only 8 in Nebraska.

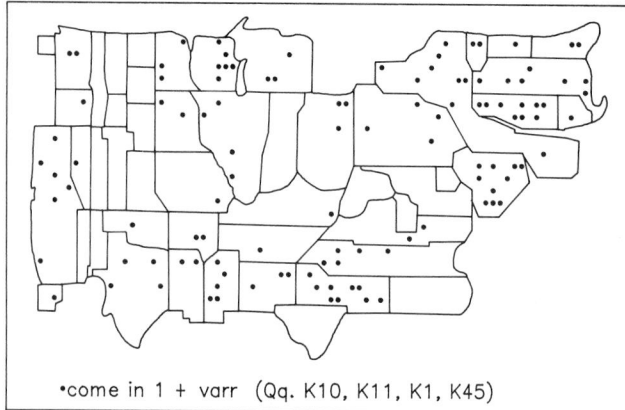

•come in 1 + varr (Qq. K10, K11, K1, K45)

2 Of animals: to come in heat.

1912 *DN* 3.573 **wIN**, *Come in*. . . Applied to animals. "Since the colt is weaned now, she (the mare) will probably come in next month."

3 Of weather: to become. Cf **come B4**

1933 *Hanley Disks* **seMA**, It come in very cold that night.

come in an ace of, come in a one See **come within one of**

come in fresh See **come fresh**

come in one (of) See **come within one of**

come in profit v phr

1917 *DN* 4.390 **CT**, *Come in profit* [To calve].

comeny v [Prob *come* + *ny* nigh; cf *OED comether*] *prob obs*

1895 *DN* 1.386 **ceKY**, *Comeny:* = *haw;* turn to the left (in driving oxen).

come off v phr

1 imper: Quit! Stop! Cut it out!

1892 *N.Y. Mercury* Feb (Ware) *(DA)*, "How much does yez ax for this book?" "Six dollars" replied the smiling clerk. "Six dollars! Oh, come off!" **1927** *AmSp* 2.351 **WV**, *Come off.* . conveys the idea of surprise or ridicule. "Come off such notions!" **1935** Sandoz *Jules* 139 **wNE** (as of 1880–1930), "We come to get your rifle," he said. "But I have not got any," he pleaded, rubbing his bony hands together. "Oh, come off! Didn't I repair it for your boy this spring?" **1969** *DARE* (Qu. II22, *Expressions to tell somebody to keep to himself and mind his own business*) Inf **NY206,** Come off it.

2 Of the weather: to become, to turn out.

1944 Walker *Winter Wheat* 41, Dad had not intended to go. But Saturday came off so warm the winter wheat showed bright apple-green. **1966–67** *DARE* Tape **ME18,** Then it come off kinda warm, warm enough so that snow would melt; **MA5C,** If it comes off cold, they [=the maple trees] won't run for three or four days.

3 In the process of hatching chicks:

a Of the hen: to finish her hatch.

1878 in 1937 Ruede *Sod-House* 225, Another hen is sitting on 15 eggs. She will come off in a week.

b Of the chicks: to hatch.

1959 Sanders *Echoes* 38 **swAR**, She gave me a "setting" of the eggs and when they "came off", I wouldn't let them associate with other chickens. **1968** *DARE* Tape **IA38,** We had incubators going and chicks coming off [i.e. hatching and being moved].

come-off n

1 A circumstance, an outcome, or some particular behavior, often unfortunate. **Sth, S Midl**

1884 Harrison *Negro Engl.* 274, Sech er come off ez dis = such behavior. **1887** (1967) Harris *Free Joe* 128 **GA**, "Well, well, well!" exclaimed the old man, . . "What kind of a come-off is this?" **1909** *DN* 3.359 **eAL, wGA**, *Pretty come-off* . . . An unfortunate circumstance, a regrettable condition. "It's a pretty come-off that you are not ready for meetin'." **1950** *PADS* 14.78 **cwFL**, That's some come-off! An odd way to behave, or an unfortunate occurrence. **1960** Criswell *Resp. to PADS* 20 **Ozarks**, *Come-off* . . . A happening, a result. "Well, that's a fine come-off. I thought he was going to leave the country." (Probably still current).

2 See quot.

1899 (1912) Green *VA Folk-Speech, Come-off* . . . Evasion, escape; means of escape. "It was a great come-off."

3 A thing or creature. Cf **come off** v phr **3b**

1934 Vines *Green Thicket* 181 **cnAL**, And he took the fish to a hole . . dumped them in, and told them to find company with the others like them already there. They were all *purty*-looking come-offs.

come on v phr

1a Of weather: to develop into (a different and freq disagreeable condition); to begin (to be). See also **come B4, come up 2**

1799 (1898) Hunt *Diary* 3 **PA**, In the afternoon it came on a severe storm of wind & snow. **1806** (1904) Roe *Diary* 28 **Long Island NY**, It came on to rain about ten o'clock. **1887** *Scribner's Mag.* 2.484 **AR**, "An' ef do come on ter rain," remarked the widow, . . "it'll holp ter clean 'em all the mo'!" **1903** *DN* 2.294 **seMA**, *Come on*. . . Of the weather, to begin or begin to be. "It come on to blow a gale of wind." "It come on thick" i.e. foggy. **1933** Rawlings *South Moon* 194 **FL**, My God, if it comes on to rain, hit'll wash out Kezzy's tracks. **1939** *LANE* Map 90 **seME**, *Clouding up* . . . [coming on to storm]. **1939** Coffin *Capt. Abby* 150 **ME** (as of c1860s), And it came on to pour. It rained cats and dogs. **1940** (1942) Clark *Ox-Bow* 68 **NV** (as of 1885), The sky was really changing now, fast; it was coming on to storm, or I didn't know signs. **1966** *DARE* Tape **MI20,** When it come on cold weather, they'd go back.

b Of other natural phenomena: to approach, develop into, begin.

1926 Roberts *Time of Man* 364 **KY**, He'll be right glad he took Elbertas when they come on to ripen, two or three years from now. **1931–33** *LANE Worksheets* **swCT**, When it comes on dusk. **1939** Coffin *Capt.*

Abby 139 **ME** (as of c1860s), It was coming on fairtime now, a quarter of the globe away. **1968** *DARE* FW Addit **CT**15, 'Twas coming on Fall. **1970** *DARE* (Qu. A5, *The time . . before it becomes all dark*) Inf **NJ**67, Coming on night. [Inf old]

2 To make a visit that involves a journey. **chiefly MA**

1817 (1910) Ayer *Diary* 219 **neMA**, We had a letter from my father . . informing us that it was necessary for me to come on directly. **1931–33** *LANE Worksheets* **seMA**, A visitor comes on [=to visit]. *Ibid* **seMA**, He comes on. *Ibid* **seMA**, He hasn't been on in 20 years. He came on last summer. **1960** *DE Folkl. Bulletin* Oct 36/2, Coming on (coming for a visit). **1978** *DARE* File **cnMA** (as of c1915), I knew the expression "to come on." It was used in such sentences as, "She came on last summer when her mother died." I think it was used only of people who came from a distance: people "came on" only from the west, from Omaha, say, or San Francisco; you couldn't "come on" from New York City.

3 in phr *How (do) you come on?:* To feel, get on. **chiefly S Midl**

a1883 (1911) Bagby *VA Gentleman* 261, "Ah!" Said I, turning around, "how do you do, sir?" "Right peart; how'd y' come on yourself?" **1895** *DN* 1.371 **neTN**, *Come on:* for *do.* (Most common salutation.) "How do you come on?" **1905** *DN* 3.75 **nwAR**, *Come on . . .* Get on, get along. "How do you come on?" Common. **1908** *DN* 3.300 **eAL, wGA**. **1912** Green *VA Folk-Speech* 123, *Come on . . .* A mode of salutation: "How you come on." **1937** (1963) Hyatt *Kiverlid* 35 **KY**, "How do you come on this evenin' Granny?" inquired Nancy, as she entered the big house. **1967–70** *DARE* (Qu. NN10a, *Expressions . . used when you meet somebody you know quite well*) Inf **TN**1, How do you come on today?

4 To act or work vigorously or superbly.

1946 (1972) Mezzrow *Really Blues* 331, *Come on:* give a terrific performance, be superb. **1967–70** *DARE* (Qu. KK29, *To start working very hard*) Infs **IN**61, **KY**75, **LA**17, **MO**11, Coming on; (Qu. EE21b, . . *Boys . . fighting very actively*) Inf **VA**71, Came on.

5 To mature, grow up. Cf **come up 2**

1966–70 *DARE* Tape **NC**23, I have fresh squash an' fresh cucumbers coming on; **TN**51, They don't love you as well now as they did when I were comin' on; **VA**114, I never done much of that after I come on. **1968** *DARE* (QR, near Qu. S7) Inf **CA**70, We used to have seasons here where different things—plants—came on.

6 See quot. Cf **come around 2**

1954 *AmSp* 29.298 **TX, OK, FL**, [Terms for menstruation as producing] *Illness, inconvenience, or disability: . . come on.*

7 See **come A5b.**

come-on n, also attrib

1 An allurement; bait. **chiefly Nth**

1902 George Ade *Girl Proposition* 122 *(OEDS),* As soon as any one began to give him the old come-on about being one Man shy he would start in to back up. **1965–70** *DARE* (Qu. U15, . . *A little extra to make you feel . . you're getting a good bargain, you call that [a] _____*) 26 Infs, **Nth**, Come-on; **NY**219, Come-on gift; (Qu. P16, . . *Bits of bait . . to attract fish*) Inf **CA**80, Come-on; (Qu. HH37, *An immoral woman*) Inf **CA**110, Come-on girl.

2 also *comer-on*: A dupe, patsy, an easy mark.

1898 Stead *Satan's Invisible World* 109 **NYC**, The victim, who was known as a "Come On" . . , was swindled by a variety of methods. **1968–69** *DARE* (Qu. II34, *If you think somebody is trying to use you to his advantage: "I'm not going to be his _____."*) Inf **RI**17, Come-on; **PA**104, Comer-on.

come-on adj Cf **come on** v phr **2, come-here**

Newcome.

1952 *Jrl. Amer. Folkl.* 65.61 **IN**, He first gathered up every scrap of evidence he could, "which pinted [sic] out the come-on woman . . . " The expression "come-on" was applied to anyone moving into any neighborhood from any other neighborhood.

come one-up v phr Cf **come C2**

To get oneself in a superior position.

1968 *DARE* (Qu. II33, . . *"I don't trust him, he's always trying to _____."*) Inf **MN**30, Come one-up.

come out v phr *obs*

1 To progress.

1842 in 1956 Eliason *Tarheel Talk* 265 **NC**, She is to teach Greek and Latin dont [sic] you think our town is coming out.

2 To profess one's religious faith. Cf **come through 1**

1856 Whitcher *Bedott Papers* 108 **NEng**, I experienced religion . . at

one o' brother Armstrong's protracted meetin's . . . Them special efforts is great things—ever sence I *come out* I've felt like a new critter. **1872** Schele de Vere *Americanisms* 231, A person proposing to *join a church* is expected first openly to *come out,* that is to say, to *profess* his religion.

come outer n, also attrib

A dissenter, one who drops out of an established (usually religious, sometimes political) organization.

1860 Greeley *Overland Journey* 187, We met several wagon-loads of come-outers from Mormonism on their way to the states. **1903** *Atlantic Mth.* Sept 352/1, Dr. Holmes was rather a believer in existing institutions than a "come-outer." **1904** *DN* 2.424 **seMA**, *Come-outer . . .* One who secedes from the regular church. **1908** Lincoln *Cy Whittaker* 54 **MA**, Come-Outer religion's all right, for those that have that kind of appetite. **1955** *Seattle Daily Times* (WA) 12 Apr mag sec 11 (as of c1911), Wilson is the last remaining member of a religious colony which originated in Seattle's Ballard area. The colony had no formal name, but was known as the "Come-Outers," because members had "come out" of many other church denominations.

come over v phr

1 To pay a debt.

1954 *Harder Coll.* **cwTN**, *Come over:* Pay up; same as *shell it over.* **1969–70** *DARE* (Qu. U18, *If you force somebody to pay money that he owes you . . "I finally made him _____."*) Infs **PA**188, **SC**69, **TX**68, Come over.

2 Fig: to die. *euphem*

1968 *DARE* Tape **IN**19, When my mother died the last thing she did was to hold her arms out as if she was reaching for somebody . . . I asked my son if he was there when Grandmother came over.

comer n

1 An animal or person showing promise of full development or success.

1903 *KS State Bd. Ag. Rept. for 1901–02* 202, He has made good growth since he came before the public . . and still shows that remarkable looseness and elasticity of hide that indicates a "*comer*" when he is put next to the feed-box. **1913** *DN* 4.10 **MN**, *Comer . . .* A person with a "future," a person making rapid progress. "He's a comer in politics." **1947** *Denver Post* 2 Mar 1/2 *(DA),* Richard isn't quite that smart but he is a comer if his boorish behavior doesn't get the better of him. **1967** *DARE* (Qu. HH27a, *A very able and energetic person who gets things done*) Infs **OR**1, **WA**22, Comer.

2 A crab which is becoming fat as it approaches the moulting stage.

1879 *St. Nicholas* 7.1.84/2 **NJ**, A buckler [=a young crab] is always very poor to begin with; but he eats everything he gets hold of, which, of course, fattens him up some. Then he is called a "Comer." He keeps on eating till he is bigger still. **1980** *DARE* File, Comer. Yes, definitely. This seems to have been a common term in New Jersey, although not in the sense of a crab fattening up after moult . . . I remember *comer* as synonymous with the general term *peeler,* as used in the Chesapeake, which means any crab with a short time to go before moulting or casting off the\exoskeleton. [Private Correspondence: William Warner, author of *Beautiful Swimmers*]

comer-and-goer n

A tourist.

1899 (1912) Green *VA Folk-Speech* 123, There are comers and goers all the time. **1939** FWP *Guide NC* 303, While there are no boarding houses proper, tourists (comers n' goers) find shelter along the way. **1946** *AN&Q* 6.87/1 **NC**, "Comers 'n' Goers": tourists, in the district of the "bankers" of North Carolina.

comer-on See **come-on** n **2**

come round See **come around 2**

comes See **come A1**

come-see n

1933 *N. Amer. Rev.* 236.542 **eSC** [Gullah], A delicate child is called a Come-see. The child has come to the world, indecisively, to see whether or not it wishes to stay.

come sick v phr **Sth, S Midl**

To menstruate; hence vbl n *coming sick.*

1948 *AmSp* 23.264 **Ozarks**, To menstruate was to *come sick.* **1950** *PADS* 14.21 **SC**, *Come sick . . .* To menstruate. **1954** *AmSp* 29.298 **TX, OK, FL**, *Illness, inconvenience, or disability* [of menstruation]: . . *come* *sick* or *unwell*. **1954** *Harder Coll.* **cwTN. 1960** Criswell *Resp. to PADS* **20 Ozarks**, *Come sick* . . To menstruate. *Sick* meant menstruating. **1967** *DARE* (Qu. AA27, *What other names and expressions are used for* . . *menstruation*) Infs **TN**12, 15, Come sick; **AR**52, Coming sick. **1978** *MJLF* 4.1.38 **cTX**, My mother, in the hushed tones she used for biological discussions, called menstruation "coming sick."

comes, it comes n For varr, see quots *?old-fash*
A children's guessing game: see quots 1883, 1968.

1883 Newell *Games & Songs* 150, *Comes, it Comes*. A simple guessing-game, familiar to children in New England. One child . . says to another, "It comes, it comes." The player addressed replies, "What do you come by?" The first replies by naming the initial letter of some object in the room . . . The rest must now guess what thing. **1968** *DARE* Tape **DE**2, This is a game that we used to play when I was young . . . One person [would] go outside of the room, and then we'd all decide upon an object . . and then when we all had it in our mind . . we'd say "OK, comey comey," and the person coming in would say "What do you come by?" and we'd say "The letter p" . . . Finally he'd say "The picture" and everybody'd say yes . . . We'd call that *comey comey*. Just a guessing game. **1968–69** *DARE* (Qu. EE33, *Other outdoor games . . that children play now or that were played*) Inf **NC**82, ['kʌm si ˌkʌm]. A guessing game: A. "What do you come by?" B. "I come by a C."; **RI**1, Comes ya come—word game. [Infs old]

come through v phr

1 rarely *come across:* To experience religious conversion, esp at a revival meeting. **chiefly Sth, S Midl**

1881 Pierson *In the Brush* 172, They could scarcely speak for hoarsness —enjoyed seeing them "come through" (the vernacular for conversion). **1895** *DN* 1.371 **eTN**, *Come through:* to be converted. **1899** Chesnutt *Conjure Woman* 121 **NC** [Black], De cunjuh man had n' mo' d'n come th'oo good, befo' he wuz tuk sik wid a col'. **1906** *DN* 3.132 **nwAR**, *Come through*. **1908** *DN* 3.300 **eAL, wGA**, *Come through*. **1913** Porter *Laddie* 236 **IN**, *Leon* said our house reminded him of the mourners' bench before anyone had "come through." **1914** *DN* 4.104 **KS**, *Come through* . . . To be converted to a religious life; also, to *come across*. **1915** *DN* 4.182 **VA**, *Come through*. **1950** *PADS* 14.21 **SC**, *Come through* . . . To pass through a religious experience at a revival meeting . . . Negro usage. **c1960** *Wilson Coll.* **csKY**, *Come through*. **1983** *MJLF* 9.35 **ceKY**, *Come through*.

2 To confess fully. Cf **come clean 1**

1916 Du Puy *Uncle Sam* 169, The man that the Government wanted usually came through with all he knew. **1916** Sandburg *Chicago Poems* 63, I ask you to come through and show me where you're pouring out the blood of your life.

3 also *come across:* To pay a debt. **scattered, but chiefly West** See Map

1916 *DN* 4.321 **KS**, *Come thru* (or *across*) *with money* . . . To pay or relinquish money. Slang, general. **1965–70** *DARE* (Qu. U18, *If you force somebody to pay money . . he owes . . "I finally made him* _____.") 46 Infs, **scattered, but chiefly West**, Come through.

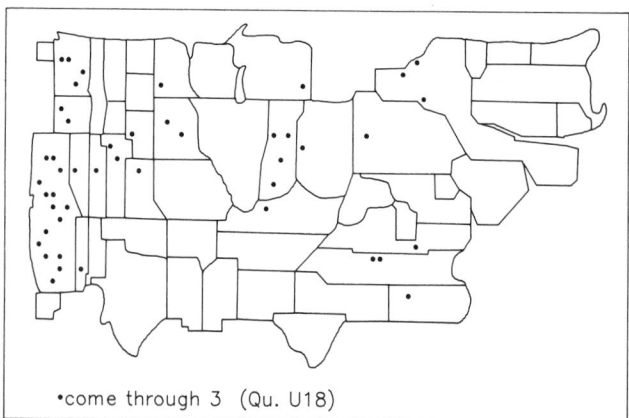

•come through 3 (Qu. U18)

come-tickle-me n
A Johnny-jump-up (here: *Viola tricolor*).
1899 (1909) Earle *Child Life* 383 **NY**, The flowers chosen to sail in these tiny crafts were those most human of all flowers, pansies, or their smaller garden sisters, the "ladies'-delights" . . . The folk names of this flower,

such as "three-faces-under-a-hood," "johnny-jump-up," "jump-up-and-kiss-me," "come-tickle-me," show the universal sense of its kinship to humanity.

come to adv phr [Ellip for *come to find out* or some similar phr]
As it turned out, as a matter of fact, actually—used as an introductory phr.

1909 *DN* 3.419 **Cape Cod MA**, *Come to* . . . Accented on *to*. Finally; come to find out. "Come to, there wasn't a mite of truth in it." **1980** *DARE* File **cnMA** (as of c1930), I suppose that *come to* with the stress on *to* derived from *come to think of it* or *come to find out* as in "Come to, they never sent me a bill" or "Come to, she lived right across the common from us."

come-together n
1968 *DARE* (Qu. Y12a, *A fight between two people, mostly with words*) Inf **NJ**39, Come-together.

come-to-heaven collar n
A wing collar.
1925 Lewis *Arrowsmith* 72, I never thought I'd have to live up to a man with a dress-suit and a come-to-Heaven collar.

come-to-Jesus coat n
1930 Williams *Logger-Talk* 20 **Pacific NW**, *Come-to-Jesus coat*: A frock, Prince Albert, morning, or any long official or ministerial looking coat.

come to one's milk v phr
To yield to authority, comply.
1927 *AmSp* 2.351 **WV**, *Come to his milk* . . to do what must be done, either willingly or unwillingly through the force of necessity. "That boy will come to his milk soon." **1928** *Ruppenthal Coll.* **KS**, *Come to one's milk* . . to yield; to cease to be stubborn; perhaps from the effects of hunger on a stubborn calf that refuses to drink. **1950** *WELS* (Show somebody you're boss: "I made him _____.") 1 Inf, **csWI**, Come to his milk.

come-too-soon n Cf **come-by-chance, sooner**
A child born outside of marriage.
1940–41 Cassidy *WI Atlas* **nwWI**, Come-too-soon—a child born out of wedlock. Not common. **1968–70** *DARE* (Qu. Z11b) Infs **KS**15, **KY**10, **NY**36, **VA**78, **WI**66, Come-too-soon.

come to time v phr
To yield to authority, comply.
1937 Sandoz *Slogum* 78 **NE** (as of 1900–20), Butch began to lag again, knowing he had his sister where the hair was short. She came to time. **1950** *WELS* (Show somebody you're boss: "I made him _____.") 7 Infs, **WI**, Come to time. **1966–70** *DARE* (Qu. JJ25, *To show somebody . . you're the boss: ". . I made him* _____.") Infs **CA**59, **MI**92, **WI**66, 67, Come to time; (Qu. JJ26, *. . The boss might say," . . he'd better* _____.") Inf **TN**65, Come to time; (Qu. JJ38, *. . "At the last minute he* _____.") Inf **NM**9, Gave in; came to time.

comet split See **split** n

come undone See **come apart**

come up v phr

1 imper: Move!—used as a call to draft animals to make them start moving or go faster. **chiefly Sth, S Midl** See Map Cf **cope v²**

1899 (1912) Green *VA Folk-Speech* 123, *Come-up* . . . Said to horses to urge them on. **1915** *DN* 4.182 **VA**. **1937** (1977) Hurston *Their Eyes* 83 **FL**, "Ah does feed 'im [=a mule]. He's jus' too mean tuh git fat. He stay poor and rawbony jus' fuh spite . . ." "Yeah, you feeds 'im. Feeds 'im offa 'come up' and seasons it wid raw-hide." **1949** Kurath *Word Geog.* 43, In addition we find the regional call *come up!* . . from the Virginia Piedmont westward and southward, but not on the Southern coast. That the Virginia Piedmont is the area from which this call was disseminated is not certain but quite probable. *Ibid* 66, In Virginia and adjoining parts of Maryland, West Virgina, and North Carolina the more usual call is *come up!*, which may be followed by *sir*. **1965–70** *DARE* (Qu. K36a, *. . To make a horse go faster*) 28 Infs, **Sth, S Midl**, Come up; **CT**39, The minister used to say "High hum Creation come up"; (Qu. K82, *. . To get horses in from pasture*) Inf **MS**46, Come up; (Qu. K33, *When you're driving horses . . how do you make them start?*—total Infs questioned, 75) 10 Infs, **Sth**, Come up. **1967** LeCompte *Word Atlas* 182 **seLA**, *(Call to horses to make them go)*, Come up. [4 of 21 Infs] **1968** *DARE* Tape

LA29, [FW:] What were the other calls for oxen? How about to get them started, to move? [Inf:] We'd tell 'em to come up.

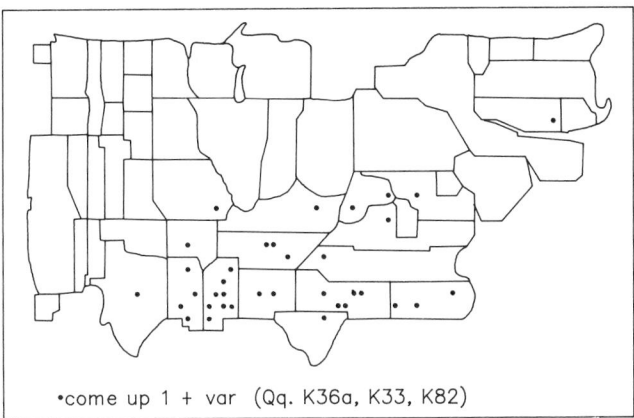

•come up 1 + var (Qq. K36a, K33, K82)

2 Of weather or other natural phenomena: to become, develop into.   See also **come B4, come on 1**

1903 *DN* 2.293 **seMA,** *Come up thick* . . . Get foggy. **1939** *LANE* Map 91 **scattered throughout NEng,** *The wind is getting stronger . . Coming up (fresh).* **1960** Criswell *Resp. to PADS 20* **Ozarks,** *Come up* . . . Used in an impersonal sort of expression in several contexts involving natural phenomena, as illustrated by the following: "It came up a big rain just as we camped." "There came up a big storm", also common form of expression . . . All these were universal in olden times and are still very frequent. **1967–70** *DARE* (Qu. B5, *When the weather looks as if it will become bad*) Infs **GA1, LA11, TX54,** Coming up a storm; **MO4,** Looks like it may come up a thunderstorm; **TN23,** Going to come up a storm; (Qu. B6) Infs **CT17, IN30,** Coming up a storm; (Qu. B12) Inf **CT17,** Come up to thunder shower; (QR, near Qu. A5, *The time right after the sun goes out of sight*) Inf **NJ67,** Come up night. **1969** *DARE* FW Addit **ceNC,** Coming up bull onions and Irish potatoes. [FW: Used, I think, to mean that some stormy clouds are forming.]

3 Of illness: to take hold.

1906 *DN* 3.132 **nwAR,** *Come up* . . . To begin, set in. "Then fever comes up."

4 Of persons: to grow up.   **chiefly Sth, S Midl**

1953 Brewer *Word Brazos* 90 **TX** [Black], In dat time comin' up, dey insult de preachuh evuhwhich way. **1967–68** *DARE* FW Addit **GA33,** When I was coming up; **csNC,** When I was coming up, no one cussed in front of women. **1967–70** *DARE* Tapes **AL13, DC11, GA79, MO8, NY55, 236, NC74, OK53, SC44,** Come up; **AL33,** They got more [population] as I come on up. **1969** *Foxfire* Winter 9 **nGA,** "We used t', when we's a' comin' up children — you see, they'd cut and thresh their wheat and rye ever'year. **1972** Claerbaut *Black Jargon* 61, *Comin' up* . . . growing up; maturing: "When I was comin' up." **1978** *Natl. Geog. Mag.* Mar 410 **AR,** Kim, who is 33, remembers a Little Rock of trolleys and busy sidewalks when he was "coming up" near the Rock Island Railroad tracks in the city's south end.

comeuppance n Also sp *come-up-ance, come-up 'ans, come-upence, come-uppin(g)s, comeuppunce, comuppance* Cf **come up with, comings**

1 One's just deserts.

1859 *Harper's Mag.* 18.277/1, Dennis once got his 'come-up-ance'. **1893** *KS Univ. Qrly.* 2.138 **neKS,** *Come-upence:* deserts, as 'He got his come-upence.' **1893** Owen *Voodoo Tales* 29, Gooses . . git dey come-uppunce (deserts) des lak folks. **1897** Higginson *Tales from Puget Sound* 155 (1912 Thornton), I can give him his come-up 'ans if he goes to foolin' around. *Ibid* 230, I'll give her her come-uppings! **1903** *DN* 2.350, *Come-up-ance.* **1907** *DN* 3.184 **seNH,** *Come-up-ance.* **1913** *DN* 4.42, *Come-uppance.* **1927** *AmSp* 2.351 **WV,** *Come-uppance.* **1967–70** *DARE* (Qu. II27 . . "*I certainly got a _____ for that.*") Infs **KS8, MN2,** Come-uppins; **MD33, MA98, NC31,** Comeuppance; (Qu. Y16, . . "*He gave the bully an awful _____.*") Inf **SC44,** Got his comeuppance. **1979** *Greenfield Recorder* (MA) 9 June, They get their comuppance.

2 An advantage: see quot.

1941 Faulkner *Men Working* 132 **MS,** That way we'll all share and share alike and won't no man have air comeuppance over no other man.

come-upper n Cf **comer 1**

1968 *DARE* (Qu. HH27a, *A very able and energetic person who gets things done*) Inf **NY54,** Come-upper.

come-uppin(g)s, comeuppunce See **comeuppance**

come up with v phr, usu passive **esp NEng**

To get even with or get the best of; to punish.

1856 *Harper's Mag.* 12.710/1 **East,** One of our smart young lawyers was well come up with the other day. **1871** (1882) Stowe *Fireside Stories* 126 **MA,** He thought he must have his say with Miry, but he got pretty well come up with. **1893** *KS Univ. Qrly.* 2.138, *Come up with:* to get even with. **1901** White *Westerners* 78, Revenge with him seemed to lie . . in the victim's realization that he was being come up with. **1907** *DN* 3.184 **seNH,** *Come up with* . . . Passively, to be overtaken by punishment, to be punished, to get one's just deserts . . . "He got come up with when he tried to skin me." **1928** *DN* 6.2 **MA** (as of 1869–1910), *Come up with* . . . Overtaken by one's match. She gets come up with occasionally, and then I'm delighted.

come within one of v phr Also *come in one (of), come in a one, come (with)in an ace of*

To barely escape (doing something).

1914 *DN* 4.155 **seMA,** *Come within one of* . . . Come near, in the sense of barely to escape . . . "I come within one of breaking my best china platter this morning." **1938** Stuart *Dark Hills* 388 **KY,** "I've come in a one havin' a lot of fights over you." **1940** Stuart *Trees of Heaven* 107 **KY,** "You come in one gittin lost." **1951** *PADS* 15.66 **cwNH,** *Come within an ace of* . . . Come nearly. **c1960** *Wilson Coll.* **csKY,** *Come in* (or *within*) *one of.* To come close to doing something that would have been embarassing or worse. **1966** Barnes–Jensen *Dict. UT Slang,* *Come in one of.* **1966–67** *DARE* (Qu. LL30, *Words and expressions meaning "nearly" or "almost"*) Inf **MS71,** Come in an ace of; **TN12,** Come within an ace of.

come with one's horns down v phr

1912 *DN* 3.573 **wIN,** *Come with one's horns down* . . . To come as if ready for a contest, as a bull when he is angry. "John is coming over here next week, and he's coming with his horns down, too."

comey comey See **comes, it comes**

comf'able See **comfortable**

comfort n

1 =**comforter 1.**   **chiefly Sth, Midl**   See Map   Cf **coverlet, hap, puff**

1834 *S. Lit. Messenger* 1.168, A lady of our party . . aptly compared it to a Yankee comfort. **1908** *DN* 3.300 **eAL, wGA.** **1930** Shoemaker *1300 Words* 12 **cPA Mts** (as of c1900). **1949** Kurath *Word Geog.* 61, The thick cotton-padded quilt is known as a *comfort* in the Midland and the South, as a *comforter* or as a *comfortable* in the North. **1950** *WELS* (*A padded covering used on a bed, mostly for warmth*) 4 Infs, **WI,** Comfort. **1962** Atwood *Vocab. TX* 47, *Comfort,* which is usual throughout the Midland and South, predominates in all parts of Texas . . . Both of these words [*comfort* and *comforter*] are apparently obsolescent. **1965–70** *DARE* (Qu. E16, *A padded covering used on a bed, mostly for warmth*) 203 Infs, **chiefly Sth, Midl,** Comfort; **NC48, PA126,** Down comfort; **NC50,** Home comfort; **VA74,** Wool comfort. **1973** Allen *LAUM* 1.228, As terms, *comfort* and *comforter* retain their eastern distribution contrast. *Comfort* is sharply confined to the Midland territory in Iowa and eastern Nebraska; Northern *comforter* dominates elsewhere.

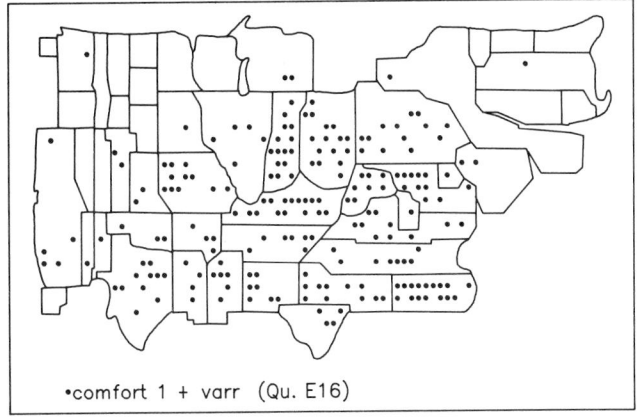

•comfort 1 + varr   (Qu. E16)

2 A storage container for **comforters.**

1967 *DARE* FW Addit **cnNY,** *Comfort*—a comfort chest.

3 A scarf: see quot. [Prob abbr for **comforter 2**]

1899 (1912) Green *VA Folk-Speech, Comfort* . . . A knitted or crochet-ted woolen scarf, long and narrow, for tying around the neck in cold weather.

4 also *comfort shoe:* A bedroom slipper.

1967 *DARE* (Qu. W21, *Soft shoes that people wear only inside the house*) Infs **OH6, SC46, TX42,** Comforts; **DE2,** Comfort shoes.

5 also *comfortweed:* =**comfrey.** [Folk-etym]

1933 Miller *Lamb in His Bosom* 76 **GA,** She poulticed Eliza-beth's face and neck with wild comfort that Vince dug out of the soggy earth. **1970** *DARE* (Qu. BB50c, . . *Remedies . . for infections*) Inf **NC83,** Comfort-weed ointment.

6 also *comfy:* A small cake; see quots. [?Folk-etym for *comfit*]

1968 *DARE* (Qu. H28, *Different shapes or types of doughnuts*) Inf **NH15,** Comfort: small—maybe holes from other doughnuts; **NJ21,** Comfort, a doughnut with no hole. Made and carried by soldiers in Revolutionary War; still made by some old ladies here; **CA59,** Comfy: dropped spoonfuls or doughnut centers. **1975** Jones *Amer. Food* 80, In Pennsylvania Dutch homes . . the final course . . is a cooked dessert, a pudding, for instance, or sugar dumplings known as "Comforts."

comfortable adj, n |ˈkʌmfə(r)təbl̩, ˈkʌmftə(r)bl̩|, occas |ˈkam-|
Pronc-spp *comf'able, comf'table, cum-f't'bl*

A Forms.

1895 (1969) Crane *Red Badge* 8, I want my boy to be jest as warm and comf'able as anybody in the army. **1907** *DN* 3.184 **seNH,** *Comf'table.* **1935** *AmSp* 10.165 **PA,** Another matter of pronunciation attributable to the German influence is the substitution of [aː] for [ʌ], noticeable especially in the words *nothing, comfortable,* and *country.* **1937** *AmSp* 12.126 **Upstate NY,** Metathesis, or reversal of the order of sounds, is common, especially when [r] is one of the affected sounds; thus: *comfortable* [ˈkʌmftrbl̩]. **1942** *AmSp* 17.153 **seNY,** *Comfortable* has [kʌmfə·təbl̩] . . [kʌmfətəbl̩] . . [kʌmftə·bl̩] . . [kʌmftəbl̩]. **1975** Gould *Me Lingo* 56, *Comfortable*—Pronounced *cum-f't'bl.*

B As noun.

1 Something that adds to one's comfort. *obs*

1786 (1888) Cutler *Life* 2.247, He appeared much pleased, and pro-poses to provide well in *comfortables* for the journey. **1838** (1925) Kemper *Trip WI* 436 **NY,** We started at 4 supplied with many comfort-ables—green veils for the hats of all three of us . . two roast ducks, crackers, smoke beef, cakes, wine, salt.

2 =**comforter 1.** **chiefly NEast** See Map Cf **comfort 1**

1842 Buckingham *E. & W. States* 3.434, Still Mr. Van Buren was not content; he longed for the 'Turkish divan' and the 'French comfort-able.' **1907** *DN* 3.184 **seNH,** *Comf'table* . . . A wadded bedquilt; a comforter. "I need another comf'table on this bed." **1949** Kurath *Word Geog.* 61, *Comforter* is the usual term in Eastern New England and in Manhattan, *comfortable* is Southwestern New England, in the Hudson Valley, on Long Island, in East Jersey, and in New York State. However *comforter* is scattered all through the *comfortable* area, and *comfortable,* in turn, is not unknown in the Delaware Valley beside *comfort.* **1965–70** *DARE* (Qu. E16, *A padded covering used on a bed, mostly for warmth*) 18 Infs, **chiefly NEast,** Comfortable. **1973** Allen *LAUM* 1.228, *Comfortable,* common in Connecticut and the Hudson Valley,

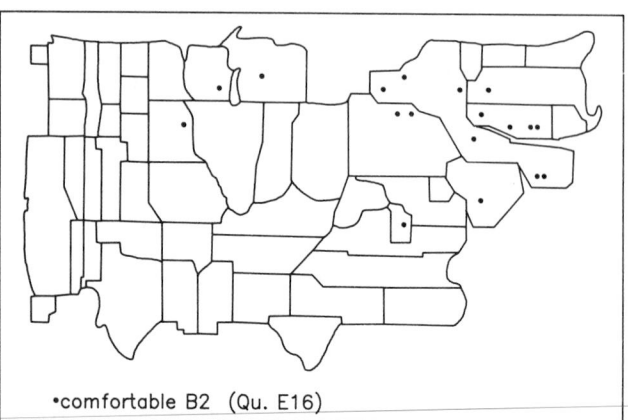

•comfortable B2   (Qu. E16)

survives with only four infs. in Iowa and western South Dakota. **1975** Gould *ME Lingo* 56, *Comfortable.* Pronounced *cum-f't'ble.* A variation for comforter, a quilt or puff for winter sleeping, but not a blanket. It's about fifty-fifty that Mainers will say comforter or *comfortable.*

comfort bag n Also *comfort kit* old-fash

A package of small personal items for soldiers; a ditty bag.

1867 Moore *Women War* 586, The little child diligently sewing with tiny fingers upon the soldiers' comfort-bag. **1870** Macrae *Americans* 1.79, They made tens of thousands of little housewives—'comfort-bags,' as the soldiers called them—with buttons, needle and thread, comb, cake of soap, and above all, a little tract or Testament. **1941** FWP *Guide IN* 73, *Comfort kit.* The women of the State put together countless "comfort kits" [for soldiers in World War I].

comforter n

1 A heavy quilt. **widespread, but least freq in Sth** See Map Cf **comfort 1, comfortable B2**

1832 S.G.Goodrich *Univ. Geog.* 107 *(DAE),* The females also have similar meetings called "quilting bees," when many assemble to work for one, in padding or quilting bed coverings or comforters. **1907** *DN* 3.242 **eME.** **1910** *DN* 3.439 **wNY,** *Comforter* . . . A quilt lined with cotton batting. **1949** Kurath *Word Geog.* 13, *Comforter* and *comfortable* are distinctive Northern words for a thick quilt. The boundary between these terms and the Midland *comfort* is well defined. **1962** Atwood *Vocab. TX* 47, The Northern form *comforter* appears also, with slightly greater frequency in Southwest Texas than elsewhere. Both of these words [*comfort* and *comforter*] are apparently obsolescent. **1965–70** *DARE* (Qu. E16, *A padded covering used on a bed, mostly for warmth*) 234 Infs, **widespread, but least freq in Sth,** Comforter; **CA11, CO26, NY8,** 65, Down comforter; **NJ5,** Quilted comforter; (Qu. E15, *The cloth . . put on top of a bed, mostly for decoration*) Inf **MA6,** Comforter. **1973** [see **comfort 1**].

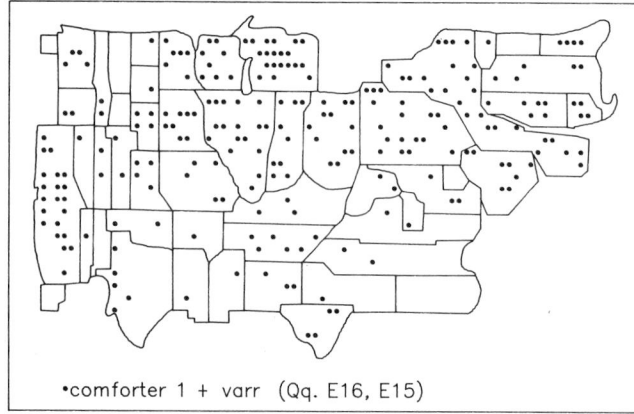

•comforter 1 + varr   (Qq. E16, E15)

2 A long, heavy, usu knitted, neck scarf. **Nth** *old-fash*

1840 (1841) Dana *2 Yrs.* 263, This added to guernsey frocks, striped comforters about the neck, . . and a strong, oily smell, . . will complete the description. **1890** Howells *Boy's Town* 79 **sOH,** When a boy had . . tied his comforter round his neck and over his ears, he was warmly dressed. **1907** *DN* 3.242 **eME,** *Comforter* . . . A long, heavy knit scarf for the neck. "His neck was all wrapped up in a comforter." **1909** *DN* 3.410 **nME,** *Comforter* . . . A scarf worn about the neck.

3 A pacifier. Cf **fooler**

1908 *DN* 3.300 **eAL, wGA,** *Comforter* . . . A rubber nipple used to soothe a baby. Also called *fooler.*

comfort kit See **comfort bag**

comfort-quilt n [**comfort** n 1]

=**comforter 1.**

1970 *DARE* (Qu. E16, *A padded covering used on a bed, mostly for warmth*) Inf **VA53,** Comfort-quilt.

comfort root n

=**coontie.**

1933 Small *Manual SE Flora* 1, *Zamia* . . . Comfortroots.

comfort shoe See **comfort 4**

comfortweed See **comfort 5**

comfrey n Also *comfrey root, comfy plant* [Etym obscure; cf *OED*] Cf also **comfort root, wild comfrey**

A plant of the genus *Symphytum*, esp *S. officinale*.   Also called **comfort 5, healing herb, slippery root**

   1737 (1911) Brickell *Nat. Hist. NC* 20, In these Parts [are found] . . Comfrey, Monks-Rhubarb, Burdock. [*DARE* Ed: This may instead refer to **wild comfrey**.]   **1773** (1957) Fithian *Jrl. & Letters* 1.61, The Hostler, when we had led him to the Stable, applied Spirits of Turpentine . . and in the Evening is to fill it with Comfrey Roots pounded Soft.   **1847** Wood *Class-Book* 560, Comfrey . . . A large, coarse-looking mucilaginous plant, in gardens and low grounds, Mid. States.   **1874** *Shaker Med. Preparations,* Comfrey Root — Symphytum Officinale.   **1877** Still *Early Recoll.* 119, Comfrey . . . Cough balsam. Take spikenard root 8 oz, comfrey root 8 oz.   **1889** *Century Dict.,* Comfrey . . . The root of the common comfrey, *S. officinale,* . . is used in decoction in dysentery, chronic diarrhea, etc.   **1899** (1912) Green *VA Folk-Speech* 123, Comfrey . . . A plant so called with reference to its medicinal qualities.   **1969** *DARE* (Qu. I28a, . . *Kinds of . . "greens" around here . . eaten raw*) Inf **PA221,** Comfrey; (Qu. S20) Inf **GA80,** Comfrey plant; comfy plant.

comf'table See **comfortable**

comfy See **comfort 6**

comfy plant See **comfrey**

comical adj Pronc-sp *commikil*   ?Sth
Strange, peculiar.
   1889 (1971) Farmer *Americanisms* 161, Dr. White, who discovered the Puncheon Run Falls, said to a mountaineer that they were a great curiosity. "I don't see nothing kewrus about 'em," replied the man disdainfully, "when the water comes over the top, it is bound to run down to the bottom, and der ain't nothin' kewrus or *comical* in that . ." . . *E.A. Pollard's Southern Scenery.*   **1899** (1912) Green *VA Folk-Speech* 123, Comical . . . Odd in appearance; having some peculiarity. "He is a comical looking person." Strange; extraordinary.   **1922** Gonzales *Black Border* 293 **sSC, GA coasts** [Gullah glossary], Commikil — comical, peculiar.

coming See **coming over**

coming appetite n
A mounting desire, usu for food; also fig.
   1853 (1854) Baldwin *Flush Times* 3, He lied with a coming appetite, growing with what it fed on.   **1898** Lloyd *Country Life* 50 **AL,** There is more than likely always somethin around home about that time to make a man feel some older, but a heap better, and give him a comin appetite.   **1978–79** *DARE* File **sCA,** "You're certainly eating with a coming appetite!"; **Upstate NY,** He ate with a coming appetite.

coming back exclam Also *come back*
=**pigtail** exclam.
   1965–70 *DARE* (Qu. EE23b, *In . . Andy-over . . if you fail to get the ball over . . and it rolls back, what do you call out?*) 15 Infs, **chiefly Sth,** Coming back; **TX33,** Coming back at you; **IL29,** Come back.

coming-out pants n [In humorous ref to *coming-out* a social debut]
   1968 *DARE* (Qu. W24b, . . *To warn a man that his pants are torn or split*) Inf **OH79,** Have you got your coming-out pants on?; **WI60,** He's got his coming-out pants on.

coming over exclam Also *coming*
=**Antony-over** exclam.
   1965–70 *DARE* (Qu. EE23a, *In . . Andy-over . . what do you call out when you throw the ball?*) Infs **FL37, GA86, MA6, NJ21, OH20, VA93,** Coming over; **MI67, NY75, VA24,** Coming.

comings n pl Cf **comeuppance 1**
One's due or just deserts.
   1947 Ballowe *The Lawd* 10 **LA,** He gwineter git his comin's. Sho's you bawn, he gwineter git 'em.

coming sick See **come sick**

comleka See **kamleika**

comma See **commie**

commandante See **comandante**

commandos n Also sp *commandoes* Cf **run sheep run**
A children's hiding game: see quots.

   1968 *DARE* (Qu. EE12, *Games in which one captain hides his team and the other team tries to find it*) Inf **TX54,** Commandos, played at night.   **1975** *Ford Times* Mar 21 **Detroit MI** (as of 1940s), Commandoes had no rules really. We just crawled around on our stomachs a lot searching out the other team who was The Enemy. When we sighted an Enemy we pointed a stick at him and made sounds like a machine gun.

commas(s) See **camas 1**

commencer n
   1931–33 *LANE Worksheets* **swME,** Commencer . . self-starter of a car.

commercial v [Prob abbr for *to fish for commercially* or perh *to commercial-fish*]
To fish professionally.
   1967 *DARE* Tape **LA5,** Around here they have got another fish they commercial a whole lot.

commeser See **camas 1**

commie n Usu |'kɑmi|, also |'kʌmi| Also *comma, common, common(e)y, commy, kimmie* [Prob abbr for *common marble* + *-ie, -(e)y* dimin suff]   **chiefly N Midl, Inland Nth**   See Map
A playing marble, esp an inexpensive clay marble.
   1890 *DN* 1.60 **wPA,** Commy: a clay marble of the kind least valued by boys . . . *Commony* is the name in Ohio.   **1890** Howells *Boy's Town* 81 **OH,** Commy.   **1934** *AmSp* 9.75 **ND,** Commies. Glass marbles, particularly the creamy ones.   **1935** *AmSp* 10.159 **seNE,** Commies. As I knew them, these were not glass marbles, but those made of common clay, painted all sorts of colors.   **1949** *PADS* 11.19 **CO,** Commy.   **1950** *WELS (Different kinds of marbles)* 7 Infs, WI, Commie(s) [small ones]; 1 Inf, Commies; 1 Inf, Clay commies [cheap ones].   **1955** *PADS* 23.14, Commie (commy, commony, commoney, kimmie) . . . 1. A cheap burnt clay playing marble . . . 2. A valuable marble . . . 3. A common or glass marble.   **1958** *PADS* 29.32, **IA, MI, NE, SD, WA, WI,** Commie.   **1965–70** *DARE* (Qu. EE6c, . . *Cheap marbles*) 81 Infs, **chiefly N Midl, Inland Nth,** Commies; **OH56,** Commons; **NC84,** Commas — made of clay; little brown marbles; (Qu. EE6b, . . *Small marbles*) 20 Infs, **chiefly N Midl,** Commies; (Qu. EE7, . . *Marble games*) Inf **PA237,** Commies.   **1966–68** *DARE* Tape **IL2,** Commies ['kɑmiz] . . were made of clay, but the real ones were agate; **IL12, MI55,** Commies ['kɑmiz] . . were made out of clay; **IA35,** The commons were cheaper marbles and that's what everybody played for; **NM6,** So many marbles, either glassies or commons.   **1973** Ferretti *Marble Book* 42 **NYC,** Commies. Pronounced "Come-ee" not "Commie" . . . The small marbles at which shooters are shot . . . [Also] *Commons.*

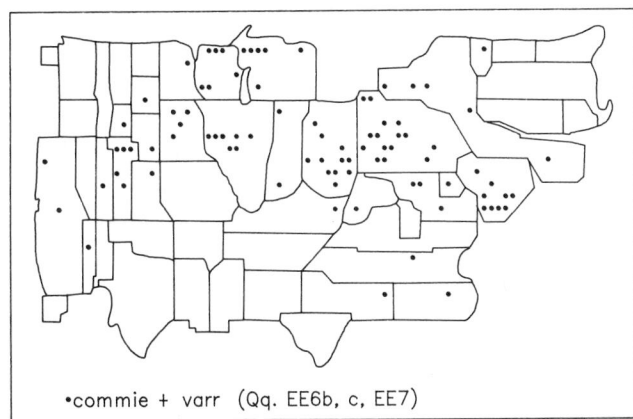

•commie + varr (Qq. EE6b, c, EE7)

commikil See **comical**

commissionate v *arch*
   1899 (1912) Green *VA Folk-Speech* 123, Commissionate . . . To give a commission; to appoint or empower a person to act for another.

commode n
1 also attrib; also rarely *commoder:* A dresser, chest of drawers. **chiefly Nth**
   1845 *Lowell Offering* 5.254, Do they have commodes, and workstands, and spoolstands, and tape-measures, and finger-nail brushes?   **1890** *Boston Journal* 25 Feb. 1/3 *(DAE),* To-day we place on sale a Bedroom Suit . . . It has the wide French bureau and the 1890 English commode.   **1902** Singleton *Social NY* 83 (as of 1773), [Joseph Cox from London]

makes . . commode dressing and toilet-tables. **1941** *LANE* Map 339 **scattered in NEng**, *Bureau . . Commode.* **1950** *WELS* (*A piece of furniture where clothes are laid flat*) 4 Infs, **WI**, Commode; 1 Inf, **swWI**, Commoder. **1965–70** *DARE* (Qu. E3) 17 Infs, **chiefly Nth**, Commode. **1970** Tarpley *Blinky* 84 **neTX**, (*Piece of furniture containing one drawer on top of another*)—Other responses: . . commode.

2 A wardrobe.

1934 *Hanley Disks* **cMA**, Commodes, as tall as a man and various sizes. [In answer to Hanley's, "Do you remember these large wardrobe closets?"] **1965–70** *DARE* (Qu. E1, *A piece of furniture that stands against the wall, and you hang clothes in it*) Infs **MI**119, **MO**11, **OH**21, 24, **OK**9, **WI**50, Commode.

3 A buffet.

1968–69 *DARE* (Qu. E5, *A piece of furniture with a flat top for keeping tablecloths, dishes, and such*) Infs **CA**36, **CT**32, Commode.

4a An indoor toilet. **chiefly Sth, Midl** See Map

1965–70 *DARE* (Qu. F37, . . *An indoor toilet*) 130 Infs, **chiefly Sth, Midl**, Commode; **GA**81, Bathroom commode; **AL**14, Commode bowl; (Qu. X17, . . *A damp cellar . . shut up for some time would smell* _____) Inf **GA**43, Like a commode. **1967–69** *DARE* FW Addit **cnNC**, *Commode:* Indoor toilet [common; seen on signs in restaurants and service stations]; **eTN**, *Commode* [kəˈmod] seems to be the commonest term for indoor toilet throughout East Tennessee, though I never receive it as a response. **1968** *State* (Columbia SC) 2 May sec B 16, 2 Piece Bath Set . . . This set includes a reverse trap commode. **1971** *Today Show Letters* **New Orleans LA**, Bathroom is never called this in Alabama, but rather is the commode. *Ibid*, I am 71. I grew up in an almost unbelievable concept of modesty and in Louisiana the term "toilet" was simply not in the vocabulary of any of us. Instead, we used the word "commode." **1978** *AP Letters* **swPA**, A commode is a toilet, not a chest.

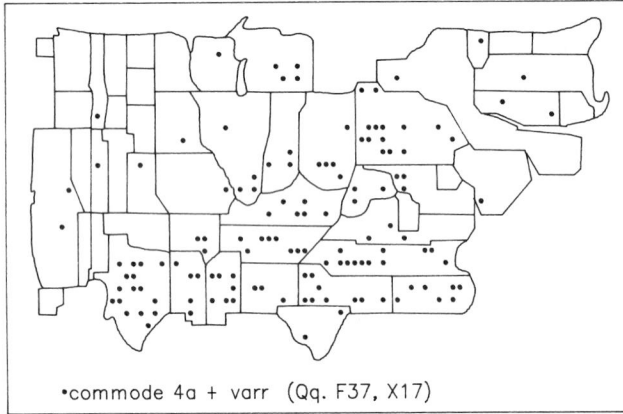

•commode 4a + varr (Qq. F37, X17)

b A chamber pot. **scattered, but esp Atl, Nth**

1950 *WELS* (*Utensil kept under a bed for use at night*) 3 Infs, **WI**, Commode. **1957** Battaglia *Resp. to PADS 20* **MD**, Commode. **1965–70** *DARE* (Qu. F38) 28 Infs, **esp freq Atl, Nth**, Commode.

common adv

Commonly, usually.

1784 (1925) Washington *Diaries* 2.297, The Land is leveller than is common to be met with in this part of the Country. **1916** Porter *Just David* 75, We don't use this room common, little boy, nor the bedroom there, either.

common adj

1 Unpretentious, affable, unassuming, approachable. **chiefly S Midl**

1913 Morley *Carolina Mts.* 175, When you hear one of your friends spoken of by a highlander as being "common" you are puzzled, to say the least, until you learn that the word is the most complimentary possible, retaining its original meaning as understood when we speak of the "common people," the "common good." **1924** Raine *Land of Saddle-Bags* 105 **sAppalachians**, "He's a mighty *common* man" (affable, mingles with folk as an equal). **1927** *DN* 5.473 **Ozarks**, *Common* . . . Devoid of snobbishness or conceit, the highest compliment that can be paid to a professional man or a *furriner*. "Doc Oakley's jes' a nice, common feller." **1930** Shoemaker *1300 Words* 13 **cPA Mts** (as of c1900). **1931** *AmSp* 7.90 **eKY**. **1950** *PADS* 14.21 **SC**. **1954** *Harder*

Coll. **cwTN**. **1968** *DARE* FW Addit **GA**30, 31, *Common* means fine, good. "He's right common" means "he's a good person, a simple man." **1975** Gould *ME Lingo* 56, *Common.* When Mainers say somebody is *common,* they mean he is unpretentious, a real sort who doesn't put on airs: "Real *common,* same as us." It is high praise.

2 Usual—used esp in phr *as common.* **chiefly S Midl, occas NEng**

1817 E. Pettigrew *Let. to Ann Pettigrew* 22 March (Pettigrew P.) *(DAE),* She is as well as common. **1834** Pike *Prose Sketches* 115, 'Busy as common, comadre!' said Lopez as he entered. **1905** *DN* 3.6 **cCT**, *Common* . . . Usual. "As well as common." **1907** *DN* 3.210 **nwAR**, *Common* . . . Usual. **1942** in 1954 *Harder Coll.* **cwTN** (Letter), How does this find you all? Fine, I hope. As for us, just about as well as common. **1943** Writers' Program NC *Bundle of Troubles* 132, Just like common, the pack quit when they hit the bald ground below the top. **1943** *LANE* Map 497 **wMA**, Noncommittal . . expressions of the type of *pretty well, fair to middling,* indicating that the speaker's health is normal [are] *as well as usual, (as) well as common* . . . [1 inf] In Andover . . they say [oh, 'bout as good as common]. **c1960** *Wilson Coll.* **csKY**, I'm as well as common. **1968** Haun *Hawk's Done Gone* 57 **eTN**, He laid there like common—stone-still save for that foot.

3 See quot.

1916 *DN* 4.268 **seLA**, *Common* . . . Monotonous. "Things here are common."

4 Of health:

a Average, fair.

1902 *DN* 2.231 **sIL**, *Common* . . . Tolerable, as applied to health. "How are you?" "Jes *common*." **1968** *DARE* FW Addit **GA**30, 31, "Oh, common" means pretty fair, above average. **1976** Garber *Mountain-ese* **sAppalachians**, *Common* . . in average health. "How air ye Jed?" "Oh, I'm jist common Seth, jist common."

b Unwell.

1968 *DARE* File **eKY**, *Common.* Unwell. "Pa's feelin' common."

5 Familiar.

1972 *Atlanta Letters, Common,* familiar: "Your face looks common."

common n

1 sometimes pl: Undeveloped land owned jointly by members of a town and freq reserved for pasturage. **chiefly NEng**

1634 in 1894 Watertown MA *Records* 1.1, No man shall fell or cutt down any timber trees vpon the Common. **1814** (1916) Thornton *Diary* 19.176 **PA**, Our wounded men . . were still on the Common. **1876** *Scribner's Mth.* 11.744/2, Sods for this purpose are, as a rule, cut from some worn-out pasture, neglected public 'common,' or may be the roadside. **1916** Macy–Hussey *Nantucket Scrap Basket* 127, *Commons* —Unlike most New England towns, Nantucket never had a Common, but it did have thousands of acres of "commons," that is, undivided lands held in common by the early proprietors and their successors. **1931–33** *LANE Worksheets* **seCT**, Commons—A piece of land owned by several people and not fenced.

2 A public park or open square usu in the center of a town. **chiefly NEng** Cf **green** n

1827 (1829) Hall *Travels* 2.126, There was, moreover, a fine Mall, or public promenade, called the Common, laid out in grass fields, surrounded and intersected by broad gravel walks. **1931–33** *LANE Worksheets* **ceCT**, *Common*—an artificial park. **1949** Kurath *Word Geog.* 20, The village green, held in common, is known as the *common* in most of Massachusetts, New Hampshire, eastern Vermont, and Maine . . . Villages that became cities often turned the *green* or *common* into a park, e.g. *Boston Common* and the *New Haven Green.* **1968** *Amherst Rec.* (MA) 27 Nov 2, Santa at the bank and reindeer on the common highlight downtown celebration. **1981** *Greenfield Recorder* (MA) 5 Dec sec A 4, Some men came and dug two holes and set up posts on the little common in front of the church.

3 usu pl: Pasture lands, usu unfenced.

1857 *Lawrence Republican* 18 June 1 *(DAE),* Two-thirds of her [Virginia's] soil that was formerly fertile and productive has been exhausted and much of it thrown into commons. **1858** Braman *Info. TX* 3.51, The rich prairies of this county afford free commons to any number of herdsmen. **1912** Green *VA Folk-Speech* 124, *Commons* . . . Unenclosed land, though having an owner, is subject to the uses of stock going at large. **1916** *DN* 4.333 **KS**, *Commons* . . . Unfenced land. **1967** *DARE* (Qu. C29, *A good-sized stretch of level land with practically no trees*) Inf **NY**1, A common: "up on the commons." **1968** *DARE* FW Addit **LA**40, *Commons:* pasture in town for use of household milk cows.

4 usu pl: A vacant lot.

1865 *Atlantic Mth.* 15.474/1, There lay numerous open lots or commons, all of which afforded abundant evidence of the extent to which this public wastefulness was carried. **1901** Robertson *Inlander* 26 *(DA)*, The three [boys] . . became . . friendly with the young barbarians on the commons.

5 in pl: The general public. *old-fash*

1934 *Hanley Disks* **swMA**, It ain't a-goin' out to the commons?

6 See **commie.**

7 See **common gas.**

common v [**common** n **1**] *obs*

To pasture on jointly owned land.

1801 in **1889** MA Hist. Soc. *Proc.* 2d ser 4.133, He had been riding, he told us, over a third of the Island to find him [his horse]. This process, to which all they who "common" their horses must submit, sometimes requires half a day to execute.

common buyer n [Prob abbr for **common-crop** + *buyer*]

One who buys low-quality tobacco.

1967 Key *Tobacco Vocab.* **MD,** *Common buyer:* A common buyer will buy anything; "buyer" means tobacco company agent who buys at auctions.

common cracker n **NEng**

=**Boston cracker.**

1939 Wolcott *Yankee Cook Book* 362, *Common Cracker.* A large old-fashioned lightly salted cracker also called Boston cracker. **1977** *Blair & Ketchum Country Jrl.* Dec 3 [Advt], Common crackers for soups, chowders, and stuffing . . . Milton, Mass. **1978** *Yankee* Oct 227 **NEng,** A good cook can make an apple pie out of nearly anything—even common crackers. **1978** *DARE* File, Common crackers (all I knew were made by the Westminster Cracker Factory in Westminster MA) were the old-fashioned oyster crackers but bigger, about 2–2½ in. in diameter. They split easily.

common-crop n Also *common tobacco*

Low-quality tobacco.

1966 *PADS* 45.10 **KY,** *Common-crop . . .* Tobacco strains of undesirable quality . . . "They grow some common-crop in the mountain counties." **1967** Key *Tobacco Vocab.* **MD, MO,** Common-crop; **TN,** Common-crop . . would be . . small tobacco; **GA,** A common-crop is when it don't make a plumb failure and then it don't make as good as it should; **NC,** Common-crop, common tobacco—of low quality; mixed grades—maybe not clean.

common doings n pl [*common* ordinary + **doing**] *obs*

Plain, ordinary fare; also fig.

1838 Flagg *Far West* 2.72 **IL,** What'll ye take: wheat-bread and *chicken fixens,* or corn-bread and *common doins?* by the latter . . being signified bacon. **1846** Levinge *Echoes from Backwoods* 2.46, We were, therefore, obliged to content ourselves with "common doings," instead of "chicken fixens"—the southern mode of expressing the difference between an *en famille* manner of feeding and the preparation for a guest. **1850** *Knickerbocker* 36.575, O, ye editors of the *'Pacific News'* of San Francisco, answer us; is that a specimen of your 'common-doin's' in agriculture, in your soil? **1852** Regan *Emigrant's Guide* 66 *(DA)*, What'll you hev, strangers? Chicken fixin's or common doin's.

commonette See **combinet**

commoney See **commie**

common gas n Also *common*

Regular (gas) as distinct from **ethyl.**

1966–69 *DARE* (Qu. N15a, *Gas stations . . usually have two kinds of gasoline: a cheaper kind that's called* _____) Inf **NH5,** The common gas; **RI4,** Common.

common pin n chiefly **NEng**

A straight pin.

c1965–78 *DARE* File **swME,** *Common pin:* a straight pin; **eMA** (as of 1960s), I recall a friend, a native of Boston, using the term *common pin.* It caught my attention because I had never heard it before and I had to ask him what it meant. I was amused to find he just meant a straight pin; **cnMA,** *Common pin* was the only term I knew for a straight pin until I came to Wisconsin [in the 1930s]. **1983** *Greenfield Recorder* (MA) 25 June (Hemenway column) (as of 1920), What kind of a pincushion is there? Who made it? It is doubtless well stuck with common pins and

needles, but long ago, a common pin was a real possession, and well taken care of.

commonplace adj

=**common** adj **1.**

1951 *DE Folkl. Bulletin* Mar 4/2, Commonplace (not stuck up—of a person).

common road n [Prob *common* shared, public]

1971 Green *Last Trail Drive* 2 **TX** (as of 1920s), That night I got a map and figured out where Paint Rock was and how to get there by common roads and highways ahorseback.

common school n

A public school.

a1651 (1899) Bradford *Plimoth Plantation* 194, Indeede, we have no comone schoole for want of a fitt person, or hithertoo means to maintaine one; though we desire now to begine. **1903** U.S. Bur. Educ. *Rept. for 1902* 1.x, Table I is . . a comparative summary . . showing the increase . . in what are called common schools, including under this designation schools of the elementary and secondary grades supported from public funds. **1950** *WELS (A school . . any child can go to without paying)* 1 Inf, **cWI,** Common school—old-fashioned. **1968** *DARE* FW Addit **seIN,** *Common school,* denotes a grammar school.

common talk n

Public knowledge.

1975 Gould *ME Lingo* 57, *Common Talk.* No longer gossip because everybody knows it: "They're always lovey-dovey in front of people, but it's common talk they don't get along."

common tell n [*common* general + **tell** n]

Accepted opinion.

1907 Lincoln *Cape Cod* 238, 'Cordin' to common tell, you was born with that same kind of lumbago.

common tobacco See **common-crop**

commony See **commie**

commune n [Span *común* toilet, see quot 1978]

An outdoor toilet.

1966 *DARE* (Qu. M21a, *An outside toilet building*) Inf **NM6,** Commune (Mexican origin). [**1978** *DARE* File, In Mexico *común* is a common peasant expression for privy. It is from *voy al común,* which is itself an abbreviation of the fuller phrase, *voy al lugar común.* The expression is of Spanish, not Mexican, origin.]

community loop n Cf **Texas loop**

An especially large lasso loop; see quots.

1936 McCarthy *Lang. Mosshorn* **SW,** *Community Loop.* A lasso loop from six to eight feet in diameter. A calf generally jumps through the large loop. **1946** *NYT Mag.* 20 Oct 35, *Community loop*—very large loop thrown by trick roper; e.g., in lassoing four riders. **1968** Adams *Western Words* 72, *Community loop*—An extra-large loop or noose thrown by a roper.

community road n Cf **common road**

1970 *DARE* (Qu. N27a, . . *Different kinds of unpaved roads*) Inf **FL48,** Community road; (Qu. N29, . . *A less important road running back from a main road*) Inf **TX98,** Community road.

commux n [Prob pronc var of *commerce* social interaction]

1977 *Yankee* Jan 73 **csME,** There are some folks in town who simply don't hobnob with each other, meaning they have no commux.

commy See **commie**

comoc n Cf **cold flour**

1915 *DN* 4.240 **MA,** *Comoc . . .* A dish eaten on whale-ships at sea. Hard-tack is put in a bag and pounded till it is about as fine as coarse meal. Then it is mixed with water, till about as thick as hasty-pudding, sweetened with molasses, and eaten with a spoon.

comp n[1] [Abbr for *compliment, complimentary*]

1 See quots.

1914 *DN* 4.122, *Comp,* from compliment. "I heard a nice comp for you the other day." **1967–68** *DARE* (Qu. KK35, . . *To pass on a compliment . . "I have a* _____ *for you."*) Infs **NE8, 10, OH10,** Comp.

2 A complimentary pass or ticket.

1909 in **1914** *DN* 4.133, 'Rag' Elliott gives comps to the Majestic. **1977** *DARE* File **NV,** *Comp:* A noun and verb. It means acquiring passes, tickets, or verbal invitations to shows or entertainment events. Usually verbal (a pit boss calls the maître d'). A *full comp* means that even the toke [tip] is taken care of by the management.

comp v [comp n[1] 2]
To give someone a complimentary pass or ticket.

1977 [see **comp** n[1] 2]. **1978** Puzo *Fools Die* 395 **Las Vegas NV,** Over the years Cully Cross had counted down the shoe perfectly and finally caught the loaded winning hand . . . He could comp everything, not only room, food and beverage, the standard RFB, but air fares from all over the world, top-price call girls, the power to make customer markers disappear. He could even dispense free gambling chips to the top-rank entertainers who played the Xanadu Hotel. *Ibid* 496, Why don't you stay at our hotel? I'll comp you. It won't cost you a penny.

comp n[2] See **compie**

compadre n [Span *compadre* godfather, friend] **SW**
A close friend, companion, or associate—used esp as a familiar term of address.

1834 Pike *Prose Sketches* 99, Nay, compadre, an American cannot steal. **1894** *DN* 1.324 **TX,** *Compádre:* friend, companion, not partner. From Sp. meaning godfather. **1948** *Chicago Tribune* (IL) 4 Feb 22/5, You, Francisco, are not only my compadre and my brother, you are the omen of my good fortune as well. **1966–69** *DARE* (Qu. II1, *Words meaning a close friend . . "He's my _____."*) Infs **NM6, TX**11, 27, 72, Compadre. **1968** Adams *Western Words* 72, Compadre—A southwestern cowboy's term for a close friend, partner, companion, or protector; from the Spanish.

compair See **compere**

compañera n [Span] **SW**
A female companion, a mistress.

1844 (1846) Kendall *Santa Fé Exped.* 2.342, That the good padres of that country have their *compañeras,* or female companions, is well known.

compañero n Also *campanyero, companyero* [Span] **chiefly SW**
A male companion, a **pardner.**

1845 Frémont *Rept. Rocky Mts.* 256, Four *compañeros* joined our guide at the pass. **1848** (1855) Ruxton *Life Far West* 147 **NM,** As several mountaineers were in company, Killbuck and LaBonté recognized more than one friend, and the former and Sublette were old compañeros. **1894** *DN* 1.342 **TX,** *Compañero:* partner; corresponds in mining slang to "pardner," "pard," etc. **1968** Adams *Western Words* 52, *Campanyero*—Friend; companion; from the Spanish *compañero.* **1968** *AmSp* 43.217, For others he [the mountain trapper] had an even larger range of epithets . . . trail companions were *companyeros.*

companion n
A wife.

1893 Shands *MS Speech,* Companion . . . Used to mean wife by a large number of educated people. **1939** *Hall Coll.* **eTN,** Companion . . . Wife. **1967** *DARE* (Qu. AA4a, . . *Words . . about a man . . eager to get married*) Inf **SC**42, Companion-crazy; (Qu. AA15b, . .*Joking ways . . of saying . . a man is getting married*) Inf **SC**42, Got himself a companion.

companion cow n Cf *DS* K23
1950 *WELS* (*Words used by women or in mixed company for a bull*) 1 Inf, **nWI,** Companion cow.

company n Usu |'kʌmp(ə)ni|, also |'kɑmp-| See Pronc Intro 3.I.4.b Pronc-sp *comp'ny*
A Forms.

1901 *DN* 2.181 **KY** [Black], Company, comp'ny. **1942** Hall *Smoky Mt. Speech* 39 **wNC, eTN,** [ʌ], without perceptible difference from the general American sound, may be heard in a number of words: . . company. *Ibid* 40, [Footnote 73:] These examples with [ɑ] for [ʌ] are interesting in view of the [ɑ] coloring of [ʌ] in British . . . Such forms as Smokies ['kɑmpnɪ] company . . possibly reflect the spelling.

B Sense.
See quot.

1914 *DN* 4.71 **ME, nNH,** Comp'ny . . . A boarder, or boarders, from the city. "Summer comp'ny."

company v
To entertain.

1942 *Sat. Eve. Post* 22 Aug 40/1 **NC,** She didn't dare company herself with thoughts of the dance, for fear her thinking might be readable to pap.

company bedroom See **company room 1**

company-clean v
1970 *DARE* (Qu. KK49, *When you don't have the time or ambition to do something thoroughly: "I'm not going to give the place a real cleaning, I'll just _____."*) Inf **MS**88, Company-clean.

‡**company coffee** n Cf **egg coffee**
1969 *DARE* (QR p50) Inf **MI**108, Company coffee—made with a raw egg.

companyero See **compañero**

company keeper n
A person of the opposite sex with whom one has a regular, intimate relationship.

1802 in 1956 Eliason *Tarheel Talk* 265 **NC,** He is lately married to his former company-keeper by whom he has many children. **1942** in 1958 Brewer *Dog Ghosts* 63 **TX** [Black], She staa't to cookin' chicken dinnuh evuh evenin' for her young comp'ny keepuh.

company line n Cf *DS* HH14
A nonexistent item used as the basis of a practical joke.

1921 *DN* 5.94, *Company line.* Young recruit sent for at Officer's Training Camp, Fort Benjamin Harrison, Indiana.

company room n **Sth, S Midl**
1 also *company bedroom:* A guest bedroom.

1886 Stapleton *Major's Christmas* 97 (*DAE*), His wife . . was kind and good to me, . . making me sleep in her company room as I'd been the best leddy in the land. **1910** C. Harris *Eve's Husband* 109 (*DAE*), He would come in the front gate, . . . creep upstairs to the 'company room,' undress and get in bed. **1932** Stribling *Store* 154 **AL,** Miltiades finally went into the company room and put on the wrapper. **c1960** Wilson *Coll.* **csKY,** Company room . . . The guest room; rarely used. **1965–70** *DARE* (Qu. D3, *A room for visitors to sleep in*) Infs **FL**26, **GA**1, 4, **MS**48, 63, Company room; **MS**65, Company bedroom.

2 The parlor, living room, front room.

1966–70 *DARE* (Qu. D13, *The room where you entertain company*) Infs **GA**4, **SC**9, 26, 43, **VA**69, Company room; **AL**11, Middle company room.

compass cactus n
=**barrel cactus.**

1961 Douglas *My Wilderness* 82 **csAZ,** Here is the short and squatty barrel cactus, sometimes called compass cactus because it almost invariably leans southwest. In the winter months its dome is decorated with yellow pods full of black seeds that squirrels and birds relish. **1973** *AZ Highways* Mar 33, The Barrel Cactus, scientifically classified under the name of *Echinocactus,* is the simplest of the cactus shapes. Mexicans call it "Visnaga" or "Bisnaga" and the early settlers knew it as "The Traveler's Friend" and the "Compass Cactus."

compass plant n [From the arrangement of the leaves or branches indicating cardinal compass directions]

1 also *compass flower:* A **rosinweed** (here: *Silphium laciniatum*).

[**1843** in 1917 Pelzer *Marches* 191, The polar plant, a rosin weed. This plant is a tall plant, perhaps 7 feet high, with a few [sic] shaped leaf which ranges, generally, north and south, affording a tolerable compass to the traveler over the prairies.] **1846** Longfellow *Poems* 1219, This is the compass-flower, that the finger of God has planted. **1882** *Amer. Naturalist* 16.629, The compass plant shows its peculiarity best in mid-summer. **1901** Mohr *Plant Life AL* 792, *Silphium laciniatum* . . Compass Plant . . . Alleghenian to Louisianian area. Dakota, Minnesota, Ohio to Missouri, Arkansas, and Colorado; south from Tennessee to Georgia, west to Texas. **1939** *Natl. Geog. Mag.* 76.220/2, Several coneflowers, the most familiar being the black-eyed Susan, those intelligent giants the compass plants, . . coreopsis and the closely related bur marigolds. **1972** Brown *Wildflowers LA* 217, Compass-plant . . . Perennial with coarse stems up to 6 feet tall.

2 A **mule-ears** (here: *Wyethia angustifolia*).

1897 Parsons *Wild Flowers CA* 157, Californian Compass-Plant. Sunflower. *Wyethia angustifolia.* **1934** Haskin *Wild Flowers Pacific Coast* 379, Compass plant. Wyethia—*Wyethia angustifolia.*

3 A Spanish clover (here: *Lotus purshianus*).

1898 *Plant World* 1.118 **KS,** We have then in this plant *[Lotus Americanus]* another example of a true compass plant . . in which it is the leaves and not the branches that are effected [sic]. **1911** *Century Dict.*, *Compass plant . . .* The prairie bird's-foot trefoil, *Lotus Americanus*, of the western United States, the numerous distichous branches of which are polarized on the stem after the manner of the leaves of other compass-plants.

4 A wild lettuce (here: *Lactuca scariola*).

1959 Carleton *Index Herb. Plants* 30, *Compass-plant:* Dodecatheon media [sic]; Lactuca scariola; Physostegia (v); Silphium laciniatum. **1971** Krochmal *Appalachia Med. Plants* 156, *Lactuca Scariola . .* (Asteraceae)—Common names: Prickly lettuce, compass plant, wild lettuce, wild opium.

5 A shooting star (here: *Dodecatheon meadia*).

1959 [see **4** above].

6 =false dragonhead.

1959 [see **4** above].

‡compeltry n [*compel* + *-try* used irreg as a noun-forming suff] Power, control.

1942 Perry *Texas* 133, An when I tried to get 'im to go on an' do right, he said I didn't have no *compeltry* over him.

compere n Also sp *compair* [Fr *compère* comrade] See quot 1983.

1927 Kennedy *Gritny* 64 **sLA** [Black], How you do, Aun' Susan? Hi! old compair Tom. **1983** Reinecke Coll. **New Orleans LA,** *Comperes* ['kʌmpæ:]—one's relatives by marriage. Mostly rural Black creole.

compersation n [Alter of *conversation*] See Pronc Intro 3.I.20

1927 Adams *Congaree* 111 **SC** [Black], *Compersation:* conversation. *Ibid* 9, But dat nigger been so busy he ain't had time to make compersation wid nobody. **1930** Stoney–Shelby *Black Genesis* 62 **seSC,** Ebe too lub compersation, an' . . it look like she got to hab sometin' for keep she company.

compie n Also *comp* **Pacific, esp CA** A marble: see quots.

1958 *PADS* 29.32 **WA,** *Compie . . .* Dim. from "composition". **1969** *DARE* Tape **CA172,** They'd go to school with their pockets full of doughbabies and compies and glassies. [FW:] What were the differences between all those kinds of marbles? [Inf:] Well, . . the compies were kind of a porcelain-like marble. **1971** Bright *Word Geog. CA & NV* 116, *Comps* 3 [infs] East Bay, North Coast, Sacramento Valley "smaller marbles." "Colored." "Glazed, tile stuff."

complaining ppl adj [*complain* to be ill, ailing] Ill, unwell.

1805 (1904) Clark *Orig. Jrls. Lewis & Clark Exped.* 2.159, The Indian woman complaining all night & excessively bad this morning. **1806** (1904) Roe *Diary* 37 **NY,** Austin & Stphn Roe . . say Justus is more complaining. **1942** Smiley *Gloss. New Paltz* **NY,** Phil Ayers had been speaking of Miss A. LeRoy's death. He asked: "Had she been complaining very long?" [Meaning "sick"]. **1954** *Harder Coll.* **cwTN,** *Complaining:* Unwell, in pain. "John's allus complainin' o' that old tooth." "He is still complaining with his feet." **c1960** *Wilson Coll.* **csKY,** *Complaining . . .* Ailing and usually enjoying it. **1967–69** *DARE* (Qu. BB41, *Not seriously ill, but sick enough to be in bed: "He's been ____ for a week.")* Infs **CT27, KS6, MD15, MI89,** 105, Complaining.

complainy adj Ill, unwell.

1887 *Harper's Mag.* 74.547/2, News come to Cousin Cynthy only yesterday that her aunt was quite complainy. **1941** Faulkner *Men Working* 26 **MS,** Hit makes us all feel ailish and complainy sort of.

complected adj Note: generally objected to as "dialectal" for many years, but now established as informal std. Complexioned.

1806 (1905) Lewis *Orig. Jrls. Lewis & Clark Exped.* 3.315, They are generally low in stature, proportionably small, reather lighter complected and much more illy formed than the Indians of the Missouri. **1890** *DN* 1.73 **NEng,** *Complected.* In *dark-complected* and *light-complected,* used of dark and fair persons respectively. **1892** *DN* 1.234 **KY.** **1902** *DN* 2.231 **sIL.** **1903** *DN* 2.310 **seMO.** **1905** *DN* 3.6 **cCT.** *Ibid* 61 **NE.** **1906** *DN* 3.116 **sIN.** **1907** *DN* 3.329 **nwAR, seMO.** **1908** *DN* 3.300 **eAL, wGA.** **1915** *DN* 4.225 **wTX,** *Complected . . .* The usual

form. One often hears such expressions as "a fat-complected man." **1923** *DN* 5.204 **swMO.** **1928** *AmSp* 5.128 **ME.** **1938** *AmSp* 13.74 **OH.** **1965–70** *DARE* (Qu. X57, *A person with light-colored hair and skin, "He's fair ____."*) 396 Infs, **widespread,** Complected.

complete adv Completely.

1940 *Sat. Eve. Post* 6 Apr 55/2 **Sth,** Just about complete crippled.

complete adj Highly proficient.

1939 *Hall Coll.* **eTN,** *Completest . . .* Best. "Tom Barnes was the completest hunter I was ever acquainted with."

‡complexion towel n **1969** *DARE* (Qu. G17, *Other kinds of towels*) Inf **NY210,** Complexion towel: a fingertip towel.

compliment n

1 A present, gift. *obs*

1859 (1968) Bartlett *Americanisms, Compliment.* A present. South-Western.

2 also pl: An invitation.

1933 *AmSp* 8.1.31 **TX,** *Compliments.* A note of invitation; e.g. "Compliments of Mr. John Hammer, requesting the pleasure of Miss Gussie Hames' company for the dance . . . " Many a cowboy has ridden miles . . to take his friend's *compliments* to a young lady. **1967** *DARE* (Qu. FF6, *Expressions used around here meaning "to be asked to go to a party": "Did you get a ____ to the party?")* Inf **TX3,** Compliment ['kɑmpləˌmɪnt].

comp'ny See **company** n

compoodle n [Alter of *caboodle*] =caboodle.

1890 *DN* 1.64 **KY,** *Compoodle* [kəm'pudl] . . . "He cleaned out (*i.e.* whipped out) the whole compoodle." **1908** *DN* 3.300 **eAL, wGA,** *Compoodle . . .* Same as caboodle. **1914** *DN* 4.104 **KS,** It would take the whole compoodle to equal him.

comport n [*compote* + intrusive *r*] A compote, serving dish.

1942 Whipple *Joshua* 500 **UT,** Amelia, with her fruit comport and old long-stemmed wineglasses on the table. **1966–68** *DARE* (Qu. G6, *Other dishes . . you might have on the table for a big dinner or special occasion*) Inf **AL6,** Comport—stem and ring handle; **OH65,** Comports —for jelly, pickles.

composant n [Alter of *corposant*] St. Elmo's fire.

1899 (1912) Green *VA Folk-Speech* 124, *Composant . . .* A ball of fire seen on a ship's rigging on a stormy night.

compoter n [Perh from *compotier*] A compote.

1969 *DARE* (Qu. G6, *Other dishes*) Inf **PA179,** Compoter—footed, cover type bowl for fruit.

comprador n [Port *compradór* buyer] **1945** Colcord *Sea Language* 58 **ME, Cape Cod, Long Island,** *Comprador.* A business agent. Portuguese, via pidgin English, brought home by sailors.

compree v Usu |kəm'pri| sometimes |ˌkɔm'pri|, |'kɑmpri| [Fr *compris* understood]

1965–70 *DARE* (Qu. NN5, *Other ways of saying, "Do you understand?"*) 11 Infs, **scattered east of Missip R,** Compree; **LA35,** [ˌkɔm'pri]; **OK42,** [kəm'pri]; **MD25,** Do you compree ['kɑmpri]?; **IN61,** You compree?; (Qu. JJ16, *. . Something you didn't understand, then suddenly you do . . , "Oh, now I ____."*) Infs **AL6, DE1, IN61,** Compree.

‡comprehende v [Appar a blend of *comprehend* + Span *comprender*]

1966 *DARE* (Qu. JJ16, *. . Something you didn't understand, then suddenly you do . . , "Oh, now I ____."*) Inf **FL28,** Comprehende ['kɔmpri'hɛndɛɪ].

compressed hay n **SW** *joc* Cow chips.

1959 Tallman *Dict. Amer. Folkl.*, *Compressed hay*—In areas of the Southwest where wood for fuel was not easily accessible this was a term used for dried cow chips—end result of much eating of hay. **1968** Adams *Western Words,* Compressed hay—A cowboy's name for dried cow chips used for fuel.

compressed yeast n Pronc-spp *compressed east, compress yeast* **chiefly Nth, N Midl** See Map
A yeast cake: see quot 1891.
1891 Chase & Clow *Industry* II.98 *(DA),* Yeast is the froth that rises to the top of malt liquor. It is thick, like cream, and after being taken off, is partly dried, pressed, washed and then cut into little blocks. Then it is called *compressed yeast,* and you have seen how it comes to us in those little blocks, rolled up in tin-foil. **1950** *WELS (What is used to raise bread before baking?)* 28 Infs, **WI,** Compressed yeast. **1965–70** *DARE* (Qu. H17, . . *Kinds [of yeast])* 61 Infs, **chiefly Nth, N Midl,** Compressed (yeast); **RI5,** Compressed east; **MS79,** Compress and loose yeast. [Of all Infs responding to the question, 72% were old; of those giving this response, 89% were old.] **1968** *DARE* Tape IN3, *Compressed east:* a form of yeast.

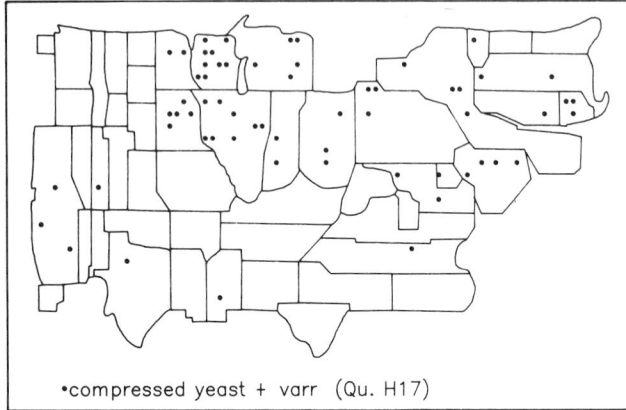

•compressed yeast + varr   (Qu. H17)

‡compromise v
1917 *DN* 4.390 **neOH, KS,** Compromise [kəmˈprɑmɪs] . . . An isolated but apparently natural pronunciation.

comptie See **coontie**

comptroller n Cf **bowler**
A large marble.
1968 *DARE* (Qu. EE6d, *Special marbles)* Inf **DE3,** Comptrollers [ˌkɑmˈtroʊləz]—great big ones.

compulshency n [Prob blend of *compulsion* + **pushency** or *urgency*]
Urgency.
1905 *DN* 3.61 **NE,** Compulshency . . . Same as *pushency.*

compulsionary adj
Compulsory.
1927 Kennedy *Gritny* 208 **sLA** [Black], It was compulsionary for him to be at the wake and go to the funeral.

compush n Also *compushency, compushity* [*com-* as in *compulsion* + *push* (+ *-ency* or *-ity)*] Cf **compulshency, pushency**
Urgency, compulsion, necessity.
1905 *DN* 3.61 **NE,** Compush, compushency, compulshency . . . Same as *pushency.* "A case of *compush.*" **1911** *DN* 3.542 **NE,** Compushity . . . Same meaning as *compush,* or *compushency,*—blends of *compulsion* and *push,* or *urgency.* **1914** *DN* 4.104 **KS,** Compushency . . . Necessity; compulsion. "It was a case of compushency; so I went."

comuppance See **comeuppance**

con n[1], also attrib [Abbr for **consumption**] **scattered, but esp NY, CA** See Map Cf **bug** n[1] **5b, miner's consumption**
Freq *the con:* Tuberculosis; silicosis.
1916 *DN* 4.357, *Con.* Consumption: among doctors. **1926** *AmSp* 4.651 [Hobo lingo], *Con*—tuberculosis. **1945** *CA Folkl. Qrly.* 4.322 **CO,** The con: Silicosis. **1949** Emrich *Wild West Custom* 205, Even when a miner died above ground, of the "con" or as the result of an accident, some miners refused to return to work. **1950** *WELS (What other names . . are there for tuberculosis?)* 9 Infs, **WI,** Con. **c1965** *DARE* FW Addit, "The con" (usually used with the article) is very common,

though somewhat old fashioned in Wisconsin. *The galloping con* and *the quick con* also heard. **1965–70** *DARE* (Qu. BB10, *What other names . . are used . . around here for tuberculosis?)* 21 Infs, **scattered, but esp NY, CA, Con; MT1, NY2, PA39,** The con; (Qu. BB11, *Speaking of a deep cough that you can't seem to get rid of)* Inf **CA158,** Con cough.

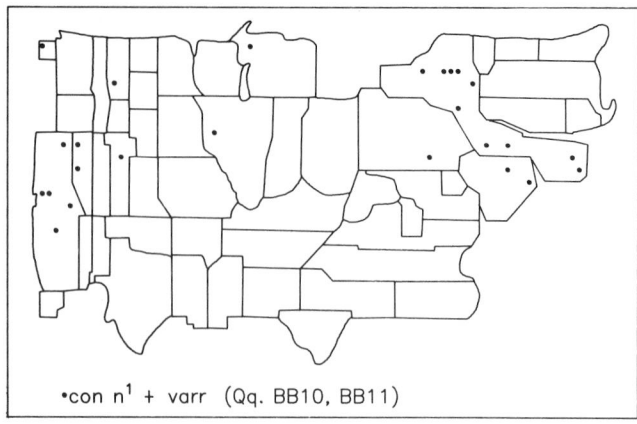

•con n[1] + varr   (Qq. BB10, BB11)

con n[2] [Abbr for *Congregationalist*]
=**Congo** n[2].
1950 *WELS (Nicknames for different religions)* 2 Infs, **sWI,** Cons.

con n[3] [Abbr for *conductor*]
A railroad conductor.
1900 in 1953 Botkin *Treas. Railroad Folkl.* 314, At a railroad wreck official investigation recently, . . the "Brakesey" on the carpet recalled . . : "The 'con' was flipping the tissue in the doghouse." **1925** *Ibid* 226, [I] used to hide under seats in the day-coaches, and old ladies would cover me up with their skirts and feed me when the con wasn't around. **1977** Adams *Lang. Railroader,* Con: Short for *conductor.*

con- See **ker-**

co'n See **co'**

co-nan(nie) v phr Also *coo-nan(nie)* Usu |ˈkoˌnæn(i), ˈkʌ-|; also|ˈkɒ-, ˈku-, ˈkɔ-, ˈkwo(ə)-; -næn, -ɨ|; rarely |ˈkɝˌnæni| Also sp *co-nanny, cu-nanny, ka-nanny, ker-nanny* [**co** v + *nan(nie)*]
chiefly east of the Missip R, esp Atlantic
Come!—used to call sheep.
1896 *DN* 1.414 **n,cNY,** *Conan* [kɒn-æn], for "Come, Nan"? **1899** (1912) Green *VA Folk-Speech* 124, *Conanny.* A sheep call. **1914** *DN* 4.182, **VA,** *Coo-sheep, interj.* A call to sheep. Also *coo-sheepy, coo-nan, coo-nannie.* **1942** Warnick *Garrett Co. MD (as of 1900–18), Conan* or *conanny,* v., a call for sheep. **1949** Kurath *Word Geog.* 42, The Rappahannock Valley has *kə-nan!* or *nannie!* **1951** Johnson *Resp. to PADS 20* **DE,** Ka-nanny-ka-nanny! Cu-nanny-cu-nanny! **1965–70** *DARE* (Qu. K85, *The call to sheep to come in from . . pasture)* **KY16, MA68, NY148, PA218, VA24, 57, SC19, WI68,** Coo-nannie; **ME9, NC1,** Co-nannie; **CT14, DE1, KY43,** [ˈkʌˌnæn(i)]; **DE5, LA2,** [ˈkoˌnæːnɪ]; **DC5,** [ˈkwoəˌnæːnɨ]; **LA7,** [ˈkwoˌnæən]; **KY39,** [ˈkuˌnæni]; **MD13,** [ˈkɔˌnæni]; **LA3,** Ker-nanny [ˈkɝˌnæni]. **1973** Allen *LAUM* 1.266, *Co-nan* and *co-nanny* . . [10% of 712 mail respondents] are clearly Northern with 16% in Minnesota, 13% in northern Iowa, and only 5% in southern Iowa.

co-nannie n [**co-nan(nie)** v phr] Cf **co-sheep(ie)** n
A children's game: see quot.
1968 *DARE* (Qu. EE27, *Games played on the ice)* Inf **NJ21,** Co-nannie —teams like Red rover on ice; yell co-nannie, co-nannie, co-nannie come over.

conbobberated ppl adj [Cf **discombobulate, conbobberation;** see also **bobbered**]
1968 *DARE* (Qu. GG2, . . *'Confused, mixed up':* "So many things were going on at the same time that he got completely _____.") Inf **WA16,** Conbobberated.

conbobberation n [*con-* + *bobber* as in Engl dial *bobbery* disturbance, quarrel + *-ation*] *obs*
A disturbance.
1845 Hooper *Daddy Biggs' Scrape* 194 *(DA),* There was something aflouncin' and sloshin', and makin' a devil of a conbobberation at the end of the line. **1852** (1854) Kennedy *Horse-Shoe Robinson* 60 **cVA** (as

of 1780), Consarn you! What are you making such a conbobberation about?

concarn See **concern** v

conceit v Pronc-sp *concait* *old-fash*

To think, suppose, imagine.

1806 (1904) Clark *Orig. Jrls. Lewis & Clark Exped.* 5.63, A canoe came down with the Indian man who had applyed for medical assistance . . he conceited himself a little better than he was at that time. **1836** (1838) Haliburton *Clockmaker* (1st ser) 305 **NEng,** I concait you'll find that no joke. **1843** (1916) Hall *New Purchase* 149 **IN,** Sometimes I conceited it [the cabin] to be ahead of me, but all at once it vanished, and I seed it was only a case of fantis-mágery [=*phantasmagoria*]. **1889** (1971) Farmer *Americanisms, Conceit, to.*—Equivalent to "reckon," "guess," "calculate"; to have in view; to form an idea; to think . . . To conceit may be regarded as a New Englandism. **1942** Greene *Papa is All* 103 **PA,** Mama: do you conceit he'll take the telephone out? *Ibid* 109, You conceited you killed me, maybe.

conceity adj Pronc-sp *consaity* Cf **self-conceity**

Hard to please.

1916 *DN* 4.337 **PA,** *Conceity* . . . Over-particular. "She's so conceity about her victuals that she's likely to go hungry." **1927** *AmSp* 2.351 **wcWV,** *Consaity* . . hard to please. "Sarah is too consaity about her kitchen."

concern v Pronc-spp *concarn, consarn, consahn, consaa'n, cunsaa'n* (reflecting archaic or old-fash varr); also *consoin* See Pronc Intro 3.I.1.f

Std senses, var forms.

1815 Humphreys *Yankey in England* 104, *Concarning,* concerning. **1841** (1952) Cooper *Deerslayer* 40, No, Jude will be just as like as not to tell you her opinion consarning your looks. **1843** (1916) Hall *New Purchase* 134 **IN,** Oh! I don't know nuther [sic] consarnin high-flow'd diksionary shapes. **1893** Shands *MS Speech* 24, *Consarned.* . . Illiterate white for *concerned.* **1901** *DN* 2.181 **KY** [Black], *Concern* consahn. *Concerning* consahnin'. **1908** *DN* 3.300 **eAL, wGA,** *Consarn* . . . concern. **1915** *DN* 4.225 **wTX,** It don't consarn me. **1922** Gonzales *Black Border* 294 **sSC, GA coasts** [Gullah glossary], *Consaa'n, cunsaa'n*—concern, concerns, concerned, concerning. **1942** *Time* 1 June 58/3 **Brooklyn NY,** Say—as far as I'm consoined, chum, why da good old days was sweller.

concern n Pronc-sp *consarn*

Esp among Quakers: a firm conviction and sense of obligation to act, based on religious insight or belief.

1707 in 1872 *PA Hist. Soc. Memoirs* 10.214, During their absence, I was under the greatest concern of mind that ever I knew in my life. **1838** Cooper *Home as Found* 2.25 **NY,** 'Have you heard that Grace is under concern?' . . 'Not under the church parson's, I'll engage; no one ever heard of a real . . conversion under *his* ministry.' **1886** *Amer. Missionary* 40.287, In a day or two Mrs. Tuttle [a Friend] "had a concern" to visit the Modocs. **1887** (1895) Robinson *Uncle Lisha* 92 **wVT,** Joel, he's got a *'consarn'* a-workin' on his mind, an' he's a-goin' off on a preachin' taower jes' 's soon 's they get through hayin' . . . The idear o' goin' shoolin' off wi' one o' his *'consarns,'* leavin' her an' them child'n an' the farm tu 'tend tu! Ketch me a-marryin' a Quaker, 'at's allus lierble tu be took with a *'consarn'!* **1978** Friends *Faith and Practice* 9, *Concern,* as Friends use the word, is a sense of obligation to do something, or to demonstrate sympathetic interest in some individual or group, as a result of what is felt to be a direct intimation of God's will.

conch n, also attrib Usu |kɑŋk|; sp-pronc |kɑnč| Also sp *con(c)k, konck* [Bahamian Engl *conch* a native Bahamian (*DBE* 1804 →) < *conch* a large edible sea snail]

1 rarely *concher*: A White resident of the Florida Keys, esp one of Bahamian descent. **sFL** *sometimes derog*

1852 *NY Tribune* 1 May 7/3 [sic *DA*—quot not found], Nearly one half of all residents [of Key West] are natives of the Bahamas Islands. They are called Conch-men or *Conchs,* by reason of their skill in diving. **1859** (1968) Bartlett *Americanisms, Koncks,* or *Conks.* Wreckers are so called, familiarly, at Key West; and the place they inhabit is called Koncktown. **1861** in 1877 Bartlett *Americanisms,* A Negro on this Key . . is a more successful cultivator of the soil than all the rebel *concks* together.—*N.Y. Tribune,* Nov. 27, 1861, *Lett. from Key West.* **c1873** Schele DeVere *MS. Notes* 45 (*DAE*), *Conch* of Fla., conchers, mostly from Key West, fr[om] large shellfish (*Strombus gigans* [sic]) on which it is pretended

they subsist. The common story is th[at] these islanders can dive to [the] bottom in 10 fathom water and crack a conch in their teeth. **1942** Kennedy *Palmetto Country* 243, In South Florida there are some 5,000 Anglo-Saxons of Bahamian descent who have come to be called Conchs, probably because the conch shellfish is an important item in their diet. **1950** *PADS* 14.75, *Conch* . . . A descendant of the early English settlers on the lower east coast of Florida. **1966** *DARE* (Qu. C36, . . *Special communities or groups*) Inf **FL24,** Conchs; (Qu. HH28, . . *People of foreign background*) Inf **FL25,** Conch; (Qu. II25, . . *The part of a town where the poorer people, special groups, or foreign groups live*) Inf **FL25,** Conch town. **1966** *DARE* Tape **FL40,** Some people say the conchs [kɑŋks] are the people who are born here. **1982** *Milwaukee Jrl.* (WI) 23 Apr 1/6 **FL,** Key West natives, known as conchs, and other residents have been especially dependent on tourists. **1984** *DARE* File **csWI,** *Conch*—I've heard people call them [kɑnčɪz] on the basis of spelling, but Floridians regularly say [kɑŋks].

2 See quots. *arch* Cf **corncracker 1**

1870 *Lippincott's* 6.458/2, The North Carolina "Conch" is unquestionably the lowest specimen of the race known. He has absolutely no virtues, and is dirtier, if possible, than the negro. But he is not so lazy. **1872** Schele de Vere *Americanisms* 45, A *corn cracker* is looked upon as so low a person that he is simply called a *cracker;* he inhabits the low, unproductive regions near the sea-shore, and besides his generic name derived from the chief article of his diet, he appears as *Conch* or *Low Downer* in North Carolina, and as *Sandhiller* or *Poor White Trash* in South Carolina and Georgia. Even in Florida he is found occasionally, leading a wretched life in the woods.

concha n Also *concho* [Span *concha* shell] **SW**

An ornament, orig shell-shaped and usu of silver, attached to chaps, belt, hatband, and other accoutrements of the cowboy.

1887 *Scribner's Mag.* 2.512/1, And listen to the *conchas,* the silver ornaments outside the spur, as they jingle and ring to the *broncho's* tread! **1894** *DN* 1.324 **TX,** *Cóncha* . . silver ornaments on the Mexican spur . . . Sp. *concha,* a shell, anything in the form of a shell. **1907** White *AZ Nights* 275, The leather chaps with the silver *conchas* hung behind the door. **1936** Barnard *Rider* 15, The Indians had blankets of bright colors, and wore buckskin leggings with fringe below the knee and silver conchos on the side, and their moccasins were brightly beaded. **1968** Adams *Western Words, Concha* . . . In the language of the cowboy it means a small, semiflat, circular metal disk, usually made of silver. It is used for decorative purposes, attached to chaps, belt, or hatband or to the saddle skirt or the browband of the bridle.

conchalagua See **canchalagua**

concher See **conch 1**

concho See **concha**

concho grass n [Prob from the *Concho* River in Texas; but cf Span *concho* corn husk] Cf **Colorado grass**

=**Texas millet.**

1884 Vasey *Ag. Grasses* 36, It . . has been called concho grass in some parts; in others Colorado bottom grass. **1911** *Century Dict., Concho-grass* . . . A name sometimes given to the *Panicum Texanum,* a Texan grass . . now cultivated in the southern United States and found to yield a large amount of valuable forage. **1967** *DARE* (Qu. L8, *Hay that grows naturally in damp places*) Inf **TX13,** Concho grass.

conch pea n **FL**

Perh a congo pea.

1942 Rawlings *Cross Creek* 52 **nFL,** She . . promised to send medicine to one, quilt scraps to another, and a pound of little conch pea seed to yet another. **1966** *DARE* (Qu. I20, . . *Beans that are grown around here*) Inf **FL33,** Conch peas. **1966** *DARE* Tape **FL41,** There's so many different kinds of peas—blackeyes, and the conchs [kɑŋks] and the crowders. **1975** Newell *If Nothin' Don't Happen* 209 **nwFL,** Uncle Wint had brought Ma a mess of fresh conch peas.

conck See **conch**

Concord See **Concord coach**

Concord buggy n Also *Concord runabout* [From the place of origin, Concord MA] **chiefly NEng** *hist*

A light, four-wheeled, one-horse carriage with side-spring suspension.

1902 Sears *Catalogue* 364/2, Our $37.95 High Grade Concord Buggy. **1934** *Hanley Disks* **csCT,** There was a buggy called a Concord buggy that was very popular . . . There was no box to it . . the flatform of the buggy was all open and often they had the straw mats to cover the bottom of the buggy. **1966–69** *DARE* (Qu. N41a, . . *Horse-drawn vehicles . . to carry people*) Infs **CT**29, **MA**6, 47, **NY**66, Concord buggy; (Qu. N41c, . . *Horse-drawn vehicles . . to carry light loads*) Inf **CT**2, Concord buggy. **1971** Sears *1908 Vehicles* 24, $43.65 For This Concord Runabout.

Concord coach n, also attrib Also *Concord (hack),* ~ *(spring) wagon,* ~ *stage* [From the place of origin, Concord NH] *hist*
A large, closed, horse-drawn coach; see quot 1968.
1853 *Shasta Courier* (Redding, Calif.) 12 Mar. *(DA),* The Proprietors of the above line . . have placed upon this route their splendid stock of American Horses and elegant Concord Coaches. **1860** (1932) *ND Hist.* 6.233, Started at 6.30 a.m. in a covered vehicle (generally known as a Concord wagon or hack) on leather slings and rather comfortable. **1940** Fergusson *Our Southwest* 100, Mr. Butterfield bought a hundred Concord spring wagons and square-bodied coaches. **1949** *AmSp* 24.259, The coach universally used in the West was known as the *Concord coach* (1855). **1966–69** *DARE* (Qu. N41a, . . *Horse-drawn vehicles . . to carry people*) Infs **CA**114, **NV**2, Concord stage. **1968** Adams *Western Words,* Concord—A common name for the coach used on the Overland Mail, made by Abbot–Downing Company, of Concord, New Hampshire. The coach had an arching roof with a railing around the outer edge. In front was the boot where the driver sat with his feet braced against the footboard . . . At the rear was another boot, a sort of projecting platform covered with a leather curtain.

Concord fight, since the adv phr [In ref to the skirmish at Concord MA, Apr 19, 1775, the first armed hostilities of the Amer Revolution]
For a very long time.
1967 *DARE* (Qu. A16, . . *"I haven't seen him _____."*) Inf **MA**72, Since the Concord fight.

Concord runabout See **Concord buggy**

Concord (spring) wagon, Concord stage See **Concord coach**

concrete beater n
1966 *DARE* (Qu. V9, *What nicknames do people have around here for a policeman*) Inf **MS**1, Concrete beater.

condemn v, hence *condemned* ppl adj Also sp *condem,* pronc-spp *condamn, condum(n)* *euphem*
To damn; damned.
1897 *KS Univ. Qrly.* 6.86, Condem: mild substitute for 'damn!' **1951** *PADS* 15.66 **NH,** Con dum it . . . Mild oaths. **1967–68** *DARE* (Qu. NN25a, . . *Substitutes for "damn" or "damned"*) Inf **MN**12, Condamn it; **NY**105, Condumn; **OH**28, Condemn; (Qu. NN17, *"That _____ fly won't go away."*) Inf **NY**105, Condumned ['kɑn,dəmd].

condemn n
A farm animal designated for sale or slaughter.
1966 *DARE* Tape **NM**14, In gathering the fall cattle we would get all the condemns [kən'dɛmz] and cripples and various things like that.

condemned ppl adj Pronc-spp *condemn, cundemn*
Guilty, culpable.
1922 Gonzales *Black Border* 295 **sSC, GA coasts** [Gullah glossary], *Cundem, condemn*—condemn, condemns, condemned, condemning; but more frequently to denote guilt or the appearance of guilt; as: "W'en uh ketch Joe wid de hog, 'e look so cundemn."

conduct v chiefly **NEng** *old-fash*
To behave, to comport oneself.
1754 (1957) Edwards *Freedom of Will* 2.17, [Footnote:] I say not only "doing," but "conducting"; because a voluntary forbearing to do, sitting still, keeping silence, etc., are instances of persons' conduct, about which liberty is exercised. **1802** (1941) Tucker *Diary* 330 **MA,** Were I thus to conduct I should be called sullen. **1828** (1936) McCoy *Jrl. Exped.* 342 **NEng,** Our sister Wiskehelaehqua, alias Mrs. Shane, I am happy to hear conducts like a Christian. **1829–30** *Dunglison's Glossary* (*DN* 5.425) **NEng,** To Conduct. Used in New England without the pronoun. "He conducts well." **1871** Binghamton *Republican* 17 Jan (Schele de Vere *Americanisms* 456), Mr. Schutt said to him, "How strangely you have conducted." **1905** *DN* 3.6 **cCT,** Conduct. To conduct oneself.

conduct n See **conductor (pipe)**

conducta n [Span "convoy"] **SW** *prob obs*
A guarded pack train, esp for the transport of bullion.

1836 (1935) Holley *Texas* 117, There are already heavy capitalists located there, and one *conducta* has arrived from Chihuahua with three hundred thousand dollars. **1844** (1846) Kendall *Santa Fé Exped.* 2.404, A large *conducta,* or escort guarding nearly a million of dollars in silver, was entering the city at the same time. **1860** *Los Angeles Star* 21 July 1/4 (1957 *Western Folkl.* 16.8), The taxes are crushing . . . On every *conducta* Miramon charges 8 per cent and Juarez 4 per cent . . . By law, specie is required to be forwarded to the capital or to the coast in Government conductas. **1910** Bronson *Red-Blooded* 234, It was a point at which *conductas* were often attacked. **1927** Fergusson *Wolf Song* 59 **NM,** Ambrosio took charge of the pack mule train that went from Taos every spring to join the *conducta* below Socorro.

conductor (pipe) n Also *conduct* **Nth, esp NEast**
A downspout.
1931–33 *LANE Worksheets* **ceMA,** Conductor—A troff that leads water to the ground. **1950** *WELS* (*The pipe that takes . . water . . to the ground or . . cistern*) 5 Infs, **chiefly swWI,** Conductor (pipe). **1965–70** *DARE* (Qu. D29) 9 Infs, **chiefly NEast,** Conductor (pipe); **MA**50, Conduct.

conductor's car n Also *conductor's castle*
A caboose n[1] 2.
1906 *Car Builders' Dict.* 31, Caboose car . . . Also, but rarely, called conductor's car, cabin car, cabin, or train car. **1950** *WELS* (*Names for the last car on a freight train*) 1 Inf, **cWI,** Conductor's castle. **1977** Adams *Lang. Railroader,* Conductor's car: A caboose.

condum(n) See **condemn** v

cone n [Alter of *comb*]
1 also *coning,* also attrib: =**comb** n B2. **chiefly W Midl** See Map
1965–70 *DARE* (Qu. D30, *The strip of wood or metal that covers the ridge of a roof*) 28 Infs, **chiefly W Midl,** Cone; **MO**16, Ridge cone; **NE**5, Coning; (Qu. M1, . . *Different . . kinds of barns*) Inf **OH**75, Cone-roofed barn.

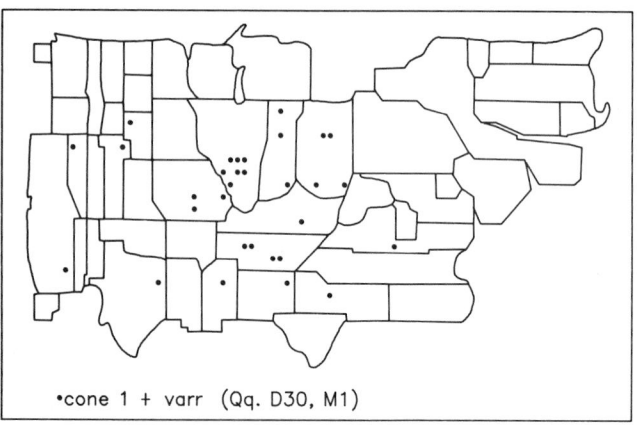

•cone 1 + varr (Qq. D30, M1)

2 A beehive; a honeycomb.
1968–69 *DARE* (Qu. R19a, *The place where* [tame] *bees live and store their honey*) Inf **CA**167, Cone; (Qu. R19b, . . *Wild bees*) Infs **CA**167, **IL**56, **KS**8, **NV**7, Cone; **IL**45, **OH**4, Honey cones.

cone corn n
Unshelled cobs of corn.
1967 Cerello *Dakota Co. MN* 49, Cone corn: Husked, unshelled maize. We always sold cone corn because father did not have a sheller . . . [7 counties; still common].

coneflower n [From the cone-shaped flower disks]
1 A plant of the genus *Rudbeckia.* For other names see **black-eyed Susan 2, goldenglow** See also **green-headed coneflower, meadow coneflower, prairie coneflower 2, sweet coneflower**
1822 Eaton *Botany* 436, *Rudbeckia laciniata* cone-flower, conedisk sunflower. **1901** Mohr *Plant Life AL* 798, *Rudbeckia fulgida* . . . Golden Cone-Flower. **1931** Harned *Wild Flowers Alleghanies* 571, Britton's Cone-flower (*R. Brittonii*). **1937** Stemen *OK Flora* 579, *Dracopis amplexicaulis* . . . Clasping-leaved Cone-flower . . . *Rudbeckia amplexicaulis* Vahl. **1948** Stevens *KS Wild Flowers* 374, *Rudbeckia grandiflora* Large-flowered Coneflower . . . Ray flowers yellow, disk flowers purplish-brown. **1960** Williams *Walk Egypt* 100 **GA,** Clusters

of wild flowers took shape at the corners of the lot . . orange coneflowers with bulging brown centers. **1961** Peck *Manual OR* 802, *R[udbeckia] californica* . . California cone-flower. **1966** *DARE* Wildfl QR Pl.253–5 Inf **OH**14, Coneflower; **CO**7, Green-headed coneflower. **1967–70** *DARE* (Qu. S26a, . . *Other wildflowers*) Infs **CO**20, **IA**8, **VA**52, Coneflower; **IL**26, **WI**12, Coneflowers; (Qu. S26e) Inf **RI**15, Coneflower; (Qu. S7, *A kind of daisy, bright yellow with a dark center, that grows along roadsides in late summer*) Infs **CO**7, **IA**3, Coneflower. [Note: some of these Infs may refer instead to sense **2** or **3** below.]

2 A plant of the genus *Ratibida*.   For other names see **prairie coneflower 1**

1900 Lyons *Plant Names* 316, *Ratibida* . . . Cone-flower. **1936** IL Nat. Hist. Surv. *Wildflowers* 367, Yellow coneflower *Lepachys pinnata* . . . The Yellow or Gray-headed Coneflower frequents dry open places. *Ibid,* The Long-headed Coneflower, *Lepachys columnaris.* **1950** Stevens *ND Plants* 283, *Ratibida columnifera* . . . Long-headed coneflower . . . The genus name *Lepachys* has been often used for this plant. **1961** Smith *MI Wildflowers* 407, Prairie Coneflower—*Ratibida pinnata.* **1972** Brown *Wildflowers LA* 213, Cone-flower, Mexican Hat—*Ratibida columnaris* . . . Also Texas, Arkansas, and Mississippi.

3 A plant of the genus *Echinacea*.   For other names see **purple coneflower**

1901 Lounsberry *S. Wild Flowers* 520, *B. pallida,* drooping coneflower, . . has rays longer, and more slender and drooping, than those of its relatives. Its cone of disk flowers is possibly higher and in outline, ovate. **1940** Steyermark *Flora MO* 536, *Cone-flower (Echinacea pallida* . . *).* Center of flower-head cone-shaped . . . *Cone-flower (Echinacea paradoxa* . . *).* Flower-heads dome-shaped. **1974** (1977) Coon *Useful Plants* 107, *Echinacea purpurea*—Cone flower . . . The large flowers usually are cone-shaped and with mostly purple petals.

conenose n Also *cone-nose bug*

=**assassin bug** (esp *Triatoma* spp).

1911 *Century Dict. Suppl., Cannibal-bug* . . . Any one of the predatory heteropterous insects of the family *Reduviidae* . . . Familiar examples are the 'conenoses'. **1957** Jaeger *N. Amer. Deserts* 170, *Western Cone-Nose Bug* . . . A representative of blood-sucking bugs found in pack rat nests. **1964** Borror–DeLong *Intro. Insects* 229, *T[riatoma] sanguisuga* . . , sometimes called the blood-sucking conenose, can inflict an extremely painful bite.

conestoga n [Ult from *Conestoga,* Pennsylvania]

1 also attrib: A large, heavy draft horse bred originally by the Pennsylvania Dutch and now extinct. *hist*

1824 Keating *Narrative* 2.24, There are several appellations by which the different breeds of this useful animal are distinguished in Pennsylvania, such as the Conestoga. **1866** Jennings *Horse* 1.61, The vast, white-topped wagons, drawn by superb teams of the stately Conestogas, were a distinguishing feature in the landscape of that great agricultural State. **1884** *Century Illustr. Mag.* 27.445/1, To the German farmers of Pennsylvania is due the credit of producing the great Conestoga horses, the finest draught animals on the continent in the colonial age. **1930** Shoemaker *1300 Words* 14 **cPA Mts** (as of c1900), *Conestoga*—A type of large and speedy horse, mostly roan colored, used in freight wagons and stage coaches in Pennsylvania, now extinct in the pure race. **1964** Smith *PA Germans* 19, The Pennsylvania Dutch can also claim the first great horse of American origin, the Conestoga horse, which was considered the most efficient draft horse and was sought by freighters before the development of the railroads.

2 Transf: see quot.

1912 Green *VA Folk-Speech, Conestoga* . . . A large, coarse, rough horse; as distinguished from a "thoroughbred;" also applied to men in the same sense.

3 A heavy work shoe.   Also called **stogie** Cf *DS* W11

1892 *DN* 1.229 **KY,** *Conostoga* [sic] . . brogans.

4 See **stogie.**

coney n[1] Also sp *cony;* pronc-spp *cooney, coony*

1 =**pika.** **chiefly CO**

1872 *Harper's Mag.* 46.32/2 **CO,** They are said to be a true cony, however, . . and no marmot, and consequently can not hibernate like the common woodchuck. **1878** (1887) Jackson *Bits of Travel* 319 **cCO,** But conies are said to be a fearless folk: and well they may be who dwell in impregnable homes in the walls of the Ute Pass. **1884** Kingsley *Std. Nat. Hist.* 5.81, The miners and hunters in the West know these oddities as "conies" and "starved rats." **1936** Thompson *High Trails* 131 **nwMT,** The conies are well protected from both the severe weather and attacks

from numerous enemies. **1941** FWP *Guide CO* 20, Perhaps the most interesting of the small mammals is the diminutive cony, or pica, an odd rabbit-like creature found only in rock slides above timberline and unknown outside the State. For its practice of curing and storing hay in small stacks for winter use, it is known as the "Haymaker of the Heights." **1961** Douglas *My Wilderness* 19 **cCO,** These clovers are choice feed for elk and deer. I have found them in the hay which the conies spread out in sheltered places among rockslides to cure and later to store for their winter use. **1966** Barnes–Jensen *Dict. UT Slang* 40, The little mammal (*pika* or *ochotona princeps; starved rat*) is also sometimes called cony or rock-rabbit. **1967** *DARE* (Qu. P32, . . *Other . . wild animals*) Inf **CO**41, Coony—a high-country animal, a guinea-pig-sized rodent.

2 A rabbit of the genus *Sylvilagus*. **chiefly nNEng**

1907 *DN* 3.184 **seNH,** Coony (rabbit) . . . Cony. "The cat has caught a coony rabbit." **1951** *PADS* 15.66 **cwNH,** Cooney: . . Corruption of *cony,* the cottontail rabbit (*Sylvilagus transitionalis*). **1965–70** *DARE* (Qu. P30, . . *Wild rabbits*) Infs **ME**6, **MA**32, **NH**4, 5, 10, Coney (rabbit); **MA**26, 35, 58, 62, **VT**4, 12, Coony (rabbit); **VT**16, ['kʌni]. **1982** Elman *Hunter's Field Guide* 369, *Sylvilagus* . . Common or Regional Names: Cooney, Coney.

coney n[2] Also sp *cony*

Any of three **groupers:**

a A tawny-colored, spotted **grouper 1** *(Cephalopholis fulva)* found in warm waters off the Florida coast.   Also called **butterfish, Jacob Evertzens, niggerfish, yellowfish**

1882 U.S. Natl. Museum *Bulletin* 16.541, *Butter-fish; Nigger-fish; Coney* . . . West Indies, north to Florida Keys. **1933** John G. Shedd Aquarium *Guide* 97, *Cephalopholis fulvus*—Yellow Coney; Butter-fish. **1960** Amer. Fisheries Soc. *List Fishes* 25 Coney . . *Cephalopholis fulva* (Linnæus).

b =**red hind 1.**

1887 Goode *Amer. Fishes* 51, The Coney of Key West, *Epinephelus apua,* the "Hind" of Bermuda, is an important food-fish. **1946** La-Monte *N. Amer. Game Fishes* 56, *Red Hind* . . . *Names:* Cabrilla, Coney [etc].

c =**graysby.**

1902 Jordan–Evermann *Amer. Fishes* 380, At Key West, where it [*Petrometopon cruentatus*] is called cony, it is rather common about the reefs. **1933** John G. Shedd Aquarium *Guide* 97, *Petrometopon cruentatus*—Graysby; Coney. **1946** LaMonte *N. Amer. Game Fishes* 57, *Coney* . . . *Petrometopon cruentatus* (Lacépède) . . . *Names:* Red Hind, Graysby.

Coney Island n Also *Coney* [From the resort in Brooklyn NY]

1 also attrib: A hot dog, usu served in a bun with condiments.

1950 *WELS* (*A small sausage that is put whole into a bun to make a sandwich*) 1 Inf, **seWI,** Coney Island. **1965–66** *DARE* (Qu. H40, *A small sausage . . put into a long roll*) Inf **AL**11, Coney; (Qu. H41, *Other . . roll or bun sandwiches*) Inf **OK**1, Coney Islands—weenie and chili. **1968** *Budget* (Sugarcreek OH) 25 July 16, Sugardale coneys . . lb. 49¢. **1968** *DARE* FW Addit **ceTX,** Coney Islands: Hot dog with a hot chili sauce, mustard, and chopped fresh onion on it. In Newburgh NY they're called Texas Hot Weenies. **1969** *Times–News* (Mt. Pulaski IL) 12 June 10, Toast master Hamburger or Coney Buns / 4 Pkgs. –8 Pak. 98¢. **1976** Flexner *America Talking* 189, By this time [1913] the main Coney Island snack was a large, spicy frankfurter on a roll, often topped with sauerkraut, this called a *Coney Island* (the term had meant fried clams in the 1870's and 80's).

2 A hamburger: see quot.

1965–68 *DARE* (Qu. H41, *Other kinds of roll or bun sandwiches favored around here—in a round bun or roll*) Inf **OH**76, Coney Island; **MO**20, Coney; **OK**1A, Conies (hamburger)—same as Coney Islands.

3 A **submarine sandwich.**

1960 Wentworth–Flexner *Slang, Coney Island* . . 1957: "Coney Islands—your choice of two meats, two cheese, tomato; topped with sauerkraut, mustard, relish and onions." Sign in front of drive-in restaurant, Wheeling, W. Va. **1966–68** *DARE* (Qu. H42, *The kind [of sandwich] in a much larger, longer bun, that's a meal in itself*) Infs **NE**8, **WA**27, Coney Island; **IN**27, **OK**26, Coney.

Coney Island butter n

1947 *AN&Q* 7.86 **NY,** "Coney Island Butter": mustard; term overheard in New York rathskeller.

confab n [Abbr for *confabulation;* by ext from std senses] Cf **conflab 3**

A serious quarrel or disagreement.

1933 Wiliamson *Woods Colt* 19 **Ozarks,** All at once their confab seems to be over. **1968** *DARE* (Qu. KK15, *A disagreement or quarrel*) Inf MI82, Confab. **1969** *DARE* FW Addit KY54, Confab—A serious argument with serious consequences. For example, the fight between Augusta and Brooksville over the county seat of Bracken County. "They had a real confab over that." Because of the grudge, some refugees from Augusta refused to be rescued to Brooksville during the flood of '37.

confectionary n Also sp *confectionery*

1 A barroom or liquor store. *arch* Cf **grocery**

1836 *Spirit of the Times* (1846 Porter *Quarter Race* 24) **KY,** I went to town last night to the confectionary, [a whiskey shop in a log pen fourteen feet square]. **1859** (1968) Bartlett *Americanisms, Confectionary.* In the South-West and some parts of the West, a barroom. **1889** (1971) Farmer *Americanisms, Confectionery . . .* Also called a *grocery.*

2 A small store; see quot.

1973 *DARE* File **Savannah GA,** *Confectionary*—A small, hole-in-the-wall store where cigarettes, bread, and other basic needs are sold. Common.

Confederate coffee n

1909 *S. Atl. Qrly.* 8.45 [Gullah], "Dat is sho' nuff po'-stuff yo' all buckra is drunk fuh brukwuss!", commented Maum' Hester, sarcastically; "Nuttn mo'na co'nfederit coffee!" [Footnote:] *Confederate coffee:* parched beans, chicory, burnt grains, used as substitute for the true coffee-bean during the deprivations of the Confederate War.

Confederate jasmine n [Because it has been cultivated in the southern states]

A **star jasmine** (here: *Trachelospermum jasminoides*).

1897 Stuart *Simpkinsville* 49, He turned . . to see the . . edge of a woman's skirt as it disappeared behind the hedge of Confederate jasmine. **1927** FL Ag. Exper. Station Gainesville *Bulletin* 202, Confederate Jasmine . . is one of the few vines bearing very fragrant flowers. **1953** Greene–Blomquist *Flowers South* 171, Confederate-Jasmine (*Trachelospermum jasminoides)* This evergreen vine from Malaya with dark, glossy-green, leathery foliage has been the stand-by of old southern gardens since colonial days. **1976** Bailey–Bailey *Hortus Third* 1119.

Confederate pintree n [See quot 1950]

=**honey locust 1.**

1897 Sudworth *Arborescent Flora* 254, *Gleditsia triacanthos . . Common Names . .* Confederate Pintree (Fla.). **1950** Peattie *Nat. Hist. Trees* 404, Down in Florida this tree is still sometimes called by the obsolete name of Confederate Pintree, because its formidable spines were used to pin together the tattered uniforms of the southern hosts in the war of the Blue and the Gray.

Confederate rose n [Cf **Confederate jasmine**]

A hibiscus (here: *Hibiscus mutabilis*). Also called **cotton rose 1**

1959 Carleton *Index Herb. Plants* 30, *Confederate-rose:* Hibiscus mutabilis. **1965–70** *DARE* (Qu. S26e, *Other wildflowers*) Infs AL20, 30, FL26, TX40, WV14, Confederate rose; (Qu. S26a, . . *Other wildflowers . . roadside*) FL6, 16, Confederate rose. **1976** Bailey–Bailey *Hortus Third* 562, *Confederate rose.* Shrub or small tree, to 15 ft.

Confederate syrup n *hist*

Sorghum syrup.

1863 *Southern Cultivator* 21.75/2 **AL,** *The Manufacture of Sorgho or Confederate Syrup.*—My directions are for farmers and planters who have not, cannot, and would not get the elaborate apparatus of a sugar-house; but there are essential fixtures, &c., which must be had, to wit: *a mill, boilers,* a bailing dipper . ., a common dipper, and perforated ladles or skimmers. **1964** Bonner *GA Ag.* 86 (as of 1860s), Sherman's bummers reported large supplies of sorghum syrup "at nearly every plantation" on the march to the sea and his soldiers developed a liking for it. During the war it was known as Confederate syrup.

Confederate violet n [From the gray-blue flower, the color of the Confederate states' army uniform] **chiefly Sth**

A **violet** (here: *Viola sororia*).

1940 FWP *Guide VA* 20, Confederate violet. **1955** Taber *Stillmeadow Daybook* 25 **swCT,** The line between fact and fancy has always been a tenuous one with me, and many a time I have gone out to see if my unicorn had come down to crop the Confederate violets. **1965–70**

DARE (Qu. S26e, *Other wildflowers*) Infs AR10, NC13, SC31, Confederate violet; (Qu. S11, . . *Other names . . for . . blue violet*) Inf GA80, Confederate violet: gray-blue and a white center; SC36, Confederate violet: grayish-blue; wild; (Qu. S26a, . . *Other wildflowers . . roadside*) Inf NC14, Confederate violet; (Qu. S26c, *Wildflowers that grow in woods*) Inf TN39, Confederate violets; (Qu. S26d, *Wildflowers . . in meadows*) Inf KY24, Confederate violet. **1976** Bailey–Bailey *Hortus Third* 1160, *[Viola] sororia . . . Woolly blue violet . . .* The color of the fls. is also variable, and . . the so-called *Confederate violet* [is] a form with gray-blue fls.

Confederate War n **chiefly S Atl**

The American Civil War.

1909 [see **Confederate coffee**]. **1966–68** *DARE* FW Addit **SC,** The Confederate War—War for Southern Rights, 1860–1865 [occasional]; **GA26,** Confederate War [used in conversation; Inf old]. **1969** McDavid *Unpleasantness* 197, *Confederate War* is not in the historical dictionaries at all, though it is perhaps the second commonest term in folk usage. It is not in the dictionaries because it is not the term of historians or politicians; it is merely a term used among the people. *Ibid* 199, Ignored by lexicographers, it *[Confederate War]* shows a striking regional pattern and, in fact, is the commonest folk term in the South Atlantic States.

confession seat n Cf **amen pew, mourners' bench**

1967–69 *DARE* (Qu. CC5, *Names for seats in a church*) Inf **CO14,** Confession seats—ones near the front; heard somewhere; **NC85,** Confession seats, same as mourners' bench.

confess the corn See **acknowledge the corn**

confidence v **chiefly S Midl**

To trust.

1917 *DN* 4.410 **NC Mts,** Confidence . . . To place confidence in. "I don't confidence them dogs much." **1931** *PMLA* 46.1320 **sAppalachians,** Big Jim won't confidence preacher-men. **1933** *AmSp* 8.1.48 **Ozarks.** **1933** Williamson *Woods Colt* 104 **Ozarks,** Uncle Joe don't confidence none o' them Starbucks. **1934** (1970) Wilson *Backwoods Amer.* 68 **AR, MO,** Colonel Bullteeters couldn't confidence no Republican. **1968** *Foxfire* Fall–Winter 24 **nGA,** "You can confidence me," means "You can trust me." Also, "Can I confidence you?" **1969** *DARE* (Qu. JJ44, *Expressions about someone who can be trusted to keep a secret*) Infs **GA72, 77,** You can confidence (him, this fellow). **1972** Cooper *NC Mt. Folkl.* 90, Can't confidence—can't trust or believe.

confidenshun adv [Alter of *confidentially*]

1927 Kennedy *Gritny* 94 **sLA** [Black], I wan' talk wid you confidenshun.

confident v [Perh back-formation from **confidence** v, understood as *confidents* v 3rd pers sg]

To trust; believe.

1937 *Hall Coll.* **wNC,** I don't confident the story.

confidential adj

Reliable, deserving of confidence.

1895 *DN* 1.371 **TN Mts,** *Confidential . . :* trusty. "Oh, that mule won't hurt you. He's a confidential mule."

confidential adv

In a manner deserving of confidence.

1895 *DN* 1.371 **TN Mts,** *Confidential . . .* honestly, well. "They will do your work confidential and right." **1942** *Amer. Mercury* 55.85 **Harlem NYC,** That's confidential right from the Bible.

confinded See **-ed** pret suff **1**

confisticate v [Alter of *confiscate*]

See quots.

1781 *PA Jrl. & Weekly Advt.* (Philadelphia) 23 May 1/3, *Confisticate,* for *confiscate.* The most ignorant of the vulgar only use this phrase. **1864** (1868) Trowbridge *Cudjo's Cave* 153, The prop'ty of these yer durned Union-shriekers is all gwine to be confisticated. **1916** *DN* 4.273 **NE.** **1972** Cooper *NC Mt. Folkl.* 90, *Confisticate*—confiscate.

conflab n [Alter of *confab,* abbr for *confabulation*]

1 A conversation.

1873 *Winfield* (Kans.) *Courier* 7 Aug 3/1 *(DA),* 'Conflabs' lively among lawyers. **1914** *DN* 4.104 **KS,** *Conflab . . . = Confab,* conversation. **1923** *DN* 5.204 **swMO.** **1928** in 1952 Crane *Letters* 25 Dec 332, After a day or two in conflab with some of these natives one does tend to lose one's "middle-western accent." **1966** *DARE* (Qu. O21, *When men out in seagoing boats get together for a visit*) Inf **FL1**, Conflab.

2 A conference, meeting. *sometimes joc*

1942 *AmSp* 17.283/2, An inquirer, citing a letter from the president of the sophomore class at the University of Colorado that gave as one of his duties 'to attend . . . *conflabs* with other schools,' asks whether 'conflab' is an error. **1950** *WELS* (*Joking words for a meeting where there is a lot of talking*) 2 Infs, **WI**, Conflab. **c1960** *Wilson Coll.* **csKY**, Confab (sometimes *conflab*) . . A humorous name for a conference. **1965–70** *DARE* (Qu. KK12, *A meeting where there's a lot of talking*) 59 Infs, **scattered**, Conflab.

3 =**confab.**

1967 *DARE* (Qu. Y12a, *A fight between two people, mostly with words*) Inf **KS5**, Conflab; (Qu. KK15, *A disagreement or quarrel*) Inf **IL17**, Conflab.

conflummox See **flummox** v, **ker-**

conflutement n [*con-* + (perh) *flute* ornamental grooving + -ment suff] **?chiefly GA** *old-fash*

A contrivance, frill.

1844 Thompson *Major Jones's Courtship* 57 **GA**, Why sich other cog-wheels, cranks and conflutements, I never did see. **1896** Harris *Sister Jane* 168 **GA**, Your Aunt Prue had saw some new-fangled bonnet . . an' pictur'd out to your Aunt Sally ev'ry flower an' folderol an' all the conflutements that the consarn had on it. **1908** *DN* 3.300 **eAL, wGA**, *Conflutement* . . . Contrivance.

‡confuddled ppl adj [Prob blend of *confused* + *befuddled*]

1966 *DARE* (Qu. GG2, *Expressions meaning "confused, mixed up"*) Inf **NC9**, Confuddled.

con-fum-it intj [?Perh alter of *confound it*] Cf **condemn** v

1959 *VT Hist.* new ser 27.130 **neVT**, Con-fum-it! . . Rare. Essex.

confusement n Cf **-ment** suff

1970 *DARE* FW Addit **VA38**, Confusement—confusion.

Cong See **Congo** n²

congaine See **coonjine** n 3

congar eelpout See **congar eel** 2

congar viper See **congo snake** 2

congealed salad n **chiefly Sth**

A gelatin salad.

1965 *Colonial Kitchens* 96 **neGA**, Mix and congeal as any congealed salad. **1967** *Refugio Co. Press* (TX) 12 Apr 4/1, *Wednesday*—Fried chicken, rice and gravy, congealed salad. **1968** *DARE* (Qu. H52, *Dishes made with fresh cabbage*) Inf **LA40**, Congealed Salad. **1968** *DARE* FW Addit **GA44**, *Congealed salad*—a gelatin salad, with or without fruit in it. Common.

congeree See **conger eel** 3

conger eel n Cf **congo eel**

1 Std: a fish of the family Congridae, but esp *Conger conger*, an often large saltwater eel. [*OED* 1602 →; also *conger, OED* c1300 →]

2 also *congar eelpout*: =**eelpout 1.** **Atl coast**

1861 *Acad. Nat. Sci. Philadelphia Proc.* 45 **NY**, *Zoarces anguillaris* . . . "Ling," "Conger Eel." **1873** Gill *Catalog Fishes* 19, *Zoarces anguillaris* . . . Eel-pout; conger-eel (*Massachusetts Bay*); lamper eel (*Eastport*). **1906** NJ State Museum *Annual Rept. for 1905* 406, *Zoarces anguillaris* . . . Eel Pout. Conger Eel Pout. **1911** *Century Dict.* Eel-pout . . . The conger-eel or lamper eel, *Zoarces anguillaris*, of North America.

3 also *congeree*: the California moray (*Gynothorax mordax*).

1882 U.S. Natl. Museum *Bulletin* 16.356, *M[uræna] mordax* . . Conger Eel . . . Reaches a length of 5 feet. Point Concepcion to Cape San Lucas; abundant about the islands, and remarkable for its ferocity. **1884** Goode *Fisheries U.S.* 1.629, This species [*Sidera mordax*] . . is always known as 'Conger Eel' or 'Congeree.' It is found among rocks about the Santa Barbara Islands, and southward along the coast of Lower California. Its flesh . . is very palatable when fried. **1902** Jordan–Evermann *Amer. Fishes* 83, The conger-eel of California . . . is a food-fish of some importance.

4 =**wrymouth 1.**

1873 Gill *Catalog Fishes* 19, *Crytacanthodes inornatus* . . . Ghost-fish; conger-eel (*Me.*) Nova Scotia to Cape Cod.

congestive chill n

A chill followed by intestinal disturbances; see quot 1965.

1871 Eggleston *Queer Stories* 108 (*DAE*), His father died of a congestive chill. **1946** *PADS* 6.9 **eNC** (as of 1900–10), Congestive chill . . . A severe chill? Pamlico, 1900. Occasional. **c1960** *Wilson Coll.* **csKY**, Congestive chill . . . A severe chill, accompanied by cramps and nausea. **1965** *Dorland's Med. Dict.* 290/2, Congestive c[hill], pernicious malaria with gastrointestinal congestion and diarrhea, preceded by a chill.

congo n¹ [*Congo* a region in Africa]

1 also attrib: A Black person; see quot 1976. **chiefly Sth** *old-fash*

[**1810** Lambert *Travels* 2.443 **Charleston SC**, All the papers are well stocked with advertisements, among which, *prime Congo, Gambia,* and *Angola slaves* for *sale* at Gadsden's Wharf, were very conspicuous.] **1855** *Putnam's Mag.* 5.79/2, Then Ethiopian Serenaders, and Congo Minstrels will draw crowded houses at three dollars a seat, and one dollar for a promenade ticket. **1880** Cable *Grandissimes* 89 **LA**, A dwarf Congo woman, as black as soot, had ushered her in. **1941** FWP *Guide LA* 687, *Congo:* A very black Negro. Formerly it meant a Negro actually from the Congo Nation. **1976** Flexner *America Talking* 55, *Congo* (1760) originally meant a slave from the Congo region . . but . . eventually came to mean any slave and then any Black.

2 By ext: anything of a very dark color. Cf **congo snake**

1931 Read *LA French* 121, *Congo*, a name first given to negroes from the Congo region of Africa, was afterwards bestowed on objects or animals of a dark or black color.

3 also attrib: A dance of Haitian origin also adapted as a ballroom dance. **Sth** *obs*

1803 Davis *Travels* 380 **VA**, My young master himself could shake a desperate foot at the fiddle; there was nobody that could face him at a *Congo Minuet*. **1835** (1847) Longstreet *GA Scenes* 160 (*DAE*), Except the minuet . . and the Congo, which is only to chase away the solemnities of the minuet, it was all a jovial . . amusement. **1886** *Century Illustr. Mag.* 31.527/2 **seLA**, The Congo . . was a kind of Fandango, they say, in which the Madras kerchief held by its tip-ends played a graceful part. **1957** Stearns *Story of Jazz* 3.26, The Congo, as such, is no longer danced in New Orleans, but it is still danced in Haiti, along with the Bamboula.

4 See **congo snake.**

5 =**green-winged teal.**

1982 Elman *Hunter's Field Guide* 178, Green-winged Teal . . . Common & Regional Names: . . congo.

6 See **congo eel 1, 2.**

Congo n², also attrib Also *Cong* [Abbr for *Congregationalist*] **chiefly NEng**

A member of a Congregational church.

1922 (1926) Cady *Rhymes* 17 (*DA*) **VT**, My! such a peaceful, fambly day, It makes you Congos Quakers. **1950** *WELS* (*Nicknames for different religions*) 2 Infs, **WI**, Congos. **1968–70** *DARE* (Qu. CC4, . . *Nicknames . . for various religions or religious groups*) Infs **CT6, 8, 16, MA50, 59**, Congos; **MA77**, Congo; **CT12**, Congo club; **OH8**, Congs.

congo eel n [?Alter of *conger*, but see **congo snake**] Cf **conger eel**

1 also *congo*: =**eelpout 1.** **Atl coast**

1884 Goode *Fisheries U.S.* 1.247, The Mutton-fish, *Zoarces anguillaris*, called Congo Eel and Ling, especially by the Maine fishermen, is often seen near the shore north of Cape Cod, and in winter especially is frequently taken with hook and line from the wharves. **1911** *Century Dict.*, Conger-eel . . . Along the Atlantic coast of the United States, *Zoarces anguillaris* . . . Also called *congo, lamper-eel, ling,* and *muttonfish.*

2 also *congo*: A large salamander, esp a **siren 1** (here: *Siren lacertina*) or the **congo snake 1.** **SE**

1889 *Century Dict.* **Sth**, *Congo* . . . Same as *congo-eel* . . . *Congo eel* . . . In the southern United States, an amphibian of the family *Sirenidae, Siren lacertina.* **1942** *Nat. Hist.* 50.249, Yet with consistent and delightful inaccuracy, the Floridians call . . one of their true salamanders, a "congo eel." **1953** Schmidt *N. Amer. Amphibians* 27, *Amphiuma means* . . . Common name.—Amphiuma, congo eel [etc]. **1958** Conant *Reptiles & Amphibians* 205, *Amphiuma means* . . . This is the "congo (conger) eel," "lamper eel," or "ditch eel," of fishermen and country folk. (The same names are often applied to both species of *Siren.*) **c1970** *DARE* FW Addit **csLA**, *Congo eel:* A large salamander

[that] gets as large as three or four feet. This is the only common local name. [Ed: prob *Amphiuma means*]

3 =**wrymouth 1** (here: *Delolepis gigantea* and *Cryptacanthodes maculatus*).

1928 Pan-Pacific Research Inst. *Jrl.* 3.15, *Delolepis giganteus* . . . "Congo eel." Taken by us south to Heceta Head, Oregon. **1960** Amer. Fisheries Soc. *List Fishes* 56, Eel, congo—see wrymouth, giant. *[Delolepis gigantea]* **1961** W3, Congo eel . . . Wrymouth. *[Cryptacanthodes maculatus]*

congolene n [Prob from **congo** n[1] **1** + -*(l)ene*, in imitation of var quasi-scientific brand names] *esp among Black speakers*
A preparation used to straighten hair.

1965 Little *Autobiog. Malcolm X* 53, Shorty soon decided that my hair was finally long enough to be conked. He had promised to school me in how to beat the barbershops' three- and four-dollar price by making up congolene, and then conking ourselves . . . I got a can of Red Devil lye, two eggs, and two medium-sized white potatoes . . . He peeled the potatoes and thin-sliced them into a quart-sized Mason fruit jar, then started stirring them with a wooden spoon as he gradually poured in a little over half the can of lye . . . A jelly-like, starchy-looking glop resulted from the lye and potatoes, and Shorty broke in the two eggs, stirring real fast—his own conk and dark face bent down close. The congolene turned pale-yellowish.

congo root n [Etym unknown]
A **scurf pea** (here: *Psoralea psoralioides*).

1953 Greene–Blomquist *Flowers South* 56, *Congo-Root* (*Psoralea psoralioides*) . . . ranges in the Coastal Plain from Fla. to Tex. n. to Ind. and Va. **1972** Brown *Wildflowers LA* 87, *Congo-root* . . . Erect, bushy perennial up to 2 feet tall.

congo snake n Also *congo* [Prob **congo** n[1] **2**]
1 An eel-like bluish-black salamander (*Amphiuma means*) of the southeastern US which has four tiny two- or three-toed limbs and grows to about one meter long. Also called **congo eel 2, ditch eel, lamp eel, lamper eel 3, mud eel 1, mud puppy, snake with legs**

1831–39 Audubon *Ornith. Biog.* 3.90, The Congo snake and the water-moccasin glide before you as they seek to elude your sight. **1892** IN Dept. Geol. & Nat. Resources *Rept. for 1891* 421, *Amphiuma; Congo-Snake* . . . This, like the Siren, appears to be a mud-loving species. **1911** *Century Dict.* 5724, Snake . . . A snake-like amphibian: as, the Congo *snake*, the North American *Amphiuma means*, a urodele amphibian . . . Congo snakes, the family *Amphiumidae*. **1925** TX Folkl. Soc. *Pub.* 4.50, The *Amphiuma means* . . has a habit of coiling . . . This attitude is very snake-like and . . . one of its English vernacular names is "Congo snake." **1931** [see **2** below]. **1947** *Chi. Tribune* (Grafic Mag.) 21 Dec. 9/3 (*DA*), There were malaria and typhus in the swamps, and many snakes: rattlers, moccasins, copperheads, and the Congo, a blue black eel, most feared of all. **1967** LeCompte *Word Atlas* 217 seLA, (*A snake-like creature with four tiny legs, usually found in ditches after a heavy rain*)—Congo [3 infs].

2 also *congar viper:* =**cottonmouth** (here: prob *Agkistrodon piscivorus leucostoma*). **LA**

1806 Berquin–Duvallon *Travels* 124 LA, The rattle snake . . is common here; but a more dreadful animal is the congar viper. **1888** Cable *Bonaventure* 284 wLA, A large moccasin—not of the dusky kind described in books, but of that yet deadlier black sort, an ell in length, which the swampers call the Congo—came up the anchor-rope. **1931** Read *LA French* 121, Congo . . . The name *Congo* is given by most Creoles and Acadians to the poisonous Water Moccasin, or Cotton-Mouth Moccasin (*Ancistrodon piscivorous* Lacépède); by others to a bluish-black eel-like amphibian (*Amphiuma means* Garden), which, though quite harmless, is considered deadly by the common folk. Both reptiles are common in Louisiana.

coning See **cone 1**

co-nin(nie) See **co-nan(nie)** v phr

conjo, conju' See **conjure** v, n

conjunct v [Prob back-formation from *conjunction*]
To conjoin.

1888 Jones *Negro Myths* 49 **GA coast** [Gullah], All de animal conjunct togedder fuh buil house.

conjure v, also ppl adj *conjuring* Also sp *conjo, conju', conjur, kunger* **chiefly SE** See Map Cf **mojo** v

To practice voodoo or other magical arts, esp to charm, bewitch, invoke spirits, or effect cures.

1847 Child *Fact & Fiction* 201 **SC**, I hear an old conjuring woman say she could conjure de Divil out of anybody. **1898** Dunbar *Folks from Dixie* 91, Sis' Williams ain't gwine conju' nobidy. **1899** (1912) Green *VA Folk-Speech* 124, *Conjur*. **1921** (1923) Greer–Petrie *Angeline Seelbach* 17 **KY**, 'Peared like he kungered them beds out of space. **1939** Hall Coll. eTN, wNC, *Conjure*, . . [kʌndʒɚ] . . . "The Indians will conjure two or three days before a ball game. The night before the game they'll have a dance and conjure all night long." **1945** FWP *Lay My Burden Down* 46 **AL** [Black], Conjuring Doc say that he done put a spell on Old Marse. **c1960** Wilson Coll. csKY, *Conjure*: To place someone under a spell. Very rare, largely now a joke. **1965–70** *DARE* (Qu. CC14, . . *One person supposedly casts a spell over another*) 31 Infs, **chiefly SE**, Conjure; **LA31**, Conjo; (Qu. BB51b, . . *"Magical" cures for corns or warts*) 10 Infs, **Sth**, Conjure (them, it, the wart) (off); **NC16**, Negroes conjure them off; **NC55**, We had them conjured; **GA9**, Conjuring. [9 of 41 Infs Black]

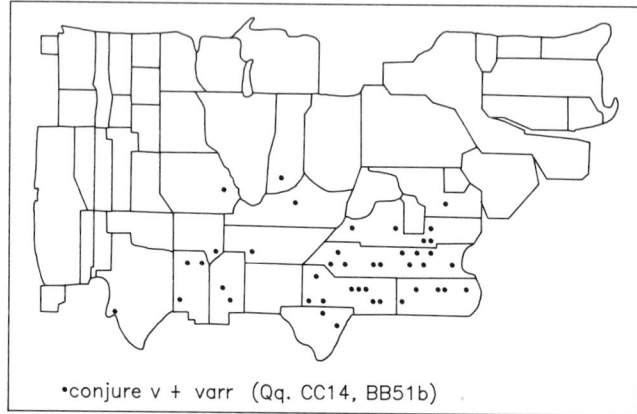

•conjure v + varr (Qq. CC14, BB51b)

conjure n, also attrib Also sp *conjo, conju', cunjer, cunjuh, cunjur, kunger* [**conjure** v] **chiefly Sth, esp S Atl**
1 Conjuration; the practice of voodoo or other magic.

1888 Jones *Negro Myths* 69 **GA coast** [Gullah], De man tell um say him bin a po man, an dat eh mek eh libbin by cunjur. **1899** Chesnutt *Conjure Woman* 146 **NC** [Black], En so w'en he did n' git no better, she . . went ter see ole Aun' Peggy, de cunjuh 'oman. **1905** Culbertson *Banjo Talks* 90 **SE**, She's a cunjer-doctah, . . 'kase she cunjer me good. **1909** *Sat. Eve. Post* 29 May 16/1, His mammy used to scare him with tales of the potent "conju'-man" who came down in this very swamp and changed skins with the devil. **1941** FWP *Guide AL* 380, There are "conjure doctors," both white and black, who make their living by selling "tricks" to the illiterate and superstitious. **1941** Writers' Program SC *Folk Tales* 97, Conjure is another name for hoodoo, voodoo, coocoo, and goofering, all of which may be found in South Carolina. **1966** *DARE* Tape **FL19**, My grandmother was a—they called her a conjure ['kʌnjɚ] doctor and . . she used herbs and made her medicines . . . She went for miles to doctor people when they were sick . . . Now they refer to a conjure doctor I think as one that's sort of a fake doctor, you know, that says he can cure cancer and things like that. **1968–70** *DARE* (Qu. BB51a, . . *Cures for corns or warts*) Inf **LA31**, Conjo ['kʌnjoʊ]; (Qu. EE41) Inf **VA39**, Conjure doctor.

2 =**conjure bag.**

1863 Gilmore *S. Friends* 153, The conjurer's bag of the Africans . . is called "waiter," or "kunger," by the Southern blacks, and is supposed to have the power to charm away evil spririts, and to do all manner of miraculously good things for its wearer. Those that I have seen are harmless little affairs, consisting only of small pieces of rags sewed up in coarse muslin.

conjure bag n Also *conjure ball* **chiefly Sth** Cf **mojo** n
A magic charm made up of a varied assortment of things and often placed under the doorstep to gain some control over the victim or to keep off evil spirits.

1898 Harris *Tales Home Folks* 65 **GA**, It seemed to be a bundle of rags. "It's his conjure-bag," the colonel said to himself. **1941** Percy *Lanterns* 305 **MS**, She . . pleaded in defense that he had placed a spell on her by means of a cunjer-bag. **1942** Rawlings *Cross Creek* 276 **FL**, "I wisht I could find me a good root man, to find out something buried under my house." "A conjur bag?" "Yessum." **1945** Saxon *Gumbo Ya-Ya* 542

LA, *A Conjure Ball*—One kind is made of a snake tooth, a piece of human flesh, and a lock of human hair. **1950** *PADS* 14.21 **SC,** *Conjure* ['kʌndʒə] *ball:* . . A ball made of such weird objects as dead lizards and bats, frog's legs, snake skins dried and tied together. The ball is then thrown under the front steps of the victim, who finds it and is conjured thereby. **c1960** *Wilson Coll.* **csKY,** *Conjure ball* . . Very rarely heard of now and chiefly as a joke. **1970** Anderson *TX Folk Med.* 31, To keep off evil spirits, make up a conjure ball and keep it under your steps. The conjure ball is made of thorns off of a locust tree, some wool or cotton from a mockingbird nest, and a piece of frog skin. Wrap all of this into a ball with goofer powder (the dust out of a dry tree in a cemetery).

conk n^1

1 also attrib: The head. *joc*

1922 Rollins *Cowboy* 105, These other names (for hat) included . . "conk cover". **1931** Queen *Dutch Shoe* 48 (1976 Flexner *America Talking*), Persistent idea has been buzzing around in my conk. **1950** WELS *(Joking names for a person's head)* 3 Infs, **WI,** Conk. **1966–68** *DARE* (Qu. X28) Infs **CA**15, **GA**15, **IN**3, **WI**19, Conk. **1970** Major *Afro–Amer. Slang, Conk:* (1940's) . . the human head itself.

2 The nose. *joc*

1966 *DARE* (Qu. X14, *Joking words for the nose*) Inf **MS**16, Conk.

conk n^2 [Prob from *conch* spiral-shelled mollusk, usu pronc [kɑŋk]]

1 also *konkus:* A saprophitic fungus of the family Polyporaceae, esp of the genera *Fomes, Ganoderma,* and *Polyperus;* also the disease caused by such fungi. Cf **beefsteak fungus**

1851 (1856) Springer *Forest Life* 99 **ME,** There is a cancerous disease peculiar to the Pine-tree, to which lumbermen give the original name of "Conk" or "Konkus." **1902** U.S. Forest Serv. *Bulletin* 33.15, The "conk" or bracket seen on affected trees is the fruiting organ. *Ibid,* Conk spores never enter through the bark, but usually through the scars of broken branches. **1948** Boyce *Forest Pathology* 403, The large annual conks with a reddish shiny lacquerlike upper surface and usually with a short thick lateral stalk are conspicuous on logs, stumps, and standing or fallen dead trees. **1966–68** *DARE* (Qu. S19, *Mushrooms that grow out like brackets from the sides of trees*) Infs **MN**14, **WA**20, 28, 30, Conk(s). **1968** Adams *Western Words, Conk wood*—A destructive tree fungus which is visible on the affected tree.

2 By ext: the decay caused by the fungus.

1905 U.S. Forest Serv. *Bulletin* 61.33, *Conk* . . [is] the decay in the wood of trees caused by a fungus. **1969** Sorden *Lumberjack Lingo* **NEng, Gt Lakes,** *Conk*—A rotten tree. The decay in the wood of a tree caused by a fungus.

3 See **conch.**

conk n^3 [Prob abbr and alter of **congolene** infl by **conk** n^1 1]

1 also *conk job:* A hairstyle in which curly hair is straightened and smoothed down or lightly waved. *esp among Black speakers* Also called **process**

1965 Little *Autobiog. Malcolm X* 54, "Going to lay on that first conk?" the drugstore man asked me. *Ibid* 55, "You took it real good, homeboy. You got a good conk." . . I'd seen some pretty conks, but when it's the first time, on your *own* head, the transformation, after a lifetime of kinks, is staggering . . I vowed that I'd never be without a conk. **1968** *Current Slang* Fall **Watts CA** [Black], *Conk job* . . A straightened lightly waved hair-style, also called a "process." **1970** *DARE* (Qu. KK38, *To put preparations on the hair to hold it close to the head and make it shiny*) Inf **NY**241, A conk—straightening hair with lye. **1983** Mebane *Mary Wayfarer* 200 **NC,** He left with a group of leather-jacketed young men, all of them with the processed hair known as a "conk." I was rather startled by that. Black college students were very much into the "black folk" tradition, yet they wore neither leather jackets nor "conks;" they wore Afros and denim.

2 See quot.

1970 Major *Afro–Amer. Slang, Conk:* (1940's) pomade for the hair.

conk v^1 [Prob from **conk** n^1 1]

To hit someone hard, esp on the head.

1951 *NEA* 13 Dec (1960 Wentworth–Flexner *Slang*), *Conk* . . . He knocked over a lamp, got conked on the head, and wound up in the hospital. **1960** Criswell *Resp. to PADS 20* **Ozarks,** *Conk* . . to hit hard, used of a person. (Still common). **1966–70** *DARE* (Qu. Y14a, *To hit somebody hard with the fist*) Infs **CA**36, **GA**89, **IA**4, **PA**237, **SD**8, Conk; (Qu. Y11, . . *A very hard blow*) Inf **IA**4, Conked him; (Qu. Y15, *To beat someone thoroughly*) Infs **MD**27, **NJ**56, Conked. **1969** *DARE* Tape

MA58, To hit anything, you'd tell him to whop it one . . . Or, especially if you hit it in the head, or tell him to hit it in the head, to conk him one . . . That'd be to conk him one—seems to be to hit him in the head . . . Conk him on the noggin.

conk v^2, also ppl adj *conked* [**conk** n^3] *esp among Black speakers*

To straighten one's hair artificially.

1965 [see **congolene**]. **1968** *NY Times* (NY) 10 April 33, Street youths with elaborately straightened or "conked" hair. **1970** *DARE* (Qu. KK38, *To put preparations on the hair to hold it close to the head and make it shiny*) Inf **MO**30, Conk.

conk-buster n [From **conk** n^1 1 + *buster* that which breaks (something)] *among Black speakers*

1 Cheap liquor. Cf **busthead**

1942 *Amer. Mercury* 55.94 **Harlem NYC,** *Conk buster*—cheap liquor.

2 A difficult problem.

1960 Wentworth–Flexner *Slang, Conkbuster* . . . Any difficult problem . . ; fig., anything so complex that one breaks one's head in thinking about it. *Primarily Negro use.* **1970** Major *Afro–Amer. Slang, Conk-buster:* (rare since 1940's) generally, anything that proved mentally difficult.

3 A Black intellectual.

1942 *Amer. Mercury* 55.84 **Harlem NYC,** Conk Buster. [Caption below a cartoon of a Black man studiously reading a book.] *Ibid* 94, *Conk buster* . . an intellectual Negro.

conker n^1 [*conk a blow* < **conk** v^1 + *-er*]

1969 *DARE* (Qu. Y11, . . *A very hard blow* . . "*Joe really hit him a ———."*) Inf **IL**110, Conker.

conker n^2 See **conquer John**

‡**conker** n^3 [Perh alter of *clunker,* infl by *conk* (of an engine) to stall]

1967 *DARE* (Qu. N5, . . *An old or broken-down car*) Inf **IL**7, Old conker.

conkerin' John See **conquer John**

conkers n [Engl dial; cf *OEDS, EDD*]

See quot 1937.

1937 (1947) Bancroft *Games* 84, *Conkers* . . . Each boy carries a store of empty horse-chestnut shells . . . Each boy has also one shell on the end of a string held in place by a knot. Two boys, as opponents, try each to break the shell of the other by banging his single shell against the opponent's. **1984** *DARE* File **neMA,** Students from U. Mass. have told me that they played conkers ['kɒŋkəz] in Lawrence and Lowell, Mass. in the 1950s.

conkhouse n [**conk** n^1 1] Cf **conkpiece**

The head, mind.

1946 (1972) Mezzrow *Really Blues* 274, One afternoon things came to a head for me; in ten frantic minutes the formless mush of my life bubbled and seethed and then jellied, in a shape I could finally recognize. Fireworks busted loose in my skull . . . It may not seem like much, frozen in cold type, but . . it'll stay locked in my conkhouse till the day I die.

conk job See **conk** n^3 1

‡**conkle** n [Prob var of *cockle* mollusk, infl by *conch* pronc [kɑŋk]]

1966 *DARE* Tape **ME**22, [FW:] What do you haul up besides lobsters in your traps? [Inf:] Oh, we get conkles and—[FW:] What kind of conkles? [Inf:] Crab conkles, and then there's some kind you can eat, and there's whore's eggs and sculpins—and we get any kind of—codfish, crabs . . . [FW:] What do you call these conkles, now? [Inf:] Crab conkles. [FW:] No, there's another kind. [Inf:] Picky-diddle conkles!

conk-onk n [Echoic]

=**bittern.**

1959 *Names* 7.120, The true sound names range from "a" to "z": . . conk-onk (Mich.).

conkpiece n [**conk** n^1]

1970 Major *Afro–Amer. Slang, Conkpiece:* (1940's) the head.

conky adj [**conk** n^2 + *-y*]

1 Of trees: affected by **conk** n^2.

1905 U.S. Forest Serv. *Bulletin* 61.33, *Conky* . . . Affected by conk. **1945** (1946) Macdonald *Egg & I* 60, We sawed fallen firs, six and seven feet in diameter and conky in the middle, for wood.   **1956** *AmSp* 31.150, *Conky* . . . Description of a log or a tree bearing wood-rotting fungi.   **1969** Sorden *Lumberjack Lingo* **NEng, Gt Lakes,** *Conky*—Affected by conk.

2 By ext: in poor condition, dried out, brittle.

1966 *DARE* (Qu. I8, *When root vegetables get old and tough . . you say they are_____*) Inf **WA**18, Conky; (Qu. KK24, *Something that breaks easily*) Inf **WA**18, Conky.

conkywine n [Alter of *concubine*]

1922 Gonzales *Black Border* 293 **sSC, GA coasts** [Gullah glossary], *Conkywine*—concubine . . used for masculine as well as for feminine affiliations.

Connecticut mile n *joc*

1962 *Western Folkl.* 21.30, *Connecticut mile*—the distance traveled in one minute. [Footnote:] The distance traveled in one minute usually is something less than 5,280 feet.

Connecticut River pork n *joc* Cf **Albany beef**

Shad (*Alosa* spp).

1907 *Springfield W. Republican* 21 March 13 *(DAE)*, Shad were formerly so plenty in this region as to be known as "Connecticut river pork."

Connecticut warbler n

A warbler (here: *Oporornis agilis*). Also called **swamp warbler, tamarack warbler**

1812 Wilson *Amer. Ornith.* 5.64, [The] *Connecticut Warbler. Sylvia Agilis* . . . is a new species, first discovered in the state of Connecticut, and twice since met with in the neighbourhood of Philadelphia.   **1868** *Amer. Naturalist* 2.174, The Connecticut Warbler (*Oporornis agilis*) . . frequents low, bushy swamps . . and utters, at times, a feeble chirp.   **1895** Minot *Land-Birds New Engl.* 87, *Oporornis agilis.* Connecticut Warbler. A migrant in New England.   **1929** Forbush *Birds MA* 3.289, *Oporornis ágilis* . . . Connecticut Warbler.   **1948** Seton *Trail of Artist* 218, I found the nest and eggs of the Connecticut warbler, and sent them safely to the Smithsonian, where now they are to be seen.

conner See cunner n¹, n²

connip v [Back-formation of *conniption* a fit of anger or hysteria]

1896 *DN* 1.415 **NYC,** Connip [kən'ɪp]: to laugh violently.

connipity adj [Prob from *conniption* infl by such words as *uppity*, **biggity** adj]

1927 *AmSp* 2.351 **wcWV,** Connipity . . . full of whims; hard to please. "That old woman is too connipity to get along with any of her neighbors."

conniption bug n

=**hellgrammite.**

1901 Howard *Insect Book* 212, In 1889 Professor W.W. Bailey . . collected the names in Rhode Island alone for this insect, and they are . . . conniption bugs, . . dragon and hell-diver.   **1948** *Field & Stream* July 42/2 *(DA)*, Various stages of the dobson are known as conniption bugs, chippers, water grampus, . . and hell-divers.

conniver n Cf **conniving**

c**1960** Wilson *Coll.* **csKY,** Conniver . . . A greedy person, a grabber.

conniver v, hence *connivering* vbl n [*connive* + -*er* affix]

To intrigue, plot, scheme.

1927 *AmSp* 3.137 **coastal ME,** "Conniver," to connive with in secret (complicity) always implies wrong.   **1968** *DARE* (Qu. V1, *When you suspect that somebody is trying to deceive you, or that something is going on behind your back, you say, "There's_____."*) Inf **LA**40, Connivering.

‡conniverate v [*conniver* v + -*ate*]

1968 *DARE* (Qu. JJ36, *To work out a plan, especially a secret plan: "Mary knows more about that, you and she can_____together."*) Inf **VA**15, Conniverate.

conniving ppl adj

Stingy, greedy.

1966–70 *DARE* (Qu. U33, . . *A stingy person*) Inf **NJ**67, Conniving; (Qu. U35, *Words meaning thrifty but not in a complimentary way: "She's not a bad housekeeper, but very_____."*) Inf **LA**40, Conniving; (Qu. U36a, *Greedy in money matters: "He's an awful_____."*) Inf **GA**28, Conniving person; (Qu. U36b, *Words . . used to describe a person*

who saves in a mean way or is greedy in money matters: "She certainly is_____.") Inf **ME**15, Conniving.

connyswaggle v [Perh blend of Engl dial *connyfogle* to dupe, cheat + **hornswoggle**] Cf **cohogle 1**

1912 *DN* 3.573 **wIN,** Conny-swaggle . . . To cheat.

‡conogracy n

Association.

1937 (1963) Hyatt *Kiverlid* 50 **KY,** Now there's Minton Sailor bin traipsin' over here to make sheep's eyes at the gal. I ain't wantin' no conogracies with his like.

conohany n [Cherokee *kanahena* sour corn gruel]

1953 Randolph *Down in Holler* 236 **Ozarks,** Conohany [kono'hænɪ] . . . Hominy cooked with meat and nuts, seasoned with wild herbs. It is still favored by old-timers in the Cookson Hills of Oklahoma, where it is said to be a Cherokee dish.

conoodle See **canoodle** v

conquain See **cooncan**

conque n [Span "wherewithal"]

1967 *DARE* (Qu. U19a, *Words used around here for money in general: "He's certainly got the_____."*) Inf **TX**28, Conque ['kon,kei].

conquedle n   Also *conquiddle, quongqueedle, quamquidle* [Echoic] **NEng, esp RI** =**bobolink B.**

1778 in 1903 *NYC Pub. Lib. Bulletin* 7.431, The Quongquéedle of Rhode-Island, Bob of Lincoln in New England, seems to be Emberiza oryzivora.   **1778** (1930) Mackenzie *Diary* 1.281 **RI,** I shot a bird here this day, which is called here, The Quamquidle, or Bob-o'-Lincoln; but properly the Rice bird.   **1783** Latham *Synop. Birds* II.189 *(DAE)*, This species is known in the country by the names of Bob-Lincoln and Conquedle.   **1796** Morse *Amer. Universal Geog.* 1.210, [Footnote:] The rice bird and pied rice bird are . . called in New England Boblincoln, Conquedle.   **1858** *Atlantic Mth.* 2.601/2 **NEng,** The Bobolink, or Conquedle, has unquestionably great talents as a musician.   **1956** *MA Audubon Soc. Bulletin* 40.130 **RI,** Bobolink . . Conquiddle (R.I. A sonic, Indian name.).

conquer v

To control.

1931 *PMLA* 46.1304 **sAppalachians,** I hain't never had a boy I couldn't conquer (control).

conquering Tom n [Perh var of **conquer John**]

1938 (1955) FWP *Guide DE* 106, Conquering Tom. "Conquerin' Tom" when rubbed on the body assures success in courting girls. [Sussex Co.]

conquer John n   Also *big* (or *high*) *John the Conqueror, conker, conkerin' John, conqueror John, John(ny) the Conqueror* **chiefly Gulf States, Lower Missip Valley**

A Solomon's seal (here: *Polygonatum biflorum*); also its root.

1893 Owen *Voodoo Tales* 67 **MO,** Er chunk ob er root ob Conquer-John (Solomon's Seal—*Polygonatum* [sic] *biflorum*).   **1894** *Jrl. Amer. Folkl.* 7.25.102, *Polygonatum biflorum* . . . conquer-John, Mo.   **1931** Ibid 44.413 **Gulf States,** Roots and herbs are used freely [for conjure magic] under wide-spread names: Big John the Conquerer.   **1934** Carmer *Stars Fell on AL* 220, Warning: Never let John the Conqueror Root come in contact with snuff or tobacco; that will kill its effect.   **1935** Hurston *Mules & Men* 233 **LA** [Black], She even throwed at *me* once, but she can't do nothin'. Ah totes mah Big John de Conqueror wid me. [Footnote:] A root, extensively used in conjure.   **1940** Clute *Amer. Plant Names* 228, *P. biflorum* . . . conquerer [sic] John.   **1942** Kennedy *Palmetto Country* 168 **FL,** European John the Conqueror—carried in pocket for good luck; 50¢. High John the Conqueror—carried in pocket to offset melancholy moods; 50¢.   **1945** Saxon *Gumbo Ya-Ya* 543 **LA,** *Conjure paraphernalia* . . . Some of the roots and herbs . . : Big John the Conqueror.   Ibid 539, *To Win Love* . . . Carry a piece of weed called 'John the Conqueror' in your pocket.   **1946** Tallant *Voodoo* 225, Thousands of Negroes carry Johnny the Conqueror roots, not only in New Orleans, but all over the country.   **1970** Hyatt *Hoodoo* 2.1391 [Black], You placed in the black bottle what they call a King Solomon—the root of *King Solomon root*, then you put the *love root*, then you put the devil's-shoestring root in there and that ~~Conker~~ what they call the *Conkerin' John*—it is known to be the *conker of the Earth*. [DARE Ed: used as part of a charm to win a lawsuit.]   **1971** Krochmal *Appalachia*

Med. Plants 202, *[Polygonatum Biflorum]* Common names: Small solo-monseal, conquer-John, dwarf solomon's seal, hairy solomon's seal, sealwort, solomon's seal.

conqueror n [Cf Engl dial *conqueror* a game played with shells or horse-chestnuts]

1955 *PADS* 23.14 **cwTN,** *Conqueror . . .* A marble game.

conqueror John See **conquer John**

conquian See **cooncan**

conquiddle See **conquedle**

consaa'n, consahn See **concern** v

consaity See **conceity**

consarn v Abbr *'sarn* [Alter of **concern** v] *somewhat old-fash, euphem*

To damn—often used as a mild oath.

[1803 Davis *Travels* 360 **VA,** Master Waring . . will make nothing of climbing a hickory after an owl's nest, and pulling out old and young by the neck. Concern it, an owl always scares me.] 1885 Green *Memoir Otey* 5 **VA** (as of c1800), As the old hen was about to pass once more through the fence, I threw my stick at her, exclaiming in my rage, *"Consarn you!"* 1914 *DN* 4.70 **ME, nNH,** Consarn ye! 1915 *DN* 4.225 **wTX,** Consarn you! 1919 *DN* 5.35 **KY,** 'Sarn his looks! 1931 *PMLA* 46.1308 **sAppalachians,** "Cuss-words," expressions of surprise and intense expressions are numerous, as one might expect. A few of them follow: . . Consarn it (or you)! 1951 *PADS* 15.66 **NH,** Con sarn it . . . Mild oaths. 1962 Atwood *Vocab. TX* 70, *Exclamations of disgust . . .* Some of those of less frequency might be of interest; they all occur more than once, and probably show no originality: . . *consarn it.* 1965–70 *DARE* (Qu. NN8b, . . *Expressions of annoyance*) 13 Infs, **scattered east of Missip R,** Consarn; [MA58, Concern it;] (Qu. NN9b) 14 Infs, **scattered, chiefly east of Missip R,** Consarn him; (Qu. NN25a, . . *Substitutes for "damn"*) Inf **GA31,** Consarn. [21 of 27 Infs old] 1966 Barnes–Jensen *Dict. UT Slang,* Consarn your picture . . damn you.

consarn n See **concern** n

consarned ppl adj, adv Pronc-spp *consarnt(ly)* *euphem*

Damned; by a damn sight—often used as an intensifier.

1834 *Life Andrew Jackson* 228, The Cherokees, who are a consarnt cute christianized sort of pagans. *Ibid* 109, They thou't tu make the brave boys from Kentuck and Tenesee take leg-bail, but they mist it consarntly. Not a man of 'em wou'd budge a peg. 1844 Stephens *High Life in NY* 1.200, It raly made me ketch my breath to look at her, she was so consarned harnsome. 1893 Shands *MS Speech* 24, Consarned . . . This is a favorite expletive among the lower classes of whites. They say: "I'll be consarned if it ain't so." 1905 *DN* 3.6 **cCT,** I'm consarned sorry for it. 1907 *DN* 3.210 **nwAR, cCT,** Consarned. 1935 Davis *Honey* 93 **OR,** The flare was consarned hot. 1967 *DARE* (Qu. NN17, . . *"That_____fly won't go away."*) Infs **CA10, SC45,** Consarned.

conscience n [nEngl dial *conscience* estimation]

Judgment, estimation.

1843 (1916) Hall *New Purchase* 147 **IN,** Sartin, indeed, a white would now and then be killed: but . . it was ginerally found the white was agressur, . . and me and Nancy had a secret conscience that the white deserved his fate. 1939 *Hall Coll.* **eTN,** Conscience . . . Opinion. "That was the best version I've read according to my conscience." (The exp[ression] 'according to my conscience' was heard two or three times).

conscious n [Alter of *conscience*]

1927 Adams *Congaree* 111 **SC** [Black], Conscious: conscience.

consecrate(d) adj [Malaprop]

Concentrated.

1869 *Atlantic Mth.* 24.482 **sePA,** The forests are being obliterated from this fertile tract, and many use what some call "consecrated" lye [in making soap]. 1922 Gonzales *Black Border* 274 **sSC, GA coasts** [Gullah], 'E tek de can wid de consecrate' lye, en' 'e pit de consecrate' lye een de hom'ny, en' fus' t'ing 'e know, 'e yent know nutt'n' 'cause 'e dead! [='He takes the can with the consecrated lye, and he puts the consecrated lye in the hominy, and first thing he knows, he doesn't know nothing, because he's dead!] *Ibid* 294 [Glossary], *Consecrate lye*—concentrated lye.

consecrated dime n

A monetary offering at a Black revival meeting.

1976 *Voices Harlem Renaissance* 127 (as of 1930s), Then "when the milleniums are quaking it's time to clap our hands." It is the moment for the "consecrated dime," and the singing begins again, but the trances are over; other preachers may speak later. 1977 Dillard *Lexicon* 54, An important part of the service is, of course, the collection, sometimes described by terms like *raise the offering* or the *consecrated dime.*

conseeder See **consider**

consentable adj

1939 FWP *Guide NC* 521 **seNC,** *Consentable:* willing.

conservation blade n

1968 *DARE* (Qu. L35, *Hand tools used for cutting underbrush and digging out roots*) Inf **NY92,** Conservation blade. [Drawing in QR shows a single-bladed mattock resembling an adz.]

consid'able See **considerable** adv

consider v Pronc-sp *conseeder*

A Form.

1927 Mason *Lure Great Smokies* 191, I jest toted my Bible in a tow sack at the handle of my bull-tongue . . and I steddied hit at the turn o' the furrer and conseedered hit throw the rows.

B Sense.

To value, appreciate.

1956 *DE Folkl. Bulletin* Oct 24/2, I consider (i.e. appreciate) your present immensely.

considerable n

1 A large amount.

1685 (1861) *MA Hist. Soc. Coll.* 4th ser 5.132, One More, of Long Island, [who hath] . . lost considerable of wheat and Indian corn. 1745 (1912) *Essex Inst. Coll.* 48.300, A Considerable of Cannon shot [was] hove att ym. 1781 *PA Jrl. & Weekly Advt.* (Philadelphia) 23 May 1/3, Considerable of it may be found in that country. 1834 in 1934 Frear *Lowell & Abigail* 96 **MA,** We begin to have considerable of rain. 1903 Wiggin *Rebecca* 126, Rebecca took her scolding . . like a soldier. There was considerable of it. 1950 Faulkner *Stories* 32 **MS,** It was a kind of mixed hound, with a little bird dog and some Collie and maybe a considerable of almost anything else.

2 Of things, events, situations: a notable example, a remarkable degree or instance.

1766 (1888) Cutler *Life* 10, This morning about 6 o'clock considerable of a shock of an earthquake was felt in Boston. 1847 Paulding *Amer. Comedies* 141, I shouldn't wonder if I could make a pretty considerable of a sharp guess. 1875 Twain *Sketches New & Old* (Hartford) 47, A brick came through the window with a splintering crash, and gave me a considerable of a jolt in the back. 1889 Jewett *Betty Leicester* 19 **swME,** I was in considerable of a hurry to get home.

3 Of people: a good example or specimen.

1781 *PA Jrl. & Weekly Advt.* (Philadelphia) 23 May 1/3, He is *considerable* of a surveyor. 1852 Bristed *Upper Ten Thousand* 142, He is really worth knowing and considerable of a man, as we say—no fool at all, except in the way he lets his wife bully him. 1909 Rice *Mr. Opp* 97, I was considerable of a performer at one time.

considerable adv Pronc-sp *consid'able*

Considerably, very, remarkably.

1834 Smith *Letters Jack Downing* 159, 'Well,' says I, 'it's no matter;' but it lifted my dander considerable. 1871 Eggleston *Hoosier Schoolmaster* 130 **sIN, sIL, sOH,** Pete picked himself up slowly, and, muttering that he felt "consid'able shuck up like," crawled away like a whipped puppy. 1905 *DN* 3.6 **cCT,** Considerable. 1907 *DN* 3.184 **seNH,** Consid'able. *Ibid* **nwAR,** Considerable. 1929 *AmSp* 5.121 **ME.** 1960 Criswell *Resp. to PADS* 20 **Ozarks,** Considerable . . . Considerably. Always the most common usage, still so. "That lick hurt me considerable for an hour or two." 1966–67 *DARE* Tape **MI23,** It cut the sod up considerable; **MI47,** Simplified loading logs considerable; **MI66,** This community has changed considerable.

considerably adv

1917 *DN* 4.410 **wNC, KY,** Considerably . . . For the most part. "My parents were considerably Scotch."

consider-lily n [Perh influenced by Matthew 6:28, Luke 12:27, "Consider the lilies of the field."]

1974 Peden *Speak to Earth* 58 **cIN,** The females [=ducks] walk about, exploring the ground as if they had never seen it before, tasting the little threads of water, inquiring into clumps of consider-lilies, weeds or deep grass that might be able to conceal a duck's nest.

consoin See **concern** v

consolate v [Prob a back-formation from *consolation*]
To console.
  1959 Lomax *Rainbow Sign* 104 **AL** [Black], I would kinda hum and sing a little and that's the only thing that would consolate me.

consound v [Prob alter of *confound*] *euphem* Cf **consarn**
  1941 Percy *Lanterns* 142 **nwMS,** When he would . . exclaim: "Consound Cam's kittycats!" I would know what had happened.

conspicious adj Also sp *conspishous* [Alter of *conspicuous*]
Conspicuous.
  1920s in 1944 *ADD* **cNY,** Conspicious. **1940** *Ibid,* He has to don a conspicious hat. **1942** *New Yorker* 11 July 18/2, The name . . would make the family look too conspishous.

constabule n [Alter of *constable,* perh infl by *mule;* cf **animule**]
joc
A constable.
  1965–70 *DARE* (Qu. V10c, . . *Joking names for a constable*) 25 Infs, **scattered,** Constabule.

constancy, as a adv phr
Habitually.
  1899 (1912) Green *VA Folk-Speech* 125, Constancy . . . To make a practice of doing something. "I don't do it as a constancy."

constant adv Cf **every constant**
Constantly, regularly.
  1805 (1905) Whitehouse *Jrl.* 151, 4 hunters were furnished horses without loads to hunt constant. **1929** *AmSp* 5.17 **Ozarks,** The touristers they puts this hyer donk [alcohol] inter their sody-pop constant.

consumpshus n Also sp *cunsumpshus*
  1922 Gonzales *Black Border* 294 **sSC, GA coasts** [Gullah glossary], Consumpshus, cunsumpshus—consumption.

consumpted ppl adj [*consumpt* v, back-formation from *consumption*] *old-fash*
Having tuberculosis.
  1894 Riley *Armazindy* 1 **IN,** The girl's mother'd *allus* ben / Sickly— wuz consumpted when / Word come 'bout her husband. **1899** (1912) Green *VA Folk-Speech* 125, Consumpted . . . Suffering with consumption. "I always thought she was consumpted." **1903** *DN* 2.310 **seMO,** Consumpted . . . Affected with consumption. 'My daughter is in bad health and I'm afraid she's consumpted.'

consumption n *somewhat old-fash* See also **galloping consumption, hasty ~, miner's ~,** and *DS* BB10, BB49
Any wasting disease, but esp tuberculosis.
  1731 Hempstead *Diary* 232 (*DAE*), Richd Morgan . . died of a Consumption. **1891** (1967) Freeman *New Engl. Nun* 156, Betsy shivered and coughed. She had coughed more or less for years. People said she had the old-fashioned consumption. **1926** *AmSp* 2.80 **ME,** Chronic colds are always "catarrh," and tuberculosis is "consumption." **1950** *WELS* (*Other names . . for tuberculosis*) 37 Infs, **WI,** Consumption. **c1960** *Wilson Coll.* **csKY,** Consumption . . . Until the younger generation learned to say tuberculosis, this was the common term. **1965–70** *DARE* (Qu. BB10, . . *Names . . for tuberculosis*) 639 Infs, **widespread,** Consumption; (Qu. BB49, . . *Other kinds of diseases*) 23 Infs, **scattered,** Consumption; (Qu. BB9) Inf **MN10,** Consumption; (Qu. BB11) Infs **MN19, OK13,** Consumption (cough); (Qu. K28, . . *Chief diseases . . cows have*) Infs **CA31, GA3,** 5, 12, 16, **MI113,** Consumption; (Qu. K47, . . *Diseases . . horses and mules . . get*) Inf **PA166,** Consumption. **1966** *DARE* Tape **MS77,** They didn't call it T.B. then . . [but rather] consumption.

consumption weed n

1 also *consumption root:* =**wintergreen 1.**
  1784 in 1785 *Amer. Acad. Arts & Sci. Memoirs* 1.444 **N Atl,** *Pyrola* . . . Consumption-root. Blossoms white. In wood land. July. **1795** Winterbotham *Amer. U.S.* 3.398, Among native and uncultivated plants of New England, the following have been employed for medical purposes: . . Consumption root, Pyrola rotundifolia. **1828** Rafinesque *Med. Flora* 72, The *P. rotundifolia, P. elliptica,* and *P. uniflora,* are called vulgarly . . *Consumption Weed* . . . Empirics employ them . . in diseases of the breast, colds, wounds, ophthalmia, bad humours, weak nerves, and externally as blisters. **1900** Lyons *Plant Names* 312, *P. rotundifolia* . . . Consumption-weed. **c1960** *Wilson Coll.* **csKY,** Consumption root . . .

Pyrola americana, false wintergreen. Nobody except one seems to have heard of it, and nobody knew the plant itself.

2 A groundsel tree (here: *Baccharis halimifolia*).
  1950 Gray–Fernald *Manual of Botany* 1448, Consumption-weed . . . The pistillate shrub conspicuous in autumn. **1960** Vines *Trees SW* 977, It [*Baccharis halimifolia*] is also known under the vernacular names of Groundsel-tree, Cottonseed-tree, Consumption-weed, Sea Myrtle, and Ploughman's Spikenard. **1970** Correll *Plants TX* 1560, *Baccharis halimifolia* . . Sea-myrtle, Consumption-weed.

consumptive's weed n Cf **consumption weed**
A yerba santa (here: *Eriodictyon californicum*).
  1889 *Century Dict.* 1221/1, Consumptive's-weed, the bear's-weed of California, *Eriodictyon Californicum,* an evergreen resinous shrub, of the family *Hydrophyllaceae.* **1900** Lyons *Plant Names* 149. **1974** (1977) Coon *Useful Plants* 152, Consumptive's weed . . . A number of references to this plant indicate its value as an expectorant.

contact n, also attrib **chiefly West**
In mining: the juncture of two different rock formations, often an indicator of ore deposits.
  1872 U.S. Treas. Dept. *Mines for 1871* 3.262 **AZ,** It is . . a contact vein, porphyry forming the hanging and syenite the foot wall. **1899** (1977) Norris *McTeague* 272 **CA,** "There's gold in them damn Panamint Mountains. If you can find a good long 'contact' of country rocks you ain't far from it." *Ibid* 277, Cribbens hunted for "contacts," closely examining country rocks and out-crops, continually on the lookout for spots where sedimentary and igneous rock came together. **1923** Bower *Parowan Bonanza* 13 (*DAE*) **West,** I'm hoping it'll run into higher values when I hit the contact. **1968** Adams *Western Words.*

contact v [For *contract* become infected with]
To catch (a disease) by exposure to someone who has it.
  1967–70 *DARE* (Qu. BB44, *Words used around here about a person just starting some sickness . . : "He _____ pneumonia."*) 40 Infs, **scattered,** Contacted. **1969** *DARE* Tape **CA166,** She contacted T.B.

contact worker n
  1977 Dillard *Lexicon* 118 [Black], But the *conjure doctor* . . performs more typically through artifacts . . . There are legions of names for these "doctors." . . They may be *contact workers, practitional doctors, . .* or *interpreters.*

‡**contage** v [Back-formation from *contagious* or *contagion*]
To transmit by contact.
  1946 McCullers *Member* 84 **GA,** I lay myself down over Ludie with my arms spread out and my face on his face. And I pray that the Lord would contage my strength to him.

contempory adj [By syncope from *contemporary*]
  1916 *DN* 4.354 **NE,** In the following shortened forms, all of frequent occurrence, two successive syllables beginning with *r* are reduced to one. They show permanent rather than accidental syncopation, in the mouths of their users . . . Contempory, contemporary.

continental n [In ref to a piece of currency issued by the Continental Congress that quickly lost value after the Revolutionary War] *somewhat old-fash*
In var phrr of negation: Something worthless.
  [**1786** (1975) Freneau *Poems & Misc. Wks.* 323, That damnable bubble the *old* continental, / That *took* people *in* at this wonderful crisis.] **1872** Twain *Roughing It* 251 **MO,** He didn't give a continental for *any*body. **1907** *DN* 3.184 **seNH,** Continental . . . Originally, a note of Continental money; secondarily, something of no value. "I don't give a continental if he don't like it." **1917** *DN* 4.390 **neOH,** I don't care a continental. **1950** *WELS* ("*I don't give _____*.") 7 Infs, **WI,** A continental; ("*It's not worth _____*.") 2 Infs, A continental. **1965–70** *DARE* (Qu. J2) Inf **IL104,** Ain't worth a continental; (Qu. U29, . . *Worthless money*) 9 Infs, **scattered,** Continental; **IL114, KY77,** Not worth a continental; (Qu. GG21b, . . *"I don't give a _____."*) 13 Infs, **scattered,** Continental; (Qu. HH20b, . . *"He doesn't amount to _____."*) Inf **MS8,** A continental; (Qu. HH20c, . . *"He isn't worth _____."*) Infs **AL27, AR28, NC9,** 61, **TX35, VA15, WI62,** A continental; (Qu. KK17, . . *"It isn't worth _____."*) Inf **OK27,** Continental; (Qu. KK19) Inf **FL6,** Doesn't sew worth a continental. [24 of 32 total Infs old, 8 mid-aged]

continental adj [**continental** n]
Usu in var phrr of negation: Of little or no value, worthless; darned.

1841 Simms *Kinsmen* 1.98 *(DA)*, I wouldn't give a continental copper for the safety of your skin. **1890** *AN&Q* 5.169, "A tinker's Dam" is equivalent to the expression, "A Continental Damn." **1908** *DN* 3.300 **eAL, wGA,** *Continental damn* . . . Used to express the trifling or worthless nature of something. "It ain't worth a *continental damn*," i.e., a plain, unequivocal damn. **1917** *DN* 4.390 **neOH,** *Continental* . . . "This continental old thing won't work." **1950** *WELS (Words and expressions meaning "worthless")* 2 Infs, **cwWI,** A continental damn. **1966–70** *DARE* (Qu. GG21b, . . *"Go ahead—I don't give a _____."*) Inf CA36, Continental darn; IL50, Continental hoot; (Qu. HH20b, . . *"He doesn't amount to _____."*) Inf MS35, Continental damn; (Qu. HH20c, . . *"He isn't worth _____."*) Infs NC38, 87, Continental damn; (Qu. KK17, . . *"It isn't worth _____."*) Inf MS14, Continental damn.

continued fever n

1937 Johnson *Ante-Bellum NC* 724, Malaria was the "periodical fever" and typhoid, the "continued fever."

contoggle v [*con-* together + *toggle* to mend, to ornament] *old-fash*

To repair or mend.

1895 Holley *Samantha in Europe* 69, Her dress . . wuz black, and old and rusty, but all contoggled up good, mended neat and smooth. *Ibid* 298, "I can glue it together with Ury's help, or we could tie it up, so's it would be jest as good as a new one." . . "I shouldn't like to wear a pin that you and Ury had contoggled up." **1939** *LANE* Map 152 *(Repair),* The map shows the terms *repair, mend, fix (up),* . . *contoggle* . . *Contoggle* is defined as an old word meaning to repair a bushel basket or a wagon.

contra dance n [Engl *country dance* altered in Fr to *contredanse:* see etym discussion in *OED* under *contre-dance*] **chiefly NEng** See also **chorus jig**

A folk dance of rural origin in which the dancers form opposing lines.

1803 Fessenden *Terrible Tractoration* 36 **NH,** So fam'd Aldini, erst in France / Led dead folks down a contradance. **1841** Buckingham *America* 3.532 **MA,** Country dances, called here, more accurately than with us in England, "contra dances." **1882** C. Waite *Adv. Far West* 101 *(DAE),* Cotillions, contra-dances and old fashioned reels are in high esteem. **1966–68** *DARE* (Qu. FF5a, *Names for different steps and figures in dancing—in past years*) Inf CA65, Contra dance ['kɒntrə danzə]; MA6, Contra [kɒntrə]—six couples in a set. **1977** Nevell *Time to Dance* 95 **eVT,** He thought it would be nice to have a group down there to demonstrate some of the old-time contra dances. So he asked my father to get a group together, . . and we danced at the Tunbridge fair just about every year since then.

contrady, contrairy See contrary adj

contrarious adj **chiefly sAppalachians**

Contrary, perverse.

1924 *Qrly. Jrl. Speech* 10.234 **sAppalachians,** When a lad calls a cow *contrarious,* he has the authority of Milton. **1931** *AmSp* 7.90 **eKY.** **1933** *AmSp* 8.2.30 **Appalachians.** **1953** Randolph *Down in Holler* 84 **Ozarks,** Chaucer also used the adjective *contrarious,* which is a common word in southwest Missouri. **1958** Campbell *Tales* 103 **seKY Mts,** But she was a contrarious cow, and got mad at the least thing. **c1960** *Wilson Coll.* **csKY,** *Contrarious* . . . Contrary, willful.

contrarisome adj *prob obs*

Perverse, **contrarious.**

1887 *Amer. Philol. Assoc. Trans. for 1886* 17.38 **eTN,** Even the adj. *contrarisome,* which [John] Jamieson gives [in *An Etymological Dictionary of the Scottish Language,* Edinburgh, 1840–41], may be heard.

contrariwise adj Also *contrary-wise*

Contrary, stubborn.

1891 Murfree *Stranger People's Country* 82 **TN,** He was . . remembering the criticisms . . on her unexpected and contrariwise conversation. **1905** *DN* 3.75 **nwAR,** *Contrary-wise* . . . At odds, at enmity. 'He's contrary-wise with the world.' **1908** *DN* 3.300 **eAL, wGA,** *Contrary-wise* . . . Contrary, stubborn.

contrary adj Usu |'kɑn,treri|; also |,kən'treri, -'treri, -'trærɪ|; less freq |'kɒn'trɛrə, 'kɑntə,ʀeri, 'kɑntri; 'kɒn-, 'kɒn-| Pronc-spp *contrady, contrairy, cont'ry, cuntrady*

Std senses, var forms.

1871 Eggleston *Hoosier Schoolmaster* 140 **IN,** They a'n't no human soul here as dares to do a thing con*trary* to Pete. **1895** *DN* 1.375 **TN,**

KY, NC, *Contráry. Ibid* 386 **eOH,** *Contráry.* **1899** (1912) Green *VA Folk-Speech* 125, *Contrary* . . . Contrairy. **1903** *DN* 2.296 **Cape Cod MA** (as of 1850s), *Contrary,* ['kɑntri] . . . Stubborn. *Ibid* 310 **seMO,** *Contrary* [kən'treri] . . . Stubborn. 'He's that *contrairy* I can't do a thing with him.' **1922** Gonzales *Black Border* 295 **sSC, GA coasts** [Gullah glossary], *Cuntrady*—contrary, provoking. **1930** Stoney–Shelby *Black Genesis* 18 **seSC,** He ought to not been so stupid an' contrady. **1930** Shoemaker *1300 Words* 13 **cPA Mts** (as of c1900), Contrairy—Wilful, unreliable. **1941** *LANE* Map 471, The map shows the adjectives *obstinate,* . . *contrary* (often pronounced as *cont'ry*) . . . Words of two or more syllables with major stress on the map have initial stress, . . [e.g.] [kɑntreri, kɒntrɛrɪ, kɒntrɪ, kɒntri, kɑntərɛ'ri]. **1942** Hall *Smoky Mt. Speech* 57 **wNC, eTN,** *Contrary* is never stressed on the initial syllable as in general American, always being pronounced [kən'træri]. A colorful example of its use is in the sentence, [hiz 'kwæə kən'træri n 'min], 'He's queer, contrary, and mean!' **c1960** *Wilson Coll.* **csKY,** *Contrary* . . . Obstinate. **1969** *DARE* (Qu. NN17, *Something that keeps on annoying you . .* "*That _____ fly won't go away.*") Inf GA77, Contrary [,kən'trerə]. **1976** Allen *LAUM* 3.287, The usual pronunciation [is] /'kɑn,treri/ . . . [less frequently] /,kən'treri/.

contrary v Also abbr *'trary* **chiefly S Midl**

1 To oppose; hence also to vex, annoy, anger.

1886 *Amer. Philol. Assoc. Trans.* 17.37 **eTN,** *To contráry,* 'to oppose.' Still used in the Cumberland Mountains in Tennessee, and elsewhere in East Tennessee perhaps. A typical expression there would be "quit contraryin' that child." **1903** *DN* 2.310 **seMO,** *Contrary* . . . "You had better not contrairy her." **1906** *DN* 3.116 **sIN,** *Contrary* . . . To oppose. **1908** *DN* 3.300 **eAL, wGA.** **1909** *DN* 3.394 **nwAR,** *Contrary* . . . To make contrary. **1927** *AmSp* 3.5 **Ozarks,** A number of good verbs are coined from adjectives, too. For example . . . *I shore did'nt aim t' contrary thet ol' heifer fr'm Hell Holler.* **1931** *PMLA* 46.1321 **sAppalachians,** Adjectives may be used as verbs: "Contrary that dog and watch him fight." **1937** (1963) Hyatt *Kiverlid* 67 **KY,** "Eh well," put in Granny, "don't be so tetchus, Marthy Lou, gittin' your self all in a dither, jist ain't no use contraryin' the young-un that away." **1967** *DARE* FW Addit TN17, Don't contrary 'em [=bulls]. **1972** Cooper *NC Mt. Folkl.* 96, *To contrary*—to vex or anger.

2 Spec: to disobey.

1946 *PADS* 6.10 **swVA** (as of 1940), *Contrary* . . . To disobey; said of children. **1954** Harder *Coll.* **cwTN,** *Contrary* . . disobey . . . "Dontchie 'trary me none. I'll slap the tar out o' ye." **c1960** *Wilson Coll.* **csKY,** *Contrary* . . . To disobey and, thus, to make one offended or contrary.

contrary-wise See contrariwise

contrayerba n [Span *contrahierba* antidote: used of var medicinal plants]

A caltrop (here: *Kallstroemia brachystylis*).

1924 Austin *Land of Journeys' Ending* 278 **NM,** In some such fashion came many herbs of healing, *yerba santa, contra yerba,* and the horehound which may be found widely escaped from mission gardens. **1947** Curtin *Healing Herbs* 67, *Contrayerba—Kallstroemia brachystylis* . . . *Contrayerba* . . is not the same plant that was formerly . . used . . as an antidote against poison. **1953** *AmSp* 28.101 **SW,** *Contra Yerba* (Sp.). Caltrop *(Kallstroemia brachystylis).*

contrite v *rare*

To abase, to make remorseful or penitent.

1793 (1890) Lindley *Exped. Detroit* 593 **PA,** Went . . to the house of John Missiner, where we had a solemn season, with a number of his neighbors, to the contriting of the hearts of divers present. **1960** Williams *Walk Egypt* 80 **GA,** If'n you humble yourself and contrite yourself enough, maybe. He'll think on it. Down on your knees!

contrive v *old-fash*

1 To convey or have (something) conveyed by whatever contrivance.

1781 *PA Jrl. & Weekly Advt.* (Philadelphia) 9 May 1/2, I wish we could contrive it to Philadelphia. The words *to carry it, to have it carried,* or some such, are wanting. [**1816** Pickering *Vocab., Contrive.* [Cites quot 1781] I doubt whether this strange expression is ever used at the present day. I never heard it myself, nor have I found any person that has heard it from any class of people in this country.] **1899** (1912) Green *VA Folk-Speech* 125, *Contrive* . . . To contrive a thing is to send it to the person. "If I see anybody going that way I will try to contrive the bundle to him." **1903** *DN* 2.310 **seMO,** *Contrive* . . . Convey. 'I wish you would contrive this letter to Mr. Smith.'

2 To devise in one's imagination, divine.

1893 *Nation* 57.67/3, We [in America] have, too, a colloquial sense for *contrive* which we do not find noticed [in the *OED*], but which must have occurred more than once in the great body of New England tales. "I can't contrive how he did it"—i.e. guess, imagine, divine. **1899** (1912) Green *VA Folk-Speech* 125, *Contrive* . . . To imagine; find out.

3 To damn—used as a mild oath. *euphem* Cf **condemn** v
1899 (1912) Green *VA Folk-Speech* 125, *Contrive* . . . "Contrive that boy."

controverse v [*OED* →1755] *rare*
To mull something over.
1948 Hurston *Seraph* 93 **wFL**, Minutes and possibly an hour passed with Jim controversing inside his mind.

cont'ry See **contrary** adj

contwisted ppl adj *euphem, obs*
Confounded.
1834 Caruthers *Kentuckian* 1.23, I wish I may be contwisted. **1845** Kirkland *Western Clearings* 71 **MI**, His father . . tore his boot almost off with what he called 'a contwisted stub of the toe.'

contwistification n *obs*
A devious maneuver.
1852 (1854) Kennedy *Horse-Shoe Robinson* 71 **cVA** (as of 1780), We hold in despise all sorts of contwistifications, either by layin of tongue-traps, or listening under eaves of houses.

conutchie n [Cf Cherokee *kanataluhi* hominy cooked with walnut kernels]
1941 FWP *Guide OK* 410, At noon a communal meal is spread . . in which the characteristic Cherokee dishes of conutchie (a hominy made of corn and nuts), bean bread, and lye-treated hominy are served.

convenant See **convenient**

convene v [Prob back-formation from *convenient*] *obs*
To suit, be agreeable to.
1816 Pickering *Vocab.* 70, *To Convene.* This is used in some parts of New England in a very strange sense; that is, *to be convenient,* fit, or suitable. *Ex.* This road will convene the public . . . The word, however, is used only by the illiterate. **1844** Uncle Sam *Peculiarities* 1.99 **IN**, It don't convene *to* my feelings to say it war a murder. *Ibid* 1.161 **KY**, The temperance movement, as they call it, don't convene to a man like *me.*

convenient adj Pronc-spp *convenant, convenunt, cunweenyunt*
Std sense, var forms.
1837 Sherwood *Gaz. GA* 69/2, *Provincialisms . . . Convenunt,* convenient. **1871** (1892) Johnston *Dukesborough Tales* 68 **GA**, Ef it war convenant, and the favor war not too much, it mout be that I mout grant it. **1922** Gonzales *Black Border* 295 **sSC, GA coasts** [Gulluh glossary], *Cunweenyunt*—convenient, conveniently. *Ibid, Cunweenyuntly*—conveniently.

conversation fluid n
Whiskey.
1944 Adams *Western Words* 38, *Conversation fluid*—Whiskey. Some Westerners drink only enough to "gather a talkin' load." **1968** *Foxfire* Fall–Winter 101 **sAppalachians**, Various names given moonshine include: . . conversation fluid. **1969** *DARE* Tape **GA**72, We have a variety of names for this homemade whiskey in this county . . . We call it coal juice, conversation fluid, sweet spirits o' cats a-fightin' [etc].

‡convexel n
1967 *DARE* (Qu. NN12b, *Things that people say to put off a child when he asks, "What are you making?"*) Inf **IL**4, Convexel [kən'vɛksl], means something that's worthless.

convict n, also attrib Also *convict fish* [From the resemblance of the striped skin to the (formerly) striped clothing of convicts]
Any of var striped fish as the **sheepshead** *(Archosargus probatocephalus)* on the Atlantic and Gulf coasts, the painted greenling *(Oxylebius pictus)* on the Pacific coast, a tang *(Acanthurus sandvicensis)* in Hawaii, or the freshwater **yellow perch.**
1928 Pan-Pacific Research Inst. *Jrl.* 3.13 **Pacific NW**, *Oxylebius pictus* . . . Convict-fish. **1933** John G. Shedd Aquarium *Guide* 126, *Convict Tang* . . . This very abundant fish receives its common name from the black stripes on the body. **1960** Gosline–Brock *Hawaiian Fishes* 245, *Convict tang* . . . Readily distinguished from other surgeonfishes by its pale color and vertical black bars. **1960** Amer. Fisheries Soc. *List Fishes*

54, Convictfish—see greenling, painted. **1969** *DARE* FW Addit **KY**65, *Convict.* A Florida fish with white and red vertical bands. In the Inf's opinion, *convict* is a Kentucky "slang" word for a Florida fish. **1972** Sparano *Outdoors Encycl.* 385, *Sheepshead . . . Common Names: . .* convict fish. **1975** Evanoff *Catch More Fish* 89, The yellow perch *(Perca flavescens)* is also called the red perch, lake perch, striped perch, and convict.

convict v, hence *convicted* ppl adj
To convince (someone) of sinfulness; to convert.
1822 (1906) Smith *First 40 Yrs.* 159, A methodist hymn, sung amidst the groans and sobs of the newly converted, or convicted as they call them. **1836** in 1934 Frear *Lowell & Abigail* 106 **MA**, May the Lord grant me his rich blessing during the year in convicting the children unto himself. **1885** Murfree *Prophet of Smoky Mts.* 5, "The boys air convicted, then?" he asked . . . "The boys hev got thar religion, too," she faltered. **c1960** Criswell *Resp. to PADS 20* **MO**, *Convicted* . . . Used of a "sinner" who realizes his wickedness and is ready to repent and be converted. Still a regular fundamentalist term. **c1960** *Wilson Coll.* **csKY**, *Convicted* . . . Conscious of sin, a protracted meeting word.

convict fish See **convict** n

conviction n Cf **convict** v
Consciousness of one's wrong-doing.
1950 *PADS* 13.16 **c,cwTX**, *Amen corner* . . . The middle front seat is kept open for those "under conviction" and is known as the mourner's bench.

convincement n [*OED convincement* 4 1617 →]
Religious conversion.
1933 *AmSp* 8.1.14 **PA** [Among Quakers], *Convincement.* Used instead of conviction. *He is a Friend by convincement.* **1984** *DARE* File **csWI**, A Friend by convincement is a member who has joined the Society as opposed to one who is a birthright Friend.

convulsion root n Also *convulsion weed* [Because formerly considered an antispasmodic] *prob obs*
=**Indian pipe 1.**
1876 Hobbs *Bot. Hdbk.* 26, Convulsion weed . . Monotropa uniflora. **1891** *Jrl. Amer. Folkl.* 4.148 **NJ**, Grandmother called Monotropa uniflora Convulsion Root. **1911** *Century Dict. Suppl., Convulsion-root . . .* The Indian-pipe . . . Also called *convulsion-weed.*

cony See **coney** n[1], n[2]

coo v See **co** v

coo exclam See **coop** n[3], exclam

coob See **coop** n[1] A

cooberlee n
1944 *PADS* 2.41 **sGA**, *Cooberlee* ['kubə,li] . . . An onomatopoeic word. A bird.

coobie n Cf **cob** n[2] 1
1958 *PADS* 29.32 **KY**, *Coobie* . . . A marble of baked clay . . . Dim. or famil. of *cob.*

cooch n [Var of **hooch**]
Liquor.
1965–68 *DARE* (Qu. DD21a, *. . Any kind of liquor*) Infs **KS**13, **OK**11, Cooch; **NY**10, Hooch; cooch; (Qu. DD21b, *. . Bad liquor*) Inf **VT**7, [kuč] or [kɔč]. [Inf uncertain]

cooch v See **crouch**

coo-chee See **co-chick**

cooch grass See **couch grass 1**

coo-chick See **co-chick**

coocoo n
1941 Writers' Program SC *Folk Tales* 97, Conjure is another name for hoodoo, voodoo, coocoo, and goofering, all of which may be found in South Carolina.

coo-coo owl n Also *coo-coo* [Echoic]
A barred owl.
1936 *Oriole* 5.8 **GA**, Barred Owl.—Coo-coo (a sonic name). **1966** *DARE* (Qu. Q1, *. . The kind of owl that makes a shrill, trembling cry*) Inf **SC**9, Coo-coo; (Qu. Q2, *Other kinds of owls*) Inf **SC**26, Coo-coo owl; (Qu. Q3, *Other birds that come out only after dark*) Inf **SC**9, Coo-coo.

cood v See **can** v[1] **2a**

cood n See **cud** n

coodle n[1] Cf **cooter** n

A terrapin.

1899 (1912) Green *VA Folk-Speech* 125, *Coodle* . . . A terrapin.

coodle n[2] [Etym unknown]

1975 Gould *ME Lingo* 57, *Coodle*—A word of unexplained origin, this is a small cove or *backwater,* most often one used by a sawmill for storing logs.

coo-ee See **co-ee**

coo-ee-waa See **cui-ui**

coof n [Perh from Scots *coof* a dolt, lout]   **Nantucket MA** *old-fash*

A person not a native of Nantucket.

1859 Willis *Convalescent* 254 **Nantucket MA,** To a "coof" like myself (all persons who have the misfortune not to have been born on Nantucket, are contemptuously called *coofs* by the happier islanders). **1890** *DN* 1.8, Mr. Daniell spoke of Nantucket usages, such as [kuf] . . applied to a native of Cape Cod. **1895** *DN* 1.386 **Nantucket MA,** *Coof:* local term for all "off-islanders." **1916** Macy–Hussey *Nantucket Scrap Basket* 127.

coogle See **kugel**

coohee See **cohee**

cook v

1 To brew (coffee). [Prob calque from Ger *kochen,* Sw *koka,* Nor *koke,* to cook, boil; to make (coffee, tea, etc)]   **chiefly Nth, esp in Ger and Scan settlement areas**   Cf **make** v[1] **B**

1934 *AmSp* 9.79 **nLA,** To cook biscuit and to cook coffee were rather common phrases. **1950** *WELS* ("I'm going to _____ some coffee.") 14 Infs, **throughout WI,** Cook. [12 of 14 Infs had at least one parent from Germany or Scandinavia, or said that the term is used by Germans or Scandinavians.] **1965–70** *DARE* (Qu. H73, *Words for preparing coffee*) 26 Infs, **chiefly Nth,** Cook; (Qu. X45, . . *Snoring*) Inf **PA**18, Cooking coffee. [16 of 27 Infs have German or Scandinavian backgrounds.] **1965** *DARE* File **csWI** (as of 1950), To make coffee is most common in Wisconsin; to cook coffee is heard in German families. **1973** Allen *LAUM* 1.296, The dominance of *make* [coffee] is consistent with its status in New England . . . But its U[pper] M[idwest] dominance has been challenged by *cook,* a cognate translation from either the German or Scandinavian population.

2 To bake (something).

1934 [see **1** above]. **1967** *DARE* (Qu. GG22a, *When you have come to the end of your patience*) Inf **TX**11, That cooks the cake. [Perh a blend of *that takes the cake* and *that cooks the goose.*] **1967** *DARE* Tape **LA**11, Our little granddaughter cooks cakes when she comes.

3 To boil (something).

1935 *AmSp* 10.170 **PA,** *Cook.* To boil. 'Cookin' water'; 'a soft-cooked egg.' **1939** Wolcott *Yankee Cook Book* 121, *Scalloped eggs and onions* . . [includes] 6 sliced hard cooked eggs. **1952** Tracy *Coast Cookery* 69 **IL,** Egg Mold with Caviar Dressing . . [includes] 12 to 14 hard-cooked eggs. **1968** *Helen Adolph Festschrift* 37 **PA,** *Cook* (Pennsylvania German *koche*) for 'boil'; for example, "a soft-cooked egg."

4 with *up:* To marinate.

1967 Cerello *Dakota Co. MN* 50, *Cook up*—Marinate, soak in brine or pickle liquid before cooking. "We always let slaw [cabbage] cook up over night before serving it." "It's best to let wild game like venison cook up over night in salt brine too, before cooking it."

5 in phrr *cook with gas* (or *butane, electricity, radar*), *cook on the front burner:* To do well, work effectively; to be up-to-date, on the right track.

1941 *Kansas City Star* 23 Feb (*OEDS*), Now you're cooking with electricity. **1942** *Time* 27 Apr 84/3, Many a student . . figured that . . Thurman Arnold was cooking with gas. **1945** Shelly *Jive Talk Dict.* 23/1 (*OEDS*), Cooking on the front burner, tops. **1946** Wakeman *Hucksters* 209 **Hollywood CA,** Vic said, "Good boy, Georgie. Now you're cooking with radar." **1950** *WELS* (*To work very hard:* "He was slow to begin with, but now he's _____.") 2 Infs, **WI,** Cooking with gas. **1966–68** *DARE* (Qu. KK28, *Feeling ambitious and eager to work*) Inf **ME**11, Cooking with gas; (Qu. KK29, . . *"He was slow at first but now he's really _____."*) Infs **CA**85, **CT**19, **ME**11, Cooking with gas. **c1970** Halpert Coll. **wKY,** Cooking on the front burner [means] doing just right. Var. Cooking with gas; cooking with Butane.

cook n

A communal meal.

1966 *DARE* (Qu. O21, *When men out in seagoing boats get together for a visit and a cup of hot coffee, that's called a _____*) Inf **FL**24, To have a cook: several fishing boats get together and cook up a meal of fresh fish.

cookania See **cackany**

cook camp n Also *cook tent*   **chiefly MI**   Also called **cookhouse, cook shanty**

A combined kitchen and dining room, esp in a logging camp.

1893 *Scribner's Mag.* 13.703/2 **MI,** There is . . a cook camp, which is a large dining-room and kitchen combined. **1902** White *Blazed Trail* 38 **eMI,** Thorpe . . found himself for the first time in a "cook camp." **1966–69** *DARE* Tape **MI**10, He got into the cook camp—part of a large camp organization; **MI**105, They would eat on the grounds . . . We'd get over and go into cook camp, cook tent what we called it. **1969** Sorden *Lumberjack Lingo* **NEng, Gt Lakes,** *Cook camp*—A building used as kitchen and dining room in a logging camp.

cook car n *old-fash*

1 In railroading: a work train's commissary car.

1910 *Sat. Eve. Post* 23 July 8/2, And quite as important as the crane is the cook-car—generally some old-time coach or sleeper descended to humble service on the road.

2 See quot.   Also called **cook shack 3**

1916 *DN* 4.273 **NE,** *Cook car.* A closed wagon belonging with a threshing outfit. It is driven to the different fields where threshing is in progress, and cooking done there, much as in a hamburger wagon. "The Moores are thrashing this week and Mrs. Moore has gone with the cook car." Term brought by contributor from Montana.

cook cheese n Also *cooked cheese* (or *käse*), *kochcase* [Calque from Ger *Kochkäse*]   **Ger settlement areas**   Cf **cup cheese**

A cheese made by heating cured skim milk curds, but see quot 1971.

1950 *WELS* (*The lumpy white cheese . . made from sour milk*) 1 Inf, **ceWI,** [Cottage cheese]—can be made into cook cheese which is like a paste; (*Different kinds of home-made cheese*) 1 Inf, **seWI,** Cook cheese; 3 Infs, **ce,seWI,** Cooked cheese; 1 Inf, **ceWI,** Cooked käse; [1 Inf, **WI,** Koch Käse]. **1962** Atwood *Vocab. TX* 61, Some thirteen informants, all of German extraction, give *kochcase,* while eight others give the translated form *cook-cheese.* These two terms designate a different type of homemade cheese, which involves the cooking of the curd. **1968** *DARE* (Qu. H65, *Foreign foods*) Inf **WI**24, Cooked cheese: German [dish] made by cooking cottage cheese. **1971** *AmSp* 46.178 **Chicago IL,** Another group of words also reflect bilingual behavior, but all of them seem more tenuously related to the influence of a second language (specifically German): *cook-cheese* . . In Chicago . . it occurred only once, in the speech of the most authoritative German bilingual in the sample . ., who insisted *cook-cheese* was the "correct" name for cottage cheese, prepared in the kitchen by hanging a cheese-cloth bag over the sink and involving no cooking. This suggests Küchenkäse 'kitchen-cheese' as a plausible source.

cook coffee See **cook turnips**

cooked over ppl adj

Reheated, warmed over.

1966–69 *DARE* (Qu. H68, *When food remains over from one meal and you heat it again for another meal, you call it _____*) Infs **GA**4, 88, **TX**35, Cooked over. **1973** Allen *LAUM* 1.301 **MN,** *Cooked over* [1 inf].

cookee n Also sp *cookey, cookie* [*cook* + *-ee, -ey, -ie* dimin suffs]   Also called **biscuit shooter 1**

Esp in logging camps:

a The chief cook.

1846 *Spirit of the Times* 4 July 218/2 (*DAE*), We embarked . . in company with . . a cookie who was lord and master of the culinary department. **1888** Billings *Hardtack* 287 (as of 1862), Not at all daunted by this experience [being almost drowned], the cookey [of an army regiment] harnessed the mule again as before. **1926** Kephart *Highlanders* 232 **sAppalachians,** The cookee [in a lumber camp] banged his poker on a piece of iron swung from a string, to call all hands to dinner. **1930** *DN* 6.86 **cWV,** *Cookee,* cook in [lumber] camp. **1942** Warnick *Garrett Co. MD* (as of 1900–18), *Cookee* . . chief cook in a lumber camp. **1950** *WELS* (*Joking names for a cook*) 3 Infs, **WI,** Cookee. **1968** *DARE* FW Addit **cMN,** *Cookee:* Used for cook and second cook.

b The cook's assistant.   **chiefly Nth**   Also called **flunky 1**

1902 White *Blazed Trail* 39 **eMI,** The cook . . directed where the provisions were to be stowed; and the "cookee," a hulking youth, assisted. **1907** *DN* 3.242 **eME,** *Cookee.* **1914** *DN* 4.70 **ME, nNH,** *Cookee.* **1930** Shoemaker *1300 Words* 11 **cPA Mts** (as of c1900), *Cookee*—The assistant cook at a lumber camp. **1938** (1939) Holbrook *Holy Mackinaw* 260, *Cookee.* Any sort of cook's helper in Lake States and Northeast. **1950** *WELS (Joking names for a cook's helper)* 20 Infs, **WI,** Cookee; 1 Inf, Cookee is a real legitimate term; 3 Infs, Cookee, a second cook. **1966–68** *DARE* Tape **ME1,** The third cook, well he gets the water and wood and just sets the table and washes the dishes . . . First cook and second cook, then cookee—he doesn't know as much as the other ones about cooking; **ME26,** Two men were cookees; they had to keep fire all night; **NH14,** They had what they called a cookee. He had to look out for wood and get it into the [logging] camp; **WI59,** You had a cook and then had what you called a cookee. He was the younger fella that peeled the potatoes and carried in the water and perhaps if there's a small camp he'd also split and carried in some wood.

cooker n [**cook** v **3**] Also called **boiler** n[1] **2, evaporator 2**
A still used in making moonshine whiskey.

1949 *AmSp* 24.5 **KY,** These stills . . do not depend on the old-time copper pot, but have a metal boiler . . from which steam is piped into one or more large *cookers,* sometimes built of staves and demountable, where vaporization takes place. **1968** *Foxfire* Fall–Winter 49, *Still*— the container into which the beer is placed for boiling. Also called Evaporator or Boiler or Kettle or Cooker. **1974** Maurer *KY Moonshine* 116, *Cooker . . .* The beer still proper . . . A tank or box to precook beer.

cookey n[1] See **cookie** n[1] **1**

cookey n[2] See **cookee**

cook fire n [Abbr for *cooking fire*]
An outdoor fire used for cooking.

1852 Stansbury *Expedition* 148 **UT,** While engaged in the survey of the Utah Valley, we were no little annoyed by numbers of the latter tribe, who hung around the camp, crowding the cook-fires, more like hungry dogs than human beings. **1894** *Harper's Mag.* 89.518/1 **swID,** Sergeant Keyser . . had adopted the troop cook fire for his camp guard after the cooks had finished their work. **1941** *Sat. Eve. Post* 1 Mar 81/1 **TX,** The taffy-haired Arkansas girl in Kerrville had been handy around a cook fire too.

cook-fish n
1968 *DARE* FW Addit **AK1,** *Cook-fish:* fish for home use.

cookhouse n Also called **cookshack 1**
A building where food is cooked and often served, esp on a farm or in a logging camp.

1831 Peck *Guide for Emigrants* 126, Around it [=a cabin] are usually put up a meat or smoke house, a kitchen or cook house, a stable and corn crib, and perhaps a spring house to keep milk cool in summer. **1897** Hough *Cowboy* 12, The cook house is also the dining hall. **1926** Kephart *Highlanders* 232 **sAppalachians,** We followed an old logging road . . to Barradale's camp. This camp was in a new location, with flume, portable mill and cook-house just finished, and shacks under construction. **1959** *AmSp* 34.77 **nCA** [Logging terms], *Cookhouse . . .* The building where the food is prepared; the dining room is also included. **1967–68** *DARE* (Qu. M22 . . *Other kinds of buildings . . on farms)* Infs **CA16, NV8, NY80, 82,** Cookhouse. **1973** Allen *LAUM* 1.169 **Upper MW,** *Cookhouse:* Separate from the house [4 infs]. On ranches used for ranch hands [3 infs].

cookie n[1]

1 also sp *cookey:* A pancake. [Prob Scots *cookie* flour cake or bun]
1899 (1912) Green *VA Folk-Speech, Cookey . . .* A small, thin cake made of corn-meal and milk and cooked on a griddle. **1968–70** *DARE* (Qu. H20b, . . *Names . . for pancakes)* Infs **MD37, VA47B,** Cookies.

2 A doughnut. [Prob Du *koekje* small sweetened cake] **Sth, S Midl**
1949 Kurath *Word Geog.* 47 **neNC,** Among the local expressions of this section are . . *cookie . . .* for a doughnut. *Ibid* 69, The unraised variety [of doughnut] has also other names: . . *cookie* (in northeastern North Carolina). **1966–67** *DARE* (Qu. H27, . . *Joking names for doughnuts)* Inf **SC43,** Cookie. **1971** Wood *Vocab. Change* 45, For the yeast doughnut the second choice . . in Tennessee, Alabama, and Mississippi . . is Dutch *cookie.* **1973** Allen *LAUM* 1.281, One southern Iowan remembered the rare North Carolina *cookie.*

3 in phrr *to (lose, spill, toss,* etc) *one's cookies:* To vomit. **scattered, but chiefly Nth, N Midl** See Map *joc, euphem*
1927 *AmSp* 2.278 **nCA** [College words], *Shoot one's cookies*—vomit. **1965–70** *DARE* (Qu. BB17, *Other words or expressions . . for vomiting)* 24 Infs, **chiefly Nth,** Toss (your, his, their, the) cookies; **IL21, PA94, 142, 165,** Spill your cookies; **IN22, MI68, PA175,** (Lose, lost) (my, your, their) cookies; **MN15, NY183, PA237,** (Throw, threw) up (my, his, your) cookies; **MN2, WI57,** Cough up your cookies; **CO27, PA130,** (Heaved up, heaving) (my, his) cookies; **HI1, WI5,** Park(ing) your cookies; **AL6,** Check your cookies; **IA45,** Dropping your cookies; **PA74,** Flash his cookies; (Qu. BB18, *To vomit a great deal at once)* 8 Infs, **chiefly Nth,** Toss (your, his, one's) cookies; **MI68, WI19,** Heave (up) (my, his) cookies; **OR1, PA223,** Lost (his, my) cookies; **FL30, IL11,** Snap (up) your cookies; **PA223,** Parked his cookies; **IL14,** Spill your cookies.

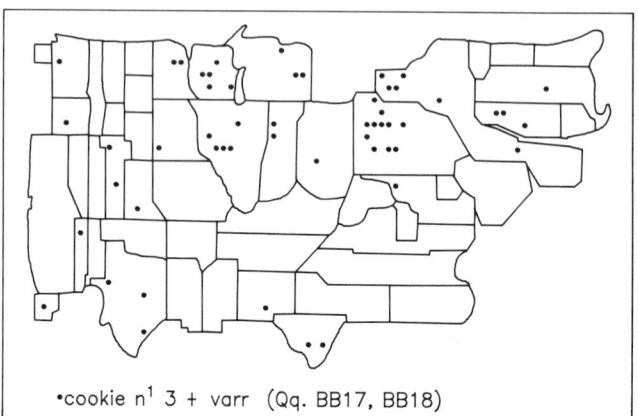

•cookie n[1] 3 + varr (Qq. BB17, BB18)

4 in phrr *to drop* (or *flip) one's cookies:* To feel strong emotion; to lose control of oneself.
1967–68 *DARE* (Qu. AA10, *A very special liking . . a boy may have for a girl . . you'd say, "He _____ her.")* Inf **WA22,** Dropped his cookies over; (Qu. GG15, *Talking about a person who became over-excited and lost control, "At that point he really _____.")* Inf **CA61,** Flipped his cookies.

5 See quot. [In allusion to **oreo**] *among Black speakers* Cf **handkerchief head, Tonto**
1972 Claerbaut *Black Jargon* 61, *Cookie . . .* A black person deemed disloyal to his race . . . A black person who tries to live exactly as white people do.

cookie n[2] See **cookee**

cookie pusher n *joc* Also called **biscuit shooter 2, hasher 1**
A waiter or waitress.
1950 *WELS (Joking names for waiters or waitresses in restaurants)* 1 Inf, **seWI,** Cookie pusher. **1958** McCulloch *Woods Words* **Pacific NW,** *Cookie pusher*—A hasher, same as biscuit shooter. **1968** Adams *Western Words, Cookie pusher*—A cowboy's name for a waitress in a restaurant.

‡**cookie, take the** v phr [Alter of *take the cake*]
1886 *The Lantern* 20 Oct 3/1 *(AmSp* 25.31) **New Orleans LA,** For keeping away from trouble a peeler takes the cookie.

cooking cheese n Cf **cook cheese**
1968 *DARE* (Qu. H60, *The lumpy white cheese . . made from sour milk)* Inf **VA9,** Cooking cheese.

cooking ear n
=**roasting ear.**
1968 *DARE* (Qu. I33, . . *Ears of corn . . just right for eating)* Inf **MN33,** Cooking ears.

cooking soda n [Prob **cook** v **2**]
?Baking soda.
1970 *DARE* (Qu. BB22, . . *Home remedies . . for constipation)* Inf **VA71,** Cooking soda.

cook off v phr [**cook** v **3**]
To boil down or distill.
1956 Hall *Coll.* **ce, neTN,** *Cook off . . .* To distill (whiskey, etc.). He was cookin' it off (making apple brandy). **1967** *DARE* FW Addit **cnLA,**

Cook off a batch, to make as much cane syrup as is normally made at one time. (Common.).

cook one's own soup v phr

1950 *WELS (Expressions used to tell somebody to keep to himself and mind his own business)* 1 Inf, **cwWI,** Cook your own soup.

cookroom n chiefly Sth, S Midl

A kitchen, orig one separate from a house.

1649 (1908) Winthrop *Jrl.* 1.25 **NEng,** A maid . . fell down at the grating by the cook-room. **1776** Leacock *Brit. Tyranny* 45, I should never be able to keep 'em out of the cook room, or their noses out of the slush-tub. **1896** Harris *Sister Jane* 54 **GA,** I made haste to go to the cook-room, intending to start the fire. **1905** *DN* 3.75 **nwAR.** **1939** FWP *Guide NC* 95, Cook-room, kitchen. **1954** *Harder Coll.* **cwTN,** Cook-room — Kitchen. Old fashioned but still understood by everyone. **c1960** *Wilson Coll.* **csKY.** **1966–67** *DARE* (Qu. D16, . . *Parts added on to the main part of a house*) Infs **SC22, 29,** Cookroom. **1968** *DARE* Tape **VA25,** They had a cookroom out yonder. **1972** *Atlanta Letters* **nwGA.**

cookshack n

1 =cookhouse.

1909 Wason *Happy Hawkins* 38 *(DA),* I felt a sting in the left shoulder, spun around and fell, but jumped up just as Jabez changed directions for the cook shack. **1966** *DARE* Tape **ME19,** [In a lumber camp] they had a cookshack where the cook was. **1968** Adams *Western Words,* Cook shack — A cowboy's name for the kitchen, especially when it is a separate building. **1973** Allen *LAUM* 1.169 **Upper MW,** Summer heat made the kitchen so uncomfortable that, particularly on the farm, cooking was frequently done in temporary quarters elsewhere . . . [2 infs gave the term] cook shack.

2 See quot.

1977 Adams *Lang. Railroader,* Cook shack: A caboose, so called because the trainmen's meals are often prepared in it.

3 =cook car 2.

1916 *DN* 4.273, Cook car. A closed wagon belonging with a threshing outfit . . . In Kan[sas], cook shack. **1973** Allen *LAUM* 1.169, Cook-shack: Dakota name for portable wagon which followed threshing crews [1 inf].

cook shanty n chiefly Gt Lakes

In logging: =cook camp.

1895 *Outing* 26.393/1, It was a blazing bonfire of hemlock bark in a deep hole, which threw a flickering warm light on the side of the cook-shanty. **1956** Sorden–Ebert *Logger's Words* **Gt Lakes,** Cook shanty, The building used as a kitchen and dining-room in a logging camp. Same as cook-camp, cook-house. **1968** *DARE* Tape **MI96,** Sometimes they would have three stoves and a cook shanty too; **WI58,** In the early days . . the lumberjacks . . would build a fire . . [and] cook their beans over this. This was in the days before cook shanties; **WI59,** The building where the cooking was done also was the area where they had their tables and the lumberjacks had their meals. They called this the cook shanty.

cookshop n

1 also *cook's shop:* An eating house. **chiefly Sth**

1663 in 1881 Boston Registry Dept. *Records* 7.18, John Lewis is allowed to kepp a Cook shopp for the refreshing of Traulers. **1834** Brackenridge *Recollections* 201 **DC,** The exterior is undoubtedly sublime; but with the exception of the handsome library room . . and the cook-shops below, it is a melancholy failure. **1837** *S. Lit. Messenger* 3.389/1 **VA,** Fortunately a sort of cook's-shop was at hand. **1870** Parton *Ginger Snaps* 24, Finally . . let China, or Africa, or Professor Blot with his travelling cook-shop . . come speedily to the rescue, and find us a way of escape. **1940** FWP *Guide VA* 253, Despite too-evident poverty, the Negroes support a theater, and many 'cook shops' and general stores. **1970** *DARE* (Qu. D39, . . *A small eating place where the food is not especially good*) Inf **NC84,** Cookshop.

2 In logging: see quot. [Perh var of **cock shop**]

1941 *AmSp* 16.233 **NW,** Cook Shop. The cook shop is the company store, which usually includes the camp offices, too.

cook's piece n Also *cook's portion*

The last piece of food on a plate.

1950 *WELS (The last piece . . on a plate)* 1 Inf, **cnWI,** Cook's piece. **1968–69** *DARE* (Qu. H71) Inf **SC51,** Cook's piece; **MA40,** Cook's portion.

cook tent See cook camp

cook turnips v phr Also *cook coffee, cook (or boil) cabbage* chiefly PA *joc*

To snore.

1967–69 *DARE* (Qu. X45, . . *Joking expressions . . about snoring*) Infs **PA142, 243,** Cooking turnips; **PA14,** Cooking cabbage; **PA18,** Cooking coffee; **MD31,** Boiling cabbage.

cook up See cook v 4

cook vessel n

A cooking utensil.

1942 Thomas *Blue Ridge Country* 52 **sAppalachians,** I've got plenty of iron cook vessels . . . A tin peddler come with his pack of shiny cook vessels in a shiny black oilcloth poke on his back.

cook woman n

1899 (1912) Green *VA Folk-Speech* 125, Cook-woman . . . A cook.

cook wood n

Wood specially cut for use in a wood-burning kitchen stove.

1904 *DN* 2.417 **nwAR,** Cook-wood . . . Kitchen stove-wood. 'I want cook-wood sixteen inches long.' **1969** *DARE* File **csKY,** Cook wood: Wood cut into very small pieces for the wood cookstove.

cool adj

1 Good, fine, pleasing.

1884 Harrison *Negro Engl.* 257, Interjections . . 'Dat's cool!' **1948** *New Yorker* 3 July 28, The bebop people have a language of their own . . . Their expressions of approval include "cool!" **1967–69** *DARE* (Qu. KK1a, *Other words meaning very good—for example, food: "That pie was _____."*) Infs **HI1, PA165,** Cool; (Qu. GG34a, *To feel depressed or in a gloomy mood*) Inf **MA1,** [He] doesn't feel so cool; (Qu. NN6b, *Expressions of joy used mostly by children*) Infs **VT4, VA99,** Cool. **1970** *Harper's Mag.* Aug 84/1, You want to have it all your way, don't you, Colonel? That's cool with me.

2 Of jazz music: restrained and more relaxed in style than earlier, traditional "hot" jazz.

1947 (record by Charlie Parker Quartet, Dial 1015) *(OEDS),* Cool Blues. **1948** *Life* 11 Oct 139, Bebop[:] New Jazz School is Led by Trumpeter Who is Hot, Cool and Gone. **1950** *Chr. Sci. Monitor* (Boston MA) 8 Feb 15, This dead, or thin tone, is more in character with bop, which is generally described as "cool jazz," in contrast to the hot variety of the Swing or Dixieland schools. **1958** *PADS* 30.44, Cool . . . Agreeing with the generally received aesthetic standards of the modern jazzman. *Ibid* 47, [Footnote:] This can best be indicated by the substitution of *cool* for *hot* as a term of approbation. Bop musicians favored a detached, intellectual approach to improvisation as opposed to the emotional approach of earlier players, and the word change was made accordingly.

3 Self-possessed, calm, sophisticated. *earlier esp among Black speakers, now more widely used*

1955 *NYT Mag.* 22 May 19/2, Maybe it's all these new buildings breeding more of these cool Brooks Brothers cats. **1965–70** *DARE* (Qu. W38, . . *A man . . in his best clothes . . you say he's _____*) Infs **FL51, KY94, VA73,** Cool; (Qu. GG23c, . . *To tell someone to be patient*) Infs **DC11, PA247,** Be cool; (Qu. GG27a, . . *"Everything's going to be all right, so _____."*) Inf **MO29,** Be cool; **LA6,** Keep it cool; **SC65,** Stay cool; (Qu. KK46, . . *Taking things as they come*) Infs **MA127, MO30, NJ70, NY114, RI6,** Cool; (Qq. AA6a, GG9b, HH24, II21, 22, JJ44, KK2, 37, NN11, 19) 14 Infs, Cool (in var phrr). [17 of 25 Infs Black] **1972** *Dict. Contemp. & Colloq. Usage* 7, Cool . . . unemotional, even though intellectually or spiritually involved. **1977** Smitherman *Talkin* 53, Cool, referring to slow tempoed music, and by extension, calm, slow, worldly posture. **1982** *Milwaukee Jrl.* (WI) 3 June Green Sheet 1/2 [Erma Bombeck column], He tries to be cool about the outfit [=white tuxedo], but you know him well enough to see the anxiety.

cool n

1 Composure, self-control. *earlier esp among young, coll educ, and Black speakers, now more widely used*

1965–70 *DARE* (Qu. GG23a, *If you speak sharply to somebody to make him be patient, you say, "Now just keep your _____."*) 102 Infs, **widespread,** Cool; (Qu. GG15, . . *A person who . . lost control, "At that point he really _____."*) 39 Infs, **widespread,** Blew (*or* lost) his cool; (Qu. GG23c, . . *To tell someone to be patient*) Infs **PA93, SC68,** Don't blow your cool; (Qu. Y2) Inf **CA113,** Didn't lose his cool; (Qu. HH6,

Someone who is out of his mind) Inf **LA3**, Lost his cool; (Qu. JJ23, *To refuse to give in or yield*) Inf **NY241**, Didn't blow my cool; (Qu. KK11, *To make . . a big fuss about something*) Infs **MO32, WI55**, Blew his cool. [Of all Infs responding to Qu. GG23a, 11% were young, 33% coll educ, 6% Black; of those giving this response, 33% were young, 48% coll educ, 21% Black.] **1966** *New Yorker* 18 June 37/1–3, [Cartoon caption:] I'll bet *that* old guy has never blown his cool. **1968** *Harper's Mag.* 236.115/2, A man was nothing in prison without his cool. **1968** *Sat. Review* 16 Nov 36/2, He ambled down Main Street in big town and small, flaunting his difference and his cool.

2 By ext: used as a stereotypical or caricaturing name: see quot.
   1968–70 *DARE* (Qu. GG19b, *When you can see from the way a person acts that he's feeling important or independent: "He seems to think he's _____."*) Infs **GA54, NY211**, Joe Cool; **WV21**, Mr. Cool.

coolcock See **coldcock**

cool-doo n [Prob echoic, but cf **pull-doo**]
   1950 *PADS* 14.22 **SC**, *Cool-doo* . . . The wood ibis. Negro usage of the Pee-Dee [River].

cooler n
   1 An icebox; less freq a refrigerator. **esp west of Missip R** See Map
   1965–70 *DARE* (Qu. D10a, *The place to keep food cool, usually with ice, so that it won't spoil*) 26 Infs, **esp West of Missip R**, Cooler; (Qu. D10b, *The place to keep food cool if it is run by electricity or gas*) Infs **CA92, GA72, IA25, MN38**, Cooler.

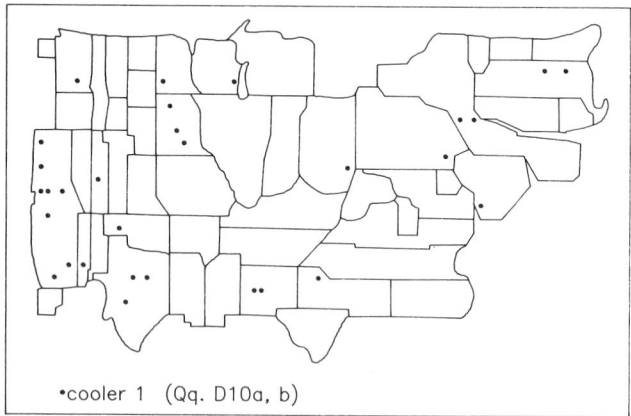

•cooler 1 (Qq. D10a, b)

2 A pantry; a cupboard or **safe** for keeping foodstuffs slightly below room temperature. **esp CA**
   1967–69 *DARE* (Qu. D8, *The small room next to the kitchen [in older houses] where dishes and sometimes foods are kept*) Infs **CA111, WA21**, Cooler; (Qu. D9, *To prevent bread and cake from drying, you put them in a _____*) Inf **CA125**, A cooler had a vent at bottom and top, and air would circulate; used before refrigerators; **DC7**, Cooler—formerly used; metal panels with holes; **CA111**, Cooler; (Qu. D10a, *The place to keep food cool*) Inf **CA107**, A cooler: inside the house but air would flow into it—no ice; (QR, near Qu. D20) Inf **CA146**, The trapdoor, usually inside in the kitchen, went down to the cellar where the "cooler" (or "safe") was kept. The cooler and safe are hanging things. **1979** *DARE* File **swCA** (as of 1950s), I remember that people in Long Beach commonly had what they called coolers in their kitchens. These were built-in cupboards with mesh gratings instead of shelves and open to the ground below. In this cooler people kept fresh fruits and such things as butter for table use—things that they wanted to keep slightly below room temperature. The homes I am thinking of were built in the early 1930s.

3 An aerated container hung in a tree, used to preserve meat.
   1967 *DARE* (QR, near Qu. M18) Inf **CA23**, *Cooler*—hung in tree, air cooled meat for two to three days. It would only keep there.

cooley See **coulee**

cool head n [**cool** adj **1** + *head* fellow, person]
   A person one likes, a "nice guy".
   1967 *DARE* FW Addit **cWA**, A *cool head*: a good person, someone you like. **1971** Landy *Underground Dict.*, *Cool head* . . . Someone whom you admire. **1979** *DARE* File **swCA** (as of 1955–65), I knew *cool head* throughout my high-school and early college years as the regular expression among my peers for a fellow you respected and liked. "Ron? He's a

cool head, man. What ya got against him?" Or: "Mrs. Rietz is a cool head, man. She didn't flunk me and she could 'av'."

coolie See **coulee**

cooling board n **Sth, Midl**
   A plank for laying out a corpse; hence v phr *lay* (or *put*) *on the cooling board:* to kill.
   1853 Simms *Sword & Distaff* 251 **SC** (as of 1780s), He wouldn't care ef I was on my cooling board to-morrow. **1896** Harris *Sister Jane* 19 **GA,** I'm old and ugly, but I don't want to be put on my cooling-board on account of driving a new set of nails in the front palings. **1931** *PMLA* 46.1308 **sAppalachians,** To "stop one's eating," [means] to kill, likewise, to "lay one on the cooling-board". **1944** *PADS* 2.41, *Cooling-board* . . . A large board used to lay a dead person on before *rigor mortis* sets in. In w.N.C. it is regarded as bad luck to allow a corpse to lie in any position other than straight. To *put* a person *on the cooling-board* means to kill him. The board itself is still in use in some sections of w.N.C. **W.N.C. Common. S.Va. Obsolescent.** **1945** Saxon *Gumbo Ya-Ya* 65 **New Orleans LA,** A 'cooling board' . . was placed on two chairs or sawhorses, and here the body lay until it was placed in the coffin. **1950** *PADS* 14.22 **SC**. **1953** Goodwin *It's Good* 41 **sIL** [Black], First, Lawd, we want to thank ya that when we rose this mornin' our bed was not our coolin' board, nor our cover our windin' sheet. **c1960** *Wilson Coll.* **csKY**. **1966–68** *DARE* Tape **AL1** [Black], [FW:] What was the thing you laid him out on? [Inf:] Coolin' board. The coolin' board, yeah; **AL11** [Black], When I was a boy and you'd died, dey'd lay ya out on de coolin' board at home . . . People would come and take him, fix him up, lay him on de coolin' board; **NJ15A**, Cooling board. [FW:] Now, what's a cooling board? [Inf:] Well years before you embalmed anyone, why, they didn't . . . I know this, I've seen it . . . It looked like an ironing board, as much as I can tell . . . Then they'd pack the body in ice and put tubs under it—cover the body with a sheet or something—and put tubs under it so when the ice melted, it would drop in, in the tub; **PA30**, The body is taken back home and laid on a cooling board. *Cooling board* is a term that goes back eighty, ninety years in the funeral industry, back to the ice-box age.

cooling room n
   1 See quot.
   1939 FWP *Guide NC* 495, *Cooling room.* There are large brick fireplaces, wide porches, . . graceful stairways, and a "cooling room" on the upper floor, in which the bodies of the dead were kept awaiting burial.
   2 also *cooling house, ~ shed:* A milk house. **esp Sth, S Midl**
   1965–70 *DARE* (Qu. M18, *The separate building where milk is kept cool*) 10 Infs, **chiefly Sth, S Midl**, Cooling room; **IL5, LA18, NC26, 81, OH67, TN53, UT3**, Cooling house; **CA114, TX89**, Cooling shed.

cooling saucer See **coffee cooler 3**

cool it v phr
   1 To calm oneself, relax, take it easy. *formerly esp among young, coll educ, and Black speakers; now more widespread*
   1954 *Time* 8 Nov 70, *Cool* . . . Relax . . . "I cooled it at a table for a while." **1965–70** *DARE* (Qu. GG23c, . . *To tell someone to be patient*) 76 Infs, **widespread**, Cool it; (Qu. GG27a, *To get somebody out of an unhappy mood, you might say . . , "Everything's going to be all right, so _____."*) Infs **IN75, LA46, MA1, SC45, 68**, Cool it; (Qu. KK46, *Other expressions for taking things as they come and not worrying: "The whole family was sort of _____."*) Infs **DC11, NY241**, Cooling it. [Of all Infs responding to Qu. GG23c, 11% were young, 33% coll educ, 6% Black; of those giving this response, 41% were young, 43% coll educ, and 28% Black.] **1972** *Dict. Contemp. & Colloq. Usage* 7, *Cool it* . . to be calm.
   2 To stop, leave off, desist.
   1965–70 *DARE* (Qu. X10b, *To tell a person to stop talking*) Infs **NY224, SC55, TX106, VA107, WA22**, Cool it; (Qu. Y17, . . *Two people agree to stop fighting*) Inf **IN75**, Cooled it; (Qu. Y51, . . *To avoid . . people*) Inf **NY240**, Cool it; (Qu. II22, . . *To tell somebody to . . mind his own business*) Infs **CA197, LA46, WA22**, Cool it; (Qu. NN12a, . . *To put a child off when he asks too may questions*) Inf **OH18**, Cool it; (Qu. NN19, *When you want people to stop talking*) Infs **CA127, IN61, NH18, PA66, SC65**, Cool it.

coolit leaf n [?Folk-etym for **coolwort 1**]
   1968 *DARE* (Qu. BB50c, *Remedies for infections*) Inf **NY92**, *Coolit leaves:* Oval-shaped leaf that grows in a swampy place—they would heat 'em and fold 'em in a cloth.

coolly See **coulee**

cool one See **cold one**

cool one's cubes v phr [*cool* (see **cool it 1**) + *cubes* dice]
To relax, take it easy.
1968 *DARE* (Qu. GG23c, . . *Other expressions [to tell someone to be patient]*) Inf **NY**81, Cool it; cool your cubes; calm down.

cool out v phr
To flee, get away fast.
1933 Rawlings *South Moon* 215 **FL**, Let's drag him off in the hammock. Then we kin cool out do we hear ary one comin'. Ma'll be here direckly.

cool water n
1974 Dabney *Mountain Spirits* 26, The people who in all likelihood currently know more about the taste of modern-day moonshine . . are the ghetto blacks of southern cities . . . They have coined such nicknames as . . "cool water." This last term got its start because many shot houses cut their white whiskey so many times with water.

coolweed n [See quots]
=**richweed 1.**
1843 Torrey *Flora NY* 2.223, *Adike pumila* . . . Richweed. Coolweed . . . Moist shady places, particularly in cool ravines. **1899** *Century Dict.*, *Coolweed* . . . The clearweed, so called from its succulent pellucid stems and its habit of growing in cool places.

coolwort n
1 =**foamflower** (esp *Tiarella cordifolia*).
1848 Bartlett *Americanisms* 90, *Cool-wort*. (*Tiarella cordifolia*) The popular name of an herb, the properties of which are diuretic and tonic. It is prepared by the Shakers. **1893** *Jrl. Amer. Folkl.* 6.142, *Tiarella cordifolia* . . . white coolwort, N.Y. **1901** Lounsberry *S. Wild Flowers* 217, With its masses of handsome flowers and usually attractive foliage the coolwort, as the mountaineers call the plant, is one of the most pleasing of early bloomers. **1933** Small *Manual SE Flora* 594, *Tiarella* . . . Cool-worts. **1952** Taylor *Plants Colonial Days* 38 **VA**, Foamflower . . . Other common names are . . coolwort, and Nancy-over-the-ground. **1973** Hitchcock–Cronquist *Flora Pacifc NW* 199, *Tiarella* . . Coolwort; Foamflower; False Mitrewort; Laceflower.

2 A **miterwort 1** (here: *Mitella diphylla*).
1891 *Jrl. Amer. Folkl.* 4.148 **NEast**, Our name for Mitella diphylla was *Coolwort*. **1961** Smith *MI Wildflowers* 170, Two-leaved Bishop's-cap, Miterwort, Coolwort *Mitella diphylla*.

coomtie See **coontie**

coomy adj
1968 *DARE* (Qu. U36a, *Words . . about a person who saves in a mean way or is greedy in money matters*) Inf **NY**41, Coomy.

coon n[1] [Aphet form of *raccoon*]
1 A person, fellow; esp a rustic. **chiefly Sth, S Midl, West** *sometimes derog*
1832 *Political Examiner* (Shelbyville KY) 8 Dec 4/1 (*OEDS*), I was always reckoned a pretty slick koon for a trade. **1848** (1855) Ruxton *Life Far West* 126, Isn't this old coon [=a trapper] putting out to save 'ee from the darned Injuns now, do 'ee hyar? **1899** (1912) Green *VA Folk-Speech*, *Coon* . . . A sly, knowing person. **1914** *DN* 4.131, *Coon*, from *raccoon*. "In the Western States, where the raccoon is plentiful, they use the abbreviation 'coon' when speaking of people." **1915** *DN* 4.196, *Coon*, a peculiar old fellow. **1939** *Hall Coll.* wNC, eTN, *Coon* . . . Raccoon, used in a derived sense: "fighter," "rascal?" "[General] Morgan fit . . there at Greeneville . . . He was a bad old coon; he was a fighter." " 'He's a bad old coon' —lots of old people use that." **c1960** *Wilson Coll.* csKY, *Coon* . . . A term of reproach, with no especial reference to a Negro as such. Cf. *skunk, buzzard, snake in the grass*. **1965–70** *DARE* (Qu. Z12, . . *A small child*) Inf **GA**77, Coon; (Qu. Z16, . . *A small child who . . doesn't obey*) Inf **GA**77, Mean little coon; (Qu. BB54, . . *A sick person . . past recovery*) Infs **NY**42, **VA**46, [A] Gone coon; (Qu. HH1, . . *A rustic or countrified person*) Inf **TN**53, Mountain coon; (Qu. HH40, *Uncomplimentary words for an old man*) Infs **FL**52, **GA**7, **MS**60, **MO**39, (Old) coon; (Qu. KK37, . . *A very sly person*) Inf **AR**55, Sly old coon.

2 A Black person —usu considered offensive.
1848 in 1950 Blesh–Janis *Ragtime* 86, Dey may talk ob dandy niggers / But dey neber see dis coon, / A prombernarding Broadway / On a Sunday afternoon. **1890** *DN* 1.64 **KY**, Coon: for *negro*. **1893** Shands *MS Speech* 24, *Coon* . . has come to be extensively used to mean also a *negro* . . . it is common to all of the Southern States, and even extends to our more northern brethren. **1905** *DN* 3.6 cCT. **1907** *DN* 3.210 nwAR. **1908** *DN* 3.300 eAL, wGA. **1928** White *Amer. Negro Folk-Songs* 8, "Jim Crow" had been preceded in 1829 by "Zip Coon" and "Long Tail Blue." **1948** *Chicago Defender* (Natl ed) (IL) 23 Oct 7/2 [Black], A lot of us are referred to as "nigger," "coon," "darky," etc., right to our faces and can't do anything about it if we want to keep our jobs, or credit, or property, or life and limbs. **c1960** *Wilson Coll.* csKY, *Coon* . . . A Negro, with no especial derogatory meaning. I have heard many a Negro use the word, humorously. **1962** Atwood *Vocab. TX* 73, *Negro* . . . Terms that are undoubtedly derogatory are *coon* . . and *burrhead*. **1965–70** *DARE* (Qu. HH28, *Names and nicknames around here for people of foreign background . . Negro*) 187 Infs, **widespread, but least common in West**, Coon; **SC**31, Black coon; **VA**71, Coon-Jacob. **1973** Allen *LAUM* 1.347, Equally demeaning [as *nigger* and *black*] are *coon, jig* . . . and *smoke*. Although they perhaps sometimes occur with what the speaker would consider jocular intent, they are never funny to a Black.

3 A thief. Cf **coon v 4**
1968–70 *DARE* (Qu. V6, . . *Any kind of thief*) Infs **SC**69, **WI**74, Coon.

4 in phr *go the whole coon*: See quots. Cf **whole hog**
1892 (1925) Walsh *Lit. Curiousities* 190, *Coon, Go the whole*, an American equivalent for "go the whole hog." **1959** Tallman *Dict. Amer. Folkl.*, *Coon, to go the whole coon*—A popular Southern expression equivalent to—to go the whole hog—to see the thing to the bitter end and never mind the consequences.

5 See **coon cat 1.**

coon n[2] See **coonass**

coon v, hence vbl n *cooning* [**coon** n[1]]
1 also *coon it:* To crawl on all fours like a raccoon, esp on a log across a stream; to straddle a log and pull oneself along it. **chiefly Sth, S Midl**
1834 Pike *Prose Sketches* 77, Irwin . . was obliged to straddle the log, and as they quaintly call it in the west, 'Coon it across.' **1893** Shands *MS Speech* 24, *Coon* . . . Used by all classes to mean *to crawl over*. If a man cannot walk a log over a creek, he gets down on his hands and knees and *coons* it; or if he get astride of the log and pull himself along with his hands, he is then also said to *coon* it. **1908** *DN* 3.300 eAL, wGA, I cooned every log we come to. **1917** *DN* 4.410 IL, KY, NC, I cooned acrost on a log. **1927** *AmSp* 2.351 WV, Coon. **1933** *AmSp* 8.1.48 **Ozarks**, Coon. **1937–56** *Hall Coll.* eTN, wNC, Coon. **1954** *Harder Coll.* cwTN, Coon, coon across. **c1960** *Wilson Coll.* csKY, Coon. **1966–70** *DARE* FW Addit ceGA, *Cooning*: crawling or shinnying horizontally as on a tree limb or log across a creek. (Inf says it was a common expression when he was young but doesn't know if it's still used); **KY**84, *Cooning* or *cooning a log*: crossing a stream by crawling across a log. You coon it *only* if you crawl across, not if you can walk across the log; **OK**42, *Cooning* across a footlog: crossing a footlog (bridge) by sitting on it and pulling yourself across with your hand. **1969** *DARE* (Qu. Y34a, *When somebody moves on his hands and knees: "He was down in the bushes, _____."*) Inf **GA**77, Coonin' on his knees.

2 To climb (a tree or pole) like a raccoon. **chiefly Sth, Midl**
1903 *DN* 2.310 seMO, *Coon* . . . To climb. 'He cooned up the tree.' **1906** *DN* 3.116 sIN. **1926** Lord *Frontier Dust* 190, I would show her how a Yankee could coon a pole. **1954** *Harder Coll.* cwTN, *Coon (up)* . . climb . . . (Common). **1965–70** *DARE* (Qu. EE36, *To climb the trunk of a tree by holding on with your legs while you pull yourself up with your hands*) 27 Infs, **chiefly Sth**, Cooning; **OH**56, **OK**18, Coon up.

3 In railroading: see quot.
1977 Adams *Lang. Railroader*, *Coon*: To move across the tops of cars of a freight train. To run a train at reduced speed. Also *coon a train, coon it*.

4 To steal something of small value; to pilfer.
1890 *Rockford* (Wash.) *Enterprise* 23 Aug. 3/1 (*DA*), One of our lads while 'cooning' apples in town this week was caught and badly scared. **1901** *DN* 2.138 nNY, NYC, *Coon* . . . Steal; "to go cooning melons." **1917** *DN* 4.410 IL, KY, NC. **1947** *AmSp* 22.74 KY. **1950** *WELS* (*To take something of small value*) 3 Infs, **WI**, Coon. **1965** Little *Autobiog. Malcolm X* 15, In the summertime . . some of us boys would slip out . . and go "cooning" watermelons. **1966–69** *DARE* (Qu. V5a, *To take something that doesn't belong to you—for example, a child taking cookies: "Who's been _____ the cookies?"*) Infs **MI**18, 103, Cooning; (Qu. V4, *Other words for stealing something valuable—for example, a watch: "Yesterday somebody _____ my watch."*) Inf **MI**76, Cooned. **1967** *DARE* Tape OH15, They used to go cooning . . for melons.

5 To act in a cunning or sly manner.

1958 McCulloch *Woods Words* **Pacific NW,** *Cooning*—Pulling some trick as smart as an old raccoon.

6 See quot.

1960 Criswell *Resp. to PADS 20* **Ozarks,** *Coon* . . . To embarrass. "When I talk about seeing him in the man's crib, that cooned him." (Always very common. Do not know about now.)

coona See **cuna 1**

coonah n, also attrib [Alter and abbr of **John Canoe;** cf *DJE John Canoe, DBE Junkanoo*] See also **coonering**

A **John Canoe** reveler.

1913 (1973) *African Times & Orient Rev.* 2.234/2 [Black], *De Coonah Man* . . . Fuh mo' welcome den ol' Santi was de ragged coonah man, / Uh dancin' an' uh capering' about; / Makin' moshuns an' uh shufflin' jes to mek de chillan run, / Whilst de older ones uh follerin' 'ud shout: — / "Show yo moshun, mister coonah, blow horn, blow! / . . . Chrismus comes but wunst uh yeah, blow horn, blow!" **1968** *DARE* FW Addit **csNC,** *Coonah* ['kunə]: false—used in the phrase a "coonah face" meaning a false face or mask.

coo-nan(nie) See **co-nan(nie)**

coonass n, also attrib Also **coon, coonie** [Folk-etym of Fr *conasse* female genitals (used insultingly); see Littré *Dictionnaire, conassière* used vulgarly for *femelots* gudgeon] **chiefly LA, seTX** See Map *orig derog; now sometimes neutral or accepted* Cf **cajun** n[1] 1, 2

A person of Acadian French heritage; also transf: see quot 1980.

1962 Atwood *Vocab. TX* 73 **seTX,** For a person of Acadian French origin . . . In keeping with their tendency to avoid "bad words," only five Texas informants gave *Coonass*, a term that I have personally heard many more times than that. **1965–70** *DARE* (Qu. HH28, . . *People of foreign background*) 14 Infs, **LA, seTX,** Coonass; **LA**2, 17, 28, 32, **TX**86, Coonie; (Qu. F39) Inf **TX**37, Coonass pistol; (Qu. H74a, *Different words for coffee according to how it's made—very strong*) Inf **TX**11, Coonass coffee. **1967** LeCompte *Word Atlas* 252 **seLA,** Acadian French . . coonass [5 of 21 infs]. **1967** *DARE* Tape **LA**14, The coonass is the lineal descendent of that group of people who were forcibly deported from Nova Scotia. **1969** *DARE* FW Addit, *Coon, coonass* ['kun‚æ·s], *coonie* ['kuni]: names for white Cajun swampers who live by trapping and fishing. Louisiana—near Baton Rouge and elsewhere. Term of derogation: implies ignorance, primitiveness. **1970** Tarpley *Blinky* 257 **neTX,** Familiarity with nicknames for the Acadian French of Louisiana depends upon the proximity of the informant's home to Louisiana . . . *Coonie* and *coon ass* are common nicknames for *Cajuns* in Louisiana which are heard occasionally in Northeast Texas in the southeastern counties near the Louisiana line. **1976** *Capital Times* (Madison WI) 22 Sept 21/3 (UPI) **csLA,** "I picked up all them songs from family. I know plenty of them—you know I'm what you call a coonass," said John "Cowboy" Trahan. **1980** *DARE* File **eKY,** *Coonass:* I first heard this term used by a corporal in my outfit from Lafayette, LA. This was in 1949. *Coonass* is still a pejorative for any low-life individual, especially Negroes. In my stay in the army if a white soldier called another trooper a coonass, we made ready for a real fistfight.

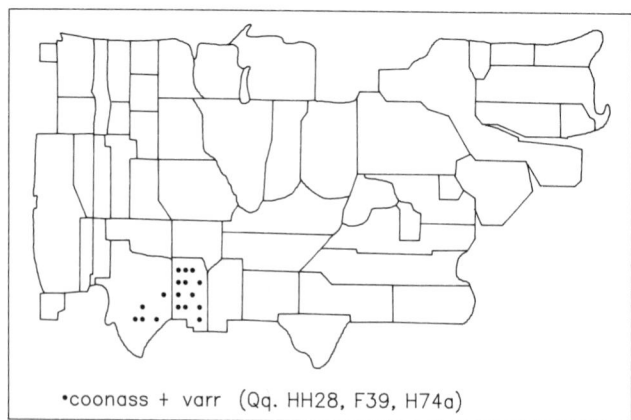

•coonass + varr (Qq. HH28, F39, H74a)

coonass pistol n *joc*

1967 *DARE* (Qu. F39, *A large pocket knife with blades that fold in and out*) Inf **TX**37, Coonass pistol.

Coon Bottom n [**coon** n[1] 2 or *coon* raccoon + **bottom** n 2] **esp FL**

A particular part of town: see quots.

1966–68 *DARE* (Qu. C34, *Nicknames for nearby settlements, villages, or districts*) Inf **FL**26, Coon Bottom; **GA**31, Coon Bottom—actual name of a nearby town; doesn't refer to the rear end of a coon; (Qu. C36, *Nicknames for special communities . . around here;* total Infs questioned, 75) Infs **FL**7, 26, Coon Bottom; (Qu. II25, . . *The part of town where the poorer people, special groups, or foreign groups live*) Inf **FL**52, Coon Bottom.

cooncan n Also sp *conquain, councan* [Folk-etym of MexSpan *con quién* with whom] **esp Sth, SW**

A card game similar to rummy.

1889 *Century Illustr. Mag.* 37.905/1 **AZ,** The men [=Black troopers] got out a pack of Mexican cards and gambled at a game called 'Coon-can' for a few nickels and dimes. **1913** Foster *Cooncan* ix, Cooncan is simply a mispronunciation of the Mexican name for a game of cards which has been a favorite in the Southwestern States of America for the past fifty years or more . . . Cooncan was played with the Spanish pack of forty cards, from which the eights, nines and tens are missing. **1913** U.S. Playing Card Co. *Official Rules* 8, Conquain (Coon-can). **1929** *Sat. Eve. Post* 17 Aug 136/2 **Lower Missip R.,** One man, stripped of all odd change in a Cooncan game. **1931** *AmSp* 7.49 **Sth, SW,** Lumberjacks are fun-loving fellows whose diversions and entertainments depend pretty much on themselves . . . Some play checkers, some read, some play "coon-can," some write letters. **1961** Oliver *Blues Fell* 154, One of the oldest card games associated almost exclusively with Negroes is Coon-can, a form of gambling rummy in which the dice are also employed. Because it needs only two hands to form a game it is widely played and extremely popular. **1966–70** *DARE* (Qu. DD35, . . *Favorite card games*) Infs **LA**26, **MO**24, Cooncan; **IL**140, [kun'ken]; (Qu. DD37, *Other table games played a lot by adults*) Inf **CA**94, Cooncan—a Mohave game. [Inf not familiar with it.] **1970** Abrahams *Deep Down* 147 **PA,** Cooncan is a favorite rummy game among the Negroes in this area (and throughout the South). It is very complicated. **1970** Berlin *Best of Families* 22 **NY** (as of 1908), On rainy days he played councan or Parcheesi with us.

coon cat n

1 also *coon, coony cat:* A large, long-haired domestic cat with a ringed tail, sometimes confused with the raccoon. **NEng, esp ME**

1902 (1904) Rowe *Maid of Bar Harbor* 331 **ME,** Yes, we have two splendid coon cats that we have hired for the occasion. **1903** Hall *Pine Grove* 12, Old Mrs. Lindsay's cooncat had a fit in Mrs. White's bedroom. **1907** *DN* 3.242 **eME,** *Coon-cat* . . . Folk-loristic name for the hybrid cat which has the long, soft fur of the Angora and the short tail of the Manx cat. Even intelligent people . . contend that the *coon-cat* is half cat and half raccoon. **1937** FWP *Guide ME* 265, *Coon* cats. It is Captain Clough who is given credit for having introduced coon cats into Maine . . . The coon cats, quite gentle and fragile, have long, frosty-gray hair; they are difficult to rear. **1957** Beck *Folkl. ME* 67, The "coon-cat," a long-haired beast, is the one [kind of cat] characteristic of the state. **1967–69** *DARE* (QR, near Qu. J5) Inf **KY**39, Coony cat—a gray cat; (Qu. P31, . . *Other names . . for the . . raccoon*) Inf **NY**35, Coon cats. [Ed: prob erron] **1975** Gould *ME Lingo,* Coon cat—The Maine *coon cat* was sometimes thought to be a cross between a cat and a raccoon. The truth is that Maine captains brought home all manner of cats from around the world, and the *coon cat* is a descendant of the Angora cats brought from Turkey. Cat fanciers like the Maine *coon cat*, but he's common enough so most Mainers aren't that much impressed. **1977** *Yankee* Feb 172 **cwMA,** There's Abyssinian and Alley, Angora and Australian . . . But none of these guys are as proud as a Maine Coon Cat! *Ibid* **ceNY,** I was owned by a Maine Coon cat for 13 years. She was beautiful, fastidious and loving. Also she was *extremely* intelligent. **1978** *Ibid* Oct 198, Breeders of Maine coon cats, a New England breed with a traditionally high frequency of polydactylism . . decided to rule the trait out of the show standard. *Ibid,* Others would like to see a separate standard developed for showing Maine coons.

2 A cacomistle. **SW**

1918 *Natl. Geog. Mag.* 33.482/2, In the United States it [the cacomistle] is known by several other names, including "civet cat," "coon cat," and "band-tailed cat." **1928** Anthony *N. Amer. Mammals* 90, *Cacomistle.—Bassariscus astutus flavus . . Names.*—Cacomistle; Cacomixtl; Ringtail; Ring-tailed Cat; Civet-cat; Coon-cat; Bassarisk. **1947** Cahalane *Mammals* 166, The other common names [of the cacomistle] arose from the bicolored tail: coon cat, band-tailed cat, and ringtail.

coon chaser n [Var of **nigger chaser**]

   1968 *DARE* (Qu. FF28, . . *Kinds of fireworks*) Inf **NJ**37, Coon chasers.

coon dick n [Etym unknown] Cf **coon juice**

Strong homemade liquor.

   1935 Hurston *Mules & Men* 32 **FL,** "What is coon dick?" "Aw, Zora, jus' somethin' to make de drunk come. Made out uh grape fruit juice, corn meal mash, beef bones and a few mo' things."

coon dog n[1] Also *cooner, coon hound* **chiefly Sth, S Midl**

A dog trained to hunt raccoon.

   1833 Hall *Harpe's Head* 230, A dog who is a veteran in such affairs, or as the hunters say, "An old coon dog," has a face covered with scars. **1920** *Outing* 76.59/3 **nwMS,** For Sale — a few as good Coon Hounds and mixed hunters as live. **1939** *Hall Coll.* **wNC, eTN,** Coon dog. **1941** *FWP Guide AR* 100, They appreciate a good pocketknife, a true rifle, and a cold-nosed coonhound. **1954** in 1962 *Catahoula Hog Dog* 5 **LA,** Coonhounds. — The black-and-tan *cooner* is big enough, sufficiently aggressive and fast enough to follow a wild boar after winding him. **1966–70** *DARE* Tape **GA**9, You go out at night with a bunch of good coon dogs . . . I've kept some good coon hounds; **IN**13, 36, 51, **MI**120, Coon dog. **1967** *Boston Sunday Herald Mag.* 26 Mar. 23/1 *(OEDS),* He got the idea of cashing in on the coons in our neighborhood by making a really fine coon dog out of Old George. *Ibid,* Old George is a coon hound.

coon dog n[2] [Alter of *corn dog*]

   1970 *DARE* FW Addit **cnLA,** *Coon dog:* a wiener rolled in cornmeal batter and deep-fried.

cooner n

   1 A person who hunts raccoon.

   1900 Bacheller *Eben Holden* 4, He was what they call in the north country "a natural cooner." After nightfall, . . he spoke in a whisper and had his ear cocked for coons.

   2 See quot. [Cf **coon** n[1] 1]

   1930 Shoemaker *1300 Words* 13 **cPA Mts** (as of c1900), *Cooner* — a cute little boy.

   3 See **coon dog** n[1].

coonering n [Alter and abbr of *John Kunering;* see **John Canoe**] Cf **coonah**

   1978 *DARE* File **seNC,** [A university professor from the region says that] "coonering" is the activity of the Blacks in Wilmington, North Carolina on Christmas Day, when they go around entertaining neighborhoods and expecting gifts in return. Sort of a combination of trick-or-treat and the English Boxing Day.

cooney n[1] See **coney** n[1]

cooney n[2] See **cuna** 2

coon-faced bird n

=**Maryland yellowthroat.**

   1955 *AmSp* 30.179 **FL,** Rather apt is the Florida cognomen, *coon-faced bird,* for the Maryland yellowthroat, with a black mask enclosing its eyes.

coon-footed adj

   1 See quot.

   1915 *DN* 4.182 **swVA,** *Coon-footed* . . . Having toes turned out.

   2 Of a horse or mule: see quot 1968.

   1968 Adams *Western Words, Coon-footed* — Said of a horse with long and very low pasterns. **1970** *Foxfire* 4.35 **nGA,** I'd bought a little old coon-footed mule.

coonfoot harrow n Also *coontooth harrow*

See quot 1954.

   1954 *Harder Coll.* **cwTN,** *Coon tooth harrow* . . . A homemade, V-shaped harrow with pointed steel spikes (teeth) driven through the two sides of the V, and used to level the freshly plowed ground in rough fields. (Old-fashioned). **1968** *DARE* (Qu. L20, *The implement used in a field after it's . . plowed to break up the lumps*) Inf **TN**26, Coonfoot harrow.

coon grape n

   1 also *raccoon grape:* A **fox grape** (here: *Vitis labrusca*).

   1920 *Torreya* 20.23, *Vitis labrusca* . . . Raccoon grape, Coatsville, Pa . . . ; coon-grape, Ashland, Del. **1957** *KY Folkl. Rec.* 3.46 **cKY,** If we were tired of civilized food, there were "coon" grapes, black and red haw, wild plum, papaw. **1966–70** *DARE* (Qu. I46, *Other kinds of fruits that grow wild around here*) Infs **VA**35, 42, 78, Coon grapes; **KY**81, **NH**5, Coon grape.

   2 usu *raccoon grape:* A **false grape** (here: *Ampelopsis cordata*).

   1920 *Torreya* 20.23, *Ampelopsis cordata* . . . Raccoon, or swamp grape, Louisiana. **1940** Steyermark *Flora MO* 349, Raccoon Grape, False Grape. **1941** Lyon *Take to Hills* 252, The coon grapes and fox grapes grow closer to the ground. **1973** Stephens *Woody Plants* 376, Raccoon grape . . . Seeds similar to those of the grape.

   3 =**supplejack.**

   1913 *Torreya* 13.232 **cLA,** *Berchemia scandens* . . coon grapes, Marksville, La.

coonheel n Cf **coon oyster**

A form of the eastern **oyster.**

   1881 Ingersoll *Oyster-Industry* 243, *Coon-heel* — A long, slim oyster. (Connecticut.)

coon hound See **coon dog** n[1]

coonhunt v **chiefly S Midl**

To hunt raccoons.

   1905 *DN* 3.75 **nwAR,** *Coonhunt* . . . To hunt racoons. 'I used to coonhunt when I was a boy.' Common. **1937** *Hall Coll.* **wNC, eTN,** *Coon-hunt* . . . To hunt raccoon. "Hit takes only one man to coon-hunt." "Me and my brother-in-law one time left the White Oak . . and went a-coon-huntin' one night." **1966** *DARE* Tape **AR**15, He likes to coonhunt; **DC**9, They coonhunt the same way; **GA**9, I used to coonhunt a good bit. **1968** *DARE* FW Addit **DE**5, *Coonhunt:* To hunt racoons; **neTN,** *Coonhunt:* To go hunting for coons.

coonie n[1] See **coonass**

coonie n[2] See **cuna** 2

cooning See **coon** v

coon it See **coon** v 1

coon-jigger n

A Black child.

   1965 *DARE* File **swPA** (as of 1920s), *Coon-jigger.* Older black people were called 'colored people' but the children were called 'coon-jiggers' . . it was never said in a nasty way.

coonjine v [Etym uncert but perh in ref to the waddling gait of the raccoon] **chiefly Missip Valley** *hist*

Esp of Black dockhands: to move with a rhythmic, swaying gait adapted to loading freight; hence n *coonjiner.*

   1896 *The Bully* (A song) *(DA),* I coonjined in the front door, the coons were dancing high. **1907** Stewart *Partners* 87 **MO River Valley,** There was Blue and Red, which was our best coonjiners. **1926** *AmSp* 1.362 (as of c1880) [Song lyrics], Ah coonjined down to the engine room. [Footnote:] *Coonjining* is a name for a peculiar gait or shuffle which the darkies of fifty years ago sometimes indulged in. **1929** *Sat. Eve. Post* 17 Aug 11/3 **LA,** The instant they receive their tickets the rousters string out and "coonjine" down the plank. **1948** *Sat. Review* 26 June 15/1, The Negro rousters who coonjined freight up and down the stage planks of our river steamers . . have gone. **1950** Blesh–Janis *Ragtime* 38 **MO** (as of 1885), The shouts of roustabouts coonjining to the plink-plank of banjos.

coonjine n [**coonjine** v] **chiefly Missip Valley** *hist*

   1 See quot 1929.

   1929 *Sat. Eve. Post* 17 Aug 11/3 **LA,** The coonjine is a step peculiar to roustabouts. It is difficult to execute and more difficult to describe. In movement it approaches something between a dog trot and a buck-and-wing dance, with interpolations and grace notes scattered throughout. The coonjiner bends forward at the hips, bends his knees until they get springy, spreads his arms and legs apart and waddles foward with exaggerated swings of his body. His muscles are relaxed and his joints are loose. It looks most awkward, except for some little something in it that makes it look extremely graceful. **1945** Saxon *Gumbo Ya-Ya* 382 **LA,** Early roustabouts were famed for their songs and their 'coonjines.' The 'coonjine' was a rhythmic shuffle affected to expedite loading and unloading; the songs were usually doleful, yet served to lighten their labors. **1947** Ballowe *The Lawd* 89 **LA,** They left doing coonjine steps and returned the same way. [Footnote:] A step practiced by rousters in carrying freight ashore from a packet boat.

   2 A song that facilitates freight loading.

   1941 *Chr. Sci. Monitor* (Boston MA) mag sec 3 May 11/5, Coonjine, a word used originally on the river for the waddling run of Negro rousters with freight across the stage or gangplank . . . From the gait the word got to mean the song and jingles to the singing of which the Negro rousters jerked themselves along. **1949** Dean *Diamond Bess* 22 **TX**, Their [=Black dock hands'] "coonjines" or singing, as it was known, had a somewhat barbaric and haunting quality, but supplied perfect rhythm for their feet and timing for loading the heavy freight.

3 sp *congaine, kunjine:* See quot. [Perh by folk-etym assoc with *conjoin*]

1975 *DARE* File, Gennett disk 20012 was recorded, Oct [1923], in Richmond, Indiana by Deppe's Serenaders under the title of *Congaine.* Deppe says that "the word covers sexual intercourse as a noun, verb, and adjective." Vocalion disk 1450 was recorded, Dec. [1929], in Chicago (?) by Tampa Red (Hudson Whittaker) under the title of *Kunjine Baby.*

coon juice n Cf **coon dick**

1965–70 *DARE* (Qu. DD21b, . . *Bad liquor*) Infs **MS59, VA61,** Coon juice.

coon-log v [Perh from *coon a log,* see **coon** v **1**; cf also **coon tree**] Perh =**coon** v **1**.

1960 Williams *Walk Egypt* 111 **GA,** First snowstorm they had in Limus, Alabama, in fifteen years, and I had to be out coon-logging.

coon muddle n [*coon* raccoon + **muddle**]
=**Brunswick stew 1.**

1952 Brown *NC Folkl.* 1.529, *Coon muddle* . . . Brunswick stew—Chapel Hill.

coonner See **cunner** n[2]

coon-on-the-log n
A dance step.

1967 *DARE* Tape **TX49,** [She] got to talking about coon-on-the-log . . . She could tear it up.

coon oyster n Also *raccoon oyster* [From their being favored by raccoons] **chiefly S Atl, esp FL** Cf **coon-heel**
Either of two small **oysters,** *Lopha frons* or *Crassostrea virginica.*

1869 *Amer. Naturalist* 3.460 **cwFL,** The small oysters . . are not generally eaten except by the raccoons, hence the common name for them of 'coon oysters.' **1881** Ingersoll *Oyster-Industry* 243 **S Atl,** *Coon oyster.*—Small, shapeless, worthless stock, growing in heavy clusters along the salt marshes, or forming great bars . . . At Cape May [NJ] the word is restricted to young oysters caught on the sedges. *Ibid* 247, *Raccoon Oysters* . . . Southern coast. **1894** *DN* 1.329 **NJ,** *Coon oyster:* small oyster attached to the sedge rather than to the usual more solid supports. **1899** (1912) Green *VA Folk-Speech.* **1937** *Natl. Geog. Mag.* 71.208 **FL,** Extensive beds of coon oysters *(Ostrea frons)* project from the white mud of low water . . . These oysters are abundant from Florida and the West Indies to North Carolina, and throughout the coast of the Southern States are much sought after by raccoons; hence their popular name. **1946** *PADS* 6.10 **seNC,** *Coon oyster* . . . A long, narrow sharp-shelled oyster found in marshes. Usually in clusters, sometimes a dozen to a cluster. **1961** Douglas *My Wilderness* 139 **sFL,** These oysters that grow in clusters as large as coral are in a state of deterioration. They are now called "coon" oysters because only the raccoons relish them. Once they were the delight of epicures. **1974** Abbott *Seashells* 457/1, *Lopha frons* . . . Frons Oyster—Florida, Louisiana . . . Formerly called the 'coon oyster.

coon root n [Abbr for *puccoon root*] **chiefly sAppalachians**
=**bloodroot 1.**

1893 *Jrl. Amer. Folkl.* 6.137, *Sanguinaria Canadensis* . . puccoon root. Anderson, Ind. coon-root. West Va. [**1910** Hodge *Hdbk. Amer. Indians* 2.315, In s.w. Virginia puccoon is locally abbreviated 'coon.'] **c1964** *Hall Coll.* **wNC, eTN,** *Coon root* . . . Plant name. For puccoon. **1971** Krochmal *Appalachia Med. Plants* 226, Sanguinaria Canadensis L. (Papaveraceae) *Common names:* . . coonroot.

coonshine n [*coon* raccoon + *shine* n, a **shining**]
A night hunt for raccoons, using bright lights.

1960 Williams *Walk Egypt* 10 **GA,** "The night you was born, he took off on a coonshine," she moaned. "And when Tessie come he was gone on a foxhunt."

coon shout v [*coon* n[1] **2** + *shout* to participate in a **shout** song]
To sing in a style used esp by Blacks, characterized by responsive calls between a leader and congregation; hence *coon shout(ing), coon shouter.*

1906 Green *Actors' Boarding House* 26 *(OEDS),* "I goes big," remarked the Coon Shouter, enviously. **1926** (1974) Whiteman–McBride *Jazz*

228, The exchange of experience between the classicist and "coon-shouter". **1945** *Newsweek* 26 Mar 108/3, She sang first in the German Village, a big, old-fashioned beer garden. Then she became a black-faced coon shouter. **1946** (1972) Mezzrow *Really Blues* 146, Look at Sophie Tucker, Al Jolson, Eddie Cantor and the rest—where'd they be without their blackface routines and corny coon-shouting and mammy numbers? *Ibid* 331/2, *Coonshout*—corny imitation of oldtime Negro style of singing.

coonskin n[1] [Perh a relic from the fur trade, when furs became a kind of tender] Cf **frogskin**

1950 *WELS (Joking names for a paper dollar)* 1 Inf, **cWI,** Coonskin—common.

coon skin n[2] [Perh var of **cooncan**]

1966 *DARE* (Qu. DD34, . . *Favorite card games people play around here*) Inf **AL4,** Coon skin.

coon skinner n [Perh ref to the wearing of a coonskin cap]
1 See quot.

1906 *DN* 3.132 **nwAR,** *Coon-skinner* . . . An uncouth countryman.

2 In lumbering: see quots; hence *coon skinning.*

1930 *DN* 6.86 **cWV,** *Coonskinner* . . a peeler of tanbark; a woodsman who cuts by the thousand feet, cutting very close, almost literally "skinning" the land. *Ibid, Coon skinning,* peeling tanbark, or cutting as above. **1964** Clarkson *Tumult* 358 **WV,** *Coon skinner*—A subcontractor cutting timber. Syn. buck wheater.

coon-striped shrimp n
A West Coast prawn *(Pendalus danae)* marked with rings similar to those on a raccoon's tail.

1935 Pratt *Manual Animals* 450, *Pendalus danae* . . Coon-striped shrimp.

coonta See **coontie**

coontail n [From the whorled leaves which give the bushy appearance of a raccoon's tail]
1 also *coontail moss:* A **hornwort,** esp *Ceratophyllum demersum.*

1913 *Torreya* 13.10.230 **AR, LA,** *Ceratophyllum demersum* . . Coontail, Big Lake, Ark.; Marksville, La.; coon-tail moss, Menasha and Lake Wapanoca, Ark. **1938** FWP *Guide IA* 16, Among plants living in diffused light under water are pondweed, coontail, and bladderwort. **1960** Williams *Walk Egypt* 106 **GA,** She hung it on a branch and looked up the race to the broad-breasted pond dotted with tree snags and coontail moss. **1968** *DARE* (Qu. S22) Inf **GA20,** Coontail moss.

2 A water milfoil: see quots.

1937 Stemen *OK Flora* 358, *Myriophyllum pinnatum* . . . Sometimes called Coontail. A good water plant for fish ponds. **1940** Steyermark *Flora MO* 377, Coontail *(Myriophyllum heterophyllum* . .).

coontail rattler n Also *coontailed ~, coontail rattlesnake* [See quots]
The western **diamondback rattlesnake** (here: *Crotalus atrox*).

1958 Conant *Reptiles & Amphibians* 195, Western diamondback rattlesnake—*Crotalus atrox* . . . *Tail strongly ringed* with black and white or light gray ("coontail rattler") . . . *Range:* Cent. Arkansas and Texas to California. **1966–70** *DARE* (Qu. P25, . . *Kinds of snakes . . found around here*) Inf **OK52,** Coontail rattler; **AR56,** Coontailed rattler. **1974** Shaw–Campbell *Snakes West* 219, Sometimes called "coontail" rattlesnake, the western diamondback is characterized by an easily identifiable tail barred in black and white like a raccoon's.

coontie n Also sp *comptie, coomtie, coonta, coonti, coonty, koonta, koontie* [Seminole *kunti*]
A plant *(Zamia floridana, Z. integrifolia,* or *Z. pumila)* native to Florida; also its root. Also called **comfort root, Florida arrowroot, Seminole bread, wild sago**

1819 *Pennsylvania Gazette* 22 June 2/3 *(OEDS),* [The Seminoles] use a root called coonty, as a substitute [for corn]. **1823** in 1868 McCall *Letters Frontiers* 60, He was absent; but today I found him digging the coonta-root. **1836** *Ibid* 295, He stated . . that the *"koonta,"* a very good species of arrow-root, grew plenteously everywhere. **1837** (1962) Williams *Territory FL* 33, The inhabitants living principally on fish, turtle, and coonti. **1939** FWP *Guide FL* 21, *Coontie.* Throughout the central and lower East coast section grows a cycad, the coontie of the genus Zamia, roots of which provide a kind of arrowroot [used by the Seminoles to make bread]. **1944** Barbour *Vanishing Eden* 49, The basis of the *sofkee* used to be the arrowroot-like starch which is made from the coomtie plant. But the coomtie does not grow abundantly where the Indians are now forced to live, and grits is the ordinary substitute. **1945** Dickinson *Jrl.* 152 **FL** (as of 1696), They obtained their food . . from the starch pith of the coontie root (one reads of "Koontie and Hunting Grounds" in southern Florida and knows that coontie starch-making later became a profitable industry). **1949** Brown *Amer. Cooks* 112 **FL**, *Coontie.* Another indigenous food the Indians passed on to the whites was the "coontie" or "comptie" as variously spelled—a plant with a palmlike leaf and a starchy root. **1976** Bailey–Bailey *Hortus Third* 1180, *Zamia . . . floridana . . .* [*Z.*] *integrifolia . . .* [*Z.*] *pumila . . .* Comptie, Coontie.

coontooth harrow See **coonfoot harrow**

coontra n [AmSpan *contra* extra, something thrown in] =**lagniappe.**
    1966 *DARE* (Qu. U15, *When you're buying something, if the seller puts in a little extra . . you call that* _____) Inf **FL**25, Gave us some coontra ['kʊntrə] to entice us back — at stores when parents paid bills, they'd give kids a handful of candy, called it coontra.

coon track n
    A marble game: =**boss-out.**
    1955 *PADS* 23.14 **cwTN**, *Coon track . .* Reg[ular] dial[ectal] var[iant] fr[om] *raccoon track.* Same as *boss out* and *boss and span. Heard.*

coon tree n
    A tree in which a raccoon would be likely to live.
    1958 McCulloch *Woods Words* **Pacific NW**, *Coon tree*—A hollow tree.

coonty See **coontie**

coony See **coney** n[1]

coony cat See **coon cat 1**

coop n[1] In **Nth, N Midl** usu |kup|; in **Sth, S Midl** usu |kʊp|; occas |kub, kʊb| Pronc-sp *coob*
    A Forms.
    1899 (1912) Green *VA Folk-Speech, Coob . . .* Coop, a small building for fowls. "Chicken-coob." **1930** *DN* 6.80 **cSC**, *Coob* [kʊb] *. . .* coop. Universal. The pen in which chickens are confined before being killed is always built on high stilts and spoken of as the "fat'nin' coob." **1930** Shoemaker *1300 Words* 9 **cPA Mts** (as of c1900), *Coob,* a pen for poultry. **1933** *AmSp* 8.2.44 **neNY**, As elsewhere usage varies widely between [u] and [ʊ] *. . .* Of those words that vary, the following generally have [u]: *. . coop.* **1936** *AmSp* 11.30 **eTX**, The following words are pronounced with [ʊ]: coop. *Ibid* 143 **nNY**, The vowels [u] and [ʊ] interchange quite freely in a few words, as will be seen in the following table. A number of speakers use both vowels in some of the words . . . coop. **1937** *AmSp* 12.286 **cnVA**, *Coop* and *cooper,* however, in spite of the general southern tendency to say [kʊp] and ['kʊpər], are usually [kup] and ['kupər]. **1942** *AmSp* 17.40 **seNY**, Coop [37 infs [u], 1 inf [ʊ]]. **1960** Criswell *Resp. to PADS 20* **Ozarks**, *Coop . . .* [kʊp]. The universal pronunciation always; [kup] never used. **1961** Kurath–McDavid *Pronc. Engl.* 153, The two different vowels occurring in *coop* (and its variant *coob*) exhibit a rather clear-cut regional dissemination: the North and the North Midland have predominantly, if not exclusively, the vowel /u/ of *two,* the South and the South Midland the /ʊ/ of *pull.* **1968** *DARE* (QR, near Qu. KK20b) Inf **MD**34, Flew the coop [kʊp].
    B Senses.
    1 A jail.   *somewhat old-fash*
    1912 *DN* 3.573 **wIN**, *Coop . . .* Penitentiary. "I think they'll send him to the coop for two or three years." **1950** *WELS* (*A county or city jail*) 7 Infs, Coop. [All Infs old] **1965–70** *DARE* (Qu. V11, *. . A city or county jail*) 57 Infs, **scattered,** Coop. [Of all Infs responding to the question, 67% were old; of those giving this response, 82% were old.] **1969** Sorden *Lumberjack Lingo* **NEng, Gt Lakes**, *Coop*—The local jail.
    2 See quot.   Also called **chicken roost 1**
    1967 *DARE* (Qu. D40, *. . The upper balcony in a theater*) Inf **OH**34, Coop.
    3 See quot.
    1977 Adams *Lang. Railroader* 26, *Caboose . .* coop.
    4 pl: One's lips, mouth.
    1966 *DARE* (Qu. GG23a, *If you speak sharply to somebody to make him be patient, you say* _____) Inf **SC**10, Shut your coops [ʃɛt jo kʊps].

coop n[2] [Prob from *OED cop* sb.[2] 5 "A conical heap . . of straw or hay. (Chiefly in Kent)"; cf *OED coop* sb.[3] "A small heap, as of manure."]
    1 A haycock.
    1968 *DARE* (Qu. L12, *. . The small piles of hay standing in the field*) Inf **WI**65, Coops.
    2 A pile of tobacco leaves; a bulk.
    1966 *PADS* 45.10 **cKY**, *Coop . . . bulk. . .* "The flunky takes the hands from the press to the coop." **1970** *DARE* Tape **VA**40, And then we would take it and carry it to the pack house and pack it down in coops [kʊps] so that stalk would stick out and the tier would be on the inside so the 'bacco wouldn' damage.

coop n[3], exclam Also *coo, coop and seek* [From **cope** v[2]] Cf **hide-and-coop**
    The game hide-and-seek; a call used in this game.
    1884 *Advance* (Chicago IL) *(DA)*, And then we play at coop and seek. **1946** *AmSp* 21.307, *C-o-o-p!* A call. Used when playing 'Hide-and-seek' in Massachusetts when I was child. When a child was well hidden, she called in a long drawn-out cry, 'C-o-o-p!' This is never heard in the Middle West. It means 'Come up!' and is recorded by Wright *[EDD]* and by Halliwell–Philips. **1967–68** *DARE* (Qu. EE13a, *Games in which every player hides except one, and that one must try to find the others*) Inf **ME**5, Coop: hiders hollered "coop" to seekers too—player hollered "coop" when he found a hider and both ran for the starting place; **MA**3, Coop; **MA**42, [hɑɪd n̩ kup]: same as hide-and-go-seek, but played a little different—when players were hidden, they would holler coo [ku·]; then player who was "it" would go to find them.

coop n[4] Pronc-sp for *coup*
    1920 *DN* 5.78, *Coop,* coup. "He made a coop in grain speculation."

coop n[5] Pronc-sp for *coupé*
    1920 *DN* 5.78, *Coop,* coupé. "He sent her home in a coop."

coop n[6] [Prob alter of Ger *kopf*]
    1968 *DARE* (Qu. X28, *. . A person's head*) Inf **WI**47, Coop. [Inf of German and Czech ancestry]

coop v[1] [**coop** n[2] 2]
    To pile tobacco leaves, to bulk them.
    1966 *PADS* 45.10 **cKY**, *Coop . . . bulk . . .* "I coop my tobacco and cover it with a tarpaulin to keep it in case." **1967** Key *Tobacco Vocab.* **MO**, *Coop:* To bulk [=pile] tobacco [leaves].

coop v[2] [Pronc var of *cup;* cf *SND coop* n.[1] "Ork. form of Eng. *cup.*"]
    1954 *Harder Coll.* **cwTN**, *Coop:* cup. "To coop the hands."

coop v[3] See **cope** v[2]

coop and seek See **coop** n[3]

‡**cooper** n [Var of **coop** n[1]]
    1968 *DARE* (Qu. M16, *The small shelter for a hen that can be moved about from place to place*) Inf **GA**68, Cooper.

coopered See **cooper up**

Cooper's hawk n Also *Cooper hawk* [After William Cooper, Amer naturalist]
    A gray hawk (*Accipiter cooperi*) marked with black and white. Also called **blue darter 2, blue hawk 3, blue hen hawk 2, blue-tail hawk, bullet hawk, chicken hawk 1, hen hawk, pheasant hawk, pigeon hawk, privateer, quail hawk, striker, swift hawk, zel rond**
    1828 Bonaparte *Amer. Ornith.* 2.1, *Cooper's Hawk . . Falco cooperii . .* The bird represented in the plate . . was a male, killed in the later part of September, near Bordentown, New-Jersey. **1917** (1923) *Birds Amer.* 67, *Cooper's hawk—Accipiter cooperi . .* Other Names.—Pigeon Hawk; Chicken Hawk; Quail Hawk; Big Blue Darter; Swift Hawk; Striker. **1948** *Pacific Discovery* Mar/Apr 18/2 **cwCA**, The Cooper hawk [is] sulking among the shrubs at the back of the Aquarium. **1950** *WELS* (*Kinds of hawks*) 6 Infs, **WI**, Cooper's hawk; 2 Infs, Cooper hawk. **c1960** *Wilson Coll.* **csKY**, *Cooper's hawk . . .* Known as a separate species to very few; usually classed with Sharpshinned as one species, the Blue-tailed or Blue-darter Hawk. **1965–70** *DARE* (Qu. Q4, *. . Kinds of hawks*) 27 Infs, **chiefly Nth,** Cooper's hawk; 13 Infs, **scattered, but chiefly CA, SW,** Cooper hawk.

cooper's reed n [See quot 1847]
    =**cattail 1.**

1847 Darlington *Weeds & Plants* 347 *(DAE)*, *Typha latifolia* . . . Broad-leafed *Typha*. Cat-tail. Cooper's Reed . . . The leaves of this plant are (or formerly were) much used, by the coopers, to secure the joints of casks, etc., from leaking. **1933** Small *Manual SE Flora* 13, *Typha* . . . Erect herbs with sheathed stems . . . Represented in our range by 2 species widely distributed . . . *Cat-tails. Reed-maces. Cooper's reed. Cat-o'-nine-tails.*

cooper up v phr, also ppl adj *coopered* [Cf *EDD cooper* v.[2] "To injure, spoil, 'do for'"]
To become or cause to become stiff, unable to move, exhausted.
1959 *VT Hist.* new ser 27.130 **VT**, *Coopered* . . . Finished; exhausted. A term from the days of barrel making or coopering. Occasional. Windsor; Chittenden. **1969** *DARE* Tape NY209, If you sat too long your leg would cooper up. **1969** *DARE* FW Addit **seNY**, *Cooper me up for fair*—stiffen me up for good.

coopie See **cope** v[2]

coopilow See **cupola**

cooser n [Scots; alter of *courser*]
An uncastrated male horse; a stallion.
1930 Shoemaker *1300 Words* 11 **cPA Mts** (as of c1900), *Cooser or codster*—An entire horse.

coosey See **coosie**

coosh See **cush** n[1]

coo-sheep(ie), coo-sheepy See **co-sheep(ie)** n, v phr

cooshion See **cushion**

coosie n Also sp *coos(e)y, cosi, cusi(e)* [Alter and abbr of AmSpan *cocinero, -a*] **SW**
1 A cook on a ranch or a cattle drive.
1933 *AmSp* 8.1.27 **wTX**, *Coosey*. Variation of *cocinera*. **1939** Wellman *Trampling Herd* 237 **West**, Long before dawn, "coosie" was at work by his winking campfire, preparing the morning meal. **1949** Emrich *Wild West Custom* 233, Into it [a folksong] the cowboy, like a *cosi* making stew, threw everything at hand. **1961** Adams *Old-Time Cowhand* 343, Once she slipped the nosebag on 'im he was like a grain-fed hoss, and was never again satisfied with the hay shoveled out by some old roundup coosie. **1977** Watts *Dict. Old West*, *Cocinero*—(Sp; SW). Also *coosie, coosy, cosi, cusi, cusie*, etc. Ranch or trail-drive cook.
2 =**cuna** 2.
1968 Adams *Western Words*, *Coosie*—A cowhide stretched under a wagon for carrying wood or other fuel.

cooster v [Perh Du *koesteren* to cherish; cf **cooter** v]
1 See quot.
1895 *DN* 1.382 **NJ**, *Cooster* . . . to caress, coddle.
2 To idle, putter around.
1895 *DN* 1.382 **NJ**, *Cooster*: to "potter around," fuss. "What you been coosterin' at all day?" **1930s** in **1944** *ADD* **eWV**, 'They're just coosterin' around' = wasting time. Common.

cooster n
1 See quot.
1930 Shoemaker *1300 Words* 12 **cPA Mts** (as of c1900), *Cooster*—An old codger; a worn out retired libertine.
2 See quot.
1968 Adams *Western Words*, Cooster—A cowboy's word for a valise or suitcase.
3 In a freighting outfit: a trailer with living quarters.
1976 Sublette Co. Artist Guild *More Tales* 160 **WY** (as of c1900), The better outfits had what was called a "Cooster", pronounced like the male chicken with a "c" instead of an "r". This was either a two-wheeled or a four-wheeled unit resembling an old fashioned sheep wagon. This was the living quarters. *Ibid* 251, Perry Bolsby came driving in with the supplies, motivated by his ten horse team pulling two wagons and a cooster behind. The cooster was his living quarters while enroute.

coosy See **coosie**

coot n[1]
1 rarely *cooty*: A bird of the family *Rallidae*, esp the American coot *(Fulica americana)* which is also called **Barnegat turkey, blacklegs, blue marsh-hen, blue peter 2, chicken duck, Chinese mallard, crowbill, crow duck 2, flusterer, fool hen, hen-bill,**

marsh hen, meadow hen, moorhead, moor hen, Mother Carey's chicken, mud crow, mud duck, mud hen, pelick, pond crow, pond hen, poule d'eau, pull-doo, quark, sea crow, shuffler, splatter, water chicken, water hen, whitebill.

1709 (1967) Lawson *New Voyage* 149, Black Flusterers . . . Some call these the great bald Coot. **1791** (1958) Bartram *Travels* 118 **S Atl**, The verges and islets of the lagoon were elegantly embellished with flowering plants and shrubs; the laughing coots with wings half spread were tripping over the little coves and hiding themselves in the tufts of grass. **1888** Trumbull *Names of Birds* 123, At St. Augustine, Fla., many class the Gallinule indiscriminately with . . [*Fulica americana*] as *Coot* . . . I showed the same specimen [=a Gallinule] to a Sanford negro who said, "Why, dat a coot," adding, after I had pointed out the difference, "Yes, but day both coots." **1899** Howe *Birds RI* 47, *Fulica americana* . . Coot. Marsh Hen. Mud Hen. **1910** Wayne *Birds SC* 38, This species [*Porzana carolina*], which is locally known as the "Coot," is also very abundant in the rice plantations. **1917** (1923) *Birds Amer.* 214, Coot—*Fulica americana*— . . Many people think that the Coot is a Duck because it is usually seen swimming. As a matter of fact, however, it belongs to the rail tribe. **1950** *WELS* (*The bird that looks like a small dull-colored duck, . . commonly found on ponds and lakes*) 13 Infs, **WI**, Coot [response alternates and appears together with *mudhen*]; (*Wild ducks*) 5 Infs, Coot; (*Other kinds of game birds*) 2 Infs, Coot. **1956** *AmSp* 31.183, A peculiarly Southern way of indicating superiority in size is exemplified in the title *mammy coot* for the Virginia rail and purple gallinule (S.C.), as being larger than the sora, there known as *coot*. **1965–70** *DARE* (Qu. Q9, *The bird that looks like a small, dull-colored duck*) 192 Infs, **widespread, but least freq in nNEng, N Midl**, Coot; **PA104**, Coot duck; **PA214**, Cooty; (Qu. Q10, *Other water birds and marsh birds*) Infs **FL27, 32, MI2, NY84, VA47**, (Bay) Coot. **1966** *DARE* Tape **SC15**, Then we take that switch and lick them at the neck, kill them, put 'em in a sack . . . And that, we call that lick coot; **SC16**, Then, another thing, we used to catch bird and lick coot and shoot duck. Now, we make money on bird, coot, and duck.
2 Any of var ducks, often named with distinguishing qualifiers, as:
a A duck of the genus *Melanitta* (also known as *Oidemia*) such as the **scoter, surf scoter,** or **white-winged scoter.**
1844 Giraud *Birds Long Is.* 330, This [=surf scoter (*Oidemia perspicillata*)] is another of those hardy sea-birds that by our gunners generally are termed "Coots." *Ibid* 331, This also [=American or common scoter (*O. americana*)] is one of the "Coots." **1872** Coues *Key to N. Amer. Birds* 293, Genus *Oedemia* . . Embracing . . the black sea-ducks, surf-ducks, scoters or "coots" as they are variously called. **1899** Howe *Birds RI* 40, *Oidemia americana* . . . Butter-bill Coot. Yellow-billed Coot. *Ibid*, *Oidemia perspicillata* . . Patch-bill Coot. Females are called *Gray Coot.* **1909** Field Mus. Nat. Hist. *Zool. Ser.* 343, *Oidemia americana* . . American Scoter Duck.—*Local name*: Butter-bill Coot. *Ibid* 344, *Oidemia deglandi* . . White-winged Scoter.—*Local names*: White-winged Coot. *Ibid* 345, *Oidemia perspicillata* . . Surf Scoter.—*Local names*: Skunk-head Coot. **1917** (1923) *Birds Amer.* 148, Scoter—*Oidemia americana* . . . We have no means of knowing the early history of any one of the Scoters as they all were generally grouped together as "Coots" or "Black Ducks" by the early historians. The Scoters or "Coots," as they are called by the gunners and fishermen, are typical diving Ducks . . . The Scoters are universally known as Coots along the New England coast, a name derived probably from the French fishermen. **1943** Musgrove *Waterfowl IA* 65, White-Winged Scoter—*Melanitta deglandi* . . Other names: sea coot, . . coot. **1955** *MA Audubon* 39.10.376, *Harlequin Duck [Histrionicus histrionicus]* . . . Rock Coot (Mass. From frequenting ledges; any sea duck may be called a coot.) *Ibid, White-winged Scoter [Oidemia deglandi]* . . . Coot (All). *Ibid* 375, *Old-Squaw [Harelda hyemalis].* Butterfly Coot (Mass. Coot is applied to most sea ducks; this one has conspicuous coloration hence "butterfly."). *Ibid* 315, Coot is applied generally to sea fowl along the New England coast. **1962** Imhof *AL Birds* 156, White-winged Scoter—*Melanitta deglandi* . . Other names: White-winged Coot, Sea Coot. *Ibid* 157, Surf Scoter—*Melanitta perspicillata* . . Other Names: Skunkhead Coot, Sea Coot. *Ibid* 158, [Common Scoter]—*Oidemia nigra* . . Other Names: . . Coot. **1965–70** *DARE* (Qu. Q5, . . *Kinds of wild ducks*) 29 Infs, **scattered**, Coot; (Qu. Q7, . . *Other kinds of game birds*) Infs **ME22, OH16**, Coot. **1966** *DARE* Tape **ME10**, The common name for these birds up here are coots, they're really scoters . . . There's horsehead coots, and bufflehead coots, and white-winged coots, little gray coots . . . different color on their bills. Butterbill coots is a very light yellow. Looks just like butter on each side of that bill. *Ibid*, Sit down to coot stew.

1975 Gould *ME Lingo, Coot*—On the Maine coast, the American scoter, a saltwater duck whose habits give us numerous similes, and whose athletic flesh is legendary. He will not fly over land, so will wing miles down one cove and up another to reach a spot 50 yards over a neck of land; hence, to be "crazy as a *coot*" is not complimentary . . . A much loved elderly man may be referred to by his friends an "an old *coot*."

b =**ruddy duck.**

1888 Trumbull *Names of Birds* 110, At Baltimore, Md., *Coot* simply. **1917** (1923) *Birds Amer.* 148, Ruddy Duck—*Erismatura jamaicensis* . . Other Names.—Dumpling Duck; . . Widgeon Coot; Creek Coot; Sleepy Coot; Booby Coot; . . Bumblebee Coot; Quill-tailed Coot; Heavy-tailed Coot.

c An **eider duck** (here: *Somateri dresseri*).

1917 (1923) *Birds Amer.* 146, Eider—*Somateri dresseri* . . Other Names . . . Black and White Coot (male).

coot n[2] See **cootie** n[1] **1**

cooter n, also attrib Usu |'kutə(r)|; in **coastal SC and GA,** |'kutə| Pronc-spp *coota, cootuh* [Afr, akin to Bambara, Malinké *kuta* turtle; also Central Afr *nkudu;* cf *DA*] **chiefly S Atl, Gulf States, esp SC** Cf **alligator cooter, box cooter, coodle** n[1]**, cow-dung cooter, hard-backed cooter**

1 A freshwater turtle of the genus *Chrysemys*, found chiefly in the eastern part of the US. **chiefly S Atl, Gulf States, esp SC** See Map Also called **slider** For other names of var spp see **hard-shell cooter, neat turtle, soft-shell cooter**

1832 Johnston *Memoirs Nullifier* 40 ?**SC**, It was a large cooter, that . . rose to the surface, only a few feet distant. **1884** Goode *Fisheries U.S.* 1.155, *Pseudemys concinna*, the "Florida Cooter," is found in all the Southern States. **1895** *DN* 1.386 **cwMS**, *Cooter:* land turtle. **1899** (1912) Green *VA Folk-Speech, Cooter* . . . A terrapin. **1908** *DN* 3.300 **eAL, wGA,** *Cooter* . . . A terrapin. **1918** *DN* 5.18 **NC**, *Cooter,* a turtle, especially a fresh-water turtle. **1922** Gonzales *Black Border* 62 **sSC, GA coasts** [Gullah glossary], Uh gone fish duh backwatuh, . . en' one limus cootuh grab de hook en' uh ketch *him* en' t'row'um'way. **1927** Adams *Congaree* 81 **sSC** [Black], I been fishin' all day and catch heap of fish 'en I try to catch coota but I ain't ketch 'em. **1928** Baylor Univ. Museum *Contrib.* 16.6 **SC**, Among the negroes of the Gullah district of South Carolina, a Cooter is any kind of hard-shelled turtle. The name has spread all over the South, but at present time principally refers to large river and pond turtles of the genus *Pseudemys*. **1938** *DAE* 614 **SC**, *Cooter* . . . 'It is never here pronounced "cooter" as spelled, but ku-duh, ku-tuh.' **1941** Percy *Lanterns* 305 **MS**, The hoodoo doctor returned. He leaned over her and said: "You've swallowed a cooter. I can't do nothing about cooters." **1944** *PADS* 2.7 **AL, GA, MS, NC, SC, VA,** *Cooter* ['kutə, -ɚ] . . . A turtle. **1949** Turner *Africanisms* 258, From dɪ kuta ɑn dɪ deə 'The Tortoise and the Deer' [Title]. **1955** *AmSp* 30.56, *Cooter* 'turtle' is not found in the Southern Appalachians, much less in the Ohio Valley. **1958** Conant *Reptiles & Amphibians* 55, Cooters and Sliders: Genus *Pseudemys*—These include most of the big basking turtles, an abundant group in ponds and streams of the Southeast, where people call them Cooters, and the Mississippi Valley, where they are known as Sliders. **1961** Kurath–McDavid *Pronc. Engl.* 153, *Goober* 'peanut' and *cooter* 'turtle,' taken from African languages spoken by the slaves in the South, have either the /ʊ/ of *book* or the /u/ of *two* . . . *Cooter* . . is confined to South Carolina and adjoining parts of North Carolina and Georgia . . . In *cooter* /ʊ/ is restricted to the coastal plain of South Carolina and Georgia. **1965–70** *DARE* (Qu. P24, . . *Kinds of turtles*) 29 Infs, **S Atl & Gulf States, but esp SC,** Cooter; 10 Infs, **Sth, but esp SC,** Yellow-belly cooter; **SC26,** Yellow-breast cooter; **SC43,** Yellow cooter; **SC7,** Terrapin cooter; **SC45,** Water cooter. **1966** *DARE* Tape SC16, Cooter, we eased off that, man . . . [FW:] What did you eat them with? [Inf:] Rice, rice and bread. — Them good eatin'. And there in that time, there ain' no' much o' sickness been here. **1971** *Today Show Letters* **MS,** Cooter. Turtle: very much in use in Mississippi. **1972** Ernst–Barbour *Turtles* 161, *Chrysemys Floridana* . . Cooter . . There are three subspecies. *C.f. floridana* . . the Florida cooter . . . *C.f. peninsularis* . . the peninsula cooter. *Ibid* 155, *Chrysemys Concinna* . . River Cooter . . Five subspecies are recognized. *C.c. concinna* . . the river cooter . . . *C.c. suwanniensis* . . the Suwanee cooter. *C.c. mobiliensis* . . the Mobile cooter [etc].

2 A box turtle.

1889 *Century Dict.* **Sth,** Cooter . . . The common box-turtle, *Cistudo carolina.* **1950** *PADS* 14.22 **sSC,** Cooter ['kutə, 'kʊtə]: . . The box tortoise; the fresh-water turtle. **1976** Flexner *America Talking* 32, *Cooter* (from a West African word *kuta* or the Kongo *nkuda*) a box turtle, 1832. The word came into our Southern dialect through Gullah and is mainly heard in Georgia and Alabama.

3 =**gopher tortoise.**

1967–68 *DARE* (Qu. P29, *Do you have "gophers" around here? If so, what other name do they have?*) Infs **GA28, SC63,** Highland cooter; (QR, near Qu. V1) Inf **GA44,** A gopher is called a "cooter."

4 in phr *drunk as a cooter:* Very drunk. Cf **Cooter Brown, drunk as**

1827 *Mass. Spy* 22 Aug *(DAE),* A few jolly topers, who wallowed in the sand, 'as drunk as a cooter.' **1908** *DN* 3.307 **eAL, wGA,** Drunk as a *coot(er)* . . . Very drunk.

5 A lazy, indolent person. Cf **cooter** v **1**

1868 in 1945 Easterby *SC Rice Plantation* 242, I am not surprised, because he is a "coota" generally and loves inaction for its own sake.

6 A louse. [Prob var of **cootie** n[1] **1**] joc

1968 *DARE* (Qu. R25, *Joking names for a head louse, or body louse*) Infs **LA18, VA15,** Cooter.

7 A small child.

1967 *DARE* (Z12, *Nicknames and joking words meaning "a small child": "He's a healthy little _____."*) Inf **SC34,** Cooter.

cooter v Also sp *cuter* [Prob Scots, nEngl dial: see *SND cuiter, coot(h)er* "To nurse . . ; to pamper . . ; nurse oneself" and *queeter* "to work lazily . . , waste time . . . Appar. a . . variant of *cuiter*." See also *EDD couther, cutter*. Perh also infl by **cooter** n **1** through similarity of form and assoc with the indolent habit of the turtle] Cf **cooster** v

1 often with *around:* To loiter or move about aimlessly; to putter about. **chiefly sAppalachians** Cf **cooster** v **2**

1926 Kephart *Highlanders* 277 **sAppalachians,** Yes, I'm jest cooterin' around. **1933** Williamson *Woods Colt* 128 **Ozarks,** "What was you a-doin' up to that Chinkapin Point church-house, anyway?" . . . "Oh, I was jest a-cooterin' aroun' up there." **1944** *PADS* 2.41 **wNC,** Cooter ['kutə, -ɚ] . . . To travel about aimlessly. **1966–69** *DARE* (Qu. A10, *[What do you call] doing little unimportant things*) Infs **KY20, NC34,** Cootering around. **1968** *Asheville Citizen* (NC) 10 Mar, These news-spreaders and news-gatherers had a way of trying to cover up their mission by saying they were "jes' cooterin' around." **1972** Cooper *NC Mt. Folkl.* 90, *Cooter around*—to walk aimlessly or idly.

2 See quot.

1933 *AmSp* 8.1.48 **Ozarks,** Cuter . . . To debate fruitlessly. A man once said to me [=Vance Randolph]: *Wal, it aint no use for us t' stand hyar a-cuterin' 'bout that money, 'cause I aint a-goin' t' pay nohow!*

3 To spoil or pamper (a child). Cf **cooster** v **1**

1966 *DARE* (Qu. Z14a, *To give a child its own way, or to pay too much attention to it: "Everyone _____ that child."*) Inf **AL4,** Cooter ['kutər].

cooter-backed adj

1950 *PADS* 14.22 **SC,** *Cooter-backed* . . . Highly arched, as the back of a cooter. Applied especially to dirt roads which are so constructed as to shed the rainfall and thus to prevent water from standing in the driveway and puddling the road.

Cooter Brown, drunk as adj phr Also *drunk as Cooter,* ~ *Cooty Brown* **chiefly Sth**
Very intoxicated.

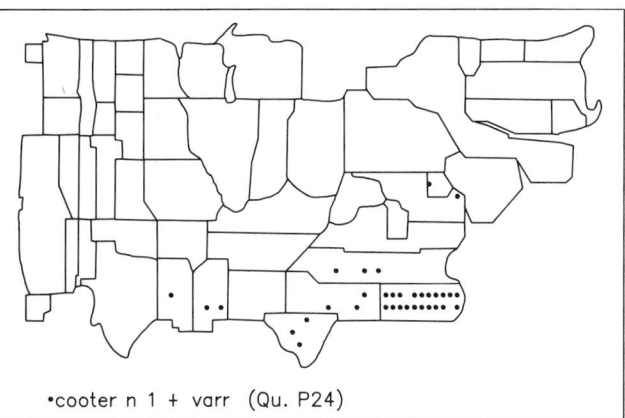

•cooter n 1 + varr (Qu. P24)

1967–70 *DARE* (Qu. DD15, *A person who is thoroughly drunk*) Infs **GA**77, **SC**40, Drunk as Cooter; **AL**8, **TX**100, Drunk as Cooter Brown. **1978** *DARE* File, *Drunk as Cooty Brown.* This is a Black expression very familiar to the informant, who is from New Jersey. She says it is current and, so far as she knows, it "came up with the Blacks from the Carolinas." She thinks it probably derives from some proverbial drunkard.

cooter grass n

1 =**water shield 1.**

1916 *Torreya* 16.237 **eSC**, *Cabomba caroliniana* . . . Cooter grass. **1950** *PADS* 14.22 **SC**, *Cooter grass* . . . The water-shield, a plant kin to the water-lily, growing in ponds and sluggish streams.

2 A **purslane** (here: *Portulaca oleracea*).

1950 *PADS* 14.22 **SC**, *Cooter grass* . . . Portulaca or purslane, gathered by children as food for small captive tortoises, the succulent stems and leaves being considered choice for that purpose.

cooter-hash v

1968 *DARE* (Qu. V1, *When you suspect somebody is trying to deceive you, or that something is going on behind your back*) Inf **GA**44, [Somebody is] trying to cooter-hash me; a gopher [tortoise] is called a "cooter."

cooter liver, eat v phr

To tell a secret.

1967 *DARE* (Qu. JJ43, *To give away a secret or tell a piece of news too soon: "He wasn't supposed to know. Somebody must have _____."*) Inf **SC**40, Been eating cooter liver; (Qu. JJ44, *Expressions about someone who can be trusted to keep a secret: "Don't worry about him, he'll _____."*) Inf **SC**40, Doesn't eat cooter liver.

cooter log n Cf **cooter** v **1**

1950 *PADS* 14.22 **eSC**, *Cooter log* . . . Any log or bench used as a seat for chronic idlers and loafers. The *cooter* is well known for crawling out of the water on a log and lying by the hour without moving.

cooter up v phr [Perh var of **coot up**]

To stir up.

1969 *DARE* FW Addit **AL**, *Cooter up the fire* ['kudər] means to stir up, warm up; and down south where I come from we also talk about *cooterin' up* the girls.

cooter wampee n Cf **wampee**

1 A **pickerelweed 1** (here: *Pontederia cordata*).

1896 in **1913** *Torreya* 13.229 **SC**, *Pontederia cordata* . . . Santee Club, S.C. Called cooter wampee because cooters or fresh-water terrapins eat the leaves.

2 =**arrow arum.**

1896 in **1913** *Torreya* 13.229, Cooter wampee . . . Gerard also notes the use of this name in South Carolina and states that it is . . applied to . . . *Pontederia* and *Peltandra*.

3 A **jack-in-the-pulpit 1** (here: *Arisaema triphyllum*).

1896 in **1913** *Torreya* 13.229, Cooter wampee . . . Gerard also notes the use of this name in South Carolina and states that it is sometimes applied to *Arisaema triphyllum*.

cootie n¹ [?Malay *kutu* a biting insect]

1 also *coot (louse):* A body louse.

1918 Depew *Gunner Depew* 46, Of course you know what the word "cooties" means . . . When you get in or near the trenches, you take a course in the natural history of bugs, lice, rats and every kind of pest that has ever been invented. **1926** Essig *Insects N. Amer.* 193 **West**, The *body louse, grayback* or *cootie, Pediculus corporis* . . is grayish in color. **1954** Borror–DeLong *Intro. Insects* 190, The body louse (also called "cootie" or "seam squirrel") is an important vector of human disease. **1965–70** *DARE* (Qu. R25, *Joking names . . for a head louse or body louse*) 378 Infs, **scattered**, Cootie; **AZ**10, **FL**6, Coot; **AZ**2, Coot lice.

2 The bedbug (*Cimex lectularius*).

1965–70 *DARE* (Qu. R24, *Joking names . . for a bedbug*) 9 Infs, **scattered**, Cootie.

3 A table game similar to hangman.

1968–70 *DARE* (Qu. EE39, *Other games played on paper by two people*) Infs **CA**126, **IN**68, **PA**167, **WI**47, Cootie; **OH**98, Cootie—similar to hangman—you draw a "cootie" (i.e. a louse); **PA**130, Cootie—roll dice and add features and limbs to animal being drawn.

4 in phr *drunk as a cootie:* Very drunk. [Cf **cooter** n **4; Cooter Brown, drunk as**]

1969 *DARE* (Qu. DD15, *A person who is thoroughly drunk*) Inf **GA**82, Drunk as a cootie.

cootie n² [*coot* + *-ie* dimin suff]

=**ruddy duck.**

1956 *AmSp* 30.184, Cootie—Ruddy duck—Mich.

cootie cage n [**cootie** n¹ **1**] *joc*

A bed or bunk, esp one in crowded quarters.

1930 Irwin *Amer. Tramp* 55, *Cootie cage.*—A berth in a carnival or circus sleeping car. A bunk in a construction camp or logging camp. The term was used before the World War had made the word "cootie" so familiar. **1968** Adams *Western Words, Cootie cage*—What the logger called a bunk or berth in camp quarters.

cootie garage n [**cootie** n¹ **1**] *joc*

Human hair (esp in a particular puffy hairstyle) where lice might live.

1922 Lewis *Babbitt* 342, Hey, leggo, quit crushing me cootie-garage. **1953** *New Yorker* 3 Jan 15/1 **RI** (as of 1920), A hairdress of those unlovely puffs we used to call "cootie garages." **1966–68** *DARE* (QR, near Qu. R25) Inf **OK**23, Cootie garage: a moustache was sometimes called this; **CA**40, Cootie garage—a very ratted [hair] style; (Qu. X1a, . . *False hair, used by men*) Inf **AK**1, Cootie garage (American Expeditionary Force word after World War I). **1975** Gould *ME Lingo* 107, In the early 1920s the ladies and girls affected a new hair-do which was inelegantly dubbed the "cootie garage." Puffs of hair over each ear suggested a stabling place for the troublesome cooties (lice) of the trenches in World War I.

coot louse See **cootie** n¹ **1**

cootuh See **cooter** n

coot up v phr

1917 *DN* 4.410 **sAppalachians**, *Coot up* . . . To revive. "After the rope broke they cooted him up and hung him sure enough next time."

cooty See **coot** n¹ **1**

Cooty Brown, drunk as See **Cooter Brown, drunk as**

coo-way See **co-ee**

coo-wench See **co-wench**

coozie, coozy See **cozy**

cop n [*cop* top, summit]

1967 *DARE* (Qu. X28, . . *A person's head*) Infs **MA**2, **MO**14, Cop.

cop v [*cop* to take, seize; cf **cob** v⁴] *among Black speakers*

1 To understand.

1958 Hughes–Bontemps *Negro Folkl.* 482, *Cop:* To take, receive, understand. **1970** *DARE* (Qu. NN5, *Other ways of saying 'do you understand?': "You take hold of it this way, _____?"*) Inf **FL**52, Cop. [Inf Black]

2 in var phrr: See quots.

1958 Hughes–Bontemps *Negro Folkl.* 482, *Cop a deuceways:* To buy two dollars worth of something. "Let's cop a deuceways of barbecue." *Cop a nod:* Take a quick nap. "Between acts he cops a nod." *Cop a slave:* To go to work. "It's time to cop a slave." *Cop a squat:* To take a seat. "Cop a squat and stay awhile." **1970** *DARE* Tape NY242, "I gotta cop a slave" means "I gotta go to work." . . Cop *the* job you happen to be on. [Inf remarked that expressions like this went back thirty to forty years and derived largely from Black musicians.] **1972** Claerbaut *Black Jargon* 61, *Cop a squat* . . to take a seat; sit down.

copacetic adj Also sp *copasetic, copasetty, copesetic, copisettic, kopasetee* [Etym unknown; see quots]

Fine and dandy; hunky-dory.

1919 Bacheller *Man for Ages* 69 **cwIL** (as of 1830s), "As to looks I'd call him, as ye might say, real copasetic." Mrs. Lukins expressed this opinion solemnly . . . Its last word stood for nothing more than an indefinite depth of meaning. **1926** Van Vechten *Nigger Heaven* 286, *Kopasetee:* an approbatory epithet somewhat stronger than *all right.* **1933** Ersine *Underworld and Prison Slang* 29 (*OEDS*), *Copissettic,* all right, okay. **1936** in **1943** *AN&Q* 3.91/1, "Copacetic" is a Harlem and gangster corruption of an Italian word. I don't know how to spell the Italian, but it's something like copasetti. In American it means all right. Bill Robinson, whose favorite word it is, has an expression: "Everything is copasetic, everything is rosy and the goose hangs high." **1948** Hurston *Seraph* 292 **FL**, "Shake your rusty-dusty down there! I'm hungry as hell." "It's on the fire and your name's done called . . ." "Copasetty! I'm rearing to go." **1953** *AmSp* 28.230 **LA** (as of 1880s), *Copesetic* . . was originally spelled *coupersètique* which was derived from Old French *couper, colper*, to strike . . . The term, also spelled *coupesètique, coupe-sètique,* or *copesètique,* was Creole-French . . . It is his belief . . that 'the word was not used outside the Cajun or Bayou region by those not speaking Creole or the Creole-French Patois.' **1965–70** *DARE* (Qu. KK4, *When things turn out just right, you might say, "Everything is _____ now."*) 13 Infs, **scattered,** Copacetic; (Qu. GG23c, *Any other expressions to tell someone to be patient*) Inf **PA**239, Be copacetic [ˌkopəˈsɛtɪk]. **1980** Safire *On Language* 54, Plenty of mail on the origin of "copacetic." *Ibid* 55, One group holds that it was a gangland term . . . a lookout would say "The cop is on the settee," which meant "all clear." In time, the sentence ran together as "copasettee," or "copacetic." . . A more likely explanation . . is the Hebrew term *"hakol b'seder,"* a frequently used phrase meaning "all in order." A slight corruption, *"kol b'tzedek,"* means "all with justice."

cop-cop See **cap-cap**

cope v[1] *old-fash*

    1899 (1912) Green *VA Folk-Speech, Cope* . . . To strive or contend; meet in combat; oppose.

cope v[2] Usu |kop| also |kwop|; less freq |ˈko-əp|; in **Nth,** also |kʌp, kʊp, kup| Pronc-spp *coop(ie), co-up, cup, kope, kup, kwoip, kwope, kworp, quoby, quop(e), quopy, quowa, quup* [From *come up;* cf **co** v] **chiefly Midl, scattered Sth** See Map

Come! — used to call horses and sometimes other farm animals.

    1893 *DN* 1.264, Another similar call is [ko-əp], seldom, if ever, modified to [kop] for cows. *Ibid* 266, **VA,** [kop] is also reported as in use for hogs. *Ibid* **KS,** The only long call I have heard for horses is [kop], undoubtedly a contraction of [ko-əp]. **1899** (1912) Green *VA Folk-Speech, Coop.* Word used for calling a horse. Contraction for "come up." *Cope.* **1915** *DN* 4.188 **swVA,** *Quop* . . . Call to a horse. Also *quopy, quoby, quowa.* **1949** Kurath *Word Geog.* 23, *Coop!* . . a call to chickens (on lower Narragansett Bay and eastern Long Island). **1949** *PADS* 11.4, **wTX,** *Cope.* **1954** *Harder Coll.* **cwTN,** *Cope:* Call to get the mules from pasture: "Cope, cope, co-up, and then whistle." Common. **1960** Williams *Walk Egypt* 151 **GA,** Nearer a woman called a cow, "Coop! Cush, cush!" **c1960** *Wilson Coll.* **csKY,** *Quope* (or *quup*) To call horses. **1965–70** *DARE* (Qu. K82, *The call used . . to get horses in from the pasture*) 72 Infs, **chiefly Midl, scattered Sth,** Cope [gop]; **IN**8, Cope [gop]; 31 Infs, **chiefly Midl,** Kwope; **IN**49, [kwok]; **MO**8, Kworp kwoip [kworp kwoɪp kwoɪ·p]; **PA**71, Coop boy [kup bɔɪ]; **MN**7, 12, Cup [kʌp]; **MN**16, Cup [kʊp]; (Qu. K83, *To call a calf . . at feeding time*) Inf **NC**49, Cope; (Qu. K84, *The call . . to get the pigs in*) Infs **GA**1, 5, Kwope; **GA**77, Coopie. [Of all Infs responding to Qu. K82, 74% were old; of those giving these responses, 84% were old.] **c1970** *DARE* FW Addit **VA**15, *Cupcollee* [ˈkʌːp koˌli] — a call used to get mules in from the pasture. Old-fashioned. **1971** Wood *Vocab. Change* 46 **Gulf States,** If he wishes to use a customary word [in calling horses from pasture], he calls *kope.* **1973** Allen *LAUM* 1.262, Three probably related calls [to horses] are *kope, kwope,* and *kup* /kup/. The first two are surely Midland, for they occur only in Iowa . . and Nebraska . . . *Kup,* however, may be Northern, since 3 of the 4 instances are in Northern speech territory in Minnesota and Iowa, and it was found 4 times in Wisconsin (but *kope* and *kwope* not at all).

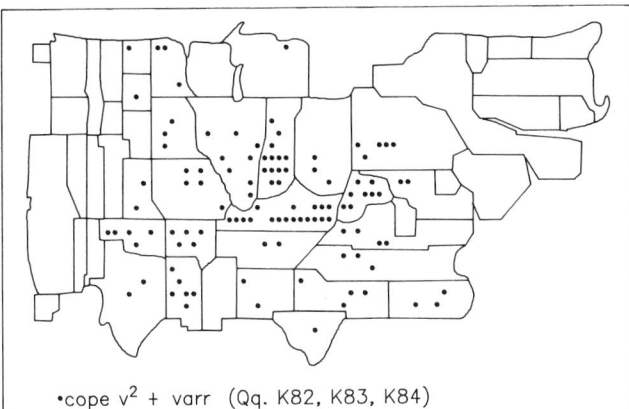

•cope v[2] + varr (Qq. K82, K83, K84)

cope v[3] See **keep**

cope bet See **coat bet**

copee-pee-pee v

    1899 (1912) Green *VA Folk-Speech, Copee-pee-pee.* A call used for turkeys.

Copenhagen n [From *Copenhagen* the capital of Denmark] **prob NEng** *old-fash*

A children's kissing game: see quot 1899.

    1873 Bailey *Life in Danbury* 77 **CT,** The only people saved are those who drink lemonade out of a dipper and play copenhagen with their aunts. **1899** Champlin *Young Folks' Games* 205, *Copenhagen,* a game played by any number of persons, who stand in a circle holding a rope whose ends are tied together. One of the players stands in the middle of the ring, and tries to slap the hands that hold the rope, using only one of his hands at a time . . . If any one's hand is slapped or he lets the rope go altogether, he must take the place of the one in the ring. As the game is often played, a girl tries to slap only boys' hands and a boy only girls' . . and when a hand is slapped the players kiss as they change places. **1907** *DN* 3.184 **seNH.** **1908** Lincoln *Cy Whittaker* 175 **MA,** The children played "Post Office" and "Copenhagen" and "Clap in, Clap out," while the grown folks looked on.

coperas See **copperas**

coperosity See **corporosity**

copesetic, copisettic See **copacetic**

‡**cop-out, on the** adv

Slightly unwell, under the weather.

    1970 *DARE* (Qu. BB39, *On a day when you don't feel just right, though not actually sick, you might say, "I'll be all right tomorrow — I'm just feeling _____ today."*) Inf **TX**92, On the cop-out.

copper n

1 also *copper cent, ~ coin, ~ penny:* A penny; hence, something of little value. *old-fash*

    1767 (1849) Smith *Jrls.* 276, We had smelts to-day, two coppers a dozen. **1815** Humphreys *Yankey in England* 104, *Copper,* formerly current money of the value of a halfpenny in England. **1890** *DN* 1.73 **NEng,** *Copper:* a cent . . . Seems to be going out of use. **1905** *DN* 3.6 **cCT,** *Copper* . . . A copper cent. **1909** *DN* 3.394 **nwAR.** **1940** (1944) Kahn *Cable Car* 70 **San Francisco CA,** A well-known lady living on Nob Hill . . boarded a California Street cable car and produced five coppers in payment of her fare. **1946** in 1954 *Harder Coll.* **cwTN** (Letter), He's not got any fence that is worth a copper. **1950** *WELS (Nicknames for: $.01)* 33 Infs, **WI,** Copper. **c1960** *Wilson Coll.* **csKY,** Copper (or *copper cent*) . . . Now a humorous name for a one-cent piece. Younger people have grown up using penny almost exclusively. **1965–70** *DARE* (Qu. U21, *Other words for "one cent"*) 205 Infs, **widespread,** Copper; **IL**117, **MO**39, **TX**51, 89, Copper cent; **NJ**9, **NY**24, Copper penny; **GA**77, Copper coin; (Qu. HH22c, *Talking about a very mean person, you might say, "He's mean enough to _____."*) Infs **GA**84, **ME**16, **NY**24, Get (or steal, take) the coppers out of a dead man's eye(s).

2 See **copperskin.**

3 A whiskey still or its copper parts.

    1917 *DN* 4.410 **wNC,** *Cut up copper* . . . To destroy a still. "Last winter there come a revenue in here and cut up a lot of copper on Jones' Creek." **1949** *AmSp* 24.9 **S Midl,** *Copper* . . . The still pot . . . The condenser . . . All copper parts of the moonshiner's equipment. "Pull out the copper and leave the rest be." **1968** *DARE* (Qu. DD28b, *What fermented drinks are made at home around here?*) Inf **GA**30, Copper-run liquor.

4 By ext: see quot.

    1970 *DARE* (Qu. DD21c, *. . Whiskey, especially illegally made whiskey*) Inf **TX**86, Copper — from the copper tubes used in the distilling process.

copperas n attrib Also sp *coperas, coppers, coppras* **chiefly Sth, S Midl** *old-fash*

Of trousers: dyed with copperas.

    1840 *Spirit of Times* 7 March 8/2 *(DA),* Copperas trowsers; Copperas breeches. **1851** Burke *Polly Peablossom* 29 **GA,** The first step upon arriving in the city was to lay aside their "copperas-coloureds," fabrics of the wife or daughter's loom, and purchase a new suit of "store-clothes." **1898** Lloyd *Country Life* 25 **AL,** By this time some of the folks at home had fixed me up with a pair of new 'coperas' breeches for Sunday. [**1900** Harris *On the Wing* 65 **GA,** He wore brogans of undressed leather, his copperas-colored breeches short enough to show his woollen socks.] **1908** *DN* 3.301 **eAL, wGA,** Copp(e)ras britches . . . Home-made trousers of coarse domestic dyed with copperas. **1954** *Harder Coll.* **cwTN,** *Coppers' britches*—brown clothing. (Old-fashioned).

copper-back snake n Cf **copper-belly 2**

Perh the red-bellied **water snake** *(Natrix erythrogaster).*

1967 *DARE* (Qu. P25, . . *Kinds of snakes . . around here*) Inf **NY10,** Copper-back snake.

copper-belly n

1 also *copper-bellied snake:* =**copperhead snake 1.**

1705 Beverley *Hist. VA* 4.64, The black Viper-Snake, and the Copper-bellied Snake, are said to be as venemous [sic] as the Rattle-Snake. **1788** Schöpf *Reise Staaten* 1.485, Ich habe mich überall nach der Klapperschlange und dem Kupferbauch (Copper belly, auch Moccoson-Snake genannt,) . . erkundiget. [I gathered information everywhere about the rattlesnake and the copperbelly (Copper belly, also called Moccasin snake).] **1842** DeKay *Zool. NY* 3.54, The Copper-head . . has various popular names in different districts; the most common of these are, in this State, *Copper-head, Red Adder,* and *Dumb Rattle-head.* In other districts, it is called *Copper-belly, Red Viper, Deaf Adder,* and *Chunk-head.* **1872** Schele de Vere *Americanisms* 387, [The Copperhead *(Trigonocephalus contortrix)*] is known as Copperbelly and Chunkhead.

2 also *copper-belly* (or *bellied) moccasin, copper-belly snake, copper-bottom, coppy-belly moccasin:* The red-bellied water snake *(Natrix erythrogaster erythrogaster).*

1736 (1754) Catesby *Nat. Hist. Carolina* 2.46, *Anguis ventre cuprei coloris, The Copper-belly Snake . . .* They are of a brown Colour, except their Bellies, which are of a muddy Red or Copper Colour. **1872** Schele de Vere *Americanisms* 387, The true *Copperbelly* (Nerodia erythrogaster [sic]) is perfectly harmless and of aquatic habits. **1909** Biol. Soc. DC *Proc.* 22.135, These Copperbellies, as they are called in North Carolina, are uniform rusty red above, and yellowish red below. **1952** Ditmars *N. Amer. Snakes* 112, Red-bellied Water Snake, Copper-bellied "Mocca-sin," *Natrix erythrogaster erythrogaster.* **1957** Wright *Hdbk. Snakes* 1.480, Does the recent school know from sufficient live firsthand experience with each region that the Mississippi Valley yellow belly is the same as the Atlantic coastal copper belly? **1958** Conant *Reptiles & Amphibians* 115, Copperbelly. **1965–68** *DARE* (Qu. P25, . . *Snakes . . found around here*) Infs **FL35, GA16, NC49, SC40, 57,** Copper-belly mocca-sin; **GA1, MI32, MS60,** Copper-belly; **MI20,** Copper-bellies (or "cop-per-bottoms"): the biggest ones get to be eight inches; **MS47,** Coppy-belly moccasin. **1974** Shaw–Campbell *Snakes West* 130, Over much of its range the plain-bellied water snake *(Natrix erythrogaster)* is called "copperbelly," because its faintly spotted belly is often a dull, reddish color.

3 =**ringneck snake.**

1969 *DARE* (Qu. P25, . . *Snakes . . found around here*) Inf **GA72,** Copper-belly: small, copper ring about the neck.

copper-belly moccasin, copper-belly snake See **copper-belly 2**

copperbill See **coppernose 1**

copper blister n

A piece of peacock ore.

1967 *DARE* (Qu. C26, *What special kinds of stone or rock are there in this part of the state?*) Inf **NV1,** Copper blister—(peacock), copper with heat bubbles.

copper-bottom See **copper-belly 2**

copper cent See **copper 1**

copper chip See **copperhead** n[1] **4**

copper coin See **copper 1**

copper-face bream See **coppernose 2**

copperhead n[1]

1 See **copperhead snake 1.**

2 A goldeneye (here: *Glaucionetta clangula).*

1917 (1923) *Birds Amer.* 1.138, Golden-Eye—*Clangula clangula americana* . . Other Names . . Copperhead. **1918** Grinnell *Game Birds CA* 167, American Golden-eye—*Clangula clangula americana* . . Other names . . Copperhead (female only). **1923** U.S. Dept. Ag. *Misc. Circular* 13.22, Golden-eye *(Glaucionetta clangula) . . . In local use . . .* copperhead (for female and young) (Oreg., Calif.). **1946** Hausman *Eastern Birds* 157, American Goldeneye *Glaucionetta clangula americana* . . Other Names . . Copperhead.

3 =**yellow-headed blackbird.**

1911 *Century Dict.,* Copperhead . . . The yellow-headed blackbird, *Xanthocephalus xanthocephalus,* of the western United States: so called from the reddish-yellow color of its head. **1917** (1923) *Birds Amer.* 2.246, Yellow-headed Blackbird—*Xanthocephalus xanthocephalus* . . Other Name.—Copperhead. **1946** Hausman *Eastern Birds* 551.

4 also *copper chip:* A **ground squirrel** (here: *Citellus lateralis).*

1934 *W2,* Copperhead . . . A ground squirrel *(Callospermophilus lateralis)* of the western United States, having a yellowish head and shoulders and conspicuously striped body. **1943** Gordon *W. Chipmunk* 8, The mantled ground squirrels are now placed in the genus *Citellus,* and most of them in the species *lateralis* . . . These animals have been given many common names in addition to the ponderous book name of mantled ground squirrel . . . Among these common names are big chipmunk, golden chipmunk, copperhead, copper chip, yellow head, callico [sic] chip, Callo, bummer, rock squirrel, and tiger squirrel.

5 also *copperhead bream:* =**bluegill 1.**

1935 Caine *Game Fish* 11, Bluegill—*Lepomis pallidus* . . . Copper-head Bream. **1961** *W3,* Copperhead . . or *copperhead bream:* bluegill. **1968** *DARE* Tape **GA20,** We get what we call a copperhead brim—most people call it a bluegill.

copperhead n[2] [Perh blend of **copper** n **1** + *Indian head*]

1968 *DARE* (Qu. U21, *Other words for "one cent"*) Inf **PA66,** Copper-head.

copperhead bream See **copperhead** n[1] **5**

copperhead snake n Also *copper snake*

1 also *copperhead, copperhead(ed) moccasin, copperhead pilot:* A venomous snake *(Agkistrodon contortrix).* **chiefly Sth, Midl** See Map Also called **chunkhead, copper-belly 1, coppermouth, deaf adder, dumb rattlesnake, highland moccasin, pilot snake, poplar leaf, rattlesnake pilot, red adder, red viper, thunder snake**

1764 in 1925 Fries *Rec. Moravians* 2.580 **NC,** *Copper Snake* is not so brown as the Rattlesnake, and I have not seen large ones. **1765** Timberlake *Memoirs* 46, The copper-snake, whose bite is very difficult to cure. **1775** (1934) Fithian *Jrl.* 2.54 **PA,** The Snake that wounded her they call a *"Copper-Head."* **1842** [see **copper-belly 1**]. **1872** Schele de Vere *Americanisms* 387, The rival of this formidable snake [=rattlesnake] is the *Copperhead (Trigonocephalus contortrix),* which rejoices in nearly a dozen names, having apparently a different one in every part of the country. **1905** *DN* 3.6 **cCT,** Copperhead . . . A kind of snake. **1907** *DN* 3.210 **nwAR, cCT,** Copperhead. **1913** Porter *Laddie* 288 **OH,** Through the rough puncheon floor a copperhead stuck up its gleam of bronzy gold, and shot its darting tongue within a foot of her bare leg. **1931** (1946) Ditmars *Snakes* 97, Two species of moccasins must be considered—the Water Moccasin and the Copperhead Snake (highland moccasin, pilot snake, or chunk-head), which are members of the same family as the rattlers. **1949** *Scientific Mth.* 68.55/1, Thus, the belief goes, whenever one sees a copperhead, a rattlesnake may appear on its trail. **c1960** *Wilson Coll.* **csKY,** Copperhead . . . One of the two poison-ous snakes in the area, fairly common as such snakes go; the other one is the rattlesnake. In spite of the wild stories told of the number of such snakes in the region, 28 seasons of walking and camping in the park have brought into my experience only 6 poisonous snakes, 2 of them copper-heads. **1963** Snedigar *Small Native Animals* 192, Although . . capable of inflicting a severe and potent bite, the copperhead . . is shy and retiring. **1965–70** *DARE* (Qu. P25, . . *Kinds of snakes . . around here*) 337 Infs, **chiefly Sth, Midl,** Copperhead; 7 Infs, **Sth,** Copperhead moc-

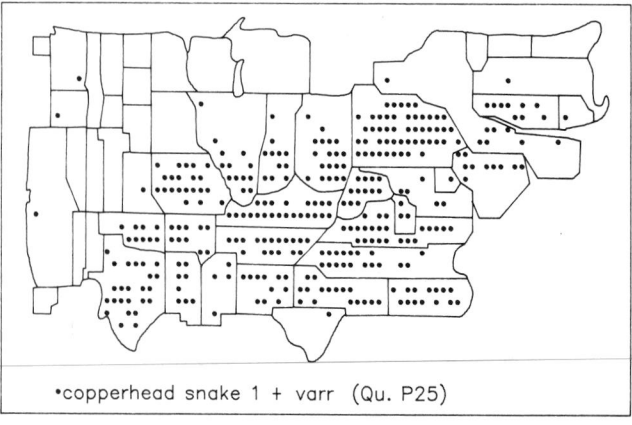

•copperhead snake 1 + varr (Qu. P25)

casin; **NJ**1, 8, **NC**41, Copperhead pilot; **MD**15, 22, Copper snake; **LA**40, Copperheaded moccasin.

2 =fox snake. chiefly **WI, MI**

1949 Dickinson *Lizards & Snakes WI* 7, The rufous head of the fox snake has given many people the impression that it is the copperhead. *Ibid* 36, Occasionally it [=the fox snake] is referred to as "copperhead". **1950** *WELS (Kinds of snakes found in your neighborhood)* 4 Infs, **WI,** Copper snake; 2 Infs, Copperhead. **1958** Conant *Reptiles & Amphibians* 157, *Fox Snake Elaphe vulpina . . .* A serpent with many aliases . . . The reddish head frequently causes it to be killed as a "copperhead." **1965–70** *DARE* (Qu. P25, . . *Kinds of snakes . . around here*) Infs **MI**67, **WI**6, 22, 38, 50, 78, Copperhead; **MI**76, Fox snake—also called wood snake and copperhead, but it's not a true copperhead.

3 =red-bellied snake *(Storeria occipitomaculata).*

1949 Dickinson *Lizards & Snakes WI* 7, I have also heard the little red-bellied snake called copperhead. *Ibid* 52, Due to the red underside, this species *[Storeria occipitomaculata]* is sometimes called "copperhead" though it is harmless. **1966–69** *DARE* (Qu. P25, . . *Kinds of snakes . . around here*) Inf **MI**2, Copper snake or copper-belly; **MI**27, Copper snake, small—6″–12″ long; **MI**44, Copper snake; **MI**47, Copper snake, 6″ or 7″ long, black on back, copper-colored on the belly—streaks on 'im; **VT**12, Copper snake, harmless, not copperhead, about a foot long. [Note: some Infs may instead refer to **copper-belly 2.**] **1974** Shaw–Campbell *Snakes West* 132, The red-bellied snake *(Storeria occipitomaculata)* is also called . . *copper snake.*

copperleaf n

=**three-seeded mercury.**

1948 Stevens *KS Wild Flowers* 104, *Acalypha*—Copperleaf. *Ibid, Acalypha virginica*—Virginia Copperleaf. *Ibid, Acalypha gracilens*—Slender Copperleaf. *Ibid, Acalypha ostryaefolia*—Hop-hornbeam Copperleaf. **1948** (1965) Neal *Gardens HI* 508, *Copper leaf. . .* Acalypha wilkesiana. **1953** Greene–Blomquist *Flowers South* 163, Copperleaf . . *(Acalypha Wilkesiana).*

copper lily n [From the color]

A small bulbous plant *(Habranthus texanus)* native to Louisiana and Texas, which has orange-yellow flowers sometimes tinged with red. Also called **atamasco (lily) 2, rain lily 3, stagger grass 2**

1951 *PADS* 15.29 **TX,** *Atamasco texana* Herbert.—Copper-lily; stagger-grass; yellow rain-lily. **1970** Correll *Plants TX* 418, *Copper Lily . . .* In water among grasses, swales, moist pasturelands and other such places. **1972** Brown *Wildflowers LA* 24, *Copper-lily . . .* Very abundant on lawns of several residences in Natchitoches.

coppermouth n [Prob a blend of **copperhead** and **cottonmouth**]

=**copperhead snake 1.**

1966 *DARE* (Qu. P25, . . *Kinds of snakes . . around here*) Inf **OK**23, Coppermouth, same as copperhead.

copper nickel n Cf **wooden nickel**

A nonexistent coin which would be of no value if it existed.

1969 *DARE* (Qu. HH20c, *Of an idle, worthless person you might say, "He isn't worth _____."*) Inf **NY**206, [A] copper nickel.

coppernose n

1 also *copperbill:* A scoter (here: *Oidemia americana*).

1888 Trumbull *Names of Birds* 107, *Oidemia americana—American scoter . .* formerly believed identical with very similar European species *(Oidemia nigra) . . .* In Massachusetts . . at North Plymouth, Fairhaven, and New Bedford, Copper-nose and Copper-bill. **1925** (1928) Forbush *Birds MA* 1.271, *Oidémia americana . .* Scoter.—*Other names: . .* copperbill; copper-nose.

2 also *copper-face bream, copper-nosed bream, copper-nose(d) sunfish:* =**bluegill 1.**

1882 U.S. Natl. Museum *Bulletin* 16.479, *Blue Sunfish; Copper-nosed Bream; Dollardee.* **1889** *Century Dict.* 1255/3, *Coppernose . . .* The copper-nosed sunfish, *Lepomis pallidus.* **1902** Jordan–Evermann *Amer. Fishes* 349, The bluegill . . is known also as . . copper-nosed sunfish. **1935** Caine *Game Fish* 11, *Bluegill . . . Synonyms: . .* Copper-face Bream. **1946** LaMonte *N. Amer. Game Fishes* 138, *Bluegill Sunfish . . .* Names: . . Copper-nosed Bream. **1949** Caine *N. Amer. Sport Fish* 38, *Colloquial Names . . .* Coppernose Sunfish. **1975** Evanoff *Catch More Fish* 88, The bluegill *(Lepomis macrochirus)* is . . also called the . . copper-nosed bream.

copper penny See **copper 1**

copper pox n [From the copper-colored skin eruptions of secondary syphilis]

Syphilis.

1931 *Jrl. Amer. Folkl.* 44.395 **FL** [Black], If a woman wishes to give a man syphillis [*sic*], so that he will die of it . . . When she goes to bed with the man she must take two pennies and hold them under her tongue while having intercourse . . . Wrap up . . the pennies in the cloth and place the bundle up over the door and he will have the copper pox (syphillis) which is incurable.

copper rag n

1966 *DARE* (Qu. G14, *The rough metal pad that's used to scour pots and pans*) Inf **GA**10, Copper rag.

coppers See **copperas**

copperskin n, hence *copper-skinned* adj Also abbr *copper*

An American Indian.

1772 in 1916 Mereness *Travels* 523 **FL,** He said there would be Copers and White people present at the meeting. **1840** Hoffman *Greyslaer* 2.26, "Go on, go on, Kit; d'ye say a dozen Injuns?" "Yes, uncle, not a Copperskin less." **1907** Cook *Border & Buffalo* 80 **KS,** Come on, you copper-skinned devils; I'm good for the whole Cheyenne tribe! **1966** *DARE* (Qu. HH28, . . *People of foreign background*) Inf **WA**16, Coppers, copperskins [American Indians].

copper snake See **copperhead snake**

copperweed n

A shrubby plant *(Iva acerosa)* native chiefly to the Southwest.

1960 Vines *Trees SW* 999, The genus name, *Oxytenia,* is from the Greek and refers to the pointed leaves, meaning literally "pointed thread." The species name, *acerosa,* means "needle-shaped," also referring to the leaves. A vernacular name is Copperweed.

coppras See **copperas**

coppy-belly moccasin See **copper-belly 2**

coppy woods n [*coppy,* Engl dial var of *coppice,* taken as adj]

1890 *AN&Q* 5.115/1 **sePA,** Dialect Forms . . . Among other expressions . . are . . "Coppy woods," for a small grove.

copsal See **copsil**

cops and thieves n [Var of *cops and robbers*]

A children's game.

1903 *Independent* (US) 15 Jan 146/1 *(OEDS),* When I was a youngster one of my favorite games was what we children called 'Cops and Thieves.' **1970** *DARE* (Qu. EE12, *Games in which one captain hides his team and the other team tries to find it*) Inf **DC**12, Cops and thieves.

copse n

1965–70 *DARE* (Qu. T1, . . *A bunch of trees growing together in open country, especially on a hill*) 16 Infs, **scattered, but chiefly Nth, N Midl,** Copse; (Qu. T2a, . . *A piece of land covered with trees—if it's only a few acres*) Inf **WA**11, Copse.

copsil n Also sp *copsal* [Alter of *copsole*] arch

1899 (1912) Green *VA Folk-Speech,* Copsil . . . A cuff at the end of a plough beam to which the singletree is fastened. *Copsal.*

coquina n, also attrib [Span "cockle, soft shelly stone"]

A soft calcareous rock composed of accreted shells and corals used for construction in the southern US, esp Florida.

1837 (1962) Williams *Territory FL* 44, The quarries of Coquina stone are extensive. **1883** Shields *Hunting* 178, The old Spanish residences are built of coquina, a species of shell-rock. **1911** *Century Dict., Coquina . . .* The name is chiefly applied to a rock of this kind occurring on the east coast of Florida, and used to some extent as a building material. **1932** Lovell *Golden Isles* 11, The material used for these buildings was coquina. **1942** Amer. Philos. Soc. *Trans.* 33.58/1 **SC,** Beds of fossiliferous rocks (coquina) . . may be seen near high-tide mark at Hurl Rock Beach. **1966–70** *DARE* (Qu. C26, . . *Special kinds of stone or rock*) Inf **FL**1, Coquina rock; (Qu. N27a, . . *Different kinds of unpaved roads*) Inf **FL**51, Coquina road.

cor- See **ker-**

coral See **corral**

coral-and-pearl n

=**red baneberry.**

1900 Lyons *Plant Names* 14, *A[ctæa] rubra . . .* Coral-and-pearl.

coral bead n Also *coral seed* [From the color of the drupe]
A **moonseed** (here: *Cocculus carolinus*).

1903 Small *Flora SE U.S.* 454, *Cébatha* . . Coral-bead. **1942** Tehon
Fieldbook IL Shrubs 77, *Cocculus carolinus* . . . Carolina Moonseed.
Coral Bead. **1960** Vines *Trees SW* 275, *Carolina Snailseed-vine—Cocculus carolinus* . . . Vernacular names are Coral-bead, Coral-seed, Coral-vine . . Carolina Moonseed. **1973** Stephens *Woody Plants* 176, *Cocculus carolinus*—Snailseed, coral berry, coral bead.

coral bean n

1 =**coral tree.**

1931 U.S. Dept. Ag. *Misc. Pub.* 101.86, *Western coralbean* . . is the only
species of the large tropical-subtropical coraltree . . occurring in the
West. **1938** Van Dersal *Native Woody Plants* 124, *Erythrina flabelliformis* . . . Coralbean. **1960** Vines *Trees SW* 558/2, Western Coral
Bean—*Erythrina flabelliformis. Ibid* 559/1, Eastern Coral Bean—
Erythrina herbacea. **1970** Correll *Plants TX* 880, *Erythrina* L.—Coral
Bean. Colorín. **1972** Brown *Wildflowers LA* 79, Coral Bean—*Erythrina herbacea* L.—Legume family . . . It is widely distributed in
Louisiana from the beach at Cameron Parish to the northern portion of
the state . . . Also Texas, Arkansas, and Mississippi. **1975** Duncan–
Foote *Wildflowers SE* 84, Cardinal-spear; Coral Bean—*Erythrina herbacea.*

2 A sp of *Sophora*: usu **frijolillo 1,** but also **Eve's necklace.**

1886 Havard *Flora W. & S. TX for 1885* 500, *Sophora secundiflora,*
Lag. (Frijolillo; Coral Bean.) Stout ornamental shrub, with deep green
foliage, common from the Gulf Coast to the Pecos. **1900** Lyons *Plant
Names* 351 **TX,** *Sophora* . . *secundiflora* . . . Coral-bean. **1938** Van
Dersal *Native Woody Plants* 263, *Sophora affinis* . . . Coralbean. **1979**
Little *Checklist U.S. Trees* 276, *Sophora affinis* . . . *Other common
names*—coralbean . . . *Sophora secundiflora* . . . *Other common names*
—coralbean.

coralbells n

=**alumroot 1.**

1942 Hylander *Plant Life* 263, Alum Root *(Heuchera)* . . . One species,
native to New Mexico and Arizona, has bright red flowers; it is often
found in gardens under the name of Coral Bells. **1948** (1965) Neal
Gardens HI 380, Coral Bells. *Heuchera sanguinea.* **1949** Moldenke
Amer. Wild Flowers 55, Showiest [of the alumroots *(Heuchera)*] is the
coralbells, *H. sanguinea,* of New Mexico and Arizona, with bright red
flowers. **1968** *DARE* Tape IN14, I have an unusual flower that everyone likes is the coralbells. They're small, pink flower [sic]. The leaf looks
very much like a geranium.

coralberry n

1 A **snowberry,** esp *Symphoricarpos orbiculatus* which is also
called **buckberry 1, buckbrush 3a, buckbush, devil's shoestrings,
Indian currant, shoestring weed, snapberry, turkey berry, turkey
bush, waxberry, wolfberry.**

1859 (1968) Bartlett *Americanisms,* Coral Berry. *(Symphoricarpus
vulgaris.)* The Indian Currant of Missouri. **1937** U.S. Forest Serv.
Range Plant Hdbk. B151, With one exception, all the United States
species have white or slightly pink berries . . . The single red-fruited
species *(S. orbiculatus)* is dubbed coralberry. **1942** Tehon *Fieldbook IL
Shrubs* 265, *Symphoricarpos* . . . The coralberries are shrubs with opposite, short-petioled leaves, and they bear white or pink flowers in small
terminal or axillary clusters . . . There are about 10 species of coralberries, all of them North American. **1944** Harper *Weeds AL* 131, *S[ymphoricarpos] orbiculatus* . . (Coral-berry.) A medium-sized shrub, presumably native on dry limestone rocks in the Tennessee Valley, and also
common on roadsides in that region, and occasional in the neighboring
regions which are not calcareous. **1948** Stevens *KS Wild Flowers* 357,
Symphoricarpos—Snowberry, Coralberry— . . Berry white (snowberry) or purple-red (coralberry). **1960** Vines *Trees SW* 948/2, It
[*Symphoricarpos orbiculatus*] is also known under the vernacular names
of Coralberry, Snapberry, [etc]. **1967** *WI Conserv. Bulletin* 32.1.21/1
The shrubs include wild plum, . . corralberry [sic], . . and hazel.

2 =**red baneberry.**

1933 Small *Manual SE Flora* 513, *A[ctaea] rubra* . . . Coralberry.
1959 Carleton *Index Herb. Plants* 30.

3 The Carolina **moonseed.**

1951 *PADS* 15.31 **TX,** *Menispermaceæ—Epibaterium carolinum* L.
—Red-berried moonseed; coralberry; coral-vine; margil. **1973** Stephens *Woody Plants* 176, *Cocculus carolinus*—Snailseed, coral berry,
coral bead.

coral evergreen n

A **club moss** (here: *Lycopodium clavatum*).

1892 *Jrl. Amer. Folkl.* 5.105, *Lycopodium clavatum,* coral evergreen.
Stratham, N.H. **1950** Gray–Fernald *Manual of Botany* 14.

coral greenbrier n

Either of two **greenbriers,** *Smilax walteri* or *S. lanceolata.*

1933 Small *Manual SE Flora* 313, *S[milax] Walteri* . . . Coral-greenbrier. **1960** Vines *Trees SW* 71, Redbeard Greenbrier—*Smilax walteri*
. . . The plant is also known under the vernacular names of Red-berry
Bamboo, Coral Greenbrier, and Sarsaparilla. *Ibid* 76, *Lanceleaf Greenbrier—Smilax lanceolata* . . . Also known under the vernacular names
of Coral Greenbrier [etc]. **1966** Grimm *Recognizing Native Shrubs* 75,
Red-Berried Greenbrier *Smilax walteri* . . . Also known as the Coral
Greenbrier.

coral honeysuckle n

=**trumpet honeysuckle.**

1864 *Harper's Mag.* 30.43/1 **sePA,** I stepped up on the shaky old
wooden porch, covered with the same coral honey-suckle. **1900** Lyons
Plant Names 229, *L[onicera] sempervirens* . . . Eastern U.S., west to
Nebraska. Trumpet or Coral Honeysuckle. **1933** Small *Manual SE
Flora* 1274, *P[henianthus] sempervirens* . . . [*Lonicera sempervirens*
L.]—*(Trumpet-honeysuckle. Coral-honeysuckle. Woodbine.)* . . . Fla. to
Tex., Nebr., and Me. **1941** Walker *Lookout* 58 **TN,** Trumpet, or coral
honeysuckle with its scarlet and yellow flowers that open in April and
May, is one of the most popular wild flowers in the mountain.

coralito n

A **coral bean 1** (here: *Erythrina herbacea*).

1951 *PADS* 15.35 **TX,** *Erythrina herbacea* L.—Coralito.

coral orchid n

=**coralroot 1.**

1953 Greene–Blomquist *Flowers South* 25, Coral-Orchids . . . are
generally pink or brownish in color.

coral plant See **coral tree**

coralroot n

1 A saprophytic plant of the genus *Corallorhiza.* Also called
coral orchid, crawley root, dragon's claws For other names of
var spp see **Adam-and-Eve 1, coral teeth**

1821 in 1832 MA Hist. Soc. *Coll.* 2.9.149, Plants, which are indigenous
in the township of Middlebury, [Vt., include] . . Cymbidium . . corallorhizum, Coral-root. **1889** *Century Dict.,* *Corallorhiza* . . . The species
are popularly known as *coralroot,* from the coral-like rootstocks. **1901**
Mohr *Plant Life AL* 458, *Corallorhiza odontorhiza* . . . Small-flowered
Coral-root. *Ibid, Corallorhiza wisteriana* . . . Wister's Coral-root.
1941 FWP *Guide CO* 17, The coral-root orchid is frequently found in the
woods. **1949** Peattie *Cascades* 234, Another kind of orchid is the
coral-root, Corallorhiza. Coral-roots get their name from their coral-like
branching roots. Generally they have pinkish or purplish stalks and
lovely little orchids on short stems. **1967** *DARE* File **CO,** Coralroot—a
parasite; the flowers are colored but [have] no green. **1971** Krochmal
Appalachia Med. Plants 104, *Corallorhiza* (Chat.) (Orchidaceae) Common names: Coralroot, crawleyroot.

2 usu *crested coralroot:* A somewhat similar saprophytic plant
(Hexalectris spicata). Cf **Texas purple-spike**

1901 Lounsberry *S. Wild Flowers* 94, *Crested coral-root.*—*Hexaléctris
aphýllus* . . . Through southeastern America. **1953** Greene–Blomquist
Flowers South 25, Another saprophytic orchid in the South is crested
coralroot *(Hexalectris spicata)* which has relatively large flowers and
blooms in summer. **1970** Correll *Plants TX* 446, *Hexalectris spicata* . .
Crested coral-root.

coral seed See **coral bead**

coral snake n

1 Either of two venomous elapid snakes:

a A relatively small, secretive snake *(Micrurus fulvius)* with
brightly colored alternating rings of red, yellow and black and a
black snout, which is found chiefly in the South Atlantic and
Gulf States. Also called **candystick, harlequin snake, king
snake 2, stinging snake 2, thunder snake 3**

1883 *Harper's Mag.* 67.708/1, None of my venomous acquaintances,
whether . . black-snake, whip-snake, coral-snake, or viper, has ever . .
[sprung] off the ground at me. **1948** *Nat. Hist.* 57.187/2, Venomous

relatives of the cobra, coral snakes in the United States have the red bands bordered by yellow, in contrast to the false coral (king) snakes, which have the red bordered by black. **1965–70** *DARE* (Qu. P25) 54 Infs, **chiefly S Atl and Gulf States,** Coral snake. [Note: some of these Infs may be referring to **coral snake 2.**] **1972** GA Dept. Ag. *Farmers Market Bulletin* 24 May 8/1, The coral snake, the only poisonous species in Georgia which is not a pit viper, can be identified by its coloration . . . It is only found in South Georgia.

b A snake *(Micruroides euryxanthus)* similar to **1a** above, but with red, white (sometimes cream) and black rings, which is found in Arizona and New Mexico and southward.

1937 Pope *Snakes Alive* 220. **1961** Douglas *My Wilderness* 85 **AZ,** Arizona has some poisonous snakes—at least eight species of rattlesnake, the Mexican moccasin snake, and the coral snake, with red, whitish, and black bands (in that order) encircling the body. **1969–70** *DARE* (Qu. P25) Infs **AZ**13, 15, Coral snake. **1974** Shaw–Campbell *Snakes West* 191, Several snakes in the Southwest . . sometimes are confused with the coral snake. Chief among these are the shovel-nosed snake, the long-nosed snake, the California mountain kingsnake, and the Sonora mountain kingsnake.

2 Any of several nonvenomous snakes which resemble the above in coloring as:

a A **king snake 1,** in particular the Sonora mountain king snake *(Lampropeltis pyromelana)* found in Arizona, New Mexico, Nevada and Utah, the coral king snake *(L. zonata)* found chiefly in California, and the **milk snake 1.**

1899 *Century Dict.* 1261/1, *Coral-snake* . . . Marked with red zones, suggesting the color of coral . . . Various innocuous colubrine serpents, as of the genera *Oxyrhopus, Ophibolus, Erythrolampris,* and *Pliocercus.* **1952** Ditmars *N. Amer. Snakes* 147, California "Coral" Snake, *Lampropeltis zonatus* . . . Arizona "Coral" Snake, *Lampropeltis pyromelana pyromelana. Ibid* 203, As the Western "Milk" Snake . ., Cope's "Milk" Snake . . and the Mexican Ringed "Milk" Snake . . closely contact the ranges of the poisonous Coral Snakes . . in the South and Southwest, and are commonly called "Coral" Snakes, a word about differentiation is important. **1967–68** *DARE* (Qu. P25) Inf **CA**87, Coral snake—one or two; **CO**12, Coral snake—black, white, red spots —a few.

b =**scarlet snake.**

1952 Ditmars *N. Amer. Snakes* 146, Scarlet Snake, "Coral" Snake . . . Southeastern states to eastern Oklahoma and eastern Texas.

coral sumac n Also sp *coral sumach*

A **poisonwood** (here: *Metopium toxiferum*).

1884 Sargent *Forests of N. Amer.* 54, *Rhus Metopium* . . . Poison Wood. Coral Sumach. **1953** Greene–Blomquist *Flowers South* 68, Poison-Wood, Coral-Sumac *(Metopium toxiferum).*

coral teeth n

A **coral root 1** (here: *Corallorrhiza odontorrhiza*).

1959 Carleton *Index Herb. Plants* 30/2, Coral teeth: Corallorrhiza odontorrhiza.

coral tree n Also *coral plant*

A shrub or tree of the genus *Erythrina* characterized by trifoliate leaves and racemes of usu red or orange flowers followed by pods inclosing usu red seeds, that is native in the US to the South and Southwest. Also called **coral bean 1, Cherokee bean, dragon's teeth, snakeweed** For other names of var spp see **cardinalspear, crybaby tree, fireman's cap, Indian bean, mamou, manroot, wiliwili, woman root**

1863 *Harper's Mag.* 26.532/2 **FL,** Here, too . . I found the gay "Coraltree" (Erythrina), with its lance-like scarlet banners. **1876** Hobbs *Bot. Hdbk.* 26, Coral tree, Erythrina crista galli. **1901** Mohr *Plant Life AL* 579, *Erythrina herbacea* . . . Coral Plant. **1949** Moldenke *Amer. Wild Flowers* 131, A great many of these [Fabaceæ] are trees and shrubs, some of spectacular beauty, such as coraltrees (Erythrina). *Ibid* 242, In our cultivated flower gardens everyone knows how popular red cannas, . . coraltree . . and poinciana are with hummingbirds. **1981** Benson–Darrow *Trees SW Deserts* 253, Erythrina . . . Coral Tree.

coral vine n

1 =**coralbean 1.**

1913 *Torreya* 13.231 **FL,** *Erythrina herbacea* . . Coral vine, St. Vincent I[slan]d.

2 =**dodder.**

1932 Rydberg *Flora Prairies* 651, *Cuscuta* . . Dodder, . . Coral-vine. **1936** Winter *Plants NE* 112, *Cuscuta* . . Dodder, . . Coral-vine. **1973** Hitchcock–Cronquist *Flora Pacific NW* 365, *Cuscuta* . . Dodder; . . Coral-vine.

3 A perennial vine *(Antigonon leptopus)* from tuberlike roots which has alternate heart-shaped leaves and pendulous clusters of pink or less often white flowers; commonly planted as an ornamental in the Gulf States, esp Texas. Also called **Confederate rose, hearts on a chain, Mexican creeper, mountain rose, pink vine, privy vine, queen's wreath**

1942 Amer. Joint Comm. Horticult. Nomenclature *Std. Plant Names* 137, Coralvine . . . *Antigonon.* **1959** Carleton *Index Herb. Plants* 30, Coral-vine: Antigonon leptopus. **1966** *DARE* Wildfl QR (Wills–Irwin) Pl.214a Inf **TX**34, Coral vine.

4 =**trumpet honeysuckle.**

1967 *DARE* Wildfl QR Pl.214a Inf **TX**34, Coral vine or red honeysuckle.

coram n[1] [Perh pronc-sp for *quorum,* but infl by Lat *coram* before, in the presence of; cf *W3 coram judice*]

1899 (1912) Green *VA Folk-Speech,* Coram . . . For *quorum,* certain magistrates who were necessary to form a court.

coram n[2]

Prob a children's game.

1911 Shute *Plupy* 236 **seNH** (as of 1860s), Beany dodged under the old gentleman's extended arm like a boy playing "coram" and went through the front door like a shot.

corberater n Pronc-sp for *carburetor*

1976 Garber *Mountain-ese,* Corberater . . carburetor. "Lige's lizzie won't run till he gits the corberater fixed."

corbie n [*corbie* a raven]

1930 Shoemaker *1300 Words* 14 **cPA Mts** (as of c1900), Corbie—A Roman Catholic Priest.

corbina See **corvina e**

corcajou See **carcajou**

corcus See **caucus**

cord n

1 also sp *corde:* A large amount; a great many. [*cord* a quantity of cut wood]

1843 Field *Drama Pokerville* 13 **MO,** Manager Dust was just nat'rally bound to make "a corde of money!" **1871** (1882) Stowe *Fireside Stories* 35 **NEng,** Ruth . . kept true, and wouldn't have nothin' to say to nobody that came arter her, for there was lots and cords o' fellows as did come arter her.

2 See quot. [*EDD cord* sb. "*pl.* A contraction of the muscles of the neck"]

1967 *DARE* (Qu. BB3a, *What do you call a pain that strikes you suddenly in the neck?*) Inf **PA**4, Cord. Oh, I've got it so in my neck.

cordal See **cordelle**

corde See **cord 1**

cordelle n, v Also sp *cordal, cordel* [Fr] **chiefly Missip Valley** *hist*

A towline, esp one used on a riverboat; to tow something with such a line; hence vbl n *cordelling.*

1812 (1920) Luttig *Jrl.* 31 July 62, Departed early . . cordelled all Morning. **1814** Brackenridge *Views of LA* 214, Continued until eleven, with *cordelle,* or towing line—the banks being favorable. **1816** Ker *Travels* 36 **seLA,** After getting above their cordaling ground, in swift water they make use of their warp. **1817** (1889) Long *Jrl.* 34 **MN,** We could make no headway by all these means, and were obliged to substitute the cordel in place of the poles and oars. **1836** (1932) Chardon *Jrl.* 71, He [a bull] lay with his head down the hill untill the whole "jolly crew" Cordelled the Cart to the top and again returned to him . . and after cordelling him up, they proceeded without any further difficulty. **1941** Baldwin *Keelboat Age* 65 **Missip R,** When the bottom of the river was too soft for poling and the shores on both sides were unsuitable for cordelling, resort was made to warping. **1968** Adams *Western Words,* Cordelle—In steamboating, a towline used to pull a boat from shore . . . It took from twenty to forty men, walking in single file, to cordelle a boat along average stretches of river, and the work was always very difficult. A boat could also be towed by using a line fastened upstream to an anchor or *deadman,* a beam or log buried in the sand. In this case the line was wound up by a steam capstan on the boat.

corder strap n

The girth or bellyband of a horse's harness.

1967 *DARE* (Qu. L53b, *The band that goes under a horse's middle to hold a saddle on—what is it called if it's part of a work harness?*) Inf **OR**10, Corder strap.

cordgrass n

Std: any of the reedlike grasses of the genus *Spartina* found commonly in both fresh and salt-water areas. Also called **alkali cordgrass, bull grass, cane grass, corn grass, corn sedge, couch grass 2, cow grass, creek sedge, creekstuff, creek thatch, ditch grass, fox grass, high-water grass, hog cane, lowland grass, meadow grass, prairie cordgrass, quill cane, ramrod grass, ripgut, sacahuista, salt-marsh grass, salt-meadow grass, salt reed grass, salt thatch, saltwater grass, sawgrass, sea cane, sloughgrass, thatch grass, wildcat grass, wire grass**

corduroy hedge n [By analogy with *corduroy road*]

1871 U.S. Dept. Ag. *Rept. of Secy.* 505, The worm-fence again predominates in Missouri, amounting to 74 per per [sic] cent., while there is 26 per cent. of board-fence, and "corduroy" (poles nailed to posts) hedge.

corduvant n [Alter of *cordovan*]

1899 (1912) Green *VA Folk-Speech, Corduvant . . .* Thin leather named from the town Córdoba in Spain where it was made. "Corduvant gloves".

cordwinder n [Folk-etym for *cordwainer*] *arch*

A shoemaker.

1644 (1880) Suffolk Co. MA *Deeds* 1.51, I Richard Cranniwell of Woodbridge in the County of Suff‍ Cordwinder. **1790** in 1929 Summers *Annals* 1.440, Thomas McGinnis bound to Philip Cole, (cord winder). **1899** (1912) Green *VA Folk-Speech, Cordwinder . . .* Cordwainer. A shoemaker.

cordwood n *joc*

1 also *cordwood match:* A kitchen match.

1943 *AN&Q* 3.120/1, Household Matches. Regional Names. What local or regional names have been given to common household matches? I myself have heard them referred to as "cordwood," "fence posts," and "railroad ties." **1967–69** *DARE* (Qu. F46, *. . The kind of matches you can strike anywhere*) Infs **CT**2, **NV**2, **SC**32, Cordwood matches; **MA**57, Cordwood.

2 A toothpick. Also called **dining room lumber, timber**

1967 *DARE* (Qu. G11) Inf **NV**2, Cordwood.

3 See quot.

1966 *DARE* (Qu. HH1, *Names and nicknames for a rustic or countrified person*) Inf **NC**33, Cordwood from the sticks.

core n

1959 *VT Hist.* new ser 27.131, Core . . . The pile of snow left after plowing; a balk. Occasional.

corel See **corral**

coreline, to the adv phr

1967 *DARE* (Qu. LL26b, *Other words meaning "entirely"—for example, "He's Irish _____."*) Inf **NJ**1, To the coreline.

corell See **corral**

corfish n [Prob assim of *corft, corved* ppl adj, preserved in salt, + *fish*; SND *corft*, OED *corved* "Obs.*'*]

1975 Gould *ME Lingo* 59, *Corfish*—Whole cod pickled in brine; the "soft cure" of early English colonists and Maine's major export for a long time.

cork n[1] [*cork* a stopper for a container] *obs* Cf **cork** v[1], **curl** n **B**2

See quots.

1851 Hall *College Words* 85, *Cork. Calk.* In some of the Southern colleges, this word, with a derived meaning, signifies a *complete stopper.* Used in the sense of a complete failure in reciting; an utter inability to answer an instructor's interrogatories. **1888** *Corks and Curls* 11 (1980 *DARE* File) [University of Virginia Annual], The real agony of the unprepared student, who, when called upon to recite . . sitteth and

openeth not his mouth, even as a bottle is corked up, so that our gracious founder . . did bestow upon such like the name of 'Cork.'

cork v[1] [**cork** n[1]]

To baffle; see quots.

1906 *DN* 3.132 **nwAR**, *Cork . . .* To get the better of. "It certainly did cork me." **1920** Bruce *Univ. VA* 4.83, [Footnote:] The student who flagrantly failed to reply correctly to the questions of his professor in the classroom was said to have been *corked.* **1960** Criswell *Resp. to PADS* 20 **Ozarks**, *Cork . . .* To give (one) pause, to baffle. "Now wouldn't that cork you?" (Very common; still used a good deal.)

cork n[2] [Folk-etym for *calk*]

1 A wedge or similar projection on a horseshoe to prevent slipping.

1806 (1970) Webster *Compendious Dict., Cork . .* a sharp point on a horse shoe. **1846** Porter *Quarter Race* 162 **IL**, I then just took my old mare down to a blacksmith's shop, and had some shoes made with corks about four inches long, and had 'em nailed on to her hind feet. **1922** (1926) Cady *Rhymes VT* 41, Old shoes with corks as sharp as forks / Are kicking 'round the stable; / The nags are wearing mud-corks now / That wouldn't dent a table. **1931–33** *LANE Worksheets* **Boston MA**, *Corks:* Always pitch them [=horseshoes] with the pegs up—want to slide a ringer. Pegs would interfere; pegs are called corks. **1968** *DARE* File **neAL**. **1969** Sorden *Lumberjack Lingo* **NEng, Gt Lakes. 1970** *DARE* Tape **MI**125, He'd take that shoe off, put it in the fire and he'd pound that, them corks out. The toe cork he'd pry off and weld a new cork on there.

2 A sharp metal point on a boot sole to prevent slipping, used esp in logging. **chiefly Nth**

1902 White *Blazed Trail* 187 **eMI**, His face and flesh were ripped and torn everywhere by the "corks" on the boots. **c1922** Titus *Timber* 286 *(DAE),* There'll never be a Michigan man who is lonesome for white pine who can't . . feel the corks in his boots biting into the bark. **1950** *WELS* (*Heavy pieces of metal under the soles of boots to keep them from slipping*) 4 Infs, **WI**, Corks; 1 Inf, **cWI**, Metal corks—this is what the lumberjacks call them. **1954** *Harder Coll.* **cwTN. 1956** *AmSp* 31.150 **nwCA. 1965–70** *DARE* (Qu. W12a) 22 Infs, **chiefly Nth**, Corks. [19 of 22 Infs old] **1969** Sorden *Lumberjack Lingo* **NEng, Gt Lakes. 1977** *WI State Jrl.* (Madison) 16 Jan sec 5 5/1 **AK**, "Caulks" (pronounced "corks") . . steel pegs in the soles of heavy logger boots.

3 also *cork boot, ~ shoe:* A men's work shoe fitted with calks and used esp in logging. **chiefly Nth**

1950 *WELS* (*Men's low, rough work shoes*) 1 Inf, **cwWI**, In logging days, cork shoes. **1950** *Western Folkl.* 9.116 **nwOR**, *Corks* or *cork boots.* Boots having steel caulks screwed into the soles. **1958** McCulloch *Woods Words* **Pacific NW. 1966–67** *DARE* Tape **ME**19, [They] had cork shoes—had corks on 'em—worn by river drivers in logging; **MI**47, We just got drove out of one house because we had cork shoes on . . . Ha, ha, she [the landlady] said, cork shoes put this house up and cork shoes can tear it down. **1968** *DARE* (Qu. W11, *Men's low rough work shoes*) Inf **WV**2, Cork; (Qu. W12a) Inf **NY**96, Cork shoes; (Qu. W43) Inf **CA**106, Cork boots, logging boots with calks—sticker boots. **1977** Churchill *Don't Call* 144 **nwOR** (as of c1920), The linoleum in most logging camp homes was pock-marked by the pointed calks loggers wore in the soles of their shoes ("cork" shoes in logger terminology instead of "calk" shoes). Dad never wore his calk shoes in the house.

4 A toe cap for a shoe or boot.

1954 *Harder Coll.* **cwTN.**

cork v[2] [Folk-etym for *calk, caulk*]

1 To provide a horseshoe or a boot with **corks** n[2] **1** or **2**.

1776 (1901) *Documents Revol. Hist. NJ* 1.168, A chestnut sorrel *mare, . .* shod before, shoes are steel corked. **1797** in 1956 Eliason *Tarheel Talk* 266 **NC**, Pr cork'd shoes. **1829** *Va. Lit. Museum* 16 Dec 419 *(DAE),* To cork. 'To shoe a horse with points—or with frost nails.' **1966** *DARE* Tape **ID**4, Lumberjacks with their corked boots.

2 Of a horse or mule: to strike with the **corks** n[2] **1**.

1907 *DN* 3.230 **nwAR, seMO**, *Cork . . .* Calk. "That horse corks itself." **1912** *DN* 3.567 **cNY**, *Cork . . .* "The horse has corked himself": struck one of his legs with the iron calk on one of his shoes. **1941** Heydrick *Americans All* 239, He corked me! . . Jammed his spikes into me. **c1960** Wilson *Coll.* **csKY. 1968** *DARE* File **neAL**, The mule corked hisself. **1970** *DARE* Tape **KY**84, If a horse corked hisself, an' that is bumping his opposite ankle with the other foot . . he'd . . get a sore on his ankle . . an' that was caused from improper shoeing.

3 By ext: to injure oneself; to make oneself ridiculous.

1905 *DN* 3.75 **nwAR,** *Cork one's self . . .* To make one's self ridiculous. "He corks himself." Rare. **1907** *DN* 3.230 **nwAR, seMO,** *Cork . . .* to make oneself ridiculous. "A feller only corks hisself that jaws a man while hot."—J.W. Riley. **1909** *DN* 3.394 **nwAR,** *Cork one's self . . .* To injure one's self.

4 To make tight against leakage; to caulk. *esp among old speakers and those with less than high school educ*

1823 (1928) Kennerly *Diary* 55 **VA,** Making attempt to get boat out of water to cork her. **1903** *DN* 2.310 **seMO.** **1906** *DN* 3.116 **sIN,** *Cork . . .* Common pronunciation of *calk*. "We corked the boat." **1909** *DN* 3.394 **nwAR.** **1912** *DN* 3.567 **cNY,** *Cork . . .* Calk: to fill up a seam with something, usually with cloth or oakum. "Cork up the door for winter." **1946** *PADS* 6.10 **NC.** **1954** *Harder Coll.* **cwTN.** **1965–70** *DARE* (Qu. O6, *If a wooden boat is leaking*) 134 Infs, **widespread,** Cork (it, her, them, the seams). [Of all Infs responding to the question, 65% were old, 30% had less than high school educ; of those giving these responses, 84% were old, 48% had less than high school educ.]

cork n³, also attrib [From *Cork* county in Ireland]

A person of Irish descent.

1950 *WELS* (*Common nicknames for people living in nearby settlements or places*) 1 Inf, **swWI,** Cork Hollow (the Irish). **1966–68** *DARE* (Qu. HH28, *Names and nicknames around here for people of foreign background . . Irish*) Inf **DE3,** Corks; (Qu. C35, *Nicknames for the different parts of your town or city*) Infs **MI49, 67,** Corktown; (Qu. II25, *Names or nicknames for the part of a town where . . foreign groups live*) Inf **NY139,** Cork Hill: the Irish section.

cork v³ [Prob var of **cock** v², but cf **cork** v² 2]

To strike (someone).

1968 *DARE* (Qu. Y14a, *To hit somebody hard with the fist*) Infs **NY123, PA83,** Cork. **1978** *DARE* File **sCA** (as of c1940–70), I am familiar with *cork* through my mother and father. It means to strike someone sharply and quickly on the arm (especially just behind and to the side of the elbow) with the upraised knuckle of the middle finger. It was usually done in a playful and joking manner.

cork ball n *chiefly sIL*

A bat-and-ball game: see quot 1965.

1965 *DARE* FW Addit, *Cork ball*—A game played (as of the middle 1930s and 40s, and probably still going on) in the St. Louis, Missouri—Belleville, Illinois area. A minimum of four players use a ball made of cork, sometimes covered with horsehide, and a thin bat. The ball is a little larger than a golf ball in size. There is a pitcher, a batter, a catcher, and one or more fielders. Upon hitting the ball, the batter tries to run to first base and back to home plate before the fielder can throw the ball back to the catcher. However, if the fielder catches a fly, the batter is out and another player takes his place at bat. The fielder, pitcher, and batter rotate. **1967–69** *DARE* (Qu. EE11, *Bat-and-ball games for just a few players*) Infs **IL26, 68, 77, 78, 85, 86, MO21,** Cork ball.

corkbark elm See **cork elm** 1, 4

corkbark fir n Also *cork fir*

A subsp of the **alpine fir** (*Abies lasiocarpa arizonica*).

1898 Sudworth *Forest Trees* 26, *Abies arizonica . .* Arizona cork fir. **1938** Van Dersal *Native Woody Plants* 35, *Abies arizonica*—Corkbark fir. **1960** Vines *Trees SW* 6, Alpine Corkbark Fir, *A. lasiocarpa var. arizonica.* **1979** Little *Checklist U.S. Trees* 35, *Abies lasiocarpa* var. *arizonica . .* corkbark fir.

cork boot See **cork** n² 3

corked adj

1 Drunk.

1912 *DN* 3.573 **wIN,** *Corked . . .* Drunk. **1927** *New Republic* 9 Mar 71/2, The following is a partial list of words denoting drunkenness now in common use in the United States . . . canned, corked, corned. **1967–69** *DARE* (Qu. DD15, *A person who is thoroughly drunk*) Infs **NY23, PA199,** Corked. **1969** *DARE* FW Addit **PA199,** Boy, when we got back in camp, it took him about a half an hour and he was so corked that he didn't know whether he was in Pittsburgh or Shoeshoe.

2 freq with *up*: See quot.

1967–70 *DARE* (Qu. BB21, *Other words for being constipated*) Infs **MO5, PA205, 214, SC40,** Corked up; **MO36,** Corked.

3 See quot.

1970 *DARE* (Qu. X47, *. . Other ways . . of saying, "I'm very tired, at the end of my strength"*) Inf **CA212,** Corked.

cork elm n

1 also *corkbark elm, corky white elm:* =**rock elm.** **eUS**

1847 Wood *Class-Book* 483, *U[lmus] racemosa . .* Cork Elm. **1850** *New Engl. Farmer* 2.142 **neMA,** We have grafted the Slippery and the Cork-bark Elm on the White Elm. **1857** Gray *Manual of Botany* 396, Corky White Elm. **1969** *DARE* (Qu. T11) Infs **MS38, TN22,** Cork elm. **1979** Little *Checklist U.S. Trees* 291, *Ulmus thomasii . .* Other common name—cork elm.

2 also *corky elm:* =**winged elm.**

1813 Muhlenberg *Catalogus Plantarum* 29, *Ulmus . . .* U. alata (Waho). Elm . . . Cork elm. **1897** Sudworth *Arborescent Flora* 182, Cork Elm (Fla., S.C., Tex.) . . Corky Elm (Tex.). **1979** Little *Checklist U.S. Trees* 290, *Ulmus alata . .* Other common names—cork elm.

3 =**cedar elm.**

1950 Moore *Trees AR* 62, Cedar Elm—(*Ulmus crassifolia . .*)—Local Names: Cork [Elm].

4 also *corkbark elm:* =**Siberian elm.** **West**

1966–69 *DARE* (Qu. T11) Infs **CA130, 163, WA8,** Cork elm; **NV8,** Chinese elm, cork elm; **WA12,** Corkbark elm.

corker n [Etym uncert; perh from **cork** v³ + *-er* agentive: one who strikes forcefully, impressively]

1 A person or thing of remarkable quality or strength. **chiefly Nth, N Midl** See Map

1902 Day *Pine Tree Ballads* 242 **ME,** Them fellers on the trick trapeze was corkers in their line. **1908** *DN* 3.301 **eAL, wGA,** *Corker . . .* A knock-out blow, a good blow. **1927** *AmSp* 2.351 **WV,** *Corker . .* a story that is hard to believe. **1938** Farrell *No Star* 85 **Chicago** (as of 1914–15), Poor thing, she's had a hard time, but God, Mike, she's a corker. **1960** Criswell *Resp. to PADS* 20 **Ozarks,** *Corker . . .* Something extraordinary. May be said of a story, or an animal (as to size) or of an unpredictable person. (Once very common; still used.) **1965–70** *DARE* (Qu. B3, *If a day is very hot, you say it's [a]* ———) 17 Infs, **Nth,** Corker; (Qu. Y11, *. . A very hard blow: " . . Joe really hit him a* ———." ') Infs **NJ59, VA26,** Corker; (Qu. Z14b, *If a child expects to have its own way . . you might say, "That child is* ———." ') Inf **MI51,** [A] corker; (Qu. Z16, *A small child who is rough, misbehaves, and doesn't obey, you'd call him a* ———) Inf **OH44,** Corker; (Qu. KK11, *To make . . a big fuss about something*) Inf **MA79,** Put up a corker; (Qu. KK41, *. . "I managed to get through it, but it was a* ———." ') Inf **CA127,** Corker; (Qu. LL5, *Something impressively big: "That cabbage is really a* ———." ') Infs **NY206, 223,** Corker. **1966–67** *DARE* Tape **MI28,** We used to have lots of fun with 'em 'cause the little billy [goat] was a corker; **OH16,** I had a Russian wolfhound to kill it—seven cats, the first week I got it. He was a corker.

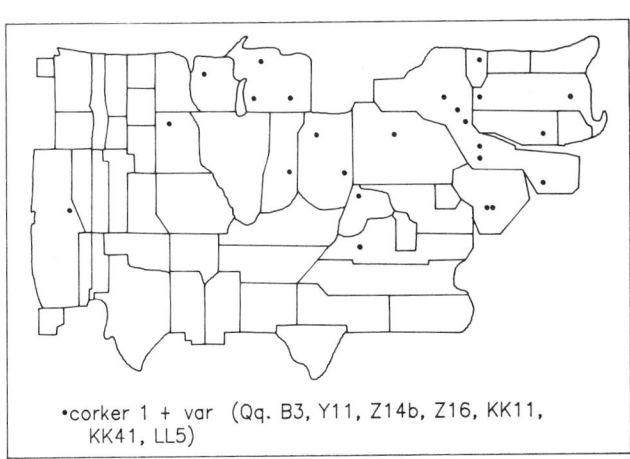

•corker 1 + var (Qq. B3, Y11, Z14b, Z16, KK11, KK41, LL5)

‡**2** See quot.

1968 *DARE* (Qu. EE41, *A hobgoblin that is used to threaten children and make them behave*) Inf **GA33,** Old corker.

corker plum n [Var of **coco plum**]

1896 *Garden and Forest* 9.263/1, Hickok. (Chrysobalanus Icaco.)—Through Carib–Span., from *ikákoo,* the name of the plum-like fruit in the female dialect of the Caribs of the Lesser Antilles. Cocoa in the name Cocoa-plum (Corker-plum in Fla.), is a variant of the word.

cork fir See **corkbark fir**

‡cork high and bottle deep adj phr

Drunk.

1960 Williams *Walk Egypt* 9 **GA,** A group of Atlanta fishermen nearly suffocated when the chimney, stopped up by swallows and bats, drove smoke back upon them. "They was cork-high and bottle deep," Aunt Baptist said, "or they'da smelled it."

corking-pin n *arch*

1899 (1912) Green *VA Folk-Speech, Corking-pin* . . . A pin of the largest size. Manikin pin, the smallest size.

cork leg n

1912 Green *VA Folk-Speech* 127, *Cork-leg* . . . An artificial leg made of light wood usually *willow,* but never of *cork.* Not a *peg-leg.*

cork-legged limited n [*cork-legged* crippled] *joc*

1950 *WELS* (*Joking names for a branch railroad that is not very important or does not give the best service*) 1 Inf, **seWI,** Cork-legged limited.

cork off v [Var of **caulk B** + *off*]

1968 *DARE* (Qu. X40, . . *Ways . . of saying, "I'm going to bed"*) Inf **AK1,** Cork off.

Corkonian n [*Cork* county in Ireland] Cf **cork** n³, **Fardown**

An Irish-American whose family came from the south of Ireland.

1834 *Amer. Railroad Jrl.* 21 June 384/1 **MD,** The parties arrayed against each other are known as the *Fardowns* and the *Corkonians.* **1905** Valentine *Hecla Sandwith* 180 **cPA,** The 'Corkonians' employed on the Dunkirk branch of the Pennsylvania and Erie Canal [in 1856] became more notorious. **1950** *Western Folkl.* 9.46 **swMT** [Song lyrics], Mighty Pat pulled him back with a Corkonian's rage.

cork pine n

1 =**white pine 1** (*Pinus strobus*). **chiefly MI**

1865 in 1959 *MI Hist.* 43.401, Much of this "would be termed cork pine." **1873** Walling *Atlas MI* 20/1, Michigan pine . . is what is known as white pine, and of this there are several varieties. The soft or "cork" pine, so called from the resemblance in softness and texture of the wood to the cork of commerce, is the least plentiful of all. **1902** White *Blazed Trail* 119 **eMI,** Often in the hollows it shaded gradually into the rough-skinned cork pine. **1930** Shoemaker *1300 Words* 14 **cPA Mts** (as of c1900), *Cork-pine*—An original growth white pine with large plates of gold-colored bark, reputed to have the softest and finest grade of lumber. **1958** [see **2** below]. **1968** *DARE* (Qq. T16, 17) Inf **MI76,** Cork pine. **1969** Sorden *Lumberjack Lingo* **NEng, Gt Lakes,** *Cork pine*—A white pine tree yielding a superior grade of lumber. It floated better than other kinds of pine. Found in Maine and in the lake states.

2 =**white pine 2** (*Pinus monticola*).

1958 McCulloch *Woods Words* **Pacific NW,** *Cork pine*—As used in the Northwest means fine old growth Idaho white pine. The term is taken directly from the Lake States loggers who used it to mean top quality eastern white pine.

corkscrew n **Pacific NW**

A geared engine on a logging railroad.

1905 U.S. Forest Serv. *Bulletin* 61.33 **Pacific NW,** *Corkscrew* . . . A geared logging locomotive. **1958** McCulloch *Woods Words* 39 **Pacific NW,** *Corkscrew*—A geared engine on a logging railroad, particularly a Shay. **1962** *AmSp* 32.132 **Pacific NW.**

corkscrew bush n

=**granjeno.**

1951 *PADS* 15.30 **TX,** *Momisia pallida* . . . Corkscrew bush.

corkscrew plant n Also *corkscrew orchid* [Prob from the twisted flowering stem]

=**ladies' tresses.**

1900 Lyons *Plant Names* 180, *S[piranthes] gracilis* . . Corkscrew plant. **1911** *Century Dict.* 5839, *Spiranthes* . . . They are known as *lady's-tresses,* . . also locally as *wild tuberose,* and *G. gracilis* as *corkscrew-plant.* **1972** Brown *Wildflowers LA* 42, Corkscrew Orchids . . *Spiranthes grayi* . . *S. gracilis* . . *S. praecox* . . *S. vernalis* . . *S. longilabris.*

corkscrew snake n

=**ringneck snake.**

1958 Conant *Reptiles & Amphibians* 141, *Southern Ringneck Snake—Diadophis punctatus punctatus* . . . When alarmed, Ringnecks of this species and of the Prairie Ringneck sometimes twist their tails upward in

a tight spiral, thus exposing the bright colors to view. This habit has earned them the name of "corkscrew" and "thimble snakes."

corkscrew willow n [From the twisted branches]

The contorted Hankow willow (*Salix matsudana* var. *tortuosa*).

1965 *DARE* (Qu. T15, . . *Kinds of swamp trees*) Inf **UT3,** Corkscrew willow. **1969** *SC Market Bulletin* 11 Sept 4, Cork screw willows . . 25¢ each.

cork shoe See **cork** n² **3**

‡cork the duration v phr

1967 *DARE* (Qu. GG22b, *When you have come to the end of your patience, you might say, "Well, that certainly _____."*) Inf **OH18,** Corks the duration.

corkus See **caucus**

corkwood n [From the lightweight wood] **chiefly Gulf States**

1 Std: a small tree (*Leitneria floridana*) native chiefly to the southeastern US.

2 A blolly.

1897 Sudworth *Arborescent Flora* 192, Cork Wood (Fla.). **1900** Lyons *Plant Names* 293, *P[isonia] obtusata* . . Corkwood.

3 =**queen's delight.**

1960 Vines *Trees SW* 623, Corkwood Stillingia—*Stillingia aquatica* . . . The plant is rather short-lived, and the wood is lighter than cork.

4 See quots.

1969 *DARE* Tape KY34, There used to be a corkwood growing in the garden . . . It looked like a, a hollyhock blossom . . . [FW:] What color flower did it have? [Inf:] It had a red 'un and a blue 'un, maybe a white one. **1969** *DARE* FW Addit KY34, *Corkwood*—an old-fashioned garden-flower. It put up a single stalk with one white or blue flower on it.

corky adj Pronc-sp *cawky* [Cf *OED corky* 2 "fig. Dry and stiff, withered, sapless. *Obs.*" and *EDD corky* 3 "Soft through exposure, as wood that has suffered through lying too long with the bark on."] **chiefly NEast**

Of vegetables: tough, pithy.

1966 *DARE* FW Addit ME, [kɔki]—of turnips, old and not good to eat. **1967–69** *DARE* (Qu. I8, *When root vegetables get old and tough and are not good to eat, you say they are _____*) Infs **MA5, NJ1, VT13,** Corky; **ME23,** Cawky; [**NC12,** Cork—of potatoes with black spots].

corky elm See **cork elm 2**

corky white elm See **cork elm 1**

cormorant n

Std: a water bird of the genus *Phalacrocorax.* Also called **crow duck 1, shag, Taunton turkey** For other names see **double-crested cormorant**

corn n Usu |korn, kɔ(r)n|, occas |korən, karn| See Pronc Intro 3.I.1.e, 3.II.26 Pronc-spp *cawn, corrun*

A Forms.

1843 (1916) Hall *New Purchase* 459, Git what cawn you like. **1890** *DN* 1.64 **KY,** Corn [kɔn]. **1914** *DN* 4.159 **cVA,** Carry the hawse ovah tuh neah thu cawn-haouse. **1922** Gonzales *Black Border* 292 **sSC, GA coasts** [Gullah glossary], *Cawn*—corn. **1934** (1970) Wilson *Backwoods Amer.* 70, That cawn gets so on-handy big and shady that you can see the lightnin' bugs in amongst it in the daytime. **1961** *Mt. Life* Spring 7 **sAppalachians,** Often *r* is rolled so that a spurious syllable appears: . . *corrun* (corn). **1968–70** *DARE* FW Addit swKY, cs,seMD, ['karn]; ceVA, ['kaərn].

B Senses.

1 Corn liquor, moonshine.

1820 *Chillicothe* (*O.*) *Supporter* 5 July (*DA*), If we go to town . . . we are invited to try a little corn as usual. **1908** *DN* 3.301 **eAL, wGA. 1934** Carmer *Stars Fell on AL* 5, We've drunk up all the corn waitin' for you. **1965–70** *DARE* (Qu. DD21a, . . *Liquor*) Infs **FL16, TN53, VA24,** Corn; (Qu. DD21b, . . *Bad liquor*) Infs **IL7, NY94, OK58, SC69, TX42, VA73,** Corn; (Qu. DD21c, . . *Whiskey, especially illegally made whiskey*) 11 Infs, **scattered,** Corn; (Qu. DD28b, *What fermented drinks are made at home around here?*) Inf **TX79,** Corn.

2 in phr *plant the corn before they build the fence:* See **build the fence.**

3 Money.

1969 *DARE* (Qu. U19a, . . *Money in general: "He's certainly got the _____."*) Inf **NY**156, Corn. **1970** Major *Afro–Amer. Slang*, Corn: (1940's) money.

4 Cornmeal.

1966 *DARE* Tape **GA**1, And ground [it] up into corn to make cornbread.

5 pl: An ear of maize. Note: also in Caribbean; see *DJE*

1972 Carr *Da Kine Talk* 128 **HI**, *Corns* vs. *corn on the cob* — "Hot corns for sale!" This was on a sign at a vegetable stand on Windward Oahu in the 1940s, where youngsters were selling cooked corn on the cob. Taking orders for products of school gardens, secretaries will still often ask the teachers, "Do you want any corns today?" The usual Mainland meaning of *corns* finds little use in the Islands.

corn v

1 To plant with corn. *?chiefly S Midl*

1886 U.S. Bur. Foreign Commerce *Consular Repts.* 18.40, What possibilities, through this crude mineral, await the redemption of those hundreds of thousands of acres of once valuable Southern lands, "corned to death." **1906** *DN* 3.132 **nwAR**, *Corn* . . . To cause to produce corn continuously year after year. **1940** Stuart *Trees of Heaven* 129 **neKY**, I'd corn this land three years, then I'd sow it in wheat and orchard grass. **1962** *Mt. Life* Spring 17 **sAppalachians**, He grasses a field after he has corned it for a few years.

2 See quot. [Back-formation from **corned**]

1899 (1912) Green *VA Folk-Speech*, *Corn* . . . To make drunk with whiskey.

3 To vote for someone by casting corn as a ballot. *hist*

1937 FWP *Guide MA* 556, At early island elections corn and beans were used as ballots. 'The freeman shall use Indian corn and beans, the corn to manifest Election, the Beanes Contrary' — which explains the phrase 'to corn a man.' [**1970** League Women Voters MA *MA State Govt.* 3, A law passed in 1643 directed that, in voting for assistants (or directors), the freemen were to use Indian corn for a favorable vote and a bean for a blank.]

corn ball n

A popcorn ball.

1874 E. S. Phelps *Trotty's Wedding* i *(DA)*, They were eating a corn-ball at recess. **1877** Bartlett *Americanisms* 779, *Corn-Balls*. Balls made of pop-corn and molasses, of which children are very fond. **1950** Farmer *Handy Cook Book* 704, Corn Balls: 5 quarts popped corn, 2 cups sugar . . . Make into balls, let stand in cold place until brittle.

corn barn n esp NEng, S Atl *somewhat old-fash*

A corncrib; see quot 1852.

1780 (1899) Parkman *Diary* 278 **MA**, Dr. Hawes . . took ye whole care of husking ye Corn, & carrying it into the Corn Barn. **1852** *Harper's Mag.* 4.590/2 **NEng**, A corn-barn is a small square building, standing upon high posts at the four corners. **1907** *DN* 3.184 **seNH**, *Corn-barn* . . . Shed, the floor of which is mounted on posts and in which Indian corn is stored. **1965–70** *DARE* (Qu. M1, . . *Different or special kinds of barns*) 8 Infs, **chiefly S Atl**, Corn barn; (Qu. M8, *The building where corn is kept*) 9 Infs, **chiefly S Atl**, Corn barn; (Qu. M22, . . *Other kinds of buildings . . on farms*) Inf **VT**2, Corn barns (years ago). [10 Infs old, 7 mid-aged]

corn bead (seed) n [From the resemblance of the stem and leaves to those of corn and from the beadlike seeds] Gulf States

=**Job's tears 1.**

1927 *Jrl. Amer. Folkl.* 40.166 **LA**, Wear cornbeads to prevent or cure headache. **1970** GA Dept. Ag. *Farmers Market Bulletin* 5 Aug, Corn bead seed, 25¢ pkg. **1982** *DARE* File, Corn bead seed . . . According to our specialist [at the Georgia Department of Agriculture], the scientific name of the plant is *"Coix lacryma-jobi"* or "Job's Tears."

corn bean See cornfield bean

corn, beans, and succotash n

1968 *DARE* (Qu. EE33, *Other outdoor games not yet mentioned that children play now, or that were played in your childhood*) Inf **OH**87, Corn, beans, and succotash — It's a game with numbers, multiples of five are corn, multiples of seven are beans, multiples of twelve are succotash.

corn beer n chiefly Sth

Fermented maize, either drunk like beer or distilled into corn whiskey.

[**c1662** in 1937 *New Engl. Qrly.* 10.131, The English have found out a way to make very good Beere of this Graine which they doe either out of Bread made of it, or by Maulting of it.] **1891** *Century Illustr. Mag.* 41.706/2 **LA** (as of 1863), I . . carried with me some of the corn beer brewed in the camp. **1939** *Hall Coll.* **wNC, eTN**, Corn beer. Same as *beer:* fermented mash which is distilled in the making of whiskey. **1967** *DARE* (Qu. DD28b, *What fermented drinks are made at home around here?*) Inf **AL**20, Corn beer: Boil corn, put in big jar, put in syrup, put in sun; ferment; at a certain stage it is good. Let it stay; it will turn to whiskey; **LA**12, Corn beer.

corn beetle n

Either the corn flea beetle *(Chaetocnema pulicaria)* or the corn seed beetle *(Agonoderus pallipes)*.

1966–68 *DARE* (Qu. R30, . . *Other kinds of beetles . . around here*) Infs **NC**44, **OH**88, **SC**57, Corn beetle.

corn bin n chiefly Sth, Midl See Map Cf corn barn

A structure for storing shelled corn, either freestanding or in a barn; also sometimes a corncrib.

c1960 *Wilson Coll.* **csKY**, Corn bin . . . A place to store corn, usually shelled corn. **1965–70** *DARE* (Qu. M8, *The building where corn is kept*) 37 Infs, **chiefly Sth, Midl**, Corn bin; (Qu. M12, *What do you keep food for the cattle in over winter?*) Infs **MO**7, **NC**54, **OK**1, Corn bin; (Qu. M22, *What other kinds of buildings would there be on farms around here?*) Infs **GA**87, **IL**90, Corn bin; (Qu. M6, *The place where grain is kept in a barn*) Inf **DC**2, Corn bin; **LA**18, Corncrib — most common; also corn [bɪnd].

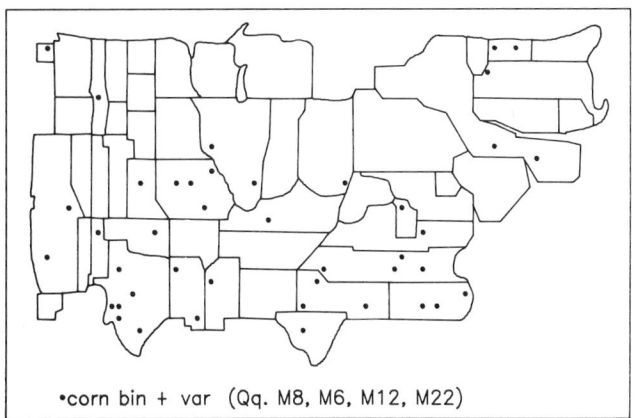

•corn bin + var (Qq. M8, M6, M12, M22)

cornbind n

1 =**bindweed 1.**

1900 Lyons *Plant Names* 115, *Convolvulus arvensis* . . Corn-bind. **1949** Moldenke *Amer. Wild Flowers* 270, It *[Convolvulus arvensis]* possesses scores of common names including such picturesque ones as *hedgebells . . cornbind . .* and *sheepbine.*

2 See **corn bindweed.**

cornbinder n [Alter of *cornerbind*, infl by *corn binder* harvesting machine]

1958 McCulloch *Woods Words* **Pacific NW**, *Cornbinder* . . . A term for a railroad logging truck equipped with cornerbind chains to hold logs on the truck.

corn bindweed n Also cornbind

=**black bindweed.**

1900 Lyons *Plant Names* 300, *Polygonum Convolvulus* . . Corn Bindweed. **1910** Graves *Flowering Plants* 163 **CT**, *Polygonum Convolvulus* . . Corn Bindweed. **1936** McDougall *Plants of Yellowstone* 52, Cornbind *(P[olygonum] convolvulus).*

corn bird n Cf corn thief 2

=**blue jay 1.**

1857 U.S. Patent Office *Annual Rept. for 1856: Ag.* 140, The blue-jay or "Corn Bird," as it is called in some localities. **1956** *MA Audubon* 40.84, *Blue Jay.* Corn Bird (Mass. From picking up newly planted corn.). **1970** *DARE* (Qu. Q16) Inf **TN**53, Corn bird.

corn bluebottle n Also cornbottle

=**cornflower 1.**

1900 Lyons *Plant Names* 89, *C[entaurea] Cyanus* . . Corn Blue-bottle . . Corn-bottle. **1910** Shreve et al *MD Plant Life* 497, Corn Blue Bottle. **1959** Carleton *Index Herb. Plants* 30, *Corn-blue-bottle:* Centaurea cyanus. *Corn bottle:* Centaurea cyanus.

corn boiling n Also *corn boil*

A festivity at which fresh corn is boiled and eaten.

1929 *Randolph Enterprise* (Elkins, W.Va.) 26 Sep. 1/1 *(DA),* Tygart Lodge of the Knights of Pythias had a most enjoyable corn boiling and weiner roast last Thursday night. **1966–67** *DARE* (Qu. FF2, . . *Kinds of parties . . around here*) Inf **SC**11, Corn boiling; (Qu. FF16, . . *Local contests or celebrations*) Inf **IL**4, Corn boil.

cornbottle See **corn bluebottle**

corn bread n

1 =**corn pone 1. esp Sth**

c1960 *Wilson Coll.* **csKY,** *Cornbread . . .* The generic name for bread made of cornmeal, but often restricted to bread cooked in a pan. **1965–70** *DARE* (Qu. H25, . . *Fried cornmeal*) Infs **FL**11, 31, **LA**16, 43, **MA**3, **NC**51, 76, **OK**44, **RI**3, Corn bread.

2 attrib: Cornmeal.

1869 in 1884 Lanier *Poems* 172 **GA,** And his hogs was flat as his corn-bread pones. **1965–70** *DARE* (Qu. H14, *Bread that's made with cornmeal*) 9 Infs, **chiefly Sth,** Corn bread muffins; **KY**22, **LA**3, 11, 24, Corn bread sticks; **GA**3, Corn bread dodgers; **KY**62, Corn bread cakes; **LA**11, Corn bread pone; **NC**76, Corn bread dumplings; (Qu. H18, . . *Special kinds of bread*) Inf **MO**38, Corn bread patties, corn bread sticks; (Qu. H23, . . *Hot cooked breakfast cereal*) Inf **AR**47, Corn bread mush; (Qu. H24, . . *Boiled cornmeal*) Inf **AR**47, Corn bread mush; (Qu. H25, . . *Fried cornmeal*) Inf **MS**46, Corn bread patties; **VA**56, Corn bread cakes; (Qu. H32, . . *Fancy rolls*) Inf **FL**49, Corn bread muffins.

corn bread adj

Ordinary, common.

1951 Porter *Ragged Roads* 116, In plain old corn-bread language we would just call them [=fat people] "hog fat."

corn bread consumption n *joc*

An excessive predilection for corn bread.

1940 *AmSp* 15.447 **eTN,** *Cornbread consumption.* To eat cornbread excessively. 'Lida's man has cornbread consumption.'

corn break See **break** n[1] **8**

corn broom n Also *corn-sage broom, corn-straw broom* **scattered, but chiefly NEast** See Map *old-fash*

A broom made from broomcorn.

a1817 (1822) Dwight *Travels* 4.485, [Manufactures of Massachusetts include] Straw bonnets, Brushes, Corn Brooms. **1899** (1912) Green *VA Folk-Speech,* Corn-broom . . . Brooms made from the tops of broom-corn. **1935** CT Bd. Educ. *Colony of CT* 11, Corn brooms . . . These were made about 1798. **1950** *WELS* (*Different kinds of brooms used around the house*) 7 Infs, **WI,** Corn broom. **1965–70** *DARE* (Qu. F36, *Other kinds of brooms that people use around here*) 69 Infs, **chiefly NEast,** Corn broom; **AR**17, Corn-sage broom—just a sweeping broom; **PA**217, Corn-straw broom; (Qu. F35, *A small broom that you hold in one hand, and use . . in places that are hard to get at*) Infs **ME**5, **MA**40, 72, 98, **OR**13, Corn broom. [59 Infs old, 15 mid-aged]

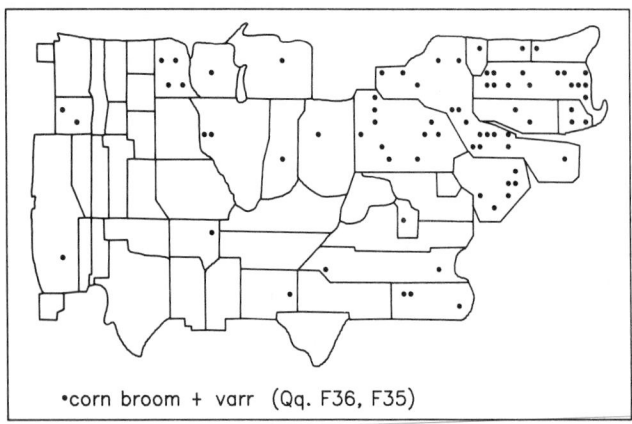

•corn broom + varr (Qq. F36, F35)

corn cake n Also *cornmeal cake* **chiefly Sth, Midl** See Map Cf **hoecake, johnnycake**

Cornbread shaped in a flat cake and fried on a griddle or sometimes baked in a pan.

1791 (1958) Bartram *Travels* 38, It (shellbarked hiccory) . . is an ingredient in most of their cookery, especially homony and corn cakes. **1852** Stowe *Uncle Tom's Cabin* 39, Her corn-cake, in all its varieties of hoe-cake, dodgers, muffins, and other species . ., was a sublime mystery to all less practised compounders. **1903** *N.Y. Sun* 1 Nov. *(DA),* Corn cakes as a substitute for bread are popular in the South. **1946** *PADS* 5.16 **VA,** *Corn cakes . . .* Cornmeal griddle cakes; fairly common. **1949** Kurath *Word Geog.* 68, On the lower Susquehanna and in northern Delaware griddle cakes made of cornmeal are known as *corn cakes,* and this term now competes in Maryland with *johnny cake,* in the Shenandoah valley and the Northern Neck of Virginia with *hoe cake.* **1958** *PADS* 29.8 **TN,** *Corn cake.* c1960 *Wilson Coll.* **csKY,** *Corn cakes . . .* Griddle cakes made of cornmeal. **1965–70** *DARE* (Qu. H14, *Bread . . made with cornmeal*) 45 Infs, **chiefly Sth, S Midl,** Corn cake(s); (Qu. H20b, . . *Other names . . for pancakes*) 12 Infs, **chiefly Appalachians, wPA,** Corn cakes; (Qu. H25, . . *Fried cornmeal*) 55 Infs, **chiefly Midl, Sth,** Corn cakes; **OK**56, Cornmeal cakes.

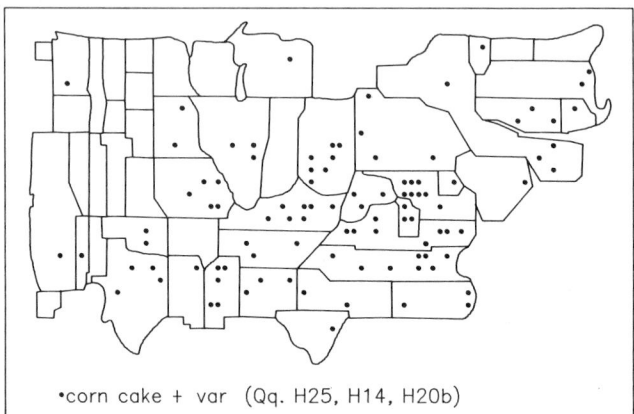

•corn cake + var (Qq. H25, H14, H20b)

corn campion n

=**corn cockle.**

1900 Lyons *Plant Names* 20, *A[grostemma] Githago* . . Corn Campion. **1932** Rydberg *Flora Prairies* 323, *Agrostemma . . .* Corn Cockle, Corn Campion.

corn chuck n [?Alter of *corn shuck*] *hist*

A minstrel dance or dance step.

c1830 in 1962 Nathan *Dan Emmett* 89, [Minstrel broadside:] Here's Virginia double trouble, / Where dey dance de corn chuck, / And here's de real scientific, / What dey hab in Kentuck.

corncob n

=**yellow rail.**

1923 U.S. Dept. Ag. *Misc. Circular* 13.44, *Yellow Rail . . . Vernacular names . . .* corncob. **1956** *AmSp* 31.184 **LA,** Corn cob—Yellow rail.

corncob jelly n Cf **corn jelly**

A kind of jelly made from cobs of corn; see quot 1968.

1967 *Good Old Days* June 24/1 **swMO,** *Corn Cob Jelly*—12 bright red cobs / 3 pints water / 1 pkg. pectin / 3 cups sugar. **1968** *Rockport Democrat* (IN) Sept np, Mrs. Wallace F. Crews . . recently was "written-up" in the Daily Times . . as a result of her recipe for the unusual corn cob jelly . . . "It is actually made," she said, "by boiling regular horse corn cobs in water, with sugar and pectin, and has an amber color and a pleasant fruity taste much like plum or apple jelly."

corncob wine n

1969–70 *DARE* (Qu. DD28b, *What fermented drinks are made at home around here?*) Infs **GA**77, **KY**80, **OK**52, Corncob wine.

corn cockle n

Std: a tall silky weed (*Agrostemma githago*) with purplish-red flowers, naturalized in the US, and common in grainfields. Also called **corn campion, corn pink 1, corn rose, mullen pink, old-maid's-pink, rose campion, rose pink**

corn coffee n

1 A coffee substitute brewed with parched corn or acorns.

1844 Featherstonhaugh *Excursion Slave States* 114, The supper consisted of . . coffee made of burnt acorns and maize . . . He laughed at our fastidiousness, and advised us to drink some of the *corn*-coffee. **1894** Robley *Hist. Bourbon Co.* 68 **KS** (as of 1857), The "menu" consisted of cornbread, bacon, fried potatoes and corn coffee with "long sweetnin'[".]

2 Corn whiskey, moonshine.

1939 *AmSp* 14.90 **TN**, Corn *coffee*. Mountain liquor. 'He's full up on corn coffee.' **1941** *AmSp* 16.70, *Liquor* . . . Corn coffee. **c1970** Halpert *Coll.* 13 **wKY**, Corn *coffee*—mountain liquor.

corn cookie n

A kind of **corn cake**.

1970 *DARE* (Qu. H25, . . *Fried cornmeal*) Inf **VA**48, Corn cookies; like a pancake but made with cornmeal.

corncracker n

1 A poor White farmer; a rustic — often used to refer to a person from a specific state: see quots. *sometimes derog* See also **cracker 2**

1835 *Western Review* June 342 *(DA)*, There is neither wit nor meaning in the terms *Hoosier, Sucker, Corncracker,* and *Buckeye,* which have become so current; and it is not without mortification that we hear strangers inquiring the origin and meaning of these names. **1848** (1855) Ruxton *Life Far West* 26, But them diggings get too over crowded nowadays, and it is hard to fetch breath amongst them big bands of corncrackers to Missoura. **1908** *DN* 3.302 **eAL, wGA**, *Cracker* . . . A Georgian. Sometimes called *corn-cracker*. **1938** *AmSp* 13.22, *Hog and hominy* was considered fit food for *Corn-crackers,* the poor whites of Florida, Georgia, Kentucky, and Tennessee. **1940** Hatcher *Buckeye Country* 298, I never in my life heard a Buckeye get into his voice that quiver of ecstasy that is second nature to a Corncracker when he mentions his bluegrass and his mountains and his folks. **1968** *DARE* (Qu. HH1, . . *A rustic or countrified person*) Inf **MD**31, Corncracker. **1968** *DARE* File **swNJ**, *Corncracker,* a person from Delaware.

2 A kind of gristmill. *hist*

1844 Lee–Frost *10 Yrs. OR* 134, At the mission we had a small cast-iron corncracker, in which we ground wheat after a fashion. **1911** Shute *Plupy* 42 **seNH** (as of 1860s), Pewt was also in the most astonishing condition possible, and looked as if he had been shaken up in a corncracker. **1933** *AmSp* 8.1.48 **Ozarks**, Corn *cracker* . . . A primitive gristmill. **1948** *NW Ohio Qrly.* 20.84, They built a dam and mill race and the little corncracker began to turn. **1968** *DARE* Tape **IN**3, They [Indians] had at one time camped in through here, and we have evidence of that . . . Indian relics, tommyhawks and peace pipes and arrowheads and corncrackers and lots of things.

3 See quot.

1905 *DN* 3.6 **cCT**, *Corn-cracker* . . . Slang for a good thing.

4 =**cownose ray.**

1884 Goode *Fisheries U.S.* 1.666, Of the Eagle Ray family, *Myliobatidae,* . . only one [species] seems to be found in Florida and the Gulf; this is the "Whipparee" or "Corn-Cracker" of the South (*Rhinoptera quadriloba).*

corn crib n Cf *DS* K44

See quot.

1969 Sorden *Lumberjack Lingo* 27 **NEng, Gt Lakes**, *Corncrib*—A very thin horse in poor physical condition. With ribs showing, it reminded men from the farms of a corncrib.

corn-crib pipe n

1970 *DARE* FW Addit **TX**99, *Corn-crib pipe*—old-fashioned but common term for "corncob pipe."

corn crow n [Perh folk-etym or pronc-sp for **carrion crow**] **Sth** Cf **Jim Crow, John Crow**

=**black vulture.**

1966–68 *DARE* (Qu. Q13, . . *The vulture*) Infs **GA**1, **TX**35, Corn crow; (Qu. Q14, . . *Other names . . for these birds*) Inf **NC**49, Corn crow; (Qu. Q12, . . *Kinds of crows*) Inf **MS**6, Corn crow.

corn-crust bread n

Cornmeal bread baked in a thin layer.

1965–68 *DARE* (Qu. H18, . . *Special kinds of bread*) Infs **IN**16, **MS**25, Corn-crust bread; **AL**11, Corn-crust bread; [make it of] meal and bake thin—like a crust.

cornder See **corner** n[1]

corn doctor n *often derisive*

One who removes corns from the feet.

1839 Pencil *White Sulphur* 40, There are several resident physicians here; . . and a corn-doctor's card . . have been posted up for several days. **1923** Watts *Luther Nichols* 69 *(DAE),* Mrs. Siefert's establishment . . with the corn-doctor in the basement, and the I.W.W. agitator in the garret. **1958** Randolph *Sticks* 86 **Ozarks**, There was a corn-doctor doing tricks to draw the crowd . . . The corn-doctor slammed the dollar on the counter.

corn dodger n Occas *cornmeal dodger* [**dodger** n[1]]

1 A corn bread cake often shaped by hand and fried on a griddle or baked in an oven. **chiefly Sth, S Midl** Cf **corn cake, corn pone**

1839 in 1882 Kimball *President Jrl.* 87, The next morning I had to go till twelve o'clock before I had anything to eat, and then it was transparent pork and corn dodger. **1847** Rutledge *Carolina Housewife* 25 **SC**, *Corn Dodgers*—One quart of corn meal, a little salt, and water enough to make the batter just stiff enough to make the mixture into cakes with the hands. Bake in a Dutch oven, on tin sheets. **1903** *DN* 2.310 **seMO**, *Corndodger* . . . A kind of cornbread baked in a skillet. It is not sweetened or shortened and is very hard, but quite palatable. **1907** *DN* 3.230 **nwAR**. **1908** *DN* 3.301 **eAL, wGA**. **1912** *DN* 3.573 **wIN**. **1949** Kurath *Word Geog.* 68, In the South Midland (most of West Virginia, western Virginia, western North Carolina), and in the Northern Neck and the northern Piedmont of Virginia the term *corn dodger* is applied to a small corn cake (two or three in one pan). **1958** *PADS* 29.8 **TN**. **1965–70** *DARE* (Qu. H14, *Bread that's made with cornmeal*) 24 Infs, **chiefly S Midl, eTX**, Corn dodger(s). **1972** Hilliard *Hog Meat* 39 **Sth**, I have never fallen in with any cooking so villainous. Rusty salt pork, boiled or fried . . . and musty cornmeal dodgers, rarely a vegetable of any description, no milk, butter, eggs, or the semblance of a condiment.

2 A cornmeal dumpling steamed or boiled with meat and vegetables. **chiefly S Atl, eVA** Cf **corn dumpling, poorsoul**

1899 (1912) Green *VA Folk-Speech, Corn-dodger* . . . A dumplin' made of corn meal and boiled in a pot with ham and cabbage. **1949** Kurath *Word Geog.* 68, In the eastern part of the Carolinas and on the Eastern Shore of Maryland *corn dodger* means a dumpling, usually steamed with vegetables. **1950** *PADS* 14.22 **SC**, *Corn dodger* . . . A lump of cornmeal dough, flavored with onions and black or red pepper, dropped into a pot of greens and boiled for half an hour. **1966** *DARE* Tape **FL**31, Corn dodgers . . . You take your cornmeal and you have your greens boiling and take some cold water and mix this cornmeal up. I make mine up in little pones and lay them on top of this greens, where you have the bacon and the greens and it's boiling and when that gets done, why, you eat that right along with your greens.

corn dog n Also *corny dog* **esp Gulf States, SW**

A frankfurter on a stick, dipped in cornmeal batter, and deep fried.

1967 *Refugio Co. Press* (TX) 12 April 4/1, *School Menus* . . Monday—Corn dogs. **1967–69** *DARE* (Qu. H40, *A small sausage that is put into a long roll or bun to make a sandwich*) Inf **MO**15, Corn dog; **TX**9, Corn dog—hot dog covered with corn batter fried in deep fat; **TX**69, Corn dog, dipped in batter; **TX**104, Corny dog; (Qu. H42) Inf **AZ**8, Corn dog, weenie on a stick; **TX**36, Corny dog; (Qu. H41) Inf **AL**30, Corn dog, cooked in cornmeal; (Qu. H31, *Other foods made with dough and cooked in deep fat*) Inf **OK**47, Corn dogs, cornmeal & onions. **1967–69** *DARE* FW Addit **cnLA**, *Corn dog*—a wiener rolled in cornmeal batter and deep fried; **cwIL**, *Corn dog*—a hot dog on a stick, dipped in corn batter and deep-fat fried. **1973** *Valdez Copper-Basin News* (AK) 16 Aug 1/1, The American Legion Auxiliary, Unit 27 operated the food concession and sold Corn Dogs. **1979** *Starkville Daily News* (MS) 17 Mar 10/6, School Menus. Elementary Schools . . Monday—Corn Dog, Mustard.

corn drill n **esp KY**

A farm implement for planting corn (maize) in rows.

1853 MI State Ag. Soc. *Trans. for 1852* 4.84, Corn drill, an excellent article. **1872** (1876) Knight *Amer. Mech. Dict.* 624/2, *Corn-drill.* A planter for sowing corn in rows. The corn planter, properly speaking, places the seed in hills in a row. When the rows are *checked,* so called, the corn may be worked one way and then across . . . Corn in drills can be tended but one way. **c1960** Wilson *Coll.* **csKY**, *Corn drill* . . . A regular farm implement in all the later years of the area; dropping the grains of corn by hand is still remembered by all the older people and many younger ones. **1966–70** *DARE* (Qu. L23, *What machinery is used* *around here in putting in the seed?*) Infs **KY**29, 35, 49, 76, 90, **MO**10, **NC**30, Corn drill.

corn dumpling n Also *cornmeal dumpling* **chiefly Sth** See Map

=**corn dodger 2.**

1880 *Harper's Mag.* 60.330/1 **cNY** (as of 1743), Here were they "lustily entertained" . . feasting on "corn dumplings," venison, and hominy. **1912** in 1914 Stewart *Letters* 150 **WY** (as of 1909–13), They [Mexicans] had a most wonderful pot-roast with potatoes and corn dumplings that were delicious. **1939** FWP *These are Our Lives* 352 **SE**, She'd cook up a big pot of greens with corn dumplin's, fix sausage and gravy to eat with the yams, and maybe bake a sweetcake, if she had time, or pies. **1965–70** *DARE* (Qu. H24, . . *Boiled cornmeal*) 10 Infs, **Sth**, Corn dumpling(s); **FL**26, **GA**8, **MD**14, **MS**72, **NC**79, **VA**45, Cornmeal dumplings; (Qu. H14, *Bread that's made with cornmeal*) Infs **AL**1, **MD**12, **NC**25, 55, 84, **SC**19, Corn dumplin(g)s; **VA**39, Cornmeal dumplings; (Qu. H45, *Dishes made with meat, fish, or poultry*) Inf **AL**33, Corn dumplings; (Qu. H50, *Dishes made with beans, peas, or corn*) Inf **GA**75, Corn dumplings.

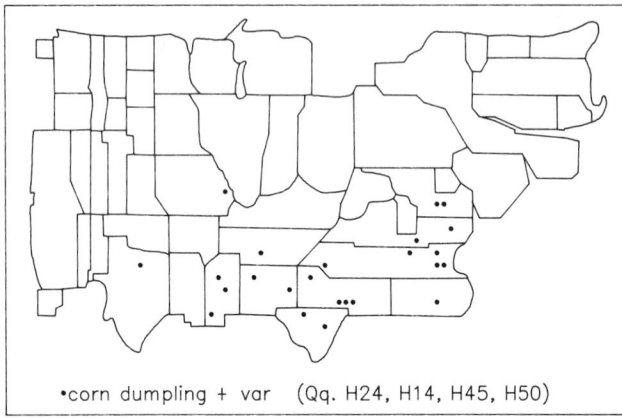

•corn dumpling + var   (Qq. H24, H14, H45, H50)

corn earworm n Also *corn worm, earworm*

A moth larva (*Heliothis zea*), which is a pest on var plants including corn, cotton, and tomato. Also called **tassel worm, tobacco bollworm, tomato worm**

1802 MA Hist. Soc. *Coll.* 1st ser 8.190, Five [worms] . . are very destructive to Indian corn . . . The fifth is the *ear worm;* which, after the ear is formed, eats the grains and between them; about an inch long. **1899** (1962) Cushman *Hist. Choctaw* 210, The corn-worms were usually numerous and were committing great depredations upon their fields of green corn. **1900** Bailey *Cyclop. Horticulture* 1.376, The corn worm is also known south as the cotton-boll worm. It is destructive to sweet corn especially. **1911** *Century Dict., Boll-worm* . . also molests other plants, and is known, under varying circumstances, as the *bod-worm, corn-worm, ear-worm, tassel-worm,* and *tomato-fruit worm.* **1967–70** *DARE* (Qu. R27, . . *Kinds of caterpillars or similar worms*) Infs **CT**2, **IN**67, **KY**80, **MA**47, 58, **MI**93, **RI**15, **VA**46, Earworm; **HI**14, **IA**6, **OH**4, **SC**63, Corn earworm.

corned adj [Prob from **corn** n **B1**]   Cf *DS* DD14, 15

Intoxicated, drunk.

1823 *Mass. Spy* 22 Dec *(DAE)*, "Pretty well corned" and "up to everything." Drunk as a lord and happy as a king. **1880** *Harper's Mag.* 60.636/2 **MD**, Living near him were two farmers named Jervis and Dixon, who commonly got well "corned" when they came to town. **1899** (1912) Green *VA Folk-Speech* 127, Corned = drunk. **1907** *DN* 3.184 **seNH**. **1909** *DN* 3.410 **cnME**. **1930** Shoemaker *1300 Words* 12 **cPA Mts** (as of c1900), *Corned*—Intoxicated.

cornelia(n) See **carnelian**

corner n[1] Pronc-spp *cawnuh, cyorner,* and **esp in Sth, S Midl**, *cawnder, cornder*

A Forms.

1795 Dearborn *Columbian Grammar* 135, [In a list of improprieties:] Cornder for Corner. **1890** *DN* 1.64 **KY**, *Cornder:* for *corner.* **1899** (1912) Green *VA Folk-Speech,* Put that broom in the cornder. **1908** *DN* 3.301 **eAL, wGA**, *Cornder.* **1909** *DN* 3.394 **nwAR**, We set up a stob at the cornder of your lot. **1916** *Scribner's Mag.* 59.351/2 **Blue Ridge Mts**

VA [Black], De clover-patch over by de fur cornder o' de yard. **1922** Gonzales *Black Border* 292 **sSC, GA coasts** [Gullah glossary], *Cawnuh.* **1927** Kennedy *Gritny* 131 **LA** [Black], You gotta fetch a bucket o' water from de well, yonder to de cawnder. **1928** *AmSp* 3.406 **Ozarks**, *Corner* is frequently turned into *cornder.* **1963** *Mt. Life* Summer 51 **KY**, I'd be willin' . . to bet ye a double handful of hullgull ches'nits he couldn't hem a blind pig in a fence cyorner.

B Senses.

1 also attrib: A small parcel (of land).

1650 in 1926 Warwick RI *Early Rec.* 86, Henry Townsend shall have a corner of land in the front. **1854** (1923) Melville *Works* 11.192 **MA** (as of 1790s), The d----d soul had not a corner-lot on earth! **1970** *DARE* (Qu. L6a, . . *A piece of land under cultivation—less than an acre*) Inf **TN**53, Corner.

2 See quot.

1953 *AmSp* 28.248 **csPA**, *Corner* . . . A topographical term designating the dead end of a valley resulting from the intersection of two mountains. The angle thus formed must be less than 90 degrees. In general use.

3 also pl: A small locality, such as a village or part of a village; see quots. **chiefly NEng**

1825 Neal *Brother Jonathan* 2.10, They continued watching him, until he came to the "corner;" the west end of every Yankee village, or settlement. **1841** (1973) Gurney *Journey* 216, The small villages in New England are often called *corners.* **1892** VT State Bd. Ag. *Report* 12.130, Each town has a small village or "corners," where the churches, post-office, store, and various shops are located. **1942** Rawson *NH Borns a Town* 15, To the east of these falls and spreading out as though sown by some generous hand, certain little villages today lie comfortably among the breathing hills where they were given birth one hundred and eighty years ago as "clearings," "hollows," "notches," or "corners." **1968–69** *DARE* (Qu. C34, *Nicknames for nearby settlements, villages, or districts*) Infs **NY**66, **RI**12, Corners. **1975** Gould *ME Lingo* 60, *Corner*—Certain Maine towns where the business section formed at the meeting of highways (a *corner*) have retained this term for the complex of stores, post office, barber shop, etc. "Going to the *corner*" means going to the store.

‡**4** See quot.

1970 *DARE* (QR, near Qu. DD18) Inf **NY**241, The corner—the last drop in the bottle.

5 in phrr *cut* (or *trim*) *one's corners sharp* (or *closely*): To get away with as much as a situation allows.

1904 (1916) Porter *Freckles* 125, Freckles was trimming his corners as closely as he dared. **1949** *Western Folkl.* 8.100 **CA**, *To cut one's corners pretty sharp*—To fulfill only the minimum obligations.

6 in phr *keep one's corners up*: To be meticulous about one's work; to attend to the less important tasks.

1903 *DN* 2.310 **seMO**, *Corners* . . . In expression, to 'keep the *corners* up,' to keep in repair. Applied particularly to farms. 'He is a good farmer and always keeps his corners up.'

corner v

1 In turpentine production: to make additional cuts in a **box** n **1** with an ax; hence vbl n *cornering.*

1893 *Outing* 21.269/2, Then he "cornered" the old "boxes" in the pines, and "chipped" with a vengeance till they ran full of turpentine. **1904** *DN* 2.396, *Corner* . . . In the turpentine industry. "The next step is *cornering,* which is done with an ordinary axe, a left-handed and a right-handed man working together. A slanting cut is made through the bark and about one inch into the sapwood, rising slightly from the top of the back of the *box* to a point perpendicularly above the corner of the box. By a side blow of the axe the wood is then split out between the cut and the rounding edge of the box." **1968** *DARE* Tape **GA**22, [Inf:] After they got the boxes cut, they went back over and cornered 'em. [FW:] What does that mean? [Inf:] Well, that just means they cut it on each side there, just above the box, and fix it right for chippin'.

2 See quot.

1969 Sorden *Lumberjack Lingo* 27 **NEng, Gt Lakes**, *Corner* . . . In felling timber, to cut through the sapwood on all sides to prevent the trunk from splitting as it falls from its stump.

corner n[2] Pronc-sp for *coroner*

1976 Garber *Mountain-ese, Corner* . . coroner.

cornerball n [See quot 1954] **esp PA**

A children's outdoor game: see quot 1883.

1848 (1870) Drake *Pioneer Life* 149 **KY,** This was the case with that admirable game, a favorite at all country schools, corner ball. **1883** Newell *Games & Songs* 183, *Corner-Ball.* This is also an old game kept up by the Pennsylvania Germans . . . Four players stand on the four angles of a square, and the four adversaries in the centre. The ball is passed from one to another of the players in the corners, and finally thrown at the central players . . . If the player in the corner hits a central player, the latter is out, and *vice versâ.* **1940** Yoder *Rosanna* 124 **PA,** The boys played corner ball very well . . . The valley boys drew corners first and as they passed the ball around swiftly and then threw it at one of the two Pequea boys in the "middle" they were surprised to see how those Pequea boys could dodge the ball . . . When the valley boys had exhausted their corner force, they had to take their turns in the "middle." **1954** *AmSp* 29.48, *Corner ball* looks suspiciously like a translation of PaG [Pennsylvania German] /egbɑlə/. That the reverse is not the case is amply demonstrated by the fact that both the noun *Eckball* (in its various dialect forms) as well as the verb *eckballen* 'to play corner ball' are current in the dialects of Alsace, the Palatinate, and the Saar. **1968** *DARE* (Qu. EE33, *Other outdoor games . . that children play now, or that were played in your childhood*) Inf **OH82,** Cornerball.

corner, carry a v phr Cf **corner man**
In constructing a log building: to notch and fit the ends of logs together to form a corner.
1878 Guild *Old Times in TN* 160, The principal workmen in making notches in the logs (carrying up corners), were Hon John Bell and Dr. Boyd McNairy. **1945** Wilson *Passing Institutions* 47, It took skill to carry a corner. Only the most agile young men could do this. The rabble could tote logs and push them up the skids. c**1960** *Wilson Coll.* **csKY,** *Carry a corner* . . . To notch logs and fit them *in situ,* at a house- or barn-raising; a very skillful job.

corner gal n Cf **fence-corner**
1970 *DARE* (Qu. HH37, *An immoral woman*) Inf **TN53,** Corner gal.

‡**corner house** n
1968 *DARE* (Qu. M21b, *Joking names for an outside toilet building*) Inf **WI24,** Corner house.

cornering See **corner** v 1

corner man n
See quot 1905.
1905 U.S. Forest Serv. *Bulletin* 61.34, *Corner man.* In building a camp or barn of logs, one who notches the logs so that they will fit closely and make a square corner. **1926** Kephart *Highlanders* 314 **sAppalachians,** The mountain home of to-day is the log cabin of the American pioneer —not such a lodge as well-to-do people affect . . , but a pen that can be erected by four "corner men" in one day and is finished by the owner at his leisure. **1969** Sorden *Lumberjack Lingo* 28 **NEng, Gt Lakes.**

corners n
=**pussy wants a corner.**
1970 *DARE* (Qu. EE2, *Games that have one extra player—when a signal is given, the players change places, and the extra one tries to get a place*) Inf **NY250,** Corners—a game similar to musical chairs. The person in the center of the square tries to get a position in one of the corners.

corner the market n
A marbles game.
1973 Ferretti *Marble Book* 106, *Corner the market*—A "for keeps" game. Each player puts a designated number of marbles in a square or a hexagon, drawn in the dirt. Often played with shooters . . but just as often played with oversized *steelies* or *scaboulders* with which the shooter simply bowls, attempting to wham target marbles out of the drawn figure. With a good eye and a hot streak one could . . "corner the market" in *immies* in one's neighborhood.

corn-fed adj
1 Large, strong; clumsy, dull-witted.
1915 *DN* 4.218, *Corn-fed,* large and clumsy. "Those fellows are corn-fed." Colloquial. **1938** *AmSp* 13.23 **NE,** *Corn-fed,* used colloquially today in reference to persons, may mean plump, or it may mean heavy, dull, and slow-witted. **1967** *DARE* (Qu. X50, . . *A person who is very fat*) Inf **LA11,** Corn-fed. **1972** Cooper *NC Mt. Folkl.* 90, *Corn-fed*—husky; strong.
2 Rural.
1936 *AmSp* 11.275 **cTN,** *Corn fed* (person). One who lives in the country. "She is a corn fed girl."

3 Of music: countrified or out-of-style.
1929 *Melody Maker* Mar. 285/1 *(OEDS),* This peculiar . . style of melody, the appeal of which lies in the fact that it is purposely so utterly corn-fed. **1935** *Peabody* (Mass.) *Bull.* Dec. 42/2 *(OEDS),* Corny—Derived from cornfed, meaning [music] played in country style, out of date, hill-billy, or in a style of pre-1925. **1937** L. Feather in *Radio Times* 2 Apr. 10/3 *(OEDS),* Corn, old-fashioned style: out-of-date idiom and technique in jazz. Hence *corny* or *cornfed* applied to musicians and their style.

corn, feel one's v phr [Var of *feel one's oats*]
To feel frisky, energetic.
1890 *DN* 1.64 **KY,** Corn . . . Of a frisky horse, we say, "He feels his corn." [*DN* ed.: In New England, "He feels his *oats.*" Also used metaphorically of persons.]

‡**cornfield** v
1968 *DARE* FW Addit **nIN,** Cornfield—used in connection with catching fish: to play the fish and land it slowly. "You had better cornfield that one in."

cornfield bean n Also *corn bean, cornfield pole bean, cornfield snap, cornhill bean* [See quot 1906] **chiefly Sth**
A common bean (*Phaseolus* spp).
1906 *DN* 3.132 **nwAR,** *Cornfield bean* . . . A kind of climbing bean planted with field corn, the stalks of which serve as poles. **1932** *Hanley Disks* **cnCT,** This season [there is] a new variety . . . They call them the cornhill . . . They are a peculiar looking little thing . . they look like peas, short, round and fat . . that is, the fruits are crowded in the pods. **1939** Harris *Purslane* 129 **NC,** Jessie farmed about as he pleased, planted cabbage in the cotton rows, corn-field beans among the corn. **1948** *WELS Suppl.* **cIN,** Corn beans. **1956** *Harder Coll.* **cwTN,** *Cornfield bean:* A bean that is dark red when dry. Also known as *cut short beans, striped crease black beans.* **1960** Criswell *Resp. to PADS* 20 **Ozarks,** *Cornfield beans* . . . Any kind of climbing beans, pole beans, which will climb a cornstalk. (Very frequent from long ago.). c**1960** *Wilson Coll.* **csKY,** *Cornfield bean* . . . A variety of climbing bean planted with corn, especially in the later "roasnear" [=roasting ear] patches. **1962** *Hall Coll.* **wNC,** A panther almost caught my great grandmother. On her way home from pickin' cornfield beans, she saw this panther and it started follerin' her. **1965–70** *DARE* (Qu. I20, *Other kinds of beans that are grown around here*) 26 Infs, **chiefly Appalachians,** Cornfield beans; **VA35,** Cornfield snaps; (Qu. I14, *Kinds of beans that you eat in the pod before they're dry*) Infs **AR17, NC55, TN4,** Cornfield beans; (Qu. I18, *The smaller beans that are white when they are dry*) Infs **GA72, MD35,** Cornfield beans; (Qu. I19, *Small white beans with a black spot where they were joined to the pod*) Inf **VA24,** Cornfield beans. **1969** *DARE* Tape **GA77,** [FW:] What kind of beans would you have? [Inf:] . . Well, it would be mostly cornfield beans or butter beans. **1970** *DARE* FW Addit **cwTN,** *Cornfield bean:* a kidney-type bean, brown background with dark brown lengthwise stripey blotches. **1976** *Wanigan Catalog* 7, Cornfield Pole [Bean], Cornhill [Bean].

cornfield darky See **cornfield negro**

cornfield duck n esp **TX**
=**tree duck 2.**
1878 U.S. Geol. & Geog. Surv. *Bulletin* 4.62, By the inhabitants it is called "Corn-field Duck", from its habit of frequenting corn-fields for the grain. **1879** U.S. Natl. Museum *Proc. for 1878* 1.169 **csTX,** *Dendrocygna autumnalis* . . . Called by the Mexicans *patos maizal,* or Corn-field Duck, from its habit of frequenting those localities. *Ibid* 170, *Dendrocygna fulva* . . . Like the Corn-field Duck, it is a summer visitant. **1923** U.S. Dept. Ag. *Misc. Circular* 13.38, *Black-bellied Tree-duck (Dendrocygna autumnalis)* . . . cornfield duck. *Ibid, Fulvous Tree-duck (Dendrocygna bicolor)* . . . In local use.—Cornfield duck (Tex.).

cornfield hand See **cornfield negro**

cornfield meet n [**meet** n]
A head-on train collision or one that is narrowly averted.
1943 *AmSp* 18.164, *Cornfield meet.* Head-on collision between two trains using the same track. **1945** Hubbard *Railroad Ave.* 338, *Cornfield meet*—Head-on collision or one that is narrowly averted. **1969** *AmSp* 44.255.

cornfield negro n, also attrib Also *cornfield darky, ~ hand, ~ nigger* **Sth**
1 A slave assigned to field labor.

1851 Burke *Polly Peablossom* 117, We worked like a cornfield nigger. **1881** Hammond *Georgians* 95, That infectious, good natured, "cornfield darky" laugh arose again. **1899** (1912) Green *VA Folk-Speech* 127, *Corn-field hand*. . . A negro who worked in the field, to distinguish from others who were house-servants, boatmen and so on. **1950** *PADS* 14.23 **SC**, *Cornfield Negro*. . . In slavery days, a Negro who was suitable only for work in the field; the same general meaning obtains today.

2 Transf: non-standard speech.

1948 Mencken *Amer. Lang. Suppl. 2* 124/1, The late W.J. Cash . . noted [in 1937] . . a tendency among educated Southerners to drop, on informal and especially jovial occasions, into what he termed *cornfield nigger*.

cornfield pea n Sth, S Midl
=black-eyed pea.

1820 *Western Carolinian* (NC) 1 Aug. *(DA)*, He will find its component parts to consist of corn field peas. **1895** Murfree *Mystery of Witch-Face* 157 **TN**, I would n't hev trested him with a handful o' cornfield peas. **1902** *Everybody's Mag.* 6.70/1 **Sth**, I dun et 'bout two quarts uv cawnfiel' peas cooked right greasy wid er poun' er two er bac'n. **1906** *DN* 3.132 **nwAR**, *Cornfield pea* . . . Field pea. "Cornfield peas are good for the land." **1966** *DARE* (Qu. I9, *Small white beans with a black spot where they were joined to the pod*) Inf **MS54**, Cornfield peas; (Qu. I20, *Other kinds of beans that are grown around here*) Inf **NC15**, Cornfield peas; (Qu. L9b, *Hay from other kinds of plants [not grass]*) Inf **NC15**, Cornfield peas.

cornfield plover n
=upland plover.

1888 Trumbull *Names of Birds* 172, Upland Plover . . We hear *Cornfield Plover* among other names at Washington, D.C. **1923** U.S. Dept. Ag. *Misc. Circular* 13.64, *Vernacular Names. In general use* . . . Upland plover . . . *In local use* . . . Cornfield plover (Md.).

cornfield pole bean See cornfield bean

cornfield preacher n Cf old-field preacher
1970 Tarpley *Blinky* 237 **neTX**, Among these *other responses, cornfield preacher* refers either to men who preach on Sunday and farm during the week or to the tales of men who had religious experiences and decided to become preachers while plowing in the field.

cornfield school n Sth hist
=old-field school.

1872 Schele de Vere *Americanisms* 48, Even the *cornfield* plays naturally a prominent part in Southern life, and as schoolhouses were apt to be erected in or near them, so-called self-made men are to this day fond of boasting that they never received any other education but in an *old cornfield school*. **1940** FWP *Guide TX* 100, Many private schools appeared during the period 1823–36. They were called "old field" or "cornfield" schools. **1954** *AmSp* 29.225 **SC**, I would go a step further and suggest that both of these words *[old field school, cornfield school]* are derived from *Indian old field* because the only man-made clearings found on the frontier were of Indian origin.

cornfield snap See cornfield bean

corn fish n [corn corned, salted]
See quot 1969.

1833 Neal *Down-Easters* 1.91 **ME**, Dod butter it all! . . That aint the kind o' sarse I wanted, puddin'-gravy to corn-fish! . . I wanted cabbage or potaters, or most any sort o' garden sarse. **1969** *DARE* (Qu. H45, *Dishes made with meat, fish, or poultry that everybody around here would know, but that people in other places might not*) Inf **NH16**, Corn fish: small fish split, laid in pan with salt; let lay for two or three days; rinse off; make bread stuffing; bake in the oven—a Seabrook special dish.

cornflake bush n
A **saltbush** (here: prob *Atriplex canescens*).

1967 *DARE* FW Addit **CO15**, *Cornflake bush*—name for salt sage; **CO29**, *Cornflake bush*—name for salt sage because it looks like it's strung with cornflakes.

cornflower n
1 A **star thistle**, esp *Centaurea cyanus* which is also called **barbeau, bluebonnet 2, bluebottle 1, blue sailors 2, bunk n¹ 3, corn bluebottle, French pink, hurtsickle, Kaiser's buttonhole flower, knapweed, ragged robin, ragged sailor.**

1825 Neal *Brother Jonathan* 1.346, One would have thought . . the cruel storm had been spoiling bright birds of their plummage [sic]—instead of the red poppy, and blue corn flower. **1900** Lyons *Plant Names* 89, *C[entaurea] Cyanus* . . Cornflower. **1950** Stevens *ND Plants* 295, *Centaurea* Cornflower. **1950** *WELS* 12 Infs, **WI**, Cornflower. **1965–70** *DARE* (Qu. S11, . . *Bachelor button*) 250 Infs, **widespread, but esp freq N Cent, PA**, Cornflower; (Qu. S26d) Infs **MD18, VA30**, Cornflower; (Qu. S5) Inf **OH37**, Cornflower; (Qu. S23) Inf **MT2**, Cornflower; (Qu. S25) Inf **NY30**, Cornflower; (Qu. S26a, . . *Roadside flowers*) Inf **NY30**, Cornflower; **MI82**, Wild cornflowers; (Qu. S26e) Inf **NY199**, Cornflower; **CA40**, Blue cornflower.

2 =bead lily.

1897 *Jrl. Amer. Folkl.* 10.145, *Clintonia borealis* . . corn flower.

3 =dogtooth violet.

1897 *Jrl. Amer. Folkl.* 10.145, *Erythronium Americanum* . . corn-flower.

4 A **bellwort** (here: *Uvularia sessilifolia* and *U. grandifolia*).

1897 *Jrl. Amer. Folkl.* 10.145 **ME**, *Oakesia sessilifolia* . . corn-flower. **1959** Carleton *Index Herb. Plants* 31, Corn-flower . . . *Uvularia grandifolia.*

5 A **false foxglove.**

1892 *Jrl. Amer. Folkl.* 5.101, *Gerardia quercifolia* (?), corn-flower. Hillsborough Co., N.H. *[Gerardia] pedicularia* (?).

corn fly n
A **midge.**

1966–70 *DARE* (Qu. R10, *Very small flies that don't sting*) Infs **AL38, IN45, KY88**, Corn fly.

corn freight n Cf grass freight
1968 Adams *Western Words* 75, *Corn freight*—Goods shipped by mule team; so called because corn had to be carried to feed the mules, reducing the amount of space available for freight and thus increasing cost. However, mule-team freight was much speedier than bull-team freight.

corn grass n
1 A **foxtail grass**: see quot. *obs*

1806 (1905) Lewis *Orig. Jrls. Lewis & Clark Exped.* 5.107, A harsh course grass; it appears to be the same which is called the Corn grass in the Southern states, and the foxtail in Virginia.

2 A **panic grass** (here: *Panicum clandestinum*).

1910 Graves *Flowering Plants* 55 **CT**, *Panicum clandestinum* . . Corn Grass. **1966–69** *DARE* (Qu. S9, *Other kinds of grass*) Infs **MA74, NJ52**, Corn grass; (Qu. S21, . . *Other weeds*) Inf **NC1**, Corn grass.

3 =barnyard grass.

1910 Graves *Flowering Plants* 56 **CT**, *Echinochloa crusgalli* . . . Barnyard Grass. Corn Grass . . . Useful as a forage plant and for the silo.

4 A **cordgrass** (here: *Spartina cynosuroides*).

1916 *Torreya* 16.237 **SC**, *Spartina cynosuroides* . . . Corn grass.

corn grub n
Prob a moth larva of the family Noctuidae.

1817 *Natl. Intelligencer* 7 June 1/5, What modes of previous preparation of the soil have been found to prevent the Corn Grub, or Cutworm. **1967** *DARE* (Qu. R27, . . *Kinds of caterpillars or similar worms*) Inf **NY24**, Corn grub.

cornhill bean See cornfield bean

corn-horse n
1910 *DN* 3.453 **seVT**, *Corn-horse* . . . A frame consisting of a pole with two legs at one end, and a small transverse stick. Used in "stoocking" [=bundling] corn.

cornhouse n chiefly NEng, Mid Atl See Map
A **corncrib.**

1696 (1977) Dickinson *God's Providence* 82, The People . . having . . large Cropps of Corn, as We could tell by their Corn-houses. **1772** in 1916 Mereness *Travels* 555, Some other Chiefs were Smoking and talking with me on a Cornhouse Scaffold. **1931–33** *LANE Worksheets* c**MA**, A corn crib is a compartment in a corn house. **1934** *Hanley Disks* s**ME**, Some would have a regular corn house. It would be set apart in the ground four feet or so. The sides of it and the middle would be slats. There'd be walks through the middle and slats. **1945** FWP *Lay My Burden Down* 211 **NC**, Start to set the cornhouse afire, but ma say: "Please sir, don't burn the cornhouse." **1946** *PADS* 5.17 **VA**, Corn house . . . Corn crib; everywhere east of the Blue Ridge except south of the lower James. **1949** Kurath *Word Geog.* 54, The Virginia Piedmont, the Tidewater area north of the James, and the Western Shore of Maryland have the distinctive term *corn house* to the exclusion of *corn crib.* In New England the two expressions stand side by side, but only scattered relics of *corn house* are found in the New England settlement area. **c1960** *Wilson Coll.* **csKY,** Corn house . . . Rare word for storage place for corn; usually crib or corncrib. **1965–70** *DARE* (Qu. M8, *The building where corn is kept*) 34 Infs, **chiefly NEng, Mid Atl,** Cornhouse; (Qu. M22, *What other kinds of buildings would there be on farms around here?*) Infs **DC8, GA16, VA32,** Cornhouse; (Qu. M6, *The place where grain is kept in a barn*) Infs **CT36, VA38,** Cornhouse; (Qu. M12, *What do you keep food for the cattle in over winter?*) Inf **NC80,** Cornhouses.

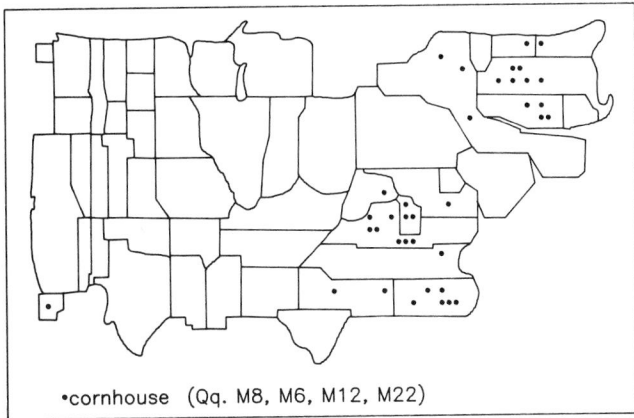

•cornhouse (Qq. M8, M6, M12, M22)

‡**cornhusk** n

A corncob.

1899 (1912) Green *VA Folk-Speech,* Corn-husk . . . The spike on which the grains of corn grow. [*DARE* Ed. questions accuracy]

corn husker n Cf *DS* HH1

A rustic.

1973 Allen *LAUM* 1.349 **IA,** Corn husker. [1 inf]

corn husker's peg n Also *corn peg*

See quot 1912.

a1872 Talmadge *Sermons* 1st ser 164, Corn-husker's peg never ripped out fuller ear. **1912** Green *VA Folk-Speech,* Corn-peg . . . A peg of some hard wood, or bone, about six inches long, held in the right hand, fastened to the middlefinger by a string, or leather loop, and the point used for shucking corn.

corn husking See **husking**

cornice n Usu |ˈkɔrnəs|; also freq |ˈkɔrnɪš| Pronc-spp *cornish, carnish*

Std senses, var forms.

1867 Lowell *Biglow* xxv **NEng,** Our *cornish* (which I find also in Herrick) remembers French better than *cornice* does. **1907** *DN* 3.242 **eME,** *Cornish* . . . Cornice. Used by carpenters. **1914** *DN* 4.104 **KS,** *Cornish, carnish* . . . Cornice. **1921** *DN* 5.204 **swMO,** *Cornish,* or *carnish.* **1942** McAtee *Dial. Grant Co. IN* 7/1 (as of 1890s), *Cornish* (cornice). **1950** *WELS* (*Under edge of a roof*) 33 Infs, **WI,** Cornish. **1960** Criswell *Resp. to PADS 20* **Ozarks,** *Cornice* . . . [ˈkɔrnɪš]. Practically universal pronc, used by country and small city carpenters and, of course, by those who hire them and work with them. **1968** *DARE* (Qu. D30, *The strip of wood or metal that covers the ridge of a roof*) Inf **IA17,** Called *cornish* by a repairman — he doesn't know it's wrong.

‡**corning** n [?Error for **horning**]

1969 *DARE* (Qu. AA18, *What do you call a noisy neighborhood celebration after a wedding, where the married couple is expected to give a treat?*) Inf **NY135,** Corning.

corn in the ear See **ear corn**

cornish See **cornice**

corn jelly n

1967 *DARE* (Qu. H57, *Tasty or spicy side-dishes served with meat*) Inf **IL9,** Corn jelly.

corn John n Cf **johnnycake**

1952 Brown *NC Folkl.* 1.529, Corn John . . . A hoecake.

corn juice n Cf **corn** n B1

Whiskey, esp that made of corn (maize).

1846 Porter *Quarter Race* 83 **TN,** He . . only axes a "fip" for a reel, and two "bits" fur what corn-juice you suck. **1878** *Appleton's Jrl.* 5.416/2 **West,** Western people . . prefer to call whiskey *corn-juice,* because therein is the conception of the *make* of the article. **1907** Mulford *Bar-20* 364 **West,** Tex swaggered over to the bar and tossed a quarter upon it: "Corn juice," he laconically exclaimed. **1926** Kephart *Highlanders* 123 **sAppalachians,** Corn *juice* is about all we can tote around over the country and git cash money for. **1938** *AmSp* 13.23 **NE.** **1967** *DARE* FW Addit **cwNC,** Corn juice — illegally made whiskey. **1969** *DARE* (Qu. DD21c, *Nicknames for whiskey, especially illegally made whiskey*) Inf **NC61,** Corn juice.

corn light bread n **Sth, S Midl** Cf **corn yeast, light bread**

Leavened bread formed in loaves and consisting largely or wholly of cornmeal rather than wheat flour.

1932 Stribling *Store* 399 **AL,** Drusilla was in the kitchen, going into the higher mysteries of corn lightbread with Jinny Lou. **1952** Tracy *Coast Cookery* 229 **TN,** Corn Light Bread . . . Moisten 2 cups [water-ground] cornmeal with cold water. Add boiling water and allow to work in a warm place . . overnight. In the morning add buttermilk, flour, soda, sugar, salt, warm water, and . . more meal. [Footnote:] Ordinary cornmeal is degerminated and therefore will not "work" as the water-ground meal will. **1969–70** *DARE* (Qu. H18, *Are there any special kinds of bread made now or in past years around here?*) Infs **TN31, 61, 64,** Corn light bread; **KY85,** Corn light bread — made with meal and flour, baked in loaf form; raised.

corn lightning n

1968 Coatsworth *ME Memories* 155, She turned the subject to other days on the island . . . Old words live on in out-of-the-way places . . . Heat lightning is "corn lightning."

corn lily n

1 =**spiderwort.**

1897 *Jrl. Amer. Folkl.* 10.146, *Tradescantia,* sp., . . corn lily, Sulphur Grove, Ohio.

2 A **bindweed 1** (here: *Convolvulus arvensis*).

1900 Lyons *Plant Names* 115, *C. arvensis* . . . Corn-lily, Corn-bind. **1949** Moldenke *Amer. Wild Flowers* 270, The *field bindweed* . . . possesses scores of common names, including . . *hedgebells, cornlily* [etc.].

3 Any of var plants of the lily family, as:

a =**false hellebore,** esp *Veratrum californicum* and *V. viride.* **West, esp CA**

1923 in 1925 Jepson *Manual Plants CA* 213, *V. californicum* . . . Corn Lily . . . Often reported as poisonous to stock and sometimes called False Hellebore. **1937** U.S. Forest Serv. *Range Plant Hdbk.* W201, *Veratrum* spp . . . The common name cornlily indicates the similarity of its leaves and their stalk arrangement to corn. **1947** *Southern Sierran* Aug 2/2 *(DA)* **CA,** Two miles beyond this point the Baden–Powell group descended 500 feet to Lily Springs (8060 feet) where ice cold water, masses of corn lilies . . made the side trip worth while. **1951** *PADS* 15.9, *Veratrum viride* . . . Corn-lily, southern California. **1963** Craighead *Rocky Mt. Wildflowers* 31, *False Hellebore* . . . Other names: Cornlily . . . The numerous flowers are yellowish green . . arranged in a large, dense panicle at top of plant.

b =**trillium.**

1920 *Torreya* 20.19, *Trillium* spp.—Corn lilies, Traverse City, Mich.

c A **bead lily** (here: *Clintonia borealis*).

1940 Clute *Amer. Plant Names* 221, *Clintonia borealis.* Blue bead, corn-lily, wood lily. **1961** Smith *MI Wildflowers* 48, Corn Lily — *Clintonia borealis.* **1975** Duncan–Foote *Wildflowers SE* 254, *C[lintonia] borealis* . . Corn-lily.

d A **day lily** (here: *Hemerocallis fulva*).

1966 *DARE* Wildfl QR Pl.12 Inf **MI57,** Corn lily.

corn malt n ?**S Midl** Cf **malt corn**

See quot 1974.

1967–69 *DARE* Tape **GA72,** Corn malt is whole corn grains that are dampened and sprouted; **TN9,** Take . . corn, soaked in water, then bury in leaves or sawdust and let sprout. Take out and dry, and grind. This makes corn malt. **1974** Maurer *KY Moonshine* 120, Corn malt . . .

Universally used in the eastern Kentucky mountains, made by burying a sack of corn under damp leaves until the corn has sprouted, then grinding the sprouted grain. Used principally by small operators. Large operators buy barley malt in larger quantities. "Yeah, I got a gunny sack of malt corn sprouted."

cornmeal bread n chiefly Nth, CA See Map
Cornbread.

1965 *PADS* 43.25 **seMA,** *Corn meal bread.* [1 inf] **1965–70** *DARE* (Qu. H14, *Bread that's made with cornmeal*) 47 Infs, **chiefly Nth, CA,** Cornmeal bread. **1968** *DARE* Tape **IN**30, The corn pone or the cornmeal bread . . . These were placed in this little . . three-legged skillet. **1971** *AmSp* 46.172 **Chicago IL,** 'Bread made of corn meal' . . *cornmeal bread.* [2 infs]

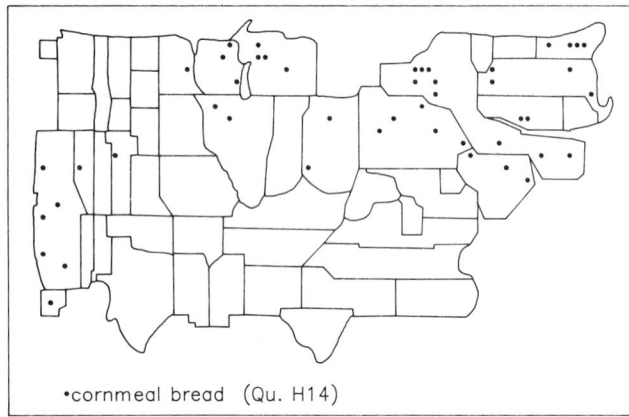

•cornmeal bread (Qu. H14)

cornmeal cake, ~ dodger, ~ dumpling, ~ muffin, ~ pone, ~ slapper, ~ yeast See **corn cake, ~ dodger, ~ dumpling, ~ muffin, ~ pone, ~ slapper, ~ yeast**

corn muffin n Also *cornmeal muffin* **scattered, but chiefly Mid and S Atl** See Map
A bread made of cornmeal and baked in a cup-shaped container.

1872 (1973) Thompson *Major Jones's Courtship* 189 **GA,** When we got in the dinin room, thar the old woman was, keeled over in her cheer, with her eyes sot in her head and a corn muffin stickin in her mouth. **1947** Croy *Corn Country* 200 **cnMO,** She is especially famous for her corn muffins. **1950** *WELS* (*Bread made with corn meal*) 1 Inf, **WI,** Corn muffin; 2 Infs, Cornmeal muffins. **1965–70** *DARE* (Qu. H14, *Bread that's made with cornmeal*) 80 Infs, **scattered, but esp S Atl,** Corn muffins; 19 Infs, **widely scattered,** Cornmeal muffins; (Qu. H18, . . *Special kinds of bread*) Inf **DC**11, Corn muffins; (Qu. H50) Inf **NJ**56, Corn muffins. **1973** Allen *LAUM* 1.280, Although *Boston brown bread, corn gems,* and *corn muffins* all occur in New England, they and other minor variants are almost entirely restricted to Midland speech territory in the U[pper] M[idwest] field records. This distribution probably reflects the relatively uncommon use of cornmeal in home baking in the northern areas.

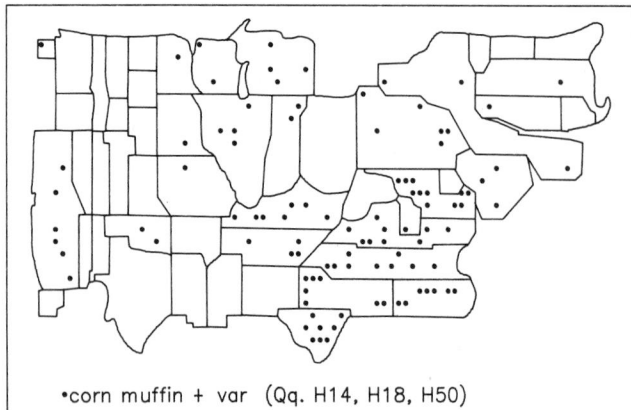

•corn muffin + var (Qq. H14, H18, H50)

corn mule n Cf **white mule** and *DS* DD21a, b, c
Corn liquor.

1929 *AmSp* 4.385 **KS,** It appears that the ordinary liquor of the region is a white distillate of corn or rye, variously known as *corn, corn-mule, . . corn-juice.* **1960** Wentworth–Flexner *Slang, Corn mule*—Corn whiskey; specif., home-made or bootleg or inferior corn whiskey.

corn mush n esp Nth Cf **hasty pudding**
Boiled cornmeal.

1846 in 1942 *CA Hist. Soc. Qrly.* 21.216, They [horse drovers] had nothing to eat but penolas & corn mush—no shelter. **1860** (1863) Goode *Outposts of Zion* 329 **neKS,** The main article of diet for our evening and morning meal was "hasty pudding," or, in Western parlance, "corn-mush," without any of the accompaniments usually considered appropriate. **1917** Alsaker *Eating for Health* 131, Corn mush: Cook corn meal in plain water until it is done, using moderate amount of salt. **1941** in 1964 Huxley *Letters* 465, Most of the southern farmers still prefer corn mush . . to vegetables. **1965–70** *DARE* (Qu. H24, . . *Boiled cornmeal*) 22 Infs, **esp freq in Nth,** Corn mush; (Qu. H23, . . *Hot cooked breakfast cereal*) Infs **CT**16, **MD**21, **MN**3, Corn mush.

corn nettle n
Prob a caterpillar with stinging hairs.

1970 *DARE* (Qu. R27, . . *Kinds of caterpillars or similar worms*) Inf **VA**79, Corn nettle.

corn night n
The night before Halloween, **cabbage night.**

1980 *DARE* File **neOH,** When I was . . living near Ashtabula, Ohio, in the late 1930's, we had a custom with which we celebrated the night before Halloween. We called it "Corn Night," and pelted the porches or doors of future Halloween "victims" with dried, shelled corn.

corn oyster n esp NEast
A small fritter made with grated fresh corn.

1847 (1855) *House & Home* 85 **SC,** *Corn Oysters*—Grate the corn, while green and tender, with a coarse grater, in a deep dish. To two ears of corn allow one egg; beat the whites and yolks separately, and add them to the corn, with one table-spoonful of wheat flour and one of butter. **1862** (1882) Stowe *Pearl of Orr's Is.* 321 **ME,** In this secret direction about the *mace* lay the whole mystery of corn-oysters. **1942** in 1957 Old Farmer's Almanac *Sampler* 255 **NH.** **1968** *DARE* (Qu. H50, *Dishes made with beans, peas, or corn*) Inf **PA**74, Corn oysters. **1979** *DARE* File **cnMA** (as of c1915), My mother made both corn fritters and corn oysters. Corn oysters were made from raw corn, scored and then scraped.

corn patty n chiefly Sth, S Midl Cf **corn cake, ~ dodger 1, ~ muffin**
A kind of cornmeal cake.

1950 *WELS* (*Dishes made with corn*) 2 Infs, **WI,** Corn patties. **1966–68** *DARE* (Qu. H14, *Bread that's made with cornmeal*) Infs **GA**4, **MO**17, **NC**18, Corn patties; (Qu. H25, . . *Fried cornmeal*) Infs **GA**4, 62, **MO**22, **TX**40, Corn patties.

corn peg See **corn husker's peg**

corn pen n
=**crib** n[1] 1.

1860 Claiborne *Life Dale* 26 **neGA** (as of 1783), We ran to the corn-pen, pulled down the rails, and let the high pile of corn slip down on the blazing shucks. **1864** (1938) Cate *Two Soldiers* 47 **nwGA,** I moved our lodging for the night from Sweet Gum Hotel to a corn pen in order to keep dry in case of falling weather. **1969–70** *DARE* (Qu. M8, *The building where corn is kept*) Infs **IL**80, 114, **NC**85, Corn pen.

corn pie n

1965–70 *DARE* (Qu. H50, *Dishes made with beans, peas, or corn*) Infs **PA**1, **SC**4, 9, 11, 22, 26, **WI**49, Corn pie; (Qu. H48, *Baked dishes made of potatoes cut up with meat or cheese*) Inf **PA**18, Corn pie.

corn pink n [*corn* from its freq occurrence in cornfields + *pink* from its resemblance to "pinks" (*Dianthus* spp)]

1 =**corn cockle** (*Agrostemma githago*).
1900 Lyons *Plant Names* 20, A[grostemma] Githago . . Corn Pink. **1959** Carleton *Index Herb. Plants* 31, Corn-pink: Agrostemma githago.
2 =**cornflower 1.**
1951 *PADS* 15.20, *Centaurea cyanus* . . Corn pinks.

corn planter n
=**brown thrasher.**

1955 *MA Audubon* 39.128, *Brown thrasher* [*Toxostoma rufum*] . . Corn-planter (Mass. From singing at corn-planting time; country people say that it sings: "Drop it, drop it, cover it, cover it, I'll pull it up, I'll pull it up.").

corn pone n [corn + pone]

1 also *cornmeal pone, corn pone bread, corn pony:* A cornmeal cake or bread sometimes formed into ovals and baked or fried. **orig chiefly Sth, Midl, now widespread exc NEng Cf ashcake, corn bread 1, corn cake, corn dodger 1, johnnycake**

1859 (1968) Bartlett *Americanisms, Corn Pone.* A superior kind of corn-bread, made with milk and eggs and baked in a pan. **1885** Twain *Huck. Finn* 62 **MO,** It was "baker's bread"—what the quality eat—none of your low-down corn-pone. **1946** PADS 5.17 **VA,** *Corn pone.* **1949** Kurath *Word Geog.* 67, In the valley of the Susquehanna, in all of Pennsylvania lying to the west of it, and in all the Atlantic states south of Pennsylvania *pone, corn pone,* and *pone bread* are widely used. **1950** WELS (*Bread made with corn meal*) 10 Infs, **WI,** Corn pone. **1958** PADS 29.8 **TN,** Corn pone, plain corn bread—the little pones cooked inside the stove. **c1960** *Wilson Coll.* **csKY,** *Corn-pone.* **1962** Atwood *Vocab. TX* 102, *Corn pone* is often associated with times when only meal and water were available for its preparation, whereas *corn bread* refers to bread made by more sumptuous recipes. *Ibid* 113, A considerable number of obsolescent terms have to do with food . . : (corn) pone. **1965–70** DARE (Qu. H14, *Bread that's made with cornmeal*) 166 Infs, **scattered throughout US, with heavy concentration in WV, MD, DC,** Corn pone; **GA**36, **KY**63, **MO**1, 17, **VA**69, Corn pones; **TX**42, Corn pone bread; **MA**48, Cornmeal pone; (Qu. H25, . . *Fried cornmeal*) 10 Infs, **chiefly Sth,** Corn pone; **VA**88, Corn ponies; **AL**25, Fried corn pone; (Qu. H18, . . *Special kinds of bread*) Infs **AR**38, **GA**70, **MO**20, 37, **NC**34, Corn pone; (Qu. H50, *Dishes made with beans, peas, or corn*) Inf **MA**40, Corn pone. **1967–68** DARE Tape **IN**30, After your corn pone . . was placed in the spider . . it would bake from above and from below; **SC**46, Corn pone would be baked inside the stove and . . hoe cakes on top the stove.

2 See quot. Cf **corn dodger 2, corn dumpling**

1967–68 DARE (Qu. H24, . . *Boiled cornmeal*) Inf **AZ**1, **LA**43, Corn pone.

3 Transf: see quots.

1967 DARE (Qu. HH1, . . *A rustic or countrified person*) Inf **TX**41, Corn pone. **1970** Major *Afro–Amer. Slang, Corn pone:* personality with the flavor of a Southeasterner.

corn pone bread, corn pony See corn pone 1

cornpout n

Prob =**brown bullhead 1.**

1972 NYT *Article Letters, Cornpout:* Bull head, catfish. Local name in Maine.

corn pudding n scattered, but esp PA, VA, KY See Map

A baked dish made with corn, milk, eggs, and sugar.

1823 (1922) Anthony *New Bedford* 55/2 **MA,** At brother William T., at a corn pudding party. **1848** Mitchell *Nantucketisms* (AmSp 10.40), *Corn-pudding.* Corn pounded or grated with milk, eggs & sugar & baked. **1932** (1946) Hibben *Amer. Regional Cookery* 210 **KY,** Corn Pudding. **1950** WELS (*Dishes made with corn*) 3 Infs, **WI,** Corn pudding (with sausage). **1952** Tracy *Coast Cookery* 86 **KY,** Now, to show you that we appreciate all ways of using corn, here is a corn pudding that originated in Kentucky and wound up recently winning a national prize. **1965–70** DARE (Qu. H50, *Dishes made with beans, peas, or corn*) 84 Infs, **scattered, but esp PA, VA, KY,** Corn pudding; (Qu. H48,

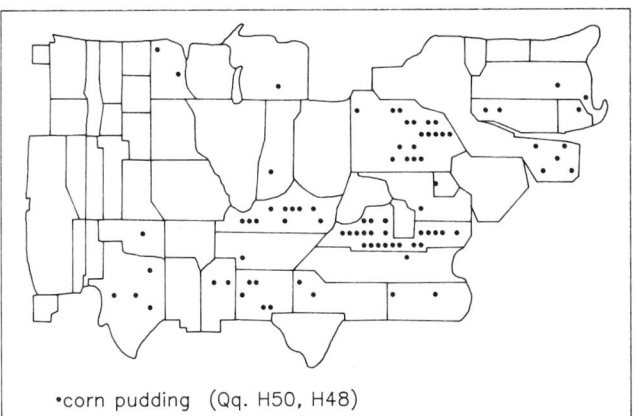

•corn pudding (Qq. H50, H48)

Baked dishes made of potatoes cut up with meat or cheese) Inf **VA**66, Corn pudding. **1972** *Complete World Cookery* 425, West Virginia Corn Pudding.

corn rock n

A millstone for grinding corn.

1968 DARE Tape **VA**5, I saw . . in Ash County, North Carolina, a turbine actually made out of wood, [it] ran and pulled the corn rock that ground meal.

corn rose n

=**corn cockle.**

1903 Small *Flora SE U.S.* 428, *Agrostemma Githago* . . Corn Rose. **1930** OK Univ. Biol. Surv. *Pub.* 2.61, Corn Rose. **1959** Carleton *Index Herb. Plants* 31, Corn-rose.

cornrow n, v esp among Blacks

A hairstyle having rows of tight braids close to the scalp, worn orig by Black women; to fashion one's hair in such a way.

1946 PADS 6.10 **eNC** (as of 1900–10), *Corn rows* . . . Braids formerly used by Negro women in their hair-dos. **1971** *Tuscaloosa News* 8 Nov 10/4 (AmSp 46.293) **AL,** The first thing little black girls once did when they got to be big girls was to unbraid their 'cornrowed' hair. Now big black girls borrow back this childhood coiffure. Cornrowing . . is high style. **1972** *New York Post* 8 March 15 (1973 Barnhart *New English*), "We all suffered through our mothers cornrowing our hair when we were little," Miss Taylor said, "and we couldn't wait to get out of it." But cornrowing is back. **1976** Flexner *America Talking* 45, It [the Afro] has been followed by a variety of African hair styles, including the *cornrow,* rows of small flat braids separated by half-inch parts. **1980** DARE File, On February 5 the Today Show (NBC-TV) featured a "new" hairstyle, the cornrow, once worn by Black women, now being adopted as high style by white women in imitation of Bo Derek's coiffure in the movie "10."

corn sack n

A **burlap bag.**

1850 (1926) Sawyer *Way Sketches* 21 May 36, We . . filled two corn sacks which we happened to have with us for saddle blankets. **1851** Hall *Manhattaner* 5, It was a modest commercial plain . . with . . corn sacks, in quantities. **1966–69** DARE (Qu. F19, *A cloth container for grain*) Inf **MS**72, Corn sack; (Qu. F23, *A container made of rough, loosely-woven, brown cloth; commonly used for potatoes, etc.*) Inf **NC**63, Corn sack. **1971** Wood *Vocab. Change* 371 **Sth,** [Footnote 82:] Volunteered: *paper bag, paper sack, . . corn sack, peat sack.*

corn-sage broom See corn broom

corn sedge n

A **cordgrass** (here: *Spartina cynosuroides*).

1933 *Torreya* 33.82, *Spartina cynosuroides* . . Corn sedge, Poplar Branch, N.C.

corn sheller n joc

1950 WELS (*Large front teeth that stick out of the mouth*) 1 Inf, **ceWI,** Corn shellers.

corn shucking n

1 also *corn shuck:* A social gathering at which corn is picked or husked. **chiefly Sth, S Midl**

1823 Faux *Memorable Days* 211 **swIN,** My host had a large party of distant neighbors assembled to effect a corn shucking, something like an English hawkey, or harvest home . . . Corn shucking means plucking the ears of Indian corn from the stalk, and then housing it in cribs . . for winter use. **1859** *Russell's Mag.* 5.552/1 **SC,** One night, very late, about one o'clock, returning on foot from a corn-shuck or quilting party, he encountered a herd of cattle in the road. **1874** (1937) Nichols *40 Yrs.* 11, The Indian corn . . is still upon the stalk . . and the . . ears . . are still enclosed in their tough, fibrous husks, or shucks, from which latter name this pleasant gathering is sometimes called a "corn-shucking." This is the western and southern term. **1895** DN 1.371 **eTN,** Corn-shucking. **1908** DN 3.301 **eAL, wGA,** *Corn-shuckin(g).* **1915** DN 4.182 **swVA,** Corn-shucking. **1944** Duncan *Mentor Graham* 181 **IL** (as of 1840s), Almira had had her share of merrymakings: apple stirrings and parings, corn shuckings, and fulling bees. **1950** PADS 14.23 **SC,** Corn shucking. **c1960** *Wilson Coll.* **csKY,** Corn-shucking. **1965–70** DARE (Qu. FF2, *What kinds of parties do people favor around here?*) 12 Infs, **chiefly Sth,** Corn shuckings; (Qu. FF1, . . *A "social" or "sociable"*) Infs **LA**11, **NC**49, Corn shucking; (Qu. FF16, . . *Local contests or celebrations*) Inf **AL**32, Corn shucking.

2 Harvest time.

1944 Howard *Walkin' Preacher* 23 **Ozarks,** He gave our names and ages and his birthday correctly [to the schoolmaster] but he couldn't remember my birthday. "He was borned in corn-shuckin'," he said.

corn silk n

1 See **silk.**

2 =**dodder.**

1897 *Jrl. Amer. Folkl.* 10.51 **NY,** *Cuscuta* . . . Corn silk, Southold, L.I.

corn slapper n Also *cornmeal slapper* Cf **slapjack**

See quot 1957.

1939 Wolcott *Yankee Cook Book* 134, Fried Indian Cakes . . *Also called Cornmeal Slappers* . . . Mix cornmeal, soda and salt quickly with boiling water . . to form into inch-thick cakes with the hands. Fry in skillet. **1957** *DE Folkl. Bulletin* 1.7.28, Corn slappers (griddle cakes made of corn meal).

corn smoke n [From appearance of the black spores]

Corn smut.

1950 *WELS (The blackish lumps that sometimes grow on ears of corn)* 1 Inf, **ceWI,** Corn smoke.

corn snake n [See quots]

A **rat snake** *(Elaphe guttata),* esp the subsp *E.g. guttata* which is marked dorsally with black-bordered red blotches on a gray or reddish ground and found throughout most of the South and as far north as southern New Jersey. Also called **chicken snake 1, house snake 2, red rat snake**

1676 *Royal Soc. London Philos. Trans.* 11.631, There is another sort called the *Corn-Snake,* because he is usually found in Corn-fields. **1743** (1754) Catesby *Nat. Hist. Carolina* 2.55, *Anguis e rubro & albo varius. The Corn Snake* . . . is all over beautifully marked with red, and white, which seems to have given it the Name of Corn-Snake; there being some *Maize* or *Indian* corn much resembling this Colour: they are Robbers of Hen-Roosts, otherwise they are harmless. **1896** Bruce *Economic Hist. VA* 1.129, Other varieties of snake were common, such as the puff adder, the moccasin, the corn, . . and the horn. **1966–70** *DARE* (Qu. P25, . . *Snakes . . around here)* Infs **GA93, NC13, 21, 27, 82, 85, VA55,** Corn snake. **1968** McPhee *Pine Barrens* 137 **sNJ,** There are . . beautiful corn snakes, five feet long, with red eyes, red tongues, and red bodies. **1974** Shaw–Campbell *Snakes West* 100, The corn snake *(Elaphe guttata)* . . . ranges from Eastern Utah and central New Mexico to the Gulf and Atlantic coasts . . . It has received its common name . . from its presence near cornfields.

corn snakeroot n [From somewhat cornlike leaves and use of root against snakebite]

A **button snakeroot 2** (here: either *Eryngium aquaticum* or *E. yuccifolium*).

1830 Rafinesque *Med. Flora* 218, *E. yucefolium,* mostly used, this last also called *Corn Snakeroot,* said to be the best cure for rattle snake bites, chewed and laid on the wound. **1901** Mohr *Plant Life AL* 643, *Eryngium yuccifolium* . . . Button Snakeroot . . . The root, called "corn snakeroot," is used medicinally. **1953** Greene–Blomquist *Flowers South* 84, Corn snakeroot *(Eryngium aquaticum)* has simple, yucca-like leaves with bristles on the margins. **1971** Krochmal *Appalachia Med. Plants* 114, *Eryngium Aquaticum* L. (Apiaceae) Common Names: . . corn snakeroot.

corn snapper n

A farm implement that breaks the ear of corn from the stalk but does not husk it.

1966 *DARE* (Qu. L29, *Machines now used for cutting grain)* Inf **AL7,** Corn snapper. **1969** *SC Market Bulletin* 11 Sept 4, C11 International corn snapper, good condition fits all C Super C200 and some 230 Farmall Tractors $250.

corn snow n

A granular snow produced by successive thawing and freezing.

1955 U.S. Arctic Info. Center *Gloss., Corn snow.* Spring snow. **1968–69** *DARE* (Qu. B39, *A very light fall of snow)* Inf **PA74,** Corn snow; [MI108, The kernel-shaped snow crystals are called *corn.*] **1982** *Sunset* July 27 **OR,** [Caption:] *Bikini-clad skier* carves turn in corn snow on the mile-wide, mile-long Palmer Snowfield high on Mount Hood.

corn song n chiefly Sth esp among Blacks

A melody, often with chorus, sung while harvesting or shucking corn.

1834 Caruthers *Kentuckian* 2.24, Here was the sooty patent-sweeper, with our southern corn-songs converted into the monotonous twang of business. **1867** Allen *Slave Songs of U.S.* x **eSC,** In other parts of the South, "fiddle-sings," "devil-songs," "corn-songs," "jig-tunes," and what not, are common. **1882** *Century Illustr. Mag.* 24.874/2 **GA** [Black], The corn-song is almost always a song with a chorus . . . These songs are kept up continously during the entire time the work [of corn-shucking] is going on, and though extremely simple, yet, when sung by fifty pairs of lusty lungs, there are few things more stirring. **1912** Green *VA Folk-Speech, Corn-song* . . . The song sung at the corn-shucking. The neighbours' hands come, with consent of their masters, to shuck corn until about midnight. The "captain of the corn-pile" marched up and down on the heap of corn with a shuck in his hat, gave out the song and led the chorus. The shuckers were given supper, and one or two drinks of whiskey. Boys and women were not allowed. It was a great frolic. **1938** *AmSp* 13.20 **NE,** The guests at a 'bee' enjoyed a social time while helping their host perform his work, singing *corn songs.*

corn speedwell n

A **speedwell** (here: *Veronica arvensis*).

1847 Wood *Class-Book* 406, *V. arvensis. Field Veronica. Corn Speedwell* . . . Frequent in dry fields. **1895** Gray–Bailey *Field Botany* 324, *V. arvensis* . . . Corn S[peedwell]. **1941** Walker *Lookout* 45 **TN,** A man may . . pluck the tiny blue flowers of corn speedwell. **1961** Peck *Manual OR* 715, Corn Speedwell . . . Abundant and widely distributed in fields, lawns and waste ground.

corn squeezings n esp Midl

Corn liquor, moonshine.

1956 *Hall Coll.* **TN,** *Corn squeezin's* . . . Moonshine whiskey. "You double it back and run it again. Then you get your good whiskey, which the old people called 'corn squeezin's.'" **c1960** *Wilson Coll.* **csKY,** *Corn squeezings* . . . Home-made whiskey. **1965–70** *DARE* (Qu. DD21c, *Nicknames for whiskey, especially illegally made whiskey)* 23 Infs, scattered, but esp **Midl,** Corn squeezin's; (Qu. DD21a, . . *Any kind of liquor)* Infs **TN36, WA19, GA72,** Corn squeezings; (Qu. DD31, *Joking names for home-made hard liquor)* Infs **GA9, MS8,** Corn squeezings. **1967** *DARE* FW Addit **cwNC,** *Corn squeezin's:* illegally made whiskey. **1968** *Foxfire* Fall–Winter 101 **neGA, cwNC,** Various names given moonshine include . . corn squeezin's.

corn stabber n Cf **jobber**

1969 *DARE* (Qu. L23, *What machinery is used around here in putting in the seed?)* Inf **MA15,** He has a corn stabber—you stab the ground with it and it lets a few grains out at a time. About two feet high. Tied to a wooden stick is a metal seed container that opens at the bottom as the stick is stabbed—jabbed—into the ground.

corn stack n **Delmarva**

A corncrib.

1946 *PADS* 5.17 **VA,** Corn stack . . . Corn crib; on the Eastern Shore. **1949** Kurath *Word Geog.* 54, Two local expressions are worth noting, the *crib house* of southern New Jersey and the *corn stack* of southern Delamarvia (southern Delaware to Cape Charles). **1968–70** *DARE* (Qu. M8, *The building where corn is kept)* Infs **MD38, VA49,** Corn stack.

cornstalk fiddle n Also *cornstick fiddle old-fash*

A toy fiddle made by lifting the outer fibers of a section of cornstalk and inserting a bridge under them at each end.

1824 *Historical Colls.* (Concord, N.H.) May 159 *(DA),* And there they'd *fife away like fun,* And play on cornstalk fiddles. **1856** (1857) Goodrich *Recollections* 2.96 **CT,** His corn-stalk fiddle, and the deeper tone / That murmurs from his pumpkin-leaf trombone, / Conspire to teach the boy. **1899** (1912) Green *VA Folk-Speech, Corn-stalk fiddle.* **1932** *Hanley Disks* **nwCT,** They had what they called cornstalk fiddles, hell-bells, shot-guns—most anything to make a disagreeable noise, at a horning. **1943** Holt *G. W. Carver* 18, Little boys made cornstalk fiddles the same way little girls made rag dolls. "Cornstick fiddle and rausum bow makes best old music you ever did know." **c1960** *Wilson Coll.* **csKY,** *Cornstalk fiddle* . . . A child's toy made from a joint of cornstalk, with the strings of the fiddle and the bow propped up with a small piece of the stalk. A queer noise can be produced on the fiddle, too.

cornstalk gun n

1927 *DN* 5.473 **Ozarks,** Cornstalk gun . . . A weapon used by the hill children in hunting small birds. A handful of fine gravel is thrown sling-fashion from the hollow end of a cornstalk.

cornstalk horse n

A hobbyhorse made of a length of cornstalk.

1886 Poore *Reminiscences* 1.175 **DE** (as of 1830s), You gentlemen were riding cornstalk horses in your fathers' barnyards. **1953** *Hall Coll.* **cwNC,** Corn-stalk horses . . . Toys made with corn stalks for children. "[Jake Sutton] would take a length of corn stalk between two joints. Jake would make corn-stalk horses for toys."

cornstalk pine n

=loblolly pine 1.

1897 Sudworth *Arborescent Flora* 26, *Pinus taeda* [Loblolly pine] . . Cornstalk Pine (Va.). **1908** Britton *N. Amer. Trees* 35, This tree *[Pinus taeda]* is known under many common names, as . . . Cornstalk pine, . . and Long straw pine. **1923** Dallimore–Jackson *Coniferae* 463, *Loblolly Pine* . . . Cornstalk Pine.

cornstalk shoot n

1941 FWP *Guide OK* 402, Annually in June, the Cherokees meet at Stillwell for a cornstalk shoot. In this tournament, bundles of cornstalks are set up at a certain distance from the shooters armed with bows and arrows; and the winner is the bowman whose arrow has pierced most stalks in a bundle. The game is one of the most ancient played by men of the tribe.

cornstalk weed n

A pondweed (here: *Potamogeton lucens*).

1894 *Outing* 24.302/1, We are near the bar and the 'cornstalk' weeds are here to our right.

cornstarch air n

1916 Macy–Hussey *Nantucket Scrap Basket* **Cape Cod MA,** "Cornstarch airs" — Stiff, formal manners.

cornstarch pudding n chiefly NEast

A type of pudding made with milk and eggs, thickened with cornstarch.

1877 Henderson *Practical Cooking* 323, *Corn-starch* and Rice Puddings are explained among the regular receipts for puddings. **1942** Rich *We Took to Woods* 115 **ME,** I use it to take the lumps out of gravy or chocolate cornstarch pudding or cream sauce. **1965–70** *DARE* (Qu. H63, *Kinds of desserts especially favored by people around here*) Infs **ME7, 19, MA14, NH2, NY36, 37, 209, PA126,** Cornstarch pudding. **1979** *DARE* File **cnMA** (as of c1915), In addition to pies and cakes, we had for dessert many varieties of bread puddings (to use up bread) and many custards and cornstarch puddings — secret weapons, I now realize, to provide milk in the diet of children who didn't like to drink it.

corn stick n chiefly S Atl, Inland Sth See Map

A long slender piece of corn bread often baked in a special pan having indentations shaped like ears of corn.

1944 Fast *Freedom Road* 44 **Charleston SC,** She piled a dish high with the stuff and threw in two corn sticks for good measure. **1950** *WELS* (*Bread made with corn meal*) 3 Infs, **WI,** Corn sticks. **1952** Tracy *Coast Cookery* 233 **TX,** Corn Sticks. **1965–70** *DARE* (Qu. H14, *Bread that's made with cornmeal*) 66 Infs, **chiefly S Atl, Inland Sth,** Corn sticks; (Qu. H25, . . *Fried cornmeal*) Infs **FL17, 33, MO15, NC51,** Corn sticks; (Qu. H15) Inf **SC32,** Corn sticks. **1967** *DARE* Tape **SC46,** We make corn sticks now occasionally . . . I've got some irons . . that you put it [the batter] in.

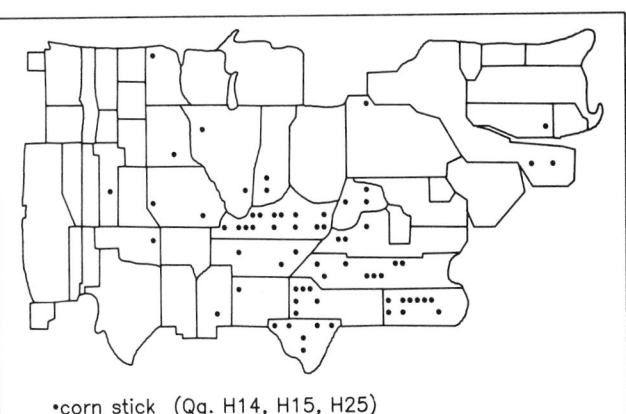

•corn stick (Qq. H14, H15, H25)

cornstick fiddle See cornstalk fiddle

corn-straw broom See corn broom

corn sweat n

1975 Gould *ME Lingo* 60, *Corn Sweat* — Today, a *corn sweat* is an effort by cajolement and insistence to persuade somebody to your way of thinking: "The folks on Birch Hill really put on a *corn sweat* to get their road paved." The expression comes from an old home remedy for a fever. Steamed or boiled ears of yellow corn were laid alongside a patient with a fever, and when the patient was well covered with blankets he'd burst into a sweat in no time.

cornswoggled adj [Alter of hornswoggled]

1969 *DARE* (Qu. NN25b, *Weakened substitutes for . . 'damned':* "*Well, I'll be _____.*") Inf **CA127,** Cornswoggled.

corn tassel n

1931–33 *LANE Worksheets* **cCT,** Corn tassel . . nickname for a rustic.

corn thief n

1 =redwing blackbird. Cf maize thief

1811 Wilson *Amer. Ornith.* 4.37, [Red-winged Starlings] are known by various names . . such as . . Corn or *Maize thief.* **1844** DeKay *Zool. NY* 2.141, The *Red-winged Blackbird [=Icterus phœniceus]* is equally well known in every part of the State under the names of *Swamp Blackbird* and *Corn-thief.*

2 =blue jay 1.

1917 (1923) *Birds Amer.* 2.217, Corn thief. **1946** Hausman *Eastern Birds* 420, Northern Blue Jay . . . Corn Thief.

corn thistle n

=Canada thistle.

1900 Lyons *Plant Names* 81, *[Cirsium] arvensis* . . Corn-Thistle. **1959** Carleton *Index Herb. Plants* 31, Corn-Thistle: *Cirsium arvense.*

corn-tossel bird n

=goldfinch.

1970 *DARE* (Qu. Q14, . . *Goldfinch*) Inf **KY86,** Corn-tossel bird.

corn twister n Also corn-twisting weather

A hot, dry spell.

1954 *Harder Coll.* **cwTN,** Corn-twister, a drouth. *Corn-twisting weather,* very hot weather . . . Common; somewhat humorous.

cornubble See curnubble

cornucopia n HI Cf angel's trumpet 1, jimson weed

The garden datura *(Datura metel).*

1929 Neal *Honolulu Gardens* 279, From the Tropics of the Eastern Hemisphere comes a datura popularly known as "cornucopia" or "horn of plenty." Its flowers tend to consist of two or three nested trumpets. **1948** (1965) Neal *Gardens HI* 750, *Garden Datura, cornucopia. Datura metel* L. form *pleniflora* . . . A garden form of a species native to India, is grown for its ornamental flowers and in Hawaii is also found wild.

corn wagon n [Imit] Cf breadwagon 2

A clap of rolling thunder.

1915 *DN* 4.182 **swVA,** *Corn-wagon* . . . Thunder clap. **1952** Brown *NC Folkl.* 1.529, *Corn-wagons* . . . The rattle of thunder. — Central and east.

corn weather n

1975 Gould *ME Lingo* 60, *Corn weather* — Hot July and August weather, just right for forcing the sweetcorn so important to Maine farmers. *Corn weather* is when the farmer sleeps "nekkid," without even a sheet. 'Twas said he could lie abed and hear the corn grow.

corn wind n

Practically no wind at all — the ideal condition for growth of corn.

1938 FWP *Guide IA* 395, Flags hang limply from their poles, or stir faintly in the hot August "corn-wind."

corn worker n

1968–69 *DARE* (Qu. L25, *The implement used to clean out weeds and loosen the earth between rows of corn*) Infs **MD48, PA163, 191,** Corn worker.

corn worm See corn earworm

corny dog See corn dog

corn yeast n Also *cornmeal yeast*

Yeast made by allowing moistened cornmeal to ferment.

1968 *DARE* (Qu. H17, . . *Kinds of yeast . . used around here*) Inf MD21, Corn yeast [ɪst]: Homemade; hops used — no longer made now; VA30, Hops and cornmeal yeast.

corn yuck n Cf **cedar fever**

1978 *Freeman* (Waukesha WI) 4 Aug mag sec 18/1, Bagby . . said "corn yuck" is a rash of little red bumps that afflicts a few of the tassel pickers when the humidity is high.

corona n [Span "crown"] **SW**

See quots.

1892 *DN* 1.247, *Coróna:* a crown. Specifically, in western Texas, New Mexico, and Arizona, the highly decorated piece of canvas used to put over each pack. **1933** White *Dog Days* 198, Under the saddle were ordinary folded blankets for padding; but over them was the corona, which offered wide play to the fancy — pigskin, embroidered broadcloth, bright Navajo blankets, woven horsehair, were a few possibilities. **1968** Adams *Western Words, Corona* — A cowman's name for a shaped pad placed under the skirt of a saddle. In packing, a pad placed upon the mule's back before the blanket and aparejo are put on; a numeral is placed on one side of the pad to indicate the owner. From the Spanish, meaning *crown*.

corona de Cristo n Also *corona de Jesús, crown of thorns* **SW**

=**allthorn 1.**

1924 Austin *Land of Journeys' Ending* 125 **SW**, The ocotilla is not a true cactus, but belongs rather by nature of its adaptations to the fellowship of the mesquite and that leafless thorny shrub often found in its neighborhood, called *corona de Jesús.* **1953** *AmSp* 28.101 **SW**, *Corona de Cristo* (Mex. Sp.). **1960** Vines *Trees SW* 299, Common names for the plant are Junco, Corona de Cristo, and Crucifixion Thorn. **1979** Little *Checklist U.S. Trees* 158, *Allthorn . . Other common names* — crown-of-thorns, crucifixion-thorn, junco, corona de Cristo.

coronado n

=**amberjack 2.**

1975 Evanoff *Catch More Fish* 215, The amberjack *(Seriola dumerili)* is also called the . . coronado . . . The Florida Keys are especially noted for the amberjack prevalent in those waters.

corp n [Back-formation from *corpse,* understood as pl]

1917 *DN* 4.410 **NC, SC,** *Corp* . . . Corpse.

‡**corple out** v phr

1912 *DN* 4.43, *Corple out* . . . To take out (piece of pie). "You corple it out," seeming to imply difficulty. I [Francis Wood] can think of no word that could have suggested this.

corporacity See **corporosity**

corporal n¹ See **caporal**

corporal n² [Appar from Du *korporaal*]

=**fallfish.**

1887 Goode *Amer. Fishes* 427, The name Corporal seems to have derived from the Dutch or German settlers of the Middle States. "Corporaalen" is one of its common names in that region. **1896** U.S. Natl. Museum *Bulletin* 47.221, Mitchell calls the fish *Corporal* or *Corporaalen.* **1946** LaMonte *N. Amer. Game Fishes* 158. **1964** Walden *Familiar Freshwater Fishes Amer.* 184 *(OEDS),* The fallfish is known to many anglers as chub, silver chub, chivin, windfish, and corporal.

corporal oath n [*OED* at corporal a. 5a 1534–1755]

1899 (1912) Green *VA Folk-Speech, Corporal,* adj. Corporal oath, an oath ratified by touching a sacred object, especially the New Testament, as distinguished from a merely spoken or written oath.

corporation n **Nth** Cf **alderman**

An oversize belly, paunch.

1931–33 *LANE Worksheets* (Stout, paunchy) 1 inf, **nwCT,** Big corporation; 1 inf, **nwCT,** Quite a corporation; *(A big stomach)* 1 inf, **nwCT,** He's getting a big corporation. **1967–69** *DARE* (Qu. X53a, . . *An oversize stomach*) Infs CA15, IL30, NJ25, NY37, 179, Corporation.

corporosity n Also sp *coperosity, corporacity* [Quasi-Lat as if from **corporositas* corpulence < Lat *corpus* body] **chiefly Sth, S Midl** *joc, old-fash*

One's body or health.

1838 Neal *Charcoal Sketches* 100 **NEng,** Should he, however, chance to trip, . . before he achieves a fair start from the perpendicular, his "corporosity" touches the ground which his hands in vain attempt to reach. **1883** (1971) Harris *Nights with Remus* 80 **GA,** [Footnote:] How does yo' corporosity seem ter segashuate? **1898** Lloyd *Country Life* 30 **AL,** "How does your coperosity seem to egashuate?" says I. "Tolerable fermently accordin to our doxology, how does yours seem to redoshiate?" says he. **1908** *DN* 3.301 **eAL, wGA,** Corporacity . . . Body, corporal or physical make-up. Often heard in the humorous expression, "How does your corporacity seem to segashuate?" **1945** Street *Gauntlet* 125 **MO** (as of 1920s), "Well, well, hello, Preacher," he said, and slipped into the chair next to London. "How's your corporosity segaciating?" **1950** *PADS* 14.23 **SC,** Corporosity. **1960** Criswell *Resp. to PADS* 20 **Ozarks,** Corporosity. **c1960** Wilson *Coll.* **csKY,** Corporosity . . . Body, health. A mock-learned word formerly used for fun: "How does your corporosity segaciate?" **1979** *DARE* File **cnMA** (as of c1915), I remember my aunt's using some of the high-falutin' talk heard in minstrel shows — considered most amusing — when she talked to children. "And how is the state of your high corporosity this morning?" she might say. We would giggle and answer "Pretty good."

corpse candle n

1975 Gould *ME Lingo* 60, *Corpse Candles* — St. Elmo's fire; a slow discharge of atmospheric electricity making a glow at mastheads of vessels and other tall objects. The macabre attitude of Maine mariners to the glow, making it a bad omen, is inconsistent with the older name of St. Elmo's fire. Early Mediterranean sailors believed the glow proved their patron saint was on guard.

corpse flower See **corpse plant**

corpse maker n Cf **widow maker**

1969 *DARE* (Qu. FF15, *When a firecracker doesn't go off, and you break it in the middle and light the powder, you call it a _____*) Inf NY213, Corpse maker — real big ones.

corpse plant n Also *corpse flower* [See quot 1931]

=**Indian pipe 1.**

1857 Gray *Manual of Botany* 262, Corpse-Plant . . Smooth, waxy-white . . . Dark and rich woods. **1901** Lounsberry *S. Wild Flowers* 375, Corpse plant . . . [is] white, turning to black after being picked. **1931** Harned *Wild Flowers Alleghanies* 36, The name, Corpse plant, was assigned to it *[Monotropa uniflora]* because of its colorless appearance and disposition to turn black when handled. **1940** Richter *Trees* 49 **OH,** She . . was white and waxy as the corpse plants that come up under the beech trees. **1942** (1960) Robertson *Red Hills* 138 **SC,** We had fine sunsets and the west wind, and polecats and corpse flowers and mica and wild lilies in the field. **1951** Hough *Singing in Morning* 126 **seMA,** The only thing against the Indian pipe, so far as we know, is that some people choose to call it the corpse flower.

corral n, also attrib Usu |kəˈræl|, also |kəˈrɛl|; occas |kɔˈræl, kərɑl, krɛl| Pronc-spp *coral, corel(l), corrale, correll, coural* [Span]

1 A pen or enclosure for livestock; any similar enclosure. **chiefly West** See Map

1829 *Amer. Turf Reg.* Oct. 101 *(DA),* They procure from a great distance, and by almost incredible labour, a quantity of wood palisades, with which they form a *corral,* of great size. **1845** Stapp *Prisoners* 71, We entered our former quarters (the coural of the ranch). **1892** *DN* 1.190 **TX,** *Corrál.* **1929** *AmSp* 5.54 **NE,** The "corral," sometimes the "branding pen," is the most conspicuous and largest of ranch accessories. Formerly all "corrals" were circular areas fenced by horizontal, wooden rails, supported by posts set firmly in the ground . . . By far the greater number now . . are square or rectangular enclosures. **1932** Bentley *Spanish Terms, Corral* (*Spanish,* koː rráːl; *English,* kəˈrɛl *and* krɛl). **1941** Smith *Going to God's Country* 90 **MO** (as of 1890), We had just built us a shed for our teams and a chicken house for a cow corell. **1959** Pearce in 1980 *DARE* File (paper read at Amer. Dial. Soc. meeting), *Corral* dots the map in every Rocky Mountain State, being dominant in Arizona and New Mexico, and a rival to *barnyard* everywhere, even in Utah usually so impregnable to any term not born within its North Midland cultural matrix. *Corral,* like *ranch,* as a term has shifted in semantic scope from its early associations with the range and range animals to almost any outdoors location. **1962** Atwood *Vocab. TX* 50, *General enclosure about the barn . . . Corral . .* is confined to West and Northwest Texas. *Ibid* 125, *Corral.* A barnyard, or enclosure for any kind of animals — cows, horses, sheep, poultry . . . The specialization to the idea of a pen for horses evidently occurred after the adoption of the word into Texas English. **1965–70** *DARE* (Qu. M13,

The space near the barn with a fence around it where you keep the livestock) 189 Infs, **chiefly West,** Corral; (Qu. M14, *The open area around or next to the barn*) Infs CA99, 124, 131, 195, 207, **FL27, IA39, MI101, WA25,** Corral; (Qu. L64, *. . Wooden fence . . around a garden or near a house*) Infs **AZ2, MO11, TX6,** Corral; **NJ3, NY205,** Corral fence; **NM13,** Picket corral, Pole corral; (Qu. L65, *. . Other kinds of fences*) Inf **OR1,** Corral fence; **OR10,** Stockade corral; willow corral; (Qu. L61, *Fences made of solid logs*) Inf **CA87,** Corral fence; **SC8,** Log corral; (Qu. L60, *A fence made of stone or rock without mortar*) Inf **CA131,** Rock corral, stone corral. **1977** Watts *Dict. Old West,* Corral—A pen or enclosure to confine horses or cattle. Commonly . . composed of posts and poles, but there were many varieties, including temporary corrals of rope; in the Southwest they were frequently made of high adobe walls to keep out marauding Indians . . . This Spanish word had many (some unbelievable) Anglo variants (*coral, corel, corrale,* etc.).

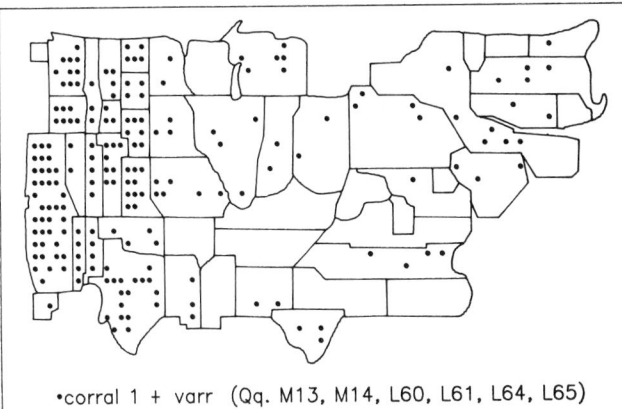

•corral 1 + varr (Qq. M13, M14, L60, L61, L64, L65)

2 A group of wagons drawn into a defensive formation. *hist*
1848 Ruxton *Advent. Rocky Mts.* 177, Among the trees, in open spaces, were drawn up the wagons, formed into a corral or square, and close together, so that the whole made a most formidable fort. **1859** Marcy *Prairie Traveler* 55, Should hostile Indians be discovered, the fact should be at once reported to the commander, who . . will rapidly form his wagons into a circle or *"corral,"* with the animals toward the centre, and the men on the inside, with their arms in readiness to repel an attack from without. **1859** (1942) Patterson *Travel Diary* 162 **VA,** Today we formed a correll of our wagons.

3 See quot.
1859 (1942) Patterson *Travel Diary* 173, We cut down a large pine, and taking the branches built a neat correll or hedge around our sleeping place, which protected us against the wind.

corral snake n **CA**
=**king snake.**
1967–68 *DARE* (Qu. P25) Inf **CA23,** Corral snake—speckled and spotted—around corrals; **CA31,** Corral snakes [korǣl]; **CA65,** King snake or corral snake—it's just marked like a corral snake—brown and yellow.

correll See **corral**

correosa n **TX**
A **prickly ash 1** (here: *Zanthoxylum fagara*).
[**1942** Santamaría *Dicc. Americanismos, Colima . . .* Los tejanos le dicen igualmente *correosa.* [*Colima . . .* The Texans call it equally *correosa.*]] **1970** Correll *Plants TX* 911, Zanthoxylum Fagara . . . Correosa. Shrub, rounded, very prickly.

correspond the idea v phr
1930 *DN* 6.80 **cSC,** Correspond the idea . . . Relinquish the plan. "Why, Uncle, I thought you were going over the river today?" "Yap 'm, Uh sesso; but Uh done curryspon de aideah o' goin'." This expression is used by all negroes in a very small locality.

corrida n [Span "race"]
A cattle ranching outfit.
1929 Dobie *Vaquero* 1, Thus in one *corrida,* or outfit, may be found "Mexican vaqueros," "white vaqueros," and "nigger vaqueros." **1932** Bentley *Spanish Terms* 129, Corrida . . A cattle ranching outfit. **1968** Adams *Western Words.*

corrugate n, v Also *corrugation* n **West**
A small irrigation furrow; to make such a furrow.
1967 *DARE* Tape **ID** 8, You have a corrugate ['korǝgeɪt], a little ditch, beside each row [of the garden]; **ID**10, Before a man could irrigate he had to corrugate his land, which simply means he plowed ditches through all his fields so that he could run the water down . . . In the corrugations, just a shovelful of mud would stop up one that was running too fast. **1967** *DARE* FW Addit **CO**12, Corrugates: little furrows about 3′ apart—water is turned out of a head ditch, then cuts are made at the corrugates and the water runs down. Also called *corrugate fields. Ibid,* Corrugate crops ['korǝgeɪt]: From two irrigations you get pretty good corrugate crops. **1968** Adams *Western Words,* Corrugate—To make small irrigation ditches in a field.

corrun See **corn**

corrupted ppl adj
1 Tainted, polluted. *arch*
1963 Adamson *Household Hints* 79 **NEng** (as of late 1800s), *Purifying "Corrupted Water"*—1½ oz. of powdered charcoal will suffice for the purification of 3½ pts. of corrupted water. This discovery has been largely carried into execution, at sea, on long voyages and with great success.
2 Ruptured. [*EDD corrupted* 1]
1944 *PADS* 2.33 **cnNC,** Corrupted . . . Ruptured. "I done been corrupted several year." . . Negro.

corruption n
1 Pus, matter. **chiefly Sth, S Midl** See Map *esp among speakers with little formal educ*
1899 (1912) Green *VA Folk-Speech,* Corruption . . . Putrid matter; pus. **1902** *DN* 2.231 **sIL.** **1903** *DN* 2.310 **seMO.** **1907** *DN* 3.230 **nwAR, seMO.** **1908** *DN* 3.301 **eAL, wGA.** **1915** *DN* 4.182 **swVA.** **1930** *DN* 6.84 **cSC.** **1946** *PADS* 5.17 **VA,** Corruption: Pus; common. **1950** *WELS* (*What do you call the kind of stuff that sometimes comes from a sore?*) 2 Infs, **sWI,** Corruption. **c1960** *Wilson Coll.* **csKY,** Corruption: pus. More often called matter. **1965–70** *DARE* (Qu. BB35, *The yellowish stuff that comes out of a boil when the head breaks*) 119 Infs, **chiefly Sth, S Midl,** Corruption; **AL6,** Pus and corruption; **MA58,** Guts and corruption; (Qu. BB36, *When there's an open sore and this yellowish stuff is coming out of it, you say it's _____*) Inf **GA44,** There's corruption; **VA42,** Got corruption. [Of all Infs responding to Qu. BB35, 26% were grade school educ or less, 32% coll educ; of those giving this response, 41% were grade school educ or less, 15% were coll educ.]

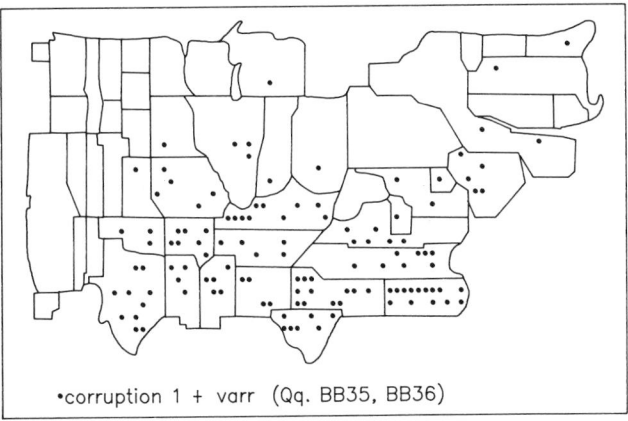

•corruption 1 + varr (Qq. BB35, BB36)

2 A rupture. Cf **corrupted 2**
1944 *PADS* 2.33 **cnNC,** Corruption . . . Rupture. "I'se turned down by the draft board on account of corruption." . . Negro.
3 See quot.
1959 *VT Hist.* new ser 27.131, Corruption . . . Junk; waste iron; any scrap or trash. Rare.

corset-stretcher See **stretcher**

corshin See **caution**

corten See **certain**

‡**cortenion** n [Perh alter of *cortina* or *curtain,* as in agaric fungi]
An unidentified plant.

1899 (1912) Green *VA Folk-Speech*, *Cortenions* . . . Curtenemous? Like capers. "Gathering Tuckahoe, Cortenions and other Wild Fruits," from the Englishman's land.

corvina n [Span]

Any of various fish of the family Sciaenidae:

a A **mademoiselle** (here: *Bairdiella chrysura*). **Atl coast**

1842 DeKay *Zool. NY* 4.74, The Silvery Corvina. Corvina argyroleuca . . . This fish . . is frequently called *Silvery Perch* by the fishermen. *Ibid* 77, The Sharp-Finned Corvina. Corvina oxyptera . . . Pectoral fins long and pointed.

b also *caravina*: Any of three Pacific coast fish of the genus *Cynoscion*, esp **white sea bass.**

[**1787** Clavijero *Hist. Mexico* (transl Cullen) 1.65, The Curvina is about a foot and a half long, of a slender, round shape, and of a blackish purple colour.] **1882** U.S. Natl. Museum *Bulletin* 16.579, *A. nobile* . . . White Sea Bass; Sea Trout; Corvina. *Ibid* 580, *C. parvipinne* . . . Blue-fish; Corvina. **1887** Goode *Amer. Fishes* 121, Both [*Cynoscion nobile,* young and mature] are frequently called 'Corvina' and 'Caravina.' . . *Cynoscion parvipinne,* is usually known as the 'Corvina' or 'Caravina.' **1960** Amer. Fisheries Soc. *List Fishes* 31, Shortfin corvina . . P[acific] . . *Cynoscion parvipinnis* . . Orangemouth corvina . . P[acific] . . *Cynoscion xanthulus.* **1972** Sparano *Outdoors Encycl.* 381, *California White Sea Bass*—Common Names: . . sea bass, . . croaker, white corvina. Scientific Name: *Cynoscion nobilis.*

c =**croaker** n[1] **1a(1)** (here: *Micropogon undulatus*). **Atl and Gulf coasts**

1898 U.S. Natl. Museum *Bulletin* 47.1461, *Micropogon undulatus* . . . (Croaker; Roncadina; Corvina). **1946** LaMonte *N. Amer. Game Fishes* 83, *Croaker*—*Micropogon undulatus* . . . Names: Corvina, Roncadina, Ronco, Crocus.

d The reef **croaker** n[1] **1a(1)** (*Odontoscion dentex*).

1898 U.S. Natl. Museum *Bulletin* 47.1425, *Odontoscion dentex* . . . Corvina.

e also *corbina*: The California **whiting** (*Menticirrhus undulatus*). **Pacific coast**

1955 Zim *Fishes* 157, Corbina: M[enticirrhus] undulatus. **1960** Amer. Fisheries Soc. *List Fishes* 31, California corbina . . P[acific] . . *Menticirrhus undulatus.* **1968–70** DARE (Qu. P1) Infs CA91, 191, Corvina; (Qu. P2) Infs CA36, 52, 65, 181, Corvina; (Qu. H45) Inf CA91, Corvina. [Note: some of these Infs may be referring instead to **corvina b.**] **1972** Sparano *Outdoors Encycl.* 386, *California Corbina*—Common Names: . . corbina, corvina, whiting, sea trout. Scientific Name: *Menticirrhus undulatus.*

cos See **because** conj

cose adv See **course**

cose conj See **because** conj

cose v [Back-formation from *cosy*]

To enjoy ease and comfort.

1914 DN 4.141, Back-formations from words with initial accent . . . *Cose,* from *cosy.*

coshaw See **cushaw**

co-sheep(ie) v phr Usu |'ko‚šip(i), 'ku‚šip(i)|; less freq |'kʌ‚šip(i), 'kʊ-, 'kɝ-; 'ku‚ši| Also *coo-sheep(ie),* ~ *sheepy, cu-sheep(ie)* [**co** v] **chiefly S Midl** See Map

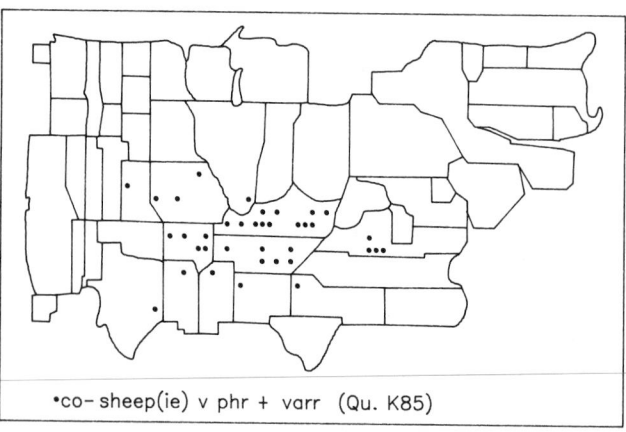

•co-sheep(ie) v phr + varr (Qu. K85)

Come!—used to call sheep.

1893 DN 1.267, In Illinois the long call for sheep is ['ko šip], sung like [ke bɑs]. **1914** DN 4.182 **VA,** *Coo-sheep, interj.* A call to sheep. Also *coo-sheepy, coo-nan, coo-nannie.* **1949** Kurath *Word Geog.* 30, In the Appalachians south of the Kanawha the Virgina Piedmont call *co-sheep!* now competes with the Midland call [*Sheep!, Sheepie!].* **c1960** Wilson *Coll.* **csKY,** *Cu-sheep (or -sheepie)*—regular call to sheep; ['kʌ‚šip]. **1965–70** DARE (Qu. K85, *The call to sheep*) 14 Infs, **chiefly S Midl,** Co-sheep(ie); 19 Infs, **chiefly S Midl,** Coo-sheep(ie); **GA77, MO38,** ['ku‚ši]; **VA14,** ['kʌ‚šip]; **MO37,** ['kʊ‚šipi]; **VA95,** ['kɝ‚šip]. **1969** DARE FW Addit **NC,** [kwu] sheepie. **1971** Wood *Vocab. Change* 46 **Sth,** The call to get sheep in from the pasture is *coo-sheep* or *sheepie, co-sheep.* [Not found in Florida or Oklahoma]

co-sheep(ie) n Also sp *coo-sheep(ie),* **cu-sheepy** [**co-sheep(ie)** v phr] **chiefly S Midl** Cf **run sheep run**

A children's game: see quot 1952.

1906 DN 3.133 **nwAR,** *Cu, sheepy* [kʊ šipɪ] . . . A boys' and girls' game. **1908** DN 3.303 **eAL, wGA,** *Cu-sheepy* . . . A children's game. The leader continually cries *cu-sheepy*[,] the other children follow and answer each time *baa-a-a.* In the end the leader turns and tries to catch a sheep before all get back home. **1952** Brown *NC Folkl.* 1.81, *Co-sheep* . . . All the players except one stand inside a large circle drawn on the ground. The player outside the ring is the shepherd, and he walks away calling: "Co-sheep, co-sheep, co-sheep!" All must follow slowly and bleat: "Baa-baa. . . ." Suddenly the shepherd turns around and chases them. All that are caught before they reach the ring must help catch the others. The last player caught becomes shepherd. **1966–67** DARE (Qu. EE12, *Games in which one captain hides his team and the other team tries to find it*) Inf **IL20,** Coo-sheepie; (Qu. EE33, *Other outdoor games*) Inf **AR13,** Coo-sheep.

coshinera See **cocinero**

cosi See **coosie**

cosinero See **cocinero**

coslush, cosouse See **ker-**

cosses See **cost** A1

cosset n [Perh ult from OE *cotsetla* cottager, but ME evidence is lacking; see *OED*] **chiefly NEng**

1 also attrib: A pet lamb.

1806 (1970) Webster *Compendious Dict., Cosset* . . . a lamb brought up by the hand. **1897** Barton *Sim Galloway* 35 (DAE), He'd ruther take yon little cosset lamb right outen the chimbley corner an' throw it out to the wolves. **1931–33** LANE *Worksheets* **sRI,** *Cosset sheep,* a pet sheep; **cnCT,** *Cattle cosset,* a lamb that is brought up with cows. **1939** LANE Map 202 **throughout NEng,** A tame lamb, defined variously as 'brought up by hand' . . or as nourished from a bottle . . , is called *cosset, cosset lamb, cosset sheep.* **1950** WELS (*A sheep that is kept as a pet*) 2 Infs, **WI,** Cosset. **1966** DARE (Qu. K62) Inf **ME5,** Cosset lamb—a young sheep. **1970** *AmSp* 45.65, Two of the regional terms for a pet lamb documented in the SED [*Survey of English Dialects*] struck root in New England, *cosset* and *cade.* The former, current in all parts of New England, where sheep are, or were, raised, doubtless came from East Anglia.

2 A spoiled child or pet; a favorite.

1816 Pickering *Vocab.* 72, *Cosset* . . is used in *New England* . . to signify a favourite or darling. **1884** Jewett *Country Dr.* 1.9 **ME,** She's [a cat] a proper cosset, ain't she? **1902** (1904) Rowe *Maid of Bar Harbor* 18 **ME,** "Ma'am's cosset," he delighted to call her, and the knowledge that this species of sister-baiting was a sport in which their father might be counted on not to interfere lent an added zest to their enjoyment of it. **1931–33** LANE *Worksheets* **csCT,** *Cosset,* a pet of any kind; inf later said that cosset applied to lambs; **seCT,** *Cosset,* of a child, if spoiled. "He's a regular cosset"; **nwMA,** Cosset, tame calf.

cosset v esp **NEng**

To treat as a pet, to pamper.

1860 Emerson *Conduct* 4 **MA,** Nature is no sentimentalist—does not cosset or pamper us. **1939** LANE Map 202 **swCT,** Cosseting, 'pampering,' of persons; **seMA,** Cosset . . 'to pet' (a child or animal).

cossie v Also sp *cussie, cussy* esp **Mid Atl, S Atl** Cf **cush** v

Come!—used to summon calves.

1949 Kurath *Word Geog.* 46, The Eastern Shore of Maryland and southern Delaware have many local expressions. Here we find . . *cossie!* or *cussie!* . . as a call to calves. *Ibid* 64, There are three regional calls:

bossie! in New England and the New England settlements, *sookie!* in the Midland, and *cossie!* or *cussie!* in the South. **1966–70** *DARE* (Qu. K83, *To call a calf*) Infs **AL**62, **MN**16, **NC**6, 87, **SC**69, Cussie; (Qu. K80, *The call . . to get the cows in*) Inf **NC**6, Cussie. **1973** Allen *LAUM* 1.260, *Cussy,* a minor variant found in eastern South Carolina, apparently survives in southern Nebraska, where it has been acquired by an inf. of Swedish parentage; a possibly related *kissy* is the term of a North Dakota inf. both of whose parents came from The Netherlands.

cost v

A Forms.

1 pres 3rd pers sg: usu *costs;* also, **esp in S Midl,** pronc-spp *costes, costies, costus;* less freq *cosses.* Cf **-es** suff[1]

1895 *DN* 1.375 **eTN,** The most interesting thing . . is the use of a vowel in plurals and the third singular of verbs, giving such forms as *costes.* **1908** *DN* 3.301 **eAL, wGA,** *Costes,* 3rd sing. of *cost.* **1924** *Qrly. Jrl. Speech* 10.234 **sAppalachians,** "Hit costes a lot." **1942** Hall *Smoky Mt. Speech* 82, The following verbal forms were pronounced with [ə] in the final syllable: *costs* ['kɔstəs]. **1942** *Sat. Eve. Post* 16 May 84/4 **eTN,** But, Mr. Hurley, mules costes money! **1953** Atwood *Survey of Verb Forms* 28/2, A variation from the usual inflectional pattern (/s/ after voiceless consonants) is seen in the form *costes* /kɔstəz/, which occurs occasionally in the Chesapeake Bay area, s.W.Va., N.C., S.C., and Ga. All together, 54 informants (51 of them in Type I [having little education]) use this form. A similar form, *cosses* /kɔsəz/, is used by nine additional Southern informants. **1954** *Harder Coll.* **cwTN,** Cost. "Ey puttin' in black top right down creek. Costies ['kɔstɪz] sixty-thousand dollars." **c1960** *Wilson Coll.* **csKY,** Costs: often *costes.* **1977** Miles *Ozark Dict.* 2, It costus ten cents.

2 past: usu *cost;* sometimes *costed.* Cf **-ed** pret suff **2**

1908 *DN* 3.283 **eAL, wGA,** Abnormal preterits . . . costed. **1965–70** *DARE* (Qu. U8a, *Other ways of saying, "It cost me ten dollars."*) 12 Infs, **scattered,** Costed me. **1966** *Wilson Coll.* **csKY,** It cost me ten dollars. **1976** Garber *Mountain-ese* 17 **sAppalachians,** My galluses costed two dollars.

B Sense.

In phr *to cost more than it comes to:* To be more expensive than a thing is worth. *arch*

1854 (1969) Thoreau *Walden* 63 **MA,** It costs more than it comes to. **1884** Harrison *Negro Engl.* 262, To cos' mo' an it come ter — not to be worth the trouble.

costes See **cost A1**

costic adj [Used for *costive*]

1966–68 *DARE* (Qu. BB21, *Other words for being constipated*) Infs **IN**38, **MS**15, Costic ['kɔstɪk].

costies See **cost A1**

costive adj [*cost* expense + *-ive*]

Costly.

1933 *AmSp* 8.1.48 **Ozarks,** Costive . . . Expensive, costly. **1947** Ballowe *The Lawd* 197 **LA,** Ah got hit f'um a fust-class obeah man, long time ago an' hit was costive. He say it was wuth the money.

‡costly adj [Used for *costive*]

1966 *DARE* (Qu. BB21, *Other words for being constipated*) Inf **SC**27, Costly.

costus See **cost A1**

cot n[1]

A sofa, couch.

c1770 in 1833 Boucher *Glossary* 49, A Cot; a sopha. **1835** (1838) *S. Lit. Messenger* 4.89/2, I should not like to occupy one of those settees or cots as they call them, all conglomerated as they are into a dense mass. **1965–70** *DARE* (Qu. E7, *The piece of upholstered furniture that you can stretch out on to rest*) Infs **AL**11, **CA**36, **LA**24, **MA**6, **MO**38, **NY**92, **PA**235, Cot. [6 of 7 Infs old]

cot n[2] [Abbr for *apricot*]

1921 *DN* 5.109 **CA,** Cot . . . Apricot. [Used by] Newspapers and orchard people. **1966** *DARE* FW Addit **CA,** Cots — short for apricots. "Cots are $1.49 a lug." **1967–68** *DARE* (Qu. I53, *Other fruits grown around here*) Inf **CA**62, Cots or apricots; **NE**3, Apricots are often called just cots too.

‡cot n[3] [Prob alter of *cock* n[2]]

1970 *DARE* (Qu. L12, . . *Small piles of hay standing in the field*) Inf **KY**90, Cots [kats].

cot bed n Also sp *cott bed* [Redund]

A narrow light single bed.

1838 Ingraham *Burton* 2.175, A narrow cott bed, with a military cloak thrown over it, constituted the sole furniture of the warrior's abode. **1892** Gunter *Miss Dividends* 177, She goes up to her room, where she finds a clean cot-bed. **1926** Roberts *Time of Man* 21 **KY,** He came back with some iron cooking utensils, a kitchen table, and a cot bed for Ellen. **1943** Lewis *Gideon Planish* 11 **Chicago IL,** Hatche's room was a stable, . . a cot-bed in one stall, and in the other an old wood-stove. **1967** *DARE* Tape **MA**5, You just had two bunks or two cot beds and a stove [in a logging shanty]. **1970** *DARE* (Qu. E18, *A temporary or emergency bed made up on the floor*) Inf **MA**98, Cot bed.

cotbetty n [*cot* a cottage + *OED Betty* sb. 2] *obsolescent, derog*

A man who likes to do "women's work."

1859 (1968) Bartlett *Americanisms,* Cotbetty. A man who meddles in the woman's part of household affairs. North and East. It is probably of English origin. Halliwell and Wright give both *cot* and *cot-quean* with the same meaning. **1870** *Nation* 4 Aug 73/1 **NJ,** "Cot-betty," not "cot," was what our old cook called us when we bothered her in the kitchen. **1930** Shoemaker *1300 Words* 15 **cPA Mts** (as of c1900), Cot-betty — A man fond of doing women's work.

cotch v See **catch v A1,3**

cotch n Also sp *kotch* [Perh alter of *catch*] **LA** *among Blacks*

A card game.

1935 Hurston *Mules & Men* 280 **LA,** He spend up all my money playing coon-can and kotch and then expect me to buy him a suit of clothes. **1954** Armstrong *Satchmo* 100 **LA,** Several times I went to the pawnshop and picked up some loot on my horn. Once it was to play cotch and be around the good old hustlers and gamblers. *Ibid* 129, George . . was running the cotch game, and he was sore as hell at Benny because he was winning all the money. **1968** *DARE* (Qu. DD35, . . *Favorite card games*) Inf **LA**26, Cotch [kač]; **LA**45, [kač], perhaps spelled *cotch;* played by Negroes.

cotched, cotcht See **catch v A3**

cote See **quote**

cote-house See **courthouse**

cottage n chiefly **NEast**

1965–70 *DARE* (Qu. L2, *The extra house on a large farm where a hired man and his family live*) 11 Infs, **chiefly NEast,** Cottage; **MI**73, **MA**4, Gardener's cottage; **RI**12, Farmer's cottage.

cottage curds n pl

1969 *DARE* (Qu. H60, *The lumpy white cheese that is made from sour milk*) Inf **VT**16, Cottage curds.

cottage fried potatoes n pl Also *cottage fries* chiefly **Nth, N Midl** See Map Cf **American fried potatoes, fresh fried potatoes, home fried potatoes**

Potatoes sliced and fried.

1965–70 *DARE* (Qu. H47, *Kinds of fried potatoes favored around here*) 13 Infs, **scattered Nth, N Midl,** Cottage fried; **IL**13, **MN**1, **OH**61, **PA**95, Cottage fries.

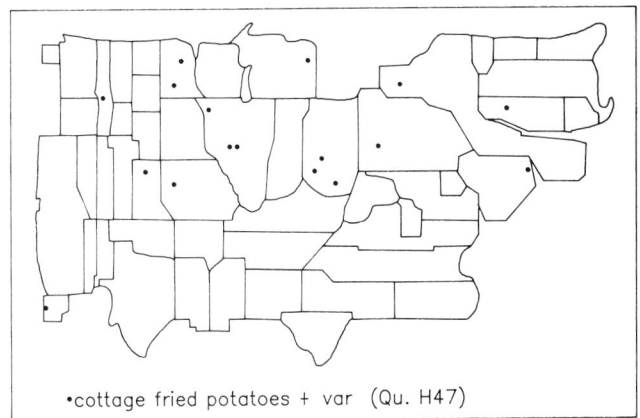

•cottage fried potatoes + var (Qu. H47)

cottage pudding n chiefly **Nth, esp NEast**

Cake covered with a sweet sauce.

1896 (c1973) Farmer *Orig. Cook Book* 331, Cottage Pudding [Plain cake recipe] Serve with Vanilla or Hard Sauce. *Ibid* 332, Strawberry and Peach Cottage Pudding.   **1909** Porter in *Munsey's Mag.* 41.18/2 **VA**, We had browsed . . on local topics, and then parted, after . . Irish stew, flannel cakes, cottage pudding, and coffee.   **1950** *WELS* (*Kinds of pudding*) 5 Infs, **WI**, Cottage pudding.   **1965–70** *DARE* (Qu. H63, *Kinds of desserts especially favored by people around here*) 9 Infs, **chiefly NEast**, Cottage pudding; (QR, near Qu. H66) Inf **CO**27, Lemon-flavored sauce over cake is cottage pudding.   **1969** *DARE* FW Addit **ceNY**, *Cottage pudding:* white pudding with egg-white sauce.

cott bed See **cot bed**

cotted cheese n [Assim of *cottage cheese*]
  1949 *AmSp* 24.107 **neFL, ceGA**, Cotted cheese . . . Cottage cheese.

cottige See **cartridge**

cotton n
  1 also *cotton canvas:* In tobacco farming: see quots.
  1966 *PADS* 45.10 **cKY**, Cotton. . . Cotton canvas . . = canvas. "Cotton canvas comes in twelve-foot widths."   **1967** Key *Tobacco Vocab.* **MD, MO**, Cotton: A covering for a tobacco seed-bed. "After the plants get up to a certain size, they take the cottons off."
  2 attrib: A cheap imitation.
  1914 *DN* 4.154 **NH**, Cotton . . . In a *cotton waggon, house,* etc., a cheaply made waggon, etc., made in imitation of a costly one.
  3 See quot.
  1930 Shoemaker *1300 Words* 12 **cPA Mts** (as of c1900), Cotton—An old man who tries to act youthful.
  4 in var phrr, esp *cotton is low:* See quot.   **chiefly Sth**   See Map
  1965–70 *DARE* (Qu. W24a, . . *Expressions . . to warn a woman slyly that her slip is showing*) 21 Infs, **Sth**, (Your) cotton is (getting, hanging) low; **AL**30, **FL**6, 10, 31, **GA**28, **LA**18, 40, **NC**10, Cotton is (getting) cheap; **GA**86, **SC**6, 26, Cotton is (hanging) below the market; **FL**19, **MO**29, Cotton (is) below (the) price; **GA**9, 77, **TX**32, (Your) cotton is (coming) down; **GA**28, Cotton is going down; **GA**67, **NC**50, (Your) cotton is (a-)hanging; **AL**33, **FL**15, **GA**44, **LA**2, **MS**6, (Your) cotton is (high, pretty *or* showing).

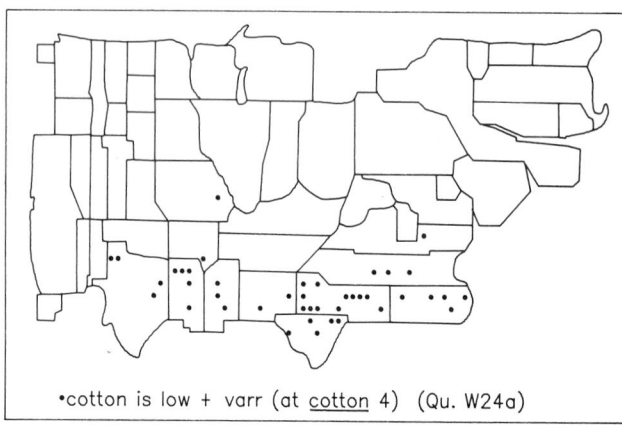

•cotton is low + varr (at <u>cotton</u> 4) (Qu. W24a)

cotton balls n Also *sheet cotton*
  The mineral ulexite.
  1953 Pough *Rocks & Minerals* 178, Ulexite . . . Also known as "cotton balls" or "sheet cotton" . . . Ulexite forms in borax deposits and salt beds in loose fragile balls or crusts . . . Found in 3- to 4-inch balls in the Mohave Desert in southern Nevada and California.

cotton basket n Cf **hamper 1**
  A large basket, used esp for cotton.
  1852 Stowe *Uncle Tom's Cabin* 2.23, Poor, shiftless dogs put stones at the bottom of their cotton-baskets to make them weigh heavier.   **1908** *DN* 3.318 **eAL, wGA**, Hamper basket . . . A hamper, a large open basket made of white-oak splits for holding cotton, corn, etc. Also called *cotton-basket.*   **1939** FWP *These are Our Lives* 381 **Sth**, I remember distinctly mother takin' me to the fields when I was just a little fellow and placin' me on a blanket or in the cotton basket while she worked.

cotton bird n
  =**killdeer**.
  1970 *DARE* (Qu. Q14, . . *Other names . . for . . killdeer*) Inf **TN**53, Cotton bird.

cotton blossom n
  Perh a hibiscus.
  1970 *DARE* (QR, near Qu. T16) Inf **NC**87, Cotton blossom. [Name for a bush]

cotton bollworm See **bollworm**

cotton box n **Sth** *hist*
  A type of barge: see quots.
  1940 FWP *Guide GA* 77, Great one way "cottonboxes," which were actually shallow wooden barges, were floated down the rivers of the coastal plain to the market towns, where they were broken up and sold for lumber.   **1941** FWP *Guide AL* 89, A development of the flatboat peculiar to Alabama was the "cotton box," a huge cumbersome craft whose high sides provided cargo space for hundreds of bales.

cotton bush n Also *cotton plant* [Prob from resemblance of flower heads to cotton]
  =**groundsel tree**.
  1898 *Jrl. Amer. Folkl.* 11.229, *Baccharis pilularis* . . cotton plant, Cal.   **1937** *Torreya* 37.101, *Baccharis* spp.—Cotton-bush . . Georgia.   **1951** *PADS* 15.42 **TX**, *Baccharis halimifolia* . . . Cotton bush.

cotton canvas See **cotton 1**

cotton caterpillar n Also *cotton moth*
  Prob a corn borer, but cf **corn earworm**.
  1846 *DeBow's Rev.* 2.278, Cotton moth.   **1856** U.S. Patent Office *Annual Rept. for 1855: Ag.* 66, If it or any similar method should lead to the destruction of the cotton caterpillar and boll-worm, . . it will be of incalculable benefit.   **1967–69** *DARE* (Qu. R27, . . *Kinds of caterpillars*) Infs **GA**89, **LA**10, 15, 18, Cotton caterpillar.

cotton eater See **cotton leafworm**

cotton-eyed adj Also *cotton-eye*
  See quot 1905.
  1905 *DN* 3.75 **nwAR**, Cotton-eyed . . . Having the whites of the eyes prominent.   **1934** Carmer *Stars Fell on AL* 275, Fiddlers' Tunes—Cotton-eyed Joe.   **1940** FWP *Guide TX* 558, There are also dances popular locally, such as Cotton-eye Joe.

cotton fern n [From its being covered with densely matted hairs]
  A cloak fern (here: *Notholæna newberryi*) native to southern California.
  1925 Jepson *Manual Plants CA* 27, *Notholæna newberryi* . . Cotton Fern.   **1974** Munz *Flora S. CA* 29, *Notholæna newberryi* . . Cotton Fern.

cottonfish n **LA**
  =**bowfin**.
  1851 *DeBow's Rev.* 11.56 **LA**, Gaspagon [sic for *gaspergou*]; Cotton Fish Trout [occur].   **1933** LA Dept. of Conserv. *Fishes* 383, Louisianians also know the Grindle as the Cottonfish.   **1946** LaMonte *N. Amer. Game Fishes* 102.   **1968** *DARE* (Qu. P3, *Freshwater fish that are not good to eat*) Inf **LA**40, Cottonfish.

cotton flower n
  1 A cottonweed.
  1967 *DARE* (Qu. S26a) Inf **NC**49, Cotton flower.
  2 =**cotton grass 1**.
  1968 *DARE* (Qu. S26b) Inf **MI**42, Cotton flower.

cotton gin n [Transf] *obsolescent* Cf **gin house**
  A structure for housing a cotton gin.
  1807 U.S. Congress *Debates & Proc.* 460/2 **LA**, I went into the cotton gin that was near the house.   **1966–67** *DARE* (Qu. M22, . . *Other kinds of buildings . . on farms*) Infs **SC**24, 47, Cotton gin.

cotton grass n [*OED* 1597 →]
  1 also *cotton rush, cottontop grass:* A sedge of the genus *Eriophorum* with bristles producing large white cotton-like heads in fruit.   Also called **Alaska cotton, bog cotton, cotton flower 2, cotton sedge**   For other names of var spp see **frog hair, hare's tail 1, niggerhead**
  1784 in 1785 Amer. Acad. Arts & Sci. *Memoirs* 1.407, *Eriophorum. Cottongrass. Pussy.*   **1864** (1922) Jackson *Col.'s Diary* 155 **PA**, Colonel Swayne so often repeats the order to graze our animals, which means to turn them out on the fields that have nothing more on them than dry cotton grass which is about as good as pine shavings.   **1899** Going *Field, Forest & Wayside Flowers* 193 (*DAE*), The calyx and corolla of the

pretty "cotton-grass" are changed . . into long streamers. **1938** *Torreya* 38.63 **Pine Barrens NJ,** There are rushes and cotton grass. **1955** *U.S. Arctic Info. Center Gloss., Cotton grass.* Any plant of the genus *Eriophorum,* perennial, grass-like, growing on sphagnum bogs and tundra, bearing terminal tufts or balls of whitish, soft bristles. Also called 'sedge,' 'cotton rush,' 'cotton-sedge,' 'cotton-top grass.' Cf. *nigger-head.* **1978** *UpCountry* Nov 34 **NH,** Cotton grass . . . is misnamed since it is a sedge, a plant that looks like grass, but its blossom looks like cotton.

2 =**wool grass.**

1814 Bigelow *Florula Bostoniensis* 16 **MA,** *Eriophorum Cyperinum . . . Red cotton grass . . .* A common and very tall meadow grass . . . Spikelets . . covered with dull reddish wool. **1840** MA Zool. & Bot. Surv. *Herb. Plants & Quadrupeds* 259, S[cirpus] . . . Red Cotton-Grass. Named Trichophorum *cyperinum,* by Persoon, on account of the hairs in its flowers, and its resemblance to Cyperus. **1959** Carleton *Index Herb. Plants* 31, Cotton-grass . . Scirpus cyperinus.

cotton gum n

=**tupelo gum.**

1860 Curtis *Cat. Plants NC* 62, *Cotton gum. . .* As it does not split and is very easily worked, it is manufactured into light bowls and trays. **1884** Sargent *Forests of N. Amer.* 93, Large Tupelo. Cotton Gum. Tupelo gum. Southern Virginia, south near the coast to the valley of the Saint Mary's river, Georgia, through the Gulf states to the valley of the Neches river, Texas, and through Arkansas and southern and southeastern Missouri to the valley of the lower Wabash river, Illinois. **1969** *DARE* (Qu. T15, . . *Kinds of swamp trees*) Inf **TN**31, Cotton gum; (Qu. T16, . . *Kinds of trees . . "special" around here*) Inf **TN**33, Cotton gum. **1979** Little *Checklist U.S. Trees* 178.

cottonhead n

1 A person with light-colored hair; hence adj *cotton-headed.* **esp Sth, S Midl** See also **cottontop 1**

1861 *Harper's Mag.* 22.292/1 **NV,** John . . was the father of a thriving little family of "cotton-heads." **1885** Cable *Dr. Sevier* 417 **MS,** A Confederate deserter, fed his ague-shaken wife and cotton-headed children. **1960** Criswell *Resp. to PADS 20* **Ozarks,** *Cotton-headed. . .* Used of young children, especially boys, who have very light blond hair. Sometimes such children are called *cottontops.* Long use of both. **c1960** Wilson *Coll.* **csKY,** *Cotton-headed:* with light-colored hair, tow-headed. **1965** *DARE* FW Addit **neOK,** *Cottonhead*—a person with very light-colored hair.

2 See quot.

1969 *DARE* (Qu. HH9, *A very silly or light-headed person*) Inf **CA**169, Cottonhead.

cotton house n Sth ?obsolescent

A building for storing cotton.

1796 in 1916 Hawkins *Letters* 30 **GA,** I viewed his cotton house, the staple of the cotton [being] good. **1930** Faulkner *As I Lay Dying* 3 **MS,** The path runs straight as a plumb-line . . to the cottonhouse in the center of the field . . . The cottonhouse is of rough logs, from between which the chinking has long fallen. **1965–68** *DARE* (Qu. M22, . . *Other kinds of buildings . . . on farms*) Infs **GA**5, **MS**46, 63, **TX**32, Cotton house; (Qu. M1, . . *Special kinds of barns*) Infs **GA**28, **SC**40, 57, Cotton house. [5 of 7 Infs old] **1967** *PADS* 47.26, Cotton houses . . on the hill farms of Mississippi are usually built of logs or very plain lumber and covered with wooden shingles or tin. Cotton pickers carry their sacks of cotton to the cotton house, where it is stored until at least one bale . . can be taken to be ginned. **1971** Wood *Vocab. Change* 47 **Sth,** *Storage Places . . .* The range of volunteered words is impressively long and shows a complex of changing influences. *Cotton house, pump house,* and *wash house* for example, reflect earlier domestic requirements which have doubtless vanished; the building may now be used as a garage or for some other purpose.

cotton leafworm n Also *cotton eater, cotton worm*

A moth larva *(Alabama argillacea)* which strips or rags the leaves of cotton, esp late in the season.

1847 U.S. Patent Office *Annual Rept.: Ag.* 170, There has been some complaint respecting the cotton worm in the early part of the season. **1851** *DeBow's Rev.* 11.57 **LA,** They were supposed by some to be the *Cotton Eater (Ophiusa Xylina).* Ibid, [Footnote:] Much has been written about the *cotton eater* caterpillar. **1890** *Boston Journal* 7 March 4/1 *(DA),* An average annual loss of $30,000,000 has been occasioned in the South by the cotton-worm alone. **1966–70** *DARE* (Qu. R27, . . *Kinds of caterpillars or similar worms*) Infs **NC**85, **SC**24, **TX**35, 37, **VA**70, Cotton worm; **TX**13, Cotton leafworm.

cotton louse n

A cotton aphid *(Aphis gossypii).*

1846 *DeBow's Rev.* 2.141 **MS,** The *insects,* we are most troubled with, are the *"cotton lice."* **1856** U.S. Patent Office *Annual Rept. for 1855: Ag.* 68, When the cotton-plant is very young and tender, it is particularly subject to the attacks of the cotton-louse. **1966** *DARE* (Qu. R26, . . *The small greenish lice that come on plants*) Inf **GA**7, Cotton lice.

cotton marais n [cotton + Fr *marais* swamp]

Perh =**sweet flag.**

1977 *Mais Jamais* 17 **LA** (as of 1921), The herbs and roots they had to collect [to make a cough syrup] were mamou roots, Bull Sickle roots, Prickly Ash bark, Sea Merkle roots, Blue Brier roots, and Cotton Marais roots.

cotton milkweed n [In ref to the white down of the mature seedpods]

The common **milkweed** *(Asclepias syriaca).*

1948 Wherry *Wild Flower Guide* 105, Many additional *Milkweeds* occur in our area; commonest is the *Cotton Milkweed (A. syriaca),* a coarse plant spreading rapidly by underground stems.

cotton mink n

A mink *(Mustela vison)* having white underhair.

1968 *DARE* Tape **MN**42, Their [=cotton minks'] guard hair is brown and underneath it . . is white instead of brown all the way through. [FW:] What do they do with those? Are they prime or not so good? [Inf:] They're prime but they're just a freak mink or something. I don't think they use them for anything maybe outside of pins and stuff where they cut 'em up. They don't go into good coats because the fur'd have to be dyed. Oh, he [=a trapper] hates it when he comes home with a cotton mink. Day spoiler.

cotton moccasin See **cottonmouth**

cotton moth See **cotton caterpillar**

cotton mouse n [See quot 1928]

A **white-footed mouse** (here: *Peromyscus gossypinus*).

1928 Anthony *N. Amer. Mammals* 361, *Cotton Mouse . . .* Upperparts from bright cinnamon-rufous to deep russet . . . Underparts white. **1957** Blair et al *Vertebrates U.S.* 709, Cotton mouse . . . Forests throughout peninsular Florida and mostly on coastal plain from southeastern Virginia to southeastern Oklahoma and eastern Texas.

cottonmouth n, also attrib Also *cotton moccasin, cottonmouth(ed) moccasin, cottontooth moccasin*

A venomous snake *(Ancistrodon piscivorus)* with a mouth white inside, native to the South and Lower Mississippi Valley. Also called **congo snake 2, gapper, moccasin, trapjaw, water moccasin**

1832 in 1868 McCall *Letters Frontiers* 259, On reaching the spot, I found a large *moccason* or *cotton-mouth* snake writhing on the ground, with its head crushed . . but there it stood . . disclosing the whole of the interior of his immense dead-white, or, as it is well named, "cotton-mouth." **1879** *Scribner's Mth.* 18.882/1, A wilderness of briars, vines, and young forest trees; affording shelter to innumerable rabbits, opossums, . . rattlesnakes and "cotton-mouth" moccasins. **1906** *DN* 3.132 **nwAR,** *Cottonmouth . . .* A kind of moccasin snake. **1922** *DN* 5.160 **nwAR. 1938** Matschat *Suwannee R.* 22, Freeman, with the free, effortless movements of the swamp folk, trotted ahead across the rickety planks as casually as though no alligators, alligator snappers, and cottonmouths inhabited the waters of the marsh. **1947** *Prairie Schooner* 21.433, A cottonmouthed moccasin lay on the sand. **1965–70** *DARE* (Qu. P25, *What kinds of snakes are found around here?*) 96 Infs, **chiefly Gulf, Inland Sth, SW, Missip Valley,** Cottonmouth; 22 Infs, **S Atl, Gulf States,** Cottonmouth moccasin; **OK**3, Cotton moccasin; **NC**80, Cottontooth moccasin.

cottonmouth garter snake n

A snake of the genus *Thamnophis.*

1954 *Harder Coll.* **cwTN,** *Cottonmouth garter snake:* A type of garter snake with a white mouth.

cottonmouth moccasin See **cottonmouth**

cotton mule n

A small mule especially fit for cultivating cotton.

1908 U.S. Dept. Ag. *Farmers' Bulletins* 334/24, Cotton mules are lighter boned than miners and not so compactly built. **1960** Williams *Walk Egypt* 71 **GA,** Cotton mules were small and light and often old, and most of the farmers hereabouts had them, for they were cheaper, cheaper to buy and cheaper to feed. **1969** Kantor *MO Bittersweet* 83, Missouri mules used to be bred as sugar mules or cotton mules (depending on whether they were going to work in cane or cotton) and also as all-purpose draft animals.

cottonpatch loop n

1968 Adams *Western Words, Cotton-patch loop*—In roping, an extra-large loop; also called *community loop.*

cottonpatch rabbit n

A rabbit of the genus *Sylvilagus.*

1966 *DARE* Tape **AR**15, We call 'em cottonpatch rabbits 'cause they run out in the cottonpatch a whole lot. **1967–70** *DARE* (Qu. P30, . . *Wild rabbits*) Infs **AL**28, **GA**84, **MS**89, **MO**24, Cottonpatch rabbit.

cotton picker n

1 One's hand.

1966–69 *DARE* (Qu. X32, *Joking or uncomplimentary words for the hands—you might say, "Those are mine. You keep your_____(out of them)."*) Infs **MO**27, **SC**19, Cotton pickers.

2 In logging: see quots.

1930 Williams *Logger-Talk* 15 **Pacific NW,** *Cotton-picker:* A negro. **1958** McCulloch *Woods Words* 39 **Pacific NW,** *Cotton picker*—A dark logger.

3 See quots—generalized as a disparaging epithet.

1937 Coolidge *TX Cowboys* 15, Eastern Texas, according to the punchers, is given over to cotton and corn; and their favorite term of reproach is to call a man a cotton-picker. **1950** *Western Folkl.* 9.158, *Cotton picker.* An ignorant, foolish, or uninitiated person. A "rube." **1969** *DARE* FW Addit **CA,** Cotton picker, a Texan.

cotton-picking adv esp Sth, SW Note: *cotton-picking* adj is widespread as a term of disparagement.

Damned, darned.

1965–70 *DARE* (Qu. LL37, *To make a statement as strong as you can: "I could have wrung her neck, I was so_____mad."*) 11 Infs, **esp Sth, SW,** Cotton-picking.

cotton plant See cotton bush

cotton plow n NC

1966–70 *DARE* (Qu. L18, *Kinds of plows used around here, at present and in the past*) Inf **NC**15, Cotton plow; **NC**81, Cotton plow—throws dirt two ways; **NC**85, Cotton plow—horse drawn, but farmer had to walk; **NC**49, Walking cotton plow.

cotton poplar n

=cottonwood 1.

1970 *DARE* (Qu. T12, *The kind of poplar that has sticky, sweet-smelling buds*) Inf **VA**46, Cotton poplar; (Qu. T13, . . *Other names . . for . . poplar*) Inf **VA**46, Cotton poplar.

cotton rat n

A rodent of the genus *Sigmodon,* esp *S. hispidus.*

1831 Audubon *Ornith. Biog.* 1.298, I have never seen them [=Red-shouldered hawks] chase any other small birds than those mentioned, or quadrupeds of smaller size than the *Cotton Rat.* **1948** *NY Times* (NY) 12 Sept sec E 9/6, A dormant virus . . attacks the muscle-controlling nerves of the cotton rat.

cotton red-bug See cotton stainer

cotton rock n

A soft whitish type of limestone.

1855 MO Geol. Surv. *Rept. for 1854* 115, But the lower part of this Formation is made up of thin regular strata, of a soft earthy, light drab or cream-colored silicoargillaceous magnesian limestone . . . [Footnote:] This variety of Magnesian Limestone is generally called *"Cotton Rock"* in many parts of the State. **1941** FWP *Guide MO* 205, The *Wathen-Ranney* house is a two and one half story, ten room . . structure of buff colored "cotton rock."

cotton rose n

1 =Confederate rose.

1831 Audubon *Ornith. Biog.* 1.104 **LA,** Large-flowered Hibiscus, Cotton Rose, or Wild Althaea. **1933** Small *Manual SE Flora* 857, *H. mutabilis . . . Cotton-rose.* **1976** Bailey–Bailey *Hortus Third* 562, *Cotton rose . . .* Shrub or small tree, to 15 ft.

2 A filago (here: *Filago germanica*). [From the woolly heads] Also called **herba impia, rabbit tobacco**

1857 Gray *Manual of Botany* 229, *Filago . . . Cotton-Rose.* **1933** Small *Manual SE Flora* 1404, *Herba-impia.* Cotton-rose. **1959** Carleton *Index Herb. Plants* 31, *Cotton-rose:* Gifola germanica (Filago germanica).

3 A plant of the genus *Evax.* [See quot] Also called **rabbit tobacco**

1970 Correll *Plants TX* 1613, *Evax . . . Rabbit-tobacco.* Cotton-rose. Low taprooted annuals, gray floccose-woolly all over.

cotton rush See cotton grass 1

cotton sedge n [*OED* 1872 →] West

=cotton grass 1.

1889 *Century Dict., Cotton-sedge . . .* Same as *cotton-grass.* **1911** Jepson *Flora CA* 84, *Eriophorum* L. Cotton-sedge . . . E. gracile . . . Slender Cotton-sedge. **1936** McDougall *Plants of Yellowstone* 36, The most conspicuous member of the family is a *cotton-sedge . . .* readily recognized by its large, cottony head when in fruit. **1961** Douglas *My Wilderness* 21 **CO,** Cotton sedge (Eriophorum Chamissonis) is not common, but it can be found in wet meadows.

cotton shower n

1970 Tarpley *Blinky* 55 **neTX,** *Other responses* [for a short hard rain] . . reflect regional interest in farming, i.e. *cotton-shower, clod-buster, clod-melter.*

cotton spider n

An unidentified spider.

1966–68 *DARE* (Qu. R28, . . *Different kinds of spiders . . around here*) Infs **AL**41, **GA**6, Cotton spider.

cotton spinner n

A sea cucumber (*Holothuria* spp).

1962 Nichols *Echinoderms* 6.81, The process [=extrusion of cuvierian organs] has given rise to the common name 'cotton-spinner' for *Holothuria.*

cotton stainer n Also *cotton red-bug* [See quot 1856]

A red bug (*Dysdercus suturellus*) which is a serious pest of cotton in the southern US.

1856 U.S. Patent Office *Annual Rept.: Ag.* 103, The Red-Bug, or Cotton-Stainer . . is found by millions in East Florida, on the cotton plantations, where it does immense damage by staining the fibre of the cotton in the bolls. **1868** U.S. Dept. Ag. *Rept. of Secy.* 71, They hibernate in the perfect state concealed beneath bark, under brush-heaps, or stones, like the cotton red-bug. **1964** Borror–DeLong *Intro. Insects* 233, The most important pest species in this family [Pyrrhocoridæ] is the cotton stainer, *Dysdercus suturellus.* **1965** Blickenstaff *Insects* 291, Cotton stainer.

cottontail bluebill n Cf creamy ass

=lesser scaup.

1917 *Wilson Bulletin* 29.2.77, *Marila affinis.*—Cotton-tail bluebill, Wallops I[slan]d, Va. **1923** U.S. Dept. Ag. *Misc. Circular* 13.20, *Lesser Scaup Duck . . . Vernacular Names . . . In local use . . .* cottontail bluebill (Va.)

cottontail deer n

=whitetail deer.

1940 *Jrl. Mammalogy* 21.271 **OR, WA,** The existence, near the mouth of the Columbia River, of a population of Pacific white-tailed deer, *Odocoileus virginianus leucurus . . ,* has been recently called to our attention . . . To the farmers and fishermen . . of the river, the "tideland deer" or "cottontail deer" are well known. *Ibid* 273, The colloquial names "cottontail deer" and "tideland deer" . . have tended to conceal the true identity of the animal. **1970** *DARE* (Qu. P32, . . *Wild animals . . around here*) Infs **AR**56, **LA**2, Cottontail deer.

cotton thistle n [See quot 1931]

The scotch thistle (*Onopordum acanthium*).

1822 Eaton *Botany* 366, *Onopordum . . acanthium* (cotton thistle . .). Dr. Bigelow says, this exotic is now naturalized about Boston. **1872** VT State Bd. Ag. *Report* 1.283, *Onopordon acanthium,* Cotton Thistle is naturalized in a few places. **1931** Harned *Wild Flowers Alleghanies* 611, Scotch Thistle (*Onopordum Acanthium . .*)—A species known also as Cotton Thistle, probably because the whole plant has a cottony appearance.

cottontooth moccasin See cottonmouth

cottontop n

1 A person with light-colored hair; hence adj *cotton-topped.* Cf **cottonhead 1**

1922 *DN* 5.160, *Cotton-top . . .* A white-haired man. **1930** Shoemaker *1300 Words* 12 **cPA Mts** (as of c1900), *Cotton-top*—A white-haired old woman. **1935** Sandoz *Jules* 275 **wNE** (as of 1880–1930), That was after one of his wives . . left him . . . And here he had raised this crop of little cotton-tops growing up about him from another. **1949** Guthrie *Way West* 43 (as of 1847), A little boy, cotton-topped and thin, was following them. **1960** Criswell *Resp. to PADS 20* **Ozarks,** Cotton-headed . . . Used of young children, especially boys, who have very light blond hair. Sometimes such children are called *cottontops.* Long use of both. **1967** *DARE* (Qu. HH28, . . *Nicknames . . for people of foreign background . . Swedish*) Inf **ID5,** Cottontop.

2 =**scaled quail. chiefly SW**

1917 (1923) *Birds Amer.* 2.7, *Scaled Quail . . . Other Names.*—Blue Quail; Cotton Top. **1928** Bailey *Birds NM* 217, So well do its pale colors and scale-like markings conceal it . . that the white tip of its crest, which gives it the local name of White-top or Cotton-top, is often all that catches one's eye. **1965** Teale *Wandering Through Winter* 62 **AZ,** We recalled . . little "cottontops," scaled quail, feeding beneath them at sunset.

3 A perennial grass *(Trichachne califonia)* native to the Southwest. [See quot 1960]

1950 Hitchock *Manual Grasses* 573, *Cottontop . . .* Texas and Oklahoma to Colorado, Arizona, and Mexico. **1960** Correll *Plants TX* 149, *Arizona Cottontop . . .* Second glume . . densely covered with long silky whitish or purplish hairs that before drying are antrorse . . but after drying are widely spreading and fluffy. **1970** in 1983 *Carleton Coll.,* Cottontop = *Trichachne californica.* SW USA.

cottontop cactus n

A **barrel cactus** (here: *Echinocactus polycephalus*).

1941 Jaeger *Wildflowers* 165 **Desert SW,** *Cottontop Cactus . . . Echinocactus polycephalus . . .* The name "cottontop" refers to the generous tufts of cottony hairs enveloping the flower base and fruit.

cottontop grass See **cotton grass 1**

cottontop gravy n Cf **red-eye gravy**

1969 *DARE* (Qu. H37, . . *Gravy*) Inf **KY66,** Cottontop gravy: joking name for gravy made with milk and flour for thickening.

cotton tree n

Prob var spp of the genus *Populus,* as **cottonwood 1.**

1602 Brereton *Discouerie VA* 12, Walnut trees great store. Elmes. Beech. Hollie. Haslenut trees. Cherry trees. Cotten trees. Other fruit trees to us vnknown. **1763** LePage du Pratz *Hist. LA* 2.30, The *Cotton-tree* (a *poplar*) is a large tree which no wise deserves the name it bears, unless for some beards that it throws out. **1836** Hall *Statistics* 27 **Ohio R Valley,** The deep gloom with which they envelop the soil, gives a wild, pensive, and solemn character, to the *cotton tree grove.* **1899** (1962) Cushman *Hist. Choctaw* 170, For fresh wounds they made a poultice of the root of the cotton-tree which proved very efficacious. **1967–70** *DARE* (Qu. T13, . . *Other names . . for . . poplar*) Infs **LA20, SC32, VA40,** Cotton tree; **MI72,** Cotton; (Qu. T15, . . *Kinds of swamp trees*) Infs **LA20, SC57,** Cotton tree.

cotton-tree plover n

=**upland plover.**

1951 Pough *Audubon Water Bird* 325, Cotton-tree plover. *See* Upland plover.

cotton vacation n

Release-time from school in order to harvest the cotton crop.

1975 Thomas *Hear the Lambs* 132 **nwAL,** The cotton vacation came to a close, and the county schools were reopened in October.

cottonweed n [See quots] Cf **wild cotton**

1 Any of several woolly or hairy composite plants as:

a Various plants of any of three widely distributed, somewhat similar genera: 1) *Gnaphalium* (more at **cudweed 1**); 2) *Antennaria* (more at **ladies' tobacco**); 3) *Anaphalis* (more at **pearly everlasting**).

1876 Hobbs *Bot. Hdbk.* 27, Cotton weed, Pearl flow'd life everlasting, Gnaphalium margaritaceum. **1900** Lyons *Plant Names* 32, *A[naphalis] margaretacea . . .* Pearly Everlasting, . . Cotton-weed. *Ibid* 37, *A[ntennaria] dioica . . .* Cotton-weed. **1959** Carleton *Index Herb. Plants* 31,

Cotton-weed . . Gnaphalium sylvaticum. **1966** *DARE* (Qu. S21) Inf **NM2,** Cottonweed grows in cotton, has a little pod full of seeds and a purplish flower. **1974** (1977) Coon *Useful Plants* 102, *Anaphalis margaritacea . .* cotton-weed. *Ibid* 109, *Gnaphalium obtusifolium . .* cotton weed.

b Either of two rather small, woolly annual plants: *Stylocline amphibola,* found in California, or *Micropus californicus,* native from California to Oregon.

1961 Peck *Manual OR* 794, *M[icropus] californicus . . .* Slender Cotton-weed. Whole plant densely white-lanate. **1961** Thomas *Flora Santa Cruz* 356 **CA,** *M[icropus] californicus . . .* Slender Cottonweed. *Ibid* 357, *S[tylocline] amphibola . . .* Mount Diablo Cottonweed. **1973** Hitchcock–Cronquist *Flora Pacific NW* 540, *M. californicus . . .* Slender cottonweed.

2 The common **milkweed** *(Asclepias syriaca).*

1815–16 *Niles' Natl. Reg.* Supp. 9.189, The circumstance of a young school girl effecting a cure of one by rubbing it every day . . with the juice of *Milk or Wild Cotton Weeds* which finally destroyed the wen. **1971** Krochmal *Appalachia Med. Plants* 68, *Asclepias syriaca . . .* Cottonweed . . . In Appalachia it is used to treat warts and moles.

3 =**velvetleaf 1.**

1900 Lyons *Plant Names* 8, *Abutilon . . .* Velvet-leaf, . . Cotton-weed, . . Pie-marker. **1959** Carleton *Index Herb. Plants* 31, *Cotton-weed:* Abutilon theoprasti [sic]. **1967** *DARE* (Qu. S21) Inf **IL19,** Cottonweed, pie marker, buttonweed, velvetleaf—all refer to the same weed; **MO**11, Cottonweeds; **MO**18, Cottonweeds or buttonweeds.

4 =**willow herb 1.**

1932 Rydberg *Flora Prairies* 568, *Epilobium . . .* Cotton-weed. **1933** Small *Manual SE Flora* 946, *Epilobium . . .* Seeds comose . . . Willowherbs. Cotton-weeds.

5 =**snake cotton. Sth**

1933 Small *Manual SE Flora* 478, *Froelichia . . .* Cottonweed.—Pinelands, sandhills, and sandy old fields. **1953** Greene–Blomquist *Flowers South* 29, Cotton-Weed . . gets its common name from the dense hairiness of the underside of the leaves and the outside of the flowers. **1961** Wills–Irwin *Flowers TX* 104, Snake-cotton or Cotton-weed, a plant of the eastern half of Texas, is sometimes rather conspicuous by numbers. **1975** Duncan–Foote *Wildflowers SE* 30, Cottonweed . . [is a] loosely hairy annual.

6 The long-fruited anemone *(Anemone cylindrica).*

1950 Stevens *ND Plants* 143, *Anemone cylindrica . . .* The fruit heads remain all winter breaking up in spring, each achene covered with a fine tuft of crinkly hairs. This loose, cottony mass suggested the name "cottonweed."

7 =**bladder campion.**

1966 *DARE* Wildfl QR Pl.52 Inf **NC28,** Cottonweed.

cotton-white n

=**gray fox.**

1934 (1970) Wilson *Backwoods Amer.* 106 **Ozarks,** A cotton-white is a gray fox that happens to be white, a sort of albino of the species, usually swifter and more cunning than the general run of foxes.

cottonwood n

1 also *cottonwood poplar:* A tree of the genus *Populus.* **chiefly west of Appalachians** See Map Also called **alamo, aspen poplar, cotton poplar, cotton tree, poplar, popple** For other

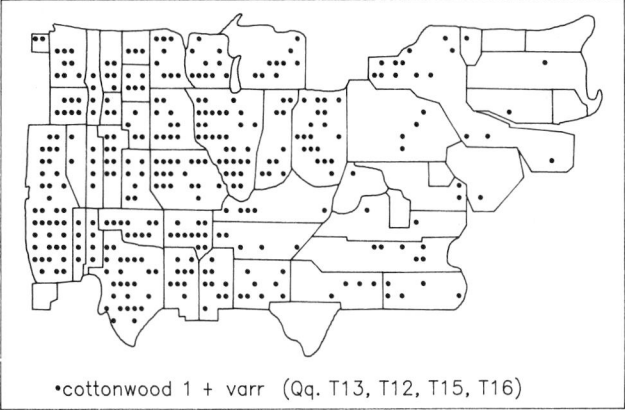

•cottonwood 1 + varr (Qq. T13, T12, T15, T16)

names of var spp see **balsam poplar, California poplar, Carolina poplar 1, quaking aspen, swamp cottonwood, white poplar**

1802 (1803) Ellicott *Jrl.* 123 **Missip Valley,** A boat may at all times come to with safety at . . any of the points that are covered with young cotton wood. **1824** (1928) MO Hist. Soc. *Coll.* 6.60, Nothing for horses to eat, except cotton wood bark. **1945** Wallace *Barington* 1 *(DA),* There is no fragrance on earth like the incense of burning cottonwood. **1948** *Chr. Sci. Monitor* 8 April 6 *(DA),* Buds on the cottonwood trees and the willows burst open. **1965–70** *DARE* (Qu. T13, *. . Other names . . for . . poplar*) 313 Infs, **chiefly west of Appalachians,** Cottonwood; **MI79,** Cottonwood poplar; **NM2,** Mountain cottonwood; **MO2,** Poplar cottonwood; (Qu. T15, *. . Kinds of swamp trees*) 39 Infs, **chiefly west of Appalachians,** Cottonwood; (Qu. T16, *. . Kinds of trees . . special*) 27 Infs, **chiefly West,** Cottonwood (tree); (Qu. T12, *The kind of poplar that has sticky, sweet-smelling buds*) 19 Infs, **chiefly Inland Nth,** Cottonwood. **1971** Krochmal *Appalachia Med. Plants* 206, *Populus Balsamifera* L. (Salicaceae) Common Names: . . cottonwood.

2 Perh =catalpa B1.

1965–70 *DARE* (Qu. T9, *The common shade tree with large heart-shaped leaves, clusters of white blossoms, and long thin seed pods or "beans"*) Infs GA80, MS47, 86, NC55, OR5, VA47, Cottonwood.

cottonwood blossom n [*cottonwood* tree]

See quot 1968.

1961 Adams *Old-Time Cowhand* 186, They made a cottonwood blossom out of 'im. **1968** Adams *Western Words,* Cottonwood blossom—A cowboy's term for a man hanged from the limb of a tree.

cottonwood ice cream n *hist*

1941 FWP *Guide UT* 23, In the spring the inner bark of cottonwood trees was sometimes scraped into a white pulpy mass which the early settlers called "cottonwood ice cream."

cottonwood on one, have the v phr Also *get the cottonwood over on one* [Perh in ref to the cottonwood as a gallows tree]

To have an advantage over one.

1888 *Detroit Free Press* Nov 3 (Farmer *Americanisms*), I jess reckoned she was blowin' around, an' yere she had de cottonwood on me all de time! **1977** Watts *Dict. Old West* 99, To *get the cottonwood over on somebody* was to have the advantage of them.

cottonwood poplar See **cottonwood 1**

cotton worm See **cotton leafworm**

‡cotty n

1967 *DARE* (Qu. L17, *Other names . . for manure*) Inf WA23, Cow cotty [ˈkɑdi].

couac See **quawk**

cou blanc n Also *pluvier à cou blanc* [See quot 1923]

=semipalmated plover.

1916 *DN* 4.424 **LA,** *Cou blanche* [sic]. The semipalmated plover (Aegialitis semipalmata). **1923** U.S. Dept. Ag. *Misc. Circular* 13.70, *Semipalmated Plover . . . Vernacular Names . . . In local use . . .* Cou blanc (white-neck) (Que., La.). **1951** Pough *Audubon Water Bird* 341, Pluvier á cou blanc. *See* Ringed plover.

couch See **couch grass 1**

couche-couche See **cush** n[1]

couch grass n [Var of *quitch grass: OED* 1578 →]

1 also *couch, cooch grass, cutch ~:* **=quack grass. chiefly NEast** Cf Map at **quack grass**

1790 Deane *New Engl. Farmer* 230/2, Quitch-Grass, called also . . *Couch-Grass.* **1868** U.S. Dept. Ag. *Rept. of Secy.* 347, For pastures and meadows on wet clay soil, redtop, couch or twitch grass. **1872** VT State Bd. Ag. *Report* 1.290, Three years ago I found couch in one end of my young pear orchard. **1913** *DN* 4.6 **ME** [at *witch grass*], The Century Dict. gives *quitch grass,* or *couch grass.* The forms *quick grass, cooch grass,* and *cutch grass,* are also known. Doubtless the original of all these forms is *quick* or its palatalized form *quitch,* and the other forms are merely instances of popular etymology. **1965–70** *DARE* (Qu. S8) Infs IN1, ME3, MA78, OH64, PA6, 44, SC41, VT12, WA28, Couch grass; (Qu. S21) Inf CA101, Couch grass.

2 A **cordgrass** (here: *Spartina patens*).

1933 *Torreya* 33.82, *Spartina patens . . .* Couch grass, southwestern Louisiana.

cou collier n [See quot 1931] **LA**

=killdeer.

1916 *DN* 4.425 **LA,** *Cou collier.* The killdeer (Oxyechus vociferus). **1923** U.S. Dept. Ag. *Misc. Circular* 13.69, *Kildeer* [sic] *. . In local use.*—Cou collier (ringneck) (La.). **1931** Read *LA French* 30, Killdeer . . owes its name *cou collier,* "neck band," to the fact that the lower part of the bird's neck is encircled by a broad brownish-black collar.

cougar n Also *croger* **chiefly NW, CA, UT** See Map

=mountain lion.

[**1774** Goldsmith *Hist. Earth* 13.244, There is an animal of America, which is usually called the Red Tiger, but Mr. Buffon calls it the Cougar.] **1809** Henry *Travels Indian Terr.* 299 **MT, ND** (as of 1760s), I saw also the skins . . of panthers, sometimes called tigers, and most properly *cougars.* **1893** Roosevelt *Wilderness Hunter* 292, There have been instances in which five or six . . huge, fierce, ban-dogs . . have by themselves mastered the cougar. **1897** Hough *Cowboy* 25 **SW,** A cowboy came into camp with the tails of four "crogers" (cougar—the mountain lion) which he said he had met in a body at a little piece of chaparral. **1965–70** *DARE* (Qu. P31, *. . Other names . . for the . . panther*) 39 Infs, **chiefly NW, CA, UT,** Cougar; (Qu. P32, *. . Other kinds of wild animals*) Infs IA5, OR3, UT3, WA17, Cougar. **1966** Barnes–Jensen *Dict. UT Slang* 31, [Mountain Lion:] The puma *(Felis concolor).* Although this large cat is known by almost fifty different names, in Utah it is . . called . . less frequently, cougar. **1966** *Port Townsend Leader* (WA) 1 Dec 2/8, I think it is also a terrible custom of training cougar dogs with the gentle coon. **1969** *DARE* Tape CA172, Cougars. **1977** Watts *Dict. Old West,* Cougar—In the West, *Panthera concolor* was known by many names, among them cougar, from the French *couguar.*

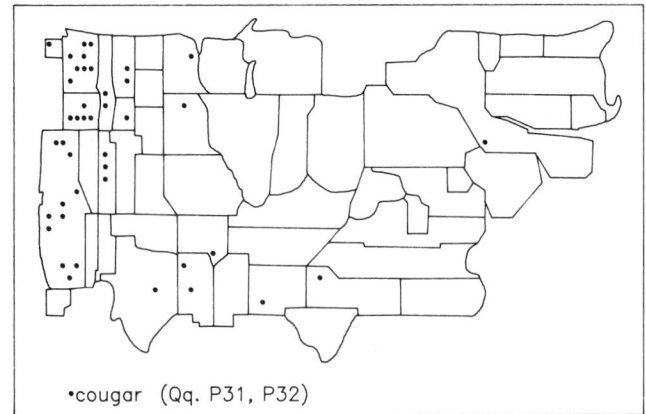

•cougar (Qq. P31, P32)

cougar den n *joc*

In logging: a bunkhouse.

1958 McCulloch *Woods Words* 39 **Pacific NW,** Cougar den—A bunkhouse. **1969** Sorden *Lumberjack Lingo* **NEng, Gt Lakes,** Cougar den.

cougar juice n

Kerosene.

1958 McCulloch *Woods Words* 36 **Pacific NW,** Coal oil—Kerosene; also called saw oil . . . Also known as cougar juice.

cougar milk n Also *cougar juice, ~ run* *joc*

See quot 1958.

1958 McCulloch *Woods Words* 39 **Pacific NW,** Cougar "juice" . . . A measure of strength, particularly the kind of whiskey which will rot the bottle. *Ibid,* Cougar milk—Any kind of stout home brew or other raw liquor. **1965** *DARE* (Qu. DD31, *Joking names for homemade hard liquor*) Inf OK7, Cougar run. **1969** Sorden *Lumberjack Lingo* **NEng, Gt Lakes,** Cougar milk—Prohibition-era woods liquor.

coughing sickness n

1968 *DARE* (Qu. BB10, *What other names . . are used, or used to be used, around here for tuberculosis?*) Inf MN28, Coughing sickness.

coughroot n

1 =nodding trillium.

1876 Hobbs *Bot. Hdbk.* 27, Cough root . . *Trillium pendulum.* **1900** Lyons *Plant Names* 378, *T[rillium] cernuum* . . Cough-root.

2 =lovage.

1900 Lyons *Plant Names* 223, *L[igusticum] filicinum* . . Colorado cough-root. **1937** U.S. Forest Serv. *Range Plant Hdbk.* W106, Two Rocky Mountain species *[Ligusticum filicinum; L. porteri]* are called coughroots because of their medicinal uses.

cough up v phr
To vomit violently.
1966–68 *DARE* (Qu. BB18, *To vomit a great deal at once*) Inf **PA**1, Cough up your guts; **NY**123, Cough up your toenails; (Qu. BB17, *Other words or expressions used around here for vomiting*) Inf **WI**64, Cough up.

coughweed n
1 =golden ragwort.
1876 Hobbs *Bot. Hdbk.* 27, *Coughweed*, Life root plant, *Senecio aureus*. **1971** Krochmal *Appalachia Med. Plants* 234, *Senecio aureus* . . . As the common name, "coughweed", would indicate, the herb is an expectorant.
2 =horehound.
1951 *PADS* 15.40 **TX**, *Marrubium vulgare* . . cough weed.

coughwort n
=coltsfoot 1.
1900 Lyons *Plant Names* 381, *T[ussilago] Farfara* . . Coughwort. **1903** Porter *Flora PA* 338, Coughwort. **1976** Miller *Shaker Herbs* 159 (as of 1800s), Coltsfoot – *Tussilago farfara* . . Coughwort. **1910** Graves *Flowering Plants* 402 **CT**, Coughwort.

couia See cui-ui

couillon n [Fr] **seLA**
1 also adj: A fool, hick, rube; stupid, inept.
1967 LeCompte *Word Atlas* 257 **seLA**, (*Somebody from the country who doesn't know much*), Couillon [1 inf]. *Ibid* 347, (*Stupid*), Couillon [1 inf]. *Ibid* 353, (*Dressed in bad taste*), Couillon [1 inf]. **1968** *DARE* FW Addit **seLA**, Couillon [ˌkwiˈjɔ̃]: fool (as an epithet and sometimes as a plain noun). **1983** Reinecke *Coll.* **New Orleans LA**, *Couillon* n. [ˈkujɔ̃] or [kuˈjɔ̃] — a foolish or inept person; *adj.* inept.
2 By ext: see quot. *derog*
1968 *DARE* (Qu. HH28, *Names and nicknames around here for people of foreign background: Creole*) Inf **LA**46, Cajun, cop-cops, couillons [ˈkuˌjɔnz].

couldn See can v¹ 2b

coulee n Also sp *cooley, coolie, coolly, coulé(e), couley, coulie* [Fr *coulée* a flow; see quot 1931]
1 Any of var types of watercourse:
a A stream bed, often one that runs dry according to the season; also the steam itself. **scattered, but esp LA**
1807 in 1832 U.S. Congress *Amer. State Papers* (Public Lands) 1.313, Bounded in front by the river Detroit, and in rear by a *coulée,* or small run. **1808** *Ibid* 346, Bounded . . above by a creek, (or coulée, called ventre de beouf.) **1920** *DN* 5.81 **eWA**, Coulee. Creek beds and gullies. Usually dry in summer. **1931** Read *LA French* 166, *Coulée,* a substantive from the feminine past participle of French *couler,* "to flow," is generally used in Louisiana of a small stream that may become dry in summer. *Coulée* is also written *coulee, -ie, coolie, -ey,* as an English word. **1941** FWP *Guide LA* 687, *Coulée*: a small stream, generally dry in summer. **1966–68** *DARE* (Qu. C1, . . *A small stream of water not big enough to be a river*) Infs **MN**16, **ND**3, Coulee. **1971** Wood *Vocab. Change* 34, For a slight depression, . . Louisiana choices are between *draw* and *coulee*, the latter being Canadian French in origin. **1971** Detro *Generic Terms* 135, In areas of Louisiana, *coulée* was anglicized and appeared spelled as an English word: coulie, coolie, cooley, and couley. These variant forms appeared primarily in settlement names. Only one variant, couley, which was recorded applied to a physical landscape feature. *Ibid* 138, Though the meaning of the term *"coulée"* was definitely extended to signify various types of streams and the characteristics of many *"coulees"* were altered through time, there still remained a conflict between map symbolization and local usage of the term *"coulée."* **1973** Allen *LAUM* 1.234, In North Dakota and extreme northwestern Minnesota it *[coulee]* typically denotes a shallower depression, dry except during wet weather or spring thaws, that may extend for miles across the prairie.
b A small bayou or canal in marshland. **esp LA**
1917 *DN* 4.420 **New Orleans LA**, *Coulie* . . . A little bayou . . . Also N. Dak. **1967** LeCompte *Word Atlas* 225 **seLA**, (*A very small, shallow canal through the marsh*), Coulee [1 inf].

c A valley or depression between hills. **chiefly WI, MN, MT, ND, WY**
1891 Garland *Main-Travelled Roads* 82 **WI**, The dazzling sunlight flamed along the luscious velvety grass . . and streamed in bars of gold and crimson across the blue mist of the narrower upper Coulés. *Ibid* 83, "There's our old house, ain't it?" Howard broke out, pointing to one of the houses farther up the Coulé . . . "Where's Grant living, anyhow?" "Farther up the Coolly." **1939** FWP *Guide MT* 414, Coulee — A small valley in prairie country. **1950** *WELS* (*Low land running between hills: small or narrow*) 3 Infs, **WI**, Coulee. **1966** *WI Conserv. Bulletin* July – Aug 23, Southwestern Wisconsin offers thousands of scenic miles for our motoring pleasure. This is coulee country. A land of rolling bluffs, bold cliffs, rock monuments, deep sheer-walled valleys. **1966–68** *DARE* (Qu. C19, *What do you call low land running between hills [with and without water]?*) Infs **MT**3, 5, **ND**5, 9, **WI**57, **WY**2, Coulee. **1973** Allen *LAUM* 1.234, *Coulee* . . occurs in two distinct areas. In southeastern Minnesota it denotes a small gently sloping valley leading into either the Mississippi River or an immediate tributary.
d A ravine or valley with sloping sides. **chiefly West**
1895 *DN* 1.386, *Coulee*: ravine . . . West. **1913** *DN* 4.10 **MN**, Coulee . . . A ravine. "We were riding in the coulee below the hill." **1921** Thorp *Songs Cowboys* 150 **NM, TX**, If you want to see some bad lands, / Go over on the Dry; / You will bog down in the coulees / Where the mountains reach the sky. **1947** Jones *Evergreen Land* 57 **WA**, Although *coulee* is a French word, Washingtonians have little truck with Continental pronunciations, and from Territorial days the deep, dry river beds of lava rock, whose inclining sides distinguish them from *canyons* have been simply "coolies." **1966** *DARE* (Qu. C21, *A deep place cut in sloping ground by running water*) Inf **ND**3, Coulee. **1966** *DARE* FW Addit **ceWA**, Coulee: a ravine. **1968** Adams *Western Words*, *Coulee* . . a ravine; used in the Northwest as a synonym for the Southwest's *arroyo*.
2 Transf: see quot.
1933 *AmSp* 8.4.51/1 **NE**, An excessive drinker of whiskey was frequently called a *coulee*.

councan See cooncan

count v Usu |kaʊnt|, also |k(j)æʊnt| and varr — see quot 1936. Pronc-sp *kyount*
A Forms.
1905 Culbertson *Banjo Talks* 69 **SE**, Kyountin' on dem ol' nine lives fer ter up an' do me? **1936** *AmSp* 11.34, If a norm may be said to exist for this diphthong in East Texas, it is [æʊ] . . . Examples: . . account . . count . . . When this diphthong follows [k] or [g], the [k] or [g] is palatalized, and the diphthong frequently becomes [eaʊ], [eæʊ]; [ɛaʊ], [ɛæʊ]; [æaʊ], [æːːʊ]; [ɪaʊ], [ɪæʊ]. The initial sounds of these triphthongs is always an on-glide preceding the stress. **1941** *AmSp* 16.7 **eTX**, In Negro speech this diphthong [=aʊ] is not often flattened to [æʊ] as in 'hill type' speech, but retains its standard form, with lengthening of the first element. A lighter [j] than 'hill type' speech develops after [k], [g]. Examples: . . *count* . . [kjãʊnt]. **c1970** *DARE* FW Addit **neKY**, Count [kæʊnt].
B Sense.
To expect, reckon. *arch*
1815 Humphreys *Yankey in England* 29, I should be glad to know, what kind of way you count to improve me in. *Ibid* 104, Count, (in provincial use,) estimate, reckon. **1899** (1912) Green *VA Folk-Speech*, Count . . . To expect or think.

count n, also attrib [Abbr for *countable*; cf *OED countable* 2] **chiefly C Atl** Cf counter n¹ 1
A shellfish or terrapin of an established market size; also the numerical equivalent of such a size.
1881 Ingersoll *Oyster-Industry* 243 **PA, NY**, Count . . . Method of selling oysters in Philadelphia and New York, by enumeration instead of measurement. *Ibid*, In respect to terrapins, one of full size, i.e., six inches long; two or three small ones will make a "count". (Savannah [GA].) *Ibid* **ceNJ**, Count-clams. — Quahaugs large enough to count 800 to the barrel. **1883** U.S. Natl. Museum *Bulletin* 27.234, "Count" Clams, the largest size, . . sell for $3 per barrel, wholesale. It takes 800 "counts" to make a barrel. **1894** *DN* 1.329 **NJ**, Count: terrapin six inches across belly, fit for market. *Ibid, Count clams*: quahaugs, 800 to the barrel. **1940** FWP *Guide MD* 169, Today the smallest count sells for $3 (counts are terrapin not less than five inches from end to end of the under shell). **1949** Brown *Amer. Cooks* 351 **MD**, The short six inch diamond backs (Terrapin) called counts are the pick of the market, and the female sex is deemed more tasty; they're called cow terrapin.

'count See **account** n **A**

count base n

Home base.

1967 *DARE* (Qu. EE14, . . *The place where the player who is "it" has to wait and count while the others hide*) Inf **TX**35, Count base.

counter n¹

1 A lobster of legal catch size. **ME** Cf **count** n

1966 *DARE* Tape **ME**17, One or two counters in it and maybe seven or eight lobsters in it but the rest of 'em are small . . three and an eighth across his back. Counters are between three and an eighth and five and an eighth; under or over these limits are illegal. **1975** Gould *ME Lingo,* Counter—A legal lobster, or *keeper.* **1978** Merriam *Illustr. Lobstering* **ME,** *Counter*—A lobster of legal size. A legally-sized lobster must have a carapace that measures between 3 3/16 and 5 inches in length.

2 In marble play: see quot.

1958 *PADS* 29.32 **WA,** *Counter* . . . A marble not used in playing, but "fine for stakes."

3 In certain children's games, the one who is "it" and must count while others hide.

1966–70 *DARE* (Qu. EE13b, *In games in which all the others hide, the one who must try to find them, he's [the]* ———) Infs **GA**42, 72, **KY**85, **LA**8, **NC**30, **SC**69, Counter.

‡counter n² [Abbr for *counterpane*]

1968 *DARE* (Qu. E15, *The cloth that is put on top of a bed, mostly for decoration*) Inf **PA**102, Counter.

counterbrand n, v chiefly **SW**

A brand put on livestock to indicate transfer of ownership; to apply such a brand.

1859 (1968) Bartlett *Americanisms* 103 **SW,** *Counter-brand.* To destroy a brand by branding on the opposite side . . . When cattle are a year old, they are branded; and if afterwards sold, the same brand is burnt in on the opposite side, thus destroying the original title. **1874** McCoy *Cattle Trade* 8 **TX,** When a stock is purchased it is usual, if it be not very large, that each animal is counterbranded; i.e., the first brand burned out and the purchaser's brand burned on instead. **1922** Rollins *Cowboy* 236, The brute might be given one which was known interchangeably as the "vent brand" (from Spanish "venta," meaning a sale) or "counter brand," and which was the seller's admission of the fact of sale. **1955** *AmSp* 30.57 **TX** (as of 1824), The safest rule is not to purchase from them at all unless the Horse or mule is counter-branded for otherwise the purchaser runs the risk of losing him. **1968** Adams *Western Words, Counterbrand*—A brand placed on an animal to supersede an earlier one.

counterdict v [Alter of *contradict*]

See quots.

1905 *DN* 3.58 **eNE,** A sort of metathesis, or perhaps slurring of the middle syllable, is very frequent in *counterdict, interduce.* **1968** *DARE* (Qu. GG16, *Words for finding fault* . . *"You just can't please him—he's always* ———.'') Inf **MO**35, Counterdicting.

counterjumper n Also *counterhopper*

A store clerk.

1845 *Knickerbocker* 25.126, Fourteen days are still to elapse before the time when the ardent apprentice and the constant counter-hopper indite their amatory lays. **1859** (1968) Bartlett *Americanisms, Counterjumper.* A clerk in a retail "store," whose place is behind a counter. **1899** (1912) Green *VA Folk-Speech, Counter-jumper* . . . A salesman in a dry-goods store. **1919** *DN* 5.63 **NM,** *Counter-jumper.* **1927** *Ruppenthal Coll.* **KS,** Counter hopper . . a clerk in a retail store, esp. a clerk who has many and varied duties. **1968** Adams *Western Words, Counterjumper*—The logger's name for a commissary clerk.

counterpiece n [Alter of *counterpane*]

1968 *DARE* (Qu. E15, *The cloth that is put on top of a bed, mostly for decoration*) Inf **NJ**28, Counterpiece.

counterpin n Also pronc-sp *county pin* [Alter of *counterpane*] chiefly **Sth, S Midl** See Map

A bedspread.

1836 (1937) Poole *Yankee School Teacher* 668 **MA,** In the dormitory there are perhaps 150 beds standing in rows, all with white counterpins looking as nice as possible. **1917** *DN* 4.410 **wNC, KY,** *Counterpin* . . . Variant of *counterpane.* **1937** Eaton *Handicrafts* 113, The counterpanes or "county-pins," or "dimities," as they were sometimes called,

represent a very old form of weaving with fine cotton thread in both warp and weft and are usually in one color. **1954** *Harder Coll.* **cwTN,** *Counterpin.* Bedspread. **1899** (1912) Green *VA Folk-Speech, Counterpin* . . . Covering for a bed; counterpane. **1965–70** *DARE* (Qu. E15, *The cloth that is put on top of a bed, mostly for decoration*) 106 Infs, **chiefly Sth, S Midl,** Counterpin. [Of all Infs responding to the question, 70% were old; of those giving this response, 84% were old.] **1970** Tarpley *Blinky* 108 **neTX,** *(Fancy daytime cover for the bed),* Counterpin, counterpane, countypin. **1971** Wood *Vocab. Change* 49 **Sth,** A fancy daytime cover ordinarily removed before the bed is used. The preferred name is *bedspread* followed by the phonological variants of a synonym, *counterpane, counterpin.*

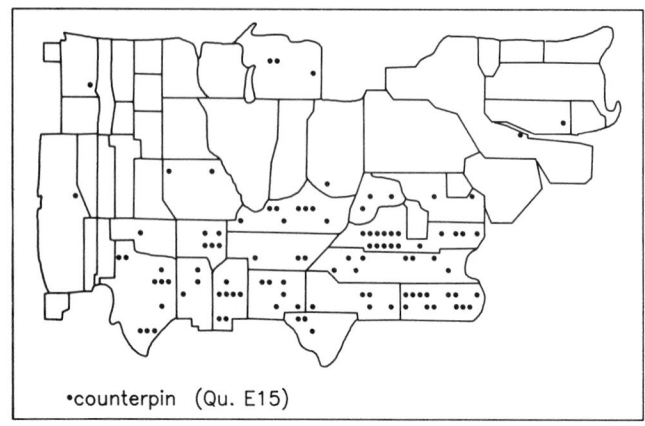

•counterpin (Qu. E15)

counting n

1966–67 *DARE* (Qu. EE13a, *Games in which every player hides except one, and that one must try to find the others*) Inf **LA**8, Counting: The one that be at the base, he counts—they call it "gettin' your hundred"; (Qu. EE17, *Hiding games that start with a special, elaborate method of sending the players out to hide*) Inf **WA**9, Counting.

counting apple-seeds See **apple-seed fortune**

count one's potatoes See **brag the potatoes**

count out v phr

To tally up to a particular number.

1903 (1965) Adams *Log Cowboy* 13, Just so the herd don't count out shy on the day of delivery.

count over v phr

To count a herd of cattle in the process of transferring it to a new owner.

1920 Hunter *Trail Drivers TX* 67, We reached the Tusler Ranch on August 19th and on the 20th we counted the old herd over to the ranch boss.

country n Usu |'kʌntri|; also |'kentri|, |'kɑntri| See Pronc Intro 3.I.4.b Pronc-spp *countree, kentry*

A Forms.

1858 (1892) Holmes *One Hoss Shay* 15 **NEng,** 'N' the keounty 'n' all the kentry raoun'. **1895** (1969) Crane *Red Badge* 48, He was dumbed if he was goin' t' have every dumb bushwacker in th' kentry walkin' round on it. **1901** *Century Illustr. Mag.*62.906/2 **TN,** De odder niggers kin mek er place in er new kentry. **1916** *DN* 4.273 **NE,** *Coun-tree* . . . Country. "We had headed for a new coun-tree." Usage brought to Southeastern Nebraska by men who had been Klondike prospectors. **1926** Kephart *Highlanders* 429 **sAppalachians,** "Borned in the kentry and ain't never been out o' hit" is all that most of them can say for themselves. **1935** *AmSp* 10.165 **PA,** Another matter of pronunciation attributable to the German influence is the substitution of [a:] for [ʌ], noticeable especially in the words *nothing, comfortable,* and *country.*

B Senses.

1 esp in phr *in one's country:* The particular region to which one belongs. **esp S Midl**

1835 Crockett *Account* 45 **TN,** If you was to talk that way to a white man in my country, he'd give you first-rate hell. **1894** *Congressional Record* 14 Feb 2186/1 **KY,** The "commercial tourists," as I believe they are called now—down in my country we call them "drummers." **1939–56** Hall Coll. **cwNC,** He was give up to be the best bear dog in this country. **1967–70** *DARE* FW Addit **seGA,** *Country* is used meaning "area of the country." Hence, 1) "our country" means the swamp area nearby; 2) "your country up there" refers to wherever the person spoken to happens to be from; **swGA,** *Country* is used for the immediate area. "We don't have them in this country." This usage was noticed throughout southern Georgia; **TX89,** *Country* means area. **1969** *DARE* (Qu. MM22, *If you are talking to a friend who lives in another place and you want to inquire about his neighborhood, you might ask, "How are things _____?"*) Infs **KY36, NY219,** In your country.

2 attrib in var usu derog combs in ref to a rustic, yokel, hick:

a *country jake,* infreq ~ *jack.* [jake] **scattered, but chiefly W Midl** See Map *somewhat old-fash*

  1856 Kelly *Humors* 136 (*OEDS*), You're a pooty looking country jake, you are, to advertise for a *dog,* and don't know Chiney Terrier from a singed possum. **1885** Twain *Huck. Finn* 171 **MO,** These country jakes won't ever think of that. **1919** *DN* 5.65 **NM,** *Country-jake.* **1931–33** *LANE Worksheets* **seRI,** Country jake—a rustic. **1950** *WELS* 4 Infs, **WI,** Country jake. **1958** *AmSp* 33.265 **Upper MW,** Country jake, country jay. **1960** Criswell *Resp. to PADS 20* **Ozarks,** *Country Jake . . .* A yokel. Widely used even by country people, but especially by small town residents. **c1960** *Wilson Coll.* **csKY,** Country jake. **1965–70** *DARE* (Qu. HH1, *. . A rustic or countrified person*) 56 Infs, **chiefly W Midl,** Country jake; **HI6, 13, VA25,** Country jack; (Qu. II21, *. . Somebody . . without manners*) Inf **HI13,** Country jack. [Of all Infs responding to Qu. HH1, 63% were old; of those giving these responses, 84% were old.] **1968** Kellner *Aunt Serena* 81 **sIN** (as of c1910), Albert was right, I decided. We *were* ignorant Country Jakes, and this was just a hick place nobody would want to live in.

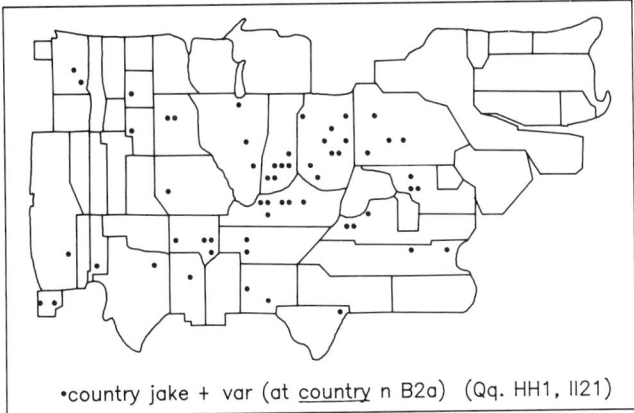

  •country jake + var (at <u>country</u> n B2a)   (Qq. HH1, II21)

b *country jay,* infreq ~ *jayhawk.* [jay, jayhawk] **chiefly Nth**
  1899 A.H. Quinn *Pa. Stories* 45 (*DA*), Well, you all know what a country jay Dutch was when he came to college. **1919** O'Neill *Moon Caribbees* 204, You country jays oughter wake up and see what's goin' on. **1950** *WELS* 1 Inf, **csWI,** Country jay. **1958** *AmSp* 33.265 **Upper MW,** Pejorative Designations of Rural Dwellers . . . Country jay. **1968–69** *DARE* (Qu. HH1, *. . A rustic or countrified person*) Infs **AZ10, MA55,** Country jay; **WI13,** Country jayhawk.

c *country gawk.* [gawk] **esp NEng**
  1931–33 *LANE Worksheets* **nwMA,** Country gawk—a rustic. **1941** *LANE* Map 450, The map shows a great variety of terms, largely derogatory and jocular applied to a person who lives in the country . . . The following terms were recorded in more than one community . . *Country gawk.* **1958** *AmSp* 33.265 **Upper MW,** Pejorative Designations of Rural Dwellers . . . Country gawk. **1966–69** *DARE* (Qu. HH1, *. . A rustic or countrified person*) Infs **MA11, 47,** Country gawk.

d *countryman.* **chiefly S Atl, esp SC** See Map
  1931–33 *LANE Worksheets* **csME,** *Countryman.* Name supplied by inf for those who live "out back from the ocean." A countryman is supposed to be a farmer. Those near shore take part in water businesses. **1958** *AmSp* 33.265 **Upper MW,** Pejorative Designations of Rural Dwellers . . . countryman. **c1960** *Wilson Coll.* **csKY,** Countryman . . . Yokel, boor. Rare. **1965–70** *DARE* (Qu. HH1, *. . A rustic or countrified person*) 18 Infs, **chiefly S Atl,** Countryman; **SC40,** Hick countryman. **c1970** Pederson *Dial. Survey Rural GA,* (*If a country person goes into town, what might the city people call him behind his back?*) 15 infs, **seGA,** Countryman. [11 of 15 infs Black]

e *country cracker.* [cracker 2] **S Atl**
  1865 (1905) Chesnut *Diary from Dixie* 401 **SC,** Everybody in our walk of life gave Milly a helping hand. She was a perfect specimen of the

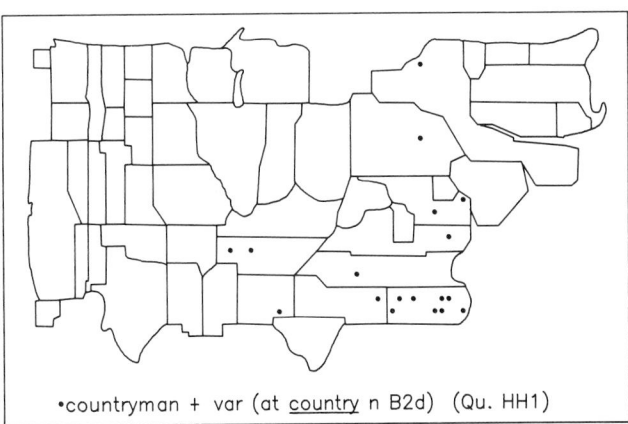

  •countryman + var (at <u>country</u> n B2d)   (Qu. HH1)

Sandhill "tackey" race, sometimes called "country crackers." **1908** *DN* 3.301 **eAL, wGA,** *Country-cracker.* A backwoodsman, a rustic. **1965–70** *DARE* (Qu. HH1, *. . A rustic or countrified person*) Infs **FL26, 52, GA7, 74, SC5, 31, 34, 44,** Country cracker.

f in numerous other combs: See quots.

  1949 *AmSp* 24.107 **cnGA,** *Country sager . . A rustic* ('new'). **1950** *WELS* (*City person's nicknames for a country person*) 7 Infs, **WI,** Country bumpkin; 6 Infs, Country cousin; 1 Inf, Country jerk; 1 Inf, Country hick. **1958** *AmSp* 33.265 **Upper MW,** Pejorative Designations of Rural Dwellers [20 different combs with *country* are recorded, including] country boob . . country gawk . . country ike . . country 'punkin.' **1965–70** *DARE* (Qu. HH1, *. . A rustic or countrified person*) 49 Infs, **scattered,** Country bumpkin; 30 Infs, **scattered,** Country hick; 12 infs, **scattered,** Country boy; **AL20, OH8, PA27, 242, VT7,** Country rube; **CA76, MN6, NY48, 76,** Country cousin; **MN38, NY141, WI49,** Country gentleman; **LA40, MS6, 71, MO4,** Country hoosier; **KY91, 94, TX91,** Country hunk; **IN35, VA103,** Country bum; **CT42, NJ1, NY149, NC61,** Country (pumpkin, punkin); **MO8, NH14,** Country guy; **MA30,** Country boob; 17 Infs, **scattered,** Country (buck, gink, joker, peck, slicker, squash, etc). **1970** *Thompson Coll.* **cwGA,** One of them thought it [=a word] was something used only by country sagers until he checked it in Webster's. **1970** Tarpley *Blinky* 266 **neTX,** (*A poor white from the back country*), Other responses . . country hunk. **1973** Allen *LAUM* 1.349 **Upper MW,** (A rustic)—Several additional terms of limited use appear in the detailed list below: . . Country boy . . ~ bum . . ~ bumpkin . . ~ cousin . . ~ farmer . . ~ folk . . ~ gook . . ~ guy . . ~ hayseed . . ~ hick . . ~ hunk . . ~ ike . . ~ jig . . ~ jigger . . ~ punk . . ~ pumpkin . . ~ rube.

3 See quot.
  1939 *FWP Guide NC* 98, To the banker [=inhabitant of the Outer Banks] the mainland is "the country."

4 A large number, a mass.
  1966 *DARE* (Qu. LL8b, *A large number, for example, of cousins: "She has a whole _____ of cousins."*) Inf **MO1,** Country.

country adj **chiefly Sth, Atlantic** See Map *esp among Black speakers* Cf **country** n 2
  Countrified, uncultured, rustic—used predicatively.

  [**1834** Caruthers *Kentuckians* 32, One of 'em popped his head out of the window, and says to me as they went by, 'Country,' says he, 'there's

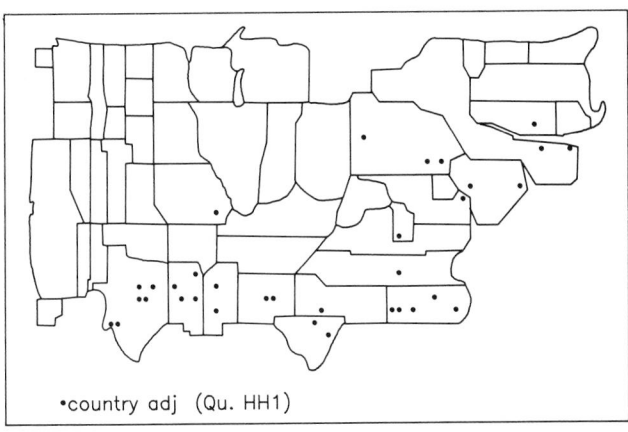

  •country adj   (Qu. HH1)

something on your horse's tail.'] **1958** Humphrey *Home from the Hill* 268 **TX,** She hoped he would not think she was vulgar, country. **1965–70** *DARE* (Qu. HH1, . . *A rustic or countrified person*) 34 Infs, **chiefly Sth,** Country. [18 of 34 Infs Black] **c1970** Pederson *Dial. Survey Rural GA,* (*If a country person goes into town, what might the city people call him behind his back?*) 5 infs, **seGa,** [He's] country. [3 infs Black]

country ball n Cf **country job**

    1967–69 *DARE* (Qu. EE11, *Bat-and-ball games for just a few players [when there aren't enough for a regular game]*) Inf **GA**86, Country ball.

country bank n [*country* + **bank** n[1] 2]

    1943 Korson *Coal Dust* 4 **PA,** Some farmers . . overcame this fear [of the darkness of a coal mine] and operated small mines variously called "country banks," "wagon mines," "dog holes," "gopher holes," or "father-and-son" mines.

country block n Cf **country mile**

An indefinite distance, relatively long.

    1928 *Ruppenthal Coll.* **KS,** *Country block* . . . an indefinite distance. "We couldn't get within a country block of the spot. You did much better; you had him skinned by a country block." **1954** TN Folk Lore Soc. *Bulletin* 20.38 **eTN,** As long as a country block.

country boy match See **country match**

country buying n *obsolescent*

In tobacco farming: see quots.

    1966 *PADS* 45.10 **cnKY,** *Country buying* . . . The practice of buying from farmers by visiting the farm and offering a price for the whole lot while it is in the barn. (archaic) . . "Country buying is only practiced in the mountain areas." **1967** Key *Tobacco Vocab., Country buying,* buying tobacco in the barn from the farmer. Going out of use.

country clod See **clod** n 1

country coin n Cf **country** adj

    1970 *DARE* (Qu. HH1, . . *A rustic or countrified person*) Inf **KY**84, Country coin.

country cousin n *euphem*

Menstruation.

    1908 *DN* 3.301 **eAL, wGA,** *Country cousin* . . . Menses. **1948** *Word* 4.183 ["Vocabulary of Menstruation" — euphemisms], Female anthropomorphisms . . are numerous . . *little sister's here, Aunt Jane, my country cousin.* **1966–70** *DARE* (Qu. AA27, . . *A woman's menstruation*) Infs **MI**24, **NY**167, My country cousin is coming; **VA**100, Country cousin came; **TX**23, Country cousin is here.

country cracker See **country** n B2e

country cut n

    1968 *DARE* (Qu. MM16, *If you're walking with somebody to the other corner of a square, and you want to save steps, you might say: "It'll be shorter if we _____."*) Inf **NJ**16, Make a country cut.

country fever n *old-fash*

Malaria.

    1822 *Christian Observer* 22.630 *(DA),* Their apprehensions being confined to what they term the "country fever" and "fever and ague." **1882** Eggleston *Wreck Red Bird* 6, "What 's country fever?" asked Jack . . "It's a very severe and fatal form of bilious fever, which one night's exposure — or even a few hours' exposure after sunset — brings on." **1941** FWP *Guide SC* 349, Plantation owners, plagued every summer by malaria, which they called "country fever" . ., flocked here [Gaffney SC] to drink the water. **1950** *PADS* 14.23 **SC,** *Country fever* . . . Malaria.

country fries n pl Also *country fried, country style (fried)*

Raw or cooked potatoes that are sliced and fried.

    1965–70 *DARE* (Qu. H47, *Kinds of fried potatoes*) Infs **CA**210, **IL**9, **MI**68, **MO**17, **NE**11, **NC**31, **OH**44, **VA**72, Country fried; **CA**54, Country fried — sliced, cooked, fried; **KY**63, Country fried — sliced and fried raw; **FL**11, Country fries; **CT**6, Country style fried — also called kitchen fried; potatoes cut up after they are cooked, and fried in grease; **IN**65, **MD**41, Country style. **1979** *New Yorker* 5 Mar 98/2 **NM,** Breakfast in West also offers side order of pancakes. (Country fries come anyway.)

country gawk See **country** n B2c

country ham n chiefly **KY, NC, VA**

See quot 1949.

    1949 Brown *Amer. Cooks* 630 **NC,** This section of the south has "country hams" which should be distinguished from country-cured

hams smoked on farms . . the North Carolina "country ham" is merely salt cured. **1965–70** *DARE* (Qu. H45, *Dishes made with meat, fish, or poultry that everybody around here would know, but that people in other places might not*) 9 Infs, **KY, VA,** Country ham; **SC**46, Fresh ham — one not cured; country — cured ham; **KY**41, Country ham and biscuits; (Qu. H37, . . *Gravy*) Infs **KY**74, 84, Country ham.

country jack, country jake See **country** n B2a

country jay(hawk) See **country** n B2b

country job n

    1967 *DARE* (Qu. EE11, *Bat-and-ball games for just a few players [when there aren't enough for a regular game]*) Inf **AL**19, Country job: Three players — a pitcher, a catcher, and a hitter.

country light n Cf **city light**

The high beam of an automobile headlight.

    1950 *WELS Suppl.* **WI,** Country lights — bright lights on a car. **1965–70** *DARE* (Qu. N10, *What other words are used around here for the bright and dim lights on a car?*) 12 Infs, **scattered,** Country lights; **IL**78, 83, **NJ**36, **TN**31, **TX**53, Country lights and city lights.

countryman See **country** n B2d

country match n Also *country boy match*

    1968–70 *DARE* (Qu. F46, . . *Matches you can strike anywhere*) Infs **IL**94, **IA**30, **VA**47, Country matches; **IL**117, Country boy matches; **VA**22, Old, country matches.

country mile n

An indefinitely long distance.

    1951 TN Folk Lore Soc. *Bulletin* 17.58 **wTN,** Long as a country mile. **1957** *KY Folkl. Rec.* 3.53 **cwKY,** My mother's family lived about four "country miles" from the church. **1967–70** *DARE* (Qu. KK52, *To do something in an indirect and complicated way: "I don't know why he had to go _____ to do that."*) Inf **NV**3, Around the country mile; (Qu. KK55a, *To deny something very firmly: "No, not by a _____."*) Inf **WI**34, Country mile; (Qu. MM25, . . *A long distance: "Texas is a _____ [from here]."*) Inf **TX**81, Country mile. **1968** *DARE* File **nePA.** **1968** *Foxfire* Fall–Winter 112 **nGA,** Doodle . . grabbed him [a possum] up by his naked tail and slung him a country mile across the creek.

country mouse n

=**white-footed mouse.**

    1965 Teale *Wandering Through Winter* 313 **RI,** Throughout the swamp . . such . . mice, sometimes called country mice . ., fill a niche in many habitats.

country pie n

    1949 *AmSp* 24.107 **ceGA,** *Country pie* . . . Deep pie.

‡**country rough** n

    1965–69 *DARE* (Qu. AA6b, *What do you call a man who is fond of being with women and tries to attract their attention — if he's rude or not respectful?*) Infs **GA**70, **MS**59, Country rough.

country style (fried) See **country fries**

count (the) ties v phr

1 In railroading: to reduce a train's speed.

    1945 Hubbard *Railroad Ave.* 338, *Counting the ties* — Reducing speed. **1977** Adams *Lang. Railroader, Count the ties:* To reduce speed.

2 To walk on a railroad track.

    1893 *KS Univ. Qrly.* 1.138, *Count ties:* to walk on the railroad track. **1908** *DN* 3.302 **eAL, wGA,** *Count the ties* . . . To walk the railroad track when one hasn't the money to ride. **1912** *DN* 3.573 **wIN.**

3 In logging and railroading: to be fired or quit a job.

    1958 McCulloch *Woods Words* **Pacific NW,** *Count ties* — To be fired, or to quit. From the days when the only way to leave camp was to walk down the railroad. **1969** Sorden *Lumberjack Lingo* **NEng, Gt Lakes.** **1977** Adams *Lang. Railroader.*

county n Usu |ˈkaʊntɪ, -tɪ|, sometimes |ˈkæʊntɪ, ˈkjæʊntɪ| See Pronc Intro 3.I.16, 3.II.14 Pronc-spp *caounty, ceounty, keounty, kyounty*

Std sense, var forms.

    1858 (1892) Holmes *One Hoss Shay* 15 **NEng,** He would build one shay to beat the taown / 'n' the keounty 'n' all the kentry raoun'. **1861** Holmes *Venner* 1.168 **NEng,** You'll be known through the taown 'n' through the caounty . . as the Principal of the Broken-Victuals Institoot! **1871** Eggleston *Hoosier Schoolmaster* 133 **IN**, Ole Pearson . . died a fightin' thieves on Rocky Branch in Hoopole Kyounty, State of Injeanny. **1899** Garland *Boy Life* 152 **nwIA**, The next one came from Tama County . . . and became famous for his boastful references to "Tamy Caounty." **1926** Kephart *Highlanders* 468 **sAppalachians**, She got, I reckon, about the toughest deestric' in the ceounty, which is sayin' a good deal. **1941** *AmSp* 16.7 **eTX** [Black], [aʊ] In Negro speech this diphthong is not often flattened to [æʊ] as in 'hill type' speech, but retains its standard form, with lengthening of the first element. A lighter [j] than in 'hill type' speech develops after [k], [g]. Examples: . . *county.* **1942** Hall *Smoky Mt. Speech* 46 **eTN, wNC**, After [k], the diphthong [aʊ] is often preceded by a palatal glide, which is more or less marked. The less extreme variety may be represented as in *cow* [kæʊ], *county* ['kæʊntɪ], etc.; the more extreme as in [kjæʊ], ['kjæʊntɪ] . . . The consonantal type, [kj], is not at all rare. **c1960** *Wilson Coll.* **csKY**, *County* is regularly ['kæʊntɪ] somewhat slurred. Some older people said ['kjæʊntɪ].

county attorney n
=**son-of-a-bitch stew.**
   1933 *AmSp* 8.1.27 **nwTX**, *County attorney* or *son-of-a-gun* . . . The term *county attorney* used as the name of a dish called many unmentionable names is an interesting sidelight on the general opinion of that official. **1977** Watts *Dict. Old West* 308, *Son-of-a-bitch stew* . . . included sweetbreads, marrow gut, and kidneys added to the best meat of the calf . . . Also, in the later days, known among cattlemen as *district attorney* . . and *county attorney.*

county beef n Cf **government beef**
   1967 *DARE* (Qu. P35a, . . *Any deer shot illegally*) Inf **MN2**, County beef.

county boarding house See **county hotel**

county capital n Cf **county site, county town**
   A county seat.
   [**1854** White *Hist. Coll. GA* 460, *Gilmer County* . . . Ellijay is the capital. *Ibid* 495, *Henry County* . . . McDonough is the capital.] **1970** Tarpley *Blinky* 294 **neTX**, *(Town where the county government is located)* County capital. [.5% of responses]

county hotel n Also *county (boarding) house* joc
   A county jail.
   1965–70 *DARE* (Qu. V11, . . *Joking names . . for a county or city jail*) 10 Infs, **scattered**, County hotel; **CA36, GA72, MI78**, County boarding house; **SC45**, County house. **1968** Adams *Western Words*, *County hotel*—What the logger calls the county jail.

county pin See **counterpin**

county site n chiefly **sAppalachians**
   A county seat.
   1828 Sherburne *Memoirs* 184 **ME** (as of 1782), The town of Cornish appointed me as their delegate, but restricted me with respect to the county site. **1851** Burke *Polly Peablossom* 98, Many persons in the county of Hall, State of Georgia, recollect a queer old customer who used to visit the county site regularly on "General Muster" days and Court Week. **1917** *DN* 4.410 **wNC**, *County site.* County seat. **1926** Kephart *Highlanders* 396 **sAppalachians**, I'd haffter walk nineteen miles out to the railroad, pay seventy cents the round-trip to the county-site, pay my board thar fer mebbe a week. **1966** *PMLA* 81.2.14/1 **GA**, Yet *county site*, for the more usual *county seat*, is common in Georgia but unknown in South Carolina. **1979** *McDavid Coll.* **GA**, In [George] White's *Historical Collections of Georgia*, there seems to be free variation between *county site* (which I have heard frequently in Ga., and only in Ga., and where the only Atlas cite outside Ga. was in a Lowman record in western NC), *county town, county seat,* and *seat of justice.*

county town n Cf **courthouse 1**
   A county seat.
   1670 in 1852 CT *(Colony) Pub. Rec.* 2.140, Waightes and measures . . [are] to be preserued and kept in the county townes as standards for the respectiue countyes. **1887** Amer. Philol. Assoc. *Trans. for 1886* 17.45, *[Court-house]* (County-town in Virginia and South Carolina). **1905** Valentine *Hecla Sandwith* 36 **cPA**, The Sandwith Meeting House stood . . on the edge of the county town of Dunkirk. **1931–33** *LANE Worksheets* **Boston MA**, *County town:* county seat. **1943** *LANE* Map 548, *County Town* is described as a rare term . . and as older or old fashioned though still in use. **1949** *AmSp* 24.107 **neFL**, *County town* . . . County seat. **1979** [see **county site**].

co-up See **cope** v[2]

coupe n [Fr *coupe* a cut] **LA**
1 A notch or channel made by excavation or erosion.
   [**1811** in 1814 Brackenridge *Views of LA* 229, Passed *la coupe à L'Oiselle*. This name originated, in the circumstance of a trader having made a narrow escape, being in the river at the very moment that this cut-off was forming. It was a bend of fifteen miles round, and perhaps not more than a few hundred yards across, the neck, which was suddenly cut through by the river, became the main channel.] **1967** [see **2** below]. **1968** *DARE* (Qu. C1, *What do you call a small stream of water not big enough to be a river?*) Inf **LA31**, Coupe [kup], connection between two marshes through a ridge. **1971** Detro *Generic Terms* 191 **LA**, Though the toponymic generic *"coupe"* was not recorded in Louisiana until the period 1901–1968, it was observed that it occurred in the same area in which the English variants "cut" and "cut-off" were recorded during the period 1801–1850.
2 A break in a levee.
   1967 LeCompte *Word Atlas* **seLA**, (Break in the levee) . . *coupe* [1 inf] . . . *Coup* (cut) is also standard French, and is used in place of *crevasse* in the St. Martinsville area.

couple-cap n
=**three-seeded mercury.**
   1933 Small *Manual SE Flora* 785, Acalypha . . . Couple-caps.

couple-three, (a) adj phr Also *couple or three, couple of* (or *a*) *three* chiefly **Nth** See Map
   Two or three; a few, several.
   1935 Davis *Honey* 1 **OR**, There was a run-down old tollbridge station . . where Uncle Preston Shiveley had lived for fifty years, outlasting . . a couple or three invasions of land-hunting settlers. **1939** *AmSp* 14.156 **cwWV**, *Couple a three.* Two or three. 'I saw him a couple a three weeks ago.' Used almost invariably for 'two or three' in colloquial speech. **1965–70** *DARE* (Qu. LL19, *A few, anywhere from two to four: "Just put in _____ onions."*) 21 Infs, **chiefly Nth**, Couple-three; **CO47, MO20**, Couple or three. **1967** *DARE* FW Addit **neNY**, A couple-three—several. **1968–70** *DARE* Tape **CA36**, After a couple-three years; **CA161**, I smoked for over 60 years and didn't quit 'til a couple-three years ago; **CA181**, There are over a thousand, a couple-of-three thousand maybe. **1968–69** *DARE* File **neOH**, "How many do you want?" "Oh, a couple-three;" **ceNC**, A couple or three. **1973** *Patrick Coll.* **Sth**, *Couple or three, a.* A few. Also Western.

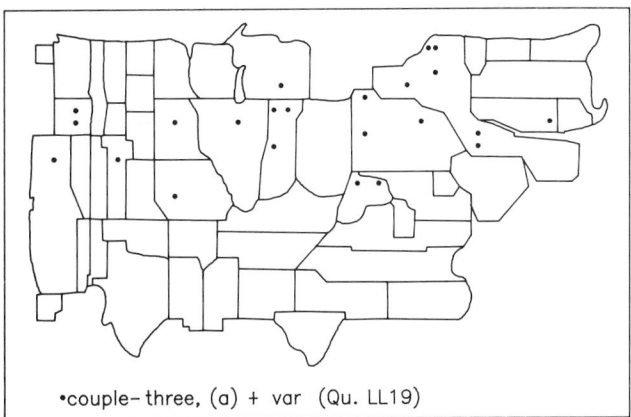

•couple-three, (a) + var (Qu. LL19)

courage n [*OED* →1615]
   Sexual vigor or desire.
   1981 *Broaddus Coll.* **ceKY** (as of 1958), Courage—sexual desire. **1982** *NADS Letters* **swVA** (as of c1950), A male, white farmer, 55–60 years of age, no more than grade school education, went to see a psychiatrist in Richmond, VA, about a sexual problem, and explained to the nurse [informant's mother] that he "couldn't get his courage up." *Ibid*, As a boy in southern Virginia, I heard *courage* used to refer to . . potency as well as to sexual desire.

courage bump n [**courage**] Cf **love bump, nature bump**
   A pimple.
   1966–67 *DARE* (Qu. X59, . . *Small infected pimples that form, usually on the face*) Infs **GA3, 13, SC40**, Courage bumps.

coural See **corral**

‡courier boat n
  1966 *DARE* (Qu. B10, . . *Long trailing clouds high in the sky*) Inf **MA6**, Courier boats.

course adv Also pronc-spp *co(a)se* Cf *in course* under **in** prep **B2**
  Of course.
    1901 Merwin *Calumet "K"* 13, "Have you tried to get any of it here in Chicago?" "Course not. It's all ordered and cut out up to Ledyard." **1908** *DN* 3.301 **eAL, wGA,** *Cose*. . . Of course. Common. Frequently *in cose.* **1917** McCutcheon *Green Fancy* 158, Course I couldn't tell her what I told the sheeny, seein' as she's a female. **1922** Gonzales *Black Border* 294 **sSC, GA coasts** [Gullah glossary], *'Co'se*—course, of course. **1927** Adams *Congaree* 111 **SC,** *Coase:* of course. **1960** Criswell *Resp. to PADS 20* **Ozarks,** *Course* . . Of course. Almost invariable usage . . "Course he didn't have any money, he never has." **c1960** *Wilson Coll.* **csKY,** *Course:* Often used for *of course.* **1966–67** *DARE* (Qu. NN1, *Other words like "yes"*) Inf **WA22,** Course; (Qu. NN4, *Other ways of answering "no"*) Inf **ME1,** Course not; (Qu. NN14, *When you doubt something that somebody has said, and you want to be sure that it is true . . "Is that really so?" He answers: "_____."*) Inf **NM4,** Course it's true.

court v, hence vbl n *courting* **chiefly sAppalachians**
  To attend court; to take (someone) to court.
    1917 *DN* 4.410 **wNC, KS,** *Courting* . . . Attending court; litigating. "Bill, are they courtin' up there yit?" **1927** *AmSp* 2.352 **WV,** *Courting* . . attending the circuit court. "My brother has been at courting for two weeks." **1976** Garber *Mountain-ese* **sAppalachians,** *Court* . . sue at law. "I'm agoin' to court you iffen you don't move that dadburn fence."

court ball n
  1970 *DARE* (Qu. EE11, *Bat-and-ball games for just a few players [when there aren't enough for a regular game]*) Inf **MO23,** Court ball.

court bouillon n Pronc-sp *cubie yon* [Fr *court* condensed + *bouillon*] **esp LA**
  A highly seasoned fish stock usually containing vegetables and wine.
    1931 Read *LA French* 32, *Courtbouillon* . . A fish stew, generally made of redfish—less often of red snapper—with tomatoes, onions, and spices. **1932** (1946) Hibben *Amer. Regional Cookery* 97 **NC,** *Curried Shrimp* . . . Combine all the ingredients of the court bouillon [onion, garlic, salt, water] and bring slowly to a boil. Simmer . . throw in the well washed shrimp and boil. **1941** FWP *Guide LA* 687, *Courtbouillon* . . . Redfish stew cooked with highly-seasoned gravy. **1945** Saxon *Gumbo Ya-Ya* 202 **LA,** Food, its preparation and consumption, must be classified as a Cajun pleasure . . . Favorites are oysters, . . crawfish bisque, courtbouillon. **1954** Armstrong *Satchmo* 85 **LA,** When she sent me . . to get fifteen cents' worth of fish heads she made a big pot of "cubie yon" which she served with tomato sauce and fluffy white rice with every grain separate. **1968** *DARE* (Qu. H45, *Dishes made with meat, fish, or poultry that everybody around here would know, but that people in other places might not*) Infs **LA23, 33, 38, 43,** Court bouillon; **LA20, 28, 40,** Fish court bouillon.

court cupboard n
  1899 (1912) Green *VA Folk-Speech, Court-cupboard* . . . A sideboard with a number of shelves for the display of plate, and distinguished from the "livery cupboard," or wardrobe.

court day n **KY**
  A festival day, a fair.
    1969 *DARE* (Qu. FF16 . . *Local contests or celebrations*) Infs **KY50, 59,** Court day. **1970** *DARE* File **neKY** [Poster announcement], *Mason County Court Day*—Maysville, Kentucky—Buy-sell-trade-enjoy; [Newspaper publicity], All roads will lead to Maysville next Monday, October 6 [1969], when the fifth annual Mason County Court Day festivities will get underway at an early hour and continue throughout the day.

courtesey See **curtsy**

courtesy n
  A party at which gifts are given; a shower.
    1966 *Clinton Herald* (IA) 13 Aug Women's Page 3/2, A miscellaneous pre-nuptial courtesy was given Aug. 4 for . . [the] bride-elect. **1966** *Carroll Daily Times Herald* (IA) 6 Sept 4/1, *Courtesy for Jean Schrad* A miscellaneous bridal shower Sunday afternoon in the home of Mr. and Mrs. Earl Schrad honored their daughter. **1968** *Hammond Vindicator*

(LA) 4 Apr sec B 7/7, Approximately 25 ladies attended the seven o'clock courtesy.

courthouse n Pronc-spp *cawt-house, cote-house* Also abbr **C.H.**
  1 A county seat—used esp in place names. **chiefly Mid Atl**
    1804 *Guardian of Freedom* (Frankfort, Ky.) 14 Sep. 3/4 *(DA),* Extract of a letter from a gentleman at Wythe Court-house (Virginia) to his friend in Frederick Town, (Md.) dated July 30, 1804. **1886** Amer. Philol. Assoc. *Trans.* 45, *Court-house* (county-town [=county seat] in Virginia and South Carolina). **1888** Trumbull *Names of Birds* 79, *Golden-eye* . . . At Cape May C.H. [NJ], Cob-head. **1899** (1912) Green *VA Folk-Speech, Cote-house* . . . For courthouse. *Ibid, Court-house* . . . County seat. Shortened to C.H., often having no other name. **1914** *DN* 4.159 **cVA,** *Cawt-house* . . . County-seat. **1948** *Chi. Tribune* 5 Dec. I.24/3 *(DA),* Greene, however, crossed into North Carolina . . ., offering battle at Guilford courthouse. **1982** Heat Moon *Blue Highways* 71 **SC,** Old Ninety Six was the courthouse town, but they moved it out here after the Revolutionary War and renamed it. Even had a college. Then the courthouse was moved two miles north where the railroad passed through.
  2 See quot. Cf **government house, post office**
    1969 *DARE* (Qu. M21b, *Joking names for an outside toilet building*) Inf **IL38,** Courthouse.

‡courting alcove n Cf **courting block**
  1937 (1966) FWP *Guide VT* 297, The parlor is distinguished by recesses on either side of the fireplace, one known as the "courting alcove," the other as the "marriage arch."

courting apple n *joc*
  1976 Garber *Mountain-ese* **sAppalachians,** *Courtin'-apple* . . onion— "I shore raised a good crop uv courtin' apples this year."

courting block n Cf **courting alcove**
  1930 Shoemaker *1300 Words* 14 **cPA Mts** (as of c1900), *Courting blocks*—Blocks on either side of an old-fashioned open fire place, occupied by lovers at night for their up-sitting.

courting buggy n
  1966 *DARE* (Qu. N41a, *What kinds of horse-drawn vehicles are used around here, or used to be, to carry people?*) Inf **ID1,** Courting buggy, sweetheart buggy. [Inf old]

courting man n
  A rake, womanizer.
    1966 Maddux *Spring Rain* 15 **WV,** "And you watch out for Will Workman," she said . . . "He's reputed to be a devil with the ladies." "What they call a courtin man," Evans said.

courting pistol n *old-fash*
  1967 Cerello *Dakota Co. MN* 50, Courting pistol—A small caliber gun with ten to eighteen inch barrel used by women for protection when alone in the house. ["]My maiden auntie always had a courting pistol about the house. She used to hide its barrel in the side of her favorite chair . . some women carried a courting pistol in a long pocket in the fullness of their skirts . . I guess the courting pistol became a fashion from my grandmother's time to about the turn of the century . . my mother said the fashion of having a courting pistol came to these parts from down east and was brought here by women of questionable character.["]

courting room n
  c1960 *Wilson Coll.* **csKY,** *Courting room* . . . Facetious name for parlor or front room, where the girl received her beau on Sunday afternoon.

courting seat n
  1983 *MJLF* 9.36 **ceKY,** *Courting seat* . . a love seat.

court whist n **WI**
  A card game.
    1966 *Tomahawk Leader* (WI) 3 Mar 3/1, A pink and blue shower . . was held. Five tables of Court Whist were played. **1968** *DARE* (Qu. EE39) Inf **WI24,** Court whist; (Qu. EE40) Inf **WI20,** Court whist.

cous n Also *caious, couse, cowas, cowish, cows, kouse* **Pacific NW**
  =**biscuit root 1,** esp *Lomatium ambiguum, L. cous,* and *L. utriculatum.*
    1806 (1808) Gass *Jrl.* 308 **NW,** We also got bread made of roots, which the natives call Cow-as. **1847** (1978) Smet *OR Missions* 116, The bitter root . . grows in light, dry, sandy soil, as also the caious or biscuit root.

1885 Onderdonk *Idaho* 134, The favorite roots are the camas, couse, and bitter root. **1893** (1965) Lewis–Clark *Hist. Lewis–Clark Exped.* 3.1000, [Footnote by Coues:] The plant whose root is here called *cows,* elsewhere *cowas,* is the same as *cowish,* given in the Century Dictionary as a plant found in the valley of the Columbia river . . . But it certainly is the well-known *Peucedanum cous.* **1911** Curtis *N. Amer. Indian* 8.41, In May all the bands would congregate at Tipahlíwan (Camas prairie) to dig kouse. **1964** Jackman–Long *OR Desert* 301, There are innumerable cases of starvation among whites in favorite food-gathering spots for Indians—where cous grows along a dry ridge, for example.

cousen in v *obs*

1935 *AmSp* 10.40 **Nantucket MA** (as of 1848), *Cousen in.* To ingratiate one's self into favor. [Note in text: No doubt from the archaic 'cozen,' with semantic freshening from the word of relationship, 'cousin.']

coush-coush See **cush** n[1]

cousin n Cf **cud'n**

1 A dupe. [*W3 "obs"*]

1938 *AmSp* 13.5 **seAR,** *Cousin* . . . An easy victim. This is possibly a descendant from the Elizabethan *cozen* to beguile.

2 See quot. *joc*

1970 *DARE* (Qu. R15a, . . *Nicknames* . . *for mosquitoes*) Inf **VA70,** Cousins, because they are so many and they stick so close.

3 See quot. *euphem*

1968 *DARE* (Qu. AA19, *Words or expressions about a man and woman who are not married but live together as if they were*) Inf **NJ48,** Cousins.

cousin v Also sp *cozen* **NEng** *old-fash*

To visit one's relatives or friends; hence vbl n *cousining.*

1774 in 1875 J. & A. Adams *Familiar Letters* 10 **MA,** You know I never get or save anything by cozening or classmating. **1863** Dodge *Gala-Days* 36 **MA,** I stop for the night a-cousining. **1901** (1961) Greenough–Kittredge *Words* 68, 'To go a-cousining' is an old-fashioned New England phrase applied to one who quarters himself on his distant relatives. **1917** *DN* 4.377 **MA,** Cousin. **1926** *AmSp* 2.83 **ME,** "I hear you've taken on a wife . .," remarks an acquaintance just returned from a "cousining" ("cousining" means a visit to distant relatives). **1926** *DN* 5.386 **ME,** Cousin. **1973** *DARE* File **VT, MA,** Cousin, to travel inexpensively by stopping with relatives or friends. "They cousined their way across the country."

cousin Anne n Cf **cousin Jenny**

A Welsh woman.

1968 Adams *Western Words* 78, *Cousin Anne*—A miner's name for the wife of a Welsh miner.

‡**cousin-close** adj

1970 Angelou *Caged Bird* 24 **MO,** We took our meals from the smokehouse, the little garden that lay cousin-close to the store and from the shelves of canned foods.

cousin Jack n, also attrib **chiefly nMI, scattered West** See Map Cf **cousin Jenny**

A Cornishman.

1899 (1977) Norris *McTeague* 215 **CA,** "Are you a 'cousin Jack'?" The dentist grinned. This prejudice against Cornishmen he remembered too. **1929** *AmSp* 5.147 **CO.** **1944** Nute *Lake Superior* 251 **MI,** Copper Harbor, Eagle Harbor and Eagle River were settled soon after Ontonagon . . . To these villages and to others came miners of all nationalities,

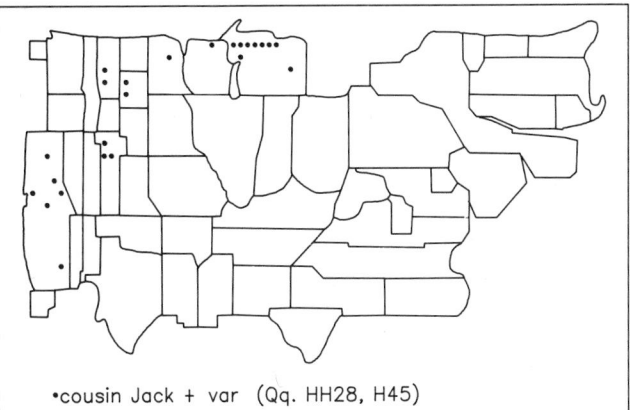

•cousin Jack + var (Qq. HH28, H45)

but those who stamped their impress on the region more than others were the "Cousin Jacks," the Cornishmen. **1965–70** *DARE* (Qu. HH28, *Names and nicknames around here for people of foreign background . . Cornish*) 23 Infs, **chiefly nMI, West,** Cousin Jack; (Qu. H45, *Dishes made with meat, fish, or poultry that everybody around here would know, but that people in other places might not*) Infs **CO40, 47,** Cousin Jack pasty. **1966–69** *DARE* Tape **MI32,** Every time there's a joke about a cousin Jacks I'm the blunt [sic] of it, so I switch 'em [the jokes] around for dem; **CA151,** Cousin Jack. **1968** *DARE* FW Addit **csCA,** Cousin Jacks wouldn't work a mine with tommy-knockers [=ghosts of men killed there] in it. **1973** Allen *LAUM* 1.277 **MN,** Cousin Jack Pasties [1 inf].

cousin Jenny n **chiefly nMI, scattered West** Cf **cousin Jack**

A Cornishwoman.

1918 *DN* 5.24 **nID,** *Cousin Jennie* . . . A Cornishwoman. Companion to the universal Cousin Jack for a Cornishman. Coeur d'Alenes. **1929** *AmSp* 5.147 **CO.** **1965–70** *DARE* (Qu. HH28, *Names and nicknames around here for people of foreign background . . Cornish*) Infs **CA149, MI10, 13, 17, 26, 44, WI52,** Cousin Jenny. **1968** Adams *Western Words* 78, *Cousin Jenny*—A miner's name for a Cornish girl or woman.

cousin on v phr [Cf **cousin** v]

1917 *DN* 4.377 **neOH,** *Cousin on,* to live with (one) as a relative.

cousin trout n [See quot 1887]

=**fallfish.**

1839 MA *Zool. & Bot. Surv. Fishes Reptiles* 91, *L[euciscus] pulchellus* . . . In some portions of the State it receives the name of *"Cousin Trout."* **1887** Goode *Amer. Fishes* 428, In Massachusetts it *[Semotilus bullaris]* is often called the "Cousin Trout" in allusion to its trout-like habits.

cousin up v phr

1967 *DARE* (Qu. II20b, *A person who tries too hard to gain somebody else's favor: "He's always trying to _____ the boss."*) Inf **ID5,** Cousin up.

co-ut See **co-ets**

couthy adj Also sp *couthie* [Scots *couth* familiar + *-ie, -y*]

Amiable, genial.

1938 Matschat *Suwannee R.* 161 **nFL, sGA,** He couldn't read ary word, but he got hisself a couthy woman . . to share his homesite. *Ibid* 289, *Couthy:* from couthie, agreeable.

covault See **cavort** 1

cove n[1]

1a A small body of usually fresh water adjoining or flowing into a larger body; a body of water cut off from the larger body.

1650 in 1940 McJimsey *Topog. VA* 167, Three hundred acres of Land, lying on the North Side of Rappaha. river Up the west branch of the west Side thereof bounded Vizt from a marked tree by the side of a Cove. **1785** *Ibid* The place where the Water passes when the River is full it is quite easy and safe to descend to, being in a cove of still Water. **1899** (1912) Green *VA Folk-Speech,* Cove . . . A small inlet, creek, or bay; a nook in the shore of any considerable body of water. **1940** McJimsey *Topog. VA* 167, *Cove* . . . Extended in Virginia to small streams emptying into a tidal water. **1968** *DARE* (Qu. C4a, *A fairly large body of fresh water*) Inf **NC49,** Coves. Coves and old runs are parts of rivers that have been isolated due to low water or something else.

b Floodland, marsh, or still water adjoining a body of water. **scattered, but chiefly NEast, Mid Atl** See Map on p. 806

1637 in 1856 RI (Colony) *Records* 1.46, The grasse upon the rivers and coves about Kitickamuckqutt. **1667** in 1940 McJimsey *Topog. VA* 167, Crossing the mouth of pasuhetank [?] Creek to a Cove of Sunken Land. **1765** (1942) Bartram *Diary of a Journey* 21, There is many coves & very rich low swamps up ye coves. **1940** McJimsey *Topog. VA* 167, *Cove* . . . A nook of marsh or sunken ground indenting the shore of a body of water. **1965–70** *DARE* (Qu. C14, *A stretch of still water going off to the side from a river or lake*) 48 Infs, **scattered, but chiefly NEast, Mid Atl,** Cove.

c A shallow lake or swamp. **FL**

1836 in 1861 U.S. Congress *Amer. State Papers (Military Affairs)* 7.146 **FL,** The cove appeared to me, from the knowledge I had of it, to be a large shallow lake . . occupying a bend of the river, and communicating with the river by cypress swamps on its banks at many places. The breadth of the lake is generally from one to five miles, interspersed with islands of

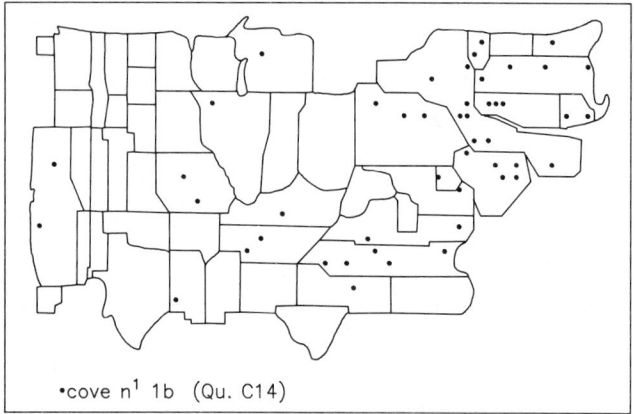

•cove n¹ 1b (Qu. C14)

hammock growth and apparent fertility. *Ibid* 258, And thus . . enclose the Seminoles in their stronghold in the cove, or big swamp of the Withlacooche. **1837** (1962) Williams *Territory FL* 242, The Seminoles since the commencement of the war, have concentrated about the great cove of Ouithlacooche. **1953** McMullen *Topog. Terms FL* 92, Cove. In the sing. the term signifies a shallow lake containing hammock islands . . or a swamp.

2 See **cove oyster.**

3 A sheltered recess or valley partly enclosed by mountains. **esp S Midl**

1762 in 1940 McJimsey *Topog. VA* 167, On the ridges and in the coves of a Mountain. **1890** *Appalachia* 6.140, A "cove" is a valley that lies between two mountain ridges, generally ending in a point like a cove on the sea-shore. **1927** *DN* 5.473 **Ozarks. 1937** *Hall Coll.* **ceTN,** Cove: only the enclosed valleys are called 'coves'. "From the Ace Cove we clum up out on top, Hughes Ridge, come back to the bald." **1950** *AmSp* 25.163 **CO,** Another interesting mountain word is *cove* . . . In Colorado it means a small lateral valley hidden in the mountains. **1966–69** *DARE* (Qu. C19, . . *Low land running between hills*) Infs **NC34, PA205, TN11, 37,** Cove. **1968** *Foxfire* Fall–Winter 45 **nGA,** Mickey Justice studies a still-house built high up in a rocky cove. **1969** *DARE* FW Addit **NC.**

4 See quot.

1859 (1968) Bartlett *Americanisms,* Cove. A strip of prairie extending into the woodland.

5 A grove or copse.

1969–70 *DARE* (Qu. T1, *A bunch of trees growing together in open country, especially on a hill*) Infs **OH90, OK58,** Cove.

6 See quot.

1970 *DARE* (Qu. D7, *A small space anywhere in a house where you can hide things or get them out of the way*) Inf **AZ12,** Cove.

cove n² [Brit *cove* chap, bloke; prob from Romany *kova* thing, person] Cf **covey**

1915 *DN* 4.198, Cove, peculiar, eccentric person. "What's the matter with the old cove? Did he jump his bond?"

cove-cull n [Prob **cove** n¹ **3**]

1952 Brown *NC Folkl.* 1.530, Cove-cull . . . A mountaineer.

cove juice n [**cove** n¹ **3**] *joc*

Illegally distilled whiskey, moonshine.

1952 Brown *NC Folkl.* 1.530, Cove-juice . . . Whisky. **1968** *Foxfire* Fall–Winter 101 **neGA, cwNC,** Various names given moonshine include: . . cove juice. **1969** *DARE* (Qu. DD21c, . . *Whiskey, especially illegally made whiskey*) Inf **GA72,** Cove juice.

covena n **AZ**

A **brodiaea** (here: *Brodiaea pulchella*).

1912 Lumholtz *New Trails* 213, There is a certain tuberous plant growing on the plains called *covena,* which furnishes a favorite food supply. **1915** (1926) Armstrong *Western Wild Flowers* 16, *Brodiæa capitata* . . Covena is the Arizona name. **1942** Castetter *Pima & Papago Ag.* 60 *(DA),* Bulbs of *covenas* . . (*Brodiæa capitata* var. *pauciflora*) were of less importance.

cove oyster n Also *cove*

See quot 1881.

1876 *Harper's Weekly* 20.307/2, The "Morris Coves" of Philadelphia,

while very insipid, are the plumpest bivalves brought to market. **1881** Ingersoll *Oyster-Industry* 243, Cove-oyster . . . The packer, by cove-oysters, simply means steamed oysters packed in hermetically sealed cans . . . By 'cove-oysters' the oysterman means the single oysters scattered through the bays and creeks and old planting-grounds, occurring too sparsely to be taken by the ordinary methods of tonging. **1898** Canfield *Maid of Frontier* 181 **TX,** When we get to town we'll go to Burr's store and get some cove oysters, pepper-vinegar and crackers. **1946** Wilson *Fidelity Folks* 89 **swKY,** Many old-timers would prefer the grocery, such as one of ours at Fidelity, with its cheese and crackers, its cove oysters and pepper sauce. **1976** Warner *Beautiful Swimmers* 226 **MD, VA,** He held up a small oyster, round and well formed . . . The oyster sat up plump and round in the shell . . . Fortunately we began to take more of these beautiful round "cove" oysters.

cover n, v Usu |'kʌvə(r)|; also in **Sth, Midl, occas NEng,** |'kɪvɚ| (Note: this pronc is also common in Engl dial; see *SND, EDD kiver*); rarely |kjɪvə| Pronc-spp *civer, kever, kiver, kyiver*

A Forms.

1815 Humphreys *Yankey in England* 106, Kiver, cover. **1837** Sherwood *Gaz. GA* 70, Kiver, for cover. **1856** in 1956 Eliason *Tarheel Talk* 309 **csNC,** Civered. **1902** *DN* 2.231 **sIL,** *Cover* [kɪvər]. **1907** *DN* 3.192 **seNH,** *Kiver* . . . Pronunciation of older generation. *Ibid* 221 **nwAR, sIL,** *Cover* . . . Pronounced often [kɪvɚ]. *Ibid* 230 **nwAR, seMO,** *Cover* . . . Pronounced kiver. **1908** *DN* 3.327 **eAL, wGA,** *Kiver* . . . Sometimes *kyiver.* **1912** *DN* 3.580 **wIN,** *Kiver.* **1924** Raine *Land of Saddle-Bags* 78 **sAppalachians,** On bright summer days, Aunt Sally brings out her store of "bed kivers" and "kiverlids." **1930** Shoemaker *1300 Words* 35 **cPA Mts** (as of c1900), *Kivers*—Bed clothes. **1941** *AmSp* 16.6 **eTX** [Black], *Cover* is both ['kʌvə] and ['kjɪvə]. **1954** *Harder Coll.* **cwTN,** *Kiver:* cover, seldom used. Formerly thought to be more elegant than cover. The two world wars caused the boys to take cover instead of take kiver. **1965–69** *DARE* FW Addit **MS, ceNC, cwNC, neTX,** ['kɪvɚ]. **1966** *DARE* Tape **ID2,** He . . kevered ['kɛvɚd] 'em up.

B As noun.

1 A roof. *old-fash* Cf **C1** below

1939 Hall Coll. **eTN, wNC,** "That's an old-timey *cover* [kɪvɚ] on that house." "[kɪvɚ] is used for roof by old people; you never hear it from the young generation." "It would be an old board roof made of split boards; it's used by old people lots."

2 also *stove cover, hole cover:* The round, flat lid of a wood-burning stove. **chiefly Nth, esp NEng** See Map and Map Section

1965–70 *DARE* (Qu. F10, . . *The round flat pieces [of a wood-burning stove] that you take out to put in the wood*) 22 Infs, **Nth, esp NEng,** Cover; 12 Infs, **chiefly Nth, esp NEng,** Stove cover; **CA6,** Hole cover; (Qu. F11, *The thing you use to remove the lids from a wood-burning stove*) Inf **LA2,** Cover lifter.

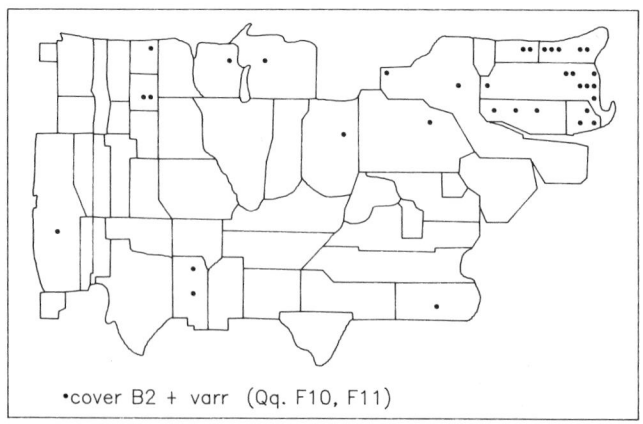

•cover B2 + varr (Qq. F10, F11)

3 also *cover bundle, covering:* The top bundle of a stack or set of sheaves. Cf **cap** n¹ **1**

1965–70 *DARE* (Qu. L31, . . *The top bundle of a shock*) 8 Infs, **Midl,** Cover; **OH77,** Cover bundle; **MS19,** Covering.

4 See **coverclip.**

C As verb.

1 To roof; hence vbl n *covering,* ppl adj *covered.*

1775 (1971) Calk *Jrl.* 38 **VA,** We git out [sic] house kivered with Bark and move our things into it at Night and Begin housekeeping. **1933** Rawlings *South Moon* 15 **FL,** She told them, "Pa promises . . him and the boys'll put a blow-way here . . . " They approved the prospect. "Hain't nothin' like a kivered blow-way for comfort." **1968** *DARE* (Qu. FF2 . . *Kinds of parties*) Inf **SC58,** House covering: To put a roof on a house—feed the workers, dance, etc.

2 Of a forest fire: to burn in the tree tops; to **crown v 1.** Cf **crown fire**

1956 Sorden–Ebert *Logger's Words* **Gt Lakes,** Crown-fire, A forest fire that goes into the tops, or crowns of trees. When it does that, the woodsmen say "she's covering."

cover a rain See **cover up**

coverclip n Also *cover*
=**hogchoker.**
1842 DeKay *Zool. NY* 4.304, The New-York Sole, *Achirus mollis* . . is common in our waters . . . They abound on the shallow flats on the Jersey shore opposite New-York, where they are called *Calico* and *Coverclip.* **1872** Schele de Vere *Americanisms* 384, *Coverclip* is the curious name by which the sole is known in the waters of New York; but even more mysterious is that of *Calico* which may be heard quite as frequently. **1906** NJ State Museum *Annual Rept. for 1905* 397, *Achirus fasciatus* . . Cover Clip. **1945** McAtee *Nomina Abitera* 20, *American Sole (Achirus fasciatus)*—Making proper allowance for their older names, DeKay . . notes this as being called "coverclip" and . . Goode . . as "coverclip" or "cover," in New Jersey . . the relationship of these terms to "cunt-kiver" for the sunfishes is obvious.

covered cars n pl *old-fash*
A passenger train.
1960 Criswell *Resp. to PADS 20* **Ozarks,** Covered cars . . . Very early designation of railway coaches when they first appeared. (Common sixty or seventy years ago.) **1977** Miles *Ozark Dict.* 5, *Kivered cars*—A train. "Clyde tuk the kivered cars to the West."

covered-dish meal n Also *coverdish (luncheon, supper), covered-dish (dinner, lunch, luncheon, party, picnic, social, supper), covered supper* **widespread exc Pacific, Upper MW, WI, MI** See Map
A community meal to which people bring a dish to share; a **potluck.**
1931 *Durant* (Okla.) *D. Democrat* 3 June 4/5 *(DA),* The ladies of the Durant country club enjoyed a covered dish luncheon Thursday. **1950** *WELS* (*When people bring hot dishes to a meeting place and share them together, you call that a _____ meal*) 6 Infs, **WI,** Covered dish; 1 Inf, **seWI,** Covered dish supper. **1965–70** *DARE* (Qu. H70, *When people bring baked dishes, salads, and so forth to a meeting-place and share them together, that's a _____ meal*) 371 Infs, **widespread exc Pacific, Upper MW, WI, MI,** Covered-dish; 33 Infs, **scattered, but esp Atlantic,** Covered-dish supper; 15 Infs, **scattered,** Covered-dish (dinner, lunch, luncheon, party, social); **NC79, 82, TX73, VA94,** Coverdish (supper); (Qq. FF1, 2, 3) 20 Infs, **chiefly Atlantic,** Covered-dish supper(s); 9 Infs, **chiefly Atlantic,** Covered-dish (dinners, luncheon, parties, socials). **1967** *Independence Enterprise* (OR) 12 Jan 2/4, Covered dish dinner at noon; bring own table service. **1967** *Madison Star–Mail* (NE) 5 Oct 5/2, A covered supper will be held Tuesday evening. **1968** *Burlington Co. Herald* (Mt. Holly NJ) 8 Aug sec A 8/5, The Jr. Grange planned covered dish picnic will be held Aug. 14 beginning at 6 p.m. at the

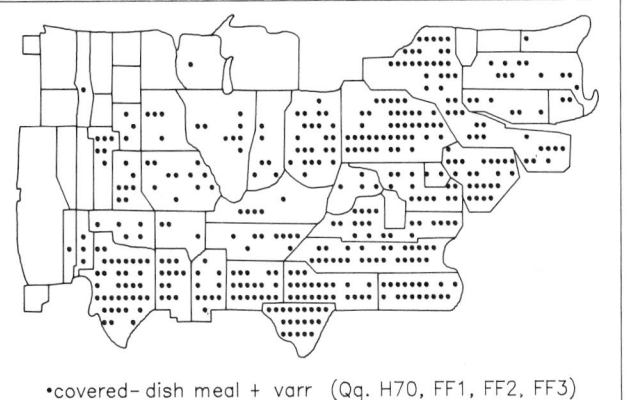

•covered-dish meal + varr (Qq. H70, FF1, FF2, FF3)

Grange Hall. **1968** *E. Liverpool Rev.* (OH) 19 June 9/7, The Town and Country Club held a coverdish luncheon. **1980** *Prairie Drummer* (Colby KS) 24 May 9/1, Shelly Brock . . entertained T.O.B. Club in her home Wednesday with a covered dish lunch at noon.

covered up ppl adj
Booked up; busy.
1980 *DARE* File **cwIN** (as of 1950s), When we lived in Terre Haute, if we called a serviceman to come repair something but he was too busy, he'd say, "I'm sorry, I can't come. I'm all covered up."

covered wagon n
1 In railroading: see quot.
1969 *AmSp* 44.250, One of the first questions which the engine crew on a freight train asks . . is, "What do we have for *power*?" The answer might be, "Two two-hundreds and a *covered wagon.*" Covered wagons are older locomotives that have the diesel engine entirely enclosed.
‡2 See quot.
1966 *DARE* (Qu. M21b, *Joking names for an outside toilet building*) Inf **SC21,** Covered wagon.

coverhauls n [Blend of *coveralls* + *overhauls*]
1966–70 *DARE* (Qu. W9, *A work garment, usually of blue cloth, covering the legs and sometimes the chest, worn by farmers*) Infs **ME6, 9, MO23, NJ7, OH2,** Coverhauls.

coverlet n Also sp *coverle(a)d, coverlid;* pronc-spp *coverlit, cubbahlet, kiverlet, kiverlid*
1 A bedspread or **comforter 1. widespread, but least freq in West and Atlantic** See Map
1636 in 1914 Essex Inst. *Coll.* 50.220, A Coverlet. **1640** in 1850 CT (Colony) *Pub. Rec.* 1.449, 3 ruggs, one Couerled. **1767** in 1860 Essex Inst. *Coll.* 2.87/1, Sarah Veary . . hath one good feather Bed, one Bolster, one Piller, . . one Coverlead. **1843** (1916) Hall *New Purchase* 80 **IN,** There was a night-cap peering above the "kiver-lid," and Mrs. Major Billy Westland's head on it! **1901** *DN* 2.181 **KY** [Black], Coverlets—cubbahlets. **1905** *DN* 3.75 **nwAR,** Coverlid. **1908** *DN* 3.302 **eAL, wGA,** Coverlid. **1910** *DN* 3.439 **wNY,** Coverlid. **1926** *DN* 5.399 **Ozarks,** Coverlid. **1937** Eaton *Handicrafts* 122 **KY,** It's . . watchin' the blossoms come out and smile at ye in the kiverlet. **c1960** *Wilson Coll.* **csKY,** Coverlid /ˈkɪvɚˌlɪd/ sometimes; occasionally, among the elderly /ˈkɪvɚˌlɪd/. **1965–70** *DARE* (Qu. E15, *The cloth that is put on top of a bed, mostly for decoration*) 55 Infs, **scattered, but least freq in West and Atlantic,** Coverlet; 18 Infs, **scattered,** Coverlid; (Qu. E16, *A padded covering used on a bed, mostly for warmth*) Infs **GA63, KS18, LA23, PA184, TN60, TX87, WI47,** Coverlet; **IA25, NY72, VA28,** Coverlid; **NY20,** Coverlit. **1973** Allen *LAUM* 1.228, Almost obsolete in the U[pper] M[idwest] is the eastern *coverlet* or *coverlid,* reportedly in use by only three informants in Iowa.

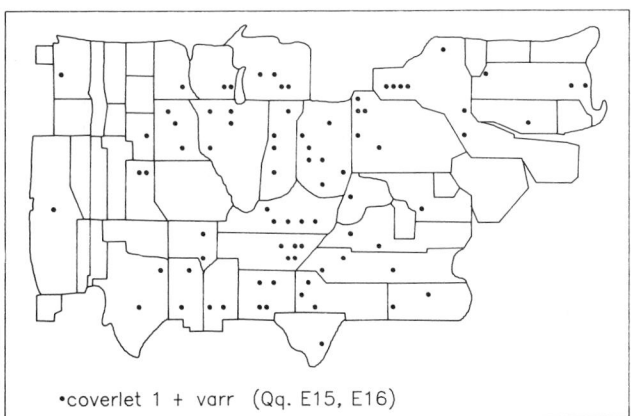

•coverlet 1 + varr (Qq. E15, E16)

2 See quot.
1968 *DARE* (Qu. E10, *Knitted or crocheted pieces placed on the back and arms of a chair for decoration and cleanliness*) Inf **OH44,** Coverlets.
3 Fig: see quot.
1940 in 1944 *ADD* 138 **WV,** 3 kinds of pies: open-face, crossbarred, & kiverlid.

cover one's back with one's belly v phr
To lack adequate covering.

1929 Dobie *Vaquero* 160 **TX,** But I was tired of "covering my back with my belly" and shivering all night. **1968** Adams *Western Words* 78, *Covered his back with his belly*—A cowboy's phrase for a man forced to sleep in the open without blankets. Such a situation is also spoken of as "usin' his back for a mattress and his belly for a blanket."

cover one's dog v phr

1961 Adams *Old-Time Cowhand* 251, When the wagon boss had gathered all the cattle in a given region, he was said to have "covered his dog."

cover piece n

A **coverlet 1.**

1937 (1963) Hyatt *Kiverlid* 15 **KY,** I 'llowed hit would be a leetle more partic'lar warpin' for a kiver piece than hit would be in jist the plain weave like I allus done.

cover the waterfront v phr

1 To menstruate. *euphem* Cf *DS* AA27

1948 *Word* 4.183, Synonym for menstruation . . *manhole covers* [for sanitary napkins] and *she's covering the waterfront,* have been reported.

2 To diaper a baby. *joc*

1984 *DARE* File **wNC,** I have heard the phrase *cover the waterfront* used for "attend to or provide for a baby's lower frontal area, esp by the use of diapers."

cover up v phr Also *cover a rain*

To become cloudy.

1966–68 *DARE* (Qu. B6, *When clouds begin to increase, you say it's* ———) Infs **AL41, WA11,** Covering up; **VA1,** Covering a rain.

covey n Cf **cove** n[2]

1851 Burke *Polly Peablossom* 94 **GA,** Bill Sweeney and Tom Culpepper is the two greatest old coveys in our settlement for coon-huntin. The fact is, they don't do much of anything else.

covia See **cobia**

coving vbl n Cf **cove oyster**

1881 Ingersoll *Oyster-Industry* 243 **Chesapeake Bay,** Coving.—The business of picking up "cove-oysters" . . with nippers.

cow n Usu |kaʊ, kæʊ, kɑʊ|; also **esp in NEng, Midl,** |kjaʊ, kjæʊ|; rarely |kjɛə, kaɪ|; for further varr see quots Pronc-spp *caow, keow*

A Forms.

1815 Humphreys *Yankey in England* 106, *Keow,* cow. **1866** *Beadle's Monthly* 2.283/2, Whenever an immigrant sought to cross into the new . . Territory, [the Missourians] asked him to say "cow." If he pronounced it, "keow," he was voted a Yankee and . . was not permitted to enter the desired paradise. **1871** Eggleston *Hoosier Schoolmaster* 39 **IN,** Squire Hawkins was a poar Yankee School-master, that said 'pail' instid of bucket, and that called a cow a 'caow.' **1907** *DN* 3.192 **seNH,** *Keow* [kjaʊ] . . . Cow. Now rare. **1916** *DN* 4.340 **seOH,** *Cow* [kiɑʊ]. **1939** *LANE* Map 191, [Pronunciations include [k(ɪ)æo, k(ɪ)ɑʊ, kɑo, kæo, kaʊ].] **1941** *AmSp* 16.7 **eTX** [Black], In Negro speech this diphthong [aʊ] is not often flattened to [æʊ] as in 'hill type' speech, but retains its standard form, with lengthening of the first element. A lighter [j] than in 'hill type' speech develops after [k], [g]. Examples: *about, . . cow.* **1942** Hall *Smoky Mt. Speech* 46 **eTN, wNC,** After [k], the diphthong is often preceded by a palatal glide, which is more or less marked. The less extreme variety may be represented as in *cow* [kæʊ] . . the more extreme as in [kjæʊ]. **1944** *PADS* 2.28 **eKY, nwNC,** Cow [kjɛə] . . . Usual meaning. "I haf to melk the keow." **1967** *DARE* (QR p64) Inf **KY32,** *Cow, cows* [kaɪ, kaɪz]. Inf reports these as heard, not used by herself. **1969** *DARE* FW Addit **MA42,** Cow [kjaʊ].

B Senses.

1 also attrib: See quots.

1894 *DN* 1.329 **sNJ,** *Cow:* six-inch female terrapin . . . (One "count."). **1949** Brown *Amer. Cooks* 351 **MD,** The short six inch diamond backs [=terrapins] called counts are the pick of the market, and the female sex is deemed more tasty; they're called cow terrapin.

2 A woman's breast. Cf **milk can**

1968–70 *DARE* (X31, *Other words . . for a woman's breasts*) Infs **MD21,** Cows; **SC66,** Coburg's cows.

3 See quot. [Cf **holy cow**] *euphem*

1968 *DARE* (Qu. NN27a, *Weakened substitutes for "God": "My* ———*!"*) Infs **NC51, VA15,** Cow.

4 See **cow bug.**

‡5 The buttocks. *euphem*

1970 *DARE* (Qu. X35, *Joking words for the part of the body . . you sit on . . "He slipped and came down hard on his* ———*."*) Inf **KY94,** Cow.

cowallop, cowalloping, cowallup See **ker-**

cow ant n

1 See **cow-killer ant.**

2 An aphid. Cf **ant cow**

1970 *DARE* (Qu. R26, *Other names for the small greenish lice . . on plants*) Inf **PA242,** Cow ants.

cowardy calf n

A timid or easily frightened person.

1897 *KS Univ. Qrly.* 6.86 **KS,** *Cowardy calf:* a young coward. Used chiefly by youths. **1912** *DN* 3.574 **wIN,** *Cowardy-calf, bull and a half* . . . A term applied by one child to another who is afraid to do something the first wants done. **1942** McAtee *Dial. Grant Co. IN* (as of 1890s), "*Cowardy calf, bull and a half*", child's taunt. (Western Ind.).

cowardy cat n [Perh infl by **cowardy calf** and **fraidy-cat**]

1969 *DARE* (Qu. HH10, *A very timid or cowardly person: "He's* ———*."*) Inf **MO15,** Cowardy cat.

cowas See **cous**

cow ate the cabbage, tell one how the v phr

To speak one's mind; hence adv phr *like the cow ate the cabbage* with firm or harsh words.

1965–70 *DARE* (Qu. JJ22, *To express your opinion—for example . . : "I went to the meeting and* ———*."*) Inf **TX75,** Told 'em how the cow ate the cabbage; (Qu. JJ35b, *Other expressions . . when you . . are just about ready to tell somebody what you think*) Inf **TX81,** Tell him how the cow ate the cabbage; (Qu. LL27, *Words meaning "thoroughly": "The boss bawled him out* ———*."*) Inf **OK45,** Like the cow eat the cabbage.

co-way See **co-ee**

cowbane n

1 =**water hemlock,** esp **spotted cowbane.**

1791 in 1793 Amer. Philos. Soc. Philadelphia *Trans.* 3.165, *Cicuta, maculata.* Cowbane. **1876** Hobbs *Bot. Hdbk.* 27, Cowbane. **1913** (1979) Barnes *Western Grazing* 267, Water Hemlock (*Cicuta occidentalis, C. maculata* . . . This plant sometimes is called cowbane or wild parsnip. **1940** (1951) FWP *Guide OR* 21, The juice of the deadly cowbane augmented the supply of rattlesnake virus as a poison for [the Indians'] arrows.

2 An umbelliferous plant of the genus *Oxypolis,* esp *O. rigidior* which is also called **hemlock, pig potato, water-dropwort, wild potato.** For names of other spp see **hog fennel, sanicle, snakeroot**

1900 Lyons *Plant Names* 272, *O[xypolis] rigida* . . Cowbane. **1913** *Torreya* 13.253 **Staten Island NY,** The cowbane, *Oxypolis rigidius.* **1950** Gray–Fernald *Manual of Botany* 1102, *O[xypolis] rigidior* . . Cowbane. **1970** Correll *Plants TX* 1161, *Oxypolis rigidior* . . Cowbane.

cowbane parsnip n

Prob **cow parsnip 1.**

1968 *DARE* (Qu. S26a, *Other wildflowers . . around here . . roadside flowers*) Inf **PA70,** Cowbane parsnip.

cow barn is open phr Cf **barn door 2b, cow lot gate is open**

1966–68 *DARE* (Qu. W24c, *Sayings to warn a man that his trouser-fly is open*) Infs **IN1, NJ16, OR1,** Cow barn's open.

cow bean n Cf **cowpea**

=**black-eyed pea.**

1968 *DARE* (Qu. I19, *Small white beans with a black spot where they were joined to the pod*) Inf **NJ67,** Cow bean.

cow beast See **beast B2**

cow beef n

1975 Gould *ME Lingo* 61, *Cow beef* . . . The Superannuated Maine dairy cow, readied for table, was not always a blessing.

cow beet n Also *cow turnip*

=**rutabaga.**

1950 *WELS* (*Names or nicknames for large yellow turnips*) 1 Inf, **ceWI,** Cow beet; 2 Infs, **c,ceWI,** Cow turnips. **1967** *DARE* (Qu. I3, *The large yellowish root vegetable, similar to a turnip, with a strong taste*) Inf **OH8,** Cow beet; **MI68,** Cow turnip.

cowbell n [From the shape of the flower]
=bladder campion.

1900 Lyons *Plant Names* 345, *S[ilene] Cucubalus* . . . Bladder Campion . . Cow-bell. **1911** *Century Dict.,* Cow-bell . . . A Scotch and American name of the bladder-campion. **1968** Barkley *Plants KS* 144, Cowbell Silene. Fields and waste places.

cowbell frog See **bell frog**

‡cowbell phosphate n [Perh *cowbell* something characteristically rural + *phosphate* a soft drink]

1969 *DARE* (Qu. DD21c, *Nicknames for whiskey, especially illegally made whiskey*) Inf **KY**35, Cowbell phosphate [laughter].

cowbelly n **chiefly LA**

1 Soft river mud; see quots.

1968 *DARE* Tape **LA**46 (as of 1950s), We used to have a lot of fun in the cowbellies, we call 'em. Cowbellies are the soft mud out by de river . . . And it's about as soft as jello—not quite, but almost. We had a lot of experiences with that . . . We used to dive into 'em, but only from standin' on the groun'. **1980** *DARE* File **LA,** Cowbelly—Soft river mud often used for play. [10 Infs]

2 Transf: a kind of workshoe.

1966 *DARE* (Qu. W11, *Men's low, rough work shoes*) Inf **SC**10, Cowbelly. **1980** *DARE* File **LA,** Whenever daddy tells Danny to go out to do any work outside and it's raining or muddy or something, Danny always says, "I can't go 'till I put my cowbellies on"—he means his old brogans or his boots.

cowberry n

1 **=mountain cranberry. NEng**

1824 Bigelow *Florula Bostoniensis* 154, *Vaccinium Vitis Idæa* . . Cow Berry. **a1862** (1864) Thoreau *Maine Woods* 311, *Vaccinium vitis-idæa* (cow-berry). **1900** Lyons *Plant Names* 386, Cow-berry. **1961** Douglas *My Wilderness* 228 **NH,** I was busy examining the dainty pinkish bloom and tiny leaves of the cowberry (*Vaccinium Vitis-idaea*).

2 **=partridgeberry 1.**

1892 *Jrl. Amer. Folkl.* 5.98, *Mitchella repens,* . . cow-berry. Ulster Co., N.Y. **1900** Lyons *Plant Names* 249, *M[itchella] repens* . . Cow-berry.

3 A cinquefoil (here: *Potentilla palustris*). **West**

1925 Jepson *Manual Plants CA* 485, *P[otentilla] palustris* . . Cowberry. **1932** Rydberg *Flora Prairies* 415, Cowberry.

4 A nannyberry (here: *Viburnum lentago*).

1941 *Torreya* 41.52, *Viburnum lentago* . . . Cow-berry, New England.

cowbird n

1 A dark-colored passerine bird *(Molothrus ater)* native to the US and noted esp for its habit of depositing its eggs in the nest of other birds. [From its association with cattle] Also called **buffalo bird, cow blackbird, cow bunting, cow-pen bird, cow-pen bunting, cow tick 2, cuckold 2, horse bird, lazy bird, tick bird**

1810 Wilson *Amer. Ornith.* 2.40, I placed a young unfledged Cow-bird (the *Fringilla pecoris* of Turton) . . in the same cage with a Red-bird, which fed and reared it with great tenderness. **1903** *Eve. Post* (NY NY) 24 Oct sec 3 1/3, The cowbird is not aggressively intrusive, like the sparrow. **1916** *DN* 4.425 **LA,** Cowbird (Molothrus ater). **c1960** *Wilson Coll.* **csKY,** Cowbird . . . A common bird of the area, known to very few people except as a little blackbird. A few call it a Horse Bird, from its being seen in the pastures among the stock. **1964** Jackman–Long *OR Desert* 96, There are little brown birds, smaller than blackbirds, that like to ride on the cows' backs . . . They usually come in pairs and often stay with a herd all day. We called them "cow birds." **1965–70** *DARE* (Qu. Q14, . . *Other names* . . *for* . . *cowbird*) 330 Infs, **scattered,** Cowbirds; (Qu. Q11, *Kinds of blackbirds*) 115 Infs, **scattered,** Cowbird; (Qu. Q10) Inf **NJ**12, Cowbird; (Qu. Q15) Inf **MO**5, Cowbird.

2 also *kow-bird:* Either of two similar birds: the **yellow-billed cuckoo** or the **black-billed cuckoo.** [Echoic]

1810 Wilson *Amer. Ornith.* 2.145, The American Cuckoo (Cuculus Carolinensis) is by many people called the Cow-bird, from the sound of its notes resembling the words *cow, cow.* **1844** DeKay *Zool. NY* 2.194, The Yellow-Billed Cuckoo—*Coccyzus Americanus* . . . It is called . . *Cow-bird.* **1888** (1890) Warren *Birds PA* 161, *Coccyzus erythrophthalmus* . . Kow-bird. **1936** *Oriole* 1.8, Yellow-billed cuckoo.—*Cowbird* ("cow" from a common call) . . *Black-billed cuckoo* . . . (doubtless this closely similar bird shares all the names of the yellow-bill. .). **1945** *Chicago Daily News* (IL) 2 Feb 14/6, He was chirping as merrily as a cowbird in a robin's nest.

3 **=boat-tailed grackle.**

1932 Howell *FL Bird Life* 432, Boat-tailed Grackle . . . Other Names: Jackdaw; Cowbird (female). **1955** Forbush–May *Birds* 473, Boat-tailed Grackle . . . Other names: . . Cowbird (female).

4 **=cattle egret.**

1969 Longstreet *Birds FL* 22, Cattle egret—Other name: Cowbird.

cow blackbird n
=cowbird 1.

1810 Wilson *Amer. Ornith.* 2.151, Hence the [cow buntings] have pretty generally obtained the name of *Cow-pen birds, Cow-birds,* or *Cow Blackbirds.* **1965–70** *DARE* (Qu. Q14, . . *Other names* . . *for* . . *cowbird*) 22 Infs, **chiefly Inland Nth, N Midl,** Cow blackbird; (Qu. Q11, *Kinds of blackbirds*) Infs **DE**3, **IL**14, **MI**2, **MO**19, **NY**191, Cow blackbird.

cow boss n
The foreman of a cattle ranch.

1900 Garland *Eagle's Heart* 156, We'll ride over to the round-up to-morrow, and I'll introduce you to the cow boss, and you can go right into the mess. **1966** Barnes–Jensen *Dict. UT Slang,* Cow-boss . . . the foreman in charge of a cattle ranch.

cow boss v phr See **co-boss(ie)**

cowboy n

1 also *cowboy driver:* A reckless driver; an inexperienced driver. **chiefly NEast** See Map

1942 *AmSp* 17.103 [Among truck drivers], Cowboy. Reckless driver. **1951** *AmSp* 26.308 **WI** [Among truck drivers], Cowboy . . . A new driver, one who has much to learn. **1961** *AmSp* 36.272 **Midwest, East,** Cowboy . . . A reckless driver. **1962** *AmSp* 37.268 **sCA,** Cowboy . . . A highway 'cutup' who weaves in and out of traffic as if he were riding the range. **1965–70** *DARE* (Qu. N12, *Names for somebody who drives carelessly or not well*) 44 Infs, **chiefly NEast,** Cowboy; **CT**17, Drugstore cowboy; (Qu. GG42, *A reckless person*) Inf **NY**18, Cowboy. **1965** *DARE* File **nNH** (as of 1953), Cowboy driver. A careless or reckless driver, especially a very young one. "There's so many cowboy drivers on the roads these days it isn't safe for a good driver."

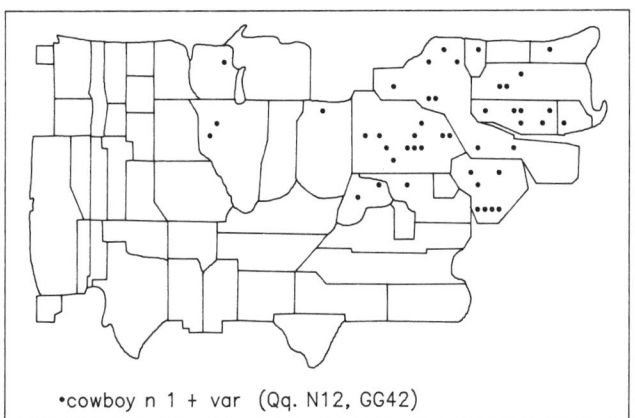

•cowboy n 1 + var (Qq. N12, GG42)

2 See quot.

1965 *DARE* (Qu. II10b, *Asking directions of somebody on the street when you don't know his name—what you'd say to a man:* "Say, _____, *how far is it to the next town?*") Inf **OK**48, Cowboy.

3 A policeman.

1968 *DARE* (Qu. V9, . . *Nicknames* . . *for a policeman*) Infs **LA**32, **NY**92, Cowboy.

cowboy v [**cowboy** n **1**]
To drive a car in a reckless manner.

1980 *DARE* File **Madison WI** (as of 1953), Fred had to let him go; he got caught cowboying the customers' cars.

cowboy bible n

1980 *AZ Highways* Feb 8, Roll-your-own cigarettes were so popular that the little books of paper were called "cowboy bibles." They hated pipes and couldn't afford cigars or expensive manufactured cigarettes.

cowboy box n

1958 Blasingame *Dakota Cowboy* 18 **SD** (as of 1900–10), The cowboy box on the chuck wagon usually held our guns, ammunition, razors, soap, and perhaps a can of talcum powder and a comb, although some of us kept these in the little canvas "war-bag" in our bedroll.

cowboy bread n

1967 *DARE* (Qu. H18, . . *Special kinds of bread made now or in past years*) Inf **OR**1, Cowboy bread: camp bread (like sourdough); **TX**4, Cowboy breads: cooked over a campfire, tallow for shortening.

cowboy-broke ppl adj Cf **Indian-broke**

1946 Mora *Trail Dust* 201, Oh, yes, they [the horses] are all broken. That is "cowboy broke." If you can saddle and bridle and get aboard one without too much outside help, he's broke. What may happen after that does not count: he's broke just the same.

cowboy change n

1968 Adams *Western Words* 79, *Cowboy Change*—Gun cartridges of various sizes used for small change . . . A silver fifty-cent piece was the smallest coin in circulation, but it was sometimes necessary to make change to the value of quarters and dimes. For this the standard sizes of cartridges were used, and they became known as *cowboy change.*

cowboy cocktail n

1968 Adams *Western Words* 79, *Cowboy cocktail*—Straight whiskey, because that is the way the cowboy wanted it.

cowboy coffee n

Boiled or very strong coffee.

1967 *DARE* (Qu. H74a, . . *Coffee . . very strong*) Inf **KS**1, Cowboy coffee. **1967** *DARE* FW Addit **CO**29, Cowboy coffee—boiled coffee.

cowboy driver See **cowboy** n 1

cowboy fountain pen See **cowboy pen**

cowboy leg n

A bowleg.

1967–70 *DARE* (Qu. X37, *Words . . to describe people's legs if they're noticeably bent, or uneven, or not right*) Infs **CO**7, **KY**94, **OH**43, Cowboy legs; **MN**2, Cowboy; **IN**82, Cowboy's legs.

cowboy lily n West

1 A stickleaf (here: *Mentzelia decapetala*).

1938 FWP *Guide ND* 177, In June the large white open flowers of the low-growing gumbo lily, also known as the cowboy lily . . appear in the otherwise barren soil at the foot of the buttes.

2 A western species of evening primrose (here: *Oenothera caespitosa*).

1959 Carleton *Index Herb. Plants* 31, *Cow-boy-Lily:* Oenothera caespitosa.

cowboy match n [In ref to moving-picture cowboys' striking matches on the seat of their pants] Cf **country match, farmer match**

1967 *DARE* (Qu. F46, . . *The kind of matches you can strike anywhere*) Infs **HI**6, 9, Cowboy matches.

cowboy pants n pl

1967–68 *DARE* (Qu. W10, *Work trousers made of rough cloth, usually blue*) Inf **CO**27, Cowboy pants; **MN**33, Cowboy pants, the real tight buggers. [Inf distinguished these pants from *Levi's* and *riding breeches*.]

cowboy pen n Also *cowboy fountain pen* joc

A plant stalk used for doodling in the soil.

1961 Adams *Old-Time Cowhand* 19, They'd hunker down on their boot heels, twist a cigarette, and mighty soon be fishin' 'round for a cowboy fountain pen, which was a broomweed stalk with plenty of loose dirt to draw in. Seems like a cowhand could talk better when he was a-scratchin' in the sand like a hen in a barnyard. **1968** Adams *Western Words* 80, Cowboy pen.

‡cowboy potatoes n pl

1967 *DARE* (Qu. H47, *Kinds of fried potatoes favored around here*) Inf **TX**4, Cowboy potatoes: cut up, round slices, onion, bacon—boiled.

cowboy preacher n

1967 *DARE* (Qu. CC10, *Words . . for an unprofessional, part-time lay preacher*) Inf **CO**42, Cowboy preacher.

cowboy saddle See **cow saddle**

cowboy's delight n

1960 Teale *Journey into Summer* 196 **WY**, Another plant they [=prairie dogs] seemed to favor at Devils Tower is a miniature mallow with the picturesque name of cowboy's-delight.

cowboy stew n Cf **county attorney**

=**son-of-a-bitch stew.**

1967 *DARE* (Qu. H43, *Foods made from parts of the head and inner organs of an animal*) Inf **TX**1, Cowboy stew: beef haslets; some with pork; **TX**29, Cowboy stew: Same thing as son-of-a-gun stew.

cow brake See **brake** n[4] 1

cowbrute n chiefly Midl, SW Cf **brute**

A cow or steer—sometimes used euphem for a bull.

1828 *Cherokee Phoenix* (New Echoto GA) 24 Apr 1/3, Any person or persons finding a dead cow brute and skinning the same, such person or persons shall receive from the owner of such beast, the sum of fifty cents. **1903** (1965) Adams *Log Cowboy* 159 **SW,** We usually wanted the herd thirsty when reaching a large river. But any cow brute that halted in fording the Canadian that day was doomed to sink into quicksands. **1906** *DN* 3.116 **sIN,** Cow-brute . . . A cow. **1916** *DN* 4.322 **KS.** **1923** *DN* 5.204 **swMO,** Cow brute . . . Any member of the ox family, but specifically a bull. **1934** (1970) Wilson *Backwoods Amer.* 70 **AR, MO,** A cow is likely to be, but not invariably, a *cow-brute;* while a mule or a horse is a *critter.* **1939** Hall Coll. **eTN,** Robert McClure, 23, born and raised near Waynesville, well-educated, says that it is still not good form to use the word *bull* in the presence of women; *cow-brute* is used instead. **1940** *AmSp* 15.46, Whereas in the Smokies, Cumberlands and Ozarks the usual variant for cow is *cow-brute,* in the Blue Ridge it is commonly a *she-cow.* **1966** *DARE* Tape **OK**30, A cowbrute, after they get used to . . being on the trail, they're very easily handled at night. They will lay down soon after you put them on the bed-ground, and lay there 'til about 12 o'clock. **1969** *DARE* (Qu. K23, *Words used by women or in mixed company for a bull*) Inf **KY**46, Cowbrute.

cow bug n Also *cow* Cf **ant cow**

An aphid.

1968–70 *DARE* (Qu. R26, *Other names for the small greenish lice that come on plants*) Inf **CA**65, Cow bug; **GA**11, Cows; (Qu. R30) Inf **VA**64, Cow bug.

cowbuncle See **carbuncle**

cow bunting n

=**cowbird 1.**

1810 Wilson *Amer. Ornith.* 2.145, [The] Cow Bunting. Emberiza Pecoris . . . winters regularly in the lower parts of North and South Carolina and Georgia. **1903** *Eve. Post* (NY NY) 24 Oct sec 3 1/2, Flocks of redwinged blackbirds, with an occasional cow-bunting and perhaps a rusty grackle. **1969** *DARE* (Qu. Q14, . . *Other names . . for . . cowbird*) Inf **IL**32, Cow bunting.

cow business n

1 The handling of cattle, as on a roundup or drive.

1907 White *AZ Nights* 94, Always in a cowboy's "string" of from six to ten animals the boss assigns him two or three broncos to break in to the cow business. **1947** Westerners Los Angeles Corral *Brand Book* 55 **WY,** No man ever learned the cow business easily or quickly. **1956** Almirall *From College* 63 **CO,** To have ridden and talked with this old-timer, I believe, stands out predominantly in the life I led, learning the cow business.

2 See quot.

1966 Barnes–Jensen *Dict. UT Slang, Cow-business* . . . cattle raising on a large scale.

cow butter n

1976 Garber *Mountain-ese* 18, *Cow-Butter* . . homemade butter[.] We allers serve real cow butter atter the cows cum fresh.

cow cabbage n

A **false hellebore** (here: *Veratrum californicum*).

1966 Barnes–Jensen *Dict. UT Slang, Cow cabbage* . . . a name sometimes given to White Hellebore (*Veratrum speciosum*).

cow cake n, also attrib Also *cow pancake* [By analogy with *cow pie*]

Cow dung.

1968 *DARE* (Qu. HH20c, *Of an idle, worthless person . . "He doesn't amount to _____."*) Inf **TX**54, Cow cake; (Qu. BB50c, *Favorite remedies . . for infections*) Inf **MD**30, Cow-cake poultice. **1971** Today Show Letters **swPA** (as of c1925), *Cow pancake:* a dropping of cow manure. [Among children]

cow camp n, also attrib **West**

The headquarters of a cattle roundup; a cowboy's camp.

1873 in 1931 *Annals WY* 8.495, Had supper with them and learned that . . . Mr. Richards . . has a cow camp [on Red Creek] three miles north. **1945** James *Cherokee Strip* 8 **CO,** Mr. Howell knew a cow-camp cook in Colorado who was bitten on the thumb by a rattler. **1969** *DARE* Tape **CA**163, An old cow camp that's always been in my family, where [the] headquarters [were] for camping and we [would] go out there buckeroo-ing during the year while the cattle were out there grazing. **1977** Watts *Dict. Old West, Cowcamp*—It could mean a relatively permanent settlement in cattle-country; if a man built himself a shack or a soddy . . and corral, that was a cowcamp. The term could also be applied to a temporary camp of cowhunters (in Texas) or to a camp of trail-drivers.

cow-camp stew n

=cowboy stew.

1949 Trahey *Taste TX* 12, Cow camp stew. Stew made of beef, heart, liver, sweetbreads and brains.

cowcatcher n

1 A cattle guard at a railroad crossing.

1968 *DARE* Tape **CT**17, They used to have the cowcatchers—an open place under the track to keep the cattle from walkin' across.

2 See quots. [Transf from *cowcatcher* a frame on the front of a railroad engine]

1967–70 *DARE* (Qu. X15, . . *Kinds of noses, according to shape or size*) Inf **AR**55, Cowcatcher; (Qu. X53a, . . *An oversize stomach*) Inf **CA**202, Cowcatcher.

3 =cow-killer ant.

1966 *DARE* (Qu. R18, . . *Kinds of ants*) Inf **FL**35, Cowcatcher: big, red on each end and dark in the middle.

4 =beggar ticks 1.

1969 *DARE* (Qu. S14, *Other prickly seeds, small and flat, with two prongs at one end*) Inf **TX**71, Cowcatchers.

cow-chip beetle n

=dung beetle.

1966 *DARE* (Qu. R30, . . *Kinds of beetles*) Inf **SD**5, Cow-chip beetle.

cowc'late See **calculate**

cowc'lation See **calculation**

cow clover n

1 A **red clover** (here: *Trifolium pratense*).

1900 Lyons *Plant Names* 377, T[rifolium] pratense . . . Broad-leaved or Cow Clover. **1971** Krochmal *Applachia Med. Plants* 252, *Trifolium Pratense* L. (Fabaceae) Common names: . . cow clover.

2 also *cow grass:* =zigzag clover.

1900 Lyons *Plant Names* 377, T[rifolium] medium . . . Zigzag Clover, Cow-grass. **1961** *W3,* Cow clover . . Zigzag clover.

cow cockle n chiefly **Plains States, Pacific NW**

=cowherb.

1889 *Century Dict., Cockle[1]* . . . Cow-cockle, the cow-herb, *Vaccaria Vaccaria* . . . is . . a bad weed in the northwestern States and adjacent Canada, west of the main range of the corn-cockle. **1932** Rydberg *Flora Prairies* 327, *Vaccaria* . . . Cow-herb, Cow Cockle. **1940** Gates *Flora KS* 163, *Vaccaria vulgaris* . . . Cow Cockle . . . Waste places. **1950** Stevens *ND Plants* 138, Cow Cockle . . . Common in fields, especially westward; frequently grown as an ornamental. **1973** Hitchcock–Cronquist *Flora Pacific NW* 122.

cow corn n Also *cattle corn* [From its use as livestock feed] chiefly **Nth,** esp **NEast** See Map

Field corn.

1965–70 *DARE* (Qu. I34, *If you don't have sweet corn, you can always eat young _____*) 29 Infs, **chiefly Nth,** esp **NEast,** Cow corn; 7 Infs, **esp NEast,** Cattle corn.

cow country n **West** *somewhat old-fash*

Open range, good cattle-raising land.

1881 (1882) Chase *Editor's Run* 160 **CO, NM,** There is no excuse in a cow country like this for a landlord to set before his guests oleomargarine or condensed milk. **1927** James *Cow Country* vii, When we speak of cow country out here, we mean range country—a country where cattle run loose in open territory and are identified by brands and earmarks, not by names and spots. **1942** *AmSp* 17.74, **nwNE,** Natives [of the

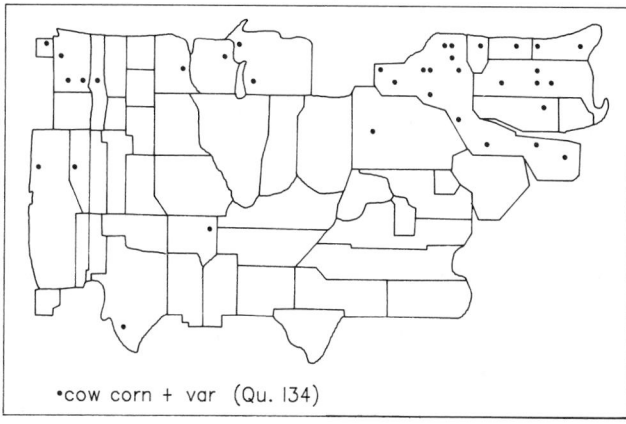

•cow corn + var (Qu. I34)

sandhill region] will tell you that it is God's own cow country. **1969** Laine *Cow Country* ix, Anybody with any "cow sense" at all, knows that "cow country" is not just any area that has a cow. No! It has to be West Texas—the Panhandle; the Plains; . . the scenic Hill Country; extending on to the foot of the peaks in Big Bend. That's cow country. It spawned the greatest ranch spreads in the world. **1969** *DARE* Tape **CA**160, There's so much difference between southern California and northern California. It should be two different states, actually . . . northern California . . is old mining country, cow country, sheep country.

cow county n **CA, NV** Cf *DS* C33

A rural place, "the sticks."

1850 *S.F. Herald* 16 Jan 2/4 (*AmSp* 21.116) **CA,** The last spell of rain and wind, lasting some thirty days, has brought the subject home to every man's mind in the "cow counties." **1895** Harte *Clarence* 13, I'm not the kind to be fooled by anybody from the Cow counties. **1946** *AmSp* 21.116, Cow county . . . Phrase still used in Calif., referring to rural districts in general, 'the sticks.' **1980** *DARE* File **NV,** In Nevada, the distinction is made between The North and The South. You can hear the capital letters in conversation. The North is Reno, usually; sometimes Reno and Carson City. The South is Clark County—Las Vegas and the surrounding townships that make up the metropolitan area. The rest of the state is referred to as The Cow Counties, whether or not cattle or whores are the primary source of income.

cow cousin n

1944 *PADS* 2.33 **NC,** Cow-cousins . . . Cousins weaned on the milk of the same cow.

cow-cow n [Echoic] Cf **skeow**

1 =green heron.

1917 *Wilson Bulletin* 29.2.78, *Butorides virecens* [sic] . . . cow-cow, Marksville, La. All these names are onomatopoeic. **1959** *AmSp* 34.74, Cow-cow (green heron; yellow-billed cuckoo).

2 also sp *kow-kow:* Either of two birds: the **yellow-billed cuckoo** or the **black-billed cuckoo.**

1917 (1923) *Birds Amer.* 2.128, Yellow-Billed Cuckoo . . . Kow-Kow . . . Black-Billed Cuckoo . . . Kow-Kow. **1927** Forbush *Birds MA* 2.244, Black-bill Cuckoo. Other names: . . cow-cow. **1956** *MA Audubon* 40.80, Black-billed cuckoo . . . Cow-cow. **1959** [see **1** above].

cow critter n Also *cow creature* chiefly **S Midl** *old-fash* Cf **cowbrute**

A cow or steer—sometimes used euphem for a bull.

1859 (1968) Bartlett *Americanisms* xxvi, The essentially English word *bull* is refined beyond the mountains, and perhaps elsewhere, into *cow-creature, male-cow,* and even *gentle-man cow!* **1865** *Atlantic Mth.* 15.671, He knowed I was apt to buy cow-critters along in the spring. **1923** *DN* 5.204 **swMO,** Cow critter . . . Specifically, a bull, though the term may refer to any other member of the ox family. **1931** Randolph *Ozarks* 19, Me and Sis made two craps 'ith a yoke o' cow-critters. **1931–33** *LANE Worksheets* **cwCT,** Cow critter: Bull. (Old-fashioned euphemism.) **1960** *Wilson Coll.* **csKY,** Cow critter . . . Any member of the cattle family—usually humorous. **1976** Garber *Mountain-ese* 18, Cow-critter . . bovine animal.

cow crowd n **SW**

See quot 1968.

1929 Dobie *Vaquero* 104, Wherever he rode, alone or in a cow crowd, death was reaching for his bridle reins. **1968** Adams *Western Words* 79, *Cow crowd*—An outfit or unit of cowboys.

‡cow cud n

A wad or roll of paper money.

1966 *DARE* (Qu. U19b, *Talking of paper money: "He always carries a big _____."*) Inf **MS**1, Cow cud.

cowcumber n *scattered, but esp* **W Midl, LA** See Map *somewhat old-fash*

A cucumber.

1685 (1902) Budd *Good Order* 31 **PA, NJ**, Garden Fruits groweth well, as Cabbage, . . Cowcumbers. **1742** (1850) Pinckney *Jrl. Eliza Lucas* 20, Sent for Cowcumber seed. **1838** Cooper *Amer. Democrat* 119, Many words are in a state of mutation, the pronunciation being unsettled even in the best society . . . To this class belong "clerk," "cucumber" and "gold," which are often pronounced as spelt, though it were better and more in conformity with polite usage to say "clark," "cow-cumber," (not cow*cumber*,) and "goold." **1867** Lowell *Biglow* xx, I obtained . . three diverse pronunciations of a single word, —cow*cumber*, coo*cumber*, and *cucumber*. Of these the first, which is Yankee also, comes nearest to the nasality of *concombre*. **1890** *DN* 1.64 **KY**, *Cowcumber*: for *cucumber*; used now more as a reminder of how the old folks pronounced the word. **1893** Shands *MS Speech.* **1909** *DN* 3.394 **nwAR**, *Cowcumber* . . . Jocose pronunciation of cucumber. Infrequently heard in serious use. **1925** *AmSp* 1.137 **Nth** [Loggers' speech], Pickles are "cow-cumbers." **1936** *AmSp* 11.314 **Ozarks**, *Cowcumber* . . . Cucumber. Nearly all of the old-timers cling to this archaic pronunciation. **1965–70** *DARE* (Qu. I25, . . *Cucumbers*) 40 Infs, **scattered, but esp W Midl, LA**, Cowcumbers.

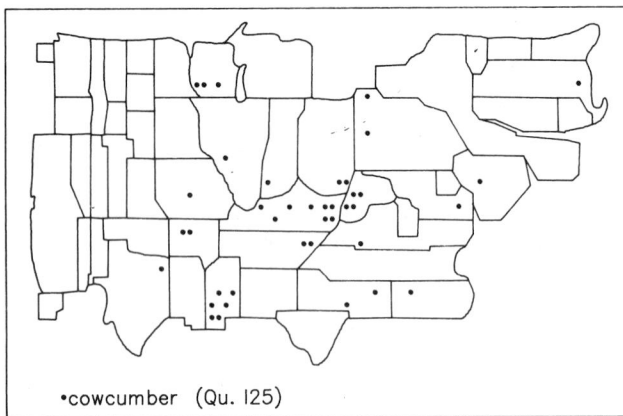

•cowcumber (Qu. I25)

cow cup n

1960 Williams *Walk Egypt* 241 **GA**, The flush of the Milky Way, which children called "The Cow Cup," was gone.

cow cuppen, cow cuppin See **cuppen**

cow dab n [*dab* a lump, small amount]

A piece of cow dung.

1899 (1912) Green *VA Folk-Speech, Cow-dab* . . . A lump of cowdung. **1949** Guthrie *Way West* 102 (as of 1847), She walked away and stopped and stooped, somehow pitiful and somehow dignified, and fingered for a cow dab. **1956** Rayford *Whistlin' Woman* 34 **AL**, In those days, when there were no screens, mosquitoes were repelled by burning cowdabs in buckets. **1960** Criswell *Resp. to PADS* 20 **Ozarks**, Cowdab . . . Cow manure, particularly a pile. Common term among women and children—possibly still used.

cow daisy n

=**black-eyed Susan 2.**

1968 *DARE* (Qu. S7, *A kind of daisy, bright yellow with a dark center, that grows along roadsides in late summer*) Inf **WI**37, Cow daisy.

cow doctor n [By analogy with *horse doctor*]

1967 *DARE* (Qu. BB53b, *A doctor who is not very capable or doesn't have a very good reputation*) Inf **SC**32, Cow doctor.

cowdog n

A cowboy.

1921 Thorp *Songs Cowboys* 12 **NM**, I hope the settlers will be glad /

When rain hits the land, / And all us cowdogs are in hell / With a "set" joined hand in hand.

cow-down See **cow-dung cooter**

cow drive n

A cattle roundup.

1961 Adams *Old-Time Cowhand* 246, The primitive Western forerunner of the roundup was a gettin' together of a few neighborin' stockmen to look over each other's herds for strays . . . Them neighborly gatherin's were called "cow hunts," "cow drives," or were spoken of as 'runnin' cattle.'

cow driver n

A cattle herder.

1771 in 1919 *MD Hist. Mag.* 14.136, I have order'd Squires to go downe to morrow with the Cow driver. **1856** in 1859 Willis *Convalescent* 112 **NY**, With no accomplishments except for his own pleasure—no rat-catcher, no cow-driver, no pig-chaser—he love *me!* **1932** Kelley *Inchin' Along* 211 *(DA)*, The ox-drivers—'cow-drivers,' they were called. **1968** Fletcher *Up the Trail* 8 **West** (as of 1879), "Mister, is you a Christian?" "I hope so," was the reply. "And a cow driver?" "Yes, why not?" **1977** Watts *Dict. Old West, Cow driver*—(Texas). One who drove cows on the trail north from Texas or who trailed them west into Colorado and California; essentially, a man who drove cattle on a long trail.

cow dumpling See **dumpling**

cow-dung cooter n Also *cow-down, cow-turd cooter*

Either a **box turtle** or the striped **mud turtle**.

1952 Carr *Turtles* 93, It [the striped mud turtle] shares with *Terrapene* [the box turtle] the name "cow-dung cooter" in some places, and I have several times seen individuals eating manure. **1966–67** *DARE* (Qu. P24, . . *Kinds of turtles*) Inf **SC**19, Cow-dung cooter [kʊtə]—black belly; **SC**43, Cow-down; **GA**3, Cow-turd cooter—small, black; stinks.

cow egret n

=**cattle egret.**

1968 *DARE* Tape **GA**30, You know you got the snowy egret and the cow egret.

co-wench v phr |ˌkoˈ(w)ɛn(č), -ˈın(č), ˈko-|, rarely |kwo-|, |-wæn|, |-ıŋk| Also sp *co-inch, coo-wench, co-wen, co-wenchie, co-wink, cow-wench, cur-winch, ker-(w)inch* [**co** v + Engl dial *wench* cow] *chiefly* **S Atl** See Map

Come!—used to call cows.

1899 (1912) Green *VA Folk-Speech, Coo-wench.* A word used for calling cows, repeated several times. **1908** *DN* 3.303 **eAL, wGA**, *Cur-winch* . . . The common call for cows. *Ibid* 326, *Ker-(w)inch* . . . The call for cows. *Ker-inch* is also heard. **1946** *PADS* 6.10 **eNC**, *Co, wench* [ko] . . . A call used for a cow when she is only a short distance away . . . Common. **1949** Kurath *Word Geog.* 63, Co-wench!, co-inch!, co-ee! in the South, from Delaware Bay to Georgia. **1965–70** *DARE* (Qu. K80, *The call that's used . . to get the cows in from the pasture*) 15 Infs, **S Atl**, Co-wench (sometimes repeated); **GA**28, Co-wenchie; **FL**26, [ˈkoˌwıŋk]; **GA**39A, Co-wen [ˈkoˌɛn]; **SC**12, [ˈko:wæn]; **GA**5, Cow-wench; (Qu. K83, *To call a calf . . at feeding time*) Infs **FL**7, **GA**22, 39, **NC**3, 8, **SC**1, 43, Co-wench (co-wench); **FL**26, Co-wink. **1971** Wood *Vocab. Change* 46 **Sth**, *Co-wench* occurs less often as a call for cows than does *bossie* or *here bossie. Ibid* 336, [Map shows *co-wench* to occur within a limited area in southern Georgia and northern Florida].

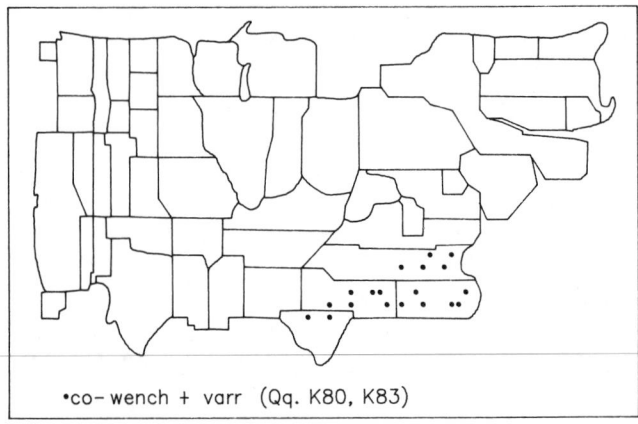

•co-wench + varr (Qq. K80, K83)

cowetch See **cowitch**

cow express n Cf **ankle express** and *DS* Y24
   1970 Major *Afro–Amer. Slang* 41, *Cow express:* (1940's) shoe leather.

cow eye n Also *cow's eye*
   A very round sometimes protruding eye; hence adj *cow-eyed* having such eyes.
   1965–70 *DARE* (Qu. X21c, *If the eyes are very round*) Infs **IL**35, 69, 77, **IN**42, **LA**23, **MI**103, **MN**28, **NY**217, Cow eyes; **CA**157, **KS**7, **NJ**53, 54, **NY**145, **OH**68, **OK**54, 57, Cow-eyed; **OH**4, Cow's eyes; (Qu. X21a, *. . If they stick out*) Inf **GA**59, Cow eyes.

cowfish n Cf **sea cow**
   1 A **trunkfish** (here: *Lactophrys quadricornis*). Also called **cuckold 3, toro**
   1870 *Amer. Naturalist* 3.467, The odd-looking trigonal Trunk-fish (*Lactophrys camelinus* DeKay), sometimes called Cow-fish, a profile view of the head much resembling that of a cow. **1902** Jordan–Evermann *Amer. Fishes* 490, The family [Ostraciidae] contains one genus, *Ostracion,* with 4 American species . . . They are known variously as trunk-fish, chapin, rock shellfish, plate-fish, cow-fish, and the like. **1960** Amer. Fisheries Soc. *List Fishes* 49, Cowfish . . *Lactophrys quadricornis.*
   2 A **grampus,** esp Risso's dolphin.
   1884 Goode *Fisheries U.S.* 1.14, The oil of the Cowfish, particularly that of its jaws, is highly prized. **1955** U.S. Arctic Info. Center *Gloss.,* Cowfish . . . A New England name for Risso's dolphin.
   3 See quot.
   1968 *DARE* File **c, ceDE,** Cowfish: A female sturgeon full of eggs.

cowflower n
   1 A **bachelor's button** (here: *Centaurea cyanus*).
   1968 *DARE* (Qu. S11) Inf **MN**42, Cowflower.
   2 Prob =**marsh marigold.**
   1969 *DARE* (Qu. S26e) Inf **WI**78, Cowflower.

cow fly n
   1 A large biting fly of the family Tabanidae.
   1851 *DeBow's Rev.* 11.56, Cow Fly, Tabani—Large black, large gray, small gray and green. **1879** U.S. Dept. Ag. *Special Rept.* 12.208 **TX,** Ticks, screw-worm, and the large horse or cow fly have destroyed many animals. **1965–70** *DARE* (Qu. R12, *. . Flies . . around animals*) 167 Infs, **throughout US, but least freq west of Rocky Mts,** Cow fly. **1968** Abbey *Desert Solitaire* 35 **seUT,** The cowfly, or deerfly if you prefer, loves blood. Human blood especially. Persistent as a mosquito, it will keep attacking until either it samples your blood or you succeed in killing it, or both.
   2 A small gnat-like fly or midge.
   1967–69 *DARE* (Qu. R10, *Very small flies that don't sting, often seen hovering in large groups . . in summer*) Infs **IL**93, **LA**15, **OH**53, **PA**29, Cow fly; (Qu. R11, *A very tiny fly that you can hardly see, but that stings*) Infs **AR**5, **TX**52, Cow fly.

cow foot n
   A large foot; hence adj *cow footed* clumsy.
   1965 Will *Okeechobee Boats* 39 **FL,** Did you ever have a barge break loose . . with nobody . . but some cow footed backwoods deckhand who didn't know a towing bitt from a bilge pump? **1968** *DARE* (Qu. X38, *Joking names for unusually big or clumsy feet*) Inf **OH**40, Cow foot.

cow freshener n [That which causes a cow to **freshen,** or produce a calf and milk]
   1968 *DARE* (Qu. K22) Inf **PA**103, A cheap bull was called a cow freshener [rather than a sire], since the calf wasn't important.

cow frog n
   1 See quots.
   1950 *WELS Suppl.* **seWI,** Cow frog—a big frog. **1968** *DARE* (Qu. P22) Inf **CT**14, Cow frog—a medium-sized bullfrog; **NJ**22, Cow frog; **OH**79, Cow frogs are smaller [than bullfrogs]. **1981** *DARE* File **OK,** Cow frog—a small, striped frog.
   2 =**shoveler.**
   1888 Trumbull *Names of Birds* 43, Shoveller . . . Another odd title, of much less recent origin, encountered at Morehead, N.C., is *cow-frog.* Though no one attempts to give a reason for the term, the oldest inhabitants tell of hearing it in use from early childhood. **1917** (1923) *Birds Amer.* 1.126, Shoveller (Spatula clypeata) . . . Other Names . . . Butter Duck; Cow-frog.

cow grass n
   1 A **cordgrass.**
   1889 (1971) Farmer *Americanisms, Cow-grass.*—A weed which constitutes one of the plagues of farming in the Southern States. **1937** *Torreya* 37.95 **DE,** *Spartina alterniflora . . .* Cow-grass. **1966** *DARE* (Qu. S8, *A common . . wild grass*) Inf **SC**7, Cow grass.
   2 See **cow clover 2.**

cow grease n Also *cow paste, ~ salve* **chiefly Midl** *joc*
   Butter.
   1930 *DN* 6.87 **eWV, OH,** Cow grease, butter. (This expression is not limited to this section, but is used, generally facetiously, in rural sections in Ohio, for instance). **1936** *AmSp* 11.275 **cn,neTN,** Cow paste. Butter. **1944** *PADS* 2.58 **nwMO, NC, SC, TN, VA,** Cow-grease . . . Butter . . . Vulgar. Rare. **1965–68** *DARE* FW Addit **neNM, GA**24, Cow salve. **1968** Adams *Western Words* 80, Cow grease—A cowboy's name for butter. *Ibid* 81, Cow salve.

cowhalloping See **ker-**

cowhand n [**hand** n B1] **chiefly SW**
   One who assists with ranch work and the care of cattle; a cowboy.
   1886 *Outing* 8.3/1, Though a first-rate cow hand, he very shortly proved himself to be wholly incapable of acting as head. **1936** McCarthy *Lang. Mosshorn* **SW,** Cow-hand . . . One who has had extensive experience with cattle. **1937** *DN* 6.620 **swTX,** Even for the cowboy there are different names. He is indifferently called *cow-hand, ranch-hand, cow-puncher, rawhide, waddie,* or *cow-waddie.* **1962** Atwood *Vocab. TX* 53, The ordinary hired hand on a ranch is generally known as a *cowhand . . ,* particularly in the areas of the early ranches [i.e., in southwestern Texas]. **1967** *DARE* (Qu. L1, *A man who is employed to help with work on a farm*) Infs **LA**3, **TX**22, Cowhand. **1973** Allen *LAUM* 1.406, The more diversified employee on a modern mechanized ranch is increasingly likely to be called by *cowhand* or *ranchhand.*

cowhanded adj [*cow* alter of *car* left-handed, awkward; from Gael and Ir *cearr* + (redund) *handed;* see *EDD* car adj]
   1 Awkward, clumsy. *obs*
   1834 *Life Andrew Jackson* 101, The gineral . . was never . . a hum-durgeon when danger was near, or cow-handed on the turf, wasn't backward, when his country needed him.
   2 Of a batter in baseball: having the hands in reversed position; cross-handed.
   1931 *Collier's* 9 May 32/3, He batted cow-handed! That's what the kids call it, and even kids don't do it. Being a right-hand hitter, he should have gripped his bat with his right hand above his left; but he gripped it with his left hand above his right . . so that when he swung and missed he was apt to hit himself across the shoulders. **1962** *AN&Q* 1.39/1 **NY,** Visitors to Highland, N.Y., are surprised when they call the one youngster in hundreds who holds the bat with crossed hands a "cross-handed batter" and natives ask, "Don't you mean *cowhanded?*" All over the United States the expression "crosshanded" is used . . . Highlanders concede that they can't explain why they use "cowhanded," but even Mr. Rufe Fraino, the oldest ex-semi-pro ball player around here says it was used by Highlanders when he was a boy. Mr. Frank Kozloski, who played pro baseball in minor leagues in 39 states, says he never heard the term anywhere but in Highland. **1963** *AN&Q* 1.73, Perhaps, as *butterfingers* was brought to this country by cricketers, *caw-handed* appears to have been modified to *cow-handed* by little-folk etymology.

cow hay n
   1967 TN Folk Lore Soc. *Bulletin* 33.44, *Cow hay . . .* Hay made from cowpeas. *Cowpea hay . . .* Same as *cow hay.*

cowherb n
   An annual weed (*Vaccaria segetalis*), often found in grainfields, which has opposite sessile leaves and open cymes of rose-colored flowers. Also called **cockle 1, cow cockle, cow rattle, dairy-pink, flytrap**
   1857 Gray *Manual of Botany* 55, Vaccària . . Cow-Herb. **1901** Mohr *Plant Life AL* 498, Vaccaria vaccaria . . . Cowherb. **1940** Steyermark *Flora MO* 184, Cow-herb . . . Begins to bloom the last of May. **1973** Hitchcock–Cronquist *Flora Pacific NW* 122, Cowcockle, cowherb . . . Mostly in waste areas and along roadsides and railroads.

‡cow-hick n
   1969 *DARE* (Qu. HH1, *. . A rustic or countrified person*) Inf **MO**18, Old cow-hick.

cowhide n

1 A whip made of rawhide strips.

1818 Birkbeck *Letters IL* 90 **VA,** The enraged barrister, with a hand-whip, or cow-hide as they are called, . . actually cut his jacket to ribbons. **1905** *DN* 3.7 **cCT,** *Cowhide* . . . A whip made of straps of rawhide. **1907** *DN* 3.210 **nwAR, cCT. 1908** *DN* 3.315 **eAL, wGA,** I'll take a cowhide and give you bringer [*DARE* Ed: =severe punishment; see **brinjer 1**] if you don't mind. **1912** Green *VA Folk-Speech.*

2 A shoe or boot made of cowhide. Cf **cowbelly 2**

1841 *Spirit of Times* 6 Feb. 583/1 *(DA),* Inch-soaled cowhides on a pine flooring. **1905** *DN* 3.7 **cCT,** *Cowhide* . . . Pl. heavy boots. **1907** *DN* 3.184 **NH,** *Cowhides* . . . Cowhide boots with long legs. "He had on a pair of cow-hides." *Ibid* 211 **nwAR, cCT,** *Cowhides* . . . Heavy boots. **1919** Cady *Rhymes of Vt.* (1923) 22 *(DA),* Each boy was taught a-what to do / To make his cowhides winter through.

cowhide v

To beat with a cowhide whip.

1794 *KY Gaz.* 1 Mar 2/3, In November 1792 . . a justice of the peace was cited to appear before the house of Delegates . . some he had horse-whipped; others he had cow-hided. **1818** in 1822 Flint *Letters* 116, The happy Kentuckian slave lives under the danger of being cow-hided (a term signifying a whipping, with a stripe of half tanned leather, which is twisted into the form of a tapered switch of a very rigid texture,) for the slightest . . offence. **1905** *DN* 3.7 **cCT,** *Cowhide* . . . To flog. **1907** *DN* 3.211 **nwAR, cCT. 1912** Green *VA Folk-Speech,* *Cowhide* . . . To whip with a cowhide: "She tried to cowhide him in the street."

cow-hocked adj

Of a horse: see quot 1968.

1964 Jackman–Long *OR Desert* 394 [Horse buyers' jargon], *Cow-hocked*—hocks together, toes out. **1968** Adams *Western Words* 80, *Cow-hocked*—Said of a horse whose hind legs almost touch at the hocks and then spread at the pastern joints, like those of a cow.

cowhollop, cowhollup See ker-

cow hook n Cf goose hook, poke

A yoke or frame placed on a cow's neck to prevent passage through a fence.

1933 *Hanley Disks* **swCT,** I'd seen cow hooks, but I'd never seen a goose hook.

cowhorn n [From the shape]

1 also *cowhorn pepper:* An unspecified *Capsicum:* see quot.

1966–67 *DARE* (Qu. I22b, *Kinds of peppers—large hot*) Infs **FL37, SC32,** Cowhorn peppers; **TX35,** Cowhorns; (Qu. I22d, *Kinds of peppers—large sweet*) Inf **LA12,** Cowhorn peppers; (Qu. I22a, *Kinds of peppers—small hot*) Inf **AL34,** Cowhorns; **GA1,** ['kɑʊæn].

2 See **cowhorn turnip.**

cowhorn orchid n [See quot 1975]

An epiphytic orchid (*Cyrtopodium punctatum*) with brown-spotted yellow flowers native to southern Florida. Also called **cigar orchid, tree orchid**

1933 Small *Manual SE Flora* 394, *Cowhorn-orchid. Butterfly-orchid* . . . Plants with as many as 200 pseudobulbs have been found. **1950** Correll *Native Orchids* 349, If it is desired to grow the Cowhorn Orchid in clay pots, about one third of the pot should be filled with potsherds. **1975** Natl. Audubon Soc. *Corkscrew* 27, *Cow-horn Orchid* . . . Its long conical pseudobulbs are responsible for its common names.

cowhorn pepper See cowhorn 1

cowhorn squash n

Perh a crookneck squash.

1866 *Eastern Slope* (Washoe, Nev.) 15 Dec 1/2 *(DA),* His nose is just like dad's, crooked as a cowhorn squash.

cowhorn turnip n Also *cowhorn* [From the shape]

See quots.

1906 *DN* 3.132 **nwAR,** *Cowhorn turnip* . . . A long, bow-shaped turnip, which grows to be approximately one and one-half inches in diameter, and over a foot in length, and is used to fertilize the soil or to feed to stock. **1966** *DARE* (Qu. I4c, *Any other names . . for turnips*) Inf **FL37,** Cowhorn.

cow horse n Also *cow pony* chiefly SW

A saddle horse adapted and especially trained for herding cattle.

1853 Hammett *Stray Yankee in TX* 97, The dogs that had returned were cared for, the very best cow horses . . selected. **1907** White *AZ Nights* 277, He jingled loosely along on his cow-horse. **1945** Mathews *Talking Moon* 156 **KS, OK,** I appreciate the feeling which inspires a cowhorse to buck on a frosty morning. **1968** Adams *Western Words* 80, *Cow horse*—A horse the cowhand rides while working cattle. A good cow horse has to possess strength and intelligence, both qualities well trained. *Ibid, Cow pony*—A cow horse . . . Occasionally a westerner uses this term in speaking of his horse, but it is used mostly by easterners and writers who have never lived in the West. The cowman usually calls him a *hoss,* and *cow hoss* is the almost universal term for him. **1969** *DARE* FW Addit **neCT,** Cow horse: a horse bred for herding cattle.

cow house n *obsolescent*

A building or part of a building where cows are kept.

1635 in 1896 Cambridge MA Proprietors *Records* 3, One Cow house and yeard. **1780** *NJ Jrl.* (Chatham NJ) 13 Dec 4/1, On said farm is a large two story dwelling house, . . a good barn, cider, chair, and cow houses. **1885** Warner *Wide World* 163 **NY,** There were the milky mothers, . . standing about, each in her own corner of the yard or cowhouse. **1966** *DARE* (Qu. M10, *The part of the barn where cows are kept*) Inf **SC19,** Cow house.

cow hunt n Cf cow drive, cow work

A cattle roundup; hence v *cowhunt* to round-up livestock.

1853 Hammett *Stray Yankee in TX* 108, Everything in the shape of a man . . had left the settlement, and engaged in a general "cow-hunt." **1920** Hunter *Trail Drivers TX* 104 (as of c1858), The cattle began to mix with other cattle and then began to stray off, some drifting as far as the Rio Grande or the coast. Soon the settlers began to organize cow hunts and work the cattle. **1929** Dobie *Vaquero* 13, When we gathered cattle, we said that we were on a "cow hunt," a "cow work," a "work," or a "cow drive," or maybe we said we were out "running cattle." **1966** *DARE* Tape **MS72,** All my life I've cowhunted in winter ground.

cowie See co-ee

cow-in n *old-fash*

A stanchion.

1933 *Hanley Disks* **neMA,** The hay bays on one side of the barn door and the cow tie-ups on the other. The old-fashioned name is cow-in.

co-wink See co-wench

cowish See cous

cowitch n Also *cowitch plant,* ~ *vine;* also sp *cowetch* [Folketym for *cowage*]

1 A woody vine (*Mucuna pruriens*) which produces pods covered with short stiff hairs that cause severe itching.

1840 MA Zool. & Bot. Surv. *Herb. Plants & Quadrupeds* 65, *D[olichos] pruriens* . . . Cowitch . . . Does not reach maturity in Berkshire County, although the *irritating* hairs on the pods, by which it is useful in certain diseases, are pretty full grown. **1876** Hobbs *Bot. Hdbk.* 27, Cowitch,—Cowhage,—Mucuna pruriens. **1900** Lyons *Plant Names* 254, *M[ucuna] pruriens* . . . Cowitch. **1933** Small *Manual SE Flora* 717, *Mucuna . . Cowitch-vine* . . The hairs of the pod are exceedingly irritating to the skin—hence "cowitch." **1959** Carleton *Index Herb. Plants* 32, *Cow itch:* Stizolobium pruritum.

2 =**trumpet creeper.** chiefly SE See Map

1901 Lounsberry *S. Wild Flowers* 472, But the southern natives have no such poetical idea of it *[Campsis radicans]:* they call it . . even more

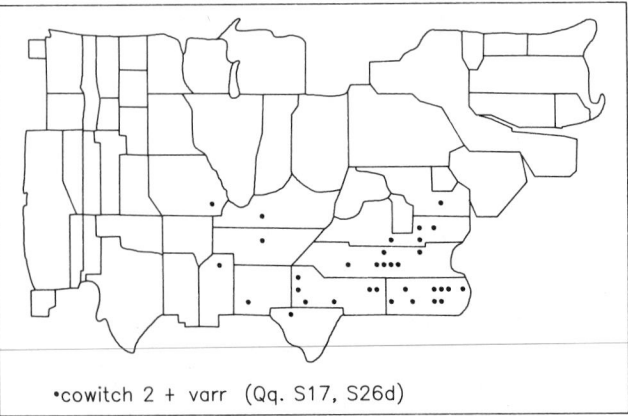

•cowitch 2 + varr (Qq. S17, S26d)

contemptuously, "cowitch," in reference to the belief that when cows eat of it the effect on their milk is harmful. **1933** Small *Manual SE Flora* 1241, *Bignonia radicans . . .* The leaves of this plant are often mistaken for those of *Toxicodendron*, whence the name "cow-itch." **1941** Walker *Lookout* 57 **TN**, It [trumpet-creeper] is known by the undignified name of cow-itch vine. **c1960** *Wilson Coll.* **csKY**, *Cow-itch . . .* The trumpet creeper *(Campsis radicans); also called devil's shoestring.* **1965–70** *DARE* (Qu. S17, *. . Other . . plants . . that . . cause itching*) 32 Infs, **chiefly SE**, Cowitch (vine); NC24, Cowitch plant; (Qu. S26d) Inf **NC21**, Cowitch vine. **1972** *DARE* File **nwFL**, 3 Infs, Cowitch — looks like the trumpet vine, by some confused with poison ivy.

3 =poison ivy. esp S Atl

1927 Boston Soc. Nat. Hist. *Proc.* 38.239 **GA**, A great deal of climbing 'cow-itch' (*Rhus [toxicodendron]*) adds to the inconvenience of getting about. **1966–68** *DARE* (Qu. S16, *A three-leaved plant that . . makes people's skin itch and swell*) Infs **FL9, 35, SC43**, Cowitch; **GA20, OK52**, Cowitch vine.

4 Transf: a skin irritation such as that caused by the aforementioned plants.

1805 Parkinson *Tour* 2.484 **MD**, The heat is frequently so great that, if sand get into your shoes, it will compel you to take them off, otherwise your toes will become excoriated. By working, ploughing, harrowing, sowing, &c. I have had my feet in that state, and which the working-people call the cow-itch. **a1883** (1911) Bagby *VA Gentleman* 48, He must . . Get the cow-itch, and live on milk and brimstone for a time. **1954** *Harder Coll.* **cwTN**, *Cow-itch:* A disease of the skin, especially of cows. Also applied to humans who have skin diseases, usually facetiously.

cow ivy n

Perh =**trumpet creeper.**

1960 Williams *Walk Egypt* 131 **GA**, She pointed to the change-house . . . It was a hut of gray scantlings just beyond the baptistry. Cow ivy veiled the roof; hickory limbs hung over each door.

cow jockey n

1 See **jockey.**

2 See quot.

1968 *DARE* (Qu. HH1, *. . A rustic or countrified person*) Inf **WI65**, Cow jockey.

cow-kicked, I'll be exclam **chiefly Nth** *often joc*

See quots.

1950 *WELS* (*Weakened substitutes for "damned": "Well I'll be _____."*) 2 Infs, **csWI**, Cow-kicked (by a mule); 1 inf, **seWI**, Cow-kicked by a grasshopper. **1965–70** *DARE* (Qu. NN7, *Exclamations of surprise*) Infs **MD20, MI51, PA104, 234, WI6, 12, 65**, I'll be cow-kicked; **MI28**, I'll be cow-kicked by a jackass; (Qu. NN25b, *Weakened substitutes for "damn" or "damned": "Well, I'll be _____."*) Infs **MI93, WA1, WI65**, Cow-kicked; **IL39**, Cow-kicked by a mule.

cow-killer ant n Also *cow ant, cow killer, cow stinger, cow wasp*

=**velvet ant.**

1889 *Century Dict.* 1321/1, *Cow-killer ant*, a Texan species of hymenopterous insects . . so called from the popular belief that these wasps, which superficially resemble ants, kill cattle by their stinging. **1899** Bergen *Animal Lore* 63, Cow-killer, cow-killer-ant, *Mutilla, Clerus* or *Trichodes. South. Ibid* 93, A hymenopterous insect, which somewhat resembles a red ant, is known as "cow-killer," from the (imaginary) effects of its sting upon cattle. *Alabama and Texas.* **1905** Kellogg *Amer. Insects* 498, Interesting wasps living habitually in nests of other wasps or bees are the Mutillidæ, popularly known as velvet-ants, cow-ants, or cow-killers. **1914** *Jrl. Amer. Folkl.* 27.246 **SC**, *Cow-ant*. The sting of the big "cow-ant" (*Sphaerophthalma occidentalis*) is deadly poison. *Ibid* **TX**, In Texas it is known as the "cow-killer ant," because of a popular superstition that its sting is very dangerous to live stock. **1933** Jaeger *CA Deserts* 58, Those furry-backed insects which so energetically wander about on the sands, and which are known as fuzzy ants or cow-killers, are really solitary, parasitic wasps. **1954** *Harder Coll.* **cwTN**, *Cow ant:* A big black ant. **1965–70** *DARE* (Qu. R17, *. . Big black ants that sting*) 15 Infs, **Sth**, Cow ant; **GA7**, Cow killer; **NC49**, Cow stinger [appears] alone, not in groups; looks like a piss-ant; (Qu. R18, *. . Kinds of ants*) 11 Infs, **Sth**, Cow ant; **AL17, FL34, IL119, NC24, 41, SC43**, Cow killer; **VA35**, Cow wasp; (Qu. R12) Inf **TX68**, Cow killers.

cow kine n pl [*cow* + uncertain element, perh *kine* or *kind*]

Cattle.

1970 *DARE* (Qu. L34) Inf **VA43**, Cow kine — milk cows and beef cows.

cow lice n

=**beggar ticks.**

1873 in 1976 Miller *Shaker Herbs* 163, *Bidens frondosa . . .* Cow Lice. **1900** Lyons *Plant Names* 63, *B[idens] frondosa . .* Cow-lice.

cowlick n

1 A lock of hair that is naturally unruly or out of place as if licked by a cow.

1889 Murfree *Despot* 36 **TN**, Her hair waved backward with a deep undulation which he called a "cow-lick," from a brow smooth and white and broad. **1905** in 1925 Moses *Repr. Amer. Dramas* 58/1, He combs his hair over his forehead in a cowlick. **1908** *DN* 3.302 **eAL, wGA**, *Cow-lick . . .* A tuft of hair on the forehead, which seems to have been licked backward. This is ordinarily considered a mark of comeliness.

2 A bald spot.

1976 *DARE* File **Baton Rouge LA** [Black], He has cowlicks.

3 A piece of cotton left in the field after picking; hence n *cowlicking* an incomplete job of picking.   Cf **goosepicking**

1968 *DARE* FW Addit **nAL**, When he was ready to go back over the field after the initial picking, he always said that he was "going back after the cowlicks." *. . Cowlicking* is synonymous with *gooselocking* or *goosepicking . . .* I am told that it is not uncommon for cotton farmers to turn geese or cattle into the fields of cotton to eat jimson weed. If the bolls are mature, the geese or cows often pick at or lick an occasional boll, pulling some of the fiber loose. This . . is why these terms are used to describe a poor job of picking cotton.

4 Fig: illegible handwriting; see quot. [From fancied resemblance to unruly tufts of hair]

1970 *DARE* (Qu. JJ11, *Joking names for handwriting that's hard to read: "I can't make anything out of his _____."*) Inf **TN53**, Cowlicks.

cowlicks n pl but sg or pl in constr

=**silverbell.**

1897 Sudworth *Arborescent Flora* 324, *Mohrodendron dipterum . .* Cow Licks (La.). **1903** Small *Flora SE U.S.* 915, *Mohrodendron dipterum . .* Cow Licks. **1960** Vines *Trees SW* 843, *Halesia diptera . .* Cowlicks.

cow lily n

1 =**spatterdock. chiefly NEng**

1862 in 1867 Lowell *Biglow* 112 'Upcountry' **MA**, There was a pool . . spotted with cow-lilies garish. **1892** *Jrl. Amer. Folkl.* 5.91 **ME**, *Nuphar advena*, cow lily. **1907** *DN* 3.185 **NH**, *Cow-lily . . .* Common *yellow* lily or spatter-dock growing in pools and ponds and bearing some resemblance to the white water-lily. "I wish those cow-lilies were pond-lilies." **1931** Clute *Common Plants* 97, The cow-lily (*Nymphæa advena*) is a coarse relative of the water-lily. **1966** *DARE* Wildfl QR Pl.56 Infs **MI57, NH4**, Cow lily. **1969–70** *DARE* (Qu. S22) Inf **CA117**, Cow lilies; (Qu. S26b) Inf **MA100**, Cow lily; **RI15**, Yellow cow lily. **1976** Bruce *How to Grow Wildflowers* 277, *Nuphar* — Spatterdocks or Cowlilies. These have leaves like their relatives the true waterlilies, but these usually stand above the water rather than float upon it.

2 A **marsh marigold** (here: *Caltha palustris*).

1959 Carleton *Index Herb. Plants* 32, *Cow-lily:* Caltha palustris.

cowlip n [Perh alter of **cowslip**]

Prob =**marsh marigold.**

1970 *DARE* (Qu. S26b, *. . Wildflowers . . that grow in wet places*) Inf **VA75**, Cowlips; (Qu. S26c, *. . Wildflowers . . that grow in meadows*) Inf **VA75**, Cowlips.

cow load n

A piece of dried cow manure.

c1937 in 1970 Yetman *Voices* 230 **NC** (as of 1860), De yer before de War started Marse Jim died. He was out in de pasture pickin' up cow loads, a-throwin' 'em in de garden. And he just drop over.

cow lot n [**lot** n] **chiefly Sth, Midl**   See Map   Cf **barn lot, cow yard**

An enclosed area where cows are kept, usu near the barn.

1896 (1909) White *Real Issue* 156 **OH**, Colonel Hucks went for a prowl down in the cow lot. **1905** *DN* 3.76 **nwAR**, *Cow-lot . . .* Cow-yard. "Our cow-lot isn't big enough." **1933** Miller *Lamb in His Bosom* 43 **GA**, They simpered at you; they were tongue-tied when you spoke to 'em, like so many heifers starin' from a cow-lot. **1949** Kurath *Word Geog.* 55, *Cow lot* and *milk lot* turn up in scattered fashion in different parts of the South and the South Midland. **c1960** *Wilson Coll.* **csKY**, *Cowlot* — uncommon in the area. **1962** Atwood *Vocab. TX* 49, *Place to enclose cows. Cow pen .* . is slightly more common than *(cow) lot* . . both, however, are current in all areas and age groups. **1965–70** *DARE* (Qu. M13, *The space near the barn with a fence around it where you keep the livestock*) 38 Infs, **chiefly Sth,** Cow lot; (Qu. M14, *The open area around or next to the barn*) 18 Infs, **chiefly east of Missip R,** Cow lot; (Qu. M22) Inf **GA**68, Cow lot.

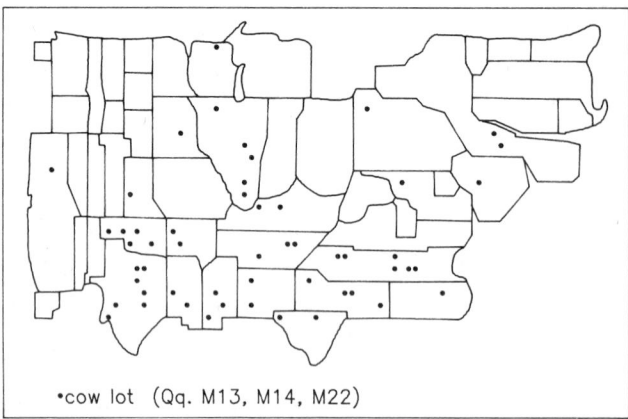

•cow lot (Qq. M13, M14, M22)

cow lot gate is open phr Cf **barn door 2b**

1954 *Harder Coll.* **cwTN,** *Cow lot gate is open.* Warning statement that a trouser fly is open.

cow mullein n

=**mullein.**

1968 *DARE* (Qu. S20, *A common weed .* . *on open hillsides:* . . *velvety green leaves .* . *tall stalk with small yellow flowers*) Inf **DE**3, Cow mullein.

cow nettle n Cf **bull nettle 1**

Perh a **spurge nettle.**

1967 *DARE* (Qu. S17, . . *Other kinds of plants .* . *that will cause itching and swelling*) Inf **TX**35, Bull nettle, cow nettle.

cownose ray n Also *cownosed ray*

An **eagle ray** (here: *Rhinoptera bonasus*).

1814 in 1815 *Lit. & Philos. Soc. NY Trans.* 1.479, Cow-nosed Ray. *(Raja bonasus.)* With a blunt snout resembling the nose of an ox . . . A shoal of cow-noses roots on the salt waterflats as completely as a drove of hogs would do. **1842** DeKay *Zool. NY* 4.375, The Cow-nosed Ray . . is an exceedingly common species about New York in the autumn. **1896** U.S. Natl. Museum *Bulletin* 47.1.90, *Rhinoptera Bonasus* . . Cow-nose Ray. **1960** Amer. Fisheries Soc. *List Fishes* 9, Cownose ray . . *Rhinoptera bonasus.*

cow oak n

Either of two similar oaks: the **basket oak 1** or the **swamp chestnut oak.**

1884 Sargent *Forests of N. Amer.* 141, *Quercus Michauxii* . . . Cow Oak. **1903** Small *Flora SE U.S.* 354, *Quercus Michauxii* . . . Cow Oak. **1930** OK Univ. Biol. Surv. *Pub.* 2.1.58, *Quercus prinus* . . . Cow Oak. **1960** Vines *Trees SW* 153, Swamp Chestnut Oak. *Quercus prinus* . . . Cow Oak. **1979** Little *Checklist U.S. Trees* 236, *Quercus michauxii* . . cow oak.

cow onion n

1968 *DARE* (Qu. I5, *The kind of onions that come up fresh early in the year, and you eat them raw*) Inf **NY**83, Cow onions.

cow pancake See **cow cake**

cow pap n [From the shape of the flower]

=**bladder campion.**

1923 W.N. Clute *American Plant Names* 63 *(DAE),* Bladder Campion. —Cow-paps, cow-bell, bull-rattle . . . maiden's tears.

cow parlor n

1969 *DARE* (Qu. M1, . . *Different or special kinds of barns*) Inf **IL**63, Cow parlor—three sides: the cows are loose inside, not in stanchions.

cow parsley n

Prob =**cow parsnip 1.**

[**1876** Hobbs *Bot. Hdbk.* 27, Cow parsley . . Heracleum sphondylium.] **1937** *Torreya* 37.6, Cowbane, cow parsley, cow parsnip, all poisonous umbelliferous plants. **1969** *DARE* (Qu. I28a, *What kinds of things do you call "greens"—those that are eaten raw*) Inf **MO**37, Cow parsley.

cow parsnip n

1 An umbelliferous plant of the genus *Heracleum* (esp *H. lanatum*) with large compound leaves and broad umbels of white flowers. Also called **cow cabbage, eltrot, Hercules' parsnip, hogweed, masterwort**

1796 Morse *Amer. Universal Geog.* 1.188, Cow parsnep (Heracleum foliis ternatis). **1950** Gray–Fernald *Manual of Botany* 1104, *Heracleum .* . Cow-parsnip. **1961** Douglas *My Wilderness* 20 **CO,** Cow parsnip also grows to giant proportions. **1966** *DARE* Wildfl QR Pl.149 Infs **MI**7, **MN**14, **OR**12, Cow parsnip. **1966–67** *DARE* (Qu. S26e, *Other wildflowers*) Infs **DC**2, **MI**31, Cow parsnip.

2 =**golden alexanders.**

1864 *Catalogue of Herbs,* Cowparsnip, Royal. *(Zizia aurea).*

cow pass n chiefly NEast See Map

A cattle crossing.

1965–70 *DARE* (Qu. N31, *A place in a road where animals regularly go across*) 19 Infs, **chiefly NEast,** Cow pass.

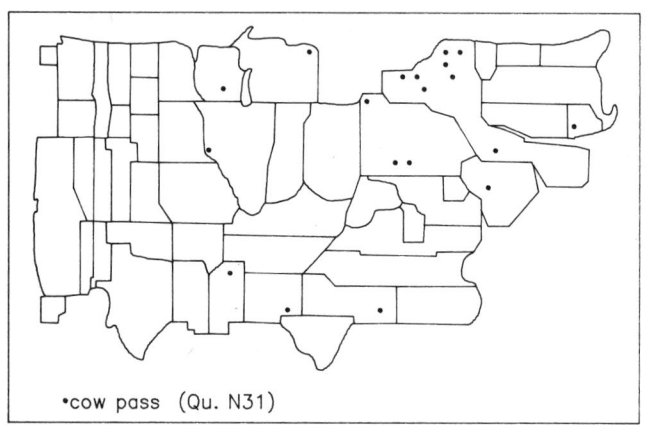

•cow pass (Qu. N31)

cow paste See **cow grease**

‡cowpasture line n

A local and perhaps primitive telephone line.

1934 (1970) Wilson *Backwoods Amer.* 11 **AR, MO,** The old lawyer let him have a try at the phone. Uncle Homer proceeded to call over the cowpasture line to the Brentwood store.

cow pathies exclam

1967 *DARE* FW Addit **seNY,** *Cow pathies*—a call used in marble play to allow the player to draw a path to the opponent's marble.

cowpea n, also attrib **chiefly Sth, Midl**

=**black-eyed pea.**

1776 in 1908 *William & Mary Qrly.* 17.17, The ground . . must be got ready . . as soon as it is run over with the cow-pease. **1844** Thompson *Major Jones's Courtship* 31 **GA,** Thar's rich land, pore land what can be made tolerable good, and some bominable shaller, rollin truck what all the manure in creation wouldn't make grow cow peas. **1912** U.S. Dept. Ag. *Farmers' Bulletins* 509.28, Cowpea hay is often cured by stacking the wilted vines around poles. **1934** Carmer *Stars Fell on AL* 40, We went back to the kitchen and sat down to a steaming mess of salt pork, collard greens, cowpeas and corn bread. **1942** (1960) Robertson *Red Hills* 65 **SC,** I never heard this invocation varied except once when one of our cousins, who did not care for cowpeas and fat back, bowed his head and said: "Good God, look at this." **1965–70** *DARE* (Qu. I19, *Small white bean with a black spot where they were joined to the pod*) 24 Infs, **esp Midl,** Cowpeas; **MI**116, Black-eyed cowpeas; (Qu. I20) 14 Infs, **chiefly S Atl,** Cowpeas; (Qu. L9b) Infs **GA**84, **IN**35, **KY**58, **OH**44, **SC**63, **VA**77, Cowpea(s); **NC**33, **VA**26, Cowpea hay. **1970** Correll *Plants TX* 889, *Vigna unguiculata* . . Cowpea. **1970** Major *Afro-Amer. Slang,* Cow pea soup: soul-food vegetable often cooked with ham bones and onions. **1970** *DARE* File **swKY,** Cowpeas—speckled: a variety of field pea not usually grown in the garden; used for pea hay, though also used for human consumption.

cowpen v *esp* **VA** *old-fash*

To fertilize land by enclosing cattle on it; hence vbl n *cowpenning*.

1688 in 1693 *Royal Soc. London Philos. Trans.* 17.979 **VA,** So that after they have cleared a fresh piece of Ground out in the Woods, it will not bear Tobacco past two or three Years, unless Cow-pen'd. *Ibid* 984, Hitherto, as I have said, they used none [i.e. no system of fertilization] but that of Cowpenning. **1786** (1925) Washington *Diaries* 3.131 **VA,** [I] plowed a poor ½ acre to Cowpen on. **1870** *TX Almanac* 12, Cow-penning, in successive lots, . . is a good plan for manuring. **1899** (1912) Green *VA Folk-Speech*, Cowpen . . . To manure land by penning cattle on it.

cow-pen bird n

=**cowbird 1.**

1731 (1754) Catesby *Nat. Hist. Carolina* 1.34, *Passer fusca. The Cowpen Bird* . . . They delight much to feed in the Pens of Cattle, which has given them their Name. **1844** Giraud *Birds Long Is.* 139, Cow-pen Bird. **1887** C. C. Abbot *Waste-Land Wand.* 55 (DA), The cowpen-bird, which is never mated, and for several months in the year deposits fertile eggs in the nests of other birds. **1955** *Oriole* 20.13, Cowbird . . . Cowpen Bird.

cow-pen bunting n

=**cowbird 1.**

1857 U.S. Patent Office *Annual Rept. for 1856: Ag.* 129, Associating partially with reed-birds, grackles, and cow-pen buntings . . they [=red-winged starlings] move to the Southern States. **1895** Minot *Land-Birds New Engl.* 254, *Molothrus ater* . . . Cow-pen Bunting.

cow-pen daisy n

A **crownbeard** (here: *Verbesina encelioides*).

1970 Correll *Plants TX* 1656, *Verbesina encelioides* . . . Cowpen daisy.

cow-pen Spanish n **SW**

Colloquial Mexican Spanish.

1930 Dobie *Coronado* 117 **TX,** The Texans talked "Mexican," or "cowpen Spanish," as fluently as though they were natives. **1977** Watts *Dict. Old West*, Cowpen Spanish—Bad Spanish such as that picked up by cowhands in the Southwest from Mexican vaqueros.

cow-pen tea n

A medicinal drink made from cow manure.

1897 (1952) McGill *Narrative* 45 **SC** (as of 1820s), These toddies were now substituted for Pride America root tea, boiled down quite thick, and given to both white and colored children before eating in the morning, which the writer was dosed with in his earliest years as a prophylactic, and which vermifuge must have been quite an improvement in elegance, if not in remedy, on Cow Pen tea, used however before his time, yet nevertheless true.

cowpile n

A dropping of cow manure.

c1960 *Wilson Coll.* **csKY,** Cowpile is the regular term; cowflop has always been unknown when I have suggested it as a synonym. **1968** *DARE* FW Addit **LA**11, Cow manure was called cowpiles and it stunk like polecats on cow stomps.

cow plant n

A **rosebay** (here: *Rhododendron maximum*).

1894 *Jrl. Amer. Folkl.* 7.93, *Rhododendron maximum* . . cow-plant, Montpelier, Vt.

cow poison n [See quot 1949] *chiefly* **CA**

A delphinium (here: *D. trolliifolium*).

1911 *Century Dict.*, Cow-poison . . . The *Delphinium trolliifolium* of California, a native larkspur. **1925** Jepson *Manual Plants CA* 377, Cow Poison. **1949** Moldenke *Amer. Wild Flowers* 13, All larkspurs contain a poisonous principle . . . A related species along the California and Oregon coast, *D[elphinium] trolliifolium*, is called *cowpoison* for this reason.

cow-poison vine n

An unidentified plant.

1851 *DeBow's Rev.* 11.48, Cow Poison Vine grows short and jointed.

cow poke n[1]

Prob =**pokeweed 1.**

1968 *DARE* (Qu. I28b, *Kinds of greens that are cooked*) Inf **NH**14, Cow poke.

cowpoke n[2] [Prob alter of **cowpuncher** infl by *poke* to punch]

1 A cowboy, but see quot 1977.

1881 in 1944 *ADD* **CO,** Cowpoke. **1928** *Lariat Mag.* Jan. (DA), I camped there once, and a cowpoke told me why they were named that. **1936** McCarthy *Lang. Mosshorn* [Rodeo Terms], Cowpolk [sic]. An amateur bronc rider. **1949** *PADS* 11.20 **CO.** **1962** Atwood *Vocab. TX* 53, Cowpuncher . . and cowpoke . . are also in occasional use, the latter particularly in the Northwest. **1966** *News & Observer* (Raleigh NC) 22 Aug 8, [Photo caption:] Cowpokes Mary Ann Whitty and Benny Brenn . . get together with Indians Betsy Smith . . Barbara Todd, and Willie Taylor [at a "Western" party]. **1973** Allen *LAUM* 1.406, A ranch employee who works with cattle is still widely identified . . in Nebraska by *cowpoke*. **1977** Watts *Dict. Old West*, Cowpoke—Originally—say, from the late 1860s through the 1880s, at a guess—it meant those men who were employed on the cattle-trains carrying live cattle to the East and who kept the cows on their feet during the journey by the use of a long goad. In later years, it was applied to a cowhand.

2 See quots. Cf **cow hook**

1968 Adams *Western Words*, Cow poke—A device to prevent fence crawling, made of a green sapling about 4 feet long and with a forked prong. This was put on top of the animal's neck and lashed with a piece of rope well up on the neck. **1984** *MJLF* 10.148 **WI,** Cow poke. A metal collar with spurs top and bottom, and put around a cow's neck to keep her from pushing her head out through the fence.

cow pony See **cow horse**

cow pound n *esp* **Delmarva** Cf **cuppen**

An enclosure for cows.

1946 *PADS* 5.17 **VA,** Cow pound . . . Pen for cows; on the Eastern Shore and on the point of land east of Norfolk. **1949** Kurath *Word Geog.* 55/1, In Delamarvia and on Albemarle Sound *(cow) pound* still predominates, and in a belt directly west of the *pound* area on Albemarle Sound one hears *cow brake*. **1971** Wood *Vocab. Change* 47/1 **Sth,** Cow brake, cow pound, cuppin, and *farm lot* are chosen more often east of the Mississippi than west of it.

cow prod n Also *cow prodder* Cf **cowpoke** n[2] **1**, **cowpuncher 1**

A cowboy.

1930 Henry *Conquering Plains* 51 **SW** (as of 1868), For the cowprodders, and sometimes the drovers, to go about fully armed, presumably ready to shoot men on sight, soon grew to be the well-known disposition in this unorganized, humming, little universe. **1961** Adams *Old-Time Cowhand* 191, Most all good cow prods love their hosses. **1977** Watts *Dict. Old West*, Cowprod—A cowboy.

cow pumpkin n Also *cow punkin* [From its use as cattle feed]

A field pumpkin (*Cucurbita pepo* var *pepo*).

1935 *AmSp* 170/2 **PA,** The round yellow things, good for making jack-o'-lanterns, are here called *cow-punkins* and are not in great favor. **1968** *DARE* (Qu. I23 . . *Kinds of squash*) Inf **CT**6, Cow pumpkin; **MD**30, Cow punkin: round, yellow—children make jack-o-lanterns of them; (Qu. I24, . . *Kinds of pumpkins*) Inf **MS**16, Cow pumpkin.

cowpunch v **SW**

To herd cattle; hence vbl n *cowpunching*.

1881 Romspert *W. Echo* 189, Some of them have been cowpunching —as it is called—for many years, and know every water for hundreds of miles around. **1918** Lomax *Cowboy Songs* 368, He's sold him his saddle, his spurs and his rope, / And there's no more cow punching, and that's what I hope. **1921** Gillett *TX Rangers* 27 (as of 1874), I had cow-punched and seen Indian raids.

cowpuncher n

1 A cowboy. *chiefly* **West** Cf **cowpoke** n[2] **1**, **cow prod**

1878 in 1939 *Colorado Mag.* 16.152, At Hugo the cow-punchers were assembling for the round-up. **1913** *DN* 4.10 **MN.** **1920** *Hunter Trail Drivers TX* 50 **OK** (as of 1882), At this time a general roundup was in progress and I believe there were a hundred and fifty cow-punchers in the place. **1937** *DN* 6.620 **swTX,** The cowboy . . is indifferently called *cow-hand, ranch-hand, cowpuncher, rawhide, waddie,* or *cow-waddie.* **1962** Atwood *Vocab. TX* 53, Ranch employee. The ordinary hired hand on a ranch is generally known as a *cowhand* . . . Cowpuncher . . and *cowpoke* . . are also in occasional use. **1966** *DARE* Tape **OK**30, In the fall . . they wouldn't have the use for all these cowpunchers. **1968** Adams *Western Words*, Cowpuncher—A more recent name for a cowboy, derived from the metal-pointed rod employed to drive cattle into stock cars . . . *Cowpuncher* is usually shortened to *puncher.* **1973** Allen

LAUM 1.406, A ranch employee who works with cattle is still widely identified by *cowboy* or, less often, by *cowpuncher.*

2 One who prods cattle; the prod itself.

1966 *DARE* (Qu. K27, *Sharp-pointed stick . . to get oxen to move*) Inf **AR**21, Cowpuncher. **1968** *DARE* Tape **WV**2, They called 'em [=men who goaded oxen while plowing] cowpunchers. [FW:] I thought that was strictly a western term. [Inf:] Well, it was. They called 'em that, but they called 'em that along the South Branch River in nineteen and nineteen.

3 A veterinarian.

1975 Gould *ME Lingo* 61, *Cow puncher*—A doctor of veterinary medicine . . . The term was used in Maine long before they had cows in Wyoming. The first stomach of a cow is called the rumen, and sometimes from eating apples or perhaps some fermented grain or pomace a cow would bloat . . . Standard treatment was to "punch" the cow with an awl or the small blade of a jackknife. This released the gas . . . As recently as the 1920s a Maine veterinarian was referring to himself pleasantly as "one of the last real old *cow punchers* left in the state!"

cow punkin See **cow pumpkin**

‡cow-pusher n Cf **cow train**

1950 *WELS* (A train that stops at every station) 1 Inf, **seWI**, Cow-pusher.

cow rattle n Cf **bull rattle**

Either of two related plants: the **white campion 1** or the **cowherb.**

1900 Lyons *Plant Names* 231, *L[ychnis] alba* . . . Bull-rattle, Cow-rattle. **1910** Graves *Flowering Plants* 180 **CT**, *Saponaria Vaccaria* . . . Cow-herb. Field Soapwort. Cow-rattle. Cockle. **1959** Carleton *Index Herb. Plants* 32, *Cow Rattle:* Lychnis alba.

cow rigging n

1968 Adams *Western Words*, Cow rigging—Clothes, or the costume, worn by the cowman when he is working. As one cowhand said, "You'd have to be some persuader to get a puncher to shed his cow riggin' for any of that gearin' of the shorthorn."

cow run n

1967–70 *DARE* (Qu. M13, *The space near the barn with a fence around it where you keep the livestock*) Inf **MA**75, Cow run; (Qu. M14, *The open area around or next to the barn*) Inf **MN**2, Cow run.

cows See **cous**

cow saddle n Also *cowboy saddle* **West**

A heavy saddle built for roping and holding livestock.

1881 Romspert *W. Echo* 173, The average cow-boy saddle weighs forty pounds, and *some* weigh *sixty-five pounds.* **1895** Remington *Pony Tracks* 1, I inspected them (=horses), and saw that one had a "cow saddle." **1903** *Forest & Stream* 60.147, A bit farther on we saw some cowpunchers, or what seemed such, for they sat in cow saddles and wore chaparejos. **1966** Barnes–Jensen *Dict. UT Slang*, Cow-saddle . . a heavy saddle suitable for use in roping cattle.

cow sailor n

1942 *ME Univ. Studies* 67, Before the end of the War of the States coasting vessels were small and often unseaworthy . . . They were looked down upon by deep water sailors who called their crews "cow sailors," because along the coast of Maine they farmed it part of the year.

cow salve See **cow grease**

cow's brother See **cow's husband**

cow sense n [By analogy with *horse sense*] **West**

1 Practical knowledge of cattle-handling.

1903 (1965) Adams *Log Cowboy* 309, The wisdom of mounting us well for just such an emergency reflected the good cow sense of our employer. **1941** FWP *Guide WY* 122, The tales 'traded' give life and currency to such expressions as 'cow sense' . . and 'running iron'. **1968** Adams *Western Words*, Cow sense—Such sense as is needed for success in cattle raising. **1977** Watts *Dict. Old West*, Cow sense—A man, a horse, or a dog could have cow sense, but it was applied particularly to a good *cutting horse* . . . The term implied that they understood cows and possibly anticipated their moves.

2 Common sense.

1942 *AmSp* 17.75 **nwNE**, A sandhiller who shows a lack of judgment or is careless is said *not to have cow sense.* **1968** Adams *Western Words*, Cow sense—Common sense.

cow's eye See **cow eye**

cow's foot n

Perh =**coltsfoot 1.**

1965 *DARE* (Qu. S21, . . *Weeds . . that are a trouble in gardens and fields*) Inf **MS**59, Cow's foot.

cow's husband n Also *cow's brother,* ~ *gentleman friend,* ~ *spouse* *euphem* or *joc*

A bull.

1834 *Life Andrew Jackson* 120, In one place, the gineral seed the Bullites [=English soldiers], every one with a cag-mag [=inferior meat], a piece of cow's spouse [=bull], or an Essex lion [=calf] in his wallet. **1942** Berrey–Van den Bark *Amer. Slang* 120.15, Bull . . . Cow's husband. **1966–68** *DARE* (Qu. K22, . . *A bull*) Inf **NY**65, Cow's husband; (Qu. K23, *Words used by women in mixed company for a bull*) Inf **CA**3, Cow's husband; **DC**8, Cow's brother; **MD**48, Cow's gentleman friend.

cowskin n

=**cowhide** n **1.**

1738 (1960) Franklin *Papers* 2.225 **PA**, A good Cowskin, Crabtree or Bulls pizzle may be plentifully bestow'd on your outward Man. **1838** (1852) Gilman *S. Matron* 260, I unthinkingly drew my scented pocket-handkerchief from my bag, when out flew the ratan with a bound. My deep and inextinguishable blush probably helped on any uncharitable surmises that she might have made, . . that Charleston ladies carried cowskins in their pockets! **1854** in 1957 Old Farmer's Almanac *Sampler* 160, Some schoolmasters know no other way but to fret and scold, and use the cowskin or ferule. **1947** *Western PA Hist. Mag.* 30.34 (as of 1805), Tarleton avoided this scheme by attacking Pentland and giving him a chastisement with a "cowskin," or what is now known as a rawhide whip.

cow skinner n

1968 Adams *Western Words*, Cow skinner—A severe winter storm which kills cattle and from which all the owner can salvage is the hides.

cowslip n

1 =**marsh marigold. chiefly Nth, esp NEast**

1778 Carver *Travels N. Amer.* 520, Flowers. Heart's Ease . . . Cowslips. **1822** Eaton *Botany* 215, *Caltha palustris* . . . American cowslip. **1907** *DN* 3.185 **NH**, Cowslip . . . Marsh marigold (Caltha). A yellow flower growing in spring in the swamps of southeastern New Hampshire. Before it blossoms the plant has very delicate greens. "It's fun to pick cowslips and then peddle 'em." Same as *coltsfoot.* **1951** Voss *IL Wild Flowers* 15, American Cowslip—*Caltha palustris* . . . Cowslips, many people call them. The young shoots are used for greens in some parts of the country. **1965–70** *DARE* (Qu. S22) 258 Infs, **chiefly Nth**, Cowslip(s); **RI**10, English cowslip; (Qu. S26b) 9 Infs, **chiefly NY, PA**, Cowslip(s); (Qu. S26c) Inf **IN**17, Cowslip; (Qu. S26d) Inf **ID**1, Cowslip; (Qu. S26e) Infs **MA**25, **SC**36, Cowslip(s); (Qu. I28b) 23 Infs, **chiefly NY, NEng**, Cowslip(s); (Qu. I28a) Infs **MA**5, 15, **NY**21, 176, **PA**128, Cowslip; **ME**5, Cowslip greens; **CT**12, 17, Cowslips; (Qu. BB22) Inf **NY**2, Cowslip.

2 as *American cowslip, false* ~: =**shooting star** (esp *Dodecatheon meadia*).

1822 Eaton *Botany* 268, *Dodecatheon meadia* . . false-cowslip. **1840** MA Zool. & Bot. Surv. *Herb. Plants & Quadrupeds* 153, *D[odecatheon] Meadia* . . . False Cowslip. American Cowslip. **1903** Small *Flora SE U.S.* 905, *Dodecatheon* . . . American cowslip. **1937** Stemen *OK Flora* 386, *Dodecatheon Meadia* . . . American Cowslip. **1970** Correll *Plants TX* 1183, *Dodecatheon* . . . American cowslip.

3 often with a qualifier: =**bluebell 1g** (esp *Mertensia virginica*).

1837 Darlington *Flora Cestrica* 117, *P[ulmonaria] virginica* . . . Virginian Cowslip. **1857** Gray *Manual of Botany* (rev.) 323, *M[ertensia] Virginica* . . . (Virginian Cowslip or Lungwort). **1900** Lyons *Plant Names* 246, Virginia Cowslip, American Cowslip. **1933** Small *Manual SE Flora* 1123, Virginia-cowslip. **1946** Tatnall *Flora DE* 217, *M. virginica* . . . Virginia (or Brandywine) Cowslip. **1951** Voss *IL Wild Flowers* 55, Cowslips. **1966** *DARE* Wildfl QR Pl.181 Inf **CO**11, Bluebell—Colorado cowslip.

4 A trillium.

1897 *Jrl. Amer. Folkl.* 10.145 **IN**, *Trillium recurvatum* . . cowslip. **1965** *DARE* (Qu. S2, *What do you call the flower that comes up in the woods early in spring, with three white petals that turn pink as the flower grows older*) Inf **FL**22, Cowslip.

5 A false lily of the valley (here: *Maianthemum canadense*).

1892 *Jrl. Amer. Folkl.* 5.104, *Maianthemum Canadense,* cowslip. Dennysville, Me. **1940** Clute *Amer. Plant Names* 13, *M. Canadense* . . . Cowslip.

cowslip vine n

A **ground cherry** (here: *Physalis mollis*).

1951 *PADS* 15.38 **TX,** *Physalis mollis* . . . Cowslip vines; paper hearts.

cowslop n [Evid preservation of OE and ME var form of *cow-slip*] **NEng**

=**marsh marigold.**

1869 Fuller *Uncle John* 26, She said, "Cowslops is Cowslops, and noffin else; and theys good for noffin in the world but to bile for greens." **1871** (1882) Stowe *Fireside Stories* 34 **NEng,** She was jest as chirk and chipper as a wren, . . a black-berryin' and diggin' sweet-flag, and gettin cowslops and dandelions. **1893** *Jrl. Amer. Folkl.* 6.136 **VT,** *Caltha palustris* . . cowslops. **1907** *DN* 3.185 **seNH,** Cowslops. Facetious for cowslips (*Caltha*). An archaic form.

cow's mouth n

A notch put in a tree to direct the fall; the felling notch.

1927 *AmSp* 2.351 **cwWV,** *Cow's mouth, to put in the* . . to cut the felling notch in a tree for the sawyer. "Put the cow's mouth on the north side of that tree, and it will not fall over the haul road." **1968** Adams *Western Words, Cow's mouth*—What the logger calls the falling notch in a tree.

cow snake n Cf **cowsucker**

1 =**bull snake.**

1804 (1905) Lewis *Orig. Jrls. Lewis & Clark Exped.* 6.124, This snake is vulgarly called the cow or bull snake from a bellowing nois which it is said sometimes to make resembling that anamal. **1946** Stuart *Tales Plum Grove* 227 **KY,** I ran upstairs and killed two cow-snakes restin' on the wall plate.

2 A **king snake 1,** but esp the **milk snake 1.**

1965–70 *DARE* (Qu. P25, *What kinds of snakes are found around here?*) 9 Infs, **KY, IN, OH,** Cow snake. [All Infs old or mid-aged]

cow snipe n

=**pectoral sandpiper.**

1888 Trumbull *Names of Birds* 176, [Pectoral Sandpiper] At Alexandria, Va., Cow-snipe. **1923** U.S. Dept. Ag. *Misc. Circular* 13.54, *Pectoral Sandpiper* . . . *Vernacular Names* . . . *In local use* . . . Cow snipe (Va.). **1946** Hausman *Eastern Birds* 278, *Pectoral Sandpiper* . . *Other Names* . . Cow Snipe.

cow spider n

An unidentified spider.

1969 *DARE* (Qu. R28, *Different kinds of spiders . . around here*) Inf **CA**155, Cow spiders; **CA**165, Cow spider: great fat yellow one.

cow squash n Cf **cow pumpkin**

Perh a field pumpkin (*Cucurbita pepo* var *pepo*).

1966 *DARE* (Qu. I23, *Kinds of squash . . around here*) Inf **DC**8, Cow squash.

cow's spouse See **cow's husband**

cow stable n **widespread exc in West** See Map

A cow barn.

1796 Barton *Disappointment* 63 **PA,** Hide yourself in the cow-stable. **1883** Eggleston *Hoosier Schoolboy* 21, He found "King Milkmaid" written on the door of his father's cow-stable. **1965–70** *DARE* (Qu. M10, *Part of the barn where cows are kept*) 185 Infs, **widespread exc in West,** Cow stable(s).

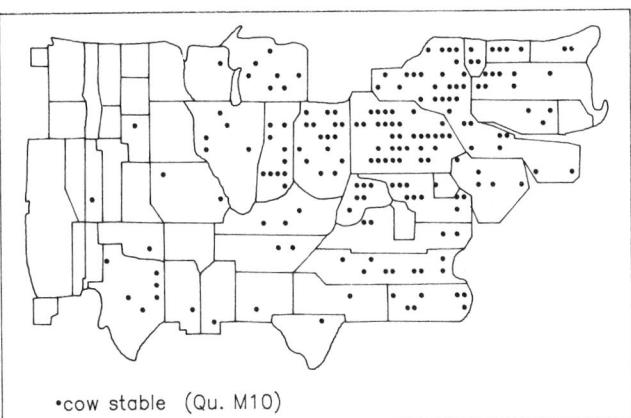
•cow stable (Qu. M10)

cow's tail n

1 =**horseweed 1.**

1876 Hobbs *Bot. Hdbk.* 27, Cows' tail, Canada fleabane, Erigeron Canadense. **1930** Sievers *Amer. Med. Plants* 37, Horseweed . . . *Other common names* . . . Cow's-tail. **1959** Carleton *Index Herb. Plants* 32.

2 also *cow tail:* The last one to arrive; a tagalong. **esp Midl, Sth**

1908 *DN* 3.302 **eAL, wGA,** *Cow's tail* . . . The last one. "He is always the cow's tail." "You are always the old cow's tail." **1939** Harris *Purslane* 76 **cNC,** He left the other fodder pullers and didn't even stop to holler—to "crow," they called it, at the cow's tail—at the end of the row, but hurried into another. **1942** Whipple *Joshua* 469 **UT,** There was a knock at the door and Erastus and his three wives bundled in . . . 'The cow's tail!' someone greeted him. **1950** *WELS (Somebody who always follows along behind)* 3 Infs, **WI,** Cow's tail. **c1960** *Wilson Coll.* **csKY,** *Cow's tail:* Humorous reference to someone who is always behind, like a cow's tail. **1965–70** *DARE* (Qu. Y9, *Somebody who always follows along behind others: "His little brother is an awful _____."*) Infs **CA**36, **DE**2, **LA**2, **MD**17, **PA**1, **SC**44, Cow's tail; **SC**10, 40, Cow tail.

3 A frayed rope; fig, unkempt hair.

1970 *DARE* Tape **PA**235, Then we had what they called a cat's tail, or cow's tail, which was used—it was only odds and ends [of rope], maybe some of 'em six feet long . . it was used more on a yawl to haul anybody off the dam that we found. **1975** Gould *ME Lingo, Cow's tail*—The frayed ends of a rope, looking very like a cow's tail. The straggly hair of a child may be called a *cow's tail. Irish pennants.*

4 See quot. [Prob infl by **mare's tail 1**]

1968 *DARE* (Qu. B10, . . *Long trailing clouds high in the sky*) Inf **WV**13, Cows' tails.

cow stinger See **cow-killer ant**

cow stomp See **stomp** n

cow's tongue n

1 A prickly pear.

1982 *NY Times* (NY) 3 Jan sec 10 17/2 **AZ,** Clusters of hedgehog cactus, and prickly pear with names like clockface and cows-tongue, have wedged roots into the rock.

2 Fig: see quot.

1975 Gould *ME Lingo, Cow's tongue*—From the rough and smooth sides of a cow's tongue; a two-faced person. A hypocrite. Also, a gruff old codger who is soft-hearted.

cow storm n Cf **chicken rain**

1914 *DN* 4.155 **Cape Cod MA,** *Cow-storm* . . . A drizzling rain unaccompanied by wind. "'T ain't really rainin', —just a reg'lar cow-storm."

cowsucker n [So called because these snakes were thought to suck milk from cows] Cf **cow snake**

1 =**racer 1.**

1904 Conway *Autobiog.* 1.22 **ceVA,** Any deficiency of milk in a cow was ascribed to the "cowsucker" (black snake). **1925** TX Folkl. Soc. *Pub.* 4.45, The milk snake, or cow-sucker, is supposed to visit cow lots and clandestinely to relieve cows of their milk . . . In Louisiana . . the name has been shifted to the southern phase of the blue racer. **1968** *DARE* (Qu. P25) Inf **MO**38, Black snakes—the old 'cowsucker' they call 'em.

2 A **king snake 1,** esp the **milk snake 1. esp KY, Delmarva**

1925 TX Folkl. Soc. *Pub.* 4.45, *The Milk Snake or Cow-Sucker* . . . In some states, the name is applied to a variety of king snake; in Indiana, to *Lampropeltis triangulum* . . and in southeastern Missouri, to its scarlet cousin, *Lampropeltis triangulum amaura.* **1948** *Atlantic Mth.* Feb 88/1 **KY,** To the last, though, the little cowsucker would coil and vibrate his tail and strike savagely but harmlessly at our hands. **1965–70** *DARE* (Qu. P25) Infs **DE**4, **IN**13, **KY**9, 11, 53, 65, 72, **VA**75, 79, 89, Cowsucker(s); **DE**3, King snake or cowsucker—black and white—old-fashioned; **KY**35, Cowsucker or cow snake; **MD**42, Cowsucker—like black snake, but has lots of white splotches; nonpoisonous, reputed to suck milk from cow. [12 of 13 Infs old or mid-aged]

3 See quot.

1969 *DARE* (Qu. O2, *Nicknames . . for an old, clumsy boat*) Inf **PA**231, Cowsucker.

cow tail n See **cow's tail 2**

cowtail v

See quots.

1970 *Thompson Coll.* **cnAL** (as of 1920s), *Cowtail:* To drive a baseball away out yonder—"I told you I was gonna cowtail it if you didn't." **1982** *DARE* File, Our Red Sox TV game announcers . . employ some colorful usage which makes listening great fun. The other night during one of our magnificent victories one of them, Mr. Martin, I believe, said, possibly after a home run: "That ball was really *cow-tailed* out of here."

cow thistle n

Prob a *sow thistle*.

1967–68 *DARE* (Qu. I28b, *Kinds of greens that are cooked*) Inf **KY**34, Cow thistle; (Qu. S26d, *Wildflowers that grow in meadows*) Inf **DE**3, Cow thistle.

cowthump, cowthumpi(a)n See **callithumpian**

cow tick n

1 The cattle tick *(Boophilus annulatus).* **Sth**

1966–68 *DARE* (Qu. R23a, *Insects . . that fasten themselves to the skin and suck blood—on land*) Infs **AL**10, **GA**28, **LA**10, **MS**6, **SC**43, **TX**17, Cow ticks.

2 =**cowbird 1.**

1936 *Oriole* 1.13, Cowbird *[Molothrus ater]* . . . Cow-tick (perhaps from its clambering over cattle in search of ticks).

cow time n

Feeding or chore time on a farm.

1968 *DARE* (Qu. L4b, *The time early in the morning or at night . . to feed livestock, clean stalls, and so on*) Inf **NJ**53, Cow time. **1973** Allen *LAUM* 1.258 **ND**, *Feeding time . . .* cow time. [1 inf]

cowtongue n

1 =**bead lily.** [Perh from the shape of the leaf]

1892 *Jrl. Amer. Folkl.* 5.104, *Clintonia borealis,* cow-tongue.

2 See quot.

1978 *DARE* File **neSC**, *Cowtongue,* a candy much like the present sugar daddy, which would keep a child quiet for hours. [Inventory from an old country store]

cow-tongue prickly pear n

A **prickly pear** (here: *Opuntia linguiformis*).

1960 Vines *Trees SW* 778, Cow-tongue Prickly Pear. *Opuntia linguiformis. . .* The species name, *linguiformis,* refers to the "tongue-shaped" joints.

cow topper n [*top* v to copulate with + *-er*] *euphem*

A bull.

1939 *LANE* Map 190 1 inf, **seNH**, *Bull*—Cow topper, 'kids use it'.

cow town n Rarely *cattle town* **chiefly West**

A community based largely on the cattle industry; a small town, sometimes assumed by city dwellers to be provincial.

1885 *Santa Fe W. New Mexican* 3 Dec 4/1 *(DA),* St. Louis is the biggest cowtown on earth just at present. **1935** *AmSp* 10.80 **seMO**, In a county where no stock law exists, [the terms] *Cowtown, Hog Wallow,* or *Hog-Eye* may be applied [to a nondescript place]. **1947** *Time* 3 Feb 82/2 **TX**, His father was a well-fixed cattleman, banker and hotel proprietor in the little cow town of Canadian. **1961** Sackett–Koch *KS Folkl.* 112, *Cow town . . .* A town such as Abilene on the Union Pacific or Dodge City on the Santa Fe from which were shipped the cattle from the great ranges of the west. These towns are still often called cow towns. **1967** *DARE* Tape **TX**11, Well, it was a cow town, was all it was. A small cow town. **1967–69** *DARE* FW Addit **CO**21, Cow towns: Dallas, Ft. Worth, and Denver, before they lost their charm and uniqueness; **swTX**, Cow Town—a nickname of Ft. Worth.

cow train n [Perh by analogy with *milk train*]

1951 Johnson *Resp. to PADS 20* **DE**, *(Names for a train that stops at every station along the way)* Cow train.

cow trap n

1967 *DARE* (Qu. M14, *The open area around or next to the barn*) Inf **TX**3, Cow trap. [FW: Sometimes these are enormous.]

cow-turd cooter See **cow-dung cooter**

cow turnip See **cow beet**

cow vetch n

=**Canada pea 1.**

1953 Greene–Blomquist *Flowers South* 61, Canada-pea or cow-vetch *(V. Cracca)* is . . naturalized in fields and waste places. **1959** Anderson

Flora AK 324, *Vicia cracca . .* Cow Vetch. **1961** Peck *Manual OR* 492, *Vicia Cracca . .* Cow Vetch. **1976** Bailey–Bailey *Hortus Third* 1155, *Vicia Cracca . .* Cow vetch.

cow vine n

=**bindweed 1.**

1970 *DARE* (Qu. S5, . . *The wild morning glory*) Infs **KY**71, 77, Cow vine.

cow waddy n Also sp *cow waddie* [**waddy**] **chiefly SW**

A cowboy.

1923 Cook *50 Yrs.* 19 **TX**, Trouble would come to the "cow waddie" who had caused it. **1928** French *Ranchman NM* 243 (as of 1880s), He said: 'Hell, fellows, we common cow-waddies ain't got but one vote nohow!' **1937** *DN* 6.620 **wTX**, *Cow-waddie.* **1942** Perry *Texas* 12, His [Frank Dobie's] intimately felt past goes beyond his birth, reaches out to the Rangers, the cow waddies, . . and the outlaw men who roamed this hard land. **1949** *PADS* 11.20 **CO**, Cow waddy. **1973** Allen *LAUM* 1.406, In the Nebraska sandhill country are also found *hay-waddy* and *cow-waddy.*

cow-walkers n pl

Stilts.

1968 *DARE* (Qu. EE35, *Long wooden poles with a footpiece that children walk around on to make them tall*) Inf **MO**9, Cow-walkers.

cow wampee n Cf **wampee**

A **pickerelweed 1** (here: *Pontederia cordata*).

1896 in 1913 *Torreya* 13.229 **SC**, *Pontederia cordata . .* cow . . wampee, Santee Club, S.C.

cow wasp See **cow-killer ant**

cow weed n

=**milkvetch.**

1938 (1958) Sharples *AK Wild Flowers* 21, *Astragalus . . .* "Milk Vetch," "Cow Weed."

cow-wench See **co-wench**

cowwheat n

A small, inconspicuous plant *(Melampyrum lineare).*

1784 in 1785 Amer. Acad. Arts & Sci. *Memoirs* 1.464, *Melampyrum . . . Cow-wheat.* Blossoms yellowish white. In woods. June. **1881** *Amer. Naturalist* 15.101 **NJ**, The only other leaf carried by them [=ants] . . is the leaf of cow wheat *(Melampyrum americanum),* a plant which abounds in the woods. **1913** *Torreya* 13.11.253, Cowwheat, *Melampyrum lineare.* **1931** Harned *Wild Flowers Alleghanies* 452. **1938** Madison *Wild Flowers OH* 104, Narrow-leaved Cow-wheat. *Melampyrum lineare.* **1961** Smith *MI Wildflowers* 349.

cow wood n, also attrib **SW** Cf **chip** n[1] **1, cow dab**

Dried cow dung used as fuel.

1850 Garrard *Wah-to-yah* 2.27 **NM**, We huddled around the miserable 'cow wood' fires. **1940** FWP *Guide NM* 112, Cow-wood—dried manure chips used for fuel. **1941** *AmSp* 16.181 **SW**, English slang metaphor also has its place, as *bark* for a scalp . . , *cow wood* for dried buffalo manure which would burn, a *prairie oyster* for the testicles of a steer.

cow work n **SW**

Cattle handling; a cattle roundup.

1886 *Century Illustr. Mag.* 32.341/1, It is even more laughable to see some young fellow from the East or from England . . attempt in his turn to do cow-work with his ordinary riding or hunting rig. **1907** White *AZ Nights* 53, He kept his own mount of horses, took care of them, hunted, and took part in all the cow work. **1921** Thorp *Songs Cowboys* 127 **NM**, She goes to every round-up, every cow-work without fail, / Looking out for all her cattle branded "walking hog on rail." **1929** Dobie *Vaquero* 13, When we gathered cattle, we said that we were on a "cow hunt," a "cow work," a "work," or a "cow drive." **1966** Barnes–Jensen *Dict. UT Slang,* Cow-work . . work in caring for cattle on a ranch.

cowy adj

1907 *DN* 3.185 **seNH**, *Cowy . . .* Tainted by unsanitary conditions in a cow-stable. "This milk tastes cowy."

cow yard n **chiefly Nth, N Midl, esp NEng**

A barnyard.

1637 in 1896 Cambridge MA Proprietors *Records* 42, My dwelling howse . . with the yardes cowhouse cowyarde & my parte in the oxm[a]rsh. *Ibid* 3, One the northwest cow yard lane. **1784** (1877)

Belknap *Papers* 5th ser 2.397 **NH,** The people made little smokes in their cow-yards to defend their cows against the flies and mosquitoes. **1836** Simms *Mellichampe* 47.393 [Black], Da's some of you sodger bin . . breck down de gate of de cow-yard. **1867** Hill *Homespun* 321 **NEng,** He . . hurries off to the cow-yard to help about the milking. **1907** *DN* 3.185 se**NH. 1914** *DN* 4.155 **Cape Cod MA. 1949** Kurath *Word Geog.* 55, In the North only Eastern New England and eastern Long Island have local expressions for the cowpen, the former *cow yard,* the latter *pightle.* **1965–70** *DARE* (Qu. M13, *The space near the barn with a fence around it where you keep the livestock*) 31 Infs, **chiefly Nth, N Midl,** Cow yard; (Qu. M12, *What do you keep food for the cattle in over . . winter?*) Inf **MD3,** Cow yard; (Qu. M14, *The open area around or next to the barn*) Infs **CA9, ME5,** Cow yard. [All Infs old or mid-aged]

cow yard tar n **ME** Cf **cow sailor**
A person who is both farmer and sailor according to the season.
1905 Wasson *Green Shay* 195 (*AmSp* 37.251) **ME,** They'll make out to cast loose their dinky all right, unless'n they're complete farmers, an ef they're nothin' only a pair of plague-gone cow-yard tars . . this 'ere breeze o' wind will show 'em the nighest way to the turf pretty quick! **1975** Gould *ME Lingo, Cow yard tar*—One of many Maine-isms for a saltwater farmer. A fisherman who grows a good garden or a farmer who goes clamming. "Hayfied lobsterman" and "straw-sailor" are similar terms. Depending on context, these terms may be either complimentary or not, and the combination is so important to Maine that the farmer and sailor share prominence on the official state seal.

coxcomb See **cockscomb**

coy v |kɔɪ, kwɔɪ, kɔɪə| [Var of **co-ee**] **C Atl**
Come!—used to call cows from pasture.
1965–70 *DARE* (Qu. K80, *The call that's used . . to get cows in from the pasture*) Inf **DC5,** [kɔ·ɪ, kwɔɪ]; **DE5,** Coy; **VA38,** ['kɔːɔɪ]; **VA40,** ['kɔɪə]; **VA82,** [kɔɪ]; (Qu. K83) Inf **VA38,** Coy.

coydog n [Blend of *coyote* + *dog*] **Nth, esp NEast**
A hybrid of a coyote and a wild dog.
1966–68 *DARE* (Qu. P32, . . *Kinds of wild animals . . around here*) Infs **MI32, NY6, 23, 92, 93, VT10,** Coydog. **1969** *Living Museum* 31.115, Coincident with the recent eastward shift in the range of the coyote, numerous reports of wolf-like animals have occurred . . . These hybrids, referred to as coy-dogs, have in the past 20 years become quite numerous throughout Illinois. **1975** Gould *ME Lingo, Coydog*—A coined Maine word to describe an animal found in the woods—this one real. Western coyotes came via Canada, and crossing with domestic dogs they entered Maine along the Québec border. When first sighted they were thought to belong to the *Shagimaw* and *Fillieloo* category, but biologists studied the cranium structure and confirmed that they truly are coyote-dogs, or *coydogs.* **1978** *UpCountry* Oct 35 **NEng,** Many species of wildlife are rare or endangered in New England, and it is unlawful to hunt them. This is true of . . Eastern coyote (or coydog) among others.

coyer n
Prob =**coot** n[1] 1.
1970 *DARE* (Qu. Q9, *The bird that looks like a small, dull-colored duck and is commonly found on ponds and lakes*) Inf **MA122,** Coyer ['kɔjə].

coyote n Usu |'kaɪ(ˌj)oʊt|, also |ˌkaɪ'(j)oti|; less freq |'kaɪ(ˌj)oti, 'kaɪjut|; rarely |'kaɪˌhot, -ˌhut, 'kɔɪjot, -ət| Pronc-spp *cayeute, cayota, cayote, collote, coyoto, cuiota, cyote, kiote* [MexSpan] **chiefly West**
A Forms.
1826 in 1831 Beechey *Narrative* 79 **nCA,** The *cuiotas,* or jackalls . . prove very destructive to the sheep. **1834** Pike *Prose Sketches* 14 **West,** The little gray collotes or prairie wolves. **1848** (1855) Ruxton *Life Far West* 78 **NM,** Round the camp, during the night, the cayeute keeps unremitting watch. **1850** *Calif. Courier* (S.F.) 29 July *(DA),* Cayotas are to be employed to search . . for sheep. **1850** [see B2 below]. **1892** *DN* 1.190, *Coyote:* prairie wolf. Often improperly spelled and pronounced *cayote.* From Mexican *coyotl.* **1898** *South Dakotan* 1.65/2, Thenceforward the Dakotans were called "kiotes." **1941** Smith *Going to God's Country* 78 **MO** (as of 1890), We were there with the cyotes, prarie chickens, ratle snakes. **1965–70** *DARE* (Qu. P32) 192 Infs, **chiefly West,** Coyote. [Usu pronounced ['kaɪ(j)oʊt]; also fairly frequently [ˌkaɪ'(j)oti]; occasionally ['kaɪ(j)oti, 'kaɪˌjut]; rarely ['kaɪˌhot, 'kaɪˌhut, 'kɔɪˌjot, 'kɔɪˌət].] **1968** Adams *Western Words* 81, *Coyote*—A prairie wolf; pronounced *kí-yote* by the westerner.
B Senses.

1 Std: a small American wolf *(Canis latrans).* Also called **brush wolf, medicine wolf, prairie wolf**
2 attrib in var combs referring to mining: A shallow tunnel or excavation. **West**
1850 *S.F. Picayune* 31 Aug. 3/1 *(DA),* There are Coyoto Diggins, near this place, from which, at the depth of from 17 to 25 feet, $23,000 have been taken out in two days. **1851** *Ibid* 14 Oct. 2/4, The beds of the streams have proved very rich, the banks richer, the cayote shafts richest of all. **1877** Wright *Big Bonanza* 133 **NV,** Large and substantially constructed tunnels took the place of the "coyote holes" that were at first run into the hills. **1940** FWP *Guide NV* 60, A coyote hole is shallow diggin's not large enough or deep enough to establish proof of a favorable prospect. **1964** Jackman–Long *OR Desert* 395, Coyote gold—fine gold obtained near the surface in small mining operations. *Ibid* 396, *Coyote diggins*—rundown excavations . . . *Coyote hole*—prospector's hole . . . *Coyote placers*—hillside placers . . . *Coyote shaft*—hillside shafts. **1968** Adams *Western Words, Coyote*—In mining, an excavation suggestive of those made by coyotes. *Ibid, Coyote hole*—In mining, a small tunnel driven into the rock horizontally at right angles to the face of the mine. **1979** *DARE* File **WA** (as of 1904), Blasting 'coyote holes' into the sides of the cliff, which were filled with black powder to blast off huge portions of the mountain.
3 Of persons: an Indian or person with one Indian parent; a squatter. **West**
1872 Powers *Afoot* 277 **sCA,** Many slouching fellows make that pretense [i.e., pretend to be looking for government lands], while they are really squatters or "coyotes." **1948** *NM Qrly. Rev.* 18.198, Often *coyote* is used as a synonym for *native,* and is applied to Indians and *mestizos* (mixed-bloods) as readily as to plants. **1964** Jackman–Long *OR Desert* 395, *Coyote* . . . To apply to persons—squatters, half-breeds of any kind.
4 also *coyote dun:* A dun-colored horse often having a dark stripe down the back. **West** Cf **bayo 2, buckskin 1**
1903 (1965) Adams *Log Cowboy* 14, It was my good fortune that morning to get a good mount of horses,—three sorrels, two grays, two coyotes, a black, a brown, and a *grulla.* **1964** Jackman–Long *OR Desert* 395, *Coyote* . . . A horse the color of coyotes, a buckskin. **1968** Adams *Western Words, Coyote dun*—A dun horse with a dark stripe running down its back, sometimes into the tail, and often marking the legs.
5 See **coyote house.**

coyote v **West**
1 In mining: see quot 1906; also vbl n *coyoting.* **esp CA** Cf **drift** v B
1851 (1922) Clappe *Shirley Letters* 82 **CA,** I intend, some day, . . to bore you with some profound remarks upon the claiming, drifting, sluicing, ditching, fluming, and coyoting politics of the "diggins." **1906** Canfield *Diary Forty-Niner* 41 **CA,** [Footnote:] Coyoting was a local descriptive term of a mining method which meant the sinking of shafts, and running small drifts from the bottom in the bedrock in all directions. **1928** Ritchie *Forty-Niners* 81 **CA,** Their example was followed by hundreds who began "coyoteing"—the name taken from the domicile holes of the despised animal—wherever gravel outcrop showed on the mountain side. **1964** Jackman–Long *OR Desert* 396, Coyoting—sink a shaft, thereafter digging small shafts from the bottom in all directions.
2 also with *around:* To dig one's way out; to get away or move surreptitiously.
1857 *Phoenix* (Sacramento) 13 Sep. 1/3 *(DA)* **CA,** And I, why I cayotied. **1861** Stone *Pacific Song Book* 21 *(DA),* I did as I had done before, / Coyoted out from 'neath the floor. **1964** Jackman–Long *OR Desert* 396, Coyote . . . To get out of there surreptitiously or hurriedly. **1968** Adams *Western Words, Coyotin' round*—Sneaking.
3 also with *around:* To wander about, drift.
1948 *NM Qrly. Rev.* 18.199, Nowadays in the Southwest, 'coyoting around' means drifting loosely from one place or occupation to another, without anchor or responsibility. **1964** Jackman–Long *OR Desert* 396, Coyote . . . To drift from place to place. **1968** Adams *Western Words, Coyotin' round*—Drifting aimlessly from one place to another.
4 See quot.
1964 Jackman–Long *OR Desert* 396, Coyote . . . To chase a wild horse until he can be handled.
5 in phr *coyote around the rim:* See quot.
1968 Adams *Western Words* 81, *Coyotin' round the rim*—Touching a subject on the edges, as in a conversation or speech; hinting.

coyote berry n

A type of **currant**.

1964 Jackman–Long *OR Desert* 396, Coyote berries—wild currants.

coyote brush n Also *coyote bush* **SW**

A **groundsel tree** (here: *Baccharis pilularis*).

1925 Jepson *Manual Plants CA* 1058, *B. pilularis . . . Coyote Brush.* **1931** U.S. Dept. Ag. *Misc. Pub.* 101.160, *Kidneywort . .* also known as . . coyote bush . . is a smooth . . evergreen shrub. **1940** *Jrl. Mammalogy* 21.388 **CA,** This farm was originally covered with such plants as . . coyote brush (*Baccharis pilularis*). **1967** Stegner *Little Live Things* 126 **cwCA,** The coyote brush, hardy and forehanded, has been blooming white since November.

coyote cactus n Also sp *cayote cactus*

A **prickly pear** (here: *Opuntia leptocaulis*).

1936 NM Univ. *Biol. Ser.* 4.5.59, Cactus, cayote or turkey, tessajo, *xuclogo*—'crazy cactus' (*Opuntia leptocaulis* DC.). **1953** *AmSp* 28.101 **SW,** *Coyote cactus . . . Opuntia leptocaulis.*

coyote dog n Cf **coydog**

A dog related to, or possessing traits of, the coyote.

1868 Whymper *Travel AK* 20, These people appeared to be very bare of provisions, and disputed with their wretched 'cayota' dogs anything that we threw out of our camp, in the shape of bones, bacon rind, or tea leaves, and similar luxuries. **1964** Jackman–Long *OR Desert* 395, Coyote dog—a domestic dog that acts like a coyote.

coyote dun See **coyote** n **B4**

coyote farming n [Perh **coyote** n **B2**]

1964 Jackman–Long *OR Desert* 182, In the Columbia basin, before scientific dry farming, every now and then someone with a gambling nature would drill wheat into the stubble, with no summer fallow or other land preparation at all. If it rained frequently, such a person might harvest a crop at very little expense. This was "coyote farming."

coyote house n Also *coyote* **West** *hist*

A **dugout**.

1870 Pine *Beyond the West* 307 **UT,** A coyote house is a small cellar dug in the ground with a few boards placed up over the hole as a roof. **1885** Jackson *Zeph* 7 **CO,** Especially lucky were those who came in the beginning, in the "tent and coyote" days, as they were called, and had seen the lots they bought then for hundreds of dollars boom up into value rated by thousands. **1938** *AmSp* 13.44, *Coyote house* is another name for the dugout, or artificial cave, in which the pioneer on the western plains of America often lived with his family until he could afford a better habitation. **1964** Jackman–Long *OR Desert* 395, *Coyote days*— early days of the West when many homesteaders, trappers, and others lived in dugouts . . . *Coyote house*—a dugout.

coyote melon n

=**calabacilla**.

1907 Mearns *Mammals* 474, This rat also feeds upon the seeds of a gourd known by the name of "Coyote melon." **1948** *NM Qrly. Rev.* 18.198, A desert gourd common to the Southwest as well as Mexico is called coyote melon and is said to be eaten by coyotes. **1964** Jackman–Long *OR Desert* 395, Coyote melon—calabagilla [sic], a wild plant of the southwest.

coyote's tobacco See **coyote tobacco**

coyote thistle n

=**button snakeroot 2**.

1922 Smiley *Weeds CA* 160, Button snakeroot or Coyote thistle (*Eryngium armatum . .*) . . . This is but one of several so-called 'coyote thistles' found in California. **1964** Jackman–Long *OR Desert* 396, Coyote thistle—species of Eryngium. **1973** Hitchcock–Cronquist *Flora Pacific NW* 324, *Eryngium . . . Coyote-thistle.*

coyote tobacco n Also *coyote's tobacco*

A **wild tobacco** (here: *Nicotiana trigonophylla*).

1912 Lumholtz *New Trails* 52 **sAZ,** The name for tobacco . . used for certain sacred purposes . . is . . coyote tobacco (*pan vívuka*). **1942** Castetter *Pima & Papago Ag.* 108 *(DA),* The first tobacco smoked by the Papago and Pima was *Nicotiana trigonophylla* Dunal, known as 'Coyote's tobacco.' **1964** Jackman–Long *OR Desert* 396, Coyote tobacco.

coyote well n **West**

A usu hidden desert spring.

1933 Jaeger *CA Deserts* 29, Even the insects are aware of the location of these "coyote" wells, as they are often called, and several times . . I have located such places by watching converging lines of thirsty bees. **1964** Jackman–Long *OR Desert* 396, Coyote well—a hidden water hole. **1966** Barnes–Jensen *Dict. UT Slang,* Coyote-well . . . a water hole.

coyote willow n

=**sandbar willow**.

1960 Vines *Trees SW* 97, Silver-leaf Willow—*Salix argophylla . . .* Also known under the vernacular name of Coyote Willow. *Ibid* 101, Coyote Willow—*Salix exigua.* **1979** Little *Checklist U.S. Trees* 261, *Salix exigua . .* sandbar willow (coyote willow).

coyotey adj [*coyote* n + *-y*] Cf **coyote** n **B4**

Mangy-looking.

1937 Sandoz *Slogum* 42 **NE** (as of 1900–20), And as Gulla pounded her coyotey old ponies onward, he scowled upon the fondness growing up between the two. *Ibid* 275, Several times he tried to speak . . a friendly word, about ordinary things, like . . a coyotey team of bronchs hitched to an old top buggy they passed.

coyotillo n [MexSpan *coyot(e)* + *-illo*, dimin]

A shrub (*Karwinskia humboldtiana*) native to Texas.

1892 DN 1.190 **wTX,** *Coyotillo:* a shrub of Western Texas, with blackish poisonous berries and beautiful pinnate-veined leaves (*Karwinskia Humboldtiana*). *Ibid* 247, Captain Bourke informs me that the berry itself is edible, but that people believe that if the small round seed is swallowed it will cause paralysis of the lower extremities. The Mexicans along the lower Rio Grande say that the *coyote* knows this . . and . . invariably rejects the seed, hence the name [coyotíllo]. **1948** *NM Qrly. Rev.* 18.198, The beautiful-leafed *coyotillo* plant (*Karwinskia humboldtiana*) makes up for lack of thorns by containing an ingredient poisonous to goats, which sometimes eat it; coyotes delight in and thrive on its berries. **1953** *AmSp* 28.101 **SW,** *Coyotillo . . . Karwinskia humboldtiana.* **1967** *DARE* Tape **TX29,** [FW:] What are the native brushes . . . ? [Inf:] [kɔjoʻtijo]—this will make goats very sick. **1969** *DARE* (Qu. S21, *Other weeds . . that are a trouble in gardens and fields*) Inf **TX68,** Coyotillo.

coyoto See **coyote** n

coz n See **co'**

coz conj See **because** conj

cozen See **cousin** v

cozy adj Pronc-spp *coozie, coozy*

Std sense, var forms.

1911 DN 3.542 **NE,** *Coozy* . . . Occasional for *cozy.* "Sit there in the coozy corner." **1956** *AmSp* 31.39 **MA,** Variants like *coozie* and *cozy, doosie* and *dosie* are not uncommon.

C.P.T. See **colored people's time**

crab n

1 also *water crab:* =**crawfish** n **B1**. [Cf Ger *Flusskrebs*] **chiefly Nth, N Midl, esp Gt Lakes** See Map

1890 *Manti* (Utah) *Sentinel* 28 Nov. 1/2 *(DA),* We call crawfish 'crabs' in Penn Yan [N.Y.]. **1944** *ADD* **cNY** (as of 1914–22), Crab . . . A crayfish . . . Common. **c1950** *Atlas Checklists* **IL, PA, WI,** *Crabs:* freshwater shellfish with claws; swim backwards. [6 infs] **1965–70**

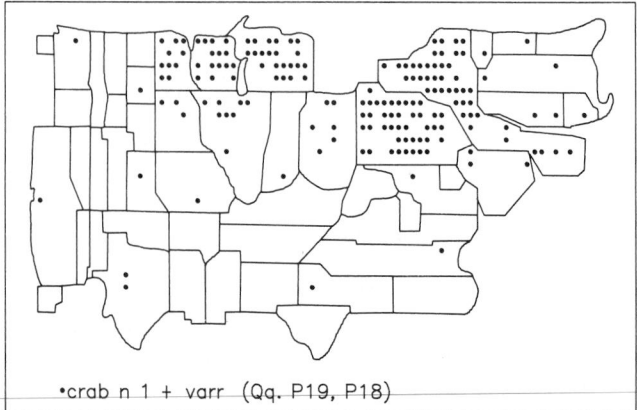

•crab n 1 + varr (Qq. P19, P18)

DARE (Qu. P19, *What do you call the small, freshwater crayfish*) 170 Infs, **chiefly Nth, N Midl, esp Gt Lakes,** Crab(s); **PA**205, Water crabs; (Qu. P18, *. . Kinds of shellfish . . common around here*) Inf **NY**164, Crayfish—called crabs.

2 A louse, esp a pubic louse.

1889 *Century Dict., Crab* . . . A crab-louse. **1930** Irwin *Amer. Tramp,* Crab.—A body louse, especially of that variety infesting the pubic region; short for "crab louse." **1934** Wylie *Finnley Wren* 130 **NYC,** She would have flown into a rage of protest if someone had bluntly said that her friends slobbered, ripped off girls' dresses at parties, had crabs. **1949** Palmer *Nat. Hist.* 389, "Crab" is pubic louse. **1964** Borror–DeLong *Intro. Insects* 189, The family Phthiriidae includes a single species, the crab or pubic louse of man, *Phthirius pubis*. **1965–70** *DARE* (Qu. R25, *Joking terms . . for a head louse or body louse*) 172 Infs, **scattered,** Crab.

crab v[1] [Cf *OED crab* v.[1] "To go counter to, . . to irritate, anger, . . provoke"] **scattered, but chiefly Nth** See Map
To complain, grouse, argue.

1906 *Westm. Gaz.* 11 Aug 1/2 *(OEDS),* The difference between us and you, said an American who had watched Mr. Chamberlain's Fiscal campaign, is that 'we boom, and you crab.' **1925** Fitzgerald *Gatsby* 152 **seNY,** The thing to do is to forget about the heat . . . You make it ten times worse by crabbing about it. **1965–70** *DARE* (Qu. GG16, *Words for finding fault or complaining: "You just can't please him—he's always _____."*) 25 Infs, **chiefly Nth,** Crabbing; (Qu. GG35a, *To sulk or pout: "It won't do any good to _____ about it."*) Infs **CA**22, **MN**6, 36, **NC**38, **NY**108, 209, **OH**5, Crab; (Qu. GG35b, *. . "Because she couldn't go, she's been _____ all day."*) Infs **MD**2, **MI**68, **MN**36, **NY**108, Crabbing; (Qu.HH12, *A person who is always finding fault about unimportant things*) Infs **CA**107, **ME**9, **NY**1, (Always) crabbing; (Qu. KK13, *. . Arguing*) Inf **IL**59, Crabbing.

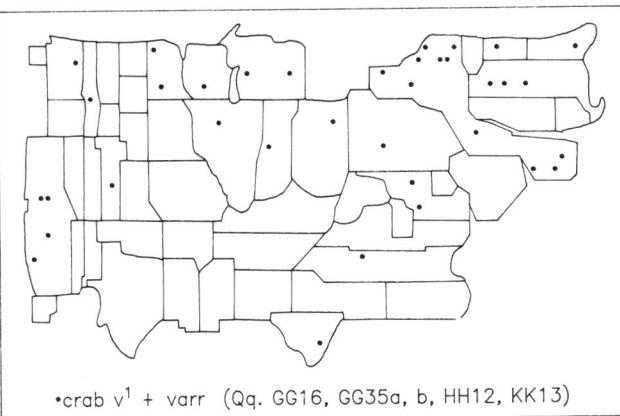

•crab v[1] + varr (Qq. GG16, GG35a, b, HH12, KK13)

crab v[2] [Etym uncert; perh *OED crab* v.[2] "To criticize adversely"]
To criticize, insult; to annoy.

1969 *DARE* (Qu. Y3, *To say uncomplimentary things about somebody*) Inf **RI**12, Crab him; (Qu. Y7, *When one person never misses a chance to be mean to another or to annoy another: "I don't know why she keeps _____ me all the time!"*) Infs **NY**24, 80, Crabbing.

‡crab v[3] [Perh folk-etym for *crib*]
1970 *DARE* (Qu. JJ7, *Words . . for cheating in school examinations*) Inf **SC**69, Crabbing.

crab-apple switch n [By ext from *crab apple* + *switch* a slender flexible rod or twig, perh infl by *switchblade*] **Sth, S Midl, esp MS** *esp among Black speakers* Cf **peach-tree tea**
A large pocket knife.

1941 Percy *Lanterns* 305 **nwMS,** A woman had cut her husband to shreds with a long knife the Negroes call a crab-apple switch. **1965–70** *DARE* (Qu. F39, *A large pocket knife with blades that fold in and out*) Infs **MS**1, 60, 79, 80, **MO**22, **TN**52, Crab-apple switch; **MO**17, Crab-apple switch. [Inf and her husband said this is what colored people call them.] [5 of 7 Infs Black] **1980** *DARE* File **cSC,** Another young lady . . thinks that she had heard her uncle refer to his knife as a crab-apple switch. It is the kind of knife that has half a dozen or more blades of different sizes or shapes in one handle into which they fold.

crab-apple two-step n Cf **green-apple quickstep**
1967 *DARE* (Qu. BB19, *Joking names for looseness of the bowels*) Inf **OH**2, Crab-apple two-step.

crabbing hook n
1967 *DARE* (Qu. L35, *Hand tools used for cutting underbrush and digging out roots*) Inf **AL**15, Crabbing hook.

crab bottom n
An undersea area where crabs flourish; a crab bed.

1976 Warner *Beautiful Swimmers* 227 **Chesapeake Bay,** Bloodsworth Island's Northeast Cove is one among some fifty "crab bottoms" set aside by the state of Maryland solely for crab scraping. Scrapers may work outside these bottoms if they wish, but they are out of bounds for . . any exploitation other than crabbing.

crabburger n **LA**
A round sandwich like a hamburger but made with crab meat.

1968 *DARE* (Qu. H41, *Kinds of roll or bun sandwiches . . in a round bun or roll*) Infs **LA**24, 38, Crabburger. **1968** *DARE* FW Addit **csLA,** *Crabburger:* A round sandwich featured on a menu at a drive-in restaurant.

crab cactus n Also *claw cactus*
The Thanksgiving cactus (*Schlumbergera truncata*).

1900 Bailey *Cyclop. Horticulture* 2.536/2, *Epiphyllum . . . Cactàceæ.* Crab Cactus. **1942** Weygandt *Plenty* 173, They love whitewash on the dooryard palings; wrens in bird boxes by the back stoop; crab cactuses in the south windows. **1976** Bailey–Bailey *Hortus Third* 1019, *Crab cactus, claw cactus . . .* Many hybrids and cvs. [=cultivated varieties] are grown.

crab cake n **chiefly Delmarva**
A fried patty made with crabmeat; see quot 1952.

1952 Tracy *Coast Cookery* 96 **MD,** *Crab cakes*—Trim crusts from bread and pour melted butter over them . . . To these add crabmeat . . . Mix lightly with a fork . . and shape the mixture into cakes. Brown in a hot skillet that has been brushed with fat. **1964** *Amer. Heritage Cookbook* 463 **MD,** *Maryland Crab Cakes.* **1965–70** *DARE* (Qu. H45, *Dishes made with . . fish . . that everybody around here would know, but . . people in other places might not*) 10 Infs, **chiefly Delmarva,** Crab cakes.

crabcatcher n
=green heron.
1939 Forbush–May *Birds* 34, *Eastern Green Heron . . . Other names:* Little Green Heron; Green Bittern; Poke; Fly-up-the-creek; Crabcatcher; Indian Pullet. **1946** Hausman *Eastern Birds* 107, *Eastern Green Heron . . . Other Names . .* Crabcatcher, Indian Pullet, Minnow Fisher, Kelly Fisher. **1969** Longstreet *Birds FL* 21, Green Heron . . . Crabcatcher.

crabeater n Cf **crabcatcher**
=cobia.
1814 in 1815 *Lit. & Philos. Soc. NY Trans.* 1.490, Crab-eater. *Centronotus spinosus.* **1887** Goode *Amer. Fishes* 144, The Cobia or crab-eater, *Elacate canada . . .* The name "Crab-eater" appears to have been ascribed to the fish by Dr. Mitchill. **1976** Warner *Beautiful Swimmers* 35 **Chesapeake Bay,** The rapacious bluefish no longer maraud crab pots. By now they are far down the Carolina beaches. Accompanying them are . . the huge cobias, also called "northern bonita" or crab-eaters.

‡crab eye n
A protuberant or prominent eye.

1968 *DARE* (Qu. X21a, *Words . . used to describe people according to their eyes—for example, if they stick out*) Inf **NY**66, Crab eyes.

crabfish n
=crawfish n **B1.**
1966–68 *DARE* (Qu. P19, *What do you call the small, freshwater crayfish around here?*) Infs **SC**26, 57, Crabfish.

crabgrass n
1 also *crapgrass* (**chiefly S Midl**), *crop grass:* A grass of the genus *Digitaria.* For other names of var spp see **finger grass, hurrah grass**
1743 (1946) Gronovius *Flora Virginica* 134, Panicum spicis alternis opositisve [etc] . . Crab-grass. **1908** *DN* 3.302 **eAL, wGA,** *Crap-grass . . .* Crab-grass. **1944** Harper *Weeds AL* 62, When this [=*Syntherisma sanguinale*] first came to the notice of English-speaking people it was

called 'crop grass.' **1948** *Holland's* June 47/3 *(DA)*, If permitted to grow high enough, Bermuda grass will shade out crab grass and protect it from gaining much headway. **1954** *Harder Coll.* **cwTN**, *Crap grass:* crab grass. **1965–70** *DARE* (Qu. S9, *Kinds of grass that are hard to get rid of*) 550 Infs, **widespread**, Crabgrass; **KY**21, 28, 53, 83, **OK**58, **VA**43, Crapgrass; (Qu. S8, *A common kind of wild grass . . it spreads by sending out long underground roots and it's hard to get rid of*) 222 Infs, **widespread**, Crabgrass; **AR**56, **KY**40, 53, 60, 63, **LA**25, **MO**36, Crapgrass; **IL**110, Wild crabgrass; (Qu. S21, *Other weeds . . around here that are a trouble in gardens and fields*) 30 Infs, **scattered**, Crabgrass; **KY**9, 35, 40, Crapgrass; (Qu. L9a, *Kinds of grass . . grown for hay*) Infs **AR**36, **FL**37, **GA**16, 74, **LA**7, 40, **NC**81, **SC**63, Crabgrass; (Qu. L8, *Hay that grows naturally in damp places*) Infs **FL**7, **LA**40, **SC**40, 47, **TN**62, Crabgrass; **LA**18, Crapgrass; (Qu. L9b, *Hay from other kinds of plants*) Inf **NC**1, Crabgrass; **NC**24, Crabgrass hay. [Note: some of these Infs may refer instead to **crabgrass 2** or **3**.] **1968–69** *DARE* Tape **GA**22, After we'd lay by the corn, . . that crabgrass would come up here and that'd be about this high. [FW:] . . . A yard high. [Inf:] That'd make good hay; **GA**77, Maybe the crapgrass was about to take over that field.

2 also *crop grass:* A **goose grass** (here: *Eleusine* spp, esp *E. indica*).

1775 (1962) Romans *Nat. Hist. FL* 128, The artificial *grasses* found here are 1st: That kind of grass known in the islands by the name of dog grass, and in Carolina and Georgia by that of crop grass. **1857** Gray *Manual of Botany* 554, *Eleusine* . . . Crab-grass. Yard-grass. **1884** Vasey *Ag. Grasses* 58, *Eleusine Indica* (Yard-grass . . Crab-grass . .).

3 A **knotweed** (here: *Polygonum aviculare*).

1910 Graves *Flowering Plants* 160 **CT**, *Polygonum aviculare* . . Crab Grass.

crab hawk n

=**Mexican black hawk.**

1957 Pough *Audubon Water Bird* 55, *Buteogallus anthracinus* . . . Crab Hawk.

crab house n

1976 Warner *Beautiful Swimmers* 84 **Chesapeake Bay**, Shortly after World War I . . Virginia could boast over forty hard crab-picking plants or "crab houses" which specialized in the cooking and packing of crabmeat. *Ibid* 186, In the Chesapeake an establishment performing this difficult function [hand extraction of crabmeat] is known as a picking plant or more often simply a "crab house."

crab imperial See imperial crab

crab lantern n Also sp *crab lanthorn, ~ lanton* [Prob *crab* crab apple + *lantern,* from the ventilating slashes that expose the fruit filling; cf *EDD* at *crab* sb.² 2] **?Midl old-fash**

A fruit pie shaped like a half-moon and fried.

c1770 in 1833 Boucher *Glossary* l **MD**, At night *crab-lanthorn,* and *fried cucumbers. Ibid* Footnote 59, *Crab-lanthorn.* To the best of my recollection, fried apples are so called. **1801** in 1926 *William & Mary Qrly.* 2d ser 6.183 **VA**, Had some peaches stewed in order to make Crab Lanterns for dinner. **1818** in 1824 Knight *Letters* 106 **KY**, At the oven, children wait for their crablanterns, and cobble. **1904** Derville *Other Side of Story* 45 *(DAE)*, I ate my drumstick and then a 'crablanton,' and was hesitating as to the propriety of finishing with a wing. **1908** *DN* 3.302 **eAL, wGA**, *Crab-lantern* . . . A half-moon pie made of dried fruit and fried.

crab pot v

To catch crabs by setting crab pots; hence n *crab potter.*

1968–70 *DARE* Tape **MD**45, I was the third man who crab potted in this area; **VA**112, After they [=crabs] start comin' out of that mud . . then that's when the crab potter takes over [from the dredger].

crab's claws n

=**lady's thumb.**

1900 Lyons *Plant Names* 300, *P[olygonum] Persicaria* . . Crab's-claws.

crab scrape n Chesapeake Bay

A kind of dredging apparatus used in crabbing; see quots.

1968–70 *DARE* Tape **VA**112, They got a four foot scrape, see, that's got a bar on it . . and a frame, and they got big long knitted bag behind it, see? . . They're not what you call real heavy, but they're made out of iron . . that's a crab scrape; **MD**36, A crab scrape . . is the same as the oyster dredge, only it has no teeth and it's lighter; **MD**43, In the peeler [crab] business . . it's legal to use power to drag your crab scrape. **1976** Warner

Beautiful Swimmers 23 **Chesapeake Bay**, At six, he clearly remembers, there was a blacksmith on the island who made him a little crab scrape, or a specialized device of steel rods and twine net for the catching of peelers and softs. *Ibid* 206, Two crab scrapes were up-ended and chocked into convenient spaces in the forward washboard coamings. Their triangular steelrod foreparts pointed to the sky.

crab scraper n

A boat used to dredge for crabs; one who operates such a boat.

1976 Warner *Beautiful Swimmers* 204 **Chesapeake Bay**, It was a workboat unlike any other I had ever seen on the Bay . . . The boat was small, about thirty feet length overall, I guessed. Its freeboard amidships was questionable, being not more than eighteen inches from the waterline to the rail . . . "Funny looking things, ain't they?" . . "They're crab scrapers. Here we call them 'Jenkins creekers'; over on Tangier they call them 'bar cats.'" *Ibid* 205 **Chesapeake Bay**, Friends had arranged for me to go out with Morris Goodwin Marsh . . a widely respected crab scraper.

crab's eye n

A woody vine (*Abrus precatorius*); also its scarlet seed with a black spot at the base. Also called **Indian licorice, licorice vine, love peas, prayer beads, red-bean vine, rosary pea, weather vine, wild licorice**

1876 Hobbs *Bot. Hdbk.* 27, Crabs' eyes, the seeds of Abrus precatorius. **1900** Lyons *Plant Names* 8, *A. precatorius* . . . *Seeds* . . Crab's-eyes. **1933** Small *Manual SE Flora* 743, Seed oval . . scarlet except the black base . . . *Crab's-eye.* **1953** Greene–Blomquist *Flowers South* 61, *Crab's-Eye* . . . The outstanding characteristic of this extensively climbing vine is the scarlet seeds with a black base which are used for beads and novelties wherever it grows. **1976** Fleming *Wild Flowers FL* 76, Crab's eye blooms from May to September from Central Florida to the West Indies and Mexico.

crab shanty n

1976 Warner *Beautiful Swimmers* 186 **Chesapeake Bay**, A "crab shanty" . . is the shacklike structure used by soft crab pound operators to watch over their shedding floats.

crab-shed n

1899 (1912) Green *VA Folk-Speech*, *Crab-shed* . . . The dead shell thrown off by a crab when he sheds.

crab soup n chiefly Mid Atl, esp MD Cf she-crab soup

A cream soup having crabmeat as its main ingredient.

1932 (1946) Hibben *Amer. Regional Cookery* 50 **VA**, *Mrs. Washington's Crab Soup.* **1965–70** *DARE* (Qu. H36, *Kinds of soups favored around here*) Infs **MD**7, 8, 12, 14, 37, **MS**54, **VA**98, Crab soup; **GA**15, Crab cream soup; (Qu. H45, *Dishes made with . . fish . . that everybody around here would know, but that people in other places might not*) Infs **MD**14, 35B, 37, 41, 50, Crab soup.

crab spider n

A spider of the family Thomisidae, esp *Misumena calycina*.

1964 Borror–DeLong *Intro. Insects* 805, The Thomisidæ, or crab spiders, are somewhat crablike in shape and walk sideways or backward. **1966–68** *DARE* (Qu. R28, *Different kinds of spiders*) Infs **CA**26, **FL**9, **HI**2, **NJ**45, **NY**22, **SC**43, 63, Crab spider.

crabwood n

An evergreen tree (*Gymnanthes lucida*) native to southern Florida. Also called **oysterwood, poisonwood**

1884 Sargent *Forests of N. Amer.* 121, *Sebastiania lucida* . . . Crab Wood. Poison Wood. **1897** Sudworth *Arborescent Flora* 271, *Gymnanthes lucida* . . . Crabwood . . . (Fla.). **1939** *FWP Guide FL* 328, On the keys grow 27 varieties of hardwood, some so heavy they will not float in water—notably, the madeira, tamarind, mahogany, crabwood, sarilla, granadilla, and black ironwood. **1979** Little *Checklist U.S. Trees* 143, *Gymnanthes lucida* . . . Other common name—crabwood.

crack v

1 To break wind.

1967–68 *DARE* (Qu. X55b, *Words for breaking wind from the bowels*) Infs **MD**19, **OH**53, **SC**40, **VA**31, Crack; **MD**9, Crack one; **OH**72, Cracking.

2 To taunt, tease, play tricks on.

1942 Hurston *Dust Tracks* 112 **FL**, She demanded that Papa "handle" some of the sisters of the church who kept cracking her about it, but he explained that there was nothing he could do. **1970** *DARE* (Qu.

GG32a, *To habitually play tricks or jokes on people: "He's always
————."*) Inf **NJ**69, Cracking me.

3 To open slightly; hence ppl adj *cracked* ajar.

1899 (1912) Green *VA Folk-Speech, Crack* . . . To open a short distance: as, "Crack the door a little to let out the smoke." **1927** *Ruppenthal Coll.* **KS,** *Cracked* . . . (of a door) slightly ajar. **1941** Faulkner
Men Working 169 **MS,** The inner hall doors cracked open and the men
in the rooms peered at the committee in the hall through the cracks.
1946 *PADS* 6.10 **eNC** (as of 1900–10), *Crack the door* . . . To open the
door slightly. **1968** *DARE* FW Addit **Brooklyn NY.** **1980** *DARE* File
(as of c1965), A middle-aged friend of mine from south of the Western
Reserve asked me, when I was driving, if I would "crack the window" on
my side. She was amazed to discover that to a Yankee it meant only to
break the glass; **sCA,** I have known the phrase *crack the window* (or *door*)
for as long as I can remember. **1983** Mebane *Mary Wayfarer* 118 **NC,**
"Who is it?" I asked, partly cracking the door.

4 in phr *crack day:* To dawn. Cf **crack of day**

1970 *Foxfire* Spring–Summer 35, An' it was just begin' t' crack day
when th' gobbler settin' on a roost a'raised up an' gobbled.

5 See **crack one's side(s).**

crack n

1 An expulsion of intestinal gas. [**crack** v 1]

1968 *DARE* (Qu. X55b, *Words for breaking wind from the bowels*) Inf
PA70, Let a crack; **CA**85, **OH**40, Cracks.

2 A very hard blow. **chiefly NEast, C Atl** See Map

1965–70 *DARE* (Qu. Y11, *A very hard blow: ". . Joe really hit him a
————."*) 15 Infs, **chiefly NEast,** Crack; **ME**16, **MI**68, **NY**122, **RI**1,
Good crack; **MD**21, **NY**219, **OH**16, Hard crack; **NY**190, Crack on the
head; **NY**209, Smashing crack; (Qu. Y14a, *To hit somebody hard*) Inf
NY14, Good crack; (Qu. Y16, *A thorough beating*) Inf **CA**2, Crack.

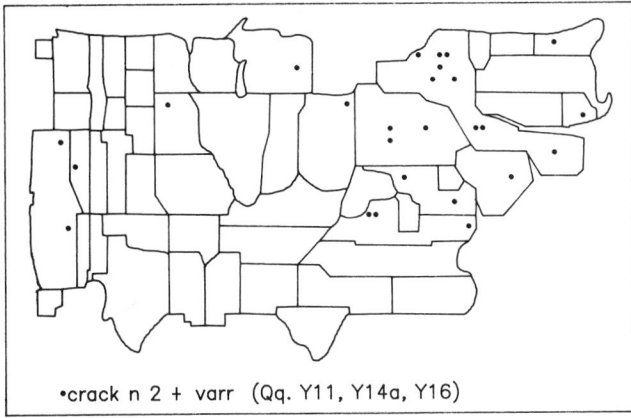

•crack n 2 + varr (Qq. Y11, Y14a, Y16)

3 See quot.

1931–33 *LANE Worksheets* **ceMA,** *Crack*—soot, when you get it on
your hands; **sVT,** You got your fingers all crack after touching the inside
of a stove.

4 A cracked egg.

1966 *DARE* Tape **NJ**7, You always get more cracks when you use old
hens; **NC**6, You take out the cracks.

5 A small quantity of something, a bit.

1967 *DARE* (Qu. LL1, *Something very small*) Inf **NY**9, Little cracks.

6 Assistance.

1969–70 *DARE* FW Addit **seMA,** Crack: help or hint. "Give me a little
crack on that."

7 A coat vent.

1971 *Thompson Coll.* **cnAL** (as of 1930s), *Crack:* The vent in a coat or
jacket. "He was a short, fat man and he had on one of them real fancy
sport coats, and the crack wouldn't stay to."

8 in phr *on the crack:* Slightly open, ajar. Cf **crack v 3**

1892 Harris *Uncle Remus & Friends* 143 **GA,** When he got little nigher,
he tuck notice dat de front door was on de crack. **1911** Saunders *Col.
Todhunter* 161 **MO,** Then the front door was opened on the crack.

crack adv [?Infl by *chock*]

1967 *DARE* (Qu. LL28, *Expressions meaning entirely full*) Inf **MO**38,
Crack full.

---

crack a gut See **crack one's side(s)**

crackajack See **crackerjack**

crackaloo See **crackloo**

crack a rib See **crack one's side(s)**

crack-buster n Cf **buster 5**

The soft-shell crab in the beginning of the moulting process.

1879 *St. Nicholas* Nov 84/2 **ceNJ** (*AmSp* 6.465), He [the soft-shell crab]
keeps on eating till he is bigger still; then he is called a "Shedder"; and he
still keeps on eating and gets bigger still, and then cracks a little, and is
called a "Crack-buster." [**1980** *DARE* File, I [=Wm. W. Warner,
author of *Beautiful Swimmers*] have never heard *crack-buster*, but it is
obviously a good descriptive term for the same phase [the beginning of
the moulting process], since the blue crab starts the moult in the "crack"
or separation of the dorsal and ventral plates, on the back side.]

crack corn v phr *joc*

To snore.

1968 *DARE* (Qu. X45, *Joking expressions . . around here about snoring*) Inf **IN**13, Crackin' corn.

crack day See **crack** v 4

crack down v phr

To lower and shoot a gun.

1938 Rawlings *Yearling* 70 **FL,** There was two shells in the gun, and
there stood the buck, jest waitin'. I cracked down and he dropped.

cracked See **crack** v 3

crackee See **cracky** intj

cracker n

1 Any of var kinds of small dry baked goods: see quots. Cf
Boston cracker

1907 *DN* 3.185 **seNH,** *Cracker* . . . A round brittle biscuit three inches
in diameter, consisting of two separable layers. "I bought a barrel of
crackers." Such crackers are common only in New England. Called in
New York *Boston crackers.* **1930** *DN* 6.79 **cSC,** *Cracker* . . . Any kind
of commercial biscuit, cookie or small cake. Cookies are sometime
differentiated by the term "sweet crackers." Universal. **1942** Whipple
Joshua 27 **UT,** Willie, bending over the grub box, was filling a pan from a
huge sack of 'crackers' (oven-dried bread slices). **1968** *DARE* Tape
AK11, They were just, you've seen them, big round crackers, and thick.
Hard. 'Saloon Pilot' they called it . . . Like a sea biscuit . . . Sailors used to
carry that when they couldn't take bread.

2 often in combs: A backwoodsman, rustic, countrified person;
a poor White person. [Prob orig from *cracker* a braggart, but cf
corncracker 1] **chiefly S Atl** Cf **country** n B2e See Map

1766 Lett. from Gavin Cochrane to Earl of Dartmouth 27 June
(Dartmouth MSS) *(DA)*, I should explain to your Lordship what is meant
by Crackers; a name they have got from being great boasters; they are a
lawless set of rascals on the frontiers of Virginia, Maryland, the Carolinas, and Georgia, who often change their places of abode. **1836**
Knickerbocker 7.453, It is the killing of the cattle of the 'crackers'—as
the southern back-woodsmen are called—that is the most fruitful source
of disputes. **1886** *Amer. Philol. Assoc. Trans.* 17.45, List of common
Southern expressions . . *cracker* (poor white). **1908** *DN* 3.302 **eAL,**
wGA, *Cracker* . . . A Georgian. Sometimes called *corn-cracker,* which

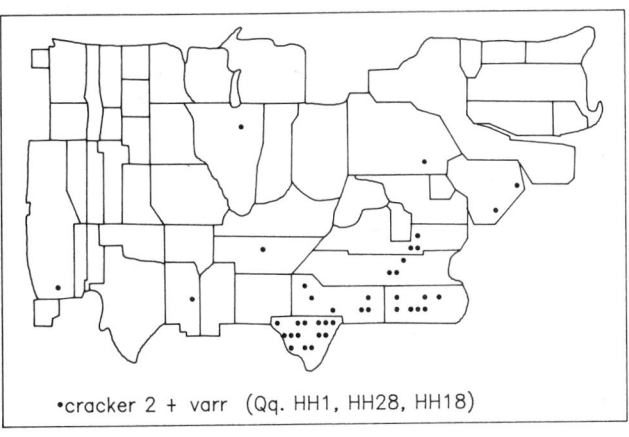

•cracker 2 + varr (Qq. HH1, HH28, HH18)

was probably the original form of the word. **1926** Kephart *Highlanders* 433 **sAppalachians,** As the plantations expanded, these [White] freedmen [formerly bond-servants] were pushed further and further back upon more and more sterile soil. They became "pine-landers" . . , "corn-crackers" or "crackers." **1965–70** DARE (Qu. HH1, . . *A rustic or countrified person*) 22 Infs, **chiefly S Atl,** Cracker; **FL**26, 52, **GA**7, 74, **SC**5, 31, 34, 44, Country cracker; **FL**10, 11, 16, 20, 28, 38, Florida cracker; **FL**38, Backwoods cracker; **FL**17, Georgia cracker; (Qu. HH18, *Very insignificant or low-grade people*) Infs **LA**6, **SC**26, **VA**69, Crackers; (Qu. HH28) Inf **LA**6, Cracker—for poor White folks, poorer than we are; **SC**26, Cracker—White (especially of the no-good sort); **PA**66, Cracker—Caucasian; **CA**81, **GA**83, **VA**41, Cracker [used by Blacks for Whites]; **VA**71, Blacks call Whites of whatever origin "pecks" or "crackers." **1968** DARE Tape **GA**21, You was raised in the swamp, don't act like you a damned old city cracker.

3 By ext: a White racist. *among Black speakers; derog*

1928 McKay *Home to Harlem* 49, Buddy, I'll tell you this and I'll tell the wo'l'—all the crackers, all the poah white trash, all the nigger-hitting and nigger-breaking white folks—I loves life and I got to live and I'll scab through hell to live. *Ibid* 169, He bitterly hated the whites he served ("crackers" he called them all). **1932** Stribling *Store* 473 **AL,** "We would do very well with white folks if it weren't for these miserable crackers!" declared the tan girl passionately. **1965** Little *Autobiog. Malcolm X* 78, A big beefy, redfaced cracker soldier got up in front of me . . and announced . . "I'm going to fight you, nigger." **1977** Smitherman *Talkin* 252, *Cracker,* negative term for whites, especially those who are extremely racist. **1980** *Sun Times* (Chicago IL) 5 Mar Letters [From R.I. McDavid], I must deplore . . Jay McMullen's tactless, racist designation of President Carter as a "Georgia cracker." It is one of the most offensive terms that can be used about whites, and it has been traditionally used by blacks to designate the poorest, most degraded whites with whom they come in contact.

4 An extreme or outstanding example of its kind. Cf **crackerjack**

1914 DN 4.70 **ME, nNH,** *Cracker* . . . A fine-looking, stylish, lively person. "She's a cracker!" **1938** AmSp 13.5 **AR,** *Cracker* . . . 'He's the cracker on this team.' That is, he is the player who inspires the team to do its best. Possibly a descendant of the use of the word for the whip used by the Georgia cracker. **1970** DARE (Qu. B3, *If a day is very hot, you say it's a _____*) Inf **NC**83, Cracker. Cracker can also mean very bitter cold—both extremes, then; (Qu. Y11, *Words for a very hard blow: "You should have seen Bill go down. Joe really hit him a _____."*) Inf **VA**46, Cracker.

5 also *cracker line:* A railroad.

1887 in 1953 Botkin *Treas. Railroad Folkl.* 105 **IN,** "Now we're goin' ter have some fun, Shorty!" exclaimed Si, as the 200th Indiana stacked arms beside the track . . . "I hain't never fergot the time the Johnnies cut our cracker-line." **1966** DARE (Qu. N37, *Joking names for a branch railroad that is not very important or gives poor service*) Inf **GA**11, Cracker.

cracker-ass n

1 A slender person. *derog*

1966 DARE FW Addit **MA**6, *Cracker-ass:* a skinny person. **1970** *Current Slang* 5 **CA** [Railroad jargon], *Crackerass* . . . A slender or skinny person.—Hurry up, crackerass!

2 =**killdeer.**

1945 McAtee *Nomina Abitera* 34, Killdeer (*Oxyechus vociferus*)— Cracker-ass.

cracker ball n

A kind of percussion firecracker.

1967–68 DARE (Qu. FF14, *Different kinds of firecrackers . . around here*) Inf **HI**6, Cracker ball—a small wadded ball; flung on the ground and it explodes; **HI**9, Cracker balls; **LA**35, Cracker balls: firecrackers you throw against the ground; **SC**44, Cracker balls; **SC**65, Cracker balls—percussion [firecrackers].

cracker benders See cracky benders

crackerberry n [See quots] chiefly Nth

1 =**bunchberry 1.**

1900 Lyons *Plant Names* 118, *C[ornus] Canadensis* . . . Crackerberry. **1963** Craighead *Rocky Mt. Wildflowers* 132, Bunchberry . . . Other names: . . Crackerberry . . . *Cornus* fruits contain a hard 2-celled stone with 2 seeds.

2 A **lowbush blueberry 1** (here: *Vaccinium angustifolium*).

1867 DeVoe *Market Ass't* 393 *(DA),* The common lowbush blueberry or *huckleberry* is commonly known among the Jersey pickers or gatherers as the 'cracker-berry,' as they crack or snap in the mouth on account of their tough skin.

cracker bomb n Cf cracker ball

1968 DARE (Qu. FF14, *Kinds of firecrackers*) Inf **LA**46, Cracker bombs; these are like small torpedoes [a kind of firecracker]—you step on them.

cracker bread n

1967–69 DARE (Qu. H18, *Special kinds of bread made now or in past years around here*) Inf **CA**24, An Armenian bread called cracker bread—looks like a pizza-sized round cracker; **CA**118, Cracker bread: 15″–20″ in diameter, round, a little thicker than a soda cracker; made by Armenians here.

cracker broth n

1970 DARE (Qu. H36, *Kinds of soup favored around here*) Inf **PA**234, Cracker broth—butter, salt and pepper, water with crackers.

cracker custard pudding See cracker pudding 2

cracker-fed adj Cf corn-fed 2

Urban.

1936 AmSp 11.275 **cTN,** *Cracker fed (person).* One who lives in a city. 'He is a cracker fed school teacher.'

crackerjack n, also attrib Also sp crackajack scattered, but chiefly Nth See Map Cf cracker 4

Something that is exceptionally fine; someone who is especially expert or skillful.

1895 *Inlander* Nov 62 *(OEDS),* He got a crackerjack when he bought that horse. *Ibid,* As a pitcher he's a crackerjack. **1905** DN 3.61 **NE,** *Crackajack, crackerjack* . . . Term of admiration. "His new gun is a crackajack." **1956** Hall Coll. **ceTN,** *Crackerjack.* **1959** VT Hist. new ser 27.131, *Cracker jack* . . . A person of marked ability. Common. **1960** Criswell *Resp. to PADS 20* **Ozarks,** *Crackerjack* . . . Something of excellent quality. Used commonly for at least fifty-five years, not so common now as formerly. **c1960** Wilson Coll. **csKY,** *Crackerjack.* **1965–70** DARE (Qu. KK5, *A very skilled or expert person*) 21 Infs, **chiefly Nth,** A crackerjack; (Qu. BB53b) Inf **DE**2, A crackerjack doctor—if he's a good one; (Qu. HH27a, *A very able and energetic person*) Inf **NY**60, Crackerjack; (Qu. KK18, . . *In good running order*) Inf **FL**19, In crackerjack condition; (Qu. LL5, *Something impressively big*) Inf **KY**55, Crackerjack.

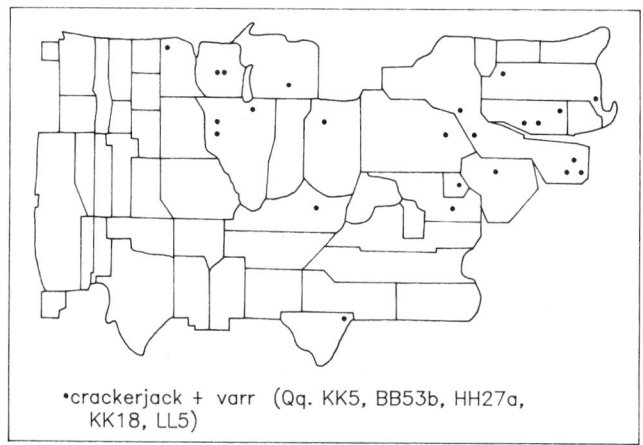

•crackerjack + varr (Qq. KK5, BB53b, HH27a, KK18, LL5)

crackerjack preacher n

1970 DARE (Qu. CC10, *An unprofessional part-time lay preacher*) Inf **OK**55, Crackerjack preacher.

cracker line See cracker n 5

cracker-over-enny n [Prob for Fr *cracovienne* a Polish dance]

1872 (1973) Thompson *Major Jones's Courtship* 35 **GA,** They tuck him to New York, whar he seed Fanny Elsler dance the *cracker-over-enny,* as they call it.

cracker pudding n

1 also *cracker plum pudding:* A dessert consisting largely of crackers, eggs, raisins, milk, and butter. **NEng**

1939 Wolcott *Yankee Cook Book* 196 **swME**, *Cracker pudding*... The pudding is the consistency of curds and all the sweetness is derived from the raisins and the sweet foamy sauce served with it. **1947** Bowles-Towle *New Engl. Cooking* 177, But dancing or not [at the second-day wedding celebration], there was always an elaborate collation in which a rich cracker plum pudding had a place of honor. **1967** *DARE* (Qu. H45) Inf **MA83**, Cracker plum pudding, made with common crackers, soaked over night. **1980** *DARE* File **cnMA** (as of c1915), One of the night-before-Thanksgiving preparations in our household was making the cracker pudding, served along with mince and squash pies because it was traditional, not because anyone liked it. We put common crackers (broken in half) inside up in a baking dish and sprinkled them with raisins. A custard was then poured over them and the dish allowed to stand over night. It was served hot in small portions with lots of foamy sauce.

2 also *cracker custard pudding:* A custard thickened with cracker crumbs.

1896 (1973) Farmer *Orig. Cook Book* 330, *Cracker Custard Pudding.* Make same as Bread Pudding, using .. cracker crumbs in place of bread crumbs; after baking, cover with meringue. **1970** *DARE* Tape **PA242**, Cracker pudding was just milk-egg custard thickened with crackers. Then she'd bake it in the oven. **1972** Hewitt *NYT Heritage Cookbook* 134, *Cracker Pudding.* Pennsylvania. 4 cups milk, 2 eggs separated, ½ cup plus three tablespoons sugar, 2 cups coarse cracker crumbs, 1 cup .. coconut, 1 teaspoon vanilla. [Crumbs and coconut are added to the custard ... Pudding baked in oven, egg whites making meringue.]

crackers intj Also *cracks* [Euphem for *Christ*] Cf **cheese and crackers 1**

1967–68 *DARE* (Qu. NN31, *Exclamations beginning with the sound of* "*cr-*") Infs **NJ35, NY34**, Crackers; **MD5**, Cracks.

crackers and benders See **cracky benders**

crackety intj [Var of **cracky** intj]

1970 *DARE* (Qu. NN31, *Exclamations beginning with the sound of* "*cr-*") Inf **NY234**, Oh crackety.

crackey See **cracky** intj

crackie n

1963 *KY Folkl. Rec.* 9.59 **ceKY**, [A] broken or chipped [playing] marble ... *crackie.*

crackie intj See **cracky** intj

cracking of day See **crack of day**

crackle n[1] See **crackly ice**

crackle n[2] See **grackle**

crackle willow See **crack willow**

crackling n, usu pl Pronc-spp *cracklin(s)*

1 A crisp piece of skin or other tissue remaining after fat (usu of a hog) has been rendered, used as food or in making soap; also fig. **chiefly Sth, Midl**

1834 Crockett *Narrative* 106, I looked like a pretty cracklin ever to get to Congress!!! **1899** (1912) Green *VA Folk-Speech, Cracklings*... The crisp residue of hogs' fat after the lard has been *dried out.* **1903** *DN* 2.310 **seMO. 1906** *DN* 3.116 **sIN.** *Ibid* 132 **nwAR. 1908** *DN* 3.302 **eAL, wGA. 1935** Sandoz *Jules* 304 **wNE** (as of 1880–1930), She should be learning to do the more useful things—making soap from cracklings after butcherings. **1939** Hall *Coll.* **eTN, wNC. 1965–70** *DARE* (Qu. H19) Inf **VA69**, Cracklin biscuit; (Qu. H37, .. *Gravy*) Inf **CO27**, Crackling; (Qu. H43, *Foods made from parts of the head and inner organs of an animal*) Infs **SC42, TN5**, Cracklins; **IL57, MD19, VA26**, Cracklings; **SC34**, Crackling; **SC3**, Cornmeal with cracklings only; (QR, near Qu. F4) Inf **AL1**, Boil cracklins—the skin of a hog—in a wash pot; (Qu. K44, *A bony or poor-looking horse*) Inf **GA77**, Bundle of cracklins; (Qu. HH20c, *Of an idle, worthless person you might say, "He isn't worth _____."*) Inf **KY91**, Crackling. **1968** *DARE* Tape **IN3**, Nowdays when we make the cold water soap, it has to be made out of grease. But then they used their cracklings and their meat rinds. This soap-making come early in the spring, after all the butchering was through, when they'd have their cracklings; **LA28**, My folks didn't go for that crackling bread ... We didn't eat the crackling [sic], we made soap out of 'em! .. You make it in a pot. You take it and put 'bout a bucket of water in that pot and about two boxes of lye and get that melted and you put—I believe it was five pounds of cracklings to a box of lye. **1970** Major

Afro-Amer. Slang, Crackling biscuits (bread): oven-cooked bread containing dried pork skin, a soul food. **1972** *Foxfire Book* 207 **nGA**, In the morning, the fat [of a hog] is cut up into pieces about the size of hens' eggs and put in a pot containing just enough water to keep it from sticking to the sides when cooked ... By evening, the grease will have boiled out, the water evaporated, and the hard residue called "cracklin's" will have fallen to the bottom ... The cracklin's are saved for bread.

2 Matter that collects in the eyes.

1899 (1912) Green *VA Folk-Speech, Cracklings*... Hardened mucus in the corners of the eyes in the morning. **1963** Watkins *Yesterday Hills* 23 **cnGA**, Sim Walker .. was so weak-eyed that matter, or "cracklings," gathered in the corners of his eyes.

crackling bread n Also *crackling corn bread* [**crackling 1**] **chiefly Sth, S Midl** See Map Cf **chitterling bread, fatty-bread 1, goody-bread, scrap johnnycake**

Corn bread made with cracklings.

1842 in Thompson *M. Jones* (1872) 70 *(DA)*, I haint eat nothin but back-bone and turnips, and spare-ribs, and sassingers, and cracklin-bread ever sense the killin commenced. **1890** *DN* 1.64 **KY**, Crackling bread. **1903** *DN* 2.310 **seMO**, *Cracklin-bread.* **1905** *DN* 3.76 **nwAR**, *Cracklin' bread.* **1908** *DN* 3.302 **eAL, wGA**, *Cracklin-bread.* **1914** *DN* 4.159 **cVA**, *Cracklin-bread.* **1938** *AmSp* 13.22 **NE**, *Cracklin' bread.* **1958** *PADS* 29.8 **TN**, *Crackling bread.* **1960** (1962) Lee *Mockingbird* 33 **AL**, It was not often that she made crackling bread, she said she never had time. **1962** Atwood *Vocab. TX* 114, Since corn bread is not offered in stores, many people are no longer familiar with .. *cracklin bread.* **1965–70** *DARE* (Qu. H18, *Special kinds of bread*) 16 Infs, **Sth, S Midl**, Cracklin bread; 13 Infs, **Sth, S Midl**, Crackling bread; **FL6, KY85, MO38**, Crackling corn bread; (Qu. H14, *Bread that's made with cornmeal*) 12 Infs, **Sth**, Cracklin bread; **LA19, OK21**, Crackling bread; **SC42, 51, VA42**, Cracklin corn bread; **FL6, NC8**, Crackling corn bread; (Qu. H43, *Foods made from parts of the head and inner organs of an animal*) Infs **GA55, MO3**, Cracklin bread; (Qu. H45, *Dishes made with meat*) Inf **TN5**, Cracklin bread.

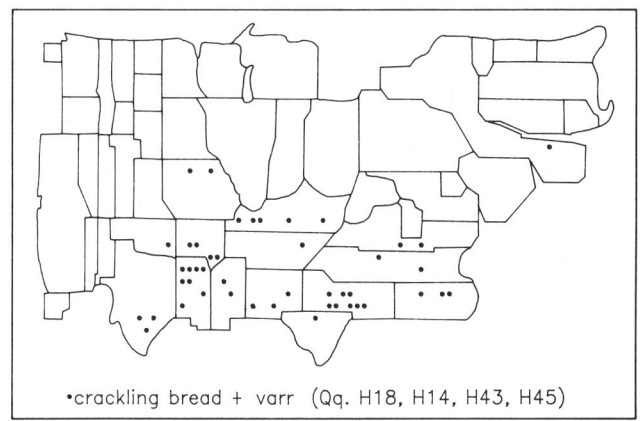

•crackling bread + varr (Qq. H18, H14, H43, H45)

crackling corn pone n Also *crackling pone*
=**crackling bread.**

1967 *DARE* (Qu. H18, *Special kinds of bread*) Inf **LA11**, Cracklin corn pone—with fried cracklins in it; (Qu. H43, *Foods made from .. inner organs of an animal*) Inf **MD35**, Crackling pone.

crackling ice See **crackly ice**

crackling pone See **crackling corn pone**

cracklins See **crackling**

crackloo n Also *crackaloo* [*crack* a narrow break or split + *loo* a card game of chance] **chiefly Sth, S Midl**

A game orig played by pitching coins so as to fall on or near cracks.

1843 (1973) Porter *Big Bear AR* 176, It may be crack-loo, poker, brag, or set-back-euchre. **1902** *Everybody's Mag.* 7.83/2 **TX**, In those times cattlemen played at crack-loo on the sidewalks with double-eagles. **1940** (1978) Still *River of Earth* 209 **KY**, While Mother washed the dishes we played crackaloo, pitching beans at a floor seam. **1946** *PADS* 6.10 **neNC** (as of 1900–10), *Crack-a-loo* ... A game played with pennies, nickels, or dimes. The coin is pitched against the ceiling and falls to the floor. The person whose coin comes to rest on or nearest a chosen crack

wins. **1967–70** *DARE* (Qu. EE40, *Table games . . played around here,
using dice*) Inf **VA42**, Crackaloo—throw dice, bet for pennies; (Qu.
EE33, *Other outdoor games . . that children play now, or that were played
in your childhood*) Inf **LA14**, Crackaloo—with bottle tops. You lag for
place to see who goes first, then one throws up a handful—the other calls
heads or tails and gets all those that land according to his call. Then the
other takes his turn, and so on. **1968** Adams *Western Words*, Crack-a-
loo.

crack loose v phr Cf **cut loose**

1 See quots.

1902 *DN* 2.231 **sIL**, *Crack loose . . .* To execute a threat . . to proceed
against. **1906** *DN* 3.116 **sIN**, *Crack loose . . .* To let one's self loose; to
act in a threatening manner. "Crack loose if you dare."

2 See quot.

1902 *DN* 2.231 **sIL**, *Crack loose . . .* In a command, to act instantly.

crackly ice n Also *crackle, crackling ice*
=**rubber ice.**

1954 *Harder Coll.* **cwTN**, *Crackly ice:* Ice that will bend but not break
when stepped on. **1966–70** *DARE* (Qu. B35, *Ice that will bend when
you step on it, but not break*) Infs **IL34, IN75**, Crackly ice; **VA105,
WA18**, Crackling ice; **PA128, 165**, Crackle(s).

cracknel n
=**crackling 1.**

1889 *Century Dict.* 1326/2, *Cracknel . . pl.* Small bits of fat pork fried
crisp.—*Cracknel bread,* bread in which pork cracknels are mixed: a
luxury among the negroes of the southern United States. Also called
goody-bread. **1953** Piercy *Shaker Cook Book* 138, *Cracknels,* cracklings.

crack of day n Also *cracking of day* **chiefly Sth**
Dawn, daybreak.

1887 *Outing* 10.7/1, At "crack of day," as the sergeant of the guard
expressed it, the stir of camp was started by waking up the cook. **1899**
(1912) Green *VA Folk-Speech, Crack of day . . .* Break of day. The
narrow crack of light on the horizon which is the first appearance of
dawn. "He was up by the crack of day." **1908** *DN* 3.302 **eAL, wGA**,
Crack of day. **1922** Gonzales *Black Border* 294 **sSC, GA coasts** [Gullah
glossary], *Crack-uh-day.* **1927** Kennedy *Gritny* 101 **sLA** [Black], Looks
like I could hyeah evvy rooster . . crowin' an' 'nouncin' de crackin' o' day
all over Gritny. **1970** *Foxfire* Spring–Summer 35 **nGA**, So we pulled
out before day an' went up above Barker's Creek there a piece, an' got up
there before crack a' day. **1970** Tarpley *Blinky* 46 **neTX**, Crack of day.
1970 *DARE* (Qu. A1, . . *The time in the early morning before the sun
comes into sight*) Inf **VA47**, Crack of day. **1972** Cooper *NC Mt. Folkl.*
90, *Crack of day.*

crack one's breath See **crack one's teeth**

crack one's side(s) v phr Also *crack, ~ a gut, ~ a rib* esp
among Black speakers Cf **crack up**
To hurt oneself (with violent laughter): see quots.

1953 Brewer *Word Brazos* 66 **eTX** [Black], Dey gonna . . crack dey sides
laffin' when de young preachuh an' his wife come runnin' outen de
chu'ch house when de lamps goes out an' de ghostes staa'ts to comin' in.
1965–70 *DARE* (Qu. GG31, *To laugh very hard: "I thought I'd
_____."*) 18 Infs, **chiefly Atlantic**, Crack my side(s); **LA3, VA50**,
Crack my sides laughing; **AL60, MD47, MO23, VA37**, Crack; **NC63,
PA118**, Crack a rib; (Qu. FF21b, *About old jokes . . "The first time I
heard that one I _____."*) Inf **NC84**, I almost cracked; **FL48, MS86**, I
cracked my side(s); (Qu. GG30, *To suddenly break out laughing: "When
he told her that, she just _____."*) Inf **MS45**, Almost cracked her side;
IL99, Cracked a gut. [19 of 31 Infs Black]

crack one's teeth v phr Also *crack one's breath* [Afr calque; see
also **crack** v **3**] **SC, GA coasts** *Gullah* Cf **break a breath**
To speak—usu in neg constrs.

1867 Allen *Slave Songs* xxxv **eSC**, " 'E nebber crack 'e bret," *i.e.,* say a
word. **1888** Jones *Negro Myths* 156 **GA coast**, Dem walk up tarrur side
de fire an look at we, but dem yent bin crack eh teet ter we. **1922**
Gonzales *Black Border* 294 **sSC, GA coasts** [Gullah glossary], *Crack 'e
bre't'*—crack his or her breath; same as "crack 'e teet'." *Ibid, Crack 'e
teet' . .* meaning opened her or his mouth to speak; as: " 'E yent crack 'e
teet' "—She never opened her mouth. *Ibid* 344, Buh Rabbit . . say:
"Wuh you hole me han fuh? Lemme go . . ." De Tar Baby yent crack eh
teet. **1928** Peterkin *Scarlet Sister Mary* 211 **SC** [Gullah], Ben would
make such a fine one. E would scare de women so bad dey couldn' crack

dey teeth, to holler. **1941** Writers' Program SC *Folk Tales* 107, W'en
dey lef' by deyself you could hear a tappin', tappin', tappin' all day an' all
night. An' dey wouldn' crack dey teet' to dem. **1949** Turner *Africanisms*
233, [krak tit] 'to speak,' i.e., 'to crack the teeth.'

cracks See **crackers** intj

crack seed n [Chinese calque] **HI**
A dried fruit; see quot 1972.

c1970 *DARE* File **HI**, *Crack seed:* Chinese dried fruit sold by the pound
as a snack. **1972** Carr *Da Kine Talk* 99 **HI**, Children from all ethnic
groups consider *crack seed* and *see mui* . . to be better than candy. The
terms have become generic ones for a variety of preparations of dried
plums or other fruits, salty, sour, or sweet, and sometime with the seed
actually cracked to give additional flavor. *Ibid* 128, *Crack seed* vs
cracked seed or *see mui*—"Crack-Seed Center" is the name of a small
but popular store not far from the Manoa campus of the University of
Hawaii . . . Many Island youngsters use the Chinese words *see mui,*
pronouncing them "see moy."

crack up v phr [Fig from *crack up* to lose control esp when under
pressure] *esp among young, urban, coll educ, and Black
speakers* Cf **crack one's side(s)**
To laugh suddenly or very hard.

1965–70 *DARE* (Qu. GG30, *To suddenly break out laughing: "When
he told her that, she just _____."*) 35 Infs, **widely scattered,** Cracked
up; (Qu. GG31, *To laugh very hard: "I thought I'd _____."*) 11 Infs,
scattered, Crack up; (Qu. FF21b, *About old jokes . . "The first time I
heard that one I _____."*) Infs **CT35, FL51, IL138, NC63, 84, SC67,
VA67**, Cracked up. [Of all Infs responding to Qq. GG30 and GG31, 12%
were young, 7% comm type 1, 34% coll educ, and 6% Black; of those
giving this response, 62% were young, 34% comm type 1, 51% coll educ,
and 32% Black.] **1970** Major *Afro–Amer. Slang, Crack up:* (1950's) [To
be] convulsive with laughter.

crack willow n Also *crackle willow*
The brittle **willow** *(Salix fragilis).*

1892 Apgar *Trees Nth. U.S.* 163, (Brittle Willow. Crack-willow.) . . A
tall . . handsome Willow . . cultivated from Europe for basket-work, and
extensively naturalized. **1897** Sudworth *Arboreous Flora* 127, *Salix
fragilis* . . . Crack Willow. **1936** *Torreya* 36.78, The season . . is
continued with the tree willows such as the crackle willow *(S. fragilis)*
and the black willow *(S. nigra).* **1970** Correll *Plants TX* 453, *Salix
fragilis . .* Crack willow.

cracky adj

1930 Shoemaker *1300 Words* 12 **cPA Mts** (as of c1900), *Cracky*—Odd
or eccentric.

cracky intj Also sp *crackee, crackey, crackie* [Prob euphem for
Christ; cf **crickey** intj]
Freq in phr *by cracky:* Used as a mild oath.

1830 *Painesville* (Ohio) *Telegraph* 15 June 3/2 (*DA*), Oh! Crackee what
luck! **1856** Holmes *Lena Rivers* 69, That's so, by cracky. You've hit her
this time, granny. **1880** Pierce *Zachariah* 37 (*DAE*), "Oh, crackey!"
exclaimed Peggy, clapping her hands. **1903** *DN* 2.296 **Cape Cod MA**,
Crackie! Exclamation of sudden surprise. **1907** *DN* 3.206 **nwAR. 1950**
WELS (*Exclamations beginning with the sound of "cr-"*) 3 Infs, **WI**, (By)
cracky. **1959** *VT Hist.* new ser 27.131 **cn,neVT**, *By cracky! . .* Common. *Ibid, Cracky-be-darn! . .* Rare. **1960** Criswell *Resp. to PADS* 20
Ozarks, *Cracky . . .* In this section always used with *by* as a mild
substitute for profanity. (Not extremely common, probably rarely used
now.) **1966–70** *DARE* (Qu. NN31, *Exclamations beginning with the
sound of "cr-"*) Infs **NH5, NY230, VT7**, By cracky; (Qu. NN27a,
Weakened substitutes for "God") Inf **NH5**, By cracky.

cracky n See **cracky wagon**

cracky benders n Also *cracker benders, crackers and benders*
CT, RI Cf **bender, crackly ice**
=**rubber ice**; a game played on such ice.

1943 *LANE* Map 575 1 inf, **seCT**, [krækɨ bendəz, krækə ~], the game of
running and sliding on thin ice. **1969** *DARE* (Qu. B35, *Ice that will bend
when you step on it, but not break*) Inf **RI12**, Cracky benders; **RI8**,
Crackers and benders.

cracky wagon n Also *cracky* [*crack* noise + *-y*] **esp PA, WV**
old-fash
A small, lightweight wagon.

1890 *DN* 1.60 **wPA**, *Cracky-wagon:* a one-horse wagon, without springs. **1940** *AmSp* 15.83 **swPA, WV,** *Cracky,* a small light wagon, sometimes called a 'spring wagon.' **1946** Driscoll *Country Jake* 179 **csKS,** Frank Yaw, who raised peaches on a sandy tract, . . went about his lawful occasions in what was called a cracky wagon, drawn by two little donkeys. **1967–70** *DARE* (Qu. N41c, *Horse-drawn vehicles to carry light loads*) Infs **PA**187, 234, **WV**4, Cracky wagon; (Qu. N41b, *Horse-drawn vehicles to carry heavy loads*) Inf **OH**92, Cracky wagon (this may be an expression from my husband's Illinois background); (QR p102) Inf **CO**7, *Cracky wagon:* a one-horse Pennsylvania wagon — one seat, no cover.

cradle n

1 In railroading: a kind of freight car.

1943 *AmSp* 18.164 [Railroad language], *Cradle.* A gondola or open-top car. **1945** Hubbard *Railroad Ave.* 338.

2 =sawbuck 1.

1966–69 *DARE* (Qu. L59, *An implement with an X-frame . . to hold firewood for sawing*) Infs **FL**12, **SC**63, Cradle; **IL**31, Log cradle.

‡3 A stoneboat.

1967 *DARE* (Qu. L57, *A low wooden platform used for bringing stones or heavy things out of the fields*) Inf **NJ**2, Cradle.

4 A rope hitch: see quot.

1975 Gould *ME Lingo, Cradle* — Besides its usual meanings, this is a term Mainers use for a Y-shaped rope hitch when towing a canoe. A line directly off the bow causes a keelless canoe to sideweave; the *cradle* does the towing from the forward gunwales just abaft the bow, and the craft will follow steadily. Lobstermen also use a *cradle* hitch to attach warps to their traps to gain a direct pull.

cradle hole n

A large hole or rut (in a road).

1982 *Greenfield Recorder* (MA) 27 Feb sec A 4, If you drove a horse and sleigh in spring, you must remember the "cradle holes" that had to be avoided. They were about the same as the present-day holes.

cradle knoll n chiefly Nth, esp NEng

A small mound or hummock with a cradle-like depression beside it.

1887 (1895) Robinson *Uncle Lisha* 40 **VT,** During the season of sugar-making . . . Stumps, logs, and wintergreen-clad cradle knolls began to show above the snow. **1905** U.S. Forest Serv. *Bulletin* 61.34, *Cradle knolls,* small knolls which require grading in the construction of logging roads. (N[orth] W[oods], L[ake] S[tates].) **1939** *LANE* Map 38 **sME,** The map shows terms for a small elevation in land . . . *knoll,* either a round-topped elevation in a field, meadow or pasture, or a small hump (=*cradle knoll, hummock*). *Ibid,* 1 inf, **eME,** *Cradle-knoll,* in a pasture; 1 inf, **sNH,** *Cradle-knoll,* a very small knoll. **1940–41** Cassidy *WI Atlas.* **1968** *DARE* (Qu. C17, . . *A small rounded hill*) Inf **NY**92, Cradle knoll. **1969** *DARE* Tape **MA**58, Cradle knoll is a hump . . . The land's never plowed. And that'd be a New Englander, probably, because in the west they wouldn't have those cradle knolls . . . It's a small hump in the ground, not more than two or three feet high, not a hill; there'd be hollers between, just kind of undulating.

‡cradle leg n

1970 *DARE* (Qu. X37, *Words . . to describe people's legs if they are noticeably bent, or uneven, or not right*) Inf **NJ**67, Cradle legs.

cradle rock n [*cradle* device attached to a scythe + **rock** whetstone]

A whetstone.

1949 *AmSp* 24.107 **ceGA, nwSC.** **1967** *DARE* (Qu. L38, *What do you use around here to sharpen tools in the field?*) Inf **SC**34, Cradle rock for [a] grain cradle.

craft n [By ext from *craft* ship]

A person: see quot.

1916 Macy–Hussey *Nantucket Scrap Basket* **MA,** "Craft" — This word is often given a personal application. Respect or contempt are expressed by such terms as "She's quite a craft," or "He's a poor craft." Eccentricity is implied in the term "a queer craft."

craftman n Hence also *craftmanship* [Alter of *craftsman*]

1967–70 *DARE* (Qu. KK5b, *A very skilled or expert person*) Infs **KY**84, **VA**2, Craftman; **LA**40, **NY**75, ['kræfmən]; **NJ**7, ['kræftmɪn]; (Qu. KK3b, *Something done perfectly . . "It _____."*) Inf **MA**1, Shows good craftmanship.

crag-jangle n [Prob from its preference for a rocky habitat and the bell-shaped flower]

=alumroot 1.

1933 Small *Manual SE Flora* 592, *Heuchera* . . . Alumroots. Rock-geraniums. Crag-jangles.

cragrock n

Perh a type of shale; see quot.

1969 *DARE* (Qu. C26, *Special kinds of stone or rock . . in this part of the state*) Inf **TN**30, Cragrock ['krɛg,rɑk] is in layers something like limestone.

‡craig myrtle n [?Alter of *crape myrtle*]

1970 *DARE* (Qu. T16, *What kinds of trees are special around here?*) Inf **CA**185, Craig myrtle [kreg mʌrdəl].

crake See **creek** n[1]

cram n See **cramp** n

cram v

1930 Shoemaker *1300 Words* 15 **cPA Mts** (as of c1900), *Cram* — To co-habit.

cramberry n Also sp *crambry* [By assim from *cranberry*]

A cranberry.

1670 (1937) Denton *Brief Descr.* 4 **NYC,** The Fruits natural to the Island are . . *Huckelberries, Cramberries.* **1808** *Mth. Anthol. & Boston Rev.* 5.536/1, Cranberry Sauce, vulgarly called cramberry sauce, from the voracious manner in which they eat it, is made from a berry. **1902** Rice *Mrs. Wiggs* 24 **KY,** I think I would n't 'a' minded so much . . ef they had n't 'a' sent the cramberries, too! **1908** *DN* 3.302 **eAL, wGA,** *Cramberry* . . . Cranberry. **1927** *AmSp* 3.139 **ME,** "*Crambry*" (cramberry). **1941** *LANE* Map 274, 1 inf, **swCT,** [kræmbɪriz], not common here; 1 inf, **ceMA,** [kræmbɪrɪz]. **1959** *VT Hist.* new ser 27.131, *Cranberry* ['kræm,berɪ] . . . Occasional.

cram-jam v

To fill to overflowing.

1905 *East Coast Visitor* 17 Aug 7/3 (*OEDS*), I've seen these flats cram-jammed with fowl of all sorts.

cram-jam full adj

As full as possible.

1903 *DN* 3.296 **Cape Cod MA,** *Cram jam full* . . . Crammed full. **1907** *DN* 3.206 **nwAR, Cape Cod MA.** **1908** *DN* 3.302 **eAL, wGA,** The jar was cram-jam full. **1953** *PADS* 19.10 **Appalachia, eNC,** *Cram-jam-full* . . . Very full. **1954** *Harder Coll.* **cwTN,** *Cram-jam full:* as full as possible.

‡crammer n [*cram* to stuff, prob infl by Ger *Kramkammer* cubbyhole]

1968 *DARE* (Qu. D7, *A small space anywhere in a house where you can hide things or get them out of the way*) Inf **NY**116, Crammer. [Inf of German parentage]

crammus See **crimus**

cramp v

1 To curve or turn sharply (toward).

1875 Twain in *Atlantic Mth.* 35.286/2, A boat hates shoal water . . . Now cramp her down! Snatch her! **1883** Twain *Life on Missip.* (Boston) 223, I *told* you not to cramp that reef. **1914** *DN* 4.154 **NH** (as of 1858–c1900), *Cramp* . . . To turn around (a waggon) so as to leave a space to get off; also, "the road cramps around a building." **1919** (1923) Cady *Rhymes of Vt.* 50 (*DA*), They cramp and back and cramp again And out a-come the helper men. **1924** Raine *Troubled Waters* iii (*OEDS*), She tried to cramp to the left.

2 To exert pressure on; to affect strongly; hence ppl adj *cramped* strongly affected by.

1969 *DARE* (Qu. U18, *If you force somebody to pay money that he owes you . . you might say: "I finally made him _____."*) Inf **NC**76, Cramped him [into paying it]; (Qu. AA10, *A very special liking . . a boy may have for a girl . . "He _____ her."*) Inf **CA**158, He's cramped on her; (Qu. II29b, *You might try to explain the unpleasant effect . . [a] person has on you: "He just _____."*) Inf **NY**76, Cramps me.

cramp n Also *cram, crum, crump* [Euphem for *Christ*]

1950 *WELS* (*Exclamations beginning with the sound of "cr-"*) 2 Infs, **WI,** Cram sakes; 1 Inf, Cram; 1 Inf, Cramp's sake; 1 Inf, For crump's sake; 1 Inf, Crumps. **1966–70** *DARE* (Qu. NN31) Inf **NY**234, By cramp; Oh cramps; **NY**73, Cramp's sakes; **WI**55, Cram sakes; **MI**28, 43, For (the) crump's sake; (Qu. NN27b, *Weakened substitutes for "God": "For _____ sakes.'*) Inf **NY**73, Cramp's; **MI**28, Crump's. **1967** *DARE* File nw**MI**, For crum(p)'s sake.

crampass See **grampus**

cramp bark n [See quot 1848]

Usu the **highbush cranberry,** but also a **black haw 1** (here: *Viburnum prunifolium*).

1848 Bartlett *Americanisms,* Cramp-bark. (*Viburnum oxycoccus.*) The popular name of a medicinal plant; its properties anti-spasmodic. It bears a fruit intensely acid. In New England it is called the tree cranberry. **1942** Van Dersal *Ornamental Amer. Shrubs* 109 *(DA),* It is frequently listed as *Viburnum americanum,* and called cramp bark, highbush cranberry, pembina, and wild guelder-rose. **1971** Krochmal *Appalachia Med. Plants* 272, *Viburnum Prunifolium* L. . . Common *Names:* . . cramp bark.

cramp-colic n Also sp *cramp-cholic* [Redund] **scattered Sth, S Midl**

Abdominal spasms; appendicitis.

1857 *Harper's Mag.* 15.860/2, Jack hath eaten four large potatoes, three big drop dumplings, one boiled fowl, and bread according . . . It was fair to conclude that Jack was dead from cramp-cholic. **1894** *Jrl. Amer. Folkl.* 7.112 **Alleghenies,** Rattlesnake venom cures cramp-colic. **1944** Clark *Pills* 236, One of the mortal diseases of the South was "cramp colic," and many a southerner . . tried to relieve his abdominal pains with large doses of calomel, salts or castor oil. **1960** Criswell *Resp. to PADS* 20 **Ozarks,** *Cramp colic* . . . Colic accompanied by cramps. Common ailment in earlier days. **1967** *DARE* (Qu. BB3c, *A sudden pain that comes in the side*) Inf **TX**40, Cramp-colic. **1973** *Foxfire* 2.382 n**GA,** I never heard tell of 'pendicitis till I was growed . . I didn't know there was such a thing. People called it th' cramp colic.

crampfish n [See quot 1860]

An electric ray of the family Torpedinidae, esp *Narcine brasiliensis.*

1793 MA Hist. Soc. *Coll.* 3.119, There are but few towns so well supplied with fish of all kinds as Wellfleet; among which are some that are uncommon, such as the sword-fish and cramp-fish. **1860** Prescott *Telegraph* 37 *(DAE),* The torpedo . . is known by the inhabitants of that locality [=Cape Cod] as *Cramp-fish,* from the manner in which the muscles of the hands and arms are cramped when in contact with this singular animal. **1939** Natl. Geog. Soc. *Book of Fishes* 250, The electric ray, or crampfish, . . occurs along our Pacific coast . . in moderately deep to shallow water. **1960** Amer. Fisheries Soc. *List Fishes* 55, Crampfish . . lesser electric ray *[Narcine brasiliensis].*

cramp knot n [*cramp* muscular spasm + *knot* lump in wood caused by a branch growing from a tree trunk; cf *OED cramp-stone* "a stone used as a charm against cramp" 1629 →]

A knot of wood carried as a supposed preventive of muscle cramp.

1978 *Yankee* Oct 56/1 **NH,** *Dear Oracle: My father used to carry what he called a "cramp knot" in his pocket . . . can you tell me what they were? . . . Answer:* The knot is from a cranberry tree, sometimes called a snowball tree. It is said to be anti-spasmodic. **[1982** *DNE* 119 **Newfoundland,** *Cramp* n Attrib *cramp knot:* small knot cut from a tree and worn as a charm against muscular contractions . . . "Cramp was believed to be prevented by a 'cramp knot' worn on the person. A cramp knot is a small round knob of wood varying in size from one to two inches in diameter and larger. It grows mainly on fir trees" . . . "It was a belief that by wearing a cramp knot (a node cut from a tree) around your neck you would have no cramps."]

crampois, crampush See **grampus**

cramp weed n Cf **cramp bark**

A **silverweed 1** (here: *Potentilla anserina*).

1873 in 1976 Miller *Shaker Herbs* 232, *Potentilla anserina* . . Cramp Weed . . . As a tea it is used for diarrhea.

cranberry bean n Also *cranberry* **scattered, but esp NEast, S Atl**

Any of var beans (*Phaseolus* spp) with deep red markings; see quots.

1790 Deane *New Engl. Farmer* 20/1, The cranberry-bean is so called from the resemblance it bears, when ripe, to that fruit. **1884** Baldwin

Yankee School-Teacher 213 **VA,** The fus' time I seed it hauled out an' the beans (most used up they was then) rattlin' roun' in it, it give me a start. 'The mortal suz!' I yelled out, 'what's that?' 'Why, cranberries, these be,' says he; 'I hain't got no kidneys now.' **1941** *LANE* Map 259, 2 infs, **NH,** Cranberry beans; 1 inf, c**VT,** Cranberry beans, a special variety; 1 inf, ce**VT,** Cranberry beans, the usual local variety; 1 inf, se**NH,** Cranberry beans, speckled, smaller and more round than Lima beans. **1965–70** *DARE* (Qu. I17, *Beans that are dark red . . dry*) 17 Infs, **chiefly NEast, also S Atl,** Cranberry bean(s); (Qu. I20, *Other kinds of beans*) 15 Infs, **chiefly NEast,** Cranberry beans; **CA**138, Cranberries; (Qu. I14, *Kinds of beans you eat in the pod . . before dry*) Inf **CT**12, Cranberry beans; (Qu. I16, *Large flat beans . . not eaten in the pod*) Inf **VT**16, Cranberry beans. **1971** Bright *Word Geog.* **CA** & **NV** 184, *Pinto beans* . . cranberry beans. **1976** *Wanigan Catalog* 7, *Cranberry [Bean]*—This name has been synonymous with horticultural, in California early, and now pretty much everywhere. Horticultural, or shell beans are a class having full pods streaked with red, and seed similarly marked with buff and red. However, the earliest descriptions of cranberry referred to seed that looked like the berry, i.e. true red cranberry. **1982** *Smithsonian Letters* cn**WV,** Enclosed please find evidence for cranberry bean [some beans enclosed], alias October beans. One of my students found this in a super market in Morgantown.

cranberry bush See **cranberry tree**

cranberry pusher n *joc* Cf *DS* N37

1950 *WELS* (*A small train that runs on a narrow track*) 1 Inf, cw**WI,** Cranberry pusher. Occasional.

cranberry tree n Also *cranberry bush, tree cranberry*
=**highbush cranberry.**

1814 Pursh *Flora Americae* 1.203 [sic *DA*—quot not found]. **1824** Bigelow *Florula Bostoniensis* 117, *Tree Cranberry* . . . Fruit large, red, ripening late, and remaining after the leaves have fallen, intensely acid and somewhat bitter. **1857** Gray *Manual of Botany* 168, *Cranberry-tree* . . . The acid fruit is used as a (poor) substitute for cranberries. **1892** Apgar *Trees Nth. U.S.* 114, Fruit is peduncled clusters, light red and quite sour (whence the name "Cranberry-tree"). **1931** U.S. Dept. Ag. *Misc. Pub.* 101.153, *American cranberrybush* . . . is not known to have material browse significance. **1960** Teale *Journey into Summer* 10 **NH,** At the top of the bank nearby . . . a cranberry tree spread its broad, three-pointed leaves. This north-country viburnum, *Viburnum opulus,* is variously known as the squaw bush, the water elder, the high-bush cranberry and the pincushion tree. **1976** Bailey–Bailey *Hortus Third* 1155, *[Viburnum] trilobum* . . . Cranberry bush, cranberry tree, . . tree c[ranberry].

cranch See **craunch**

crane n

1 Std: a bird of the family Gruidae.

2 A bird of the family Ardeidae, esp the **great blue heron.**

1858 Baird *Birds* 668, *Ardea herodias* . . . Great Blue Heron, or Crane. **1913** *Pacific Coast Avifauna* 9.21, *Great Blue Heron* . . . Known to nearly everyone as "Crane," . . it seems fortunate that the impression prevails everywhere to the effect that this bird is strictly protected. **1949** Sprunt–Chamberlain *SC Bird Life* 85, *Louisiana Heron* . . . *Hydranassa tricolor ruficollis* . . *Local Names:* Crane. **1951** Teale *North with Spring* 111 **LA,** Our rushing advance frightened individuals up from time to time, . . Louisiana herons and little blue "cranes" and American bitterns flapping out of the vegetation. **1955** *MA Audubon Soc. Bulletin* 39.312, Herons are frequently mis-called cranes.

3 pronc-sp *crene:* A pain or crick (in the neck). [*crane* to stretch the neck forward] Cf *DS* BB3a

1972 *Atlanta Letters,* Ever have "crene" in your neck? . . every part of our nation uses colloquialisms that can't be understood in another region. *Ibid* ne**GA,** Yes, I have cranes in my neck, you bet. . . . When you work like we did, anything can happen to you. *Ibid* cn**GA,** I've often heard my mother give a remedy for a crene, only she called it a crick in the neck. **1980** *DARE* File c**TX,** One of my students said her father would speak of having a [kri:n] in his neck—a word she never used. I checked it with students in other classes and found about five or six (out of about eighty) who knew or used the word . . . All who knew and used the word were from central Texas and were white.

craneberry n Also *crane's berry*

A cranberry (here: *Vaccinium* spp).

1824 Bigelow *Florula Bostoniensis* 154, *Vaccinium macrocarpon* . . . *Craneberry* . . . The craneberry vine spreads in large beds at the bottom of the grass in boggy meadows. **1900** Lyons *Plant Names* 271, *V. macrocarpon* . . . Crane's-berry. **1961** Smith *MI Wildflowers* 283, Cranberries . . . The plant was originally called "crane berry" because the shape of the flowers suggests the head and neck of a crane.

cranebill See **cranesbill 1**

crane fisher n
A wading bird: see quot.
1954 *Harder Coll.* **cwTN**, *Crane fisher*—A bird that commonly stays on ponds or around streams.

crane fly n
Std: a long-legged insect of the family Tipulidae. Also called **daddy-long-legs, gallinipper, weaver**

cranefly orchid n Also *crippled cranefly, mottled cranefly*
An orchid *(Tipularia discolor)* which produces flowers thought to resemble craneflies. Also called **elfin spur, tallow root**
1900 Lyons *Plant Names* 372, Cranefly Orchis . . . From . . an insect which the flowers resemble. **1933** Small *Manual SE Flora* 387, *Cranefly-orchid.* **1950** Correll *Native Orchids* 277, Crippled Crane-fly . . . One of the petals distinctly overlaps the dorsal sepal for about half its width, resulting in a "crippled" appearance of the flower. **1976** Bailey-Bailey *Hortus Third* 1116, Cranefly orchid, . . crippled-cranefly, mottled cranefly.

crane's berry See **craneberry**

cranesbill n
1 also *cranebill, cranesbill geranium*: A plant of the genus *Geranium.* Also called **wild geranium** For other names of var spp see **chocolate flower, dove's foot geranium, herb Robert, spotted geranium**
1784 in 1785 *Amer. Acad. Arts & Sci. Memoirs* 1.469, Geranium . . . Common cranesbill . . . The root is astringent, and frequently used in gargles for cankerous sores in the mouth. **1883** *Century Illustr. Mag.* 26.727/1, The strictest utilitarian cannot find fault with the way in which the crane's-bill and the meadow-violet expend their surplus revenue in adding to their attractiveness. **1911** Porter *Harvester* 314 **IN**, On and on they slowly drove through the woods, past the big beds of cranesbill, violets, and lilies. **1931–33** *LANE Worksheets* **nwRI**, Crane's bill [Geranium]. **1966** *DARE* (Qu. S26c, *Wildflowers that grow in woods*) Inf **MI**92, Cranesbills; (Qu. S26e, *Other wildflowers*) Inf **WA**15, Cranebill. **1967** *DARE* FW Addit **VA**15, Cranesbill—named after the seed pod which resembles a crane's bill. **1967** *DARE* Wildfl QR Pl.119,120 Inf **OR**12, Cranebill; **CO**7, **MI**57, **OH**37, Wild cranesbill. **1971** Krochmal *Appalachian Med. Plants* 134, *Geranium Maculatum L.* (Geraniaceæ) Common names: . . common crane's bill, cranesbill, cranesbill geranium.
2 An **alumroot 1** (here: *Heuchera pubescens*).
1873 in 1976 Miller *Shaker Herbs* 127, Alum Root. *Heuchera pubescens.* Cranesbill. Splitrock.
3 Alfilaria.
1963 Craighead *Rocky Mt. Wildflowers* 105, *Erodium cicutarium* . . . Other names: Cranesbill, . . Alfilaria.

cranesbill geranium See **cranesbill 1**

crane willow n Cf **button willow**
=**buttonbush 1.**
1900 Lyons *Plant Names* 90, *C. occidentalis* . . . Crane-willow. **1960** Vines *Trees SW* 938, Vernacular names for the shrub are . . Crane-willow [etc].

craney adj Cf *DS* X49
1899 (1912) Green *VA Folk-Speech, Craney* . . . A person is said to be *craney,* when he is tall and slender.

craney crow n Also sp *crany crow* [See quot 1908]
In the game of **chickamy chickamy craney crow:** the hawk, witch, or other predatory character.
1877 *Lumberman's Gaz.* 24 May sec 9 1/1 **MI**, [Cartoon:] Chickie! My chickie! My craney crow. You've had your "day" and down you go out through the smalley end of the horn. **1906** *DN* 3.132 **nwAR**, *Crany-crow* . . . Expression used in the game of "*old witch.*" **1908** *DN* 3.296 **eAL, wGA**, Carion-crow . . . Also commonly called *kyarny-crow.* Perhaps by metathesis, the form *crany-crow* occurs in the familiar rime in the game of Old Witch: "Chicky-ma, chicky-ma, crany-crow, / I went to the well to wash my toe." **1941** *Sat. Eve. Post* 10 May 111/2, It was hard not to gobble them down like an old craney crow.

crang n [Alter of Du *kreng* carcass of a whale; a skeleton]
1895 *DN* 1.386 **cNY**, *Crang:* a scrawny animal.

crank v
1 Of an engine: to turn over, start.
1967 *DARE* FW Addit **sGA**, *Crank* [kræŋk]—To start a car. People *never* talk of "starting a car." "The damned car won't crank." "It oughta crank good now." And a teenager, in preparing to ride a Honda: "How do you crank it?" *Ibid* **swNC**, *Crank:* Used of a car engine turning over—"After it set for a couple of hours, it wouldn't crank."
2 By ext: to cause to accelerate.
c1970 *DARE* File **swPA, SC**, *Crank the car:* Tramp on the gas.
3 To draw out with a rotary pump.
1970 *DARE* FW Addit **ceVA**, The molasses came in barrels and they cranked it out. (*Crank*—to pump). Occasional.

crank adj Also *cranky* [Abbr for *crank-sided*] **Atlantic**
Of a boat or ship: liable to tip or capsize; unsteady.
1702 (1870) *PA Hist. Soc. Memoirs* 9.82, A jealousy of the vessel being crank, and weak by her beating when on ground in the bay. **1830** Ames *Mariner's Sketches* 50 **MA**, I saw the lovely neophyte of Bacchus a few evenings afterwards, with a cloud of mounted beaux, civil, military and ecclesiastical around her carriage, but she was apparently less 'crank in the upper works' then, than when I first saw her. **1899** (1912) Green *VA Folk-Speech, Crank* . . . Cranky; liable to lurch or capsize. Cranksided. Unsteady; not firm. **1903** *DN* 2.294 **Cape Cod MA**. **1939** Coffin *Capt. Abby* 110 **ME** (as of c1860s), They took in 2725 boxes and 333 barrels of sugar. Abby was afraid of it. It was a cranky cargo, sugar . . . "Capt. Curtis," she wrote her mother, "says every ship is crank loaded with sugar." **1942** ME Univ. *Studies* 12, Ships . . when light were too *crank* or *cranky,* i.e., unstable, to sail with safety. **1967** *DARE* (Qu. KK70, *Something . . out of proper shape: "That house is all _____."*) Inf **LA**6, Cranky. **1975** Gould *ME Lingo, Crank, cranky*—Said of a vessel which doesn't handle properly, whether from poor design, dirty bottom, poorly stowed cargo, or whatever.

crank n [?Perh a blend of *crick* and *cramp;* cf **crane 3**]
1966–68 *DARE* (Qu. BB3a, *A pain that strikes you suddenly in the neck*) Infs **GA**17, **SC**7, Crank; **SC**19, [kreŋk].

crank doctor n Cf *DS* BB53b
1981 *Broaddus Coll.* **ceKY** (as of 1958), Crank doctor—a quack.

crankpot n [Perh blend of *crank + crackpot*]
1966–70 *DARE* (Qu. GG38, *Somebody . . usually mean and bad-tempered: "He's an awful _____."*) Inf **LA**17, Crankpot; (Qu. HH4, *Someone who has odd or peculiar ideas or notions*) Inf **CA**202, Crankpot; (Qu. HH5, *Someone . . queer but harmless*) Inf **MS**21, Crankpot; (Qu. HH22a, *An idle, worthless person: "He's a _____."*) Inf **OK**45, Crankpot.

crank-sided adj Also *crankside* [*crank* bent, out of kilter; cf **crank** adj] **chiefly Sth**
Askew, lopsided.
a1883 (1911) Bagby *VA Gentleman* 51, Here and there is an opening in the woods, with a lonely, crank-sided tobacco-house in the midst, looking as if it were waiting resignedly for the end of the world to come. **1891** *PMLA* 6.173 **TN**, *Cranksided* means twisted or careened to one side. **1893** Shands *MS Speech, Crank-sided* . . . Used by all classes to mean *twisted* or *bent to one side.* A man may be *cranksided* physically, mentally, or morally. The word is, of course, also used of inanimate objects. Frequently heard in Tennessee. **1908** *DN* 3.302 **eAL, wGA**, *Crank-sided.* **1965–70** *DARE* (Qu. MM13, *The table was nice and straight until he came along and knocked it _____*) Infs **MS**69, **NC**15, 88, **SC**40, **VA**69, Crank-sided; (Qu. KK70, *Something . . out of proper shape: "That house is all _____."*) Inf **LA**6, Crank-sided; (Qu. MM3, *When someone does something the wrong way round . . "You've got the whole thing turned _____."*) Inf **NC**38, Crank-sided; (Qu. MM15, *If a carpenter nails a board crossing another board at an angle, you might say: "He nailed the board on _____."*) Inf **LA**7, Crankside.

cranky adj[1]
1 Overly fastidious, fussy.
1965–70 *DARE* (Qu. HH11b, *Someone . . too particular or fussy—if it's a woman*) 16 Infs, **scattered, but esp Midl, Sth**, Cranky; (Qu. HH11a, *Someone . . too particular or fussy—if it's a man*) 12 Infs, **scattered**, Cranky.
2 Eccentric.

1966–70 *DARE* (Qu. HH4, *Someone who has odd or peculiar ideas or notions*) Infs **DC**13, **SC**24, 34, Cranky; **GA**19, Rather cranky; (Qu. II7, *Somebody who doesn't seem to 'fit in'. . you might say. . "He's kind of . . ———.")* Infs **LA**28, **VA**29, Cranky.

3 with *about:* Enamored of, infatuated with.

1967 *DARE* (Qu. AA10, *A very special liking. . a boy may have for a girl . . you'd say, "He ——— her.")* Inf **SC**34, Is cranky about.

cranky adj² See **crank** adj

cranky adj³ [Engl dial *cranky* sprightly, merry, sportive]
1930 Shoemaker *1300 Words* 15 **cPA Mts** (as of c1900), Cranky— High-spirited, cheerful.

cranky n Also *big cranky* [See quot 1917] chiefly **VA**
=**great blue heron.**
1913 Bailey *Birds VA* 38, *Ardea herodias herodias* . . . Big Blue Crane. Cranky. **1917** *Wilson Bulletin* 29.2.78, *Ardea herodias.*—Cranky (a good name for this species, which scolds so vehemently when disturbed), Wallops Revels and Cobbs I[slan]ds., Va. **1951** Pough *Audubon Water Bird* 319, Big cranky. See Great blue heron. **1970** *DARE* (Qu. Q10, *Water and marsh birds common around here*) Inf **VA**52A, Cranky (Great Blue Heron).

cranky adv [**cranky** adj¹ **1**] Cf **nasty neat**
Fastidiously, fussily.
1963 North *Rascal* 100 **WI** (as of c1918), Yes, I live alone. Can't stand womenfolks around—cranky clean.

cranny n
A privy or toilet.
1968 *DARE* (Qu. F37, *Indoor toilet*) Inf **UT**4, Cranny; (Qu. M21a, *An outside toilet building*) Inf **UT**4, Cranny. **c1971** Hall *Snake River Valley* **sID**, 3 infs, Cranny.

crany crow See **craney crow**

craowner See **crowner** n¹

crap n¹ See **crop** n

crap n² See **crappie**

crap v See **crop** v

crape myrtle n Also sp *crepe* ~; also infreq *crape murder, crape tree* [See quot 1952]
A commonly cultivated shrub or small tree (*Lagerstroemia indica*). Also called **Indian lilac, ladies' streamer, laggerstreamer**
1850 (1968) Taylor *Eldorado* 6, The houses of the planters . . are buried among orange trees, acacias and the pink blossoms of the crape myrtle. **1910** C. Harris *Eve's Husb.* 113 *(DA)*, We were sitting upon a bench near a flowering pink crape tree. **1948** *Dly. Ardmoreite* (Ardmore, OK) 18 April 16/2 *(DA)*, Ardmore folk became crape myrtle conscious a few years ago and this city has many lovely crape myrtles as a result. **1952** Taylor *Plants Colonial Days* 30, Crape myrtle . . . The common name comes from the crapelike flower petals and the resemblance of the leaves to the true myrtle. **1965–70** *DARE* (Qu. T16, *Trees. . "special" around here*) 8 Infs, **chiefly Sth**, Crape myrtle; (Qu. S26e, *Wildflowers not yet mentioned*) Inf **DE**2, Crape myrtle; **SC**67, Wild crape myrtle; **MS**82, Crape murder, has a pink flower that grows in a bush—the flowers are very small; (Qu. T5, *Kinds of evergreens, other than pine*) Inf **SC**63, Crape myrtle. **1968** *Budget* (Sugarcreek OH) 18 July, The beautiful flowering crepe myrtle are just beginning to flower . . . the colors range from pale pink to a deep purple. **1969** *Big Sandy News & Lawrence Co. Recorder* (Louisa KY) 18 Sept 3/8, Crape Myrtle (Lagerstroemia indica) is considered by many to be the most magnificent midsummer (late summer in Kentucky) flowering shrub in cultivation. **1969** *SC Market Bulletin* 9 Jan 4, Crepe myrtles. **1970** *DARE* Tape **TX**85, Then we have crape myrtle that comes along and blooms.

crapgrass See **crabgrass 1**

crapout See **cropout**

crappé(e), crapper n¹ See **crappie**

crapper n² [Perh *crap* pronc-sp for *crop* + *-er*]
1901 *DN* 2.138 **cnNY**, Crapper . . . A wealthy but stingy man.

crapper n³ See **cropper 1**

crappie n Also *crap, crappé(e), crapper, croppie, croppy* [Prob CanFr *crapais, crapet* sunfish]

Either of two similar fishes of the sunfish family: the black crappie *(Pomoxis nigromaculatus)* or the white crappie *(Pomoxis annularis).* Also called **calico** n **B3b, calico bass, chinquapin B5, goggle-eye, grass bass, lamplighter, papermouth, speckled perch, strawberry bass, strawberry perch, tinmouth** For other names of the black crappie see **banklick bass, barfish 1, bigfin bass, bitterhead 1, goggle-eye perch, razorback, rock bass, silver bass, speckled bass, speckled crappie** For other names of the white crappie see **bachelor, bridge perch, campbellite, goldring, John Demon, newlight, pale crappie, ringed crappie, sac-a-lait, sago, shad, silver crappie, silver perch, suckley perch, timber crappie, tin perch, white bass, white perch**
1827 in 1969 *Living Museum* 30.28, Black Crappie (C.A. LeSueur), Wabash River, New Harmony, Indiana. **1856** *Porter's Spirit of Times* 20 Sept 43/1 **IL**, Our best fish are the pike and salmon, . . striped, rock and black bass, croppy, and the common sunfish. **1861** Berkeley *English Sportsman* 41 **NYC**, A fish they call the "crappeè." *Ibid* 363 **MO**, They also had the crappè, so pronounced, which was very like our freshwater bream. **1906** *DN* 3.132 **nwAR**, Crappie ['krɔpi] . . Common edible centrachoid fish (Pomoxys annularis). **1914** *DN* 4.163 **NW**, Croppie . . . A Southern fresh water fish resembling perch. **1965–70** *DARE* (Qu. P1, *Freshwater fish . . caught around here that are good to eat*) 137 Infs, **widespread exc NEng**, Crappie(s); 170 Infs, **chiefly Cent, West**, Croppie(s); **OK**25, Black croppie; white croppie; **MD**40, Crap [kræp]; **GA**16, Crappers; (Qu. P7, *Small fish used as bait*) Infs **MN**21, **MO**20, Crappie minnow; **GA**89, Crappie; (Qu. P3, *Freshwater fish . . not good to eat*) Inf **NY**219, Crappie; **WA**31, Croppie; (Qu. P14, . . *Commercial fishing*) Inf **AR**36, Crappie; **KY**86, Croppie; (Qu. P2, *Saltwater fish . . good to eat*) Inf **TX**9, Crappie; (Qu. P4, *Saltwater fish . . not good to eat*) Inf **CA**95, Croppie; (Qu. P16) Inf **GA**42, Fishing for crappies. **1966–67** *DARE* Tape **IL**9, All kinds of panfish . . . croppies, bluegills, ring perch, catfish; **SD**3, Now, then, we've got walleyes moved in here, and croppies. **1968** *Sumter Co. Jrl.* (York AL) 13 June 2/7, We did catch two striped bass and crappie below the dam in the swift water. **1968** *DARE* FW Addit **OK**, Crappie: Invariably spelled this way, but invariably pronounced "croppie." **1975** Evanoff *Catch More Fish* 90, The black crappie has also been called the Calico bass, strawberry bass, grass bass, papermouth, tinmouth, and just plain crappie . . . The black crappie is most numerous in northern waters in Canada, the Great Lakes to New Jersey and south to Texas. It has also been introduced along the Pacific Coast.

crapping See **crop** v **3**

crash v [Prob blend of *crush* and *smash*]
1 To break or squash.
1965–70 *DARE* (Qu. KK21, *When something hollow is crushed by a heavy weight, or by a fall: "They ran the wagon over the coffee pot and ———.")* Infs **IN**45, **MO**1, 17, Crashed (it); (Qu. KK22, . . *Completely shattered: "The jug fell out of the window and was ———.")* Infs **IL**39, **NY**88, Crashed; (Qu. Y33, *Words for squeezing or crushing something —for example, your finger in a door: "I ——— my finger.")* Inf **VT**16, Crashed.

2 To court, to woo.
1973 Allen *LAUM* 1.371 **MN**, *(He is courting her)* Other more or less colorful expressions . . *crashing her* [1 inf].

cratch n¹ [Engl dial *cratch* a rack or crib for fodder]
1981 Hardeman *Shucks* 114, Another Indian corn-storage creation, which immigrants copied and maintained as their most important system, was the cratch or crib. Hernando de Soto's company of explorers found it in use in the Mississippi Valley during the 1540s. It was a little house with bark or thatched roof, sides of slightly separated slats, and a cane floor, and it stood on four posts. While not rodent proof, it resisted the little varmints somewhat. The crib at once kept the ears of corn aired and shielded from direct downpours.

Cratch n² [Alter of *scratch,* itself a blend of *scrat* and *cratch* v to scratch] Cf Pronc Intro 3.I.22
=**Scratch.**
1965 *DARE* (Qu. EE41, *A hobgoblin . . used to threaten children and make them behave*) Inf **NY**205, Old Cratch. [Inf old]

cratch n³ See **crutch**

cratch n⁴ See **crotch** n¹

cratch v [Reduction of *scratch*] Cf Pronc Intro 3.I.22
1922 Gonzales *Black Border* 294 **sSC, GA coasts** [Gullah glossary], 'Cratch . . scratch, scratches, scratched, scratching.

crate n

1 See quot.
1975 Gould *ME Lingo*, *Crate*—A container, and its amount. A lobster *crate* is designed for 100 pounds, and a *crate* can thus mean 100 pounds. Transferred to many metaphors: "He talked for an hour, biggest *crate* of hogwash I ever heard."

2 A bony horse.
1969 *DARE* (Qu. K44, *A bony or poor-looking horse*) Infs **MA**42, 47, Crate.

craul See **crawl** n[2]

craunch v Also sp *cronch;* pronc-sp *cranch*

1 To crush under foot; hence vbl n, ppl adj *craunching,* adv *craunchingly.* **Nth**
1854 (1969) Thoreau *Walden* 285 **MA**, He [a barred owl] could hear me when I moved and cronched the snow with my feet. *Ibid* 287, I heard the cronching of the snow made by the step of a long-headed farmer. **1873** Harte *Mrs. Skaggs* 135 **CA**, At this point there was a pause, of which Mr. Folinsbee availed himself to walk very grimly and craunchingly down the gravel-walk toward the gate. **1904** Day *Kin o' Ktaadn* 182 **ME**, The driving crews who cranched there with spike-soled shoes. **1917** Garland *Son Middle Border* 87 **WI**, The steel [plowshare] running steadily with a crisp craunching ripping sound which I rather liked to hear.

2 To crunch, chew noisily. **chiefly Nth, esp NEng**
1903 *DN* 2.296 **Cape Cod MA** (as of 1850s), *Craunch* [krɔntš] . . . To crunch. **1916** *DN* 4.265 **Cape Cod MA**, She [the Cape housewife] tells her son not to "craunch" his toast. **1941** *LANE* Map 315, Jocular and derogatory terms meaning 'to chew noisily' were systematically recorded in the early stages of the field work. The material is presented below . . . krɔntʃ . . krɔntʃ, kroˑntʃ, of animals . . krauntʃ, of cows eating pumpkins. **1967–68** *DARE* (Qu. H11a, *If somebody eats noisily and rapidly*) Inf **MI**96, Craunches his food; (Qu. H11b, *If he makes a noise with his food, he _____*) Inf **MD**14, Craunch.

3 To **scrunch**.
1967 *DARE* (Qu. Y32, *To squeeze yourself into a small space*) Inf **HI**9, Craunch down.

4 To **chum** v **1**.
1968 *DARE* (Qu. P16, *When fishermen throw bits of bait in the water to attract fish*) Inf **MD**40, Craunching ['krɔnčn̩].

crauncher n [craunch 2]
1968 *DARE* (Qu. X13a, . . *Joking names . . for teeth*) Inf **MD**19, Crauncher.

crave n
A craving, desire.
1966 *DARE* Tape **MS**61, That was my crave when I got grown, to be a blacksmith.

craw n[1]
One's stomach.
1859 Taliaferro *Fisher's R.* 86 **nwNC** (as of 1820s), My craw's full. **1909** *DN* 3.394 **nwAR**, *Craw* . . . Jocosely, a human being's stomach or neck. "I feel sick at the craw this morning." **1967** *DARE* (Qu. BB16a, *If something a person ate didn't agree with him, he might be sick _____ his stomach*) Inf **LA**2, Sick at the craw.

craw n[2] See **crawfish** n

crawcrab See **crawdad** n

craw-craw v [Echoic]
To make the distinctive sound of a hen.
1871 (1882) Stowe *Fireside Stories* 87 **NEng**, There wa'n't nothin' a goin' on but jest the hens a craw-crawin'. *Ibid* 104, A drowsy, dreamy October day, when the hens were lazily "craw, crawing," in a soft, conversational undertone with each other.

crawdab See **crawdad** v **2**

crawdad n Also *crawcrab, crawdab(ber), crawdaddy, crawjinny, crawldaddy, crawpappy, craydad*

1 =**crawfish** n **B1**. **chiefly west of Appalachians** See Map
1905 *DN* 3.76 **nwAR**, *Crawdad* . . . Crawfish. **1911** *DN* 3.537 **eKY**, *Craw-dad.* **1912** Ade *Knocking* 39, The Alsatian Nobleman . . substituted a Tid-Bit with Cray-Fish as the principal ornament . . . "It's a Craw-Dabber!" exclaimed the Man from the Prairies. **1914** *DN* 4.163

LA, TX, *Crawdad.* **1923** *DN* 5.204 **swMO**, *Craw dad* . . . Also *Craw dab, Craw pappy.* **1931** Randolph *Ozarks* 99, I have known hillmen to spend hours and even days in searching for large "craw-pappies" in order to get the two circular "lucky-bones" found in their bodies, which are carried in the pocket to ward off syphilis. **1940** Stong *Hawkeyes* 249 **IA**, We seined "crawjinnies" for bait in quiet pools and let these minuscule freshwater shrimps try out the strength of their claws on our little fingers. **1944** Howard *Walkin' Preacher* 155 **Ozarks**, "What a grand day to fish," I thought as I garnered a dozen crawdaddies. **1944** *PADS* 1.55 **cnMO**, *Crawdad* . . . A crawfish. *Ibid* **nwMO, nwAR**, *Crawdaddy.* **1949** Brown *Amer. Cooks* 269 **LA**, [Red bones are] people of mixed Indian, negro and white blood who live in the Louisiana swamps and subsist on crawfish, called craw-daddy and crawl-daddy. **1954** Harder *Coll.* **cwTN**, *Crawdad:* Crawfish. Also *crawdaddy.* **c1960** Wilson *Coll.* **csKY**, *Crawdad* or *crawdaddy:* . . Crayfish . . . Crawdad is largely humorous. **1963** North *Rascal* 38 **WI**, His catch was a particularly large crayfish (or "crawdad" in the terminology of the region). **1965–70** *DARE* (Qu. P19, *What do you call the small, freshwater crayfish around here?*) 202 Infs, **chiefly west of Appalachians**, Crawdad(s); 26 Infs, **scattered, but esp IL, IA, MO, KS**, Crawdaddy; **NY**93, Craydad; **WV**13A, Crawdabber [FW: the Inf once heard a child say this]; **WV**14, Crawcrab; **OK**52, Crawpappy; (Qu. P18, *Shellfish . . common around here*) Infs **IL**27, **IN**58, **NY**52, **TX**33, **WA**6, Crawdad; **KS**10, Crawdaddy; (Qu. P7, *Small fish used as bait*) Infs **CO**4, **IN**22, **IA**32, Crawdad; **WA**28, Crawdaddy; (Qu. P13, *Other ways of fishing*) Inf **KY**6, Crawdads. **1970** *DARE* Tape **WV**14, Crawcrabs around here—some people call 'em crawdads . . . They're crayfish.

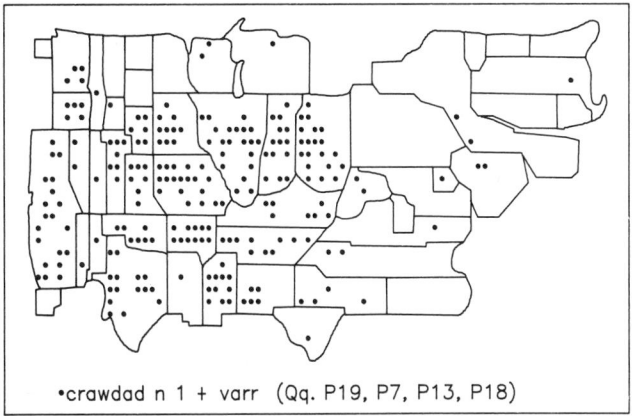

•*crawdad* n 1 + varr (Qq. P19, P7, P13, P18)

2 A lift loader; see quot.
1958 McCulloch *Woods Words* **Pacific NW**, Crawdad—A lift loader mounted on a cat [tractor]; looks like a crawfish waving a pincher in the air.

crawdad v Cf **crawfish** v

1 To catch **crawfish** n **B1**.
1933 Williamson *Woods Colt* 138 **Ozarks**, Mighty small taters an' few in the hill, I says to him, so don't you go to crawdaddin'.

2 also *crawdab:* To move in the manner of a **crawfish**.
1933 *AmSp* 8.1.48 **Ozarks**, *Crawdad* . . . To crawl on one's belly, like a crawfish. "Ab had t' crawdad purty near half a mile t' git a shot at them geese." **1940** *Amer. Mercury* 50.210/2 **eKY**, I craw-dabbed from under the house. **1954** Harder *Coll.* **cwTN**, *Crawdad:* To go slow.

3 =**crawfish** v **2**.
1968 *DARE* (Qu. JJ45, *When someone avoids giving a definite answer: "We tried to pin him down, but he just kept _____."*) Inf **OH**87, Crawdadding.

crawdad adj See **crawfish** adj

crawdaddy n

1 See **crawdad** n.

2 also attrib: See quot.
1967 Cerello *Dakota Co. MN* 51, *Crawdaddy*—A kind of wine made from cranberry juice, sometimes with beet juice added. "Some people . . would not let crawdaddy juice ferment too long." "It was best to not bottle but rather to keg crawdaddy after it had been allowed to properly ferment." *Crawdaddy* may also mean cranberry: "We've always made a rich red wine from crawdaddy berries and grapes."

crawdad eye n

A protruding or prominent eye.

1969 *DARE* (Qu. X21a, *Words . . used to describe people according to their eyes . . if they stick out*) Inf **TX**61, Crawdad eyes.

crawder pea See **crowder (pea)**

crawfish n Also *crayfish*, rarely *craw*, *crowfish*

A Forms.   Note: the form *crawfish* is **widespread, but chiefly Sth, Midl**, while *crayfish* is **scattered, but least freq in Midl**   See Maps   Cf **crawdad**

1624 Smith *Genl. Hist. VA* 175 **VA**, Great craw-fishes . . they have taken in great quantity.   **1791** (1958) Bartram *Travels* 28 **GA**, In this eddy shoal were a number of little gravelly pyramidal hills . . very artfully constructed by a species of small cray-fish (Cancer macrourus) which inhabited them.   **1905** *DN* 3.76 **nwAR**, Craw . . . Crawfish.   **1965–70** *DARE* (Qu. P19, *The small, freshwater crayfish around here*) 454 Infs, **widespread, but chiefly Sth, Midl**, Crawfish; 58 Infs, **scattered, but least freq Midl**, Crayfish; **IN**18, Craws; **FL**26, Crowfish ['krou͵fiš]; (Qu. P18, *Kinds of shellfish . . common around here*) 19 Infs, **scattered**, Crawfish; 12 Infs, **scattered**, Crayfish; (Qu. P3) Infs **CA**105, **KY**93, **NC**33, Crawfish; **NJ**45, Crayfish; (Qu. P6) Infs **AR**48, **IN**3, Crawfish; (Qu. P7) Infs **IL**69, **IN**39, **MA**62, **NC**38, 48, **SC**40, Crawfish; (Qu. P14) Infs **CA**65, **FL**24, Crawfish; (Qu. H45, *Dishes made with . . fish*) Infs **LA**23, 24, (Boiled) crawfish; **LA**20, 23, Crawfish etouffee.   **1971** Kieran *Nat. Hist. NYC* 47, However, our swamp and adjacent lake can produce . . crayfish (colloquially spelled and pronounced "crawfish").   **1971** Bright *Word Geog. CA & NV* 186, *Crawfish* 40% M[inor] G[eneral] D[istribution] in Northern California; S[cattered] otherwise . . . Thirteen percent of the [300] informants were also familiar with the terms *crawdad* and *crayfish*, both scattered throughout the state.

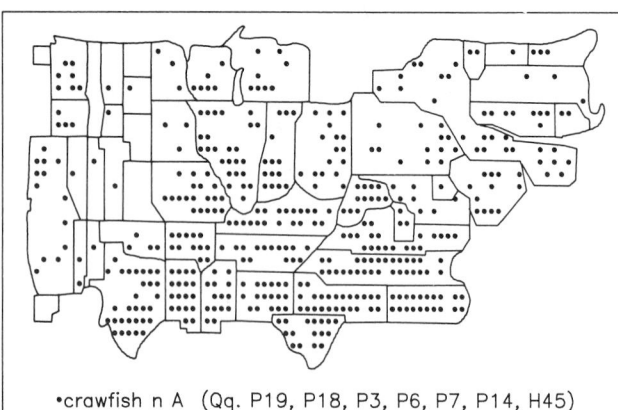

•crawfish n A   (Qq. P19, P18, P3, P6, P7, P14, H45)

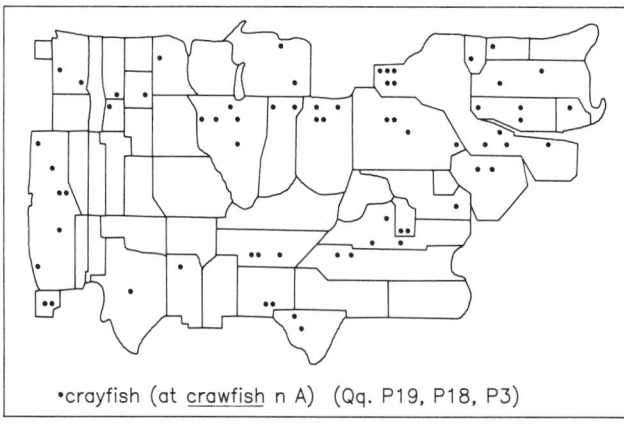

•crayfish (at <u>crawfish</u> n A)   (Qq. P19, P18, P3)

B Senses.

1 Std: a crustacean of the family Astacidae, esp of the genus *Cambarus*.   Also called **clawfish, crawdad** n 1, **crawler** n¹ 5

2 The spiny lobster (family Palinuridæ).

1935 Pratt *Manual Animals* 452, *Palinurus argus* . . Sea crawfish.   **1937** *Natl. Geog. Mag.* 71.215 **FL**, Although the *spiny lobster*, or *crayfish*, of Florida and the West Indies has no pincer claws, as does its northern cousin, long, lancelike antennae and sharp spines help protect

it against enemies.   **1968** *DARE* File **New Orleans LA**, Crayfish — the spiny lobster.

3 A person of French descent.   Cf **frog** n¹ **B2**

1968 *DARE* (Qu. HH28, *Names . . for people of foreign background . . French*) Inf **IN**5, Crawfish.

crawfish v Also *crayfish*

1 To move or crawl backwards; to back away.

1848 *Ladies' Repository* 8.292/2 **MI**, We had just time to crawfish out into deep water, and get the proper course, before it [=a storm] fully broke upon us.   **1872** (1973) Thompson *Major Jones's Courtship* 22 **GA**, I was in the galls [=girls'] room! But there was no time for apologisin . . I crawfished out of that place monstrous quick.   **1877** Wright *Big Bonanza* 213, As my hand approached, his moon eyes rapidly grew moonier, and he began crawfishing, as though determined, if possible, to retreat in good order and with his face to the foe.   **1968** Adams *Western Words*, Crawfish . . . To back away.

2 Fig: to back out (of an agreement); to yield or back down (from a position); to be evasive; hence vbl n *crawfishing*.   **chiefly Sth, W Midl, Pacific NW**   See Map

1844 *Whig Battering Ram* (U.S.) 9 Aug. 4/1 (*OEDS*), Look out for such a specimen of crawfishing as the Locofocos alone can practice.   **1848** U.S. Congress *Congressional Globe* 1 Feb 277/3, No sooner did they see the old British Lion rising up . . than they crawfished back to 49°.   **1890** *DN* 1.64 **KY**, Crawfish . . . To back out . . . "He will crawfish out of it."   **1892** *KS Univ. Qrly.* 1.95, *Crawfish*: same as *crawl*.   *Ibid*, *Crawl*: To try to escape from an embarassing situation without admitting one's mistake.   **1903** *DN* 2.310 **seMO**, We made fair trade but he crawfished.   **1906** *DN* 3.116 **sIN**, *Crawfish*.   **1907** *DN* 3.230 **nwAR, seMO**, *Crawfish*.   **1908** *DN* 3.302 **eAL, wGA**, *Crawfish*.   **1922** *DN* 5.160 **AL, AR, IN, KY, MO, NE**, *Crawfish*.   **c1940** Eliason *Word Lists FL* 7, *Crawfish* . . . To back out of some trade, or promise to do something and then go back on one's word.   **c1960** *Wilson Coll.* **csKY**, *Crawfish* . . . To back out of something attempted.   **1965–70** *DARE* (Qu. II31, . . *"He saw that he was wrong, so he started to _____."*) 85 Infs, **chiefly Sth, W Midl, Pacific NW**, Crawfish; **IL**126, **SC**2, Crawfish out of it; **LA**8, Crawfish back; **LA**46, Crawfish out; **LA**17, **MS**63, **WV**3, Crawfishing; **MI**4, Crayfish; (Qu. II32, . . *"He said it wasn't his fault and tried to _____."*) Infs **IL**40, 96, 126, **PA**135, **TN**1, Crawfish (out *or* out of it); (Qu. JJ25, . . *"He thought he could take the place over, but I made him _____."*) Inf **WA**18, Crawfish; (Qu. JJ40, . . *"It was my fault and I'm willing to _____."*) Inf **LA**32, Crawfish; (Qu. JJ45, . . *"We tried to pin him down, but he just kept _____."*) Infs **IN**58, **MS**56, **TX**5, **WA**18, Crawfishing; (Qu. A11, *When somebody takes too long about coming to a decision . . "I wish he'd quit _____."*) Inf **FL**7, Crawfishing.

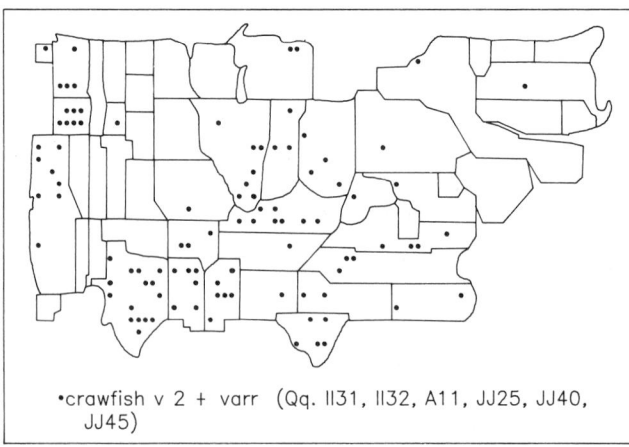

•crawfish v 2 + varr   (Qq. II31, II32, A11, JJ25, JJ40, JJ45)

3 Of a horse, to buck backwards.

1933 *AmSp* 8.1.28 **TX**, Crawfish. To pitch backwards.   **1961** Adams *Old-Time Cowhand* 301, When a hoss bucked backward he was said to be "crawfishin'."

crawfish adj Also *crawdad, crawfishy*   **chiefly Sth, S Midl**

Of land: low, wet.

1857 (1859) Olmsted *Journey TX* 360, Having a wet, sandy or "crawfish" soil.   **1883** Smith *Rept. for 1881 & 1882* 363 **AL**, In wet lowlands there is much . . 'crawfishy' land, which is worthless unless improved; but by thorough ditching . . the crawfishy character disappears.   **1903**

DN 2.310 **seMO**, *Crawfishy* (land) . . . Low ground in which water rises nearly to the surface. This is the kind of ground in which crawfishes make their home. **1906** *DN* 4.132 **nwAR**, *Crawfish land.* **1936** *AmSp* 11.314 **Ozarks**, *Crawdad bottom* . . . Swampy land near seeps or springs, too wet for cultivation. **1954** *Harder Coll.* **cwTN**, *Crawfish bottom.* **1965–70** *DARE* (Qu. C6, *A piece of land that's often wet and has grass and weeds*) Infs **GA77**, **KY60**, **OK21**, Crawfish land; **AL52**, **56**, **GA65**, Crawfish land; [**AR53**, Crawfishing land]; (Qu. C31, *Heavy, sticky soil*) Infs **AL11**, **VA44**, Crawfish land; **TX100**, Crawfish soil; [**LA7**, Crawfishing].

crawfish bisque n Also *crayfish bisque* **LA**

A soup made with crawfish.

1932 (1946) Hibben *Amer. Regional Cookery* 45 **New Orleans LA**, Crayfish Bisque. **1968** *DARE* (Qu. H36, *Kinds of soup favored around here—any specialties*) Inf **LA23**, Crawfish bisque. **1968** *DARE* Tape **LA22**, You clean the head out, get the shell, you understand? You take the tail and cut up the tail, . . stuff it, and fix it, and serve with lemons and stuff like . . parsley, you know. That's what you call a crawfish bisque; **LA35**, Crawfish bisque, you take and grind your tails, and you . . put a little bread crumbs in and put all your seasoning in it, and stuff the head again . . . Restuff the tails and you'll have some on the side that you haven't ground up . . and make a little stew with it, and then put your stuffed tails back into this. **1980** *DARE* File **New Orleans LA**, I lived five years in New Orleans between 1965 and 1971, and in that time I regularly met with *crawfish bisque* in conversation among natives and on local menus. It was clearly a local favorite. Outside Louisiana, I cannot recall ever having heard it referred to. **1983** *Reinecke Coll.* **New Orleans LA**, *Bisque* [bɪsk] . . . A soup made with a roux, crawfish, and red pepper, and containing stuffed crawfish heads which are removed and sucked or scooped out. Often "crawfish bisque" but no other soup is called thus in New Orleans.

crawfish boil n **LA**

1 A social gathering at which boiled crawfish are eaten. **Cf fish boil**

1972 *DARE* File **New Orleans LA**, *Crawfish boil:* A Louisiana social activity at which "crawdads" are boiled (and there's drinking along with the eating). **1980** *Ibid*, The Louisiana crawfish boil is a meal the likes of which I have never encountered outside Louisiana. The boiled crawfish are heaped in the middle of the table, which has previously been liberally spread with newspapers. The people around the table proceed to shell and eat the crawfish with deftness and aplomb and at a rate that leaves the non-native gaping. In the homes in which I took part in crawfish boils, I never saw fork, knife, or plate, and beer was often the complementary beverage. Napkins were in plentiful supply.

2 See quot.

1980 *DARE* File **New Orleans LA**, Crawfish boil was a special mix of seasonings commercially prepared in the New Orleans area when I lived there between 1965 and 1971. Most people used it; and it was recommended I take it with me when I flew home with a "mess of crawfish" in order to hold a regular Louisiana "crawfish boil" at my home in California.

crawfish chimney n

A cylindrical pile of mud or clay that a crawfish throws up around the entrance to its hole.

1940 Wilson *Wabash* 201, There he is—old Mr. Coon—running along the bank . . . He is inspecting crawfish chimneys; and, when he finds one that suits him, he pushes it over and, with great deliberation, runs his arm down into the hole. **1946** *PADS* 6.10 **eNC** (as of 1900–10), *Crawfish chimney* . . . The mud or clay cylinder-shaped structure made by a lobster-like crustacean that lives in low, damp places. The chimney is about six inches high and three inches in diameter . . . Common. **1954** *Harder Coll.* **cwTN**, *Crawfish chimley:* The mud structure over the hole that the crayfish lives in. **c1960** *Wilson Coll.* **csKY**, *Crawfish chimney* . . . Mud pushed up by a crawfish to form a sort of chimney-like pile.

crawfish clay n **Cf crawfish adj**

1975 McDonough *Garden Sass* 51 **AR**, There's a mud they call "post oak" mud . . . (Mr. Simpson, who was from the same region, called this "crawfish clay" or "post oak flat," and said that this was a white clay.)

crawfishy See crawfish adj

craw hammer n [By rhotacism, from *claw hammer*]

1972 *Atlanta Letters*, Craw hammer: claw hammer.

crawjinny See crawdad n

crawl v Also *crawl on, crawl over* **chiefly Sth, S Midl** Cf **crawl one's hump**

To rebuke or reprove severely; sometimes, to attack physically.

1905 *DN* 3.76 **nwAR**, *Crawl* . . . To whip, to reprove . . . 'The professor crawled him for cutting recitations.' **1938** Rawlings *Yearling* 16 **FL**, He would like to slip from his bed and perhaps . . finish the hoeing that Jody had left undone. "I reckon I'd ought to of crawled him about it," he thought. *Ibid* 70, "Me bringin' in venison," I figgered, "Ma won't crawl me for leavin' Jody with Fodderwing." **1940** *Sat. Eve. Post* 3 Feb 55/3 **sMS**, I may have to crawl on you about extravagance. **1960** Criswell *Resp. to PADS* 20 **Ozarks**, *Crawl* . . . To attack, either physically or verbally. (Very common always.) "I'll crawl the bastard as soon as I see him even if I don't feel very good after bein' sick." **c1970** *Halpert Coll.* **wKY**, **eTN**, "Oh! Did she crawl all over me about that!"

crawl n¹

1881 Ingersoll *Oyster-Industry* 243 **FL**, *Crawl* . . . The track of a sea-turtle to its nest.

crawl n² Also sp *craul* [Alter of colonial Du *kraal*] **S Atl**

An enclosure for keeping var sea creatures alive in shallow water.

1682 (1836) Ash *Carolina* 76, They bring them [turtles] in Sloops alive, and afterwards keep them in Crauls, which is a particular place of Salt Water of Depth and Room for them to swim in, pallisado'd or staked, in round above the Water's surface. **1881** Ingersoll *Oyster-Industry* 243 **FL**, *Crawl* . . . A pen or *corral* made of upright stakes wattled together, intended to hold sponges while being cleaned; or turtle awaiting a market. **1906** Bell *Carolina Lee* 191, I sold some timber to a Yankee firm who wanted fine cypress, and with the money I constructed a terrapin crawl. **1966** *DARE* Tape **FL9**, And then they had what they called crawls, that was places fixed where they could come in with their sponge and put 'em in them places. And then they'd clean 'em; **FL10**, They had places fixed around the edge of the water . . . they'd put the sponges in there. Then they'd clean them in there, [in] the crawls, the sponge crawls [krɔɔlz]. **1981** *DARE* File, The word *crawl* is in current use as a noun in Key West, Florida. I saw sea turtles in crawls there in 1979. Perhaps other sea creatures are also kept in crawls.

crawl-a-bottom n [For *crawl-on-the-bottom*, from its habitual method of feeding]

=hog sucker.

1882 U.S. Natl. Museum *Bulletin* 16.130, *Catostomus nigricans* . . . Crawl-a-bottom. **1896** U.S. Natl. Museum *Bulletin* 47.181, *Hypentelium nigricans* . . Crawl-a-Bottom.

crawldaddy See crawdad n

crawler n¹

1 In fishing: the common earthworm used as bait. **chiefly Nth** Cf **night crawler**

1965–70 *DARE* (Qu. P6, *Other kinds of worms also used for bait*) 9 Infs, **Nth**, Crawler; (Qu. P5, *The common worm used as bait*) Infs **MA35**, **MI10**, **26**, **MN10**, **OK46**, Crawler; (Qu. R27) Inf **MI67**, Crawlers—same as angleworms.

2 A head or body louse.

1965–68 *DARE* (Qu. R25, *A head louse, or body louse*) Infs **IN3**, **OK46**, **VA30**, Crawler.

3 A caterpillar or similar larva.

1967 *DARE* (Qu. R27, *Kinds of caterpillars or similar worms*) Inf **MN7**, Crawler.

4 =wriggler.

1968 *DARE* (Qu. R14, *Small worm-like things . . that hatch into mosquitoes*) Inf **MI51**, Crawlers.

5 =crawfish n B1.

1968 *DARE* (Qu. P19, *Small, freshwater crayfish*) Inf **NJ10**, Crawlers.

6 =hellgrammite.

1884 *Standard Nat. Hist.* 2.156 (*DA*), They [*Corydalus cornutus*] are called by fishermen "crawlers."

7 See quot 1958.

1958 McCulloch *Woods Words* **Pacific NW**, *Crawler*—A tractor operating on endless treads instead of wheels; also refers to an arch [=a trailer pulled behind a tractor] on the same type treads. *Crawlers*. The endless treads. **1966** *Cynthiana Democrat* (KY) 28 Apr sec 3 6/6, The equipment consists of the following: John Deere 420 crawler tractor with front and rear control. **1970** *DARE* (Qu. L42, *What kind of thing do you call a "rig"?*) Inf **NC85**, A crawler—something that pulled logs out of the woods; called a "rig" sometimes.

8 See quot.

1966 *DARE* (Qu. FF14, *Kinds of firecrackers*) Inf **MT4**, Crawler.

9 See quot.

1968 *DARE* (Qu. W8, *Low canvas-top shoes with rubber soles*) Inf **KS16**, Crawlers.

10 A part of a horse harness.

1969 *DARE* Tape **NJ56**, A crawler is a parted harness that fastens to the shaft so the single horse is in between two shafts and the crawler is fastened to the shaft—also fastened to the britches of the harness so the horse can back to the wagon. There must be some leeway between the trace length and the crawler.

11 See quot.

1967 *DARE* (Qu. N43, *Vehicles for a small child—the kind it has to sit up in*) Inf **TX11**, Crawler.

12 A kind of outboard motor. Cf **kicker**

1967 *DARE* (Qu. O11, *Other names . . for an outboard motor*) Inf **OR13**, Crawler.

crawler n² See **cruller**

crawley root n Also *crawley, crawly ~* [Perh folk-etym]
=**coralroot 1.**

1876 Hobbs *Bot. Hdbk.* 26, Coral root,—Crawley root,—Corallorhiza odontorhiza. **1894** *Jrl. Amer. Folkl.* 7.100, *Corallorhiza,* sp., crawley, N.C. **1895** *DN* 1.396 **cNY**, *Crawly root:* folk-etymology for coral root. **1971** Krochmal *Appalachia Med. Plants* 104, *Corallorhiza* (Chat.)—Common Names: Coralroot, crawley root, dragon's claws.

crawling cedar n
=**creeping juniper.**

1966 *DARE* (Qu. T5, *Kinds of evergreens, other than pine*) Inf **MT3**, Crawling cedar.

crawling company n Also *crawling elephant joc*
A bedbug.

1936 *AmSp* 11.275 **cTN**, *Crawling elephants.* Bed bugs. 'The crawling elephants bit me last night.' **1969** *DARE* (Qu. R24, *Other names . . for a bedbug*) Inf **IN67**, Crawling company.

crawling dandruff See **galloping dandruff**

crawling grass n
An unidentified plant: see quot.

1965–70 *DARE* (Qu. S15, *Other weed seeds that cling to clothing*) 9 Infs, **chiefly Sth**, Crawling grass.

crawling phlox See **creeping phlox**

crawling pussy n
Prob a puss caterpillar *(Megalopyge opercularis).*

1967 *DARE* (Qu. R27, *Kinds of caterpillars or similar worms*) Inf **OH28**, Crawling pussies.

crawl on See **crawl** v

crawl one's hump v phr Also *crawl one's frame* Cf **crawl** v
To attack, assault one.

1905 *DN* 3.76 **nwAR**, *Crawl . . .* To whip, to reprove. 'He crawled his frame.' **1907** White *AZ Nights* 171, Here I pick you up . . and save your worthless carcass, and the first chance you get you try to crawl my hump. **1923** *DN* 5.204 **swMO**, *Crawl one's hump . . .* To assault. **1940** White *Wild Geese* 381 **AK** (as of 1890s), I got to brag to tell you that you're plenty fast with that thing [a revolver] . . . I reckon nobody in this country will crawl your hump. **1942** McAtee *Dial. Grant Co. IN* 19 (as of 1890s), *Crawl one's frame . .* attack comprehensively. **1950** *PADS* 14.78, *Crawl* your frame. **1968** Adams *Western Words, Crawl his hump*—To start a bodily attack upon someone. **c1970** Halpert Coll. **wKY, eTN**, Somebody ought to crawl that guy's frame.

crawl over See **crawl** v

‡**crawl under the dog's belly** v phr
To live in poverty.

1935 Wolfe *Of Time* 263 **PA** (as of c1885), I was left a widow with seven children to bring up, but I never took charity from no one; as I told 'em all, I've crawled under the dog's belly all my life; now I guess I can get over its back.

crawly adj
Covered with, or as if covered with, insects; creepy; uncomfortable.

1857 *Putnam's Mag.* 10.355/1 **NEng**, I guess I shan't, but I do feel kinder crawly about bein' resigned. **1880** Twain *Tramp Abroad* 206, It makes one feel crawly even to think of it. **1944** *PADS* 2.33 **NC**, *Crawly . . .* Infested with bugs. "This time o' year [September] all meal's crawly." . . Common. **1954** *Harder Coll.* **cwTN**, *Crawly:* Covered with fleas, bugs; itchy. Common.

crawly-bottom n Cf **crawler** n¹ **5, 6**

1954 *Harder Coll.* **cwTN**, *Crawly-bottom:* small insect or creature that moves around on the bottom of streams and ponds.

crawl yoke n Cf **cowpoke** n² **2**
=**cow hook.**

1944 Wellman *Bowl* 86 **KS**, "Old Egypt busted out an' cut her bag on the wire." "Better put a crawl yoke on her, Tilford."

crawly root See **crawley root**

crawm n, also attrib |krɒm, krɔm| Also sp *crom, krawm, krom* [Etym uncert, but cf Scots, nEngl dial *crame* booth for sale of small wares, the wares themselves; also cognate Ger *kram* rubbish] **sME, seNH** Cf **kram** n
Rubbish, refuse; waste, esp from food.

1890 *DN* 1.73 **seNH**, *Crawm* [krɒm]: a pile of old straw or rubbish (not structural rubbish, however). "Clear out that lot (or mess) of crawm." **1903** Wasson *Cap'n Simeon's Store* 59 **swME** (as of c1850), She [=an oil-can] laid there on that krawm-heap, atop of other ole rubbidge. **1927** *AmSp* 3.137 **ME coast**, "Crom" or "krom" (. . as applied to waste, as "lobster or fish crom") came to denote *any* waste or refuse, especially pertaining to food. **1931–33** *LANE Worksheets* **sME**, *Crom:* Rubbish. "Where you haul a load of old crom." **1941** *LANE* Map 346 **sME, seNH**, Old, broken, useless things (furniture, tools, machinery, boxes, tin cans and the like) such as accumulate in the house or yard and are eventually thrown away or otherwise disposed of . . . *Crom.* [7 infs variously pronounced it [krɒm, krɒəm, krɔm].] **1975** Gould *ME Lingo* 155, *Krawm*—For crum; a lot of rubbish. *Culch* does not suggest the uselessness and offensiveness of *krawm. Culch* may have value; *krawm* is to be hove out. The word is used to downgrade excellence: after a bountiful meal of delicious goodies opulently served, a sated guest may say, "There! That's about all of that *krawm* I can take!"

crawney-bone n [Perh infl by *scrawny, rawboned*]

1966 *DARE* (Qu. K15, *A thin, bony, or poor-looking cow*) Inf **SC9**, Crawney-bone.

crawpappy See **crawdad** n

crawthumper n Also *claw thumper* [*craw* breast + *thumper* beater, in allusion to Roman Catholics and their role in founding Maryland; *OED* 1785 → (at *craw* sb.4)] *old-fash*
A native of Maryland.

1845 (1965) *Broadway Jrl.* 1.286/2, The inhabitants of . . Maryland, [are called] Craw-thumpers. **1863** *Walla Walla* (Wash.) *Statesman* 6 June 1/7 *(DA)*, The inhabitants of Maryland are called Claw Thumpers. **1888** Whitman *November Boughs* 70, Those [soldiers] from . . Maryland, [were called] Claw Thumpers. **1948** *Dly. Ardmoreite* (Ardmore, Okla.) 11 July 21/5 *(DA)*, Nebraskans have been dubbed 'Bug Eaters'; Marylanders as 'Craw Thumpers.'

craydad See **crawdad** n

crayfish See **crawfish** n,v

crayon n
A piece of blackboard chalk.

1967 *DARE* Tape **TX35**, We had to have crayons to write on the board with.

craythur See **creature**

crazy adj

1 See quot 1837. *arch*

1837 Sherwood *Gaz. GA* 69 [In a list of Provincialisms to be avoided], *Crazy,* for sickly or weakly. **1899** (1912) Green *VA Folk-Speech* 132, *Crazy . . .* condition of health.

2 Askew, out of line; ramshackle.

1899 (1912) Green *VA Folk-Speech, Crazy . . .* Broken; delapidated [sic]; weak; applied to any structure, but especially to a building or to a boat, or a carriage. **1968–70** *DARE* (Qu. MM13, *The table was nice and straight until he came along and knocked it* ———) Infs **AL48, TN42**, Crazy.

crazy ace n

   1969 *DARE* (Qu. EE40, . . *Table games . . played around here using dice*) Inf **WI**77, Crazy ace: Played at the bar—First ace names it [the drink], second ace pays for it, third ace drinks it.

crazy ant n Cf *DJE* **mad-ants**

   An ant *(Paratrechina longicornis)* characterized by esp busy activity.

   1965 Blickenstaff *Insects* 291, Crazy ant . . . *Paratrechina longicornis.* **1966** *DARE* (Qu. R18, *Other kinds of ants . . around here*) Inf **FL**23, Crazy ants.

crazy bait n

   See quots.

   1867 PA Laws *Laws Genl. Assembly* 1068, Any person, or persons, found guilty of throwing crazy bait, cocculus indicus . . or any other poisonous drug, or substance, into any of the streams aforesaid: shall . . pay a fine of forty dollars. **1942** *AmSp* 17.133, In *American Speech* for February 1936 (XI, 98) Sir William Craigie asked for an explanation of 'crazy bait,' mentioned . . in *Pennsylvania Laws* for 1867 . . . It seems clear . . that crazy bait is not the poisonous berry *cocculus indicus* but that is it similarly intoxicating. I should like to suggest the herb devil's-shoestring, goat's rue, cat gut, or wild sweet pea, *Cracca virginiana.* This plant grows widely in Pennsylvania, where it was outlawed.

crazy bet n Also *crazy beth*

   A **marsh marigold** (here: *Caltha palustris*).

   1900 Lyons *Plant Names* 77, C[altha] palustris . . . Crazy-Bet. **1959** Carleton *Index Herb. Plants* 32, Crazy Beth: Caltha palustris.

crazy bone n **widespread, but least freq in Sth, NYC** See Map
=**funny bone.**

   1876 Whitney *Sights & Insights* 1.148, Do you remember the old "Boston days?" When we went into the city shopping . . holding on to . . our accumulated packages with our "crazy-bones?" **1899** (1912) Green *VA Folk-Speech, Crazy-bone* . . . The point of the elbow, where the ulnar nerve comes near the surface and is hurt by a casual blow. **1965–70** *DARE* (Qu. X33, *The place in the elbow that gives you a strange feeling if you hit it*) 493 Infs, **widespread, but least freq in Sth, NYC area,** Crazy bone.

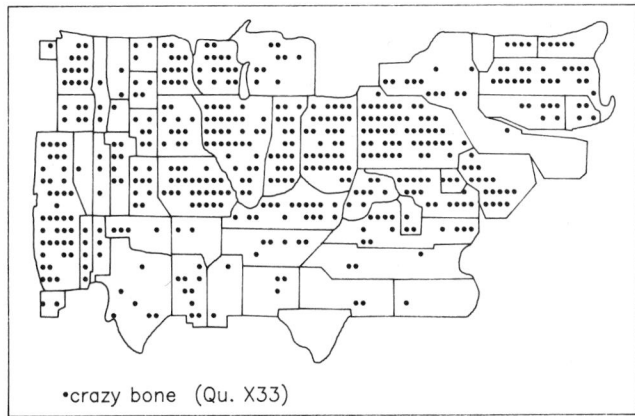

•crazy bone (Qu. X33)

crazy bug n [Perh from its seemingly erratic habits]

   A **water strider** of the family Gerridae.

   1890 in 1896 IL Ag. Exper. Sta. Urbana *Bulletin* 3.172, *Crazy Bugs* . . . The eggs . . are attached to aquatic plants, and the young pupae resemble the grown insect except for the wings and increased size.

crazy clean adj Cf **nasty neat**

   1965–70 *DARE* (Qu. HH11b, *Too particular or fussy—if it's a woman*) **MI**33, **MN**33, **PA**138, 167, 245, **SC**19, **VA**67, **WI**47, 60, 71, **WV**1, Crazy clean; (Qu. HH11a, . . *If it's a man*) Inf **PA**138, Crazy clean.

crazy crane n

   =**snowy egret.**

   1962 Imhof *AL Birds* 93, Snowy Egret . . . Other Names: . . Crazy Crane.

crazy day n esp **MN**

   A special day when merchants display their goods on the street at bargain prices.

   1967 *DARE* Tape **MN**11, The merchants here have certain days they call crazy days, or bargain days, when they have sidewalk sales. **1967–68** *DARE* (Qu. FF16, *Local contests or celebrations*) Infs **MN**12, 22, 38, 42, **MO**2, Crazy day. **1982** *DARE* File **St. Paul MN** [Heard on radio], They'd go into town for crazy days.

crazy dray n Also *crazy drag*

   In logging: see quots.

   1966 *DARE* (Qu. N40a, . . *Sleighs . . for hauling loads*) Inf **MI**2, Crazy dray—so designed that the runners can "collapse" somewhat on a turn to get through narrow places; for hauling logs. **1969** Sorden *Lumberjack Lingo* **NEng, Gt Lakes,** *Crazy drag*—A dray used to haul logs from woods to skidway. One end of the log is on the dray and the other end drags on the ground. Same as go-devil, snow snake, travois.

‡**crazy elbow** n
=**crazy bone.**

   1967 *DARE* (Qu. X33, *The place in the elbow that gives you a strange feeling if you hit it*) Inf **PA**14, Crazy elbow.

crazy fly n

   A **midge.**

   1966 *DARE* (Qu. R10, *Very small flies that don't sting, often seen hovering in large groups or bunches outdoors in summer*) Inf **WA**15, Crazy fly.

crazy grass n

   Sudan grass *(Sorghum lanceolatum).*

   1968 *DARE* (Qu. L22, *This year I'm going to* ———— *a crop of* ————) Inf **PA**163, Sow a crop of crazy grass—"sudan sorghum grass;" this is the technical name for what they call "crazy grass."

crazy Ike See **Ike** n[1]

crazy Jane n

   1978 *DARE* File **cnMA,** My grandmother, born near Salem, Massachusetts, about 1860, used *crazy Jane* to mean a person without good judgment, someone lacking know-how. "Why, if I went downtown wearing a straw hat in winter someone would say 'Who's that crazy Jane?' "

crazy jay n

   =**northern shrike.**

   1956 *MA Audubon Soc. Bulletin* 40.129, *Northern Shrike* . . . Crazy Jay (Maine. Perhaps from its medley of squalls or screeches.)

crazy quail n

   =**harlequin quail.**

   1982 Elman *Hunter's Field Guide* 102, It is the harlequin . . quail . . , also called . . crazy quail.

crazyweed n Cf **locoweed**

   Any of var plants which cause aberrant behavior: see quots.

   1889 *Century Dict.* 1337/2, *Crazy-weed* . . . A name given to various plants growing in the western United States . . often called *loco-weed* . . . Among them are species of *Astragalus, Oxytropis* and perhaps some plants of other genera. **1939** *Natl. Geog. Mag.* 76.247/1, **Upper MW, Rocky Mts,** This is eminently true of this section of the pea family, known as 'locoweeds' or 'crazyweeds,' for death by slow poison lies in wait for man or beast that may be inclined to feast upon the foliage. **1945** Thorp *Pardner* 57 **SW,** These tough little pioneer horses have largely disappeared . . No doubt many thousands of them were victims of the "crazy weed." **1959** Carleton *Index Herb. Plants* 32, Crazy-weed: Astragalus (v); Crotalaria sagittalis; Datura (v); Oxytropis lamberti. **1966** *DARE* Wildfl QR Inf **CO**7, Crazyweed.

creachy adj [Var of Engl dial *craichy* infirm ailing]

   1967 *DARE* FW Addit **sePA,** She [=a woman who was ill and no longer wanted to live] is getting [kriči].

creaker n[1]

   An old person.

   1958 Hughes–Bontemps *Negro Folkl.* 482, Creaker: An aged person. "I hate to see a creaker act so chippyfied." **1970** Major *Afro–Amer. Slang, Creaker:* (1940's) an old person.

creaker n[2] See **krieker**

cream n, also attrib Cf **ice-cream supper**

   Ice cream.

   1851 Northall *Before Curtain* 113 **NYC,** The concerts and other entertainments . . were looked upon as something thrown in with the punch and cream . . . The old temple being consecrated to bad music and excellent cream. **1858** (1930) DeLong *Jrls.* 9.263 **NY,** Went to the theatre with her in the evening, afterward went to a cream saloon had some strawberrie's. **1910** *Sat. Eve. Post* 13 Aug 35/3 **Chicago IL,** It makes a smoother, better grade of cream than ordinary freezers. **1966** *DARE* (Qu. FF1, . . *Kinds [of 'socials']*) Inf **AL2,** Cream supper; (Qu. FF2, *Kinds of parties*) Inf **MS1,** Cream suppers.

cream v

1 To take or remove the best of something; hence n *creamer,* one who does this.

1958 McCulloch *Woods Words* **Pacific NW,** *Cream*— To high grade a stand, taking only the best logs. **1959** *AmSp* 34.67 **ceWI,** It is often a great temptation to a [cherry-] picker whose ladder is placed so that he can reach into two trees to *cream* the tree adjoining the one he is officially picking. This involves simply reaching over and taking the best and most easily reached fruit from the other tree. By most pickers creaming is considered unethical, if not downright mean . . . The *creamer* is seized and restrained. **1969** Sorden *Lumberjack Lingo* **NEng, Gt Lakes,** *Creaming*—Taking only the best trees in the stand.

2 To beat thoroughly; to drub; to crush.

1945 O'Hara *Pipe Night* 45 **PA,** She had sat there and had seen him just *cream* Ned Work. He *creamed* him: 6–4, 6–2. **1965–70** *DARE* (Qu. Y15, *To beat somebody thoroughly*) Infs **CA177, HI8, NJ6, NY1,** 157, **PA161,** Creamed; (Qu. Y16, *A thorough beating*) Inf **HI9,** Creamed him; (Qu. KK21, *When something hollow is crushed by a heavy weight*) Infs **CA80, NY109,** Creamed it.

cream-and-molasses n

1965 *DARE* (Qu. K38, *A horse of a dirty white color*) Inf **MA55,** Cream-'n-molasses.

creambush n [From the color of the flowers: see quot 1954] =ocean spray.

1925 Jepson *Manual Plants CA* 479, H[*olodiscus*] *discolor* . . . Cream Bush . . . Shrub 3 to 6 ft. high. **1941** Jaeger *Wildflowers* 88, *Shrubby cream-bush* . . . Low, compact shrub, with arching twigs. **1954** Sharpe *101 Wildflowers* 16, *Creambush* . . . Flowers creamy white, numerous, small, forming plumed, pendant clusters. **1973** Hitchcock–Cronquist *Flora Pacific NW* 213.

cream cabbage See **creamed cabbage**

cream-can cash n

1967 *DARE* FW Addit **seND,** Farmers who are distrustful of banks . . keep money buried in a cream can. Thus, when one planks down a wad of musty bills, he pays cold cream-can cash. Also applied figuratively.

cream cheese n

1 Cottage cheese. **esp LA** See Map

1941 *LANE* Map 299, The map shows the terms *cottage cheese* . . *cream ch*. . . and *Irish ch*. . . denoting a kind of cheese made of the curds of whole or skim milk, curdled either naturally or artificially . . . *Cream cheese* is often described as finer and smoother than the other varieties. **1962** Atwood *Vocab. TX* 61, The southern Louisiana *cream cheese* (also meaning cottage cheese) has penetrated into, but not much beyond, the southeastern counties of Texas. **1965–70** *DARE* (Qu. H60, *The lumpy white cheese that is made from sour milk*) 25 Infs, **esp LA,** Cream cheese. **1967** LeCompte *Word Atlas* 290 **seLA,** (*Homemade cheese made out of milk curd*) — Cream cheese [17 of 21 infs].

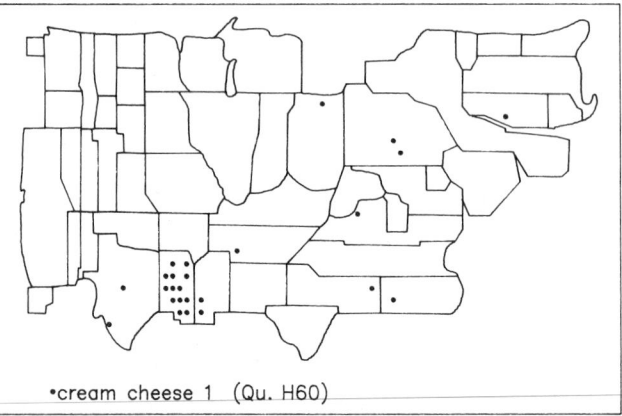

•cream cheese 1 (Qu. H60)

2 See quot.

1968 *DARE* FW Addit **New Orleans LA,** *Cream cheese:* A breakfast dessert with cream over sour cheese — sugar is spread over it. [FW: This is neither cottage cheese nor what is sold commercially as "cream cheese".]

cream-colored fall bean See **cream pea**

creamcups n

1 A plant (*Platystemon californicus*) with cream-colored flowers. **Pacific**

1888 Lindley *Calif. of South* 328 (*DA*), Two weeks later rank patches, with open, bright-yellow flowers, appear in company with blue *Nemophilas,* nodding cream-cups, purple *Calendrinias,* and yellow violets. **1902** (1974) Chestnut *Plants Indian* 351, The common "cream cup" of the region, a slender hairy annual with . . erect cream-colored flowers an inch or so in diameter. **1915** (1926) Armstrong *Western Wild Flowers* 166, *Cream-cups* . . . Pretty graceful plants, their creamy blossoms often whitening the spring meadows. **1946** Peattie *Pacific Coast* 53 **CA,** One could go on to speak . . of dainty creamcups and tidytips. **1965–70** *DARE* (Qu. S26d, *Wildflowers that grow in meadows*) Infs **CA20, 24, 41,** Creamcups; (Qu. S26e, *Wildflowers not yet mentioned*) Infs **CA2, 115,** Creamcup(s); (Qu. S22, *Bright yellow flowers that bloom in clusters in marshes in early springtime*) Inf **CA20,** Creamcups; (Qu. S26a, *Wildflowers . . roadside*) Inf **CA87,** Creamcups. **1968** *DARE* File **CA,** Creamcups — lighter colored than buttercups.

2 A primrose-like plant (*Calylophus drummondianus*).

1936 Whitehouse *TX Flowers* 83, *Creamcups* (*Meriolix spinulosa*) has yellow cup-shaped flowers.

cream day n

Saturday; see quots.

1928 *AmSp* 4.132 **NE,** Saturday is "cream day," the day for taking cream, eggs and other produce to the "hangout," which is generally the inland store and post-office. **1939** FWP *Guide NE* 111, *Cream day.* Saturday, when cream and eggs are taken to the store.

cream doughnut n Also *cream-filled doughnut* **esp MD**

A custard-filled doughnut.

1968 *DARE* (Qu. H29, *A round cake, cooked in deep fat, with jelly inside*) Infs **MD33, 39, 41,** Cream doughnut; **DE4, MD21, 37,** Cream-filled doughnut.

creamed cabbage n Also *cream cabbage, cream slaw* **esp PA**

A cabbage dish with a cream dressing.

1965–70 *DARE* (Qu. H52, *Dishes made with fresh cabbage*) Infs **PA22, 26, 49, 52,** Cream cabbage; **NC36, 38, PA2, 40, 110, TN5,** Creamed cabbage; **PA13,** Cream cabbage — whip cream; **MD27,** Cream slaw — cabbage with mayonnaise or sour cream dressing.

creamed potatoes n pl

Mashed potatoes.

1930 *DN* 6.80 **ceSC,** *Creamed potatoes* (more usually *creamed I'sh potatoes*) . . . Mashed potatoes. Universal. **1967** *DARE* FW Addit **LA9,** *Creamed potatoes* — the most frequent term for mashed potatoes. *Ibid* **TN,** *Creamed potatoes:* the same as mashed potatoes. A restaurant cook explained that there is a distinction — creamed potatoes have milk in them; but he admitted that, milk or not, on the menu mashed potatoes are always "creamed." Common.

creamer See **cream** v **1**

creamery n **chiefly NEast**

A separate building or room for cooling and storing dairy products.

1858 *Harper's Mag.* 17.44/2, **CT,** Come down with me to the creamery and we'll cool off before dinner. **1965–70** *DARE* (Qu. M18, *The separate building where milk is kept cold*) Infs **ME14, MA34, NJ65, NY23, 41, 66, PA13, WA11,** Creamery; (Qu. D16, *Names . . for parts added on to the main part of a house*) Inf **ME20,** Creamery.

cream-filled doughnut See **cream doughnut**

cream gland n

1950 *PADS* 14.23 **SC,** *Cream glands* . . . The highly prized thymus glands of calves and lambs. Also called *sweetbreads.*

cream gravy n **chiefly Sth, S Midl**

A gravy made with animal fat, flour, and milk or cream.

1932 (1946) Hibben *Amer. Regional Cookery* 152 **VA,** Fried Chicken with Cream Gravy and Mush. **1942** Rawlings *Cross Creek Cookery* 136

FL, Turn out all but two tablespoons of the [bacon] fat, and to the two tablespoons add one and one-half tablespoons of flour. Stir until browned. Add one cup of milk, salt and pepper to taste . . . Dot the dish of potatoes and cream gravy with butter. **1960** Criswell *Resp. to PADS 20* **Ozarks,** *Cream gravy* . . . Gravy made in a skillet with grease left from frying by addition of flour, water, milk. Staple diet of the growing pioneer child . . . (Still common). **1965–70** *DARE* (Qu. H37, . . *Words . . for gravy*) Infs DC1, GA55, LA12, 19, NJ54, SC56, TN1, 37, TX43, VA42, Cream gravy. **1967** *DARE* Tape SC46, We called it cream gravy . . [made with] flour and milk, just like chicken gravy.

creamie See **creamy**

cream of the pot n Also *cream of the soup* [*cream* the choicest part of something]
The best of its kind.
1953 *PADS* 19.10 **cnNC,** *Cream of the pot* . . . The best of its kind. "Our minister is the cream of the pot." **c1960** *Wilson Coll.* **csKY,** *Cream of the pot:* The very best; often used about someone who is decidedly superior to his family or neighbors. **1968** *DARE* (Qu. II23, *Joking names for the people who are, or think they are, the best society*) Inf NY69, Cream of the soup.

cream pea n Also *cream-colored fall bean, lady cream pea*
A **black-eyed pea** (here: *Vigna unguiculata*).
1965–70 *DARE* (Qu. I20, *Beans . . grown around here*) Infs FL18, TX105, Cream peas; KY40, Cream-colored fall beans; TX33, Lady cream peas; (Qu. I18, *Smaller beans . . white when . . dry*) Infs TX62, 102, Cream peas. **1970** Correll *Plants TX* 889, *Vigna unguiculata* . . . Cream-pea.

cream pitcher n
=**hog sucker.**
1915 *DN* 4.181 **swVA,** *Cream-pitcher* . . . The hog perch (?): often called *hog-molly.*

cream roll See **cream stick**

cream-shitter n [From its defecatory habits] Cf **chalk-line**
Either of two herons: the **great blue heron** or the **green heron.**
1945 McAtee *Nomina Abitera* 26, Great Blue Heron . . cream-shitter, southeastern Alaska. *Ibid* 27, Green Heron . . . cream-shitter, Iowa.

cream slaw See **creamed cabbage**

cream stick n Also *cream roll* Cf **cream doughnut**
A deep-fried oblong cake with a sweet creamy filling.
1967–69 *DARE* (Qu. H30, *An oblong cake, cooked in deep fat*) Infs MI72, NY94, OH21, 81, **PA221,** Cream stick; AL11, Cream roll; (Qu. H28, *Different shapes or types of doughnuts*) Inf CA94, Cream sticks; (Qu. H32, . . *Fancy rolls*) Inf KY74, Cream rolls.

cream supper See **ice-cream supper**

cream tartar n, also attrib *?old-fash*
Cream of tartar.
1790 *PA Packet & Daily Advt.* 1 Jan 4/1, A Fresh and General Assortment of Drugs and Medicines: among which are . . Cream Tartar, Jalap. **1857** Collins *Great West. Cook Book* 59 *(DA)*, Cream Tartar Biscuit. **1879** Whitney *Just How* 14 *(DA)*, Two teaspoonfuls of cream-tartar to one of soda. **1968** *DARE* (Qu. H19) Inf NY75, Cream tartar and soda biscuits. [Inf old] **1982** *Greenfield Recorder* (MA) 27 Mar sec A 4/2 (as of c1910), The cream tartar was [in] a larger red shaker box.

cream toast n
Toast served with a cream sauce over it.
1856 Holmes *Lena Rivers* 297 **NEng,** On entering the kitchen, she found Aunt Milly preparing a rich cream toast. **1891** *Harper's Mag.* 84.49/2 **NYC,** My cousin Flagg, with his mind undistracted by relays of cream toast, could give his entire attention to the Lost Cause. **1980** *DARE* File **cnMA** (as of c1910), In addition to plain toast, my grandmother made cream toast, that is, toast covered with cream sauce and served from a covered dish—a supper food. It was probably a way of using up bread that had become dry.

creamy n Also sp *creamie* Cf **ivory** n¹ **2**
An opaque, usu white, glass playing marble.
1934 *AmSp* 9.75 **cND,** Creamies. A term generally applied to all glass marbles. **1955** *PADS* 23.14, *Creamy (creamie)* . . . A cream-colored glass marble. **1963** *KY Folkl. Rec.* 9.59, *White colored marble:* creamy. **c1970** Wiersma *Marbles Terms* **csMI,** Creamie: A cream-colored glass playing marble.

creamy ass n
=**old-squaw.**
1945 McAtee *Nomina Abitera* 32, Old Squaw . . . The bird is reported as being called "creamy-ass" on Hatteras Island, North Carolina.

crease n¹
1 A part in one's hair.
1935 *AmSp* 10.167 **sePA,** He wears his crease in the middle (he parts his hair in the middle).
2 A mountain pass or gap.
1967 *DARE* (Qu. C15, *A place in mountains or high hills where you can get through without climbing over the top*) Inf **MO**18, A crease.

crease n² See **creece**

crease-back bean n Also *crease-back (pea)*
A cultivated bean (*Phaseolus* spp.)
1967–69 *DARE* (Qu. I20, *Kinds of beans . . grown around here*) Inf IL76, Crease-back beans; TN13, Crease-backs; KY40, White crease-back peas. **1976** *Wanigan Catalog* 7, Creaseback [bean]. **1983** Montell *Don't Go Up* 27 **csKY, cnTN,** In their gardens, frontier families grew . . black crease-back beans.

creassy green, creasy, creasy green See **creece**

creater See **creature**

creation intj [Prob euphem for *Christ*] *old-fash*
Used as a mild expletive.
1843 (1846) Haliburton *Attaché* (1st ser) 2.159, "Creation, man," said Mr. Slick, "I have done it . . and you didn't know it." **1847** (1962) Robb *Squatter Life* 138, Cre-*a*-tion, how tough he war. **1926** Kephart *High-landers* 101 **sAppalachians,** I halted to listen. Creation, what a rumpus!

creature n Usu |ˈkriˌčə(r)|, also in **Sth, S Midl,** and **NEng,** |ˈkritə(r)|; rarely |ˈkrečə˞| Pronc-spp *craythur, creater, creatoore, creatur', creeter, creetuh, creetur, cretur, crutter* See also **critter**
A Forms.
1848 Cooper *Oak-Openings* 1.20, Ben would say ac*tyve* and *sar*tain, though he was above saying creatoore, or creatur'. This is the difference between a Pennsylvanian and a Yankee. **1857** *Putnam's Mag.* 10.347/1 **NEng,** "Sakes alive!" said "Miss" Ranney. "I never did see sech a cretur as that are boy in all my days!" **1871** Eggleston *Hoosier Schoolmaster* 128 **IN,** You're a coward and a thief to be a-beatin' a little creetur like him! **1878** *Atlantic Mth.* 41.307/1 **ME,** I never made pretensions to being younger than I am, but you'd 'a' thought I was a topplin' old creatur' going on a hundred. **1894** *DN* 1.341 **wCT,** Creeter [kritr]. **1899** (1912) Green *VA Folk-Speech*, Creetur. **1903** *DN* 2.296 **Cape Cod MA** (as of c1850s), *Creature* [kritər]. **1914** *DN* 4.70 **ME,** Crutter . . . Creature. **1922** Gonzales *Black Border* 294 **sSC, GA coasts** [Gullah glossary], *Creetuh.* **1928** Ruppenthal Coll. **KS,** Craythur. **1938** Rawlings *Yearling* 26 **FL,** A creetur that kills and eats what he needs, why, he's jest like the rest of us, makin' out the best he kin. **1940** Richter *Trees* 57 **sOH,** Them varmints kin smell death furder than a she-creater in heat. **1968** [see B3 below].
B Senses.
1 Any farm animal. *somewhat old-fash*
1662 (1896) Hempstead *NY Records* 1.105, This Day (at a generall Towne meeting) was given to Caleb Carman two hollowes; . . hee is to Secure them from all Creatures. **1746** (1915) NH (Colony) Probate Court *Records* 3.448, I also give him halfe my stock of Creturs that I shall Dye seasd of that is both neat Cattel sheep horses and swine. **1818** in 1822 Flint *Letters* 94, She told us further, that travelers commonly hire a creature (a horse) at her house. **1872** *Harper's Mag.* 45.861/1, It was a cheerful old place, one building tumbling into another, mixed with a delightful familiarity of weeds, flowers, poultry, 'creatures,' and people. **1931–33** *LANE Worksheets* **nwCT,** A tongue is the piece of wood between the two creatures; **cnCT,** *Creatures:* Farm animals; **seMA,** *Creature:* A beef cow. **1933** Rawlings *South Moon* 30 **FL,** The chickens were asleep in their coop . . . They untethered the mule and cow and removed the rails from around the hogs. The creatures snorted but did not stir.
2 See quot.
1975 Gould *ME Lingo,* Creatures—The womenfolks. English-speaking Mainers borrowed this from the archaic French of the St. John Valley, where it is still the generic word for ladies—*les créatures* . . . "Run and tell the creatures (i.e., your mother, aunts, and sisters) that Uncle Josh is staying for supper!"

3 with *the:* Liquor; less freq tobacco. [Orig in allusion to I Tim. 4:4; cf *OED creature* 1c, d] *old-fash* See also **critter B5**

1737 *Penna. Gazette* 13 Jan 1/2 *(DAE)*, He's been too free with the Creature. **1760** (1765) Hutchinson *Hist. MA Bay* 1.107, The good creature tobacco. **1832** Hawthorne in *Token* 94, Nearly all, in short, evinced a predilection for the Good Creature in some of its various shapes. **1843** (1916) Hall *New Purchase* 65 **PA,** It is known he left town yesterday in a state of intoxicated inebriety, and with a jug of the creature. **1968** *DARE* Tape **PA**84, They could have drinks there [=at wakes], mostly cider, or a drop of the creature ['krečɚ] . . . It's a little alcoholic beverage. Well, it's Irish . . . "The creature's the divil himself."

credit n, v Usu |'krɛdɪt|; also, *esp among Black speakers,* |krɛdɪk| Cf Pronc Intro 3.I.14 Pronc-spp *credi(c)k*

A Forms.

1922 Gonzales *Black Border* 294 **sSC, GA coasts** [Gullah glossary], *Credik.* **1929** *Sat. Eve. Post* 17 Aug 136/2 **LA** [Black], And the rousters, who have "credik" at the bar for their needs, like bananas. **1939** McGuire *FL Cracker Dial.* 145, *Credit:* [krɛdɪk] . . heard . . "chiefly among Negroes." **1942** *Sat. Eve. Post* 14 Feb 20/3 [Black], I don't do business on credick. **1944** *ADD* **FL,** *Credit* . . . |krɛdɪk|. Reported as chiefly negro. **1968** *DARE* (Qu. U11, *If you buy something but don't pay cash for it . . "I _____."*) Inf **LA**20, Got it on credik.

B As noun.

Used as a count noun: See quots. **chiefly Sth, S Midl** See Map

1908 *DN* 3.285 **eAL, wGA,** On a credit. **1941** Faulkner *Men Working* 75 **MS,** I might talk to some of 'em today and git a credit fixed up fer us. **1942** *Sat. Eve. Post* 3 Jan 16/3 **TN,** Every penny he takes in is pure profit because he buys on a credit. **1965–70** *DARE* (Qu. U11, *If you buy something but don't pay cash for it, you might say, "I _____."*) 25 Infs, **chiefly Sth, S Midl,** Bought (*or* got) it on a credit; **AR**48, **GA**28, **MO**15, **NC**37, **TX**45, 106, Bought (*or* got) it on the credit.

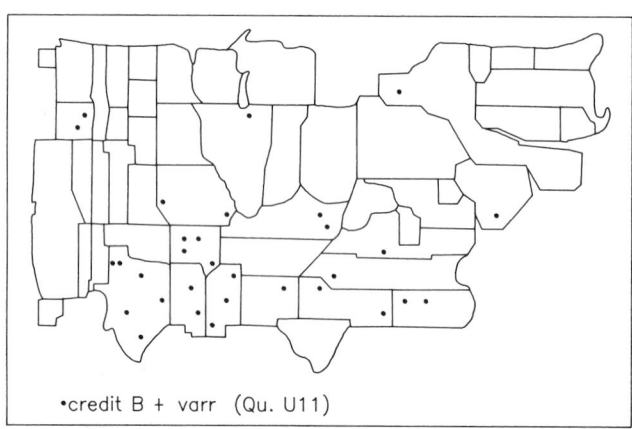

•credit B + *varr* (Qu. U11)

C As verb.

See quot.

1965–70 *DARE* (Qu. U11, *If you buy something but don't pay cash for it, you might say, "I _____."*) Infs **MO**4, 6, 18, **WA**8, Credit; **SC**26, 68, 69, Credit it; **FL**51, **NY**156, Credited it.

creece n Also *crease, creassy green, creasy (green), creecy ~, creese, creesie* (or *creesy*) *salad* [Varr of *cress*] **chiefly S Midl** =**cress.**

1937 (1963) Hyatt *Kiverlid* 79 **KY,** We picked wild mustard . . an' I don't know what all—I think maybe some creeces, too. **1942** Hall *Smoky Mt. Speech* 21, Examples of [i] for [ɛ]: *cress* ['krisɚz] (apparently the usual form). *Ibid* 24, [Footnote:] Some of these are probably cases of modern English [i] for ME [ɛ:] . . although *cress* may have had ME [e:]. **1946** *PADS* 6.10 **sVA, cNC,** *Creeses* ['krisɪz] . . . Cress or cress greens . . . Common . . . *Creesy salad* . . . Same as *cresses.* **1952** Giles *Forty Acres* 116 **KY,** To hunt dry land creases! . . . It was a small, flat plant growing close to the ground, with leaves very similar to our water cress. Creases? Cress, of course. Dry land cress. **1954** *PADS* 19.10 **NC,** *Creasy-greens.* *Ibid* 21.24 **SC,** *Creasy greens:* n. pl. Watercress. **1961** *Mt. Life* Spring 57, In almost any old field can be found wild lettuce . . creasies, crow's foot, and a hundred others. **1963** Watkins *Yesterday Hills* 79 **cnGA,** Food was plentiful in the spring; creases grew in the creek bottom, and the "salet" of creases boiled with a piece of fat meat was good. **1965–70** *DARE* (Qu. I28b) Infs **NC**31, 33, 36, 37, 44, 63, Creases; **NC**72, **TN**11,

Creasy greens; **GA**72, **KY**34, 40, 42, [krisɪz]; **KY**8, [kris]; **VA**104, ['krisi]; (Qu. I28a) Inf **VA**9, ['krisɛz]; **TN**13, Crease; **MD**37, Winter crease. **1973** *Foxfire 2* 79 **nGA,** "They bloom yeller all over a cornfield, that's creases." . . Cress salad: toss together lightly, two cups finely cut creases. **1976** Garber *Mountain-ese* 19 **NC,** *Creesie-salad* . . cress greens—"The wimmern air down in the bottom pickin' creesie salad fer dinner." **1981** *Greensboro Daily News* (NC) 22 July sec 1 B1, Technically, creecy greens are dry land cress . . . They grow wild in North Carolina and other southern states, often in cleared cornfields. They were especially welcome in former days because they grew in winter when other greens were scarce . . . The plant grows close to the ground with distinctive, ragged, dark green leaves. Eaten raw, it has a hot, radishy taste. The preferred way of eating creecies, however, is boiled with fatback or streak-o-lean.

creed n

1950 *PADS* 14.23 **SC,** *Creed* . . . In the expression: "my creed," a term of endearment. Gaelic: *mo cridhe,* my heart.

creek n[1], *also attrib* Usu |krik|; also, **esp Inland Nth, N Midl, West,** |krɪk| Pronc-spp *crick, crik, krick,* rarely *crake* See Map and Map Section

A Forms.

1608 Smith *True Relation* [19] **VA,** The Bay where he dwelleth hath in it 3 cricks. **1677** (1900) Manning *Sea Jrl.* 182 **ME,** Stood to ye n.ward of ye road & see several cricks. **1843** (1916) Hall *New Purchase* 437 **sIN,** He seed a crik a runnin across tother end. **1845** Hooper *Advent. Simon Suggs* 136, Sometimes I goes a-fishin on the krick. **1892** *DN* 1.238 **MO, MI,** Always [krɪk]. **1906** *DN* 3.116 **sIN,** *Crick.* **1909** *DN* 3.407 **nME,** *Crick.* **1933** *AmSp* 8.1.24 **sAppalachians,** Creek in one place may be *crick,* and in another place not far away *crake,* or it may rime with Greek. **1961** Kurath–McDavid *Pronc. Engl.* 148, *Creek* has either the vowel /i/ of *peak* or the /ɪ/ of *pick* . . . /i/ is in general use in the South . . . The vowel /ɪ/ of *pick* predominates throughout the North Midland and the North, except for southern New England and, perhaps, Metropolitan New York. It has nearly universal currency in New Jersey, Delaware, Pennsylvania, and northern West Virginia, as well as in the valleys of the Hudson and the Mohawk in New York State and in northeastern New England and New Brunswick. **1965–70** *DARE* (Qu. C1, *A small stream of water not big enough to be a river*) 581 Infs, **throughout US, but infreq in NEng and NW,** Creek; 292 Infs, **chiefly Inland Nth, N Midl, West,** Crick. **1970** *DARE* Tape IL126, You're getting over into crick ground, so to speak, with waterways.

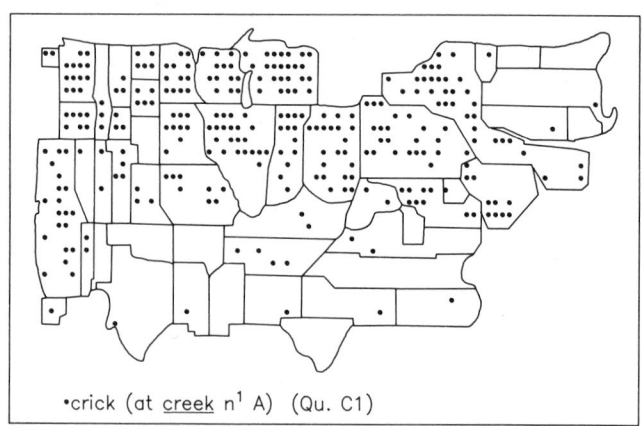

•crick (at <u>creek</u> n[1] A) (Qu. C1)

B Senses.

1 An inlet from the sea, an estuary. **Atlantic, esp Mid and N Atl**

1608 [see A above]. **1766** Bartram in 1953 McMullen *Topog. Terms FL* 93, Past by Trout-creek, 300 yards broad, salt to its head. **1771** in 1887 Franklin *Complete Wks.* 1.61 **sPA,** We put toward the shore, got into a creek, landed near an old fence. **1838** Cooper *Amer. Democrat* 118, "Creek," a word that signifies an *inlet* of the sea, or of a lake, is misapplied to running streams, and frequently to the *outlets* of lakes. **1939** *LANE* Map 40, *Creek* is in general use along the seashore for a salt water stream emptying into the sea or into a salt river, but also for a salt water pond formed by the stream . . . At some distance from the sea *creek* is not commonly used, and the meanings associated with it are often vague and confused. **1946** *PADS* 5.17 **VA,** *Creek* . . . a narrow salt water inlet, on the Tidewater and Eastern Shore. **1949** Kurath *Word Geog.* 61, The salt-water inlets of small streams that empty into the sea are known as *creeks* from Maine to Cape Fear in North Carolina. **1950** *PADS* 14.23 **SC,** *Crick* . . . A salt water inlet; a creek.

2 A freshwater stream generally smaller than a river. **widespread exc in NEng** See Map Cf **brook**

1638 (1837) *MA Hist. Soc. Coll.* 3d ser 6.42, They . . are dispersed securely in their plantations sixty miles along the coast, and within the land also, along some small creeks and rivers. **1724** (1865) Jones *Present State VA* 34, Into these Rivers run abundance of great *Creeks* or short Rivers, navigable for *Sloops*. **1817** Paulding *Letters from South* 2.39, It abounds in iron-ore, and is finely watered by the different branches of James river, which are here called creeks. **1912** *DN* 3.567 cNY, *Creek* . . . Any stream larger than a brook. In Central Vermont, *branch* is used; and in Mississippi *creek* is . . anything smaller than a river and larger than a branch. **1931–33** *LANE Worksheets* cCT, I heard a man speak about creeks in York State. I wondered how they got creeks that far from salt water. **1949** Kurath *Word Geog.* 61, *Creek* is the most common word for a small fresh-water stream in the Eastern States. It is current everywhere except in the greater part of New England, where *brook* or *river* are the usual terms . . . In Pennsylvania and the northern half of West Virginia *creek* is now the common noun. **1953** McMullen *Topog. Terms FL* 93, *Creek* . . . A stream tributary to a larger river; a small stream, a brook or rivulet . . . Called a *branch* . . and a *run*. **1965–70** *DARE* (Qu. C1, *A small stream of water not big enough to be a river*) 581 Infs, **throughout US, but infreq in NEng and NW,** Creek; 292 Infs, **chiefly Inland Nth, N Midl, West,** Crick.

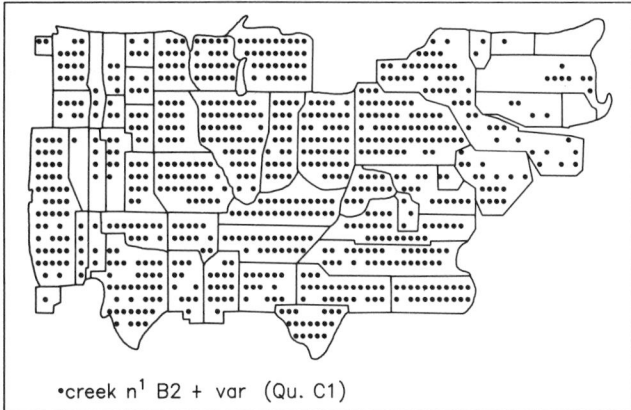

•creek n¹ B2 + var (Qu. C1)

3 A body of still water off to the side of a river or lake. **chiefly S Atl** Cf **bayou B3**

1828 in 1953 McMullen *Topog. Terms FL* 93, Which tract . . is situated . . on the south side of a creek known by the name of Bayou Grande, about seven miles west-southwest from Pensacola. **1864** (1922) Jackson *Col.'s Diary* 167 **GA,** The sloughs are called creeks but they spread out like swamps. **1965–70** *DARE* (Qu. C14, *A stretch of still water going off to the side from a river or lake*) 10 Infs, **chiefly S Atl,** Creek. [8 Infs old]

4 See quot. [*OED* →1856; *W3* "archaic"]

1968–70 *DARE* (Qu. C19, . . *Low land running between hills*) Infs IL69, 93, MN38, OK56, Creek.

creek n² [Perh hypercorrection]
A crick (in one's back or neck).

1966–70 *DARE* (Qu. BB3a, *A pain that strikes you suddenly in the neck*) Infs NC7, OH98, [krik]; (Qu. BB3b, *A sudden pain that strikes you in the back*) Inf IL61, [krik]; MI81, Creek.

‡creekbank coffee n
1970 *DARE* (Qu. H74a, *Coffee according to how it's made—very strong*) Inf IL117, Regular creekbank coffee.

creek blackhead See **creek broadbill**

creek boat n
1966–70 *DARE* (Qu. O1, *A small rowboat, not big enough to hold more than two people*) Infs FL51, IL67, OK52, TN35, VA70, 73, Creek boat.

creek boy n Pronc-sp *crick boy*
1950 *PADS* 14.23 **SC,** *Creek boy* [krik] . . . A boy employed to bring in crabs and other sea food from the creeks of the coastal area to boarding houses, hotels, etc. *Ibid,* *Crickboy* . . . Same as *creek boy,* low country pronunciation.

creek broadbill n Also *creek blackhead*
=**lesser scaup.**

1844 DeKay *Zool. NY* 2.324, This *Creek Broadbill* . . appears to prefer the creeks and smaller streams of the interior. **1888** Trumbull *Names of Birds* 58, *Aythya affinis* . . at Shinnecock Bay, L.I., and Tuckerton, N.J., *Creek Broad-bill;* and Giraud . . mentions this name as "well-known to the bay gunners." . . Many duckers of the Chesapeake know it as *Creek Blackhead.* **1899** Howe *Birds RI* 38, *Aythya affinis* . . . Creek Broadbill. **1917** (1923) *Birds Amer.* 1.136, Lesser Scaup Duck—*Marila affinis* . . . Other Names . . . Creek Broadbill. **1923** U.S. Dept. Ag. *Misc. Circular* 13.20, *Lesser Scaup Duck (Fulix affinis [Marila affinis]) . . In local use . . .* creek blackhead (Md.); creek broadbill (R.I., Long Island, N.Y., N.J.). **1925** (1928) Forbush *Birds MA* 1.241, *Marila affinis* . . . Creek Broad-bill.

creek cat n [**cat** n 8]
Perh a **bullhead 1.**

1969–70 *DARE* (Qu. P1, *Freshwater fish . . that are good to eat*) Infs KY43, VA46, Creek cat.

creek chubsucker n Also *creekfish*
A sucker (here: *Erimyzon oblongus*).

1884 Goode *Fisheries U.S.* 1.614, The Chub Sucker—*Erimyzon sucetta*. The 'Chub Sucker,' 'Sweet Sucker,' or 'Creek-fish' is one of the most abundant and widely diffused of the Suckers, being found from Maine to Texas. **1889** *Century Dict., Creek-fish* . . . A local name in the United States of the chub-sucker. **1970** WI State Hist. Soc. *Coll.* 58.281, *Erimyzon oblongus* . . . Creek chubsucker—*Erimyzon sucetta oblongus* . . . Rare. Taken only twice in the southeastern corner of Wisconsin during the late 1920's from the Des Plaines R. (Kenosha Co.) and a tributary.

creek duck n [From its habitat]
=**gadwall.**

1888 Trumbull *Names of Birds* 24, Though rather a rare visitant on Long Island, it [gadwall] is known . . as creek duck . . a common name also at Morehead, N.C., and in the vicinity of Savannah. **1909** Field Mus. Nat. Hist. *Zool. Ser.* 9.322, The Gadwall is known to gunners as Gray Widgeon and Creek Duck. **1928** Bailey *Birds NM* 116, The name of Creek Duck suggests the habits of the Gadwall, . . feeding along the reedy or grassy shores of creeks, shallow ponds, and lakes. **1955** *Oriole* 20.3, Gadwall.—Creek Duck (from its preference for small waters).

creeker n¹
A backwoodsman, rustic, hick.

1872 Flagg *Good Investment* iv *(DA),* A 'creeker'—as they [people along the Ohio R.] called backwoodsmen. **1970** Tarpley *Blinky* 266 **neTX,** *A poor white from the back country* . . . Other responses . . . creekers.

creeker n² See **krieker**

‡creekers intj [Euphem for *Christ;* cf *creepers, crikey,* etc]
1970 *DARE* (Qu. NN31, *Exclamations beginning with the sound of "cr-"*) Inf MA75, Creekers [krikəz].

creekfish See **creek chubsucker**

creek ivy n
=**mountain laurel 1.**

1966–67 *DARE* (Qu. S26b, *Wildflowers that grow in water or wet places*) Inf AL33, Creek ivy; (Qu. S26c, *Wildflowers that grow in woods*) Inf NC16, Creek ivy or mountain laurel.

creek maple n
A **silver maple** (here: *Acer saccharinum*).

1960 Vines *Trees SW* 673, Silver Maple—*Acer saccharinum* . . . Vernacular names are . . Creek Maple. **1968** *DARE* (Qu. T14, *Kinds of maples . . around here*) Inf VA34, Creek maple.

creek mussel n [Prob **creek** n¹ **B1**]
A mussel.

1968 *DARE* (Qu. P18, *Kinds of shellfish . . common around here*) Inf VA8, Creek mussels.

creek plum n **SW**
A shrubby plum *(Prunus rivularis).* Also called **hog plum**

1886 Havard *Flora W. & S. TX for 1885* 512, *Prunus rivularis* . . . (Creek Plum.) Small shrub, not uncommon on the Colorado and its tributaries, bearing excellent red plums in August and September. **1891** Coulter *Botany W. TX* 102, *Prunus rivularis* Creek plum . . . Not uncommon on the Colorado and its tributaries and extending to the upper Guadalupe and the Leona. **1938** Van Dersal *Native Woody*

Plants 206, *Prunus rivularis*... Creek plum. **1960** Vines *Trees SW* 400, Creek Plum—*Prunus rivularis.* **1970** Correll *Plants TX* 760, *Prunus rivularis*.. Creek plum.

creek redhead n Cf redhead

The female of the **ring-necked duck.**

1888 Trumbull *Names of Birds* 60, Ring-necked duck... At the mouth of the Susquehanna.. many of the local gunners regard the female as a distinct species, and term it *creek redhead,* because of its resemblance to female No. 16 [=redhead]. **1923** U.S. Dept. Ag. *Misc. Circular* 13.21, *Ring-necked Duck ... Vernacular Names ... In local use* .. creek redhead (applied to the female) (Md.).

creek road n

A rough back road usu following alongside a creek.

1954 *Harder Coll.* **cwTN,** *Creek road.* A road that follows a creek bank very closely. **1968–70** *DARE* (Qu. N27b, *When unpaved roads get very rough, you call them* _____) Inf **OH**58, Creek roads; (Qu. N29, *A less important road running back from a main road*) Inf **KY**72, Creek road.

creek sedge n

A **cordgrass** (here: *Spartina glabra alterniflora*).

1911 *Century Dict., Creek-sedge* ... A salt-marsh grass, *Spartina glabra,* abounding particularly along the edge of creeks and estuaries on the Atlantic coast. **1912** Baker *Book of Grasses* 162, Creek Sedge ... *Spartina glàbra.*

creek snake n

Perh a **water snake.**

1970 *DARE* (Qu. P25, *Kinds of snakes.. around here*) Inf **KY**72, Creek snake.

creekstuff n [From its habitat]

=**cordgrass,** esp *Spartina cynosuroides.*

1669 in 1901 Essex Inst. *Coll.* 37.219, On[e] aker more for Capt. Gardner & Thomas Macy.. for the mill and creek stuff proportionable. **1807** in 1846 MA Hist. Soc. *Coll.* 2d ser 3.51, Another kind of grass, called creek stuff, grows on the borders of the ponds, and the greatest part of it in the water. **1911** *Century Dict., Spartina ... S. polystachya,* the largest species.. is known locally on the coast as .. *creek stuff.*

creek thatch n [See quot 1911]

=**cordgrass,** esp *Spartina cynosuroides* and *S. glabra.*

1673 (1901) Essex Inst. *Coll.* 37.220, 2 acres meadow, and his proportion of creek thatch. **1794** (1801) Society Useful Arts *Trans.* 1.143 **NY,** He informed me that he gave the horse no grain of any kind, but kept him in a very poor pasture adjoining a creek where creek-thatch grew on sand-flats. **1911** *Century Dict., Spartina ... S. polystachya,* the largest species, .. is known locally on the coast as *creek-thatch* .., from its growth in creeks or inlets of salt water, and from its use, when cut, as a cover for stacks of salt-hay and as bedding in stables. **1912** Baker *Book of Grasses* 162, Creek Thatch ... *Spartina glabra* ... On the Atlantic and Pacific coasts.

creek water n

=**branch water 2.**

1967 *DARE* (Qu. H74b, *Words for coffee according to how it's made—very weak*) Inf **TX**42, Creek water.

creel v [Cf *EDD creel* v.² 2 "To lame by beating"] ?**S Midl**

To twist or wrench (usu a part of one's body); to become twisted, to lean; hence ppl adj *creeled* twisted or wrenched.

1917 *DN* 4.410 **wNC,** *Creel* ... To wrench. "I creeled my knee (neck, back)." **1966** *DARE* (Qu. BB3b, *A sudden pain that strikes you in the back*) Inf **AR**21, A creel back [=assim form of *creeled back*]. **1976** Garber *Mountain-ese* 19 **sAppalachians,** *Creel*.. turn, twist. "Be keerful uv the chug-holes or you might creel yore ankle." **1983** *MJLF* 9.36 **ceKY,** *Creel*.. to sprain (an ankle). **1984** *DARE* File **KY,** "That pile of tobacco slats is creeling," meaning it's beginning to fall over.

Creel n [See quot 1947]

A member of a mixed-race group in South Carolina.

1947 *AmSp* 22.83, The need for distinguishing names for tri-racial mixed-blood groups was met in part at first by the use of clan or family names. Illustrations.. are *Bones*.., *Chavises, Creels* ... [Footnote:] A possible variant of Creoles? **1963** Berry *Almost White* 34 **SC,** There are .. the Collinses in Tennessee, the Chavises and Creels in South Carolina.

‡creelin water n

1969 *DARE* (Qu. BB50c, *Remedies for infections*) Inf **MO**27, Wash it off with creelin [krɪˑilən] water.

creen v¹ See careen

creen v² [Alter of *crane*] Cf crane n 3

To stretch and turn the neck.

1944 *PADS* 2.41 **VA, NC,** Creen [krin] ... To turn partly around and look, to bend over. "When I walked into the church, she creened around and looked at me." .. Somewhat rare now. **1954** *Harder Coll.* **cwTN,** *Creen* ... To turn the head partly around. To creen the neck at something. From *crane.*

creep v

A Forms.

Past and past pple: usu *crept,* freq also *crep;* by analogy with other verbs, also *creeped,* sometimes *crope, crup;* rarely double pret *crepted.* All var forms **chiefly Sth, S Midl**

1848 (1894) Lowell *Biglow* 10 **NEng,** Zekle crep' up, quite unbeknown, An' peeked in thru the winder. **1881** Harris *Uncle Remus Songs* 55 **GA,** Brer Tarrypin, he crope under de bed. **1884** Amer. Philol. Assoc. *Trans. for 1883* 14.47, *Crope* .. is common among the negroes and poorer whites. It was once used by a pupil of mine ... South. **1892** *DN* 1.238 **MO,** *Crept.* In *crept* ... the *t* is generally left off in Kansas City. [*DN:* So in New England.] **1893** Shands *MS Speech* 25, *Crep* [krɛp]. Used largely by all classes for *crept* ... *Crope* [krop] ... is marked obsolete by Webster; it is, however, still preserved in negro speech. **1899** (1912) Green *VA Folk-Speech, Crope* ... Crept. **1908** *DN* 3.302 **eAL, wGA,** *Crep.* **1927** *AmSp* 2.2 **Ozarks,** Creep—crope—crope, crep. **1943** *LANE* Map 643, The following preterites .. were incidentally noted in the informants' conversation ... [krep] [1 inf, **CT**] **1965–70** *DARE* (Qu. Y26b, *"The children* _____ *out the back way."*) 23 Infs, **scattered,** Crept; **AL**20, **GA**77, 82, Creeped; **NY**67, Crepted; (Qu. Y34a, *When somebody moves on his hands and knees*) Inf **CA**70, Crep' around. **1966** *Wilson Coll.* **csKY,** He crup up behind me. **1970** *DARE* Tape **TN**46, Somebody .. had creeped under the tent. **1972** *Atlanta Letters* **cGA,** *Crope:* crept.

B Senses.

1 To move on all fours, to crawl. **widespread, but chiefly NEast, N Cent** See Map Note: *DARE* evidence shows *crawl* to be widespread throughout the US.

1943 *LANE* Map 582 **throughout NEng,** The baby *creeps.* **c1960** *Wilson Coll.* **csKY,** *Creep* ... To go on all fours, like a baby. Not common at all until lately. Crawl is the standard word in the area. **1965–70** *DARE* (Qu. Y34b, *What babies do before they walk*) 307 Infs, **scattered, but chiefly NEast, N Cent,** Creep; **SC**24, Crept; (Qu. Y34a, *When somebody moves on his hands and knees*) 111 Infs, **scattered, but esp NEast,** Creeping; **GA**82, **OK**1, Creeping on all fours; **CA**97, Creeping about; **NY**75, Creeping along. **1971** Wood *Vocab. Change* 41 **Sth,** A baby moving across the floor ordinarily *crawls,* though in a few instances outside of Louisiana he *creeps.* **1973** *AmSp* 48.60, Still another instance [i.e. of "semantic specialization induced by dialect overlapping"] comes from the contact of Northern *creep* and Midland *crawl* ... Typically, Northern babies do the first and, Midland babies do the second. An old Iowa farmer.. knew both terms. Clearly, he once must have thought that if both terms exist they mean different things. His conclusion was neat: babies creep on their bellies before they crawl on their knees. *Ibid* 64, A[n] .. Iowa farmer living just south of the Minnesota state line told the

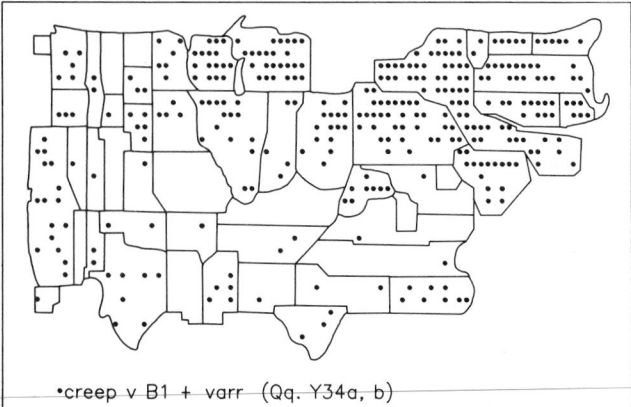

•creep v B1 + varr (Qq. Y34a, b)

fieldworker, "Well some people say *crawl,* but *creep* is right." **1973** Allen *LAUM* 1.393, (The baby *crawls* on all fours.)—Although this item was added to the UM worksheets only after the Minnesota survey was virtually completed, evidence from the other states strongly supports the inference, based upon the dominance of *creep* in New England, that creep is primarily Northern and *crawl* is primarily Midland. Creep dominates northern Iowa and the northern counties of Nebraska. *Crawl* is almost exclusively in southern Iowa and most of Nebraska, with scattered occurrences in the Dakotas. **1981** *Greenfield Recorder* (MA) 8 Aug sec A 7, Ivory soap had very attractive baby pictures, some creeping and one large one in color of the young mother giving a bath to a little child who is standing in a tub on the floor in the nursery.

2 also with *about, along, around:* To move lethargically or listlessly. **chiefly Sth, scattered Midl** See Map
1965–70 *DARE* (Qu. Y21, *To move about slowly and without energy*) 36 Infs, **scattered Sth, KY, sIN,** Creep; **GA**28, **IL**76, 116, **LA**3, **NC**62, **TX**43, **VA**74, Creep around; **MS**37, Creep around like dead lice were falling off him; **AR**51, **FL**11, **LA**6, **PA**24, **TX**9, 18, Creep along; **CT**15, **KY**33, **MS**10, **SC**3, Creep about; **NC**55, Creep easy; **IA**27, **MS**30, **NM**9, **TX**4, 76, (Barely) creeping around; **MA**6, **MI**2 **MS**86, Creeping; **NJ**15, Creeping serious; **CT**19, He's a creeping Moses; (Qu. Y23, *"I was so stiff I could hardly _____."*) Infs **MS**10, 23, **TX**4, Creep; (Qu. BB39, *When you don't feel just right, though not acutally sick . . "I'm just _____."*) Inf **KY**51A, Creeping around.

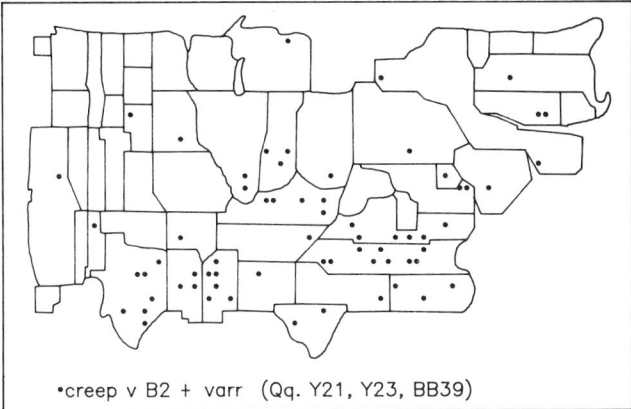

•creep v B2 + varr (Qq. Y21, Y23, BB39)

3 To move quietly or stealthily. [*OED* c1340 →] **scattered, but chiefly Sth, Midl** See Map
1965–70 *DARE* (Qu. Y26a, *To walk very quietly: "She came _____ to the baby's bed."*) 45 Infs, **chiefly Sth, Midl,** Creeping; **VT**8, Creeping in like a mouse; **VA**2, Creep; **OH**48, Crept; (Qu. Y26b, . . *"The children filled their pockets and _____ out the back way."*) 23 Infs, **scattered,** Crept; **AL**20, **GA**77, 82, Creeped; **NY**67, Crepted. **1968** *DARE* Tape **CA**80, Like if they're [=a kind of ant] on a potholder and it would drop, you know, they'd lay there and pretend they're dead. And then afterwards they'd creep off.

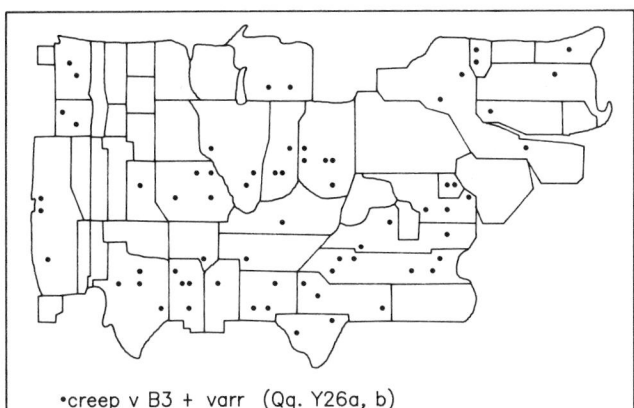

•creep v B3 + varr (Qq. Y26a, b)

4 in phr *creep the goose:* See quot.
1945 Saxon *Gumbo Ya-Ya* 200 **LA,** 'Creeping the goose' is the Cajun's method of hunting geese. They believe geese always leave a member of a flock posted as a sentinel, and that this sentinel is alert for only one thing, the appearance of any watching human eyes. So the Cajuns, when they

have spotted geese feeding in a pond or bay, begin to creep toward them, snaking through the sawgrass and holding their heads down so that their eyes cannot be seen by the sentinel bird. When they are near the geese, one of the Cajuns, who has been previously selected, claps his hands, and at this signal all the hunters spring up and fire.

5 esp in phr *creep on (someone):* See quots. *among Black speakers* See also **creep** n², **creeper 9**
1971 Roberts *Third Ear* [3] [Black], *Creep* . . to cheat on a friend; to two-time a person; e.g. She's trying to creep on him. **1972** Claerbaut *Black Jargon* 61, *Creeping* . . . To be unfaithful to one's spouse, fiancé, or regular dating partner. **1980** Folb *Runnin' Down* 140 swCA [Black], "To creep on someone" has multiple references . . . It can mean to catch someone unawares by sneaking up behind them, usually with the intention of doing physical harm. It can mean deliberately and slowly to follow another person . . . But . . the most common meaning relates to some kind of covert sexual move, making a quiet play for another's mate or lover: "*Creep* on a *nigger's woman!* One of yo' partners got a broad and you jus creep, go over dere and don't let nobody know—on the quiet side. Tha's like committing adultery . . . " It may refer to cheating on your mate or lover . . . Or it can mean to lie about your whereabouts: "Creep on yo' old man. You say you goin' out wid d' girls to d' movies. Really, you be out wid 'nother brother."

creep n¹ [Engl, Scots dial *creepie* a low stool] *?obs*
A stool.
1889 (1971) Farmer *Americanisms* 182, *Creep.*—In Pennsylvania a stool.

creep n² *among Black speakers* Cf **creep v B5, creeper 9**
See quots.
1960 Wentworth–Flexner *Slang* 129, *Creep,* A clandestine meeting or mission. *Some Negro use.* **1970** Major *Afro–Amer. Slang* 42, *Creep:* a clandestine mission usually referring to a romantic meeting between male and female.

‡**creep-about** n [**creep v B1**]
A baby at the crawling stage.
1968 *DARE* Tape **NY**123, My younger sister was very curious and she was a creep-about at that time.

creep about, creep along, creep around See **creep v B2**

creep chequerberry n [*creep* creeping + **checkerberry 3**]
=**partridgeberry 1.**
1971 Krochmal *Appalachia Med. Plants* 176, *Mitchella Repens L. (Rubiaceæ)*—Common names: Partridgeberry . . creep-chequer berry.

creep-coat n Cf **crawling grass**
An unidentified plant: see quot.
1912 Green *VA Folk-Speech* 133, *Creep-coat* . . . A kind of light grass that is said to *creep* up the women's coats.

creeped See **creep v A**

creeper n

1 A creeping or twining plant of any of var genera such as *Campsis, Ipomoea, Convolvulus, Parthenocissus.*
1800 in 1803 Elliott *Jrl.* 288 **FL,** Many of the trees in the low grounds are loaded with a variety of vines, the most conspicuous of which are the creeper, or trumpet flower, (begonia radicans,) and common poison vine, (rhus radicans). **1894** *Jrl. Amer. Folkl.* 7.95, *Calystegia sepium* . . creeper. **1900** Lyons *Plant Names* 115, *Convolvulus Sepium* . . . Creeper. **1935** Sandoz *Jules* 114 wNE (as of 1880–1930), Along the Niobrara the silvery-gray strips of buffalo-berry bushes flaunted clumps of blood-red creeper. **1965–70** *DARE* (Qu. S5, *The wild morning glory*) Infs **CA**41, **MI**92, **MA**68, **NY**10, 68, 88, Creeper; (Qu. S21, *Weeds . . that are a trouble in gardens and fields*) Inf **MN**2, Creeper—spread along the ground; **IL**52, Creepers, a vine with little leaves on each side, looks like the garden flower called portulaca—creeps all over the lawn.

2 Any of var small creeping birds such as the **titmouse** and **nuthatch,** but esp the American brown creeper *(Certhia familiaris).*
1731 (1754) Catesby *Nat. Hist. Carolina* 1.62, *Parus Americanus gutture luteo.* The Yellow-throated Creeper. **1902** White *Blazed Trail* 292, Over the way a creeper was droning sleepily a little chant. **1965–70** *DARE* (Qu. Q23, *The insect-eating bird that goes headfirst down a tree trunk*) 14 Infs, **chiefly Nth,** Brown creeper; 12 Infs, **scattered,** Creeper; **PA**44, Black-and-white creeper; **NY**103, Creeper nuthatch; **CA**78, Sierra creeper; **CA**140, Western creeper; (Qu. Q17, *Woodpeckers . . around here*) Infs **AR**48, 49, **GA**25, **SC**4, Creeper.

3 A louse. Cf **crawler** n[1] **2**

1899 (1912) Green *VA Folk-Speech* 133, *Creepers* . . . Head-lice. **1950** *WELS* (Names for body and head lice) 2 Infs, **WI**, *Creepers*. **1965–70** *DARE* (Qu. R25, *Joking names for a head . . or body louse*) Infs **IN**3, 17, **KY**34, **MO**15, **VA**7, 30, *Creeper*.

4 A dipterous larva.

1965 *DARE* FW Addit **KY**47, *Creepers*—maggots or fly larvæ. Common.

5 Perh a **spring peeper**.

1966–70 *DARE* (Qu. P21, *Small frogs that sing or chirp loudly in spring*) Infs **AR**41, **IL**100, **NC**36, **NY**231, *Creepers*.

6 An earthworm. Cf **crawler** n[1] **1**

1967 *DARE* (Qu. P5, *The common worm used as bait*) Inf **LA**8, *Creeper*.

7 also *ice creeper*: A fixture with iron points that is attached to footgear to prevent slipping on ice. **chiefly Nth, esp NEast** See Map *somewhat old-fash*

1859 (1968) Bartlett *Americanisms* 107, *Creepers*. Pieces of iron, furnished with sharp points and strapped under the feet, to prevent one falling when walking upon ice. **1927** Sears *Catalogue* 344/1, *Ice Creepers*. Adjustable straps. Easily attached to boots, rubbers, etc. **1945** Hatcher *Lake Erie* 285 **Gt Lakes**, The fisherman, with sharp-cleated ice creepers strapped to his boots, goes forth to his day's fishing pushing his sled with a box full of equipment. **1948** Peattie *Berkshires* 234, We had not yet learned about sealskins or creepers for climbing, and waxing was still largely a matter of merely preventing the skis from sticking. **1950** *WELS* (Heavy pieces of metal under the soles of boots to keep them from slipping) 4 Infs, **WI**, *Ice creepers*. **1965–70** *DARE* (Qu. W12a, *Heavy pieces of metal fastened under the soles of boots to keep them from slipping*) 41 Infs, **chiefly NEast**, *Creepers*; 17 Infs, **chiefly Nth**, *Ice creepers*.

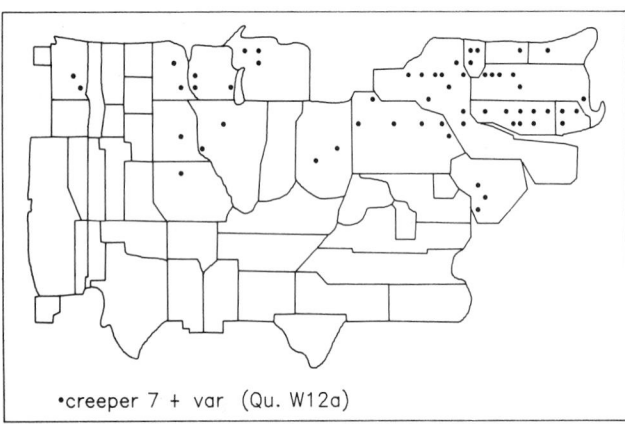

•creeper 7 + var (Qu. W12a)

8 A skillet or heavy frying pan. **chiefly MA** *obsolescent* Cf **spider**

1877 Bartlett *Americanisms*, *Creeper*. A shallow iron dish used in frying; a spider. New England. **1933** *Hanley Disks* **neMA**, We always say creepers, while you would say frying pans. **1949** Kurath *Word Geog.* 23/1, The Merrimack Valley, including the northern parts of the counties of Essex and Middlesex in Massachusetts and the southeastern counties of New Hampshire, has retained some striking localisms . . . *creeper* . . for the cast-iron frying pan (only in Essex county, now rare). **1963** Pilgrim Sóc. Plymouth MA *Notes* 4 (as of 18th, 19th cent), They parched corn in the creeper.

9 An adulterer; one who covertly loves another's lover or spouse. *among Black speakers* Cf **creep** v **B5**, n[2]

1911 *Jrl. Amer. Folkl.* 24.354 **Sth** [Black], The "creeper" watches his chance to get admittance into a home, unknown to the husband. **1926** Van Vechten *Nigger Heaven* 285, *Creeper*: a man who invades another's marital rights. **1977** Dillard *Lexicon* 36 [Black], The man doing the cuckolding may be a *creeper*, a term which occurs frequently in many contexts; one of the congregation shouts the word when the sermon turns to adultery in "Satan Is a Dirty Fighter."

10 See quot.

1916 *DN* 4.340, *Creeper* . . . A narrow guage [sic] railroad.

11 A kind of diaper.

1970 *DARE* (Qu. W19, *The folded cloth worn by a baby in place of pants*) Inf **NJ**67, *Creeper*: like a diaper, but it buttons on.

creeper milkweed n

A spurge.

1971 Green *Village Horse Doctor* 43 **TX** (as of 1940s), I compounded in my laboratory a full treatment for sheep that were stiff from grazing creeper milkweed.

creepified ppl adj [*creepy* + *-ified*]

Frightened; frightening, eerie.

1942 Rawlings *Cross Creek* 158 **FL**, Night overtakened me and I begun to feel a mite creepified. **1967** Will *Dredgeman* 18 **FL**, A right boogerish place, this dark swamp looked to be, for sure, plumb creepified!

creeping ppl adj

Taking effect slowly, gradually, or insidiously.

1939 FWP *Guide TN* 426, Certain brands were known as "creeping likker," because they kicked slow and powerful. **1965–70** *DARE* (Qu. BB28, . . *Imaginary diseases*) Infs **CA**1, 82, **LA**23, **NJ**34, Creeping crud; (Qu. A18, . . *A very slow person*) Inf **IL**7, As slow as creeping paralysis; (Qu. Y21, *To move . . without energy*) Inf **TX**98, Looks like he's got creeping paralysis; (Qu. BB5, *A general feeling of discomfort*) Inf **AR**47, Creeping paralysis; (Qu. DD27, *Nicknames . . for wine*) Inf **NY**80, Sneaky Pete, creeping Lucy.

creeping alkali grass n

A low-growing grass (*Puccinellia phryganodes*).

1955 U.S. Arctic Info. Center *Gloss.*, Creeping alkali grass. A plant *Puccinellia phryganodes*, commonly found on brackish flats. Cf. *alkali grass*. **1959** Anderson *Flora AK* 74, *Puccinellia phryganodes* . . Creeping Alkali-grass.

creeping bent n [*bent* abbr for *bentgrass*]

=**redtop 1**.

1966 *DARE* (Qu. S9, *Kinds of grass that are hard to get rid of*) Inf **WA**12, Creeping bent.

creeping buttercup n Also *creeping crowfoot*

A **crowfoot 1** (here: *Ranunculus repens*).

1840 MA Zool. & Bot. Surv. *Herb. Plants & Quadrupeds* 26, *Ranunculus repens* . . . Creeping Crowfoot. **1900** Lyons *Plant Names* 316, *Ranunculus repens* . . . Creeping Buttercup. **1931** Harned *Wild Flowers Alleghanies* 189, Creeping Buttercup (*Ranunculus repens* . .). **1938** Madison *Wild Flowers OH* 26, Creeping Buttercup. *Ranunculus repens*. **1970** Correll *Plants TX* 646, *Ranunculus repens* . . Creeping Buttercup.

creeping cedar See **creeping juniper**

creeping Charlie n Also sp *creeping Charley*

1 =**wallpepper**.

1900 Lyons *Plant Names* 340, *S[edum] acre* . . . Creeping-Charlie. **1959** Carleton *Index Herb. Plants* 32, Creeping Charley: Lysimachia nummularia; Nepta [sic] hederacea . . . Sedum acre.

2 =**ground ivy**.

1900 Lyons *Plant Names* 174, *G[lechoma] hederacea* . . . Creeping-Charlie. **1950** Stevens *ND Plants* 241, Ground Ivy . . . Sometimes called "creeping charley," a name applied to various plants of creeping habit. **1965–70** *DARE* (Qu. S21, *Weeds . . that are a trouble in gardens and fields*) Infs **FL**4, **NY**165, 233, **WI**8, 20, 64, 66, Creeping Charlie; (Qu. S9, *Grass . . hard to get rid of*) Infs **MI**45, **MN**11, **OH**37, **WI**50, Creeping Charlie; (Qu. S26d, *Wildflowers that grow in meadows*) Inf **MN**19, Creeping Charlie. [Note: some of these Infs may refer instead to other senses.] **1973** Hitchcock–Cronquist *Flora Pacific NW* 402, Ground Ivy . . . Creeping Charlie.

3 =**ponyfoot**.

1951 *PADS* 15.38 **TX**, *Dichondra* spp.—Creeping Charley.

4 =**moneywort**.

1959 [see **1** above]. **1966** *DARE* Wildfl QR Pl.164a Infs **NY**91, **OH**14, Creeping Charlie. **1967** *DARE* FW Addit **MA**5, Creeping Charlie—moneywort. **1976** Bailey–Bailey *Hortus Third* 691, Creeping Charlie.

creeping crowfoot See **creeping buttercup**

creeping cucumber n

A vine (*Melothria pendula*) that bears a somewhat cucumber-like fruit.

1840 Phelps *Lectures on Botany* App 116, *Melothria* . . *pendula*, (small creeping cucumber). **1937** Stemen *OK Flora* 516, *Melothria pendula* . . . Creeping Cucumber. **1939** Tharp *Vegetation TX* 70, Creeping Cucumber (*Melothria*).

creeping hemlock See **ground hemlock**

creeping Jack n

=**wallpepper**.

1900 Lyons *Plant Names* 340, *S. acre* . . . Creeping-Jack. **1914** Georgia *Manual Weeds* 200, Wall Pepper . . Creeping Jack. **1959** Carleton *Index Herb. Plants* 32, *Creeping Jack:* Sedum acre.

creeping Jennie n Also sp *creeping Jenn(e)y*

1 =**moneywort**. [*OED* 1882 →]

1900 Lyons *Plant Names* 234, *L. Nummularia* . . . Creeping-Jenny. **1902** Earle *Old Time Gardens* 60, One garden owner has set his edgings of Moneywort, otherwise Creeping-jenny. **1965–70** *DARE* (Qu. S5, *The wild morning glory*) 44 Infs, **chiefly Nth, esp nwPlains States**, Creeping Jennie; (Qu. S21, *Weeds . . that are a trouble in gardens and fields*) Infs **MN6, NE11, WI17,** 72, Creeping Jennie; (Qu. S9, *Grass . . hard to get rid of*) Infs **IL40,** 113, **WI12,** Creeping Jennie; (Qu. T5, *Kinds of evergreens, other than pine*) Infs **RI4,** 10, 17, Creeping Jennie. [Note: some of these Infs may refer instead to other senses.] **1966** *DARE* Wildfl QR Pl.164a Inf **OH14,** Creeping Jennie.

2 A **ground pine**.

1892 *Jrl. Amer. Folkl.* 5.105, *Lycopodium complanatum,* creeping Jenny, Bedford, Mass. **1898** *Jrl. Amer. Folkl.* 11.283, Creeping Jenny. **1900** Lyons *Plant Names* 233, *L. clavatum* . . . Creeping-Jennie . . . *L. complanatum* . . . Creeping-Jennie.

3 A **wild cucumber** (here: *Echinocystis lobata*).

1896 *Jrl. Amer. Folkl.* 9.188, *Echinocystis lobata* . . creeper, creeping Jenny, Oxford County, Me. **1959** Carleton *Index Herb. Plants* 32, *Creeping Jenney:* Echinocystis lobata; Helxine soleiri; Lysimachia nummularia; Nepeta hederacea (N. glechoma, Glechoma h.).

4 =**ground ivy**.

1940 Clute *Amer. Plant Names* 26, Ground Ivy . . . Creeping Jenny. **1959** [see **3** above].

5 A **bindweed 1** (here: *Convolvulus arvensis*).

1950 Stevens *ND Plants* 229, *Convolvulus arvensis* L. Field Bindweed. "Creeping Jennie."

creeping juniper n Also *creeping cedar, ~ savin (juniper)*

A procumbent trailing **juniper** (here: *Juniperus horizontalis*). Also called **crawling cedar, ground cedar, ground juniper, running cedar, slinkweed, trailing yew, Waukegan juniper**

1928 Rosendahl–Butters *Trees MN* 49, Creeping Savin . . . Prostrate evergreen shrub, often spreading over a considerable area. **1942** Tehon *Fieldbook IL Shrubs* 28, The Creeping Juniper or Creeping Savin . . was seeded on the Waukegan moorland nearly three-quarters of a century ago. **1950** Stevens *ND Plants* 45, Creeping Cedar . . . Forming dense mats on buttes, hills and slopes. **1955** U.S. Arctic Info. Center *Gloss.,* Creeping juniper. An evergreen tree or shrub, *Juniperus horizontalis.* Also called 'ground juniper.' **1976** Bailey–Bailey *Hortus Third* 616, *[Juniperus] horizontalis* . . . Creeping j., creeping savin j., creeping cedar.

creeping myrtle n

A **periwinkle** n[1] **1** (here: *Vinca minor*).

1972 GA Dept. Ag. *Farmers Market Bulletin* 29 Mar 8, The most popular ground cover of all, Vinca Minor, also known as Creeping Myrtle, Running Myrtle and Periwinkle, was known in Medieval England as "Joye of the Grounde."

creeping palmetto n

=**blue palmetto 1**.

1791 (1958) Bartram *Travels* 181 **FL,** We behold . . a . . plain . . covered by a fine short grass, with extensive parterres of the dwarf creeping Palmetto, their stipes sharply toothed or serrated. **1942** Kennedy *Palmetto Country* 5, Another low-lying palmetto—variously called the dwarf, needle, porcupine, blue, or creeping palmetto—has an even wider range than the saw palmetto, extending from Florida to North Carolina and Texas.

creeping phlox n Also *crawling phlox*

A **phlox** (here: *Phlox stolonifera*).

1931 Harned *Wild Flowers Alleghanies* 406, Crawling Phlox (*Phlox stolonifera . .*). **1964** Campbell *Great Smoky Wildflowers* 16, Creeping Phlox—*Phlox stolonifera.* **1968** *DARE* (Qu. S26c, *Wildflowers that grow in woods*) Inf **PA99,** Creeping phlox. **1976** Bailey–Bailey *Hortus Third* 862, *Creeping phlox.*

creepings n pl

1899 (1912) Green *VA Folk-Speech* 133, *Creepings* . . . Shivery sensations from dread, or cold.

creeping savin (juniper) See **creeping juniper**

creeping snowberry n Cf **snowberry**

A **wintergreen 2** (here: *Gaultheria hispidula*).

1848 Gray *Manual of Botany* 262, *Chiógenes,* Salisb. Creeping Snowberry. **1853** (1864) Thoreau *ME Woods* 211, The Creeping Snowberry (*Chiogenes hispidula*) . . was quite common there. **1952** Blackburn *Trees* 112, Evergreen creeping plant with brilliant white berries . . . creeping snowberry. **1966** Grimm *Recognizing Native Shrubs* 232, *Creeping-snowberry . . . Leaves* with a wintergreen odor when bruised . . . *Fruits . .* with wintergreen odor when crushed.

creeping spike rush n

A **spike rush** (here: *Eleocharis palustris*).

1959 Anderson *Flora AK* 109, *Eleocharis palustris . .* Creeping Spike-rush. **1961** Peck *Manual OR* 144, *Eleocharis palustris* . . . Creeping Spike-rush.

creeping thistle n

=**Canada thistle**.

1900 Lyons *Plant Names* 81, *Carduus arvense* . . . Creeping thistle. **1903** Porter *Flora PA* 341. **1912** Blatchley *IN Weed Book* 166, *Carduus arvensis* . . . Creeping Thistle. **1950** Gray–Fernald *Manual of Botany* 1542, *Cirsium arvense* . . . Canada thistle . . . *Perennial by extensively creeping and too freely sprouting roots.* **1963** Craighead *Rocky Mt. Wildflowers* 203, Canada Thistle *Cirsium arvense . .* Other Names: Creeping Thistle. **1973** Hitchcock–Cronquist *Flora Pacific NW* 503, *Cirsium arvense . .* creeping thistle.

creeping-up n Cf **crowhop** n **3**

In marble play: see quot.

1963 *KY Folkl. Rec.* 9.64 **eKY,** *Trying to get closer shot by placing the hand in a position nearer to the marble being shot at* . . . Creeping-up.

creeping Veronica n

A **speedwell**.

1969 *DARE* (Qu. S21, *Weeds . . that are a trouble in gardens and fields*) Inf **NY171,** Creeping Veronica.

creeping warbler n Also *black-and-white creeping warbler, tree-~, varied ~*

=**black-and-white warbler**.

1844 Giraud *Birds Long Is.* 70, *Mniotilta varia* . . . Creeping warbler. **1898** (1900) Davie *Nests N. Amer. Birds* 426, The little Black-and-white Creeping Warbler . . climbs around the trunks of trees. **1917** (1923) *Birds Amer.* 3.112, *Mniotilta varia. . Other Names . . .* Black and White Creeping Warbler; Creeping Warbler; . . Varied Creeping Warbler. **1923** Dawson *Birds CA* 437, *Mniotilta varia* . . . Tree-creeping Warbler. **1946** Hausman *Eastern Birds* 497, *Mniotilta varia* . . . Other Names—Black and White Creeping Warbler, Creeping Warbler.

creeping wintergreen n

1 =**wintergreen 2**.

1822 Eaton *Botany* 287, *Gaultheria . . . hispidula . .* creeping wintergreen. **1848** Gray *Manual of Botany* 264, *G. procumbens* . . . Creeping Wintergreen. **1906** Rydberg *Flora CO* 260, *Gaultheria* . . . Creeping Wintergreen. **1924** Deam *Shrubs IN* 258, The Creeping Wintergreens . . . Prostrate, creeping shrubs with underground stems from which arise erect branches. **1971** Krochmal *Appalachia Med. Plants* 128, *Gaultheria Procumbens L.* (Ericaceæ)—Common names: Checkerberry wintergreen . . creeping wintergreen.

2 The soapwort **gentian** (*Gentiana saponaria*). obs

1821 in 1832 *MA Hist. Soc. Coll.* 2d ser 9.150 **VT,** Gentiana saponaria . . . Creeping wintergreen.

creepmouse n, also attrib Also *creep-mousey, creep-mousie, creepy-mouse*

A tickling game usu played with a small child; see quots.

1899 (1912) Green *VA Folk-Speech* 133, *Creep-mouse* . . . To tickle babies to make them laugh by moving the fingers rapidly on their bodies as if a mouse was running over them. **1914** *Lippincott's* Dec 55 **NY,** Personally, I think it much more dignified for a woman to admit frankly that she loves a particular man and to start out openly to win him, than to stalk him in the creep-mousy fashion of some of your so called 'nice girls.' **1954** Welty *Ponder Heart* 140 **TN,** He went right to the top with "creep-mousie," up between those bony little shoulder blades to the nape of her neck and her ear. **1983** *NADS Letters* se**LA** (as of 1920s), As a tot in the twenties I was a victim of creepy-mouse. In the fifties I inflicted it on my own children. [**1983** *DARE* File s**IN** (as of c1900), As fingers "walk" up a bare arm, or leg, or stomach, the following rhyme is repeated: "Here comes a little mousie-mouse, creeping up to baby's house." (The baby's given name is used in the rhyme.)]

Cree potato n Also *Cree turnip*

=**Indian breadroot.**

1900 Lyons *Plant Names* 309, *P[soralea] esculenta* . . . Cree potato, Cree turnip. **1931** Clute *Common Plants* 30, A species of *Psoralea*, Otherwise known as Indian bread-root *(P. esculenta),* is the Cree potato. **1959** Carleton *Index Herb. Plants* 33, *Cree-potato:* Psoralea esculenta.

creese, creesie salad, creesy salad See **creece**

creeter See **creature, critter**

creetuh See **creature**

creetur See **creature, critter**

Cree turnip See **Cree potato**

crene See **crane 3**

creole n See **creole pony**

creole adj Usu |ˈkriol| Pronc-spp *creowl, creyall* [LaFr; see quot 1931] **chiefly LA**

Of or pertaining to the Creoles, either of two groups, the descendants of the French or Spanish colonists, or persons of mixed French or Spanish and Black heritage; by ext: of native origin or production, homemade and old-fashioned, hence locally considered excellent.

1834 (1878) Aime *Plantation Diary* 37 **LA,** A creole cow from plantation pasture, having never been fed on corn. Gave seventy-one pounds of melted tallow. **1841** *Daily Picayune* (New Orleans LA) 16 Apr 1/6, Creowl hoss. **1852** (1878) Aime *Plantation Diary* 159 **LA,** A creole potatoe, from the plantation of Mr. S. Roman, weighs four and a half pounds. **1912** Green *VA Folk-Speech* 133, *Cre'owl* . . . For *creole.* **1927** Kennedy *Gritny* 215 **sLA** [Black], Sho will make you rear back an' smack yo' lips manful, after you done sopped some o' dese light biscuits in dis good ole-time Creyall gravy. [**1931** Read *LA French* 32, *Créole* designates anything manufactured or produced by the Creoles and considered therefore of peculiar excellence.] **1941** FWP *Guide LA* 562, The Creole lily is generally called the Easter lily; its local name merely exemplifies the tendency of this section to apply the term "Creole" to both people and things. **1945** Saxon *Gumbo Ya-Ya* 177 **LA,** There are Creole cabbages, Creole lilies and Creole horses. And a thousand other little things, little inbred habits, superstitions, proverbs, all with derivations springing from that past that belonged to the Creoles. **1952** Tracy *Coast Cookery* 88, They [New Orleans chefs and housewives] have a rich background in the art of preparing food. The French who settled here brought their roux . . . The Spanish arrived with their crushed garlic . . . The Indians . . contributed their knowledge . . . And the Negroes added their genius . . . Then the American know-how combined them all into the fabulous Creole cooking. *Ibid* 89, The oysters, shrimp, crayfish, and . . crabs all are challenges that the Creole cook takes in his stride. **1967** LeCompte *Word Atlas* 253 **seLA,** A specialized meaning for *Creole* is becoming noticeable, i.e., the use of word [sic] as an adjective to mean "excellent" or "old fashioned" or "like mother used to make." *Cf.* Creole cream cheese, Creole onions, Creole cooking, Creole pralines. **1968** *DARE* (Qu. H74a, *Coffee . . very strong*) Inf **LA16,** Creole coffee; (Qu. I34, *If you don't have sweet corn, you can always eat young _____*) Inf **LA20,** Creole corn—like sweet corn but it comes twenty or thirty days later; it is bigger than sweet corn; (Qu. HH30, *Things that are nicknamed for different nationalities*) Inf **LA32,** Creole stew.

creole pony n Also *creole, ~ horse, ~ tackey* **LA, TX**

Perh an **appaloosa** n[1], but see quots.

1841 *Daily Picayune* (New Orleans LA) 16 Apr 2/5, There are nineteen entries, among them some of the first "Creoles of Louisiana." *Ibid* 1/6, He got on to a creowl hoss that never'd ben rid much, and was as fiery as a rattlesnake. [**1849** Bracht *TX im Jahre 1848* 85, Nach diesen kommt das sogenannte Kreolen-pferdchen, auch Opelousas poney genannt, ein ausgezeichnetes Damenpferd. [After these comes the so-called creole pony, also called the Opelousas pony, an excellent horse for ladies.]] **1853** Hammett *Stray Yankee in TX* 378, Planters and stock-raisers in Texas keep many horses, but they are usually of the small breed of Louisiana Creole ponies, or those of the Spanish kind. **1941** FWP *Guide LA* 432, *Creole pony.* These small and hardy ponies, with their flashing eyes, long manes and tails, and fuzzy varicolored coats are known by a variety of names: Creole pony (most common), Cajun pony, Creole tackey, prairie pony, and coco pony (they feed on the wild coco grass).

1944 *AmSp* 19.69 **TX,** Creole pony. **1967** *DARE* (Qu. HH30, *Things that are nicknamed for different nationalities—for example, a "Dutch treat"*) Inf **LA2,** Creole pony.

creole skiff n Cf **esquif**

1956 Knipmeyer *Settlement Succession* 168 **LA,** The smallest and lightest is actually called the "Creole skiff" wherever it is in a minority to the other types. The name occurs from Bayou Bonfuca, near Slidell, to Bayou Boeuf, near Morgan City. The Creole skiff characteristically occurs on small, interior water bodies, and attains its most typical development in the Atchafalaya Basin, where it is specifically *esquif*. The distinguishing features are a narrow beam, considerable sheer, and a high, slightly overhanging V-shaped stern.

creole tackey See **creole pony**

creosote bush n Also *creosote (plant)*

A resinous, ill-smelling, yellow-flowered shrub *(Larrea tridentata)* native to the Southwest. Also called **gobernadora, greasewood, hedionilla**

1848 Emory *Notes Reconnoissance* 612, The vegetation on the jornada is the creosote bush, the mesquite, the Fremontia, and occasionally patches of thin grass. **1853** U.S. Army Corps Topog. Engineers *Rept. Sitgreaves* 34, Up the Rio Grande . . the vegetation alters but little, the timber being principally . . the creosote plant, *(Larrea Mexicana,)* . . and various species of artemisia. **1903** (1950) Austin *Land of Little Rain* 10, If you have any doubt about it, know that the desert begins with the creosote. This immortal shrub spreads down into Death Valley and up to the lower timber-line, odorous and medicinal. **1942** Whipple *Joshua* 95 **UT,** A sprinkling of creosote bush with its pungent aroma and resinous-covered leaves, always so green against the universal drabness of winter: creosote seldom grew where there was alkali. **1965** Teale *Wandering Through Winter* 31 **CA,** We fed dry twigs from creosote bushes to a campfire. *Ibid* 124, Dr. Jaeger . . . was of the opinion that the plant had been named about the time creosote was being introduced widely and the fact that both had strong chemical smells led to the choice of the name. **1967–68** *DARE* (Qu. S26e, *Other wildflowers*) Inf **CA4,** Creosote bush. **1973** *AZ Highways* Mar 4/2, Waxy-leaf plants like the Creosote bush *(greasewood)* have a varnish-like, shiny coating which reflects heat.

creowl See **creole** adj

crep See **creep** v A

crepe moss n

=**Spanish moss 1.**

1949 Moldenke *Amer. Wild Flowers* 310, A venerable old live oak, its branches abundantly bearded with tumbling cascades of gently swaying *crepemoss* or *Floridamoss*, forms a sight of such unique beauty.

crepe myrtle See **crape myrtle**

crepted See **creep** v A

‡**crescent** n joc Cf **moonhouse**

A privy.

1967 *DARE* (Qu. M21b, *Joking names for an outside toilet*) Inf **MN2,** Crescent, because of the moon-shaped ventilation hole cut in the wall.

cress n Also *cressy (salad)* **chiefly Appalachians, esp wVA**

Any of var plants of the mustard family, esp **wintercress.** Also called **creece**

1965–70 *DARE* (Qu. I28b, *Greens that are cooked*) Infs **KY8, VA9,** 13, 68, 78, 88, 93, Cress(es); **IN39, MD27, VA26,** 104, Land cress; **DE1,** 3, **MD39,** Winter cress; **VA30,** Dry land cress; **MD30,** Field cress; **VA33,** Wild cress; **OH2, PA198,** Land cress; **VA35,** 42, Cressy sallet; **VA71,** Cressy; (Qu. I28a, *Things . . you call "greens" . . eaten raw*) Infs **IA41, PA203, VA9,** 24, 74, 101, 108, **WA18,** Cress(es); **VA24,** Curly cress, field cress; **OH78,** Land cress; **PA163,** Winter cress, yellow cress; [**PA248,** Crest]; (Qu. S26d, *Wildflowers . . in meadows*) Inf **VA59,** Cress; (Qu. S21, *Other weeds*) Inf **PA191,** Winter cress. **1981** Mebane *Mary* 11 **cnNC,** Mama . . and I . . picked gunnysacks full of cressy salad.

crested coralroot See **coralroot 2**

crested flycatcher n

Any of var flycatchers with prominent crests, but esp *Myiarchus crinitus,* which is also called **Christian flycatcher, freightbird, race bird, snakebird, snakeskin bird, wheep, yellowhammer, yellow kingbird, yellow snapper, yellow-tailed beebird.**

1731 (1754) Catesby *Nat. Hist. Carolina* 1.52, The crested Fly-Catcher

. . . It breeds in *Carolina* and *Virginia,* but retires in Winter. **1810** Wilson *Amer. Ornith.* 2.75, The *Great Crested Flycatcher, Muscicapa crinita* . . arrives in Pennsylvania early in May and builds his nest in a hollow tree deserted by the Blue-bird or Woodpecker. **1948** *Press Gazette* (Green Bay WI) 13 July 11/4, Birds that sang in the afternoon were the . . scarlet tanager, indigo bunting, red-eyed vireo and crested flycatcher.

crest grass n

Prob crested **wheatgrass** *(Agropyron cristatum).*

1966 *DARE* (Qu. L9a, *Grass . . grown for hay*) Inf **WA**1, Crest grass.

cretter See **critter**

cretur See **creature**

creuple See **cripple** n[1]

crevalle n Also sp *crevally* [Prob Fr *crevale* a fish (Littré)] Cf **cavalla, cavally**

A fish of the family Carangidae as:

a A fish of the genus *Caranx,* as the **hardtail 1,** but esp *C. hippos* which is also called **cavalla 2, cavally, horse crevalle, jack** n[1]**, jack crevalle, toro, tourist tarpon, yellow mackerel. esp S Atl, but also Pacific coast**

1879 U.S. Natl. Museum *Bulletin* 14.41, *Paratractus pisquetus* . . . Yellow Crevallé. **1882** U.S. Natl. Museum *Bulletin* 16.920, *Caranx hippos* . . . (Crevallé; Toro; Horse Crevallé; Cavally; Jack . .). *Ibid* 920, *Caranx crysos* . . . (Hard Tail . . Crevalle). **1897** U.S. Bur. Fisheries *Report* 236 **FL,** The crevallé is probably common in the Indian River at all times, but is not highly esteemed by commercial fishermen. **1939** Natl. Geog. Soc. *Fishes* 151, Among them are . . certain species of the carangidae, or crevally family. **1947** Dalrymple *Panfish* 264 **FL,** Most of the time these fishermen take small Jack (Crevalle) of two or three pounds. **1972** Sparano *Outdoors Encycl.* 377, *Caranx hippos* . . . The crevalle seems to prefer shallow flats, though large solitary specimens are often taken in deep off-shore waters.

b =**rainbow runner.**

1946 Stilwell *Hunting in TX* 31, Now, while you are angling . . along the coast of Texas you will encounter one fish that those of us who know the ropes consider a prime nuisance . . . This fish is the jackfish, or crevallé, or yellowtail as he is called down on the coast of Mexico.

crevalle jack See **jack crevalle**

crevally See **crevalle**

crevasse n Missip Valley

A break in a levee.

1813 *Pittsburgh Alman. 1814* 57 *(DA),* The numerous crevasses (breaks) above are supposed to have added to the safety and perhaps prevented the city from experiencing inundation. **1826** (1878) Aime *Plantation Diary* 9 **LA,** A crevasse on the 26th between the DeLogny and Choppin's plantations. **1941** Baldwin *Keelboat Age* 77 **Missip R** (as of 19th c), A similar danger was the crevasse, formed in time of high water when the river broke through a levee. **1967** *Good Old Days* June 15 **New Orleans LA** (as of 1900), But the river [Mississippi] also had a sinister side . . . We were forced to yield to the break in the levee, called a "crevasse", which meant loss of crops and living in a very inconvenient way until the waters receded.

crevey n [Fr *crevé* a break, broken place]

A water channel in a swamp.

1979 Hallowell *People Bayou* 134 **sLA,** Randall Stelly goes out with a flashlight to "bull-eye" some alligators in the crevey back of the camp . . . The garfish in the crevey are turning cartwheels of excitement in the murky water where young shrimps are abundant.

crevice n Usu |ˈkrɛvəs|, sometimes |ˈkrɪvɪs|

A Form.

1942 Hall *Smoky Mt. Speech* 19, The raising of [ɛ] to [ɪ] was observed also in: crevice [ˈkrɪvɪs].

B Sense.

A mountain pass.

1967–69 *DARE* (Qu. C15, *A place in mountains or high hills where you can get through without climbing over the top*) Infs **IL**29, 93, **MN**38, **OR**4, 13, 14, Crevice.

crevice v, hence vbl n *crevicing* **esp CA** *hist*

See quot 1968.

1851 *Alta Californian* 17 July *(DA),* The early adventures in the gold-diggings required simply . . a strong sheath-knife for crevicing. **1853** *Ore. Statesman* 6 Dec. 1/2 *(DA),* One claim thou may'st own, and then drive your stake. And coyote and crevice till you make or you break. **1928** Ritchie *Forty-Niners* 8 **CA,** Men who were panning their fifteen or twenty ounces a day or "crevicing" that much out of stream banks with butcher knives and iron spoons whooped into line. **1968** Adams *Western Words* 82, *Crevice*—In mining, to work or explore rock crevices for gold. *Crevicing*—In mining, picking out gold with a knife from cracks in rocks.

creyall See **creole**

crib n[1]

1 A barred or slatted structure in a barn: a manger; a storage place for corn, a corncrib. **chiefly W Midl, Gulf States** See Map

1939 *LANE* Map 106, *Corn Crib*—The map shows the terms *(corn) crib, corn house* . . and *corn chamber,* denoting the building, room or compartment in which . . corn is stored. **1965–70** *DARE* (Qu. M6, *The place where grain is kept in a barn*) 62 Infs, **chiefly W Midl, Gulf States,** Crib; **CA**7, **GA**77, **ME**24, **VA**27, **WA**11, Grain crib; **AR**56, Corn in crib; (Qu. M3, *The place inside a barn for storing hay*) Infs **TX**26, 99, Crib; (Qu. M12) Infs **IL**93, **TN**37, Corn in crib; **GA**1, Crib in barn.

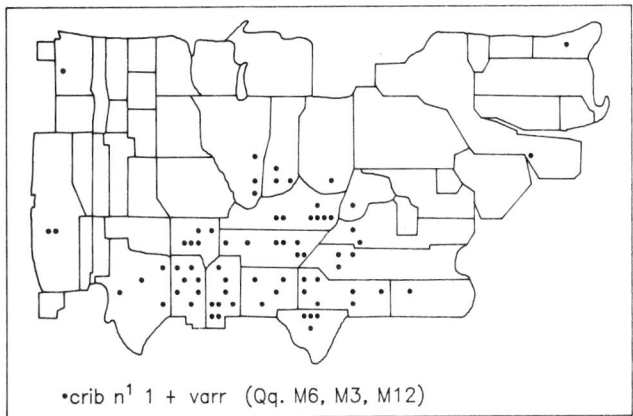

•crib n[1] 1 + varr (Qq. M6, M3, M12)

2 The place where one dwells. [Perh orig thieves' jargon] *esp among Black speakers*

1859 Matsell *Vocabulum, Crib.* A house. **1958** Hughes–Bontemps *Negro Folkl.* 482, *Crib:* House, home, where you can not only hang your hat, but raise hell. **1967** *DARE* Tape LA3, I wish you would go by my crib and get my blood [kinfolk] to raise [free] me. [Heard by Inf from New Orleans' Blacks at the Louisiana State Penitentiary] **1970** *DARE* (Qu. AA21, *Joking expressions . . about a wife who gives the orders and a husband who takes them from her*) Inf **FL**51, She runs that crib. [Inf Black] **c1970** *DARE* File **CT, MA,** *Crib*—Used frequently by some young people for one's home or apartment. **1972** Claerbaut *Black Jargon* 62, *Crib* . . a house; living quarters; place to live: Got to get back to my crib. **1980** Folb *Runnin' Down* 84 **swCA** [Black], The two environments most often referred to were one's *crib* (apartment or home) and one's *ride* (car).

3 A jail. [Orig criminal jargon] *joc*

1938 Stuart *Dark Hills* 257 **KY,** Yes, Jailer Adams locks many of them in the crib . . . The good wives often take care of the tobacco when the men are put in the Greenup crib for "misorderly conduct." **1969** *DARE* (Qu. V11, . . *A county or city jail*) Inf **NY**219, Crib.

4 In railroading: a caboose.

1945 Hubbard *Railroad Ave.* 338, *Crib*—Caboose. **1977** Adams *Lang. Railroader.*

5 also *cribby:* See quot.

1966–69 *DARE* (Qu. M21a, *An outside toilet building*) Inf **WA**1, Crib; (Qu. M21b, *Joking names for an outside toilet building*) Inf **IL**90, Cribby.

6 Something used to cheat in an examination; one who cheats in an examination.

1856 Hall *College Words* 144, *Crib.* Probably a translation; a pony. **1915** *DN* 4.233 [Western Reserve Univ., Harvard], *Crib* . . . One who cheats. "He's a dirty crib." **1927** *AmSp* 3.219 [Kansas Univ. slang], *Crib* . . some object or material used in cribbing. **1930** *AmSp* 5.238 **NY**

[Colgate Univ. slang], *Crib* . . a paper or set of notes used in cheating in an examination. **1931** *AmSp* 6.203 [Univ. of Missouri], *Crib:* a paper on which material unlearned but needed on an examination is written and taken to class.

7 A buoy.

1968 *DARE* (Qu. O14a, *A floating structure out in a large lake or the sea usually marking a channel for boats*) Inf **LA**15, Cribs.

8 A kind of fishnet.

1968 *DARE* Tape **MD**15, Pound net is a big, long leader that runs off of the net on to it, and then they have what they call a crib. The fish will come up against this leader, and then they'll follow that back and they get caught in this crib and then the fisherman goes there with a big net and he can dip 'em out.

9 The cupola or ventilator on a barn.

1969 *DARE* (Qu. M2, *The small wooden construction on top of a barn with slats for ventilation*) Inf **IN**80, Crib.

crib n² See **cribbage**

crib v

1 To cheat on a school examination; hence vbl n *cribbing.* [*OED* 1748 →] **chiefly Nth, N Midl, West** See Map

1927 *AmSp* 3.219 [Kansas Univ. slang], *Crib* . . . To cheat during an examination. The word is also used as a noun meaning some object or material used in cribbing. **1930** *AmSp* 5.238 NY [Colgate Univ. slang]. **1931** *AmSp* 6.203 [Univ. of Missouri slang]. **1965–70** *DARE* (Qu. JJ7, *. . Cheating in school examinations*) 242 Infs, **chiefly Nth, N Midl, West,** Cribbing. [Of all Infs responding to the question, 35% were coll educ; of those giving this response, 57% were coll educ.]

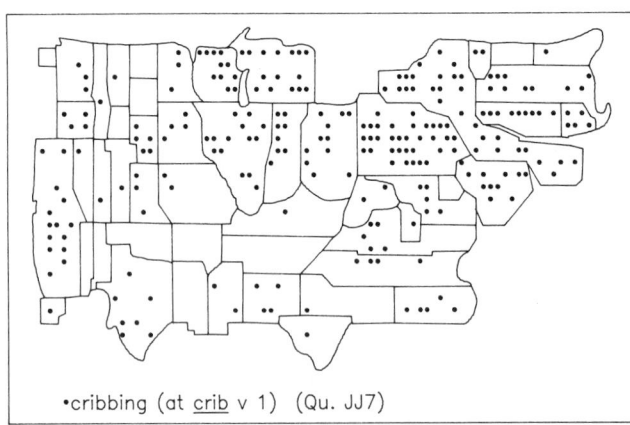

•cribbing (at <u>crib</u> v 1) (Qu. JJ7)

2 To form floating logs into a raft by enclosing them in a boom (a string of logs fastened end to end); also, by ext, to tow a raft so formed. **chiefly Nth**

1878 in 1888 MN Laws *Genl. Statutes* 1.342, Any person who may do . . any manual labor in cutting, . . cribbing, or towing any logs or timber in this state, shall have a lien thereon. **1905** U.S. Forest Serv. *Bulletin* 61.35, *Crib logs, to.* To surround floating logs with a boom and draw them by a windlass on a raft (a *crab*), or to tow them with a steamboat. [North Woods, Lake States Forests.]

cribbage n, also attrib Also *crib* **chiefly Nth, West** See Map A card game for two to four players, the score being kept by inserting pegs in holes in rows on a board.

1965–70 *DARE* (Qu. DD35, *Favorite card games . . people play around here*) 83 Infs, **chiefly Nth, West,** Cribbage; **CA**160, Crib; **WA**18, Cribbage or crib; (Qu. DD37, *Other table games played a lot by adults around here*) 16 Infs, **chiefly Nth,** Cribbage; (Qu. FF2) Inf **MI**45, Cribbage parties; (Qu. FF22a) Inf **MI**9, Cribbage league; **MI**18, Women's cribbage league; (Qu. FF22b) Inf **MI**55, Cribbage club.

crib basket n

See quots.

1933 *AmSp* 8.1.48 **Ozarks,** Crib basket . . . A stout basket made of oak splints, used to carry corn. **1954** *Harder Coll.* **cwTN,** Crib basket: A basket used to carry corn.

crib bed n

1930 Shoemaker *1300 Words* 13 **cPA Mts** (as of c1900), *Crib-bed*—A single bed, a bed for one person, "spool" bed.

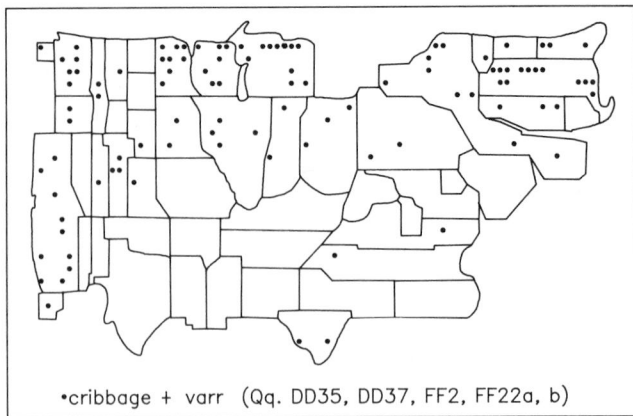

•cribbage + varr (Qq. DD35, DD37, FF2, FF22a, b)

cribben n pl [Ger *Grieben* leavings of rendered fat]

1914 *DN* 4.104 KS, *Cribben* . . . Pork cracklings: used by persons of German extraction.

cribber n [crib n¹ **1** + *-er*] **chiefly S Midl**

See quot 1923.

1923 *DN* 5.204 **swMO,** Cribber . . . An animal, specifically a horse, addicted to the habit of gnawing or sucking at the manger or at trees or stumps. [Also] . . stump sucker. **1929** *AmSp* 4.204 **Ozarks,** Come can'le-light he geared up his ol' piedy cribber an' lit a shuck fer Gotham Holler. **1947** Steed *KY Tobacco Patch* 103, The only pedigreed horse I could ever boast of was a saddle horse, but when I discovered he was a cribber, I sold him for thirty-five dollars. **1972** Green *More Horse Tradin'* 114, The old storekeeper laughed and said: "Young fellow, you've got a stump sucker." Then I remembered about the man hollering and using the word cribber; so I asked . . what was the difference between a cribber and a stump sucker. He said: "There ain't any difference in the vice—the difference is in the location. If he's in Kentucky, he's a cribber—and if he's in Texas, he's a stump sucker."

cribbing See **crib** v **1**

crib burner n

1954 *Harder Coll.* **cwTN,** Crib burner: A very dishonest person.

‡**crib buster** n

1971 WI Statist. Reporting Serv. *Report* 13 Sept, Many farmers are expecting a bumper corn crop . . "Looks like a crib buster," said a Fond du Lac County man.

cribby See **crib** n¹ **5**

‡**crib fence** n

1968 *DARE* (Qu. L60, *A fence made of stone or rock without mortar*) Inf **UT**7, Crib fence.

cribway n

1966 *DARE* (Qu. O4, *A much larger and solider structure [than a dock] where ships can come to land*) Inf **ME**16, Cribway, used by some summer people, made of timbers criss-crossed and bolted together in a square frame then sunk and filled with rocks; a top is put on and a walkaway [sic] to shore. Many of these are used as bases for a large wharf. Each structure or base is a crib. When many are covered over together they make a cribway.

crick See **creek** n¹

crick boy See **creek boy**

cricket n¹

1 A roller in a horse's bit; see quot. **SW**

1961 Adams *Old-Time Cowhand* 118, The "roller" in such a bit's ["half-breed bit"] called a "cricket" because it makes a chirpin' noise, givin' the hoss somethin' with which to amuse 'imself with his tongue and creatin' a music the cowboy loves to hear.

2 A frying pan, skillet. Cf **creeper** n **8, spider**

1970 *DARE* Tape **WV**14, They would bake 'em in a cricket . . that's a black iron skillet with a long handle on it and a cover for it, and it stands on legs.

cricket n² Also *cricket(y) stick* [*OED* 1598 →] **chiefly Nth** See *DS* EE10 for numerous varr

A children's game in which usu a short piece of wood (**cat** n **3b**) is flipped into the air, then struck with a long stick or bat, the methods of play differing locally.

1950 *WELS Suppl.* **WI,** Cricket—a game in which a short stick is hit with a longer one. **1965–70** *DARE* (Qu. EE10, *A game in which a short stick lying on the ground is flipped into the air and then hit with a longer stick, that's _____*) 24 Infs, **scattered, but esp Upper MW, C Atl, sNY,** Cricket; **GA**15, Cricket stick; **MN**11, Crickety stick. **1966** *DARE* File **nWI, nMI,** Cricket—a children's game played with two sticks. One stick stuck in a crack, hit with second stick.

cricket n³ [*OED* a1643 →]
A small four-legged stool.

1788 *MA Centinel* (Boston) 21 June 114 [sic for 113], Detached at a considerable distance, it [the *New Hampshire pillar*] rests on something similar to a *cricket,* quite *forlorn* and *dejected.* **1899** (1912) Green *VA Folk-Speech, Cricket* . . . A small, low stool of wood, with four legs like a bench; a seat for one person. **1904** (1969) Robins *Magnetic North* 136 **AK,** The child stooped to pick up his wooden cricket . . . In less than five minutes Kaviak was once more seated on the cricket. *Ibid* 126, He was sitting on his cricket by the fire waiting for dinner. **1906** Churchill *Coniston* 68 **NEng,** The high pulpit, taken from the old meeting house, and the cricket on which he used to stand and the Bible from which he used to preach. **1931–33** *LANE Worksheets* **Boston MA,** Cricket, footstool; **swRI,** Cricket, a little square stool, higher than a footstool. Same as ottoman.

cricket n⁴ [Perh alter of *pricket*]
A young deer.

1969 *DARE* (Qu. P32, *Other kinds of wild animals*) Inf **IL**32, Cricket—a deer born in late May or early June that is killed in early November; very tender meat.

cricket intj [Euphem for *Christ*]
1965–68 *DARE* (Qu. NN31, *Exclamations beginning with the sound of "cr-"*) Inf **VA**29, Crickets; **OK**1, For cricket's sake.

cricket frog n Also *cricket toad* [From its chirping]
A frog of the genus *Acris.* Also called **peeper, rattler, Savannah cricket**

1891 in 1896 *IL Ag. Exper. Sta.* Urbana *Bulletin* 3.342, Its note is a rapidly repeated grating noise, thought to resemble the trilling of a cricket, whence the name cricket-frog. **1892** *IN Dept. Geol. & Nat. Resources Rept. for 1891* 461, *Acris gryllus* . . . Cricket Frog . . . Though belonging to the "tree frogs" it never ascends trees. **1930** *Copeia* 4.153 **GA,** Cricket frogs were heard calling at the mill pond every few days from March 20 to April 6. **1932** Wright *Life-Hist. Frogs* 156, *Acris gryllus* . . . Common Names. Cricket-Frog . . . Cricket Toad. **1968** *DARE* (Qu. P21, *Small frogs that sing or chirp loudly in spring*) Inf **GA**54, Cricket frogs.

cricket hawk n
=**loggerhead shrike.**

1956 *MA Audubon Soc. Bulletin* 40.129, Southern Shrike . . . Cricket Hawk (Maine).

cricket stick See cricket n² 1

cricket stomper n [In ref to the Mormons' struggle against swarms of locusts during the early settlement of Utah]
A Mormon.

1968 *DARE* File **seID,** Cricket stompers—Mormons. **c1971** Hall *Snake River Valley,* 2 infs, **cs,seID,** Cricket stompers.

cricket toad See cricket frog

crickety See crickey

crickety stick See cricket n²

crickey n |ˈkrɪki| [*crick* var of **creek** n¹ + *-ey*]
A dry creek bed.

1978 *DARE* File **eTN** (as of 1950), Drive down the crickey.

crickey intj Also sp *cricky* Also *crickety* [Euphem for *Christ*] Cf **cracky** intj
Used as a mild oath—freq in phr *by crickey.*

1884 *Harper's Mag.* 69.693/1, Cricky! didn't she go it, though! **1944** *AmSp* 19.243, Walter's list of words [M.R. Walter, "A Dictionary of Profanity and Its Substitutes" (typescript, Princeton University Library)] is especially rich in euphemisms. Some of them follow . . . For *Christ:* . . *crickey,* . . *cracky.* **1959** *VT Hist.* new ser 27.131, *By crickety!*

. . . Occasional. **1960** Criswell *Resp. to PADS 20* **Ozarks,** *Cricky* . . . Often used with *by* as a mild oath. Fairly common, more so than *cracky.* **1969** *DARE* (Qu. NN31, *Exclamations beginning with the sound of "cr-"*) Inf **RI**17, Crickey.

crickled adj [Prob for *crippled*]
1906 *DN* 3.116 **sIN,** Crickled . . . Disabled. Rare. "The man is crickled."

cricksand n [Folk-etym for *quicksand;* cf **creek** n¹]
Quicksand.

1921 *DN* 5.110 **cCA,** Crick-sand . . . Quicksand. A popular etymology resulting from the almost universal pronunciation of creek as crick. **1934** Weseen *Dict. Amer. Slang* 95, ["Cowboys and Westerners"] Cricksand—Quicksand. **1966** *DARE* (Qu. C11, *Soft, wet sand in streams or wet places, that draws people and things down into it*) Inf **DC**8, Cricksand [ˈkrɪksænd]—on land.

cricky See crickey

cried up ppl adj
1899 (1912) Green *VA Folk-Speech, Cried up* . . . Well spoken of; much praised.

crik See creek n¹

crim n |krɪm| Folk-etym sp *cream* [Engl dial *creem* a shiver, chill] Cf **crimmy**
1931–33 *LANE Worksheets* **neMA,** Cream [krɪm] A chilly feeling. Cream is a chilly feeling with goose flesh that's creamy.

crimanetly intj Also freq sp *crimanently* For other varr, see quot [Prob alter of **criminy**] **chiefly Inland Nth, N Midl, West** See Map
Used as an expression of surprise or annoyance.

1965–70 *DARE* (Qu. NN31, *Exclamations beginning with the sound of "cr-"*) 42 Infs, **chiefly Inland Nth, N Midl, West,** Crimanetly; 13 Infs, **Nth, N Midl,** Crimanently; **CA**170, Crimanentle; **IN**40, Crimanetlies; **IA**38, Crimanightie; **MN**2, Crimanattly; **NJ**53, Crimamental; **NY**14, Crimanenty; **NY**92, Crimanetty; **NY**109, Criminy-ently; **OH**49, Crimanentny; **WI**48, Crimaneatly; (Qu. NN29c, *Exclamations beginning with 'holy'*) Inf **IA**5, Crimanetly; (Qu. NN30, *Exclamations beginning with the sound of 'J'*) Inf **CA**61, Jesus crimanently.

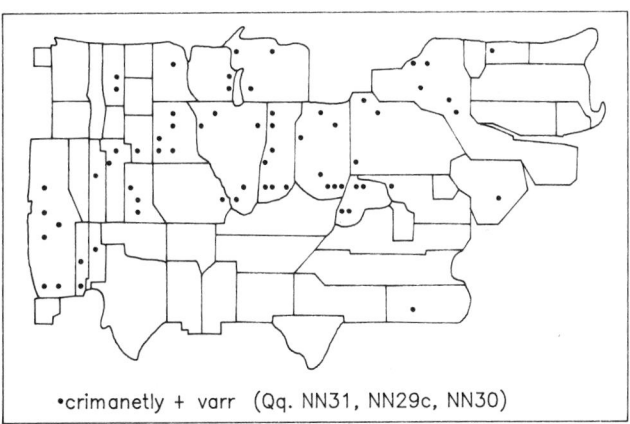

•crimanetly + varr (Qq. NN31, NN29c, NN30)

crimast intj Also *crimast jees* [Euphem for *Christ*]
1969 *DARE* (Qu. NN31, *Exclamations beginning with the sound of "cr-"*) Inf **NY**157, Crimast [ˈkraɪmɛst]; **MA**30, Crimast jees [ˈkraɪmast jis].

criminy intj Also sp *crimeny* [Prob euphem for *Christ,* but cf *OED,* "perh. It. *crimine* crime, etc., as an ejaculation;" 1681 →] **chiefly Nth, N Midl, West** See Map on p. 850 Cf **jiminy**
Used as an expression of surprise or annoyance.

1924 *DN* 5.265 **ME,** Crimeny . . . _____ sakes alive. **1965–70** *DARE* (Qu. NN31, *Exclamations beginning with the sound of "cr-"*) 171 Infs, **chiefly Nth, N Midl, West,** criminy; 25 Infs, **scattered Nth, N Midl, West,** Criminy('s) sake(s); **MI**3, Criminies; **SC**67, **SD**5, Criminy Christmas; **MD**32, **MI**10, Criminy crickets; **SC**69, Criminy creeps; **MI**55, Criminy oh crumb; **NY**109, Criminy-ickets; (Qu. NN8a) Inf **LA**32, Criminy; (Qu. NN27b, . . *"For _____ sakes."*) Infs **CA**145, **IL**14, **IN**32, Crimeny('s); (Qu. NN29c) Inf **NJ**57, Crimeny.

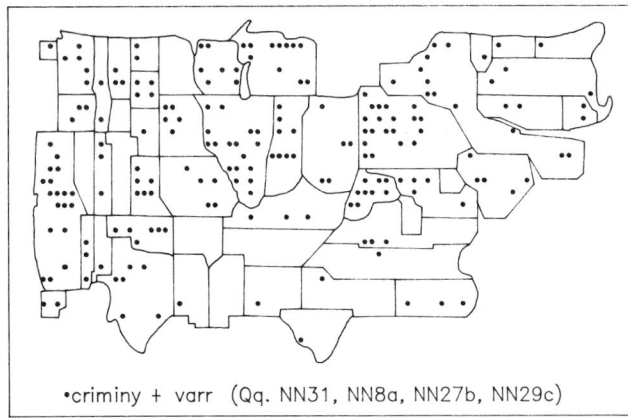

•criminy + varr (Qq. NN31, NN8a, NN27b, NN29c)

crimmy adj |ˈkrɪmɪ| [Engl dial *creemy* chilly] **chiefly MA** Cf
crim, crimpy
Cold, chilly.
  1886 Bynner *Agnes Surriage* 58 **MA** (as of 1742), Ye're crimmy wi' th'
fog Job. Ye'd best get some grog. **1891** *Jrl. Amer. Folkl.* 4.159 **neMA**,
An old fisherman says: "Ain't it too crimmy to go sailen'?" **1895** *DN*
1.386 **neMA**, *Crimmy:* chilly, out of sorts, "under the weather."
1931–33 *LANE Worksheets* **neMA**, [krɪmɪ]. **1934** *Hanley Disks*
neMA, We still use the word crimmy [krɪmɪ]. **1981** *DARE* File,
Crimmy . . . Chilly, cold, even clammy. Used by family, including
grandparents, in Merion township near Fennimore in southwestern
Wisconsin. The word is still known and familiar.

crimp v
  1 To double up in pain; to cramp.
  1927 *DN* 5.473 **Ozarks**, *Crimp* . . . To writhe in agony, to collapse.
"Tom shore did crimp up when thet 'ar bigges' gal kicked him in th'
stummick." **1983** *MJLF* 9.36 **ceKY**, *Crimp* . . to cramp (suffer an
involuntary muscle spasm).
  2 To castrate or sterilize an animal; hence ppl adj *crimped*
castrated.
  1967 *DARE* (Qu. K70, *Words . . for castrating an animal*) Inf **CO**38,
Crimped cow. **c1970** *DARE* FW Addit **MD**42, *Crimp:* To tie off the
testes of a steer as a means of sterilization.
  3 To crush or break the stems of hay to promote drying and
curing. **chiefly N Cent, PA, NY** See Map
  1965–70 *DARE* (Qu. L11, *What do you do to hay in the field after it's
cut*) 23 Infs, **scattered, but chiefly N Cent, PA, NY**, Crimp it; **MN**23,
TX5, Crimp; **PA**51, Crimping; **HI**12, Crimp it—put it through the
crimping machine which mangles the stalk so that it will dry faster; **IA**6,
Crimp it—crushes stems, like a washing machine wringer; **MA**25,
Today hay is crimped in the field to take the moisture out of it; **PA**103,
Crush or crimp after it was cut.

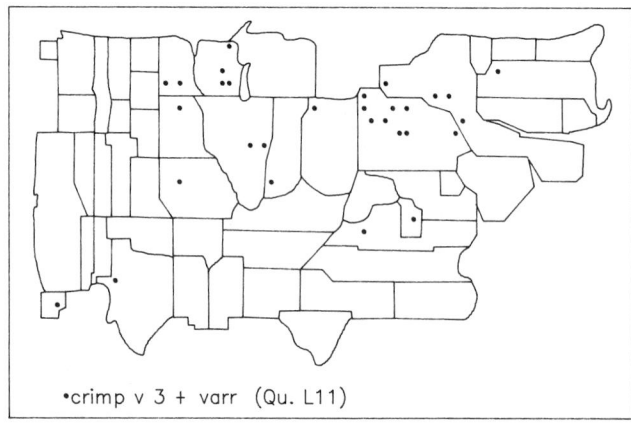

•crimp v 3 + varr (Qu. L11)

crimp n [**crimp** v 1]
  A sudden sharp pain or cramp.
  1966–70 *DARE* (Qu. BB3a, *A pain that strikes . . suddenly in the neck*)
Infs **IN**35, **MO**1, **OH**8, 43, Crimp; (Qu. BB3c, *A sudden pain that comes
in the side*) Inf **OH**95, Crimp.

crimper n Also *crimp machine, cripper* [**crimp** v 3] **scattered,
but chiefly N Cent, PA, NY** See Map
A machine used to **crimp** hay.
  1965–70 *DARE* (Qu. L16, *Machines used around here in handling hay*)
39 Infs, **scattered, but chiefly N Cent, PA, NY**, Crimper; **GA**84, **NY**150,
216, **PA**193, 232, Hay crimper; **IA**22, Crimp machine; **PA**29, Cripper;
(Qu. L11, *What do you do to hay in the field after it's cut?*) Inf **IL**33, Goes
through crimper; **MI**12, Run your crimper through; **NY**150, Put it
through a crimper.

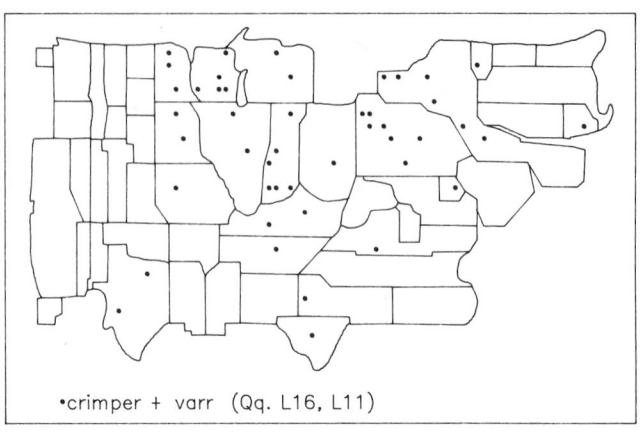

•crimper + varr (Qq. L16, L11)

crimple v
  1 See quot. [Perh var of *crumple*]
  1899 (1912) Green *VA Folk-Speech, Crimple* . . . To contract or draw
together; cause to shrink or pucker.
  2 To walk lamely, to hobble. [Cf **cripple** v]
  1966 *Wilson Coll.* **csKY**, *Crimple.* To walk as a cripple does.

crimp machine See **crimper**

crimps intj Also *crimpst* [Prob euphem for *Christ*]
  Used as an expression of surprise or dismay.
  1924 *DN* 5.265, For [crimp]'s sake (surp[rise]). **1966–69** *DARE* (Qu.
NN31, *Exclamations beginning with the sound of "cr-"*) Inf **MO**1,
Crimps; **MA**58, By crimpst.

crimps on, put the v phr
  1970 *DARE* (Qu. Y6, *To put pressure on somebody to do something*) Inf
VA74, Put the crimps on.

crimpst See **crimps**

crimpy adj **esp S Midl** Cf **crimmy**
  Of weather: cold; disagreeable.
  1905 *DN* 3.76 **nwAR**, *Crimpy* . . . Inferior, disagreeable. 'How's this for
crimpy weather?' Rare. **1953** Randolph *Down in Holler* 237 **Ozarks**,
Crimpy: . . Cool, chilly. "It gits pretty crimpy on these high ridges of a
mornin'." **1954** *Harder Coll.* **cwTN**. **1958** McCulloch *Woods Words*
Pacific NW, *Crimpy*—Cold weather. **1960** Criswell *Resp. to PADS 20*
Ozarks, *Crimpy* . . . Chilly. "The air is a little crimpy out there." (Always
common.) **1983** *MJLF* 9.36 **ceKY**, *Crimpy* . . cool (referring to the
weather).

crimson n Usu |ˈkrɪmzən|; also |-sən, -səm, -zɛn, -zn̩|
  Std sense, var forms.
  1927 *AmSp* 12.124 **NY**, There are a few miscellaneous variations
between [s] and [z] . . . *Crimson* has [z] 101 times, [s] 23 times. [666 total
infs interviewed] **1942** *AmSp* 17.155 **seNY**, Another frequent variation
in the voicing is that between [s] and [z] . . . Crimson . . 2 [infs] [s] . . 25
[infs] [z]. **1944** *ADD* **cNY** (as of 1920s), /krɪmzn̩/. **1969** *DARE* (QR,
near Qu. T14) Inf **KY**65, [ˈkrɪmsəm]; **NY**142, [ˈkrɪmzɛn].

crimson beak n
  A plant: the white **ratany** (here: *Krameria grayi*).
  1960 Vines *Trees SW* 549, *Gray's Krameria* . . . Also it is known under
the vernacular names of . . White Ratany, and Crimson Beak.

crimson rambler n [In ref to the well-known climbing rose of
that name] *joc*
  A bedbug.
  1906 *DN* 3.132 **nwAR**, *Crimson rambler* . . . Bed-beg [sic]. "At that
hotel they have great beds of crimson ramblers." Rare. **1927** *DN* 5.160

AR, *Crimson rambler* . . . Bed bug. **1928** *Ruppenthal Coll.* **KS,** *Crimson rambler* . . . euphemistic for: a bedbug. **1967** *DARE* (Qu. R24, *Other names . . for a bedbug*) Inf **IA**1, Crimson ramblers, common in older days.

crimus intj Also *crammus, crimulus, crymus* [Prob euphem for *Christ*]
Used as an expression of surprise or dismay.
1914 [see **cripe**]. **1959** *VT Hist.* new ser 27.131, Crammus! . . Rare . . . Crimulus! . . Rare. By Crimus! . . Rare . . . By Crymus!: . . Rare. **1967–69** *DARE* (Qu. NN31, *Exclamations beginning with the sound of "cr-"*) Inf **NY**1, By crimus ['kraɪməs]; **VT**16, Crimus ['kraɪməs]; **VT**7, Crimus to fishhooks.

cringe v, n Usu |krɪnǰ|; occas, esp **Sth, S Midl,** |skrɪnǰ| Pronc-sp *scringe*
A Forms.
1867 Lowell *Biglow* 61 **NEng,** 'T wun't pay to scringe to England: will it pay / To fear thet meaner bully, old "They'll say"? **1869** *Overland Mth.* 3.131, In Texas "scringe" means *to flinch*. **1895** *DN* 1.376 **seKY, eTN, wNC,** *Scringe* = cringe. **1915** *DN* 4.189 **swVA,** *Scringe* . . . To cringe. **1936** *AmSp* 11.239 **eTX,** In East Texas speech there are very few words in which intrusive sounds regularly appear in general use . . . The other pronunciations in my list belong properly to illiterate or low colloquial speech . . . *Cringe* . . . [skrɪndʒ]. **1941** *Sat. Eve. Post* 22 Mar 125/1 **TX,** How a woman would scringe away from him. **c1960** *Wilson Coll.* **csKY,** Cringe is sometimes /skrɪndʒ/.
‡B Sense.
=crink.
1969 *DARE* (Qu. BB3a, . . *A pain that strikes you suddenly in the neck*) Inf **MA**69, Cringe [krɪnǰ].

cringle n [*cringle* ring or loop for fastening]
1946 *PADS* 6.10 **eNC** (as of 1900–10), *Cringle* . . . The glass insulator to which a telephone or telegraph wire is attached.

crink n [Perh alter of *crick* a sharp pain in the back or neck; but cf *EDD crink* sb.[1] "A twist or sprain in the neck"] **scattered, but esp S Atl** See Map Cf **crimp** n
A sudden sharp pain, a cramp.
1965–70 *DARE* (Qu. BB3a, *A pain that strikes you suddenly in the neck*) 31 Infs, **scattered, but esp S Atl,** Crink; (Qu. BB3b, *A sudden pain that strikes you in the back*) Infs **FL**31, 33, **NC**13, 18, 22, **NY**146, **WA**1, 11, Crink; (Qu. BB3c, *A sudden pain that comes in the side*) Inf **NC**4, Crink.

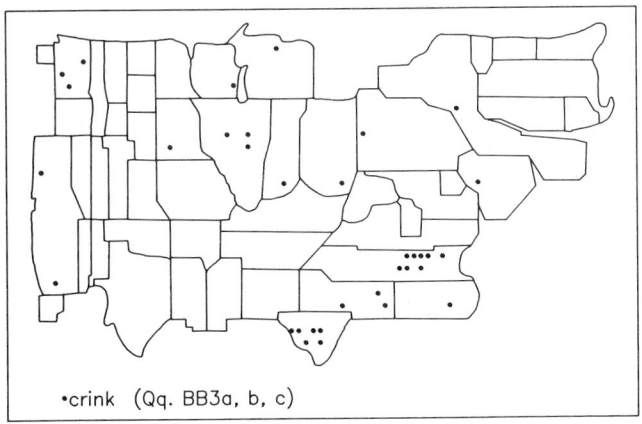

•crink (Qq. BB3a, b, c)

crinkleawn n
A perennial grass *(Trachypogon secundus)* with plumose awns.
1942 *Amer. Joint Comm. Horticult. Nomenclature Std. Plant Names* 144, Crinkleawn. *Trachypogon montufari.* **1950** Hitchcock *Manual Grasses* 781, *Trachypogon secundus* . . . Crinkle-awn.

crinkleburr n
=cockleburr 1.
1970 *DARE* (Qu. S13) Inf **VA**40, Crinkleburrs.

crinkleroot n
=toothwort *(Dentaria* spp).
1847 *Knickerbocker* 29.377, Sassafras is 'coming good' now too in the woods; and so is 'crinkle-root'. **1899** (1900) Van Dyke *Fisherman's*

Luck 74 **Alleghany Mts,** Crinkle-root is spicy, but you must partake of it delicately, or it will bite your tongue. **1937** *Torreya* 37.64 **NY,** Only a few herbs were seen in flower namely: Bloodroot, Fawn Lily, . . Crinkle-root, . . and Pale Violet. **1968** *DARE* (Qu. S26c, *Wildflowers that grow in woods*) Inf **PA**99, Crinkleroot; also pepperroot.

crinklety adj Also redup form *crinklety-cranklety*
Wrinkled, creased.
1906 *DN* 3.132 **nwAR,** *Crinklety* (cranklety) . . . Crinkly; creased. **1908** *DN* 3.302 **eAL, wGA,** *Crinklety-cranklety* . . . Crinkled, roughly creased. "My clothes are all crinklety-cranklety."

crip n, adj **prob chiefly Sth**
A thing easily done, a snap, cinch; easy.
1923 *DN* 5.243 **LA,** *Crip* . . . A cinch; a set up. **1959** *AmSp* 34.156 **FL,** A *crip* is an easy course. **1970** *DARE* (Qu. KK42a, *Expressions about a person who does things very easily: "For him that would be _____."*) Inf **VA**86, Crip [krɪp]. **1980** *DARE* File **NC** (as of c1930), [A student at Chapel Hill] had apparently signed up for [the Professor's] large, popular course in the ballad under the misapprehension that it was a crip. He was too busy with extracurricular activities to spare the time for a real course.

crip around v phr [Prob from **cripple,** but cf *creep*]
1960 Criswell *Resp. to PADS 20* **Ozarks,** *Crip around* . . . To walk or creep around like a cripple, usually from some injury or rheumatism. Many times a man would also say that he was "just crippin' around" when he was not actually disabled at all in his means of locomotion but was only feeling bad, not up to par, "under the weather."

cripe intj Also *cripers, cripes, cripity, cripus* For var phrr, see quots [Euphem for *Christ*] **chiefly Nth, Midl, West** See Map
Used as an expression of dismay, anger, etc.
1914 *DN* 4.69 **ME, nNH,** By cripes, or crimus . . . Common expletives. *Ibid* 70, Cripes, by. A common exclamation, probably corrupted from "By Christ!" **1924** *DN* 5.265 **NY,** Cripe: [in phr] sleeping _____. **1924** Marks *Plastic Age* 6, Sweet! Cripes, that old hen made him sick. *Ibid* 103, Cripes! what a title! *Ibid* 79/2, Cripus, do you know her? *Ibid* 88/1, By cripus, it's a crazy business. **1944** *AmSp* 19.243, [Euphemisms]: For *Christ:* cripes. **1959** *VT Hist.* new ser 27.131, By Cripes! . . By Cripity! interj. Rare. **1965–70** *DARE* (Qu. NN31, *Exclamations beginning with the sound of "cr-"*) 69 Infs, **chiefly Nth, N Midl, West,** (For) cripe sake(s); 62 Infs, **chiefly Nth, N Midl, West,** Cripes (a'mighty); **NY**163, **OH**48, Cripe(s) almighty; **AK**8, Cripe, yes; **IA**4, Cripes, no; **IA**46, Cripe Maria; **TN**23, Cripes a-livin'; **CT**22, By cripers; (Qu. NN27b, *Weakened substitutes for 'God': "For _____ sakes."*) 16 Infs, **chiefly Nth, N Midl,** Cripe; (Qu. NN8a, . . *"Oh _____. I've lost my glasses again."*) Inf **CO**15, For cripe's sake; **PA**66, Cripes; (Qu. NN9a, . . *"_____. The electric power is off again."*) Inf **CT**3, Cripes; **WI**34, Cripe's sake; (Qu. NN28a, *Exclamations beginning with 'good': "Good _____!"*) Inf **MI**63, Cripes.

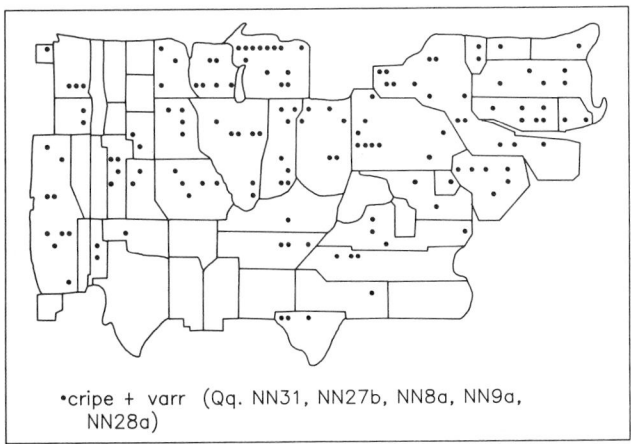

•cripe + varr (Qq. NN31, NN27b, NN8a, NN9a, NN28a)

cripper See **crimper**

cripper bone See **crupper bone**

cripple v [*OED* c1220 →; "Now chiefly *Sc.*"] **S Midl**
To move as if crippled, to limp or hobble.
1926 *DN* 5.399 **Ozarks,** *Cripple* . . . To limp. "I got so's I caint hardly cripple 'round." **1942** Whipple *Joshua* 111 **UT** (as of 1860), 'We'll need 'ot water, too, agin they gits back,' said Willie; crippling around to help.

1963 Edwards *Gravel* 123 **eTN** (as of early 1880s), Wal, they come cripplin on up to fernent the shop and the cap'm said "Halt." **1966** *Wilson Coll.* **csKY,** He went crippling along.

cripple n¹ Also *creuple* Formerly (17th–18th cent) *cripple-bush* [Abbr for *cripplebush* from Amer colonial Du *Kreuple-bush* swamp (see quot 1929) < Du *kreupelbos* thicket, under-growth] **eNY, ePA, NJ** Cf **spung**

Low swampy ground usu covered with trees or underbrush.

1675 in 1880 *Documents Colonial & Post-Revol. Hist. NJ* 1.115, The sd land . . lyeth between two Small gutts or Run's, and streatches into the woods as far as the great Swamp or Cripple wch backs the said two Necks of land. **1676** in 1877 *Documents Colonial Hist. NY* 12.556, Martin Garritson was Imployed by Mr. Hans Block (Deceased) to make a way from his Plantation over ye valley & Creuple, into his Backward Land wch Lyeth behinde the Sayd Valley & Creuple. **1765** in 1883 Pearson *Hist. Schenectady Patent* 118 **eNY,** The cripplebush . . lying between the lake and the river. **1769** (1906) Smith *Tour Great Rivers* 12 **eNY,** A Quantity of low cripple Land may be seen . . & this reaches 4 miles to the Kaatskill. **1890** *Hist. Mag. & Notes & Queries* 5.30, In parts of Connecticut even the low *swale,* or wet land about the backset, is sometimes called a *creek;* near Philadelphia it would be called a *cripple.* **1929** *AmSp* 5.159 **eNY** (as of 17th cent), *Cripple bush* . . a direct borrowing from the Dutch (Kreuple bush) seems to have been current in common speech. The first occurrences are Dutch, and already the word means *swamp* instead of *underbrush.* "Eastward to a certain swamp (kreuple-bush)" is a translation from a patent of 1637. **1940** Weygandt *Down Jersey* 48 **sNJ,** The cripple that is the head of a brushed or timbered swamp I have known these forty years . . . Long Cripple was an unlumbered swamp of white cedar when I first visited it. **1942** *Sat. Eve. Post* 5 Sept 9/1 **sNJ,** When they came to the cripple he sloshed straight through. **1968** McPhee *Pine Barrens* 61 **NJ,** A low, wet area where the Atlantic white cedars grow are called a cripple.

cripple n² [Perh alter of **scrapple** by folk-etym] **Sth, esp SC**

Headcheese or scrapple.

1950 *PADS* 14.23 **SC,** Cripple . . . Scrapple. Orangeburg. Origin undetermined. **1967** *PADS* 47.6 **eGA, wSC,** Cripple—'scrapple.' **1967** *DARE* (Qu. H43, *Foods made from parts of the head and inner organs of an animal*) Inf **SC34,** Cripple—press meat with meal in it; **SC38,** Cripple—made from liver, thickened with corn meal; fried. **1971** Wood *Vocab. Change* 44/2, *Scrapple* is a general name for a loaf made of corn meal, meat scraps, and meat juice. *Cripple,* reported everywhere [in the Sth] but in Louisiana, has its greatest preference in Alabama and Mississippi.

cripplebush See **cripple** n¹

crippled cranefly See **cranefly orchid**

cripple down v phr

To walk lamely; to crouch.

1840 in 1934 Frear *Lowell & Abigail* 147 **MA,** The latter part of our journey [in Hawaii] it rained very hard and oh the sharp lava—it did seem that I must cripple down and stop. **1909** *DN* 3.410 **nME,** Cripple down . . . To crouch.

cripplety-crumplety adj

=**crinklety.**

1908 *DN* 3.302 **eAL, wGA,** Cripplety-crumplety . . . Crumpled.

crips v [Metath of *crisp*]

1917 *DN* 4.410 **wNC,** Crips . . . To crisp. "Smoke come in and cripsed up the aidges of the leaves."

cripsy adj Also *crips(e)* [Metath]

Crispy; crisp.

1889 (1971) Farmer *Americanisms,* Crispse [sic] and *cripsy.*—Crisp; crispy. A vulgarism formed on the same lines as "wopse" for wasp. **1917** *DN* 4.410 **NH, MA,** Crips, cripsy . . [crisp].

cripus See **cripe**

crischul See **crystal**

Cris'mus gif' See **Christmas gift**

crispied ppl adj [From *crisp* v or inferred *crispy* v]

1969 *DARE* FW Addit **cTX,** Crispied ['krɪspid]: Slightly burnt around the edges.

crisscross n

Tick-tack-toe.

1848 Bartlett *Americanisms,* Criss-cross. A game played on slates by children, at school. **1905** *DN* 3.17 **cCT,** Criss-cross . . . A game played by children. **1950** *WELS* (Tick-tack-toe) 2 Infs, **sWI,** Crisscross. **1967–68** *DARE* (Qu. EE38a, *A game played with pencil and paper where the players try to get three x's or three o's in a row*) Infs **IA7, MD25, MA27,** Crisscross.

criss-crossedness n Pronc-sp *criss-crossedniss*

Contrariness.

1898 Westcott *Harum* 324 **nNY,** I noticed that she'd pined and pindled some, but I thought the' was some natural criss-crossedniss mixed up into it too.

cristial See **crystal**

critical-looking adj Eye-dial sp *crittacul-lookin'*

?Subject to criticism.

1927 Kennedy *Gritny* 181 **sLA** [Black], Callin' people tenshun to you, crittacul-lookin' as you is. [Said to a woman with her skirt lifted to avoid mud.]

critter n Usu |ˈkrɪtə(r)|; occas |ˈkrɪtɚ(r)|; also |krɛtər|; sometimes, esp in ME, |ˈkʌtər| Also sp *crit(t)ur* Pronc-spp *creeter, creetur, cretter, cutter* See also **creature**

A Forms.

1905 *DN* 3.56 **eNE,** In *creek, clique, sleek, creature,* (*critter,* sometimes *creetur*), [ɪ] prevails for [i]. **1926** *DN* 5.386 **sME,** [*Creatures*] (critters; cutters in southern Maine) . . . Any domestic animal; a disreputable person, especially a female. **1927** *AmSp* 3.139 **sME,** "Critter," or "cutter" for creature. **1950** *PADS* 14.23 **SC,** Critter . . . Sometimes pronounced creeter. **c1960** *Wilson Coll.* **csKY,** *Creature* is sometimes ['krɪtə] or [krɪtə]. Chiefly now humorous. **1966** *DARE* FW Addit **ME5,** Cutter: a young farm animal (an older one was a critter). *Cutter* also applied to a young girl as a term of endearment. **1969** *DARE* FW Addit **GA19,** Cretter ['krɛtɚ]—a work animal. Common [among country people].

B Senses.

1 Any animal, but esp a domestic animal. *sometimes derog* Cf **creature B1**

1815 Humphreys *Yankee in England* 41, I compounded the matter to work my way, by cooking for the crew, and taking care of the dum critturs. **1867** Hill *Homespun* 298, If many of our farmers are asked by a travelling drover what they will take for such or such a "beef critter," they will show in a moment their disinclination . . to sell. **1907** *DN* 3.185 **NH,** Critter . . . Creature. Older generation. **1908** *DN* 3.302 **eAL, wGA,** Critter . . . Applied to animals or older persons. **1910** *DN* 3.440 **wNY,** Critter . . . Animal. **1939** Thompson *Body & Britches* 191, No other boat had been near when the whale was harpooned. Looking more closely, he realized that the critter had pulled Mulford's boat so fast. **1950** *PADS* 14.23 **SC,** Critter . . . A creature, especially a domestic animal. **1966** *DARE* Tape **ME18,** All critters [=farm animals] have it. **1969–70** *DARE* (Qu. J1, *A dog of mixed breed*) Inf **MA16,** Critter; (Qu. R24, *A bedbug*) Inf **PA242,** Critter; (Qu. NN17, *Something that keeps on annoying you—for example, a fly*) Inf **GA73,** That critter. **1972** Cooper *NC Mt. Folkl.* 90, Critter . . a wild or vicious animal. **1976** Garber *Mountain-ese* **sAppalachians,** Critter . . any farm animal.

2 Specifically:

a A domestic bovine animal. **chiefly Nth, N Midl, West**

1894 *DN* 1.341 **wCT,** Critter: a neat animal; sing. of *cattle.* "Is that a horse out in the road?" "No, it's a critter." . . This use of *critter* is so well fixed that the natives, when they are trying to "talk polite" with strangers, use *creature* with the same meaning. **1905** *DN* 3.7 **cCT,** Creature . . . Cows and oxen, etc. Among farmers called *critter.* **1910** *DN* 3.440 **wNY. 1928** *AmSp* 4.129 **NE. 1961** Adams *Old-Time Cowhand* 153, "Critter" was 'nother word he used to designate cow as a general term. **1965–70** *DARE* (Qu. K16, *A cow with a bad temper*) 34 Infs, **chiefly Nth, N Midl, West,** Ornery critter; **TX7, WI21,** Mean critter; **NY35,** Critter; (Qu. K15, *A thin, bony, or poor-looking cow*) Infs **KS9, MI56, 74, NJ44, UT4, WI21,** Poor critter; **PA3,** Skinny old critter. **1966** *DARE* Tape **SC10,** I don't raise no feed and I go over there to get the feed for the critter ['krɪdə]; **SD3,** The Angus is a good beef critter. **1969** *DARE* FW Addit **MA58,** Critter—Cattle.

b A bull. **chiefly Nth** *euphem*

1892 *DN* 1.210 **swNH,** Cross critter: a bull. **1912** *DN* 3.567 **cNY. 1923** *DN* 5.204 **swMO,** Critter . . . Usually applied to any male animal, especially a bull, which is kept exclusively for breeding purposes. **1939** *LANE* Map 190 **throughout NEng,** Bull . . . Euphemisms used when a direct reference to the bull is avoided on grounds of delicacy . . *the brute, the critter* or *creature.* **1950** *WELS Suppl.* **cwWI,** Critter—euphemism for bull. Used by women more than men. Common. **1959** *VT Hist.* new ser 27.131, *Critter* . . var. beef critter. Fomerly, a common euphemism for *bull.* Common. Orleans; Addison; Bennington; Grand Isle. **1965–70** *DARE* (Qu. K22, *Words . . for a bull*) 19 Infs, **chiefly Nth,** Critter; **AZ2,** Beef critter; **CA**101, Male critter; (Qu. K23, *Words used by women or in mixed company for a bull*) Infs **IL**33, **IA**19, **MI**78, **PA**174, Critter. **1967** Schilla *Prairies* 99 **ND** (as of 1880–1965), The Dohrmanns called a bull a "booman." Others would use the word "critter" or "gentleman cow."

c A horse or occas a mule. **esp Midl**

1827 in 1927 *DN* 5.415 **GA,** *Beast* or *crittur,* for horse. **1861** Holmes *Venner* 2.187 **wMA,** Y' won't curry that 'ere long-tailed black hoss no more . . . Th' critter's gone, sure enough! **1890** *DN* 1.64 **KY,** *Critter* [krita] was used for horse by old people. **1939** *Hall Coll.* **eTN, wNC,** *Critter* . . . Creature (?especially of a horse or mule). "He was a ugly old critter." **1944** *PADS* 2.7 **neGA, LA,** *Critter* . . . A horse. **1950** *PADS* 14.23 **SC,** *Critter* . . . In some localities applied only to a horse. **c1960** *Wilson Coll.* **csKY,** *Critter* . . . A patronizing name for a horse, especially, or any other animal. **1968–69** *DARE* (Qu. K44, *A bony or poor-looking horse*) Infs **IL**78, **IA**19, **MD**15, Critter; (Qu. K42, *A horse that is rough, wild, or dangerous*) Infs **CT**32, **NY**176, Critter; (Qu. K50, *Joking nicknames for mules*) Inf **KY**16, Long-eared critter. **1972** Cooper *NC Mt. Folkl.* 90, *Critter*—a riding mare.

3 A person. (Note: this sense has a broad range of uses—from *jocose* and *affectionate* to *patronizing* and *disparaging*)

1843 (1916) Hall *New Purchase* 121 **IN,** Yes, we don't ax pay in cash nor trade nither for the Gospel . . but as the Lord freely give us, we freely give our fellow critturs. **1871** Eggleston *Hoosier Schoolmaster* 63 **IN,** You allers take sides with that air hussy agin your own flesh and blood . . . I may be disgraced by that air ongrateful critter, and you set right here in my own house and sass me about it. **1908** [see **1** above]. **1941** *LANE* Map 379 *(Kid, tot),* 1 Inf, **nNH,** Critter. **1942** Faulkner *Go Down* 52 **MS,** Maybe that's why you done it: because what you and your pa got from old Carothers had to come to you through a woman—a critter not responsible like men are responsible. **1950** *PADS* 14.23 **SC,** *Critter* . . . Also applied to persons in a patronizing and commiserating sense: "old *critter,*" "poor *critter,*" "poor old *critter.*" **1958** McCulloch *Woods Words* **Pacific NW,** *Critter* . . . A worthless man. **1960** Criswell *Resp. to PADS 20* **Ozarks,** *Critter* . . . It was fairly common to call a person *that critter* . . in disparagement, especially a woman. **1961** Adams *Old-Time Cowhand* 22, As a rule he was a plumb truthful critter unless he was tryin' to protect some friend. **1965–70** *DARE* (Qu. Z12, *Nicknames and joking words meaning "a small child"*) Infs **AR**40, **CA**10, **IL**47, 126, **MO**11, **TX**23, 40, Critter; **GA**77, Cutter; (Qu. HH40, *Uncomplimentary words for an old man*) Infs **CT**16, **TN**24, Critter; (Qu. HH2, *A citified person*) Inf **NY**121, City critter; (Qu. HH32, *Words meaning "a person"* . . ". . . what's _____ to do?"* total Infs questioned, 75) Inf **AR**39, [A] Critter; (Qu. KK27, *A very lively, active old person*) Inf **NJ**4, Lively old critter; (Qu. AA3, *. . Affectionate names for a sweetheart*) Inf **ME**5, Dear sweet cutter. **1966** *DARE* FW Addit **ME**19, Critter: A feller, guy.

4 Anything to which a balky or contrary personality may be attributed.

1834 Smith *Letters Jack Downing* 189, Now there is a few things we must look into a little . . What kind of a critur the bank of the United States raly is. **1843** (1916) Hall *New Purchase* 467, The spiteful critter [=a shotgun] kick'd so powerful. **1893** *Harper's Mag.* 88.81/1 **eTN,** Few folks kem this way nowadays . . sence harnts an' sech unlikely critters hev been viewed a-crossin' the foot-bredge. **1942** *Morgantown Post* (VA) 19 May 6 (Editorial) *(ADD),* You are more concerned in making the critter [typewriter] work than in having it work for you. **1958** McCulloch *Woods Words* **Pacific NW,** *Critter* . . . Any machine or piece of equipment. **1968** *DARE* (Qu. W25, *When a woman is cutting out a dress to sew, what do you call the little scraps of cloth left over?*) Inf **CA**106, Critters—applies to cookie-dough scraps also.

5 =**creature B3.** *arch*

1848 *Knickerbocker* 31.56 **cnVT,** Not a drop of the 'critter' is to be found in this place. **1887** Eggleston *Graysons* 150, I got a fresh jug full uv the critter yisterday, un I 'low you're purty consid'able dry agin this time. **1928** *Ruppenthal Coll.* **KS,** He had a drop of the critter on him. **1939** in 1944 *ADD* **nWV,** 'A box of critter' = snuff. Freq. 'Prob. people knew snuff was a contemptible habit.'

critter-back adv [**critter B2c**] **Cf beast-back**

Horseback.

1890 *DN* 1.64 **KY,** I went to church critter-back.

critter-flung ppl adj [**critter B2c**]

Thrown by a horse.

1937 (1963) Hyatt *Kiverlid* 13 **KY,** I come as a pea agittin' critter-flung. Old Dorie shied at a sow . . All suddent she fetched a lunge and bolted . . and busted one of the saddle gyrts.

critter-house n [**critter B1**]

1941 FWP *Guide SC* 335, The farm animals or 'critters' roam the countryside, foraging as they can. Most of them have no shelter, but a few are kept in 'critter houses' of poles and palmetto leaves.

crit(t)ur See **critter**

crivice n

1950 *PADS* 14.75 **FL,** *Crivice* . . . A small enclosure for cattle; a corral.

cro n See **Croatan**

cro v [?Var of **co** v]

1969 *DARE* (Qu. K80, *The call . . to get the cows in from the pasture*) Inf **NJ**56, Cro ['kro].

croak See **croaker** n[1] **2**

croaken-oil n Pronc-sp for *croton oil* Cf Pronc Intro 3.I.14

1938 Stuart *Dark Hills* 383 **KY,** Druggist MacDonald wouldn't sell me croton oil . . . Had to stay in the toilet all night. It's been two days since I got that pie and I'm still goin' . . . It must a-been high-powered croaken-oil or some kind of poison one.

croaker n[1]

1 Any of var fish that make croaking or grunting noises, as:

a A fish of the family Sciaenidae, as:

(1) In the Atlantic and Gulf of Mexico such fish as the **mademoiselle** or the **spot** (here: *Leiostomus xanthurus*), but esp a common food fish *(Micropogon undulatus)* which is also called **corvina c, crocus** n[2], **golden croaker, hardhead, roncadina, ronco.** See also **post croaker**

1676 Royal Soc. London *Philos. Trans.* 11.625 **VA,** In the Creeks are great store of small fish, as *Perches, Crokers, Taylors, Eels.* **1772** in 1924 Phillips *Notes B. Romans* 123 **FL,** It Abounds here in fish of all kinds . . the Hog Fish, the Croaker, the Glen Fish. **1875** *Fur Fin & Feather* 157 **DE,** Croakers appear on the steamer's table; and croakers, fresh, salt, and under all conceivable circumstances, are a constant feature of the place. This fish, which is known to science as *Micropogon undulatus,* seldom exceeds six or eight inches in length, and is of the most beautiful iridescent coloring, looking as though carved out of mother-of-pearl, with transverse darker bands. It is excellent eating, being very finely flavored, and with very few bones. **1899** (1912) Green *VA Folk-Speech, Croaker* . . . A small fish getting its name from a peculiar croaking sound it makes when caught. **1960** Amer. Fisheries Soc. *List Fishes* 31, Reef croaker . . *Odontoscion dentex* . . . Blue croaker . . *Vacuoqua sialis.* **1965–70** *DARE* (Qu. P2) 36 Infs, **chiefly S Atl and Gulf coasts,** Croaker; **NC**49, Red-fin croaker; (Qu. P14) Infs **LA**40, **MD**34, 42, **NJ**60, **NC**82, **SC**66, **VA**55, Croaker(s); (Qu. P7) Infs **LA**37, 44, **TX**88, Croaker(s); (Qu. P4) Infs **AL**22, **TX**17, Croaker; (Qu. P1) Inf **NC**8, Croaker.

(2) On the Pacific coast such fish as the **queenfish** (here: *Seriphus politus*), **little roncador, red roncador 1, roncador,** or **white sea bass.** See also **black croaker, Chinese croaker, golden croaker, white croaker**

1887 Goode *Amer. Fishes* 134, *Corvina saturna,* is known wherever found as the "Red Roncador," less commonly as "Black Roncador" or "Croaker." **1898** U.S. Natl. Museum *Bulletin* 47.1460, *Genyonemus lineatus* . . . Little roncador; Kingfish; Croaker. **1902** Jordan–Evermann *Amer. Fishes* 455, This is *S[eriphus] politus,* the queenfish or white croaker. **1946** LaMonte *N. Amer. Game Fishes* 83, Yellowfin Croaker . . . *Umbrina roncador.* **1947** Dalrymple *Panfish* 26, He stood on the beach at Santa Monica, California, watching the surf fishermen scramble for Yellowtail, Sand Sharks, and Croakers. **1955** Zim *Fishes* 120, Spotfin Croaker . . . is often caught by Pacific Coast surf-fishers. **1960** Amer. Fisheries Soc. *List Fishes* 31, Catalina croaker . . *Ophioscion thompsoni.* **1968–70** *DARE* (Qu. P2) Infs **CA**36, 181, Croaker; (Qu. P1) Inf **CA**52, Spotfin croaker. **1972** Sparano *Outdoors Encycl.* 381, *California White Sea Bass*—Common Names . . . *croaker* . . [etc]. Scientific Name: *Cynoscion nobilis.*

(3) =**freshwater drum.**

1882 U.S. Natl. Museum *Bulletin* 16.567, *H. grunniens* . . . Drum; White Perch; Croaker. **1887** Goode *Amer. Fishes* 143, These names,

"Croaker," "Drum," "Thunder-pumper," . . refer to the croaking or grunting noise made by this species. **1945** *AmSp* 20.277, Other common names [for the fresh-water drum, *Aplodinotus grunniens* Rafinesque] are *bubbler, croaker, crocus* (probably a corruption of *croakers*). **1972** Sparano *Outdoors Encycl.* 369, Croaker . . . make a weird "drumming" noise which, when they feed near the surface on calm evenings, seems to come from everywhere.

b A fish of the family Pomadasyidae, esp of the genera *Haemulon* and *Conodon;* see also **grunt.**

1889 *Century Dict.,* Croaker . . . A fish of the genus *Haemulon.* Also called *grunter.* [Local, U.S.]. **1931** *Copeia* 48, *Conodon nobilis* . . . The "mango croaker" was common in a fisherman's haul from the Gulf surf near Corpus Christi Pass on July 21.

c =**black perch 2b** (here: *Embiotoca jacksoni*).

1882 U.S. Natl. Museum *Bulletin* 16.595, *D. jacksoni* . . . Surf-fish; Croaker; Black Perch. **1911** *Century Dict.,* Croaker . . . A Californian embiotocoid fish, *Embiotoca jacksoni;* a kind of surf-fish.

2 also *croak:* A frog. [*OED* 1651 →] **esp Nth, N Midl**

1965 *PADS* 43.21 **MA,** *A big, deep-voiced bullfrog* . . . Croakers [4 infs]. **1965–70** *DARE* (Qu. P22, . . *A very large frog that makes a deep, loud sound*) 87 Infs, **esp Nth, N Midl,** Croaker; **MD5,** Night croaker; **FL20,** Croak; (Qu. P21, *Small frogs that sing or chirp loudly in spring*) 21 Infs, **scattered, but chiefly Nth,** Croaker; **MD29,** Croaks.

3 An insect such as a cicada or cricket. [*OED* 1868 →]

1966–68 *DARE* (Qu. R7, *Insects . . in trees or bushes in hot weather . . [that] make a sharp, buzzing sound*) Inf **NJ27,** Croakers; (Qu. R8, . . *Creatures that make a clicking or shrilling or chirping kind of sound*) Inf **OK25,** Croaker.

4 See quot.

1912 *DN* 3.574 **wIN,** Croaker . . . One who talks loudly and too much.

5 See quot.

1905 *DN* 3.7 **cCT,** Croaker . . . Slang for one who backs out of an undertaking.

6 See quot.

1930 Shoemaker *1300 Words* 12 **cPA Mts** (as of c1900), Croaker—A person who takes a gloomy view of things.

croaker n[2] [Alter of *crocus*]

1970 *DARE* (Qu. S2) Inf **OK58,** Croakers.

croaker n[3] Also *croaky* Cf **crockery**

1968 *DARE* (Qu. EE6a, . . *The big one [marble] that's used to knock others out of the ring*) Inf **NJ28,** The croaker was the shooter; **NY82,** Croaker; (Qu. EE6c, *Cheap marbles*) Inf **NJ27,** Croakies.

croaker sack See **croker sack**

croaky See **croaker** n[3]

croase See **clothes**

Croatan n Also abbr *cro* [*Croatan* an island off the coast of NC] **NC, SC** *usu derog*

A person of mixed Indian, White and Black ancestry in southeastern North Carolina and eastern South Carolina.

1907 Hodge *Hdbk. Amer. Indians* 1.365/2, *Croatan Indians* . . . In North Carolina . . a people evidently of mixed Indian and White blood, found in various E. sections of the state, but chiefly in Robeson co., and numbering approximately 5,000. For many years they were classed with the free negroes, but steadily refused to accept such classification . . . About 20 years ago their claim was officially recognized and they were given a separate legal existence under the title of "Croatan Indians," on the theory of descent from Raleigh's lost colony of Croatan. **1939** *Amer. Sociol. Rev.* 4.520, The name "Croatan" soon went sour. For the first time, the whites and Negroes had a term which they could apply to these hitherto nameless people. They pronounced it with a sort of sneer or they shortened it to "Cro" . . . It soon became a fighting term, and . . virtually taboo in the presence of Indians. **1946** *Social Forces* 24.4.439, Brass ankles and allied groups of South Carolina . . . These peoples are located mainly on the coastal plain area of the State. They are called by a variety of names, depending upon the county . . . Croatans or Cros in Marlboro, Dillon, Marion and Horry counties. **1947** *Time* 3 Nov 24/3 **NC,** A 33-year-old member of the Croatan Indians . . was jailed for slashing two of his fellow tribesmen and drinking their blood. **1963** Berry *Almost White* 33 **NC,** It is an unpardonable sin to refer to them [=Lumbees, people of mixed race in NC] by the older and commoner term Croatans. And nothing inflames them more than to hear the shortened form "cro," which the Negroes thereabouts use with obvious relish. **1967–70**

DARE (Qu. HH29a, *Names . . for people of mixed blood—part Indian*) Infs **NC41, 51,** Croatan; **SC68,** ['krɪətæn]; (Qu. HH29b, . . *Part Negro*) Inf **SC7,** Croatan ['kroɪtæn].

croater n [Var of **croaker** n[3]]

In marble play: =**crockery.**

1890 *DN* 1.76, Mr. E.F. Griffing sends the following New York and Jersey City words used in playing at marbles: . . "croaters" are burned alleys, brown with blistered spots. **1955** *PADS* 23.14 **cwTN,** Croater . . . See **crockery.**

crochet n [Prob alter of *croquet*]

1968–70 *DARE* (Qu. EE33, *[Outdoor games] . . that were played in your childhood*) Infs **MS90, TX33, WV1,** Crochet.

crock n[1]

1 See quot.

1946 *PADS* 6.10 **eNC,** Crock . . . A terra cotta drain pipe . . . Common.

2 A container for keeping bread. **chiefly Nth** *rural, old-fash*

1965–70 *DARE* (Qu. D9, *To prevent bread and cake from drying, you put them in a* _____) 14 Infs, **chiefly Nth,** Crock; **NY43, 105, RI1,** Stone crock; **IL42,** Earthen crock; **MI106,** Ten-gallon crock; **OH15,** Bread crock. [18 Infs old, 2 mid-aged; all Infs rural]

3 See **crockery.**

crock n[2] [Etym uncertain; *OED* "obs. exc. dial."] *prob obsolescent*

Soot or dirt, esp from something burned or charred.

1806 (1970) Webster *Compendious Dict.,* Crock . . an earthen pot, pan, black of a pot. **1883** *Harper's Mag.* 66.665/1, New England expressions here are . . "you have *crock* on your nose" for a smut. **1968** *DARE* FW Addit **NY,** Crock ['krɑk]—the black soot on your hands from burnt wood. (Common).

crock n[3] [Scots *crock* an old ewe]

1 A hypochondriac; a malingerer. [*OEDS* 1880 →]

1961 *AmSp* 36.146, Crock . . . A patient who complains continually of multiple symptoms, many of which are either imaginary or of psychic origin; one whose complaints are out of proportion to his illness. **1967** *DARE* (Qu. BB27, *When somebody pretends to be sick . . you'd say he's* _____) Inf **NC47,** A crock. **1968** *DARE* FW Addit **nwLA,** Crock: A hypochondriac. Used especially by interns at the Shreveport hospital, but also by younger people in northwestern Louisiana. **1969** *Scientific Amer.* Feb 69/2, Physicians . . blame the patient by labeling him a 'crock'—medical slang for a neurotic complainer.

2 An old man, codger. *sometimes derog*

1943 Mitchell *McSorley* 143 **NJ,** Old man Hollinan . . was good company . . . He was a funny old crock. **1968** *DARE* (Qu. HH40, *Uncomplimentary words for an old man*) Infs **KS13, NY100,** Old crock.

3 See quots. [*OEDS* 1905 →]

1950 *WELS* (*An old broken-down car*) 1 Inf, **ceWI,** Old crock. **1969** *DARE* (Qu. N5, . . *An automobile, especially an old or broken-down car*) Inf **MA19,** Crocks [krɑks]—kids call 'em this today.

4 A drunkard. [Prob infl by *crock* jug]

1939 *AmSp* 14.239 (Hotel slang), Crock. Bottle; drunken person. **1941** *AmSp* 16.70 **NYC,** Drunken person (or Habitual Drunkard) crock. **1969** *DARE* (Qu. DD12, . . *A person who drinks steadily or a great deal*) Inf **NY202,** Crock.

5 An insane person.

1967 *DARE* (Qu. HH6, *Someone who is out of his mind*) Inf **SC54,** A crock.

crock n[4] [Perh abbr for *crocodile;* cf **alligator** n[1] **B3**] =**hellgrammite.**

1901 Howard *Insect Book* 212, In 1889 Professor W.W. Bailey . . collected the names in use in Rhode Island alone for this insect, and they are . . . crock, hell devils, flip-flaps [etc].

crock v[1]

1 To soil with soot. *obs* Cf **crock** n[2]

1781 (1884) Hutchinson *Diary* 1.145 **Boston MA,** The thunder cloud gathered black enough to crock charcoal. **1806** (1970) Webster *Compendious Dict.,* Crock . . To blacken with foul matter. **1872** in 1919 Hale *Letters* 101 **Boston MA,** Then "the Professor" came and sandpapered the box himself where the black had crocked it.

2 Of dyed fabric or leather: to transfer color, to bleed or run. *somewhat old-fash*

1855 *Knickerbocker* 45.566 **wPA,** A pair of green gloves . . had 'crocked off' very generously to what ever was in contact with them. **1905** *DN* 3.7 **cCT,** *Crock* . . . To blacken with the coloring matter in cloth. **1942** Whipple *Joshua* 64 **UT** (as of 19th cent), Finally the bead-embroidered plush cape, badly crocked, but with a deep collar to be turned up around the ears. **1950** *WELS Suppl.* **WI,** Of fabric colors: to run. "If the color runs out of a dress onto your slip, you'd say it crocked." **1951** in 1965 *DARE* File **cwWI,** My red calico pinnies always crocked the first few times. We used it *(crock)* to mean that it bled onto the next garment.

crock v[2]
1 To cheat.
    1966 *DARE* (Qu. LL23, . . *"These apples are wormy, I think you got* _____.") Inf **ME22,** Crocked.
2 To steal, swipe.
    1969 *DARE* (Qu. V4, . . *"Yesterday somebody* _____ *my watch."*) Inf **PA182,** Crocked.

crock v[3]
=**coldcock 1.**
    1960 Criswell *Resp. to PADS 20* **Ozarks,** *Cold-cock* . . . To knock out . . . Also *cold-crock* is very often used, as is also *crock*.

crock cut n Also *crock haircut, soup-crock cut*
A haircut which looks as if a bowl has been placed on the head as a guide for the shears.
    1947 *AmSp* 22.73 (Mennonite), 'Crock hair-cuts' were the result of inverting a crock over the cranium and cutting the hair off squarely below the edge of the vessel, instead of shingling it. Hair cut in such fashion might be parted in the middle, but not on either side. **1968–69** *DARE* (Qu. X5, . . *Kinds of men's haircuts*) Infs **IL96, OH61,** Crock (cut); **OH82,** Crock—that's Amish originally; **LA40,** Soup-crock—looked like they put a crock on the head and cut what hung down.

crocked ppl adj [Prob from *crock* to cause to become impaired]
1 Drunk. **esp Nth, N Midl** Cf **crock** n[3] **4**
    1927 *New Republic* 9 Mar 71/2, The following is a partial list of words denoting drunkenness . . crocked. **1958** Kerouac *On Road* 76 **San Francisco CA,** I had traveling money and got crocked in the bar. **1963** *AmSp* 38.174 **ceKS** (Kansas University), *Drunk* . . *crocked* (6 infs). **1965–70** *DARE* (Qu. DD15, *A person who is thoroughly drunk*) 12 Infs, **chiefly Nth,** Crocked; (Qu. DD14, *When a person is partly drunk, "He's* _____.") Infs **CA14, 36,** Crocked; **LA45, MI103, PA76, SC54,** Half-crocked; (Qu. DD13, *When a drinker is just beginning to show the effects of the liquor*) Inf **MN35,** Getting crocked.
2 Insane, crazy. Cf **crock** n[3] **5**
    1970 *DARE* (Qu. HH6, *Someone who is out of his mind*) Inf **OH94,** Crocked.

crocker See **crockery**

crocker sack See **croker sack**

crockery n Also *crock, crocker, crockett, crockie, crookie* somewhat old-fash Cf **commie, dobie**
Orig a glazed clay marble; more recently a large glass marble.
    1935 *AmSp* 10.159 **seNE,** *Crockeries* or *Crockies.* Marbles with a baked glazed finish, usually blue or brown in color. These vary greatly in size. **1955** *PADS* 23.14 **cwTN,** *Crockery.* **1958** *PADS* 29.32, *Crocker* . . . A cheap marble (Wis.). Cf. *crockery, crockie. Ibid, Crockery* . . . A crockery marble "with blue and brown flecks, 3 for a nickel" (Neb.). (Also Wash., Wis.). *Ibid, Crockie* . . . Dim. of *crockery.* "Looks like drats with paint off" (Ky.). (Also Ind., Neb., Wis.). *Ibid, Crookie* . . . Same as *crockie* (Neb.). **1962** *PADS* 37.1 **cKS,** *Crockie.* A colored marble with flecks of darker color in it. **1965–70** *DARE* (Qu. EE6c, *Cheap marbles*) 9 Infs, **scattered, but chiefly Nth,** Crockeries; **CA65, OH23, 38, OR4,** Crockies; **IN5, KY36, MS15, MO27, OR1,** Crocks; **OH37,** Crockers; (Qu. EE6b, *Small marbles or marbles in general*) Inf **LA15,** Crocketts; **MO13,** Crockies; **MS15,** Crocks; (Qu. EE6d, *Special marbles*) Inf **NE9, OK28,** Crockies; **KY66,** Crocks. [19 of 22 Infs old, 3 mid-aged] **1966–68** *DARE* Tape **IA42,** We had what they called a crockie; they're usually a big marble about ¾ of an inch in diameter; **WA6,** Crocks—they were like little brown and blue enamel things. **c1970** Wiersma *Marbles Terms* **IA, csMI,** *Crockie:* A large glass marble formerly made from pottery or baked clay. **1971** Bright *Word Geog. CA & NV* 116, *Crocker(ies)* 4 infs Los Angeles and San Diego "Cheap." "Porcelainized."

crock haircut See **crock cut**

crocus n[1]
1 Std: a plant of the genus *Crocus.*
2 Any of var other plants, as:
a also *wild crocus:* A **pasqueflower,** usu *Anemone patens.* **chiefly Nth, esp Inland Nth**
    1893 *Jrl. Amer. Folkl.* 6.136, *Anemone patens* . . crocus. Minnesota. **1896** *Jrl. Amer. Folkl.* 9.179, *Anemone patens* . . wild crocus, Madison, Wis. **1898** *Jrl. Amer. Folkl.* 11.98, *Anemone patens* . . crocus, Wyo. **1950** Stevens *ND Plants* 143, *Anemone patens* . . . Commonly called "crocus" to which the flowers have only superficial resemblance. **1950** *WELS* 3 Infs, **WI,** Crocus. **1965–70** *DARE* (Qu. S23) 16 Infs, **Inland Nth,** Crocus; **ID5, WI8,** Wild crocus; (Qu. S3) Infs **MD9, NE11, NY39, ND9,** Crocus; **OH49,** Wild crocus; (Qu. S26c) Infs **KY63, MN34, UT3,** Crocus; (Qu. S26d) Infs **NJ26, SC67,** Crocus; (Qu. S21) Inf **ID1,** Crocus.
b A **flag** (here: *Iris pumila*).
    1892 *Jrl. Amer. Folkl.* 5.103, *Iris pumila,* crocus. Stratham, N.H.
c =**arbutus.**
    1900 Lyons *Plant Names* 146, *E[pigaea] repens* . . . Crocus (N. Carolina). **1959** Carleton *Index Herb. Plants* 33, *Crocus:* Anemone pulsatilla; Crocus (v); Epigaea repens.
d A **yellow bells** (here: *Fritillaria pudica*).
    1915 (1926) Armstrong *Western Wild Flowers* 38, *Fritillaria pudica* . . . The local Utah names, Crocus, Snowdrop, and Buttercup are absurd. **1966** Barnes–Jensen *Dict. UT Slang, Crocus* . . the orange fritillaria *(Fritillaria pudica),* snowdrop or yellow bells is sometimes called crocus.
e =**trillium.**
    1965–70 *DARE* (Qu. S2, . . *The flower that comes up in the woods early in spring, with three white petals that turn pink as the flower grows older*) 11 Infs, **scattered,** Crocus; **TX60,** Purple crocus.

crocus n[2] [Alter of *croaker(s)*]
Either of two **croakers 1a:**
a The Atlantic croaker (here: *Micropogon undulatus*).
    1887 Goode *Amer. Fishes* 133, The Croaker, *Micropogon undulatus,* ranges from New York at least to the Gulf of Mexico, although rarely seen north of Delaware . . . Its name refers to the peculiar grunting sound which it utters. *Ibid,* In the Chesapeake this name [croaker] has been corrupted into "Crocus." **1946** LaMonte *N. Amer. Game Fishes* 83, *Croaker . . . Names . .* Crocus, Hardhead, Chut. **1968** *DARE* (Qu. P2) Infs **MD34, 45,** Crocus.
b =**freshwater drum.**
    1887 Goode *Amer. Fishes* 142, In the lakes of Northern Indiana it is called "Crocus," evidently a corruption of "Croaker." **1945** *AmSp* 20.277, Other common names [for the fresh-water drum, *Aplodinotus grunniens* Rafinesque] are *bubbler, croaker, crocus* (probably a corruption of *croakers*). **1972** Sparano *Outdoors Encycl.* 369, *Freshwater Drum . . . Common Names . .* croaker, crocus, jewelhead, grunter.

crocus sack n Also *crocus bag* Also sp *crokass* ~ [Prob from use of the material for sacks in which *crocus,* saffron, was shipped; see 1955 *AmSp* 30.14–16] **chiefly S and Mid Atl** See Map Cf **croker sack** and *DJE*
A container made of coarse, loosely woven material; a **gunny sack.**
    1696 (1977) Dickinson *God's Providence* 35, My *Wife* had two pieces of *Sail-Canvas* given her; and I with others had each a *Crocus Ginger-*

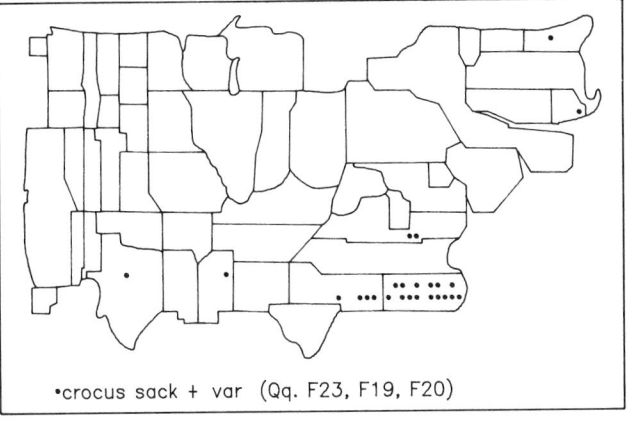

•crocus sack + var (Qq. F23, F19, F20)

Bagg. **1790** in 1912 *Augusta Co. VA Chronicles* 1.509 **VA,** James McPheeters opened a negro grave and took therefrom the body, in order to dissect the same . . and after doing so, did sew him up in a crokass bag and put him in the cave within mentioned. **1888** Jones *Negro Myths* 123 **GA,** Eh graff um an eh pit um een one crocus bag. [=He grabbed him and he put him in a crocus bag.] **1927** Adams *Congaree* 25 **cSC** [Black], Dey put her in a crocus sack an' dragged her to de back door of heaven. **1945** *AmSp* 20.309 **VA, NC, SC, GA,** Crocus sack. **1949** Kurath *Word Geog.* 57/1, *Croker sack, crocus sack* is in common use (1) in the southern part of the Virginia Piedmont, (2) in South Carolina and Georgia (also in Wilmington at the mouth of the Cape Fear), and (3) on Martha's Vineyard off Cape Cod. **1958** *PADS* 29.9 **TN,** *Crocus sack:* A burlap bag. **1959** *VT Hist.* new ser 27.131 **swVT, NC, VA,** *Crocus bag* . . Occasional. Bennington. Also Va. and N.C. **1965–70** *DARE* (Qu. F23, *A container made of rough, loosely woven, brown cloth; commonly used for potatoes*) 15 Infs, **chiefly SC, GA,** Crocus sack; 12 Infs, **chiefly SC, GA,** Crocus bag; (Qu. F20, *A cloth container for feed*) Inf **RI**14, Crocus bag; **ME**11, Crocus sack; (Qu. F19) Inf **ME**11, Crocus sack.

croger See **cougar**

croiller See **cruller**

crokass sack See **crocus sack**

croker sack n Also *croker bag* Also sp *croaker ~*, pronc-spp *coker ~, crocker ~, crokie ~* [Alter of **crocus sack**] **chiefly Gulf States, S Atl** See Map
=**crocus sack.**

1895 *DN* 1.386 **wFL,** *Coker-sack:* a sack of heavy stuff for corn, bran, etc. **1908** *DN* 3.302 **eAL, wGA,** *Crôker sack.* **1942** (1960) Robertson *Red Hills* 226 **SC,** Whole families would appear with crocker sacks slung over one shoulder—old and young would take to the cotton patch. **1953** Brewer *Word Brazos* 75 **eTX** [Black], He hangs his ole frock-tail coat an' preachin' breeches on a nail in de wall an' th'ows his ol croakersack full of bed clothes in one of de room corners. **1965–70** *DARE* (Qu. F23, *A container made of rough, loosely woven, brown cloth*) 70 Infs, **chiefly Gulf States,** Croker sack; **AL**14, **FL**36, **GA**3, 79, **SC**29, 51, Croker bag; (Qu. F19, *A cloth container for grain*) Infs **AL**21, **AR**52, **MS**1, 13, 63, 73, 85, **TN**44, Croker sack; (Qu. F20, *A cloth container for feed*) Infs **AL**1, **FL**11, **GA**23, **MS**22, 37, 63, 73, 85, Croker sack; **FL**31, Croker bag; **MO**9, Crokie sack. **1966–68** *DARE* Tape **FL**26A, Pile on burlap, croker sacks ['kroka sæks]; **GA**50A, I've seen his cousin come out one evenin' with a whole croker sack ['krokæ·sæk] full of ducks. **1968** Fox *Southern Fried Plus* 6 20 **SC, GA** (as of c1940), Look at it [a woman wearing a tight sweater], will you. I say, look at it. It's like two bobcats in a croker sack. **1972** GA Dept. Ag. *Farmers Market Bulletin* 8 Mar 8/2, You should try wrapping the trunks of the trees with croker sacks.

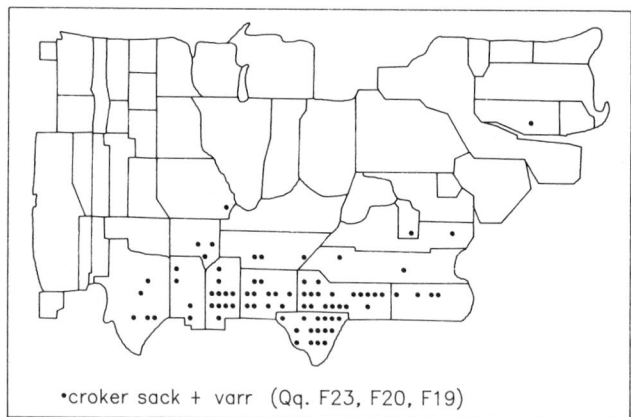
•croker sack + varr (Qq. F23, F20, F19)

croker sack, hacked to the ppl adj phr
1950 *AmSp* 25.230 **nwMS,** *Hacked to the crocker sack.* Extremely humiliated or embarassed.

crokie sack See **croker sack**

croller See **cruller**

crom See **crawm**

crome v Also sp *cromb* [Perh from *crome, cromb* to seize with a hook]
See quot 1981.

1922 in 1981 Harper–Presley *Okefinokee* 166 **seGA,** I broke me off a "light-'ood knot" and "crombed" it [a snake]. **1950** *PADS* 14.24 **SC,** *Crome* . . To overpower, to subdue. **1981** Harper–Presley *Okefinokee* 138 **seGA** (as of a1951), *Cromb* . . To catch or kill something . . by hooking or hitting it with a stick or implement.

cronch See **craunch**

crooch See **crouch**

crook n[1] [Prob alter of *crick* a painful muscle spasm, perh coalescing with Engl dial *crook* 'pain or twinge' *(EDD); OED* 1828] *esp among Black speakers*
A sudden sharp pain, a **crink.**

1965–70 *DARE* (Qu. BB3a, . . *A pain that strikes you suddenly in the neck*) 32 Infs, **scattered,** Crook; (Qu. BB3b, *A sudden pain that strikes you in the back*) Infs **CA**118, **FL**51, **MI**33, **OK**31, Crook; (Qu. BB4, *Other words for a pain* . . *"He's had a _____ in his arm for a week."*) Infs **FL**2, **IA**22, **NY**241, **VA**71, Crook. [22 of 40 Infs Black]

crook n[2]
1 A handle for lifting the lid of a wood-burning stove. Cf *DS* F11
1921 *DN* 5.118 **KY,** *Crook* . . . A short, crooked instrument for lifting caps from a kitchen stove. Otherwise called *ketch* by the hillsman.
‡2 A staple.
1967 LeCompte *Word Atlas* 166 **seLA,** (*U-shaped nail*) . . . A crook [1 inf].
3 An out-of-the-way space, a nook.
1967 *DARE* (Qu. Y48, *To look in every possible place for something you've mislaid*) Inf **TX**43, Looked in every crook and cranny. **1968** *DARE* Tape **WI**23, That house sure has a lot of crooks and corners.
4 A cucumber.
1969 *DARE* (Qu. I25, *Names or nicknames for cucumbers*) Inf **IN**67, Crooks.
5 See quot.
1972 *DARE* FW Addit **nwFL,** *Crook:* Wood discarded after barrel heads are cut; used for kindling.

crook v, hence vbl n *crooking*
To cheat; steal.
1841 (1969) Emerson *Essays* 197 **NEng,** Shuffle they will, and crow, crook, and hide, feign to confess here, only that they may brag and conquer there. **1883** (1970) Lewis *Lime-Kiln Club* 216 **Detroit MI,** But for a jury of six good men he would once have gone to jail on the charge of 'crooking' six hens. **1931–33** *LANE Worksheets* **seMA,** *Crooked,* stole. "Kids would say crooked." **1939** *Sat. Eve. Post* 10 June 122/3, He's gonna crook us out of our chance. **1941** Percy *Lanterns* 300 **MS** [Black], Well, s'pose some nigger crooks you in a crap game—you sho ain't goin' to let him get away with that and with your thin dime too, is you? **1957** Battaglia *Resp. to PADS* 20 **eMD,** (*I don't trust him, he's always trying to _____*) Crook somebody. **1966–69** *DARE* (Qu. II33, . . *"I don't trust him, he's always trying to _____."*) Infs **AR**41, **KY**10, **MD**24, Crook you; **GA**77, **TN**15, Crook me; **MO**16, Crook somebody; (Qu. V4, . . *Stealing* . . *"Yesterday somebody _____ my watch."*) Infs **LA**23, **NH**18, **NJ**1, **NY**59, Crooked; (Qu. V5a, *To take something of small value that doesn't belong to you* . . *"Who's been _____ the cookies?"*) Inf **NJ**1, Crooking; (Qu. JJ7, . . *Expressions for cheating in school examinations*) Infs **GA**13, **HI**6, Crooking.

crooked brush n
1 also *crooked bush:* A **forestiera.**
1921 Deam *Trees IN* 282, *Crooked Brush* . . . Small trees, or shrub like, . . branchlets numerous and somewhat spiny. **1939** Tharp *Vegetation TX* 10, Prairie relicts . . indicate the stages of the progressive invasion by mesquite, Acacia, . . crooked-bush . . and other species which compose the chaparral.
2 A thicket.
1969 *DARE* (Qu. C28, *A place where underbrush, weeds, vines and small trees grow together so that it's nearly impossible to get through*) Inf **IL**93, Crooked brush.

crooked crab n
1905 *DN* 3.76 **nwAR,** *Crooked crab* . . . Name of a game.

crooked rail fence n Also *crooked fence*
A **worm fence.**
1830 (1831) Fowler *Jrl.* 79, The usual description of fences are *worm,* or

crooked rail fences. **1856** U.S. Dept. Ag. *Rept. of Secy. for 1855* 20, Formerly, cattle were kept here through the winter with very little protection except a crooked rail fence. **1909** *DN* 3.410 **nME**, *Crooked fence* . . . A Virginia fence. **c1960** *Wilson Coll.* **csKY**, *Crooked rail fence*—the ordinary, zigzag type, the rail fence par excellence. **1968–70** *DARE* (Qu. L62, *A fence made of split logs*) Infs **VA**27, 77, Crooked rail fence; **SC**30, Crooked fence; (Qu. L65, . . *Other kinds of fences*) Inf **NY**122, Crooked rail fence.

crooked steel n

In logging: a cant hook.

1956 Sorden–Ebert *Logger's Words* **Gt Lakes**, *Crooked-steel*, A cant-hook or a peavey. **1958** McCulloch *Woods Words* **Pacific NW**. **1966** *DARE* Tape **MI**10, When they [=lumberjacks] were out in the woods working, a cant hook, the most useful tool they employed with heavy timber, became the flip or the crooked steel.

crooked stick n

A worthless, undependable person; a dishonest person.

1828 (1936) McCoy *Jrl. Exped.* 349 **PA**, Knowing that there were many crooked sticks about St. Louis, I had the precaution to take a copy. **1848** Lowell *Biglow* 9.124 'Upcountry' **MA**, So, ez I aint a crooked stick, jest like—like ole (I swow, / I dunno ez I know his name)—I'll go back to my plough. **1905** *DN* 3.7 **cCT**, *Crooked stick* . . . A dishonest person. **1907** *DN* 3.211 **nwAR**. **1923** *DN* 5.234 **swWI**, *Crooked stick* . . . A man who has turned out to be more or less a failure in life. No dishonesty of character is implied. "She was very partikler who she was goin' to marry, but she finally picked up a crooked stick." **c1960** *Wilson Coll.* **csKY**, *Crooked stick* . . . A failure, undependable. **1965** *DARE* File **MN, ND**, *Crooked stick:* a worthless mate (husband or wife).

crooked swamp-bush n [From the zigzag branches and its habitat]

=pond spice.

1960 Vines *Trees SW* 293, *Glabraria geniculata* . . . Common names include . . Crooked Swamp-bush.

crooked wood n

=buttonbush 1.

1916 *Torreya* 16.239, *Cephalanthus occidentalis* . . . Button willow, crooked wood, Ballard Co., Ky.

crookedy adj Also sp crookety

Crooked, misshapen; see also quot 1922.

1922 Gonzales *Black Border* 295 **sSC, GA coasts** [Gullah glossary], *Crookety*—crooked; also tricky, unreliable. **1938** Rawlings *Yearling* 203 **FL**, I've lost my boy. My pore crookedy boy.

crookie See crockery

crook nose n prob chiefly Sth, S Midl

A hooked nose.

1965–70 *DARE* (Qu. X15, . . *Different kinds of noses*) Infs **AL**33, **GA**72, **MD**41, 44, **MI**96, **SC**3, **TN**52, **TX**37, Crook nose.

crooks intj [From crook an angle]

A call used in marble play; see quots.

1922 *DN* 5.186 **KY**, *Crooks* . . . A term in the "keeps" game. When one of the "stakes," inside the ring, is knocked out near the edge, the boy shooting next may cry out "crooks," and be allowed to shoot "crooked" at it from the angle that will send it the nearest way out of the ring. If the boy who first knocked the "man" near the edge first cries out "Vence ye crooks," the next player must shoot at it in a diametric line. **1955** *PADS* 23.14 **TN**, *Crooks* . . . A call granting permission to the shooter to move around a ring to a more favorable position nearer the target. The counter call is *no crooks*, or *vence ye crooks* . . heard, *crooks* and *no crooks*.

crootsed up ppl adj [Cf PaGer gruunselt wrinkled]

1965 *DARE* File **swPA** (as of 1920s), *Crootsed up:* wrinkled, crushed. "When my mother dressed me to go to Sunday school, she'd say, 'Now you sit down til I'm ready, so you don't get all crootsed up.' "

crop n Usu |krɔp, krɑp|; sometimes, chiefly Sth, S Midl, |kræp| Pronc-sp crap

A Forms.

c1770 in 1833 Boucher *Glossary* 1, My *new crap's pitch'd*, from which I hope to *share* / At least *two thousand*, all good *notes*, next year. **1853** Hammett *Stray Yankee in TX* 114, North Carolina is notorious for a peculiar flatness of pronunciation in such words as *crap* for "crop". **1893** Shands *MS Speech*, *Crap* (kræp). Negro pronunciation of crop.

1899 (1912) Green *VA Folk-Speech*, *Crap* . . . A crop of grain. **1902** *DN* 2.231 **sIL**, *Crap* . . . Pronunciation of crop. **1903** *DN* 2.310 **seMO**, *Crap*. **1907** *DN* 3.221 **nwAR**, [kræp]. **1908** *DN* 3.302 **eAL, wGA**, *Crap*. **1915** *DN* 4.225 **wTX**, *Craps* . . for crops. **1922** Gonzales *Black Border* 294 **sSC, GA coasts** [Gullah glossary], *Crap* . . crop, crops; crops, cropped, cropping. **1954** *Harder Coll.* **cwTN**, *Crop* [kræp], occasional pronunciation. **c1960** *Wilson Coll.* **csKY**, Crop is sometimes [kræp], now largely humorous. **1961** Kurath–McDavid *Pronc. Engl.* 143, The /æ/ of *cat* appears in *crop* in the folk speech of two areas: (1) the Atlantic coast from Chesapeake Bay to the Neuse River in North Carolina, and (2) the Appalachians south of the Kanawha River. It is rather more common along the Atlantic coast than in the Appalachians. Scattered instances survive in Pennsylvania and elsewhere. **1967** Key *Tobacco Vocab.* 10 **NC, TN**, *Crop* [kræp, krɔp].

B Senses.

1 An earmark. prob chiefly Sth, S Midl, West

1653 in 1889 Plymouth **MA** *Records* 1.2, The marke of his Cattle is a cropp on the left eare. **1801** *NC Mercury & Salisbury Advt.* (Salisbury) 29 Jan 4/3, A gang of hogs . . having two smooth craps and a hole in the right ear. **1889** (1971) Farmer *Americanisms*, *Crop* . . . In the bucolic dialect of the plains an ear mark. **1906** *DN* 3.132 **nwAR**. **1961** Adams *Old-Time Cowhand* 263, A "crop" is made by cuttin' 'bout one half of the ear off smoothly, straight from the upper side. **1967–68** *DARE* (Qu. K18, . . *Mark* . . *to identify a cow*) Infs **AL**20, **CO**4, **LA**40, **NC**26, **TX**43, Crop; **LA**2, 27, **SC**43, Smooth crop; **LA**29, Crop and saw-set mark; **LA**18, Crop and slip. **1967** *DARE* Tape **TX**24, Our earmark was a crop; we cropped the right; **TX**47, [Looking at pictures:] There's an overbit . . . That's a crop . . there's an under-half crop.

2 The throat; sometimes the stomach.

1899 (1977) Norris *McTeague* 161 **CA**, Sunday he . . spent the afternoon lying full length upon the bed, crop-full, stupid, warm, smoking his huge pipe. **1965–70** *DARE* (Qu. X7, . . *Some food got stuck in his ___*) 9 Infs, **scattered Nth**, Crop.

3 See quot.

1967 Key *Tobacco Vocab.* 16 **MD**, *Crop:* The best grade of tobacco leaves.

4 also cropper: See quot.

1968 *DARE* (Qu. K41, *A horse with its tail cut short*) Inf **TX**52, A crop; **WA**23, A cropper.

crop v Pronc-sp crap

1 To earmark an animal.

c1960 *Wilson Coll.* **csKY**, *Crop* . . . To cut the tip of the ear of a pig, esp, as a mark of the owner.

2 To pick or cut (flowers, greens, etc); to be cut or harvested; hence vbl n cropping.

1910 *DN* 3.456 **seKY**, Crop [kræp] . . To pick flowers. "Nanny didn't have time to *cräp* the daffodils for you." **1933** Miller *Lamb in His Bosom* 12 **GA** (as of 18th cent), The greens would soon be ready to crap. **1966–68** *DARE* Tape **NC**8, Some call it cropping the tobacco; **NC**51, You got to go in there every week an' crop or break those leaves off as they are ready; **SC**17, When it [the tobacco] got . . mature enough we'd crop it, put it in the barn, and cure it out . . . After you leave two first cropping, then you get it [the tobacco] thicker and heavier . . . It do now—used to, our best cropping was our first. **1982** *DARE* File **NC**, From a 30-ish woman, Black, from Winterville, N.C . . . She "crops" tobacco (works with the tobacco harvest).

3 To plant or raise a crop; to farm; hence vbl n crapping, cropping. ?S Midl

1838 (1930) W. Sewall *Diary* 202 **MA**, Cleaning up, and burning up stubble ground preparatory to cropping. **1899** (1912) Green *VA Folk-Speech*, *Crap* . . . To raise a crop. *Crapping*, farming. *Ibid*, *Cropping* . . . Farming; raising crops. **1903** *DN* 2.310 **seMO**, *Crop* (often crap) . . . Cultivate. 'I am cropping with Mr. Brown this year.' **1919** *DN* 5.33 **seKY**, Lish's Rob's jist cleverly begun to crap (farm). **1940–41** Cassidy *WI Atlas* **swWI**, *Crop:* Plant a crop in (a field). "(We'll) crop it." **1954** *Harder Coll.* **cwTN**, Crop. **c1960** *Wilson Coll.* **csKY**, We cropped the Smith place that year. **1968** *DARE* Tape **MD**34, They used to crop 100–160 acres.

4 in phr crop on shares: To sharecrop.

1879 (1880) Tourgée *Fool's Errand* 91, They didn't require me to leave, only to stop selling horses to niggers and letting them crop on shares. **1895** *DN* 1.386 **cwIN**, *Crapping it on the sheers:* farming on rented land. **1954** *Harder Coll.* **cwTN**, *Crop on shares:* To live on a farm, do the work, and share expenses and profits with the owner. (Occasional).

5 with *out:* To wear the soil out with planting.

1947 Croy *Corn Country* 39 **IA**, My Uncle Jim had been a hard-pan farmer but had "cropped out" and had moved back to our section.

crop bean n [*crop* craw]

1961 *Midland Cooperator* 20 Nov 7/1, According to legend, one of the Pilgrim forefathers, while cleaning a wild turkey for the feast, discovered a strange bean in the bird's crop . . . The bean was named the "crop bean" because of the strange place it was discovered. The beans were planted every year and seeds were passed down to the next generations . . . The bean grows and looks something like a cross between a lima and navy bean. Unlike these beans, however, the pod and all is cooked like green beans.

crop cabbage n [Prob from **crop** v 2]

1967 *DARE* (Qu. H52, *Dishes made with fresh cabbage*) Inf **TN**5, Crap [kræp] cabbage, [you] cut the cabbage before it begins to head.

crope See **creep** v A

crop egg n

1958 *Hand Coll.* **csOH**, Did you ever hear of the bad luck egg? Some people call them 'crop eggs,' as I think the hens lay them when they have finished laying a crop of eggs. They are very small and have no yolks and the whites will not spoil and can be used for mucilage.

crop grass See **crabgrass** 1, 2

croping adj [Engl dial] *obsolescent*

See quots.

1914 *DN* 4.70 **ME, nNH**, Cropin' . . . Stingy, niggardly, mean. **1927** *AmSp* 3.136 **sME**, A "croping" person was stingy, penurious, or "nigh."

crop on shares See **crop** v 4

cropout n Pronc-sp *crapout* [Metath of *outcrop*]

1966 *PADS* 46.25 **cnAR**, Crapout . . . ['kræpaut] Outcropping; exposed vein. — "They's crapouts of coal out here on the mountain."

crop out v phr See **crop** v 5

cropper n

1 also attrib, pronc-sp *crapper:* A sharecropper or tenant farmer. **chiefly Sth, S Midl, occas NEng**

1800 Tatham *Tobacco* 101 *(DAE)*, He tills the ground with his own negroes, with hireling labourers, or with independent cultivators, termed *croppers.* **1859** IL State Ag. Soc. *Trans. for 1857–58* 3.408, Absence from home . . compelled me to depend . . on annual "croppers," who were accustomed to skim over the ground with the "bar-share" plow. **1908** *DN* 3.354 **eAL, wGA**, A third of the corn and a fourth of the cotton crop, is a frequent method of renting to small farmers, who are usually called *croppers.* **1923** *DN* 5.204 **swMO**, *Crapper.* **1926** Roberts *Time of Man* 58 **cKY**, They say his pap come to this country withouten a cent, a cropper. And now look, he owns a right good farm. **1941** Percy *Lanterns* 280 **nwMS**, Those hundred and twenty-four families of mine with $437.64 in their jeans worked "on the shares" and called themselves "croppers," but I wasn't familiar with the term "share-croppers." **1942** (1960) Robertson *Red Hills* 164 **SC**, In our state only a third of the farmers owned the land. A third were renters, a third were croppers. **c1960** *Wilson Coll.* **csKY**, *Cropper* (share-cropper): A tenant farmer who uses the implements and stock of his employer and gets a certain percentage of the crops for his own, the rest going as rent. Usually he is distinguished from the renter, who uses his own tools and stock. **1965–69** *DARE* (Qu. L3, *A man who lives on the farm and does the work, but divides the expenses and profits with the owner*) Inf **LA**29, Cropper; **FL**7, **GA**22, 33, **NC**49, Half cropper; **MA**47, Field cropper; **MA**55, Farm cropper; **MS**58, Third and fourth cropper; **NC**49, Third cropper; (Qu. L2, *The extra house on a large farm where a hired man and his family live*) Inf **NC**63, Cropper house. **1966** *DARE* Tape **AL**1, He had a lot of croppers on his hand, and I don't know what got wrong with them people down there.

2 In tobacco farming: one who harvests tobacco leaves. [**crop** v 2]

1966 *DARE* Tape **NC**7, Some of 'em call 'em croppers, also called primers; **SC**17, That's the croppers; **SC**24, You have to have the pickers . . the croppers.

3 See quot.

1969 *DARE* (Qu. W14, *Names for underwear, including joking names . . Men's — short*) Inf **TX**72, Cropper, i.e., Jockey shorts.

4 See **crop** n **B4.**

croppercrown n

1899 (1912) Green *VA Folk-Speech, Croppercrown* . . . A top-knot on a fowl's head.

croppie n[1] Also sp *croppy* [*crop* cut]

1 See quot.

1930 Shoemaker *1300 Words* 13 **cPA Mts** (as of c1900), *Croppie* — A bob-haired girl, an Indian girl.

2 See quot.

1968 Adams *Western Words, Croppy* — An outlaw horse with his ears cropped to identify him as such.

croppie n[2], croppy See **crappie**

crop tramp n

?A migrant farm worker.

1935 Davis *Honey* 153 **OR**, None of the hoboes knew her, and none of the crop tramps had ever seen her along the road they followed regularly.

cross v

1 freq with *up:* To oppose, go counter to, be at odds with; hence ppl adj *crossed (up).* [*OED* c1555 →] **chiefly Sth, S Midl** Cf **crossways 2**

1945 Saxon *Gumbo Ya-Ya* 551 **New Orleans LA** [Black], If you play lottery in August, you will lose, because 'It was on the 1st of August dat God put de Devil out of heaven . . an' since dat happen, de Devil crosses everything we does in August.' **1965–70** *DARE* (Qu. II11b, *If two people can't bear each other at all . . "Those two are _____."*) Infs **AL**43, **AR**52, **GA**9, (All) crossed up; (Qu. KK68, *When people don't think alike about something: "We agree on most things, but on politics we're _____."*) Infs **GA**89, **MS**1, **SC**40, Crossed (up); (Qu. Y51, *Other ways of saying 'to avoid' things or people — for example: "He's not your kind — you'd better _____ him."*) Inf **GA**77, Not get crossed up with; (Qu. BB40, . . *About somebody acting strangely: "All of a sudden he got up and left. What do you suppose _____ him?"*) Inf **VA**30, Crossed; (Qu. GG3, *To tease: "See those big boys trying to _____ [that little one]."*) Inf **TN**1, Cross up.

2 usu with *up:* To deceive, confuse. [*OEDS* 1823 →]

1934 Cain *Postman* 74 **CA**, That's to cross them up. **1965–70** *DARE* (Qu. GG2, . . *"Confused, mixed up": "So many things were going on at the same time that he got completely _____."*) Infs **IL**136, **ME**9, **MI**26, **MO**7, **WI**9, Crossed up; **LA**8, Crossed; (Qu. II33, *To get an advantage over somebody by tricky means: "I don't trust him, he's always trying to _____."*) Inf **LA**32, Cross you up. **1970** Major *Afro-Amer. Slang, Cross* . . . to deceive or mislead or confuse.

3 freq with *out:* In **cat** n 3c or similar children's ball games: see quots.

1883 Eggleston *Hoosier Schoolboy* 10 **IN**, The larger boys . . were having a game of "three old cat" . . . When the ball was struck, it was called a "tick," and when there was a tick, all the batters were obliged to run one base to the left, and then the ball thrown between a batter and the base to which he was running "crossed him out," and obliged him to give up his "paddle" to the one who threw the ball. **1966** *Wilson Coll.* **csKY**, *Cross out* . . . In elementary baseball-type games, to put a base-runner out by throwing the ball between him and the base — in cat ball. **1966** *DARE* Tape **AL**4, If he knocked this ball, or if he got the ball, and crossed you — threw it in front of you — ah, you were out.

4 See quot.

1922 Rollins *Cowboy* 53, At each shot he "crossed" his rifle, that is he fired alternately from his right and left shoulder.

5 freq *cross over* and in var expanded phrr: To die. *euphem*

1942 *AmSp* 17.72/2, Cross over the range — the old-timer's euphemism for dying. **1943** *LANE* Map 520 3 infs, **eMA, seNH**, Crossed over, crossed the river. **1948** *AN&Q* 8.167, To "Cross the Ties": in hobo language, to die (coming from the fact that a hobo, traditionally, spends most of his life riding the box cars). **1950** *WELS* (*Way . . for saying someone died*) 1 Inf, **ceWI**, Crossed the veil; 1 Inf, **csWI**, Crossed the river. **1967–68** *DARE* (Qu. BB56, *Joking expressions for dying: "He _____."*) Inf **SC**40, Crossed Jordan; **SC**55, Crossed over Jordan; **GA**44, Crossed over to the other side; (Qu. BB54, *When a sick person is past hope of recovery, you'd say he's _____*) Inf **MI**96, Gonna cross over. **1969** Emmons *Deep Rivers* 94 **eTX** [Black], Us is got two spirits, a good one and a bad one; and that when we die, one o' them spirits don't never leave this earth. It may be the good one, or it may be the bad one that don't cross over. **1982** *NY Times* (NY) 29 Aug sec 10 9/5 **csME**, As time passes, the dialect of the time and place becomes infectious. There are reports of so-and-so who "crossed over" (died) or "passed away" (married — not died).

cross-and-Bible door n Also *cross-of-Christ door*
A six-panel door; see quot 1966.
1966 *DARE* File (in 1966 *Boston Record* 7 May), The famous six-panel Colonial door found in millions of American homes is also known as a "Cross-and-Bible" door. This is because the center stile and crossbar which divide the upper four panels outline a cross, while the lower two panels represent the open pages of a Bible . . . Six-panel doors of ponderosa pine are available today as stock items at lumber dealers. **1969** *Foxfire* 3.2.7 **SC,** Restoration began at once . . . Two original cross and Bible doors will go back into the house. **1969** *DARE* Tape **MA**69, This house was built in the late 1700s . . . It has the cross-of-Christ doors and those huge locks with their brass handles.

cross-angle adv Also *cross-angles*
Diagonally.
1966–70 *DARE* (Qu. MM15, *If a carpenter nails a board crossing another board at an angle, you might say, "He nailed the board on _____."*) Infs **MO**20, **NY**181, Cross-angle; **PA**242, **WA**1, Cross-angles.

cross-back n [In allusion to the Christian cross] *usu derog*
A Roman Catholic.
1964 *PADS* 42.34 **Chicago IL,** The Catholic is identified by multiple responses of *papist, cross-back, Turk,* and *Roman* . . . All three instances of cross-back were elicited from Protestant informants . . all of whom are closely similar in age, education, and ancestry. Further, all grew up on the North Side of Chicago and remember the expression from childhood. **1965–70** *DARE* (Qu. CC4, . . *Nicknames . . for various religions or religious groups*) Infs **AL**20, **IN**19, **KY**11, 60, 70 **MD**9, 15, **MI**110, **NY**36, 42, 49, 57, Cross-backs. **1971** *AmSp* 46.80 **Chicago IL,** Social Relations: terms of abuse . . Catholic . . . *crossback.*

‡**cross-ball** n Cf **cross out 1, one-eyed cat, three old cat, work-up**
1968 *DARE* (Qu. EE11, *Bat-and-ball games for just a few players [when there aren't enough for a regular game]*) Inf **WV**3, Cross-ball.

crossbar n **chiefly east of Missip R, esp Atlantic**
A **singletree** or **doubletree**.
1940–41 Cassidy *WI Atlas* **seWI,** Cross-bar: Doubletree. **1965–70** *DARE* (Qu. L47, *The two movable bars behind a team of horses are fastened to a longer piece; this is a _____*) 47 Infs, **scattered, but esp Atlantic,** Crossbar; (Qu. L46, *Behind each horse there's a movable bar . . [called:]*) Infs **FL**1, **NC**52, Crossbar.

crossbar hotel n Also *crossbar inn, ~ motel joc*
A jail or guardhouse.
1941 *AmSp* 16.164 (Army slang), Cross Bar Hotel. Guard House. **1966–70** *DARE* (Qu. V11, . . *Joking names . . for a county or city jail*) Infs **IL**12, **KY**84, **TX**37, 54, **WI**57, Crossbar hotel; **NC**30, Crossbar inn; **NC**41, Crossbar motel. [All Infs male] **1970** Tarpley *Blinky* 270 **neTX,** *Other names for the jail . . crossbar hotel.*

crossbone n
1 pl: The pelvic bones.
1949 Arnow *Hunter's Horn* 232 **KY,** A body wanted it [childbirth] over with, but, oh, God, so many things could go wrong. What if it got caught on the crossbones like Vadie Anderson's third one.
2 The **wishbone** of a chicken.
1967 *DARE* (Qu. K74, *A bone from the breast of a chicken, shaped like a horseshoe*) Inf **SC**43, Crossbone.

cross-brand v **West** Cf **counterbrand**
To re-brand cattle upon sale to show the change of ownership; hence n *cross-brander* one who changes brands, usu illegally.
1877 Cozzens *Crossing Quicksands* 302, Each animal purchased must be "cross-branded," i.e., the seller re-brands upon the shoulder, as a sign that his title to the animal has passed. **1912** Wason *Friar Tuck* 377, There must be at least fifteen cross-branders in the neighbourhood, and probaby more. **1977** Watts *Dict. Old West, Cross-brand*—The seller of a cow re-branded the animal to show that his brand was vented, or canceled . . . *Cross-brander*—A cow-thief who altered brands.

crossbuck n
1 =**sawbuck 1.**
1956 Ker *Vocab. W. TX* 173, Wooden device for sawing logs for firewood . . . crossbuck. **1968–69** *DARE* (Qu. L59, *An implement with an X-frame . . to hold firewood for sawing*) Infs **CA**45, **NY**66, Crossbuck.
2 An X-shaped railroad crossing sign.

1966 *Aroostook Republican* (Caribou ME) 8 June 4/4, Railroad tracks may be marked with a crossbuck, but not always a bell or flasher signal.
3 See quot. Cf **sawbuck**
1968 *DARE* (Qu. U28b, . . *A ten-dollar bill*) Inf **NY**66, Crossbuck.

crossbuck saddle n Also *crossbuck* [**crossbuck 1**] Cf **aparejo**
A pack saddle that resembles a small sawhorse.
1922 Rollins *Cowboy* 153, The West employed two types of pack-saddle, respectively designated as the "cross-buck saddle" (usually contracted into "cross-buck") and the "aparéjo." **1947** *Trail & Timberline* May 75/1 *(DA),* You will need . . a wooden cross-buck pack saddle, a pad and a saddle blanket. **1968** Adams *Western Words, Cross-buck saddle*—A packsaddle, so called because of its similarity to the woodcutter's cross-buck sawhorse. It consists of two short, parallel planks connected at each end by a short wooden cross. Of necessity it has two cinches and is used to carry equipment or freight.

cross cleavers n [*cross* from the arrangement of the leaves + **cleavers**]
A **bedstraw,** usu a **wild licorice** (here: *Galium circaezans*).
1814 Bigelow *Florula Bostoniensis* 37, *Galium brachiatum . . . Cross Cleavers . . .* Found in woods . . . Fruit a little burr. **1900** Lyons *Plant Names* 167, *G. circaezans . . .* Cross Cleavers. **1936** Winter *Plants NE* 133, Cross-cleavers. In woods in eastern Nebr. **1946** Reeves–Bain *Flora TX* 234, Crosscleavers . . . Leaves usually 4 in each whorl.

cross-corners adj, adv Also *cross-corner(wise)*
Catercorner, in a diagonal position; diagonal.
1968–70 *DARE* (Qu. MM14, *If a drugstore is on one corner of a square and a gas station is on the far corner you might say, "The drugstore is _____ the gas station."*) Infs **DE**7, **IL**138, **MN**19, Cross-corners from; **MA**61, Cross-corner; **MO**10, Cross-cornerwise from; [**GA**77, On the cross-corner from].

crosscut v
To take a shortcut.
1903 (1965) Adams *Log Cowboy* 49 **TX,** I cross-cut the country and was soon on another trail of our stampeded cattle. **1969** *DARE* (Qu. MM16, *If you're walking with somebody to the other corner of a square, and you want to save steps, you might say, "It'll be shorter if we _____."*) Inf **PA**216, Crosscut.

crosscut n [*OED* 1800 →]
A direct route, a shortcut.
1879 Bancroft *Hist. U.S.* 5.492, He knew the by-ways . . and the cross-cuts and roads as far as Brunswick. **1968–69** *DARE* (Qu. MM16, *If you're walking with somebody to the other corner of a square, and you want to save steps, you might say, "It'll be shorter if we _____."*) Infs **NY**59, **WI**66, Take a crosscut; **NY**103, Take the crosscut.

crossed See **cross 1**

crossed fox See **cross fox**

crossed up See **cross 1**

‡**crosser** n
=**cross-back.**
1966 *DARE* (Qu. CC4, . . *Nicknames . . for various religions or religious groups*) Inf **NM**9, Crossers: Catholics—they button their collars in the back.

crosses n pl Cf **cross out 2**
1954 *Harder Coll.* **cwTN,** Crosses: A game of zeros and crosses played on paper.

cross-eye adj [For *cross-eyed*]
1966–67 *DARE* (Qu. X26a, *If a person's eyes look in different directions, looking inward, he's _____*) Infs **MS**73, **SC**10, 26, 42, 44, Cross-eye.

cross fence n Cf **crossrail fence**
?A fence which crosses (rather than encloses) a field.
1967 *DARE* (Qu. L62, *A fence made of split logs*) Inf **CO**38, A cross fence—on the order of a drift fence, a separating fence; (Qu. L63, . . *Fences made with wire*) Inf **TN**7, Cross fence—separates two fields; (Qu. L64, . . *Wooden fence that's built around a garden or near a house*) Inf **TN**14, Cross fence.

cross fox n Also *crossed fox* [See quot 1917]
A color phase of the **red fox;** see quots.

[**1792** (1911) Cartwright *Labrador Jrl.* 374, Cross-fox. A fox which is bred between a silver and yellow.] **1917** Anthony *Mammals Amer.* 75, The Cross Fox gets its name from the large cross-mark formed by two dark stripes; one across the shoulders, and the other running down the middle of the back . . . It occurs . . occasionally in the northwestern States. **1955** U.S. Arctic Info. Center *Gloss., Cross fox.* Alternate name for an 'American red fox' which has reddish yellow fur with one dark band across the shoulders and another down the dorsal line forming a rough cross. **1966–69** *DARE* (Qu. P32, . . *Other kinds of wild animals . . around here*) Infs MI2, MN15, Cross fox; MA58, Crossed fox. **1982** Elman *Hunter's Field Guide* 362, In the same regions [northern US] is a slightly more common intermediate color phase, the cross fox, which at shooting distance looks like an ordinary red but has a dark brown, sometimes almost black, cross on its back—a stripe from nape to rump, transected behind the withers.

crosshaul n, also attrib

1 In logging: see quot 1905. Cf **crosshaul** v
1905 U.S. Forest Serv. *Bulletin* 61.34, Cross haul. The cleared space in which a team moves in cross hauling. (N[orthern] F[orest]). **1969** Sorden *Lumberjack Lingo* **NEng, Gt Lakes,** Cross haul.

2 Among loggers: a non-existent item used as the basis for practical jokes.
1913 *DN* 4.2 **ME,** Crosshaul. . . An imaginary article used in logging. A greenhorn is often sent to the boss to get one. **1924** Shephard *Paul Bunyan* 80, He sent Bud to Ashland over forty miles away to get a crosshaul, and the kid didn't know no better than to start out to go after it. **1966–68** (Qu. HH14, *Ways of teasing a beginner or inexperienced person—for example, by sending him for a "left-handed monkey wrench": "Go get me _____."*) Inf MI10, Round crosshaul [Inf is a sawmill owner and operator]; WI59, A crosshaul—used at logging camp. **1969** Sorden *Lumberjack Lingo* **NEng, Gt Lakes,** Cross haul.

3 A chain or cable used to load a log onto a car or sled. Cf **parbuckle**
1926 Rickaby *Ballads Shanty-Boy* 234, Cross-haul. A line (chain) used in the early days in loading logs. Cross-haul loading . . served the shanty-boy long and well. **1967** *DARE* Tape MI47, Them days, everything was loaded with cant hooks and chain gang. It was three men to a gang—a top-loader, and a man to send up logs with a cant hook to keep the logs straight on the skids, and a teamster, and of course a team and the crosshaul. *Ibid,* Crosshaul team—these logs, as they put skids on the sleighs . . they'd have to roll the logs up at that time then and they would have to use a team to roll the logs up. **1969** Sorden *Lumberjack Lingo* **NEng, Gt Lakes,** Cross haul . . A chain around a log to roll a log up the skids onto the load. Sometimes called a parbuckle.

4 See quot.
1969 Sorden *Lumberjack Lingo* **NEng, Gt Lakes,** Cross haul . . A road built for a team that was pulling the cable or chain used to load logs with a jammer or gin pole.

crosshaul v

1 In logging: to load logs with chains or cables; see quots.
1905 U.S. Forest Serv. *Bulletin* 61.34, Cross haul, to. To load cars or sleds with logs by horsepower and crotch or loading chain. **1958** McCulloch *Woods Words* **Pacific NW,** Crosshaul. . . To parbuckle, or load a log by passing a line over and under, then pulling on it to roll the log up a set of skids . . . To pull at right angles to the main haul . . . To get a payload on a return trip.

2 Fig: see quot.
1958 McCulloch *Woods Words* **Pacific NW,** Crosshaul . . To work at cross purposes.

cross-hobble n
1961 Adams *Old-Time Cowhand* 130, Some men used the "cross-hobble". . . This meant hobblin' one front foot to a hind one on the opposite side. If the hoss was . . nervous . . this method was dangerous because it throwed 'im into a panic. If this happened, he'd fight the hobbles, throw 'imself, and be injured.

cross-hobbled ppl adj Also *cross-hoppled* Cf **cross-hobble**
Uneven, twisted, askew.
1951 Johnson *Resp. to PADS 20* **DE,** (*Uneven,* . . *"That house is all _____."*), Cross-hoppled. **1960** *DE Folkl. Bulletin* Oct 36, Cross-hobbled (said of corn twisted by the wind).

cross-horse n Also *cross-saw* Cf **crossbuck 1**
A sawbuck.

1965–67 *DARE* (Qu. L59, *An implement with an X-frame . . to hold firewood for sawing*) Infs FL7, OH20, Cross-horse; FL22, Cross-saw.

crossing light n Also *crosslight*
A traffic signal at a street intersection.
1970 *DARE* (Qu. N9, *The colored lights that control the cars at busy road crossings*) Infs CA23, GA6, LA15, ME5, TX89, WI18, Crossing lights; NY236, Crosslights.

‡**cross, in the** adv phr
1901 *DN* 2.142 **MD,** In the cross . . . Unwillingly. "I did it in the cross."

‡**cross iron** n
An andiron.
1970 *DARE* (Qu. D32, *The metal stands in a fireplace that the logs are laid on*) Inf VA39, Cross irons.

cross-jaw v [*cross* adv, from side to side + *jaw* to talk]
1946 *PADS* 6.10 **eNC,** Cross-jaw. . . To chatter, palaver, clatterwhack. Used mainly in reference to women.

cross-jostle n, v
1899 (1912) Green *VA Folk-Speech,* Cross-jostle . . . A wrangle. To cross-jostle.

crosslight See **crossing light**

cross-lot(s) adv [Abbr for **across lot(s)**] **chiefly NEast** See Map
By a short-cut, directly.
1825 Neal *Brother Jonathan* 1.138 **CT,** They could push on, a pooty, tedious, clever bit furder, cross lots. **1904** Day *Kin o' Ktaadn* 197 **ME,** To walk down 'cross lots to the lake. **1922** Brown *Old Crow* 469 **NEng,** They might even go over to Mountain Brook by the path "cross lots." **1942** Whipple *Joshua* 325 **UT,** Sinners have been sent to hell 'cross-lots before. **1965–70** *DARE* (Qu. MM16, . . *Walking . . to the other corner of a square, . . you want to save steps . . "It'll be shorter if we _____."*) 15 Infs, **NEast,** Cut cross-lot(s); 13 Infs, **NEast,** Go cross-lot(s); CT36, Beat it cross-lots; NH14, Went cross-lots. **1968** *DARE* FW Addit NY73, They went down cross-lots to the train to get the mail.

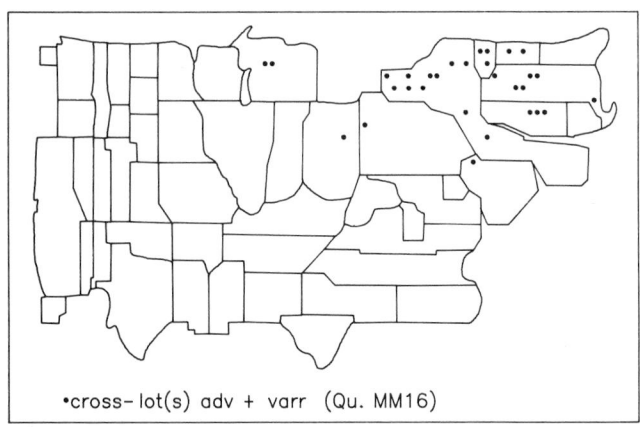

•cross-lot(s) adv + varr (Qu. MM16)

cross lots v phr
To go by the most direct route.
1967–69 *DARE* (Qu. MM16, . . *Walking . . to the other corner of a square, . . you want to save steps . . "It'll be shorter if we _____."*) Infs CT39, MA41, NY35, 69, 201, Cross lots.

cross-mouthed adj
1966 Wilson *Coll.* **csKY,** Cross-mouthed: Having a jaw slanting aside.

cross oak n Cf **cross timbers**
=**post oak.**
1960 Vines *Trees SW* 155, *Q. stellata* . . . Vernacular names are Iron Oak, Cross Oak, . . and Box Oak.

cross-of-Christ door See **cross-and-Bible door**

cross one's track v phr
1905 *DN* 3.7 **cCT,** Cross one's track . . . To oppose one's plans.

cross out v phr See **cross** v 3

cross out n

1 also *cross over:* A bat-and-ball game for a few players. Cf **cat** n **3, cross 3, cross-ball, work-up**

1950 *WELS (Bat-and-ball games for a few players)* 1 Inf, swWI, *Cross out:* throw the ball between the runner and the base to put him out; 1 Inf, scWI, Cross over. **1965–69** *DARE* (Qu. EE11) Infs IL96, MO11, OK6, Cross out. **1966** *DARE* File neIN, *Cross out:* A kind of ball game.

2 Tick-tack-toe. Cf **crosses**

1966 *DARE* (Qu. EE38a, *A game played with pencil and paper where the players try to get three x's or three o's in a row*) Inf WA13, Cross out.

crossover n

1 In railroading: a length of track connecting two main lines, but see quot 1958; in a canal, a connecting channel between two main channels.

1884 *Harper's Mag.* 69.272/2, The incoming trains approach the city on the western track until they reach the "cross-over," which throws them to the eastern track. **1947** Beebe *Mixed Train* 236, Thirsty colored folk and parched but hopeful hillbillies are forever dreaming that one of its cars, awash with barrels of wonderful, expensive bonded whisky, may roll down an embankment or come to grief at the Southern crossover at Georgetown. **1958** McCulloch *Woods Words* **Pacific NW,** *Crossover* . . A switch from one track to another; or a railroad crossing. **1965** Will *Okeechobee Boats* 113 **FL,** Before he'd made many trips Ziegler ripped her [=his boat's] bottom out at the Cross Over up the canal. **1969** *AmSp* 44.255 [Railroad jargon], *Crossover*—Section of track between two main lines with switches at each end, permitting a train to cross from one main line to the other.

2 See **cross out** n 1.

cross over v phr See **cross 5**

cross questions and crooked answers n Also *cross questions, ~ and crazy* (or *silly*) *answers*

A question-and-answer game; see quots.

1899 Champlin *Young Folks' Games,* Cross questions, a game played by any number of persons who sit in a circle. Each puts a question to his right hand neighbor, and receives an answer. Each . . then repeats aloud the question that his left hand neighbor asked . . and the answer that his right hand neighbor gave. **1905** *DN* 3.76 nwAR, *Cross questions and crooked answers* . . . Name of a game. Common. **1941** *Jrl. Amer. Folkl.* 54.69 eTN, "Cross Questions and Crooked Answers" was similar. Each player was provided in advance with a question and with an answer to his partner's question. Each question and answer were repeated three times, the idea being not to laugh at the humorous and sometimes embarrassing incongruities which would develop. **1950** *WELS Suppl.* WI, Cross Questions and Crazy Answers: Two equal rows, a leader for each. One row assigned a question each, the other an answer each by their respective leaders. Then the question and answer opposite each other are matched. The mismatching makes "much glee." **1953** Brewster *Amer. Nonsinging Games* 37 **IA,** *Cross Questions and Silly Answers*—All the players seat themselves in a circle, their chairs close enough together that they can converse with each other in whispers. Each player is asked a question by his neighbor on the left and given an answer to his own question by the player on his right. He must remember both the question and the answer. Then each player in turn is asked to repeat aloud the question and the answer given him by his neighbors. If he fails to give them correctly, he must pay a forfeit. **1966–69** *DARE* (Qu. EE39, *Other games played on paper by two people*) Inf GA80, Cross questions and crooked answers—the answer was written and the question drawn out of a box and then matched; (Qu. EE40, *What table games are played around here, using dice?*) Inf MS15, Cross questions and silly answers. **1967** *DARE* Tape TX36, Cross questions . . . One would give you a question and one on the other side'd give the answers . . . One old boy . . asked a girl if her feet wasn't matched and she told [him] his eyes looked like two fried eggs in a mudhole. Now that was a cross question, you see. That was just plumb silly.

crossrail fence n

1969 *DARE* (Qu. L62, *A fence made of split logs*) Inf GA80, Crossrail fence—logs getting shorter at the top.

cross-saw See **cross-horse**

cross-section n [Blend of *crossroads* and *intersection*]

An intersection.

1967–70 *DARE* (Qu. N32, *A place where roads cross at right angles*) Infs MI85, NJ1, NY236, Cross-section.

cross-set adj

Crisscrossed.

1960 Williams *Walk Egypt* 300 **GA,** The world beyond his animals was cross-set with traps.

cross tag n

A variation of the game of tag in which the player who is "it" must chase whoever moves between himself and the player under pursuit.

1891 *Jrl. Amer. Folkl.* 4.223 **Brooklyn NY,** *Cross Tag.*—The player who is "it" selects one of the others whom he will chase. The pursued is given a short start, and, while both are running, another player will try to cross between them. If successful, he becomes the object of pursuit, and this is continued until one of the players is tagged. He becomes "it," and the game is continued. **1909** (1923) Bancroft *Games* 75, *Cross Tag.* **1953** Brewster *Amer. Nonsinging Games* 66 **IN,** *Cross Tag* . . In the South the game is sometimes known as Turn Tag. **1969** *DARE* (Qu. EE33, . . *Outdoor games* . . *that children play now, or that were played in your childhood*) Inf CT23, Cross tag—if someone cuts between "it" and the guy he's after, the one who cut between has to be chased instead.

cross-talk v

To interrupt a speaker or contradict him before he has finished.

1963 Wright *Lawd Today* 19 **Chicago IL** [Black], Don't cross-talk me, woman!

cross the mark n

A children's game: see quot.

1968 *DARE* (Qu. EE33, *Other outdoor games* . . *that children play now, or that were played in your childhood*) Inf MD33, Cross the mark—also called Prisoner's Base—two teams, each on the opposite side of a line. One team had to cross the line without being tagged by the other team. Tagged people had to stay in prison until another member of their team rescued them by tagging them.

cross-the-road n

1901 *DN* 2.138 seNY, *Cross-the-road* . . . A game, the same as mosey . . and mossy. [*Ibid* 144, *Mossy* . . . The same as pom-pom-pull-away.]

crosstie v

To make railroad ties from.

1962 *Mt. Life* Spring 18 sAppalachians, The ease with which mountain folk convert nouns and adjectives to verbs has long fascinated outsiders . . . He cradles his oats and . . "cross-ties" his white oaks.

cross timbers n

A belt of chiefly oak timberland stretching across grasslands; also the **blackjack oak. TX, OK** *hist*

1820 in 1858 Dewees *Letters TX* 15, I joined a party of about thirty men, who were going up Red river to the Cross Timbers on a buffalo hunt. **1834** Pike *Prose Sketches* 13, These Cross Timbers are a belt of timber, extending from the Canadian . . to an unknown distance south of Red River. The belt is in width from fifteen to fifty miles, composed of black-jack and post oak, with a thick undergrowth of small bushy oak and briers. **1941** FWP *Guide OK* 8, Interesting and important in the history of Oklahoma, is a north- and south-trending strip of rough country known as the Cross Timbers, varying from five to thirty miles in width across the central part of the state. **1945** Mathews *Talking Moon* 22 **OK,** As a matter of fact, they [=blackjacks] go by any number of names, such as scrub-oak, jack-oak, and Cross Timbers.

cross-tracks n

1958 *PADS* 29.32 WI, *Cross-tracks* . . . A marble game played between railroad tracks, in which the marbles are shot at directly.

crosstree n

=**doubletree.**

1966 *DARE* (Qu. L47, *The two movable bars behind a team of horses are fastened to a longer piece; this is a* _____) Inf FL37, Crosstree.

cross up See **cross 1, 2**

cross vine n

1 A woody, evergreen climber (*Bignonia capreolata*). [See quot c1960] Also called **quarter vine, smoke vine, trumpet creeper 2, trumpet flower**

1785 Marshall *Arbustrum* 21, *Bignonia crucigera. Cross-vine.* This rises with slender trailing stalks, which must be supported . . being impatient of much cold. **1908** *DN* 3.303 eAL, wGA, *Cross-vine* . . . A porous vine much used by boys for smoking. **1941** Walker *Lookout* 56 **TN**, Cross-vine thrives at the top of the mountain as well as . . on both sides. **1944** Harper *Weeds AL* 204, In Small's Manual it is made the type of *Bignonia*, a name long used for our well-known native cross-vine. **1946** *PADS* 6.10 **eNC**, Cross-vine . . . A scaly-bark porous vine that twists around trees. Boys cut it into pieces and smoke it. (*Bignonia capreolata*.) . . Perhaps obsolete now. **1954** *Harder Coll.* **cwTN**. **c1960** *Wilson Coll.* **csKY**, Cross-vine . . . *Bignonia capreolata*, a vine with a porous stem and with pith shaped like a cross; dried vines were smoked by boys. **1976** Bailey–Bailey *Hortus Third* 162.

2 A **trumpet creeper 1** (here: *Campsis radicans*).

1900 Lyons *Plant Names* 366, *T. radicans* . . . Cross-vine.

crossway v [Etym uncert: logs were laid across roads to give a firm surface; perh infl also by *causeway*]
To surface a road with logs laid from side to side.

1794 in 1971 Denny *Military Jrl.* 199, Near five miles was cross-way'd, and no road can be had from the lake to French creek with less. **1959** Sanders *Echoes* 10 **swAR** (as of early 1900s), Most of the work consisted of filling up the low places . . and if a place got too bad, they cut pine poles and cross-wayed it.

crossway n
A causeway.

1837 Sherwood *Gaz. GA* 69, Crossway, causeway. **1968** *DARE* Tape **NJ51**, We also call 'em a crossway, but the right name is causeway.

crossways adj Also *crosswise* chiefly **Sth, S Midl**
1 Ill-tempered, cross; in a bad humor.

1906 *DN* 3.132 **nwAR**, Crossways . . . In an ill-humor. "He's all crossways." **c1960** *Wilson Coll.* **csKY**, Crossways or *crosswise* . . . Frustrated, ill-tempered, hard to get along with. **1966** *DARE* (Qu. GG18, . . *Obstinate*) Inf **NC4**, Crossways.

2 In disagreement, at cross purposes. Cf **cross 1**

1965–70 *DARE* (Qu. GG39, *Somebody who seems to be looking for reasons to be angry*) Inf **TX65**, He's crosswise with the world; (Qu. II11b, *If two people can't bear each other at all, "Those two are _____."*) Infs **NM4, TX43**, Crossways; **WY5**, Crosswise; (Qu. KK15, *A disagreement or quarrel: "They had _____ about where the fence was to be."*) Inf **TX1**, Got crossways; (Qu. KK68, *When people don't think alike about something: "We agree on most things, but on politics we're _____."*) Infs **KY84, NM4, TX1, 19**, Crossways; **KY85**, Plumb crossways about it; **GA73**, Crossways.

crossways adv Also *crosswise*
1 In a bad humor.

1927 *Ruppenthal Coll.* **KS**, Crosswise, get up . . . to be ill-humored, esp. in the morning. "Johnny got up crosswise this morning."

2 Disapprovingly.

1956 Gipson *Old Yeller* 55 **TX**, What if he did fall over and yell bloody murder every time I looked crossways at him?

crost adv, prep [Aphet form of *across* + excr *t*] Cf **acrost**
Across.

1904 Day *Kin o' Ktaadn* 55 **ME**, From his shop, clear crost the kitchen, on the cook stove. **1966–68** *DARE* (Qu. MM1, *Words meaning "opposite to"*) Infs **MD5, 20, NY122**, Crost from; (Qu. MM14, . . *"The drugstore is _____ the gas station."*) Inf **MD5**, Crost the street from; (Qu. MM16, . . *"It'll be shorter if we _____."*) Infs **GA28, MA6**, Cut crost; **MD13**, Go crost. **1976** Garber *Mountain-ese* **sAppalachians**, Crost . . across "They live crost the road from us."

crotch n¹ Pronc-spp *cratch, crouch*
A Forms.

1899 (1912) Green *VA Folk-Speech* 132, Cratch . . . Crotch, fork of a tree. **1941** *Sat. Eve. Post* 5 Apr 10/2, "He's comin' along as masket," says Magrew, holdin' the midget in the crouch of his arm like a football.
B Senses.
1 A notch as an **earmark** for cattle.

1653 in 1889 New Plymouth Colony *Records* 1.2, The marke of his Cattle is a croch on the left eare. **1970** *DARE* (Qu. K18, . . *Kind of mark . . used around here to identify a cow*) Inf **TX89**, An earmark is a crotch in the ear.

2 A fork in a road.

1752 in 1893 Duxbury MA *Copy of Rec.* 311, The New Meeting house at the Northerly corner of John Chanlers 2d Homestead by the crotch of the ways, or where the ways do part and meet. **1857** Holland *Bay-path*

265 **NEng**, I'm standing right in the crotch of the roads. **1966** *DARE* (QR, near Qu. N32) Inf **ME5**, Where roads branch, it's the *crotch in the road* and the triangular piece of land is the *flatiron piece*.

3 A sled used in hauling logs; see quot 1968. Cf **go-devil, lizard**

1905 U.S. Forest Serv. *Bulletin* 61.34, Crotch . . . See Dray. *Ibid* 36 **Gt Lakes, NEng**, Dray . . . A single sled used in dragging logs . . . Syn.: . . crotch. **1950** *WELS* (*Different kinds of sleighs*) 1 Inf, **cwWI**, Crotch. **1968** Adams *Western Words* 84, Crotch—A small sled, without a tongue, often made from the natural fork of a tree, with a crosspiece nailed midway through the V and pulled by horses as an aid in skidding logs on stony or bare ground; also called *crazy dray, go-devil*, and *lizard*.

crotch n² See **crutch**

crotch v¹
To notch a log.

1905 U.S. Forest Serv. *Bulletin* 61.34 **Pacific NW**, Crotch . . . To cut notches on opposite sides of a log near the end, into which dogs [q.v.] are fastened.

crotch v² See **crouch**

crotch beetle See **crotch pheasant**

crotch chain n
1 A tackle or hauling apparatus for loading logs.

1905 U.S. Forest Serv. *Bulletin* 61.34, Crotch chain. A tackle for loading logs on sleds, cars, or skidways by cross hauling.

2 Part of the harnessing apparatus for a team of horses.

1966 *DARE* (Qu. L47, *The two movable bars behind a team of horses are fastened to a long piece; this is a _____*) Infs **ME1**, Crotch chain [a V-shaped chain]; **ME9**, Crotch chain, if no pole is used.

crotch harrow n
1909 *DN* 3.410 **nME**, Crotch harrow . . . A light, one-horse harrow made in the shape of a V, and used on new land.

crotch-horn n
1968 *DARE* FW Addit **NY98**, Crotch-horn: a buck with antlers forked only once, making a total of four points. [FW: Everywhere I have been in the South, this is a *forkhorn* or *four-point*.]

crotch line n Cf **crotch chain 1**
In logging: see quot 1967.

1938 (1939) Holbrook *Holy Mackinaw* 260, Crotch line. Device for loading logs onto railroad cars. **1967** *DARE* Tape **WA24**, First they loaded them [=logs] with a crotch line . . . That was on another donkey that had a hook, a big hook on each end . . . They was about six feet long, with them big hooks on them and they'd put that on each end of the log to pick it up. That's the way they loaded them when they first started, and when they got the duplex, they used the duplex instead.

crotch pheasant n Also *crotch beetle*
1967–69 *DARE* (Qu. R25, *Joking names for a head louse, or body louse*) Infs **IL26, PA223**, Crotch pheasant; **PA3**, Crotch beetle.

croton bug n Also *croton-water bug, kroton* [See quot 1980]
The German cockroach (*Blatella germanica*).

1857 T. B. Gunn *N.Y. Boarding-houses* 53 (DA), The buckwheat cakes . . . sometimes had insects (known as Croton-water bugs) in them. **1876** *Billings' Farmer's Allminax* 12 (DA), Thare is only one sure way to git the krotons out ov a house, burn up the house. **1907** Hodge *Hdbk. Amer. Indians* 1.367/1, Croton-bug. The water cockroach (Blatta germanica), from Croton, the name of a river in Westchester co., N.Y. **1980** Milne *Audubon Field Guide Insects* 124, Its common name "Croton Bug" derives from the fact that the insect first became a household pest in 1890, when water from the Croton Reservoir began augmenting New York City's municipal supply.

crouch v Usu |ˈkrauč|; occas |krač| Pronc-spp *cooch, crooch, crotch, cruh-ooch*
Std senses, var forms.

1914 *DN* 4.104 **KS**, Crocht [kračt] . . . Crouched. **1927** Shewmake *Engl. Pronc. VA* 42, Crouched. Cruh-ooched is the typical Virginia pronunciation. **1941** *Sat. Eve. Post* 5 Apr 114/1, He crotches down in what was prob'ly the most fearsome stanch in organized ball. *Ibid* 114/4, Even in a crotchin' position, the ketcher towers over the midget. **1943** *LANE* Map 581 (*Crouch*), The map shows the expressions *crouch (down), crooch (down)* . . . usually meaning 'crouch down out of sight . . .', especially as used by children when playing hide-and-seek . . . *crooch*, 'a man's word' . . *cooch* . . [down], 'a girl's word.' **1968** *DARE* (Qu. Y32,

. . *"If you're going to fit in there you'll have to _____."*) Inf **WI**70, Crotch [krač].

crounar See **crowner** n[2]

croup n Pronc-sp *crowp*
Std sense, var form.
1887 *Scribner's Mag.* 2.474/2 **AR** [Black], "An' now de onlies' chile she got dyin' of [sic]. Was hit sick long, sah?" "On'y two days. 'T hed crowp."

crouper bush n Also *crouper brush* [Prob ref to use of the root against "lung diseases," as croup]
=**buttonbush 1.**
1894 *Jrl. Amer. Folkl.* 7.90, *Cephalanthus occidentalis . .* crouper-bush. Ferrisburgh, Vt. **1960** Vines *Trees SW* 938, Vernacular names for this shrub are Spanish Pincushion . . and Crouper-brush.

croup kettle n
See quot 1884.
1884 Knight *New Mech. Dict., Croup kettle,* a small kettle and alcohol lamp for quickly raising a steam for inhalation in cases of croup. **1889** Twain *CT Yankee* 516, I rousted out the croup-kettle myself; for I don't sit down and wait for doctors. **1966** *DARE* (Qu. BB50b, *Remedies for chest colds*) Infs **MS**33, 51, Croup kettle.

croup string n
1984 *DARE* File **cUT** (as of 1917), Wear a black velvet ribbon (a croup string) around your neck to prevent getting the croup.

croupweed n Cf **coughweed 2**
=**horehound.**
1951 *PADS* 15.40 **TX,** *Marrubium vulgare . .* croup weed.

crouse around v phr
1952 Brown *NC Folkl.* 1.531, *Crouse around . . .* To walk stealthily.

crow n[1]
1 A Black person. Cf *cro* at **Croatan;** see also **Jim Crow**
1823 Cooper *Pioneers* 1.249, Shut your oven, you crow! Where is the man that can hit a turkey's head at a hundred yards? **1924** *Amer. Mercury* 1.130/2, I wish I was black like you . . . No you don't. Dey'd call you Crow, den—or Chocolate—or Smoke. **1965–70** *DARE* (Qu. HH28, . . *Nicknames . . for people of foreign background . . Negro*) Infs **CA**66, **PA**76, 94, 167, **RI**6, **SC**21, 26, Crow; **LA**20, **SC**7, Black crow.
2 See quots.
1930 Shoemaker *1300 Words* 13 **cPA Mts** (as of c1900), *Crow*—A rather attractive girl. **1968** *DARE* (Qu. HH34, *General words . . for a woman, not necessarily uncomplimentary*) Inf **NY**87, Crow.

crow n[2] [Back-formation from *croze,* taken as pl]
1899 (1912) Green *VA Folk-Speech* 136, *Crow . . .* Groove in the head of a barrel into which the head is fitted. **1968** *DARE* FW Addit **swVA,** Crow cutter—A cooper's tool that makes a groove on the top of a barrel for the lid.

crow n[3] Cf **crocus** n[1] **2a**
=**pasqueflower.**
1968 *DARE* (Qu. S23, *Pale blue flowers with downy leaves and cups that come up on open, stony hillsides in March or early April*) Inf **MN**42, Crows.

crow intj [Euphem for *Christ*]
1965–70 *DARE* (Qu. NN29c, *Exclamations beginning with "holy"*) 10 Infs, **chiefly east of Missip R,** Crow; (Qu. NN30, *Exclamations beginning with the sound of "J"*) Inf **VT**16, Jeezum Crow; (Qu. NN31, *Exclamations beginning with the sound of "cr-"*) Inf **MA**71, For crow mike.

crow and chicken n
1905 *DN* 3.76 **nwAR,** *Crow and chicken . . .* The name of a children's out-door game. Cf. 'cat and mouse' and 'kitten and mouse.'

crowbait n, also attrib Also *crow feed* [See quot c1960] **chiefly Nth, N Midl, West** See Map Cf **fox bait**
An emaciated, worn-out horse or cow; by ext, a worthless person.
1851 Kelly *Excursion* 2.98, I hired a mule of a most Rozenantish pattern from one of the traders, such an animal as is called a "Crowbait" in Yankeeland. **1898** Westcott *Harum* 228 **nNY,** Oh, yes, it was the first hoss I ever owned. I give fifteen dollars for him . . . Crowbait wa'n't no name fer him. **1905** *DN* 3.76 **nwAR,** *Crow-bait.* **1907** White *AZ Nights*

34, Texas Pete had bored one of them poor old crowbait hosses plumb through the head. **1912** *DN* 3.574 **wIN,** Crow-bait. **1928** Ruppenthal *Coll.* **KS,** Crowbait. **1928** *AmSp* 4.129 **NE,** Crowbait. **1944** *PADS* 2.55 **cnMO,** Crow-bait. **1949** *PADS* 11.20 **CO,** *Crow bait . . .* A worthless horse . . . A worthless person; an ugly, repulsive person. **1958** *AmSp* 33.269 **eWA,** Crowbait. **c1960** *Wilson Coll.* **csKY,** Crowbait . . . A sorry old horse or cow, probably about ready to die and become food for crows. **1963** Burroughs *Head-First* 173 **CO,** She was built more like a crow-bait mare than a cow. **1965–70** *DARE* (Qu. K44, *A bony or poor-looking horse*) 92 Infs, **widespread, but esp Nth, N Midl, West,** Crowbait; **NY**9, Crow feed; **CA**87, Old crowbait; **MI**116, Piece of crowbait; (Qu. K15, *A thin, bony, or poor-looking cow*) 48 Infs, **Nth, N Midl, NW,** Crowbait; (Qu. HH40, *Uncomplimentary words for an old man*) Inf **CA**158, Crowbait. **1983** *DARE* File **nwNJ,** Father never kept crowbait. He always had good horses.

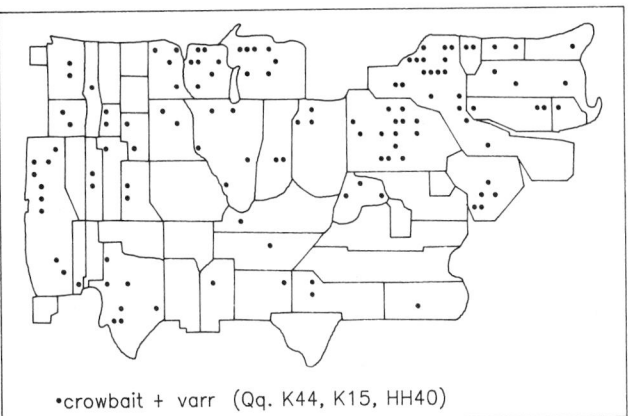

•crowbait + varr (Qq. K44, K15, HH40)

crowbar hotel n *joc*
1968–70 *DARE* (Qu. V11, . . *A county or city jail*) Infs **CA**210, **NY**92, 224, **PA**104, **VT**8, Crowbar hotel.

crowberry n
1 A low shrub of the genus *Empetrum,* esp *E. nigrum* which is also called **curlewberry, hog cranberry, mossberry, pigeonberry, squirt plum.**
1806 (1808) Gass *Jrl.* 309 **NW,** [Footnote:] The herbage had scarce begun to spring, and the crowberry bushes were just beginning to blossom. **1938** FWP *Guide MN* 282, The crowberry grows in rocky places on the island. **1955** U.S. Arctic Info. Center *Gloss., Crowberry . . .* Also called 'curlewberry,' 'black crowberry,' 'blackberry.' **1961** Douglas *My Wilderness* 217 **NH,** At times the crowberry, mountain cranberry, and billberry take possession. I was to learn on later trips that this austere and wind-blown slope can produce an arctic garden that is bright and gay. **1977** *New Yorker* 9 May 94/1 **AK,** The trails would go along, well cut and stamped out through moss campion, reindeer moss, sedge tussocks, crowberries . . ; then, abruptly, . . the trails would disappear.
2 A bearberry 2 (here: *Arctostaphylos uva-ursi*).
1892 *Jrl. Amer. Folkl.* 5.99, *Arctostaphylos uva-ursi,* crowberry. **1930** U.S. Dept. Ag. *Misc. Pub.* 77.10, *Bearberry . . . Other common names . . .* Crowberry. **1974** (1977) Coon *Useful Plants* 133, Crowberry . . . As a food plant, the lovely red berries are listed in some books as being edible when cooked.

crow-biddy n [*crow* the cry of a rooster + **biddy** n[1] **1;** *EDD* "gen. used by children"]
1907 *DN* 3.185 **seNH,** *Crow-biddy . . .* Children's language. A rooster.

crowbill n **Mid Atl**
=**coot** n[1] **1.**
1888 Trumbull *Names of Birds* 118, [*Fulica americana*] At Baltimore, Md., Crow-bill. **1949** Sprunt–Chamberlain *SC Bird Life* 206, *American coot:* Fulica americana americana . . . Local Names: . . . Crowbill. **1950** *PADS* 14.24 **SC,** Crowbill . . . The American coot. **1968** *DARE* (Qu. Q5, . . *Kinds of wild duck . . around here*) Inf **MD**42, Crowbill.

crow blackbird n Also *crowblack, crow-billed blackbird*
Usu the **purple grackle** (and its races), but also the **boat-tailed grackle.**

1778 Carver *Travels N. Amer.* 473, The crow blackbird . . is quite black, and of the same size and shape of those in Europe. **1825** Bonaparte *Amer. Ornith.* 1.42, Female Common Crow-Blackbird. *Quiscalus Versicolor.* **1899** (1912) Green *VA Folk-Speech* 136, Crow-blackbird . . . A large black bird. **1917** *DN* 4.423, Boat-tailed grackle . . . Crow Black-bird. **1947** *Collier's* 29 Mar 92/2, There is the purple grackle which is most frequently known as the blackbird or as the crow blackbird, the marsh blackbird, and the red-winged blackbird. **1955** *AmSp* 30.181, Crow blackbird (the purple grackle, generally) and the great grackle (Fla., La.). **1955** Forbush–May *Birds* 474, Purple Grackle . . . Other names: Crow Blackbird, Crow-billed Blackbird . . . Bronzed Grackle . . . Other names: Crow Blackbird, Crow-billed Blackbird . . . The three races of *Quiscalus quiscula* found in eastern North America are . . alike in habits and haunts. **1965–70** *DARE* (Qu. Q11, . . Kinds of blackbirds . . around here) 12 Infs, **chiefly C Atl, Nth,** Crow blackbird; **RI4,** Crow-black, larger than a regular blackbird.

crowbones n

=**crowbait.**

1968 *DARE* (Qu. K15, A thin, bony, or poor-looking cow) Inf **CT**17, Old crowbones; (Qu. K44, A bony or poor-looking horse) Inf **CT**17, Crow-bones.

crow cord n

1931–33 *LANE Worksheets* **cwCT,** Crow cord: Wrapping twine stretched on poles to keep the crows away from the corn.

crow corn n [See quot 1889]

A **colicroot 2** (here: *Aletris farinosa*).

1876 Hobbs *Bot. Hdbk.* 28, Crow corn . . . Aletris farinosa. **1889** *Century Dict.,* Crow-corn . . . The colic-root, *Aletris farinosa,* the white mealy flowers of which somewhat resemble kernels of grain. **1930** Sievers *Amer. Med. Plants* 4. **1971** Krochmal *Appalachia Med. Plants* 40, Aletris farinosa . . . Common Names: . . crow corn.

crow-crackling n [*crow* the mesentery of an animal + **crackling**]

1899 (1912) Green *VA Folk-Speech* 136, Crow-cracklings are the brown, crisp pieces left after drying out the lard from the fat of the mesentery, or "gut-fat."

crow cress n

A **cress** (here: *Lepidium campestre*).

1931 Harned *Wild Flowers Alleghanies* 200, Crow Cress (*Lepidium campestre* . .).

crowd v

1 To embarrass financially; to press to pay a debt.

1775 in 1889 *NH Hist. Soc. Coll.* 9.88, I have Several Debts that crowd much. **1776** *Ibid* 97, I am crowded for money beyond what I can well discribe [sic]. **1853** in 1912 Thornton *Amer. Gloss.* 1.227, [I have never] distressed a man for what he owes me, or *crowded* any person in the least. **1928** Ruppenthal *Coll.* **KS,** Crowd, . . to urge strongly and persistently upon one, as: to crowd him to pay his debts.

2 To rush or hurry (someone).

1838 *Knickerbocker* 12.506 **GA,** Well, children, don't *crowd* the old man so; give him time. **1876** Twain *Tom Sawyer* 34 **MO,** There was a gate, but as a general thing he was too crowded for time to make use of it. **1951** *PADS* 15.66 **NH,** Crowd . . . Hurry. "Don't crowd me!" **c1960** Wilson *Coll.* **csKY,** Crowd . . . Hurry, rush, push. **c1965** *DARE* FW Addit **cwTN,** Crowd . . . rush, hurry (someone). "Don't crowd me." **1968–69** *DARE* (Qu. A21, When someone is in too much of a hurry . . "Now just slow down! Don't _____.") Inf **CA**160, Crowd me.

3 To pursue closely.

c1871 Twain *Screamers* 131, A beaver can't climb a tree? By gosh, he *had* to climb a tree, the dog was a crowdin' him so! **1924** Mulford *Rustlers' Valley* 107 (*DAE*), Matt rolled down the slope of a ravine . . . . Milt crowded him. **1950** Stuart *Hie Hunters* 36 **eKY,** Then they heard Shooting Star barking every breath on a warm track. "He's crowdin' somethin'," Sparkie shouted. "Be ready any time to hear him tree."

4 To put pressure on.

1874 Taylor *World on Wheels* 1.124, We are apt to crowd the rhetoric sometimes, and say that railroads have taken America. **1950** Stuart *Hie Hunters* 57 **eKY,** Don't push the crosscut fornenst the tree. Don't try to crowd it. It'll eat into the wood fast enough. **1961** Adams *Old-Time Cowhand* 7, This short trot was a natural gait for the cow hoss, and he'd maintain it for a long time if not crowded too hard. **1966–70** *DARE* (Qu. Y6, . . To put pressure on somebody to do something he ought to have done but hasn't: He's a whole week late. I'm going to _____.")

Infs **CT**36, **NY**68, Crowd him; (Qu. Y5, . . To urge somebody to do something he shouldn't: "Johnny wouldn't have tried that if the other boys hadn't _____.") Inf **NY**75, Crowded him.

5 See quot. (Cf *cram* in same sense)

1969–70 *DARE* (Qu. JJ8, To study very hard the last minute before an exam) Inf **PA**230, Crowd it all in; **VA**46, Crowding.

crowdad n Also *crowdab, crow pappy*

=**crawdad** n **1.**

1923 *DN* 5.204 **swMO,** Craw dad . . . Cray fish. Also *Craw dab, Craw pappy, Crow dab, Crow dad* and *Crow pappy.*

crowder n Also *crowder bean, ~ pea* **chiefly Sth, S Midl**

A **black-eyed pea** or any other bean or pea in which the seeds fit tightly against each other in the pod.

1787 (1925) Washington *Diaries* 3.161 **VA,** Sorts of Seeds . . . Crowder. **1797** Imlay *Western Terr.* 240, The white crowder, and many others, are undoubtedly at least as good [as the European]. **1855** Davis *Farm Book* 188 **AL** (*DA*), First next the ditch are the Harper peas to a peach tree and then come the gray crowder or poor mans pea. *Ibid,* The peas here are the Mountain crowder—2d the white crowder and then the gray crowder. **1859** Taliaferro *Fisher's R.* 143 **nwNC** (as of 1820s), To make a bully crap o' Crowders and all other sorts o' peas uver hearn on, I pitched them in the best spot uv the little bit uv yeth [=earth]. **1899** (1912) Green *VA Folk-Speech,* Crowder . . . A kind of pea; many in the hull. **1949** *Natl. Geog. Mag.* 96.211/1 **Sth,** Present varieties called "crowders," as Brown Crowder, Cream Crowder. **1965–70** *DARE* (Qu. I20, Other kinds of beans . . grown around here) 27 Infs, **chiefly Sth,** Crowder peas; **NJ**39, **VA**46, Crowder beans; **GA**81, **TN**24, Purple crowder peas; **OK**18, **TN**52, Yellow crowder peas; **GA**9, Brown crowder peas, purple-hull crowder peas, spotted crowder peas; **TN**24, White crowder beans; **GA**16, Crowders, **NC**81, Black (brown *or* gray) crowder beans; (Qu. I19, Small white beans with a black spot) Infs **AR**17, **IL**117, **OK**1, 51, **SC**11, **TN**4, Crowder peas; **IL**117, **LA**15, Black-eyed crowder peas; **VA**24, Gray crowder; **MS**1, White crowder peas; (Qu. I4, . . Vegetables . . less commonly grown around here) Inf **GA**13, Crowders; **VA**78, Sugar crowder; (Qu. I17, Beans . . that are dark red when they are dry) Infs **GA**90, 92, **OK**3, Crowder; (Qu. I18, The smaller beans that are white when . . dry) Infs **GA**9, **KY**85, White crowder peas. **1970** *DARE* FW Addit **KY**85, Crowder peas: white—a variety of field peas not usually grown in the garden; used for pea hay, though also used for human consumption; old-fashioned; **cwTN,** Brown crowder—a kind of bean of somewhat squashed shape from crowding together in the pod—dark brown. **1972** Hilliard *Hog Meat* 275, There were several varieties of peas grown in the southeastern states. Known locally by such names as "crowders," or "blackeyes," they were much more commonly grown than green peas or any of the beans. The species was *Vigna sinensis.*

crowding pen n

A small enclosure used to concentrate cattle closely together in the process of branding them.

1933 (1950) Allen *Cowboy Lore,* Crowding pen, Small pen where stock are crowded at branding time. **1968** Adams *Western Words* 84, Crowding pen—A small corral used for branding grown cattle.

crowd the mourners v phr

1 To add to someone's embarrassment or discomfiture.

1842 *Spirit of the Times* 12.426 (*OEDS*), In the second mile, however, Fashion commenced 'crowding the mourners' by brushing down both straight sides. **1868** U.S. Congress *Congressional Globe* 19 Feb 1263/3 **MI,** It is true that I voted money . . to raise the means of supporting rebel prisoners captured by our arms . . . Will that Senator tell me . . that my act in doing this office of humanity . . is just as guilty as the conduct of Thomas in giving his son $100 to enable him to join the rebel ranks . . ? Sir, this is "crowding the mourners." **1905** *DN* 3.14 **cCT,** In the expression 'crowding the *mourners*,' i.e. putting some further embarrassment upon a person already laboring under difficulties.

2 To act in haste, to be precipitate.

1912 *DN* 3.574 **wIN,** Crowd the mourners . . . To be in a hurry. Used only in the expression, "Don't crowd the mourners." **1914** *DN* 4.104 **KS,** Crowd the mourners . . . To be premature or forward. **1923** *DN* 5.205 **swMO,** Crowd the mourners . . . To be in a hurry, premature. "Keep ca'm now, an' don't crowd the mourners," i.e., don't be precipitate. **1936** *AmSp* 11.314 **Ozarks.**

crow duck n [See quots]

1 A **cormorant,** esp the **double-crested cormorant. chiefly NEast, Gt Lakes**

[**1792** in 1934 Hearne *Jrls. Hearne Turnor* 476 **Canada,** This day we took some eggs of the Crow duck its a large black kind of duck with a beak like a crow and lives upon fish.] **1898** (1900) Davie *Nests N. Amer. Birds* 66, In Eastern North America the Double-crested Cormorant or "Crow Duck" is a common species. **1951** Pough *Audubon Water Bird* 325, Crow-duck. *See* Cormorants and Coot. **1955** *MA Audubon* 39.311, *European Cormorant.* Crow-duck (Maine. From its black color and resemblance to a duck in shape.). **1955** *AmSp* 30.180, In a good many . . bird names, the object has been to indicate color. Thus *crow duck* (double-crested cormorant, Lake Huron, Wis., Man., Minn. . .) describes black or blackish birds.

2 A coot n¹ 1 (here: *Fulica americana*). **esp C Atl**

1888 Trumbull *Names of Birds* 118, *[Coot]* In New Jersey at Manasquan, Barnegat, and Tuckerton, Washington, D.C., Alexandria, Va., and Crisfield, Md., *Crow-duck.* **1925** (1928) Forbush *Birds MA* 1.369, *Fúlica americána* . . . Coot. Other names . . . Crow duck. **1955** *AmSp* 30.180, *Crow duck* (. . common coot, N.J., Md., D.C., Va. . .) describes black or blackish birds. **1970** *DARE* (Qu. Q9, *The bird that looks like a small, dull-colored duck and is commonly found on ponds and lakes*) Inf **VA**75, Crow duck.

3 Brünnich's murre.

1955 *AmSp* 30.180, *Crow duck* (. . thick-billed murre, Conn.) describes black or blackish birds. **1956** *MA Audubon* 40.80, *Bruennich's Murre.* Crow Duck (Conn. "Crow" from its color and shape of bill; "duck" from its general resemblance to a bird of that group.).

crowdweed n

A **cress** (here: *Lepidium campestre*).

1893 *Jrl. Amer. Folkl.* 6.137, *Brassica sinapistrum,* crowd-weed . . . West Va.

crower n *euphem*

A rooster, cock.

1891 (1967) Freeman *New Engl. Nun* 221, Well, old Eph he jest goes out in the yard, an' he ketches a nice fat crower, an' he kills him, an' picks him. **1923** *DN* 5.205 **swMO** *Crower* . . . A rooster, a cock. **1931** Randolph *Ozarks* 80, The male fowl is usually called a crower—the word cock is altogether impossible, since it is used to designate the genitals. **1953** Piercy *Shaker Cook Book* 100 (as of c1871), All young crowers should be gotten ready for the pot, sold or exchanged for several roosters of some good outside flock.

crow feed See **crowbait**

crow flower n

=**crocus** n¹ 1.

1954 *Harder Coll.* **cwTN,** *Crow flower* . . . Crocus.

crowfoot n Also *crow's-foot*

1 Any of numerous plants of the family Ranunculaceae with leaves shaped somewhat like a bird's foot as:

a =**buttercup 1.** [*OED* c1440 →]

1784 in 1785 *Amer. Acad. Arts & Sci. Memoirs* 1.458, *Ranunculus . . .* Crowfoot, Buttercup. **1967** *DARE* Wildfl QR Pl.79a Inf **OH**37, Crowfoot.

b An anemone, such as the **Canada anemone** or a **pasqueflower.**

1896 *Jrl. Amer. Folkl.* 9.179, *Anemone Pennsylvanica* . . crowfoot, Burnside, S. Dak. **1900** Lyons *Plant Names* 34, *A. Canadensis* . . . White-flowered . . Crowfoot . . . *A. nemorosa* . . . Wood Crowfoot. **1968** *DARE* (Qu. S23, *Pale blue flowers with downy leaves and cups that come up on open stony hillsides in March or early April*) Inf **OH**49, Crow's-feet.

c =**marsh marigold.**

1896 *Jrl. Amer. Folkl.* 9.179, *Caltha palustris* . . . Crowfoot, South Berwick, Me. **1900** Lyons *Plant Names* 77, *C[altha] palustris* . . . Crowfoot. **1959** Carleton *Index Herb. Plants* 33, Crow-foot: *Caltha palustris.* **1966–69** *DARE* (Qu. I28a, . . *Things . . you call greens . . eaten raw*) Infs **KY**66, **NC**84, Crow's-foot; (Qu. I28b, . . *Greens that are cooked*) Infs **KY**28, 40, 44, Crow's-foot. **1968–69** *DARE* Tape **IN**14, Crow's-foot is about the first flower that comes up in the hills and blooms; **KY**50, Crow's-foot was one of the earliest [plants] . . it's real flat and it's got fancy-like leaves [and is used for greens]; **IN**32, Crowfoot.

d A globeflower (here: *Trollius laxus*).

1967 *DARE* Wildfl QR Pl.61 Inf **MI**57, Crowfoot.

2 also *crowfoot geranium:* =**spotted geranium.** Cf *OED* crowfoot 2a

1822 Eaton *Botany* 289, *Geranium . . . maculatum* (crowfoot geranium . .). The root is a powerful astringent. **1828** Rafinesque *Med. Flora* 215, *Geranium maculatum* . . . *Vulgar Names*—Crowfoot, Alum-root, . . Storkbill. **1900** Lyons *Plant Names* 172, *G. maculatum* . . . Crowfoot. **1930** U.S. Dept. Ag. *Misc. Pub.* 77.62, *Wild Geranium . . . Other common names . . .* Crowfoot. **1974** (1977) Coon *Useful Plants* 144, Crowfoot.

3 also *crowfoot grass:* Any of var grasses, as **Dallis grass, goose grass** (here: *Eleusine* spp), or a mat-forming grass *(Dactyloctenium aegyptium)* common in the South.

1855 Simms *Forayers* 515 **SC,** The green bosom of their mother earth—at this season covered with . . crab-grass and crowfoot, to say nothing of . . a pretty variety of wild flowers. **1889** Vasey *Ag. Grasses* 58, Two species of grass [of the genus *Eleusine*] in the Southern States have received the name of crow-foot. **1926** *Torreya* 26.4, *Paspalum dilatatum* . . . Crow-foot, Morton, Miss. **1933** Small *Manual SE Flora* 118, *D[actyloctenium] ægyptium* . . Crowfoot-grass. **1965–70** *DARE* (Qu. S9, *Other kinds of grass . . hard to get rid of*) Infs **AR**52, **GA**84, **IN**83, **KY**49, 53, 75A, **MS**82, **TX**38, **VA**105, Crowfoot grass; **GA**80, **IA**8, Crow's-foot; (Qu. S8, *A common kind of wild grass that grows in fields: it spreads by . . long underground roots*) Inf **GA**77, Crowfoot grass; **MD**29, Crow's-foot; (Qu. S21, . . *Other weeds . . that are a trouble in gardens and fields*) Inf **GA**7, Crowfoot grass; (Qu. L9a, . . *Kinds of grass . . grown for hay*) Inf **GA**33, Crowfoot grass. **1970** Correll *Plants TX* 236, *Dactyloctenium aegyptium* . . . Crowfoot.

4 A ground pine.

1892 *Jrl. Amer. Folkl.* 5.105, *Lycopodium dendroideum* . . crowfoot. Chestertown, Md. **1900** Lyons *Plant Names* 233, *L. complanatum* . . . Crow-foot . . . *L. obscurum* . . . Crow-foot. **1968** *DARE* (Qu. T5, . . *Kinds of evergreens, other than pine, . . around here*) Inf **NJ**21, Ground pine or crow's-foot.

5 also *crowtoes:* A toothwort (here: *Dentaria laciniata*).

1893 *Jrl. Amer. Folkl.* 6.137, *Dentaria laciniata,* crow's foot. Anderson, Ind. **1896** *Jrl. Amer. Folkl.* 9.181, *Dentaria laciniata* . . crow-toes, Sulphur Grove, Ohio. **1967** *DARE* Wildfl QR Pl.81a Inf **OH**14, Crowfoot.

6 See **crowfoot violet.**

7 See quot.

1940–41 Cassidy *WI Atlas* **cWI,** *Crowfoot:* One of the grooves cut in a nether millstone, deeper toward the center and spreading toward the edges—grooves called crowfoots.

8 See quot.

1908 *DN* 3.303 **eAL, wGA,** *Crow's-foot* . . . A form made on the fingers with a string.

9 See quot.

1941 FWP *Guide WI* 482, All summer, men in hip boots, using long rakes called "crow's feet," take clams from the Wolf and its tributaries.

10 A type of cattle brand.

1967 *DARE* (Qu. K18, . . *Kind of mark . . used . . to identify a cow*) Inf **LA**3, Crowfoot.

11 See quot.

1968 *DARE* (Qu. W42a, . . *Nicknames . . for men's sharp-pointed shoes*) Inf **PA**142, Crow's-feet.

12 A crowbar.

1968–69 *DARE* (Qu. L39, *An iron bar with a bent end, used for pulling nails, opening boxes, and so on*) Infs **MD**26, **PA**207, Crowfoot.

crowfoot blackbird n Cf **crow blackbird**

Prob =**boat-tailed grackle.**

1968 *DARE* (Qu. Q11, . . *Kinds of blackbirds*) Inf **NY**71, Crowfoot blackbird or spackle—they got quite a fantail onto 'em. [FW: this is the grackle.]

crowfooted adj

Tangled.

1935 Davis *Honey* 118 **OR,** It left the girl to manage the loose horses alone . . . They were still roped head to tail, and the smell of feed . . made them all try to get through the gate at once. The opening couldn't be expanded . . so they jammed up in it with their ropes crossed and crowfooted so they couldn't get loose.

crowfoot geranium See **crowfoot 2**

crowfoot grass See **crowfoot 3**

crowfoot lily n
Prob a **crow poison.**

1967 *DARE* (Qu. S26e, *Other wildflowers*) Inf **SC**31, Crowfoot lily—white flower—poison.

crowfoot violet n Also *crowfoot, crow's-foot (violet)*
=**bird's foot violet 1.**

1892 *Jrl. Amer. Folkl.* 5.92, *Viola pedata* . . . Crowfoot violet. New England. **1933** Small *Manual SE Flora* 886, *V[iola] pedata* . . Crowfoot-violet. **1942** Weygandt *Plenty* 270, I think of the pike-side over the Welsh Mountain blue with crowfoot violets. **1965–70** *DARE* (Qu. S3, *A flower like a large violet with a yellow center and small ragged leaves*) 46 Infs, **scattered, but chiefly east of Missip R,** Crowfoot violet; **CT**11, **KY**11, **NC**49, **PA**89, **VA**11, 96, Crowfoot; **KY**42A, 43, 47, **MI**108, **OH**16, 37, Crow's-foot; **VA**2, Crow's-foot violet; (Qu. S11, . . *Other names . . for . . blue violet*) Inf **RI**17, Crowfoot; (Qu. S26d, *Wildflowers that grow in meadows*) Inf **KY**82, Crowfoot.

crow hobble n Also called **Scotch hobble**
A rope shackle contrived to prevent a horse from kicking by suspending the back foot.

1961 Adams *Old-Time Cowhand* 132, This hobble [the "Scotch hobble"] was used to keep a hoss still while sackin' 'im out, gettin' 'im used to throwin' the saddle on, and other breakin' maneuvers. It's called a "Crow hobble" in the Northwest.

crowhop v [From the awkward vertical jumps of a crow]
1 To back out (of an agreement, commitment, etc); to **crawfish** v **2.**

1897 *Chicago Tribune* (IL) 25 July 15/2, Crow Hop to 'crawfish'—'Leedy has crow hopped out of the special session of the Legislature.' **1897** *KS Univ. Qrly.* 6.86, Crow-hop,: To 'crawfish,' to back out.

2 Of a horse: to buck mildly; see quots. **West**
1935 Davis *Honey* 24 **OR,** The horses were forehobbled and easy to catch, and Simmons had . . the canvas *alforjas* packed by the time they came crow-hopping in. **1937** Sandoz *Slogum* 9 **NE** (as of 1900–20), Sidesaddles were so dangerous on these wild Western horses, she sometimes said as she saw them go, the well-fed young colts crow-hopping a little, fine necks bowed. **1939** FWP *ID Lore* 244, The old bronc might crow hop (jump in a straight line) or unwind (twist and turn). **1939** FWP *Guide MT* 414, Crow hop—Straight jump made by a bucking horse, especially in leaving the chute (at a rodeo). **1941** FWP *Guide WY* 461. **1949** *PADS* 11.20 **CO.** **1962** Atwood *Vocab.* **TX** 56, When a bronc wants to dislodge the rider, he is usually said to *pitch* . . or to *buck* . . . Only an occasional informant speaks specifically of *goating, crow-hopping, sunfishing,* and so on—terms that are probably familiar in rodeo circles.

3 In athletic competition: see quots.
1906 *DN* 3.132 **nwAR,** Crow-hop . . . To take a short step after leaving one's position and before making the full leap in jumping. "Get back there, you crowhopped." **1916** *DN* 4.268 **New Orleans LA,** Crow hop . . . To step over the starting mark in a standing broad jump. "He crowhopped on the jump." **1927** *AmSp* 2.351 **WV,** Crowhop . . . to take an unfair advantage in the start of any sort of athletic contest. "He crowhopped on the other men, and the judges set him back three feet." **1949** *PADS* 11.20 **CO,** Crow hop . . . To fudge in a game, esp. to get across the line set for a race before the race begins.

4 See quot. Cf **crowhop** n **2**
1949 *PADS* 11.20 **CO,** Crow hop . . . To go to a barn dance.

5 To move lamely, to limp.
1965–70 *DARE* (Qu. BB1, *When a person has been injured so that when he walks he steps more heavily on one foot than the other,* "He _____.") Infs **GA**74, 77, **FL**22, **NC**82, **WV**16, Is crowhopping; **AR**55, Crowhops.

crowhop n
1 Of a horse: a short leap with arched back; mild bucking. **West** Cf **crowhop** v **2**
1903 *Wide World Magazine* 548 *(DA),* The ways they try to throw their riders may be classed under three heads. The first is known as the crow-hop. **1933** (1950) Allen *Cowboy Lore* 58, Crow-hops, A term applied in contempt to mild bucking motions. **1939** Wellman *Trampling Herd* 238 **West,** When the man assigned to carry the bucket mounted his horse, that animal . . objected . . . About the second crow-hop every drop of hard-won milk was spattered over the prairie.

2 A kind of barn dance; see quots.

1949 *PADS* 11.20 **CO,** Crow hop . . . A barn dance, a type of jerky dancing or Dutch hop, a square dance. **c1960** *Wilson Coll.* **csKY,** Crow-hop . . . A sort of corny, humorous, barn dance, usually a solo.

3 In marble play: see quot. Cf **crowhop** v **3**
1963 *KY Folkl. Rec.* 9.64 **neKY,** *Trying to get closer shot by placing the hand in a position nearer to the marble being shot at:* . . Crow-hops.

4 See quot. Cf **crow's fly**
1969 *DARE* (Qu. MM24, . . *A short distance*) Inf **GA**72, Crowhop.

crow-jack n [*crow* + *jack* something like, but smaller than, the thing to which it is likened]
=**boat-tailed grackle.**

1917 *DN* 4.423, Boat-tailed grackle . . . Crow-jack. **1968** *DARE* (Qu. Q11, . . *Kinds of blackbirds . . around here*) Inf **DE**4, Crow-jacks—like a little crow. [FW: a grackle]

crown v

1 Of a forest fire: to burn in the tops of the trees. Cf **cover** C2, **crown fire**
1916 *Outing* 67.406/2, Burning rapidly up hill in the dry ground cover and windfalls, the fire was threatening every minute to crown. **1938** [see **crown fire**]. **1947** *Time* 3 Nov 26/1, The fire crowned into the tops of trees and leaped forward "as fast as a race horse could run." **1976** Maclean *River Runs Through* 140 **wMT** (as of 1919), For a lot of years a prospective ranger taking his exam had said the last word on crown fires . . . When asked on his examination, "What do you do when a fire crowns?" he had answered, "Get out of the way and pray like hell for rain."

2 In tobacco farming: see quot.
1967 Key *Tobacco Vocab.* 21 **MD,** Crown—To hang tobacco on the comb rails. "We crown the top of the barn first."

crown n See **crown cap**

crownbeard n [Because the flowers seem to have a crown and a beard]
A plant of the genus *Verbesina.* Also called **wingstem** For other names of var spp see **cow-pen daisy, frostweed, goldweed**
1848 Gray *Manual of Botany* 232, *Verbesina* . . . Crownbeard. **1941** Walker *Lookout* 55 **TN,** Among the common weeds of the mountain, yellow crown beard is the most abundant. **1947** *Desert Mag.* April 12/3 *(DA),* April possibilities: . . . prickly pear, brittle bush, apricot mallow, . . . and crownbeard. **1975** Duncan–Foote *Wildflowers SE* 214, Crown-beard . . . *Verbesina occidentalis* . . . Single-stemmed perennial to 2.5m tall.

crown block n
1903 *DN* 2.340 [Oil-drilling terms], Crown-block . . . A strong timber structure holding together the upper ends of the four derrick corner-posts.

crown cap n Also *crown*
1967–70 *DARE* (Qu. D30, *The strip of wood or metal that covers the ridge of a roof*) Infs **VA**75, **WA**27, Crown; **KY**83, Crown cap.

crow needle n [From the needlelike fruit]
=**Venus' comb.**

1900 Lyons *Plant Names* 336, *Scandix* . . crow needles. **1933** Small *Manual SE Flora* 968, *S[candix] Pectens-Veneris* . . Crow-Needles. **1970** Correll *Plants TX* 1154, *Scandix Pectens-Veneris* . . Crow-needles.

crowner n[1] Pronc-sp *craowner*
The thing or event in a series which outdoes or is a climax to all those preceding.
1815 *Mass. Spy* 31 May *(DAE),* This is the crowner, the cap-sheaf. **1861** Holmes *Venner* 2.175 **NEng,** Ketched ye 'ith a slippernoose, hey? Wal, if that a'n't the craowner! **1922** Brown *Old Crow* 320, Isn't that a joke, Rookie? Charlotte would say it's the crowner.

crowner n[2] Obs sp *crounar* relic
A coroner.
1656 in 1900 RI Hist. Soc. Pub. 8.144, The Scot within named hath bene taken up, drowned (as is brought in by the Crowners Inquest). **1661** in 1901 Portsmouth RI *Early Rec.* 107, The Crounars inquest beinge panneled thay made inquirey hou he Came by his death. **1844** *Knickerbocker* 24.266 **VT,** The 'crowners' at length gave a verdict. **1899** (1912) Green *VA Folk-Speech* 136, Crowner . . . For coroner. **1922** Brown *Old Crow* 482, I asked him if the crowner'd come, an' I'd have to swear to't.

crown fire n Cf **crown** v **1**

A forest fire that rapidly advances in the tree tops, often well ahead of the ground fire.

1921 *Outing* 79.109/2 **MN,** If the fire is a crown fire there is little that the canoe crews can do toward putting it out. **1938** (1939) Holbrook *Holy Mackinaw* 260, *Crown fire.* Forest fire that goes into tops, or crowns, of trees. When it does that, the boys say "she's crowning." **1955** U.S. Arctic Info. Center *Gloss., Crown fire.* A forest fire confined to the tops of living trees. **1964** Clarkson *Tumult* 359 **WV,** *Crown fire*—A forest fire in the tops or crowns of trees. **1967** *DARE* Tape **MI** 42, Did you ever see a crown fire? That's when a little twig or a branch from a tree that's burning flies through the air and maybe it'll lodge up in top of a hemlock or any coniferous tree that has so much pitch in 'em . . . the fire will start. **1976** [see **crown** v **1**].

crown flower n

A large native Hawaiian shrub (*Calotropis gigantea*).   Also called **giant milkweed**

1929 Neal *Honolulu Gardens* 254, *Crown flower . . (Calotropis gigantea . .).* A large shrub reaching a height of ten feet . . is called in Honolulu the "crown flower."

crown of thorns See **corona de Cristo**

crown out v phr

Of pine trees: to grow full tops.

1969 *DARE* Tape **GA**51, It's time to thin 'em [=pine trees] . . . so the others'll do better, them 'at's left, you see, give 'em more room to crown out.

crown squash n [From the shape]

A buttercup squash.

1968 *DARE* (Qu. I23, *. . Kinds of squash . . around here*) Inf **WI**20, Crown squash, same as buttercup squash. **1980** *DARE* File **csWI,** Living in Madison over the past nine years, I have regularly heard buttercup squash referred to as crown squash, never buttercup.

crow out (of something) v phr

1969 *DARE* (Qu. II32, *To manage some way to shift the responsibility: "He said it wasn't his fault and tried to _____."*) Inf **GA**82, Crow out of it.

crowp See **croup**

crow pappy See **crowdad**

crow-pecker See **crow woodpecker 2**

crow poison n

1 =**fly poison 1.**

1837 (1966) Martineau *Soc. in America* 1.290, The ground was gay with violets, may-apple, . . and crow-poison. The last is like the white lily, growing close to the ground. **1894** *Jrl. Amer. Folkl.* 7.101, *Amianthium muscætoxicum . .* crow-poison, Banner Elk, N.C. **1959** Carleton *Index Herb. Plants* 33, *Crow-poison:* Amianthium muscatoxicum; Veratrum viride.

2 A **death camas** (usu *Zigadenus densus*).

1903 Small *Flora SE U.S.* 251, *Tracyanthus angustifolius . . .* In low grounds, North Carolina to Florida. Spring. *Crow-poison.* **1938** Matschat *Suwannee R.* 216 **GA,** Along the borders of the marsh crow poison opened tall racemes of tiny lily-like bloom, the older flowers faded in tints of pink and purple beneath the pure white of the flowering buds. **1939** FWP *Guide FL* 423, Among them [=flowers] is Osceola's plume, also known as 'crow poison', identified by its slender leafless stem. It bears a conical cluster of small white flowers which change to pink and purple before seeding. **1975** Duncan–Foote *Wildflowers SE* 246, *Crow-poison . . . Zigadenus densus . . .* Probably not poisonous . . . The above species is often confused with *Amianthium muscaetoxicum.*

3 A **false garlic** (here: *Nothoscordum bivalve*).   **TX**

1936 Whitehouse *TX Flowers* 8, *Crow Poison. False Garlic (Nothoscordum bivalve)* is one of the first flowers to appear in the spring. **1951** *PADS* 15.28 **TX,** *Nothoscordum bivalve . . .* Crow poison. **1970** Correll *Plants TX* 391, *Crow-poison.*

4 =**Indian poke 1.**

1959 [see **1** above].

crow scratching, crow's feet See **crow tracks**

‡**crow's fly** n Cf **crowhop** n **4**

A short distance.

1969 *DARE* (Qu. MM24, *Other expressions meaning "a short distance"*) Inf **KY**19, A crow's fly away.

crow's-foot n

1 See **crowfoot.**

2 See **crowfoot violet.**

3 See **crow tracks.**

crow's-foot violet See **crowfoot violet**

crow's marks See **crow tracks**

crow snatcher n

=**kingbird.**

1967 *DARE* (Qu. Q14, *. . Other names . . for . . kingbird*) Inf **KS**5, Crow snatcher.

crow's nest n

1 A **wild carrot** (here: *Daucus carota*).   Cf **bird's nest 4**

1959 Carleton *Index Herb. Plants* 33, *Crow's nest:* Daucus carota.

2 =**bird's nest 1.**

1896 *DN* 1.415 **NYC,** *Crow's-nest:* apple pudding. **1941** *LANE* Map 292, (*Apple dumpling*), An old-fashioned dish made of apples and biscuit dough . . . 3 infs, **nVT,** *Crow's nest.*

3 An enclosed or semi-enclosed platform or vantage point, spec:

a On a house; see quot.

1937 Sandoz *Slogum* 3 **NE** (as of 1900–20), The house, a two-story block topped by a crow's nest not much larger than a smokehouse, was a patchwork of used lumber.

b The cupola or observation tower on a railroad caboose.

1940 Cottrell *Railroader* 124, *Crow's nest*—The cupola or box-like structure raised above the rest of the roof of a caboose from which a trainman may see along the train while it is in motion. **1947** Beebe *Mixed Train* 355, *Crow's nest:* Caboose cupola. **1977** Adams *Lang. Railroader, Crow's nest:* The cupola of a caboose.

4 also *crow's roost:* The upper balcony of a theater.   Cf **buzzard roost 2**

1965–70 *DARE* (Qu. D40) 15 Infs, **chiefly east of Missip R exc NEng,** Crow's nest; **MS**22, **OH**38, **SC**43, Crow's roost.

5 Kindling wood.

1966–70 *DARE* (Qu. D34, *. . Small pieces of wood and other stuff that are used to start a fire*) Inf **MS**1, Crow's nest—old term; **IL**117, Crow's nest [sugg].

6 See quot 1950.   *joc*

1950 *WELS* (*When a woman puts her hair up on her head in a bunch, you call this a _____*) 1 Inf, **seWI,** Crow's nest. **1970** *DARE* (Qu. X3) Inf **MI**120, Crow's nest.

crow's tracks See **crow tracks**

crowtoes See **crowfoot 5**

crow to pick, have a v phr [Cf *have a bone to pick*] **chiefly Sth, Midl** See Map Cf **chicken** n **C2a**

To have a disagreement or dispute to settle.

[**1896** *DN* 1.422 **NC, AL,** *Pick a crow.*] **1905** *DN* 3.76 **nwAR,** *Crow to pick . . .* Explanation to ask, something to settle. 'I have a crow to pick with you.' **1927** *AmSp* 2.361 **WV,** We have a crow to pick over that affair. **1938** *AmSp* 14.267 **swIN,** To 'have a crow to pick' with someone

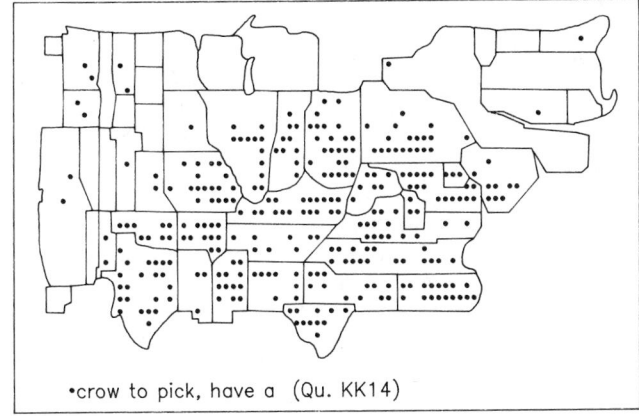

•crow to pick, have a (Qu. KK14)

is to have something to talk over, usually an unfriendly act or a derogatory remark of the latter directed against the speaker. **c1960** *Wilson Coll.* **csKY**. **1965–70** *DARE* (Qu. KK14, *Something . . people disagree about: "I have a _____ to pick with you."*) 303 Infs, **chiefly Sth, Midl**, Crow. **1967** *DARE* Tape **AZ**1, I have a crow to pick with you.

crow tracks n Also *crow scratching, crow's (feet, foot, marks, tracks)* Cf **chicken scratch 1, hen tracks, turkey tracks**
Illegible handwriting.

1875 (1969) Coffin *Caleb Krinkle* 133 **MA**, He remembered . . how, before he reached the bottom of the page he became disgusted with the copy and wrote as fast as he could, without paying any attention to the hair strokes and shaded lines; and how Miss Hyssop, as a punishment for making such crow's tracks, reset it on the next page, and he had to write it a second time. **c1960** *Wilson Coll.* **csKY**, Crow-tracks . . . Bad or illegible penmanship; used humorously. **1967–69** *DARE* (Qu. JJ11, . . *Handwriting that's hard to read*) Infs **IL**53, **MN**21, **RI**17, Crow tracks; **AR**52, Crow scratching; **AR**52, **KY**47, Crow's foot; **NY**66, Crow's feet; **GA**73, Crow's marks.

crow woodpecker n

1 =**Lewis's woodpecker.**

1917 (1923) *Birds Amer.* 2.159, Lewis's Woodpecker . . . is likely to proceed by regular and rather heavy wingbeats, resembling those of the Crow. (On the Pacific coast he is called the Crow Woodpecker.)

2 also *crow-pecker:* =**pileated woodpecker.**

1955 *AmSp* 30.180 **IL, MA, PA**, In a good many of the compounds of bird names, the object has been to indicate color. Thus *crow duck* . . describes black or blackish birds; as does *crow woodpecker* . . for the pileated with, doubtless, allusion to size also. **1956** *MA Audubon* 40.83, *Pileated Woodpecker* . . . Crow-pecker (Mass. Telescoping of crow and woodpecker; from its large size and chiefly black coloration.). **1966** *DARE* (Qu. Q17, . . *Kinds of woodpeckers . . around here*) Inf **ME**14, Crow woodpecker—large as a crow—black; the law is on 'em. [FW: They are protected.]

crucifixion thorn n **chiefly Desert SW**

1 A spiny, intricately branched shrub or small tree of the genus *Castela* (formerly *Holacantha*). [From the crown of thorns placed on Christ's head before the crucifixion (Mark 15:17)] See also **corona de Cristo, goatbush**

1920 *Torreya* 20.22, *Holacantha emoryi* . . . Crucifixion thorn, Higley, Ariz. **1941** Jaeger *Wildflowers* 123, Crucifixion Thorn . . . A southern Arizona plant which has spread westward to the low, hot deserts of eastern Calif . . . The leaves are reduced to mere scales, and the flowers are of separate sexes . . . Donkeys and goats are said to relish the clusters of small, dry, nut-like fruits but decline to eat the thorny branchlets. **1960** Vines *Trees SW* 601, Stewart Crucifixion-thorn. *Holacantha stewartii* . . . Twigs. Forming a mass of divaricate thorns. **1981** Benson–Darrow *Trees SW Deserts* 129, *Castela. Crucifixion Thorn* . . . This is one of the three crucifixion thorns occurring within the Southwestern Deserts. The others are *Canotia Holacantha* and *Koeberlinia spinosa.*

2 =**allthorn 1.**

1944 *AZ Univ. Biol. Sci. Bulletin* 6.239, *Koeberlinia spinosa* . . . This crucifixion thorn . . forms dense, low thickets. **1957** Jaeger *N. Amer. Deserts* 232, Crucifixion Thorn . . . Rigid spiny branched shrub . . . The fruit is a shiny black berry. **1981** [see **1** above].

3 A small spiny tree (*Canotia holacantha*) with yellowish-green trunk and branches. Also called **Mohave thorn, palo verde, tree of Christ**

1931 U.S. Dept. Ag. *Misc. Pub.* 101.116, *Canotia (Canotia holacantha),* also called crucifixion thorn . . . although worthless as browse . . is hard and makes good fuel. **1944** *AZ Univ. Biol. Sci. Bulletin* 6.238, *Canotia Holacantha* . . . This is the most abundant of the three crucifixion thorns in the Southwestern deserts. **1981** [see **1** above].

crucilla See **crucillo 2**

crucillo n [Span "little cross"]

1 A plant of the genus *Condalia.* For other names of var spp see **abrojo, bluewood, chamise 2, chaparral B1, javelina bush, lotebush, squawbush, wild plum**

1944 *AZ Univ. Biol. Sci. Bulletin* 6.244, *Condalia lycioides* . . . White Crucillo. *Ibid* 245, *Condalia spathulata* . . . Mexican Crucillo. **1953** *AmSp* 28.101 **SW**, (White) crucillo (Amer. Sp.). Lote bush (*Condalia lycioides*). **1959** Munz–Keck *CA Flora* 970, *Condalia* . . . Crucillo. **1981** Benson–Darrow *Trees SW Deserts* 148, *Condalia Warnockii* . . . Mexican Crucillo.

2 also *crucilla:* A thorny shrub (*Randia rhagocarpa*) native to southern Texas.

1960 Vines *Trees SW* 940, *R. rhagocarpa* . . . The crosslike paired thorns are a conspicuous feature supporting the name of Crucilla ("little cross"). **1970** Correll *Plants TX* 1486, *Randia rhagocarpa* . . . Crucillo. Shrub to 2 m. high, bearing numerous pairs of spines scattered along the branches.

crud n Usu |krʌd|; sometimes |krʌt| Pronc-sp *crut*
A Forms.

1937 Hemingway *To Have* 131, You miserable little crut. **1967** [see quots at **B** below]. **1967–69** *DARE* (Qu. Y40b, *"I've got to wash my hands. They're all covered with _____."*) Inf **PA**199, Crut [krʌt]; (Qu. NN31, *Exclamations beginning with the sound of "cr-"*) Inf **MI**55, Crut; (Qu. X16, *Sticky mucus that forms in the nose*) Inf **NY**10, Cruts ['krʌts].
B Senses.

1 =**curd** n **1**; cottage cheese. [Scots and Engl dial] *obsolescent*

1901 *DN* 2.138 **Detroit MI**, Crud . . . Curd. **1903** *DN* 2.350 **sePA**, Crud . . . Curdled milk, as in 'cruds and whey.' **1949** Kurath *Word Geog.* 36, Among the local words we may mention . . *cruds* for cottage cheese . . from the Alleghenies to the Ohio State line. **1967** Cerello *Dakota Co. MN* 52, It wasn't hard to make cruds provided you had the proper ingredients, i.e., good, whole sour milk . . I still get a hankering for good old home made cruts. **1967** *Good Old Days* Feb 25/1 **MA**, Cottage cheese was called "smearcase." Sometimes called "cruts."

2 See **cruddled milk.**

crud adj [Perh in the sense of *curd, curdled,* "stirred up"; cf **crud** n **B1**]

1968 Coatsworth *ME Memories* 155, A light snow is "enough to track a cat"; you "flank" a sick person when you look after him; "glarmy" means clumsy; and "crud," annoyed.

crudded milk See **cruddled milk**

cruddle v, hence ppl adj *cruddled* [Scots and Engl dial] *old-fash* Cf **cruddled milk**
To curdle.

1901 *DN* 2.138 **c,sPA**, Cruddle . . . To curdle. **1903** *DN* 2.350, Cruddled . . . Curdled. **1930s** in 1944 *ADD* **eWV**, Cruddle. **1968** *DARE* (Qu. H59, *Milk that becomes thick as it turns sour*) Inf **NJ**37, It cruddles.

cruddle n

1940–41 Cassidy *WI Atlas* **csWI**, Cruddles: Small lumps of mixed flour, sugar, and butter, scattered on coffee cake.

cruddled milk n Also *crud, crudded milk, cruddy ~* [Scots and Engl dial]
=**clabber** n[1] **1.**

1949 Kurath *Word Geog.* 36, Among the local words we may mention . . *crudded milk* for curdled milk (of Ulster Scot origin), from the Alleghenies to the Ohio State line. *Ibid* 71, *Cruddled milk (crudded milk, cruddy milk)* in western Pennsylvania and to some extent also on the Susquehanna. *Cruddled milk* is almost certainly of Scotch-Irish origin. **1971** Wood *Vocab. Change* 300 **Sth**, 8 [infs] Cruddled milk. **1973** Allen *LAUM* 1.291, *Curdled milk . . . Cruddled milk and crud . .* do not in the U[pper] M[idwest] reflect their importance in western Pennsylvania. Two northwestern Minnesotans use *cruddled milk* and one North Dakotan has overheard *crud* in his community, Fargo.

cruddly adj [*EDD crudly*] Cf **curdled sky**

1949 *AmSp* 24.107 **cnGA**, Cruddly . . . Thick, as of clouds. 'Clouds git cruddly' (sign of rain).

cruddy n
=**crud** n **B1.**

1940–41 Cassidy *WI Atlas* **swWI**, When milk sours the cruddy will come to the top.

cruddy adj
Coagulating into curds; curdy.

1968 *DARE* (Qu. H58, *Milk that's just beginning to become sour is _____*) Inf **OH**48, Cruddy.

cruddy milk See **cruddled milk**

cruel adv *old-fash*
Very.

1803 *Thomas' MA Spy or Worcester Gaz.* (MA) 9 Feb 4/2, [A person who had been invited out, said] Mr. _____ was *dreadful* polite, and his daughters were *cruel* pretty, and *abominable* fine. **1859** (1968) Bartlett *Americanisms* 110, *Cruel.* One of the numerous substitutes for very, exceedingly. **1904** (1916) Porter *Freckles* 99 **cnIN,** It's cut cruel deep. It might be making a scar. **1947** Adams *Banner* 55 **NY** (as of 1817–1847), I'm cruel handy. Your figures need a touch of the paintbrush.

cruelize v *esp* **NEng** *old-fash*
    To treat brutally, torture.
    1847 Child *Fact & Fiction* 199, **Charleston SC,** They don't all cruellize [sic] their slaves. **1903** *DN* 2.296 **Cape Cod MA** (as of 1850s), *Cruelize* . . To treat cruelly, formed by the analogy of realize. **1908** Lincoln *Cy Whittaker* 227 **MA,** I'd learned enough . . to know that he was . . a drunken, good-for-nothin' scamp who had cruelized his wife. **1927** *AmSp* 3.137 **ME,** A man who beat his horses was said to "cruelize" them. **1974** *AmSp* 49.62 **swME** (as of c1890s), *Cruelize* . . Torture.

crueller See **cruller**

cruel plant n
    =**spreading dogbane.**
    1931 Clute *Common Plants* 43, One of the dogbanes *(Apocynum androsaemifolium)* . . catches small insects by the tongue and holds them fast until they starve to death. It is frequently called by the appropriate name of cruel plant.

cruh-ooch See **crouch**

cruise v, hence vbl n *cruising*
    In logging: to survey and estimate the amount and value of standing timber.
    [**1879** Vivian *Wanderings* 53 **New Brunswick,** Experienced men are sent out into the forests exploring, or to use their own term "cruising;" their object being . . to find suitable lumber for chopping.] **1919** *DN* 5.54 **WA,** Should their cruising operations again take them that way. **1947** *Sierra Club Bulletin* Sept–Oct 4/2, Logging companies, however, are now cutting on the edges and have already cruised the heart of the virgin forest. **1958** McCulloch *Woods Words* **Pacific NW,** *Cruise* . . To estimate the quantity and quality of standing timber on a given area. **1969** Sorden *Lumberjack Lingo* **NEng, Gt Lakes.**

cruise n
    In logging: a survey or estimate taken of standing timber.
    1911 J. F. Wilson *Land Claimers* viii.112 *(DA),* I finished the cruise today. **1948** *Sat. Eve. Post* 31 July 86/2, Boss wants you to look over this cruise on some timber. **1958** McCulloch *Wood Words* **Pacific NW. 1959** *AmSp* 34.77 **nCA,** *Cruise* . . A survey of forest land to locate and estimate the volume of standing timber.

cruiser n
    1 In logging: one who surveys and estimates standing timber. [*cruise* v] **Nth** Also called **landlooker**
    1893 *Scribner's Mag.* 13.695/1, My first day's experience as a 'Cruiser' or 'Landlooker'. **1919** *DN* 5.54 **WA,** As neither of the cruisers had a gun, it is lucky for them that the mother bear failed to show up. **1930** Shoemaker *1300 Words* 15 **cPA Mts** (as of 1900). **1938** (1939) Holbrook *Holy Mackinaw* 260 **MI. 1945** Colcord *Sea Language* 62 **ME, Cape Cod and Long Island,** A timber cruiser is an expert woodsman who estimates stumpage in advance. **1946** Peattie *Pacific Coast* 232, With his cruiser's eye, he could measure the quantity and the quality of the timber from the water's edge. **1968** *DARE* Tape MN29, A cruiser would judge the quality of the land [for logging].
    2 A lumberman's high-topped laced boot.
    1902 White *Blazed Trail* 131 **MI,** They were . . dressed in broad hats, flannel shirts, coarse trousers tucked in high laced "cruisers". **1946** *Sat. Eve. Post* 11 May 41/1, He was wearing Tillamook light cruisers from Portland.
    3 also attrib, also *cruising car:* A police vehicle. **chiefly NEng, N Cent, Mid Atl** See Map
    1929 *Sat. Eve. Post* 7 Dec 68/2, The cruisers are high-powered seven-passenger touring cars manned by a crew of four. **1965–70** *DARE* (Qu. N4, *A police vehicle with a red, blue, or yellow flashing light on top*) 38 Infs, **chiefly NEng, wN Midl,** Cruiser; 14 Infs, **chiefly NEng, N Cent, Mid Atl,** Police cruiser; MA40, Cruiser car; VA20, Cruising car. **1967** *Boston Sunday Globe* 23 Apr. 25/1 *(OEDS),* In Weymouth Patrolmen Richard McDonald and Ralph Campbell were injured when a car hit their cruiser.

cruiser coat n Also *cruiser jacket* [**cruiser 1**]
    See quot 1958.

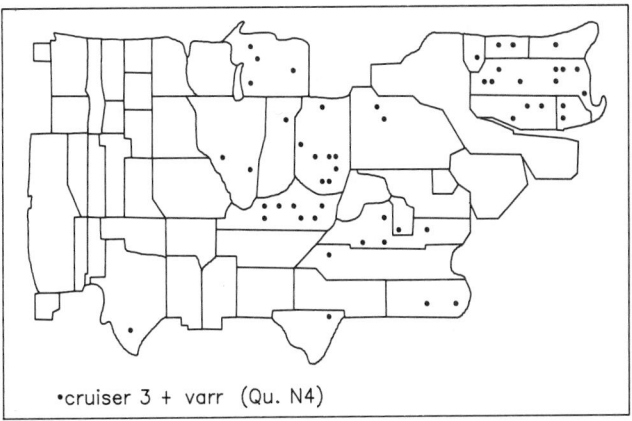

•cruiser 3 + varr (Qu. N4)

1958 McCulloch *Woods Words* **Pacific NW,** *Cruiser coat*—A short wool coat, shower repellant, with many special pockets and a double back lunch or game pocket. Much favored in the Northwest woods. Also worn by a large percentage of the male population in the Coos Bay region of Oregon—doctors and lawyers as well as cruisers and loggers. **1967** *DARE* (Qu. W4, . . *Men's coats or jackets for work and outdoor wear*) Inf CO9, Cruiser jacket, a professional forester's jacket.

cruiser vest n [**cruiser 1**]
    1958 McCulloch *Woods Words* **Pacific NW,** *Cruiser vest*—A canvas vest with double back and many pockets; preferred by logging engineers and cruisers.

cruising car See **cruiser 3**

cruller n *Usu* |krʌlə(r)|; for var proncs see quots 1941, 1965–70 Also *crull* *Pronc-spp* crawler, croiller, croller, crueller [Du *krulle* a kind of curled cake] **scattered, but chiefly NEast, N Cent, C Atl** See Map *Cf* **friedcake 1**
    A small sweet cake made from a rich egg batter, formed variously but often into twisted strips, and deep-fried until brown; sometimes a **cake doughnut.**
    1820 Irving *Sketch Book Crayon* 1.386 **NY,** The doughty dough-nut, . . the crisp and crumbling cruller. **1831** Peck *Guide for Emigrants* 152, The Yankee . . tell us of their pies, dough-nuts, and crulls. **1855** *Harper's Mag.* 10.421/1, Up to two o'clock he had redeemed two crollers and a dough-nut. **1895** *DN* 1.387, In Dutch-settled districts the word . . *crullers* is also common for . . [a deep-fried cake] raised with baking soda or saleratus; sweetened; cut in rings or twisted. **1896** (c1973) Farmer *Orig. Cook Book* 83 **NEng,** Crullers. **1905** *DN* 3.7 **cCT,** Cruller. **1906** *Pocumtuc Housewife* 34 **MA,** Crullers, Matrimony or Love Knots . . Roll thin, cut in strips and tie in knots, or braid three strips together. **1907** *DN* 3.211 **nwAR,** Cruller. **1941** *LANE* Map 284 **throughout NEng,** [Most common pronc [krʌlə]; also [krɔlə], [krʌlr], [krolr], [kraulə], [krɒlə].] *Cruller,* made of 'unraised' dough. It is usually described as twisted; but a ring-shaped variety is mentioned regularly . . and an oblong one. **1953** *AmSp* 28.246 **csPA,** The sweetened, unraised, doughnut-shaped cake fried in deep fat is here called by the Dutch term, *cruller,* not the PaG [Pennsylvania German] *fossnock* or *fatcake* or the more generally known *fried cake.* **1962** Atwood *Vocab. TX* 63, *Cruller* . . is also in limited use, but informants are in agreement that this is different from a *doughnut*—it has no hole, it is long, the dough is twisted, and so on. **c1965** Randle *Cookbooks* (Ask Neighbor) 1.109 **OH,** Slovenian Cruellers. **1965–70** *DARE* (Qu. H28, *Different shapes or types of doughnuts*) 152 Infs, **chiefly Nth, esp NEng,** Cruller; CA184, CT12, 18, MA57, 69, NY237, OH98, (Dainty, French, twisted, raised) cruller(s); MO16, Crulls—made around Easter and Christmas time; CA54, Crueller; OH21, Croiller; MA43, ['krɛlɚz]; NY152, ['krɪlɚ]; CA144, NY181, ['krulɚ]; VA60, ['krʌlɚ]; WI24, ['krulə]; (Qu. H26, *A round cake of dough, cooked in deep fat, with a hole in the center*) 96 Infs, **chiefly NEast,** Cruller; PA239, French crullers; (Qu. H30, *An oblong cake, cooked in deep fat*) 45 Infs, **chiefly NEast,** Cruller; NY194, PA248, (Long, stick) cruller; CT37, Croller; NJ54, NY58, ['krolə]; (Qu. H27, . . *Joking names for doughnuts*) 12 Infs, **chiefly NEast,** Cruller; (Qu. H32, . . *Fancy rolls and pastries*) Infs AR8, CA22, CT42, MD12, NJ1, NY205, SD3, Crullers; (Qu. H31, *Other foods made with dough and cooked in deep fat;* total Infs questioned, 75) Infs MS17, 73, Crullers. **1971** *AmSp* 46.79 **Chicago,** (Twisted sugared doughnut) . . crawler. **1973** Allen *LAUM* 1.281, *Doughnut* . . . For the twisted variety a

scattered half dozen [infs] retain the Dutch *cruller* that had spread from New York to the Philadelphia and Baltimore areas.

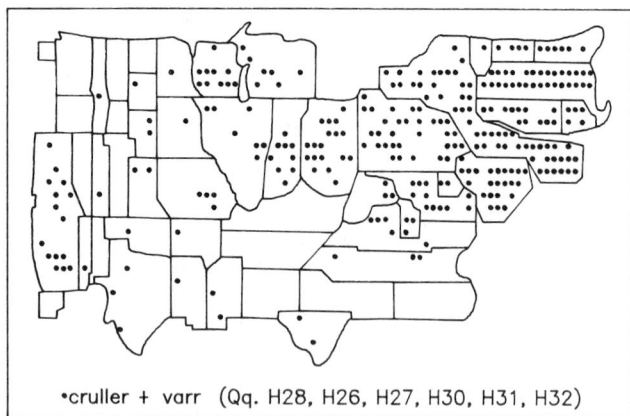

•cruller + varr (Qq. H28, H26, H27, H30, H31, H32)

crum See **cramp** n

crumb n Also sp *crum*
A louse or bedbug.
1863 in 1903 Norton *Army Letters* 175 **PA,** Fortunately, I am not troubled with the 'crumbs' now. **1918** *DN* 5.24 **NW,** Crumb . . . Bed-bug. Rare. **1927** *DN* 5.443 [Underworld jargon], Crum . . . A louse. **1950** *WELS (Body and head lice)* 1 Inf, **cnWI,** Crumbs. **1966–68** *DARE* (Qu. R25, *Joking names for a head louse, or body louse*) Infs **CA15, CT13, ID4, MN29,** Crumb. **1968** Adams *Western Words,* Crumb—A logger's name for a louse. Also sometimes used by the cowboy.

crumb v
1 To clean up crumbs, to wipe off (a table).
1920 *DN* 5.81 **Seattle WA,** Crumb the table, to. To remove the crumbs from the table. **1966–70** *DARE* (Qu. G10, *When the meal is all over, what do you have to do to the table?*) Infs **NJ9, NY41,** Crumb it; **MD50, MA69,** Crumb the table; **AR8,** Crumb; **GA90,** Crumb it off.
2 See quot.
1941 *FWP Guide OK* 121, Crumb: Infringing upon the work or rights of others. "Stop crumbing on me."

crumb boss n Also sp *crum boss* Cf **crumb** n
1 A janitor or clean-up man in a construction or logging camp, or on a railroad work train.
1926 *AmSp* 1.651 [Hobo lingo], Crum boss—a janitor in a camp "bunkhouse." **1938** (1939) Holbrook *Holy Mackinaw* 260, Crumb boss. Low name for a bullcook. **1945** Hubbard *Railroad Ave.* 339, Crumb boss—Man in charge of camp cars.
2 See quot.
1958 McCulloch *Woods Words* **Pacific NW,** Crumb boss . . . Another name for a conductor on a log train.

crumb box n Also sp *crum box*
A caboose.
1945 Hubbard *Railroad Ave.* 339, [Crummy—Caboose.] Also called *crum box, crib,* and many other names. **1977** Adams *Lang. Railroader,* Crumb box.

crumb castle n
=**chuck wagon 1.**
1942 Berrey–Van den Bark *Amer. Slang* 915.14, Western . . . Ranch equipment . . . Chow *or* chuck wagon, crumb castle, mess wagon, *a* dinner wagon. **1968** Adams *Western Words,* Crumb castle—A cowboy's name for the chuck wagon.

crumb catcher n
1970 *DARE* (Qu. Q22, *Joking names . . for the common sparrow*) Inf **NC85,** Crumb catcher—what the young 'uns call 'em.

crumb chaser n Cf **crumb boss 1**
In logging: a cook's helper.
1958 McCulloch *Woods Words* **Pacific NW,** Crumb chaser—A cook's helper. **1969** Sorden *Lumberjack Lingo* **NEng, Gt Lakes.**

crumb crusher n *esp among Black speakers; joc*
1 also *crumb cruncher, ~ picker, ~ snatcher:* A small child.

1967–70 *DARE* (Qu. Z12, *"A small child": "He's a healthy little ———."*) Infs **FL51, NY241,** Crumb crusher; **TN13,** Crumb picker; (Qu. Z16, *A small child who is rough, misbehaves, and doesn't obey, you'd call him a ———*) Inf **AL1,** Crumb snatcher; **PA94,** No-good little crumb snatcher. [3 of 5 Infs Black] **1967–76** *DARE* File **SC** [Black], *Crumb snatcher:* A small child; **seLA** [Black], He has two crumb crushers. **1970** Major *Afro–Amer. Slang,* Crumb crusher (snatcher): (1930's and after) a baby or small child. *Ibid,* Crumb cruncher . . a child; an infant. **1972** Claerbaut *Black Jargon,* Crumb snatcher . . a small child: Got to take care of my crumb snatcher.
2 pl: The lips. Cf **coffee cooler** n **4, jibs**
1972 Claerbaut *Black Jargon,* Crumb crushers . . lips.
3 pl, also *crumb crunchers:* Teeth.
1947 Berrey–Van den Bark *Amer. Slang Suppl.* 7.28, Crumb crunchers, *teeth.* **1970** *DARE* (Qu. X13a, . . *Teeth*) Inf **FL51,** Crumb crushers. [Inf Black]

crumbie See **crummy** n

crumble n Also *crumbling*
A crumb.
1903 *DN* 2.296 **Cape Cod MA,** Crumblings . . . Crums. **1909** *DN* 3.410 **nME,** Crumbles . . . Crums. *Ibid* 422 **Cape Cod MA,** *Corrigenda* [for *DN* 2.296] Crumblings is more commonly *crumbles.* **1960** Criswell *Resp. to PADS 20* **Ozarks,** Crumblings . . . Very small crumbs. (Common).

crumble in n Also *crumbled in*
1 See quot.
1958 *PADS* 29.9 **TN,** Crumbled in: Biscuits in sweetened coffee.
2 also *crumb up:* See quots.
1958 *PADS* 29.9 **TN,** Crumb up: Corn bread crumbled in sweet milk. **1981** Howell *Surv. Folklife* 100 **cTN,** "Crumble in" (corn bread crumbled into sweet milk and eaten like cereal) is still a favorite light supper of several informants.

crumbling See **crumble**

‡**crumbling worm** n
1971 Wood *Vocab. Change* 368 **Sth,** [Footnote 18:] Additional volunteered words [for a worm used for bait]: *bait(s), big worm, . . crumbling worm,* and the generic *worm(s).*

crumb picker See **crumb crusher 1**

crumb roll n [**crumb** n + *roll* portable bedding]
See quots.
1918 *DN* 5.24 **NW,** Crumb-roll . . . A bed roll; sometimes a bed . . . Woodsmen; ranchmen. **1968** Adams *Western Words,* Crumb roll—A logger's name for his bedroll; also called *balloon.*

crumb snatcher n
1 See **crumb crusher 1.**
2 A hand. *joc*
1970 *DARE* (QR, near Qu. Y40a) Inf **NY249,** Crumb snatchers [=hands].

crumb up v phr Also sp *crum up* [**crumb** n]
To wash or boil the lice out of clothes.
1926 *AmSp* 1.651 [Hobo lingo], Crum-up—washing one's under clothing. **1933** *AmSp* 8.3.26 [Prison argot], Crumbing up: boiling lousy clothes. **1968** Adams *Western Words,* Crumb up—To get rid of body lice.

crumb up n See **crumble in 2**

crummy n Also sp *crumbie, crummie*
1 A caboose or bunk car. Cf **crumb box**
1926 *AmSp* 1.651 [Hobo lingo], Crummy—a caboose. **1938** *AmSp* 13.70, Crummy. Bunk car. **1950** *WELS (The last car on a freight train, usually used as headquarters for the crew)* 2 Infs, **WI,** Crummy; 1 Inf, Crummy car (so called by brakies [brakemen]). **1953** Botkin *Treas. Railroad Folkl.* 344, One hot day, while I was straightening up the crummy, I found a bunch of torpedoes. **1962** *AmSp* 37.132 **nCA** [Logging railroad language], Crummy . . . Originally a transportation car on a railroad (usually a caboose), so called because of its usual condition. **1966** *DARE* Tape **SD5,** The way car is the crummy . . . That's the one that's . . on the back end of the train. **1970** *Current Slang* 1.5.5 **cCA,** Crummy . . . Caboose.
2 also *crummy car;* In logging: a vehicle used to transport

loggers to and from the work site. **chiefly Pacific NW Cf candy wagon**

1946 Peattie *Pacific Coast* 279, In the woods gasoline and Diesel engines have largely replaced steam and gone is the "crummy" car that used to bring loggers into town on Saturday night. **1950** *AmSp* 25.88 **OR,** Many terms used by loggers are similar to those used by railroaders, probably because logging once depended upon a network of railroads manned by 'boomers' . . who used the lingo of railroading and introduced it to the woods. So *crummy,* the railroader's unflattering description of his caboose or crewcar, appeared on logging railroads and then became the logger's word to mean any railroad car or motorbus used to transport workers to and from the cuttings. In advertising it sometimes appears as *crumbie.* **1956** *AmSp* 31.150 **nwCA** [Logger lingo], *Crummie* . . . A station wagon or bus that transports men to and from work in the woods. Originally, a transportation car on a railroad, so-called because of its usual condition. **1962** *AmSp* 37.132 **Pacific NW,** *Crummy.* **1965** *Perrin Coll.* **WA,** *Crummy:* a bus, usually an old one, which takes loggers to work . . . Any vehicle used in transporting loggers to work.

3 A lice-infested shirt. **[crumb n]**
1958 McCulloch *Woods Words* 42 **Pacific NW,** *Crummy* . . . A shirt occupied by others than its owner [i.e. by lice].

4 =crumb boss 1.
1968 Adams *Western Words, Crummie*—In logging, the man who takes care of the logger's bunkhouse.

5 See quot.
1968 Adams *Western Words, Crummie* . . . A bed in the bunkhouse.

crummy adj **[crumb n]**
Infested with lice, lousy.
1918 *DN* 5.24 **NW,** *Crummy* . . . Full of, infested with, body lice. Lumbermen. **1919** *DN* 5.41 (Hobo cant). **1927** *DN* 5.443 (Underworld jargon). **1939** (1962) Thompson *Body & Britches* 494 **NY,** Crummy (lousy) as a pet coon.

crump n[1] See **cramp** n

crump n[2] See **crumplety horns**

crump v
1895 *DN* 1.386 **seMA,** *Crump* (for dandelions): to dig . . . "O[ld]." and "R[are]."

crumple-horned ppl adj **[crumpled** twisted]
1 also *crumplety-horned:* See quot.
1908 *DN* 3.303 **eAL, wGA,** *Crumple(ty)-horned* . . . Having irregular or twisted horns.
‡**2** Of a cow: dehorned.
1965 *DARE* (Qu. K13, *A cow that has had her horns cut off*) Inf **FL21,** Crumple-horned.

crumplety horns n Also *crump* **[EDD** *crumpledy horn* (at *crumpled*)]
A **crumple-horned** cow.
1908 *DN* 3.303 **eAL, wGA,** A cow with such horns [irregular or twisted horns] is often called *Crumplety horns,* or simply *Crump.*

crum up See **crumb up**

crunge v **[Echoic]**
Of a bullfrog: to make its characteristic sound.
1966 *DARE* (QR, near Qu. P22) Inf **ME8,** They say these frogs are crungin' ['krʌnjɪn] when they make a loud sound.

crup See **creep** v A

crupper bone n Also *cripper bone* **[OED** a1652, 1882 at *crupper* sb. 5]
The sacrum.
1899 (1912) Green *VA Folk-Speech* 136, *Crupper-bone* . . . The lower end of the backbone. **1942** Warnick *Garrett Co. MD* (as of 1900–18), *Cripper-bone* . . crupper bone (lower end of backbone). **1968** *DARE* (Qu. X35, *Joking words for the part of the body you sit on*) Inf **MI96,** ['krupɚ] bone.

cruppered ppl adj
1959 *VT Hist.* new ser 27.131, *Cruppered* . . . Finished. Occasional. Orleans.

crushaw See **cushaw**

crusher n
1 A boorish intruder. **[Cf** *(gate)crasher]*
1965–68 *DARE* (Qu. II18, *Someone who joins himself on to you and your group without being asked and won't leave*) Infs **MS30, NY83,** Crusher.

2 One who makes unwelcome advances to women, a rude flirt. **[Perh by analogy with masher]**
1967 *DARE* (Qu. AA6b, . . *A man who is fond of . . women and tries to attract their attention—if he's rude or not respectful*) Inf **ID5,** Crusher.

crusie n **[From Middle Fr** *creuset;* see *OED*] hist
A kind of oil-burning lamp.
1930 Shoemaker *1300 Words* 14 **cPA Mts** (as of 1900), *Crusie*—A small oil-burning lamp. **1966** *Weekly Monadnock Ledger* (Jaffrey NH) 7 July 4/3, For students of history, the exhibit will have special interest. More than 100 items are displayed, ranging from tinder boxes, . . *Crusie's* and Betty lamps to fishing lights.

cruso n **[Perh alter of Span** *cruz* tail of a coin]
1969 *DARE* (Qu. EE33, *Other outdoor games . . that children play now, or . . were played in your childhood*) Inf **CA107,** Cruso ['kruso]—a game played with coins tossed to a line and then all thrown into the air and whatever came down heads belonged to you.

crust n
A Forms.
Pl usu *crusts,* sometimes *crusses, crustes.* **Cf -es** suff[1]
1899 (1912) Green *VA Folk-Speech, Crusses* . . . For *crusts.* "Promises like pie-crusses are made to be broken." **1954** in 1958 Brewer *Dog Ghosts* 33 **TX** [Black], Dey fin'ly runned 'cross some bread crustes.
B Senses.
1 Impudence, insensitive aggressiveness. **chiefly Nth, West** See Map
1900 *DN* 2.31 **csWI, cCT,** *Crust* . . . Forwardness. **1915** *DN* 4.233 **neOH,** *Crust* . . . Selfish aggressiveness. [From imperiousness to delicate suggestions or hints.—*[DN]* Ed.] "That guy certainly has some crust." **1950** *WELS* (When a person does something . . bold or forward: "Well, she certainly has a lot of _____.") 16 Infs, **WI,** Crust. **1965–70** *DARE* (Qu. GG5) 39 Infs, **chiefly Nth, West,** Crust; **NY202,** More crust than a pie factory; (Qu. II36b, *Of somebody who talks back or gives rude answers:* "She certainly _____.") Inf **TN1,** Has got a lot of crust; (Qu. JJ19, *If somebody has dishonest intentions, or is up to no good . .* "I think he's got _____.") Inf **UT8,** His crust. **1970** *DARE* FW Addit **nwPA,** Lot of *crust:* lot of nerve. **1979** *DARE* File **cnMA** (as of 1920s), When I was in high school one of the nastiest things you could say to a bold, pushy sort of person was "You tell em, pie-face—you've got the crust."

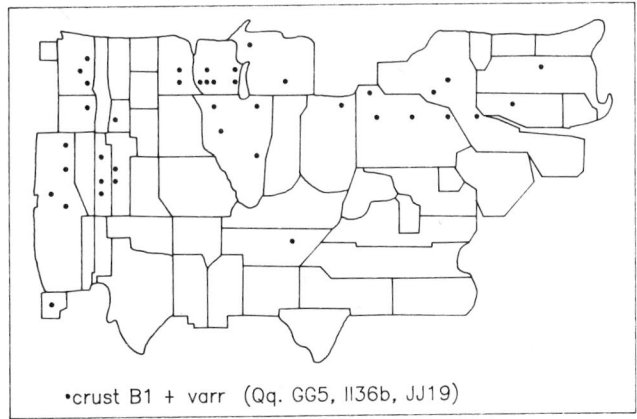

•crust B1 + varr (Qq. GG5, II36b, JJ19)

2 One's head. **Cf** *DS* X28
1915 *DN* 4.244 **MT,** *Crust* . . . Head. "Look out, boys. You'll fall and break your crust."

3 See quot.
1940 *AmSp* 15.447 **eTN,** *Crust.* A meal. "Have you had your crust?"

crust coffee n *old-fash*
A beverage made with toasted bread crusts and hot water.
1863 *Ladies' Repository* 23.90/1 **AR** (as of 1842), For supper we had fried sweet potatoes, a little crust coffee, and venison. **1934** *Hanley Disks* **csNH,** Take the crusts from your brownbread . . put it into a dish

.. and put in some water and set it .. on the stove . . . It's called crust coffee. That won't hurt anybody to drink if they're sick. **1939** Wolcott *Yankee Cook Book* 187 **seMA,** A beverage called Crust Coffee was made from the hard crusts from brown bread. Hot water was poured over the crusts and the resulting liquid was served as a coffee substitute. **1942** Whipple *Joshua* 29 **UT,** Free .. preferred 'crust' coffee; so .. the girl browned a piece of bread on a fork over the coals .. crumbled the toasted crusts into a tin cup which, filled with water, she put to boil on the heated rock. **1967** *DARE* (QR, near Qu. H18) Inf **MA5,** Brown bread .. used to be made .. with one to one and a half inch crust all over . . . Crust coffee was made from this, dried and sweetened with molasses, hot water poured on it.

crustes See **crust A**

crut n¹ [Perh from Engl dial *crut* a dwarf, a stunted person]
1 See quot.
  1950 *PADS* 14.24 **SC,** *Crut* . . . A term of endearment. A father says to his wife or daughter: "My little crut."
2 See quot.
  1968 *DARE* (Qu. K41, *A horse with its tail cut short is called a _____*) Inf **NY66,** Crut.

crut n² See **crud** n

crut n³ [Prob echoic, but see **crut** n¹]
A frog.
  1940 in 1944 *ADD* **swPA, nWV,** A spring peeper . . . [krʌts] cruts, pl. Old illit[erate] speaker. **1949** *AmSp* 24.107 **SC,** *Cruts* . . . Bullfrogs.

crutch n Pronc-spp *cratch, crotch*
Std senses, var forms.
  1899 (1912) Green *VA Folk-Speech, Cratch* . . . *Cratches,* crutches. **1914** *DN* 4.154 **NH,** *Crotch* . . . crutch.

crutch-stick n
A crutch.
  1931 *AmSp* 6.270 **KY,** Crutch stick. **1940** *AmSp* 15.51 **sAppalachians, Ozarks,** A characteristic of mountain dialect is its abundance of noun compounds in which an initial noun is used attributively .. crutch-stick.

crute up v phr [Perh *EDD croot* v. "Fig. to recover from illness;" but perh aphet form of *recruit*] *?obs*
  1914 *DN* 4.150 **NH,** *Crute up.* My wife *cruted up,* has recovered.

crutter See **creature**

crutty adj [Alter of *cruddy* dirty, soiled; cf **crud** n]
  1950 *PADS* 14.24 **SC,** *Crutty* ['krʌtɪ] . . . Very dirty, so that the dirt almost forms a crust.

cry v
1 usu with *off* or in phr *cry sales:* To sell at auction.
  1723 in 1880 Brookhaven NY *Records* 1.114, Itt was cryed off to him att twenty one shilling pr acre. **1847** (1962) Robb *Squatter Life* 135, I . . was comin' along, slow and easy, by the St. Louis Exchange, when I heerd Major Beard cryin' off a lot of field hands. **1941** FWP *Guide IN* 416, After one week of instruction [in the Auctioneering School] the students are given practical experience, 'crying' public sales in the streets of Decatur. **1955** Warren *Angels* 51 **KY** (as of 1850s), "Yeah, you niggers," Mr. Marmaduke yelled to them across the distance of lawn. "I aim to sell all of you, ever one—ever last one, you hear!—vendue or dicker—vendue or dicker—cry-off or jew-down—ever last one!" **1958** Randolph *Sticks* 101 **Ozarks,** One of 'em was a doctor, and the other fellow used to cry sales. **1960** Criswell *Resp. to PADS 20* **Ozarks,** *Cry a sale.* **1967** Jacobs *Rejoicing* 156 **IN** (as of 1920–40), I appreciate being asked to cry a pie supper. **1970** *DARE* Tape **VA105,** He joined with this guy and furnished his truck and his address system, for to cry the prices and one would cry for a while and then the other one would cry for a while.
2 To announce the banns of marriage. *old-fash*
  1804 Fessenden *Poems* 82 **NEng,** Next Sabbath-day we will be cried. **1874** Lowell *Courtin'* [22] **MA,** An' all I know is they was cried / In meetin' come nex' Sunday. **1905** *DN* 3.7 **cCT,** *Cry* . . . To publish the banns of marriage.

crybaby n
A type of cookie: see quots.
  1968 *DARE* (Qu. H32) Inf **NJ21,** Delaware crybaby—molasses cookie from Beaver Valley, Delaware. **1975** Gould *ME Lingo* 65, *Cry-baby—*

A soft sugar cookie with a filling of mince-meat, raisins, nuts, jam, etc. A filled cookie.

crybaby tree n [Etym unknown]
An introduced **coral tree** (here: *Erythrina crista-galli*) often planted for ornament esp in the Gulf States.
  1960 Vines *Trees SW* 561, *Erythrina crista-galli* . . . Some of the vernacular names in use are .. Crybaby-tree, Dragon's Teeth. **1976** Bailey–Bailey *Hortus Third* 445, *Cockspur* c[oral] tree, cry-baby tree.

cry-eye exclam Also *cry-eye-eye* [Ellip euphem for *Christ,* perh infl by *for crying out loud*] **esp MI, WI**
Usu in phrr *for (the) cry-eye:* An expression of surprise, annoyance, etc.
  1950 *WELS* (Exclamations beginning with the sound of "cr-") 6 Infs, **WI,** Cry-eye; 2 Infs, For (the) cry-eye. **1966–70** *DARE* (Qu. NN31) Infs **MI3, 28, 43, 46, NH1, TX97, WI48, 61,** For (the) cry-eye; **MI13,** Cry-eye; **MI18,** Cry-eye-eye.

crying ppl adj
  1952 Brown *NC Folkl.* 1.531, *Crying* . . . Least, any. Generally modifies *thing.* "I haven't a *crying* thing to wear." "I don't know a *crying* thing."

crying bird n [See quot 1917] **esp FL**
=**limpkin.**
  1791 (1958) Bartram *Travels* 49 **SE,** The crying-bird, another faithful guardian, screaming in the gloomy thickets, warns the feathered tribes of approaching peril. **1872** Coues *Key to N. Amer. Birds* 271 **FL,** *Scolopaceous Courlan.* Crying-bird. **1917** (1923) *Birds Amer.* 202 **FL,** Limpkins at times are very noisy creatures. Their usual call possesses a quality of unutterable sadness . . . For this reason the name "Crying-bird" is usually given them by the natives. **1937** *Torreya* 37.71, Okefenokee Wildlife Refuge . . . to protect such wild life as the .. limpkin or "crying bird," otter, alligator, and other birds and animals has recently been established. **1948** *Outdoor Life* July 72/2, The limpkin, or crying bird, of Florida and points south, has a weird, desolate cry. **1951** Teale *North with Spring* 90 **FL,** Hardly had we stopped at the wooden bridge before we heard the wailing of the "crying bird" up and down the river.

‡crying pew n
  1967 *DARE* (Qu. CC5, *Names for seats in a church*) Inf **NY27,** Crying pews—the seats for children in the back.

crying Willy n
  1968 *DARE* (Qu. CC4, . . *Nicknames* . . *for various* . . *religious groups*) Inf **MD5,** Crying Willies—the Baptists.

crymus See **crimus**

cry one's wife down v phr [*OED cry down* 1457 →] Cf **cry 2**
To publish a disclaimer of financial responsibility.
  1980 *DARE* File **MA,** *Cry (one's) wife down in the paper:* A New England expression for publishing such a notice as the following from *The Fitchburg Sentinel* (MA) 2 Sept 1966, "After this date I will not be responsible for any debts contracted by anyone but myself."

crystal n Usu |'krɪstəl|; in **S Midl** occas |'krɪstɪəl, -jəl| Pronc-spp *christial, crischul, cristial, crystial*
A Forms.
  1899 (1912) Green *VA Folk-Speech* 137, *Crystal* . . . The glass cover of a watch face. Cristial. **1903** *DN* 2.310 **seMO,** *Cristial* . . . Crystal. **1907** *DN* 3.230 **nwAR,** *Cristial.* **1912** Green *VA Folk-Speech* 114, *Christial.* **1944** *PADS* 2.33 **w,cNC,** *Crystal* ['krɪstəl]: Common pronunciation among semieducated. **1946** *AmSp* 21.270 **KY,** *Crystial* . . . Crystal. Current. **c1960** *Wilson Coll.* **csKY,** *Crystal* is commonly ['krɪstjəl], as in ['krɪstjəl] Cave. **1983** Allin *Sthn. Legislative Dict.* 4 **AR,** *Crischul:* fine glass. "Senator Nosegay suffered a broke ankle when he fell from the crischul chandelier."
B Sense.
A kind of marble. Cf **glassie**
  1958 *PADS* 29.32 **WI,** *Crystal* . . . A crystal bowler. *Ibid* 30 **WI,** Bowler, crystal . . . A bowler made of crystal or similar material. **1963** *KY Folkl. Rec.* 9.59 **ne,seKY,** Clear Glass Marble, Transparent: . . . Crystal. **1965–70** *DARE* (Qu. EE6d, *Special marbles*) 14 Infs, **scattered,** Crystals. **c1970** Wiersma *Marbles Terms* **TX** (as of 1925), *Crystal:* A clear glass playing marble.

crystallized (cucumber) pickle n
  1967 *DARE* (Qu. H56, . . *Different kinds of pickles*) Inf **SC34,** Crystallized cucumber pickle; **SC46,** Crystallized pickle; **AL15,** Crystallized.

crystial See **crystal**

Cuban See **Cuban sandwich**

Cuban itch n *joc*

1967–68 *DARE* (Qu. BB25, *What are some common skin diseases around here?*) Inf **MO**38, Cuban itch — treated with sulfur, lard, and carbolic acid; **NY**23, Cuban itch — (not common) from handling money; (Qu. R25, *Joking names for a head louse, or body louse*) Inf **MN**14, Cuban itch — in lumber camps.

Cuban pine n

=**slash pine 1.**

1883 Smith *Rept. for 1881 & 1882* 289, Toward the Gulf coast the . . tree-growth consists of the long-leaf pine and the so-called Cuban pine. **1901** Mohr *Plant Life AL* 131, Open groves of Cuban pines cover the flats behind the dunes, merging frequently into the pine meadows of the coast plain. **1967** *DARE* (Qu. T17, *. . Different kinds of pine trees around here*) Inf **SC**63, Cuban.

Cuban sandwich n Also *Cuban* chiefly **FL** See Map Section

=**submarine sandwich.**

1965–70 *DARE* (Qu. H42, *The kind [of sandwich] in a much larger, longer bun, that's a meal in itself*) 11 Infs, chiefly **FL,** Cuban sandwich; **FL**37, Cuban. **1967** *AmSp* 42.283 **FL,** *The Submarine Sandwich* . . Cuban Sandwich — Miami. **1976** *NYT Mag.* 17 Oct 82/2, What Tampa calls "Cuban sandwiches" are made of Cuban bread, sliced open and filled overpoweringly with ham, pork, sausage, cheese and dill pickles.

cubbage See **cubbitch**

cubbahlet See **coverlet**

cubbidge See **cubbitch**

cubbie v |'kʌbi| Also sp *cubby, kibby* [Perh alter by shift in stress of **co-boy**] chiefly **Delmarva**

Come! — used to call calves.

1949 Kurath *Word Geog.* 64, Cubbie! predominates on the Eastern Shore of Virginia and in the Norfolk area. **1965–70** *DARE* (Qu. K83, *To call a calf . . at feeding time*) Inf **MD**38, ['kʌbɪ]; **VA**49, 57, ['kʌbi]; **PA**166, Kibby. **1973** Allen *LAUM* 1.260, *Kibby,* which may be a variant of the *cubby* known in the Norfolk area of Virginia, also is the term of an inf. of Swedish parentage in northwestern North Dakota. **1978** *DARE* File **Delmarva** [Black], ['kʌbɪ] repeated several times — a call to calves to feed.

cubbitch adj Also sp *cubbage, cubbidge* [From *covetous; DJE* 1862 →]

1 Stingy, tight-fisted. *Gullah*

1930 Stoney–Shelby *Black Genesis* 68 **seSC,** But Br' Guinea-fowl is too cubbitch (miserly) to lend it to anybody. **1966** *DARE* (Qu. U33, *. . A stingy person*) Inf **SC**10, He [kʌbɪč]. **c1970** Pederson *Dial. Survey Rural GA,* 1 inf, **seGA,** *(A person who doesn't like to spend his money might be called a close person or a _____ person)* Cubbidge. [Inf Black]

2 Transf: characteristic of a stingy person. [Cf *DJE* cubbitch-hole "the hollow below the skull at the back of the neck, which, if pronounced, is taken as a sign that one is *cubbitch*"]

1950 *PADS* 14.24 **SC,** Cubbage ['kʌbɪǰ] . . . Cubbage pot, a small pot, the idea being that it will hold only enough food for one person . . . Cubbage hole . . . The depression in the middle of the back of the neck at the base of the skull.

cubby See **cubbie**

cubbyhouse n

1 A small house; a play house. Cf **cuddy**

1828 Neal *Rachel Dyer* 192 **MA** (as of c1690), And so you'd better come out o' your cubby-house. **1890** *Harper's Mag.* 80.713/2 **NEng,** We hadn't hardly got into that lonesome, empty little cubby-house afore we all three took sick.

2 See quot. Cf *DS* M2

1969 *DARE* FW Addit **cnTX** [Black], *Cubbyhouse:* The cupola on an old house (common; old-fashioned).

cube lead n

In lead mining: a lead ore which shows large, distinct crystals.

1967 *DARE* Tape **CO**47, There's also a fine grain in here [=in piece of ore]. They call that galena . . . Then there's also some cube lead in there. See this square foundation of lead, that's called cube lead. That's not the

technical name for it but that's what we call it in the mine . . . [FW:] Now what's the difference between cube lead and galena? I always thought galena was in crystal or cube shape. [Inf:] Well it could be I suppose under a magnifying glass, but just looking at it with the naked eye it's just a — well — finer grade, it's more tightly packed, or tighter together, more like sugar or something like that. It's tighter, where flour would be tighter than sugar.

cubert See **culvert**

cube-seed iris n

A flag.

1968 *DARE* (Qu. S26b, *Wildflowers that grow in water or wet places*) Inf **PA**99, Cube-seed iris.

cubhead n [See prob etym at **cobb** n²] Cf **cobhead**

A goldeneye (here: *Glaucionetta clangula*).

1888 Trumbull *Names of Birds* 79, Golden-eye . . . In New Jersey at Barnegat, Tuckerton, Pleasantville (Atlantic Co.), Atlantic City, and Somers Point, Cub-head. **1923** U.S. Dept. Ag. *Misc. Circular* 13.22, Goldeneye . . . *Vernacular Names* . . . *In local use* . . . Cubhead (N.J., Va.). **1946** Hausman *Eastern Birds* 157, American Goldeneye . . . *Other Names* . . Cubhead, Copperhead.

cubie yon See **court bouillon**

cucaracha n [Span]

A cockroach.

1887 in 1921 Thorp *Songs Cowboys* 93 **SW,** Centipedes and Tarantulas / Crawl o'er me while I sleep . . Cucarachas on the wall. **1967** *DARE* (Qu. R30, *. . Other kinds of beetles . . known around here*) Inf **TX**1, Cucarachas [ˌkuˌku'račɪz].

cuch See **culch 1**

cuckatoo owl n [Echoic]

=**great horned owl.**

1909 *S. Atl. Qrly.* 8.48 **sSC coast** [Gullah], The Great Horned Owl is called, from his cry . . the *cuckatoo owl*. **1950** *PADS* 14.24 **SC,** Cuckatoo owl . . . The great horned owl, so called in imitation of its hoot (?).

cuckle n See **cockle 2, 3**

cuckle v See **cuckold v**

cuckleberry See **cockleberry**

cuckleburr n [Var of **cockleburr**]

1 =**cockleburr 1.** chiefly **Sth, S Midl, SW** See Map Cf **burr n¹ 1**

1845 Hooper *Advent. Simon Suggs* 148, They was as thick all round me, as cuckle-burrs in a colt's tail. **1884** Smith *Bill Arp's Scrap Book* 72 **GA** (*AmSp* 48.90), Then there is briars and nettles and tread softs and smartsweed and pison oak and Spanish needles and cuckle burrs and dog fennel and snakes. **1892** *Auk* 9.54 **IN,** The special food of the Parrakeet was the 'cuckle-burr' . . . Parrakeets will leave any other kind of food for cuckle-burrs. **1903** *DN* 2.310 **seMO,** Cuckle-burr. Cockle-burr. **1905** *DN* 3.56 **eNE,** In *cockelburr . .* [ʌ] is likely to appear; if not the vowel . . is a. **c1906** *DN* 3.116 **sIN,** Cockle-bur. Regularly pronounced [kʌklbɚ]. **1907** *DN* 3.230 **nwAR,** Cuckle-burr. **1908** *DN* 3.303 **eAL, wGA,** Cuckleburr. **1949** *PADS* 11.5 **wTX,** Cuckle-burr ['kʌklˌbɚ]. Almost never *cockleburr* ['kɑkˌbɚ] even among the educated. **c1960** *Wilson Coll.* **csKY,** Cocklebur is always *Xanthium strumarium. Ibid,* Cucklebur. Universal for cocklebur. **1965–70** *DARE* (Qu. S13) 258 Infs, chiefly

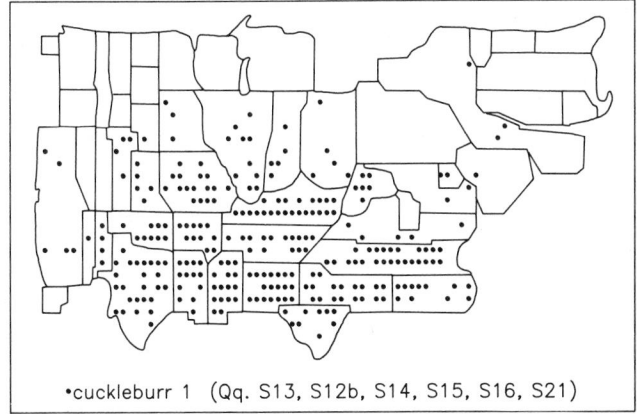

•cuckleburr 1 (Qq. S13, S12b, S14, S15, S16, S21)

Sth, S Midl, SW, Cuckleburrs; (Qu. S21) 19 Infs, **chiefly Sth, S Midl**, Cuckleburr(s); (Qu. S14) Infs **CO**37, **NY**68, Cuckleburrs; (Qu. S15) Infs **FL**16, **GA**28, 46, **IL**69, 76, 78, **MO**10, **NJ**69, **TN**52, Cuckleburr(s); (Qu. S16) Inf **TX**35, Cuckleburrs; (Qu. S12b) Inf **FL**17, Cuckleburrs. **1968** *DARE* Tape **IN**42, We can get a cuckleburr with post-emerge [herbicide] now.

2 See **cockleburr 4.**

cuckle button See **cockle button**

cuckold n

1 also *cockhold herb*: =**beggar ticks.**

1784 in 1785 *Amer. Acad. Arts & Sci. Memoirs* 1.478, *Bidens* . . . *Harvest-Lice*. Cuckold. Blossoms yellow. In cornfields. September. **1840** MA *Zool. & Bot. Surv. Herb. Plants & Quadrupeds* 137, *B[idens] frondosa* . . . Cuckold. **1873** in 1976 Miller *Shaker Herbs* 163, Cuckold *Bidens frondosa. Ibid* 182, *Bidens connata* Cockhold Herb. **1950** Gray–Fernald *Manual of Botany* 1499, *Bidens* . . . Cuckold. **1959** Carleton *Index Herb. Plants* 34, *Cuckolds: Bidens bipinnata.*

2 =**cowbird 1.**

1903 Dawson *Birds OH* 14, *Cowbird. Molothrus ater* . . . Synonyms . . . Cuckold. **1917** (1923) *Birds Amer.* 2.243, Cuckold. **1953** Jewett *Birds WA* 592, Cuckold.

3 =**cowfish 1.**

1898 U.S. Natl. Museum *Bulletin* 47.1724, *Lactophrys Tricornis* . . Cuckold.

cuckold v Usu |ˈkʌkəld|; also, **chiefly sAppalachians**, |ˈkʌkəl| (by back-formation, |ˈkʌkəld| being taken as pret) Pronc-spp *cuckle, cuckol* **chiefly sAppalachians, Ozarks**

A Forms.

1895 *DN* 1.371 eTN, *Cuckold:* "She cuckold 'em" —of an unscrupulous but pretty woman, who made fools of neighbors' husbands. **1936** *AmSp* 11.314 Ozarks, *Cuckle* . . . To commit adultery with a married woman. The injured husband is said to be *cuckled.* **1942** Hall *Smoky Mt. Speech* 91, [d] is frequently unsounded after [n] or [l], as in . . . cuckold. **1944** *PADS* 2.18 sAppalachians, *Cuckol* [ˈkʌkəl]. **1945** *PADS* 3.9, In the Kentucky mountains *cuckol'* is used mainly as a verb. **1949** Webber *Backwoods Teacher* 227 sAppalachians, Whur does the old bitch think her man is at? I'll cuckle her 'fore she's a day older if I have to backslide to do it.

B Senses.

1 To date or spend time with another fellow's sweetheart.

1939 Hall *Coll.* wNC, *Cuckold* . . . Used jocularly by CCC boys; for example, when one boy goes out with another boy's girl. The unlucky boy may ask, "You didn't cuckold me last night, did you?" According to [an inf], in CCC language it might mean "beat his time" and nothing more. **1969** *DARE* FW Addit WV, *Cuckold* . . . [ˈkʌkl]. To go out with another fellow's girl friend is to cuckold him. No actual sexual activity necessary or implied. (Among young people of high-school, or "dating," age).

2 See quot. Cf *cack'late* at **calculate**

1945 *PADS* 3.9, In the Kentucky mountains *cuckol'* . . . Used figuratively . . means to reach the wrong conclusion through faulty reason or prejudice.

cuckold dock n

=**burdock 1.**

1900 Lyons *Plant Names* 43, *A[rctium] Lappa* . . Cuckold-dock. **1930** Sievers *Amer. Med. Plants* 17, *Arctium minus* . . Other common names . . . cuckold dock. **1959** Carleton *Index Herb. Plants* 34, *Cuckold-dock: Arctium lappa.*

cuckoo-button n

=**burdock 1.**

1900 Lyons *Plant Names* 43, *A[rctium] Lappa* . . Cuckoo-button. **1931** Harned *Wild Flowers Alleghanies* 602, In this country the name Cuckoo-button is sometimes applied to it *[Arctium minus].* **1971** Krochmal *Appalachia Med. Plants* 60, *Arctium minus* . . cuckoo button.

cuckoo fly See **cuckoo wasp**

cuckoo owl n [Echoic]

=**burrowing owl.**

1923 Dawson *Birds CA* 1120, *Burrowing Owl* . . . Synonyms . . . Cuckoo Owl. [*Ibid* 1125, One may hear at evening a soft and melodious love song, *coo coo-oo, coo coo-oo,* which the male repeats by the hour.] **1953** Jewett *Birds WA* 361, *Western Burrowing Owl* . . . Other names: . . Cuckoo Owl.

cuckoo plant n

A **jack-in-the-pulpit 1** (here: *Arisaema triphyllum*).

1971 Krochmal *Appalachia Med. Plants* 62, *Arisaema triphyllum* . . . Common Names: . . cuckoo plant. **1974** (1977) Coon *Useful Plants* 67, *Arisaema triphyllum* —Jack-in-the-pulpit, . . cuckoo plant, and others.

cuckoo plum n

=**bunchberry 1.**

1898 *Jrl. Amer. Folkl.* 11.228, *Cornus Canadensis* . . . cuckoo plum, Oxford Co., Me.

cuckoo wasp n Also *cuckoo fly*

A small metallic-green or blue wasp of the family Chrysididae which lays its eggs on other insects.

1901 Howard *Insect Book* 25, All of the social wasps belong to this super-family . . as well as the so-called cuckoo flies of the old family Chrysididae. **1905** Kellogg *Amer. Insects* 498, The brilliant metallic-green little bee-like cuckoo-flies (Chrysididae) are not unfamiliar to collectors. **1928** Metcalf–Flint *Destructive & Useful Insects* 218, Cuckoo wasps, Family Chrysididae. **1964** Borror–DeLong *Intro. Insects* 721, Most of the cuckoo wasps are external parasites of full-grown wasp or bee larvae.

cucu n

=**yellowlegs 1.**

1917 (1923) *Birds Amer.* 1.242, *Totanus melanoleucus* . . . Other Names . . . Cucu; Big Cucu. **1946** Hausman *Eastern Birds* 274, *Totanus melanoleucus* . . Cucu. *Ibid* 275, *Totanus flavipes:* Small Cucu.

cucumber n Usu |ˈkju,kəmbə(r)|; infreq |ˈkʊkəmɚ| Pronc-spp *curcumber, kewcumber* See also **cowcumber**

A Forms.

a1883 (1911) Bagby *VA Gentleman* 71, There is always some household business going on here —some slicing of curcumbers (call 'em kewcumbers? Never!), shelling of peas, washing of butter. **1899** (1912) Green *VA Folk-Speech, Curcumber* . . . A cucumber. **1968** *DARE* (Qu. I25, *Names or nicknames for cucumbers*) Inf **MD**28, Some people say [ˈkʊkəmɚ].

B Senses.

1 See quot.

1941 FWP *Guide AR* 207, *Cucumber* . . . a type of mussel shell.

2 See **wild cucumber.**

3 See **cucumber tree 1.**

cucumber exclam [From homophony of 2d syll with *come*]

In the game of hide-and-seek: =**all (in) free.**

1967 *DARE* (Qu. EE15, *When he has caught the first of those . . hiding what does the player who is "it" call out?*) Inf **PA**16, Cucumber [means] come in, come in; *tobacco* means go back and hide. **1984** *DARE* File **csWI** (as of 1930), In hide-and-go-seek we'd call to the kids who were still out, "Tobacco, tobacco" (stay *back!*) or "Cucumber, cucumber" (*come on in!*).

cucumber beetle n Also *cucumber bug*

A beetle (*Diabrotica* spp).

1838 MA *Zool. & Bot. Surv. Repts. Zool.* 100, The cucumber-bug . . is called *Galeruca vittata.* At first sight it appears much like the potato-insect (*Crioceris trilineata*). **1856** U.S. Dept. Ag. *Rept. of Secy. for 1855* 90 **PA**, Among the remedies suggested for destroying the striped cucumber-beetle, *(Galereuca vittata,)* Dr. B.S. Barton . . recommends "sprinkling the vines with a mixture of red pepper and tobacco." **1928** Metcalf–Flint *Destructive & Useful Insects* 311, Cucumber Beetle . . . *Diabrotica duodecimpunctata.* **1948** *Ada* (Okla.) *Ev. News* 2 July 4/4 *(DA),* [It] is a powerful insecticide that will kill such stubborn pests as Cucumber Beetles. **1964** Borror–DeLong *Intro. Insects* 407, Cucumber beetle, *Diabrotica 12-punctata* . . . feed[s] on cucumbers and related plants. **1965–70** *DARE* (Qu. R30, *Other kinds of beetles . . around here*) 12 Infs, **chiefly Nth**, Cucumber beetle; **MD**22, **WI**12, Cucumber bug.

cucumber fish n

A **burfish** (here: *Chilomycterus schoepfi*).

1906 NJ State Museum *Annual Rept. for 1905* 366, *Chilomycterus schoepfi* . . . Burr Fish. Cucumber Fish.

cucumber flea beetle n

A flea beetle (here: *Epitrix cucumeris*).

1877 VT State Bd. Ag. *Report* 4.154, The Cucumber Flea Beetle, . . a little black beetle . . sometimes attacks the raspberry.

cucumber floor n [Prob the wood of **cucumber tree 1** or **2**]
 1949 *McDavid Coll.* **wNY,** Cucumber floors—parquet.

cucumber magnolia See **cucumber tree 1**

cucumber poplar See **cucumber tree 2**

cucumber pump n Also *cucumber-top pump*
 See quots.
 1939 *Sun* (Baltimore MD) 4 Oct 10/5 **cnMD,** A cucumber pump is usually square, made of four boards, 6 to 8 inches wide, and about four feet high . . . Cucumber pumps are seldom seen nowadays. 1946 Gould *Yankee Storekeeper* 151 **ME,** Some people had a newfangled cucumber pump, but father stuck to the old chain pump. 1968 *DARE* FW Addit **csDE,** *Cucumber-top pump:* A wooden water pump with an oval protector fitted on top of the [pump] rod to keep birds from perching there and fouling the water.

cucumber root n
 1 =**Indian cucumber root.** [See quot 1931]
 1814 Bigelow *Florula Bostoniensis* 85, *Medeola Virginica.* Cucumber root. 1931 Clute *Common Plants* 41, The cucumber-root *(Mediola Virginica)* was more accurately named, for the underground root-stock has a strong flavor of cucumber. 1968 *DARE* (Qu. S26c, *Wildflowers that grow in woods*) Inf **PA99,** Cucumber root. 1970 GA Dept. Ag. *Farmers Market Bulletin* 19 Aug 8/1, Indian cucumber-root . . is a perennial woodland herb of the Lily Family growing in eastern North America. It gets its more common name of cucumber-root because of its tuberous root shaped like a cucumber and with a suggestion of its flavor.
 2 A **twisted-stalk** (here: *Streptopus amplexifolius*).
 1959 Anderson *Flora AK* 156, *S. amplexifolius* . . . Cucumber-root. Clasping Twisted-stalk. Rootstock short, stout, horizontal, with thick fibrous roots.

cucumber-top pump See **cucumber pump**

cucumber tree n
 1 also *cowcumber, cucumber, ~ magnolia, mountain cucumber, wild ~:* Any of several **magnolias,** but esp *Magnolia acuminata* which is also called **blue magnolia, elkwood, Indian bitter, mountain magnolia, yellow linn.** [See quot 1964]
 a1782 (1788) Jefferson *Notes VA* 38, Cucumber-tree. Magnolia acuminata. 1797 (1856) Baily *Jrl.* 178 **nwNY, wPA, sOH,** The sugar maple [trees] . . . are generally found on the richest land, and frequently in stony ground, and mixed with . . elm, oak, cucumber, and other trees. 1822 Eaton *Botany* 347, *[Magnolia] acuminata* . . cucumber tree. 1831 Audubon *Ornith. Biog.* 1.198, This species *[Magnolia auriculata],* which is remarkable for the beauty of its foliage, is known in America by the names of *White Cucumber Tree, Long-leaved Cucumber Tree,* and *Indian Physic.* 1860 Curtis *Cat. Plants NC* 68, Long-leaved cucumber tree *(M. Fraseri)*. . . The flowers are 3 or 4 inches broad, pure white, and of agreeable fragrance . . . Heart-leaved cucumber tree *(M. cordata)*. . . This is smaller than the *Cucumber Tree,* but is equally desireable. 1897 Sudworth *Arborescent Flora* 196, Cucumber. 1919 Cunningham *Chronicle of an Old Town* 283 *(DA),* We cut down cucumbers and white woods and split 'em and hollowed 'em out with an adz. 1943 Peattie *Great Smokies* 155, The Canadian hemlock in the Great Smokies reaches a maximum of 100 feet . . and even the cucumber tree soars up, in some of the rich coves, to 90 feet. c1960 *Wilson Coll.* **csKY,** Cucumber tree (called *Cowcumber* by most older people). The wild magnolia *(Magnolia acuminata),* quite common in wild areas north of Green River, as in the Wet-Buffalo gorges. 1961 Douglas *My Wilderness* 172 **wNC,** Here were cucumber magnolia trees whose pale yellow, fragrant flowers bring the woods to life, come springtime, and turn to dark red cucumbers that break open at maturity and expose the seeds on their surface. 1964 Campbell *Great Smoky Wildflowers* 78, The cucumber tree is so named because its large fruits resemble a cucumber. 1965–70 *DARE* (Qu. T16, *What kinds of trees are "special" around here?*) Infs **KY39, 47, MD22, 26, NY103, NC36, PA176, VA42,** Cucumber tree; **WV4,** Mountain cucumber; **AR48,** Wild cucumber; **AR48, LA2,** Cucumber tree. 1969 *DARE* FW Addit **csKY,** Cowcumber is a later term for "Wahoo"—some say a tree with leaves like a tobacco leaf. 1979 Little *Checklist U.S. Trees* 166, *Magnolia acuminata* . . . Cucumbertree . . . Other common names—cucumber magnolia, . . yellow cucumbertree . . . *Magnolia fraseri* . . . Earleaf cucumbertree . . . *Magnolia macrophylla* . . . Large-leaf cucumbertree, white cucumbertree . . . *Magnolia pyramidata* . . . Southern cucumbertree.
 2 also *cucumber poplar, cucumber wood, wild cucumber:* =**tulip tree.**

1873 in 1976 Miller *Shaker Herbs* 252, *Liriodendron tulipifera.* Tulip Tree. Cucumber Tree. Tulip Poplar. 1893 *Jrl. Amer. Folkl.* 6.136, *Liriodendron tulipifera* . . . Cucumber-tree. N.Y. 1897 Sudworth *Arborescent Flora* 198, Cucumber Tree (N.Y.). 1939 FWP *Guide TN* 441, During the spring this gap is notable for its gorgeous stands of mountain laurel and wild honey-suckle and for its flowering cucumber trees. 1940 Richter *Trees* 104 **sOH,** She told him to fetch along fresh mint and cucumber tree leaves, for they made it smell good and welcome over a swept dirt floor. 1960 Vines *Trees SW* 281, *Liriodendron tulipifera* . . . Cucumber-tree. 1965–70 *DARE* (Qu. T13, . . *Other names . . for . . tulip tree*) Infs **NY113, 115, NC30, OH16, 82,** Cucumber tree; **NY105,** Cucumber wood; **OH41,** Is that the wild cucumber tree? (Qu. T12, . . *Poplar tree that has sticky, sweet-smelling buds*) Infs **OH72, PA49, 70,** Cucumber tree; **NJ56,** Cucumber poplar.
 3 Also occas other trees: see quot.
 1967–69 *DARE* (Qu. T9, *The common shade tree with large heart-shaped leaves, clusters of white blossoms, and long thin seed pods*) Inf **OH6,** Cucumber trees; (Qu. T13) Inf **OH12,** Cucumber [Linden]; **NY227,** Cucumber tree [Sycamore].

cucumber wood See **cucumber tree 2**

cud n Usu |kʌd|; also, **Sth, Midl,** |kʊd, kud| Pronc-sp *cood* [Cf Scots *cood, cuid* cud]
 Std senses, var forms.
 1903 *DN* 2.311 **seMO,** *Cud* . . . Pronounced cood [kʊd] almost universally. 1906 *DN* 3.117 **sIN,** *Cud* . . . Regularly pronounced [kʊd]. 1908 *DN* 3.303 **eAL, wGA,** *Cud* . . . Pronounced [kʊd]. "The cow chews its *cood.*" 1944 *PADS* 2.18 **sAppalachians,** *Cud* [kʊd]. 1950 *PADS* 13.17 **cTX,** *Cud* [kʊd]. 1965–70 *DARE* (Qu. DD2) 330 Infs, **widespread,** [kʌd]; 87 Infs, **Sth, Midl,** [kʊ(ə)d]; 10 Infs, **Sth, Midl,** [kud]; (Qu. K28) Inf **DC8,** When she'd lose a cud [kʊd]; (Qu. U19b) Inf **MS1,** Cow cud [kud]. 1967 *DARE* FW Addit **c,cnLA,** *Cud* [kʊd]—what a cow chews.

cud v See **can** v[1] **2a**

cuda n [Abbr]
 =**barracuda.**
 1946 LaMonte *N. Amer. Game Fishes* 15, Great Barracuda *Sphyræna barracuda* . . . Cuda. 1966 *Palm Beach Co. Sun Press* (Lake Park FL) 31 Mar 9/3, The Kembe, Jessinda, Em K, and Okeh [=fishing boats] have been doing exceptionally well on Kings, Dolphin, Amberjacks, Cuda, and [sic] well as some bottom fishing. 1966 *Carteret Co. News–Times* (Morehead City & Beaufort NC) 16 Aug 2/4, Sunday, Boats continued to have good luck and the catches were like this: Bunny Too, 20 kings, 2 cuda. 1972 Sparano *Outdoors Encycl.* 380, Great Barracuda—Common Names: . . cuda.—Scientific Name: *Sphyræna barracuda.* 1975 Evanoff *Catch More Fish* 215, The great barracuda *(Sphyraena barracuda)* is also called . . cuda.

cud-buddy See **cut-buddy**

cuddle v
 1903 *DN* 2.297 **Cape Cod MA,** *Cuddle* . . . To tickle.

cuddy n Also *cuddy-hole old-fash*
 A small room, closet, or cupboard.
 a1641 (1908) Winthrop *Jrl.* 2.34, He threw himself in at the door of the cuddy. 1793 (1853) Jefferson *Writings* 4.74, Then we must give him from four to six or eight dollars a week for cuddies without a bed, and sometimes without a chair or table. 1848 *S. Lit. Messenger* 14.494/2, Every nook and corner was diligently examined: not a cuddy-hole, closet, chest . . escaped the general scrutiny. a1883 (1911) Bagby *VA Gentleman* 13, In cold weather the old house was often miserably uncomfortable . . . Then there were dark closets, cuddies, and big old chests that came mayhap from England. 1899 (1912) Green *VA Folk-Speech, Cuddy* . . . A small cupboard, or storeroom for odds and ends. 1930 *AmSp* 6.99 **cNY,** *Sleeping-cuddy:* The sleeping cabin of a bargeboat. "The sleeping-cuddy was forward in the boat." 1939 Harris *Purslane* 84 **cNC,** The wrapping and spreading of winesaps in the cuddy. 1975 Gould *ME Lingo* 65, *Cuddy*—A storage space forward in a small boat, never so large as a cabin or a house. Thus, any cupboard or closet usually thought of as a catch-all. Mainers usually call it a cuddy-hole.

cudjo n [Perh alter of Engl *cudgel* a game similar to **catty** n[1] **1**]
 1906 *DN* 3.132 **nwAR,** *Cudjo* . . . A boys' game played in the evening or by moonlight.

cudjoe-wood n [*Cudjoe* African day-name for a male born on Monday + *wood*]
 =**joewood.**

1933 Small *Manual SE Flora* 1028, *J[acquinia]. keyensis . . . Cudjoewood . . .* Hammocks along the coast, S. pen. Fla., . . and Florida Keys. **1953** Greene–Blomquist *Flowers South* 94, *Cudjoe-Wood . . .* The opposite, evergreen leaves are thick and very brittle. Small, straw-colored flowers are very fragrant. **1979** Little *Checklist U.S. Trees* 151, *Joewood . . . Other common name*—cudjoe-wood.

cud'n n [Alter of *cousin*] Cf Pronc Intro 3.I.17

1965–70 DARE (Qu. Z7, *Nicknames and affectionate words for any other relatives*) 18 Infs, **chiefly S Atl & Gulf States,** Cud'n.

cudn't See **can** v[1] **2b**

cudweed n

1 Std: a plant of the genus *Gnaphalium.* [From the use of leaves to replace a cow's lost cud] Also called **balsam 3, balsamweed 2, everlasting, ladies' tobacco, life everlasting** For other names of var spp see **catfoot 2, dysentery weed, featherweed, fuzzy-guzzy, Indian posy, life-of-man, moonshine, mouse-ear, pincushions, povertyweed, rabbit tobacco, wild lavender**

2 =**pussytoes,** usu *Antennaria dioica.*

1837 Darlington *Flora Cestrica* 494, *Antennaria dioica . . . Vulgò*—Mouse-ear Cud-weed. **1959** Carleton *Index Herb. Plants* 34, *Cudweed:* Antennaria (v); Artemisia purshiana; Gifolia germanica (Filago germanica); Gnaphalium.

3 also *cudweed mugwort, cudweed sagebrush:* A **sagebrush** (here: *Artemisia ludoviciana*).

1900 Lyons *Plant Names* 47, *A. Ludoviciana . . .* Prairie or Cudweed Mugwort. **1936** McDougall *Plants of Yellowstone* 133, Heads small and numerous. *Cudweed sagebrush.* **1976** Bailey–Bailey *Hortus Third* 112, *Western m[ugwort],* cudweed, white sage.

4 =**cotton rose 2.**

1959 [see **2** above].

cue n[1] [Abbr]

A barbecue; barbecued food.

1908 DN 3.303 **eAL, wGA,** *Cue . . .* Barbecue. "Judge Denson gave a cue to a number of his friends on Monday evening [afternoon]." **1949** Brown *Amer. Cooks* 632, *"Cue"*— The real barbecue in North Carolina, known as "cue" whether referring to the occasion or the food, is a pig roast.

cue n[2] See **q-ter**

cue n[3] [Abbr for *cucumber*]

1 See quot.

1969 DARE (Qu. I25, *Names or nicknames for cucumbers*) Inf **NJ56,** Cues.

2 A muskmelon. [Perh from its shape]

1954 *Harder Coll.* **cwTN,** A cue is another type of musk melon, tastes like it a little bit, about a foot and a half long; doesn't grow much bigger than ye [=your] arm. **1968** DARE (Qu. I26, . . *Kinds of melons . . around here*) Infs **TN26, VA24, 26,** Cues; **MO9,** ['kjuˑuːz].

cue n[4] [Prob abbr for *curlicue*]

1970 DARE (Qu. JJ12, *Little flourishes . . on . . handwriting or signature to make it look fancy*) Inf **WV21,** Cues ['kjuz].

cue n[5]

A crick.

1968 DARE (Qu. BB3a, . . *A pain that strikes you suddenly in the neck*) Inf **KS16,** Cue ['kju].

cue-whiff n [**cue** n[4] + *whiff,* perh in transf sense, a short, light stroke of the pen]

1968 DARE (Qu. JJ12, *Little flourishes . . on . . handwriting or signature to make it look fancy*) Inf **MD47,** Cue-whiffs ['kju,wɪfs].

cuff n[1]

1965 DARE (Qu. I47, *When you pull the stem out of a strawberry, what do you call the green part that comes off with the stem?*) Inf **MS60,** Cuff.

cuff n[2], **cuffee, cuffey** See **cuffy**

cuffing vbl n Also *cuff-cheating* [From a student's secretly writing information on his cuff]

Cheating.

1968 DARE (Qu. JJ7, . . *Cheating in school examinations*) Inf **IN41,** Cuffing; **IN32,** Cuff-cheating.

cuff up v phr

To strike, hit, beat up.

1940 White *Wild Geese* 278 **WA** (as of 1890s), He had half a mind to go right now and hunt up that son of a bitch and cuff him up to a peak. His fists clenched. **1966** DARE FW Addit **ME22,** *Cuff 'em up:* To beat them up (fighting).

cuffy n Also sp *cuffee, cuffey;* abbr *cuff* [Twi *kofi* the day-name for a male born on Friday; see also quot 1949] **chiefly Sth** Cf DJE

Orig a Black man's name; later, any Black male; transf: something thought to be characteristic of Black people.

1713 (1879) S. Sewall *Diary* 2.386 **ME,** I press'd him, and came away with some hope; obliged Cuffee to call for him. **1755** (1901) Hempstead *Diary* 656 **CT,** An Indian freewoman wife to Mr. Tilley's Negro Cuff died. **1855** Wise *Tales Marines* 246, In burst a laughing-eyed little cuffee, as black and shining as his master's varnished boots. *Ibid* 253, We secured the boat, and leaving her to be protected by the little cuffy, we walked along the shingly beach. **1867** *Atlantic Mth.* 20.609/1 **PA** (as of 1830), After the play, Rice, having shaded his own countenance to the "contraband" hue, ordered Cuff [=a proper name] to disrobe. **1904** Day *Kin o' Ktaadn* 100 **ME,** As straight as Cuffy. **1925** Krapp *Engl. Lang.* 1.256, The name Cuffy is recorded in the *Century Dictionary* as a general name for a negro in the South. It is said to be derived from Dutch Koffi, in Guiana a common name for negroes and by custom applies to any one born on Friday. It is this name probably which has given rise to the phrase "proud as Cuffy," that is, proud as a negro tricked out in gaudy splendor. **1929** *AmSp* 5.119 **ME,** Someone conceited . . . "bigger than Cuffy". **1937** *AmSp* 12.243, Nickname for a negro, *'cuffy.'* **1942** Hurston *Dust Tracks* 229 [Black], Old cuffy just got to cut de fool, you know. *Ibid* 241, Any definitely negroid thing was just not done . . if it was old cuffy, down with it. [**1949** Turner *Africanisms* 117, Gullah Personal Names . . . *'kufi . .* K[ongo (Angola)], *kufi* pers. n. 'shortness'; Ki[=Kikongo (Belgian Congo)], ŋkufi.] **1950** PADS 14.24 **SC,** Cuffey ['kʌfi] . . . A Negro. Patronizing, sometimes with a shade of derision . . . Obsolete. **1964** PADS 42.29 **Chicago IL,** Most of the terms collected exclusively from Negro informants are rare within the Caucasian social dialects of Chicago, e.g. Cuff, Ned, blue, . . and black fay. **1966** DARE (Qu. C36, *Nicknames for special communities or groups of people living around here*) Inf **GA9,** Cuffy ['kʌfi]—Negroes. **1970** Major *Afro-Amer. Slang,* Cuffee: (African word) black person. **1971** Roberts *Third Ear* [Black], Cuff . . a black man.

cuhn'l See **colonel**

cuidado v, usu imper |ˌkwiˈðao, ˌkwiˈdao| Pronc-spp *cuidáo, quidow* [Span] **SW** *old-fash*

To be careful, watch out—usu used in exclams of warning.

1846 (1962) Magoffin *Down Santa Fé* 172 **NM,** Will he walk into the calabozo, rather a different place from the *mint* into which they are going "cuindado [sic] . . I think should rather be their motto. **1855** in 1948 *Western Folkl.* 7.9 **sCA,** A complainant, subscribing himself "Cuidado" protests against the frequenting of rum shops by the city guards. **1855** Wise *Tales Marines* 139, "*Quidow!* marm! don't make lub to a baby, when dere is a full-grown young gentleman, like dis little nigger, in de room." *Ibid* 276, "O! *cuidado!*" screamed the factor. **1894** DN 1.324 **TX,** *Cuidádo:* take care! look out! mind! A common explanation [sic] of warning. Often pronounced *cuidáo.* **1903** (1950) Austin *Land of Little Rain* 101 **sCA,** At this time when . . the young quail cry "cuidado." **1932** Bentley *Spanish Terms* 131, *Cuidado (. . English,* |kwi: ðáːo| *also* |kwi: dáːo|) . . An exclamation of warning . . . It is also used . . by Americans in such expressions as . . "If you do not carry out his instructions you had better *cuidado*" or "Better *cuidado* or you will be hurt." The occurrence of *cuidado* is fairly well restricted to spoken English.

cuiota See **coyote** n **A**

cuissome See **curioussome**

cuitan n [Chinook Jargon] **Pacific NW**

An Indian pony.

1922 Rollins *Cowboy* 78, In the extreme Northwest a few words were borrowed from the Chinook jargon of the coastal trappers and traders. The words most commonly taken . . were "skookum" (great) . . "cuitan," (a horse) and "heehee" (fun or a joke). [**1935** (1970) Thomas *Chinook* 78, *kuˈ-i-tan . . .* Horse.] **1942** Berrey–Van den Bark *Amer. Slang* 916.10, Cuitan, *an Indian pony.* **1968** Adams *Western Words* 85, *Cuitan*—An Indian pony; pronounced *coo-ee-tan'.* The first coastal

Indian tribe to see a horse called him *e-cu-i-ton;* in the later trade jargon or Chinook it became *qui-tan;* hence the present word.

cuite n Also *lacuite* [Fr; see quot 1931] **LA**
Thick syrup.
    1931 Read *LA French* 33, *Cuite*. . Thick syrup, the last drawn in the sugar house before the syrup turns to sugar. *Cuite,* the past participle of *cuire,* "cook," is shortened from *la masse cuite.* **1941** FWP *Guide LA* 688, *Cuite*. . thick syrup, drawn just before it turns to sugar. "Sugarhouse candy." **1961** Folk *Word Atlas N. LA* 195, Cane syrup. . [the French term] *cuite* [occurred] in East Carroll and Franklin. **1969** *DARE* FW Addit **sLA**, *Lacuite* [lɐˈkwiːt] heavy molasses remaining from sugar-making process. Used in recipes.

cui-ui n For proncs see quots 1960, 1968 Also sp *coo-ee-waa, couia, kuyui, kwee-wee, quee-wee* [AmInd] **NV**
A freshwater **sucker** *(Chasmistes cujus).*
    1877 *Territorial Enterprise* (Va. City, Nevada) 27 Dec. *(DA),* There is found in the waters [of Pyramid Lake] fish the like of which has never been seen in any other part of the world. This is what is called by the Indians the 'Coo-ee-waa.' It has a tremendous head, with a sucker mouth, and is so covered with ugly, shaggy fins that the fish must be trimmed of them. . before being sent to market. **1896** U.S. Natl. Museum *Bulletin* 47.1.183, *Chasmistes Cujus*. . (Couia.). . Pyramid Lake, Nevada, in deep water. . . *(couia,* the Indian name.) **1918** U.S. Fish & Wildlife Serv. *Fishery Bulletin* 35 Doc. 843.53 **NV**, In former times the coming of the "cui-ui" was a great event. **1940** FWP *Guide NV* 140, Neither trout nor cui-ui (kwee-wee) angling in Pyramid Lake was practiced by Paiutes before white men came. **1942** Lillard *Desert Challenge* 104, Far outnumbering them are ten thousand or so white pelicans, which stay during the warmer half of the year and eat tons of chub minnows, suckers, and quee-wee. **1951** *DA, Cui-ui*. . The spelling *kuyui* is found. **1960** Amer. Fisheries Soc. *List Fishes* 17, Cui-ui. . . *Chasmistes cujus*. . . Pronounced kweé-wee. **1968** *DARE* (QR p107) Inf **NV8A**, Cui-ui [ˈkjuwi, ˈkiwi]: a freshwater sucker in Nevada (in Pyramid Lake only).

cul- See **ker-**

culantro See **cilantro**

culbert See **culvert**

culch n, also attrib Also sp *cultch*
    1 also *cu(t)ch, clutch:* Refuse used in oyster beds for oyster spat to grow on.
    1881 Goode *Fisheries U.S.* 243, *Cultch.* —The shells, gravel, fragments of brick, or any other material placed in the water to catch the spawn of the oyster. See *Cutch.* **1948** *AmSp* 23.297 **Puget Sound WA,** *Cuch* (riming with 'much'), *cutch, culch* (riming with 'mulch') is the debris, such as empty clam shells or gravel, that is spread over the oyster beds for the *spat* (oysters in the swimming stage) to grow on after they settle down. **1950** *AmSp* 25.151 **Puget Sound WA,** The Washington State Shellfish Laboratory biologists in their *Bulletin* issued weekly during the spawning and setting season spell the word *cultch.* But the oyster farmers, obviously influenced by the similar automotive term, now call it the *clutch.* **1955** *Seattle Daily Times* (WA) 18 Sept mag sec 2, Brush is the oldest type of cultch (material to attract the larvæ [of oysters]). **1976** Warner *Beautiful Swimmers* 88 **Chesapeake Bay,** This is because there is no better "cultch" or hard surface for the spat to strike on than another oyster, and too many Maryland oysters are shucked out of state to provide a good supply of fresh shell. **1982** Heat Moon *Blue Highways* 391 **Chesapeake Bay,** Don't ask me what the machines do to the culch—the [oyster] beds. Couldn't say. But I know nothing lasts long when you turn the machinery on.
    2 Transf: any kind of trash or rubbish; occas used of a person held in low esteem. [OED "South of Engl. and U.S." 1736 →] **chiefly eNEng, esp ME Cf sculch**
    1890 *Jrl. Amer. Folkl.* 3.64 **ME,** *Culch.* —A domestic in my household, from Maine, uses this word as a synonym for rubbish. . . "Old culch" is used in connection with stuff, household goods, etc., which are valueless. **1891** *Ibid* 4.159 **neMA,** *Culch*—This word, when applied to human beings, has a secondary sense of disgust. "He's a mean old culch!" **1909** *DN* 3.410 **nME,** *Culch*. . Refuse. **1913** *DN* 4.1 **swME,** *Culch.* **1926** *DN* 5.386 **ME,** Culch. **1926** *AmSp* 2.79 **ME,** Cultch. **1927** *AmSp* 3.139 **ME,** Culch. **1929** *AmSp* 5.124 **ME,** Culch. **1941** *LANE* Map 346 **throughout eNEng,** *Rubbish*. . . culch, sculch. **1950** Moore *Candlemas Bay* 126 **ME,** What a rude ignorant woman! she thought. And Candace was thinking, Common cultch! **1951** *PADS*

15.66 **NH,** *Culch*. . . Junk, trash. **1952** Brown *NC Folkl.* 1.531, *Culch* . . . Clean rubbish—paper, strings, cloth, etc. **1959** *VT Hist.* new ser 27.131, *Culch.* **c1965** *DARE* FW Addit **nNH** (as of 1920s), We always had a culch box around. Neither rubbish nor junk. A box of odds and ends, pieces of useable wire, bolts with no nuts to fit or vice versa, empty spools, wooden or metal, string, fish line. . . in fact anything that a fertile imagination and a Jack-of-all-trades could imagine might possibly be used. **1975** Gould *ME Lingo* 66, *Culch, cultch*—This word's basic meaning is the debris to which young oysters attach themselves but in Maine it has always meant rubbish, junk, and any accumulation in attic, shed, and cellar. It may or may not have value. Children may be told to pick up their *culch* and get to bed. Reading matter in bad taste is *culch.* Po' white trash can be *culch.* A poor cook's unsavory offering is *culch.* Silly speech is *culch.* Many times Maine attics have yielded *culch* which antique buyers are happy to pay for. **1977** *Yankee* Jan 112 **csME,** Anything that's not fit to eat is called culch.

culinary water n **UT**
Potable water; see quot 1984.
    [**1883** *Deseret News* (Salt Lake City UT) 28 Aug, One of the most important questions. . is the supply of water for the residents on the dry benches. No one denies or can deny their great need of water for culinary and irrigating purposes.] **1983** *Cent. UT Jrl.* (Orem) 6 Nov 3/3, [Letter to Editor:] The mayor stated the water would be brought to my property line, but culinary and irrigation water would still have to be paid. **1983** *Daily UT Chron.* (Salt Lake City) 27 May 3/2, The University's water supply. . is being used by Fort Douglas as an emergency measure. . . For[t] Douglas. . will use only culinary water; there will be no irrigation. **1983** *Deseret News* (Salt Lake City UT) 2 Sept sec A 8/3, Jacob/Welby is a water exchange that will trade low-grade irrigation water for high-grade culinary water. **1984** *DARE* File **cUT**, Water coming down from the canyons is divided into two sorts: the portion that is treated (for various human uses) is subsequently known as "culinary water," and the portion that remains untreated is called "irrigation water."

cullah-cullah n [Prob echoic]
    1950 *PADS* 14.24 **SC,** *Cullah-cullah* [ˈkʌlə-ˈkʌlə] . . . The wild duck. "Gen. Alexander listed this word as American Indian."

cull board See **culling board**

culling n Also sp *cullen, cullin* Cf **cullinteen**
A small or poor oyster (that has been separated from those of higher quality).
    1894 *DN* 1.329 **NJ,** Poor oysters are *cullins*. . . *Cullinteens:* bushel oysters; like *cullings* or *cullens.* **1931–33** *LANE Worksheets* **swCT,** A regular oyster basket would hold two hundred cullings [small oysters].

culling board n Also *cull board*
A flat surface or table used for grading oysters for market.
    1968–70 *DARE* Tape **MD41,** The oysters are culled out on a culling board; **VA112,** They bring 'em up by hand an' dump 'em [oysters] on the cull board, an' then they go through 'em to separate 'em.

cullinteen n [Etym uncert; cf **culling**]
A small oyster.
    1881 Goode *Fisheries U.S.* 243 **swCT,** *Cullinteens.* —The smaller grade left after "extra", "box", and "cull" oysters have been picked out. (Norwalk.) Formerly called "bushel oysters". **1894** *DN* 1.329 **NJ,** *Cullinteens:* bushel oysters.

cullion n [*cullion* a round or bulbous root, an orchid, from obs sense "testis"]
A wild green onion.
    c1960 Wilson *Coll.* **csKY,** *Cullions*. . . Winter onions or volunteer onions of any kind. **1964** *PADS* 42.15 **csKY,** *Cullions* [ˈkʌljənz]. A name used all over the region for *volunteer* or *winter onions,* which usually grow, without cultivation, around the edges of the garden. **1967–69** *DARE* (Qu. I5, *The kind of onions that keep coming up without replanting year after year)* Infs **IA43, KY5, PA52,** Cullions; (Qu. I6, *The kind of onions that come up fresh early in the year, and you eat them raw)* Inf **KY5,** Cullions, winter onions.

cull list, on the adj phr [*cull* something rejected as inferior] **S Midl**
Of a young woman: unmarried (and presumed rejected).
    1933 *AmSp* 8.1.48 **Ozarks,** *Cull list*. . . When a mountain girl reaches the age of 19 or 20 without being married, she is said to be on the cull list. **1942** (1971) Campbell *Cloud-Walking* 122 **seKY,** Hetty was nigh

twenty and had been on the cull list a long spell. **1951** Craig *Singing Hills* 111 **swVA, nwNC,** A nicer-turned woman we never saw than you, but you'll be on the cull list if you don't get yourself a man soon. **1952** Brown *NC Folkl.* 1.531, *Cull list, be on the* . . . To be no longer on the marriage list. West. [**1967** *DARE* FW Addit **TN**12, *Cull list:* Unmarried girls over twenty. Old-fashioned term used by the country people around here.]

cullowhee n [Cherokee *gûlâhí* a plant eaten as greens in the spring]

=**atamasco (lily) 1.**

[**1953** Greene–Blomquist *Flowers South* 14, *Zephyranthes Atamasco* . . . The Cherokee Indian name for this lily was Cullowhee for which the town of Cullowhee, N.C. was named.] **1964** Batson *Wild Flowers SC* 35, *Atamasco Lily, Fairy Lily, Cullowhee* . . . Broad, grass-like, shining leaves and a flowering stalk . . arise from an underground bulb. **1980** *DARE* File **wNC,** Cullowhee [ˌkəloˈwiː] was thought to mean "valley of the lilies." Now the usual translation is "swampy hunting ground". The lilies are rather rare in this part of North Carolina.

cullud See **colored** n

cullumpus See **ker-**

cully n [Cf *cully* one easily tricked, a dupe; to make a fool of] Cf *DS* B35

An informal children's game the object of which is to walk on thin ice without breaking through.

1968 *DARE* (Qu. B33a, *The first thin ice that forms over the surface of a pond or pool*) Inf **CT**17, Skim—a good place to play cully [ˈkʌli], see who can get across without going in; (Qu. EE27, *Games played on the ice*) Inf **CT**19, Play cully [ˈkʌli]—see how much you could bend without going in. **1968** *DARE* Tape **CT**17, We used to go down there an' play cully on the ice as kids . . . You go down on the ice an' bend an' run around until it broke.

cullyflower See **cauliflower**

cully line See **cunny line**

cultch See **culch**

cultus adj Also sp *kultus* [Chinook Jargon] **Pacific NW**
Bad, worthless.

[**1849** Ross *Adventures* 346 *(DCan)* **Pacific NW,** Idle talk . . . Kaltash wa-wa.] **1851** *Ore. Statesman* 28 Mar. 2/3 *(DA),* They did not award him the work—a work which he is just as incompetent to perform as though he was not possessed of a *cultus* old printing establishment. **1855** in 1912 Thornton *Amer. Gloss.* 228 **OR,** The eggs were examined, pronounced cultus, and found no sale. **1894** *Harper's Mag.* 88.784/1 **NW,** He can't bile water without burnin' it . . . He's jest kultus, he is. **1907** Hodge *Hdbk. Amer. Indians* 1.371 [at *cultus-cod*], So called from *cultus,* signifying 'worthless,' in the Chinook jargon, a word ultimately derived from the Chinook dialect of the Chinookan stock and in frequent use on the Pacific coast. **1930** Williams *Logger-Talk* 22 **Pacific NW,** *Cultus:* Bad; from the Chinook jargon. **1945** *Senior Scholastic Teachers' Ed.* 23 Apr 19/3, *Cultus*—Worthless. A degree of worthlessness not expressed by English. For example, a 'cultus siwash' is the last word in no-accountedness. **1964** Jackman–Long *OR Desert* 180, In Oregon one hears "skookum," "cultus," "potlatch," but you don't hear those words in Pennsylvania. **1966** *DARE* (Qu. II21, . . *"The way he behaves, you'd think he was _____."*) Inf **WA**11, Cultus [ˈkʌltɪs]—Indian for no good. **1966** *DARE* FW Addit **nwWA,** Cultus wawa [ˈkʌltɪs ˈwaˌwa]—Useless folk, from the Indian. [FW: I have only heard this from one Inf in Port Townsend, but she claims it is more widely in use.]

cultus cod n [*cultus*] **Pacific coast**
=**lingcod 1.**

1882 U.S. Natl. Museum *Bulletin* 16.646, *O[phiodon] elongatus* . . . Cultus Cod . . . Pacific coast, Alaska to Santa Barbara. **1907** Hodge *Hdbk. Amer. Indians* 1.371, *Cultus-cod.* A name of the blue, or buffalo, cod. *(Ophiodon elongatus)* . . so called from *cultus,* signifying 'worthless,' in the Chinook jargon. **1960** *Amer. Fisheries Soc. List Fishes* 55, Cultus, Pacific—see lingcod.

culver's root n [From Dr. Culver, early Amer. physician]

1 also *culver root, culver's physic, culvert root:* A tall perennial plant *(Veronicastrum virginicum)* known for its medicinal root. Also called **blackroot 1, bowman's root 3, physic root, whorly-wort**

1716 in 1868 MA Hist. Soc. *Coll.* 4th ser 8.420, There is a fine plant, in your vicinity at Lebanon, known by the name of *Culver's Root;*—

Famous for the cure of Consumptions. **1828** Rafinesque *Med. Flora* 20, *Names* . . . *Vulgar* . . . Culvert-root . . . The local names of Bowman, Brinton, Culvert, were given from men who used the roots in practice. **1838** MA Zool. & Bot. Surv. *Repts. Zool.* 162, Culver's Physic. Culver Root. Grows in alluvial meadows; . . July. Root bitter and offensive. **1901** Mohr *Plant Life AL* 724, *Leptandra virginica* . . . Culver's-Root. *Veronica virginica.*

2 =**lizard's tail.**

1966 *DARE* Wildfl QR Pl.44 Inf **MI**57, Culver's root.

culvert n Usu |ˈkʌlvə(r)t|; also, **esp Midl,** |ˈkʌlbə(r)t| Pronc-spp *culbert, cubert*

A Forms.

1908 *DN* 3.303 **eAL, wGA,** *Culbert* . . . Culvert. **1912** *DN* 3.574 **wNE,** *Culbert* . . . Culvert. Very common. **1927** Ruppenthal *Coll.* **KS,** *Culbert.* **1940–41** Cassidy *WI Atlas* **nwWI,** *Culbert:* culvert. **1942** McAtee *Dial. Grant Co. IN* 21 **AL, wIN, MO** (as of 1890s), *Culbert* . . [for] culvert, the latter never heard. **1949** *PADS* 11.5 **wTX,** *Culbert.* **1950** *PADS* 13.22 **sKY,** *Culbert.* **1954** Harder *Coll.* **cwTN,** *Cubert, culbert:* culvert. "Them two cuberts 'll git 'im two more votes . . . " "Sunday night it rained so hard the culberts did not hold the water." **1960** Criswell *Resp. to PADS 20* **Ozarks,** *Culvert* . . . [ˈkʌlbət]. Invariable pronunciation from the last fifty years up through the present. c**1960** *Wilson Coll.* **csKY,** *Culvert* is often /kʌlbət/. **1968** *DARE* (Qu. N24, *A ditch along the side of a graded road*) Inf **OH**39, Culbert.

B Sense.

An underpass or road crossing used as a place for animals to pass.

1966–69 *DARE* (Qu. N31, *A place in a road where animals regularly go across*) Inf **IL**42, Culvert [ˈkʌlvərt]; **IA**4, Large underpasses or culverts are commonly used to allow cattle to pass beneath the road; **RI**4, Cattle culvert.

culvert root See **culver's root 1**

cum See **come**

cumaro n Also *cumaru, cumero* [AmSpan *cumbio, cumbro* hackberry]

A **hackberry** (here: *Celtis reticulata*).

1869 Browne *Adventures* 274 **AZ,** The country is well wooded in this vicinity, abounding in fine specimens of cumero, a tree resembling the hackleberry. **1913** Wooton *Trees NM* 62, The Elm Family *(Ulmaceae)* is represented in New Mexico by a single species of Hackberry or Cumaro *(Celtis reticulata).* **1925** Bryan *Papago Country* 46 **swAZ,** A smaller species, *Celtis reticulata,* is included under the popular name hackberry or cumaru.

cumber n Also *cummer* [Abbr for **cucumber** n]

1968–69 *DARE* (Qu. H56, . . *Different kinds of pickles favored around here*) Inf **NC**60, Pickled cumbers; (Qu. I25, . . *Nicknames for cucumbers*) Inf **CA**63, Cumbers; **OK**53, Cummers.

cumbo n [Perh alter of **gumbo** a heavy sticky soil]

1966 *DARE* (Qu. EE6c, *Cheap marbles*) Inf **OK**52, Gumboes or cumboes (lopsided and made of clay).

cumero See **cumaro**

cumeshaw See **cumshaw**

cumfluttered adj [Scots *cum-,* intensive + *flutter* to show agitation + *-ed*] **old-fash**
Flustered, excited.

1928 Chapman *Happy Mt.* 173 **seTN,** "Nothing there to get cumfluttered over," Barsha comforted. **1952** Brown *NC Folkl.* 1.531, *Cumfluttered* . . . Excited.—Caldwell county.

cum-f't'bl See **comfortable**

cummer See **cumber**

‡**cumoldiction** n, hence *cumoldictious* adj [Fanciful formation]

1944 *PADS* 2.18 **Sth,** *Cumoldiction* [kɪuməlˈdɪkʃən] . . . A curiosity, something ususual. *Cumoldictious* [kɪuməldɪkʃɛs] . . . Curious, unusual.

cumshaw n Also sp *cumeshaw, cumsha* [Chinese (Amoy) pidgin]

A bonus, gift; **lagniappe.**

[**1935** *AmSp* 10.40/2 **Nantucket** (as of 1848), *Cumsha kute.* Excellent.] **1945** Colcord *Sea Language* 62 **ME, Cape Cod, and Long Island,** *Cumshaw.* Chinese; a beggar's term meaning alms. In pidgin English it means, however, an honorable gift; something thrown in on a trade. The term was brought home by sailors. **1958** McCulloch *Woods Words Pacific NW*, *Cumsha*—A handout (from Indian); also spelled cumeshaw. **1962** Faulkner *Reivers* 45 **MS**, So all his clumsy machinations to seduce and corrupt me were only corroboration. They were not even cumshaw, lagniappe.

cun See **co'**

cuna n [Span "cradle"] **SW**

1 also sp *coona:* A folk dance characterized by a swinging, cradle-like motion.

1848 Emory *Notes Reconnoissance* 43, This cold and formal dance soon gave way to the more joyous dances of the country, the Coona, the Bolero, and the Italiana. **1902** *Out West Mag.* 17.283, The Favorite Dance of Old California. (The Cuna, or "Cradle-Waltz.") **1930** Duffus *Santa Fe Trail* 169, There was an ordinary waltz, a slow waltz, which may have resembled the tango, and the *cuna*, or cradle dance, in which there was a beautiful figure danced with arms locked and head thrown back. **1939** Vestal *Old Santa Fe* 272, The Mexicans did most of the prancing, engaged in such 'lascivious' dances as the waltz, or in some of their charming folk dances such as the *cuna*, or cradle dance. **1940** FWP *Guide NM* 112, *Cuna*—Cradle; also a kind of dance. **1968** Adams *Western Words*, *Coona*—A New Mexico dance which starts out like a country dance but turns into an Indian swing, in which the dancers copy the manner in which an Indian dancer swings his body.

2 also sp *cooney, coonie:* A cowhide stretched under a wagon as a carrying device, esp for fuel. Also called **bitch** n **2, caboose** n[1] **4, coosie 2, possum belly**

1913 (1979) Barnes *Western Grazing* 380, *Cooney.*—A raw hide slung under the rear axle and reach of the chuck wagon in which the cook carries his iron dutch-ovens and other heavy utensils. Often the brands are carried in it also. **1941** Dobie *Longhorns* 226, A trail outfit usually had a dry cowhide slung under the bed of the chuck wagon for carrying wood or cow chips in, for fuel on the plains. This hide was called a "cooney" (for *cuna*, cradle); movers with numerous children sometimes placed the little ones in this cowhide sling and then it was truly a *cuna*. Other names for it were "caboose" and "possum belly." **1966** *DARE* Tape NM14, We'd take and stretch a beef hide under the wagon and call that a coonie and that's tied in four different places and hangs open . . we'd take and pitch it [=scrub brush] in that coonie. **1968** Adams *Western Words*, *Cuna*—A green cowhide stretched to the running gear of a chuck wagon . . It is tied lower at the back to make it easier of access, and while it is drying is filled with rocks or something heavy to make it bag down, thus increasing its carrying capacity. It is used to carry wood or other fuel . . . Also called *bitch, caboose, coosie,* and *possum belly.* **1977** Watts *Dict. Old West, Cooney*—Also *coonie.*

cu-nanny See **co-nan(nie)**

cungeons intj Also *cungeon roots* [Alter of *conjure (roots)*]

1892 *DN* 1.219 **DC**, *Cungeons!* or *cungeon roots!* An exclamation supposed to prevent one's marble from being hit.

cunicum See **coakum**

cunjer, cunjuh, cunjur See **conjure** n

cunjurum n [Alter of *condom,* perh infl by **conjure** n, v]

1968 *DARE* FW Addit **GA23,** *Cunjurum* [Inf's sp] ['kʌnjrəm]: A rubber (i.e., a condom). This term originated with the Negroes; it is now used also by Whites. (Common).

cunnal See **canal** A

cunner n[1] **NEng**

1 also *conner:* A perchlike saltwater fish *(Tautogolabrus adspersus).* Also called **bait-stealer 1, bergall, chogset, nibbler, nipper, sea perch, sea roach, thornback**

1672 Josselyn *New-Englands Rarities* 25, Fish . . to be seen between the English Coast and *America,* and those proper to the Countrey . . [include the] Cunner or Sea Roach. **1685** in 1878 S. Sewall *Diary* 1.93 **MA,** Sup̄ed with a new sort of Fish called Coñers, my wife had bought. **1832** Williamson *Hist. ME* 1.163, The *Thornback,* or *Cunner,* is a brown coloured, scaled salt water fish, as large as a white perch, and is a good pan-fish. **1839** MA *Zool. & Bot. Surv. Fishes Reptiles* 16, The *Greenland Sculpin* . . I have . . often taken, while fishing from the rocks there [at Nahant, Mass.], for the *Sea-perch* or *Conner.* **1859** (1968) Bartlett *Americanisms* 58, Other names for the same fish [Burgall *(Ctenolabrus ceruleus)*] are Nibbler . . . Chogset, the Indian name; and in New England, those of Blue Perch and Conner. **1877** Jewett *Deephaven* 151 **ME,** It was one of the days when, in spite of twitching the line and using

all the tricks we could think of, the cunners would either eat our bait or keep away altogether. **1905** *DN* 3.7 **cCT,** *Cunner.* **1920** Packard *Old Plymouth* 163, In the beginning of things were the cunners, known along Massachusetts Bay mainly as perch. Names are good only in certain localities . . . Down at Newport, R.I., they catch cunners and if you talk salt-water perch to them it is at your peril. **1931–33** *LANE Worksheets* **swRI,** *Cunner*—A variety of fish (same as tautog). **1966** *DARE* (Qu. P2, . . *Saltwater fish caught around here . . good to eat)* Infs **ME6, 16,** Cunner. **1978** Merriam *Illustr. Lobstering* **ME,** Cunner (Tautogolabrus adspersus). Small fish formerly caught and used for bait in the old hoop net traps.

2 A limpet.

1889 (1971) Farmer *Americanisms, Cunner.*—A univalve found in New England waters. Genus *Patella.*

cunner n[2] Also sp *conner, coonner, cun'r* [Perh by coalescence of *canoe,* ult from Arawak, with Gullah *'kunu,* ult Afr, perh from Bambara] *old-fash*

A kind of log sailing canoe formerly common in the Chesapeake Bay.

1877 *Harper's Mag.* 54.706/2 **Chesapeake Bay,** An unpainted dirty dugout, known in the vernacular of the district as a cunner, and by persons of education called a canoe. **1880** in 1956 Eliason *Tarheel Talk* 135 **eNC,** In the East . . . they say 'Cun'r for Canoe.' **1881** Ingersoll *Oyster-Industry* 243 **Chesapeake Bay,** *Cunner.*—A canoe. **1893** *Outing* 22.94/2, We embarked in the keeper's large 30-foot 'cunner'—the local pronunciation of canoe, so called on account of its being constructed from the hollowed trunks of three large trees joined together somewhat in the form of a canoe or dugout. **1899** (1912) Green *VA Folk-Speech, Coonner* . . . A canoe. Hard to express by letters. Not *cunner,* nor *conner.* **1930** *AmSp* 6.96 **eVA,** ['kʌnəɹ], the Chesapeake canoe, formerly hollowed out of a great log, now distinguished from [kə'nu] *canoe.* **1939** FWP *Guide NC* 303, *Cunner:* canoe. **1959** Tallman *Dict. Amer. Folkl., Conner*—A variation of the word canoe. The term is still used in tidal Virginia and along the Eastern Shore of Maryland.

cunnle See **colonel**

Cunnuck See **Canuck**

cunny-fingered adj [Prob obs *cunny* var of *coney* a rabbit, a woman; cf *EDD* cunny-fingered at *cunny* sb.[1]]

1 also *cunny-thumbed;* In marble play: using a weak method of shooting the taw by holding it between the thumb and middle of the forefinger; also adv *cunny-thumb* with such a method of shooting.

1892 *DN* 1.219 **DC,** *Cunny-thumb:* used in the phrase "to shoot cunny-thumb"; that is, with the marble held between the thumb and the middle of the forefinger. This kind of shot is much feebler than when the marble rests on the end of the forefinger. **1899** (1912) Green *VA Folk-Speech, Cunny-fingered* . . . A peculiar way of using the fingers in shooting a marble, it being held on the thumb nail with the end of the fore-finger. A way of bending the thumb into the closed hand to shoot the taw, in playing marbles. **1955** *PADS* 23.15, *Cunny-fingered* . . . See *cunny-thumbed* . . . Also America. *Ibid, Cunny-thumbed* . . . Said of holding the taw or shooter before the thumb which is turned inward under the fingers of the closed fist; the way a girl shoots marbles . . . In general use in American speech.

2 See quot.

1931 Hench *Coll., Cunny-fingered*—butter-fingered, unable to hold things.

cunny line n Also *cully line* [Perh rel to **cunny-fingered** and the Scots, Engl dial var *cully-thumb (EDD Suppl., SND);* cf *EDD cunny-hole* "a hole in the ground, aimed at in the game of marbles."] Cf **taw line**

1967 *DARE* (Qu. EE8, *The line toward which the players roll their marbles before beginning a game, to determine the order of shooting)* Inf **HI6A,** The cully or cunny line (men up to sixty play marbles).

cunny-thumb adv See **cunny-fingered 1**

cunny-thumb v phr [See **cunny-fingered**]

In marble play: see quot.

1973 Ferretti *Marble Book* 42, *Cunny thumb.* To shoot with the knuckles off the ground. Regarded as a "sissy" way of shooting.

cunny-thumbed See **cunny-fingered 1**

cunnywobble n Cf **collywobbles 2**
=**mayapple.**
    1968 *DARE* (Qu. S4, *Other words . . for the mayapple*) Inf **DE3,** Cunnywobble [ˈkʌnɪˌwɑbl̩].

cun'r See **cunner** n²

cunsaa'n See **concern** v

cunsumpshus See **consumpshus**

cunterman n Also *cutterman*
    See quots.
    1981 *Seventeen Letters* **PA,** In East Stroudsburg, and some of the surrounding areas, we use the word *cunterman* or *cutterman,* to describe a person who is a slob. I am not sure about the origin of this word, but I believe it may have evolved from a similar sounding family name from this area. **1982** *DARE* File ce**PA,** The word "cunterman" (also "cutterman," but less often used) originated from the family name *Counterman.* A cunterman is a dirty, sloppy, often poor person. It . . can be applied to someone who forgot to clean under his fingernails or a wino in New York. I have heard this word used everywhere (supermarkets, church, you name it!) by all age groups, although it's mainly used by junior high and high schoolers. I have only heard this word used in Stroudsburg and East Stroudsburg and the surrounding villages.

cunt-hair grass n
    Either an **oatgrass** (here: *Danthonia spicata*) or a spike rush (here: *Eleocharis acicularis*).
    1945 McAtee *Nomina Abitera* 7, Oat Grass (*Danthonia spicata*)— Cunt-hair grass (West Virginia) . . . Needle Rush (*Eleocharis acicularis*) —Cunt-hair grass (Mount Desert, Maine, where seen as a dense stand under shallow water.)

cuntrady See **contrary** adj

cunt splice n
    1956 *AmSp* 31.150 **nwCA** [Loggers' argot], *Cunt splice . . .* A makeshift splice for temporary use.

cunweenyunt See **convenient** adj

cup n
    1 A depression below a level ground surface: a low-lying area of (sometimes wet) land; a dip in a road.
    1819 in 1823 Faux *Memorable Days* 284 **IL,** He would have bought [land] from Mr. Birkbeck, but could get only a "cup," that is, a swamp. **1886** *Outing* 9.107/1 **Rocky Mts,** [The grizzly] had passed the end of the butte, and descended into a shallow cup in the plain. **1914** Steele *Storm* 27 **NEng,** After that the two men started back up the slope toward the rim of the Handkerchief Lady's cup. **1970** *DARE* (Qu. N30, . . *A sudden short dip in a road*) Inf **TN53,** A cup.
    2 =**slipper shell.**
    1955 *Seattle Daily Times* (WA) 18 Sept mag sec 2, We'd like to insure freedom from parasites. When we import sets from Japan or the East Coast we bring in barnacles, drills and slipper shells, or cups . . . When a cup settles on an oyster shell it is a male; next year it turns into a female. Then a male settles on it. They pile up that way on an oyster.

cup v¹
    1 Of wood: to warp; hence ppl adj *cupped.*
    1902 *DN* 2.232 **sIL,** *Cup . . .* To warp. **1903** *DN* 2.311 **seMO,** *Cup . . .* To warp. (Applied to lumber.) **1906** *DN* 3.117 **sIN,** *Cupped . . .* Warped. "The planks are cupped." **1907** *DN* 3.230 **nwAR, seMO,** *Cup . . .* To warp. "The shingles are cupped on the roof, and it leaks like a sieve."
    2 with *up:* See quot.
    1906 *DN* 3.133 **nwAR,** *Cup up . . .* To become uneven, to draw up unevenly. "That cloth cups up."

cup v² See **cope** v²

cupalo See **cupola**

cup-and-line n
    1968 *DARE* Tape **WV4,** [A carpenter] strikes a line with a chalk line, and goes by that; they called it a cup-and-line . . because way back yonder they had a cup and they'd gather these pokeberries to make a juice and they'd dip their string down in that—in that cup—and . . if you wanted to mark anything with a line, why, they had a cup and a line.

cup-and-saucer n
    1 Any of var plants, as:

    a A cultivated **bellflower** (here: *Campanula medium* cv. *calycanthema*).
    1959 Carleton *Index Herb. Plants* 34, Cups-and-saucers: Campanula medium (C. calycanthema); Cobaea scandens. **1967** *DARE* FW Addit sw**WA,** *Cup-and-saucer:* Also called Canterbury bell. The same as Canterbury bell, but with a saucer-like form below the bell. Common.
    b also *cup-and-saucer vine:* A climbing plant (*Cobaea scandens*) often used in gardens.
    1909 Doubleday *Amer. Flower Garden* 330, Another very rapid grower is the cup-and-saucer vine (*Cobaea scandens*). **1959** [see **1a** above]. **1976** Bailey–Bailey *Hortus Third* 288, [*Cobaea*] *scandens . . .* Cup-and-saucer vine. Glabrous climber, to 25 ft.
    c =**butter-and-eggs 1.**
    1967 *DARE* (Qu. S11, . . *Other names . . for . . wild snapdragon*) Inf **PA40,** Cup-and-saucer.
    d An anemone.
    1968–69 *DARE* (Qu. S23, *Pale blue flowers with downy leaves and cups . . come up on open, stony hillsides in March or early April*) Inf **PA213,** Cup-and-saucer; **MD24,** Cups-and-saucers.
    2 An acorn.
    1899 (1912) Green *VA Folk-Speech, Cups and saucers . . .* A child's term of acorns, and the cups that hold them.

cup-and-saucer vine See **cup-and-saucer 1b**

cupberry n
    Perh a **thimbleberry,** but see quot.
    1818 (1920) Clark *Diary* 2315 **CT,** Found cup-berries & blackberries.

cupboard n scattered, but chiefly **Nth, N Midl** See Map
    A wardrobe or dresser; a clothes closet.
    1941 *LANE* Map 338 scattered **NEng,** Clothes closet . . . (Clothes) cupboard. **1965–70** *DARE* (Qu. E2, *A built-in space in a room for hanging clothes*) 25 Infs, scattered, but chiefly **Nth, N Midl,** Cupboard; **MD21, MI68, MT5, OH8, PA163, 196,** Clothes cupboard; **MI68,** Storage cupboard; (Qu. E1, *A piece of furniture that stands against the wall, and you hang clothes in it*) Infs **AR7, 17, 34, FL21, IL82, 141, MI68, OK13, RI16,** Cupboard; **AR47, CA115, IL53, MD21, MI68, NY48, WA11,** Clothes cupboard; (Qu. E3, *A piece of furniture in which you lay clothes flat*) Inf **IN54,** Cupboard. **1973** Allen *LAUM* 1.168, *Wardrobe . . .* A hybrid variant, *clothes cupboard,* occurred once each in three Midland speech states, Iowa, South Dakota, and Nebraska.

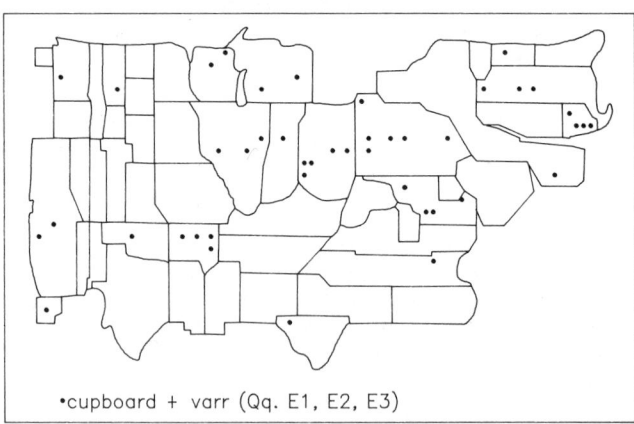

•cupboard + varr (Qq. E1, E2, E3)

cup cheese n Cf **cook cheese**
    Cottage cheese that has been kneaded until fine, heated until smooth, and molded in a cup.
    1939 Berolzheimer *U.S. Cookbook* 291 **PA,** *Cup cheese*—a soft cheese made from sour milk and molded in cups or bowls. **1957** Sun (Baltimore MD) 29 Mar Ed. B 15/1 se**PA** (Hench Coll.), Everyday items, these, to the Pennsylvania Dutch, their chicken corn soup, . . the smearcase and cup cheese. **1968–70** *DARE* (Qu. H60, *The lumpy white cheese that is made from sour milk*) Inf **MD28,** Cup cheese—in old days—cottage cheese kneaded until fine, over several days—melt—becomes smooth; **PA242,** Cup cheese.

cupen See **cuppen**

cuperler See **cupola**

cup grass n [See quot 1950]

A grass of the genus *Eriochloa*.

1950 Hitchcock *Manual Grasses* 587, *Eriochloa . . . Cupgrass . . .* The species are called cupgrasses because of the tiny cup made by the first glume at the base of the spikelet. **1970** Correll *Plants TX* 153, *Eriochloa . . Cupgrass.* **1976** Bailey–Bailey *Hortus Third* 440, *Eriochloa . . . Cup grass.*

Cupid's cramp n

Amorous infatuation.

1961 Adams *Old-Time Cowhand* 337, If there was a pretty daughter the whole range would soon be sufferin' with Cupid's cramp.

Cupid's delight n

A **Johnny-jump-up** (here: *Viola tricolor*).

1892 *Jrl. Amer. Folkl.* 5.92, *Viola tricolor . . .* Cupid's delight. Salem, Mass. **1900** Lyons *Plant Names* 394, *V[iola] tricolor . . .* Cupid's delight.

cupid's flower n

1 A **cypress vine 1** (here: *Quamoclit vulgaris*).

1949 Moldenke *Amer. Wild Flowers* 266, These are the *cypressvine . . .* and the *small red morning-glory . . .* The former [is] also called *cupids-flower* and *redjasmine.* **1959** Carleton *Index Herb. Plants* 34, *Cupid's-flower:* Quamoclit pennata (Ipomaea quamoclit).

2 A **Johnny-jump-up** (here: *Viola tricolor*).

1959 Carleton *Index Herb. Plants* 34, *Cupid's-flower . .* Viola tricolor.

cupilo See cupola

cup of flame n

=**California poppy**.

1891 *Jrl. Amer. Folkl.* 4.92 **NEng**, *Eschscholtzia . .* cups-of-flame.

cup of gold n

=**California poppy**.

1896 *Jrl. Amer. Folkl.* 9.181, *Eschscholtzia Californica . .* cups of gold. **1915** (1926) Armstrong *Western Wild Flowers* 164, California Poppy *Eschscholtzia Californica . . .* "Cup of gold." **1916** Parsons *Wild Flowers CA* 120, "California poppy" . . "cup of gold".

cupola n Usu |'kjupələ, 'kupələ|; also freq |'kjupələ, 'ku-|; occas |'k(j)upolə, 'kjupjələ(r)|. For numerous other varr see quot 1965–70 Pronc-spp *coopilow, cupalo, cuperler, cupilo, cupolo, cupoly*

A Forms.

1848 (1936) Thorne *Jrl. of Boy's Trip* 39 **seNY**, The Capitol . . is a neat building being built of brick with a cupilo on the top. **1848** Bartlett *Americanisms, Cupalo,* for *cupola,* is a common error of pronunciation. It is also a very old one. **1856** in 1870 *Overland Mth.* 4.570 **West**, That house with the coopilow's his'n—which the same isn't bad for a Pike. **1875** (1886) Woolson *Castle Nowhere* 257 **ceOH**, He lived in that big brick house with dormel-winders and a cuperler. **1892** *DN* 1.233 **KY**, *Cupola* ['kjupələ (-o?)] . . . ['kjupələu] or [-o], with the accent on the first syllable, is common in New England and Michigan. *Ibid* 238 **MO**, *Cupola.* Universally [kjupələ]. **1893** Shands *MS Speech* 71, *Cupola.* Very commonly pronounced ['kjupələ] by the illiterate. **1903** *DN* 2.296 **Cape Cod MA**, *Cupola . . .* Pronounced cupalo. **1904** [see **B1** below]. **1905** *DN* 3.7 **cCT**, *Cupalo* [kjupələ]. **1907** *DN* 3.206 **nwAR**, *Cupola . . .* Pronounced cupalo. **1909** *DN* 3.410 **nME**, *Cupolo.* **1910** *DN* 3.440 **cwNY**, *Cupola . . .* Pronounced cupalo. **1912** *DN* 3.574 **wIN**, *Cupola . . .* Pronounced cupolo or cupalo. **1918** *DN* 5.24 **NW**, *Cupolo . . .* General. **1936** *AmSp* 11.314 **Ozarks**, *Cupola . .* the hill-people always pronounce it *cu-pa-lo.* **1944** Kenyon–Knott *Pronc. Dict., Cupalo, -olo* ['kjupə,lo] . . represents a 17c variant still widely heard in US. **1965–70** *DARE* (Qu. M2, . . *The small wooden construction on top of a barn with slats for ventilation*) 246 Infs, **chiefly Nth, N Midl, West,** ['kjupələ]; 53 Infs, **chiefly Nth, N Midl,** ['kjupələ]; 48 Infs, **chiefly Inland Nth, N Midl, West,** ['kupələ]; 15 Infs, **esp IA, NE,** ['kjupo(ʊ)lə]; 12 Infs, **scattered,** ['kupələ]; **CT**39, **DE**1, **MD**20, 24, 42, **MO**32, **NJ**16, **NY**209, **OH**81, ['kjubələ]; **ME**5, 14, **NH**3, 12, **VT**2, ['kjubʊlə]; **NJ**2, **NY**211, **WA**4, ['kjupɛlo]; **PA**178, ['kjubɛlo]; **IL**114, **MT**3, ['kjupjələ]; **CA**99, ['kjupjulo]; **IL**125, **NJ**8, ['kjupolo]; **IA**32, [,kju'polo]; **ND**1, ['kjuplo]; **PA**230, ['kjubɪlo]; **CA**182, **IL**69, **MI**107, **NH**16, ['kubələ]; **NE**8, ['kupo,lo]; **VT**10, ['kupʊlo]; **MD**34, **NY**40, ['kjubələ]; **AL**43, **KS**20, **MO**12, 14, 27, **OH**47, **PA**147, **WY**5, ['kjupjələ]; **RI**7, **WI**10, **NJ**12, ['kjupjulə]; **NY**37, 123, **NE**2, ['kjupolə]; **AL**19, **LA**33, **NC**30, [,kju'polə]; **MI**73, [kjupʊlə]; **WI**6, [kjuplə]; **OH**78, [kjupələ];

MN2, **PA**72, ['kupoʊlə]; **FL**18, **IA**43, **NY**86, [kə'polə]; **IL**33, **WI**54, [kuplə]; **NJ**17, [kupɛlə]; **FL**18, **IL**29, **WA**5, ['kupjulə]; **AL**20, [kwupələ]; **NJ**1, [kublo]; **NY**82, ['kjubɪ,o]; **PA**212, ['kuləpə]; **MI**23, ['kopələ]. **1983** *DARE* File **Boston MA**, [kjupjələ].

B Senses.

1 A ventilating structure on the roof of a barn. **chiefly Nth, N Midl, West** See Map

1845 *Knickerbocker* 25.123 **GA**, Two red-brick pillars guard the door, / And for a splendid show, / To hold the weathercock on top / They've clapped up a cu-pa-lo. **1874** **VT** *State Bd. Ag. Rept. for 1873–74* 2.515, The roof is slated, and on this I have a fine cupola for ventilation of barn. **1904** Day *Kin o' Ktaadn* 91 **ME**, I hop up and run to see whether the cupoly of my barn is still there. **c1960** *Wilson Coll.* **csKY**, *Cupalo . . .* A small wooden structure on a barn or other roof for ventilation. **1965–70** *DARE* (Qu. M2, . . *The small wooden construction on top of a barn with slats for ventilation*) 465 Infs, **chiefly Nth, N Midl, West,** Cupola (and varr: see **A** above).

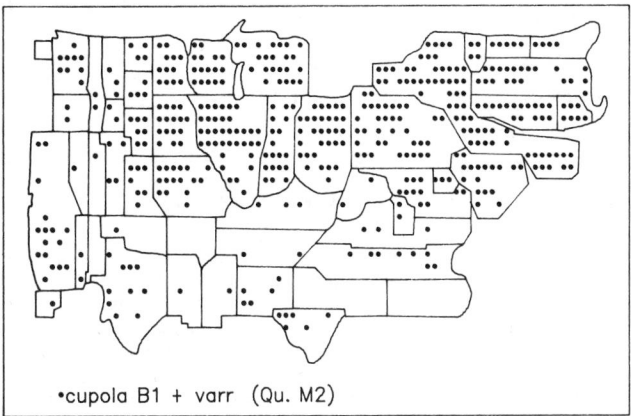

•cupola B1 + varr (Qu. M2)

2 In railroading: see quots.

1944 *Sun* (Baltimore MD) 17 Apr 9/3, [The] conductor . . in the caboose cupola had been in almost regular touch with the engine. **1945** Hubbard *Railroad Ave.* 339, *Cupola*—Observation tower on caboose. **1962** *AmSp* 37.132 **Pacific NW**, *Cupola . . .* The lookout hatch on a caboose. **1977** Adams *Lang. Railroader, Cupola:* The observation tower of a caboose. From that vantage point it was possible for the brakeman to spot hot journals, brake beams that had dropped down, and other dangers.

cupola wrench n Also *cupola key*

An imaginary item used as the basis for a practical joke.

1966 *DARE* (Qu. HH14, *Ways of teasing a beginner . . for example, by sending him for a "left-handed monkey wrench"*) Inf **AL**10, A cupola wrench; **NC**52, A [kjubɪlo] key.

cupolo, cupoly See cupola

cupped See cup v[1] 1

cuppen n |'kʌpɪn| Also sp *cupen, cuppin* Also *cow cuppen, ~ cuppin* [Alter of *cow pen*] **chiefly VA Piedmont**

An enclosure for cows, usu adjoining a barn.

1823 *Natl. Intelligencer* 1 May (*DN* 4.47), *Cuppen . . .* The enclosure within which milch cows are kept. **1834** in 1954 Smith *Yazoo River* 46 **MS**, I heard the crack of his rifle as I was comin' to the cup-pen. **a1883** (1911) Bagby *VA Gentleman* 25, The drowsy tinkle of the cow-bells in the "cup-pen" smote softly on your ear. **1891** Page *Elsket* 120 **VA** [Black], He boldly declared that he "would 'a' recognized me for one of de rail quality ef he had foun' me in a cuppen." **1895** *DN* 1.386 **ceKY**, *Cuppin':* milking yard. **1899** (1912) Green *VA Folk-Speech* 138, *Cuppen . . .* Pen for cattle. Cowpen. *Ibid* 171, Come, you had better go to the 'cuppen,' it is feeding-time. **1944** *PADS* 2.42 **sVA**, *Cupen* ['kʌpɪn] . . . Cowpen. **1946** *PADS* 5.18 **VA**, *Cuppen, cow-cuppen . . .* A pen for cows; the Piedmont and the Northern Neck. **1949** Kurath *Word Geog.* 55, In the Virginia Piedmont and the adjoining parts of Maryland and North Carolina the old compound *cuppin* (sometimes *cow cuppin*) is still current, and many remember it as an older word for the cowpen. **1966–70** *DARE* (Qu. M10, *The part of the barn where cows are kept*) Inf **VA**111, Cuppen ['kʌpɪn]; (Qu. M13, *The space near the barn with a fence around it where you keep the livestock*) Infs **VA**77, 89, Cuppen; **DC**5, [kʌpm̩]. **1967** *PADS* 47.6 **VA Piedmont,** Cow cuppin 'cowpen'. **1971** Wood *Vocab. Change* 47 **Sth,** Fenced yards or lots for certain animals . . *cuppin,* and *farm lot* are chosen more often east of the Mississippi than west of it.

cup plant n

1 also *cup rosinweed:* A tall **rosinweed** (*Silphium perfoliatum*), the upper leaves of which form a cup around the stem, native chiefly to the central third of the US. Also called **Indian cup 1, pitcher plant 3, ragged cup**

1847 Wood *Class-Book* 336, *S[ilphium] perfoliatum* . . Cup-plant . . . Along streams, &c., Mich.! to Tenn. **1870** *Amer. Naturalist* 4.580 **IL, IA,** Another species of the same genus, called the cup plant . . is common in the moist ravines. **1901** Lounsberry *S. Wild Flowers* 519, Indian-cup or cup-plant, may be known by its square stem and by its leaves that are united, about the stem, at their bases. **1936** IL Nat. Hist. Surv. *Wildflowers* 360, The Cup Plant . . . The upper leaves . . forming cup-shaped receptacles . . are often partly filled with water and drowned insects. **1968** Barkley *Plants KS* 362, Cup plant. Cup Rosinweed. Moist prairies and thickets.

2 =**pitcher plant 1.**

1899 *Plant World* 2.199 **Pine Barrens NJ,** Cup-plant for *Sarracenia purpurea* . . from the shape of the leaves.

cup rosinweed See **cup plant 1**

cup-stretcher See **stretcher**

cup towel n **chiefly TX, Inland Sth** See Map
A dish towel.

1899 (1912) Green *VA Folk-Speech, Cup-towel* . . . The last yard or so of a piece of cotton cloth in a loom had spaces of an inch cut out of the warp, the filling going all the way across, the thrums were tied so as to form lozenge shaped spaces, and tossels at the ends; used for wiping cups. **1904** Glasgow *Deliverance* 267 **VA,** Cynthia, standing at the kitchen window with a cup-towel slung across her arm, watched the chatting merrily in the sunshine. **1914** *DN* 4.151 **ME. 1939** *LANE* Map 140 *(Dish towel)* 15 infs, **chiefly ME,** Cup towel. [3 infs regard this as older or old-fashioned; 3 infs regard it as the modern term.] **1940–41** Cassidy *WI Atlas* **ceWI,** Cup towel: Dish towel. Some said [it]. For example, my grandmother, born in Baltimore. **1948** Faulkner *Intruder* 108 **MS,** The sheriff stood over a sputtering skillet . . a battercake turner in one hand and a cuptowel in the other. **1958** *PADS* 29.9 **TN.** c**1960** Wilson *Coll.* **csKY,** *Cup towel* . . . Known but not widely used. **1962** Atwood *Vocab. TX* 46, The cloth with which women used to dry and polish dishes is known as a *cup towel. Ibid* 96, Some of the common Texas words come to an end in the vicinity of the Texas-Louisiana border, and do not occur farther eastward. These are *tank, cup towel.* **1965–70** *DARE* (Qu. G16, *What do you dry the dishes with?*) 61 Infs, **chiefly TX, Inland Sth,** Cup towel; (Qu. G17, *Other kinds of towels*) Inf **MS22,** Cup towel. **1968** *DARE* FW Addit **CA101,** Cup towel: for the very best china. My mama wouldn't leave me call them anything else. **1970** Tarpley *Blinky* 91, In Northeast Texas, the most common term for a cloth used for drying dishes is *cup towel,* particularly among non-city women and in the two highest educational divisions.

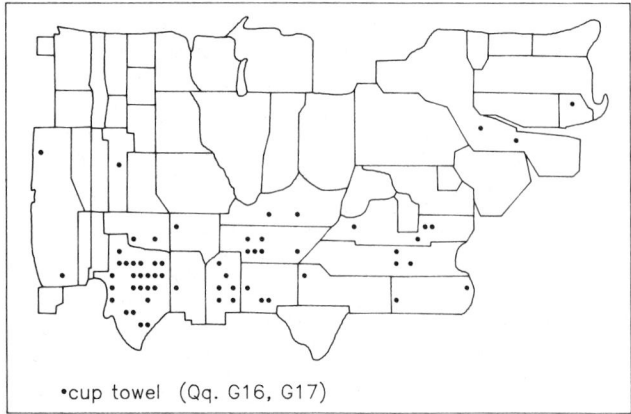

•cup towel (Qq. G16, G17)

cup turn n
=**jug-handle turn.**

~~**1981** *DARE* File **swNH** [From a young service station employee], To make a cup turn you pull to the right, swing around 90 degrees facing~~

into the cross road (this is the cup shape), then cross when there's a break in the traffic.

cup up See **cup** v¹ **2**

cur n [*OED* 1621–51 →]
A **goldeneye** (here: *Glaucionetta clangula*).

1888 Trumbull *Names of Birds* 79, The name Cob-head is again heard at Cape May City [NJ], where the species is also very generally known as *Cur;* a name that may have come from likening the bird's note to that of a dog . . . Since writing the above, I have found that in portions of Great Britain the name "Curre" is given to the Golden-eye . . and Swainson says in his Provincial Names of British Birds, that this is "from the bird's croaking cry." **1923** U.S. Dept. Ag. *Misc. Circular* 13.22, Goldeneye . . . *Vernacular Names* . . . *In local use* . . . Cur (N.J.).

cur v See **co**

cur- See **ker-**

curage n [Fr "persicaria, water pepper"]
=**lady's thumb.**

1828 Rafinesque *Med. Flora* 66, The *Polygonum persicaria* . . called *Curage* in Louisiana, and much esteemed. **1942** *Torreya* 42.159, *Polygonum* spp.—Curage, Louisiana.

curb n Pronc-sp *kearb*

1 also *curbing:* A rim or framework around the mouth of a well.
1899 (1912) Green *VA Folk-Speech* 248, *Kearb* . . . A stone, brick, or other casing in a well, or spring. **1903** *DN* 2.311 **seMO,** Curb . . . Pronounced kearb. The wall or frame about a well. **1906** *DN* 3.117 **sIN,** Curb . . . Well trough. "The curb is rotten." **1977** Foxfire 4 368 **sAppalachians,** [Caption:] Note the wooden curb built up over the hole to keep things from the surface from falling into it. *Ibid* 372, There's a well up here in town where me and my daddy walled it up to the top and put a rock curbing on it.

2 also *curbing, curb lawn,* ~ *line,* ~ *side,* ~ *strip,* ~ *way:* The strip of grass between curb and sidewalk. **scattered, but chiefly Nth, N Midl**

1960 *PADS* 34.57 **CO,** Curbing 'curb lawn'. [46 infs, all old] **1965–70** *DARE* (Qu. N44, . . *The strip of grass and trees between the sidewalk and the curb*) 16 Infs, **chiefly Nth, N Midl,** Curb: 14 Infs, **chiefly Nth, Midl,** Curb line; 11 Infs, **chiefly Nth, N Midl,** Curbing; 10 Infs, **chiefly Inland Nth,** Curb strip; **OH**50, 71, **OR**10, Curb lawn; **TN**47, Curb side; **IA**7, Curb way; **NY**62, Grass curbing. **1971** Wood *Vocab. Change* 371 **Sth,** [Footnote 88:] *(Grass strip between walk and street)* Volunteered: Curb. **1973** Allen *LAUM* 1.381, The strip of grass between a sidewalk and the street . . . Central and west central Nebraska . . is marked by the use of *curb,* which appears also in northern Iowa . . . *curb lawn* [1 inf, South Dakota], *curbing* [2 infs, Iowa] . . . *curb strip* [scattered, but esp South Dakota, Nebraska].

3 In marble play: =**bomber** n **1.**
1973 Ferretti *Marble Book* 66, In the United States it [=the marble game *boss-out*] is called *chasies* but is also known as *trails* or *trailing, bomber, curb, span* and, in Massachusetts, *plumpers.*

curb ball n
A children's street game.
1968 *DARE* (Qu. EE11, *Bat-and-ball games for just a few players*) Inf **MD2,** Curb ball: Throw the ball against the curb; as it bounces back, someone catches it, runs to places designated as bases; the other players try to tag him before he finishes the bases; (Qu. EE33, *Other outdoor games*) Inf **NY**119, Curb ball. **1979** *DARE* File **NYC** (as of c1925), *Curb ball* . . similar to *stoop ball,* played by throwing the ball against the curb when a stoop was not available.

curb hop n Also *curb boy,* ~ *girl,* ~ *hostess, curbie*
One who serves food and drink to customers in their cars; a carhop; hence *curb hopping* serving such food.
1937 *Variety* 29 Sept 63 **UT,** Curb hopping is strictly an American enterprise. It originated during the 1925 Miami land boom, but since then has gained hundreds of protagonists in practically every city of the United States. **1938** *New Yorker* 8 Jan 48 **FL,** Us curbies . . don't get no salary for banging these trays. **1939** FWP *These are Our Lives* 342 **TN,** The first job I had when I came to Memphis was being curb hop for a drugstore. **1960** Wentworth–Flexner *Slang* 134, *Curbie* . . . A waitress who serves food and drink to patrons in their automobiles parked at the curb; a carhop. **1966** *Lexington Herald & Leader* (KY) 27 Aug 15/5, *Waitresses* and *Curb Hostesses*—Experience preferred. Will train. **1968** *State* (Columbia SC) 3 May sec C 4, Neat, attractive curb girl

wanted. *Ibid* 4 May sec B 4, *Curb Boy*—work weekends, salary, good tips.

curbing n

1 See **curb 1**.

2 See **curb 2**.

curb lawn, curb line See curb 2

curb market n

An open-air market.

1940 Faulkner *Hamlet* 63 **MS,** He called on the twelfth customer, a distant kinsman, and found that he had departed a week ago with a string of mules to sell at the mule curb-market at Columbia, Tennessee. **1940** FWP *Guide PA* 100, *Curb market:* Open air or curb markets are found in most of the smaller cities. **1966** DARE Tape **FL38,** Curb market—a market in town; the farmers would come and line up on the curb every Saturday morning. **1971** Thompson *Coll.* **cnAL** (as of 1920s), *Curb market:* A market at which farmers, along with some ringers, sell produce. The ringers buy from farmers and from produce wholesalers. Open-air; **cwGA,** On a building: so-and-so's "curb market."

curb side See curb 2

curbstone-setter n Also *curb-setter, curbstone-sitter* [By analogy, as in *Irish setter*] *joc*

A mongrel dog.

1935 *AmSp* 10.51, Calling names seems to be a favorite pastime of the comic-strip actors . . . I quote only a few of the many examples I collected . . . That curb setter (applied to a dog). **1968** DARE (Qu. J1, . . *A dog of mixed breed*) Inf **WI47,** Curbstone-setter; **MN15,** Curbstone-sitter; (Qu. J2, . . *Joking or uncomplimentary words . . for dogs*) Inf **OH60,** Curbstone-setter.

curb strip See curb 2

curb wash n

An outdoor faucet.

1968 DARE (Qu. F27b, *What you turn on and off outside the house to get running water*) Inf **DE3,** Curb wash. Occasional.

curb way See curb 2

curchey, curchy See curtsy

curcumber See cucumber

curd n

1 freq pl, also *curd cheese:* Cottage cheese. **scattered, but chiefly Gulf States, S Atl, NEast** See Map

1697 (1878) S. Sewall *Diary* 1.460 **MA,** Had first Butter, Honey, Curds and Cream. **1940** Hench *Coll.* **VA,** *Smear case . .* is often used to refer to cottage cheese. In Baltimore I have heard the word *curd* used in the same way. **1941** *LANE* Map 299 **scattered, but esp neNEng,** *Cottage cheese* —Curd ch[eese] or curd. **1946** *PADS* 5.19 **VA,** Curds, curd cheese . . . Cheese made of the drained curd of sour milk, especially that fed to turkeys or chickens; mostly in the Tidewater area. **1949** Kurath *Word Geog.* 22/2, Other "Down East" expressions are: . . curd, curd cheese . . for cottage cheese (in Maine and on the New Hampshire coast). **1950** *WELS (The lumpy white cheese . . made from sour milk)* 1 Inf, **cWI,** Curd cheese; 1 Inf, **cWI,** Curds. **1951** *AmSp* 26.251 **Upstate NY,** One finds sporadic examples of such eastern New England words as . . *curds* (cottage cheese). **1962** Atwood *Vocab. TX* 61, Homemade curd cheese

. . . In Texas, as elsewhere, the creamery term *cottage cheese . .* has gone far toward replacing the older regional usages . . . A few informants, also predominantly older, use *curd.* **1965–70** DARE (Qu. H60, . . *Lumpy white cheese . . made from sour milk*) 25 Infs, **chiefly Gulf States, S Atl,** Curd; **ME16, 19, MA4, 98, NY158, 181,** Curd cheese; **AL52, FL1, PA229, UT8,** Curds; **[MO15,** Large curd cheese;**] OH76,** Heavy curd. **1968** DARE Tape **MD3,** Cottage cheese. We called it curd. **1971** *AmSp* 46.172 **Chicago IL,** 'Cheese made with the curds from sour milk': . . [4 infs] *curds.* **1971** Wood *Vocab. Change* 44, *Cottage cheese . . . Curds* is an important synonym in Florida only. *Ibid* 210 **Sth,** *Curd cheese* [scattered instances].

2 freq pl: Sour milk that has thickened; **clabber** n[1] **1.**

1962 Atwood *Vocab. TX* 62, Milk that has turned sour and thick . . . *Sour milk* and *curds* occur very sporadically. **1965–70** DARE (Qu. H58, *Milk that's just beginning to become sour*) Inf **OH40,** Curd; (Qu. H59, *Milk that becomes thick as it turns sour*) Infs **CA165, MD7, OH40, SC56,** Curd; **IN70, NY48, SC43,** Curds. **1970** Tarpley *Blinky* 190 **neTX,** *(Milk that has soured and thickened),* Curds [occurs infrequently].

3 A dust ball. Cf **curdle** n[2]

1968–69 DARE (Qu. E20, *Soft rolls of dust . . under beds and other furniture*) Infs **IL63, MN23,** Curds.

curd v See curdle v

cur dawg See cur dog

curd cheese See curd n 1

curded See curdled

curdle v Also *curd* **chiefly Nth, N Midl** See also **curdled**

Of milk: to sour and thicken.

1806 (1970) Webster *Compendious Dict.* 74, *Curd, curdle . .* to turn or shoot into curds. **1828** Webster *Amer. Dict.,* *Curdle . . .* Milk *curdles* by a mixture of runnet . . . Runnet or brandy *curdles* milk. **1965–70** DARE (Qu. H58, *Milk that's just beginning to become sour is* _____) 24 Infs, **scattered Nth, N Midl,** Curdling; **NJ54, WA30,** Starting to curdle; **MO38,** First curdles, then clabbers; (Qu. H59, *Milk that becomes thick as it turns sour*) Infs **MA43, 44, MN3, NY81, OH42,** Curdles; **CA112,** Curdling.

curdle n[1] Cf curd n 2

Sour milk that has thickened; **clabber** n[1] **1.**

1965–70 DARE (Qu. H58, *Milk that's just beginning to become sour is* _____) Infs **AL43, NC39, WA3,** Curdle; (Qu. H59, *Milk that becomes thick as it turns sour*) Infs **MA2, OK9, PA71,** Curdle.

curdle n[2] [*EDD curdle sb.*[2] 1 "A curl of hair, a ringlet"] Cf curd n 3

1973 *Examiner & Chron.* (San Francisco CA) 2 Dec Sunday Punch sec 1/1, Those little rolls . . of crud that form under beds . . are "gerfingles," whereas "curdles" are the curly hairs found in bathrooms.

curdled ppl adj Also *curded* [curdle v; *OED* 1596 →] **chiefly Nth, N Midl, West** See Map

Of milk: sour and usu thick or coagulated; also fig.

1860 Worcester *Dict.* 349, *Curdled . . .* Turned into curds; coagulated; as, "Curdled milk." **1940** Faulkner *Hamlet* 33 **MS,** "Old man Ab aint naturally mean. He's just soured." . . . "How soured?" . . . "Why, just soured." . . . "Then he run into Pat Stamper. And Pat eliminated him

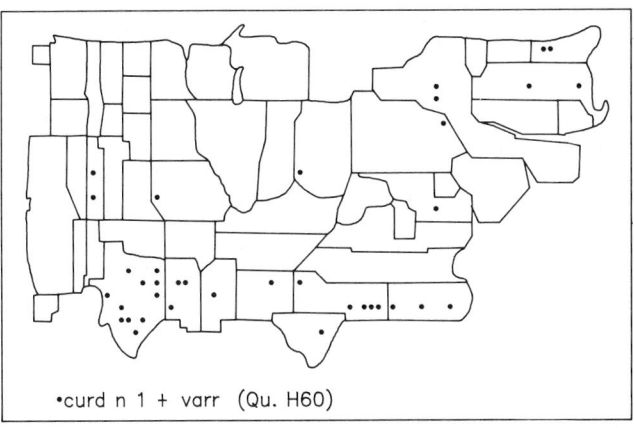

•curd n 1 + varr (Qu. H60)

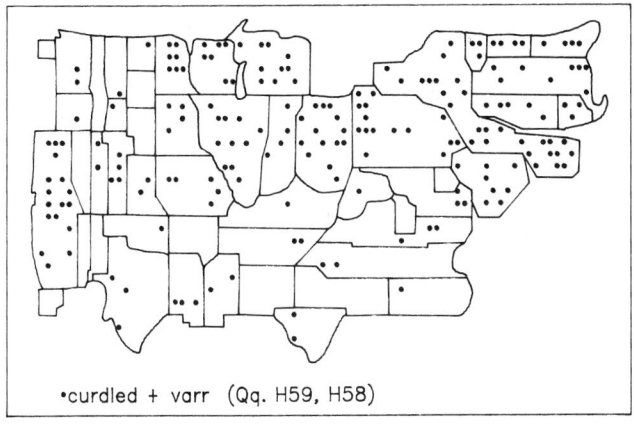

•curdled + varr (Qq. H59, H58)

from horse-trading. And so he just went plumb curdled." **1941** *LANE* Map 298 *(Sour Milk)* **throughout NEng,** The map presents the words for naturally soured and curdled milk: . . *curdled milk.* . . Thick sour milk is not a favorite article of food in New England . . . In cities and urbanized areas it is hardly known nowadays. For this reason the usage of many informants is unsettled and their notions are often vague. **1949** Kurath *Word Geog.* 71, There is no national or literary term for curdled sour milk . . . *Curdled milk* occurs in eastern Pennsylvania and Metropolitan New York. **c1960** *Wilson Coll.* **csKY,** *Curdled milk* is known and sometimes used; clabber is common. **1965–70** *DARE* (Qu. H59, *Milk that becomes thick as it turns sour*) 124 Infs, **scattered, but chiefly Nth, N Midl, West,** Curdled (milk); **OH24,** Curdled and set; **CA77, NY28,** Curded (milk); (Qu. H58, *Milk that's just beginning to become sour is _____*) 85 Infs, **scattered Nth, N Midl, West,** Curdled (milk); **CA77, NJ9, 55,** Curded (milk). **1971** *AmSp* 46.172 **Chicago IL,** 'Thick, sour milk': . . [4 infs] *curdled milk.* **1973** Allen *LAUM* 1.291, Milk that has become so sour as to form curds . . . In the U[pper] M[idwest] *curdled milk* . . has extended into much of the northern speech area . . . A variant *curded milk* appears in northern Iowa.

curdled sky n Also *curdle sky, curdly ~* [From the resemblance of the clouds to milk curd] Cf **buttermilk sky, clabber** adj, **mackerel sky**

A cloud-filled sky usu presaging rain.

[**1925** *Jrl. Amer. Folkl.* 38.621, "Curdly" (i.e., mottled) sky is a sign of rain. [*DARE* ed: The inf is a Canadian Black whose father immigrated there from Virginia in the 1860s].] **c1930** in 1966 Goldstein–Byington *Two Penny Ballads* 158 **cnPA,** A curdled sky never leaves the ground dry . . . ("Everyone knew it in the area.") **1950** *WELS* 1 Inf, **cWI,** A curdled sky never lets the earth go dry. **1968–69** *DARE* (Qu. B11, . . *Kinds of clouds*) Inf **CT10,** Curdle sky (=mackerel or herringbone sky)—all little puffs of clouds; it indicates rain; **NY146,** Curdled sky (looks like sheeps' heads); **NY227,** Curdly sky—the clouds look like curdled milk; [**NY213,** Curdly clouds].

curdled udder n

Prob chronic bovine mastitis.

1967 *DARE* (Qu. K7, *What sickness can a cow get in her udder?*) Inf **MO38,** Curdled udder.

curdle sky, curdly sky See **curdled sky**

cur dog n Eye-dial *cur dawg* [ME *curre-dog* < *curre* to growl] **chiefly Sth, S Midl** See Map

A worthless dog, mongrel.

1791 (1958) Bartram *Travels* 252 **PA,** This creature was about half the size of a small cur-dog, and quite black. **1830** *Collegian* (Harvard) 11 **MA,** The cur-dog growled an ugly growl, and grinned a bitter grin. **1892** Johnston *Mr. Billy Downs* 74 **GA,** His meanness about that cur-dog and them hound-puppies. **1899** (1912) Green *VA Folk-Speech,* Cur-dog . . . A cur, a worthless dog. A dog of unknown breed or blood, but of mean stock. **1902** *DN* 2.232 **sIL,** Cur-dog . . . A mongrel. **1906** *DN* 3.117 **sIN,** Cur-dog. **1907** *DN* 3.221 **nwAR,** Cur-dog. **1939** *LANE* Map 212 *(Mongrel)* 2 infs, **cwVT, seCT,** Cur dog. **1941** Stuart *Men of Mts.* 201 **seKY,** He brought a cur dog that would run a human being like a polecat. **1954** *Harder Coll.* **cwTN,** Cur-dog. **1954** in 1962 *Catahoula Hog Dog* 5/2 **neLA,** *"Cur dawgs".*—In no other type of hunting does a nondescript-looking mongrel shine more than when he's after wild boar. **1965–70** *DARE* (Qu. J1, . . *A dog of mixed breed*) 32 Infs, **chiefly Sth, S Midl,** Cur dog; **LA2,** A cur dog is a special kind—short-haired

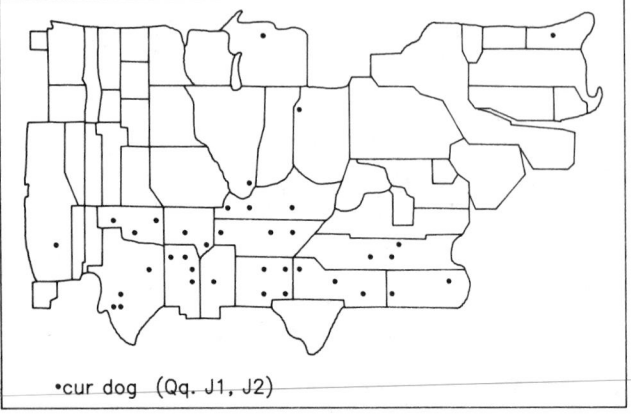

•cur dog (Qq. J1, J2)

and short eared; (Qu. J2, . . *Joking or uncomplimentary words . . for dogs*) Infs **GA11, 13, KY86, MI19, NC18, OK49,** Cur dog. **1971** Wood *Vocab. Change* 45 **Sth,** A dog of mixed and uncertain breed is ordinarily a *cur* or a *mongrel* . . . Next [in frequency] are *cur dog* and *no count.*

cure n, v Usu |kjʊr, kjʊə(r)|; also, **chiefly Sth, S Midl,** |kjo(r)| Pronc-spp *cyo', cyore, kyo(re)*

Std senses, var forms.

1892 *DN* 1.233 **KY,** Cure [kjoʊr]. **1893** Shands *MS Speech* 12, *u* has the (ô) sound in the two negro words (kyô) for *cure,* and (pyô) for *pure.* **1899** Chesnutt *Conjure Woman* 156 **NC** [Black], Mebbe he could kyo' 'im en fetch 'im roun' all right. **1908** *DN* 3.328 **eAL, wGA,** *Kyore,* n. and v. Cure. **1919** *DN* 5.34 **seKY,** *Kyore.* **1922** Gonzales *Black Border* 296 **sSC, GA coasts** [Gullah glossary], *Cyo'*—cure, cures, cured, curing. **1929** Sale *Tree Named John* 88 **MS** [Black], Dey ain' nothin' in de worl' dat'll cyore hit any quicker den dat will. **1941** Faulkner *Men Working* 92 **MS,** I managed to cyore them up with some powders. **1942** Hall *Smoky Mt. Speech* 37, Combined with a following *r,* [ʊ] becomes [ʊɚ], as in *cure* [kjʊɚ] . . . In the speech of elderly or uneducated people, the vowel may become [o]; for example, *cure* [kjoɚ]. **1950** Faulkner *Stories* 78 **MS** [Black], I wuz jest helping you kyo him of dem hiccups. **c1960** *Wilson Coll.* **csKY,** Cure /kjor/—used by many elderly people. **1966–67** *DARE* FW Addit **cwNC,** Cure: [kjor]. (Common).

cure-all n

1 =**water avens.**

1784 *Amer. Acad. Arts & Sci. Memoirs* 1.454, *Geum* . . . Water Avens. Throat-root. Cureall. **1842** Buckingham *E. & W. States* 1.162, Among these [=medicinal plants] are the heal-all, the heart's ease, the cure-all. **1873** in 1976 Miller *Shaker Herbs* 130 **PA,** Avens, Water—*Geum rivale*—Chocolate Root. Throat root. Cure-All. Evans Root. **1974** (1977) Coon *Useful Plants* 226, *Geum rivale* . . cureall. This is a three-foot herb with purple flowers found growing in bogs or wet meadows all over the United States, except for the West Coast area.

2 An **evening primrose** (here: *Oenothera biennis*).

1847 Griffith *Med. Botany* 304, *Œ[nothera] biennis* . . . Common Names.—Evening Primrose, Cure-all, &c. **1892** (1974) Millspaugh *Amer. Med. Plants* 60, *Evening Primrose* . . . Com. Names.—Common Evening Primrose, . . Cure-all. **1959** Carleton *Index Herb. Plants* 34, *Cure All:* Geum rivale; Oenothera biennis.

3 =**lemon balm.**

1873 in 1976 Miller *Shaker Herbs* 131, *Melissa officinalis.* Bee Balm . . . Cure-All. **1876** Hobbs *Bot. Hdbk.* 29, Cureall, Balm lemon, Melissa officinalis. **1940** Clute *Amer. Plant Names* 264, Citronelle, garden balm, . . cure-all. **1974** (1977) Coon *Useful Plants* 160.

4 A **self-heal** (here: *Prunella vulgaris*).

1897 *Jrl. Amer. Folkl.* 10.53, *Brunella* [sic] *vulgaris* . . cure-all, West.

cured beef n

Dried beef.

1865 *Atlantic Mth.* 15.85/1 **NYC,** We find a remainder, for annual metropolitan consumption, amounting, in the case of . . Cured Beef . . [to] 89,209 pkgs. **1966–70** *DARE* (Qu. H44, *Beef . . dried to preserve it*) Infs **AL33, LA9, MS17, 46, VA35,** Cured beef.

cured out See **cure out**

cure down v phr

Of tobacco: =**cure out.**

1967 Key *Tobacco Vocab.* **MD, NC,** Cure down; **TN,** Cure down: as the curing process takes place down the stalk. **1969** *DARE* Tape **KY9,** They [=tobacco leaves] cure down . . from the green down to the red, and it's just as thin. Course it's thick when it's green.

cure out v phr, hence ppl adj *cured out* **Sth, S Midl**

Of tobacco, hay, meat, etc: to become suitable for use, esp by drying and aging; to make usable in such a way.

1941 Stuart *Men of Mts.* 49 **neKY,** Got some cured-out burley out there in the barn-shed. **1966–69** *DARE* Tape **AR50,** If it's [=gumwood] cured out right it's pretty; **FL26,** It takes about a week to cure it [=tobacco] out; **KY9,** Then when it [=broom corn] cures out; **KY23,** It [=tobacco] hangs there 'til it all cures out; **NC7,** Then we're ready to start . . curing it [=tobacco] out; **NC8,** They [=certain tobacco leaves] don't cure out as well as the other; **TN16,** I like dry weather to kill hogs . . because the meat cures out better; **WV5,** Hang it in . . a tobacco barn and let it cure out. **1967** Key *Tobacco Vocab.* **GA, KY, MO, NC, TN,** *Cure out:* To allow tobacco to dry and exhaust its plant food reserves. **1969** *DARE* (Qu. L11, *What do you do to hay in the field after it's cut?*) Inf **GA87,** It cures out; **KY43,** Let it lay and cure out.

cure up v phr **chiefly S Midl**
Of tobacco: =**cure out.**
  1949 *PADS* 45.11 **cnKY**, *Cure up . . .* To cure fully . . . "It cures up in about eight weeks." **1966–69** *DARE* Tape **IN11**, It [=tobacco] just cures up; **KY9, 56**, They [=tobacco leaves] cure up; **SC17**, You take that green tobacco, you can cure it up, it'll be slick. **1967** Key *Tobacco Vocab.* **KY, MO, NC, TN**, *Cure up:* To allow tobacco to dry and exhaust its plant food reserves. **1967–70** *DARE* (Qu. L11, *What do you do to hay in the field after it's cut?*) Inf **KY86**, Let it cure up; **MO3**, Cure it up.

curf See **kerf**

curiosity n Usu |ˌkjuriˈɑs(ə)ti|; also **esp Sth, S Midl**, |ˌk(j)urˈɑs(ə)ti|; occas, |kjuˈɑstɪ| Pronc-spp *cur'os(s)ity*
Std senses, var forms.
  1861 Holmes *Venner* 2.175 **wMA**, Th' ol' Doctor, he's got a gre't cur'osity t' see ye. **1891** *DN* 1.117 **cwNY**, [kurˈɑsəti] . . 'curiosity'. **1936** *AmSp* 11.152 **eTX**, Curiosity . . [kjurɪˈɑstɪ], [kjurˈɑstɪ]. **1938** Rawlings *Yearling* 76 **FL**, Look at him. He's white. He's a cur'ossity. **1941** *AmSp* 16.9 **eTX** [Black], *Curiosity* [kjuˈɑstɚ]. **1941** Faulkner *Men Working* 68 **MS**, He's a monst'ous cur'osity. **1942** Hall *Smoky Mt. Speech* 65 **wNC, eTN**, Omission of [ɪ] is usual in the following words: . . curiosity [kjurˈɑstɪ]. **1966** *DARE* Tape **AL3**, Curiosity [ˌkjuˈrɑstɪ].

curious adj Usu |ˈkjuriəs|; also, **chiefly Sth, S Midl, NEng**, |ˈk(j)urəs|; occas |ˈkju(ə)s|; infreq |ˈkɪr(ə)s| Pronc-spp *curi⁽ʰ⁾'s, cur'o's, cur⁽ʰ⁾ous, cur⁽ʰ⁾us(s), cuse, cu'us, kewrus, kuse, ku'yus*
A Forms.
  1848 Lowell *Biglow* 3 **NEng**, My ant Keziah used to say it's nater to be curus. **1873** Harte *Mrs. Skaggs* 147, It's a mighty cur'o's thing that nobody gets hit so often. **1880** *Appletons' Summer Book* 131/1 **eTN**, "I likes yer better nor any gal I ever see.". . "Yer hev got a mighty cur'ous way o' showin' it," Cynthia replied. **1884** Jewett *Mate of Daylight* 200 **ME**, It did look kind of curi's. **1887** (1967) Harris *Free Joe* 110 **GA**, Folks 'roun' here is mighty kuse. **1887** *Scribner's Mag.* 2.474/2 **AR** [Black], By gum, ain't dat cuse! **1888** Jones *Negro Myths* 99 **GA coast**, De Cunjur Man larne um heap er curous ting. **1889** (1971) Farmer *Americanisms* 161 **Sth**, *Comical . . .* [He] said . . that they were a great curiosity. 'I don't see nothing kewrus about 'em,' replied the man disdainfully. **1891** *DN* 1.149 **cwNY**, [ˈkjurɪs] < *curious*. **1891** (1967) Freeman *New Engl. Nun* 82, It's cur'us how them oak leaves hang on arter the others have all fell off. **1891** (1900) French *Otto* 162 **AR**, When it [a loaf of bread] come out so sad an' curis lookin' he said for me to come here to-day. **1900** Day *Up in ME* 54, 'Twas sort of curi's, I confess, but still I slept complete. **1901** *DN* 2.181 **neKY** [Black], *Curious* ku'yus. **1905** Culbertson *Banjo Talks* 122 **SE**, *Cur'ous,* now, dis trouble. **1914** *DN* 4.70 **ME, nNH**, *Cur'us . . .* Curious. **1927** Kennedy *Gritny* 19 **sLA** [Black], Yo' curuss clo'se. **1929** Sale *Tree Named John* 121 **MS** [Black], Hit's makin' me feel cu'us, hit do. **1933** Rawlings *South Moon* 6 **FL**, She's a perfeckly cur'ous young un. **1941** *AmSp* 16.10 **eTX** [Black], *Curious . .* [ˈkju:əs]. **1941** Faulkner *Men Working* 68 **MS**, Hit's a cur'ous thing the way Buddy's face gits all shiny like ever' time he looks at Hub. **1942** Hall *Smoky Mt. Speech* 65 **wNC, eTN**, Omission of [ɪ] is usual in . . curious [ˈkjurəs]. **1954** *Harder Coll.* **cwTN**, Curious [kɪrs; kɪrəs]. **1959** *VT Hist.* new ser 27.132, Curious [kūr'ŭs] . . . Common.
B Senses.
1 Particularly fine; nice; interesting. *obs*
  1816 Pickering *Vocab.* 74, *Curious.* This word . . is often heard among the common farmers of New England, in the sense of *excellent,* or *peculiarly excellent* . . "These are *curious* apples; this is *curious* cider," &c . . This use of the word is hardly known in our sea-port towns. **1861** Holmes *Venner* 2.189 **wMA**, They a'n't good f'r much, but they're cur'ous t' keep t'look at. **1867** Lowell *Biglow* lvi **'Upcountry' MA**, *Curious,* meaning nice, occurs continually in old writers, and is as old as Pecock's "Repressor."
2 Of persons: strange, odd, eccentric. **chiefly Sth, S Midl**
  1938 Rawlings *Yearling* 84 **FL**, I reckon we be as cur'ous to the creeturs as they be to us. **1954** *Harder Coll.* **cwTN**, *Curious . . .* Odd or not quite right mentally. **c1960** Wilson *Coll.* **csKY**, *Curious . . .* Queer rather than inquisitive. **1965–70** *DARE* (Qu. HH4, *Someone who has odd or peculiar ideas*) Infs **IL32, LA12, MS49, NC2, TN15, 26, VA35, 42**, Curious (guy, person); (Qu. HH5, *Someone . . queer but harmless*) Infs **KY6, VA35**, Curious; (Qu. HH11a, *Someone who is too particular or fussy—if it's a man*) Inf **GA28**, Curious; (Qu. II7, *Somebody who doesn't seem to fit in . . "He's kind of a _____."*) Infs **MO23, VA38**, Curious (person).

curious adv Pronc-sp *kuse*
1 With curiosity, inquisitively.
  1885 Twain *Huck. Finn* 86 **MO**, When the woman stopped talking, I looked up, and she was looking at me pretty curious. **1887** (1967) Harris *Free Joe* 222 **cGA** [Black], De white mens look at me mighty kuse w'en I ax um 'bout my young marster.
2 Strangely, oddly.
  1926 Roberts *Time of Man* 47 **KY**, "A dog barks curious," she said again, "curious now."

curious-minded adj
  1954 *Harder Coll.* **cwTN**, *Curious-minded:* Odd, not quite right mentally. "All them Jones's curious minded's 'ey can be. Better leave 'em 'lone."

curious ointment n [Folk-etym for aphet form of *mercurous*]
  1930 *DN* 6.80 **cSC**, *Curious intment . . .* Mercurial ointment, used to destroy "boogers" [lice] in the hair.

curioussome adj Pronc-spp *cuissome, curisome* **chiefly Sth** *esp among Black speakers* Cf **-some**
Curious, odd, strange.
  1884 Harrison *Negro Engl.* 273 **Sth**, Mighty curisome noshuns 'bout = to have curious ideas about. **1891** Page *Elsket* 138 **VA** [Black], Dat's a curisome thing, suh. **1901** *Century Illustr. Mag.* 62.903/2 **TN** [Black], But hit gittin' too hot here wid all dem quare-talkin', cuissome folks dat ain' know de business eend uv er muel f'om t'other. **1916** *Scribner's Mag.* 59.353/2 **VA** [Black], He look at me, kinder curisome. **1957** *DE Folkl. Bulletin* Oct 28, Curioussome (odd, peculiar).

curis See **curious** adj **A**

curisome See **curioussome**

curl n, v Usu |ˈkɜ˞(ə)l, kɜl|; also, **esp Sth, S Midl**, *somewhat old-fash*, |kwɜ˞l| (cf **coil** v); occas, **chiefly in NYC**, *decreasing currency*, |kɔɪl| See Pronc Intro 3.II.12 Pronc-spp *kwirl, quirl* Cf *OED querl* sb.
A Forms.
  c1853 (1860) Taylor *January & June* 23, [The grapevine's] aspirations were soon manifested in the display of divers mermaidish-looking ringlets, with two or three dainty "quirls" therein. **1889** Cooke *Steadfast* 162 **CT**, A hundred resolute little quirls above the low forehead. **1890** *DN* 1.75 **Cape Cod MA**, Quirl [kwɚl]: curl, v. "Quirled way up." . . . [DN editor:] "Quirl, both noun and verb, is familiar to me." **1893** Shands *MS Speech, Quirl* [kwɜ˞l]. This word is largely used by negroes, and to some extent by white people, for *curl.* It is also thus used in New England. **1899** (1912) Green *VA Folk-Speech, Quirl,* v. Curl. "The dog was quirled up on the mat." **1908** *DN* 3.303 **eAL, wGA**, *Curl . . .* Often pronounced *kwirl* by the negroes. *Ibid* 361, *Quirl,* v. and n. Curl. **1940** *AmSp* 15.372 **NYC**, *Variants of* [ɜ/ɚ] *as in 'curl' . . .* The diphthongal form, despite the efforts of the schools and despite the ridicule to which it has been subjected, is employed by a majority of New York's seven-and-a-half millions . . . It is today by no means confined to the level of uncultivated speech, but is often found in the speech of the educated, especially among older people. The exact quality of the diphthong is somewhat variable. Most commonly it would be transcribed as [ɜɪ] or [ʌɪ], but I have also occasionally heard a pronunciation for which I have been tempted to write [ʊɪ] and another, not very common, [ɚɪ]. Several of my colleagues have reported a rounded diphthong. The pronunciation [ɔɪ] is very rare, if it occurs at all. **1941** *AmSp* 16.15 **eTX** [Black], Curl . . . [kɜ:l]. **1944** *PADS* 2.30 **eKY**, Quirl [kwɜ:l] . . . To curl. "Does hit quirl like a pig's tail?" . . Common. **1950** *PADS* 14.55 **SC**, Quirl . . . A *curl,* as on a watermelon vine. **1966** Labov *Social Stratification NYC* 337, The most well known example of a stigmatized New York City trait is the up-gliding central diphthong [ɜɪ] in words like *third, bird* and *shirt, curl* and *worm . . .* This sound is still frequently heard in New York City for the words just listed. **1968** *DARE* (QR, near Qu. P25) Inf **SC9**, A rattler gets into a [kwɛrl].
B As noun.
1 also sp *curle:* A nearly circular bend in a stream—sometimes used as a place name. **VA**
  1638 in 1940 *AmSp* 15.169 **VA**, Within the four Mile Creek near Curles. **1899** (1912) Green *VA Folk-Speech, Curles . . .* Name of a place on the James river from the "Curles of the river," 1612. From an Indian word meaning "a sinuous tidal estuary;" "the curles of the river." **1929** Wilstach *Tidewater VA* 144, These bends are often called the Curles of the River, and in olden times this section was also often called The

Corkscrew. So nearly completely circular are some of these "curles" that to go the six miles . . the river takes a sinuous course of sixteen miles.

2 Among students: one who recites well; an excellent recitation. **VA** Cf **C** below

1888 in 1980 *DARE* File [From University of Virginia annual called *Corks and Curls*], And it is said that, even untoe this day, when a student reciteth passing well, he is called a "Curl." **1901** *DN* 2.138 c**VA** [College Words], *Curl* . . . Fine recitation . . . Charlottesville, Va.

3 A wave, esp the concave face of a cresting breaker.

1962 Masters *Surfing Made Easy* 64 *(OEDS)*, *Curl*, the curved top of a breaking wave. **1963** Kuhns *Surfing* 111, *Curl:* The concave part of a wave just as it is breaking; the face of a breaker as the crest curls forward; the hook; the tunnel; the tube. **1966** *DARE* (Qu. O15, . . *Different kinds of waves*) Inf **GA**11, Curl. **1970** *DARE* FW Addit **CA**191, *In the curl:* Surfing lingo meaning the steepest part of the wave before it breaks. [FW: the Inf, a surfer for thirty years, says the term is long-established and still current.]

4 A flourish that ornaments handwriting; a curlicue.

1962 [see **C** below]. **1965–70** *DARE* (Qu. JJ12, *Little flourishes . . on . . handwriting . . to make it look fancy*) 16 Infs, **esp Mid Atl**, Curls; **LA**28, Curls & tails.

5 See quot. **esp Nth, N Midl**

1965–70 *DARE* (Qu. E20, *Soft rolls of dust that collect on the floor under beds or other furniture*) 10 Infs, **esp Nth, N Midl**, Dust curls: **MA**4, **MI**34, **NJ**2, 19, 30, **PA**225, **VA**98, Curls; **IL**50, Curls of dust.

C As verb.

Among students: to recite with excellence; hence n *curler* one who recites well. **VA**

1851 Hall *College Words* 89, *Curl*. In the University of Virginia, to make a perfect recitation; to overwhelm a Professor with student learning. **1900** *DN* 2.31 ce**VA** [College words], *Curl* . . . To pass a perfect recitation or examination. R[andolph]–M[acon College]. **1921** Bruce *Univ. VA* 4.83, [Footnote:] The student who flagrantly failed to reply correctly to the questions . . in the classroom was said to have been *corked*. If . . he answered with a grand flourish of pertinent information, he was said to have *curled*. **1926** in 1960 Wentworth–Flexner *Slang* 135, Even the indigenous ancient verb, 'to curl,' i.e., to confound a professor by a perfect recitation, is in good repute [at the Univ. of Virginia]. **1962** *Cavalier Daily* (Univ of VA) 1 Mar 2/3 *(Hench Coll.)* (as of c1900), To curl meant to do well, or to speak eloquently. A curler was one who knew his studies and could recite well. Often a student who curled would be applauded by his classmates . . . Mr. H. has a theory about its derivation. He thinks that it comes from Spencerian penmanship which was taught in the 19th century. Since it is characterized by many loops and curves, the handwriting of one skilled in it would contain many curls.

curle See **curl B1**

curled ppl adj [Prob ellip for or folk-etym from *curdled*, but cf *EDD curlings* curds]

Of milk: sour, curdled.

1968–70 *DARE* (Qu. H58, *Milk that's just beginning to . . sour*) Infs **DC**12, **MO**16, Curled; (Qu. H59, *Milk that becomes thick as it turns sour*) Inf **DC**11, Curled.

curled dock n

Std: a dock *(Rumex crispus)* which has leaves with strongly wavy or curled margins. Also called **coffeeweed 2b, garden patience, narrow dock, sour dock, yellow dock**

curled maple See **curly maple**

curler n¹ See **curl C**

curler n² [Metath or transl of **cruller**] Cf **twister**

A kind of doughnut or **friedcake 1.**

1967–70 *DARE* (Qu. H26, *A round cake of dough, cooked in deep fat, with a hole in the center*) Inf **PA**242, Curler; (Qu. H28, *Different shapes or types of doughnuts*) Inf **NY**28, Curlers; **OH**47, Curlers. [FW: not crullers.]

curlew n

1 Std: any of a number of birds of the family Scolopacidæ.
2 A bird of the family Threskiornithidæ, esp the **white ibis.**

1913 *Auk* 30.490, *Guara alba*. White Ibis; 'Curlew'. **1936** *Oriole* 1.3, White Ibis.—Curlew. **1938** Rawlings *Yearling* 312 n**FL**, The curlews were coming south. They came every winter from Georgia. The old ones

were white with long curved bills. The young ones, from the spring hatching, were gray-brown in color. The young curlews made fine eating. **1954** Sprunt *FL Bird Life* 46, The "curlews" mentioned by Mrs. Rawlings in her great novel, *The Yearling*, were of course White Ibis. **1968** *DARE* FW Addit **GA**25, *Curlew*—a nickname for the white ibis.

curlewberry n

A **crowberry 1** (here: *Empetrum nigrum*).

1900 Lyons *Plant Names* 145, *E. nigrum* . . . Curlew-berry. **1950** Gray–Fernald *Manual of Botany* 975, *Black C[rowberry]*, Curlew-berry. **1972** Viereck *AK Trees* 201, Curlewberry . . . Low, creeping or spreading evergreen heatherlike shrub.

curley flower See **curly flower**

curl flower, curl-flowered clematis See **curly clematis**

curlicue See **curly n¹ 2**

curlimacue n [*curlicue* + **-ma-** infix]

A curlicue.

1951 Johnson *Resp. to PADS 20* **DE**, *(Little flourishes that some people put on their handwriting to make it look fancy)* Curlimacues—old fashioned. **1965–70** *DARE* (Qu. JJ12, *Little flourishes . . on . . handwriting . . to make it look fancy*) 15 Infs, **scattered**, Curlimacues.

curling tin n

A hair curler.

1937 Sandoz *Slogum* 184 **NE** (as of 1900–20), Gulla was at the inner screen door, her corset on, the curling tins out of her bangs.

curl-leaf n, also attrib Also *curl-leaf mountain-mahogany* [See quot 1937] **West**

A **mountain mahogany** (here: *Cercocarpus ledifolius*).

1931 Dayton *Important Browse* 45, *Curlleaf mountain-mahogany (C. ledifolius)*, frequently known simply as curlleaf or mountain-mahogany . ., is much the commonest, most widely distributed, and best known of the narrow-leaved and hard-leaved species. **1937** U.S. Forest Serv. *Range Plant Hdbk.* B50, Curlleaf mountain-mahogany, also known as curlleaf and desert mahogany, is usually a shrub . . . The leaves are rolled under (revolute) at the margins which accounts for the common name, curlleaf. **1941** Jaeger *Wildflowers* 92 **Desert SW**, Go into the curl-leaf thickets when you will during the summer, and you will always find them much frequented by birds. **1973** Hitchcock–Cronquist *Flora Pacific NW* 209, Curl-l[ea]f m[ountain-mahogany].

curl maple See **curly maple**

curls n [Prob from the turned-back leaves]

An **amaranth** (here: *Amaranthus retroflexus*).

1897 *Jrl. Amer. Folkl.* 10.53, *Amaranthus retroflexus* . . . curls, red root, Sulphur Grove, Ohio.

curly n¹

1 A curlicue. Cf **curl B4**

1965–70 *DARE* (Qu. JJ12, *Little flourishes . . on . . handwriting . . to make it look fancy*) Infs **KY**72, **LA**16, **MS**25, **TX**10, Curlies.

2 also *curlicue:* A dust ball. Cf **curl B5**

1969 *DARE* (Qu. E20, *Soft rolls of dust . . on the floor under beds or other furniture*) Inf **NY**162, Curlies; **MI**28, Curlicues.

3 A caterpillar with stinging hairs.

1969 *DARE* (Qu. R21, . . *Kinds of stinging insects*) Inf **IL**58, Curlies— These are a kind of caterpillar that stings.

curly n² See **quirley**

curly birch n [*curly* having variegated grain + *birch;* cf **curly maple**]

=**yellow birch.**

1939 *Hall Coll.* w**NC**, Curly birch . . . A kind of birch.

curly clematis n Also *curl flower, curl-flowered clematis* Cf **curly-heads**

A clematis (here: *Clematis crispa*).

1900 Lyons *Plant Names* 106, *C. crispa* . . . Curl-flowered Clematis. **1953** Greene–Blomquist *Flowers South* 35, Of the woody vines, one of the most attractive is curly- or marsh-clematis *(C. crispa)*. **1960** Vines *Trees SW* 260, Curly Clematis. *Clematis crispa* . . . Also known under the vernacular names of Curl Flower. **1976** Bailey–Bailey *Hortus Third* 282, *[Clematis] crispa . . . Curly c[lematis], curlflower* . . . Calyx . . with broad, wavy, thin margins.

curlycup gumweed n

A **gum plant** (here: *Grindelia squarrosa*).

 1937 U.S. Forest Serv. *Range Plant Hdbk.* W86 (leaf 2), Fluid extract of grindelia . . is obtained from the flowering tops and leaves of . . curlycup gumweed. **1967** *DARE* FW Addit **CO,** Curlycup gumweed (*or* tarweed) [*Grindelia squarrosa*]. **1976** Dodge *Roadside Wildflowers* 72, *Curlycup Gumweed* . . . Leaves and flower buds of gumweed are covered with a clear, sticky substance for which the plants are named.

curly dirt n Cf *DS* E20

=**curly** n[1] 2.

 1953 *Hench Coll.* ceVA, Friends were talking about fuzzy balls of lint, etc. which collect on floors, especially under beds. Two of them said that they call such balls *curly dirt.*

curly-end pepper n Cf **bird pepper**

A pepper of the genus *Capsicum.*

 1966 *DARE* (Qu. I22a, . . *Different kinds of peppers—small hot*) Inf **SC26,** Curly-end peppers—little-finger sized.

curly flower n Also sp *curley flower* [Folk-etym; cf *EDD curly-flower* at *curly* adj. 1 (9)] **SC**

The cauliflower.

 1909 *S. Atl. Qrly.* 8.45 sSC coast [Gullah], *Cauliflower* is universally known by the descriptive of *curly-flowers.* **1941** FWP *Guide SC* 108 [Gullah], *Curly flower.* Cauliflower. **1950** *PADS* 14.24 SC, *Curley flowers:* The cauliflower; survival of an English usage.

curly grass n

A small grasslike fern (*Schizæa pusilla*).

 1938 *Torreya* 38.64 cNJ, I have found Curly Grass . . in a hollow where rainwater collects. **1939** FWP *Guide NJ* 18, On damp sandy spots near cedar swamps at 30 known places throughout the pine barrens is found the little fern, *Schizæa pusilla* (curly grass), the outstanding rarity of the State. **1950** Gray–Fernald *Manual of Botany* 25, Curly-grass. **1976** Bailey–Bailey *Hortus Third* 1017, *Schizæa pusilla* . . . Curly grass.

curly hair n [From the fibers at the edges of the leaf]

An **Adam's needle (and thread)** (here: *Yucca filamentosa*).

 1933 Small *Manual SE Flora* 303, *Y. filamentosa* . . . Bear-grass. Adam's-needle. Curly-hair. Yucca.

curly-heads n Also *curly head* [See quot 1851] Cf **curly clematis**

A clematis (here: *Clematis ochroleuca*).

 1851 *DeBow's Rev.* 11.49, *Curly head,* a vine resembling the other [*Morning Glory*], but the bloom is a whorl or curly plevus [sic, perh for *plexus*] of whitish fibrils. **1900** Lyons *Plant Names* 107, *C. ochroleuca* . . . Curly-heads. **1950** Gray–Fernald *Manual of Botany* 665, Curly-heads. **1976** Bailey–Bailey *Hortus Third* 284, [*Clematis*] *ochroleuca* . . . Curly-heads.

curly lily n

A **dogtooth violet** (here: *Erythronium giganteum*).

 1934 Haskin *Wild Flowers Pacific Coast* 25, *Erythronium giganteum* . . . Other local names are . . curly lily.

curly maple n Also *curl(ed) maple* [See quot 1965]

The wood of a maple tree (such as the **sugar maple**) which has a grain with distinctive whorls.

 1778 in 1907 *PA Archives* 6th ser 12.860, *Invantary* . . . A Curl'd maple Teatable. **1818** Fearon *Sketches* 24 **NY,** Curl maple, a native and most beautiful wood, is also much approved. **1832** Williamson *Hist. ME* 2.703, Our indigenous cherry, black-birch, and curl maple . . were shoved from the parlour and setting-room, to admit articles of foreign mahogany. **1909** Porter *Girl Limberlost* 2.218 **cnIN,** In an expressed crate was a fine curly-maple dressing table. **1916** Seton *Woodcraft Manual Girls* 291, Bird's-eye and curled Maple are freaks of the grain. **1942** (1960) Robertson *Red Hills* 104 **SC,** Our beautiful curly maple and solid walnut furniture was made by hand. **1942** Weygandt *Plenty* 29, Curly maple is hard to come by and is jealously husbanded in what cabinet making shops have the luck to hold a supply of it. **1965** (1973) Sloane *Wood* 106, Bird's-eye and curly maple are not distinct varieties, but rather are common maple with grain irregularities that give them these names. **1967–69** *DARE* (Qu. T14) Infs **OH6, WV3,** Curly maple; (Qu. T16) Inf **CT28,** Curly maple.

curly mesquite n

1 also *Texas curly mesquite grass:* A forage grass (*Hilaria belangeri*) native to the Southwest.

 1877 McDanield *Coming Empire* 100, There are several varieties of mesquite grass in Texas . . but the curly mesquite . . excels them all. **1912** Wooton–Standley *Grasses NM* 36, *Texas Curly Mesquite Grass* . . is a small grass which spreads over the ground by means of runners forming a pretty compact sod. **1937** U.S. Forest Serv. *Range Plant Hdbk.* G69, Curly-mesquite cures well on the ground and is highly palatable to all classes of livestock for both winter and summer use. **1967** *DARE* (Qu. L9a, . . *Kinds of grass . . grown for hay*) Inf **TX42,** Curly mesquite (native).

2 A **buffalo grass a** (here: *Buchloë dactyloides*).

 1941 *Torreya* 41.46, *Buchloë dactyloides* . . . Curly mesquite . . Texas Panhandle.

‡**curly pudding** n

 1959 *VT Hist.* new ser 27.153, *Curly pudding* . . . Tapioca. Rare.

curly redwood n Cf **curly maple**

 1949 Powers *Redwood Country* 74 **CA,** Sometimes an accidental twist or curl was given to a young tree, continuing in the growth to form 'curly redwood,' with spiral whorls in the grain, very ornamental and much sought-after for fancy work.

curly top n

A disease of sugar beets in which the leaves become much curled.

 1902 U.S. Dept. Ag. *Yearbook for 1901* 671, Sugar beets . . suffered severely from leaf spot. In Utah, Colorado, Nebraska . . the disease known as "curly top" was prevalent and injurious. **1930** *AmSp* 6.11 [Sugar beet language], The disease injuries may include *heart rot* . . and *beet blight* or *curly top.*

curly wolf n

An objectionable or mean person.

 1919 *Amer. Magazine* Nov 69/3 [sic *DA*—quot not found], Alex was a curly wolf, they's no question about that. **1944** Adams *Western Words,* *Curly wolf*—A tough character.

curn See **currant** A1

curnubble v Also sp *cornubble* [*cor-, cur-* varr of *ker-* + *nubble* var of Engl dial *knubble, nobble* to strike; cf *SND curnoble*] *obs*

To beat, drub, pummel; hence n *cornubbler,* vbl n *curnubbling.*

 1834 *Life Andrew Jackson* 27, Hew Montgomery, a whaller of a feller follow'd the batch of cornubblers. *Ibid* 93, He thou't it best tu give those chaps a curnubblin, jist tu incourage the folks in the city. *Ibid* 169, Decatur . . axed Mr. Kemper tu dissuade the gineral from his purpose. Kemper wou'd n't; and expressin his concurrence in the design of the gineral tu cornubble every rascally member who wou'd question his conduct.

curoner n Pronc-sp for *coroner*

 1917 *DN* 4.410 **wNC,** *Curoner* . . . Variant of coroner.

cur'o's See **curious** adj

cur'osity, cur'ossity See **curiosity**

cur⁽⁾ous See **curious** adj

curp v Also *curpy* Also sp *kerp* [Var of **cope** v[2]]

Come!—used as a call to horses.

 1908 *DN* 3.303 eAL, wGA, Curp₍₎ curpy . . . The common call for horses. "*Curp! curp! Curpy,* coltie: here's your mammy!" *Ibid* 326, *Kerp* . . . The call for horses. **1966** *DARE* (Qu. K82, *The call used . . to get horses in from the pasture*) Inf **MS66,** [kʌrp].

curragh n [*OED currach, curragh* "a small boat made of wicker-work covered with hides, used from ancient times in Scotland and Ireland;" c1450 →]

 1930 Shoemaker *1300 Words* 9 **cPA Mts** (as of c1900), *Curragh*—A light canoe, the sides covered with bark or skins.

currant n

A Forms.

1 usu *currant;* infreq *curn.*

 1942 McAtee *Dial. Grant Co. IN* (as of 1890s), *Curn* . . currant, the latter never heard. **1942** Warnick *Garrett Co. MD* (as of 1900–1918), Other prevalent dialectal pronunciations were . . . *curn* (currant).

2 double pl: See quot.

1895 *DN* 1.375 **seKY, wNC, eTN,** *Currantses* (currants).

B Senses.

1 Std: any of var spp of the genus *Ribes;* also the fruit of such a plant.

2 also *wild currant:* An **agarita** (here: *Berberis trifoliata*); also its fruits. **TX**

1911 *Century Dict. Suppl., Currant . . . Wild currant,* any currant in its native state; also, other plants with currant-like fruit, as *Amelanchier Botryapium* (Dismal Swamp region), and *Berberis trifoliata* (Texas). The fruit of the latter is used for tarts, jellies, etc. **1916** *Torreya* 16.237, *Berberis trifoliata . . .* Currants, New Braunfels, Tex. **1951** *PADS* 15.32 TX, Wood and roots . . were used for making a dye almost as yellow as the . . flowers that crowd stems of the "wild currant" bushes. **1961** Wills–Irwin *Flowers TX* 116, The Agarita is usually a low shrub. . . . The red berries, sometimes called "currants," ripen in May.

3 also *wild currant:* A **serviceberry** (here: *Amelanchier canadensis*).

1911 [see **2** above].

currant grape n
=**sand grape.**

1960 Vines *Trees SW* 729, *Vitis rupestris . . .* Vernacular names are . . Currant Grape . . and Bush Grape.

currant-leaf n
=**miterwort 1.**

1822 (1832) MA Hist. Soc. *Coll.* 2d ser 9.152, Plants which are indigenous in the township of Middlebury, [Vt., include] . . *Mitella diphylla,* Currant leaf. **1882** *Harper's Mag.* 66.126/2 **NEng,** The old man drank his store tea in triumph, offering no objections to the currant-leaf beverage with which his wife and daughter saw fit to regale themselves.

currency-stretcher See **stretcher**

current adj
See quots.

1918 *DN* 5.15 **Martha's Vineyard MA,** *Current . .* In good health, active. "How are you?" "I've been sick, but I'm pretty current again now." **1941** *LANE* Map 461 *(Lively, spry)* 1 inf, **Martha's Vineyard MA,** [kə̆rənt].

currier n [From *curry favor*]
1967 *DARE* (Qu. II20a, *A person who tries too hard to gain somebody else's favor*) Inf **MI68,** A currier.

currying vbl n [*curry* to beat, drub]
A severe scolding.

c1960 *Wilson Coll.* **csKY,** *Currying . . .* A scolding, a "goingover." **1966–68** *DARE* (Qu. II27, *If somebody gives you a very sharp scolding, you might say, "I certainly got a _____ for that."*) Infs **GA**19, **MD**23, **SD**8, Currying.

curry one's jacket v phr
1914 *DN* 4.104 **KS,** *Curry (one's) jacket . . .* To whip soundly on the back.

cursed thistle n Cf **blaspheme vine**
=**Canada thistle.**

1900 Lyons *Plant Names* 81, *Carduus arvensis . . .* Cursed-thistle. **1901** Mohr *Plant Life AL* 817. **1912** Blatchley *IN Weed Book* 166, *Carduus arvensis . . .* Cursed Thistle. **1963** Craighead *Rocky Mt. Wildflowers* 203, *Canada Thistle Cirsium arvense . . . Other names: . .* Cursed thistle.

curse, the n Also *curse of Eve, Eve's curse* esp common among women, young and mid-aged speakers, and coll educ speakers
Menstruation.

1930 Dos Passos *42nd Parallel* 147, She was afraid her period was coming on. She'd only had the curse a few times yet. **1948** *Word* 4.3.183, The most consistent term [for menstruation] used by women, which is largely age-typed, almost universally used by American women under thirty-five years of age, is *the curse.* **1949** *PADS* 11.5 **wTX,** *Curse, the . . .* The menstrual period. **1954** *AmSp* 29.298, Vernacular terms pertaining to menstruation . . . *Curse of Eve* [used chiefly by women]. **1965–70** *DARE* (Qu. AA27, . . *Menstruation*) 107 Infs, **widespread,** The curse. [Of all Infs responding to the question, 60% were old, 34% coll educ, 58% female; of those giving this response, 46% were old, 53% coll educ, and 78% female.]; **WA**6, Eve's curse.

curshion See **cushion**

curtain n Pronc-spp *curtin, curting* Cf **-ing**

A Forms.

1843 (1916) Hall *New Purchase* 420 **IN,** I say, Jake ain't them danglings up there like Carltin's ole woman's curtins! **1861** Holmes *Venner* 1.119 **wMA,** Chintz curtings, — jest put up, — o' purpose for the party, I'll give ye a dollar. **1941** *AmSp* 16.15 **eTX** [Black], *Curtain . .* ['kʌtn̩].

B Senses.

1 also *curtain blind, ~ pull, ~ shade:* A roller window shade. **chiefly Nth, Midl** Cf **blind n 2**

1903 *DN* 2.350 **seIA,** *Curtain . . .* Used in the sense of 'window-shade.' **1909** *DN* 3.395 **nwAR,** *Curtain . . .* Window-shade. **1926** *DN* 5.386 ME, *Curtain . . .* Window-shade. "Pull down the curtains." Common. **1926** *AmSp* 2.79/2 ME, If you spoke of "curtains" simply, you would be understood to refer to the window *shades.* **1946** *PADS* 6.10 **seNC,** *Curtain . . .* A window shade . . . Obsolete. **1949** Kurath *Word Geog* 52, *Roller shades . . . Curtain* is widely used in this sense (1) in New England and the New England settlement area, (2) in the Philadelphia area, and (3) on Chesapeake Bay and in the coastal part of northeastern North Carolina. Scattered instances of it have also been noted in the Midland. **1950** *WELS Suppl.* **cWI,** Curtain — used for what is now called 'roller shades.' **c1960** *Wilson Coll.* **csKY,** *Curtain . . .* To all the older people curtain means window shade. What others call curtains were called lace curtains. **1962** *AmSp* 37.173 **seNC,** The typically Southern coast expressions *lightwood . .* for 'kindling wood,' and *curtain* for 'roller shade,' seem surprisingly infrequent on Ocracoke: they occur five and three times, respectively, in the Ocracoke records. **1965–70** *DARE* (Qu. E12, *Pieces of stiff material that you pull down on the inside of a window to keep the sun out*) 60 Infs, **scattered, but esp Nth, Midl,** Curtains; **NV**2, Curtain blinds; **MA**48, Curtain pulls; **IA**7, Curtain shades.

2 The caul or fetal membrane.

1958 *Hand Coll.* **cwOH,** The son of a seventh son born with a curtain (caul) on his face has the gift of insight.

curtsy n, v Pronc-spp *courtesey, curch(e)y, curtshy*
Std senses, var forms.

1899 (1912) Green *VA Folk-Speech, Curchy . . .* A gesture of reverence, respect, or civility; a kind of obeisance made by a woman, consisting in a sinking or inclination of the body, with the bending of the knee. Curtsy; curtshy; courtesey. *Ibid* 44, We curchey to the new moon when we first see it.

‡curtsy mug n [Perh alter of *courtesy*] *euphem*
A chamber pot.

1967 *DARE* (Qu. F38, *Utensil kept under the bed for use at night*) Inf **NJ**2, Curtsy ['kɜ·či] mug.

cur'us(s) See **curious** adj

curvicue n [Alter of *curlicue* infl by *curve*]
A curlicue.

1851 (1976) Melville *Moby-Dick* 426 **MA,** I'll try my hand at raising a meaning out of these queer curvicues here with the Massachusetts calendar. **1966** *DARE* (Qu. JJ12, *Little flourishes . . on . . handwriting or signature to make it look fancy*) Inf **FL**6, Curvicues.

cur-winch See **co-wench**

‡cusac pie n
1949 *AmSp* 24.108 **ceSC,** *Cusac pie* ['kju̧zæk] . . Deep pie.

cuse See **curious** adj

cush n[1] Usu |kuš|, also |kuš|; rarely |kʌš| Also *coosh, couche-couche, coush-coush, cush-cush, cushie* [Of Afr orig, ult from Arabic; see quots 1931, 1949, and cf *OED couscous*[1]] **chiefly Sth**
A dish made with cornmeal or cornbread either sweetened and fried or seasoned and cooked with meat or drippings.

c1770 in 1833 Boucher *Glossary* 1 MD, [Footnote 58:] *Cushie;* a kind of pancake, made of Indian meal. **1882** McCarthy *Soldier Life* 59 **nVA** (as of 1861–65), "Slosh" or "coosh" . . . The bacon is fried out till the pan is half full of boiling grease. The flour is mixed with water until it flows like milk, poured into the grease and rapidly stirred til the whole is a dirty brown mixture. **1899** (1912) Green *VA Folk-Speech, Cush . . .* A dish made by stirring broken corn-bread in a spider with the gravy of fried bacon, water being added, and pieces of red-pepper pods. "Coosh." **1931** Read *LA French* 122, *Couche-Couche . . .* Corn-meal dough sweetened with sugar and fried brown. It is served with milk or eaten at breakfast with coffee. St[andard].-Fr[ench]. *couscou*—in the eighteenth century written also *cuzcuz, cousse-couche* and *couche-couche*—was borrowed from the African slaves of the West Indies. The ultimate source of the word is the same as that of Fr. *couscous*, an Arabian dish of meat-balls and flour, which is borrowed from Arabic *kuskus*, itself a derivative of Arabic *kaskasa*, "to pound small." **1949** Turner *Africanisms* 197 **SC, GA coasts** [Gullah], [kuʃ, 'kuʃkuʃ] 'corn-meal dough sweetened and fried.' H[ausa]. **1949** *PADS* 11.5 **wTX,** *Cush* . . A kind of dressing, but served as a separate dish. Old fashioned. **1951** *AmSp* 26.14 **S Atl** [Black], *Cush,* 'a kind of mush,' is frequently recorded in the coastal plain. **1952** Brown *NC Folkl.* 1.531, *Cush (molly)* . . . Corn bread (generally stale) crumbled and fried or stewed in water and grease, sometimes flavored with onions.—General. *Ibid, Cush hominy* . . . Corn meal hominy. Same as *cush* (?).—Central and east. **1954** *Harder Coll.* **cwTN,** *Cush.* **1954** *PADS* 21.24 **SC,** *Cush* [kuʃ] . . . In coastal S.C., corn meal mixed with water, cooked in bacon grease. In the upcountry, corn bread mashed up in bacon grease to a homogeneous mass. In the central section, fried scrapple is called cush, also corn meal fried with meat or oysters. Always a mixture is involved. **1962** Atwood *Vocab. TX* 64, The southern Louisiana *cush-cush,* which designates some kind of mushy preparation with meal, shows up only twice in [southeast] Texas . . four other informants use the simple form *cush.* **1965–70** *DARE* (Qu. H25, . . *Fried cornmeal*) Infs **AL1, 11, TN52,** Cush [kʊš]; **KY81,** Cush [kʌš] or [kʊš]—cold mush sliced and fried; **LA28,** Cush [kʊš]—also ['kʊš,kuš]; **LA31,** Couche-couche ['kuš,kuš]—a dry cooked cornmeal; **LA35,** ['kuš,kuš]; **LA33, 38,** Cush-cush ['kʊš,kʊš]; (Qu. H24, . . *Boiled cornmeal*) Inf **AR52,** Cush [kuš]—a little coarser, it's "grits"; **KY5,** Cush—grease and meat scraps in it; **VA56,** Cush—with meat grease in it, stirred up in the spider and cooked; (Qu. H23, . . *Hot cooked breakfast cereal*) Inf **MO22,** Cush; (QR p44) Inf **GA53,** Cush [kuš]: Mash up leftover grits, add egg, milk, salt, pepper, butter; and bake. **1966** *DARE* Tape **MS75** [Black], You have cold bread, cold corn bread, 'n' pour grease over it, 'n' mash it up, 'n' put some pepper and salt on it, 'n' let it get hot good. That was cush. That was good somethin' to eat. **1979** *Cuisine* 8.70/3 **LA,** *Coush-coush.*

cush n² Also *cush cow* [Engl dial *cush, cush-cow*]
A hornless cow, a **muley.**
    1966 *DARE* (Qu. K12, *A cow that has never had horns*) Inf **ME12,** Cush; **ME23,** Cush, a cush cow.

cush v Also *kush(ie)* [Engl dial]
Come!—used as a call to cows.
    1949 Kurath *Word Geog.* 24.1, In east Jersey and on the upper Delaware, here and there also in the Hudson Valley, farmers still call their cows with a kush! (riming with *bush*) or kushie! **1960** Williams *Walk Egypt* 151 **GA,** A woman called a cow, "Coop! Cush, cush!"

‡**cush** n³ [Etym uncert]
1 Loose, raw tobacco.
    1950 *WELS (Names and nicknames for home-grown and home-cured tobacco)* 1 Inf, **csWI,** Cush [kuʃ], raw tobacco—loose in the pocket: chew, wad, or [use] in a pipe.
2 Nonsense, rubbish. [Perh rel to **cush** n¹]
    1970 *DARE* (Qu. NN13, . . *The thing somebody has just said is silly or untrue: "Oh, that's a lot of _____.")* Inf **VA69,** Cush [kuš].

cushaw n Also *cashaw, coshaw, crushaw, cusha, cushaw melon, ~ squash* [Prob Algonkian] **chiefly Sth, S Midl** Note: *DA* quot 1588 is erron.
A kind of squash *(Cucurbita mixta)* with pale-yellow edible flesh.
    1698 (1848) Thomas *Hist. & Geog. Acct.* 21, Cucumbers, Coshaws, Artichokes, with many others . . besides what grows naturally wild in the Country. **1797** Imlay *Western Terr.* 240, Cushas; cucurbita melopepo; squashes, a kind of pumpkin. **1868** White *Gardening South* 308, *Winter Squashes* are of many varieties . . . The Cashaw Pumpkin is a good substitute for the winter squash [e.g. Valparaiso, Cocoanut, Boston Marrow, Bell, Canada Crookneck, and Hubbard]. **1883** *Bot. Gaz.* 8.357 **FL,** Common Indian pumpkins are perennial, but the Cushaw will only bear one crop, and then dies, as at the north. **1933** *AmSp* 8.1.48 **Ozarks,** *Cushaw* . . . A kind of squash. **1940** Stuart *Trees of Heaven* 242 **neKY,** Crushaw vines and punkin vines air runnin all over the corn balks. **1941** *FWP Guide LA* 226, *Cushaw* . . neck pumpkin. **1947** *Democrat* 11 Sep. 1/7 *(DA)* **AL,** Grover states that he has also had cushaws and an ample supply of vegetables. **1965–70** *DARE* (Qu. I23, . . *Kinds of squash . . around here*) 20 Infs, **chiefly KY, OH, TN,** Cushaw squash; **KY52, VA2,** Cushaws; **MO38,** Long-necked cushaws; (Qu. I24, . . *Kinds of pumpkins*

. . *around here*) Infs **FL1, MS72, OK27,** Cushaw; **GA9,** Crookneck cushaw; (Qu. I26, . . *Kinds of melons . . around here*) Infs **LA3, 40, VA19,** Cushaw melons; **LA15,** Cushaws; (Qu. I4, . . *Vegetables . . less commonly grown around here*) Inf **KY34,** Cushaws. **1968** *DARE* FW Addit **LA18,** *Cushaw* ['kʊˌšɔ]—a melon or squash-like vegetable used like sweet potatoes. **1971** GA Dept. Ag. *Farmers Market Bulletin* 24 Nov 1/3, What is the difference in butternut squash, cushaw, and sugar pumpkin? . . The cushaw is 20 inches long, white with green stripes, and weighs 12 pounds.

cushawn n [Var of **goujon**]
=**flathead catfish 1.**
    1920 Forbes–Richardson *Fishes of IL* 193, It *[Pylodictis olivaris]* is . . less often referred to as the "cushawn," a corruption of the French *goujon.*

cush cow See **cush** n²

cush-cush See **cush** n¹

cu-sheep(y) See **co-sheep(ie)** v phr, n

‡**cush foot** n [Perh from **cush** n²] Cf **cow foot**
    1970 *DARE* (Qu. X38, . . *Unusually big and clumsy feet*) Inf **MS86,** Flat feet, big feet, Flat Foot Floozie, cush feet.

cushie See **cush** n¹

cushion n Usu |'kʊšən|; also, **esp in NEast,** |'kwɪšən, kwʊ-|; infreq |'kəˌšən| Pronc-spp *cooshion, curshion, cushing, cwishion, quishion* Cf Pronc Intro 3.I.20, 3.I.23
A Forms.
    1858 in 1873 Harte *Poetical Works* 82 **CA,** Take a cheer. Not that; you can't fill them theer cushings this year. **1890** *DN* 1.58 **Cape Cod MA,** *Cushion.* I have heard the pronunciation *quishion* from two persons, and it is said to be a Cape Cod pronunciation. *Ibid* 77 **MA,** [kwʊšən]. **1891** (1967) Freeman *New Engl. Nun* 95, An' she had a coach with lamps on the sides, an' blue satin cushings. **1896** *DN* 1.415, **CT, cNY,** *Cushion:* usually pron, [kwɪšən]. **1903** *DN* 2.291 **Cape Cod MA** (as of 1850s), *Cushion* was *cwishion.* **1930s** in 1944 *ADD* **WV,** *Cooshion* ['kušən] normal pron . . . **eWV,** Curshion [kəˌšn̩] . . . Less common than [kušn̩]. **1940** *AmSp* 15.333 **cNY,** In the neighborhood of Seneca Falls, New York, *cushion* was usually pronounced, thirty years ago, [kwɪšn]. **1966** *DARE* (Qu. CC5, . . *Seats in a church*) Inf **MA6,** Each one made their own [kwɪšən] to sit on.
B Senses.
1 A railroad passenger car. Cf **varnished car**
    1918 *DN* 5.29 **NW,** To ride the cushions . . . Used by college students in antithesis to bumming one's way. To ride first class. **1927** *DN* 5.457 [Underworld jargon], On the cushions, to be . . . To ride in a passenger coach. **1943** *AmSp* 18.164 [Railroad terms], Cushions. Passenger coaches. **1945** Hubbard *Railroad Ave.* 339, Cushions—Passenger cars.
2 The hind end, buttocks. *joc*
    1966–67 *DARE* (Qu. K73, . . *The rump of a cooked chicken*) Inf **DC5A,** Cushion; (Qu. X35, . . *The part of the body . . you sit on*) Infs **CT6, SC29,** Cushion.

cushion buckwheat n
=**butterball 4.**
    1973 Hitchcock–Cronquist *Flora Pacific NW* 83, Cushion buckwheat . . . *Eriogonum ovalifolium.*

cushion cactus See **pincushion cactus**

cushion pink n [From its mossy, cushion-like appearance]
=**moss campion.**
    1900 Lyons *Plant Names* 345, *S[ilene] acaulis* . . . Cushion Pink. **1915** (1926) Armstrong *Western Wild Flowers* 114, Cushion Pink—*Silene acaulis.* **1963** Craighead *Rocky Mt. Wildflowers* 50, *Moss Campion Silene acaulis* . . . Cushion Pink. **1973** Hitchcock–Cronquist *Flora Pacific NW* 118. **1976** Bailey–Bailey *Hortus Third* 1043, *Silene acaulis* . . . Cushion pink.

cushion weed n
A **milkweed.**
    1951 *PADS* 15.38 **TX,** *Asclepiadaceæ*—Asclepias . . . Rather widely known as cushion weeds; small cushions have been filled with their down from time immemorial.

cusi(e) See **coosie**

cusk n [Etym obscure; see *DA*]

1 also *cusk fish:* A saltwater fish *(Brosme brosme).* [*OED* 1624 →] Also called **torsk, tusk**

1616 Smith *Descr. New Engl.* 30, And scarce any place, but Cod, Cuske, Holybut, Mackerell, Scate, or such like, a man may take with a hooke or line. **1677** (1900) Manning *Sea Jrl.* 179 **ME,** Richard Reof. Shalop, gave us 4 pickled cusk. **1724** in 1859 Essex Inst. *Coll.* 1.72/2, [Footnote:] At 4 this morning sounded, found 65 fathom . . sand, got a cusk, saw two shallops & one Skooner. **1843** in 1857 Webster *Private Corresp.* 2.178, I will bring you also a cusk if there shall be one in our market. **1948** *Dly. Ardmoreite* (Ardmore, Okla.) 21 Mar. 8/5 *(DA),* The cusk fish lays more than 2,000,000 eggs in a season. **1955** U.S. Arctic Info. Center *Gloss.,* Cusk . . . A large edible marine fish, *Brosme brosme,* related to the cod. Also called 'torsk,' 'tusk.' **1966** *DARE* (Qu. P2, . . *Saltwater fish . . good to eat?)* Infs **ME**10, 16, 22, Cusk; (Qu. P14, . . *What do the fisherman go out after?)* Inf **ME**16, Ground fish (haddock, cod, cusk, hake).

2 also *kusk:* =**burbot. NEast, esp ME**

1839 Holmes *Rept. Aroostook R.* 33 **ME,** The large lake trout . . abound here—also the kusk, a fish somewhat similar in appearance to the salt water kusk. **1867** *Amer. Naturalist* 1.165, The donation of two species of fish from Lake Winnipisiogee, one the *Lota maculosa* (Ling, or freshwater Cusk), and the other a species of Lake Trout. **1906** *N.Y. Ev. Post* 2 June 8 *(DA),* The breeding season of the black bass, pike, perch, and cusk is past. **1946** LaMonte *N. Amer. Game Fishes* 166, *Burbot . . Names: . .* Freshwater Cusk. **1966** *Lewiston Daily Sun* (Lewiston–Auburn ME) 5 May 22, Fresh Casco Bay Cusk Fillets. **1966** *DARE* (Qu. P1, . . *Kinds of freshwater fish . . caught around here . . good to eat)* Inf **ME**8, Cusk.

cusk eel n

A saltwater fish of the family Ophidiidae. See also **slippery dick**

1898 U.S. Natl. Museum *Bulletin* 47.2481, *Ophidiidae.* (The Cusk Eels.) Body elongate, compressed, more or less eel-shaped, usually covered with very small scales. **1911** *Century Dict.,* Cusk-eel . . . Any fish of the family *Ophidiidæ.* They are marine forms, eel-shaped, but have nothing in common with true eels. **1933** John G. Shedd Aquarium *Guide* 153, In the cusk eels the ventrals are developed into long, forked barbels. **1960** Amer. Fisheries Soc. *List Fishes* 45, Ophidiidae—cusk-eels.

cusk fish See **cusk 1**

cuspitoon n [Blend of *cuspidor + spitoon*] Cf **goboon**

A cuspidor.

1950 *WELS* (Article used by tobacco chewers) 1 Inf, **csWI,** Cuspitoon. **1967–70** *DARE* (Qu. DD5, *A metal or earthenware receptacle . . tobacco chewers use)* Infs **PA**245, **SC**40, Cuspitoon.

‡cussadang exclam [Appar a contr of *cuss and dang*]

1966 *DARE* (Qu. NN21a, *Exclamations caused by sudden pain)* Inf **AZ**11, Cussadang ['kʌs,dæn].

cussed gorm exclam [*cussed* cursed + *gorm!* damn! (see *EDD gorm, garm*)] Cf **gormed**

See quot 1967.

1967 *DARE* FW Addit **ME,** Cussed gorm. A cussword. I spent many summers, as a boy, on Bailey Island, Casco Bay, Maine, and the cussword that intrigued me most was *cussed gorm.* It took me many years to discover that Gorm was a Norse Raider, hated and feared, who burned and pillaged England's East Coast many centuries ago. [**1975** Gould *ME Lingo* 114, "Ain't he the boy broke your plow, smashed your cart, . . and got your Edie in a family way?" "Ayeh." "*Gormy* cuss, ain't he?"]

cussenca See **cassena**

cussey See **causey**

cuss-fight n **chiefly Sth, S Midl** See Map

A loud and angry quarrel.

1923 *DN* 5.205 **swMO,** Cuss fight . . . A violent quarrel, unaccompanied by any other form of assault than angry words. **1926** Kephart *Highlanders* 36 **sAppalachians,** By that time the land will be so poor hit wouldn't raise a cuss-fight. **1940** FWP *Guide TX* 383, Cussfight. A quarrel without violence. **1965–70** *DARE* (Qu. Y12a, *A fight between two people, mostly with words)* 49 Infs, **chiefly Sth, S Midl,** Cuss-fight. **1976** Garber *Mountain-ese* 19 **NC,** Cuss-fight . . exchange of profanity. They had the dangedest cussfight you ever seed.

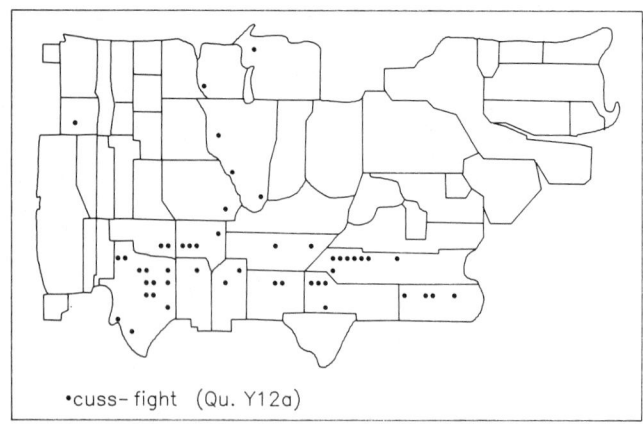

•cuss-fight (Qu. Y12a)

cuss-fired adj [Prob blend of *cussed + hell-fired*]

1929 *AmSp* 5.119 **ME,** "A cuss-fired fool" was an exasperating man.

cussie See **cossie**

cussie owl n [Prob *cuss* curse + *-ie,* famil suff] =**screech owl.**

1978 *DARE* File **Delmarva,** Cussie owl, a screech owl.

cussy See **cossie**

cussywop n Also *cuzzywop* [Fanciful formation]

See quots.

1967 *DARE* (Qu. E20, *Soft rolls of dust . . on the floor under beds)* Inf **PA**49, Cussywop ['kʊsi,wap]. **1982** *Smithsonian Letters* **?NY,** Among the samples listed for underbed lint . . the word *cuzzy-wop* was missing . . . I have used it for years. My brother says he never heard my mother use it. Perhaps I picked it up from a camp counselor in the 30's.

custard apple n [From the pulpy, custard-like fruit]

1 A tree of the genus *Annona;* also its fruit. [*OED* 1657 →] **chiefly FL, Gulf coast** For other names of var spp see **alligator apple, pond apple, sugar apple, sweetsop**

1785 Marshall *Arbustrum* 9, *Annona* . . . Custard Apple. **1868** U.S. Dept. Ag. *Rept. of Secy. for 1867* 143 **FL,** *Custard Apple,* (*Anona* [sic] *reticulata.*)—Sometimes called sugar apple. There are upwards of forty varieties of this fruit, and nearly all the species are edible. **1939** FWP *Guide FL* 23, The custard apple, a species of the Annona, often forms dense thickets here. **1965** Will *Okeechobee Boats* 113 **FL,** From the custard apple woods along the lake shore . . you'd see nothin' from the pilot house excusin' only sawgrass as far around as you could look. *Ibid* 113, Her unmuffled exhausts would wake the echos of the custard apple swamps.

2 also *custard banana:* =**papaw** (here: *Asimina* spp); also its fruit.

1830 Rafinesque *Med. Flora* 2.197, *Asimina* . . . Papaw, Custard Apple . . . The *A. triloba,* found from Ohio to Mexico. Fruit with a bad smell, but when ripe after frost, the pulp is sweet, luscious, yellow, similar to Custards. **1901** Mohr *Plant Life AL* 507, Anonaceæ. Custard Apple Family . . . Asimina triloba . . . Papaw. **1950** Moore *Trees AR* 73, *Pawpaw* . . . Local Names: Custard Apple, Arkansas Banana. **1960** Vines *Trees SW* 291, *Asimina parviflora* . . . Vernacular names are Small-fruited Pawpaw, Small Custard-apple, and Custard-banana. **1967** *DARE* (Qu. I46, *Other . . fruits that grow wild around here)* Inf **LA**14, The papaw, usually defined as the custard apple. **1973** Stephens *Woody Plants* 182, *Asimina triloba* . . . Pawpaw, custard apple.

3 Papaya.

1933 Small *Manual SE Flora* 894, *Carica L.* . . (Papaya . . . Custard-apple. Melon-tree.)

custard banana n

1 See **banana B1.**

2 See **custard apple 2.**

custom exclam *euphem*

See quots.

1903 *DN* 2.296 **Cape Cod MA** (as of 1850), *Custom* . . . Exclamation on touching something hot. **1943** *LANE* Map 600, 2 infs, **sME,** Exclamations of impatience, irritation, sudden anger and the like . . . *Custom.*

custom work n Also *custom*

Work done by one with specialized or expensive equipment for others who lack the machinery; hence *custom worker* one who performs such work.

1944 *Harper's Mag.* 188.457/2 **IA,** I did have a hired man some but the custom work I did for the neighbors with the tractor plowing and with the cornpicker picking corn just about balanced that up. **1945** *Harper's Mag.* 190.669/1 **MA,** His neighbors would like to have the use of a field ensilage harvester, a combine, a manure-loader, . . a pickup baler. No one of them can buy machines like these for himself. But a father and son doing custom work with such heavy tools will have plenty of work in the neighborhood the year around. **1952** Kolb–Brunner *Study Rural Soc.* 95, *Custom workers,* often small farmers with machinery, hire themselves and their equipment to others. **1967** *DARE* Tape **IA6,** There's some consolidation of machines between farmers, like the large combines and this sort of thing. The large combine now, that some of the fellows have around that are doing custom work, runs seventeen to eighteen thousand dollars. They certainly can't afford it for just their own operation so when they buy one, why, they go out and sign up other farmers who don't want to buy one. This is better for all of us, I guess. **1968–69** *DARE* (Qu. L5, *When a farmer gets help on a job from his neighbors in return for his help on their farms later on, you call it* _____) Inf **IL33,** Custom work—if you hire someone to bring in their machinery and do the work; **WI54,** Custom.

cut v

1 To wound with a knife, to stab; hence vbl n *cutting* a knife fight, a stabbing.　**chiefly Sth, S Midl**

1899 (1977) Norris *McTeague* 179, "Zerkow, by God! he's killed her. Cut her throat.". . "Whew!" whistled one of the officers as they came out into the kitchen, "cutting scrape? By George! *somebody's* been using his knife all right." **1902** *DN* 2.232 **sIL,** *Cuttin* . . . A personal encounter where knives are used. **1907** *DN* 3.221 **nwAR, sIL,** Cuttin'. **1936** Stuart *'Uncle Fonse' (ADD)* **neKY,** Them Perkins boys got cut the other night. **1937** (1977) Hurston *Their Eyes* 155 **FL** [Black], "Is he bad 'bout totin' pistols and knives tuh hurt people wid?" "Dey don't say he ever cut nobody or shot nobody neither." **1941** Percy *Lanterns* 300 **LA** [Black], To tell the truth, most scrappin' and cuttin' and sech comes from checkin' [=offensive joking]. **1941** *Post* (Morgantown WV) 23 Apr *(ADD),* [Title:] Negro Convicted in Cutting Case . . indicted for feloniously cutting his friend. **1966** *Haines City Herald* (FL) 31 Mar 5/5, Three "Cuttings" Saturday, One Proved Fatal. **1970** *DARE* (Qu. Y12b, *A real fight in which blows are struck*) Inf **FL48,** Cutting spree—with knives.

2 Of a rodent: to chew, gnaw.

1899 (1912) Green *VA Folk-Speech, Cut* . . . To gnaw as a rat. "I heard a rat cutting in the closet." **1944** *Hall Coll.* **NC** *Cut* . . . Of squirrels, to eat. "The squirrels is cuttin' on hickory nuts now." **1963** Edwards *Gravel* 141 **eTN** (as of 1920s), "Gonna kill some squirrels, I 'spect," ventured Uncle Stevey. "Yes, Alvis Hale says they're cuttin on hickory nuts now."

3 To spay.　[By ext of *cut* castrate]

1967–69 *DARE* (Qu. J3a, *To make a female dog so she can't breed*) Infs **AR47, CA113, OH82,** Cut; (Qu. J3b, . . *A female cat*) Infs **CA113, NJ53, NY75, 216,** Cut.

4 See quots.

1938 *AmSp* 13.152 (Indiana University slang), *Cut* . . To have sexual intercourse. **c1940** in **1944** *ADD* **swWV,** *Cut* . . . To have coition . . . Reported as frequent. **1950** *PADS* 13.17 **cTX,** *Cut* or *cut meat* may also mean to copulate. **1954** *Harder Coll.* **cwTN,** *Cut* . . . To deflower. In the expression, "old enough to bleed, old enough to cut," of a young girl reaching puberty.

5 freq with *out:* To separate or remove (one or more animals) from a herd; hence vbl n *cutting* the act of removing certain animals from a herd.　**West**　Addit quots at **cutting horse**

1869 *Overland Mth.* 3.126 **TX,** Another rides in, selects a stray brand, and "cuts it out," by chasing it out with his horse. **1874** McCoy *Cattle Trade* 81, Whilst from six to ten cow boys hold the herd together the ranchman with one or two assistants separate such as are suitable. This process is termed "cutting out". **1903** (1965) Adams *Log Cowboy* 358 **NM,** That cow never lived that he couldn't cut. **1907** Love *Deadwood Dick* 47 **SD, ND,** All the large cattle raisers had their squad of brand readers whose duty it was to attend all the big round-ups and cuttings throughout the country. **1912** Porter *Rolling Stones* 88, Saunders had assigned him to a place holding the herd during the cuttings. **1920** Hunter *Trail Drivers TX* 297, When fences became more common the calves were cut out through a cutting chute or "dodged out" so they

could be counted. **1935** Sandoz *Jules* 371 **wNE** (as of 1880–1930), The range bosses gathered on a high knoll, their horses in a circle, manes blowing. The cutting began. **1937** Coolidge *TX Cowboys* 88, With a big herd they cut from both sides at once. **1939** FWP *Guide MT* 414, *Cut out*—To separate (an animal) from the herd. **1952** *Argosy* (NY) June 99/1 **neLA,** If a Lynch hog or steer crosses the river and gets mixed up in with another man's stock, one of Lynch's dogs can be sent across to find it, cut it out, bring it home. **1966** [see **cut** n 3]. **1972** Green *More Horse Tradin'* 251 **TX,** I had rounded up my trading stock and cut out a few of the very best ones.

6 also with *off;* In railroading: to detach a car or locomotive from a train.

1953 Botkin *Treas. Railroad Folkl.* 326, It was the usual practice of Uncle Henry's crew to head in on the wye at Appalachia, cut off their engine, do their station switching and then come back and pick up their train. **1969** *AmSp* 44.255 (Railroad language), *Cut*—Separate (a locomotive or car) from a train. *Ibid,* Cut off [=*cut*].

7 To beat or whip (eggs) vigorously.

1902 (1968) Clapin *Americanisms, Cut* (to) . . . In New England, to beat in speaking of eggs. **1963** Adamson *Household Hints* 214 **NEng** (as of late 1800s), *In warm weather chill your eggs* in cold water some time before you are ready to break them. They cut into a much finer froth for being cold. For some kinds of cake the whites should be cut to a stiff froth.

8 To gather (abalone).

1968 *DARE* Tape **CA103,** They cut abalones all along the coast.

9 See quot.

1972 Carr *Da Kine Talk* 128 **HI,** *Cut* . . . vs. the causative form of the verb. — "I cut my tonsils," rather than the causative expression, "I had my tonsils removed" . . is probably a loan translation from the Japanese or Korean, where parallel forms are used.

10 in var phrr: To expel intestinal gas.

1899 (1912) Green *VA Folk-Speech, Cut* . . . To cut one's finger, is to break wind. "Somebody has cut his finger." **1965–70** *DARE* (Qu. X55b, . . *Breaking wind from the bowels*) Infs **CA85, IA27, MO26, MA1, PA94,** Cut one; **CA170,** Cut a melon; **MD9,** Cut one loose; **IL98,** Cut a fart; **WA22,** Cut the cheese; **MD15, 25,** Cutting one; **CA1,** Cutting the cheese. **1980** *DARE* File **sCA,** My husband was amused when, before a party, I asked if he would cut the cheese. To him that meant to break wind. *Ibid* **CA** (as of 1950s & 60s), I knew *cut the cheese,* meaning to expel intestinal gas, through all my growing up years in southern and central California. It was mainly a jocose and mildly euphemistic expression—one to be used, if appropriate, even in mixed company. **1981** *Verbatim Letters* **CA,** I have heard teenage and young adult male children of blue collar workers ask, "Who cut the cheese?" when the deed [=passing gas] is done in crowded unventilated rooms. *Ibid* **NY,** I am familiar with the phrase "to cut the cheese." As children, we used this idiom to mean "to pass wind." . . This must date back to the early 1970's . . at least that's when I used it liberally! . . . I was born & raised in Rochester, New York . . . Friends of mine from Southern Connecticut used it as children as well.

11 in neg constr: To tolerate.　Cf **hack** v

1965 *DARE* FW Addit **OK,** I just can't cut cream cheese. [FW: i.e., stand].

12 To understand.

1966 *DARE* (Qu. NN5, . . *Ways of saying: "Do you understand?"*) Inf **WA16,** Can you cut it?

13 with *down* or *up;* Transf: to decrease or increase the volume or intensity.　Cf **cut off** v phr

1967 *DARE* FW Addit **cwNC,** *Cut down:* to turn down the volume of a radio, or the intensity of heat; *cut up:* to turn up the volume or intensity. **1970** *DARE* Tape **TX100,** Can you cut that thing [=tape recorder] down?

14 See **cut behind.**

cut n

1 A passageway or channel; spec:

a A ravine, gully or gorge; a mountain pass.　**chiefly east of Rocky Mts**　Cf **canyon**

1821 in **1940** *AmSp* 15.169 **VA,** Beginning at a white oak on the side of a hill . . . crossing a deep cut and Panters creek to a large white oak on the side of a hill. **1939** *LANE* Map 36, 6 infs, **scattered,** *Notch,* A pass between mountains or hills. . *cut* = *notch* but smaller. **1956** Ker *Vocab. W. TX* 72, Deeply cut valley or gully . . . [1 inf:] cut. **1965–70** *DARE* (Qu. C15, *A place in mountains or high hills where you can get through* *without climbing over the top*) 48 Infs, **east of Rocky Mts,** Cut; **SC**32, Mud cut; (Qu. C19, . . *Low land running between hills*) Inf **MI**67, Cut; (Qu. C21, *A deep place cut in sloping ground by running water*) 24 Infs, **chiefly east of Rocky Mts,** Cut; **NC**71, Deep cut; **MN**15, Rock cut. **1971** Bright *Word Geog.* CA & NV 166, *Notch* (between mountains) . . . *Cut.* **1973** Allen *LAUM* 1.235 **csMN,** A small depression with a usually dry watercourse . . . Cut [1 inf].

b A way cut through a hill or mountain, esp for a railroad.

1862 in 1864 Moore *Rebellion Rec.* 5.1.403 **MD,** On Friday morning we held the ridge, in front of which runs an incomplete railroad-cut and embankment. **1897** Brodhead *Bound in Shadows* 265 *(DAE),* The North-bound train dashed from the cut below the hotel. **1904** *Phil. Ev. Telegraph* 15 Nov. 5 *(DA),* Snowdrifts covered railroad tracks in the deep cuts. **1945** Hubbard *Railroad Ave.* 339, *Cut* . . . That part of the right-of-way which is excavated out of a hill or mountain instead of running up over it or being tunneled through it. **1958** McCulloch *Woods Words* **Pacific NW,** *Cut* . . . A truck road or railroad excavation through a rise of ground. **1967** *Chadron Rec.* (NE) 4 Sept 4/8, Snow plows were sent out to open rail lines. Twenty-seven head of cattle were killed by a snow plow in a deep cut into which they had drifted. **1970** *DARE* Tape **PA**233, [FW:] What does a railroad cut mean? [Inf:] It means a cut . . well, they cut through the mountains.

2 A portion of cultivated land. **chiefly Sth, S Midl**

1765 (1925) Washington *Diaries* 1.216 **VA,** Finishd sowing Wheat at the Mill—viz 19 Bushls. in ye large cut within the Post and Rail fence and 6 B. in ye small cut. **1887** *Century Illustr. Mag.* 35.115/1 **LA,** A *sugar* plantation is divided by main ditches and roads into sections known in some parishes as "cuts," in others as "strips." **1890** *DN* 1.64 **KY,** With tobacco-raisers *cut* means a portion of a tobacco field. "Did you finish worming that cut you were on?" **1946** *PADS* 6.10 **eNC,** Cut . . . A piece of arable land enclosed by ditches, generally from one-half to three acres . . . Common. **1966–70** *DARE* (Qu. L6a, . . *A piece of land under cultivation—less than an acre*) Inf **NC**8, A cut of land; (Qu. L6b, . . *If it's several acres*) Inf **MS**81, Cut.

3 also attrib: A group of cattle separated out of the main herd; see quot 1961. [**cut** v **5**] **West**

1884 Aldridge *Ranch Notes* 89, One of our party goes in, and whenever he sees an animal bearing one of our brands he runs it out . . until we have collected a little bunch . . which a second man herds . . to prevent them straying off and mixing with the other 'cuts.' **1907** White *AZ Nights* 117, Occasionally some particularly enterprising cow would conclude that one or another of the cut-herds would suit her better than this mill of turmoil. *Ibid* 112, The round-up captain appointed two men to hold the cow-and-calf cut, and two more to hold the steer cut. **1935** Sandoz *Jules* 371 **wNE** (as of 1880–1930), In pockets in the chop-hills solitary horsemen guarded the little cuts. **1940** *FWP Guide NV* 76. **1961** Adams *Old-Time Cowhand* 249, A "cut" was a group of cattle separated from the main herd for any definite purpose, as for shippin' or for brandin' . . . The men keepin' the cut under control were said to be "holdin' the cut." **1966** *DARE* Tape **NM**13, Sometimes they'd have as many as four cuts coming out of that roundup . . . They would cut their cows and unbranded calves at one place and then . . other cuts were started.

4 In logging: the amount of timber harvested within a specified period or by a specified unit of loggers. **chiefly Inland Nth, NW**

1876 *Lumberman's Gaz.* 10 Jan 24/1, As usual there is a large amount of talk being indulged in as to . . the probable winter's cut of logs. **1948** *Popular Western* June 69/1 *(DA),* The best you can hope for is a long jerkline haul of your entire cut. **1956** Sorden–Ebert *Logger's Words* **Gt Lakes.** **1958** McCulloch *Woods Words* **Pacific NW,** Cut . . . The output of logs per day, per side, per season, etc. **1969** *DARE* Tape **CA**158, They just have a yearly cut now to support what mills we have around here.

5 In railroading: a short string of cars; see quots.

1945 Hubbard *Railroad Ave.* 399, Cut—Several cars attached to an engine or coupled together by themselves. **1953** Botkin *Treas. Railroad Folkl.* 326, The yard crew [was] shoving a cut of cars onto a spur. **1958** McCulloch *Woods Words* **Pacific NW,** Cut . . . A string of cars in a switching operation. **1969** *AmSp* 44.255 (Railroading language), *Cut of cars*—Portion of a train. **1970** *Current Slang* 1.5.5 **cCA,** Cut . . . Approximately four or more railroad cars coupled to each other, but with no engine or caboose attached.

6 also *cutoff:* See quot.

1968 *DARE* (Qu. N30, . . *A sudden short dip in a road*) Inf **VA**13, Cut; **MD**4, Cutoff.

7 See **cutthroat trout.**

cut ppl adj

1 also in phrr *cut in the craw* (or *eye*): Drunk; hence *half-cut* partly drunk.

1722 *New Engl. Courant* 3 Sept 1/2, [Drunkards] are seldom known to be *drunk,* tho they are very often *boozey, cogey, tipsey, fox'd, merry,* . . *Confoundedly cut,* [etc]. **1857** Quinland 1.134 **NY,** You are as *balmy* as a summer evening, as *shiney* as a new boot; you are *sprung* and *cut in the eye;* come, rouse yourself. **1859** Matsell *Vocabulum,* Cut . . . Drunk; "Half cut," half drunk. **1927** *AmSp* 2.276 [Stanford Univ. jargon], *Cut*—intoxicated. **1963** Carson *Social Hist. Bourbon* 9, Toward the end of the [18th] century rum slipped in popularity but left behind a legacy of quaint and slangy names for the various stages of intoxication; . . "boozy, . . cut, . . cut in the craw." **1966–69** *DARE* (Qu. DD14, . . *Partly drunk*) Infs **ME**10, **NY**23, **PA**199, Half-cut; (Qu. DD15, . . *Thoroughly drunk*) Inf **HI**9, Cut.

2 Embarrassed.

1968 *DARE* FW Addit **Salt Lake City UT,** "He's too cut [FW: embarrassed] to come in." This was said of a man who wouldn't enter the house (where women were) wearing shorts, since he had very hairy legs.

cut a big figure See **figure** n B

cut a buck(-and-wing) See **cut the buck 1**

cut across v phr

To interrupt.

1970 *DARE* FW Addit **VA**41, I don't like to cut across you. (Common).

cut a curf See **kerf**

cut a duel v phr

To fight with knives.

1942 Hurston *Dust Tracks* 195 **FL,** She can handle a knife with anybody. She'll join hands and cut a duel.

cut a fart See **cut** v **10**

cut a fat pig in the hip v phr Cf **cut a hog 2**

To do something noteworthy.

1979 *Verbatim Letters* **MO,** When I've done something clever, I congratulate myself for having *cut a fat pig in the hip.*

cut a figure See **figure** n B

cut a flip v phr

To do a *flip* n² **2.**

1967–68 *DARE* (Qu. EE9b, *If children jump forward, land on the hands, and turn over*) Inf **SC**54, Cut a flip; **NC**52, Cutting a flip.

cut a forked stick v phr

1958 McCulloch *Woods Words* 43 **Pacific NW,** *Cut a forked stick*—To open up the throttle wide (from the old trick of placing a forked stick under the throttle on a steam donkey).

cut a gut v phr Cf **cut a hog 1**

To make a mistake, esp an embarrassing one; to do something silly.

1923 *DN* 5.234 **swWI,** Cut a gut . . . To make a mistake, or to fail in a task. (From dressing an animal.) "Oh yes, he said he'd do it, and then he cut a gut." **1933** *AmSp* 8.1.48 **Ozarks,** Cut a big gut . . . To do something foolish, to make oneself ridiculous. **1939** *AmSp* 14.90 **eTN,** *Cut a big gut.* To act foolish or appear ridiculous. 'He cut a big gut at the dance.' **1969** *DARE* (Qu. JJ41, *An embarrassing mistake: "Last night she . . _____."*) Inf **TX**72, Cut a gut. **c1970** *Halpert Coll.* **wKY.**

cut a hog v phr

1 =**cut a gut.**

1937 (1977) Hurston *Their Eyes* 149 **FL** [Black], B'lieve Ah done cut uh hawg, so Ah guess Ah better ketch air. **1966** *DARE* (Qu. JJ41, *An embarrassing mistake*) Inf **DC**3, Cut a hog.

2 in var extended phrr: To undertake something beyond one's ability.

1912 *DN* 3.574 **wIN,** *Cut a big hog in the mouth with a small knife* . . . To attempt something beyond one's capacity. **1947** *AmSp* 22.299 **WI,** *Cut a hog in two* . . . The meaning is uncertain . . . Example: 'Dan started for Portage, where he met his brother H.W. "I've come up to study law with you, by thunder." H.W. replied sharply, "You have? You are a darned fool; you'd better stick to printing. You'll cut a hog in two studying law? But if you are bound to stick to law, you can see what you can do." ' **1968** *DARE* (Qu. KK9) Inf **IN**31, Cutting a big hog with a small knife.

cut along v phr

To hasten away, run along.

1927 *AmSp* 3.139 **ME coast**, A neighbor often said "Well, I must be mogging along," mog meaning to move slowly, to depart. If [in] a hurry he must "cut along" or "marvel" or go "quick as scat." **1954** Forbes *Rainbow* 210 **VT**, "Your servant, ma'am," bowing with old-fashioned courtesy. And to me, "You cut along, Eddy."

cut a melon v phr

1 To divide or share something.

1927 *Ruppenthal Coll.* **KS**, Cut a melon . . . To divide or distribute gains, esp. very large gains, or dishonest gain. **1966** Barnes–Jensen *Dict. UT Slang*, Cut a melon . . to divide or share a profit.

2 See **cut** v **10.**

cut-and-come-again n

Any of several flowers:

a A stock (*Matthiola* spp).

1936 Morehouse *Rain on Just* 41 **NC**, Cut-and-come-again was bushing up properly. Piny roses were . . gone. **1959** Carleton *Index Herb. Plants* 35, Cut-and-come-again: Matthiola.

b A **black-eyed Susan 2** (here: *Rudbeckia hirta*).

1966 *DARE* Wildfl QR Pl.254 Inf **NC28**, Black-eyed Susan — cut-and-come-again.

c A zinnia.

1968 *DARE* (Qu. S11, . . *Other names . . for zinnia*) Inf **VA34**, Cut-and-come-again.

cut and cover v phr

To plow carelessly so that the unturned earth between furrows is covered with loose dirt; also fig.

1839 Buel *Farmer's Companion* 302 (*DAE*), Cut and cover, in plowing, to make wide furrows, turning over the sod upon a part not ploughed, and covering it up. **1902** *DN* 2.232 **sIL**, Cut and cover . . . To plow carelessly; to leave balks in plowing. **1903** *DN* 2.311 **seMO**, Cut and cover . . . In plowing to throw furrows on unplowed land so all appears to be plowed when only half is really broken. **1906** *DN* 3.117 **sIN**. **1927** *AmSp* 2.352 **WV**, Cut and cover . . to leave a part of the balk unturned in plowing, but to cover that part with loose dirt. "Instead of plowing that field well, it is only cut and covered." **1927** *Ruppenthal Coll.* **KS**, Cut and cover . . to do slovenly work — from the farm term, wherein a plow runs so far away from the preceding furrow that it . . cuts part way and covers a strip of uncut earth close to the preceding furrow, regarded as very poor farming.

cut-and-split n

1930 *AmSp* 5.419 **csNH**, Cut-and-split: firewood sawed into lengths and split up. "The cut-and-split is in the woodshed."

cut-and-try adv phr

By trial and error.

1969 *DARE* (Qu. KK48, . . "*I didn't have anything to go by, so I just did it _____.*") Inf **MO39**, Cut-and-try.

cut-ant See **cutting ant**

cut a pigeon wing See **cut the pigeon('s) wing**

cut around v phr

1 To frisk about; to flirt.

1843 (1916) Hall *New Purchase* 392 **IN**, "Well, Glenville, what do you say to Miss Smythe?" . . "She would do . . But Carlton, the Squire, has been cutting round there the last six months." **1856** Whitcher *Bedott Papers* 91 **NEng**, They say she cut round and hollered and laffed and tried to be wonderful interestin'. **1879** Stockton *Rudder Grange* 100, [The dog] was only cuttin' round because he was so glad to get loose. **1942** Warnick *Garrett Co. MD* (as of 1900–18), Cutting around . . flirting or courting.

2 See quot.

1906 *DN* 3.133 **nwAR**, Cut around . . . To show anger in an unbecoming manner. "He got mad and just cut around."

cut a rusty v phr [Perh *cut* to play or act + *rusty* alter of *rustic* an uncouth, unsophisticated person] **chiefly Sth, S Midl**

1 also *cut some rusty, cut up one's rusties:* To caper, show off, or behave in a silly, boisterous manner.

1838 Neal *Charcoal Sketches* 111 **sePA**, It won't do for us to be cutting rusties here at this time o' night. **1853** *S. Lit. Messenger* 19.602/2 **AL**, We cut up our rusties at his hotel. **1911** *DN* 3.539 **eKY**, Rusty . . . A

prank or caper; used chiefly in the phrase "cut a rusty," meaning play a prank or do a "stunt." **1927** *DN* 5.473 **Ozarks**, Cut a rusty . . . To do something foolish or improper. "I shore did cut a rusty when I showed th' ol' woman thet 'ar letter." **1933** *AmSp* 8.1.31 **nwTX**, Cut a rusty. To do something clever or pert. **1944** *PADS* 2.48, **NC, TN, NJ**, *Rusty, to cut a.* **1946** Stuart *Tales Plum Grove* 113 **KY**, The last spell I took was one night I's out with the men fox huntin'. . . I cussed and laughed. I called my dogs. I tooted my fox horn. I cut some rusty. **1954** *Harder Coll.* **cwTN**, *Cut a rusty.* **c1960** *Wilson Coll.* **csKY**, *Cut a rusty.* **1966** *DARE* (QR, near Qu. A6) Inf **AL15**, Cut a rusty [means] the kids had a big time. **1976** Garber *Mountain-ese* 19 **Appalachians**, *Cut-a-rusty.*

2 also *cut up rusty:* To have an emotional outburst, usu of anger.

1899 (1912) Green *VA Folk-Speech* 362, Unruly; ill-humoured; "he cut up *rusty*"; applied to persons or horses. **1939** *AmSp* 14.90 **eTN**, Cut a rusty. To have an outburst of anger. "He cut a rusty when he was talking to his papa." **1940** *AmSp* 15.215 **FL**, Cut a rusty may refer to a 'fit of anger,' . . but more often, in talk I have heard, it refers to a fit of joy. **1959** McAtee *Oddments* 4 **cNC**, Cut a rusty: . . have a conniption fit or tantrum, as a little boy did when they threatened to take his cat away. **1960** Criswell *Resp. to PADS 20* **Ozarks**, Cut a rusty . . . To go into an emotional display of anger. "When he took the other girl to town she really cut a rusty." Very common once. **1966–68** *DARE* (Qu. KK11, *To make great objections or a big fuss about something*) Infs **AL3, WV3**, Cut a rusty.

3 See quots.

1920 Hunter *Trail Drivers TX* 300 **wTX**, "Cutting a rusty" means doing your best. **1944** Adams *Western Words* 86, Cut a rusty — To do one's best.

cut a stick See **cut stick**

cutaway n

A landslide.

1969 *DARE* (Qu. C16, *When a mass of earth and rock comes loose from a high place and rushes down, you call it a _____*) Inf **VT16**, Cutaway.

cutaway dam n

In logging: see quot.

1956 Sorden–Ebert *Logger's Words* 10 **Gt Lakes**, Cut-away-dam, A temporary dam, built on a tributary to a larger stream to hold back the water. It was usually built of slash and removed after the drive had passed.

cutaway harrow n Also *cutout harrow* Cf **cut harrow**

A harrow with discs that have notches cut out for a deeper bite.

1903 Bailey *Cyclop. Horticulture* 1969 **GA**, After breaking, two harrowings, one with a cutaway, the other with an Acme harrow, should follow. **1940** Gilbert *Country Preacher* 103, Then I got . . a cutaway harrow. **1965–70** *DARE* (Qu. L20, *The implement used in a field after it's been plowed to break up the lumps*) 17 Infs, **chiefly NEng, S Atl**, Cutaway (harrow); **CT14**, Double cutaway harrow. **1980** *DARE* File **csWI**, Cutout harrow — not used in Wisconsin, but probably in parts of the South.

cutback n **West**

1 Of livestock, usu cattle: a reject, a cull; transf: a worthless person. Cf **cut** v **5**

1909 *Sat. Eve. Post* 5 June 19/1, Why don't you buy cut-backs (these are the cattle that, at Kansas City, are found to be unfit for killing), or Texas stock, and feed 'em? **1933** *AmSp* 8.1.29 **nwTX**, Cut-back. An inferior animal left after those worthy of selling have been cut out; figuratively, an inferior person. **1938** (1952) FWP *Guide SD* 85, Cut-back: a lamb or ewe that is rejected on account of size or condition. **1961** Adams *Old-Time Cowhand* 158, A scrawny, poorly developed animal was a "rusty," "rough steer," "scrag," "cull," . . or "cutback."

2 also attrib: =**cutout 1.**

1943 Hough *Snow Above Town* 135 **WY**, Frank spots an animal he wants, and moves his horse among the steers. He moves slowly, carefully, worms his way into a position directly behind the cutback . . . The nearest cowboy . . picks up the steer . . and scoots it down the field to that lone cowboy . . who now takes charge of it, forming the nucleus of the cutback herd.

3 A sharp bend or loop in a river. Cf **curl B1**

1966 *DARE* Tape **SD8**, There's cutbacks along it . . . Lots of places where you can ford it.

cut-bait n **chiefly Sth**

Fish cut up and used for bait; **chum.**

1965–70 *DARE* (Qu. P8, . . *"White bait" . . what is it?*—total Infs questioned, 75) Infs **FL17, GA5, MS66,** Cut-bait; **FL21,** Cut-bait—a mullet sliced up and used for bait; (Qu. P7, *Small fish used as bait for bigger fish*) Infs **NC21, SC57,** Cut-bait; (Qu. P13, . . *Other ways of fishing . . besides . . hook and line*) Inf **FL48,** Cut-bait; **SC45,** Fish deep with cut-bait. **1966–67** *DARE* Tape **LA5,** You can bait with any kind of cut-bait or crawfish; **MI21,** Even when we used to use cut-bait, we'd very seldom get any fish on the tail part; it would either be the head part or the middle part.

cutbank n, also attrib **scattered, but chiefly West**

A nearly perpendicular slope usu produced by stream erosion.

1819 (1965) *N. Amer. Rev.* 8.11 **VA,** A level was then taken . . over the intermediate ridge between Rose creek and Sturgeon creek to the Nottoway at Cut Bank Bridge. **1885** Twain *Huck. Finn* 115 **MO,** I passed the line around one of them [=saplings] right on the edge of the cut bank. **1925** Evarts *Spanish Acres* 286 **TX,** Sheltered by a cutbank draw . . opening into the little bottom on the far side . . , another man viewed this uncanny spectacle. **1932** *DN* 6.228 **MT, NE, ND, SD, WY,** Cutbank. This word (variously spelled *cutbank, cut-bank,* and *cut bank*) is often used for the outer bank at the bend of a stream, the bank which the stream cuts into, leaving the opposite side flat. It is perhaps curious that such a natural name for so general a thing should be found in a limited area. *Cutbank,* however, seems to be commonly heard only in the region of Montana, Dakota, Wyoming, and Nebraska. **1938** (1952) FWP *Guide SD* 86, Cut-bank . . a perpendicular bank of earth, originally cut by running water, but may be any distance from existing stream bed. **1957** Trautman *Fishes* 193 **OH,** The Brook [trout] hides quickly under "cut banks" and other cover when frightened. **1967** *DARE* (Qu. C21, *A deep place cut in sloping ground by running water*) Inf **CO28,** Cutbanks —in Montana; [you] never hear [it] here. **1968** Adams *Western Words* 86, Cut-bank—A precipitous hillside or jump-off. Cut-banks . . . are caused by the wind's whipping around some point and eroding the soil until precipitous banks, sometimes yards high, have been formed.

cut behind v phr Also *cut old-fash*

To run behind or catch a ride on (the back of a wagon or sleigh)—often used as an exclam to warn the driver that someone is cutting behind.

1848 *Popular Songs* 36 *(DA),* Another calls out 'cut behind.' **1860** Holmes *Professor* 171 **MA,** Here is a boy that loves to . . chalk doorsteps, "cut behind" anything on wheels or runners. **1892** *DN* 1.212 **MA,** The expression *cut, cut behind,* was used to call the attention of a driver to boys running behind his wagon. **1963** Pilgrim Soc. Plymouth **MA** *Notes* 7 (as of late 1800s), Small boys, who stood to watch the procession sweep along, cried out to the man with the whip, "Cut behind, Mister," if a dare-devil dashed out and stole a ride on the sleigh runner, or hitched his sled behind for a tow.

cutbones n Cf **bone** n **3**

=sawbones.

1966 *DARE* (Qu. BB53a, . . *Joking names . . for a doctor*) Inf **AR39,** Cutbones.

cut-buddy n, adj Also *cud-buddy* [Prob *cut* to give or receive a share + *buddy* friend, pal]

A close friend; friendly.

1970 *DARE* (Qu. II1, . . *A close friend*) Inf **NC84,** Cut-buddy; (Qu. II3, . . *Expressions to say . . people are very friendly*) Inf **SC69,** Cut-buddy; **NY238,** Cud-buddies. [All Infs Black]

cut buddy short v phr Cf *DS* MM16

To take a shortcut.

1953 Brewer *Word Brazos* 18 **eTX** [Black], He doin' what dey calls "cuttin' buddy short." (Dat mean, teckin' a short cut thoo de woods, so you git whar you goin' lots quicker'n goin' way 'roun' de dirt road.) *Ibid* 55, She set im down rat by her so de triflin' rascal cain't slip outen de chu'ch house an' cut buddy short back home.

cut butter v phr

1912 Green *VA Folk-Speech* 139, Cut butter . . . When two boys are riding on a see-saw they try to throw each other off by suddenly moving the end of the see-saw to one side.

cut buttonholes in v phr

To use a whip with exceptional precision.

1967 *DARE* Tape **MI56,** [In reply to the FW's question whether the Inf had been proficient with a whip when he was a teamster, he said] "Yea, I used to cut buttonholes in a lot of 'em [=horses]."

cut cabbage v phr Also *cut up cabbage* [Humorous substitute for *cut capers*] Cf **cut a rusty 3**

1938 *AmSp* 13.5 **seAR,** Cutting cabbage. 'He is really cutting up cabbage.' That is, he is doing something in a spectacular manner.

cutch See **culch 1**

cut cheese, not to v phr

To have no importance.

1896 *DN* 1.414 **cNY,** Cheese: "That don't cut any cheese," that has no weight. **1922** *DN* 5.158 **NE, NY.**

cutch grass n¹ See **couch grass 1**

cutch grass n² See **scutch grass**

cut corners v phr

To take a shortcut.

1965–70 *DARE* (Qu. MM16, . . *Walking . . to the other corner of a square . . to save steps, you might say; "It'll be shorter if we _____."*) 13 Infs, **scattered,** Cut corners.

cut cross-lots v phr [*cut* go abruptly or swiftly + **cross-lot(s)** adv]

1969 *DARE* FW Addit **MA61,** Cut cross-lots: Fig: get to the point.

cut curlicues See **cut up a curlicue**

cut down v phr

1 To lower (a gun) in the direction of a target object; to shoot (at).

1918 Mulford *Man from Bar-20* 90 *(DA),* He wheeled like a flash, his upraised gun cutting down swiftly. *Ibid* 96, Bein' in a pocket made by them fool boulders I couldn't get out, so I had to cut down on you with both hands. **1939** Hall *Coll.* **eTN, wNC,** Cut down . . . To lower a gun from an upright position preparatory to firing. "He cut down and shot at it." *Ibid, Cut down (on, at)* . . . Sometimes to shoot at. "He cut down on it with a muzzle-loadin' rifle." . . . "He cut down at 'im and out he fetched 'im." **1943** Writers' Program NC *Bundle of Troubles* 80, Next time I went hunting I loaded Ole Bessie with half buckshot and half rocksalt. I were way back of Ole Roan when I sighted a deer with the spyglass. Same as usual I cut down, and the deer kicked over. **1970** *Foxfire* 4.28 **nGA,** When a hunter says, "I cut down on him," he means he opened fire.

2 In a spelling bee: see quot 1946.

1899 (1912) Green *VA Folk-Speech,* Cut down . . . At the last hour just before the school breaking up all the children who were big enough to spell were made to stand up and the master gave out the words. The scholar who spelt a word missed by those ahead of him *cut them down,* and went ahead of them. **1946** *PADS* 6.11 **seNC,** Cut down . . . To go up one place in a spelling class; that is, to take the place of the student who has just misspelled a word.

3 To reduce the speed of (something in motion).

1939 Hall *Coll.* **eTN, wNC,** Cut down . . . To slow (a horse). "I cut down my horse a little bit."

4 See quot. Cf **cut-down** n **2, cut over** v phr **1**

c1960 Wilson *Coll.* **csKY,** Cut down . . . To alter clothes, esp. for the next-younger child. *Cut-down* is also an adjective for such clothes.

5 See quots.

1966 *DARE* FW Addit **MA6,** Cut down . . to cut through [bread dough] with a knife to break the air bubbles. **c1969** *DARE* File **MA,** I am familiar with *cut down* meaning to cut through bread in order to release air bubbles.

6 See **cut** v **13.**

cut down ppl adj

1 Troubled, frustrated, dejected. **chiefly SE**

1843 Field *Drama Pokerville* 117 **AL,** Sure enough, there was no mistake about it, till, finally, terribly cut down, he was obliged to say: "Well, gentlemen, it *is* gone, by gracious." **1883** Cooke *Somebody's Neighbors* 198 **NEng,** He was cut down dreadful: the consolations of religion wa'n't of no account to him. **1888** Jones *Negro Myths* 92 **GA coast,** Wen Buh Rabbit fine eh cant git no saterfaction outer Buh Elephunt, eh cut down, an eh berry bex [=and he (is) very vexed], an eh mek plan fuh git eeben wid Buh Elephunt. **1922** Gonzales *Black Border* 295 **sSC, GA coasts** [Gullah glossary], Cut'down, or tek'down—dejected, chagrined. **1950** *PADS* 14.25 **SC,** Cut down . . . Vexed, troubled or disconcerted by some disagreeable occurrence.

2 Of clothing: made smaller. Cf **cut down** v phr **4, cut-down** n **2**

1932 Faulkner *Light in August* 143 **MS,** The small figure in cutdown underwear. *Ibid* 145, He returned to the bed, carrying the empty tray as though it were a monstrance and he the bearer, his surplice the cutdown undergarment. **c1960** [see **cut down** v phr **4**].

cut-down n

1 Potential farmland on which the trees, though felled, have not yet been removed. *arch* Cf **fallow B, fell-piece**

1851 Sibley *Hist. Union* 98 **csME,** After the trees had been left to dry through a considerable part of the season, the 'cut-down,' or 'fell-piece,' was set on fire. *Ibid* 99, And even when such ravages were not made . . the fire continued to burn in the 'cut-down' for many days. **1891** in 1949 *PADS* 11.31 **ME,** You know that "cut-down" little west / And little east of Henry Hill's.

2 also *cut-me-down:* A hand-me-down garment altered for a younger or smaller person. Cf **cut down** v phr **4**

1939 Coffin *Capt. Abby* 11 **ME** (as of c1860s), Children went to school for arithmetic to their own mothers . . [who] became distant . . taskmasters and allowed no boy at the beginning of his multiplication table to rest his cut-me-downs from his father's trousers on her prim lap. **1967** *DARE* (Qu. U3, . . *Garment that is passed on from one person to another*) Inf **MA5,** Cut-down.

3 An old automobile modified to increase speed; a hot rod or jalopy.

1966–67 *DARE* (Qu. N6, *An old car . . fixed up to . . go fast or make a lot of noise*) Infs **GA12, 13, SC63,** Cut-down.

cute adj [Aphet form of *acute*]

1 Clever, smart; shrewd.

1718 in 1909 Earle *Child Life* 87, He is a brisk child & grows very cute. **1834** *Life Andrew Jackson* 190, Major, says the gineral, that are augural address was the cutest thing I ever rit. **1855** Wise *Tales Marines* 153, My partner . . is tarnation cute in all his investments. **1905** *DN* 3.7 **cCT,** Cute . . . Sharp, keen. **1907** *DN* 3.211 **nwAR. 1909** *DN* 3.410 **ME,** Cute . . . Sharp-witted. **1926** *DN* 5.383 **NEng** (as of 1818). **1951** Porter *Ragged Roads* 54 **KS, OK,** Well, here's whur ye been goin'. Work hard and be cute. **1967–68** *DARE* (Qu. KK37, . . *A very sly person:* "He's _____.") Infs **MA45, MN12,** Cute.

2 Bow-legged. *euphem*

1905 *DN* 3.76 **nwAR,** Cute . . . Bow-legged. The latter adjective is regarded as indelicate. The euphemism is used by women. **1950** *WELS Suppl.* **neWI,** Cute means bow-legged—used by older members of the family; **csWI,** Cute means bow-legged—revived around 1940. **1983** *MJLF* 9.39 **ceKY,** Cute . . bowlegged.

3 Haughty, self-important.

1966–70 *DARE* (Qu. HH35, *A woman who puts on a lot of airs:* "She's too _____ for me.") Infs **KY94, MS45, NC84,** Cute. [All Infs Black]

cute adv [**cute** adj **1**]

Cleverly, shrewdly.

1834 Davis *Letters Downing* 286, This 'Protest' is pretty cute written. **1940** (1942) Clark *Ox-Bow* 24 **NY** (as of 1885), They drew around, Gil dropping Farnley's cards where he had to reach for them. Farnley looked at them longer this time. Then he put one down very slowly, like he wasn't sure. Four of a kind played cute, or keeping one for luck, I thought.

cute v [**cute** adj]

1953 Randolph *Down in Holler* 166 **Ozarks,** As a verb, cute means to flatter, to praise excessively. O.O. McIntyre [in a 1930 syndicated column] told of an Arkansawyer who said that his daughter had been "*cuted* too much" by her admirers. He also mentioned a girl who peeked around the corner of an Ozark cabin at Riley Cooper. "She's tryin' to *cute* you," an old man explained to the visitor.

cuter See **cooter** v

cut-eye n, v [Caribbean Creole (Cf Haitian *kout je,* Jamaican and Bahamian *cut-eye*); prob loan transl of an Afr idiom; see *DBE*] *among Black speakers* Cf **cut one's eyes**

A scornful gesture made with the eyes; to make such a gesture; see quot 1976.

[**1942** Hurston *Dust Tracks* 55 **FL** [Black], She would cut her eyes and give us a glare that meant trouble.] **1976** *Jrl. Amer. Folkl.* 89.296, The basic *cut-eye* gesture is initiated by directing a hostile look or glare in the other person's direction . . . After the initial glare, the eyeballs are moved . . down or diagonally across the line of the person's body. This "cut"

with the eyes is the heart of the gesture . . . [It is] generally completed by a final glare, and then the entire head may be turned away contemptuously from the person. *Ibid* 299, Cut-eye . . . Almost all the Black informants were familiar with the term. Among the "meanings" volunteered were "a look of disgust"; "expression of hostility"; "to threaten"; "act of defiance or disapproval"; "bad feelings"; "when you're mad at someone"; "to show you don't like somebody." . . *Cut-eye* as a lexical item and as a cultural form of behavior is almost totally unknown to White Americans.

cut-eye adj, adv *among Black speakers*

Of someone's glance or look: questioning; askance, suspiciously.

1937 (1977) Hurston *Their Eyes* 149 **FL** [Black], He gave her a little cut-eye look to get her meaning. **1942** Hurston *Dust Tracks* 127 **FL** [Black], She looked at me cut-eye first thing because the madam had hired me without asking her about it.

cut eyes See **cut one's eyes**

cut felt v phr

To clear a field.

1970 *DARE* Tape **WV14,** Cuttin' felt . . [you] take your scythe and go cut the briars and weeds and all, off the fields.

cut from the same cloth adj phr Also *cut out of* ~ chiefly **Nth**

Very much alike; "like two peas in a pod."

[**1950** *WELS* (*I knew they'd get along all right; they're* _____) 2 Infs, **WI,** Cut off the same piece (of goods); 1 Inf, **seWI,** Cut out of the same material.] [**1961** Cole *Idioms New Engl.,* To have been *cut* out of the same piece of goods as another person.] **1965–70** *DARE* (Qu. KK65, . . *'The same sort':* "If you like Bob, I'm sure you'll like his brother— They're _____.") Infs **CT39, MA79, NE11, NJ28, NY92, OR1,** (Both) cut from (*or* out of) the same cloth; [**UT6,** Made in the same piece of cloth; **NE6,** Made of the same cloth; **IN22,** Of the same cut of cloth; **OH49,** Same kind of cloth].

cut glass sledgehammer n Cf *DS* HH14

An imaginary object used as the basis for a practical joke.

c1960 Bailey *Resp. to PADS 20* **KS,** (*Ways of teasing a beginner . . :* "Go get me a _____.") Cut glass sledgehammer.

cut-grass n [For *cutting* that cuts + *grass*]

1 A grass of the genus *Leersia.* See also **rice cutgrass, white grass**

1822 Eaton *Botany* 332, *Leersia—virginica* . . (cut grass . .) . . . A very rough harsh grass. **1901** Mohr *Plant Life AL* 363, *Homalocenchrus oryzoides* . . . Rice-like cutgrass . . . *Homalocenchrus hexandrus* . . . Southern cutgrass. **1912** Baker *Book of Grasses* 90, Cut-grass. *Leersia oryzoides.*

2 =**tearthumb.**

1913 *Torreya* 13.230, *Polygonum sagittatum* . . . Cut grass . . S.C.

3 =**wild rice 2.**

1911 *Torreya* 11.227, *Zizaniopsis miliacea* . . . Cut grass, Mississippi Delta, La. **1967** LeCompte *Word Atlas* 233 **seLA,** [1 inf] Cut grass . . . *Jonc coupant* (cut grass) belongs to the family of rushes.

cut-hair n

An Indian who has cut his hair short, like a White man's.

1967 Cerello *Dakota Co. MN* 53, Cut-hair: An Indian or part-Indian who is farming the white man's way. "Old Indian John was a kind, trustworthy and industrious old cut-hair." "There were several old cut-hairs who lived by us when we were kids." "My folks never did trust those old cut-hairs that lived down on the bottom-lands."

cut harrow n Also *cutting harrow*

=**cutaway harrow.**

1968–69 *DARE* (Qu. L20, *The implement used in a field after it's been plowed to break up the lumps*) Infs **NJ16, 20, 22, 58,** Cut harrow; **GA84, NC54,** Cutting harrow.

cut-horse See **cutting horse**

cut in v phr

1 See quot. Cf **cut** v **5**

1944 Adams *Western Words* 47, Cut in—To drive stragglers or wandering cattle back into the herd from which they had strayed.

2 To use a harrow or similar implement to cover seed or work stubble into the soil.

1966 *DARE* (Qu. L22, . . *About a crop he intends to plant . . a farmer* might say, "This year, I'm going to _____ a crop of oats / corn / cotton, etc.'') Inf **FL**7, Cut in; harrow in. **1966** DARE Tape **NC**3, We usually cut the tobacco stalks in and then plant a cover crop. **1967** DARE FW Addit **cwNC**, Cut in: after a field has been harvested, to plow up the ground.

cut in the craw, cut in the eye See **cut** ppl adj **1**

cut it down v phr Cf **break down** v phr

To dance with flamboyant skill.

1940 FWP Guide NY 664, When the fiddles were brought out no one could 'cut it down' like Ed Horton: an original jitterbug, he put in somersaults and other improvisations, all in perfect time.

cut jackets v phr

To play the game of **yellow jacket**, in which players strike each other with switches or cornstalks until one gives up.

a1883 (1911) Bagby VA Gentleman 49, He must now learn to cut jackets, play hard-ball, choose partners for cat and chermany, be kept in, fight every other day, and be turned out for painting his face with pokeberry juice and grinning at the school-master. **1899** (1912) Green VA Folk-Speech, Cut-jackets . . . Two boys or young men, white or black, each armed with a hickory switch gave it to each other on the shoulders and back as long as they could stand it. The one who gave in first lost the game.

cutleaf daisy See **cut-leaved daisy b**

cutleaf maple n Also cut-leafed maple, cut-leaved ~

=**box elder.**

1897 Sudworth Arborescent Flora 291, Acer negundo . . . Cut-leaved Maple (Colo.). **1900** Lyons Plant Names 11, Acer Negundo . . . Cut-leaved Maple. **1965–70** DARE (Qu. T14, . . Different kinds of maples) 20 Infs, **Nth**, Cutleaf maple; **NY**75, Cutleaf soft maple; **PA**242, Cut-leafed maple; **MA**78, Silver cutleaf maple; (Qu. T3, The tree that produces syrup and sugar) Inf **MI**102, Cutleaf maple; (Qu. T13, . . Other names . . for . . : box elder) Inf **MI**108, Cutleaf maple. **1974** (1977) Coon Useful Plants 48, Acer negundo . . cut-leaved maple . . . This tree, which is not usually identified as a maple because of its cut-leaved appearance, is a short-lived, coarse tree.

cut-leaved daisy n

Either of two composite plants:

a A perennial yellow-flowered plant (Engelmannia pinnatifida).

1936 Whitehouse TX Flowers 171, Cut-leaved Daisy . . . is closely related to the sunflowers but has the daisy habit of closing the flower heads at night and opening them in bright sunlight. **1961** Wills–Irwin Flowers TX 232, A very common plant of plains and prairies, the Cut-leaved Daisy is found over most of the state.

b also cutleaf daisy: A **fleabane** (here: Erigeron compositus).

1953 Nelson Plants Rocky Mt. Park 165, Cut-leaved daisy . . , Erigeron compositus . . . Hairy leaves three-forked at the apex. **1963** Craighead Rocky Mt. Wildflowers 209, The Cutleaf Daisy increases with overgrazing and is used as an indicator of range abuse. **1973** Hitchcock–Cronquist Flora Pacific NW 516, Widespread sp.; cut-lvd d[aisy].

cut-leaved maple See **cutleaf maple**

cutlips minnow n Also cutlips

A cyprinid fish with a tripartite lower lip (Exoglossum maxilingua).

1880 Günther Introd. to Study of Fishes 596 (DAE), From the fresh waters of North America . . Exoglossum (the 'Stone-toter' or 'Cut-lips'). **1887** Goode Amer. Fishes 427, The "Cut-lips," . . . Exoglossum maxilingua [sic]. **1960** Amer. Fisheries Soc. List Fishes 13, Cutlips minnow . . Exoglossum maxillingua [sic].

cut loose v phr Also cut one's dog (or wolf) loose

To act energetically or suddenly, without restraint.

1809 (1814) Weems F. Marion 231, The enemy . . all at once cut loose upon them with a thundering clap. **1902** DN 2.232 **sIL**, Cut loose . . . The same as crack loose. [Crack loose . . . 1. To execute a threat. 2. To proceed against. 3. In a command, to act instantly.] **1903** (1965) Adams Log Cowboy 81 **SW**, Any time that you have the leisure and want to shoot me, just cut loose your dog. **1906** DN 3.117 **sIN**, Cut loose . . . Same as crack loose. [Crack loose . . . To let one's self loose; to act in a threatening manner.] **1907** DN 3.221 **nwAR, sIL**, Cut loose. **1912** Wason Friar Tuck 167, So Kit cut loose and told me her story. **1939** Hall Coll. **eTN, wNC**, Cut loose . . . Shoot . . . "Bowles says, 'I'll shoot if

it catches us both.' I says, 'Cut loose after I take care of myself and you take care of yourn.' " **c1960** Wilson Coll. **csKY**, Cut loose . . . To explode, usually with anger, though occasionally with a determination to do something. **1961** Adams Old-Time Cowhand 7, If, when he got to town, after long months out in the brush, on the lone prairie, or on the long, long trail, the cowboy cut his wolf loose and had a little fun, he could hardly be blamed. Ibid 323, It was kinda natural that when he hit town after the roundup he cut his wolf loose and freighted his crop with likker. **1967** DARE Tape **CA**13, He decided to cut loose [=quit].

cut-me-down n

1 See **cut-down** n **2**.

2 Among loggers: see quot.

1956 Sorden–Ebert Logger's Words 11 **Gt Lakes**, Cut-me-down, A cross cut saw.

cut mud v phr

1936 AmSp 11.314 **Ozarks**, Cut mud . . . To make haste. One of our neighbors told her ten-year-old boy: 'You jest cut mud for home, afore I take a hick'ry to you!'

cut off v phr Also cut out **chiefly Sth, S Midl** See Map Cf **cut** v **13, cut on**

To turn or switch (something) off; to extinguish (a lamp or fire).

1941 Faulkner Men Working 73 **MS**, She cut the light out. Ibid 140, And the City cut the lights off and last of all the water. [Ibid 174, And I'm going over to the City Hall right now and tell them to cut this water back on.] **1950** Faulkner Stories 177 **MS**, The second car came up and stopped . . . "Cut the lights off!" McLendon said. **1965–70** DARE (Qu. Y42, Expressions for putting out a lamp or light) 42 Infs, **Sth, S Midl**, Cut off (the light or the lamp); **KY**10, Cut off light; **FL**8, **MS**51, Cut it off; 14 Infs, **chiefly Sth**, Cut out (the light); **GA**7, Cut it out; **NC**49, Cut that light out; (Qu. Y43b, . . To put out a fire) Inf **TX**86, Cut the fire out. **1967** DARE Tape **TX**23, Cut that damn thing [=tape recorder] off a minute. **1968** DARE FW Addit **GA**44, "Cut this off!" (An acquaintance telling the Inf to unplug an electric coffeepot.)

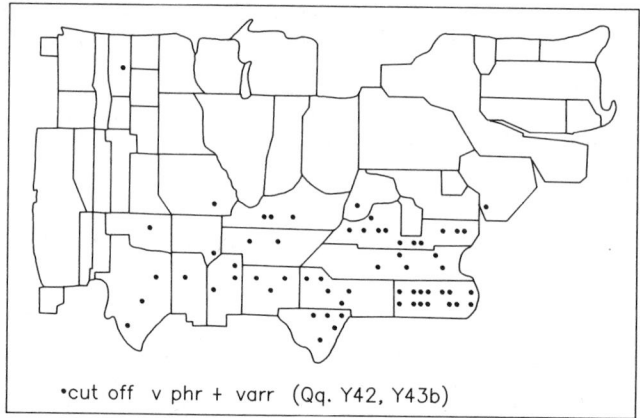

•cut off v phr + varr (Qq. Y42, Y43b)

cutoff n

1 A channel, cut by high water, that shortens the course of a stream; also the part of the former stream so separated, forming a slough. **chiefly Sth**

1773 in 1953 McMullen Topog. Terms FL 96, Plan of Nassau Inlet & of the Stream as far N.W. as the cut-off situated in Latde. 30°, 13' 24". **1814** Brackenridge Views of LA 229, This name originated in the circumstance of a trader . . being in the river at the very moment that this cut-off was forming. **1890** Townsend U.S. Index 137, Cutoffs are applied to lakelets on the banks of the Mississippi and of the Red River, formed of the parts of the river left by the change in the channel, which gradually become insulated through the deposit of silt. **1914** DN 4.154 **NH**, Cut-off . . . A small, ditchlike washout. **1918** Giles Country Camp Lee 15 **VA**, In time the streams will cut entirely through these necks, producing new and shorter channels known as cut-offs. **1945** Saxon Gumbo Ya-Ya 275 **LA**, At Raccourci Cut-Off, there is an even stranger phenomenon. **1965–69** DARE (Qu. C1, . . A small stream of water not big enough to be a river) Inf **FL**21, Cutoff; (Qu. C14, A stretch of still water going off to the side from a river or lake) Inf **LA**12, Cutoff—that's where there's a low place where the water flows through when the water gets too high; (Qu. C21) Inf **IL**32, Cutoff.

2 =**cut** n **3**.

1895 Remington *Pony Tracks* 87, Fresh horses are saddled . . but before high noon the work is done, and the various 'cut-offs' are herded in different directions.
3 See quot.
1969 *DARE* (Qu. CC4, . . *Various religions or religious groups*) Inf MI103, Cutoffs—Dutch reformed who broke away from the original Holland group because of the strictness of the rules.
4 See **cut** n **6**.

‡**cut off one's jib** v phr
1913 *DN* 4.26 NW, Cut off one's jib . . . To keep one from talking.

cut on v phr **chiefly Sth, S Midl** See Map
To turn or switch (something) on.
1941 [see **cut off** v phr]. **1965–70** *DARE* (Qu. Y41a, . . *To light a lamp or lantern: "_____ the lamp."*) Infs AL60, MS51, OK54, SC44, TX27, WV5, Cut on; NJ21, Cut the lamp on; (Qu. Y41b, . . *To light an electric light: "_____ the light."*) 28 Infs, **chiefly Sth, S Midl**, Cut on; NC76, SC44, Cut it on; KY94, Cut 'em on. **1966–67** Baltimore MD Dept. Educ. *Bulletin* 43.2–4.62, Cut . . . To turn or switch [a light] on or off. Washington [Black] kids don't *switch* or *turn* a light off, they *cut* it on or off.

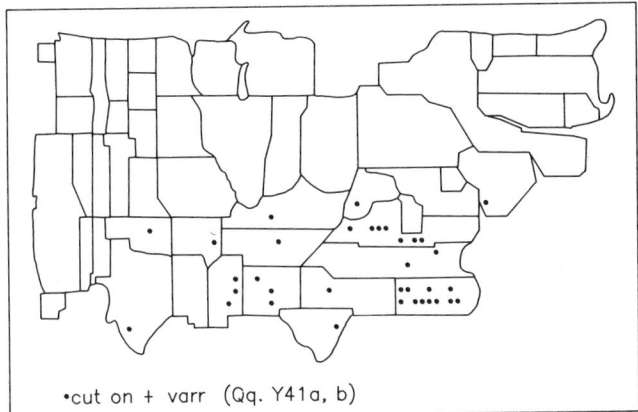

•cut on + varr (Qq. Y41a, b)

cut one down v phr
=**beat one down.**
1966–69 *DARE* (Qu. U12, *If you were buying something and you argued with the person selling it till you made him lower the price, you might say, "I _____."*) Infs MA15, NH14, RI4, WA11, Cut him down (on the deal).

‡**cut one into** v phr
To introduce one to.
1970 *DARE* (Qu. II4, *When people . . ask to be introduced to someone . . "I'd like to _____ John Smith."*) Inf NY238, Cut me into. [New expression used here among Blacks]

cut one's comb v phr Also *cut the comb* [In ref to a cock's *comb*, symbolic of pride or arrogance; *OED comb* sb.[1] 5, 1548 →] **chiefly Sth, NEng** *old-fash*
To humble someone; to lower someone's pride.
1741 in 1930 Winslow *Amer. Broadside* 117/1 NEng, Resolv'd to cut the *Spaniards* Comb. **1770** (1965) Carter *Diary* 1.458 VA, I wish he would send down a cargo of it [=flour] that I might cut Mr. Ritchie's comb a little. **1845** Thompson *Pineville* 141 GA, "Now's the time to cut his comb, major." "Challenge him right here, now?" "Yes, and you'll see how he'll drop his feathers." **1890** *Nation* 50.352/3, His reckoning it a proud thing to cut the comb of an American at all hazards. **1899** (1912) Green *VA Folk-Speech, Cut the comb* . . . To humiliate; abase. **1903** *DN* 2.311 seMO, *Cut the comb* . . . To humiliate. 'It cut his comb mightily when she refused his company.'

cut one's dog loose See **cut loose**

cut one's eye down v phr
1927 *AmSp* 2.352 WV, Cut his eye down . . to blacken one's eye. "Several of the boys got their eyes cut down at the fair."

cut one's eyes v phr Also *cut eyes, cut one's eye* [Prob coalescence of two forms: *cut* to cleave, slash; snub; change the direction; and **cut-eye** n, v] **chiefly Sth, S Midl**
To glance out of the corners of one's eyes; to look furtively.

1827 in 1939 Thornton *Amer. Gloss.* 3.103, Went to New York, took steamboat to New Brunswick, thence Stage No. 7, strangers crossed words and cut eyes. **1839** *S. Lit. Messenger* 5.377 GA, Billy . . said . . "She was the most beautifulest I ever seen . . excepting *one*"—cutting his eyes, as he spoke, at Rachel. **1898** Smith *Caleb West* 70 NY, "We come purty nigh leavin' everybody on the Ledge las' night," . . said Captain Joe, "cutting" his eye at the skipper as he spoke. **1899** (1912) Green *VA Folk-Speech, Cut* . . . To cast or turn stealthily: as, "She cut her eyes at him." **1903** *DN* 2.311 seMO, *Cut (the eyes)* . . . To glance furtively. "He cut his eyes at the girl." **1907** *DN* 3.230 nwAR, *Cut one's eyes.* **1928** Peterkin *Scarlet Sister Mary* 345 SC, He cut his eyes all round to be certain Maum Hannah could not hear him. **1933** *Scribner's Mag.* 94.196 FL, But when we got to the porch, here lay the bird-dogs in the rocking chairs. There was one to every chair, rocking away and cutting their eyes at her. **1956** McAtee *Some Dialect NC*, Cut eyes . . . Glance sidewise without turning the head. **c1960** Wilson Coll. **csKY**, *Cut eyes at* . . . To flirt with; to roll the eyes. **1981** Harper–Presley *Okefinokee* 65 (as of a1948), He could see Wes cutting his eye at every dark hole and under the bushes and all the corners around. He was looking for alligators all around.

cut one's finger See **cut** v **10**

cut one's foot v phr **esp S Midl** *euphem*
To step in dung.
1899 (1912) Green *VA Folk-Speech, Cut* . . . To cut the foot. A person "cuts his foot" when he treads on dung. **1931** *PMLA* 46.1307 **sAppalachians**, He cut his foot (stepped in excrement) behind the barn. **1939** Hench Coll. **csPA**, Recorded Jan. 19, 1939, but heard from 1898 on. When I was a boy and visited my country cousins each summer in Bedford County, Penna., all the youngsters spoke of stepping in a pile of cow manure . . as "cutting your foot." As a city boy I cut my foot a lot before I learned to watch my step. **1953** Randolph *Down in Holler* 118 **Ozarks**, When a well-bred country boy is walking with his girl, and sees that she is about to step into some cow dung, he says, "Don't cut your foot!" This euphemism is known to everybody in the backwoods and is sometimes used figuratively even in the pulpit. **1960** Criswell *Resp. to PADS 20* **Ozarks**, Cut (one's) foot . . . To step into a pile of cow manure. Extremely common euphemistic way to avoid the plain truth. "Look out, boy, you're about to cut your foot. These old cows have dumped manure all over this lot." This has been reported from elsewhere as, "cut one's foot on a Chinese razor." **1975** Gould *ME Lingo, Cut your foot*—On the farm, to step inadvertently on a pasture cow dropping or flap is to cut your foot.

cut one's own weeds v phr Cf **kill one's own snakes**
See quot 1953.
1953 Randolph *Down in Holler* 238 **Ozarks**, Cut your own weeds . . . To mind one's own business. **1954** Harder Coll. **cwTN**, *Cut your own weeds.*

cut one's stick See **cut stick**

cut one's string v phr Cf **cut loose, cut-the-buckle**
To cease to restrain oneself, to let go.
1913 LaFollette *Autobiog.* 537, Don Hanna of Ohio . . had urged that it was time for him [=Theodore Roosevelt] to 'cut the string' and turn his candidacy loose.

cut one's suspenders v phr
1944 Adams *Western Words* 86, Cut his suspenders—Said of one who leaves one place for another, to leave the country.

cut one's water off v phr
1954 Harder Coll. **cwTN**, Cut his water off . . . To stop someone from doing something.

cut one's wolf loose See **cut loose**

cutout n

1 also attrib: The action of separating selected cattle from a herd; an animal so separated (cf **cut** n **3**); the place where such animals are temporarily kept. **West** Cf **cut** v **5**
1874 McCoy *Cattle Trade* 81, In the beginning of the cut-out, a few gentle cows or working oxen are driven a short space from the round-up and held, to form a nucleus, to which those cut out gather. **1890** *Gate City Herald* (Deep Creek Falls, Wash.) 23 Oct. 1/4 (*DA*), All this time the 'cut-out' experts leading these extra horses came up leisurely in the rear. **1907** Mulford *Bar-20* 120 (*DA*), In this contest Hopalong Cassidy led his nearest rival, Red Connors . . by twenty cut-outs. **1920** Hunter *Trail Drivers TX* 98, Our camp was the catch and cut-out for all the other bosses. **1943** Hough *Snow Above Town* 144 WY, Frank is wondering

about the steers. Sometimes after the cutout they get restless and mill around far into the night.

2 =**cut** n **1a.**

1966 *DARE* (Qu. C21, *A deep place cut in sloping ground by running water*) Infs ME22, MT5, Cutout.

3 See quot.

1979 *DARE* File **swNC** [Black], *Cutouts:* Summer sandals. "She's wearing a pair of cutouts."

cut out v phr See **cut off** v phr

cut out fence rows v phr

1954 *Harder Coll.* **cwTN**, *Cut out fence rows* . . . To remove bushes from fence rows.

cutout harrow See **cutaway harrow**

cut out of the same cloth See **cut from the same cloth**

cut over v phr

1 Of clothing: to refashion, alter. Cf **cut down** v phr **4**

1895 Wiggin *Village Watch-Tower* 161, She cut over Dr. Berry's old trousers into briefer ones for Tommy Berry. **1904** in 1913 Pringle *Woman Rice Planter* 73 **SC coast**, We . . watch with interest the successful and ingenious remodelling of sleeves—I being the only recalcitrant who will not cut over sleeves.

2 Of timberland: to remove all the marketable trees.

1905 U.S. Forest Serv. *Bulletin* 61.9, *Cut over, to.* To cut most or all of the merchantable timber in a forest. **1917** (1923) *Birds Amer.* 2.154, When found they [=woodpeckers] are usually in regions of original forest growth, rarely being seen where the woods have been once cut over. **1966–70** *DARE* Tape MI20, Cutting over considerable territory; VA75, They've cut most all of the timberland over, there's not too much more timber there. **1970** *DARE* FW Addit MI121, *Cut over:* To cut down the tall trees in an area.

3 To convert (to a different system), to change over. See also **cutover** n **2**

1967 *DARE* Tape MI46, We cut over to dial phones.

cutover ppl adj [**cut over** v phr **2**]

Of timberland: having had the marketable trees removed.

1899 *Westminster Gaz.* 6 Jan 10/2 (*DAE*), At least 90 per cent. of the cut-over lands [on the Pacific coast] are of absolutely no value for agricultural purposes. **1905** U.S. Forest Serv. *Bulletin* 61.9, *Cut-over forest.* Forest in which most or all of the merchantable timber has been cut. **1911** Quick *Yellowstone Nights* 12.338, The solitary guest which is the only thing that brings the haunch to the spit in the Minnesota cut-over forest. **1939** Towne *Her Majesty Montana* 102 (*Hench Coll.*), More than 7,000 acres are cut-over, burned or young growth. **1940** *Sun* (Baltimore MD) 3 Dec 6/2 (*Hench Coll.*), [He] estimated there were 5,000,000 acres of "fertile, but poorly drained, underdeveloped, cutover land" in the Mississippi Delta area. **1966** *DARE* (Qu. C29, *A good-sized stretch of level land with practically no trees*) Inf MS73, Cutover land (trees had been on it). **1966–69** *DARE* Tape MI8, Each one has still 1600 acres. Course, it's not all farmland, it's cutover land, and there's a lot of deer country on it; CA158, MN29, Cutover land.

cutover n [**cut over** v phr]

1 Land from which all or most of the marketable timber has been removed.

1922 Titus *Timber* vi.60 (*DA*), If we had known we could have gone north . . into the hardwood cutover and made a go of it. **1969** Sorden *Lumberjack Lingo* 31 **NEng, Gt Lakes**, *Cutover*—Any area that has been logged, devoid of trees and possibly burned over. **1969** *DARE* Tape CA158, It used to be just cutover, the most of this timber and so forth, and now this sells for so much more, that the taxes have been raised.

2 A conversion or change (to a different system).

1947 *Progress* (Charlottesville VA) 22 Feb 2/2 (*Hench Coll.*), [He] explained the "cut-over" from manual to dial operation will be effected between 9 and 11 A.M.

3 =**cut-down** n **2.**

1967 *DARE* (Qu. U3, . . *Garment that is passed on from one person to another*) Inf MA5, Cutover.

cut paper n

The paper mulberry (*Broussonetia papyrifera*).

1894 *Jrl. Amer. Folkl.* 7.98, *Broussonetia papyrifera,* . . cut paper, West Va.

cut short v phr Also *cut shorts* [Metath of *shortcut*]

1967 *DARE* (Qu. MM16, *If . . you want to save steps, you might say, "It'll be shorter if we_____."*) Inf HI13, Cut short. [FW: Inf's husband says *cut shorts.*]

cutshort n [Metath of *shortcut*]

1981 *DARE* File **HI**, In Hawaii on Maui we were told to take a *"cut short"* instead of a "shortcut".

cutshort bean n Cf **French bean**

A type of bean (*Phaseolus* spp).

c1960 *Wilson Coll.* **csKY**, *Cutshort beans* . . . A variety of pole beans that has seeds, crowded in a short pod; often raised as a cornfield bean. **1966–68** *DARE* (Qu. I20, . . *Kinds of beans . . grown around here*) Inf NC33, Cutshort beans (snap beans); VA24, Cutshort bean: brown, three inches long, hangs in bunches, and is squared. **1976** *Wanigan Catalog* 7, Cutshort bean. **1981** *Broaddus Coll.* **ceKY** (as of 1958), Cut-short bean—a variety of green beans.

cut shorts See **cut short** v phr

cutsie n Also sp *kutsie*

1950 *PADS* 14.25 **SC**, *Cutsie, kutsie* ['kʌtsɪ] . . . A twinge in the throat caused by swallowing something sour. Supposed to be a symptom of mumps. Origin undetermined.

cut some rusty See **cut a rusty 1**

cut stick v phr Also *cut a stick, cut one's stick old-fash*

To prepare to leave; to depart quickly, run away.

1832 Paulding *Westward Ho* 1.180, You or I must cut a stick and quit this hunting-ground. **1834** *Life Andrew Jackson* 67, The fellers seeing their danger cut stick and run. **1865** in 1875 Twain *Sketches New & Old* (Hartford) 299, Go to the door-keeper and get your money, and cut your stick—vamose the ranche! **1883** Eggleston *Hoosier Schoolboy* 69 **IN**, "Run," spelled out Susan on her fingers. "The school-house is on fire!" called out Bob . . . Bob whispered to Jack to "cut sticks," but Jack only went to his seat. **1899** (1912) Green *VA Folk-Speech, Cut stick* . . . To be off; to go away. **1905** *DN* 3.6 **cCT**, *Cut stick* . . . To be off. **1936** *AmSp* 11.314 **Ozarks**, *Cut a stick* . . . To run rapidly.

cut straw and molasses n

Fig: poor food.

1857 (1923) Beadle *To Nebraska* 173, Their supper smelled delicious and would be a luxury to some families here who live on "cut straw and molasses." **1944** Adams *Western Words, Cut straw and molasses*— Poor food.

cutter n[1]

1 A light horse-drawn sleigh used primarily for passengers and having a single set of runners. **chiefly Nth, exc eNEng** See Map

1803 Fessenden *Terrible Tractoration* 80, Guide my wild Parnassian pony, Till our aerial chariot runs Athwart 'a wilderness of suns!' **1885** Howells *Rise Lapham* 2 **Boston MA**, The Colonel and his wife were driving slowly down Beacon Street in the light, high-seated cutter. **1905** *DN* 3.7 **cCT**, *Cutter* . . . A light sleigh, or a sled. **1943** *LANE* Maps 573–574, Sleighs, horse-drawn and metal-shod, for passengers: [1 inf, neMA,] cutter, ~ sleigh. **1963** Pilgrim Soc. Plymouth MA *Notes* 13.7, The company would all set out in sleighs for the six-mile ride from town: cutters for two, and pungs with a load. **1965–70** *DARE* (Qu. N40b, . . *Sleighs for carrying people*) 242 Infs, **chiefly Nth, exc eNEng**, Cutter; MD48, MI118, Cutter sleigh; MI64, NY233, Swell-back cutter; CO46, Double cutter, single cutter; NY93, Horse and cutter; NY97, One-horse cutter; MI11, Open cutter; NJ3, Portland cutter; ID5, Swell-bodied cutter; (Qu. N40a, . . *Sleighs . . for hauling loads*) Infs CT2, MI81, ND2, NY66, 216, WI5, Cutter; (Qu. N40c, . . *Sleighs for carrying other things*) Inf NH5, Cutter; NY148, Dickey double cutter; (Qu. N41a, . . *Horse-drawn vehicles . . to carry people*) Infs NJ16, NY66, OH3, Cutter; (Qu. N41c, *Horse-drawn vehicles to carry light loads*) Inf MI85, Cutter, sleigh. **1966–67** *DARE* Tape IA2, He was fortunate enough to hang to the reins and didn't lose his horse and we got back into the cutter; MI8, We had to take a horse and cutter in the wintertime; MI49, In the winters he'd have the hired man do the chores, and he'd take his horse and buggy or horse and cutter and go teach in school; MI71, A cutter is . . a two-passenger . . open rig; NY27, We had a cutter in the wintertime. **1968** *ID Enterprise* (Malad City) 1 Feb 8/1, We are sincerely appreciative of the support given by the business firms and individuals to our cutter racing program this winter. **1973** Allen *LAUM* 1.220 **MN, IA, NE**, Horse-drawn vehicles for traversing snow are principally of two kinds, those with two sets of runners and those with one set . . . The latter type, generally called *cutter*, or, less frequently, *sleigh*, consists of a box or compartment large enough for two or three passengers, supported on two runners, and drawn by a single horse.

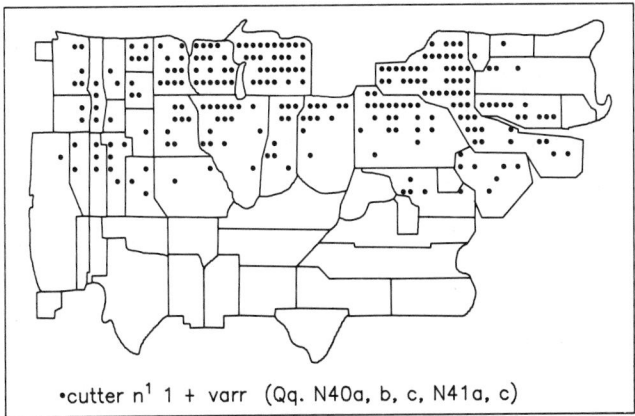

•cutter n¹ 1 + varr (Qq. N40a, b, c, N41a, c)

2 An inferior grade of beef animal, a cull or reject; inferior beef from such an animal. **scattered, but chiefly Midl** See Map

1905 *Chicago Daily News* (IL) 3 July 7/7, Canners and cutters were rather slow, as packers did not care to secure them, to-morrow being a holiday. **1936** *Sun* (Baltimore MD) 2 Nov 13/6 *(Hench Coll.),* Low cutter and cutter cows brought $3a4; medium grades around $4.50, a few good kinds up to $5.50. **1947** *Chi. Tribune* 17 July 23/1 *(DA),* Canners sold steady and losses in cutters ranged up to 50 cents. **1965–70** *DARE* (Qu. K15, *A thin, bony, or poor-looking cow*) 28 Infs, **scattered, but chiefly Midl,** Cutter; **OR**1, Cutter cow.

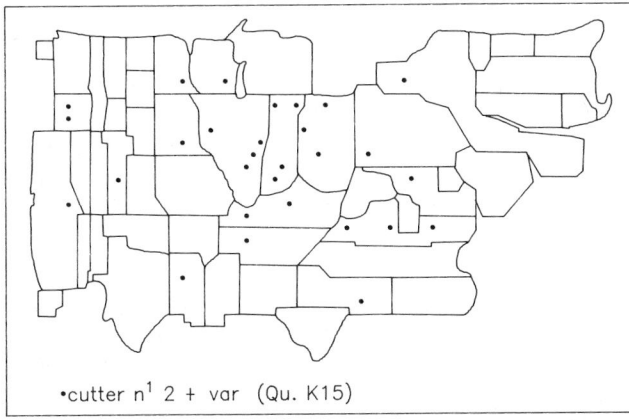

•cutter n¹ 2 + var (Qu. K15)

3 A fine fellow; also transf to an animal. Cf *cutter* at **critter**

1911 *DN* 3.537 **eKY,** Cutter . . . A term of approval; e.g., "He's a cutter," meaning "a good fellow." **1930** Vines *River Goes with Heaven* 215 *(DA),* I was a young cutter then, Jake. **1940** *Sat. Eve. Post* 6 Jan 32/2 **MS,** I got him [=a goat], papa. He's a cutter! **c1960** *Wilson Coll.* **csKY,** Cutter . . . A good fellow, a "jim-dandy."

4 also *cutter-out:* One who separates cattle from a herd; a horse used in separating cattle. **[cut v 5]** **West** Cf **cutting horse**

1910 Mulford *Hopalong* 24 **West,** Each of the cutters-out rode after some calf. **1942** *AmSp* 17.75 **NE,** A *fine cutter* is a horse with exceptional ability in *cutting,* or separating cattle from a herd. **1944** Adams *Western Words* 47, Cutter . . one engaged in cutting out cattle, a good cutting horse.

5 One who **earmarks** cattle.

1944 Adams *Western Words.* **1961** Adams *Old-Time Cowhand* 259, The men who cut the ear-marks, dewlaps, wattles, and other marks of identification on the animal's anatomy were knowed as the "butchers," or "knife men," or "cutters."

6 A revolver. Cf **cut down** v phr **1**

1913 (1979) Barnes *Western Grazing* 381, Cutter.—Slang for six-shooter. **1944** Adams *Western Words* 47, Cutter—A slang name for the pistol.

7 also attrib: A sharp blade in front of a plowshare to cut roots or other impediments; a colter; hence *cutter* the plow itself. **chiefly S Midl**

1902 (1969) Sears *Catalogue* 678, Gauge Wheels and Fin Cutters, for Pony Plows. **1950** Faulkner *Stories* 16 **MS,** Did you put the cutter back in that straight stock like I told you? **1968–69** *DARE* (Qu. L18, . . *Kinds of plows used . . at present and in the past*) Inf **GA**14, Cutters; **KY**53, Cutter plows—V-shaped; **KY**58, Cutter plow—old-fashioned; **WV**5, Cutter stocks—two handles, a root-cutter in front, plow behind. **1981** *Broaddus Coll.* **ceKY** (as of 1958), Cutter plow—a plow with a thin, knife-like blade for cutting roots.

8 Perh =**cutaway harrow.**

1968 *DARE* (Qu. L20, *The implement used in a field after it's been plowed, to break up the lumps*) Inf **OH**62, Cutter.

cutter n² See **critter**

cutterman See **cunterman**

cutter-out See **cutter** n¹ **4**

cut the alkali in one's drinking water v phr *joc*

To reduce the proportion of alkali in a drink of water by adding liquor to it.

1903 (1965) Adams *Log Cowboy* 130, He had produced a black bottle used for cutting the alkali in your drinking water. *Ibid* 194, McCann had not forgotten us, but had smuggled out a quart bottle to cut the alkali in our drinking water. But a quart among eight of us was not dangerous, so the night passed without incident.

cut the blood out of v phr

To whip severely.

1953 *PADS* 19.10 **sAppalachians,** Cut the blood out of . . . To whip severely. "Paw cut the blood out of Bill when he laid out [i.e., stayed out . .] of school." **1954** *Harder Coll.* **cwTN,** Cut the blood out of someone . . . To switch severely. "Iffen ye don't cut out 'at air squallin', I jist a-gonna cuttabloodouttaye with a switch."

cut the buck v phr [*cut* to engage in, perform + *buck* abbr for **buck-and-wing** n]

1 also *cut a buck(-and-wing):* To dance vigorously and usu solo with much improvisation; spec to dance the **buck-and-wing.** Cf **cut-the-buckle**

1927 Adams *Congaree* 9 **cSC** [Black], He started to takin' long steps, skippin' 'roun', an' jumpin'. Look like he was cuttin' the buck. *Ibid* 52, And as de night wored on you ought er seen some of dem niggers cut de buck and de buzzard lope, and sidin' 'round dem sisters like er rooster 'round er hen. **1938** Rawlings *Yearling* 350 **neFL,** He slapped Jody on the back and cut a buck-and-wing. **1975** Thomas *Hear the Lambs* 104 **nwAL,** "Your sister here can dance," the man said. "How about you, Tom?" "I can cut a few buck."

2 Transf: to work efficiently; to perform rapidly or successfully.

1927 *AmSp* 2.352 **wcWV,** Cut the buck . . to accomplish any effort. "He was not able to cut the buck that time." **1946** *PADS* 6.11 **swVA,** Cut the buck . . To move rapidly, as in driving a car. Salem. Reported, 1940. **1950** *WELS* (To work very hard: "He was slow to begin with, but now he's _____.") 1 Inf, **cwWI,** Cutting the buck (and wing). **1967** *DARE* (Qu. JJ26, *If somebody has been doing poor work or not enough, the boss might say, "If he wants to keep his job he'd better _____."*) Inf **CA**15, Cut the buck; (Qu. LL32, . . *One man's ability is not nearly as great as another man's: "John can't . . _____ Bill.")* Inf **CA**15A, Can't cut the buck like.

3 In railroading: see quots.

1942 Berrey–Van den Bark *Amer. Slang* 781.5, Cut the buck . . *said of a [railroad] fireman when the steam gauge shows full working pressure.* **1977** Adams *Lang. Railroader* 40, Cut the buck: To build steam to full working pressure.

4 Prob by ext from **1**: see quot.

1968 *DARE* (Qu. GG15, *Talking about a person who became over-excited and lost control, "At that point he really _____."*) Inf **SC**58, Flew to pieces; cut the buck.

cut-the-buckle adj Cf **cut the buck 1**

Of dancing: unrestrained, extremely vigorous.

1835 Crockett *Account* 34, It would do you good to see our boys and girls dancing. None of your stradling, mincing, sadying: but a regular sifter, cut-the-buckle, chicken-flutter set-to.

cut the cake v phr

To get married.

1970 *DARE* (Qu. AA15a, . . *Joking ways . . of saying that people got married: "They _____."*) Inf **SC**69, Cut the cake; (Qu. AA15b,c . .

Ways of saying . . getting married: "He _____." . . "She _____.") Inf **WV**20, Cut the cake. [Both Infs Black]

cut the cheese v phr See **cut** v **10**

cut the cheese n Cf **red light**

A children's game: see quot.

1968 *DARE* Tape **IA**34, I remember playing . . we used to call it cut the cheese and nowadays they call it . . red light . . . Same rules.

cut the comb See **cut one's comb**

cut the cord v phr

To be the "last straw."

1967 *DARE* (Qu. GG22b, *When you have come to the end of your patience, you might say, "Well, that certainly_____.")* Inf **NY**12, Cuts the cord.

cut the corner n

1967 *DARE* (Qu. EE28, *Games played in water*) Inf **SC**44, Cut the corner—a tag game played at a pool—you can run on the sides but you must dive and swim the corners.

cut the fool v phr **chiefly S Atl**

To joke around, behave mischievously, act up.

1933 Rawlings *South Moon* 34 **FL**, Ma, 'pears to me like you'd be used to them cuttin' the fool. **1940** *Sat. Eve. Post* 23 Nov 104 **sGA**, He died without no hollering ner cutting the fool, just like a natural man. **1942** Hurston *Dust Tracks* 229 **FL** [Black], Old cuffy just got to cut de fool, you know. **1942** in 1959 Lomax *Rainbow Sign* 186 **nMS** [Black], The young want to . . walk home . . hanging around outside, skylarking and cutting the fool. **1966** *Sumter Co. Times* (Bushnel FL) 31 Mar 6/3, When we drove on the ferry boat the mules began to cut the fool. **1966** *DARE* (Qu. GG32a, . . *Habitually play tricks or jokes on people*) Infs **SC**7, 21, Cutting the fool.

cut the pie n

1 =**fox and geese** n **2**.

1945 Boyd *Hdbk. Games* 15, Fox and Geese, or Cut the Pie—This game is played in the snow. **1966–70** *DARE* (Qu. EE26, . . *Games . . children play in the snow*) Inf **MI**123, Cut the pie (same as fox and goose); **MT**1, Cut the pie.

2 See quot.

1950 *WELS (Hiding games that start with some special, elaborate way of sending the players out to hide)* 1 Inf, **cwWI**, Cut the pie.

cut the pigeon('s) wing v phr Also *cut a pigeon wing* [*cut* to dance + *pigeon wing* a dance movement imitative of pigeons] **esp S Midl**

To execute intricate dance steps gracefully.

1897 (1952) McGill *Narrative* 139, In many of these dances an opportunity is given for the display of much grace and artistic coquetry by the young ladies, and of activity by some of the young men, as they "cut the pigeon wing." **1898** Lloyd *Country Life* 15 **AL**, I use to cut the pigeon wing around Miss Tildy some myself. **1912** *DN* 3.574 **wIN**, Cut a pigeon wing . . . To dance with graceful steps. **1927** *AmSp* 2.352 **WV**, Cut the pigeon's wing. **1940** FWP *Guide TX* 114 (as of 1828), When young people danced in those days, . . they 'shuffled' and 'double-shuffled,' and 'wired' and 'cut the pigeon's wing,' making the splinters fly. **1946** Greer–Petrie *Angeline Steppin'* 35 **csKY**, He'd jump out in the middle of the floor and cut the pidgeon wing. **1954** *Harder Coll.* **cwTN**, Cut the pigeon wing . . . To dance in a fancy way. " 'At air girl shore is a-cuttin' the pigeon wing." **1966** *DARE* (Qu. FF5a, . . *Steps and figures in dancing—in past years*) Inf **DC**8, Cut the pigeon's wing.

cut the throttle v phr

See quot 1958.

1958 McCulloch *Woods Words* 43 **Pacific NW**, Cut the throttle—To coast, take it easy. **1962** *AmSp* 37.132.

‡**cut the wind** v phr

1968 *DARE* (Qu. K48, *When a horse is short of breath, you say it's _____*) Inf **MD**20, Cutting the wind.

cutthroat trout n Also *cut, cutthroat, ~ steelhead*

A trout *(Salmo clarkii)* distinguished by a red mark near the gills. **chiefly West** Also called **black-spotted trout, harvest trout, mountain trout, native trout, salmon trout, silver trout, trout 1**

1902 Jordan–Evermann *Amer. Fishes* 176, Cut-throat Trout—*Salmo clarkii*. **1939** Natl. Geog. Soc. *Fishes* 270, When the species *[Salmo*

clarkii] runs to the sea, it is called a *Cutthroat Steelhead.* **1955** U.S. Arctic Info. Center *Gloss., Cutthroat* trout. A trout, *Salmo clarkii,* in streams and lakes of western North America, with rather coarse scales, heavily spotted with black, and usually red under each side of the jaw. The cutthroat trout . . . occasionally runs to salt water and is then called a 'steelhead' or 'salmon trout.' **1961** Douglas *My Wilderness* 21 **CO**, One September I was at Geneva Lake, which rests in a graceful bowl near timber line. Native cutthroat trout were spawning; and the males, in honor of the sacred ritual, had acquired brilliant red streaks over their entire bodies. **1965–70** *DARE* (Qu. P1, . . *Freshwater fish . . good to eat*) Infs **AK**1, **CO**41, **NM**6, **NV**8, **WY**1, 5, Cutthroat trout; **CO**9, 22, **ID**3, **WA**24, **WY**4, Cutthroat(s); (Qu. P2, . . *Saltwater fish . . good to eat*) Inf **WA**24, Cutthroat. **1968** *Hungry Horse News* (Columbia Falls MT) 20 Dec 23, Cutthroat trout. **1972** Sparano *Outdoors Encycl.* 356, *Cutthroat Trout—Common Names . . . cut . . . Scientific Name: Salmo clarki.*

cut timber See **saw wood**

cutting vbl n

1 See **cut** v **1**.

2 A stand of trees fit to be cut for timber; also an area where the trees have been logged off.

1902 White *Blazed Trail* 191 **MI**, It's a fine country . . with a great cutting of white pine. **1907** *DN* 3.242 **eME**, *Cutting . . .* Woodland the trees of which have been cut out and removed. "You see that old spruce cutting." **1942** Rich *We Took to the Woods* (1948) 131 *(DA),* If we . . scramble up a steep, spruce-covered slope to the foot of the pumpkin pine, we'll come out in an old, overgrown birch cutting. **1943** *Sun* (Baltimore MD) 9 July 12/2 **MD**, Teams snaking logs from the cutting to the mill.

3 See **cut** v **5**.

cutting ant n Also *cut-ant*

Perh a **harvester ant.**

1862 Acad. Nat. Sci. Philadelphia *Proc. for 1861* 9, *Notes on Ants in Texas . . .* I had been told that "cutting ants" could carry the largest grains of corn . . [and] at that time I saw some big grains of corn move slowly along the ant path, and on close scrutiny could see that said grains were carried on the backs of the little ants. **1947** Ballowe *The Lawd* 140 **LA**, Men came out with loads on their backs, took out up the road, like a string of giant cut-ants. **1967** *DARE* (Qu. R18, . . *Other kinds of ants . . around here*) Inf **TX**1, Cutting ant (cuts leaves); **TX**13, Cutting ants.

cutting bee n [**bee** n²]

1967 *DARE* Tape **HI**2, We have these pilot tests all over the United States, you know, what they would call cutting bees in which they go into a supermarket and test these new varieties [of pineapple] to see how well they go over with the public . . . [FW:] Why "cutting" bees? [Inf:] Because you cut open the can . . . Someone goes into the warehouses and randomly selects cans from that year's pack from all the canneries and then . . these are coded and then we have a cutting bee and these are all opened and put in these pans—display pans—and they're looked at for appearance, blemishes, and for taste—some slices are cut up . . . A cutting bee is held every October.

cutting gate n [**cut** v **5**]

A gate used to separate cattle from a herd; see quot 1944.

1890 in 1942 *AmSp* 71.208/2, New cutting gates put in and new wings thrown out, so that now cattle with much less worry, can be loaded. **1942** *AmSp* 17.208/2, Cutting gate. A gate used to help cut an animal from a herd. **1944** Adams *Western Words, Cutting gate*—A wide, swinging gate so arranged that it can be operated with a long extension by a man sitting on top of the fence. It is used like the switch of a railroad track to shunt cattle into one of several pens which it serves.

cutting harrow See **cut harrow**

cutting horse n Also *cut-horse, cutting pony* [**cut** v **5**] **West** Cf **carving, chopping horse, cutter** n¹ **4**

A horse trained to cut cattle from the herd.

1881 Romspert *W. Echo* 177, Each firm has particular horses trained for this business, and they are called "cutting horses." **1907** White *AZ Nights* 157, We finished cutting the herd . . . We jogged homeward, our cutting ponies, tired with the quick, sharp work, shuffling knee deep in . . dusk. **1920** Hunter *Trail Drivers TX* 297, Those [=cattle] cut out are called the "cut;" the specially trained horses used for this work, so intelligent that you can remove the bridle after the animal to be cut out is indicated, and the horse will separate the cow from the bunch with unerring instinct, are called "cutting horses," "carving horses" or "chopping horses." **1933** *AmSp* 8.1.29 **TX,** *Cuttin' horse.* A horse expert at *cutting* cattle, always an intelligent, agile, and sure-footed pony. This term came to be used in the figure *as frisky as a cuttin' horse,* and *as smart as a cuttin' horse.* Variations: *carvin' horse, choppin' horse.* **1937** *DN* 6.618 **wTX,** A *cutting* horse is one especially trained to separate or "cut" a single animal from a whole herd. (I have seen one "cutting" horse who could "cut" a hen from a big flock of chickens.) **1939** FWP *Guide MT* 414, *Cutting horse*—Quick horse, good at cutting out. **1941** FWP *Guide WY* 461, *Cut-horse.* **1956** Ker *Vocab. W. TX* 243, *Cuttin' horse.* **1966** *DARE* Tape NM13, You had to stay at the wagon unless you were goin' to ride your roundup horse or your cuttin' horse, as they called it; **OK30,** They'd have a cutting horse that they'd use for . . cutting cattle.

cutting house n

A processing plant for herring.

1976 Warner *Beautiful Swimmers* 130 **Chesapeake Bay,** Twenty-five years ago there were many processing plants, called "striking houses" or "cutting houses," where herring were swiftly beheaded and gutted by skillful black hands, and the roe collected in gleaming tin pails. Today there are only two such places on the Bay where herring is still prepared for the table.

cutting machine n

In coal mining: see quot 1973.

1968–69 *DARE* Tape KY39, Then they got the cuttin' machine, they'd cut . . square . . rooms and then they'd drill these holes in one; **VA2,** The other brother run a cutting machine in the mine. **1973** *PADS* 59.33 **sIL, WV, eKY, TN, AL,** *Cutting machine* . . a coal *face* opening machine which advances into the coal by means of a chain saw arranged around a solid bar usually about three feet in width.

‡cutting-off saw n

A crosscut saw.

1965 Needham–Mussey *Country Things* 110 **VT** (as of c1900), Gramp began showing me how to use a cutting-off saw . . . I started to hang up the cutting-off saw (they call them crosscuts at the hardware store) on the nearest peg in the wall.

cutting plow n

A plow with a **cutter** n[1] 7.

1969–70 *DARE* (Qu. L18, *Kinds of plows*) Infs **KY72, NC63,** Cutting plow.

cutting pony See **cutting horse**

cutting worm n

1 Prob a **sawfly** larva.

1859 Perry *Turpentine Farming* 104, Cutting Worm.—This insect is produced by the bug aforementioned: when hatched or spawned, they are not larger than a tobacco seed, are perfectly white, and commence feeding upon the sour, moist bust which is made by the parent bug; when they attain a length of from half an inch to an inch, they are found to be flat, larger at the head than any where else, with ridges around them, and a dark brown . . bill . . with two prongs, uniting at the points, which are very hard, and used to cut with.

2 A cutworm.

1968–70 *DARE* (Qu. R27, . . *Caterpillars or similar worms*) Inf **NJ35,** Cutting worm—cuts stem of the bean plant; **VA47,** Cutting worm.

cutty adj [Scots]

1930 Shoemaker *1300 Words* 15 **cPA Mts** (as of c1900), *Cutty*—short.

cuttyhole n [Alter of **cuddy** + *hole*]

1946 *PADS* 6.11 **eNC,** *Cuttyhole* . . . A small room or corner for holding plunder . . . Occasional.

cutty pipe n [**cutty**] *arch*

A short-stemmed pipe.

1857 *Putnam's Mag.* 10.348/1 **CT,** He would smoke a cutty-pipe. [**1968** *DARE* (Qu. DD1, . . *Different forms of chewing tobacco*) Inf **PA165,** Cutty pipe. [*DARE* ed: trademark: *Cutty Pipe Smoking Tobacco.*]]

cut under v phr [?Metath of *undercut*]

To insult.

1954 Armstrong *Satchmo* 212 **LA,** I did not like the way he cut under me.

cut-under n, also attrib *old-fash*

A horse-drawn vehicle; see quot 1948.

1887 A. Hayes *Jesuit's Ring* 61 (*DAE*), I have chartered a cut-under.

1902 (1969) Sears *Catalogue* 373, *Our new acme model cut under extension top surrey* . . . Latest style cut under extension body. **1948** Rittenhouse *Amer. Horse-Drawn Vehicles* 13, *Cut Under Runabout.* City driving required sharp turns into driveways and alleys, and this necessitated the 'cut under' construction which gave clearance to the front wheels when turning in a small radius. **1953** Johnson *Sullivan* 138 **ME,** Sunday afternoons found the family together, riding perhaps in a surrey or cut-under drawn by a span of horses. **1966–68** *DARE* (Qu. N41a, . . *Kinds of horse-drawn vehicles . . used . . to carry people*) Inf **ME10,** Cut-under—has a cloth top with pieces cut out to wave in the breeze; (Qu. N41b, . . *To carry heavy loads*) Inf **OH56,** Cut-unders—to turn short.

cut up v phr

1 See quot.

1912 *DN* 3.574 **wIN,** *Cut up* . . . To experience menstruation [prob erron for *estrus*]. Applied especially to cows.

2 To complain.

1968 *DARE* Tape NY61 [Black], [FW:] Was it all a Negro neighborhood when you were little? [Inf:] No. That's the reason I can't understand why the people just cuttin' up 'bout the White people. I never had no trouble with White people. White people used to come my house [sic], friends would come to my house and have tea or somethin' other, and I'd go to their house and have somethin' to eat.

cut up a curlicue v phr Also *cut (up) curlicues* *obs*

To act in a devious manner; to play a trick or prank.

1840 Hoffman *Greyslaer* 2.27, I soon saw, by the way in which the white man's track doubled and doubled again . . that the fellow could not be cutting such carlicues for nothing. **1848** Bartlett *Americanisms* 394, *Carlacue.* A caper; a boyish trick. *'To cut up carlacues,'* is a common expression, equivalent to 'cutting up didoes.' Used in New York. **1858** Hammett *Piney Woods Tavern* 35, Most a powerful rough-lookin' flat-boat captain, sold him out a bargain and cut up a most amazin' slick curlecue with him, I guess.

cut up cabbage See **cut cabbage**

cut up curlicues See **cut up a curlicue**

cut up Jack (and kill Jinny) See **jack** n[1]

cut up lard v phr

See quots.

1946 *PADS* 6.11 **eNC** *Cut up lard* . . . To cut hog fat into small pieces to be fried . . . Common. **c1960** *Wilson Coll.* **csKY,** *Cut up lard* . . . Cut hog fat into small pieces to be "rendered" into lard.

cut up one's rusties, cut up rusty See **cut a rusty** 1, 2

cutwater n

1 The black skimmer (*Rynchops nigra*). Cf **shearwater**

1731 (1754) Catesby *Nat. Hist. Carolina* 1.90, *Larus Major Rostro inæquali.* The Cut Water . . . These Birds frequent near the Sea-coasts of Carolina. **1872** Coues *Key to N. Amer. Birds* 324, Genus *Rhynchops* . . . *Black Skimmer. Cut-water.* **1946** Hausman *Eastern Birds* 332, Black Skimmer *Rynchops nigra nigra* . . Other Names . . . Cutwater. **1951** Teale *North Spring* 32, As we passed one reef, fifty black skimmers—the 'cut-waters' of Old Mark Catesby—leaped into the air, barking like puppies.

2 Fig: the nose.

1942 ME Univ. *Studies* 26, *Cut water.* [Footnote 74:] Fig. The nose (facetious).

cut wood See **saw wood**

cut Z's See **Z's**

cu'us See **curious**

cuyamaca bush n

A **ceanothus** (here: *Ceanothus palmeri*).

1938 Van Dersal *Native Woody Plants* 89, *Ceanothus palmeri* . . . *Cuyamaca bush* . . . Browsed by cattle in times of scarcity of other feed.

cuzzywop See **cussywop**

cwishion See **cushion**

cwoil See **coil** v

cya' See **carry** A1

cyaa See **car** n[1]

cyaaf See **calf** n[1]

cya(a)r n See **car** n[1]

cyar v See **carry** A1

cyard See **card** n[1]

cyarn See **carrion**

cycle bean n

An unidentified bean.

1969 *DARE* (Qu. I20, . . *Kinds of beans*) Inf **PA203**, Cycle beans.

cyclone n Pronc-sp *cyclome*

1 A tornado. *somewhat old-fash*

[**1856** Kane *Arctic Explor.* 2.220, [The gale] had the character . . of a cyclone.] **1871** *Scribner's Mth.* 1.402, I purpose . . to determine the tracks and behavior of the cyclones that sweep over and desolate our land. **1883** *Harper's Mag.* 67.967/1, One-third of the city of Rochester, Minnesota, destroyed by a cyclone. **1891** *Pomona* (Cal.) *Times–Courier* 13 Sept. 4/4 *(DAE)*, The word 'cyclone' is incorrectly applied by great newspapers to a tornado. **c1960** *Wilson Coll.* **csKY**, Cyclone . . . Universally used by older people for tornado. Some younger people merely say storm. **1965–70** *DARE* (Qu. B16, *A destructive wind that comes with a funnel-shaped cloud*) 263 Infs, **widespread**, Cyclone. [Of all Infs responding to the question, 69% were old; of those giving this response, 81% were old.] **1967** *Chadron Rec.* (NE) 4 Sept 4/4, July 10, 1894, Chadron was visited by a small cyclone; outbuildings were turned over, a few buildings were unroofed.

2 A strong, non-rotating wind; a gale. *somewhat old-fash*

1965–70 *DARE* (Qu. B17, *A destructive wind that blows straight*) 56 Infs, **widespread, exc Pacific and Atlantic**, Cyclone; (Qu. O19, *Different kinds or degrees of wind that are important when you're in a boat*) Infs **MI76, MN12**, Cyclone. [All Infs old or mid-aged]

cyclone cellar n Also *cyclone shelter, ~ cave* [cyclone] **chiefly wGt Lakes, West** See Map

An underground refuge from a tornado or other destructive storm.

1887 Custer *Tenting* 652 **KS**, Those women who take refuge in these days in their cyclone-cellar . . will know. **1945** James *Cherokee Strip* 7 **OK** (as of 1890s), In the winter it was snug and cozy; and in summertime as cool and nice as our cyclone cellar in the creek bank. **1960** Bailey *Resp. to PADS 20* **KS**, Cyclone cellar. **1965–70** *DARE* (Qu. D22, *Underground place to go to in case of a violent windstorm*) 53 Infs, **chiefly wGt Lakes, West**, Cyclone cellar; **CA153, MA83**, Cyclone shelter; **KS5**, Cyclone cave.

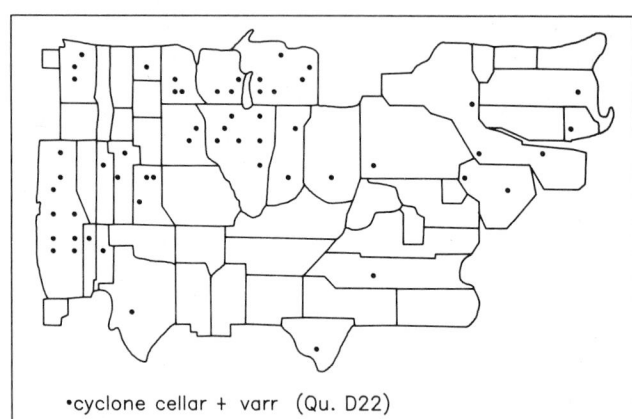

•cyclone cellar + varr (Qu. D22)

cyclone door n

1969 *DARE* (Qu. D20, . . *A sloping outside cellar door*) Inf **MI91**, Cyclone door.

cyclone shelter See **cyclone cellar**

cyclops n Cf *DS* FF27

=**one-eyed monster.**

1972 Claerbaut *Black Jargon* 62, Cyclops . . a television set; TV: The dude's got an old cyclops.

cymbal n Also sp *cimbal, cymball, simball* **NEng** *old-fash*

A kind of doughnut or **friedcake 1.**

1828 Webster *Amer. Dict.*, Cimbal, a kind of cake. **1865** (1889) Whitney *Gayworthys* 36 **NEng**, After they had popped corn, and roasted

apples, and eaten simballs, . . they had all gone to bed. **1895** *DN* 1.394 **seMA**, *Simball:* one of the varieties of doughnut. **1899** Freeman *In Colonial Times* 19 *(DA)*, Here's a piece of sweet cake and a couple of simballs. **1915** *DN* 4.239 **MA**, Cymballs . . . Jumbles made with caraway seed and rose water. **1931–33** *LANE Worksheets* **seMA**, Cymbal . . . a doughnut without a hole. Cymbal used to be universal. But the center didn't cook through. A sea captain down on the coast got the idea of the hole. **1947** Bowles–Towle *New Engl. Cooking* 202, The simball or cymbal, known both in Massachusetts and Connecticut, was as Oliver Wendell Holmes put it "a kind of genteel doughnut."

cymblin(g) See **cymling**

cymblin-head See **cymling-head**

cymling n Also sp *cimlin, cymblin(g), cymlin(ʾ), cymnel, cynmon, simblin, simlin(g)* **chiefly Sth, S Midl**

1 Any of several varieties of gourds or squash. Cf **pattypan squash**

1839 Randolph *VA Housewife* 110, Squash or Cimlin. **1844** Thompson *Major Jones's Courtship* 39 **GA**, One feller had . . cowcumbers, simblins . . and every other vegetable you could think of. **1886** Amer. Philol. Assoc. *Trans.* 17.38 **Sth**, Cymbling or simlin, a 'variety of squash.' This and not squash is the universal name for the fruit in the South, as a professor at Vanderbilt University, from New York, found out when he ordered a *squash* and failed utterly to make the huckster understand. **1899** (1912) Green *VA Folk-Speech*, Cymblin . . . A sort of eatable gourd. The dried shell of the cymblin that is used for dipping water, and many other household purposes. **1926** *DN* 5.399 **Ozarks**, Cymblin . . . A small, hard, striped gourd. Tucker spells the word *cimlin*, and says it is a kind of squash. Bartlett gives the forms *cymbling* and *cymnel*. **1938** (1955) FWP *Guide DE* 363, Fried cymlin' squash. **1950** *PADS* 14.25 **SC**, Cymlin', cymling, simlin . . . A variety of squash, the pan squash. **1953** Randolph *Down in Holler* 238 **Ozarks**, Cymlin . . . Any small gourd, also a kind of summer squash. **1954** *Harder Coll.* **cwTN**, Cymlin . . . A type of gourd, usually small. **1960** Criswell *Resp. to PADS 20* **Ozarks**, Cymling . . . pron [sɪmlɪn, sɪmlən]. **c1960** *Wilson Coll.* **csKY**, Cymbling . . . A summer squash. **1965–70** *DARE* (Qu. I23) 32 Infs, **chiefly C Atl**, Cymling squash; **VA46**, White cymling; **CA87, NC12, 14, 44**, Cymlings. **1968** *DARE* FW Addit **MD13**, Cynmon ['sɪnmən]—used for a round, pale green vegetable called summer squash by the FW. I think this is a variant of cymling which I later heard people use in the area.

2 An unidentified watermelon.

1950 *PADS* 14.23 **SC**, Cymlin', cymling, simlin ['sɪmlɪn, 'sɪmlɪŋ] . . . A small dwarf watermelon often found in cotton fields. Also called a *cotton field watermelon*. **1954** *PADS* 21.25 **SC**, Cymling, simling, simlin . . . A variety of dwarf watermelon found in cotton fields. It seldom grows bigger than the double fist, with seeds correspondingly small. The flesh is of a yellowish or pale pink color and far inferior in taste to the watermelon.

cymling-head n Also *cymblin-head, cymlin-, sim(b)lin-* **chiefly Sth, S Midl**

A small, round head; hence transf: a stupid person; a dunce; hence adj *cymling-headed* stupid, simple.

1909 *DN* 3.370 **eAL, wGA**, Sim(b)lin-headed . . . Foolish, simple. "You simlin-headed idiot!" **1926** *DN* 5.399 **Ozarks**, Cymblin-head . . . A fool, a dunce, a squash-head. **1953** Randolph *Down in Holler* 238 **Ozarks**, Cymlin-head . . . A fool, a dunce, a gourd-head. **1954** *Harder Coll.* **cwTN**, Cymlin-head . . . A stupid person. **1954** *PADS* 21.25 **cSC**, Cymling-head . . . A silly person; a dolt. **1965–70** *DARE* (Qu. X28, *Joking words . . for a person's head*) Infs **MS23, NC33, OK51, VA35, 46**, Cymlin-head; **KY65, NC55**, Cymling-head—a small head. **1973** Allen *LAUM* 1.315, This item [=*squash*] was added . . to ascertain whether the southern folk word *simlin* appears in the U[pper] M[idwest]. Its only occurrence is . . in the derogatory personal epithet, *simlin head* [1 North Dakota inf].

cymnel, cynmon See **cymling**

cyo', cyore See **cure**

cyorner See **corner** n[1]

cyote See **coyote** n

cypher See **cipher** n, v

cypress n

1 Std: a tree of the family Cupressaceæ.

2 Any of var trees thought to resemble those of **1** above, as:

a =**bald cypress.** [Note: early quots may perh refer instead to **1** above.]

1587 (1964) Laudonnière *Notable History* (transl Hakluyt) 2ʳ, There is great store of Cedars, Cypresses, Bayes, Palme trees, Hollies, and wilde Vines. **1612** Smith *Map VA* 10, There is a kinde of wood we called Cypres, because both the wood, the fruit, and leafe did most resemble it. [**1640** Parkinson *Theatrum Botanicum* 1476, *Cupressus Americana.* The Cipresse tree of America . . . I do not take this to be a true Cipresse tree.] **1728** in **1886** NC *Colonial Rec.* 2.752, The ground . . was overgrown with Gall bushes and the trees which grew here & there amongst them were generally Cypresses. **1859** Perry *Turpentine Farming* 161, Cypress.—This tree will live with its roots continually in the water; its leaf, or straw, partakes somewhat of the nature of both, with large pulp and small fibre, which shows it is intended to separate a large quantity of water from the sap: the tree is thus furnished with ample natural protection. **1933** Rawlings *South Moon* 41 **FL,** Scrub met swamp in a twisting moil of briers and rattan and moccasins . . . Only cypresses reared their feathery heads from gigantic bases. **1965–70** *DARE* (Qu. T15, . . *Kinds of swamp trees*) 14 Infs, **chiefly Sth,** Cypress; (Qu. T5, . . *Kinds of evergreens other than pines*) 16 Infs, **chiefly Sth,** Cypress.

b =**jack pine 1.**

1908 Britton *N. Amer. Trees* 44, *Pinus Banksiana* . . . It is also known as . . Jack pine . . and erroneously as Juniper and Cypress.

3 See *cypress brake* at **brake** n² **d.**

4 See **cypress spurge.**

cypress brake See **brake** n² **d**

cypress bucket n Also *cypress knee bucket*

A pail fashioned from a **cypress knee.**

1857 *Harper's Mag.* 15.746/1 **eNC,** There are besides four characteristic indispensables to every cottage: a well-sweep with a cypress-knee bucket, in shape and size like a slouched hat. [**1903** *DN* 2.311 **seMO,** *Cypress-knee*. . . These knobs or knees are hollow and are often used for well buckets in primitive localities.] **1938** Rawlings *Yearling* 77 **FL,** It was Penny himself who slung the ox yoke across his narrow shoulders, hung the great hewn cypress buckets at either end, and trudged up and down the sandy road. [**1946** Wilson *Fidelity Folks* 113 **csKY,** The old mill had . . a toll cup made into a bucket-like shape by cutting off a section of a cypress knee.]

cypress gall See **gall 1**

cypress holly n [Prob from its growing in cypress ponds and swamps]

A **holly** (here: *Ilex myrtifolia*).

1960 Vines *Trees SW* 651, *Ilex myrtifolia* . . . Common names are Small-leaf Dahoon, Myrtle Holly, and Cypress Holly.

cypress knee n Pronc-sp *cypuss-knee*

A large hollow process or outgrowth from the roots of a **bald cypress.**

1784 Smyth *Tour U.S.A.* 1.107 **NC,** Down this way I also observed . . multitudes of singular excrescences, named cypress knees, . . arising in the form of knees, out of the most miry places. **1837** (1962) Williams *Territory FL* 89, Cypress knees are hollow cones, which rise from roots of the cypress tree, from one to six feet high, and terminate in a blunt point. **1903** *DN* 2.311 **seMO,** *Cypress-knee* . . . A peculiar growth or process upward from the roots of cypress trees. **1907** *DN* 3.230 **nwAR,** *Cypress-knee.* **1908** *DN* 3.304 **eAL, wGA,** The cypuss-knees are thick in this swamp. **1946** *PADS* 6.11 **eNC,** *Cypress knee* . . . The branchless and top root-growth of the cypress tree from one to three feet high. The top is round and looks like the nub of a finger or an amputated leg . . . Common. **1950** Faulkner *Stories* 328 **MS,** The drums began after dark. They kept them hidden in the creek bottom. They were made of hollowed cypress knees, and the Negroes kept them hidden; why, none knew. **1966** *DARE* Tape **FL39,** There [in the swamp] you see all those old curious strange cypress knees coming up. **1975** Natl. Audubon Soc. *Corkscrew* 17, *Cypress Knees*—Growing through the water, up from roots of the cypress trees, are many short, conical bark-covered projections called "knees." The true function of these knees has long been under debate by naturalists. One theory calls them "breathers" for the tree, but they may also provide structural support for the Cypress where it grows in unstable sites of deep muck or organic debris. It has been further conjectured that in such sites the knees emerge as "pegs" through the shallow overlapping root system further securing one tree to the next.

cypress knee bucket See **cypress bucket**

cypress moss n

1 Prob =**Spanish moss 1.**

1847 *Knickerbocker* 29.331 **AL,** Another curiosity of the southern forest is the cypress moss, which abounds in the swamps. **1862** Gilmore *Among the Pines* 211 **SC,** We passed . . now and then a horned animal browsing on the cypress-moss where it hung low on the trees.

2 A **club moss:** see quots.

1900 Lyons *Plant Names* 233, *L. Alpinum* . . Alpine Club-moss, . . Cypress Moss. **1959** Carleton *Index Herb. Plants* 35, *Cypress-moss:* Lycopodium clavatum.

cypress spurge n Also *cypress*

A **spurge** (here: *Euphorbia cyparissias*). Also called **balsam 4, butternut 2, graveyard moss, graveyard weed, Irish moss, love-in-a-huddle, milkweed, squib-knocket, tree moss**

1857 Gray *Manual of Botany* 388, *E[uphorbia] Cyparissias* . . . (Cypress Spurge). **1892** *Jrl. Amer. Folkl.* 5.102 **NH,** *Euphorbia Cyparissias,* cypress. **1898** *Jrl. Amer. Folkl.* 11.278 **ME,** Cypress. **1931** Clute *Common Plants* 133, It [=cypress spurge *(Euphorbia cyparissias)*] is a close-set little plant, much resembling an evergreen.

cypress trout n chiefly **LA**

=**bowfin.**

1933 LA Dept. of Conserv. *Fishes* 383, Louisianians also know the Grindle as the Cottonfish, the Speckled Cat and the Cypress Trout, which last becomes among the French speaking inhabitants the "Cypress Truite." **1968** *DARE* (Qu. P1, . . *Freshwater fish . . caught around here that are good to eat*) Inf **LA20,** Cypress trout or choupique or bowfin; **LA44,** Cypress trout (same as grindle); **LA22,** Choupique or cypress trouts; (Qu. P3, *Freshwater fish that are not good to eat*) Inf **LA26,** Cypress trout. **1968** *DARE* Tape **GA20,** Mudfish, he's known as a grinny, boatfin, dogfish . . we call them cypress trout, too.

cypress vine n

1 A low-climbing, red-flowered convolvulaceous vine (usu *Quamoclit vulgaris,* but occas *Q. coccinea*) native to the southeastern US. [See quot 1944] *Quamoclit vulgaris* is also called **cupid's flower 1, Indian pink, jasmine, red jasmine** *Q. coccinea* is also called **jasmine, red morning glory, scarlet creeper**

1819 A. Pettigrew *Lett.* 7 Jan. (Pettigrew P.) *(DAE),* Inquire of Sam for the cypress vine seed which I forgot to bring with me. **1853** Hammett *Stray Yankee in TX* 57, The cypress vine, with its dazzling gem-like blossoms, whose form is said to have suggested the pentagonal star of the Texas flag. **1901** Lounsberry *S. Wild Flowers* 439, Cypress vine . . is known from the small, red morning-glory by its leaves being pinnately divided. **1940** Gates *Flora KS* 177, Quamoclit coccinea . . . Cypress Vine, Red Morning-glory . . . Quamoclit vulgaris . . . Cypress Vine. **1944** AL Geol. Surv. *Bulletin* 53.182, *Q. vulgaris* . . *(Ipomoea Quamoclit . .)*, the cypress vine, is more commonly cultivated, on account of its attractive feathery foliage. **1972** Brown *Wildflowers LA* 148, Cypress Vine . . . Frequently a weed in cultivated fields.

2 =**mountain fringe 1.**

1900 Lyons *Plant Names* 16, *A[dlumia] fungosa* . . . Cypress-vine, Fairy-creeper. **1959** Carleton *Index Herb. Plants* 35.

cypress-weed n [Perh for the cypress-like foliage]

A **dog fennel** (here: *Eupatorium capillifolium*).

1972 Brown *Wildflowers LA* 202, Cypress-weed. Eupatorium capillifolium . . . Stem much-branched with a panicle-like arrangement of cascading arched branches.

cypuss-knee See **cypress knee**

czarnina n Pronc-spp *chalina, charnina, czarina* [Pol *czernina*] **Pol** settlement areas, esp **WI**

A kind of **duck's blood soup;** see quot 1980.

1941 FWP *Guide WI* 484, After the church ceremony, the guests return to the bride's home to eat boiled chicken, roast pork, vegetables, cookies, pies, cakes, biscuits and, most indispensable of all, czarina, or blood soup. **1950** *WELS* (*Foreign foods*) 1 Inf, **Milwaukee WI,** Chalina [tʃɑ'linə] = blood soup, [for] Thanksgiving, Christmas. **1968** *DARE* (Qu. H45, *Dishes made with meat, fish, or poultry*) Inf **WI47,** Charnina; (Qu. H65, *Foreign foods*) Inf **WI47,** Charnina [čɑr'ninə] = duck's blood soup. **1980** *DARE* File **Chicago IL,** Czarnina [čɑr'ninə], traditional Polish soup made with duck's blood, pork, prunes, apples, and seasonings. [Our correspondent's] husband knew it from his youth in Easthampton, Massachusetts.

czezski See **chesky**